Profiles of California

2015

Fourth Edition

Profiles of California

A Universal Reference Book

Grey House Publishing

PUBLISHER: Leslie Mackenzie
EDITORIAL DIRECTOR: Laura Mars
EDITOR: David Garoogian
MARKETING DIRECTOR: Jessica Moody

Grey House Publishing, Inc.
4919 Route 22
Amenia, NY 12501
518.789.8700
FAX 845.373.6390
www.greyhouse.com
e-mail: books @greyhouse.com

First edition published 2007
Printed in Canada

ISBN: 978-1-61925-815-0

Table of Contents

Introduction

This is the fourth edition of *Profiles of California—Facts, Figures & Statistics for 1,712 Populated Places in California.* As with the other titles in our *State Profiles* series, it was built with content from Grey House Publishing's award-winning *Profiles of America*—a 4-volume compilation of data on more than 43,000 places in the United States. We have updated and included the California chapter from *Profiles of America,* and added several new chapters of demographic information and ranking sections, so that *Profiles of California* is the most comprehensive portrait of the state of California ever published.

Profiles of California provides data on all populated communities and counties in the state of California for which the US Census provides individual statistics. This edition also includes profiles of 216 unincorporated places based on US Census data by zip code.

This premier reference work includes seven major sections that cover everything from **Education** to **Ethnic Backgrounds** to **Climate**. All sections include **Comparative Statistics** or **Rankings**. **About California** at the front of the book, is comprised of detailed narrative and colorful photos and maps. Here is an overview of each section:

1. About California
This 4-color section gives the researcher a real sense of the state and its history. It includes a Photo Gallery, and comprehensive sections on California's Government, Land and Natural Resources, State Energy Profile, and Demographic Maps. With charts and maps, these 38 pages help to anchor the researcher to the state, both physically and politically.

2. Profiles
This section, organized by county, gives detailed profiles of 1,712 places plus 58 counties, based on Census 2010 and data from the American Community Survey. We have added current government statistics and original research, so that these profiles pull together statistical and descriptive information on every Census-recognized place in the state. Major fields of information include:

Geography	*Housing*	*Education*	*Religion*
Ancestry	*Transportation*	*Population*	*Climate*
Economy	*Industry*	*Health*	

NEW categories to this edition include public and private health insurance, language spoken at home, people with disabilities and veterans. In addition to place profiles, this section includes an **Alphabetical Place Index**.

3. Comparative Statistics
This section includes tables that compare California's 100 largest communities by dozens of data points.

4. Community Rankings
This NEW section includes tables that rank the top 150 and bottom 150 communities with popultion over 10,000, in dozens of categories.

5. Education
This section begins with an **Educational State Profile,** summarizing number of schools, students, diplomas granted and educational dollars spent. Following the state profile are **School District Rankings** on 16 topics ranging from *Teacher/Student Ratios* to *High School Drop-Out Rates.* Following these rankings are statewide *National Assessment of Educational Progress (NAEP)* results and data from the *California Assessment of Student Performance and Progress (CAASPP)*—an overview of student performance by subject.

6. Ancestry and Ethnicity
This section provides a detailed look at the ancestral, Hispanic and racial makeup of California's 200+ ethnic categories. Profiles are included for the state, for all 58 counties, and for all places with 50,000 or more

residents. In the ranking section, data is displayed three ways: 1) by number, based on all places regardless of population; 2) by percent, based on all places regardless of population; 3) by percent, based on places with populations of 50,000 or more. You will discover, for example, that San Jose has the greatest number of people reporting Portuguese ancestry in the state (15,480), and that 34.1% of the population of Glendale are of Armenian ancestry.

7. Climate

This section includes a State Summary, three colorful maps and profiles of both National and Cooperative Weather Stations. In addition, you'll find Weather Station Rankings with hundreds of interesting details, such as Donner Memorial State Park reporting the highest annual snowfall with 185.4 inches.

This section also includes Significant Storm Event data from January 2000 through December 2009. Here you will learn that a wildfire caused over $1 billion in property damage in San Diego County in October 2003 and that excessive heat was responsible for 46 deaths in interior central California in July 2006.

Note: The extensive **User Guide** that follows this introduction is segmented into four sections and examines, in some detail, each data field in the individual profiles and comparative sections for all chapters. It provides sources for all data points and statistical definitions as necessary.

User Guide

Places Covered

All 58 counties.

482 incorporated municipalities. Comprised of 461 cities and 21 towns.

1,014 Census Designated Places (CDP). The U.S. Bureau of the Census defines a CDP as "a statistical entity, defined for each decennial census according to Census Bureau guidelines, comprising a densely settled concentration of population that is not within an incorporated place, but is locally identified by a name. CDPs are delineated cooperatively by state and local officials and the Census Bureau, following Census Bureau guidelines.

216 unincorporated communities. The communities included have statistics for their ZIP Code Tabulation Area (ZCTA) available from the Census Bureau. They are referred to as "postal areas." "Postal areas" can span multiple ZCTAs. A ZCTA is a statistical entity developed by the Census Bureau to approximate the delivery area for a US Postal Service 5-digit or 3-digit ZIP Code in the US and Puerto Rico. A ZCTA is an aggregation of census blocks that have the same predominant ZIP Code associated with the mailing addresses in the Census Bureau's Master Address File. Thus, the Postal Service's delivery areas have been adjusted to encompass whole census blocks so that the Census Bureau can tabulate census data for the ZCTAs. ZCTAs do not include all ZIP Codes used for mail delivery and therefore do not precisely depict the area within which mail deliveries associated with that ZIP Code occur. Additionally, some areas that are known by a unique name, although they are part of a larger incorporated place, are also included as "postal areas."

For a more in-depth discussion of geographic areas, please refer to the Census Bureau's Geographic Areas Reference Manual at http://www.census.gov/geo/www/garm.html.

IMPORTANT NOTES

- Since the last decennial census, the U.S. Census replaced the long-form sample with the American Community Survey (ACS), which uses a series of monthly samples to produce annually updated estimates for the same areas. ACS estimates are based on data from a sample of housing units (3.54 million in 2013) and people in the population, not the full population. ACS sampling error (uncertainty of data) is greater for those areas with smaller populations. In an effort to provide the most accurate data, *Profiles of California* reports ACS data for counties and communities with populations of 2,500 or more. The profiles for these places (2,500 or more population) also include data from Census 2010, including: population; population growth; population density; race; Hispanic origin; average household size; median age; age under 18; age 65 and over; males per 100 females; homeownership rate; homeowner vacancy rate; and rental vacancy rate. Profiles for counties and communities with 2,500 or less population show data from the Census 2010 only.
- *Profiles of California* uses the term "community" to refer to all places except counties. The term "county" is used to refer to counties and county-equivalents. All places are defined as of the 2010 Census.
- If a community spans multiple counties, the community will be shown in the county that contains its largest population.
- When a county and city are coextensive (occupying the same geographic area and sharing the same government), they are given a single entry.
- In each community profile, only school districts that have schools that are physically located within the community are shown. In addition, statistics for each school district cover the entire district, regardless of the physical location of the schools within the district.
- Special care should be taken when interpreting certain statistics for communities containing large colleges or universities. College students were counted as residents of the area in which they were living while attending college (as they have been since the 1950 census). One effect this may have is skewing the figures for population, income, housing, and educational attainment.
- Some information (e.g. income) is available for both counties and individual communities. Other information is available for just counties (e.g. election results), or just individual communities (e.g. local newspapers). Refer to the "Data Explanation and Sources" section for a complete listing.
- Some statistical information is available only for larger communities. In addition, the larger places are more apt to have services such as newspapers, airports, school districts, etc.
- For the most complete information on any community, users should also check the entry for the county in which the community is located. In addition, more information and services will be listed under the larger places in the county.

Data Explanation and Sources: County Profiles

PHYSICAL AND GEOGRAPHICAL CHARACTERISTICS

Physical Location: Describes the physical location of the county. *Source: Columbia University Press, The Columbia Gazetteer of North America and original research.*

Land and Water Area: Land and water area in square miles. *Source: U.S. Census Bureau, Census 2010*

Latitude and Longitude: Latitude and longitude in degrees. *Source: U.S. Census Bureau, Census 2010*

Time Zone: Lists the time zone. *Source: Original research*

Year Organized: Year the county government was organized. *Source: National Association of Counties*

County Seat: Lists the county seat. If a county has more than one seat, then both are listed. *Source: National Association of Counties*

Metropolitan Area: Indicates the metropolitan area the county is located in. Also lists all the component counties of that metropolitan area. The Office of Management and Budget (OMB) defines metropolitan and micropolitan statistical areas. The most current definitions are as of February 2013. *Source: U.S. Census Bureau*

Climate: Includes all weather stations located within the county. Indicates the station name and elevation as well as the monthly average high and low temperatures, average precipitation, and average snowfall. The period of record is generally 1980-2009, however, certain weather stations contain averages going back as far as 1900. *Source: Grey House Publishing, Weather America: A Thirty-Year Summary of Statistical Weather Data and Rankings, 2010*

POPULATION

Population: 2010 figures are a 100% count of population. *Source: U.S. Census Bureau, Census 2010*

Population Growth: The increase or decrease in population between 2000 and 2010. *Source: U.S. Census Bureau, Census 2000, Census 2010*

Population Density: Total 2010 population divided by the land area in square miles. *Source: U.S. Census Bureau, U.S. Census Bureau, Census 2010*

Race/Hispanic Origin: Figures include the U.S. Census Bureau categories of White alone; Black/African American alone; Asian alone; American Indian/Alaska Native alone; Native Hawaiian/Other Pacific Islander alone; two or more races; and Hispanic of any race. Alone refers to the fact that these figures are not in combination with any other race. *Source: U.S. Census Bureau, Census 2010*

The concept of race, as used by the Census Bureau, reflects self-identification by people according to the race or races with which they most closely identify. These categories are socio-political constructs and should not be interpreted as being scientific or anthropological in nature. Furthermore, the race categories include both racial and national-origin groups.

- **White.** A person having origins in any of the original peoples of Europe, the Middle East, or North Africa. It includes people who indicated their race(s) as "White" or reported entries such as Irish, German, Italian, Lebanese, Arab, Moroccan, or Caucasian.
- **Black/African American.** A person having origins in any of the Black racial groups of Africa. It includes people who indicated their race(s) as "Black, African Am., or Negro" or reported entries such as African American, Kenyan, Nigerian, or Haitian.
- **Asian.** A person having origins in any of the original peoples of the Far East, Southeast Asia, or the Indian subcontinent, including, for example, Cambodia, China, India, Japan, Korea, Malaysia, Pakistan, the Philippine Islands, Thailand, and Vietnam. It includes people who indicated their race(s) as "Asian" or reported entries such as "Asian Indian," "Chinese," "Filipino," "Korean," "Japanese," "Vietnamese," and "Other Asian" or provided other detailed Asian responses.
- **American Indian/Alaska Native.** A person having origins in any of the original peoples of North and South America (including Central America) and who maintains tribal affiliation or community attachment. This category includes people who indicated their race(s) as "American Indian or Alaska Native" or

reported their enrolled or principal tribe, such as Navajo, Blackfeet, Inupiat, Yup'ik, or Central American Indian groups or South American Indian groups.

- **Native Hawaiian/Other Pacific Islander.** A person having origins in any of the original peoples of Hawaii, Guam, Samoa, or other Pacific Islands. It includes people who indicated their race(s) as "Pacific Islander" or reported entries such as "Native Hawaiian," "Guamanian or Chamorro," "Samoan," and "Other Pacific Islander" or provided other detailed Pacific Islander responses..
- **Two or More Races.** People may choose to provide two or more races either by checking two or more race response check boxes, by providing multiple responses, or by some combination of check boxes and other responses. The race response categories shown on the questionnaire are collapsed into the five minimum race groups identified by OMB, and the Census Bureau's "Some Other Race" category.
- **Hispanic.** The data on the Hispanic or Latino population were derived from answers to a question that was asked of all people. The terms "Spanish," "Hispanic origin," and "Latino" are used interchangeably. Some respondents identify with all three terms while others may identify with only one of these three specific terms. Hispanics or Latinos who identify with the terms "Spanish," "Hispanic," or "Latino" are those who classify themselves in one of the specific Spanish, Hispanic, or Latino categories listed on the questionnaire ("Mexican," "Puerto Rican," or "Cuban") as well as those who indicate that they are "other Spanish/Hispanic/Latino." People who do not identify with one of the specific origins listed on the questionnaire but indicate that they are "other Spanish/Hispanic/Latino" are those whose origins are from Spain, the Spanish-speaking countries of Central or South America, the Dominican Republic, or people identifying themselves generally as Spanish, Spanish-American, Hispanic, Hispano, Latino, and so on. All write-in responses to the "other Spanish/Hispanic/Latino" category were coded. Origin can be viewed as the heritage, nationality group, lineage, or country of birth of the person or the person's parents or ancestors before their arrival in the United States. People who identify their origin as Spanish, Hispanic, or Latino may be of any race.

Average Household Size: Number of persons in the average household. *Source: U.S. Census Bureau, Census 2010*

Median Age: Median age of the population. *Source: U.S. Census Bureau, Census 2010*

Age Under 18: Percent of the total population under 18 years old. *Source: U.S. Census Bureau, Census 2010*

Age 65 and Over: Percent of the total population age 65 and over. *Source: U.S. Census Bureau, Census 2010*

Males per 100 Females: Number of males per 100 females. *Source: U.S. Census Bureau, Census 2010*

Marital Status: Percentage of population never married, now married, separated, widowed, or divorced. *Source: U.S. Census Bureau, American Community Survey, 2009-2013 Five-Year Estimates*

The marital status classification refers to the status at the time of enumeration. Data on marital status are tabulated only for the population 15 years old and over. Each person was asked whether they were "Now married," "Widowed," "Separated," "Divorced," or "Never married." Couples who live together (for example, people in common-law marriages) were able to report the marital status they considered to be the most appropriate.

- **Never married.** Never married includes all people who have never been married, including people whose only marriage(s) was annulled.
- **Now married.** All people whose current marriage has not ended by widowhood or divorce. This category includes people defined as "separated."
- **Separated.** Includes people legally separated or otherwise absent from their spouse because of marital discord. Those without a final divorce decree are classified as "separated." This category also includes people who have been deserted or who have parted because they no longer want to live together, but who have not obtained a divorce.
- **Widowed**. This category includes widows and widowers who have not remarried.
- **Divorced.** This category includes people who are legally divorced and who have not remarried.

Foreign Born: Percentage of population who were not U.S. citizens at birth. Foreign-born people are those who indicated they were either a U.S. citizen by naturalization or they were not a citizen of the United States. *Source: U.S. Census Bureau, American Community Survey, 2009-2013 Five-Year Estimates*

Speak English Only: Percent of population that reported speaking only English at home. *Source: U.S. Census Bureau, American Community Survey, 2009-2013 Five-Year Estimates*

With Disability: Percent of the civilian noninstitutionalized population that reported having a disability. Disability status is determined from from six types of difficulty: vision, hearing, cognitive, ambulatory, self-care, and independent living. For children under 5 years old, hearing and vision difficulty are used to determine disability status. For children between the ages of 5 and 14, disability status is determined from hearing, vision, cognitive, ambulatory, and self-care difficulties. For people aged 15 years and older, they are considered to have a disability if they have difficulty with any one of the six difficulty types. *Source: U.S. Census Bureau, American Community Survey, 2009-2013 Five-Year Estimates*

Veterans: Percent of the civilian population 18 years and over who have served (even for a short time), but are not currently serving, on active duty in the U.S. Army, Navy, Air Force, Marine Corps, or the Coast Guard, or who served in the U.S. Merchant Marine during World War II. People who served in the National Guard or Reserves are classified as veterans only if they were ever called or ordered to active duty, not counting the 4-6 months for initial training or yearly summer camps. All other civilians are classified as nonveterans. Note: While it is possible for 17 year olds to be veterans of the Armed Forces, ACS data products are restricted to the population 18 years and older. *Source: U.S. Census Bureau, American Community Survey, 2009-2013 Five-Year Estimates*

Ancestry: Largest ancestry groups reported (up to five). The data includes persons who report multiple ancestries. For example, if a person reported being Irish and Italian, they would be included in both categories. Thus, the sum of the percentages may be greater than 100%. *Source: U.S. Census Bureau, American Community Survey, 2009-2013 Five-Year Estimates*

The data represent self-classification by people according to the ancestry group or groups with which they most closely identify. Ancestry refers to a person's ethnic origin or descent, "roots," heritage, or the place of birth of the person, the person's parents, or their ancestors before their arrival in the United States. Some ethnic identities, such as Egyptian or Polish, can be traced to geographic areas outside the United States, while other ethnicities such as Pennsylvania German or Cajun evolved in the United States.

The ancestry question was intended to provide data for groups that were not included in the Hispanic origin and race questions. Therefore, although data on all groups are collected, the ancestry data shown in these tabulations are for non-Hispanic and non-race groups. *See* Race/Hispanic Origin for information on Hispanic and race groups.

RELIGION

Religion: Lists the largest religious groups (up to six) based on the number of adherents divided by the population of the county. Adherents are defined as "all members, including full members, their children and the estimated number of other regular participants who are not considered as communicant, confirmed or full members." *Source: American Religious Bodies, 2010 U.S. Religion Census: Religious Congregations & Membership Study*

ECONOMY

Unemployment Rate: Unemployment rate as of October 2014. Includes all civilians age 16 or over who were unemployed and looking for work. *Source: U.S. Department of Labor, Bureau of Labor Statistics, Local Area Unemployment Statistics*

Leading Industries: Lists the three largest industries (excluding government) based on the number of employees. *Source: U.S. Census Bureau, County Business Patterns 2012*

Farms: The total number of farms and the total acreage they occupy. *Source: U.S. Department of Agriculture, National Agricultural Statistics Service, 2012 Census of Agriculture*

Company Size: The numbers of companies at various employee headcounts. Includes private employers only. *Source: U.S. Census Bureau, County Business Patterns 2012*

- **Employ 1,000 or more persons.** The numbers of companies that employ 1,000 or more persons.
- **Employ 500-999 persons.** The numbers of companies that employ 500 to 999 persons.
- **Employ 100-499 persons.** The numbers of companies that employ 100 to 499 persons.
- **Employ 1-99 persons.** The numbers of companies that employ 1 to 99 persons.

Business Ownership: Number of businesses that are majority-owned by women or various minority groups. *Source: U.S. Census Bureau, 2007 Economic Census, Survey of Business Owners: Black-Owned Firms, 2007 (latest statistics available at time of publication)*

- **Women-Owned.** Number of businesses that are majority-owned by a woman. Majority ownership is defined as having 51 percent or more of the stock or equity in the business.
- **Black-Owned.** Number of businesses that are majority-owned by a Black or African-American person(s). Majority ownership is defined as having 51 percent or more of the stock or equity in the business. Black or African American is defined as a person having origins in any of the black racial groups of Africa, including those who consider themselves to be "Haitian."
- **Hispanic-Owned.** Number of businesses that are majority-owned by a person(s) of Hispanic or Latino origin. Majority ownership is defined as having 51 percent or more of the stock or equity in the business. Hispanic or Latino origin is defined as a person of Cuban, Mexican, Puerto Rican, South or Central American, or other Spanish culture or origin, regardless of race.
- **Asian-Owned.** Number of businesses that are majority-owned by an Asian person(s). Majority ownership is defined as having 51 percent or more of the stock or equity in the business.

EMPLOYMENT

Employment by Occupation: Percentage of the employed civilian population 16 years and over in management, professional, service, sales, farming, construction, and production occupations. *Source: U.S. Census Bureau, American Community Survey, 2009-2013 Five-Year Estimates*

- Management, business, and financial occupations include:
  - Management occupations
  - Business and financial operations occupations
- Computer, engineering, and science occupations include:
  - Computer and mathematical occupations
  - Architecture and engineering occupations
  - Life, physical, and social science occupations
- Education, legal, community service, arts, and media occupations include:
  - Community and social service occupations
  - Legal occupations
  - Education, training, and library occupations
  - Arts, design, entertainment, sports, and media occupations
- Healthcare practitioners and technical occupations include:
  - Health diagnosing and treating practitioners and other technical occupations
  - Health technologists and technicians
- Service occupations include:
  - Healthcare support occupations
  - Protective service occupations:
    - Fire fighting and prevention, and other protective service workers including supervisors
    - Law enforcement workers including supervisors
  - Food preparation and serving related occupations
  - Building and grounds cleaning and maintenance occupations
  - Personal care and service occupations
- Sales and office occupations include:
  - Sales and related occupations
  - Office and administrative support occupations
- Natural resources, construction, and maintenance occupations include:
  - Farming, fishing, and forestry occupations
  - Construction and extraction occupations
  - Installation, maintenance, and repair occupations
- Production, transportation, and material moving occupations include:
  - Production occupations
  - Transportation occupations
  - Material moving occupations

INCOME

Per Capita Income: Per capita income is the mean income computed for every man, woman, and child in a particular group. It is derived by dividing the total income of a particular group by the total population in that group. Per capita income is rounded to the nearest whole dollar. *Source: U.S. Census Bureau, American Community Survey, 2009-2013 Five-Year Estimates*

Median Household Income: Includes the income of the householder and all other individuals 15 years old and over in the household, whether they are related to the householder or not. The median divides the income distribution into two equal parts: one-half of the cases falling below the median income and one-half above the median. For households, the median income is based on the distribution of the total number of households including those with no income. Median income for households is computed on the basis of a standard distribution and is rounded to the nearest whole dollar. *Source: U.S. Census Bureau, American Community Survey, 2009-2013 Five-Year Estimates*

Average Household Income: Average household income is obtained by dividing total household income by the total number of households. *Source: U.S. Census Bureau, American Community Survey, 2009-2013 Five-Year Estimates*

Percent of Households with Income of $100,000 or more: Percent of households with income of $100,000 or more. *Source: U.S. Census Bureau, American Community Survey, 2009-2013 Five-Year Estimates*

Poverty Rate: Percentage of population with income below the poverty level. Based on individuals for whom poverty status is determined. Poverty status was determined for all people except institutionalized people, people in military group quarters, people in college dormitories, and unrelated individuals under 15 years old. *Source: U.S. Census Bureau, American Community Survey, 2009-2013 Five-Year Estimates*

EDUCATIONAL ATTAINMENT

Figures show the percent of population age 25 and over with the following levels of educational attainment. *Source: U.S. Census Bureau, American Community Survey, 2009-2013 Five-Year Estimates*

- **High school diploma or higher.** Includes people whose highest degree is a high school diploma or its equivalent (GED), people who attended college but did not receive a degree, and people who received a college, university, or professional degree.
- **Bachelor's degree or higher.** Includes people who received a bachelor's, master's, doctorate, or professional degree.
- **Graduate/professional degree or higher.** Includes people who received a master's, doctorate, or professional degree.

HOUSING

Homeownership Rate: Percentage of housing units that are owner-occupied. *Source: U.S. Census Bureau, Census 2010*

Median Home Value: Median value in dollars of all owner-occupied housing units as reported by the owner. *Source: U.S. Census Bureau, American Community Survey, 2009-2013 Five-Year Estimates*

Median Year Structure Built: Year structure built refers to when the building was first constructed, not when it was remodeled, added to, or converted. For mobile homes, houseboats, RVs, etc, the manufacturer's model year was assumed to be the year built. The data relate to the number of units built during the specified periods that were still in existence at the time of enumeration. *Source: U.S. Census Bureau, American Community Survey, 2009-2013 Five-Year Estimates*

Homeowner Vacancy Rate: Proportion of the homeowner inventory that is vacant "for sale." It is computed by dividing the number of vacant units "for sale only" by the sum of the owner-occupied units, vacant units that are "for sale only," and vacant units that have been sold but not yet occupied, and then multiplying by 100. This measure is rounded to the nearest tenth. *Source: U.S. Census Bureau, Census 2010*

Median Gross Rent: Median monthly gross rent in dollars on specified renter-occupied and specified vacant-for-rent units. Specified renter-occupied and specified vacant-for-rent units exclude 1-family houses on 10 acres or more. Gross rent is the contract rent plus the estimated average monthly cost of utilities (electricity, gas, and water and sewer) and fuels (oil, coal, kerosene, wood, etc.) if these are paid by the renter (or paid for the renter by someone else). Gross rent is intended to eliminate differentials that result from varying practices with respect to the inclusion of utilities and fuels as part of the rental payment. Contract rent is the monthly rent agreed to or contracted for, regardless of any furnishings, utilities, fees, meals, or services that may be included. For vacant units, it is the monthly rent asked for the rental unit at the time of enumeration. *Source: U.S. Census Bureau, American Community Survey, 2009-2013 Five-Year Estimates*

Rental Vacancy Rate: Proportion of the rental inventory that is vacant "for rent." It is computed by dividing the number of vacant units "for rent" by the sum of the renter-occupied units, vacant units that are "for rent," and vacant units that have been rented but not yet occupied, and then multiplying by 100. This measure is rounded to the nearest tenth. *Source: U.S. Census Bureau, Census 2010*

VITAL STATISTICS

Birth Rate: Estimated number of births per 10,000 population in 2013. *Source: U.S. Census Bureau, Annual Components of Population Change, July 1, 2010 - July 1, 2013*

Death Rate: Estimated number of deaths per 10,000 population in 2013. *Source: U.S. Census Bureau, Annual Components of Population Change, July 1, 2010 - July 1, 2013*

Age-adjusted Cancer Mortality Rate: Number of age-adjusted deaths from cancer per 100,000 population in 2011. Cancer is defined as International Classification of Disease (ICD) codes C00–D48.9 Neoplasms. *Source: Centers for Disease Control, CDC Wonder, 2011*

Age-adjusted death rates are weighted averages of the age-specific death rates, where the weights represent a fixed population by age. They are used because the rates of almost all causes of death vary by age. Age adjustment is a technique for "removing" the effects of age from crude rates, so as to allow meaningful comparisons across populations with different underlying age structures. For example, comparing the crude rate of heart disease in Virginia to that of California is misleading, because the relatively older population in Virginia will lead to a higher crude death rate, even if the age-specific rates of heart disease in Virginia and California are the same. For such a comparison, age-adjusted rates would be preferable. Age-adjusted rates should be viewed as relative indexes rather than as direct or actual measures of mortality risk.

Death rates based on counts of twenty or less (≤ 20) are flagged as "Unreliable". Death rates based on fewer than three years of data for counties with populations of less than 100,000 in the 2000 Census counts, are also flagged as "Unreliable" if the number of deaths is five or less (≤ 5).

HEALTH INSURANCE

Health insurance coverage in the ACS and other Census Bureau surveys define coverage to include plans and programs that provide comprehensive health coverage. Plans that provide insurance for specific conditions or situations such as cancer and long-term care policies are not considered coverage. Likewise, other types of insurance like dental, vision, life, and disability insurance are not considered health insurance coverage.

For reporting purposes, the Census Bureau broadly classifies health insurance coverage as private health insurance or public coverage. Private health insurance is a plan provided through an employer or union, a plan purchased by an individual from a private company, or TRICARE or other military health care. Public health coverage includes the federal programs Medicare, Medicaid, and VA Health Care (provided through the Department of Veterans Affairs); the Children's Health Insurance Program (CHIP); and individual state health plans. The types of health insurance are not mutually exclusive; people may be covered by more than one at the same time. People who had no reported health coverage, or those whose only health coverage was Indian Health Service, were considered uninsured. *Source: U.S. Census Bureau, American Community Survey, 2009-2013 Five-Year Estimates*

- **Have Insurance:** Percent of the civilian noninstitutionalized population with any type of comprehensive health insurance.
- **Have Private Insurance.** Percent of the civilian noninstitutionalized population with private health insurance. A person may report that they have both public and private health insurance, thus, the sum of the percentages may be greater than 100%.
- **Have Public Insurance.** Percent of the civilian noninstitutionalized population with public health insurance. A person may report that they have both public and private health insurance, thus, the sum of the percentages may be greater than 100%.
- **Do Not Have Insurance.** Percent of the civilian noninstitutionalized population with no health insurance.
- **Children Under 18 With No Insurance.** Percent of the civilian noninstitutionalized population under age 18 with no health insurance.

HEALTH CARE

Number of physicians, hospital beds and hospital admission per 10,000 population. *Source: Area Resource File (ARF) 2012-2013. U.S. Department of Health and Human Services, Health Resources and Services Administration, Bureau of Health Professions, Rockville, MD.*

- **Number of Physicians.** The number of active, non-federal physicians (MDs and DOs) per 10,000 population in 2011.
- **Number of Hospital Beds.** The number of hospital beds per 10,000 population in 2010.
- **Number of Hospital Admissions.** The number of hospital admissions per 10,000 population in 2010.

AIR QUALITY INDEX

The percentage of days in 2013 the AQI fell into the Good (0-50), Moderate (51-100), Unhealthy for Sensitive Groups (101-150), Unhealthy (151-200), Very Unhealthy (201-300), and Hazardous (300+) ranges. If a range does not appear, its value is zero. Data covers January 2013 through December 2013. *Source: AirData: Access to Air Pollution Data, U.S. Environmental Protection Agency, Office of Air and Radiation*

The AQI is an index for reporting daily air quality. It tells you how clean or polluted your air is, and what associated health concerns you should be aware of. The AQI focuses on health effects that can happen within a few hours or days after breathing polluted air. EPA uses the AQI for five major air pollutants regulated by the Clean Air Act: ground-level ozone, particulate matter, carbon monoxide, sulfur dioxide, and nitrogen dioxide. For each of these pollutants, EPA has established national air quality standards to protect against harmful health effects.

The AQI runs from 0 to 500. The higher the AQI value, the greater the level of air pollution and the greater the health danger. For example, an AQI value of 50 represents good air quality and little potential to affect public health, while an AQI value over 300 represents hazardous air quality. An AQI value of 100 generally corresponds to the national air quality standard for the pollutant, which is the level EPA has set to protect public health. So, AQI values below 100 are generally thought of as satisfactory. When AQI values are above 100, air quality is considered to be unhealthy—at first for certain sensitive groups of people, then for everyone as AQI values get higher. Each category corresponds to a different level of health concern. For example, when the AQI for a pollutant is between 51 and 100, the health concern is "Moderate." Here are the six levels of health concern and what they mean:

- "Good" The AQI value for your community is between 0 and 50. Air quality is considered satisfactory and air pollution poses little or no risk.
- "Moderate" The AQI for your community is between 51 and 100. Air quality is acceptable; however, for some pollutants there may be a moderate health concern for a very small number of individuals. For example, people who are unusually sensitive to ozone may experience respiratory symptoms.
- "Unhealthy for Sensitive Groups" Certain groups of people are particularly sensitive to the harmful effects of certain air pollutants. This means they are likely to be affected at lower levels than the general public. For example, children and adults who are active outdoors and people with respiratory disease are at greater risk from exposure to ozone, while people with heart disease are at greater risk from carbon monoxide. Some people may be sensitive to more than one pollutant. When AQI values are between 101 and 150, members of sensitive groups may experience health effects. The general public is not likely to be affected when the AQI is in this range.
- "Unhealthy" AQI values are between 151 and 200. Everyone may begin to experience health effects. Members of sensitive groups may experience more serious health effects.
- "Very Unhealthy" AQI values between 201 and 300 trigger a health alert, meaning everyone may experience more serious health effects.
- "Hazardous" AQI values over 300 trigger health warnings of emergency conditions. The entire population is more likely to be affected.

TRANSPORTATION

Commute to Work: Percentage of workers 16 years old and over that use the following means of transportation to commute to work: car; public transportation; walk; work from home. The means of transportation data for some areas may show workers using modes of public transportation that are not available in those areas (e.g. subway or elevated riders in a metropolitan area where there actually is no subway or elevated service). This result is largely due to people who worked during the reference week at a location that was different from their usual place of work (such as people away from home on business in an area where subway service was available) and people who used more than one means of transportation each day but whose principal means was unavailable where they lived (e.g. residents of non-metropolitan areas who drove to the fringe of a metropolitan area and took the commuter railroad most of the distance to work). *Source: U.S. Census Bureau, American Community Survey, 2009-2013 Five-Year Estimates*

Median Travel Time to Work: Median travel time to work for workers 16 years old and over. Travel time to work refers to the total number of minutes that it usually took the person to get from home to work each day during the reference week. The elapsed time includes time spent waiting for public transportation, picking up passengers in carpools, and time spent in other activities related to getting to work. *Source: U.S. Census Bureau, American Community Survey, 2009-2013 Five-Year Estimates*

PRESIDENTIAL ELECTION

2012 Presidential election results. *Source: Dave Leip's Atlas of U.S. Presidential Elections*

NATIONAL AND STATE PARKS

Lists National/State parks located in the area. *Source: U.S. Geological Survey, Geographic Names Information System*

ADDITIONAL INFORMATION CONTACTS

General telephone number and website address (if available) of local government.

Data Explanation and Sources: Community Profiles

PHYSICAL AND GEOGRAPHICAL CHARACTERISTICS

Place Type: Lists the type of place (city, town, village, borough, Census-Designated Place (CDP), township, charter township, plantation, gore, district, grant, location, purchase, municipality, reservation, unorganized territory, or unincorporated postal area). *Source: U.S. Census Bureau, Census 2010 and U.S. Postal Service, City State File*

ZCTA: *This only appears within unincorporated postal areas.* The statistics that follow cover the corresponding ZIP Code Tabulation Area (ZCTA). A ZCTA is a statistical entity developed by the Census Bureau to approximate the delivery area for a US Postal Service 5-digit or 3-digit ZIP Code in the US and Puerto Rico. A ZCTA is an aggregation of census blocks that have the same predominant ZIP Code associated with the mailing addresses in the Census Bureau's Master Address File. Thus, the Postal Service's delivery areas have been adjusted to encompass whole census blocks so that the Census Bureau can tabulate census data for the ZCTAs. ZCTAs do not include all ZIP Codes used for mail delivery and therefore do not precisely depict the area within which mail deliveries associated with that ZIP Code occur. Additionally, some areas that are known by a unique name, although they are part of a larger incorporated place, are also included as "postal areas."

Land and Water Area: Land and water area in square miles. *Source: U.S. Census Bureau, Census 2010*

Latitude and Longitude: Latitude and longitude in degrees. *Source: U.S. Census Bureau, Census 2010.*

Elevation: Elevation in feet. *Source: U.S. Geological Survey, Geographic Names Information System (GNIS)*

HISTORY

Historical information. *Source: Columbia University Press, The Columbia Gazetteer of North America; Original research*

POPULATION

Population: 2010 figures are a 100% count of population. *Source: U.S. Census Bureau, Census 2010*

Population Growth: The increase or decrease in population between 2000 and 2010. *Source: U.S. Census Bureau, Census 2000, Census 2010*

Population Density: Total 2010 population divided by the land area in square miles. *Source: U.S. Census Bureau, U.S. Census Bureau, Census 2010*

Race/Hispanic Origin: Figures include the U.S. Census Bureau categories of White alone; Black/African American alone; Asian alone; American Indian/Alaska Native alone; Native Hawaiian/Other Pacific Islander alone; two or more races; and Hispanic of any race. Alone refers to the fact that these figures are not in combination with any other race. *Source: U.S. Census Bureau, Census 2010*

The concept of race, as used by the Census Bureau, reflects self-identification by people according to the race or races with which they most closely identify. These categories are socio-political constructs and should not be interpreted as being scientific or anthropological in nature. Furthermore, the race categories include both racial and national-origin groups.

- **White.** A person having origins in any of the original peoples of Europe, the Middle East, or North Africa. It includes people who indicated their race(s) as "White" or reported entries such as Irish, German, Italian, Lebanese, Arab, Moroccan, or Caucasian.
- **Black/African American.** A person having origins in any of the Black racial groups of Africa. It includes people who indicated their race(s) as "Black, African Am., or Negro" or reported entries such as African American, Kenyan, Nigerian, or Haitian.
- **Asian.** A person having origins in any of the original peoples of the Far East, Southeast Asia, or the Indian subcontinent, including, for example, Cambodia, China, India, Japan, Korea, Malaysia, Pakistan, the Philippine Islands, Thailand, and Vietnam. It includes people who indicated their race(s) as "Asian" or reported entries such as "Asian Indian," "Chinese," "Filipino," "Korean," "Japanese," "Vietnamese," and "Other Asian" or provided other detailed Asian responses.
- **American Indian/Alaska Native.** A person having origins in any of the original peoples of North and South America (including Central America) and who maintains tribal affiliation or community attachment.

This category includes people who indicated their race(s) as "American Indian or Alaska Native" or reported their enrolled or principal tribe, such as Navajo, Blackfeet, Inupiat, Yup'ik, or Central American Indian groups or South American Indian groups.

- **Native Hawaiian/Other Pacific Islander.** A person having origins in any of the original peoples of Hawaii, Guam, Samoa, or other Pacific Islands. It includes people who indicated their race(s) as "Pacific Islander" or reported entries such as "Native Hawaiian," "Guamanian or Chamorro," "Samoan," and "Other Pacific Islander" or provided other detailed Pacific Islander responses..
- **Two or More Races.** People may choose to provide two or more races either by checking two or more race response check boxes, by providing multiple responses, or by some combination of check boxes and other responses. The race response categories shown on the questionnaire are collapsed into the five minimum race groups identified by OMB, and the Census Bureau's "Some Other Race" category.
- **Hispanic.** The data on the Hispanic or Latino population were derived from answers to a question that was asked of all people. The terms "Spanish," "Hispanic origin," and "Latino" are used interchangeably. Some respondents identify with all three terms while others may identify with only one of these three specific terms. Hispanics or Latinos who identify with the terms "Spanish," "Hispanic," or "Latino" are those who classify themselves in one of the specific Spanish, Hispanic, or Latino categories listed on the questionnaire ("Mexican," "Puerto Rican," or "Cuban") as well as those who indicate that they are "other Spanish/Hispanic/Latino." People who do not identify with one of the specific origins listed on the questionnaire but indicate that they are "other Spanish/Hispanic/Latino" are those whose origins are from Spain, the Spanish-speaking countries of Central or South America, the Dominican Republic, or people identifying themselves generally as Spanish, Spanish-American, Hispanic, Hispano, Latino, and so on. All write-in responses to the "other Spanish/Hispanic/Latino" category were coded. Origin can be viewed as the heritage, nationality group, lineage, or country of birth of the person or the person's parents or ancestors before their arrival in the United States. People who identify their origin as Spanish, Hispanic, or Latino may be of any race.

Average Household Size: Number of persons in the average household. *Source: U.S. Census Bureau, Census 2010*

Median Age: Median age of the population. *Source: U.S. Census Bureau, Census 2010*

Age Under 18: Percent of the total population under 18 years old. *Source: U.S. Census Bureau, Census 2010*

Age 65 and Over: Percent of the total population age 65 and over. *Source: U.S. Census Bureau, Census 2010*

Males per 100 Females: Number of males per 100 females. *Source: U.S. Census Bureau, Census 2010*

Marital Status: Percentage of population never married, now married, separated, widowed, or divorced. *Source: U.S. Census Bureau, American Community Survey, 2009-2013 Five-Year Estimates*

The marital status classification refers to the status at the time of enumeration. Data on marital status are tabulated only for the population 15 years old and over. Each person was asked whether they were "Now married," "Widowed," "Separated," "Divorced," or "Never married." Couples who live together (for example, people in common-law marriages) were able to report the marital status they considered to be the most appropriate.

- **Never married.** Never married includes all people who have never been married, including people whose only marriage(s) was annulled.
- **Now married.** All people whose current marriage has not ended by widowhood or divorce. This category includes people defined as "separated."
- **Separated.** Includes people legally separated or otherwise absent from their spouse because of marital discord. Those without a final divorce decree are classified as "separated." This category also includes people who have been deserted or who have parted because they no longer want to live together, but who have not obtained a divorce.
- **Widowed**. This category includes widows and widowers who have not remarried.
- **Divorced.** This category includes people who are legally divorced and who have not remarried.

Foreign Born: Percentage of population who were not U.S. citizens at birth. Foreign-born people are those who indicated they were either a U.S. citizen by naturalization or they were not a citizen of the United States. *Source: U.S. Census Bureau, American Community Survey, 2009-2013 Five-Year Estimates*

Speak English Only: Percent of population that reported speaking only English at home. *Source: U.S. Census Bureau, American Community Survey, 2009-2013 Five-Year Estimates*

With Disability: Percent of the civilian noninstitutionalized population that reported having a disability. Disability status is determined from from six types of difficulty: vision, hearing, cognitive, ambulatory, self-care, and independent living. For children under 5 years old, hearing and vision difficulty are used to determine disability status. For children between the ages of 5 and 14, disability status is determined from hearing, vision, cognitive, ambulatory, and self-care difficulties. For people aged 15 years and older, they are considered to have a disability if they have difficulty with any one of the six difficulty types. *Source: U.S. Census Bureau, American Community Survey, 2009-2013 Five-Year Estimates*

Veterans: Percent of the civilian population 18 years and over who have served (even for a short time), but are not currently serving, on active duty in the U.S. Army, Navy, Air Force, Marine Corps, or the Coast Guard, or who served in the U.S. Merchant Marine during World War II. People who served in the National Guard or Reserves are classified as veterans only if they were ever called or ordered to active duty, not counting the 4-6 months for initial training or yearly summer camps. All other civilians are classified as nonveterans. Note: While it is possible for 17 year olds to be veterans of the Armed Forces, ACS data products are restricted to the population 18 years and older. *Source: U.S. Census Bureau, American Community Survey, 2009-2013 Five-Year Estimates*

Ancestry: Largest ancestry groups reported (up to five). The data includes persons who report multiple ancestries. For example, if a person reported being Irish and Italian, they would be included in both categories. Thus, the sum of the percentages may be greater than 100%. *Source: U.S. Census Bureau, American Community Survey, 2009-2013 Five-Year Estimates*

The data represent self-classification by people according to the ancestry group or groups with which they most closely identify. Ancestry refers to a person's ethnic origin or descent, "roots," heritage, or the place of birth of the person, the person's parents, or their ancestors before their arrival in the United States. Some ethnic identities, such as Egyptian or Polish, can be traced to geographic areas outside the United States, while other ethnicities such as Pennsylvania German or Cajun evolved in the United States.

The ancestry question was intended to provide data for groups that were not included in the Hispanic origin and race questions. Therefore, although data on all groups are collected, the ancestry data shown in these tabulations are for non-Hispanic and non-race groups. *See* Race/Hispanic Origin for information on Hispanic and race groups.

EMPLOYMENT

Employment by Occupation: Percentage of the employed civilian population 16 years and over in management, professional, service, sales, farming, construction, and production occupations. *Source: U.S. Census Bureau, American Community Survey, 2009-2013 Five-Year Estimates*

- Management, business, and financial occupations include:
  - Management occupations
  - Business and financial operations occupations
- Computer, engineering, and science occupations include:
  - Computer and mathematical occupations
  - Architecture and engineering occupations
  - Life, physical, and social science occupations
- Education, legal, community service, arts, and media occupations include:
  - Community and social service occupations
  - Legal occupations
  - Education, training, and library occupations
  - Arts, design, entertainment, sports, and media occupations
- Healthcare practitioners and technical occupations include:
  - Health diagnosing and treating practitioners and other technical occupations
  - Health technologists and technicians
- Service occupations include:
  - Healthcare support occupations
  - Protective service occupations:
    - Fire fighting and prevention, and other protective service workers including supervisors
    - Law enforcement workers including supervisors
  - Food preparation and serving related occupations
  - Building and grounds cleaning and maintenance occupations
  - Personal care and service occupations

- Sales and office occupations include:
    Sales and related occupations
    Office and administrative support occupations

- Natural resources, construction, and maintenance occupations include:
    Farming, fishing, and forestry occupations
    Construction and extraction occupations
    Installation, maintenance, and repair occupations

- Production, transportation, and material moving occupations include:
    Production occupations
    Transportation occupations
    Material moving occupations

INCOME

Per Capita Income: Per capita income is the mean income computed for every man, woman, and child in a particular group. It is derived by dividing the total income of a particular group by the total population in that group. Per capita income is rounded to the nearest whole dollar. *Source: U.S. Census Bureau, American Community Survey, 2009-2013 Five-Year Estimates*

Median Household Income: Includes the income of the householder and all other individuals 15 years old and over in the household, whether they are related to the householder or not. The median divides the income distribution into two equal parts: one-half of the cases falling below the median income and one-half above the median. For households, the median income is based on the distribution of the total number of households including those with no income. Median income for households is computed on the basis of a standard distribution and is rounded to the nearest whole dollar. *Source: U.S. Census Bureau, American Community Survey, 2009-2013 Five-Year Estimates*

Average Household Income: Average household income is obtained by dividing total household income by the total number of households. *Source: U.S. Census Bureau, American Community Survey, 2009-2013 Five-Year Estimates*

Percent of Households with Income of $100,000 or more: Percent of households with income of $100,000 or more. *Source: U.S. Census Bureau, American Community Survey, 2009-2013 Five-Year Estimates*

Poverty Rate: Percentage of population with income below the poverty level. Based on individuals for whom poverty status is determined. Poverty status was determined for all people except institutionalized people, people in military group quarters, people in college dormitories, and unrelated individuals under 15 years old. *Source: U.S. Census Bureau, American Community Survey, 2009-2013 Five-Year Estimates*

EDUCATIONAL ATTAINMENT

Figures show the percent of population age 25 and over with the following levels of educational attainment. *Source: U.S. Census Bureau, American Community Survey, 2009-2013 Five-Year Estimates*

- **High school diploma or higher.** Includes people whose highest degree is a high school diploma or its equivalent (GED), people who attended college but did not receive a degree, and people who received a college, university, or professional degree.
- **Bachelor's degree or higher.** Includes people who received a bachelor's, master's, doctorate, or professional degree.
- **Graduate/professional degree or higher.** Includes people who received a master's, doctorate, or professional degree.

SCHOOL DISTRICTS

Lists the name of each school district, the grade range (PK=pre-kindergarten; KG=kindergarten), the student enrollment, and the district headquarters' phone number. In each community profile, only school districts that have schools that are physically located within the community are shown. In addition, statistics for each school district cover the entire district, regardless of the physical location of the schools within the district. *Source: U.S. Department of Education, National Center for Educational Statistics, Directory of Public Elementary and Secondary Education Agencies, 2012-13*

COLLEGES

Four-year Colleges: Lists the name of each four-year college, the type of institution (private or public; for-profit or non-profit; religious affiliation; historically black), the total estimated student enrollment in 2013, the general telephone number, and the annual tuition and fees for full-time, first-time undergraduate students (in-state and out-of-state). *Source: U.S. Department of Education, National Center for Educational Statistics, IPEDS College Data, 2013-14*

Two-year Colleges: Lists the name of each two-year college, the type of institution (private or public; for-profit or non-profit; religious affiliation; historically black), the total estimated student enrollment in 2013, the general telephone number, and the annual tuition and fees for full-time, first-time undergraduate students (in-state and out-of-state). *Source: U.S. Department of Education, National Center for Educational Statistics, IPEDS College Data, 2013-14*

Vocational/Technical Schools: Lists the name of each vocational/technical school, the type of institution (private or public; for-profit or non-profit; religious affiliation; historically black), the total estimated student enrollment in 2013, the general telephone number, and the annual tuition and fees for full-time students. *Source: U.S. Department of Education, National Center for Educational Statistics, IPEDS College Data, 2013-14*

HOUSING

Homeownership Rate: Percentage of housing units that are owner-occupied. *Source: U.S. Census Bureau, Census 2010*

Median Home Value: Median value in dollars of all owner-occupied housing units as reported by the owner. *Source: U.S. Census Bureau, American Community Survey, 2009-2013 Five-Year Estimates*

Median Year Structure Built: Year structure built refers to when the building was first constructed, not when it was remodeled, added to, or converted. For mobile homes, houseboats, RVs, etc, the manufacturer's model year was assumed to be the year built. The data relate to the number of units built during the specified periods that were still in existence at the time of enumeration. *Source: U.S. Census Bureau, American Community Survey, 2009-2013 Five-Year Estimates*

Homeowner Vacancy Rate: Proportion of the homeowner inventory that is vacant "for sale." It is computed by dividing the number of vacant units "for sale only" by the sum of the owner-occupied units, vacant units that are "for sale only," and vacant units that have been sold but not yet occupied, and then multiplying by 100. This measure is rounded to the nearest tenth. *Source: U.S. Census Bureau, Census 2010*

Median Gross Rent: Median monthly gross rent in dollars on specified renter-occupied and specified vacant-for-rent units. Specified renter-occupied and specified vacant-for-rent units exclude 1-family houses on 10 acres or more. Gross rent is the contract rent plus the estimated average monthly cost of utilities (electricity, gas, and water and sewer) and fuels (oil, coal, kerosene, wood, etc.) if these are paid by the renter (or paid for the renter by someone else). Gross rent is intended to eliminate differentials that result from varying practices with respect to the inclusion of utilities and fuels as part of the rental payment. Contract rent is the monthly rent agreed to or contracted for, regardless of any furnishings, utilities, fees, meals, or services that may be included. For vacant units, it is the monthly rent asked for the rental unit at the time of enumeration. *Source: U.S. Census Bureau, American Community Survey, 2009-2013 Five-Year Estimates*

Rental Vacancy Rate: Proportion of the rental inventory that is vacant "for rent." It is computed by dividing the number of vacant units "for rent" by the sum of the renter-occupied units, vacant units that are "for rent," and vacant units that have been rented but not yet occupied, and then multiplying by 100. This measure is rounded to the nearest tenth. *Source: U.S. Census Bureau, Census 2010*

HEALTH INSURANCE

Health insurance coverage in the ACS and other Census Bureau surveys define coverage to include plans and programs that provide comprehensive health coverage. Plans that provide insurance for specific conditions or situations such as cancer and long-term care policies are not considered coverage. Likewise, other types of insurance like dental, vision, life, and disability insurance are not considered health insurance coverage.

For reporting purposes, the Census Bureau broadly classifies health insurance coverage as private health insurance or public coverage. Private health insurance is a plan provided through an employer or union, a plan purchased by an individual from a private company, or TRICARE or other military health care. Public health coverage includes the federal programs Medicare, Medicaid, and VA Health Care (provided through the Department of Veterans Affairs); the Children's Health Insurance Program (CHIP); and individual state health plans. The types of health insurance are not mutually exclusive; people may be covered by more than one at the same time. People who had no reported health coverage, or those whose only health coverage was Indian Health Service, were considered uninsured. *Source: U.S. Census Bureau, American Community Survey, 2009-2013 Five-Year Estimates*

- **Have Insurance:** Percent of the civilian noninstitutionalized population with any type of comprehensive health insurance.
- **Have Private Insurance.** Percent of the civilian noninstitutionalized population with private health insurance. A person may report that they have both public and private health insurance, thus, the sum of the percentages may be greater than 100%.
- **Have Public Insurance.** Percent of the civilian noninstitutionalized population with public health insurance. A person may report that they have both public and private health insurance, thus, the sum of the percentages may be greater than 100%.
- **Do Not Have Insurance.** Percent of the civilian noninstitutionalized population with no health insurance.
- **Children Under 18 With No Insurance.** Percent of the civilian noninstitutionalized population under age 18 with no health insurance.

HOSPITALS

Lists the hospital name and the number of licensed beds. *Source: Grey House Publishing, The Comparative Guide to American Hospitals, 2014*

NEWSPAPERS

List of daily and weekly newspapers with circulation figures. *Source: Gebbie Press, 2015 All-In-One Media Directory*

SAFETY

Violent Crime Rate: Number of violent crimes reported per 10,000 population. Violent crimes include murder, forcible rape, robbery, and aggravated assault. *Source: Federal Bureau of Investigation, Uniform Crime Reports 2013*

Property Crime Rate: Number of property crimes reported per 10,000 population. Property crimes include burglary, larceny-theft, and motor vehicle theft. *Source: Federal Bureau of Investigation, Uniform Crime Reports 2013*

TRANSPORTATION

Commute to Work: Percentage of workers 16 years old and over that use the following means of transportation to commute to work: car; public transportation; walk; work from home. The means of transportation data for some areas may show workers using modes of public transportation that are not available in those areas (e.g. subway or elevated riders in a metropolitan area where there actually is no subway or elevated service). This result is largely due to people who worked during the reference week at a location that was different from their usual place of work (such as people away from home on business in an area where subway service was available) and people who used more than one means of transportation each day but whose principal means was unavailable where they lived (e.g. residents of non-metropolitan areas who drove to the fringe of a metropolitan area and took the commuter railroad most of the distance to work). *Source: U.S. Census Bureau, American Community Survey, 2009-2013 Five-Year Estimates*

Median Travel Time to Work: Median travel time to work for workers 16 years old and over. Travel time to work refers to the total number of minutes that it usually took the person to get from home to work each day during the reference week. The elapsed time includes time spent waiting for public transportation, picking up passengers in carpools, and time spent in other activities related to getting to work. *Source: U.S. Census Bureau, American Community Survey, 2009-2013 Five-Year Estimates*

Amtrak: Indicates if Amtrak rail or bus service is available. Please note that the cities being served continually change. *Source: National Railroad Passenger Corporation, Amtrak National Timetable, 2015*

AIRPORTS

Lists the local airport(s) along with type of service and hub size. *Source: U.S. Department of Transportation, Bureau of Transportation Statistics*

ADDITIONAL INFORMATION CONTACTS

General telephone number and website address (if available) of local government.

User Guide: Education Section

School District Rankings

Number of Schools: Total number of schools in the district. *Source: U.S. Department of Education, National Center for Education Statistics, Common Core of Data, Public Elementary/Secondary School Universe Survey: School Year 2011-2012.*

Number of Teachers: Teachers are defined as individuals who provide instruction to pre-kindergarten, kindergarten, grades 1 through 12, or ungraded classes, or individuals who teach in an environment other than a classroom setting, and who maintain daily student attendance records. Numbers reported are full-time equivalents (FTE). *Source: U.S. Department of Education, National Center for Education Statistics, Common Core of Data, Local Education Agency (School District) Universe Survey: School Year 2011-2012.*

Number of Students: A student is an individual for whom instruction is provided in an elementary or secondary education program that is not an adult education program and is under the jurisdiction of a school, school system, or other education institution. *Sources: U.S. Department of Education, National Center for Education Statistics, Common Core of Data, Local Education Agency (School District) Universe Survey: School Year 2011-2012 and Public Elementary/Secondary School Universe Survey: School Year 2011-2012*

Individual Education Program (IEP) Students: A written instructional plan for students with disabilities designated as special education students under IDEA-Part B. The written instructional plan includes a statement of present levels of educational performance of a child; statement of annual goals, including short-term instructional objectives; statement of specific educational services to be provided and the extent to which the child will be able to participate in regular educational programs; the projected date for initiation and anticipated duration of services; the appropriate objectives, criteria and evaluation procedures; and the schedules for determining, on at least an annual basis, whether instructional objectives are being achieved. *Source: U.S. Department of Education, National Center for Education Statistics, Common Core of Data, Local Education Agency (School District) Universe Survey: School Year 2011-2012*

English Language Learner (ELL) Students: Formerly referred to as Limited English Proficient (LEP). Students being served in appropriate programs of language assistance (e.g., English as a Second Language, High Intensity Language Training, bilingual education). Does not include pupils enrolled in a class to learn a language other than English. Also Limited-English-Proficient students are individuals who were not born in the United States or whose native language is a language other than English; or individuals who come from environments where a language other than English is dominant; or individuals who are American Indians and Alaskan Natives and who come from environments where a language other than English has had a significant impact on their level of English language proficiency; and who, by reason thereof, have sufficient difficulty speaking, reading, writing, or understanding the English language, to deny such individuals the opportunity to learn successfully in classrooms where the language of instruction is English or to participate fully in our society. *Source: U.S. Department of Education, National Center for Education Statistics, Common Core of Data, Local Education Agency (School District) Universe Survey: School Year 2011-2012*

Students Eligible for Free Lunch Program: The free lunch program is defined as a program under the National School Lunch Act that provides cash subsidies for free lunches to students based on family size and income criteria. *Source: U.S. Department of Education, National Center for Education Statistics, Common Core of Data, Public Elementary/Secondary School Universe Survey: School Year 2011-2012*

Students Eligible for Reduced-Price Lunch Program: A student who is eligible to participate in the Reduced-Price Lunch Program under the National School Lunch Act. *Source: U.S. Department of Education, National Center for Education Statistics, Common Core of Data, Public Elementary/Secondary School Universe Survey: School Year 2011-2012*

Student/Teacher Ratio: The number of students divided by the number of teachers (FTE). See Number of Students and Number of Teachers above for for information.

Student/Librarian Ratio: The number of students divided by the number of library and media support staff. Library and media support staff are defined as staff members who render other professional library and media services; also includes library aides and those involved in library/media support. Their duties include selecting, preparing, caring for, and making available to instructional staff, equipment, films, filmstrips, transparencies, tapes, TV programs, and similar materials maintained separately or as part of an instructional materials center. Also included are activities in the audio-visual center, TV studio, related-work-study areas, and services provided by audio-visual personnel.

Numbers are based on full-time equivalents. *Source: U.S. Department of Education, National Center for Education Statistics, Common Core of Data, Local Education Agency (School District) Universe Survey: School Year 2011-2012.*

Student/Counselor Ratio: The number of students divided by the number of guidance counselors. Guidance counselors are professional staff assigned specific duties and school time for any of the following activities in an elementary or secondary setting: counseling with students and parents; consulting with other staff members on learning problems; evaluating student abilities; assisting students in making educational and career choices; assisting students in personal and social development; providing referral assistance; and/or working with other staff members in planning and conducting guidance programs for students. The state applies its own standards in apportioning the aggregate of guidance counselors/directors into the elementary and secondary level components. Numbers reported are full-time equivalents. *Source: U.S. Department of Education, National Center for Education Statistics, Common Core of Data, Local Education Agency (School District) Universe Survey: School Year 2011-2012.*

Current Spending per Student: Expenditure for Instruction, Support Services, and Other Elementary/Secondary Programs. Includes salaries, employee benefits, purchased services, and supplies, as well as payments made by states on behalf of school districts. Also includes transfers made by school districts into their own retirement system. Excludes expenditure for Non-Elementary/Secondary Programs, debt service, capital outlay, and transfers to other governments or school districts. This item is formally called "Current Expenditures for Public Elementary/Secondary Education."

Instruction: Includes payments from all funds for salaries, employee benefits, supplies, materials, and contractual services for elementary/secondary instruction. It excludes capital outlay, debt service, and interfund transfers for elementary/secondary instruction. Instruction covers regular, special, and vocational programs offered in both the regular school year and summer school. It excludes instructional support activities as well as adult education and community services. Instruction salaries includes salaries for teachers and teacher aides and assistants.

Support Services: Relates to support services functions (series 2000) defined in Financial Accounting for Local and State School Systems (National Center for Education Statistics 2000). Includes payments from all funds for salaries, employee benefits, supplies, materials, and contractual services. It excludes capital outlay, debt service, and interfund transfers. It includes expenditure for the following functions:

- Business/Central/Other Support Services
- General Administration
- Instructional Staff Support
- Operation and Maintenance
- Pupil Support Services
- Pupil Transportation Services
- School Administration
- Nonspecified Support Services

Values shown are dollars per pupil per year. They were calculated by dividing the total dollar amounts by the fall membership. Fall membership is comprised of the total student enrollment on October 1 (or the closest school day to October 1) for all grade levels (including prekindergarten and kindergarten) and ungraded pupils. Membership includes students both present and absent on the measurement day. *Source: U.S. Department of Education, National Center for Education Statistics, Common Core of Data, School District Finance Survey (F-33), Fiscal Year 2011.*

Drop-out Rate: A dropout is a student who was enrolled in school at some time during the previous school year; was not enrolled at the beginning of the current school year; has not graduated from high school or completed a state or district approved educational program; and does not meet any of the following exclusionary conditions: has transferred to another public school district, private school, or state- or district-approved educational program; is temporarily absent due to suspension or school-approved illness; or has died. The values shown cover grades 9 through 12. *Note: Drop-out rates are no longer available to the general public disaggregated by grade, race/ethnicity, and gender at the school district level. Beginning with the 2005–06 school year the CCD is reporting dropout data aggregated from the local education agency (district) level to the state level. This allows data users to compare event dropout rates across states, regions, and other jurisdictions. Source: U.S. Department of Education, National Center for Education Statistics, Common Core of Data, Local Education Agency (School District) Universe Survey Dropout and Completion Data, 2008-2009; U.S. Department of Education, National Center for Education Statistics, Common Core of Data, State Dropout and Completion Data File, 2009-2010*

Average Freshman Graduation Rate (AFGR): The AFGR is the number of regular diploma recipients in a given year divided by the average of the membership in grades 8, 9, and 10, reported 5, 4, and 3 years earlier, respectively. For example, the denominator of the 2008–09 AFGR is the average of the 8th-grade membership in 2004–05, 9th-grade membership in 2005–06, and 10th-grade membership in 2006–07. Ungraded students are prorated into these grades. Averaging these three grades provides an estimate of the number of first-time freshmen in the class of 2005–06 freshmen in order to estimate the on-time graduation rate for 2008–09.

Caution in interpreting the AFGR. Although the AFGR was selected as the best of the available alternatives, several factors make it fall short of a true on-time graduation rate. First, the AFGR does not take into account any imbalances in the number of students moving in and out of the nation or individual states over the high school years. As a result, the averaged freshman class is at best an approximation of the actual number of freshmen, where differences in the rates of transfers, retention, and dropping out in the three grades affect the average. Second, by including all graduates in a specific year, the graduates may include students who repeated a grade in high school or completed high school early and thus are not on-time graduates in that year. *Source: U.S. Department of Education, National Center for Education Statistics, Common Core of Data, Local Education Agency (School District) Universe Survey Dropout and Completion Data, 2008-2009; U.S. Department of Education, National Center for Education Statistics, Common Core of Data, State Dropout and Completion Data File, 2009-2010*

Number of Diploma Recipients: A student who has received a diploma during the previous school year or subsequent summer school. This category includes regular diploma recipients and other diploma recipients. A High School Diploma is a formal document certifying the successful completion of a secondary school program prescribed by the state education agency or other appropriate body. *Note: Diploma counts are no longer available to the general public disaggregated by grade, race/ethnicity, and gender at the school district level. Source: U.S. Department of Education, National Center for Education Statistics, Common Core of Data, Local Education Agency (School District) Universe Survey Dropout and Completion Data, 2008-2009; U.S. Department of Education, National Center for Education Statistics, Common Core of Data, State Dropout and Completion Data File, 2009-2010*

Note: n/a indicates data not available.

State Educational Profile

Please refer to the District Rankings section in the front of this User Guide for an explanation of data for all items except for the following:

Average Salary: The average salary for classroom teachers in 2013-2014. *Source: National Education Association, Rankings & Estimates: Rankings of the States 2013 and Estimates of School Statistics 2014*

College Entrance Exam Scores:

Scholastic Aptitude Test (SAT). *Note: Data covers all students during the 2013 school year. The College Board strongly discourages the comparison or ranking of states on the basis of SAT scores alone. Source: The College Board*

American College Testing Program (ACT). *Note: Data covers all students during the 2013 school year. Source: ACT, 2013 ACT National and State Scores*

National Assessment of Educational Progress (NAEP)

The National Assessment of Educational Progress (NAEP), also known as "the Nation's Report Card," is the only nationally representative and continuing assessment of what America's students know and can do in various subject areas. As a result of the "No Child Left Behind" legislation, all states are required to participate in NAEP.

For more information, visit the U.S. Department of Education, National Center for Education Statistics at http://nces.ed.gov/nationsreportcard.

User Guide: Ancestry and Ethnicity Section

Places Covered

The ancestry and ethnicity profile section of this book covers the state, all counties, and all places with populations of 50,000 or more. Places included fall into one of the following categories:

Incorporated Places. Depending on the state, places are incorporated as either cities, towns, villages, boroughs, municipalities, independent cities, or corporations. A few municipalities have a form of government combined with another entity (e.g. county) and are listed as special cities or consolidated, unified, or metropolitan governments.

Census Designated Places (CDP). The U.S. Census Bureau defines a CDP as "a statistical entity," defined for each decennial census according to Census Bureau guidelines, comprising a densely settled concentration of population that is not within an incorporated place, but is locally identified by a name. CDPs are delineated cooperatively by state and local officials and the Census Bureau, following Census Bureau guidelines.

Minor Civil Divisions (called charter townships, districts, gores, grants, locations, plantations, purchases, reservations, towns, townships, and unorganized territories) for the states where the Census Bureau has determined that they serve as general-purpose governments. Those states are Connecticut, Maine, Massachusetts, Michigan, Minnesota, New Hampshire, New Jersey, New York, Pennsylvania, Rhode Island, Vermont, and Wisconsin. In some states incorporated municipalities are part of minor civil divisions and in some states they are independent of them.

Note: Several states have incorporated municipalities and minor civil divisions in the same county with the same name. Those communities are given separate entries (e.g. Burlington, New Jersey, in Burlington County will be listed under both the city and township of Burlington). A few states have Census Designated Places and minor civil divisions in the same county with the same name. Those communities are given separate entries (e.g. Bridgewater, Massachusetts, in Plymouth County will be listed under both the CDP and town of Bridgewater).

Source of Data

The ethnicities shown in this book were compiled from two different sources. Data for Race and Hispanic Origin was taken from Census 2010 Summary File 1 (SF1) while Ancestry data was taken from the American Community Survey (ACS) 2006-2010 Five-Year Estimate. The distinction is important because SF1 contains 100-percent data, which is the information compiled from the questions asked of all people and about every housing unit. ACS estimates are compiled from a sampling of households. The 2006-2010 Five-Year Estimate is based on data collected from January 1, 2006 to December 31, 2010.

The American Community Survey (ACS) is a relatively new survey conducted by the U.S. Census Bureau. It uses a series of monthly samples to produce annually updated data for the same small areas (census tracts and block groups) formerly surveyed via the decennial census long-form sample. While some version of this survey has been in the field since 1999, it was not fully implemented in terms of coverage until 2006. In 2005 it was expanded to cover all counties in the country and the 1-in-40 households sampling rate was first applied. The full implementation of the (household) sampling strategy for ACS entails having the survey mailed to about 250,000 households nationwide every month of every year and was begun in January 2005. In January 2006 sampling of group quarters was added to complete the sample as planned. In any given year about 2.5% (1 in 40) of U.S. households will receive the survey. Over any 5-year period about 1 in 8 households should receive the survey (as compared to about 1 in 6 that received the census long form in the 2000 census). Since receiving the survey is not the same as responding to it, the Bureau has adopted a strategy of sampling for non-response, resulting in something closer to 1 in 11 households actually participating in the survey over any 5-year period. For more information about the American Community Survey visit http://www.census.gov/acs/www.

Ancestry

Ancestry refers to a person's ethnic origin, heritage, descent, or "roots," which may reflect their place of birth or that of previous generations of their family. Some ethnic identities, such as "Egyptian" or "Polish" can be traced to geographic areas outside the United States, while other ethnicities such as "Pennsylvania German" or "Cajun" evolved in the United States.

The intent of the ancestry question in the ACS was not to measure the degree of attachment the respondent had to a particular ethnicity, but simply to establish that the respondent had a connection to and self-identified with a particular ethnic group. For example, a response of "Irish" might reflect total involvement in an Irish community or only a memory of ancestors several generations removed from the respondent.

The Census Bureau coded the responses into a numeric representation of over 1,000 categories. Responses initially were processed through an automated coding system; then, those that were not automatically assigned a code were coded by individuals trained in coding ancestry responses. The code list reflects the results of the Census Bureau's own research and consultations with many ethnic experts. Many decisions were made to determine the classification of responses. These decisions affected the grouping of the tabulated data. For example, the "Indonesian" category includes the responses of "Indonesian," "Celebesian," "Moluccan," and a number of other responses.

Ancestries Covered

- Afghan
- African, Sub-Saharan
  - African
  - Cape Verdean
  - Ethiopian
  - Ghanaian
  - Kenyan
  - Liberian
  - Nigerian
  - Senegalese
  - Sierra Leonean
  - Somalian
  - South African
  - Sudanese
  - Ugandan
  - Zimbabwean
  - Other Sub-Saharan African
- Albanian
- Alsatian
- American
- Arab
  - Arab
  - Egyptian
  - Iraqi
  - Jordanian
  - Lebanese
  - Moroccan
  - Palestinian
  - Syrian
  - Other Arab
- Armenian
- Assyrian/Chaldean/Syriac
- Australian
- Austrian
- Basque
- Belgian
- Brazilian
- British
- Bulgarian
- Cajun
- Canadian
- Carpatho Rusyn
- Celtic
- Croatian
- Cypriot
- Czech
- Czechoslovakian
- Danish
- Dutch
- Eastern European
- English
- Estonian
- European
- Finnish
- French, ex. Basque
- French Canadian
- German
- German Russian
- Greek
- Guyanese
- Hungarian
- Icelander
- Iranian
- Irish
- Israeli
- Italian
- Latvian
- Lithuanian
- Luxemburger
- Macedonian
- Maltese
- New Zealander
- Northern European
- Norwegian
- Pennsylvania German
- Polish
- Portuguese
- Romanian
- Russian
- Scandinavian
- Scotch-Irish
- Scottish
- Serbian
- Slavic
- Slovak
- Slovene
- Soviet Union
- Swedish
- Swiss
- Turkish
- Ukrainian
- Welsh
- West Indian, ex. Hispanic
  - Bahamian
  - Barbadian
  - Belizean
  - Bermudan
  - British West Indian
  - Dutch West Indian
  - Haitian
  - Jamaican
  - Trinidadian/Tobagonian
  - U.S. Virgin Islander
  - West Indian
  - Other West Indian
- Yugoslavian

The ancestry question allowed respondents to report one or more ancestry groups. Generally, only the first two responses reported were coded. If a response was in terms of a dual ancestry, for example, "Irish English," the person was assigned two codes, in this case one for Irish and another for English. However, in certain cases, multiple responses such as "French Canadian," "Scotch-Irish," "Greek Cypriot," and "Black Dutch" were assigned a single code reflecting their status as unique groups. If a person reported one of these unique groups in addition to another group, for example, "Scotch-Irish English," resulting in three terms, that person received one code for the unique group (Scotch-Irish) and another one for the remaining group (English). If a person reported "English Irish French," only English and Irish were coded. If there were more than two ancestries listed and one of the ancestries was a part of another, such as "German Bavarian Hawaiian," the responses were coded using the more detailed groups (Bavarian and Hawaiian).

The Census Bureau accepted "American" as a unique ethnicity if it was given alone or with one other ancestry. There were some groups such as "American Indian," "Mexican American," and "African American" that were coded and identified separately.

The ancestry question is asked for every person in the American Community Survey, regardless of age, place of birth, Hispanic origin, or race.

Although some people consider religious affiliation a component of ethnic identity, the ancestry question was not designed to collect any information concerning religion. Thus, if a religion was given as an answer to the ancestry question, it was listed in the "Other groups" category which is not shown in this book.

Ancestry should not be confused with a person's place of birth, although a person's place of birth and ancestry may be the same.

Hispanic Origin

The data on the Hispanic or Latino population were derived from answers to a Census 2010 question that was asked of all people. The terms "Spanish," "Hispanic origin," and "Latino" are used interchangeably. Some respondents identify with all three terms while others may identify with only one of these three specific terms. Hispanics or Latinos who identify with the terms "Spanish," "Hispanic," or "Latino" are those who classify themselves in one of the specific Spanish, Hispanic, or Latino categories listed on the questionnaire ("Mexican," "Puerto Rican," or "Cuban") as well as those who indicate that they are "other Spanish/Hispanic/Latino." People who do not identify with one of the specific origins listed on the questionnaire but indicate that they are "other Spanish/Hispanic/Latino" are those whose origins are from Spain, the Spanish-speaking countries of Central or South America, the Dominican Republic, or people identifying themselves generally as Spanish, Spanish-American, Hispanic, Hispano, Latino, and so on. All write-in responses to the "other Spanish/Hispanic/Latino" category were coded.

Hispanic Origins Covered

Hispanic or Latino
- Central American, ex. Mexican
  - Costa Rican
  - Guatemalan
  - Honduran
  - Nicaraguan
  - Panamanian
  - Salvadoran
  - Other Central American
- Cuban
- Dominican Republic
- Mexican
- Puerto Rican
- South American
  - Argentinean
  - Bolivian
  - Chilean
  - Colombian
  - Ecuadorian
  - Paraguayan
  - Peruvian
  - Uruguayan
  - Venezuelan
  - Other South American
- Other Hispanic or Latino

Origin can be viewed as the heritage, nationality group, lineage, or country of birth of the person or the person's parents or ancestors before their arrival in the United States. People who identify their origin as Hispanic, Latino, or Spanish may be of any race.

Ethnicities Based on Race

The data on race were derived from answers to the Census 2010 question on race that was asked of individuals in the United States. The Census Bureau collects racial data in accordance with guidelines provided by the U.S. Office of Management and Budget (OMB), and these data are based on self-identification.

The racial categories included in the census questionnaire generally reflect a social definition of race recognized in this country and not an attempt to define race biologically, anthropologically, or genetically. In addition, it is recognized that the categories of the race item include racial and national origin or sociocultural groups. People may choose to report more than one race to indicate their racial mixture, such as "American Indian" and "White." People who identify their origin as Hispanic, Latino, or Spanish may be of any race.

Racial Groups Covered

African-American/Black
- *Not Hispanic*
- *Hispanic*

American Indian/Alaska Native
- *Not Hispanic*
- *Hispanic*
- Alaska Athabascan *(Ala. Nat.)*
- Aleut *(Alaska Native)*
- Apache
- Arapaho
- Blackfeet
- Canadian/French Am. Indian
- Central American Indian
- Cherokee
- Cheyenne
- Chickasaw
- Chippewa
- Choctaw
- Colville
- Comanche
- Cree
- Creek
- Crow
- Delaware
- Hopi
- Houma
- Inupiat *(Alaska Native)*
- Iroquois
- Kiowa
- Lumbee
- Menominee
- Mexican American Indian
- Navajo
- Osage
- Ottawa
- Paiute
- Pima
- Potawatomi
- Pueblo
- Puget Sound Salish
- Seminole
- Shoshone
- Sioux
- South American Indian
- Spanish American Indian
- Tlingit-Haida *(Alaska Native)*
- Tohono O'Odham
- Tsimshian *(Alaska Native)*
- Ute
- Yakama
- Yaqui
- Yuman
- Yup'ik *(Alaska Native)*

Asian
- *Not Hispanic*
- *Hispanic*
- Bangladeshi
- Bhutanese
- Burmese
- Cambodian
- Chinese, ex. Taiwanese
- Filipino
- Hmong
- Indian
- Indonesian
- Japanese
- Korean
- Laotian
- Malaysian
- Nepalese
- Pakistani
- Sri Lankan
- Taiwanese
- Thai
- Vietnamese

Hawaii Native/Pacific Islander
- *Not Hispanic*
- *Hispanic*
- Fijian
- Guamanian/Chamorro
- Marshallese
- Native Hawaiian
- Samoan
- Tongan

White
- *Not Hispanic*
- *Hispanic*

African American or Black: A person having origins in any of the Black racial groups of Africa. It includes people who indicated their race(s) as "Black, African Am., or Negro" or reported entries such as African American, Kenyan, Nigerian, or Haitian.

American Indian or Alaska Native: A person having origins in any of the original peoples of North and South America (including Central America) and who maintains tribal affiliation or community attachment. This category includes people who indicated their race(s) as "American Indian or Alaska Native" or reported their enrolled or principal tribe, such as Navajo, Blackfeet, Inupiat, Yup'ik, or Central American Indian groups or South American Indian groups.

Asian: A person having origins in any of the original peoples of the Far East, Southeast Asia, or the Indian subcontinent, including, for example, Cambodia, China, India, Japan, Korea, Malaysia, Pakistan, the Philippine Islands, Thailand, and Vietnam. It includes people who indicated their race(s) as "Asian" or reported entries such as "Asian Indian," "Chinese," "Filipino," "Korean," "Japanese," "Vietnamese," and "Other Asian" or provided other detailed Asian responses.

Native Hawaiian or Other Pacific Islander: A person having origins in any of the original peoples of Hawaii, Guam, Samoa, or other Pacific Islands. It includes people who indicated their race(s) as "Pacific Islander" or reported entries such as "Native Hawaiian," "Guamanian or Chamorro," "Samoan," and "Other Pacific Islander" or provided other detailed Pacific Islander responses.

White: A person having origins in any of the original peoples of Europe, the Middle East, or North Africa. It includes people who indicated their race(s) as "White" or reported entries such as Irish, German, Italian, Lebanese, Arab, Moroccan, or Caucasian.

Profiles

Each profile shows the name of the place, the county (if a place spans more than one county, the county that holds the majority of the population is shown), and the 2010 population (based on 100-percent data from Census 2010 Summary File 1). The rest of each profile is comprised of all 218 ethnicities grouped into three sections: ancestry; Hispanic origin; and race.

Column one displays the ancestry/Hispanic origin/race name, column two displays the number of people reporting each ancestry/Hispanic origin/race, and column three is the percent of the total population reporting each ancestry/Hispanic origin/race. The population figure shown is used to calculate the value in the "%" column for ethnicities based on race and Hispanic origin. The 2006-2010 estimated population figure from the American Community Survey (not shown) is used to calculate the value in the "%" column for all other ancestries.

For ethnicities in the ancestries group, the value in the "Number" column includes multiple ancestries reported. For example, if a person reported a multiple ancestry such as "French Danish," that response was counted twice in the tabulations, once in the French category and again in the Danish category. Thus, the sum of the counts is not the total population but the total of all responses. Numbers in parentheses indicate the number of people reporting a single ancestry. People reporting a single ancestry includes all people who reported only one ethnic group such as "German." Also included in this category are people with only a multiple-term response such as "Scotch-Irish" who are assigned a single code because they represent one distinct group. For example, the count for German would be interpreted as "The number of people who reported that German was their only ancestry."

For ethnicities based on Hispanic origin, the value in the "Number" column represents the number of people who reported being Mexican, Puerto Rican, Cuban or other Spanish/Hispanic/ Latino (all written-in responses were coded). All ethnicities based on Hispanic origin can be of any race.

For ethnicities based on race data the value in the "Number" column represents the total number of people who reported each category alone or in combination with one or more other race categories. This number represents the maximum number of people reporting and therefore the individual race categories may add up to more than the total population because people may be included in more than one category. The figures in parentheses show the number of people that reported that particular ethnicity alone, not in combination with any other race. For example, in Alabama, the entry for Korean shows 8,320 in parentheses and 10,624 in the "Number" column. This means that 8,320 people reported being Korean alone and 10,624 people reported being Korean alone or in combination with one or more other races.

Rankings

In the rankings section, each ethnicity has three tables. The first table shows the top 10 places sorted by ethnic population (based on all places, regardless of total population), the second table shows the top 10 places sorted by percent of the total population (based on all places, regardless of total population), the third table shows the top 10 places sorted by percent of the total population (based on places with total population of 50,000 or more).

Within each table, column one displays the place name, the state, and the county (if a place spans more than one county, the county that holds the majority of the population is shown). Column one in the first table displays the state only. Column two displays the number of people reporting each ancestry (includes people reporting multiple ancestries), Hispanic origin, or race (alone or in combination with any other race). Column three is the percent of the total population reporting each ancestry, Hispanic origin or race. For tables representing ethnicities based on race or Hispanic origin, the 100-percent population figure from SF1 is used to calculate the value in the "%" column. For all other ancestries, the 2006-2010 five-year estimated population figure from the American Community Survey is used to calculate the value in the "%" column.

Alphabetical Ethnicity Cross-Reference Guide

Afghan *see* Ancestry–Afghan
African *see* Ancestry–African, Sub-Saharan: African
African-American *see* Race–African-American/Black
African-American: Hispanic *see* Race–African-American/Black: Hispanic
African-American: Not Hispanic *see* Race–African-American/Black: Not Hispanic
Alaska Athabascan *see* Race–Alaska Native: Alaska Athabascan
Alaska Native *see* Race–American Indian/Alaska Native
Alaska Native: Hispanic *see* Race–American Indian/Alaska Native: Hispanic
Alaska Native: Not Hispanic *see* Race–American Indian/Alaska Native: Not Hispanic
Albanian *see* Ancestry–Albanian
Aleut *see* Race–Alaska Native: Aleut
Alsatian *see* Ancestry–Alsatian
American *see* Ancestry–American
American Indian *see* Race–American Indian/Alaska Native
American Indian: Hispanic *see* Race–American Indian/Alaska Native: Hispanic
American Indian: Not Hispanic *see* Race–American Indian/Alaska Native: Not Hispanic
Apache *see* Race–American Indian: Apache
Arab *see* Ancestry–Arab: Arab
Arab: Other *see* Ancestry–Arab: Other
Arapaho *see* Race–American Indian: Arapaho
Argentinean *see* Hispanic Origin–South American: Argentinean
Armenian *see* Ancestry–Armenian
Asian *see* Race–Asian
Asian Indian *see* Race–Asian: Indian
Asian: Hispanic *see* Race–Asian: Hispanic
Asian: Not Hispanic *see* Race–Asian: Not Hispanic
Assyrian *see* Ancestry–Assyrian/Chaldean/Syriac
Australian *see* Ancestry–Australian
Austrian *see* Ancestry–Austrian
Bahamian *see* Ancestry–West Indian: Bahamian, except Hispanic
Bangladeshi *see* Race–Asian: Bangladeshi
Barbadian *see* Ancestry–West Indian: Barbadian, except Hispanic
Basque *see* Ancestry–Basque
Belgian *see* Ancestry–Belgian
Belizean *see* Ancestry–West Indian: Belizean, except Hispanic
Bermudan *see* Ancestry–West Indian: Bermudan, except Hispanic
Bhutanese *see* Race–Asian: Bhutanese
Black *see* Race–African-American/Black
Black: Hispanic *see* Race–African-American/Black: Hispanic
Black: Not Hispanic *see* Race–African-American/Black: Not Hispanic
Blackfeet *see* Race–American Indian: Blackfeet
Bolivian *see* Hispanic Origin–South American: Bolivian
Brazilian *see* Ancestry–Brazilian
British *see* Ancestry–British

British West Indian *see* Ancestry–West Indian: British West Indian, except Hispanic
Bulgarian *see* Ancestry–Bulgarian
Burmese *see* Race–Asian: Burmese
Cajun *see* Ancestry–Cajun
Cambodian *see* Race–Asian: Cambodian
Canadian *see* Ancestry–Canadian
Canadian/French American Indian *see* Race–American Indian: Canadian/French American Indian
Cape Verdean *see* Ancestry–African, Sub-Saharan: Cape Verdean
Carpatho Rusyn *see* Ancestry–Carpatho Rusyn
Celtic *see* Ancestry–Celtic
Central American *see* Hispanic Origin–Central American, except Mexican
Central American Indian *see* Race–American Indian: Central American Indian
Central American: Other *see* Hispanic Origin–Central American: Other Central American
Chaldean *see* Ancestry–Assyrian/Chaldean/Syriac
Chamorro *see* Race–Hawaii Native/Pacific Islander: Guamanian or Chamorro
Cherokee *see* Race–American Indian: Cherokee
Cheyenne *see* Race–American Indian: Cheyenne
Chickasaw *see* Race–American Indian: Chickasaw
Chilean *see* Hispanic Origin–South American: Chilean
Chinese (except Taiwanese) *see* Race–Asian: Chinese, except Taiwanese
Chippewa *see* Race–American Indian: Chippewa
Choctaw *see* Race–American Indian: Choctaw
Colombian *see* Hispanic Origin–South American: Colombian
Colville *see* Race–American Indian: Colville
Comanche *see* Race–American Indian: Comanche
Costa Rican *see* Hispanic Origin–Central American: Costa Rican
Cree *see* Race–American Indian: Cree
Creek *see* Race–American Indian: Creek
Croatian *see* Ancestry–Croatian
Crow *see* Race–American Indian: Crow
Cuban *see* Hispanic Origin–Cuban
Cypriot *see* Ancestry–Cypriot
Czech *see* Ancestry–Czech
Czechoslovakian *see* Ancestry–Czechoslovakian
Danish *see* Ancestry–Danish
Delaware *see* Race–American Indian: Delaware
Dominican Republic *see* Hispanic Origin–Dominican Republic
Dutch *see* Ancestry–Dutch
Dutch West Indian *see* Ancestry–West Indian: Dutch West Indian, except Hispanic
Eastern European *see* Ancestry–Eastern European
Ecuadorian *see* Hispanic Origin–South American: Ecuadorian
Egyptian *see* Ancestry–Arab: Egyptian
English *see* Ancestry–English
Eskimo *see* Race–Alaska Native: Inupiat
Estonian *see* Ancestry–Estonian
Ethiopian *see* Ancestry–African, Sub-Saharan: Ethiopian
European *see* Ancestry–European
Fijian *see* Race–Hawaii Native/Pacific Islander: Fijian
Filipino *see* Race–Asian: Filipino
Finnish *see* Ancestry–Finnish
French (except Basque) *see* Ancestry–French, except Basque
French Canadian *see* Ancestry–French Canadian
German *see* Ancestry–German
German Russian *see* Ancestry–German Russian
Ghanaian *see* Ancestry–African, Sub-Saharan: Ghanaian
Greek *see* Ancestry–Greek
Guamanian *see* Race–Hawaii Native/Pacific Islander: Guamanian or Chamorro
Guatemalan *see* Hispanic Origin–Central American: Guatemalan
Guyanese *see* Ancestry–Guyanese
Haitian *see* Ancestry–West Indian: Haitian, except Hispanic
Hawaii Native *see* Race–Hawaii Native/Pacific Islander
Hawaii Native: Hispanic *see* Race–Hawaii Native/Pacific Islander: Hispanic

Pueblo *see* Race–American Indian: Pueblo
Puerto Rican *see* Hispanic Origin–Puerto Rican
Puget Sound Salish *see* Race–American Indian: Puget Sound Salish
Romanian *see* Ancestry–Romanian
Russian *see* Ancestry–Russian
Salvadoran *see* Hispanic Origin–Central American: Salvadoran
Samoan *see* Race–Hawaii Native/Pacific Islander: Samoan
Scandinavian *see* Ancestry–Scandinavian
Scotch-Irish *see* Ancestry–Scotch-Irish
Scottish *see* Ancestry–Scottish
Seminole *see* Race–American Indian: Seminole
Senegalese *see* Ancestry–African, Sub-Saharan: Senegalese
Serbian *see* Ancestry–Serbian
Shoshone *see* Race–American Indian: Shoshone
Sierra Leonean *see* Ancestry–African, Sub-Saharan: Sierra Leonean
Sioux *see* Race–American Indian: Sioux
Slavic *see* Ancestry–Slavic
Slovak *see* Ancestry–Slovak
Slovene *see* Ancestry–Slovene
Somalian *see* Ancestry–African, Sub-Saharan: Somalian
South African *see* Ancestry–African, Sub-Saharan: South African
South American *see* Hispanic Origin–South American
South American Indian *see* Race–American Indian: South American Indian
South American: Other *see* Hispanic Origin–South American: Other South American
Soviet Union *see* Ancestry–Soviet Union
Spanish American Indian *see* Race–American Indian: Spanish American Indian
Sri Lankan *see* Race–Asian: Sri Lankan
Sub-Saharan African *see* Ancestry–African, Sub-Saharan
Sub-Saharan African: Other *see* Ancestry–African, Sub-Saharan: Other
Sudanese *see* Ancestry–African, Sub-Saharan: Sudanese
Swedish *see* Ancestry–Swedish
Swiss *see* Ancestry–Swiss
Syriac *see* Ancestry–Assyrian/Chaldean/Syriac
Syrian *see* Ancestry–Arab: Syrian
Taiwanese *see* Race–Asian: Taiwanese
Thai *see* Race–Asian: Thai
Tlingit-Haida *see* Race–Alaska Native: Tlingit-Haida
Tohono O'Odham *see* Race–American Indian: Tohono O'Odham
Tongan *see* Race–Hawaii Native/Pacific Islander: Tongan
Trinidadian and Tobagonian *see* Ancestry–West Indian: Trinidadian and Tobagonian, except Hispanic
Tsimshian *see* Race–Alaska Native: Tsimshian
Turkish *see* Ancestry–Turkish
U.S. Virgin Islander *see* Ancestry–West Indian: U.S. Virgin Islander, except Hispanic
Ugandan *see* Ancestry–African, Sub-Saharan: Ugandan
Ukrainian *see* Ancestry–Ukrainian
Uruguayan *see* Hispanic Origin–South American: Uruguayan
Ute *see* Race–American Indian: Ute
Venezuelan *see* Hispanic Origin–South American: Venezuelan
Vietnamese *see* Race–Asian: Vietnamese
Welsh *see* Ancestry–Welsh
West Indian *see* Ancestry–West Indian: West Indian, except Hispanic
West Indian (except Hispanic) *see* Ancestry–West Indian, except Hispanic
West Indian: Other *see* Ancestry–West Indian: Other, except Hispanic
White *see* Race–White
White: Hispanic *see* Race–White: Hispanic
White: Not Hispanic *see* Race–White: Not Hispanic
Yakama *see* Race–American Indian: Yakama
Yaqui *see* Race–American Indian: Yaqui
Yugoslavian *see* Ancestry–Yugoslavian
Yuman *see* Race–American Indian: Yuman
Yup'ik *see* Race–Alaska Native: Yup'ik
Zimbabwean *see* Ancestry–African, Sub-Saharan: Zimbabwean

User Guide: Climate Section

SOURCES OF THE DATA

The National Climactic Data Center (NCDC) has two main classes or types of weather stations; first-order stations which are staffed by professional meteorologists and cooperative stations which are staffed by volunteers. All National Weather Service (NWS) stations included in this book are first-order stations.

The data in the climate section is compiled from several sources. The majority comes from the original NCDC computer tapes (DSI-3220 Summary of Month Cooperative). This data was used to create the entire table for each cooperative station and part of each National Weather Service station. The remainder of the data for each NWS station comes from the International Station Meteorological Climate Summary, Version 4.0, September 1996, which is also available from the NCDC.

Storm events come from the NCDC Storm Events Database which is accessible over the Internet at http://www4.ncdc.noaa.gov/ cgi-win/wwcgi.dll?wwevent~storms.

WEATHER STATION TABLES

The weather station tables are grouped by type (National Weather Service and Cooperative) and then arranged alphabetically. The station name is almost always a place name, and is shown here just as it appears in NCDC data. The station name is followed by the county in which the station is located (or by county equivalent name), the elevation of the station (at the time beginning of the thirty year period) and the latitude and longitude.

The National Weather Service Station tables contain 32 data elements which were compiled from two different sources, the International Station Meteorological Climate Summary (ISMCS) and NCDC DSI-3220 data tapes. The following 13 elements are from the ISMCS: maximum precipitation, minimum precipitation, maximum snowfall, maximum 24-hour snowfall, thunderstorm days, foggy days, predominant sky cover, relative humidity (morning and afternoon), dewpoint, wind speed and direction, and maximum wind gust. The remaining 19 elements come from the DSI-3220 data tapes. The period of record (POR) for data from the DSI-3220 data tapes is 1980-2009. The POR for ISMCS data varies from station to station and appears in a note below each station.

The Cooperative Station tables contain 19 data elements which were all compiled from the DSI-3220 data tapes with a POR of 1980-2009.

WEATHER ELEMENTS (NWS AND COOPERATIVE STATIONS)

The following elements were compiled by the editor from the NCDC DSI-3220 data tapes using a period of record of 1980-2009.

The average temperatures (maximum, minimum, and mean) are the average (see Methodology below) of those temperatures for all available values for a given month. For example, for a given station the average maximum temperature for July is the arithmetic average of all available maximum July temperatures for that station. (Maximum means the highest recorded temperature, minimum means the lowest recorded temperature, and mean means an arithmetic average temperature.)

The extreme maximum temperature is the highest temperature recorded in each month over the period 1980-2009. The extreme minimum temperature is the lowest temperature recorded in each month over the same time period. The extreme maximum daily precipitation is the largest amount of precipitation recorded over a 24-hour period in each month from 1980-2009. The maximum snow depth is the maximum snow depth recorded in each month over the period 1980-2009.

The days for maximum temperature and minimum temperature are the average number of days those criteria were met for all available instances. The symbol ≥ means greater than or equal to, the symbol ≤ means less than or equal to. For example, for a given station, the number of days the maximum temperature was greater than or equal to 90°F in July, is just an arithmetic average of the number of days in all the available Julys for that station.

Heating and cooling degree days are based on the median temperature for a given day and its variance from 65°F. For example, for a given station if the day's high temperature was 50°F and the day's low temperature was 30°F, the median (midpoint) temperature was 40°F. 40°F is 25 degrees below 65°F, hence on this day there would be 25 heating degree days. This also applies for cooling degree days. For example, for a given station if the day's high temperature was 80°F and the day's low temperature was 70°F, the median (midpoint) temperature was 75°F. 75°F is 10 degrees above 65°F, hence on this day there would be 10 cooling degree days. All heating and/or cooling degree days in a month are summed for the month giving respective totals for each element for that month. These sums for a given month for a given station over the past thirty years are again summed and then arithmetically averaged. It should be noted that the heating and cooling degree days do not cancel each other out. It is possible to have both for a given station in the same month.

Precipitation data is computed the same as heating and cooling degree days. Mean precipitation and mean snowfall are arithmetic averages of cumulative totals for the month. All available values for the thirty year period for a given month for a given station are summed and then divided by the number of values. The same is true for days of greater than or equal to 0.1", 0.5",and 1.0" of precipitation, and days of greater than or equal to 1.0" of snow depth on the ground. The word trace appears for precipitation and snowfall amounts that are too small to measure.

Finally, remember that all values presented in the tables and the rankings are averages, maximums, or minimums of available data (see Methodology below) for that specific data element for the last thirty years (1980-2009).

WEATHER ELEMENTS (NWS STATIONS ONLY)

The following elements were taken directly from the International Station Meteorological Climate Summary. The periods of records vary per station and are noted at the bottom of each table.

Maximum precipitation, minimum precipitation, maximum snowfall, maximum snow depth, maximum 24-hour snowfall, thunderstorm days, foggy days, relative humidity (morning and afternoon), dewpoint, prevailing wind speed and direction, and maximum wind gust are all self-explanatory.

The word trace appears for precipitation and snowfall amounts that are too small to measure.

Predominant sky cover contains four possible entries: CLR (clear); SCT (scattered); BRK (broken); and OVR (overcast).

INCLUSION CRITERIA—HOW STATIONS WERE SELECTED

The basic criteria is that a station must have data for temperature, precipitation, heating and cooling degree days of sufficient quantity in order to create a meaningful average. More specifically, the definition of sufficiency here has two parts. First, there must be 22 values for a given data element, and second, ten of the nineteen elements included in the table must pass this sufficiency test. For example, in regard to mean maximum temperature (the first element on every data table), a given station needs to have a value for every month of at least 22 of the last thirty years in order to meet the criteria, and, in addition, every station included must have at least ten of the nineteen elements with at least this minimal level of completeness in order to fulfill the criteria. We then removed stations that were geographically close together, giving preference to stations with better data quality.

METHODOLOGY

The following discussion applies only to data compiled from the NCDC DSI-3220 data tapes and excludes weather elements that are extreme maximums or minimums.

The data is based on an arithmetic average of all available data for a specific data element at a given station. For example, the average maximum daily high temperature during July for any given station was abstracted from NCDC source tapes for the thirty Julys, starting in July, 1980 and ending in July, 2009. These thirty figures were then summed and divided by thirty to produce an arithmetic average. As might be expected, there were not thirty values for every data element on every table. For a variety of reasons, NCDC data is sometimes incomplete. Thus the following standards were established.

For those data elements where there were 26-30 values, the data was taken to be essentially complete and an average was computed. For data elements where there were 22-25 values, the data was taken as being partly complete but still valid enough to use to compute an average. Such averages are shown in ***bold italic*** type to indicate that there was less than 26 values. For the few data elements where there were not even 22 values, no average was computed and 'na' appears in the space. If any of the twelve months for a given data element reported a value of 'na', no annual average was computed and the annual average was reported as 'na' as well.

Thus the basic computational methodology used is designed to provide an arithmetic average. Because of this, such a pure arithmetic average is somewhat different from the special type of average (called a "normal") which NCDC procedures produces and appears in federal publications.

Perhaps the best outline of the contrasting normalization methodology is found in the following paragraph (which appears as part of an NCDC technical document titled, CLIM81 1961-1990 NORMALS TD-9641 prepared by Lewis France of NCDC in May, 1992):

Normals have been defined as the arithmetic mean of a climatological element computed over a long time period. International agreements eventually led to the decision that the appropriate time period would be three consecutive decades (Guttman, 1989). The data record should be consistent (have no changes in location, instruments, observation practices, etc.; these are identified here as "exposure changes") and have no missing values so a normal will reflect the actual average climatic conditions. If any significant exposure changes have occurred, the data record is said to be "inhomogeneous," and the normal may not reflect a true climatic average. Such data need to be adjusted to remove the nonclimatic inhomogeneities. The resulting (adjusted) record is then said to be "homogeneous." If no exposure changes have occurred at a station, the normal is calculated simply by averaging the appropriate 30 values from the 1961-1990 record.

In the main, there are two "inhomogeneities" that NCDC is correcting for with normalization: adjusting for variances in time of day of observation (at the so-called First Order stations data is based on midnight to midnight observation times and this practice is not necessarily followed at cooperative stations which are staffed by volunteers), and second, estimating data that is either missing or incongruent.

The editors had some concerns regarding the comparative results of the two methodologies. Would our methodology produce strikingly different results than NCDC's? To allay concerns, results of the two processes were compared for the time period normalized results are available (1971-2000). In short, what was found was that the answer to this question is no. Never the less, users should be aware that because of both the time period covered (1980-2009) and the methodology used, data is not compatible with data from other sources.

POTENTIAL CAUTIONS

First, as with any statistical reference work of this type, users need to be aware of the source of the data. The information here comes from NOAA, and it is the most comprehensive and reliable core data available. Although it is the best, it is not perfect. Most weather stations are staffed by volunteers, times of observation sometimes vary, stations occasionally are moved (especially over a thirty year period), equipment is changed or upgraded, and all of these factors affect the uniformity of the data. The editors do not attempt to correct for these factors, and this data is not intended for either climatologists or atmospheric scientists. Users with concerns about data collection and reporting protocols are both referred to NCDC technical documentation.

Second, users need to be aware of the methodology here which is described above. Although this methodology has produced fully satisfactory results, it is not directly compatible with other methodologies, hence variances in the results published here and those which appear in other publications will doubtlessly arise.

Third, is the trap of that informal logical fallacy known as "hasty generalization," and its corollaries. This may involve presuming the future will be like the past (specifically, next year will be an average year), or it may involve misunderstanding the limitations of an arithmetic average, but more interestingly, it may involve those mistakes made most innocently by generalizing informally on too broad a basis. As weather is highly localized, the data should be taken in that context. A weather station collects data about climatic conditions at that spot, and that spot may or may not be an effective paradigm for an entire town or area.

About California

Governor	**Edmund G. "Jerry" Brown, Jr. (D)**
Lt Governor	**Gavin Newsom (D)**
State Capital	Sacramento
Date of Statehood	September 9, 1850 (31st state)
State Nickname	The Golden State
Largest City	Los Angeles
Highest Point	Mount Whitney (14,505 feet)
Lowest Point	Badwater Basin in Death Valley (-282 feet)
State Animal	California Grizzly Bear *(Ursus californicus)*
State Bird	California Valley Quail *(Lophortyx californica)*
State Colors	Blue and Gold
State Dance	West Coast Swing Dance
State Fish	California Golden Trout *(Salmo aqua bonita)*
State Flower	Golden Poppy *(Eschscholzia)*
State Folk Dance	Square Dance
State Fossil	Sabre-Toothed Cat *(Smilodon californicus)*
State Gemstone	Benitoite
State Grass	Purple Needlegrass *(Nassella pulchra)*
State Insect	California Dogface Butterfly *(Zerene eurydice)*
State Marine Fish	Garibaldi *(Hypsypops rubicundus)*
State Marine Mammal	California Gray Whale *(Eschrichtius robustus)*
State Marine Reptile	Pacific Leatherback Sea Turtle *(Dermochelys coriacea)*
State Reptile	California Desert Tortoise *(Gopherus agasizzii)*
State Rock	Serpentine
State Soil	San Joaquin Soil
State Song	"I Love You, California"
State Tree	Coast Readwood *(Sequoia sempervirens)*; Giant Sequoia *(Sequoia gigantea)*

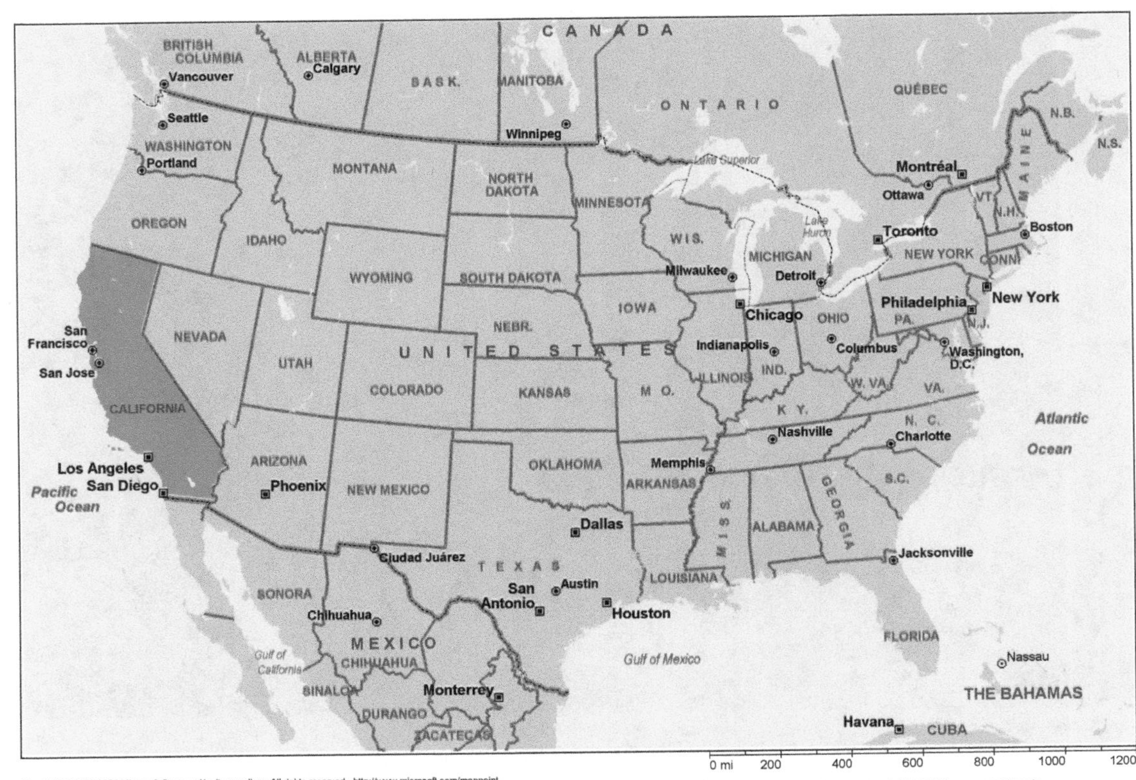

Los Angeles, top, is the most populous city in the state, and second only to New York in the U.S. Noted for the diversity of its residents, Los Angeles is nicknamed City of Angels. The Golden Gate Bridge, bottom, spans the San Francisco Bay, connecting San Francisco, the financial and cultural center of northern California, with the city of Oakland.

The California State Capitol, top, is in the city of Sacramento. The sixth largest city in the state, and the 35th largest in the U.S., Sacramento is located at the confluence of the Sacramento and American Rivers in the northern section of California's Central Valley. This Napa Valley vineyard, bottom, is located in one of nine San Francisco Bay Area counties. Napa County has been known for decades as an outstanding wine producer, winning the Judgment of Paris award in 1976.

Beaches are one of the most popular travel destinations in the world and, with over 1,000 miles of coastline and 118 beaches, California is the most visited state in the country. Due to its size and extreme geographical diversity, California beaches range from hot, sandy and tropical in the south to windy, rocky and rugged in the north. Pictured above is Santa Monica Beach in Los Angeles.

A tribute to those in the entertainment industry, the Hollywood Walk of Fame comprises more than 2,500 five-pointed terrazzo and brass stars, pictured top, embedded in a 1.3 mile stretch in Hollywood, California. The state's three main deserts, Mojave, Colorado, pictured bottom, and the Great Basin, are known for their dramatic natural features and are, along with the Hollywood Walk of Fame, popular tourist destinations.

San Diego, top, is located 120 miles south of Los Angeles. It's the oldest and second largest city in California and the eighth largest city in the United States. San Diego is known for its mild year-round climate, natural deep-water harbor, extensive beaches and, recently, as a healthcare and biotechnology development center. Laguna Beach, bottom, is a seaside resort city and artist community in southern Orange County. It sits 19 miles southeast of the city of Santa Ana, with a population of nearly 23,000.

Container shipping in the port of Oakland, top, is a major part of this northern California city's transportation and trade industries. It's the busiest port is the San Francisco Bay and all of northern California. The Redwood National Park, bottom, sits along the state's northern coast. One of four National State Parks that, together, protect 45% of all remaining coast redwood (Sequoia) old-growth forests, totaling nearly 39,000 acres.

A Brief History of California

European Exploration and Colonization

The first voyage (1542) to Alta California (Upper California), as the region north of Baja California (Lower California) came to be known, was commanded by the Spanish explorer Juan Rodríguez Cabrillo, who explored San Diego Bay and the area farther north along the coast. In 1579 an English expedition headed by Sir Francis Drake landed near Point Reyes, North of San Francisco, and claimed the region for Queen Elizabeth I. In 1602, Sebastián Vizcaíno, another Spaniard, explored the coast and Monterey Bay.

Colonization was slow, but finally in 1769 Gaspar de Portolá, governor of the Californias, led an expedition up the Pacific coast and established a colony on San Diego Bay. The following year he explored the area around Monterey Bay and later returned to establish a presidio there. Soon afterward Monterey became the capital of Alta California. Accompanying Portolá's expedition was Father Junipero Serra, a Franciscan missionary who founded a mission at San Diego. Franciscans later founded several missions that extended as far N as Sonoma, N of San Francisco. The missionaries sought to Christianize the Native Americans but also forced them to work as manual laborers, helping to build the missions into vital agricultural communities. Cattle raising was of primary importance, and hides and tallow were exported. The missions have been preserved and are now open to visitors.

In 1776, Juan Bautista de Anza founded San Francisco, where he established a military outpost. The early colonists, called the Californios, lived a pastoral life and for the most part were not interfered with by the central government of New Spain (as the Spanish empire in the Americas was called) or later (1820s) by that of Mexico. The Californios did, however, become involved in local politics, as when Juan Bautista Alvarado led a revolt (1836) and made himself governor of Alta California, a position he later persuaded the Mexicans to let him keep. Under Mexican rule the missions were secularized (1833–34) and the Native Americans released from their servitude. The degradation of Native American peoples, which continued under Mexican rule and after U.S. settlers came to the area, was described by Helen Hunt Jackson in her novel Ramona (1884). Many mission lands were subsequently given to Californios, who established the great ranchos, vast cattle-raising estates. Colonization of California remained largely Mexican until the 1840s.

Russian and U.S. Settlement

Russian fur traders had penetrated south to the California coast and established Fort Ross, north of San Francisco, in 1812. Jedediah Strong Smith and other trappers made the first U.S. overland trip to the area in 1826, but U.S. settlement did not become significant until the 1840s. In 1839, Swiss-born John Augustus Sutter arrived and established his "kingdom" of New Helvetia on a vast tract in the Sacramento valley. He did much for the overland American immigrants, who began to arrive in large numbers in 1841. Some newcomers met with tragedy, including the Donner Party, which was stranded in the Sierra Nevada after a heavy snowstorm.

Political events in the territory moved swiftly in the next few years. After having briefly asserted the independence of California in 1836, the Californios drove out the last Mexican governor in 1845. Under the influence of the American explorer John C. Frémont, U.S. settlers set up (1846) a republic at Sonoma under their unique Bear Flag. The news of war between the United States and Mexico (1846–48) reached California soon afterward. On July 7, 1846, Commodore John D. Sloat captured Monterey, the capital, and claimed California for the United States. The Californios in the north worked with U.S. soldiers, but those in the south resisted U.S. martial law. In 1847, however, U.S. Gen. Stephen W. Kearny defeated the southern Californios. By the Treaty of Guadalupe Hidalgo (1848), Mexico formally ceded the territory to the United States.

The Gold Rush

In 1848, the year that California became a part of the United States, another major event in the state's history occurred: While establishing a sawmill for John Sutter near Coloma, James W. Marshall discovered gold and touched off the California gold rush. The forty-niners, as the gold-rush miners were called, came in droves, spurred by the promise of fabulous riches from the Mother Lode. San Francisco rapidly became a boom city, and its bawdy, lawless coastal area, which became known as the Barbary Coast, gave rise to the vigilantes, extralegal community groups formed to suppress civil disorder. American writers such as Bret Harte and Mark Twain have recorded the local color as well as the violence and human tragedies of the roaring mining camps.

Statehood and Immigration

With the gold rush came a huge increase in population and a pressing need for civil government. In 1849, Californians sought statehood and, after heated debate in the U.S. Congress arising out of the slavery issue, California entered the Union as a free, nonslavery state by the Compromise of 1850. San Jose became the capital. Monterey, Vallejo, and Benicia each served as the capital before it was moved to Sacramento in 1854. In 1853, Congress authorized the survey of a railroad route to link California with the eastern seaboard, but the transcontinental railroad was not completed until 1869. In the meantime communication and transportation depended upon ships, the stagecoach, the pony express, and the telegraph.

Chinese laborers were imported in great numbers to work on railroad construction. The Burlingame Treaty of 1868 provided, among other things, for unrestricted Chinese immigration. That was at first enthusiastically endorsed by Californians; but after a slump in the state's shaky economy, the white settlers viewed the influx of the lower-paid Chinese laborers as an economic threat. Ensuing bitterness and friction led to the Chinese Exclusion Act of 1882.

A railroad-rate war (1884) and a boom in real estate (1885) fostered a new wave of overland immigration. Cattle raising on the ranchos gave way to increased grain production. Vineyards were planted by 1861, and the first trainload of oranges was shipped from Los Angeles in 1886.

Industrialization and Increased Settlement

By the turn of the century the discovery of oil, industrialization resulting from the increase of hydroelectric power, and expanding agricultural development attracted more settlers. Los Angeles grew rapidly in this period and, in population, soon surpassed San Francisco, which suffered greatly after the great earthquake and fire of 1906. Improvements in urban transportation stimulated the growth of both Los Angeles and San Francisco; the advent of the cable car and the electric railway made possible the development of previously inaccessible areas.

As industrious Japanese farmers acquired valuable land and a virtual monopoly of California's truck-farming operations, the issue of Asian immigration again arose. The bitter struggle for the exclusion of Asians plagued international relations, and in 1913 the California Alien Land Act was passed despite President Woodrow Wilson's attempts to block it. The act provided that persons ineligible for U.S. citizenship could not own agricultural land in California.

Successive waves of settlers arrived in California, attracted by a new real-estate boom in the 1920s and by the promise of work in the 1930s. The influx during the 1930s of displaced farm workers, depicted by John Steinbeck in his novel The Grapes of Wrath, caused profound dislocation in the state's economy. During World War II the Japanese in California were removed from their homes and placed in relocation centers. Industry in California expanded rapidly during the war; the production of ships and aircraft attracted many workers who later settled in the state.

Growing Pains and Natural Disasters

Prosperity and rapid population growth continued after the war. Many African Americans who came during World War II to work in the war industries settled in California. By the 1960s they constituted a sizable minority in the state, and racial tensions reached a climax. In 1964, California voters approved an initiative measure, Proposition 14, allowing racial discrimination in the sale or rental of housing in the state, a measure later declared unconstitutional by the U.S. Supreme Court. In 1965 riots broke out in Watts, a predominantly black section of Los Angeles, touching off a wave of riots across the United States. Also in the 1960s migrant farm workers in California formed a union and struck many growers to obtain better pay and working conditions. Unrest also occurred in the state's universities, especially the Univ. of California at Berkeley, where student demonstrations and protests in 1964 provoked disorders.

Republicans generally played a more dominant role than Democrats in California politics during the 20th cent., but by the early 21st cent. the state had become more Democratic. From the end of World War II through the mid-1990s, five of the seven governors were Republicans, starting with Earl Warren (1943–53). Ronald Reagan, a former movie actor and a leading conservative Republican, was elected governor in 1966 and reelected in 1970; he later served two terms as U.S president. The two Democrats were liberals Edmund G. (Pat) Brown (1959–67) and his son Jerry Brown (1975–83). In the late 1970s, Californians staged a "tax revolt" that attracted national attention, passing legislation to cut property taxes.

During the 1970s and 80s California continued to grow rapidly, with a major shift of population to the state's interior. The metropolitan areas of Riverside–San Bernardino, Modesto, Stockton, Bakersfield, and Sacramento were among the fastest growing in the nation during the 1980s. Much of the state's population growth was a result of largely illegal immigration from Mexico; there was also a heavy infux of immigrants from China, the Philippines, and SE Asia.

Population growth and immigration contributed to growing economic pressures, as did cuts in federal defense spending; meanwhile, social tensions also increased. In April, 1992, four white Los Angeles police officers were acquitted of brutality charges after they had been videotaped beating a black motorist; the verdict touched off riots in South-Central Los Angeles and other neighborhoods, resulting in 58 deaths, thousands of arrests, and approximately billion in property damage.

In addition to periodic heavy flooding and brushfires, earthquakes have caused widespread damage in California. In Oct., 1989, a major earthquake killed about 60 people and injured thousands in Santa Cruz and the San Francisco Bay area. In Jan., 1994, an earthquake hit the Northridge area of North Los Angeles, killing some 60 people and causing at least billion in damage.

In a backlash against illegal immigration, California voters in 1994 approved Proposition 187, an initiative barring the state from providing most services—including welfare, education, and nonemergency medical care—to illegal immigrants. Federal courts found much of Proposition 187 unconstitutional; the appeal of their rulings was dropped in 1999, at a time when the state's economy had rebounded and a Democratic administration was in Sacramento.

In late 2000, California began experiencing an electricity crisis as insufficient generating capacity and increasing short-term wholesale prices for power squeezed the state's two largest public utilities, who, under the "deregulation" plan they had agreed to in the early 1990s, were not allowed to pass along their increased costs. As the state worked to come up with both short-term and long-time solutions to the situation, consumers experienced sporadic blackouts and faced large rate hikes under the terms of a bailout plan. The crisis was severe enough that it was expected to slow the state's economic growth. Evidence subsequently emerged of both price gouging and market manipulation by a number of energy companies.

The economic downturn in the early 2000s resulted in enormous budget shortfalls for California's state government, and made Governor Gray Davis increasingly unpopular. A recall petition financed mainly by a Republican congressman who withdrew from the subsequent election led to a vote (Oct., 2003) that removed Davis from office. The actor Arnold Schwarzenegger, a Republican, was elected to succeed him. The year the state experienced devastating wildfires in the greater San Diego area; the area was again hit with particularly dangerous wildfires in 2007. The housing bubble that burst in 2007 and the significant recession that followed it had especially severe consequences in California, both for the state's economy (which experienced unemployment levels not seen since the early 1940s) and government (which again faced enormous budget shortfalls).

Source: The Columbia Electronic Encyclopedia, 6th ed.

California Government

Government at a Glance

The government of California is composed of three branches: the executive, consisting of the Governor of California and the other elected constitutional officers; the legislative, consisting of the California State Legislature, which includes the Assembly and the Senate; and the judicial, consisting of the Supreme Court of California and lower courts.

Government is exercised through state agencies and commissions as well as local governments consisting of counties, cities and special districts including school districts.

The state also allows direct participation of the electorate by initiative, referendum, recall and ratification.

Constitution and Law

California's constitution is one of the longest collections of laws in the world, taking up 110 pages. Part of this length is caused by the fact that many voter initiatives take the form of a constitutional amendment.

The basic form of law in California is a republic, governed by democratically elected state Senators and Assembly members. The governing law is a constitution, interpreted by the California Supreme Court, whose members are appointed by the Governor, and ratified at the next general election. The constitution can be changed by initiatives passed by voters. Initiatives can be proposed by the governor, legislature, or by popular petition, giving California one of the most flexible legal systems in the world.

Many of the individual rights clauses in the state constitution have been construed as protecting rights even broader than the Bill of Rights in the federal constitution.

Executive Branch

California's executive branch is headed by the Governor. Other executive positions are the Lieutenant Governor, Attorney General, Secretary of State, State Treasurer, State Controller, Insurance Commissioner, and the State Superintendent of Public Instruction. All offices are elected separately to concurrent four-year terms. Each officer may be elected to an office a maximum of two times.

The Governor has the powers and responsibilities to: sign or veto laws passed by the Legislature, including a line item veto; appoint judges, subject to ratification by the electorate; propose a state budget; give the annual State of the State address; command the state militia; and grant pardons for any crime, except cases involving impeachment by the Legislature. The Governor and Lieutenant Governor also serve as ex officio members of the University of California Board of Regents and of the California State University Board of Trustees.

The Lieutenant Governor is the President of the California Senate and acts as the governor when the Governor is unable to execute the office, including whenever the Governor leaves the state. As the offices are elected separately, the two could conceivably be from separate parties.

State Agencies

State government is organized into several dozen departments, of which most were, until recently, grouped into several huge Cabinet-level agencies to reduce the number of people who report directly to the Governor. The main Cabinet-level agencies are:

- California Business, Transportation and Housing Agency (BTH)
- California Environmental Protection Agency (Cal/EPA)

- California Health and Human Services Agency (CHHS)
- California Labor and Workforce Development Agency (LWDA)
- California Natural Resources Agency (CNRA)
- California State and Consumer Services Agency (SCSA)
- California Department of Corrections and Rehabilitation (CDCR)

In June 2012, Governor Jerry Brown began to implement a reorganization plan. By July 2013, the business and housing components of BTH were consolidated with the consumer components of SCSA to form the new Business, Consumer Services and Housing Agency; the remainder of SCSA and the Technology Agency merged into the new Government Operations Agency; and the transportation components of BTH along with the formerly separate California Transportation Commission became part of the new Transportation Agency.

Legislative Branch of California

The constitution makes the California legislature bicameral, with a Senate and an Assembly. Virtually all Assembly and Senate district lines are drawn in a way so as to favor one party or the other, and it is rare for a district to suddenly shift party allegiance.

As part of the system of checks and balances, the Legislature has statutory influence over the funding, organization, and procedures used by agencies of the executive branch. It also has the authority to appoint citizens to policy-making committees in the executive branch and to designate members of the Legislature to serve on agency boards. Many appointments made by the governor are subject to legislative approval.

Judicial Branch

The Judiciary of California interprets and applies the law and is defined under the California Constitution, law, and regulations. The judiciary has a hierarchical structure with the Supreme Court at the apex. The Superior Courts are the primary trial courts, and the Courts of Appeal are the primary appellate courts. The Judicial Council is the rule-making arm of the judiciary.

The California Supreme Court consists of the Chief Justice of California and six Associate Justices. The Court has original jurisdiction in a variety of cases, including habeas corpus proceedings, and has discretionary authority to review all the decisions of the California Courts of Appeal, as well as mandatory review responsibility for cases where the death penalty has been imposed.

The Courts of Appeal are the intermediate appellate courts. The state is geographically divided into six appellate districts. Notably, all published California appellate decisions are binding on all Superior Courts, regardless of appellate district.

The Superior Courts are the courts of general jurisdiction that hear and decide any civil or criminal action which is not specially designated to be heard before some other court or governmental agency, like those dealing with workers' compensation. As mandated by the California Constitution, each of the 58 counties in California has a superior court.

Independent Entities

There are many government entities and offices that are under neither executive, legislative, judicial, or local control, but operate independently on a Constitutional, statutory, or common law basis, including Regents of the University of California and California Public Utilities Commission.

California also uses grand juries, with at least one per county. These county-level grand juries are often called civil grand juries because their primary focus is on oversight of government institutions at the county level and lower. They meet at least once per year.

Local Government

California is divided into counties which are legal subdivisions of the state. There are 58 California counties, 480 California cities, and about 3,400 Special Districts and School Districts. Special Districts deliver specific public programs and public facilities to constituents, and are defined as "any agency of the state for the local performance of governmental or proprietary functions within limited boundaries." Much of the government of California is in practice the responsibility of county governments, while cities may provide additional services.

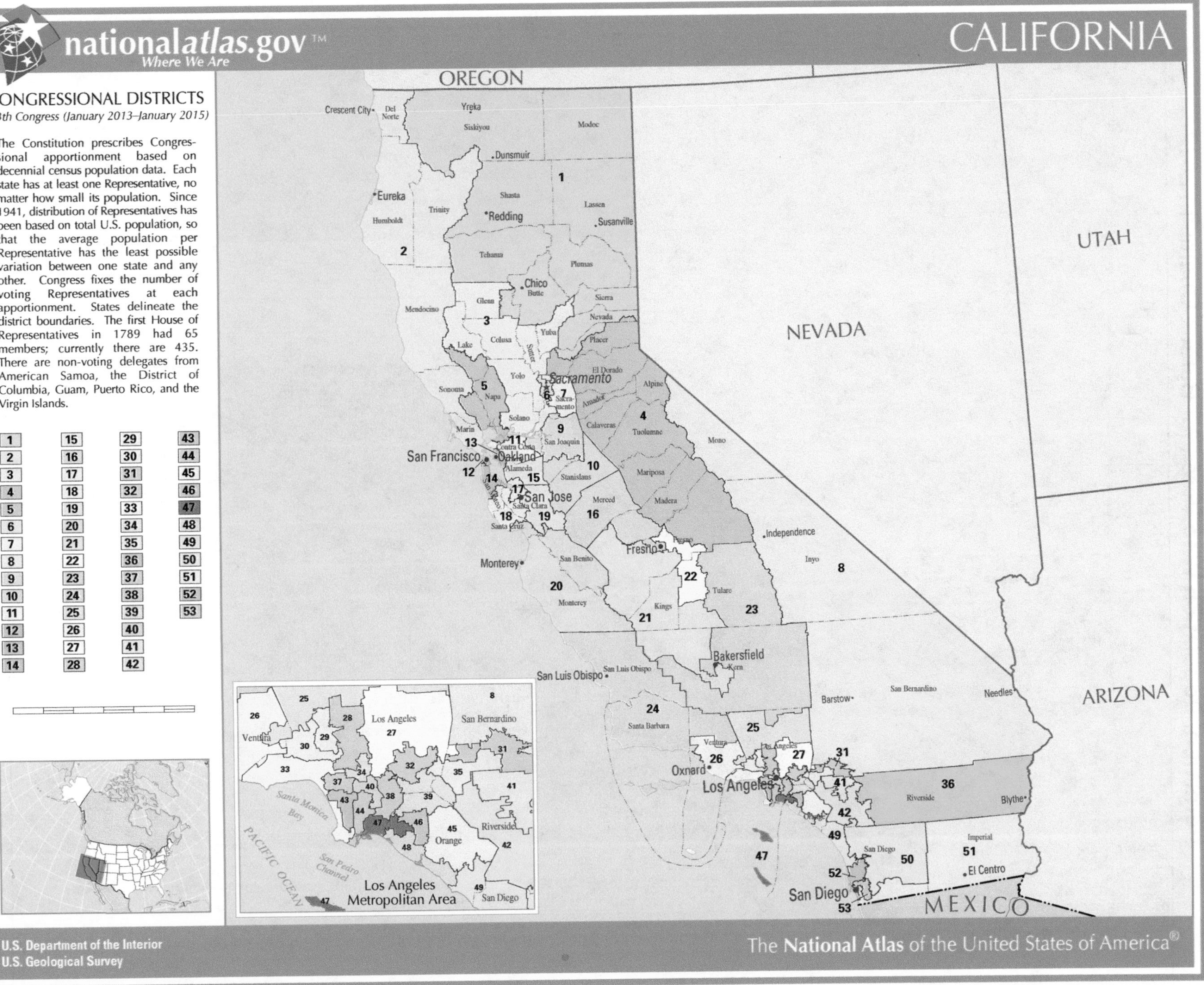
nationalatlas.gov™
Where We Are
CALIFORNIA
CONGRESSIONAL DISTRICTS
113th Congress (January 2013–January 2015)
The Constitution prescribes Congressional apportionment based on decennial census population data. Each state has at least one Representative, no matter how small its population. Since 1941, distribution of Representatives has been based on total U.S. population, so that the average population per Representative has the least possible variation between one state and any other. Congress fixes the number of voting Representatives at each apportionment. States delineate the district boundaries. The first House of Representatives in 1789 had 65 members; currently there are 435. There are non-voting delegates from American Samoa, the District of Columbia, Guam, Puerto Rico, and the Virgin Islands.
1 2 3 4 5 6 7 8 9 10 11 12 13 14
15 16 17 18 19 20 21 22 23 24 25 26 27 28
29 30 31 32 33 34 35 36 37 38 39 40 41 42
43 44 45 46 47 48 49 50 51 52 53
OREGON
NEVADA
UTAH
ARIZONA
MEXICO
Crescent City
Del Norte
Yreka
Siskiyou
Modoc
Dunsmuir
Eureka
Humboldt
Trinity
Shasta
Redding
Lassen
Susanville
Tehama
Plumas
Chico
Butte
Glenn
Mendocino
Sierra
Nevada
Lake
Colusa
Yuba
Sutter
Placer
El Dorado
Sonoma
Napa
Yolo
Sacramento
Alpine
Amador
Solano
Marin
Contra Costa
Calaveras
Tuolumne
San Joaquin
Mono
San Francisco
Oakland
Alameda
Stanislaus
Mariposa
San Mateo
San Jose
Santa Clara
Merced
Madera
Santa Cruz
Monterey
San Benito
Fresno
Independence
Inyo
Kings
Tulare
Bakersfield
Kern
San Luis Obispo
Santa Barbara
Ventura
Oxnard
Los Angeles
Barstow
San Bernardino
Needles
Riverside
Blythe
Orange
San Diego
Imperial
El Centro
Los Angeles Metropolitan Area
Santa Monica Bay
San Pedro Channel
PACIFIC OCEAN
U.S. Department of the Interior
U.S. Geological Survey
The National Atlas of the United States of America®

Percent of Population Who Voted for Barack Obama in 2012

Land and Natural Resources

Topic	Value	Time Period
Total Surface Area (acres)	101,510,200	2007
Land	99,635,300	2007
Federal Land	46,639,000	2007
Owned	4,537,255	FY 2009
Leased	11,807	FY 2009
Otherwise Managed	7,414	FY 2009
National Forest	20,822,000	September 2006
National Wilderness	14,982,645	October 2011
Non-Federal Land, Developed	6,173,800	2007
Non-Federal Land, Rural	46,822,500	2007
Water	1,874,900	2007
National Natural Landmarks	35	December 2010
National Historic Landmarks	138	December 2010
National Register of Historic Places	2,479	December 2010
National Parks	25	December 2010
Visitors to National Parks	34,915,676	2010
Historic Places Documented by the National Park Service	3,310	December 2010
Archeological Sites in National Parks	9,261	December 2010
Threatened and Endangered Species in National Parks	99	December 2010
Economic Benefit from National Park Tourism (dollars)	1,054,833,000	2009
Conservation Reserve Program (acres)	108,870	October 2011
Land and Water Conservation Fund Grants (dollars)	287,823,890	Since 1965
Historic Preservation Grants (dollars)	46,667,855	2010
Community Conservation and Recreation Projects	153	Since 1987
Federal Acres Transferred for Local Parks and Recreation	13,816	Since 1948
Crude Petroleum Production (millions of barrels)	204	2010
Crude Oil Proved Reserves (millions of barrels)	2,835	2009
Natural Gas Reserves (billions of cubic feet)	2,773	2009
Natural Gas Liquid Reserves (millions of barrels)	113	2008
Natural Gas Marketed Production (billions of cubic feet)	277	2009
Coal Reserves (millions of short tons)	Not Available	2009

Sources: *U.S. Department of the Interior, National Park Service, State Profiles, December 2010; United States Department of Agriculture, Natural Resources Conservation Service, 2007 National Resources Inventory; U.S. General Services Administration, Federal Real Property Council, FY 2009 Federal Real Property Report, September 2010; University of Montana, www.wilderness.net; U.S. Department of Agriculture, Farm Services Agency, Conservation Reserve Program, October 2011; U.S Census Bureau, 2012 Statistical Abstract of the United States*

California State Energy Profile

Quick Facts

- Excluding federal offshore areas, California ranked third in the nation in crude oil production in 2013, despite an overall decline in production rates since the mid-1980s.
- California also ranked third in the nation in refining capacity as of January 2014, with a combined capacity of almost 2 million barrels per calendar day from its 18 operable refineries.
- In 2012, California's per capita energy consumption ranked 49th in the nation; the state's low use of energy was due in part to its mild climate and its energy efficiency programs.
- In 2013, California ranked fourth in the nation in conventional hydroelectric generation, second in net electricity generation from other renewable energy resources, and first as a producer of electricity from geothermal energy.
- In 2013, California ranked 15th in net electricity generation from nuclear power after one of its two nuclear plants was taken out of service in January 2012; as of June 2013, operations permanently ceased at that plant, the San Onofre Nuclear Generating Station.
- Average site electricity consumption in California homes is among the lowest in the nation (6.9 megawatthours per year), according to EIA's Residential Energy Consumption Survey.

Source: *U.S. Energy Information Administration, State Profile and Energy Estimates, July 17, 2014*

Analysis

Overview

With the largest economy in the nation, California runs on energy. It is the most populous state and its total energy demand is second only to Texas. California state policy promotes energy efficiency. The state's extensive efforts to increase energy efficiency and the implementation of alternative technologies have restrained energy demand growth. Although it is a leader in the energy-intensive petroleum, chemical, forest product, and food product industries, California has one of the lowest per capita total energy consumption levels in the country.

Transportation dominates California's energy consumption profile. Major airports, military bases, and California's many motorists all contribute to high demand. More motor vehicles are registered in California than in any other state, and commute times in California are among the longest in the country. California leads the nation in registered alternatively fueled vehicles and requires that all California motorists use, at a minimum, a specific blend of gasoline called California Reformulated Gasoline (CaRFG). In ozone non-attainment areas motorists face even stricter requirements and must use California Oxygenated Reformulated Gasoline. As a result, California also leads the nation in retail sales of reformulated gasoline.

In much of the more densely populated areas of the state, the climate is dry and relatively mild. More than two-fifths of state households report that they do not have or do not use their air-conditioning, and residential energy use per person in the state is among the lowest in the nation.

California is also rich in energy resources. The state has an abundant supply of crude oil and is a top producer of conventional hydroelectric power. California also has extensively developed solar, wind, biomass, and geothermal resources that produce significant amounts of energy.

Petroleum

California is oil rich. Even though California's crude oil production has declined overall in the past 25 years, it is one of the top producers of crude oil in the nation, accounting for more than 7% of total U.S. production. Petroleum reservoirs in the geologic basins along the Pacific Coast and in the Central Valley contain large crude oil reserves. The most prolific oil-producing area is the San Joaquin basin in the southern half of the Central Valley.

Federal assessments of the California's offshore areas indicate the potential for large undiscovered reserves of recoverable crude oil and natural gas in the federally administered Outer Continental Shelf (OCS), possibly as much as 10 billion barrels of crude oil and 16 trillion cubic feet of natural gas. A federal moratorium on oil and gas leasing in OCS waters expired in 2008. However, no new lease sales for exploration in California federal offshore waters are currently scheduled. In California, concerns regarding the cumulative impacts and risks of offshore oil and gas development have led to a permanent state moratorium on offshore oil and gas leasing in state waters. Development of state leases acquired prior to 1969 is not affected by this moratorium.

California ranks third in the nation in petroleum refining capacity and accounts for more than one-tenth of the total U.S. capacity. A network of crude oil pipelines connects the state's oil production to the refining centers located in the Central Valley, Los Angeles, and the San Francisco Bay area. California refiners also process large volumes of Alaskan and foreign crude oil received at ports in Los Angeles, Long Beach, and the Bay Area. Crude oil production in California and Alaska has declined, and California refineries have become increasingly dependent on foreign imports to meet the state's needs. Led by Saudi Arabia, Ecuador, Iraq, and Colombia, foreign suppliers now provide more than half of the crude oil refined in California.

California's largest refineries are highly sophisticated and are capable of processing a wide variety of crude oil types. To meet strict federal and state environmental regulations, California refineries are configured to produce cleaner fuels, including reformulated gasoline and low-sulfur diesel. California refineries often operate at or near maximum capacity because of the high demand for those petroleum products. The relative isolation and specific requirements of the California fuel market make California motorists particularly vulnerable to short-term spikes in the price of motor gasoline. When unplanned refinery outages occur, replacement supplies must be brought in by marine tanker. Locating and transporting replacement motor gasoline that conforms to the state's strict fuel specifications can take from two to six weeks.

Natural Gas

As with crude oil production, California's natural gas gross production has experienced a gradual overall decline in the past two decades. Reserves and production are located primarily in geologic basins in the Central Valley, the coastal basins onshore in Northern California, and offshore along the Southern California coast. California production accounts for a very small percentage of total U.S. natural gas production and satisfies about one-tenth of state demand.

Interstate pipelines bring natural gas from Arizona, Nevada, and Oregon into California where markets are served by two key natural gas trading centers—the Golden Gate Center in Northern California and the California Energy Hub in Southern California. As of July 2011, new supply has arrived by way of the Ruby pipeline that extends from Wyoming to Oregon, linking Wyoming natural gas supplies to markets in Northern California. The state also has more than a dozen natural gas storage fields that help stabilize supply; together they have a storage capacity of more than 500 billion cubic feet of natural gas and a working gas capacity of approximately 300 billion cubic feet. California has long exported natural gas to Mexico, but since 2008 has also imported natural gas from Mexico. In May of 2008, operations began at Mexico's liquefied natural gas (LNG) import terminal in Baja, Mexico. Although Baja California in Mexico is the primary market for the terminal's natural gas supply, natural gas not consumed in Mexico will be exported to the southwestern United States, including California, until demand in Mexico reaches the terminal's full capacity.

Coal

California has no coal production and has been phasing out its use of electricity generated by coal-fired power plants. In addition to minor amounts of coal currently consumed at plants in the electric power sector, some coal is also consumed at industrial facilities. Almost all of the coal consumed in California is from mines in Utah and Colorado. Some coal also arrives by rail from western coal mines and is exported to overseas markets from port facilities located primarily in the Los Angeles and San Francisco areas.

Electricity

Because California consumes much more electricity than it generates, about one-fourth of California's electricity comes from outside the state. Overall, the state receives more electricity from outside its borders than any other state in the nation. States in the Pacific Northwest deliver power to California markets that is generated at hydroelectric power plants, and states in the Southwest have, in the past, delivered power primarily generated at coal-fired power plants. Electricity supplied from coal-fired power plants has decreased since the enactment of a state law in late 2006. The law requires California utilities to limit new long-term financial investments in base-load generation to those power plants that meet strict California emissions performance standards.

In-state natural gas-fired power plants account for more than half of California's electricity generation. Until 2012, California's two nuclear power plants with their four reactors typically provided almost one-fifth of the state's total generation. However, the two reactors at the San Onofre nuclear plant were permanently shut down in mid-2013 cutting the amount of electricity generation from nuclear power in half. With adequate snowpack, hydroelectric power typically accounts for between one-tenth and one-fourth of California's total net generation. In the past decade alone, hydroelectric power has averaged one-sixth of the state's net generation. By contrast, only a small amount of the electricity generated within the state comes from coal-fired sources.

In 2000 and 2001, California suffered an energy crisis caused by a supply and demand imbalance characterized by electricity price instability and blackouts. Many factors contributed to this imbalance, including the state's dependence on out-of-state electricity providers, a lack of generation capacity, drought, market manipulations, a pipeline rupture, increased competition with other western states for supply, and unusually high temperatures. Following the crisis, the California state government created an Energy Action Plan that was designed to eliminate outages and excessive price spikes. Its goal was to ensure that adequate, reliable, and reasonably priced electrical power and natural gas supplies, including prudent reserves, were provided. To achieve its goals, the plan called for optimizing energy conservation, building new generation, and upgrading and expanding the electricity transmission and distribution infrastructure to ensure that generation facilities could quickly come online when needed. California imports significant amounts of electricity from neighboring systems, making transmission capability a critical reliability concern. The Sunrise Powerlink Transmission project, which was put into service in June 2012, added approximately 800 megawatts of transmission capability to the Southern California electric grid. The new transmission lines bring electricity generated from renewable energy from Imperial County, in the southeastern corner of the state, to San Diego.

Renewable Energy

California is among the top states in the nation, typically second after Washington, in net electricity generation from renewable resources. A top producer of electricity from conventional hydroelectric power, California is also a leader in net electricity generation from several other renewable energy sources, including geothermal, solar, wind, and biomass. Substantial geothermal resources exist in the coastal mountain ranges and in the volcanic areas of northern California, as well as along the state's borders with Nevada and Mexico. Wind resources are found along the state's many eastern and southern mountain ranges. High solar energy potential is found in southeastern California's deserts. The California Renewable Portfolio Standard sets a goal of 33% of electricity generation from eligible renewable resources by 2020. Eligible resources include wind, solar, geothermal, biomass, biogas, and small hydroelectric generation facilities (less than 30 megawatts).

With over 2,700 megawatts of installed capacity, California is the top producer of electricity from geothermal energy in the nation. The facility known as The Geysers, located in the Mayacamas Mountains north of San Francisco, is the largest complex of geothermal power plants in the world, with more than 700 megawatts of installed capacity. Although wind power potential is widespread, almost three-fourths of the state's land is excluded from development of this resource because the land consists of wilderness area, parks, urban areas, or bodies of water. Even so, the state is a top generator of electricity from wind energy, producing almost 8% of the nation's total, ranking third behind Texas and Iowa. California also leads the nation in the generation of electricity from biomass and solar energy. The world's largest solar thermal plant, located in California's Mojave Desert, began delivering electricity to the grid in early 2014. On a smaller scale, the California Solar Initiative offers cash back for installing solar power systems on rooftops of homes and businesses.

Growing concern over the environment has spurred policy initiatives to reduce greenhouse gas emissions. California's Low Carbon Fuel Standard, issued in January 2007, called for a reduction of at least 10% in the carbon intensity of California's transportation fuels by 2020. The standard requires substitutes for fossil fuels that demonstrate lower lifecycle greenhouse gas emissions than the fuels they replace. A reduction in the carbon intensity of transportation fuels was first required in 2011. A number of alternative pathways have been identified that reduce the levels of greenhouse gas emissions in the production of ethanol, biodiesel, and renewable diesel. California has several ethanol production plants in state, but most of its ethanol supply arrives by rail from the Midwest.

California has also established an emissions cap-and-trade program as part of the state's Global Warming Solutions Act of 2006. The goal of the program is to reduce the state's greenhouse gas emissions (GHG) to their 1990 levels by 2020. Major sources of GHG emissions in the state, including refineries, power plants, industrial facilities, and transportation fuels, must meet a GHG cap that declines over time. To minimize the costs of pollution controls, a system for trading allowable emissions permits was created. The California Air Resources Board held its first auction of the tradable GHG emissions permits for the cap-and-trade program in November 2012. California also has adopted policies to promote increased energy efficiency, including introducing stricter appliance efficiency standards and setting higher standards for public buildings. The state also requires net metering and power source disclosure from utilities.
Source: *U.S. Energy Information Administration, State Profile and Energy Estimates, June 19, 2014*

Energy on Tribal Lands

California leads the nation in the size of its Native American population. The state is home to more than 100 federally recognized tribal groups. Although tribal areas are spread throughout the state, they account for less than 1% of state lands. Many of the tribal lands are small, including the nation's smallest reservation, the 1.32 acre Pit River Tribe cemetery. The Colorado River Tribe Reservation, one of the nation's 50 largest reservations, straddles the California-Arizona border, but only about 70 square miles of its almost 450 square mile area is within California.

California's diverse geography gives tribal lands access to a variety of renewable energy resources. A number of tribes are developing those resources. The Campo Kumeyaay Nation in Southern California was the first tribe in the nation to develop a large-scale wind project. Its 25 wind turbines generate enough electricity annually to supply about 30,000 homes. Several California reservations have abundant solar power potential. Others, particularly in Northern California, are in areas of abundant biomass potential. The Blue Lake Rancheria Tribe in Humboldt County uses wood waste from timber harvesting to fuel a first-of-a-kind biogas fuel cell system. Geothermal resources underlie several reservations in the state, particularly in the Imperial Valley in the southern-most part of California and along the state's eastern boundary.
Source: *U.S. Energy Information Administration, State Profile and Energy Estimates, October 16, 2014*

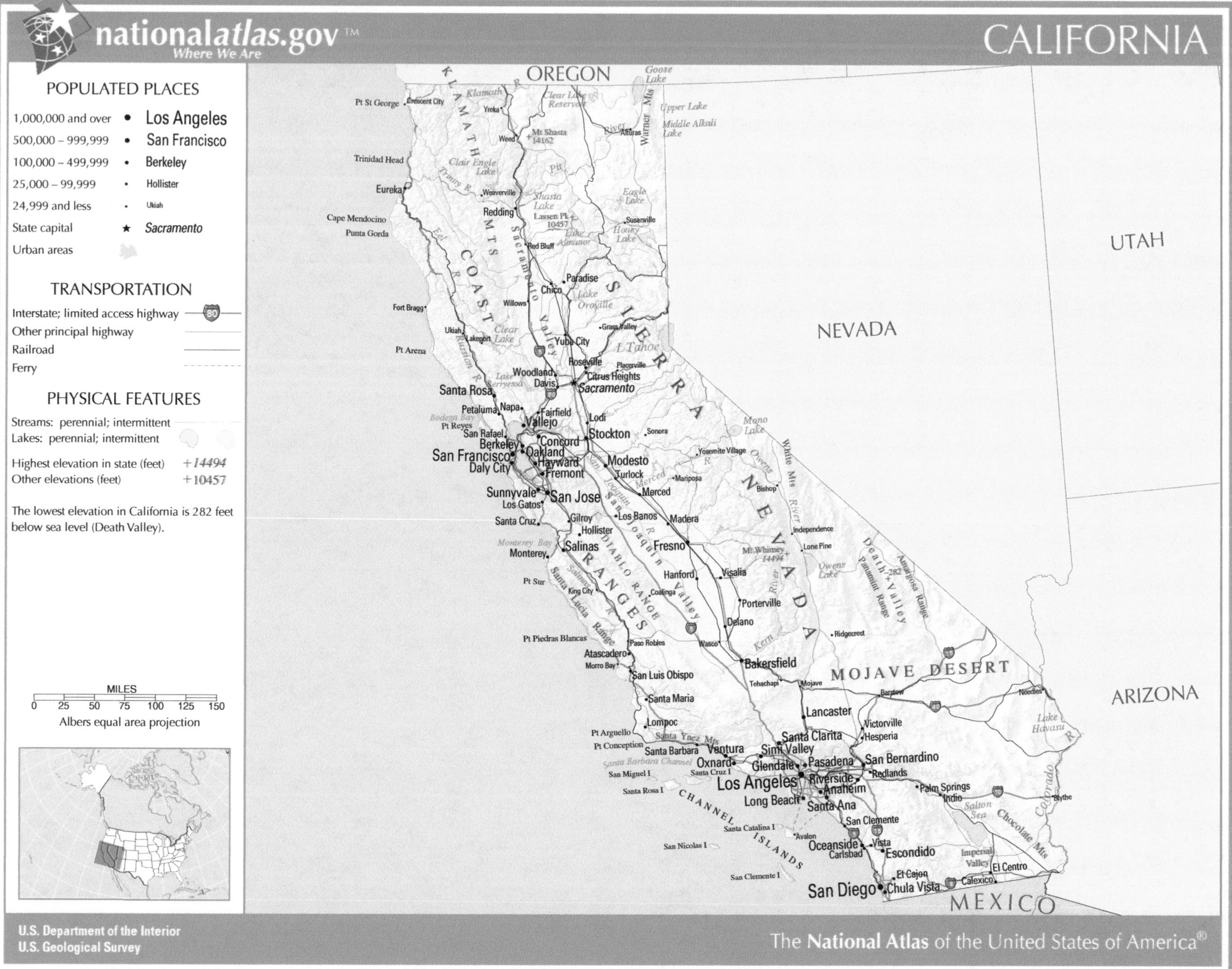
nationalatlas.gov™
Where We Are
CALIFORNIA
POPULATED PLACES
1,000,000 and over • Los Angeles
500,000 – 999,999 • San Francisco
100,000 – 499,999 • Berkeley
25,000 – 99,999 • Hollister
24,999 and less • Ukiah
State capital ★ Sacramento
Urban areas
TRANSPORTATION
Interstate; limited access highway
Other principal highway
Railroad
Ferry
PHYSICAL FEATURES
Streams: perennial; intermittent
Lakes: perennial; intermittent
Highest elevation in state (feet) +14494
Other elevations (feet) +10457
The lowest elevation in California is 282 feet below sea level (Death Valley).
MILES
0 25 50 75 100 125 150
Albers equal area projection
OREGON
NEVADA
UTAH
ARIZONA
MEXICO
KLAMATH MTS
COAST RANGES
SIERRA NEVADA
DIABLO RANGE
MOJAVE DESERT
CHANNEL ISLANDS
Death Valley
Los Angeles
San Francisco
San Diego
San Jose
Sacramento
Fresno
Bakersfield
Stockton
Modesto
Oakland
Long Beach
Santa Ana
Anaheim
Riverside
San Bernardino
Eureka
Redding
Chico
Salinas
Santa Barbara
U.S. Department of the Interior
U.S. Geological Survey
The National Atlas of the United States of America®

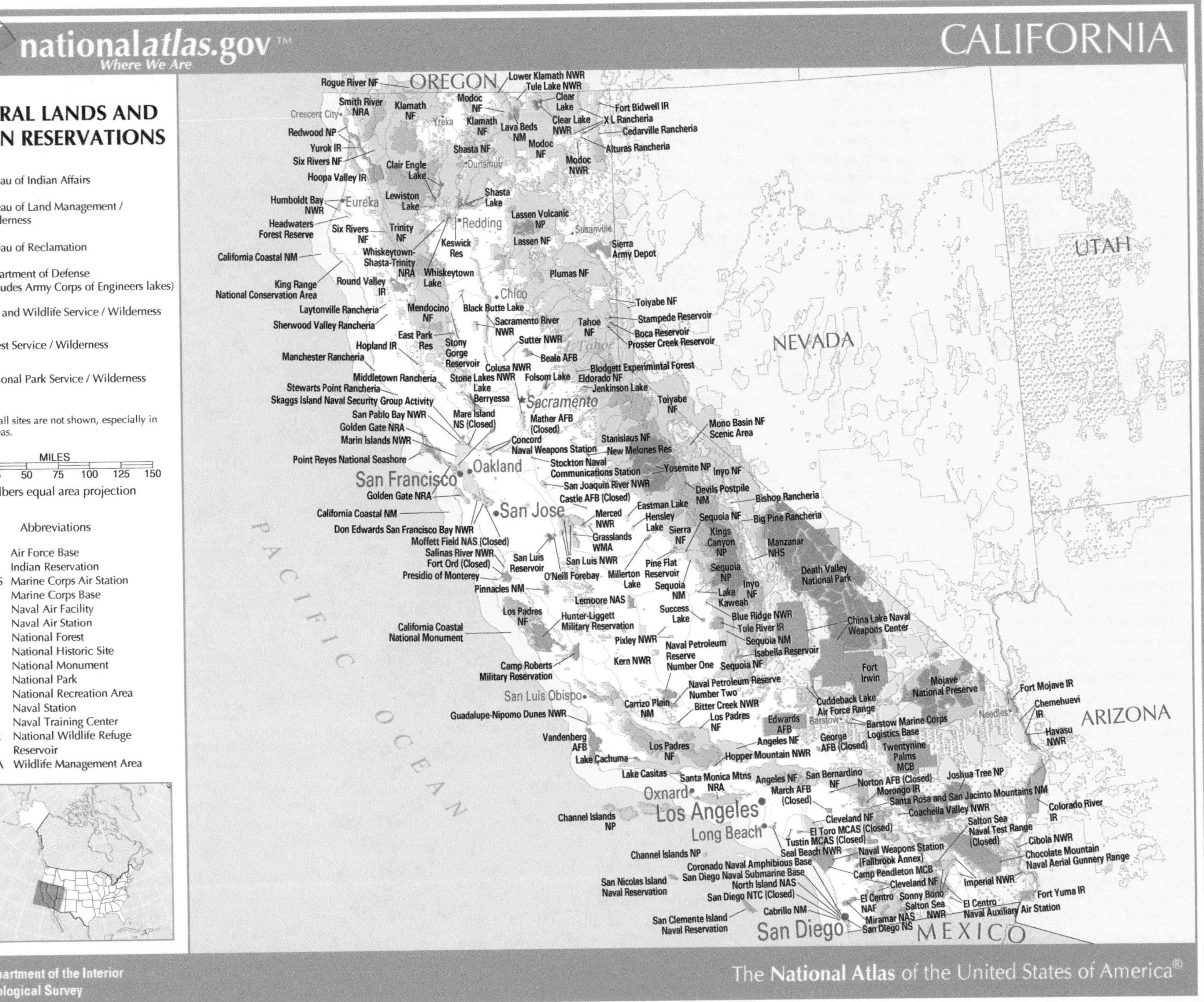
nationalatlas.gov™
Where We Are
CALIFORNIA
FEDERAL LANDS AND INDIAN RESERVATIONS
Bureau of Indian Affairs
Bureau of Land Management / Wilderness
Bureau of Reclamation
Department of Defense (includes Army Corps of Engineers lakes)
Fish and Wildlife Service / Wilderness
Forest Service / Wilderness
National Park Service / Wilderness
Some small sites are not shown, especially in urban areas.
MILES
0 25 50 75 100 125 150
Albers equal area projection
Abbreviations
AFB Air Force Base
IR Indian Reservation
MCAS Marine Corps Air Station
MCB Marine Corps Base
NAF Naval Air Facility
NAS Naval Air Station
NF National Forest
NHS National Historic Site
NM National Monument
NP National Park
NRA National Recreation Area
NS Naval Station
NTC Naval Training Center
NWR National Wildlife Refuge
Res Reservoir
WMA Wildlife Management Area
OREGON
NEVADA
UTAH
ARIZONA
MEXICO
PACIFIC OCEAN
San Francisco
Oakland
San Jose
Sacramento
Los Angeles
Long Beach
San Diego
U.S. Department of the Interior
U.S. Geological Survey
The National Atlas of the United States of America®

nationalatlas.gov™
Where We Are

CALIFORNIA

SATELLITE VIEW

In 1972, Landsat began transmitting views of our planet back to Earth. The first Landsat and its five successors (two of them are in operation now) have delivered millions of images from a satellite orbiting 438 miles above the Earth. Landsat's orbit enables a new image to be recorded every sixteen days of any area on the Earth's surface. The satellite view on this map was created from a mosaic of many Landsat images joined together. Colors were selected to better show variations in the landscape. Relief shading was added to enhance the terrain and make the landforms of each state more apparent.

Albers equal area projection

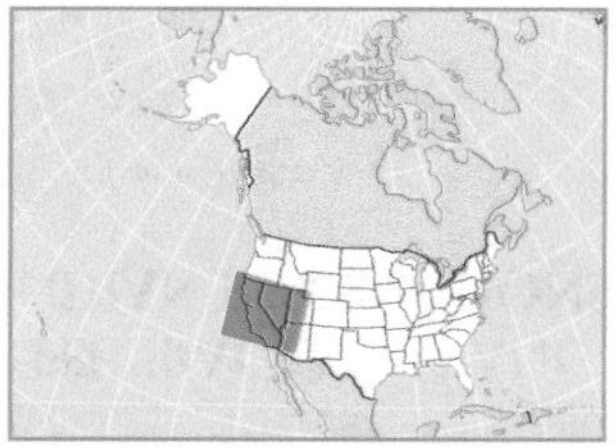

U.S. Department of the Interior
U.S. Geological Survey

The **National Atlas** of the United States of America®

Economic Losses from Hazard Events, 1960-2009

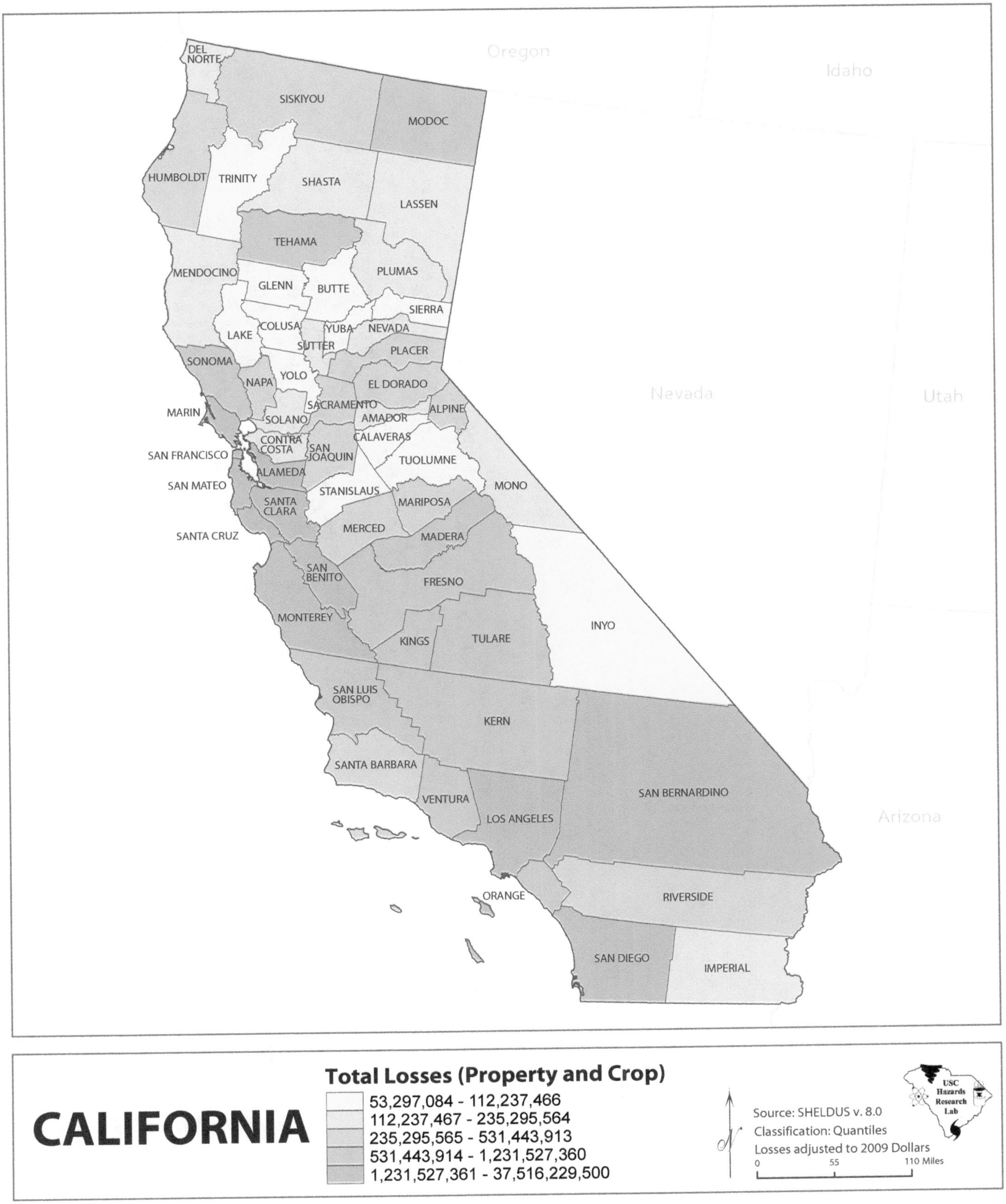

Oregon
Idaho
Nevada
Utah
Arizona
DEL NORTE
SISKIYOU
MODOC
HUMBOLDT
TRINITY
SHASTA
LASSEN
TEHAMA
MENDOCINO
GLENN
BUTTE
PLUMAS
SIERRA
LAKE
COLUSA
YUBA
NEVADA
SUTTER
PLACER
SONOMA
NAPA
YOLO
EL DORADO
MARIN
SACRAMENTO
ALPINE
SOLANO
AMADOR
CONTRA COSTA
CALAVERAS
SAN JOAQUIN
SAN FRANCISCO
TUOLUMNE
ALAMEDA
SAN MATEO
STANISLAUS
MONO
SANTA CLARA
MARIPOSA
MERCED
SANTA CRUZ
MADERA
SAN BENITO
FRESNO
INYO
MONTEREY
KINGS
TULARE
SAN LUIS OBISPO
KERN
SANTA BARBARA
SAN BERNARDINO
VENTURA
LOS ANGELES
ORANGE
RIVERSIDE
SAN DIEGO
IMPERIAL
CALIFORNIA
Total Losses (Property and Crop)
53,297,084 - 112,237,466
112,237,467 - 235,295,564
235,295,565 - 531,443,913
531,443,914 - 1,231,527,360
1,231,527,361 - 37,516,229,500
Source: SHELDUS v. 8.0
Classification: Quantiles
Losses adjusted to 2009 Dollars
0
55
110 Miles
USC Hazards Research Lab

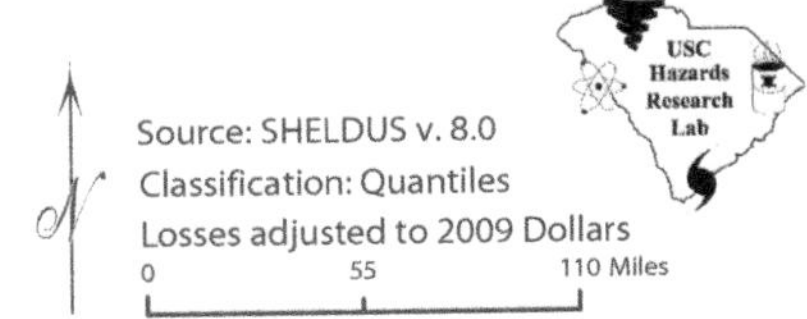

CALIFORNIA

Hazard Losses
1960-2009

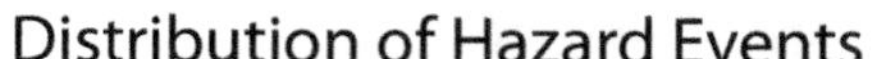

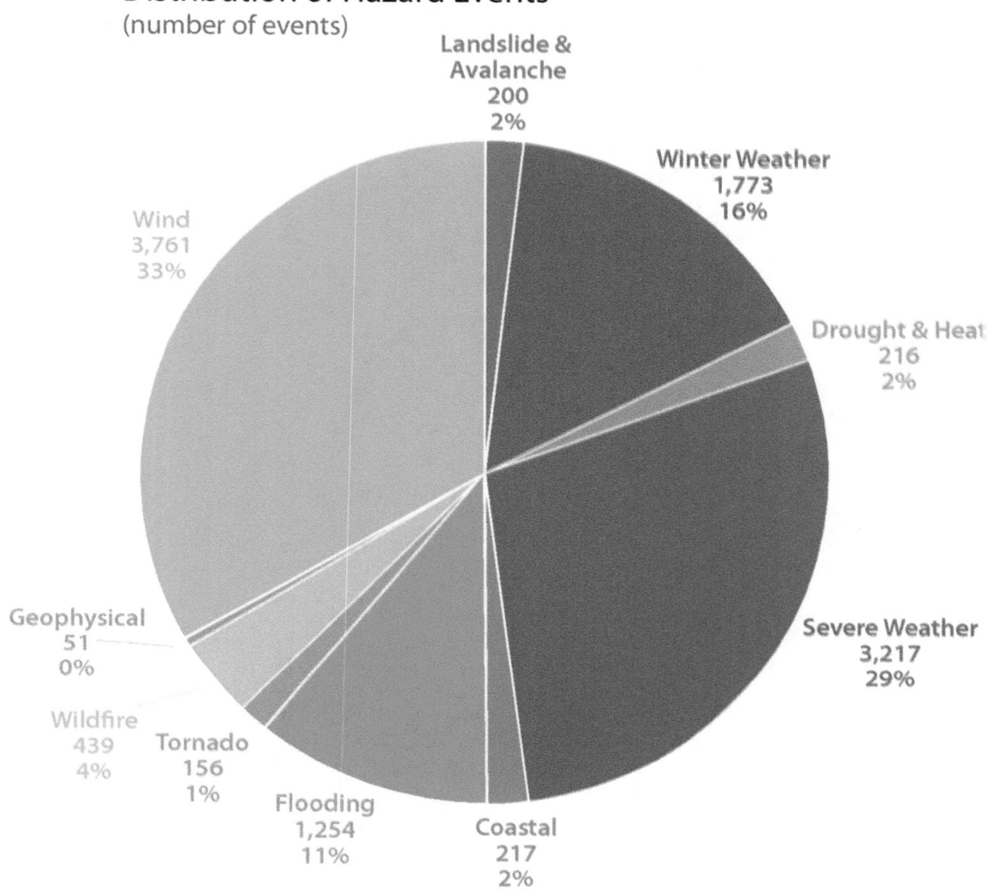

CALIFORNIA

Hazard Losses
1960-2009

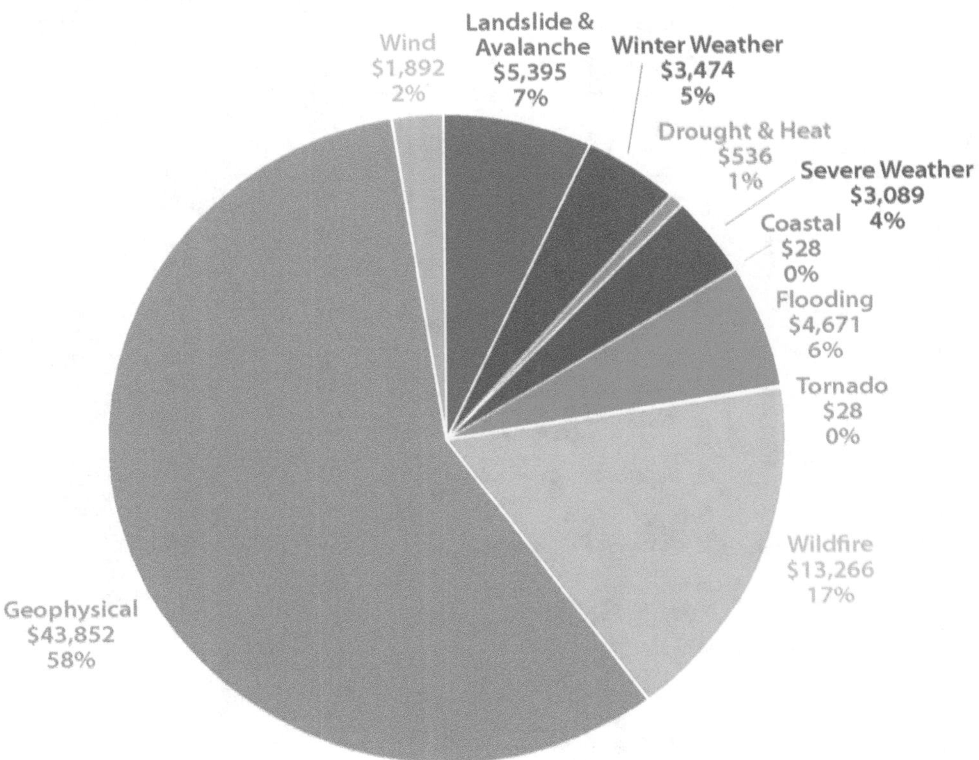

Demographic Maps

Population

Percent White

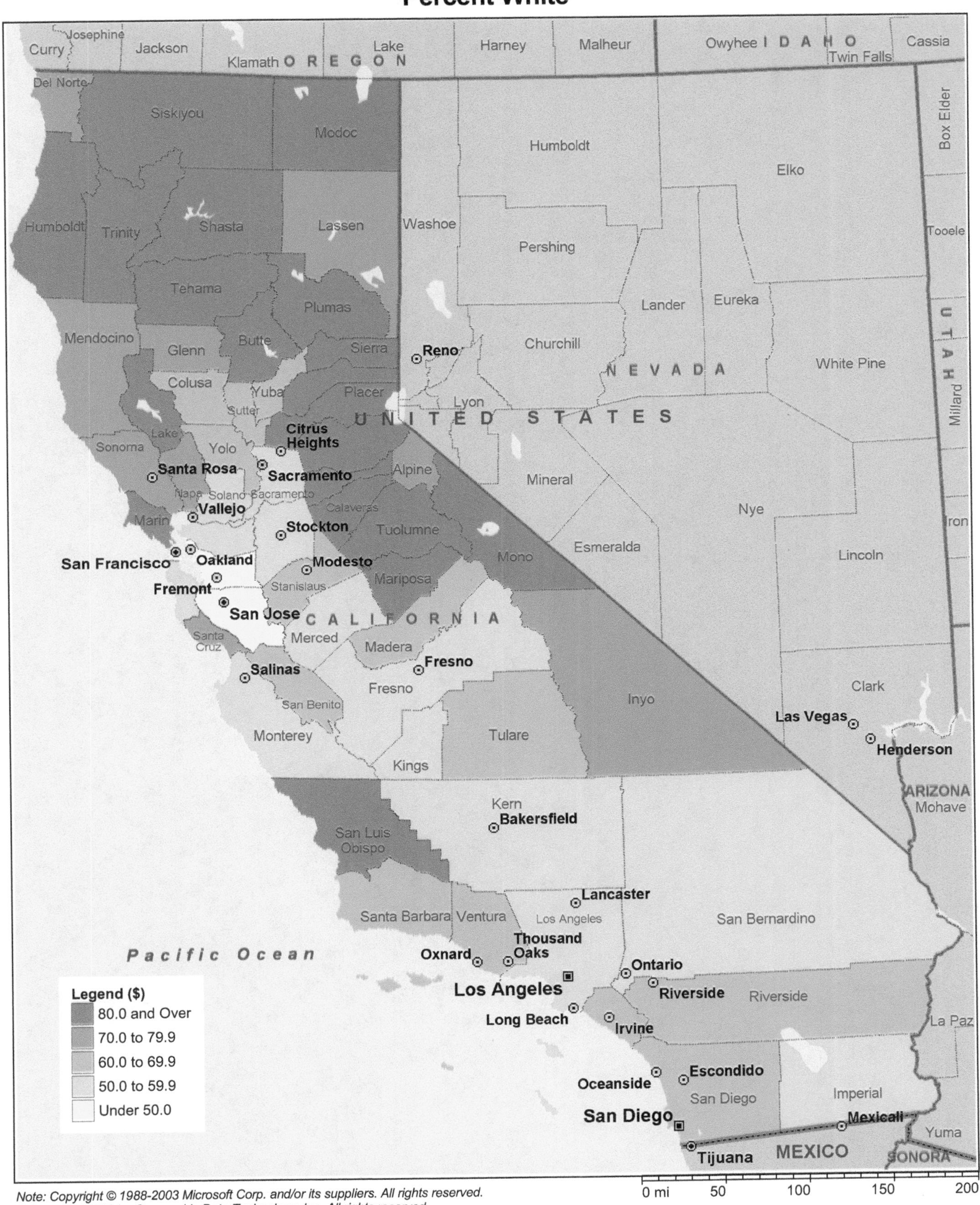

Percent Black

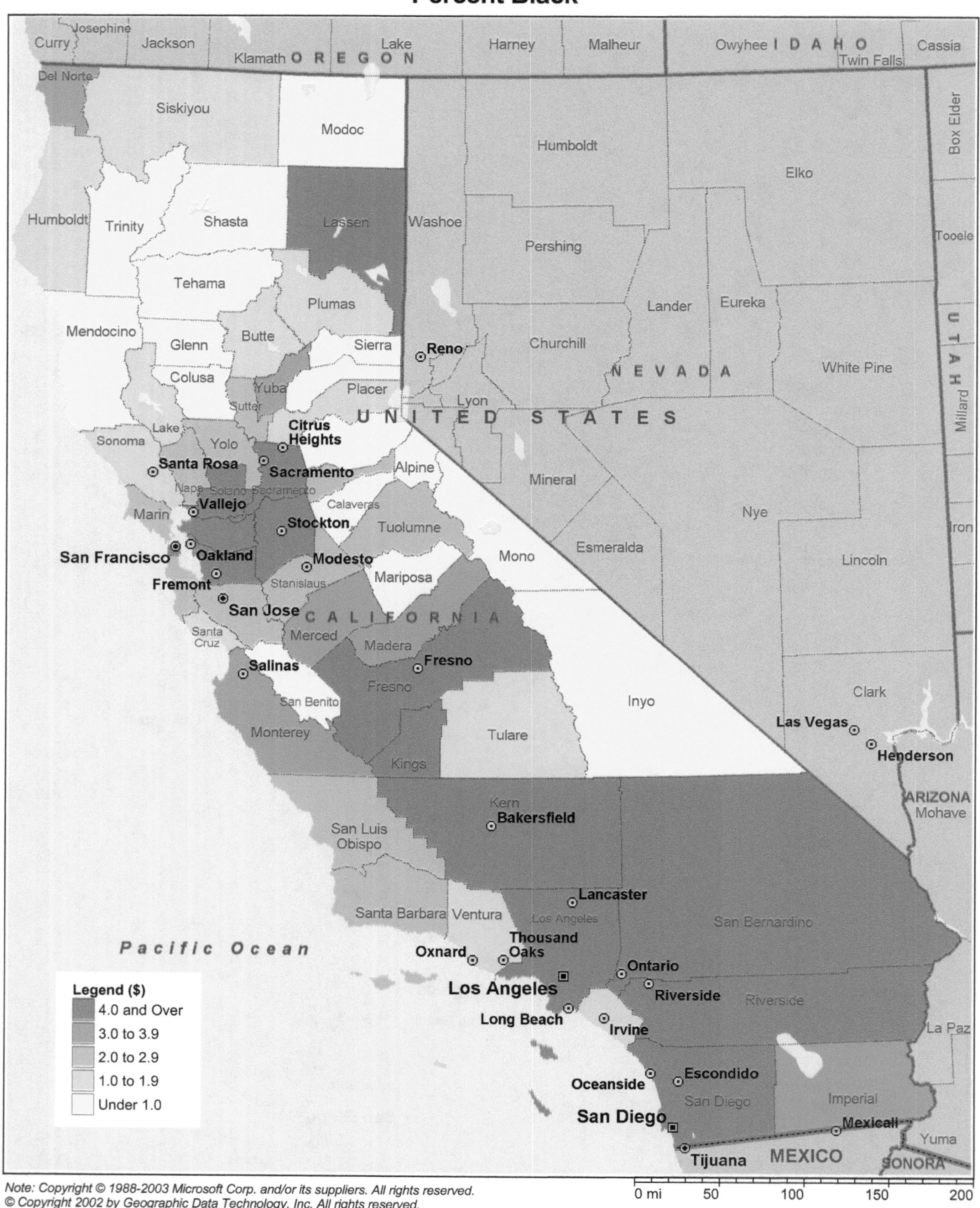

Percent Asian

Percent Hispanic

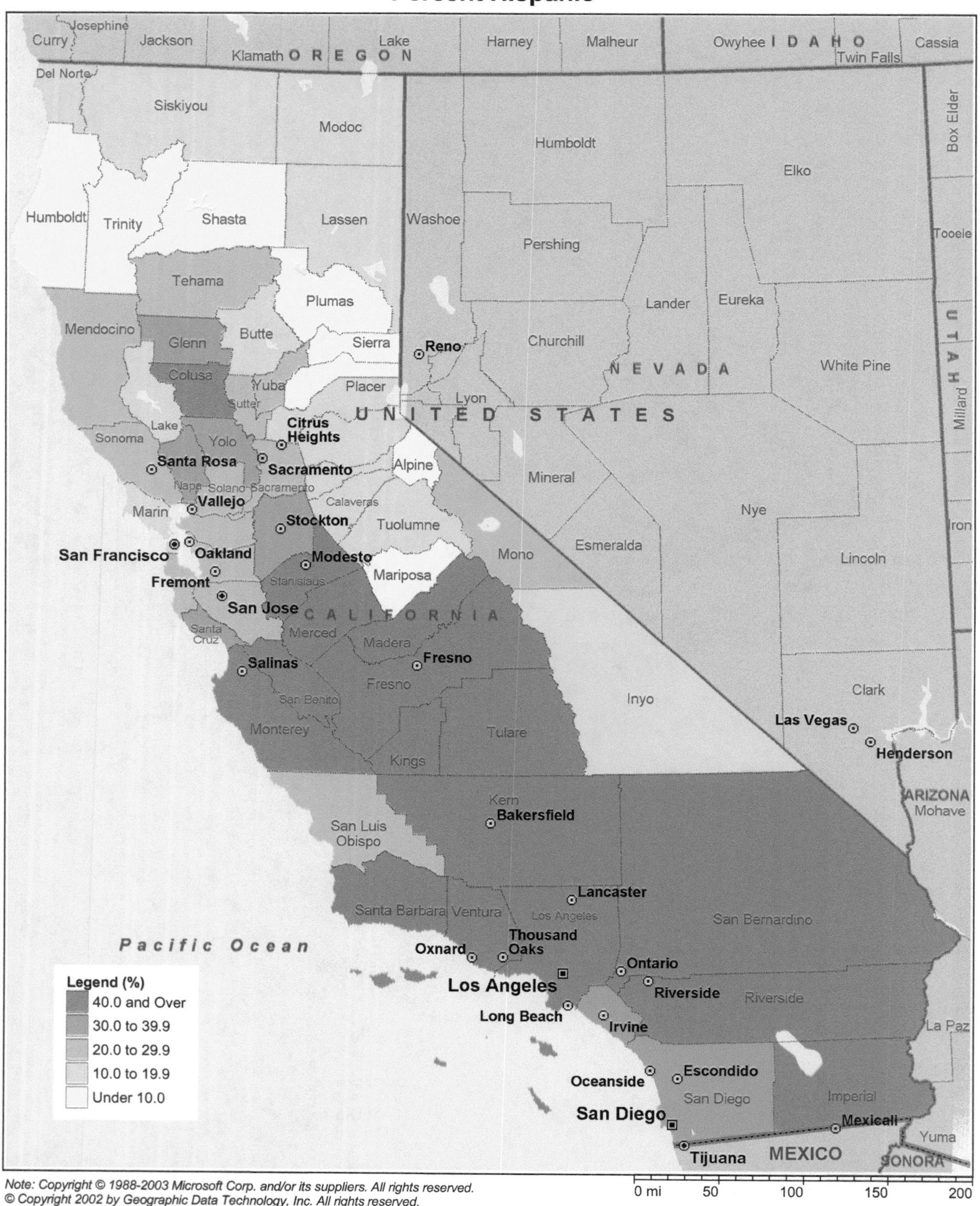

Median Age

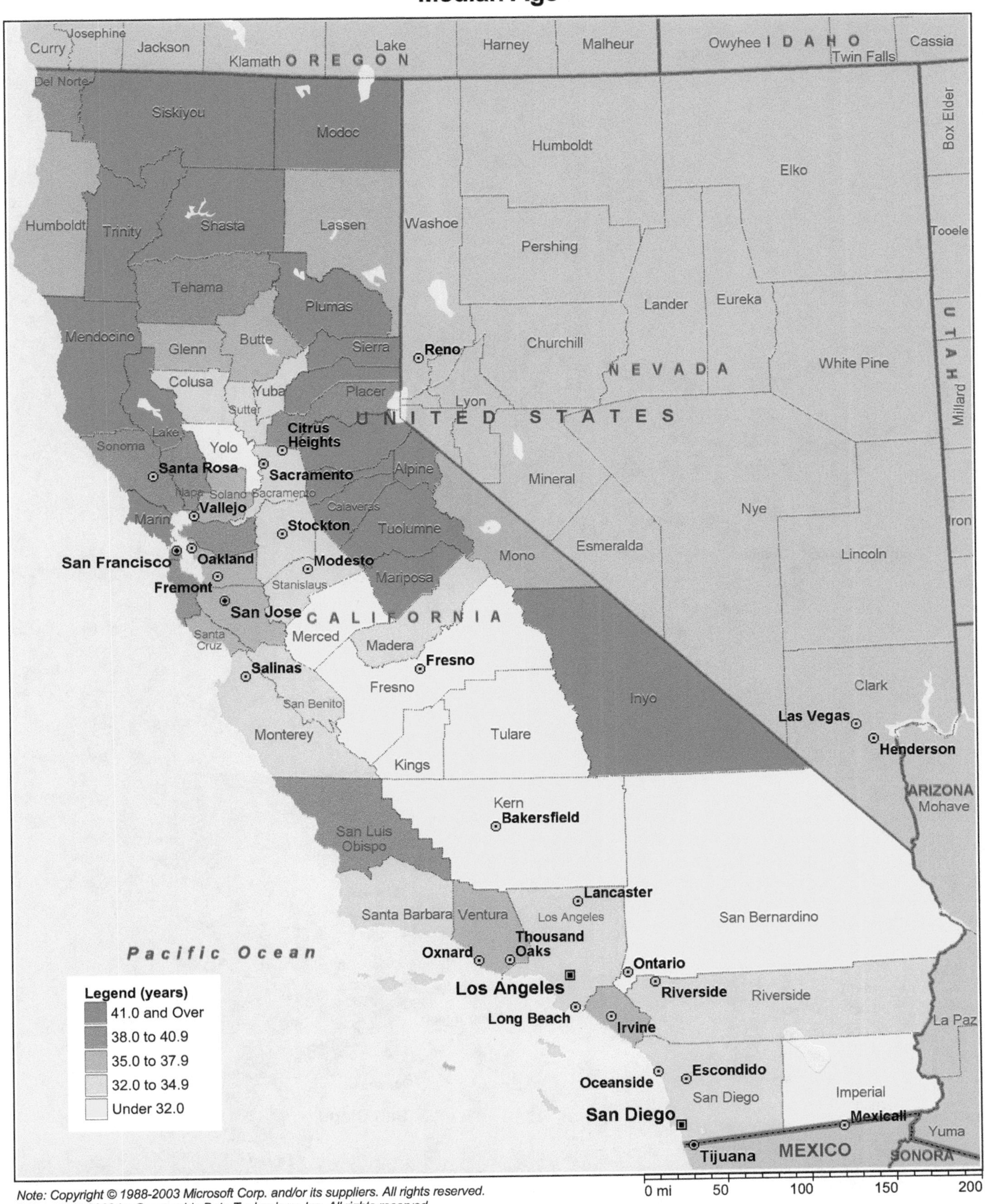
Legend (years)
41.0 and Over
38.0 to 40.9
35.0 to 37.9
32.0 to 34.9
Under 32.0
Pacific Ocean
OREGON
NEVADA
IDAHO
UTAH
ARIZONA
UNITED STATES
CALIFORNIA
MEXICO
SONORA
San Francisco
Oakland
Fremont
San Jose
Santa Rosa
Vallejo
Sacramento
Citrus Heights
Stockton
Modesto
Salinas
Fresno
Bakersfield
Lancaster
Oxnard
Thousand Oaks
Los Angeles
Long Beach
Ontario
Riverside
Irvine
Oceanside
Escondido
San Diego
Tijuana
Mexicali
Reno
Las Vegas
Henderson
0 mi 50 100 150 200

Median Household Income

Median Home Value

High School Graduates*

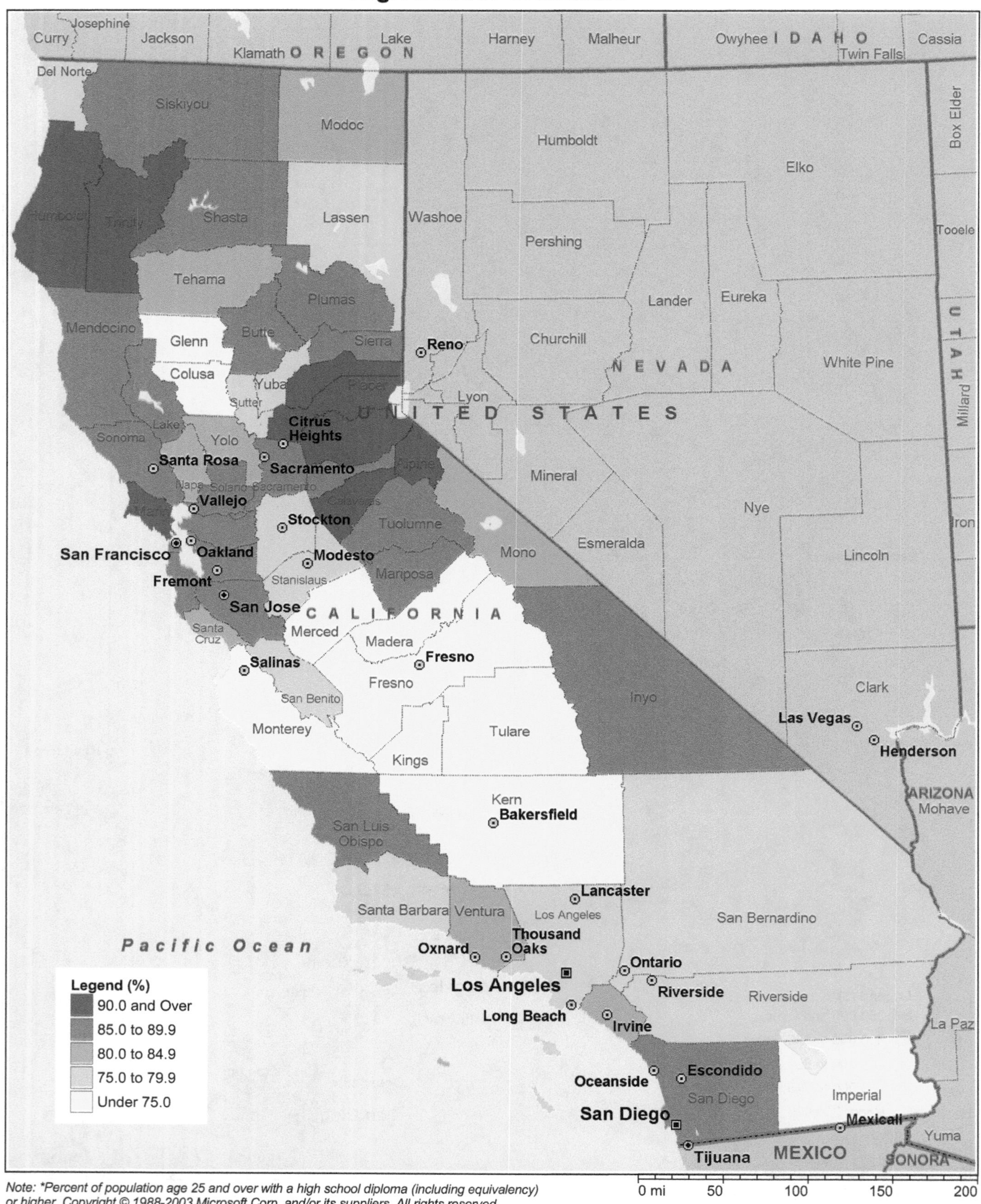

Note: *Percent of population age 25 and over with a high school diploma (including equivalency) or higher.

College Graduates*

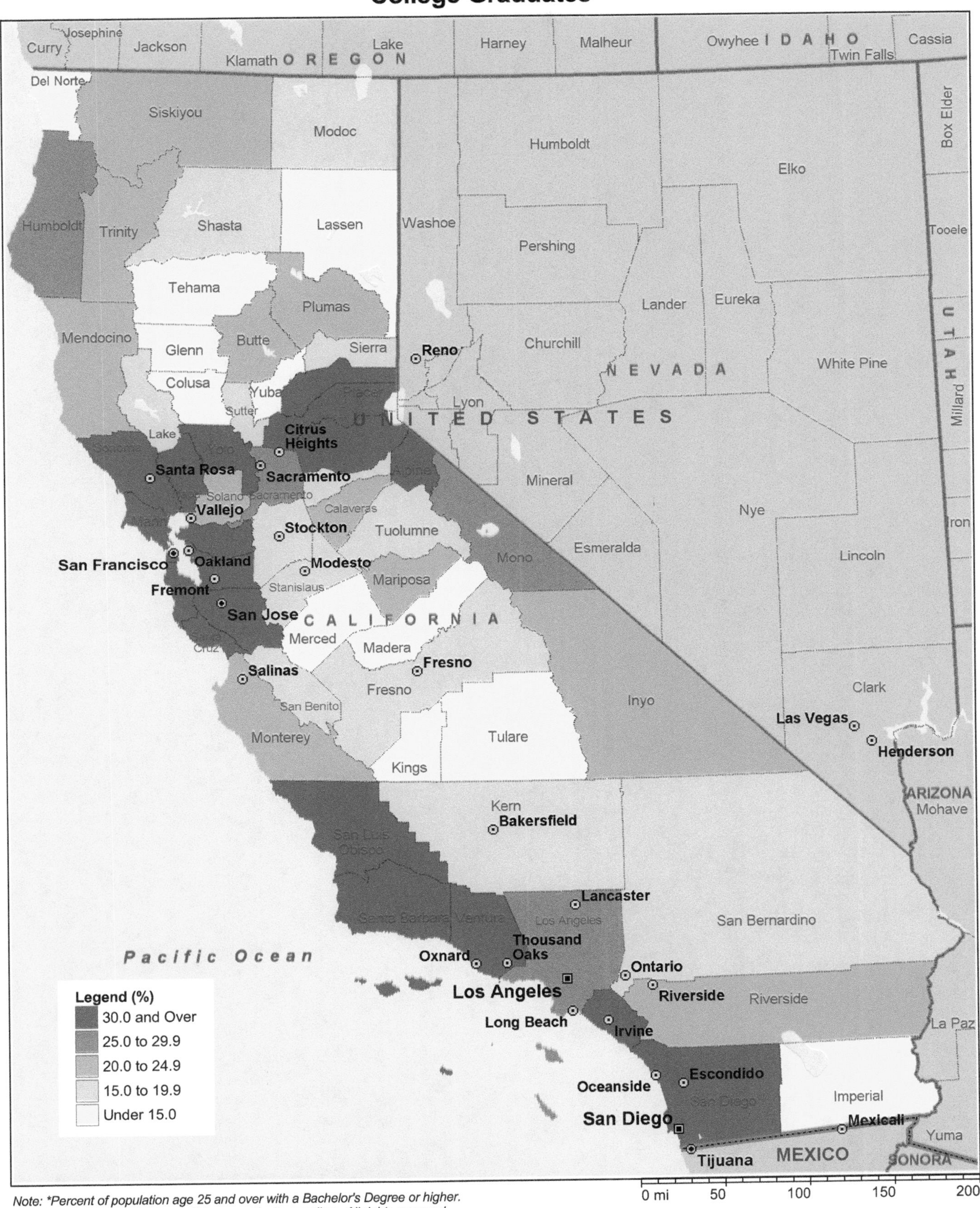

Note: *Percent of population age 25 and over with a Bachelor's Degree or higher.

Alameda County

Located in western California; stretches east from San Francisco Bay to the Coast Ranges; touches San Joaquin Valley in the northeast; includes the Livermore Valley. Covers a land area of 739.017 square miles, a water area of 82.311 square miles, and is located in the Pacific Time Zone at 37.65° N. Lat., 121.91° W. Long. The county was founded in 1853. County seat is Oakland.

Alameda County is part of the San Francisco-Oakland-Hayward, CA Metropolitan Statistical Area. The entire metro area includes: Oakland-Hayward-Berkeley, CA Metropolitan Division (Alameda County, CA; Contra Costa County, CA); San Francisco-Redwood City-South San Francisco, CA Metropolitan Division (San Francisco County, CA; San Mateo County, CA); San Rafael, CA Metropolitan Division (Marin County, CA)

Weather Station: Berkeley — Elevation: 310 feet

	Jan	Feb	Mar	Apr	May	Jun	Jul	Aug	Sep	Oct	Nov	Dec
High	57	60	63	65	68	72	73	73	73	71	63	57
Low	44	46	47	48	50	53	54	55	55	52	48	44
Precip	5.0	5.5	3.7	1.7	0.9	0.2	0.0	0.1	0.3	1.3	3.3	4.9
Snow	0.0	0.0	0.0	0.0	0.0	0.0	0.0	0.0	0.0	0.0	0.0	0.0

High and Low temperatures in degrees Fahrenheit; Precipitation and Snow in inches

Weather Station: Livermore — Elevation: 479 feet

	Jan	Feb	Mar	Apr	May	Jun	Jul	Aug	Sep	Oct	Nov	Dec
High	57	61	66	71	77	84	89	89	86	78	65	57
Low	39	41	43	46	50	54	57	56	55	49	43	39
Precip	2.9	2.9	2.4	1.0	0.5	0.1	0.0	0.1	0.2	0.8	1.8	2.5
Snow	0.0	0.0	tr	0.0	0.0	0.0	0.0	0.0	0.0	0.0	0.0	tr

High and Low temperatures in degrees Fahrenheit; Precipitation and Snow in inches

Weather Station: Newark — Elevation: 9 feet

	Jan	Feb	Mar	Apr	May	Jun	Jul	Aug	Sep	Oct	Nov	Dec
High	58	61	65	68	71	75	77	77	77	73	65	58
Low	43	46	48	50	54	56	58	59	58	54	48	43
Precip	2.9	3.1	2.3	1.0	0.5	0.1	0.0	0.0	0.2	0.8	1.6	2.5
Snow	0.0	0.0	0.0	0.0	0.0	0.0	0.0	0.0	0.0	0.0	0.0	0.0

High and Low temperatures in degrees Fahrenheit; Precipitation and Snow in inches

Weather Station: Oakland Museum — Elevation: 29 feet

	Jan	Feb	Mar	Apr	May	Jun	Jul	Aug	Sep	Oct	Nov	Dec
High	58	62	64	66	69	71	72	73	74	72	64	58
Low	45	48	49	51	54	56	57	58	58	55	50	45
Precip	4.6	4.9	3.4	1.4	0.7	0.1	0.0	0.1	0.2	1.3	2.9	4.2
Snow	0.0	0.0	0.0	0.0	0.0	0.0	0.0	0.0	0.0	0.0	0.0	0.0

High and Low temperatures in degrees Fahrenheit; Precipitation and Snow in inches

Weather Station: Tracy Pumping Plant — Elevation: 61 feet

	Jan	Feb	Mar	Apr	May	Jun	Jul	Aug	Sep	Oct	Nov	Dec
High	55	61	67	73	81	87	93	92	88	79	65	55
Low	40	42	46	49	54	58	61	61	59	53	45	39
Precip	2.5	2.4	1.8	0.8	0.5	0.1	0.0	0.0	0.2	0.7	1.5	2.1
Snow	0.0	0.0	0.0	0.0	0.0	0.0	0.0	0.0	0.0	0.0	0.0	0.0

High and Low temperatures in degrees Fahrenheit; Precipitation and Snow in inches

Population: 1,510,271; Growth (since 2000): 4.6%; Density: 2,043.6 persons per square mile; Race: 43.0% White, 12.6% Black/African American, 26.1% Asian, 0.6% American Indian/Alaska Native, 0.8% Native Hawaiian/Other Pacific Islander, 6.0% two or more races, 22.5% Hispanic of any race; Average household size: 2.70; Median age: 36.6; Age under 18: 22.6%; Age 65 and over: 11.1%; Males per 100 females: 96.2; Marriage status: 36.5% never married, 49.4% now married, 2.1% separated, 5.1% widowed, 9.1% divorced; Foreign born: 30.8%; Speak English only: 56.9%; With disability: 9.1%; Veterans: 5.3%; Ancestry: 7.5% German, 6.3% Irish, 5.4% English, 3.7% Italian, 2.0% Portuguese
Religion: Six largest groups: 15.3% Catholicism, 4.0% Non-denominational Protestant, 2.8% Baptist, 2.0% Muslim Estimate, 1.7% Latter-day Saints, 1.5% Methodist/Pietist
Economy: Unemployment rate: 5.7%; Leading industries: 14.7% professional, scientific, and technical services; 11.7% health care and social assistance; 11.5% retail trade; Farms: 452 totaling 177,798 acres; Company size: 35 employ 1,000 or more persons, 54 employ 500 to 999 persons, 826 employ 100 to 499 persons, 35,785 employ less than 100 persons; Business ownership: 45,107 women-owned, 9,583 Black-owned, 12,455 Hispanic-owned, 34,306 Asian-owned
Employment: 17.5% management, business, and financial, 11.3% computer, engineering, and science, 12.3% education, legal, community service, arts, and media, 4.6% healthcare practitioners, 15.8% service, 22.5% sales and office, 6.6% natural resources, construction, and maintenance, 9.4% production, transportation, and material moving
Income: Per capita: $35,763; Median household: $72,112; Average household: $96,982; Households with income of $100,000 or more: 36.2%; Poverty rate: 12.5%
Educational Attainment: High school diploma or higher: 86.4%; Bachelor's degree or higher: 41.8%; Graduate/professional degree or higher: 17.2%
Housing: Homeownership rate: 53.4%; Median home value: $493,800; Median year structure built: 1966; Homeowner vacancy rate: 1.8%; Median gross rent: $1,289 per month; Rental vacancy rate: 6.4%
Vital Statistics: Birth rate: 122.3 per 10,000 population; Death rate: 62.1 per 10,000 population; Age-adjusted cancer mortality rate: 147.3 deaths per 100,000 population
Health Insurance: 87.4% have insurance; 70.2% have private insurance; 25.7% have public insurance; 12.6% do not have insurance; 5.1% of children under 18 do not have insurance
Health Care: Physicians: 28.4 per 10,000 population; Hospital beds: 21.8 per 10,000 population; Hospital admissions: 936.5 per 10,000 population
Air Quality Index: 52.6% good, 45.8% moderate, 1.6% unhealthy for sensitive individuals, 0.0% unhealthy (percent of days)
Transportation: Commute: 75.5% car, 12.2% public transportation, 3.7% walk, 5.5% work from home; Median travel time to work: 28.8 minutes
Presidential Election: 78.9% Obama, 18.2% Romney (2012)
National and State Parks: Bethany Reservoir State Recreation Area; Carnegie State Vehicular Recreation Area; Don Edwards San Francisco Bay National Wildlife Refuge; Knowland State Arboretum and Park; Lake Del Valle State Recreation Area
Additional Information Contacts
Alameda Government . . . . (510) 272-6347
http://www.acgov.org

Alameda County Communities

ALAMEDA (city). Covers a land area of 10.611 square miles and a water area of 12.349 square miles. Located at 37.76° N. Lat; 122.28° W. Long. Elevation is 33 feet.
History: Named for the Spanish translation of "grove of poplar trees". Alameda was established in the 1850s on the former Rancho San Antonio, occupying a flat island separated from the mainland by an estuary that was connected by a canal with San Leandro Bay. Shipbuilding, shipping, and fishing were early industries.
Population: 73,812; Growth (since 2000): 2.1%; Density: 6,956.3 persons per square mile; Race: 50.8% White, 6.4% Black/African American, 31.2% Asian, 0.6% American Indian/Alaska Native, 0.5% Native Hawaiian/Other Pacific Islander, 7.1% Two or more races, 11.0% Hispanic of any race; Average household size: 2.40; Median age: 40.7; Age under 18: 20.7%; Age 65 and over: 13.5%; Males per 100 females: 91.7; Marriage status: 33.5% never married, 50.3% now married, 1.9% separated, 5.0% widowed, 11.2% divorced; Foreign born: 28.1%; Speak English only: 63.8%; With disability: 9.4%; Veterans: 7.2%; Ancestry: 10.2% German, 9.1% Irish, 8.1% English, 4.3% Italian, 2.4% French
Employment: 19.6% management, business, and financial, 8.3% computer, engineering, and science, 14.4% education, legal, community service, arts, and media, 5.5% healthcare practitioners, 15.8% service, 23.7% sales and office, 4.5% natural resources, construction, and maintenance, 8.2% production, transportation, and material moving
Income: Per capita: $41,340; Median household: $74,606; Average household: $100,605; Households with income of $100,000 or more: 36.0%; Poverty rate: 10.3%
Educational Attainment: High school diploma or higher: 90.6%; Bachelor's degree or higher: 48.1%; Graduate/professional degree or higher: 18.4%

School District(s)

Alameda City Unified (KG-12)
2012-13 Enrollment: 10,836 . . . . (510) 337-7000
East Bay Regional Occupational Agency (Rop)
2012-13 Enrollment: n/a . . . . (510) 337-7093

Four-year College(s)

Argosy University-San Francisco Bay Area (Private, For-profit)
Fall 2013 Enrollment: 559 . . . . (510) 217-4700
2013-14 Tuition: In-state $13,663; Out-of-state $13,663

Two-year College(s)

College of Alameda (Public)
Fall 2013 Enrollment: 5,799 . . . . (510) 522-7221
2013-14 Tuition: In-state $1,144; Out-of-state $6,256

Vocational/Technical School(s)

Avalon School of Cosmetology-Alameda (Private, For-profit)
Fall 2013 Enrollment: 186 . . . . (510) 523-1050
2013-14 Tuition: $19,200

Housing: Homeownership rate: 48.1%; Median home value: $618,800; Median year structure built: 1961; Homeowner vacancy rate: 1.1%; Median gross rent: $1,336 per month; Rental vacancy rate: 5.7%

Health Insurance: 88.5% have insurance; 73.5% have private insurance; 25.3% have public insurance; 11.5% do not have insurance; 6.2% of children under 18 do not have insurance

Hospitals: Alameda Hospital (135 beds)

Safety: Violent crime rate: 20.7 per 10,000 population; Property crime rate: 249.6 per 10,000 population

Newspapers: Alameda Sun (weekly circulation 20000); Hills Newspapers (weekly circulation 60000)

Transportation: Commute: 70.8% car, 15.2% public transportation, 4.2% walk, 6.6% work from home; Median travel time to work: 28.7 minutes

Additional Information Contacts

City of Alameda . . . . (510) 747-7400
http://alamedaca.gov

ALBANY (city). Covers a land area of 1.788 square miles and a water area of 3.677 square miles. Located at 37.89° N. Lat; 122.33° W. Long. Elevation is 43 feet.

History: Albany, incorporated in 1908 as Ocean View, was renamed in 1909 for its mayor's New York birthplace.

Population: 18,539; Growth (since 2000): 12.7%; Density: 10,367.2 persons per square mile; Race: 54.6% White, 3.5% Black/African American, 31.2% Asian, 0.5% American Indian/Alaska Native, 0.2% Native Hawaiian/Other Pacific Islander, 6.7% Two or more races, 10.2% Hispanic of any race; Average household size: 2.49; Median age: 37.0; Age under 18: 25.0%; Age 65 and over: 10.0%; Males per 100 females: 90.8; Marriage status: 26.5% never married, 61.7% now married, 2.0% separated, 2.6% widowed, 9.1% divorced; Foreign born: 31.6%; Speak English only: 62.2%; With disability: 6.8%; Veterans: 4.7%; Ancestry: 9.4% German, 8.1% Irish, 7.4% English, 5.4% Italian, 4.8% European

Employment: 15.8% management, business, and financial, 20.3% computer, engineering, and science, 24.4% education, legal, community service, arts, and media, 7.8% healthcare practitioners, 9.7% service, 16.1% sales and office, 2.9% natural resources, construction, and maintenance, 3.0% production, transportation, and material moving

Income: Per capita: $39,967; Median household: $79,926; Average household: $101,241; Households with income of $100,000 or more: 40.4%; Poverty rate: 10.6%

Educational Attainment: High school diploma or higher: 96.3%; Bachelor's degree or higher: 71.5%; Graduate/professional degree or higher: 40.5%

School District(s)

Albany City Unified (KG-12)
2012-13 Enrollment: 3,804 . . . . (510) 558-3750

Housing: Homeownership rate: 48.3%; Median home value: $621,900; Median year structure built: 1953; Homeowner vacancy rate: 1.0%; Median gross rent: $1,616 per month; Rental vacancy rate: 6.2%

Health Insurance: 92.7% have insurance; 84.4% have private insurance; 17.1% have public insurance; 7.3% do not have insurance; 3.3% of children under 18 do not have insurance

Safety: Violent crime rate: 15.2 per 10,000 population; Property crime rate: 291.6 per 10,000 population

Transportation: Commute: 57.4% car, 24.1% public transportation, 4.6% walk, 6.4% work from home; Median travel time to work: 29.9 minutes

Additional Information Contacts

City of Albany . . . . (510) 528-5710
http://www.albanyca.org

ASHLAND (CDP). Covers a land area of 1.838 square miles and a water area of 0 square miles. Located at 37.69° N. Lat; 122.12° W. Long. Elevation is 43 feet.

Population: 21,925; Growth (since 2000): 5.4%; Density: 11,926.7 persons per square mile; Race: 30.6% White, 19.5% Black/African American, 18.4% Asian, 1.1% American Indian/Alaska Native, 1.2% Native Hawaiian/Other Pacific Islander, 5.9% Two or more races, 42.8% Hispanic of any race; Average household size: 2.99; Median age: 31.4; Age under 18: 27.8%; Age 65 and over: 7.6%; Males per 100 females: 95.2; Marriage status: 41.6% never married, 43.2% now married, 2.4% separated, 5.9% widowed, 9.2% divorced; Foreign born: 34.0%; Speak English only: 46.2%; With disability: 10.0%; Veterans: 3.5%; Ancestry: 2.5% German, 2.4% English, 2.4% American, 2.2% Irish, 1.8% Italian

Employment: 11.9% management, business, and financial, 4.8% computer, engineering, and science, 5.9% education, legal, community service, arts, and media, 2.4% healthcare practitioners, 26.3% service, 21.4% sales and office, 10.4% natural resources, construction, and maintenance, 16.9% production, transportation, and material moving

Income: Per capita: $19,331; Median household: $48,085; Average household: $56,932; Households with income of $100,000 or more: 14.0%; Poverty rate: 17.0%

Educational Attainment: High school diploma or higher: 74.9%; Bachelor's degree or higher: 18.3%; Graduate/professional degree or higher: 4.3%

Housing: Homeownership rate: 34.5%; Median home value: $278,700; Median year structure built: 1964; Homeowner vacancy rate: 2.5%; Median gross rent: $1,108 per month; Rental vacancy rate: 4.5%

Health Insurance: 78.5% have insurance; 49.6% have private insurance; 33.4% have public insurance; 21.5% do not have insurance; 11.7% of children under 18 do not have insurance

Transportation: Commute: 82.4% car, 11.7% public transportation, 1.3% walk, 2.9% work from home; Median travel time to work: 29.2 minutes

---

BERKELEY (city). Covers a land area of 10.470 square miles and a water area of 7.226 square miles. Located at 37.87° N. Lat; 122.30° W. Long. Elevation is 171 feet.

History: Berkeley was named for George Berkeley, Bishop of Cloyne (1685-1753), an Irish philosopher, whose ideals were valued by Henry Durant, one of the trustees of the College of California, as being suitable for a college town. Berkeley was founded on the 1820 land grant of the Peralta family, called Rancho San Antonio. In 1853 title to some of the land was purchased by speculators, and the first building in what is now Berkeley was erected. Berkeley developed as a university town. Contra Costa Academy, begun in 1853 in Oakland by Henry Durant, became the College of California under Samuel Hopkins Willey, and then the University of California at Berkeley in 1869. Berkeley's population swelled after the 1906 San Francisco earthquake as refugees moved across the Bay.

Population: 112,580; Growth (since 2000): 9.6%; Density: 10,752.4 persons per square mile; Race: 59.5% White, 10.0% Black/African American, 19.3% Asian, 0.4% American Indian/Alaska Native, 0.2% Native Hawaiian/Other Pacific Islander, 6.2% Two or more races, 10.8% Hispanic of any race; Average household size: 2.17; Median age: 31.0; Age under 18: 12.3%; Age 65 and over: 11.7%; Males per 100 females: 95.6; Marriage status: 55.0% never married, 33.7% now married, 1.3% separated, 3.4% widowed, 7.8% divorced; Foreign born: 21.2%; Speak English only: 73.9%; With disability: 7.9%; Veterans: 3.9%; Ancestry: 9.6% German, 8.5% English, 8.1% Irish, 4.5% Italian, 3.3% Russian

Employment: 18.5% management, business, and financial, 15.2% computer, engineering, and science, 27.5% education, legal, community service, arts, and media, 4.4% healthcare practitioners, 11.0% service, 16.7% sales and office, 3.2% natural resources, construction, and maintenance, 3.5% production, transportation, and material moving

Income: Per capita: $41,308; Median household: $63,312; Average household: $97,635; Households with income of $100,000 or more: 33.6%; Poverty rate: 18.7%

Educational Attainment: High school diploma or higher: 94.9%; Bachelor's degree or higher: 69.7%; Graduate/professional degree or higher: 37.4%

School District(s)

Alameda County Office of Education (PK-12)
2012-13 Enrollment: 4,041 . . . . (510) 887-0152

Berkeley Unified (KG-12)
2012-13 Enrollment: 9,780 . . . . (510) 644-8764

Four-year College(s)

Acupuncture and Integrative Medicine College-Berkeley (Private, Not-for-profit)
Fall 2013 Enrollment: 140 . . . . (510) 666-8248

American Baptist Seminary of the West (Private, Not-for-profit, American Baptist)
Fall 2013 Enrollment: 49 . . . . (510) 841-1905

Church Divinity School of the Pacific (Private, Not-for-profit, Protestant Episcopal)
Fall 2013 Enrollment: 79 . . . . (510) 204-0700
Dominican School of Philosophy & Theology (Private, Not-for-profit, Roman Catholic)
Fall 2013 Enrollment: 89 . . . . (510) 849-2030
Franciscan School of Theology (Private, Not-for-profit, Roman Catholic)
Fall 2013 Enrollment: 44 . . . . (510) 848-5232
Graduate Theological Union (Private, Not-for-profit)
Fall 2013 Enrollment: 253 . . . . (510) 649-2400
Pacific Lutheran Theological Seminary (Private, Not-for-profit, Evangelical Lutheran Church)
Fall 2013 Enrollment: 99 . . . . (510) 524-5264
Pacific School of Religion (Private, Not-for-profit, Multiple Protestant Denomination)
Fall 2013 Enrollment: 183 . . . . (510) 849-8200
Starr King School for Ministry (Private, Not-for-profit, Unitarian Universalist)
Fall 2013 Enrollment: 90 . . . . (510) 845-6232
The Wright Institute (Private, Not-for-profit)
Fall 2013 Enrollment: 434 . . . . (510) 841-9230
University of California-Berkeley (Public)
Fall 2013 Enrollment: 36,198 . . . . (510) 642-6000
2013-14 Tuition: In-state $12,864; Out-of-state $35,742

Two-year College(s)

Berkeley City College (Public)
Fall 2013 Enrollment: 6,471 . . . . (510) 981-2800
2013-14 Tuition: In-state $1,144; Out-of-state $6,256

Housing: Homeownership rate: 41.0%; Median home value: $698,600; Median year structure built: Before 1940; Homeowner vacancy rate: 1.0%; Median gross rent: $1,298 per month; Rental vacancy rate: 4.5%

Health Insurance: 91.4% have insurance; 81.6% have private insurance; 19.6% have public insurance; 8.6% do not have insurance; 3.0% of children under 18 do not have insurance

Hospitals: Alta Bates Summit Medical Center (551 beds)

Safety: Violent crime rate: 48.4 per 10,000 population; Property crime rate: 462.7 per 10,000 population

Newspapers: Berkeley Planet (weekly circulation 25000)

Transportation: Commute: 43.5% car, 20.2% public transportation, 15.4% walk, 10.9% work from home; Median travel time to work: 26.9 minutes; Amtrak: Train service available.

Additional Information Contacts

City of Berkeley . . . . (510) 981-2489
http://www.ci.berkeley.ca.us

CASTRO VALLEY (CDP). Covers a land area of 16.635 square miles and a water area of 0.284 square miles. Located at 37.71° N. Lat; 122.06° W. Long. Elevation is 161 feet.

Population: 61,388; Growth (since 2000): 7.1%; Density: 3,690.4 persons per square mile; Race: 58.0% White, 6.9% Black/African American, 21.4% Asian, 0.5% American Indian/Alaska Native, 0.7% Native Hawaiian/Other Pacific Islander, 6.3% Two or more races, 17.4% Hispanic of any race; Average household size: 2.69; Median age: 41.2; Age under 18: 23.4%; Age 65 and over: 13.4%; Males per 100 females: 94.5; Marriage status: 29.4% never married, 54.8% now married, 1.4% separated, 6.1% widowed, 9.8% divorced; Foreign born: 22.3%; Speak English only: 67.3%; With disability: 8.7%; Veterans: 7.4%; Ancestry: 10.8% German, 8.5% Irish, 8.0% English, 5.2% Italian, 3.5% Portuguese

Employment: 21.2% management, business, and financial, 7.2% computer, engineering, and science, 10.7% education, legal, community service, arts, and media, 5.9% healthcare practitioners, 14.1% service, 26.2% sales and office, 7.0% natural resources, construction, and maintenance, 7.6% production, transportation, and material moving

Income: Per capita: $38,681; Median household: $83,211; Average household: $104,618; Households with income of $100,000 or more: 41.9%; Poverty rate: 7.8%

Educational Attainment: High school diploma or higher: 92.1%; Bachelor's degree or higher: 36.9%; Graduate/professional degree or higher: 13.3%

School District(s)

Castro Valley Unified (KG-12)
2012-13 Enrollment: 9,210 . . . . (510) 537-3000
Hayward Unified (KG-12)
2012-13 Enrollment: 21,937 . . . . (510) 784-2600

Housing: Homeownership rate: 69.0%; Median home value: $533,600; Median year structure built: 1965; Homeowner vacancy rate: 1.3%; Median gross rent: $1,379 per month; Rental vacancy rate: 5.4%

Health Insurance: 91.1% have insurance; 78.8% have private insurance; 23.2% have public insurance; 8.9% do not have insurance; 2.7% of children under 18 do not have insurance

Hospitals: Eden Medical Center (302 beds)

Transportation: Commute: 82.7% car, 9.2% public transportation, 1.4% walk, 5.8% work from home; Median travel time to work: 30.1 minutes

---

CHERRYLAND (CDP). Covers a land area of 1.197 square miles and a water area of 0 square miles. Located at 37.68° N. Lat; 122.10° W. Long. Elevation is 66 feet.

Population: 14,728; Growth (since 2000): 6.4%; Density: 12,301.9 persons per square mile; Race: 41.0% White, 11.5% Black/African American, 9.5% Asian, 1.4% American Indian/Alaska Native, 2.1% Native Hawaiian/Other Pacific Islander, 7.2% Two or more races, 54.0% Hispanic of any race; Average household size: 3.07; Median age: 32.3; Age under 18: 26.9%; Age 65 and over: 8.5%; Males per 100 females: 101.9; Marriage status: 43.6% never married, 41.9% now married, 3.0% separated, 4.8% widowed, 9.7% divorced; Foreign born: 33.7%; Speak English only: 41.9%; With disability: 11.9%; Veterans: 4.7%; Ancestry: 4.9% Portuguese, 3.7% Irish, 3.1% English, 2.8% German, 1.9% Italian

Employment: 10.0% management, business, and financial, 2.6% computer, engineering, and science, 6.5% education, legal, community service, arts, and media, 1.5% healthcare practitioners, 24.1% service, 22.1% sales and office, 11.7% natural resources, construction, and maintenance, 21.5% production, transportation, and material moving

Income: Per capita: $20,115; Median household: $49,265; Average household: $62,366; Households with income of $100,000 or more: 15.0%; Poverty rate: 25.9%

Educational Attainment: High school diploma or higher: 69.4%; Bachelor's degree or higher: 14.3%; Graduate/professional degree or higher: 3.1%

Housing: Homeownership rate: 31.4%; Median home value: $307,700; Median year structure built: 1959; Homeowner vacancy rate: 1.5%; Median gross rent: $1,153 per month; Rental vacancy rate: 5.4%

Health Insurance: 80.3% have insurance; 44.9% have private insurance; 41.7% have public insurance; 19.7% do not have insurance; 4.3% of children under 18 do not have insurance

Transportation: Commute: 84.3% car, 6.4% public transportation, 3.8% walk, 3.5% work from home; Median travel time to work: 27.8 minutes

---

DUBLIN (city). Covers a land area of 14.908 square miles and a water area of 0.004 square miles. Located at 37.71° N. Lat; 121.90° W. Long. Elevation is 367 feet.

History: Named,legend has it,for its great concentration of Irish settlers, by James Witt Dougherty in 1852. Dublin was established on land granted in 1834 to Jose Maria Amador, a private in the San Francisco Company, in recompense for his military services. The post office had been designated Dougherty's Station but, said Dougherty, there were so many Irish there, the settlement might as well be called Dublin.

Population: 46,036; Growth (since 2000): 53.6%; Density: 3,088.0 persons per square mile; Race: 51.3% White, 9.4% Black/African American, 26.8% Asian, 0.5% American Indian/Alaska Native, 0.6% Native Hawaiian/Other Pacific Islander, 6.0% Two or more races, 14.5% Hispanic of any race; Average household size: 2.70; Median age: 35.3; Age under 18: 22.4%; Age 65 and over: 7.3%; Males per 100 females: 108.8; Marriage status: 31.0% never married, 56.0% now married, 2.6% separated, 3.4% widowed, 9.5% divorced; Foreign born: 25.9%; Speak English only: 65.5%; With disability: 5.5%; Veterans: 5.2%; Ancestry: 10.2% German, 9.4% Irish, 6.3% English, 6.2% Italian, 3.6% Portuguese

Employment: 23.5% management, business, and financial, 15.4% computer, engineering, and science, 9.3% education, legal, community service, arts, and media, 4.9% healthcare practitioners, 12.2% service, 27.1% sales and office, 3.3% natural resources, construction, and maintenance, 4.4% production, transportation, and material moving

Income: Per capita: $42,660; Median household: $115,236; Average household: $127,116; Households with income of $100,000 or more: 58.7%; Poverty rate: 3.8%

Educational Attainment: High school diploma or higher: 91.5%; Bachelor's degree or higher: 50.4%; Graduate/professional degree or higher: 17.7%

School District(s)

Dublin Unified (KG-12)
2012-13 Enrollment: 7,325 . . . . (925) 828-2551

Housing: Homeownership rate: 63.2%; Median home value: $564,900; Median year structure built: 1995; Homeowner vacancy rate: 2.5%; Median gross rent: $1,786 per month; Rental vacancy rate: 5.0%

Health Insurance: 94.2% have insurance; 87.5% have private insurance; 13.6% have public insurance; 5.8% do not have insurance; 1.6% of children under 18 do not have insurance

Safety: Violent crime rate: 14.1 per 10,000 population; Property crime rate: 148.4 per 10,000 population

Transportation: Commute: 81.4% car, 9.2% public transportation, 2.1% walk, 5.9% work from home; Median travel time to work: 31.3 minutes

Additional Information Contacts

City of Dublin. . . . . (925) 833-6600
http://www.ci.dublin.ca.us

EMERYVILLE (city). Covers a land area of 1.246 square miles and a water area of 0.764 square miles. Located at 37.84° N. Lat; 122.30° W. Long. Elevation is 23 feet.

History: Incorporated 1896.

Population: 10,080; Growth (since 2000): 46.5%; Density: 8,091.7 persons per square mile; Race: 44.5% White, 17.5% Black/African American, 27.5% Asian, 0.4% American Indian/Alaska Native, 0.2% Native Hawaiian/Other Pacific Islander, 6.4% Two or more races, 9.2% Hispanic of any race; Average household size: 1.76; Median age: 35.0; Age under 18: 10.2%; Age 65 and over: 10.0%; Males per 100 females: 97.8; Marriage status: 48.5% never married, 33.1% now married, 1.8% separated, 5.9% widowed, 12.5% divorced; Foreign born: 22.6%; Speak English only: 69.1%; With disability: 11.2%; Veterans: 4.9%; Ancestry: 7.0% German, 5.9% Irish, 5.0% English, 4.6% Italian, 2.8% American

Employment: 23.3% management, business, and financial, 13.8% computer, engineering, and science, 23.1% education, legal, community service, arts, and media, 8.0% healthcare practitioners, 9.8% service, 17.2% sales and office, 2.0% natural resources, construction, and maintenance, 2.7% production, transportation, and material moving

Income: Per capita: $48,800; Median household: $65,000; Average household: $82,629; Households with income of $100,000 or more: 29.2%; Poverty rate: 9.7%

Educational Attainment: High school diploma or higher: 96.2%; Bachelor's degree or higher: 71.5%; Graduate/professional degree or higher: 35.8%

School District(s)

Emery Unified (KG-12)
2012-13 Enrollment: 751. . . . . (510) 601-4000
Piedmont City Unified (KG-12)
2012-13 Enrollment: 2,605 . . . . (510) 594-2600

Four-year College(s)

Expression College for Digital Arts (Private, For-profit)
Fall 2013 Enrollment: 574. . . . . (510) 654-2934
2013-14 Tuition: In-state $23,747; Out-of-state $23,747

Vocational/Technical School(s)

National Holistic Institute (Private, For-profit)
Fall 2013 Enrollment: 764. . . . . (510) 547-6442
2013-14 Tuition: $14,341

Housing: Homeownership rate: 35.4%; Median home value: $296,000; Median year structure built: 1984; Homeowner vacancy rate: 9.3%; Median gross rent: $1,587 per month; Rental vacancy rate: 10.2%

Health Insurance: 84.7% have insurance; 72.0% have private insurance; 22.3% have public insurance; 15.3% do not have insurance; 16.6% of children under 18 do not have insurance

Safety: Violent crime rate: 126.7 per 10,000 population; Property crime rate: 1,585.2 per 10,000 population

Transportation: Commute: 61.9% car, 19.3% public transportation, 8.0% walk, 6.3% work from home; Median travel time to work: 28.3 minutes; Amtrak: Train service available.

Additional Information Contacts

City of Emeryville. . . . . (510) 596-4300
http://www.ci.emeryville.ca.us

FAIRVIEW (CDP). Covers a land area of 2.765 square miles and a water area of 0.024 square miles. Located at 37.68° N. Lat; 122.04° W. Long. Elevation is 597 feet.

Population: 10,003; Growth (since 2000): 5.6%; Density: 3,617.8 persons per square mile; Race: 45.0% White, 21.0% Black/African American, 15.2% Asian, 0.8% American Indian/Alaska Native, 1.3% Native Hawaiian/Other Pacific Islander, 7.6% Two or more races, 21.7% Hispanic of any race; Average household size: 2.82; Median age: 41.1; Age under 18: 20.7%; Age 65 and over: 12.8%; Males per 100 females: 97.9; Marriage status: 31.2% never married, 53.6% now married, 2.4% separated, 4.8% widowed, 10.4% divorced; Foreign born: 22.5%; Speak English only: 65.5%; With disability: 13.6%; Veterans: 7.9%; Ancestry: 5.7% Irish, 5.6% German, 5.5% English, 3.8% Portuguese, 2.4% Italian

Employment: 21.6% management, business, and financial, 6.0% computer, engineering, and science, 11.2% education, legal, community service, arts, and media, 7.6% healthcare practitioners, 13.1% service, 22.8% sales and office, 6.5% natural resources, construction, and maintenance, 11.3% production, transportation, and material moving

Income: Per capita: $39,169; Median household: $91,220; Average household: $112,790; Households with income of $100,000 or more: 47.0%; Poverty rate: 7.2%

Educational Attainment: High school diploma or higher: 92.2%; Bachelor's degree or higher: 38.2%; Graduate/professional degree or higher: 12.4%

Housing: Homeownership rate: 78.0%; Median home value: $419,400; Median year structure built: 1975; Homeowner vacancy rate: 1.8%; Median gross rent: $1,495 per month; Rental vacancy rate: 5.1%

Health Insurance: 89.6% have insurance; 74.5% have private insurance; 27.2% have public insurance; 10.4% do not have insurance; 7.2% of children under 18 do not have insurance

Transportation: Commute: 87.7% car, 7.6% public transportation, 1.0% walk, 3.2% work from home; Median travel time to work: 33.2 minutes

FREMONT (city). Covers a land area of 77.459 square miles and a water area of 10.151 square miles. Located at 37.49° N. Lat; 121.94° W. Long. Elevation is 56 feet.

History: Named for John C. Fremont, explorer and military leader in early California. Long an Agriculture center, with champagne vineyards founded (1870) by Leland Stanford. Its economy was transformed in 1963, however, when General Motors opened a huge automobile-assembly plant here. Mission San Jose de Guadalupe (1797) to southeast, has been restored as a Museum. Incorporated 1956.

Population: 214,089; Growth (since 2000): 5.2%; Density: 2,763.9 persons per square mile; Race: 32.8% White, 3.3% Black/African American, 50.6% Asian, 0.5% American Indian/Alaska Native, 0.5% Native Hawaiian/Other Pacific Islander, 5.9% Two or more races, 14.8% Hispanic of any race; Average household size: 2.99; Median age: 36.8; Age under 18: 24.9%; Age 65 and over: 10.2%; Males per 100 females: 98.9; Marriage status: 26.4% never married, 62.0% now married, 1.6% separated, 4.7% widowed, 6.9% divorced; Foreign born: 43.7%; Speak English only: 41.6%; With disability: 7.2%; Veterans: 4.5%; Ancestry: 6.6% German, 5.3% Irish, 4.0% English, 3.0% Italian, 2.3% Portuguese

Employment: 20.1% management, business, and financial, 23.1% computer, engineering, and science, 8.1% education, legal, community service, arts, and media, 4.9% healthcare practitioners, 10.9% service, 20.5% sales and office, 4.8% natural resources, construction, and maintenance, 7.7% production, transportation, and material moving

Income: Per capita: $40,190; Median household: $101,535; Average household: $119,720; Households with income of $100,000 or more: 50.9%; Poverty rate: 6.0%

Educational Attainment: High school diploma or higher: 91.0%; Bachelor's degree or higher: 50.9%; Graduate/professional degree or higher: 23.0%

School District(s)

California School for the Blind (State Special Sch (KG-12)
2012-13 Enrollment: 82. . . . . (510) 794-3800
California School for the Deaf-Fremont (State Spec (PK-12)
2012-13 Enrollment: 407. . . . . (510) 794-3666
Fremont Unified (KG-12)
2012-13 Enrollment: 33,308 . . . . (510) 657-2350
Mission Valley Roc/p
2012-13 Enrollment: n/a . . . . (510) 657-1865

Four-year College(s)

Northwestern Polytechnic University (Private, Not-for-profit)
Fall 2013 Enrollment: 988. . . . . (510) 592-9688
2013-14 Tuition: In-state $8,300; Out-of-state $8,300
Unitek College (Private, For-profit)
Fall 2013 Enrollment: 904. . . . . (510) 249-1060
2013-14 Tuition: In-state $18,968; Out-of-state $18,968

Two-year College(s)

Ohlone College (Public)
Fall 2013 Enrollment: 10,310 . . . . (510) 659-6000
2013-14 Tuition: In-state $1,162; Out-of-state $6,394
Wyotech-Fremont (Private, For-profit)
Fall 2013 Enrollment: 1,199 . . . . (800) 248-8585

Housing: Homeownership rate: 62.6%; Median home value: $600,300; Median year structure built: 1976; Homeowner vacancy rate: 1.3%; Median gross rent: $1,566 per month; Rental vacancy rate: 4.5%

Health Insurance: 91.5% have insurance; 78.7% have private insurance; 19.4% have public insurance; 8.5% do not have insurance; 2.9% of children under 18 do not have insurance

Hospitals: Washington Hospital (337 beds)

Safety: Violent crime rate: 12.2 per 10,000 population; Property crime rate: 182.5 per 10,000 population

Newspapers: The Argus (daily circulation 26400); Tri-City Voice (weekly circulation 35700)

Transportation: Commute: 85.9% car, 7.4% public transportation, 1.4% walk, 3.8% work from home; Median travel time to work: 29.7 minutes; Amtrak: Train and bus service available.

Additional Information Contacts

City of Fremont . . . . (510) 284-4000
http://www.fremont.gov

HAYWARD (city). Covers a land area of 45.323 square miles and a water area of 18.425 square miles. Located at 37.63° N. Lat; 122.11° W. Long. Elevation is 105 feet.

History: Hayward was established on Rancho San Lorenzo belonging to Guillermo Castro, who laid out the town in 1854. It was named for William Hayward, a friend of Castro, who built the first hotel here in 1852.

Population: 144,186; Growth (since 2000): 3.0%; Density: 3,181.3 persons per square mile; Race: 34.2% White, 11.9% Black/African American, 22.0% Asian, 1.0% American Indian/Alaska Native, 3.1% Native Hawaiian/Other Pacific Islander, 7.1% Two or more races, 40.7% Hispanic of any race; Average household size: 3.12; Median age: 33.5; Age under 18: 24.5%; Age 65 and over: 10.2%; Males per 100 females: 97.4; Marriage status: 37.4% never married, 48.6% now married, 2.8% separated, 5.6% widowed, 8.3% divorced; Foreign born: 38.1%; Speak English only: 42.8%; With disability: 9.8%; Veterans: 5.3%; Ancestry: 4.5% German, 3.5% Irish, 2.8% Portuguese, 2.7% English, 1.8% Italian

Employment: 11.9% management, business, and financial, 5.5% computer, engineering, and science, 6.8% education, legal, community service, arts, and media, 3.9% healthcare practitioners, 18.2% service, 26.9% sales and office, 10.7% natural resources, construction, and maintenance, 16.1% production, transportation, and material moving

Income: Per capita: $25,208; Median household: $62,013; Average household: $77,320; Households with income of $100,000 or more: 26.8%; Poverty rate: 14.4%

Educational Attainment: High school diploma or higher: 79.5%; Bachelor's degree or higher: 24.2%; Graduate/professional degree or higher: 6.1%

School District(s)

Alameda County Office of Education (PK-12)
2012-13 Enrollment: 4,041 . . . . (510) 887-0152
Eden Area Rop
2012-13 Enrollment: n/a . . . . (510) 293-2900
Hayward Unified (KG-12)
2012-13 Enrollment: 21,937 . . . . (510) 784-2600
New Haven Unified (KG-12)
2012-13 Enrollment: 12,873 . . . . (510) 471-1100
San Lorenzo Unified (KG-12)
2012-13 Enrollment: 12,270 . . . . (510) 317-4600

Four-year College(s)

California State University-East Bay (Public)
Fall 2013 Enrollment: 14,526 . . . . (510) 885-3000
2013-14 Tuition: In-state $6,550; Out-of-state $17,710
Life Chiropractic College West (Private, Not-for-profit)
Fall 2013 Enrollment: 456 . . . . (510) 780-4500

Two-year College(s)

Chabot College (Public)
Fall 2013 Enrollment: 13,142 . . . . (510) 723-6600
2013-14 Tuition: In-state $1,138; Out-of-state $6,970
Heald College-Hayward (Private, For-profit)
Fall 2013 Enrollment: 1,249 . . . . (510) 783-2100
2013-14 Tuition: In-state $13,620; Out-of-state $13,620

Vocational/Technical School(s)

Everest College-Hayward (Private, For-profit)
Fall 2013 Enrollment: 170 . . . . (510) 582-9500
2013-14 Tuition: $15,009
NCP College of Nursing-Hayward (Private, For-profit)
Fall 2013 Enrollment: 88 . . . . (650) 871-0701

Housing: Homeownership rate: 52.7%; Median home value: $321,500; Median year structure built: 1971; Homeowner vacancy rate: 2.3%; Median gross rent: $1,292 per month; Rental vacancy rate: 6.6%

Health Insurance: 81.8% have insurance; 60.3% have private insurance; 29.6% have public insurance; 18.2% do not have insurance; 7.0% of children under 18 do not have insurance

Hospitals: Kaiser Foundation Hospital - Fremont/Hayward (234 beds); Saint Rose Hospital (175 beds)

Safety: Violent crime rate: 39.0 per 10,000 population; Property crime rate: 320.9 per 10,000 population

Transportation: Commute: 85.9% car, 8.1% public transportation, 2.2% walk, 2.4% work from home; Median travel time to work: 29.1 minutes; Amtrak: Train service available.

Airports: Hayward Executive (general aviation)

Additional Information Contacts

City of Hayward . . . . (510) 583-4000
http://www.ci.hayward.ca.us

LIVERMORE (city). Covers a land area of 25.173 square miles and a water area of 0.003 square miles. Located at 37.69° N. Lat; 121.76° W. Long. Elevation is 492 feet.

History: Named for Robert Livermore, English sailor who received a rancho land grant here in 1835 after leaving his ship in 1822. In 1838 Livermore and his partner, Jose Noriega, were granted the land which comprised the Rancho las Positas.

Population: 80,968; Growth (since 2000): 10.4%; Density: 3,216.5 persons per square mile; Race: 74.6% White, 2.1% Black/African American, 8.4% Asian, 0.6% American Indian/Alaska Native, 0.3% Native Hawaiian/Other Pacific Islander, 5.4% Two or more races, 20.9% Hispanic of any race; Average household size: 2.76; Median age: 38.3; Age under 18: 25.5%; Age 65 and over: 10.3%; Males per 100 females: 98.6; Marriage status: 27.7% never married, 57.8% now married, 2.0% separated, 4.2% widowed, 10.3% divorced; Foreign born: 16.6%; Speak English only: 78.3%; With disability: 7.8%; Veterans: 8.7%; Ancestry: 15.5% German, 12.7% Irish, 10.7% English, 7.8% Italian, 3.9% Portuguese

Employment: 18.9% management, business, and financial, 11.9% computer, engineering, and science, 9.7% education, legal, community service, arts, and media, 4.4% healthcare practitioners, 15.8% service, 23.8% sales and office, 7.7% natural resources, construction, and maintenance, 7.7% production, transportation, and material moving

Income: Per capita: $42,213; Median household: $99,161; Average household: $116,498; Households with income of $100,000 or more: 49.6%; Poverty rate: 5.7%

Educational Attainment: High school diploma or higher: 92.0%; Bachelor's degree or higher: 38.9%; Graduate/professional degree or higher: 13.2%

School District(s)

Livermore Valley Joint Unified (KG-12)
2012-13 Enrollment: 12,629 . . . . (925) 606-3200
Sbe - Livermore Valley Charter (KG-08)
2012-13 Enrollment: 1,089 . . . . (925) 443-1690
Sbe - Livermore Valley Charter Preparatory High (09-12)
2012-13 Enrollment: 330 . . . . (925) 456-9000
Tri-Valley Rop
2012-13 Enrollment: n/a . . . . (925) 455-4800

Two-year College(s)

Las Positas College (Public)
Fall 2013 Enrollment: 8,631 . . . . (925) 424-1000
2013-14 Tuition: In-state $1,138; Out-of-state $6,562

Housing: Homeownership rate: 70.1%; Median home value: $476,400; Median year structure built: 1977; Homeowner vacancy rate: 1.5%; Median gross rent: $1,448 per month; Rental vacancy rate: 4.8%

Health Insurance: 91.2% have insurance; 82.7% have private insurance; 18.3% have public insurance; 8.8% do not have insurance; 5.0% of children under 18 do not have insurance

Safety: Violent crime rate: 32.0 per 10,000 population; Property crime rate: 217.0 per 10,000 population

Newspapers: The Independent (weekly circulation 49000)

Transportation: Commute: 88.5% car, 3.3% public transportation, 1.2% walk, 5.1% work from home; Median travel time to work: 29.1 minutes; Amtrak: Train and bus service available.
Airports: Livermore Municipal (general aviation)
Additional Information Contacts
City of Livermore . . . . (925) 960-4000
http://www.ci.livermore.ca.us

NEWARK (city). Covers a land area of 13.875 square miles and a water area of 0.023 square miles. Located at 37.50° N. Lat; 122.03° W. Long. Elevation is 20 feet.
Population: 42,573; Growth (since 2000): 0.2%; Density: 3,068.4 persons per square mile; Race: 41.3% White, 4.7% Black/African American, 27.2% Asian, 0.7% American Indian/Alaska Native, 1.5% Native Hawaiian/Other Pacific Islander, 6.6% Two or more races, 35.2% Hispanic of any race; Average household size: 3.27; Median age: 35.4; Age under 18: 25.4%; Age 65 and over: 10.6%; Males per 100 females: 99.3; Marriage status: 33.5% never married, 52.7% now married, 2.3% separated, 4.6% widowed, 9.1% divorced; Foreign born: 33.5%; Speak English only: 49.5%; With disability: 7.8%; Veterans: 5.2%; Ancestry: 8.5% German, 6.7% Irish, 4.4% English, 3.9% Portuguese, 3.8% Italian
Employment: 15.4% management, business, and financial, 10.6% computer, engineering, and science, 6.8% education, legal, community service, arts, and media, 5.5% healthcare practitioners, 14.7% service, 22.0% sales and office, 9.0% natural resources, construction, and maintenance, 15.9% production, transportation, and material moving
Income: Per capita: $31,056; Median household: $85,847; Average household: $96,493; Households with income of $100,000 or more: 41.1%; Poverty rate: 7.7%
Educational Attainment: High school diploma or higher: 88.6%; Bachelor's degree or higher: 27.8%; Graduate/professional degree or higher: 8.8%

School District(s)

Alameda County Office of Education (PK-12)
2012-13 Enrollment: 4,041 . . . . (510) 887-0152
Newark Unified (KG-12)
2012-13 Enrollment: 6,484 . . . . (510) 818-4112
Housing: Homeownership rate: 69.0%; Median home value: $433,100; Median year structure built: 1973; Homeowner vacancy rate: 1.0%; Median gross rent: $1,543 per month; Rental vacancy rate: 4.0%
Health Insurance: 89.7% have insurance; 73.9% have private insurance; 24.4% have public insurance; 10.3% do not have insurance; 4.0% of children under 18 do not have insurance
Safety: Violent crime rate: 28.0 per 10,000 population; Property crime rate: 241.6 per 10,000 population
Transportation: Commute: 89.7% car, 4.8% public transportation, 1.3% walk, 2.7% work from home; Median travel time to work: 27.1 minutes
Additional Information Contacts
City of Newark . . . . (510) 578-4000
http://www.newark.org

OAKLAND (city). County seat. Covers a land area of 55.786 square miles and a water area of 22.216 square miles. Located at 37.77° N. Lat; 122.23° W. Long. Elevation is 43 feet.
History: Oakland was established on what was originally Rancho San Antonio, land granted in 1820 to Don Luis Maria Peralta for his service in the Spanish army. In 1842 the land was divided between Peralta's four sons, and Vincente Peralta became the owner of the area that became Oakland, maintaining his large herds of cattle here. The gold rush brought many settlers to the area, including Horace W. Carpentier who in 1852 incorporated the Town of Oakland with himself as mayor. Carpentier named his town for the many oak trees growing there. Oakland grew when train service was established in the 1860's, and when 50,000 refugees from the 1906 San Francisco earthquake moved across the bay to Oakland. In 1936 the San Francisco-Oakland Bay Bridge opened.
Population: 390,724; Growth (since 2000): -2.2%; Density: 7,004.0 persons per square mile; Race: 34.5% White, 28.0% Black/African American, 16.8% Asian, 0.8% American Indian/Alaska Native, 0.6% Native Hawaiian/Other Pacific Islander, 5.6% Two or more races, 25.4% Hispanic of any race; Average household size: 2.49; Median age: 36.2; Age under 18: 21.3%; Age 65 and over: 11.1%; Males per 100 females: 94.2; Marriage status: 44.2% never married, 39.8% now married, 2.9% separated, 5.7% widowed, 10.4% divorced; Foreign born: 27.0%; Speak English only: 60.1%; With disability: 11.4%; Veterans: 4.8%; Ancestry: 5.4% German, 4.7% Irish, 4.1% English, 2.8% Italian, 1.9% European
Employment: 16.1% management, business, and financial, 6.9% computer, engineering, and science, 15.4% education, legal, community service, arts, and media, 3.6% healthcare practitioners, 20.2% service, 20.8% sales and office, 7.2% natural resources, construction, and maintenance, 9.7% production, transportation, and material moving
Income: Per capita: $31,971; Median household: $52,583; Average household: $78,684; Households with income of $100,000 or more: 25.2%; Poverty rate: 20.5%
Educational Attainment: High school diploma or higher: 80.2%; Bachelor's degree or higher: 38.1%; Graduate/professional degree or higher: 16.6%

School District(s)

Alameda County Office of Education (PK-12)
2012-13 Enrollment: 4,041 . . . . (510) 887-0152
Oakland Unified (KG-12)
2012-13 Enrollment: 46,463 . . . . (510) 879-8582

Four-year College(s)

Academy of Chinese Culture and Health Sciences (Private, Not-for-profit)
Fall 2013 Enrollment: 132 . . . . (510) 763-7787
Holy Names University (Private, Not-for-profit, Roman Catholic)
Fall 2013 Enrollment: 1,343 . . . . (510) 436-1000
2013-14 Tuition: In-state $33,020; Out-of-state $33,020
ITT Technical Institute-Oakland (Private, For-profit)
Fall 2013 Enrollment: 169 . . . . (510) 553-2800
2013-14 Tuition: In-state $18,048; Out-of-state $18,048
Lincoln University (Private, Not-for-profit)
Fall 2013 Enrollment: 492 . . . . (510) 628-8010
2013-14 Tuition: In-state $10,105; Out-of-state $10,105
Mills College (Private, Not-for-profit)
Fall 2013 Enrollment: 1,595 . . . . (510) 430-2255
2013-14 Tuition: In-state $41,494; Out-of-state $41,494
SUM Bible College and Theological Seminary (Private, Not-for-profit, Assemblies of God Church)
Fall 2013 Enrollment: 367 . . . . (510) 567-6174
2013-14 Tuition: In-state $7,946; Out-of-state $7,946
Samuel Merritt University (Private, Not-for-profit)
Fall 2013 Enrollment: 1,542 . . . . (510) 869-6511

Two-year College(s)

Laney College (Public)
Fall 2013 Enrollment: 11,362 . . . . (510) 834-5740
2013-14 Tuition: In-state $1,144; Out-of-state $6,256
Merritt College (Public)
Fall 2013 Enrollment: 5,887 . . . . (510) 531-4911
2013-14 Tuition: In-state $1,144; Out-of-state $6,256

Vocational/Technical School(s)

International College of Cosmetology (Private, For-profit)
Fall 2013 Enrollment: 179 . . . . (510) 261-8256
2013-14 Tuition: $700
Moler Barber College (Private, For-profit)
Fall 2013 Enrollment: 76 . . . . (510) 652-4177
2013-14 Tuition: $12,999
The English Center (Private, Not-for-profit)
Fall 2013 Enrollment: 79 . . . . (510) 836-6700
2013-14 Tuition: In-state $9,705; Out-of-state $9,705
Housing: Homeownership rate: 41.0%; Median home value: $428,900; Median year structure built: 1949; Homeowner vacancy rate: 3.0%; Median gross rent: $1,087 per month; Rental vacancy rate: 8.5%
Health Insurance: 82.7% have insurance; 57.1% have private insurance; 33.6% have public insurance; 17.3% do not have insurance; 7.1% of children under 18 do not have insurance
Hospitals: Alameda County Medical Center (308 beds); Alta Bates Summit Medical Center (517 beds); Kaiser Foundation Hospital - Oakland/Richmond (348 beds)
Safety: Violent crime rate: 197.7 per 10,000 population; Property crime rate: 623.3 per 10,000 population
Newspapers: East Bay Express (weekly circulation 50000); Oakland Tribune (daily circulation 52700); Post News Group (weekly circulation 50000)
Transportation: Commute: 66.4% car, 18.3% public transportation, 4.2% walk, 6.7% work from home; Median travel time to work: 28.3 minutes; Amtrak: Train service available.
Airports: Metropolitan Oakland International (primary service/medium hub)
Additional Information Contacts

City of Oakland . . . . (510) 444-2489
http://www.oaklandnet.com

PIEDMONT (city). Covers a land area of 1.678 square miles and a water area of 0 square miles. Located at 37.82° N. Lat; 122.23° W. Long. Elevation is 331 feet.

History: Named for the Italian or French translation of "foot of the mountain". Many of its homes and streets enjoy a spectacular view of the San Francisco Bay area. Incorporated 1907.

Population: 10,667; Growth (since 2000): -2.6%; Density: 6,358.5 persons per square mile; Race: 74.2% White, 1.3% Black/African American, 18.2% Asian, 0.1% American Indian/Alaska Native, 0.1% Native Hawaiian/Other Pacific Islander, 5.2% Two or more races, 3.9% Hispanic of any race; Average household size: 2.81; Median age: 46.2; Age under 18: 28.3%; Age 65 and over: 15.4%; Males per 100 females: 94.7; Marriage status: 22.4% never married, 70.3% now married, 1.4% separated, 3.5% widowed, 3.8% divorced; Foreign born: 14.4%; Speak English only: 82.3%; With disability: 4.4%; Veterans: 5.8%; Ancestry: 17.5% English, 14.9% German, 8.8% Irish, 5.9% Russian, 4.6% Italian

Employment: 35.8% management, business, and financial, 9.9% computer, engineering, and science, 21.9% education, legal, community service, arts, and media, 9.1% healthcare practitioners, 4.0% service, 16.5% sales and office, 0.9% natural resources, construction, and maintenance, 2.0% production, transportation, and material moving

Income: Per capita: $98,949; Median household: $207,222; Average household: $293,923; Households with income of $100,000 or more: 77.9%; Poverty rate: 4.1%

Educational Attainment: High school diploma or higher: 97.9%; Bachelor's degree or higher: 82.7%; Graduate/professional degree or higher: 45.1%

School District(s)

Piedmont City Unified (KG-12)
2012-13 Enrollment: 2,605 . . . . (510) 594-2600

Housing: Homeownership rate: 88.3%; Median home value: 1 million+; Median year structure built: Before 1940; Homeowner vacancy rate: 0.5%; Median gross rent: $1,953 per month; Rental vacancy rate: 3.7%

Health Insurance: 99.0% have insurance; 95.1% have private insurance; 14.4% have public insurance; 1.0% do not have insurance; 0.3% of children under 18 do not have insurance

Safety: Violent crime rate: 18.2 per 10,000 population; Property crime rate: 266.4 per 10,000 population

Transportation: Commute: 73.4% car, 11.4% public transportation, 1.8% walk, 9.7% work from home; Median travel time to work: 25.6 minutes

Additional Information Contacts

City of Piedmont . . . . (510) 420-3040
http://www.ci.piedmont.ca.us

PLEASANTON (city). Covers a land area of 24.113 square miles and a water area of 0.153 square miles. Located at 37.67° N. Lat; 121.88° W. Long. Elevation is 351 feet.

History: Named for General Alfred Pleasonton, who served in the Mexican War. Pleasanton was founded in 1868.

Population: 70,285; Growth (since 2000): 10.4%; Density: 2,914.8 persons per square mile; Race: 67.0% White, 1.7% Black/African American, 23.2% Asian, 0.3% American Indian/Alaska Native, 0.2% Native Hawaiian/Other Pacific Islander, 4.8% Two or more races, 10.3% Hispanic of any race; Average household size: 2.77; Median age: 40.5; Age under 18: 27.1%; Age 65 and over: 10.9%; Males per 100 females: 96.1; Marriage status: 25.4% never married, 62.1% now married, 1.6% separated, 4.2% widowed, 8.3% divorced; Foreign born: 24.7%; Speak English only: 69.9%; With disability: 6.6%; Veterans: 6.8%; Ancestry: 13.6% German, 12.2% Irish, 10.1% English, 7.6% Italian, 3.0% French

Employment: 25.4% management, business, and financial, 16.5% computer, engineering, and science, 9.8% education, legal, community service, arts, and media, 5.0% healthcare practitioners, 12.4% service, 22.3% sales and office, 4.4% natural resources, construction, and maintenance, 4.2% production, transportation, and material moving

Income: Per capita: $50,540; Median household: $118,317; Average household: $142,891; Households with income of $100,000 or more: 58.2%; Poverty rate: 4.8%

Educational Attainment: High school diploma or higher: 95.0%; Bachelor's degree or higher: 56.5%; Graduate/professional degree or higher: 23.0%

School District(s)

Pleasanton Unified (KG-12)
2012-13 Enrollment: 14,932 . . . . (925) 462-5500

Two-year College(s)

Golden State College of Court Reporting (Private, For-profit)
Fall 2013 Enrollment: 68 . . . . (925) 223-6604

Housing: Homeownership rate: 70.9%; Median home value: $709,400; Median year structure built: 1982; Homeowner vacancy rate: 0.9%; Median gross rent: $1,680 per month; Rental vacancy rate: 4.1%

Health Insurance: 93.0% have insurance; 87.0% have private insurance; 15.5% have public insurance; 7.0% do not have insurance; 3.1% of children under 18 do not have insurance

Hospitals: Valleycare Medical Center

Safety: Violent crime rate: 8.2 per 10,000 population; Property crime rate: 175.5 per 10,000 population

Newspapers: Pleasanton Weekly (weekly circulation 18000); Tri-Valley Herald (daily circulation 33400)

Transportation: Commute: 81.9% car, 7.1% public transportation, 3.0% walk, 6.7% work from home; Median travel time to work: 29.6 minutes; Amtrak: Train and bus service available.

Additional Information Contacts

City of Pleasanton . . . . (925) 931-5002
http://www.ci.pleasanton.ca.us

SAN LEANDRO (city). Covers a land area of 13.343 square miles and a water area of 2.320 square miles. Located at 37.70° N. Lat; 122.16° W. Long. Elevation is 56 feet.

History: Named for the Mexican land grant, probably for St. Leander, 6th-century Archbishop of Seville. San Leandro was settled in the early 1850s by squatters who tried to drive Jose Joaquin Estudillo and his family from their Rancho San Leandro. Estudillo eventually forced the squatters to pay for their land, and laid out a town that served as the seat of Alameda County from 1855 to 1872.

Population: 84,950; Growth (since 2000): 6.9%; Density: 6,366.8 persons per square mile; Race: 37.6% White, 12.3% Black/African American, 29.7% Asian, 0.8% American Indian/Alaska Native, 0.8% Native Hawaiian/Other Pacific Islander, 5.6% Two or more races, 27.4% Hispanic of any race; Average household size: 2.74; Median age: 39.3; Age under 18: 22.3%; Age 65 and over: 13.8%; Males per 100 females: 92.3; Marriage status: 34.1% never married, 50.5% now married, 1.7% separated, 6.0% widowed, 9.4% divorced; Foreign born: 34.5%; Speak English only: 50.9%; With disability: 9.8%; Veterans: 5.8%; Ancestry: 5.0% German, 4.4% Irish, 4.3% English, 3.4% Portuguese, 3.4% Italian

Employment: 13.1% management, business, and financial, 6.9% computer, engineering, and science, 8.7% education, legal, community service, arts, and media, 3.8% healthcare practitioners, 18.5% service, 26.3% sales and office, 8.7% natural resources, construction, and maintenance, 13.9% production, transportation, and material moving

Income: Per capita: $28,801; Median household: $63,055; Average household: $77,090; Households with income of $100,000 or more: 27.8%; Poverty rate: 10.0%

Educational Attainment: High school diploma or higher: 82.0%; Bachelor's degree or higher: 27.3%; Graduate/professional degree or higher: 8.1%

School District(s)

Alameda County Office of Education (PK-12)
2012-13 Enrollment: 4,041 . . . . (510) 887-0152
San Leandro Unified (KG-12)
2012-13 Enrollment: 8,704 . . . . (510) 667-3500
San Lorenzo Unified (KG-12)
2012-13 Enrollment: 12,270 . . . . (510) 317-4600

Two-year College(s)

Carrington College California-San Leandro (Private, For-profit)
Fall 2013 Enrollment: 521 . . . . (510) 276-3888

Vocational/Technical School(s)

Northern California Institute of Cosmetology Inc (Private, For-profit)
Fall 2013 Enrollment: 44 . . . . (510) 635-4371
2013-14 Tuition: $15,000

Housing: Homeownership rate: 57.5%; Median home value: $367,300; Median year structure built: 1958; Homeowner vacancy rate: 1.4%; Median gross rent: $1,213 per month; Rental vacancy rate: 5.8%

Health Insurance: 86.0% have insurance; 67.0% have private insurance; 28.5% have public insurance; 14.0% do not have insurance; 5.2% of children under 18 do not have insurance

Hospitals: San Leandro Hospital

Safety: Violent crime rate: 45.0 per 10,000 population; Property crime rate: 452.6 per 10,000 population
Newspapers: Times (weekly circulation 46000)
Transportation: Commute: 81.9% car, 11.2% public transportation, 1.8% walk, 3.0% work from home; Median travel time to work: 28.4 minutes
Additional Information Contacts
City of San Leandro. . . . . (510) 577-3351
http://www.sanleandro.org

SAN LORENZO (CDP). Covers a land area of 2.763 square miles and a water area of 0.007 square miles. Located at 37.67° N. Lat; 122.14° W. Long. Elevation is 36 feet.
Population: 23,452; Growth (since 2000): 7.1%; Density: 8,486.6 persons per square mile; Race: 47.4% White, 4.8% Black/African American, 21.6% Asian, 1.0% American Indian/Alaska Native, 0.8% Native Hawaiian/Other Pacific Islander, 6.5% Two or more races, 37.7% Hispanic of any race; Average household size: 3.15; Median age: 37.9; Age under 18: 24.2%; Age 65 and over: 12.7%; Males per 100 females: 95.3; Marriage status: 33.4% never married, 49.9% now married, 1.7% separated, 7.1% widowed, 9.6% divorced; Foreign born: 31.8%; Speak English only: 48.6%; With disability: 12.0%; Veterans: 5.5%; Ancestry: 7.7% German, 6.0% Irish, 5.1% Portuguese, 4.3% Italian, 3.6% English
Employment: 10.3% management, business, and financial, 5.4% computer, engineering, and science, 7.0% education, legal, community service, arts, and media, 4.0% healthcare practitioners, 19.5% service, 28.1% sales and office, 11.2% natural resources, construction, and maintenance, 14.5% production, transportation, and material moving
Income: Per capita: $26,088; Median household: $71,443; Average household: $79,247; Households with income of $100,000 or more: 28.6%; Poverty rate: 9.0%
Educational Attainment: High school diploma or higher: 81.9%; Bachelor's degree or higher: 20.1%; Graduate/professional degree or higher: 3.7%

School District(s)

San Lorenzo Unified (KG-12)
2012-13 Enrollment: 12,270 . . . . (510) 317-4600
Housing: Homeownership rate: 75.0%; Median home value: $343,800; Median year structure built: 1954; Homeowner vacancy rate: 1.1%; Median gross rent: $1,524 per month; Rental vacancy rate: 4.1%
Health Insurance: 90.0% have insurance; 71.5% have private insurance; 29.2% have public insurance; 10.0% do not have insurance; 2.6% of children under 18 do not have insurance
Transportation: Commute: 86.9% car, 7.8% public transportation, 1.1% walk, 2.4% work from home; Median travel time to work: 27.7 minutes

---

SUNOL (CDP). Covers a land area of 27.751 square miles and a water area of 0.013 square miles. Located at 37.59° N. Lat; 121.88° W. Long. Elevation is 266 feet.
History: Sunol was the site in the 1840's of the ranch house of Antonio Sunol.
Population: 913; Growth (since 2000): -31.5%; Density: 32.9 persons per square mile; Race: 85.4% White, 0.1% Black/African American, 5.3% Asian, 0.7% American Indian/Alaska Native, 0.8% Native Hawaiian/Other Pacific Islander, 5.7% Two or more races, 10.0% Hispanic of any race; Average household size: 2.52; Median age: 49.3; Age under 18: 16.2%; Age 65 and over: 16.4%; Males per 100 females: 101.1

School District(s)

Sunol Glen Unified (KG-08)
2012-13 Enrollment: 273. . . . . (925) 862-2026
Housing: Homeownership rate: 75.1%; Homeowner vacancy rate: 1.1%; Rental vacancy rate: 4.1%

UNION CITY (city). Covers a land area of 19.469 square miles and a water area of 0 square miles. Located at 37.60° N. Lat; 122.02° W. Long. Elevation is 66 feet.
History: Named for its formation from the union of three towns. Population more than tripled between 1970 and 1990. Incorporated 1959, with the merger of Decoto and Alvarado districts.
Population: 69,516; Growth (since 2000): 4.0%; Density: 3,570.6 persons per square mile; Race: 23.9% White, 6.3% Black/African American, 50.9% Asian, 0.5% American Indian/Alaska Native, 1.3% Native Hawaiian/Other Pacific Islander, 6.7% Two or more races, 22.9% Hispanic of any race; Average household size: 3.38; Median age: 36.2; Age under 18: 24.2%; Age 65 and over: 11.1%; Males per 100 females: 97.5; Marriage status: 30.8% never married, 56.9% now married, 1.3% separated, 5.6% widowed, 6.7% divorced; Foreign born: 46.0%; Speak English only: 37.3%; With disability: 8.2%; Veterans: 4.6%; Ancestry: 3.7% German, 3.4% Irish, 2.0% Afghan, 1.6% English, 1.5% Portuguese
Employment: 15.6% management, business, and financial, 12.2% computer, engineering, and science, 6.8% education, legal, community service, arts, and media, 6.6% healthcare practitioners, 14.5% service, 26.2% sales and office, 6.3% natural resources, construction, and maintenance, 11.9% production, transportation, and material moving
Income: Per capita: $29,685; Median household: $82,083; Average household: $97,434; Households with income of $100,000 or more: 41.4%; Poverty rate: 8.4%
Educational Attainment: High school diploma or higher: 86.2%; Bachelor's degree or higher: 36.6%; Graduate/professional degree or higher: 10.2%

School District(s)

New Haven Unified (KG-12)
2012-13 Enrollment: 12,873 . . . . (510) 471-1100
Housing: Homeownership rate: 66.4%; Median home value: $474,300; Median year structure built: 1978; Homeowner vacancy rate: 1.5%; Median gross rent: $1,451 per month; Rental vacancy rate: 5.3%
Health Insurance: 89.2% have insurance; 71.0% have private insurance; 26.2% have public insurance; 10.8% do not have insurance; 4.7% of children under 18 do not have insurance
Safety: Violent crime rate: 30.1 per 10,000 population; Property crime rate: 225.4 per 10,000 population
Transportation: Commute: 86.7% car, 8.6% public transportation, 1.0% walk, 2.4% work from home; Median travel time to work: 30.1 minutes
Additional Information Contacts
City of Union City. . . . . (510) 471-3232
http://www.ci.union-city.ca.us

Alpine County

Located in eastern California, along the crest of the Sierra Nevada, south of Lake Tahoe; bounded on the northeast by Nevada. Covers a land area of 738.332 square miles, a water area of 4.848 square miles, and is located in the Pacific Time Zone at 38.62° N. Lat., 119.80° W. Long. The county was founded in 1864. County seat is Markleeville.
Population: 1,175; Growth (since 2000): -2.7%; Density: 1.6 persons per square mile; Race: 75.0% White, 0.0% Black/African American, 0.6% Asian, 20.4% American Indian/Alaska Native, 0.0% Native Hawaiian/Other Pacific Islander, 2.4% two or more races, 7.1% Hispanic of any race; Average household size: 2.32; Median age: 46.7; Age under 18: 21.8%; Age 65 and over: 14.1%; Males per 100 females: 106.5
Religion: Largest group: 4.3% Non-denominational Protestant
Housing: Homeownership rate: 71.9%; Homeowner vacancy rate: 6.3%; Rental vacancy rate: 32.9%
Health Care: Physicians: 8.8 per 10,000 population; Hospital beds: 0.0 per 10,000 population; Hospital admissions: 0.0 per 10,000 population
Presidential Election: 60.1% Obama, 36.5% Romney (2012)
National and State Parks: Grover Hot Springs State Park
Additional Information Contacts
Alpine Government . . . . (530) 694-2281
http://www.alpinecountyca.gov

Alpine County Communities

ALPINE VILLAGE (CDP). Covers a land area of 2.804 square miles and a water area of 0 square miles. Located at 38.79° N. Lat; 119.80° W. Long. Elevation is 5,604 feet.
Population: 114; Growth (since 2000): -16.2%; Density: 40.7 persons per square mile; Race: 79.8% White, 0.0% Black/African American, 0.9% Asian, 16.7% American Indian/Alaska Native, 0.0% Native Hawaiian/Other Pacific Islander, 0.9% Two or more races, 5.3% Hispanic of any race; Average household size: 2.19; Median age: 47.8; Age under 18: 19.3%; Age 65 and over: 13.2%; Males per 100 females: 96.6
Housing: Homeownership rate: 78.9%; Homeowner vacancy rate: 4.7%; Rental vacancy rate: 0.0%

BEAR VALLEY (CDP). Covers a land area of 5.156 square miles and a water area of 0.022 square miles. Located at 38.47° N. Lat; 120.05° W. Long. Elevation is 7,100 feet.
Population: 121; Growth (since 2000): -9.0%; Density: 23.5 persons per square mile; Race: 98.3% White, 0.0% Black/African American, 0.8%

Asian, 0.0% American Indian/Alaska Native, 0.0% Native Hawaiian/Other Pacific Islander, 0.8% Two or more races, 0.8% Hispanic of any race; Average household size: 1.81; Median age: 48.8; Age under 18: 14.9%; Age 65 and over: 14.0%; Males per 100 females: 124.1
Housing: Homeownership rate: 70.2%; Homeowner vacancy rate: 29.9%; Rental vacancy rate: 75.3%

KIRKWOOD (CDP). Covers a land area of 4.359 square miles and a water area of 0.975 square miles. Located at 38.69° N. Lat; 120.05° W. Long. Elevation is 7,687 feet.
Population: 158; Growth (since 2000): 64.6%; Density: 36.2 persons per square mile; Race: 96.8% White, 0.0% Black/African American, 0.6% Asian, 2.5% American Indian/Alaska Native, 0.0% Native Hawaiian/Other Pacific Islander, 0.0% Two or more races, 3.8% Hispanic of any race; Average household size: 1.86; Median age: 44.5; Age under 18: 12.7%; Age 65 and over: 15.8%; Males per 100 females: 150.8
Housing: Homeownership rate: 62.5%; Homeowner vacancy rate: 5.6%; Rental vacancy rate: 10.0%

MARKLEEVILLE (CDP). County seat. Covers a land area of 6.531 square miles and a water area of 0 square miles. Located at 38.68° N. Lat; 119.82° W. Long. Elevation is 5,531 feet.
History: Markleeville was settled in the 1850's along an early immigrant route. It later furnished timber for the mines of the Comstock Lode.
Population: 210; Growth (since 2000): 6.6%; Density: 32.2 persons per square mile; Race: 91.4% White, 0.0% Black/African American, 1.0% Asian, 1.9% American Indian/Alaska Native, 0.0% Native Hawaiian/Other Pacific Islander, 2.9% Two or more races, 5.2% Hispanic of any race; Average household size: 2.10; Median age: 50.8; Age under 18: 18.6%; Age 65 and over: 16.2%; Males per 100 females: 101.9

School District(s)

Alpine County Office of Education (01-12)
2012-13 Enrollment: 2. . . . . (530) 694-2230
Alpine County Unified (KG-12)
2012-13 Enrollment: 103. . . . . (530) 694-2230

Housing: Homeownership rate: 63.0%; Homeowner vacancy rate: 1.6%; Rental vacancy rate: 9.8%

MESA VISTA (CDP). Covers a land area of 4.875 square miles and a water area of 0 square miles. Located at 38.81° N. Lat; 119.80° W. Long. Elevation is 5,485 feet.
Population: 200; Growth (since 2000): 9.9%; Density: 41.0 persons per square mile; Race: 89.0% White, 0.0% Black/African American, 1.0% Asian, 7.5% American Indian/Alaska Native, 0.0% Native Hawaiian/Other Pacific Islander, 2.5% Two or more races, 5.5% Hispanic of any race; Average household size: 2.41; Median age: 50.8; Age under 18: 20.0%; Age 65 and over: 18.0%; Males per 100 females: 94.2
Housing: Homeownership rate: 88.0%; Homeowner vacancy rate: 1.3%; Rental vacancy rate: 28.6%

Amador County

Located in central and eastern California, extending from the Sacramento Valley on the west to the Sierra Nevadas on the east; bounded on the north by the Mokelumne River. Covers a land area of 594.583 square miles, a water area of 11.373 square miles, and is located in the Pacific Time Zone at 38.44° N. Lat., 120.65° W. Long. The county was founded in 1854. County seat is Jackson.
Population: 38,091; Growth (since 2000): 8.5%; Density: 64.1 persons per square mile; Race: 87.0% White, 2.5% Black/African American, 1.1% Asian, 1.8% American Indian/Alaska Native, 0.2% Native Hawaiian/Other Pacific Islander, 3.6% two or more races, 12.5% Hispanic of any race; Average household size: 2.30; Median age: 48.2; Age under 18: 16.8%; Age 65 and over: 20.6%; Males per 100 females: 119.6; Marriage status: 23.7% never married, 52.7% now married, 2.0% separated, 8.7% widowed, 15.0% divorced; Foreign born: 5.7%; Speak English only: 90.4%; With disability: 17.6%; Veterans: 14.8%; Ancestry: 18.5% German, 16.4% Irish, 13.4% English, 8.9% Italian, 6.2% French
Religion: Six largest groups: 10.2% Catholicism, 3.1% Latter-day Saints, 2.3% Holiness, 1.9% Pentecostal, 1.9% Baptist, 1.8% Non-denominational Protestant
Economy: Unemployment rate: 7.1%; Leading industries: 15.5% retail trade; 12.5% health care and social assistance; 12.5% accommodation and food services; Farms: 461 totaling 155,187 acres; Company size: 0 employ 1,000 or more persons, 1 employs 500 to 999 persons, 7 employ 100 to 499 persons, 793 employ less than 100 persons; Business ownership: 802 women-owned, n/a Black-owned, n/a Hispanic-owned, n/a Asian-owned
Employment: 12.0% management, business, and financial, 3.5% computer, engineering, and science, 10.2% education, legal, community service, arts, and media, 4.6% healthcare practitioners, 24.4% service, 23.2% sales and office, 11.2% natural resources, construction, and maintenance, 10.9% production, transportation, and material moving
Income: Per capita: $27,347; Median household: $53,684; Average household: $69,891; Households with income of $100,000 or more: 20.6%; Poverty rate: 12.6%
Educational Attainment: High school diploma or higher: 88.1%; Bachelor's degree or higher: 19.3%; Graduate/professional degree or higher: 5.1%
Housing: Homeownership rate: 74.7%; Median home value: $270,500; Median year structure built: 1981; Homeowner vacancy rate: 3.1%; Median gross rent: <$100 per month; Rental vacancy rate: 9.1%
Vital Statistics: Birth rate: 72.3 per 10,000 population; Death rate: 106.8 per 10,000 population; Age-adjusted cancer mortality rate: 183.1 deaths per 100,000 population
Health Insurance: 88.4% have insurance; 69.6% have private insurance; 40.7% have public insurance; 11.6% do not have insurance; 7.5% of children under 18 do not have insurance
Health Care: Physicians: 13.8 per 10,000 population; Hospital beds: 11.2 per 10,000 population; Hospital admissions: 586.5 per 10,000 population
Air Quality Index: 93.4% good, 6.6% moderate, 0.0% unhealthy for sensitive individuals, 0.0% unhealthy (percent of days)
Transportation: Commute: 88.6% car, 0.9% public transportation, 2.5% walk, 6.5% work from home; Median travel time to work: 30.0 minutes
Presidential Election: 39.2% Obama, 58.2% Romney (2012)
National and State Parks: Indian Grinding Rock State Historic Park; Mount Zion State Forest; Salt Springs State Game Refuge
Additional Information Contacts
Amador Government. . . . . (209) 223-6470
http://www.co.amador.ca.us

Amador County Communities

AMADOR CITY (city). Covers a land area of 0.314 square miles and a water area of 0 square miles. Located at 38.42° N. Lat; 120.82° W. Long. Elevation is 919 feet.
History: Amador City was a mining camp in 1849. In 1851 the Rev. Mr. Davison and three other preachers made the first quartz discovery in the region.
Population: 185; Growth (since 2000): -5.6%; Density: 589.6 persons per square mile; Race: 92.4% White, 0.0% Black/African American, 1.1% Asian, 2.2% American Indian/Alaska Native, 0.0% Native Hawaiian/Other Pacific Islander, 3.2% Two or more races, 5.9% Hispanic of any race; Average household size: 2.18; Median age: 43.5; Age under 18: 20.0%; Age 65 and over: 13.5%; Males per 100 females: 94.7
Housing: Homeownership rate: 63.5%; Homeowner vacancy rate: 6.9%; Rental vacancy rate: 8.8%

BUCKHORN (CDP). Covers a land area of 5.871 square miles and a water area of 0 square miles. Located at 38.45° N. Lat; 120.54° W. Long. Elevation is 3,294 feet.
Population: 2,429; Growth (since 2000): n/a; Density: 413.7 persons per square mile; Race: 93.0% White, 0.4% Black/African American, 1.0% Asian, 1.5% American Indian/Alaska Native, 0.2% Native Hawaiian/Other Pacific Islander, 2.0% Two or more races, 6.9% Hispanic of any race; Average household size: 2.13; Median age: 54.9; Age under 18: 14.4%; Age 65 and over: 28.9%; Males per 100 females: 106.0
Housing: Homeownership rate: 84.5%; Homeowner vacancy rate: 3.8%; Rental vacancy rate: 8.6%

BUENA VISTA (CDP). Covers a land area of 1.622 square miles and a water area of 0 square miles. Located at 38.30° N. Lat; 120.92° W. Long. Elevation is 295 feet.
Population: 429; Growth (since 2000): n/a; Density: 264.5 persons per square mile; Race: 85.1% White, 0.2% Black/African American, 0.0% Asian, 5.4% American Indian/Alaska Native, 0.0% Native Hawaiian/Other Pacific Islander, 6.5% Two or more races, 8.2% Hispanic of any race; Average household size: 2.38; Median age: 43.2; Age under 18: 25.4%; Age 65 and over: 16.1%; Males per 100 females: 84.9

Housing: Homeownership rate: 73.9%; Homeowner vacancy rate: 8.9%; Rental vacancy rate: 25.8%

CAMANCHE NORTH SHORE (CDP). Covers a land area of 2.306 square miles and a water area of 0 square miles. Located at 38.24° N. Lat; 120.95° W. Long.

Population: 979; Growth (since 2000): n/a; Density: 424.5 persons per square mile; Race: 87.8% White, 0.3% Black/African American, 1.2% Asian, 1.4% American Indian/Alaska Native, 0.3% Native Hawaiian/Other Pacific Islander, 5.0% Two or more races, 15.3% Hispanic of any race; Average household size: 2.50; Median age: 44.1; Age under 18: 23.5%; Age 65 and over: 13.7%; Males per 100 females: 105.7

Housing: Homeownership rate: 78.1%; Homeowner vacancy rate: 4.4%; Rental vacancy rate: 9.5%

CAMANCHE VILLAGE (CDP). Covers a land area of 5.437 square miles and a water area of 0.015 square miles. Located at 38.27° N. Lat; 120.99° W. Long. Elevation is 276 feet.

Population: 847; Growth (since 2000): n/a; Density: 155.8 persons per square mile; Race: 90.0% White, 0.0% Black/African American, 0.9% Asian, 1.1% American Indian/Alaska Native, 0.5% Native Hawaiian/Other Pacific Islander, 3.9% Two or more races, 14.3% Hispanic of any race; Average household size: 2.74; Median age: 38.7; Age under 18: 24.9%; Age 65 and over: 10.9%; Males per 100 females: 110.7

Housing: Homeownership rate: 88.6%; Homeowner vacancy rate: 3.5%; Rental vacancy rate: 10.3%

DRYTOWN (CDP). Covers a land area of 3.688 square miles and a water area of 0 square miles. Located at 38.44° N. Lat; 120.86° W. Long. Elevation is 646 feet.

Population: 167; Growth (since 2000): n/a; Density: 45.3 persons per square mile; Race: 91.6% White, 0.0% Black/African American, 0.6% Asian, 0.0% American Indian/Alaska Native, 0.0% Native Hawaiian/Other Pacific Islander, 6.6% Two or more races, 6.6% Hispanic of any race; Average household size: 2.32; Median age: 50.1; Age under 18: 18.6%; Age 65 and over: 17.4%; Males per 100 females: 111.4

Housing: Homeownership rate: 68.0%; Homeowner vacancy rate: 2.0%; Rental vacancy rate: 0.0%

FIDDLETOWN (CDP). Covers a land area of 4.636 square miles and a water area of 0 square miles. Located at 38.51° N. Lat; 120.76° W. Long. Elevation is 1,683 feet.

Population: 235; Growth (since 2000): n/a; Density: 50.7 persons per square mile; Race: 91.5% White, 0.0% Black/African American, 0.4% Asian, 2.1% American Indian/Alaska Native, 0.0% Native Hawaiian/Other Pacific Islander, 2.6% Two or more races, 9.4% Hispanic of any race; Average household size: 2.30; Median age: 51.6; Age under 18: 20.4%; Age 65 and over: 23.4%; Males per 100 females: 95.8

Housing: Homeownership rate: 75.5%; Homeowner vacancy rate: 1.3%; Rental vacancy rate: 7.4%

IONE (city). Covers a land area of 4.765 square miles and a water area of 0.015 square miles. Located at 38.36° N. Lat; 120.94° W. Long. Elevation is 299 feet.

History: Ione was called Bedbug and Freeze Out by the miners who first had a camp here. When family homes replaced miners' tents, the residents chose the name of Ione from Edward Bulwer-Lytton's novel "The Last Days of Pompeii."

Population: 7,918; Growth (since 2000): 11.1%; Density: 1,661.8 persons per square mile; Race: 73.6% White, 10.4% Black/African American, 1.4% Asian, 2.2% American Indian/Alaska Native, 0.3% Native Hawaiian/Other Pacific Islander, 3.6% Two or more races, 25.1% Hispanic of any race; Average household size: 2.56; Median age: 41.5; Age under 18: 13.4%; Age 65 and over: 9.9%; Males per 100 females: 310.5; Marriage status: 38.5% never married, 35.7% now married, 2.9% separated, 3.7% widowed, 22.1% divorced; Foreign born: 8.8%; Speak English only: 78.6%; With disability: 14.1%; Veterans: 12.0%; Ancestry: 15.1% German, 10.4% English, 10.0% Irish, 9.3% Italian, 5.1% French

Employment: 11.5% management, business, and financial, 1.3% computer, engineering, and science, 13.8% education, legal, community service, arts, and media, 1.0% healthcare practitioners, 28.9% service, 16.8% sales and office, 5.5% natural resources, construction, and maintenance, 21.2% production, transportation, and material moving

Income: Per capita: $13,515; Median household: $53,426; Average household: $72,898; Households with income of $100,000 or more: 24.5%; Poverty rate: 13.8%

Educational Attainment: High school diploma or higher: 73.8%; Bachelor's degree or higher: 11.6%; Graduate/professional degree or higher: 2.8%

School District(s)

Amador County Unified (KG-12)
2012-13 Enrollment: 3,884 . . . . (209) 223-1750

Housing: Homeownership rate: 69.9%; Median home value: $228,700; Median year structure built: 1991; Homeowner vacancy rate: 4.2%; Median gross rent: $1,063 per month; Rental vacancy rate: 9.9%

Health Insurance: 92.0% have insurance; 75.9% have private insurance; 32.6% have public insurance; 8.0% do not have insurance; 0.6% of children under 18 do not have insurance

Safety: Violent crime rate: 8.4 per 10,000 population; Property crime rate: 141.1 per 10,000 population

Transportation: Commute: 89.3% car, 1.0% public transportation, 4.3% walk, 1.3% work from home; Median travel time to work: 29.8 minutes

Additional Information Contacts

City of Ione . . . . (209) 274-2412
http://ione-ca.com/home/ione

JACKSON (city). County seat. Covers a land area of 3.730 square miles and a water area of 0 square miles. Located at 38.35° N. Lat; 120.77° W. Long. Elevation is 1,217 feet.

History: From 1848 to 1851 Jackson was a stopping point on the branch of the Carson Pass Emigrant Trail. It was first called Bottileas for the piles of bottles that collected at the crossroad, but in 1850 was named for a resident, Colonel Jackson. Jackson men stole the county records from Double Springs in 1851 and claimed the county seat. The honor was wrested from them in 1852 by Mokelumne Hill, but a decade later Jackson again became the seat of Amador County.

Population: 4,651; Growth (since 2000): 16.6%; Density: 1,246.9 persons per square mile; Race: 87.9% White, 0.7% Black/African American, 1.3% Asian, 2.0% American Indian/Alaska Native, 0.1% Native Hawaiian/Other Pacific Islander, 4.0% Two or more races, 11.2% Hispanic of any race; Average household size: 2.14; Median age: 46.0; Age under 18: 20.3%; Age 65 and over: 25.2%; Males per 100 females: 84.1; Marriage status: 30.3% never married, 38.8% now married, 3.3% separated, 14.4% widowed, 16.5% divorced; Foreign born: 4.4%; Speak English only: 91.5%; With disability: 22.6%; Veterans: 12.4%; Ancestry: 23.6% German, 14.2% Irish, 12.7% Italian, 10.6% English, 5.6% French

Employment: 18.7% management, business, and financial, 1.7% computer, engineering, and science, 9.8% education, legal, community service, arts, and media, 4.6% healthcare practitioners, 27.2% service, 27.4% sales and office, 5.4% natural resources, construction, and maintenance, 5.2% production, transportation, and material moving

Income: Per capita: $25,088; Median household: $42,959; Average household: $58,688; Households with income of $100,000 or more: 10.9%; Poverty rate: 16.6%

Educational Attainment: High school diploma or higher: 88.2%; Bachelor's degree or higher: 17.8%; Graduate/professional degree or higher: 4.2%

School District(s)

Amador County Office of Education (KG-12)
2012-13 Enrollment: 300. . . . . (209) 257-5353
Amador County Rop
2012-13 Enrollment: n/a . . . . (209) 267-5497
Amador County Unified (KG-12)
2012-13 Enrollment: 3,884 . . . . (209) 223-1750

Housing: Homeownership rate: 54.3%; Median home value: $248,100; Median year structure built: 1979; Homeowner vacancy rate: 4.9%; Median gross rent: $884 per month; Rental vacancy rate: 5.8%

Health Insurance: 84.3% have insurance; 56.5% have private insurance; 45.7% have public insurance; 15.7% do not have insurance; 3.2% of children under 18 do not have insurance

Hospitals: Sutter Amador Hospital (66 beds)

Safety: Violent crime rate: 50.6 per 10,000 population; Property crime rate: 393.5 per 10,000 population

Newspapers: Amador Ledger Dispatch (weekly circulation 8400)

Transportation: Commute: 94.9% car, 0.4% public transportation, 2.0% walk, 2.3% work from home; Median travel time to work: 15.0 minutes

Additional Information Contacts

City of Jackson . . . . (209) 223-1646
http://www.ci.jackson.ca.us

MARTELL (CDP). Covers a land area of 2.336 square miles and a water area of <.001 square miles. Located at 38.36° N. Lat; 120.80° W. Long. Elevation is 1,486 feet.

Population: 282; Growth (since 2000): n/a; Density: 120.7 persons per square mile; Race: 83.0% White, 0.0% Black/African American, 0.0% Asian, 5.0% American Indian/Alaska Native, 1.8% Native Hawaiian/Other Pacific Islander, 5.3% Two or more races, 12.8% Hispanic of any race; Average household size: 2.24; Median age: 41.7; Age under 18: 15.2%; Age 65 and over: 9.2%; Males per 100 females: 89.3

Housing: Homeownership rate: 54.6%; Homeowner vacancy rate: 0.0%; Rental vacancy rate: 16.7%

PINE GROVE (CDP). Covers a land area of 6.969 square miles and a water area of 0 square miles. Located at 38.41° N. Lat; 120.66° W. Long. Elevation is 2,513 feet.

Population: 2,219; Growth (since 2000): n/a; Density: 318.4 persons per square mile; Race: 91.3% White, 0.4% Black/African American, 0.4% Asian, 1.6% American Indian/Alaska Native, 0.3% Native Hawaiian/Other Pacific Islander, 3.7% Two or more races, 9.1% Hispanic of any race; Average household size: 2.25; Median age: 52.7; Age under 18: 16.4%; Age 65 and over: 24.8%; Males per 100 females: 99.2

Housing: Homeownership rate: 77.0%; Homeowner vacancy rate: 3.5%; Rental vacancy rate: 5.4%

PIONEER (CDP). Covers a land area of 4.321 square miles and a water area of 0 square miles. Located at 38.44° N. Lat; 120.58° W. Long. Elevation is 2,986 feet.

Population: 1,094; Growth (since 2000): n/a; Density: 253.2 persons per square mile; Race: 93.0% White, 0.0% Black/African American, 0.1% Asian, 3.1% American Indian/Alaska Native, 0.2% Native Hawaiian/Other Pacific Islander, 2.6% Two or more races, 4.8% Hispanic of any race; Average household size: 2.30; Median age: 51.3; Age under 18: 18.0%; Age 65 and over: 23.9%; Males per 100 females: 97.5

School District(s)

Amador County Unified (KG-12)
2012-13 Enrollment: 3,884 . . . . (209) 223-1750

Housing: Homeownership rate: 83.0%; Homeowner vacancy rate: 4.3%; Rental vacancy rate: 7.9%

PLYMOUTH (city). Covers a land area of 0.931 square miles and a water area of 0.013 square miles. Located at 38.48° N. Lat; 120.84° W. Long. Elevation is 1,083 feet.

History: Plymouth developed around the Plymouth Consolidated mines.

Population: 1,005; Growth (since 2000): 2.6%; Density: 1,079.7 persons per square mile; Race: 84.6% White, 0.3% Black/African American, 0.6% Asian, 1.8% American Indian/Alaska Native, 0.2% Native Hawaiian/Other Pacific Islander, 5.6% Two or more races, 18.2% Hispanic of any race; Average household size: 2.47; Median age: 40.1; Age under 18: 23.7%; Age 65 and over: 15.4%; Males per 100 females: 85.1

School District(s)

Amador County Office of Education (KG-12)
2012-13 Enrollment: 300. . . . . (209) 257-5353

Amador County Unified (KG-12)
2012-13 Enrollment: 3,884 . . . . (209) 223-1750

Housing: Homeownership rate: 64.3%; Homeowner vacancy rate: 4.0%; Rental vacancy rate: 12.0%

Additional Information Contacts

City of Plymouth . . . . (209) 245-6941
http://www.ci.plymouth.ca.us

RED CORRAL (CDP). Covers a land area of 5.842 square miles and a water area of 0 square miles. Located at 38.41° N. Lat; 120.61° W. Long.

Population: 1,413; Growth (since 2000): n/a; Density: 241.9 persons per square mile; Race: 89.1% White, 1.7% Black/African American, 0.8% Asian, 1.1% American Indian/Alaska Native, 0.2% Native Hawaiian/Other Pacific Islander, 4.7% Two or more races, 10.4% Hispanic of any race; Average household size: 2.35; Median age: 48.9; Age under 18: 17.5%; Age 65 and over: 21.0%; Males per 100 females: 106.9

Housing: Homeownership rate: 80.0%; Homeowner vacancy rate: 1.7%; Rental vacancy rate: 8.0%

RIVER PINES (CDP). Covers a land area of 0.366 square miles and a water area of 0 square miles. Located at 38.55° N. Lat; 120.75° W. Long. Elevation is 1,982 feet.

Population: 379; Growth (since 2000): n/a; Density: 1,036.3 persons per square mile; Race: 85.5% White, 0.0% Black/African American, 1.1% Asian, 1.3% American Indian/Alaska Native, 0.0% Native Hawaiian/Other Pacific Islander, 10.0% Two or more races, 8.2% Hispanic of any race; Average household size: 2.41; Median age: 45.6; Age under 18: 21.4%; Age 65 and over: 12.1%; Males per 100 females: 84.0

Housing: Homeownership rate: 70.1%; Homeowner vacancy rate: 2.6%; Rental vacancy rate: 16.1%

SUTTER CREEK (city). Covers a land area of 2.558 square miles and a water area of 0 square miles. Located at 38.39° N. Lat; 120.80° W. Long. Elevation is 1,188 feet.

History: General John Augustus Sutter, in search for a site for his sawmill, passed up this spot in favor of Coloma. Many miners settled down in Sutter Creek after the first gold fever had died. The mines in this area produced fortunes in the 1860's and 1870's for Leland Stanford, who used the money to build the Central Pacific Railroad.

Population: 2,501; Growth (since 2000): 8.6%; Density: 977.8 persons per square mile; Race: 90.8% White, 0.4% Black/African American, 2.6% Asian, 1.4% American Indian/Alaska Native, 0.2% Native Hawaiian/Other Pacific Islander, 3.0% Two or more races, 8.8% Hispanic of any race; Average household size: 2.14; Median age: 49.4; Age under 18: 18.6%; Age 65 and over: 26.0%; Males per 100 females: 84.3; Marriage status: 21.7% never married, 53.2% now married, 2.6% separated, 12.1% widowed, 13.0% divorced; Foreign born: 5.2%; Speak English only: 96.1%; With disability: 18.5%; Veterans: 12.1%; Ancestry: 29.1% Irish, 24.3% German, 9.6% English, 8.9% Italian, 6.7% French

Employment: 8.0% management, business, and financial, 2.8% computer, engineering, and science, 9.0% education, legal, community service, arts, and media, 2.0% healthcare practitioners, 32.3% service, 30.0% sales and office, 6.5% natural resources, construction, and maintenance, 9.3% production, transportation, and material moving

Income: Per capita: $28,046; Median household: $45,919; Average household: $58,679; Households with income of $100,000 or more: 18.3%; Poverty rate: 15.2%

Educational Attainment: High school diploma or higher: 92.3%; Bachelor's degree or higher: 21.2%; Graduate/professional degree or higher: 7.7%

School District(s)

Amador County Unified (KG-12)
2012-13 Enrollment: 3,884 . . . . (209) 223-1750

Housing: Homeownership rate: 53.6%; Median home value: $363,500; Median year structure built: 1974; Homeowner vacancy rate: 2.6%; Median gross rent: $1,057 per month; Rental vacancy rate: 14.6%

Health Insurance: 88.6% have insurance; 64.9% have private insurance; 46.1% have public insurance; 11.4% do not have insurance; 0.0% of children under 18 do not have insurance

Safety: Violent crime rate: 16.4 per 10,000 population; Property crime rate: 237.2 per 10,000 population

Transportation: Commute: 90.4% car, 1.0% public transportation, 5.2% walk, 3.3% work from home; Median travel time to work: 22.2 minutes

Additional Information Contacts

City of Sutter Creek. . . . . (209) 267-5647
http://www.cityofsuttercreek.org

VOLCANO (CDP). Covers a land area of 1.501 square miles and a water area of 0 square miles. Located at 38.45° N. Lat; 120.63° W. Long. Elevation is 2,070 feet.

Population: 115; Growth (since 2000): n/a; Density: 76.6 persons per square mile; Race: 94.8% White, 0.0% Black/African American, 1.7% Asian, 1.7% American Indian/Alaska Native, 0.0% Native Hawaiian/Other Pacific Islander, 1.7% Two or more races, 6.1% Hispanic of any race; Average household size: 2.09; Median age: 57.1; Age under 18: 17.4%; Age 65 and over: 24.3%; Males per 100 females: 98.3

Housing: Homeownership rate: 67.3%; Homeowner vacancy rate: 0.0%; Rental vacancy rate: 14.3%

Butte County

Located in north central California; drained by the Feather and Sacramento Rivers; includes parts of Lassen and Plumas National

Forests. Covers a land area of 1,636.464 square miles, a water area of 40.667 square miles, and is located in the Pacific Time Zone at 39.67° N. Lat., 121.60° W. Long. The county was founded in 1850. County seat is Oroville.

Butte County is part of the Chico, CA Metropolitan Statistical Area. The entire metro area includes: Butte County, CA

Weather Station: De Sabla Elevation: 2,709 feet

	Jan	Feb	Mar	Apr	May	Jun	Jul	Aug	Sep	Oct	Nov	Dec
High	53	55	60	65	74	83	90	90	84	73	58	51
Low	33	34	36	39	45	51	55	54	50	44	36	32
Precip	11.6	12.1	9.4	4.9	2.9	0.9	0.1	0.2	1.1	3.5	7.7	13.6
Snow	1.9	0.1	2.2	0.3	0.0	0.0	0.0	0.0	0.0	0.0	0.0	0.2

High and Low temperatures in degrees Fahrenheit; Precipitation and Snow in inches

Weather Station: Oroville Elevation: 170 feet

	Jan	Feb	Mar	Apr	May	Jun	Jul	Aug	Sep	Oct	Nov	Dec
High	56	61	67	72	81	90	96	94	88	78	65	55
Low	37	40	44	46	52	57	61	59	54	48	42	37
Precip	5.3	5.7	4.6	2.1	1.2	0.4	0.0	0.2	0.5	1.4	3.4	5.4
Snow	0.0	0.0	0.0	0.0	0.0	0.0	0.0	0.0	0.0	0.0	0.0	0.0

High and Low temperatures in degrees Fahrenheit; Precipitation and Snow in inches

Weather Station: Paradise Elevation: 1,750 feet

	Jan	Feb	Mar	Apr	May	Jun	Jul	Aug	Sep	Oct	Nov	Dec
High	54	57	61	67	76	84	92	91	86	75	61	54
Low	39	41	44	47	53	59	66	64	61	53	44	39
Precip	10.1	10.3	8.3	4.0	2.3	0.8	0.1	0.2	0.9	2.8	6.8	11.0
Snow	0.0	0.6	0.2	0.0	0.0	0.0	0.0	0.0	0.0	0.0	0.0	0.0

High and Low temperatures in degrees Fahrenheit; Precipitation and Snow in inches

Population: 220,000; Growth (since 2000): 8.3%; Density: 134.4 persons per square mile; Race: 81.9% White, 1.6% Black/African American, 4.1% Asian, 2.0% American Indian/Alaska Native, 0.2% Native Hawaiian/Other Pacific Islander, 4.7% two or more races, 14.1% Hispanic of any race; Average household size: 2.45; Median age: 37.2; Age under 18: 21.0%; Age 65 and over: 15.4%; Males per 100 females: 98.1; Marriage status: 34.6% never married, 45.9% now married, 2.3% separated, 6.5% widowed, 13.0% divorced; Foreign born: 7.5%; Speak English only: 86.4%; With disability: 17.4%; Veterans: 10.6%; Ancestry: 18.2% German, 13.6% Irish, 12.1% English, 7.3% American, 6.5% Italian
Religion: Six largest groups: 15.5% Catholicism, 4.3% Latter-day Saints, 3.1% Holiness, 2.0% Non-denominational Protestant, 1.8% Baptist, 1.5% Adventist
Economy: Unemployment rate: 7.3%; Leading industries: 15.7% retail trade; 15.5% health care and social assistance; 9.8% construction; Farms: 2,056 totaling 381,019 acres; Company size: 3 employ 1,000 or more persons, 3 employ 500 to 999 persons, 58 employ 100 to 499 persons, 4,551 employs less than 100 persons; Business ownership: 5,357 women-owned, 213 Black-owned, n/a Hispanic-owned, 462 Asian-owned
Employment: 12.7% management, business, and financial, 3.7% computer, engineering, and science, 11.3% education, legal, community service, arts, and media, 6.0% healthcare practitioners, 23.2% service, 24.4% sales and office, 9.0% natural resources, construction, and maintenance, 9.7% production, transportation, and material moving
Income: Per capita: $23,787; Median household: $43,752; Average household: $59,081; Households with income of $100,000 or more: 15.7%; Poverty rate: 20.4%
Educational Attainment: High school diploma or higher: 87.7%; Bachelor's degree or higher: 24.4%; Graduate/professional degree or higher: 8.2%
Housing: Homeownership rate: 58.2%; Median home value: $225,900; Median year structure built: 1977; Homeowner vacancy rate: 2.4%; Median gross rent: $890 per month; Rental vacancy rate: 6.4%
Vital Statistics: Birth rate: 107.3 per 10,000 population; Death rate: 102.2 per 10,000 population; Age-adjusted cancer mortality rate: 187.3 deaths per 100,000 population
Health Insurance: 84.3% have insurance; 59.5% have private insurance; 38.6% have public insurance; 15.7% do not have insurance; 8.4% of children under 18 do not have insurance
Health Care: Physicians: 19.9 per 10,000 population; Hospital beds: 24.1 per 10,000 population; Hospital admissions: 1,390.8 per 10,000 population
Air Quality Index: 63.6% good, 35.6% moderate, 0.8% unhealthy for sensitive individuals, 0.0% unhealthy (percent of days)
Transportation: Commute: 85.3% car, 1.1% public transportation, 3.9% walk, 6.0% work from home; Median travel time to work: 20.3 minutes
Presidential Election: 46.4% Obama, 50.3% Romney (2012)
National and State Parks: Bidwell Mansion State Historic Park; Bidwell-Sacramento River State Park; Clay Pit State Vehicular Recreation Area; Lake Oroville State Recreation Area
Additional Information Contacts
Butte Government . . . . (530) 538-7224
http://www.buttecounty.net

Butte County Communities

BANGOR (CDP). Covers a land area of 13.423 square miles and a water area of 0 square miles. Located at 39.38° N. Lat; 121.41° W. Long. Elevation is 761 feet.
Population: 646; Growth (since 2000): n/a; Density: 48.1 persons per square mile; Race: 84.1% White, 0.8% Black/African American, 0.6% Asian, 2.6% American Indian/Alaska Native, 0.2% Native Hawaiian/Other Pacific Islander, 9.0% Two or more races, 7.3% Hispanic of any race; Average household size: 2.76; Median age: 46.9; Age under 18: 26.2%; Age 65 and over: 18.1%; Males per 100 females: 92.3

School District(s)

Bangor Union Elementary (KG-08)
2012-13 Enrollment: 117. . . . . (530) 679-2434
Housing: Homeownership rate: 79.0%; Homeowner vacancy rate: 2.6%; Rental vacancy rate: 3.8%

BERRY CREEK (CDP). Covers a land area of 57.120 square miles and a water area of 0.060 square miles. Located at 39.63° N. Lat; 121.41° W. Long. Elevation is 1,995 feet.
Population: 1,424; Growth (since 2000): n/a; Density: 24.9 persons per square mile; Race: 87.7% White, 0.6% Black/African American, 0.9% Asian, 3.4% American Indian/Alaska Native, 0.2% Native Hawaiian/Other Pacific Islander, 6.3% Two or more races, 6.9% Hispanic of any race; Average household size: 2.18; Median age: 54.3; Age under 18: 12.9%; Age 65 and over: 24.2%; Males per 100 females: 111.6

School District(s)

Pioneer Union Elementary (KG-08)
2012-13 Enrollment: 64. . . . . (530) 589-1633
Housing: Homeownership rate: 80.5%; Homeowner vacancy rate: 4.5%; Rental vacancy rate: 7.1%

BIGGS (city). Covers a land area of 0.636 square miles and a water area of 0 square miles. Located at 39.41° N. Lat; 121.71° W. Long. Elevation is 98 feet.
Population: 1,707; Growth (since 2000): -4.8%; Density: 2,685.5 persons per square mile; Race: 76.3% White, 0.6% Black/African American, 0.5% Asian, 3.2% American Indian/Alaska Native, 0.1% Native Hawaiian/Other Pacific Islander, 4.6% Two or more races, 34.0% Hispanic of any race; Average household size: 3.02; Median age: 35.1; Age under 18: 28.1%; Age 65 and over: 10.9%; Males per 100 females: 94.6

School District(s)

Biggs Unified (KG-12)
2012-13 Enrollment: 548. . . . . (530) 868-1281
Housing: Homeownership rate: 69.4%; Homeowner vacancy rate: 3.2%; Rental vacancy rate: 6.5%
Safety: Violent crime rate: 93.5 per 10,000 population; Property crime rate: 198.7 per 10,000 population
Additional Information Contacts
City of Biggs . . . . (530) 868-0102
http://www.biggs-ca.gov

BUTTE CREEK CANYON (CDP). Covers a land area of 20.472 square miles and a water area of 0.027 square miles. Located at 39.74° N. Lat; 121.71° W. Long.
Population: 1,086; Growth (since 2000): n/a; Density: 53.0 persons per square mile; Race: 93.1% White, 0.0% Black/African American, 1.7% Asian, 1.8% American Indian/Alaska Native, 0.1% Native Hawaiian/Other Pacific Islander, 2.6% Two or more races, 4.4% Hispanic of any race; Average household size: 2.32; Median age: 52.6; Age under 18: 15.6%; Age 65 and over: 14.8%; Males per 100 females: 106.1
Housing: Homeownership rate: 84.2%; Homeowner vacancy rate: 1.2%; Rental vacancy rate: 7.4%

BUTTE MEADOWS (CDP). Covers a land area of 2.144 square miles and a water area of <.001 square miles. Located at 40.09° N. Lat; 121.54° W. Long. Elevation is 4,340 feet.

Population: 40; Growth (since 2000): n/a; Density: 18.7 persons per square mile; Race: 95.0% White, 0.0% Black/African American, 0.0% Asian, 0.0% American Indian/Alaska Native, 0.0% Native Hawaiian/Other Pacific Islander, 5.0% Two or more races, 0.0% Hispanic of any race; Average household size: 1.60; Median age: 58.0; Age under 18: 0.0%; Age 65 and over: 30.0%; Males per 100 females: 207.7

Housing: Homeownership rate: 72.0%; Homeowner vacancy rate: 7.7%; Rental vacancy rate: 78.8%

BUTTE VALLEY (CDP). Covers a land area of 18.290 square miles and a water area of 0.011 square miles. Located at 39.67° N. Lat; 121.65° W. Long.

Population: 899; Growth (since 2000): n/a; Density: 49.2 persons per square mile; Race: 87.0% White, 0.0% Black/African American, 1.0% Asian, 2.1% American Indian/Alaska Native, 0.1% Native Hawaiian/Other Pacific Islander, 5.1% Two or more races, 9.9% Hispanic of any race; Average household size: 2.63; Median age: 46.3; Age under 18: 20.8%; Age 65 and over: 13.3%; Males per 100 females: 102.5

Housing: Homeownership rate: 85.2%; Homeowner vacancy rate: 0.7%; Rental vacancy rate: 15.3%

CHEROKEE (CDP). Covers a land area of 1.751 square miles and a water area of 0.171 square miles. Located at 39.65° N. Lat; 121.53° W. Long. Elevation is 1,306 feet.

Population: 69; Growth (since 2000): n/a; Density: 39.4 persons per square mile; Race: 69.6% White, 0.0% Black/African American, 11.6% Asian, 2.9% American Indian/Alaska Native, 0.0% Native Hawaiian/Other Pacific Islander, 15.9% Two or more races, 1.4% Hispanic of any race; Average household size: 2.65; Median age: 42.8; Age under 18: 23.2%; Age 65 and over: 17.4%; Males per 100 females: 122.6

Housing: Homeownership rate: 73.1%; Homeowner vacancy rate: 0.0%; Rental vacancy rate: 0.0%

CHICO (city). Covers a land area of 32.923 square miles and a water area of 0.172 square miles. Located at 39.76° N. Lat; 121.82° W. Long. Elevation is 197 feet.

History: Chico had its beginnings in 1840 when John Bidwell, a member of the first overland party to cross the Sierra Nevada, planted orchards on his Rancho Chico. A pioneer in raisin growing and olive oil manufacture, Bidwell laid out the town of Chico in 1860 and offered free lots to any who would build here. In 1877 British botanist Sir Joseph Hooker judged an oak tree in Chico to be the world's largest oak (28 feet in circumference, 101 feet tall, branch spread of 147 feet).

Population: 86,187; Growth (since 2000): 43.8%; Density: 2,617.8 persons per square mile; Race: 80.8% White, 2.1% Black/African American, 4.2% Asian, 1.4% American Indian/Alaska Native, 0.2% Native Hawaiian/Other Pacific Islander, 5.0% Two or more races, 15.4% Hispanic of any race; Average household size: 2.38; Median age: 28.6; Age under 18: 19.5%; Age 65 and over: 10.6%; Males per 100 females: 98.2; Marriage status: 45.7% never married, 37.7% now married, 1.8% separated, 4.9% widowed, 11.7% divorced; Foreign born: 7.7%; Speak English only: 86.1%; With disability: 12.4%; Veterans: 7.3%; Ancestry: 17.4% German, 13.5% Irish, 11.2% English, 7.9% Italian, 6.2% American

Employment: 13.6% management, business, and financial, 5.3% computer, engineering, and science, 12.2% education, legal, community service, arts, and media, 6.2% healthcare practitioners, 23.4% service, 25.0% sales and office, 6.5% natural resources, construction, and maintenance, 7.9% production, transportation, and material moving

Income: Per capita: $24,221; Median household: $43,372; Average household: $58,659; Households with income of $100,000 or more: 16.6%; Poverty rate: 23.2%

Educational Attainment: High school diploma or higher: 91.2%; Bachelor's degree or higher: 33.8%; Graduate/professional degree or higher: 11.9%

School District(s)

Butte County Office of Education (KG-12)
2012-13 Enrollment: 1,060 . . . . (530) 532-5761
Butte County Rop
2012-13 Enrollment: n/a . . . . (530) 532-5650
Chico Unified (PK-12)
2012-13 Enrollment: 13,875 . . . . (530) 891-3000
Golden Feather Union Elementary (KG-12)
2012-13 Enrollment: 156. . . . . (530) 533-3833

Four-year College(s)

California State University-Chico (Public)
Fall 2013 Enrollment: 16,356 . . . . (530) 898-6116
2013-14 Tuition: In-state $6,972; Out-of-state $18,132

Housing: Homeownership rate: 42.7%; Median home value: $266,500; Median year structure built: 1979; Homeowner vacancy rate: 2.0%; Median gross rent: $907 per month; Rental vacancy rate: 5.8%

Health Insurance: 83.5% have insurance; 64.5% have private insurance; 28.3% have public insurance; 16.5% do not have insurance; 7.7% of children under 18 do not have insurance

Hospitals: Enloe Medical Center (369 beds)

Safety: Violent crime rate: 33.9 per 10,000 population; Property crime rate: 291.5 per 10,000 population

Newspapers: Chico Enterprise-Record (daily circulation 31000); Chico News & Review (weekly circulation 42000)

Transportation: Commute: 81.7% car, 1.3% public transportation, 5.4% walk, 5.0% work from home; Median travel time to work: 17.3 minutes; Amtrak: Train service available.

Airports: Chico Municipal (primary service/non-hub)

Additional Information Contacts

City of Chico . . . . (530) 896-7200
http://www.chico.ca.us

COHASSET (CDP). Covers a land area of 25.306 square miles and a water area of 0 square miles. Located at 39.90° N. Lat; 121.74° W. Long. Elevation is 2,828 feet.

Population: 847; Growth (since 2000): n/a; Density: 33.5 persons per square mile; Race: 90.2% White, 0.9% Black/African American, 0.2% Asian, 1.7% American Indian/Alaska Native, 0.1% Native Hawaiian/Other Pacific Islander, 4.5% Two or more races, 5.1% Hispanic of any race; Average household size: 2.39; Median age: 45.5; Age under 18: 21.0%; Age 65 and over: 12.8%; Males per 100 females: 111.8

Housing: Homeownership rate: 82.2%; Homeowner vacancy rate: 0.7%; Rental vacancy rate: 4.5%

CONCOW (CDP). Covers a land area of 27.406 square miles and a water area of 0.374 square miles. Located at 39.77° N. Lat; 121.51° W. Long. Elevation is 1,759 feet.

Population: 710; Growth (since 2000): -35.2%; Density: 25.9 persons per square mile; Race: 86.1% White, 0.0% Black/African American, 0.7% Asian, 3.4% American Indian/Alaska Native, 0.4% Native Hawaiian/Other Pacific Islander, 8.0% Two or more races, 7.9% Hispanic of any race; Average household size: 2.35; Median age: 50.4; Age under 18: 17.5%; Age 65 and over: 14.1%; Males per 100 females: 115.8

Housing: Homeownership rate: 83.1%; Homeowner vacancy rate: 4.5%; Rental vacancy rate: 3.7%

DURHAM (CDP). Covers a land area of 81.781 square miles and a water area of 0.152 square miles. Located at 39.63° N. Lat; 121.79° W. Long. Elevation is 161 feet.

History: Durham began when a tract of land, purchased by the State, was subdivided in 1918 and sold to settlers, many of them war veterans, under supervision of the State Land Settlement Board.

Population: 5,518; Growth (since 2000): 5.7%; Density: 67.5 persons per square mile; Race: 92.2% White, 0.3% Black/African American, 0.6% Asian, 1.0% American Indian/Alaska Native, 0.2% Native Hawaiian/Other Pacific Islander, 2.7% Two or more races, 11.1% Hispanic of any race; Average household size: 2.61; Median age: 43.3; Age under 18: 23.6%; Age 65 and over: 14.4%; Males per 100 females: 99.3; Marriage status: 27.8% never married, 54.5% now married, 0.7% separated, 7.1% widowed, 10.7% divorced; Foreign born: 4.0%; Speak English only: 92.8%; With disability: 9.9%; Veterans: 11.6%; Ancestry: 19.5% German, 14.9% Irish, 13.7% English, 12.6% American, 5.9% European

Employment: 20.7% management, business, and financial, 1.7% computer, engineering, and science, 16.5% education, legal, community service, arts, and media, 8.5% healthcare practitioners, 15.2% service, 22.9% sales and office, 6.8% natural resources, construction, and maintenance, 7.6% production, transportation, and material moving

Income: Per capita: $33,718; Median household: $65,033; Average household: $85,504; Households with income of $100,000 or more: 26.6%; Poverty rate: 9.9%

Educational Attainment: High school diploma or higher: 98.0%; Bachelor's degree or higher: 41.0%; Graduate/professional degree or higher: 14.3%

School District(s)

Durham Unified (KG-12)
2012-13 Enrollment: 991 . . . . (530) 895-4675

Housing: Homeownership rate: 73.9%; Median home value: $394,000; Median year structure built: 1968; Homeowner vacancy rate: 1.4%; Median gross rent: $872 per month; Rental vacancy rate: 3.5%

Health Insurance: 83.8% have insurance; 74.5% have private insurance; 22.3% have public insurance; 16.2% do not have insurance; 21.7% of children under 18 do not have insurance

Transportation: Commute: 86.1% car, 0.1% public transportation, 6.1% walk, 6.9% work from home; Median travel time to work: 21.5 minutes

FORBESTOWN (CDP). Covers a land area of 6.274 square miles and a water area of 0.006 square miles. Located at 39.53° N. Lat; 121.27° W. Long. Elevation is 2,772 feet.

Population: 320; Growth (since 2000): n/a; Density: 51.0 persons per square mile; Race: 81.9% White, 1.3% Black/African American, 3.1% Asian, 4.7% American Indian/Alaska Native, 0.0% Native Hawaiian/Other Pacific Islander, 7.8% Two or more races, 7.2% Hispanic of any race; Average household size: 2.32; Median age: 52.3; Age under 18: 17.8%; Age 65 and over: 23.4%; Males per 100 females: 105.1

Housing: Homeownership rate: 79.0%; Homeowner vacancy rate: 5.2%; Rental vacancy rate: 0.0%

FOREST RANCH (CDP). Covers a land area of 13.923 square miles and a water area of 0 square miles. Located at 39.90° N. Lat; 121.67° W. Long. Elevation is 2,415 feet.

Population: 1,184; Growth (since 2000): n/a; Density: 85.0 persons per square mile; Race: 94.3% White, 0.7% Black/African American, 0.3% Asian, 0.5% American Indian/Alaska Native, 0.1% Native Hawaiian/Other Pacific Islander, 2.4% Two or more races, 4.4% Hispanic of any race; Average household size: 2.28; Median age: 50.0; Age under 18: 17.7%; Age 65 and over: 16.5%; Males per 100 females: 99.3

School District(s)

Chico Unified (PK-12)
2012-13 Enrollment: 13,875 . . . . (530) 891-3000

Housing: Homeownership rate: 86.0%; Homeowner vacancy rate: 2.3%; Rental vacancy rate: 18.9%

GRIDLEY (city). Covers a land area of 2.071 square miles and a water area of 0 square miles. Located at 39.36° N. Lat; 121.70° W. Long. Elevation is 95 feet.

History: Incorporated 1905.

Population: 6,584; Growth (since 2000): 22.3%; Density: 3,179.1 persons per square mile; Race: 65.1% White, 0.8% Black/African American, 3.8% Asian, 1.5% American Indian/Alaska Native, 0.0% Native Hawaiian/Other Pacific Islander, 5.2% Two or more races, 45.6% Hispanic of any race; Average household size: 2.96; Median age: 33.1; Age under 18: 28.7%; Age 65 and over: 14.1%; Males per 100 females: 94.3; Marriage status: 28.6% never married, 58.2% now married, 3.4% separated, 5.5% widowed, 7.7% divorced; Foreign born: 24.3%; Speak English only: 51.6%; With disability: 12.1%; Veterans: 8.3%; Ancestry: 11.4% German, 7.4% American, 7.2% Irish, 6.2% English, 2.2% French

Employment: 7.6% management, business, and financial, 1.8% computer, engineering, and science, 13.3% education, legal, community service, arts, and media, 0.0% healthcare practitioners, 25.8% service, 21.4% sales and office, 13.9% natural resources, construction, and maintenance, 16.1% production, transportation, and material moving

Income: Per capita: $17,001; Median household: $40,682; Average household: $53,927; Households with income of $100,000 or more: 13.5%; Poverty rate: 17.1%

Educational Attainment: High school diploma or higher: 68.3%; Bachelor's degree or higher: 10.9%; Graduate/professional degree or higher: 4.3%

School District(s)

Gridley Unified (KG-12)
2012-13 Enrollment: 2,112 . . . . (530) 846-4721
Manzanita Elementary (KG-08)
2012-13 Enrollment: 300 . . . . (530) 846-5594

Housing: Homeownership rate: 57.8%; Median home value: $164,800; Median year structure built: 1969; Homeowner vacancy rate: 2.6%; Median gross rent: $752 per month; Rental vacancy rate: 6.5%

Health Insurance: 70.1% have insurance; 39.4% have private insurance; 39.0% have public insurance; 29.9% do not have insurance; 21.7% of children under 18 do not have insurance

Hospitals: Biggs Gridley Memorial Hospital (45 beds)

Safety: Violent crime rate: 109.7 per 10,000 population; Property crime rate: 291.0 per 10,000 population

Newspapers: Gridley Herald (weekly circulation 1800)

Transportation: Commute: 89.2% car, 0.5% public transportation, 6.6% walk, 3.8% work from home; Median travel time to work: 20.1 minutes

Additional Information Contacts

City of Gridley . . . . (530) 846-5695
http://www.gridley.ca.us

HONCUT (CDP). Covers a land area of 4.237 square miles and a water area of 0 square miles. Located at 39.33° N. Lat; 121.54° W. Long. Elevation is 108 feet.

Population: 370; Growth (since 2000): n/a; Density: 87.3 persons per square mile; Race: 67.0% White, 1.6% Black/African American, 1.1% Asian, 3.8% American Indian/Alaska Native, 0.0% Native Hawaiian/Other Pacific Islander, 3.5% Two or more races, 39.2% Hispanic of any race; Average household size: 3.49; Median age: 36.8; Age under 18: 30.5%; Age 65 and over: 13.2%; Males per 100 females: 104.4

Housing: Homeownership rate: 67.0%; Homeowner vacancy rate: 0.0%; Rental vacancy rate: 0.0%

KELLY RIDGE (CDP). Covers a land area of 1.951 square miles and a water area of 0 square miles. Located at 39.53° N. Lat; 121.47° W. Long.

Population: 2,544; Growth (since 2000): n/a; Density: 1,303.7 persons per square mile; Race: 89.9% White, 0.8% Black/African American, 1.4% Asian, 2.2% American Indian/Alaska Native, 0.3% Native Hawaiian/Other Pacific Islander, 3.8% Two or more races, 8.0% Hispanic of any race; Average household size: 2.08; Median age: 57.4; Age under 18: 13.2%; Age 65 and over: 37.0%; Males per 100 females: 91.6; Marriage status: 17.0% never married, 53.2% now married, 2.1% separated, 16.4% widowed, 13.4% divorced; Foreign born: 5.8%; Speak English only: 95.8%; With disability: 27.6%; Veterans: 27.1%; Ancestry: 22.3% English, 22.0% German, 19.2% Irish, 7.0% American, 5.6% Polish

Employment: 12.5% management, business, and financial, 1.1% computer, engineering, and science, 2.3% education, legal, community service, arts, and media, 10.3% healthcare practitioners, 34.1% service, 22.5% sales and office, 8.5% natural resources, construction, and maintenance, 8.7% production, transportation, and material moving

Income: Per capita: $28,228; Median household: $39,130; Average household: $52,028; Households with income of $100,000 or more: 11.8%; Poverty rate: 5.2%

Educational Attainment: High school diploma or higher: 94.2%; Bachelor's degree or higher: 20.6%; Graduate/professional degree or higher: 5.4%

Housing: Homeownership rate: 81.1%; Median home value: $151,300; Median year structure built: 1981; Homeowner vacancy rate: 3.9%; Median gross rent: $1,108 per month; Rental vacancy rate: 7.9%

Health Insurance: 88.2% have insurance; 71.7% have private insurance; 57.9% have public insurance; 11.8% do not have insurance; 8.8% of children under 18 do not have insurance

Transportation: Commute: 84.0% car, 0.0% public transportation, 10.0% walk, 1.6% work from home; Median travel time to work: 21.4 minutes

MAGALIA (CDP). Covers a land area of 14.015 square miles and a water area of 0.004 square miles. Located at 39.82° N. Lat; 121.61° W. Long. Elevation is 2,333 feet.

Population: 11,310; Growth (since 2000): 7.0%; Density: 807.0 persons per square mile; Race: 91.9% White, 0.4% Black/African American, 0.8% Asian, 1.2% American Indian/Alaska Native, 0.2% Native Hawaiian/Other Pacific Islander, 4.3% Two or more races, 6.8% Hispanic of any race; Average household size: 2.34; Median age: 49.0; Age under 18: 19.1%; Age 65 and over: 23.7%; Males per 100 females: 97.8; Marriage status: 23.6% never married, 51.9% now married, 1.8% separated, 9.3% widowed, 15.2% divorced; Foreign born: 2.7%; Speak English only: 96.2%; With disability: 23.3%; Veterans: 16.5%; Ancestry: 24.4% German, 17.1% Irish, 14.7% English, 6.7% American, 5.4% Italian

Employment: 10.5% management, business, and financial, 1.8% computer, engineering, and science, 8.5% education, legal, community service, arts, and media, 4.7% healthcare practitioners, 21.3% service, 29.7% sales and office, 9.8% natural resources, construction, and maintenance, 13.7% production, transportation, and material moving

Income: Per capita: $20,899; Median household: $38,612; Average household: $48,388; Households with income of $100,000 or more: 8.8%; Poverty rate: 16.8%

Educational Attainment: High school diploma or higher: 90.9%; Bachelor's degree or higher: 15.6%; Graduate/professional degree or higher: 3.7%

School District(s)

Paradise Unified (KG-12)
2012-13 Enrollment: 4,282 . . . . (530) 872-6400

Housing: Homeownership rate: 77.0%; Median home value: $154,600; Median year structure built: 1981; Homeowner vacancy rate: 2.7%; Median gross rent: $992 per month; Rental vacancy rate: 7.1%

Health Insurance: 86.2% have insurance; 58.1% have private insurance; 50.6% have public insurance; 13.8% do not have insurance; 5.2% of children under 18 do not have insurance

Transportation: Commute: 87.4% car, 4.0% public transportation, 1.1% walk, 7.2% work from home; Median travel time to work: 27.4 minutes

NORD (CDP). Covers a land area of 2.105 square miles and a water area of 0 square miles. Located at 39.77° N. Lat; 121.95° W. Long. Elevation is 151 feet.

Population: 320; Growth (since 2000): n/a; Density: 152.0 persons per square mile; Race: 72.8% White, 0.3% Black/African American, 5.0% Asian, 1.9% American Indian/Alaska Native, 0.0% Native Hawaiian/Other Pacific Islander, 5.0% Two or more races, 38.1% Hispanic of any race; Average household size: 3.08; Median age: 36.5; Age under 18: 25.9%; Age 65 and over: 8.1%; Males per 100 females: 117.7

Housing: Homeownership rate: 77.9%; Homeowner vacancy rate: 0.0%; Rental vacancy rate: 4.2%

OROVILLE (city). County seat. Covers a land area of 12.993 square miles and a water area of 0.018 square miles. Located at 39.50° N. Lat; 121.57° W. Long. Elevation is 167 feet.

History: Oroville sprang up in 1849 as a tent town called Ophir City, when gold was discovered here. When a canal brought water in 1856, Oroville became the seat of Butte County. Dredging on the Feather River extracted nearly thirty million dollars in gold in a 20-year period beginning in 1898. Mining was later replaced by the growing of semitropical fruits, and fruit-packing houses and an olive-oil refinery were founded in Oroville.

Population: 15,546; Growth (since 2000): 19.5%; Density: 1,196.5 persons per square mile; Race: 75.2% White, 2.9% Black/African American, 8.0% Asian, 3.7% American Indian/Alaska Native, 0.4% Native Hawaiian/Other Pacific Islander, 6.3% Two or more races, 12.5% Hispanic of any race; Average household size: 2.60; Median age: 31.5; Age under 18: 27.4%; Age 65 and over: 12.6%; Males per 100 females: 93.7; Marriage status: 36.5% never married, 39.3% now married, 3.9% separated, 6.4% widowed, 17.8% divorced; Foreign born: 7.5%; Speak English only: 82.9%; With disability: 21.8%; Veterans: 11.3%; Ancestry: 16.5% German, 13.7% Irish, 9.4% English, 9.0% American, 7.5% Italian

Employment: 12.5% management, business, and financial, 0.9% computer, engineering, and science, 9.1% education, legal, community service, arts, and media, 1.9% healthcare practitioners, 28.2% service, 25.2% sales and office, 8.3% natural resources, construction, and maintenance, 13.9% production, transportation, and material moving

Income: Per capita: $17,852; Median household: $36,857; Average household: $48,436; Households with income of $100,000 or more: 8.7%; Poverty rate: 23.3%

Educational Attainment: High school diploma or higher: 83.6%; Bachelor's degree or higher: 12.3%; Graduate/professional degree or higher: 4.0%

School District(s)

Butte County Office of Education (KG-12)
2012-13 Enrollment: 1,060 . . . . (530) 532-5761
Feather Falls Union Elementary (KG-12)
2012-13 Enrollment: 60. . . . . (530) 589-1633
Golden Feather Union Elementary (KG-12)
2012-13 Enrollment: 156. . . . . (530) 533-3833
Oroville City Elementary (KG-08)
2012-13 Enrollment: 2,622 . . . . (530) 532-3000
Oroville Union High (09-12)
2012-13 Enrollment: 2,452 . . . . (530) 538-2300
Palermo Union Elementary (KG-08)
2012-13 Enrollment: 1,297 . . . . (530) 533-4842
Thermalito Union Elementary (KG-08)
2012-13 Enrollment: 1,332 . . . . (530) 538-2900

Two-year College(s)

Butte College (Public)
Fall 2013 Enrollment: 12,163 . . . . (530) 895-2511
2013-14 Tuition: In-state $1,354; Out-of-state $6,154

Housing: Homeownership rate: 42.9%; Median home value: $156,300; Median year structure built: 1962; Homeowner vacancy rate: 3.6%; Median gross rent: $760 per month; Rental vacancy rate: 8.4%

Health Insurance: 85.0% have insurance; 44.5% have private insurance; 50.6% have public insurance; 15.0% do not have insurance; 5.5% of children under 18 do not have insurance

Hospitals: Oroville Hospital (153 beds)

Safety: Violent crime rate: 50.1 per 10,000 population; Property crime rate: 648.9 per 10,000 population

Newspapers: Mercury-Register (daily circulation 7000)

Transportation: Commute: 89.5% car, 0.9% public transportation, 3.8% walk, 4.9% work from home; Median travel time to work: 17.2 minutes; Amtrak: Bus service available.

Airports: Oroville Municipal (general aviation)

Additional Information Contacts

City of Oroville . . . . (530) 538-2401
http://www.cityoforoville.org

OROVILLE EAST (CDP). Covers a land area of 22.149 square miles and a water area of 0.175 square miles. Located at 39.49° N. Lat; 121.49° W. Long.

Population: 8,280; Growth (since 2000): -4.6%; Density: 373.8 persons per square mile; Race: 82.5% White, 1.5% Black/African American, 3.6% Asian, 5.8% American Indian/Alaska Native, 0.1% Native Hawaiian/Other Pacific Islander, 4.8% Two or more races, 8.5% Hispanic of any race; Average household size: 2.47; Median age: 48.8; Age under 18: 20.1%; Age 65 and over: 23.1%; Males per 100 females: 97.5; Marriage status: 21.0% never married, 58.4% now married, 2.3% separated, 8.4% widowed, 12.3% divorced; Foreign born: 2.8%; Speak English only: 95.5%; With disability: 22.3%; Veterans: 19.7%; Ancestry: 20.5% German, 13.9% Irish, 13.5% English, 8.7% American, 5.3% Italian

Employment: 12.5% management, business, and financial, 2.3% computer, engineering, and science, 6.9% education, legal, community service, arts, and media, 6.3% healthcare practitioners, 23.3% service, 24.4% sales and office, 10.2% natural resources, construction, and maintenance, 14.2% production, transportation, and material moving

Income: Per capita: $25,100; Median household: $54,180; Average household: $64,618; Households with income of $100,000 or more: 17.5%; Poverty rate: 13.8%

Educational Attainment: High school diploma or higher: 86.8%; Bachelor's degree or higher: 13.0%; Graduate/professional degree or higher: 3.2%

Housing: Homeownership rate: 80.6%; Median home value: $162,200; Median year structure built: 1976; Homeowner vacancy rate: 3.2%; Median gross rent: $902 per month; Rental vacancy rate: 9.0%

Health Insurance: 88.3% have insurance; 61.7% have private insurance; 50.1% have public insurance; 11.7% do not have insurance; 5.6% of children under 18 do not have insurance

Transportation: Commute: 90.7% car, 0.2% public transportation, 0.8% walk, 7.9% work from home; Median travel time to work: 19.1 minutes

PALERMO (CDP). Covers a land area of 29.162 square miles and a water area of 0.014 square miles. Located at 39.43° N. Lat; 121.52° W. Long. Elevation is 194 feet.

Population: 5,382; Growth (since 2000): -5.9%; Density: 184.6 persons per square mile; Race: 72.5% White, 0.7% Black/African American, 4.6% Asian, 4.1% American Indian/Alaska Native, 0.1% Native Hawaiian/Other Pacific Islander, 6.1% Two or more races, 23.8% Hispanic of any race; Average household size: 2.77; Median age: 40.9; Age under 18: 24.3%; Age 65 and over: 17.9%; Males per 100 females: 105.1; Marriage status: 25.4% never married, 51.7% now married, 3.1% separated, 9.0% widowed, 13.9% divorced; Foreign born: 7.6%; Speak English only: 83.8%; With disability: 24.9%; Veterans: 8.4%; Ancestry: 14.9% Irish, 13.2% German, 8.8% American, 6.5% English, 4.7% Italian

Employment: 4.6% management, business, and financial, 0.5% computer, engineering, and science, 6.2% education, legal, community service, arts, and media, 5.1% healthcare practitioners, 30.0% service, 21.3% sales and office, 14.5% natural resources, construction, and maintenance, 17.9% production, transportation, and material moving

Income: Per capita: $20,765; Median household: $44,922; Average household: $60,531; Households with income of $100,000 or more: 18.6%; Poverty rate: 21.6%

Educational Attainment: High school diploma or higher: 74.1%; Bachelor's degree or higher: 6.6%; Graduate/professional degree or higher: 1.5%

School District(s)

Palermo Union Elementary (KG-08)
2012-13 Enrollment: 1,297 . . . . (530) 533-4842

Housing: Homeownership rate: 76.3%; Median home value: $149,700; Median year structure built: 1980; Homeowner vacancy rate: 1.7%; Median gross rent: $798 per month; Rental vacancy rate: 8.0%

Health Insurance: 86.2% have insurance; 54.4% have private insurance; 48.4% have public insurance; 13.8% do not have insurance; 7.9% of children under 18 do not have insurance

Transportation: Commute: 94.5% car, 0.1% public transportation, 1.2% walk, 2.4% work from home; Median travel time to work: 24.9 minutes

PARADISE (town). Covers a land area of 18.308 square miles and a water area of 0.014 square miles. Located at 39.75° N. Lat; 121.61° W. Long. Elevation is 1,778 feet.

History: Gold was discovered nearby in 1859.

Population: 26,218; Growth (since 2000): -0.7%; Density: 1,432.0 persons per square mile; Race: 92.0% White, 0.4% Black/African American, 1.3% Asian, 1.1% American Indian/Alaska Native, 0.1% Native Hawaiian/Other Pacific Islander, 3.5% Two or more races, 7.0% Hispanic of any race; Average household size: 2.17; Median age: 50.2; Age under 18: 17.2%; Age 65 and over: 25.1%; Males per 100 females: 90.5; Marriage status: 25.3% never married, 48.5% now married, 1.6% separated, 10.2% widowed, 16.0% divorced; Foreign born: 4.5%; Speak English only: 93.3%; With disability: 22.7%; Veterans: 13.6%; Ancestry: 21.7% German, 17.3% English, 14.5% Irish, 6.4% Italian, 6.0% American

Employment: 12.5% management, business, and financial, 3.2% computer, engineering, and science, 9.4% education, legal, community service, arts, and media, 8.5% healthcare practitioners, 22.9% service, 23.1% sales and office, 10.3% natural resources, construction, and maintenance, 10.0% production, transportation, and material moving

Income: Per capita: $24,046; Median household: $40,837; Average household: $53,114; Households with income of $100,000 or more: 13.3%; Poverty rate: 17.5%

Educational Attainment: High school diploma or higher: 91.1%; Bachelor's degree or higher: 23.2%; Graduate/professional degree or higher: 6.5%

School District(s)

Paradise Unified (KG-12)
2012-13 Enrollment: 4,282 . . . . (530) 872-6400

Housing: Homeownership rate: 67.1%; Median home value: $207,400; Median year structure built: 1973; Homeowner vacancy rate: 2.8%; Median gross rent: $911 per month; Rental vacancy rate: 5.9%

Health Insurance: 86.3% have insurance; 62.9% have private insurance; 45.5% have public insurance; 13.7% do not have insurance; 10.9% of children under 18 do not have insurance

Hospitals: Feather River Hospital (101 beds)

Safety: Violent crime rate: 25.9 per 10,000 population; Property crime rate: 202.1 per 10,000 population

Newspapers: Paradise Post (weekly circulation 9300)

Transportation: Commute: 87.8% car, 1.3% public transportation, 2.2% walk, 7.2% work from home; Median travel time to work: 20.7 minutes

Additional Information Contacts

Town of Paradise . . . . (530) 872-6291
http://www.townofparadise.com

RACKERBY (CDP). Covers a land area of 2.954 square miles and a water area of 0 square miles. Located at 39.43° N. Lat; 121.35° W. Long.

Population: 204; Growth (since 2000): n/a; Density: 69.1 persons per square mile; Race: 94.6% White, 0.0% Black/African American, 0.0% Asian, 0.5% American Indian/Alaska Native, 0.0% Native Hawaiian/Other Pacific Islander, 3.4% Two or more races, 8.8% Hispanic of any race; Average household size: 2.37; Median age: 47.3; Age under 18: 19.1%; Age 65 and over: 18.1%; Males per 100 females: 100.0

Housing: Homeownership rate: 73.2%; Homeowner vacancy rate: 1.5%; Rental vacancy rate: 17.9%

RICHVALE (CDP). Covers a land area of 0.927 square miles and a water area of 0 square miles. Located at 39.49° N. Lat; 121.75° W. Long. Elevation is 108 feet.

Population: 244; Growth (since 2000): n/a; Density: 263.2 persons per square mile; Race: 88.5% White, 0.0% Black/African American, 0.0% Asian, 4.5% American Indian/Alaska Native, 0.0% Native Hawaiian/Other Pacific Islander, 2.9% Two or more races, 11.1% Hispanic of any race; Average household size: 2.74; Median age: 40.5; Age under 18: 26.2%; Age 65 and over: 18.0%; Males per 100 females: 112.2

School District(s)

Biggs Unified (KG-12)
2012-13 Enrollment: 548. . . . . (530) 868-1281

Housing: Homeownership rate: 78.7%; Homeowner vacancy rate: 1.4%; Rental vacancy rate: 0.0%

ROBINSON MILL (CDP). Covers a land area of 1.317 square miles and a water area of 0 square miles. Located at 39.49° N. Lat; 121.32° W. Long. Elevation is 2,654 feet.

Population: 80; Growth (since 2000): n/a; Density: 60.7 persons per square mile; Race: 92.5% White, 0.0% Black/African American, 0.0% Asian, 1.3% American Indian/Alaska Native, 1.3% Native Hawaiian/Other Pacific Islander, 5.0% Two or more races, 13.8% Hispanic of any race; Average household size: 2.16; Median age: 53.8; Age under 18: 10.0%; Age 65 and over: 16.3%; Males per 100 females: 95.1

Housing: Homeownership rate: 86.5%; Homeowner vacancy rate: 0.0%; Rental vacancy rate: 16.7%

SOUTH OROVILLE (CDP). Covers a land area of 2.964 square miles and a water area of 0 square miles. Located at 39.48° N. Lat; 121.54° W. Long. Elevation is 187 feet.

Population: 5,742; Growth (since 2000): -25.4%; Density: 1,937.0 persons per square mile; Race: 59.3% White, 7.1% Black/African American, 15.4% Asian, 4.3% American Indian/Alaska Native, 0.2% Native Hawaiian/Other Pacific Islander, 7.5% Two or more races, 14.8% Hispanic of any race; Average household size: 3.22; Median age: 30.0; Age under 18: 30.6%; Age 65 and over: 8.1%; Males per 100 females: 100.9; Marriage status: 32.9% never married, 45.3% now married, 6.1% separated, 6.6% widowed, 15.2% divorced; Foreign born: 16.9%; Speak English only: 70.6%; With disability: 30.1%; Veterans: 11.6%; Ancestry: 20.3% German, 11.4% American, 6.7% Czechoslovakian, 6.6% Irish, 6.4% English

Employment: 9.0% management, business, and financial, 0.6% computer, engineering, and science, 5.2% education, legal, community service, arts, and media, 0.4% healthcare practitioners, 22.5% service, 38.2% sales and office, 11.3% natural resources, construction, and maintenance, 12.7% production, transportation, and material moving

Income: Per capita: $11,981; Median household: $33,460; Average household: $39,183; Households with income of $100,000 or more: 2.3%; Poverty rate: 31.9%

Educational Attainment: High school diploma or higher: 72.8%; Bachelor's degree or higher: 3.0%; Graduate/professional degree or higher: 0.2%

Housing: Homeownership rate: 49.4%; Median home value: $105,100; Median year structure built: 1971; Homeowner vacancy rate: 3.1%; Median gross rent: $911 per month; Rental vacancy rate: 8.1%

Health Insurance: 87.7% have insurance; 31.3% have private insurance; 63.9% have public insurance; 12.3% do not have insurance; 5.1% of children under 18 do not have insurance

Transportation: Commute: 85.9% car, 0.5% public transportation, 0.4% walk, 12.4% work from home; Median travel time to work: 17.9 minutes

STIRLING CITY (CDP). Covers a land area of 1.177 square miles and a water area of <.001 square miles. Located at 39.91° N. Lat; 121.53° W. Long. Elevation is 3,570 feet.

Population: 295; Growth (since 2000): n/a; Density: 250.6 persons per square mile; Race: 89.5% White, 0.3% Black/African American, 0.0% Asian, 3.7% American Indian/Alaska Native, 0.0% Native Hawaiian/Other Pacific Islander, 6.1% Two or more races, 5.8% Hispanic of any race; Average household size: 2.52; Median age: 41.1; Age under 18: 25.8%; Age 65 and over: 14.9%; Males per 100 females: 107.7

Housing: Homeownership rate: 60.7%; Homeowner vacancy rate: 2.7%; Rental vacancy rate: 6.1%

THERMALITO (CDP). Covers a land area of 12.702 square miles and a water area of 0.168 square miles. Located at 39.51° N. Lat; 121.60° W. Long. Elevation is 223 feet.

History: Thermalito was situated in a "thermal belt" that provided a good climate for the orange groves planted here in 1886.

Population: 6,646; Growth (since 2000): 9.9%; Density: 523.2 persons per square mile; Race: 69.1% White, 0.9% Black/African American, 16.6% Asian, 3.9% American Indian/Alaska Native, 0.6% Native Hawaiian/Other Pacific Islander, 4.9% Two or more races, 10.7% Hispanic of any race; Average household size: 2.90; Median age: 37.0; Age under 18: 26.3%; Age 65 and over: 15.0%; Males per 100 females: 100.4; Marriage status: 34.0% never married, 41.9% now married, 3.1% separated, 5.8% widowed, 18.2% divorced; Foreign born: 11.2%; Speak English only: 77.3%; With disability: 24.4%; Veterans: 10.0%; Ancestry: 13.2% American, 12.8% German, 11.2% Irish, 9.0% English, 3.6% French

Employment: 6.3% management, business, and financial, 0.0% computer, engineering, and science, 8.4% education, legal, community service, arts, and media, 2.6% healthcare practitioners, 36.6% service, 20.8% sales and office, 8.8% natural resources, construction, and maintenance, 16.4% production, transportation, and material moving

Income: Per capita: $15,367; Median household: $38,650; Average household: $44,288; Households with income of $100,000 or more: 7.7%; Poverty rate: 30.9%

Educational Attainment: High school diploma or higher: 71.9%; Bachelor's degree or higher: 3.3%; Graduate/professional degree or higher: 0.4%

Housing: Homeownership rate: 67.3%; Median home value: $118,200; Median year structure built: 1971; Homeowner vacancy rate: 3.2%; Median gross rent: $878 per month; Rental vacancy rate: 5.7%

Health Insurance: 84.5% have insurance; 39.6% have private insurance; 62.0% have public insurance; 15.5% do not have insurance; 5.2% of children under 18 do not have insurance

Transportation: Commute: 82.2% car, 0.2% public transportation, 2.7% walk, 9.3% work from home; Median travel time to work: 22.3 minutes

YANKEE HILL (CDP). Covers a land area of 6.061 square miles and a water area of 0.002 square miles. Located at 39.70° N. Lat; 121.52° W. Long. Elevation is 1,982 feet.

Population: 333; Growth (since 2000): n/a; Density: 54.9 persons per square mile; Race: 91.6% White, 0.6% Black/African American, 1.2% Asian, 2.1% American Indian/Alaska Native, 0.0% Native Hawaiian/Other Pacific Islander, 3.0% Two or more races, 6.6% Hispanic of any race; Average household size: 2.15; Median age: 53.6; Age under 18: 9.9%; Age 65 and over: 24.9%; Males per 100 females: 99.4

Housing: Homeownership rate: 80.7%; Homeowner vacancy rate: 1.6%; Rental vacancy rate: 8.8%

Calaveras County

Located in central California, in the Sierra Nevada; bounded on the north by the Mokelumne River, and on the south by the Stanislaus River; includes the Stanislaus National Forest. Covers a land area of 1,020.012 square miles, a water area of 16.915 square miles, and is located in the Pacific Time Zone at 38.19° N. Lat., 120.56° W. Long. The county was founded in 1850. County seat is San Andreas.

Weather Station: Calaveras Big Trees — Elevation: 4,693 feet

	Jan	Feb	Mar	Apr	May	Jun	Jul	Aug	Sep	Oct	Nov	Dec
High	44	45	49	55	64	73	81	80	73	63	51	44
Low	29	29	31	34	41	47	54	53	48	41	33	29
Precip	10.4	10.3	8.3	4.4	2.5	0.7	0.1	0.1	0.9	3.1	6.1	9.0
Snow	22.9	25.7	23.8	11.1	1.7	0.1	0.0	0.0	tr	0.6	6.3	20.6

High and Low temperatures in degrees Fahrenheit; Precipitation and Snow in inches

Weather Station: Camp Pardee — Elevation: 658 feet

	Jan	Feb	Mar	Apr	May	Jun	Jul	Aug	Sep	Oct	Nov	Dec
High	54	60	65	71	80	89	95	94	89	78	64	55
Low	39	42	45	47	52	57	62	62	59	53	46	40
Precip	4.3	3.9	3.9	1.9	1.1	0.3	0.0	0.0	0.4	1.2	2.5	3.6
Snow	0.0	0.0	0.0	0.0	0.0	0.0	0.0	0.0	0.0	0.0	0.0	0.0

High and Low temperatures in degrees Fahrenheit; Precipitation and Snow in inches

Population: 45,578; Growth (since 2000): 12.4%; Density: 44.7 persons per square mile; Race: 88.9% White, 0.8% Black/African American, 1.3% Asian, 1.5% American Indian/Alaska Native, 0.2% Native Hawaiian/Other Pacific Islander, 3.9% two or more races, 10.3% Hispanic of any race; Average household size: 2.39; Median age: 49.2; Age under 18: 19.6%; Age 65 and over: 21.0%; Males per 100 females: 100.3; Marriage status: 21.6% never married, 61.1% now married, 1.6% separated, 6.1% widowed, 11.3% divorced; Foreign born: 4.2%; Speak English only: 93.0%; With disability: 17.6%; Veterans: 14.3%; Ancestry: 22.2% German, 17.6% Irish, 12.1% English, 9.5% Italian, 5.5% European

Religion: Six largest groups: 55.0% Catholicism, 3.5% Latter-day Saints, 2.9% Non-denominational Protestant, 2.9% Methodist/Pietist, 1.6% Baptist, 1.1% Presbyterian-Reformed

Economy: Unemployment rate: 7.6%; Leading industries: 18.7% construction; 15.0% retail trade; 11.2% accommodation and food services; Farms: 663 totaling 212,140 acres; Company size: 0 employ 1,000 or more persons, 0 employ 500 to 999 persons, 3 employ 100 to 499 persons, 888 employ less than 100 persons; Business ownership: 1,327 women-owned, n/a Black-owned, n/a Hispanic-owned, n/a Asian-owned

Employment: 13.3% management, business, and financial, 2.6% computer, engineering, and science, 12.9% education, legal, community service, arts, and media, 5.5% healthcare practitioners, 20.0% service, 21.0% sales and office, 13.9% natural resources, construction, and maintenance, 10.8% production, transportation, and material moving

Income: Per capita: $29,329; Median household: $55,295; Average household: $70,161; Households with income of $100,000 or more: 22.3%; Poverty rate: 10.9%

Educational Attainment: High school diploma or higher: 92.8%; Bachelor's degree or higher: 21.2%; Graduate/professional degree or higher: 6.2%

Housing: Homeownership rate: 76.9%; Median home value: $254,800; Median year structure built: 1985; Homeowner vacancy rate: 3.7%; Median gross rent: $1,061 per month; Rental vacancy rate: 10.4%

Vital Statistics: Birth rate: 71.2 per 10,000 population; Death rate: 106.7 per 10,000 population; Age-adjusted cancer mortality rate: 173.8 deaths per 100,000 population

Health Insurance: 88.5% have insurance; 70.8% have private insurance; 37.8% have public insurance; 11.5% do not have insurance; 4.7% of children under 18 do not have insurance

Health Care: Physicians: 9.6 per 10,000 population; Hospital beds: 5.5 per 10,000 population; Hospital admissions: 303.0 per 10,000 population

Air Quality Index: 81.3% good, 18.4% moderate, 0.3% unhealthy for sensitive individuals, 0.0% unhealthy (percent of days)

Transportation: Commute: 90.4% car, 0.5% public transportation, 2.8% walk, 5.6% work from home; Median travel time to work: 35.5 minutes

Presidential Election: 40.1% Obama, 57.1% Romney (2012)

National and State Parks: Altaville State Historic Landmark; Brownsville State Historic Landmark; Calaveras Big Trees State Park; Jenny Lind State Historic Landmark; Mokelumne Hill State Historic Landmark; Murphys State Historic Landmark; Sandy Gulch State Historic Landmark; Vallecito State Historic Landmark; Valley Springs State Historic Landmark; West Point State Historic Landmark

Additional Information Contacts

Calaveras Government . . . . (209) 754-6303
http://www.co.calaveras.ca.us

Calaveras County Communities

ANGELS (city). Covers a land area of 3.628 square miles and a water area of 0.009 square miles. Located at 38.07° N. Lat; 120.55° W. Long.

Population: 3,836; Growth (since 2000): n/a; Density: 1,057.3 persons per square mile; Race: 86.8% White, 0.3% Black/African American, 1.3% Asian, 1.3% American Indian/Alaska Native, 0.1% Native Hawaiian/Other Pacific Islander, 3.2% Two or more races, 13.0% Hispanic of any race; Average household size: 2.30; Median age: 45.9; Age under 18: 20.7%; Age 65 and over: 22.8%; Males per 100 females: 93.3; Marriage status: 25.9% never married, 51.7% now married, 2.6% separated, 12.3% widowed, 10.1% divorced; Foreign born: 4.0%; Speak English only: 93.7%; With disability: 25.4%; Veterans: 11.5%; Ancestry: 23.7% Irish, 21.6% German, 13.2% English, 11.1% Italian, 5.1% French

Employment: 13.9% management, business, and financial, 0.6% computer, engineering, and science, 8.0% education, legal, community service, arts, and media, 8.6% healthcare practitioners, 25.0% service, 15.3% sales and office, 16.7% natural resources, construction, and maintenance, 11.9% production, transportation, and material moving

Income: Per capita: $31,369; Median household: $50,948; Average household: $65,639; Households with income of $100,000 or more: 16.4%; Poverty rate: 13.0%

Educational Attainment: High school diploma or higher: 89.8%; Bachelor's degree or higher: 24.9%; Graduate/professional degree or higher: 8.1%

Housing: Homeownership rate: 64.5%; Median home value: $260,200; Median year structure built: 1983; Homeowner vacancy rate: 3.2%; Median gross rent: $927 per month; Rental vacancy rate: 10.7%

Health Insurance: 86.2% have insurance; 66.2% have private insurance; 46.6% have public insurance; 13.8% do not have insurance; 14.4% of children under 18 do not have insurance

Safety: Violent crime rate: 24.1 per 10,000 population; Property crime rate: 152.9 per 10,000 population

Transportation: Commute: 93.0% car, 0.0% public transportation, 3.0% walk, 4.0% work from home; Median travel time to work: 25.7 minutes

Additional Information Contacts

City of Angels City . . . . (209) 736-2181
http://www.angelscamp.gov

ANGELS CAMP (unincorporated postal area)

ZCTA: 95222

Covers a land area of 151.093 square miles and a water area of 3.782 square miles. Located at 38.07° N. Lat; 120.63° W. Long. Elevation is 1,378 feet.

Population: 5,292; Growth (since 2000): 24.6%; Density: 35.0 persons per square mile; Race: 88.3% White, 0.4% Black/African American, 1.1% Asian, 1.4% American Indian/Alaska Native, 0.1% Native Hawaiian/Other Pacific Islander, 3.1% Two or more races, 11.6% Hispanic of any race; Average household size: 2.34; Median age: 47.9; Age under 18: 20.1%; Age 65 and over: 22.4%; Males per 100 females: 95.3; Marriage status: 24.6% never married, 56.2% now married, 2.7% separated, 10.4% widowed, 8.9% divorced; Foreign born: 3.7%; Speak English only: 94.4%; With disability: 22.8%; Veterans: 13.4%; Ancestry: 21.9% German, 21.3% Irish, 12.3% Italian, 11.5% English, 5.3% French

Employment: 18.8% management, business, and financial, 0.5% computer, engineering, and science, 8.6% education, legal, community service, arts, and media, 7.5% healthcare practitioners, 22.8% service, 15.2% sales and office, 16.1% natural resources, construction, and maintenance, 10.6% production, transportation, and material moving

Income: Per capita: $30,506; Median household: $52,088; Average household: $67,401; Households with income of $100,000 or more: 18.1%; Poverty rate: 12.9%

Educational Attainment: High school diploma or higher: 88.9%; Bachelor's degree or higher: 25.0%; Graduate/professional degree or higher: 8.7%

School District(s)

Bret Harte Union High (09-12)
2012-13 Enrollment: 754. . . . . (209) 736-8340
Calaveras County Office of Education (KG-12)
2012-13 Enrollment: 588. . . . . (209) 736-4662
Calaveras County Rop
2012-13 Enrollment: n/a . . . . (530) 621-0123
Mark Twain Union Elementary (KG-08)
2012-13 Enrollment: 830. . . . . (209) 736-1855

Housing: Homeownership rate: 68.7%; Median home value: $274,000; Median year structure built: 1984; Homeowner vacancy rate: 2.9%; Median gross rent: $924 per month; Rental vacancy rate: 10.3%

Health Insurance: 88.1% have insurance; 70.3% have private insurance; 42.8% have public insurance; 11.9% do not have insurance; 8.9% of children under 18 do not have insurance

Transportation: Commute: 92.0% car, 0.0% public transportation, 2.4% walk, 4.2% work from home; Median travel time to work: 26.7 minutes

ARNOLD

ARNOLD (CDP). Covers a land area of 14.788 square miles and a water area of 0.062 square miles. Located at 38.25° N. Lat; 120.35° W. Long. Elevation is 4,003 feet.

Population: 3,843; Growth (since 2000): -8.9%; Density: 259.9 persons per square mile; Race: 93.4% White, 0.5% Black/African American, 1.2% Asian, 0.7% American Indian/Alaska Native, 0.1% Native Hawaiian/Other Pacific Islander, 2.5% Two or more races, 6.7% Hispanic of any race; Average household size: 2.18; Median age: 54.1; Age under 18: 16.0%; Age 65 and over: 27.2%; Males per 100 females: 104.4; Marriage status: 20.3% never married, 64.0% now married, 2.1% separated, 4.0% widowed, 11.7% divorced; Foreign born: 5.1%; Speak English only: 94.4%; With disability: 18.4%; Veterans: 14.0%; Ancestry: 18.4% Irish, 16.5% English, 14.3% European, 13.6% German, 7.3% French

Employment: 22.0% management, business, and financial, 4.1% computer, engineering, and science, 17.4% education, legal, community service, arts, and media, 0.9% healthcare practitioners, 17.5% service, 13.0% sales and office, 13.8% natural resources, construction, and maintenance, 11.3% production, transportation, and material moving

Income: Per capita: $34,087; Median household: $54,564; Average household: $68,029; Households with income of $100,000 or more: 26.8%; Poverty rate: 11.7%

Educational Attainment: High school diploma or higher: 95.3%; Bachelor's degree or higher: 37.3%; Graduate/professional degree or higher: 6.7%

School District(s)

Vallecito Union (KG-08)
2012-13 Enrollment: 599. . . . . (209) 795-8500

Housing: Homeownership rate: 80.8%; Median home value: $364,000; Median year structure built: 1982; Homeowner vacancy rate: 4.8%; Median gross rent: $807 per month; Rental vacancy rate: 16.8%

Health Insurance: 91.7% have insurance; 76.1% have private insurance; 44.6% have public insurance; 8.3% do not have insurance; 0.0% of children under 18 do not have insurance

Transportation: Commute: 78.1% car, 1.1% public transportation, 13.3% walk, 5.9% work from home; Median travel time to work: 19.2 minutes

AVERY

AVERY (CDP). Covers a land area of 4.501 square miles and a water area of 0 square miles. Located at 38.19° N. Lat; 120.38° W. Long. Elevation is 3,389 feet.

Population: 646; Growth (since 2000): -3.9%; Density: 143.5 persons per square mile; Race: 93.5% White, 0.8% Black/African American, 0.5% Asian, 1.1% American Indian/Alaska Native, 0.2% Native Hawaiian/Other Pacific Islander, 3.7% Two or more races, 5.9% Hispanic of any race; Average household size: 2.30; Median age: 48.1; Age under 18: 20.0%; Age 65 and over: 21.8%; Males per 100 females: 105.7

School District(s)

Vallecito Union (KG-08)
2012-13 Enrollment: 599. . . . . (209) 795-8500

Housing: Homeownership rate: 77.6%; Homeowner vacancy rate: 7.6%; Rental vacancy rate: 11.3%

BURSON (unincorporated postal area)

ZCTA: 95225

Covers a land area of 7.007 square miles and a water area of 0.077 square miles. Located at 38.20° N. Lat; 120.89° W. Long. Elevation is 413 feet.

Population: 672; Growth (since 2000): 4,700.0%; Density: 95.9 persons per square mile; Race: 81.8% White, 1.9% Black/African American, 1.8% Asian, 1.5% American Indian/Alaska Native, 0.0% Native Hawaiian/Other Pacific Islander, 8.9% Two or more races, 18.2% Hispanic of any race; Average household size: 2.77; Median age: 47.8; Age under 18: 21.7%; Age 65 and over: 18.5%; Males per 100 females: 102.4

Housing: Homeownership rate: 83.5%; Homeowner vacancy rate: 2.8%; Rental vacancy rate: 0.0%

CAMPO SECO (unincorporated postal area)

ZCTA: 95226

Covers a land area of 5.645 square miles and a water area of 0.152 square miles. Located at 38.23° N. Lat; 120.86° W. Long. Elevation is 564 feet.

Population: 84; Growth (since 2000): 52.7%; Density: 14.9 persons per square mile; Race: 88.1% White, 0.0% Black/African American, 1.2% Asian, 0.0% American Indian/Alaska Native, 0.0% Native Hawaiian/Other Pacific Islander, 9.5% Two or more races, 9.5% Hispanic of any race; Average household size: 2.47; Median age: 42.0; Age under 18: 22.6%; Age 65 and over: 10.7%; Males per 100 females: 100.0

Housing: Homeownership rate: 70.6%; Homeowner vacancy rate: 4.0%; Rental vacancy rate: 9.1%

COPPEROPOLIS

COPPEROPOLIS (CDP). Covers a land area of 20.789 square miles and a water area of 0.643 square miles. Located at 37.94° N. Lat; 120.63° W. Long. Elevation is 997 feet.

Population: 3,671; Growth (since 2000): 55.4%; Density: 176.6 persons per square mile; Race: 90.4% White, 0.8% Black/African American, 1.0% Asian, 1.2% American Indian/Alaska Native, 0.3% Native Hawaiian/Other Pacific Islander, 4.0% Two or more races, 12.4% Hispanic of any race; Average household size: 2.50; Median age: 46.9; Age under 18: 21.3%; Age 65 and over: 17.8%; Males per 100 females: 102.4; Marriage status:

20.1% never married, 62.1% now married, 2.8% separated, 2.9% widowed, 15.0% divorced; Foreign born: 5.4%; Speak English only: 91.6%; With disability: 11.5%; Veterans: 13.3%; Ancestry: 21.4% German, 15.3% Irish, 13.2% English, 9.0% Italian, 7.2% Portuguese
Employment: 13.8% management, business, and financial, 5.6% computer, engineering, and science, 6.6% education, legal, community service, arts, and media, 7.6% healthcare practitioners, 22.8% service, 19.7% sales and office, 12.0% natural resources, construction, and maintenance, 12.0% production, transportation, and material moving
Income: Per capita: $28,486; Median household: $57,347; Average household: $72,980; Households with income of $100,000 or more: 24.5%; Poverty rate: 10.4%
Educational Attainment: High school diploma or higher: 94.5%; Bachelor's degree or higher: 18.8%; Graduate/professional degree or higher: 6.5%

School District(s)

Mark Twain Union Elementary (KG-08)
2012-13 Enrollment: 830 . . . . (209) 736-1855
Housing: Homeownership rate: 74.3%; Median home value: $231,500; Median year structure built: 1999; Homeowner vacancy rate: 6.7%; Median gross rent: $1,361 per month; Rental vacancy rate: 8.7%
Health Insurance: 89.4% have insurance; 77.8% have private insurance; 26.8% have public insurance; 10.6% do not have insurance; 5.1% of children under 18 do not have insurance
Transportation: Commute: 96.7% car, 0.0% public transportation, 0.0% walk, 3.3% work from home; Median travel time to work: 45.5 minutes

DORRINGTON (CDP). Covers a land area of 3.653 square miles and a water area of 0.005 square miles. Located at 38.29° N. Lat; 120.27° W. Long. Elevation is 4,767 feet.
Population: 609; Growth (since 2000): -16.2%; Density: 166.7 persons per square mile; Race: 94.6% White, 0.0% Black/African American, 1.8% Asian, 0.3% American Indian/Alaska Native, 0.2% Native Hawaiian/Other Pacific Islander, 3.0% Two or more races, 5.4% Hispanic of any race; Average household size: 2.07; Median age: 57.6; Age under 18: 12.5%; Age 65 and over: 29.4%; Males per 100 females: 112.2
Housing: Homeownership rate: 91.5%; Homeowner vacancy rate: 6.2%; Rental vacancy rate: 17.1%

FOREST MEADOWS (CDP). Covers a land area of 5.655 square miles and a water area of 0 square miles. Located at 38.17° N. Lat; 120.41° W. Long. Elevation is 3,373 feet.
Population: 1,249; Growth (since 2000): 4.3%; Density: 220.9 persons per square mile; Race: 95.9% White, 0.0% Black/African American, 1.1% Asian, 0.3% American Indian/Alaska Native, 0.0% Native Hawaiian/Other Pacific Islander, 2.1% Two or more races, 4.8% Hispanic of any race; Average household size: 2.13; Median age: 58.0; Age under 18: 12.2%; Age 65 and over: 33.5%; Males per 100 females: 99.5
Housing: Homeownership rate: 83.3%; Homeowner vacancy rate: 5.4%; Rental vacancy rate: 7.4%

GLENCOE (unincorporated postal area)

ZCTA: 95232

Covers a land area of 7.899 square miles and a water area of 0 square miles. Located at 38.36° N. Lat; 120.59° W. Long. Elevation is 2,746 feet.
Population: 304; Growth (since 2000): 1,688.2%; Density: 38.5 persons per square mile; Race: 89.8% White, 0.0% Black/African American, 1.6% Asian, 3.0% American Indian/Alaska Native, 0.0% Native Hawaiian/Other Pacific Islander, 4.3% Two or more races, 6.3% Hispanic of any race; Average household size: 2.25; Median age: 53.3; Age under 18: 12.2%; Age 65 and over: 20.1%; Males per 100 females: 92.4
Housing: Homeownership rate: 77.0%; Homeowner vacancy rate: 0.9%; Rental vacancy rate: 8.8%

HATHAWAY PINES (unincorporated postal area)

ZCTA: 95233

Covers a land area of 7.003 square miles and a water area of 0.005 square miles. Located at 38.16° N. Lat; 120.37° W. Long. Elevation is 3,327 feet.
Population: 436; Growth (since 2000): 38.0%; Density: 62.3 persons per square mile; Race: 95.0% White, 0.0% Black/African American, 0.5% Asian, 0.7% American Indian/Alaska Native, 0.0% Native Hawaiian/Other Pacific Islander, 3.9% Two or more races, 6.4% Hispanic of any race; Average household size: 2.26; Median age: 49.0; Age under 18: 19.5%; Age 65 and over: 22.5%; Males per 100 females: 101.9
Housing: Homeownership rate: 74.6%; Homeowner vacancy rate: 8.9%; Rental vacancy rate: 10.9%

MOKELUMNE HILL (CDP). Covers a land area of 3.079 square miles and a water area of 0.003 square miles. Located at 38.30° N. Lat; 120.72° W. Long. Elevation is 1,470 feet.
History: Mokelumne Hill was settled in 1848 and grew into one of the Mother Lode's biggest and liveliest towns. Nearby is French Hill, scene of the French War skirmishes of 1851 in which American miners drove off Frenchmen and appropriated their claims.
Population: 646; Growth (since 2000): -16.5%; Density: 209.8 persons per square mile; Race: 88.4% White, 0.5% Black/African American, 0.6% Asian, 1.9% American Indian/Alaska Native, 0.0% Native Hawaiian/Other Pacific Islander, 4.6% Two or more races, 10.2% Hispanic of any race; Average household size: 2.16; Median age: 51.4; Age under 18: 15.8%; Age 65 and over: 21.8%; Males per 100 females: 88.9

School District(s)

Calaveras Unified (KG-12)
2012-13 Enrollment: 3,188 . . . . (209) 754-2300
Housing: Homeownership rate: 68.5%; Homeowner vacancy rate: 2.8%; Rental vacancy rate: 18.3%

MOUNTAIN RANCH (CDP). Covers a land area of 41.188 square miles and a water area of 0.056 square miles. Located at 38.25° N. Lat; 120.51° W. Long. Elevation is 2,136 feet.
Population: 1,628; Growth (since 2000): 4.6%; Density: 39.5 persons per square mile; Race: 90.4% White, 0.9% Black/African American, 1.1% Asian, 2.0% American Indian/Alaska Native, 0.1% Native Hawaiian/Other Pacific Islander, 4.5% Two or more races, 7.6% Hispanic of any race; Average household size: 2.18; Median age: 55.3; Age under 18: 13.1%; Age 65 and over: 25.6%; Males per 100 females: 105.8
Housing: Homeownership rate: 82.9%; Homeowner vacancy rate: 2.8%; Rental vacancy rate: 9.8%

MURPHYS (CDP). Covers a land area of 10.321 square miles and a water area of 0.002 square miles. Located at 38.14° N. Lat; 120.43° W. Long. Elevation is 2,175 feet.
History: The brothers Murphy, John and Daniel, were the first to discover gold here, and the town of Murphys was named for them. As with many gold-country towns, Murphys claims that outlaw Joaquin Murrieta began his lawless career here.
Population: 2,213; Growth (since 2000): 7.4%; Density: 214.4 persons per square mile; Race: 92.4% White, 0.4% Black/African American, 0.3% Asian, 0.8% American Indian/Alaska Native, 0.5% Native Hawaiian/Other Pacific Islander, 1.9% Two or more races, 10.1% Hispanic of any race; Average household size: 2.10; Median age: 54.1; Age under 18: 18.1%; Age 65 and over: 29.4%; Males per 100 females: 83.0

School District(s)

Vallecito Union (KG-08)
2012-13 Enrollment: 599 . . . . (209) 795-8500
Housing: Homeownership rate: 68.9%; Homeowner vacancy rate: 4.1%; Rental vacancy rate: 6.5%

RAIL ROAD FLAT (CDP). Covers a land area of 33.006 square miles and a water area of 0.156 square miles. Located at 38.31° N. Lat; 120.50° W. Long. Elevation is 2,608 feet.
Population: 475; Growth (since 2000): -13.5%; Density: 14.4 persons per square mile; Race: 86.5% White, 0.0% Black/African American, 0.8% Asian, 3.2% American Indian/Alaska Native, 0.4% Native Hawaiian/Other Pacific Islander, 7.2% Two or more races, 8.6% Hispanic of any race; Average household size: 2.16; Median age: 53.7; Age under 18: 16.2%; Age 65 and over: 25.7%; Males per 100 females: 93.1

School District(s)

Calaveras Unified (KG-12)
2012-13 Enrollment: 3,188 . . . . (209) 754-2300
Housing: Homeownership rate: 76.9%; Homeowner vacancy rate: 2.9%; Rental vacancy rate: 10.5%

RANCHO CALAVERAS (CDP). Covers a land area of 8.376 square miles and a water area of 0.030 square miles. Located at 38.13° N. Lat; 120.85° W. Long. Elevation is 535 feet.
Population: 5,325; Growth (since 2000): 27.3%; Density: 635.8 persons per square mile; Race: 87.2% White, 0.9% Black/African American, 1.6% Asian, 1.9% American Indian/Alaska Native, 0.2% Native Hawaiian/Other Pacific Islander, 4.4% Two or more races, 12.6% Hispanic of any race;

Average household size: 2.74; Median age: 43.6; Age under 18: 24.2%; Age 65 and over: 13.3%; Males per 100 females: 101.2; Marriage status: 22.9% never married, 64.5% now married, 0.0% separated, 6.4% widowed, 6.2% divorced; Foreign born: 3.5%; Speak English only: 93.4%; With disability: 14.2%; Veterans: 14.0%; Ancestry: 23.2% German, 16.1% Irish, 12.7% English, 8.1% French, 6.9% Italian

Employment: 7.6% management, business, and financial, 3.4% computer, engineering, and science, 9.0% education, legal, community service, arts, and media, 7.9% healthcare practitioners, 12.2% service, 23.7% sales and office, 21.3% natural resources, construction, and maintenance, 14.8% production, transportation, and material moving

Income: Per capita: $24,679; Median household: $56,964; Average household: $66,474; Households with income of $100,000 or more: 18.3%; Poverty rate: 9.2%

Educational Attainment: High school diploma or higher: 94.1%; Bachelor's degree or higher: 11.3%; Graduate/professional degree or higher: 2.3%

Housing: Homeownership rate: 87.5%; Median home value: $198,000; Median year structure built: 1991; Homeowner vacancy rate: 3.9%; Median gross rent: $1,339 per month; Rental vacancy rate: 8.2%

Health Insurance: 87.4% have insurance; 75.3% have private insurance; 29.3% have public insurance; 12.6% do not have insurance; 1.6% of children under 18 do not have insurance

Transportation: Commute: 97.5% car, 0.0% public transportation, 0.0% walk, 2.5% work from home; Median travel time to work: 43.8 minutes

---

SAN ANDREAS (CDP). County seat. Covers a land area of 8.378 square miles and a water area of 0.016 square miles. Located at 38.18° N. Lat; 120.67° W. Long. Elevation is 1,017 feet.

History: San Andreas was first a Mexican town. It developed as the seat of Calaveras County. San Andreans claim that the bandit Joaquin Murrieta began his career here.

Population: 2,783; Growth (since 2000): 6.4%; Density: 332.2 persons per square mile; Race: 88.1% White, 0.8% Black/African American, 1.0% Asian, 1.7% American Indian/Alaska Native, 0.0% Native Hawaiian/Other Pacific Islander, 5.3% Two or more races, 9.2% Hispanic of any race; Average household size: 2.26; Median age: 45.7; Age under 18: 21.0%; Age 65 and over: 22.8%; Males per 100 females: 88.6; Marriage status: 21.5% never married, 51.4% now married, 0.9% separated, 7.3% widowed, 19.7% divorced; Foreign born: 9.1%; Speak English only: 85.6%; With disability: 29.1%; Veterans: 7.7%; Ancestry: 21.6% German, 13.5% Irish, 11.2% Italian, 10.9% English, 9.2% Swedish

Employment: 6.1% management, business, and financial, 2.1% computer, engineering, and science, 24.8% education, legal, community service, arts, and media, 5.8% healthcare practitioners, 16.1% service, 23.8% sales and office, 12.5% natural resources, construction, and maintenance, 8.8% production, transportation, and material moving

Income: Per capita: $21,346; Median household: $42,388; Average household: $49,041; Households with income of $100,000 or more: 5.7%; Poverty rate: 13.7%

Educational Attainment: High school diploma or higher: 88.0%; Bachelor's degree or higher: 24.8%; Graduate/professional degree or higher: 12.9%

School District(s)

Calaveras County Office of Education (KG-12)
 2012-13 Enrollment: 588. . . . . (209) 736-4662
Calaveras Unified (KG-12)
 2012-13 Enrollment: 3,188 . . . . (209) 754-2300

Housing: Homeownership rate: 55.2%; Median home value: $168,400; Median year structure built: 1976; Homeowner vacancy rate: 1.9%; Median gross rent: $789 per month; Rental vacancy rate: 13.3%

Health Insurance: 81.7% have insurance; 60.7% have private insurance; 33.3% have public insurance; 18.3% do not have insurance; 0.0% of children under 18 do not have insurance

Hospitals: Mark Twain Medical Center

Newspapers: Calaveras Newspapers (weekly circulation 29000)

Transportation: Commute: 81.2% car, 0.0% public transportation, 14.5% walk, 3.3% work from home; Median travel time to work: 24.6 minutes

---

VALLECITO (CDP). Covers a land area of 8.561 square miles and a water area of 0.005 square miles. Located at 38.08° N. Lat; 120.45° W. Long. Elevation is 1,762 feet.

Population: 442; Growth (since 2000): 3.5%; Density: 51.6 persons per square mile; Race: 90.0% White, 0.0% Black/African American, 2.5% Asian, 1.4% American Indian/Alaska Native, 0.2% Native Hawaiian/Other Pacific Islander, 4.8% Two or more races, 7.5% Hispanic of any race; Average household size: 2.29; Median age: 47.7; Age under 18: 19.0%; Age 65 and over: 17.4%; Males per 100 females: 87.3

School District(s)

Bret Harte Union High (09-12)
 2012-13 Enrollment: 754. . . . . (209) 736-8340

Housing: Homeownership rate: 71.5%; Homeowner vacancy rate: 0.7%; Rental vacancy rate: 6.8%

VALLEY SPRINGS (CDP). Covers a land area of 9.872 square miles and a water area of 0.003 square miles. Located at 38.18° N. Lat; 120.80° W. Long. Elevation is 669 feet.

Population: 3,553; Growth (since 2000): 38.8%; Density: 359.9 persons per square mile; Race: 85.8% White, 1.0% Black/African American, 2.0% Asian, 1.1% American Indian/Alaska Native, 0.2% Native Hawaiian/Other Pacific Islander, 5.0% Two or more races, 12.8% Hispanic of any race; Average household size: 2.65; Median age: 42.7; Age under 18: 24.9%; Age 65 and over: 17.4%; Males per 100 females: 98.0; Marriage status: 31.2% never married, 57.4% now married, 0.6% separated, 1.2% widowed, 10.3% divorced; Foreign born: 8.0%; Speak English only: 92.8%; With disability: 12.8%; Veterans: 10.3%; Ancestry: 28.1% German, 10.4% Irish, 8.1% English, 7.0% Italian, 5.6% Portuguese

Employment: 12.2% management, business, and financial, 3.5% computer, engineering, and science, 5.6% education, legal, community service, arts, and media, 0.5% healthcare practitioners, 32.2% service, 21.9% sales and office, 18.7% natural resources, construction, and maintenance, 5.4% production, transportation, and material moving

Income: Per capita: $28,038; Median household: $68,958; Average household: $80,685; Households with income of $100,000 or more: 27.1%; Poverty rate: 11.0%

Educational Attainment: High school diploma or higher: 94.4%; Bachelor's degree or higher: 14.2%; Graduate/professional degree or higher: 3.1%

School District(s)

Calaveras Unified (KG-12)
 2012-13 Enrollment: 3,188 . . . . (209) 754-2300

Housing: Homeownership rate: 75.0%; Median home value: $242,000; Median year structure built: 1993; Homeowner vacancy rate: 4.0%; Median gross rent: $1,326 per month; Rental vacancy rate: 9.8%

Health Insurance: 83.9% have insurance; 67.7% have private insurance; 29.2% have public insurance; 16.1% do not have insurance; 15.5% of children under 18 do not have insurance

Newspapers: The News (weekly circulation 1100)

Transportation: Commute: 87.4% car, 0.0% public transportation, 3.6% walk, 9.0% work from home; Median travel time to work: 31.1 minutes

---

WALLACE (CDP). Covers a land area of 4.333 square miles and a water area of 0.080 square miles. Located at 38.20° N. Lat; 120.96° W. Long. Elevation is 190 feet.

Population: 403; Growth (since 2000): 83.2%; Density: 93.0 persons per square mile; Race: 86.1% White, 0.7% Black/African American, 2.5% Asian, 1.0% American Indian/Alaska Native, 0.5% Native Hawaiian/Other Pacific Islander, 3.7% Two or more races, 7.9% Hispanic of any race; Average household size: 2.62; Median age: 47.8; Age under 18: 20.1%; Age 65 and over: 20.1%; Males per 100 females: 89.2

Housing: Homeownership rate: 85.0%; Homeowner vacancy rate: 4.3%; Rental vacancy rate: 8.0%

WEST POINT (CDP). Covers a land area of 3.719 square miles and a water area of 0 square miles. Located at 38.40° N. Lat; 120.54° W. Long. Elevation is 2,769 feet.

Population: 674; Growth (since 2000): -9.7%; Density: 181.2 persons per square mile; Race: 83.5% White, 0.0% Black/African American, 0.3% Asian, 6.4% American Indian/Alaska Native, 1.0% Native Hawaiian/Other Pacific Islander, 4.5% Two or more races, 9.9% Hispanic of any race; Average household size: 2.19; Median age: 50.0; Age under 18: 19.7%; Age 65 and over: 24.2%; Males per 100 females: 94.2

School District(s)

Calaveras Unified (KG-12)
 2012-13 Enrollment: 3,188 . . . . (209) 754-2300

Housing: Homeownership rate: 69.2%; Homeowner vacancy rate: 2.3%; Rental vacancy rate: 6.9%

WILSEYVILLE (unincorporated postal area)

ZCTA: 95257

Covers a land area of 15.200 square miles and a water area of 0.062 square miles. Located at 38.38° N. Lat; 120.45° W. Long. Elevation is 2,769 feet.

Population: 413; Growth (since 2000): -0.5%; Density: 27.2 persons per square mile; Race: 91.0% White, 0.0% Black/African American, 0.5% Asian, 3.4% American Indian/Alaska Native, 0.7% Native Hawaiian/Other Pacific Islander, 2.4% Two or more races, 5.3% Hispanic of any race; Average household size: 2.08; Median age: 53.0; Age under 18: 15.3%; Age 65 and over: 25.7%; Males per 100 females: 95.7
Housing: Homeownership rate: 74.4%; Homeowner vacancy rate: 1.3%; Rental vacancy rate: 8.9%

Colusa County

Located in north central California; bounded on the east by the Sacramento River; includes part of Mendocino National Forest. Covers a land area of 1,150.731 square miles, a water area of 5.630 square miles, and is located in the Pacific Time Zone at 39.18° N. Lat., 122.24° W. Long. The county was founded in 1850. County seat is Colusa.

Weather Station: Colusa 2 SSW Elevation: 49 feet

	Jan	Feb	Mar	Apr	May	Jun	Jul	Aug	Sep	Oct	Nov	Dec
High	54	60	66	74	82	89	94	92	89	79	64	54
Low	38	41	44	46	53	58	60	58	54	48	42	38
Precip	3.5	3.2	2.5	0.9	0.7	0.2	0.0	0.1	0.3	0.9	2.1	2.9
Snow	0.0	0.0	0.0	0.0	0.0	0.0	0.0	0.0	0.0	0.0	0.0	tr

High and Low temperatures in degrees Fahrenheit; Precipitation and Snow in inches

Weather Station: East Park Reservoir Elevation: 1,205 feet

	Jan	Feb	Mar	Apr	May	Jun	Jul	Aug	Sep	Oct	Nov	Dec
High	56	59	63	69	78	86	93	93	88	78	64	57
Low	32	35	37	40	47	53	59	57	52	44	37	32
Precip	5.1	4.5	3.3	1.1	0.8	0.3	0.0	0.1	0.3	1.0	2.9	3.7
Snow	1.3	0.4	0.0	0.0	0.0	0.0	0.0	0.0	0.0	0.0	0.0	0.4

High and Low temperatures in degrees Fahrenheit; Precipitation and Snow in inches

Population: 21,419; Growth (since 2000): 13.9%; Density: 18.6 persons per square mile; Race: 64.7% White, 0.9% Black/African American, 1.3% Asian, 2.0% American Indian/Alaska Native, 0.3% Native Hawaiian/Other Pacific Islander, 3.6% two or more races, 55.1% Hispanic of any race; Average household size: 3.00; Median age: 33.5; Age under 18: 29.9%; Age 65 and over: 11.6%; Males per 100 females: 105.8; Marriage status: 31.1% never married, 54.9% now married, 1.6% separated, 5.7% widowed, 8.2% divorced; Foreign born: 23.3%; Speak English only: 53.7%; With disability: 12.5%; Veterans: 7.5%; Ancestry: 13.1% German, 8.1% English, 7.6% Irish, 3.4% American, 2.4% Italian
Religion: Six largest groups: 42.8% Catholicism, 2.1% Non-denominational Protestant, 2.1% Pentecostal, 2.0% Methodist/Pietist, 1.7% Latter-day Saints, 0.9% Presbyterian-Reformed
Economy: Unemployment rate: 11.0%; Leading industries: 15.7% retail trade; 10.6% accommodation and food services; 9.0% other services (except public administration); Farms: 782 totaling 453,061 acres; Company size: 0 employ 1,000 or more persons, 0 employ 500 to 999 persons, 7 employ 100 to 499 persons, 369 employ less than 100 persons; Business ownership: 320 women-owned, n/a Black-owned, n/a Hispanic-owned, n/a Asian-owned
Employment: 13.9% management, business, and financial, 2.2% computer, engineering, and science, 7.3% education, legal, community service, arts, and media, 1.7% healthcare practitioners, 18.8% service, 17.3% sales and office, 24.5% natural resources, construction, and maintenance, 14.4% production, transportation, and material moving
Income: Per capita: $21,579; Median household: $52,158; Average household: $63,743; Households with income of $100,000 or more: 16.4%; Poverty rate: 12.5%
Educational Attainment: High school diploma or higher: 69.4%; Bachelor's degree or higher: 13.8%; Graduate/professional degree or higher: 2.5%
Housing: Homeownership rate: 61.2%; Median home value: $181,600; Median year structure built: 1974; Homeowner vacancy rate: 2.2%; Median gross rent: $923 per month; Rental vacancy rate: 3.1%
Vital Statistics: Birth rate: 140.0 per 10,000 population; Death rate: 51.0 per 10,000 population; Age-adjusted cancer mortality rate: 207.4 deaths per 100,000 population
Health Insurance: 78.3% have insurance; 49.7% have private insurance; 38.1% have public insurance; 21.7% do not have insurance; 8.5% of children under 18 do not have insurance
Health Care: Physicians: 4.7 per 10,000 population; Hospital beds: 14.0 per 10,000 population; Hospital admissions: 464.3 per 10,000 population
Air Quality Index: 87.1% good, 12.9% moderate, 0.0% unhealthy for sensitive individuals, 0.0% unhealthy (percent of days)
Transportation: Commute: 92.8% car, 0.1% public transportation, 2.8% walk, 3.4% work from home; Median travel time to work: 21.2 minutes
Presidential Election: 38.5% Obama, 59.9% Romney (2012)
National and State Parks: Colusa National Wildlife Refuge; Colusa-Sacramento River State Recreation Area; Delevan National Wildlife Refuge
Additional Information Contacts
Colusa Government . . . . (530) 458-0508
http://www.countyofcolusa.org

Colusa County Communities

ARBUCKLE (CDP). Covers a land area of 1.759 square miles and a water area of 0 square miles. Located at 39.01° N. Lat; 122.06° W. Long. Elevation is 141 feet.
History: Almond growing in Arbuckle began in 1892 when C.H. Locke, observing that oak trees here grew large crops of acorns, planted 21 acres of almond trees, expecting rightly that they would do as well.
Population: 3,028; Growth (since 2000): 29.8%; Density: 1,721.2 persons per square mile; Race: 57.7% White, 0.6% Black/African American, 0.6% Asian, 0.8% American Indian/Alaska Native, 0.2% Native Hawaiian/Other Pacific Islander, 3.1% Two or more races, 69.9% Hispanic of any race; Average household size: 3.49; Median age: 28.3; Age under 18: 32.4%; Age 65 and over: 7.6%; Males per 100 females: 103.1; Marriage status: 35.3% never married, 53.7% now married, 2.5% separated, 5.6% widowed, 5.5% divorced; Foreign born: 28.5%; Speak English only: 34.1%; With disability: 12.2%; Veterans: 5.6%; Ancestry: 8.5% German, 6.4% Irish, 3.1% English, 2.4% French, 1.8% Scotch-Irish
Employment: 16.0% management, business, and financial, 2.3% computer, engineering, and science, 5.5% education, legal, community service, arts, and media, 0.7% healthcare practitioners, 25.3% service, 16.9% sales and office, 19.6% natural resources, construction, and maintenance, 13.7% production, transportation, and material moving
Income: Per capita: $16,465; Median household: $49,123; Average household: $59,678; Households with income of $100,000 or more: 11.1%; Poverty rate: 12.0%
Educational Attainment: High school diploma or higher: 60.3%; Bachelor's degree or higher: 11.5%; Graduate/professional degree or higher: 1.9%

School District(s)

Pierce Joint Unified (KG-12)
2012-13 Enrollment: 1,377 . . . . (530) 476-2892
Housing: Homeownership rate: 63.0%; Median home value: $202,000; Median year structure built: 1980; Homeowner vacancy rate: 4.0%; Median gross rent: $1,025 per month; Rental vacancy rate: 2.7%
Health Insurance: 71.5% have insurance; 41.0% have private insurance; 36.0% have public insurance; 28.5% do not have insurance; 12.9% of children under 18 do not have insurance
Transportation: Commute: 97.7% car, 0.0% public transportation, 0.0% walk, 2.3% work from home; Median travel time to work: 27.2 minutes

COLLEGE CITY (CDP). Covers a land area of 3.279 square miles and a water area of 0 square miles. Located at 39.01° N. Lat; 122.01° W. Long. Elevation is 72 feet.
Population: 290; Growth (since 2000): n/a; Density: 88.5 persons per square mile; Race: 71.4% White, 0.0% Black/African American, 0.3% Asian, 1.7% American Indian/Alaska Native, 0.0% Native Hawaiian/Other Pacific Islander, 9.0% Two or more races, 46.2% Hispanic of any race; Average household size: 3.15; Median age: 36.0; Age under 18: 29.0%; Age 65 and over: 13.4%; Males per 100 females: 113.2
Housing: Homeownership rate: 69.6%; Homeowner vacancy rate: 1.5%; Rental vacancy rate: 9.7%

COLUSA (city). County seat. Covers a land area of 1.834 square miles and a water area of 0 square miles. Located at 39.20° N. Lat; 122.01° W. Long. Elevation is 49 feet.
History: Colusa was founded soon after Colonel Charles D. Semple purchased land here from John Bidwell. Semple was successful in

developing river commerce between Colusa and Sacramento and San Francisco.

Population: 5,971; Growth (since 2000): 10.5%; Density: 3,255.3 persons per square mile; Race: 66.1% White, 0.9% Black/African American, 1.3% Asian, 1.8% American Indian/Alaska Native, 0.5% Native Hawaiian/Other Pacific Islander, 4.2% Two or more races, 52.4% Hispanic of any race; Average household size: 2.76; Median age: 33.5; Age under 18: 30.0%; Age 65 and over: 11.7%; Males per 100 females: 100.1; Marriage status: 35.2% never married, 48.6% now married, 2.8% separated, 6.9% widowed, 9.2% divorced; Foreign born: 21.4%; Speak English only: 56.4%; With disability: 12.8%; Veterans: 8.3%; Ancestry: 14.5% German, 8.1% English, 6.2% Irish, 2.9% American, 2.8% Italian

Employment: 10.2% management, business, and financial, 2.3% computer, engineering, and science, 10.2% education, legal, community service, arts, and media, 1.4% healthcare practitioners, 15.8% service, 21.9% sales and office, 22.2% natural resources, construction, and maintenance, 16.0% production, transportation, and material moving

Income: Per capita: $23,526; Median household: $49,487; Average household: $62,128; Households with income of $100,000 or more: 16.4%; Poverty rate: 10.0%

Educational Attainment: High school diploma or higher: 73.7%; Bachelor's degree or higher: 15.1%; Graduate/professional degree or higher: 2.7%

School District(s)

Colusa County Office of Education (KG-12)
2012-13 Enrollment: 28. . . . . (530) 458-0350

Colusa Unified (KG-12)
2012-13 Enrollment: 1,408 . . . . (530) 458-7791

Housing: Homeownership rate: 55.6%; Median home value: $167,900; Median year structure built: 1968; Homeowner vacancy rate: 1.4%; Median gross rent: $802 per month; Rental vacancy rate: 2.3%

Health Insurance: 82.0% have insurance; 55.0% have private insurance; 39.4% have public insurance; 18.0% do not have insurance; 5.7% of children under 18 do not have insurance

Hospitals: Colusa Regional Medical Center (48 beds)

Safety: Violent crime rate: 16.8 per 10,000 population; Property crime rate: 231.7 per 10,000 population

Newspapers: Sun Herald (weekly circulation 1800)

Transportation: Commute: 96.3% car, 0.4% public transportation, 0.4% walk, 2.1% work from home; Median travel time to work: 19.1 minutes

Additional Information Contacts

City of Colusa . . . . (530) 458-4740
http://www.cityofcolusa.com

GRIMES (CDP). Covers a land area of 2.261 square miles and a water area of 0 square miles. Located at 39.07° N. Lat; 121.90° W. Long. Elevation is 46 feet.

Population: 391; Growth (since 2000): n/a; Density: 172.9 persons per square mile; Race: 72.6% White, 1.8% Black/African American, 0.3% Asian, 0.8% American Indian/Alaska Native, 0.0% Native Hawaiian/Other Pacific Islander, 7.9% Two or more races, 66.0% Hispanic of any race; Average household size: 3.01; Median age: 33.6; Age under 18: 30.7%; Age 65 and over: 10.2%; Males per 100 females: 96.5

School District(s)

Pierce Joint Unified (KG-12)
2012-13 Enrollment: 1,377 . . . . (530) 476-2892

Housing: Homeownership rate: 54.6%; Homeowner vacancy rate: 4.1%; Rental vacancy rate: 9.2%

LODOGA (CDP). Covers a land area of 3.387 square miles and a water area of 0 square miles. Located at 39.30° N. Lat; 122.51° W. Long. Elevation is 1,240 feet.

Population: 197; Growth (since 2000): n/a; Density: 58.2 persons per square mile; Race: 84.8% White, 8.1% Black/African American, 1.0% Asian, 2.0% American Indian/Alaska Native, 1.0% Native Hawaiian/Other Pacific Islander, 1.5% Two or more races, 4.1% Hispanic of any race; Average household size: 2.01; Median age: 54.5; Age under 18: 13.2%; Age 65 and over: 28.4%; Males per 100 females: 116.5

Housing: Homeownership rate: 79.6%; Homeowner vacancy rate: 1.3%; Rental vacancy rate: 0.0%

MAXWELL (CDP). Covers a land area of 2.150 square miles and a water area of 0 square miles. Located at 39.28° N. Lat; 122.19° W. Long. Elevation is 92 feet.

Population: 1,103; Growth (since 2000): n/a; Density: 512.9 persons per square mile; Race: 66.5% White, 1.0% Black/African American, 0.8% Asian, 1.3% American Indian/Alaska Native, 0.2% Native Hawaiian/Other Pacific Islander, 2.4% Two or more races, 51.7% Hispanic of any race; Average household size: 3.02; Median age: 33.9; Age under 18: 32.3%; Age 65 and over: 13.7%; Males per 100 females: 108.9

School District(s)

Maxwell Unified (KG-12)
2012-13 Enrollment: 345. . . . . (530) 438-2052

Housing: Homeownership rate: 64.4%; Homeowner vacancy rate: 0.4%; Rental vacancy rate: 1.5%

PRINCETON (CDP). Covers a land area of 1.836 square miles and a water area of 0 square miles. Located at 39.40° N. Lat; 122.02° W. Long. Elevation is 82 feet.

Population: 303; Growth (since 2000): n/a; Density: 165.0 persons per square mile; Race: 71.6% White, 0.0% Black/African American, 0.3% Asian, 3.3% American Indian/Alaska Native, 0.3% Native Hawaiian/Other Pacific Islander, 1.3% Two or more races, 30.7% Hispanic of any race; Average household size: 2.44; Median age: 47.1; Age under 18: 19.8%; Age 65 and over: 16.2%; Males per 100 females: 103.4

School District(s)

Princeton Joint Unified (KG-12)
2012-13 Enrollment: 202. . . . . (530) 439-2261

Housing: Homeownership rate: 67.0%; Homeowner vacancy rate: 1.2%; Rental vacancy rate: 4.7%

STONYFORD (CDP). Covers a land area of 2.897 square miles and a water area of 0 square miles. Located at 39.37° N. Lat; 122.54° W. Long. Elevation is 1,184 feet.

Population: 149; Growth (since 2000): n/a; Density: 51.4 persons per square mile; Race: 85.2% White, 0.0% Black/African American, 0.0% Asian, 2.7% American Indian/Alaska Native, 0.7% Native Hawaiian/Other Pacific Islander, 3.4% Two or more races, 14.8% Hispanic of any race; Average household size: 2.16; Median age: 50.4; Age under 18: 16.8%; Age 65 and over: 21.5%; Males per 100 females: 93.5

School District(s)

Stony Creek Joint Unified (KG-12)
2012-13 Enrollment: 111. . . . . (530) 968-5361

Housing: Homeownership rate: 68.1%; Homeowner vacancy rate: 2.1%; Rental vacancy rate: 4.3%

WILLIAMS (city). Covers a land area of 5.444 square miles and a water area of 0 square miles. Located at 39.15° N. Lat; 122.14° W. Long. Elevation is 82 feet.

History: Williams was laid out by W.H. Williams in 1876, and became a supply and shipping center for the surrounding rice fields.

Population: 5,123; Growth (since 2000): 39.6%; Density: 941.0 persons per square mile; Race: 54.4% White, 1.2% Black/African American, 1.8% Asian, 1.1% American Indian/Alaska Native, 0.1% Native Hawaiian/Other Pacific Islander, 3.5% Two or more races, 76.0% Hispanic of any race; Average household size: 3.66; Median age: 28.3; Age under 18: 33.2%; Age 65 and over: 8.3%; Males per 100 females: 108.7; Marriage status: 34.9% never married, 56.1% now married, 0.8% separated, 3.3% widowed, 5.8% divorced; Foreign born: 34.5%; Speak English only: 35.9%; With disability: 8.7%; Veterans: 4.7%; Ancestry: 6.4% German, 5.9% Irish, 4.5% American, 4.0% English, 1.7% Portuguese

Employment: 7.1% management, business, and financial, 2.6% computer, engineering, and science, 7.4% education, legal, community service, arts, and media, 0.4% healthcare practitioners, 14.8% service, 14.7% sales and office, 36.4% natural resources, construction, and maintenance, 16.6% production, transportation, and material moving

Income: Per capita: $15,818; Median household: $53,118; Average household: $54,298; Households with income of $100,000 or more: 11.6%; Poverty rate: 12.3%

Educational Attainment: High school diploma or higher: 56.8%; Bachelor's degree or higher: 5.8%; Graduate/professional degree or higher: 1.2%

School District(s)

Williams Unified (KG-12)
2012-13 Enrollment: 1,324 . . . . (530) 473-2550

Housing: Homeownership rate: 60.8%; Median home value: $159,200; Median year structure built: 1991; Homeowner vacancy rate: 3.8%; Median gross rent: $1,013 per month; Rental vacancy rate: 4.4%
Health Insurance: 72.3% have insurance; 38.6% have private insurance; 37.3% have public insurance; 27.7% do not have insurance; 7.8% of children under 18 do not have insurance
Safety: Violent crime rate: 9.7 per 10,000 population; Property crime rate: 129.4 per 10,000 population
Transportation: Commute: 88.3% car, 0.0% public transportation, 6.9% walk, 2.9% work from home; Median travel time to work: 19.4 minutes
Additional Information Contacts
City of Williams . . . . (530) 473-2955
http://cityofwilliams.org

Contra Costa County

Located in west central California; bounded on the west by San Francisco Bay, on the north by San Pablo Bay, and on the northeast by Suisun Bay. Covers a land area of 715.937 square miles, a water area of 87.833 square miles, and is located in the Pacific Time Zone at 37.92° N. Lat., 121.95° W. Long. The county was founded in 1850. County seat is Martinez.

Contra Costa County is part of the San Francisco-Oakland-Hayward, CA Metropolitan Statistical Area. The entire metro area includes: Oakland-Hayward-Berkeley, CA Metropolitan Division (Alameda County, CA; Contra Costa County, CA); San Francisco-Redwood City-South San Francisco, CA Metropolitan Division (San Francisco County, CA; San Mateo County, CA); San Rafael, CA Metropolitan Division (Marin County, CA)

Weather Station: Antioch Pump Plant #3 Elevation: 60 feet

	Jan	Feb	Mar	Apr	May	Jun	Jul	Aug	Sep	Oct	Nov	Dec
High	54	60	65	72	79	86	92	90	86	77	64	55
Low	39	42	45	48	53	58	59	58	57	52	45	39
Precip	2.9	2.7	2.4	0.8	0.5	0.1	0.0	0.0	0.2	0.5	1.6	2.4
Snow	0.0	tr	0.0	0.0	0.0	0.0	0.0	0.0	0.0	0.0	0.0	0.0

High and Low temperatures in degrees Fahrenheit; Precipitation and Snow in inches

Weather Station: Martinez Water Plant Elevation: 40 feet

	Jan	Feb	Mar	Apr	May	Jun	Jul	Aug	Sep	Oct	Nov	Dec
High	55	61	66	72	79	85	89	88	84	76	64	55
Low	39	42	44	46	50	54	55	55	53	49	43	39
Precip	4.0	4.1	2.9	1.2	0.6	0.1	0.0	0.1	0.2	1.0	2.5	3.6
Snow	0.0	0.0	0.0	0.0	0.0	0.0	0.0	0.0	0.0	0.0	0.0	0.0

High and Low temperatures in degrees Fahrenheit; Precipitation and Snow in inches

Weather Station: Mount Diablo Junction Elevation: 2,169 feet

	Jan	Feb	Mar	Apr	May	Jun	Jul	Aug	Sep	Oct	Nov	Dec
High	55	56	59	64	70	77	85	85	82	73	62	55
Low	39	39	41	42	47	53	59	59	57	50	43	39
Precip	4.6	4.8	3.7	1.6	1.0	0.2	0.0	0.1	0.3	1.3	3.1	4.2
Snow	0.2	0.3	0.1	0.0	0.0	0.0	0.0	0.0	0.0	0.0	0.1	0.1

High and Low temperatures in degrees Fahrenheit; Precipitation and Snow in inches

Weather Station: Richmond Elevation: 20 feet

	Jan	Feb	Mar	Apr	May	Jun	Jul	Aug	Sep	Oct	Nov	Dec
High	58	61	64	67	69	72	72	72	74	72	65	58
Low	43	46	48	50	52	55	56	56	56	54	49	44
Precip	4.8	4.5	3.4	1.5	0.7	0.2	0.0	0.1	0.2	1.3	3.1	4.4
Snow	0.0	0.0	0.0	0.0	0.0	0.0	0.0	0.0	0.0	0.0	0.0	0.0

High and Low temperatures in degrees Fahrenheit; Precipitation and Snow in inches

Population: 1,049,025; Growth (since 2000): 10.6%; Density: 1,465.2 persons per square mile; Race: 58.6% White, 9.3% Black/African American, 14.4% Asian, 0.6% American Indian/Alaska Native, 0.5% Native Hawaiian/Other Pacific Islander, 5.9% two or more races, 24.4% Hispanic of any race; Average household size: 2.77; Median age: 38.5; Age under 18: 24.8%; Age 65 and over: 12.4%; Males per 100 females: 95.2; Marriage status: 30.9% never married, 53.8% now married, 2.1% separated, 5.4% widowed, 9.9% divorced; Foreign born: 23.5%; Speak English only: 66.7%; With disability: 10.2%; Veterans: 7.1%; Ancestry: 10.3% German, 9.1% Irish, 7.7% English, 6.2% Italian, 3.3% American
Religion: Six largest groups: 21.8% Catholicism, 2.9% Baptist, 2.5% Non-denominational Protestant, 2.1% Latter-day Saints, 2.0% Pentecostal, 1.3% Methodist/Pietist
Economy: Unemployment rate: 5.7%; Leading industries: 15.3% professional, scientific, and technical services; 13.1% health care and social assistance; 11.3% retail trade; Farms: 602 totaling 127,670 acres; Company size: 15 employ 1,000 or more persons, 34 employ 500 to 999 persons, 377 employ 100 to 499 persons, 21,684 employ less than 100 persons; Business ownership: 29,835 women-owned, 3,965 Black-owned, 10,447 Hispanic-owned, 14,157 Asian-owned
Employment: 19.1% management, business, and financial, 7.6% computer, engineering, and science, 10.1% education, legal, community service, arts, and media, 5.5% healthcare practitioners, 17.8% service, 24.2% sales and office, 8.1% natural resources, construction, and maintenance, 7.6% production, transportation, and material moving
Income: Per capita: $38,219; Median household: $78,756; Average household: $106,018; Households with income of $100,000 or more: 39.7%; Poverty rate: 10.5%
Educational Attainment: High school diploma or higher: 88.8%; Bachelor's degree or higher: 39.0%; Graduate/professional degree or higher: 14.1%
Housing: Homeownership rate: 67.1%; Median home value: $404,000; Median year structure built: 1975; Homeowner vacancy rate: 2.1%; Median gross rent: $1,365 per month; Rental vacancy rate: 6.8%
Vital Statistics: Birth rate: 110.7 per 10,000 population; Death rate: 68.8 per 10,000 population; Age-adjusted cancer mortality rate: 158.6 deaths per 100,000 population
Health Insurance: 88.1% have insurance; 73.6% have private insurance; 25.4% have public insurance; 11.9% do not have insurance; 6.1% of children under 18 do not have insurance
Health Care: Physicians: 26.2 per 10,000 population; Hospital beds: 14.2 per 10,000 population; Hospital admissions: 748.8 per 10,000 population
Air Quality Index: 60.0% good, 39.5% moderate, 0.5% unhealthy for sensitive individuals, 0.0% unhealthy (percent of days)
Transportation: Commute: 81.6% car, 9.3% public transportation, 1.6% walk, 5.7% work from home; Median travel time to work: 33.3 minutes
Presidential Election: 65.8% Obama, 31.9% Romney (2012)
National and State Parks: Antioch Dunes National Wildlife Refuge; Eugene O'Neil National Historic Site; Franks Tract State Recreation Area; John Muir National Historic Site; Marsh Creek State Park; Mount Diablo State Park; Port Chicago Naval Magazine National Memorial; Rosie the Riveter World War II Home Front National Historical Park
Additional Information Contacts
Contra Costa Government . . . . (925) 335-1024
http://www.co.contra-costa.ca.us

Contra Costa County Communities

ACALANES RIDGE (CDP). Covers a land area of 0.461 square miles and a water area of 0 square miles. Located at 37.90° N. Lat; 122.08° W. Long.
Population: 1,137; Growth (since 2000): n/a; Density: 2,468.2 persons per square mile; Race: 83.6% White, 0.4% Black/African American, 11.1% Asian, 0.7% American Indian/Alaska Native, 0.2% Native Hawaiian/Other Pacific Islander, 3.3% Two or more races, 4.4% Hispanic of any race; Average household size: 2.58; Median age: 46.3; Age under 18: 23.3%; Age 65 and over: 16.2%; Males per 100 females: 94.7
Housing: Homeownership rate: 89.1%; Homeowner vacancy rate: 0.3%; Rental vacancy rate: 7.5%

ALAMO (CDP). Covers a land area of 9.667 square miles and a water area of 0 square miles. Located at 37.85° N. Lat; 122.01° W. Long. Elevation is 259 feet.
History: Named for the Spanish translation of "poplar (or cottonwood) tree". Alamo had its beginnings in 1848-1849 when the first adobe was built, followed in 1854 by two stores that served the surrounding Spanish population.
Population: 14,570; Growth (since 2000): -6.8%; Density: 1,507.2 persons per square mile; Race: 86.9% White, 0.5% Black/African American, 8.2% Asian, 0.1% American Indian/Alaska Native, 0.2% Native Hawaiian/Other Pacific Islander, 3.3% Two or more races, 5.8% Hispanic of any race; Average household size: 2.82; Median age: 47.7; Age under 18: 25.7%; Age 65 and over: 17.6%; Males per 100 females: 98.6; Marriage status: 20.2% never married, 70.7% now married, 0.3% separated, 3.3% widowed, 5.8% divorced; Foreign born: 10.7%; Speak English only: 89.9%; With disability: 5.5%; Veterans: 6.5%; Ancestry: 16.8% Irish, 16.5% English, 15.1% German, 11.1% Italian, 7.8% American

Employment: 38.7% management, business, and financial, 5.9% computer, engineering, and science, 11.9% education, legal, community service, arts, and media, 7.7% healthcare practitioners, 5.6% service, 25.7% sales and office, 2.0% natural resources, construction, and maintenance, 2.5% production, transportation, and material moving
Income: Per capita: $72,984; Median household: $160,220; Average household: $209,620; Households with income of $100,000 or more: 70.4%; Poverty rate: 2.3%
Educational Attainment: High school diploma or higher: 98.7%; Bachelor's degree or higher: 72.4%; Graduate/professional degree or higher: 27.2%

School District(s)

Contra Costa County Office of Education (KG-12)
2012-13 Enrollment: 3,297 . . . . (925) 942-3388
San Ramon Valley Unified (KG-12)
2012-13 Enrollment: 30,757 . . . . (925) 552-5500

Housing: Homeownership rate: 91.4%; Median home value: 1 million+; Median year structure built: 1976; Homeowner vacancy rate: 1.2%; Median gross rent: $2,000+ per month; Rental vacancy rate: 6.5%
Health Insurance: 98.4% have insurance; 94.1% have private insurance; 17.4% have public insurance; 1.6% do not have insurance; 0.3% of children under 18 do not have insurance
Transportation: Commute: 79.8% car, 6.4% public transportation, 2.0% walk, 11.4% work from home; Median travel time to work: 30.3 minutes

ALHAMBRA VALLEY (CDP). Covers a land area of 2.155 square miles and a water area of 0 square miles. Located at 37.97° N. Lat; 122.14° W. Long.
Population: 924; Growth (since 2000): n/a; Density: 428.8 persons per square mile; Race: 90.7% White, 0.3% Black/African American, 4.5% Asian, 0.0% American Indian/Alaska Native, 0.5% Native Hawaiian/Other Pacific Islander, 2.1% Two or more races, 8.8% Hispanic of any race; Average household size: 2.57; Median age: 52.2; Age under 18: 15.5%; Age 65 and over: 23.2%; Males per 100 females: 102.2
Housing: Homeownership rate: 91.2%; Homeowner vacancy rate: 1.2%; Rental vacancy rate: 0.0%

ANTIOCH (city). Covers a land area of 28.349 square miles and a water area of 0.734 square miles. Located at 37.98° N. Lat; 121.80° W. Long. Elevation is 43 feet.
History: Named for the biblical city in Syria. Antioch's first settlers were twin brothers, Joseph H. and W.W. Smith, both carpenters and ordained ministers, who came from Boston with their families in 1849.
Population: 102,372; Growth (since 2000): 13.1%; Density: 3,611.2 persons per square mile; Race: 48.9% White, 17.3% Black/African American, 10.5% Asian, 0.9% American Indian/Alaska Native, 0.8% Native Hawaiian/Other Pacific Islander, 7.7% Two or more races, 31.7% Hispanic of any race; Average household size: 3.15; Median age: 33.8; Age under 18: 28.1%; Age 65 and over: 8.8%; Males per 100 females: 94.8; Marriage status: 35.5% never married, 49.4% now married, 2.5% separated, 5.1% widowed, 10.1% divorced; Foreign born: 20.4%; Speak English only: 66.4%; With disability: 12.8%; Veterans: 7.0%; Ancestry: 7.8% Irish, 7.5% German, 5.5% Italian, 4.5% English, 2.9% American
Employment: 12.1% management, business, and financial, 3.8% computer, engineering, and science, 8.2% education, legal, community service, arts, and media, 4.7% healthcare practitioners, 22.6% service, 27.9% sales and office, 9.9% natural resources, construction, and maintenance, 10.8% production, transportation, and material moving
Income: Per capita: $24,678; Median household: $65,254; Average household: $77,188; Households with income of $100,000 or more: 28.2%; Poverty rate: 14.9%
Educational Attainment: High school diploma or higher: 87.2%; Bachelor's degree or higher: 19.9%; Graduate/professional degree or higher: 4.6%

School District(s)

Antioch Unified (KG-12)
2012-13 Enrollment: 18,852 . . . . (925) 779-7500
Contra Costa County Office of Education (KG-12)
2012-13 Enrollment: 3,297 . . . . (925) 942-3388

Two-year College(s)

Carrington College California-Antioch (Private, For-profit)
Fall 2013 Enrollment: 49 . . . . (925) 522-7777

Housing: Homeownership rate: 64.3%; Median home value: $233,600; Median year structure built: 1983; Homeowner vacancy rate: 2.7%; Median gross rent: $1,315 per month; Rental vacancy rate: 8.2%
Health Insurance: 85.8% have insurance; 64.9% have private insurance; 30.1% have public insurance; 14.2% do not have insurance; 7.7% of children under 18 do not have insurance
Hospitals: Kaiser Foundation Hospital - Antioch; Sutter Delta Medical Center (111 beds)
Safety: Violent crime rate: 88.9 per 10,000 population; Property crime rate: 417.1 per 10,000 population
Transportation: Commute: 87.6% car, 5.8% public transportation, 1.3% walk, 4.0% work from home; Median travel time to work: 40.0 minutes; Amtrak: Train service available.
Additional Information Contacts
City of Antioch . . . . (925) 779-7000
http://www.ci.antioch.ca.us

BAY POINT (CDP). Covers a land area of 6.554 square miles and a water area of 0.817 square miles. Located at 38.03° N. Lat; 121.96° W. Long. Elevation is 62 feet.
Population: 21,349; Growth (since 2000): -0.9%; Density: 3,257.4 persons per square mile; Race: 41.4% White, 11.6% Black/African American, 9.9% Asian, 1.1% American Indian/Alaska Native, 0.7% Native Hawaiian/Other Pacific Islander, 6.5% Two or more races, 54.9% Hispanic of any race; Average household size: 3.41; Median age: 30.1; Age under 18: 30.5%; Age 65 and over: 6.5%; Males per 100 females: 99.7; Marriage status: 40.5% never married, 44.3% now married, 4.2% separated, 4.8% widowed, 10.4% divorced; Foreign born: 35.1%; Speak English only: 42.9%; With disability: 11.3%; Veterans: 6.5%; Ancestry: 3.7% German, 3.3% Irish, 3.1% American, 2.9% Italian, 1.9% English
Employment: 7.0% management, business, and financial, 2.8% computer, engineering, and science, 4.9% education, legal, community service, arts, and media, 2.2% healthcare practitioners, 33.3% service, 23.2% sales and office, 13.9% natural resources, construction, and maintenance, 12.8% production, transportation, and material moving
Income: Per capita: $17,581; Median household: $43,441; Average household: $56,923; Households with income of $100,000 or more: 13.7%; Poverty rate: 29.1%
Educational Attainment: High school diploma or higher: 67.2%; Bachelor's degree or higher: 14.7%; Graduate/professional degree or higher: 3.0%

School District(s)

Mt. Diablo Unified (KG-12)
2012-13 Enrollment: 32,001 . . . . (925) 682-8000

Housing: Homeownership rate: 56.4%; Median home value: $164,500; Median year structure built: 1976; Homeowner vacancy rate: 3.0%; Median gross rent: $1,174 per month; Rental vacancy rate: 7.6%
Health Insurance: 79.0% have insurance; 46.1% have private insurance; 38.6% have public insurance; 21.0% do not have insurance; 7.2% of children under 18 do not have insurance
Transportation: Commute: 84.4% car, 9.5% public transportation, 1.2% walk, 3.2% work from home; Median travel time to work: 36.1 minutes

BAYVIEW (CDP). Covers a land area of 0.305 square miles and a water area of 0.081 square miles. Located at 38.01° N. Lat; 122.32° W. Long. Elevation is 36 feet.
Population: 1,754; Growth (since 2000): n/a; Density: 5,758.9 persons per square mile; Race: 49.7% White, 10.6% Black/African American, 21.0% Asian, 1.0% American Indian/Alaska Native, 0.5% Native Hawaiian/Other Pacific Islander, 7.0% Two or more races, 29.7% Hispanic of any race; Average household size: 3.04; Median age: 41.0; Age under 18: 23.5%; Age 65 and over: 16.5%; Males per 100 females: 92.1
Housing: Homeownership rate: 83.3%; Homeowner vacancy rate: 1.4%; Rental vacancy rate: 3.0%

BETHEL ISLAND (CDP). Covers a land area of 5.564 square miles and a water area of 0 square miles. Located at 38.03° N. Lat; 121.64° W. Long. Elevation is 7 feet.
Population: 2,137; Growth (since 2000): -7.6%; Density: 384.1 persons per square mile; Race: 86.2% White, 1.9% Black/African American, 2.2% Asian, 0.7% American Indian/Alaska Native, 0.2% Native Hawaiian/Other Pacific Islander, 3.3% Two or more races, 13.1% Hispanic of any race; Average household size: 2.07; Median age: 52.8; Age under 18: 12.2%; Age 65 and over: 26.9%; Males per 100 females: 115.0
Housing: Homeownership rate: 78.5%; Homeowner vacancy rate: 5.6%; Rental vacancy rate: 17.0%

BLACKHAWK (CDP). Covers a land area of 5.801 square miles and a water area of 0.010 square miles. Located at 37.81° N. Lat; 121.91° W. Long. Elevation is 997 feet.

Population: 9,354; Growth (since 2000): n/a; Density: 1,612.4 persons per square mile; Race: 73.6% White, 1.8% Black/African American, 19.3% Asian, 0.2% American Indian/Alaska Native, 0.1% Native Hawaiian/Other Pacific Islander, 4.3% Two or more races, 5.0% Hispanic of any race; Average household size: 2.80; Median age: 48.0; Age under 18: 24.3%; Age 65 and over: 14.0%; Males per 100 females: 96.3; Marriage status: 15.1% never married, 74.9% now married, 0.5% separated, 4.9% widowed, 5.1% divorced; Foreign born: 24.0%; Speak English only: 73.8%; With disability: 4.6%; Veterans: 6.6%; Ancestry: 16.7% German, 13.6% English, 11.7% Irish, 9.5% Italian, 3.9% Russian

Employment: 44.7% management, business, and financial, 10.0% computer, engineering, and science, 5.3% education, legal, community service, arts, and media, 8.0% healthcare practitioners, 4.7% service, 23.8% sales and office, 2.3% natural resources, construction, and maintenance, 1.4% production, transportation, and material moving

Income: Per capita: $82,011; Median household: $170,694; Average household: $215,192; Households with income of $100,000 or more: 74.6%; Poverty rate: 2.9%

Educational Attainment: High school diploma or higher: 97.8%; Bachelor's degree or higher: 72.9%; Graduate/professional degree or higher: 32.0%

Housing: Homeownership rate: 91.0%; Median home value: $995,400; Median year structure built: 1987; Homeowner vacancy rate: 1.3%; Median gross rent: $2,000+ per month; Rental vacancy rate: 3.8%

Health Insurance: 96.5% have insurance; 93.4% have private insurance; 15.7% have public insurance; 3.5% do not have insurance; 5.0% of children under 18 do not have insurance

Transportation: Commute: 83.3% car, 2.6% public transportation, 0.2% walk, 12.4% work from home; Median travel time to work: 35.4 minutes

BRENTWOOD (city). Covers a land area of 14.786 square miles and a water area of 0.019 square miles. Located at 37.94° N. Lat; 121.72° W. Long. Elevation is 79 feet.

History: Named for Brentwood, Essex in England, by original settlers. Incorporated 1948.

Population: 51,481; Growth (since 2000): 120.9%; Density: 3,481.8 persons per square mile; Race: 67.9% White, 6.6% Black/African American, 7.9% Asian, 0.6% American Indian/Alaska Native, 0.4% Native Hawaiian/Other Pacific Islander, 6.9% Two or more races, 26.8% Hispanic of any race; Average household size: 3.11; Median age: 35.6; Age under 18: 31.2%; Age 65 and over: 11.4%; Males per 100 females: 94.2; Marriage status: 27.3% never married, 59.1% now married, 1.7% separated, 4.1% widowed, 9.5% divorced; Foreign born: 14.6%; Speak English only: 77.4%; With disability: 8.4%; Veterans: 8.9%; Ancestry: 11.3% Irish, 10.7% German, 9.5% Italian, 8.7% English, 3.5% Portuguese

Employment: 15.5% management, business, and financial, 6.2% computer, engineering, and science, 9.9% education, legal, community service, arts, and media, 5.8% healthcare practitioners, 15.0% service, 28.7% sales and office, 11.6% natural resources, construction, and maintenance, 7.3% production, transportation, and material moving

Income: Per capita: $33,524; Median household: $91,475; Average household: $104,850; Households with income of $100,000 or more: 46.7%; Poverty rate: 5.7%

Educational Attainment: High school diploma or higher: 89.4%; Bachelor's degree or higher: 28.5%; Graduate/professional degree or higher: 7.1%

School District(s)

Brentwood Union Elementary (KG-08)
2012-13 Enrollment: 8,426 . . . . (925) 513-6300
Contra Costa County Office of Education (KG-12)
2012-13 Enrollment: 3,297 . . . . (925) 942-3388
Liberty Union High (09-12)
2012-13 Enrollment: 7,704 . . . . (925) 634-2166

Housing: Homeownership rate: 76.2%; Median home value: $345,000; Median year structure built: 2001; Homeowner vacancy rate: 2.7%; Median gross rent: $1,872 per month; Rental vacancy rate: 6.0%

Health Insurance: 93.1% have insurance; 82.4% have private insurance; 20.6% have public insurance; 6.9% do not have insurance; 3.9% of children under 18 do not have insurance

Safety: Violent crime rate: 16.4 per 10,000 population; Property crime rate: 223.6 per 10,000 population

Newspapers: The Press for Antioch, Brentwood, Discovery Bay, Oakley (weekly circulation 42000)

Transportation: Commute: 88.3% car, 2.6% public transportation, 0.4% walk, 7.6% work from home; Median travel time to work: 40.9 minutes

Additional Information Contacts

City of Brentwood . . . . (925) 516-5400
http://www.ci.brentwood.ca.us

BYRON (CDP). Covers a land area of 6.487 square miles and a water area of 0 square miles. Located at 37.88° N. Lat; 121.64° W. Long. Elevation is 33 feet.

Population: 1,277; Growth (since 2000): 39.4%; Density: 196.8 persons per square mile; Race: 71.3% White, 4.8% Black/African American, 0.3% Asian, 0.9% American Indian/Alaska Native, 0.9% Native Hawaiian/Other Pacific Islander, 4.3% Two or more races, 39.4% Hispanic of any race; Average household size: 3.03; Median age: 32.0; Age under 18: 31.7%; Age 65 and over: 9.2%; Males per 100 females: 112.8

School District(s)

Byron Union Elementary (KG-08)
2012-13 Enrollment: 1,686 . . . . (925) 809-7500
Contra Costa County Office of Education (KG-12)
2012-13 Enrollment: 3,297 . . . . (925) 942-3388
Mountain House Elementary (KG-08)
2012-13 Enrollment: 31. . . . . (209) 835-2283

Housing: Homeownership rate: 65.3%; Homeowner vacancy rate: 3.0%; Rental vacancy rate: 3.6%

CAMINO TASSAJARA (CDP). Covers a land area of 1.261 square miles and a water area of 0 square miles. Located at 37.79° N. Lat; 121.88° W. Long. Elevation is 702 feet.

Population: 2,197; Growth (since 2000): n/a; Density: 1,742.6 persons per square mile; Race: 39.9% White, 2.4% Black/African American, 50.8% Asian, 0.2% American Indian/Alaska Native, 0.0% Native Hawaiian/Other Pacific Islander, 5.1% Two or more races, 6.3% Hispanic of any race; Average household size: 3.48; Median age: 35.2; Age under 18: 36.4%; Age 65 and over: 4.3%; Males per 100 females: 98.8

Housing: Homeownership rate: 81.8%; Homeowner vacancy rate: 0.6%; Rental vacancy rate: 0.9%

CANYON (unincorporated postal area)

ZCTA: 94516

Covers a land area of 0.875 square miles and a water area of 0 square miles. Located at 37.83° N. Lat; 122.17° W. Long..

Population: 211; Growth (since 2000): n/a; Density: 241.3 persons per square mile; Race: 89.1% White, 0.9% Black/African American, 5.7% Asian, 0.9% American Indian/Alaska Native, 0.0% Native Hawaiian/Other Pacific Islander, 3.3% Two or more races, 0.9% Hispanic of any race; Average household size: 2.40; Median age: 43.6; Age under 18: 19.4%; Age 65 and over: 9.0%; Males per 100 females: 122.1

School District(s)

Canyon Elementary (KG-08)
2012-13 Enrollment: 73. . . . . (925) 376-4671

Housing: Homeownership rate: 52.3%; Homeowner vacancy rate: 0.0%; Rental vacancy rate: 0.0%

CASTLE HILL (CDP). Covers a land area of 0.728 square miles and a water area of 0 square miles. Located at 37.87° N. Lat; 122.06° W. Long.

Population: 1,299; Growth (since 2000): n/a; Density: 1,784.5 persons per square mile; Race: 85.6% White, 2.2% Black/African American, 8.5% Asian, 0.1% American Indian/Alaska Native, 0.2% Native Hawaiian/Other Pacific Islander, 2.8% Two or more races, 6.0% Hispanic of any race; Average household size: 2.55; Median age: 50.3; Age under 18: 21.2%; Age 65 and over: 22.1%; Males per 100 females: 97.7

Housing: Homeownership rate: 88.7%; Homeowner vacancy rate: 1.6%; Rental vacancy rate: 8.2%

CLAYTON (city). Covers a land area of 3.836 square miles and a water area of 0 square miles. Located at 37.94° N. Lat; 121.93° W. Long. Elevation is 394 feet.

Population: 10,897; Growth (since 2000): 1.3%; Density: 2,840.7 persons per square mile; Race: 85.1% White, 1.3% Black/African American, 6.6% Asian, 0.3% American Indian/Alaska Native, 0.1% Native Hawaiian/Other Pacific Islander, 4.4% Two or more races, 9.0% Hispanic of any race; Average household size: 2.72; Median age: 45.0; Age under 18: 24.4%; Age 65 and over: 14.7%; Males per 100 females: 93.4; Marriage status:

23.5% never married, 62.9% now married, 0.8% separated, 4.9% widowed, 8.6% divorced; Foreign born: 10.6%; Speak English only: 89.4%; With disability: 6.9%; Veterans: 10.2%; Ancestry: 18.9% German, 17.5% Irish, 15.7% English, 12.7% Italian, 7.0% American
Employment: 31.8% management, business, and financial, 10.9% computer, engineering, and science, 9.4% education, legal, community service, arts, and media, 7.0% healthcare practitioners, 12.0% service, 21.3% sales and office, 1.6% natural resources, construction, and maintenance, 6.1% production, transportation, and material moving
Income: Per capita: $52,174; Median household: $127,159; Average household: $145,622; Households with income of $100,000 or more: 64.1%; Poverty rate: 3.7%
Educational Attainment: High school diploma or higher: 98.7%; Bachelor's degree or higher: 49.9%; Graduate/professional degree or higher: 16.3%

School District(s)

Mt. Diablo Unified (KG-12)
2012-13 Enrollment: 32,001 . . . . (925) 682-8000
Housing: Homeownership rate: 90.4%; Median home value: $584,700; Median year structure built: 1981; Homeowner vacancy rate: 0.7%; Median gross rent: $2,000+ per month; Rental vacancy rate: 3.8%
Health Insurance: 97.4% have insurance; 90.9% have private insurance; 20.3% have public insurance; 2.6% do not have insurance; 1.6% of children under 18 do not have insurance
Safety: Violent crime rate: 1.7 per 10,000 population; Property crime rate: 88.3 per 10,000 population
Transportation: Commute: 84.6% car, 6.6% public transportation, 0.3% walk, 7.8% work from home; Median travel time to work: 34.9 minutes
Additional Information Contacts
City of Clayton . . . . (925) 673-7300
http://www.ci.clayton.ca.us

CLYDE (CDP). Covers a land area of 0.134 square miles and a water area of 0 square miles. Located at 38.03° N. Lat; 122.03° W. Long. Elevation is 23 feet.
Population: 678; Growth (since 2000): -2.3%; Density: 5,054.5 persons per square mile; Race: 78.2% White, 1.6% Black/African American, 8.6% Asian, 0.6% American Indian/Alaska Native, 0.4% Native Hawaiian/Other Pacific Islander, 6.9% Two or more races, 14.6% Hispanic of any race; Average household size: 2.73; Median age: 38.4; Age under 18: 22.3%; Age 65 and over: 7.8%; Males per 100 females: 98.8
Housing: Homeownership rate: 77.8%; Homeowner vacancy rate: 2.5%; Rental vacancy rate: 5.2%

CONCORD (city). Covers a land area of 30.546 square miles and a water area of 0 square miles. Located at 37.97° N. Lat; 122.00° W. Long. Elevation is 75 feet.
History: Named for the hope of peace and harmony, by settlers from New England. Concord was founded on the site of Rancho del Diablo granted to Salvio Pacheco in 1834, and developed as a shipping point for farm produce from the surrounding valley.
Population: 122,067; Growth (since 2000): 0.2%; Density: 3,996.2 persons per square mile; Race: 64.5% White, 3.6% Black/African American, 11.1% Asian, 0.7% American Indian/Alaska Native, 0.7% Native Hawaiian/Other Pacific Islander, 6.4% Two or more races, 30.6% Hispanic of any race; Average household size: 2.73; Median age: 37.0; Age under 18: 22.9%; Age 65 and over: 11.8%; Males per 100 females: 98.8; Marriage status: 32.2% never married, 52.2% now married, 2.2% separated, 4.9% widowed, 10.7% divorced; Foreign born: 25.6%; Speak English only: 65.0%; With disability: 10.8%; Veterans: 7.7%; Ancestry: 11.5% German, 10.2% Irish, 8.8% English, 6.5% Italian, 3.5% American
Employment: 15.8% management, business, and financial, 6.2% computer, engineering, and science, 8.7% education, legal, community service, arts, and media, 5.0% healthcare practitioners, 21.2% service, 24.6% sales and office, 9.8% natural resources, construction, and maintenance, 8.7% production, transportation, and material moving
Income: Per capita: $31,359; Median household: $65,798; Average household: $84,220; Households with income of $100,000 or more: 31.4%; Poverty rate: 12.1%
Educational Attainment: High school diploma or higher: 87.6%; Bachelor's degree or higher: 30.5%; Graduate/professional degree or higher: 9.4%

School District(s)

Contra Costa County Office of Education (KG-12)
2012-13 Enrollment: 3,297 . . . . (925) 942-3388
Mt. Diablo Unified (KG-12)
2012-13 Enrollment: 32,001 . . . . (925) 682-8000

Four-year College(s)

ITT Technical Institute-Concord (Private, For-profit)
Fall 2013 Enrollment: 258 . . . . (925) 674-8200
2013-14 Tuition: In-state $18,048; Out-of-state $18,048

Two-year College(s)

Heald College-Concord (Private, For-profit)
Fall 2013 Enrollment: 1,503 . . . . (925) 288-5800
2013-14 Tuition: In-state $13,620; Out-of-state $13,620

Vocational/Technical School(s)

Mt Diablo Adult Education (Public)
Fall 2013 Enrollment: 176 . . . . (925) 685-7340
2013-14 Tuition: $5,889
Paris Beauty College (Private, For-profit)
Fall 2013 Enrollment: 99 . . . . (925) 685-7603
2013-14 Tuition: $10,400
Housing: Homeownership rate: 61.1%; Median home value: $356,500; Median year structure built: 1970; Homeowner vacancy rate: 1.9%; Median gross rent: $1,282 per month; Rental vacancy rate: 7.0%
Health Insurance: 85.2% have insurance; 69.4% have private insurance; 26.1% have public insurance; 14.8% do not have insurance; 7.0% of children under 18 do not have insurance
Hospitals: John Muir Medical Center - Concord Campus (267 beds)
Safety: Violent crime rate: 32.4 per 10,000 population; Property crime rate: 347.3 per 10,000 population
Transportation: Commute: 82.4% car, 9.8% public transportation, 1.8% walk, 3.6% work from home; Median travel time to work: 30.0 minutes
Airports: Buchanan Field (general aviation)
Additional Information Contacts
City of Concord . . . . (925) 671-3150
http://www.ci.concord.ca.us

CONTRA COSTA CENTRE (CDP).
Note: Statistics that would complete this profile are not available because the CDP was created after the 2010 Census was released.

CROCKETT (CDP). Covers a land area of 1.060 square miles and a water area of 0 square miles. Located at 38.05° N. Lat; 122.22° W. Long. Elevation is 128 feet.
History: Crockett developed as a company town around the California-Hawaiian Sugar Refining Corporation plant. The town was laid out when the railroad arrived in 1877 and given the name of a one-time California Supreme Court Justice. In 1882 a foundry was built, joined in 1884 by the Starr flour mill. A beet sugar refinery opened in 1898 became the C-H sugar refinery in 1906.
Population: 3,094; Growth (since 2000): -3.1%; Density: 2,918.7 persons per square mile; Race: 79.8% White, 4.7% Black/African American, 3.5% Asian, 1.0% American Indian/Alaska Native, 0.8% Native Hawaiian/Other Pacific Islander, 6.3% Two or more races, 15.8% Hispanic of any race; Average household size: 2.14; Median age: 45.7; Age under 18: 14.9%; Age 65 and over: 15.0%; Males per 100 females: 95.9; Marriage status: 30.1% never married, 51.7% now married, 2.6% separated, 5.8% widowed, 12.4% divorced; Foreign born: 7.0%; Speak English only: 87.8%; With disability: 9.7%; Veterans: 6.4%; Ancestry: 21.8% Irish, 19.6% Italian, 16.1% German, 13.4% English, 6.0% Portuguese
Employment: 15.8% management, business, and financial, 2.5% computer, engineering, and science, 7.4% education, legal, community service, arts, and media, 1.3% healthcare practitioners, 20.3% service, 34.3% sales and office, 11.4% natural resources, construction, and maintenance, 7.2% production, transportation, and material moving
Income: Per capita: $43,017; Median household: $83,716; Average household: $94,562; Households with income of $100,000 or more: 35.3%; Poverty rate: 9.0%
Educational Attainment: High school diploma or higher: 94.2%; Bachelor's degree or higher: 31.2%; Graduate/professional degree or higher: 8.6%

School District(s)

John Swett Unified (KG-12)
2012-13 Enrollment: 1,600 . . . . (510) 245-4300
Housing: Homeownership rate: 55.8%; Median home value: $361,800; Median year structure built: 1940; Homeowner vacancy rate: 1.3%; Median gross rent: $981 per month; Rental vacancy rate: 10.1%

Health Insurance: 91.8% have insurance; 80.6% have private insurance; 25.9% have public insurance; 8.2% do not have insurance; 4.4% of children under 18 do not have insurance

Transportation: Commute: 88.7% car, 6.5% public transportation, 0.9% walk, 3.9% work from home; Median travel time to work: 30.6 minutes

DANVILLE (town). Covers a land area of 18.028 square miles and a water area of 0 square miles. Located at 37.81° N. Lat; 121.97° W. Long. Elevation is 358 feet.

History: Named for Daniel Inman, who settled here in 1858. Danville stands on land once owned by Inman, who first visited the site in 1852 and took up wheat farming in 1858.

Population: 42,039; Growth (since 2000): 0.8%; Density: 2,331.9 persons per square mile; Race: 83.1% White, 0.9% Black/African American, 10.5% Asian, 0.2% American Indian/Alaska Native, 0.2% Native Hawaiian/Other Pacific Islander, 4.0% Two or more races, 6.8% Hispanic of any race; Average household size: 2.71; Median age: 44.5; Age under 18: 26.6%; Age 65 and over: 14.4%; Males per 100 females: 93.5; Marriage status: 19.9% never married, 65.9% now married, 1.1% separated, 5.3% widowed, 8.9% divorced; Foreign born: 11.8%; Speak English only: 85.7%; With disability: 7.3%; Veterans: 8.7%; Ancestry: 17.7% German, 13.7% Irish, 12.6% English, 11.1% Italian, 5.8% American

Employment: 36.6% management, business, and financial, 8.2% computer, engineering, and science, 10.8% education, legal, community service, arts, and media, 7.5% healthcare practitioners, 7.9% service, 23.4% sales and office, 2.9% natural resources, construction, and maintenance, 2.8% production, transportation, and material moving

Income: Per capita: $61,916; Median household: $136,116; Average household: $168,952; Households with income of $100,000 or more: 64.0%; Poverty rate: 4.6%

Educational Attainment: High school diploma or higher: 97.8%; Bachelor's degree or higher: 63.3%; Graduate/professional degree or higher: 22.8%

School District(s)

San Ramon Valley Unified (KG-12)
2012-13 Enrollment: 30,757 . . . . (925) 552-5500

Vocational/Technical School(s)

W Academy of Salon and Spa (Private, For-profit)
Fall 2013 Enrollment: 36 . . . . (925) 855-5551
2013-14 Tuition: $14,100

Housing: Homeownership rate: 84.4%; Median home value: $827,600; Median year structure built: 1978; Homeowner vacancy rate: 0.8%; Median gross rent: $2,000+ per month; Rental vacancy rate: 5.3%

Health Insurance: 96.6% have insurance; 92.3% have private insurance; 17.2% have public insurance; 3.4% do not have insurance; 1.8% of children under 18 do not have insurance

Safety: Violent crime rate: 3.9 per 10,000 population; Property crime rate: 95.1 per 10,000 population

Transportation: Commute: 84.1% car, 5.0% public transportation, 0.9% walk, 8.9% work from home; Median travel time to work: 30.3 minutes

Additional Information Contacts

Town of Danville . . . . (925) 314-3388
http://www.ci.danville.ca.us

DIABLO (CDP). Covers a land area of 1.357 square miles and a water area of 0 square miles. Located at 37.84° N. Lat; 121.96° W. Long. Elevation is 528 feet.

Population: 1,158; Growth (since 2000): 17.2%; Density: 853.1 persons per square mile; Race: 92.0% White, 0.1% Black/African American, 4.7% Asian, 0.2% American Indian/Alaska Native, 0.0% Native Hawaiian/Other Pacific Islander, 2.6% Two or more races, 3.4% Hispanic of any race; Average household size: 2.67; Median age: 49.3; Age under 18: 23.7%; Age 65 and over: 21.9%; Males per 100 females: 94.9

Housing: Homeownership rate: 92.2%; Homeowner vacancy rate: 1.8%; Rental vacancy rate: 3.0%

DISCOVERY BAY (CDP). Covers a land area of 6.219 square miles and a water area of 0.821 square miles. Located at 37.91° N. Lat; 121.60° W. Long. Elevation is 7 feet.

Population: 13,352; Growth (since 2000): 48.7%; Density: 2,147.0 persons per square mile; Race: 81.7% White, 4.1% Black/African American, 3.9% Asian, 0.6% American Indian/Alaska Native, 0.4% Native Hawaiian/Other Pacific Islander, 5.7% Two or more races, 15.5% Hispanic of any race; Average household size: 2.83; Median age: 39.6; Age under 18: 26.9%; Age 65 and over: 11.1%; Males per 100 females: 101.0; Marriage status: 18.3% never married, 66.9% now married, 1.0% separated, 4.8% widowed, 9.9% divorced; Foreign born: 7.7%; Speak English only: 89.2%; With disability: 7.9%; Veterans: 10.5%; Ancestry: 16.8% German, 14.2% Irish, 12.4% Italian, 7.9% English, 5.0% Norwegian

Employment: 22.9% management, business, and financial, 6.1% computer, engineering, and science, 9.2% education, legal, community service, arts, and media, 6.4% healthcare practitioners, 16.1% service, 23.1% sales and office, 8.2% natural resources, construction, and maintenance, 7.9% production, transportation, and material moving

Income: Per capita: $46,563; Median household: $111,508; Average household: $126,361; Households with income of $100,000 or more: 56.2%; Poverty rate: 5.0%

Educational Attainment: High school diploma or higher: 94.8%; Bachelor's degree or higher: 30.7%; Graduate/professional degree or higher: 8.5%

School District(s)

Byron Union Elementary (KG-08)
2012-13 Enrollment: 1,686 . . . . (925) 809-7500

Housing: Homeownership rate: 82.3%; Median home value: $375,200; Median year structure built: 1990; Homeowner vacancy rate: 3.4%; Median gross rent: $2,000+ per month; Rental vacancy rate: 6.3%

Health Insurance: 93.9% have insurance; 85.3% have private insurance; 23.6% have public insurance; 6.1% do not have insurance; 5.6% of children under 18 do not have insurance

Transportation: Commute: 89.7% car, 1.2% public transportation, 1.3% walk, 7.2% work from home; Median travel time to work: 46.0 minutes

EAST RICHMOND HEIGHTS (CDP). Covers a land area of 0.580 square miles and a water area of 0 square miles. Located at 37.95° N. Lat; 122.31° W. Long. Elevation is 387 feet.

Population: 3,280; Growth (since 2000): -2.3%; Density: 5,653.6 persons per square mile; Race: 60.8% White, 12.0% Black/African American, 12.4% Asian, 0.4% American Indian/Alaska Native, 0.2% Native Hawaiian/Other Pacific Islander, 8.4% Two or more races, 14.2% Hispanic of any race; Average household size: 2.37; Median age: 46.2; Age under 18: 17.8%; Age 65 and over: 16.4%; Males per 100 females: 94.1; Marriage status: 36.5% never married, 43.3% now married, 0.8% separated, 5.5% widowed, 14.6% divorced; Foreign born: 20.1%; Speak English only: 73.0%; With disability: 8.0%; Veterans: 9.4%; Ancestry: 14.3% German, 11.0% English, 8.5% Irish, 4.6% Other Arab, 4.4% Russian

Employment: 14.5% management, business, and financial, 7.4% computer, engineering, and science, 18.7% education, legal, community service, arts, and media, 6.1% healthcare practitioners, 16.1% service, 22.8% sales and office, 6.8% natural resources, construction, and maintenance, 7.7% production, transportation, and material moving

Income: Per capita: $31,932; Median household: $69,682; Average household: $80,296; Households with income of $100,000 or more: 37.9%; Poverty rate: 13.5%

Educational Attainment: High school diploma or higher: 95.8%; Bachelor's degree or higher: 46.3%; Graduate/professional degree or higher: 18.4%

Housing: Homeownership rate: 78.8%; Median home value: $365,000; Median year structure built: 1954; Homeowner vacancy rate: 1.8%; Median gross rent: $1,348 per month; Rental vacancy rate: 3.3%

Health Insurance: 88.7% have insurance; 79.4% have private insurance; 23.3% have public insurance; 11.3% do not have insurance; 3.8% of children under 18 do not have insurance

Transportation: Commute: 75.8% car, 12.5% public transportation, 1.1% walk, 10.2% work from home; Median travel time to work: 31.1 minutes

EL CERRITO (city). Covers a land area of 3.688 square miles and a water area of 0 square miles. Located at 37.92° N. Lat; 122.30° W. Long. Elevation is 69 feet.

History: Named for the Spanish translation of "little hill". Incorporated 1917.

Population: 23,549; Growth (since 2000): 1.6%; Density: 6,385.8 persons per square mile; Race: 53.3% White, 7.7% Black/African American, 27.3% Asian, 0.5% American Indian/Alaska Native, 0.2% Native Hawaiian/Other Pacific Islander, 6.5% Two or more races, 11.1% Hispanic of any race; Average household size: 2.31; Median age: 43.5; Age under 18: 17.4%; Age 65 and over: 17.9%; Males per 100 females: 92.3; Marriage status: 29.8% never married, 54.2% now married, 1.1% separated, 6.9% widowed, 9.1% divorced; Foreign born: 28.9%; Speak English only: 64.1%;

With disability: 10.1%; Veterans: 5.9%; Ancestry: 10.2% German, 9.5% English, 6.8% Irish, 5.4% Italian, 3.1% European
Employment: 19.7% management, business, and financial, 14.8% computer, engineering, and science, 18.4% education, legal, community service, arts, and media, 5.8% healthcare practitioners, 13.1% service, 19.2% sales and office, 5.2% natural resources, construction, and maintenance, 3.8% production, transportation, and material moving
Income: Per capita: $44,153; Median household: $85,481; Average household: $102,381; Households with income of $100,000 or more: 41.1%; Poverty rate: 8.5%
Educational Attainment: High school diploma or higher: 93.0%; Bachelor's degree or higher: 58.7%; Graduate/professional degree or higher: 28.9%

School District(s)

West Contra Costa Unified (KG-12)
2012-13 Enrollment: 30,398 . . . . (510) 231-1101
Housing: Homeownership rate: 60.6%; Median home value: $573,700; Median year structure built: 1954; Homeowner vacancy rate: 1.1%; Median gross rent: $1,424 per month; Rental vacancy rate: 5.4%
Health Insurance: 88.8% have insurance; 78.8% have private insurance; 24.3% have public insurance; 11.2% do not have insurance; 5.5% of children under 18 do not have insurance
Safety: Violent crime rate: 38.0 per 10,000 population; Property crime rate: 463.1 per 10,000 population
Transportation: Commute: 63.7% car, 22.3% public transportation, 1.6% walk, 8.5% work from home; Median travel time to work: 32.2 minutes
Additional Information Contacts
City of El Cerrito . . . . (510) 215-4300
http://www.el-cerrito.org

EL SOBRANTE (CDP). Covers a land area of 2.765 square miles and a water area of 0 square miles. Located at 37.98° N. Lat; 122.31° W. Long. Elevation is 187 feet.
Population: 12,669; Growth (since 2000): 3.3%; Density: 4,581.4 persons per square mile; Race: 50.6% White, 13.2% Black/African American, 15.7% Asian, 1.0% American Indian/Alaska Native, 0.9% Native Hawaiian/Other Pacific Islander, 7.7% Two or more races, 24.0% Hispanic of any race; Average household size: 2.65; Median age: 40.6; Age under 18: 21.3%; Age 65 and over: 12.6%; Males per 100 females: 95.1; Marriage status: 32.9% never married, 49.5% now married, 3.0% separated, 5.2% widowed, 12.4% divorced; Foreign born: 22.7%; Speak English only: 64.3%; With disability: 12.0%; Veterans: 7.3%; Ancestry: 10.4% German, 7.8% Irish, 7.8% English, 6.4% European, 4.9% Italian
Employment: 12.9% management, business, and financial, 7.7% computer, engineering, and science, 10.6% education, legal, community service, arts, and media, 2.9% healthcare practitioners, 20.5% service, 27.5% sales and office, 8.4% natural resources, construction, and maintenance, 9.5% production, transportation, and material moving
Income: Per capita: $30,668; Median household: $60,849; Average household: $79,670; Households with income of $100,000 or more: 24.1%; Poverty rate: 10.2%
Educational Attainment: High school diploma or higher: 89.6%; Bachelor's degree or higher: 27.6%; Graduate/professional degree or higher: 8.4%

School District(s)

West Contra Costa Unified (KG-12)
2012-13 Enrollment: 30,398 . . . . (510) 231-1101
Housing: Homeownership rate: 62.0%; Median home value: $315,600; Median year structure built: 1964; Homeowner vacancy rate: 2.0%; Median gross rent: $1,194 per month; Rental vacancy rate: 7.2%
Health Insurance: 85.9% have insurance; 68.1% have private insurance; 27.8% have public insurance; 14.1% do not have insurance; 7.7% of children under 18 do not have insurance
Transportation: Commute: 86.6% car, 7.0% public transportation, 0.5% walk, 4.3% work from home; Median travel time to work: 31.2 minutes

HERCULES (city). Covers a land area of 6.205 square miles and a water area of 11.974 square miles. Located at 38.02° N. Lat; 122.29° W. Long. Elevation is 79 feet.
History: Named for the Hercules Powder Company, which was established here in 1869 to manufacture dynamite for the mines.
Population: 24,060; Growth (since 2000): 23.5%; Density: 3,877.3 persons per square mile; Race: 22.0% White, 18.9% Black/African American, 45.5% Asian, 0.4% American Indian/Alaska Native, 0.4% Native Hawaiian/Other Pacific Islander, 6.2% Two or more races, 14.6% Hispanic of any race; Average household size: 2.96; Median age: 39.0; Age under 18: 22.8%; Age 65 and over: 10.5%; Males per 100 females: 90.1; Marriage status: 32.0% never married, 55.2% now married, 2.9% separated, 4.4% widowed, 8.5% divorced; Foreign born: 32.6%; Speak English only: 57.3%; With disability: 7.7%; Veterans: 5.8%; Ancestry: 3.7% German, 3.5% Italian, 2.9% Irish, 2.8% English, 2.0% Portuguese
Employment: 19.3% management, business, and financial, 11.1% computer, engineering, and science, 8.5% education, legal, community service, arts, and media, 6.9% healthcare practitioners, 15.7% service, 27.1% sales and office, 3.8% natural resources, construction, and maintenance, 7.6% production, transportation, and material moving
Income: Per capita: $36,793; Median household: $96,750; Average household: $107,025; Households with income of $100,000 or more: 48.1%; Poverty rate: 6.0%
Educational Attainment: High school diploma or higher: 92.2%; Bachelor's degree or higher: 41.0%; Graduate/professional degree or higher: 8.3%

School District(s)

West Contra Costa Unified (KG-12)
2012-13 Enrollment: 30,398 . . . . (510) 231-1101
Housing: Homeownership rate: 79.5%; Median home value: $365,900; Median year structure built: 1987; Homeowner vacancy rate: 2.3%; Median gross rent: $1,528 per month; Rental vacancy rate: 6.2%
Health Insurance: 91.1% have insurance; 80.0% have private insurance; 19.2% have public insurance; 8.9% do not have insurance; 4.0% of children under 18 do not have insurance
Safety: Violent crime rate: 8.9 per 10,000 population; Property crime rate: 110.3 per 10,000 population
Transportation: Commute: 86.6% car, 9.1% public transportation, 0.4% walk, 1.8% work from home; Median travel time to work: 38.6 minutes
Additional Information Contacts
City of Hercules. . . . . (510) 799-8200
http://www.ci.hercules.ca.us

KENSINGTON (CDP). Covers a land area of 0.947 square miles and a water area of 0.009 square miles. Located at 37.91° N. Lat; 122.28° W. Long. Elevation is 587 feet.
History: The area that is now Kensington was originally the territory of the Huichin band of the Ohlone indigenous people who occupied much of the East Bay of the San Francisco Bay Area. In 1911, the area was named "Kensington" by Robert Brousefield, a surveyor who had lived in the London borough of South Kensington at one time.
Population: 5,077; Growth (since 2000): 2.9%; Density: 5,360.1 persons per square mile; Race: 78.1% White, 2.6% Black/African American, 12.0% Asian, 0.3% American Indian/Alaska Native, 0.0% Native Hawaiian/Other Pacific Islander, 5.9% Two or more races, 5.2% Hispanic of any race; Average household size: 2.31; Median age: 49.5; Age under 18: 18.4%; Age 65 and over: 22.2%; Males per 100 females: 89.7; Marriage status: 22.3% never married, 62.8% now married, 1.4% separated, 6.5% widowed, 8.4% divorced; Foreign born: 15.0%; Speak English only: 89.1%; With disability: 7.0%; Veterans: 9.4%; Ancestry: 15.3% German, 12.0% English, 11.3% Irish, 4.7% Russian, 4.2% Polish
Employment: 26.0% management, business, and financial, 13.8% computer, engineering, and science, 30.9% education, legal, community service, arts, and media, 7.9% healthcare practitioners, 5.4% service, 11.6% sales and office, 2.9% natural resources, construction, and maintenance, 1.6% production, transportation, and material moving
Income: Per capita: $64,502; Median household: $133,036; Average household: $150,835; Households with income of $100,000 or more: 62.7%; Poverty rate: 3.4%
Educational Attainment: High school diploma or higher: 99.2%; Bachelor's degree or higher: 80.7%; Graduate/professional degree or higher: 48.4%

School District(s)

West Contra Costa Unified (KG-12)
2012-13 Enrollment: 30,398 . . . . (510) 231-1101
Housing: Homeownership rate: 82.9%; Median home value: $749,500; Median year structure built: 1947; Homeowner vacancy rate: 1.1%; Median gross rent: $2,000+ per month; Rental vacancy rate: 5.0%
Health Insurance: 97.0% have insurance; 89.5% have private insurance; 26.6% have public insurance; 3.0% do not have insurance; 1.0% of children under 18 do not have insurance
Safety: Violent crime rate: 9.6 per 10,000 population; Property crime rate: 162.5 per 10,000 population

Transportation: Commute: 67.8% car, 15.4% public transportation, 1.5% walk, 11.1% work from home; Median travel time to work: 29.6 minutes

KNIGHTSEN (CDP). Covers a land area of 8.366 square miles and a water area of 0.089 square miles. Located at 37.96° N. Lat; 121.65° W. Long. Elevation is 30 feet.

Population: 1,568; Growth (since 2000): 82.1%; Density: 187.4 persons per square mile; Race: 80.9% White, 0.9% Black/African American, 1.8% Asian, 0.5% American Indian/Alaska Native, 0.2% Native Hawaiian/Other Pacific Islander, 5.4% Two or more races, 29.0% Hispanic of any race; Average household size: 2.95; Median age: 42.6; Age under 18: 24.4%; Age 65 and over: 13.5%; Males per 100 females: 107.7

School District(s)

Knightsen Elementary (KG-08)
2012-13 Enrollment: 472 . . . . (925) 625-0073

Housing: Homeownership rate: 73.3%; Homeowner vacancy rate: 2.5%; Rental vacancy rate: 2.1%

LAFAYETTE (city). Covers a land area of 15.221 square miles and a water area of 0.166 square miles. Located at 37.89° N. Lat; 122.12° W. Long. Elevation is 308 feet.

History: Named in 1853 for the Marquis de Lafayette, a Frenchman who fought in the U.S. War of Independence. The site of Lafayette was chosen by Elam Brown in 1848 for a home site. Brown set up a horse powered mill near his house.

Population: 23,893; Growth (since 2000): -0.1%; Density: 1,569.8 persons per square mile; Race: 84.7% White, 0.7% Black/African American, 9.0% Asian, 0.3% American Indian/Alaska Native, 0.1% Native Hawaiian/Other Pacific Islander, 4.2% Two or more races, 5.8% Hispanic of any race; Average household size: 2.58; Median age: 45.2; Age under 18: 24.9%; Age 65 and over: 16.6%; Males per 100 females: 94.5; Marriage status: 21.6% never married, 65.0% now married, 1.1% separated, 5.8% widowed, 7.6% divorced; Foreign born: 13.4%; Speak English only: 86.1%; With disability: 6.4%; Veterans: 8.7%; Ancestry: 16.9% German, 14.5% English, 13.7% Irish, 7.6% Italian, 7.1% American

Employment: 31.2% management, business, and financial, 10.4% computer, engineering, and science, 19.8% education, legal, community service, arts, and media, 8.1% healthcare practitioners, 7.2% service, 17.8% sales and office, 2.4% natural resources, construction, and maintenance, 3.1% production, transportation, and material moving

Income: Per capita: $67,902; Median household: $136,207; Average household: $179,752; Households with income of $100,000 or more: 61.4%; Poverty rate: 3.4%

Educational Attainment: High school diploma or higher: 97.6%; Bachelor's degree or higher: 72.9%; Graduate/professional degree or higher: 34.4%

School District(s)

Acalanes Union High (09-12)
2012-13 Enrollment: 5,349 . . . . (925) 280-3900
Lafayette Elementary (KG-08)
2012-13 Enrollment: 3,435 . . . . (925) 927-3500

Housing: Homeownership rate: 75.2%; Median home value: $993,400; Median year structure built: 1960; Homeowner vacancy rate: 0.8%; Median gross rent: $1,561 per month; Rental vacancy rate: 5.7%

Health Insurance: 96.1% have insurance; 90.3% have private insurance; 20.1% have public insurance; 3.9% do not have insurance; 1.3% of children under 18 do not have insurance

Safety: Violent crime rate: 8.5 per 10,000 population; Property crime rate: 166.3 per 10,000 population

Transportation: Commute: 71.9% car, 15.2% public transportation, 1.4% walk, 10.4% work from home; Median travel time to work: 28.6 minutes

Additional Information Contacts

City of Lafayette . . . . (925) 284-1968
http://www.ci.lafayette.ca.us

MARTINEZ (city). County seat. Covers a land area of 12.131 square miles and a water area of 1.004 square miles. Located at 38.00° N. Lat; 122.11° W. Long. Elevation is 23 feet.

History: Martinez was named for Ignacio Martinez, comandante at the San Francisco Presidio from 1828-1831, who settled on neighboring Rancho El Pinole about 1836. Martinez developed after 1850 as the seat of Contra Costa County.

Population: 35,824; Growth (since 2000): -0.1%; Density: 2,953.1 persons per square mile; Race: 77.1% White, 3.6% Black/African American, 8.0% Asian, 0.7% American Indian/Alaska Native, 0.3% Native Hawaiian/Other Pacific Islander, 6.3% Two or more races, 14.7% Hispanic of any race; Average household size: 2.42; Median age: 42.2; Age under 18: 20.5%; Age 65 and over: 12.1%; Males per 100 females: 96.9; Marriage status: 30.9% never married, 50.8% now married, 2.2% separated, 4.7% widowed, 13.7% divorced; Foreign born: 11.4%; Speak English only: 83.8%; With disability: 10.7%; Veterans: 9.7%; Ancestry: 15.2% Irish, 15.0% German, 10.7% English, 8.2% Italian, 5.0% American

Employment: 19.8% management, business, and financial, 8.2% computer, engineering, and science, 10.3% education, legal, community service, arts, and media, 5.8% healthcare practitioners, 15.2% service, 25.8% sales and office, 9.2% natural resources, construction, and maintenance, 5.6% production, transportation, and material moving

Income: Per capita: $39,164; Median household: $83,112; Average household: $97,662; Households with income of $100,000 or more: 40.7%; Poverty rate: 6.3%

Educational Attainment: High school diploma or higher: 93.7%; Bachelor's degree or higher: 35.9%; Graduate/professional degree or higher: 11.3%

School District(s)

Contra Costa County Office of Education (KG-12)
2012-13 Enrollment: 3,297 . . . . (925) 942-3388
Martinez Unified (KG-12)
2012-13 Enrollment: 4,087 . . . . (925) 335-5800
Mt. Diablo Unified (KG-12)
2012-13 Enrollment: 32,001 . . . . (925) 682-8000

Housing: Homeownership rate: 67.3%; Median home value: $406,300; Median year structure built: 1974; Homeowner vacancy rate: 1.4%; Median gross rent: $1,410 per month; Rental vacancy rate: 4.9%

Health Insurance: 92.1% have insurance; 82.5% have private insurance; 21.3% have public insurance; 7.9% do not have insurance; 4.3% of children under 18 do not have insurance

Hospitals: Contra Costa Regional Medical Center (166 beds)

Safety: Violent crime rate: 14.4 per 10,000 population; Property crime rate: 223.2 per 10,000 population

Newspapers: Martinez News-Gazette (weekly circulation 14000)

Transportation: Commute: 84.2% car, 6.5% public transportation, 2.1% walk, 6.0% work from home; Median travel time to work: 27.9 minutes; Amtrak: Train service available.

Additional Information Contacts

City of Martinez . . . . (925) 372-3500
http://www.cityofmartinez.org

MONTALVIN MANOR (CDP). Covers a land area of 0.341 square miles and a water area of 0 square miles. Located at 38.00° N. Lat; 122.33° W. Long. Elevation is 69 feet.

Population: 2,876; Growth (since 2000): n/a; Density: 8,426.4 persons per square mile; Race: 45.0% White, 7.7% Black/African American, 10.6% Asian, 1.3% American Indian/Alaska Native, 0.9% Native Hawaiian/Other Pacific Islander, 4.7% Two or more races, 62.6% Hispanic of any race; Average household size: 3.51; Median age: 35.2; Age under 18: 25.7%; Age 65 and over: 12.7%; Males per 100 females: 93.1; Marriage status: 35.5% never married, 48.0% now married, 0.7% separated, 7.7% widowed, 8.8% divorced; Foreign born: 42.9%; Speak English only: 26.5%; With disability: 13.6%; Veterans: 3.5%; Ancestry: 3.1% German, 2.6% Norwegian, 2.5% English, 2.0% Irish, 2.0% Swedish

Employment: 7.9% management, business, and financial, 2.1% computer, engineering, and science, 1.1% education, legal, community service, arts, and media, 1.1% healthcare practitioners, 36.4% service, 18.2% sales and office, 20.6% natural resources, construction, and maintenance, 12.6% production, transportation, and material moving

Income: Per capita: $25,760; Median household: $59,615; Average household: $81,508; Households with income of $100,000 or more: 24.5%; Poverty rate: 10.9%

Educational Attainment: High school diploma or higher: 67.8%; Bachelor's degree or higher: 16.2%; Graduate/professional degree or higher: 2.9%

Housing: Homeownership rate: 75.9%; Median home value: $154,200; Median year structure built: 1958; Homeowner vacancy rate: 5.3%; Median gross rent: $1,591 per month; Rental vacancy rate: 8.4%

Health Insurance: 75.0% have insurance; 51.7% have private insurance; 31.4% have public insurance; 25.0% do not have insurance; 18.0% of children under 18 do not have insurance

Transportation: Commute: 86.0% car, 4.8% public transportation, 0.0% walk, 7.7% work from home; Median travel time to work: 38.4 minutes

MORAGA (town). Covers a land area of 9.433 square miles and a water area of 0.009 square miles. Located at 37.85° N. Lat; 122.12° W. Long. Elevation is 499 feet.

History: Named for Joaquin Moraga, the grandson of the founder of San Francisco, Joseph Joaquin Moraga. St. Mary's College is to Northeast.

Population: 16,016; Growth (since 2000): n/a; Density: 1,697.8 persons per square mile; Race: 76.2% White, 1.7% Black/African American, 14.9% Asian, 0.2% American Indian/Alaska Native, 0.2% Native Hawaiian/Other Pacific Islander, 5.0% Two or more races, 7.0% Hispanic of any race; Average household size: 2.57; Median age: 45.0; Age under 18: 21.7%; Age 65 and over: 19.1%; Males per 100 females: 89.2; Marriage status: 30.5% never married, 55.9% now married, 0.9% separated, 5.9% widowed, 7.7% divorced; Foreign born: 13.9%; Speak English only: 81.2%; With disability: 7.5%; Veterans: 7.6%; Ancestry: 14.1% German, 13.3% Irish, 12.4% English, 9.1% Italian, 5.0% American

Employment: 29.2% management, business, and financial, 8.5% computer, engineering, and science, 18.1% education, legal, community service, arts, and media, 8.0% healthcare practitioners, 11.3% service, 20.9% sales and office, 1.7% natural resources, construction, and maintenance, 2.3% production, transportation, and material moving

Income: Per capita: $57,132; Median household: $120,353; Average household: $161,686; Households with income of $100,000 or more: 58.5%; Poverty rate: 4.4%

Educational Attainment: High school diploma or higher: 97.9%; Bachelor's degree or higher: 74.3%; Graduate/professional degree or higher: 36.4%

School District(s)

Acalanes Union High (09-12)
2012-13 Enrollment: 5,349 . . . . (925) 280-3900
Moraga Elementary (KG-08)
2012-13 Enrollment: 1,856 . . . . (925) 376-5943

Four-year College(s)

Saint Mary's College of California (Private, Not-for-profit, Roman Catholic)
Fall 2013 Enrollment: 4,257 . . . . (925) 631-4000
2013-14 Tuition: In-state $39,890; Out-of-state $39,890

Housing: Homeownership rate: 83.9%; Median home value: $884,200; Median year structure built: 1971; Homeowner vacancy rate: 0.7%; Median gross rent: $1,800 per month; Rental vacancy rate: 4.1%

Health Insurance: 94.2% have insurance; 89.2% have private insurance; 19.5% have public insurance; 5.8% do not have insurance; 3.7% of children under 18 do not have insurance

Safety: Violent crime rate: 6.6 per 10,000 population; Property crime rate: 90.0 per 10,000 population

Transportation: Commute: 71.4% car, 15.5% public transportation, 3.6% walk, 8.7% work from home; Median travel time to work: 33.3 minutes

Additional Information Contacts

Town of Moraga . . . . (925) 888-7050
http://moraga.ca.us

MOUNTAIN VIEW (CDP). Covers a land area of 0.290 square miles and a water area of 0 square miles. Located at 38.01° N. Lat; 122.12° W. Long. Elevation is 112 feet.

Population: 2,372; Growth (since 2000): -3.9%; Density: 8,182.2 persons per square mile; Race: 79.9% White, 2.5% Black/African American, 3.0% Asian, 1.3% American Indian/Alaska Native, 0.8% Native Hawaiian/Other Pacific Islander, 5.9% Two or more races, 22.1% Hispanic of any race; Average household size: 2.50; Median age: 36.5; Age under 18: 20.2%; Age 65 and over: 7.7%; Males per 100 females: 99.8

Housing: Homeownership rate: 60.9%; Homeowner vacancy rate: 3.9%; Rental vacancy rate: 6.6%

NORRIS CANYON (CDP). Covers a land area of 3.536 square miles and a water area of 0 square miles. Located at 37.75° N. Lat; 121.99° W. Long.

Population: 957; Growth (since 2000): n/a; Density: 270.6 persons per square mile; Race: 49.7% White, 4.3% Black/African American, 38.9% Asian, 0.1% American Indian/Alaska Native, 0.1% Native Hawaiian/Other Pacific Islander, 4.0% Two or more races, 4.4% Hispanic of any race; Average household size: 3.86; Median age: 36.4; Age under 18: 35.2%; Age 65 and over: 3.7%; Males per 100 females: 101.5

Housing: Homeownership rate: 97.1%; Homeowner vacancy rate: 4.7%; Rental vacancy rate: 0.0%

NORTH GATE (CDP). Covers a land area of 0.658 square miles and a water area of 0 square miles. Located at 37.91° N. Lat; 122.00° W. Long.

Population: 679; Growth (since 2000): n/a; Density: 1,032.2 persons per square mile; Race: 83.4% White, 0.1% Black/African American, 9.6% Asian, 0.0% American Indian/Alaska Native, 0.0% Native Hawaiian/Other Pacific Islander, 4.1% Two or more races, 8.2% Hispanic of any race; Average household size: 2.63; Median age: 48.0; Age under 18: 21.9%; Age 65 and over: 18.0%; Males per 100 females: 84.0

Housing: Homeownership rate: 89.1%; Homeowner vacancy rate: 0.0%; Rental vacancy rate: 0.0%

NORTH RICHMOND (CDP). Covers a land area of 1.408 square miles and a water area of 0.141 square miles. Located at 37.97° N. Lat; 122.37° W. Long. Elevation is 16 feet.

Population: 3,717; Growth (since 2000): n/a; Density: 2,639.0 persons per square mile; Race: 17.1% White, 33.3% Black/African American, 11.6% Asian, 0.6% American Indian/Alaska Native, 0.5% Native Hawaiian/Other Pacific Islander, 4.9% Two or more races, 50.1% Hispanic of any race; Average household size: 3.62; Median age: 29.0; Age under 18: 31.0%; Age 65 and over: 5.6%; Males per 100 females: 98.9; Marriage status: 38.3% never married, 45.9% now married, 2.8% separated, 5.7% widowed, 10.0% divorced; Foreign born: 41.5%; Speak English only: 30.2%; With disability: 11.2%; Veterans: 2.8%; Ancestry: 3.4% African, 2.5% German, 0.7% American, 0.6% Irish, 0.6% Slavic

Employment: 5.6% management, business, and financial, 2.6% computer, engineering, and science, 4.1% education, legal, community service, arts, and media, 2.3% healthcare practitioners, 31.0% service, 25.3% sales and office, 11.0% natural resources, construction, and maintenance, 18.1% production, transportation, and material moving

Income: Per capita: $16,755; Median household: $37,396; Average household: $54,177; Households with income of $100,000 or more: 15.1%; Poverty rate: 22.1%

Educational Attainment: High school diploma or higher: 72.2%; Bachelor's degree or higher: 15.4%; Graduate/professional degree or higher: 3.0%

Housing: Homeownership rate: 45.8%; Median home value: $185,500; Median year structure built: 1997; Homeowner vacancy rate: 4.4%; Median gross rent: $946 per month; Rental vacancy rate: 14.6%

Health Insurance: 69.5% have insurance; 41.5% have private insurance; 33.3% have public insurance; 30.5% do not have insurance; 17.8% of children under 18 do not have insurance

Transportation: Commute: 87.4% car, 8.9% public transportation, 1.4% walk, 0.6% work from home; Median travel time to work: 29.5 minutes

OAKLEY (city). Covers a land area of 15.853 square miles and a water area of 0.302 square miles. Located at 37.99° N. Lat; 121.69° W. Long. Elevation is 20 feet.

Population: 35,432; Growth (since 2000): 38.3%; Density: 2,235.0 persons per square mile; Race: 63.9% White, 7.3% Black/African American, 6.3% Asian, 0.9% American Indian/Alaska Native, 0.4% Native Hawaiian/Other Pacific Islander, 7.1% Two or more races, 34.9% Hispanic of any race; Average household size: 3.29; Median age: 32.0; Age under 18: 30.5%; Age 65 and over: 6.7%; Males per 100 females: 98.8; Marriage status: 34.4% never married, 51.1% now married, 1.6% separated, 5.3% widowed, 9.2% divorced; Foreign born: 17.8%; Speak English only: 68.8%; With disability: 10.6%; Veterans: 7.3%; Ancestry: 11.1% German, 8.6% Irish, 5.4% Italian, 5.1% English, 4.0% Portuguese

Employment: 11.2% management, business, and financial, 4.1% computer, engineering, and science, 3.7% education, legal, community service, arts, and media, 6.0% healthcare practitioners, 21.3% service, 28.0% sales and office, 13.5% natural resources, construction, and maintenance, 12.3% production, transportation, and material moving

Income: Per capita: $27,718; Median household: $77,043; Average household: $89,744; Households with income of $100,000 or more: 37.0%; Poverty rate: 9.4%

Educational Attainment: High school diploma or higher: 85.4%; Bachelor's degree or higher: 14.2%; Graduate/professional degree or higher: 2.6%

School District(s)

Antioch Unified (KG-12)
2012-13 Enrollment: 18,852 . . . . (925) 779-7500
Liberty Union High (09-12)
2012-13 Enrollment: 7,704 . . . . (925) 634-2166
Oakley Union Elementary (KG-08)
2012-13 Enrollment: 4,745 . . . . (925) 625-0700

Housing: Homeownership rate: 76.1%; Median home value: $235,400; Median year structure built: 1991; Homeowner vacancy rate: 3.4%; Median gross rent: $1,519 per month; Rental vacancy rate: 5.5%
Health Insurance: 87.0% have insurance; 68.6% have private insurance; 26.5% have public insurance; 13.0% do not have insurance; 3.9% of children under 18 do not have insurance
Safety: Violent crime rate: 18.5 per 10,000 population; Property crime rate: 131.4 per 10,000 population
Transportation: Commute: 88.4% car, 3.9% public transportation, 1.1% walk, 4.6% work from home; Median travel time to work: 40.2 minutes
Additional Information Contacts
City of Oakley . . . . (925) 625-7000
http://www.ci.oakley.ca.us

ORINDA (city). Covers a land area of 12.683 square miles and a water area of 0.015 square miles. Located at 37.88° N. Lat; 122.17° W. Long. Elevation is 495 feet.
History: In the late 1800s, the land was named by Alice Marsh Cameron in honor of the poet Katherine Philips, who was also known as the "Matchless Orinda". Bisected by California State Route 24 and framed by its rolling oak-covered hills, the city of Orinda was incorporated on July 1, 1985.
Population: 17,643; Growth (since 2000): 0.3%; Density: 1,391.1 persons per square mile; Race: 82.4% White, 0.8% Black/African American, 11.4% Asian, 0.1% American Indian/Alaska Native, 0.1% Native Hawaiian/Other Pacific Islander, 4.4% Two or more races, 4.6% Hispanic of any race; Average household size: 2.69; Median age: 47.8; Age under 18: 25.6%; Age 65 and over: 20.1%; Males per 100 females: 94.4; Marriage status: 21.0% never married, 68.1% now married, 0.5% separated, 5.4% widowed, 5.5% divorced; Foreign born: 14.2%; Speak English only: 80.6%; With disability: 7.1%; Veterans: 7.6%; Ancestry: 15.3% English, 13.9% German, 12.3% Irish, 7.1% European, 6.5% Italian
Employment: 35.2% management, business, and financial, 9.0% computer, engineering, and science, 15.6% education, legal, community service, arts, and media, 8.3% healthcare practitioners, 7.7% service, 19.9% sales and office, 1.8% natural resources, construction, and maintenance, 2.4% production, transportation, and material moving
Income: Per capita: $77,530; Median household: $164,437; Average household: $215,668; Households with income of $100,000 or more: 71.6%; Poverty rate: 1.5%
Educational Attainment: High school diploma or higher: 97.8%; Bachelor's degree or higher: 77.9%; Graduate/professional degree or higher: 35.0%

School District(s)

Acalanes Union High (09-12)
2012-13 Enrollment: 5,349 . . . . (925) 280-3900
Orinda Union Elementary (KG-08)
2012-13 Enrollment: 2,488 . . . . (925) 254-4901
Housing: Homeownership rate: 89.7%; Median home value: $973,600; Median year structure built: 1959; Homeowner vacancy rate: 1.2%; Median gross rent: $2,000+ per month; Rental vacancy rate: 4.2%
Health Insurance: 97.6% have insurance; 92.0% have private insurance; 20.3% have public insurance; 2.4% do not have insurance; 0.7% of children under 18 do not have insurance
Safety: Violent crime rate: 5.4 per 10,000 population; Property crime rate: 115.6 per 10,000 population
Transportation: Commute: 68.2% car, 15.6% public transportation, 1.0% walk, 13.4% work from home; Median travel time to work: 28.6 minutes
Additional Information Contacts
City of Orinda . . . . (925) 253-4220
http://www.cityoforinda.org

PACHECO (CDP). Covers a land area of 0.740 square miles and a water area of 0 square miles. Located at 37.99° N. Lat; 122.07° W. Long. Elevation is 75 feet.
History: The first settler in Pacheco was G.L. Wallrath, who built a house here in 1853. The town was laid out in 1857 around a warehouse and a flour mill, and survived flood, fire, and earthquake in its first ten years.
Population: 3,685; Growth (since 2000): 3.5%; Density: 4,978.4 persons per square mile; Race: 76.4% White, 2.1% Black/African American, 9.9% Asian, 0.7% American Indian/Alaska Native, 0.3% Native Hawaiian/Other Pacific Islander, 5.1% Two or more races, 16.8% Hispanic of any race; Average household size: 2.35; Median age: 44.4; Age under 18: 19.2%; Age 65 and over: 15.9%; Males per 100 females: 92.5; Marriage status: 34.8% never married, 48.3% now married, 4.0% separated, 2.7% widowed, 14.2% divorced; Foreign born: 18.4%; Speak English only: 74.7%; With disability: 13.2%; Veterans: 7.1%; Ancestry: 13.4% English, 10.9% American, 9.3% German, 7.8% French, 7.6% Irish
Employment: 8.0% management, business, and financial, 2.6% computer, engineering, and science, 10.3% education, legal, community service, arts, and media, 3.7% healthcare practitioners, 18.9% service, 33.0% sales and office, 10.3% natural resources, construction, and maintenance, 13.3% production, transportation, and material moving
Income: Per capita: $29,116; Median household: $54,955; Average household: $72,016; Households with income of $100,000 or more: 21.4%; Poverty rate: 15.3%
Educational Attainment: High school diploma or higher: 89.6%; Bachelor's degree or higher: 21.0%; Graduate/professional degree or higher: 3.4%
Housing: Homeownership rate: 81.3%; Median home value: $166,700; Median year structure built: 1974; Homeowner vacancy rate: 1.5%; Median gross rent: $1,186 per month; Rental vacancy rate: 12.6%
Health Insurance: 81.6% have insurance; 65.3% have private insurance; 26.8% have public insurance; 18.4% do not have insurance; 10.0% of children under 18 do not have insurance
Transportation: Commute: 88.5% car, 4.8% public transportation, 2.7% walk, 3.1% work from home; Median travel time to work: 23.6 minutes

PINOLE (city). Covers a land area of 5.323 square miles and a water area of 8.252 square miles. Located at 38.00° N. Lat; 122.32° W. Long. Elevation is 102 feet.
History: Named for the Aztec translation of "ground and parched seeds". The town of Pinole was laid out by Samuel J. Tennant, on land that had been part of the Rancho el Pinole of Don Ignacio Martinez, comandante of the San Francisco Presidio 1822-8132.
Population: 18,390; Growth (since 2000): -3.4%; Density: 3,454.7 persons per square mile; Race: 46.2% White, 13.4% Black/African American, 22.9% Asian, 0.8% American Indian/Alaska Native, 0.3% Native Hawaiian/Other Pacific Islander, 6.9% Two or more races, 21.8% Hispanic of any race; Average household size: 2.70; Median age: 42.6; Age under 18: 20.5%; Age 65 and over: 15.5%; Males per 100 females: 90.6; Marriage status: 33.0% never married, 53.2% now married, 2.8% separated, 7.1% widowed, 6.7% divorced; Foreign born: 25.0%; Speak English only: 63.9%; With disability: 13.1%; Veterans: 8.5%; Ancestry: 8.6% German, 5.7% Irish, 5.5% Italian, 4.9% English, 2.9% American
Employment: 13.6% management, business, and financial, 9.1% computer, engineering, and science, 11.7% education, legal, community service, arts, and media, 5.4% healthcare practitioners, 17.2% service, 26.9% sales and office, 6.1% natural resources, construction, and maintenance, 10.0% production, transportation, and material moving
Income: Per capita: $34,689; Median household: $77,315; Average household: $95,373; Households with income of $100,000 or more: 36.4%; Poverty rate: 9.2%
Educational Attainment: High school diploma or higher: 89.1%; Bachelor's degree or higher: 34.7%; Graduate/professional degree or higher: 12.0%

School District(s)

West Contra Costa Unified (KG-12)
2012-13 Enrollment: 30,398 . . . . (510) 231-1101
Housing: Homeownership rate: 71.8%; Median home value: $341,700; Median year structure built: 1971; Homeowner vacancy rate: 1.5%; Median gross rent: $1,376 per month; Rental vacancy rate: 8.0%
Health Insurance: 88.5% have insurance; 73.4% have private insurance; 29.5% have public insurance; 11.5% do not have insurance; 8.1% of children under 18 do not have insurance
Safety: Violent crime rate: 36.6 per 10,000 population; Property crime rate: 363.4 per 10,000 population
Transportation: Commute: 82.4% car, 9.0% public transportation, 0.5% walk, 5.0% work from home; Median travel time to work: 34.7 minutes
Additional Information Contacts
City of Pinole . . . . (510) 724-8928
http://www.ci.pinole.ca.us

PITTSBURG (city). Covers a land area of 17.218 square miles and a water area of 1.936 square miles. Located at 38.02° N. Lat; 121.90° W. Long. Elevation is 26 feet.
History: Named for the Pittsburg Coal Company, which mined local coal. Pittsburg was laid out in 1849 by William Tecumseh Sherman for the owners of the Rancho los Medanos, who hoped the town would become a prosperous seaport on the river. For three decades after coal was discovered in the 1850s, the town was a busy coal shipping port, renamed

in 1863 as Black Diamond for one of the mines. In the early 1900s, steel replaced coal as the mainstay of the economy, and the town was renamed for its Philadelphia counterpart in the steel industry.

Population: 63,264; Growth (since 2000): 11.4%; Density: 3,674.2 persons per square mile; Race: 36.5% White, 17.7% Black/African American, 15.6% Asian, 0.8% American Indian/Alaska Native, 1.0% Native Hawaiian/Other Pacific Islander, 7.3% Two or more races, 42.4% Hispanic of any race; Average household size: 3.22; Median age: 32.5; Age under 18: 27.5%; Age 65 and over: 8.6%; Males per 100 females: 94.9; Marriage status: 38.5% never married, 45.9% now married, 2.3% separated, 4.8% widowed, 10.8% divorced; Foreign born: 31.3%; Speak English only: 52.2%; With disability: 13.6%; Veterans: 6.1%; Ancestry: 3.8% German, 3.8% Irish, 3.2% Italian, 2.6% English, 1.8% American

Employment: 11.0% management, business, and financial, 3.2% computer, engineering, and science, 5.9% education, legal, community service, arts, and media, 4.9% healthcare practitioners, 27.2% service, 25.1% sales and office, 12.8% natural resources, construction, and maintenance, 9.8% production, transportation, and material moving

Income: Per capita: $23,972; Median household: $58,866; Average household: $75,549; Households with income of $100,000 or more: 25.7%; Poverty rate: 16.8%

Educational Attainment: High school diploma or higher: 78.7%; Bachelor's degree or higher: 17.4%; Graduate/professional degree or higher: 4.9%

School District(s)

Mt. Diablo Unified (KG-12)
2012-13 Enrollment: 32,001 . . . . (925) 682-8000
Pittsburg Unified (KG-12)
2012-13 Enrollment: 10,560 . . . . (925) 473-2300

Two-year College(s)

Los Medanos College (Public)
Fall 2013 Enrollment: 8,525 . . . . (925) 439-2181
2013-14 Tuition: In-state $1,298; Out-of-state $7,038

Housing: Homeownership rate: 58.8%; Median home value: $222,700; Median year structure built: 1980; Homeowner vacancy rate: 3.8%; Median gross rent: $1,305 per month; Rental vacancy rate: 6.8%

Health Insurance: 82.0% have insurance; 58.9% have private insurance; 31.2% have public insurance; 18.0% do not have insurance; 9.1% of children under 18 do not have insurance

Safety: Violent crime rate: 27.9 per 10,000 population; Property crime rate: 304.6 per 10,000 population

Transportation: Commute: 85.0% car, 8.9% public transportation, 1.1% walk, 3.1% work from home; Median travel time to work: 35.5 minutes; Amtrak: Train service available.

Additional Information Contacts

City of Pittsburg . . . . (925) 252-4850
http://www.ci.pittsburg.ca.us

PLEASANT HILL (city). Covers a land area of 7.072 square miles and a water area of 0 square miles. Located at 37.95° N. Lat; 122.08° W. Long. Elevation is 52 feet.

History: Named for the hope that it would encourage people to settle here. First settled in 1844, the area remained rural until the housing boom of World War II. Incorporated 1961.

Population: 33,152; Growth (since 2000): 1.0%; Density: 4,688.1 persons per square mile; Race: 74.9% White, 2.1% Black/African American, 13.6% Asian, 0.4% American Indian/Alaska Native, 0.2% Native Hawaiian/Other Pacific Islander, 5.5% Two or more races, 12.1% Hispanic of any race; Average household size: 2.38; Median age: 40.7; Age under 18: 19.8%; Age 65 and over: 13.9%; Males per 100 females: 94.1; Marriage status: 29.6% never married, 50.1% now married, 1.6% separated, 7.2% widowed, 13.1% divorced; Foreign born: 19.2%; Speak English only: 77.2%; With disability: 12.4%; Veterans: 6.8%; Ancestry: 16.8% German, 14.0% Irish, 10.3% English, 7.3% Italian, 3.5% Scottish

Employment: 22.3% management, business, and financial, 8.9% computer, engineering, and science, 12.6% education, legal, community service, arts, and media, 5.5% healthcare practitioners, 14.0% service, 26.5% sales and office, 6.8% natural resources, construction, and maintenance, 3.3% production, transportation, and material moving

Income: Per capita: $43,031; Median household: $77,326; Average household: $101,587; Households with income of $100,000 or more: 39.3%; Poverty rate: 9.1%

Educational Attainment: High school diploma or higher: 95.8%; Bachelor's degree or higher: 48.8%; Graduate/professional degree or higher: 15.2%

School District(s)

Contra Costa County Rop
2012-13 Enrollment: n/a . . . . (925) 942-3368
Mt. Diablo Unified (KG-12)
2012-13 Enrollment: 32,001 . . . . (925) 682-8000

Four-year College(s)

John F Kennedy University (Private, Not-for-profit)
Fall 2013 Enrollment: 1,356 . . . . (925) 969-3300

Two-year College(s)

Carrington College California-Pleasant Hill (Private, For-profit)
Fall 2013 Enrollment: 589 . . . . (925) 609-6650
Diablo Valley College (Public)
Fall 2013 Enrollment: 20,286 . . . . (925) 685-1230
2013-14 Tuition: In-state $1,298; Out-of-state $7,038

Vocational/Technical School(s)

Paul Mitchell the School-East Bay (Private, For-profit)
Fall 2013 Enrollment: 259 . . . . (925) 691-7687
2013-14 Tuition: $18,623

Housing: Homeownership rate: 61.7%; Median home value: $507,900; Median year structure built: 1972; Homeowner vacancy rate: 1.3%; Median gross rent: $1,463 per month; Rental vacancy rate: 5.1%

Health Insurance: 91.5% have insurance; 82.7% have private insurance; 22.1% have public insurance; 8.5% do not have insurance; 3.5% of children under 18 do not have insurance

Safety: Violent crime rate: 16.2 per 10,000 population; Property crime rate: 431.5 per 10,000 population

Transportation: Commute: 77.0% car, 13.0% public transportation, 1.1% walk, 7.3% work from home; Median travel time to work: 30.7 minutes

Additional Information Contacts

City of Pleasant Hill . . . . (925) 671-5270
http://www.pleasanthill.ca.gov

PORT COSTA (CDP). Covers a land area of 0.158 square miles and a water area of 0 square miles. Located at 38.04° N. Lat; 122.18° W. Long. Elevation is 16 feet.

History: Port Costa grew around the wharves from which grain was shipped direct to Europe.

Population: 190; Growth (since 2000): -18.1%; Density: 1,200.1 persons per square mile; Race: 90.5% White, 1.1% Black/African American, 3.7% Asian, 1.1% American Indian/Alaska Native, 0.0% Native Hawaiian/Other Pacific Islander, 3.7% Two or more races, 5.3% Hispanic of any race; Average household size: 1.92; Median age: 52.5; Age under 18: 10.0%; Age 65 and over: 21.1%; Males per 100 females: 97.9

Housing: Homeownership rate: 53.6%; Homeowner vacancy rate: 5.4%; Rental vacancy rate: 2.1%

RELIEZ VALLEY (CDP). Covers a land area of 2.363 square miles and a water area of 0 square miles. Located at 37.94° N. Lat; 122.10° W. Long.

Population: 3,101; Growth (since 2000): n/a; Density: 1,312.2 persons per square mile; Race: 86.8% White, 1.0% Black/African American, 7.5% Asian, 0.1% American Indian/Alaska Native, 0.1% Native Hawaiian/Other Pacific Islander, 3.5% Two or more races, 6.2% Hispanic of any race; Average household size: 2.47; Median age: 50.5; Age under 18: 19.4%; Age 65 and over: 22.6%; Males per 100 females: 93.8; Marriage status: 18.8% never married, 67.7% now married, 0.3% separated, 5.7% widowed, 7.8% divorced; Foreign born: 15.9%; Speak English only: 83.7%; With disability: 10.6%; Veterans: 8.7%; Ancestry: 16.7% English, 13.4% Irish, 10.4% German, 7.8% Italian, 5.9% Iranian

Employment: 41.4% management, business, and financial, 11.2% computer, engineering, and science, 9.0% education, legal, community service, arts, and media, 2.1% healthcare practitioners, 9.7% service, 20.1% sales and office, 1.4% natural resources, construction, and maintenance, 5.1% production, transportation, and material moving

Income: Per capita: $82,493; Median household: $133,594; Average household: $200,386; Households with income of $100,000 or more: 62.4%; Poverty rate: 2.3%

Educational Attainment: High school diploma or higher: 97.3%; Bachelor's degree or higher: 63.4%; Graduate/professional degree or higher: 27.2%

Housing: Homeownership rate: 82.8%; Median home value: $871,900; Median year structure built: 1975; Homeowner vacancy rate: 1.1%; Median gross rent: $1,292 per month; Rental vacancy rate: 10.1%

Health Insurance: 95.0% have insurance; 90.3% have private insurance; 23.1% have public insurance; 5.0% do not have insurance; 5.6% of children under 18 do not have insurance

Transportation: Commute: 75.3% car, 9.1% public transportation, 1.4% walk, 10.5% work from home; Median travel time to work: 32.1 minutes

RICHMOND (city). Covers a land area of 30.068 square miles and a water area of 22.412 square miles. Located at 37.95° N. Lat; 122.36° W. Long. Elevation is 46 feet.

History: Named probably for Richmond, Virginia. Richmond was established in 1899 when the Santa Fe Railway purchased a right-of-way to the bayshore here. The town grew around plants of such industrial corporations as the Standard Oil Company and the Ford Motor Company.

Population: 103,701; Growth (since 2000): 4.5%; Density: 3,448.9 persons per square mile; Race: 31.4% White, 26.6% Black/African American, 13.5% Asian, 0.6% American Indian/Alaska Native, 0.5% Native Hawaiian/Other Pacific Islander, 5.6% Two or more races, 39.5% Hispanic of any race; Average household size: 2.83; Median age: 34.8; Age under 18: 24.9%; Age 65 and over: 10.2%; Males per 100 females: 94.8; Marriage status: 39.4% never married, 44.6% now married, 3.8% separated, 5.1% widowed, 10.9% divorced; Foreign born: 32.7%; Speak English only: 50.6%; With disability: 10.5%; Veterans: 5.0%; Ancestry: 3.8% German, 3.0% Irish, 2.7% English, 2.2% Italian, 1.9% African

Employment: 11.7% management, business, and financial, 4.5% computer, engineering, and science, 10.7% education, legal, community service, arts, and media, 3.7% healthcare practitioners, 25.2% service, 21.7% sales and office, 11.2% natural resources, construction, and maintenance, 11.3% production, transportation, and material moving

Income: Per capita: $25,722; Median household: $54,589; Average household: $71,818; Households with income of $100,000 or more: 22.8%; Poverty rate: 18.5%

Educational Attainment: High school diploma or higher: 77.4%; Bachelor's degree or higher: 26.2%; Graduate/professional degree or higher: 9.4%

School District(s)

Contra Costa County Office of Education (KG-12)
2012-13 Enrollment: 3,297 . . . . (925) 942-3388
West Contra Costa Unified (KG-12)
2012-13 Enrollment: 30,398 . . . . (510) 231-1101

Housing: Homeownership rate: 51.7%; Median home value: $270,200; Median year structure built: 1962; Homeowner vacancy rate: 2.5%; Median gross rent: $1,172 per month; Rental vacancy rate: 8.1%

Health Insurance: 79.3% have insurance; 55.4% have private insurance; 33.2% have public insurance; 20.7% do not have insurance; 11.6% of children under 18 do not have insurance

Safety: Violent crime rate: 103.6 per 10,000 population; Property crime rate: 449.6 per 10,000 population

Transportation: Commute: 79.9% car, 13.2% public transportation, 2.0% walk, 3.1% work from home; Median travel time to work: 31.4 minutes; Amtrak: Train service available.

Additional Information Contacts

City of Richmond . . . . (510) 620-6512
http://www.ci.richmond.ca.us

RODEO (CDP). Covers a land area of 3.747 square miles and a water area of 0.885 square miles. Located at 38.04° N. Lat; 122.25° W. Long. Elevation is 16 feet.

History: Rodeo preserves in its name the days of Spanish dominion when ranchers held their yearly cattle rodeos in nearby Rodeo Valley. The town of Rodeo began when two Irishmen, John and Patrick Tormey, started a meat-packing plant here on a cattle ranch.

Population: 8,679; Growth (since 2000): -0.4%; Density: 2,316.0 persons per square mile; Race: 44.0% White, 16.2% Black/African American, 20.3% Asian, 0.6% American Indian/Alaska Native, 0.7% Native Hawaiian/Other Pacific Islander, 7.9% Two or more races, 24.6% Hispanic of any race; Average household size: 2.96; Median age: 38.2; Age under 18: 24.5%; Age 65 and over: 12.2%; Males per 100 females: 95.3; Marriage status: 30.2% never married, 51.7% now married, 4.3% separated, 6.3% widowed, 11.8% divorced; Foreign born: 31.5%; Speak English only: 60.8%; With disability: 14.2%; Veterans: 7.7%; Ancestry: 12.1% German, 8.4% Italian, 7.0% Irish, 4.8% English, 4.2% Portuguese

Employment: 14.2% management, business, and financial, 3.6% computer, engineering, and science, 6.7% education, legal, community service, arts, and media, 1.9% healthcare practitioners, 18.4% service, 30.8% sales and office, 11.6% natural resources, construction, and maintenance, 12.8% production, transportation, and material moving

Income: Per capita: $27,112; Median household: $64,756; Average household: $78,813; Households with income of $100,000 or more: 25.6%; Poverty rate: 9.0%

Educational Attainment: High school diploma or higher: 84.5%; Bachelor's degree or higher: 24.0%; Graduate/professional degree or higher: 5.5%

School District(s)

John Swett Unified (KG-12)
2012-13 Enrollment: 1,600 . . . . (510) 245-4300

Housing: Homeownership rate: 63.7%; Median home value: $294,700; Median year structure built: 1970; Homeowner vacancy rate: 2.3%; Median gross rent: $1,147 per month; Rental vacancy rate: 7.4%

Health Insurance: 83.7% have insurance; 62.7% have private insurance; 31.8% have public insurance; 16.3% do not have insurance; 9.1% of children under 18 do not have insurance

Transportation: Commute: 90.0% car, 3.2% public transportation, 2.7% walk, 3.0% work from home; Median travel time to work: 31.5 minutes

ROLLINGWOOD (CDP). Covers a land area of 0.166 square miles and a water area of 0 square miles. Located at 37.97° N. Lat; 122.33° W. Long. Elevation is 75 feet.

Population: 2,969; Growth (since 2000): 2.4%; Density: 17,864.2 persons per square mile; Race: 38.1% White, 7.4% Black/African American, 18.0% Asian, 0.9% American Indian/Alaska Native, 0.7% Native Hawaiian/Other Pacific Islander, 4.3% Two or more races, 61.8% Hispanic of any race; Average household size: 4.06; Median age: 31.1; Age under 18: 28.6%; Age 65 and over: 8.4%; Males per 100 females: 97.5; Marriage status: 33.0% never married, 54.9% now married, 0.3% separated, 4.8% widowed, 7.4% divorced; Foreign born: 46.5%; Speak English only: 20.5%; With disability: 10.6%; Veterans: 3.2%; Ancestry: 4.7% German, 4.0% Irish, 1.6% Scotch-Irish, 1.0% Norwegian, 0.9% Italian

Employment: 4.3% management, business, and financial, 0.5% computer, engineering, and science, 1.6% education, legal, community service, arts, and media, 5.1% healthcare practitioners, 26.5% service, 29.6% sales and office, 13.4% natural resources, construction, and maintenance, 19.0% production, transportation, and material moving

Income: Per capita: $15,310; Median household: $56,384; Average household: $66,674; Households with income of $100,000 or more: 16.4%; Poverty rate: 17.2%

Educational Attainment: High school diploma or higher: 57.2%; Bachelor's degree or higher: 11.4%; Graduate/professional degree or higher: 3.9%

Housing: Homeownership rate: 67.6%; Median home value: $165,100; Median year structure built: 1949; Homeowner vacancy rate: 1.8%; Median gross rent: $1,394 per month; Rental vacancy rate: 6.3%

Health Insurance: 86.6% have insurance; 56.0% have private insurance; 41.3% have public insurance; 13.4% do not have insurance; 2.0% of children under 18 do not have insurance

Transportation: Commute: 74.7% car, 19.3% public transportation, 1.1% walk, 4.3% work from home; Median travel time to work: 31.1 minutes

SAN MIGUEL (CDP). Covers a land area of 1.050 square miles and a water area of 0 square miles. Located at 37.89° N. Lat; 122.04° W. Long.

Population: 3,392; Growth (since 2000): n/a; Density: 3,229.1 persons per square mile; Race: 88.0% White, 0.9% Black/African American, 5.6% Asian, 0.1% American Indian/Alaska Native, 0.1% Native Hawaiian/Other Pacific Islander, 4.2% Two or more races, 5.9% Hispanic of any race; Average household size: 2.70; Median age: 47.2; Age under 18: 24.5%; Age 65 and over: 16.0%; Males per 100 females: 96.0; Marriage status: 18.8% never married, 66.2% now married, 1.0% separated, 5.7% widowed, 9.2% divorced; Foreign born: 6.3%; Speak English only: 90.7%; With disability: 5.5%; Veterans: 4.8%; Ancestry: 21.1% German, 15.5% Irish, 14.4% English, 8.6% Italian, 6.1% American

Employment: 29.8% management, business, and financial, 6.7% computer, engineering, and science, 20.1% education, legal, community service, arts, and media, 6.7% healthcare practitioners, 8.8% service, 20.9% sales and office, 5.3% natural resources, construction, and maintenance, 1.6% production, transportation, and material moving

Income: Per capita: $54,589; Median household: $125,662; Average household: $152,205; Households with income of $100,000 or more: 62.8%; Poverty rate: 0.7%

Educational Attainment: High school diploma or higher: 99.7%; Bachelor's degree or higher: 64.5%; Graduate/professional degree or higher: 26.7%
Housing: Homeownership rate: 91.2%; Median home value: $824,800; Median year structure built: 1957; Homeowner vacancy rate: 1.0%; Median gross rent: $2,000+ per month; Rental vacancy rate: 6.0%
Health Insurance: 92.4% have insurance; 91.0% have private insurance; 12.5% have public insurance; 7.6% do not have insurance; 9.8% of children under 18 do not have insurance
Transportation: Commute: 72.3% car, 16.1% public transportation, 1.0% walk, 9.8% work from home; Median travel time to work: 31.9 minutes

SAN PABLO (city). Covers a land area of 2.634 square miles and a water area of 0 square miles. Located at 37.96° N. Lat; 122.34° W. Long. Elevation is 52 feet.
History: Named for a Mexican land grant, for St. Paul. Before 1820, this land was pasture for the herds of cattle and sheep belonging to Mission San Francisco de Asis, becoming part of the Rancho San Pablo grant to Francisco Maria Castro after the missions were secularized.
Population: 29,139; Growth (since 2000): -3.6%; Density: 11,063.4 persons per square mile; Race: 32.2% White, 15.8% Black/African American, 14.9% Asian, 0.8% American Indian/Alaska Native, 0.6% Native Hawaiian/Other Pacific Islander, 5.4% Two or more races, 56.5% Hispanic of any race; Average household size: 3.28; Median age: 31.6; Age under 18: 28.3%; Age 65 and over: 8.8%; Males per 100 females: 98.8; Marriage status: 42.5% never married, 44.2% now married, 2.6% separated, 4.9% widowed, 8.4% divorced; Foreign born: 42.3%; Speak English only: 32.9%; With disability: 11.6%; Veterans: 5.2%; Ancestry: 3.1% Irish, 2.4% German, 1.8% Italian, 1.3% English, 0.9% Belizean
Employment: 7.1% management, business, and financial, 2.6% computer, engineering, and science, 6.4% education, legal, community service, arts, and media, 2.7% healthcare practitioners, 31.5% service, 21.1% sales and office, 13.9% natural resources, construction, and maintenance, 14.9% production, transportation, and material moving
Income: Per capita: $17,582; Median household: $44,983; Average household: $55,348; Households with income of $100,000 or more: 13.7%; Poverty rate: 20.8%
Educational Attainment: High school diploma or higher: 63.5%; Bachelor's degree or higher: 12.7%; Graduate/professional degree or higher: 3.3%

School District(s)

West Contra Costa Unified (KG-12)
2012-13 Enrollment: 30,398 . . . . (510) 231-1101

Two-year College(s)

Contra Costa College (Public)
Fall 2013 Enrollment: 6,865 . . . . (510) 235-7800
2013-14 Tuition: In-state $1,298; Out-of-state $7,038
Housing: Homeownership rate: 46.9%; Median home value: $187,000; Median year structure built: 1964; Homeowner vacancy rate: 3.1%; Median gross rent: $1,054 per month; Rental vacancy rate: 8.3%
Health Insurance: 74.8% have insurance; 49.0% have private insurance; 31.4% have public insurance; 25.2% do not have insurance; 11.9% of children under 18 do not have insurance
Hospitals: Doctors Medical Center - San Pablo (247 beds)
Safety: Violent crime rate: 66.9 per 10,000 population; Property crime rate: 391.4 per 10,000 population
Transportation: Commute: 84.6% car, 10.0% public transportation, 1.7% walk, 2.1% work from home; Median travel time to work: 30.4 minutes
Additional Information Contacts
City of San Pablo. . . . . (510) 215-3000
http://www.ci.san-pablo.ca.us

SAN RAMON (city). Covers a land area of 18.061 square miles and a water area of 0.016 square miles. Located at 37.76° N. Lat; 121.94° W. Long. Elevation is 486 feet.
History: This city was incorporated on July 1, 1983. It is located approximately 25 miles east of Oakland in the San Francisco Bay Area and known for its temperate climate and scenic beauty.
Population: 72,148; Growth (since 2000): 61.3%; Density: 3,994.7 persons per square mile; Race: 53.6% White, 2.8% Black/African American, 35.6% Asian, 0.3% American Indian/Alaska Native, 0.2% Native Hawaiian/Other Pacific Islander, 5.3% Two or more races, 8.7% Hispanic of any race; Average household size: 2.85; Median age: 37.1; Age under 18: 29.6%; Age 65 and over: 7.8%; Males per 100 females: 96.6; Marriage status: 23.8% never married, 66.0% now married, 1.4% separated, 3.4% widowed, 6.9% divorced; Foreign born: 31.6%; Speak English only: 59.9%; With disability: 4.9%; Veterans: 5.0%; Ancestry: 9.3% German, 7.5% Irish, 7.2% English, 6.4% Italian, 3.2% American
Employment: 28.8% management, business, and financial, 18.8% computer, engineering, and science, 8.0% education, legal, community service, arts, and media, 6.7% healthcare practitioners, 8.8% service, 22.0% sales and office, 3.6% natural resources, construction, and maintenance, 3.4% production, transportation, and material moving
Income: Per capita: $51,091; Median household: $127,313; Average household: $147,573; Households with income of $100,000 or more: 64.7%; Poverty rate: 3.8%
Educational Attainment: High school diploma or higher: 97.3%; Bachelor's degree or higher: 64.5%; Graduate/professional degree or higher: 25.3%

School District(s)

San Ramon Valley Unified (KG-12)
2012-13 Enrollment: 30,757 . . . . (925) 552-5500
Housing: Homeownership rate: 71.4%; Median home value: $692,000; Median year structure built: 1990; Homeowner vacancy rate: 1.3%; Median gross rent: $1,736 per month; Rental vacancy rate: 4.0%
Health Insurance: 94.7% have insurance; 90.7% have private insurance; 10.2% have public insurance; 5.3% do not have insurance; 2.9% of children under 18 do not have insurance
Hospitals: San Ramon Regional Medical Center (123 beds)
Safety: Violent crime rate: 3.6 per 10,000 population; Property crime rate: 102.1 per 10,000 population
Transportation: Commute: 83.2% car, 6.2% public transportation, 1.6% walk, 7.8% work from home; Median travel time to work: 32.7 minutes
Additional Information Contacts
City of San Ramon . . . . (925) 973-2500
http://www.ci.san-ramon.ca.us

SARANAP (CDP). Covers a land area of 1.135 square miles and a water area of 0 square miles. Located at 37.89° N. Lat; 122.08° W. Long. Elevation is 180 feet.
Population: 5,202; Growth (since 2000): n/a; Density: 4,583.6 persons per square mile; Race: 82.2% White, 1.3% Black/African American, 8.7% Asian, 0.3% American Indian/Alaska Native, 0.2% Native Hawaiian/Other Pacific Islander, 5.2% Two or more races, 8.4% Hispanic of any race; Average household size: 2.38; Median age: 41.9; Age under 18: 22.9%; Age 65 and over: 13.0%; Males per 100 females: 96.7; Marriage status: 22.1% never married, 62.2% now married, 3.3% separated, 3.1% widowed, 12.6% divorced; Foreign born: 13.0%; Speak English only: 84.8%; With disability: 6.3%; Veterans: 7.3%; Ancestry: 20.2% Irish, 15.3% German, 9.1% English, 5.5% Italian, 5.5% Scottish
Employment: 26.4% management, business, and financial, 7.0% computer, engineering, and science, 15.0% education, legal, community service, arts, and media, 7.7% healthcare practitioners, 12.3% service, 24.6% sales and office, 2.8% natural resources, construction, and maintenance, 4.1% production, transportation, and material moving
Income: Per capita: $47,656; Median household: $88,977; Average household: $117,726; Households with income of $100,000 or more: 46.7%; Poverty rate: 7.5%
Educational Attainment: High school diploma or higher: 98.6%; Bachelor's degree or higher: 61.9%; Graduate/professional degree or higher: 24.5%
Housing: Homeownership rate: 67.8%; Median home value: $698,800; Median year structure built: 1959; Homeowner vacancy rate: 0.9%; Median gross rent: $1,436 per month; Rental vacancy rate: 4.1%
Health Insurance: 87.9% have insurance; 84.2% have private insurance; 18.0% have public insurance; 12.1% do not have insurance; 20.1% of children under 18 do not have insurance
Transportation: Commute: 69.4% car, 11.6% public transportation, 1.4% walk, 11.4% work from home; Median travel time to work: 32.7 minutes

SHELL RIDGE (CDP). Covers a land area of 0.430 square miles and a water area of 0 square miles. Located at 37.91° N. Lat; 122.03° W. Long.
Population: 959; Growth (since 2000): n/a; Density: 2,230.6 persons per square mile; Race: 85.6% White, 0.5% Black/African American, 7.6% Asian, 0.2% American Indian/Alaska Native, 0.6% Native Hawaiian/Other Pacific Islander, 4.6% Two or more races, 6.2% Hispanic of any race; Average household size: 2.69; Median age: 48.3; Age under 18: 23.9%; Age 65 and over: 18.1%; Males per 100 females: 106.2
Housing: Homeownership rate: 93.5%; Homeowner vacancy rate: 0.0%; Rental vacancy rate: 11.1%

TARA HILLS (CDP). Covers a land area of 0.639 square miles and a water area of 0 square miles. Located at 37.99° N. Lat; 122.32° W. Long. Elevation is 92 feet.

Population: 5,126; Growth (since 2000): -3.9%; Density: 8,028.2 persons per square mile; Race: 43.2% White, 13.3% Black/African American, 17.0% Asian, 0.6% American Indian/Alaska Native, 0.4% Native Hawaiian/Other Pacific Islander, 5.8% Two or more races, 38.0% Hispanic of any race; Average household size: 3.08; Median age: 36.8; Age under 18: 23.9%; Age 65 and over: 12.8%; Males per 100 females: 95.2; Marriage status: 33.9% never married, 54.7% now married, 5.5% separated, 6.8% widowed, 4.6% divorced; Foreign born: 29.7%; Speak English only: 51.6%; With disability: 15.6%; Veterans: 5.0%; Ancestry: 8.7% German, 5.0% English, 4.6% Irish, 3.2% American, 2.7% Italian

Employment: 9.0% management, business, and financial, 2.9% computer, engineering, and science, 8.4% education, legal, community service, arts, and media, 6.6% healthcare practitioners, 25.8% service, 23.4% sales and office, 10.6% natural resources, construction, and maintenance, 13.5% production, transportation, and material moving

Income: Per capita: $29,197; Median household: $57,926; Average household: $81,342; Households with income of $100,000 or more: 23.2%; Poverty rate: 13.9%

Educational Attainment: High school diploma or higher: 80.2%; Bachelor's degree or higher: 16.3%; Graduate/professional degree or higher: 4.6%

Housing: Homeownership rate: 69.7%; Median home value: $279,800; Median year structure built: 1964; Homeowner vacancy rate: 2.0%; Median gross rent: $1,216 per month; Rental vacancy rate: 3.3%

Health Insurance: 83.9% have insurance; 66.5% have private insurance; 31.8% have public insurance; 16.1% do not have insurance; 11.5% of children under 18 do not have insurance

Transportation: Commute: 90.3% car, 5.8% public transportation, 1.9% walk, 0.6% work from home; Median travel time to work: 30.2 minutes

VINE HILL (CDP). Covers a land area of 1.504 square miles and a water area of 0 square miles. Located at 38.01° N. Lat; 122.09° W. Long. Elevation is 30 feet.

History: John Muir National Historic site to West.

Population: 3,761; Growth (since 2000): 15.4%; Density: 2,501.2 persons per square mile; Race: 68.3% White, 3.0% Black/African American, 5.2% Asian, 0.9% American Indian/Alaska Native, 0.9% Native Hawaiian/Other Pacific Islander, 6.8% Two or more races, 31.1% Hispanic of any race; Average household size: 2.94; Median age: 35.1; Age under 18: 24.1%; Age 65 and over: 8.9%; Males per 100 females: 103.2; Marriage status: 38.4% never married, 38.8% now married, 1.7% separated, 8.2% widowed, 14.6% divorced; Foreign born: 18.8%; Speak English only: 59.8%; With disability: 11.7%; Veterans: 3.9%; Ancestry: 12.4% Irish, 12.1% German, 5.4% English, 4.1% Italian, 3.8% American

Employment: 10.3% management, business, and financial, 3.4% computer, engineering, and science, 13.3% education, legal, community service, arts, and media, 5.5% healthcare practitioners, 19.9% service, 23.3% sales and office, 12.6% natural resources, construction, and maintenance, 11.7% production, transportation, and material moving

Income: Per capita: $21,974; Median household: $62,708; Average household: $69,569; Households with income of $100,000 or more: 26.3%; Poverty rate: 19.1%

Educational Attainment: High school diploma or higher: 82.4%; Bachelor's degree or higher: 19.8%; Graduate/professional degree or higher: 4.8%

Housing: Homeownership rate: 66.0%; Median home value: $309,100; Median year structure built: 1964; Homeowner vacancy rate: 3.4%; Median gross rent: $1,587 per month; Rental vacancy rate: 5.7%

Health Insurance: 81.4% have insurance; 57.4% have private insurance; 29.1% have public insurance; 18.6% do not have insurance; 5.2% of children under 18 do not have insurance

Transportation: Commute: 91.2% car, 4.1% public transportation, 0.3% walk, 2.2% work from home; Median travel time to work: 27.7 minutes

WALNUT CREEK (city). Covers a land area of 19.757 square miles and a water area of 0.012 square miles. Located at 37.90° N. Lat; 122.04° W. Long. Elevation is 171 feet.

History: Named for its abundance of local walnut trees. Walnut Creek was established in the middle of walnut groves, with shipping of walnuts as the first industry.

Population: 64,173; Growth (since 2000): -0.2%; Density: 3,248.2 persons per square mile; Race: 78.7% White, 1.6% Black/African American, 12.5% Asian, 0.2% American Indian/Alaska Native, 0.2% Native Hawaiian/Other Pacific Islander, 4.2% Two or more races, 8.6% Hispanic of any race; Average household size: 2.08; Median age: 47.9; Age under 18: 16.7%; Age 65 and over: 26.6%; Males per 100 females: 86.4; Marriage status: 25.7% never married, 53.0% now married, 1.0% separated, 10.2% widowed, 11.1% divorced; Foreign born: 21.8%; Speak English only: 76.9%; With disability: 11.9%; Veterans: 8.8%; Ancestry: 15.9% German, 13.5% Irish, 13.4% English, 8.0% Italian, 3.8% American

Employment: 25.8% management, business, and financial, 11.4% computer, engineering, and science, 15.1% education, legal, community service, arts, and media, 7.1% healthcare practitioners, 11.5% service, 21.6% sales and office, 3.3% natural resources, construction, and maintenance, 4.1% production, transportation, and material moving

Income: Per capita: $51,314; Median household: $81,593; Average household: $109,950; Households with income of $100,000 or more: 40.6%; Poverty rate: 5.3%

Educational Attainment: High school diploma or higher: 97.3%; Bachelor's degree or higher: 61.0%; Graduate/professional degree or higher: 24.7%

School District(s)

Acalanes Union High (09-12)
2012-13 Enrollment: 5,349 . . . . (925) 280-3900

Mt. Diablo Unified (KG-12)
2012-13 Enrollment: 32,001 . . . . (925) 682-8000

Walnut Creek Elementary (KG-08)
2012-13 Enrollment: 3,543 . . . . (925) 944-6850

Housing: Homeownership rate: 66.6%; Median home value: $585,000; Median year structure built: 1972; Homeowner vacancy rate: 2.4%; Median gross rent: $1,423 per month; Rental vacancy rate: 6.7%

Health Insurance: 92.7% have insurance; 83.9% have private insurance; 29.6% have public insurance; 7.3% do not have insurance; 2.9% of children under 18 do not have insurance

Hospitals: John Muir Medical Center - Walnut Creek Campus (321 beds); Kaiser Foundation Hospital - Walnut Creek (362 beds)

Safety: Violent crime rate: 11.8 per 10,000 population; Property crime rate: 326.7 per 10,000 population

Newspapers: Concord Transcript (weekly circulation 27000); Contra Costa Sun & Walnut Creek Journal (weekly circulation 15000); Contra Costa Times (daily circulation 160000); Rossmoor News (weekly circulation 6800)

Transportation: Commute: 71.9% car, 15.4% public transportation, 3.3% walk, 7.5% work from home; Median travel time to work: 30.7 minutes

Additional Information Contacts

City of Walnut Creek . . . . (925) 943-5812
http://www.ci.walnut-creek.ca.us

Del Norte County

Located in northwestern California; bounded on the north by Oregon, and on the west by the Pacific Ocean; includes parts of Siskiyou and Klamath National Forests. Covers a land area of 1,006.373 square miles, a water area of 223.370 square miles, and is located in the Pacific Time Zone at 41.75° N. Lat., 123.98° W. Long. The county was founded in 1857. County seat is Crescent City.

Del Norte County is part of the Crescent City, CA Micropolitan Statistical Area. The entire metro area includes: Del Norte County, CA

Weather Station: Crescent City 3 NNW — Elevation: 68 feet

	Jan	Feb	Mar	Apr	May	Jun	Jul	Aug	Sep	Oct	Nov	Dec
High	55	56	57	58	61	63	66	66	66	63	57	54
Low	41	41	42	44	46	49	51	52	49	46	43	40
Precip	10.3	8.7	8.9	5.7	3.3	1.7	0.4	0.6	1.1	4.4	9.7	13.2
Snow	0.0	0.0	0.0	tr	0.0	0.0	0.0	0.0	0.0	0.0	0.0	0.0

High and Low temperatures in degrees Fahrenheit; Precipitation and Snow in inches

Weather Station: Klamath — Elevation: 24 feet

	Jan	Feb	Mar	Apr	May	Jun	Jul	Aug	Sep	Oct	Nov	Dec
High	55	56	57	59	62	65	67	67	67	64	58	55
Low	39	40	41	43	46	49	52	52	49	45	42	39
Precip	12.4	10.5	10.1	6.2	3.9	1.8	0.4	0.6	1.2	4.7	11.4	15.2
Snow	tr	0.7	0.0	0.0	0.0	0.0	0.0	0.0	0.0	0.0	0.0	0.1

High and Low temperatures in degrees Fahrenheit; Precipitation and Snow in inches

Population: 28,610; Growth (since 2000): 4.0%; Density: 28.4 persons per square mile; Race: 73.7% White, 3.5% Black/African American, 3.4%

Asian, 7.8% American Indian/Alaska Native, 0.1% Native Hawaiian/Other Pacific Islander, 4.5% two or more races, 17.8% Hispanic of any race; Average household size: 2.50; Median age: 39.1; Age under 18: 21.5%; Age 65 and over: 13.5%; Males per 100 females: 125.2; Marriage status: 36.7% never married, 42.9% now married, 2.8% separated, 7.2% widowed, 13.1% divorced; Foreign born: 6.5%; Speak English only: 84.7%; With disability: 21.5%; Veterans: 12.4%; Ancestry: 16.4% German, 13.0% Irish, 11.1% English, 5.3% American, 3.4% Italian
Religion: Six largest groups: 5.5% Catholicism, 4.2% Latter-day Saints, 3.1% Pentecostal, 1.8% Lutheran, 1.7% Methodist/Pietist, 1.6% Non-denominational Protestant
Economy: Unemployment rate: 8.9%; Leading industries: 15.5% health care and social assistance; 15.3% accommodation and food services; 13.3% retail trade; Farms: 121 totaling n/a acres; Company size: 0 employ 1,000 or more persons, 0 employ 500 to 999 persons, 5 employ 100 to 499 persons, 439 employ less than 100 persons; Business ownership: 449 women-owned, n/a Black-owned, n/a Hispanic-owned, n/a Asian-owned
Employment: 11.2% management, business, and financial, 2.8% computer, engineering, and science, 14.5% education, legal, community service, arts, and media, 4.2% healthcare practitioners, 31.0% service, 20.9% sales and office, 8.6% natural resources, construction, and maintenance, 6.7% production, transportation, and material moving
Income: Per capita: $19,072; Median household: $37,909; Average household: $53,185; Households with income of $100,000 or more: 14.1%; Poverty rate: 21.8%
Educational Attainment: High school diploma or higher: 79.1%; Bachelor's degree or higher: 14.0%; Graduate/professional degree or higher: 5.1%
Housing: Homeownership rate: 61.7%; Median home value: $198,400; Median year structure built: 1978; Homeowner vacancy rate: 3.0%; Median gross rent: $914 per month; Rental vacancy rate: 6.8%
Vital Statistics: Birth rate: 119.1 per 10,000 population; Death rate: 85.7 per 10,000 population; Age-adjusted cancer mortality rate: 181.9 deaths per 100,000 population
Health Insurance: 85.0% have insurance; 51.3% have private insurance; 47.6% have public insurance; 15.0% do not have insurance; 4.2% of children under 18 do not have insurance
Health Care: Physicians: 14.2 per 10,000 population; Hospital beds: 17.2 per 10,000 population; Hospital admissions: 791.6 per 10,000 population
Air Quality Index: 100.0% good, 0.0% moderate, 0.0% unhealthy for sensitive individuals, 0.0% unhealthy (percent of days)
Transportation: Commute: 86.8% car, 0.3% public transportation, 3.6% walk, 5.8% work from home; Median travel time to work: 14.2 minutes
Presidential Election: 42.8% Obama, 53.6% Romney (2012)
National and State Parks: Castle Rock National Wildlife Refuge; Del Norte Coast Redwoods State Park; Jedediah Smith Redwoods State Park; Pelican State Beach; Redwood Heritage State Wilderness; Six Rivers National Forest; Tolowa Dunes State Park
Additional Information Contacts
Del Norte Government .... (707) 464-7214
http://www.co.del-norte.ca.us

Del Norte County Communities

BERTSCH-OCEANVIEW (CDP). Covers a land area of 5.487 square miles and a water area of 0.274 square miles. Located at 41.75° N. Lat; 124.16° W. Long.
Population: 2,436; Growth (since 2000): 8.8%; Density: 444.0 persons per square mile; Race: 74.3% White, 0.1% Black/African American, 3.9% Asian, 12.1% American Indian/Alaska Native, 0.0% Native Hawaiian/Other Pacific Islander, 6.3% Two or more races, 12.7% Hispanic of any race; Average household size: 2.69; Median age: 38.5; Age under 18: 26.0%; Age 65 and over: 13.8%; Males per 100 females: 98.2
Housing: Homeownership rate: 73.7%; Homeowner vacancy rate: 4.0%; Rental vacancy rate: 5.2%

CRESCENT CITY (city). County seat. Covers a land area of 1.963 square miles and a water area of 0.452 square miles. Located at 41.77° N. Lat; 124.20° W. Long. Elevation is 43 feet.
History: Crescent City was laid out in 1852 and grew rapidly, serving for a time as the seat of Klamath County. When they lost this honor, the residents forced formation of a new county, Del Norte, so that their city could be its seat.
Population: 7,643; Growth (since 2000): 90.8%; Density: 3,892.8 persons per square mile; Race: 66.1% White, 11.9% Black/African American, 4.4% Asian, 4.8% American Indian/Alaska Native, 0.1% Native Hawaiian/Other Pacific Islander, 3.6% Two or more races, 30.6% Hispanic of any race; Average household size: 2.38; Median age: 34.9; Age under 18: 14.5%; Age 65 and over: 7.7%; Males per 100 females: 250.1; Marriage status: 53.2% never married, 27.6% now married, 3.7% separated, 4.6% widowed, 14.6% divorced; Foreign born: 8.4%; Speak English only: 76.5%; With disability: 23.1%; Veterans: 9.4%; Ancestry: 13.5% Irish, 13.1% German, 10.2% English, 3.8% American, 2.7% Swedish
Employment: 12.3% management, business, and financial, 2.5% computer, engineering, and science, 17.2% education, legal, community service, arts, and media, 4.3% healthcare practitioners, 29.5% service, 21.7% sales and office, 4.3% natural resources, construction, and maintenance, 8.3% production, transportation, and material moving
Income: Per capita: $11,152; Median household: $29,700; Average household: $40,905; Households with income of $100,000 or more: 9.8%; Poverty rate: 24.2%
Educational Attainment: High school diploma or higher: 66.2%; Bachelor's degree or higher: 10.6%; Graduate/professional degree or higher: 5.0%

School District(s)
Del Norte County Office of Education (KG-12)
2012-13 Enrollment: 602.......... (707) 464-0200
Del Norte County Rop
2012-13 Enrollment: n/a .... (707) 464-0274
Del Norte County Unified (KG-12)
2012-13 Enrollment: 3,595 .... (707) 464-0200
Housing: Homeownership rate: 31.1%; Median home value: $149,400; Median year structure built: 1965; Homeowner vacancy rate: 7.7%; Median gross rent: $827 per month; Rental vacancy rate: 4.8%
Health Insurance: 85.3% have insurance; 54.0% have private insurance; 41.4% have public insurance; 14.7% do not have insurance; 7.3% of children under 18 do not have insurance
Hospitals: Sutter Coast Hospital (49 beds)
Safety: Violent crime rate: 128.2 per 10,000 population; Property crime rate: 275.5 per 10,000 population
Newspapers: Daily Triplicate (daily circulation 5300)
Transportation: Commute: 80.1% car, 0.6% public transportation, 5.7% walk, 2.2% work from home; Median travel time to work: 16.8 minutes; Amtrak: Bus service available.
Airports: Jack McNamara Field (primary service/non-hub)
Additional Information Contacts
City of Crescent City .... (707) 464-7483
http://www.crescentcity.org

GASQUET (CDP). Covers a land area of 4.756 square miles and a water area of 0.066 square miles. Located at 41.84° N. Lat; 123.98° W. Long. Elevation is 384 feet.
Population: 661; Growth (since 2000): n/a; Density: 139.0 persons per square mile; Race: 88.5% White, 0.3% Black/African American, 0.2% Asian, 4.1% American Indian/Alaska Native, 0.2% Native Hawaiian/Other Pacific Islander, 4.5% Two or more races, 5.9% Hispanic of any race; Average household size: 2.07; Median age: 54.0; Age under 18: 14.5%; Age 65 and over: 21.2%; Males per 100 females: 103.4

School District(s)
Del Norte County Office of Education (KG-12)
2012-13 Enrollment: 602.......... (707) 464-0200
Del Norte County Unified (KG-12)
2012-13 Enrollment: 3,595 .... (707) 464-0200
Housing: Homeownership rate: 75.3%; Homeowner vacancy rate: 1.2%; Rental vacancy rate: 17.7%

HIOUCHI (CDP). Covers a land area of 0.580 square miles and a water area of 0 square miles. Located at 41.79° N. Lat; 124.07° W. Long. Elevation is 171 feet.
Population: 301; Growth (since 2000): n/a; Density: 519.1 persons per square mile; Race: 88.7% White, 0.0% Black/African American, 2.0% Asian, 3.7% American Indian/Alaska Native, 0.7% Native Hawaiian/Other Pacific Islander, 2.3% Two or more races, 3.7% Hispanic of any race; Average household size: 2.10; Median age: 54.2; Age under 18: 17.3%; Age 65 and over: 22.9%; Males per 100 females: 104.8
Housing: Homeownership rate: 70.0%; Homeowner vacancy rate: 1.0%; Rental vacancy rate: 4.3%

KLAMATH (CDP). Covers a land area of 12.541 square miles and a water area of 0 square miles. Located at 41.53° N. Lat; 124.01° W. Long. Elevation is 30 feet.

Population: 779; Growth (since 2000): 19.7%; Density: 62.1 persons per square mile; Race: 48.7% White, 0.1% Black/African American, 0.4% Asian, 41.7% American Indian/Alaska Native, 0.0% Native Hawaiian/Other Pacific Islander, 8.5% Two or more races, 11.6% Hispanic of any race; Average household size: 2.52; Median age: 43.1; Age under 18: 23.5%; Age 65 and over: 18.5%; Males per 100 females: 107.2

School District(s)

Del Norte County Office of Education (KG-12)
2012-13 Enrollment: 602. . . . . (707) 464-0200

Del Norte County Unified (KG-12)
2012-13 Enrollment: 3,595 . . . . (707) 464-0200

Housing: Homeownership rate: 56.3%; Homeowner vacancy rate: 3.9%; Rental vacancy rate: 8.8%

SMITH RIVER (CDP). Covers a land area of 3.970 square miles and a water area of 0.015 square miles. Located at 41.92° N. Lat; 124.15° W. Long. Elevation is 52 feet.

Population: 866; Growth (since 2000): n/a; Density: 218.1 persons per square mile; Race: 61.0% White, 0.1% Black/African American, 0.6% Asian, 6.8% American Indian/Alaska Native, 0.0% Native Hawaiian/Other Pacific Islander, 4.5% Two or more races, 33.8% Hispanic of any race; Average household size: 2.75; Median age: 34.8; Age under 18: 30.8%; Age 65 and over: 12.4%; Males per 100 females: 92.0

School District(s)

Del Norte County Unified (KG-12)
2012-13 Enrollment: 3,595 . . . . (707) 464-0200

Housing: Homeownership rate: 57.5%; Homeowner vacancy rate: 3.2%; Rental vacancy rate: 3.6%

El Dorado County

Located in east central California, rising from the Sierra Nevada foothills; drained by the American, Rubicon, and Cosumnes Rivers; includes Pyramid Peak (10,020 ft), part of Lake Tahoe, and part of El Dorado National Forest. Covers a land area of 1,707.883 square miles, a water area of 78.473 square miles, and is located in the Pacific Time Zone at 38.79° N. Lat., 120.53° W. Long. The county was founded in 1850. County seat is Placerville.

El Dorado County is part of the Sacramento—Roseville—Arden-Arcade, CA Metropolitan Statistical Area. The entire metro area includes: El Dorado County, CA; Placer County, CA; Sacramento County, CA; Yolo County, CA

Weather Station: Placerville Elevation: 1,850 feet

	Jan	Feb	Mar	Apr	May	Jun	Jul	Aug	Sep	Oct	Nov	Dec
High	56	59	62	68	76	85	93	92	87	77	63	55
Low	34	37	40	43	48	54	60	59	55	47	39	34
Precip	7.4	7.0	6.0	3.1	1.8	0.5	0.0	0.1	0.7	2.0	4.7	6.6
Snow	0.0	tr	tr	0.0	0.0	0.0	0.0	0.0	0.0	0.0	0.0	tr

High and Low temperatures in degrees Fahrenheit; Precipitation and Snow in inches

Population: 181,058; Growth (since 2000): 15.8%; Density: 106.0 persons per square mile; Race: 86.6% White, 0.8% Black/African American, 3.5% Asian, 1.1% American Indian/Alaska Native, 0.2% Native Hawaiian/Other Pacific Islander, 3.8% two or more races, 12.1% Hispanic of any race; Average household size: 2.55; Median age: 43.6; Age under 18: 22.7%; Age 65 and over: 14.6%; Males per 100 females: 100.1; Marriage status: 24.4% never married, 59.5% now married, 1.6% separated, 5.2% widowed, 10.8% divorced; Foreign born: 8.7%; Speak English only: 87.5%; With disability: 11.5%; Veterans: 11.9%; Ancestry: 20.3% German, 13.6% Irish, 13.5% English, 7.8% Italian, 4.5% American

Religion: Six largest groups: 12.9% Catholicism, 5.2% Non-denominational Protestant, 3.9% Latter-day Saints, 1.3% Methodist/Pietist, 0.9% Holiness, 0.8% Baptist

Economy: Unemployment rate: 6.4%; Leading industries: 14.7% construction; 12.6% retail trade; 12.3% professional, scientific, and technical services; Farms: 1,358 totaling 128,365 acres; Company size: 4 employ 1,000 or more persons, 2 employ 500 to 999 persons, 40 employ 100 to 499 persons, 4,177 employ less than 100 persons; Business ownership: 5,727 women-owned, n/a Black-owned, 1,390 Hispanic-owned, 505 Asian-owned

Employment: 17.5% management, business, and financial, 6.4% computer, engineering, and science, 9.6% education, legal, community service, arts, and media, 5.9% healthcare practitioners, 19.7% service, 24.9% sales and office, 9.0% natural resources, construction, and maintenance, 7.0% production, transportation, and material moving

Income: Per capita: $34,884; Median household: $69,297; Average household: $90,247; Households with income of $100,000 or more: 33.2%; Poverty rate: 9.0%

Educational Attainment: High school diploma or higher: 93.2%; Bachelor's degree or higher: 32.0%; Graduate/professional degree or higher: 10.4%

Housing: Homeownership rate: 73.2%; Median home value: $359,500; Median year structure built: 1981; Homeowner vacancy rate: 2.4%; Median gross rent: $1,090 per month; Rental vacancy rate: 10.2%

Vital Statistics: Birth rate: 89.4 per 10,000 population; Death rate: 78.4 per 10,000 population; Age-adjusted cancer mortality rate: 164.1 deaths per 100,000 population

Health Insurance: 89.8% have insurance; 76.2% have private insurance; 27.9% have public insurance; 10.2% do not have insurance; 3.8% of children under 18 do not have insurance

Health Care: Physicians: 18.8 per 10,000 population; Hospital beds: 12.3 per 10,000 population; Hospital admissions: 438.0 per 10,000 population

Air Quality Index: 76.7% good, 20.5% moderate, 2.7% unhealthy for sensitive individuals, 0.0% unhealthy (percent of days)

Transportation: Commute: 87.0% car, 1.2% public transportation, 2.2% walk, 7.6% work from home; Median travel time to work: 28.8 minutes

Presidential Election: 39.7% Obama, 57.8% Romney (2012)

National and State Parks: D.L. Bliss State Park; Diamond Spring State Historic Landmark; Ed Z'berg Sugar Pine Point State Park; Eight Mile House State Historic Landmark; Eldorado National Forest; Emerald Bay State Park; Folsom Lake State Recreation Area; James W Marshall State Historical Monument; Lake Valley State Recreation Area; Marshall Gold Discovery State Historic Park; Pine Hill State Ecological Reserve; Pleasant Grove House State Historic Landmark; Pony Express State Historic Landmark 703; Shingle Springs State Historic Landmark 456; Sportsmans Hall State Historic Landmark 704; Washoe Meadows State Park

Additional Information Contacts

El Dorado Government . . . . (530) 621-5390
http://www.edcgov.us

El Dorado County Communities

AUBURN LAKE TRAILS (CDP). Covers a land area of 12.727 square miles and a water area of 0.022 square miles. Located at 38.89° N. Lat; 120.98° W. Long. Elevation is 1,916 feet.

Population: 3,426; Growth (since 2000): n/a; Density: 269.2 persons per square mile; Race: 93.1% White, 0.2% Black/African American, 1.1% Asian, 0.8% American Indian/Alaska Native, 0.1% Native Hawaiian/Other Pacific Islander, 3.4% Two or more races, 6.1% Hispanic of any race; Average household size: 2.51; Median age: 48.3; Age under 18: 21.0%; Age 65 and over: 17.4%; Males per 100 females: 93.7; Marriage status: 16.4% never married, 71.8% now married, 0.5% separated, 4.8% widowed, 6.9% divorced; Foreign born: 1.2%; Speak English only: 96.7%; With disability: 9.3%; Veterans: 19.6%; Ancestry: 25.8% German, 15.8% English, 13.2% Irish, 10.1% Italian, 5.7% French

Employment: 13.4% management, business, and financial, 8.8% computer, engineering, and science, 14.4% education, legal, community service, arts, and media, 13.2% healthcare practitioners, 15.3% service, 27.2% sales and office, 6.5% natural resources, construction, and maintenance, 1.3% production, transportation, and material moving

Income: Per capita: $36,372; Median household: $91,583; Average household: $95,836; Households with income of $100,000 or more: 43.8%; Poverty rate: 4.1%

Educational Attainment: High school diploma or higher: 98.2%; Bachelor's degree or higher: 32.6%; Graduate/professional degree or higher: 12.7%

Housing: Homeownership rate: 88.5%; Median home value: $309,600; Median year structure built: 1984; Homeowner vacancy rate: 2.6%; Median gross rent: $1,877 per month; Rental vacancy rate: 3.1%

Health Insurance: 95.1% have insurance; 87.1% have private insurance; 24.1% have public insurance; 4.9% do not have insurance; 1.6% of children under 18 do not have insurance

Transportation: Commute: 89.7% car, 1.3% public transportation, 0.7% walk, 6.2% work from home; Median travel time to work: 34.3 minutes

CAMERON PARK (CDP). Covers a land area of 11.107 square miles and a water area of 0.069 square miles. Located at 38.67° N. Lat; 120.99° W. Long. Elevation is 1,204 feet.

Population: 18,228; Growth (since 2000): 25.3%; Density: 1,641.2 persons per square mile; Race: 89.1% White, 0.8% Black/African American, 2.3% Asian, 1.1% American Indian/Alaska Native, 0.2% Native Hawaiian/Other Pacific Islander, 4.0% Two or more races, 11.3% Hispanic of any race; Average household size: 2.61; Median age: 40.6; Age under 18: 25.1%; Age 65 and over: 14.4%; Males per 100 females: 94.3; Marriage status: 23.4% never married, 60.1% now married, 1.1% separated, 6.2% widowed, 10.3% divorced; Foreign born: 6.0%; Speak English only: 89.4%; With disability: 11.3%; Veterans: 14.1%; Ancestry: 19.6% German, 14.1% English, 13.6% Irish, 9.3% Italian, 5.3% French

Employment: 17.3% management, business, and financial, 9.8% computer, engineering, and science, 12.9% education, legal, community service, arts, and media, 5.7% healthcare practitioners, 16.7% service, 22.5% sales and office, 7.7% natural resources, construction, and maintenance, 7.5% production, transportation, and material moving

Income: Per capita: $34,653; Median household: $74,266; Average household: $89,827; Households with income of $100,000 or more: 34.2%; Poverty rate: 5.2%

Educational Attainment: High school diploma or higher: 94.4%; Bachelor's degree or higher: 32.4%; Graduate/professional degree or higher: 10.3%

School District(s)

Buckeye Union Elementary (KG-08)
2012-13 Enrollment: 5,099 . . . . (530) 677-2261

Housing: Homeownership rate: 68.2%; Median home value: $314,900; Median year structure built: 1986; Homeowner vacancy rate: 2.0%; Median gross rent: $1,114 per month; Rental vacancy rate: 14.6%

Health Insurance: 94.2% have insurance; 82.5% have private insurance; 26.9% have public insurance; 5.8% do not have insurance; 3.4% of children under 18 do not have insurance

Transportation: Commute: 89.1% car, 0.8% public transportation, 1.5% walk, 6.6% work from home; Median travel time to work: 29.3 minutes

CAMINO (CDP). Covers a land area of 2.250 square miles and a water area of 0 square miles. Located at 38.74° N. Lat; 120.68° W. Long. Elevation is 3,133 feet.

Population: 1,750; Growth (since 2000): n/a; Density: 777.7 persons per square mile; Race: 91.7% White, 0.4% Black/African American, 1.0% Asian, 0.8% American Indian/Alaska Native, 0.2% Native Hawaiian/Other Pacific Islander, 2.7% Two or more races, 11.3% Hispanic of any race; Average household size: 2.42; Median age: 47.8; Age under 18: 21.1%; Age 65 and over: 21.7%; Males per 100 females: 98.4

School District(s)

Camino Union Elementary (KG-08)
2012-13 Enrollment: 513. . . . . (530) 644-4552

Housing: Homeownership rate: 71.1%; Homeowner vacancy rate: 2.3%; Rental vacancy rate: 7.4%

COLD SPRINGS (CDP). Covers a land area of 0.755 square miles and a water area of 0 square miles. Located at 38.75° N. Lat; 120.88° W. Long. Elevation is 1,204 feet.

Population: 446; Growth (since 2000): n/a; Density: 590.4 persons per square mile; Race: 92.6% White, 0.9% Black/African American, 0.7% Asian, 1.1% American Indian/Alaska Native, 0.0% Native Hawaiian/Other Pacific Islander, 1.3% Two or more races, 9.6% Hispanic of any race; Average household size: 2.28; Median age: 53.1; Age under 18: 17.9%; Age 65 and over: 28.9%; Males per 100 females: 100.9

Housing: Homeownership rate: 83.7%; Homeowner vacancy rate: 1.2%; Rental vacancy rate: 11.1%

COLOMA (CDP). Covers a land area of 3.355 square miles and a water area of 0 square miles. Located at 38.80° N. Lat; 120.89° W. Long. Elevation is 764 feet.

Population: 529; Growth (since 2000): n/a; Density: 157.7 persons per square mile; Race: 87.3% White, 0.8% Black/African American, 1.5% Asian, 0.6% American Indian/Alaska Native, 0.0% Native Hawaiian/Other Pacific Islander, 7.0% Two or more races, 11.9% Hispanic of any race; Average household size: 2.29; Median age: 49.0; Age under 18: 13.0%; Age 65 and over: 19.3%; Males per 100 females: 115.9

Housing: Homeownership rate: 70.8%; Homeowner vacancy rate: 1.3%; Rental vacancy rate: 12.5%

COOL (unincorporated postal area)

ZCTA: 95614

Covers a land area of 35.498 square miles and a water area of 0.087 square miles. Located at 38.89° N. Lat; 120.98° W. Long..

Population: 3,833; Growth (since 2000): 4.8%; Density: 108.0 persons per square mile; Race: 93.0% White, 0.2% Black/African American, 1.0% Asian, 0.9% American Indian/Alaska Native, 0.1% Native Hawaiian/Other Pacific Islander, 3.4% Two or more races, 5.8% Hispanic of any race; Average household size: 2.50; Median age: 48.3; Age under 18: 20.9%; Age 65 and over: 17.1%; Males per 100 females: 93.9; Marriage status: 16.6% never married, 70.9% now married, 0.4% separated, 4.8% widowed, 7.7% divorced; Foreign born: 1.0%; Speak English only: 97.1%; With disability: 9.3%; Veterans: 20.2%; Ancestry: 23.1% German, 19.9% English, 15.6% Irish, 8.9% Italian, 5.6% French

Employment: 13.0% management, business, and financial, 9.0% computer, engineering, and science, 12.6% education, legal, community service, arts, and media, 11.6% healthcare practitioners, 17.2% service, 26.9% sales and office, 6.5% natural resources, construction, and maintenance, 3.2% production, transportation, and material moving

Income: Per capita: $35,831; Median household: $92,721; Average household: $97,135; Households with income of $100,000 or more: 45.5%; Poverty rate: 3.6%

Educational Attainment: High school diploma or higher: 98.4%; Bachelor's degree or higher: 29.9%; Graduate/professional degree or higher: 11.3%

School District(s)

Black Oak Mine Unified (KG-12)
2012-13 Enrollment: 1,422 . . . . (530) 333-8300

Housing: Homeownership rate: 88.4%; Median home value: $308,800; Median year structure built: 1984; Homeowner vacancy rate: 2.6%; Median gross rent: $1,877 per month; Rental vacancy rate: 4.8%

Health Insurance: 94.4% have insurance; 87.4% have private insurance; 23.2% have public insurance; 5.6% do not have insurance; 1.4% of children under 18 do not have insurance

Transportation: Commute: 90.9% car, 1.2% public transportation, 0.6% walk, 5.5% work from home; Median travel time to work: 34.3 minutes

DIAMOND SPRINGS (CDP). Covers a land area of 16.642 square miles and a water area of 0.070 square miles. Located at 38.69° N. Lat; 120.84° W. Long. Elevation is 1,791 feet.

History: Diamond Springs began in 1849 as a camp on the Carson Pass Emigrant Trail, and became a supply center for lumbermen.

Population: 11,037; Growth (since 2000): 125.8%; Density: 663.2 persons per square mile; Race: 88.3% White, 0.4% Black/African American, 1.0% Asian, 1.6% American Indian/Alaska Native, 0.1% Native Hawaiian/Other Pacific Islander, 4.0% Two or more races, 12.5% Hispanic of any race; Average household size: 2.38; Median age: 47.1; Age under 18: 20.4%; Age 65 and over: 22.1%; Males per 100 females: 88.9; Marriage status: 24.4% never married, 50.7% now married, 2.5% separated, 10.3% widowed, 14.6% divorced; Foreign born: 5.7%; Speak English only: 90.2%; With disability: 17.6%; Veterans: 13.6%; Ancestry: 19.1% German, 13.6% Irish, 12.2% English, 9.1% Italian, 6.1% American

Employment: 13.8% management, business, and financial, 6.0% computer, engineering, and science, 4.4% education, legal, community service, arts, and media, 4.4% healthcare practitioners, 25.1% service, 28.1% sales and office, 11.2% natural resources, construction, and maintenance, 6.9% production, transportation, and material moving

Income: Per capita: $25,510; Median household: $50,848; Average household: $64,615; Households with income of $100,000 or more: 20.2%; Poverty rate: 11.6%

Educational Attainment: High school diploma or higher: 92.9%; Bachelor's degree or higher: 20.4%; Graduate/professional degree or higher: 7.6%

School District(s)

El Dorado Union High (09-12)
2012-13 Enrollment: 6,873 . . . . (530) 622-5081

Housing: Homeownership rate: 72.1%; Median home value: $234,500; Median year structure built: 1982; Homeowner vacancy rate: 3.4%; Median gross rent: $1,291 per month; Rental vacancy rate: 5.0%

Health Insurance: 88.9% have insurance; 71.7% have private insurance; 35.4% have public insurance; 11.1% do not have insurance; 1.5% of children under 18 do not have insurance

Transportation: Commute: 92.5% car, 0.9% public transportation, 1.6% walk, 3.3% work from home; Median travel time to work: 25.4 minutes

ECHO LAKE (unincorporated postal area)

ZCTA: 95721

Covers a land area of 12.530 square miles and a water area of 0.690 square miles. Located at 38.84° N. Lat; 120.08° W. Long. Elevation is 7,536 feet.

Population: 37; Growth (since 2000): -38.3%; Density: 3.0 persons per square mile; Race: 97.3% White, 0.0% Black/African American, 0.0% Asian, 0.0% American Indian/Alaska Native, 0.0% Native Hawaiian/Other Pacific Islander, 0.0% Two or more races, 5.4% Hispanic of any race; Average household size: 1.48; Median age: 53.5; Age under 18: 2.7%; Age 65 and over: 27.0%; Males per 100 females: 146.7

Housing: Homeownership rate: 84.0%; Homeowner vacancy rate: 0.0%; Rental vacancy rate: 0.0%

EL DORADO (unincorporated postal area)

ZCTA: 95623

Covers a land area of 52.347 square miles and a water area of 0.009 square miles. Located at 38.61° N. Lat; 120.86° W. Long. Elevation is 1,608 feet.

Population: 3,806; Growth (since 2000): -7.1%; Density: 72.7 persons per square mile; Race: 91.4% White, 0.4% Black/African American, 1.4% Asian, 1.1% American Indian/Alaska Native, 0.3% Native Hawaiian/Other Pacific Islander, 3.2% Two or more races, 9.2% Hispanic of any race; Average household size: 2.49; Median age: 48.6; Age under 18: 19.0%; Age 65 and over: 18.1%; Males per 100 females: 98.6; Marriage status: 23.5% never married, 60.0% now married, 3.2% separated, 6.3% widowed, 10.1% divorced; Foreign born: 3.7%; Speak English only: 95.6%; With disability: 15.8%; Veterans: 12.1%; Ancestry: 19.8% German, 18.5% English, 10.8% Irish, 8.1% American, 6.7% European

Employment: 6.6% management, business, and financial, 5.2% computer, engineering, and science, 10.4% education, legal, community service, arts, and media, 3.3% healthcare practitioners, 17.4% service, 31.7% sales and office, 15.7% natural resources, construction, and maintenance, 9.6% production, transportation, and material moving

Income: Per capita: $31,659; Median household: $62,321; Average household: $78,448; Households with income of $100,000 or more: 30.5%; Poverty rate: 7.3%

Educational Attainment: High school diploma or higher: 93.3%; Bachelor's degree or higher: 22.1%; Graduate/professional degree or higher: 8.3%

School District(s)

El Dorado County Office of Education (KG-12)
2012-13 Enrollment: 980 . . . . (530) 622-7130
El Dorado Union High (09-12)
2012-13 Enrollment: 6,873 . . . . (530) 622-5081

Housing: Homeownership rate: 79.2%; Median home value: $338,300; Median year structure built: 1985; Homeowner vacancy rate: 1.7%; Median gross rent: $1,109 per month; Rental vacancy rate: 3.9%

Health Insurance: 87.9% have insurance; 70.9% have private insurance; 28.9% have public insurance; 12.1% do not have insurance; 0.0% of children under 18 do not have insurance

Transportation: Commute: 89.5% car, 0.0% public transportation, 4.3% walk, 3.5% work from home; Median travel time to work: 35.5 minutes

EL DORADO HILLS (CDP). Covers a land area of 48.454 square miles and a water area of 0.152 square miles. Located at 38.67° N. Lat; 121.05° W. Long. Elevation is 768 feet.

Population: 42,108; Growth (since 2000): 133.7%; Density: 869.0 persons per square mile; Race: 83.3% White, 1.5% Black/African American, 8.5% Asian, 0.5% American Indian/Alaska Native, 0.2% Native Hawaiian/Other Pacific Islander, 4.5% Two or more races, 9.0% Hispanic of any race; Average household size: 2.93; Median age: 40.6; Age under 18: 29.5%; Age 65 and over: 10.6%; Males per 100 females: 97.5; Marriage status: 22.4% never married, 66.6% now married, 1.0% separated, 3.2% widowed, 7.7% divorced; Foreign born: 12.0%; Speak English only: 86.0%; With disability: 6.4%; Veterans: 9.8%; Ancestry: 18.6% German, 13.5% English, 12.0% Irish, 8.5% Italian, 3.9% American

Employment: 26.3% management, business, and financial, 8.8% computer, engineering, and science, 11.5% education, legal, community service, arts, and media, 6.3% healthcare practitioners, 12.3% service, 25.5% sales and office, 3.9% natural resources, construction, and maintenance, 5.4% production, transportation, and material moving

Income: Per capita: $46,627; Median household: $119,025; Average household: $137,935; Households with income of $100,000 or more: 58.6%; Poverty rate: 3.8%

Educational Attainment: High school diploma or higher: 97.6%; Bachelor's degree or higher: 52.4%; Graduate/professional degree or higher: 17.4%

School District(s)

Buckeye Union Elementary (KG-08)
2012-13 Enrollment: 5,099 . . . . (530) 677-2261
El Dorado Union High (09-12)
2012-13 Enrollment: 6,873 . . . . (530) 622-5081
Rescue Union Elementary (KG-08)
2012-13 Enrollment: 3,899 . . . . (530) 677-4461

Housing: Homeownership rate: 84.7%; Median home value: $469,700; Median year structure built: 1998; Homeowner vacancy rate: 1.7%; Median gross rent: $1,768 per month; Rental vacancy rate: 4.1%

Health Insurance: 95.1% have insurance; 89.1% have private insurance; 17.1% have public insurance; 4.9% do not have insurance; 2.9% of children under 18 do not have insurance

Transportation: Commute: 84.3% car, 1.3% public transportation, 0.8% walk, 12.0% work from home; Median travel time to work: 30.4 minutes

GARDEN VALLEY (unincorporated postal area)

ZCTA: 95633

Covers a land area of 41.225 square miles and a water area of 0.039 square miles. Located at 38.84° N. Lat; 120.83° W. Long. Elevation is 1,949 feet.

Population: 3,349; Growth (since 2000): 33.0%; Density: 81.2 persons per square mile; Race: 92.4% White, 0.2% Black/African American, 0.6% Asian, 1.4% American Indian/Alaska Native, 0.1% Native Hawaiian/Other Pacific Islander, 3.9% Two or more races, 7.1% Hispanic of any race; Average household size: 2.48; Median age: 48.5; Age under 18: 18.5%; Age 65 and over: 16.9%; Males per 100 females: 103.7; Marriage status: 19.9% never married, 66.3% now married, 1.7% separated, 6.4% widowed, 7.4% divorced; Foreign born: 3.1%; Speak English only: 92.7%; With disability: 20.6%; Veterans: 11.7%; Ancestry: 28.7% German, 17.6% Irish, 16.9% English, 8.1% Scottish, 7.5% Italian

Employment: 13.1% management, business, and financial, 4.0% computer, engineering, and science, 5.9% education, legal, community service, arts, and media, 7.9% healthcare practitioners, 23.4% service, 18.2% sales and office, 20.0% natural resources, construction, and maintenance, 7.5% production, transportation, and material moving

Income: Per capita: $32,408; Median household: $65,603; Average household: $78,132; Households with income of $100,000 or more: 22.9%; Poverty rate: 6.5%

Educational Attainment: High school diploma or higher: 91.4%; Bachelor's degree or higher: 26.8%; Graduate/professional degree or higher: 9.8%

School District(s)

Black Oak Mine Unified (KG-12)
2012-13 Enrollment: 1,422 . . . . (530) 333-8300

Housing: Homeownership rate: 84.5%; Median home value: $266,100; Median year structure built: 1983; Homeowner vacancy rate: 2.1%; Median gross rent: $984 per month; Rental vacancy rate: 5.4%

Health Insurance: 83.7% have insurance; 72.4% have private insurance; 32.9% have public insurance; 16.3% do not have insurance; 7.9% of children under 18 do not have insurance

Transportation: Commute: 93.4% car, 0.0% public transportation, 0.0% walk, 6.6% work from home; Median travel time to work: 40.0 minutes

GEORGETOWN (CDP). Covers a land area of 15.128 square miles and a water area of 0.004 square miles. Located at 38.91° N. Lat; 120.83° W. Long. Elevation is 2,654 feet.

History: A group of Oregonians discovered gold in 1849 on Oregon Creek. The community that grew up was first called Growlersburg, but was renamed in 1852 to honor George Phipps who led a company of sailors here in 1850. In its prime Georgetown was the trading center for miners from almost a hundred camps.

Population: 2,367; Growth (since 2000): 146.0%; Density: 156.5 persons per square mile; Race: 89.9% White, 2.0% Black/African American, 0.8% Asian, 2.5% American Indian/Alaska Native, 0.1% Native Hawaiian/Other Pacific Islander, 2.9% Two or more races, 7.5% Hispanic of any race; Average household size: 2.45; Median age: 46.4; Age under 18: 18.6%; Age 65 and over: 17.9%; Males per 100 females: 111.0

School District(s)

Black Oak Mine Unified (KG-12)
2012-13 Enrollment: 1,422 . . . . (530) 333-8300

Housing: Homeownership rate: 77.6%; Homeowner vacancy rate: 3.5%; Rental vacancy rate: 8.1%

Newspapers: Georgetown Gazette (weekly circulation 1600)

Airports: Georgetown (general aviation)

GREENWOOD (unincorporated postal area)

ZCTA: 95635

Covers a land area of 20.277 square miles and a water area of 0.023 square miles. Located at 38.90° N. Lat; 120.91° W. Long. Elevation is 1,608 feet.

Population: 1,262; Growth (since 2000): 11.1%; Density: 62.2 persons per square mile; Race: 89.1% White, 1.4% Black/African American, 1.3% Asian, 1.7% American Indian/Alaska Native, 0.0% Native Hawaiian/Other Pacific Islander, 3.7% Two or more races, 9.0% Hispanic of any race; Average household size: 2.47; Median age: 45.8; Age under 18: 19.4%; Age 65 and over: 13.2%; Males per 100 females: 113.2

Housing: Homeownership rate: 79.9%; Homeowner vacancy rate: 0.8%; Rental vacancy rate: 4.8%

GRIZZLY FLATS (CDP).

Covers a land area of 6.629 square miles and a water area of 0 square miles. Located at 38.64° N. Lat; 120.54° W. Long.

Population: 1,066; Growth (since 2000): n/a; Density: 160.8 persons per square mile; Race: 89.5% White, 0.6% Black/African American, 0.7% Asian, 1.3% American Indian/Alaska Native, 0.2% Native Hawaiian/Other Pacific Islander, 6.0% Two or more races, 9.0% Hispanic of any race; Average household size: 2.47; Median age: 46.8; Age under 18: 22.0%; Age 65 and over: 16.5%; Males per 100 females: 109.4

School District(s)

Pioneer Union Elementary (KG-08)
2012-13 Enrollment: 312. . . . . (530) 620-3556

Housing: Homeownership rate: 85.6%; Homeowner vacancy rate: 3.1%; Rental vacancy rate: 8.8%

KYBURZ (unincorporated postal area)

ZCTA: 95720

Covers a land area of 121.080 square miles and a water area of 0.578 square miles. Located at 38.77° N. Lat; 120.21° W. Long. Elevation is 4,058 feet.

Population: 157; Growth (since 2000): -6.0%; Density: 1.3 persons per square mile; Race: 80.3% White, 0.6% Black/African American, 3.8% Asian, 1.9% American Indian/Alaska Native, 1.9% Native Hawaiian/Other Pacific Islander, 8.9% Two or more races, 8.3% Hispanic of any race; Average household size: 2.07; Median age: 53.4; Age under 18: 14.6%; Age 65 and over: 15.9%; Males per 100 females: 96.3

School District(s)

Silver Fork Elementary (KG-08)
2012-13 Enrollment: 10. . . . . (530) 644-5416

Housing: Homeownership rate: 67.1%; Homeowner vacancy rate: 1.9%; Rental vacancy rate: 3.8%

LOTUS (unincorporated postal area)

ZCTA: 95651

Covers a land area of 11.605 square miles and a water area of 0 square miles. Located at 38.82° N. Lat; 120.93° W. Long. Elevation is 722 feet.

Population: 637; Growth (since 2000): 31.9%; Density: 54.9 persons per square mile; Race: 92.6% White, 0.3% Black/African American, 0.9% Asian, 0.5% American Indian/Alaska Native, 0.0% Native Hawaiian/Other Pacific Islander, 3.5% Two or more races, 5.5% Hispanic of any race; Average household size: 2.38; Median age: 46.2; Age under 18: 17.4%; Age 65 and over: 14.1%; Males per 100 females: 111.6

Housing: Homeownership rate: 69.9%; Homeowner vacancy rate: 3.8%; Rental vacancy rate: 6.2%

PILOT HILL (unincorporated postal area)

ZCTA: 95664

Covers a land area of 37.735 square miles and a water area of 4.714 square miles. Located at 38.80° N. Lat; 121.04° W. Long. Elevation is 1,175 feet.

Population: 1,380; Growth (since 2000): 19.4%; Density: 36.6 persons per square mile; Race: 93.1% White, 0.7% Black/African American, 0.4% Asian, 1.2% American Indian/Alaska Native, 0.0% Native Hawaiian/Other Pacific Islander, 3.8% Two or more races, 6.6% Hispanic of any race; Average household size: 2.49; Median age: 48.3; Age under 18: 20.2%; Age 65 and over: 14.9%; Males per 100 females: 107.5

Housing: Homeownership rate: 88.8%; Homeowner vacancy rate: 0.8%; Rental vacancy rate: 7.4%

PLACERVILLE (city).

County seat. Covers a land area of 5.812 square miles and a water area of <.001 square miles. Located at 38.73° N. Lat; 120.80° W. Long. Elevation is 1,867 feet.

History: Placerville was born when men who found the land about Coloma well occupied plodded on to new territory. A strategic point on the overland trail and the Coloma Road, Placerville by 1854 was a contender with San Francisco and Sacramento in wealth and population. Through Placerville went the Overland Mail, the Pony Express, and the overland telegraph. Several men who were later to become industrial giants began their careers here: Mark Hopkins, later a railroad magnate, set up shop on the main street of Placerville with a wagonload of groceries; Philip D. Armour of meat-packing fame ran a butcher shop in town; John Studebaker laid the foundation for an automobile industry by building miners' wheelbarrows.

Population: 10,389; Growth (since 2000): 8.1%; Density: 1,787.6 persons per square mile; Race: 83.9% White, 0.8% Black/African American, 0.9% Asian, 1.6% American Indian/Alaska Native, 0.1% Native Hawaiian/Other Pacific Islander, 4.4% Two or more races, 17.9% Hispanic of any race; Average household size: 2.37; Median age: 40.4; Age under 18: 21.9%; Age 65 and over: 17.7%; Males per 100 females: 90.3; Marriage status: 30.6% never married, 48.0% now married, 3.4% separated, 7.9% widowed, 13.5% divorced; Foreign born: 9.5%; Speak English only: 85.2%; With disability: 16.7%; Veterans: 9.5%; Ancestry: 16.1% German, 11.3% Irish, 9.7% English, 4.8% European, 4.8% Italian

Employment: 9.7% management, business, and financial, 2.9% computer, engineering, and science, 14.8% education, legal, community service, arts, and media, 5.9% healthcare practitioners, 24.6% service, 20.3% sales and office, 10.5% natural resources, construction, and maintenance, 11.3% production, transportation, and material moving

Income: Per capita: $24,629; Median household: $44,096; Average household: $61,549; Households with income of $100,000 or more: 16.5%; Poverty rate: 18.4%

Educational Attainment: High school diploma or higher: 88.6%; Bachelor's degree or higher: 20.6%; Graduate/professional degree or higher: 8.0%

School District(s)

Central Sierra Rop
2012-13 Enrollment: n/a . . . . (530) 622-7130
El Dorado County Office of Education (KG-12)
2012-13 Enrollment: 980. . . . . (530) 622-7130
El Dorado Union High (09-12)
2012-13 Enrollment: 6,873 . . . . (530) 622-5081
Gold Oak Union Elementary (KG-08)
2012-13 Enrollment: 445. . . . . (530) 626-3150
Gold Trail Union Elementary (KG-08)
2012-13 Enrollment: 568. . . . . (530) 626-3194
Lucerne Valley Unified (KG-12)
2012-13 Enrollment: 2,668 . . . . (760) 248-6108
Mother Lode Union Elementary (KG-08)
2012-13 Enrollment: 1,142 . . . . (530) 622-6464
Placerville Union Elementary (KG-08)
2012-13 Enrollment: 1,268 . . . . (530) 622-7216

Housing: Homeownership rate: 52.4%; Median home value: $238,500; Median year structure built: 1971; Homeowner vacancy rate: 3.5%; Median gross rent: $924 per month; Rental vacancy rate: 7.8%

Health Insurance: 87.9% have insurance; 55.1% have private insurance; 48.2% have public insurance; 12.1% do not have insurance; 1.4% of children under 18 do not have insurance

Hospitals: Marshall Medical Center (105 beds)

Safety: Violent crime rate: 60.9 per 10,000 population; Property crime rate: 284.4 per 10,000 population

Newspapers: Mountain Democrat (daily circulation 12500); Village Life (weekly circulation 12000)

Transportation: Commute: 87.9% car, 0.6% public transportation, 2.4% walk, 7.0% work from home; Median travel time to work: 26.5 minutes; Amtrak: Bus service available.

Additional Information Contacts

City of Placerville. . . . . (530) 642-5531
http://www.cityofplacerville.org

POLLOCK PINES (CDP). Covers a land area of 7.928 square miles and a water area of 0.032 square miles. Located at 38.75° N. Lat; 120.60° W. Long. Elevation is 3,930 feet.
History: Pollock Pines is located in central California and named for H.R. Pollock, an early settler in the region who operated a lumber mill.
Population: 6,871; Growth (since 2000): 45.3%; Density: 866.7 persons per square mile; Race: 90.2% White, 0.3% Black/African American, 0.8% Asian, 1.9% American Indian/Alaska Native, 0.0% Native Hawaiian/Other Pacific Islander, 3.2% Two or more races, 10.4% Hispanic of any race; Average household size: 2.42; Median age: 44.8; Age under 18: 21.3%; Age 65 and over: 16.4%; Males per 100 females: 101.6; Marriage status: 18.9% never married, 63.4% now married, 2.1% separated, 7.1% widowed, 10.6% divorced; Foreign born: 3.1%; Speak English only: 93.7%; With disability: 18.3%; Veterans: 13.0%; Ancestry: 27.5% German, 17.6% Irish, 14.8% English, 7.5% Swedish, 6.5% French
Employment: 20.2% management, business, and financial, 7.0% computer, engineering, and science, 4.6% education, legal, community service, arts, and media, 2.9% healthcare practitioners, 19.8% service, 27.4% sales and office, 9.1% natural resources, construction, and maintenance, 8.9% production, transportation, and material moving
Income: Per capita: $31,427; Median household: $53,490; Average household: $72,500; Households with income of $100,000 or more: 18.9%; Poverty rate: 9.9%
Educational Attainment: High school diploma or higher: 92.8%; Bachelor's degree or higher: 16.7%; Graduate/professional degree or higher: 5.7%

School District(s)

Pollock Pines Elementary (KG-08)
2012-13 Enrollment: 694. . . . . (530) 644-2384
Housing: Homeownership rate: 74.9%; Median home value: $205,600; Median year structure built: 1976; Homeowner vacancy rate: 3.2%; Median gross rent: $1,049 per month; Rental vacancy rate: 11.9%
Health Insurance: 88.0% have insurance; 69.8% have private insurance; 36.6% have public insurance; 12.0% do not have insurance; 0.8% of children under 18 do not have insurance
Transportation: Commute: 90.8% car, 0.6% public transportation, 0.4% walk, 6.3% work from home; Median travel time to work: 31.9 minutes

RESCUE (unincorporated postal area)
ZCTA: 95672
Covers a land area of 22.570 square miles and a water area of 0.193 square miles. Located at 38.73° N. Lat; 121.00° W. Long..
Population: 4,773; Growth (since 2000): 25.5%; Density: 211.5 persons per square mile; Race: 89.9% White, 0.8% Black/African American, 3.0% Asian, 0.9% American Indian/Alaska Native, 0.3% Native Hawaiian/Other Pacific Islander, 3.3% Two or more races, 7.7% Hispanic of any race; Average household size: 2.79; Median age: 45.3; Age under 18: 24.1%; Age 65 and over: 13.9%; Males per 100 females: 102.2; Marriage status: 18.8% never married, 69.2% now married, 1.7% separated, 3.1% widowed, 8.9% divorced; Foreign born: 11.5%; Speak English only: 84.5%; With disability: 8.7%; Veterans: 11.2%; Ancestry: 20.5% German, 17.8% English, 8.9% Irish, 7.2% French, 5.7% Dutch
Employment: 27.7% management, business, and financial, 10.6% computer, engineering, and science, 9.6% education, legal, community service, arts, and media, 6.0% healthcare practitioners, 16.3% service, 19.0% sales and office, 6.3% natural resources, construction, and maintenance, 4.5% production, transportation, and material moving
Income: Per capita: $38,148; Median household: $93,209; Average household: $107,762; Households with income of $100,000 or more: 46.9%; Poverty rate: 2.2%
Educational Attainment: High school diploma or higher: 96.6%; Bachelor's degree or higher: 46.9%; Graduate/professional degree or higher: 12.5%

School District(s)

Rescue Union Elementary (KG-08)
2012-13 Enrollment: 3,899 . . . . (530) 677-4461
Housing: Homeownership rate: 86.0%; Median home value: $427,700; Median year structure built: 1989; Homeowner vacancy rate: 2.1%; Median gross rent: $1,636 per month; Rental vacancy rate: 4.0%
Health Insurance: 93.6% have insurance; 87.1% have private insurance; 18.1% have public insurance; 6.4% do not have insurance; 1.8% of children under 18 do not have insurance
Transportation: Commute: 93.1% car, 0.4% public transportation, 0.3% walk, 4.3% work from home; Median travel time to work: 30.9 minutes

SHINGLE SPRINGS (CDP). Covers a land area of 8.209 square miles and a water area of 0.029 square miles. Located at 38.67° N. Lat; 120.94° W. Long. Elevation is 1,421 feet.
History: Shingle Springs was the site of a shingle mill in 1849, and a stopping place for gold prospectors.
Population: 4,432; Growth (since 2000): 67.7%; Density: 539.9 persons per square mile; Race: 88.4% White, 0.3% Black/African American, 1.1% Asian, 2.4% American Indian/Alaska Native, 0.1% Native Hawaiian/Other Pacific Islander, 4.6% Two or more races, 10.6% Hispanic of any race; Average household size: 2.67; Median age: 44.6; Age under 18: 23.3%; Age 65 and over: 14.1%; Males per 100 females: 97.7; Marriage status: 22.7% never married, 67.4% now married, 3.2% separated, 2.5% widowed, 7.4% divorced; Foreign born: 8.1%; Speak English only: 90.9%; With disability: 12.9%; Veterans: 9.9%; Ancestry: 19.0% German, 14.8% Irish, 8.7% English, 7.9% Italian, 6.7% American
Employment: 19.1% management, business, and financial, 10.5% computer, engineering, and science, 5.8% education, legal, community service, arts, and media, 5.8% healthcare practitioners, 19.0% service, 23.0% sales and office, 10.5% natural resources, construction, and maintenance, 6.4% production, transportation, and material moving
Income: Per capita: $34,908; Median household: $78,179; Average household: $99,939; Households with income of $100,000 or more: 35.3%; Poverty rate: 12.5%
Educational Attainment: High school diploma or higher: 93.2%; Bachelor's degree or higher: 25.8%; Graduate/professional degree or higher: 10.6%

School District(s)

Buckeye Union Elementary (KG-08)
2012-13 Enrollment: 5,099 . . . . (530) 677-2261
El Dorado Union High (09-12)
2012-13 Enrollment: 6,873 . . . . (530) 622-5081
Latrobe (KG-08)
2012-13 Enrollment: 150. . . . . (530) 677-0260
Housing: Homeownership rate: 76.7%; Median home value: $400,000; Median year structure built: 1983; Homeowner vacancy rate: 1.2%; Median gross rent: $1,121 per month; Rental vacancy rate: 5.2%
Health Insurance: 82.8% have insurance; 71.9% have private insurance; 22.6% have public insurance; 17.2% do not have insurance; 11.6% of children under 18 do not have insurance
Transportation: Commute: 89.8% car, 2.3% public transportation, 0.0% walk, 7.2% work from home; Median travel time to work: 30.3 minutes

SOMERSET (unincorporated postal area)
ZCTA: 95684
Covers a land area of 145.398 square miles and a water area of 0.060 square miles. Located at 38.59° N. Lat; 120.59° W. Long. Elevation is 2,093 feet.
Population: 3,422; Growth (since 2000): 16.0%; Density: 23.5 persons per square mile; Race: 90.5% White, 0.5% Black/African American, 0.9% Asian, 1.5% American Indian/Alaska Native, 0.1% Native Hawaiian/Other Pacific Islander, 4.5% Two or more races, 7.8% Hispanic of any race; Average household size: 2.38; Median age: 50.8; Age under 18: 16.2%; Age 65 and over: 17.8%; Males per 100 females: 103.8; Marriage status: 15.8% never married, 56.1% now married, 2.2% separated, 8.4% widowed, 19.8% divorced; Foreign born: 4.9%; Speak English only: 99.1%; With disability: 9.1%; Veterans: 15.6%; Ancestry: 31.2% German, 19.6% Irish, 12.3% English, 10.9% Italian, 6.1% European
Employment: 14.3% management, business, and financial, 1.3% computer, engineering, and science, 7.8% education, legal, community service, arts, and media, 0.3% healthcare practitioners, 21.6% service, 24.2% sales and office, 20.5% natural resources, construction, and maintenance, 10.0% production, transportation, and material moving
Income: Per capita: $38,750; Median household: $53,148; Average household: $78,217; Households with income of $100,000 or more: 20.0%; Poverty rate: 9.6%
Educational Attainment: High school diploma or higher: 92.4%; Bachelor's degree or higher: 22.3%; Graduate/professional degree or higher: 5.5%

School District(s)

Indian Diggings Elementary (KG-08)
2012-13 Enrollment: 18. . . . . (530) 620-6546

Pioneer Union Elementary (KG-08)
2012-13 Enrollment: 312. . . . . (530) 620-3556

Housing: Homeownership rate: 83.4%; Median home value: $247,400; Median year structure built: 1981; Homeowner vacancy rate: 3.4%; Median gross rent: $1,116 per month; Rental vacancy rate: 3.2%

Health Insurance: 88.2% have insurance; 65.2% have private insurance; 38.8% have public insurance; 11.8% do not have insurance; 0.0% of children under 18 do not have insurance

Transportation: Commute: 84.3% car, 4.1% public transportation, 5.0% walk, 5.6% work from home; Median travel time to work: 51.6 minutes

SOUTH LAKE TAHOE (city). Covers a land area of 10.161 square miles and a water area of 6.442 square miles. Located at 38.94° N. Lat; 119.98° W. Long. Elevation is 6,237 feet.

History: Named for its location at the south end of Lake Tahoe. Seat of Lake Tahoe Community College.

Population: 21,403; Growth (since 2000): -9.3%; Density: 2,106.3 persons per square mile; Race: 73.5% White, 0.9% Black/African American, 5.5% Asian, 1.1% American Indian/Alaska Native, 0.2% Native Hawaiian/Other Pacific Islander, 3.7% Two or more races, 31.1% Hispanic of any race; Average household size: 2.36; Median age: 35.6; Age under 18: 20.6%; Age 65 and over: 9.8%; Males per 100 females: 113.6; Marriage status: 36.4% never married, 45.5% now married, 2.5% separated, 4.5% widowed, 13.6% divorced; Foreign born: 20.7%; Speak English only: 65.5%; With disability: 12.4%; Veterans: 7.6%; Ancestry: 15.0% Irish, 13.9% German, 9.2% English, 6.9% Italian, 4.0% French

Employment: 8.9% management, business, and financial, 3.7% computer, engineering, and science, 5.4% education, legal, community service, arts, and media, 3.7% healthcare practitioners, 37.2% service, 22.5% sales and office, 9.8% natural resources, construction, and maintenance, 8.9% production, transportation, and material moving

Income: Per capita: $23,224; Median household: $41,004; Average household: $55,395; Households with income of $100,000 or more: 13.6%; Poverty rate: 18.3%

Educational Attainment: High school diploma or higher: 83.5%; Bachelor's degree or higher: 22.3%; Graduate/professional degree or higher: 5.9%

School District(s)

El Dorado County Office of Education (KG-12)
2012-13 Enrollment: 980. . . . . (530) 622-7130
Lake Tahoe Unified (KG-12)
2012-13 Enrollment: 3,793 . . . . (530) 541-2850

Two-year College(s)

Lake Tahoe Community College (Public)
Fall 2013 Enrollment: 2,426 . . . . (530) 541-4660
2013-14 Tuition: In-state $1,221; Out-of-state $6,642

Housing: Homeownership rate: 38.9%; Median home value: $319,800; Median year structure built: 1971; Homeowner vacancy rate: 4.5%; Median gross rent: $890 per month; Rental vacancy rate: 14.6%

Health Insurance: 78.0% have insurance; 57.7% have private insurance; 30.4% have public insurance; 22.0% do not have insurance; 8.1% of children under 18 do not have insurance

Hospitals: Barton Memorial Hospital (75 beds)

Safety: Violent crime rate: 54.6 per 10,000 population; Property crime rate: 275.4 per 10,000 population

Newspapers: Tahoe Daily Tribune (daily circulation 7700)

Transportation: Commute: 78.8% car, 2.9% public transportation, 10.1% walk, 4.0% work from home; Median travel time to work: 14.5 minutes; Amtrak: Bus service available.

Airports: Lake Tahoe (general aviation)

Additional Information Contacts

City of South Lake Tahoe . . . . (530) 542-6000
http://www.cityofslt.us

TAHOMA (CDP). Covers a land area of 2.594 square miles and a water area of <.001 square miles. Located at 39.06° N. Lat; 120.15° W. Long.

Population: 1,191; Growth (since 2000): n/a; Density: 459.2 persons per square mile; Race: 94.8% White, 0.5% Black/African American, 1.2% Asian, 0.8% American Indian/Alaska Native, 0.0% Native Hawaiian/Other Pacific Islander, 1.7% Two or more races, 4.3% Hispanic of any race; Average household size: 2.15; Median age: 43.1; Age under 18: 17.5%; Age 65 and over: 9.2%; Males per 100 females: 124.3

Housing: Homeownership rate: 64.9%; Homeowner vacancy rate: 6.0%; Rental vacancy rate: 12.6%

TWIN BRIDGES (unincorporated postal area)

ZCTA: 95735

Covers a land area of 21.661 square miles and a water area of 0.314 square miles. Located at 38.84° N. Lat; 120.15° W. Long. Elevation is 6,115 feet.

Population: 68; Growth (since 2000): 385.7%; Density: 3.1 persons per square mile; Race: 97.1% White, 0.0% Black/African American, 0.0% Asian, 0.0% American Indian/Alaska Native, 0.0% Native Hawaiian/Other Pacific Islander, 2.9% Two or more races, 4.4% Hispanic of any race; Average household size: 2.00; Median age: 52.5; Age under 18: 13.2%; Age 65 and over: 16.2%; Males per 100 females: 142.9

Housing: Homeownership rate: 82.4%; Homeowner vacancy rate: 3.4%; Rental vacancy rate: 0.0%

Fresno County

Located in central California, in the San Joaquin Valley, stretching from the Diablo Range in the west to the crest of the Sierra Nevada in the east; drained by the Kings, San Joaquin, and Fresno Rivers; includes parts of Sierra and Sequoia National Forests. Covers a land area of 5,957.991 square miles, a water area of 53.211 square miles, and is located in the Pacific Time Zone at 36.76° N. Lat., 119.66° W. Long. The county was founded in 1856. County seat is Fresno.

Fresno County is part of the Fresno, CA Metropolitan Statistical Area. The entire metro area includes: Fresno County, CA

Weather Station: Auberry 2 NW — Elevation: 2,089 feet

	Jan	Feb	Mar	Apr	May	Jun	Jul	Aug	Sep	Oct	Nov	Dec
High	55	58	62	69	79	88	95	94	87	76	63	55
Low	37	39	42	45	53	60	68	67	62	53	42	37
Precip	5.3	4.7	4.3	2.0	1.0	0.3	0.1	0.1	0.4	1.4	2.5	3.9
Snow	0.4	0.3	0.7	0.1	0.0	0.0	0.0	0.0	0.0	0.0	tr	0.4

High and Low temperatures in degrees Fahrenheit; Precipitation and Snow in inches

Weather Station: Balch Power House — Elevation: 1,720 feet

	Jan	Feb	Mar	Apr	May	Jun	Jul	Aug	Sep	Oct	Nov	Dec
High	53	58	64	70	78	86	95	95	89	78	61	52
Low	38	40	42	46	53	60	68	68	62	53	44	38
Precip	6.1	5.7	5.0	2.6	1.3	0.5	0.2	0.0	0.7	1.6	3.0	4.4
Snow	0.0	0.0	0.0	0.0	0.0	0.0	0.0	0.0	0.0	0.0	0.0	0.0

High and Low temperatures in degrees Fahrenheit; Precipitation and Snow in inches

Weather Station: Coalinga — Elevation: 669 feet

	Jan	Feb	Mar	Apr	May	Jun	Jul	Aug	Sep	Oct	Nov	Dec
High	59	65	71	78	87	94	100	99	93	83	68	59
Low	37	41	44	47	54	61	67	65	60	51	42	36
Precip	1.9	1.7	1.5	0.5	0.3	0.1	0.0	0.0	0.2	0.4	0.5	1.1
Snow	0.0	tr	0.0	0.0	0.0	0.0	0.0	0.0	0.0	0.0	0.0	0.0

High and Low temperatures in degrees Fahrenheit; Precipitation and Snow in inches

Weather Station: Fresno Field — Elevation: 282 feet

	Jan	Feb	Mar	Apr	May	Jun	Jul	Aug	Sep	Oct	Nov	Dec
High	55	62	68	75	84	92	99	97	91	80	65	55
Low	39	42	46	49	56	62	68	66	61	53	44	38
Precip	2.3	2.0	2.1	0.9	0.4	0.2	0.0	0.0	0.2	0.6	1.0	1.6
Snow	na	na	na	na	na	na	na	na	na	na	na	na

High and Low temperatures in degrees Fahrenheit; Precipitation and Snow in inches

Weather Station: Friant Government Camp — Elevation: 410 feet

	Jan	Feb	Mar	Apr	May	Jun	Jul	Aug	Sep	Oct	Nov	Dec
High	56	62	67	75	85	93	100	99	92	82	67	56
Low	38	41	42	44	50	56	61	60	56	50	42	37
Precip	3.1	2.7	2.7	1.1	0.5	0.2	0.0	0.0	0.2	0.8	1.4	2.1
Snow	0.0	0.0	0.0	0.0	0.0	0.0	0.0	0.0	0.0	0.0	0.0	0.0

High and Low temperatures in degrees Fahrenheit; Precipitation and Snow in inches

Weather Station: Huntington Lake — Elevation: 7,020 feet

	Jan	Feb	Mar	Apr	May	Jun	Jul	Aug	Sep	Oct	Nov	Dec
High	45	45	47	51	58	66	74	74	68	59	49	45
Low	26	25	27	30	36	42	49	49	44	37	30	26
Precip	8.5	8.1	6.8	3.6	2.2	0.6	0.5	0.2	0.9	2.4	5.1	6.6
Snow	na	na	na	na	na	na	na	na	na	na	na	na

High and Low temperatures in degrees Fahrenheit; Precipitation and Snow in inches

Population: 930,450; Growth (since 2000): 16.4%; Density: 156.2 persons per square mile; Race: 55.4% White, 5.3% Black/African American, 9.6%

Asian, 1.7% American Indian/Alaska Native, 0.2% Native Hawaiian/Other Pacific Islander, 4.5% two or more races, 50.3% Hispanic of any race; Average household size: 3.15; Median age: 30.6; Age under 18: 29.8%; Age 65 and over: 10.0%; Males per 100 females: 99.8; Marriage status: 37.1% never married, 48.2% now married, 2.8% separated, 5.2% widowed, 9.5% divorced; Foreign born: 21.9%; Speak English only: 56.3%; With disability: 11.6%; Veterans: 6.5%; Ancestry: 8.3% German, 5.4% Irish, 4.7% English, 3.2% Italian, 1.9% American

Religion: Six largest groups: 31.0% Catholicism, 4.2% Pentecostal, 3.9% Non-denominational Protestant, 3.5% Baptist, 2.3% Latter-day Saints, 1.0% Buddhism

Economy: Unemployment rate: 10.2%; Leading industries: 15.4% retail trade; 14.0% health care and social assistance; 9.6% professional, scientific, and technical services; Farms: 5,683 totaling 1,721,202 acres; Company size: 10 employ 1,000 or more persons, 23 employ 500 to 999 persons, 265 employ 100 to 499 persons, 15,496 employ less than 100 persons; Business ownership: 17,261 women-owned, 2,289 Black-owned, 12,553 Hispanic-owned, 6,650 Asian-owned

Employment: 10.7% management, business, and financial, 2.7% computer, engineering, and science, 10.0% education, legal, community service, arts, and media, 5.2% healthcare practitioners, 19.0% service, 23.8% sales and office, 15.8% natural resources, construction, and maintenance, 13.0% production, transportation, and material moving

Income: Per capita: $20,208; Median household: $45,563; Average household: $63,079; Households with income of $100,000 or more: 17.9%; Poverty rate: 26.0%

Educational Attainment: High school diploma or higher: 73.1%; Bachelor's degree or higher: 19.6%; Graduate/professional degree or higher: 6.5%

Housing: Homeownership rate: 54.8%; Median home value: $195,400; Median year structure built: 1978; Homeowner vacancy rate: 2.4%; Median gross rent: $875 per month; Rental vacancy rate: 7.0%

Vital Statistics: Birth rate: 169.5 per 10,000 population; Death rate: 69.4 per 10,000 population; Age-adjusted cancer mortality rate: 156.2 deaths per 100,000 population

Health Insurance: 80.4% have insurance; 48.9% have private insurance; 40.2% have public insurance; 19.6% do not have insurance; 6.8% of children under 18 do not have insurance

Health Care: Physicians: 19.0 per 10,000 population; Hospital beds: 19.1 per 10,000 population; Hospital admissions: 1,063.9 per 10,000 population

Air Quality Index: 17.3% good, 53.4% moderate, 25.2% unhealthy for sensitive individuals, 4.1% unhealthy (percent of days)

Transportation: Commute: 89.1% car, 1.2% public transportation, 2.1% walk, 4.0% work from home; Median travel time to work: 22.1 minutes

Presidential Election: 48.1% Obama, 50.1% Romney (2012)

National and State Parks: Kings Canyon National Park; Sierra National Forest

Additional Information Contacts

Fresno Government . . . . (559) 488-3529
http://www.co.fresno.ca.us

Fresno County Communities

AUBERRY (CDP). Covers a land area of 19.144 square miles and a water area of 0.061 square miles. Located at 37.08° N. Lat; 119.50° W. Long. Elevation is 2,018 feet.

Population: 2,369; Growth (since 2000): 15.4%; Density: 123.7 persons per square mile; Race: 86.4% White, 0.4% Black/African American, 1.0% Asian, 4.4% American Indian/Alaska Native, 0.1% Native Hawaiian/Other Pacific Islander, 4.7% Two or more races, 13.0% Hispanic of any race; Average household size: 2.63; Median age: 46.0; Age under 18: 22.4%; Age 65 and over: 20.3%; Males per 100 females: 98.4

School District(s)

Pine Ridge Elementary (KG-08)
2012-13 Enrollment: 95. . . . . (559) 841-2444
Sierra Unified (KG-12)
2012-13 Enrollment: 1,402 . . . . (559) 855-3662

Housing: Homeownership rate: 76.1%; Homeowner vacancy rate: 2.7%; Rental vacancy rate: 3.7%

BIG CREEK (CDP). Covers a land area of 0.460 square miles and a water area of 0 square miles. Located at 37.20° N. Lat; 119.25° W. Long. Elevation is 4,984 feet.

Population: 175; Growth (since 2000): n/a; Density: 380.4 persons per square mile; Race: 90.3% White, 0.6% Black/African American, 2.9% Asian, 0.6% American Indian/Alaska Native, 0.0% Native Hawaiian/Other Pacific Islander, 4.0% Two or more races, 15.4% Hispanic of any race; Average household size: 2.78; Median age: 37.6; Age under 18: 34.3%; Age 65 and over: 9.1%; Males per 100 females: 86.2

School District(s)

Big Creek Elementary (KG-08)
2012-13 Enrollment: 52. . . . . (559) 893-3314

Housing: Homeownership rate: 34.9%; Homeowner vacancy rate: 0.0%; Rental vacancy rate: 31.1%

BIOLA (CDP). Covers a land area of 0.647 square miles and a water area of 0 square miles. Located at 36.80° N. Lat; 120.02° W. Long. Elevation is 253 feet.

Population: 1,623; Growth (since 2000): 56.5%; Density: 2,508.4 persons per square mile; Race: 31.4% White, 0.4% Black/African American, 19.5% Asian, 2.6% American Indian/Alaska Native, 0.1% Native Hawaiian/Other Pacific Islander, 3.3% Two or more races, 73.7% Hispanic of any race; Average household size: 4.75; Median age: 23.8; Age under 18: 38.3%; Age 65 and over: 6.5%; Males per 100 females: 102.4

Housing: Homeownership rate: 63.2%; Homeowner vacancy rate: 0.9%; Rental vacancy rate: 3.1%

BOWLES (CDP). Covers a land area of 0.381 square miles and a water area of 0 square miles. Located at 36.61° N. Lat; 119.75° W. Long. Elevation is 279 feet.

Population: 166; Growth (since 2000): -8.8%; Density: 436.0 persons per square mile; Race: 65.1% White, 3.6% Black/African American, 0.6% Asian, 0.6% American Indian/Alaska Native, 0.0% Native Hawaiian/Other Pacific Islander, 4.2% Two or more races, 42.8% Hispanic of any race; Average household size: 3.29; Median age: 59.0; Age under 18: 15.7%; Age 65 and over: 37.3%; Males per 100 females: 90.8

Housing: Homeownership rate: 64.7%; Homeowner vacancy rate: 4.3%; Rental vacancy rate: 14.3%

CALWA (CDP). Aka formerly Calwa City.

Note: Statistics that would complete this profile are not available because the CDP was created after the 2010 Census was released.

CANTUA CREEK (CDP). Covers a land area of 3.797 square miles and a water area of 0 square miles. Located at 36.50° N. Lat; 120.32° W. Long. Elevation is 295 feet.

Population: 466; Growth (since 2000): -28.9%; Density: 122.7 persons per square mile; Race: 52.4% White, 1.1% Black/African American, 0.2% Asian, 0.6% American Indian/Alaska Native, 0.0% Native Hawaiian/Other Pacific Islander, 3.0% Two or more races, 98.9% Hispanic of any race; Average household size: 4.08; Median age: 28.0; Age under 18: 30.9%; Age 65 and over: 7.9%; Males per 100 females: 130.7

School District(s)

Golden Plains Unified (KG-12)
2012-13 Enrollment: 1,865 . . . . (559) 693-1115

Housing: Homeownership rate: 42.5%; Homeowner vacancy rate: 0.0%; Rental vacancy rate: 8.5%

CARUTHERS (CDP). Covers a land area of 2.023 square miles and a water area of 0 square miles. Located at 36.54° N. Lat; 119.85° W. Long. Elevation is 246 feet.

Population: 2,497; Growth (since 2000): 18.7%; Density: 1,234.6 persons per square mile; Race: 49.0% White, 0.6% Black/African American, 8.9% Asian, 1.5% American Indian/Alaska Native, 0.0% Native Hawaiian/Other Pacific Islander, 3.8% Two or more races, 63.7% Hispanic of any race; Average household size: 3.89; Median age: 29.7; Age under 18: 31.8%; Age 65 and over: 9.7%; Males per 100 females: 101.0

School District(s)

Alvina Elementary (KG-08)
2012-13 Enrollment: 212. . . . . (559) 864-9411
Caruthers Unified (KG-12)
2012-13 Enrollment: 1,347 . . . . (559) 864-6500

Housing: Homeownership rate: 66.7%; Homeowner vacancy rate: 1.6%; Rental vacancy rate: 3.2%

CENTERVILLE (CDP). Covers a land area of 8.138 square miles and a water area of 0 square miles. Located at 36.74° N. Lat; 119.50° W. Long. Elevation is 394 feet.

Population: 392; Growth (since 2000): n/a; Density: 48.2 persons per square mile; Race: 81.9% White, 0.3% Black/African American, 5.1%

Asian, 2.3% American Indian/Alaska Native, 0.0% Native Hawaiian/Other Pacific Islander, 2.0% Two or more races, 25.3% Hispanic of any race; Average household size: 2.55; Median age: 46.6; Age under 18: 19.9%; Age 65 and over: 18.1%; Males per 100 females: 111.9
Housing: Homeownership rate: 61.7%; Homeowner vacancy rate: 2.0%; Rental vacancy rate: 1.7%

CLOVIS (city). Covers a land area of 23.278 square miles and a water area of 0 square miles. Located at 36.83° N. Lat; 119.69° W. Long. Elevation is 361 feet.
History: Clovis developed as a trading center for a wine-producing, lumbering, and dairying area.
Population: 95,631; Growth (since 2000): 39.7%; Density: 4,108.2 persons per square mile; Race: 70.9% White, 2.7% Black/African American, 10.7% Asian, 1.4% American Indian/Alaska Native, 0.2% Native Hawaiian/Other Pacific Islander, 4.8% Two or more races, 25.6% Hispanic of any race; Average household size: 2.85; Median age: 34.1; Age under 18: 28.1%; Age 65 and over: 10.6%; Males per 100 females: 93.2; Marriage status: 31.4% never married, 52.5% now married, 2.4% separated, 5.2% widowed, 10.9% divorced; Foreign born: 11.2%; Speak English only: 76.9%; With disability: 10.7%; Veterans: 8.9%; Ancestry: 14.9% German, 10.3% Irish, 9.4% English, 6.1% Italian, 2.6% American
Employment: 13.2% management, business, and financial, 4.9% computer, engineering, and science, 13.3% education, legal, community service, arts, and media, 8.3% healthcare practitioners, 17.7% service, 27.3% sales and office, 7.9% natural resources, construction, and maintenance, 7.5% production, transportation, and material moving
Income: Per capita: $27,906; Median household: $65,260; Average household: $80,267; Households with income of $100,000 or more: 27.9%; Poverty rate: 13.2%
Educational Attainment: High school diploma or higher: 89.0%; Bachelor's degree or higher: 30.2%; Graduate/professional degree or higher: 10.3%

School District(s)

Clovis Unified (KG-12)
2012-13 Enrollment: 39,894 . . . . (559) 327-9100
Sanger Unified (KG-12)
2012-13 Enrollment: 10,916 . . . . (559) 524-6521

Four-year College(s)

ITT Technical Institute-Clovis (Private, For-profit)
Fall 2013 Enrollment: 439 . . . . (559) 325-5400
2013-14 Tuition: In-state $18,048; Out-of-state $18,048
San Joaquin College of Law (Private, Not-for-profit)
Fall 2013 Enrollment: 194 . . . . (559) 323-2100

Two-year College(s)

Institute of Technology Inc (Private, For-profit)
Fall 2013 Enrollment: 1,989 . . . . (559) 297-4500
Kaplan College-Fresno (Private, For-profit)
Fall 2013 Enrollment: 312 . . . . (559) 325-5100

Vocational/Technical School(s)

Clovis Adult Education (Public)
Fall 2013 Enrollment: 608 . . . . (559) 327-2800
2013-14 Tuition: $10,500
Milan Institute-Clovis (Private, For-profit)
Fall 2013 Enrollment: 488 . . . . (559) 323-2800
2013-14 Tuition: $16,789

Housing: Homeownership rate: 62.2%; Median home value: $247,000; Median year structure built: 1989; Homeowner vacancy rate: 2.3%; Median gross rent: $1,039 per month; Rental vacancy rate: 6.4%
Health Insurance: 86.9% have insurance; 70.6% have private insurance; 26.8% have public insurance; 13.1% do not have insurance; 5.6% of children under 18 do not have insurance
Hospitals: Clovis Community Medical Center (109 beds)
Safety: Violent crime rate: 18.2 per 10,000 population; Property crime rate: 342.2 per 10,000 population
Transportation: Commute: 93.6% car, 0.3% public transportation, 1.3% walk, 3.1% work from home; Median travel time to work: 20.5 minutes
Additional Information Contacts
City of Clovis . . . . (559) 324-2000
http://www.ci.clovis.ca.us

COALINGA (city). Covers a land area of 6.119 square miles and a water area of 0.031 square miles. Located at 36.13° N. Lat; 120.34° W. Long. Elevation is 673 feet.
History: R.C. Baker Memorial Museum. Incorporated 1906.
Population: 13,380; Growth (since 2000): 14.7%; Density: 2,186.7 persons per square mile; Race: 57.8% White, 4.1% Black/African American, 3.0% Asian, 1.3% American Indian/Alaska Native, 0.3% Native Hawaiian/Other Pacific Islander, 4.1% Two or more races, 53.5% Hispanic of any race; Average household size: 3.02; Median age: 31.9; Age under 18: 28.1%; Age 65 and over: 7.9%; Males per 100 females: 123.1; Marriage status: 42.6% never married, 43.3% now married, 3.2% separated, 3.7% widowed, 10.3% divorced; Foreign born: 18.2%; Speak English only: 59.8%; With disability: 10.1%; Veterans: 6.4%; Ancestry: 7.8% Irish, 7.4% German, 4.2% American, 3.5% English, 1.7% Italian
Employment: 10.6% management, business, and financial, 1.5% computer, engineering, and science, 8.5% education, legal, community service, arts, and media, 7.6% healthcare practitioners, 17.5% service, 21.8% sales and office, 18.6% natural resources, construction, and maintenance, 13.9% production, transportation, and material moving
Income: Per capita: $18,737; Median household: $46,500; Average household: $63,244; Households with income of $100,000 or more: 19.7%; Poverty rate: 22.8%
Educational Attainment: High school diploma or higher: 73.3%; Bachelor's degree or higher: 12.9%; Graduate/professional degree or higher: 5.6%

School District(s)

Coalinga-Huron Joint Unified (KG-12)
2012-13 Enrollment: 4,322 . . . . (559) 935-7500

Two-year College(s)

West Hills College-Coalinga (Public)
Fall 2013 Enrollment: 3,055 . . . . (559) 934-2000
2013-14 Tuition: In-state $1,380; Out-of-state $8,490

Housing: Homeownership rate: 51.2%; Median home value: $149,600; Median year structure built: 1978; Homeowner vacancy rate: 3.8%; Median gross rent: $788 per month; Rental vacancy rate: 8.4%
Health Insurance: 85.1% have insurance; 56.7% have private insurance; 34.8% have public insurance; 14.9% do not have insurance; 7.5% of children under 18 do not have insurance
Hospitals: Coalinga Regional Medical Center (78 beds)
Safety: Violent crime rate: 79.9 per 10,000 population; Property crime rate: 295.8 per 10,000 population
Transportation: Commute: 90.9% car, 0.3% public transportation, 3.6% walk, 3.0% work from home; Median travel time to work: 19.1 minutes
Airports: New Coalinga Municipal (general aviation)
Additional Information Contacts
City of Coalinga . . . . (559) 935-1533
http://www.coalinga.com

DEL REY (CDP). Covers a land area of 1.217 square miles and a water area of 0 square miles. Located at 36.66° N. Lat; 119.60° W. Long. Elevation is 344 feet.
Population: 1,639; Growth (since 2000): 72.5%; Density: 1,346.6 persons per square mile; Race: 45.1% White, 0.4% Black/African American, 2.1% Asian, 0.7% American Indian/Alaska Native, 0.0% Native Hawaiian/Other Pacific Islander, 2.0% Two or more races, 93.6% Hispanic of any race; Average household size: 4.31; Median age: 27.3; Age under 18: 35.6%; Age 65 and over: 8.1%; Males per 100 females: 100.9

School District(s)

Sanger Unified (KG-12)
2012-13 Enrollment: 10,916 . . . . (559) 524-6521

Housing: Homeownership rate: 54.9%; Homeowner vacancy rate: 0.0%; Rental vacancy rate: 4.4%

DUNLAP (unincorporated postal area)

ZCTA: 93621

Covers a land area of 65.984 square miles and a water area of 3.940 square miles. Located at 36.79° N. Lat; 119.14° W. Long. Elevation is 1,919 feet.
Population: 464; Growth (since 2000): -5.3%; Density: 7.0 persons per square mile; Race: 75.4% White, 1.1% Black/African American, 1.3% Asian, 7.3% American Indian/Alaska Native, 0.0% Native Hawaiian/Other Pacific Islander, 6.3% Two or more races, 15.7% Hispanic of any race; Average household size: 2.62; Median age: 44.0; Age under 18: 20.9%; Age 65 and over: 18.8%; Males per 100 females: 92.5

School District(s)

Kings Canyon Joint Unified (KG-12)
2012-13 Enrollment: 9,954 . . . . (559) 305-7005

Housing: Homeownership rate: 79.1%; Homeowner vacancy rate: 0.7%; Rental vacancy rate: 9.8%

EASTON (CDP). Covers a land area of 3.011 square miles and a water area of 0 square miles. Located at 36.65° N. Lat; 119.79° W. Long. Elevation is 276 feet.

Population: 2,083; Growth (since 2000): 6.0%; Density: 691.7 persons per square mile; Race: 59.9% White, 0.6% Black/African American, 3.3% Asian, 2.8% American Indian/Alaska Native, 0.0% Native Hawaiian/Other Pacific Islander, 4.9% Two or more races, 62.8% Hispanic of any race; Average household size: 3.31; Median age: 35.1; Age under 18: 27.2%; Age 65 and over: 13.4%; Males per 100 females: 104.0

Housing: Homeownership rate: 67.3%; Homeowner vacancy rate: 1.2%; Rental vacancy rate: 5.5%

FIREBAUGH (city). Covers a land area of 3.462 square miles and a water area of 0.057 square miles. Located at 36.85° N. Lat; 120.45° W. Long. Elevation is 151 feet.

Population: 7,549; Growth (since 2000): 31.4%; Density: 2,180.4 persons per square mile; Race: 62.5% White, 0.9% Black/African American, 0.5% Asian, 1.5% American Indian/Alaska Native, 0.0% Native Hawaiian/Other Pacific Islander, 3.1% Two or more races, 91.2% Hispanic of any race; Average household size: 3.93; Median age: 26.4; Age under 18: 36.0%; Age 65 and over: 6.5%; Males per 100 females: 106.3; Marriage status: 45.2% never married, 44.8% now married, 2.0% separated, 3.3% widowed, 6.7% divorced; Foreign born: 39.8%; Speak English only: 14.7%; With disability: 8.6%; Veterans: 1.2%; Ancestry: 3.6% Arab, 1.2% German, 1.1% Italian, 0.8% Irish, 0.8% English

Employment: 9.4% management, business, and financial, 1.3% computer, engineering, and science, 6.1% education, legal, community service, arts, and media, 0.0% healthcare practitioners, 14.0% service, 9.1% sales and office, 39.8% natural resources, construction, and maintenance, 20.2% production, transportation, and material moving

Income: Per capita: $12,370; Median household: $35,000; Average household: $44,716; Households with income of $100,000 or more: 9.4%; Poverty rate: 35.2%

Educational Attainment: High school diploma or higher: 40.8%; Bachelor's degree or higher: 5.5%; Graduate/professional degree or higher: 0.6%

School District(s)

Firebaugh-Las Deltas Joint Unified (KG-12)
2012-13 Enrollment: 2,291 . . . . (559) 659-1476

Housing: Homeownership rate: 52.5%; Median home value: $117,200; Median year structure built: 1982; Homeowner vacancy rate: 1.6%; Median gross rent: $669 per month; Rental vacancy rate: 3.6%

Health Insurance: 71.9% have insurance; 29.7% have private insurance; 50.6% have public insurance; 28.1% do not have insurance; 9.2% of children under 18 do not have insurance

Safety: Violent crime rate: 86.8 per 10,000 population; Property crime rate: 60.8 per 10,000 population

Transportation: Commute: 94.6% car, 0.0% public transportation, 0.4% walk, 1.1% work from home; Median travel time to work: 21.8 minutes

Additional Information Contacts

City of Firebaugh . . . . (559) 659-2043
http://www.ci.firebaugh.ca.us

FIVE POINTS (unincorporated postal area)

ZCTA: 93624

Covers a land area of 112.063 square miles and a water area of 0.142 square miles. Located at 36.38° N. Lat; 120.12° W. Long. Elevation is 223 feet.

Population: 1,134; Growth (since 2000): -38.6%; Density: 10.1 persons per square mile; Race: 36.7% White, 0.6% Black/African American, 0.0% Asian, 0.4% American Indian/Alaska Native, 0.0% Native Hawaiian/Other Pacific Islander, 1.8% Two or more races, 96.7% Hispanic of any race; Average household size: 4.25; Median age: 24.8; Age under 18: 39.9%; Age 65 and over: 2.1%; Males per 100 females: 114.4

School District(s)

Westside Elementary (KG-12)
2012-13 Enrollment: 609 . . . . (559) 884-2494

Housing: Homeownership rate: 14.6%; Homeowner vacancy rate: 0.0%; Rental vacancy rate: 7.2%

FORT WASHINGTON (CDP). Covers a land area of 0.124 square miles and a water area of 0 square miles. Located at 36.88° N. Lat; 119.76° W. Long.

Population: 233; Growth (since 2000): n/a; Density: 1,879.0 persons per square mile; Race: 89.7% White, 1.7% Black/African American, 3.0% Asian, 0.4% American Indian/Alaska Native, 0.0% Native Hawaiian/Other Pacific Islander, 4.7% Two or more races, 11.2% Hispanic of any race; Average household size: 2.40; Median age: 57.8; Age under 18: 14.2%; Age 65 and over: 36.9%; Males per 100 females: 104.4

Housing: Homeownership rate: 90.7%; Homeowner vacancy rate: 0.0%; Rental vacancy rate: 0.0%

FOWLER (city). Covers a land area of 2.531 square miles and a water area of 0 square miles. Located at 36.62° N. Lat; 119.67° W. Long. Elevation is 308 feet.

History: Incorporated 1908.

Population: 5,570; Growth (since 2000): 40.0%; Density: 2,200.3 persons per square mile; Race: 47.3% White, 1.9% Black/African American, 11.0% Asian, 2.4% American Indian/Alaska Native, 0.1% Native Hawaiian/Other Pacific Islander, 5.0% Two or more races, 66.2% Hispanic of any race; Average household size: 3.21; Median age: 31.6; Age under 18: 29.8%; Age 65 and over: 10.0%; Males per 100 females: 99.5; Marriage status: 33.6% never married, 49.5% now married, 3.6% separated, 7.9% widowed, 9.1% divorced; Foreign born: 20.5%; Speak English only: 51.3%; With disability: 9.6%; Veterans: 4.7%; Ancestry: 5.7% Irish, 5.1% German, 3.4% Italian, 2.9% English, 1.7% Armenian

Employment: 13.1% management, business, and financial, 3.4% computer, engineering, and science, 5.8% education, legal, community service, arts, and media, 2.3% healthcare practitioners, 25.1% service, 25.2% sales and office, 12.7% natural resources, construction, and maintenance, 12.4% production, transportation, and material moving

Income: Per capita: $20,326; Median household: $49,663; Average household: $64,137; Households with income of $100,000 or more: 19.0%; Poverty rate: 23.2%

Educational Attainment: High school diploma or higher: 66.3%; Bachelor's degree or higher: 14.5%; Graduate/professional degree or higher: 3.9%

School District(s)

Fowler Unified (KG-12)
2012-13 Enrollment: 2,393 . . . . (559) 834-6080

Housing: Homeownership rate: 64.0%; Median home value: $211,900; Median year structure built: 1977; Homeowner vacancy rate: 2.6%; Median gross rent: $845 per month; Rental vacancy rate: 5.2%

Health Insurance: 83.9% have insurance; 56.8% have private insurance; 31.5% have public insurance; 16.1% do not have insurance; 3.1% of children under 18 do not have insurance

Safety: Violent crime rate: 61.3 per 10,000 population; Property crime rate: 274.9 per 10,000 population

Transportation: Commute: 86.9% car, 0.0% public transportation, 6.6% walk, 3.7% work from home; Median travel time to work: 18.7 minutes

Additional Information Contacts

City of Fowler . . . . (559) 834-3113
http://www.fowlercity.org

FRESNO (city). County seat. Covers a land area of 111.957 square miles and a water area of 0.351 square miles. Located at 36.78° N. Lat; 119.79° W. Long. Elevation is 308 feet.

History: A.J. Manssen, a Hollander, settled on the site of Fresno in the 1860's, but it was in 1872 when the Central Pacific Railroad built a station here that a town was laid out and called Fresno, (Spanish, meaning "ash tree"). Having the railroad resulted in the new town of Fresno being named the county seat. Fresno became a raisin-growing region in the 1870's, with the Raisin Growers Association cooperative organized in 1898 to protect and manage the industry. Fresno received a city charter in 1900.

Population: 494,665; Growth (since 2000): 15.7%; Density: 4,418.4 persons per square mile; Race: 49.6% White, 8.3% Black/African American, 12.6% Asian, 1.7% American Indian/Alaska Native, 0.2% Native Hawaiian/Other Pacific Islander, 5.0% Two or more races, 46.9% Hispanic of any race; Average household size: 3.07; Median age: 29.3; Age under 18: 30.1%; Age 65 and over: 9.3%; Males per 100 females: 96.7; Marriage status: 39.7% never married, 44.7% now married, 3.0% separated, 5.1% widowed, 10.5% divorced; Foreign born: 20.9%; Speak English only: 58.3%; With disability: 12.3%; Veterans: 6.2%; Ancestry: 7.8% German, 5.1% Irish, 4.3% English, 3.2% Italian, 1.5% American

Employment: 10.6% management, business, and financial, 2.7% computer, engineering, and science, 10.3% education, legal, community service, arts, and media, 5.7% healthcare practitioners, 20.9% service, 25.7% sales and office, 11.4% natural resources, construction, and maintenance, 12.7% production, transportation, and material moving

Income: Per capita: $19,455; Median household: $42,015; Average household: $58,850; Households with income of $100,000 or more: 15.7%; Poverty rate: 28.9%

Educational Attainment: High school diploma or higher: 75.0%; Bachelor's degree or higher: 20.3%; Graduate/professional degree or higher: 6.5%

School District(s)

Central Unified (KG-12)
2012-13 Enrollment: 15,262 . . . . (559) 274-4700
Clovis Unified (KG-12)
2012-13 Enrollment: 39,894 . . . . (559) 327-9100
Fowler Unified (KG-12)
2012-13 Enrollment: 2,393 . . . . (559) 834-6080
Fresno County Office of Education (KG-12)
2012-13 Enrollment: 2,094 . . . . (559) 265-3000
Fresno Rop
2012-13 Enrollment: n/a . . . . (559) 497-3860
Fresno Unified (KG-12)
2012-13 Enrollment: 73,689 . . . . (559) 457-3000
Monroe Elementary (KG-08)
2012-13 Enrollment: 208. . . . . (559) 834-2895
Orange Center (KG-12)
2012-13 Enrollment: 966. . . . . (559) 237-0437
Pacific Union Elementary (KG-08)
2012-13 Enrollment: 374. . . . . (559) 834-2533
Raisin City Elementary (KG-12)
2012-13 Enrollment: 580. . . . . (559) 233-0128
Sanger Unified (KG-12)
2012-13 Enrollment: 10,916 . . . . (559) 524-6521
Washington Colony Elementary (KG-08)
2012-13 Enrollment: 424. . . . . (559) 233-0706
Washington Unified (KG-12)
2012-13 Enrollment: 3,103 . . . . (559) 495-5600
West Park Elementary (KG-12)
2012-13 Enrollment: 672. . . . . (559) 233-6501
Westside Elementary (KG-12)
2012-13 Enrollment: 609. . . . . (559) 884-2494

Four-year College(s)

California Christian College (Private, Not-for-profit, Free Will Baptist Church)
Fall 2013 Enrollment: 30 . . . . (559) 251-4215
2013-14 Tuition: In-state $8,275; Out-of-state $8,275
California State University-Fresno (Public)
Fall 2013 Enrollment: 23,060 . . . . (559) 278-4240
2013-14 Tuition: In-state $6,287; Out-of-state $17,447
Fresno Pacific University (Private, Not-for-profit, Mennonite Brethren Church)
Fall 2013 Enrollment: 3,393 . . . . (559) 453-2000
2013-14 Tuition: In-state $25,716; Out-of-state $25,716
University of Phoenix-Central Valley Campus (Private, For-profit)
Fall 2013 Enrollment: 2,725 . . . . (866) 766-0766
2013-14 Tuition: In-state $11,309; Out-of-state $11,309

Two-year College(s)

Fresno City College (Public)
Fall 2013 Enrollment: 21,344 . . . . (559) 442-4600
2013-14 Tuition: In-state $1,142; Out-of-state $6,782
Heald College-Fresno (Private, For-profit)
Fall 2013 Enrollment: 1,791 . . . . (559) 438-4222
2013-14 Tuition: In-state $13,620; Out-of-state $13,620
San Joaquin Valley College-Fresno (Private, For-profit)
Fall 2013 Enrollment: 686 . . . . (559) 448-8282
2013-14 Tuition: In-state $16,023; Out-of-state $16,023
San Joaquin Valley College-Fresno Aviation (Private, For-profit)
Fall 2013 Enrollment: 87 . . . . (559) 453-0123
2013-14 Tuition: In-state $13,620; Out-of-state $13,620
Sierra Valley College of Court Reporting (Private, For-profit)
Fall 2013 Enrollment: 137 . . . . (559) 222-0947
2013-14 Tuition: In-state $12,000; Out-of-state $12,000

Vocational/Technical School(s)

Lyles Fresno College of Beauty (Private, For-profit)
Fall 2013 Enrollment: 56 . . . . (559) 431-6060
2013-14 Tuition: $16,084
Manchester Beauty College (Private, For-profit)
Fall 2013 Enrollment: 67 . . . . (559) 224-4242
2013-14 Tuition: $10,000
Paul Mitchell the School-Fresno (Private, For-profit)
Fall 2013 Enrollment: 248 . . . . (559) 224-2700
2013-14 Tuition: $15,000
UEI College-Fresno (Private, For-profit)
Fall 2013 Enrollment: 1,014 . . . . (949) 272-7200
2013-14 Tuition: $18,300

Housing: Homeownership rate: 49.1%; Median home value: $180,100; Median year structure built: 1977; Homeowner vacancy rate: 2.6%; Median gross rent: $884 per month; Rental vacancy rate: 7.6%

Health Insurance: 80.4% have insurance; 47.0% have private insurance; 41.5% have public insurance; 19.6% do not have insurance; 6.9% of children under 18 do not have insurance

Hospitals: Community Regional Medical Center (452 beds); Fresno Heart & Surgical Hospital (66 beds); Fresno Surgical Hospital; Fresno VA Medical Center - VA Central California (157 beds); Kaiser Foundation Hospital - Fresno (169 beds); Saint Agnes Medical Center (330 beds)

Safety: Violent crime rate: 50.2 per 10,000 population; Property crime rate: 443.8 per 10,000 population

Newspapers: Fresno Bee (daily circulation 149000)

Transportation: Commute: 89.3% car, 2.0% public transportation, 1.8% walk, 3.7% work from home; Median travel time to work: 21.7 minutes; Amtrak: Train service available.

Airports: Fresno Yosemite International (primary service/small hub)

Additional Information Contacts

City of Fresno . . . . (559) 621-7770
http://www.fresno.gov/default.htm

FRIANT (CDP). Covers a land area of 1.275 square miles and a water area of 0.050 square miles. Located at 36.98° N. Lat; 119.71° W. Long. Elevation is 344 feet.

Population: 509; Growth (since 2000): -1.9%; Density: 399.1 persons per square mile; Race: 85.1% White, 0.8% Black/African American, 1.4% Asian, 2.8% American Indian/Alaska Native, 0.0% Native Hawaiian/Other Pacific Islander, 7.9% Two or more races, 12.4% Hispanic of any race; Average household size: 2.27; Median age: 51.8; Age under 18: 16.3%; Age 65 and over: 27.5%; Males per 100 females: 111.2

Housing: Homeownership rate: 76.3%; Homeowner vacancy rate: 5.5%; Rental vacancy rate: 8.6%

HELM (unincorporated postal area)

ZCTA: 93627

Covers a land area of 35.658 square miles and a water area of 0 square miles. Located at 36.47° N. Lat; 120.06° W. Long. Elevation is 187 feet.

Population: 123; Growth (since 2000): -16.9%; Density: 3.4 persons per square mile; Race: 52.0% White, 5.7% Black/African American, 9.8% Asian, 0.0% American Indian/Alaska Native, 0.0% Native Hawaiian/Other Pacific Islander, 2.4% Two or more races, 86.2% Hispanic of any race; Average household size: 4.39; Median age: 26.5; Age under 18: 33.3%; Age 65 and over: 4.1%; Males per 100 females: 95.2

School District(s)

Golden Plains Unified (KG-12)
2012-13 Enrollment: 1,865 . . . . (559) 693-1115

Housing: Homeownership rate: 14.3%; Homeowner vacancy rate: 0.0%; Rental vacancy rate: 0.0%

HUME (unincorporated postal area)

ZCTA: 93628

Covers a land area of 35.877 square miles and a water area of 0.134 square miles. Located at 36.78° N. Lat; 118.94° W. Long. Elevation is 5,344 feet.

Population: 327; Growth (since 2000): 255.4%; Density: 9.1 persons per square mile; Race: 93.9% White, 0.6% Black/African American, 0.6% Asian, 1.5% American Indian/Alaska Native, 0.0% Native Hawaiian/Other Pacific Islander, 3.1% Two or more races, 5.2% Hispanic of any race; Average household size: 2.48; Median age: 24.6; Age under 18: 26.6%; Age 65 and over: 3.7%; Males per 100 females: 94.6

School District(s)

Fresno County Office of Education (KG-12)
2012-13 Enrollment: 2,094 . . . . (559) 265-3000

Housing: Homeownership rate: 12.1%; Homeowner vacancy rate: 0.0%; Rental vacancy rate: 0.0%

HURON (city). Covers a land area of 1.591 square miles and a water area of 0 square miles. Located at 36.20° N. Lat; 120.10° W. Long. Elevation is 374 feet.

Population: 6,754; Growth (since 2000): 7.1%; Density: 4,245.0 persons per square mile; Race: 34.1% White, 1.0% Black/African American, 0.6% Asian, 1.1% American Indian/Alaska Native, 0.1% Native Hawaiian/Other Pacific Islander, 4.5% Two or more races, 96.6% Hispanic of any race; Average household size: 4.41; Median age: 24.7; Age under 18: 37.1%; Age 65 and over: 4.9%; Males per 100 females: 111.6; Marriage status: 50.4% never married, 41.7% now married, 3.8% separated, 3.7% widowed, 4.2% divorced; Foreign born: 52.6%; Speak English only: 2.6%; With disability: 7.0%; Veterans: 1.5%; Ancestry: 0.2% Swedish, 0.1% English, 0.1% Irish

Employment: 3.9% management, business, and financial, 0.0% computer, engineering, and science, 1.3% education, legal, community service, arts, and media, 1.8% healthcare practitioners, 11.5% service, 14.2% sales and office, 58.4% natural resources, construction, and maintenance, 8.7% production, transportation, and material moving

Income: Per capita: $8,928; Median household: $22,684; Average household: $35,102; Households with income of $100,000 or more: 3.2%; Poverty rate: 39.8%

Educational Attainment: High school diploma or higher: 27.6%; Bachelor's degree or higher: 1.9%; Graduate/professional degree or higher: 0.8%

School District(s)

Coalinga-Huron Joint Unified (KG-12)
2012-13 Enrollment: 4,322 . . . . (559) 935-7500

Housing: Homeownership rate: 32.2%; Median home value: $120,400; Median year structure built: 1990; Homeowner vacancy rate: 1.8%; Median gross rent: $604 per month; Rental vacancy rate: 3.9%

Health Insurance: 64.0% have insurance; 9.7% have private insurance; 57.4% have public insurance; 36.0% do not have insurance; 7.0% of children under 18 do not have insurance

Safety: Violent crime rate: 104.2 per 10,000 population; Property crime rate: 397.8 per 10,000 population

Transportation: Commute: 81.8% car, 5.5% public transportation, 4.5% walk, 3.1% work from home; Median travel time to work: 28.8 minutes

Additional Information Contacts

City of Huron . . . . (559) 945-2241
http://www.webconnections.net/huron

KERMAN (city). Covers a land area of 3.233 square miles and a water area of 0 square miles. Located at 36.73° N. Lat; 120.06° W. Long. Elevation is 220 feet.

History: Incorporated 1946.

Population: 13,544; Growth (since 2000): 58.4%; Density: 4,189.9 persons per square mile; Race: 50.6% White, 0.5% Black/African American, 8.1% Asian, 1.3% American Indian/Alaska Native, 0.1% Native Hawaiian/Other Pacific Islander, 4.9% Two or more races, 71.7% Hispanic of any race; Average household size: 3.67; Median age: 28.2; Age under 18: 34.3%; Age 65 and over: 7.2%; Males per 100 females: 99.6; Marriage status: 36.5% never married, 51.3% now married, 1.5% separated, 6.6% widowed, 5.5% divorced; Foreign born: 34.7%; Speak English only: 28.7%; With disability: 9.1%; Veterans: 2.4%; Ancestry: 2.8% American, 2.6% Irish, 2.1% German, 1.8% English, 1.1% Portuguese

Employment: 10.6% management, business, and financial, 0.0% computer, engineering, and science, 7.2% education, legal, community service, arts, and media, 2.9% healthcare practitioners, 20.9% service, 16.8% sales and office, 20.8% natural resources, construction, and maintenance, 20.7% production, transportation, and material moving

Income: Per capita: $16,494; Median household: $49,748; Average household: $62,775; Households with income of $100,000 or more: 18.4%; Poverty rate: 23.4%

Educational Attainment: High school diploma or higher: 57.4%; Bachelor's degree or higher: 10.6%; Graduate/professional degree or higher: 2.8%

School District(s)

Kerman Unified (KG-12)
2012-13 Enrollment: 4,799 . . . . (559) 846-5383

Housing: Homeownership rate: 58.7%; Median home value: $165,400; Median year structure built: 1994; Homeowner vacancy rate: 3.3%; Median gross rent: $818 per month; Rental vacancy rate: 4.9%

Health Insurance: 74.7% have insurance; 42.6% have private insurance; 36.0% have public insurance; 25.3% do not have insurance; 8.8% of children under 18 do not have insurance

Safety: Violent crime rate: 30.9 per 10,000 population; Property crime rate: 299.8 per 10,000 population

Newspapers: Kerwest Inc (weekly circulation 12000)

Transportation: Commute: 95.7% car, 0.0% public transportation, 0.2% walk, 2.5% work from home; Median travel time to work: 23.8 minutes

Additional Information Contacts

City of Kerman. . . . . (559) 846-9384
http://www.cityofkerman.net

KINGSBURG (city). Covers a land area of 2.828 square miles and a water area of 0 square miles. Located at 36.52° N. Lat; 119.56° W. Long. Elevation is 302 feet.

History: Many of Kingsburg early residents were of Swedish descent, part of a colony from Michigan that settled here in the 1870's as farmers.

Population: 11,382; Growth (since 2000): 23.7%; Density: 4,024.3 persons per square mile; Race: 75.3% White, 0.5% Black/African American, 3.4% Asian, 1.3% American Indian/Alaska Native, 0.2% Native Hawaiian/Other Pacific Islander, 4.3% Two or more races, 42.9% Hispanic of any race; Average household size: 2.96; Median age: 33.7; Age under 18: 29.6%; Age 65 and over: 12.8%; Males per 100 females: 92.9; Marriage status: 30.1% never married, 56.6% now married, 4.5% separated, 5.9% widowed, 7.4% divorced; Foreign born: 18.9%; Speak English only: 62.3%; With disability: 10.5%; Veterans: 8.0%; Ancestry: 10.4% German, 7.6% Irish, 6.0% Swedish, 5.5% English, 3.8% Italian

Employment: 12.7% management, business, and financial, 3.0% computer, engineering, and science, 9.8% education, legal, community service, arts, and media, 4.9% healthcare practitioners, 14.6% service, 26.9% sales and office, 14.0% natural resources, construction, and maintenance, 14.2% production, transportation, and material moving

Income: Per capita: $23,970; Median household: $56,563; Average household: $70,452; Households with income of $100,000 or more: 20.3%; Poverty rate: 17.9%

Educational Attainment: High school diploma or higher: 82.4%; Bachelor's degree or higher: 25.6%; Graduate/professional degree or higher: 8.9%

School District(s)

Clay Joint Elementary (KG-08)
2012-13 Enrollment: 258. . . . . (559) 897-4185

Kings River Union Elementary (KG-08)
2012-13 Enrollment: 451. . . . . (559) 897-7209

Kingsburg Elementary Charter (KG-08)
2012-13 Enrollment: 2,388 . . . . (559) 897-2331

Kingsburg Joint Union High (09-12)
2012-13 Enrollment: 1,194 . . . . (559) 897-7721

Housing: Homeownership rate: 66.4%; Median home value: $212,600; Median year structure built: 1984; Homeowner vacancy rate: 2.8%; Median gross rent: $901 per month; Rental vacancy rate: 6.5%

Health Insurance: 82.7% have insurance; 58.4% have private insurance; 36.2% have public insurance; 17.3% do not have insurance; 4.4% of children under 18 do not have insurance

Safety: Violent crime rate: 19.7 per 10,000 population; Property crime rate: 280.7 per 10,000 population

Newspapers: Kingsburg Recorder (weekly circulation 3300)

Transportation: Commute: 88.2% car, 0.1% public transportation, 3.8% walk, 2.7% work from home; Median travel time to work: 22.4 minutes

Additional Information Contacts

City of Kingsburg. . . . . (559) 897-5821
http://cityofkingsburg-ca.gov

LAKESHORE (unincorporated postal area)

ZCTA: 93634

Covers a land area of 1,184.712 square miles and a water area of 22.727 square miles. Located at 37.22° N. Lat; 119.00° W. Long. Elevation is 6,995 feet.

Population: 33; Growth (since 2000): -28.3%; Density: <0.1 persons per square mile; Race: 72.7% White, 0.0% Black/African American, 0.0% Asian, 12.1% American Indian/Alaska Native, 3.0% Native Hawaiian/Other Pacific Islander, 9.1% Two or more races, 18.2% Hispanic of any race;

Average household size: 2.75; Median age: 40.3; Age under 18: 33.3%; Age 65 and over: 3.0%; Males per 100 females: 175.0
Housing: Homeownership rate: 41.7%; Homeowner vacancy rate: 0.0%; Rental vacancy rate: 94.8%

LANARE (CDP). Covers a land area of 2.018 square miles and a water area of 0 square miles. Located at 36.44° N. Lat; 119.93° W. Long. Elevation is 207 feet.
Population: 589; Growth (since 2000): 9.1%; Density: 291.8 persons per square mile; Race: 30.7% White, 9.7% Black/African American, 0.3% Asian, 0.8% American Indian/Alaska Native, 0.0% Native Hawaiian/Other Pacific Islander, 7.5% Two or more races, 88.1% Hispanic of any race; Average household size: 4.21; Median age: 28.5; Age under 18: 33.8%; Age 65 and over: 8.3%; Males per 100 females: 95.0
Housing: Homeownership rate: 62.2%; Homeowner vacancy rate: 0.0%; Rental vacancy rate: 1.8%

LATON (CDP). Covers a land area of 1.937 square miles and a water area of 0 square miles. Located at 36.43° N. Lat; 119.69° W. Long. Elevation is 259 feet.
Population: 1,824; Growth (since 2000): 47.6%; Density: 941.5 persons per square mile; Race: 54.9% White, 0.2% Black/African American, 0.5% Asian, 0.7% American Indian/Alaska Native, 0.0% Native Hawaiian/Other Pacific Islander, 2.9% Two or more races, 76.4% Hispanic of any race; Average household size: 3.85; Median age: 29.4; Age under 18: 32.0%; Age 65 and over: 8.8%; Males per 100 females: 108.7

School District(s)

Laton Joint Unified (KG-12)
2012-13 Enrollment: 702. . . . . (559) 922-4015
Housing: Homeownership rate: 61.1%; Homeowner vacancy rate: 1.4%; Rental vacancy rate: 2.6%

MALAGA (CDP). Covers a land area of 0.274 square miles and a water area of 0 square miles. Located at 36.68° N. Lat; 119.73° W. Long. Elevation is 295 feet.
Population: 947; Growth (since 2000): n/a; Density: 3,457.2 persons per square mile; Race: 44.1% White, 1.3% Black/African American, 1.2% Asian, 1.6% American Indian/Alaska Native, 0.2% Native Hawaiian/Other Pacific Islander, 2.6% Two or more races, 94.1% Hispanic of any race; Average household size: 3.93; Median age: 27.9; Age under 18: 33.7%; Age 65 and over: 9.7%; Males per 100 females: 97.7
Housing: Homeownership rate: 53.9%; Homeowner vacancy rate: 1.5%; Rental vacancy rate: 2.6%

MAYFAIR (CDP). Covers a land area of 0.518 square miles and a water area of 0 square miles. Located at 36.77° N. Lat; 119.76° W. Long.
Population: 4,589; Growth (since 2000): n/a; Density: 8,860.5 persons per square mile; Race: 44.2% White, 3.7% Black/African American, 6.8% Asian, 2.2% American Indian/Alaska Native, 0.3% Native Hawaiian/Other Pacific Islander, 5.0% Two or more races, 65.6% Hispanic of any race; Average household size: 3.28; Median age: 29.7; Age under 18: 31.9%; Age 65 and over: 9.0%; Males per 100 females: 99.8; Marriage status: 38.2% never married, 47.3% now married, 2.1% separated, 3.0% widowed, 11.5% divorced; Foreign born: 25.1%; Speak English only: 51.6%; With disability: 20.9%; Veterans: 7.8%; Ancestry: 10.3% Irish, 5.2% German, 3.5% American, 2.7% New Zealander, 2.6% Italian
Employment: 3.7% management, business, and financial, 0.6% computer, engineering, and science, 8.9% education, legal, community service, arts, and media, 0.5% healthcare practitioners, 22.2% service, 23.6% sales and office, 19.6% natural resources, construction, and maintenance, 20.9% production, transportation, and material moving
Income: Per capita: $16,135; Median household: $42,500; Average household: $51,862; Households with income of $100,000 or more: 10.1%; Poverty rate: 28.9%
Educational Attainment: High school diploma or higher: 72.3%; Bachelor's degree or higher: 10.2%; Graduate/professional degree or higher: 4.2%
Housing: Homeownership rate: 55.4%; Median home value: $109,600; Median year structure built: 1955; Homeowner vacancy rate: 1.8%; Median gross rent: $764 per month; Rental vacancy rate: 5.3%
Health Insurance: 77.3% have insurance; 40.8% have private insurance; 44.7% have public insurance; 22.7% do not have insurance; 4.7% of children under 18 do not have insurance
Transportation: Commute: 95.1% car, 0.0% public transportation, 1.3% walk, 0.6% work from home; Median travel time to work: 23.0 minutes

MENDOTA (city). Covers a land area of 3.278 square miles and a water area of 0.003 square miles. Located at 36.76° N. Lat; 120.38° W. Long. Elevation is 174 feet.
History: Incorporated 1942.
Population: 11,014; Growth (since 2000): 39.6%; Density: 3,359.6 persons per square mile; Race: 52.9% White, 1.0% Black/African American, 0.7% Asian, 1.4% American Indian/Alaska Native, 0.0% Native Hawaiian/Other Pacific Islander, 3.4% Two or more races, 96.6% Hispanic of any race; Average household size: 4.54; Median age: 26.2; Age under 18: 33.9%; Age 65 and over: 4.7%; Males per 100 females: 123.6; Marriage status: 52.8% never married, 41.1% now married, 2.1% separated, 3.1% widowed, 3.0% divorced; Foreign born: 55.1%; Speak English only: 11.5%; With disability: 7.1%; Veterans: 0.6%; Ancestry: 0.8% German, 0.3% Ethiopian, 0.1% American
Employment: 3.5% management, business, and financial, 0.3% computer, engineering, and science, 1.8% education, legal, community service, arts, and media, 2.0% healthcare practitioners, 9.4% service, 7.2% sales and office, 61.8% natural resources, construction, and maintenance, 14.0% production, transportation, and material moving
Income: Per capita: $8,781; Median household: $24,264; Average household: $32,067; Households with income of $100,000 or more: 1.8%; Poverty rate: 47.4%
Educational Attainment: High school diploma or higher: 29.0%; Bachelor's degree or higher: 1.6%; Graduate/professional degree or higher: 0.7%

School District(s)

Mendota Unified (KG-12)
2012-13 Enrollment: 2,978 . . . . (559) 655-4942
Housing: Homeownership rate: 43.6%; Median home value: $110,600; Median year structure built: 1981; Homeowner vacancy rate: 1.9%; Median gross rent: $635 per month; Rental vacancy rate: 4.1%
Health Insurance: 60.6% have insurance; 17.1% have private insurance; 46.9% have public insurance; 39.4% do not have insurance; 7.9% of children under 18 do not have insurance
Safety: Violent crime rate: 33.1 per 10,000 population; Property crime rate: 256.3 per 10,000 population
Transportation: Commute: 90.0% car, 1.4% public transportation, 2.8% walk, 0.2% work from home; Median travel time to work: 29.3 minutes
Additional Information Contacts
City of Mendota . . . . (559) 655-3291
http://www.ci.mendota.ca.us

MINKLER (CDP). Covers a land area of 5.864 square miles and a water area of 0 square miles. Located at 36.73° N. Lat; 119.46° W. Long. Elevation is 397 feet.
Population: 1,003; Growth (since 2000): n/a; Density: 171.1 persons per square mile; Race: 81.6% White, 0.4% Black/African American, 2.3% Asian, 2.0% American Indian/Alaska Native, 0.0% Native Hawaiian/Other Pacific Islander, 3.0% Two or more races, 30.1% Hispanic of any race; Average household size: 2.62; Median age: 47.6; Age under 18: 20.4%; Age 65 and over: 20.7%; Males per 100 females: 95.5
Housing: Homeownership rate: 72.3%; Homeowner vacancy rate: 3.1%; Rental vacancy rate: 14.4%

MIRAMONTE (unincorporated postal area)

ZCTA: 93641

Covers a land area of 31.927 square miles and a water area of 0.146 square miles. Located at 36.70° N. Lat; 119.02° W. Long. Elevation is 3,094 feet.
Population: 595; Growth (since 2000): 6.4%; Density: 18.6 persons per square mile; Race: 88.2% White, 3.7% Black/African American, 0.7% Asian, 1.8% American Indian/Alaska Native, 0.3% Native Hawaiian/Other Pacific Islander, 2.2% Two or more races, 8.9% Hispanic of any race; Average household size: 2.16; Median age: 47.6; Age under 18: 13.6%; Age 65 and over: 15.8%; Males per 100 females: 144.9
Housing: Homeownership rate: 70.8%; Homeowner vacancy rate: 6.4%; Rental vacancy rate: 7.9%

MONMOUTH (CDP). Covers a land area of 0.308 square miles and a water area of 0 square miles. Located at 36.57° N. Lat; 119.74° W. Long. Elevation is 276 feet.
Population: 152; Growth (since 2000): n/a; Density: 493.4 persons per square mile; Race: 53.9% White, 3.9% Black/African American, 3.3% Asian, 0.7% American Indian/Alaska Native, 0.0% Native Hawaiian/Other

Pacific Islander, 7.2% Two or more races, 70.4% Hispanic of any race; Average household size: 3.62; Median age: 34.0; Age under 18: 24.3%; Age 65 and over: 18.4%; Males per 100 females: 90.0
Housing: Homeownership rate: 66.7%; Homeowner vacancy rate: 0.0%; Rental vacancy rate: 6.7%

OLD FIG GARDEN (CDP). Covers a land area of 1.652 square miles and a water area of 0 square miles. Located at 36.80° N. Lat; 119.81° W. Long.
Population: 5,365; Growth (since 2000): n/a; Density: 3,247.5 persons per square mile; Race: 74.6% White, 2.0% Black/African American, 3.9% Asian, 1.0% American Indian/Alaska Native, 0.2% Native Hawaiian/Other Pacific Islander, 4.7% Two or more races, 28.6% Hispanic of any race; Average household size: 2.52; Median age: 44.7; Age under 18: 21.9%; Age 65 and over: 17.2%; Males per 100 females: 96.2; Marriage status: 29.5% never married, 44.6% now married, 1.6% separated, 11.5% widowed, 14.5% divorced; Foreign born: 10.5%; Speak English only: 79.9%; With disability: 13.6%; Veterans: 7.4%; Ancestry: 13.5% German, 10.9% Irish, 8.5% Italian, 6.4% English, 5.5% Armenian
Employment: 12.1% management, business, and financial, 9.6% computer, engineering, and science, 18.4% education, legal, community service, arts, and media, 10.2% healthcare practitioners, 13.3% service, 25.2% sales and office, 5.7% natural resources, construction, and maintenance, 5.5% production, transportation, and material moving
Income: Per capita: $38,663; Median household: $62,744; Average household: $96,389; Households with income of $100,000 or more: 29.1%; Poverty rate: 25.7%
Educational Attainment: High school diploma or higher: 90.6%; Bachelor's degree or higher: 38.8%; Graduate/professional degree or higher: 19.5%
Housing: Homeownership rate: 71.9%; Median home value: $294,800; Median year structure built: 1955; Homeowner vacancy rate: 2.0%; Median gross rent: $900 per month; Rental vacancy rate: 6.7%
Health Insurance: 81.3% have insurance; 62.0% have private insurance; 31.8% have public insurance; 18.7% do not have insurance; 8.9% of children under 18 do not have insurance
Transportation: Commute: 92.2% car, 0.0% public transportation, 2.6% walk, 4.4% work from home; Median travel time to work: 17.2 minutes

ORANGE COVE (city). Covers a land area of 1.912 square miles and a water area of 0 square miles. Located at 36.62° N. Lat; 119.32° W. Long. Elevation is 423 feet.
History: Incorporated 1948.
Population: 9,078; Growth (since 2000): 17.6%; Density: 4,748.6 persons per square mile; Race: 43.4% White, 0.8% Black/African American, 1.1% Asian, 1.4% American Indian/Alaska Native, 0.0% Native Hawaiian/Other Pacific Islander, 3.9% Two or more races, 92.7% Hispanic of any race; Average household size: 4.39; Median age: 23.6; Age under 18: 39.9%; Age 65 and over: 5.7%; Males per 100 females: 100.9; Marriage status: 44.1% never married, 45.5% now married, 5.6% separated, 5.3% widowed, 5.2% divorced; Foreign born: 37.7%; Speak English only: 21.5%; With disability: 6.9%; Veterans: 2.4%; Ancestry: 1.7% American, 1.2% German, 0.6% English, 0.5% Irish, 0.3% Scottish
Employment: 3.9% management, business, and financial, 0.5% computer, engineering, and science, 2.7% education, legal, community service, arts, and media, 2.1% healthcare practitioners, 16.1% service, 14.5% sales and office, 37.0% natural resources, construction, and maintenance, 23.2% production, transportation, and material moving
Income: Per capita: $9,161; Median household: $26,799; Average household: $35,445; Households with income of $100,000 or more: 2.8%; Poverty rate: 49.2%
Educational Attainment: High school diploma or higher: 38.4%; Bachelor's degree or higher: 4.1%; Graduate/professional degree or higher: 0.8%

School District(s)

Kings Canyon Joint Unified (KG-12)
2012-13 Enrollment: 9,954 . . . . (559) 305-7005
Housing: Homeownership rate: 43.2%; Median home value: $124,800; Median year structure built: 1982; Homeowner vacancy rate: 0.8%; Median gross rent: $697 per month; Rental vacancy rate: 9.5%
Health Insurance: 79.1% have insurance; 20.8% have private insurance; 62.4% have public insurance; 20.9% do not have insurance; 1.2% of children under 18 do not have insurance
Safety: Violent crime rate: 217.4 per 10,000 population; Property crime rate: 902.6 per 10,000 population
Transportation: Commute: 83.8% car, 0.0% public transportation, 3.7% walk, 2.5% work from home; Median travel time to work: 25.6 minutes
Additional Information Contacts
City of Orange Cove . . . . (559) 626-4488
http://www.cityoforangecove.com

PARLIER (city). Covers a land area of 2.194 square miles and a water area of 0 square miles. Located at 36.61° N. Lat; 119.54° W. Long. Elevation is 344 feet.
Population: 14,494; Growth (since 2000): 30.0%; Density: 6,606.9 persons per square mile; Race: 50.0% White, 0.6% Black/African American, 0.5% Asian, 1.2% American Indian/Alaska Native, 0.1% Native Hawaiian/Other Pacific Islander, 3.5% Two or more races, 97.5% Hispanic of any race; Average household size: 4.40; Median age: 25.1; Age under 18: 37.1%; Age 65 and over: 5.5%; Males per 100 females: 104.9; Marriage status: 45.6% never married, 47.8% now married, 3.3% separated, 2.4% widowed, 4.1% divorced; Foreign born: 40.6%; Speak English only: 17.4%; With disability: 7.7%; Veterans: 2.4%; Ancestry: 0.7% Irish, 0.7% German, 0.3% Arab, 0.2% American, 0.2% English
Employment: 1.6% management, business, and financial, 1.9% computer, engineering, and science, 4.2% education, legal, community service, arts, and media, 0.3% healthcare practitioners, 17.0% service, 13.3% sales and office, 28.6% natural resources, construction, and maintenance, 33.1% production, transportation, and material moving
Income: Per capita: $11,092; Median household: $35,327; Average household: $43,598; Households with income of $100,000 or more: 7.1%; Poverty rate: 35.5%
Educational Attainment: High school diploma or higher: 41.8%; Bachelor's degree or higher: 3.9%; Graduate/professional degree or higher: 1.1%

School District(s)

Kings Canyon Joint Unified (KG-12)
2012-13 Enrollment: 9,954 . . . . (559) 305-7005
Parlier Unified (KG-12)
2012-13 Enrollment: 3,320 . . . . (559) 646-2731
Housing: Homeownership rate: 46.2%; Median home value: $110,000; Median year structure built: 1991; Homeowner vacancy rate: 1.3%; Median gross rent: $737 per month; Rental vacancy rate: 3.7%
Health Insurance: 69.5% have insurance; 23.4% have private insurance; 50.4% have public insurance; 30.5% do not have insurance; 9.3% of children under 18 do not have insurance
Safety: Violent crime rate: 61.3 per 10,000 population; Property crime rate: 252.4 per 10,000 population
Transportation: Commute: 82.6% car, 0.2% public transportation, 3.2% walk, 2.8% work from home; Median travel time to work: 23.7 minutes
Additional Information Contacts
City of Parlier. . . . . (559) 646-3545
http://www.parlier.ca.us

PRATHER (unincorporated postal area)
ZCTA: 93651
Covers a land area of 28.729 square miles and a water area of 0.027 square miles. Located at 37.00° N. Lat; 119.52° W. Long. Elevation is 1,657 feet.
Population: 1,674; Growth (since 2000): 27.9%; Density: 58.3 persons per square mile; Race: 89.2% White, 0.5% Black/African American, 1.3% Asian, 1.7% American Indian/Alaska Native, 0.3% Native Hawaiian/Other Pacific Islander, 4.4% Two or more races, 10.0% Hispanic of any race; Average household size: 2.72; Median age: 46.4; Age under 18: 21.9%; Age 65 and over: 14.6%; Males per 100 females: 99.0

School District(s)

Sierra Unified (KG-12)
2012-13 Enrollment: 1,402 . . . . (559) 855-3662
Housing: Homeownership rate: 83.8%; Homeowner vacancy rate: 1.9%; Rental vacancy rate: 7.4%

RAISIN CITY (CDP). Covers a land area of 0.760 square miles and a water area of 0 square miles. Located at 36.60° N. Lat; 119.91° W. Long. Elevation is 236 feet.
Population: 380; Growth (since 2000): 130.3%; Density: 500.3 persons per square mile; Race: 32.4% White, 1.3% Black/African American, 1.6% Asian, 8.2% American Indian/Alaska Native, 0.0% Native Hawaiian/Other Pacific Islander, 3.2% Two or more races, 81.1% Hispanic of any race; Average household size: 4.69; Median age: 24.8; Age under 18: 36.3%; Age 65 and over: 6.6%; Males per 100 females: 128.9

School District(s)

Raisin City Elementary (KG-12)
2012-13 Enrollment: 580. . . . . (559) 233-0128

Housing: Homeownership rate: 50.6%; Homeowner vacancy rate: 0.0%; Rental vacancy rate: 8.9%

REEDLEY (city). Covers a land area of 5.084 square miles and a water area of 0.072 square miles. Located at 36.60° N. Lat; 119.45° W. Long. Elevation is 348 feet.

History: Founded 1889, incorporated 1913.

Population: 24,194; Growth (since 2000): 16.6%; Density: 4,759.2 persons per square mile; Race: 58.3% White, 0.7% Black/African American, 3.3% Asian, 1.1% American Indian/Alaska Native, 0.0% Native Hawaiian/Other Pacific Islander, 4.1% Two or more races, 76.3% Hispanic of any race; Average household size: 3.65; Median age: 29.1; Age under 18: 32.5%; Age 65 and over: 9.5%; Males per 100 females: 104.0; Marriage status: 34.5% never married, 54.6% now married, 1.7% separated, 3.2% widowed, 7.8% divorced; Foreign born: 33.2%; Speak English only: 36.7%; With disability: 9.3%; Veterans: 4.4%; Ancestry: 5.8% German, 3.5% English, 2.6% Irish, 1.9% Dutch, 1.7% American

Employment: 7.6% management, business, and financial, 0.9% computer, engineering, and science, 9.9% education, legal, community service, arts, and media, 2.7% healthcare practitioners, 14.5% service, 17.2% sales and office, 32.9% natural resources, construction, and maintenance, 14.3% production, transportation, and material moving

Income: Per capita: $15,944; Median household: $47,145; Average household: $59,753; Households with income of $100,000 or more: 14.3%; Poverty rate: 24.2%

Educational Attainment: High school diploma or higher: 61.1%; Bachelor's degree or higher: 14.5%; Graduate/professional degree or higher: 4.2%

School District(s)

Kings Canyon Joint Unified (KG-12)
2012-13 Enrollment: 9,954 . . . . (559) 305-7005

Two-year College(s)

Reedley College (Public)
Fall 2013 Enrollment: 13,807 . . . . (559) 638-3641
2013-14 Tuition: In-state $1,142; Out-of-state $6,782

Housing: Homeownership rate: 59.1%; Median home value: $168,400; Median year structure built: 1980; Homeowner vacancy rate: 1.8%; Median gross rent: $854 per month; Rental vacancy rate: 3.7%

Health Insurance: 76.9% have insurance; 38.6% have private insurance; 45.6% have public insurance; 23.1% do not have insurance; 7.3% of children under 18 do not have insurance

Hospitals: Adventist Medical Center - Reedley (44 beds)

Safety: Violent crime rate: 62.8 per 10,000 population; Property crime rate: 211.4 per 10,000 population

Newspapers: Orange Cove & Mtn. Times (weekly circulation 14000); Parlier Post (weekly circulation 14000); Reedley Exponent (weekly circulation 14000)

Transportation: Commute: 88.1% car, 0.9% public transportation, 2.0% walk, 2.5% work from home; Median travel time to work: 22.3 minutes

Additional Information Contacts

City of Reedley . . . . (559) 637-4200
http://www.reedley.com

RIVERDALE (CDP). Covers a land area of 3.925 square miles and a water area of 0 square miles. Located at 36.43° N. Lat; 119.87° W. Long. Elevation is 223 feet.

Population: 3,153; Growth (since 2000): 30.5%; Density: 803.3 persons per square mile; Race: 57.9% White, 1.0% Black/African American, 0.9% Asian, 1.9% American Indian/Alaska Native, 0.2% Native Hawaiian/Other Pacific Islander, 4.8% Two or more races, 66.8% Hispanic of any race; Average household size: 3.73; Median age: 27.6; Age under 18: 35.2%; Age 65 and over: 8.3%; Males per 100 females: 99.7; Marriage status: 34.2% never married, 52.8% now married, 4.6% separated, 3.7% widowed, 9.2% divorced; Foreign born: 34.5%; Speak English only: 41.9%; With disability: 9.7%; Veterans: 6.8%; Ancestry: 14.0% Portuguese, 7.3% German, 5.6% Irish, 2.8% English, 1.5% American

Employment: 7.0% management, business, and financial, 0.0% computer, engineering, and science, 6.1% education, legal, community service, arts, and media, 3.7% healthcare practitioners, 15.7% service, 9.5% sales and office, 37.2% natural resources, construction, and maintenance, 20.8% production, transportation, and material moving

Income: Per capita: $14,402; Median household: $44,018; Average household: $52,559; Households with income of $100,000 or more: 7.9%; Poverty rate: 29.1%

Educational Attainment: High school diploma or higher: 63.6%; Bachelor's degree or higher: 5.4%; Graduate/professional degree or higher: 0.3%

School District(s)

Burrel Union Elementary (KG-08)
2012-13 Enrollment: 119. . . . . (559) 866-5634

Riverdale Joint Unified (KG-12)
2012-13 Enrollment: 1,568 . . . . (559) 867-8200

Housing: Homeownership rate: 60.2%; Median home value: $148,500; Median year structure built: 1975; Homeowner vacancy rate: 3.4%; Median gross rent: $893 per month; Rental vacancy rate: 9.9%

Health Insurance: 76.4% have insurance; 37.9% have private insurance; 46.3% have public insurance; 23.6% do not have insurance; 1.6% of children under 18 do not have insurance

Transportation: Commute: 86.9% car, 0.0% public transportation, 3.1% walk, 4.8% work from home; Median travel time to work: 21.3 minutes

SAN JOAQUIN (city). Covers a land area of 1.148 square miles and a water area of 0 square miles. Located at 36.61° N. Lat; 120.19° W. Long. Elevation is 174 feet.

History: San Joaquin was incorporated on February 14, 1920 and it is the smallest city in Fresno County. San Joaquin is also located about 11 miles southwest of Kerman.

Population: 4,001; Growth (since 2000): 22.4%; Density: 3,485.3 persons per square mile; Race: 49.1% White, 0.8% Black/African American, 0.9% Asian, 1.3% American Indian/Alaska Native, 0.0% Native Hawaiian/Other Pacific Islander, 3.7% Two or more races, 95.6% Hispanic of any race; Average household size: 4.54; Median age: 23.6; Age under 18: 41.3%; Age 65 and over: 4.4%; Males per 100 females: 103.0; Marriage status: 37.9% never married, 56.9% now married, 3.4% separated, 2.6% widowed, 2.6% divorced; Foreign born: 49.0%; Speak English only: 7.4%; With disability: 4.4%; Veterans: 0.7%; Ancestry: 2.6% Arab, 0.4% German

Employment: 9.1% management, business, and financial, 0.0% computer, engineering, and science, 2.3% education, legal, community service, arts, and media, 0.3% healthcare practitioners, 8.8% service, 4.8% sales and office, 67.2% natural resources, construction, and maintenance, 7.4% production, transportation, and material moving

Income: Per capita: $7,366; Median household: $26,181; Average household: $30,023; Households with income of $100,000 or more: 0.4%; Poverty rate: 51.7%

Educational Attainment: High school diploma or higher: 25.3%; Bachelor's degree or higher: 4.0%; Graduate/professional degree or higher: n/a

School District(s)

Golden Plains Unified (KG-12)
2012-13 Enrollment: 1,865 . . . . (559) 693-1115

Housing: Homeownership rate: 46.0%; Median home value: $107,200; Median year structure built: 1983; Homeowner vacancy rate: 1.9%; Median gross rent: $447 per month; Rental vacancy rate: 6.3%

Health Insurance: 73.7% have insurance; 14.7% have private insurance; 61.7% have public insurance; 26.3% do not have insurance; 8.4% of children under 18 do not have insurance

Transportation: Commute: 94.4% car, 0.0% public transportation, 2.0% walk, 0.7% work from home; Median travel time to work: 20.4 minutes

Additional Information Contacts

City of San Joaquin . . . . (559) 693-4311
http://www.cityofsanjoaquin.org

SANGER (city). Covers a land area of 5.524 square miles and a water area of 0 square miles. Located at 36.70° N. Lat; 119.56° W. Long. Elevation is 371 feet.

History: Sanger developed around farms producing semi-tropical fruits, grapes, and plums.

Population: 24,270; Growth (since 2000): 28.2%; Density: 4,393.7 persons per square mile; Race: 59.6% White, 0.9% Black/African American, 3.1% Asian, 1.3% American Indian/Alaska Native, 0.2% Native Hawaiian/Other Pacific Islander, 3.5% Two or more races, 80.5% Hispanic of any race; Average household size: 3.62; Median age: 29.2; Age under 18: 33.6%; Age 65 and over: 9.4%; Males per 100 females: 97.4; Marriage status: 34.3% never married, 49.8% now married, 3.2% separated, 6.6% widowed, 9.3% divorced; Foreign born: 25.1%; Speak English only: 41.8%;

With disability: 9.6%; Veterans: 4.6%; Ancestry: 3.8% German, 2.6% Irish, 2.0% English, 1.1% American, 0.9% Armenian
Employment: 8.3% management, business, and financial, 1.7% computer, engineering, and science, 8.8% education, legal, community service, arts, and media, 2.0% healthcare practitioners, 22.1% service, 22.1% sales and office, 18.1% natural resources, construction, and maintenance, 16.9% production, transportation, and material moving
Income: Per capita: $15,978; Median household: $42,415; Average household: $56,087; Households with income of $100,000 or more: 15.6%; Poverty rate: 22.7%
Educational Attainment: High school diploma or higher: 60.4%; Bachelor's degree or higher: 10.8%; Graduate/professional degree or higher: 2.7%

School District(s)

Sanger Unified (KG-12)
2012-13 Enrollment: 10,916 . . . . (559) 524-6521
Valley Rop
2012-13 Enrollment: n/a . . . . (559) 876-2122
Housing: Homeownership rate: 58.2%; Median home value: $158,500; Median year structure built: 1982; Homeowner vacancy rate: 3.1%; Median gross rent: $887 per month; Rental vacancy rate: 5.3%
Health Insurance: 78.3% have insurance; 46.5% have private insurance; 37.4% have public insurance; 21.7% do not have insurance; 9.7% of children under 18 do not have insurance
Safety: Violent crime rate: 59.2 per 10,000 population; Property crime rate: 294.5 per 10,000 population
Newspapers: Fowler Ensign (weekly circulation 1200); Sanger Herald (weekly circulation 2500)
Transportation: Commute: 85.4% car, 0.1% public transportation, 2.1% walk, 5.3% work from home; Median travel time to work: 22.9 minutes
Additional Information Contacts
City of Sanger . . . . (559) 876-6300
http://www.ci.sanger.ca.us

SELMA (city). Covers a land area of 5.136 square miles and a water area of 0 square miles. Located at 36.57° N. Lat; 119.62° W. Long. Elevation is 308 feet.
History: Selma grew as a packing center for the muscat grape belt.
Population: 23,219; Growth (since 2000): 19.4%; Density: 4,520.6 persons per square mile; Race: 55.4% White, 1.2% Black/African American, 4.6% Asian, 2.1% American Indian/Alaska Native, 0.0% Native Hawaiian/Other Pacific Islander, 3.8% Two or more races, 77.6% Hispanic of any race; Average household size: 3.59; Median age: 29.5; Age under 18: 32.1%; Age 65 and over: 9.9%; Males per 100 females: 100.3; Marriage status: 34.8% never married, 51.5% now married, 3.6% separated, 4.8% widowed, 8.9% divorced; Foreign born: 29.6%; Speak English only: 42.1%; With disability: 9.5%; Veterans: 4.9%; Ancestry: 3.6% German, 2.4% English, 2.0% Irish, 1.2% American, 0.8% Portuguese
Employment: 6.0% management, business, and financial, 2.1% computer, engineering, and science, 7.2% education, legal, community service, arts, and media, 3.1% healthcare practitioners, 17.7% service, 17.7% sales and office, 25.3% natural resources, construction, and maintenance, 20.8% production, transportation, and material moving
Income: Per capita: $15,724; Median household: $43,324; Average household: $54,475; Households with income of $100,000 or more: 12.0%; Poverty rate: 23.3%
Educational Attainment: High school diploma or higher: 58.5%; Bachelor's degree or higher: 10.4%; Graduate/professional degree or higher: 3.3%

School District(s)

Selma Unified (KG-12)
2012-13 Enrollment: 6,453 . . . . (559) 898-6500
Housing: Homeownership rate: 59.7%; Median home value: $159,600; Median year structure built: 1978; Homeowner vacancy rate: 2.4%; Median gross rent: $777 per month; Rental vacancy rate: 5.5%
Health Insurance: 75.0% have insurance; 38.7% have private insurance; 43.8% have public insurance; 25.0% do not have insurance; 10.8% of children under 18 do not have insurance
Safety: Violent crime rate: 79.8 per 10,000 population; Property crime rate: 441.2 per 10,000 population
Newspapers: Selma Enterprise (weekly circulation 11700)
Transportation: Commute: 86.6% car, 0.1% public transportation, 1.0% walk, 4.0% work from home; Median travel time to work: 25.0 minutes
Additional Information Contacts
City of Selma . . . . (559) 891-2200
http://www.cityofselma.com

SHAVER LAKE (CDP). Covers a land area of 32.214 square miles and a water area of 2.277 square miles. Located at 37.10° N. Lat; 119.33° W. Long. Elevation is 5,627 feet.
Population: 634; Growth (since 2000): -10.1%; Density: 19.7 persons per square mile; Race: 96.4% White, 0.0% Black/African American, 0.5% Asian, 0.8% American Indian/Alaska Native, 0.0% Native Hawaiian/Other Pacific Islander, 1.1% Two or more races, 6.9% Hispanic of any race; Average household size: 2.17; Median age: 54.3; Age under 18: 14.7%; Age 65 and over: 24.1%; Males per 100 females: 110.6

School District(s)

Sierra Unified (KG-12)
2012-13 Enrollment: 1,402 . . . . (559) 855-3662
Housing: Homeownership rate: 80.8%; Homeowner vacancy rate: 12.0%; Rental vacancy rate: 39.3%

SQUAW VALLEY (CDP). Covers a land area of 56.559 square miles and a water area of 0.051 square miles. Located at 36.70° N. Lat; 119.19° W. Long. Elevation is 1,631 feet.
Population: 3,162; Growth (since 2000): 17.5%; Density: 55.9 persons per square mile; Race: 85.4% White, 0.9% Black/African American, 1.5% Asian, 2.4% American Indian/Alaska Native, 0.1% Native Hawaiian/Other Pacific Islander, 4.6% Two or more races, 16.6% Hispanic of any race; Average household size: 2.66; Median age: 46.3; Age under 18: 22.4%; Age 65 and over: 17.2%; Males per 100 females: 103.2; Marriage status: 18.0% never married, 71.3% now married, 2.9% separated, 3.0% widowed, 7.7% divorced; Foreign born: 5.3%; Speak English only: 87.3%; With disability: 16.9%; Veterans: 24.3%; Ancestry: 20.5% German, 17.8% Irish, 9.8% English, 5.8% American, 4.9% European
Employment: 12.1% management, business, and financial, 1.3% computer, engineering, and science, 38.2% education, legal, community service, arts, and media, 2.4% healthcare practitioners, 6.7% service, 10.8% sales and office, 14.4% natural resources, construction, and maintenance, 14.2% production, transportation, and material moving
Income: Per capita: $27,086; Median household: $62,230; Average household: $62,698; Households with income of $100,000 or more: 14.8%; Poverty rate: 5.4%
Educational Attainment: High school diploma or higher: 91.5%; Bachelor's degree or higher: 21.7%; Graduate/professional degree or higher: 10.8%
Housing: Homeownership rate: 84.9%; Median home value: $163,500; Median year structure built: 1988; Homeowner vacancy rate: 3.6%; Median gross rent: $847 per month; Rental vacancy rate: 5.7%
Health Insurance: 83.7% have insurance; 59.1% have private insurance; 39.5% have public insurance; 16.3% do not have insurance; 11.7% of children under 18 do not have insurance
Transportation: Commute: 83.2% car, 0.0% public transportation, 4.9% walk, 11.9% work from home; Median travel time to work: 39.2 minutes

---

SUNNYSIDE (CDP). Covers a land area of 1.932 square miles and a water area of 0 square miles. Located at 36.73° N. Lat; 119.69° W. Long. Elevation is 328 feet.
Population: 4,235; Growth (since 2000): n/a; Density: 2,191.7 persons per square mile; Race: 63.4% White, 4.2% Black/African American, 11.0% Asian, 1.4% American Indian/Alaska Native, 0.1% Native Hawaiian/Other Pacific Islander, 4.7% Two or more races, 36.0% Hispanic of any race; Average household size: 2.84; Median age: 43.1; Age under 18: 23.2%; Age 65 and over: 20.0%; Males per 100 females: 98.5; Marriage status: 30.0% never married, 60.8% now married, 1.8% separated, 4.8% widowed, 4.5% divorced; Foreign born: 14.6%; Speak English only: 66.7%; With disability: 21.6%; Veterans: 15.7%; Ancestry: 13.9% German, 9.0% English, 6.6% Irish, 5.4% Armenian, 3.4% Italian
Employment: 12.3% management, business, and financial, 2.4% computer, engineering, and science, 16.1% education, legal, community service, arts, and media, 6.2% healthcare practitioners, 24.5% service, 22.4% sales and office, 8.6% natural resources, construction, and maintenance, 7.5% production, transportation, and material moving
Income: Per capita: $32,291; Median household: $64,473; Average household: $91,011; Households with income of $100,000 or more: 32.6%; Poverty rate: 11.2%
Educational Attainment: High school diploma or higher: 88.6%; Bachelor's degree or higher: 25.5%; Graduate/professional degree or higher: 7.5%

Housing: Homeownership rate: 80.4%; Median home value: $257,500; Median year structure built: 1964; Homeowner vacancy rate: 1.5%; Median gross rent: $899 per month; Rental vacancy rate: 5.5%

Health Insurance: 91.1% have insurance; 67.1% have private insurance; 45.0% have public insurance; 8.9% do not have insurance; 1.4% of children under 18 do not have insurance

Transportation: Commute: 86.9% car, 1.6% public transportation, 0.0% walk, 9.4% work from home; Median travel time to work: 22.4 minutes

TARPEY VILLAGE (CDP). Covers a land area of 0.805 square miles and a water area of 0 square miles. Located at 36.79° N. Lat; 119.70° W. Long. Elevation is 351 feet.

Population: 3,888; Growth (since 2000): n/a; Density: 4,829.4 persons per square mile; Race: 73.8% White, 2.0% Black/African American, 6.7% Asian, 1.5% American Indian/Alaska Native, 0.1% Native Hawaiian/Other Pacific Islander, 4.3% Two or more races, 31.4% Hispanic of any race; Average household size: 3.03; Median age: 38.8; Age under 18: 25.2%; Age 65 and over: 15.9%; Males per 100 females: 98.6; Marriage status: 28.7% never married, 50.6% now married, 0.5% separated, 7.3% widowed, 13.4% divorced; Foreign born: 2.4%; Speak English only: 90.7%; With disability: 14.6%; Veterans: 12.8%; Ancestry: 20.3% German, 11.4% Irish, 7.9% American, 7.3% English, 5.4% Italian

Employment: 8.6% management, business, and financial, 3.4% computer, engineering, and science, 11.6% education, legal, community service, arts, and media, 2.4% healthcare practitioners, 18.4% service, 33.1% sales and office, 14.3% natural resources, construction, and maintenance, 8.3% production, transportation, and material moving

Income: Per capita: $21,683; Median household: $57,246; Average household: $61,752; Households with income of $100,000 or more: 15.9%; Poverty rate: 12.3%

Educational Attainment: High school diploma or higher: 89.1%; Bachelor's degree or higher: 19.0%; Graduate/professional degree or higher: 7.6%

Housing: Homeownership rate: 80.1%; Median home value: $154,100; Median year structure built: 1959; Homeowner vacancy rate: 1.9%; Median gross rent: $1,154 per month; Rental vacancy rate: 6.2%

Health Insurance: 89.8% have insurance; 70.5% have private insurance; 43.7% have public insurance; 10.2% do not have insurance; 0.0% of children under 18 do not have insurance

Transportation: Commute: 88.3% car, 1.0% public transportation, 0.8% walk, 9.3% work from home; Median travel time to work: 27.0 minutes

THREE ROCKS (CDP). Covers a land area of 0.750 square miles and a water area of 0 square miles. Located at 36.51° N. Lat; 120.39° W. Long. Elevation is 423 feet.

Population: 246; Growth (since 2000): n/a; Density: 328.2 persons per square mile; Race: 52.4% White, 0.0% Black/African American, 0.0% Asian, 0.4% American Indian/Alaska Native, 0.0% Native Hawaiian/Other Pacific Islander, 5.7% Two or more races, 95.5% Hispanic of any race; Average household size: 4.47; Median age: 31.0; Age under 18: 30.9%; Age 65 and over: 8.1%; Males per 100 females: 117.7

Housing: Homeownership rate: 56.4%; Homeowner vacancy rate: 3.1%; Rental vacancy rate: 0.0%

TOLLHOUSE (unincorporated postal area)

ZCTA: 93667

Covers a land area of 111.340 square miles and a water area of 0.886 square miles. Located at 36.96° N. Lat; 119.34° W. Long. Elevation is 1,919 feet.

Population: 2,604; Growth (since 2000): -0.9%; Density: 23.4 persons per square mile; Race: 82.6% White, 0.5% Black/African American, 0.4% Asian, 9.1% American Indian/Alaska Native, 0.2% Native Hawaiian/Other Pacific Islander, 4.9% Two or more races, 10.3% Hispanic of any race; Average household size: 2.83; Median age: 42.0; Age under 18: 26.7%; Age 65 and over: 14.4%; Males per 100 females: 106.2; Marriage status: 19.1% never married, 59.7% now married, 1.0% separated, 7.8% widowed, 13.4% divorced; Foreign born: 2.8%; Speak English only: 95.7%; With disability: 20.6%; Veterans: 16.9%; Ancestry: 26.8% German, 11.9% American, 8.9% Irish, 5.6% English, 2.4% Swedish

Employment: 19.4% management, business, and financial, 1.3% computer, engineering, and science, 13.0% education, legal, community service, arts, and media, 1.2% healthcare practitioners, 6.7% service, 39.1% sales and office, 12.5% natural resources, construction, and maintenance, 6.7% production, transportation, and material moving

Income: Per capita: $26,976; Median household: $54,459; Average household: $72,017; Households with income of $100,000 or more: 23.9%; Poverty rate: 12.0%

Educational Attainment: High school diploma or higher: 83.9%; Bachelor's degree or higher: 21.1%; Graduate/professional degree or higher: 6.7%

School District(s)

Sierra Unified (KG-12)
2012-13 Enrollment: 1,402 . . . . (559) 855-3662

Housing: Homeownership rate: 76.8%; Median home value: $286,000; Median year structure built: 1987; Homeowner vacancy rate: 2.5%; Median gross rent: $1,290 per month; Rental vacancy rate: 4.4%

Health Insurance: 83.7% have insurance; 63.5% have private insurance; 41.9% have public insurance; 16.3% do not have insurance; 9.4% of children under 18 do not have insurance

Transportation: Commute: 89.4% car, 0.0% public transportation, 2.7% walk, 5.7% work from home; Median travel time to work: 35.4 minutes

TRANQUILLITY (CDP). Covers a land area of 0.617 square miles and a water area of 0 square miles. Located at 36.65° N. Lat; 120.25° W. Long. Elevation is 164 feet.

Population: 799; Growth (since 2000): -1.7%; Density: 1,294.1 persons per square mile; Race: 63.1% White, 1.1% Black/African American, 0.3% Asian, 1.6% American Indian/Alaska Native, 0.0% Native Hawaiian/Other Pacific Islander, 2.5% Two or more races, 79.7% Hispanic of any race; Average household size: 3.49; Median age: 32.7; Age under 18: 33.4%; Age 65 and over: 11.8%; Males per 100 females: 106.5

School District(s)

Golden Plains Unified (KG-12)
2012-13 Enrollment: 1,865 . . . . (559) 693-1115

Housing: Homeownership rate: 63.4%; Homeowner vacancy rate: 2.0%; Rental vacancy rate: 13.3%

WEST PARK (CDP). Covers a land area of 1.792 square miles and a water area of 0 square miles. Located at 36.71° N. Lat; 119.85° W. Long. Elevation is 266 feet.

Population: 1,157; Growth (since 2000): n/a; Density: 645.8 persons per square mile; Race: 52.0% White, 2.8% Black/African American, 4.7% Asian, 2.8% American Indian/Alaska Native, 0.1% Native Hawaiian/Other Pacific Islander, 5.7% Two or more races, 76.0% Hispanic of any race; Average household size: 3.94; Median age: 29.8; Age under 18: 32.9%; Age 65 and over: 9.5%; Males per 100 females: 111.5

Housing: Homeownership rate: 59.2%; Homeowner vacancy rate: 1.7%; Rental vacancy rate: 6.2%

Glenn County

Located in north central California, partly in the Sacramento Valley, rising in the west to the Coast Ranges; watered by the Sacramento River; includes part of Mendocino National Forest. Covers a land area of 1,313.947 square miles, a water area of 13.031 square miles, and is located in the Pacific Time Zone at 39.60° N. Lat., 122.40° W. Long. The county was founded in 1891. County seat is Willows.

Weather Station: Orland — Elevation: 253 feet

	Jan	Feb	Mar	Apr	May	Jun	Jul	Aug	Sep	Oct	Nov	Dec
High	56	61	66	73	81	89	94	93	89	79	65	55
Low	37	40	43	47	54	60	63	61	57	50	42	37
Precip	4.4	4.1	3.2	1.3	1.0	0.5	0.0	0.1	0.4	1.1	2.7	3.8
Snow	0.0	0.0	0.0	0.0	0.0	0.0	0.0	0.0	0.0	0.0	0.0	0.0

High and Low temperatures in degrees Fahrenheit; Precipitation and Snow in inches

Weather Station: Stony Gorge Reservoir — Elevation: 799 feet

	Jan	Feb	Mar	Apr	May	Jun	Jul	Aug	Sep	Oct	Nov	Dec
High	56	59	64	71	80	89	96	95	90	79	64	56
Low	34	36	38	41	48	55	60	59	54	46	38	33
Precip	4.6	4.1	3.0	1.2	1.0	0.6	0.1	0.1	0.3	1.0	2.2	4.1
Snow	0.2	0.0	0.0	0.0	0.0	0.0	0.0	0.0	0.0	0.0	0.0	tr

High and Low temperatures in degrees Fahrenheit; Precipitation and Snow in inches

Weather Station: Willows 6 W — Elevation: 232 feet

	Jan	Feb	Mar	Apr	May	Jun	Jul	Aug	Sep	Oct	Nov	Dec
High	57	62	67	74	82	89	94	93	90	80	65	57
Low	37	39	42	44	51	57	60	58	56	49	41	36
Precip	4.0	3.8	2.9	1.1	0.9	0.4	0.0	0.1	0.3	1.0	2.3	3.2
Snow	tr	0.0	0.0	0.0	0.0	0.0	0.0	0.0	0.0	0.0	0.0	0.2

High and Low temperatures in degrees Fahrenheit; Precipitation and Snow in inches

Population: 28,122; Growth (since 2000): 6.3%; Density: 21.4 persons per square mile; Race: 71.1% White, 0.8% Black/African American, 2.6% Asian, 2.2% American Indian/Alaska Native, 0.1% Native Hawaiian/Other Pacific Islander, 3.6% two or more races, 37.5% Hispanic of any race; Average household size: 2.84; Median age: 35.3; Age under 18: 28.0%; Age 65 and over: 13.3%; Males per 100 females: 101.9; Marriage status: 28.7% never married, 54.9% now married, 2.8% separated, 5.8% widowed, 10.6% divorced; Foreign born: 17.2%; Speak English only: 63.9%; With disability: 15.8%; Veterans: 7.5%; Ancestry: 12.0% German, 9.5% Irish, 7.5% American, 6.6% English, 3.7% Portuguese
Religion: Six largest groups: 21.7% Catholicism, 3.7% Methodist/Pietist, 2.9% Latter-day Saints, 2.3% Non-denominational Protestant, 2.3% Baptist, 2.2% Pentecostal
Economy: Unemployment rate: 8.0%; Leading industries: 15.9% retail trade; 11.7% accommodation and food services; 10.0% other services (except public administration); Farms: 1,311 totaling 668,784 acres; Company size: 0 employ 1,000 or more persons, 0 employ 500 to 999 persons, 6 employ 100 to 499 persons, 454 employ less than 100 persons; Business ownership: 496 women-owned, n/a Black-owned, 315 Hispanic-owned, n/a Asian-owned
Employment: 10.2% management, business, and financial, 0.9% computer, engineering, and science, 8.6% education, legal, community service, arts, and media, 3.5% healthcare practitioners, 20.4% service, 19.7% sales and office, 21.7% natural resources, construction, and maintenance, 15.0% production, transportation, and material moving
Income: Per capita: $22,148; Median household: $43,023; Average household: $62,856; Households with income of $100,000 or more: 15.2%; Poverty rate: 18.8%
Educational Attainment: High school diploma or higher: 72.3%; Bachelor's degree or higher: 14.6%; Graduate/professional degree or higher: 4.5%
Housing: Homeownership rate: 62.2%; Median home value: $217,700; Median year structure built: 1973; Homeowner vacancy rate: 1.9%; Median gross rent: $720 per month; Rental vacancy rate: 6.4%
Vital Statistics: Birth rate: 136.4 per 10,000 population; Death rate: 75.5 per 10,000 population; Age-adjusted cancer mortality rate: 173.6 deaths per 100,000 population
Health Insurance: 79.4% have insurance; 51.5% have private insurance; 39.4% have public insurance; 20.6% do not have insurance; 8.7% of children under 18 do not have insurance
Health Care: Physicians: 2.5 per 10,000 population; Hospital beds: 5.3 per 10,000 population; Hospital admissions: 124.2 per 10,000 population
Air Quality Index: 93.6% good, 6.4% moderate, 0.0% unhealthy for sensitive individuals, 0.0% unhealthy (percent of days)
Transportation: Commute: 87.4% car, 0.0% public transportation, 3.8% walk, 7.4% work from home; Median travel time to work: 21.8 minutes
Presidential Election: 35.8% Obama, 61.3% Romney (2012)
National and State Parks: Bidwell-Sacramento River State Park; Mendocino National Forest; Sacramento National Wildlife Refuge
Additional Information Contacts
Glenn Government . . . . (530) 934-6400
http://www.countyofglenn.net

Glenn County Communities

ARTOIS (CDP). Covers a land area of 2.880 square miles and a water area of 0 square miles. Located at 39.63° N. Lat; 122.19° W. Long. Elevation is 167 feet.
Population: 295; Growth (since 2000): n/a; Density: 102.4 persons per square mile; Race: 83.1% White, 0.0% Black/African American, 1.0% Asian, 2.7% American Indian/Alaska Native, 0.0% Native Hawaiian/Other Pacific Islander, 4.7% Two or more races, 18.3% Hispanic of any race; Average household size: 2.92; Median age: 40.4; Age under 18: 26.1%; Age 65 and over: 15.9%; Males per 100 females: 102.1
Housing: Homeownership rate: 78.2%; Homeowner vacancy rate: 0.0%; Rental vacancy rate: 0.0%

BUTTE CITY (unincorporated postal area)
ZCTA: 95920
Covers a land area of 69.079 square miles and a water area of 0.238 square miles. Located at 39.45° N. Lat; 121.94° W. Long. Elevation is 89 feet.
Population: 274; Growth (since 2000): -5.8%; Density: 4.0 persons per square mile; Race: 70.8% White, 1.5% Black/African American, 0.4% Asian, 3.3% American Indian/Alaska Native, 0.0% Native Hawaiian/Other Pacific Islander, 0.4% Two or more races, 40.9% Hispanic of any race; Average household size: 2.69; Median age: 34.8; Age under 18: 27.7%; Age 65 and over: 11.3%; Males per 100 females: 130.3
Housing: Homeownership rate: 51.0%; Homeowner vacancy rate: 0.0%; Rental vacancy rate: 2.0%

ELK CREEK (CDP). Covers a land area of 1.449 square miles and a water area of 0.031 square miles. Located at 39.60° N. Lat; 122.53° W. Long. Elevation is 745 feet.
Population: 163; Growth (since 2000): n/a; Density: 112.5 persons per square mile; Race: 88.3% White, 0.0% Black/African American, 0.6% Asian, 4.3% American Indian/Alaska Native, 0.0% Native Hawaiian/Other Pacific Islander, 1.8% Two or more races, 4.9% Hispanic of any race; Average household size: 2.23; Median age: 52.5; Age under 18: 15.3%; Age 65 and over: 26.4%; Males per 100 females: 101.2
School District(s)
Stony Creek Joint Unified (KG-12)
2012-13 Enrollment: 111 . . . . (530) 968-5361
Housing: Homeownership rate: 79.5%; Homeowner vacancy rate: 3.3%; Rental vacancy rate: 0.0%

GLENN (unincorporated postal area)
ZCTA: 95943
Covers a land area of 63.299 square miles and a water area of 2.168 square miles. Located at 39.58° N. Lat; 122.03° W. Long. Elevation is 98 feet.
Population: 879; Growth (since 2000): -38.8%; Density: 13.9 persons per square mile; Race: 88.9% White, 0.0% Black/African American, 1.0% Asian, 0.1% American Indian/Alaska Native, 0.0% Native Hawaiian/Other Pacific Islander, 3.9% Two or more races, 19.7% Hispanic of any race; Average household size: 2.67; Median age: 37.3; Age under 18: 27.4%; Age 65 and over: 15.5%; Males per 100 females: 111.3
Housing: Homeownership rate: 60.8%; Homeowner vacancy rate: 1.9%; Rental vacancy rate: 13.3%

HAMILTON CITY (CDP). Covers a land area of 0.312 square miles and a water area of 0 square miles. Located at 39.74° N. Lat; 122.01° W. Long. Elevation is 151 feet.
Population: 1,759; Growth (since 2000): -7.6%; Density: 5,642.8 persons per square mile; Race: 47.4% White, 1.0% Black/African American, 0.9% Asian, 1.3% American Indian/Alaska Native, 0.0% Native Hawaiian/Other Pacific Islander, 3.7% Two or more races, 84.7% Hispanic of any race; Average household size: 3.45; Median age: 29.6; Age under 18: 30.1%; Age 65 and over: 9.9%; Males per 100 females: 103.8
School District(s)
Hamilton Unified (KG-12)
2012-13 Enrollment: 710 . . . . (530) 826-3261
Housing: Homeownership rate: 56.7%; Homeowner vacancy rate: 2.0%; Rental vacancy rate: 5.1%

ORLAND (city). Covers a land area of 2.971 square miles and a water area of 0 square miles. Located at 39.75° N. Lat; 122.19° W. Long. Elevation is 259 feet.
History: Orland was the site of the Reclamation Service Orland Irrigation Project, the first organized in California after the passage of the Wright Irrigation Act in 1887. Orland grew as the center of wheat and barley farms.
Population: 7,291; Growth (since 2000): 16.1%; Density: 2,453.8 persons per square mile; Race: 66.2% White, 0.5% Black/African American, 2.9% Asian, 1.7% American Indian/Alaska Native, 0.0% Native Hawaiian/Other Pacific Islander, 3.6% Two or more races, 44.8% Hispanic of any race; Average household size: 2.89; Median age: 32.0; Age under 18: 30.3%; Age 65 and over: 11.8%; Males per 100 females: 96.6; Marriage status: 33.3% never married, 51.7% now married, 3.6% separated, 6.1% widowed, 8.9% divorced; Foreign born: 15.9%; Speak English only: 57.3%; With disability: 16.9%; Veterans: 5.5%; Ancestry: 7.3% Irish, 7.0% American, 6.8% German, 5.9% English, 3.8% Dutch
Employment: 8.4% management, business, and financial, 0.6% computer, engineering, and science, 9.7% education, legal, community service, arts, and media, 3.6% healthcare practitioners, 26.9% service, 14.9% sales and office, 14.7% natural resources, construction, and maintenance, 21.2% production, transportation, and material moving

Income: Per capita: $16,017; Median household: $37,118; Average household: $49,526; Households with income of $100,000 or more: 6.5%; Poverty rate: 26.7%

Educational Attainment: High school diploma or higher: 69.0%; Bachelor's degree or higher: 11.4%; Graduate/professional degree or higher: 4.0%

School District(s)

Capay Joint Union Elementary (KG-08)
2012-13 Enrollment: 199. . . . . (530) 865-1222
Lake Elementary (KG-08)
2012-13 Enrollment: 157. . . . . (530) 865-1255
Orland Joint Unified (KG-12)
2012-13 Enrollment: 2,163 . . . . (530) 865-1200
Plaza Elementary (KG-08)
2012-13 Enrollment: 134. . . . . (530) 865-1250

Housing: Homeownership rate: 58.0%; Median home value: $172,700; Median year structure built: 1972; Homeowner vacancy rate: 2.2%; Median gross rent: $692 per month; Rental vacancy rate: 3.5%

Health Insurance: 82.1% have insurance; 44.3% have private insurance; 47.3% have public insurance; 17.9% do not have insurance; 6.7% of children under 18 do not have insurance

Safety: Violent crime rate: 36.4 per 10,000 population; Property crime rate: 235.8 per 10,000 population

Transportation: Commute: 92.3% car, 0.0% public transportation, 2.8% walk, 4.4% work from home; Median travel time to work: 24.6 minutes

Additional Information Contacts

City of Orland . . . . (530) 865-1600
http://www.cityoforland.com

WILLOWS (city). County seat. Covers a land area of 2.847 square miles and a water area of 0.026 square miles. Located at 39.51° N. Lat; 122.20° W. Long. Elevation is 138 feet.

History: Willows was named for a clump of willow trees bordering the creek. The town grew as the seat of Glenn County.

Population: 6,166; Growth (since 2000): -0.9%; Density: 2,166.1 persons per square mile; Race: 69.8% White, 1.3% Black/African American, 5.1% Asian, 2.2% American Indian/Alaska Native, 0.2% Native Hawaiian/Other Pacific Islander, 3.6% Two or more races, 32.8% Hispanic of any race; Average household size: 2.75; Median age: 32.6; Age under 18: 28.9%; Age 65 and over: 12.7%; Males per 100 females: 97.4; Marriage status: 26.9% never married, 50.9% now married, 2.4% separated, 7.8% widowed, 14.4% divorced; Foreign born: 18.4%; Speak English only: 66.0%; With disability: 17.5%; Veterans: 5.5%; Ancestry: 12.3% Irish, 10.1% German, 8.5% English, 8.4% American, 5.6% Italian

Employment: 5.8% management, business, and financial, 1.3% computer, engineering, and science, 10.6% education, legal, community service, arts, and media, 5.1% healthcare practitioners, 19.5% service, 25.4% sales and office, 21.4% natural resources, construction, and maintenance, 10.8% production, transportation, and material moving

Income: Per capita: $24,292; Median household: $43,807; Average household: $62,706; Households with income of $100,000 or more: 17.5%; Poverty rate: 17.6%

Educational Attainment: High school diploma or higher: 77.8%; Bachelor's degree or higher: 18.8%; Graduate/professional degree or higher: 9.7%

School District(s)

Glenn County Office of Education (KG-12)
2012-13 Enrollment: 372. . . . . (530) 934-6575
Glenn County Rop
2012-13 Enrollment: n/a . . . . (530) 934-6575
Willows Unified (KG-12)
2012-13 Enrollment: 1,467 . . . . (530) 934-6600

Housing: Homeownership rate: 52.8%; Median home value: $189,100; Median year structure built: 1970; Homeowner vacancy rate: 2.3%; Median gross rent: $732 per month; Rental vacancy rate: 8.8%

Health Insurance: 82.0% have insurance; 60.5% have private insurance; 34.0% have public insurance; 18.0% do not have insurance; 8.0% of children under 18 do not have insurance

Hospitals: Glenn Medical Center

Safety: Violent crime rate: 27.8 per 10,000 population; Property crime rate: 292.4 per 10,000 population

Newspapers: Orland Press-Register (weekly circulation 2400); Sacramento Valley Mirror (weekly circulation 2900); Willows Journal (weekly circulation 8000)

Transportation: Commute: 84.7% car, 0.0% public transportation, 6.9% walk, 7.3% work from home; Median travel time to work: 20.6 minutes

Additional Information Contacts

City of Willows. . . . . (530) 934-7041
http://www.cityofwillows.org

Humboldt County

Located in northwestern California, on the Pacific Coast; drained by the Klamath, Trinity, Mad, Eel, and Mattole Rivers; mainly in the Coast Range, including part of the Klamath Mountains in the east and northeast, and part of Trinity National Forest ; includes redwood forests. Covers a land area of 3,567.987 square miles, a water area of 484.271 square miles, and is located in the Pacific Time Zone at 40.71° N. Lat., 123.93° W. Long. The county was founded in 1853. County seat is Eureka.

Humboldt County is part of the Eureka-Arcata-Fortuna, CA Micropolitan Statistical Area. The entire metro area includes: Humboldt County, CA

Weather Station: Eureka — Elevation: 20 feet

	Jan	Feb	Mar	Apr	May	Jun	Jul	Aug	Sep	Oct	Nov	Dec
High	56	57	57	58	61	63	64	65	64	62	59	55
Low	42	43	43	45	48	51	53	54	51	48	44	41
Precip	6.3	5.6	5.3	3.2	1.7	0.7	0.2	0.3	0.6	2.1	5.5	8.0
Snow	tr	0.2	tr	tr	0.0	tr	0.0	0.0	0.0	0.0	tr	0.1

High and Low temperatures in degrees Fahrenheit; Precipitation and Snow in inches

Weather Station: Orleans — Elevation: 399 feet

	Jan	Feb	Mar	Apr	May	Jun	Jul	Aug	Sep	Oct	Nov	Dec
High	51	57	63	70	77	84	92	92	87	73	57	50
Low	36	38	40	42	47	51	55	54	50	45	41	36
Precip	8.8	7.5	6.4	3.6	2.3	0.9	0.2	0.4	0.7	3.3	7.7	10.8
Snow	0.9	1.1	0.3	tr	tr	0.0	0.0	0.0	0.0	0.0	0.1	1.4

High and Low temperatures in degrees Fahrenheit; Precipitation and Snow in inches

Weather Station: Richardson Gr St Pk — Elevation: 500 feet

	Jan	Feb	Mar	Apr	May	Jun	Jul	Aug	Sep	Oct	Nov	Dec
High	50	54	59	65	71	77	85	86	83	70	55	49
Low	38	39	40	42	46	50	53	53	49	45	41	38
Precip	12.1	11.1	9.6	4.5	2.3	0.9	0.0	0.2	0.7	3.6	9.0	14.2
Snow	0.0	0.0	tr	0.0	0.0	0.0	0.0	0.0	0.0	0.0	0.0	0.2

High and Low temperatures in degrees Fahrenheit; Precipitation and Snow in inches

Weather Station: Scotia — Elevation: 139 feet

	Jan	Feb	Mar	Apr	May	Jun	Jul	Aug	Sep	Oct	Nov	Dec
High	57	58	59	61	64	67	70	71	72	68	61	56
Low	41	42	42	44	48	51	53	53	51	47	44	40
Precip	8.2	7.7	7.1	3.6	1.8	0.6	0.1	0.2	0.5	2.5	6.3	9.9
Snow	tr	0.3	tr	tr	0.0	0.0	0.0	0.0	0.0	0.0	0.0	0.2

High and Low temperatures in degrees Fahrenheit; Precipitation and Snow in inches

Population: 134,623; Growth (since 2000): 6.4%; Density: 37.7 persons per square mile; Race: 81.7% White, 1.1% Black/African American, 2.2% Asian, 5.7% American Indian/Alaska Native, 0.3% Native Hawaiian/Other Pacific Islander, 5.3% two or more races, 9.8% Hispanic of any race; Average household size: 2.31; Median age: 37.1; Age under 18: 20.1%; Age 65 and over: 13.2%; Males per 100 females: 100.8; Marriage status: 37.7% never married, 43.7% now married, 2.3% separated, 5.5% widowed, 13.1% divorced; Foreign born: 5.7%; Speak English only: 90.3%; With disability: 15.7%; Veterans: 9.7%; Ancestry: 13.7% German, 11.5% Irish, 10.5% English, 6.1% Italian, 4.5% European

Religion: Six largest groups: 7.4% Catholicism, 2.8% Latter-day Saints, 2.3% Baptist, 1.9% Pentecostal, 1.6% Methodist/Pietist, 0.9% Presbyterian-Reformed

Economy: Unemployment rate: 6.6%; Leading industries: 18.1% retail trade; 13.7% health care and social assistance; 11.6% accommodation and food services; Farms: 930 totaling 593,597 acres; Company size: 1 employs 1,000 or more persons, 0 employ 500 to 999 persons, 30 employ 100 to 499 persons, 3,194 employ less than 100 persons; Business ownership: 3,953 women-owned, n/a Black-owned, n/a Hispanic-owned, n/a Asian-owned

Employment: 12.3% management, business, and financial, 3.7% computer, engineering, and science, 12.0% education, legal, community service, arts, and media, 5.0% healthcare practitioners, 22.9% service, 23.9% sales and office, 11.6% natural resources, construction, and maintenance, 8.6% production, transportation, and material moving

Income: Per capita: $23,540; Median household: $41,426; Average household: $56,127; Households with income of $100,000 or more: 13.3%; Poverty rate: 20.4%
Educational Attainment: High school diploma or higher: 90.4%; Bachelor's degree or higher: 27.5%; Graduate/professional degree or higher: 8.8%
Housing: Homeownership rate: 55.0%; Median home value: $288,300; Median year structure built: 1971; Homeowner vacancy rate: 1.5%; Median gross rent: $889 per month; Rental vacancy rate: 3.6%
Vital Statistics: Birth rate: 104.5 per 10,000 population; Death rate: 94.5 per 10,000 population; Age-adjusted cancer mortality rate: 188.4 deaths per 100,000 population
Health Insurance: 80.6% have insurance; 56.6% have private insurance; 36.4% have public insurance; 19.4% do not have insurance; 10.2% of children under 18 do not have insurance
Health Care: Physicians: 18.6 per 10,000 population; Hospital beds: 17.5 per 10,000 population; Hospital admissions: 834.3 per 10,000 population
Air Quality Index: 87.1% good, 12.9% moderate, 0.0% unhealthy for sensitive individuals, 0.0% unhealthy (percent of days)
Transportation: Commute: 83.1% car, 1.3% public transportation, 6.0% walk, 6.5% work from home; Median travel time to work: 17.5 minutes
Presidential Election: 60.0% Obama, 33.8% Romney (2012)
National and State Parks: Azalea State Natural Reserve; Benbow Lake State Recreation Area; Bull Creek State Wilderness; Fort Humboldt State Historic Park; Grizzly Creek Redwoods State Park; Harry A. Merlo State Recreation Area; Humboldt Bay National Wildlife Refuge; Humboldt Lagoons State Park; Humboldt Redwoods State Park; John B Dewitt Redwoods State Natural Reserve; Little River State Beach; Murrelet State Wilderness; Patrick's Point State Park; Prairie Creek Redwoods State Park; Redwood National Park; Richardson Grove State Park; Trinidad State Beach; Horse Ridge National Scenic Trail
Additional Information Contacts
Humboldt Government .... (707) 476-2396
http://www.co.humboldt.ca.us

Humboldt County Communities

ALDERPOINT (CDP). Covers a land area of 2.429 square miles and a water area of 0 square miles. Located at 40.16° N. Lat; 123.62° W. Long. Elevation is 472 feet.
Population: 186; Growth (since 2000): n/a; Density: 76.6 persons per square mile; Race: 91.4% White, 0.0% Black/African American, 0.5% Asian, 4.8% American Indian/Alaska Native, 0.0% Native Hawaiian/Other Pacific Islander, 2.7% Two or more races, 5.4% Hispanic of any race; Average household size: 2.33; Median age: 47.0; Age under 18: 17.2%; Age 65 and over: 13.4%; Males per 100 females: 111.4
Housing: Homeownership rate: 72.5%; Homeowner vacancy rate: 0.0%; Rental vacancy rate: 0.0%

ARCATA (city). Covers a land area of 9.097 square miles and a water area of 1.897 square miles. Located at 40.86° N. Lat; 124.07° W. Long. Elevation is 23 feet.
History: Arcata was called Uniontown when it was founded in 1850 as a shipping center for lumber. The town served briefly as the seat of Humboldt County. An early resident here was author Bret Harte who worked as an assistant to the newspaper editor and as a Wells, Fargo & Company agent from 1857-1859.
Population: 17,231; Growth (since 2000): 3.5%; Density: 1,894.2 persons per square mile; Race: 81.8% White, 2.0% Black/African American, 2.6% Asian, 2.3% American Indian/Alaska Native, 0.2% Native Hawaiian/Other Pacific Islander, 6.6% Two or more races, 11.6% Hispanic of any race; Average household size: 2.10; Median age: 26.1; Age under 18: 12.6%; Age 65 and over: 8.2%; Males per 100 females: 99.2; Marriage status: 60.1% never married, 25.5% now married, 1.8% separated, 3.8% widowed, 10.6% divorced; Foreign born: 6.2%; Speak English only: 89.0%; With disability: 10.6%; Veterans: 5.8%; Ancestry: 13.4% Irish, 13.0% German, 10.1% English, 6.9% European, 5.4% Italian
Employment: 10.1% management, business, and financial, 6.1% computer, engineering, and science, 16.7% education, legal, community service, arts, and media, 6.3% healthcare practitioners, 23.4% service, 25.0% sales and office, 5.7% natural resources, construction, and maintenance, 6.8% production, transportation, and material moving
Income: Per capita: $18,829; Median household: $31,336; Average household: $46,187; Households with income of $100,000 or more: 11.1%; Poverty rate: 34.1%
Educational Attainment: High school diploma or higher: 92.2%; Bachelor's degree or higher: 44.2%; Graduate/professional degree or higher: 17.5%

School District(s)

Arcata Elementary (KG-08)
2012-13 Enrollment: 932........................ (707) 822-0351
Humboldt County Office of Education (PK-12)
2012-13 Enrollment: 467........................ (707) 445-7000
Northern Humboldt Union High (KG-12)
2012-13 Enrollment: 1,722 .... (707) 839-6470
Pacific Union Elementary (KG-08)
2012-13 Enrollment: 542........................ (707) 822-4619

Four-year College(s)

Humboldt State University (Public)
Fall 2013 Enrollment: 8,293 .... (707) 826-3011
2013-14 Tuition: In-state $7,144; Out-of-state $18,304
Housing: Homeownership rate: 34.2%; Median home value: $335,100; Median year structure built: 1972; Homeowner vacancy rate: 1.2%; Median gross rent: $902 per month; Rental vacancy rate: 2.2%
Health Insurance: 79.1% have insurance; 64.0% have private insurance; 24.8% have public insurance; 20.9% do not have insurance; 6.3% of children under 18 do not have insurance
Hospitals: Mad River Community Hospital (78 beds)
Safety: Violent crime rate: 37.6 per 10,000 population; Property crime rate: 472.3 per 10,000 population
Newspapers: Arcata Eye (weekly circulation 4000)
Transportation: Commute: 67.0% car, 1.6% public transportation, 16.0% walk, 5.9% work from home; Median travel time to work: 14.9 minutes; Amtrak: Bus service available.
Airports: Arcata (primary service/non-hub)
Additional Information Contacts
City of Arcata.................................. (707) 822-5951
http://www.cityofarcata.org

BAYSIDE (unincorporated postal area)
ZCTA: 95524
Covers a land area of 10.420 square miles and a water area of 0.010 square miles. Located at 40.83° N. Lat; 124.05° W. Long. Elevation is 30 feet.
Population: 1,787; Growth (since 2000): 6.2%; Density: 171.5 persons per square mile; Race: 89.3% White, 0.4% Black/African American, 2.6% Asian, 2.4% American Indian/Alaska Native, 0.3% Native Hawaiian/Other Pacific Islander, 4.1% Two or more races, 4.9% Hispanic of any race; Average household size: 2.31; Median age: 47.6; Age under 18: 18.4%; Age 65 and over: 16.2%; Males per 100 females: 98.8

School District(s)

Jacoby Creek Elementary (KG-08)
2012-13 Enrollment: 427........................ (707) 822-4896
Housing: Homeownership rate: 75.0%; Homeowner vacancy rate: 0.3%; Rental vacancy rate: 3.0%

BAYVIEW (CDP). Covers a land area of 0.732 square miles and a water area of 0 square miles. Located at 40.77° N. Lat; 124.18° W. Long. Elevation is 66 feet.
Population: 2,510; Growth (since 2000): 6.4%; Density: 3,429.8 persons per square mile; Race: 78.0% White, 1.1% Black/African American, 3.5% Asian, 4.7% American Indian/Alaska Native, 0.2% Native Hawaiian/Other Pacific Islander, 5.0% Two or more races, 16.9% Hispanic of any race; Average household size: 2.43; Median age: 36.2; Age under 18: 23.9%; Age 65 and over: 11.7%; Males per 100 females: 96.9; Marriage status: 37.8% never married, 42.4% now married, 3.8% separated, 6.6% widowed, 13.3% divorced; Foreign born: 12.0%; Speak English only: 79.3%; With disability: 18.9%; Veterans: 5.4%; Ancestry: 12.6% Irish, 9.9% German, 8.0% English, 7.5% American, 5.5% Italian
Employment: 19.7% management, business, and financial, 1.3% computer, engineering, and science, 9.4% education, legal, community service, arts, and media, 6.3% healthcare practitioners, 21.3% service, 17.9% sales and office, 22.3% natural resources, construction, and maintenance, 1.7% production, transportation, and material moving
Income: Per capita: $25,130; Median household: $31,071; Average household: $54,229; Households with income of $100,000 or more: 8.8%; Poverty rate: 28.9%
Educational Attainment: High school diploma or higher: 81.9%; Bachelor's degree or higher: 17.9%; Graduate/professional degree or higher: 7.3%

Housing: Homeownership rate: 63.4%; Median home value: $240,600; Median year structure built: 1964; Homeowner vacancy rate: 1.4%; Median gross rent: $957 per month; Rental vacancy rate: 2.3%
Health Insurance: 80.8% have insurance; 50.0% have private insurance; 40.0% have public insurance; 19.2% do not have insurance; 13.4% of children under 18 do not have insurance
Transportation: Commute: 94.7% car, 1.1% public transportation, 0.2% walk, 1.6% work from home; Median travel time to work: 19.4 minutes

BENBOW (CDP). Covers a land area of 4.881 square miles and a water area of 0 square miles. Located at 40.06° N. Lat; 123.77° W. Long. Elevation is 440 feet.
Population: 321; Growth (since 2000): n/a; Density: 65.8 persons per square mile; Race: 91.6% White, 0.0% Black/African American, 0.3% Asian, 0.6% American Indian/Alaska Native, 0.0% Native Hawaiian/Other Pacific Islander, 3.4% Two or more races, 7.8% Hispanic of any race; Average household size: 2.13; Median age: 46.2; Age under 18: 18.4%; Age 65 and over: 17.4%; Males per 100 females: 101.9
Housing: Homeownership rate: 79.3%; Homeowner vacancy rate: 2.4%; Rental vacancy rate: 0.0%

BIG LAGOON (CDP). Covers a land area of 0.599 square miles and a water area of 0 square miles. Located at 41.16° N. Lat; 124.13° W. Long. Elevation is 56 feet.
Population: 93; Growth (since 2000): n/a; Density: 155.2 persons per square mile; Race: 78.5% White, 0.0% Black/African American, 0.0% Asian, 11.8% American Indian/Alaska Native, 0.0% Native Hawaiian/Other Pacific Islander, 8.6% Two or more races, 11.8% Hispanic of any race; Average household size: 1.75; Median age: 56.3; Age under 18: 12.9%; Age 65 and over: 26.9%; Males per 100 females: 72.2
Housing: Homeownership rate: 71.7%; Homeowner vacancy rate: 0.0%; Rental vacancy rate: 0.0%

BLOCKSBURG (unincorporated postal area)
ZCTA: 95514
Covers a land area of 86.698 square miles and a water area of 0.217 square miles. Located at 40.29° N. Lat; 123.65° W. Long. Elevation is 1,591 feet.
Population: 254; Growth (since 2000): 28.3%; Density: 2.9 persons per square mile; Race: 88.2% White, 0.0% Black/African American, 0.4% Asian, 4.7% American Indian/Alaska Native, 0.4% Native Hawaiian/Other Pacific Islander, 5.5% Two or more races, 9.1% Hispanic of any race; Average household size: 2.37; Median age: 44.0; Age under 18: 20.1%; Age 65 and over: 12.6%; Males per 100 females: 126.8
School District(s)
Southern Humboldt Joint Unified (KG-12)
2012-13 Enrollment: 742. . . . . (707) 943-1789
Housing: Homeownership rate: 75.7%; Homeowner vacancy rate: 0.0%; Rental vacancy rate: 7.1%

BLUE LAKE (city). Covers a land area of 0.592 square miles and a water area of 0.030 square miles. Located at 40.88° N. Lat; 123.99° W. Long. Elevation is 131 feet.
History: Blue Lake developed as the trading center of a farming and dairying area.
Population: 1,253; Growth (since 2000): 10.4%; Density: 2,116.6 persons per square mile; Race: 87.3% White, 0.4% Black/African American, 1.0% Asian, 4.4% American Indian/Alaska Native, 0.3% Native Hawaiian/Other Pacific Islander, 4.6% Two or more races, 6.5% Hispanic of any race; Average household size: 2.31; Median age: 38.3; Age under 18: 19.8%; Age 65 and over: 10.1%; Males per 100 females: 95.8
School District(s)
Blue Lake Union Elementary (KG-08)
2012-13 Enrollment: 152. . . . . (707) 668-5674
Green Point Elementary (KG-08)
2012-13 Enrollment: 5. . . . . (707) 668-5921
Four-year College(s)
Dell'Arte International School of Physical Theatre (Private, Not-for-profit)
Fall 2013 Enrollment: 29 . . . . (707) 668-5663
2013-14 Tuition: In-state $12,750; Out-of-state $12,750
Housing: Homeownership rate: 55.6%; Homeowner vacancy rate: 1.0%; Rental vacancy rate: 2.8%
Additional Information Contacts
City of Blue Lake . . . . (707) 668-5655
http://bluelake.ca.gov

BRIDGEVILLE (unincorporated postal area)
ZCTA: 95526
Covers a land area of 110.080 square miles and a water area of 0.181 square miles. Located at 40.46° N. Lat; 123.67° W. Long. Elevation is 633 feet.
Population: 378; Growth (since 2000): -44.8%; Density: 3.4 persons per square mile; Race: 85.7% White, 0.3% Black/African American, 0.8% Asian, 8.2% American Indian/Alaska Native, 0.0% Native Hawaiian/Other Pacific Islander, 4.5% Two or more races, 5.8% Hispanic of any race; Average household size: 1.95; Median age: 48.5; Age under 18: 14.8%; Age 65 and over: 14.0%; Males per 100 females: 129.1
School District(s)
Bridgeville Elementary (KG-08)
2012-13 Enrollment: 37. . . . . (707) 777-3311
Southern Trinity Joint Unified (KG-12)
2012-13 Enrollment: 97. . . . . (707) 574-6237
Housing: Homeownership rate: 73.8%; Homeowner vacancy rate: 0.7%; Rental vacancy rate: 11.3%

CARLOTTA (unincorporated postal area)
ZCTA: 95528
Covers a land area of 102.587 square miles and a water area of 0.158 square miles. Located at 40.50° N. Lat; 123.93° W. Long. Elevation is 131 feet.
Population: 1,139; Growth (since 2000): 6.6%; Density: 11.1 persons per square mile; Race: 89.2% White, 0.2% Black/African American, 0.8% Asian, 3.8% American Indian/Alaska Native, 0.4% Native Hawaiian/Other Pacific Islander, 3.2% Two or more races, 9.2% Hispanic of any race; Average household size: 2.55; Median age: 45.0; Age under 18: 21.3%; Age 65 and over: 14.0%; Males per 100 females: 105.2
School District(s)
Cuddeback Union Elementary (KG-08)
2012-13 Enrollment: 122. . . . . (707) 768-3372
Housing: Homeownership rate: 75.1%; Homeowner vacancy rate: 2.0%; Rental vacancy rate: 4.2%

CUTTEN (CDP). Covers a land area of 1.294 square miles and a water area of 0 square miles. Located at 40.77° N. Lat; 124.14° W. Long. Elevation is 200 feet.
Population: 3,108; Growth (since 2000): 6.0%; Density: 2,401.8 persons per square mile; Race: 84.6% White, 0.9% Black/African American, 2.6% Asian, 3.8% American Indian/Alaska Native, 0.4% Native Hawaiian/Other Pacific Islander, 5.3% Two or more races, 8.2% Hispanic of any race; Average household size: 2.37; Median age: 37.9; Age under 18: 23.1%; Age 65 and over: 15.5%; Males per 100 females: 96.2; Marriage status: 24.6% never married, 48.8% now married, 3.6% separated, 10.9% widowed, 15.7% divorced; Foreign born: 1.7%; Speak English only: 96.5%; With disability: 22.4%; Veterans: 9.2%; Ancestry: 16.2% German, 14.5% English, 13.2% Irish, 9.8% Italian, 4.8% Polish
Employment: 22.5% management, business, and financial, 2.0% computer, engineering, and science, 7.2% education, legal, community service, arts, and media, 10.1% healthcare practitioners, 8.0% service, 37.4% sales and office, 7.9% natural resources, construction, and maintenance, 4.9% production, transportation, and material moving
Income: Per capita: $30,625; Median household: $56,676; Average household: $62,892; Households with income of $100,000 or more: 16.4%; Poverty rate: 16.8%
Educational Attainment: High school diploma or higher: 98.0%; Bachelor's degree or higher: 34.6%; Graduate/professional degree or higher: 6.8%
Housing: Homeownership rate: 54.7%; Median home value: $312,400; Median year structure built: 1973; Homeowner vacancy rate: 2.3%; Median gross rent: $986 per month; Rental vacancy rate: 3.4%
Health Insurance: 91.6% have insurance; 68.3% have private insurance; 40.8% have public insurance; 8.4% do not have insurance; 0.0% of children under 18 do not have insurance
Transportation: Commute: 86.1% car, 0.0% public transportation, 2.6% walk, 7.5% work from home; Median travel time to work: 13.3 minutes

EUREKA (city). County seat. Covers a land area of 9.384 square miles and a water area of 5.070 square miles. Located at 40.79° N. Lat; 124.16° W. Long. Elevation is 39 feet.
History: Eureka was laid out and named in 1850 by James Ryan, who jubilantly shouted "Eureka" ("I have found it!") when he landed at the site.

U.S. troops occupied Fort Humboldt between 1853 and 1865, with Ulysses S. Grant serving as captain of the Fourth U.S. Infantry here in 1854. The town developed as a mill town, processing redwoods from the surrounding forests.

Population: 27,191; Growth (since 2000): 4.1%; Density: 2,897.5 persons per square mile; Race: 79.3% White, 1.9% Black/African American, 4.2% Asian, 3.7% American Indian/Alaska Native, 0.6% Native Hawaiian/Other Pacific Islander, 5.9% Two or more races, 11.6% Hispanic of any race; Average household size: 2.27; Median age: 36.2; Age under 18: 20.0%; Age 65 and over: 11.8%; Males per 100 females: 106.0; Marriage status: 41.0% never married, 39.4% now married, 4.3% separated, 5.4% widowed, 14.2% divorced; Foreign born: 8.0%; Speak English only: 88.9%; With disability: 17.6%; Veterans: 12.1%; Ancestry: 14.3% German, 13.0% Irish, 10.6% English, 6.0% Italian, 4.3% American

Employment: 8.9% management, business, and financial, 3.1% computer, engineering, and science, 10.0% education, legal, community service, arts, and media, 4.0% healthcare practitioners, 27.8% service, 27.1% sales and office, 10.0% natural resources, construction, and maintenance, 9.2% production, transportation, and material moving

Income: Per capita: $20,930; Median household: $36,618; Average household: $47,527; Households with income of $100,000 or more: 9.4%; Poverty rate: 23.8%

Educational Attainment: High school diploma or higher: 87.7%; Bachelor's degree or higher: 22.8%; Graduate/professional degree or higher: 7.3%

School District(s)

Cutten Elementary (KG-06)
2012-13 Enrollment: 561 . . . . (707) 441-3900

Eureka City Schools (KG-12)
2012-13 Enrollment: 3,669 . . . . (707) 441-2400

Fortuna Union High (09-12)
2012-13 Enrollment: 1,075 . . . . (707) 725-4461

Freshwater Elementary (KG-08)
2012-13 Enrollment: 332 . . . . (707) 442-2969

Garfield Elementary (KG-06)
2012-13 Enrollment: 62 . . . . (707) 442-5471

Humboldt County Office of Education (PK-12)
2012-13 Enrollment: 467 . . . . (707) 445-7000

Humboldt County Rop
2012-13 Enrollment: n/a . . . . (707) 445-7018

Loleta Union Elementary (KG-12)
2012-13 Enrollment: 284 . . . . (707) 733-5705

South Bay Union Elementary (KG-12)
2012-13 Enrollment: 849 . . . . (707) 476-8549

Two-year College(s)

College of the Redwoods (Public)
Fall 2013 Enrollment: 4,938 . . . . (707) 476-4100
2013-14 Tuition: In-state $1,140; Out-of-state $1,140

Vocational/Technical School(s)

Fredrick and Charles Beauty College (Private, For-profit)
Fall 2013 Enrollment: 83 . . . . (707) 443-2733
2013-14 Tuition: $10,500

Housing: Homeownership rate: 43.3%; Median home value: $241,400; Median year structure built: 1954; Homeowner vacancy rate: 2.0%; Median gross rent: $802 per month; Rental vacancy rate: 3.7%

Health Insurance: 79.0% have insurance; 47.7% have private insurance; 42.1% have public insurance; 21.0% do not have insurance; 9.5% of children under 18 do not have insurance

Hospitals: Saint Joseph Hospital (189 beds)

Safety: Violent crime rate: 71.4 per 10,000 population; Property crime rate: 776.4 per 10,000 population

Newspapers: Humboldt Beacon (weekly circulation 4500); North Coast Journal (weekly circulation 21000); Times-Standard (daily circulation 19900)

Transportation: Commute: 84.1% car, 1.6% public transportation, 6.0% walk, 4.1% work from home; Median travel time to work: 13.3 minutes; Amtrak: Bus service available.

Additional Information Contacts

City of Eureka . . . . (707) 441-4144
http://www.ci.eureka.ca.gov/default.asp

FERNDALE (city). Covers a land area of 1.027 square miles and a water area of 0 square miles. Located at 40.58° N. Lat; 124.26° W. Long. Elevation is 56 feet.

History: An April 1992 earthquake of 7.0 magnitude, centered near here, destroyed many 19th-century Victorian houses. Town again badly damaged, by floods, in 1995, which killed much livestock.

Population: 1,371; Growth (since 2000): -0.8%; Density: 1,335.5 persons per square mile; Race: 93.4% White, 0.1% Black/African American, 1.5% Asian, 1.6% American Indian/Alaska Native, 0.1% Native Hawaiian/Other Pacific Islander, 2.0% Two or more races, 5.6% Hispanic of any race; Average household size: 2.24; Median age: 47.2; Age under 18: 20.6%; Age 65 and over: 22.5%; Males per 100 females: 89.6

School District(s)

Ferndale Unified (KG-12)
2012-13 Enrollment: 515 . . . . (707) 786-5900

Housing: Homeownership rate: 63.5%; Homeowner vacancy rate: 1.8%; Rental vacancy rate: 3.0%

Safety: Violent crime rate: 29.3 per 10,000 population; Property crime rate: 190.6 per 10,000 population

Newspapers: Ferndale Enterprise (weekly circulation 1500)

Additional Information Contacts

City of Ferndale . . . . (707) 786-4224
http://ci.ferndale.ca.us

FIELDBROOK (CDP). Covers a land area of 10.468 square miles and a water area of 0.004 square miles. Located at 40.97° N. Lat; 124.03° W. Long. Elevation is 203 feet.

Population: 859; Growth (since 2000): n/a; Density: 82.1 persons per square mile; Race: 88.8% White, 0.5% Black/African American, 0.6% Asian, 2.2% American Indian/Alaska Native, 0.0% Native Hawaiian/Other Pacific Islander, 6.3% Two or more races, 5.9% Hispanic of any race; Average household size: 2.48; Median age: 47.0; Age under 18: 18.9%; Age 65 and over: 11.8%; Males per 100 females: 100.2

Housing: Homeownership rate: 80.9%; Homeowner vacancy rate: 0.4%; Rental vacancy rate: 6.8%

FIELDS LANDING (CDP). Covers a land area of 0.277 square miles and a water area of 0.003 square miles. Located at 40.72° N. Lat; 124.22° W. Long. Elevation is 13 feet.

Population: 276; Growth (since 2000): n/a; Density: 997.4 persons per square mile; Race: 76.1% White, 2.2% Black/African American, 7.6% Asian, 4.7% American Indian/Alaska Native, 0.4% Native Hawaiian/Other Pacific Islander, 6.9% Two or more races, 6.5% Hispanic of any race; Average household size: 2.03; Median age: 36.8; Age under 18: 15.6%; Age 65 and over: 11.2%; Males per 100 females: 133.9

Housing: Homeownership rate: 31.6%; Homeowner vacancy rate: 2.3%; Rental vacancy rate: 5.1%

FORTUNA (city). Covers a land area of 4.845 square miles and a water area of <.001 square miles. Located at 40.59° N. Lat; 124.14° W. Long. Elevation is 66 feet.

History: Fortuna was first called Springville because of the numerous nearby springs. The name was changed to Slide, and then to Fortuna by a landowner who hoped to attract more residents.

Population: 11,926; Growth (since 2000): 13.6%; Density: 2,461.4 persons per square mile; Race: 81.2% White, 0.6% Black/African American, 0.9% Asian, 3.7% American Indian/Alaska Native, 0.1% Native Hawaiian/Other Pacific Islander, 4.6% Two or more races, 17.0% Hispanic of any race; Average household size: 2.49; Median age: 38.1; Age under 18: 24.6%; Age 65 and over: 17.3%; Males per 100 females: 93.1; Marriage status: 30.0% never married, 50.4% now married, 2.0% separated, 7.7% widowed, 11.9% divorced; Foreign born: 8.6%; Speak English only: 85.2%; With disability: 17.0%; Veterans: 10.7%; Ancestry: 14.4% European, 12.3% German, 9.5% English, 8.6% Irish, 3.6% Italian

Employment: 11.2% management, business, and financial, 2.8% computer, engineering, and science, 11.1% education, legal, community service, arts, and media, 3.4% healthcare practitioners, 24.4% service, 28.4% sales and office, 10.0% natural resources, construction, and maintenance, 8.6% production, transportation, and material moving

Income: Per capita: $21,383; Median household: $41,026; Average household: $58,853; Households with income of $100,000 or more: 12.4%; Poverty rate: 20.3%

Educational Attainment: High school diploma or higher: 86.7%; Bachelor's degree or higher: 16.1%; Graduate/professional degree or higher: 4.8%

School District(s)

Fortuna Union High (09-12)
2012-13 Enrollment: 1,075 . . . . (707) 725-4461
Humboldt County Office of Education (PK-12)
2012-13 Enrollment: 467. . . . . (707) 445-7000

Housing: Homeownership rate: 58.6%; Median home value: $269,600; Median year structure built: 1978; Homeowner vacancy rate: 1.7%; Median gross rent: $819 per month; Rental vacancy rate: 6.2%

Health Insurance: 82.7% have insurance; 56.3% have private insurance; 42.3% have public insurance; 17.3% do not have insurance; 8.0% of children under 18 do not have insurance

Hospitals: Redwood Memorial Hospital (25 beds)

Safety: Violent crime rate: 34.7 per 10,000 population; Property crime rate: 363.5 per 10,000 population

Transportation: Commute: 81.9% car, 2.7% public transportation, 5.4% walk, 6.8% work from home; Median travel time to work: 20.6 minutes; Amtrak: Bus service available.

Airports: Rohnerville (general aviation)

Additional Information Contacts

City of Fortuna. . . . . (707) 725-7600
http://www.friendlyfortuna.com

GARBERVILLE (CDP). Covers a land area of 2.705 square miles and a water area of 0.057 square miles. Located at 40.10° N. Lat; 123.79° W. Long. Elevation is 535 feet.

Population: 913; Growth (since 2000): n/a; Density: 337.5 persons per square mile; Race: 89.3% White, 1.5% Black/African American, 1.9% Asian, 3.2% American Indian/Alaska Native, 0.0% Native Hawaiian/Other Pacific Islander, 3.4% Two or more races, 5.9% Hispanic of any race; Average household size: 2.01; Median age: 40.0; Age under 18: 17.5%; Age 65 and over: 13.7%; Males per 100 females: 109.9

School District(s)

Humboldt County Office of Education (PK-12)
2012-13 Enrollment: 467. . . . . (707) 445-7000
Southern Humboldt Joint Unified (KG-12)
2012-13 Enrollment: 742. . . . . (707) 943-1789

Housing: Homeownership rate: 44.8%; Homeowner vacancy rate: 2.2%; Rental vacancy rate: 2.3%

Hospitals: Jerold Phelps Community Hospital (9 beds)

HONEYDEW (unincorporated postal area)

ZCTA: 95545

Covers a land area of 47.945 square miles and a water area of 0 square miles. Located at 40.28° N. Lat; 124.06° W. Long. Elevation is 322 feet.

Population: 153; Growth (since 2000): 109.6%; Density: 3.2 persons per square mile; Race: 91.5% White, 0.7% Black/African American, 1.3% Asian, 0.7% American Indian/Alaska Native, 0.7% Native Hawaiian/Other Pacific Islander, 5.2% Two or more races, 2.6% Hispanic of any race; Average household size: 2.15; Median age: 46.3; Age under 18: 21.6%; Age 65 and over: 7.8%; Males per 100 females: 125.0

School District(s)

Mattole Unified (KG-12)
2012-13 Enrollment: 794. . . . . (707) 629-3311

Housing: Homeownership rate: 71.8%; Homeowner vacancy rate: 0.0%; Rental vacancy rate: 4.8%

HOOPA (unincorporated postal area)

ZCTA: 95546

Covers a land area of 136.502 square miles and a water area of 1.505 square miles. Located at 41.09° N. Lat; 123.68° W. Long. Elevation is 328 feet.

Population: 3,494; Growth (since 2000): 14.9%; Density: 25.6 persons per square mile; Race: 13.2% White, 0.1% Black/African American, 0.1% Asian, 80.5% American Indian/Alaska Native, 0.2% Native Hawaiian/Other Pacific Islander, 5.4% Two or more races, 7.1% Hispanic of any race; Average household size: 3.06; Median age: 28.5; Age under 18: 34.9%; Age 65 and over: 8.8%; Males per 100 females: 98.0; Marriage status: 44.4% never married, 39.7% now married, 4.3% separated, 4.8% widowed, 11.1% divorced; Foreign born: 4.6%; Speak English only: 92.2%; With disability: 14.5%; Veterans: 6.8%; Ancestry: 1.8% German, 1.6% Italian, 1.5% Irish, 0.9% European, 0.7% Swedish

Employment: 16.9% management, business, and financial, 7.8% computer, engineering, and science, 23.5% education, legal, community service, arts, and media, 1.3% healthcare practitioners, 12.8% service, 15.7% sales and office, 15.5% natural resources, construction, and maintenance, 6.4% production, transportation, and material moving

Income: Per capita: $13,777; Median household: $26,786; Average household: $39,958; Households with income of $100,000 or more: 7.2%; Poverty rate: 34.3%

Educational Attainment: High school diploma or higher: 82.1%; Bachelor's degree or higher: 17.6%; Graduate/professional degree or higher: 5.8%

School District(s)

Klamath-Trinity Joint Unified (KG-12)
2012-13 Enrollment: 1,040 . . . . (530) 625-5600

Housing: Homeownership rate: 69.5%; Median home value: $120,400; Median year structure built: 1981; Homeowner vacancy rate: 0.6%; Median gross rent: $464 per month; Rental vacancy rate: 7.3%

Health Insurance: 79.5% have insurance; 41.6% have private insurance; 43.5% have public insurance; 20.5% do not have insurance; 7.0% of children under 18 do not have insurance

Transportation: Commute: 92.3% car, 0.0% public transportation, 0.9% walk, 6.4% work from home; Median travel time to work: 13.7 minutes

---

HUMBOLDT HILL (CDP). Covers a land area of 4.153 square miles and a water area of 0.015 square miles. Located at 40.72° N. Lat; 124.20° W. Long. Elevation is 194 feet.

History: College of the Redwoods to South.

Population: 3,414; Growth (since 2000): 5.2%; Density: 822.1 persons per square mile; Race: 83.6% White, 1.2% Black/African American, 3.0% Asian, 3.5% American Indian/Alaska Native, 0.1% Native Hawaiian/Other Pacific Islander, 4.9% Two or more races, 8.7% Hispanic of any race; Average household size: 2.41; Median age: 42.2; Age under 18: 18.9%; Age 65 and over: 17.5%; Males per 100 females: 94.6; Marriage status: 34.5% never married, 45.9% now married, 1.4% separated, 5.6% widowed, 14.1% divorced; Foreign born: 6.2%; Speak English only: 88.8%; With disability: 21.6%; Veterans: 8.2%; Ancestry: 16.1% German, 11.9% Irish, 10.0% English, 5.2% Italian, 4.9% Scottish

Employment: 14.0% management, business, and financial, 0.0% computer, engineering, and science, 9.8% education, legal, community service, arts, and media, 3.5% healthcare practitioners, 17.9% service, 32.3% sales and office, 12.8% natural resources, construction, and maintenance, 9.7% production, transportation, and material moving

Income: Per capita: $21,899; Median household: $47,736; Average household: $55,577; Households with income of $100,000 or more: 8.2%; Poverty rate: 13.6%

Educational Attainment: High school diploma or higher: 86.2%; Bachelor's degree or higher: 15.7%; Graduate/professional degree or higher: 3.3%

Housing: Homeownership rate: 76.7%; Median home value: $257,700; Median year structure built: 1976; Homeowner vacancy rate: 1.4%; Median gross rent: $887 per month; Rental vacancy rate: 3.4%

Health Insurance: 81.7% have insurance; 61.0% have private insurance; 32.8% have public insurance; 18.3% do not have insurance; 16.0% of children under 18 do not have insurance

Transportation: Commute: 88.3% car, 0.7% public transportation, 5.0% walk, 1.0% work from home; Median travel time to work: 24.1 minutes

---

HYDESVILLE (CDP). Covers a land area of 7.500 square miles and a water area of 0 square miles. Located at 40.56° N. Lat; 124.08° W. Long. Elevation is 364 feet.

Population: 1,237; Growth (since 2000): 2.3%; Density: 164.9 persons per square mile; Race: 89.6% White, 0.3% Black/African American, 0.5% Asian, 2.7% American Indian/Alaska Native, 0.0% Native Hawaiian/Other Pacific Islander, 4.5% Two or more races, 5.7% Hispanic of any race; Average household size: 2.55; Median age: 46.2; Age under 18: 21.2%; Age 65 and over: 15.2%; Males per 100 females: 102.8

School District(s)

Hydesville Elementary (KG-08)
2012-13 Enrollment: 164. . . . . (707) 768-3610

Housing: Homeownership rate: 75.1%; Homeowner vacancy rate: 1.9%; Rental vacancy rate: 3.2%

INDIANOLA (CDP). Covers a land area of 1.416 square miles and a water area of <.001 square miles. Located at 40.81° N. Lat; 124.08° W. Long. Elevation is 43 feet.

Population: 823; Growth (since 2000): n/a; Density: 581.1 persons per square mile; Race: 86.6% White, 0.2% Black/African American, 1.3% Asian, 5.1% American Indian/Alaska Native, 0.1% Native Hawaiian/Other

Pacific Islander, 5.1% Two or more races, 5.3% Hispanic of any race; Average household size: 2.31; Median age: 43.9; Age under 18: 19.1%; Age 65 and over: 14.5%; Males per 100 females: 96.4
Housing: Homeownership rate: 75.5%; Homeowner vacancy rate: 0.7%; Rental vacancy rate: 2.2%

KNEELAND (unincorporated postal area)
ZCTA: 95549
Covers a land area of 112.336 square miles and a water area of 0.071 square miles. Located at 40.67° N. Lat; 123.91° W. Long. Elevation is 2,129 feet.
Population: 805; Growth (since 2000): 229.9%; Density: 7.2 persons per square mile; Race: 89.4% White, 0.7% Black/African American, 1.1% Asian, 1.6% American Indian/Alaska Native, 0.0% Native Hawaiian/Other Pacific Islander, 4.1% Two or more races, 3.7% Hispanic of any race; Average household size: 2.36; Median age: 46.7; Age under 18: 18.1%; Age 65 and over: 13.5%; Males per 100 females: 112.4

School District(s)

Kneeland Elementary (KG-08)
2012-13 Enrollment: 32. . . . . (707) 442-5472
Housing: Homeownership rate: 77.1%; Homeowner vacancy rate: 0.4%; Rental vacancy rate: 6.0%

KORBEL (unincorporated postal area)
ZCTA: 95550
Covers a land area of 134.932 square miles and a water area of 0.194 square miles. Located at 40.78° N. Lat; 123.83° W. Long. Elevation is 154 feet.
Population: 128; Growth (since 2000): -12.9%; Density: 0.9 persons per square mile; Race: 78.1% White, 0.0% Black/African American, 3.9% Asian, 11.7% American Indian/Alaska Native, 0.0% Native Hawaiian/Other Pacific Islander, 4.7% Two or more races, 2.3% Hispanic of any race; Average household size: 2.61; Median age: 34.7; Age under 18: 26.6%; Age 65 and over: 9.4%; Males per 100 females: 100.0

School District(s)

Maple Creek Elementary (KG-08)
2012-13 Enrollment: 11. . . . . (707) 668-5596
Housing: Homeownership rate: 40.8%; Homeowner vacancy rate: 0.0%; Rental vacancy rate: 0.0%

LOLETA (CDP). Covers a land area of 2.125 square miles and a water area of 0 square miles. Located at 40.64° N. Lat; 124.22° W. Long. Elevation is 46 feet.
Population: 783; Growth (since 2000): n/a; Density: 368.5 persons per square mile; Race: 82.1% White, 1.5% Black/African American, 0.6% Asian, 2.0% American Indian/Alaska Native, 0.0% Native Hawaiian/Other Pacific Islander, 5.4% Two or more races, 14.6% Hispanic of any race; Average household size: 2.49; Median age: 36.5; Age under 18: 23.8%; Age 65 and over: 8.7%; Males per 100 females: 90.0

School District(s)

Loleta Union Elementary (KG-12)
2012-13 Enrollment: 284. . . . . (707) 733-5705
Housing: Homeownership rate: 56.7%; Homeowner vacancy rate: 2.7%; Rental vacancy rate: 4.2%

MANILA (CDP). Covers a land area of 0.654 square miles and a water area of 0.050 square miles. Located at 40.85° N. Lat; 124.16° W. Long. Elevation is 13 feet.
Population: 784; Growth (since 2000): n/a; Density: 1,198.3 persons per square mile; Race: 87.5% White, 1.8% Black/African American, 0.6% Asian, 3.2% American Indian/Alaska Native, 0.0% Native Hawaiian/Other Pacific Islander, 5.4% Two or more races, 3.8% Hispanic of any race; Average household size: 2.11; Median age: 38.1; Age under 18: 19.4%; Age 65 and over: 8.5%; Males per 100 females: 117.2
Housing: Homeownership rate: 43.5%; Homeowner vacancy rate: 1.2%; Rental vacancy rate: 3.6%

MCKINLEYVILLE (CDP). Covers a land area of 20.796 square miles and a water area of 0.218 square miles. Located at 40.95° N. Lat; 124.07° W. Long. Elevation is 144 feet.
Population: 15,177; Growth (since 2000): 11.6%; Density: 729.8 persons per square mile; Race: 85.7% White, 0.7% Black/African American, 1.4% Asian, 4.6% American Indian/Alaska Native, 0.1% Native Hawaiian/Other Pacific Islander, 5.3% Two or more races, 7.1% Hispanic of any race; Average household size: 2.40; Median age: 36.3; Age under 18: 22.7%; Age 65 and over: 12.4%; Males per 100 females: 95.9; Marriage status: 35.1% never married, 47.4% now married, 1.3% separated, 5.3% widowed, 12.2% divorced; Foreign born: 4.1%; Speak English only: 90.7%; With disability: 13.9%; Veterans: 10.6%; Ancestry: 15.0% German, 12.2% Irish, 10.0% English, 8.9% Italian, 7.5% American
Employment: 14.5% management, business, and financial, 3.4% computer, engineering, and science, 12.4% education, legal, community service, arts, and media, 6.3% healthcare practitioners, 22.0% service, 22.1% sales and office, 10.5% natural resources, construction, and maintenance, 8.9% production, transportation, and material moving
Income: Per capita: $25,445; Median household: $49,001; Average household: $61,911; Households with income of $100,000 or more: 17.2%; Poverty rate: 13.2%
Educational Attainment: High school diploma or higher: 90.4%; Bachelor's degree or higher: 31.9%; Graduate/professional degree or higher: 9.8%

School District(s)

Fieldbrook Elementary (KG-08)
2012-13 Enrollment: 139. . . . . (707) 839-3201
Mckinleyville Union Elementary (KG-08)
2012-13 Enrollment: 1,145 . . . . (707) 839-1549
Northern Humboldt Union High (KG-12)
2012-13 Enrollment: 1,722 . . . . (707) 839-6470
Housing: Homeownership rate: 60.0%; Median home value: $294,900; Median year structure built: 1985; Homeowner vacancy rate: 1.1%; Median gross rent: $923 per month; Rental vacancy rate: 2.7%
Health Insurance: 83.4% have insurance; 63.7% have private insurance; 33.8% have public insurance; 16.6% do not have insurance; 7.6% of children under 18 do not have insurance
Transportation: Commute: 91.5% car, 1.8% public transportation, 1.3% walk, 4.5% work from home; Median travel time to work: 18.6 minutes; Amtrak: Bus service available.

MIRANDA (CDP). Covers a land area of 1.491 square miles and a water area of 0.008 square miles. Located at 40.23° N. Lat; 123.82° W. Long. Elevation is 348 feet.
Population: 520; Growth (since 2000): n/a; Density: 348.7 persons per square mile; Race: 84.4% White, 0.8% Black/African American, 0.8% Asian, 2.5% American Indian/Alaska Native, 0.2% Native Hawaiian/Other Pacific Islander, 5.4% Two or more races, 14.4% Hispanic of any race; Average household size: 2.11; Median age: 41.3; Age under 18: 22.5%; Age 65 and over: 11.5%; Males per 100 females: 94.0

School District(s)

Southern Humboldt Joint Unified (KG-12)
2012-13 Enrollment: 742. . . . . (707) 943-1789
Housing: Homeownership rate: 55.2%; Homeowner vacancy rate: 0.7%; Rental vacancy rate: 0.0%

MYERS FLAT (CDP). Covers a land area of 0.432 square miles and a water area of 0.055 square miles. Located at 40.27° N. Lat; 123.88° W. Long. Elevation is 203 feet.
Population: 146; Growth (since 2000): n/a; Density: 337.8 persons per square mile; Race: 85.6% White, 0.0% Black/African American, 0.7% Asian, 4.1% American Indian/Alaska Native, 0.0% Native Hawaiian/Other Pacific Islander, 6.8% Two or more races, 7.5% Hispanic of any race; Average household size: 1.83; Median age: 46.7; Age under 18: 13.7%; Age 65 and over: 10.3%; Males per 100 females: 97.3
Housing: Homeownership rate: 50.0%; Homeowner vacancy rate: 9.1%; Rental vacancy rate: 0.0%

MYRTLETOWN (CDP). Covers a land area of 2.099 square miles and a water area of 0.082 square miles. Located at 40.79° N. Lat; 124.13° W. Long. Elevation is 112 feet.
Population: 4,675; Growth (since 2000): 4.8%; Density: 2,227.2 persons per square mile; Race: 84.9% White, 1.1% Black/African American, 3.3% Asian, 3.0% American Indian/Alaska Native, 0.4% Native Hawaiian/Other Pacific Islander, 4.5% Two or more races, 8.3% Hispanic of any race; Average household size: 2.25; Median age: 41.3; Age under 18: 19.6%; Age 65 and over: 20.8%; Males per 100 females: 89.1; Marriage status: 30.7% never married, 50.0% now married, 2.1% separated, 9.7% widowed, 9.6% divorced; Foreign born: 4.7%; Speak English only: 94.6%; With disability: 20.2%; Veterans: 9.9%; Ancestry: 12.9% German, 9.2% English, 6.8% American, 6.8% Italian, 6.5% Irish
Employment: 6.0% management, business, and financial, 3.1% computer, engineering, and science, 20.1% education, legal, community service, arts,

and media, 6.9% healthcare practitioners, 18.1% service, 22.0% sales and office, 12.9% natural resources, construction, and maintenance, 10.9% production, transportation, and material moving

Income: Per capita: $28,386; Median household: $61,587; Average household: $66,626; Households with income of $100,000 or more: 19.9%; Poverty rate: 8.9%

Educational Attainment: High school diploma or higher: 91.3%; Bachelor's degree or higher: 34.6%; Graduate/professional degree or higher: 10.3%

Housing: Homeownership rate: 51.8%; Median home value: $274,900; Median year structure built: 1968; Homeowner vacancy rate: 0.9%; Median gross rent: $1,012 per month; Rental vacancy rate: 3.5%

Health Insurance: 84.6% have insurance; 61.3% have private insurance; 33.6% have public insurance; 15.4% do not have insurance; 24.9% of children under 18 do not have insurance

Transportation: Commute: 90.8% car, 0.0% public transportation, 3.7% walk, 4.9% work from home; Median travel time to work: 14.1 minutes

ORICK (CDP). Covers a land area of 4.746 square miles and a water area of 0.104 square miles. Located at 41.29° N. Lat; 124.07° W. Long. Elevation is 26 feet.

Population: 357; Growth (since 2000): n/a; Density: 75.2 persons per square mile; Race: 80.7% White, 0.0% Black/African American, 0.0% Asian, 10.9% American Indian/Alaska Native, 0.8% Native Hawaiian/Other Pacific Islander, 5.9% Two or more races, 5.6% Hispanic of any race; Average household size: 2.08; Median age: 48.1; Age under 18: 16.8%; Age 65 and over: 18.2%; Males per 100 females: 113.8

School District(s)

Orick Elementary (KG-08)
2012-13 Enrollment: 21 . . . . (707) 488-2821

Housing: Homeownership rate: 53.6%; Homeowner vacancy rate: 2.2%; Rental vacancy rate: 8.2%

ORLEANS (unincorporated postal area)

ZCTA: 95556

Covers a land area of 136.991 square miles and a water area of 0.700 square miles. Located at 41.31° N. Lat; 123.59° W. Long. Elevation is 404 feet.

Population: 605; Growth (since 2000): 6.3%; Density: 4.4 persons per square mile; Race: 56.5% White, 0.0% Black/African American, 1.3% Asian, 28.9% American Indian/Alaska Native, 0.0% Native Hawaiian/Other Pacific Islander, 12.4% Two or more races, 8.1% Hispanic of any race; Average household size: 2.33; Median age: 40.7; Age under 18: 22.3%; Age 65 and over: 14.7%; Males per 100 females: 113.8

School District(s)

Klamath-Trinity Joint Unified (KG-12)
2012-13 Enrollment: 1,040 . . . . (530) 625-5600

Housing: Homeownership rate: 60.8%; Homeowner vacancy rate: 3.0%; Rental vacancy rate: 0.9%

PETROLIA (unincorporated postal area)

ZCTA: 95558

Covers a land area of 200.912 square miles and a water area of 0.294 square miles. Located at 40.30° N. Lat; 124.24° W. Long. Elevation is 121 feet.

Population: 425; Growth (since 2000): 46.0%; Density: 2.1 persons per square mile; Race: 91.3% White, 0.9% Black/African American, 1.2% Asian, 0.9% American Indian/Alaska Native, 0.0% Native Hawaiian/Other Pacific Islander, 4.2% Two or more races, 2.6% Hispanic of any race; Average household size: 2.01; Median age: 48.4; Age under 18: 15.3%; Age 65 and over: 16.2%; Males per 100 females: 122.5

School District(s)

Mattole Unified (KG-12)
2012-13 Enrollment: 794 . . . . (707) 629-3311

Housing: Homeownership rate: 60.1%; Homeowner vacancy rate: 1.6%; Rental vacancy rate: 4.5%

PHILLIPSVILLE (CDP). Covers a land area of 0.715 square miles and a water area of 0.028 square miles. Located at 40.21° N. Lat; 123.78° W. Long. Elevation is 282 feet.

Population: 140; Growth (since 2000): n/a; Density: 195.8 persons per square mile; Race: 86.4% White, 0.0% Black/African American, 0.7% Asian, 2.9% American Indian/Alaska Native, 0.0% Native Hawaiian/Other Pacific Islander, 10.0% Two or more races, 2.1% Hispanic of any race; Average household size: 1.87; Median age: 48.5; Age under 18: 10.0%; Age 65 and over: 9.3%; Males per 100 females: 105.9

Housing: Homeownership rate: 57.3%; Homeowner vacancy rate: 2.3%; Rental vacancy rate: 0.0%

PINE HILLS (CDP). Covers a land area of 10.118 square miles and a water area of 0.042 square miles. Located at 40.73° N. Lat; 124.16° W. Long. Elevation is 420 feet.

Population: 3,131; Growth (since 2000): 0.7%; Density: 309.5 persons per square mile; Race: 84.6% White, 0.7% Black/African American, 3.7% Asian, 2.7% American Indian/Alaska Native, 0.1% Native Hawaiian/Other Pacific Islander, 5.8% Two or more races, 7.0% Hispanic of any race; Average household size: 2.47; Median age: 45.6; Age under 18: 20.6%; Age 65 and over: 17.1%; Males per 100 females: 99.9; Marriage status: 28.3% never married, 56.8% now married, 3.2% separated, 3.4% widowed, 11.5% divorced; Foreign born: 5.8%; Speak English only: 90.0%; With disability: 18.9%; Veterans: 9.0%; Ancestry: 22.7% German, 12.8% English, 8.6% Italian, 7.5% Irish, 5.5% Swedish

Employment: 15.7% management, business, and financial, 4.2% computer, engineering, and science, 6.8% education, legal, community service, arts, and media, 5.9% healthcare practitioners, 22.9% service, 26.1% sales and office, 8.7% natural resources, construction, and maintenance, 9.6% production, transportation, and material moving

Income: Per capita: $32,263; Median household: $62,981; Average household: $79,312; Households with income of $100,000 or more: 31.9%; Poverty rate: 12.3%

Educational Attainment: High school diploma or higher: 88.2%; Bachelor's degree or higher: 27.5%; Graduate/professional degree or higher: 7.4%

Housing: Homeownership rate: 73.9%; Median home value: $339,300; Median year structure built: 1979; Homeowner vacancy rate: 1.2%; Median gross rent: $1,330 per month; Rental vacancy rate: 3.8%

Health Insurance: 91.2% have insurance; 68.3% have private insurance; 37.9% have public insurance; 8.8% do not have insurance; 15.2% of children under 18 do not have insurance

Transportation: Commute: 88.5% car, 0.9% public transportation, 0.0% walk, 8.2% work from home; Median travel time to work: 17.7 minutes

REDCREST (CDP). Covers a land area of 0.598 square miles and a water area of 0 square miles. Located at 40.40° N. Lat; 123.95° W. Long. Elevation is 377 feet.

Population: 89; Growth (since 2000): n/a; Density: 148.8 persons per square mile; Race: 82.0% White, 0.0% Black/African American, 0.0% Asian, 5.6% American Indian/Alaska Native, 0.0% Native Hawaiian/Other Pacific Islander, 9.0% Two or more races, 4.5% Hispanic of any race; Average household size: 2.12; Median age: 50.8; Age under 18: 16.9%; Age 65 and over: 20.2%; Males per 100 females: 71.2

Housing: Homeownership rate: 69.1%; Homeowner vacancy rate: 3.3%; Rental vacancy rate: 7.1%

REDWAY (CDP). Covers a land area of 1.250 square miles and a water area of 0.021 square miles. Located at 40.12° N. Lat; 123.82° W. Long. Elevation is 538 feet.

Population: 1,225; Growth (since 2000): 3.1%; Density: 979.7 persons per square mile; Race: 89.2% White, 0.4% Black/African American, 0.5% Asian, 2.9% American Indian/Alaska Native, 0.1% Native Hawaiian/Other Pacific Islander, 5.7% Two or more races, 7.8% Hispanic of any race; Average household size: 2.16; Median age: 40.8; Age under 18: 22.7%; Age 65 and over: 11.8%; Males per 100 females: 93.8

School District(s)

Southern Humboldt Joint Unified (KG-12)
2012-13 Enrollment: 742 . . . . (707) 943-1789

Housing: Homeownership rate: 55.7%; Homeowner vacancy rate: 1.6%; Rental vacancy rate: 1.2%

RIO DELL (city). Covers a land area of 2.282 square miles and a water area of 0.136 square miles. Located at 40.50° N. Lat; 124.11° W. Long. Elevation is 161 feet.

Population: 3,368; Growth (since 2000): 6.1%; Density: 1,475.9 persons per square mile; Race: 85.9% White, 0.4% Black/African American, 0.7% Asian, 3.7% American Indian/Alaska Native, 0.1% Native Hawaiian/Other Pacific Islander, 5.0% Two or more races, 11.4% Hispanic of any race; Average household size: 2.45; Median age: 38.3; Age under 18: 23.8%; Age 65 and over: 13.2%; Males per 100 females: 96.7; Marriage status: 35.4% never married, 48.1% now married, 3.7% separated, 3.5%

widowed, 13.0% divorced; Foreign born: 4.4%; Speak English only: 90.4%; With disability: 21.1%; Veterans: 12.2%; Ancestry: 14.0% English, 9.5% German, 9.0% Irish, 5.1% Italian, 4.8% French

Employment: 9.7% management, business, and financial, 1.7% computer, engineering, and science, 7.4% education, legal, community service, arts, and media, 2.6% healthcare practitioners, 26.5% service, 24.0% sales and office, 18.7% natural resources, construction, and maintenance, 9.4% production, transportation, and material moving

Income: Per capita: $25,279; Median household: $42,127; Average household: $62,747; Households with income of $100,000 or more: 11.7%; Poverty rate: 11.7%

Educational Attainment: High school diploma or higher: 89.5%; Bachelor's degree or higher: 11.9%; Graduate/professional degree or higher: 2.1%

School District(s)

Rio Dell Elementary (KG-08)
2012-13 Enrollment: 303. . . . . (707) 764-5694

Housing: Homeownership rate: 56.6%; Median home value: $215,300; Median year structure built: 1961; Homeowner vacancy rate: 0.6%; Median gross rent: $808 per month; Rental vacancy rate: 2.8%

Health Insurance: 83.2% have insurance; 49.5% have private insurance; 44.6% have public insurance; 16.8% do not have insurance; 2.8% of children under 18 do not have insurance

Safety: Violent crime rate: 32.7 per 10,000 population; Property crime rate: 136.6 per 10,000 population

Transportation: Commute: 94.2% car, 0.0% public transportation, 0.9% walk, 4.8% work from home; Median travel time to work: 21.8 minutes

Additional Information Contacts

City of Rio Dell. . . . . (707) 764-3532
http://www.riodellcity.com

SAMOA (CDP). Covers a land area of 0.837 square miles and a water area of 0 square miles. Located at 40.81° N. Lat; 124.19° W. Long. Elevation is 23 feet.

Population: 258; Growth (since 2000): n/a; Density: 308.4 persons per square mile; Race: 76.7% White, 0.4% Black/African American, 0.0% Asian, 3.5% American Indian/Alaska Native, 0.0% Native Hawaiian/Other Pacific Islander, 7.4% Two or more races, 20.2% Hispanic of any race; Average household size: 2.84; Median age: 28.1; Age under 18: 18.2%; Age 65 and over: 3.5%; Males per 100 females: 126.3

School District(s)

Peninsula Union (KG-08)
2012-13 Enrollment: 34. . . . . (707) 443-2731

Housing: Homeownership rate: 1.1%; Homeowner vacancy rate: 0.0%; Rental vacancy rate: 2.2%

SCOTIA (CDP). Covers a land area of 0.746 square miles and a water area of 0.096 square miles. Located at 40.48° N. Lat; 124.10° W. Long. Elevation is 194 feet.

Population: 850; Growth (since 2000): n/a; Density: 1,139.3 persons per square mile; Race: 79.3% White, 0.4% Black/African American, 0.4% Asian, 4.1% American Indian/Alaska Native, 1.1% Native Hawaiian/Other Pacific Islander, 4.2% Two or more races, 17.6% Hispanic of any race; Average household size: 3.20; Median age: 26.0; Age under 18: 37.9%; Age 65 and over: 2.7%; Males per 100 females: 104.8

School District(s)

Scotia Union Elementary (KG-08)
2012-13 Enrollment: 238. . . . . (707) 764-2212

Housing: Homeownership rate: n/a; Homeowner vacancy rate: 0.0%; Rental vacancy rate: 1.5%

SHELTER COVE (CDP). Covers a land area of 5.830 square miles and a water area of 0 square miles. Located at 40.04° N. Lat; 124.06° W. Long. Elevation is 138 feet.

Population: 693; Growth (since 2000): n/a; Density: 118.9 persons per square mile; Race: 90.9% White, 0.4% Black/African American, 1.0% Asian, 0.7% American Indian/Alaska Native, 0.1% Native Hawaiian/Other Pacific Islander, 4.9% Two or more races, 6.8% Hispanic of any race; Average household size: 1.99; Median age: 43.1; Age under 18: 17.0%; Age 65 and over: 14.7%; Males per 100 females: 118.6

Housing: Homeownership rate: 71.3%; Homeowner vacancy rate: 10.6%; Rental vacancy rate: 13.8%

TRINIDAD (city). Covers a land area of 0.485 square miles and a water area of 0.186 square miles. Located at 41.06° N. Lat; 124.14° W. Long. Elevation is 174 feet.

History: Trinidad developed about 1850 as a distribution point for the Trinity County mines. Nearby is Trinidad Head, where in 1775 explorers Bruno Heceta and Juan Francisco Bodega y Cuadra took possession of the territory in the name of Charles III of Spain. The Spaniards named the region Trinidad because they were there on the day after the feast of the Holy Trinity.

Population: 367; Growth (since 2000): 18.0%; Density: 757.3 persons per square mile; Race: 90.2% White, 0.5% Black/African American, 0.5% Asian, 4.1% American Indian/Alaska Native, 0.3% Native Hawaiian/Other Pacific Islander, 4.1% Two or more races, 3.0% Hispanic of any race; Average household size: 1.96; Median age: 45.9; Age under 18: 16.3%; Age 65 and over: 19.3%; Males per 100 females: 98.4

School District(s)

Big Lagoon Union Elementary (KG-08)
2012-13 Enrollment: 63. . . . . (707) 677-3688

Trinidad Union Elementary (KG-08)
2012-13 Enrollment: 172. . . . . (707) 677-3631

Housing: Homeownership rate: 60.4%; Homeowner vacancy rate: 4.2%; Rental vacancy rate: 12.9%

Additional Information Contacts

City of Trinidad . . . . (707) 677-0223
http://www.trinidad.ca.gov

WEOTT (CDP). Covers a land area of 0.753 square miles and a water area of 0.019 square miles. Located at 40.32° N. Lat; 123.92° W. Long. Elevation is 289 feet.

Population: 288; Growth (since 2000): n/a; Density: 382.7 persons per square mile; Race: 87.5% White, 0.0% Black/African American, 0.3% Asian, 4.5% American Indian/Alaska Native, 0.0% Native Hawaiian/Other Pacific Islander, 6.6% Two or more races, 6.9% Hispanic of any race; Average household size: 2.15; Median age: 45.6; Age under 18: 18.7%; Age 65 and over: 12.8%; Males per 100 females: 102.8

School District(s)

Southern Humboldt Joint Unified (KG-12)
2012-13 Enrollment: 742. . . . . (707) 943-1789

Housing: Homeownership rate: 65.7%; Homeowner vacancy rate: 1.1%; Rental vacancy rate: 4.2%

WESTHAVEN-MOONSTONE (CDP). Covers a land area of 8.092 square miles and a water area of 0.037 square miles. Located at 41.04° N. Lat; 124.09° W. Long. Elevation is 328 feet.

Population: 1,205; Growth (since 2000): 15.4%; Density: 148.9 persons per square mile; Race: 89.9% White, 0.7% Black/African American, 1.5% Asian, 3.2% American Indian/Alaska Native, 0.0% Native Hawaiian/Other Pacific Islander, 3.8% Two or more races, 4.4% Hispanic of any race; Average household size: 2.20; Median age: 45.6; Age under 18: 19.4%; Age 65 and over: 15.4%; Males per 100 females: 106.0

Housing: Homeownership rate: 66.6%; Homeowner vacancy rate: 0.8%; Rental vacancy rate: 3.1%

WHITETHORN (unincorporated postal area)

ZCTA: 95589

Covers a land area of 186.678 square miles and a water area of 9.028 square miles. Located at 40.06° N. Lat; 123.97° W. Long. Elevation is 1,024 feet.

Population: 1,612; Growth (since 2000): 118.7%; Density: 8.6 persons per square mile; Race: 89.5% White, 1.1% Black/African American, 1.1% Asian, 0.8% American Indian/Alaska Native, 0.1% Native Hawaiian/Other Pacific Islander, 5.3% Two or more races, 6.0% Hispanic of any race; Average household size: 2.05; Median age: 45.0; Age under 18: 16.3%; Age 65 and over: 12.6%; Males per 100 females: 118.1

School District(s)

Leggett Valley Unified (KG-12)
2012-13 Enrollment: 116. . . . . (707) 925-6285

Southern Humboldt Joint Unified (KG-12)
2012-13 Enrollment: 742. . . . . (707) 943-1789

Housing: Homeownership rate: 74.4%; Homeowner vacancy rate: 5.3%; Rental vacancy rate: 9.9%

WILLOW CREEK (CDP). Covers a land area of 30.310 square miles and a water area of 0.300 square miles. Located at 40.94° N. Lat; 123.64° W. Long. Elevation is 610 feet.

Population: 1,710; Growth (since 2000): -1.9%; Density: 56.4 persons per square mile; Race: 80.4% White, 0.4% Black/African American, 0.8% Asian, 9.8% American Indian/Alaska Native, 0.4% Native Hawaiian/Other Pacific Islander, 6.6% Two or more races, 6.3% Hispanic of any race; Average household size: 2.09; Median age: 49.5; Age under 18: 16.8%; Age 65 and over: 18.4%; Males per 100 females: 101.4

School District(s)

Klamath-Trinity Joint Unified (KG-12)
2012-13 Enrollment: 1,040 . . . . (530) 625-5600

Housing: Homeownership rate: 64.7%; Homeowner vacancy rate: 1.7%; Rental vacancy rate: 5.2%

Imperial County

Located in southern California, in the Colorado Desert; bounded on the south by the Mexican border, and on the east by the Colorado River and the Arizona border. Covers a land area of 4,176.603 square miles, a water area of 305.116 square miles, and is located in the Pacific Time Zone at 33.04° N. Lat., 115.36° W. Long. The county was founded in 1907. County seat is El Centro.

Imperial County is part of the El Centro, CA Metropolitan Statistical Area. The entire metro area includes: Imperial County, CA

Weather Station: Brawley 2 SW — Elevation: -100 feet

	Jan	Feb	Mar	Apr	May	Jun	Jul	Aug	Sep	Oct	Nov	Dec
High	71	74	80	86	95	103	107	107	102	92	79	70
Low	41	44	48	53	60	67	75	76	70	59	47	40
Precip	0.5	0.6	0.4	0.1	0.0	tr	0.1	0.3	0.2	0.2	0.2	0.4
Snow	0.0	0.0	0.0	0.0	0.0	0.0	0.0	0.0	0.0	0.0	0.0	0.0

High and Low temperatures in degrees Fahrenheit; Precipitation and Snow in inches

Weather Station: El Centro 2 SSW — Elevation: -29 feet

	Jan	Feb	Mar	Apr	May	Jun	Jul	Aug	Sep	Oct	Nov	Dec
High	71	74	80	86	94	103	107	106	101	91	78	70
Low	43	46	51	56	63	70	77	78	72	61	49	42
Precip	0.5	0.5	0.3	0.0	0.0	tr	0.1	0.3	0.3	0.3	0.2	0.4
Snow	0.0	0.0	0.0	0.0	0.0	0.0	0.0	0.0	0.0	0.0	0.0	0.0

High and Low temperatures in degrees Fahrenheit; Precipitation and Snow in inches

Weather Station: Imperial — Elevation: -63 feet

	Jan	Feb	Mar	Apr	May	Jun	Jul	Aug	Sep	Oct	Nov	Dec
High	70	74	80	86	94	103	106	106	101	90	78	69
Low	43	47	51	56	63	70	77	78	72	61	50	42
Precip	0.4	0.5	0.4	0.1	0.0	tr	0.1	0.2	0.3	0.2	0.2	0.4
Snow	0.0	0.0	0.0	0.0	0.0	0.0	0.0	0.0	0.0	0.0	0.0	0.0

High and Low temperatures in degrees Fahrenheit; Precipitation and Snow in inches

Population: 174,528; Growth (since 2000): 22.6%; Density: 41.8 persons per square mile; Race: 58.8% White, 3.3% Black/African American, 1.6% Asian, 1.8% American Indian/Alaska Native, 0.1% Native Hawaiian/Other Pacific Islander, 4.4% two or more races, 80.4% Hispanic of any race; Average household size: 3.34; Median age: 31.9; Age under 18: 29.3%; Age 65 and over: 10.4%; Males per 100 females: 105.6; Marriage status: 35.6% never married, 50.1% now married, 3.4% separated, 5.6% widowed, 8.6% divorced; Foreign born: 32.3%; Speak English only: 25.5%; With disability: 13.1%; Veterans: 5.2%; Ancestry: 3.2% German, 2.7% Irish, 1.6% English, 1.4% American, 1.1% Italian

Religion: Six largest groups: 28.2% Catholicism, 2.9% Baptist, 2.3% Pentecostal, 1.8% Latter-day Saints, 1.2% Non-denominational Protestant, 0.7% Adventist

Economy: Unemployment rate: 23.6%; Leading industries: 18.7% retail trade; 11.3% health care and social assistance; 10.7% accommodation and food services; Farms: 421 totaling 515,783 acres; Company size: 2 employ 1,000 or more persons, 3 employ 500 to 999 persons, 28 employ 100 to 499 persons, 2,364 employ less than 100 persons; Business ownership: 2,915 women-owned, 261 Black-owned, 5,283 Hispanic-owned, n/a Asian-owned

Employment: 9.7% management, business, and financial, 1.7% computer, engineering, and science, 9.4% education, legal, community service, arts, and media, 2.9% healthcare practitioners, 23.9% service, 24.8% sales and office, 14.6% natural resources, construction, and maintenance, 12.9% production, transportation, and material moving

Income: Per capita: $16,763; Median household: $41,807; Average household: $57,847; Households with income of $100,000 or more: 16.4%; Poverty rate: 23.3%

Educational Attainment: High school diploma or higher: 64.5%; Bachelor's degree or higher: 13.3%; Graduate/professional degree or higher: 4.1%

Housing: Homeownership rate: 55.9%; Median home value: $147,300; Median year structure built: 1983; Homeowner vacancy rate: 3.5%; Median gross rent: $744 per month; Rental vacancy rate: 7.5%

Vital Statistics: Birth rate: 174.9 per 10,000 population; Death rate: 51.6 per 10,000 population; Age-adjusted cancer mortality rate: 130.6 deaths per 100,000 population

Health Insurance: 78.7% have insurance; 45.0% have private insurance; 39.8% have public insurance; 21.3% do not have insurance; 12.4% of children under 18 do not have insurance

Health Care: Physicians: 7.1 per 10,000 population; Hospital beds: 15.5 per 10,000 population; Hospital admissions: 738.5 per 10,000 population

Air Quality Index: 59.5% good, 34.2% moderate, 5.8% unhealthy for sensitive individuals, 0.5% unhealthy (percent of days)

Transportation: Commute: 89.6% car, 1.3% public transportation, 2.2% walk, 4.6% work from home; Median travel time to work: 20.8 minutes

Presidential Election: 63.6% Obama, 34.8% Romney (2012)

National and State Parks: Cibola National Wildlife Refuge; Heber Dunes State Vehicular Recreation Area; Imperial National Wildlife Refuge; Picacho State Recreation Area; Salton Sea State Recreation Area; Sonny Bono Salton Sea National Wildlife Refuge

Additional Information Contacts

Imperial Government. . . . . (760) 339-4220
http://www.co.imperial.ca.us

Imperial County Communities

BOMBAY BEACH (CDP). Covers a land area of 0.941 square miles and a water area of 0 square miles. Located at 33.35° N. Lat; 115.73° W. Long. Elevation is -223 feet.

Population: 295; Growth (since 2000): -19.4%; Density: 313.5 persons per square mile; Race: 75.6% White, 12.5% Black/African American, 0.3% Asian, 2.7% American Indian/Alaska Native, 0.0% Native Hawaiian/Other Pacific Islander, 1.4% Two or more races, 20.0% Hispanic of any race; Average household size: 1.69; Median age: 58.5; Age under 18: 10.2%; Age 65 and over: 39.0%; Males per 100 females: 113.8

Housing: Homeownership rate: 65.7%; Homeowner vacancy rate: 14.5%; Rental vacancy rate: 16.4%

BRAWLEY (city). Covers a land area of 7.682 square miles and a water area of 0 square miles. Located at 32.98° N. Lat; 115.53° W. Long. Elevation is -112 feet.

History: Brawley developed as a shipping center for the surrounding agricultural area, and as a trading town in the Imperial Valley.

Population: 24,953; Growth (since 2000): 13.2%; Density: 3,248.4 persons per square mile; Race: 54.4% White, 2.0% Black/African American, 1.4% Asian, 1.0% American Indian/Alaska Native, 0.1% Native Hawaiian/Other Pacific Islander, 4.0% Two or more races, 81.5% Hispanic of any race; Average household size: 3.25; Median age: 30.2; Age under 18: 32.6%; Age 65 and over: 10.1%; Males per 100 females: 94.3; Marriage status: 35.7% never married, 47.2% now married, 2.4% separated, 6.0% widowed, 11.1% divorced; Foreign born: 23.3%; Speak English only: 33.7%; With disability: 13.2%; Veterans: 5.0%; Ancestry: 3.7% German, 2.8% Irish, 1.7% English, 1.0% Danish, 0.9% American

Employment: 11.8% management, business, and financial, 1.4% computer, engineering, and science, 7.4% education, legal, community service, arts, and media, 2.9% healthcare practitioners, 25.7% service, 23.4% sales and office, 13.3% natural resources, construction, and maintenance, 14.2% production, transportation, and material moving

Income: Per capita: $18,467; Median household: $41,784; Average household: $59,291; Households with income of $100,000 or more: 14.2%; Poverty rate: 24.1%

Educational Attainment: High school diploma or higher: 68.9%; Bachelor's degree or higher: 10.6%; Graduate/professional degree or higher: 3.3%

School District(s)

Brawley Elementary (KG-08)
2012-13 Enrollment: 3,807 . . . . (760) 344-2330
Brawley Union High (09-12)
2012-13 Enrollment: 1,834 . . . . (760) 312-5819

Magnolia Union Elementary (KG-08)
2012-13 Enrollment: 135. . . . . (760) 344-2494
Mulberry Elementary (KG-08)
2012-13 Enrollment: 91. . . . . (760) 344-8600

Housing: Homeownership rate: 52.1%; Median home value: $147,500; Median year structure built: 1978; Homeowner vacancy rate: 2.0%; Median gross rent: $732 per month; Rental vacancy rate: 8.0%

Health Insurance: 85.1% have insurance; 47.9% have private insurance; 44.3% have public insurance; 14.9% do not have insurance; 3.7% of children under 18 do not have insurance

Hospitals: Pioneers Memorial Healthcare District (99 beds)

Safety: Violent crime rate: 23.7 per 10,000 population; Property crime rate: 470.2 per 10,000 population

Transportation: Commute: 89.7% car, 1.6% public transportation, 2.4% walk, 2.8% work from home; Median travel time to work: 19.1 minutes

Additional Information Contacts

City of Brawley . . . . (760) 351-3059
http://www.brawley-ca.gov

CALEXICO (city).

Covers a land area of 8.391 square miles and a water area of 0 square miles. Located at 32.68° N. Lat; 115.49° W. Long. Elevation is 3 feet.

History: A tent city of the Imperial Land Company was the first Calexico. The town developed as a border town with neighboring Mexicali, just across the Mexican border. The site was formerly owned by George Chaffey, a promoter of the first irrigation projects in the Imperial Valley.

Population: 38,572; Growth (since 2000): 42.3%; Density: 4,596.7 persons per square mile; Race: 60.0% White, 0.3% Black/African American, 1.3% Asian, 0.5% American Indian/Alaska Native, 0.1% Native Hawaiian/Other Pacific Islander, 4.2% Two or more races, 96.8% Hispanic of any race; Average household size: 3.80; Median age: 31.8; Age under 18: 31.1%; Age 65 and over: 11.4%; Males per 100 females: 89.6; Marriage status: 34.7% never married, 53.5% now married, 5.3% separated, 6.4% widowed, 5.4% divorced; Foreign born: 47.7%; Speak English only: 3.5%; With disability: 13.6%; Veterans: 1.8%; Ancestry: 0.4% American, 0.4% Italian, 0.2% German, 0.2% Irish, 0.2% Palestinian

Employment: 8.4% management, business, and financial, 1.2% computer, engineering, and science, 8.5% education, legal, community service, arts, and media, 1.7% healthcare practitioners, 23.0% service, 28.7% sales and office, 14.4% natural resources, construction, and maintenance, 14.0% production, transportation, and material moving

Income: Per capita: $13,137; Median household: $36,236; Average household: $49,473; Households with income of $100,000 or more: 10.7%; Poverty rate: 25.4%

Educational Attainment: High school diploma or higher: 55.4%; Bachelor's degree or higher: 13.4%; Graduate/professional degree or higher: 3.7%

School District(s)

Calexico Unified (KG-12)
2012-13 Enrollment: 9,203 . . . . (760) 768-3888

Four-year College(s)

San Diego State University-Imperial Valley Campus (Public)
Fall 2013 Enrollment: 883. . . . . (760) 768-5500
2013-14 Tuition: In-state $5,706; Out-of-state $16,866

Vocational/Technical School(s)

International Polytechnic Institute (Private, Not-for-profit)
Fall 2013 Enrollment: 33. . . . . (760) 357-2995
2013-14 Tuition: $5,582

Housing: Homeownership rate: 53.7%; Median home value: $153,500; Median year structure built: 1992; Homeowner vacancy rate: 2.6%; Median gross rent: $789 per month; Rental vacancy rate: 3.1%

Health Insurance: 73.0% have insurance; 37.8% have private insurance; 39.3% have public insurance; 27.0% do not have insurance; 19.5% of children under 18 do not have insurance

Safety: Violent crime rate: 23.3 per 10,000 population; Property crime rate: 372.9 per 10,000 population

Transportation: Commute: 86.7% car, 2.8% public transportation, 2.1% walk, 4.9% work from home; Median travel time to work: 24.5 minutes

Airports: Calexico International (general aviation)

Additional Information Contacts

City of Calexico . . . . (760) 768-2110
http://www.calexico.ca.gov/index.php

CALIPATRIA (city).

Covers a land area of 3.716 square miles and a water area of 0 square miles. Located at 33.17° N. Lat; 115.49° W. Long. Elevation is -180 feet.

History: Calipatria developed as a center for a green pea growing area, with a mill that ground alfalfa into cattle fodder.

Population: 7,705; Growth (since 2000): 5.7%; Density: 2,073.6 persons per square mile; Race: 41.7% White, 20.9% Black/African American, 1.2% Asian, 1.0% American Indian/Alaska Native, 0.3% Native Hawaiian/Other Pacific Islander, 2.9% Two or more races, 64.1% Hispanic of any race; Average household size: 3.51; Median age: 32.9; Age under 18: 16.2%; Age 65 and over: 4.6%; Males per 100 females: 330.9; Marriage status: 41.4% never married, 44.2% now married, 3.3% separated, 5.3% widowed, 9.1% divorced; Foreign born: 26.6%; Speak English only: 26.3%; With disability: 13.0%; Veterans: 5.9%; Ancestry: 2.0% German, 1.7% Irish, 1.5% French, 1.3% African, 1.0% English

Employment: 4.1% management, business, and financial, 0.0% computer, engineering, and science, 9.7% education, legal, community service, arts, and media, 1.2% healthcare practitioners, 21.8% service, 18.3% sales and office, 20.3% natural resources, construction, and maintenance, 24.5% production, transportation, and material moving

Income: Per capita: $12,089; Median household: $33,893; Average household: $51,350; Households with income of $100,000 or more: 12.5%; Poverty rate: 23.1%

Educational Attainment: High school diploma or higher: 56.3%; Bachelor's degree or higher: 4.6%; Graduate/professional degree or higher: 1.3%

School District(s)

Calipatria Unified (KG-12)
2012-13 Enrollment: 1,191 . . . . (760) 348-2151

Housing: Homeownership rate: 53.2%; Median home value: $85,000; Median year structure built: 1978; Homeowner vacancy rate: 5.9%; Median gross rent: $729 per month; Rental vacancy rate: 10.6%

Health Insurance: 83.5% have insurance; 42.3% have private insurance; 44.6% have public insurance; 16.5% do not have insurance; 2.9% of children under 18 do not have insurance

Transportation: Commute: 83.1% car, 0.8% public transportation, 4.7% walk, 8.2% work from home; Median travel time to work: 21.6 minutes

Additional Information Contacts

City of Calipatria . . . . (706) 348-4141
http://www.calipatria.com

DESERT SHORES (CDP).

Covers a land area of 0.682 square miles and a water area of 0 square miles. Located at 33.40° N. Lat; 116.04° W. Long. Elevation is -200 feet.

Population: 1,104; Growth (since 2000): 39.4%; Density: 1,619.9 persons per square mile; Race: 64.2% White, 0.7% Black/African American, 0.4% Asian, 2.4% American Indian/Alaska Native, 0.1% Native Hawaiian/Other Pacific Islander, 4.4% Two or more races, 76.8% Hispanic of any race; Average household size: 3.21; Median age: 29.9; Age under 18: 31.9%; Age 65 and over: 13.3%; Males per 100 females: 108.7

Housing: Homeownership rate: 65.4%; Homeowner vacancy rate: 4.2%; Rental vacancy rate: 2.4%

EL CENTRO (city).

County seat. Covers a land area of 11.081 square miles and a water area of 0.018 square miles. Located at 32.79° N. Lat; 115.56° W. Long. Elevation is -39 feet.

History: El Centro was founded in 1905 by W.F. Holt, and developed as the trade, storage and shipping center of Imperial Valley and the seat of Imperial County. Irrigation provided by Boulder Dam on the Colorado River, brought to the valley by the All-American Canal, created an agricultural area from former desert.

Population: 42,598; Growth (since 2000): 12.6%; Density: 3,844.2 persons per square mile; Race: 59.6% White, 2.5% Black/African American, 2.3% Asian, 1.3% American Indian/Alaska Native, 0.1% Native Hawaiian/Other Pacific Islander, 5.2% Two or more races, 81.6% Hispanic of any race; Average household size: 3.19; Median age: 31.8; Age under 18: 29.7%; Age 65 and over: 10.7%; Males per 100 females: 94.7; Marriage status: 36.5% never married, 50.3% now married, 3.6% separated, 5.1% widowed, 8.2% divorced; Foreign born: 31.9%; Speak English only: 23.9%; With disability: 12.5%; Veterans: 5.1%; Ancestry: 4.1% German, 3.0% Irish, 2.0% English, 1.5% American, 1.4% Italian

Employment: 10.3% management, business, and financial, 1.2% computer, engineering, and science, 12.2% education, legal, community service, arts, and media, 4.2% healthcare practitioners, 24.4% service,

23.8% sales and office, 11.9% natural resources, construction, and maintenance, 12.0% production, transportation, and material moving

Income: Per capita: $18,877; Median household: $42,166; Average household: $60,391; Households with income of $100,000 or more: 18.7%; Poverty rate: 24.9%

Educational Attainment: High school diploma or higher: 67.2%; Bachelor's degree or higher: 17.3%; Graduate/professional degree or higher: 6.0%

School District(s)

Central Union High (09-12)
2012-13 Enrollment: 4,113 . . . . (760) 336-4500
El Centro Elementary (KG-08)
2012-13 Enrollment: 5,996 . . . . (760) 352-5712
Imperial County Office of Education (KG-12)
2012-13 Enrollment: 540. . . . . (760) 312-6464
Imperial Unified (KG-12)
2012-13 Enrollment: 3,711 . . . . (760) 355-3200
Imperial Valley Rop
2012-13 Enrollment: n/a . . . . (760) 482-2600
Mccabe Union Elementary (KG-08)
2012-13 Enrollment: 1,267 . . . . (760) 335-5200
Meadows Union Elementary (KG-08)
2012-13 Enrollment: 475. . . . . (760) 352-7512

Vocational/Technical School(s)

CET-El Centro (Private, Not-for-profit)
Fall 2013 Enrollment: 234 . . . . (408) 287-7924
2013-14 Tuition: $7,958

Housing: Homeownership rate: 49.5%; Median home value: $149,200; Median year structure built: 1976; Homeowner vacancy rate: 2.8%; Median gross rent: $741 per month; Rental vacancy rate: 7.2%

Health Insurance: 80.3% have insurance; 44.4% have private insurance; 42.2% have public insurance; 19.7% do not have insurance; 9.8% of children under 18 do not have insurance

Hospitals: El Centro Regional Medical Center (165 beds)

Safety: Violent crime rate: 33.3 per 10,000 population; Property crime rate: 471.5 per 10,000 population

Newspapers: Imperial Valley Press (daily circulation 12000)

Transportation: Commute: 90.1% car, 1.0% public transportation, 2.2% walk, 5.2% work from home; Median travel time to work: 19.0 minutes

Airports: El Centro NAF (general aviation)

Additional Information Contacts

City of El Centro . . . . (760) 337-4510
http://www.cityofelcentro.org

HEBER (CDP). Covers a land area of 1.485 square miles and a water area of 0 square miles. Located at 32.73° N. Lat; 115.52° W. Long. Elevation is -10 feet.

History: Heber was founded in 1901 by the Imperial Land Company and named Paringa. When the Southern Pacific Railway was completed in 1903, the town was moved to the railroad line and renamed for a president of the California Development Company.

Population: 4,275; Growth (since 2000): 43.1%; Density: 2,878.3 persons per square mile; Race: 50.9% White, 0.1% Black/African American, 0.4% Asian, 0.8% American Indian/Alaska Native, 0.0% Native Hawaiian/Other Pacific Islander, 6.8% Two or more races, 98.2% Hispanic of any race; Average household size: 3.91; Median age: 28.7; Age under 18: 34.0%; Age 65 and over: 9.9%; Males per 100 females: 89.9; Marriage status: 28.3% never married, 63.0% now married, 2.2% separated, 4.7% widowed, 3.9% divorced; Foreign born: 46.5%; Speak English only: 1.9%; With disability: 11.8%; Veterans: 1.7%; Ancestry: 0.4% English

Employment: 8.1% management, business, and financial, 1.3% computer, engineering, and science, 4.7% education, legal, community service, arts, and media, 7.4% healthcare practitioners, 23.3% service, 17.5% sales and office, 24.2% natural resources, construction, and maintenance, 13.5% production, transportation, and material moving

Income: Per capita: $13,641; Median household: $47,578; Average household: $50,172; Households with income of $100,000 or more: 12.1%; Poverty rate: 16.0%

Educational Attainment: High school diploma or higher: 53.6%; Bachelor's degree or higher: 6.3%; Graduate/professional degree or higher: 2.8%

School District(s)

Heber Elementary (KG-08)
2012-13 Enrollment: 1,170 . . . . (760) 337-6530

Housing: Homeownership rate: 62.0%; Median home value: $120,200; Median year structure built: 1997; Homeowner vacancy rate: 2.0%; Median gross rent: $1,014 per month; Rental vacancy rate: 6.3%

Health Insurance: 71.0% have insurance; 43.6% have private insurance; 31.9% have public insurance; 29.0% do not have insurance; 23.2% of children under 18 do not have insurance

Transportation: Commute: 88.8% car, 0.0% public transportation, 2.6% walk, 8.6% work from home; Median travel time to work: 24.7 minutes

HOLTVILLE (city). Covers a land area of 1.148 square miles and a water area of 0.005 square miles. Located at 32.81° N. Lat; 115.38° W. Long. Elevation is -10 feet.

History: Holtville was named for W.F. Holt, who bought large blocks of stock in the Imperial Water Companies. Many of Holtville's first settlers were people of Swiss descent who established dairy farms.

Population: 5,939; Growth (since 2000): 5.8%; Density: 5,172.6 persons per square mile; Race: 61.5% White, 0.6% Black/African American, 0.8% Asian, 0.7% American Indian/Alaska Native, 0.1% Native Hawaiian/Other Pacific Islander, 2.9% Two or more races, 81.8% Hispanic of any race; Average household size: 3.30; Median age: 32.1; Age under 18: 31.2%; Age 65 and over: 12.3%; Males per 100 females: 93.5; Marriage status: 32.2% never married, 49.0% now married, 3.6% separated, 9.4% widowed, 9.3% divorced; Foreign born: 31.5%; Speak English only: 25.4%; With disability: 19.2%; Veterans: 7.8%; Ancestry: 3.7% German, 2.3% Swiss, 2.1% Scottish, 2.0% American, 1.9% English

Employment: 9.2% management, business, and financial, 0.0% computer, engineering, and science, 8.3% education, legal, community service, arts, and media, 1.4% healthcare practitioners, 21.3% service, 23.1% sales and office, 22.0% natural resources, construction, and maintenance, 14.6% production, transportation, and material moving

Income: Per capita: $18,083; Median household: $32,628; Average household: $51,641; Households with income of $100,000 or more: 15.0%; Poverty rate: 25.9%

Educational Attainment: High school diploma or higher: 57.2%; Bachelor's degree or higher: 10.9%; Graduate/professional degree or higher: 2.3%

School District(s)

Holtville Unified (KG-12)
2012-13 Enrollment: 1,586 . . . . (760) 356-2974

Housing: Homeownership rate: 50.3%; Median home value: $130,200; Median year structure built: 1974; Homeowner vacancy rate: 1.6%; Median gross rent: $702 per month; Rental vacancy rate: 6.5%

Health Insurance: 71.7% have insurance; 38.2% have private insurance; 41.5% have public insurance; 28.3% do not have insurance; 19.5% of children under 18 do not have insurance

Safety: Violent crime rate: 19.9 per 10,000 population; Property crime rate: 169.4 per 10,000 population

Newspapers: Hometown Publishing (weekly circulation 11000)

Transportation: Commute: 94.5% car, 1.2% public transportation, 1.3% walk, 2.9% work from home; Median travel time to work: 19.4 minutes

Additional Information Contacts

City of Holtville. . . . . (760) 356-2912
http://www.holtville.ca.gov

IMPERIAL (city). Covers a land area of 5.856 square miles and a water area of 0 square miles. Located at 32.84° N. Lat; 115.57° W. Long. Elevation is -59 feet.

History: Founded 1902, incorporated 1904.

Population: 14,758; Growth (since 2000): 95.2%; Density: 2,519.9 persons per square mile; Race: 63.0% White, 2.2% Black/African American, 2.5% Asian, 1.0% American Indian/Alaska Native, 0.1% Native Hawaiian/Other Pacific Islander, 5.5% Two or more races, 74.8% Hispanic of any race; Average household size: 3.34; Median age: 29.9; Age under 18: 33.4%; Age 65 and over: 6.5%; Males per 100 females: 95.6; Marriage status: 28.9% never married, 58.3% now married, 2.0% separated, 4.4% widowed, 8.4% divorced; Foreign born: 26.7%; Speak English only: 36.6%; With disability: 7.1%; Veterans: 10.1%; Ancestry: 3.8% German, 3.5% Irish, 2.7% American, 2.5% Italian, 2.4% English

Employment: 10.6% management, business, and financial, 4.5% computer, engineering, and science, 9.7% education, legal, community service, arts, and media, 4.8% healthcare practitioners, 25.0% service, 30.5% sales and office, 8.9% natural resources, construction, and maintenance, 6.0% production, transportation, and material moving

Income: Per capita: $23,397; Median household: $66,552; Average household: $76,341; Households with income of $100,000 or more: 26.5%; Poverty rate: 11.8%

Educational Attainment: High school diploma or higher: 81.3%; Bachelor's degree or higher: 20.9%; Graduate/professional degree or higher: 6.5%

School District(s)

Imperial Unified (KG-12)
2012-13 Enrollment: 3,711 . . . . (760) 355-3200

Two-year College(s)

Imperial Valley College (Public)
Fall 2013 Enrollment: 7,701 . . . . (760) 352-8320
2013-14 Tuition: In-state $1,326; Out-of-state $6,926

Housing: Homeownership rate: 71.1%; Median home value: $175,100; Median year structure built: 2000; Homeowner vacancy rate: 4.5%; Median gross rent: $1,055 per month; Rental vacancy rate: 4.5%

Health Insurance: 83.9% have insurance; 66.3% have private insurance; 24.2% have public insurance; 16.1% do not have insurance; 10.0% of children under 18 do not have insurance

Safety: Violent crime rate: 4.4 per 10,000 population; Property crime rate: 53.9 per 10,000 population

Transportation: Commute: 96.5% car, 0.0% public transportation, 0.7% walk, 2.4% work from home; Median travel time to work: 19.2 minutes

Airports: Imperial County (commercial service–non-primary)

Additional Information Contacts

City of Imperial . . . . (760) 355-4371
http://www.imperial.ca.gov

NILAND (CDP). Covers a land area of 0.402 square miles and a water area of 0 square miles. Located at 33.24° N. Lat; 115.51° W. Long. Elevation is -141 feet.

History: Niland developed around ranches raising grapefruit, oranges, lemons, and tangerines.

Population: 1,006; Growth (since 2000): -12.0%; Density: 2,504.8 persons per square mile; Race: 53.6% White, 3.6% Black/African American, 3.6% Asian, 2.0% American Indian/Alaska Native, 0.0% Native Hawaiian/Other Pacific Islander, 6.0% Two or more races, 61.4% Hispanic of any race; Average household size: 2.74; Median age: 39.6; Age under 18: 24.7%; Age 65 and over: 15.9%; Males per 100 females: 96.9

School District(s)

Calipatria Unified (KG-12)
2012-13 Enrollment: 1,191 . . . . (760) 348-2151

Housing: Homeownership rate: 51.5%; Homeowner vacancy rate: 7.4%; Rental vacancy rate: 23.3%

OCOTILLO (CDP). Covers a land area of 8.857 square miles and a water area of 0 square miles. Located at 32.74° N. Lat; 116.00° W. Long. Elevation is 377 feet.

Population: 266; Growth (since 2000): -10.1%; Density: 30.0 persons per square mile; Race: 91.0% White, 0.4% Black/African American, 0.8% Asian, 0.4% American Indian/Alaska Native, 0.0% Native Hawaiian/Other Pacific Islander, 1.1% Two or more races, 22.9% Hispanic of any race; Average household size: 1.93; Median age: 56.1; Age under 18: 16.5%; Age 65 and over: 26.7%; Males per 100 females: 111.1

Housing: Homeownership rate: 71.0%; Homeowner vacancy rate: 2.8%; Rental vacancy rate: 14.9%

PALO VERDE (CDP). Covers a land area of 0.590 square miles and a water area of 0 square miles. Located at 33.43° N. Lat; 114.73° W. Long. Elevation is 233 feet.

Population: 171; Growth (since 2000): -27.5%; Density: 289.6 persons per square mile; Race: 72.5% White, 1.2% Black/African American, 0.6% Asian, 2.9% American Indian/Alaska Native, 0.0% Native Hawaiian/Other Pacific Islander, 7.6% Two or more races, 19.3% Hispanic of any race; Average household size: 2.04; Median age: 54.5; Age under 18: 14.6%; Age 65 and over: 25.1%; Males per 100 females: 119.2

Housing: Homeownership rate: 41.7%; Homeowner vacancy rate: 16.7%; Rental vacancy rate: 16.9%

SALTON CITY (CDP). Covers a land area of 21.431 square miles and a water area of 0 square miles. Located at 33.30° N. Lat; 115.96° W. Long. Elevation is -125 feet.

Population: 3,763; Growth (since 2000): 284.8%; Density: 175.6 persons per square mile; Race: 60.1% White, 2.1% Black/African American, 1.6% Asian, 1.6% American Indian/Alaska Native, 0.1% Native Hawaiian/Other Pacific Islander, 3.6% Two or more races, 62.9% Hispanic of any race; Average household size: 3.13; Median age: 31.3; Age under 18: 33.1%; Age 65 and over: 12.3%; Males per 100 females: 101.4; Marriage status: 34.1% never married, 48.2% now married, 5.1% separated, 3.8% widowed, 13.9% divorced; Foreign born: 21.4%; Speak English only: 45.6%; With disability: 15.8%; Veterans: 9.6%; Ancestry: 14.0% Irish, 4.5% German, 2.4% American, 2.0% French Canadian, 1.9% British

Employment: 5.2% management, business, and financial, 2.2% computer, engineering, and science, 0.8% education, legal, community service, arts, and media, 0.0% healthcare practitioners, 15.8% service, 25.1% sales and office, 19.8% natural resources, construction, and maintenance, 31.1% production, transportation, and material moving

Income: Per capita: $16,128; Median household: $29,387; Average household: $44,116; Households with income of $100,000 or more: 9.1%; Poverty rate: 31.9%

Educational Attainment: High school diploma or higher: 69.8%; Bachelor's degree or higher: 10.9%; Graduate/professional degree or higher: 2.0%

School District(s)

Coachella Valley Unified (KG-12)
2012-13 Enrollment: 18,720 . . . . (760) 399-5137

Housing: Homeownership rate: 69.2%; Median home value: $75,800; Median year structure built: 2002; Homeowner vacancy rate: 18.0%; Median gross rent: $795 per month; Rental vacancy rate: 20.3%

Health Insurance: 69.8% have insurance; 39.6% have private insurance; 36.9% have public insurance; 30.2% do not have insurance; 14.6% of children under 18 do not have insurance

Transportation: Commute: 92.3% car, 0.0% public transportation, 2.5% walk, 5.2% work from home; Median travel time to work: 36.0 minutes

---

SALTON SEA BEACH (CDP). Covers a land area of 0.301 square miles and a water area of 0 square miles. Located at 33.38° N. Lat; 116.01° W. Long. Elevation is -217 feet.

Population: 422; Growth (since 2000): 7.7%; Density: 1,400.9 persons per square mile; Race: 73.2% White, 1.4% Black/African American, 0.5% Asian, 0.9% American Indian/Alaska Native, 0.5% Native Hawaiian/Other Pacific Islander, 4.0% Two or more races, 54.3% Hispanic of any race; Average household size: 2.38; Median age: 40.0; Age under 18: 25.8%; Age 65 and over: 25.6%; Males per 100 females: 128.1

Housing: Homeownership rate: 70.6%; Homeowner vacancy rate: 3.4%; Rental vacancy rate: 12.9%

SEELEY (CDP). Covers a land area of 1.219 square miles and a water area of 0.023 square miles. Located at 32.79° N. Lat; 115.69° W. Long. Elevation is -36 feet.

History: Seeley was founded in 1911 near the site of Silsbee, a town destroyed by a flood in 1907.

Population: 1,739; Growth (since 2000): 7.1%; Density: 1,426.8 persons per square mile; Race: 42.9% White, 1.1% Black/African American, 1.2% Asian, 0.4% American Indian/Alaska Native, 0.1% Native Hawaiian/Other Pacific Islander, 8.7% Two or more races, 85.6% Hispanic of any race; Average household size: 3.53; Median age: 28.5; Age under 18: 33.2%; Age 65 and over: 9.9%; Males per 100 females: 95.4

School District(s)

Seeley Union Elementary (KG-08)
2012-13 Enrollment: 345. . . . . (760) 352-3571

Housing: Homeownership rate: 49.9%; Homeowner vacancy rate: 5.3%; Rental vacancy rate: 10.5%

WESTMORLAND (city). Covers a land area of 0.590 square miles and a water area of 0 square miles. Located at 33.04° N. Lat; 115.62° W. Long. Elevation is -164 feet.

History: Westmorland was founded in 1910, and served the surrounding agricultural area.

Population: 2,225; Growth (since 2000): 4.4%; Density: 3,769.7 persons per square mile; Race: 46.7% White, 0.9% Black/African American, 0.5% Asian, 1.7% American Indian/Alaska Native, 0.0% Native Hawaiian/Other Pacific Islander, 3.4% Two or more races, 87.1% Hispanic of any race; Average household size: 3.53; Median age: 29.2; Age under 18: 34.4%; Age 65 and over: 11.2%; Males per 100 females: 87.8

School District(s)

Westmorland Union Elementary (KG-08)
2012-13 Enrollment: 364. . . . . (760) 344-4364

Housing: Homeownership rate: 47.4%; Homeowner vacancy rate: 1.6%; Rental vacancy rate: 5.9%

Safety: Violent crime rate: 8.8 per 10,000 population; Property crime rate: 26.3 per 10,000 population

Additional Information Contacts

City of Westmorland . . . . (760) 344-3411
http://www.cityofwestmorland.net

WINTERHAVEN (CDP). Covers a land area of 0.238 square miles and a water area of 0 square miles. Located at 32.74° N. Lat; 114.64° W. Long. Elevation is 131 feet.

History: Winterhaven began as headquarters for the All-American Canal construction workers.

Population: 394; Growth (since 2000): -25.5%; Density: 1,655.3 persons per square mile; Race: 62.2% White, 1.0% Black/African American, 0.3% Asian, 9.4% American Indian/Alaska Native, 0.0% Native Hawaiian/Other Pacific Islander, 5.8% Two or more races, 66.2% Hispanic of any race; Average household size: 2.61; Median age: 39.0; Age under 18: 29.4%; Age 65 and over: 16.8%; Males per 100 females: 86.7

School District(s)

San Pasqual Valley Unified (KG-12)
2012-13 Enrollment: 770. . . . . (760) 572-0222

Housing: Homeownership rate: 41.1%; Homeowner vacancy rate: 3.1%; Rental vacancy rate: 8.1%

Inyo County

Located in eastern California; bounded on the west by the crest of the Sierra Nevada; includes Mt. Whitney, highest point in the state (14,495 ft) and nine other peaks over 14,000 ft, and Death Valley, lowest point in the Western Hemisphere (280 ft b elow sea level). Covers a land area of 10,180.878 square miles, a water area of 46.026 square miles, and is located in the Pacific Time Zone at 36.56° N. Lat., 117.40° W. Long. The county was founded in 1866. County seat is Independence.

Weather Station: Bishop Arpt Elevation: 4,102 feet

	Jan	Feb	Mar	Apr	May	Jun	Jul	Aug	Sep	Oct	Nov	Dec
High	54	58	65	72	82	91	98	96	87	76	62	53
Low	23	26	31	36	44	51	56	54	47	37	27	22
Precip	1.0	0.9	0.5	0.3	0.2	0.2	0.2	0.1	0.2	0.3	0.5	0.7
Snow	na	na	na	na	na	na	na	na	na	na	na	na

High and Low temperatures in degrees Fahrenheit; Precipitation and Snow in inches

Weather Station: Death Valley Elevation: -193 feet

	Jan	Feb	Mar	Apr	May	Jun	Jul	Aug	Sep	Oct	Nov	Dec
High	67	73	82	91	101	110	116	115	106	93	77	65
Low	39	45	54	61	72	80	87	85	75	61	47	38
Precip	0.4	0.5	0.3	0.1	0.1	0.0	0.1	0.1	0.2	0.1	0.2	0.2
Snow	0.0	0.0	0.0	0.0	0.0	0.0	0.0	0.0	0.0	0.0	0.0	0.0

High and Low temperatures in degrees Fahrenheit; Precipitation and Snow in inches

Weather Station: Haiwee Elevation: 3,825 feet

	Jan	Feb	Mar	Apr	May	Jun	Jul	Aug	Sep	Oct	Nov	Dec
High	54	58	65	72	82	91	97	96	88	78	64	54
Low	29	32	37	42	50	58	64	63	55	46	36	29
Precip	1.3	1.6	1.1	0.3	0.2	0.1	0.4	0.3	0.3	0.2	0.6	0.9
Snow	0.4	0.3	0.0	0.1	0.0	0.0	0.0	0.0	0.0	0.0	0.1	0.4

High and Low temperatures in degrees Fahrenheit; Precipitation and Snow in inches

Weather Station: Independence Elevation: 3,943 feet

	Jan	Feb	Mar	Apr	May	Jun	Jul	Aug	Sep	Oct	Nov	Dec
High	56	59	66	74	84	93	100	98	90	78	65	55
Low	29	33	38	43	52	60	66	63	57	46	35	28
Precip	1.1	1.2	0.6	0.2	0.1	0.2	0.1	0.1	0.2	0.2	0.7	0.8
Snow	0.4	0.2	tr	tr	0.0	0.0	0.0	0.0	0.0	0.0	tr	0.3

High and Low temperatures in degrees Fahrenheit; Precipitation and Snow in inches

Population: 18,546; Growth (since 2000): 3.3%; Density: 1.8 persons per square mile; Race: 74.1% White, 0.6% Black/African American, 1.3% Asian, 11.4% American Indian/Alaska Native, 0.1% Native Hawaiian/Other Pacific Islander, 3.5% two or more races, 19.4% Hispanic of any race; Average household size: 2.25; Median age: 45.6; Age under 18: 21.0%; Age 65 and over: 19.1%; Males per 100 females: 101.8; Marriage status: 28.5% never married, 51.2% now married, 3.0% separated, 7.1% widowed, 13.2% divorced; Foreign born: 10.4%; Speak English only: 85.1%; With disability: 12.5%; Veterans: 11.8%; Ancestry: 17.5% German, 13.7% Irish, 12.0% English, 4.5% French, 4.2% American

Religion: Six largest groups: 26.0% Catholicism, 3.9% Methodist/Pietist, 3.3% Latter-day Saints, 3.0% Non-denominational Protestant, 2.3% Pentecostal, 1.2% Lutheran

Economy: Unemployment rate: 6.4%; Leading industries: 17.1% accommodation and food services; 16.6% retail trade; 10.5% health care and social assistance; Farms: 125 totaling 330,840 acres; Company size: 0 employ 1,000 or more persons, 0 employ 500 to 999 persons, 9 employ 100 to 499 persons, 522 employ less than 100 persons; Business ownership: n/a women-owned, n/a Black-owned, n/a Hispanic-owned, n/a Asian-owned

Employment: 11.7% management, business, and financial, 5.2% computer, engineering, and science, 8.1% education, legal, community service, arts, and media, 4.3% healthcare practitioners, 23.7% service, 27.3% sales and office, 9.9% natural resources, construction, and maintenance, 9.8% production, transportation, and material moving

Income: Per capita: $27,441; Median household: $44,796; Average household: $61,137; Households with income of $100,000 or more: 17.7%; Poverty rate: 12.8%

Educational Attainment: High school diploma or higher: 88.1%; Bachelor's degree or higher: 21.4%; Graduate/professional degree or higher: 8.3%

Housing: Homeownership rate: 63.6%; Median home value: $236,100; Median year structure built: 1974; Homeowner vacancy rate: 1.7%; Median gross rent: $829 per month; Rental vacancy rate: 5.8%

Vital Statistics: Birth rate: 117.5 per 10,000 population; Death rate: 96.9 per 10,000 population; Age-adjusted cancer mortality rate: 121.6 deaths per 100,000 population

Health Insurance: 84.9% have insurance; 62.2% have private insurance; 38.7% have public insurance; 15.1% do not have insurance; 8.7% of children under 18 do not have insurance

Health Care: Physicians: 17.9 per 10,000 population; Hospital beds: 33.7 per 10,000 population; Hospital admissions: 529.8 per 10,000 population

Air Quality Index: 74.0% good, 21.4% moderate, 1.6% unhealthy for sensitive individuals, 1.9% unhealthy, 1.1% very unhealthy (% of days)

Transportation: Commute: 81.7% car, 0.6% public transportation, 7.1% walk, 5.5% work from home; Median travel time to work: 14.8 minutes

Presidential Election: 42.7% Obama, 54.5% Romney (2012)

National and State Parks: Death Valley National Park; Manzanar National Historic Site

Additional Information Contacts

Inyo Government. . . . . (760) 878-0366
http://www.inyocounty.us

Inyo County Communities

BIG PINE (CDP). Covers a land area of 2.954 square miles and a water area of 0.002 square miles. Located at 37.17° N. Lat; 118.30° W. Long. Elevation is 3,989 feet.

History: Big Pine developed as an outfitting center for fishing, packing, and hiking groups bound for the high Sierra.

Population: 1,756; Growth (since 2000): 30.1%; Density: 594.4 persons per square mile; Race: 67.9% White, 0.2% Black/African American, 0.7% Asian, 24.9% American Indian/Alaska Native, 0.1% Native Hawaiian/Other Pacific Islander, 3.2% Two or more races, 10.4% Hispanic of any race; Average household size: 2.30; Median age: 46.6; Age under 18: 19.4%; Age 65 and over: 19.6%; Males per 100 females: 97.1

School District(s)

Big Pine Unified (KG-12)
2012-13 Enrollment: 186. . . . . (760) 938-2005
Bishop Unified (KG-12)
2012-13 Enrollment: 1,985 . . . . (760) 872-3680

Housing: Homeownership rate: 76.7%; Homeowner vacancy rate: 1.5%; Rental vacancy rate: 6.3%

BISHOP (city). Covers a land area of 1.864 square miles and a water area of 0.047 square miles. Located at 37.37° N. Lat; 118.40° W. Long. Elevation is 4,147 feet.

History: Bishop was named for Bishop Creek, which in turn was named for Samuel A. Bishop, a Fort Tejon stockman who drove the first herd of cattle into Owens Valley in 1861. By 1863 settlers had come into the valley and a village had sprung up near Bishop's ranch. Bishop became a supply point for stockraisers and miners.

Population: 3,879; Growth (since 2000): 8.5%; Density: 2,081.3 persons per square mile; Race: 73.9% White, 0.6% Black/African American, 1.6% Asian, 2.3% American Indian/Alaska Native, 0.0% Native Hawaiian/Other

Pacific Islander, 2.9% Two or more races, 30.9% Hispanic of any race; Average household size: 2.16; Median age: 38.9; Age under 18: 23.8%; Age 65 and over: 15.8%; Males per 100 females: 99.8; Marriage status: 28.7% never married, 45.9% now married, 4.5% separated, 5.5% widowed, 19.9% divorced; Foreign born: 18.5%; Speak English only: 77.6%; With disability: 13.5%; Veterans: 12.0%; Ancestry: 17.2% Irish, 15.2% English, 13.1% German, 5.9% French, 5.0% American
Employment: 12.2% management, business, and financial, 5.6% computer, engineering, and science, 7.7% education, legal, community service, arts, and media, 6.7% healthcare practitioners, 32.6% service, 21.2% sales and office, 6.9% natural resources, construction, and maintenance, 7.0% production, transportation, and material moving
Income: Per capita: $26,081; Median household: $30,813; Average household: $53,265; Households with income of $100,000 or more: 14.5%; Poverty rate: 16.8%
Educational Attainment: High school diploma or higher: 85.4%; Bachelor's degree or higher: 24.6%; Graduate/professional degree or higher: 6.2%

School District(s)

Bishop Unified (KG-12)
2012-13 Enrollment: 1,985 . . . . (760) 872-3680
Inyo County Office of Education (KG-12)
2012-13 Enrollment: 1,657 . . . . (760) 878-2426
Inyo County Rop
2012-13 Enrollment: n/a . . . . (760) 873-3262
Round Valley Joint Elementary (KG-08)
2012-13 Enrollment: 146. . . . . (760) 387-2525

Housing: Homeownership rate: 38.7%; Median home value: $293,700; Median year structure built: 1967; Homeowner vacancy rate: 0.3%; Median gross rent: $807 per month; Rental vacancy rate: 5.8%
Health Insurance: 82.9% have insurance; 60.1% have private insurance; 31.7% have public insurance; 17.1% do not have insurance; 6.4% of children under 18 do not have insurance
Hospitals: Northern Inyo Hospital (32 beds)
Safety: Violent crime rate: 72.5 per 10,000 population; Property crime rate: 279.7 per 10,000 population
Newspapers: Inyo Register (weekly circulation 5900)
Transportation: Commute: 73.8% car, 0.8% public transportation, 7.6% walk, 4.3% work from home; Median travel time to work: 15.3 minutes
Airports: Eastern Sierra Regional (general aviation)
Additional Information Contacts
City of Bishop . . . . (760) 873-5863
http://www.ca-bishop.us

CARTAGO (CDP). Covers a land area of 1.169 square miles and a water area of 0.003 square miles. Located at 36.31° N. Lat; 118.03° W. Long. Elevation is 3,629 feet.
Population: 92; Growth (since 2000): -15.6%; Density: 78.7 persons per square mile; Race: 68.5% White, 0.0% Black/African American, 0.0% Asian, 7.6% American Indian/Alaska Native, 0.0% Native Hawaiian/Other Pacific Islander, 12.0% Two or more races, 17.4% Hispanic of any race; Average household size: 2.09; Median age: 45.0; Age under 18: 20.7%; Age 65 and over: 17.4%; Males per 100 females: 124.4
Housing: Homeownership rate: 63.6%; Homeowner vacancy rate: 0.0%; Rental vacancy rate: 0.0%

DARWIN (CDP). Covers a land area of 1.345 square miles and a water area of 0 square miles. Located at 36.27° N. Lat; 117.59° W. Long. Elevation is 4,790 feet.
Population: 43; Growth (since 2000): -20.4%; Density: 32.0 persons per square mile; Race: 88.4% White, 0.0% Black/African American, 2.3% Asian, 4.7% American Indian/Alaska Native, 2.3% Native Hawaiian/Other Pacific Islander, 2.3% Two or more races, 4.7% Hispanic of any race; Average household size: 1.54; Median age: 63.5; Age under 18: 0.0%; Age 65 and over: 48.8%; Males per 100 females: 168.8
Housing: Homeownership rate: 85.7%; Homeowner vacancy rate: 4.0%; Rental vacancy rate: 0.0%

DEATH VALLEY (unincorporated postal area)

ZCTA: 92328

Covers a land area of 701.083 square miles and a water area of 5.052 square miles. Located at 36.60° N. Lat; 116.83° W. Long..
Population: 445; Growth (since 2000): 0.7%; Density: 0.6 persons per square mile; Race: 90.3% White, 1.6% Black/African American, 0.4% Asian, 3.6% American Indian/Alaska Native, 0.9% Native Hawaiian/Other Pacific Islander, 1.3% Two or more races, 10.8% Hispanic of any race; Average household size: 1.54; Median age: 47.9; Age under 18: 5.2%; Age 65 and over: 10.1%; Males per 100 females: 141.8

School District(s)

Death Valley Unified (KG-12)
2012-13 Enrollment: 28. . . . . (760) 852-4303

Housing: Homeownership rate: 25.5%; Homeowner vacancy rate: 0.0%; Rental vacancy rate: 4.6%

DIXON LANE-MEADOW CREEK (CDP). Covers a land area of 3.360 square miles and a water area of 0 square miles. Located at 37.39° N. Lat; 118.42° W. Long. Elevation is 4,190 feet.
Population: 2,645; Growth (since 2000): -2.1%; Density: 787.3 persons per square mile; Race: 86.5% White, 0.2% Black/African American, 1.8% Asian, 1.2% American Indian/Alaska Native, 0.1% Native Hawaiian/Other Pacific Islander, 2.1% Two or more races, 18.6% Hispanic of any race; Average household size: 2.27; Median age: 48.4; Age under 18: 22.2%; Age 65 and over: 23.7%; Males per 100 females: 93.6; Marriage status: 21.0% never married, 59.4% now married, 2.1% separated, 11.1% widowed, 8.5% divorced; Foreign born: 11.8%; Speak English only: 76.5%; With disability: 16.6%; Veterans: 11.4%; Ancestry: 22.1% German, 12.7% Irish, 11.8% English, 4.1% American, 3.5% Dutch
Employment: 8.1% management, business, and financial, 5.6% computer, engineering, and science, 8.0% education, legal, community service, arts, and media, 5.6% healthcare practitioners, 22.0% service, 31.9% sales and office, 5.5% natural resources, construction, and maintenance, 13.2% production, transportation, and material moving
Income: Per capita: $28,074; Median household: $51,827; Average household: $60,387; Households with income of $100,000 or more: 14.0%; Poverty rate: 7.9%
Educational Attainment: High school diploma or higher: 82.5%; Bachelor's degree or higher: 16.0%; Graduate/professional degree or higher: 6.0%
Housing: Homeownership rate: 84.9%; Median home value: $56,300; Median year structure built: 1979; Homeowner vacancy rate: 1.5%; Median gross rent: $1,090 per month; Rental vacancy rate: 0.6%
Health Insurance: 90.8% have insurance; 64.1% have private insurance; 48.0% have public insurance; 9.2% do not have insurance; 0.8% of children under 18 do not have insurance
Transportation: Commute: 91.7% car, 0.0% public transportation, 0.0% walk, 3.2% work from home; Median travel time to work: 14.2 minutes

---

FURNACE CREEK (CDP). Covers a land area of 31.203 square miles and a water area of 0.260 square miles. Located at 36.41° N. Lat; 116.88° W. Long. Elevation is -190 feet.
Population: 24; Growth (since 2000): -22.6%; Density: 0.8 persons per square mile; Race: 25.0% White, 0.0% Black/African American, 0.0% Asian, 66.7% American Indian/Alaska Native, 0.0% Native Hawaiian/Other Pacific Islander, 8.3% Two or more races, 0.0% Hispanic of any race; Average household size: 1.60; Median age: 52.0; Age under 18: 8.3%; Age 65 and over: 25.0%; Males per 100 females: 71.4
Housing: Homeownership rate: 73.4%; Homeowner vacancy rate: 0.0%; Rental vacancy rate: 0.0%

HOMEWOOD CANYON (CDP). Covers a land area of 10.250 square miles and a water area of 0 square miles. Located at 35.89° N. Lat; 117.39° W. Long.
Population: 44; Growth (since 2000): n/a; Density: 4.3 persons per square mile; Race: 84.1% White, 0.0% Black/African American, 0.0% Asian, 0.0% American Indian/Alaska Native, 0.0% Native Hawaiian/Other Pacific Islander, 4.5% Two or more races, 13.6% Hispanic of any race; Average household size: 1.83; Median age: 56.0; Age under 18: 9.1%; Age 65 and over: 22.7%; Males per 100 females: 144.4
Housing: Homeownership rate: 87.5%; Homeowner vacancy rate: 0.0%; Rental vacancy rate: 0.0%

INDEPENDENCE (CDP). County seat. Covers a land area of 4.867 square miles and a water area of 0.003 square miles. Located at 36.83° N. Lat; 118.21° W. Long. Elevation is 3,930 feet.
History: Independence developed as an outfitting center for pack trips into the Sierras via Kearsarge Pass, a shipping point for farm products, and the seat of Inyo County.
Population: 669; Growth (since 2000): 16.6%; Density: 137.5 persons per square mile; Race: 73.7% White, 0.9% Black/African American, 1.2% Asian, 14.6% American Indian/Alaska Native, 0.1% Native Hawaiian/Other

Pacific Islander, 5.2% Two or more races, 13.9% Hispanic of any race; Average household size: 2.00; Median age: 51.1; Age under 18: 14.9%; Age 65 and over: 20.8%; Males per 100 females: 105.8

School District(s)

Bishop Unified (KG-12)
2012-13 Enrollment: 1,985 . . . . (760) 872-3680
Inyo County Office of Education (KG-12)
2012-13 Enrollment: 1,657 . . . . (760) 878-2426
Owens Valley Unified (KG-12)
2012-13 Enrollment: 71. . . . . (760) 878-2405

Housing: Homeownership rate: 69.8%; Homeowner vacancy rate: 5.8%; Rental vacancy rate: 6.1%

KEELER (CDP). Covers a land area of 1.302 square miles and a water area of 0 square miles. Located at 36.48° N. Lat; 117.87° W. Long. Elevation is 3,602 feet.

Population: 66; Growth (since 2000): 0.0%; Density: 50.7 persons per square mile; Race: 95.5% White, 0.0% Black/African American, 3.0% Asian, 0.0% American Indian/Alaska Native, 0.0% Native Hawaiian/Other Pacific Islander, 1.5% Two or more races, 9.1% Hispanic of any race; Average household size: 1.65; Median age: 59.3; Age under 18: 13.6%; Age 65 and over: 33.3%; Males per 100 females: 120.0

Housing: Homeownership rate: 82.5%; Homeowner vacancy rate: 2.9%; Rental vacancy rate: 22.2%

LONE PINE (CDP). Covers a land area of 19.034 square miles and a water area of 0.181 square miles. Located at 36.57° N. Lat; 118.08° W. Long. Elevation is 3,727 feet.

History: The community of Lone Pine, settled in the early 1850's, grew as a supply center for tourists and as an outfitter for trips to Mount Whitney.

Population: 2,035; Growth (since 2000): 23.0%; Density: 106.9 persons per square mile; Race: 65.6% White, 0.3% Black/African American, 0.8% Asian, 10.1% American Indian/Alaska Native, 0.0% Native Hawaiian/Other Pacific Islander, 4.7% Two or more races, 34.1% Hispanic of any race; Average household size: 2.37; Median age: 41.9; Age under 18: 24.2%; Age 65 and over: 18.9%; Males per 100 females: 98.5

School District(s)

Inyo County Office of Education (KG-12)
2012-13 Enrollment: 1,657 . . . . (760) 878-2426
Lone Pine Unified (KG-12)
2012-13 Enrollment: 385. . . . . (760) 876-5579

Housing: Homeownership rate: 54.3%; Homeowner vacancy rate: 2.6%; Rental vacancy rate: 7.1%

Hospitals: Southern Inyo Hospital (37 beds)

Airports: Lone Pine (general aviation)

MESA (CDP). Covers a land area of 3.503 square miles and a water area of 0.153 square miles. Located at 37.42° N. Lat; 118.54° W. Long.

Population: 251; Growth (since 2000): 17.3%; Density: 71.7 persons per square mile; Race: 87.6% White, 0.0% Black/African American, 1.2% Asian, 4.0% American Indian/Alaska Native, 0.0% Native Hawaiian/Other Pacific Islander, 1.6% Two or more races, 10.4% Hispanic of any race; Average household size: 2.41; Median age: 50.0; Age under 18: 13.1%; Age 65 and over: 15.9%; Males per 100 females: 97.6

Housing: Homeownership rate: 75.0%; Homeowner vacancy rate: 0.0%; Rental vacancy rate: 0.0%

OLANCHA (CDP). Covers a land area of 7.841 square miles and a water area of 0.031 square miles. Located at 36.27° N. Lat; 118.00° W. Long. Elevation is 3,658 feet.

Population: 192; Growth (since 2000): 43.3%; Density: 24.5 persons per square mile; Race: 69.3% White, 0.0% Black/African American, 4.2% Asian, 2.1% American Indian/Alaska Native, 0.0% Native Hawaiian/Other Pacific Islander, 4.7% Two or more races, 24.5% Hispanic of any race; Average household size: 2.46; Median age: 47.2; Age under 18: 22.9%; Age 65 and over: 17.2%; Males per 100 females: 115.7

Housing: Homeownership rate: 56.4%; Homeowner vacancy rate: 2.2%; Rental vacancy rate: 2.9%

PEARSONVILLE (CDP). Covers a land area of 4.141 square miles and a water area of 0.081 square miles. Located at 35.82° N. Lat; 117.88° W. Long. Elevation is 2,513 feet.

Population: 17; Growth (since 2000): -37.0%; Density: 4.1 persons per square mile; Race: 94.1% White, 0.0% Black/African American, 0.0% Asian, 0.0% American Indian/Alaska Native, 0.0% Native Hawaiian/Other Pacific Islander, 0.0% Two or more races, 5.9% Hispanic of any race; Average household size: 1.89; Median age: 59.8; Age under 18: 0.0%; Age 65 and over: 35.3%; Males per 100 females: 70.0

Housing: Homeownership rate: 77.8%; Homeowner vacancy rate: 12.5%; Rental vacancy rate: 0.0%

ROUND VALLEY (CDP). Covers a land area of 13.809 square miles and a water area of 0.012 square miles. Located at 37.41° N. Lat; 118.57° W. Long. Elevation is 4,692 feet.

Population: 435; Growth (since 2000): 56.5%; Density: 31.5 persons per square mile; Race: 76.6% White, 8.7% Black/African American, 0.7% Asian, 4.8% American Indian/Alaska Native, 0.0% Native Hawaiian/Other Pacific Islander, 3.0% Two or more races, 15.9% Hispanic of any race; Average household size: 2.30; Median age: 39.8; Age under 18: 14.5%; Age 65 and over: 6.7%; Males per 100 females: 155.9

Housing: Homeownership rate: 31.9%; Homeowner vacancy rate: 0.0%; Rental vacancy rate: 4.0%

SHOSHONE (CDP). Covers a land area of 28.711 square miles and a water area of <.001 square miles. Located at 35.97° N. Lat; 116.31° W. Long. Elevation is 1,585 feet.

Population: 31; Growth (since 2000): -40.4%; Density: 1.1 persons per square mile; Race: 90.3% White, 3.2% Black/African American, 0.0% Asian, 3.2% American Indian/Alaska Native, 0.0% Native Hawaiian/Other Pacific Islander, 3.2% Two or more races, 0.0% Hispanic of any race; Average household size: 1.82; Median age: 44.5; Age under 18: 9.7%; Age 65 and over: 16.1%; Males per 100 females: 93.8

School District(s)

Death Valley Unified (KG-12)
2012-13 Enrollment: 28. . . . . (760) 852-4303

Housing: Homeownership rate: 29.4%; Homeowner vacancy rate: 16.7%; Rental vacancy rate: 20.0%

TECOPA (CDP). Covers a land area of 18.589 square miles and a water area of 0.068 square miles. Located at 35.82° N. Lat; 116.20° W. Long. Elevation is 1,339 feet.

History: Death Valley National Monument to West.

Population: 150; Growth (since 2000): 51.5%; Density: 8.1 persons per square mile; Race: 79.3% White, 0.7% Black/African American, 1.3% Asian, 5.3% American Indian/Alaska Native, 0.0% Native Hawaiian/Other Pacific Islander, 12.7% Two or more races, 5.3% Hispanic of any race; Average household size: 1.63; Median age: 57.5; Age under 18: 12.7%; Age 65 and over: 33.3%; Males per 100 females: 138.1

School District(s)

Death Valley Unified (KG-12)
2012-13 Enrollment: 28. . . . . (760) 852-4303

Housing: Homeownership rate: 62.0%; Homeowner vacancy rate: 6.6%; Rental vacancy rate: 10.3%

WEST BISHOP (CDP). Covers a land area of 8.759 square miles and a water area of 0.001 square miles. Located at 37.36° N. Lat; 118.48° W. Long. Elevation is 4,403 feet.

Population: 2,607; Growth (since 2000): -7.1%; Density: 297.7 persons per square mile; Race: 91.0% White, 0.4% Black/African American, 1.7% Asian, 1.1% American Indian/Alaska Native, 0.0% Native Hawaiian/Other Pacific Islander, 3.0% Two or more races, 10.0% Hispanic of any race; Average household size: 2.30; Median age: 52.6; Age under 18: 17.5%; Age 65 and over: 25.4%; Males per 100 females: 97.2; Marriage status: 25.5% never married, 63.2% now married, 2.4% separated, 5.9% widowed, 5.3% divorced; Foreign born: 6.3%; Speak English only: 89.8%; With disability: 8.9%; Veterans: 11.4%; Ancestry: 16.4% German, 15.8% Irish, 13.5% English, 9.0% American, 4.8% French

Employment: 12.4% management, business, and financial, 7.5% computer, engineering, and science, 11.5% education, legal, community service, arts, and media, 4.2% healthcare practitioners, 13.5% service, 29.3% sales and office, 9.1% natural resources, construction, and maintenance, 12.5% production, transportation, and material moving

Income: Per capita: $37,102; Median household: $86,089; Average household: $90,795; Households with income of $100,000 or more: 41.2%; Poverty rate: 4.1%

Educational Attainment: High school diploma or higher: 96.7%; Bachelor's degree or higher: 33.0%; Graduate/professional degree or higher: 18.4%

Housing: Homeownership rate: 86.0%; Median home value: $412,700; Median year structure built: 1972; Homeowner vacancy rate: 1.0%; Median gross rent: $1,556 per month; Rental vacancy rate: 4.2%

Health Insurance: 92.0% have insurance; 82.5% have private insurance; 38.0% have public insurance; 8.0% do not have insurance; 3.9% of children under 18 do not have insurance

Transportation: Commute: 93.1% car, 0.8% public transportation, 0.0% walk, 4.7% work from home; Median travel time to work: 13.3 minutes

WILKERSON (CDP). Covers a land area of 5.727 square miles and a water area of <.001 square miles. Located at 37.28° N. Lat; 118.39° W. Long.

Population: 563; Growth (since 2000): 0.2%; Density: 98.3 persons per square mile; Race: 93.1% White, 0.0% Black/African American, 0.9% Asian, 2.3% American Indian/Alaska Native, 0.2% Native Hawaiian/Other Pacific Islander, 2.7% Two or more races, 9.4% Hispanic of any race; Average household size: 2.31; Median age: 51.2; Age under 18: 17.8%; Age 65 and over: 20.4%; Males per 100 females: 101.1

Housing: Homeownership rate: 82.0%; Homeowner vacancy rate: 1.5%; Rental vacancy rate: 4.3%

Kern County

Located in south central California; in the San Joaquin Valley, with the Tehachapi Mountains in the south, the Sierra Nevadas in the east, and the Coast Range in the west; includes part of the Mojave Desert, and part of Sequoia National Forest. Covers a land area of 8,131.916 square miles, a water area of 30.725 square miles, and is located in the Pacific Time Zone at 35.35° N. Lat., 118.73° W. Long. The county was founded in 1866. County seat is Bakersfield.

Kern County is part of the Bakersfield, CA Metropolitan Statistical Area. The entire metro area includes: Kern County, CA

Weather Station: Bakersfield Meadows Field — Elevation: 488 feet

	Jan	Feb	Mar	Apr	May	Jun	Jul	Aug	Sep	Oct	Nov	Dec
High	57	64	69	76	84	92	98	96	91	80	66	57
Low	39	42	46	49	57	63	69	68	63	54	44	38
Precip	1.2	1.2	1.2	0.5	0.2	0.1	tr	0.1	0.1	0.3	0.6	0.8
Snow	0.1	na	na	na	na	na	na	na	na	na	na	na

High and Low temperatures in degrees Fahrenheit; Precipitation and Snow in inches

Weather Station: Buttonwillow — Elevation: 269 feet

	Jan	Feb	Mar	Apr	May	Jun	Jul	Aug	Sep	Oct	Nov	Dec
High	56	64	70	76	85	92	97	96	91	81	67	57
Low	37	41	45	48	55	61	66	64	59	50	40	35
Precip	1.2	1.2	1.3	0.5	0.2	0.1	0.0	0.0	0.1	0.3	0.6	0.7
Snow	0.0	0.0	0.0	0.0	0.0	0.0	0.0	0.0	0.0	0.0	0.0	0.0

High and Low temperatures in degrees Fahrenheit; Precipitation and Snow in inches

Weather Station: Glennville — Elevation: 3,140 feet

	Jan	Feb	Mar	Apr	May	Jun	Jul	Aug	Sep	Oct	Nov	Dec
High	57	58	60	66	74	83	90	89	83	73	62	56
Low	30	32	34	36	41	46	52	51	46	39	33	29
Precip	4.0	3.7	3.4	1.6	0.8	0.2	0.1	0.1	0.3	0.8	2.3	2.9
Snow	2.1	1.5	1.4	0.6	0.0	0.0	0.0	0.0	0.0	0.0	0.6	1.3

High and Low temperatures in degrees Fahrenheit; Precipitation and Snow in inches

Weather Station: Inyokern — Elevation: 2,439 feet

	Jan	Feb	Mar	Apr	May	Jun	Jul	Aug	Sep	Oct	Nov	Dec
High	61	65	72	78	88	97	103	102	95	83	70	60
Low	32	36	40	46	54	61	66	66	59	49	38	31
Precip	0.8	1.3	0.6	0.2	0.1	0.0	0.2	0.3	0.2	0.1	0.3	0.5
Snow	0.3	tr	0.0	0.0	0.0	0.0	0.0	0.0	0.0	0.0	0.0	0.3

High and Low temperatures in degrees Fahrenheit; Precipitation and Snow in inches

Weather Station: Kern River Ph 3 — Elevation: 2,703 feet

	Jan	Feb	Mar	Apr	May	Jun	Jul	Aug	Sep	Oct	Nov	Dec
High	60	63	67	73	81	90	98	97	91	81	68	61
Low	33	35	38	43	50	58	64	63	57	48	37	32
Precip	2.8	2.7	2.1	0.7	0.3	0.1	0.2	0.2	0.2	0.6	1.4	1.8
Snow	0.2	0.0	0.0	0.0	0.0	0.0	0.0	0.0	0.0	0.0	0.0	tr

High and Low temperatures in degrees Fahrenheit; Precipitation and Snow in inches

Weather Station: Mojave — Elevation: 2,734 feet

	Jan	Feb	Mar	Apr	May	Jun	Jul	Aug	Sep	Oct	Nov	Dec
High	59	61	67	73	81	90	97	97	90	79	65	57
Low	34	38	42	47	55	64	69	68	61	51	40	33
Precip	1.2	1.6	0.9	0.2	0.1	0.1	0.2	0.3	0.2	0.3	0.4	0.7
Snow	0.3	0.1	0.1	0.0	0.0	0.0	0.0	0.0	0.0	0.0	0.0	0.4

High and Low temperatures in degrees Fahrenheit; Precipitation and Snow in inches

Weather Station: Randsburg — Elevation: 3,569 feet

	Jan	Feb	Mar	Apr	May	Jun	Jul	Aug	Sep	Oct	Nov	Dec
High	55	58	64	72	82	91	98	96	89	76	63	54
Low	36	38	41	46	55	62	68	67	61	52	42	36
Precip	1.4	1.7	1.2	0.3	0.1	0.0	0.2	0.2	0.2	0.5	0.6	0.9
Snow	0.6	0.4	0.4	0.0	0.0	0.0	0.0	0.0	0.0	0.0	0.1	1.5

High and Low temperatures in degrees Fahrenheit; Precipitation and Snow in inches

Weather Station: Tejon Rancho — Elevation: 1,424 feet

	Jan	Feb	Mar	Apr	May	Jun	Jul	Aug	Sep	Oct	Nov	Dec
High	59	63	68	75	84	91	98	97	91	81	67	59
Low	34	38	41	45	52	59	65	63	59	50	40	34
Precip	2.2	2.1	2.2	1.1	0.5	0.1	0.0	0.1	0.2	0.5	1.6	1.4
Snow	0.0	0.0	0.0	0.0	0.0	0.0	0.0	0.0	0.0	0.0	0.0	tr

High and Low temperatures in degrees Fahrenheit; Precipitation and Snow in inches

Weather Station: Wasco — Elevation: 345 feet

	Jan	Feb	Mar	Apr	May	Jun	Jul	Aug	Sep	Oct	Nov	Dec
High	57	65	71	79	87	94	99	98	93	82	67	57
Low	37	40	44	48	54	60	65	63	59	49	40	35
Precip	1.4	1.3	1.4	0.7	0.2	0.1	0.0	0.0	0.1	0.4	0.6	0.8
Snow	0.1	0.0	0.0	0.0	0.0	0.0	0.0	0.0	0.0	0.0	0.0	0.0

High and Low temperatures in degrees Fahrenheit; Precipitation and Snow in inches

Population: 839,631; Growth (since 2000): 26.9%; Density: 103.3 persons per square mile; Race: 59.5% White, 5.8% Black/African American, 4.2% Asian, 1.5% American Indian/Alaska Native, 0.1% Native Hawaiian/Other Pacific Islander, 4.5% two or more races, 49.2% Hispanic of any race; Average household size: 3.15; Median age: 30.7; Age under 18: 30.3%; Age 65 and over: 9.0%; Males per 100 females: 106.5; Marriage status: 35.3% never married, 50.1% now married, 3.1% separated, 4.8% widowed, 9.8% divorced; Foreign born: 20.6%; Speak English only: 57.9%; With disability: 11.8%; Veterans: 7.6%; Ancestry: 8.6% German, 7.3% Irish, 5.4% English, 3.4% American, 2.6% Italian

Religion: Six largest groups: 29.3% Catholicism, 4.6% Non-denominational Protestant, 4.4% Baptist, 2.9% Pentecostal, 2.6% Latter-day Saints, 0.7% Holiness

Economy: Unemployment rate: 9.0%; Leading industries: 15.2% retail trade; 12.7% health care and social assistance; 10.4% accommodation and food services; Farms: 1,938 totaling 2,330,233 acres; Company size: 14 employ 1,000 or more persons, 13 employ 500 to 999 persons, 260 employ 100 to 499 persons, 11,979 employ less than 100 persons; Business ownership: 16,676 women-owned, 2,309 Black-owned, 12,751 Hispanic-owned, n/a Asian-owned

Employment: 9.9% management, business, and financial, 3.5% computer, engineering, and science, 8.6% education, legal, community service, arts, and media, 4.1% healthcare practitioners, 19.0% service, 21.8% sales and office, 19.9% natural resources, construction, and maintenance, 13.3% production, transportation, and material moving

Income: Per capita: $20,295; Median household: $48,552; Average household: $64,677; Households with income of $100,000 or more: 19.4%; Poverty rate: 22.9%

Educational Attainment: High school diploma or higher: 72.4%; Bachelor's degree or higher: 15.0%; Graduate/professional degree or higher: 5.1%

Housing: Homeownership rate: 60.0%; Median home value: $161,700; Median year structure built: 1981; Homeowner vacancy rate: 3.2%; Median gross rent: $885 per month; Rental vacancy rate: 8.7%

Vital Statistics: Birth rate: 167.5 per 10,000 population; Death rate: 65.7 per 10,000 population; Age-adjusted cancer mortality rate: 156.2 deaths per 100,000 population

Health Insurance: 79.8% have insurance; 51.5% have private insurance; 36.3% have public insurance; 20.2% do not have insurance; 9.8% of children under 18 do not have insurance

Health Care: Physicians: 12.7 per 10,000 population; Hospital beds: 19.1 per 10,000 population; Hospital admissions: 980.3 per 10,000 population

Air Quality Index: 20.5% good, 52.3% moderate, 21.4% unhealthy for sensitive individuals, 5.5% unhealthy, 0.3% very unhealthy (% of days)

Transportation: Commute: 91.9% car, 1.0% public transportation, 1.8% walk, 3.0% work from home; Median travel time to work: 23.6 minutes
Presidential Election: 39.4% Obama, 58.4% Romney (2012)
National and State Parks: Bitter Creek National Wildlife Refuge; Cesar E Chavez National Monument; Fort Tejon State Historic Park; Kern National Wildlife Refuge; Old Town State Historic Landmark; Red Rock Canyon State Park; Tomo-Kahni State Historic Park; Tule Elk State Natural Reserve
Additional Information Contacts
Kern Government . . . . (661) 868-3601
http://www.co.kern.ca.us

Kern County Communities

ARVIN (city). Covers a land area of 4.819 square miles and a water area of 0 square miles. Located at 35.19° N. Lat; 118.83° W. Long. Elevation is 449 feet.
Population: 19,304; Growth (since 2000): 49.0%; Density: 4,005.5 persons per square mile; Race: 53.1% White, 1.0% Black/African American, 0.8% Asian, 1.2% American Indian/Alaska Native, 0.0% Native Hawaiian/Other Pacific Islander, 4.2% Two or more races, 92.7% Hispanic of any race; Average household size: 4.48; Median age: 24.0; Age under 18: 38.4%; Age 65 and over: 5.1%; Males per 100 females: 108.2; Marriage status: 40.9% never married, 50.9% now married, 2.6% separated, 3.2% widowed, 5.0% divorced; Foreign born: 45.8%; Speak English only: 12.3%; With disability: 7.9%; Veterans: 1.2%; Ancestry: 1.0% Arab, 0.8% English, 0.7% Irish, 0.7% American, 0.6% German
Employment: 1.7% management, business, and financial, 0.7% computer, engineering, and science, 3.3% education, legal, community service, arts, and media, 1.1% healthcare practitioners, 13.0% service, 11.4% sales and office, 50.6% natural resources, construction, and maintenance, 18.1% production, transportation, and material moving
Income: Per capita: $10,304; Median household: $32,999; Average household: $42,272; Households with income of $100,000 or more: 7.3%; Poverty rate: 32.7%
Educational Attainment: High school diploma or higher: 36.8%; Bachelor's degree or higher: 3.3%; Graduate/professional degree or higher: 0.5%

School District(s)

Arvin Union Elementary (KG-08)
2012-13 Enrollment: 3,159 . . . . (661) 854-6500
Di Giorgio Elementary (KG-08)
2012-13 Enrollment: 204. . . . . (661) 854-2604
Kern County Office of Education (KG-12)
2012-13 Enrollment: 4,552 . . . . (661) 636-4621
Kern Union High (09-12)
2012-13 Enrollment: 37,070 . . . . (661) 827-3100

Housing: Homeownership rate: 53.5%; Median home value: $98,700; Median year structure built: 1986; Homeowner vacancy rate: 2.5%; Median gross rent: $812 per month; Rental vacancy rate: 4.8%
Health Insurance: 64.4% have insurance; 28.8% have private insurance; 39.2% have public insurance; 35.6% do not have insurance; 15.6% of children under 18 do not have insurance
Safety: Violent crime rate: 75.0 per 10,000 population; Property crime rate: 364.9 per 10,000 population
Transportation: Commute: 91.8% car, 0.3% public transportation, 1.4% walk, 1.9% work from home; Median travel time to work: 25.6 minutes
Additional Information Contacts
City of Arvin. . . . . (661) 854-3134
http://www.arvin.org

BAKERSFIELD (city). County seat. Covers a land area of 142.164 square miles and a water area of 1.445 square miles. Located at 35.32° N. Lat; 119.02° W. Long. Elevation is 404 feet.
History: Bakersfield was named for Colonel Thomas Baker, who arrived in 1862 to direct a reclamation project and remained to lay out the townsite in 1869. The new town soon claimed the county seat from nearby Havilah. The citizens incorporated their town briefly in 1873 in order to oust an unpopular marshall, but disincorporated immediately afterwards. In 1898, when the town had become an agricultural trade center, it was reincorporated. The discovery of gold in Kern River Canyon in 1885 brought a boom, as did the discovery of oil in 1899.
Population: 347,483; Growth (since 2000): 40.6%; Density: 2,444.2 persons per square mile; Race: 56.8% White, 8.2% Black/African American, 6.2% Asian, 1.5% American Indian/Alaska Native, 0.1% Native Hawaiian/Other Pacific Islander, 4.9% Two or more races, 45.5% Hispanic of any race; Average household size: 3.10; Median age: 30.0; Age under 18: 31.5%; Age 65 and over: 8.4%; Males per 100 females: 96.0; Marriage status: 35.4% never married, 50.2% now married, 3.1% separated, 4.7% widowed, 9.7% divorced; Foreign born: 18.7%; Speak English only: 62.1%; With disability: 10.9%; Veterans: 6.5%; Ancestry: 8.2% German, 6.9% Irish, 5.6% English, 3.6% American, 2.8% Italian
Employment: 11.5% management, business, and financial, 3.6% computer, engineering, and science, 10.4% education, legal, community service, arts, and media, 5.4% healthcare practitioners, 19.2% service, 23.6% sales and office, 13.1% natural resources, construction, and maintenance, 13.1% production, transportation, and material moving
Income: Per capita: $23,316; Median household: $56,204; Average household: $72,299; Households with income of $100,000 or more: 23.3%; Poverty rate: 20.4%
Educational Attainment: High school diploma or higher: 78.5%; Bachelor's degree or higher: 20.0%; Graduate/professional degree or higher: 6.7%

School District(s)

Bakersfield City (KG-08)
2012-13 Enrollment: 28,987 . . . . (661) 631-4600
Beardsley Elementary (KG-08)
2012-13 Enrollment: 1,730 . . . . (661) 393-8550
Edison Elementary (KG-08)
2012-13 Enrollment: 1,136 . . . . (661) 363-5394
Fairfax Elementary (KG-08)
2012-13 Enrollment: 2,363 . . . . (661) 366-7221
Fruitvale Elementary (KG-08)
2012-13 Enrollment: 2,945 . . . . (661) 589-3830
General Shafter Elementary (KG-08)
2012-13 Enrollment: 142. . . . . (661) 837-1931
Greenfield Union (KG-08)
2012-13 Enrollment: 9,057 . . . . (661) 837-6000
Kern County Office of Education (KG-12)
2012-13 Enrollment: 4,552 . . . . (661) 636-4621
Kern High Roc
2012-13 Enrollment: n/a . . . . (661) 831-3327
Kern Union High (09-12)
2012-13 Enrollment: 37,070 . . . . (661) 827-3100
Lakeside Union (KG-08)
2012-13 Enrollment: 1,314 . . . . (661) 836-6658
Norris Elementary (KG-08)
2012-13 Enrollment: 3,884 . . . . (661) 387-7000
Panama-Buena Vista Union (KG-08)
2012-13 Enrollment: 17,325 . . . . (661) 831-8331
Rio Bravo-Greeley Union Elementary (KG-08)
2012-13 Enrollment: 1,041 . . . . (661) 589-2696
Rosedale Union Elementary (KG-08)
2012-13 Enrollment: 5,408 . . . . (661) 588-6000
Standard Elementary (KG-08)
2012-13 Enrollment: 2,979 . . . . (661) 392-2110
Vineland Elementary (KG-08)
2012-13 Enrollment: 762. . . . . (661) 845-3713

Four-year College(s)

California State University-Bakersfield (Public)
Fall 2013 Enrollment: 8,371 . . . . (661) 654-2782
2013-14 Tuition: In-state $6,775; Out-of-state $17,935
Santa Barbara Business College-Bakersfield (Private, For-profit)
Fall 2013 Enrollment: 543 . . . . (661) 835-1100
2013-14 Tuition: In-state $12,464; Out-of-state $12,464

Two-year College(s)

Bakersfield College (Public)
Fall 2013 Enrollment: 17,770 . . . . (661) 395-4011
2013-14 Tuition: In-state $1,324; Out-of-state $7,008
California College of Vocational Careers (Private, For-profit)
Fall 2013 Enrollment: 69 . . . . (661) 323-6791
Kaplan College-Bakersfield (Private, For-profit)
Fall 2013 Enrollment: 512 . . . . (661) 836-6300
San Joaquin Valley College-Bakersfield (Private, For-profit)
Fall 2013 Enrollment: 642 . . . . (661) 834-0126
2013-14 Tuition: In-state $16,492; Out-of-state $16,492

Vocational/Technical School(s)

Lyles Bakersfield College of Beauty (Private, For-profit)
Fall 2013 Enrollment: 67 . . . . (661) 327-9784
2013-14 Tuition: $16,000

Milan Institute-Bakersfield (Private, For-profit)
Fall 2013 Enrollment: 411 . . . . (661) 335-5900
2013-14 Tuition: $16,664

Housing: Homeownership rate: 59.7%; Median home value: $179,700; Median year structure built: 1986; Homeowner vacancy rate: 3.2%; Median gross rent: $979 per month; Rental vacancy rate: 9.0%

Health Insurance: 81.8% have insurance; 57.5% have private insurance; 31.8% have public insurance; 18.2% do not have insurance; 9.0% of children under 18 do not have insurance

Hospitals: Bakersfield Heart Hospital (47 beds); Bakersfield Memorial Hospital (355 beds); Good Samaritan Hospital (64 beds); Kern Medical Center (243 beds); Mercy Hospital (260 beds); San Joaquin Community Hospital (252 beds)

Safety: Violent crime rate: 51.3 per 10,000 population; Property crime rate: 464.7 per 10,000 population

Newspapers: Bakersfield Californian (daily circulation 144000); Bakersfield Voice (weekly circulation 55000); Lamont Reporter (weekly circulation 5600); Observer Group (weekly circulation 97000)

Transportation: Commute: 92.9% car, 1.2% public transportation, 1.4% walk, 2.8% work from home; Median travel time to work: 22.9 minutes; Amtrak: Train service available.

Airports: Meadows Field (primary service/non-hub)

Additional Information Contacts

City of Bakersfield . . . . (661) 326-3000
http://www.bakersfieldcity.us

BEAR VALLEY SPRINGS (CDP). Covers a land area of 41.485 square miles and a water area of 0.066 square miles. Located at 35.18° N. Lat; 118.63° W. Long. Elevation is 4,121 feet.

Population: 5,172; Growth (since 2000): 22.2%; Density: 124.7 persons per square mile; Race: 92.3% White, 1.4% Black/African American, 1.1% Asian, 0.9% American Indian/Alaska Native, 0.1% Native Hawaiian/Other Pacific Islander, 2.5% Two or more races, 7.7% Hispanic of any race; Average household size: 2.43; Median age: 51.0; Age under 18: 20.6%; Age 65 and over: 23.8%; Males per 100 females: 99.2; Marriage status: 17.0% never married, 69.7% now married, 2.2% separated, 7.2% widowed, 6.1% divorced; Foreign born: 2.8%; Speak English only: 93.9%; With disability: 11.8%; Veterans: 16.9%; Ancestry: 18.4% German, 16.6% Irish, 13.5% English, 8.6% Italian, 6.6% Dutch

Employment: 16.1% management, business, and financial, 11.1% computer, engineering, and science, 8.4% education, legal, community service, arts, and media, 9.0% healthcare practitioners, 19.3% service, 24.5% sales and office, 6.0% natural resources, construction, and maintenance, 5.6% production, transportation, and material moving

Income: Per capita: $36,313; Median household: $77,077; Average household: $92,535; Households with income of $100,000 or more: 37.5%; Poverty rate: 5.0%

Educational Attainment: High school diploma or higher: 97.2%; Bachelor's degree or higher: 38.2%; Graduate/professional degree or higher: 19.9%

Housing: Homeownership rate: 87.6%; Median home value: $292,300; Median year structure built: 1987; Homeowner vacancy rate: 4.6%; Median gross rent: $1,305 per month; Rental vacancy rate: 10.5%

Health Insurance: 97.2% have insurance; 92.9% have private insurance; 25.3% have public insurance; 2.8% do not have insurance; 0.0% of children under 18 do not have insurance

Transportation: Commute: 95.7% car, 0.0% public transportation, 0.0% walk, 4.3% work from home; Median travel time to work: 47.7 minutes

BODFISH (CDP). Covers a land area of 7.971 square miles and a water area of 0.012 square miles. Located at 35.57° N. Lat; 118.48° W. Long. Elevation is 2,687 feet.

History: Bodfish began as a mining camp during the Kern River Canyon gold rush of the 1880's.

Population: 1,956; Growth (since 2000): 7.3%; Density: 245.4 persons per square mile; Race: 89.9% White, 0.2% Black/African American, 0.7% Asian, 2.6% American Indian/Alaska Native, 0.2% Native Hawaiian/Other Pacific Islander, 4.0% Two or more races, 9.7% Hispanic of any race; Average household size: 2.22; Median age: 50.1; Age under 18: 19.4%; Age 65 and over: 25.1%; Males per 100 females: 102.7

Housing: Homeownership rate: 74.9%; Homeowner vacancy rate: 3.5%; Rental vacancy rate: 11.0%

BORON (CDP). Covers a land area of 13.800 square miles and a water area of 0.021 square miles. Located at 35.02° N. Lat; 117.67° W. Long. Elevation is 2,467 feet.

Population: 2,253; Growth (since 2000): 11.3%; Density: 163.3 persons per square mile; Race: 77.5% White, 7.2% Black/African American, 2.1% Asian, 2.2% American Indian/Alaska Native, 0.2% Native Hawaiian/Other Pacific Islander, 4.6% Two or more races, 18.0% Hispanic of any race; Average household size: 2.53; Median age: 39.3; Age under 18: 27.6%; Age 65 and over: 13.1%; Males per 100 females: 106.9

School District(s)

Muroc Joint Unified (KG-12)
2012-13 Enrollment: 2,071 . . . . (760) 769-4821

Housing: Homeownership rate: 56.6%; Homeowner vacancy rate: 3.2%; Rental vacancy rate: 31.4%

BUTTONWILLOW (CDP). Covers a land area of 6.927 square miles and a water area of 0 square miles. Located at 35.41° N. Lat; 119.44° W. Long. Elevation is 269 feet.

Population: 1,508; Growth (since 2000): 19.1%; Density: 217.7 persons per square mile; Race: 35.4% White, 2.4% Black/African American, 0.7% Asian, 0.7% American Indian/Alaska Native, 0.0% Native Hawaiian/Other Pacific Islander, 1.8% Two or more races, 78.4% Hispanic of any race; Average household size: 3.98; Median age: 26.5; Age under 18: 37.2%; Age 65 and over: 6.1%; Males per 100 females: 110.0

School District(s)

Buttonwillow Union Elementary (KG-08)
2012-13 Enrollment: 342. . . . . (661) 764-5166

Housing: Homeownership rate: 48.6%; Homeowner vacancy rate: 1.6%; Rental vacancy rate: 4.4%

CALIENTE (unincorporated postal area)

ZCTA: 93518

Covers a land area of 298.135 square miles and a water area of 0.083 square miles. Located at 35.38° N. Lat; 118.47° W. Long. Elevation is 1,312 feet.

Population: 1,146; Growth (since 2000): 13.6%; Density: 3.8 persons per square mile; Race: 87.3% White, 0.5% Black/African American, 1.0% Asian, 2.3% American Indian/Alaska Native, 0.0% Native Hawaiian/Other Pacific Islander, 5.4% Two or more races, 9.5% Hispanic of any race; Average household size: 2.23; Median age: 53.6; Age under 18: 16.8%; Age 65 and over: 26.0%; Males per 100 females: 101.1

School District(s)

Caliente Union Elementary (KG-08)
2012-13 Enrollment: 61. . . . . (661) 867-2301

Housing: Homeownership rate: 84.4%; Homeowner vacancy rate: 6.4%; Rental vacancy rate: 11.1%

CALIFORNIA CITY (city). Covers a land area of 203.523 square miles and a water area of 0.108 square miles. Located at 35.15° N. Lat; 117.86° W. Long. Elevation is 2,405 feet.

Population: 14,120; Growth (since 2000): 68.4%; Density: 69.4 persons per square mile; Race: 65.1% White, 15.2% Black/African American, 2.6% Asian, 0.9% American Indian/Alaska Native, 0.4% Native Hawaiian/Other Pacific Islander, 5.6% Two or more races, 38.1% Hispanic of any race; Average household size: 2.80; Median age: 34.8; Age under 18: 24.4%; Age 65 and over: 8.4%; Males per 100 females: 144.0; Marriage status: 31.3% never married, 53.6% now married, 2.2% separated, 4.1% widowed, 11.0% divorced; Foreign born: 11.7%; Speak English only: 80.5%; With disability: 15.0%; Veterans: 19.4%; Ancestry: 12.5% German, 8.0% Irish, 7.1% English, 5.2% American, 2.3% Dutch

Employment: 15.3% management, business, and financial, 10.2% computer, engineering, and science, 6.5% education, legal, community service, arts, and media, 2.3% healthcare practitioners, 21.8% service, 22.9% sales and office, 12.4% natural resources, construction, and maintenance, 8.6% production, transportation, and material moving

Income: Per capita: $22,293; Median household: $51,131; Average household: $60,768; Households with income of $100,000 or more: 22.3%; Poverty rate: 24.0%

Educational Attainment: High school diploma or higher: 78.9%; Bachelor's degree or higher: 12.0%; Graduate/professional degree or higher: 5.0%

School District(s)

Mojave Unified (KG-12)
2012-13 Enrollment: 2,691 . . . . (661) 824-4001

Housing: Homeownership rate: 60.3%; Median home value: $93,600; Median year structure built: 1992; Homeowner vacancy rate: 8.3%; Median gross rent: $898 per month; Rental vacancy rate: 22.5%

Health Insurance: 84.3% have insurance; 51.8% have private insurance; 44.6% have public insurance; 15.7% do not have insurance; 7.6% of children under 18 do not have insurance

Safety: Violent crime rate: 65.2 per 10,000 population; Property crime rate: 512.0 per 10,000 population

Newspapers: Mojave Desert News (weekly circulation 5000)

Transportation: Commute: 89.0% car, 0.6% public transportation, 0.4% walk, 9.3% work from home; Median travel time to work: 32.8 minutes

Additional Information Contacts

City of California City. . . . . (760) 373-8661
http://www.californiacity.com

CANTIL (unincorporated postal area)

ZCTA: 93519

Covers a land area of 78.741 square miles and a water area of 0.554 square miles. Located at 35.29° N. Lat; 117.93° W. Long. Elevation is 2,018 feet.

Population: 101; Growth (since 2000): n/a; Density: 1.3 persons per square mile; Race: 73.3% White, 2.0% Black/African American, 12.9% Asian, 4.0% American Indian/Alaska Native, 0.0% Native Hawaiian/Other Pacific Islander, 6.9% Two or more races, 3.0% Hispanic of any race; Average household size: 2.02; Median age: 53.8; Age under 18: 12.9%; Age 65 and over: 30.7%; Males per 100 females: 114.9

Housing: Homeownership rate: 82.0%; Homeowner vacancy rate: 4.5%; Rental vacancy rate: 18.2%

CHEROKEE STRIP (CDP). Covers a land area of 0.091 square miles and a water area of 0 square miles. Located at 35.47° N. Lat; 119.26° W. Long. Elevation is 331 feet.

Population: 227; Growth (since 2000): n/a; Density: 2,504.6 persons per square mile; Race: 37.0% White, 0.0% Black/African American, 0.0% Asian, 1.8% American Indian/Alaska Native, 0.0% Native Hawaiian/Other Pacific Islander, 9.7% Two or more races, 82.4% Hispanic of any race; Average household size: 4.05; Median age: 27.3; Age under 18: 35.2%; Age 65 and over: 7.9%; Males per 100 females: 100.9

Housing: Homeownership rate: 58.9%; Homeowner vacancy rate: 5.7%; Rental vacancy rate: 4.2%

CHINA LAKE ACRES (CDP). Covers a land area of 5.210 square miles and a water area of <.001 square miles. Located at 35.64° N. Lat; 117.77° W. Long. Elevation is 2,431 feet.

Population: 1,876; Growth (since 2000): 6.5%; Density: 360.1 persons per square mile; Race: 85.3% White, 1.9% Black/African American, 0.9% Asian, 1.5% American Indian/Alaska Native, 0.4% Native Hawaiian/Other Pacific Islander, 5.5% Two or more races, 14.1% Hispanic of any race; Average household size: 2.48; Median age: 44.0; Age under 18: 23.1%; Age 65 and over: 16.7%; Males per 100 females: 102.2

Housing: Homeownership rate: 74.3%; Homeowner vacancy rate: 1.6%; Rental vacancy rate: 6.2%

DELANO (city). Covers a land area of 14.303 square miles and a water area of 0.052 square miles. Located at 35.76° N. Lat; 119.26° W. Long. Elevation is 315 feet.

History: Colonel Allensworth State Historical Park to Northwest. Incorporated 1915.

Population: 53,041; Growth (since 2000): 36.6%; Density: 3,708.4 persons per square mile; Race: 36.4% White, 7.9% Black/African American, 12.7% Asian, 0.9% American Indian/Alaska Native, 0.1% Native Hawaiian/Other Pacific Islander, 3.7% Two or more races, 71.5% Hispanic of any race; Average household size: 4.11; Median age: 28.5; Age under 18: 28.4%; Age 65 and over: 6.1%; Males per 100 females: 149.1; Marriage status: 44.4% never married, 43.9% now married, 2.9% separated, 4.3% widowed, 7.3% divorced; Foreign born: 38.1%; Speak English only: 24.4%; With disability: 7.9%; Veterans: 2.8%; Ancestry: 1.8% Irish, 1.7% German, 1.0% English, 0.6% Italian, 0.4% Scottish

Employment: 4.0% management, business, and financial, 0.3% computer, engineering, and science, 4.9% education, legal, community service, arts, and media, 2.9% healthcare practitioners, 17.4% service, 17.1% sales and office, 38.3% natural resources, construction, and maintenance, 15.2% production, transportation, and material moving

Income: Per capita: $10,453; Median household: $35,122; Average household: $46,755; Households with income of $100,000 or more: 9.3%; Poverty rate: 29.9%

Educational Attainment: High school diploma or higher: 53.4%; Bachelor's degree or higher: 6.8%; Graduate/professional degree or higher: 1.4%

School District(s)

Columbine Elementary (KG-08)
2012-13 Enrollment: 184. . . . . (661) 725-8501
Delano Joint Union High (09-12)
2012-13 Enrollment: 4,323 . . . . (661) 725-4000
Delano Union Elementary (KG-08)
2012-13 Enrollment: 7,636 . . . . (661) 721-5000
Kern County Office of Education (KG-12)
2012-13 Enrollment: 4,552 . . . . (661) 636-4621

Housing: Homeownership rate: 56.2%; Median home value: $140,100; Median year structure built: 1985; Homeowner vacancy rate: 1.6%; Median gross rent: $760 per month; Rental vacancy rate: 3.5%

Health Insurance: 72.6% have insurance; 36.5% have private insurance; 41.0% have public insurance; 27.4% do not have insurance; 14.0% of children under 18 do not have insurance

Hospitals: Delano Regional Medical Center (156 beds)

Safety: Violent crime rate: 59.2 per 10,000 population; Property crime rate: 373.3 per 10,000 population

Newspapers: Delano Record (weekly circulation 4600)

Transportation: Commute: 94.0% car, 0.6% public transportation, 1.5% walk, 1.5% work from home; Median travel time to work: 21.4 minutes

Additional Information Contacts

City of Delano . . . . (661) 720-2269
http://www.cityofdelano.org

DERBY ACRES (CDP). Covers a land area of 3.581 square miles and a water area of 0 square miles. Located at 35.24° N. Lat; 119.60° W. Long. Elevation is 1,371 feet.

Population: 322; Growth (since 2000): -14.4%; Density: 89.9 persons per square mile; Race: 89.8% White, 0.0% Black/African American, 0.0% Asian, 0.3% American Indian/Alaska Native, 0.0% Native Hawaiian/Other Pacific Islander, 2.8% Two or more races, 11.2% Hispanic of any race; Average household size: 2.62; Median age: 41.5; Age under 18: 19.6%; Age 65 and over: 14.6%; Males per 100 females: 92.8

Housing: Homeownership rate: 79.7%; Homeowner vacancy rate: 6.7%; Rental vacancy rate: 19.4%

DUSTIN ACRES (CDP). Covers a land area of 3.676 square miles and a water area of 0 square miles. Located at 35.22° N. Lat; 119.37° W. Long. Elevation is 384 feet.

Population: 652; Growth (since 2000): 11.5%; Density: 177.4 persons per square mile; Race: 82.7% White, 0.6% Black/African American, 0.2% Asian, 1.4% American Indian/Alaska Native, 0.0% Native Hawaiian/Other Pacific Islander, 4.3% Two or more races, 19.8% Hispanic of any race; Average household size: 2.91; Median age: 37.6; Age under 18: 26.8%; Age 65 and over: 12.6%; Males per 100 females: 107.6

Housing: Homeownership rate: 83.5%; Homeowner vacancy rate: 4.6%; Rental vacancy rate: 5.1%

EDISON (unincorporated postal area)

ZCTA: 93220

Covers a land area of 26.365 square miles and a water area of <.001 square miles. Located at 35.40° N. Lat; 118.76° W. Long. Elevation is 568 feet.

Population: 211; Growth (since 2000): n/a; Density: 8.0 persons per square mile; Race: 44.5% White, 0.0% Black/African American, 10.0% Asian, 0.5% American Indian/Alaska Native, 0.0% Native Hawaiian/Other Pacific Islander, 0.9% Two or more races, 70.1% Hispanic of any race; Average household size: 3.20; Median age: 26.5; Age under 18: 33.6%; Age 65 and over: 8.5%; Males per 100 females: 104.9

Housing: Homeownership rate: 22.8%; Homeowner vacancy rate: 0.0%; Rental vacancy rate: 1.9%

EDMUNDSON ACRES (CDP). Covers a land area of 0.066 square miles and a water area of 0 square miles. Located at 35.23° N. Lat; 118.82° W. Long. Elevation is 486 feet.

Population: 279; Growth (since 2000): n/a; Density: 4,195.6 persons per square mile; Race: 38.7% White, 1.8% Black/African American, 0.4% Asian, 1.1% American Indian/Alaska Native, 0.0% Native Hawaiian/Other

Pacific Islander, 6.8% Two or more races, 80.6% Hispanic of any race; Average household size: 3.93; Median age: 27.5; Age under 18: 31.9%; Age 65 and over: 11.5%; Males per 100 females: 105.1

Housing: Homeownership rate: 59.1%; Homeowner vacancy rate: 2.3%; Rental vacancy rate: 6.3%

EDWARDS AFB (CDP). Covers a land area of 17.134 square miles and a water area of <.001 square miles. Located at 34.90° N. Lat; 117.92° W. Long.

Population: 2,063; Growth (since 2000): -65.1%; Density: 120.4 persons per square mile; Race: 73.6% White, 8.0% Black/African American, 4.8% Asian, 0.8% American Indian/Alaska Native, 0.5% Native Hawaiian/Other Pacific Islander, 7.7% Two or more races, 17.2% Hispanic of any race; Average household size: 3.20; Median age: 23.0; Age under 18: 37.4%; Age 65 and over: 0.5%; Males per 100 females: 106.5

School District(s)

Muroc Joint Unified (KG-12)
2012-13 Enrollment: 2,071 . . . . (760) 769-4821

Housing: Homeownership rate: 1.4%; Homeowner vacancy rate: 0.0%; Rental vacancy rate: 0.2%

FELLOWS (CDP). Covers a land area of 0.656 square miles and a water area of 0 square miles. Located at 35.18° N. Lat; 119.55° W. Long. Elevation is 1,316 feet.

Population: 106; Growth (since 2000): -30.7%; Density: 161.5 persons per square mile; Race: 88.7% White, 0.9% Black/African American, 0.0% Asian, 4.7% American Indian/Alaska Native, 0.0% Native Hawaiian/Other Pacific Islander, 3.8% Two or more races, 10.4% Hispanic of any race; Average household size: 2.86; Median age: 40.0; Age under 18: 27.4%; Age 65 and over: 11.3%; Males per 100 females: 116.3

School District(s)

Midway Elementary (KG-08)
2012-13 Enrollment: 101 . . . . (661) 768-4344

Housing: Homeownership rate: 89.2%; Homeowner vacancy rate: 2.9%; Rental vacancy rate: 0.0%

FORD CITY (CDP). Covers a land area of 1.535 square miles and a water area of 0 square miles. Located at 35.16° N. Lat; 119.46° W. Long. Elevation is 892 feet.

History: Ford City began as a boom town when oil was found. It was named for the many Model-T Fords on the streets of the early tent city.

Population: 4,278; Growth (since 2000): 21.8%; Density: 2,787.6 persons per square mile; Race: 63.9% White, 0.7% Black/African American, 0.8% Asian, 3.6% American Indian/Alaska Native, 0.7% Native Hawaiian/Other Pacific Islander, 4.2% Two or more races, 46.1% Hispanic of any race; Average household size: 3.40; Median age: 27.4; Age under 18: 31.6%; Age 65 and over: 8.2%; Males per 100 females: 110.1; Marriage status: 36.8% never married, 44.8% now married, 2.6% separated, 5.1% widowed, 13.3% divorced; Foreign born: 19.4%; Speak English only: 61.6%; With disability: 18.3%; Veterans: 10.1%; Ancestry: 11.7% German, 11.5% Irish, 7.8% English, 4.0% American, 3.5% French

Employment: 0.8% management, business, and financial, 1.9% computer, engineering, and science, 3.0% education, legal, community service, arts, and media, 0.6% healthcare practitioners, 18.5% service, 19.2% sales and office, 30.9% natural resources, construction, and maintenance, 25.2% production, transportation, and material moving

Income: Per capita: $15,797; Median household: $37,171; Average household: $46,782; Households with income of $100,000 or more: 8.0%; Poverty rate: 32.2%

Educational Attainment: High school diploma or higher: 66.4%; Bachelor's degree or higher: 2.7%; Graduate/professional degree or higher: n/a

Housing: Homeownership rate: 49.2%; Median home value: $90,500; Median year structure built: 1954; Homeowner vacancy rate: 2.8%; Median gross rent: $849 per month; Rental vacancy rate: 5.3%

Health Insurance: 79.1% have insurance; 46.7% have private insurance; 41.3% have public insurance; 20.9% do not have insurance; 14.8% of children under 18 do not have insurance

Transportation: Commute: 89.7% car, 1.0% public transportation, 6.4% walk, 0.0% work from home; Median travel time to work: 19.5 minutes

FRAZIER PARK (CDP). Covers a land area of 5.064 square miles and a water area of 0.002 square miles. Located at 34.81° N. Lat; 118.96° W. Long. Elevation is 4,639 feet.

Population: 2,691; Growth (since 2000): 14.6%; Density: 531.4 persons per square mile; Race: 85.4% White, 0.6% Black/African American, 0.8% Asian, 1.2% American Indian/Alaska Native, 0.1% Native Hawaiian/Other Pacific Islander, 4.1% Two or more races, 19.6% Hispanic of any race; Average household size: 2.48; Median age: 40.4; Age under 18: 23.9%; Age 65 and over: 11.7%; Males per 100 females: 100.7; Marriage status: 21.7% never married, 54.4% now married, 1.8% separated, 2.9% widowed, 21.0% divorced; Foreign born: 5.7%; Speak English only: 91.3%; With disability: 14.4%; Veterans: 20.0%; Ancestry: 23.3% German, 18.4% English, 9.8% French, 8.9% Irish, 7.8% American

Employment: 3.1% management, business, and financial, 0.0% computer, engineering, and science, 15.6% education, legal, community service, arts, and media, 0.9% healthcare practitioners, 26.4% service, 26.7% sales and office, 17.6% natural resources, construction, and maintenance, 9.6% production, transportation, and material moving

Income: Per capita: $21,577; Median household: $54,070; Average household: $60,049; Households with income of $100,000 or more: 16.4%; Poverty rate: 11.9%

Educational Attainment: High school diploma or higher: 90.2%; Bachelor's degree or higher: 26.7%; Graduate/professional degree or higher: 5.9%

School District(s)

El Tejon Unified (KG-12)
2012-13 Enrollment: 919. . . . . (661) 248-6247

Housing: Homeownership rate: 61.9%; Median home value: $201,300; Median year structure built: 1972; Homeowner vacancy rate: 4.5%; Median gross rent: $927 per month; Rental vacancy rate: 10.0%

Health Insurance: 82.9% have insurance; 58.6% have private insurance; 34.6% have public insurance; 17.1% do not have insurance; 6.9% of children under 18 do not have insurance

Newspapers: Mountain Enterprise (weekly circulation 3100)

Transportation: Commute: 94.1% car, 1.3% public transportation, 3.6% walk, 1.0% work from home; Median travel time to work: 42.5 minutes

FULLER ACRES (CDP). Covers a land area of 0.754 square miles and a water area of 0 square miles. Located at 35.30° N. Lat; 118.91° W. Long. Elevation is 420 feet.

Population: 991; Growth (since 2000): n/a; Density: 1,313.7 persons per square mile; Race: 61.3% White, 1.3% Black/African American, 0.1% Asian, 1.2% American Indian/Alaska Native, 0.0% Native Hawaiian/Other Pacific Islander, 2.9% Two or more races, 77.5% Hispanic of any race; Average household size: 4.06; Median age: 27.2; Age under 18: 34.9%; Age 65 and over: 6.4%; Males per 100 females: 113.6

Housing: Homeownership rate: 50.0%; Homeowner vacancy rate: 2.3%; Rental vacancy rate: 3.9%

GLENNVILLE (unincorporated postal area)

ZCTA: 93226

Covers a land area of 93.607 square miles and a water area of 0.088 square miles. Located at 35.74° N. Lat; 118.74° W. Long. Elevation is 3,176 feet.

Population: 282; Growth (since 2000): 0.7%; Density: 3.0 persons per square mile; Race: 84.4% White, 1.4% Black/African American, 1.4% Asian, 2.1% American Indian/Alaska Native, 0.0% Native Hawaiian/Other Pacific Islander, 4.6% Two or more races, 8.2% Hispanic of any race; Average household size: 2.17; Median age: 54.7; Age under 18: 16.0%; Age 65 and over: 24.1%; Males per 100 females: 91.8

School District(s)

Linns Valley-Poso Flat Union (KG-08)
2012-13 Enrollment: 30. . . . . (661) 536-8811

Housing: Homeownership rate: 67.7%; Homeowner vacancy rate: 8.3%; Rental vacancy rate: 4.4%

GOLDEN HILLS (CDP). Covers a land area of 12.249 square miles and a water area of 0.017 square miles. Located at 35.15° N. Lat; 118.50° W. Long. Elevation is 3,917 feet.

Population: 8,656; Growth (since 2000): 16.4%; Density: 706.6 persons per square mile; Race: 83.6% White, 1.5% Black/African American, 1.4% Asian, 1.4% American Indian/Alaska Native, 0.2% Native Hawaiian/Other Pacific Islander, 4.2% Two or more races, 19.3% Hispanic of any race; Average household size: 2.69; Median age: 38.6; Age under 18: 25.9%;

Age 65 and over: 12.4%; Males per 100 females: 99.9; Marriage status: 23.4% never married, 61.3% now married, 3.7% separated, 5.2% widowed, 10.1% divorced; Foreign born: 12.1%; Speak English only: 81.6%; With disability: 10.8%; Veterans: 9.7%; Ancestry: 18.0% German, 14.3% Irish, 8.0% English, 5.9% American, 3.4% Scottish

Employment: 9.3% management, business, and financial, 4.0% computer, engineering, and science, 10.5% education, legal, community service, arts, and media, 5.4% healthcare practitioners, 26.1% service, 16.9% sales and office, 17.2% natural resources, construction, and maintenance, 10.5% production, transportation, and material moving

Income: Per capita: $26,683; Median household: $59,353; Average household: $68,948; Households with income of $100,000 or more: 25.2%; Poverty rate: 16.8%

Educational Attainment: High school diploma or higher: 90.1%; Bachelor's degree or higher: 19.0%; Graduate/professional degree or higher: 7.2%

Housing: Homeownership rate: 68.6%; Median home value: $204,400; Median year structure built: 1988; Homeowner vacancy rate: 2.3%; Median gross rent: $870 per month; Rental vacancy rate: 9.5%

Health Insurance: 85.7% have insurance; 70.6% have private insurance; 28.8% have public insurance; 14.3% do not have insurance; 7.8% of children under 18 do not have insurance

Transportation: Commute: 95.2% car, 0.9% public transportation, 0.5% walk, 2.2% work from home; Median travel time to work: 28.8 minutes

---

GREENACRES (CDP). Covers a land area of 1.992 square miles and a water area of 0 square miles. Located at 35.38° N. Lat; 119.12° W. Long. Elevation is 381 feet.

Population: 5,566; Growth (since 2000): n/a; Density: 2,793.5 persons per square mile; Race: 82.9% White, 0.9% Black/African American, 1.3% Asian, 2.1% American Indian/Alaska Native, 0.1% Native Hawaiian/Other Pacific Islander, 3.6% Two or more races, 20.1% Hispanic of any race; Average household size: 2.87; Median age: 37.9; Age under 18: 25.2%; Age 65 and over: 13.1%; Males per 100 females: 99.8; Marriage status: 27.3% never married, 52.9% now married, 1.6% separated, 5.5% widowed, 14.4% divorced; Foreign born: 6.5%; Speak English only: 89.6%; With disability: 15.4%; Veterans: 11.5%; Ancestry: 16.3% German, 13.4% Irish, 10.7% English, 5.9% Italian, 5.1% European

Employment: 14.3% management, business, and financial, 0.7% computer, engineering, and science, 12.2% education, legal, community service, arts, and media, 7.5% healthcare practitioners, 20.8% service, 23.3% sales and office, 9.7% natural resources, construction, and maintenance, 11.5% production, transportation, and material moving

Income: Per capita: $29,226; Median household: $62,411; Average household: $73,811; Households with income of $100,000 or more: 20.5%; Poverty rate: 5.8%

Educational Attainment: High school diploma or higher: 89.0%; Bachelor's degree or higher: 13.7%; Graduate/professional degree or higher: 2.7%

Housing: Homeownership rate: 75.0%; Median home value: $165,700; Median year structure built: 1975; Homeowner vacancy rate: 1.9%; Median gross rent: $1,202 per month; Rental vacancy rate: 5.3%

Health Insurance: 89.2% have insurance; 74.1% have private insurance; 28.7% have public insurance; 10.8% do not have insurance; 6.0% of children under 18 do not have insurance

Transportation: Commute: 92.7% car, 0.0% public transportation, 1.1% walk, 5.3% work from home; Median travel time to work: 25.5 minutes

---

GREENFIELD (CDP). Covers a land area of 1.488 square miles and a water area of 0 square miles. Located at 35.27° N. Lat; 119.01° W. Long. Elevation is 351 feet.

Population: 3,991; Growth (since 2000): n/a; Density: 2,681.4 persons per square mile; Race: 62.9% White, 1.8% Black/African American, 1.1% Asian, 1.6% American Indian/Alaska Native, 0.0% Native Hawaiian/Other Pacific Islander, 4.7% Two or more races, 56.7% Hispanic of any race; Average household size: 3.21; Median age: 34.4; Age under 18: 28.2%; Age 65 and over: 9.6%; Males per 100 females: 106.3; Marriage status: 34.7% never married, 57.5% now married, 1.4% separated, 1.4% widowed, 6.5% divorced; Foreign born: 20.6%; Speak English only: 56.2%; With disability: 10.1%; Veterans: 11.2%; Ancestry: 6.4% Irish, 4.8% American, 3.4% German, 2.1% French, 1.8% Scotch-Irish

Employment: 4.3% management, business, and financial, 1.9% computer, engineering, and science, 1.8% education, legal, community service, arts, and media, 4.3% healthcare practitioners, 9.4% service, 26.9% sales and office, 31.4% natural resources, construction, and maintenance, 20.0% production, transportation, and material moving

Income: Per capita: $20,729; Median household: $47,759; Average household: $66,205; Households with income of $100,000 or more: 13.1%; Poverty rate: 6.2%

Educational Attainment: High school diploma or higher: 70.7%; Bachelor's degree or higher: 2.1%; Graduate/professional degree or higher: 0.4%

Housing: Homeownership rate: 69.9%; Median home value: $152,700; Median year structure built: 1980; Homeowner vacancy rate: 3.0%; Median gross rent: $906 per month; Rental vacancy rate: 8.5%

Health Insurance: 73.2% have insurance; 55.8% have private insurance; 22.4% have public insurance; 26.8% do not have insurance; 29.9% of children under 18 do not have insurance

Transportation: Commute: 90.7% car, 3.2% public transportation, 0.0% walk, 5.7% work from home; Median travel time to work: 23.4 minutes

---

INYOKERN (CDP). Covers a land area of 10.917 square miles and a water area of 0.001 square miles. Located at 35.65° N. Lat; 117.82° W. Long. Elevation is 2,434 feet.

History: Sequoia National Forest and Pacific Crest Trail to West.

Population: 1,099; Growth (since 2000): 11.7%; Density: 100.7 persons per square mile; Race: 84.6% White, 1.3% Black/African American, 2.3% Asian, 2.2% American Indian/Alaska Native, 0.2% Native Hawaiian/Other Pacific Islander, 5.0% Two or more races, 10.6% Hispanic of any race; Average household size: 2.27; Median age: 48.2; Age under 18: 20.2%; Age 65 and over: 17.8%; Males per 100 females: 108.5

School District(s)

Sierra Sands Unified (KG-12)
2012-13 Enrollment: 5,008 . . . . (760) 499-1604

Housing: Homeownership rate: 73.4%; Homeowner vacancy rate: 1.9%; Rental vacancy rate: 5.7%

Airports: Inyokern (commercial service–non-primary)

JOHANNESBURG (CDP). Covers a land area of 2.415 square miles and a water area of 0 square miles. Located at 35.37° N. Lat; 117.64° W. Long. Elevation is 3,517 feet.

History: Johannesburg was named for the city in the Transvaal, South Africa.

Population: 172; Growth (since 2000): -2.3%; Density: 71.2 persons per square mile; Race: 88.4% White, 1.2% Black/African American, 4.7% Asian, 1.2% American Indian/Alaska Native, 0.0% Native Hawaiian/Other Pacific Islander, 4.7% Two or more races, 4.7% Hispanic of any race; Average household size: 1.81; Median age: 55.0; Age under 18: 12.2%; Age 65 and over: 26.7%; Males per 100 females: 109.8

School District(s)

Sierra Sands Unified (KG-12)
2012-13 Enrollment: 5,008 . . . . (760) 499-1604

Housing: Homeownership rate: 76.9%; Homeowner vacancy rate: 2.7%; Rental vacancy rate: 14.8%

KEENE (CDP). Covers a land area of 9.660 square miles and a water area of 0.005 square miles. Located at 35.23° N. Lat; 118.61° W. Long. Elevation is 2,602 feet.

Population: 431; Growth (since 2000): 27.1%; Density: 44.6 persons per square mile; Race: 89.3% White, 0.5% Black/African American, 1.9% Asian, 2.3% American Indian/Alaska Native, 0.0% Native Hawaiian/Other Pacific Islander, 2.3% Two or more races, 10.9% Hispanic of any race; Average household size: 2.32; Median age: 53.0; Age under 18: 14.6%; Age 65 and over: 17.2%; Males per 100 females: 95.9

Housing: Homeownership rate: 84.4%; Homeowner vacancy rate: 1.9%; Rental vacancy rate: 14.7%

KERNVILLE (CDP). Covers a land area of 12.368 square miles and a water area of 0.308 square miles. Located at 35.76° N. Lat; 118.43° W. Long. Elevation is 2,667 feet.

History: Kernville began in 1885 as Whiskey Flat when a man named Hamilton opened a saloon consisting of a plank laid across two whisky barrels. The community soon developed into a mining center and changed its name to Kernville. Later Kernville became a trading center for cattle raisers and an outfitting point for hunters and fishermen.

Population: 1,395; Growth (since 2000): -19.6%; Density: 112.8 persons per square mile; Race: 90.1% White, 0.1% Black/African American, 0.5% Asian, 1.4% American Indian/Alaska Native, 0.0% Native Hawaiian/Other Pacific Islander, 5.6% Two or more races, 5.9% Hispanic of any race;

Average household size: 1.92; Median age: 55.8; Age under 18: 13.2%; Age 65 and over: 30.0%; Males per 100 females: 97.3

School District(s)

Hot Springs Elementary (KG-08)
2012-13 Enrollment: 14. . . . . (661) 548-6544
Kernville Union Elementary (KG-08)
2012-13 Enrollment: 755. . . . . (760) 379-3651

Housing: Homeownership rate: 73.6%; Homeowner vacancy rate: 5.1%; Rental vacancy rate: 13.5%

LAKE ISABELLA (CDP). Covers a land area of 21.714 square miles and a water area of 0.424 square miles. Located at 35.64° N. Lat; 118.48° W. Long. Elevation is 2,513 feet.

Population: 3,466; Growth (since 2000): 4.6%; Density: 159.6 persons per square mile; Race: 88.5% White, 0.2% Black/African American, 0.5% Asian, 2.8% American Indian/Alaska Native, 0.2% Native Hawaiian/Other Pacific Islander, 5.7% Two or more races, 9.8% Hispanic of any race; Average household size: 2.14; Median age: 47.2; Age under 18: 19.2%; Age 65 and over: 21.4%; Males per 100 females: 95.2; Marriage status: 30.5% never married, 44.6% now married, 0.9% separated, 10.1% widowed, 14.8% divorced; Foreign born: 1.8%; Speak English only: 97.6%; With disability: 32.2%; Veterans: 12.7%; Ancestry: 30.2% Irish, 21.0% German, 16.5% French, 10.9% English, 5.2% Scottish

Employment: 3.4% management, business, and financial, 0.0% computer, engineering, and science, 5.4% education, legal, community service, arts, and media, 2.0% healthcare practitioners, 20.5% service, 39.0% sales and office, 11.9% natural resources, construction, and maintenance, 17.8% production, transportation, and material moving

Income: Per capita: $16,412; Median household: $20,678; Average household: $32,160; Households with income of $100,000 or more: 3.5%; Poverty rate: 29.3%

Educational Attainment: High school diploma or higher: 88.5%; Bachelor's degree or higher: 4.5%; Graduate/professional degree or higher: n/a

School District(s)

Kern Union High (09-12)
2012-13 Enrollment: 37,070 . . . . (661) 827-3100
Kernville Union Elementary (KG-08)
2012-13 Enrollment: 755. . . . . (760) 379-3651

Housing: Homeownership rate: 62.9%; Median home value: $87,000; Median year structure built: 1968; Homeowner vacancy rate: 5.6%; Median gross rent: $640 per month; Rental vacancy rate: 8.5%

Health Insurance: 70.4% have insurance; 32.3% have private insurance; 53.2% have public insurance; 29.6% do not have insurance; 0.0% of children under 18 do not have insurance

Hospitals: Kern Valley Healthcare District (101 beds)

Newspapers: Kern Valley Sun (weekly circulation 6500)

Transportation: Commute: 91.0% car, 0.0% public transportation, 2.5% walk, 0.0% work from home; Median travel time to work: 27.6 minutes

LAKE OF THE WOODS (CDP). Covers a land area of 3.522 square miles and a water area of <.001 square miles. Located at 34.83° N. Lat; 119.00° W. Long. Elevation is 5,121 feet.

Population: 917; Growth (since 2000): 10.1%; Density: 260.4 persons per square mile; Race: 89.4% White, 0.3% Black/African American, 1.2% Asian, 2.0% American Indian/Alaska Native, 0.0% Native Hawaiian/Other Pacific Islander, 3.4% Two or more races, 13.4% Hispanic of any race; Average household size: 2.26; Median age: 45.7; Age under 18: 19.8%; Age 65 and over: 13.1%; Males per 100 females: 113.3

Housing: Homeownership rate: 67.7%; Homeowner vacancy rate: 2.8%; Rental vacancy rate: 7.1%

LAMONT (CDP). Covers a land area of 4.590 square miles and a water area of 0.036 square miles. Located at 35.27° N. Lat; 118.92° W. Long. Elevation is 404 feet.

Population: 15,120; Growth (since 2000): 13.7%; Density: 3,294.0 persons per square mile; Race: 44.2% White, 0.9% Black/African American, 0.5% Asian, 1.5% American Indian/Alaska Native, 0.1% Native Hawaiian/Other Pacific Islander, 4.3% Two or more races, 94.5% Hispanic of any race; Average household size: 4.44; Median age: 24.7; Age under 18: 35.8%; Age 65 and over: 5.4%; Males per 100 females: 111.7; Marriage status: 41.9% never married, 49.7% now married, 2.9% separated, 4.0% widowed, 4.4% divorced; Foreign born: 43.0%; Speak English only: 13.3%; With disability: 8.8%; Veterans: 1.2%; Ancestry: 0.9% Irish, 0.6% American, 0.3% English, 0.3% German, 0.1% Belgian

Employment: 2.4% management, business, and financial, 0.5% computer, engineering, and science, 3.4% education, legal, community service, arts, and media, 0.7% healthcare practitioners, 13.7% service, 14.7% sales and office, 47.1% natural resources, construction, and maintenance, 17.5% production, transportation, and material moving

Income: Per capita: $10,735; Median household: $34,672; Average household: $45,041; Households with income of $100,000 or more: 10.0%; Poverty rate: 28.8%

Educational Attainment: High school diploma or higher: 36.7%; Bachelor's degree or higher: 2.0%; Graduate/professional degree or higher: 1.0%

School District(s)

Kern Union High (09-12)
2012-13 Enrollment: 37,070 . . . . (661) 827-3100
Lamont Elementary (KG-08)
2012-13 Enrollment: 2,862 . . . . (661) 845-0751

Housing: Homeownership rate: 45.1%; Median home value: $89,800; Median year structure built: 1971; Homeowner vacancy rate: 1.5%; Median gross rent: $724 per month; Rental vacancy rate: 3.3%

Health Insurance: 65.8% have insurance; 28.5% have private insurance; 40.5% have public insurance; 34.2% do not have insurance; 17.4% of children under 18 do not have insurance

Newspapers: Arvin Tiller (weekly circulation 2500)

Transportation: Commute: 91.5% car, 0.4% public transportation, 1.3% walk, 1.3% work from home; Median travel time to work: 23.8 minutes

LEBEC (CDP). Covers a land area of 15.329 square miles and a water area of <.001 square miles. Located at 34.84° N. Lat; 118.90° W. Long. Elevation is 3,481 feet.

History: Site of Fort Tejon State Historical Park.

Population: 1,468; Growth (since 2000): 14.2%; Density: 95.8 persons per square mile; Race: 78.5% White, 1.0% Black/African American, 1.2% Asian, 3.1% American Indian/Alaska Native, 0.0% Native Hawaiian/Other Pacific Islander, 6.2% Two or more races, 26.9% Hispanic of any race; Average household size: 2.75; Median age: 40.6; Age under 18: 26.1%; Age 65 and over: 13.5%; Males per 100 females: 108.2

School District(s)

El Tejon Unified (KG-12)
2012-13 Enrollment: 919. . . . . (661) 248-6247

Housing: Homeownership rate: 71.1%; Homeowner vacancy rate: 2.8%; Rental vacancy rate: 7.1%

LOST HILLS (CDP). Covers a land area of 5.552 square miles and a water area of 0.012 square miles. Located at 35.63° N. Lat; 119.68° W. Long. Elevation is 305 feet.

Population: 2,412; Growth (since 2000): 24.5%; Density: 434.5 persons per square mile; Race: 5.5% White, 0.2% Black/African American, 0.7% Asian, 0.0% American Indian/Alaska Native, 0.0% Native Hawaiian/Other Pacific Islander, 1.0% Two or more races, 97.6% Hispanic of any race; Average household size: 5.38; Median age: 22.6; Age under 18: 40.2%; Age 65 and over: 2.5%; Males per 100 females: 134.6

School District(s)

Lost Hills Union Elementary (KG-08)
2012-13 Enrollment: 573. . . . . (661) 797-2626

Housing: Homeownership rate: 39.7%; Homeowner vacancy rate: 2.7%; Rental vacancy rate: 1.8%

MARICOPA (city). Covers a land area of 1.502 square miles and a water area of 0 square miles. Located at 35.06° N. Lat; 119.40° W. Long. Elevation is 883 feet.

Population: 1,154; Growth (since 2000): 3.9%; Density: 768.4 persons per square mile; Race: 83.0% White, 0.1% Black/African American, 1.4% Asian, 2.3% American Indian/Alaska Native, 0.2% Native Hawaiian/Other Pacific Islander, 3.3% Two or more races, 20.1% Hispanic of any race; Average household size: 2.79; Median age: 39.4; Age under 18: 26.5%; Age 65 and over: 11.7%; Males per 100 females: 101.7

School District(s)

Maricopa Unified (KG-12)
2012-13 Enrollment: 2,366 . . . . (661) 769-8231

Housing: Homeownership rate: 64.8%; Homeowner vacancy rate: 1.8%; Rental vacancy rate: 9.8%

Additional Information Contacts

City of Maricopa . . . . (661) 769-8279
http://cityofmaricopa.org

MCFARLAND (city). Covers a land area of 2.668 square miles and a water area of 0 square miles. Located at 35.67° N. Lat; 119.23° W. Long. Elevation is 354 feet.

History: McFarland was founded in 1877 by people opposed to the whisky drinking tolerated in nearby towns. All land deeds contained a clause prohibiting the selling of liquor, a condition nullified by the courts in 1934. McFarland grew around five cotton gins.

Population: 12,707; Growth (since 2000): 32.1%; Density: 4,762.7 persons per square mile; Race: 42.8% White, 1.9% Black/African American, 0.7% Asian, 1.3% American Indian/Alaska Native, 0.0% Native Hawaiian/Other Pacific Islander, 3.5% Two or more races, 91.5% Hispanic of any race; Average household size: 4.42; Median age: 25.7; Age under 18: 35.2%; Age 65 and over: 4.6%; Males per 100 females: 128.3; Marriage status: 40.8% never married, 50.3% now married, 3.8% separated, 4.1% widowed, 4.8% divorced; Foreign born: 42.9%; Speak English only: 14.8%; With disability: 7.8%; Veterans: 0.9%; Ancestry: 1.6% Other Arab, 1.0% German, 0.9% Irish, 0.7% American, 0.4% English

Employment: 4.8% management, business, and financial, 0.0% computer, engineering, and science, 3.8% education, legal, community service, arts, and media, 0.0% healthcare practitioners, 13.2% service, 11.7% sales and office, 54.6% natural resources, construction, and maintenance, 11.9% production, transportation, and material moving

Income: Per capita: $8,903; Median household: $35,433; Average household: $39,697; Households with income of $100,000 or more: 3.9%; Poverty rate: 32.9%

Educational Attainment: High school diploma or higher: 41.0%; Bachelor's degree or higher: 3.9%; Graduate/professional degree or higher: 1.3%

School District(s)

Mcfarland Unified (KG-12)
2012-13 Enrollment: 3,306 . . . . (661) 792-3081

Housing: Homeownership rate: 57.3%; Median home value: $115,600; Median year structure built: 1989; Homeowner vacancy rate: 0.9%; Median gross rent: $800 per month; Rental vacancy rate: 2.6%

Health Insurance: 65.2% have insurance; 24.5% have private insurance; 42.1% have public insurance; 34.8% do not have insurance; 15.1% of children under 18 do not have insurance

Safety: Violent crime rate: 52.9 per 10,000 population; Property crime rate: 223.0 per 10,000 population

Transportation: Commute: 93.2% car, 0.7% public transportation, 2.4% walk, 0.6% work from home; Median travel time to work: 23.6 minutes

Additional Information Contacts

City of McFarland . . . . (661) 792-3091
http://www.mcfarlandcity.org/index.html

MCKITTRICK (CDP). Covers a land area of 2.617 square miles and a water area of 0 square miles. Located at 35.30° N. Lat; 119.62° W. Long. Elevation is 1,053 feet.

Population: 115; Growth (since 2000): -28.1%; Density: 43.9 persons per square mile; Race: 87.8% White, 0.9% Black/African American, 0.0% Asian, 0.9% American Indian/Alaska Native, 0.0% Native Hawaiian/Other Pacific Islander, 4.3% Two or more races, 7.8% Hispanic of any race; Average household size: 2.74; Median age: 45.4; Age under 18: 18.3%; Age 65 and over: 12.2%; Males per 100 females: 101.8

School District(s)

Belridge Elementary (KG-08)
2012-13 Enrollment: 32. . . . . (661) 762-7381

Mckittrick Elementary (KG-08)
2012-13 Enrollment: 72. . . . . (661) 762-7303

Housing: Homeownership rate: 64.2%; Homeowner vacancy rate: 0.0%; Rental vacancy rate: 6.3%

METTLER (CDP). Covers a land area of 0.233 square miles and a water area of 0 square miles. Located at 35.06° N. Lat; 118.97° W. Long. Elevation is 541 feet.

Population: 136; Growth (since 2000): -13.4%; Density: 584.8 persons per square mile; Race: 54.4% White, 0.0% Black/African American, 0.0% Asian, 0.0% American Indian/Alaska Native, 0.0% Native Hawaiian/Other Pacific Islander, 14.0% Two or more races, 80.1% Hispanic of any race; Average household size: 4.39; Median age: 28.5; Age under 18: 27.2%; Age 65 and over: 8.1%; Males per 100 females: 109.2

Housing: Homeownership rate: 58.1%; Homeowner vacancy rate: 0.0%; Rental vacancy rate: 0.0%

MEXICAN COLONY (CDP). Covers a land area of 0.032 square miles and a water area of 0 square miles. Located at 35.47° N. Lat; 119.27° W. Long. Elevation is 331 feet.

Population: 281; Growth (since 2000): n/a; Density: 8,841.8 persons per square mile; Race: 57.7% White, 0.0% Black/African American, 0.0% Asian, 5.3% American Indian/Alaska Native, 0.0% Native Hawaiian/Other Pacific Islander, 3.9% Two or more races, 80.8% Hispanic of any race; Average household size: 3.96; Median age: 24.3; Age under 18: 40.9%; Age 65 and over: 7.1%; Males per 100 females: 105.1

Housing: Homeownership rate: 43.7%; Homeowner vacancy rate: 3.1%; Rental vacancy rate: 2.4%

MOJAVE (CDP). Covers a land area of 58.290 square miles and a water area of 0.085 square miles. Located at 35.02° N. Lat; 118.19° W. Long. Elevation is 2,762 feet.

History: In Mojave in 1883, J.W.S. Perry built ten huge wagons to haul borax out of Death Valley, and for the next five years 20-mule teams make the trip repeatedly between Death Valley and Mojave.

Population: 4,238; Growth (since 2000): 10.5%; Density: 72.7 persons per square mile; Race: 56.2% White, 15.1% Black/African American, 1.3% Asian, 1.3% American Indian/Alaska Native, 0.4% Native Hawaiian/Other Pacific Islander, 5.3% Two or more races, 37.6% Hispanic of any race; Average household size: 2.78; Median age: 31.0; Age under 18: 30.6%; Age 65 and over: 10.4%; Males per 100 females: 102.3; Marriage status: 38.7% never married, 42.3% now married, 4.0% separated, 9.3% widowed, 9.7% divorced; Foreign born: 14.3%; Speak English only: 57.7%; With disability: 13.4%; Veterans: 6.5%; Ancestry: 7.7% Irish, 5.6% English, 5.2% German, 4.9% American, 1.8% Polish

Employment: 12.0% management, business, and financial, 2.3% computer, engineering, and science, 2.8% education, legal, community service, arts, and media, 0.0% healthcare practitioners, 29.8% service, 16.1% sales and office, 17.5% natural resources, construction, and maintenance, 19.5% production, transportation, and material moving

Income: Per capita: $16,540; Median household: $32,039; Average household: $43,536; Households with income of $100,000 or more: 7.3%; Poverty rate: 34.8%

Educational Attainment: High school diploma or higher: 69.0%; Bachelor's degree or higher: 5.0%; Graduate/professional degree or higher: 1.7%

School District(s)

Kern County Rop
2012-13 Enrollment: n/a . . . . (661) 824-9313

Mojave Unified (KG-12)
2012-13 Enrollment: 2,691 . . . . (661) 824-4001

Housing: Homeownership rate: 47.2%; Median home value: $65,800; Median year structure built: 1971; Homeowner vacancy rate: 5.3%; Median gross rent: $615 per month; Rental vacancy rate: 13.7%

Health Insurance: 79.7% have insurance; 34.3% have private insurance; 50.8% have public insurance; 20.3% do not have insurance; 11.0% of children under 18 do not have insurance

Transportation: Commute: 92.4% car, 0.0% public transportation, 5.4% walk, 0.0% work from home; Median travel time to work: 20.1 minutes; Amtrak: Bus service available.

Airports: Mojave (general aviation)

MOUNTAIN MESA (CDP). Covers a land area of 0.831 square miles and a water area of 0 square miles. Located at 35.64° N. Lat; 118.40° W. Long. Elevation is 2,641 feet.

Population: 777; Growth (since 2000): 8.5%; Density: 934.7 persons per square mile; Race: 88.4% White, 0.9% Black/African American, 0.8% Asian, 2.1% American Indian/Alaska Native, 0.3% Native Hawaiian/Other Pacific Islander, 4.1% Two or more races, 9.9% Hispanic of any race; Average household size: 2.35; Median age: 49.8; Age under 18: 19.9%; Age 65 and over: 27.8%; Males per 100 females: 101.3

Housing: Homeownership rate: 77.3%; Homeowner vacancy rate: 2.9%; Rental vacancy rate: 18.6%

NORTH EDWARDS (CDP). Covers a land area of 12.746 square miles and a water area of 0 square miles. Located at 35.05° N. Lat; 117.81° W. Long. Elevation is 2,293 feet.

Population: 1,058; Growth (since 2000): -13.8%; Density: 83.0 persons per square mile; Race: 80.1% White, 4.1% Black/African American, 1.9% Asian, 2.5% American Indian/Alaska Native, 0.1% Native Hawaiian/Other Pacific Islander, 5.8% Two or more races, 16.9% Hispanic of any race;

Average household size: 2.54; Median age: 41.0; Age under 18: 26.7%; Age 65 and over: 15.0%; Males per 100 females: 102.3

Housing: Homeownership rate: 67.2%; Homeowner vacancy rate: 8.1%; Rental vacancy rate: 20.3%

OILDALE (CDP). Covers a land area of 6.533 square miles and a water area of 0 square miles. Located at 35.42° N. Lat; 119.03° W. Long. Elevation is 469 feet.

History: Oildale is located north of Bakersfield and was founded in 1909. Originally called Waits, Oildale is next to three large oil fields known as Kern River Oil Field, Kern Front Oil Field, and Fruitvale Oil Field.

Population: 32,684; Growth (since 2000): 17.2%; Density: 5,003.2 persons per square mile; Race: 84.0% White, 0.8% Black/African American, 1.0% Asian, 1.8% American Indian/Alaska Native, 0.1% Native Hawaiian/Other Pacific Islander, 4.3% Two or more races, 19.3% Hispanic of any race; Average household size: 2.71; Median age: 31.4; Age under 18: 28.8%; Age 65 and over: 10.0%; Males per 100 females: 94.9; Marriage status: 36.4% never married, 41.6% now married, 3.8% separated, 5.4% widowed, 16.6% divorced; Foreign born: 4.9%; Speak English only: 89.0%; With disability: 18.2%; Veterans: 9.2%; Ancestry: 17.2% German, 14.4% Irish, 8.0% English, 6.0% American, 5.5% Italian

Employment: 8.3% management, business, and financial, 1.8% computer, engineering, and science, 6.8% education, legal, community service, arts, and media, 3.8% healthcare practitioners, 21.3% service, 30.2% sales and office, 12.4% natural resources, construction, and maintenance, 15.5% production, transportation, and material moving

Income: Per capita: $17,488; Median household: $33,305; Average household: $45,732; Households with income of $100,000 or more: 7.4%; Poverty rate: 30.8%

Educational Attainment: High school diploma or higher: 79.2%; Bachelor's degree or higher: 9.3%; Graduate/professional degree or higher: 2.3%

Housing: Homeownership rate: 43.4%; Median home value: $124,800; Median year structure built: 1965; Homeowner vacancy rate: 4.0%; Median gross rent: $824 per month; Rental vacancy rate: 10.5%

Health Insurance: 81.3% have insurance; 42.9% have private insurance; 45.5% have public insurance; 18.7% do not have insurance; 7.4% of children under 18 do not have insurance

Transportation: Commute: 91.0% car, 2.3% public transportation, 1.8% walk, 2.5% work from home; Median travel time to work: 22.5 minutes

ONYX (CDP). Covers a land area of 11.451 square miles and a water area of 0.078 square miles. Located at 35.67° N. Lat; 118.23° W. Long. Elevation is 2,795 feet.

Population: 475; Growth (since 2000): -0.2%; Density: 41.5 persons per square mile; Race: 85.5% White, 0.8% Black/African American, 0.0% Asian, 1.9% American Indian/Alaska Native, 0.0% Native Hawaiian/Other Pacific Islander, 8.4% Two or more races, 6.3% Hispanic of any race; Average household size: 2.22; Median age: 51.4; Age under 18: 17.3%; Age 65 and over: 23.8%; Males per 100 females: 98.7

Housing: Homeownership rate: 72.0%; Homeowner vacancy rate: 8.8%; Rental vacancy rate: 14.3%

PINE MOUNTAIN CLUB (CDP). Covers a land area of 16.853 square miles and a water area of 0.007 square miles. Located at 34.85° N. Lat; 119.17° W. Long. Elevation is 5,653 feet.

Population: 2,315; Growth (since 2000): 44.7%; Density: 137.4 persons per square mile; Race: 89.8% White, 1.3% Black/African American, 1.9% Asian, 1.1% American Indian/Alaska Native, 0.0% Native Hawaiian/Other Pacific Islander, 3.4% Two or more races, 10.0% Hispanic of any race; Average household size: 2.18; Median age: 51.6; Age under 18: 17.8%; Age 65 and over: 22.2%; Males per 100 females: 102.9

School District(s)

El Tejon Unified (KG-12)
2012-13 Enrollment: 919 . . . . (661) 248-6247

Housing: Homeownership rate: 82.8%; Homeowner vacancy rate: 6.1%; Rental vacancy rate: 17.8%

RANDSBURG (CDP). Covers a land area of 1.906 square miles and a water area of 0.039 square miles. Located at 35.37° N. Lat; 117.66° W. Long. Elevation is 3,504 feet.

History: Randsburg was named for the Rand gold-mining district in the Transvaal, South Africa. Gold was discovered nine miles from Randsburg in 1893, and camps sprang up. The richest mine was the Yellow Aster on the side of Rand Mountain.

Population: 69; Growth (since 2000): -10.4%; Density: 36.2 persons per square mile; Race: 89.9% White, 0.0% Black/African American, 2.9% Asian, 5.8% American Indian/Alaska Native, 0.0% Native Hawaiian/Other Pacific Islander, 1.4% Two or more races, 2.9% Hispanic of any race; Average household size: 1.64; Median age: 59.1; Age under 18: 2.9%; Age 65 and over: 33.3%; Males per 100 females: 68.3

Housing: Homeownership rate: 92.8%; Homeowner vacancy rate: 2.4%; Rental vacancy rate: 50.0%

RED MOUNTAIN (unincorporated postal area)

ZCTA: 93558

Covers a land area of 3.669 square miles and a water area of 0 square miles. Located at 35.35° N. Lat; 117.62° W. Long..

Population: 125; Growth (since 2000): n/a; Density: 34.1 persons per square mile; Race: 80.8% White, 0.0% Black/African American, 0.8% Asian, 6.4% American Indian/Alaska Native, 0.0% Native Hawaiian/Other Pacific Islander, 9.6% Two or more races, 12.0% Hispanic of any race; Average household size: 1.89; Median age: 57.1; Age under 18: 5.6%; Age 65 and over: 31.2%; Males per 100 females: 145.1

Housing: Homeownership rate: 80.3%; Homeowner vacancy rate: 3.3%; Rental vacancy rate: 7.1%

RIDGECREST (city). Covers a land area of 20.766 square miles and a water area of 0.651 square miles. Located at 35.63° N. Lat; 117.66° W. Long. Elevation is 2,290 feet.

History: Death Valley National Monument c.60 miles Northeast.

Population: 27,616; Growth (since 2000): 10.8%; Density: 1,329.9 persons per square mile; Race: 77.4% White, 4.0% Black/African American, 4.4% Asian, 1.2% American Indian/Alaska Native, 0.5% Native Hawaiian/Other Pacific Islander, 5.7% Two or more races, 17.9% Hispanic of any race; Average household size: 2.54; Median age: 33.8; Age under 18: 27.3%; Age 65 and over: 12.4%; Males per 100 females: 100.3; Marriage status: 28.9% never married, 51.8% now married, 2.9% separated, 7.1% widowed, 12.2% divorced; Foreign born: 8.8%; Speak English only: 86.9%; With disability: 13.4%; Veterans: 18.6%; Ancestry: 12.7% German, 10.1% Irish, 8.6% English, 8.5% American, 4.5% Italian

Employment: 14.5% management, business, and financial, 15.4% computer, engineering, and science, 9.7% education, legal, community service, arts, and media, 4.4% healthcare practitioners, 14.5% service, 19.5% sales and office, 11.6% natural resources, construction, and maintenance, 10.5% production, transportation, and material moving

Income: Per capita: $27,583; Median household: $60,182; Average household: $69,123; Households with income of $100,000 or more: 23.9%; Poverty rate: 13.2%

Educational Attainment: High school diploma or higher: 89.8%; Bachelor's degree or higher: 27.8%; Graduate/professional degree or higher: 9.7%

School District(s)

Sbe - Ridgecrest Charter (KG-08)
2012-13 Enrollment: 350 . . . . (760) 375-1010

Sierra Sands Unified (KG-12)
2012-13 Enrollment: 5,008 . . . . (760) 499-1604

Two-year College(s)

Cerro Coso Community College (Public)
Fall 2013 Enrollment: 4,523 . . . . (760) 384-6100
2013-14 Tuition: In-state $1,290; Out-of-state $6,974

Housing: Homeownership rate: 60.6%; Median home value: $181,900; Median year structure built: 1980; Homeowner vacancy rate: 2.9%; Median gross rent: $860 per month; Rental vacancy rate: 9.2%

Health Insurance: 88.7% have insurance; 71.7% have private insurance; 29.6% have public insurance; 11.3% do not have insurance; 3.6% of children under 18 do not have insurance

Safety: Violent crime rate: 54.0 per 10,000 population; Property crime rate: 199.7 per 10,000 population

Newspapers: Daily Independent (daily circulation 7000); News Review (weekly circulation 7500)

Transportation: Commute: 92.1% car, 0.3% public transportation, 1.9% walk, 2.2% work from home; Median travel time to work: 14.9 minutes

Additional Information Contacts

City of Ridgecrest . . . . (760) 499-5000
http://ridgecrest-ca.gov

ROSAMOND (CDP). Covers a land area of 52.121 square miles and a water area of 0.215 square miles. Located at 34.87° N. Lat; 118.21° W. Long. Elevation is 2,342 feet.

Population: 18,150; Growth (since 2000): 26.5%; Density: 348.2 persons per square mile; Race: 62.2% White, 8.1% Black/African American, 3.6% Asian, 1.2% American Indian/Alaska Native, 0.4% Native Hawaiian/Other Pacific Islander, 6.5% Two or more races, 34.3% Hispanic of any race; Average household size: 2.93; Median age: 32.0; Age under 18: 29.1%; Age 65 and over: 8.2%; Males per 100 females: 100.6; Marriage status: 33.9% never married, 51.3% now married, 2.5% separated, 4.4% widowed, 10.4% divorced; Foreign born: 12.5%; Speak English only: 72.5%; With disability: 11.7%; Veterans: 14.8%; Ancestry: 9.7% German, 8.3% Irish, 6.5% American, 4.9% English, 3.2% Italian

Employment: 8.8% management, business, and financial, 7.5% computer, engineering, and science, 6.6% education, legal, community service, arts, and media, 4.7% healthcare practitioners, 19.9% service, 23.6% sales and office, 20.8% natural resources, construction, and maintenance, 8.0% production, transportation, and material moving

Income: Per capita: $22,780; Median household: $60,540; Average household: $68,744; Households with income of $100,000 or more: 23.3%; Poverty rate: 17.7%

Educational Attainment: High school diploma or higher: 79.4%; Bachelor's degree or higher: 11.9%; Graduate/professional degree or higher: 4.0%

School District(s)

Southern Kern Unified (KG-12)
2012-13 Enrollment: 3,035 . . . . (661) 256-5000

Housing: Homeownership rate: 67.8%; Median home value: $124,200; Median year structure built: 1991; Homeowner vacancy rate: 4.5%; Median gross rent: <$100 per month; Rental vacancy rate: 12.7%

Health Insurance: 80.1% have insurance; 59.7% have private insurance; 30.4% have public insurance; 19.9% do not have insurance; 14.5% of children under 18 do not have insurance

Newspapers: Rosamond News (weekly circulation 11000)

Transportation: Commute: 95.3% car, 0.4% public transportation, 1.5% walk, 1.9% work from home; Median travel time to work: 30.0 minutes

ROSEDALE (CDP). Covers a land area of 33.964 square miles and a water area of 0 square miles. Located at 35.39° N. Lat; 119.20° W. Long. Elevation is 364 feet.

Population: 14,058; Growth (since 2000): 66.5%; Density: 413.9 persons per square mile; Race: 83.2% White, 1.5% Black/African American, 2.8% Asian, 1.1% American Indian/Alaska Native, 0.2% Native Hawaiian/Other Pacific Islander, 4.2% Two or more races, 17.7% Hispanic of any race; Average household size: 3.08; Median age: 40.1; Age under 18: 27.1%; Age 65 and over: 8.9%; Males per 100 females: 99.0; Marriage status: 22.3% never married, 64.5% now married, 1.5% separated, 3.3% widowed, 9.9% divorced; Foreign born: 5.8%; Speak English only: 86.9%; With disability: 9.9%; Veterans: 9.4%; Ancestry: 15.9% German, 13.1% English, 10.9% Irish, 7.4% Italian, 4.0% American

Employment: 20.4% management, business, and financial, 3.7% computer, engineering, and science, 11.2% education, legal, community service, arts, and media, 7.8% healthcare practitioners, 14.9% service, 29.6% sales and office, 7.2% natural resources, construction, and maintenance, 5.3% production, transportation, and material moving

Income: Per capita: $39,976; Median household: $99,958; Average household: $122,481; Households with income of $100,000 or more: 50.0%; Poverty rate: 7.6%

Educational Attainment: High school diploma or higher: 90.9%; Bachelor's degree or higher: 27.0%; Graduate/professional degree or higher: 10.2%

Housing: Homeownership rate: 90.0%; Median home value: $329,700; Median year structure built: 1993; Homeowner vacancy rate: 1.6%; Median gross rent: $1,044 per month; Rental vacancy rate: 9.4%

Health Insurance: 92.9% have insurance; 83.4% have private insurance; 20.6% have public insurance; 7.1% do not have insurance; 5.7% of children under 18 do not have insurance

Transportation: Commute: 95.1% car, 0.5% public transportation, 0.1% walk, 3.7% work from home; Median travel time to work: 23.0 minutes

SHAFTER (city). Covers a land area of 27.945 square miles and a water area of 0 square miles. Located at 35.48° N. Lat; 119.20° W. Long. Elevation is 348 feet.

History: Incorporated 1938.

Population: 16,988; Growth (since 2000): 33.4%; Density: 607.9 persons per square mile; Race: 48.0% White, 1.3% Black/African American, 0.7% Asian, 1.2% American Indian/Alaska Native, 0.1% Native Hawaiian/Other Pacific Islander, 3.8% Two or more races, 80.3% Hispanic of any race; Average household size: 3.86; Median age: 25.9; Age under 18: 36.0%; Age 65 and over: 6.6%; Males per 100 females: 105.6; Marriage status: 34.0% never married, 56.1% now married, 3.6% separated, 3.0% widowed, 7.0% divorced; Foreign born: 29.4%; Speak English only: 28.7%; With disability: 11.3%; Veterans: 3.8%; Ancestry: 4.6% German, 3.8% Irish, 2.2% English, 1.7% American, 1.1% Italian

Employment: 6.6% management, business, and financial, 1.1% computer, engineering, and science, 7.1% education, legal, community service, arts, and media, 0.8% healthcare practitioners, 14.4% service, 20.2% sales and office, 33.3% natural resources, construction, and maintenance, 16.4% production, transportation, and material moving

Income: Per capita: $15,471; Median household: $41,974; Average household: $55,151; Households with income of $100,000 or more: 11.1%; Poverty rate: 19.1%

Educational Attainment: High school diploma or higher: 58.8%; Bachelor's degree or higher: 7.5%; Graduate/professional degree or higher: 1.8%

School District(s)

Kern Union High (09-12)
2012-13 Enrollment: 37,070 . . . . (661) 827-3100

Maple Elementary (KG-08)
2012-13 Enrollment: 276. . . . . (661) 746-4439

Richland Union Elementary (PK-08)
2012-13 Enrollment: 3,374 . . . . (661) 746-8600

Housing: Homeownership rate: 58.4%; Median home value: $129,500; Median year structure built: 1978; Homeowner vacancy rate: 2.2%; Median gross rent: $732 per month; Rental vacancy rate: 6.9%

Health Insurance: 77.7% have insurance; 45.3% have private insurance; 37.7% have public insurance; 22.3% do not have insurance; 9.5% of children under 18 do not have insurance

Safety: Violent crime rate: 33.8 per 10,000 population; Property crime rate: 318.0 per 10,000 population

Newspapers: Shafter Press & Wasco Tribune (weekly circulation 2300)

Transportation: Commute: 92.5% car, 0.4% public transportation, 2.4% walk, 2.9% work from home; Median travel time to work: 22.4 minutes

Airports: Shafter-Minter Field (general aviation)

Additional Information Contacts

City of Shafter . . . . (661) 746-5000
http://www.shafter.com

SMITH CORNER (CDP). Covers a land area of 0.220 square miles and a water area of 0 square miles. Located at 35.48° N. Lat; 119.28° W. Long. Elevation is 331 feet.

Population: 524; Growth (since 2000): n/a; Density: 2,386.7 persons per square mile; Race: 43.3% White, 1.9% Black/African American, 0.4% Asian, 0.6% American Indian/Alaska Native, 0.6% Native Hawaiian/Other Pacific Islander, 3.1% Two or more races, 84.0% Hispanic of any race; Average household size: 4.09; Median age: 23.6; Age under 18: 36.8%; Age 65 and over: 5.5%; Males per 100 females: 107.9

Housing: Homeownership rate: 50.8%; Homeowner vacancy rate: 0.0%; Rental vacancy rate: 4.5%

SOUTH TAFT (CDP). Covers a land area of 1.076 square miles and a water area of 0 square miles. Located at 35.13° N. Lat; 119.46° W. Long. Elevation is 1,017 feet.

History: South Taft was first called Jameson for its owner, J.S. Jameson, who battled with the Southern Pacific Railway over the location of a post office. When a fire destroyed Jameson, the post office was located at Taft and Jameson was rebuilt as South Taft.

Population: 2,169; Growth (since 2000): 14.3%; Density: 2,015.5 persons per square mile; Race: 64.7% White, 1.0% Black/African American, 0.2% Asian, 2.5% American Indian/Alaska Native, 0.5% Native Hawaiian/Other Pacific Islander, 3.6% Two or more races, 42.9% Hispanic of any race; Average household size: 3.35; Median age: 27.1; Age under 18: 33.7%; Age 65 and over: 6.4%; Males per 100 females: 116.9

Housing: Homeownership rate: 44.6%; Homeowner vacancy rate: 3.8%; Rental vacancy rate: 8.9%

SQUIRREL MOUNTAIN VALLEY (CDP). Covers a land area of 0.713 square miles and a water area of 0 square miles. Located at 35.62° N. Lat; 118.41° W. Long. Elevation is 2,900 feet.
Population: 547; Growth (since 2000): 9.8%; Density: 766.7 persons per square mile; Race: 93.1% White, 0.4% Black/African American, 0.2% Asian, 1.6% American Indian/Alaska Native, 0.0% Native Hawaiian/Other Pacific Islander, 2.4% Two or more races, 4.0% Hispanic of any race; Average household size: 2.15; Median age: 58.3; Age under 18: 12.4%; Age 65 and over: 34.7%; Males per 100 females: 104.1
Housing: Homeownership rate: 90.2%; Homeowner vacancy rate: 3.4%; Rental vacancy rate: 16.7%

STALLION SPRINGS (CDP). Covers a land area of 16.429 square miles and a water area of 0.024 square miles. Located at 35.09° N. Lat; 118.64° W. Long. Elevation is 3,783 feet.
Population: 2,488; Growth (since 2000): 63.5%; Density: 151.4 persons per square mile; Race: 90.0% White, 1.2% Black/African American, 1.3% Asian, 1.0% American Indian/Alaska Native, 0.3% Native Hawaiian/Other Pacific Islander, 3.0% Two or more races, 11.5% Hispanic of any race; Average household size: 2.48; Median age: 46.7; Age under 18: 21.0%; Age 65 and over: 20.7%; Males per 100 females: 95.8
Housing: Homeownership rate: 85.8%; Homeowner vacancy rate: 5.4%; Rental vacancy rate: 10.0%
Safety: Violent crime rate: 35.1 per 10,000 population; Property crime rate: 62.5 per 10,000 population

TAFT (city). Covers a land area of 15.113 square miles and a water area of 0 square miles. Located at 35.13° N. Lat; 119.42° W. Long. Elevation is 955 feet.
History: Taft grew around the West Side Oil Field. It was first called Moron by the Southern Pacific Railroad, but the name was changed to honor President Taft when the post office was established here.
Population: 9,327; Growth (since 2000): 45.7%; Density: 617.1 persons per square mile; Race: 79.2% White, 4.2% Black/African American, 1.0% Asian, 1.3% American Indian/Alaska Native, 0.7% Native Hawaiian/Other Pacific Islander, 2.6% Two or more races, 35.9% Hispanic of any race; Average household size: 2.83; Median age: 34.9; Age under 18: 19.8%; Age 65 and over: 8.4%; Males per 100 females: 186.5; Marriage status: 37.8% never married, 47.3% now married, 3.3% separated, 3.9% widowed, 10.9% divorced; Foreign born: 25.6%; Speak English only: 64.2%; With disability: 13.3%; Veterans: 9.1%; Ancestry: 13.4% German, 9.1% Irish, 8.0% English, 3.2% American, 2.8% Italian
Employment: 14.2% management, business, and financial, 3.0% computer, engineering, and science, 11.7% education, legal, community service, arts, and media, 0.2% healthcare practitioners, 9.4% service, 22.0% sales and office, 29.9% natural resources, construction, and maintenance, 9.7% production, transportation, and material moving
Income: Per capita: $18,158; Median household: $50,441; Average household: $67,865; Households with income of $100,000 or more: 21.5%; Poverty rate: 16.8%
Educational Attainment: High school diploma or higher: 72.5%; Bachelor's degree or higher: 9.9%; Graduate/professional degree or higher: 4.3%

School District(s)

Taft City (KG-08)
2012-13 Enrollment: 2,083 . . . . (661) 763-1521
Taft Union High (09-12)
2012-13 Enrollment: 1,032 . . . . (661) 763-2330
West Side Rop
2012-13 Enrollment: n/a . . . . (661) 763-2390

Two-year College(s)

Taft College (Public)
Fall 2013 Enrollment: 5,444 . . . . (661) 763-7700
2013-14 Tuition: In-state $1,380; Out-of-state $7,170
Housing: Homeownership rate: 61.0%; Median home value: $158,900; Median year structure built: 1963; Homeowner vacancy rate: 2.6%; Median gross rent: $778 per month; Rental vacancy rate: 10.8%
Health Insurance: 80.1% have insurance; 58.3% have private insurance; 33.0% have public insurance; 19.9% do not have insurance; 15.4% of children under 18 do not have insurance
Safety: Violent crime rate: 67.9 per 10,000 population; Property crime rate: 374.5 per 10,000 population
Newspapers: Midway Driller (weekly circulation 4600)
Transportation: Commute: 94.4% car, 0.4% public transportation, 1.7% walk, 2.4% work from home; Median travel time to work: 25.2 minutes
Additional Information Contacts
City of Taft. . . . . (661) 763-1222
http://www.cityoftaft.org

TAFT HEIGHTS (CDP). Covers a land area of 0.303 square miles and a water area of 0 square miles. Located at 35.13° N. Lat; 119.47° W. Long. Elevation is 1,178 feet.
Population: 1,949; Growth (since 2000): 4.5%; Density: 6,430.2 persons per square mile; Race: 82.2% White, 0.8% Black/African American, 0.6% Asian, 1.8% American Indian/Alaska Native, 0.0% Native Hawaiian/Other Pacific Islander, 3.4% Two or more races, 22.6% Hispanic of any race; Average household size: 2.89; Median age: 29.3; Age under 18: 30.2%; Age 65 and over: 8.9%; Males per 100 females: 98.9
Housing: Homeownership rate: 51.2%; Homeowner vacancy rate: 3.9%; Rental vacancy rate: 9.5%

TEHACHAPI (city). Covers a land area of 9.874 square miles and a water area of 0.097 square miles. Located at 35.14° N. Lat; 118.45° W. Long. Elevation is 3,970 feet.
History: Tehachapi was first settled in 1854 by gold prospectors attracted to China Hill. The town grew as the business center for a surrounding fruit-growing area.
Population: 14,414; Growth (since 2000): 31.6%; Density: 1,459.8 persons per square mile; Race: 65.4% White, 9.0% Black/African American, 1.7% Asian, 1.4% American Indian/Alaska Native, 0.1% Native Hawaiian/Other Pacific Islander, 3.5% Two or more races, 37.9% Hispanic of any race; Average household size: 2.72; Median age: 34.4; Age under 18: 18.0%; Age 65 and over: 8.8%; Males per 100 females: 234.8; Marriage status: 39.0% never married, 42.3% now married, 3.5% separated, 5.7% widowed, 12.9% divorced; Foreign born: 10.8%; Speak English only: 72.9%; With disability: 13.9%; Veterans: 8.8%; Ancestry: 18.3% German, 13.8% Irish, 6.3% English, 4.2% Italian, 3.8% American
Employment: 7.0% management, business, and financial, 5.5% computer, engineering, and science, 3.6% education, legal, community service, arts, and media, 6.0% healthcare practitioners, 36.5% service, 17.7% sales and office, 13.4% natural resources, construction, and maintenance, 10.3% production, transportation, and material moving
Income: Per capita: $15,986; Median household: $43,949; Average household: $54,970; Households with income of $100,000 or more: 16.6%; Poverty rate: 12.4%
Educational Attainment: High school diploma or higher: 73.8%; Bachelor's degree or higher: 9.2%; Graduate/professional degree or higher: 2.0%

School District(s)

Tehachapi Unified (KG-12)
2012-13 Enrollment: 4,446 . . . . (661) 822-2100
Housing: Homeownership rate: 59.0%; Median home value: $156,300; Median year structure built: 1977; Homeowner vacancy rate: 3.2%; Median gross rent: $804 per month; Rental vacancy rate: 12.2%
Health Insurance: 85.0% have insurance; 63.8% have private insurance; 35.2% have public insurance; 15.0% do not have insurance; 8.6% of children under 18 do not have insurance
Hospitals: Tehachapi Hospital (28 beds)
Safety: Violent crime rate: 30.1 per 10,000 population; Property crime rate: 282.9 per 10,000 population
Newspapers: Tehachapi News (weekly circulation 6000)
Transportation: Commute: 79.8% car, 0.0% public transportation, 14.6% walk, 1.5% work from home; Median travel time to work: 20.5 minutes; Amtrak: Bus service available.
Additional Information Contacts
City of Tehachapi . . . . (661) 822-2200
http://www.liveuptehachapi.com

TUPMAN (CDP). Covers a land area of 0.528 square miles and a water area of 0 square miles. Located at 35.30° N. Lat; 119.36° W. Long. Elevation is 331 feet.
Population: 161; Growth (since 2000): -29.1%; Density: 305.0 persons per square mile; Race: 92.5% White, 0.0% Black/African American, 0.0% Asian, 0.0% American Indian/Alaska Native, 0.0% Native Hawaiian/Other Pacific Islander, 6.2% Two or more races, 7.5% Hispanic of any race; Average household size: 2.93; Median age: 32.5; Age under 18: 28.0%; Age 65 and over: 10.6%; Males per 100 females: 106.4

School District(s)

Elk Hills Elementary (KG-08)
2012-13 Enrollment: 201. . . . . (661) 765-7431

Housing: Homeownership rate: 61.8%; Homeowner vacancy rate: 0.0%; Rental vacancy rate: 12.5%

VALLEY ACRES (CDP). Covers a land area of 4.123 square miles and a water area of 0 square miles. Located at 35.21° N. Lat; 119.41° W. Long. Elevation is 420 feet.
Population: 527; Growth (since 2000): 2.9%; Density: 127.8 persons per square mile; Race: 81.2% White, 0.2% Black/African American, 0.2% Asian, 1.9% American Indian/Alaska Native, 0.0% Native Hawaiian/Other Pacific Islander, 8.5% Two or more races, 23.0% Hispanic of any race; Average household size: 3.01; Median age: 39.8; Age under 18: 25.4%; Age 65 and over: 14.2%; Males per 100 females: 105.1
Housing: Homeownership rate: 78.3%; Homeowner vacancy rate: 1.4%; Rental vacancy rate: 5.0%

WASCO (city). Covers a land area of 9.426 square miles and a water area of 0 square miles. Located at 35.59° N. Lat; 119.37° W. Long. Elevation is 328 feet.
History: Wasco grew as a community center for nearby ranchers.
Population: 25,545; Growth (since 2000): 20.1%; Density: 2,710.1 persons per square mile; Race: 49.2% White, 7.6% Black/African American, 0.7% Asian, 1.1% American Indian/Alaska Native, 0.0% Native Hawaiian/Other Pacific Islander, 3.2% Two or more races, 76.7% Hispanic of any race; Average household size: 3.86; Median age: 28.3; Age under 18: 28.8%; Age 65 and over: 5.1%; Males per 100 females: 160.3; Marriage status: 47.2% never married, 41.0% now married, 3.4% separated, 3.6% widowed, 8.1% divorced; Foreign born: 28.9%; Speak English only: 30.8%; With disability: 8.1%; Veterans: 3.8%; Ancestry: 3.6% German, 2.6% Irish, 1.9% English, 1.2% American, 1.2% Italian
Employment: 2.9% management, business, and financial, 0.7% computer, engineering, and science, 4.1% education, legal, community service, arts, and media, 0.5% healthcare practitioners, 18.3% service, 15.1% sales and office, 36.7% natural resources, construction, and maintenance, 21.8% production, transportation, and material moving
Income: Per capita: $10,501; Median household: $39,061; Average household: $46,608; Households with income of $100,000 or more: 8.7%; Poverty rate: 32.4%
Educational Attainment: High school diploma or higher: 53.6%; Bachelor's degree or higher: 4.0%; Graduate/professional degree or higher: 1.7%

School District(s)

North Kern Vocational Training Center
2012-13 Enrollment: n/a . . . . (661) 758-3045
Pond Union Elementary (KG-08)
2012-13 Enrollment: 239. . . . . (661) 792-2545
Semitropic Elementary (KG-12)
2012-13 Enrollment: 571. . . . . (661) 758-6412
Wasco Union Elementary (KG-08)
2012-13 Enrollment: 3,466 . . . . (661) 758-7100
Wasco Union High (09-12)
2012-13 Enrollment: 1,760 . . . . (661) 758-8447

Housing: Homeownership rate: 52.2%; Median home value: $127,600; Median year structure built: 1979; Homeowner vacancy rate: 5.1%; Median gross rent: $655 per month; Rental vacancy rate: 4.0%
Health Insurance: 73.3% have insurance; 35.0% have private insurance; 42.8% have public insurance; 26.7% do not have insurance; 10.3% of children under 18 do not have insurance
Transportation: Commute: 91.0% car, 0.5% public transportation, 1.3% walk, 0.7% work from home; Median travel time to work: 25.1 minutes; Amtrak: Train service available.

Additional Information Contacts

City of Wasco . . . . (661) 758-7214
http://www.ci.wasco.ca.us

WEEDPATCH (CDP). Covers a land area of 3.557 square miles and a water area of 0.004 square miles. Located at 35.24° N. Lat; 118.91° W. Long. Elevation is 387 feet.
Population: 2,658; Growth (since 2000): -2.5%; Density: 747.3 persons per square mile; Race: 45.6% White, 0.3% Black/African American, 0.5% Asian, 2.9% American Indian/Alaska Native, 0.0% Native Hawaiian/Other Pacific Islander, 4.1% Two or more races, 93.5% Hispanic of any race; Average household size: 4.26; Median age: 24.4; Age under 18: 36.2%; Age 65 and over: 5.2%; Males per 100 females: 116.4; Marriage status: 44.5% never married, 42.6% now married, 2.7% separated, 4.8% widowed, 8.0% divorced; Foreign born: 42.1%; Speak English only: 13.1%; With disability: 12.6%; Veterans: 1.3%; Ancestry: 1.8% German, 1.5% Irish, 1.2% American, 0.7% English, 0.5% Scotch-Irish
Employment: 2.9% management, business, and financial, 0.0% computer, engineering, and science, 3.6% education, legal, community service, arts, and media, 0.4% healthcare practitioners, 17.5% service, 7.4% sales and office, 57.8% natural resources, construction, and maintenance, 10.4% production, transportation, and material moving
Income: Per capita: $9,109; Median household: $28,508; Average household: $33,183; Households with income of $100,000 or more: 2.6%; Poverty rate: 46.8%
Educational Attainment: High school diploma or higher: 26.9%; Bachelor's degree or higher: 1.1%; Graduate/professional degree or higher: 0.5%
Housing: Homeownership rate: 44.4%; Median home value: $66,500; Median year structure built: 1968; Homeowner vacancy rate: 1.8%; Median gross rent: $618 per month; Rental vacancy rate: 3.9%
Health Insurance: 57.2% have insurance; 13.9% have private insurance; 44.9% have public insurance; 42.8% do not have insurance; 17.4% of children under 18 do not have insurance
Transportation: Commute: 95.0% car, 0.6% public transportation, 0.7% walk, 2.8% work from home; Median travel time to work: 28.2 minutes

WELDON (CDP). Covers a land area of 26.642 square miles and a water area of 0.151 square miles. Located at 35.64° N. Lat; 118.31° W. Long. Elevation is 2,654 feet.
Population: 2,642; Growth (since 2000): 10.7%; Density: 99.2 persons per square mile; Race: 89.9% White, 0.2% Black/African American, 0.4% Asian, 3.1% American Indian/Alaska Native, 0.0% Native Hawaiian/Other Pacific Islander, 4.4% Two or more races, 8.2% Hispanic of any race; Average household size: 2.26; Median age: 50.7; Age under 18: 18.3%; Age 65 and over: 25.8%; Males per 100 females: 98.3; Marriage status: 18.6% never married, 54.8% now married, 4.4% separated, 9.0% widowed, 17.6% divorced; Foreign born: 1.5%; Speak English only: 96.4%; With disability: 32.1%; Veterans: 26.3%; Ancestry: 25.2% German, 19.3% English, 12.4% Irish, 11.3% French, 6.3% Swedish
Employment: 12.1% management, business, and financial, 0.0% computer, engineering, and science, 7.7% education, legal, community service, arts, and media, 7.0% healthcare practitioners, 17.6% service, 26.2% sales and office, 9.4% natural resources, construction, and maintenance, 20.0% production, transportation, and material moving
Income: Per capita: $17,158; Median household: $24,972; Average household: $36,291; Households with income of $100,000 or more: 4.0%; Poverty rate: 32.7%
Educational Attainment: High school diploma or higher: 82.4%; Bachelor's degree or higher: 8.8%; Graduate/professional degree or higher: 3.8%

School District(s)

South Fork Union (KG-08)
2012-13 Enrollment: 274. . . . . (760) 378-4000

Housing: Homeownership rate: 77.2%; Median home value: $85,600; Median year structure built: 1978; Homeowner vacancy rate: 4.2%; Median gross rent: $774 per month; Rental vacancy rate: 7.8%
Health Insurance: 84.7% have insurance; 47.5% have private insurance; 55.9% have public insurance; 15.3% do not have insurance; 0.0% of children under 18 do not have insurance
Transportation: Commute: 65.8% car, 3.3% public transportation, 9.9% walk, 21.0% work from home; Median travel time to work: 33.7 minutes

WOFFORD HEIGHTS (CDP). Covers a land area of 6.057 square miles and a water area of <.001 square miles. Located at 35.72° N. Lat; 118.47° W. Long. Elevation is 2,684 feet.
Population: 2,200; Growth (since 2000): -3.3%; Density: 363.2 persons per square mile; Race: 92.6% White, 0.3% Black/African American, 0.5% Asian, 1.9% American Indian/Alaska Native, 0.0% Native Hawaiian/Other Pacific Islander, 3.6% Two or more races, 7.1% Hispanic of any race; Average household size: 1.92; Median age: 58.3; Age under 18: 12.7%; Age 65 and over: 37.1%; Males per 100 females: 97.0
Housing: Homeownership rate: 75.8%; Homeowner vacancy rate: 4.7%; Rental vacancy rate: 15.9%

WOODY (unincorporated postal area)

ZCTA: 93287

Covers a land area of 55.867 square miles and a water area of 0 square miles. Located at 35.76° N. Lat; 118.99° W. Long. Elevation is 1,654 feet.

Population: 119; Growth (since 2000): 75.0%; Density: 2.1 persons per square mile; Race: 86.6% White, 0.0% Black/African American, 0.8% Asian, 4.2% American Indian/Alaska Native, 0.0% Native Hawaiian/Other Pacific Islander, 5.0% Two or more races, 5.9% Hispanic of any race; Average household size: 2.43; Median age: 50.2; Age under 18: 15.1%; Age 65 and over: 18.5%; Males per 100 females: 124.5

School District(s)

Blake Elementary (KG-08)
2012-13 Enrollment: 6. . . . . (661) 536-8559

Housing: Homeownership rate: 89.8%; Homeowner vacancy rate: 2.1%; Rental vacancy rate: 0.0%

Kings County

Located in south central California, in the San Joaquin Valley; drained by the Kings and Tule Rivers; includes Tulare Lake. Covers a land area of 1,389.420 square miles, a water area of 2.111 square miles, and is located in the Pacific Time Zone at 36.07° N. Lat., 119.82° W. Long. The county was founded in 1893. County seat is Hanford.

Kings County is part of the Hanford-Corcoran, CA Metropolitan Statistical Area. The entire metro area includes: Kings County, CA

Weather Station: Corcoran Irrig Dist — Elevation: 200 feet

	Jan	Feb	Mar	Apr	May	Jun	Jul	Aug	Sep	Oct	Nov	Dec
High	55	63	69	77	86	93	98	97	91	81	66	55
Low	38	41	45	48	54	59	64	63	58	50	42	37
Precip	1.6	1.4	1.3	0.6	0.3	0.1	tr	0.0	0.1	0.4	0.7	1.0
Snow	0.1	0.0	0.0	0.0	0.0	0.0	0.0	0.0	0.0	0.0	0.0	0.0

High and Low temperatures in degrees Fahrenheit; Precipitation and Snow in inches

Weather Station: Hanford 1 S — Elevation: 245 feet

	Jan	Feb	Mar	Apr	May	Jun	Jul	Aug	Sep	Oct	Nov	Dec
High	54	61	67	75	84	91	96	95	90	80	65	54
Low	37	40	44	48	55	60	65	63	58	50	41	35
Precip	1.8	1.5	1.7	0.7	0.3	0.1	0.0	0.0	0.1	0.5	0.7	1.2
Snow	0.0	tr	0.0	0.0	0.0	0.0	0.0	0.0	0.0	0.0	0.0	tr

High and Low temperatures in degrees Fahrenheit; Precipitation and Snow in inches

Population: 152,982; Growth (since 2000): 18.2%; Density: 110.1 persons per square mile; Race: 54.3% White, 7.2% Black/African American, 3.7% Asian, 1.7% American Indian/Alaska Native, 0.2% Native Hawaiian/Other Pacific Islander, 4.9% two or more races, 50.9% Hispanic of any race; Average household size: 3.19; Median age: 31.1; Age under 18: 27.8%; Age 65 and over: 7.9%; Males per 100 females: 129.6; Marriage status: 34.9% never married, 50.5% now married, 3.4% separated, 4.5% widowed, 10.2% divorced; Foreign born: 20.1%; Speak English only: 57.2%; With disability: 10.4%; Veterans: 10.1%; Ancestry: 6.7% German, 6.1% Irish, 4.9% American, 4.4% English, 4.1% Portuguese
Religion: Six largest groups: 43.2% Catholicism, 2.3% Baptist, 1.9% Pentecostal, 1.7% Non-denominational Protestant, 1.5% Latter-day Saints, 0.9% Adventist
Economy: Unemployment rate: 10.7%; Leading industries: 18.2% retail trade; 14.8% health care and social assistance; 11.1% accommodation and food services; Farms: 1,056 totaling 673,634 acres; Company size: 3 employ 1,000 or more persons, 1 employs 500 to 999 persons, 19 employ 100 to 499 persons, 1,536 employ less than 100 persons; Business ownership: 2,165 women-owned, n/a Black-owned, 1,678 Hispanic-owned, 423 Asian-owned
Employment: 9.0% management, business, and financial, 1.8% computer, engineering, and science, 9.5% education, legal, community service, arts, and media, 4.5% healthcare practitioners, 23.0% service, 18.9% sales and office, 19.8% natural resources, construction, and maintenance, 13.4% production, transportation, and material moving
Income: Per capita: $18,429; Median household: $48,133; Average household: $63,130; Households with income of $100,000 or more: 17.7%; Poverty rate: 21.0%
Educational Attainment: High school diploma or higher: 71.0%; Bachelor's degree or higher: 12.9%; Graduate/professional degree or higher: 3.4%
Housing: Homeownership rate: 54.2%; Median home value: $176,900; Median year structure built: 1981; Homeowner vacancy rate: 2.0%; Median gross rent: $871 per month; Rental vacancy rate: 5.3%
Vital Statistics: Birth rate: 167.5 per 10,000 population; Death rate: 53.4 per 10,000 population; Age-adjusted cancer mortality rate: 143.9 deaths per 100,000 population
Health Insurance: 81.1% have insurance; 55.5% have private insurance; 33.6% have public insurance; 18.9% do not have insurance; 10.3% of children under 18 do not have insurance
Health Care: Physicians: 8.3 per 10,000 population; Hospital beds: 11.8 per 10,000 population; Hospital admissions: 775.0 per 10,000 population
Air Quality Index: 25.5% good, 54.8% moderate, 15.9% unhealthy for sensitive individuals, 3.8% unhealthy (percent of days)
Transportation: Commute: 91.3% car, 1.7% public transportation, 2.5% walk, 2.8% work from home; Median travel time to work: 21.4 minutes
Presidential Election: 40.8% Obama, 57.0% Romney (2012)
Additional Information Contacts
Kings Government. . . . . (559) 582-3211
http://www.countyofkings.com

Kings County Communities

ARMONA (CDP). Covers a land area of 1.904 square miles and a water area of 0 square miles. Located at 36.32° N. Lat; 119.71° W. Long. Elevation is 239 feet.
History: Armona developed as a shipping point for spinach, grapes, and other fruit.
Population: 4,156; Growth (since 2000): 28.3%; Density: 2,182.5 persons per square mile; Race: 49.5% White, 2.4% Black/African American, 2.0% Asian, 1.5% American Indian/Alaska Native, 0.3% Native Hawaiian/Other Pacific Islander, 5.8% Two or more races, 67.0% Hispanic of any race; Average household size: 3.61; Median age: 28.7; Age under 18: 34.2%; Age 65 and over: 7.4%; Males per 100 females: 92.3; Marriage status: 37.8% never married, 48.7% now married, 3.3% separated, 5.6% widowed, 7.9% divorced; Foreign born: 28.8%; Speak English only: 42.0%; With disability: 9.4%; Veterans: 6.3%; Ancestry: 4.4% Irish, 3.9% American, 3.0% Portuguese, 2.9% German, 2.5% English
Employment: 4.6% management, business, and financial, 1.2% computer, engineering, and science, 4.9% education, legal, community service, arts, and media, 1.5% healthcare practitioners, 27.3% service, 21.4% sales and office, 18.0% natural resources, construction, and maintenance, 21.1% production, transportation, and material moving
Income: Per capita: $12,090; Median household: $40,181; Average household: $43,724; Households with income of $100,000 or more: 2.6%; Poverty rate: 23.8%
Educational Attainment: High school diploma or higher: 63.3%; Bachelor's degree or higher: 4.2%; Graduate/professional degree or higher: 2.4%

School District(s)

Armona Union Elementary (KG-12)
2012-13 Enrollment: 2,060 . . . . (559) 583-5000

Housing: Homeownership rate: 63.2%; Median home value: $124,100; Median year structure built: 1974; Homeowner vacancy rate: 1.1%; Median gross rent: $916 per month; Rental vacancy rate: 4.1%
Health Insurance: 73.3% have insurance; 39.8% have private insurance; 40.0% have public insurance; 26.7% do not have insurance; 17.5% of children under 18 do not have insurance
Transportation: Commute: 96.7% car, 0.0% public transportation, 0.0% walk, 1.5% work from home; Median travel time to work: 17.8 minutes

AVENAL (city). Covers a land area of 19.422 square miles and a water area of 0 square miles. Located at 36.03° N. Lat; 120.12° W. Long. Elevation is 807 feet.
Population: 15,505; Growth (since 2000): 5.7%; Density: 798.3 persons per square mile; Race: 39.0% White, 10.5% Black/African American, 0.7% Asian, 1.2% American Indian/Alaska Native, 0.0% Native Hawaiian/Other Pacific Islander, 2.2% Two or more races, 71.8% Hispanic of any race; Average household size: 4.09; Median age: 34.2; Age under 18: 21.4%; Age 65 and over: 4.0%; Males per 100 females: 262.5; Marriage status: 39.0% never married, 46.4% now married, 5.0% separated, 3.9% widowed, 10.7% divorced; Foreign born: 40.1%; Speak English only: 28.0%; With disability: 8.1%; Veterans: 4.6%; Ancestry: 2.9% Irish, 2.3% English, 1.8% German, 0.8% American, 0.8% Arab
Employment: 0.9% management, business, and financial, 0.0% computer, engineering, and science, 1.9% education, legal, community service, arts, and media, 0.0% healthcare practitioners, 23.9% service, 13.5% sales and office, 48.5% natural resources, construction, and maintenance, 11.2% production, transportation, and material moving
Income: Per capita: $8,013; Median household: $28,794; Average household: $36,247; Households with income of $100,000 or more: 5.6%; Poverty rate: 40.4%

Educational Attainment: High school diploma or higher: 44.5%; Bachelor's degree or higher: 4.0%; Graduate/professional degree or higher: 0.6%

School District(s)

Reef-Sunset Unified (KG-12)
2012-13 Enrollment: 2,643 . . . . (559) 386-9083

Housing: Homeownership rate: 45.5%; Median home value: $121,300; Median year structure built: 1978; Homeowner vacancy rate: 2.9%; Median gross rent: $701 per month; Rental vacancy rate: 5.1%

Health Insurance: 69.6% have insurance; 28.5% have private insurance; 43.6% have public insurance; 30.4% do not have insurance; 13.6% of children under 18 do not have insurance

Safety: Violent crime rate: 42.1 per 10,000 population; Property crime rate: 99.9 per 10,000 population

Transportation: Commute: 85.7% car, 7.3% public transportation, 1.8% walk, 1.5% work from home; Median travel time to work: 32.1 minutes

Additional Information Contacts

City of Avenal . . . . (559) 386-5766

CORCORAN (city). Covers a land area of 7.467 square miles and a water area of 0 square miles. Located at 36.08° N. Lat; 119.56° W. Long. Elevation is 207 feet.

History: Colonel Allensworth State Historical Park to Southeast. Incorporated 1914.

Population: 24,813; Growth (since 2000): 71.6%; Density: 3,323.2 persons per square mile; Race: 36.0% White, 15.0% Black/African American, 0.8% Asian, 1.4% American Indian/Alaska Native, 0.1% Native Hawaiian/Other Pacific Islander, 2.5% Two or more races, 62.6% Hispanic of any race; Average household size: 3.50; Median age: 35.0; Age under 18: 17.9%; Age 65 and over: 5.3%; Males per 100 females: 294.8; Marriage status: 44.9% never married, 36.6% now married, 4.6% separated, 3.9% widowed, 14.6% divorced; Foreign born: 21.1%; Speak English only: 49.4%; With disability: 12.0%; Veterans: 7.0%; Ancestry: 4.0% Irish, 3.7% German, 2.6% English, 2.1% American, 1.6% Italian

Employment: 4.0% management, business, and financial, 0.7% computer, engineering, and science, 4.4% education, legal, community service, arts, and media, 2.7% healthcare practitioners, 20.8% service, 19.2% sales and office, 32.6% natural resources, construction, and maintenance, 15.6% production, transportation, and material moving

Income: Per capita: $8,182; Median household: $32,914; Average household: $43,907; Households with income of $100,000 or more: 7.0%; Poverty rate: 28.7%

Educational Attainment: High school diploma or higher: 55.8%; Bachelor's degree or higher: 3.1%; Graduate/professional degree or higher: 0.9%

School District(s)

Corcoran Joint Unified (KG-12)
2012-13 Enrollment: 3,334 . . . . (559) 992-8888

Housing: Homeownership rate: 51.5%; Median home value: $123,400; Median year structure built: 1978; Homeowner vacancy rate: 1.7%; Median gross rent: $754 per month; Rental vacancy rate: 11.8%

Health Insurance: 80.3% have insurance; 34.7% have private insurance; 49.3% have public insurance; 19.7% do not have insurance; 10.3% of children under 18 do not have insurance

Hospitals: Corcoran District Hospital (32 beds)

Safety: Violent crime rate: 30.5 per 10,000 population; Property crime rate: 156.3 per 10,000 population

Newspapers: Corcoran Journal (weekly circulation 2400)

Transportation: Commute: 91.4% car, 0.9% public transportation, 2.8% walk, 2.4% work from home; Median travel time to work: 16.8 minutes; Amtrak: Train service available.

Additional Information Contacts

City of Corcoran . . . . (559) 992-2151
http://www.cityofcorcoran.com

GRANGEVILLE (CDP). Covers a land area of 0.640 square miles and a water area of 0 square miles. Located at 36.34° N. Lat; 119.71° W. Long. Elevation is 249 feet.

Population: 469; Growth (since 2000): n/a; Density: 733.1 persons per square mile; Race: 83.8% White, 3.2% Black/African American, 1.1% Asian, 1.1% American Indian/Alaska Native, 0.0% Native Hawaiian/Other Pacific Islander, 2.1% Two or more races, 30.9% Hispanic of any race; Average household size: 2.90; Median age: 37.1; Age under 18: 30.9%; Age 65 and over: 11.1%; Males per 100 females: 112.2

Housing: Homeownership rate: 69.1%; Homeowner vacancy rate: 0.0%; Rental vacancy rate: 1.9%

HANFORD (city). County seat. Covers a land area of 16.589 square miles and a water area of 0 square miles. Located at 36.33° N. Lat; 119.65° W. Long. Elevation is 249 feet.

History: Hanford developed as the seat of Kings County and the trading center for ranchers who specialized in stock-raising and dairying. The Mussell Slough feud between the ranchers and the Southern Pacific Railroad, upon which Frank Norris based his novel "The Octopus," came to a climax in Hanford.

Population: 53,967; Growth (since 2000): 29.5%; Density: 3,253.1 persons per square mile; Race: 62.5% White, 4.9% Black/African American, 4.3% Asian, 1.3% American Indian/Alaska Native, 0.1% Native Hawaiian/Other Pacific Islander, 5.4% Two or more races, 47.1% Hispanic of any race; Average household size: 3.03; Median age: 30.9; Age under 18: 31.0%; Age 65 and over: 9.9%; Males per 100 females: 96.3; Marriage status: 30.0% never married, 54.6% now married, 3.1% separated, 5.3% widowed, 10.1% divorced; Foreign born: 16.1%; Speak English only: 63.8%; With disability: 11.4%; Veterans: 10.8%; Ancestry: 7.5% German, 6.7% Irish, 6.2% American, 5.2% English, 5.0% Portuguese

Employment: 9.2% management, business, and financial, 2.6% computer, engineering, and science, 10.9% education, legal, community service, arts, and media, 6.0% healthcare practitioners, 25.1% service, 21.8% sales and office, 13.3% natural resources, construction, and maintenance, 11.0% production, transportation, and material moving

Income: Per capita: $22,302; Median household: $52,614; Average household: $66,610; Households with income of $100,000 or more: 21.0%; Poverty rate: 19.5%

Educational Attainment: High school diploma or higher: 80.2%; Bachelor's degree or higher: 18.0%; Graduate/professional degree or higher: 5.2%

School District(s)

Armona Union Elementary (KG-12)
2012-13 Enrollment: 2,060 . . . . (559) 583-5000
Hanford Elementary (KG-08)
2012-13 Enrollment: 5,771 . . . . (559) 585-3600
Hanford Joint Union High (09-12)
2012-13 Enrollment: 3,892 . . . . (559) 583-5901
Kings County Office of Education (KG-12)
2012-13 Enrollment: 428. . . . . (559) 584-1441
Kings County Rop
2012-13 Enrollment: n/a . . . . (559) 589-7026
Kings River-Hardwick Union Elementary (KG-08)
2012-13 Enrollment: 744. . . . . (559) 584-4475
Kit Carson Union Elementary (KG-08)
2012-13 Enrollment: 427. . . . . (559) 582-2843
Lakeside Union Elementary (KG-08)
2012-13 Enrollment: 302. . . . . (559) 582-2868
Pioneer Union Elementary (KG-08)
2012-13 Enrollment: 1,577 . . . . (559) 585-2400

Vocational/Technical School(s)

Lawrence & Company College of Cosmetology (Private, For-profit)
Fall 2013 Enrollment: 57 . . . . (559) 584-1192
2013-14 Tuition: $10,506

Housing: Homeownership rate: 58.3%; Median home value: $178,800; Median year structure built: 1982; Homeowner vacancy rate: 2.4%; Median gross rent: $908 per month; Rental vacancy rate: 4.6%

Health Insurance: 84.2% have insurance; 59.7% have private insurance; 34.4% have public insurance; 15.8% do not have insurance; 8.8% of children under 18 do not have insurance

Hospitals: Adventist Medical Center (60 beds); Central Valley General Hospital (49 beds)

Safety: Violent crime rate: 54.9 per 10,000 population; Property crime rate: 356.3 per 10,000 population

Newspapers: Hanford Sentinel (daily circulation 14000); Lemoore Advance (weekly circulation 7000)

Transportation: Commute: 94.3% car, 0.8% public transportation, 1.7% walk, 2.2% work from home; Median travel time to work: 20.3 minutes; Amtrak: Train service available.

Airports: Hanford Municipal (general aviation)

Additional Information Contacts

City of Hanford . . . . (559) 585-2500
http://www.ci.hanford.ca.us

HARDWICK (CDP). Covers a land area of 0.139 square miles and a water area of 0 square miles. Located at 36.40° N. Lat; 119.72° W. Long. Elevation is 249 feet.

Population: 138; Growth (since 2000): n/a; Density: 994.6 persons per square mile; Race: 45.7% White, 3.6% Black/African American, 0.0% Asian, 0.0% American Indian/Alaska Native, 0.0% Native Hawaiian/Other Pacific Islander, 2.2% Two or more races, 62.3% Hispanic of any race; Average household size: 4.03; Median age: 25.5; Age under 18: 37.7%; Age 65 and over: 10.1%; Males per 100 females: 112.3

Housing: Homeownership rate: 52.9%; Homeowner vacancy rate: 0.0%; Rental vacancy rate: 5.9%

HOME GARDEN (CDP). Covers a land area of 0.617 square miles and a water area of 0 square miles. Located at 36.30° N. Lat; 119.64° W. Long. Elevation is 246 feet.

Population: 1,761; Growth (since 2000): 3.5%; Density: 2,854.0 persons per square mile; Race: 37.0% White, 12.5% Black/African American, 2.8% Asian, 3.6% American Indian/Alaska Native, 0.5% Native Hawaiian/Other Pacific Islander, 5.1% Two or more races, 67.5% Hispanic of any race; Average household size: 4.01; Median age: 27.9; Age under 18: 34.1%; Age 65 and over: 8.5%; Males per 100 females: 100.8

Housing: Homeownership rate: 48.1%; Homeowner vacancy rate: 4.5%; Rental vacancy rate: 2.6%

KETTLEMAN CITY (CDP). Covers a land area of 0.211 square miles and a water area of 0 square miles. Located at 36.01° N. Lat; 119.96° W. Long. Elevation is 253 feet.

Population: 1,439; Growth (since 2000): -4.0%; Density: 6,819.9 persons per square mile; Race: 33.2% White, 0.3% Black/African American, 0.1% Asian, 0.6% American Indian/Alaska Native, 0.0% Native Hawaiian/Other Pacific Islander, 4.2% Two or more races, 96.1% Hispanic of any race; Average household size: 4.11; Median age: 25.5; Age under 18: 38.4%; Age 65 and over: 5.5%; Males per 100 females: 105.0

School District(s)

Reef-Sunset Unified (KG-12)
2012-13 Enrollment: 2,643 . . . . (559) 386-9083

Housing: Homeownership rate: 38.5%; Homeowner vacancy rate: 0.7%; Rental vacancy rate: 1.4%

LEMOORE (city). Covers a land area of 8.517 square miles and a water area of 0 square miles. Located at 36.30° N. Lat; 119.80° W. Long. Elevation is 230 feet.

History: Lemoore developed as a dairying and fruit growing trade center.

Population: 24,531; Growth (since 2000): 24.4%; Density: 2,880.4 persons per square mile; Race: 56.8% White, 6.4% Black/African American, 8.2% Asian, 1.4% American Indian/Alaska Native, 0.4% Native Hawaiian/Other Pacific Islander, 6.8% Two or more races, 40.0% Hispanic of any race; Average household size: 2.99; Median age: 28.6; Age under 18: 30.8%; Age 65 and over: 7.3%; Males per 100 females: 99.1; Marriage status: 36.3% never married, 49.7% now married, 2.5% separated, 4.4% widowed, 9.6% divorced; Foreign born: 16.2%; Speak English only: 66.2%; With disability: 9.5%; Veterans: 16.0%; Ancestry: 7.3% American, 6.8% Irish, 6.8% German, 6.5% English, 4.5% Portuguese

Employment: 8.7% management, business, and financial, 2.6% computer, engineering, and science, 16.1% education, legal, community service, arts, and media, 5.9% healthcare practitioners, 22.5% service, 17.1% sales and office, 12.5% natural resources, construction, and maintenance, 14.7% production, transportation, and material moving

Income: Per capita: $24,002; Median household: $53,711; Average household: $70,428; Households with income of $100,000 or more: 21.9%; Poverty rate: 14.5%

Educational Attainment: High school diploma or higher: 83.1%; Bachelor's degree or higher: 19.1%; Graduate/professional degree or higher: 5.0%

School District(s)

Central Union Elementary (PK-08)
2012-13 Enrollment: 1,818 . . . . (559) 924-3405
Island Union Elementary (KG-08)
2012-13 Enrollment: 314 . . . . (559) 924-6424
Lemoore Union Elementary (KG-08)
2012-13 Enrollment: 3,186 . . . . (559) 924-6800
Lemoore Union High (09-12)
2012-13 Enrollment: 2,282 . . . . (559) 924-6610

Two-year College(s)

West Hills College-Lemoore (Public)
Fall 2013 Enrollment: 4,102 . . . . (559) 925-3000
2013-14 Tuition: In-state $1,380; Out-of-state $9,000

Housing: Homeownership rate: 52.7%; Median home value: $193,700; Median year structure built: 1986; Homeowner vacancy rate: 2.0%; Median gross rent: $872 per month; Rental vacancy rate: 5.1%

Health Insurance: 82.5% have insurance; 65.4% have private insurance; 26.0% have public insurance; 17.5% do not have insurance; 11.4% of children under 18 do not have insurance

Safety: Violent crime rate: 44.8 per 10,000 population; Property crime rate: 245.1 per 10,000 population

Transportation: Commute: 94.5% car, 0.6% public transportation, 1.6% walk, 1.3% work from home; Median travel time to work: 23.9 minutes; Amtrak: Bus service available.

Additional Information Contacts

City of Lemoore . . . . (559) 924-6700
http://www.lemoore.com

LEMOORE STATION (CDP). Covers a land area of 4.205 square miles and a water area of 0 square miles. Located at 36.26° N. Lat; 119.90° W. Long.

Population: 7,438; Growth (since 2000): 29.4%; Density: 1,768.7 persons per square mile; Race: 65.6% White, 9.8% Black/African American, 7.5% Asian, 0.9% American Indian/Alaska Native, 0.7% Native Hawaiian/Other Pacific Islander, 9.7% Two or more races, 19.4% Hispanic of any race; Average household size: 3.47; Median age: 22.5; Age under 18: 32.4%; Age 65 and over: 0.2%; Males per 100 females: 144.2; Marriage status: 30.0% never married, 68.8% now married, 1.0% separated, 0.0% widowed, 1.2% divorced; Foreign born: 7.7%; Speak English only: 78.8%; With disability: 3.1%; Veterans: 30.7%; Ancestry: 21.1% German, 11.4% Irish, 8.9% American, 5.4% English, 4.7% Polish

Employment: 3.3% management, business, and financial, 3.5% computer, engineering, and science, 2.5% education, legal, community service, arts, and media, 7.5% healthcare practitioners, 27.7% service, 22.9% sales and office, 23.5% natural resources, construction, and maintenance, 9.2% production, transportation, and material moving

Income: Per capita: $17,904; Median household: $41,845; Average household: $49,834; Households with income of $100,000 or more: 7.6%; Poverty rate: 13.1%

Educational Attainment: High school diploma or higher: 98.3%; Bachelor's degree or higher: 23.1%; Graduate/professional degree or higher: 5.0%

Housing: Homeownership rate: 0.3%; Median home value: n/a; Median year structure built: 2001; Homeowner vacancy rate: 0.0%; Median gross rent: $1,203 per month; Rental vacancy rate: 2.1%

Health Insurance: 100.0% have insurance; 99.7% have private insurance; 3.0% have public insurance; 0.0% do not have insurance; 0.0% of children under 18 do not have insurance

Transportation: Commute: 77.4% car, 8.4% public transportation, 5.2% walk, 5.4% work from home; Median travel time to work: 16.3 minutes

STRATFORD (CDP). Covers a land area of 0.683 square miles and a water area of 0 square miles. Located at 36.19° N. Lat; 119.82° W. Long. Elevation is 203 feet.

Population: 1,277; Growth (since 2000): 1.0%; Density: 1,870.0 persons per square mile; Race: 44.9% White, 1.3% Black/African American, 1.5% Asian, 1.3% American Indian/Alaska Native, 0.1% Native Hawaiian/Other Pacific Islander, 2.6% Two or more races, 83.7% Hispanic of any race; Average household size: 4.09; Median age: 27.6; Age under 18: 33.9%; Age 65 and over: 7.2%; Males per 100 females: 101.4

School District(s)

Central Union Elementary (PK-08)
2012-13 Enrollment: 1,818 . . . . (559) 924-3405

Housing: Homeownership rate: 66.0%; Homeowner vacancy rate: 1.9%; Rental vacancy rate: 2.7%

Lake County

Located in northwestern California; mountain and valley region, in the Coast Ranges; drained by Cache Creek and headstreams of the Eel River; includes Clear Lake, Hull Mountain, Mt. Konochti, and part of Mendocino National Forest. Covers a land area of 1,256.464 square miles, a water area of 72.959 square miles, and is located in the Pacific Time Zone at

39.09° N. Lat., 122.75° W. Long. The county was founded in 1861. County seat is Lakeport.

Lake County is part of the Clearlake, CA Micropolitan Statistical Area. The entire metro area includes: Lake County, CA

Weather Station: Clearlake 4 SE Elevation: 1,349 feet

	Jan	Feb	Mar	Apr	May	Jun	Jul	Aug	Sep	Oct	Nov	Dec
High	55	58	62	68	75	84	92	91	85	76	62	55
Low	32	34	36	39	45	51	55	53	49	42	35	32
Precip	5.8	5.6	4.4	1.7	1.1	0.2	0.0	0.1	0.5	1.4	3.4	6.0
Snow	0.2	0.2	tr	tr	0.0	0.0	0.0	0.0	0.0	tr	tr	tr

High and Low temperatures in degrees Fahrenheit; Precipitation and Snow in inches

Population: 64,665; Growth (since 2000): 10.9%; Density: 51.5 persons per square mile; Race: 80.5% White, 1.9% Black/African American, 1.1% Asian, 3.2% American Indian/Alaska Native, 0.2% Native Hawaiian/Other Pacific Islander, 4.7% two or more races, 17.1% Hispanic of any race; Average household size: 2.39; Median age: 45.0; Age under 18: 21.1%; Age 65 and over: 17.7%; Males per 100 females: 100.8; Marriage status: 28.2% never married, 49.2% now married, 2.3% separated, 7.6% widowed, 15.0% divorced; Foreign born: 8.6%; Speak English only: 85.8%; With disability: 20.9%; Veterans: 13.3%; Ancestry: 17.5% German, 15.9% Irish, 13.0% English, 7.0% Italian, 4.4% American
Religion: Six largest groups: 10.6% Catholicism, 3.8% Latter-day Saints, 2.5% Baptist, 2.3% Pentecostal, 1.9% Non-denominational Protestant, 1.5% Methodist/Pietist
Economy: Unemployment rate: 8.8%; Leading industries: 16.1% retail trade; 14.6% health care and social assistance; 12.9% construction; Farms: 838 totaling 150,721 acres; Company size: 0 employ 1,000 or more persons, 0 employ 500 to 999 persons, 12 employ 100 to 499 persons, 1,035 employ less than 100 persons; Business ownership: 1,570 women-owned, 43 Black-owned, n/a Hispanic-owned, n/a Asian-owned
Employment: 11.5% management, business, and financial, 3.2% computer, engineering, and science, 9.7% education, legal, community service, arts, and media, 3.3% healthcare practitioners, 25.2% service, 24.3% sales and office, 14.1% natural resources, construction, and maintenance, 8.7% production, transportation, and material moving
Income: Per capita: $21,537; Median household: $36,548; Average household: $51,573; Households with income of $100,000 or more: 13.0%; Poverty rate: 25.0%
Educational Attainment: High school diploma or higher: 85.4%; Bachelor's degree or higher: 16.2%; Graduate/professional degree or higher: 4.7%
Housing: Homeownership rate: 65.9%; Median home value: $183,600; Median year structure built: 1977; Homeowner vacancy rate: 4.5%; Median gross rent: $900 per month; Rental vacancy rate: 9.8%
Vital Statistics: Birth rate: 111.3 per 10,000 population; Death rate: 117.3 per 10,000 population; Age-adjusted cancer mortality rate: 185.9 deaths per 100,000 population
Health Insurance: 80.9% have insurance; 49.0% have private insurance; 46.7% have public insurance; 19.1% do not have insurance; 15.2% of children under 18 do not have insurance
Health Care: Physicians: 11.6 per 10,000 population; Hospital beds: 7.8 per 10,000 population; Hospital admissions: 593.4 per 10,000 population
Air Quality Index: 98.4% good, 1.6% moderate, 0.0% unhealthy for sensitive individuals, 0.0% unhealthy (percent of days)
Transportation: Commute: 83.9% car, 0.7% public transportation, 3.1% walk, 11.3% work from home; Median travel time to work: 27.5 minutes
Presidential Election: 56.3% Obama, 39.8% Romney (2012)
National and State Parks: Anderson Marsh State Historic Park; Boggs Mountain State Forest; Clear Lake State Park
Additional Information Contacts
Lake Government . . . . (707) 263-2368
http://www.co.lake.ca.us

Lake County Communities

CLEARLAKE (city). Covers a land area of 10.129 square miles and a water area of 0.452 square miles. Located at 38.96° N. Lat; 122.63° W. Long. Elevation is 1,417 feet.
Population: 15,250; Growth (since 2000): 16.0%; Density: 1,505.6 persons per square mile; Race: 73.8% White, 4.0% Black/African American, 1.1% Asian, 2.6% American Indian/Alaska Native, 0.2% Native Hawaiian/Other Pacific Islander, 6.4% Two or more races, 21.3% Hispanic of any race; Average household size: 2.48; Median age: 39.9; Age under 18: 24.0%; Age 65 and over: 15.0%; Males per 100 females: 99.9; Marriage status: 35.2% never married, 39.8% now married, 2.3% separated, 8.4% widowed, 16.6% divorced; Foreign born: 9.2%; Speak English only: 81.7%; With disability: 26.4%; Veterans: 14.3%; Ancestry: 16.1% Irish, 12.6% German, 11.1% English, 7.3% Italian, 4.3% American
Employment: 5.6% management, business, and financial, 0.7% computer, engineering, and science, 9.0% education, legal, community service, arts, and media, 2.2% healthcare practitioners, 30.2% service, 24.8% sales and office, 16.6% natural resources, construction, and maintenance, 10.8% production, transportation, and material moving
Income: Per capita: $16,177; Median household: $25,061; Average household: $35,392; Households with income of $100,000 or more: 4.6%; Poverty rate: 36.3%
Educational Attainment: High school diploma or higher: 80.6%; Bachelor's degree or higher: 6.5%; Graduate/professional degree or higher: 2.1%

School District(s)

Konocti Unified (KG-12)
2012-13 Enrollment: 3,071 . . . . (707) 994-6475
Lake County Office of Education (KG-12)
2012-13 Enrollment: 67. . . . . (707) 262-4100
Housing: Homeownership rate: 53.4%; Median home value: $95,100; Median year structure built: 1975; Homeowner vacancy rate: 5.9%; Median gross rent: $811 per month; Rental vacancy rate: 12.1%
Health Insurance: 78.0% have insurance; 32.3% have private insurance; 56.8% have public insurance; 22.0% do not have insurance; 12.8% of children under 18 do not have insurance
Hospitals: Saint Helena Hospital - Clearlake (32 beds)
Safety: Violent crime rate: 83.6 per 10,000 population; Property crime rate: 461.5 per 10,000 population
Transportation: Commute: 79.3% car, 1.1% public transportation, 5.7% walk, 12.4% work from home; Median travel time to work: 21.1 minutes
Additional Information Contacts
City of Clearlake . . . . (707) 994-8201
http://clearlake.ca.us

CLEARLAKE OAKS (CDP). Covers a land area of 1.977 square miles and a water area of 0.139 square miles. Located at 39.02° N. Lat; 122.66° W. Long. Elevation is 1,335 feet.
Population: 2,359; Growth (since 2000): -1.8%; Density: 1,193.4 persons per square mile; Race: 87.1% White, 2.3% Black/African American, 1.4% Asian, 1.9% American Indian/Alaska Native, 0.0% Native Hawaiian/Other Pacific Islander, 4.7% Two or more races, 8.1% Hispanic of any race; Average household size: 2.00; Median age: 54.9; Age under 18: 13.7%; Age 65 and over: 31.3%; Males per 100 females: 98.9

School District(s)

Konocti Unified (KG-12)
2012-13 Enrollment: 3,071 . . . . (707) 994-6475
Housing: Homeownership rate: 69.9%; Homeowner vacancy rate: 5.9%; Rental vacancy rate: 9.8%

CLEARLAKE RIVIERA (CDP). Covers a land area of 5.224 square miles and a water area of 0.002 square miles. Located at 38.95° N. Lat; 122.72° W. Long. Elevation is 1,755 feet.
Population: 3,090; Growth (since 2000): n/a; Density: 591.5 persons per square mile; Race: 85.5% White, 1.2% Black/African American, 1.3% Asian, 2.4% American Indian/Alaska Native, 0.2% Native Hawaiian/Other Pacific Islander, 4.1% Two or more races, 13.7% Hispanic of any race; Average household size: 2.52; Median age: 40.3; Age under 18: 24.2%; Age 65 and over: 13.2%; Males per 100 females: 96.2; Marriage status: 27.2% never married, 48.7% now married, 3.3% separated, 3.9% widowed, 20.2% divorced; Foreign born: 4.7%; Speak English only: 92.5%; With disability: 16.5%; Veterans: 11.0%; Ancestry: 22.8% German, 15.6% Irish, 13.9% Italian, 13.8% English, 9.2% French
Employment: 5.9% management, business, and financial, 3.0% computer, engineering, and science, 17.9% education, legal, community service, arts, and media, 4.5% healthcare practitioners, 25.6% service, 27.9% sales and office, 5.1% natural resources, construction, and maintenance, 10.0% production, transportation, and material moving
Income: Per capita: $25,869; Median household: $48,781; Average household: $65,011; Households with income of $100,000 or more: 21.0%; Poverty rate: 20.7%
Educational Attainment: High school diploma or higher: 91.9%; Bachelor's degree or higher: 23.8%; Graduate/professional degree or higher: 3.4%

Housing: Homeownership rate: 71.7%; Median home value: $157,000; Median year structure built: 1991; Homeowner vacancy rate: 5.3%; Median gross rent: $1,300 per month; Rental vacancy rate: 9.4%
Health Insurance: 72.8% have insurance; 52.9% have private insurance; 33.0% have public insurance; 27.2% do not have insurance; 24.2% of children under 18 do not have insurance
Transportation: Commute: 91.8% car, 0.0% public transportation, 1.1% walk, 7.1% work from home; Median travel time to work: 26.6 minutes

COBB (CDP). Covers a land area of 4.980 square miles and a water area of 0.009 square miles. Located at 38.84° N. Lat; 122.72° W. Long. Elevation is 2,631 feet.
Population: 1,778; Growth (since 2000): 8.5%; Density: 357.0 persons per square mile; Race: 91.4% White, 0.8% Black/African American, 0.7% Asian, 1.7% American Indian/Alaska Native, 0.1% Native Hawaiian/Other Pacific Islander, 3.8% Two or more races, 6.4% Hispanic of any race; Average household size: 2.25; Median age: 50.1; Age under 18: 17.2%; Age 65 and over: 15.0%; Males per 100 females: 105.1

School District(s)

Kelseyville Unified (KG-12)
2012-13 Enrollment: 1,697 . . . . (707) 279-1511
Housing: Homeownership rate: 78.0%; Homeowner vacancy rate: 3.4%; Rental vacancy rate: 8.9%

FINLEY (unincorporated postal area)
ZCTA: 95435
Covers a land area of 0.154 square miles and a water area of 0 square miles. Located at 39.01° N. Lat; 122.87° W. Long. Elevation is 1,352 feet.
Population: 82; Growth (since 2000): n/a; Density: 531.6 persons per square mile; Race: 43.9% White, 0.0% Black/African American, 0.0% Asian, 1.2% American Indian/Alaska Native, 0.0% Native Hawaiian/Other Pacific Islander, 0.0% Two or more races, 56.1% Hispanic of any race; Average household size: 3.42; Median age: 30.7; Age under 18: 35.4%; Age 65 and over: 9.8%; Males per 100 females: 82.2
Housing: Homeownership rate: 75.0%; Homeowner vacancy rate: 0.0%; Rental vacancy rate: 0.0%

GLENHAVEN (unincorporated postal area)
ZCTA: 95443
Covers a land area of 4.186 square miles and a water area of 0.007 square miles. Located at 39.05° N. Lat; 122.75° W. Long. Elevation is 1,345 feet.
Population: 233; Growth (since 2000): 46.5%; Density: 55.7 persons per square mile; Race: 86.3% White, 4.7% Black/African American, 1.3% Asian, 0.9% American Indian/Alaska Native, 0.4% Native Hawaiian/Other Pacific Islander, 6.0% Two or more races, 7.7% Hispanic of any race; Average household size: 1.85; Median age: 54.7; Age under 18: 7.7%; Age 65 and over: 30.0%; Males per 100 females: 111.8
Housing: Homeownership rate: 58.7%; Homeowner vacancy rate: 6.3%; Rental vacancy rate: 7.1%

HIDDEN VALLEY LAKE (CDP). Covers a land area of 9.734 square miles and a water area of 0.154 square miles. Located at 38.80° N. Lat; 122.55° W. Long. Elevation is 1,188 feet.
Population: 5,579; Growth (since 2000): 47.7%; Density: 573.1 persons per square mile; Race: 86.6% White, 1.1% Black/African American, 1.3% Asian, 1.4% American Indian/Alaska Native, 0.2% Native Hawaiian/Other Pacific Islander, 3.5% Two or more races, 13.1% Hispanic of any race; Average household size: 2.63; Median age: 41.2; Age under 18: 25.1%; Age 65 and over: 13.7%; Males per 100 females: 97.2; Marriage status: 21.4% never married, 60.4% now married, 0.2% separated, 4.0% widowed, 14.2% divorced; Foreign born: 11.6%; Speak English only: 80.6%; With disability: 10.9%; Veterans: 9.3%; Ancestry: 27.0% German, 13.1% Irish, 11.9% English, 7.6% Italian, 4.2% Scottish
Employment: 12.6% management, business, and financial, 5.3% computer, engineering, and science, 11.1% education, legal, community service, arts, and media, 3.2% healthcare practitioners, 24.6% service, 21.2% sales and office, 14.1% natural resources, construction, and maintenance, 7.9% production, transportation, and material moving
Income: Per capita: $25,446; Median household: $63,281; Average household: $69,784; Households with income of $100,000 or more: 21.8%; Poverty rate: 11.8%
Educational Attainment: High school diploma or higher: 93.8%; Bachelor's degree or higher: 25.7%; Graduate/professional degree or higher: 8.7%

Housing: Homeownership rate: 79.6%; Median home value: $195,300; Median year structure built: 1988; Homeowner vacancy rate: 6.1%; Median gross rent: $1,394 per month; Rental vacancy rate: 8.2%
Health Insurance: 89.4% have insurance; 68.9% have private insurance; 34.5% have public insurance; 10.6% do not have insurance; 7.5% of children under 18 do not have insurance
Transportation: Commute: 89.4% car, 1.0% public transportation, 0.5% walk, 7.9% work from home; Median travel time to work: 39.9 minutes

KELSEYVILLE (CDP). Covers a land area of 2.885 square miles and a water area of 0.006 square miles. Located at 38.97° N. Lat; 122.83° W. Long. Elevation is 1,384 feet.
History: Kelseyville was the location of a log cabin built by Salvador and Antonio Vallejo for the vaqueros who herded cattle on their Rancho Laguna de Lu-Pi-Yo-Mi. In 1847 the land was sold to Benjamin Kelsey and others.
Population: 3,353; Growth (since 2000): 14.5%; Density: 1,162.3 persons per square mile; Race: 66.0% White, 0.7% Black/African American, 1.0% Asian, 1.5% American Indian/Alaska Native, 0.1% Native Hawaiian/Other Pacific Islander, 4.3% Two or more races, 39.9% Hispanic of any race; Average household size: 2.74; Median age: 38.0; Age under 18: 26.3%; Age 65 and over: 14.2%; Males per 100 females: 101.3; Marriage status: 35.4% never married, 55.1% now married, 0.9% separated, 4.9% widowed, 4.6% divorced; Foreign born: 23.4%; Speak English only: 65.3%; With disability: 19.5%; Veterans: 6.6%; Ancestry: 19.2% Irish, 14.9% German, 7.0% English, 3.6% Italian, 3.5% Scottish
Employment: 17.3% management, business, and financial, 3.9% computer, engineering, and science, 8.7% education, legal, community service, arts, and media, 1.5% healthcare practitioners, 21.4% service, 14.4% sales and office, 24.9% natural resources, construction, and maintenance, 8.0% production, transportation, and material moving
Income: Per capita: $15,513; Median household: $36,702; Average household: $45,980; Households with income of $100,000 or more: 6.9%; Poverty rate: 39.2%
Educational Attainment: High school diploma or higher: 68.6%; Bachelor's degree or higher: 7.1%; Graduate/professional degree or higher: 0.5%

School District(s)

Kelseyville Unified (KG-12)
2012-13 Enrollment: 1,697 . . . . (707) 279-1511
Housing: Homeownership rate: 64.1%; Median home value: $155,500; Median year structure built: 1978; Homeowner vacancy rate: 1.7%; Median gross rent: $924 per month; Rental vacancy rate: 7.0%
Health Insurance: 78.0% have insurance; 42.3% have private insurance; 39.0% have public insurance; 22.0% do not have insurance; 12.9% of children under 18 do not have insurance
Transportation: Commute: 93.3% car, 0.0% public transportation, 4.8% walk, 1.9% work from home; Median travel time to work: 20.8 minutes

LAKEPORT (city). County seat. Covers a land area of 3.058 square miles and a water area of 0.140 square miles. Located at 39.04° N. Lat; 122.92° W. Long. Elevation is 1,355 feet.
History: Lakeport was once known as Forbestown for William Forbes, who deeded land for a county seat in 1861.
Population: 4,753; Growth (since 2000): -1.4%; Density: 1,554.3 persons per square mile; Race: 82.7% White, 1.0% Black/African American, 2.1% Asian, 3.1% American Indian/Alaska Native, 0.1% Native Hawaiian/Other Pacific Islander, 3.9% Two or more races, 16.8% Hispanic of any race; Average household size: 2.31; Median age: 44.2; Age under 18: 21.7%; Age 65 and over: 20.1%; Males per 100 females: 90.8; Marriage status: 32.3% never married, 39.2% now married, 0.8% separated, 8.7% widowed, 19.8% divorced; Foreign born: 5.0%; Speak English only: 93.9%; With disability: 17.5%; Veterans: 8.2%; Ancestry: 15.8% German, 15.0% English, 10.4% Irish, 5.6% Italian, 5.6% Portuguese
Employment: 18.2% management, business, and financial, 3.9% computer, engineering, and science, 10.4% education, legal, community service, arts, and media, 5.4% healthcare practitioners, 25.4% service, 23.2% sales and office, 6.4% natural resources, construction, and maintenance, 7.1% production, transportation, and material moving
Income: Per capita: $26,435; Median household: $34,764; Average household: $58,286; Households with income of $100,000 or more: 19.3%; Poverty rate: 15.9%
Educational Attainment: High school diploma or higher: 85.4%; Bachelor's degree or higher: 21.4%; Graduate/professional degree or higher: 6.1%

School District(s)

Lake County Office of Education (KG-12)
2012-13 Enrollment: 67. . . . . (707) 262-4100
Lake County Rop
2012-13 Enrollment: n/a . . . . (707) 262-4162
Lakeport Unified (KG-12)
2012-13 Enrollment: 1,536 . . . . (707) 262-3000

Housing: Homeownership rate: 59.8%; Median home value: $204,000; Median year structure built: 1970; Homeowner vacancy rate: 5.1%; Median gross rent: $865 per month; Rental vacancy rate: 8.4%

Health Insurance: 90.2% have insurance; 58.7% have private insurance; 47.2% have public insurance; 9.8% do not have insurance; 5.9% of children under 18 do not have insurance

Hospitals: Sutter Lakeside Hospital (25 beds)

Safety: Violent crime rate: 30.0 per 10,000 population; Property crime rate: 581.9 per 10,000 population

Newspapers: Lake County Record-Bee (daily circulation 7300); Lake County Record-Bee (weekly circulation 1800)

Transportation: Commute: 86.9% car, 0.0% public transportation, 1.6% walk, 9.3% work from home; Median travel time to work: 28.4 minutes

Additional Information Contacts

City of Lakeport. . . . . (707) 263-5615
http://www.cityoflakeport.com

LOWER LAKE (CDP). Covers a land area of 2.667 square miles and a water area of 0.025 square miles. Located at 38.91° N. Lat; 122.61° W. Long. Elevation is 1,371 feet.

History: The community of Lower Lake was settled in 1858.

Population: 1,294; Growth (since 2000): -26.3%; Density: 485.3 persons per square mile; Race: 79.7% White, 1.5% Black/African American, 1.0% Asian, 1.4% American Indian/Alaska Native, 0.1% Native Hawaiian/Other Pacific Islander, 6.6% Two or more races, 16.9% Hispanic of any race; Average household size: 2.34; Median age: 46.5; Age under 18: 20.0%; Age 65 and over: 18.2%; Males per 100 females: 99.7

School District(s)

Konocti Unified (KG-12)
2012-13 Enrollment: 3,071 . . . . (707) 994-6475

Housing: Homeownership rate: 70.5%; Homeowner vacancy rate: 6.2%; Rental vacancy rate: 13.7%

LUCERNE (CDP). Covers a land area of 4.978 square miles and a water area of 0.010 square miles. Located at 39.06° N. Lat; 122.77° W. Long. Elevation is 1,329 feet.

Population: 3,067; Growth (since 2000): 6.9%; Density: 616.2 persons per square mile; Race: 84.2% White, 2.0% Black/African American, 0.8% Asian, 3.4% American Indian/Alaska Native, 0.3% Native Hawaiian/Other Pacific Islander, 6.3% Two or more races, 12.0% Hispanic of any race; Average household size: 2.21; Median age: 48.5; Age under 18: 18.1%; Age 65 and over: 21.4%; Males per 100 females: 100.5; Marriage status: 26.8% never married, 42.0% now married, 4.2% separated, 12.4% widowed, 18.7% divorced; Foreign born: 2.0%; Speak English only: 94.8%; With disability: 23.8%; Veterans: 17.2%; Ancestry: 21.7% Irish, 20.4% English, 12.4% German, 3.4% Australian, 2.7% Dutch

Employment: 10.7% management, business, and financial, 0.0% computer, engineering, and science, 9.8% education, legal, community service, arts, and media, 2.3% healthcare practitioners, 31.8% service, 33.0% sales and office, 11.4% natural resources, construction, and maintenance, 1.0% production, transportation, and material moving

Income: Per capita: $13,450; Median household: $25,375; Average household: $34,149; Households with income of $100,000 or more: 4.3%; Poverty rate: 42.3%

Educational Attainment: High school diploma or higher: 85.0%; Bachelor's degree or higher: 7.9%; Graduate/professional degree or higher: 2.8%

School District(s)

Lucerne Elementary (KG-08)
2012-13 Enrollment: 249. . . . . (707) 274-5578

Housing: Homeownership rate: 61.8%; Median home value: $118,600; Median year structure built: 1971; Homeowner vacancy rate: 3.8%; Median gross rent: $875 per month; Rental vacancy rate: 8.0%

Health Insurance: 65.8% have insurance; 29.6% have private insurance; 45.6% have public insurance; 34.2% do not have insurance; 54.3% of children under 18 do not have insurance

Transportation: Commute: 91.9% car, 0.0% public transportation, 3.4% walk, 3.2% work from home; Median travel time to work: 26.9 minutes

---

MIDDLETOWN (CDP). Covers a land area of 1.844 square miles and a water area of 0 square miles. Located at 38.75° N. Lat; 122.62° W. Long. Elevation is 1,099 feet.

History: Middletown was so named because of its location midway between Lower Lake and Calistoga. It developed as a center for poultry and dairy farms in the Loconomi Valley.

Population: 1,323; Growth (since 2000): 29.7%; Density: 717.4 persons per square mile; Race: 74.5% White, 0.4% Black/African American, 1.4% Asian, 2.1% American Indian/Alaska Native, 0.0% Native Hawaiian/Other Pacific Islander, 4.7% Two or more races, 31.2% Hispanic of any race; Average household size: 2.59; Median age: 37.4; Age under 18: 28.4%; Age 65 and over: 11.3%; Males per 100 females: 102.9

School District(s)

Middletown Unified (KG-12)
2012-13 Enrollment: 1,641 . . . . (707) 987-4100

Housing: Homeownership rate: 49.5%; Homeowner vacancy rate: 3.8%; Rental vacancy rate: 4.1%

Newspapers: Middletown Times-Star (weekly circulation 2500)

NICE (CDP). Covers a land area of 1.728 square miles and a water area of 0 square miles. Located at 39.13° N. Lat; 122.85° W. Long. Elevation is 1,362 feet.

History: Bloody Island Massacre Historic Marker to Northwest.

Population: 2,731; Growth (since 2000): 8.8%; Density: 1,580.9 persons per square mile; Race: 80.1% White, 2.4% Black/African American, 1.5% Asian, 5.8% American Indian/Alaska Native, 0.3% Native Hawaiian/Other Pacific Islander, 5.4% Two or more races, 14.1% Hispanic of any race; Average household size: 2.20; Median age: 46.6; Age under 18: 18.5%; Age 65 and over: 18.8%; Males per 100 females: 99.2; Marriage status: 27.0% never married, 44.0% now married, 5.5% separated, 9.8% widowed, 19.2% divorced; Foreign born: 4.0%; Speak English only: 96.0%; With disability: 25.3%; Veterans: 22.7%; Ancestry: 25.1% Irish, 23.6% German, 18.9% English, 5.8% French, 4.7% Italian

Employment: 16.9% management, business, and financial, 2.2% computer, engineering, and science, 6.0% education, legal, community service, arts, and media, 3.2% healthcare practitioners, 39.4% service, 26.0% sales and office, 1.4% natural resources, construction, and maintenance, 4.8% production, transportation, and material moving

Income: Per capita: $17,019; Median household: $24,138; Average household: $32,269; Households with income of $100,000 or more: 1.0%; Poverty rate: 24.7%

Educational Attainment: High school diploma or higher: 85.6%; Bachelor's degree or higher: 9.0%; Graduate/professional degree or higher: 2.7%

Housing: Homeownership rate: 57.7%; Median home value: $154,700; Median year structure built: 1973; Homeowner vacancy rate: 2.7%; Median gross rent: $647 per month; Rental vacancy rate: 7.6%

Health Insurance: 80.0% have insurance; 35.7% have private insurance; 54.0% have public insurance; 20.0% do not have insurance; 0.0% of children under 18 do not have insurance

Transportation: Commute: 86.1% car, 1.5% public transportation, 1.5% walk, 10.1% work from home; Median travel time to work: 26.9 minutes

---

NORTH LAKEPORT (CDP). Covers a land area of 3.845 square miles and a water area of 2.705 square miles. Located at 39.09° N. Lat; 122.91° W. Long.

Population: 3,314; Growth (since 2000): 15.1%; Density: 861.9 persons per square mile; Race: 81.0% White, 0.8% Black/African American, 1.2% Asian, 3.8% American Indian/Alaska Native, 0.1% Native Hawaiian/Other Pacific Islander, 4.8% Two or more races, 17.2% Hispanic of any race; Average household size: 2.34; Median age: 44.5; Age under 18: 21.6%; Age 65 and over: 20.4%; Males per 100 females: 96.1; Marriage status: 24.2% never married, 55.5% now married, 2.7% separated, 7.0% widowed, 13.3% divorced; Foreign born: 10.8%; Speak English only: 81.9%; With disability: 15.1%; Veterans: 15.0%; Ancestry: 22.6% German, 13.0% Irish, 9.4% English, 5.8% French, 5.5% Italian

Employment: 9.1% management, business, and financial, 4.0% computer, engineering, and science, 3.2% education, legal, community service, arts, and media, 3.5% healthcare practitioners, 17.4% service, 44.4% sales and office, 13.7% natural resources, construction, and maintenance, 4.7% production, transportation, and material moving

Income: Per capita: $29,342; Median household: $52,990; Average household: $66,091; Households with income of $100,000 or more: 24.4%; Poverty rate: 17.3%

Educational Attainment: High school diploma or higher: 85.1%; Bachelor's degree or higher: 18.5%; Graduate/professional degree or higher: 5.4%
Housing: Homeownership rate: 67.3%; Median home value: $174,200; Median year structure built: 1982; Homeowner vacancy rate: 4.6%; Median gross rent: $865 per month; Rental vacancy rate: 11.7%
Health Insurance: 90.8% have insurance; 66.8% have private insurance; 41.5% have public insurance; 9.2% do not have insurance; 1.2% of children under 18 do not have insurance
Transportation: Commute: 85.3% car, 0.0% public transportation, 7.2% walk, 7.0% work from home; Median travel time to work: 20.6 minutes

SODA BAY (CDP). Covers a land area of 1.285 square miles and a water area of 0 square miles. Located at 39.00° N. Lat; 122.78° W. Long. Elevation is 1,398 feet.
Population: 1,016; Growth (since 2000): n/a; Density: 790.7 persons per square mile; Race: 83.0% White, 1.6% Black/African American, 1.2% Asian, 1.4% American Indian/Alaska Native, 0.0% Native Hawaiian/Other Pacific Islander, 2.9% Two or more races, 16.8% Hispanic of any race; Average household size: 2.18; Median age: 54.0; Age under 18: 16.6%; Age 65 and over: 25.7%; Males per 100 females: 99.6
Housing: Homeownership rate: 72.3%; Homeowner vacancy rate: 5.8%; Rental vacancy rate: 14.1%

SPRING VALLEY (CDP). Covers a land area of 4.935 square miles and a water area of 0.040 square miles. Located at 39.08° N. Lat; 122.58° W. Long.
Population: 845; Growth (since 2000): n/a; Density: 171.2 persons per square mile; Race: 90.7% White, 1.8% Black/African American, 0.7% Asian, 1.2% American Indian/Alaska Native, 0.4% Native Hawaiian/Other Pacific Islander, 2.5% Two or more races, 8.4% Hispanic of any race; Average household size: 2.34; Median age: 51.9; Age under 18: 14.8%; Age 65 and over: 23.3%; Males per 100 females: 106.6
Housing: Homeownership rate: 88.9%; Homeowner vacancy rate: 4.1%; Rental vacancy rate: 2.4%

UPPER LAKE (CDP). Covers a land area of 1.682 square miles and a water area of 0.005 square miles. Located at 39.17° N. Lat; 122.91° W. Long. Elevation is 1,345 feet.
History: Upper Lake developed as a trading and resort village.
Population: 1,052; Growth (since 2000): 6.4%; Density: 625.3 persons per square mile; Race: 80.0% White, 0.7% Black/African American, 0.7% Asian, 3.1% American Indian/Alaska Native, 0.0% Native Hawaiian/Other Pacific Islander, 5.6% Two or more races, 23.0% Hispanic of any race; Average household size: 2.67; Median age: 36.3; Age under 18: 26.6%; Age 65 and over: 13.1%; Males per 100 females: 91.3

School District(s)

Upper Lake Union Elementary (KG-08)
2012-13 Enrollment: 533. . . . . (707) 275-2357
Upper Lake Union High (09-12)
2012-13 Enrollment: 351. . . . . (707) 275-2655

Housing: Homeownership rate: 68.5%; Homeowner vacancy rate: 3.2%; Rental vacancy rate: 6.8%

WITTER SPRINGS (unincorporated postal area)
ZCTA: 95493
Covers a land area of 4.531 square miles and a water area of 0.023 square miles. Located at 39.18° N. Lat; 122.97° W. Long..
Population: 198; Growth (since 2000): -12.8%; Density: 43.7 persons per square mile; Race: 96.5% White, 0.0% Black/African American, 0.0% Asian, 1.5% American Indian/Alaska Native, 0.0% Native Hawaiian/Other Pacific Islander, 1.0% Two or more races, 3.5% Hispanic of any race; Average household size: 2.28; Median age: 53.4; Age under 18: 17.2%; Age 65 and over: 26.3%; Males per 100 females: 117.6
Housing: Homeownership rate: 85.0%; Homeowner vacancy rate: 0.0%; Rental vacancy rate: 0.0%

Lassen County

Located in northeastern California, on a high volcanic plateau extending east from the Cascade Range; the Sierra Nevada Range is along the southwest and south borders; includes Modoc, Plumas, and Tahoe National Forests, and Eagle and Honey Lakes; dra ined by the Pit and Susan Rivers. Covers a land area of 4,541.184 square miles, a water area of 178.935 square miles, and is located in the Pacific Time Zone at 40.72° N. Lat., 120.63° W. Long. The county was founded in 1864. County seat is Susanville.

Lassen County is part of the Susanville, CA Micropolitan Statistical Area. The entire metro area includes: Lassen County, CA

Weather Station: Doyle 4 SSE Elevation: 4,390 feet

	Jan	Feb	Mar	Apr	May	Jun	Jul	Aug	Sep	Oct	Nov	Dec
High	43	48	56	62	71	80	88	87	79	67	52	42
Low	24	27	31	34	40	45	50	48	43	35	28	23
Precip	2.2	2.3	1.9	0.9	1.0	0.7	0.4	0.3	0.7	1.0	2.3	2.4
Snow	7.3	4.0	3.9	1.5	0.1	tr	0.0	0.0	0.2	0.2	2.5	6.8

High and Low temperatures in degrees Fahrenheit; Precipitation and Snow in inches

Population: 34,895; Growth (since 2000): 3.2%; Density: 7.7 persons per square mile; Race: 73.2% White, 8.1% Black/African American, 1.0% Asian, 3.5% American Indian/Alaska Native, 0.5% Native Hawaiian/Other Pacific Islander, 3.5% two or more races, 17.5% Hispanic of any race; Average household size: 2.50; Median age: 37.1; Age under 18: 18.0%; Age 65 and over: 10.0%; Males per 100 females: 179.6; Marriage status: 36.2% never married, 44.0% now married, 2.6% separated, 5.1% widowed, 14.6% divorced; Foreign born: 7.0%; Speak English only: 82.3%; With disability: 17.3%; Veterans: 10.9%; Ancestry: 16.4% Irish, 15.0% German, 8.8% English, 4.4% Italian, 4.2% American
Religion: Six largest groups: 9.7% Catholicism, 3.8% Latter-day Saints, 2.2% Pentecostal, 2.1% Methodist/Pietist, 1.9% Non-denominational Protestant, 1.5% Baptist
Economy: Unemployment rate: 7.2%; Leading industries: 19.1% retail trade; 14.7% health care and social assistance; 11.1% accommodation and food services; Farms: 448 totaling 482,680 acres; Company size: 0 employ 1,000 or more persons, 0 employ 500 to 999 persons, 5 employ 100 to 499 persons, 409 employ less than 100 persons; Business ownership: 372 women-owned, n/a Black-owned, n/a Hispanic-owned, n/a Asian-owned
Employment: 12.1% management, business, and financial, 2.1% computer, engineering, and science, 13.8% education, legal, community service, arts, and media, 4.9% healthcare practitioners, 28.7% service, 19.6% sales and office, 8.8% natural resources, construction, and maintenance, 10.1% production, transportation, and material moving
Income: Per capita: $19,931; Median household: $53,107; Average household: $63,149; Households with income of $100,000 or more: 17.4%; Poverty rate: 16.9%
Educational Attainment: High school diploma or higher: 79.4%; Bachelor's degree or higher: 13.1%; Graduate/professional degree or higher: 4.1%
Housing: Homeownership rate: 65.5%; Median home value: $185,500; Median year structure built: 1977; Homeowner vacancy rate: 3.6%; Median gross rent: $867 per month; Rental vacancy rate: 9.3%
Vital Statistics: Birth rate: 89.9 per 10,000 population; Death rate: 65.9 per 10,000 population; Age-adjusted cancer mortality rate: 149.6 deaths per 100,000 population
Health Insurance: 89.5% have insurance; 66.6% have private insurance; 36.3% have public insurance; 10.5% do not have insurance; 4.3% of children under 18 do not have insurance
Health Care: Physicians: 8.0 per 10,000 population; Hospital beds: 7.3 per 10,000 population; Hospital admissions: 394.6 per 10,000 population
Transportation: Commute: 87.1% car, 1.3% public transportation, 5.3% walk, 4.6% work from home; Median travel time to work: 19.4 minutes
Presidential Election: 28.7% Obama, 68.5% Romney (2012)
National and State Parks: Ash Creek State Wildlife Area; Biscar State Wildlife Area; Doyle State Wildlife Area; Hayden Hill-Silva Flat State Game Refuge; Honey Lake State Wildlife Area; Lassen National Forest
Additional Information Contacts
Lassen Government . . . . (530) 251-8333
http://www.co.lassen.ca.us

Lassen County Communities

BIEBER (CDP). Covers a land area of 1.637 square miles and a water area of 0.057 square miles. Located at 41.13° N. Lat; 121.14° W. Long. Elevation is 4,124 feet.
Population: 312; Growth (since 2000): n/a; Density: 190.6 persons per square mile; Race: 84.6% White, 0.0% Black/African American, 0.3% Asian, 4.8% American Indian/Alaska Native, 0.0% Native Hawaiian/Other Pacific Islander, 2.6% Two or more races, 23.1% Hispanic of any race;

Average household size: 2.54; Median age: 38.4; Age under 18: 25.0%; Age 65 and over: 13.5%; Males per 100 females: 93.8

School District(s)

Big Valley Joint Unified (KG-12)
2012-13 Enrollment: 200. . . . . (530) 294-5266

Housing: Homeownership rate: 73.1%; Homeowner vacancy rate: 4.2%; Rental vacancy rate: 10.8%

CLEAR CREEK (CDP). Covers a land area of 1.133 square miles and a water area of 0.006 square miles. Located at 40.31° N. Lat; 121.06° W. Long. Elevation is 4,970 feet.

Population: 169; Growth (since 2000): n/a; Density: 149.2 persons per square mile; Race: 88.2% White, 0.0% Black/African American, 0.0% Asian, 3.0% American Indian/Alaska Native, 1.2% Native Hawaiian/Other Pacific Islander, 7.1% Two or more races, 8.9% Hispanic of any race; Average household size: 2.32; Median age: 49.7; Age under 18: 17.2%; Age 65 and over: 20.1%; Males per 100 females: 101.2

Housing: Homeownership rate: 75.4%; Homeowner vacancy rate: 5.2%; Rental vacancy rate: 14.3%

DOYLE (CDP). Covers a land area of 6.107 square miles and a water area of <.001 square miles. Located at 40.03° N. Lat; 120.12° W. Long. Elevation is 4,275 feet.

Population: 678; Growth (since 2000): n/a; Density: 111.0 persons per square mile; Race: 86.0% White, 2.1% Black/African American, 0.4% Asian, 5.5% American Indian/Alaska Native, 0.3% Native Hawaiian/Other Pacific Islander, 4.0% Two or more races, 8.1% Hispanic of any race; Average household size: 2.60; Median age: 41.6; Age under 18: 23.2%; Age 65 and over: 12.7%; Males per 100 females: 104.2

School District(s)

Sbe - Long Valley Charter (KG-12)
2012-13 Enrollment: 381. . . . . (530) 827-2395

Housing: Homeownership rate: 68.2%; Homeowner vacancy rate: 6.8%; Rental vacancy rate: 10.8%

HERLONG (CDP). Covers a land area of 1.628 square miles and a water area of 0 square miles. Located at 40.14° N. Lat; 120.14° W. Long. Elevation is 4,114 feet.

Population: 298; Growth (since 2000): n/a; Density: 183.0 persons per square mile; Race: 62.8% White, 12.8% Black/African American, 0.3% Asian, 5.4% American Indian/Alaska Native, 1.0% Native Hawaiian/Other Pacific Islander, 14.8% Two or more races, 15.4% Hispanic of any race; Average household size: 2.53; Median age: 31.5; Age under 18: 30.5%; Age 65 and over: 3.0%; Males per 100 females: 101.4

School District(s)

Fort Sage Unified (KG-12)
2012-13 Enrollment: 299. . . . . (530) 827-2129

Housing: Homeownership rate: n/a; Homeowner vacancy rate: 0.0%; Rental vacancy rate: 14.1%

JANESVILLE (CDP). Covers a land area of 13.187 square miles and a water area of 0.012 square miles. Located at 40.27° N. Lat; 120.55° W. Long. Elevation is 4,239 feet.

Population: 1,408; Growth (since 2000): n/a; Density: 106.8 persons per square mile; Race: 91.1% White, 0.9% Black/African American, 0.8% Asian, 2.3% American Indian/Alaska Native, 0.2% Native Hawaiian/Other Pacific Islander, 2.8% Two or more races, 8.4% Hispanic of any race; Average household size: 2.62; Median age: 45.0; Age under 18: 24.4%; Age 65 and over: 13.9%; Males per 100 females: 106.1

School District(s)

Janesville Union Elementary (KG-08)
2012-13 Enrollment: 357. . . . . (530) 253-3660

Housing: Homeownership rate: 86.0%; Homeowner vacancy rate: 2.5%; Rental vacancy rate: 9.6%

JOHNSTONVILLE (CDP). Covers a land area of 8.357 square miles and a water area of 0.041 square miles. Located at 40.38° N. Lat; 120.59° W. Long. Elevation is 4,131 feet.

Population: 1,024; Growth (since 2000): n/a; Density: 122.5 persons per square mile; Race: 90.7% White, 0.7% Black/African American, 1.3% Asian, 1.6% American Indian/Alaska Native, 0.0% Native Hawaiian/Other Pacific Islander, 3.2% Two or more races, 7.1% Hispanic of any race; Average household size: 2.77; Median age: 39.9; Age under 18: 28.3%; Age 65 and over: 12.8%; Males per 100 females: 103.6

Housing: Homeownership rate: 77.3%; Homeowner vacancy rate: 1.0%; Rental vacancy rate: 1.2%

LITCHFIELD (CDP). Covers a land area of 3.945 square miles and a water area of 0 square miles. Located at 40.39° N. Lat; 120.38° W. Long. Elevation is 4,065 feet.

Population: 195; Growth (since 2000): n/a; Density: 49.4 persons per square mile; Race: 90.3% White, 0.0% Black/African American, 0.0% Asian, 0.0% American Indian/Alaska Native, 0.0% Native Hawaiian/Other Pacific Islander, 2.6% Two or more races, 12.8% Hispanic of any race; Average household size: 2.53; Median age: 43.9; Age under 18: 23.6%; Age 65 and over: 15.4%; Males per 100 females: 97.0

School District(s)

Shaffer Union Elementary (KG-08)
2012-13 Enrollment: 189. . . . . (530) 254-6577

Housing: Homeownership rate: 67.6%; Homeowner vacancy rate: 0.0%; Rental vacancy rate: 24.2%

MADELINE (unincorporated postal area)

ZCTA: 96119

Covers a land area of 162.142 square miles and a water area of 2.037 square miles. Located at 41.02° N. Lat; 120.52° W. Long. Elevation is 5,321 feet.

Population: 90; Growth (since 2000): 28.6%; Density: 0.6 persons per square mile; Race: 86.7% White, 5.6% Black/African American, 0.0% Asian, 1.1% American Indian/Alaska Native, 0.0% Native Hawaiian/Other Pacific Islander, 1.1% Two or more races, 11.1% Hispanic of any race; Average household size: 2.50; Median age: 54.0; Age under 18: 16.7%; Age 65 and over: 26.7%; Males per 100 females: 136.8

Housing: Homeownership rate: 75.0%; Homeowner vacancy rate: 0.0%; Rental vacancy rate: 10.0%

MILFORD (CDP). Covers a land area of 5.292 square miles and a water area of 0.006 square miles. Located at 40.15° N. Lat; 120.37° W. Long. Elevation is 4,222 feet.

Population: 167; Growth (since 2000): n/a; Density: 31.6 persons per square mile; Race: 89.8% White, 0.6% Black/African American, 0.6% Asian, 0.6% American Indian/Alaska Native, 0.6% Native Hawaiian/Other Pacific Islander, 5.4% Two or more races, 6.6% Hispanic of any race; Average household size: 2.42; Median age: 43.8; Age under 18: 19.8%; Age 65 and over: 12.6%; Males per 100 females: 111.4

Housing: Homeownership rate: 69.5%; Homeowner vacancy rate: 4.0%; Rental vacancy rate: 8.7%

NUBIEBER (CDP). Covers a land area of 0.749 square miles and a water area of 0.007 square miles. Located at 41.10° N. Lat; 121.18° W. Long. Elevation is 4,121 feet.

Population: 50; Growth (since 2000): n/a; Density: 66.8 persons per square mile; Race: 52.0% White, 0.0% Black/African American, 0.0% Asian, 26.0% American Indian/Alaska Native, 0.0% Native Hawaiian/Other Pacific Islander, 10.0% Two or more races, 20.0% Hispanic of any race; Average household size: 2.78; Median age: 35.0; Age under 18: 24.0%; Age 65 and over: 8.0%; Males per 100 females: 163.2

Housing: Homeownership rate: 55.6%; Homeowner vacancy rate: 0.0%; Rental vacancy rate: 11.1%

PATTON VILLAGE (CDP). Covers a land area of 3.322 square miles and a water area of 0 square miles. Located at 40.14° N. Lat; 120.18° W. Long. Elevation is 4,111 feet.

Population: 702; Growth (since 2000): n/a; Density: 211.3 persons per square mile; Race: 78.6% White, 6.8% Black/African American, 0.6% Asian, 3.8% American Indian/Alaska Native, 0.7% Native Hawaiian/Other Pacific Islander, 6.8% Two or more races, 8.8% Hispanic of any race; Average household size: 2.43; Median age: 44.3; Age under 18: 21.9%; Age 65 and over: 17.2%; Males per 100 females: 97.7

Housing: Homeownership rate: 62.6%; Homeowner vacancy rate: 5.2%; Rental vacancy rate: 15.0%

RAVENDALE (unincorporated postal area)

ZCTA: 96123

Covers a land area of 204.448 square miles and a water area of 2.542 square miles. Located at 40.73° N. Lat; 120.40° W. Long. Elevation is 5,305 feet.

Population: 48; Growth (since 2000): 9.1%; Density: 0.2 persons per square mile; Race: 83.3% White, 0.0% Black/African American, 2.1%

Asian, 2.1% American Indian/Alaska Native, 0.0% Native Hawaiian/Other Pacific Islander, 2.1% Two or more races, 12.5% Hispanic of any race; Average household size: 2.40; Median age: 44.5; Age under 18: 18.7%; Age 65 and over: 18.8%; Males per 100 females: 108.7

Housing: Homeownership rate: 50.0%; Homeowner vacancy rate: 9.1%; Rental vacancy rate: 16.7%

SPAULDING (CDP). Covers a land area of 3.329 square miles and a water area of 0 square miles. Located at 40.66° N. Lat; 120.79° W. Long.

Population: 178; Growth (since 2000): n/a; Density: 53.5 persons per square mile; Race: 94.4% White, 0.0% Black/African American, 0.6% Asian, 1.7% American Indian/Alaska Native, 0.0% Native Hawaiian/Other Pacific Islander, 2.8% Two or more races, 3.4% Hispanic of any race; Average household size: 1.89; Median age: 63.0; Age under 18: 5.6%; Age 65 and over: 44.4%; Males per 100 females: 107.0

Housing: Homeownership rate: 86.1%; Homeowner vacancy rate: 18.0%; Rental vacancy rate: 53.3%

STANDISH (unincorporated postal area)

ZCTA: 96128

Covers a land area of 31.415 square miles and a water area of 0.046 square miles. Located at 40.36° N. Lat; 120.41° W. Long. Elevation is 4,049 feet.

Population: 752; Growth (since 2000): 93.8%; Density: 23.9 persons per square mile; Race: 86.0% White, 0.0% Black/African American, 0.3% Asian, 3.7% American Indian/Alaska Native, 0.0% Native Hawaiian/Other Pacific Islander, 4.5% Two or more races, 14.4% Hispanic of any race; Average household size: 2.64; Median age: 39.1; Age under 18: 24.6%; Age 65 and over: 11.0%; Males per 100 females: 119.9

Housing: Homeownership rate: 75.2%; Homeowner vacancy rate: 3.8%; Rental vacancy rate: 7.0%

SUSANVILLE (city). County seat. Covers a land area of 7.931 square miles and a water area of 0.086 square miles. Located at 40.43° N. Lat; 120.63° W. Long. Elevation is 4,186 feet.

History: Susanville had its beginnings in 1853 when Isaac N. Roop, alone and penniless, arrived on horseback, staked out a claim, and built a cabin. The following year Peter Lassen and a handful of prospectors struck gold. The town of Susanville was created in 1856 by the residents, who also set up the independent territory of Nataqua. The territory was short-lived, as California claimed jurisdiction over the area and reinforced its claim in the Sagebrush War. The boundary dispute between California and Nevada was settled, but hard feelings persisted until 1864 when the California Legislature created Lassen County with Susanville as the county seat.

Population: 17,947; Growth (since 2000): 32.5%; Density: 2,262.9 persons per square mile; Race: 62.8% White, 12.5% Black/African American, 1.1% Asian, 3.4% American Indian/Alaska Native, 0.6% Native Hawaiian/Other Pacific Islander, 3.2% Two or more races, 23.7% Hispanic of any race; Average household size: 2.46; Median age: 33.6; Age under 18: 14.3%; Age 65 and over: 6.6%; Males per 100 females: 273.7; Marriage status: 42.0% never married, 36.8% now married, 3.0% separated, 4.7% widowed, 16.5% divorced; Foreign born: 7.4%; Speak English only: 78.0%; With disability: 17.7%; Veterans: 8.8%; Ancestry: 15.5% Irish, 14.2% German, 7.2% English, 4.5% American, 4.1% Portuguese

Employment: 9.2% management, business, and financial, 1.6% computer, engineering, and science, 18.5% education, legal, community service, arts, and media, 7.5% healthcare practitioners, 37.2% service, 18.2% sales and office, 3.6% natural resources, construction, and maintenance, 4.2% production, transportation, and material moving

Income: Per capita: $16,530; Median household: $50,735; Average household: $59,975; Households with income of $100,000 or more: 14.7%; Poverty rate: 22.1%

Educational Attainment: High school diploma or higher: 74.8%; Bachelor's degree or higher: 10.4%; Graduate/professional degree or higher: 3.2%

School District(s)

Johnstonville Elementary (KG-08)
2012-13 Enrollment: 226. . . . . (530) 257-2471
Lassen County Office of Education (KG-12)
2012-13 Enrollment: 41. . . . . (530) 257-2196
Lassen Rop
2012-13 Enrollment: n/a . . . . (530) 252-1673
Lassen Union High (07-12)
2012-13 Enrollment: 981. . . . . (530) 257-5134
Richmond Elementary (KG-08)
2012-13 Enrollment: 233. . . . . (530) 257-2338
Susanville Elementary (KG-08)
2012-13 Enrollment: 1,036 . . . . (530) 257-8200

Two-year College(s)

Lassen Community College (Public)
Fall 2013 Enrollment: 2,494 . . . . (530) 257-6181
2013-14 Tuition: In-state $1,127; Out-of-state $5,903

Housing: Homeownership rate: 51.5%; Median home value: $171,400; Median year structure built: 1976; Homeowner vacancy rate: 3.4%; Median gross rent: $813 per month; Rental vacancy rate: 7.7%

Health Insurance: 90.9% have insurance; 64.7% have private insurance; 37.3% have public insurance; 9.1% do not have insurance; 3.0% of children under 18 do not have insurance

Hospitals: Banner Lassen Medical Center

Safety: Violent crime rate: 51.0 per 10,000 population; Property crime rate: 236.0 per 10,000 population

Newspapers: Lassen County Times (weekly circulation 11000)

Transportation: Commute: 83.0% car, 1.8% public transportation, 8.9% walk, 4.6% work from home; Median travel time to work: 15.6 minutes

Additional Information Contacts

City of Susanville. . . . . (530) 257-1000
http://www.cityofsusanville.org

TERMO (unincorporated postal area)

ZCTA: 96132

Covers a land area of 388.396 square miles and a water area of 2.301 square miles. Located at 40.91° N. Lat; 120.40° W. Long. Elevation is 5,305 feet.

Population: 119; Growth (since 2000): 95.1%; Density: 0.3 persons per square mile; Race: 76.5% White, 1.7% Black/African American, 0.0% Asian, 0.8% American Indian/Alaska Native, 0.8% Native Hawaiian/Other Pacific Islander, 10.1% Two or more races, 16.8% Hispanic of any race; Average household size: 2.05; Median age: 56.3; Age under 18: 15.1%; Age 65 and over: 31.1%; Males per 100 females: 105.2

School District(s)

Ravendale-Termo Elementary (KG-12)
2012-13 Enrollment: 335. . . . . (530) 257-2196

Housing: Homeownership rate: 69.0%; Homeowner vacancy rate: 9.1%; Rental vacancy rate: 0.0%

WENDEL (unincorporated postal area)

ZCTA: 96136

Covers a land area of 148.133 square miles and a water area of 0.560 square miles. Located at 40.35° N. Lat; 120.08° W. Long. Elevation is 4,012 feet.

Population: 104; Growth (since 2000): -30.2%; Density: 0.7 persons per square mile; Race: 93.3% White, 0.0% Black/African American, 1.0% Asian, 1.0% American Indian/Alaska Native, 0.0% Native Hawaiian/Other Pacific Islander, 2.9% Two or more races, 11.5% Hispanic of any race; Average household size: 2.21; Median age: 45.3; Age under 18: 20.2%; Age 65 and over: 13.5%; Males per 100 females: 116.7

Housing: Homeownership rate: 57.5%; Homeowner vacancy rate: 6.7%; Rental vacancy rate: 9.1%

WESTWOOD (CDP). Covers a land area of 5.436 square miles and a water area of 0.074 square miles. Located at 40.31° N. Lat; 121.00° W. Long. Elevation is 5,128 feet.

History: Westwood was created as a company town around the mills of the Red River Lumber Company.

Population: 1,647; Growth (since 2000): -17.6%; Density: 303.0 persons per square mile; Race: 86.8% White, 0.2% Black/African American, 0.6% Asian, 6.3% American Indian/Alaska Native, 0.1% Native Hawaiian/Other Pacific Islander, 3.0% Two or more races, 10.9% Hispanic of any race; Average household size: 2.30; Median age: 41.3; Age under 18: 23.9%; Age 65 and over: 13.4%; Males per 100 females: 104.9

School District(s)

Westwood Unified (KG-12)
2012-13 Enrollment: 367. . . . . (530) 256-2311

Housing: Homeownership rate: 61.5%; Homeowner vacancy rate: 5.3%; Rental vacancy rate: 15.1%

Newspapers: Westwood Pine Press (weekly circulation 1400)

Los Angeles County

Located in southern California; bounded on the west by the Pacific Ocean; mountainous on the north, east, and south, including the San Gabriel, Santa Monica, and Santa Susana Mountains; includes Antelope Valley (part of the Mojave Desert), and Santa Catalina Island. Covers a land area of 4,057.883 square miles, a water area of 693.058 square miles, and is located in the Pacific Time Zone at 34.20° N. Lat., 118.26° W. Long. The county was founded in 1850. County seat is Los Angeles.

Los Angeles County is part of the Los Angeles-Long Beach-Anaheim, CA Metropolitan Statistical Area. The entire metro area includes: Anaheim-Santa Ana-Irvine, CA Metropolitan Division (Orange County, CA); Los Angeles-Long Beach-Glendale, CA Metropolitan Division (Los Angeles County, CA)

Weather Station: Canoga Park Pierce College Elevation: 790 feet

	Jan	Feb	Mar	Apr	May	Jun	Jul	Aug	Sep	Oct	Nov	Dec
High	69	70	73	78	82	89	95	97	93	85	75	69
Low	40	41	43	45	50	54	57	58	55	50	42	39
Precip	3.7	5.2	3.3	1.0	0.4	0.1	0.0	0.1	0.2	0.9	1.4	2.6
Snow	0.0	tr	0.0	0.0	0.0	0.0	0.0	0.0	0.0	0.0	0.0	tr

High and Low temperatures in degrees Fahrenheit; Precipitation and Snow in inches

Weather Station: Culver City Elevation: 55 feet

	Jan	Feb	Mar	Apr	May	Jun	Jul	Aug	Sep	Oct	Nov	Dec
High	66	67	69	72	73	76	80	80	79	76	70	66
Low	48	48	50	53	56	60	63	63	62	57	51	47
Precip	3.1	3.7	2.4	0.6	0.2	0.0	0.0	0.0	0.1	0.6	1.0	1.9
Snow	tr	0.0	0.0	0.0	0.0	0.0	0.0	0.0	0.0	0.0	0.0	0.0

High and Low temperatures in degrees Fahrenheit; Precipitation and Snow in inches

Weather Station: Fairmont Elevation: 3,060 feet

	Jan	Feb	Mar	Apr	May	Jun	Jul	Aug	Sep	Oct	Nov	Dec
High	55	57	62	68	75	84	91	92	86	75	63	54
Low	37	38	42	45	52	60	66	66	61	52	43	37
Precip	3.6	4.4	2.3	1.0	0.4	0.1	0.1	0.1	0.2	0.7	1.2	2.2
Snow	tr	0.9	0.2	0.0	0.0	0.0	0.0	0.0	0.0	0.0	tr	1.9

High and Low temperatures in degrees Fahrenheit; Precipitation and Snow in inches

Weather Station: Hollywood-Burbank Arpt Elevation: 725 feet

	Jan	Feb	Mar	Apr	May	Jun	Jul	Aug	Sep	Oct	Nov	Dec
High	69	70	71	75	77	82	88	90	87	82	74	69
Low	42	44	46	50	55	58	62	63	60	54	46	42
Precip	3.5	4.8	3.2	1.1	0.3	0.1	0.0	0.1	0.2	0.9	1.0	2.2
Snow	0.0	0.0	0.0	0.0	0.0	0.0	0.0	0.0	0.0	0.0	0.0	0.0

High and Low temperatures in degrees Fahrenheit; Precipitation and Snow in inches

Weather Station: Lancaster Gen Wm Fox Field Elevation: 2,338 feet

	Jan	Feb	Mar	Apr	May	Jun	Jul	Aug	Sep	Oct	Nov	Dec
High	58	61	66	72	81	90	97	96	90	79	66	57
Low	31	35	40	45	54	61	67	64	57	46	36	29
Precip	1.5	1.9	1.2	0.3	0.1	0.1	0.1	0.1	0.2	0.4	0.5	1.1
Snow	na	na	na	na	na	na	na	na	na	na	na	na

High and Low temperatures in degrees Fahrenheit; Precipitation and Snow in inches

Weather Station: Long Beach Daugherty Fld Elevation: 24 feet

	Jan	Feb	Mar	Apr	May	Jun	Jul	Aug	Sep	Oct	Nov	Dec
High	67	67	69	72	74	77	82	84	82	77	72	67
Low	46	48	51	53	58	61	65	65	63	58	51	46
Precip	2.6	3.3	2.0	0.6	0.2	0.1	0.0	0.0	0.2	0.6	1.0	1.7
Snow	na	na	na	na	na	na	na	na	na	na	na	na

High and Low temperatures in degrees Fahrenheit; Precipitation and Snow in inches

Weather Station: Los Angeles Civic Center Elevation: 270 feet

	Jan	Feb	Mar	Apr	May	Jun	Jul	Aug	Sep	Oct	Nov	Dec
High	69	69	70	73	75	79	84	85	83	79	73	68
Low	50	51	53	56	59	62	65	66	65	60	54	49
Precip	3.2	4.1	2.6	0.9	0.3	0.1	0.0	0.0	0.2	0.6	1.0	2.0
Snow	na	na	na	na	na	na	na	na	na	na	na	na

High and Low temperatures in degrees Fahrenheit; Precipitation and Snow in inches

Weather Station: Los Angeles Intl Arpt Elevation: 100 feet

	Jan	Feb	Mar	Apr	May	Jun	Jul	Aug	Sep	Oct	Nov	Dec
High	66	66	66	68	69	72	75	76	76	74	70	66
Low	49	50	52	54	57	60	64	64	63	59	53	49
Precip	2.8	3.5	2.0	0.7	0.2	0.1	0.0	0.1	0.2	0.5	1.1	1.8
Snow	na	na	na	na	na	na	na	na	na	na	na	na

High and Low temperatures in degrees Fahrenheit; Precipitation and Snow in inches

Weather Station: Mt Wilson No 2 Elevation: 5,708 feet

	Jan	Feb	Mar	Apr	May	Jun	Jul	Aug	Sep	Oct	Nov	Dec
High	54	53	56	61	69	77	83	83	78	70	61	54
Low	38	37	39	42	49	57	64	64	59	52	43	38
Precip	6.9	9.2	6.3	2.3	0.9	0.3	0.1	0.2	0.6	1.7	3.0	4.6
Snow	na	tr	1.1	0.3	tr	0.0	0.0	0.0	0.0	0.0	0.5	tr

High and Low temperatures in degrees Fahrenheit; Precipitation and Snow in inches

Weather Station: Palmdale Elevation: 2,596 feet

	Jan	Feb	Mar	Apr	May	Jun	Jul	Aug	Sep	Oct	Nov	Dec
High	60	63	69	76	84	92	98	98	92	81	68	58
Low	34	37	41	45	53	59	66	65	59	49	39	33
Precip	1.4	2.0	1.2	0.4	0.1	0.1	0.1	0.1	0.2	0.4	0.5	1.1
Snow	0.0	0.0	0.0	0.0	0.0	0.0	0.0	0.0	0.0	0.0	0.0	0.0

High and Low temperatures in degrees Fahrenheit; Precipitation and Snow in inches

Weather Station: Pasadena Elevation: 863 feet

	Jan	Feb	Mar	Apr	May	Jun	Jul	Aug	Sep	Oct	Nov	Dec
High	68	70	72	76	79	84	90	91	89	82	74	67
Low	46	47	48	51	55	58	62	63	62	56	50	45
Precip	4.6	5.7	3.5	1.3	0.4	0.2	0.1	0.1	0.4	0.9	1.6	2.6
Snow	0.0	0.0	0.0	0.0	0.0	0.0	0.0	0.0	0.0	0.0	0.0	0.0

High and Low temperatures in degrees Fahrenheit; Precipitation and Snow in inches

Weather Station: San Gabriel Fire Dept Elevation: 450 feet

	Jan	Feb	Mar	Apr	May	Jun	Jul	Aug	Sep	Oct	Nov	Dec
High	70	71	73	77	79	84	89	91	89	83	76	70
Low	44	45	48	51	56	59	63	63	61	55	48	43
Precip	3.8	4.9	3.2	1.0	0.4	0.2	0.0	0.1	0.4	0.7	1.3	1.8
Snow	0.0	0.0	0.0	0.0	0.0	0.0	0.0	0.0	0.0	0.0	0.0	0.0

High and Low temperatures in degrees Fahrenheit; Precipitation and Snow in inches

Weather Station: Santa Monica Pier Elevation: 14 feet

	Jan	Feb	Mar	Apr	May	Jun	Jul	Aug	Sep	Oct	Nov	Dec
High	64	63	63	64	65	67	70	70	71	70	67	64
Low	51	52	53	54	57	60	63	63	63	60	55	51
Precip	3.1	3.7	1.9	0.5	0.2	0.1	0.0	0.0	0.2	0.5	1.1	1.8
Snow	0.0	0.0	0.0	0.0	0.0	0.0	0.0	0.0	0.0	0.0	0.0	0.0

High and Low temperatures in degrees Fahrenheit; Precipitation and Snow in inches

Weather Station: Torrance Municipal Arpt Elevation: 109 feet

	Jan	Feb	Mar	Apr	May	Jun	Jul	Aug	Sep	Oct	Nov	Dec
High	67	67	68	71	72	75	78	79	78	76	71	67
Low	46	48	49	51	55	58	61	62	61	56	50	46
Precip	3.4	3.9	2.4	0.7	0.2	0.1	0.1	0.0	0.2	0.6	1.2	1.9
Snow	0.0	0.0	0.0	0.0	0.0	0.0	0.0	0.0	0.0	0.0	0.0	0.0

High and Low temperatures in degrees Fahrenheit; Precipitation and Snow in inches

Weather Station: U C L A Elevation: 430 feet

	Jan	Feb	Mar	Apr	May	Jun	Jul	Aug	Sep	Oct	Nov	Dec
High	67	67	67	70	70	73	77	79	78	75	71	67
Low	51	51	51	53	56	58	62	62	62	59	55	51
Precip	4.1	5.5	3.0	1.0	0.3	0.1	0.0	0.1	0.3	0.9	1.3	2.4
Snow	0.0	tr	tr	0.0	0.0	0.0	0.0	0.0	0.0	0.0	0.0	0.0

High and Low temperatures in degrees Fahrenheit; Precipitation and Snow in inches

Population: 9,818,605; Growth (since 2000): 3.1%; Density: 2,419.6 persons per square mile; Race: 50.3% White, 8.7% Black/African American, 13.7% Asian, 0.7% American Indian/Alaska Native, 0.3% Native Hawaiian/Other Pacific Islander, 4.5% two or more races, 47.7% Hispanic of any race; Average household size: 2.98; Median age: 34.8; Age under 18: 24.5%; Age 65 and over: 10.9%; Males per 100 females: 97.2; Marriage status: 41.0% never married, 45.5% now married, 2.7% separated, 5.0% widowed, 8.5% divorced; Foreign born: 35.1%; Speak English only: 43.2%; With disability: 9.5%; Veterans: 4.4%; Ancestry: 5.1% German, 4.2% Irish, 3.7% English, 2.7% Italian, 2.6% American
Religion: Six largest groups: 36.1% Catholicism, 3.5% Non-denominational Protestant, 2.6% Baptist, 1.8% Pentecostal, 1.5% Latter-day Saints, 1.1% Methodist/Pietist
Economy: Unemployment rate: 7.9%; Leading industries: 12.6% professional, scientific, and technical services; 11.9% health care and social assistance; 11.4% retail trade; Farms: 1,294 totaling 91,689 acres; Company size: 222 employ 1,000 or more persons, 330 employ 500 to 999 persons, 4,663 employ 100 to 499 persons, 244,410 employ less than 100 persons; Business ownership: 316,571 women-owned, 59,680 Black-owned, 225,812 Hispanic-owned, 183,090 Asian-owned
Employment: 14.0% management, business, and financial, 4.4% computer, engineering, and science, 12.5% education, legal, community

service, arts, and media, 4.4% healthcare practitioners, 18.9% service, 25.0% sales and office, 7.9% natural resources, construction, and maintenance, 12.8% production, transportation, and material moving
Income: Per capita: $27,749; Median household: $55,909; Average household: $81,416; Households with income of $100,000 or more: 26.1%; Poverty rate: 17.8%
Educational Attainment: High school diploma or higher: 76.6%; Bachelor's degree or higher: 29.7%; Graduate/professional degree or higher: 10.2%
Housing: Homeownership rate: 47.7%; Median home value: $420,200; Median year structure built: 1962; Homeowner vacancy rate: 1.7%; Median gross rent: $1,204 per month; Rental vacancy rate: 5.8%
Vital Statistics: Birth rate: 130.1 per 10,000 population; Death rate: 61.8 per 10,000 population; Age-adjusted cancer mortality rate: 152.2 deaths per 100,000 population
Health Insurance: 77.8% have insurance; 54.3% have private insurance; 29.7% have public insurance; 22.2% do not have insurance; 9.6% of children under 18 do not have insurance
Health Care: Physicians: 26.0 per 10,000 population; Hospital beds: 25.5 per 10,000 population; Hospital admissions: 1,113.3 per 10,000 population
Air Quality Index: 6.8% good, 72.3% moderate, 19.7% unhealthy for sensitive individuals, 1.1% unhealthy (percent of days)
Transportation: Commute: 83.0% car, 7.1% public transportation, 2.9% walk, 5.0% work from home; Median travel time to work: 29.3 minutes
Presidential Election: 68.6% Obama, 29.1% Romney (2012)
National and State Parks: Alamitos Bay State Park; Angeles National Forest; Antelope Valley California Poppy State Natural Reserve; Antelope Valley Indian Museum State Historic Park; Arthur B. Ripley Desert Woodland State Park; Castaic Lake State Recreation Area; Dockweiler State Beach; El Matador State Beach; El Pescador State Beach; Hungry Valley State Vehicular Recreation Area; Kenneth Hahn State Recreation Area; La Piedra State Beach; Leo Carrillo State Park; Los Angeles County and State Arboretum; Los Angeles State Historic Park; Los Encinos State Historic Park; Malibu Creek State Park; Malibu Lagoon State Beach; Pío Pico State Historic Park; Placerita Canyon State Park; Point Dume State Beach; Rio de Los Angeles State Park; Robert H Meyer Memorial State Beach; Saddleback Butte State Park; Santa Monica Mountains National Recreation Area; Santa Monica State Beach; Santa Susana Pass State Historic Park; Topanga State Park; Watts Towers of Simon Rodia State Historic Park; Will Rogers State Beach; Will Rogers State Historic Park; Gabrielino National Scenic Trail

Additional Information Contacts

Los Angeles Government . . . . (213) 974-1311
http://www.lacounty.gov

Los Angeles County Communities

ACTON (CDP). Covers a land area of 39.256 square miles and a water area of 0.023 square miles. Located at 34.50° N. Lat; 118.18° W. Long. Elevation is 2,710 feet.
Population: 7,596; Growth (since 2000): 217.8%; Density: 193.5 persons per square mile; Race: 86.4% White, 0.8% Black/African American, 2.0% Asian, 0.9% American Indian/Alaska Native, 0.1% Native Hawaiian/Other Pacific Islander, 3.9% Two or more races, 18.1% Hispanic of any race; Average household size: 2.86; Median age: 45.5; Age under 18: 22.0%; Age 65 and over: 11.0%; Males per 100 females: 100.0; Marriage status: 25.0% never married, 63.6% now married, 1.4% separated, 3.3% widowed, 8.1% divorced; Foreign born: 10.4%; Speak English only: 88.4%; With disability: 9.5%; Veterans: 11.0%; Ancestry: 16.7% German, 14.1% English, 13.1% Irish, 6.8% Italian, 4.5% Dutch
Employment: 14.4% management, business, and financial, 5.9% computer, engineering, and science, 10.1% education, legal, community service, arts, and media, 3.3% healthcare practitioners, 13.3% service, 29.0% sales and office, 11.8% natural resources, construction, and maintenance, 12.3% production, transportation, and material moving
Income: Per capita: $34,546; Median household: $89,886; Average household: $98,678; Households with income of $100,000 or more: 41.3%; Poverty rate: 11.7%
Educational Attainment: High school diploma or higher: 90.0%; Bachelor's degree or higher: 26.1%; Graduate/professional degree or higher: 10.0%

School District(s)

Acton-Agua Dulce Unified (KG-12)
2012-13 Enrollment: 1,542 . . . . (661) 269-5999
Housing: Homeownership rate: 89.7%; Median home value: $434,100; Median year structure built: 1988; Homeowner vacancy rate: 1.7%; Median gross rent: $1,862 per month; Rental vacancy rate: 7.4%
Health Insurance: 89.9% have insurance; 77.4% have private insurance; 22.3% have public insurance; 10.1% do not have insurance; 1.3% of children under 18 do not have insurance
Transportation: Commute: 89.4% car, 0.9% public transportation, 0.4% walk, 8.8% work from home; Median travel time to work: 43.4 minutes

AGOURA HILLS (city). Covers a land area of 7.793 square miles and a water area of 0.029 square miles. Located at 34.15° N. Lat; 118.76° W. Long. Elevation is 1,683 feet.
History: Agoura Hills is located north of the Santa Monica Mountains and was first inhabited by the Chumash Indians. This city was incorporated on December 8, 1982.
Population: 20,330; Growth (since 2000): -1.0%; Density: 2,608.7 persons per square mile; Race: 84.3% White, 1.3% Black/African American, 7.5% Asian, 0.3% American Indian/Alaska Native, 0.1% Native Hawaiian/Other Pacific Islander, 3.6% Two or more races, 9.5% Hispanic of any race; Average household size: 2.76; Median age: 42.4; Age under 18: 24.1%; Age 65 and over: 11.3%; Males per 100 females: 97.2; Marriage status: 28.1% never married, 56.7% now married, 1.0% separated, 3.1% widowed, 12.1% divorced; Foreign born: 18.1%; Speak English only: 78.6%; With disability: 6.6%; Veterans: 5.5%; Ancestry: 12.9% German, 10.8% Irish, 7.9% Russian, 7.1% English, 7.1% Italian
Employment: 25.3% management, business, and financial, 7.7% computer, engineering, and science, 17.6% education, legal, community service, arts, and media, 5.8% healthcare practitioners, 11.9% service, 26.4% sales and office, 3.1% natural resources, construction, and maintenance, 2.1% production, transportation, and material moving
Income: Per capita: $50,492; Median household: $107,885; Average household: $139,613; Households with income of $100,000 or more: 54.7%; Poverty rate: 7.1%
Educational Attainment: High school diploma or higher: 95.7%; Bachelor's degree or higher: 54.4%; Graduate/professional degree or higher: 23.1%

School District(s)

Las Virgenes Unified (KG-12)
2012-13 Enrollment: 11,200 . . . . (818) 880-4000
Housing: Homeownership rate: 78.0%; Median home value: $678,000; Median year structure built: 1979; Homeowner vacancy rate: 0.5%; Median gross rent: $1,924 per month; Rental vacancy rate: 6.8%
Health Insurance: 93.1% have insurance; 84.4% have private insurance; 17.9% have public insurance; 6.9% do not have insurance; 1.4% of children under 18 do not have insurance
Safety: Violent crime rate: 9.2 per 10,000 population; Property crime rate: 147.4 per 10,000 population
Newspapers: Acorn Newspapers (weekly circulation 144000)
Transportation: Commute: 87.4% car, 0.8% public transportation, 3.0% walk, 6.8% work from home; Median travel time to work: 29.2 minutes

Additional Information Contacts

City of Agoura Hills . . . . (818) 597-7300
http://ci.agoura-hills.ca.us

AGUA DULCE (CDP). Covers a land area of 22.835 square miles and a water area of 0.006 square miles. Located at 34.50° N. Lat; 118.32° W. Long. Elevation is 2,526 feet.
Population: 3,342; Growth (since 2000): n/a; Density: 146.4 persons per square mile; Race: 85.4% White, 1.8% Black/African American, 2.3% Asian, 0.7% American Indian/Alaska Native, 0.1% Native Hawaiian/Other Pacific Islander, 3.0% Two or more races, 18.3% Hispanic of any race; Average household size: 2.76; Median age: 47.3; Age under 18: 19.3%; Age 65 and over: 13.9%; Males per 100 females: 101.7; Marriage status: 20.2% never married, 67.0% now married, 1.0% separated, 2.4% widowed, 10.4% divorced; Foreign born: 7.8%; Speak English only: 87.1%; With disability: 16.0%; Veterans: 12.1%; Ancestry: 19.1% English, 17.2% German, 16.7% Irish, 6.0% West Indian, 5.1% Scottish
Employment: 21.3% management, business, and financial, 6.3% computer, engineering, and science, 12.1% education, legal, community service, arts, and media, 2.4% healthcare practitioners, 13.6% service, 34.1% sales and office, 6.5% natural resources, construction, and maintenance, 3.6% production, transportation, and material moving
Income: Per capita: $37,311; Median household: $103,333; Average household: $111,132; Households with income of $100,000 or more: 53.9%; Poverty rate: 2.5%

Educational Attainment: High school diploma or higher: 93.1%; Bachelor's degree or higher: 32.3%; Graduate/professional degree or higher: 8.5%

School District(s)

Acton-Agua Dulce Unified (KG-12)
2012-13 Enrollment: 1,542 . . . . (661) 269-5999

Housing: Homeownership rate: 88.1%; Median home value: $552,500; Median year structure built: 1987; Homeowner vacancy rate: 1.2%; Median gross rent: $871 per month; Rental vacancy rate: 3.4%

Health Insurance: 90.7% have insurance; 79.4% have private insurance; 26.7% have public insurance; 9.3% do not have insurance; 8.3% of children under 18 do not have insurance

Transportation: Commute: 80.9% car, 0.0% public transportation, 0.7% walk, 18.4% work from home; Median travel time to work: 44.8 minutes

Airports: Agua Dulce (general aviation)

ALHAMBRA (city). Covers a land area of 7.631 square miles and a water area of 0.001 square miles. Located at 34.08° N. Lat; 118.14° W. Long. Elevation is 492 feet.

History: Named for the Moorish fortress in Spain. Incorporated 1903.

Population: 83,089; Growth (since 2000): -3.2%; Density: 10,889.0 persons per square mile; Race: 28.3% White, 1.5% Black/African American, 52.9% Asian, 0.6% American Indian/Alaska Native, 0.1% Native Hawaiian/Other Pacific Islander, 3.5% Two or more races, 34.4% Hispanic of any race; Average household size: 2.82; Median age: 39.3; Age under 18: 18.9%; Age 65 and over: 14.3%; Males per 100 females: 89.9; Marriage status: 36.7% never married, 49.3% now married, 1.9% separated, 6.1% widowed, 7.9% divorced; Foreign born: 50.5%; Speak English only: 25.5%; With disability: 8.4%; Veterans: 3.1%; Ancestry: 4.4% American, 2.1% Irish, 2.1% German, 1.8% Italian, 1.4% English

Employment: 14.3% management, business, and financial, 6.1% computer, engineering, and science, 11.5% education, legal, community service, arts, and media, 5.1% healthcare practitioners, 19.4% service, 29.5% sales and office, 5.1% natural resources, construction, and maintenance, 9.0% production, transportation, and material moving

Income: Per capita: $25,703; Median household: $54,148; Average household: $70,002; Households with income of $100,000 or more: 22.9%; Poverty rate: 13.9%

Educational Attainment: High school diploma or higher: 80.4%; Bachelor's degree or higher: 32.8%; Graduate/professional degree or higher: 10.9%

School District(s)

Alhambra Unified (KG-12)
2012-13 Enrollment: 18,076 . . . . (626) 943-3000

Four-year College(s)

Platt College-Los Angeles (Private, For-profit)
Fall 2013 Enrollment: 608 . . . . (626) 300-5444
2013-14 Tuition: In-state $14,572; Out-of-state $14,572

Two-year College(s)

Pinnacle College (Private, For-profit)
Fall 2013 Enrollment: 147 . . . . (626) 284-0050

Vocational/Technical School(s)

Alhambra Beauty College (Private, For-profit)
Fall 2013 Enrollment: 159 . . . . (626) 282-7765
2013-14 Tuition: $9,518

Everest College-Alhambra (Private, For-profit)
Fall 2013 Enrollment: 561 . . . . (626) 979-4940
2013-14 Tuition: $21,388

Paul Mitchell The School-Pasadena (Private, For-profit)
Fall 2013 Enrollment: 174 . . . . (626) 284-2863
2013-14 Tuition: $18,000

Housing: Homeownership rate: 40.8%; Median home value: $478,500; Median year structure built: 1956; Homeowner vacancy rate: 1.3%; Median gross rent: $1,211 per month; Rental vacancy rate: 5.3%

Health Insurance: 81.1% have insurance; 60.7% have private insurance; 27.3% have public insurance; 18.9% do not have insurance; 6.4% of children under 18 do not have insurance

Hospitals: Alhambra Hospital Medical Center (144 beds)

Safety: Violent crime rate: 19.2 per 10,000 population; Property crime rate: 209.4 per 10,000 population

Transportation: Commute: 89.5% car, 4.1% public transportation, 1.5% walk, 3.9% work from home; Median travel time to work: 29.3 minutes

Additional Information Contacts

City of Alhambra . . . . (626) 570-5007
http://www.cityofalhambra.org

ALONDRA PARK (CDP). Covers a land area of 1.107 square miles and a water area of 0.036 square miles. Located at 33.89° N. Lat; 118.34° W. Long. Elevation is 52 feet.

Population: 8,592; Growth (since 2000): -0.3%; Density: 7,764.5 persons per square mile; Race: 43.2% White, 9.4% Black/African American, 16.2% Asian, 0.4% American Indian/Alaska Native, 0.6% Native Hawaiian/Other Pacific Islander, 5.0% Two or more races, 50.1% Hispanic of any race; Average household size: 3.14; Median age: 33.7; Age under 18: 27.1%; Age 65 and over: 9.0%; Males per 100 females: 97.7; Marriage status: 40.3% never married, 47.7% now married, 1.9% separated, 6.6% widowed, 5.4% divorced; Foreign born: 36.0%; Speak English only: 39.8%; With disability: 9.2%; Veterans: 3.8%; Ancestry: 5.2% American, 3.6% German, 3.6% Irish, 2.7% Italian, 2.0% English

Employment: 15.2% management, business, and financial, 2.1% computer, engineering, and science, 7.9% education, legal, community service, arts, and media, 2.2% healthcare practitioners, 18.7% service, 32.1% sales and office, 11.1% natural resources, construction, and maintenance, 10.8% production, transportation, and material moving

Income: Per capita: $22,142; Median household: $54,484; Average household: $67,575; Households with income of $100,000 or more: 22.9%; Poverty rate: 20.7%

Educational Attainment: High school diploma or higher: 73.6%; Bachelor's degree or higher: 19.2%; Graduate/professional degree or higher: 6.9%

Housing: Homeownership rate: 50.1%; Median home value: $418,900; Median year structure built: 1957; Homeowner vacancy rate: 0.7%; Median gross rent: $1,015 per month; Rental vacancy rate: 4.1%

Health Insurance: 73.7% have insurance; 49.9% have private insurance; 29.9% have public insurance; 26.3% do not have insurance; 10.6% of children under 18 do not have insurance

Transportation: Commute: 87.1% car, 6.3% public transportation, 1.4% walk, 2.2% work from home; Median travel time to work: 24.9 minutes

ALTADENA (CDP). Covers a land area of 8.713 square miles and a water area of 0.016 square miles. Located at 34.19° N. Lat; 118.14° W. Long. Elevation is 1,358 feet.

History: Named for the Spanish translation of "high" — its location above Pasadena. Founded 1887.

Population: 42,777; Growth (since 2000): 0.4%; Density: 4,909.7 persons per square mile; Race: 52.8% White, 23.7% Black/African American, 5.4% Asian, 0.7% American Indian/Alaska Native, 0.2% Native Hawaiian/Other Pacific Islander, 5.9% Two or more races, 26.9% Hispanic of any race; Average household size: 2.78; Median age: 41.8; Age under 18: 22.2%; Age 65 and over: 14.2%; Males per 100 females: 93.1; Marriage status: 34.2% never married, 49.8% now married, 1.5% separated, 5.4% widowed, 10.5% divorced; Foreign born: 21.7%; Speak English only: 65.3%; With disability: 10.7%; Veterans: 6.0%; Ancestry: 6.7% English, 6.2% German, 5.0% Armenian, 4.7% Irish, 3.8% American

Employment: 17.1% management, business, and financial, 5.2% computer, engineering, and science, 23.1% education, legal, community service, arts, and media, 5.5% healthcare practitioners, 16.1% service, 20.4% sales and office, 6.5% natural resources, construction, and maintenance, 6.2% production, transportation, and material moving

Income: Per capita: $41,612; Median household: $82,895; Average household: $116,857; Households with income of $100,000 or more: 41.4%; Poverty rate: 10.7%

Educational Attainment: High school diploma or higher: 87.3%; Bachelor's degree or higher: 44.4%; Graduate/professional degree or higher: 18.8%

School District(s)

Los Angeles County Office of Education (KG-12)
2012-13 Enrollment: 9,136 . . . . (562) 922-6111

Pasadena Unified (KG-12)
2012-13 Enrollment: 19,540 . . . . (626) 396-3600

Housing: Homeownership rate: 71.6%; Median home value: $560,000; Median year structure built: 1947; Homeowner vacancy rate: 0.9%; Median gross rent: $1,394 per month; Rental vacancy rate: 4.9%

Health Insurance: 83.6% have insurance; 67.2% have private insurance; 25.5% have public insurance; 16.4% do not have insurance; 9.4% of children under 18 do not have insurance

Transportation: Commute: 86.9% car, 3.9% public transportation, 1.5% walk, 4.9% work from home; Median travel time to work: 27.5 minutes

ARCADIA (city). Covers a land area of 10.925 square miles and a water area of 0.208 square miles. Located at 34.13° N. Lat; 118.04° W. Long. Elevation is 482 feet.
History: Named for a Greek place celebrated for its rural simplicity. Arcadia developed as a residential community for Los Angeles commuters.
Population: 56,364; Growth (since 2000): 6.2%; Density: 5,159.1 persons per square mile; Race: 32.3% White, 1.2% Black/African American, 59.2% Asian, 0.3% American Indian/Alaska Native, 0.0% Native Hawaiian/Other Pacific Islander, 2.8% Two or more races, 12.1% Hispanic of any race; Average household size: 2.83; Median age: 43.1; Age under 18: 21.8%; Age 65 and over: 16.3%; Males per 100 females: 91.2; Marriage status: 29.1% never married, 58.8% now married, 1.8% separated, 6.4% widowed, 5.7% divorced; Foreign born: 48.8%; Speak English only: 37.4%; With disability: 6.7%; Veterans: 4.4%; Ancestry: 4.2% German, 3.7% English, 2.8% Irish, 2.5% Italian, 1.6% American
Employment: 23.3% management, business, and financial, 9.3% computer, engineering, and science, 13.8% education, legal, community service, arts, and media, 6.9% healthcare practitioners, 10.3% service, 28.8% sales and office, 3.2% natural resources, construction, and maintenance, 4.3% production, transportation, and material moving
Income: Per capita: $39,137; Median household: $77,704; Average household: $110,030; Households with income of $100,000 or more: 39.4%; Poverty rate: 9.6%
Educational Attainment: High school diploma or higher: 91.3%; Bachelor's degree or higher: 52.5%; Graduate/professional degree or higher: 20.4%

School District(s)

Arcadia Unified (KG-12)
2012-13 Enrollment: 9,667 . . . . (626) 821-8300
El Monte City Elementary (KG-08)
2012-13 Enrollment: 9,304 . . . . (626) 453-3700

Housing: Homeownership rate: 63.2%; Median home value: $802,400; Median year structure built: 1966; Homeowner vacancy rate: 1.1%; Median gross rent: $1,402 per month; Rental vacancy rate: 6.7%
Health Insurance: 87.6% have insurance; 73.5% have private insurance; 22.0% have public insurance; 12.4% do not have insurance; 7.1% of children under 18 do not have insurance
Hospitals: Methodist Hospital of Southern California (460 beds)
Safety: Violent crime rate: 13.3 per 10,000 population; Property crime rate: 262.4 per 10,000 population
Transportation: Commute: 89.5% car, 3.1% public transportation, 1.1% walk, 5.7% work from home; Median travel time to work: 29.3 minutes
Additional Information Contacts
City of Arcadia . . . . (626) 574-5400
http://www.ci.arcadia.ca.us/home

ARTESIA (city). Covers a land area of 1.621 square miles and a water area of 0 square miles. Located at 33.87° N. Lat; 118.08° W. Long. Elevation is 52 feet.
History: Named for the many artesian wells in the vicinity. Now a suburb Southeast of Los Angeles. Founded 1875. Incorporated 1959.
Population: 16,522; Growth (since 2000): 0.9%; Density: 10,194.7 persons per square mile; Race: 39.0% White, 3.6% Black/African American, 37.1% Asian, 0.6% American Indian/Alaska Native, 0.2% Native Hawaiian/Other Pacific Islander, 3.6% Two or more races, 35.8% Hispanic of any race; Average household size: 3.51; Median age: 38.2; Age under 18: 22.5%; Age 65 and over: 13.6%; Males per 100 females: 98.4; Marriage status: 36.6% never married, 52.0% now married, 3.1% separated, 5.4% widowed, 5.9% divorced; Foreign born: 48.1%; Speak English only: 32.9%; With disability: 11.4%; Veterans: 2.7%; Ancestry: 7.2% Portuguese, 3.2% American, 2.6% Dutch, 2.3% Irish, 1.7% French
Employment: 11.7% management, business, and financial, 4.0% computer, engineering, and science, 5.2% education, legal, community service, arts, and media, 6.8% healthcare practitioners, 24.8% service, 32.8% sales and office, 4.8% natural resources, construction, and maintenance, 9.9% production, transportation, and material moving
Income: Per capita: $21,865; Median household: $59,845; Average household: $73,275; Households with income of $100,000 or more: 26.6%; Poverty rate: 13.5%
Educational Attainment: High school diploma or higher: 78.6%; Bachelor's degree or higher: 24.9%; Graduate/professional degree or higher: 7.0%

School District(s)

ABC Unified (KG-12)
2012-13 Enrollment: 20,835 . . . . (562) 926-5566

Vocational/Technical School(s)

Angeles Institute (Private, For-profit)
Fall 2013 Enrollment: 105 . . . . (562) 531-4100
2013-14 Tuition: $25,245

Housing: Homeownership rate: 55.6%; Median home value: $401,800; Median year structure built: 1963; Homeowner vacancy rate: 0.7%; Median gross rent: $1,361 per month; Rental vacancy rate: 3.7%
Health Insurance: 76.2% have insurance; 54.9% have private insurance; 27.0% have public insurance; 23.8% do not have insurance; 10.2% of children under 18 do not have insurance
Safety: Violent crime rate: 37.6 per 10,000 population; Property crime rate: 193.0 per 10,000 population
Transportation: Commute: 87.5% car, 2.8% public transportation, 2.0% walk, 1.4% work from home; Median travel time to work: 24.5 minutes
Additional Information Contacts
City of Artesia . . . . (562) 865-6262
http://www.cityofartesia.us

AVALON (city). Covers a land area of 2.935 square miles and a water area of 0.002 square miles. Located at 33.33° N. Lat; 118.33° W. Long. Elevation is 39 feet.
History: Avalon became the center of resort and sports activites of Santa Catalina Island, which was visited by Cabrillo in 1542 and by Viscaino in 1602. Gold prospectors were here between 1834 and 1863, and Northern troops occupied the island briefly during the Civil War. In 1919 William Wrigley, Jr., bought the land and made the island a commercial success by constructing a casino and other improvements, and conducting a publicity campaign.
Population: 3,728; Growth (since 2000): 19.2%; Density: 1,270.1 persons per square mile; Race: 62.0% White, 0.5% Black/African American, 1.3% Asian, 0.6% American Indian/Alaska Native, 0.3% Native Hawaiian/Other Pacific Islander, 4.7% Two or more races, 55.8% Hispanic of any race; Average household size: 2.53; Median age: 37.7; Age under 18: 25.8%; Age 65 and over: 10.9%; Males per 100 females: 102.8; Marriage status: 31.9% never married, 52.5% now married, 3.7% separated, 5.1% widowed, 10.4% divorced; Foreign born: 29.8%; Speak English only: 41.8%; With disability: 10.7%; Veterans: 3.2%; Ancestry: 10.3% Irish, 9.7% English, 7.8% German, 4.4% Italian, 2.6% Scottish
Employment: 9.8% management, business, and financial, 1.5% computer, engineering, and science, 5.6% education, legal, community service, arts, and media, 2.5% healthcare practitioners, 37.8% service, 29.6% sales and office, 8.1% natural resources, construction, and maintenance, 5.2% production, transportation, and material moving
Income: Per capita: $27,964; Median household: $65,433; Average household: $82,472; Households with income of $100,000 or more: 28.9%; Poverty rate: 12.5%
Educational Attainment: High school diploma or higher: 74.0%; Bachelor's degree or higher: 19.8%; Graduate/professional degree or higher: 8.0%
Housing: Homeownership rate: 26.0%; Median home value: $679,400; Median year structure built: 1970; Homeowner vacancy rate: 4.7%; Median gross rent: $1,373 per month; Rental vacancy rate: 10.7%
Health Insurance: 64.0% have insurance; 49.9% have private insurance; 20.3% have public insurance; 36.0% do not have insurance; 36.3% of children under 18 do not have insurance
Hospitals: Catalina Island Medical Center (12 beds)
Safety: Violent crime rate: 10.6 per 10,000 population; Property crime rate: 233.0 per 10,000 population
Newspapers: Avalon Bay News (weekly circulation 3000); Catalina Islander (weekly circulation 5000)
Transportation: Commute: 24.1% car, 3.7% public transportation, 45.5% walk, 4.8% work from home; Median travel time to work: 10.8 minutes
Additional Information Contacts
City of Avalon . . . . (310) 510-0220
http://www.cityofavalon.com

AVOCADO HEIGHTS (CDP). Covers a land area of 2.706 square miles and a water area of 0.136 square miles. Located at 34.04° N. Lat; 118.00° W. Long. Elevation is 338 feet.
Population: 15,411; Growth (since 2000): 1.7%; Density: 5,695.6 persons per square mile; Race: 55.6% White, 0.9% Black/African American, 8.8% Asian, 0.7% American Indian/Alaska Native, 0.1% Native Hawaiian/Other Pacific Islander, 3.3% Two or more races, 82.1% Hispanic of any race; Average household size: 4.02; Median age: 33.7; Age under 18: 27.3%; Age 65 and over: 10.9%; Males per 100 females: 98.5; Marriage status:

39.2% never married, 47.5% now married, 2.6% separated, 5.3% widowed, 7.9% divorced; Foreign born: 33.8%; Speak English only: 27.6%; With disability: 9.2%; Veterans: 4.2%; Ancestry: 1.7% German, 1.4% Irish, 1.2% American, 1.2% English, 0.7% Dutch

Employment: 11.3% management, business, and financial, 3.6% computer, engineering, and science, 6.9% education, legal, community service, arts, and media, 2.1% healthcare practitioners, 24.9% service, 23.5% sales and office, 9.0% natural resources, construction, and maintenance, 18.7% production, transportation, and material moving

Income: Per capita: $22,151; Median household: $72,240; Average household: $80,735; Households with income of $100,000 or more: 30.4%; Poverty rate: 14.1%

Educational Attainment: High school diploma or higher: 73.7%; Bachelor's degree or higher: 18.1%; Graduate/professional degree or higher: 6.1%

Housing: Homeownership rate: 77.0%; Median home value: $370,400; Median year structure built: 1966; Homeowner vacancy rate: 0.7%; Median gross rent: $1,395 per month; Rental vacancy rate: 3.1%

Health Insurance: 74.5% have insurance; 55.2% have private insurance; 25.5% have public insurance; 25.5% do not have insurance; 14.4% of children under 18 do not have insurance

Transportation: Commute: 89.2% car, 2.4% public transportation, 1.2% walk, 3.6% work from home; Median travel time to work: 30.9 minutes

AZUSA (city). Covers a land area of 9.656 square miles and a water area of 0.013 square miles. Located at 34.14° N. Lat; 117.91° W. Long. Elevation is 610 feet.

History: Named for the Indian translation of "skunk hill". Azusa was founded in 1887, and grew as a citrus-shipping center.

Population: 46,361; Growth (since 2000): 3.7%; Density: 4,801.1 persons per square mile; Race: 57.6% White, 3.2% Black/African American, 8.7% Asian, 1.2% American Indian/Alaska Native, 0.2% Native Hawaiian/Other Pacific Islander, 4.7% Two or more races, 67.6% Hispanic of any race; Average household size: 3.43; Median age: 29.3; Age under 18: 26.8%; Age 65 and over: 7.7%; Males per 100 females: 96.0; Marriage status: 48.6% never married, 40.7% now married, 2.1% separated, 4.1% widowed, 6.5% divorced; Foreign born: 31.9%; Speak English only: 41.9%; With disability: 6.7%; Veterans: 3.0%; Ancestry: 4.8% German, 3.3% Irish, 2.9% English, 2.4% Italian, 1.3% American

Employment: 9.1% management, business, and financial, 3.0% computer, engineering, and science, 10.4% education, legal, community service, arts, and media, 3.1% healthcare practitioners, 25.5% service, 23.7% sales and office, 10.8% natural resources, construction, and maintenance, 14.4% production, transportation, and material moving

Income: Per capita: $18,047; Median household: $52,001; Average household: $65,749; Households with income of $100,000 or more: 18.9%; Poverty rate: 20.1%

Educational Attainment: High school diploma or higher: 75.2%; Bachelor's degree or higher: 19.5%; Graduate/professional degree or higher: 5.9%

School District(s)

Azusa Unified (KG-12)
2012-13 Enrollment: 9,755 . . . . (626) 967-6211

Four-year College(s)

Azusa Pacific University (Private, Not-for-profit, Undenominational)
Fall 2013 Enrollment: 10,755 . . . . (626) 969-3434
2013-14 Tuition: In-state $32,256; Out-of-state $32,256

Housing: Homeownership rate: 53.5%; Median home value: $305,200; Median year structure built: 1969; Homeowner vacancy rate: 1.4%; Median gross rent: $1,202 per month; Rental vacancy rate: 6.6%

Health Insurance: 77.0% have insurance; 53.8% have private insurance; 26.9% have public insurance; 23.0% do not have insurance; 9.9% of children under 18 do not have insurance

Safety: Violent crime rate: 51.5 per 10,000 population; Property crime rate: 229.9 per 10,000 population

Transportation: Commute: 82.7% car, 6.0% public transportation, 7.1% walk, 2.1% work from home; Median travel time to work: 28.4 minutes

Additional Information Contacts

City of Azusa . . . . (626) 812-5200
http://www.ci.azusa.ca.us

BALDWIN PARK (city). Covers a land area of 6.631 square miles and a water area of 0.155 square miles. Located at 34.08° N. Lat; 117.97° W. Long. Elevation is 374 feet.

History: Named for E.J. "Lucky" Baldwin, former owner of the ranch lands on which the city is built. Settled 1870. Incorporated 1956.

Population: 75,390; Growth (since 2000): -0.6%; Density: 11,369.2 persons per square mile; Race: 43.9% White, 1.2% Black/African American, 14.2% Asian, 0.9% American Indian/Alaska Native, 0.1% Native Hawaiian/Other Pacific Islander, 3.7% Two or more races, 80.1% Hispanic of any race; Average household size: 4.36; Median age: 30.5; Age under 18: 29.9%; Age 65 and over: 8.0%; Males per 100 females: 98.5; Marriage status: 42.0% never married, 46.5% now married, 2.9% separated, 5.2% widowed, 6.3% divorced; Foreign born: 45.6%; Speak English only: 16.4%; With disability: 9.2%; Veterans: 2.3%; Ancestry: 1.1% American, 1.1% German, 1.0% Irish, 0.4% English, 0.3% Italian

Employment: 6.5% management, business, and financial, 2.2% computer, engineering, and science, 6.0% education, legal, community service, arts, and media, 2.6% healthcare practitioners, 21.3% service, 23.0% sales and office, 12.2% natural resources, construction, and maintenance, 26.1% production, transportation, and material moving

Income: Per capita: $15,314; Median household: $51,153; Average household: $61,649; Households with income of $100,000 or more: 14.8%; Poverty rate: 17.5%

Educational Attainment: High school diploma or higher: 58.3%; Bachelor's degree or higher: 11.3%; Graduate/professional degree or higher: 2.5%

School District(s)

Baldwin Park Unified (KG-12)
2012-13 Enrollment: 18,845 . . . . (626) 962-3311

Vocational/Technical School(s)

Baldwin Park Adult & Community Education (Public)
Fall 2013 Enrollment: 495 . . . . (626) 856-4101
2013-14 Tuition: $2,280

Housing: Homeownership rate: 60.2%; Median home value: $285,000; Median year structure built: 1964; Homeowner vacancy rate: 1.3%; Median gross rent: $1,194 per month; Rental vacancy rate: 3.3%

Health Insurance: 72.4% have insurance; 39.7% have private insurance; 35.5% have public insurance; 27.6% do not have insurance; 8.8% of children under 18 do not have insurance

Hospitals: Kaiser Foundation Hospital - Baldwin Park (222 beds)

Safety: Violent crime rate: 28.7 per 10,000 population; Property crime rate: 178.5 per 10,000 population

Transportation: Commute: 87.6% car, 4.6% public transportation, 1.8% walk, 3.9% work from home; Median travel time to work: 31.4 minutes

Additional Information Contacts

City of Baldwin Park . . . . (626) 960-4011
http://www.baldwinpark.com

BELL (city). Covers a land area of 2.501 square miles and a water area of 0.119 square miles. Located at 33.98° N. Lat; 118.18° W. Long. Elevation is 141 feet.

History: Named for J.G. and Alphonso Bell, founders of the town. Incorporated 1927.

Population: 35,477; Growth (since 2000): -3.2%; Density: 14,188.0 persons per square mile; Race: 53.8% White, 0.9% Black/African American, 0.7% Asian, 0.9% American Indian/Alaska Native, 0.0% Native Hawaiian/Other Pacific Islander, 4.4% Two or more races, 93.1% Hispanic of any race; Average household size: 3.93; Median age: 28.9; Age under 18: 32.0%; Age 65 and over: 6.8%; Males per 100 females: 101.7; Marriage status: 46.1% never married, 44.1% now married, 3.3% separated, 4.5% widowed, 5.3% divorced; Foreign born: 44.4%; Speak English only: 11.5%; With disability: 9.4%; Veterans: 2.1%; Ancestry: 1.8% American, 1.4% Lebanese, 0.8% German, 0.7% Irish, 0.6% Other Arab

Employment: 4.4% management, business, and financial, 1.1% computer, engineering, and science, 7.2% education, legal, community service, arts, and media, 0.6% healthcare practitioners, 19.7% service, 24.6% sales and office, 12.9% natural resources, construction, and maintenance, 29.4% production, transportation, and material moving

Income: Per capita: $12,076; Median household: $35,985; Average household: $43,447; Households with income of $100,000 or more: 6.9%; Poverty rate: 30.2%

Educational Attainment: High school diploma or higher: 45.3%; Bachelor's degree or higher: 5.9%; Graduate/professional degree or higher: 1.2%

School District(s)

Los Angeles Unified (PK-12)
2012-13 Enrollment: 655,455 . . . . (213) 241-1000

Housing: Homeownership rate: 29.0%; Median home value: $282,700; Median year structure built: 1955; Homeowner vacancy rate: 1.6%; Median gross rent: $996 per month; Rental vacancy rate: 3.3%

Health Insurance: 64.5% have insurance; 30.7% have private insurance; 35.5% have public insurance; 35.5% do not have insurance; 15.0% of children under 18 do not have insurance

Safety: Violent crime rate: 57.9 per 10,000 population; Property crime rate: 148.9 per 10,000 population

Transportation: Commute: 84.1% car, 6.8% public transportation, 3.7% walk, 3.3% work from home; Median travel time to work: 28.8 minutes

Additional Information Contacts

City of Bell . . . . (323) 588-6211
http://www.cityofbell.org

BELL GARDENS (city). Covers a land area of 2.459 square miles and a water area of 0.004 square miles. Located at 33.96° N. Lat; 118.15° W. Long. Elevation is 121 feet.

History: Named for the nearby town of Bell, and the local vegetable gardens. Incorporated 1961.

Population: 42,072; Growth (since 2000): -4.5%; Density: 17,112.4 persons per square mile; Race: 49.5% White, 0.9% Black/African American, 0.6% Asian, 1.1% American Indian/Alaska Native, 0.1% Native Hawaiian/Other Pacific Islander, 3.1% Two or more races, 95.7% Hispanic of any race; Average household size: 4.31; Median age: 27.3; Age under 18: 34.0%; Age 65 and over: 5.2%; Males per 100 females: 99.7; Marriage status: 48.8% never married, 44.0% now married, 3.7% separated, 3.6% widowed, 3.7% divorced; Foreign born: 44.5%; Speak English only: 8.2%; With disability: 7.2%; Veterans: 0.9%; Ancestry: 1.1% American, 0.4% Italian, 0.3% Irish, 0.3% English, 0.2% German

Employment: 3.6% management, business, and financial, 0.7% computer, engineering, and science, 5.7% education, legal, community service, arts, and media, 1.1% healthcare practitioners, 18.7% service, 23.0% sales and office, 15.2% natural resources, construction, and maintenance, 31.9% production, transportation, and material moving

Income: Per capita: $11,632; Median household: $38,170; Average household: $46,419; Households with income of $100,000 or more: 7.2%; Poverty rate: 27.6%

Educational Attainment: High school diploma or higher: 41.6%; Bachelor's degree or higher: 5.2%; Graduate/professional degree or higher: 1.1%

School District(s)

Montebello Unified (KG-12)
2012-13 Enrollment: 30,564 . . . . (323) 887-7900

Housing: Homeownership rate: 24.0%; Median home value: $275,200; Median year structure built: 1961; Homeowner vacancy rate: 2.1%; Median gross rent: $1,109 per month; Rental vacancy rate: 2.6%

Health Insurance: 61.8% have insurance; 27.7% have private insurance; 36.3% have public insurance; 38.2% do not have insurance; 15.9% of children under 18 do not have insurance

Safety: Violent crime rate: 27.9 per 10,000 population; Property crime rate: 177.5 per 10,000 population

Transportation: Commute: 83.8% car, 8.1% public transportation, 3.1% walk, 2.8% work from home; Median travel time to work: 28.1 minutes

Additional Information Contacts

City of Bell Gardens . . . . (562) 806-7700
http://www.bellgardens.org

BELLFLOWER (city). Covers a land area of 6.117 square miles and a water area of 0.053 square miles. Located at 33.89° N. Lat; 118.13° W. Long. Elevation is 72 feet.

History: Named for the local bellflower apples. Incorporated 1957.

Population: 76,616; Growth (since 2000): 5.1%; Density: 12,525.0 persons per square mile; Race: 42.2% White, 14.0% Black/African American, 11.6% Asian, 1.0% American Indian/Alaska Native, 0.8% Native Hawaiian/Other Pacific Islander, 4.7% Two or more races, 52.3% Hispanic of any race; Average household size: 3.21; Median age: 31.9; Age under 18: 28.4%; Age 65 and over: 8.6%; Males per 100 females: 94.4; Marriage status: 39.0% never married, 46.0% now married, 3.4% separated, 5.0% widowed, 9.9% divorced; Foreign born: 28.8%; Speak English only: 47.0%; With disability: 11.0%; Veterans: 5.3%; Ancestry: 3.6% German, 2.6% Dutch, 2.5% Irish, 2.1% American, 2.1% Italian

Employment: 10.2% management, business, and financial, 2.4% computer, engineering, and science, 7.6% education, legal, community service, arts, and media, 4.4% healthcare practitioners, 19.5% service, 28.7% sales and office, 10.2% natural resources, construction, and maintenance, 16.9% production, transportation, and material moving

Income: Per capita: $20,397; Median household: $49,637; Average household: $63,549; Households with income of $100,000 or more: 18.8%; Poverty rate: 17.1%

Educational Attainment: High school diploma or higher: 78.0%; Bachelor's degree or higher: 16.0%; Graduate/professional degree or higher: 3.6%

School District(s)

Bellflower Unified (KG-12)
2012-13 Enrollment: 13,721 . . . . (562) 866-9011

Housing: Homeownership rate: 40.0%; Median home value: $337,100; Median year structure built: 1964; Homeowner vacancy rate: 1.7%; Median gross rent: $1,179 per month; Rental vacancy rate: 5.1%

Health Insurance: 78.5% have insurance; 53.1% have private insurance; 31.1% have public insurance; 21.5% do not have insurance; 10.3% of children under 18 do not have insurance

Safety: Violent crime rate: 36.0 per 10,000 population; Property crime rate: 242.5 per 10,000 population

Transportation: Commute: 89.5% car, 4.6% public transportation, 1.8% walk, 2.6% work from home; Median travel time to work: 28.9 minutes

Additional Information Contacts

City of Bellflower . . . . (562) 804-1424
http://www.bellflower.org/home/index.asp

BEVERLY HILLS (city). Covers a land area of 5.708 square miles and a water area of 0.002 square miles. Located at 34.08° N. Lat; 118.40° W. Long. Elevation is 259 feet.

History: Beverly Hills was laid out in 1907 by a former resident of Beverly, Massachusetts. Surrounded by the boundaries of the city of Los Angeles, Beverly Hills became known as the location of the estates of many motion picture stars.

Population: 34,109; Growth (since 2000): 1.0%; Density: 5,975.5 persons per square mile; Race: 82.4% White, 2.2% Black/African American, 8.9% Asian, 0.1% American Indian/Alaska Native, 0.0% Native Hawaiian/Other Pacific Islander, 4.9% Two or more races, 5.7% Hispanic of any race; Average household size: 2.29; Median age: 43.6; Age under 18: 19.4%; Age 65 and over: 19.1%; Males per 100 females: 84.3; Marriage status: 34.2% never married, 50.3% now married, 2.0% separated, 6.4% widowed, 9.1% divorced; Foreign born: 37.4%; Speak English only: 48.4%; With disability: 10.5%; Veterans: 4.1%; Ancestry: 25.4% Iranian, 8.7% Russian, 7.2% English, 7.1% German, 6.4% Polish

Employment: 27.3% management, business, and financial, 4.8% computer, engineering, and science, 20.1% education, legal, community service, arts, and media, 8.0% healthcare practitioners, 9.3% service, 26.2% sales and office, 1.7% natural resources, construction, and maintenance, 2.6% production, transportation, and material moving

Income: Per capita: $75,890; Median household: $86,141; Average household: $177,485; Households with income of $100,000 or more: 45.3%; Poverty rate: 8.8%

Educational Attainment: High school diploma or higher: 94.7%; Bachelor's degree or higher: 58.6%; Graduate/professional degree or higher: 27.2%

School District(s)

Beverly Hills Unified (KG-12)
2012-13 Enrollment: 4,515 . . . . (310) 551-5100

Four-year College(s)

Academy of Couture Art (Private, For-profit)
Fall 2013 Enrollment: 21 . . . . (310) 360-8888
2013-14 Tuition: In-state $22,338; Out-of-state $22,338

Two-year College(s)

West Coast Ultrasound Institute (Private, For-profit)
Fall 2013 Enrollment: 796 . . . . (310) 289-5123
2013-14 Tuition: In-state $32,900; Out-of-state $32,900

Housing: Homeownership rate: 44.1%; Median home value: 1 million+; Median year structure built: 1952; Homeowner vacancy rate: 2.2%; Median gross rent: $1,893 per month; Rental vacancy rate: 8.0%

Health Insurance: 90.8% have insurance; 79.7% have private insurance; 23.1% have public insurance; 9.2% do not have insurance; 6.0% of children under 18 do not have insurance

Safety: Violent crime rate: 22.1 per 10,000 population; Property crime rate: 339.0 per 10,000 population

Newspapers: Beverly Hills Weekly (weekly circulation 15000); Canyon News (weekly circulation 40000); The Beverly Hills Courier (weekly circulation 40000)

Transportation: Commute: 78.1% car, 2.4% public transportation, 5.8% walk, 12.0% work from home; Median travel time to work: 24.2 minutes

Additional Information Contacts

City of Beverly Hills . . . . (310) 285-1000
http://www.beverlyhills.org

BRADBURY (city). Covers a land area of 1.957 square miles and a water area of 0.001 square miles. Located at 34.15° N. Lat; 117.97° W. Long. Elevation is 676 feet.

Population: 1,048; Growth (since 2000): 22.6%; Density: 535.4 persons per square mile; Race: 62.2% White, 2.1% Black/African American, 26.3% Asian, 0.4% American Indian/Alaska Native, 0.0% Native Hawaiian/Other Pacific Islander, 3.3% Two or more races, 20.8% Hispanic of any race; Average household size: 2.96; Median age: 49.1; Age under 18: 16.5%; Age 65 and over: 19.9%; Males per 100 females: 94.1

Housing: Homeownership rate: 86.7%; Homeowner vacancy rate: 1.0%; Rental vacancy rate: 7.8%

Safety: Violent crime rate: 9.3 per 10,000 population; Property crime rate: 148.1 per 10,000 population

Additional Information Contacts

City of Bradbury. . . . . (626) 358-3218
http://www.cityofbradbury.org

BURBANK (city). Covers a land area of 17.341 square miles and a water area of 0.038 square miles. Located at 34.19° N. Lat; 118.32° W. Long. Elevation is 607 feet.

History: Named in 1887 for David Burbank, a Los Angeles dentist who purchased some of the land during a real estate boom. Burbank was built on land acquired from the Rancho la Providencia.

Population: 103,340; Growth (since 2000): 3.0%; Density: 5,959.3 persons per square mile; Race: 72.7% White, 2.5% Black/African American, 11.6% Asian, 0.5% American Indian/Alaska Native, 0.1% Native Hawaiian/Other Pacific Islander, 4.8% Two or more races, 24.5% Hispanic of any race; Average household size: 2.45; Median age: 38.9; Age under 18: 19.8%; Age 65 and over: 13.3%; Males per 100 females: 93.6; Marriage status: 34.4% never married, 49.8% now married, 1.9% separated, 6.2% widowed, 9.5% divorced; Foreign born: 35.2%; Speak English only: 52.0%; With disability: 9.9%; Veterans: 5.0%; Ancestry: 13.3% Armenian, 9.1% German, 7.9% Irish, 6.2% Italian, 6.2% English

Employment: 18.8% management, business, and financial, 6.3% computer, engineering, and science, 17.9% education, legal, community service, arts, and media, 6.1% healthcare practitioners, 12.4% service, 25.5% sales and office, 4.9% natural resources, construction, and maintenance, 8.0% production, transportation, and material moving

Income: Per capita: $33,663; Median household: $66,240; Average household: $82,531; Households with income of $100,000 or more: 29.9%; Poverty rate: 9.4%

Educational Attainment: High school diploma or higher: 88.0%; Bachelor's degree or higher: 37.5%; Graduate/professional degree or higher: 10.8%

School District(s)

Burbank Unified (KG-12)
2012-13 Enrollment: 16,481 . . . . (818) 729-4400

Four-year College(s)

Woodbury University (Private, Not-for-profit)
Fall 2013 Enrollment: 1,607 . . . . (818) 767-0888
2013-14 Tuition: In-state $33,150; Out-of-state $33,150

Vocational/Technical School(s)

CES College (Private, Not-for-profit)
Fall 2013 Enrollment: 166. . . . . (818) 563-9822
2013-14 Tuition: $24,561

InterCoast Colleges-Burbank (Private, For-profit)
Fall 2013 Enrollment: 30 . . . . (818) 500-8400
2013-14 Tuition: $20,115

Make-up Designory (Private, For-profit)
Fall 2013 Enrollment: 241 . . . . (818) 729-9420
2013-14 Tuition: $19,376

Marinello Schools of Beauty-Burbank (Private, For-profit)
Fall 2013 Enrollment: 397. . . . . (562) 945-2211
2013-14 Tuition: $18,511

Video Symphony EnterTraining Inc (Private, For-profit)
Fall 2013 Enrollment: 78. . . . . (818) 557-7200
2013-14 Tuition: $29,995

Housing: Homeownership rate: 44.0%; Median home value: $554,700; Median year structure built: 1957; Homeowner vacancy rate: 1.6%; Median gross rent: $1,365 per month; Rental vacancy rate: 5.3%

Health Insurance: 84.9% have insurance; 69.9% have private insurance; 22.1% have public insurance; 15.1% do not have insurance; 5.7% of children under 18 do not have insurance

Hospitals: Providence Saint Joseph Medical Center (431 beds)

Safety: Violent crime rate: 16.3 per 10,000 population; Property crime rate: 232.0 per 10,000 population

Newspapers: The Burbank Times (weekly circulation 20000)

Transportation: Commute: 86.7% car, 2.9% public transportation, 2.9% walk, 5.0% work from home; Median travel time to work: 24.8 minutes; Amtrak: Train service available.

Airports: Bob Hope (primary service/medium hub)

Additional Information Contacts

City of Burbank . . . . (818) 238-5850
http://www.burbankca.gov

CALABASAS (city). Covers a land area of 12.901 square miles and a water area of 0.049 square miles. Located at 34.13° N. Lat; 118.67° W. Long. Elevation is 928 feet.

History: It is generally accepted that Calabasas means "pumpkin squash or gourd" derived from the Spanish calabaza. Some historians hold the theory that Calabasas is a translation of the Chumash word calahoosa.

Population: 23,058; Growth (since 2000): 15.1%; Density: 1,787.2 persons per square mile; Race: 83.9% White, 1.6% Black/African American, 8.6% Asian, 0.2% American Indian/Alaska Native, 0.0% Native Hawaiian/Other Pacific Islander, 4.0% Two or more races, 6.4% Hispanic of any race; Average household size: 2.70; Median age: 41.6; Age under 18: 25.3%; Age 65 and over: 12.6%; Males per 100 females: 93.6; Marriage status: 26.1% never married, 60.2% now married, 1.9% separated, 4.3% widowed, 9.4% divorced; Foreign born: 26.4%; Speak English only: 72.5%; With disability: 6.4%; Veterans: 5.7%; Ancestry: 11.0% Russian, 9.5% Iranian, 9.1% German, 7.3% English, 6.7% Irish

Employment: 32.9% management, business, and financial, 7.1% computer, engineering, and science, 18.6% education, legal, community service, arts, and media, 7.1% healthcare practitioners, 6.7% service, 22.9% sales and office, 1.9% natural resources, construction, and maintenance, 2.8% production, transportation, and material moving

Income: Per capita: $66,731; Median household: $124,583; Average household: $179,670; Households with income of $100,000 or more: 59.9%; Poverty rate: 6.6%

Educational Attainment: High school diploma or higher: 97.4%; Bachelor's degree or higher: 62.0%; Graduate/professional degree or higher: 29.2%

School District(s)

Las Virgenes Unified (KG-12)
2012-13 Enrollment: 11,200 . . . . (818) 880-4000

Los Angeles County Office of Education (KG-12)
2012-13 Enrollment: 9,136 . . . . (562) 922-6111

Housing: Homeownership rate: 73.6%; Median home value: $868,700; Median year structure built: 1983; Homeowner vacancy rate: 1.2%; Median gross rent: $2,000+ per month; Rental vacancy rate: 5.2%

Health Insurance: 93.3% have insurance; 85.5% have private insurance; 18.2% have public insurance; 6.7% do not have insurance; 4.5% of children under 18 do not have insurance

Safety: Violent crime rate: 8.3 per 10,000 population; Property crime rate: 129.8 per 10,000 population

Transportation: Commute: 88.5% car, 0.5% public transportation, 0.8% walk, 9.5% work from home; Median travel time to work: 31.4 minutes

Additional Information Contacts

City of Calabasas . . . . (818) 224-1600
http://www.cityofcalabasas.com

CANOGA PARK (unincorporated postal area)

ZCTA: 91303

Covers a land area of 2.163 square miles and a water area of 0.016 square miles. Located at 34.20° N. Lat; 118.60° W. Long. Elevation is 797 feet.

Population: 26,855; Growth (since 2000): 14.2%; Density: 12,412.9 persons per square mile; Race: 48.6% White, 4.2% Black/African American, 10.4% Asian, 0.8% American Indian/Alaska Native, 0.2% Native

Hawaiian/Other Pacific Islander, 4.9% Two or more races, 61.1% Hispanic of any race; Average household size: 3.08; Median age: 31.1; Age under 18: 26.1%; Age 65 and over: 6.3%; Males per 100 females: 107.4; Marriage status: 42.7% never married, 44.5% now married, 4.0% separated, 3.4% widowed, 9.4% divorced; Foreign born: 46.2%; Speak English only: 30.1%; With disability: 8.1%; Veterans: 2.3%; Ancestry: 4.1% German, 2.8% Irish, 2.4% English, 2.0% Italian, 1.9% Iranian

Employment: 9.7% management, business, and financial, 4.6% computer, engineering, and science, 9.0% education, legal, community service, arts, and media, 3.8% healthcare practitioners, 27.4% service, 24.4% sales and office, 10.3% natural resources, construction, and maintenance, 10.8% production, transportation, and material moving

Income: Per capita: $20,550; Median household: $47,484; Average household: $58,470; Households with income of $100,000 or more: 15.9%; Poverty rate: 18.0%

Educational Attainment: High school diploma or higher: 70.8%; Bachelor's degree or higher: 23.6%; Graduate/professional degree or higher: 6.4%

School District(s)

Los Angeles Unified (PK-12)
2012-13 Enrollment: 655,455 . . . . (213) 241-1000
Sbe - Ingenium Charter (KG-06)
2012-13 Enrollment: 383. . . . . (818) 456-4590

Four-year College(s)

Academy for Salon Professionals (Private, For-profit)
Fall 2013 Enrollment: 83 . . . . (818) 992-9901
California Career College (Private, For-profit)
Fall 2013 Enrollment: 78 . . . . (818) 710-1310

Two-year College(s)

Academy for Salon Professionals (Private, For-profit)
Fall 2013 Enrollment: 83 . . . . (818) 992-9901
California Career College (Private, For-profit)
Fall 2013 Enrollment: 78 . . . . (818) 710-1310

Vocational/Technical School(s)

Academy for Salon Professionals (Private, For-profit)
Fall 2013 Enrollment: 83 . . . . (818) 992-9901
2013-14 Tuition: $18,150
California Career College (Private, For-profit)
Fall 2013 Enrollment: 78 . . . . (818) 710-1310

Housing: Homeownership rate: 28.0%; Median home value: $330,900; Median year structure built: 1976; Homeowner vacancy rate: 1.8%; Median gross rent: $1,211 per month; Rental vacancy rate: 8.9%

Health Insurance: 71.5% have insurance; 44.6% have private insurance; 30.3% have public insurance; 28.5% do not have insurance; 9.6% of children under 18 do not have insurance

Transportation: Commute: 76.2% car, 9.4% public transportation, 2.6% walk, 4.8% work from home; Median travel time to work: 27.6 minutes

ZCTA: 91304

Covers a land area of 9.406 square miles and a water area of 0.019 square miles. Located at 34.22° N. Lat; 118.63° W. Long. Elevation is 797 feet.

Population: 50,231; Growth (since 2000): 2.0%; Density: 5,340.6 persons per square mile; Race: 57.5% White, 5.1% Black/African American, 13.5% Asian, 0.6% American Indian/Alaska Native, 0.1% Native Hawaiian/Other Pacific Islander, 5.1% Two or more races, 40.1% Hispanic of any race; Average household size: 3.00; Median age: 35.9; Age under 18: 24.9%; Age 65 and over: 11.5%; Males per 100 females: 97.7; Marriage status: 35.9% never married, 49.5% now married, 3.1% separated, 5.6% widowed, 9.1% divorced; Foreign born: 38.0%; Speak English only: 45.4%; With disability: 8.5%; Veterans: 5.3%; Ancestry: 5.5% German, 5.5% Irish, 5.1% English, 4.0% American, 3.1% Russian

Employment: 15.5% management, business, and financial, 4.9% computer, engineering, and science, 9.4% education, legal, community service, arts, and media, 4.8% healthcare practitioners, 20.4% service, 25.2% sales and office, 8.4% natural resources, construction, and maintenance, 11.4% production, transportation, and material moving

Income: Per capita: $25,531; Median household: $58,889; Average household: $77,386; Households with income of $100,000 or more: 27.1%; Poverty rate: 18.7%

Educational Attainment: High school diploma or higher: 80.6%; Bachelor's degree or higher: 27.9%; Graduate/professional degree or higher: 9.6%

Housing: Homeownership rate: 52.9%; Median home value: $442,900; Median year structure built: 1971; Homeowner vacancy rate: 1.3%; Median gross rent: $1,197 per month; Rental vacancy rate: 7.4%

Health Insurance: 80.1% have insurance; 57.3% have private insurance; 30.8% have public insurance; 19.9% do not have insurance; 8.6% of children under 18 do not have insurance

Transportation: Commute: 83.9% car, 6.2% public transportation, 1.7% walk, 4.9% work from home; Median travel time to work: 28.5 minutes

CANYON COUNTRY (unincorporated postal area)

ZCTA: 91351

Covers a land area of 9.571 square miles and a water area of 0.001 square miles. Located at 34.44° N. Lat; 118.45° W. Long. Elevation is 1,342 feet.

Population: 32,362; Growth (since 2000): -45.4%; Density: 3,381.2 persons per square mile; Race: 63.2% White, 4.0% Black/African American, 7.0% Asian, 0.7% American Indian/Alaska Native, 0.2% Native Hawaiian/Other Pacific Islander, 5.6% Two or more races, 40.7% Hispanic of any race; Average household size: 3.22; Median age: 33.9; Age under 18: 27.8%; Age 65 and over: 7.5%; Males per 100 females: 98.8; Marriage status: 35.3% never married, 49.1% now married, 2.5% separated, 4.1% widowed, 11.4% divorced; Foreign born: 24.2%; Speak English only: 61.1%; With disability: 10.0%; Veterans: 5.8%; Ancestry: 11.0% German, 9.3% Irish, 6.5% English, 5.6% Italian, 3.2% American

Employment: 14.5% management, business, and financial, 3.9% computer, engineering, and science, 9.9% education, legal, community service, arts, and media, 6.2% healthcare practitioners, 13.3% service, 30.0% sales and office, 9.6% natural resources, construction, and maintenance, 12.6% production, transportation, and material moving

Income: Per capita: $28,023; Median household: $71,153; Average household: $84,825; Households with income of $100,000 or more: 31.3%; Poverty rate: 11.7%

Educational Attainment: High school diploma or higher: 82.8%; Bachelor's degree or higher: 22.3%; Graduate/professional degree or higher: 6.5%

School District(s)

Saugus Union (KG-06)
2012-13 Enrollment: 10,178 . . . . (661) 294-5300
Sulphur Springs Union (KG-06)
2012-13 Enrollment: 5,553 . . . . (661) 252-5131
William S. Hart Union High (KG-12)
2012-13 Enrollment: 26,373 . . . . (661) 259-0033

Four-year College(s)

Charter College-Canyon Country (Private, For-profit)
Fall 2013 Enrollment: 1,317 . . . . (661) 252-1864
2013-14 Tuition: In-state $18,313; Out-of-state $18,313
Flair Beauty College (Private, For-profit)
Fall 2013 Enrollment: 60. . . . . (661) 251-3261

Two-year College(s)

Charter College-Canyon Country (Private, For-profit)
Fall 2013 Enrollment: 1,317 . . . . (661) 252-1864
2013-14 Tuition: In-state $18,313; Out-of-state $18,313
Flair Beauty College (Private, For-profit)
Fall 2013 Enrollment: 60. . . . . (661) 251-3261

Vocational/Technical School(s)

Charter College-Canyon Country (Private, For-profit)
Fall 2013 Enrollment: 1,317 . . . . (661) 252-1864
2013-14 Tuition: In-state $18,313; Out-of-state $18,313
Flair Beauty College (Private, For-profit)
Fall 2013 Enrollment: 60. . . . . (661) 251-3261
2013-14 Tuition: $12,081

Housing: Homeownership rate: 73.2%; Median home value: $311,600; Median year structure built: 1983; Homeowner vacancy rate: 2.3%; Median gross rent: $1,431 per month; Rental vacancy rate: 5.6%

Health Insurance: 83.3% have insurance; 66.4% have private insurance; 22.7% have public insurance; 16.7% do not have insurance; 12.8% of children under 18 do not have insurance

Transportation: Commute: 88.6% car, 3.6% public transportation, 1.3% walk, 5.4% work from home; Median travel time to work: 33.6 minutes

ZCTA: 91387

Covers a land area of 49.525 square miles and a water area of 0.086 square miles. Located at 34.40° N. Lat; 118.37° W. Long. Elevation is 1,342 feet.

Population: 40,328; Growth (since 2000): n/a; Density: 814.3 persons per square mile; Race: 61.6% White, 6.5% Black/African American, 10.5% Asian, 0.6% American Indian/Alaska Native, 0.2% Native Hawaiian/Other Pacific Islander, 5.4% Two or more races, 33.4% Hispanic of any race; Average household size: 3.13; Median age: 33.0; Age under 18: 29.1%;

Age 65 and over: 6.3%; Males per 100 females: 99.4; Marriage status: 34.4% never married, 50.7% now married, 2.6% separated, 3.3% widowed, 11.6% divorced; Foreign born: 22.6%; Speak English only: 64.4%; With disability: 9.0%; Veterans: 6.7%; Ancestry: 10.9% German, 9.1% Irish, 7.3% English, 6.2% Italian, 2.7% Scottish

Employment: 17.7% management, business, and financial, 6.1% computer, engineering, and science, 10.4% education, legal, community service, arts, and media, 6.4% healthcare practitioners, 15.4% service, 27.0% sales and office, 7.6% natural resources, construction, and maintenance, 9.3% production, transportation, and material moving

Income: Per capita: $33,071; Median household: $83,484; Average household: $100,603; Households with income of $100,000 or more: 37.7%; Poverty rate: 8.8%

Educational Attainment: High school diploma or higher: 88.1%; Bachelor's degree or higher: 29.2%; Graduate/professional degree or higher: 9.5%

Housing: Homeownership rate: 62.8%; Median home value: $371,100; Median year structure built: 1988; Homeowner vacancy rate: 2.1%; Median gross rent: $1,599 per month; Rental vacancy rate: 10.5%

Health Insurance: 85.1% have insurance; 70.9% have private insurance; 20.8% have public insurance; 14.9% do not have insurance; 8.4% of children under 18 do not have insurance

Transportation: Commute: 90.4% car, 3.2% public transportation, 0.3% walk, 5.2% work from home; Median travel time to work: 37.4 minutes

---

CARSON (city). Covers a land area of 18.724 square miles and a water area of 0.244 square miles. Located at 33.84° N. Lat; 118.25° W. Long. Elevation is 39 feet.

Population: 91,714; Growth (since 2000): 2.2%; Density: 4,898.2 persons per square mile; Race: 23.8% White, 23.8% Black/African American, 25.6% Asian, 0.6% American Indian/Alaska Native, 2.6% Native Hawaiian/Other Pacific Islander, 4.8% Two or more races, 38.6% Hispanic of any race; Average household size: 3.56; Median age: 37.6; Age under 18: 24.0%; Age 65 and over: 13.8%; Males per 100 females: 91.9; Marriage status: 38.7% never married, 46.7% now married, 2.3% separated, 6.3% widowed, 8.3% divorced; Foreign born: 35.0%; Speak English only: 46.0%; With disability: 10.4%; Veterans: 6.0%; Ancestry: 4.2% African, 2.3% German, 1.9% English, 1.5% Irish, 1.3% Nigerian

Employment: 11.4% management, business, and financial, 3.8% computer, engineering, and science, 7.6% education, legal, community service, arts, and media, 7.7% healthcare practitioners, 18.1% service, 26.8% sales and office, 7.7% natural resources, construction, and maintenance, 16.9% production, transportation, and material moving

Income: Per capita: $23,762; Median household: $72,235; Average household: $82,086; Households with income of $100,000 or more: 30.9%; Poverty rate: 10.0%

Educational Attainment: High school diploma or higher: 80.1%; Bachelor's degree or higher: 24.0%; Graduate/professional degree or higher: 5.6%

School District(s)

Compton Unified (KG-12)
 2012-13 Enrollment: 24,710 . . . . (310) 639-4321
Long Beach Unified (KG-12)
 2012-13 Enrollment: 82,256 . . . . (562) 997-8000
Los Angeles Unified (PK-12)
 2012-13 Enrollment: 655,455 . . . . (213) 241-1000

Four-year College(s)

California State University-Dominguez Hills (Public)
 Fall 2013 Enrollment: 14,670 . . . . (310) 243-3300
 2013-14 Tuition: In-state $6,100; Out-of-state $17,260

Vocational/Technical School(s)

California Healing Arts College (Private, For-profit)
 Fall 2013 Enrollment: 9 . . . . (310) 826-7622
 2013-14 Tuition: $15,428
InterCoast Colleges-Carson (Private, For-profit)
 Fall 2013 Enrollment: 33 . . . . (310) 847-8400
 2013-14 Tuition: $20,115
RWM Fiber Optics (Private, For-profit)
 Fall 2013 Enrollment: 73 . . . . (310) 769-0968
 2013-14 Tuition: $13,525

Housing: Homeownership rate: 76.8%; Median home value: $340,900; Median year structure built: 1965; Homeowner vacancy rate: 1.3%; Median gross rent: $1,347 per month; Rental vacancy rate: 3.7%

Health Insurance: 83.3% have insurance; 62.2% have private insurance; 29.3% have public insurance; 16.7% do not have insurance; 7.9% of children under 18 do not have insurance

Safety: Violent crime rate: 42.8 per 10,000 population; Property crime rate: 241.0 per 10,000 population

Transportation: Commute: 90.9% car, 3.1% public transportation, 1.5% walk, 3.6% work from home; Median travel time to work: 26.4 minutes

Additional Information Contacts

City of Carson . . . . (310) 830-7600
 http://ci.carson.ca.us

CASTAIC (CDP). Covers a land area of 7.261 square miles and a water area of 0.017 square miles. Located at 34.48° N. Lat; 118.63° W. Long. Elevation is 1,227 feet.

Population: 19,015; Growth (since 2000): n/a; Density: 2,618.8 persons per square mile; Race: 71.6% White, 3.3% Black/African American, 11.4% Asian, 0.6% American Indian/Alaska Native, 0.1% Native Hawaiian/Other Pacific Islander, 5.3% Two or more races, 24.8% Hispanic of any race; Average household size: 3.29; Median age: 35.6; Age under 18: 30.3%; Age 65 and over: 5.7%; Males per 100 females: 101.2; Marriage status: 31.3% never married, 58.1% now married, 2.2% separated, 2.9% widowed, 7.8% divorced; Foreign born: 19.6%; Speak English only: 70.4%; With disability: 7.0%; Veterans: 5.7%; Ancestry: 14.5% German, 12.6% Irish, 7.2% English, 7.2% Italian, 4.1% American

Employment: 20.5% management, business, and financial, 6.4% computer, engineering, and science, 12.3% education, legal, community service, arts, and media, 4.4% healthcare practitioners, 15.1% service, 24.6% sales and office, 7.5% natural resources, construction, and maintenance, 9.2% production, transportation, and material moving

Income: Per capita: $36,657; Median household: $103,811; Average household: $115,256; Households with income of $100,000 or more: 53.9%; Poverty rate: 8.6%

Educational Attainment: High school diploma or higher: 91.2%; Bachelor's degree or higher: 33.7%; Graduate/professional degree or higher: 8.8%

School District(s)

Castaic Union Elementary (KG-08)
 2012-13 Enrollment: 2,864 . . . . (661) 257-4500
William S. Hart Union High (KG-12)
 2012-13 Enrollment: 26,373 . . . . (661) 259-0033

Housing: Homeownership rate: 84.2%; Median home value: $402,000; Median year structure built: 1994; Homeowner vacancy rate: 1.2%; Median gross rent: $1,387 per month; Rental vacancy rate: 6.7%

Health Insurance: 88.8% have insurance; 80.5% have private insurance; 12.9% have public insurance; 11.2% do not have insurance; 10.6% of children under 18 do not have insurance

Transportation: Commute: 93.4% car, 1.7% public transportation, 0.9% walk, 3.1% work from home; Median travel time to work: 30.8 minutes

---

CERRITOS (city). Covers a land area of 8.725 square miles and a water area of 0.131 square miles. Located at 33.87° N. Lat; 118.07° W. Long. Elevation is 46 feet.

History: Cerritos was initially incorporated in 1956 as an agricultural community and was formerly known as Dairy Valley.

Population: 49,041; Growth (since 2000): -4.8%; Density: 5,620.7 persons per square mile; Race: 23.1% White, 6.9% Black/African American, 61.9% Asian, 0.3% American Indian/Alaska Native, 0.3% Native Hawaiian/Other Pacific Islander, 3.8% Two or more races, 12.0% Hispanic of any race; Average household size: 3.15; Median age: 44.0; Age under 18: 20.4%; Age 65 and over: 17.7%; Males per 100 females: 92.6; Marriage status: 29.5% never married, 57.7% now married, 1.2% separated, 6.5% widowed, 6.3% divorced; Foreign born: 45.1%; Speak English only: 39.5%; With disability: 8.0%; Veterans: 5.3%; Ancestry: 3.3% German, 2.6% Irish, 2.5% English, 2.2% American, 1.1% Italian

Employment: 18.9% management, business, and financial, 11.3% computer, engineering, and science, 9.5% education, legal, community service, arts, and media, 12.9% healthcare practitioners, 10.3% service, 28.1% sales and office, 3.0% natural resources, construction, and maintenance, 6.0% production, transportation, and material moving

Income: Per capita: $34,238; Median household: $89,594; Average household: $108,016; Households with income of $100,000 or more: 44.6%; Poverty rate: 5.5%

Educational Attainment: High school diploma or higher: 93.1%; Bachelor's degree or higher: 48.6%; Graduate/professional degree or higher: 17.2%

School District(s)

ABC Unified (KG-12)
2012-13 Enrollment: 20,835 . . . . (562) 926-5566

Four-year College(s)

Fremont College (Private, For-profit)
Fall 2013 Enrollment: 344 . . . . (562) 809-5100

Vocational/Technical School(s)

PCI College (Private, For-profit)
Fall 2013 Enrollment: 104 . . . . (562) 916-5055
2013-14 Tuition: $29,190

Housing: Homeownership rate: 81.9%; Median home value: $592,600; Median year structure built: 1974; Homeowner vacancy rate: 0.7%; Median gross rent: $1,970 per month; Rental vacancy rate: 3.1%

Health Insurance: 87.5% have insurance; 74.4% have private insurance; 23.2% have public insurance; 12.5% do not have insurance; 7.0% of children under 18 do not have insurance

Safety: Violent crime rate: 16.5 per 10,000 population; Property crime rate: 361.7 per 10,000 population

Newspapers: Community News (weekly circulation 35000)

Transportation: Commute: 92.9% car, 2.6% public transportation, 0.3% walk, 3.6% work from home; Median travel time to work: 30.8 minutes

Additional Information Contacts

City of Cerritos. . . . . (562) 860-0311
http://www.ci.cerritos.ca.us

CHARTER OAK (CDP). Covers a land area of 0.928 square miles and a water area of 0 square miles. Located at 34.10° N. Lat; 117.86° W. Long. Elevation is 761 feet.

Population: 9,310; Growth (since 2000): 3.1%; Density: 10,034.6 persons per square mile; Race: 60.2% White, 4.4% Black/African American, 11.1% Asian, 0.9% American Indian/Alaska Native, 0.2% Native Hawaiian/Other Pacific Islander, 5.1% Two or more races, 48.8% Hispanic of any race; Average household size: 3.02; Median age: 35.4; Age under 18: 25.3%; Age 65 and over: 9.9%; Males per 100 females: 94.6; Marriage status: 36.1% never married, 47.7% now married, 2.3% separated, 5.5% widowed, 10.6% divorced; Foreign born: 14.2%; Speak English only: 69.4%; With disability: 8.6%; Veterans: 6.9%; Ancestry: 11.4% German, 9.0% Irish, 8.3% Italian, 7.1% English, 4.0% French

Employment: 12.6% management, business, and financial, 4.3% computer, engineering, and science, 9.0% education, legal, community service, arts, and media, 5.8% healthcare practitioners, 22.2% service, 26.2% sales and office, 8.1% natural resources, construction, and maintenance, 11.9% production, transportation, and material moving

Income: Per capita: $23,623; Median household: $66,087; Average household: $73,472; Households with income of $100,000 or more: 26.0%; Poverty rate: 11.1%

Educational Attainment: High school diploma or higher: 84.2%; Bachelor's degree or higher: 17.6%; Graduate/professional degree or higher: 5.3%

Housing: Homeownership rate: 65.6%; Median home value: $342,400; Median year structure built: 1966; Homeowner vacancy rate: 1.5%; Median gross rent: $1,401 per month; Rental vacancy rate: 4.0%

Health Insurance: 86.8% have insurance; 63.7% have private insurance; 29.7% have public insurance; 13.2% do not have insurance; 3.8% of children under 18 do not have insurance

Transportation: Commute: 89.4% car, 4.9% public transportation, 0.8% walk, 3.4% work from home; Median travel time to work: 32.3 minutes

CHATSWORTH (unincorporated postal area)

ZCTA: 91311

Covers a land area of 32.078 square miles and a water area of 0.931 square miles. Located at 34.29° N. Lat; 118.60° W. Long. Elevation is 978 feet.

Population: 36,557; Growth (since 2000): 3.5%; Density: 1,139.6 persons per square mile; Race: 66.0% White, 4.2% Black/African American, 16.5% Asian, 0.6% American Indian/Alaska Native, 0.2% Native Hawaiian/Other Pacific Islander, 4.7% Two or more races, 21.7% Hispanic of any race; Average household size: 2.66; Median age: 42.7; Age under 18: 19.7%; Age 65 and over: 15.4%; Males per 100 females: 95.3; Marriage status: 32.3% never married, 51.1% now married, 1.8% separated, 5.9% widowed, 10.7% divorced; Foreign born: 29.2%; Speak English only: 59.1%; With disability: 10.1%; Veterans: 6.5%; Ancestry: 9.6% German, 6.5% Irish, 6.1% English, 4.4% Italian, 3.8% Russian

Employment: 19.9% management, business, and financial, 7.7% computer, engineering, and science, 15.4% education, legal, community service, arts, and media, 5.3% healthcare practitioners, 13.7% service, 24.7% sales and office, 5.2% natural resources, construction, and maintenance, 8.0% production, transportation, and material moving

Income: Per capita: $37,547; Median household: $78,414; Average household: $101,967; Households with income of $100,000 or more: 35.9%; Poverty rate: 8.2%

Educational Attainment: High school diploma or higher: 90.6%; Bachelor's degree or higher: 39.8%; Graduate/professional degree or higher: 13.7%

School District(s)

Los Angeles Unified (PK-12)
2012-13 Enrollment: 655,455 . . . . (213) 241-1000

Four-year College(s)

Phillips Graduate Institute (Private, Not-for-profit)
Fall 2013 Enrollment: 206 . . . . (818) 386-5600

Two-year College(s)

Phillips Graduate Institute (Private, Not-for-profit)
Fall 2013 Enrollment: 206 . . . . (818) 386-5600

Vocational/Technical School(s)

Phillips Graduate Institute (Private, Not-for-profit)
Fall 2013 Enrollment: 206 . . . . (818) 386-5600

Housing: Homeownership rate: 69.8%; Median home value: $438,500; Median year structure built: 1973; Homeowner vacancy rate: 1.6%; Median gross rent: $1,376 per month; Rental vacancy rate: 6.0%

Health Insurance: 85.9% have insurance; 71.7% have private insurance; 25.0% have public insurance; 14.1% do not have insurance; 5.0% of children under 18 do not have insurance

Transportation: Commute: 86.6% car, 3.7% public transportation, 1.5% walk, 6.2% work from home; Median travel time to work: 29.0 minutes

CITRUS (CDP). Covers a land area of 0.887 square miles and a water area of 0.002 square miles. Located at 34.11° N. Lat; 117.89° W. Long. Elevation is 584 feet.

Population: 10,866; Growth (since 2000): 2.7%; Density: 12,251.8 persons per square mile; Race: 54.3% White, 2.2% Black/African American, 7.9% Asian, 1.1% American Indian/Alaska Native, 0.0% Native Hawaiian/Other Pacific Islander, 4.1% Two or more races, 72.8% Hispanic of any race; Average household size: 4.15; Median age: 30.7; Age under 18: 28.4%; Age 65 and over: 7.8%; Males per 100 females: 102.2; Marriage status: 42.0% never married, 47.3% now married, 0.9% separated, 5.9% widowed, 4.9% divorced; Foreign born: 36.4%; Speak English only: 34.4%; With disability: 8.0%; Veterans: 3.4%; Ancestry: 4.1% Irish, 3.3% Egyptian, 3.0% German, 2.6% Italian, 1.8% English

Employment: 7.3% management, business, and financial, 3.6% computer, engineering, and science, 6.9% education, legal, community service, arts, and media, 2.8% healthcare practitioners, 24.5% service, 31.5% sales and office, 10.2% natural resources, construction, and maintenance, 13.2% production, transportation, and material moving

Income: Per capita: $18,578; Median household: $59,919; Average household: $70,586; Households with income of $100,000 or more: 20.1%; Poverty rate: 10.9%

Educational Attainment: High school diploma or higher: 76.1%; Bachelor's degree or higher: 13.4%; Graduate/professional degree or higher: 3.9%

Housing: Homeownership rate: 70.9%; Median home value: $309,000; Median year structure built: 1957; Homeowner vacancy rate: 1.7%; Median gross rent: $1,378 per month; Rental vacancy rate: 3.5%

Health Insurance: 72.0% have insurance; 48.1% have private insurance; 28.0% have public insurance; 28.0% do not have insurance; 12.9% of children under 18 do not have insurance

Transportation: Commute: 90.6% car, 4.0% public transportation, 2.3% walk, 2.6% work from home; Median travel time to work: 29.5 minutes

CLAREMONT (city). Covers a land area of 13.348 square miles and a water area of 0.138 square miles. Located at 34.13° N. Lat; 117.71° W. Long. Elevation is 1,168 feet.

History: Named for Claremont, New Hampshire, by an employee of the land company that plotted the town, and who had lived in Claremont. Claremont developed as a college town, with Pomona College founded in 1887 becoming the nucleus of a group of affilitated colleges known as the Claremont Colleges.

Population: 34,926; Growth (since 2000): 2.7%; Density: 2,616.5 persons per square mile; Race: 70.6% White, 4.7% Black/African American, 13.1% Asian, 0.5% American Indian/Alaska Native, 0.1% Native Hawaiian/Other Pacific Islander, 5.2% Two or more races, 19.8% Hispanic of any race;

Average household size: 2.57; Median age: 38.6; Age under 18: 18.5%; Age 65 and over: 16.5%; Males per 100 females: 88.4; Marriage status: 38.0% never married, 49.4% now married, 1.7% separated, 5.6% widowed, 7.0% divorced; Foreign born: 18.2%; Speak English only: 72.4%; With disability: 8.8%; Veterans: 7.2%; Ancestry: 13.3% German, 11.5% English, 8.8% Irish, 5.7% Italian, 3.0% French

Employment: 19.5% management, business, and financial, 5.0% computer, engineering, and science, 26.9% education, legal, community service, arts, and media, 4.6% healthcare practitioners, 12.1% service, 23.8% sales and office, 3.7% natural resources, construction, and maintenance, 4.4% production, transportation, and material moving

Income: Per capita: $36,822; Median household: $87,324; Average household: $109,342; Households with income of $100,000 or more: 44.2%; Poverty rate: 7.2%

Educational Attainment: High school diploma or higher: 92.7%; Bachelor's degree or higher: 55.0%; Graduate/professional degree or higher: 28.7%

School District(s)

Claremont Unified (KG-12)
2012-13 Enrollment: 7,018 . . . . (909) 398-0609

Four-year College(s)

Claremont Graduate University (Private, Not-for-profit)
Fall 2013 Enrollment: 2,204 . . . . (909) 621-8000
Claremont McKenna College (Private, Not-for-profit)
Fall 2013 Enrollment: 1,328 . . . . (909) 621-8000
2013-14 Tuition: In-state $45,625; Out-of-state $45,625
Claremont School of Theology (Private, Not-for-profit, United Methodist)
Fall 2013 Enrollment: 272 . . . . (909) 447-2500
Harvey Mudd College (Private, Not-for-profit)
Fall 2013 Enrollment: 807 . . . . (909) 621-8000
2013-14 Tuition: In-state $46,509; Out-of-state $46,509
Keck Graduate Institute (Private, Not-for-profit)
Fall 2013 Enrollment: 169 . . . . (909) 607-7855
Pitzer College (Private, Not-for-profit)
Fall 2013 Enrollment: 1,081 . . . . (909) 621-8000
2013-14 Tuition: In-state $45,018; Out-of-state $45,018
Pomona College (Private, Not-for-profit)
Fall 2013 Enrollment: 1,610 . . . . (909) 621-8131
2013-14 Tuition: In-state $43,580; Out-of-state $43,580
Scripps College (Private, Not-for-profit)
Fall 2013 Enrollment: 1,009 . . . . (909) 621-8000
2013-14 Tuition: In-state $45,564; Out-of-state $45,564

Housing: Homeownership rate: 66.4%; Median home value: $533,600; Median year structure built: 1967; Homeowner vacancy rate: 0.9%; Median gross rent: $1,233 per month; Rental vacancy rate: 5.5%

Health Insurance: 93.4% have insurance; 79.5% have private insurance; 24.3% have public insurance; 6.6% do not have insurance; 4.5% of children under 18 do not have insurance

Safety: Violent crime rate: 10.4 per 10,000 population; Property crime rate: 251.0 per 10,000 population

Newspapers: Claremont Courier (weekly circulation 6000)

Transportation: Commute: 76.0% car, 4.0% public transportation, 9.6% walk, 7.8% work from home; Median travel time to work: 27.4 minutes; Amtrak: Train service available.

Additional Information Contacts

City of Claremont. . . . . (909) 399-5460
http://www.ci.claremont.ca.us

COMMERCE (city). Covers a land area of 6.537 square miles and a water area of 0.001 square miles. Located at 33.99° N. Lat; 118.15° W. Long. Elevation is 141 feet.

History: Named for the town's aspiration of being a thriving business community. Incorporated 1960.

Population: 12,823; Growth (since 2000): 2.0%; Density: 1,961.7 persons per square mile; Race: 54.0% White, 0.7% Black/African American, 1.1% Asian, 1.3% American Indian/Alaska Native, 0.1% Native Hawaiian/Other Pacific Islander, 4.7% Two or more races, 94.5% Hispanic of any race; Average household size: 3.77; Median age: 31.2; Age under 18: 29.8%; Age 65 and over: 10.7%; Males per 100 females: 96.4; Marriage status: 42.7% never married, 45.0% now married, 2.0% separated, 5.7% widowed, 6.6% divorced; Foreign born: 36.4%; Speak English only: 23.1%; With disability: 11.1%; Veterans: 3.0%; Ancestry: 1.0% Irish, 0.7% American, 0.6% German, 0.3% Scotch-Irish, 0.2% Italian

Employment: 5.6% management, business, and financial, 0.7% computer, engineering, and science, 6.7% education, legal, community service, arts, and media, 2.3% healthcare practitioners, 20.8% service, 26.8% sales and office, 12.7% natural resources, construction, and maintenance, 24.3% production, transportation, and material moving

Income: Per capita: $15,963; Median household: $48,729; Average household: $57,350; Households with income of $100,000 or more: 15.4%; Poverty rate: 16.5%

Educational Attainment: High school diploma or higher: 53.6%; Bachelor's degree or higher: 5.9%; Graduate/professional degree or higher: 2.1%

School District(s)

Los Angeles County Office of Education (KG-12)
2012-13 Enrollment: 9,136 . . . . (562) 922-6111
Montebello Unified (KG-12)
2012-13 Enrollment: 30,564 . . . . (323) 887-7900

Two-year College(s)

National Polytechnic College (Private, For-profit)
Fall 2013 Enrollment: 234 . . . . (323) 728-9636

Housing: Homeownership rate: 47.9%; Median home value: $325,300; Median year structure built: 1957; Homeowner vacancy rate: 1.0%; Median gross rent: $879 per month; Rental vacancy rate: 1.8%

Health Insurance: 73.7% have insurance; 42.9% have private insurance; 36.3% have public insurance; 26.3% do not have insurance; 11.2% of children under 18 do not have insurance

Safety: Violent crime rate: 63.9 per 10,000 population; Property crime rate: 687.2 per 10,000 population

Transportation: Commute: 91.6% car, 3.4% public transportation, 1.6% walk, 2.0% work from home; Median travel time to work: 26.5 minutes

Additional Information Contacts

City of Commerce . . . . (323) 722-4805
http://www.ci.commerce.ca.us

COMPTON (city). Covers a land area of 10.012 square miles and a water area of 0.104 square miles. Located at 33.89° N. Lat; 118.23° W. Long. Elevation is 69 feet.

History: Named for Griffith D. Compton, one of the founders of the University of Southern California. Incorporated 1888.

Population: 96,455; Growth (since 2000): 3.2%; Density: 9,633.7 persons per square mile; Race: 25.9% White, 32.9% Black/African American, 0.3% Asian, 0.7% American Indian/Alaska Native, 0.7% Native Hawaiian/Other Pacific Islander, 3.4% Two or more races, 65.0% Hispanic of any race; Average household size: 4.15; Median age: 28.0; Age under 18: 33.1%; Age 65 and over: 7.5%; Males per 100 females: 94.8; Marriage status: 46.8% never married, 40.8% now married, 3.0% separated, 4.9% widowed, 7.4% divorced; Foreign born: 30.2%; Speak English only: 36.8%; With disability: 12.3%; Veterans: 3.7%; Ancestry: 2.3% African, 1.5% American, 0.3% Belizean, 0.3% Irish, 0.3% English

Employment: 6.0% management, business, and financial, 1.0% computer, engineering, and science, 5.5% education, legal, community service, arts, and media, 2.7% healthcare practitioners, 21.4% service, 26.9% sales and office, 10.8% natural resources, construction, and maintenance, 25.7% production, transportation, and material moving

Income: Per capita: $13,548; Median household: $42,953; Average household: $52,123; Households with income of $100,000 or more: 11.5%; Poverty rate: 26.3%

Educational Attainment: High school diploma or higher: 59.2%; Bachelor's degree or higher: 6.7%; Graduate/professional degree or higher: 1.8%

School District(s)

Compton Unified (KG-12)
2012-13 Enrollment: 24,710 . . . . (310) 639-4321
Compton Unified Rop
2012-13 Enrollment: n/a . . . . (310) 639-4321
Sbe - Lifeline Education Charter (06-12)
2012-13 Enrollment: 376. . . . . (310) 605-2510

Two-year College(s)

El Camino College-Compton Center (Public)
Fall 2013 Enrollment: 7,693 . . . . (310) 900-1600
2013-14 Tuition: In-state $1,142; Out-of-state $5,222

Housing: Homeownership rate: 55.2%; Median home value: $237,800; Median year structure built: 1954; Homeowner vacancy rate: 2.9%; Median gross rent: $1,043 per month; Rental vacancy rate: 5.9%

Health Insurance: 73.2% have insurance; 34.8% have private insurance; 43.0% have public insurance; 26.8% do not have insurance; 9.7% of children under 18 do not have insurance

Safety: Violent crime rate: 126.9 per 10,000 population; Property crime rate: 259.2 per 10,000 population
Transportation: Commute: 87.5% car, 6.2% public transportation, 1.6% walk, 3.0% work from home; Median travel time to work: 27.6 minutes
Additional Information Contacts
City of Compton. . . . . (310) 605-5530
http://www.comptoncity.org

COVINA (city). Covers a land area of 7.026 square miles and a water area of 0.015 square miles. Located at 34.09° N. Lat; 117.88° W. Long. Elevation is 558 feet.
History: Named for a local ranch, and means "place of vines". Covina grew up around packing houses where oranges, lemons, grapefruit, and tangerines were readied for shipment.
Population: 47,796; Growth (since 2000): 2.0%; Density: 6,803.0 persons per square mile; Race: 58.5% White, 4.2% Black/African American, 11.9% Asian, 1.1% American Indian/Alaska Native, 0.2% Native Hawaiian/Other Pacific Islander, 4.8% Two or more races, 52.4% Hispanic of any race; Average household size: 2.99; Median age: 35.7; Age under 18: 24.9%; Age 65 and over: 11.7%; Males per 100 females: 93.3; Marriage status: 35.0% never married, 48.9% now married, 2.8% separated, 5.3% widowed, 10.8% divorced; Foreign born: 21.2%; Speak English only: 59.1%; With disability: 9.2%; Veterans: 6.2%; Ancestry: 7.4% Irish, 7.0% German, 6.3% English, 4.1% Italian, 1.9% American
Employment: 12.7% management, business, and financial, 4.3% computer, engineering, and science, 11.4% education, legal, community service, arts, and media, 4.3% healthcare practitioners, 16.6% service, 31.1% sales and office, 8.9% natural resources, construction, and maintenance, 10.8% production, transportation, and material moving
Income: Per capita: $25,955; Median household: $66,726; Average household: $78,628; Households with income of $100,000 or more: 28.8%; Poverty rate: 11.3%
Educational Attainment: High school diploma or higher: 85.8%; Bachelor's degree or higher: 24.2%; Graduate/professional degree or higher: 7.0%

School District(s)

Azusa Unified (KG-12)
2012-13 Enrollment: 9,755 . . . . (626) 967-6211
Charter Oak Unified (KG-12)
2012-13 Enrollment: 5,544 . . . . (626) 966-8331
Covina-Valley Unified (KG-12)
2012-13 Enrollment: 12,978 . . . . (626) 974-7000

Housing: Homeownership rate: 58.4%; Median home value: $371,000; Median year structure built: 1960; Homeowner vacancy rate: 1.1%; Median gross rent: $1,225 per month; Rental vacancy rate: 6.4%
Health Insurance: 85.7% have insurance; 64.9% have private insurance; 26.4% have public insurance; 14.3% do not have insurance; 5.6% of children under 18 do not have insurance
Hospitals: Citrus Valley Medical Center - IC Campus (252 beds)
Safety: Violent crime rate: 28.4 per 10,000 population; Property crime rate: 277.0 per 10,000 population
Transportation: Commute: 89.3% car, 4.8% public transportation, 0.8% walk, 2.5% work from home; Median travel time to work: 31.4 minutes
Additional Information Contacts
City of Covina . . . . (626) 384-5400
http://www.ci.covina.ca.us

CUDAHY (city). Covers a land area of 1.175 square miles and a water area of 0.051 square miles. Located at 33.96° N. Lat; 118.18° W. Long. Elevation is 121 feet.
History: Cudahy was incorporated on November 10, 1960 and named after its founder, Michael Cudahy, who was a tycoon in the meat-packing industry.
Population: 23,805; Growth (since 2000): -1.7%; Density: 20,259.3 persons per square mile; Race: 49.2% White, 1.4% Black/African American, 0.6% Asian, 1.0% American Indian/Alaska Native, 0.1% Native Hawaiian/Other Pacific Islander, 4.3% Two or more races, 96.0% Hispanic of any race; Average household size: 4.24; Median age: 27.0; Age under 18: 35.0%; Age 65 and over: 5.1%; Males per 100 females: 98.3; Marriage status: 52.0% never married, 42.7% now married, 4.2% separated, 2.3% widowed, 3.0% divorced; Foreign born: 47.9%; Speak English only: 7.3%; With disability: 8.8%; Veterans: 1.2%; Ancestry: 1.8% American, 0.4% Italian, 0.3% Irish, 0.2% German, 0.1% French
Employment: 3.6% management, business, and financial, 0.5% computer, engineering, and science, 2.9% education, legal, community service, arts, and media, 0.8% healthcare practitioners, 20.6% service, 22.4% sales and office, 17.1% natural resources, construction, and maintenance, 32.1% production, transportation, and material moving
Income: Per capita: $11,298; Median household: $38,267; Average household: $44,605; Households with income of $100,000 or more: 5.5%; Poverty rate: 31.8%
Educational Attainment: High school diploma or higher: 42.8%; Bachelor's degree or higher: 3.5%; Graduate/professional degree or higher: 0.9%

School District(s)

Los Angeles Unified (PK-12)
2012-13 Enrollment: 655,455 . . . . (213) 241-1000

Housing: Homeownership rate: 18.0%; Median home value: $206,400; Median year structure built: 1967; Homeowner vacancy rate: 1.3%; Median gross rent: $1,126 per month; Rental vacancy rate: 2.3%
Health Insurance: 61.2% have insurance; 25.2% have private insurance; 37.9% have public insurance; 38.8% do not have insurance; 16.3% of children under 18 do not have insurance
Safety: Violent crime rate: 46.1 per 10,000 population; Property crime rate: 132.8 per 10,000 population
Transportation: Commute: 85.5% car, 7.1% public transportation, 3.4% walk, 2.5% work from home; Median travel time to work: 32.4 minutes
Additional Information Contacts
City of Cudahy. . . . . (323) 773-5143
http://www.cityofcudahy.com

CULVER CITY (city). Covers a land area of 5.111 square miles and a water area of 0.028 square miles. Located at 34.01° N. Lat; 118.40° W. Long. Elevation is 95 feet.
History: Named for Harry H. Culver, an immigrant from Nebraska in 1914. The U.S. motion-picture industry began in the city c.1915. Incorporated 1917.
Population: 38,883; Growth (since 2000): 0.2%; Density: 7,607.2 persons per square mile; Race: 60.3% White, 9.5% Black/African American, 14.8% Asian, 0.5% American Indian/Alaska Native, 0.2% Native Hawaiian/Other Pacific Islander, 6.1% Two or more races, 23.2% Hispanic of any race; Average household size: 2.30; Median age: 40.5; Age under 18: 18.8%; Age 65 and over: 14.9%; Males per 100 females: 89.1; Marriage status: 34.8% never married, 48.4% now married, 1.8% separated, 5.9% widowed, 10.9% divorced; Foreign born: 23.7%; Speak English only: 62.8%; With disability: 8.2%; Veterans: 4.8%; Ancestry: 8.1% German, 8.1% English, 6.5% Irish, 4.5% Italian, 4.0% Russian
Employment: 19.8% management, business, and financial, 7.5% computer, engineering, and science, 23.1% education, legal, community service, arts, and media, 6.0% healthcare practitioners, 14.6% service, 21.0% sales and office, 4.0% natural resources, construction, and maintenance, 4.0% production, transportation, and material moving
Income: Per capita: $45,003; Median household: $77,333; Average household: $103,034; Households with income of $100,000 or more: 39.0%; Poverty rate: 7.1%
Educational Attainment: High school diploma or higher: 92.6%; Bachelor's degree or higher: 50.6%; Graduate/professional degree or higher: 20.8%

School District(s)

Culver City Unified (KG-12)
2012-13 Enrollment: 6,741 . . . . (310) 842-4220
Los Angeles Unified (PK-12)
2012-13 Enrollment: 655,455 . . . . (213) 241-1000

Four-year College(s)

Antioch University-Los Angeles (Private, Not-for-profit)
Fall 2013 Enrollment: 986 . . . . (310) 578-1080
ITT Technical Institute-Culver City (Private, For-profit)
Fall 2013 Enrollment: 319 . . . . (310) 417-5800
2013-14 Tuition: In-state $18,048; Out-of-state $18,048

Two-year College(s)

West Los Angeles College (Public)
Fall 2013 Enrollment: 10,767 . . . . (310) 287-4200
2013-14 Tuition: In-state $1,221; Out-of-state $6,161

Housing: Homeownership rate: 54.3%; Median home value: $609,600; Median year structure built: 1961; Homeowner vacancy rate: 0.7%; Median gross rent: $1,606 per month; Rental vacancy rate: 4.1%
Health Insurance: 87.8% have insurance; 76.3% have private insurance; 22.2% have public insurance; 12.2% do not have insurance; 4.7% of children under 18 do not have insurance

Safety: Violent crime rate: 40.8 per 10,000 population; Property crime rate: 409.6 per 10,000 population

Newspapers: Culver City News (weekly circulation 11000); Culver City Observer (weekly circulation 10000); LA Weekly (weekly circulation 214000)

Transportation: Commute: 84.5% car, 3.1% public transportation, 2.0% walk, 7.3% work from home; Median travel time to work: 24.8 minutes

Additional Information Contacts

City of Culver City . . . . (310) 253-6000
http://www.culvercity.org

DEL AIRE (CDP). Covers a land area of 1.014 square miles and a water area of 0 square miles. Located at 33.92° N. Lat; 118.37° W. Long. Elevation is 102 feet.

Population: 10,001; Growth (since 2000): 11.0%; Density: 9,864.4 persons per square mile; Race: 60.5% White, 4.6% Black/African American, 9.2% Asian, 0.6% American Indian/Alaska Native, 1.3% Native Hawaiian/Other Pacific Islander, 5.6% Two or more races, 47.2% Hispanic of any race; Average household size: 3.04; Median age: 36.0; Age under 18: 23.3%; Age 65 and over: 10.6%; Males per 100 females: 100.5; Marriage status: 34.6% never married, 50.9% now married, 1.9% separated, 5.9% widowed, 8.6% divorced; Foreign born: 28.8%; Speak English only: 47.6%; With disability: 8.5%; Veterans: 4.2%; Ancestry: 18.8% American, 5.7% German, 4.4% English, 3.9% Irish, 2.5% Italian

Employment: 18.5% management, business, and financial, 6.4% computer, engineering, and science, 7.6% education, legal, community service, arts, and media, 4.6% healthcare practitioners, 22.3% service, 23.7% sales and office, 7.8% natural resources, construction, and maintenance, 9.0% production, transportation, and material moving

Income: Per capita: $31,494; Median household: $80,833; Average household: $92,401; Households with income of $100,000 or more: 36.3%; Poverty rate: 9.1%

Educational Attainment: High school diploma or higher: 82.0%; Bachelor's degree or higher: 26.8%; Graduate/professional degree or higher: 10.4%

Housing: Homeownership rate: 68.9%; Median home value: $444,100; Median year structure built: 1951; Homeowner vacancy rate: 0.5%; Median gross rent: $1,446 per month; Rental vacancy rate: 5.2%

Health Insurance: 82.6% have insurance; 71.5% have private insurance; 17.0% have public insurance; 17.4% do not have insurance; 13.1% of children under 18 do not have insurance

Transportation: Commute: 92.9% car, 2.1% public transportation, 1.1% walk, 2.9% work from home; Median travel time to work: 22.5 minutes

---

DESERT VIEW HIGHLANDS (CDP). Covers a land area of 0.440 square miles and a water area of 0 square miles. Located at 34.59° N. Lat; 118.15° W. Long. Elevation is 2,713 feet.

Population: 2,360; Growth (since 2000): 1.0%; Density: 5,364.0 persons per square mile; Race: 54.5% White, 7.7% Black/African American, 2.1% Asian, 1.2% American Indian/Alaska Native, 0.0% Native Hawaiian/Other Pacific Islander, 6.1% Two or more races, 53.1% Hispanic of any race; Average household size: 3.47; Median age: 31.1; Age under 18: 31.6%; Age 65 and over: 8.7%; Males per 100 females: 99.2

Housing: Homeownership rate: 65.3%; Homeowner vacancy rate: 4.1%; Rental vacancy rate: 10.3%

DIAMOND BAR (city). Covers a land area of 14.880 square miles and a water area of 0.005 square miles. Located at 34.00° N. Lat; 117.82° W. Long. Elevation is 696 feet.

Population: 55,544; Growth (since 2000): -1.3%; Density: 3,732.9 persons per square mile; Race: 33.2% White, 4.1% Black/African American, 52.5% Asian, 0.3% American Indian/Alaska Native, 0.2% Native Hawaiian/Other Pacific Islander, 3.9% Two or more races, 20.1% Hispanic of any race; Average household size: 3.10; Median age: 41.0; Age under 18: 21.4%; Age 65 and over: 11.7%; Males per 100 females: 95.2; Marriage status: 31.9% never married, 56.6% now married, 1.2% separated, 5.2% widowed, 6.4% divorced; Foreign born: 42.4%; Speak English only: 43.9%; With disability: 7.2%; Veterans: 4.5%; Ancestry: 6.2% American, 4.5% German, 3.8% Irish, 3.0% English, 2.1% Italian

Employment: 23.7% management, business, and financial, 8.4% computer, engineering, and science, 10.9% education, legal, community service, arts, and media, 8.1% healthcare practitioners, 12.6% service, 25.9% sales and office, 3.5% natural resources, construction, and maintenance, 6.9% production, transportation, and material moving

Income: Per capita: $34,313; Median household: $88,422; Average household: $105,652; Households with income of $100,000 or more: 43.5%; Poverty rate: 5.9%

Educational Attainment: High school diploma or higher: 92.0%; Bachelor's degree or higher: 48.4%; Graduate/professional degree or higher: 17.3%

School District(s)

Pomona Unified (PK-12)
2012-13 Enrollment: 27,186 . . . . (909) 397-4800
Walnut Valley Unified (KG-12)
2012-13 Enrollment: 14,661 . . . . (909) 595-1261

Four-year College(s)

California InterContinental University (Private, For-profit)
Fall 2013 Enrollment: n/a . . . . (909) 718-7016
2013-14 Tuition: In-state $6,000; Out-of-state $6,000

Housing: Homeownership rate: 81.2%; Median home value: $521,900; Median year structure built: 1980; Homeowner vacancy rate: 0.9%; Median gross rent: $1,761 per month; Rental vacancy rate: 5.2%

Health Insurance: 87.7% have insurance; 75.4% have private insurance; 18.6% have public insurance; 12.3% do not have insurance; 5.5% of children under 18 do not have insurance

Safety: Violent crime rate: 11.0 per 10,000 population; Property crime rate: 156.5 per 10,000 population

Transportation: Commute: 88.7% car, 2.2% public transportation, 1.5% walk, 6.7% work from home; Median travel time to work: 33.9 minutes

Additional Information Contacts

City of Diamond Bar . . . . (909) 839-7000
http://www.ci.diamond-bar.ca.us

DOWNEY (city). Covers a land area of 12.408 square miles and a water area of 0.160 square miles. Located at 33.94° N. Lat; 118.13° W. Long. Elevation is 118 feet.

History: Named for John G. Downey, governor of California from 1860 to 1862. Incorporated 1957.

Population: 111,772; Growth (since 2000): 4.1%; Density: 9,008.0 persons per square mile; Race: 56.6% White, 3.9% Black/African American, 7.0% Asian, 0.7% American Indian/Alaska Native, 0.2% Native Hawaiian/Other Pacific Islander, 4.1% Two or more races, 70.7% Hispanic of any race; Average household size: 3.27; Median age: 33.3; Age under 18: 26.8%; Age 65 and over: 10.4%; Males per 100 females: 94.1; Marriage status: 38.6% never married, 47.6% now married, 2.6% separated, 5.2% widowed, 8.6% divorced; Foreign born: 35.3%; Speak English only: 30.9%; With disability: 8.7%; Veterans: 4.4%; Ancestry: 3.4% German, 2.4% American, 2.3% Irish, 2.2% English, 1.4% Italian

Employment: 13.2% management, business, and financial, 2.8% computer, engineering, and science, 9.7% education, legal, community service, arts, and media, 4.7% healthcare practitioners, 16.9% service, 29.7% sales and office, 8.4% natural resources, construction, and maintenance, 14.5% production, transportation, and material moving

Income: Per capita: $23,055; Median household: $60,939; Average household: $75,200; Households with income of $100,000 or more: 24.2%; Poverty rate: 11.8%

Educational Attainment: High school diploma or higher: 77.0%; Bachelor's degree or higher: 20.6%; Graduate/professional degree or higher: 6.1%

School District(s)

Downey Unified (KG-12)
2012-13 Enrollment: 22,848 . . . . (562) 469-6500
Los Angeles County Office of Education (KG-12)
2012-13 Enrollment: 9,136 . . . . (562) 922-6111
Los Angeles County Rop
2012-13 Enrollment: n/a . . . . (562) 922-6850

Two-year College(s)

Downey Adult School (Public)
Fall 2013 Enrollment: 1,317 . . . . (562) 940-6200

Housing: Homeownership rate: 50.5%; Median home value: $409,800; Median year structure built: 1958; Homeowner vacancy rate: 1.4%; Median gross rent: $1,214 per month; Rental vacancy rate: 4.9%

Health Insurance: 78.3% have insurance; 56.6% have private insurance; 26.8% have public insurance; 21.7% do not have insurance; 9.2% of children under 18 do not have insurance

Hospitals: Kaiser Foundation Hospital - Downey; LAC/Rancho Los Amigos National Rehab Center (395 beds); PIH Hospital - Downey (199 beds)

Safety: Violent crime rate: 28.8 per 10,000 population; Property crime rate: 290.8 per 10,000 population
Newspapers: Downey Patriot (weekly circulation 25000)
Transportation: Commute: 92.1% car, 2.9% public transportation, 1.8% walk, 2.4% work from home; Median travel time to work: 27.7 minutes
Additional Information Contacts
City of Downey . . . . (562) 904-7246
http://www.downeyca.org

DUARTE (city). Covers a land area of 6.690 square miles and a water area of 0 square miles. Located at 34.16° N. Lat; 117.95° W. Long. Elevation is 512 feet.
History: Named for Andres Duarte, owner of Rancho Azusa which was subdivided to form the town. Settled c.1841. Incorporated 1957.
Population: 21,321; Growth (since 2000): -0.8%; Density: 3,186.8 persons per square mile; Race: 51.9% White, 7.4% Black/African American, 15.8% Asian, 0.8% American Indian/Alaska Native, 0.1% Native Hawaiian/Other Pacific Islander, 4.6% Two or more races, 47.8% Hispanic of any race; Average household size: 2.98; Median age: 39.9; Age under 18: 22.2%; Age 65 and over: 15.8%; Males per 100 females: 89.6; Marriage status: 31.2% never married, 48.4% now married, 2.0% separated, 10.2% widowed, 10.3% divorced; Foreign born: 34.9%; Speak English only: 46.4%; With disability: 10.1%; Veterans: 3.9%; Ancestry: 4.8% German, 3.7% English, 3.1% Irish, 2.5% Armenian, 1.8% Italian
Employment: 10.8% management, business, and financial, 6.2% computer, engineering, and science, 12.5% education, legal, community service, arts, and media, 4.7% healthcare practitioners, 19.4% service, 27.7% sales and office, 8.9% natural resources, construction, and maintenance, 9.7% production, transportation, and material moving
Income: Per capita: $24,583; Median household: $62,250; Average household: $72,810; Households with income of $100,000 or more: 25.9%; Poverty rate: 13.4%
Educational Attainment: High school diploma or higher: 81.8%; Bachelor's degree or higher: 28.0%; Graduate/professional degree or higher: 9.7%

School District(s)

Duarte Unified (KG-12)
2012-13 Enrollment: 3,749 . . . . (626) 599-5000

Four-year College(s)

Irell & Manella Graduate School of Biological Sciences at City of Hope (Private, Not-for-profit)
Fall 2013 Enrollment: 82 . . . . (626) 256-8735
Housing: Homeownership rate: 67.1%; Median home value: $362,600; Median year structure built: 1966; Homeowner vacancy rate: 1.1%; Median gross rent: $1,214 per month; Rental vacancy rate: 4.4%
Health Insurance: 82.3% have insurance; 54.8% have private insurance; 33.1% have public insurance; 17.7% do not have insurance; 8.1% of children under 18 do not have insurance
Hospitals: City of Hope Helford Clinical Research Hospital
Safety: Violent crime rate: 18.8 per 10,000 population; Property crime rate: 168.2 per 10,000 population
Transportation: Commute: 87.9% car, 4.3% public transportation, 2.9% walk, 2.9% work from home; Median travel time to work: 28.4 minutes
Additional Information Contacts
City of Duarte . . . . (626) 357-7931
http://www.accessduarte.com

EAST LOS ANGELES (CDP). Covers a land area of 7.448 square miles and a water area of 0.004 square miles. Located at 34.03° N. Lat; 118.17° W. Long. Elevation is 200 feet.
Population: 126,496; Growth (since 2000): 1.8%; Density: 16,983.2 persons per square mile; Race: 50.5% White, 0.6% Black/African American, 0.9% Asian, 1.2% American Indian/Alaska Native, 0.0% Native Hawaiian/Other Pacific Islander, 3.3% Two or more races, 97.1% Hispanic of any race; Average household size: 4.09; Median age: 29.1; Age under 18: 31.5%; Age 65 and over: 8.6%; Males per 100 females: 98.9; Marriage status: 47.8% never married, 41.6% now married, 3.3% separated, 5.1% widowed, 5.4% divorced; Foreign born: 42.9%; Speak English only: 12.4%; With disability: 8.8%; Veterans: 1.8%; Ancestry: 1.1% American, 0.4% German, 0.3% Italian, 0.2% French, 0.2% Irish
Employment: 5.0% management, business, and financial, 1.4% computer, engineering, and science, 5.7% education, legal, community service, arts, and media, 1.3% healthcare practitioners, 21.1% service, 25.6% sales and office, 14.1% natural resources, construction, and maintenance, 25.9% production, transportation, and material moving
Income: Per capita: $12,511; Median household: $37,982; Average household: $46,658; Households with income of $100,000 or more: 8.4%; Poverty rate: 26.9%
Educational Attainment: High school diploma or higher: 45.6%; Bachelor's degree or higher: 5.5%; Graduate/professional degree or higher: 1.3%
Housing: Homeownership rate: 35.7%; Median home value: $288,900; Median year structure built: 1950; Homeowner vacancy rate: 1.2%; Median gross rent: $968 per month; Rental vacancy rate: 3.2%
Health Insurance: 63.8% have insurance; 31.3% have private insurance; 35.4% have public insurance; 36.2% do not have insurance; 17.9% of children under 18 do not have insurance
Transportation: Commute: 78.8% car, 12.7% public transportation, 4.0% walk, 2.3% work from home; Median travel time to work: 29.0 minutes

EAST PASADENA (CDP). Covers a land area of 1.318 square miles and a water area of 0.005 square miles. Located at 34.14° N. Lat; 118.08° W. Long. Elevation is 725 feet.
Population: 6,144; Growth (since 2000): 1.6%; Density: 4,663.1 persons per square mile; Race: 51.8% White, 3.0% Black/African American, 25.9% Asian, 0.8% American Indian/Alaska Native, 0.1% Native Hawaiian/Other Pacific Islander, 4.5% Two or more races, 34.8% Hispanic of any race; Average household size: 2.92; Median age: 40.5; Age under 18: 21.2%; Age 65 and over: 15.6%; Males per 100 females: 97.3; Marriage status: 30.0% never married, 57.9% now married, 5.1% separated, 3.2% widowed, 8.8% divorced; Foreign born: 38.8%; Speak English only: 42.4%; With disability: 9.6%; Veterans: 5.3%; Ancestry: 6.3% German, 3.8% English, 3.5% Irish, 3.5% American, 3.1% Armenian
Employment: 15.9% management, business, and financial, 3.0% computer, engineering, and science, 13.0% education, legal, community service, arts, and media, 7.0% healthcare practitioners, 20.8% service, 25.2% sales and office, 5.8% natural resources, construction, and maintenance, 9.3% production, transportation, and material moving
Income: Per capita: $47,889; Median household: $71,151; Average household: $136,504; Households with income of $100,000 or more: 39.7%; Poverty rate: 16.0%
Educational Attainment: High school diploma or higher: 87.7%; Bachelor's degree or higher: 38.1%; Graduate/professional degree or higher: 15.5%
Housing: Homeownership rate: 68.4%; Median home value: $621,700; Median year structure built: 1945; Homeowner vacancy rate: 1.3%; Median gross rent: $1,465 per month; Rental vacancy rate: 2.4%
Health Insurance: 85.6% have insurance; 65.7% have private insurance; 27.9% have public insurance; 14.4% do not have insurance; 4.9% of children under 18 do not have insurance
Transportation: Commute: 84.7% car, 5.3% public transportation, 3.9% walk, 4.5% work from home; Median travel time to work: 26.2 minutes

EAST RANCHO DOMINGUEZ (CDP). Covers a land area of 0.822 square miles and a water area of 0 square miles. Located at 33.89° N. Lat; 118.20° W. Long. Elevation is 72 feet.
Population: 15,135; Growth (since 2000): n/a; Density: 18,412.3 persons per square mile; Race: 31.5% White, 15.9% Black/African American, 0.2% Asian, 0.9% American Indian/Alaska Native, 0.7% Native Hawaiian/Other Pacific Islander, 3.5% Two or more races, 82.0% Hispanic of any race; Average household size: 4.99; Median age: 26.1; Age under 18: 35.1%; Age 65 and over: 5.3%; Males per 100 females: 98.0; Marriage status: 50.5% never married, 38.4% now married, 3.3% separated, 4.0% widowed, 7.1% divorced; Foreign born: 39.7%; Speak English only: 23.0%; With disability: 11.8%; Veterans: 3.2%; Ancestry: 4.6% American, 1.2% Italian, 0.9% African, 0.6% Scottish, 0.6% German
Employment: 2.4% management, business, and financial, 1.3% computer, engineering, and science, 5.2% education, legal, community service, arts, and media, 1.3% healthcare practitioners, 20.6% service, 22.7% sales and office, 16.4% natural resources, construction, and maintenance, 30.1% production, transportation, and material moving
Income: Per capita: $12,878; Median household: $44,727; Average household: $54,607; Households with income of $100,000 or more: 12.2%; Poverty rate: 20.0%
Educational Attainment: High school diploma or higher: 51.7%; Bachelor's degree or higher: 4.9%; Graduate/professional degree or higher: 1.3%
Housing: Homeownership rate: 54.7%; Median home value: $238,800; Median year structure built: 1952; Homeowner vacancy rate: 3.3%; Median gross rent: $1,096 per month; Rental vacancy rate: 5.1%

Health Insurance: 64.7% have insurance; 26.6% have private insurance; 40.7% have public insurance; 35.3% do not have insurance; 13.7% of children under 18 do not have insurance

Transportation: Commute: 92.2% car, 4.1% public transportation, 1.4% walk, 1.2% work from home; Median travel time to work: 24.6 minutes

EAST SAN GABRIEL (CDP). Covers a land area of 1.561 square miles and a water area of 0.014 square miles. Located at 34.12° N. Lat; 118.08° W. Long. Elevation is 377 feet.

Population: 14,874; Growth (since 2000): 2.5%; Density: 9,526.6 persons per square mile; Race: 33.9% White, 1.6% Black/African American, 49.9% Asian, 0.4% American Indian/Alaska Native, 0.0% Native Hawaiian/Other Pacific Islander, 3.4% Two or more races, 24.9% Hispanic of any race; Average household size: 2.90; Median age: 40.2; Age under 18: 21.9%; Age 65 and over: 13.6%; Males per 100 females: 94.0; Marriage status: 28.2% never married, 58.9% now married, 1.3% separated, 5.6% widowed, 7.3% divorced; Foreign born: 44.4%; Speak English only: 38.3%; With disability: 6.9%; Veterans: 4.3%; Ancestry: 4.5% German, 3.4% English, 2.7% Irish, 2.1% American, 1.7% Italian

Employment: 21.6% management, business, and financial, 10.3% computer, engineering, and science, 13.3% education, legal, community service, arts, and media, 4.8% healthcare practitioners, 15.9% service, 22.9% sales and office, 6.3% natural resources, construction, and maintenance, 4.9% production, transportation, and material moving

Income: Per capita: $34,658; Median household: $72,734; Average household: $101,202; Households with income of $100,000 or more: 36.3%; Poverty rate: 7.8%

Educational Attainment: High school diploma or higher: 89.2%; Bachelor's degree or higher: 44.9%; Graduate/professional degree or higher: 17.0%

Housing: Homeownership rate: 57.3%; Median home value: $600,900; Median year structure built: 1959; Homeowner vacancy rate: 1.0%; Median gross rent: $1,224 per month; Rental vacancy rate: 5.8%

Health Insurance: 83.3% have insurance; 66.9% have private insurance; 23.4% have public insurance; 16.7% do not have insurance; 8.4% of children under 18 do not have insurance

Transportation: Commute: 87.7% car, 5.0% public transportation, 0.3% walk, 5.6% work from home; Median travel time to work: 31.8 minutes

EAST WHITTIER (CDP).

Note: Statistics that would complete this profile are not available because the CDP was created after the 2010 Census was released.

EL MONTE (city). Covers a land area of 9.562 square miles and a water area of 0.086 square miles. Located at 34.07° N. Lat; 118.03° W. Long. Elevation is 299 feet.

History: Named for the Spanish translation of "thicket" for the local, dense willows. Urbanization has replaced the walnut groves it was once known for. The population here has increased by more than 40% 1970—1990. El Monte was founded in 1852 by westward-bound pioneers on the Santa Fe Trail. Incorporated 1912.

Population: 113,475; Growth (since 2000): -2.1%; Density: 11,866.9 persons per square mile; Race: 38.8% White, 0.8% Black/African American, 25.1% Asian, 1.0% American Indian/Alaska Native, 0.1% Native Hawaiian/Other Pacific Islander, 3.2% Two or more races, 69.0% Hispanic of any race; Average household size: 4.04; Median age: 31.6; Age under 18: 28.4%; Age 65 and over: 9.3%; Males per 100 females: 100.9; Marriage status: 40.3% never married, 48.1% now married, 3.0% separated, 5.5% widowed, 6.1% divorced; Foreign born: 51.4%; Speak English only: 13.9%; With disability: 8.7%; Veterans: 2.3%; Ancestry: 1.3% American, 1.2% German, 0.8% Irish, 0.7% English, 0.4% Italian

Employment: 6.9% management, business, and financial, 3.2% computer, engineering, and science, 5.0% education, legal, community service, arts, and media, 2.2% healthcare practitioners, 24.0% service, 22.6% sales and office, 11.5% natural resources, construction, and maintenance, 24.5% production, transportation, and material moving

Income: Per capita: $14,735; Median household: $39,535; Average household: $52,809; Households with income of $100,000 or more: 12.1%; Poverty rate: 24.3%

Educational Attainment: High school diploma or higher: 56.8%; Bachelor's degree or higher: 12.0%; Graduate/professional degree or higher: 2.1%

School District(s)

El Monte City Elementary (KG-08)
 2012-13 Enrollment: 9,304 . . . . (626) 453-3700
El Monte Union High (09-12)
 2012-13 Enrollment: 9,812 . . . . (626) 444-9005
Mountain View Elementary (KG-08)
 2012-13 Enrollment: 7,618 . . . . (626) 652-4000

Vocational/Technical School(s)

Diamond Beauty College (Private, For-profit)
 Fall 2013 Enrollment: 122 . . . . (626) 350-1195
 2013-14 Tuition: $263
Palladium Technical Academy (Private, For-profit)
 Fall 2013 Enrollment: 73 . . . . (626) 444-0880
 2013-14 Tuition: $10,298
Professional Institute of Beauty (Private, For-profit)
 Fall 2013 Enrollment: 108 . . . . (626) 443-9401
 2013-14 Tuition: $12,882

Housing: Homeownership rate: 42.2%; Median home value: $345,200; Median year structure built: 1962; Homeowner vacancy rate: 1.4%; Median gross rent: $1,071 per month; Rental vacancy rate: 4.6%

Health Insurance: 69.6% have insurance; 32.6% have private insurance; 40.0% have public insurance; 30.4% do not have insurance; 8.8% of children under 18 do not have insurance

Safety: Violent crime rate: 29.4 per 10,000 population; Property crime rate: 188.8 per 10,000 population

Newspapers: Mid-Valley News (weekly circulation 15000)

Transportation: Commute: 86.1% car, 6.2% public transportation, 2.6% walk, 3.5% work from home; Median travel time to work: 30.3 minutes

Additional Information Contacts

City of El Monte . . . . (626) 580-2016
 http://www.elmonte.org

EL SEGUNDO (city). Covers a land area of 5.463 square miles and a water area of 0.002 square miles. Located at 33.92° N. Lat; 118.40° W. Long. Elevation is 115 feet.

History: Named for the Spanish translation of "second," as the site of the second Standard Oil Company refinery, around which the town grew.

Population: 16,654; Growth (since 2000): 3.9%; Density: 3,048.7 persons per square mile; Race: 78.0% White, 2.0% Black/African American, 8.8% Asian, 0.4% American Indian/Alaska Native, 0.2% Native Hawaiian/Other Pacific Islander, 5.7% Two or more races, 15.7% Hispanic of any race; Average household size: 2.34; Median age: 39.2; Age under 18: 22.3%; Age 65 and over: 10.1%; Males per 100 females: 99.4; Marriage status: 34.4% never married, 48.9% now married, 1.1% separated, 3.9% widowed, 12.7% divorced; Foreign born: 13.4%; Speak English only: 78.0%; With disability: 5.7%; Veterans: 6.7%; Ancestry: 19.9% German, 14.0% Irish, 13.3% American, 12.3% English, 8.0% Italian

Employment: 21.9% management, business, and financial, 9.9% computer, engineering, and science, 15.7% education, legal, community service, arts, and media, 4.2% healthcare practitioners, 13.0% service, 24.2% sales and office, 4.4% natural resources, construction, and maintenance, 6.8% production, transportation, and material moving

Income: Per capita: $43,218; Median household: $84,341; Average household: $105,466; Households with income of $100,000 or more: 42.3%; Poverty rate: 4.8%

Educational Attainment: High school diploma or higher: 96.0%; Bachelor's degree or higher: 48.5%; Graduate/professional degree or higher: 16.5%

School District(s)

Bayshore Elementary (KG-12)
 2012-13 Enrollment: 389 . . . . (415) 467-5443
El Segundo Unified (KG-12)
 2012-13 Enrollment: 3,415 . . . . (310) 615-2650
Semitropic Elementary (KG-12)
 2012-13 Enrollment: 571 . . . . (661) 758-6412
Tracy Joint Unified (KG-12)
 2012-13 Enrollment: 17,405 . . . . (209) 830-3200

Housing: Homeownership rate: 42.9%; Median home value: $736,500; Median year structure built: 1962; Homeowner vacancy rate: 0.4%; Median gross rent: $1,490 per month; Rental vacancy rate: 4.1%

Health Insurance: 91.7% have insurance; 84.3% have private insurance; 14.0% have public insurance; 8.3% do not have insurance; 2.9% of children under 18 do not have insurance

Safety: Violent crime rate: 21.9 per 10,000 population; Property crime rate: 318.1 per 10,000 population

Newspapers: Herald Publications (weekly circulation 42000)

Transportation: Commute: 87.8% car, 1.2% public transportation, 3.6% walk, 6.1% work from home; Median travel time to work: 22.0 minutes; Amtrak: Bus service available.

Additional Information Contacts

City of El Segundo. . . . . (310) 524-2300
http://www.elsegundo.org

ELIZABETH LAKE (CDP). Covers a land area of 6.246 square miles and a water area of 0.297 square miles. Located at 34.66° N. Lat; 118.38° W. Long.

Population: 1,756; Growth (since 2000): n/a; Density: 281.1 persons per square mile; Race: 90.6% White, 1.2% Black/African American, 1.3% Asian, 0.5% American Indian/Alaska Native, 0.1% Native Hawaiian/Other Pacific Islander, 3.6% Two or more races, 13.2% Hispanic of any race; Average household size: 2.61; Median age: 42.4; Age under 18: 22.9%; Age 65 and over: 8.4%; Males per 100 females: 109.3

Housing: Homeownership rate: 83.3%; Homeowner vacancy rate: 3.1%; Rental vacancy rate: 5.8%

ENCINO (unincorporated postal area)

ZCTA: 91316

Covers a land area of 5.007 square miles and a water area of 0.268 square miles. Located at 34.16° N. Lat; 118.52° W. Long. Elevation is 774 feet.

Population: 26,898; Growth (since 2000): -2.5%; Density: 5,371.9 persons per square mile; Race: 79.5% White, 3.7% Black/African American, 6.1% Asian, 0.2% American Indian/Alaska Native, 0.1% Native Hawaiian/Other Pacific Islander, 5.8% Two or more races, 12.4% Hispanic of any race; Average household size: 2.26; Median age: 42.1; Age under 18: 16.9%; Age 65 and over: 18.7%; Males per 100 females: 89.7; Marriage status: 30.9% never married, 50.2% now married, 2.0% separated, 5.6% widowed, 13.3% divorced; Foreign born: 41.1%; Speak English only: 49.7%; With disability: 12.7%; Veterans: 4.7%; Ancestry: 13.7% Iranian, 11.4% Russian, 6.2% German, 5.1% Israeli, 4.9% Irish

Employment: 18.3% management, business, and financial, 6.1% computer, engineering, and science, 16.6% education, legal, community service, arts, and media, 7.6% healthcare practitioners, 10.0% service, 30.4% sales and office, 5.5% natural resources, construction, and maintenance, 5.4% production, transportation, and material moving

Income: Per capita: $42,960; Median household: $59,199; Average household: $95,321; Households with income of $100,000 or more: 28.5%; Poverty rate: 15.0%

Educational Attainment: High school diploma or higher: 94.0%; Bachelor's degree or higher: 49.5%; Graduate/professional degree or higher: 17.2%

School District(s)

Los Angeles Unified (PK-12)
2012-13 Enrollment: 655,455 . . . . (213) 241-1000

Housing: Homeownership rate: 52.9%; Median home value: $487,700; Median year structure built: 1967; Homeowner vacancy rate: 1.5%; Median gross rent: $1,434 per month; Rental vacancy rate: 6.7%

Health Insurance: 83.6% have insurance; 65.8% have private insurance; 26.3% have public insurance; 16.4% do not have insurance; 10.3% of children under 18 do not have insurance

Hospitals: Encino Hospital Medical Center (151 beds)

Transportation: Commute: 87.2% car, 3.5% public transportation, 1.8% walk, 6.2% work from home; Median travel time to work: 29.4 minutes

ZCTA: 91436

Covers a land area of 5.696 square miles and a water area of 0.054 square miles. Located at 34.15° N. Lat; 118.49° W. Long. Elevation is 774 feet.

Population: 14,372; Growth (since 2000): 9.6%; Density: 2,523.3 persons per square mile; Race: 87.9% White, 2.1% Black/African American, 5.2% Asian, 0.1% American Indian/Alaska Native, 0.1% Native Hawaiian/Other Pacific Islander, 3.6% Two or more races, 5.9% Hispanic of any race; Average household size: 2.57; Median age: 46.5; Age under 18: 22.2%; Age 65 and over: 21.6%; Males per 100 females: 92.1; Marriage status: 24.1% never married, 62.6% now married, 1.4% separated, 7.0% widowed, 6.2% divorced; Foreign born: 25.5%; Speak English only: 68.9%; With disability: 8.9%; Veterans: 7.4%; Ancestry: 15.1% Russian, 12.3% Iranian, 8.9% Polish, 7.5% American, 6.8% German

Employment: 22.8% management, business, and financial, 5.5% computer, engineering, and science, 26.9% education, legal, community service, arts, and media, 10.9% healthcare practitioners, 6.8% service, 24.1% sales and office, 1.4% natural resources, construction, and maintenance, 1.6% production, transportation, and material moving

Income: Per capita: $75,744; Median household: $132,520; Average household: $189,277; Households with income of $100,000 or more: 62.6%; Poverty rate: 4.8%

Educational Attainment: High school diploma or higher: 95.9%; Bachelor's degree or higher: 61.7%; Graduate/professional degree or higher: 29.7%

Housing: Homeownership rate: 84.7%; Median home value: 1 million+; Median year structure built: 1961; Homeowner vacancy rate: 0.9%; Median gross rent: $2,000+ per month; Rental vacancy rate: 7.8%

Health Insurance: 95.5% have insurance; 85.3% have private insurance; 24.0% have public insurance; 4.5% do not have insurance; 2.3% of children under 18 do not have insurance

Transportation: Commute: 85.4% car, 2.3% public transportation, 1.3% walk, 10.0% work from home; Median travel time to work: 28.8 minutes

FLORENCE-GRAHAM (CDP). Covers a land area of 3.580 square miles and a water area of 0 square miles. Located at 33.97° N. Lat; 118.24° W. Long. Elevation is 141 feet.

Population: 63,387; Growth (since 2000): 5.3%; Density: 17,704.2 persons per square mile; Race: 37.7% White, 9.2% Black/African American, 0.2% Asian, 0.8% American Indian/Alaska Native, 0.0% Native Hawaiian/Other Pacific Islander, 3.6% Two or more races, 90.0% Hispanic of any race; Average household size: 4.56; Median age: 26.3; Age under 18: 35.0%; Age 65 and over: 5.4%; Males per 100 females: 100.2; Marriage status: 49.1% never married, 42.9% now married, 3.9% separated, 3.5% widowed, 4.4% divorced; Foreign born: 43.8%; Speak English only: 11.9%; With disability: 7.6%; Veterans: 1.2%; Ancestry: 2.0% American, 0.5% African, 0.3% German, 0.3% Irish, 0.1% French

Employment: 3.9% management, business, and financial, 0.4% computer, engineering, and science, 3.8% education, legal, community service, arts, and media, 1.2% healthcare practitioners, 21.4% service, 24.3% sales and office, 13.9% natural resources, construction, and maintenance, 31.0% production, transportation, and material moving

Income: Per capita: $11,136; Median household: $35,543; Average household: $44,818; Households with income of $100,000 or more: 7.4%; Poverty rate: 30.7%

Educational Attainment: High school diploma or higher: 40.9%; Bachelor's degree or higher: 3.3%; Graduate/professional degree or higher: 0.8%

Housing: Homeownership rate: 36.7%; Median home value: $243,000; Median year structure built: 1951; Homeowner vacancy rate: 2.9%; Median gross rent: $969 per month; Rental vacancy rate: 4.5%

Health Insurance: 64.5% have insurance; 25.8% have private insurance; 41.2% have public insurance; 35.5% do not have insurance; 13.2% of children under 18 do not have insurance

Transportation: Commute: 79.4% car, 14.7% public transportation, 2.5% walk, 2.2% work from home; Median travel time to work: 31.0 minutes

GARDENA (city). Covers a land area of 5.829 square miles and a water area of 0.036 square miles. Located at 33.89° N. Lat; 118.31° W. Long. Elevation is 49 feet.

History: Named for its fertile land, using the poetic form of "garden". Incorporated 1930.

Population: 58,829; Growth (since 2000): 1.9%; Density: 10,092.2 persons per square mile; Race: 24.6% White, 24.4% Black/African American, 26.2% Asian, 0.6% American Indian/Alaska Native, 0.7% Native Hawaiian/Other Pacific Islander, 4.5% Two or more races, 37.7% Hispanic of any race; Average household size: 2.82; Median age: 37.9; Age under 18: 22.8%; Age 65 and over: 14.1%; Males per 100 females: 92.6; Marriage status: 37.8% never married, 45.9% now married, 3.8% separated, 6.7% widowed, 9.6% divorced; Foreign born: 33.8%; Speak English only: 47.9%; With disability: 9.9%; Veterans: 5.9%; Ancestry: 3.5% American, 2.0% German, 1.3% English, 1.3% Irish, 0.8% Italian

Employment: 10.2% management, business, and financial, 4.6% computer, engineering, and science, 9.8% education, legal, community service, arts, and media, 4.2% healthcare practitioners, 18.1% service, 29.8% sales and office, 7.4% natural resources, construction, and maintenance, 16.0% production, transportation, and material moving

Income: Per capita: $23,376; Median household: $48,251; Average household: $62,822; Households with income of $100,000 or more: 18.6%; Poverty rate: 15.5%

Educational Attainment: High school diploma or higher: 81.0%; Bachelor's degree or higher: 24.5%; Graduate/professional degree or higher: 6.3%

School District(s)

Los Angeles Unified (PK-12)
2012-13 Enrollment: 655,455 . . . . (213) 241-1000

Vocational/Technical School(s)

American Auto Institute (Private, For-profit)
Fall 2013 Enrollment: 1,444 . . . . (949) 272-7200
2013-14 Tuition: $18,300

Everest College-Gardena (Private, For-profit)
Fall 2013 Enrollment: 494 . . . . (310) 527-7105
2013-14 Tuition: $21,388

Trinity Vocational Center (Private, For-profit)
Fall 2013 Enrollment: 90 . . . . (310) 834-3065
2013-14 Tuition: $25,054

Housing: Homeownership rate: 47.9%; Median home value: $341,400; Median year structure built: 1960; Homeowner vacancy rate: 1.3%; Median gross rent: $1,100 per month; Rental vacancy rate: 4.6%

Health Insurance: 79.3% have insurance; 56.0% have private insurance; 30.7% have public insurance; 20.7% do not have insurance; 8.5% of children under 18 do not have insurance

Hospitals: Memorial Hospital of Gardena (180 beds)

Safety: Violent crime rate: 41.0 per 10,000 population; Property crime rate: 222.9 per 10,000 population

Newspapers: Gardena Valley News (weekly circulation 5000)

Transportation: Commute: 90.8% car, 3.9% public transportation, 2.8% walk, 1.2% work from home; Median travel time to work: 26.2 minutes

Additional Information Contacts

City of Gardena . . . . (310) 217-9500
http://www.ci.gardena.ca.us

GLENDALE (city). Covers a land area of 30.453 square miles and a water area of 0.130 square miles. Located at 34.18° N. Lat; 118.25° W. Long. Elevation is 522 feet.

History: Named for the Celtic translation of "narrow valley". Glendale was built on part of the former Rancho San Rafael, an early Spanish land grant. The townsite was laid out in 1867, and the town grew when the Pacific Electric Railroad from Los Angeles arrived in 1902.

Population: 191,719; Growth (since 2000): -1.7%; Density: 6,295.5 persons per square mile; Race: 71.1% White, 1.3% Black/African American, 16.4% Asian, 0.3% American Indian/Alaska Native, 0.1% Native Hawaiian/Other Pacific Islander, 4.5% Two or more races, 17.4% Hispanic of any race; Average household size: 2.63; Median age: 41.0; Age under 18: 18.6%; Age 65 and over: 15.6%; Males per 100 females: 91.1; Marriage status: 32.4% never married, 53.2% now married, 2.1% separated, 6.7% widowed, 7.7% divorced; Foreign born: 54.8%; Speak English only: 30.1%; With disability: 12.9%; Veterans: 3.2%; Ancestry: 37.3% Armenian, 5.0% German, 4.9% Iranian, 4.1% English, 4.0% Irish

Employment: 15.9% management, business, and financial, 5.4% computer, engineering, and science, 14.7% education, legal, community service, arts, and media, 6.3% healthcare practitioners, 16.1% service, 26.7% sales and office, 5.4% natural resources, construction, and maintenance, 9.4% production, transportation, and material moving

Income: Per capita: $29,290; Median household: $53,020; Average household: $77,174; Households with income of $100,000 or more: 25.5%; Poverty rate: 14.2%

Educational Attainment: High school diploma or higher: 84.4%; Bachelor's degree or higher: 38.2%; Graduate/professional degree or higher: 12.1%

School District(s)

Glendale Unified (KG-12)
2012-13 Enrollment: 26,179 . . . . (818) 241-3111

Two-year College(s)

American Medical Sciences Center (Private, For-profit)
Fall 2013 Enrollment: 77 . . . . (818) 240-6900

Glendale Community College (Public)
Fall 2013 Enrollment: 15,744 . . . . (818) 240-1000
2013-14 Tuition: In-state $1,175; Out-of-state $5,663

Vocational/Technical School(s)

Brand College (Private, For-profit)
Fall 2013 Enrollment: 14 . . . . (818) 550-0770
2013-14 Tuition: $24,050

Glendale Career College (Private, For-profit)
Fall 2013 Enrollment: 293 . . . . (818) 243-1131
2013-14 Tuition: $28,525

North-West College-Glendale (Private, For-profit)
Fall 2013 Enrollment: 177 . . . . (818) 242-0205
2013-14 Tuition: $13,408

Housing: Homeownership rate: 38.1%; Median home value: $587,800; Median year structure built: 1962; Homeowner vacancy rate: 1.3%; Median gross rent: $1,294 per month; Rental vacancy rate: 5.5%

Health Insurance: 80.4% have insurance; 53.6% have private insurance; 32.7% have public insurance; 19.6% do not have insurance; 9.1% of children under 18 do not have insurance

Hospitals: Glendale Adventist Medical Center (448 beds); Glendale Memorial Hospital & Health Center (334 beds); USC Verdugo Hills Hospital (158 beds)

Safety: Violent crime rate: 9.3 per 10,000 population; Property crime rate: 163.7 per 10,000 population

Newspapers: Glendale News-Press (daily circulation 36000)

Transportation: Commute: 84.4% car, 4.5% public transportation, 3.8% walk, 5.8% work from home; Median travel time to work: 26.5 minutes; Amtrak: Train service available.

Additional Information Contacts

City of Glendale . . . . (818) 548-4000
http://www.ci.glendale.ca.us

GLENDORA (city). Covers a land area of 19.393 square miles and a water area of 0.165 square miles. Located at 34.15° N. Lat; 117.85° W. Long. Elevation is 774 feet.

History: Glendora was founded in 1887 by George Whitcomb, a Chicago manufacturer, who coined the name from the word "glen" and his wife's name, Ledora. In 1866 John Cook planted the first commercial orange grove here.

Population: 50,073; Growth (since 2000): 1.3%; Density: 2,582.0 persons per square mile; Race: 75.1% White, 1.9% Black/African American, 8.0% Asian, 0.7% American Indian/Alaska Native, 0.1% Native Hawaiian/Other Pacific Islander, 4.8% Two or more races, 30.7% Hispanic of any race; Average household size: 2.88; Median age: 40.2; Age under 18: 23.5%; Age 65 and over: 14.1%; Males per 100 females: 93.7; Marriage status: 32.6% never married, 51.9% now married, 1.7% separated, 6.3% widowed, 9.2% divorced; Foreign born: 16.0%; Speak English only: 74.1%; With disability: 10.3%; Veterans: 7.5%; Ancestry: 13.1% German, 10.4% English, 9.0% Irish, 7.1% Italian, 2.9% French

Employment: 17.9% management, business, and financial, 4.6% computer, engineering, and science, 13.4% education, legal, community service, arts, and media, 4.4% healthcare practitioners, 14.0% service, 29.2% sales and office, 7.4% natural resources, construction, and maintenance, 9.2% production, transportation, and material moving

Income: Per capita: $31,455; Median household: $74,615; Average household: $93,002; Households with income of $100,000 or more: 33.9%; Poverty rate: 7.8%

Educational Attainment: High school diploma or higher: 90.4%; Bachelor's degree or higher: 30.6%; Graduate/professional degree or higher: 11.8%

School District(s)

Azusa Unified (KG-12)
2012-13 Enrollment: 9,755 . . . . (626) 967-6211

Charter Oak Unified (KG-12)
2012-13 Enrollment: 5,544 . . . . (626) 966-8331

Glendora Unified (KG-12)
2012-13 Enrollment: 7,559 . . . . (626) 963-1611

Four-year College(s)

Azusa Pacific Online University (Private, Not-for-profit, Undenominational)
Fall 2013 Enrollment: 726 . . . . (877) 816-6546
2013-14 Tuition: In-state $10,300; Out-of-state $10,300

Two-year College(s)

Citrus College (Public)
Fall 2013 Enrollment: 12,920 . . . . (626) 963-0323
2013-14 Tuition: In-state $1,174; Out-of-state $5,086

Housing: Homeownership rate: 72.3%; Median home value: $448,600; Median year structure built: 1963; Homeowner vacancy rate: 1.0%; Median gross rent: $1,440 per month; Rental vacancy rate: 5.5%

Health Insurance: 88.6% have insurance; 72.9% have private insurance; 23.9% have public insurance; 11.4% do not have insurance; 4.3% of children under 18 do not have insurance

Hospitals: East Valley Hospital Medical Center (128 beds); Foothill Presbyterian Hospital (106 beds)
Safety: Violent crime rate: 12.8 per 10,000 population; Property crime rate: 263.3 per 10,000 population
Transportation: Commute: 91.5% car, 2.7% public transportation, 1.2% walk, 3.6% work from home; Median travel time to work: 31.5 minutes
Additional Information Contacts
City of Glendora . . . . (626) 914-8200
http://www.ci.glendora.ca.us

GRANADA HILLS (unincorporated postal area)

ZCTA: 91344

Covers a land area of 16.414 square miles and a water area of 0.344 square miles. Located at 34.29° N. Lat; 118.51° W. Long. Elevation is 1,033 feet.
Population: 51,747; Growth (since 2000): 5.9%; Density: 3,152.6 persons per square mile; Race: 63.1% White, 3.5% Black/African American, 17.5% Asian, 0.5% American Indian/Alaska Native, 0.1% Native Hawaiian/Other Pacific Islander, 4.6% Two or more races, 28.7% Hispanic of any race; Average household size: 3.03; Median age: 41.0; Age under 18: 21.7%; Age 65 and over: 14.8%; Males per 100 females: 95.0; Marriage status: 30.0% never married, 54.6% now married, 1.6% separated, 7.0% widowed, 8.4% divorced; Foreign born: 33.5%; Speak English only: 49.8%; With disability: 10.6%; Veterans: 6.3%; Ancestry: 7.5% Armenian, 6.7% German, 5.4% Irish, 4.8% English, 4.5% Italian
Employment: 16.8% management, business, and financial, 5.2% computer, engineering, and science, 14.9% education, legal, community service, arts, and media, 5.3% healthcare practitioners, 14.1% service, 27.3% sales and office, 8.3% natural resources, construction, and maintenance, 7.9% production, transportation, and material moving
Income: Per capita: $30,945; Median household: $77,604; Average household: $93,656; Households with income of $100,000 or more: 37.4%; Poverty rate: 8.0%
Educational Attainment: High school diploma or higher: 89.3%; Bachelor's degree or higher: 34.5%; Graduate/professional degree or higher: 11.3%

School District(s)

Los Angeles Unified (PK-12)
2012-13 Enrollment: 655,455 . . . . (213) 241-1000

Four-year College(s)

Newberry School of Beauty (Private, For-profit)
Fall 2013 Enrollment: 153 . . . . (818) 366-3211

Two-year College(s)

Newberry School of Beauty (Private, For-profit)
Fall 2013 Enrollment: 153 . . . . (818) 366-3211

Vocational/Technical School(s)

Newberry School of Beauty (Private, For-profit)
Fall 2013 Enrollment: 153 . . . . (818) 366-3211
2013-14 Tuition: $14,483
Housing: Homeownership rate: 74.7%; Median home value: $449,600; Median year structure built: 1963; Homeowner vacancy rate: 1.0%; Median gross rent: $1,546 per month; Rental vacancy rate: 4.6%
Health Insurance: 85.2% have insurance; 69.5% have private insurance; 25.8% have public insurance; 14.8% do not have insurance; 7.1% of children under 18 do not have insurance
Transportation: Commute: 90.2% car, 2.7% public transportation, 0.7% walk, 5.3% work from home; Median travel time to work: 30.4 minutes

GREEN VALLEY (CDP). Covers a land area of 12.809 square miles and a water area of <.001 square miles. Located at 34.62° N. Lat; 118.41° W. Long. Elevation is 2,936 feet.
Population: 1,027; Growth (since 2000): n/a; Density: 80.2 persons per square mile; Race: 87.7% White, 0.8% Black/African American, 1.2% Asian, 1.1% American Indian/Alaska Native, 0.1% Native Hawaiian/Other Pacific Islander, 5.7% Two or more races, 12.0% Hispanic of any race; Average household size: 2.32; Median age: 47.0; Age under 18: 19.0%; Age 65 and over: 13.0%; Males per 100 females: 113.5
Housing: Homeownership rate: 81.0%; Homeowner vacancy rate: 4.5%; Rental vacancy rate: 2.3%

HACIENDA HEIGHTS (CDP). Covers a land area of 11.175 square miles and a water area of 0.007 square miles. Located at 34.00° N. Lat; 117.97° W. Long. Elevation is 453 feet.
Population: 54,038; Growth (since 2000): 1.7%; Density: 4,835.5 persons per square mile; Race: 40.5% White, 1.4% Black/African American, 37.1% Asian, 0.6% American Indian/Alaska Native, 0.2% Native Hawaiian/Other Pacific Islander, 3.2% Two or more races, 45.5% Hispanic of any race; Average household size: 3.33; Median age: 40.1; Age under 18: 22.0%; Age 65 and over: 15.4%; Males per 100 females: 94.8; Marriage status: 31.6% never married, 55.0% now married, 1.8% separated, 6.2% widowed, 7.3% divorced; Foreign born: 42.7%; Speak English only: 33.3%; With disability: 8.3%; Veterans: 5.1%; Ancestry: 3.5% German, 2.3% Irish, 2.1% English, 2.1% American, 1.9% Italian
Employment: 19.1% management, business, and financial, 4.7% computer, engineering, and science, 9.6% education, legal, community service, arts, and media, 4.6% healthcare practitioners, 15.7% service, 29.3% sales and office, 5.3% natural resources, construction, and maintenance, 11.7% production, transportation, and material moving
Income: Per capita: $28,339; Median household: $76,839; Average household: $93,925; Households with income of $100,000 or more: 35.6%; Poverty rate: 8.1%
Educational Attainment: High school diploma or higher: 84.7%; Bachelor's degree or higher: 35.1%; Graduate/professional degree or higher: 10.3%

School District(s)

Hacienda La Puente Unified (KG-12)
2012-13 Enrollment: 20,358 . . . . (626) 933-1000
Housing: Homeownership rate: 78.6%; Median home value: $458,800; Median year structure built: 1969; Homeowner vacancy rate: 1.0%; Median gross rent: $1,585 per month; Rental vacancy rate: 3.6%
Health Insurance: 82.6% have insurance; 64.6% have private insurance; 25.5% have public insurance; 17.4% do not have insurance; 6.6% of children under 18 do not have insurance
Transportation: Commute: 90.7% car, 2.9% public transportation, 0.8% walk, 4.9% work from home; Median travel time to work: 35.2 minutes

HARBOR CITY (unincorporated postal area)

ZCTA: 90710

Covers a land area of 2.358 square miles and a water area of <.001 square miles. Located at 33.80° N. Lat; 118.30° W. Long. Elevation is 49 feet.
Population: 25,457; Growth (since 2000): 3.3%; Density: 10,796.5 persons per square mile; Race: 41.9% White, 13.3% Black/African American, 18.1% Asian, 0.6% American Indian/Alaska Native, 0.9% Native Hawaiian/Other Pacific Islander, 5.6% Two or more races, 44.9% Hispanic of any race; Average household size: 2.91; Median age: 36.7; Age under 18: 24.7%; Age 65 and over: 13.0%; Males per 100 females: 93.4; Marriage status: 38.4% never married, 46.6% now married, 2.1% separated, 5.7% widowed, 9.2% divorced; Foreign born: 34.4%; Speak English only: 44.8%; With disability: 10.0%; Veterans: 5.9%; Ancestry: 6.8% German, 4.0% English, 4.0% Irish, 3.4% Italian, 2.8% French
Employment: 13.0% management, business, and financial, 5.2% computer, engineering, and science, 8.8% education, legal, community service, arts, and media, 5.3% healthcare practitioners, 23.6% service, 25.2% sales and office, 6.8% natural resources, construction, and maintenance, 12.2% production, transportation, and material moving
Income: Per capita: $24,892; Median household: $54,065; Average household: $71,612; Households with income of $100,000 or more: 24.6%; Poverty rate: 13.4%
Educational Attainment: High school diploma or higher: 80.3%; Bachelor's degree or higher: 25.6%; Graduate/professional degree or higher: 8.1%

School District(s)

Los Angeles Unified (PK-12)
2012-13 Enrollment: 655,455 . . . . (213) 241-1000
Housing: Homeownership rate: 56.8%; Median home value: $400,400; Median year structure built: 1972; Homeowner vacancy rate: 1.2%; Median gross rent: $1,045 per month; Rental vacancy rate: 4.6%
Health Insurance: 80.4% have insurance; 57.5% have private insurance; 32.2% have public insurance; 19.6% do not have insurance; 5.1% of children under 18 do not have insurance
Hospitals: Kaiser Foundation Hospital - South Bay (251 beds)
Transportation: Commute: 89.3% car, 4.2% public transportation, 2.8% walk, 2.6% work from home; Median travel time to work: 26.4 minutes

HASLEY CANYON (CDP). Covers a land area of 5.740 square miles and a water area of 0.001 square miles. Located at 34.48° N. Lat; 118.67° W. Long.
Population: 1,137; Growth (since 2000): n/a; Density: 198.1 persons per square mile; Race: 85.0% White, 1.3% Black/African American, 2.3%

Asian, 0.2% American Indian/Alaska Native, 0.1% Native Hawaiian/Other Pacific Islander, 4.6% Two or more races, 21.5% Hispanic of any race; Average household size: 2.97; Median age: 43.0; Age under 18: 24.9%; Age 65 and over: 10.7%; Males per 100 females: 112.5

Housing: Homeownership rate: 90.9%; Homeowner vacancy rate: 2.0%; Rental vacancy rate: 7.7%

HAWAIIAN GARDENS (city). Covers a land area of 0.946 square miles and a water area of 0.010 square miles. Located at 33.83° N. Lat; 118.07° W. Long. Elevation is 33 feet.

Population: 14,254; Growth (since 2000): -3.6%; Density: 15,069.5 persons per square mile; Race: 45.4% White, 3.8% Black/African American, 10.6% Asian, 1.2% American Indian/Alaska Native, 0.4% Native Hawaiian/Other Pacific Islander, 3.9% Two or more races, 77.2% Hispanic of any race; Average household size: 4.00; Median age: 28.4; Age under 18: 32.1%; Age 65 and over: 7.9%; Males per 100 females: 99.4; Marriage status: 40.4% never married, 46.6% now married, 4.3% separated, 5.3% widowed, 7.6% divorced; Foreign born: 44.7%; Speak English only: 20.9%; With disability: 9.7%; Veterans: 2.8%; Ancestry: 2.3% English, 1.8% American, 1.6% German, 1.5% Irish, 1.0% Italian

Employment: 7.6% management, business, and financial, 1.4% computer, engineering, and science, 3.9% education, legal, community service, arts, and media, 2.2% healthcare practitioners, 27.4% service, 23.5% sales and office, 13.3% natural resources, construction, and maintenance, 20.6% production, transportation, and material moving

Income: Per capita: $14,520; Median household: $42,017; Average household: $52,173; Households with income of $100,000 or more: 11.3%; Poverty rate: 24.4%

Educational Attainment: High school diploma or higher: 56.1%; Bachelor's degree or higher: 11.3%; Graduate/professional degree or higher: 1.6%

School District(s)

ABC Unified (KG-12)
2012-13 Enrollment: 20,835 . . . . (562) 926-5566

Housing: Homeownership rate: 44.2%; Median home value: $243,800; Median year structure built: 1968; Homeowner vacancy rate: 1.7%; Median gross rent: $1,231 per month; Rental vacancy rate: 4.3%

Health Insurance: 65.3% have insurance; 32.4% have private insurance; 38.2% have public insurance; 34.7% do not have insurance; 17.2% of children under 18 do not have insurance

Hospitals: Tri - City Regional Medical Center (137 beds)

Safety: Violent crime rate: 38.8 per 10,000 population; Property crime rate: 142.0 per 10,000 population

Transportation: Commute: 84.7% car, 5.7% public transportation, 4.8% walk, 1.4% work from home; Median travel time to work: 25.9 minutes

Additional Information Contacts

City of Hawaiian Gardens . . . . (562) 420-2641
http://hgcity.org

HAWTHORNE (city). Covers a land area of 6.081 square miles and a water area of 0.011 square miles. Located at 33.91° N. Lat; 118.35° W. Long. Elevation is 72 feet.

History: Named for Nathaniel Hawthorne, 19th century American novelist. Incorporated 1922.

Population: 84,293; Growth (since 2000): 0.2%; Density: 13,861.2 persons per square mile; Race: 32.8% White, 27.7% Black/African American, 6.7% Asian, 0.7% American Indian/Alaska Native, 1.2% Native Hawaiian/Other Pacific Islander, 4.7% Two or more races, 52.9% Hispanic of any race; Average household size: 2.94; Median age: 31.5; Age under 18: 27.5%; Age 65 and over: 7.4%; Males per 100 females: 93.2; Marriage status: 45.7% never married, 40.5% now married, 3.4% separated, 4.1% widowed, 9.7% divorced; Foreign born: 33.2%; Speak English only: 43.6%; With disability: 7.9%; Veterans: 3.8%; Ancestry: 13.9% American, 2.1% German, 1.6% Irish, 1.4% African, 1.2% English

Employment: 10.2% management, business, and financial, 2.6% computer, engineering, and science, 7.5% education, legal, community service, arts, and media, 3.2% healthcare practitioners, 26.6% service, 26.6% sales and office, 8.9% natural resources, construction, and maintenance, 14.3% production, transportation, and material moving

Income: Per capita: $20,162; Median household: $44,649; Average household: $57,114; Households with income of $100,000 or more: 12.9%; Poverty rate: 19.2%

Educational Attainment: High school diploma or higher: 74.4%; Bachelor's degree or higher: 18.0%; Graduate/professional degree or higher: 4.4%

School District(s)

Centinela Valley Union High (09-12)
2012-13 Enrollment: 6,637 . . . . (310) 263-3200
Hawthorne (KG-12)
2012-13 Enrollment: 9,027 . . . . (310) 676-2276
Lawndale Elementary (KG-12)
2012-13 Enrollment: 6,325 . . . . (310) 973-1300
Los Angeles County Office of Education (KG-12)
2012-13 Enrollment: 9,136 . . . . (562) 922-6111
Los Angeles Unified (PK-12)
2012-13 Enrollment: 655,455 . . . . (213) 241-1000
Wiseburn Elementary (KG-12)
2012-13 Enrollment: 3,876 . . . . (310) 643-3025

Housing: Homeownership rate: 26.7%; Median home value: $386,500; Median year structure built: 1967; Homeowner vacancy rate: 1.5%; Median gross rent: $1,021 per month; Rental vacancy rate: 4.6%

Health Insurance: 74.4% have insurance; 49.1% have private insurance; 30.5% have public insurance; 25.6% do not have insurance; 11.6% of children under 18 do not have insurance

Safety: Violent crime rate: 67.3 per 10,000 population; Property crime rate: 260.3 per 10,000 population

Transportation: Commute: 85.8% car, 7.3% public transportation, 1.8% walk, 2.7% work from home; Median travel time to work: 27.6 minutes

Airports: Jack Northrop Field/Hawthorne Municipal (general aviation)

Additional Information Contacts

City of Hawthorne . . . . (310) 349-2960
http://www.cityofhawthorne.com

HERMOSA BEACH (city). Covers a land area of 1.427 square miles and a water area of 0 square miles. Located at 33.87° N. Lat; 118.40° W. Long. Elevation is 26 feet.

History: Named for the Spanish translation of "beautiful," by the land company that developed the land. Incorporated 1907.

Population: 19,506; Growth (since 2000): 5.1%; Density: 13,673.6 persons per square mile; Race: 86.8% White, 1.2% Black/African American, 5.7% Asian, 0.3% American Indian/Alaska Native, 0.2% Native Hawaiian/Other Pacific Islander, 4.2% Two or more races, 8.4% Hispanic of any race; Average household size: 2.04; Median age: 37.0; Age under 18: 15.9%; Age 65 and over: 9.0%; Males per 100 females: 111.3; Marriage status: 44.8% never married, 40.6% now married, 0.6% separated, 3.2% widowed, 11.4% divorced; Foreign born: 10.5%; Speak English only: 89.1%; With disability: 5.3%; Veterans: 6.4%; Ancestry: 19.8% German, 17.2% Irish, 13.1% English, 7.7% Italian, 6.5% American

Employment: 34.5% management, business, and financial, 10.4% computer, engineering, and science, 14.2% education, legal, community service, arts, and media, 4.0% healthcare practitioners, 10.6% service, 20.8% sales and office, 1.2% natural resources, construction, and maintenance, 4.3% production, transportation, and material moving

Income: Per capita: $69,606; Median household: $101,655; Average household: $142,705; Households with income of $100,000 or more: 51.0%; Poverty rate: 3.4%

Educational Attainment: High school diploma or higher: 99.0%; Bachelor's degree or higher: 70.9%; Graduate/professional degree or higher: 23.6%

School District(s)

Hermosa Beach City Elementary (KG-12)
2012-13 Enrollment: 2,667 . . . . (310) 937-5877

Housing: Homeownership rate: 44.6%; Median home value: 1 million+; Median year structure built: 1966; Homeowner vacancy rate: 1.0%; Median gross rent: $1,845 per month; Rental vacancy rate: 4.4%

Health Insurance: 92.9% have insurance; 88.0% have private insurance; 14.2% have public insurance; 7.1% do not have insurance; 1.8% of children under 18 do not have insurance

Safety: Violent crime rate: 13.6 per 10,000 population; Property crime rate: 276.5 per 10,000 population

Newspapers: Beach Reporter (weekly circulation 52000); Easy Reader Inc (weekly circulation 58000)

Transportation: Commute: 85.1% car, 1.5% public transportation, 1.9% walk, 9.3% work from home; Median travel time to work: 29.9 minutes

Additional Information Contacts

City of Hermosa Beach . . . . (310) 318-0239
http://www.hermosabch.org

HIDDEN HILLS (city). Covers a land area of 1.689 square miles and a water area of 0 square miles. Located at 34.16° N. Lat; 118.66° W. Long. Elevation is 1,076 feet.

Population: 1,856; Growth (since 2000): -1.0%; Density: 1,099.1 persons per square mile; Race: 92.3% White, 2.0% Black/African American, 2.3% Asian, 0.2% American Indian/Alaska Native, 0.1% Native Hawaiian/Other Pacific Islander, 1.6% Two or more races, 6.6% Hispanic of any race; Average household size: 3.13; Median age: 45.8; Age under 18: 28.6%; Age 65 and over: 15.9%; Males per 100 females: 96.0

Housing: Homeownership rate: 93.1%; Homeowner vacancy rate: 1.4%; Rental vacancy rate: 4.7%

Safety: Violent crime rate: 10.5 per 10,000 population; Property crime rate: 36.7 per 10,000 population

Additional Information Contacts

City of Hidden Hills . . . . (818) 888-9281
http://www.hiddenhillscity.org

HUNTINGTON PARK (city). Covers a land area of 3.013 square miles and a water area of 0.003 square miles. Located at 33.98° N. Lat; 118.22° W. Long. Elevation is 171 feet.

History: Named for Henry E. Huntington by the subdivider, E.V. Baker. Founded 1856. Incorporated 1906.

Population: 58,114; Growth (since 2000): -5.3%; Density: 19,290.7 persons per square mile; Race: 51.2% White, 0.8% Black/African American, 0.7% Asian, 1.3% American Indian/Alaska Native, 0.0% Native Hawaiian/Other Pacific Islander, 3.8% Two or more races, 97.1% Hispanic of any race; Average household size: 3.96; Median age: 28.9; Age under 18: 31.7%; Age 65 and over: 6.6%; Males per 100 females: 99.6; Marriage status: 47.7% never married, 43.3% now married, 4.4% separated, 4.1% widowed, 4.9% divorced; Foreign born: 50.5%; Speak English only: 4.8%; With disability: 7.8%; Veterans: 1.3%; Ancestry: 0.8% American, 0.1% English, 0.1% Irish, 0.1% Italian, 0.1% Dutch

Employment: 5.3% management, business, and financial, 0.8% computer, engineering, and science, 4.5% education, legal, community service, arts, and media, 1.2% healthcare practitioners, 21.8% service, 25.6% sales and office, 9.9% natural resources, construction, and maintenance, 31.0% production, transportation, and material moving

Income: Per capita: $12,064; Median household: $36,397; Average household: $44,986; Households with income of $100,000 or more: 6.7%; Poverty rate: 28.7%

Educational Attainment: High school diploma or higher: 40.0%; Bachelor's degree or higher: 5.8%; Graduate/professional degree or higher: 1.2%

School District(s)

Los Angeles Unified (PK-12)
2012-13 Enrollment: 655,455 . . . . (213) 241-1000
Sbc - Aspire Public Schools (KG-12)
2012-13 Enrollment: 1,972 . . . . (510) 434-5000

Two-year College(s)

American College of Healthcare (Private, For-profit)
Fall 2013 Enrollment: 73 . . . . (323) 585-9000
ICDC College (Private, For-profit)
Fall 2013 Enrollment: 3,265 . . . . (310) 482-6996
United Education Institute-Huntington Park Campus (Private, For-profit)
Fall 2013 Enrollment: 2,732 . . . . (949) 272-7200

Housing: Homeownership rate: 27.0%; Median home value: $294,000; Median year structure built: 1950; Homeowner vacancy rate: 1.5%; Median gross rent: $936 per month; Rental vacancy rate: 3.2%

Health Insurance: 66.0% have insurance; 28.3% have private insurance; 39.8% have public insurance; 34.0% do not have insurance; 9.9% of children under 18 do not have insurance

Hospitals: Community Hospital of Huntington Park (81 beds)

Safety: Violent crime rate: 61.0 per 10,000 population; Property crime rate: 307.9 per 10,000 population

Transportation: Commute: 76.7% car, 13.2% public transportation, 5.5% walk, 2.5% work from home; Median travel time to work: 29.9 minutes

Additional Information Contacts

City of Huntington Park . . . . (323) 582-6161
http://www.huntingtonpark.org

INDUSTRY (city). Covers a land area of 11.785 square miles and a water area of 0.279 square miles. Located at 34.03° N. Lat; 117.94° W. Long. Elevation is 322 feet.

Population: 219; Growth (since 2000): -71.8%; Density: 18.6 persons per square mile; Race: 58.9% White, 0.5% Black/African American, 8.2% Asian, 0.0% American Indian/Alaska Native, 0.0% Native Hawaiian/Other Pacific Islander, 3.7% Two or more races, 52.5% Hispanic of any race; Average household size: 3.10; Median age: 37.5; Age under 18: 26.9%; Age 65 and over: 10.0%; Males per 100 females: 108.6

Housing: Homeownership rate: 31.8%; Homeowner vacancy rate: 0.0%; Rental vacancy rate: 6.0%

Additional Information Contacts

City of Industry . . . . (626) 333-2211
http://www.cityofindustry.org

INGLEWOOD (city). Covers a land area of 9.068 square miles and a water area of 0.025 square miles. Located at 33.96° N. Lat; 118.34° W. Long. Elevation is 131 feet.

History: Named for Inglewood, Canada, by an early visitor to the community. Inglewood was founded on land granted in 1844 to Ignacio Machado and called Rancho Aguaje de la Centinela. When Daniel Freeman acquired it in 1873, he laid out a town and sold lots.

Population: 109,673; Growth (since 2000): -2.6%; Density: 12,094.7 persons per square mile; Race: 23.3% White, 43.9% Black/African American, 1.4% Asian, 0.7% American Indian/Alaska Native, 0.3% Native Hawaiian/Other Pacific Islander, 4.1% Two or more races, 50.6% Hispanic of any race; Average household size: 2.97; Median age: 33.4; Age under 18: 26.7%; Age 65 and over: 9.4%; Males per 100 females: 90.6; Marriage status: 45.0% never married, 39.7% now married, 4.1% separated, 4.9% widowed, 10.4% divorced; Foreign born: 27.8%; Speak English only: 48.7%; With disability: 10.9%; Veterans: 5.6%; Ancestry: 1.8% American, 1.6% African, 0.9% Belizean, 0.6% French, 0.5% Irish

Employment: 10.5% management, business, and financial, 1.8% computer, engineering, and science, 8.6% education, legal, community service, arts, and media, 3.3% healthcare practitioners, 25.9% service, 27.8% sales and office, 8.8% natural resources, construction, and maintenance, 13.4% production, transportation, and material moving

Income: Per capita: $20,150; Median household: $43,394; Average household: $57,780; Households with income of $100,000 or more: 14.1%; Poverty rate: 22.4%

Educational Attainment: High school diploma or higher: 71.8%; Bachelor's degree or higher: 17.4%; Graduate/professional degree or higher: 6.1%

School District(s)

Inglewood Unified (KG-12)
2012-13 Enrollment: 14,207 . . . . (310) 419-2700
Lennox (KG-12)
2012-13 Enrollment: 7,043 . . . . (310) 695-4000
Los Angeles County Office of Education (KG-12)
2012-13 Enrollment: 9,136 . . . . (562) 922-6111
Los Angeles Unified (PK-12)
2012-13 Enrollment: 655,455 . . . . (213) 241-1000

Two-year College(s)

Crimson Technical College (Private, For-profit)
Fall 2013 Enrollment: 458 . . . . (310) 642-5440

Housing: Homeownership rate: 36.9%; Median home value: $328,200; Median year structure built: 1959; Homeowner vacancy rate: 1.5%; Median gross rent: $1,076 per month; Rental vacancy rate: 5.5%

Health Insurance: 73.9% have insurance; 49.2% have private insurance; 30.8% have public insurance; 26.1% do not have insurance; 13.3% of children under 18 do not have insurance

Hospitals: Centinela Hospital Medical Center (400 beds)

Safety: Violent crime rate: 66.2 per 10,000 population; Property crime rate: 243.4 per 10,000 population

Transportation: Commute: 84.1% car, 7.6% public transportation, 2.0% walk, 4.2% work from home; Median travel time to work: 28.5 minutes

Additional Information Contacts

City of Inglewood . . . . (310) 412-5111
http://www.cityofinglewood.org/default.asp

IRWINDALE (city). Covers a land area of 8.826 square miles and a water area of 0.787 square miles. Located at 34.11° N. Lat; 117.96° W. Long. Elevation is 469 feet.

Population: 1,422; Growth (since 2000): -1.7%; Density: 161.1 persons per square mile; Race: 58.6% White, 0.8% Black/African American, 2.4% Asian, 2.0% American Indian/Alaska Native, 0.6% Native Hawaiian/Other Pacific Islander, 4.1% Two or more races, 90.6% Hispanic of any race; Average household size: 3.67; Median age: 34.0; Age under 18: 26.2%; Age 65 and over: 10.6%; Males per 100 females: 93.5

Two-year College(s)

Premiere Career College (Private, For-profit)
Fall 2013 Enrollment: 557 . . . . (626) 814-2080

Housing: Homeownership rate: 69.7%; Homeowner vacancy rate: 0.8%; Rental vacancy rate: 2.6%

Safety: Violent crime rate: 138.9 per 10,000 population; Property crime rate: 1,590.3 per 10,000 population

Additional Information Contacts

City of Irwindale. . . . . (626) 430-2217
http://ci.irwindale.ca.us/home.html

LA CAÑADA FLINTRIDGE (city). Covers a land area of 8.628 square miles and a water area of 0.017 square miles. Located at 34.21° N. Lat; 118.20° W. Long. Elevation is 1,188 feet.

History: The name has nothing to do with the country Canada. During the Spanish era, the area was known as Rancho La Ca±ada. Prior to the city's incorporation in 1976, the area consisted of two distinct communities, La Ca±ada and Flintridge (the latter named after developer and United States Senator Frank P. Flint). Flintridge comprises the southern part of the city, covering the northern flank of the San Rafael Hills, but more generally including most areas south of Foothill Blvd.

Population: 20,246; Growth (since 2000): -0.4%; Density: 2,346.5 persons per square mile; Race: 68.9% White, 0.5% Black/African American, 25.8% Asian, 0.1% American Indian/Alaska Native, 0.0% Native Hawaiian/Other Pacific Islander, 3.4% Two or more races, 6.3% Hispanic of any race; Average household size: 2.95; Median age: 45.9; Age under 18: 26.3%; Age 65 and over: 15.7%; Males per 100 females: 94.7; Marriage status: 26.2% never married, 65.1% now married, 0.7% separated, 3.8% widowed, 4.9% divorced; Foreign born: 25.3%; Speak English only: 64.7%; With disability: 5.6%; Veterans: 5.8%; Ancestry: 12.2% English, 11.2% German, 8.9% Irish, 5.6% Armenian, 5.3% European

Employment: 34.5% management, business, and financial, 8.2% computer, engineering, and science, 21.4% education, legal, community service, arts, and media, 6.2% healthcare practitioners, 6.2% service, 20.5% sales and office, 1.4% natural resources, construction, and maintenance, 1.5% production, transportation, and material moving

Income: Per capita: $76,656; Median household: $156,952; Average household: $232,943; Households with income of $100,000 or more: 71.2%; Poverty rate: 1.8%

Educational Attainment: High school diploma or higher: 98.1%; Bachelor's degree or higher: 75.2%; Graduate/professional degree or higher: 35.5%

School District(s)

Baldwin Park Unified (KG-12)
2012-13 Enrollment: 18,845 . . . . (626) 962-3311
Hermosa Beach City Elementary (KG-12)
2012-13 Enrollment: 2,667 . . . . (310) 937-5877
La Canada Unified (KG-12)
2012-13 Enrollment: 4,119 . . . . (818) 952-8304
Mariposa County Unified (KG-12)
2012-13 Enrollment: 1,843 . . . . (209) 742-0250
William S. Hart Union High (KG-12)
2012-13 Enrollment: 26,373 . . . . (661) 259-0033

Housing: Homeownership rate: 89.4%; Median home value: 1 million+; Median year structure built: 1955; Homeowner vacancy rate: 0.8%; Median gross rent: $1,906 per month; Rental vacancy rate: 5.4%

Health Insurance: 94.1% have insurance; 89.1% have private insurance; 17.0% have public insurance; 5.9% do not have insurance; 4.2% of children under 18 do not have insurance

Safety: Violent crime rate: 5.8 per 10,000 population; Property crime rate: 147.3 per 10,000 population

Newspapers: La Canada Outlook (weekly circulation 11500); Pasadena Outlook (weekly circulation 19600)

Transportation: Commute: 90.2% car, 0.9% public transportation, 0.8% walk, 7.2% work from home; Median travel time to work: 26.3 minutes

Additional Information Contacts

City of La Canada Flintridge . . . . (818) 790-8880
http://www.lcf.ca.gov

LA CRESCENTA-MONTROSE (CDP). Covers a land area of 3.426 square miles and a water area of 0.011 square miles. Located at 34.23° N. Lat; 118.24° W. Long. Elevation is 1,572 feet.

Population: 19,653; Growth (since 2000): 6.0%; Density: 5,736.4 persons per square mile; Race: 65.2% White, 0.7% Black/African American, 27.3% Asian, 0.4% American Indian/Alaska Native, 0.1% Native Hawaiian/Other Pacific Islander, 3.6% Two or more races, 11.4% Hispanic of any race; Average household size: 2.77; Median age: 41.6; Age under 18: 23.5%; Age 65 and over: 12.4%; Males per 100 females: 92.9; Marriage status: 30.3% never married, 58.0% now married, 2.0% separated, 4.2% widowed, 7.5% divorced; Foreign born: 34.1%; Speak English only: 54.2%; With disability: 6.8%; Veterans: 4.7%; Ancestry: 9.4% Armenian, 9.2% German, 7.2% Irish, 6.5% Italian, 6.1% English

Employment: 21.6% management, business, and financial, 5.6% computer, engineering, and science, 20.2% education, legal, community service, arts, and media, 6.2% healthcare practitioners, 9.8% service, 26.2% sales and office, 4.9% natural resources, construction, and maintenance, 5.6% production, transportation, and material moving

Income: Per capita: $39,440; Median household: $89,375; Average household: $109,266; Households with income of $100,000 or more: 44.1%; Poverty rate: 7.4%

Educational Attainment: High school diploma or higher: 94.8%; Bachelor's degree or higher: 51.8%; Graduate/professional degree or higher: 18.3%

School District(s)

Glendale Unified (KG-12)
2012-13 Enrollment: 26,179 . . . . (818) 241-3111

Housing: Homeownership rate: 64.5%; Median home value: $624,100; Median year structure built: 1956; Homeowner vacancy rate: 0.6%; Median gross rent: $1,375 per month; Rental vacancy rate: 4.1%

Health Insurance: 89.7% have insurance; 78.7% have private insurance; 20.0% have public insurance; 10.3% do not have insurance; 4.6% of children under 18 do not have insurance

Transportation: Commute: 89.0% car, 1.4% public transportation, 3.2% walk, 5.0% work from home; Median travel time to work: 28.5 minutes; Amtrak: Bus service available.

LA HABRA HEIGHTS (city). Covers a land area of 6.159 square miles and a water area of 0.003 square miles. Located at 33.96° N. Lat; 117.95° W. Long. Elevation is 738 feet.

History: La Habra means a low pass in the mountains, and the city was incorporated on December 4, 1978.

Population: 5,325; Growth (since 2000): -6.8%; Density: 864.7 persons per square mile; Race: 72.4% White, 0.9% Black/African American, 15.8% Asian, 0.5% American Indian/Alaska Native, 0.1% Native Hawaiian/Other Pacific Islander, 4.1% Two or more races, 23.5% Hispanic of any race; Average household size: 2.94; Median age: 47.6; Age under 18: 19.1%; Age 65 and over: 19.5%; Males per 100 females: 99.1; Marriage status: 23.0% never married, 63.3% now married, 0.5% separated, 6.5% widowed, 7.1% divorced; Foreign born: 22.4%; Speak English only: 69.7%; With disability: 10.3%; Veterans: 7.1%; Ancestry: 13.6% English, 12.3% German, 7.1% Irish, 4.7% Italian, 3.1% Portuguese

Employment: 22.3% management, business, and financial, 8.7% computer, engineering, and science, 10.7% education, legal, community service, arts, and media, 12.0% healthcare practitioners, 9.8% service, 25.0% sales and office, 8.3% natural resources, construction, and maintenance, 3.3% production, transportation, and material moving

Income: Per capita: $49,672; Median household: $118,871; Average household: $148,465; Households with income of $100,000 or more: 62.8%; Poverty rate: 2.8%

Educational Attainment: High school diploma or higher: 95.3%; Bachelor's degree or higher: 47.3%; Graduate/professional degree or higher: 22.3%

Housing: Homeownership rate: 93.2%; Median home value: $776,200; Median year structure built: 1967; Homeowner vacancy rate: 0.5%; Median gross rent: $2,000+ per month; Rental vacancy rate: 5.3%

Health Insurance: 92.5% have insurance; 81.0% have private insurance; 27.9% have public insurance; 7.5% do not have insurance; 6.7% of children under 18 do not have insurance

Safety: Violent crime rate: 5.5 per 10,000 population; Property crime rate: 101.2 per 10,000 population

Transportation: Commute: 92.6% car, 1.1% public transportation, 0.0% walk, 4.8% work from home; Median travel time to work: 29.0 minutes

Additional Information Contacts

City of La Habra Heights . . . . (562) 694-6302
http://www.la-habra-heights.org

LA MIRADA (city). Covers a land area of 7.840 square miles and a water area of 0.017 square miles. Located at 33.90° N. Lat; 118.01° W. Long. Elevation is 194 feet.

History: La Mirada derives from the Spanish for "the view," referring to the panoramic view of the surrounding valleys from atop the city's hills. It was the original site of California's olive industry. The city is the seat of Biola College. Incorporated 1960.

Population: 48,527; Growth (since 2000): 3.7%; Density: 6,189.4 persons per square mile; Race: 60.7% White, 2.3% Black/African American, 17.8% Asian, 0.8% American Indian/Alaska Native, 0.3% Native Hawaiian/Other Pacific Islander, 4.3% Two or more races, 39.7% Hispanic of any race; Average household size: 3.11; Median age: 37.9; Age under 18: 21.1%; Age 65 and over: 15.2%; Males per 100 females: 92.2; Marriage status: 34.1% never married, 53.1% now married, 1.5% separated, 5.5% widowed, 7.4% divorced; Foreign born: 23.5%; Speak English only: 57.9%; With disability: 9.4%; Veterans: 6.3%; Ancestry: 8.9% German, 6.2% Irish, 5.6% English, 3.2% Italian, 1.9% French

Employment: 17.4% management, business, and financial, 5.1% computer, engineering, and science, 13.7% education, legal, community service, arts, and media, 4.2% healthcare practitioners, 13.3% service, 27.8% sales and office, 7.5% natural resources, construction, and maintenance, 11.0% production, transportation, and material moving

Income: Per capita: $28,956; Median household: $81,961; Average household: $94,977; Households with income of $100,000 or more: 39.0%; Poverty rate: 7.0%

Educational Attainment: High school diploma or higher: 88.0%; Bachelor's degree or higher: 28.7%; Graduate/professional degree or higher: 10.8%

School District(s)

Norwalk-La Mirada Unified (KG-12)
2012-13 Enrollment: 19,770 . . . . (562) 868-0431

Four-year College(s)

Biola University (Private, Not-for-profit, Undenominational)
Fall 2013 Enrollment: 6,301 . . . . (562) 903-6000
2013-14 Tuition: In-state $32,142; Out-of-state $32,142

Housing: Homeownership rate: 79.1%; Median home value: $401,300; Median year structure built: 1959; Homeowner vacancy rate: 0.8%; Median gross rent: $1,461 per month; Rental vacancy rate: 4.0%

Health Insurance: 86.7% have insurance; 71.9% have private insurance; 23.4% have public insurance; 13.3% do not have insurance; 10.3% of children under 18 do not have insurance

Safety: Violent crime rate: 14.6 per 10,000 population; Property crime rate: 171.1 per 10,000 population

Transportation: Commute: 90.2% car, 2.1% public transportation, 3.5% walk, 3.1% work from home; Median travel time to work: 29.3 minutes

Additional Information Contacts

City of La Mirada . . . . (562) 943-0131
http://www.cityoflamirada.org

LA PUENTE (city). Covers a land area of 3.479 square miles and a water area of <.001 square miles. Located at 34.03° N. Lat; 117.95° W. Long. Elevation is 351 feet.

History: Named for the Spanish translation of "bridge". Laid out 1841. Incorporated 1956.

Population: 39,816; Growth (since 2000): -3.0%; Density: 11,445.4 persons per square mile; Race: 49.4% White, 1.4% Black/African American, 8.4% Asian, 1.1% American Indian/Alaska Native, 0.1% Native Hawaiian/Other Pacific Islander, 3.7% Two or more races, 85.1% Hispanic of any race; Average household size: 4.21; Median age: 31.5; Age under 18: 28.7%; Age 65 and over: 9.2%; Males per 100 females: 99.7; Marriage status: 42.7% never married, 47.7% now married, 3.6% separated, 4.9% widowed, 4.7% divorced; Foreign born: 41.3%; Speak English only: 21.7%; With disability: 10.9%; Veterans: 3.1%; Ancestry: 1.4% Irish, 1.4% American, 1.2% German, 0.7% Italian, 0.6% English

Employment: 6.2% management, business, and financial, 1.8% computer, engineering, and science, 7.1% education, legal, community service, arts, and media, 3.9% healthcare practitioners, 19.4% service, 26.2% sales and office, 13.2% natural resources, construction, and maintenance, 22.3% production, transportation, and material moving

Income: Per capita: $15,541; Median household: $53,794; Average household: $62,083; Households with income of $100,000 or more: 16.2%; Poverty rate: 14.3%

Educational Attainment: High school diploma or higher: 60.0%; Bachelor's degree or higher: 9.4%; Graduate/professional degree or higher: 2.6%

School District(s)

Bassett Unified (KG-12)
2012-13 Enrollment: 4,194 . . . . (626) 931-3000
Hacienda La Puente Unified (KG-12)
2012-13 Enrollment: 20,358 . . . . (626) 933-1000
Rowland Unified (KG-12)
2012-13 Enrollment: 15,501 . . . . (626) 965-2541

Vocational/Technical School(s)

Hacienda La Puente Adult Education (Public)
Fall 2013 Enrollment: 4,151 . . . . (626) 934-2801
2013-14 Tuition: $3,300

Housing: Homeownership rate: 60.3%; Median home value: $284,800; Median year structure built: 1959; Homeowner vacancy rate: 1.0%; Median gross rent: $1,162 per month; Rental vacancy rate: 3.9%

Health Insurance: 73.8% have insurance; 43.8% have private insurance; 33.9% have public insurance; 26.2% do not have insurance; 6.7% of children under 18 do not have insurance

Safety: Violent crime rate: 35.4 per 10,000 population; Property crime rate: 122.0 per 10,000 population

Transportation: Commute: 90.3% car, 2.8% public transportation, 1.3% walk, 3.1% work from home; Median travel time to work: 31.3 minutes

Additional Information Contacts

City of La Puente . . . . (626) 855-1500
http://www.lapuente.org

LA VERNE (city). Covers a land area of 8.430 square miles and a water area of 0.132 square miles. Located at 34.12° N. Lat; 117.77° W. Long. Elevation is 1,060 feet.

History: La Verne originated as Lordsburg during the 1890 land boom. In 1891 the Santa Fe Railway induced new settlers to come to the region, including a group of Dunkards who founded Lordsburg College. In 1916 the town and the college changed their names to La Verne, after a local ranch, whose owner thought that "verne" was Spanish for "green."

Population: 31,063; Growth (since 2000): -1.8%; Density: 3,684.8 persons per square mile; Race: 74.2% White, 3.4% Black/African American, 7.7% Asian, 0.9% American Indian/Alaska Native, 0.2% Native Hawaiian/Other Pacific Islander, 4.5% Two or more races, 31.0% Hispanic of any race; Average household size: 2.70; Median age: 42.9; Age under 18: 21.3%; Age 65 and over: 16.9%; Males per 100 females: 89.9; Marriage status: 32.4% never married, 50.1% now married, 1.8% separated, 7.3% widowed, 10.3% divorced; Foreign born: 15.2%; Speak English only: 76.5%; With disability: 10.5%; Veterans: 8.7%; Ancestry: 13.8% German, 9.5% Irish, 8.9% English, 6.6% Italian, 3.1% American

Employment: 18.5% management, business, and financial, 4.5% computer, engineering, and science, 13.7% education, legal, community service, arts, and media, 6.1% healthcare practitioners, 16.0% service, 27.0% sales and office, 6.0% natural resources, construction, and maintenance, 8.2% production, transportation, and material moving

Income: Per capita: $33,640; Median household: $77,040; Average household: $94,754; Households with income of $100,000 or more: 37.6%; Poverty rate: 7.9%

Educational Attainment: High school diploma or higher: 91.5%; Bachelor's degree or higher: 35.4%; Graduate/professional degree or higher: 13.0%

School District(s)

Bonita Unified (KG-12)
2012-13 Enrollment: 9,870 . . . . (909) 971-8200
Los Angeles County Office of Education (KG-12)
2012-13 Enrollment: 9,136 . . . . (562) 922-6111

Four-year College(s)

University of La Verne (Private, Not-for-profit)
Fall 2013 Enrollment: 8,796 . . . . (909) 593-3511
2013-14 Tuition: In-state $35,000; Out-of-state $35,000

Housing: Homeownership rate: 74.5%; Median home value: $448,300; Median year structure built: 1975; Homeowner vacancy rate: 1.7%; Median gross rent: $1,288 per month; Rental vacancy rate: 5.4%

Health Insurance: 91.5% have insurance; 75.4% have private insurance; 29.1% have public insurance; 8.5% do not have insurance; 3.1% of children under 18 do not have insurance

Safety: Violent crime rate: 11.8 per 10,000 population; Property crime rate: 239.5 per 10,000 population

Transportation: Commute: 88.6% car, 2.5% public transportation, 2.3% walk, 4.6% work from home; Median travel time to work: 29.3 minutes

Airports: Brackett Field (general aviation)

Additional Information Contacts

City of La Verne . . . . (909) 596-8726
http://www.ci.la-verne.ca.us

LADERA HEIGHTS (CDP). Covers a land area of 2.966 square miles and a water area of <.001 square miles. Located at 34.00° N. Lat; 118.38° W. Long. Elevation is 305 feet.

History: The area was historically mixed until the early 1980s, when the neighborhood became a mecca for wealthy black families. The Southern California real estate boom of the late 1990s and early 2000s brought into the area a few more upper middle-class families of other races. It is said that Ladera Heights is the "black Brentwood" also a community in Los Angeles.

Population: 6,498; Growth (since 2000): -1.1%; Density: 2,191.2 persons per square mile; Race: 15.1% White, 73.7% Black/African American, 3.6% Asian, 0.3% American Indian/Alaska Native, 0.0% Native Hawaiian/Other Pacific Islander, 5.3% Two or more races, 5.5% Hispanic of any race; Average household size: 2.36; Median age: 49.0; Age under 18: 17.3%; Age 65 and over: 23.5%; Males per 100 females: 79.7; Marriage status: 39.9% never married, 37.8% now married, 2.2% separated, 8.2% widowed, 14.0% divorced; Foreign born: 8.7%; Speak English only: 87.6%; With disability: 11.5%; Veterans: 8.7%; Ancestry: 6.5% African, 6.0% American, 4.6% Ethiopian, 3.7% Irish, 2.1% German

Employment: 21.0% management, business, and financial, 4.4% computer, engineering, and science, 17.0% education, legal, community service, arts, and media, 12.3% healthcare practitioners, 8.1% service, 27.0% sales and office, 0.6% natural resources, construction, and maintenance, 9.6% production, transportation, and material moving

Income: Per capita: $55,099; Median household: $99,563; Average household: $131,488; Households with income of $100,000 or more: 49.4%; Poverty rate: 4.7%

Educational Attainment: High school diploma or higher: 97.7%; Bachelor's degree or higher: 56.9%; Graduate/professional degree or higher: 28.3%

Housing: Homeownership rate: 73.7%; Median home value: $734,600; Median year structure built: 1959; Homeowner vacancy rate: 1.1%; Median gross rent: $1,700 per month; Rental vacancy rate: 6.7%

Health Insurance: 92.7% have insurance; 83.1% have private insurance; 28.0% have public insurance; 7.3% do not have insurance; 5.6% of children under 18 do not have insurance

Transportation: Commute: 93.4% car, 0.1% public transportation, 0.9% walk, 4.9% work from home; Median travel time to work: 27.3 minutes

LAKE HUGHES (CDP). Covers a land area of 10.623 square miles and a water area of 0.064 square miles. Located at 34.68° N. Lat; 118.45° W. Long. Elevation is 3,228 feet.

Population: 649; Growth (since 2000): n/a; Density: 61.1 persons per square mile; Race: 83.8% White, 2.9% Black/African American, 0.8% Asian, 1.1% American Indian/Alaska Native, 0.2% Native Hawaiian/Other Pacific Islander, 2.9% Two or more races, 16.0% Hispanic of any race; Average household size: 2.09; Median age: 46.9; Age under 18: 16.2%; Age 65 and over: 11.6%; Males per 100 females: 104.1

School District(s)

Hughes-Elizabeth Lakes Union Elementary (KG-08)
2012-13 Enrollment: 281 . . . . (661) 724-1231
Los Angeles County Office of Education (KG-12)
2012-13 Enrollment: 9,136 . . . . (562) 922-6111

Housing: Homeownership rate: 58.3%; Homeowner vacancy rate: 4.9%; Rental vacancy rate: 9.9%

LAKE LOS ANGELES (CDP). Covers a land area of 9.741 square miles and a water area of 0.049 square miles. Located at 34.61° N. Lat; 117.83° W. Long. Elevation is 2,661 feet.

History: Named for the city of Los Angeles. Antelope Valley Indian Museum is here.

Population: 12,328; Growth (since 2000): 7.0%; Density: 1,265.6 persons per square mile; Race: 55.7% White, 11.3% Black/African American, 0.9% Asian, 1.4% American Indian/Alaska Native, 0.2% Native Hawaiian/Other Pacific Islander, 5.6% Two or more races, 53.6% Hispanic of any race; Average household size: 3.76; Median age: 29.9; Age under 18: 33.2%; Age 65 and over: 7.6%; Males per 100 females: 100.8; Marriage status: 41.0% never married, 47.5% now married, 4.4% separated, 2.4% widowed, 9.1% divorced; Foreign born: 14.8%; Speak English only: 66.0%; With disability: 12.7%; Veterans: 8.6%; Ancestry: 8.5% Irish, 6.9% German, 5.0% English, 4.1% Italian, 1.9% African

Employment: 7.7% management, business, and financial, 3.0% computer, engineering, and science, 7.1% education, legal, community service, arts, and media, 4.0% healthcare practitioners, 24.3% service, 19.1% sales and office, 16.8% natural resources, construction, and maintenance, 18.0% production, transportation, and material moving

Income: Per capita: $16,919; Median household: $43,750; Average household: $59,280; Households with income of $100,000 or more: 14.7%; Poverty rate: 26.6%

Educational Attainment: High school diploma or higher: 69.8%; Bachelor's degree or higher: 9.2%; Graduate/professional degree or higher: 3.1%

Housing: Homeownership rate: 72.7%; Median home value: $83,200; Median year structure built: 1984; Homeowner vacancy rate: 4.5%; Median gross rent: $1,159 per month; Rental vacancy rate: 7.4%

Health Insurance: 78.3% have insurance; 41.7% have private insurance; 42.8% have public insurance; 21.7% do not have insurance; 14.5% of children under 18 do not have insurance

Transportation: Commute: 95.9% car, 1.0% public transportation, 0.0% walk, 2.1% work from home; Median travel time to work: 45.8 minutes

LAKEWOOD (city). Covers a land area of 9.415 square miles and a water area of 0.051 square miles. Located at 33.85° N. Lat; 118.12° W. Long. Elevation is 46 feet.

History: Named for its location near Bouton Lake in 1934, by the developer. Archtypical American suburb; first of 17,500 houses built on assembly line principles between 1950 and 1952. Incorporated 1954.

Population: 80,048; Growth (since 2000): 0.9%; Density: 8,502.4 persons per square mile; Race: 56.0% White, 8.7% Black/African American, 16.4% Asian, 0.7% American Indian/Alaska Native, 0.9% Native Hawaiian/Other Pacific Islander, 5.7% Two or more races, 30.1% Hispanic of any race; Average household size: 3.01; Median age: 37.5; Age under 18: 24.3%; Age 65 and over: 11.4%; Males per 100 females: 94.3; Marriage status: 32.9% never married, 50.7% now married, 1.7% separated, 5.8% widowed, 10.6% divorced; Foreign born: 21.1%; Speak English only: 65.7%; With disability: 10.1%; Veterans: 6.7%; Ancestry: 9.3% German, 6.5% Irish, 6.4% English, 3.4% American, 3.1% Italian

Employment: 15.2% management, business, and financial, 5.4% computer, engineering, and science, 10.2% education, legal, community service, arts, and media, 6.1% healthcare practitioners, 16.0% service, 27.2% sales and office, 7.5% natural resources, construction, and maintenance, 12.4% production, transportation, and material moving

Income: Per capita: $29,354; Median household: $77,786; Average household: $86,509; Households with income of $100,000 or more: 35.1%; Poverty rate: 8.1%

Educational Attainment: High school diploma or higher: 87.4%; Bachelor's degree or higher: 27.5%; Graduate/professional degree or higher: 7.7%

School District(s)

ABC Unified (KG-12)
2012-13 Enrollment: 20,835 . . . . (562) 926-5566
Bellflower Unified (KG-12)
2012-13 Enrollment: 13,721 . . . . (562) 866-9011
Long Beach Unified (KG-12)
2012-13 Enrollment: 82,256 . . . . (562) 997-8000
Paramount Unified (KG-12)
2012-13 Enrollment: 15,846 . . . . (562) 602-6000

Housing: Homeownership rate: 72.1%; Median home value: $413,000; Median year structure built: 1957; Homeowner vacancy rate: 1.1%; Median gross rent: $1,537 per month; Rental vacancy rate: 5.7%

Health Insurance: 87.7% have insurance; 73.2% have private insurance; 22.3% have public insurance; 12.3% do not have insurance; 5.5% of children under 18 do not have insurance

Hospitals: Lakewood Regional Medical Center (161 beds)

Safety: Violent crime rate: 27.7 per 10,000 population; Property crime rate: 254.3 per 10,000 population

Transportation: Commute: 92.0% car, 2.1% public transportation, 1.5% walk, 3.1% work from home; Median travel time to work: 27.7 minutes

Additional Information Contacts

City of Lakewood . . . . (562) 866-9771
http://www.lakewoodcity.org

LANCASTER (city). Covers a land area of 94.276 square miles and a water area of 0.271 square miles. Located at 34.69° N. Lat; 118.18° W. Long. Elevation is 2,359 feet.

History: Named for the homestead in Pennsylvania of two early settlers, in 1877. It developed as a trade center for an irrigated farming area, and has since become an important site for many industries. Antelope Valley Indian Museum with prehistoric artifacts. Laid out 1894.

Population: 156,633; Growth (since 2000): 31.9%; Density: 1,661.4 persons per square mile; Race: 49.6% White, 20.5% Black/African American, 4.3% Asian, 1.0% American Indian/Alaska Native, 0.2% Native Hawaiian/Other Pacific Islander, 5.4% Two or more races, 38.0% Hispanic of any race; Average household size: 3.16; Median age: 30.4; Age under 18: 30.1%; Age 65 and over: 8.1%; Males per 100 females: 100.6; Marriage status: 37.6% never married, 47.6% now married, 3.0% separated, 4.9% widowed, 10.0% divorced; Foreign born: 14.6%; Speak English only: 74.4%; With disability: 9.9%; Veterans: 8.1%; Ancestry: 6.7% German, 4.7% English, 4.6% Irish, 2.7% Italian, 2.2% American

Employment: 10.5% management, business, and financial, 4.6% computer, engineering, and science, 10.5% education, legal, community service, arts, and media, 5.9% healthcare practitioners, 20.0% service, 26.9% sales and office, 10.5% natural resources, construction, and maintenance, 11.1% production, transportation, and material moving

Income: Per capita: $20,156; Median household: $50,193; Average household: $63,569; Households with income of $100,000 or more: 18.0%; Poverty rate: 21.5%

Educational Attainment: High school diploma or higher: 79.8%; Bachelor's degree or higher: 15.7%; Graduate/professional degree or higher: 5.4%

School District(s)

Antelope Valley Union High (09-12)
2012-13 Enrollment: 24,816 . . . . (661) 948-7655
Eastside Union Elementary (KG-08)
2012-13 Enrollment: 3,386 . . . . (661) 952-1200
Lancaster Elementary (KG-08)
2012-13 Enrollment: 14,713 . . . . (661) 948-4661
Los Angeles County Office of Education (KG-12)
2012-13 Enrollment: 9,136 . . . . (562) 922-6111
Westside Union Elementary (KG-08)
2012-13 Enrollment: 8,645 . . . . (661) 722-0716
Wilsona Elementary (KG-08)
2012-13 Enrollment: 1,393 . . . . (661) 264-1111

Four-year College(s)

University of Antelope Valley (Private, For-profit)
Fall 2013 Enrollment: 804 . . . . (661) 726-1911

Two-year College(s)

Antelope Valley College (Public)
Fall 2013 Enrollment: 14,262 . . . . (661) 722-6300
2013-14 Tuition: In-state $1,104; Out-of-state $5,664
San Joaquin Valley College-Lancaster (Private, For-profit)
Fall 2013 Enrollment: 167 . . . . (661) 974-8282
2013-14 Tuition: In-state $16,659; Out-of-state $16,659

Vocational/Technical School(s)

Career Care Institute (Private, For-profit)
Fall 2013 Enrollment: 615 . . . . (661) 942-6204
2013-14 Tuition: $28,026
Lancaster Beauty School (Private, For-profit)
Fall 2013 Enrollment: 93 . . . . (661) 948-1672
2013-14 Tuition: $15,500

Housing: Homeownership rate: 60.4%; Median home value: $159,200; Median year structure built: 1985; Homeowner vacancy rate: 3.8%; Median gross rent: $1,069 per month; Rental vacancy rate: 9.4%

Health Insurance: 83.9% have insurance; 59.8% have private insurance; 30.9% have public insurance; 16.1% do not have insurance; 10.2% of children under 18 do not have insurance

Hospitals: Antelope Valley Hospital (378 beds)

Safety: Violent crime rate: 52.1 per 10,000 population; Property crime rate: 218.7 per 10,000 population

Transportation: Commute: 94.1% car, 1.6% public transportation, 1.1% walk, 2.4% work from home; Median travel time to work: 30.6 minutes; Amtrak: Train service available.

Airports: General Wm J Fox Airfield (general aviation)

Additional Information Contacts

City of Lancaster . . . . (661) 723-6000
http://www.cityoflancasterca.org

LAWNDALE (city). Covers a land area of 1.974 square miles and a water area of 0 square miles. Located at 33.89° N. Lat; 118.35° W. Long. Elevation is 59 feet.

History: Named by Charles Hopper, founder of the town, in 1905. The population of Lawndale grew in the 1950s, but has been stable since early 1960s. Incorporated 1959.

Population: 32,769; Growth (since 2000): 3.3%; Density: 16,599.0 persons per square mile; Race: 43.6% White, 10.1% Black/African American, 10.0% Asian, 0.9% American Indian/Alaska Native, 1.1% Native Hawaiian/Other Pacific Islander, 5.7% Two or more races, 61.0% Hispanic of any race; Average household size: 3.37; Median age: 31.9; Age under 18: 27.2%; Age 65 and over: 6.9%; Males per 100 females: 101.3; Marriage status: 43.4% never married, 43.4% now married, 2.3% separated, 4.6% widowed, 8.5% divorced; Foreign born: 40.2%; Speak English only: 34.5%; With disability: 8.6%; Veterans: 3.5%; Ancestry: 12.0% American, 4.1% German, 2.7% Irish, 1.9% English, 1.1% Italian

Employment: 9.4% management, business, and financial, 3.1% computer, engineering, and science, 6.0% education, legal, community service, arts, and media, 2.1% healthcare practitioners, 32.2% service, 24.3% sales and office, 10.1% natural resources, construction, and maintenance, 12.8% production, transportation, and material moving

Income: Per capita: $17,814; Median household: $47,769; Average household: $57,581; Households with income of $100,000 or more: 12.6%; Poverty rate: 16.7%

Educational Attainment: High school diploma or higher: 71.4%; Bachelor's degree or higher: 15.9%; Graduate/professional degree or higher: 4.4%

School District(s)

Centinela Valley Union High (09-12)
2012-13 Enrollment: 6,637 . . . . (310) 263-3200
Lawndale Elementary (KG-12)
2012-13 Enrollment: 6,325 . . . . (310) 973-1300

Housing: Homeownership rate: 34.3%; Median home value: $362,500; Median year structure built: 1967; Homeowner vacancy rate: 1.7%; Median gross rent: $1,332 per month; Rental vacancy rate: 3.8%

Health Insurance: 69.1% have insurance; 43.8% have private insurance; 29.2% have public insurance; 30.9% do not have insurance; 11.1% of children under 18 do not have insurance

Safety: Violent crime rate: 48.7 per 10,000 population; Property crime rate: 126.1 per 10,000 population

Transportation: Commute: 88.1% car, 4.5% public transportation, 1.7% walk, 2.5% work from home; Median travel time to work: 24.1 minutes

Additional Information Contacts

City of Lawndale . . . . (310) 973-3200
http://www.lawndalecity.org/home.asp

LENNOX (CDP). Covers a land area of 1.093 square miles and a water area of 0 square miles. Located at 33.94° N. Lat; 118.36° W. Long. Elevation is 72 feet.

Population: 22,753; Growth (since 2000): -0.9%; Density: 20,809.4 persons per square mile; Race: 37.9% White, 3.4% Black/African American, 0.8% Asian, 0.9% American Indian/Alaska Native, 0.8% Native Hawaiian/Other Pacific Islander, 4.4% Two or more races, 93.0% Hispanic of any race; Average household size: 4.33; Median age: 27.7; Age under 18: 33.2%; Age 65 and over: 5.4%; Males per 100 females: 105.6; Marriage status: 45.3% never married, 46.8% now married, 3.7% separated, 2.9% widowed, 4.9% divorced; Foreign born: 48.1%; Speak English only: 11.1%; With disability: 5.9%; Veterans: 0.9%; Ancestry: 2.7% American, 0.6% Ethiopian, 0.6% Jamaican, 0.4% Belizean, 0.4% German

Employment: 3.3% management, business, and financial, 0.5% computer, engineering, and science, 7.0% education, legal, community service, arts, and media, 1.7% healthcare practitioners, 33.2% service, 22.2% sales and office, 13.3% natural resources, construction, and maintenance, 18.9% production, transportation, and material moving

Income: Per capita: $11,793; Median household: $37,659; Average household: $46,273; Households with income of $100,000 or more: 8.1%; Poverty rate: 32.3%

Educational Attainment: High school diploma or higher: 47.1%; Bachelor's degree or higher: 5.3%; Graduate/professional degree or higher: 1.0%

School District(s)

Lennox (KG-12)
2012-13 Enrollment: 7,043 . . . . (310) 695-4000

Housing: Homeownership rate: 29.9%; Median home value: $304,700; Median year structure built: 1957; Homeowner vacancy rate: 0.9%; Median gross rent: $990 per month; Rental vacancy rate: 4.5%

Health Insurance: 61.7% have insurance; 33.8% have private insurance; 30.1% have public insurance; 38.3% do not have insurance; 21.1% of children under 18 do not have insurance

Transportation: Commute: 82.5% car, 9.5% public transportation, 3.7% walk, 2.0% work from home; Median travel time to work: 24.5 minutes

---

LEONA VALLEY (CDP). Covers a land area of 18.551 square miles and a water area of 0.027 square miles. Located at 34.61° N. Lat; 118.30° W. Long. Elevation is 3,153 feet.

Population: 1,607; Growth (since 2000): n/a; Density: 86.6 persons per square mile; Race: 90.6% White, 0.7% Black/African American, 1.7% Asian, 0.2% American Indian/Alaska Native, 0.0% Native Hawaiian/Other Pacific Islander, 3.5% Two or more races, 12.3% Hispanic of any race; Average household size: 2.72; Median age: 47.4; Age under 18: 20.8%; Age 65 and over: 15.6%; Males per 100 females: 104.2

School District(s)

Westside Union Elementary (KG-08)
2012-13 Enrollment: 8,645 . . . . (661) 722-0716

Housing: Homeownership rate: 87.3%; Homeowner vacancy rate: 4.1%; Rental vacancy rate: 13.8%

LITTLEROCK (CDP). Covers a land area of 1.842 square miles and a water area of 0.001 square miles. Located at 34.53° N. Lat; 117.98° W. Long. Elevation is 2,890 feet.

Population: 1,377; Growth (since 2000): -1.8%; Density: 747.6 persons per square mile; Race: 58.7% White, 5.4% Black/African American, 1.7% Asian, 1.2% American Indian/Alaska Native, 0.8% Native Hawaiian/Other Pacific Islander, 5.1% Two or more races, 54.1% Hispanic of any race; Average household size: 3.30; Median age: 32.3; Age under 18: 30.4%; Age 65 and over: 7.9%; Males per 100 females: 98.7

School District(s)

Antelope Valley Union High (09-12)
2012-13 Enrollment: 24,816 . . . . (661) 948-7655

Keppel Union Elementary (KG-08)
2012-13 Enrollment: 2,747 . . . . (661) 944-2155

Housing: Homeownership rate: 64.5%; Homeowner vacancy rate: 2.5%; Rental vacancy rate: 10.3%

LLANO (unincorporated postal area)

ZCTA: 93544

Covers a land area of 109.553 square miles and a water area of 0.212 square miles. Located at 34.50° N. Lat; 117.76° W. Long. Elevation is 3,202 feet.

Population: 1,259; Growth (since 2000): 4.8%; Density: 11.5 persons per square mile; Race: 75.3% White, 4.1% Black/African American, 1.7% Asian, 0.7% American Indian/Alaska Native, 0.6% Native Hawaiian/Other Pacific Islander, 4.1% Two or more races, 24.6% Hispanic of any race; Average household size: 2.20; Median age: 52.4; Age under 18: 14.7%; Age 65 and over: 23.4%; Males per 100 females: 120.9

Housing: Homeownership rate: 78.7%; Homeowner vacancy rate: 4.4%; Rental vacancy rate: 6.2%

LOMITA (city). Covers a land area of 1.911 square miles and a water area of 0 square miles. Located at 33.79° N. Lat; 118.32° W. Long. Elevation is 95 feet.

Population: 20,256; Growth (since 2000): 1.0%; Density: 10,601.3 persons per square mile; Race: 59.2% White, 5.3% Black/African American, 14.4% Asian, 0.9% American Indian/Alaska Native, 0.7% Native Hawaiian/Other Pacific Islander, 6.3% Two or more races, 32.8% Hispanic of any race; Average household size: 2.49; Median age: 39.6; Age under 18: 21.6%; Age 65 and over: 12.5%; Males per 100 females: 93.3; Marriage status: 30.6% never married, 51.6% now married, 2.6% separated, 5.6% widowed, 12.2% divorced; Foreign born: 27.7%; Speak English only: 60.7%; With disability: 10.7%; Veterans: 7.6%; Ancestry: 9.7% German, 7.2% Irish, 6.2% Italian, 5.5% English, 4.5% French

Employment: 13.9% management, business, and financial, 5.4% computer, engineering, and science, 9.9% education, legal, community service, arts, and media, 3.6% healthcare practitioners, 20.4% service, 29.3% sales and office, 8.9% natural resources, construction, and maintenance, 8.6% production, transportation, and material moving

Income: Per capita: $29,443; Median household: $60,398; Average household: $73,633; Households with income of $100,000 or more: 23.8%; Poverty rate: 12.2%

Educational Attainment: High school diploma or higher: 85.6%; Bachelor's degree or higher: 27.3%; Graduate/professional degree or higher: 8.3%

School District(s)

Los Angeles Unified (PK-12)
2012-13 Enrollment: 655,455 . . . . (213) 241-1000

Housing: Homeownership rate: 46.3%; Median home value: $452,900; Median year structure built: 1963; Homeowner vacancy rate: 0.7%; Median gross rent: $1,213 per month; Rental vacancy rate: 3.4%

Health Insurance: 81.8% have insurance; 63.1% have private insurance; 25.2% have public insurance; 18.2% do not have insurance; 7.7% of children under 18 do not have insurance

Safety: Violent crime rate: 32.0 per 10,000 population; Property crime rate: 200.8 per 10,000 population

Transportation: Commute: 86.1% car, 3.6% public transportation, 2.0% walk, 6.0% work from home; Median travel time to work: 26.0 minutes

Additional Information Contacts

City of Lomita . . . . (310) 325-7110
http://www.lomita.com/cityhall

LONG BEACH (city). Covers a land area of 50.293 square miles and a water area of 1.144 square miles. Located at 33.81° N. Lat; 118.16° W. Long. Elevation is 30 feet.

History: Named for its location on San Pedro Bay. The site of Long Beach was part of a 1784 land grant by the King of Spain to Manuel Nieto in payment for his service in the royal army. In 1840 the land was divided into Rancho los Alamitos (little cottonwoods) and Rancho los Cerritos (little hills), owned by John Temple and Abel Stearns. By 1881 parcels were being subdivided and sold by W.E. Willmore, who called his community Willmore City. It was renamed Long Beach in 1888 when the city began to promote itself as a seaside resort to the new settlers attracted to southern California. Discovery of the Signal Hill oil field in 1921 brought rapid growth to Long Beach.

Population: 462,257; Growth (since 2000): 0.2%; Density: 9,191.2 persons per square mile; Race: 46.1% White, 13.5% Black/African American, 12.9% Asian, 0.7% American Indian/Alaska Native, 1.1% Native Hawaiian/Other Pacific Islander, 5.3% Two or more races, 40.8% Hispanic of any race; Average household size: 2.78; Median age: 33.2; Age under 18: 24.9%; Age 65 and over: 9.3%; Males per 100 females: 96.1; Marriage status: 44.1% never married, 40.7% now married, 3.2% separated, 4.7% widowed, 10.4% divorced; Foreign born: 26.0%; Speak English only: 55.2%; With disability: 9.9%; Veterans: 6.0%; Ancestry: 6.9% German, 6.0% Irish, 4.8% English, 2.7% Italian, 2.3% American

Employment: 14.0% management, business, and financial, 4.4% computer, engineering, and science, 12.3% education, legal, community service, arts, and media, 4.3% healthcare practitioners, 19.6% service, 25.8% sales and office, 7.1% natural resources, construction, and maintenance, 12.4% production, transportation, and material moving

Income: Per capita: $27,040; Median household: $52,711; Average household: $73,779; Households with income of $100,000 or more: 23.3%; Poverty rate: 20.2%

Educational Attainment: High school diploma or higher: 79.3%; Bachelor's degree or higher: 28.5%; Graduate/professional degree or higher: 10.1%

School District(s)

Long Beach Unified (KG-12)
2012-13 Enrollment: 82,256 . . . . (562) 997-8000

Long Beach Unified Rop
2012-13 Enrollment: n/a . . . . (562) 595-8893

Los Angeles Unified (PK-12)
2012-13 Enrollment: 655,455 . . . . (213) 241-1000

Paramount Unified (KG-12)
2012-13 Enrollment: 15,846 . . . . (562) 602-6000

Sbe - Doris Topsy-Elvord Academy (06-08)
2012-13 Enrollment: 111. . . . . (909) 910-1529

Four-year College(s)

California State University-Long Beach (Public)
Fall 2013 Enrollment: 35,586 . . . . (562) 985-4111
2013-14 Tuition: In-state $6,240; Out-of-state $17,400

Two-year College(s)

Long Beach City College (Public)
Fall 2013 Enrollment: 24,020 .... (562) 938-4111
2013-14 Tuition: In-state $1,182; Out-of-state $6,702
Wyotech-Long Beach (Private, For-profit)
Fall 2013 Enrollment: 1,400 .... (562) 624-9530

Vocational/Technical School(s)

American Career College-Long Beach (Private, For-profit)
Fall 2013 Enrollment: 401 .... (949) 783-4800
2013-14 Tuition: $16,950
John Wesley International Barber and Beauty College (Private, For-profit)
Fall 2013 Enrollment: 89 .... (562) 435-7060
2013-14 Tuition: $11,456

Housing: Homeownership rate: 41.6%; Median home value: $417,600; Median year structure built: 1956; Homeowner vacancy rate: 2.0%; Median gross rent: $1,106 per month; Rental vacancy rate: 7.2%

Health Insurance: 80.4% have insurance; 55.4% have private insurance; 31.8% have public insurance; 19.6% do not have insurance; 7.6% of children under 18 do not have insurance

Hospitals: Community Hospital of Long Beach (256 beds); Long Beach Memorial Medical Center (716 beds); Miller Children's Hospital; Pacific Hospital of Long Beach (184 beds); Saint Mary Medical Center (389 beds); VA Long Beach Healthcare System (237 beds)

Safety: Violent crime rate: 50.0 per 10,000 population; Property crime rate: 276.8 per 10,000 population

Newspapers: Beachcomber (weekly circulation 42000); Downtown Gazette (weekly circulation 23000); Grunion Gazette (weekly circulation 42500); Long Beach Times (weekly circulation 45000); Press-Telegram (daily circulation 87600); The Reporter (weekly circulation 8000)

Transportation: Commute: 82.7% car, 7.7% public transportation, 2.6% walk, 4.7% work from home; Median travel time to work: 28.7 minutes; Amtrak: Bus service available.

Airports: Long Beach /Daugherty Field/ (primary service/small hub)

Additional Information Contacts

City of Long Beach .... (562) 570-6711
http://www.longbeach.gov

LOS ANGELES (city). County seat. Covers a land area of 468.670 square miles and a water area of 34.023 square miles. Located at 34.02° N. Lat; 118.41° W. Long. Elevation is 292 feet.

History: The city of Los Angeles had its beginnings in 1781 when Don Felipe de Neve, Spanish Governor of California, brought eleven families from Mexico and founded El Pueblo de Nuestra Senora la Reina de Los Angeles de Porciuncula (The Town of Our Lady the Queen of the Angels of Porciuncula). When the United States took control of California in 1848 and gold was discovered to the north, Los Angeles acquired a reputation for violence. The Southern Pacific Railroad reached Los Angeles in 1876, followed by the Santa Fe in 1885, and a fare war between the two lines made it possible for many people to come west. Land speculation was rampant as everyone tried to get rich fast. Oil wells drilled in the 1890's contributed to the boom. The constant need for an adequate water supply led in 1913 to the diversion of Owens River (238 miles away in the Sierras). Towns in the San Fernando Valley who wanted to take advantage of the water had to become part of the city of Los Angeles.

Population: 3,792,621; Growth (since 2000): 2.6%; Density: 8,092.3 persons per square mile; Race: 49.8% White, 9.6% Black/African American, 11.3% Asian, 0.7% American Indian/Alaska Native, 0.1% Native Hawaiian/Other Pacific Islander, 4.6% Two or more races, 48.5% Hispanic of any race; Average household size: 2.81; Median age: 34.1; Age under 18: 23.1%; Age 65 and over: 10.5%; Males per 100 females: 99.2; Marriage status: 45.1% never married, 41.8% now married, 2.9% separated, 4.7% widowed, 8.4% divorced; Foreign born: 38.8%; Speak English only: 39.8%; With disability: 9.5%; Veterans: 3.6%; Ancestry: 4.5% German, 3.8% Irish, 3.2% English, 2.7% Italian, 2.4% Russian

Employment: 13.3% management, business, and financial, 3.9% computer, engineering, and science, 14.2% education, legal, community service, arts, and media, 4.0% healthcare practitioners, 21.0% service, 23.3% sales and office, 8.2% natural resources, construction, and maintenance, 12.1% production, transportation, and material moving

Income: Per capita: $27,829; Median household: $49,497; Average household: $77,102; Households with income of $100,000 or more: 22.9%; Poverty rate: 22.0%

Educational Attainment: High school diploma or higher: 74.5%; Bachelor's degree or higher: 31.1%; Graduate/professional degree or higher: 10.4%

School District(s)

Compton Unified (KG-12)
2012-13 Enrollment: 24,710 .... (310) 639-4321
Inyo County Office of Education (KG-12)
2012-13 Enrollment: 1,657 .... (760) 878-2426
Los Angeles County Office of Education (KG-12)
2012-13 Enrollment: 9,136 .... (562) 922-6111
Los Angeles Unified (PK-12)
2012-13 Enrollment: 655,455 .... (213) 241-1000
Los Angeles Unified Rocp
2012-13 Enrollment: n/a .... (213) 745-1940
Montebello Unified (KG-12)
2012-13 Enrollment: 30,564 .... (323) 887-7900
Nevada County Office of Education (KG-12)
2012-13 Enrollment: 3,418 .... (530) 478-6400
Sbe - Barack Obama Charter (KG-06)
2012-13 Enrollment: 333 .... (323) 566-1965
Sbe - New West Charter Middle (06-08)
2012-13 Enrollment: 573 .... (310) 943-5444
Sbe - Today's Fresh Start Charter (KG-08)
2012-13 Enrollment: 680 .... (323) 293-9826

Four-year College(s)

Abraham Lincoln University (Private, For-profit)
Fall 2013 Enrollment: 144 .... (213) 252-5100
2013-14 Tuition: In-state $7,750; Out-of-state $7,750
Academy for Jewish Religion-California (Private, Not-for-profit, Jewish)
Fall 2013 Enrollment: 63 .... (213) 884-4133
American Film Institute Conservatory (Private, Not-for-profit)
Fall 2013 Enrollment: 348 .... (323) 856-7600
American Jewish University (Private, Not-for-profit, Jewish)
Fall 2013 Enrollment: 229 .... (310) 476-9777
2013-14 Tuition: In-state $27,900; Out-of-state $27,900
Angeles College (Private, For-profit)
Fall 2013 Enrollment: 145 .... (213) 487-2211
Argosy University-Los Angeles (Private, For-profit)
Fall 2013 Enrollment: 620 .... (310) 866-4000
2013-14 Tuition: In-state $13,663; Out-of-state $13,663
Bryan University (Private, For-profit)
Fall 2013 Enrollment: 927 .... (213) 484-8850
2013-14 Tuition: In-state $11,850; Out-of-state $11,850
California State University-Los Angeles (Public)
Fall 2013 Enrollment: 23,258 .... (323) 343-3000
2013-14 Tuition: In-state $6,344; Out-of-state $17,504
Charles R Drew University of Medicine and Science (Private, Not-for-profit)
Fall 2013 Enrollment: 515 .... (323) 563-4800
2013-14 Tuition: In-state $11,956; Out-of-state $11,956
Dongguk University-Los Angeles (Private, Not-for-profit)
Fall 2013 Enrollment: 179 .... (213) 487-0110
Fashion Institute of Design & Merchandising-Los Angeles (Private, For-profit)
Fall 2013 Enrollment: 3,459 .... (213) 624-1200
2013-14 Tuition: In-state $28,920; Out-of-state $28,920
Los Angeles Film School (Private, For-profit)
Fall 2013 Enrollment: 2,218 .... (877) 952-3456
Loyola Marymount University (Private, Not-for-profit, Roman Catholic)
Fall 2013 Enrollment: 9,661 .... (310) 338-2700
2013-14 Tuition: In-state $40,265; Out-of-state $40,265
Mount St Mary's College (Private, Not-for-profit, Roman Catholic)
Fall 2013 Enrollment: 3,274 .... (310) 954-4000
2013-14 Tuition: In-state $33,852; Out-of-state $33,852
Musicians Institute (Private, For-profit)
Fall 2013 Enrollment: 1,204 .... (323) 462-1384
2013-14 Tuition: In-state $23,985; Out-of-state $23,985
Occidental College (Private, Not-for-profit)
Fall 2013 Enrollment: 2,128 .... (323) 259-2500
2013-14 Tuition: In-state $46,652; Out-of-state $46,652
Otis College of Art and Design (Private, Not-for-profit)
Fall 2013 Enrollment: 1,086 .... (800) 527-6847
2013-14 Tuition: In-state $39,430; Out-of-state $39,430
Pacific States University (Private, Not-for-profit)
Fall 2013 Enrollment: 173 .... (323) 731-2383
2013-14 Tuition: In-state $19,340; Out-of-state $19,340
Southern California Institute of Architecture (Private, Not-for-profit)
Fall 2013 Enrollment: 493 .... (213) 613-2200
2013-14 Tuition: In-state $37,300; Out-of-state $37,300

Southern California University SOMA (Private, For-profit)
Fall 2013 Enrollment: 116 . . . . (213) 413-9500
Southwestern Law School (Private, Not-for-profit)
Fall 2013 Enrollment: 1,146 . . . . (213) 738-6700
The Chicago School of Professional Psychology at Los Angeles (Private, Not-for-profit)
Fall 2013 Enrollment: 2,006 . . . . (213) 627-2580
The Chicago School of Professional Psychology at Westwood (Private, Not-for-profit)
Fall 2013 Enrollment: 267 . . . . (310) 208-4240
University of California-Los Angeles (Public)
Fall 2013 Enrollment: 40,795 . . . . (310) 825-4321
2013-14 Tuition: In-state $12,697; Out-of-state $35,575
University of Southern California (Private, Not-for-profit)
Fall 2013 Enrollment: 41,368 . . . . (213) 740-2311
2013-14 Tuition: In-state $46,298; Out-of-state $46,298
Westwood College-Los Angeles (Private, For-profit)
Fall 2013 Enrollment: 672 . . . . (213) 739-9999
2013-14 Tuition: In-state $15,080; Out-of-state $15,080
World Mission University (Private, Not-for-profit, Other (none of the above))
Fall 2013 Enrollment: 261 . . . . (213) 388-1000
2013-14 Tuition: In-state $4,900; Out-of-state $4,900
Yeshiva Ohr Elchonon Chabad West Coast Talmudical Seminary (Private, Not-for-profit)
Fall 2013 Enrollment: 131 . . . . (323) 937-3763
2013-14 Tuition: In-state $13,300; Out-of-state $13,300
Yo San University of Traditional Chinese Medicine (Private, Not-for-profit)
Fall 2013 Enrollment: 211 . . . . (310) 577-3000

Two-year College(s)

Advanced Computing Institute (Private, For-profit)
Fall 2013 Enrollment: 211 . . . . (213) 383-8999
American Academy of Dramatic Arts-Los Angeles (Private, Not-for-profit)
Fall 2013 Enrollment: 258 . . . . (323) 464-2777
2013-14 Tuition: In-state $30,650; Out-of-state $30,650
American Career College-Los Angeles (Private, For-profit)
Fall 2013 Enrollment: 1,770 . . . . (949) 783-4800
CBD College (Private, Not-for-profit)
Fall 2013 Enrollment: 230 . . . . (323) 937-7772
Central Nursing College (Private, For-profit)
Fall 2013 Enrollment: 33 . . . . (213) 384-4789
Coast Career Institute (Private, For-profit)
Fall 2013 Enrollment: 169 . . . . (213) 747-6289
Everest College-LA Wilshire (Private, For-profit)
Fall 2013 Enrollment: 232 . . . . (213) 388-9950
2013-14 Tuition: In-state $11,424; Out-of-state $11,424
Everest College-West Los Angeles (Private, For-profit)
Fall 2013 Enrollment: 422 . . . . (310) 840-5777
2013-14 Tuition: In-state $14,328; Out-of-state $14,328
Gnomon School of Visual Effects (Private, For-profit)
Fall 2013 Enrollment: 135 . . . . (323) 466-6663
2013-14 Tuition: In-state $26,025; Out-of-state $26,025
Los Angeles City College (Public)
Fall 2013 Enrollment: 19,635 . . . . (323) 953-4000
2013-14 Tuition: In-state $1,221; Out-of-state $6,161
Los Angeles County College of Nursing and Allied Health (Public)
Fall 2013 Enrollment: 185 . . . . (323) 226-4911
Los Angeles ORT College-Los Angeles Campus (Private, Not-for-profit)
Fall 2013 Enrollment: 396 . . . . (323) 966-5444
Los Angeles Southwest College (Public)
Fall 2013 Enrollment: 7,864 . . . . (323) 241-5225
2013-14 Tuition: In-state $1,221; Out-of-state $6,161
Los Angeles Trade Technical College (Public)
Fall 2013 Enrollment: 13,879 . . . . (213) 763-7000
2013-14 Tuition: In-state $1,221; Out-of-state $6,161
Los Angeles Valley College (Public)
Fall 2013 Enrollment: 18,762 . . . . (818) 947-2600
2013-14 Tuition: In-state $1,221; Out-of-state $6,161

Vocational/Technical School(s)

Associated Technical College-Los Angeles (Private, For-profit)
Fall 2013 Enrollment: 404 . . . . (213) 413-6808
2013-14 Tuition: $14,900
Aveda Institute-Los Angeles (Private, For-profit)
Fall 2013 Enrollment: 175 . . . . (513) 576-9333
2013-14 Tuition: $21,035
Borner's Barber College (Private, For-profit)
Fall 2013 Enrollment: 23 . . . . (323) 820-9600
2013-14 Tuition: $12,007
Career College Consultants (Private, For-profit)
Fall 2013 Enrollment: 146 . . . . (323) 254-2203
2013-14 Tuition: $15,975
Career Development Institute (Private, For-profit)
Fall 2013 Enrollment: 69 . . . . (310) 559-0225
2013-14 Tuition: $26,427
Diversified Vocational College (Private, For-profit)
Fall 2013 Enrollment: 913 . . . . (213) 413-6808
2013-14 Tuition: $7,542
Elegance International (Private, For-profit)
Fall 2013 Enrollment: 205 . . . . (323) 871-8318
2013-14 Tuition: $16,750
International College of Beauty Arts & Sciences (Private, For-profit)
Fall 2013 Enrollment: 35 . . . . (818) 548-3560
2013-14 Tuition: $16,143
Joe Blasco Makeup Artist Training Center (Private, For-profit)
Fall 2013 Enrollment: n/a . . . . (323) 467-4949
2013-14 Tuition: $14,100
Ladera Career Paths Training Centers (Private, For-profit)
Fall 2013 Enrollment: n/a . . . . (310) 568-0244
Marian Health Careers Center-Los Angeles Campus (Private, For-profit)
Fall 2013 Enrollment: 108 . . . . (213) 388-3566
2013-14 Tuition: $23,010
Marinello Schools of Beauty-Los Angeles (Private, For-profit)
Fall 2013 Enrollment: 2,405 . . . . (562) 945-2211
2013-14 Tuition: $18,510
Palace Beauty College (Private, For-profit)
Fall 2013 Enrollment: 148 . . . . (323) 731-2075
2013-14 Tuition: $14,400
Preferred College of Nursing-Los Angeles (Private, For-profit)
Fall 2013 Enrollment: 159 . . . . (323) 857-5000
2013-14 Tuition: $25,688
SAE Institute of Technology-Los Angeles (Private, For-profit)
Fall 2013 Enrollment: 225 . . . . (404) 526-9366
2013-14 Tuition: $19,397
Universal College of Beauty Inc-Los Angeles 1 (Private, For-profit)
Fall 2013 Enrollment: 33 . . . . (323) 750-5750
2013-14 Tuition: $16,200
Universal College of Beauty Inc-Los Angeles 2 (Private, For-profit)
Fall 2013 Enrollment: 32 . . . . (323) 298-0045
2013-14 Tuition: $16,150
Virginia Sewing Machines and School Center (Private, For-profit)
Fall 2013 Enrollment: 66 . . . . (213) 747-8292
2013-14 Tuition: $11,295

Housing: Homeownership rate: 38.2%; Median home value: $446,100; Median year structure built: 1960; Homeowner vacancy rate: 2.1%; Median gross rent: $1,175 per month; Rental vacancy rate: 6.1%

Health Insurance: 74.4% have insurance; 49.3% have private insurance; 30.9% have public insurance; 25.6% do not have insurance; 10.6% of children under 18 do not have insurance

Hospitals: California Hospital Medical Center Los Angeles (313 beds); Cedars - Sinai Medical Center (930 beds); Children's Hospital of Los Angeles (286 beds); East Los Angeles Doctors Hospital (127 beds); Good Samaritan Hospital (408 beds); Hollywood Presbyterian Medical Center (434 beds); Kaiser Foundation Hospital - Los Angeles (737 beds); Kaiser Foundation Hospital - West La (306 beds); Keck Hospital of USC (411 beds); LAC+USC Medical Center (1395 beds); Los Angeles Community Hospital; Miracle Mile Medical Center; Olympia Medical Center (204 beds); Pacific Alliance Medical Center (122 beds); Providence Holy Cross Medical Center (257 beds); Ronald Reagan UCLA Medical Center (581 beds); Saint Vincent Medical Center (131 beds); Silver Lake Medical Center; Southern California Hospital at Hollywood (160 beds); Temple Community Hospital (170 beds); USC Kenneth Norris Jr Cancer Hospital (60 beds); VA Greater Los Angeles Healthcare System (945 beds); White Memorial Medical Center (369 beds)

Safety: Violent crime rate: 42.6 per 10,000 population; Property crime rate: 221.3 per 10,000 population

Newspapers: Beverly Press & Park LaBrea News (weekly circulation 13000); Burbank Leader (weekly circulation 21500); Eastern Group Publications (weekly circulation 116000); LA Downtown News (weekly circulation 49000); La Cañada Valley Sun (weekly circulation 10000); Los Angeles Times (daily circulation 723000)

Transportation: Commute: 77.2% car, 11.0% public transportation, 3.7% walk, 5.6% work from home; Median travel time to work: 29.2 minutes; Amtrak: Train and bus service available.

Airports: Los Angeles International (primary service/large hub)

Additional Information Contacts

City of Los Angeles . . . . (213) 978-1023
http://www.lacity.org

LYNWOOD (city). Covers a land area of 4.840 square miles and a water area of 0 square miles. Located at 33.92° N. Lat; 118.20° W. Long. Elevation is 92 feet.

History: Named for a local dairy, which was named for Lynn Wood Sessions, the wife of the owner. Founded 1896. Incorporated 1921.

Population: 69,772; Growth (since 2000): -0.1%; Density: 14,415.7 persons per square mile; Race: 39.3% White, 10.3% Black/African American, 0.7% Asian, 0.7% American Indian/Alaska Native, 0.3% Native Hawaiian/Other Pacific Islander, 3.4% Two or more races, 86.6% Hispanic of any race; Average household size: 4.57; Median age: 27.8; Age under 18: 32.9%; Age 65 and over: 5.4%; Males per 100 females: 94.7; Marriage status: 48.1% never married, 42.6% now married, 3.3% separated, 4.0% widowed, 5.3% divorced; Foreign born: 39.3%; Speak English only: 16.4%; With disability: 8.3%; Veterans: 1.8%; Ancestry: 1.1% American, 0.4% German, 0.4% Italian, 0.4% African, 0.3% Irish

Employment: 3.9% management, business, and financial, 1.0% computer, engineering, and science, 5.3% education, legal, community service, arts, and media, 2.1% healthcare practitioners, 20.2% service, 24.6% sales and office, 11.4% natural resources, construction, and maintenance, 31.4% production, transportation, and material moving

Income: Per capita: $12,187; Median household: $40,740; Average household: $50,676; Households with income of $100,000 or more: 9.9%; Poverty rate: 25.3%

Educational Attainment: High school diploma or higher: 51.0%; Bachelor's degree or higher: 5.6%; Graduate/professional degree or higher: 1.5%

School District(s)

Lynwood Unified (KG-12)
2012-13 Enrollment: 15,029 . . . . (310) 886-1600

Vocational/Technical School(s)

American Career College at St Francis (Private, For-profit)
Fall 2013 Enrollment: 47 . . . . (949) 783-4800
2013-14 Tuition: $34,450

Housing: Homeownership rate: 46.5%; Median home value: $273,200; Median year structure built: 1954; Homeowner vacancy rate: 1.9%; Median gross rent: $1,011 per month; Rental vacancy rate: 3.7%

Health Insurance: 66.6% have insurance; 34.1% have private insurance; 35.2% have public insurance; 33.4% do not have insurance; 17.4% of children under 18 do not have insurance

Hospitals: Saint Francis Medical Center (328 beds)

Safety: Violent crime rate: 61.3 per 10,000 population; Property crime rate: 215.0 per 10,000 population

Transportation: Commute: 87.6% car, 5.7% public transportation, 3.1% walk, 1.5% work from home; Median travel time to work: 28.4 minutes

Additional Information Contacts

City of Lynwood. . . . . (310) 603-0220
http://www.lynwood.ca.us

MALIBU (city). Covers a land area of 19.785 square miles and a water area of 0.043 square miles. Located at 34.04° N. Lat; 118.78° W. Long. Elevation is 105 feet.

History: Malibu was originally settled by the Chumash, Native Americans whose territory extended loosely from the San Joaquin Valley to San Luis Obispo to Malibu, as well as several islands off the southern coast of California. They named it "Humaliwo" or "the surf sounds loudly". The city's name derives from this, as the "Hu" syllable isn't stressed.

Population: 12,645; Growth (since 2000): 0.6%; Density: 639.1 persons per square mile; Race: 91.5% White, 1.2% Black/African American, 2.6% Asian, 0.2% American Indian/Alaska Native, 0.1% Native Hawaiian/Other Pacific Islander, 3.1% Two or more races, 6.1% Hispanic of any race; Average household size: 2.37; Median age: 47.8; Age under 18: 18.7%; Age 65 and over: 18.4%; Males per 100 females: 100.6; Marriage status: 30.1% never married, 53.4% now married, 2.7% separated, 5.9% widowed, 10.7% divorced; Foreign born: 16.3%; Speak English only: 85.0%; With disability: 8.4%; Veterans: 6.8%; Ancestry: 17.2% English, 16.3% German, 12.4% Irish, 7.1% Italian, 6.2% Russian

Employment: 26.7% management, business, and financial, 7.7% computer, engineering, and science, 24.4% education, legal, community service, arts, and media, 6.8% healthcare practitioners, 10.4% service, 19.6% sales and office, 2.9% natural resources, construction, and maintenance, 1.4% production, transportation, and material moving

Income: Per capita: $99,276; Median household: $133,869; Average household: $245,202; Households with income of $100,000 or more: 62.7%; Poverty rate: 10.6%

Educational Attainment: High school diploma or higher: 98.3%; Bachelor's degree or higher: 61.2%; Graduate/professional degree or higher: 31.3%

School District(s)

Los Angeles County Office of Education (KG-12)
2012-13 Enrollment: 9,136 . . . . (562) 922-6111

Santa Monica-Malibu Unified (KG-12)
2012-13 Enrollment: 11,417 . . . . (310) 450-8338

Four-year College(s)

Pepperdine University (Private, Not-for-profit, Churches of Christ)
Fall 2013 Enrollment: 7,315 . . . . (310) 506-4000
2013-14 Tuition: In-state $44,902; Out-of-state $44,902

Housing: Homeownership rate: 70.5%; Median home value: 1 million+; Median year structure built: 1975; Homeowner vacancy rate: 2.8%; Median gross rent: $2,000+ per month; Rental vacancy rate: 11.9%

Health Insurance: 96.1% have insurance; 89.1% have private insurance; 20.9% have public insurance; 3.9% do not have insurance; 0.2% of children under 18 do not have insurance

Safety: Violent crime rate: 21.7 per 10,000 population; Property crime rate: 271.5 per 10,000 population

Newspapers: Malibu Surfside News (weekly circulation 13500); Malibu Times (weekly circulation 12000)

Transportation: Commute: 68.7% car, 0.6% public transportation, 5.0% walk, 24.2% work from home; Median travel time to work: 32.6 minutes

Additional Information Contacts

City of Malibu. . . . . (310) 456-2489
http://www.ci.malibu.ca.us

MANHATTAN BEACH (city). Covers a land area of 3.937 square miles and a water area of 0.004 square miles. Located at 33.89° N. Lat; 118.40° W. Long. Elevation is 66 feet.

History: Named for Manhattan Island, New York, at the suggestion of town founder Stewart Merrill. Manhattan Beach developed as a family seaside resort.

Population: 35,135; Growth (since 2000): 3.8%; Density: 8,923.8 persons per square mile; Race: 84.5% White, 0.8% Black/African American, 8.6% Asian, 0.2% American Indian/Alaska Native, 0.1% Native Hawaiian/Other Pacific Islander, 4.6% Two or more races, 6.9% Hispanic of any race; Average household size: 2.50; Median age: 40.9; Age under 18: 24.8%; Age 65 and over: 12.7%; Males per 100 females: 100.4; Marriage status: 30.1% never married, 58.0% now married, 0.9% separated, 4.0% widowed, 7.9% divorced; Foreign born: 10.9%; Speak English only: 85.7%; With disability: 5.2%; Veterans: 7.1%; Ancestry: 18.4% German, 17.0% Irish, 15.9% English, 9.3% Italian, 5.4% American

Employment: 32.6% management, business, and financial, 8.3% computer, engineering, and science, 18.0% education, legal, community service, arts, and media, 7.3% healthcare practitioners, 7.0% service, 21.9% sales and office, 1.9% natural resources, construction, and maintenance, 3.0% production, transportation, and material moving

Income: Per capita: $81,090; Median household: $139,259; Average household: $200,982; Households with income of $100,000 or more: 65.4%; Poverty rate: 3.4%

Educational Attainment: High school diploma or higher: 98.2%; Bachelor's degree or higher: 74.0%; Graduate/professional degree or higher: 31.8%

School District(s)

Manhattan Beach Unified (KG-12)
2012-13 Enrollment: 6,832 . . . . (310) 318-7345

Housing: Homeownership rate: 67.1%; Median home value: 1 million+; Median year structure built: 1960; Homeowner vacancy rate: 0.8%; Median gross rent: $1,995 per month; Rental vacancy rate: 5.3%

Health Insurance: 96.0% have insurance; 91.9% have private insurance; 14.5% have public insurance; 4.0% do not have insurance; 1.7% of children under 18 do not have insurance

Safety: Violent crime rate: 17.8 per 10,000 population; Property crime rate: 237.4 per 10,000 population

Transportation: Commute: 84.8% car, 1.5% public transportation, 2.4% walk, 9.4% work from home; Median travel time to work: 28.2 minutes

Additional Information Contacts

City of Manhattan Beach . . . . (310) 802-5000
http://www.ci.manhattan-beach.ca.us

MARINA DEL REY (CDP). Covers a land area of 0.860 square miles and a water area of 0.595 square miles. Located at 33.98° N. Lat; 118.45° W. Long. Elevation is 16 feet.

History: Marina del Rey is an unincorporated seaside community with the world's largest man-made small craft harbor.

Population: 8,866; Growth (since 2000): 8.4%; Density: 10,313.9 persons per square mile; Race: 79.8% White, 5.2% Black/African American, 8.4% Asian, 0.3% American Indian/Alaska Native, 0.1% Native Hawaiian/Other Pacific Islander, 4.4% Two or more races, 7.7% Hispanic of any race; Average household size: 1.58; Median age: 40.0; Age under 18: 6.4%; Age 65 and over: 13.4%; Males per 100 females: 103.5; Marriage status: 36.2% never married, 44.6% now married, 5.4% separated, 2.8% widowed, 16.4% divorced; Foreign born: 27.2%; Speak English only: 68.6%; With disability: 5.6%; Veterans: 5.9%; Ancestry: 14.2% German, 12.4% Irish, 8.1% English, 7.1% Italian, 5.4% Swedish

Employment: 32.8% management, business, and financial, 6.1% computer, engineering, and science, 16.0% education, legal, community service, arts, and media, 9.8% healthcare practitioners, 6.7% service, 24.6% sales and office, 2.7% natural resources, construction, and maintenance, 1.4% production, transportation, and material moving

Income: Per capita: $69,187; Median household: $95,248; Average household: $111,866; Households with income of $100,000 or more: 45.8%; Poverty rate: 9.9%

Educational Attainment: High school diploma or higher: 98.3%; Bachelor's degree or higher: 64.8%; Graduate/professional degree or higher: 25.5%

School District(s)

Los Angeles Unified (PK-12)
2012-13 Enrollment: 655,455 . . . . (213) 241-1000

Housing: Homeownership rate: 11.5%; Median home value: $422,000; Median year structure built: 1974; Homeowner vacancy rate: 0.5%; Median gross rent: $2,000+ per month; Rental vacancy rate: 11.4%

Health Insurance: 82.3% have insurance; 75.6% have private insurance; 15.0% have public insurance; 17.7% do not have insurance; 34.7% of children under 18 do not have insurance

Hospitals: Marina Del Rey Hospital

Newspapers: The Argonaut (weekly circulation 42000)

Transportation: Commute: 79.6% car, 1.5% public transportation, 1.5% walk, 15.0% work from home; Median travel time to work: 28.3 minutes

MAYFLOWER VILLAGE (CDP). Covers a land area of 0.687 square miles and a water area of 0 square miles. Located at 34.12° N. Lat; 118.01° W. Long. Elevation is 367 feet.

Population: 5,515; Growth (since 2000): 8.5%; Density: 8,030.1 persons per square mile; Race: 53.1% White, 1.5% Black/African American, 31.4% Asian, 0.5% American Indian/Alaska Native, 0.1% Native Hawaiian/Other Pacific Islander, 4.5% Two or more races, 27.6% Hispanic of any race; Average household size: 2.89; Median age: 41.1; Age under 18: 21.7%; Age 65 and over: 13.7%; Males per 100 females: 92.5; Marriage status: 27.5% never married, 58.6% now married, 2.1% separated, 7.5% widowed, 6.4% divorced; Foreign born: 29.5%; Speak English only: 60.0%; With disability: 9.0%; Veterans: 6.6%; Ancestry: 8.7% German, 5.0% Irish, 4.9% English, 3.7% Italian, 2.8% American

Employment: 18.3% management, business, and financial, 11.6% computer, engineering, and science, 12.7% education, legal, community service, arts, and media, 3.6% healthcare practitioners, 15.6% service, 22.8% sales and office, 6.5% natural resources, construction, and maintenance, 8.9% production, transportation, and material moving

Income: Per capita: $30,820; Median household: $78,242; Average household: $88,001; Households with income of $100,000 or more: 31.7%; Poverty rate: 3.1%

Educational Attainment: High school diploma or higher: 87.8%; Bachelor's degree or higher: 35.9%; Graduate/professional degree or higher: 15.3%

Housing: Homeownership rate: 81.8%; Median home value: $476,100; Median year structure built: 1952; Homeowner vacancy rate: 1.0%; Median gross rent: $1,571 per month; Rental vacancy rate: 6.0%

Health Insurance: 88.7% have insurance; 74.1% have private insurance; 19.9% have public insurance; 11.3% do not have insurance; 2.4% of children under 18 do not have insurance

Transportation: Commute: 94.8% car, 2.2% public transportation, 0.9% walk, 1.5% work from home; Median travel time to work: 30.6 minutes

MAYWOOD (city). Covers a land area of 1.178 square miles and a water area of 0 square miles. Located at 33.99° N. Lat; 118.19° W. Long. Elevation is 151 feet.

History: Named by popular vote of the citizens at the time of incorporation, 1924. Incorporated 1924.

Population: 27,395; Growth (since 2000): -2.4%; Density: 23,247.5 persons per square mile; Race: 52.0% White, 0.6% Black/African American, 0.3% Asian, 0.8% American Indian/Alaska Native, 0.1% Native Hawaiian/Other Pacific Islander, 4.3% Two or more races, 97.4% Hispanic of any race; Average household size: 4.16; Median age: 27.9; Age under 18: 32.6%; Age 65 and over: 6.0%; Males per 100 females: 104.5; Marriage status: 49.6% never married, 43.7% now married, 3.3% separated, 2.4% widowed, 4.3% divorced; Foreign born: 46.3%; Speak English only: 8.2%; With disability: 6.5%; Veterans: 0.9%; Ancestry: 2.2% American, 0.2% Irish, 0.2% Czech, 0.2% German, 0.1% Russian

Employment: 3.1% management, business, and financial, 0.3% computer, engineering, and science, 6.3% education, legal, community service, arts, and media, 0.8% healthcare practitioners, 18.9% service, 21.0% sales and office, 15.2% natural resources, construction, and maintenance, 34.5% production, transportation, and material moving

Income: Per capita: $11,890; Median household: $37,114; Average household: $47,121; Households with income of $100,000 or more: 8.6%; Poverty rate: 28.3%

Educational Attainment: High school diploma or higher: 39.0%; Bachelor's degree or higher: 4.4%; Graduate/professional degree or higher: 0.7%

School District(s)

Los Angeles Unified (PK-12)
2012-13 Enrollment: 655,455 . . . . (213) 241-1000

Housing: Homeownership rate: 30.2%; Median home value: $268,100; Median year structure built: 1950; Homeowner vacancy rate: 1.2%; Median gross rent: <$100 per month; Rental vacancy rate: 2.6%

Health Insurance: 62.0% have insurance; 28.3% have private insurance; 35.9% have public insurance; 38.0% do not have insurance; 13.9% of children under 18 do not have insurance

Safety: Violent crime rate: 40.4 per 10,000 population; Property crime rate: 115.3 per 10,000 population

Transportation: Commute: 80.8% car, 7.5% public transportation, 5.2% walk, 3.2% work from home; Median travel time to work: 28.0 minutes

Additional Information Contacts

City of Maywood . . . . (323) 562-5700
http://www.cityofmaywood.com

MONROVIA (city). Covers a land area of 13.605 square miles and a water area of 0.109 square miles. Located at 34.16° N. Lat; 117.98° W. Long. Elevation is 571 feet.

History: Named for William N. Monroe, a railroad construction engineer who laid out the town in 1886. Monrovia was laid out in an area of orange, lemon, and avocado groves.

Population: 36,590; Growth (since 2000): -0.9%; Density: 2,689.5 persons per square mile; Race: 59.9% White, 6.8% Black/African American, 11.2% Asian, 0.8% American Indian/Alaska Native, 0.2% Native Hawaiian/Other Pacific Islander, 5.1% Two or more races, 38.4% Hispanic of any race; Average household size: 2.65; Median age: 37.9; Age under 18: 23.3%; Age 65 and over: 11.6%; Males per 100 females: 91.6; Marriage status: 34.8% never married, 50.3% now married, 2.3% separated, 5.4% widowed, 9.5% divorced; Foreign born: 26.0%; Speak English only: 59.9%; With disability: 7.7%; Veterans: 5.6%; Ancestry: 7.8% German, 6.1% Irish, 5.3% English, 3.8% Italian, 2.3% American

Employment: 20.5% management, business, and financial, 6.3% computer, engineering, and science, 12.4% education, legal, community service, arts, and media, 6.1% healthcare practitioners, 16.7% service, 25.0% sales and office, 5.6% natural resources, construction, and maintenance, 7.5% production, transportation, and material moving

Income: Per capita: $32,542; Median household: $71,768; Average household: $87,686; Households with income of $100,000 or more: 34.8%; Poverty rate: 9.8%

Educational Attainment: High school diploma or higher: 88.5%; Bachelor's degree or higher: 35.5%; Graduate/professional degree or higher: 13.1%

School District(s)

Monrovia Unified (KG-12)
2012-13 Enrollment: 5,936 . . . . (626) 471-2010

Four-year College(s)

Mt Sierra College (Private, For-profit)
Fall 2013 Enrollment: 538 . . . . (626) 873-2144
2013-14 Tuition: In-state $13,361; Out-of-state $13,361

Housing: Homeownership rate: 49.5%; Median home value: $505,700; Median year structure built: 1960; Homeowner vacancy rate: 1.3%; Median gross rent: $1,276 per month; Rental vacancy rate: 4.9%

Health Insurance: 83.2% have insurance; 66.5% have private insurance; 22.6% have public insurance; 16.8% do not have insurance; 7.2% of children under 18 do not have insurance

Safety: Violent crime rate: 15.4 per 10,000 population; Property crime rate: 217.4 per 10,000 population

Newspapers: Beacon Media News (weekly circulation 99000)

Transportation: Commute: 87.3% car, 2.8% public transportation, 2.7% walk, 5.5% work from home; Median travel time to work: 28.3 minutes

Additional Information Contacts

City of Monrovia . . . . (626) 932-5550
http://www.ci.monrovia.ca.us

MONTEBELLO (city)

MONTEBELLO (city). Covers a land area of 8.333 square miles and a water area of 0.040 square miles. Located at 34.02° N. Lat; 118.11° W. Long. Elevation is 200 feet.

History: Named for the Italian translation of "beautiful mountain". Early industry in Montebello was the growing of ornamental shurbs and flowers. Oil wells later supplemented the economy.

Population: 62,500; Growth (since 2000): 0.6%; Density: 7,500.7 persons per square mile; Race: 53.8% White, 0.9% Black/African American, 11.0% Asian, 1.0% American Indian/Alaska Native, 0.1% Native Hawaiian/Other Pacific Islander, 3.7% Two or more races, 79.3% Hispanic of any race; Average household size: 3.27; Median age: 34.7; Age under 18: 25.8%; Age 65 and over: 13.6%; Males per 100 females: 93.3; Marriage status: 38.9% never married, 45.7% now married, 3.6% separated, 6.8% widowed, 8.6% divorced; Foreign born: 37.3%; Speak English only: 27.5%; With disability: 14.3%; Veterans: 4.1%; Ancestry: 2.9% Armenian, 2.1% American, 1.4% Italian, 1.0% German, 0.6% Irish

Employment: 11.7% management, business, and financial, 3.4% computer, engineering, and science, 10.4% education, legal, community service, arts, and media, 3.5% healthcare practitioners, 18.0% service, 27.6% sales and office, 8.3% natural resources, construction, and maintenance, 17.1% production, transportation, and material moving

Income: Per capita: $20,986; Median household: $47,488; Average household: $64,037; Households with income of $100,000 or more: 19.5%; Poverty rate: 15.4%

Educational Attainment: High school diploma or higher: 69.8%; Bachelor's degree or higher: 18.1%; Graduate/professional degree or higher: 5.5%

School District(s)

Montebello Unified (KG-12)
2012-13 Enrollment: 30,564 . . . . (323) 887-7900

Vocational/Technical School(s)

Montebello Beauty College (Private, For-profit)
Fall 2013 Enrollment: n/a . . . . (323) 727-7851

Housing: Homeownership rate: 46.1%; Median home value: $385,400; Median year structure built: 1960; Homeowner vacancy rate: 0.9%; Median gross rent: $1,114 per month; Rental vacancy rate: 4.1%

Health Insurance: 76.7% have insurance; 49.4% have private insurance; 34.5% have public insurance; 23.3% do not have insurance; 8.0% of children under 18 do not have insurance

Hospitals: Beverly Hospital (223 beds)

Safety: Violent crime rate: 28.8 per 10,000 population; Property crime rate: 276.2 per 10,000 population

Transportation: Commute: 87.0% car, 5.9% public transportation, 2.0% walk, 4.5% work from home; Median travel time to work: 33.6 minutes

Additional Information Contacts

City of Montebello . . . . (323) 887-1363
http://www.cityofmontebello.com

MONTEREY PARK (city)

MONTEREY PARK (city). Covers a land area of 7.672 square miles and a water area of 0.061 square miles. Located at 34.05° N. Lat; 118.13° W. Long. Elevation is 384 feet.

History: Named for its proximity to the Monterey Pass, west of the city. Monterey Park was incorporated in 1916.

Population: 60,269; Growth (since 2000): 0.4%; Density: 7,855.8 persons per square mile; Race: 19.4% White, 0.4% Black/African American, 66.9% Asian, 0.4% American Indian/Alaska Native, 0.0% Native Hawaiian/Other Pacific Islander, 2.9% Two or more races, 26.9% Hispanic of any race; Average household size: 3.01; Median age: 43.1; Age under 18: 18.1%; Age 65 and over: 19.3%; Males per 100 females: 92.2; Marriage status: 33.3% never married, 52.3% now married, 1.9% separated, 7.7% widowed, 6.7% divorced; Foreign born: 54.4%; Speak English only: 21.7%; With disability: 10.2%; Veterans: 3.8%; Ancestry: 4.5% American, 1.0% German, 0.8% Irish, 0.7% Italian, 0.6% French

Employment: 15.4% management, business, and financial, 6.3% computer, engineering, and science, 9.9% education, legal, community service, arts, and media, 4.7% healthcare practitioners, 20.4% service, 27.6% sales and office, 5.5% natural resources, construction, and maintenance, 10.1% production, transportation, and material moving

Income: Per capita: $24,990; Median household: $56,014; Average household: $75,772; Households with income of $100,000 or more: 24.9%; Poverty rate: 15.2%

Educational Attainment: High school diploma or higher: 76.8%; Bachelor's degree or higher: 28.3%; Graduate/professional degree or higher: 8.9%

School District(s)

Alhambra Unified (KG-12)
2012-13 Enrollment: 18,076 . . . . (626) 943-3000
Garvey Elementary (KG-08)
2012-13 Enrollment: 5,259 . . . . (626) 307-3444
Los Angeles County Office of Education (KG-12)
2012-13 Enrollment: 9,136 . . . . (562) 922-6111
Los Angeles Unified (PK-12)
2012-13 Enrollment: 655,455 . . . . (213) 241-1000
Montebello Unified (KG-12)
2012-13 Enrollment: 30,564 . . . . (323) 887-7900

Two-year College(s)

East Los Angeles College (Public)
Fall 2013 Enrollment: 36,606 . . . . (323) 265-8650
2013-14 Tuition: In-state $1,221; Out-of-state $6,161

Housing: Homeownership rate: 55.4%; Median home value: $475,600; Median year structure built: 1962; Homeowner vacancy rate: 0.5%; Median gross rent: $1,203 per month; Rental vacancy rate: 4.1%

Health Insurance: 80.0% have insurance; 56.7% have private insurance; 31.0% have public insurance; 20.0% do not have insurance; 6.0% of children under 18 do not have insurance

Hospitals: Garfield Medical Center (210 beds); Monterey Park Hospital (101 beds)

Safety: Violent crime rate: 17.0 per 10,000 population; Property crime rate: 190.0 per 10,000 population

Transportation: Commute: 87.9% car, 3.6% public transportation, 1.6% walk, 5.4% work from home; Median travel time to work: 28.8 minutes

Additional Information Contacts

City of Monterey Park . . . . (626) 307-1458
http://www.ci.monterey-park.ca.us

MOUNT BALDY (unincorporated postal area)

ZCTA: 91759

Covers a land area of 82.290 square miles and a water area of <.001 square miles. Located at 34.26° N. Lat; 117.70° W. Long..

Population: 476; Growth (since 2000): 1,260.0%; Density: 5.8 persons per square mile; Race: 91.4% White, 0.2% Black/African American, 2.5% Asian, 1.7% American Indian/Alaska Native, 0.0% Native Hawaiian/Other Pacific Islander, 1.7% Two or more races, 9.7% Hispanic of any race; Average household size: 2.20; Median age: 47.2; Age under 18: 16.4%; Age 65 and over: 16.2%; Males per 100 females: 100.8

School District(s)

Mt. Baldy Joint Elementary (KG-08)
2012-13 Enrollment: 116. . . . . (909) 985-0991

Housing: Homeownership rate: 75.5%; Homeowner vacancy rate: 6.3%; Rental vacancy rate: 11.7%

NEWHALL (unincorporated postal area)

ZCTA: 91321

Covers a land area of 25.881 square miles and a water area of 0.025 square miles. Located at 34.37° N. Lat; 118.49° W. Long. Elevation is 1,257 feet.

Population: 34,882; Growth (since 2000): 13.5%; Density: 1,347.8 persons per square mile; Race: 64.9% White, 3.0% Black/African American, 6.1% Asian, 0.8% American Indian/Alaska Native, 0.2% Native Hawaiian/Other Pacific Islander, 4.2% Two or more races, 45.7% Hispanic of any race; Average household size: 3.04; Median age: 33.3; Age under 18: 26.0%; Age 65 and over: 12.0%; Males per 100 females: 99.6; Marriage status: 34.9% never married, 49.7% now married, 1.9% separated, 5.4% widowed, 9.9% divorced; Foreign born: 27.8%; Speak English only: 57.0%; With disability: 10.1%; Veterans: 5.4%; Ancestry: 10.9% German, 8.5% Irish, 7.4% English, 5.4% Italian, 3.1% American

Employment: 13.5% management, business, and financial, 3.3% computer, engineering, and science, 9.7% education, legal, community service, arts, and media, 4.5% healthcare practitioners, 21.4% service, 23.5% sales and office, 12.7% natural resources, construction, and maintenance, 11.3% production, transportation, and material moving

Income: Per capita: $26,453; Median household: $56,079; Average household: $80,515; Households with income of $100,000 or more: 26.3%; Poverty rate: 16.9%

Educational Attainment: High school diploma or higher: 76.7%; Bachelor's degree or higher: 23.2%; Graduate/professional degree or higher: 7.0%

School District(s)

Newhall (KG-06)
2012-13 Enrollment: 6,947 . . . . (661) 291-4000
Sulphur Springs Union (KG-06)
2012-13 Enrollment: 5,553 . . . . (661) 252-5131
William S. Hart Union High (KG-12)
2012-13 Enrollment: 26,373 . . . . (661) 259-0033

Housing: Homeownership rate: 58.4%; Median home value: $340,000; Median year structure built: 1978; Homeowner vacancy rate: 1.6%; Median gross rent: $1,334 per month; Rental vacancy rate: 7.1%

Health Insurance: 77.4% have insurance; 59.6% have private insurance; 26.9% have public insurance; 22.6% do not have insurance; 10.6% of children under 18 do not have insurance

Transportation: Commute: 85.9% car, 5.4% public transportation, 1.6% walk, 6.2% work from home; Median travel time to work: 28.1 minutes

NORTH EL MONTE (CDP).

Covers a land area of 0.423 square miles and a water area of 0 square miles. Located at 34.10° N. Lat; 118.02° W. Long. Elevation is 331 feet.

Population: 3,723; Growth (since 2000): 0.5%; Density: 8,794.7 persons per square mile; Race: 47.5% White, 0.9% Black/African American, 38.6% Asian, 0.3% American Indian/Alaska Native, 0.1% Native Hawaiian/Other Pacific Islander, 3.5% Two or more races, 26.9% Hispanic of any race; Average household size: 2.93; Median age: 42.2; Age under 18: 19.9%; Age 65 and over: 16.4%; Males per 100 females: 92.1; Marriage status: 23.8% never married, 61.9% now married, 0.7% separated, 9.0% widowed, 5.3% divorced; Foreign born: 37.4%; Speak English only: 41.9%; With disability: 10.6%; Veterans: 4.4%; Ancestry: 7.0% Irish, 6.0% German, 4.0% English, 3.4% Italian, 2.9% French

Employment: 11.9% management, business, and financial, 5.6% computer, engineering, and science, 11.4% education, legal, community service, arts, and media, 1.1% healthcare practitioners, 23.4% service, 30.3% sales and office, 5.5% natural resources, construction, and maintenance, 10.8% production, transportation, and material moving

Income: Per capita: $26,009; Median household: $64,408; Average household: $75,505; Households with income of $100,000 or more: 29.6%; Poverty rate: 6.0%

Educational Attainment: High school diploma or higher: 82.9%; Bachelor's degree or higher: 22.0%; Graduate/professional degree or higher: 7.0%

Housing: Homeownership rate: 75.3%; Median home value: $454,000; Median year structure built: 1955; Homeowner vacancy rate: 0.6%; Median gross rent: $1,500 per month; Rental vacancy rate: 5.2%

Health Insurance: 87.3% have insurance; 66.3% have private insurance; 30.6% have public insurance; 12.7% do not have insurance; 2.8% of children under 18 do not have insurance

Transportation: Commute: 88.6% car, 4.0% public transportation, 1.7% walk, 5.7% work from home; Median travel time to work: 31.5 minutes

NORTH HILLS (unincorporated postal area)

ZCTA: 91343

Covers a land area of 5.911 square miles and a water area of 0.013 square miles. Located at 34.24° N. Lat; 118.48° W. Long. Elevation is 843 feet.

Population: 60,254; Growth (since 2000): 5.7%; Density: 10,193.1 persons per square mile; Race: 47.3% White, 4.4% Black/African American, 14.2% Asian, 0.7% American Indian/Alaska Native, 0.2% Native Hawaiian/Other Pacific Islander, 4.6% Two or more races, 58.8% Hispanic of any race; Average household size: 3.55; Median age: 32.3; Age under 18: 27.8%; Age 65 and over: 9.1%; Males per 100 females: 100.1; Marriage status: 39.2% never married, 49.6% now married, 2.9% separated, 4.4% widowed, 6.8% divorced; Foreign born: 44.2%; Speak English only: 30.0%; With disability: 8.0%; Veterans: 3.4%; Ancestry: 3.5% German, 3.0% Irish, 2.3% English, 2.0% Italian, 1.8% Armenian

Employment: 10.7% management, business, and financial, 2.6% computer, engineering, and science, 8.0% education, legal, community service, arts, and media, 5.5% healthcare practitioners, 22.1% service, 24.2% sales and office, 13.3% natural resources, construction, and maintenance, 13.5% production, transportation, and material moving

Income: Per capita: $21,048; Median household: $54,166; Average household: $73,247; Households with income of $100,000 or more: 24.8%; Poverty rate: 21.8%

Educational Attainment: High school diploma or higher: 71.2%; Bachelor's degree or higher: 22.9%; Graduate/professional degree or higher: 6.2%

School District(s)

Los Angeles Unified (PK-12)
2012-13 Enrollment: 655,455 . . . . (213) 241-1000

Housing: Homeownership rate: 54.0%; Median home value: $380,400; Median year structure built: 1965; Homeowner vacancy rate: 1.7%; Median gross rent: $1,141 per month; Rental vacancy rate: 5.7%

Health Insurance: 73.1% have insurance; 44.2% have private insurance; 33.5% have public insurance; 26.9% do not have insurance; 11.8% of children under 18 do not have insurance

Transportation: Commute: 83.6% car, 8.6% public transportation, 2.1% walk, 2.7% work from home; Median travel time to work: 32.2 minutes

NORTH HOLLYWOOD (unincorporated postal area)

ZCTA: 91601

Covers a land area of 2.650 square miles and a water area of <.001 square miles. Located at 34.17° N. Lat; 118.37° W. Long. Elevation is 643 feet.

Population: 37,180; Growth (since 2000): 1.5%; Density: 14,028.0 persons per square mile; Race: 59.2% White, 7.8% Black/African American, 6.7% Asian, 0.8% American Indian/Alaska Native, 0.2% Native Hawaiian/Other Pacific Islander, 5.1% Two or more races, 43.8% Hispanic of any race; Average household size: 2.32; Median age: 32.9; Age under 18: 17.8%; Age 65 and over: 7.4%; Males per 100 females: 103.7; Marriage status: 51.3% never married, 36.8% now married, 3.4% separated, 3.2% widowed, 8.7% divorced; Foreign born: 35.8%; Speak English only: 48.3%; With disability: 8.9%; Veterans: 2.5%; Ancestry: 7.7% German, 6.7% Irish, 4.5% Armenian, 4.2% Italian, 4.0% English

Employment: 13.1% management, business, and financial, 4.5% computer, engineering, and science, 18.9% education, legal, community service, arts, and media, 2.2% healthcare practitioners, 22.3% service, 23.2% sales and office, 6.5% natural resources, construction, and maintenance, 9.3% production, transportation, and material moving

Income: Per capita: $28,040; Median household: $48,638; Average household: $63,358; Households with income of $100,000 or more: 18.5%; Poverty rate: 19.2%

Educational Attainment: High school diploma or higher: 82.1%; Bachelor's degree or higher: 36.7%; Graduate/professional degree or higher: 9.7%

School District(s)

Los Angeles Unified (PK-12)
2012-13 Enrollment: 655,455 . . . . (213) 241-1000

Four-year College(s)

Concorde Career College-North Hollywood (Private, For-profit)
Fall 2013 Enrollment: 925 . . . . (818) 766-8151
Galaxy Medical College (Private, For-profit)
Fall 2013 Enrollment: 31 . . . . (818) 509-9970
Kaplan College-North Hollywood (Private, For-profit)
Fall 2013 Enrollment: 792 . . . . (818) 763-2563

Southern California Health Institute (Private, For-profit)
Fall 2013 Enrollment: 272 . . . . (818) 980-8990
The Art Institute of California-Argosy University Hollywood (Private, For-profit)
Fall 2013 Enrollment: 1,906 . . . . (818) 299-5100
2013-14 Tuition: In-state $18,748; Out-of-state $18,748
West Coast University-Los Angeles (Private, For-profit)
Fall 2013 Enrollment: 1,435 . . . . (818) 299-5500
2013-14 Tuition: In-state $32,525; Out-of-state $32,525

Two-year College(s)

Concorde Career College-North Hollywood (Private, For-profit)
Fall 2013 Enrollment: 925 . . . . (818) 766-8151
Galaxy Medical College (Private, For-profit)
Fall 2013 Enrollment: 31 . . . . (818) 509-9970
Kaplan College-North Hollywood (Private, For-profit)
Fall 2013 Enrollment: 792 . . . . (818) 763-2563
Southern California Health Institute (Private, For-profit)
Fall 2013 Enrollment: 272 . . . . (818) 980-8990
The Art Institute of California-Argosy University Hollywood (Private, For-profit)
Fall 2013 Enrollment: 1,906 . . . . (818) 299-5100
2013-14 Tuition: In-state $18,748; Out-of-state $18,748
West Coast University-Los Angeles (Private, For-profit)
Fall 2013 Enrollment: 1,435 . . . . (818) 299-5500
2013-14 Tuition: In-state $32,525; Out-of-state $32,525

Vocational/Technical School(s)

Concorde Career College-North Hollywood (Private, For-profit)
Fall 2013 Enrollment: 925 . . . . (818) 766-8151
2013-14 Tuition: $14,695
Galaxy Medical College (Private, For-profit)
Fall 2013 Enrollment: 31 . . . . (818) 509-9970
2013-14 Tuition: $9,760
Kaplan College-North Hollywood (Private, For-profit)
Fall 2013 Enrollment: 792 . . . . (818) 763-2563
2013-14 Tuition: $19,760
Southern California Health Institute (Private, For-profit)
Fall 2013 Enrollment: 272 . . . . (818) 980-8990
2013-14 Tuition: $12,792
The Art Institute of California-Argosy University Hollywood (Private, For-profit)
Fall 2013 Enrollment: 1,906 . . . . (818) 299-5100
2013-14 Tuition: In-state $18,748; Out-of-state $18,748
West Coast University-Los Angeles (Private, For-profit)
Fall 2013 Enrollment: 1,435 . . . . (818) 299-5500
2013-14 Tuition: In-state $32,525; Out-of-state $32,525

Housing: Homeownership rate: 19.8%; Median home value: $464,200; Median year structure built: 1972; Homeowner vacancy rate: 4.8%; Median gross rent: $1,268 per month; Rental vacancy rate: 7.1%
Health Insurance: 68.0% have insurance; 50.1% have private insurance; 21.8% have public insurance; 32.0% do not have insurance; 12.3% of children under 18 do not have insurance
Transportation: Commute: 78.4% car, 11.4% public transportation, 1.7% walk, 5.5% work from home; Median travel time to work: 31.0 minutes

ZCTA: 91602

Covers a land area of 2.047 square miles and a water area of 0.026 square miles. Located at 34.15° N. Lat; 118.37° W. Long. Elevation is 643 feet.
Population: 17,473; Growth (since 2000): 2.9%; Density: 8,534.8 persons per square mile; Race: 76.8% White, 6.4% Black/African American, 6.9% Asian, 0.5% American Indian/Alaska Native, 0.1% Native Hawaiian/Other Pacific Islander, 4.8% Two or more races, 14.8% Hispanic of any race; Average household size: 1.88; Median age: 38.0; Age under 18: 12.3%; Age 65 and over: 9.7%; Males per 100 females: 99.7; Marriage status: 50.3% never married, 35.7% now married, 1.5% separated, 2.3% widowed, 11.6% divorced; Foreign born: 18.2%; Speak English only: 74.8%; With disability: 6.5%; Veterans: 5.3%; Ancestry: 13.9% German, 11.6% Irish, 9.4% Italian, 8.7% English, 7.4% Russian
Employment: 21.8% management, business, and financial, 5.9% computer, engineering, and science, 27.6% education, legal, community service, arts, and media, 3.9% healthcare practitioners, 10.1% service, 25.8% sales and office, 1.9% natural resources, construction, and maintenance, 3.1% production, transportation, and material moving
Income: Per capita: $47,889; Median household: $66,652; Average household: $91,242; Households with income of $100,000 or more: 31.8%; Poverty rate: 9.5%
Educational Attainment: High school diploma or higher: 95.4%; Bachelor's degree or higher: 55.9%; Graduate/professional degree or higher: 14.1%
Housing: Homeownership rate: 33.2%; Median home value: $600,000; Median year structure built: 1968; Homeowner vacancy rate: 3.5%; Median gross rent: $1,399 per month; Rental vacancy rate: 5.7%
Health Insurance: 87.2% have insurance; 78.0% have private insurance; 16.3% have public insurance; 12.8% do not have insurance; 2.3% of children under 18 do not have insurance
Transportation: Commute: 86.6% car, 3.8% public transportation, 1.4% walk, 7.2% work from home; Median travel time to work: 26.8 minutes

ZCTA: 91605

Covers a land area of 5.464 square miles and a water area of 0.015 square miles. Located at 34.21° N. Lat; 118.40° W. Long. Elevation is 643 feet.
Population: 56,343; Growth (since 2000): -1.4%; Density: 10,312.0 persons per square mile; Race: 48.9% White, 3.4% Black/African American, 9.8% Asian, 0.7% American Indian/Alaska Native, 0.1% Native Hawaiian/Other Pacific Islander, 4.6% Two or more races, 63.3% Hispanic of any race; Average household size: 3.61; Median age: 31.9; Age under 18: 26.3%; Age 65 and over: 8.5%; Males per 100 females: 101.8; Marriage status: 42.3% never married, 45.9% now married, 3.0% separated, 4.1% widowed, 7.6% divorced; Foreign born: 51.0%; Speak English only: 19.2%; With disability: 10.4%; Veterans: 2.7%; Ancestry: 9.8% Armenian, 3.0% American, 1.9% German, 1.4% Irish, 1.2% Italian
Employment: 7.3% management, business, and financial, 2.0% computer, engineering, and science, 8.1% education, legal, community service, arts, and media, 3.1% healthcare practitioners, 26.0% service, 22.1% sales and office, 14.3% natural resources, construction, and maintenance, 16.9% production, transportation, and material moving
Income: Per capita: $16,886; Median household: $43,301; Average household: $56,089; Households with income of $100,000 or more: 15.3%; Poverty rate: 23.6%
Educational Attainment: High school diploma or higher: 64.4%; Bachelor's degree or higher: 17.3%; Graduate/professional degree or higher: 3.8%
Housing: Homeownership rate: 40.6%; Median home value: $339,100; Median year structure built: 1962; Homeowner vacancy rate: 1.6%; Median gross rent: $1,074 per month; Rental vacancy rate: 5.3%
Health Insurance: 66.0% have insurance; 34.9% have private insurance; 35.4% have public insurance; 34.0% do not have insurance; 15.7% of children under 18 do not have insurance
Transportation: Commute: 83.1% car, 8.1% public transportation, 2.6% walk, 3.0% work from home; Median travel time to work: 28.2 minutes

ZCTA: 91606

Covers a land area of 3.333 square miles and a water area of 0.010 square miles. Located at 34.19° N. Lat; 118.39° W. Long. Elevation is 643 feet.
Population: 44,958; Growth (since 2000): -0.9%; Density: 13,490.7 persons per square mile; Race: 57.9% White, 3.7% Black/African American, 5.2% Asian, 0.7% American Indian/Alaska Native, 0.2% Native Hawaiian/Other Pacific Islander, 4.9% Two or more races, 57.1% Hispanic of any race; Average household size: 3.00; Median age: 34.3; Age under 18: 23.6%; Age 65 and over: 10.1%; Males per 100 females: 99.1; Marriage status: 43.2% never married, 45.2% now married, 3.1% separated, 4.5% widowed, 7.0% divorced; Foreign born: 46.7%; Speak English only: 27.4%; With disability: 9.9%; Veterans: 2.9%; Ancestry: 9.9% Armenian, 3.9% American, 3.8% German, 2.9% English, 2.4% Irish
Employment: 10.4% management, business, and financial, 1.8% computer, engineering, and science, 8.9% education, legal, community service, arts, and media, 3.3% healthcare practitioners, 25.8% service, 27.6% sales and office, 10.2% natural resources, construction, and maintenance, 12.0% production, transportation, and material moving
Income: Per capita: $19,231; Median household: $42,521; Average household: $54,596; Households with income of $100,000 or more: 13.0%; Poverty rate: 21.1%
Educational Attainment: High school diploma or higher: 70.6%; Bachelor's degree or higher: 21.8%; Graduate/professional degree or higher: 4.9%
Housing: Homeownership rate: 33.6%; Median home value: $363,400; Median year structure built: 1962; Homeowner vacancy rate: 1.8%; Median gross rent: $1,103 per month; Rental vacancy rate: 4.6%
Health Insurance: 67.1% have insurance; 39.1% have private insurance; 32.6% have public insurance; 32.9% do not have insurance; 15.1% of children under 18 do not have insurance

Transportation: Commute: 80.9% car, 8.4% public transportation, 2.7% walk, 4.9% work from home; Median travel time to work: 28.1 minutes

NORTHRIDGE (unincorporated postal area)

ZCTA: 91324

Covers a land area of 4.391 square miles and a water area of 0.025 square miles. Located at 34.24° N. Lat; 118.55° W. Long. Elevation is 807 feet.

Population: 27,669; Growth (since 2000): 7.5%; Density: 6,300.8 persons per square mile; Race: 55.8% White, 4.9% Black/African American, 17.6% Asian, 0.5% American Indian/Alaska Native, 0.2% Native Hawaiian/Other Pacific Islander, 4.9% Two or more races, 36.2% Hispanic of any race; Average household size: 2.95; Median age: 36.5; Age under 18: 22.0%; Age 65 and over: 13.2%; Males per 100 females: 95.9; Marriage status: 40.0% never married, 45.9% now married, 3.0% separated, 5.2% widowed, 8.9% divorced; Foreign born: 36.5%; Speak English only: 44.4%; With disability: 9.8%; Veterans: 5.3%; Ancestry: 5.1% German, 4.2% Italian, 4.1% Irish, 3.3% English, 2.6% Armenian

Employment: 18.2% management, business, and financial, 4.6% computer, engineering, and science, 11.8% education, legal, community service, arts, and media, 4.4% healthcare practitioners, 16.7% service, 28.0% sales and office, 6.9% natural resources, construction, and maintenance, 9.5% production, transportation, and material moving

Income: Per capita: $28,013; Median household: $58,663; Average household: $81,817; Households with income of $100,000 or more: 28.0%; Poverty rate: 16.0%

Educational Attainment: High school diploma or higher: 85.2%; Bachelor's degree or higher: 35.7%; Graduate/professional degree or higher: 11.2%

School District(s)

Los Angeles Unified (PK-12)
2012-13 Enrollment: 655,455 . . . . (213) 241-1000

Four-year College(s)

California State University-Northridge (Public)
Fall 2013 Enrollment: 38,310 . . . . (818) 677-1200
2013-14 Tuition: In-state $6,525; Out-of-state $17,685

Two-year College(s)

California State University-Northridge (Public)
Fall 2013 Enrollment: 38,310 . . . . (818) 677-1200
2013-14 Tuition: In-state $6,525; Out-of-state $17,685

Vocational/Technical School(s)

California State University-Northridge (Public)
Fall 2013 Enrollment: 38,310 . . . . (818) 677-1200
2013-14 Tuition: In-state $6,525; Out-of-state $17,685

Housing: Homeownership rate: 54.6%; Median home value: $454,800; Median year structure built: 1967; Homeowner vacancy rate: 1.0%; Median gross rent: $1,374 per month; Rental vacancy rate: 11.2%

Health Insurance: 80.5% have insurance; 59.9% have private insurance; 28.3% have public insurance; 19.5% do not have insurance; 9.0% of children under 18 do not have insurance

Hospitals: Northridge Hospital Medical Center (411 beds)

Transportation: Commute: 85.3% car, 4.6% public transportation, 2.3% walk, 5.1% work from home; Median travel time to work: 28.1 minutes

ZCTA: 91325

Covers a land area of 4.821 square miles and a water area of 0.003 square miles. Located at 34.24° N. Lat; 118.52° W. Long. Elevation is 807 feet.

Population: 32,417; Growth (since 2000): 0.4%; Density: 6,723.8 persons per square mile; Race: 57.8% White, 5.7% Black/African American, 16.9% Asian, 0.6% American Indian/Alaska Native, 0.3% Native Hawaiian/Other Pacific Islander, 5.2% Two or more races, 32.2% Hispanic of any race; Average household size: 2.72; Median age: 35.4; Age under 18: 19.8%; Age 65 and over: 13.0%; Males per 100 females: 95.3; Marriage status: 42.4% never married, 44.0% now married, 2.0% separated, 4.6% widowed, 9.0% divorced; Foreign born: 32.6%; Speak English only: 54.2%; With disability: 10.7%; Veterans: 5.6%; Ancestry: 6.8% German, 6.0% English, 4.5% Irish, 2.9% American, 2.8% Italian

Employment: 14.7% management, business, and financial, 6.3% computer, engineering, and science, 13.6% education, legal, community service, arts, and media, 5.9% healthcare practitioners, 14.1% service, 29.9% sales and office, 6.7% natural resources, construction, and maintenance, 8.8% production, transportation, and material moving

Income: Per capita: $30,570; Median household: $59,646; Average household: $81,930; Households with income of $100,000 or more: 26.0%; Poverty rate: 17.1%

Educational Attainment: High school diploma or higher: 88.6%; Bachelor's degree or higher: 38.0%; Graduate/professional degree or higher: 13.1%

Housing: Homeownership rate: 47.8%; Median home value: $485,800; Median year structure built: 1971; Homeowner vacancy rate: 1.3%; Median gross rent: $1,291 per month; Rental vacancy rate: 6.1%

Health Insurance: 83.2% have insurance; 66.5% have private insurance; 25.7% have public insurance; 16.8% do not have insurance; 7.6% of children under 18 do not have insurance

Transportation: Commute: 85.9% car, 5.1% public transportation, 3.1% walk, 4.2% work from home; Median travel time to work: 29.3 minutes

ZCTA: 91330

Covers a land area of 0.341 square miles and a water area of 0 square miles. Located at 34.25° N. Lat; 118.53° W. Long. Elevation is 807 feet.

Population: 2,702; Growth (since 2000): n/a; Density: 7,931.4 persons per square mile; Race: 41.9% White, 26.4% Black/African American, 12.2% Asian, 0.7% American Indian/Alaska Native, 0.3% Native Hawaiian/Other Pacific Islander, 6.6% Two or more races, 32.1% Hispanic of any race; Average household size: 2.50; Median age: 19.6; Age under 18: 0.7%; Age 65 and over: 0.0%; Males per 100 females: 69.0; Marriage status: 95.4% never married, 4.3% now married, 0.3% separated, 0.0% widowed, 0.3% divorced; Foreign born: 15.8%; Speak English only: 61.6%; With disability: 3.6%; Veterans: 1.3%; Ancestry: 7.1% German, 5.1% Irish, 4.9% American, 4.2% Italian, 3.6% English

Employment: 3.1% management, business, and financial, 3.1% computer, engineering, and science, 28.1% education, legal, community service, arts, and media, 0.0% healthcare practitioners, 28.8% service, 31.0% sales and office, 2.6% natural resources, construction, and maintenance, 3.4% production, transportation, and material moving

Income: Per capita: $3,835; Median household: n/a; Average household: n/a; Households with income of $100,000 or more: n/a; Poverty rate: 100.0%

Educational Attainment: High school diploma or higher: 97.2%; Bachelor's degree or higher: 54.7%; Graduate/professional degree or higher: 16.2%

Housing: Homeownership rate: 50.0%; Median home value: n/a; Median year structure built: n/a; Homeowner vacancy rate: 0.0%; Median gross rent: n/a per month; Rental vacancy rate: 0.0%

Health Insurance: 91.7% have insurance; 84.3% have private insurance; 9.0% have public insurance; 8.3% do not have insurance; 20.0% of children under 18 do not have insurance

Transportation: Commute: 38.9% car, 6.7% public transportation, 44.5% walk, 6.1% work from home; Median travel time to work: 14.6 minutes

NORWALK (city). Covers a land area of 9.707 square miles and a water area of 0.039 square miles. Located at 33.91° N. Lat; 118.08° W. Long. Elevation is 92 feet.

History: Named for Norwalk, Connecticut, former home of the city's settlers. With the arrival (1875) of the Southern Pacific Railroad, it became a center for the dairy and logging industries. Norwalk's main growth occurred after World War II, with rapid industrialization. Settled in the 1850s. Incorporated 1957.

Population: 105,549; Growth (since 2000): 2.2%; Density: 10,873.5 persons per square mile; Race: 49.4% White, 4.4% Black/African American, 12.0% Asian, 1.1% American Indian/Alaska Native, 0.4% Native Hawaiian/Other Pacific Islander, 4.3% Two or more races, 70.1% Hispanic of any race; Average household size: 3.83; Median age: 32.5; Age under 18: 27.6%; Age 65 and over: 9.9%; Males per 100 females: 98.5; Marriage status: 39.6% never married, 46.9% now married, 2.8% separated, 5.7% widowed, 7.7% divorced; Foreign born: 35.5%; Speak English only: 32.0%; With disability: 9.5%; Veterans: 4.4%; Ancestry: 2.0% German, 2.0% American, 1.9% English, 1.9% Irish, 1.1% Italian

Employment: 8.5% management, business, and financial, 2.5% computer, engineering, and science, 7.8% education, legal, community service, arts, and media, 3.6% healthcare practitioners, 18.9% service, 28.2% sales and office, 10.7% natural resources, construction, and maintenance, 19.7% production, transportation, and material moving

Income: Per capita: $19,449; Median household: $60,770; Average household: $70,938; Households with income of $100,000 or more: 22.7%; Poverty rate: 12.9%

Educational Attainment: High school diploma or higher: 72.4%; Bachelor's degree or higher: 14.8%; Graduate/professional degree or higher: 4.5%

School District(s)

Little Lake City Elementary (KG-08)
2012-13 Enrollment: 4,642 . . . . (562) 868-8241
Norwalk-La Mirada Unified (KG-12)
2012-13 Enrollment: 19,770 . . . . (562) 868-0431
Southeast Rop
2012-13 Enrollment: n/a . . . . (562) 403-7382

Two-year College(s)

Cerritos College (Public)
Fall 2013 Enrollment: 21,404 . . . . (562) 860-2451
2013-14 Tuition: In-state $1,346; Out-of-state $7,114

Vocational/Technical School(s)

ATI College-Norwalk (Private, For-profit)
Fall 2013 Enrollment: 120 . . . . (562) 864-0506
2013-14 Tuition: $28,825

Housing: Homeownership rate: 65.1%; Median home value: $315,500; Median year structure built: 1957; Homeowner vacancy rate: 1.4%; Median gross rent: $1,306 per month; Rental vacancy rate: 3.8%

Health Insurance: 75.8% have insurance; 51.5% have private insurance; 29.1% have public insurance; 24.2% do not have insurance; 9.7% of children under 18 do not have insurance

Hospitals: Coast Plaza Hospital

Safety: Violent crime rate: 38.2 per 10,000 population; Property crime rate: 210.9 per 10,000 population

Transportation: Commute: 91.1% car, 3.9% public transportation, 1.8% walk, 1.9% work from home; Median travel time to work: 28.2 minutes

Additional Information Contacts

City of Norwalk . . . . (562) 929-5700
http://www.ci.norwalk.ca.us

PACIFIC PALISADES (unincorporated postal area)

ZCTA: 90272

Covers a land area of 22.832 square miles and a water area of 0.550 square miles. Located at 34.09° N. Lat; 118.54° W. Long. Elevation is 328 feet.

Population: 22,986; Growth (since 2000): 2.0%; Density: 1,006.8 persons per square mile; Race: 90.0% White, 0.8% Black/African American, 5.3% Asian, 0.1% American Indian/Alaska Native, 0.0% Native Hawaiian/Other Pacific Islander, 3.0% Two or more races, 4.5% Hispanic of any race; Average household size: 2.49; Median age: 47.3; Age under 18: 24.4%; Age 65 and over: 20.2%; Males per 100 females: 91.0; Marriage status: 19.3% never married, 67.3% now married, 1.4% separated, 5.8% widowed, 7.6% divorced; Foreign born: 16.5%; Speak English only: 82.1%; With disability: 6.6%; Veterans: 7.4%; Ancestry: 14.9% English, 14.6% German, 13.3% Irish, 9.7% Russian, 6.5% Polish

Employment: 34.0% management, business, and financial, 5.3% computer, engineering, and science, 28.4% education, legal, community service, arts, and media, 7.9% healthcare practitioners, 4.5% service, 16.1% sales and office, 1.7% natural resources, construction, and maintenance, 2.1% production, transportation, and material moving

Income: Per capita: $110,892; Median household: $159,696; Average household: $278,435; Households with income of $100,000 or more: 66.1%; Poverty rate: 4.6%

Educational Attainment: High school diploma or higher: 98.8%; Bachelor's degree or higher: 77.0%; Graduate/professional degree or higher: 39.7%

School District(s)

Los Angeles Unified (PK-12)
2012-13 Enrollment: 655,455 . . . . (213) 241-1000

Housing: Homeownership rate: 81.5%; Median home value: 1 million+; Median year structure built: 1963; Homeowner vacancy rate: 1.0%; Median gross rent: $2,000+ per month; Rental vacancy rate: 6.0%

Health Insurance: 96.1% have insurance; 89.2% have private insurance; 22.4% have public insurance; 3.9% do not have insurance; 2.1% of children under 18 do not have insurance

Newspapers: Palisadian-Post (weekly circulation 4800)

Transportation: Commute: 79.0% car, 2.0% public transportation, 2.0% walk, 15.5% work from home; Median travel time to work: 28.5 minutes

PACOIMA (unincorporated postal area)

ZCTA: 91331

Covers a land area of 8.853 square miles and a water area of 0.046 square miles. Located at 34.26° N. Lat; 118.42° W. Long. Elevation is 991 feet.

Population: 103,689; Growth (since 2000): 6.6%; Density: 11,712.7 persons per square mile; Race: 44.4% White, 3.3% Black/African American, 4.4% Asian, 0.9% American Indian/Alaska Native, 0.1% Native Hawaiian/Other Pacific Islander, 4.0% Two or more races, 87.8% Hispanic of any race; Average household size: 4.60; Median age: 29.5; Age under 18: 30.3%; Age 65 and over: 7.6%; Males per 100 females: 102.0; Marriage status: 43.6% never married, 46.5% now married, 3.7% separated, 4.3% widowed, 5.7% divorced; Foreign born: 46.1%; Speak English only: 15.2%; With disability: 10.9%; Veterans: 2.7%; Ancestry: 0.6% Irish, 0.6% Italian, 0.6% English, 0.6% German, 0.4% American

Employment: 6.3% management, business, and financial, 1.8% computer, engineering, and science, 6.2% education, legal, community service, arts, and media, 2.7% healthcare practitioners, 24.7% service, 23.0% sales and office, 15.0% natural resources, construction, and maintenance, 20.2% production, transportation, and material moving

Income: Per capita: $14,095; Median household: $51,477; Average household: $59,275; Households with income of $100,000 or more: 14.6%; Poverty rate: 21.0%

Educational Attainment: High school diploma or higher: 50.6%; Bachelor's degree or higher: 8.3%; Graduate/professional degree or higher: 2.2%

School District(s)

Los Angeles Unified (PK-12)
2012-13 Enrollment: 655,455 . . . . (213) 241-1000

Housing: Homeownership rate: 60.0%; Median home value: $283,000; Median year structure built: 1958; Homeowner vacancy rate: 2.0%; Median gross rent: $1,299 per month; Rental vacancy rate: 3.4%

Health Insurance: 70.4% have insurance; 37.4% have private insurance; 36.7% have public insurance; 29.6% do not have insurance; 11.4% of children under 18 do not have insurance

Transportation: Commute: 88.4% car, 6.0% public transportation, 2.0% walk, 2.3% work from home; Median travel time to work: 27.4 minutes

PALMDALE (city). Covers a land area of 105.961 square miles and a water area of 0.255 square miles. Located at 34.59° N. Lat; 118.11° W. Long. Elevation is 2,657 feet.

History: Named for the Joshua tree, sometimes called a yucca palm. Palmdale developed as the busines center of southern Antelope Valley, a fruit and alfalfa growing district that specialized in Bartlett pears.

Population: 152,750; Growth (since 2000): 30.9%; Density: 1,441.6 persons per square mile; Race: 49.0% White, 14.8% Black/African American, 4.3% Asian, 0.9% American Indian/Alaska Native, 0.2% Native Hawaiian/Other Pacific Islander, 5.4% Two or more races, 54.4% Hispanic of any race; Average household size: 3.55; Median age: 29.7; Age under 18: 33.1%; Age 65 and over: 6.6%; Males per 100 females: 95.3; Marriage status: 39.0% never married, 48.4% now married, 2.8% separated, 3.6% widowed, 9.0% divorced; Foreign born: 25.1%; Speak English only: 58.2%; With disability: 10.6%; Veterans: 6.8%; Ancestry: 6.1% German, 5.3% Irish, 4.1% English, 2.6% Italian, 1.8% American

Employment: 9.8% management, business, and financial, 4.2% computer, engineering, and science, 7.6% education, legal, community service, arts, and media, 4.3% healthcare practitioners, 20.5% service, 27.2% sales and office, 11.4% natural resources, construction, and maintenance, 15.0% production, transportation, and material moving

Income: Per capita: $18,797; Median household: $53,922; Average household: $67,093; Households with income of $100,000 or more: 21.5%; Poverty rate: 21.2%

Educational Attainment: High school diploma or higher: 74.2%; Bachelor's degree or higher: 15.3%; Graduate/professional degree or higher: 4.9%

School District(s)

Antelope Valley Rop
2012-13 Enrollment: n/a . . . . (661) 575-1026
Antelope Valley Union High (09-12)
2012-13 Enrollment: 24,816 . . . . (661) 948-7655
Keppel Union Elementary (KG-08)
2012-13 Enrollment: 2,747 . . . . (661) 944-2155
Palmdale Elementary (KG-08)
2012-13 Enrollment: 21,264 . . . . (661) 947-7191
Westside Union Elementary (KG-08)
2012-13 Enrollment: 8,645 . . . . (661) 722-0716
Wilsona Elementary (KG-08)
2012-13 Enrollment: 1,393 . . . . (661) 264-1111

Housing: Homeownership rate: 67.9%; Median home value: $172,000; Median year structure built: 1989; Homeowner vacancy rate: 3.2%; Median gross rent: $1,155 per month; Rental vacancy rate: 9.4%
Health Insurance: 81.2% have insurance; 50.1% have private insurance; 36.6% have public insurance; 18.8% do not have insurance; 8.0% of children under 18 do not have insurance
Hospitals: Palmdale Regional Medical Center (121 beds)
Safety: Violent crime rate: 48.5 per 10,000 population; Property crime rate: 213.6 per 10,000 population
Newspapers: Antelope Valley Journal (weekly circulation 1000); Antelope Valley Press (daily circulation 21000)
Transportation: Commute: 91.0% car, 2.8% public transportation, 0.8% walk, 4.6% work from home; Median travel time to work: 40.5 minutes; Amtrak: Bus service available.
Additional Information Contacts
City of Palmdale . . . . (661) 267-5100
http://www.cityofpalmdale.org

PALOS VERDES ESTATES (city). Covers a land area of 4.774 square miles and a water area of <.001 square miles. Located at 33.79° N. Lat; 118.39° W. Long. Elevation is 210 feet.
History: Named for the Spanish translation of "green trees". Incorporated 1939.
Population: 13,438; Growth (since 2000): 0.7%; Density: 2,815.0 persons per square mile; Race: 77.0% White, 1.2% Black/African American, 17.3% Asian, 0.2% American Indian/Alaska Native, 0.1% Native Hawaiian/Other Pacific Islander, 3.6% Two or more races, 4.7% Hispanic of any race; Average household size: 2.65; Median age: 49.9; Age under 18: 23.2%; Age 65 and over: 24.2%; Males per 100 females: 95.2; Marriage status: 19.1% never married, 69.5% now married, 0.6% separated, 4.9% widowed, 6.5% divorced; Foreign born: 17.4%; Speak English only: 75.9%; With disability: 6.4%; Veterans: 8.3%; Ancestry: 14.1% English, 13.5% German, 10.2% Irish, 8.6% Italian, 6.0% American
Employment: 28.4% management, business, and financial, 8.6% computer, engineering, and science, 17.7% education, legal, community service, arts, and media, 8.9% healthcare practitioners, 5.9% service, 25.1% sales and office, 2.7% natural resources, construction, and maintenance, 2.6% production, transportation, and material moving
Income: Per capita: $89,351; Median household: $163,889; Average household: $247,171; Households with income of $100,000 or more: 67.0%; Poverty rate: 3.2%
Educational Attainment: High school diploma or higher: 97.9%; Bachelor's degree or higher: 76.4%; Graduate/professional degree or higher: 37.0%

School District(s)

Palos Verdes Peninsula Unified (KG-12)
2012-13 Enrollment: 11,864 . . . . (310) 378-9966
Housing: Homeownership rate: 88.8%; Median home value: 1 million+; Median year structure built: 1962; Homeowner vacancy rate: 0.7%; Median gross rent: $2,000+ per month; Rental vacancy rate: 5.6%
Health Insurance: 96.3% have insurance; 89.5% have private insurance; 23.3% have public insurance; 3.7% do not have insurance; 3.8% of children under 18 do not have insurance
Safety: Violent crime rate: 4.4 per 10,000 population; Property crime rate: 107.6 per 10,000 population
Transportation: Commute: 85.3% car, 0.3% public transportation, 1.3% walk, 11.1% work from home; Median travel time to work: 35.0 minutes
Additional Information Contacts
City of Palos Verdes Estates. . . . . (310) 378-0383
http://www.palosverdes.com/pve

PALOS VERDES PENINSULA (unincorporated postal area)
ZCTA: 90274
Covers a land area of 11.970 square miles and a water area of 1.016 square miles. Located at 33.78° N. Lat; 118.37° W. Long. Elevation is 1,204 feet.
Population: 25,209; Growth (since 2000): 0.9%; Density: 2,106.0 persons per square mile; Race: 73.5% White, 1.4% Black/African American, 19.9% Asian, 0.2% American Indian/Alaska Native, 0.1% Native Hawaiian/Other Pacific Islander, 3.9% Two or more races, 5.7% Hispanic of any race; Average household size: 2.66; Median age: 49.4; Age under 18: 23.0%; Age 65 and over: 23.9%; Males per 100 females: 93.8; Marriage status: 19.6% never married, 68.4% now married, 0.5% separated, 5.3% widowed, 6.7% divorced; Foreign born: 20.2%; Speak English only: 75.4%; With disability: 7.4%; Veterans: 8.4%; Ancestry: 14.2% German, 14.1% English, 9.6% Irish, 7.2% Italian, 5.4% American
Employment: 30.0% management, business, and financial, 9.6% computer, engineering, and science, 17.1% education, legal, community service, arts, and media, 9.7% healthcare practitioners, 6.0% service, 23.2% sales and office, 2.2% natural resources, construction, and maintenance, 2.2% production, transportation, and material moving
Income: Per capita: $81,968; Median household: $151,469; Average household: $220,299; Households with income of $100,000 or more: 65.4%; Poverty rate: 3.1%
Educational Attainment: High school diploma or higher: 97.9%; Bachelor's degree or higher: 73.0%; Graduate/professional degree or higher: 34.9%
Housing: Homeownership rate: 89.4%; Median home value: 1 million+; Median year structure built: 1965; Homeowner vacancy rate: 1.2%; Median gross rent: $2,000+ per month; Rental vacancy rate: 5.6%
Health Insurance: 96.6% have insurance; 89.1% have private insurance; 24.1% have public insurance; 3.4% do not have insurance; 3.4% of children under 18 do not have insurance
Transportation: Commute: 85.8% car, 0.5% public transportation, 1.4% walk, 10.3% work from home; Median travel time to work: 32.4 minutes

PANORAMA CITY (unincorporated postal area)
ZCTA: 91402
Covers a land area of 3.727 square miles and a water area of 0.030 square miles. Located at 34.22° N. Lat; 118.44° W. Long. Elevation is 817 feet.
Population: 69,817; Growth (since 2000): 5.4%; Density: 18,732.8 persons per square mile; Race: 40.4% White, 3.1% Black/African American, 14.1% Asian, 0.7% American Indian/Alaska Native, 0.1% Native Hawaiian/Other Pacific Islander, 4.3% Two or more races, 72.1% Hispanic of any race; Average household size: 3.81; Median age: 30.1; Age under 18: 29.3%; Age 65 and over: 7.3%; Males per 100 females: 101.1; Marriage status: 42.4% never married, 47.0% now married, 3.2% separated, 4.2% widowed, 6.4% divorced; Foreign born: 53.9%; Speak English only: 15.3%; With disability: 9.9%; Veterans: 1.7%; Ancestry: 2.5% Armenian, 1.3% American, 1.0% German, 0.8% Irish, 0.6% English
Employment: 7.2% management, business, and financial, 1.3% computer, engineering, and science, 5.1% education, legal, community service, arts, and media, 4.0% healthcare practitioners, 29.2% service, 22.3% sales and office, 14.2% natural resources, construction, and maintenance, 16.8% production, transportation, and material moving
Income: Per capita: $14,249; Median household: $40,186; Average household: $51,243; Households with income of $100,000 or more: 12.2%; Poverty rate: 27.7%
Educational Attainment: High school diploma or higher: 60.1%; Bachelor's degree or higher: 15.7%; Graduate/professional degree or higher: 2.6%

School District(s)

Los Angeles Unified (PK-12)
2012-13 Enrollment: 655,455 . . . . (213) 241-1000
Housing: Homeownership rate: 35.2%; Median home value: $279,100; Median year structure built: 1970; Homeowner vacancy rate: 2.5%; Median gross rent: $1,077 per month; Rental vacancy rate: 5.2%
Health Insurance: 67.0% have insurance; 32.7% have private insurance; 38.2% have public insurance; 33.0% do not have insurance; 14.1% of children under 18 do not have insurance
Hospitals: Kaiser Foundation Hospital - Panorama City (325 beds); Mission Community Hospital (120 beds)
Transportation: Commute: 77.8% car, 12.5% public transportation, 3.1% walk, 3.7% work from home; Median travel time to work: 32.5 minutes

PARAMOUNT (city). Covers a land area of 4.729 square miles and a water area of 0.111 square miles. Located at 33.90° N. Lat; 118.17° W. Long. Elevation is 69 feet.
History: Named for its main street, Paramount Blvd, which had been named for the motion picture company. Originally a dairy region, it has become highly industrialized since the 1950s. The city grew in 1950s and 1960s. Incorporated 1957.
Population: 54,098; Growth (since 2000): -2.1%; Density: 11,438.4 persons per square mile; Race: 42.5% White, 11.7% Black/African American, 3.0% Asian, 0.8% American Indian/Alaska Native, 0.8% Native Hawaiian/Other Pacific Islander, 4.2% Two or more races, 78.6% Hispanic of any race; Average household size: 3.87; Median age: 28.6; Age under 18: 32.6%; Age 65 and over: 6.3%; Males per 100 females: 94.7; Marriage

status: 44.4% never married, 44.6% now married, 2.7% separated, 3.8% widowed, 7.2% divorced; Foreign born: 37.8%; Speak English only: 24.0%; With disability: 8.8%; Veterans: 2.8%; Ancestry: 1.4% American, 1.1% English, 1.0% German, 0.7% Irish, 0.6% Italian

Employment: 7.8% management, business, and financial, 1.8% computer, engineering, and science, 6.0% education, legal, community service, arts, and media, 2.4% healthcare practitioners, 21.6% service, 24.9% sales and office, 9.7% natural resources, construction, and maintenance, 26.0% production, transportation, and material moving

Income: Per capita: $14,476; Median household: $44,934; Average household: $53,169; Households with income of $100,000 or more: 11.1%; Poverty rate: 22.1%

Educational Attainment: High school diploma or higher: 57.0%; Bachelor's degree or higher: 7.9%; Graduate/professional degree or higher: 1.7%

School District(s)

Paramount Unified (KG-12)
2012-13 Enrollment: 15,846 . . . . (562) 602-6000

Vocational/Technical School(s)

InfoTech Career College (Private, For-profit)
Fall 2013 Enrollment: 181 . . . . (562) 804-1239
2013-14 Tuition: $14,225

Housing: Homeownership rate: 43.4%; Median home value: $254,100; Median year structure built: 1968; Homeowner vacancy rate: 1.8%; Median gross rent: $1,172 per month; Rental vacancy rate: 4.8%

Health Insurance: 70.0% have insurance; 38.8% have private insurance; 34.3% have public insurance; 30.0% do not have insurance; 14.2% of children under 18 do not have insurance

Safety: Violent crime rate: 40.5 per 10,000 population; Property crime rate: 297.6 per 10,000 population

Transportation: Commute: 87.4% car, 5.2% public transportation, 3.3% walk, 2.7% work from home; Median travel time to work: 26.7 minutes

Additional Information Contacts

City of Paramount . . . . (562) 220-2000
http://www.paramountcity.com

PASADENA (city). Covers a land area of 22.970 square miles and a water area of 0.158 square miles. Located at 34.16° N. Lat; 118.14° W. Long. Elevation is 863 feet.

History: Named for the Chippewa Indian translation of "crown of the valley". The site of Pasadena was once part of the lands of the San Gabriel Mission, founded in 1771. After many changes of ownership, the land was purchased by a group called the California Colony of Indiana, led by Dr. Thomas B. Elliott of Indianapolis. In 1875 the group named their new townsite Pasadena. The city was incorporated in 1886, and received a charter in 1901. Pasadena soon became a center of culture and learning, with Throop University (later California Insitute of Technology) founded in 1891, and the Mt. Wilson Observatory established in 1904. Pasadena 's Tournament of Roses began in 1890 as a village festival celebrating the midwinter flowering season.

Population: 137,122; Growth (since 2000): 2.4%; Density: 5,969.6 persons per square mile; Race: 55.8% White, 10.7% Black/African American, 14.3% Asian, 0.6% American Indian/Alaska Native, 0.1% Native Hawaiian/Other Pacific Islander, 4.9% Two or more races, 33.7% Hispanic of any race; Average household size: 2.42; Median age: 37.2; Age under 18: 19.3%; Age 65 and over: 13.5%; Males per 100 females: 95.1; Marriage status: 39.5% never married, 45.2% now married, 2.6% separated, 6.1% widowed, 9.2% divorced; Foreign born: 30.5%; Speak English only: 55.4%; With disability: 9.7%; Veterans: 5.1%; Ancestry: 7.3% German, 6.2% Irish, 6.1% English, 3.8% Armenian, 3.3% Italian

Employment: 18.3% management, business, and financial, 8.7% computer, engineering, and science, 19.2% education, legal, community service, arts, and media, 6.5% healthcare practitioners, 15.4% service, 20.6% sales and office, 5.2% natural resources, construction, and maintenance, 6.0% production, transportation, and material moving

Income: Per capita: $41,152; Median household: $69,302; Average household: $99,695; Households with income of $100,000 or more: 34.9%; Poverty rate: 13.2%

Educational Attainment: High school diploma or higher: 85.8%; Bachelor's degree or higher: 48.7%; Graduate/professional degree or higher: 21.9%

School District(s)

Pasadena Unified (KG-12)
2012-13 Enrollment: 19,540 . . . . (626) 396-3600

Four-year College(s)

Art Center College of Design (Private, Not-for-profit)
Fall 2013 Enrollment: 1,985 . . . . (626) 396-2200
2013-14 Tuition: In-state $36,480; Out-of-state $36,480

California Institute of Technology (Private, Not-for-profit)
Fall 2013 Enrollment: 2,181 . . . . (626) 395-6811
2013-14 Tuition: In-state $41,538; Out-of-state $41,538

Fuller Theological Seminary in California (Private, Not-for-profit, Multiple Protestant Denomination)
Fall 2013 Enrollment: 2,694 . . . . (626) 584-5200

Pacific Oaks College (Private, Not-for-profit)
Fall 2013 Enrollment: 1,072 . . . . (626) 529-8500

Providence Christian College (Private, Not-for-profit, Undenominational)
Fall 2013 Enrollment: 66 . . . . (626) 696-4000
2013-14 Tuition: In-state $24,222; Out-of-state $24,222

Two-year College(s)

Le Cordon Bleu College of Culinary Arts-Pasadena (Private, For-profit)
Fall 2013 Enrollment: 1,739 . . . . (626) 229-1300
2013-14 Tuition: In-state $13,049; Out-of-state $13,049

Los Angeles Music Academy (Private, For-profit)
Fall 2013 Enrollment: 148 . . . . (626) 568-8850
2013-14 Tuition: In-state $22,575; Out-of-state $22,575

Pasadena City College (Public)
Fall 2013 Enrollment: 25,268 . . . . (626) 585-7123
2013-14 Tuition: In-state $1,152; Out-of-state $6,168

Vocational/Technical School(s)

North-West College-Pasadena (Private, For-profit)
Fall 2013 Enrollment: 193 . . . . (626) 796-5815
2013-14 Tuition: $28,650

Housing: Homeownership rate: 45.0%; Median home value: $601,500; Median year structure built: 1957; Homeowner vacancy rate: 2.3%; Median gross rent: $1,348 per month; Rental vacancy rate: 6.6%

Health Insurance: 82.9% have insurance; 65.6% have private insurance; 25.1% have public insurance; 17.1% do not have insurance; 9.3% of children under 18 do not have insurance

Hospitals: Huntington Memorial Hospital (606 beds)

Safety: Violent crime rate: 31.2 per 10,000 population; Property crime rate: 271.9 per 10,000 population

Newspapers: Pasadena Star-News (daily circulation 29700); Pasadena Weekly (weekly circulation 35000)

Transportation: Commute: 80.4% car, 6.4% public transportation, 4.6% walk, 5.6% work from home; Median travel time to work: 26.1 minutes; Amtrak: Bus service available.

Additional Information Contacts

City of Pasadena . . . . (626) 744-4000
http://www.ci.pasadena.ca.us

PEARBLOSSOM (unincorporated postal area)

ZCTA: 93553

Covers a land area of 86.491 square miles and a water area of 0.103 square miles. Located at 34.41° N. Lat; 117.91° W. Long. Elevation is 3,048 feet.

Population: 2,138; Growth (since 2000): 33.6%; Density: 24.7 persons per square mile; Race: 76.1% White, 3.8% Black/African American, 2.0% Asian, 1.3% American Indian/Alaska Native, 0.1% Native Hawaiian/Other Pacific Islander, 4.1% Two or more races, 25.8% Hispanic of any race; Average household size: 2.62; Median age: 43.3; Age under 18: 21.9%; Age 65 and over: 14.7%; Males per 100 females: 110.2

School District(s)

Keppel Union Elementary (KG-08)
2012-13 Enrollment: 2,747 . . . . (661) 944-2155

Housing: Homeownership rate: 68.3%; Homeowner vacancy rate: 2.3%; Rental vacancy rate: 8.5%

PICO RIVERA (city). Covers a land area of 8.296 square miles and a water area of 0.586 square miles. Located at 33.99° N. Lat; 118.09° W. Long. Elevation is 164 feet.

History: Named for the union of the towns of Pico (for Pio Pico, Mexican governor of California) and Rivera. Pio Pico State Historical Park to East. Incorporated 1958 with the union of Pico and Rivera into one community.

Population: 62,942; Growth (since 2000): -0.8%; Density: 7,587.5 persons per square mile; Race: 59.4% White, 1.0% Black/African American, 2.6% Asian, 1.4% American Indian/Alaska Native, 0.1% Native Hawaiian/Other Pacific Islander, 3.7% Two or more races, 91.2% Hispanic of any race; Average household size: 3.77; Median age: 34.0; Age under 18: 26.7%;

Age 65 and over: 12.1%; Males per 100 females: 95.5; Marriage status: 39.6% never married, 46.6% now married, 3.1% separated, 5.5% widowed, 8.3% divorced; Foreign born: 33.2%; Speak English only: 26.0%; With disability: 10.4%; Veterans: 4.9%; Ancestry: 1.5% American, 0.9% German, 0.9% Irish, 0.6% Italian, 0.5% French

Employment: 8.8% management, business, and financial, 1.5% computer, engineering, and science, 7.6% education, legal, community service, arts, and media, 2.4% healthcare practitioners, 20.9% service, 28.6% sales and office, 9.0% natural resources, construction, and maintenance, 21.2% production, transportation, and material moving

Income: Per capita: $18,971; Median household: $57,550; Average household: $67,116; Households with income of $100,000 or more: 20.1%; Poverty rate: 13.0%

Educational Attainment: High school diploma or higher: 67.5%; Bachelor's degree or higher: 10.9%; Graduate/professional degree or higher: 2.4%

School District(s)

El Rancho Unified (KG-12)
2012-13 Enrollment: 9,648 . . . . (562) 942-1500
Montebello Unified (KG-12)
2012-13 Enrollment: 30,564 . . . . (323) 887-7900

Vocational/Technical School(s)

David's Academy of Beauty (Private, For-profit)
Fall 2013 Enrollment: 199 . . . . (562) 949-1100
2013-14 Tuition: $11,480

Housing: Homeownership rate: 69.1%; Median home value: $330,100; Median year structure built: 1956; Homeowner vacancy rate: 1.0%; Median gross rent: $1,256 per month; Rental vacancy rate: 4.1%

Health Insurance: 75.5% have insurance; 51.6% have private insurance; 29.4% have public insurance; 24.5% do not have insurance; 10.1% of children under 18 do not have insurance

Safety: Violent crime rate: 32.5 per 10,000 population; Property crime rate: 238.7 per 10,000 population

Transportation: Commute: 89.2% car, 3.3% public transportation, 1.7% walk, 3.8% work from home; Median travel time to work: 29.1 minutes

Additional Information Contacts

City of Pico Rivera. . . . . (562) 942-2000
http://www.ci.pico-rivera.ca.us

PLAYA DEL REY (unincorporated postal area)

ZCTA: 90293

Covers a land area of 2.865 square miles and a water area of 1.539 square miles. Located at 33.95° N. Lat; 118.44° W. Long. Elevation is 20 feet.

Population: 12,132; Growth (since 2000): 7.8%; Density: 4,234.6 persons per square mile; Race: 76.0% White, 5.7% Black/African American, 10.0% Asian, 0.3% American Indian/Alaska Native, 0.2% Native Hawaiian/Other Pacific Islander, 5.4% Two or more races, 10.6% Hispanic of any race; Average household size: 1.83; Median age: 40.4; Age under 18: 9.6%; Age 65 and over: 13.0%; Males per 100 females: 94.4; Marriage status: 42.4% never married, 38.8% now married, 1.0% separated, 4.4% widowed, 14.3% divorced; Foreign born: 20.0%; Speak English only: 77.7%; With disability: 7.2%; Veterans: 6.3%; Ancestry: 11.4% German, 10.5% Irish, 8.2% Italian, 6.7% English, 5.6% American

Employment: 23.1% management, business, and financial, 11.3% computer, engineering, and science, 24.4% education, legal, community service, arts, and media, 5.0% healthcare practitioners, 10.3% service, 19.8% sales and office, 3.0% natural resources, construction, and maintenance, 3.1% production, transportation, and material moving

Income: Per capita: $62,160; Median household: $87,308; Average household: $112,339; Households with income of $100,000 or more: 42.9%; Poverty rate: 6.7%

Educational Attainment: High school diploma or higher: 96.8%; Bachelor's degree or higher: 64.2%; Graduate/professional degree or higher: 24.2%

School District(s)

Los Angeles Unified (PK-12)
2012-13 Enrollment: 655,455 . . . . (213) 241-1000

Housing: Homeownership rate: 45.6%; Median home value: $496,400; Median year structure built: 1974; Homeowner vacancy rate: 1.1%; Median gross rent: $1,838 per month; Rental vacancy rate: 5.3%

Health Insurance: 88.1% have insurance; 82.4% have private insurance; 15.6% have public insurance; 11.9% do not have insurance; 2.8% of children under 18 do not have insurance

Transportation: Commute: 86.7% car, 1.3% public transportation, 0.8% walk, 9.2% work from home; Median travel time to work: 26.6 minutes

PLAYA VISTA (unincorporated postal area)

ZCTA: 90094

Covers a land area of 0.611 square miles and a water area of 0 square miles. Located at 33.98° N. Lat; 118.42° W. Long. Elevation is 7 feet.

Population: 5,464; Growth (since 2000): n/a; Density: 8,942.0 persons per square mile; Race: 57.2% White, 11.4% Black/African American, 22.1% Asian, 0.3% American Indian/Alaska Native, 0.2% Native Hawaiian/Other Pacific Islander, 6.4% Two or more races, 10.0% Hispanic of any race; Average household size: 1.85; Median age: 33.7; Age under 18: 12.8%; Age 65 and over: 6.8%; Males per 100 females: 88.1; Marriage status: 45.4% never married, 41.6% now married, 0.6% separated, 2.1% widowed, 10.9% divorced; Foreign born: 23.6%; Speak English only: 70.9%; With disability: 3.4%; Veterans: 2.4%; Ancestry: 13.0% German, 8.2% Irish, 7.0% English, 6.1% Italian, 5.1% Polish

Employment: 37.9% management, business, and financial, 6.2% computer, engineering, and science, 23.0% education, legal, community service, arts, and media, 7.5% healthcare practitioners, 4.8% service, 19.0% sales and office, 1.2% natural resources, construction, and maintenance, 0.4% production, transportation, and material moving

Income: Per capita: $72,234; Median household: $91,042; Average household: $144,437; Households with income of $100,000 or more: 49.3%; Poverty rate: 7.7%

Educational Attainment: High school diploma or higher: 99.3%; Bachelor's degree or higher: 80.8%; Graduate/professional degree or higher: 40.1%

Housing: Homeownership rate: 45.3%; Median home value: $645,900; Median year structure built: 2005; Homeowner vacancy rate: 3.1%; Median gross rent: $2,000+ per month; Rental vacancy rate: 5.5%

Health Insurance: 89.4% have insurance; 85.3% have private insurance; 10.4% have public insurance; 10.6% do not have insurance; 14.1% of children under 18 do not have insurance

Transportation: Commute: 92.1% car, 1.9% public transportation, 1.4% walk, 3.3% work from home; Median travel time to work: 27.0 minutes

POMONA (city). Covers a land area of 22.952 square miles and a water area of 0.012 square miles. Located at 34.06° N. Lat; 117.76° W. Long. Elevation is 850 feet.

History: Named for the Roman goddess of orchards and gardens, the result of a name contest. Pomona was founded in 1875. It developed as a fruit-shipping point for the surrounding citrus-growing area after the Pomona Land and Water Company was formed in 1882.

Population: 149,058; Growth (since 2000): -0.3%; Density: 6,494.5 persons per square mile; Race: 48.0% White, 7.3% Black/African American, 8.5% Asian, 1.2% American Indian/Alaska Native, 0.2% Native Hawaiian/Other Pacific Islander, 4.5% Two or more races, 70.5% Hispanic of any race; Average household size: 3.77; Median age: 29.5; Age under 18: 29.4%; Age 65 and over: 7.6%; Males per 100 females: 100.0; Marriage status: 42.9% never married, 44.9% now married, 3.1% separated, 4.5% widowed, 7.7% divorced; Foreign born: 34.5%; Speak English only: 35.3%; With disability: 8.1%; Veterans: 3.5%; Ancestry: 3.3% German, 2.8% Irish, 1.8% English, 1.7% Italian, 1.5% American

Employment: 8.7% management, business, and financial, 2.9% computer, engineering, and science, 7.8% education, legal, community service, arts, and media, 2.7% healthcare practitioners, 21.7% service, 25.8% sales and office, 11.0% natural resources, construction, and maintenance, 19.5% production, transportation, and material moving

Income: Per capita: $17,035; Median household: $49,474; Average household: $61,755; Households with income of $100,000 or more: 16.2%; Poverty rate: 21.6%

Educational Attainment: High school diploma or higher: 66.3%; Bachelor's degree or higher: 16.5%; Graduate/professional degree or higher: 4.9%

School District(s)

Los Angeles County Office of Education (KG-12)
2012-13 Enrollment: 9,136 . . . . (562) 922-6111
Nuview Union (KG-12)
2012-13 Enrollment: 2,345 . . . . (951) 928-0066
Pomona Unified (PK-12)
2012-13 Enrollment: 27,186 . . . . (909) 397-4800
San Antonio Rop
2012-13 Enrollment: n/a . . . . (909) 469-2304

Sbe - the School of Arts and Enterprise (09-12)
2012-13 Enrollment: 419 . . . . (909) 622-0699

Four-year College(s)

California State Polytechnic University-Pomona (Public)
Fall 2013 Enrollment: 22,501 . . . . (909) 869-7659
2013-14 Tuition: In-state $6,350; Out-of-state $17,510
DeVry University-California (Private, For-profit)
Fall 2013 Enrollment: 9,156 . . . . (909) 622-8866
2013-14 Tuition: In-state $16,010; Out-of-state $16,010
St Luke University (Private, Not-for-profit)
Fall 2013 Enrollment: n/a . . . . (909) 623-0302
Western University of Health Sciences (Private, Not-for-profit)
Fall 2013 Enrollment: 3,748 . . . . (909) 623-6116

Two-year College(s)

Carrington College California-Pomona (Private, For-profit)
Fall 2013 Enrollment: 301 . . . . (909) 868-5800

Vocational/Technical School(s)

North-West College-Pomona (Private, For-profit)
Fall 2013 Enrollment: 280 . . . . (909) 623-1552
2013-14 Tuition: $28,525
Pomona Unified School District Adult and Career Education (Public)
Fall 2013 Enrollment: 471 . . . . (909) 469-2333
2013-14 Tuition: $7,000
Thuy Princess Beauty College (Private, For-profit)
Fall 2013 Enrollment: 77 . . . . (909) 620-6893
2013-14 Tuition: $1,150

Housing: Homeownership rate: 55.1%; Median home value: $258,700; Median year structure built: 1965; Homeowner vacancy rate: 2.0%; Median gross rent: $1,104 per month; Rental vacancy rate: 5.9%

Health Insurance: 74.0% have insurance; 44.4% have private insurance; 33.4% have public insurance; 26.0% do not have insurance; 10.0% of children under 18 do not have insurance

Hospitals: Pomona Valley Hospital Medical Center (453 beds)

Safety: Violent crime rate: 53.4 per 10,000 population; Property crime rate: 290.3 per 10,000 population

Transportation: Commute: 88.6% car, 3.4% public transportation, 2.5% walk, 3.6% work from home; Median travel time to work: 29.1 minutes; Amtrak: Train service available.

Additional Information Contacts

City of Pomona . . . . (909) 620-2311
http://www.ci.pomona.ca.us

PORTER RANCH (unincorporated postal area)

ZCTA: 91326

Covers a land area of 8.159 square miles and a water area of 0.008 square miles. Located at 34.28° N. Lat; 118.56° W. Long..

Population: 33,708; Growth (since 2000): 20.2%; Density: 4,131.4 persons per square mile; Race: 58.7% White, 3.5% Black/African American, 29.6% Asian, 0.2% American Indian/Alaska Native, 0.1% Native Hawaiian/Other Pacific Islander, 4.0% Two or more races, 13.4% Hispanic of any race; Average household size: 2.86; Median age: 42.7; Age under 18: 21.2%; Age 65 and over: 15.5%; Males per 100 females: 94.7; Marriage status: 26.9% never married, 61.0% now married, 1.5% separated, 5.0% widowed, 7.1% divorced; Foreign born: 36.4%; Speak English only: 51.1%; With disability: 8.6%; Veterans: 5.2%; Ancestry: 7.8% Armenian, 6.3% German, 4.8% Italian, 4.4% Irish, 4.1% English

Employment: 23.5% management, business, and financial, 7.5% computer, engineering, and science, 17.5% education, legal, community service, arts, and media, 6.7% healthcare practitioners, 9.0% service, 26.8% sales and office, 3.3% natural resources, construction, and maintenance, 5.7% production, transportation, and material moving

Income: Per capita: $42,685; Median household: $99,230; Average household: $122,968; Households with income of $100,000 or more: 49.3%; Poverty rate: 7.3%

Educational Attainment: High school diploma or higher: 94.4%; Bachelor's degree or higher: 53.3%; Graduate/professional degree or higher: 17.9%

Housing: Homeownership rate: 77.8%; Median home value: $611,800; Median year structure built: 1977; Homeowner vacancy rate: 1.2%; Median gross rent: $1,692 per month; Rental vacancy rate: 7.0%

Health Insurance: 89.2% have insurance; 76.6% have private insurance; 22.2% have public insurance; 10.8% do not have insurance; 6.3% of children under 18 do not have insurance

Transportation: Commute: 88.5% car, 2.4% public transportation, 0.9% walk, 6.2% work from home; Median travel time to work: 33.0 minutes

QUARTZ HILL (CDP).

Covers a land area of 3.762 square miles and a water area of <.001 square miles. Located at 34.65° N. Lat; 118.22° W. Long. Elevation is 2,497 feet.

Population: 10,912; Growth (since 2000): 10.3%; Density: 2,900.8 persons per square mile; Race: 75.3% White, 7.3% Black/African American, 2.8% Asian, 1.3% American Indian/Alaska Native, 0.3% Native Hawaiian/Other Pacific Islander, 4.4% Two or more races, 24.6% Hispanic of any race; Average household size: 2.93; Median age: 36.6; Age under 18: 26.7%; Age 65 and over: 10.1%; Males per 100 females: 97.4; Marriage status: 33.6% never married, 49.3% now married, 2.4% separated, 6.0% widowed, 11.1% divorced; Foreign born: 8.0%; Speak English only: 85.9%; With disability: 9.5%; Veterans: 12.3%; Ancestry: 12.3% German, 10.4% English, 8.2% Irish, 5.9% Italian, 5.4% American

Employment: 11.2% management, business, and financial, 4.7% computer, engineering, and science, 12.6% education, legal, community service, arts, and media, 4.9% healthcare practitioners, 23.9% service, 22.8% sales and office, 13.8% natural resources, construction, and maintenance, 6.0% production, transportation, and material moving

Income: Per capita: $22,652; Median household: $51,821; Average household: $65,286; Households with income of $100,000 or more: 20.0%; Poverty rate: 19.1%

Educational Attainment: High school diploma or higher: 87.9%; Bachelor's degree or higher: 16.5%; Graduate/professional degree or higher: 7.0%

School District(s)

Antelope Valley Union High (09-12)
2012-13 Enrollment: 24,816 . . . . (661) 948-7655
Westside Union Elementary (KG-08)
2012-13 Enrollment: 8,645 . . . . (661) 722-0716

Housing: Homeownership rate: 69.6%; Median home value: $192,400; Median year structure built: 1978; Homeowner vacancy rate: 2.0%; Median gross rent: $976 per month; Rental vacancy rate: 8.5%

Health Insurance: 83.1% have insurance; 64.5% have private insurance; 28.4% have public insurance; 16.9% do not have insurance; 11.0% of children under 18 do not have insurance

Transportation: Commute: 94.3% car, 1.6% public transportation, 0.0% walk, 3.4% work from home; Median travel time to work: 30.1 minutes

RANCHO PALOS VERDES (city).

Covers a land area of 13.465 square miles and a water area of <.001 square miles. Located at 33.75° N. Lat; 118.37° W. Long. Elevation is 220 feet.

History: This city was incorporated on September 7, 1973 and is considered a wealthy suburb of Los Angeles. Its name means "Ranch of Green Trees" or "Ranch of the Green Sticks."

Population: 41,643; Growth (since 2000): 1.2%; Density: 3,092.7 persons per square mile; Race: 61.7% White, 2.4% Black/African American, 29.0% Asian, 0.2% American Indian/Alaska Native, 0.1% Native Hawaiian/Other Pacific Islander, 4.8% Two or more races, 8.5% Hispanic of any race; Average household size: 2.65; Median age: 47.8; Age under 18: 22.2%; Age 65 and over: 23.2%; Males per 100 females: 94.3; Marriage status: 20.8% never married, 64.3% now married, 1.2% separated, 7.5% widowed, 7.4% divorced; Foreign born: 27.2%; Speak English only: 68.2%; With disability: 9.4%; Veterans: 9.3%; Ancestry: 11.2% German, 9.8% English, 8.3% Irish, 7.2% Italian, 4.3% American

Employment: 27.7% management, business, and financial, 10.5% computer, engineering, and science, 14.8% education, legal, community service, arts, and media, 9.5% healthcare practitioners, 6.4% service, 23.7% sales and office, 2.4% natural resources, construction, and maintenance, 5.1% production, transportation, and material moving

Income: Per capita: $57,733; Median household: $118,893; Average household: $154,268; Households with income of $100,000 or more: 58.3%; Poverty rate: 4.5%

Educational Attainment: High school diploma or higher: 97.7%; Bachelor's degree or higher: 64.9%; Graduate/professional degree or higher: 29.8%

School District(s)

Los Angeles Unified (PK-12)
2012-13 Enrollment: 655,455 . . . . (213) 241-1000
Palos Verdes Peninsula Unified (KG-12)
2012-13 Enrollment: 11,864 . . . . (310) 378-9966

Four-year College(s)

Marymount California University (Private, Not-for-profit, Roman Catholic)
Fall 2013 Enrollment: 1,037 . . . . (310) 377-5501
2013-14 Tuition: In-state $30,579; Out-of-state $30,579

Housing: Homeownership rate: 80.2%; Median home value: $945,400; Median year structure built: 1967; Homeowner vacancy rate: 0.6%; Median gross rent: $2,000+ per month; Rental vacancy rate: 6.4%
Health Insurance: 95.5% have insurance; 87.0% have private insurance; 25.4% have public insurance; 4.5% do not have insurance; 1.5% of children under 18 do not have insurance
Safety: Violent crime rate: 7.1 per 10,000 population; Property crime rate: 136.3 per 10,000 population
Transportation: Commute: 89.0% car, 1.6% public transportation, 0.3% walk, 8.2% work from home; Median travel time to work: 32.2 minutes
Additional Information Contacts
City of Rancho Palos Verdes . . . . (310) 377-0360
http://www.palosverdes.com/rpv

REDONDO BEACH (city). Covers a land area of 6.198 square miles and a water area of 0.010 square miles. Located at 33.86° N. Lat; 118.38° W. Long. Elevation is 62 feet.
History: Named for the Spanish translation of "round". Redondo Beach began in 1905 when rumors spread that railroad tycoon Henry E. Huntington would pour millions into improvements. Those who were successful in their bids for lots were disappointed when the rumor proved untrue.
Population: 66,748; Growth (since 2000): 5.5%; Density: 10,768.7 persons per square mile; Race: 74.6% White, 2.8% Black/African American, 12.0% Asian, 0.4% American Indian/Alaska Native, 0.3% Native Hawaiian/Other Pacific Islander, 5.8% Two or more races, 15.2% Hispanic of any race; Average household size: 2.29; Median age: 39.3; Age under 18: 19.3%; Age 65 and over: 10.5%; Males per 100 females: 99.1; Marriage status: 31.8% never married, 52.2% now married, 1.8% separated, 4.2% widowed, 11.8% divorced; Foreign born: 18.8%; Speak English only: 75.0%; With disability: 6.7%; Veterans: 6.1%; Ancestry: 14.7% German, 12.0% Irish, 9.4% English, 6.9% Italian, 6.4% American
Employment: 26.7% management, business, and financial, 10.2% computer, engineering, and science, 13.7% education, legal, community service, arts, and media, 5.5% healthcare practitioners, 11.1% service, 24.3% sales and office, 3.9% natural resources, construction, and maintenance, 4.5% production, transportation, and material moving
Income: Per capita: $53,689; Median household: $99,496; Average household: $124,292; Households with income of $100,000 or more: 49.7%; Poverty rate: 5.4%
Educational Attainment: High school diploma or higher: 95.7%; Bachelor's degree or higher: 58.0%; Graduate/professional degree or higher: 22.5%

School District(s)
Redondo Beach Unified (KG-12)
2012-13 Enrollment: 8,967 . . . . (310) 379-5449
Housing: Homeownership rate: 51.4%; Median home value: $715,000; Median year structure built: 1971; Homeowner vacancy rate: 0.9%; Median gross rent: $1,679 per month; Rental vacancy rate: 5.3%
Health Insurance: 91.3% have insurance; 82.1% have private insurance; 16.6% have public insurance; 8.7% do not have insurance; 2.8% of children under 18 do not have insurance
Safety: Violent crime rate: 23.5 per 10,000 population; Property crime rate: 233.6 per 10,000 population
Transportation: Commute: 86.8% car, 1.3% public transportation, 1.6% walk, 7.3% work from home; Median travel time to work: 28.0 minutes
Additional Information Contacts
City of Redondo Beach . . . . (310) 372-1171
http://www.redondo.org/default.asp

RESEDA (unincorporated postal area)
ZCTA: 91335
Covers a land area of 6.565 square miles and a water area of 0.031 square miles. Located at 34.20° N. Lat; 118.54° W. Long. Elevation is 738 feet.
Population: 74,363; Growth (since 2000): 9.4%; Density: 11,328.0 persons per square mile; Race: 53.8% White, 4.1% Black/African American, 12.4% Asian, 0.7% American Indian/Alaska Native, 0.1% Native Hawaiian/Other Pacific Islander, 5.2% Two or more races, 50.6% Hispanic of any race; Average household size: 3.21; Median age: 35.5; Age under 18: 23.7%; Age 65 and over: 11.1%; Males per 100 females: 96.9; Marriage status: 39.2% never married, 44.3% now married, 2.7% separated, 6.4% widowed, 10.1% divorced; Foreign born: 46.1%; Speak English only: 30.8%; With disability: 10.7%; Veterans: 2.9%; Ancestry: 3.9% German, 3.1% Armenian, 3.0% Irish, 3.0% Iranian, 2.8% Italian
Employment: 11.0% management, business, and financial, 4.1% computer, engineering, and science, 9.2% education, legal, community service, arts, and media, 4.0% healthcare practitioners, 25.6% service, 25.0% sales and office, 10.2% natural resources, construction, and maintenance, 10.8% production, transportation, and material moving
Income: Per capita: $20,674; Median household: $51,266; Average household: $64,448; Households with income of $100,000 or more: 20.7%; Poverty rate: 17.2%
Educational Attainment: High school diploma or higher: 74.7%; Bachelor's degree or higher: 22.6%; Graduate/professional degree or higher: 6.3%

School District(s)
Los Angeles Unified (PK-12)
2012-13 Enrollment: 655,455 . . . . (213) 241-1000

Four-year College(s)
Annenberg School of Nursing (Private, Not-for-profit)
Fall 2013 Enrollment: 12 . . . . (818) 757-4431
Everest College-Reseda (Private, For-profit)
Fall 2013 Enrollment: 696 . . . . (818) 774-0550
2013-14 Tuition: In-state $14,365; Out-of-state $14,365

Two-year College(s)
Annenberg School of Nursing (Private, Not-for-profit)
Fall 2013 Enrollment: 12 . . . . (818) 757-4431
Everest College-Reseda (Private, For-profit)
Fall 2013 Enrollment: 696 . . . . (818) 774-0550
2013-14 Tuition: In-state $14,365; Out-of-state $14,365

Vocational/Technical School(s)
Annenberg School of Nursing (Private, Not-for-profit)
Fall 2013 Enrollment: 12 . . . . (818) 757-4431
2013-14 Tuition: $28,390
Everest College-Reseda (Private, For-profit)
Fall 2013 Enrollment: 696 . . . . (818) 774-0550
2013-14 Tuition: In-state $14,365; Out-of-state $14,365
Housing: Homeownership rate: 51.5%; Median home value: $332,900; Median year structure built: 1961; Homeowner vacancy rate: 1.6%; Median gross rent: $1,186 per month; Rental vacancy rate: 6.5%
Health Insurance: 72.7% have insurance; 45.9% have private insurance; 31.8% have public insurance; 27.3% do not have insurance; 11.0% of children under 18 do not have insurance
Transportation: Commute: 82.6% car, 6.8% public transportation, 2.7% walk, 4.9% work from home; Median travel time to work: 29.0 minutes

ROLLING HILLS (city). Covers a land area of 2.991 square miles and a water area of 0 square miles. Located at 33.76° N. Lat; 118.35° W. Long. Elevation is 1,276 feet.
Population: 1,860; Growth (since 2000): -0.6%; Density: 622.0 persons per square mile; Race: 77.3% White, 1.6% Black/African American, 16.3% Asian, 0.3% American Indian/Alaska Native, 0.1% Native Hawaiian/Other Pacific Islander, 3.2% Two or more races, 5.5% Hispanic of any race; Average household size: 2.81; Median age: 51.7; Age under 18: 21.7%; Age 65 and over: 27.6%; Males per 100 females: 91.8

School District(s)
Palos Verdes Peninsula Unified (KG-12)
2012-13 Enrollment: 11,864 . . . . (310) 378-9966
Housing: Homeownership rate: 95.8%; Homeowner vacancy rate: 1.4%; Rental vacancy rate: 3.4%
Safety: Violent crime rate: 0.0 per 10,000 population; Property crime rate: 58.1 per 10,000 population
Additional Information Contacts
City of Rolling Hills . . . . (310) 377-1521
http://www.rolling-hills.org

ROLLING HILLS ESTATES (city). Covers a land area of 3.569 square miles and a water area of 0.044 square miles. Located at 33.78° N. Lat; 118.33° W. Long. Elevation is 469 feet.
History: Officially a part of Los Angeles County's 60th municipality on September 18, 1957, The incorporation of other areas, especially between the years of 1959 and 1982, into the city lines of Rolling Hills Estates began in the city's early years. At the time, such expansion seemed to threaten the atmosphere its citizens cherished and wanted to preserve.
Population: 8,067; Growth (since 2000): 5.1%; Density: 2,260.1 persons per square mile; Race: 67.7% White, 1.4% Black/African American, 24.9% Asian, 0.2% American Indian/Alaska Native, 0.1% Native Hawaiian/Other Pacific Islander, 4.2% Two or more races, 6.2% Hispanic of any race; Average household size: 2.72; Median age: 48.5; Age under 18: 23.4%;

Age 65 and over: 23.2%; Males per 100 females: 93.0; Marriage status: 19.2% never married, 68.8% now married, 0.4% separated, 5.8% widowed, 6.3% divorced; Foreign born: 25.0%; Speak English only: 73.4%; With disability: 8.2%; Veterans: 8.4%; Ancestry: 14.6% English, 13.3% German, 10.0% Irish, 6.3% Italian, 4.6% American
Employment: 32.4% management, business, and financial, 11.3% computer, engineering, and science, 16.5% education, legal, community service, arts, and media, 9.7% healthcare practitioners, 4.1% service, 22.7% sales and office, 1.5% natural resources, construction, and maintenance, 1.7% production, transportation, and material moving
Income: Per capita: $67,043; Median household: $143,958; Average household: $183,111; Households with income of $100,000 or more: 62.2%; Poverty rate: 3.5%
Educational Attainment: High school diploma or higher: 97.6%; Bachelor's degree or higher: 69.1%; Graduate/professional degree or higher: 30.9%

School District(s)

Palos Verdes Peninsula Unified (KG-12)
2012-13 Enrollment: 11,864 . . . . (310) 378-9966
Housing: Homeownership rate: 91.5%; Median home value: $997,900; Median year structure built: 1967; Homeowner vacancy rate: 1.8%; Median gross rent: $2,000+ per month; Rental vacancy rate: 4.9%
Health Insurance: 97.2% have insurance; 87.9% have private insurance; 23.7% have public insurance; 2.8% do not have insurance; 3.1% of children under 18 do not have insurance
Safety: Violent crime rate: 3.6 per 10,000 population; Property crime rate: 143.4 per 10,000 population
Newspapers: Peninsula News (weekly circulation 15000)
Transportation: Commute: 87.6% car, 0.5% public transportation, 1.1% walk, 9.1% work from home; Median travel time to work: 29.1 minutes
Additional Information Contacts
City of Rolling Hills Estates . . . . (310) 377-1577
http://www.ci.rolling-hills-estates.ca.us

ROSE HILLS (CDP). Covers a land area of 0.439 square miles and a water area of 0 square miles. Located at 34.01° N. Lat; 118.04° W. Long.
Population: 2,803; Growth (since 2000): n/a; Density: 6,386.4 persons per square mile; Race: 56.1% White, 1.9% Black/African American, 15.7% Asian, 0.3% American Indian/Alaska Native, 0.0% Native Hawaiian/Other Pacific Islander, 9.1% Two or more races, 58.8% Hispanic of any race; Average household size: 2.76; Median age: 41.7; Age under 18: 19.3%; Age 65 and over: 13.4%; Males per 100 females: 92.5; Marriage status: 32.6% never married, 48.4% now married, 2.9% separated, 5.6% widowed, 13.5% divorced; Foreign born: 19.5%; Speak English only: 51.8%; With disability: 9.1%; Veterans: 3.5%; Ancestry: 7.8% Irish, 7.7% English, 5.7% German, 4.6% Armenian, 4.2% Other Arab
Employment: 24.9% management, business, and financial, 3.6% computer, engineering, and science, 17.3% education, legal, community service, arts, and media, 3.2% healthcare practitioners, 11.9% service, 28.1% sales and office, 7.1% natural resources, construction, and maintenance, 3.9% production, transportation, and material moving
Income: Per capita: $44,014; Median household: $94,913; Average household: $127,311; Households with income of $100,000 or more: 47.9%; Poverty rate: 8.5%
Educational Attainment: High school diploma or higher: 91.6%; Bachelor's degree or higher: 37.2%; Graduate/professional degree or higher: 19.5%
Housing: Homeownership rate: 88.1%; Median home value: $543,000; Median year structure built: 1981; Homeowner vacancy rate: 1.1%; Median gross rent: $1,600 per month; Rental vacancy rate: 5.5%
Health Insurance: 86.9% have insurance; 71.3% have private insurance; 23.8% have public insurance; 13.1% do not have insurance; 4.3% of children under 18 do not have insurance
Transportation: Commute: 96.8% car, 0.9% public transportation, 0.0% walk, 0.6% work from home; Median travel time to work: 31.8 minutes

---

ROSEMEAD (city). Covers a land area of 5.162 square miles and a water area of 0.014 square miles. Located at 34.07° N. Lat; 118.08° W. Long. Elevation is 318 feet.
History: Named for Leonard J. Rose's horse farm, which was located on his Sunny Slope estate in the city. Rosemead grew in the 1960s and 1970s. Founded 1867. Incorporated 1959.
Population: 53,764; Growth (since 2000): 0.5%; Density: 10,414.9 persons per square mile; Race: 21.1% White, 0.5% Black/African American, 60.7% Asian, 0.7% American Indian/Alaska Native, 0.1% Native Hawaiian/Other Pacific Islander, 2.2% Two or more races, 33.8% Hispanic of any race; Average household size: 3.74; Median age: 38.1; Age under 18: 22.7%; Age 65 and over: 13.0%; Males per 100 females: 97.3; Marriage status: 35.5% never married, 52.2% now married, 2.3% separated, 5.9% widowed, 6.4% divorced; Foreign born: 56.9%; Speak English only: 18.2%; With disability: 8.1%; Veterans: 2.5%; Ancestry: 1.4% American, 0.9% Italian, 0.9% German, 0.7% Irish, 0.6% English
Employment: 10.4% management, business, and financial, 4.0% computer, engineering, and science, 5.5% education, legal, community service, arts, and media, 3.4% healthcare practitioners, 25.0% service, 28.3% sales and office, 7.4% natural resources, construction, and maintenance, 16.0% production, transportation, and material moving
Income: Per capita: $17,669; Median household: $45,760; Average household: $61,340; Households with income of $100,000 or more: 15.8%; Poverty rate: 18.8%
Educational Attainment: High school diploma or higher: 62.9%; Bachelor's degree or higher: 14.4%; Graduate/professional degree or higher: 3.3%

School District(s)

El Monte Union High (09-12)
2012-13 Enrollment: 9,812 . . . . (626) 444-9005
Garvey Elementary (KG-08)
2012-13 Enrollment: 5,259 . . . . (626) 307-3444
Rosemead Elementary (KG-08)
2012-13 Enrollment: 2,778 . . . . (626) 312-2900

Four-year College(s)

University of the West (Private, Not-for-profit)
Fall 2013 Enrollment: 362 . . . . (626) 571-8811
2013-14 Tuition: In-state $9,486; Out-of-state $9,486

Vocational/Technical School(s)

Rosemead Beauty School (Private, For-profit)
Fall 2013 Enrollment: 210 . . . . (626) 286-2146
2013-14 Tuition: $9,139
Housing: Homeownership rate: 49.0%; Median home value: $421,700; Median year structure built: 1958; Homeowner vacancy rate: 0.9%; Median gross rent: $1,197 per month; Rental vacancy rate: 3.2%
Health Insurance: 74.3% have insurance; 43.3% have private insurance; 34.7% have public insurance; 25.7% do not have insurance; 11.2% of children under 18 do not have insurance
Safety: Violent crime rate: 27.3 per 10,000 population; Property crime rate: 195.5 per 10,000 population
Transportation: Commute: 89.1% car, 3.4% public transportation, 1.6% walk, 4.3% work from home; Median travel time to work: 27.8 minutes
Additional Information Contacts
City of Rosemead . . . . (626) 569-2100
http://www.cityofrosemead.org

ROWLAND HEIGHTS (CDP). Covers a land area of 13.076 square miles and a water area of 0.006 square miles. Located at 33.97° N. Lat; 117.89° W. Long. Elevation is 525 feet.
Population: 48,993; Growth (since 2000): 0.9%; Density: 3,746.8 persons per square mile; Race: 23.5% White, 1.6% Black/African American, 59.8% Asian, 0.4% American Indian/Alaska Native, 0.1% Native Hawaiian/Other Pacific Islander, 3.1% Two or more races, 27.0% Hispanic of any race; Average household size: 3.36; Median age: 40.2; Age under 18: 20.3%; Age 65 and over: 13.1%; Males per 100 females: 96.6; Marriage status: 33.5% never married, 54.7% now married, 1.4% separated, 4.9% widowed, 6.9% divorced; Foreign born: 57.0%; Speak English only: 26.6%; With disability: 7.7%; Veterans: 3.9%; Ancestry: 3.2% American, 2.0% English, 1.9% Irish, 1.5% German, 0.8% Italian
Employment: 17.0% management, business, and financial, 6.3% computer, engineering, and science, 6.8% education, legal, community service, arts, and media, 4.4% healthcare practitioners, 19.8% service, 31.4% sales and office, 4.7% natural resources, construction, and maintenance, 9.7% production, transportation, and material moving
Income: Per capita: $26,163; Median household: $62,631; Average household: $85,607; Households with income of $100,000 or more: 28.8%; Poverty rate: 10.6%
Educational Attainment: High school diploma or higher: 85.3%; Bachelor's degree or higher: 36.9%; Graduate/professional degree or higher: 9.0%

School District(s)

Rowland Unified (KG-12)
2012-13 Enrollment: 15,501 . . . . (626) 965-2541

Housing: Homeownership rate: 67.5%; Median home value: $472,900; Median year structure built: 1975; Homeowner vacancy rate: 0.8%; Median gross rent: $1,329 per month; Rental vacancy rate: 7.2%
Health Insurance: 77.1% have insurance; 56.0% have private insurance; 26.2% have public insurance; 22.9% do not have insurance; 6.9% of children under 18 do not have insurance
Transportation: Commute: 86.2% car, 4.2% public transportation, 2.6% walk, 5.1% work from home; Median travel time to work: 33.3 minutes

SAN DIMAS (city). Covers a land area of 15.037 square miles and a water area of 0.390 square miles. Located at 34.11° N. Lat; 117.81° W. Long. Elevation is 955 feet.
History: Named for St. Dismas, by the San Jose Land Company in 1886. Pacific Coast Baptist College; LaVerne College; California State Polytechnic University, Pomona, to south. Incorporated 1960.
Population: 33,371; Growth (since 2000): -4.6%; Density: 2,219.2 persons per square mile; Race: 72.0% White, 3.2% Black/African American, 10.5% Asian, 0.7% American Indian/Alaska Native, 0.1% Native Hawaiian/Other Pacific Islander, 4.9% Two or more races, 31.4% Hispanic of any race; Average household size: 2.73; Median age: 42.6; Age under 18: 20.9%; Age 65 and over: 15.5%; Males per 100 females: 90.5; Marriage status: 31.6% never married, 52.1% now married, 2.0% separated, 5.9% widowed, 10.3% divorced; Foreign born: 21.3%; Speak English only: 71.5%; With disability: 10.1%; Veterans: 9.0%; Ancestry: 10.5% German, 9.7% American, 7.2% English, 7.1% Irish, 6.0% Italian
Employment: 20.1% management, business, and financial, 6.7% computer, engineering, and science, 12.4% education, legal, community service, arts, and media, 3.6% healthcare practitioners, 14.3% service, 29.6% sales and office, 6.7% natural resources, construction, and maintenance, 6.7% production, transportation, and material moving
Income: Per capita: $35,232; Median household: $78,685; Average household: $97,756; Households with income of $100,000 or more: 38.0%; Poverty rate: 6.6%
Educational Attainment: High school diploma or higher: 92.3%; Bachelor's degree or higher: 34.4%; Graduate/professional degree or higher: 12.8%

School District(s)

Bonita Unified (KG-12)
2012-13 Enrollment: 9,870 . . . . (909) 971-8200
Los Angeles County Office of Education (KG-12)
2012-13 Enrollment: 9,136 . . . . (562) 922-6111

Four-year College(s)

ITT Technical Institute-San Dimas (Private, For-profit)
Fall 2013 Enrollment: 534 . . . . (909) 971-2300
2013-14 Tuition: In-state $18,048; Out-of-state $18,048
ITT Technical Institute-West Covina (Private, For-profit)
Fall 2013 Enrollment: 148 . . . . (909) 971-2300
2013-14 Tuition: In-state $18,048; Out-of-state $18,048
Life Pacific College (Private, Not-for-profit, Other Protestant)
Fall 2013 Enrollment: 627 . . . . (909) 599-5433
2013-14 Tuition: In-state $12,500; Out-of-state $12,500

Housing: Homeownership rate: 72.8%; Median home value: $424,700; Median year structure built: 1976; Homeowner vacancy rate: 1.1%; Median gross rent: $1,571 per month; Rental vacancy rate: 5.6%
Health Insurance: 86.9% have insurance; 72.2% have private insurance; 22.6% have public insurance; 13.1% do not have insurance; 5.0% of children under 18 do not have insurance
Hospitals: San Dimas Community Hospital (93 beds)
Safety: Violent crime rate: 19.2 per 10,000 population; Property crime rate: 208.5 per 10,000 population
Transportation: Commute: 86.9% car, 2.7% public transportation, 2.4% walk, 6.0% work from home; Median travel time to work: 32.6 minutes
Additional Information Contacts
City of San Dimas . . . . (909) 394-6200
http://www.cityofsandimas.com

SAN FERNANDO (city). Covers a land area of 2.374 square miles and a water area of 0 square miles. Located at 34.29° N. Lat; 118.44° W. Long. Elevation is 1,070 feet.
History: Named for Mission San Fernando Rey de Espana, which was named for Ferdinand III. San Fernando had its beginnings when Mission San Fernando Rey de Espana was founded in 1797 by Fathers Fermin de Lasuen and Francisco Dumetz. The town of San Fernando was once surrounded by citrus orchards.
Population: 23,645; Growth (since 2000): 0.3%; Density: 9,959.9 persons per square mile; Race: 51.0% White, 0.9% Black/African American, 1.0% Asian, 1.3% American Indian/Alaska Native, 0.1% Native Hawaiian/Other Pacific Islander, 3.7% Two or more races, 92.5% Hispanic of any race; Average household size: 3.94; Median age: 30.7; Age under 18: 29.4%; Age 65 and over: 8.4%; Males per 100 females: 100.7; Marriage status: 43.4% never married, 44.8% now married, 2.3% separated, 4.2% widowed, 7.5% divorced; Foreign born: 35.2%; Speak English only: 23.6%; With disability: 11.2%; Veterans: 3.1%; Ancestry: 1.5% Italian, 1.4% German, 1.1% Polish, 0.6% Scottish, 0.6% English
Employment: 9.4% management, business, and financial, 1.3% computer, engineering, and science, 9.2% education, legal, community service, arts, and media, 3.2% healthcare practitioners, 17.2% service, 28.6% sales and office, 14.7% natural resources, construction, and maintenance, 16.5% production, transportation, and material moving
Income: Per capita: $17,621; Median household: $55,192; Average household: $63,272; Households with income of $100,000 or more: 16.6%; Poverty rate: 16.9%
Educational Attainment: High school diploma or higher: 57.8%; Bachelor's degree or higher: 11.4%; Graduate/professional degree or higher: 3.3%

School District(s)

Los Angeles Unified (PK-12)
2012-13 Enrollment: 655,455 . . . . (213) 241-1000

Vocational/Technical School(s)

Academy of Esthetics and Cosmetology (Private, For-profit)
Fall 2013 Enrollment: 23 . . . . (818) 361-5501
2013-14 Tuition: $14,350

Housing: Homeownership rate: 54.5%; Median home value: $285,500; Median year structure built: 1956; Homeowner vacancy rate: 1.1%; Median gross rent: $1,158 per month; Rental vacancy rate: 3.9%
Health Insurance: 75.0% have insurance; 45.8% have private insurance; 33.0% have public insurance; 25.0% do not have insurance; 8.2% of children under 18 do not have insurance
Safety: Violent crime rate: 35.5 per 10,000 population; Property crime rate: 166.6 per 10,000 population
Newspapers: San Fernando Sun (weekly circulation 10000)
Transportation: Commute: 90.3% car, 4.0% public transportation, 2.9% walk, 1.6% work from home; Median travel time to work: 26.6 minutes
Additional Information Contacts
City of San Fernando . . . . (818) 898-1200
http://www.ci.san-fernando.ca.us

SAN GABRIEL (city). Covers a land area of 4.145 square miles and a water area of <.001 square miles. Located at 34.09° N. Lat; 118.10° W. Long. Elevation is 420 feet.
History: Named for Mission San Gabriel, which was named for the Holy Archangel St. Gabriel. San Gabriel grew up around Mission San Gabriel, founded in 1771 by the Franciscans. The town developed as a residential community.
Population: 39,718; Growth (since 2000): -0.2%; Density: 9,583.1 persons per square mile; Race: 25.4% White, 1.0% Black/African American, 60.7% Asian, 0.6% American Indian/Alaska Native, 0.1% Native Hawaiian/Other Pacific Islander, 2.9% Two or more races, 25.7% Hispanic of any race; Average household size: 3.13; Median age: 40.3; Age under 18: 19.8%; Age 65 and over: 14.0%; Males per 100 females: 93.2; Marriage status: 34.3% never married, 52.7% now married, 1.3% separated, 5.8% widowed, 7.2% divorced; Foreign born: 56.1%; Speak English only: 26.8%; With disability: 7.9%; Veterans: 3.1%; Ancestry: 2.4% German, 2.3% Italian, 1.4% American, 1.4% Irish, 1.1% English
Employment: 13.4% management, business, and financial, 5.2% computer, engineering, and science, 8.8% education, legal, community service, arts, and media, 4.9% healthcare practitioners, 21.8% service, 28.4% sales and office, 6.7% natural resources, construction, and maintenance, 10.7% production, transportation, and material moving
Income: Per capita: $24,808; Median household: $56,388; Average household: $75,306; Households with income of $100,000 or more: 25.6%; Poverty rate: 13.3%
Educational Attainment: High school diploma or higher: 76.8%; Bachelor's degree or higher: 28.0%; Graduate/professional degree or higher: 8.2%

School District(s)

Alhambra Unified (KG-12)
2012-13 Enrollment: 18,076 . . . . (626) 943-3000

Garvey Elementary (KG-08)
2012-13 Enrollment: 5,259 . . . . (626) 307-3444
San Gabriel Unified (KG-12)
2012-13 Enrollment: 6,573 . . . . (626) 451-5400
Temple City Unified (KG-12)
2012-13 Enrollment: 5,799 . . . . (626) 548-5000

Housing: Homeownership rate: 49.2%; Median home value: $552,900; Median year structure built: 1956; Homeowner vacancy rate: 1.0%; Median gross rent: $1,251 per month; Rental vacancy rate: 5.7%

Health Insurance: 77.6% have insurance; 55.0% have private insurance; 28.4% have public insurance; 22.4% do not have insurance; 6.8% of children under 18 do not have insurance

Hospitals: San Gabriel Valley Medical Center (274 beds)

Safety: Violent crime rate: 25.6 per 10,000 population; Property crime rate: 179.7 per 10,000 population

Transportation: Commute: 87.4% car, 3.2% public transportation, 3.6% walk, 3.9% work from home; Median travel time to work: 28.1 minutes

Additional Information Contacts

City of San Gabriel . . . . (626) 308-2800
http://www.sangabrielcity.com

SAN MARINO (city). Covers a land area of 3.767 square miles and a water area of 0.007 square miles. Located at 34.12° N. Lat; 118.11° W. Long. Elevation is 564 feet.

History: San Marino was named by railroad magnate Henry E. Huntington for the estate of James de Barth Shorb and his homestead in Emmitsburg, Maryland. Nearby is the Huntington Library and Art Gallery founded by Collis P. Huntington in 1919.

Population: 13,147; Growth (since 2000): 1.6%; Density: 3,489.8 persons per square mile; Race: 41.3% White, 0.4% Black/African American, 53.5% Asian, 0.0% American Indian/Alaska Native, 0.0% Native Hawaiian/Other Pacific Islander, 3.1% Two or more races, 6.5% Hispanic of any race; Average household size: 3.02; Median age: 45.3; Age under 18: 26.0%; Age 65 and over: 17.6%; Males per 100 females: 92.4; Marriage status: 21.4% never married, 67.9% now married, 0.7% separated, 5.3% widowed, 5.4% divorced; Foreign born: 38.4%; Speak English only: 47.1%; With disability: 6.5%; Veterans: 5.1%; Ancestry: 8.1% English, 7.3% German, 5.5% Irish, 2.4% Italian, 2.1% Swedish

Employment: 30.7% management, business, and financial, 8.6% computer, engineering, and science, 14.3% education, legal, community service, arts, and media, 15.7% healthcare practitioners, 4.9% service, 22.7% sales and office, 0.3% natural resources, construction, and maintenance, 2.7% production, transportation, and material moving

Income: Per capita: $76,240; Median household: $131,758; Average household: $225,497; Households with income of $100,000 or more: 62.1%; Poverty rate: 5.4%

Educational Attainment: High school diploma or higher: 94.8%; Bachelor's degree or higher: 72.7%; Graduate/professional degree or higher: 35.5%

School District(s)

San Marino Unified (KG-12)
2012-13 Enrollment: 3,150 . . . . (626) 299-7000

Housing: Homeownership rate: 91.5%; Median home value: 1 million+; Median year structure built: Before 1940; Homeowner vacancy rate: 0.5%; Median gross rent: $2,000+ per month; Rental vacancy rate: 6.5%

Health Insurance: 95.9% have insurance; 87.0% have private insurance; 20.3% have public insurance; 4.1% do not have insurance; 2.6% of children under 18 do not have insurance

Safety: Violent crime rate: 15.0 per 10,000 population; Property crime rate: 168.3 per 10,000 population

Newspapers: San Marino Tribune (weekly circulation 15000)

Transportation: Commute: 85.6% car, 0.9% public transportation, 1.5% walk, 11.7% work from home; Median travel time to work: 27.1 minutes

Additional Information Contacts

City of San Marino. . . . . (626) 300-0700
http://www.ci.san-marino.ca.us

SAN PASQUAL (CDP). Covers a land area of 0.255 square miles and a water area of 0 square miles. Located at 34.14° N. Lat; 118.10° W. Long.

Population: 2,041; Growth (since 2000): n/a; Density: 8,001.1 persons per square mile; Race: 65.9% White, 3.1% Black/African American, 21.5% Asian, 0.3% American Indian/Alaska Native, 0.0% Native Hawaiian/Other Pacific Islander, 4.1% Two or more races, 17.7% Hispanic of any race; Average household size: 2.25; Median age: 41.3; Age under 18: 17.9%; Age 65 and over: 13.9%; Males per 100 females: 91.8

Housing: Homeownership rate: 58.6%; Homeowner vacancy rate: 0.7%; Rental vacancy rate: 7.6%

SAN PEDRO (unincorporated postal area)

ZCTA: 90731

Covers a land area of 9.190 square miles and a water area of 6.439 square miles. Located at 33.73° N. Lat; 118.28° W. Long. Elevation is 112 feet.

Population: 59,662; Growth (since 2000): 1.8%; Density: 6,491.8 persons per square mile; Race: 58.4% White, 7.3% Black/African American, 4.6% Asian, 1.2% American Indian/Alaska Native, 0.6% Native Hawaiian/Other Pacific Islander, 6.6% Two or more races, 53.2% Hispanic of any race; Average household size: 2.62; Median age: 35.6; Age under 18: 24.6%; Age 65 and over: 10.3%; Males per 100 females: 100.8; Marriage status: 40.9% never married, 41.7% now married, 4.1% separated, 5.1% widowed, 12.3% divorced; Foreign born: 24.9%; Speak English only: 55.5%; With disability: 12.2%; Veterans: 6.2%; Ancestry: 8.1% Irish, 7.5% Italian, 6.9% German, 4.5% English, 3.8% Croatian

Employment: 10.2% management, business, and financial, 3.2% computer, engineering, and science, 10.3% education, legal, community service, arts, and media, 3.4% healthcare practitioners, 22.7% service, 23.3% sales and office, 10.2% natural resources, construction, and maintenance, 16.7% production, transportation, and material moving

Income: Per capita: $24,750; Median household: $50,210; Average household: $65,639; Households with income of $100,000 or more: 22.2%; Poverty rate: 20.6%

Educational Attainment: High school diploma or higher: 76.1%; Bachelor's degree or higher: 21.2%; Graduate/professional degree or higher: 6.0%

School District(s)

Los Angeles Unified (PK-12)
2012-13 Enrollment: 655,455 . . . . (213) 241-1000

Housing: Homeownership rate: 32.9%; Median home value: $440,700; Median year structure built: 1959; Homeowner vacancy rate: 3.3%; Median gross rent: $1,109 per month; Rental vacancy rate: 6.9%

Health Insurance: 81.3% have insurance; 55.1% have private insurance; 33.3% have public insurance; 18.7% do not have insurance; 5.1% of children under 18 do not have insurance

Hospitals: Providence Little Co of Mary Medical Center San Pedro (387 beds)

Newspapers: Random Lengths (weekly circulation 30000)

Transportation: Commute: 86.2% car, 3.6% public transportation, 4.9% walk, 3.2% work from home; Median travel time to work: 25.1 minutes

ZCTA: 90732

Covers a land area of 3.438 square miles and a water area of 0.370 square miles. Located at 33.74° N. Lat; 118.31° W. Long. Elevation is 112 feet.

Population: 21,115; Growth (since 2000): -0.7%; Density: 6,142.5 persons per square mile; Race: 72.9% White, 4.4% Black/African American, 8.2% Asian, 0.7% American Indian/Alaska Native, 0.2% Native Hawaiian/Other Pacific Islander, 5.9% Two or more races, 26.5% Hispanic of any race; Average household size: 2.38; Median age: 45.0; Age under 18: 19.3%; Age 65 and over: 20.6%; Males per 100 females: 87.3; Marriage status: 26.1% never married, 54.3% now married, 2.6% separated, 8.3% widowed, 11.2% divorced; Foreign born: 19.0%; Speak English only: 72.6%; With disability: 12.1%; Veterans: 9.3%; Ancestry: 11.2% German, 10.1% Irish, 9.3% Italian, 9.0% English, 6.9% Croatian

Employment: 14.7% management, business, and financial, 5.4% computer, engineering, and science, 12.0% education, legal, community service, arts, and media, 5.8% healthcare practitioners, 12.5% service, 27.5% sales and office, 8.3% natural resources, construction, and maintenance, 13.7% production, transportation, and material moving

Income: Per capita: $40,282; Median household: $80,172; Average household: $92,555; Households with income of $100,000 or more: 38.7%; Poverty rate: 7.7%

Educational Attainment: High school diploma or higher: 90.8%; Bachelor's degree or higher: 33.1%; Graduate/professional degree or higher: 11.7%

Housing: Homeownership rate: 72.2%; Median home value: $483,600; Median year structure built: 1967; Homeowner vacancy rate: 0.8%; Median gross rent: $1,624 per month; Rental vacancy rate: 5.0%

Health Insurance: 91.7% have insurance; 79.9% have private insurance; 25.5% have public insurance; 8.3% do not have insurance; 2.1% of children under 18 do not have insurance

Transportation: Commute: 91.9% car, 2.1% public transportation, 0.8% walk, 4.2% work from home; Median travel time to work: 26.5 minutes

SANTA CLARITA (city). Covers a land area of 52.716 square miles and a water area of 0.065 square miles. Located at 34.40° N. Lat; 118.50° W. Long. Elevation is 1,207 feet.

History: Santa Clarita was incorporated in December 1987.

Population: 176,320; Growth (since 2000): 16.7%; Density: 3,344.7 persons per square mile; Race: 70.9% White, 3.2% Black/African American, 8.5% Asian, 0.6% American Indian/Alaska Native, 0.2% Native Hawaiian/Other Pacific Islander, 4.7% Two or more races, 29.5% Hispanic of any race; Average household size: 2.94; Median age: 36.2; Age under 18: 26.2%; Age 65 and over: 9.6%; Males per 100 females: 97.1; Marriage status: 32.3% never married, 53.2% now married, 1.8% separated, 4.3% widowed, 10.2% divorced; Foreign born: 20.5%; Speak English only: 69.5%; With disability: 9.1%; Veterans: 6.4%; Ancestry: 12.8% German, 10.7% Irish, 8.8% English, 7.0% Italian, 4.0% American

Employment: 17.2% management, business, and financial, 5.4% computer, engineering, and science, 12.1% education, legal, community service, arts, and media, 5.7% healthcare practitioners, 16.3% service, 27.0% sales and office, 8.0% natural resources, construction, and maintenance, 8.3% production, transportation, and material moving

Income: Per capita: $33,818; Median household: $82,607; Average household: $99,137; Households with income of $100,000 or more: 38.5%; Poverty rate: 9.5%

Educational Attainment: High school diploma or higher: 88.1%; Bachelor's degree or higher: 31.9%; Graduate/professional degree or higher: 10.0%

School District(s)

Hart Rop
2012-13 Enrollment: n/a . . . . (661) 259-0033
Los Angeles County Office of Education (KG-12)
2012-13 Enrollment: 9,136 . . . . (562) 922-6111
Saugus Union (KG-06)
2012-13 Enrollment: 10,178 . . . . (661) 294-5300
Sulphur Springs Union (KG-06)
2012-13 Enrollment: 5,553 . . . . (661) 252-5131
William S. Hart Union High (KG-12)
2012-13 Enrollment: 26,373 . . . . (661) 259-0033

Four-year College(s)

The Master's College and Seminary (Private, Not-for-profit, Interdenominational)
Fall 2013 Enrollment: 1,499 . . . . (661) 259-3540
2013-14 Tuition: In-state $28,800; Out-of-state $28,800

Two-year College(s)

College of the Canyons (Public)
Fall 2013 Enrollment: 18,508 . . . . (661) 259-7800
2013-14 Tuition: In-state $1,154; Out-of-state $5,450

Housing: Homeownership rate: 71.2%; Median home value: $373,700; Median year structure built: 1983; Homeowner vacancy rate: 1.4%; Median gross rent: $1,509 per month; Rental vacancy rate: 6.0%

Health Insurance: 86.8% have insurance; 74.4% have private insurance; 20.2% have public insurance; 13.2% do not have insurance; 6.9% of children under 18 do not have insurance

Safety: Violent crime rate: 13.5 per 10,000 population; Property crime rate: 132.4 per 10,000 population

Newspapers: The Signal (daily circulation 9200)

Transportation: Commute: 88.4% car, 3.2% public transportation, 1.5% walk, 5.7% work from home; Median travel time to work: 32.2 minutes; Amtrak: Train service available.

Additional Information Contacts

City of Santa Clarita . . . . (661) 259-2489
http://www.santa-clarita.com

SANTA FE SPRINGS (city). Covers a land area of 8.874 square miles and a water area of 0.040 square miles. Located at 33.93° N. Lat; 118.06° W. Long. Elevation is 135 feet.

History: Named by the Santa Fe Railroad Company when they purchased the mineral springs. They purchased the newly platted town of Fulton Sulphur Springs in 1886 and renamed it. The area grew around the oil fields.

Population: 16,223; Growth (since 2000): -7.0%; Density: 1,828.1 persons per square mile; Race: 58.6% White, 2.3% Black/African American, 4.2% Asian, 1.4% American Indian/Alaska Native, 0.2% Native Hawaiian/Other Pacific Islander, 4.2% Two or more races, 81.0% Hispanic of any race; Average household size: 3.38; Median age: 35.3; Age under 18: 26.4%; Age 65 and over: 13.3%; Males per 100 females: 93.0; Marriage status: 36.9% never married, 44.8% now married, 2.4% separated, 8.0% widowed, 10.3% divorced; Foreign born: 21.1%; Speak English only: 40.9%; With disability: 11.7%; Veterans: 5.9%; Ancestry: 2.6% German, 1.9% American, 1.5% Nigerian, 1.4% Irish, 1.4% French

Employment: 11.4% management, business, and financial, 3.4% computer, engineering, and science, 10.1% education, legal, community service, arts, and media, 3.3% healthcare practitioners, 16.9% service, 29.4% sales and office, 8.0% natural resources, construction, and maintenance, 17.5% production, transportation, and material moving

Income: Per capita: $20,772; Median household: $54,081; Average household: $68,935; Households with income of $100,000 or more: 21.2%; Poverty rate: 9.1%

Educational Attainment: High school diploma or higher: 73.1%; Bachelor's degree or higher: 11.7%; Graduate/professional degree or higher: 3.5%

School District(s)

Little Lake City Elementary (KG-08)
2012-13 Enrollment: 4,642 . . . . (562) 868-8241
Los Nietos (KG-08)
2012-13 Enrollment: 1,925 . . . . (562) 692-0271
Whittier Union High (09-12)
2012-13 Enrollment: 13,486 . . . . (562) 698-8121

Vocational/Technical School(s)

Beyond 21st Century Beauty Academy (Private, For-profit)
Fall 2013 Enrollment: 46 . . . . (562) 404-6193
2013-14 Tuition: $14,395
Medical Allied Career Center (Private, For-profit)
Fall 2013 Enrollment: 65 . . . . (562) 807-2420
2013-14 Tuition: $27,790
NTMA Training Centers of Southern California (Private, Not-for-profit)
Fall 2013 Enrollment: 242 . . . . (562) 404-4295
2013-14 Tuition: $10,950

Housing: Homeownership rate: 61.0%; Median home value: $343,100; Median year structure built: 1959; Homeowner vacancy rate: 2.1%; Median gross rent: $1,231 per month; Rental vacancy rate: 5.5%

Health Insurance: 78.2% have insurance; 56.7% have private insurance; 29.6% have public insurance; 21.8% do not have insurance; 14.1% of children under 18 do not have insurance

Safety: Violent crime rate: 44.3 per 10,000 population; Property crime rate: 712.1 per 10,000 population

Transportation: Commute: 92.6% car, 4.9% public transportation, 0.3% walk, 1.1% work from home; Median travel time to work: 29.2 minutes

Additional Information Contacts

City of Santa Fe Springs . . . . (562) 868-0511
http://www.santafesprings.org

SANTA MONICA (city). Covers a land area of 8.415 square miles and a water area of 0.001 square miles. Located at 34.02° N. Lat; 118.48° W. Long. Elevation is 105 feet.

History: Named for the Santa Monica Mountains, named by Portola for St. Monica, mother of St. Augustine. Santa Monica was founded on land once belonging to two ranchos called San Vicente and Santa Monica. The beach-front location was purchased in 1872 by Colonel R.S. Baker, a wool grower, who pastured his sheep here. Two years later Baker teamed up with Senator John P. Jones to plan a town, a wharf, and a railroad.

Population: 89,736; Growth (since 2000): 6.7%; Density: 10,664.1 persons per square mile; Race: 77.6% White, 3.9% Black/African American, 9.0% Asian, 0.4% American Indian/Alaska Native, 0.1% Native Hawaiian/Other Pacific Islander, 4.4% Two or more races, 13.1% Hispanic of any race; Average household size: 1.87; Median age: 40.4; Age under 18: 14.0%; Age 65 and over: 15.0%; Males per 100 females: 93.2; Marriage status: 44.5% never married, 37.9% now married, 2.0% separated, 5.4% widowed, 12.3% divorced; Foreign born: 23.3%; Speak English only: 72.3%; With disability: 9.9%; Veterans: 4.7%; Ancestry: 12.4% German, 11.7% Irish, 9.3% English, 7.3% Italian, 5.8% Russian

Employment: 25.1% management, business, and financial, 7.2% computer, engineering, and science, 27.1% education, legal, community service, arts, and media, 5.9% healthcare practitioners, 10.3% service,

20.0% sales and office, 1.9% natural resources, construction, and maintenance, 2.6% production, transportation, and material moving

Income: Per capita: $57,390; Median household: $73,649; Average household: $109,645; Households with income of $100,000 or more: 38.1%; Poverty rate: 11.2%

Educational Attainment: High school diploma or higher: 95.1%; Bachelor's degree or higher: 64.7%; Graduate/professional degree or higher: 28.8%

School District(s)

Los Angeles Unified (PK-12)
2012-13 Enrollment: 655,455 . . . . (213) 241-1000
Santa Monica-Malibu Unified (KG-12)
2012-13 Enrollment: 11,417 . . . . (310) 450-8338

Four-year College(s)

Emperor's College of Traditional Oriental Medicine (Private, For-profit)
Fall 2013 Enrollment: 203 . . . . (310) 453-8300
Pardee RAND Graduate School (Private, Not-for-profit)
Fall 2013 Enrollment: 102 . . . . (310) 393-0411
The Art Institute of California-Argosy University Los Angeles (Private, For-profit)
Fall 2013 Enrollment: 1,808 . . . . (412) 918-5568
2013-14 Tuition: In-state $18,748; Out-of-state $18,748

Two-year College(s)

Santa Monica College (Public)
Fall 2013 Enrollment: 29,999 . . . . (310) 434-4000
2013-14 Tuition: In-state $1,176; Out-of-state $7,596

Vocational/Technical School(s)

Toni & Guy Hairdressing Academy-Santa Monica (Private, For-profit)
Fall 2013 Enrollment: 268 . . . . (310) 451-0101
2013-14 Tuition: $16,900

Housing: Homeownership rate: 28.4%; Median home value: $999,900; Median year structure built: 1964; Homeowner vacancy rate: 1.1%; Median gross rent: $1,533 per month; Rental vacancy rate: 5.1%

Health Insurance: 88.9% have insurance; 76.3% have private insurance; 21.3% have public insurance; 11.1% do not have insurance; 5.6% of children under 18 do not have insurance

Hospitals: Providence Saint John's Health Center (237 beds); Santa Monica - UCLA Medical Center & Orthopaedic Hospital (600 beds)

Safety: Violent crime rate: 35.0 per 10,000 population; Property crime rate: 383.2 per 10,000 population

Newspapers: Observer (weekly circulation 20000); Santa Monica Daily Press (daily circulation 19000); Santa Monica Mirror (weekly circulation 20000)

Transportation: Commute: 76.0% car, 3.8% public transportation, 5.6% walk, 9.5% work from home; Median travel time to work: 26.2 minutes

Airports: Santa Monica Municipal (general aviation)

Additional Information Contacts

City of Santa Monica . . . . (310) 458-8411
http://www.smgov.net

SHERMAN OAKS (unincorporated postal area)

ZCTA: 91403

Covers a land area of 3.631 square miles and a water area of 0.015 square miles. Located at 34.15° N. Lat; 118.46° W. Long. Elevation is 663 feet.

Population: 23,484; Growth (since 2000): 6.4%; Density: 6,467.1 persons per square mile; Race: 79.4% White, 5.1% Black/African American, 7.4% Asian, 0.2% American Indian/Alaska Native, 0.1% Native Hawaiian/Other Pacific Islander, 4.4% Two or more races, 10.8% Hispanic of any race; Average household size: 2.06; Median age: 39.4; Age under 18: 15.9%; Age 65 and over: 14.5%; Males per 100 females: 92.4; Marriage status: 33.3% never married, 47.2% now married, 2.1% separated, 6.5% widowed, 13.1% divorced; Foreign born: 27.7%; Speak English only: 68.8%; With disability: 10.6%; Veterans: 5.3%; Ancestry: 11.5% Russian, 10.3% German, 8.4% Italian, 8.2% Irish, 6.3% English

Employment: 23.4% management, business, and financial, 6.2% computer, engineering, and science, 21.8% education, legal, community service, arts, and media, 6.8% healthcare practitioners, 9.7% service, 26.8% sales and office, 2.5% natural resources, construction, and maintenance, 2.8% production, transportation, and material moving

Income: Per capita: $56,485; Median household: $69,956; Average household: $115,901; Households with income of $100,000 or more: 38.1%; Poverty rate: 9.4%

Educational Attainment: High school diploma or higher: 97.6%; Bachelor's degree or higher: 59.1%; Graduate/professional degree or higher: 22.1%

School District(s)

Los Angeles Unified (PK-12)
2012-13 Enrollment: 655,455 . . . . (213) 241-1000

Four-year College(s)

Paul Mitchell the School-Sherman Oaks (Private, For-profit)
Fall 2013 Enrollment: 280 . . . . (800) 761-8006

Two-year College(s)

Paul Mitchell the School-Sherman Oaks (Private, For-profit)
Fall 2013 Enrollment: 280 . . . . (800) 761-8006

Vocational/Technical School(s)

Paul Mitchell the School-Sherman Oaks (Private, For-profit)
Fall 2013 Enrollment: 280 . . . . (800) 761-8006
2013-14 Tuition: $17,925

Housing: Homeownership rate: 45.8%; Median home value: $740,200; Median year structure built: 1970; Homeowner vacancy rate: 1.4%; Median gross rent: $1,516 per month; Rental vacancy rate: 6.1%

Health Insurance: 86.6% have insurance; 76.6% have private insurance; 21.6% have public insurance; 13.4% do not have insurance; 8.0% of children under 18 do not have insurance

Hospitals: Sherman Oaks Hospital (153 beds)

Transportation: Commute: 84.3% car, 2.6% public transportation, 1.4% walk, 10.2% work from home; Median travel time to work: 30.9 minutes

ZCTA: 91423

Covers a land area of 4.363 square miles and a water area of 0.024 square miles. Located at 34.15° N. Lat; 118.43° W. Long. Elevation is 663 feet.

Population: 30,991; Growth (since 2000): 5.5%; Density: 7,103.3 persons per square mile; Race: 80.0% White, 5.2% Black/African American, 6.4% Asian, 0.3% American Indian/Alaska Native, 0.1% Native Hawaiian/Other Pacific Islander, 4.2% Two or more races, 12.0% Hispanic of any race; Average household size: 2.07; Median age: 39.2; Age under 18: 17.0%; Age 65 and over: 12.8%; Males per 100 females: 91.3; Marriage status: 36.2% never married, 46.6% now married, 2.7% separated, 3.5% widowed, 13.7% divorced; Foreign born: 23.3%; Speak English only: 68.8%; With disability: 6.8%; Veterans: 5.0%; Ancestry: 10.2% German, 9.5% Irish, 8.8% English, 8.5% Russian, 4.6% Italian

Employment: 24.1% management, business, and financial, 5.1% computer, engineering, and science, 24.6% education, legal, community service, arts, and media, 6.2% healthcare practitioners, 11.8% service, 22.3% sales and office, 2.7% natural resources, construction, and maintenance, 3.1% production, transportation, and material moving

Income: Per capita: $54,682; Median household: $74,011; Average household: $114,926; Households with income of $100,000 or more: 37.0%; Poverty rate: 8.8%

Educational Attainment: High school diploma or higher: 95.6%; Bachelor's degree or higher: 54.9%; Graduate/professional degree or higher: 19.3%

Housing: Homeownership rate: 40.9%; Median home value: $755,300; Median year structure built: 1966; Homeowner vacancy rate: 1.4%; Median gross rent: $1,466 per month; Rental vacancy rate: 5.7%

Health Insurance: 87.9% have insurance; 77.5% have private insurance; 18.6% have public insurance; 12.1% do not have insurance; 3.1% of children under 18 do not have insurance

Transportation: Commute: 85.5% car, 2.7% public transportation, 1.2% walk, 9.0% work from home; Median travel time to work: 31.1 minutes

SIERRA MADRE (city)

Covers a land area of 2.953 square miles and a water area of 0.004 square miles. Located at 34.17° N. Lat; 118.05° W. Long. Elevation is 827 feet.

History: Named for the Spanish translation of "mother range". Incorporated 1907.

Population: 10,917; Growth (since 2000): 3.2%; Density: 3,697.5 persons per square mile; Race: 82.1% White, 1.8% Black/African American, 7.6% Asian, 0.4% American Indian/Alaska Native, 0.1% Native Hawaiian/Other Pacific Islander, 4.3% Two or more races, 14.9% Hispanic of any race; Average household size: 2.26; Median age: 46.6; Age under 18: 19.2%; Age 65 and over: 17.4%; Males per 100 females: 89.8; Marriage status: 25.9% never married, 56.3% now married, 1.0% separated, 5.6% widowed, 12.1% divorced; Foreign born: 16.1%; Speak English only: 80.0%; With disability: 7.1%; Veterans: 7.6%; Ancestry: 12.9% German, 11.2% Irish, 10.1% English, 4.9% Italian, 3.5% Dutch

Employment: 20.8% management, business, and financial, 10.1% computer, engineering, and science, 21.6% education, legal, community service, arts, and media, 6.3% healthcare practitioners, 8.1% service, 26.1% sales and office, 4.9% natural resources, construction, and maintenance, 2.2% production, transportation, and material moving

Income: Per capita: $49,626; Median household: $88,837; Average household: $117,826; Households with income of $100,000 or more: 44.1%; Poverty rate: 8.3%

Educational Attainment: High school diploma or higher: 96.8%; Bachelor's degree or higher: 59.1%; Graduate/professional degree or higher: 28.6%

School District(s)

Pasadena Unified (KG-12)
2012-13 Enrollment: 19,540 . . . . (626) 396-3600

Housing: Homeownership rate: 61.8%; Median home value: $780,300; Median year structure built: 1956; Homeowner vacancy rate: 1.0%; Median gross rent: $1,483 per month; Rental vacancy rate: 5.0%

Health Insurance: 95.1% have insurance; 85.7% have private insurance; 19.1% have public insurance; 4.9% do not have insurance; 2.8% of children under 18 do not have insurance

Safety: Violent crime rate: 11.8 per 10,000 population; Property crime rate: 116.8 per 10,000 population

Newspapers: Mountain Views News (weekly circulation 20000)

Transportation: Commute: 88.4% car, 3.6% public transportation, 0.0% walk, 7.6% work from home; Median travel time to work: 30.2 minutes

Additional Information Contacts

City of Sierra Madre . . . . (626) 355-7135
http://www.cityofsierramadre.com

SIGNAL HILL (city). Covers a land area of 2.189 square miles and a water area of 0.002 square miles. Located at 33.80° N. Lat; 118.17° W. Long. Elevation is 148 feet.

History: Covered with many oil wells (first gusher in 1921) within municipality. Incorporated 1924.

Population: 11,016; Growth (since 2000): 18.0%; Density: 5,032.9 persons per square mile; Race: 42.2% White, 13.6% Black/African American, 20.4% Asian, 0.8% American Indian/Alaska Native, 1.2% Native Hawaiian/Other Pacific Islander, 5.7% Two or more races, 31.5% Hispanic of any race; Average household size: 2.64; Median age: 36.0; Age under 18: 23.8%; Age 65 and over: 8.3%; Males per 100 females: 97.3; Marriage status: 44.8% never married, 42.2% now married, 1.5% separated, 3.2% widowed, 9.8% divorced; Foreign born: 32.3%; Speak English only: 54.7%; With disability: 8.1%; Veterans: 5.8%; Ancestry: 7.0% German, 4.8% English, 4.8% Irish, 3.7% Italian, 2.3% African

Employment: 16.9% management, business, and financial, 6.5% computer, engineering, and science, 12.8% education, legal, community service, arts, and media, 5.0% healthcare practitioners, 17.9% service, 23.7% sales and office, 5.4% natural resources, construction, and maintenance, 11.7% production, transportation, and material moving

Income: Per capita: $32,254; Median household: $70,442; Average household: $86,913; Households with income of $100,000 or more: 30.2%; Poverty rate: 14.1%

Educational Attainment: High school diploma or higher: 85.5%; Bachelor's degree or higher: 35.9%; Graduate/professional degree or higher: 12.1%

School District(s)

Long Beach Unified (KG-12)
2012-13 Enrollment: 82,256 . . . . (562) 997-8000

Four-year College(s)

American University of Health Sciences (Private, For-profit)
Fall 2013 Enrollment: 287 . . . . (562) 988-2278
2013-14 Tuition: In-state $22,684; Out-of-state $22,684

Housing: Homeownership rate: 51.5%; Median home value: $375,200; Median year structure built: 1977; Homeowner vacancy rate: 1.9%; Median gross rent: $1,122 per month; Rental vacancy rate: 5.7%

Health Insurance: 77.4% have insurance; 60.3% have private insurance; 26.1% have public insurance; 22.6% do not have insurance; 13.7% of children under 18 do not have insurance

Safety: Violent crime rate: 28.5 per 10,000 population; Property crime rate: 492.9 per 10,000 population

Newspapers: Signal Tribune (weekly circulation 25000)

Transportation: Commute: 84.7% car, 2.4% public transportation, 2.6% walk, 8.6% work from home; Median travel time to work: 26.3 minutes

Additional Information Contacts

City of Signal Hill . . . . (562) 989-7302
http://www.cityofsignalhill.org

SOUTH EL MONTE (city). Covers a land area of 2.843 square miles and a water area of 0.005 square miles. Located at 34.05° N. Lat; 118.05° W. Long. Elevation is 249 feet.

History: Named for its location south of El Monte. Incorporated 1958.

Population: 20,116; Growth (since 2000): -4.9%; Density: 7,075.0 persons per square mile; Race: 50.4% White, 0.5% Black/African American, 11.0% Asian, 1.2% American Indian/Alaska Native, 0.1% Native Hawaiian/Other Pacific Islander, 3.4% Two or more races, 84.9% Hispanic of any race; Average household size: 4.39; Median age: 30.4; Age under 18: 30.0%; Age 65 and over: 8.9%; Males per 100 females: 101.9; Marriage status: 40.5% never married, 48.2% now married, 4.3% separated, 5.4% widowed, 6.0% divorced; Foreign born: 46.0%; Speak English only: 12.8%; With disability: 12.2%; Veterans: 2.6%; Ancestry: 0.7% American, 0.7% German, 0.5% Italian, 0.4% Irish, 0.2% English

Employment: 4.7% management, business, and financial, 1.5% computer, engineering, and science, 5.2% education, legal, community service, arts, and media, 2.1% healthcare practitioners, 23.8% service, 21.1% sales and office, 14.1% natural resources, construction, and maintenance, 27.4% production, transportation, and material moving

Income: Per capita: $14,291; Median household: $44,104; Average household: $56,062; Households with income of $100,000 or more: 12.9%; Poverty rate: 19.4%

Educational Attainment: High school diploma or higher: 49.0%; Bachelor's degree or higher: 8.0%; Graduate/professional degree or higher: 1.6%

School District(s)

El Monte Union High (09-12)
2012-13 Enrollment: 9,812 . . . . (626) 444-9005
Valle Lindo Elementary (KG-08)
2012-13 Enrollment: 1,240 . . . . (626) 580-0610

Housing: Homeownership rate: 48.4%; Median home value: $331,300; Median year structure built: 1957; Homeowner vacancy rate: 0.7%; Median gross rent: $1,088 per month; Rental vacancy rate: 3.5%

Health Insurance: 69.3% have insurance; 32.8% have private insurance; 40.3% have public insurance; 30.7% do not have insurance; 10.6% of children under 18 do not have insurance

Hospitals: Greater El Monte Community Hospital (117 beds)

Safety: Violent crime rate: 43.2 per 10,000 population; Property crime rate: 218.1 per 10,000 population

Transportation: Commute: 82.3% car, 4.6% public transportation, 7.0% walk, 5.0% work from home; Median travel time to work: 32.0 minutes

Additional Information Contacts

City of South El Monte. . . . . (626) 579-6540
http://www.ci.south-el-monte.ca.us

SOUTH GATE (city). Covers a land area of 7.236 square miles and a water area of 0.117 square miles. Located at 33.94° N. Lat; 118.19° W. Long. Elevation is 115 feet.

History: Named for the South Gate Gardens on the city's Cudahy Ranch, opened to the public in 1917. Incorporated 1923.

Population: 94,396; Growth (since 2000): -2.1%; Density: 13,045.0 persons per square mile; Race: 50.5% White, 0.9% Black/African American, 0.8% Asian, 0.9% American Indian/Alaska Native, 0.1% Native Hawaiian/Other Pacific Islander, 3.7% Two or more races, 94.8% Hispanic of any race; Average household size: 4.05; Median age: 29.4; Age under 18: 31.1%; Age 65 and over: 7.0%; Males per 100 females: 96.4; Marriage status: 44.1% never married, 46.3% now married, 3.7% separated, 3.7% widowed, 5.9% divorced; Foreign born: 43.3%; Speak English only: 9.7%; With disability: 8.5%; Veterans: 1.6%; Ancestry: 0.9% American, 0.7% Irish, 0.5% English, 0.5% Italian, 0.4% German

Employment: 6.2% management, business, and financial, 1.1% computer, engineering, and science, 6.7% education, legal, community service, arts, and media, 1.9% healthcare practitioners, 17.3% service, 28.8% sales and office, 10.8% natural resources, construction, and maintenance, 27.2% production, transportation, and material moving

Income: Per capita: $14,259; Median household: $42,776; Average household: $53,366; Households with income of $100,000 or more: 11.4%; Poverty rate: 21.1%

Educational Attainment: High school diploma or higher: 52.5%; Bachelor's degree or higher: 6.2%; Graduate/professional degree or higher: 1.4%

School District(s)

Los Angeles Unified (PK-12)
2012-13 Enrollment: 655,455 . . . . (213) 241-1000
Paramount Unified (KG-12)
2012-13 Enrollment: 15,846 . . . . (562) 602-6000

Two-year College(s)

Advanced College (Private, For-profit)
Fall 2013 Enrollment: 227 . . . . (562) 408-6969

Housing: Homeownership rate: 45.8%; Median home value: $292,100; Median year structure built: 1950; Homeowner vacancy rate: 1.5%; Median gross rent: $984 per month; Rental vacancy rate: 3.6%

Health Insurance: 69.1% have insurance; 39.1% have private insurance; 33.1% have public insurance; 30.9% do not have insurance; 11.8% of children under 18 do not have insurance

Safety: Violent crime rate: 51.9 per 10,000 population; Property crime rate: 282.2 per 10,000 population

Transportation: Commute: 87.2% car, 6.9% public transportation, 2.3% walk, 2.3% work from home; Median travel time to work: 29.0 minutes

Additional Information Contacts

City of South Gate . . . . (323) 563-9500
http://www.cityofsouthgate.org

SOUTH MONROVIA ISLAND (CDP). Covers a land area of 0.548 square miles and a water area of 0 square miles. Located at 34.12° N. Lat; 118.00° W. Long.

Population: 6,777; Growth (since 2000): n/a; Density: 12,372.2 persons per square mile; Race: 50.7% White, 8.4% Black/African American, 6.2% Asian, 0.7% American Indian/Alaska Native, 0.1% Native Hawaiian/Other Pacific Islander, 4.4% Two or more races, 74.0% Hispanic of any race; Average household size: 4.27; Median age: 32.0; Age under 18: 28.6%; Age 65 and over: 8.1%; Males per 100 females: 99.2; Marriage status: 40.4% never married, 46.8% now married, 2.4% separated, 4.3% widowed, 8.5% divorced; Foreign born: 37.7%; Speak English only: 33.9%; With disability: 10.6%; Veterans: 4.9%; Ancestry: 3.1% German, 3.0% English, 2.6% Irish, 1.0% Italian, 1.0% Polish

Employment: 8.3% management, business, and financial, 2.1% computer, engineering, and science, 7.9% education, legal, community service, arts, and media, 3.9% healthcare practitioners, 19.3% service, 26.0% sales and office, 8.8% natural resources, construction, and maintenance, 23.8% production, transportation, and material moving

Income: Per capita: $17,263; Median household: $52,778; Average household: $63,486; Households with income of $100,000 or more: 22.6%; Poverty rate: 18.0%

Educational Attainment: High school diploma or higher: 66.3%; Bachelor's degree or higher: 8.1%; Graduate/professional degree or higher: 2.9%

Housing: Homeownership rate: 74.2%; Median home value: $342,000; Median year structure built: 1953; Homeowner vacancy rate: 2.1%; Median gross rent: $1,549 per month; Rental vacancy rate: 2.2%

Health Insurance: 71.4% have insurance; 44.2% have private insurance; 31.5% have public insurance; 28.6% do not have insurance; 10.1% of children under 18 do not have insurance

Transportation: Commute: 88.0% car, 3.8% public transportation, 0.2% walk, 5.8% work from home; Median travel time to work: 28.8 minutes

SOUTH PASADENA (city). Covers a land area of 3.405 square miles and a water area of 0.012 square miles. Located at 34.11° N. Lat; 118.16° W. Long. Elevation is 659 feet.

History: Named for its location south of Pasadena. Incorporated 1888.

Population: 25,619; Growth (since 2000): 5.5%; Density: 7,523.0 persons per square mile; Race: 54.3% White, 3.0% Black/African American, 31.1% Asian, 0.4% American Indian/Alaska Native, 0.0% Native Hawaiian/Other Pacific Islander, 5.5% Two or more races, 18.6% Hispanic of any race; Average household size: 2.43; Median age: 40.1; Age under 18: 23.4%; Age 65 and over: 12.1%; Males per 100 females: 90.3; Marriage status: 32.4% never married, 53.6% now married, 2.1% separated, 3.5% widowed, 10.5% divorced; Foreign born: 27.5%; Speak English only: 61.8%; With disability: 7.1%; Veterans: 4.4%; Ancestry: 7.1% English, 7.0% German, 6.8% Irish, 5.8% Italian, 3.2% European

Employment: 22.5% management, business, and financial, 8.7% computer, engineering, and science, 24.8% education, legal, community service, arts, and media, 9.3% healthcare practitioners, 8.8% service, 17.9% sales and office, 3.7% natural resources, construction, and maintenance, 4.4% production, transportation, and material moving

Income: Per capita: $47,043; Median household: $85,058; Average household: $115,518; Households with income of $100,000 or more: 42.0%; Poverty rate: 6.7%

Educational Attainment: High school diploma or higher: 96.3%; Bachelor's degree or higher: 63.0%; Graduate/professional degree or higher: 29.7%

School District(s)

South Pasadena Unified (KG-12)
2012-13 Enrollment: 4,652 . . . . (626) 441-5810

Housing: Homeownership rate: 45.7%; Median home value: $820,200; Median year structure built: 1951; Homeowner vacancy rate: 1.1%; Median gross rent: $1,406 per month; Rental vacancy rate: 6.1%

Health Insurance: 88.0% have insurance; 80.6% have private insurance; 15.0% have public insurance; 12.0% do not have insurance; 9.8% of children under 18 do not have insurance

Safety: Violent crime rate: 11.2 per 10,000 population; Property crime rate: 219.0 per 10,000 population

Newspapers: South Pasadena Review (weekly circulation 4000)

Transportation: Commute: 86.4% car, 5.4% public transportation, 1.0% walk, 5.8% work from home; Median travel time to work: 28.0 minutes

Additional Information Contacts

City of South Pasadena. . . . . (626) 403-7200
http://www.ci.south-pasadena.ca.us

SOUTH SAN GABRIEL (CDP). Covers a land area of 0.833 square miles and a water area of <.001 square miles. Located at 34.05° N. Lat; 118.10° W. Long. Elevation is 272 feet.

Population: 8,070; Growth (since 2000): 6.3%; Density: 9,687.7 persons per square mile; Race: 27.2% White, 1.0% Black/African American, 49.4% Asian, 0.7% American Indian/Alaska Native, 0.0% Native Hawaiian/Other Pacific Islander, 3.9% Two or more races, 42.7% Hispanic of any race; Average household size: 3.48; Median age: 40.5; Age under 18: 20.4%; Age 65 and over: 16.8%; Males per 100 females: 92.9; Marriage status: 34.8% never married, 48.9% now married, 2.2% separated, 9.6% widowed, 6.7% divorced; Foreign born: 43.0%; Speak English only: 21.7%; With disability: 10.1%; Veterans: 3.6%; Ancestry: 2.0% American, 1.0% English, 0.7% Dutch, 0.4% Irish, 0.3% Italian

Employment: 16.0% management, business, and financial, 8.1% computer, engineering, and science, 10.5% education, legal, community service, arts, and media, 5.4% healthcare practitioners, 16.7% service, 24.1% sales and office, 10.9% natural resources, construction, and maintenance, 8.1% production, transportation, and material moving

Income: Per capita: $22,413; Median household: $61,528; Average household: $78,658; Households with income of $100,000 or more: 28.2%; Poverty rate: 13.3%

Educational Attainment: High school diploma or higher: 76.6%; Bachelor's degree or higher: 24.0%; Graduate/professional degree or higher: 8.2%

School District(s)

Montebello Unified (KG-12)
2012-13 Enrollment: 30,564 . . . . (323) 887-7900

Housing: Homeownership rate: 71.0%; Median home value: $394,500; Median year structure built: 1963; Homeowner vacancy rate: 1.1%; Median gross rent: $1,110 per month; Rental vacancy rate: 4.8%

Health Insurance: 82.2% have insurance; 55.7% have private insurance; 35.6% have public insurance; 17.8% do not have insurance; 14.8% of children under 18 do not have insurance

Transportation: Commute: 88.9% car, 2.0% public transportation, 1.5% walk, 5.0% work from home; Median travel time to work: 28.7 minutes

SOUTH SAN JOSE HILLS (CDP). Covers a land area of 1.508 square miles and a water area of 0 square miles. Located at 34.01° N. Lat; 117.90° W. Long. Elevation is 417 feet.

Population: 20,551; Growth (since 2000): 1.6%; Density: 13,628.8 persons per square mile; Race: 45.3% White, 1.5% Black/African American, 8.0% Asian, 0.9% American Indian/Alaska Native, 0.1% Native Hawaiian/Other Pacific Islander, 3.0% Two or more races, 86.2% Hispanic of any race; Average household size: 4.99; Median age: 29.7; Age under 18: 30.4%; Age 65 and over: 8.0%; Males per 100 females: 101.4; Marriage status: 42.7% never married, 45.5% now married, 4.7% separated, 5.1% widowed, 6.7% divorced; Foreign born: 41.2%; Speak English only: 16.2%; With disability: 9.6%; Veterans: 2.7%; Ancestry: 2.2% German, 1.3% American, 1.1% Irish, 0.8% English, 0.3% Dutch

Employment: 5.2% management, business, and financial, 1.9% computer, engineering, and science, 4.0% education, legal, community service, arts,

and media, 2.3% healthcare practitioners, 21.2% service, 22.4% sales and office, 13.3% natural resources, construction, and maintenance, 29.6% production, transportation, and material moving
Income: Per capita: $13,406; Median household: $53,750; Average household: $60,752; Households with income of $100,000 or more: 14.8%; Poverty rate: 16.6%
Educational Attainment: High school diploma or higher: 52.4%; Bachelor's degree or higher: 7.8%; Graduate/professional degree or higher: 1.2%
Housing: Homeownership rate: 76.1%; Median home value: $250,000; Median year structure built: 1960; Homeowner vacancy rate: 1.0%; Median gross rent: $1,265 per month; Rental vacancy rate: 3.2%
Health Insurance: 68.7% have insurance; 33.8% have private insurance; 38.5% have public insurance; 31.3% do not have insurance; 6.9% of children under 18 do not have insurance
Transportation: Commute: 89.1% car, 3.7% public transportation, 1.4% walk, 3.3% work from home; Median travel time to work: 33.1 minutes

SOUTH WHITTIER (CDP). Covers a land area of 5.337 square miles and a water area of 0.009 square miles. Located at 33.93° N. Lat; 118.03° W. Long. Elevation is 177 feet.
Population: 57,156; Growth (since 2000): 3.6%; Density: 10,708.9 persons per square mile; Race: 58.9% White, 1.5% Black/African American, 4.0% Asian, 1.3% American Indian/Alaska Native, 0.3% Native Hawaiian/Other Pacific Islander, 4.1% Two or more races, 77.1% Hispanic of any race; Average household size: 3.77; Median age: 32.0; Age under 18: 28.5%; Age 65 and over: 8.7%; Males per 100 females: 98.5; Marriage status: 38.1% never married, 48.0% now married, 2.7% separated, 4.8% widowed, 9.1% divorced; Foreign born: 25.9%; Speak English only: 40.8%; With disability: 8.6%; Veterans: 5.7%; Ancestry: 3.8% German, 3.0% Irish, 2.4% English, 1.4% Italian, 1.4% American
Employment: 10.6% management, business, and financial, 3.4% computer, engineering, and science, 8.0% education, legal, community service, arts, and media, 2.5% healthcare practitioners, 19.6% service, 27.8% sales and office, 9.4% natural resources, construction, and maintenance, 18.7% production, transportation, and material moving
Income: Per capita: $19,896; Median household: $64,029; Average household: $72,165; Households with income of $100,000 or more: 25.6%; Poverty rate: 12.9%
Educational Attainment: High school diploma or higher: 72.5%; Bachelor's degree or higher: 14.3%; Graduate/professional degree or higher: 4.1%
Housing: Homeownership rate: 63.4%; Median home value: $339,500; Median year structure built: 1958; Homeowner vacancy rate: 1.1%; Median gross rent: $1,271 per month; Rental vacancy rate: 3.7%
Health Insurance: 78.4% have insurance; 55.3% have private insurance; 28.7% have public insurance; 21.6% do not have insurance; 8.9% of children under 18 do not have insurance
Transportation: Commute: 91.5% car, 3.0% public transportation, 0.5% walk, 2.9% work from home; Median travel time to work: 28.2 minutes

STEVENSON RANCH (CDP). Covers a land area of 6.361 square miles and a water area of <.001 square miles. Located at 34.39° N. Lat; 118.59° W. Long.
Population: 17,557; Growth (since 2000): n/a; Density: 2,760.0 persons per square mile; Race: 64.2% White, 3.5% Black/African American, 22.9% Asian, 0.4% American Indian/Alaska Native, 0.2% Native Hawaiian/Other Pacific Islander, 4.5% Two or more races, 16.1% Hispanic of any race; Average household size: 3.10; Median age: 36.5; Age under 18: 32.2%; Age 65 and over: 6.3%; Males per 100 females: 95.2; Marriage status: 29.1% never married, 59.9% now married, 2.1% separated, 3.2% widowed, 7.7% divorced; Foreign born: 19.8%; Speak English only: 71.9%; With disability: 6.1%; Veterans: 5.1%; Ancestry: 14.9% German, 10.4% English, 8.7% Irish, 6.4% Italian, 4.4% Russian
Employment: 28.7% management, business, and financial, 9.8% computer, engineering, and science, 14.4% education, legal, community service, arts, and media, 6.7% healthcare practitioners, 9.1% service, 24.2% sales and office, 3.2% natural resources, construction, and maintenance, 3.9% production, transportation, and material moving
Income: Per capita: $47,909; Median household: $116,655; Average household: $146,933; Households with income of $100,000 or more: 58.8%; Poverty rate: 4.2%
Educational Attainment: High school diploma or higher: 95.0%; Bachelor's degree or higher: 54.0%; Graduate/professional degree or higher: 21.3%

School District(s)

Newhall (KG-06)
2012-13 Enrollment: 6,947 . . . . (661) 291-4000
William S. Hart Union High (KG-12)
2012-13 Enrollment: 26,373 . . . . (661) 259-0033
Housing: Homeownership rate: 73.6%; Median home value: $583,900; Median year structure built: 1998; Homeowner vacancy rate: 1.3%; Median gross rent: $1,786 per month; Rental vacancy rate: 5.1%
Health Insurance: 92.6% have insurance; 87.3% have private insurance; 10.1% have public insurance; 7.4% do not have insurance; 5.0% of children under 18 do not have insurance
Transportation: Commute: 87.4% car, 2.4% public transportation, 1.4% walk, 8.2% work from home; Median travel time to work: 36.7 minutes

STUDIO CITY (unincorporated postal area)

ZCTA: 91604

Covers a land area of 5.152 square miles and a water area of 0.074 square miles. Located at 34.14° N. Lat; 118.39° W. Long. Elevation is 610 feet.
Population: 29,034; Growth (since 2000): 11.1%; Density: 5,635.6 persons per square mile; Race: 82.7% White, 4.1% Black/African American, 6.7% Asian, 0.3% American Indian/Alaska Native, 0.1% Native Hawaiian/Other Pacific Islander, 4.0% Two or more races, 8.5% Hispanic of any race; Average household size: 2.01; Median age: 40.2; Age under 18: 16.1%; Age 65 and over: 13.4%; Males per 100 females: 96.7; Marriage status: 39.4% never married, 42.8% now married, 2.0% separated, 4.0% widowed, 13.7% divorced; Foreign born: 19.9%; Speak English only: 75.7%; With disability: 6.4%; Veterans: 4.9%; Ancestry: 12.0% Irish, 11.5% German, 9.0% English, 8.6% Russian, 6.9% Italian
Employment: 24.2% management, business, and financial, 6.5% computer, engineering, and science, 29.2% education, legal, community service, arts, and media, 5.1% healthcare practitioners, 9.7% service, 19.4% sales and office, 2.1% natural resources, construction, and maintenance, 3.9% production, transportation, and material moving
Income: Per capita: $67,802; Median household: $88,579; Average household: $136,336; Households with income of $100,000 or more: 44.7%; Poverty rate: 7.1%
Educational Attainment: High school diploma or higher: 96.7%; Bachelor's degree or higher: 59.7%; Graduate/professional degree or higher: 21.5%

School District(s)

Los Angeles Unified (PK-12)
2012-13 Enrollment: 655,455 . . . . (213) 241-1000
Housing: Homeownership rate: 47.9%; Median home value: $824,000; Median year structure built: 1969; Homeowner vacancy rate: 2.9%; Median gross rent: $1,652 per month; Rental vacancy rate: 6.3%
Health Insurance: 89.1% have insurance; 84.2% have private insurance; 15.7% have public insurance; 10.9% do not have insurance; 4.6% of children under 18 do not have insurance
Transportation: Commute: 83.6% car, 2.4% public transportation, 1.3% walk, 11.6% work from home; Median travel time to work: 27.8 minutes

SUN VALLEY (unincorporated postal area)

ZCTA: 91352

Covers a land area of 11.669 square miles and a water area of 0.228 square miles. Located at 34.23° N. Lat; 118.37° W. Long. Elevation is 810 feet.
Population: 47,807; Growth (since 2000): 2.5%; Density: 4,097.0 persons per square mile; Race: 51.9% White, 1.8% Black/African American, 6.3% Asian, 0.8% American Indian/Alaska Native, 0.2% Native Hawaiian/Other Pacific Islander, 4.0% Two or more races, 73.9% Hispanic of any race; Average household size: 3.95; Median age: 32.1; Age under 18: 27.4%; Age 65 and over: 9.0%; Males per 100 females: 100.6; Marriage status: 41.3% never married, 46.4% now married, 2.8% separated, 4.9% widowed, 7.4% divorced; Foreign born: 46.1%; Speak English only: 19.8%; With disability: 10.8%; Veterans: 2.4%; Ancestry: 5.1% Armenian, 2.7% German, 1.9% Irish, 1.6% English, 1.3% Italian
Employment: 8.9% management, business, and financial, 2.5% computer, engineering, and science, 6.4% education, legal, community service, arts, and media, 4.0% healthcare practitioners, 21.8% service, 25.0% sales and office, 14.4% natural resources, construction, and maintenance, 17.1% production, transportation, and material moving
Income: Per capita: $18,191; Median household: $48,844; Average household: $63,358; Households with income of $100,000 or more: 18.1%; Poverty rate: 19.2%

Educational Attainment: High school diploma or higher: 64.2%; Bachelor's degree or higher: 14.4%; Graduate/professional degree or higher: 3.8%

School District(s)

Los Angeles Unified (PK-12)
2012-13 Enrollment: 655,455 . . . . (213) 241-1000

Housing: Homeownership rate: 55.9%; Median home value: $338,300; Median year structure built: 1959; Homeowner vacancy rate: 1.6%; Median gross rent: $1,145 per month; Rental vacancy rate: 4.9%

Health Insurance: 72.4% have insurance; 43.3% have private insurance; 34.7% have public insurance; 27.6% do not have insurance; 10.1% of children under 18 do not have insurance

Hospitals: Pacifica Hospital of the Valley (248 beds)

Transportation: Commute: 85.9% car, 6.6% public transportation, 1.9% walk, 3.5% work from home; Median travel time to work: 28.2 minutes

SUN VILLAGE (CDP). Covers a land area of 10.686 square miles and a water area of <.001 square miles. Located at 34.56° N. Lat; 117.96° W. Long.

Population: 11,565; Growth (since 2000): n/a; Density: 1,082.3 persons per square mile; Race: 58.8% White, 7.0% Black/African American, 1.1% Asian, 1.4% American Indian/Alaska Native, 0.2% Native Hawaiian/Other Pacific Islander, 4.5% Two or more races, 63.2% Hispanic of any race; Average household size: 3.85; Median age: 31.4; Age under 18: 31.0%; Age 65 and over: 8.6%; Males per 100 females: 106.6; Marriage status: 36.9% never married, 46.7% now married, 2.7% separated, 5.9% widowed, 10.5% divorced; Foreign born: 22.3%; Speak English only: 57.7%; With disability: 11.0%; Veterans: 4.8%; Ancestry: 7.0% Irish, 5.9% German, 4.7% English, 2.4% French, 2.3% American

Employment: 6.2% management, business, and financial, 3.8% computer, engineering, and science, 12.4% education, legal, community service, arts, and media, 2.3% healthcare practitioners, 18.0% service, 22.7% sales and office, 20.7% natural resources, construction, and maintenance, 13.9% production, transportation, and material moving

Income: Per capita: $16,444; Median household: $55,609; Average household: $59,783; Households with income of $100,000 or more: 12.3%; Poverty rate: 15.1%

Educational Attainment: High school diploma or higher: 62.9%; Bachelor's degree or higher: 9.1%; Graduate/professional degree or higher: 2.8%

Housing: Homeownership rate: 74.5%; Median home value: $150,500; Median year structure built: 1984; Homeowner vacancy rate: 2.9%; Median gross rent: $1,483 per month; Rental vacancy rate: 5.4%

Health Insurance: 76.3% have insurance; 40.9% have private insurance; 41.1% have public insurance; 23.7% do not have insurance; 11.2% of children under 18 do not have insurance

Transportation: Commute: 92.6% car, 1.9% public transportation, 1.1% walk, 3.8% work from home; Median travel time to work: 47.0 minutes

SUNLAND (unincorporated postal area)

ZCTA: 91040

Covers a land area of 8.202 square miles and a water area of 0.005 square miles. Located at 34.26° N. Lat; 118.34° W. Long. Elevation is 1,512 feet.

Population: 20,372; Growth (since 2000): 8.7%; Density: 2,483.7 persons per square mile; Race: 75.6% White, 1.3% Black/African American, 8.5% Asian, 0.6% American Indian/Alaska Native, 0.1% Native Hawaiian/Other Pacific Islander, 4.2% Two or more races, 24.4% Hispanic of any race; Average household size: 2.72; Median age: 43.3; Age under 18: 19.1%; Age 65 and over: 14.2%; Males per 100 females: 98.7; Marriage status: 31.0% never married, 49.2% now married, 2.7% separated, 5.7% widowed, 14.2% divorced; Foreign born: 28.9%; Speak English only: 60.7%; With disability: 12.8%; Veterans: 7.2%; Ancestry: 11.8% German, 10.0% Irish, 9.8% Armenian, 8.4% English, 6.0% Italian

Employment: 15.5% management, business, and financial, 7.0% computer, engineering, and science, 14.8% education, legal, community service, arts, and media, 4.4% healthcare practitioners, 12.6% service, 29.0% sales and office, 9.2% natural resources, construction, and maintenance, 7.6% production, transportation, and material moving

Income: Per capita: $32,778; Median household: $69,312; Average household: $86,031; Households with income of $100,000 or more: 32.6%; Poverty rate: 10.4%

Educational Attainment: High school diploma or higher: 86.5%; Bachelor's degree or higher: 29.4%; Graduate/professional degree or higher: 9.0%

School District(s)

Los Angeles Unified (PK-12)
2012-13 Enrollment: 655,455 . . . . (213) 241-1000

Housing: Homeownership rate: 72.0%; Median home value: $414,200; Median year structure built: 1958; Homeowner vacancy rate: 1.6%; Median gross rent: $1,193 per month; Rental vacancy rate: 4.9%

Health Insurance: 86.8% have insurance; 66.4% have private insurance; 29.5% have public insurance; 13.2% do not have insurance; 6.1% of children under 18 do not have insurance

Transportation: Commute: 93.3% car, 1.3% public transportation, 1.1% walk, 3.0% work from home; Median travel time to work: 30.4 minutes

SYLMAR (unincorporated postal area)

ZCTA: 91342

Covers a land area of 55.101 square miles and a water area of 0.274 square miles. Located at 34.33° N. Lat; 118.38° W. Long. Elevation is 1,253 feet.

Population: 91,725; Growth (since 2000): 11.9%; Density: 1,664.7 persons per square mile; Race: 49.9% White, 5.0% Black/African American, 5.6% Asian, 1.1% American Indian/Alaska Native, 0.1% Native Hawaiian/Other Pacific Islander, 4.1% Two or more races, 74.6% Hispanic of any race; Average household size: 3.83; Median age: 31.9; Age under 18: 28.4%; Age 65 and over: 8.7%; Males per 100 females: 99.7; Marriage status: 40.3% never married, 48.2% now married, 3.2% separated, 4.4% widowed, 7.2% divorced; Foreign born: 36.6%; Speak English only: 29.7%; With disability: 10.7%; Veterans: 4.7%; Ancestry: 3.3% German, 2.0% Irish, 1.9% Italian, 1.9% English, 1.4% American

Employment: 11.2% management, business, and financial, 2.8% computer, engineering, and science, 8.4% education, legal, community service, arts, and media, 4.1% healthcare practitioners, 20.9% service, 26.1% sales and office, 12.5% natural resources, construction, and maintenance, 14.0% production, transportation, and material moving

Income: Per capita: $19,296; Median household: $59,329; Average household: $69,872; Households with income of $100,000 or more: 22.7%; Poverty rate: 16.7%

Educational Attainment: High school diploma or higher: 66.9%; Bachelor's degree or higher: 17.1%; Graduate/professional degree or higher: 4.5%

School District(s)

Los Angeles County Office of Education (KG-12)
2012-13 Enrollment: 9,136 . . . . (562) 922-6111

Los Angeles Unified (PK-12)
2012-13 Enrollment: 655,455 . . . . (213) 241-1000

Four-year College(s)

ITT Technical Institute-Sylmar (Private, For-profit)
Fall 2013 Enrollment: 557 . . . . (818) 364-5151
2013-14 Tuition: In-state $18,048; Out-of-state $18,048

Los Angeles Mission College (Public)
Fall 2013 Enrollment: 8,990 . . . . (818) 364-7600
2013-14 Tuition: In-state $1,221; Out-of-state $6,161

Two-year College(s)

ITT Technical Institute-Sylmar (Private, For-profit)
Fall 2013 Enrollment: 557 . . . . (818) 364-5151
2013-14 Tuition: In-state $18,048; Out-of-state $18,048

Los Angeles Mission College (Public)
Fall 2013 Enrollment: 8,990 . . . . (818) 364-7600
2013-14 Tuition: In-state $1,221; Out-of-state $6,161

Vocational/Technical School(s)

ITT Technical Institute-Sylmar (Private, For-profit)
Fall 2013 Enrollment: 557 . . . . (818) 364-5151
2013-14 Tuition: In-state $18,048; Out-of-state $18,048

Los Angeles Mission College (Public)
Fall 2013 Enrollment: 8,990 . . . . (818) 364-7600
2013-14 Tuition: In-state $1,221; Out-of-state $6,161

Housing: Homeownership rate: 68.4%; Median home value: $322,400; Median year structure built: 1970; Homeowner vacancy rate: 2.1%; Median gross rent: $1,313 per month; Rental vacancy rate: 5.4%

Health Insurance: 77.0% have insurance; 50.4% have private insurance; 31.8% have public insurance; 23.0% do not have insurance; 9.8% of children under 18 do not have insurance

Hospitals: LAC/Olive View - UCLA Medical Center (377 beds)

Transportation: Commute: 90.4% car, 3.8% public transportation, 1.0% walk, 3.5% work from home; Median travel time to work: 28.7 minutes

TARZANA (unincorporated postal area)

ZCTA: 91356

Covers a land area of 7.334 square miles and a water area of 0 square miles. Located at 34.16° N. Lat; 118.55° W. Long. Elevation is 787 feet.
Population: 29,458; Growth (since 2000): 7.5%; Density: 4,016.4 persons per square mile; Race: 77.4% White, 4.3% Black/African American, 6.5% Asian, 0.3% American Indian/Alaska Native, 0.2% Native Hawaiian/Other Pacific Islander, 5.2% Two or more races, 13.9% Hispanic of any race; Average household size: 2.50; Median age: 41.7; Age under 18: 20.7%; Age 65 and over: 16.7%; Males per 100 females: 93.3; Marriage status: 30.1% never married, 52.2% now married, 3.2% separated, 5.4% widowed, 12.3% divorced; Foreign born: 37.8%; Speak English only: 52.0%; With disability: 11.7%; Veterans: 5.5%; Ancestry: 11.4% Iranian, 9.5% Russian, 5.0% Polish, 4.8% German, 4.3% English
Employment: 21.7% management, business, and financial, 5.4% computer, engineering, and science, 13.7% education, legal, community service, arts, and media, 7.8% healthcare practitioners, 14.9% service, 28.4% sales and office, 4.4% natural resources, construction, and maintenance, 3.7% production, transportation, and material moving
Income: Per capita: $42,149; Median household: $70,759; Average household: $109,123; Households with income of $100,000 or more: 34.6%; Poverty rate: 12.9%
Educational Attainment: High school diploma or higher: 92.8%; Bachelor's degree or higher: 45.7%; Graduate/professional degree or higher: 15.1%

School District(s)

Los Angeles Unified (PK-12)
2012-13 Enrollment: 655,455 . . . . (213) 241-1000

Four-year College(s)

Columbia College-Hollywood (Private, Not-for-profit)
Fall 2013 Enrollment: 314 . . . . (818) 345-8414
2013-14 Tuition: In-state $18,804; Out-of-state $18,804
Hypnosis Motivation Institute (Private, Not-for-profit)
Fall 2013 Enrollment: 111 . . . . (818) 758-2720

Two-year College(s)

Columbia College-Hollywood (Private, Not-for-profit)
Fall 2013 Enrollment: 314 . . . . (818) 345-8414
2013-14 Tuition: In-state $18,804; Out-of-state $18,804
Hypnosis Motivation Institute (Private, Not-for-profit)
Fall 2013 Enrollment: 111 . . . . (818) 758-2720

Vocational/Technical School(s)

Columbia College-Hollywood (Private, Not-for-profit)
Fall 2013 Enrollment: 314 . . . . (818) 345-8414
2013-14 Tuition: In-state $18,804; Out-of-state $18,804
Hypnosis Motivation Institute (Private, Not-for-profit)
Fall 2013 Enrollment: 111 . . . . (818) 758-2720
2013-14 Tuition: $15,539

Housing: Homeownership rate: 59.0%; Median home value: $704,700; Median year structure built: 1971; Homeowner vacancy rate: 1.5%; Median gross rent: $1,224 per month; Rental vacancy rate: 8.3%
Health Insurance: 85.9% have insurance; 69.6% have private insurance; 27.0% have public insurance; 14.1% do not have insurance; 6.2% of children under 18 do not have insurance
Hospitals: Providence Tarzana Medical Center (396 beds)
Transportation: Commute: 82.5% car, 5.3% public transportation, 2.3% walk, 8.3% work from home; Median travel time to work: 33.5 minutes

TEMPLE CITY (city). Covers a land area of 4.006 square miles and a water area of 0 square miles. Located at 34.10° N. Lat; 118.06° W. Long. Elevation is 400 feet.
History: Named for Water P. Temple, founder of the town and president of Temple Townsite Company. Settled 1827. Incorporated 1960.
Population: 35,558; Growth (since 2000): 6.5%; Density: 8,877.2 persons per square mile; Race: 33.6% White, 0.8% Black/African American, 55.7% Asian, 0.4% American Indian/Alaska Native, 0.1% Native Hawaiian/Other Pacific Islander, 2.9% Two or more races, 19.3% Hispanic of any race; Average household size: 3.03; Median age: 42.0; Age under 18: 21.2%; Age 65 and over: 15.1%; Males per 100 females: 90.5; Marriage status: 29.3% never married, 55.9% now married, 1.2% separated, 7.5% widowed, 7.3% divorced; Foreign born: 46.6%; Speak English only: 34.6%; With disability: 8.7%; Veterans: 4.1%; Ancestry: 4.9% German, 3.9% Irish, 3.3% Italian, 2.6% English, 1.7% American
Employment: 16.8% management, business, and financial, 8.1% computer, engineering, and science, 12.7% education, legal, community service, arts, and media, 4.5% healthcare practitioners, 14.8% service, 30.5% sales and office, 5.8% natural resources, construction, and maintenance, 6.8% production, transportation, and material moving
Income: Per capita: $26,939; Median household: $66,075; Average household: $81,423; Households with income of $100,000 or more: 30.0%; Poverty rate: 10.0%
Educational Attainment: High school diploma or higher: 85.9%; Bachelor's degree or higher: 37.0%; Graduate/professional degree or higher: 12.9%

School District(s)

El Monte City Elementary (KG-08)
2012-13 Enrollment: 9,304 . . . . (626) 453-3700
Temple City Unified (KG-12)
2012-13 Enrollment: 5,799 . . . . (626) 548-5000

Housing: Homeownership rate: 64.2%; Median home value: $575,500; Median year structure built: 1957; Homeowner vacancy rate: 0.7%; Median gross rent: $1,368 per month; Rental vacancy rate: 5.2%
Health Insurance: 83.0% have insurance; 64.8% have private insurance; 25.3% have public insurance; 17.0% do not have insurance; 6.3% of children under 18 do not have insurance
Safety: Violent crime rate: 13.2 per 10,000 population; Property crime rate: 131.2 per 10,000 population
Transportation: Commute: 89.7% car, 3.6% public transportation, 1.0% walk, 4.8% work from home; Median travel time to work: 29.6 minutes

Additional Information Contacts

City of Temple City . . . . (626) 285-2171
http://www.ci.temple-city.ca.us

TOPANGA (CDP). Covers a land area of 19.129 square miles and a water area of 0.008 square miles. Located at 34.10° N. Lat; 118.61° W. Long. Elevation is 840 feet.
History: Topanga was named by the indigenous Native American Tongva tribe and means "a place above," "sky," or "heaven." It is located in the Santa Monica Mountains, a place for inspiration for many artists.
Population: 8,289; Growth (since 2000): n/a; Density: 433.3 persons per square mile; Race: 88.2% White, 1.4% Black/African American, 4.3% Asian, 0.4% American Indian/Alaska Native, 0.0% Native Hawaiian/Other Pacific Islander, 4.1% Two or more races, 6.4% Hispanic of any race; Average household size: 2.41; Median age: 46.1; Age under 18: 20.3%; Age 65 and over: 14.1%; Males per 100 females: 97.9; Marriage status: 23.4% never married, 62.2% now married, 2.8% separated, 2.7% widowed, 11.7% divorced; Foreign born: 16.7%; Speak English only: 82.1%; With disability: 5.0%; Veterans: 7.3%; Ancestry: 18.2% German, 13.6% English, 10.5% Irish, 6.3% American, 5.0% Italian
Employment: 29.4% management, business, and financial, 7.7% computer, engineering, and science, 28.7% education, legal, community service, arts, and media, 6.9% healthcare practitioners, 5.3% service, 17.3% sales and office, 2.6% natural resources, construction, and maintenance, 2.1% production, transportation, and material moving
Income: Per capita: $58,626; Median household: $120,711; Average household: $155,643; Households with income of $100,000 or more: 58.6%; Poverty rate: 5.9%
Educational Attainment: High school diploma or higher: 97.1%; Bachelor's degree or higher: 61.1%; Graduate/professional degree or higher: 30.3%

School District(s)

Los Angeles Unified (PK-12)
2012-13 Enrollment: 655,455 . . . . (213) 241-1000

Housing: Homeownership rate: 75.2%; Median home value: $973,000; Median year structure built: 1969; Homeowner vacancy rate: 2.2%; Median gross rent: $2,000 per month; Rental vacancy rate: 3.8%
Health Insurance: 91.8% have insurance; 80.3% have private insurance; 19.4% have public insurance; 8.2% do not have insurance; 2.1% of children under 18 do not have insurance
Transportation: Commute: 80.8% car, 0.0% public transportation, 1.2% walk, 15.9% work from home; Median travel time to work: 33.7 minutes

TORRANCE (city). Covers a land area of 20.478 square miles and a water area of 0.075 square miles. Located at 33.83° N. Lat; 118.34° W. Long. Elevation is 89 feet.
History: Named for Jared Sidney Torrance, a financier and philanthropist, in 1911, when he founded the city. Torrance, a wealthy Pasadena utilities magnate, laid out the industrial and residential community after studying city plans around the world.
Population: 145,438; Growth (since 2000): 5.4%; Density: 7,102.2 persons per square mile; Race: 51.1% White, 2.7% Black/African

American, 34.5% Asian, 0.4% American Indian/Alaska Native, 0.4% Native Hawaiian/Other Pacific Islander, 5.5% Two or more races, 16.1% Hispanic of any race; Average household size: 2.58; Median age: 41.3; Age under 18: 21.9%; Age 65 and over: 14.9%; Males per 100 females: 94.7; Marriage status: 28.7% never married, 54.8% now married, 1.7% separated, 6.3% widowed, 10.2% divorced; Foreign born: 29.5%; Speak English only: 61.5%; With disability: 9.1%; Veterans: 6.9%; Ancestry: 10.4% German, 8.3% Irish, 7.4% English, 4.6% Italian, 3.9% American

Employment: 20.2% management, business, and financial, 10.8% computer, engineering, and science, 12.0% education, legal, community service, arts, and media, 6.3% healthcare practitioners, 12.0% service, 25.9% sales and office, 5.3% natural resources, construction, and maintenance, 7.5% production, transportation, and material moving

Income: Per capita: $36,234; Median household: $77,061; Average household: $92,415; Households with income of $100,000 or more: 36.2%; Poverty rate: 7.4%

Educational Attainment: High school diploma or higher: 93.0%; Bachelor's degree or higher: 44.7%; Graduate/professional degree or higher: 15.0%

School District(s)

Los Angeles Unified (PK-12)
2012-13 Enrollment: 655,455 . . . . (213) 241-1000
Southern California Roc
2012-13 Enrollment: n/a . . . . (310) 320-6700
Torrance Unified (KG-12)
2012-13 Enrollment: 24,324 . . . . (310) 972-6500

Four-year College(s)

ITT Technical Institute-Torrance (Private, For-profit)
Fall 2013 Enrollment: 457 . . . . (310) 380-1555
2013-14 Tuition: In-state $18,048; Out-of-state $18,048
Westwood College-South Bay (Private, For-profit)
Fall 2013 Enrollment: 571 . . . . (310) 525-1260
2013-14 Tuition: In-state $15,122; Out-of-state $15,122

Two-year College(s)

El Camino Community College District (Public)
Fall 2013 Enrollment: 23,996 . . . . (310) 532-3670
2013-14 Tuition: In-state $1,142; Out-of-state $5,222

Vocational/Technical School(s)

Everest College-Torrance (Private, For-profit)
Fall 2013 Enrollment: 167 . . . . (310) 320-3200
2013-14 Tuition: $21,388
Homestead Schools (Private, Not-for-profit)
Fall 2013 Enrollment: 166 . . . . (310) 791-9975
2013-14 Tuition: $28,500

Housing: Homeownership rate: 56.4%; Median home value: $613,600; Median year structure built: 1963; Homeowner vacancy rate: 0.8%; Median gross rent: $1,432 per month; Rental vacancy rate: 5.3%

Health Insurance: 88.0% have insurance; 75.0% have private insurance; 23.0% have public insurance; 12.0% do not have insurance; 7.4% of children under 18 do not have insurance

Hospitals: LAC/Harbor - UCLA Medical Center (553 beds); Providence Little Co of Mary Medical Center Torrance (317 beds); Torrance Memorial Medical Center (335 beds)

Safety: Violent crime rate: 12.7 per 10,000 population; Property crime rate: 188.8 per 10,000 population

Newspapers: Daily Breeze (daily circulation 65600)

Transportation: Commute: 89.4% car, 2.5% public transportation, 1.8% walk, 4.5% work from home; Median travel time to work: 25.8 minutes; Amtrak: Bus service available.

Airports: Zamperini Field (general aviation)

Additional Information Contacts

City of Torrance. . . . . (310) 328-5310
http://www.torranceca.gov

TUJUNGA (unincorporated postal area)

ZCTA: 91042

Covers a land area of 49.883 square miles and a water area of 0.060 square miles. Located at 34.32° N. Lat; 118.24° W. Long. Elevation is 1,772 feet.

Population: 27,585; Growth (since 2000): 3.2%; Density: 553.0 persons per square mile; Race: 72.9% White, 1.7% Black/African American, 9.4% Asian, 0.6% American Indian/Alaska Native, 0.1% Native Hawaiian/Other Pacific Islander, 5.1% Two or more races, 25.9% Hispanic of any race; Average household size: 2.74; Median age: 40.7; Age under 18: 19.7%; Age 65 and over: 12.1%; Males per 100 females: 99.2; Marriage status: 33.6% never married, 52.1% now married, 2.8% separated, 4.1% widowed, 10.2% divorced; Foreign born: 42.1%; Speak English only: 41.4%; With disability: 10.7%; Veterans: 4.9%; Ancestry: 24.3% Armenian, 7.4% German, 5.4% Irish, 5.2% English, 3.6% Italian

Employment: 12.1% management, business, and financial, 5.1% computer, engineering, and science, 13.8% education, legal, community service, arts, and media, 3.5% healthcare practitioners, 18.9% service, 27.2% sales and office, 10.9% natural resources, construction, and maintenance, 8.4% production, transportation, and material moving

Income: Per capita: $26,892; Median household: $57,500; Average household: $73,694; Households with income of $100,000 or more: 24.7%; Poverty rate: 16.1%

Educational Attainment: High school diploma or higher: 83.4%; Bachelor's degree or higher: 24.8%; Graduate/professional degree or higher: 9.0%

School District(s)

Los Angeles Unified (PK-12)
2012-13 Enrollment: 655,455 . . . . (213) 241-1000

Housing: Homeownership rate: 56.5%; Median home value: $404,600; Median year structure built: 1960; Homeowner vacancy rate: 1.4%; Median gross rent: $1,133 per month; Rental vacancy rate: 5.3%

Health Insurance: 77.2% have insurance; 54.2% have private insurance; 28.7% have public insurance; 22.8% do not have insurance; 7.6% of children under 18 do not have insurance

Transportation: Commute: 89.8% car, 2.0% public transportation, 3.1% walk, 3.4% work from home; Median travel time to work: 30.5 minutes

---

VAL VERDE (CDP). Covers a land area of 2.565 square miles and a water area of 0 square miles. Located at 34.45° N. Lat; 118.67° W. Long. Elevation is 1,188 feet.

Population: 2,468; Growth (since 2000): 67.7%; Density: 962.1 persons per square mile; Race: 56.9% White, 4.3% Black/African American, 1.9% Asian, 1.1% American Indian/Alaska Native, 0.0% Native Hawaiian/Other Pacific Islander, 6.2% Two or more races, 61.1% Hispanic of any race; Average household size: 3.68; Median age: 31.7; Age under 18: 28.6%; Age 65 and over: 5.0%; Males per 100 females: 102.1

Housing: Homeownership rate: 77.7%; Homeowner vacancy rate: 3.2%; Rental vacancy rate: 2.6%

VALENCIA (unincorporated postal area)

ZCTA: 91354

Covers a land area of 8.724 square miles and a water area of 0.002 square miles. Located at 34.47° N. Lat; 118.55° W. Long. Elevation is 1,017 feet.

Population: 28,722; Growth (since 2000): 61.0%; Density: 3,292.2 persons per square mile; Race: 71.8% White, 3.2% Black/African American, 16.0% Asian, 0.3% American Indian/Alaska Native, 0.1% Native Hawaiian/Other Pacific Islander, 4.6% Two or more races, 15.6% Hispanic of any race; Average household size: 3.01; Median age: 36.4; Age under 18: 30.3%; Age 65 and over: 6.9%; Males per 100 females: 95.7; Marriage status: 25.1% never married, 64.0% now married, 1.3% separated, 3.4% widowed, 7.4% divorced; Foreign born: 20.8%; Speak English only: 73.6%; With disability: 6.4%; Veterans: 5.9%; Ancestry: 11.7% German, 10.9% English, 10.6% Irish, 9.0% Italian, 3.3% Russian

Employment: 23.2% management, business, and financial, 7.9% computer, engineering, and science, 13.5% education, legal, community service, arts, and media, 8.1% healthcare practitioners, 12.8% service, 26.4% sales and office, 3.9% natural resources, construction, and maintenance, 4.2% production, transportation, and material moving

Income: Per capita: $40,182; Median household: $107,654; Average household: $123,006; Households with income of $100,000 or more: 55.2%; Poverty rate: 4.8%

Educational Attainment: High school diploma or higher: 97.5%; Bachelor's degree or higher: 50.1%; Graduate/professional degree or higher: 16.4%

School District(s)

Newhall (KG-06)
2012-13 Enrollment: 6,947 . . . . (661) 291-4000
Saugus Union (KG-06)
2012-13 Enrollment: 10,178 . . . . (661) 294-5300
William S. Hart Union High (KG-12)
2012-13 Enrollment: 26,373 . . . . (661) 259-0033

Four-year College(s)

California Institute of the Arts (Private, Not-for-profit)
Fall 2013 Enrollment: 1,489 . . . . (661) 255-1050
2013-14 Tuition: In-state $40,536; Out-of-state $40,536

Two-year College(s)

California Institute of the Arts (Private, Not-for-profit)
Fall 2013 Enrollment: 1,489 . . . . (661) 255-1050
2013-14 Tuition: In-state $40,536; Out-of-state $40,536

Vocational/Technical School(s)

California Institute of the Arts (Private, Not-for-profit)
Fall 2013 Enrollment: 1,489 . . . . (661) 255-1050
2013-14 Tuition: In-state $40,536; Out-of-state $40,536

Housing: Homeownership rate: 79.8%; Median home value: $454,800; Median year structure built: 1997; Homeowner vacancy rate: 1.8%; Median gross rent: $1,914 per month; Rental vacancy rate: 8.3%

Health Insurance: 92.5% have insurance; 87.0% have private insurance; 12.5% have public insurance; 7.5% do not have insurance; 1.9% of children under 18 do not have insurance

Hospitals: Henry Mayo Newhall Memorial Hospital (217 beds)

Transportation: Commute: 88.8% car, 3.1% public transportation, 0.3% walk, 7.1% work from home; Median travel time to work: 35.5 minutes

ZCTA: 91355

Covers a land area of 15.475 square miles and a water area of 0.157 square miles. Located at 34.44° N. Lat; 118.63° W. Long. Elevation is 1,017 feet.

Population: 32,605; Growth (since 2000): 30.6%; Density: 2,107.0 persons per square mile; Race: 76.7% White, 2.8% Black/African American, 10.7% Asian, 0.4% American Indian/Alaska Native, 0.1% Native Hawaiian/Other Pacific Islander, 4.3% Two or more races, 17.5% Hispanic of any race; Average household size: 2.51; Median age: 38.8; Age under 18: 22.6%; Age 65 and over: 11.5%; Males per 100 females: 93.7; Marriage status: 33.2% never married, 51.7% now married, 1.9% separated, 4.4% widowed, 10.7% divorced; Foreign born: 17.1%; Speak English only: 78.9%; With disability: 8.5%; Veterans: 7.2%; Ancestry: 14.7% German, 12.1% Irish, 10.3% English, 7.0% Italian, 5.2% American

Employment: 19.0% management, business, and financial, 7.2% computer, engineering, and science, 17.5% education, legal, community service, arts, and media, 6.5% healthcare practitioners, 13.5% service, 25.5% sales and office, 5.0% natural resources, construction, and maintenance, 5.9% production, transportation, and material moving

Income: Per capita: $41,681; Median household: $88,415; Average household: $106,389; Households with income of $100,000 or more: 40.7%; Poverty rate: 6.7%

Educational Attainment: High school diploma or higher: 92.9%; Bachelor's degree or higher: 41.5%; Graduate/professional degree or higher: 14.0%

Housing: Homeownership rate: 63.7%; Median home value: $420,700; Median year structure built: 1984; Homeowner vacancy rate: 0.9%; Median gross rent: $1,670 per month; Rental vacancy rate: 5.1%

Health Insurance: 90.8% have insurance; 82.4% have private insurance; 17.0% have public insurance; 9.2% do not have insurance; 3.4% of children under 18 do not have insurance

Transportation: Commute: 88.2% car, 1.7% public transportation, 3.5% walk, 5.6% work from home; Median travel time to work: 30.6 minutes

VALINDA (CDP).

Covers a land area of 2.014 square miles and a water area of 0 square miles. Located at 34.04° N. Lat; 117.93° W. Long. Elevation is 348 feet.

Population: 22,822; Growth (since 2000): 4.8%; Density: 11,330.9 persons per square mile; Race: 48.5% White, 1.9% Black/African American, 11.9% Asian, 1.1% American Indian/Alaska Native, 0.2% Native Hawaiian/Other Pacific Islander, 3.5% Two or more races, 78.8% Hispanic of any race; Average household size: 4.61; Median age: 31.7; Age under 18: 29.2%; Age 65 and over: 8.7%; Males per 100 females: 100.5; Marriage status: 38.6% never married, 49.7% now married, 2.1% separated, 4.3% widowed, 7.5% divorced; Foreign born: 39.1%; Speak English only: 25.5%; With disability: 9.6%; Veterans: 3.5%; Ancestry: 1.4% Irish, 1.2% Italian, 1.1% American, 1.0% English, 0.9% French

Employment: 7.7% management, business, and financial, 1.5% computer, engineering, and science, 5.8% education, legal, community service, arts, and media, 6.0% healthcare practitioners, 19.8% service, 28.6% sales and office, 8.3% natural resources, construction, and maintenance, 22.3% production, transportation, and material moving

Income: Per capita: $17,541; Median household: $67,859; Average household: $75,690; Households with income of $100,000 or more: 26.4%; Poverty rate: 12.5%

Educational Attainment: High school diploma or higher: 67.5%; Bachelor's degree or higher: 13.4%; Graduate/professional degree or higher: 3.2%

School District(s)

Hacienda La Puente Unified (KG-12)
2012-13 Enrollment: 20,358 . . . . (626) 933-1000

Housing: Homeownership rate: 76.2%; Median home value: $318,200; Median year structure built: 1957; Homeowner vacancy rate: 0.9%; Median gross rent: $1,378 per month; Rental vacancy rate: 3.3%

Health Insurance: 75.1% have insurance; 48.1% have private insurance; 30.9% have public insurance; 24.9% do not have insurance; 9.6% of children under 18 do not have insurance

Transportation: Commute: 92.3% car, 2.9% public transportation, 1.1% walk, 3.1% work from home; Median travel time to work: 32.4 minutes

VALLEY VILLAGE (unincorporated postal area)

ZCTA: 91607

Covers a land area of 2.439 square miles and a water area of 0.022 square miles. Located at 34.17° N. Lat; 118.40° W. Long..

Population: 27,927; Growth (since 2000): 1.8%; Density: 11,447.9 persons per square mile; Race: 75.8% White, 5.3% Black/African American, 5.7% Asian, 0.5% American Indian/Alaska Native, 0.1% Native Hawaiian/Other Pacific Islander, 4.4% Two or more races, 19.6% Hispanic of any race; Average household size: 2.15; Median age: 38.2; Age under 18: 17.5%; Age 65 and over: 12.2%; Males per 100 females: 95.4; Marriage status: 39.0% never married, 40.9% now married, 3.4% separated, 4.7% widowed, 15.4% divorced; Foreign born: 27.0%; Speak English only: 65.4%; With disability: 9.0%; Veterans: 3.8%; Ancestry: 8.8% German, 8.3% English, 7.1% Irish, 6.0% Russian, 5.4% Italian

Employment: 15.2% management, business, and financial, 3.8% computer, engineering, and science, 23.1% education, legal, community service, arts, and media, 5.0% healthcare practitioners, 15.3% service, 26.8% sales and office, 4.9% natural resources, construction, and maintenance, 6.0% production, transportation, and material moving

Income: Per capita: $39,607; Median household: $56,635; Average household: $84,829; Households with income of $100,000 or more: 25.9%; Poverty rate: 11.1%

Educational Attainment: High school diploma or higher: 91.8%; Bachelor's degree or higher: 45.5%; Graduate/professional degree or higher: 13.4%

Housing: Homeownership rate: 32.3%; Median home value: $594,100; Median year structure built: 1965; Homeowner vacancy rate: 3.4%; Median gross rent: $1,259 per month; Rental vacancy rate: 6.6%

Health Insurance: 81.1% have insurance; 69.2% have private insurance; 18.6% have public insurance; 18.9% do not have insurance; 9.8% of children under 18 do not have insurance

Transportation: Commute: 84.3% car, 6.0% public transportation, 1.1% walk, 6.5% work from home; Median travel time to work: 30.5 minutes

VALYERMO (unincorporated postal area)

ZCTA: 93563

Covers a land area of 40.190 square miles and a water area of 0.035 square miles. Located at 34.40° N. Lat; 117.77° W. Long. Elevation is 3,711 feet.

Population: 388; Growth (since 2000): -4.4%; Density: 9.7 persons per square mile; Race: 77.1% White, 10.1% Black/African American, 2.3% Asian, 1.3% American Indian/Alaska Native, 0.8% Native Hawaiian/Other Pacific Islander, 2.3% Two or more races, 15.5% Hispanic of any race; Average household size: 2.53; Median age: 44.5; Age under 18: 14.2%; Age 65 and over: 12.6%; Males per 100 females: 210.4

Housing: Homeownership rate: 77.6%; Homeowner vacancy rate: 2.4%; Rental vacancy rate: 8.0%

VAN NUYS (unincorporated postal area)

ZCTA: 91401

Covers a land area of 3.453 square miles and a water area of 0.009 square miles. Located at 34.18° N. Lat; 118.43° W. Long. Elevation is 712 feet.

Population: 39,285; Growth (since 2000): -2.7%; Density: 11,376.6 persons per square mile; Race: 65.3% White, 4.7% Black/African American, 5.4% Asian, 0.7% American Indian/Alaska Native, 0.1% Native Hawaiian/Other Pacific Islander, 4.5% Two or more races, 42.4% Hispanic of any race; Average household size: 2.70; Median age: 36.0; Age under 18: 22.2%; Age 65 and over: 10.2%; Males per 100 females: 99.7; Marriage status: 42.6% never married, 42.8% now married, 3.3% separated, 4.1% widowed, 10.5% divorced; Foreign born: 40.4%; Speak English only: 39.3%; With disability: 9.8%; Veterans: 3.5%; Ancestry: 10.2% Armenian, 5.1% Irish, 5.1% German, 4.0% English, 3.9% Russian

Employment: 13.2% management, business, and financial, 3.0% computer, engineering, and science, 15.9% education, legal, community service, arts, and media, 4.5% healthcare practitioners, 22.3% service, 22.9% sales and office, 8.8% natural resources, construction, and maintenance, 9.5% production, transportation, and material moving

Income: Per capita: $25,395; Median household: $46,420; Average household: $66,643; Households with income of $100,000 or more: 20.9%; Poverty rate: 22.6%

Educational Attainment: High school diploma or higher: 77.9%; Bachelor's degree or higher: 30.9%; Graduate/professional degree or higher: 9.4%

School District(s)

Hermosa Beach City Elementary (KG-12)
2012-13 Enrollment: 2,667 . . . . (310) 937-5877

Los Angeles Unified (PK-12)
2012-13 Enrollment: 655,455 . . . . (213) 241-1000

Four-year College(s)

Capstone College (Private, For-profit)
Fall 2013 Enrollment: 50 . . . . (818) 908-9912

Casa Loma College-Van Nuys (Private, Not-for-profit)
Fall 2013 Enrollment: 606 . . . . (818) 785-2726

King's University (Private, Not-for-profit, Interdenominational)
Fall 2013 Enrollment: 598 . . . . (817) 552-3600
2013-14 Tuition: In-state $11,475; Out-of-state $11,475

Los Angeles ORT College-Van Nuys Campus (Private, Not-for-profit)
Fall 2013 Enrollment: 43 . . . . (818) 382-6000

Marian Health Careers Center-Van Nuys Campus (Private, For-profit)
Fall 2013 Enrollment: 94 . . . . (818) 782-6163

National Career College (Private, For-profit)
Fall 2013 Enrollment: 43 . . . . (818) 988-2300

Preferred College of Nursing-Van Nuys (Private, For-profit)
Fall 2013 Enrollment: 18 . . . . (818) 902-3708

Two-year College(s)

Capstone College (Private, For-profit)
Fall 2013 Enrollment: 50 . . . . (818) 908-9912

Casa Loma College-Van Nuys (Private, Not-for-profit)
Fall 2013 Enrollment: 606 . . . . (818) 785-2726

King's University (Private, Not-for-profit, Interdenominational)
Fall 2013 Enrollment: 598 . . . . (817) 552-3600
2013-14 Tuition: In-state $11,475; Out-of-state $11,475

Los Angeles ORT College-Van Nuys Campus (Private, Not-for-profit)
Fall 2013 Enrollment: 43 . . . . (818) 382-6000

Marian Health Careers Center-Van Nuys Campus (Private, For-profit)
Fall 2013 Enrollment: 94 . . . . (818) 782-6163

National Career College (Private, For-profit)
Fall 2013 Enrollment: 43 . . . . (818) 988-2300

Preferred College of Nursing-Van Nuys (Private, For-profit)
Fall 2013 Enrollment: 18 . . . . (818) 902-3708

Vocational/Technical School(s)

Capstone College (Private, For-profit)
Fall 2013 Enrollment: 50 . . . . (818) 908-9912
2013-14 Tuition: $11,500

Casa Loma College-Van Nuys (Private, Not-for-profit)
Fall 2013 Enrollment: 606 . . . . (818) 785-2726
2013-14 Tuition: $27,757

King's University (Private, Not-for-profit, Interdenominational)
Fall 2013 Enrollment: 598 . . . . (817) 552-3600
2013-14 Tuition: In-state $11,475; Out-of-state $11,475

Los Angeles ORT College-Van Nuys Campus (Private, Not-for-profit)
Fall 2013 Enrollment: 43 . . . . (818) 382-6000
2013-14 Tuition: $18,060

Marian Health Careers Center-Van Nuys Campus (Private, For-profit)
Fall 2013 Enrollment: 94 . . . . (818) 782-6163
2013-14 Tuition: $23,010

National Career College (Private, For-profit)
Fall 2013 Enrollment: 43 . . . . (818) 988-2300
2013-14 Tuition: $11,106

Preferred College of Nursing-Van Nuys (Private, For-profit)
Fall 2013 Enrollment: 18 . . . . (818) 902-3708
2013-14 Tuition: $23,487

Housing: Homeownership rate: 36.8%; Median home value: $506,100; Median year structure built: 1961; Homeowner vacancy rate: 2.4%; Median gross rent: $1,144 per month; Rental vacancy rate: 5.9%

Health Insurance: 72.9% have insurance; 47.2% have private insurance; 30.8% have public insurance; 27.1% do not have insurance; 7.0% of children under 18 do not have insurance

Hospitals: Valley Presbyterian Hospital (350 beds)

Transportation: Commute: 79.1% car, 10.0% public transportation, 2.6% walk, 6.4% work from home; Median travel time to work: 29.9 minutes

Airports: Van Nuys (general aviation)

ZCTA: 91405

Covers a land area of 3.309 square miles and a water area of 0.007 square miles. Located at 34.20° N. Lat; 118.45° W. Long. Elevation is 712 feet.

Population: 51,145; Growth (since 2000): -0.4%; Density: 15,456.7 persons per square mile; Race: 52.2% White, 5.2% Black/African American, 8.1% Asian, 0.6% American Indian/Alaska Native, 0.2% Native Hawaiian/Other Pacific Islander, 4.8% Two or more races, 60.5% Hispanic of any race; Average household size: 3.11; Median age: 32.6; Age under 18: 25.9%; Age 65 and over: 8.5%; Males per 100 females: 99.4; Marriage status: 43.2% never married, 45.5% now married, 3.7% separated, 4.1% widowed, 7.1% divorced; Foreign born: 49.5%; Speak English only: 23.5%; With disability: 8.2%; Veterans: 2.7%; Ancestry: 8.2% Armenian, 3.8% German, 3.0% Irish, 2.0% English, 2.0% American

Employment: 8.9% management, business, and financial, 2.4% computer, engineering, and science, 7.8% education, legal, community service, arts, and media, 3.3% healthcare practitioners, 28.0% service, 21.6% sales and office, 12.8% natural resources, construction, and maintenance, 15.1% production, transportation, and material moving

Income: Per capita: $17,645; Median household: $38,847; Average household: $54,147; Households with income of $100,000 or more: 13.8%; Poverty rate: 26.3%

Educational Attainment: High school diploma or higher: 67.7%; Bachelor's degree or higher: 19.7%; Graduate/professional degree or higher: 5.5%

Housing: Homeownership rate: 27.8%; Median home value: $342,100; Median year structure built: 1970; Homeowner vacancy rate: 1.9%; Median gross rent: $1,078 per month; Rental vacancy rate: 7.3%

Health Insurance: 68.0% have insurance; 36.0% have private insurance; 35.4% have public insurance; 32.0% do not have insurance; 10.4% of children under 18 do not have insurance

Transportation: Commute: 76.8% car, 13.2% public transportation, 3.5% walk, 3.9% work from home; Median travel time to work: 33.0 minutes

ZCTA: 91406

Covers a land area of 8.132 square miles and a water area of 0.016 square miles. Located at 34.20° N. Lat; 118.49° W. Long. Elevation is 712 feet.

Population: 51,558; Growth (since 2000): 3.0%; Density: 6,340.1 persons per square mile; Race: 56.0% White, 5.4% Black/African American, 7.8% Asian, 0.8% American Indian/Alaska Native, 0.1% Native Hawaiian/Other Pacific Islander, 5.5% Two or more races, 55.6% Hispanic of any race; Average household size: 3.02; Median age: 33.6; Age under 18: 25.3%; Age 65 and over: 8.3%; Males per 100 females: 101.4; Marriage status: 41.0% never married, 45.2% now married, 3.3% separated, 4.9% widowed, 8.9% divorced; Foreign born: 40.4%; Speak English only: 35.6%; With disability: 8.2%; Veterans: 3.4%; Ancestry: 4.9% Armenian, 4.7% Irish, 4.3% German, 3.7% Italian, 3.2% English

Employment: 10.6% management, business, and financial, 2.6% computer, engineering, and science, 10.1% education, legal, community service, arts, and media, 3.1% healthcare practitioners, 25.2% service, 25.2% sales and office, 11.8% natural resources, construction, and maintenance, 11.4% production, transportation, and material moving

Income: Per capita: $21,853; Median household: $49,231; Average household: $63,348; Households with income of $100,000 or more: 19.1%; Poverty rate: 19.1%

Educational Attainment: High school diploma or higher: 76.0%; Bachelor's degree or higher: 22.6%; Graduate/professional degree or higher: 6.5%

Housing: Homeownership rate: 42.8%; Median home value: $361,600; Median year structure built: 1962; Homeowner vacancy rate: 1.9%; Median gross rent: $1,125 per month; Rental vacancy rate: 6.1%

Health Insurance: 76.8% have insurance; 49.0% have private insurance; 32.9% have public insurance; 23.2% do not have insurance; 8.2% of children under 18 do not have insurance
Transportation: Commute: 81.1% car, 8.7% public transportation, 1.9% walk, 5.6% work from home; Median travel time to work: 31.1 minutes

ZCTA: 91411

Covers a land area of 2.042 square miles and a water area of 0 square miles. Located at 34.18° N. Lat; 118.46° W. Long. Elevation is 712 feet.
Population: 24,628; Growth (since 2000): 4.2%; Density: 12,058.9 persons per square mile; Race: 58.0% White, 5.7% Black/African American, 6.5% Asian, 0.8% American Indian/Alaska Native, 0.1% Native Hawaiian/Other Pacific Islander, 4.7% Two or more races, 51.6% Hispanic of any race; Average household size: 2.63; Median age: 33.8; Age under 18: 22.7%; Age 65 and over: 9.2%; Males per 100 females: 103.0; Marriage status: 43.3% never married, 41.7% now married, 3.4% separated, 5.0% widowed, 9.9% divorced; Foreign born: 41.0%; Speak English only: 38.7%; With disability: 9.4%; Veterans: 4.9%; Ancestry: 5.4% German, 5.1% Irish, 3.9% English, 3.6% Italian, 3.2% Russian
Employment: 13.0% management, business, and financial, 3.4% computer, engineering, and science, 13.8% education, legal, community service, arts, and media, 3.2% healthcare practitioners, 24.3% service, 21.9% sales and office, 10.1% natural resources, construction, and maintenance, 10.3% production, transportation, and material moving
Income: Per capita: $24,510; Median household: $44,570; Average household: $62,191; Households with income of $100,000 or more: 18.4%; Poverty rate: 21.0%
Educational Attainment: High school diploma or higher: 75.1%; Bachelor's degree or higher: 29.9%; Graduate/professional degree or higher: 7.2%
Housing: Homeownership rate: 26.6%; Median home value: $456,400; Median year structure built: 1968; Homeowner vacancy rate: 2.8%; Median gross rent: $1,156 per month; Rental vacancy rate: 6.5%
Health Insurance: 67.6% have insurance; 43.7% have private insurance; 29.3% have public insurance; 32.4% do not have insurance; 12.2% of children under 18 do not have insurance
Transportation: Commute: 80.4% car, 8.1% public transportation, 3.1% walk, 6.6% work from home; Median travel time to work: 30.7 minutes

VENICE (unincorporated postal area)

ZCTA: 90291

Covers a land area of 2.495 square miles and a water area of 0.337 square miles. Located at 33.99° N. Lat; 118.47° W. Long. Elevation is 13 feet.
Population: 28,341; Growth (since 2000): -8.6%; Density: 11,358.9 persons per square mile; Race: 77.0% White, 5.3% Black/African American, 4.4% Asian, 0.7% American Indian/Alaska Native, 0.2% Native Hawaiian/Other Pacific Islander, 4.6% Two or more races, 20.0% Hispanic of any race; Average household size: 1.95; Median age: 37.6; Age under 18: 13.0%; Age 65 and over: 8.8%; Males per 100 females: 108.6; Marriage status: 52.6% never married, 33.3% now married, 1.7% separated, 2.7% widowed, 11.4% divorced; Foreign born: 17.2%; Speak English only: 77.3%; With disability: 7.3%; Veterans: 3.4%; Ancestry: 12.4% German, 12.1% Irish, 8.7% Italian, 7.9% English, 5.2% Russian
Employment: 23.4% management, business, and financial, 5.7% computer, engineering, and science, 29.0% education, legal, community service, arts, and media, 3.9% healthcare practitioners, 12.5% service, 19.2% sales and office, 3.2% natural resources, construction, and maintenance, 3.0% production, transportation, and material moving
Income: Per capita: $59,717; Median household: $79,736; Average household: $113,225; Households with income of $100,000 or more: 39.3%; Poverty rate: 13.2%
Educational Attainment: High school diploma or higher: 92.6%; Bachelor's degree or higher: 60.7%; Graduate/professional degree or higher: 21.2%

School District(s)

Los Angeles Unified (PK-12)
2012-13 Enrollment: 655,455 . . . . (213) 241-1000
Housing: Homeownership rate: 32.2%; Median home value: $992,700; Median year structure built: 1955; Homeowner vacancy rate: 1.6%; Median gross rent: $1,618 per month; Rental vacancy rate: 4.8%
Health Insurance: 84.2% have insurance; 73.1% have private insurance; 17.6% have public insurance; 15.8% do not have insurance; 2.8% of children under 18 do not have insurance
Transportation: Commute: 69.5% car, 4.3% public transportation, 4.2% walk, 15.0% work from home; Median travel time to work: 26.2 minutes

VERDUGO CITY (unincorporated postal area)

ZCTA: 91046

Covers a land area of 0.010 square miles and a water area of 0 square miles. Located at 34.21° N. Lat; 118.24° W. Long. Elevation is 1,270 feet.
Population: 156; Growth (since 2000): n/a; Density: 15,590.6 persons per square mile; Race: 85.3% White, 0.0% Black/African American, 5.1% Asian, 0.0% American Indian/Alaska Native, 0.0% Native Hawaiian/Other Pacific Islander, 5.8% Two or more races, 13.5% Hispanic of any race; Average household size: 1.37; Median age: 74.0; Age under 18: 7.1%; Age 65 and over: 69.2%; Males per 100 females: 48.6
Housing: Homeownership rate: 7.9%; Homeowner vacancy rate: 0.0%; Rental vacancy rate: 3.7%

VERNON (city). Covers a land area of 4.973 square miles and a water area of 0.184 square miles. Located at 34.00° N. Lat; 118.21° W. Long. Elevation is 203 feet.

Population: 112; Growth (since 2000): 23.1%; Density: 22.5 persons per square mile; Race: 88.4% White, 3.6% Black/African American, 1.8% Asian, 0.0% American Indian/Alaska Native, 0.0% Native Hawaiian/Other Pacific Islander, 0.0% Two or more races, 42.9% Hispanic of any race; Average household size: 4.00; Median age: 36.5; Age under 18: 18.7%; Age 65 and over: 12.5%; Males per 100 females: 96.5
Housing: Homeownership rate: 14.3%; Homeowner vacancy rate: 0.0%; Rental vacancy rate: 4.0%
Additional Information Contacts
City of Vernon . . . . (323) 583-8811
http://www.cityofvernon.org

VIEW PARK-WINDSOR HILLS (CDP). Covers a land area of 1.841 square miles and a water area of <.001 square miles. Located at 33.99° N. Lat; 118.35° W. Long. Elevation is 322 feet.

Population: 11,075; Growth (since 2000): 1.1%; Density: 6,015.1 persons per square mile; Race: 6.0% White, 84.8% Black/African American, 1.3% Asian, 0.4% American Indian/Alaska Native, 0.0% Native Hawaiian/Other Pacific Islander, 5.2% Two or more races, 6.5% Hispanic of any race; Average household size: 2.43; Median age: 47.1; Age under 18: 18.9%; Age 65 and over: 21.3%; Males per 100 females: 80.6; Marriage status: 32.1% never married, 45.9% now married, 2.5% separated, 7.4% widowed, 14.5% divorced; Foreign born: 7.2%; Speak English only: 90.2%; With disability: 12.4%; Veterans: 9.9%; Ancestry: 6.2% African, 2.1% American, 1.3% Moroccan, 1.0% Jamaican, 1.0% German
Employment: 19.2% management, business, and financial, 3.1% computer, engineering, and science, 31.3% education, legal, community service, arts, and media, 5.5% healthcare practitioners, 11.9% service, 20.7% sales and office, 3.4% natural resources, construction, and maintenance, 4.9% production, transportation, and material moving
Income: Per capita: $46,215; Median household: $79,896; Average household: $107,718; Households with income of $100,000 or more: 40.8%; Poverty rate: 8.3%
Educational Attainment: High school diploma or higher: 95.7%; Bachelor's degree or higher: 50.0%; Graduate/professional degree or higher: 26.7%
Housing: Homeownership rate: 72.3%; Median home value: $504,400; Median year structure built: 1949; Homeowner vacancy rate: 1.3%; Median gross rent: $1,215 per month; Rental vacancy rate: 5.2%
Health Insurance: 89.6% have insurance; 79.6% have private insurance; 26.2% have public insurance; 10.4% do not have insurance; 1.5% of children under 18 do not have insurance
Transportation: Commute: 87.9% car, 2.1% public transportation, 0.9% walk, 7.8% work from home; Median travel time to work: 28.8 minutes

VINCENT (CDP).

Note: Statistics that would complete this profile are not available because the CDP was created after the 2010 Census was released.

WALNUT (city). Covers a land area of 8.992 square miles and a water area of 0.004 square miles. Located at 34.04° N. Lat; 117.86° W. Long. Elevation is 561 feet.

Population: 29,172; Growth (since 2000): -2.8%; Density: 3,244.1 persons per square mile; Race: 23.7% White, 2.8% Black/African American, 63.6% Asian, 0.2% American Indian/Alaska Native, 0.1% Native Hawaiian/Other Pacific Islander, 3.5% Two or more races, 19.1% Hispanic of any race; Average household size: 3.41; Median age: 43.1; Age under 18: 20.9%; Age 65 and over: 12.2%; Males per 100 females: 96.2; Marriage status: 32.9% never married, 58.2% now married, 0.8% separated, 5.0%

widowed, 3.9% divorced; Foreign born: 47.8%; Speak English only: 36.8%; With disability: 6.1%; Veterans: 3.7%; Ancestry: 6.0% American, 2.4% German, 2.2% English, 1.5% Irish, 1.0% Italian

Employment: 20.1% management, business, and financial, 9.0% computer, engineering, and science, 10.2% education, legal, community service, arts, and media, 11.4% healthcare practitioners, 10.5% service, 29.7% sales and office, 3.6% natural resources, construction, and maintenance, 5.7% production, transportation, and material moving

Income: Per capita: $35,205; Median household: $101,250; Average household: $118,053; Households with income of $100,000 or more: 50.5%; Poverty rate: 6.2%

Educational Attainment: High school diploma or higher: 93.2%; Bachelor's degree or higher: 52.3%; Graduate/professional degree or higher: 16.0%

School District(s)

Rowland Unified (KG-12)
2012-13 Enrollment: 15,501 . . . . (626) 965-2541
Walnut Valley Unified (KG-12)
2012-13 Enrollment: 14,661 . . . . (909) 595-1261

Two-year College(s)

Mt San Antonio College (Public)
Fall 2013 Enrollment: 28,481 . . . . (909) 594-5611
2013-14 Tuition: In-state $1,346; Out-of-state $7,422

Housing: Homeownership rate: 88.3%; Median home value: $625,100; Median year structure built: 1982; Homeowner vacancy rate: 0.8%; Median gross rent: $1,955 per month; Rental vacancy rate: 4.4%

Health Insurance: 88.5% have insurance; 77.1% have private insurance; 16.0% have public insurance; 11.5% do not have insurance; 6.4% of children under 18 do not have insurance

Safety: Violent crime rate: 12.2 per 10,000 population; Property crime rate: 152.9 per 10,000 population

Transportation: Commute: 90.7% car, 2.7% public transportation, 0.6% walk, 5.4% work from home; Median travel time to work: 35.1 minutes

Additional Information Contacts

City of Walnut . . . . (909) 595-7543
http://www.ci.walnut.ca.us

WALNUT PARK (CDP). Covers a land area of 0.748 square miles and a water area of 0 square miles. Located at 33.97° N. Lat; 118.22° W. Long. Elevation is 148 feet.

Population: 15,966; Growth (since 2000): -1.3%; Density: 21,352.0 persons per square mile; Race: 56.7% White, 0.4% Black/African American, 0.6% Asian, 1.7% American Indian/Alaska Native, 0.0% Native Hawaiian/Other Pacific Islander, 3.3% Two or more races, 97.4% Hispanic of any race; Average household size: 4.42; Median age: 30.2; Age under 18: 29.7%; Age 65 and over: 8.1%; Males per 100 females: 101.5; Marriage status: 42.5% never married, 49.1% now married, 5.0% separated, 3.8% widowed, 4.6% divorced; Foreign born: 47.3%; Speak English only: 8.7%; With disability: 11.1%; Veterans: 1.8%; Ancestry: 0.9% American, 0.4% German, 0.4% English, 0.2% French, 0.2% Irish

Employment: 3.0% management, business, and financial, 0.4% computer, engineering, and science, 6.1% education, legal, community service, arts, and media, 0.8% healthcare practitioners, 21.1% service, 24.6% sales and office, 10.0% natural resources, construction, and maintenance, 33.9% production, transportation, and material moving

Income: Per capita: $12,637; Median household: $42,270; Average household: $52,035; Households with income of $100,000 or more: 13.0%; Poverty rate: 21.7%

Educational Attainment: High school diploma or higher: 45.5%; Bachelor's degree or higher: 4.6%; Graduate/professional degree or higher: 1.3%

School District(s)

Los Angeles Unified (PK-12)
2012-13 Enrollment: 655,455 . . . . (213) 241-1000

Housing: Homeownership rate: 53.3%; Median home value: $284,300; Median year structure built: 1943; Homeowner vacancy rate: 1.1%; Median gross rent: $965 per month; Rental vacancy rate: 3.6%

Health Insurance: 68.2% have insurance; 34.0% have private insurance; 37.1% have public insurance; 31.8% do not have insurance; 11.9% of children under 18 do not have insurance

Transportation: Commute: 82.5% car, 8.8% public transportation, 3.4% walk, 3.5% work from home; Median travel time to work: 30.1 minutes

WEST ATHENS (CDP). Covers a land area of 1.336 square miles and a water area of 0 square miles. Located at 33.92° N. Lat; 118.30° W. Long. Elevation is 190 feet.

Population: 8,729; Growth (since 2000): -4.1%; Density: 6,531.5 persons per square mile; Race: 18.1% White, 52.4% Black/African American, 1.3% Asian, 0.4% American Indian/Alaska Native, 0.1% Native Hawaiian/Other Pacific Islander, 3.3% Two or more races, 44.0% Hispanic of any race; Average household size: 3.44; Median age: 32.1; Age under 18: 29.1%; Age 65 and over: 10.3%; Males per 100 females: 91.5; Marriage status: 48.7% never married, 36.9% now married, 5.3% separated, 6.6% widowed, 7.8% divorced; Foreign born: 34.9%; Speak English only: 46.4%; With disability: 11.3%; Veterans: 3.1%; Ancestry: 2.3% African, 1.6% Belizean, 1.0% European, 0.4% American, 0.3% French

Employment: 10.1% management, business, and financial, 1.8% computer, engineering, and science, 9.1% education, legal, community service, arts, and media, 2.0% healthcare practitioners, 21.6% service, 23.5% sales and office, 5.9% natural resources, construction, and maintenance, 26.1% production, transportation, and material moving

Income: Per capita: $17,111; Median household: $38,649; Average household: $53,090; Households with income of $100,000 or more: 14.1%; Poverty rate: 28.6%

Educational Attainment: High school diploma or higher: 64.3%; Bachelor's degree or higher: 17.5%; Graduate/professional degree or higher: 5.1%

Housing: Homeownership rate: 52.6%; Median home value: $334,100; Median year structure built: 1958; Homeowner vacancy rate: 1.8%; Median gross rent: $940 per month; Rental vacancy rate: 8.4%

Health Insurance: 68.0% have insurance; 32.8% have private insurance; 41.1% have public insurance; 32.0% do not have insurance; 16.9% of children under 18 do not have insurance

Transportation: Commute: 80.5% car, 11.8% public transportation, 1.0% walk, 5.1% work from home; Median travel time to work: 29.9 minutes

WEST CARSON (CDP). Covers a land area of 2.266 square miles and a water area of 0.013 square miles. Located at 33.82° N. Lat; 118.29° W. Long. Elevation is 43 feet.

Population: 21,699; Growth (since 2000): 2.7%; Density: 9,576.0 persons per square mile; Race: 35.2% White, 10.7% Black/African American, 31.0% Asian, 0.9% American Indian/Alaska Native, 1.4% Native Hawaiian/Other Pacific Islander, 5.1% Two or more races, 32.7% Hispanic of any race; Average household size: 2.86; Median age: 42.1; Age under 18: 18.7%; Age 65 and over: 18.0%; Males per 100 females: 94.9; Marriage status: 30.4% never married, 48.8% now married, 2.2% separated, 8.5% widowed, 12.3% divorced; Foreign born: 36.9%; Speak English only: 48.1%; With disability: 11.9%; Veterans: 7.4%; Ancestry: 5.3% German, 3.8% English, 3.4% Irish, 2.0% French, 1.7% Italian

Employment: 16.3% management, business, and financial, 7.0% computer, engineering, and science, 10.1% education, legal, community service, arts, and media, 7.6% healthcare practitioners, 16.6% service, 25.5% sales and office, 5.2% natural resources, construction, and maintenance, 11.7% production, transportation, and material moving

Income: Per capita: $29,562; Median household: $63,948; Average household: $80,044; Households with income of $100,000 or more: 29.2%; Poverty rate: 9.6%

Educational Attainment: High school diploma or higher: 84.6%; Bachelor's degree or higher: 33.3%; Graduate/professional degree or higher: 9.4%

Housing: Homeownership rate: 76.2%; Median home value: $354,500; Median year structure built: 1969; Homeowner vacancy rate: 1.6%; Median gross rent: $1,146 per month; Rental vacancy rate: 4.3%

Health Insurance: 84.8% have insurance; 66.8% have private insurance; 29.1% have public insurance; 15.2% do not have insurance; 10.9% of children under 18 do not have insurance

Transportation: Commute: 91.1% car, 1.8% public transportation, 1.7% walk, 3.4% work from home; Median travel time to work: 28.0 minutes

WEST COVINA (city). Covers a land area of 16.041 square miles and a water area of 0.049 square miles. Located at 34.06° N. Lat; 117.91° W. Long. Elevation is 384 feet.

History: Named for its location west of Covina. Before World War II, West Covina was a small rural community where walnuts, wheat and livestock were raised. Urban and economic growth occurred after 1945, as the Los Angeles metropolitan area began intense development. The city increased in population by more than 40% between 1970 and 1990. Settled 1905. Incorporated 1923.

Population: 106,098; Growth (since 2000): 1.0%; Density: 6,614.3 persons per square mile; Race: 42.8% White, 4.5% Black/African American, 25.8% Asian, 1.0% American Indian/Alaska Native, 0.2% Native Hawaiian/Other Pacific Islander, 4.4% Two or more races, 53.2% Hispanic of any race; Average household size: 3.34; Median age: 36.0; Age under 18: 24.6%; Age 65 and over: 12.1%; Males per 100 females: 93.1; Marriage status: 35.5% never married, 50.4% now married, 2.3% separated, 5.9% widowed, 8.2% divorced; Foreign born: 34.3%; Speak English only: 44.5%; With disability: 10.4%; Veterans: 5.5%; Ancestry: 4.0% German, 3.1% Irish, 2.7% English, 1.8% Italian, 1.2% American
Employment: 14.3% management, business, and financial, 4.1% computer, engineering, and science, 8.3% education, legal, community service, arts, and media, 6.2% healthcare practitioners, 16.4% service, 30.4% sales and office, 7.5% natural resources, construction, and maintenance, 12.9% production, transportation, and material moving
Income: Per capita: $24,859; Median household: $67,088; Average household: $80,897; Households with income of $100,000 or more: 28.6%; Poverty rate: 10.0%
Educational Attainment: High school diploma or higher: 83.1%; Bachelor's degree or higher: 27.3%; Graduate/professional degree or higher: 6.7%

School District(s)

Covina-Valley Unified (KG-12)
2012-13 Enrollment: 12,978 . . . . (626) 974-7000
East San Gabriel Valley Rop
2012-13 Enrollment: n/a . . . . (626) 472-5121
Rowland Unified (KG-12)
2012-13 Enrollment: 15,501 . . . . (626) 965-2541
West Covina Unified (KG-12)
2012-13 Enrollment: 14,460 . . . . (626) 939-4600

Vocational/Technical School(s)

American Beauty College (Private, For-profit)
Fall 2013 Enrollment: 45 . . . . (626) 472-7402
2013-14 Tuition: $16,100
East San Gabriel Valley Regional Occupational Program (Public)
Fall 2013 Enrollment: 983 . . . . (626) 472-5134
2013-14 Tuition: $5,650
InterCoast Colleges-West Covina (Private, For-profit)
Fall 2013 Enrollment: 37 . . . . (626) 337-6800
2013-14 Tuition: $19,395
North-West College-West Covina (Private, For-profit)
Fall 2013 Enrollment: 550 . . . . (626) 960-5046
2013-14 Tuition: $28,525

Housing: Homeownership rate: 65.5%; Median home value: $378,200; Median year structure built: 1965; Homeowner vacancy rate: 1.1%; Median gross rent: $1,375 per month; Rental vacancy rate: 4.8%
Health Insurance: 82.1% have insurance; 62.1% have private insurance; 26.1% have public insurance; 17.9% do not have insurance; 7.7% of children under 18 do not have insurance
Hospitals: Doctors Hospital of West Covina (51 beds)
Safety: Violent crime rate: 21.4 per 10,000 population; Property crime rate: 312.4 per 10,000 population
Newspapers: San Gabriel Valley Tribune (daily circulation 42600); San Gabriel Valley Tribune (weekly circulation 40000)
Transportation: Commute: 91.0% car, 3.4% public transportation, 0.6% walk, 3.5% work from home; Median travel time to work: 33.2 minutes
Additional Information Contacts
City of West Covina . . . . (626) 939-8400
http://www.westcovina.org

WEST HILLS (unincorporated postal area)

ZCTA: 91307

Covers a land area of 8.045 square miles and a water area of 0.009 square miles. Located at 34.20° N. Lat; 118.66° W. Long..
Population: 24,474; Growth (since 2000): 3.6%; Density: 3,042.1 persons per square mile; Race: 74.9% White, 2.9% Black/African American, 12.9% Asian, 0.3% American Indian/Alaska Native, 0.1% Native Hawaiian/Other Pacific Islander, 4.6% Two or more races, 13.6% Hispanic of any race; Average household size: 2.91; Median age: 43.4; Age under 18: 22.8%; Age 65 and over: 16.3%; Males per 100 females: 95.2; Marriage status: 27.0% never married, 58.3% now married, 1.8% separated, 5.4% widowed, 9.2% divorced; Foreign born: 23.1%; Speak English only: 72.7%; With disability: 10.0%; Veterans: 6.2%; Ancestry: 10.1% German, 8.6% Italian, 8.2% English, 7.3% Irish, 6.8% Russian
Employment: 19.2% management, business, and financial, 9.0% computer, engineering, and science, 17.8% education, legal, community service, arts, and media, 5.8% healthcare practitioners, 11.4% service, 28.3% sales and office, 4.4% natural resources, construction, and maintenance, 4.2% production, transportation, and material moving
Income: Per capita: $40,029; Median household: $97,081; Average household: $116,216; Households with income of $100,000 or more: 47.7%; Poverty rate: 6.2%
Educational Attainment: High school diploma or higher: 94.8%; Bachelor's degree or higher: 46.9%; Graduate/professional degree or higher: 18.3%

School District(s)

Los Angeles Unified (PK-12)
2012-13 Enrollment: 655,455 . . . . (213) 241-1000

Four-year College(s)

Valley College of Medical Careers (Private, For-profit)
Fall 2013 Enrollment: 90 . . . . (818) 883-9002

Two-year College(s)

Valley College of Medical Careers (Private, For-profit)
Fall 2013 Enrollment: 90 . . . . (818) 883-9002

Vocational/Technical School(s)

Valley College of Medical Careers (Private, For-profit)
Fall 2013 Enrollment: 90 . . . . (818) 883-9002
2013-14 Tuition: $27,292

Housing: Homeownership rate: 85.0%; Median home value: $495,300; Median year structure built: 1965; Homeowner vacancy rate: 0.9%; Median gross rent: $2,000+ per month; Rental vacancy rate: 4.9%
Health Insurance: 90.6% have insurance; 80.2% have private insurance; 21.9% have public insurance; 9.4% do not have insurance; 7.8% of children under 18 do not have insurance
Hospitals: West Hills Hospital & Medical Center (220 beds)
Transportation: Commute: 86.1% car, 1.9% public transportation, 0.9% walk, 9.5% work from home; Median travel time to work: 30.9 minutes

WEST HOLLYWOOD (city). Covers a land area of 1.887 square miles and a water area of 0 square miles. Located at 34.09° N. Lat; 118.37° W. Long. Elevation is 282 feet.

History: West Hollywood, known as "WeHo" by its residents, was formerly the home of the Gabrielino Indians and became incorporated on November 29, 1984.
Population: 34,399; Growth (since 2000): -3.7%; Density: 18,225.6 persons per square mile; Race: 84.2% White, 3.2% Black/African American, 5.4% Asian, 0.3% American Indian/Alaska Native, 0.1% Native Hawaiian/Other Pacific Islander, 3.6% Two or more races, 10.5% Hispanic of any race; Average household size: 1.52; Median age: 40.4; Age under 18: 4.6%; Age 65 and over: 14.9%; Males per 100 females: 128.4; Marriage status: 61.4% never married, 21.2% now married, 1.4% separated, 5.5% widowed, 11.9% divorced; Foreign born: 27.8%; Speak English only: 63.8%; With disability: 14.0%; Veterans: 2.9%; Ancestry: 13.3% German, 11.2% Irish, 10.1% Russian, 9.4% Italian, 8.2% English
Employment: 22.8% management, business, and financial, 4.8% computer, engineering, and science, 23.1% education, legal, community service, arts, and media, 4.4% healthcare practitioners, 15.9% service, 24.3% sales and office, 1.7% natural resources, construction, and maintenance, 2.9% production, transportation, and material moving
Income: Per capita: $54,193; Median household: $52,649; Average household: $82,982; Households with income of $100,000 or more: 25.3%; Poverty rate: 15.8%
Educational Attainment: High school diploma or higher: 95.2%; Bachelor's degree or higher: 58.6%; Graduate/professional degree or higher: 17.2%

School District(s)

Los Angeles Unified (PK-12)
2012-13 Enrollment: 655,455 . . . . (213) 241-1000

Housing: Homeownership rate: 22.1%; Median home value: $601,900; Median year structure built: 1960; Homeowner vacancy rate: 3.6%; Median gross rent: $1,357 per month; Rental vacancy rate: 5.9%
Health Insurance: 82.6% have insurance; 67.9% have private insurance; 21.7% have public insurance; 17.4% do not have insurance; 10.5% of children under 18 do not have insurance
Safety: Violent crime rate: 61.9 per 10,000 population; Property crime rate: 411.2 per 10,000 population
Transportation: Commute: 75.7% car, 4.9% public transportation, 5.7% walk, 12.0% work from home; Median travel time to work: 25.1 minutes
Additional Information Contacts

City of West Hollywood . . . . (323) 848-6400
http://www.weho.org

WEST PUENTE VALLEY (CDP). Covers a land area of 1.761 square miles and a water area of <.001 square miles. Located at 34.05° N. Lat; 117.97° W. Long. Elevation is 322 feet.
Population: 22,636; Growth (since 2000): 0.2%; Density: 12,851.8 persons per square mile; Race: 50.3% White, 2.1% Black/African American, 7.3% Asian, 1.1% American Indian/Alaska Native, 0.1% Native Hawaiian/Other Pacific Islander, 4.0% Two or more races, 85.5% Hispanic of any race; Average household size: 4.71; Median age: 32.6; Age under 18: 27.9%; Age 65 and over: 11.0%; Males per 100 females: 97.0; Marriage status: 41.5% never married, 46.4% now married, 2.8% separated, 6.1% widowed, 6.1% divorced; Foreign born: 39.2%; Speak English only: 22.3%; With disability: 12.5%; Veterans: 3.7%; Ancestry: 2.1% American, 2.1% Irish, 1.2% English, 1.1% German, 0.6% Italian
Employment: 6.9% management, business, and financial, 1.6% computer, engineering, and science, 7.6% education, legal, community service, arts, and media, 2.6% healthcare practitioners, 19.0% service, 27.0% sales and office, 9.6% natural resources, construction, and maintenance, 25.6% production, transportation, and material moving
Income: Per capita: $16,778; Median household: $65,139; Average household: $70,486; Households with income of $100,000 or more: 21.9%; Poverty rate: 11.9%
Educational Attainment: High school diploma or higher: 62.0%; Bachelor's degree or higher: 8.8%; Graduate/professional degree or higher: 2.0%
Housing: Homeownership rate: 81.2%; Median home value: $293,600; Median year structure built: 1956; Homeowner vacancy rate: 1.2%; Median gross rent: $1,464 per month; Rental vacancy rate: 2.1%
Health Insurance: 76.7% have insurance; 48.4% have private insurance; 32.8% have public insurance; 23.3% do not have insurance; 6.1% of children under 18 do not have insurance
Transportation: Commute: 90.1% car, 3.4% public transportation, 0.8% walk, 4.2% work from home; Median travel time to work: 32.3 minutes

WEST RANCHO DOMINGUEZ (CDP). Covers a land area of 1.652 square miles and a water area of 0 square miles. Located at 33.89° N. Lat; 118.27° W. Long. Elevation is 82 feet.
Population: 5,669; Growth (since 2000): n/a; Density: 3,430.8 persons per square mile; Race: 18.6% White, 52.5% Black/African American, 0.8% Asian, 0.6% American Indian/Alaska Native, 0.4% Native Hawaiian/Other Pacific Islander, 3.3% Two or more races, 44.6% Hispanic of any race; Average household size: 3.68; Median age: 32.9; Age under 18: 29.3%; Age 65 and over: 12.0%; Males per 100 females: 88.7; Marriage status: 47.7% never married, 35.9% now married, 4.4% separated, 7.1% widowed, 9.2% divorced; Foreign born: 19.3%; Speak English only: 65.3%; With disability: 13.4%; Veterans: 5.1%; Ancestry: 5.9% African, 1.8% American, 0.8% Scottish, 0.8% Swedish, 0.4% English
Employment: 12.8% management, business, and financial, 1.3% computer, engineering, and science, 7.8% education, legal, community service, arts, and media, 1.3% healthcare practitioners, 24.6% service, 28.5% sales and office, 7.4% natural resources, construction, and maintenance, 16.3% production, transportation, and material moving
Income: Per capita: $16,975; Median household: $45,373; Average household: $55,282; Households with income of $100,000 or more: 13.5%; Poverty rate: 17.2%
Educational Attainment: High school diploma or higher: 72.8%; Bachelor's degree or higher: 10.9%; Graduate/professional degree or higher: 2.4%
Housing: Homeownership rate: 72.5%; Median home value: $246,700; Median year structure built: 1954; Homeowner vacancy rate: 1.1%; Median gross rent: $1,087 per month; Rental vacancy rate: 2.1%
Health Insurance: 77.8% have insurance; 46.8% have private insurance; 39.1% have public insurance; 22.2% do not have insurance; 8.0% of children under 18 do not have insurance
Transportation: Commute: 83.9% car, 8.7% public transportation, 2.9% walk, 2.6% work from home; Median travel time to work: 29.7 minutes

WEST WHITTIER-LOS NIETOS (CDP). Covers a land area of 2.519 square miles and a water area of 0 square miles. Located at 33.98° N. Lat; 118.07° W. Long.
Population: 25,540; Growth (since 2000): 1.6%; Density: 10,138.5 persons per square mile; Race: 59.4% White, 1.0% Black/African American, 1.5% Asian, 1.5% American Indian/Alaska Native, 0.2% Native Hawaiian/Other Pacific Islander, 3.5% Two or more races, 87.6% Hispanic of any race; Average household size: 3.80; Median age: 33.7; Age under 18: 27.0%; Age 65 and over: 11.2%; Males per 100 females: 97.0; Marriage status: 38.9% never married, 46.0% now married, 2.6% separated, 6.4% widowed, 8.7% divorced; Foreign born: 27.3%; Speak English only: 35.6%; With disability: 12.4%; Veterans: 5.8%; Ancestry: 2.6% German, 1.6% American, 1.5% Irish, 1.3% English, 1.3% Italian
Employment: 10.3% management, business, and financial, 1.5% computer, engineering, and science, 8.3% education, legal, community service, arts, and media, 3.6% healthcare practitioners, 15.9% service, 28.2% sales and office, 11.4% natural resources, construction, and maintenance, 20.9% production, transportation, and material moving
Income: Per capita: $19,776; Median household: $60,246; Average household: $70,608; Households with income of $100,000 or more: 23.6%; Poverty rate: 10.1%
Educational Attainment: High school diploma or higher: 68.2%; Bachelor's degree or higher: 10.2%; Graduate/professional degree or higher: 2.6%

School District(s)

Los Nietos (KG-08)
2012-13 Enrollment: 1,925 . . . . (562) 692-0271

Housing: Homeownership rate: 73.1%; Median home value: $323,500; Median year structure built: 1955; Homeowner vacancy rate: 1.0%; Median gross rent: $1,232 per month; Rental vacancy rate: 5.5%
Health Insurance: 79.4% have insurance; 54.6% have private insurance; 30.0% have public insurance; 20.6% do not have insurance; 9.4% of children under 18 do not have insurance
Transportation: Commute: 89.6% car, 3.0% public transportation, 1.5% walk, 2.3% work from home; Median travel time to work: 30.0 minutes

WESTLAKE VILLAGE (city). Covers a land area of 5.185 square miles and a water area of 0.320 square miles. Located at 34.14° N. Lat; 118.82° W. Long. Elevation is 922 feet.
History: The area located in Ventura County, or roughly two-thirds of the community, was annexed by the City of Thousand Oaks in two portions, in 1968 and 1972. In 1981, the remaining third eventually incorporated as the City of Westlake Village.
Population: 8,270; Growth (since 2000): -1.2%; Density: 1,594.9 persons per square mile; Race: 88.6% White, 1.2% Black/African American, 5.9% Asian, 0.1% American Indian/Alaska Native, 0.2% Native Hawaiian/Other Pacific Islander, 2.6% Two or more races, 6.4% Hispanic of any race; Average household size: 2.50; Median age: 48.7; Age under 18: 21.0%; Age 65 and over: 21.2%; Males per 100 females: 94.8; Marriage status: 22.9% never married, 58.5% now married, 1.7% separated, 6.0% widowed, 12.7% divorced; Foreign born: 12.2%; Speak English only: 85.9%; With disability: 8.8%; Veterans: 8.7%; Ancestry: 18.6% German, 14.4% English, 13.4% Irish, 10.2% Italian, 6.5% Russian
Employment: 31.7% management, business, and financial, 6.7% computer, engineering, and science, 14.9% education, legal, community service, arts, and media, 6.2% healthcare practitioners, 7.9% service, 29.0% sales and office, 2.0% natural resources, construction, and maintenance, 1.5% production, transportation, and material moving
Income: Per capita: $61,766; Median household: $112,083; Average household: $153,005; Households with income of $100,000 or more: 55.1%; Poverty rate: 3.9%
Educational Attainment: High school diploma or higher: 97.5%; Bachelor's degree or higher: 59.8%; Graduate/professional degree or higher: 27.4%

School District(s)

Conejo Valley Unified (KG-12)
2012-13 Enrollment: 20,595 . . . . (805) 497-9511
Las Virgenes Unified (KG-12)
2012-13 Enrollment: 11,200 . . . . (818) 880-4000
Ventura County Office of Education (KG-12)
2012-13 Enrollment: 2,590 . . . . (805) 383-1902

Housing: Homeownership rate: 84.2%; Median home value: $743,900; Median year structure built: 1976; Homeowner vacancy rate: 1.0%; Median gross rent: $2,000+ per month; Rental vacancy rate: 4.4%
Health Insurance: 95.7% have insurance; 86.9% have private insurance; 27.0% have public insurance; 4.3% do not have insurance; 1.7% of children under 18 do not have insurance
Safety: Violent crime rate: 13.0 per 10,000 population; Property crime rate: 175.4 per 10,000 population
Transportation: Commute: 91.3% car, 0.0% public transportation, 0.4% walk, 8.0% work from home; Median travel time to work: 26.7 minutes

Additional Information Contacts
City of Westlake Village . . . . (818) 706-1613
http://www.wlv.org

WESTMONT (CDP). Covers a land area of 1.848 square miles and a water area of 0 square miles. Located at 33.94° N. Lat; 118.30° W. Long. Elevation is 217 feet.
Population: 31,853; Growth (since 2000): 0.7%; Density: 17,239.9 persons per square mile; Race: 15.8% White, 51.1% Black/African American, 0.4% Asian, 0.6% American Indian/Alaska Native, 0.1% Native Hawaiian/Other Pacific Islander, 3.2% Two or more races, 46.7% Hispanic of any race; Average household size: 3.27; Median age: 29.9; Age under 18: 31.0%; Age 65 and over: 8.4%; Males per 100 females: 86.8; Marriage status: 52.6% never married, 33.8% now married, 3.8% separated, 5.1% widowed, 8.4% divorced; Foreign born: 23.8%; Speak English only: 55.5%; With disability: 12.3%; Veterans: 5.7%; Ancestry: 2.3% African, 1.2% American, 0.6% Belizean, 0.3% Irish, 0.2% Nigerian
Employment: 5.7% management, business, and financial, 1.8% computer, engineering, and science, 5.2% education, legal, community service, arts, and media, 2.9% healthcare practitioners, 27.6% service, 30.1% sales and office, 10.0% natural resources, construction, and maintenance, 16.7% production, transportation, and material moving
Income: Per capita: $14,635; Median household: $30,654; Average household: $43,256; Households with income of $100,000 or more: 9.1%; Poverty rate: 34.4%
Educational Attainment: High school diploma or higher: 68.3%; Bachelor's degree or higher: 9.5%; Graduate/professional degree or higher: 2.5%
Housing: Homeownership rate: 31.1%; Median home value: $291,100; Median year structure built: 1953; Homeowner vacancy rate: 2.5%; Median gross rent: $978 per month; Rental vacancy rate: 8.8%
Health Insurance: 73.6% have insurance; 33.4% have private insurance; 47.3% have public insurance; 26.4% do not have insurance; 10.5% of children under 18 do not have insurance
Transportation: Commute: 79.3% car, 14.3% public transportation, 0.7% walk, 4.2% work from home; Median travel time to work: 34.6 minutes

WHITTIER (city). Covers a land area of 14.649 square miles and a water area of 0.016 square miles. Located at 33.97° N. Lat; 118.02° W. Long. Elevation is 367 feet.
History: Named for John Greenleaf Whittier, the Quaker poet. Whittier was founded in 1881 by members of the Friends and grew around Whittier College.
Population: 85,331; Growth (since 2000): 2.0%; Density: 5,824.9 persons per square mile; Race: 64.6% White, 1.3% Black/African American, 3.8% Asian, 1.3% American Indian/Alaska Native, 0.1% Native Hawaiian/Other Pacific Islander, 4.4% Two or more races, 65.7% Hispanic of any race; Average household size: 2.96; Median age: 35.4; Age under 18: 25.4%; Age 65 and over: 11.7%; Males per 100 females: 94.0; Marriage status: 38.1% never married, 46.7% now married, 2.5% separated, 5.4% widowed, 9.8% divorced; Foreign born: 19.0%; Speak English only: 55.9%; With disability: 9.7%; Veterans: 5.9%; Ancestry: 6.5% German, 4.9% English, 4.7% Irish, 2.9% Italian, 1.7% American
Employment: 13.3% management, business, and financial, 3.9% computer, engineering, and science, 13.6% education, legal, community service, arts, and media, 4.3% healthcare practitioners, 16.3% service, 29.8% sales and office, 6.4% natural resources, construction, and maintenance, 12.3% production, transportation, and material moving
Income: Per capita: $28,149; Median household: $68,522; Average household: $85,281; Households with income of $100,000 or more: 31.7%; Poverty rate: 12.4%
Educational Attainment: High school diploma or higher: 83.6%; Bachelor's degree or higher: 24.5%; Graduate/professional degree or higher: 9.1%

School District(s)

East Whittier City Elementary (KG-08)
2012-13 Enrollment: 9,104 . . . . (562) 907-5900
Los Angeles County Office of Education (KG-12)
2012-13 Enrollment: 9,136 . . . . (562) 922-6111
Los Nietos (KG-08)
2012-13 Enrollment: 1,925 . . . . (562) 692-0271
Lowell Joint (KG-08)
2012-13 Enrollment: 3,169 . . . . (562) 943-0211
Norwalk-La Mirada Unified (KG-12)
2012-13 Enrollment: 19,770 . . . . (562) 868-0431
South Whittier Elementary (KG-08)
2012-13 Enrollment: 3,303 . . . . (562) 944-6231
Tri-Cities Rop
2012-13 Enrollment: n/a . . . . (562) 698-9571
Whittier City Elementary (KG-08)
2012-13 Enrollment: 5,849 . . . . (562) 789-3000
Whittier Union High (09-12)
2012-13 Enrollment: 13,486 . . . . (562) 698-8121

Four-year College(s)

Southern California University of Health Sciences (Private, Not-for-profit)
Fall 2013 Enrollment: 968 . . . . (562) 947-8755
Whittier College (Private, Not-for-profit)
Fall 2013 Enrollment: 2,339 . . . . (562) 907-4205
2013-14 Tuition: In-state $40,296; Out-of-state $40,296

Two-year College(s)

Rio Hondo College (Public)
Fall 2013 Enrollment: 16,548 . . . . (562) 692-0921
2013-14 Tuition: In-state $1,178; Out-of-state $5,738
Housing: Homeownership rate: 57.3%; Median home value: $418,800; Median year structure built: 1956; Homeowner vacancy rate: 1.3%; Median gross rent: $1,180 per month; Rental vacancy rate: 5.1%
Health Insurance: 84.9% have insurance; 66.8% have private insurance; 25.5% have public insurance; 15.1% do not have insurance; 8.0% of children under 18 do not have insurance
Hospitals: Presbyterian Intercommunity Hospital (444 beds); Whittier Hospital Medical Center (181 beds)
Safety: Violent crime rate: 25.8 per 10,000 population; Property crime rate: 275.7 per 10,000 population
Newspapers: Whittier Daily News (daily circulation 16300)
Transportation: Commute: 90.0% car, 2.7% public transportation, 2.2% walk, 2.8% work from home; Median travel time to work: 29.8 minutes
Additional Information Contacts
City of Whittier . . . . (562) 567-9300
http://www.cityofwhittier.org

WILLOWBROOK (CDP). Covers a land area of 3.762 square miles and a water area of 0.008 square miles. Located at 33.92° N. Lat; 118.26° W. Long. Elevation is 95 feet.
Population: 35,983; Growth (since 2000): 5.4%; Density: 9,564.6 persons per square mile; Race: 22.9% White, 34.4% Black/African American, 0.3% Asian, 0.8% American Indian/Alaska Native, 0.1% Native Hawaiian/Other Pacific Islander, 2.9% Two or more races, 63.9% Hispanic of any race; Average household size: 4.08; Median age: 28.2; Age under 18: 32.8%; Age 65 and over: 8.1%; Males per 100 females: 92.1; Marriage status: 49.2% never married, 40.7% now married, 5.3% separated, 4.4% widowed, 5.7% divorced; Foreign born: 33.7%; Speak English only: 30.2%; With disability: 10.7%; Veterans: 2.1%; Ancestry: 4.2% African, 1.7% American, 0.5% Belizean, 0.4% Irish, 0.3% French
Employment: 8.0% management, business, and financial, 0.5% computer, engineering, and science, 3.8% education, legal, community service, arts, and media, 1.0% healthcare practitioners, 18.3% service, 26.2% sales and office, 12.6% natural resources, construction, and maintenance, 29.7% production, transportation, and material moving
Income: Per capita: $11,060; Median household: $36,332; Average household: $42,864; Households with income of $100,000 or more: 7.5%; Poverty rate: 33.1%
Educational Attainment: High school diploma or higher: 53.7%; Bachelor's degree or higher: 5.2%; Graduate/professional degree or higher: 1.4%
Housing: Homeownership rate: 51.9%; Median home value: $219,800; Median year structure built: 1957; Homeowner vacancy rate: 2.5%; Median gross rent: <$100 per month; Rental vacancy rate: 5.9%
Health Insurance: 68.6% have insurance; 26.4% have private insurance; 45.0% have public insurance; 31.4% do not have insurance; 14.8% of children under 18 do not have insurance
Transportation: Commute: 86.2% car, 6.4% public transportation, 3.5% walk, 2.8% work from home; Median travel time to work: 28.4 minutes

WILMINGTON (unincorporated postal area)
ZCTA: 90744
Covers a land area of 8.337 square miles and a water area of 1.145 square miles. Located at 33.78° N. Lat; 118.26° W. Long. Elevation is 23 feet.
Population: 53,815; Growth (since 2000): 1.0%; Density: 6,454.8 persons per square mile; Race: 44.2% White, 3.2% Black/African American, 2.4%

Asian, 1.1% American Indian/Alaska Native, 0.8% Native Hawaiian/Other Pacific Islander, 5.0% Two or more races, 88.8% Hispanic of any race; Average household size: 3.83; Median age: 28.7; Age under 18: 32.0%; Age 65 and over: 7.0%; Males per 100 females: 102.9; Marriage status: 44.9% never married, 42.9% now married, 3.3% separated, 4.4% widowed, 7.8% divorced; Foreign born: 38.6%; Speak English only: 24.2%; With disability: 8.2%; Veterans: 3.1%; Ancestry: 1.6% German, 1.2% Irish, 0.7% Italian, 0.7% English, 0.7% French

Employment: 6.1% management, business, and financial, 1.9% computer, engineering, and science, 6.0% education, legal, community service, arts, and media, 1.7% healthcare practitioners, 26.1% service, 20.2% sales and office, 12.7% natural resources, construction, and maintenance, 25.4% production, transportation, and material moving

Income: Per capita: $14,383; Median household: $41,920; Average household: $54,791; Households with income of $100,000 or more: 13.1%; Poverty rate: 28.8%

Educational Attainment: High school diploma or higher: 56.8%; Bachelor's degree or higher: 6.9%; Graduate/professional degree or higher: 1.0%

School District(s)

Los Angeles Unified (PK-12)
2012-13 Enrollment: 655,455 . . . . (213) 241-1000

Four-year College(s)

Los Angeles Harbor College (Public)
Fall 2013 Enrollment: 10,098 . . . . (310) 233-4000
2013-14 Tuition: In-state $1,221; Out-of-state $6,161

Two-year College(s)

Los Angeles Harbor College (Public)
Fall 2013 Enrollment: 10,098 . . . . (310) 233-4000
2013-14 Tuition: In-state $1,221; Out-of-state $6,161

Vocational/Technical School(s)

Los Angeles Harbor College (Public)
Fall 2013 Enrollment: 10,098 . . . . (310) 233-4000
2013-14 Tuition: In-state $1,221; Out-of-state $6,161

Housing: Homeownership rate: 39.7%; Median home value: $307,700; Median year structure built: 1959; Homeowner vacancy rate: 1.3%; Median gross rent: $988 per month; Rental vacancy rate: 4.3%

Health Insurance: 70.5% have insurance; 36.5% have private insurance; 37.5% have public insurance; 29.5% do not have insurance; 10.1% of children under 18 do not have insurance

Transportation: Commute: 85.4% car, 6.1% public transportation, 3.0% walk, 1.8% work from home; Median travel time to work: 23.9 minutes

WINNETKA (unincorporated postal area)

ZCTA: 91306

Covers a land area of 4.138 square miles and a water area of 0.024 square miles. Located at 34.21° N. Lat; 118.58° W. Long. Elevation is 801 feet.

Population: 45,061; Growth (since 2000): 2.8%; Density: 10,888.8 persons per square mile; Race: 49.1% White, 4.6% Black/African American, 17.9% Asian, 0.6% American Indian/Alaska Native, 0.1% Native Hawaiian/Other Pacific Islander, 5.3% Two or more races, 47.4% Hispanic of any race; Average household size: 3.28; Median age: 35.4; Age under 18: 24.1%; Age 65 and over: 10.2%; Males per 100 females: 101.3; Marriage status: 38.5% never married, 48.5% now married, 3.3% separated, 5.1% widowed, 7.9% divorced; Foreign born: 45.2%; Speak English only: 35.8%; With disability: 9.3%; Veterans: 3.8%; Ancestry: 5.0% German, 4.3% Irish, 3.7% English, 2.8% Italian, 2.5% American

Employment: 10.6% management, business, and financial, 4.7% computer, engineering, and science, 8.2% education, legal, community service, arts, and media, 4.5% healthcare practitioners, 23.5% service, 25.4% sales and office, 11.2% natural resources, construction, and maintenance, 11.8% production, transportation, and material moving

Income: Per capita: $22,708; Median household: $61,112; Average household: $73,084; Households with income of $100,000 or more: 25.8%; Poverty rate: 16.2%

Educational Attainment: High school diploma or higher: 74.4%; Bachelor's degree or higher: 23.1%; Graduate/professional degree or higher: 6.2%

School District(s)

Los Angeles Unified (PK-12)
2012-13 Enrollment: 655,455 . . . . (213) 241-1000

Housing: Homeownership rate: 60.0%; Median home value: $357,500; Median year structure built: 1963; Homeowner vacancy rate: 1.3%; Median gross rent: $1,140 per month; Rental vacancy rate: 7.5%

Health Insurance: 74.1% have insurance; 49.0% have private insurance; 30.5% have public insurance; 25.9% do not have insurance; 8.3% of children under 18 do not have insurance

Transportation: Commute: 84.4% car, 6.0% public transportation, 1.6% walk, 4.3% work from home; Median travel time to work: 29.0 minutes

WOODLAND HILLS (unincorporated postal area)

ZCTA: 91364

Covers a land area of 7.593 square miles and a water area of 0.006 square miles. Located at 34.15° N. Lat; 118.59° W. Long. Elevation is 896 feet.

Population: 25,851; Growth (since 2000): -0.5%; Density: 3,404.6 persons per square mile; Race: 81.2% White, 4.0% Black/African American, 6.4% Asian, 0.3% American Indian/Alaska Native, 0.1% Native Hawaiian/Other Pacific Islander, 5.3% Two or more races, 9.8% Hispanic of any race; Average household size: 2.47; Median age: 44.0; Age under 18: 20.1%; Age 65 and over: 17.5%; Males per 100 females: 97.2; Marriage status: 27.7% never married, 56.1% now married, 2.5% separated, 6.0% widowed, 10.2% divorced; Foreign born: 24.9%; Speak English only: 69.2%; With disability: 9.6%; Veterans: 6.9%; Ancestry: 10.4% German, 9.3% Irish, 8.7% English, 8.2% Iranian, 6.8% Russian

Employment: 25.1% management, business, and financial, 6.8% computer, engineering, and science, 18.3% education, legal, community service, arts, and media, 6.2% healthcare practitioners, 9.1% service, 26.2% sales and office, 5.2% natural resources, construction, and maintenance, 3.1% production, transportation, and material moving

Income: Per capita: $49,578; Median household: $91,100; Average household: $124,603; Households with income of $100,000 or more: 47.2%; Poverty rate: 7.7%

Educational Attainment: High school diploma or higher: 96.3%; Bachelor's degree or higher: 52.1%; Graduate/professional degree or higher: 20.3%

School District(s)

Las Virgenes Unified (KG-12)
2012-13 Enrollment: 11,200 . . . . (818) 880-4000
Los Angeles County Office of Education (KG-12)
2012-13 Enrollment: 9,136 . . . . (562) 922-6111
Los Angeles Unified (PK-12)
2012-13 Enrollment: 655,455 . . . . (213) 241-1000

Four-year College(s)

Los Angeles Pierce College (Public)
Fall 2013 Enrollment: 20,080 . . . . (818) 719-6401
2013-14 Tuition: In-state $1,221; Out-of-state $6,161

Two-year College(s)

Los Angeles Pierce College (Public)
Fall 2013 Enrollment: 20,080 . . . . (818) 719-6401
2013-14 Tuition: In-state $1,221; Out-of-state $6,161

Vocational/Technical School(s)

Los Angeles Pierce College (Public)
Fall 2013 Enrollment: 20,080 . . . . (818) 719-6401
2013-14 Tuition: In-state $1,221; Out-of-state $6,161

Housing: Homeownership rate: 70.6%; Median home value: $646,400; Median year structure built: 1964; Homeowner vacancy rate: 1.2%; Median gross rent: $1,811 per month; Rental vacancy rate: 7.9%

Health Insurance: 90.5% have insurance; 79.3% have private insurance; 23.3% have public insurance; 9.5% do not have insurance; 4.6% of children under 18 do not have insurance

Hospitals: Kaiser Foundation Hospital - Woodland Hills (218 beds); Motion Picture & Television Hospital (256 beds)

Newspapers: Daily News (daily circulation 151000); Valley News Group (weekly circulation 20000)

Transportation: Commute: 84.8% car, 0.7% public transportation, 2.1% walk, 10.8% work from home; Median travel time to work: 30.7 minutes

ZCTA: 91367

Covers a land area of 7.441 square miles and a water area of 0.012 square miles. Located at 34.18° N. Lat; 118.62° W. Long. Elevation is 896 feet.

Population: 39,499; Growth (since 2000): 9.4%; Density: 5,308.3 persons per square mile; Race: 73.8% White, 4.6% Black/African American, 12.4% Asian, 0.4% American Indian/Alaska Native, 0.1% Native Hawaiian/Other Pacific Islander, 5.0% Two or more races, 11.1% Hispanic of any race; Average household size: 2.35; Median age: 41.0; Age under 18: 18.3%; Age 65 and over: 16.5%; Males per 100 females: 94.3; Marriage status: 31.5% never married, 50.4% now married, 2.5% separated, 5.7% widowed, 12.4% divorced; Foreign born: 28.3%; Speak English only:

65.0%; With disability: 9.6%; Veterans: 6.5%; Ancestry: 9.2% German, 8.6% Iranian, 7.5% Irish, 6.0% English, 6.0% Russian
Employment: 23.8% management, business, and financial, 9.6% computer, engineering, and science, 14.7% education, legal, community service, arts, and media, 5.9% healthcare practitioners, 13.4% service, 26.8% sales and office, 3.1% natural resources, construction, and maintenance, 2.8% production, transportation, and material moving
Income: Per capita: $43,265; Median household: $76,548; Average household: $101,895; Households with income of $100,000 or more: 37.5%; Poverty rate: 8.6%
Educational Attainment: High school diploma or higher: 95.8%; Bachelor's degree or higher: 52.5%; Graduate/professional degree or higher: 18.4%
Housing: Homeownership rate: 56.6%; Median home value: $552,000; Median year structure built: 1971; Homeowner vacancy rate: 3.9%; Median gross rent: $1,705 per month; Rental vacancy rate: 9.1%
Health Insurance: 89.5% have insurance; 77.1% have private insurance; 23.2% have public insurance; 10.5% do not have insurance; 5.3% of children under 18 do not have insurance
Transportation: Commute: 85.1% car, 2.7% public transportation, 3.5% walk, 7.1% work from home; Median travel time to work: 29.4 minutes

Madera County

Located in central California; in the San Joaquin Valley in the west, stretching northeast to the crest of the Sierra Nevada; watered by the San Joaquin, Chowchilla, and Fresno Rivers; includes part of Sierra National Forest. Covers a land area of 2,137.069 square miles, a water area of 16.200 square miles, and is located in the Pacific Time Zone at 37.21° N. Lat., 119.75° W. Long. The county was founded in 1893. County seat is Madera.

Madera County is part of the Madera, CA Metropolitan Statistical Area. The entire metro area includes: Madera County, CA

Weather Station: Madera Elevation: 270 feet

	Jan	Feb	Mar	Apr	May	Jun	Jul	Aug	Sep	Oct	Nov	Dec
High	54	61	67	74	83	90	97	95	90	79	65	54
Low	37	39	43	47	53	58	63	62	57	48	40	35
Precip	2.3	2.1	2.2	0.9	0.5	0.1	tr	0.0	0.1	0.8	1.1	1.7
Snow	0.0	0.0	0.0	0.0	0.0	0.0	0.0	0.0	0.0	0.0	0.0	0.0

High and Low temperatures in degrees Fahrenheit; Precipitation and Snow in inches

Population: 150,865; Growth (since 2000): 22.5%; Density: 70.6 persons per square mile; Race: 62.6% White, 3.7% Black/African American, 1.9% Asian, 2.7% American Indian/Alaska Native, 0.1% Native Hawaiian/Other Pacific Islander, 4.2% two or more races, 53.7% Hispanic of any race; Average household size: 3.28; Median age: 33.0; Age under 18: 28.4%; Age 65 and over: 11.4%; Males per 100 females: 93.0; Marriage status: 35.5% never married, 50.6% now married, 2.6% separated, 5.1% widowed, 8.8% divorced; Foreign born: 21.5%; Speak English only: 55.9%; With disability: 12.1%; Veterans: 7.6%; Ancestry: 6.9% German, 6.1% Irish, 5.3% English, 2.5% Italian, 2.2% American
Religion: Six largest groups: 37.5% Catholicism, 4.1% Non-denominational Protestant, 2.4% Baptist, 2.2% Latter-day Saints, 1.5% Pentecostal, 1.1% Lutheran
Economy: Unemployment rate: 8.9%; Leading industries: 17.3% retail trade; 11.7% construction; 10.9% health care and social assistance; Farms: 1,507 totaling 653,584 acres; Company size: 2 employ 1,000 or more persons, 1 employs 500 to 999 persons, 24 employ 100 to 499 persons, 1,857 employ less than 100 persons; Business ownership: 2,512 women-owned, n/a Black-owned, 2,260 Hispanic-owned, 483 Asian-owned
Employment: 11.5% management, business, and financial, 2.1% computer, engineering, and science, 8.2% education, legal, community service, arts, and media, 3.5% healthcare practitioners, 17.3% service, 21.5% sales and office, 23.7% natural resources, construction, and maintenance, 12.2% production, transportation, and material moving
Income: Per capita: $17,847; Median household: $45,625; Average household: $60,240; Households with income of $100,000 or more: 16.6%; Poverty rate: 22.8%
Educational Attainment: High school diploma or higher: 68.5%; Bachelor's degree or higher: 13.6%; Graduate/professional degree or higher: 4.0%
Housing: Homeownership rate: 64.0%; Median home value: $182,000; Median year structure built: 1985; Homeowner vacancy rate: 3.1%; Median gross rent: $914 per month; Rental vacancy rate: 6.3%
Vital Statistics: Birth rate: 155.2 per 10,000 population; Death rate: 62.8 per 10,000 population; Age-adjusted cancer mortality rate: 144.4 deaths per 100,000 population
Health Insurance: 79.4% have insurance; 45.3% have private insurance; 43.5% have public insurance; 20.6% do not have insurance; 10.1% of children under 18 do not have insurance
Health Care: Physicians: 11.3 per 10,000 population; Hospital beds: 31.4 per 10,000 population; Hospital admissions: 1,244.1 per 10,000 population
Air Quality Index: 20.8% good, 65.8% moderate, 11.2% unhealthy for sensitive individuals, 2.2% unhealthy (percent of days)
Transportation: Commute: 89.7% car, 0.2% public transportation, 1.9% walk, 6.1% work from home; Median travel time to work: 25.5 minutes
Presidential Election: 39.2% Obama, 58.7% Romney (2012)
National and State Parks: Devils Postpile National Monument; Millerton Lake State Recreation Area; Wassama Round House State Historic Park
Additional Information Contacts
Madera Government . . . . (559) 675-7700
http://www.madera-county.com

Madera County Communities

AHWAHNEE (CDP). Covers a land area of 10.024 square miles and a water area of 0 square miles. Located at 37.37° N. Lat; 119.72° W. Long. Elevation is 2,326 feet.
Population: 2,246; Growth (since 2000): n/a; Density: 224.1 persons per square mile; Race: 91.9% White, 0.3% Black/African American, 0.7% Asian, 1.3% American Indian/Alaska Native, 0.0% Native Hawaiian/Other Pacific Islander, 4.1% Two or more races, 8.7% Hispanic of any race; Average household size: 2.49; Median age: 49.4; Age under 18: 18.7%; Age 65 and over: 24.8%; Males per 100 females: 93.8

School District(s)

Bass Lake Joint Union Elementary (KG-08)
2012-13 Enrollment: 820. . . . . (559) 642-1555
Housing: Homeownership rate: 79.2%; Homeowner vacancy rate: 4.2%; Rental vacancy rate: 6.9%

BASS LAKE (CDP). Covers a land area of 1.926 square miles and a water area of 0.567 square miles. Located at 37.33° N. Lat; 119.57° W. Long. Elevation is 3,415 feet.
Population: 527; Growth (since 2000): n/a; Density: 273.6 persons per square mile; Race: 95.4% White, 0.2% Black/African American, 0.2% Asian, 1.9% American Indian/Alaska Native, 0.0% Native Hawaiian/Other Pacific Islander, 1.9% Two or more races, 4.2% Hispanic of any race; Average household size: 1.92; Median age: 62.3; Age under 18: 10.8%; Age 65 and over: 43.3%; Males per 100 females: 86.9
Housing: Homeownership rate: 83.6%; Homeowner vacancy rate: 11.1%; Rental vacancy rate: 48.9%

BONADELLE RANCHOS-MADERA RANCHOS (CDP). Covers a land area of 11.585 square miles and a water area of 0 square miles. Located at 36.98° N. Lat; 119.87° W. Long.
Population: 8,569; Growth (since 2000): 17.4%; Density: 739.7 persons per square mile; Race: 82.1% White, 1.3% Black/African American, 2.4% Asian, 1.4% American Indian/Alaska Native, 0.0% Native Hawaiian/Other Pacific Islander, 3.3% Two or more races, 26.9% Hispanic of any race; Average household size: 3.05; Median age: 41.5; Age under 18: 24.8%; Age 65 and over: 11.7%; Males per 100 females: 102.1; Marriage status: 29.9% never married, 58.4% now married, 2.5% separated, 5.2% widowed, 6.5% divorced; Foreign born: 7.4%; Speak English only: 82.5%; With disability: 11.2%; Veterans: 11.6%; Ancestry: 14.2% German, 10.6% Irish, 8.9% English, 4.7% American, 4.5% Italian
Employment: 13.4% management, business, and financial, 3.3% computer, engineering, and science, 10.1% education, legal, community service, arts, and media, 7.7% healthcare practitioners, 15.9% service, 27.1% sales and office, 14.2% natural resources, construction, and maintenance, 8.1% production, transportation, and material moving
Income: Per capita: $30,386; Median household: $77,325; Average household: $89,280; Households with income of $100,000 or more: 37.3%; Poverty rate: 9.4%
Educational Attainment: High school diploma or higher: 92.1%; Bachelor's degree or higher: 23.4%; Graduate/professional degree or higher: 5.0%
Housing: Homeownership rate: 89.9%; Median home value: $256,900; Median year structure built: 1986; Homeowner vacancy rate: 1.7%; Median gross rent: $1,592 per month; Rental vacancy rate: 5.0%

Health Insurance: 84.5% have insurance; 69.4% have private insurance; 25.1% have public insurance; 15.5% do not have insurance; 15.9% of children under 18 do not have insurance

Transportation: Commute: 93.7% car, 0.4% public transportation, 0.2% walk, 5.5% work from home; Median travel time to work: 25.7 minutes

CHOWCHILLA (city). Covers a land area of 7.661 square miles and a water area of 0 square miles. Located at 37.11° N. Lat; 120.23° W. Long. Elevation is 239 feet.

History: Chowchilla developed around cotton gins, creameries, concrete pipe factories, and a cottonseed oil mill.

Population: 18,720; Growth (since 2000): 68.2%; Density: 2,443.5 persons per square mile; Race: 61.6% White, 12.6% Black/African American, 2.1% Asian, 2.0% American Indian/Alaska Native, 0.2% Native Hawaiian/Other Pacific Islander, 3.8% Two or more races, 37.8% Hispanic of any race; Average household size: 3.08; Median age: 34.7; Age under 18: 19.1%; Age 65 and over: 7.0%; Males per 100 females: 42.7; Marriage status: 37.7% never married, 42.1% now married, 4.4% separated, 5.7% widowed, 14.5% divorced; Foreign born: 13.6%; Speak English only: 66.6%; With disability: 15.1%; Veterans: 4.6%; Ancestry: 6.1% German, 5.4% Irish, 3.3% Portuguese, 2.7% English, 2.3% Italian

Employment: 15.8% management, business, and financial, 1.4% computer, engineering, and science, 10.8% education, legal, community service, arts, and media, 1.6% healthcare practitioners, 20.7% service, 25.4% sales and office, 12.9% natural resources, construction, and maintenance, 11.4% production, transportation, and material moving

Income: Per capita: $13,135; Median household: $37,466; Average household: $53,767; Households with income of $100,000 or more: 13.5%; Poverty rate: 27.7%

Educational Attainment: High school diploma or higher: 68.9%; Bachelor's degree or higher: 9.3%; Graduate/professional degree or higher: 2.6%

School District(s)

Alview-Dairyland Union Elementary (KG-08)
2012-13 Enrollment: 367 . . . . (559) 665-2394

Chowchilla Elementary (KG-08)
2012-13 Enrollment: 2,088 . . . . (559) 665-8000

Chowchilla Union High (09-12)
2012-13 Enrollment: 1,016 . . . . (559) 665-3662

Madera County Office of Education (KG-12)
2012-13 Enrollment: 962 . . . . (559) 673-6051

Housing: Homeownership rate: 53.5%; Median home value: $138,600; Median year structure built: 1985; Homeowner vacancy rate: 6.2%; Median gross rent: $905 per month; Rental vacancy rate: 7.9%

Health Insurance: 80.4% have insurance; 44.3% have private insurance; 43.9% have public insurance; 19.6% do not have insurance; 12.3% of children under 18 do not have insurance

Safety: Violent crime rate: 45.8 per 10,000 population; Property crime rate: 255.4 per 10,000 population

Newspapers: Chowchilla News (weekly circulation 2200)

Transportation: Commute: 86.8% car, 0.4% public transportation, 2.4% walk, 7.8% work from home; Median travel time to work: 23.3 minutes

Additional Information Contacts

City of Chowchilla . . . . (559) 665-8615
http://www.ci.chowchilla.ca.us

COARSEGOLD (CDP). Covers a land area of 10.988 square miles and a water area of 0 square miles. Located at 37.25° N. Lat; 119.70° W. Long. Elevation is 2,218 feet.

Population: 1,840; Growth (since 2000): n/a; Density: 167.5 persons per square mile; Race: 87.9% White, 0.6% Black/African American, 1.7% Asian, 2.7% American Indian/Alaska Native, 0.3% Native Hawaiian/Other Pacific Islander, 4.2% Two or more races, 8.5% Hispanic of any race; Average household size: 2.40; Median age: 52.3; Age under 18: 18.4%; Age 65 and over: 27.5%; Males per 100 females: 91.1

School District(s)

Yosemite Unified (KG-12)
2012-13 Enrollment: 2,123 . . . . (559) 683-8801

Housing: Homeownership rate: 80.6%; Homeowner vacancy rate: 2.8%; Rental vacancy rate: 5.7%

FAIRMEAD (CDP). Covers a land area of 8.360 square miles and a water area of 0 square miles. Located at 37.08° N. Lat; 120.20° W. Long. Elevation is 253 feet.

Population: 1,447; Growth (since 2000): n/a; Density: 173.1 persons per square mile; Race: 52.8% White, 6.1% Black/African American, 0.5% Asian, 1.6% American Indian/Alaska Native, 0.0% Native Hawaiian/Other Pacific Islander, 4.7% Two or more races, 68.0% Hispanic of any race; Average household size: 4.02; Median age: 29.0; Age under 18: 34.3%; Age 65 and over: 7.3%; Males per 100 females: 112.5

Housing: Homeownership rate: 57.0%; Homeowner vacancy rate: 2.4%; Rental vacancy rate: 8.3%

LA VINA (CDP). Covers a land area of 0.101 square miles and a water area of 0 square miles. Located at 36.88° N. Lat; 120.11° W. Long. Elevation is 230 feet.

Population: 279; Growth (since 2000): n/a; Density: 2,770.0 persons per square mile; Race: 41.9% White, 1.1% Black/African American, 0.0% Asian, 0.0% American Indian/Alaska Native, 0.0% Native Hawaiian/Other Pacific Islander, 3.2% Two or more races, 95.0% Hispanic of any race; Average household size: 4.43; Median age: 27.6; Age under 18: 28.0%; Age 65 and over: 11.1%; Males per 100 females: 103.6

Housing: Homeownership rate: 61.9%; Homeowner vacancy rate: 2.5%; Rental vacancy rate: 11.1%

MADERA (city). County seat. Covers a land area of 15.789 square miles and a water area of 0 square miles. Located at 36.96° N. Lat; 120.08° W. Long. Elevation is 272 feet.

History: Madera was laid out in 1876 by the California Lumber Company. It grew as the seat of Madera County.

Population: 61,416; Growth (since 2000): 42.1%; Density: 3,889.7 persons per square mile; Race: 49.9% White, 3.4% Black/African American, 2.2% Asian, 3.1% American Indian/Alaska Native, 0.1% Native Hawaiian/Other Pacific Islander, 4.4% Two or more races, 76.7% Hispanic of any race; Average household size: 3.82; Median age: 26.6; Age under 18: 34.7%; Age 65 and over: 7.6%; Males per 100 females: 104.0; Marriage status: 42.8% never married, 45.5% now married, 2.4% separated, 4.2% widowed, 7.5% divorced; Foreign born: 31.2%; Speak English only: 37.0%; With disability: 10.1%; Veterans: 4.7%; Ancestry: 3.2% German, 2.3% Irish, 1.8% English, 1.2% American, 1.2% Italian

Employment: 8.4% management, business, and financial, 1.8% computer, engineering, and science, 6.0% education, legal, community service, arts, and media, 3.6% healthcare practitioners, 14.6% service, 18.7% sales and office, 32.0% natural resources, construction, and maintenance, 14.9% production, transportation, and material moving

Income: Per capita: $14,459; Median household: $41,845; Average household: $51,352; Households with income of $100,000 or more: 11.9%; Poverty rate: 27.7%

Educational Attainment: High school diploma or higher: 56.7%; Bachelor's degree or higher: 9.4%; Graduate/professional degree or higher: 2.4%

School District(s)

Golden Valley Unified (KG-12)
2012-13 Enrollment: 1,967 . . . . (559) 645-7500

Madera County Office of Education (KG-12)
2012-13 Enrollment: 962 . . . . (559) 673-6051

Madera Unified (KG-12)
2012-13 Enrollment: 19,984 . . . . (559) 675-4500

Vocational/Technical School(s)

Madera Beauty College (Private, For-profit)
Fall 2013 Enrollment: 55 . . . . (559) 673-9201
2013-14 Tuition: $10,000

Housing: Homeownership rate: 50.8%; Median home value: $151,600; Median year structure built: 1986; Homeowner vacancy rate: 3.5%; Median gross rent: $893 per month; Rental vacancy rate: 5.1%

Health Insurance: 76.9% have insurance; 36.0% have private insurance; 47.1% have public insurance; 23.1% do not have insurance; 8.4% of children under 18 do not have insurance

Hospitals: Madera Community Hospital (106 beds)

Safety: Violent crime rate: 90.2 per 10,000 population; Property crime rate: 294.6 per 10,000 population

Newspapers: Madera Tribune (daily circulation 5300)

Transportation: Commute: 90.4% car, 0.4% public transportation, 3.0% walk, 3.8% work from home; Median travel time to work: 22.8 minutes; Amtrak: Train service available.

Airports: Madera Municipal (general aviation)

Additional Information Contacts
City of Madera . . . . (559) 661-5400
http://www.cityofmadera.org

MADERA ACRES (CDP). Covers a land area of 7.278 square miles and a water area of 0 square miles. Located at 37.01° N. Lat; 120.08° W. Long. Elevation is 292 feet.
Population: 9,163; Growth (since 2000): 18.4%; Density: 1,259.0 persons per square mile; Race: 63.7% White, 2.6% Black/African American, 1.2% Asian, 1.8% American Indian/Alaska Native, 0.1% Native Hawaiian/Other Pacific Islander, 3.9% Two or more races, 65.3% Hispanic of any race; Average household size: 3.80; Median age: 31.0; Age under 18: 31.7%; Age 65 and over: 8.5%; Males per 100 females: 101.1; Marriage status: 31.2% never married, 59.2% now married, 1.2% separated, 4.4% widowed, 5.2% divorced; Foreign born: 22.1%; Speak English only: 51.5%; With disability: 8.2%; Veterans: 9.9%; Ancestry: 6.3% German, 4.9% Irish, 4.0% English, 2.9% Italian, 1.7% French
Employment: 9.8% management, business, and financial, 1.6% computer, engineering, and science, 11.2% education, legal, community service, arts, and media, 1.2% healthcare practitioners, 17.5% service, 21.0% sales and office, 20.4% natural resources, construction, and maintenance, 17.3% production, transportation, and material moving
Income: Per capita: $18,933; Median household: $62,155; Average household: $74,545; Households with income of $100,000 or more: 23.8%; Poverty rate: 11.6%
Educational Attainment: High school diploma or higher: 68.6%; Bachelor's degree or higher: 14.4%; Graduate/professional degree or higher: 4.1%
Housing: Homeownership rate: 81.6%; Median home value: $166,300; Median year structure built: 1988; Homeowner vacancy rate: 1.9%; Median gross rent: $1,288 per month; Rental vacancy rate: 5.5%
Health Insurance: 85.1% have insurance; 57.5% have private insurance; 38.0% have public insurance; 14.9% do not have insurance; 6.5% of children under 18 do not have insurance
Transportation: Commute: 95.7% car, 0.0% public transportation, 0.1% walk, 2.8% work from home; Median travel time to work: 23.6 minutes

NIPINNAWASEE (CDP). Covers a land area of 3.062 square miles and a water area of 0 square miles. Located at 37.40° N. Lat; 119.73° W. Long. Elevation is 2,930 feet.
Population: 475; Growth (since 2000): n/a; Density: 155.1 persons per square mile; Race: 88.8% White, 0.4% Black/African American, 0.0% Asian, 1.9% American Indian/Alaska Native, 0.0% Native Hawaiian/Other Pacific Islander, 8.2% Two or more races, 10.5% Hispanic of any race; Average household size: 2.47; Median age: 49.5; Age under 18: 18.9%; Age 65 and over: 20.8%; Males per 100 females: 93.1
Housing: Homeownership rate: 75.0%; Homeowner vacancy rate: 1.4%; Rental vacancy rate: 11.1%

NORTH FORK (unincorporated postal area)
ZCTA: 93643
Covers a land area of 124.516 square miles and a water area of 0.494 square miles. Located at 37.22° N. Lat; 119.47° W. Long. Elevation is 2,638 feet.
Population: 3,171; Growth (since 2000): -5.6%; Density: 25.5 persons per square mile; Race: 76.8% White, 1.0% Black/African American, 0.9% Asian, 12.6% American Indian/Alaska Native, 0.1% Native Hawaiian/Other Pacific Islander, 5.9% Two or more races, 11.5% Hispanic of any race; Average household size: 2.41; Median age: 51.0; Age under 18: 19.3%; Age 65 and over: 21.9%; Males per 100 females: 98.8; Marriage status: 24.7% never married, 60.9% now married, 6.2% separated, 4.6% widowed, 9.9% divorced; Foreign born: 0.5%; Speak English only: 97.0%; With disability: 21.6%; Veterans: 12.0%; Ancestry: 17.1% Irish, 13.2% German, 8.3% English, 5.7% American, 5.2% Italian
Employment: 16.1% management, business, and financial, 2.6% computer, engineering, and science, 7.2% education, legal, community service, arts, and media, 10.9% healthcare practitioners, 34.5% service, 9.2% sales and office, 13.2% natural resources, construction, and maintenance, 6.3% production, transportation, and material moving
Income: Per capita: $23,082; Median household: $41,875; Average household: $55,035; Households with income of $100,000 or more: 7.3%; Poverty rate: 8.8%
Educational Attainment: High school diploma or higher: 91.4%; Bachelor's degree or higher: 22.2%; Graduate/professional degree or higher: 9.9%

School District(s)
Chawanakee Unified (KG-12)
2012-13 Enrollment: 1,069 . . . . (559) 877-6209
Housing: Homeownership rate: 74.8%; Median home value: $284,300; Median year structure built: 1974; Homeowner vacancy rate: 2.4%; Median gross rent: $740 per month; Rental vacancy rate: 7.2%
Health Insurance: 72.2% have insurance; 60.0% have private insurance; 27.0% have public insurance; 27.8% do not have insurance; 41.8% of children under 18 do not have insurance
Transportation: Commute: 89.6% car, 0.0% public transportation, 0.0% walk, 8.4% work from home; Median travel time to work: 33.5 minutes

O NEALS (unincorporated postal area)
ZCTA: 93645
Covers a land area of 53.475 square miles and a water area of 0.036 square miles. Located at 37.17° N. Lat; 119.64° W. Long..
Population: 318; Growth (since 2000): 84.9%; Density: 5.9 persons per square mile; Race: 89.3% White, 0.0% Black/African American, 0.9% Asian, 4.4% American Indian/Alaska Native, 0.0% Native Hawaiian/Other Pacific Islander, 1.6% Two or more races, 9.4% Hispanic of any race; Average household size: 2.41; Median age: 49.0; Age under 18: 19.8%; Age 65 and over: 19.5%; Males per 100 females: 96.3

School District(s)
Chawanakee Unified (KG-12)
2012-13 Enrollment: 1,069 . . . . (559) 877-6209
Housing: Homeownership rate: 76.6%; Homeowner vacancy rate: 1.0%; Rental vacancy rate: 3.0%

OAKHURST (CDP). Covers a land area of 5.999 square miles and a water area of 0.007 square miles. Located at 37.35° N. Lat; 119.65° W. Long. Elevation is 2,274 feet.
Population: 2,829; Growth (since 2000): -1.4%; Density: 471.6 persons per square mile; Race: 89.5% White, 0.8% Black/African American, 1.6% Asian, 2.2% American Indian/Alaska Native, 0.1% Native Hawaiian/Other Pacific Islander, 3.6% Two or more races, 16.7% Hispanic of any race; Average household size: 2.26; Median age: 48.4; Age under 18: 18.6%; Age 65 and over: 26.5%; Males per 100 females: 90.5; Marriage status: 30.3% never married, 35.0% now married, 0.7% separated, 18.2% widowed, 16.4% divorced; Foreign born: 4.6%; Speak English only: 95.1%; With disability: 20.2%; Veterans: 11.6%; Ancestry: 14.8% German, 9.7% Irish, 9.2% European, 8.9% English, 7.5% Italian
Employment: 19.6% management, business, and financial, 1.0% computer, engineering, and science, 7.3% education, legal, community service, arts, and media, 0.0% healthcare practitioners, 27.3% service, 32.7% sales and office, 6.0% natural resources, construction, and maintenance, 6.2% production, transportation, and material moving
Income: Per capita: $22,918; Median household: $39,142; Average household: $52,152; Households with income of $100,000 or more: 11.0%; Poverty rate: 7.1%
Educational Attainment: High school diploma or higher: 84.4%; Bachelor's degree or higher: 16.2%; Graduate/professional degree or higher: 6.0%

School District(s)
Bass Lake Joint Union Elementary (KG-08)
2012-13 Enrollment: 820 . . . . (559) 642-1555
Yosemite Unified (KG-12)
2012-13 Enrollment: 2,123 . . . . (559) 683-8801
Housing: Homeownership rate: 56.4%; Median home value: $190,000; Median year structure built: 1980; Homeowner vacancy rate: 3.5%; Median gross rent: $1,073 per month; Rental vacancy rate: 5.5%
Health Insurance: 87.0% have insurance; 67.8% have private insurance; 40.2% have public insurance; 13.0% do not have insurance; 2.9% of children under 18 do not have insurance
Newspapers: Sierra Star (weekly circulation 5000)
Transportation: Commute: 94.1% car, 0.0% public transportation, 2.1% walk, 2.3% work from home; Median travel time to work: 13.9 minutes

PARKSDALE (CDP). Covers a land area of 1.811 square miles and a water area of 0 square miles. Located at 36.95° N. Lat; 120.02° W. Long. Elevation is 279 feet.
Population: 2,621; Growth (since 2000): -2.5%; Density: 1,447.2 persons per square mile; Race: 44.1% White, 2.1% Black/African American, 0.7% Asian, 2.5% American Indian/Alaska Native, 0.1% Native Hawaiian/Other Pacific Islander, 3.5% Two or more races, 86.9% Hispanic of any race; Average household size: 4.61; Median age: 25.4; Age under 18: 36.6%;

Age 65 and over: 6.6%; Males per 100 females: 111.2; Marriage status: 42.8% never married, 45.1% now married, 1.9% separated, 3.2% widowed, 9.0% divorced; Foreign born: 33.4%; Speak English only: 23.9%; With disability: 17.0%; Veterans: 2.5%; Ancestry: 1.3% English, 1.0% Irish, 0.7% Scottish, 0.7% Polish, 0.2% Italian
Employment: 7.2% management, business, and financial, 0.0% computer, engineering, and science, 3.3% education, legal, community service, arts, and media, 0.0% healthcare practitioners, 20.6% service, 23.0% sales and office, 34.7% natural resources, construction, and maintenance, 11.3% production, transportation, and material moving
Income: Per capita: $8,247; Median household: $33,083; Average household: $35,676; Households with income of $100,000 or more: n/a; Poverty rate: 32.3%
Educational Attainment: High school diploma or higher: 46.5%; Bachelor's degree or higher: 3.0%; Graduate/professional degree or higher: n/a
Housing: Homeownership rate: 64.4%; Median home value: $88,900; Median year structure built: 1989; Homeowner vacancy rate: 1.3%; Median gross rent: $724 per month; Rental vacancy rate: 3.8%
Health Insurance: 70.8% have insurance; 15.4% have private insurance; 57.8% have public insurance; 29.2% do not have insurance; 14.4% of children under 18 do not have insurance
Transportation: Commute: 90.2% car, 0.0% public transportation, 0.0% walk, 3.0% work from home; Median travel time to work: 29.9 minutes

PARKWOOD (CDP). Covers a land area of 0.698 square miles and a water area of 0 square miles. Located at 36.93° N. Lat; 120.05° W. Long. Elevation is 262 feet.
Population: 2,268; Growth (since 2000): 7.0%; Density: 3,251.2 persons per square mile; Race: 50.2% White, 5.4% Black/African American, 1.0% Asian, 2.1% American Indian/Alaska Native, 0.0% Native Hawaiian/Other Pacific Islander, 5.4% Two or more races, 78.7% Hispanic of any race; Average household size: 4.01; Median age: 26.9; Age under 18: 35.0%; Age 65 and over: 7.4%; Males per 100 females: 102.3
Housing: Homeownership rate: 56.1%; Homeowner vacancy rate: 1.6%; Rental vacancy rate: 7.1%

RAYMOND (unincorporated postal area)

ZCTA: 93653

Covers a land area of 237.365 square miles and a water area of 3.661 square miles. Located at 37.25° N. Lat; 119.94° W. Long. Elevation is 948 feet.
Population: 1,229; Growth (since 2000): 26.6%; Density: 5.2 persons per square mile; Race: 87.5% White, 1.9% Black/African American, 0.7% Asian, 3.0% American Indian/Alaska Native, 0.0% Native Hawaiian/Other Pacific Islander, 4.4% Two or more races, 9.5% Hispanic of any race; Average household size: 2.42; Median age: 49.5; Age under 18: 19.6%; Age 65 and over: 20.6%; Males per 100 females: 104.2

School District(s)

Raymond-Knowles Union Elementary (KG-08)
2012-13 Enrollment: 82. . . . . (559) 689-3336
Yosemite Unified (KG-12)
2012-13 Enrollment: 2,123 . . . . (559) 683-8801
Housing: Homeownership rate: 76.2%; Homeowner vacancy rate: 2.3%; Rental vacancy rate: 5.5%

ROLLING HILLS (CDP). Covers a land area of 0.592 square miles and a water area of 0 square miles. Located at 36.90° N. Lat; 119.80° W. Long. Elevation is 371 feet.
Population: 742; Growth (since 2000): n/a; Density: 1,253.5 persons per square mile; Race: 86.5% White, 2.2% Black/African American, 3.4% Asian, 1.5% American Indian/Alaska Native, 0.3% Native Hawaiian/Other Pacific Islander, 1.6% Two or more races, 19.3% Hispanic of any race; Average household size: 2.52; Median age: 53.0; Age under 18: 16.4%; Age 65 and over: 24.3%; Males per 100 females: 100.5
Housing: Homeownership rate: 94.6%; Homeowner vacancy rate: 0.0%; Rental vacancy rate: 5.6%

WISHON (unincorporated postal area)

ZCTA: 93669

Covers a land area of 6.805 square miles and a water area of 0.774 square miles. Located at 37.29° N. Lat; 119.55° W. Long..
Population: 295; Growth (since 2000): -4.8%; Density: 43.3 persons per square mile; Race: 86.1% White, 0.0% Black/African American, 0.0% Asian, 3.4% American Indian/Alaska Native, 0.0% Native Hawaiian/Other Pacific Islander, 8.8% Two or more races, 13.2% Hispanic of any race; Average household size: 2.25; Median age: 50.9; Age under 18: 17.6%; Age 65 and over: 22.7%; Males per 100 females: 96.7
Housing: Homeownership rate: 74.0%; Homeowner vacancy rate: 1.0%; Rental vacancy rate: 5.6%

YOSEMITE LAKES (CDP). Covers a land area of 20.902 square miles and a water area of 0.097 square miles. Located at 37.19° N. Lat; 119.77° W. Long. Elevation is 1,263 feet.
History: Yosemite Lakes is a non-gated community located in the Central California Sierra Mountain foothills between Yosemite National Park and Fresno. It became a popular vacation spot in the early 1970s.
Population: 4,952; Growth (since 2000): 19.0%; Density: 236.9 persons per square mile; Race: 89.0% White, 0.8% Black/African American, 1.0% Asian, 1.8% American Indian/Alaska Native, 0.2% Native Hawaiian/Other Pacific Islander, 4.5% Two or more races, 10.4% Hispanic of any race; Average household size: 2.60; Median age: 47.2; Age under 18: 22.5%; Age 65 and over: 19.3%; Males per 100 females: 98.9; Marriage status: 17.8% never married, 73.6% now married, 1.7% separated, 3.5% widowed, 5.1% divorced; Foreign born: 4.1%; Speak English only: 95.3%; With disability: 16.7%; Veterans: 13.2%; Ancestry: 17.2% German, 15.0% Irish, 11.5% English, 5.9% Scottish, 5.1% Italian
Employment: 15.1% management, business, and financial, 3.7% computer, engineering, and science, 14.5% education, legal, community service, arts, and media, 6.4% healthcare practitioners, 13.7% service, 33.7% sales and office, 4.4% natural resources, construction, and maintenance, 8.5% production, transportation, and material moving
Income: Per capita: $31,775; Median household: $55,563; Average household: $85,516; Households with income of $100,000 or more: 27.3%; Poverty rate: 11.5%
Educational Attainment: High school diploma or higher: 92.0%; Bachelor's degree or higher: 30.3%; Graduate/professional degree or higher: 14.7%
Housing: Homeownership rate: 84.7%; Median home value: $229,600; Median year structure built: 1990; Homeowner vacancy rate: 3.6%; Median gross rent: $1,351 per month; Rental vacancy rate: 9.3%
Health Insurance: 87.0% have insurance; 65.5% have private insurance; 41.3% have public insurance; 13.0% do not have insurance; 7.7% of children under 18 do not have insurance
Transportation: Commute: 87.6% car, 0.0% public transportation, 0.9% walk, 7.3% work from home; Median travel time to work: 37.8 minutes

Marin County

Located in western California, on a hilly peninsula; bounded on the west by the Pacific Ocean, and on the east and south by San Pablo and San Francisco Bays and the Golden Gate; includes Angel Island, and Mt. Tamalpais. Covers a land area of 520.306 square miles, a water area of 307.886 square miles, and is located in the Pacific Time Zone at 38.05° N. Lat., 122.75° W. Long. The county was founded in 1850. County seat is San Rafael.

Marin County is part of the San Francisco-Oakland-Hayward, CA Metropolitan Statistical Area. The entire metro area includes: Oakland-Hayward-Berkeley, CA Metropolitan Division (Alameda County, CA; Contra Costa County, CA); San Francisco-Redwood City-South San Francisco, CA Metropolitan Division (San Francisco County, CA; San Mateo County, CA); San Rafael, CA Metropolitan Division (Marin County, CA)

Weather Station: Kentfield — Elevation: 127 feet

	Jan	Feb	Mar	Apr	May	Jun	Jul	Aug	Sep	Oct	Nov	Dec
High	57	61	66	70	75	81	84	84	82	75	64	56
Low	41	43	44	46	49	52	53	53	52	49	45	41
Precip	9.0	9.2	6.5	2.5	1.4	0.3	0.0	0.1	0.3	2.1	6.3	9.7
Snow	0.0	0.0	0.0	0.0	0.0	0.0	0.0	0.0	0.0	0.0	0.0	0.0

High and Low temperatures in degrees Fahrenheit; Precipitation and Snow in inches

Weather Station: San Rafael Civic Center — Elevation: 120 feet

	Jan	Feb	Mar	Apr	May	Jun	Jul	Aug	Sep	Oct	Nov	Dec
High	55	60	64	67	72	77	81	81	79	74	64	55
Low	42	44	45	47	50	53	55	55	54	51	46	41
Precip	7.1	7.4	4.0	1.8	1.0	0.2	tr	0.1	0.1	1.2	3.4	6.2
Snow	0.0	0.0	0.0	0.0	0.0	0.0	0.0	0.0	0.0	0.0	0.0	0.0

High and Low temperatures in degrees Fahrenheit; Precipitation and Snow in inches

Population: 252,409; Growth (since 2000): 2.1%; Density: 485.1 persons per square mile; Race: 80.0% White, 2.8% Black/African American, 5.5% Asian, 0.6% American Indian/Alaska Native, 0.2% Native Hawaiian/Other Pacific Islander, 4.2% two or more races, 15.5% Hispanic of any race; Average household size: 2.36; Median age: 44.5; Age under 18: 20.7%; Age 65 and over: 16.7%; Males per 100 females: 96.7; Marriage status: 27.0% never married, 54.4% now married, 1.8% separated, 5.3% widowed, 13.2% divorced; Foreign born: 19.0%; Speak English only: 77.0%; With disability: 8.9%; Veterans: 7.6%; Ancestry: 14.3% Irish, 13.9% German, 12.5% English, 9.6% Italian, 3.8% French

Religion: Six largest groups: 30.6% Catholicism, 2.0% Baptist, 1.8% Judaism, 1.4% Episcopalianism/Anglicanism, 1.3% Presbyterian-Reformed, 1.0% Buddhism

Economy: Unemployment rate: 3.9%; Leading industries: 18.3% professional, scientific, and technical services; 11.6% health care and social assistance; 10.9% retail trade; Farms: 323 totaling 170,876 acres; Company size: 3 employ 1,000 or more persons, 10 employ 500 to 999 persons, 98 employ 100 to 499 persons, 9,523 employ less than 100 persons; Business ownership: 14,487 women-owned, 367 Black-owned, n/a Hispanic-owned, n/a Asian-owned

Employment: 23.7% management, business, and financial, 6.0% computer, engineering, and science, 15.8% education, legal, community service, arts, and media, 6.1% healthcare practitioners, 15.9% service, 22.4% sales and office, 5.6% natural resources, construction, and maintenance, 4.4% production, transportation, and material moving

Income: Per capita: $56,791; Median household: $90,839; Average household: $137,795; Households with income of $100,000 or more: 46.3%; Poverty rate: 7.7%

Educational Attainment: High school diploma or higher: 92.4%; Bachelor's degree or higher: 54.6%; Graduate/professional degree or higher: 23.4%

Housing: Homeownership rate: 62.6%; Median home value: $781,900; Median year structure built: 1966; Homeowner vacancy rate: 1.3%; Median gross rent: $1,628 per month; Rental vacancy rate: 5.2%

Vital Statistics: Birth rate: 88.5 per 10,000 population; Death rate: 69.6 per 10,000 population; Age-adjusted cancer mortality rate: 144.9 deaths per 100,000 population

Health Insurance: 91.1% have insurance; 79.4% have private insurance; 26.2% have public insurance; 8.9% do not have insurance; 3.8% of children under 18 do not have insurance

Health Care: Physicians: 50.1 per 10,000 population; Hospital beds: 15.2 per 10,000 population; Hospital admissions: 734.8 per 10,000 population

Air Quality Index: 71.2% good, 28.2% moderate, 0.5% unhealthy for sensitive individuals, 0.0% unhealthy (percent of days)

Transportation: Commute: 75.0% car, 8.9% public transportation, 3.3% walk, 10.3% work from home; Median travel time to work: 28.6 minutes

Presidential Election: 74.0% Obama, 23.5% Romney (2012)

National and State Parks: Angel Island State Park; China Camp State Park; Corte Madera State Ecological Reserve; Golden Gate National Recreation Area; Marconi Conference Center State Historic Park; Marin Headlands State Park; Marin Islands National Wildlife Refuge; Mount Tamalpais State Park; Muir Woods National Monument; Olompali State Historic Park; Point Reyes National Seashore; Samuel P. Taylor State Park; Tomales Bay State Park

Additional Information Contacts

Marin Government. . . . . (415) 499-7331
http://www.marincounty.org

Marin County Communities

ALTO (CDP). Covers a land area of 0.126 square miles and a water area of 0 square miles. Located at 37.91° N. Lat; 122.52° W. Long. Elevation is 16 feet.

Population: 711; Growth (since 2000): n/a; Density: 5,654.1 persons per square mile; Race: 87.1% White, 1.1% Black/African American, 4.2% Asian, 0.3% American Indian/Alaska Native, 0.1% Native Hawaiian/Other Pacific Islander, 4.9% Two or more races, 7.2% Hispanic of any race; Average household size: 2.39; Median age: 41.0; Age under 18: 24.9%; Age 65 and over: 8.9%; Males per 100 females: 81.8

Housing: Homeownership rate: 52.9%; Homeowner vacancy rate: 0.6%; Rental vacancy rate: 4.1%

BELVEDERE (city). Covers a land area of 0.519 square miles and a water area of 1.887 square miles. Located at 37.87° N. Lat; 122.47° W. Long. Elevation is 59 feet.

Population: 2,068; Growth (since 2000): -2.7%; Density: 3,981.2 persons per square mile; Race: 93.8% White, 0.1% Black/African American, 2.8% Asian, 0.0% American Indian/Alaska Native, 0.3% Native Hawaiian/Other Pacific Islander, 2.0% Two or more races, 3.5% Hispanic of any race; Average household size: 2.23; Median age: 54.0; Age under 18: 21.4%; Age 65 and over: 31.6%; Males per 100 females: 80.9

Housing: Homeownership rate: 74.9%; Homeowner vacancy rate: 2.1%; Rental vacancy rate: 4.5%

Safety: Violent crime rate: 0.0 per 10,000 population; Property crime rate: 122.6 per 10,000 population

Additional Information Contacts

City of Belvedere. . . . . (415) 435-3838
http://www.cityofbelvedere.org

BELVEDERE TIBURON (unincorporated postal area)

ZCTA: 94920

Covers a land area of 6.532 square miles and a water area of 5.282 square miles. Located at 37.89° N. Lat; 122.47° W. Long..

Population: 12,474; Growth (since 2000): -4.4%; Density: 1,909.7 persons per square mile; Race: 89.3% White, 0.7% Black/African American, 5.1% Asian, 0.1% American Indian/Alaska Native, 0.1% Native Hawaiian/Other Pacific Islander, 3.7% Two or more races, 4.4% Hispanic of any race; Average household size: 2.33; Median age: 49.0; Age under 18: 23.2%; Age 65 and over: 23.0%; Males per 100 females: 86.8; Marriage status: 17.9% never married, 63.0% now married, 2.5% separated, 7.2% widowed, 11.9% divorced; Foreign born: 15.6%; Speak English only: 83.2%; With disability: 8.4%; Veterans: 10.4%; Ancestry: 19.7% German, 16.6% English, 16.5% Irish, 9.2% Italian, 4.0% Polish

Employment: 32.2% management, business, and financial, 4.4% computer, engineering, and science, 20.3% education, legal, community service, arts, and media, 8.5% healthcare practitioners, 6.6% service, 21.6% sales and office, 3.3% natural resources, construction, and maintenance, 3.2% production, transportation, and material moving

Income: Per capita: $102,524; Median household: $138,884; Average household: $236,163; Households with income of $100,000 or more: 63.1%; Poverty rate: 5.1%

Educational Attainment: High school diploma or higher: 97.6%; Bachelor's degree or higher: 77.4%; Graduate/professional degree or higher: 36.9%

Housing: Homeownership rate: 67.0%; Median home value: 1 million+; Median year structure built: 1967; Homeowner vacancy rate: 2.0%; Median gross rent: $2,000+ per month; Rental vacancy rate: 4.8%

Health Insurance: 95.7% have insurance; 87.5% have private insurance; 25.7% have public insurance; 4.3% do not have insurance; 1.7% of children under 18 do not have insurance

Transportation: Commute: 66.5% car, 11.2% public transportation, 2.1% walk, 15.8% work from home; Median travel time to work: 32.3 minutes

BLACK POINT-GREEN POINT (CDP). Covers a land area of 2.687 square miles and a water area of 0.012 square miles. Located at 38.11° N. Lat; 122.52° W. Long.

Population: 1,306; Growth (since 2000): 14.3%; Density: 486.1 persons per square mile; Race: 90.7% White, 0.5% Black/African American, 3.4% Asian, 0.5% American Indian/Alaska Native, 0.0% Native Hawaiian/Other Pacific Islander, 2.7% Two or more races, 8.6% Hispanic of any race; Average household size: 2.26; Median age: 53.2; Age under 18: 15.1%; Age 65 and over: 22.3%; Males per 100 females: 94.6

Housing: Homeownership rate: 79.9%; Homeowner vacancy rate: 0.6%; Rental vacancy rate: 4.9%

BOLINAS (CDP). Covers a land area of 5.826 square miles and a water area of 0 square miles. Located at 37.92° N. Lat; 122.71° W. Long. Elevation is 10 feet.

History: The first settler in Bolinas was Gregorio Briones, owner of the large cattle domain of Baulinas Rancho in the 1850's.

Population: 1,620; Growth (since 2000): 30.0%; Density: 278.0 persons per square mile; Race: 86.8% White, 1.7% Black/African American, 1.0% Asian, 0.6% American Indian/Alaska Native, 0.9% Native Hawaiian/Other Pacific Islander, 5.1% Two or more races, 16.0% Hispanic of any race; Average household size: 2.05; Median age: 49.3; Age under 18: 14.4%; Age 65 and over: 17.5%; Males per 100 females: 115.1

School District(s)

Bolinas-Stinson Union (KG-08)
2012-13 Enrollment: 110 . . . . (415) 868-1603

Housing: Homeownership rate: 57.5%; Homeowner vacancy rate: 1.7%; Rental vacancy rate: 2.6%

CORTE MADERA (town). Covers a land area of 3.164 square miles and a water area of 1.242 square miles. Located at 37.93° N. Lat; 122.51° W. Long. Elevation is 26 feet.

History: Muir Woods National Monument to Southwest. Incorporated 1916.

Population: 9,253; Growth (since 2000): 1.7%; Density: 2,924.9 persons per square mile; Race: 84.4% White, 0.9% Black/African American, 6.8% Asian, 0.2% American Indian/Alaska Native, 0.3% Native Hawaiian/Other Pacific Islander, 4.6% Two or more races, 8.3% Hispanic of any race; Average household size: 2.44; Median age: 44.2; Age under 18: 25.2%; Age 65 and over: 16.0%; Males per 100 females: 87.4; Marriage status: 23.2% never married, 56.9% now married, 1.7% separated, 6.7% widowed, 13.2% divorced; Foreign born: 16.6%; Speak English only: 78.2%; With disability: 9.2%; Veterans: 6.5%; Ancestry: 18.2% German, 13.3% English, 13.1% Irish, 10.1% Italian, 5.1% French

Employment: 26.4% management, business, and financial, 8.0% computer, engineering, and science, 18.0% education, legal, community service, arts, and media, 6.7% healthcare practitioners, 9.6% service, 24.5% sales and office, 3.3% natural resources, construction, and maintenance, 3.4% production, transportation, and material moving

Income: Per capita: $64,729; Median household: $107,193; Average household: $151,640; Households with income of $100,000 or more: 53.5%; Poverty rate: 3.7%

Educational Attainment: High school diploma or higher: 93.2%; Bachelor's degree or higher: 64.6%; Graduate/professional degree or higher: 23.4%

School District(s)

Larkspur-Corte Madera (KG-08)
2012-13 Enrollment: 1,404 . . . . (415) 927-6960

Housing: Homeownership rate: 69.9%; Median home value: $878,000; Median year structure built: 1963; Homeowner vacancy rate: 0.8%; Median gross rent: $1,680 per month; Rental vacancy rate: 5.8%

Health Insurance: 94.1% have insurance; 84.2% have private insurance; 24.8% have public insurance; 5.9% do not have insurance; 2.6% of children under 18 do not have insurance

Transportation: Commute: 81.3% car, 8.5% public transportation, 0.4% walk, 7.8% work from home; Median travel time to work: 29.8 minutes

Additional Information Contacts

Town of Corte Madera. . . . . (415) 927-5086
http://www.ci.corte-madera.ca.us

DILLON BEACH (CDP). Covers a land area of 2.984 square miles and a water area of 0 square miles. Located at 38.24° N. Lat; 122.96° W. Long. Elevation is 95 feet.

Population: 283; Growth (since 2000): -11.3%; Density: 94.8 persons per square mile; Race: 94.0% White, 0.0% Black/African American, 1.4% Asian, 1.1% American Indian/Alaska Native, 0.0% Native Hawaiian/Other Pacific Islander, 3.5% Two or more races, 3.2% Hispanic of any race; Average household size: 1.93; Median age: 57.4; Age under 18: 9.9%; Age 65 and over: 27.2%; Males per 100 females: 95.2

Housing: Homeownership rate: 85.1%; Homeowner vacancy rate: 5.3%; Rental vacancy rate: 59.3%

FAIRFAX (town). Covers a land area of 2.204 square miles and a water area of 0 square miles. Located at 37.99° N. Lat; 122.60° W. Long. Elevation is 112 feet.

History: Incorporated 1931.

Population: 7,441; Growth (since 2000): 1.7%; Density: 3,376.9 persons per square mile; Race: 88.9% White, 1.5% Black/African American, 2.7% Asian, 0.5% American Indian/Alaska Native, 0.1% Native Hawaiian/Other Pacific Islander, 4.0% Two or more races, 6.8% Hispanic of any race; Average household size: 2.20; Median age: 45.9; Age under 18: 19.3%; Age 65 and over: 12.8%; Males per 100 females: 94.2; Marriage status: 28.8% never married, 51.2% now married, 1.8% separated, 5.3% widowed, 14.8% divorced; Foreign born: 8.6%; Speak English only: 91.7%; With disability: 8.0%; Veterans: 4.8%; Ancestry: 22.1% Irish, 21.8% English, 15.3% German, 12.2% Italian, 5.1% Russian

Employment: 20.6% management, business, and financial, 8.8% computer, engineering, and science, 22.9% education, legal, community service, arts, and media, 6.1% healthcare practitioners, 12.6% service, 19.2% sales and office, 6.4% natural resources, construction, and maintenance, 3.4% production, transportation, and material moving

Income: Per capita: $53,255; Median household: $88,043; Average household: $115,515; Households with income of $100,000 or more: 47.0%; Poverty rate: 7.8%

Educational Attainment: High school diploma or higher: 98.4%; Bachelor's degree or higher: 61.6%; Graduate/professional degree or higher: 23.5%

School District(s)

Ross Valley Elementary (KG-08)
2012-13 Enrollment: 2,230 . . . . (415) 454-2162

Housing: Homeownership rate: 62.2%; Median home value: $668,600; Median year structure built: 1957; Homeowner vacancy rate: 0.9%; Median gross rent: $1,597 per month; Rental vacancy rate: 4.9%

Health Insurance: 90.9% have insurance; 83.6% have private insurance; 17.2% have public insurance; 9.1% do not have insurance; 1.8% of children under 18 do not have insurance

Safety: Violent crime rate: 17.2 per 10,000 population; Property crime rate: 137.5 per 10,000 population

Transportation: Commute: 73.3% car, 6.4% public transportation, 3.2% walk, 13.4% work from home; Median travel time to work: 30.8 minutes

Additional Information Contacts

Town of Fairfax . . . . (415) 453-1584
http://www.town-of-fairfax.org

GREENBRAE (unincorporated postal area)

ZCTA: 94904

Covers a land area of 7.245 square miles and a water area of 0.160 square miles. Located at 37.95° N. Lat; 122.56° W. Long. Elevation is 26 feet.

Population: 11,995; Growth (since 2000): 0.0%; Density: 1,655.7 persons per square mile; Race: 87.7% White, 1.3% Black/African American, 4.5% Asian, 0.2% American Indian/Alaska Native, 0.1% Native Hawaiian/Other Pacific Islander, 3.8% Two or more races, 6.6% Hispanic of any race; Average household size: 2.21; Median age: 48.8; Age under 18: 21.5%; Age 65 and over: 22.8%; Males per 100 females: 84.7; Marriage status: 24.4% never married, 55.8% now married, 2.8% separated, 6.6% widowed, 13.2% divorced; Foreign born: 15.3%; Speak English only: 83.9%; With disability: 8.7%; Veterans: 9.0%; Ancestry: 17.8% German, 17.2% Irish, 15.8% English, 8.6% Italian, 5.0% Russian

Employment: 26.9% management, business, and financial, 6.0% computer, engineering, and science, 17.4% education, legal, community service, arts, and media, 10.0% healthcare practitioners, 12.2% service, 19.6% sales and office, 4.2% natural resources, construction, and maintenance, 3.8% production, transportation, and material moving

Income: Per capita: $82,093; Median household: $102,538; Average household: $181,203; Households with income of $100,000 or more: 51.2%; Poverty rate: 4.9%

Educational Attainment: High school diploma or higher: 97.5%; Bachelor's degree or higher: 64.7%; Graduate/professional degree or higher: 34.7%

Housing: Homeownership rate: 62.4%; Median home value: 1 million+; Median year structure built: 1962; Homeowner vacancy rate: 1.3%; Median gross rent: $1,726 per month; Rental vacancy rate: 6.1%

Health Insurance: 93.2% have insurance; 85.7% have private insurance; 28.1% have public insurance; 6.8% do not have insurance; 2.8% of children under 18 do not have insurance

Hospitals: Marin General Hospital (235 beds)

Transportation: Commute: 77.9% car, 7.7% public transportation, 2.5% walk, 9.2% work from home; Median travel time to work: 27.0 minutes

INVERNESS (CDP). Covers a land area of 6.399 square miles and a water area of 0.436 square miles. Located at 38.08° N. Lat; 122.85° W. Long. Elevation is 33 feet.

History: James Black, a native of Inverness, Scotland, settled here in 1832. When the town was founded in 1908, it was named Inverness for Black's home.

Population: 1,304; Growth (since 2000): -8.2%; Density: 203.8 persons per square mile; Race: 92.9% White, 1.2% Black/African American, 1.2% Asian, 0.6% American Indian/Alaska Native, 0.2% Native Hawaiian/Other Pacific Islander, 2.5% Two or more races, 6.1% Hispanic of any race; Average household size: 1.87; Median age: 57.3; Age under 18: 10.7%; Age 65 and over: 26.9%; Males per 100 females: 82.9

School District(s)

Shoreline Unified (KG-12)
2012-13 Enrollment: 554. . . . . (707) 878-2266

Housing: Homeownership rate: 64.7%; Homeowner vacancy rate: 2.2%; Rental vacancy rate: 9.8%

KENTFIELD (CDP). Covers a land area of 3.025 square miles and a water area of 0.016 square miles. Located at 37.94° N. Lat; 122.56° W. Long. Elevation is 138 feet.

History: The place was founded by James Ross as Ross Landing. The named was changed to Kent in the 1890s, and finally to Kentfield with the opening of the first post office in 1905.

Population: 6,485; Growth (since 2000): 2.1%; Density: 2,143.6 persons per square mile; Race: 91.1% White, 0.5% Black/African American, 3.5% Asian, 0.2% American Indian/Alaska Native, 0.1% Native Hawaiian/Other Pacific Islander, 3.2% Two or more races, 4.6% Hispanic of any race; Average household size: 2.51; Median age: 47.0; Age under 18: 25.6%; Age 65 and over: 19.5%; Males per 100 females: 91.1; Marriage status: 23.6% never married, 64.0% now married, 2.4% separated, 2.6% widowed, 9.9% divorced; Foreign born: 9.0%; Speak English only: 90.4%; With disability: 7.5%; Veterans: 9.5%; Ancestry: 18.9% German, 18.0% Irish, 15.8% English, 8.6% Italian, 6.8% European

Employment: 30.1% management, business, and financial, 5.4% computer, engineering, and science, 18.3% education, legal, community service, arts, and media, 8.1% healthcare practitioners, 9.9% service, 19.4% sales and office, 3.1% natural resources, construction, and maintenance, 5.6% production, transportation, and material moving

Income: Per capita: $101,001; Median household: $158,693; Average household: $251,901; Households with income of $100,000 or more: 64.1%; Poverty rate: 3.8%

Educational Attainment: High school diploma or higher: 98.5%; Bachelor's degree or higher: 74.0%; Graduate/professional degree or higher: 39.8%

School District(s)

Kentfield Elementary (KG-08)
2012-13 Enrollment: 1,217 . . . . (415) 458-5130

Two-year College(s)

College of Marin (Public)
Fall 2013 Enrollment: 6,077 . . . . (415) 457-8811
2013-14 Tuition: In-state $1,420; Out-of-state $7,570

Housing: Homeownership rate: 75.8%; Median home value: 1 million+; Median year structure built: 1956; Homeowner vacancy rate: 0.8%; Median gross rent: $1,450 per month; Rental vacancy rate: 8.1%

Health Insurance: 94.2% have insurance; 87.2% have private insurance; 25.4% have public insurance; 5.8% do not have insurance; 2.1% of children under 18 do not have insurance

Transportation: Commute: 75.0% car, 8.2% public transportation, 3.0% walk, 11.2% work from home; Median travel time to work: 29.4 minutes

LAGUNITAS-FOREST KNOLLS (CDP). Covers a land area of 4.247 square miles and a water area of 0 square miles. Located at 38.02° N. Lat; 122.69° W. Long. Elevation is 249 feet.

Population: 1,819; Growth (since 2000): -0.9%; Density: 428.3 persons per square mile; Race: 91.1% White, 1.4% Black/African American, 0.6% Asian, 0.6% American Indian/Alaska Native, 0.1% Native Hawaiian/Other Pacific Islander, 3.8% Two or more races, 7.3% Hispanic of any race; Average household size: 2.22; Median age: 48.9; Age under 18: 18.8%; Age 65 and over: 13.0%; Males per 100 females: 94.8

Housing: Homeownership rate: 66.7%; Homeowner vacancy rate: 1.6%; Rental vacancy rate: 3.2%

LARKSPUR (city). Covers a land area of 3.027 square miles and a water area of 0.216 square miles. Located at 37.94° N. Lat; 122.53° W. Long. Elevation is 33 feet.

History: Named for the blue larkspur that grows profusely in this area. Muir Woods National Monument to West. Incorporated 1908.

Population: 11,926; Growth (since 2000): -0.7%; Density: 3,940.0 persons per square mile; Race: 86.5% White, 1.6% Black/African American, 4.7% Asian, 0.2% American Indian/Alaska Native, 0.1% Native Hawaiian/Other Pacific Islander, 4.1% Two or more races, 7.7% Hispanic of any race; Average household size: 2.00; Median age: 48.5; Age under 18: 18.2%; Age 65 and over: 21.5%; Males per 100 females: 81.9; Marriage status: 23.4% never married, 53.2% now married, 1.8% separated, 7.3% widowed, 16.1% divorced; Foreign born: 18.8%; Speak English only: 80.8%; With disability: 8.8%; Veterans: 8.9%; Ancestry: 14.7% Irish, 14.6% German, 12.9% English, 9.4% Italian, 5.2% American

Employment: 25.5% management, business, and financial, 8.2% computer, engineering, and science, 16.3% education, legal, community service, arts, and media, 10.6% healthcare practitioners, 10.0% service, 22.7% sales and office, 3.8% natural resources, construction, and maintenance, 2.9% production, transportation, and material moving

Income: Per capita: $69,756; Median household: $89,137; Average household: $142,660; Households with income of $100,000 or more: 44.1%; Poverty rate: 4.0%

Educational Attainment: High school diploma or higher: 97.5%; Bachelor's degree or higher: 62.6%; Graduate/professional degree or higher: 29.4%

School District(s)

Larkspur-Corte Madera (KG-08)
2012-13 Enrollment: 1,404 . . . . (415) 927-6960
Tamalpais Union High (09-12)
2012-13 Enrollment: 3,907 . . . . (415) 945-3600

Housing: Homeownership rate: 49.0%; Median home value: 1 million+; Median year structure built: 1967; Homeowner vacancy rate: 1.5%; Median gross rent: $1,824 per month; Rental vacancy rate: 7.1%

Health Insurance: 94.3% have insurance; 86.6% have private insurance; 26.7% have public insurance; 5.7% do not have insurance; 0.8% of children under 18 do not have insurance

Transportation: Commute: 76.2% car, 12.6% public transportation, 2.1% walk, 7.8% work from home; Median travel time to work: 27.7 minutes

Additional Information Contacts

City of Larkspur . . . . (415) 927-5110
http://www.ci.larkspur.ca.us

LUCAS VALLEY-MARINWOOD (CDP). Covers a land area of 5.727 square miles and a water area of 0 square miles. Located at 38.04° N. Lat; 122.58° W. Long. Elevation is 108 feet.

History: In April 1845 James Miller of Irish decent arrived in San Rafael after enduring the first overland migration over the Sierra without fatalities. Then, in 1846 he purchased 680 acres (2.8 sq. km.) of land from Timothy Murphy, grantee of San Rafael. The land encompassed present day Marinwood and a creek which was later named Miller Creek.

Population: 6,094; Growth (since 2000): -4.1%; Density: 1,064.2 persons per square mile; Race: 85.7% White, 1.1% Black/African American, 7.0% Asian, 0.3% American Indian/Alaska Native, 0.1% Native Hawaiian/Other Pacific Islander, 3.9% Two or more races, 7.3% Hispanic of any race; Average household size: 2.56; Median age: 47.3; Age under 18: 23.9%; Age 65 and over: 20.1%; Males per 100 females: 89.6; Marriage status: 16.8% never married, 62.8% now married, 1.0% separated, 5.5% widowed, 14.8% divorced; Foreign born: 16.8%; Speak English only: 84.7%; With disability: 8.8%; Veterans: 8.5%; Ancestry: 18.1% German, 15.1% Irish, 12.3% English, 7.7% Italian, 6.9% Swedish

Employment: 27.0% management, business, and financial, 9.3% computer, engineering, and science, 17.1% education, legal, community service, arts, and media, 10.0% healthcare practitioners, 10.7% service, 15.0% sales and office, 0.9% natural resources, construction, and maintenance, 10.0% production, transportation, and material moving

Income: Per capita: $58,100; Median household: $130,949; Average household: $153,537; Households with income of $100,000 or more: 66.8%; Poverty rate: 5.0%

Educational Attainment: High school diploma or higher: 98.3%; Bachelor's degree or higher: 61.3%; Graduate/professional degree or higher: 24.8%

Housing: Homeownership rate: 85.3%; Median home value: $777,000; Median year structure built: 1965; Homeowner vacancy rate: 0.7%; Median gross rent: $2,000+ per month; Rental vacancy rate: 4.9%

Health Insurance: 93.5% have insurance; 84.4% have private insurance; 23.5% have public insurance; 6.5% do not have insurance; 11.9% of children under 18 do not have insurance

Transportation: Commute: 74.4% car, 11.7% public transportation, 0.5% walk, 11.0% work from home; Median travel time to work: 32.8 minutes

MARIN CITY (CDP). Covers a land area of 0.537 square miles and a water area of 0 square miles. Located at 37.87° N. Lat; 122.51° W. Long. Elevation is 26 feet.

Population: 2,666; Growth (since 2000): n/a; Density: 4,967.0 persons per square mile; Race: 38.9% White, 38.1% Black/African American, 10.8% Asian, 0.6% American Indian/Alaska Native, 0.8% Native Hawaiian/Other Pacific Islander, 6.3% Two or more races, 13.7% Hispanic of any race;

Average household size: 2.23; Median age: 35.6; Age under 18: 23.7%; Age 65 and over: 9.3%; Males per 100 females: 83.1; Marriage status: 45.6% never married, 32.4% now married, 3.6% separated, 3.9% widowed, 18.1% divorced; Foreign born: 17.8%; Speak English only: 78.9%; With disability: 13.5%; Veterans: 3.0%; Ancestry: 11.3% Irish, 8.9% American, 5.9% German, 4.9% English, 4.4% Italian

Employment: 17.4% management, business, and financial, 3.4% computer, engineering, and science, 11.0% education, legal, community service, arts, and media, 9.2% healthcare practitioners, 18.3% service, 32.8% sales and office, 2.3% natural resources, construction, and maintenance, 5.5% production, transportation, and material moving

Income: Per capita: $28,008; Median household: $39,083; Average household: $61,151; Households with income of $100,000 or more: 21.7%; Poverty rate: 30.9%

Educational Attainment: High school diploma or higher: 91.5%; Bachelor's degree or higher: 36.6%; Graduate/professional degree or higher: 14.1%

School District(s)

Sausalito Marin City (KG-08)
2012-13 Enrollment: 411 . . . . (415) 332-3190

Housing: Homeownership rate: 30.7%; Median home value: $487,000; Median year structure built: 1982; Homeowner vacancy rate: 2.1%; Median gross rent: $1,475 per month; Rental vacancy rate: 8.6%

Health Insurance: 79.7% have insurance; 50.3% have private insurance; 37.9% have public insurance; 20.3% do not have insurance; 19.3% of children under 18 do not have insurance

Transportation: Commute: 54.2% car, 24.3% public transportation, 9.1% walk, 12.4% work from home; Median travel time to work: 22.7 minutes

MARSHALL (unincorporated postal area)

ZCTA: 94940

Covers a land area of 22.771 square miles and a water area of 3.751 square miles. Located at 38.18° N. Lat; 122.88° W. Long. Elevation is 13 feet.

Population: 268; Growth (since 2000): -32.0%; Density: 11.8 persons per square mile; Race: 88.8% White, 0.0% Black/African American, 0.4% Asian, 1.1% American Indian/Alaska Native, 0.0% Native Hawaiian/Other Pacific Islander, 1.1% Two or more races, 14.2% Hispanic of any race; Average household size: 2.03; Median age: 54.0; Age under 18: 14.6%; Age 65 and over: 18.7%; Males per 100 females: 106.2

Housing: Homeownership rate: 48.5%; Homeowner vacancy rate: 4.5%; Rental vacancy rate: 10.5%

MILL VALLEY (city). Covers a land area of 4.763 square miles and a water area of 0.084 square miles. Located at 37.91° N. Lat; 122.54° W. Long. Elevation is 82 feet.

History: Mill Valley was founded on land belonging to the Rancho Saucelito and named for the sawmill built here by Juan Read in 1834.

Population: 13,903; Growth (since 2000): 2.2%; Density: 2,919.0 persons per square mile; Race: 88.8% White, 0.8% Black/African American, 5.4% Asian, 0.2% American Indian/Alaska Native, 0.1% Native Hawaiian/Other Pacific Islander, 3.6% Two or more races, 4.5% Hispanic of any race; Average household size: 2.27; Median age: 46.6; Age under 18: 23.7%; Age 65 and over: 18.9%; Males per 100 females: 85.3; Marriage status: 22.5% never married, 60.2% now married, 1.1% separated, 5.2% widowed, 12.2% divorced; Foreign born: 14.9%; Speak English only: 84.1%; With disability: 8.6%; Veterans: 7.6%; Ancestry: 17.4% German, 14.0% English, 11.8% Irish, 8.9% Italian, 4.9% Russian

Employment: 27.5% management, business, and financial, 9.3% computer, engineering, and science, 18.1% education, legal, community service, arts, and media, 9.6% healthcare practitioners, 8.6% service, 22.7% sales and office, 2.6% natural resources, construction, and maintenance, 1.6% production, transportation, and material moving

Income: Per capita: $82,019; Median household: $121,921; Average household: $184,635; Households with income of $100,000 or more: 57.9%; Poverty rate: 2.6%

Educational Attainment: High school diploma or higher: 97.3%; Bachelor's degree or higher: 74.7%; Graduate/professional degree or higher: 38.1%

School District(s)

Mill Valley Elementary (KG-08)
2012-13 Enrollment: 3,159 . . . . (415) 389-7700
Tamalpais Union High (09-12)
2012-13 Enrollment: 3,907 . . . . (415) 945-3600

Housing: Homeownership rate: 65.3%; Median home value: 1 million+; Median year structure built: 1959; Homeowner vacancy rate: 1.2%; Median gross rent: $1,794 per month; Rental vacancy rate: 4.5%

Health Insurance: 97.5% have insurance; 87.8% have private insurance; 25.4% have public insurance; 2.5% do not have insurance; 0.7% of children under 18 do not have insurance

Safety: Violent crime rate: 7.7 per 10,000 population; Property crime rate: 160.8 per 10,000 population

Transportation: Commute: 70.1% car, 8.5% public transportation, 4.4% walk, 13.9% work from home; Median travel time to work: 29.0 minutes

Additional Information Contacts

City of Mill Valley . . . . (415) 388-4033
http://www.cityofmillvalley.org

MUIR BEACH (CDP). Covers a land area of 0.493 square miles and a water area of 0 square miles. Located at 37.86° N. Lat; 122.58° W. Long. Elevation is 312 feet.

Population: 310; Growth (since 2000): 5.1%; Density: 629.0 persons per square mile; Race: 91.3% White, 1.6% Black/African American, 3.9% Asian, 0.3% American Indian/Alaska Native, 0.0% Native Hawaiian/Other Pacific Islander, 2.6% Two or more races, 2.3% Hispanic of any race; Average household size: 2.11; Median age: 52.6; Age under 18: 12.3%; Age 65 and over: 21.9%; Males per 100 females: 102.6

Housing: Homeownership rate: 73.8%; Homeowner vacancy rate: 1.0%; Rental vacancy rate: 2.6%

NICASIO (CDP). Covers a land area of 1.305 square miles and a water area of 0 square miles. Located at 38.06° N. Lat; 122.70° W. Long. Elevation is 194 feet.

Population: 96; Growth (since 2000): n/a; Density: 73.6 persons per square mile; Race: 97.9% White, 2.1% Black/African American, 0.0% Asian, 0.0% American Indian/Alaska Native, 0.0% Native Hawaiian/Other Pacific Islander, 0.0% Two or more races, 7.3% Hispanic of any race; Average household size: 2.74; Median age: 42.5; Age under 18: 29.2%; Age 65 and over: 13.5%; Males per 100 females: 113.3

School District(s)

Nicasio (KG-08)
2012-13 Enrollment: 46 . . . . (415) 662-2184

Housing: Homeownership rate: 80.0%; Homeowner vacancy rate: 0.0%; Rental vacancy rate: 12.5%

NOVATO (city). Covers a land area of 27.440 square miles and a water area of 0.517 square miles. Located at 38.08° N. Lat; 122.55° W. Long. Elevation is 20 feet.

History: Named for the local valley where Mission San Rafael sheep grazed. Novato grew as a trading center for the surrounding fruit-raising and dairying region.

Population: 51,904; Growth (since 2000): 9.0%; Density: 1,891.6 persons per square mile; Race: 76.0% White, 2.7% Black/African American, 6.6% Asian, 0.6% American Indian/Alaska Native, 0.2% Native Hawaiian/Other Pacific Islander, 4.9% Two or more races, 21.3% Hispanic of any race; Average household size: 2.53; Median age: 42.6; Age under 18: 22.7%; Age 65 and over: 15.7%; Males per 100 females: 93.6; Marriage status: 24.6% never married, 56.7% now married, 1.4% separated, 5.7% widowed, 13.0% divorced; Foreign born: 19.9%; Speak English only: 75.6%; With disability: 8.9%; Veterans: 7.5%; Ancestry: 15.5% Irish, 12.9% German, 11.3% Italian, 10.8% English, 3.3% French

Employment: 22.3% management, business, and financial, 5.6% computer, engineering, and science, 12.5% education, legal, community service, arts, and media, 5.0% healthcare practitioners, 18.2% service, 24.8% sales and office, 6.4% natural resources, construction, and maintenance, 5.3% production, transportation, and material moving

Income: Per capita: $44,000; Median household: $77,702; Average household: $109,213; Households with income of $100,000 or more: 40.1%; Poverty rate: 7.2%

Educational Attainment: High school diploma or higher: 92.3%; Bachelor's degree or higher: 43.9%; Graduate/professional degree or higher: 16.9%

School District(s)

Novato Unified (KG-12)
2012-13 Enrollment: 8,049 . . . . (415) 897-4201

Housing: Homeownership rate: 67.0%; Median home value: $560,300; Median year structure built: 1974; Homeowner vacancy rate: 1.0%; Median gross rent: $1,569 per month; Rental vacancy rate: 4.7%

Health Insurance: 90.3% have insurance; 77.1% have private insurance; 26.1% have public insurance; 9.7% do not have insurance; 6.1% of children under 18 do not have insurance

Hospitals: Novato Community Hospital (47 beds)

Safety: Violent crime rate: 19.9 per 10,000 population; Property crime rate: 155.6 per 10,000 population

Newspapers: Commuter Times (weekly circulation 12000); Marin Scope Newspapers (weekly circulation 33000); Novato Advance (weekly circulation 16500)

Transportation: Commute: 83.9% car, 5.6% public transportation, 1.7% walk, 7.6% work from home; Median travel time to work: 28.7 minutes

Airports: Gnoss Field (general aviation)

Additional Information Contacts

City of Novato . . . . (415) 899-8900
http://www.ci.novato.ca.us

OLEMA (unincorporated postal area)

ZCTA: 94950

Covers a land area of 8.602 square miles and a water area of 0 square miles. Located at 38.02° N. Lat; 122.76° W. Long. Elevation is 75 feet.

Population: 89; Growth (since 2000): -63.7%; Density: 10.3 persons per square mile; Race: 80.9% White, 0.0% Black/African American, 1.1% Asian, 0.0% American Indian/Alaska Native, 0.0% Native Hawaiian/Other Pacific Islander, 2.2% Two or more races, 15.7% Hispanic of any race; Average household size: 2.00; Median age: 51.5; Age under 18: 15.7%; Age 65 and over: 19.1%; Males per 100 females: 107.0

Housing: Homeownership rate: 44.2%; Homeowner vacancy rate: 0.0%; Rental vacancy rate: 0.0%

POINT REYES STATION (CDP). Covers a land area of 3.616 square miles and a water area of 0 square miles. Located at 38.08° N. Lat; 122.81° W. Long. Elevation is 36 feet.

History: The town of Point Reyes Station grew around dairy farms which produced butter, shipped to San Francisco by schooner from Point Reyes. Dairy farming began here in the 1850's.

Population: 848; Growth (since 2000): 3.7%; Density: 234.5 persons per square mile; Race: 85.5% White, 0.8% Black/African American, 1.2% Asian, 0.4% American Indian/Alaska Native, 0.0% Native Hawaiian/Other Pacific Islander, 3.5% Two or more races, 18.3% Hispanic of any race; Average household size: 2.06; Median age: 51.1; Age under 18: 18.3%; Age 65 and over: 22.9%; Males per 100 females: 81.2

School District(s)

Shoreline Unified (KG-12)
2012-13 Enrollment: 554. . . . . (707) 878-2266

Housing: Homeownership rate: 50.2%; Homeowner vacancy rate: 0.0%; Rental vacancy rate: 6.8%

Newspapers: Point Reyes Light (weekly circulation 3300); West Marin Citizen (weekly circulation 1900)

ROSS (town). Covers a land area of 1.556 square miles and a water area of 0 square miles. Located at 37.96° N. Lat; 122.56° W. Long. Elevation is 30 feet.

History: Muir Woods National Monument to South. Incorporated 1908.

Population: 2,415; Growth (since 2000): 3.7%; Density: 1,551.8 persons per square mile; Race: 93.8% White, 0.2% Black/African American, 1.9% Asian, 0.1% American Indian/Alaska Native, 0.1% Native Hawaiian/Other Pacific Islander, 3.1% Two or more races, 3.9% Hispanic of any race; Average household size: 2.96; Median age: 45.1; Age under 18: 30.3%; Age 65 and over: 17.1%; Males per 100 females: 92.0

School District(s)

Ross Elementary (KG-08)
2012-13 Enrollment: 350. . . . . (415) 457-2705

Housing: Homeownership rate: 85.9%; Homeowner vacancy rate: 1.0%; Rental vacancy rate: 5.7%

Safety: Violent crime rate: 4.1 per 10,000 population; Property crime rate: 196.2 per 10,000 population

Additional Information Contacts

Town of Ross . . . . (415) 453-1453
http://www.townofross.org

SAN ANSELMO (town). Covers a land area of 2.677 square miles and a water area of 0 square miles. Located at 37.98° N. Lat; 122.57° W. Long. Elevation is 46 feet.

History: Named for a valley in the town, which was probably named for an Indian translation. San Francisco Theological Seminary (1871) is here. Muir Woods National monument to South. Incorporated 1907.

Population: 12,336; Growth (since 2000): -0.3%; Density: 4,607.9 persons per square mile; Race: 90.3% White, 0.9% Black/African American, 3.5% Asian, 0.3% American Indian/Alaska Native, 0.2% Native Hawaiian/Other Pacific Islander, 3.5% Two or more races, 5.8% Hispanic of any race; Average household size: 2.34; Median age: 44.9; Age under 18: 23.3%; Age 65 and over: 13.5%; Males per 100 females: 87.4; Marriage status: 26.0% never married, 55.9% now married, 3.3% separated, 4.4% widowed, 13.8% divorced; Foreign born: 9.2%; Speak English only: 88.9%; With disability: 8.0%; Veterans: 8.2%; Ancestry: 18.9% Irish, 17.7% English, 16.0% German, 8.4% Italian, 5.8% Russian

Employment: 26.8% management, business, and financial, 6.3% computer, engineering, and science, 20.0% education, legal, community service, arts, and media, 7.9% healthcare practitioners, 10.4% service, 17.8% sales and office, 5.9% natural resources, construction, and maintenance, 4.8% production, transportation, and material moving

Income: Per capita: $55,595; Median household: $100,379; Average household: $130,238; Households with income of $100,000 or more: 50.1%; Poverty rate: 7.0%

Educational Attainment: High school diploma or higher: 96.2%; Bachelor's degree or higher: 62.8%; Graduate/professional degree or higher: 24.0%

School District(s)

Ross Valley Elementary (KG-08)
2012-13 Enrollment: 2,230 . . . . (415) 454-2162
Tamalpais Union High (09-12)
2012-13 Enrollment: 3,907 . . . . (415) 945-3600

Four-year College(s)

San Francisco Theological Seminary (Private, Not-for-profit, Presbyterian Church (USA))
Fall 2013 Enrollment: 167 . . . . (415) 451-2800

Housing: Homeownership rate: 66.5%; Median home value: $827,200; Median year structure built: 1951; Homeowner vacancy rate: 1.2%; Median gross rent: $1,560 per month; Rental vacancy rate: 4.5%

Health Insurance: 94.0% have insurance; 86.7% have private insurance; 20.0% have public insurance; 6.0% do not have insurance; 1.1% of children under 18 do not have insurance

Transportation: Commute: 72.4% car, 11.3% public transportation, 3.6% walk, 9.5% work from home; Median travel time to work: 32.4 minutes

Additional Information Contacts

Town of San Anselmo . . . . (415) 258-4600
http://www.townofsananselmo.org

SAN GERONIMO (CDP). Covers a land area of 1.508 square miles and a water area of 0 square miles. Located at 38.01° N. Lat; 122.66° W. Long. Elevation is 302 feet.

Population: 446; Growth (since 2000): 2.3%; Density: 295.8 persons per square mile; Race: 94.4% White, 0.7% Black/African American, 0.7% Asian, 0.4% American Indian/Alaska Native, 0.0% Native Hawaiian/Other Pacific Islander, 3.1% Two or more races, 4.7% Hispanic of any race; Average household size: 2.24; Median age: 50.0; Age under 18: 16.1%; Age 65 and over: 17.0%; Males per 100 females: 97.3

School District(s)

Lagunitas Elementary (KG-08)
2012-13 Enrollment: 292. . . . . (415) 488-4118

Housing: Homeownership rate: 73.4%; Homeowner vacancy rate: 0.0%; Rental vacancy rate: 0.0%

SAN QUENTIN (unincorporated postal area)

ZCTA: 94964

Covers a land area of 0.390 square miles and a water area of 0 square miles. Located at 37.94° N. Lat; 122.49° W. Long. Elevation is 36 feet.

Population: 5,094; Growth (since 2000): -20.9%; Density: 13,066.7 persons per square mile; Race: 40.4% White, 39.3% Black/African American, 1.4% Asian, 2.4% American Indian/Alaska Native, 0.3% Native Hawaiian/Other Pacific Islander, 1.9% Two or more races, 19.5% Hispanic of any race; Average household size: 2.42; Median age: 40.8; Age under 18: 0.8%; Age 65 and over: 1.7%; Males per 100 females: ***.*; Marriage status: 49.7% never married, 30.0% now married, 5.7% separated, 1.8% widowed, 18.6% divorced; Foreign born: 11.5%; Speak English only:

69.6%; With disability: 0.0%; Veterans: 8.5%; Ancestry: 11.9% German, 11.1% Irish, 4.9% English, 4.2% European, 2.8% French
Employment: 46.3% management, business, and financial, 0.0% computer, engineering, and science, 25.8% education, legal, community service, arts, and media, 0.0% healthcare practitioners, 27.9% service, 0.0% sales and office, 0.0% natural resources, construction, and maintenance, 0.0% production, transportation, and material moving
Income: Per capita: $4,654; Median household: n/a; Average household: n/a; Households with income of $100,000 or more: 47.0%; Poverty rate: n/a
Educational Attainment: High school diploma or higher: 68.4%; Bachelor's degree or higher: 4.5%; Graduate/professional degree or higher: 2.7%
Housing: Homeownership rate: 6.1%; Median home value: n/a; Median year structure built: n/a; Homeowner vacancy rate: 0.0%; Median gross rent: n/a per month; Rental vacancy rate: 5.1%
Health Insurance: 100.0% have insurance; 100.0% have private insurance; 20.3% have public insurance; 0.0% do not have insurance; 0.0% of children under 18 do not have insurance
Transportation: Commute: 53.7% car, 0.0% public transportation, 46.3% walk, 0.0% work from home; Median travel time to work: n/a minutes

---

SAN RAFAEL (city). County seat. Covers a land area of 16.470 square miles and a water area of 5.952 square miles. Located at 37.98° N. Lat; 122.51° W. Long. Elevation is 43 feet.
History: Named for the Mission San Rafael, which was named for the Holy Archangel St. Raphael. San Rafael grew up around Mission San Rafael Arcangel, founded in 1817 by Father Ventura Fortuni as a hospital clinic for people from other nearby missions.
Population: 57,713; Growth (since 2000): 2.9%; Density: 3,504.1 persons per square mile; Race: 70.6% White, 2.0% Black/African American, 6.1% Asian, 1.2% American Indian/Alaska Native, 0.2% Native Hawaiian/Other Pacific Islander, 5.1% Two or more races, 30.0% Hispanic of any race; Average household size: 2.44; Median age: 40.2; Age under 18: 19.3%; Age 65 and over: 15.8%; Males per 100 females: 99.7; Marriage status: 33.2% never married, 49.4% now married, 2.3% separated, 5.5% widowed, 11.8% divorced; Foreign born: 28.7%; Speak English only: 63.8%; With disability: 9.9%; Veterans: 6.3%; Ancestry: 11.3% Irish, 10.0% German, 9.2% English, 8.5% Italian, 3.4% European
Employment: 17.9% management, business, and financial, 5.3% computer, engineering, and science, 13.1% education, legal, community service, arts, and media, 4.4% healthcare practitioners, 24.2% service, 22.5% sales and office, 7.2% natural resources, construction, and maintenance, 5.4% production, transportation, and material moving
Income: Per capita: $45,069; Median household: $73,953; Average household: $111,422; Households with income of $100,000 or more: 37.2%; Poverty rate: 12.2%
Educational Attainment: High school diploma or higher: 85.4%; Bachelor's degree or higher: 45.1%; Graduate/professional degree or higher: 19.6%

School District(s)

Dixie Elementary (KG-08)
2012-13 Enrollment: 1,863 . . . . (415) 492-3700
Marin County Office of Education (KG-12)
2012-13 Enrollment: 374. . . . . (415) 472-4110
Marin County Rop
2012-13 Enrollment: n/a . . . . (415) 499-5892
San Rafael City Elementary (PK-08)
2012-13 Enrollment: 4,295 . . . . (415) 492-3233
San Rafael City High (09-12)
2012-13 Enrollment: 2,066 . . . . (415) 492-3233

Four-year College(s)

Dominican University of California (Private, Not-for-profit)
Fall 2013 Enrollment: 2,147 . . . . (415) 457-4440
2013-14 Tuition: In-state $40,600; Out-of-state $40,600

Housing: Homeownership rate: 52.3%; Median home value: $695,800; Median year structure built: 1965; Homeowner vacancy rate: 1.6%; Median gross rent: $1,428 per month; Rental vacancy rate: 5.1%
Health Insurance: 86.6% have insurance; 70.1% have private insurance; 31.4% have public insurance; 13.4% do not have insurance; 3.4% of children under 18 do not have insurance
Hospitals: Kaiser Foundation Hospital (120 beds)
Safety: Violent crime rate: 35.1 per 10,000 population; Property crime rate: 308.6 per 10,000 population
Newspapers: Marin Independent Journal (daily circulation 33000); Pacific Sun (weekly circulation 36000)
Transportation: Commute: 72.4% car, 11.4% public transportation, 4.8% walk, 8.1% work from home; Median travel time to work: 25.4 minutes

Additional Information Contacts

City of San Rafael . . . . (415) 485-3070
http://www.cityofsanrafael.org

SANTA VENETIA (CDP). Covers a land area of 3.661 square miles and a water area of 0.019 square miles. Located at 38.01° N. Lat; 122.50° W. Long. Elevation is 59 feet.
Population: 4,292; Growth (since 2000): -0.1%; Density: 1,172.4 persons per square mile; Race: 77.7% White, 2.1% Black/African American, 7.1% Asian, 0.6% American Indian/Alaska Native, 0.4% Native Hawaiian/Other Pacific Islander, 4.0% Two or more races, 19.0% Hispanic of any race; Average household size: 2.47; Median age: 47.7; Age under 18: 18.7%; Age 65 and over: 20.4%; Males per 100 females: 90.2; Marriage status: 34.4% never married, 44.2% now married, 0.8% separated, 8.7% widowed, 12.7% divorced; Foreign born: 31.8%; Speak English only: 59.0%; With disability: 14.0%; Veterans: 7.1%; Ancestry: 12.4% English, 8.0% Italian, 7.3% German, 6.4% Irish, 6.2% Russian
Employment: 13.4% management, business, and financial, 1.6% computer, engineering, and science, 11.7% education, legal, community service, arts, and media, 5.6% healthcare practitioners, 29.2% service, 23.0% sales and office, 8.9% natural resources, construction, and maintenance, 6.6% production, transportation, and material moving
Income: Per capita: $32,602; Median household: $80,978; Average household: $86,555; Households with income of $100,000 or more: 28.9%; Poverty rate: 6.3%
Educational Attainment: High school diploma or higher: 85.5%; Bachelor's degree or higher: 36.2%; Graduate/professional degree or higher: 12.7%
Housing: Homeownership rate: 71.8%; Median home value: $513,900; Median year structure built: 1961; Homeowner vacancy rate: 1.1%; Median gross rent: $1,786 per month; Rental vacancy rate: 2.1%
Health Insurance: 82.1% have insurance; 69.9% have private insurance; 24.3% have public insurance; 17.9% do not have insurance; 0.0% of children under 18 do not have insurance
Transportation: Commute: 77.9% car, 12.3% public transportation, 0.3% walk, 6.0% work from home; Median travel time to work: 24.6 minutes

---

SAUSALITO (city). Covers a land area of 1.771 square miles and a water area of 0.486 square miles. Located at 37.86° N. Lat; 122.49° W. Long. Elevation is 10 feet.
History: The name of Sausalito (from the Spanish for willow) was chosen because of the willow trees growing around a spring here in early times. Fresh water from this spring was for a time transported in barrels on rafts to San Francisco. First settled by English Captain William Richardson who worked as a pilot for trading and whaling ships anchoring in San Francisco Bay, Sausalito developed as a fishing village, residential suburb, and literary art colony.
Population: 7,061; Growth (since 2000): -3.7%; Density: 3,987.4 persons per square mile; Race: 90.6% White, 0.9% Black/African American, 4.8% Asian, 0.2% American Indian/Alaska Native, 0.1% Native Hawaiian/Other Pacific Islander, 2.5% Two or more races, 4.1% Hispanic of any race; Average household size: 1.71; Median age: 51.1; Age under 18: 8.7%; Age 65 and over: 21.2%; Males per 100 females: 90.2; Marriage status: 24.9% never married, 50.7% now married, 1.1% separated, 3.6% widowed, 20.8% divorced; Foreign born: 12.9%; Speak English only: 85.2%; With disability: 7.6%; Veterans: 12.5%; Ancestry: 25.5% German, 16.2% English, 15.1% Italian, 14.9% Irish, 6.1% French
Employment: 40.3% management, business, and financial, 9.1% computer, engineering, and science, 14.7% education, legal, community service, arts, and media, 6.4% healthcare practitioners, 4.0% service, 20.4% sales and office, 2.7% natural resources, construction, and maintenance, 2.4% production, transportation, and material moving
Income: Per capita: $86,829; Median household: $114,861; Average household: $154,729; Households with income of $100,000 or more: 56.8%; Poverty rate: 5.9%
Educational Attainment: High school diploma or higher: 97.8%; Bachelor's degree or higher: 71.5%; Graduate/professional degree or higher: 25.5%

School District(s)

Sausalito Marin City (KG-08)
2012-13 Enrollment: 411. . . . . (415) 332-3190

Housing: Homeownership rate: 50.8%; Median home value: 1 million+; Median year structure built: 1963; Homeowner vacancy rate: 2.1%; Median gross rent: $2,000+ per month; Rental vacancy rate: 5.8%
Health Insurance: 94.1% have insurance; 87.8% have private insurance; 25.3% have public insurance; 5.9% do not have insurance; 0.0% of children under 18 do not have insurance
Safety: Violent crime rate: 14.2 per 10,000 population; Property crime rate: 437.3 per 10,000 population
Transportation: Commute: 63.9% car, 15.7% public transportation, 2.4% walk, 15.3% work from home; Median travel time to work: 31.4 minutes
Additional Information Contacts
City of Sausalito . . . . (415) 289-4100
http://www.ci.sausalito.ca.us

SLEEPY HOLLOW (CDP). Covers a land area of 2.987 square miles and a water area of 0 square miles. Located at 38.01° N. Lat; 122.59° W. Long. Elevation is 190 feet.
Population: 2,384; Growth (since 2000): n/a; Density: 798.1 persons per square mile; Race: 90.6% White, 0.6% Black/African American, 4.7% Asian, 0.4% American Indian/Alaska Native, 0.3% Native Hawaiian/Other Pacific Islander, 3.0% Two or more races, 2.9% Hispanic of any race; Average household size: 2.78; Median age: 48.1; Age under 18: 26.8%; Age 65 and over: 17.0%; Males per 100 females: 94.5
Housing: Homeownership rate: 90.8%; Homeowner vacancy rate: 0.3%; Rental vacancy rate: 8.3%

STINSON BEACH (CDP). Covers a land area of 1.441 square miles and a water area of 0.018 square miles. Located at 37.91° N. Lat; 122.64° W. Long. Elevation is 10 feet.
History: The settlement at Stinson Beach began as a campground on the beach, and became a family resort center for vacationers.
Population: 632; Growth (since 2000): -15.8%; Density: 438.7 persons per square mile; Race: 92.1% White, 0.5% Black/African American, 2.2% Asian, 1.3% American Indian/Alaska Native, 0.2% Native Hawaiian/Other Pacific Islander, 2.4% Two or more races, 5.2% Hispanic of any race; Average household size: 1.86; Median age: 54.4; Age under 18: 12.0%; Age 65 and over: 21.4%; Males per 100 females: 94.5
Housing: Homeownership rate: 61.7%; Homeowner vacancy rate: 2.3%; Rental vacancy rate: 9.7%

STRAWBERRY (CDP). Covers a land area of 1.317 square miles and a water area of 0.015 square miles. Located at 37.89° N. Lat; 122.51° W. Long. Elevation is 223 feet.
History: The site of the Golden Gate Baptist Theological Seminary on Strawberry Point was considered for the headquarters for the United Nations. This was because in the forties when the UN was established in San Francisco, Strawberry was undeveloped. It was seen as a tranquil and peaceful setting. New York City was eventually chosen.
Population: 5,393; Growth (since 2000): 1.7%; Density: 4,095.0 persons per square mile; Race: 80.2% White, 2.1% Black/African American, 10.9% Asian, 0.3% American Indian/Alaska Native, 0.3% Native Hawaiian/Other Pacific Islander, 4.3% Two or more races, 6.5% Hispanic of any race; Average household size: 2.05; Median age: 44.0; Age under 18: 19.9%; Age 65 and over: 17.5%; Males per 100 females: 90.8; Marriage status: 30.5% never married, 48.3% now married, 0.6% separated, 3.3% widowed, 17.9% divorced; Foreign born: 18.3%; Speak English only: 81.4%; With disability: 7.2%; Veterans: 8.3%; Ancestry: 14.6% Irish, 12.3% English, 8.9% German, 5.6% Scottish, 4.9% European
Employment: 28.9% management, business, and financial, 5.0% computer, engineering, and science, 19.4% education, legal, community service, arts, and media, 4.5% healthcare practitioners, 11.5% service, 25.1% sales and office, 4.8% natural resources, construction, and maintenance, 0.8% production, transportation, and material moving
Income: Per capita: $63,096; Median household: $83,750; Average household: $144,310; Households with income of $100,000 or more: 42.9%; Poverty rate: 10.6%
Educational Attainment: High school diploma or higher: 99.1%; Bachelor's degree or higher: 66.5%; Graduate/professional degree or higher: 32.8%
Housing: Homeownership rate: 39.2%; Median home value: 1 million+; Median year structure built: 1970; Homeowner vacancy rate: 1.4%; Median gross rent: $1,658 per month; Rental vacancy rate: 2.4%
Health Insurance: 92.2% have insurance; 84.2% have private insurance; 21.1% have public insurance; 7.8% do not have insurance; 6.2% of children under 18 do not have insurance
Transportation: Commute: 77.8% car, 3.2% public transportation, 6.8% walk, 11.8% work from home; Median travel time to work: 25.9 minutes

TAMALPAIS-HOMESTEAD VALLEY (CDP). Covers a land area of 4.637 square miles and a water area of 0.015 square miles. Located at 37.88° N. Lat; 122.54° W. Long.
History: Coastal Miwok Indians lived in the area for thousands of years before Europeans arrived. In 1770, two explorers named the mountain La Sierra de Nuestro Padre de San Francisco, which was later changed to the Miwok word Tamalpais.
Population: 10,735; Growth (since 2000): 0.4%; Density: 2,315.0 persons per square mile; Race: 88.0% White, 0.8% Black/African American, 5.5% Asian, 0.2% American Indian/Alaska Native, 0.3% Native Hawaiian/Other Pacific Islander, 4.0% Two or more races, 4.6% Hispanic of any race; Average household size: 2.41; Median age: 45.5; Age under 18: 23.9%; Age 65 and over: 14.1%; Males per 100 females: 94.4; Marriage status: 24.5% never married, 59.7% now married, 1.2% separated, 3.5% widowed, 12.3% divorced; Foreign born: 11.2%; Speak English only: 86.2%; With disability: 6.9%; Veterans: 6.1%; Ancestry: 16.1% Irish, 13.7% English, 13.7% German, 7.9% Italian, 7.9% European
Employment: 31.3% management, business, and financial, 4.7% computer, engineering, and science, 22.1% education, legal, community service, arts, and media, 4.1% healthcare practitioners, 9.0% service, 23.6% sales and office, 2.7% natural resources, construction, and maintenance, 2.6% production, transportation, and material moving
Income: Per capita: $64,289; Median household: $115,840; Average household: $159,264; Households with income of $100,000 or more: 59.0%; Poverty rate: 5.2%
Educational Attainment: High school diploma or higher: 98.1%; Bachelor's degree or higher: 72.8%; Graduate/professional degree or higher: 33.0%
Housing: Homeownership rate: 76.0%; Median home value: $974,900; Median year structure built: 1963; Homeowner vacancy rate: 1.3%; Median gross rent: $2,000+ per month; Rental vacancy rate: 4.6%
Health Insurance: 95.9% have insurance; 90.4% have private insurance; 17.0% have public insurance; 4.1% do not have insurance; 1.7% of children under 18 do not have insurance
Transportation: Commute: 75.3% car, 7.1% public transportation, 1.9% walk, 13.2% work from home; Median travel time to work: 29.2 minutes

TIBURON (town). Covers a land area of 4.446 square miles and a water area of 8.736 square miles. Located at 37.89° N. Lat; 122.46° W. Long. Elevation is 7 feet.
History: The city's name derives from the Spanish word tibur_n, which means "shark". The name was first given to the peninsula on which the city is situated, and probably inspired by the prevalence of locally native leopard sharks in the surrounding waters.
Population: 8,962; Growth (since 2000): 3.4%; Density: 2,015.7 persons per square mile; Race: 88.1% White, 0.9% Black/African American, 5.6% Asian, 0.2% American Indian/Alaska Native, 0.1% Native Hawaiian/Other Pacific Islander, 4.1% Two or more races, 4.6% Hispanic of any race; Average household size: 2.39; Median age: 48.0; Age under 18: 24.0%; Age 65 and over: 21.2%; Males per 100 females: 87.9; Marriage status: 20.1% never married, 61.5% now married, 2.7% separated, 7.2% widowed, 11.2% divorced; Foreign born: 18.0%; Speak English only: 82.2%; With disability: 8.6%; Veterans: 9.5%; Ancestry: 20.4% German, 17.2% English, 17.2% Irish, 9.9% Italian, 4.1% Polish
Employment: 28.8% management, business, and financial, 4.0% computer, engineering, and science, 18.5% education, legal, community service, arts, and media, 9.5% healthcare practitioners, 8.3% service, 22.9% sales and office, 3.9% natural resources, construction, and maintenance, 4.1% production, transportation, and material moving
Income: Per capita: $98,011; Median household: $131,791; Average household: $231,429; Households with income of $100,000 or more: 62.3%; Poverty rate: 4.9%
Educational Attainment: High school diploma or higher: 96.7%; Bachelor's degree or higher: 76.9%; Graduate/professional degree or higher: 36.7%

School District(s)

Reed Union Elementary (KG-08)
2012-13 Enrollment: 1,508 . . . . (415) 381-1112
Housing: Homeownership rate: 67.8%; Median home value: 1 million+; Median year structure built: 1968; Homeowner vacancy rate: 1.5%; Median gross rent: $2,000+ per month; Rental vacancy rate: 5.0%

Health Insurance: 96.1% have insurance; 87.5% have private insurance; 24.9% have public insurance; 3.9% do not have insurance; 0.0% of children under 18 do not have insurance
Safety: Violent crime rate: 2.2 per 10,000 population; Property crime rate: 95.3 per 10,000 population
Newspapers: The Ark (weekly circulation 3200)
Transportation: Commute: 66.6% car, 11.0% public transportation, 1.9% walk, 16.4% work from home; Median travel time to work: 31.6 minutes
Additional Information Contacts
Town of Tiburon . . . . (415) 435-7373
http://www.townoftiburon.org

TOMALES (CDP). Covers a land area of 0.332 square miles and a water area of 0 square miles. Located at 38.25° N. Lat; 122.91° W. Long. Elevation is 89 feet.
Population: 204; Growth (since 2000): -2.9%; Density: 614.9 persons per square mile; Race: 94.6% White, 0.0% Black/African American, 2.0% Asian, 1.5% American Indian/Alaska Native, 0.0% Native Hawaiian/Other Pacific Islander, 2.0% Two or more races, 4.4% Hispanic of any race; Average household size: 2.06; Median age: 50.5; Age under 18: 10.8%; Age 65 and over: 16.7%; Males per 100 females: 85.5

School District(s)

Shoreline Unified (KG-12)
2012-13 Enrollment: 554. . . . . (707) 878-2266
Housing: Homeownership rate: 59.6%; Homeowner vacancy rate: 1.6%; Rental vacancy rate: 7.0%

WOODACRE (CDP). Covers a land area of 1.797 square miles and a water area of 0 square miles. Located at 38.01° N. Lat; 122.64° W. Long. Elevation is 361 feet.
Population: 1,348; Growth (since 2000): -3.2%; Density: 750.3 persons per square mile; Race: 91.3% White, 0.2% Black/African American, 2.0% Asian, 0.3% American Indian/Alaska Native, 0.3% Native Hawaiian/Other Pacific Islander, 5.1% Two or more races, 5.7% Hispanic of any race; Average household size: 2.27; Median age: 50.5; Age under 18: 17.7%; Age 65 and over: 16.3%; Males per 100 females: 92.0
Housing: Homeownership rate: 74.7%; Homeowner vacancy rate: 0.7%; Rental vacancy rate: 2.6%

Mariposa County

Located in central California, on the western slope of the Sierra Nevada; drained by the Merced, Tuolumne, and Chowchilla Rivers; includes parts of Sierra and Stanislaus National Forests, and the Merced and Mariposa Groves of sequoias. Covers a land area of 1,448.816 square miles, a water area of 14.004 square miles, and is located in the Pacific Time Zone at 37.57° N. Lat., 119.91° W. Long. The county was founded in 1850. County seat is Mariposa.

Weather Station: South Entr Yosemite Np — Elevation: 5,119 feet

	Jan	Feb	Mar	Apr	May	Jun	Jul	Aug	Sep	Oct	Nov	Dec
High	45	46	49	55	64	72	79	79	73	63	52	45
Low	26	27	28	32	38	44	50	49	45	37	30	26
Precip	8.7	8.1	6.6	3.2	1.9	0.6	0.1	0.1	0.7	2.5	4.2	5.9
Snow	14.6	19.7	14.5	5.3	0.5	0.1	0.0	0.0	tr	0.4	3.7	14.6

High and Low temperatures in degrees Fahrenheit; Precipitation and Snow in inches

Weather Station: Yosemite Park Hdqtrs — Elevation: 3,965 feet

	Jan	Feb	Mar	Apr	May	Jun	Jul	Aug	Sep	Oct	Nov	Dec
High	48	52	57	64	71	81	89	89	82	72	56	47
Low	29	30	33	38	44	51	56	56	50	42	33	28
Precip	6.7	6.7	5.6	2.7	1.7	0.6	0.5	0.1	0.7	2.0	4.4	5.4
Snow	13.5	4.9	5.5	0.7	tr	0.0	0.0	0.0	0.0	tr	3.0	4.6

High and Low temperatures in degrees Fahrenheit; Precipitation and Snow in inches

Population: 18,251; Growth (since 2000): 6.5%; Density: 12.6 persons per square mile; Race: 88.2% White, 0.8% Black/African American, 1.1% Asian, 2.9% American Indian/Alaska Native, 0.1% Native Hawaiian/Other Pacific Islander, 4.1% two or more races, 9.2% Hispanic of any race; Average household size: 2.28; Median age: 49.2; Age under 18: 17.8%; Age 65 and over: 20.9%; Males per 100 females: 103.2; Marriage status: 24.8% never married, 54.8% now married, 1.2% separated, 8.6% widowed, 11.8% divorced; Foreign born: 4.7%; Speak English only: 91.4%; With disability: 18.5%; Veterans: 14.4%; Ancestry: 14.8% German, 14.5% English, 14.2% Irish, 4.1% American, 3.6% French
Religion: Six largest groups: 25.6% Catholicism, 8.2% Non-denominational Protestant, 2.2% Methodist/Pietist, 2.1% Latter-day Saints, 1.1% Holiness, 0.9% Lutheran
Economy: Unemployment rate: 6.3%; Leading industries: 17.6% retail trade; 15.9% accommodation and food services; 12.2% construction; Farms: 364 totaling 283,611 acres; Company size: 0 employ 1,000 or more persons, 0 employ 500 to 999 persons, 7 employ 100 to 499 persons, 346 employ less than 100 persons; Business ownership: n/a women-owned, n/a Black-owned, n/a Hispanic-owned, n/a Asian-owned
Employment: 13.0% management, business, and financial, 3.4% computer, engineering, and science, 8.6% education, legal, community service, arts, and media, 4.2% healthcare practitioners, 30.3% service, 18.6% sales and office, 11.9% natural resources, construction, and maintenance, 9.8% production, transportation, and material moving
Income: Per capita: $26,988; Median household: $49,820; Average household: $62,748; Households with income of $100,000 or more: 20.0%; Poverty rate: 16.1%
Educational Attainment: High school diploma or higher: 87.7%; Bachelor's degree or higher: 21.3%; Graduate/professional degree or higher: 6.7%
Housing: Homeownership rate: 68.0%; Median home value: $235,000; Median year structure built: 1980; Homeowner vacancy rate: 2.7%; Median gross rent: $866 per month; Rental vacancy rate: 7.4%
Vital Statistics: Birth rate: 70.4 per 10,000 population; Death rate: 88.4 per 10,000 population; Age-adjusted cancer mortality rate: 154.1 deaths per 100,000 population
Health Insurance: 87.6% have insurance; 64.7% have private insurance; 41.1% have public insurance; 12.4% do not have insurance; 3.6% of children under 18 do not have insurance
Health Care: Physicians: 3.9 per 10,000 population; Hospital beds: 18.7 per 10,000 population; Hospital admissions: 149.0 per 10,000 population
Air Quality Index: 72.6% good, 26.3% moderate, 1.1% unhealthy for sensitive individuals, 0.0% unhealthy (percent of days)
Transportation: Commute: 73.9% car, 3.8% public transportation, 6.8% walk, 12.5% work from home; Median travel time to work: 32.0 minutes
Presidential Election: 39.0% Obama, 57.3% Romney (2012)
National and State Parks: Yosemite National Park
Additional Information Contacts
Mariposa Government. . . . . (209) 966-3222
http://www.mariposacounty.org

Mariposa County Communities

BEAR VALLEY (CDP). Covers a land area of 7.237 square miles and a water area of 0.008 square miles. Located at 37.56° N. Lat; 120.13° W. Long. Elevation is 2,054 feet.
Population: 125; Growth (since 2000): n/a; Density: 17.3 persons per square mile; Race: 93.6% White, 0.0% Black/African American, 1.6% Asian, 0.8% American Indian/Alaska Native, 0.0% Native Hawaiian/Other Pacific Islander, 3.2% Two or more races, 6.4% Hispanic of any race; Average household size: 2.16; Median age: 47.6; Age under 18: 20.0%; Age 65 and over: 24.8%; Males per 100 females: 92.3
Housing: Homeownership rate: 75.8%; Homeowner vacancy rate: 0.0%; Rental vacancy rate: 6.7%

BOOTJACK (CDP). Covers a land area of 7.001 square miles and a water area of 0.063 square miles. Located at 37.47° N. Lat; 119.89° W. Long. Elevation is 2,238 feet.
Population: 960; Growth (since 2000): -39.5%; Density: 137.1 persons per square mile; Race: 84.5% White, 0.2% Black/African American, 1.1% Asian, 3.5% American Indian/Alaska Native, 0.0% Native Hawaiian/Other Pacific Islander, 7.4% Two or more races, 7.9% Hispanic of any race; Average household size: 2.44; Median age: 49.6; Age under 18: 21.7%; Age 65 and over: 20.7%; Males per 100 females: 95.1
Housing: Homeownership rate: 72.5%; Homeowner vacancy rate: 0.3%; Rental vacancy rate: 7.7%

BUCK MEADOWS (CDP). Covers a land area of 1.743 square miles and a water area of 0 square miles. Located at 37.81° N. Lat; 120.07° W. Long. Elevation is 3,015 feet.
Population: 31; Growth (since 2000): n/a; Density: 17.8 persons per square mile; Race: 74.2% White, 0.0% Black/African American, 0.0% Asian, 0.0% American Indian/Alaska Native, 0.0% Native Hawaiian/Other Pacific Islander, 9.7% Two or more races, 22.6% Hispanic of any race;

Average household size: 2.07; Median age: 44.5; Age under 18: 22.6%; Age 65 and over: 22.6%; Males per 100 females: 210.0

Housing: Homeownership rate: 26.7%; Homeowner vacancy rate: 0.0%; Rental vacancy rate: 63.3%

CATHEYS VALLEY (CDP). Covers a land area of 23.415 square miles and a water area of 0.049 square miles. Located at 37.46° N. Lat; 120.09° W. Long. Elevation is 1,325 feet.

Population: 825; Growth (since 2000): n/a; Density: 35.2 persons per square mile; Race: 88.5% White, 0.7% Black/African American, 1.5% Asian, 1.5% American Indian/Alaska Native, 0.1% Native Hawaiian/Other Pacific Islander, 3.8% Two or more races, 9.7% Hispanic of any race; Average household size: 2.61; Median age: 47.2; Age under 18: 22.3%; Age 65 and over: 16.8%; Males per 100 females: 109.4

School District(s)

Mariposa County Unified (KG-12)
2012-13 Enrollment: 1,843 . . . . (209) 742-0250

Housing: Homeownership rate: 70.9%; Homeowner vacancy rate: 2.2%; Rental vacancy rate: 16.7%

COULTERVILLE (unincorporated postal area)

ZCTA: 95311

Covers a land area of 239.566 square miles and a water area of 3.001 square miles. Located at 37.71° N. Lat; 120.08° W. Long. Elevation is 1,699 feet.

Population: 2,197; Growth (since 2000): -2.6%; Density: 9.2 persons per square mile; Race: 91.9% White, 0.6% Black/African American, 0.6% Asian, 1.5% American Indian/Alaska Native, 0.1% Native Hawaiian/Other Pacific Islander, 4.2% Two or more races, 8.5% Hispanic of any race; Average household size: 2.24; Median age: 53.0; Age under 18: 15.7%; Age 65 and over: 23.7%; Males per 100 females: 103.4

School District(s)

Mariposa County Unified (KG-12)
2012-13 Enrollment: 1,843 . . . . (209) 742-0250

Housing: Homeownership rate: 75.4%; Homeowner vacancy rate: 3.6%; Rental vacancy rate: 7.6%

COULTERVILLLE (CDP). Covers a land area of 4.215 square miles and a water area of <.001 square miles. Located at 37.71° N. Lat; 120.20° W. Long. Elevation is 1,699 feet.

Population: 201; Growth (since 2000): n/a; Density: 47.7 persons per square mile; Race: 90.0% White, 0.0% Black/African American, 0.5% Asian, 2.5% American Indian/Alaska Native, 0.0% Native Hawaiian/Other Pacific Islander, 7.0% Two or more races, 10.0% Hispanic of any race; Average household size: 2.12; Median age: 52.9; Age under 18: 14.9%; Age 65 and over: 21.9%; Males per 100 females: 116.1

Housing: Homeownership rate: 68.5%; Homeowner vacancy rate: 5.6%; Rental vacancy rate: 11.4%

EL PORTAL (CDP). Covers a land area of 1.592 square miles and a water area of 0.047 square miles. Located at 37.68° N. Lat; 119.79° W. Long. Elevation is 1,939 feet.

Population: 474; Growth (since 2000): n/a; Density: 297.7 persons per square mile; Race: 91.6% White, 0.2% Black/African American, 1.1% Asian, 1.9% American Indian/Alaska Native, 0.0% Native Hawaiian/Other Pacific Islander, 4.2% Two or more races, 5.9% Hispanic of any race; Average household size: 2.06; Median age: 39.4; Age under 18: 15.4%; Age 65 and over: 7.4%; Males per 100 females: 95.1

School District(s)

Mariposa County Unified (KG-12)
2012-13 Enrollment: 1,843 . . . . (209) 742-0250

Housing: Homeownership rate: 38.2%; Homeowner vacancy rate: 0.0%; Rental vacancy rate: 4.1%

FISH CAMP (CDP). Covers a land area of 0.904 square miles and a water area of 0.002 square miles. Located at 37.48° N. Lat; 119.64° W. Long. Elevation is 5,062 feet.

Population: 59; Growth (since 2000): n/a; Density: 65.2 persons per square mile; Race: 96.6% White, 0.0% Black/African American, 1.7% Asian, 0.0% American Indian/Alaska Native, 0.0% Native Hawaiian/Other Pacific Islander, 1.7% Two or more races, 5.1% Hispanic of any race; Average household size: 1.90; Median age: 49.2; Age under 18: 15.3%; Age 65 and over: 23.7%; Males per 100 females: 90.3

Housing: Homeownership rate: 64.5%; Homeowner vacancy rate: 4.8%; Rental vacancy rate: 0.0%

GREELEY HILL (CDP). Covers a land area of 21.051 square miles and a water area of 0.046 square miles. Located at 37.76° N. Lat; 120.13° W. Long. Elevation is 3,140 feet.

Population: 915; Growth (since 2000): n/a; Density: 43.5 persons per square mile; Race: 92.6% White, 0.8% Black/African American, 0.1% Asian, 1.5% American Indian/Alaska Native, 0.7% Native Hawaiian/Other Pacific Islander, 3.2% Two or more races, 5.8% Hispanic of any race; Average household size: 2.19; Median age: 53.8; Age under 18: 15.2%; Age 65 and over: 23.7%; Males per 100 females: 102.4

Housing: Homeownership rate: 74.4%; Homeowner vacancy rate: 1.0%; Rental vacancy rate: 11.5%

HORNITOS (CDP). Covers a land area of 1.166 square miles and a water area of 0 square miles. Located at 37.50° N. Lat; 120.24° W. Long. Elevation is 843 feet.

Population: 75; Growth (since 2000): n/a; Density: 64.3 persons per square mile; Race: 88.0% White, 0.0% Black/African American, 1.3% Asian, 2.7% American Indian/Alaska Native, 0.0% Native Hawaiian/Other Pacific Islander, 8.0% Two or more races, 6.7% Hispanic of any race; Average household size: 2.21; Median age: 52.3; Age under 18: 18.7%; Age 65 and over: 29.3%; Males per 100 females: 97.4

Housing: Homeownership rate: 50.0%; Homeowner vacancy rate: 0.0%; Rental vacancy rate: 10.5%

LAKE DON PEDRO (CDP). Covers a land area of 12.557 square miles and a water area of 0.013 square miles. Located at 37.64° N. Lat; 120.34° W. Long.

Population: 1,077; Growth (since 2000): n/a; Density: 85.8 persons per square mile; Race: 90.9% White, 0.6% Black/African American, 1.1% Asian, 1.7% American Indian/Alaska Native, 0.2% Native Hawaiian/Other Pacific Islander, 3.8% Two or more races, 10.1% Hispanic of any race; Average household size: 2.44; Median age: 50.2; Age under 18: 18.6%; Age 65 and over: 19.7%; Males per 100 females: 107.5

Housing: Homeownership rate: 83.4%; Homeowner vacancy rate: 6.2%; Rental vacancy rate: 3.9%

MARIPOSA (CDP). County seat. Covers a land area of 12.850 square miles and a water area of 0.030 square miles. Located at 37.48° N. Lat; 119.97° W. Long. Elevation is 1,949 feet.

History: In 1854 Mariposa was named the seat of Mariposa County. The courthouse that was built in 1854 was fastened together with wooden pegs.

Population: 2,173; Growth (since 2000): 58.3%; Density: 169.1 persons per square mile; Race: 87.2% White, 0.5% Black/African American, 1.4% Asian, 4.8% American Indian/Alaska Native, 0.0% Native Hawaiian/Other Pacific Islander, 3.4% Two or more races, 9.9% Hispanic of any race; Average household size: 2.07; Median age: 49.3; Age under 18: 20.0%; Age 65 and over: 27.1%; Males per 100 females: 85.7

School District(s)

Mariposa County Office of Education (KG-12)
2012-13 Enrollment: 73. . . . . (209) 742-0250

Mariposa County Unified (KG-12)
2012-13 Enrollment: 1,843 . . . . (209) 742-0250

Housing: Homeownership rate: 52.2%; Homeowner vacancy rate: 3.4%; Rental vacancy rate: 5.8%

Hospitals: John C Fremont Healthcare District (34 beds)

Newspapers: Mariposa Gazette (weekly circulation 5400)

Airports: Mariposa-Yosemite (general aviation)

MIDPINES (CDP). Covers a land area of 24.529 square miles and a water area of 0.020 square miles. Located at 37.55° N. Lat; 119.96° W. Long. Elevation is 2,585 feet.

Population: 1,204; Growth (since 2000): n/a; Density: 49.1 persons per square mile; Race: 82.2% White, 0.3% Black/African American, 0.6% Asian, 5.2% American Indian/Alaska Native, 0.0% Native Hawaiian/Other Pacific Islander, 3.6% Two or more races, 17.3% Hispanic of any race; Average household size: 2.36; Median age: 45.4; Age under 18: 19.0%; Age 65 and over: 18.4%; Males per 100 females: 107.9

Housing: Homeownership rate: 62.2%; Homeowner vacancy rate: 1.5%; Rental vacancy rate: 10.4%

WAWONA (CDP). Covers a land area of 6.345 square miles and a water area of 0 square miles. Located at 37.55° N. Lat; 119.64° W. Long. Elevation is 3,999 feet.

Population: 169; Growth (since 2000): n/a; Density: 26.6 persons per square mile; Race: 81.7% White, 1.2% Black/African American, 2.4% Asian, 1.8% American Indian/Alaska Native, 0.0% Native Hawaiian/Other Pacific Islander, 8.3% Two or more races, 7.1% Hispanic of any race; Average household size: 2.30; Median age: 43.6; Age under 18: 18.9%; Age 65 and over: 8.9%; Males per 100 females: 141.4

Housing: Homeownership rate: 31.0%; Homeowner vacancy rate: 4.3%; Rental vacancy rate: 2.0%

YOSEMITE NATIONAL PARK (unincorporated postal area)

ZCTA: 95389

Covers a land area of 236.041 square miles and a water area of 1.361 square miles. Located at 37.63° N. Lat; 119.68° W. Long..

Population: 1,272; Growth (since 2000): -26.9%; Density: 5.4 persons per square mile; Race: 81.3% White, 2.4% Black/African American, 2.8% Asian, 2.7% American Indian/Alaska Native, 0.6% Native Hawaiian/Other Pacific Islander, 4.2% Two or more races, 11.1% Hispanic of any race; Average household size: 1.90; Median age: 38.1; Age under 18: 9.4%; Age 65 and over: 3.6%; Males per 100 females: 143.7

School District(s)

Mariposa County Unified (KG-12)
2012-13 Enrollment: 1,843 . . . . (209) 742-0250

Housing: Homeownership rate: 10.1%; Homeowner vacancy rate: 2.5%; Rental vacancy rate: 3.6%

YOSEMITE VALLEY (CDP). Covers a land area of 2.059 square miles and a water area of 0.061 square miles. Located at 37.74° N. Lat; 119.58° W. Long.

Population: 1,035; Growth (since 2000): 290.6%; Density: 502.6 persons per square mile; Race: 80.3% White, 2.7% Black/African American, 3.0% Asian, 3.0% American Indian/Alaska Native, 0.7% Native Hawaiian/Other Pacific Islander, 3.6% Two or more races, 11.9% Hispanic of any race; Average household size: 1.81; Median age: 37.6; Age under 18: 7.8%; Age 65 and over: 2.2%; Males per 100 females: 148.8

Housing: Homeownership rate: 0.7%; Homeowner vacancy rate: 0.0%; Rental vacancy rate: 1.8%

Mendocino County

Located in northwestern California, on the Pacific Coast; mountain and valley area, crossed by the Coast Ranges; includes part of Mendocino National Forest; drained by the Eel, Russian, Big, Noyo, and Navarro Rivers. Covers a land area of 3,506.343 square miles, a water area of 371.798 square miles, and is located in the Pacific Time Zone at 39.43° N. Lat., 123.44° W. Long. The county was founded in 1850. County seat is Ukiah.

Mendocino County is part of the Ukiah, CA Micropolitan Statistical Area. The entire metro area includes: Mendocino County, CA

Weather Station: Covelo Elevation: 1,410 feet

	Jan	Feb	Mar	Apr	May	Jun	Jul	Aug	Sep	Oct	Nov	Dec
High	54	58	63	69	77	85	93	93	88	76	59	52
Low	32	34	36	38	43	48	52	50	45	39	35	32
Precip	7.7	7.2	5.5	2.8	1.7	0.5	0.0	0.2	0.4	2.1	5.6	8.5
Snow	0.6	0.5	0.1	0.1	0.0	0.0	0.0	0.0	0.0	0.0	0.1	0.4

High and Low temperatures in degrees Fahrenheit; Precipitation and Snow in inches

Weather Station: Fort Bragg 5 N Elevation: 120 feet

	Jan	Feb	Mar	Apr	May	Jun	Jul	Aug	Sep	Oct	Nov	Dec
High	55	56	58	59	62	64	66	66	66	63	58	54
Low	40	41	42	43	45	48	49	50	49	46	43	40
Precip	7.1	7.1	5.9	3.1	1.7	0.6	0.1	0.2	0.5	2.3	5.3	8.3
Snow	0.0	tr	tr	0.0	0.0	0.0	0.0	0.0	0.0	0.0	0.0	0.0

High and Low temperatures in degrees Fahrenheit; Precipitation and Snow in inches

Weather Station: Potter Valley P H Elevation: 1,015 feet

	Jan	Feb	Mar	Apr	May	Jun	Jul	Aug	Sep	Oct	Nov	Dec
High	56	60	64	69	77	84	93	92	87	77	62	54
Low	35	37	38	40	45	49	54	52	48	43	38	34
Precip	8.2	7.8	6.3	3.2	1.8	0.4	0.0	0.1	0.6	2.3	6.1	9.1
Snow	0.0	0.0	0.0	0.0	0.0	0.0	0.0	0.0	0.0	0.0	0.0	0.0

High and Low temperatures in degrees Fahrenheit; Precipitation and Snow in inches

Weather Station: Ukiah Elevation: 632 feet

	Jan	Feb	Mar	Apr	May	Jun	Jul	Aug	Sep	Oct	Nov	Dec
High	57	60	65	69	76	83	91	90	86	76	63	56
Low	37	39	41	43	48	52	56	55	52	46	41	37
Precip	7.3	7.3	5.4	2.6	1.2	0.4	0.0	0.1	0.5	2.0	5.0	7.8
Snow	tr	0.0	0.0	0.0	0.0	0.0	0.0	0.0	0.0	0.0	0.0	tr

High and Low temperatures in degrees Fahrenheit; Precipitation and Snow in inches

Weather Station: Willits 1 NE Elevation: 1,350 feet

	Jan	Feb	Mar	Apr	May	Jun	Jul	Aug	Sep	Oct	Nov	Dec
High	55	58	60	64	70	77	84	84	81	73	61	54
Low	32	34	35	37	40	44	47	45	42	37	35	31
Precip	8.9	8.1	6.6	3.0	1.9	0.4	0.1	0.1	0.6	2.6	6.3	9.7
Snow	0.3	0.4	0.3	0.0	0.0	0.0	0.0	0.0	0.0	0.0	0.0	0.1

High and Low temperatures in degrees Fahrenheit; Precipitation and Snow in inches

Population: 87,841; Growth (since 2000): 1.8%; Density: 25.1 persons per square mile; Race: 76.5% White, 0.7% Black/African American, 1.7% Asian, 4.9% American Indian/Alaska Native, 0.1% Native Hawaiian/Other Pacific Islander, 4.5% two or more races, 22.2% Hispanic of any race; Average household size: 2.46; Median age: 41.5; Age under 18: 22.2%; Age 65 and over: 15.4%; Males per 100 females: 100.3; Marriage status: 29.6% never married, 48.3% now married, 2.2% separated, 7.4% widowed, 14.7% divorced; Foreign born: 12.5%; Speak English only: 78.8%; With disability: 16.1%; Veterans: 10.0%; Ancestry: 14.4% German, 11.8% Irish, 11.4% English, 5.7% Italian, 4.5% American

Religion: Six largest groups: 17.2% Catholicism, 3.5% Buddhism, 2.7% Latter-day Saints, 2.2% Baptist, 1.2% Non-denominational Protestant, 1.2% Methodist/Pietist

Economy: Unemployment rate: 5.7%; Leading industries: 18.4% retail trade; 13.5% accommodation and food services; 11.0% construction; Farms: 1,220 totaling 770,257 acres; Company size: 0 employ 1,000 or more persons, 1 employs 500 to 999 persons, 22 employ 100 to 499 persons, 2,484 employ less than 100 persons; Business ownership: 3,046 women-owned, 28 Black-owned, n/a Hispanic-owned, n/a Asian-owned

Employment: 11.7% management, business, and financial, 3.0% computer, engineering, and science, 10.1% education, legal, community service, arts, and media, 3.9% healthcare practitioners, 21.4% service, 25.4% sales and office, 15.4% natural resources, construction, and maintenance, 9.1% production, transportation, and material moving

Income: Per capita: $23,306; Median household: $43,469; Average household: $57,774; Households with income of $100,000 or more: 14.9%; Poverty rate: 20.0%

Educational Attainment: High school diploma or higher: 85.2%; Bachelor's degree or higher: 22.0%; Graduate/professional degree or higher: 8.4%

Housing: Homeownership rate: 59.0%; Median home value: $323,600; Median year structure built: 1974; Homeowner vacancy rate: 2.2%; Median gross rent: $953 per month; Rental vacancy rate: 5.3%

Vital Statistics: Birth rate: 117.8 per 10,000 population; Death rate: 92.0 per 10,000 population; Age-adjusted cancer mortality rate: 159.9 deaths per 100,000 population

Health Insurance: 81.5% have insurance; 51.1% have private insurance; 42.7% have public insurance; 18.5% do not have insurance; 9.8% of children under 18 do not have insurance

Health Care: Physicians: 20.0 per 10,000 population; Hospital beds: 12.8 per 10,000 population; Hospital admissions: 749.1 per 10,000 population

Air Quality Index: 83.1% good, 16.9% moderate, 0.0% unhealthy for sensitive individuals, 0.0% unhealthy (percent of days)

Transportation: Commute: 83.8% car, 0.6% public transportation, 5.8% walk, 7.8% work from home; Median travel time to work: 18.6 minutes

Presidential Election: 66.2% Obama, 28.6% Romney (2012)

National and State Parks: Admiral William Standley State Recreation Area; Caspar Headlands State Beach; Caspar Headlands State Natural Reserve; Greenwood State Beach; Hendy Woods State Park; Jackson State Forest; Jug Handle State Natural Reserve; MacKerricher State Park; Mailliard Redwoods State Natural Reserve; Manchester State Park; Mendocino Headlands State Park; Mendocino Woodlands State Park; Montgomery Woods State Natural Reserve; Navarro River Redwoods State Park; Point Cabrillo Light Station State Historic Park; Russian Gulch State Park; Schooner Gulch State Beach; Sinkyone State Wilderness; Sinkyone Wilderness State Park; Smithe Redwoods State Natural Reserve; Standish-Hickey State Recreation Area; Van Damme State Park; Westport-Union Landing State Beach

Additional Information Contacts

Mendocino Government . . . . (707) 463-4441
http://www.co.mendocino.ca.us

Mendocino County Communities

ALBION (CDP). Covers a land area of 1.815 square miles and a water area of 0.037 square miles. Located at 39.23° N. Lat; 123.76° W. Long. Elevation is 174 feet.

Population: 168; Growth (since 2000): n/a; Density: 92.5 persons per square mile; Race: 89.3% White, 0.6% Black/African American, 3.0% Asian, 2.4% American Indian/Alaska Native, 0.0% Native Hawaiian/Other Pacific Islander, 4.8% Two or more races, 2.4% Hispanic of any race; Average household size: 1.90; Median age: 50.3; Age under 18: 11.9%; Age 65 and over: 20.2%; Males per 100 females: 115.4

School District(s)

Mendocino Unified (KG-12)
2012-13 Enrollment: 548. . . . . (707) 937-5868

Housing: Homeownership rate: 65.8%; Homeowner vacancy rate: 1.8%; Rental vacancy rate: 17.6%

ANCHOR BAY (CDP). Covers a land area of 3.513 square miles and a water area of 0 square miles. Located at 38.81° N. Lat; 123.57° W. Long. Elevation is 105 feet.

Population: 340; Growth (since 2000): n/a; Density: 96.8 persons per square mile; Race: 88.5% White, 0.6% Black/African American, 0.6% Asian, 1.5% American Indian/Alaska Native, 0.3% Native Hawaiian/Other Pacific Islander, 5.0% Two or more races, 8.5% Hispanic of any race; Average household size: 1.95; Median age: 57.3; Age under 18: 11.5%; Age 65 and over: 25.0%; Males per 100 females: 96.5

Housing: Homeownership rate: 73.6%; Homeowner vacancy rate: 3.6%; Rental vacancy rate: 2.1%

BOONVILLE (CDP). Covers a land area of 5.542 square miles and a water area of 0 square miles. Located at 39.01° N. Lat; 123.37° W. Long. Elevation is 381 feet.

Population: 1,035; Growth (since 2000): n/a; Density: 186.7 persons per square mile; Race: 60.9% White, 0.9% Black/African American, 0.7% Asian, 1.7% American Indian/Alaska Native, 0.2% Native Hawaiian/Other Pacific Islander, 2.8% Two or more races, 50.2% Hispanic of any race; Average household size: 2.77; Median age: 36.8; Age under 18: 25.9%; Age 65 and over: 12.8%; Males per 100 females: 112.1

School District(s)

Anderson Valley Unified (KG-12)
2012-13 Enrollment: 556. . . . . (707) 895-3774

Housing: Homeownership rate: 51.1%; Homeowner vacancy rate: 0.0%; Rental vacancy rate: 4.2%

Newspapers: Anderson Valley Advertiser (weekly circulation 3000)

BRANSCOMB (unincorporated postal area)

ZCTA: 95417

Covers a land area of 75.327 square miles and a water area of 0 square miles. Located at 39.69° N. Lat; 123.61° W. Long. Elevation is 1,565 feet.

Population: 297; Growth (since 2000): 78.9%; Density: 3.9 persons per square mile; Race: 85.9% White, 0.0% Black/African American, 0.0% Asian, 3.4% American Indian/Alaska Native, 0.0% Native Hawaiian/Other Pacific Islander, 7.1% Two or more races, 11.4% Hispanic of any race; Average household size: 2.52; Median age: 48.6; Age under 18: 17.5%; Age 65 and over: 15.5%; Males per 100 females: 107.7

Housing: Homeownership rate: 76.2%; Homeowner vacancy rate: 0.0%; Rental vacancy rate: 3.4%

BROOKTRAILS (CDP). Covers a land area of 7.272 square miles and a water area of 0.047 square miles. Located at 39.44° N. Lat; 123.39° W. Long. Elevation is 1,634 feet.

Population: 3,235; Growth (since 2000): n/a; Density: 444.8 persons per square mile; Race: 87.1% White, 0.7% Black/African American, 0.8% Asian, 2.7% American Indian/Alaska Native, 0.1% Native Hawaiian/Other Pacific Islander, 5.2% Two or more races, 10.2% Hispanic of any race; Average household size: 2.45; Median age: 38.4; Age under 18: 23.2%; Age 65 and over: 12.0%; Males per 100 females: 108.2; Marriage status: 24.2% never married, 55.8% now married, 0.8% separated, 6.4% widowed, 13.6% divorced; Foreign born: 1.6%; Speak English only: 95.7%; With disability: 15.3%; Veterans: 8.7%; Ancestry: 26.3% German, 14.9% English, 14.3% Irish, 7.0% Swedish, 4.9% French

Employment: 15.8% management, business, and financial, 3.7% computer, engineering, and science, 9.6% education, legal, community service, arts, and media, 2.4% healthcare practitioners, 26.7% service, 20.6% sales and office, 13.9% natural resources, construction, and maintenance, 7.5% production, transportation, and material moving

Income: Per capita: $26,012; Median household: $50,086; Average household: $61,535; Households with income of $100,000 or more: 9.7%; Poverty rate: 8.2%

Educational Attainment: High school diploma or higher: 91.2%; Bachelor's degree or higher: 20.9%; Graduate/professional degree or higher: 8.0%

Housing: Homeownership rate: 72.2%; Median home value: $239,300; Median year structure built: 1986; Homeowner vacancy rate: 3.9%; Median gross rent: $1,648 per month; Rental vacancy rate: 5.9%

Health Insurance: 75.1% have insurance; 55.5% have private insurance; 33.5% have public insurance; 24.9% do not have insurance; 16.6% of children under 18 do not have insurance

Transportation: Commute: 86.7% car, 0.9% public transportation, 0.9% walk, 11.5% work from home; Median travel time to work: 26.6 minutes

CALPELLA (CDP). Covers a land area of 2.537 square miles and a water area of 0.024 square miles. Located at 39.23° N. Lat; 123.19° W. Long. Elevation is 682 feet.

Population: 679; Growth (since 2000): n/a; Density: 267.6 persons per square mile; Race: 68.5% White, 0.4% Black/African American, 0.4% Asian, 3.7% American Indian/Alaska Native, 0.0% Native Hawaiian/Other Pacific Islander, 5.6% Two or more races, 37.7% Hispanic of any race; Average household size: 2.68; Median age: 36.2; Age under 18: 25.2%; Age 65 and over: 10.2%; Males per 100 females: 108.9

Housing: Homeownership rate: 49.0%; Homeowner vacancy rate: 1.6%; Rental vacancy rate: 4.4%

CASPAR (CDP). Covers a land area of 2.992 square miles and a water area of 0 square miles. Located at 39.36° N. Lat; 123.80° W. Long. Elevation is 82 feet.

Population: 509; Growth (since 2000): n/a; Density: 170.1 persons per square mile; Race: 93.1% White, 0.6% Black/African American, 1.6% Asian, 0.0% American Indian/Alaska Native, 0.0% Native Hawaiian/Other Pacific Islander, 4.1% Two or more races, 2.9% Hispanic of any race; Average household size: 2.01; Median age: 57.1; Age under 18: 10.0%; Age 65 and over: 29.1%; Males per 100 females: 90.6

Housing: Homeownership rate: 65.1%; Homeowner vacancy rate: 4.0%; Rental vacancy rate: 7.4%

CLEONE (CDP). Covers a land area of 1.593 square miles and a water area of 0.024 square miles. Located at 39.49° N. Lat; 123.78° W. Long. Elevation is 79 feet.

Population: 618; Growth (since 2000): n/a; Density: 387.9 persons per square mile; Race: 83.8% White, 0.2% Black/African American, 0.5% Asian, 0.5% American Indian/Alaska Native, 0.0% Native Hawaiian/Other Pacific Islander, 2.3% Two or more races, 20.1% Hispanic of any race; Average household size: 2.17; Median age: 49.6; Age under 18: 17.3%; Age 65 and over: 21.2%; Males per 100 females: 104.0

Housing: Homeownership rate: 73.7%; Homeowner vacancy rate: 2.8%; Rental vacancy rate: 11.6%

COMPTCHE (CDP). Covers a land area of 1.154 square miles and a water area of 0 square miles. Located at 39.27° N. Lat; 123.59° W. Long. Elevation is 187 feet.

Population: 159; Growth (since 2000): n/a; Density: 137.8 persons per square mile; Race: 91.8% White, 0.0% Black/African American, 0.6% Asian, 0.6% American Indian/Alaska Native, 0.0% Native Hawaiian/Other Pacific Islander, 3.8% Two or more races, 6.3% Hispanic of any race; Average household size: 2.37; Median age: 47.3; Age under 18: 22.0%; Age 65 and over: 13.8%; Males per 100 females: 127.1

School District(s)

Mendocino Unified (KG-12)
2012-13 Enrollment: 548. . . . . (707) 937-5868

Housing: Homeownership rate: 58.2%; Homeowner vacancy rate: 0.0%; Rental vacancy rate: 9.7%

COVELO (CDP). Covers a land area of 7.095 square miles and a water area of 0.043 square miles. Located at 39.80° N. Lat; 123.25° W. Long. Elevation is 1,398 feet.

Population: 1,255; Growth (since 2000): 6.8%; Density: 176.9 persons per square mile; Race: 48.7% White, 1.1% Black/African American, 0.8% Asian, 37.8% American Indian/Alaska Native, 0.0% Native Hawaiian/Other Pacific Islander, 7.6% Two or more races, 13.0% Hispanic of any race; Average household size: 2.59; Median age: 35.8; Age under 18: 27.0%; Age 65 and over: 15.3%; Males per 100 females: 97.3

School District(s)

Round Valley Unified (KG-12)
2012-13 Enrollment: 421 . . . . (707) 983-6171

Housing: Homeownership rate: 65.3%; Homeowner vacancy rate: 2.2%; Rental vacancy rate: 3.4%

DOS RIOS (unincorporated postal area)

ZCTA: 95429

Covers a land area of 39.965 square miles and a water area of 0.158 square miles. Located at 39.72° N. Lat; 123.30° W. Long. Elevation is 961 feet.

Population: 70; Growth (since 2000): -10.3%; Density: 1.8 persons per square mile; Race: 75.7% White, 1.4% Black/African American, 1.4% Asian, 10.0% American Indian/Alaska Native, 0.0% Native Hawaiian/Other Pacific Islander, 11.4% Two or more races, 2.9% Hispanic of any race; Average household size: 1.79; Median age: 55.5; Age under 18: 7.1%; Age 65 and over: 17.1%; Males per 100 females: 125.8

Housing: Homeownership rate: 79.5%; Homeowner vacancy rate: 0.0%; Rental vacancy rate: 20.0%

ELK (unincorporated postal area)

ZCTA: 95432

Covers a land area of 72.924 square miles and a water area of 0.465 square miles. Located at 39.11° N. Lat; 123.65° W. Long. Elevation is 135 feet.

Population: 426; Growth (since 2000): 16.4%; Density: 5.8 persons per square mile; Race: 88.0% White, 0.5% Black/African American, 1.4% Asian, 1.4% American Indian/Alaska Native, 0.2% Native Hawaiian/Other Pacific Islander, 7.0% Two or more races, 9.9% Hispanic of any race; Average household size: 2.10; Median age: 50.9; Age under 18: 17.1%; Age 65 and over: 18.8%; Males per 100 females: 105.8

School District(s)

Mendocino Unified (KG-12)
2012-13 Enrollment: 548. . . . . (707) 937-5868

Housing: Homeownership rate: 60.6%; Homeowner vacancy rate: 1.6%; Rental vacancy rate: 6.9%

FORT BRAGG (city). Covers a land area of 2.749 square miles and a water area of 0.033 square miles. Located at 39.44° N. Lat; 123.80° W. Long. Elevation is 85 feet.

History: Fort Bragg was established in 1857 by Lieutenant Horatio Gates Gibson as a military post, and named for General Braxton Bragg. When the area was opened to purchase in 1867, a lumber town developed.

Population: 7,273; Growth (since 2000): 3.5%; Density: 2,645.6 persons per square mile; Race: 74.8% White, 0.7% Black/African American, 1.5% Asian, 2.2% American Indian/Alaska Native, 0.2% Native Hawaiian/Other Pacific Islander, 4.6% Two or more races, 31.8% Hispanic of any race; Average household size: 2.45; Median age: 37.4; Age under 18: 24.7%; Age 65 and over: 13.7%; Males per 100 females: 95.8; Marriage status: 30.5% never married, 46.5% now married, 3.6% separated, 9.4% widowed, 13.5% divorced; Foreign born: 24.3%; Speak English only: 63.0%; With disability: 19.0%; Veterans: 9.6%; Ancestry: 14.0% German, 12.2% Irish, 9.3% English, 6.0% Italian, 3.3% French

Employment: 13.4% management, business, and financial, 1.7% computer, engineering, and science, 5.6% education, legal, community service, arts, and media, 2.4% healthcare practitioners, 29.5% service, 26.9% sales and office, 7.6% natural resources, construction, and maintenance, 12.8% production, transportation, and material moving

Income: Per capita: $20,545; Median household: $36,641; Average household: $48,197; Households with income of $100,000 or more: 10.6%; Poverty rate: 23.5%

Educational Attainment: High school diploma or higher: 83.1%; Bachelor's degree or higher: 21.2%; Graduate/professional degree or higher: 7.9%

School District(s)

Fort Bragg Unified (PK-12)
2012-13 Enrollment: 1,917 . . . . (707) 961-2850

Housing: Homeownership rate: 40.4%; Median home value: $303,400; Median year structure built: 1964; Homeowner vacancy rate: 2.5%; Median gross rent: $996 per month; Rental vacancy rate: 4.8%

Health Insurance: 80.4% have insurance; 42.2% have private insurance; 50.2% have public insurance; 19.6% do not have insurance; 5.4% of children under 18 do not have insurance

Hospitals: Mendocino Coast District Hospital (25 beds)

Safety: Violent crime rate: 73.2 per 10,000 population; Property crime rate: 539.7 per 10,000 population

Newspapers: Advocate-News (weekly circulation 5400); Mendocino Beacon (weekly circulation 2500)

Transportation: Commute: 82.3% car, 0.0% public transportation, 10.7% walk, 5.1% work from home; Median travel time to work: 12.6 minutes

Additional Information Contacts

City of Fort Bragg . . . . (707) 961-2823
http://ci.fort-bragg.ca.us

GUALALA (unincorporated postal area)

ZCTA: 95445

Covers a land area of 85.544 square miles and a water area of 2.843 square miles. Located at 38.83° N. Lat; 123.47° W. Long. Elevation is 49 feet.

Population: 2,093; Growth (since 2000): 9.5%; Density: 24.5 persons per square mile; Race: 84.4% White, 0.3% Black/African American, 1.0% Asian, 0.8% American Indian/Alaska Native, 0.4% Native Hawaiian/Other Pacific Islander, 3.7% Two or more races, 19.2% Hispanic of any race; Average household size: 2.23; Median age: 51.8; Age under 18: 16.2%; Age 65 and over: 20.6%; Males per 100 females: 100.5

Housing: Homeownership rate: 73.3%; Homeowner vacancy rate: 4.0%; Rental vacancy rate: 8.0%

Newspapers: Independent Coast Observer (weekly circulation 3000)

HOPLAND (CDP). Covers a land area of 3.525 square miles and a water area of 0.048 square miles. Located at 38.97° N. Lat; 123.12° W. Long. Elevation is 502 feet.

Population: 756; Growth (since 2000): n/a; Density: 214.5 persons per square mile; Race: 68.9% White, 0.5% Black/African American, 1.3% Asian, 5.0% American Indian/Alaska Native, 0.0% Native Hawaiian/Other Pacific Islander, 5.4% Two or more races, 34.8% Hispanic of any race; Average household size: 2.81; Median age: 34.6; Age under 18: 25.8%; Age 65 and over: 7.5%; Males per 100 females: 124.3

Housing: Homeownership rate: 41.4%; Homeowner vacancy rate: 2.7%; Rental vacancy rate: 6.1%

LAYTONVILLE (CDP). Covers a land area of 5.367 square miles and a water area of 0.067 square miles. Located at 39.66° N. Lat; 123.50° W. Long. Elevation is 1,670 feet.

History: Laytonville developed as a trading center for the nearby cattle and sheep ranches.

Population: 1,227; Growth (since 2000): -5.7%; Density: 228.6 persons per square mile; Race: 68.4% White, 1.3% Black/African American, 0.8% Asian, 19.9% American Indian/Alaska Native, 0.1% Native Hawaiian/Other Pacific Islander, 4.6% Two or more races, 11.5% Hispanic of any race; Average household size: 2.49; Median age: 40.0; Age under 18: 22.1%; Age 65 and over: 12.2%; Males per 100 females: 108.3

School District(s)

Laytonville Unified (KG-12)
2012-13 Enrollment: 408. . . . . (707) 984-6414

Housing: Homeownership rate: 54.7%; Homeowner vacancy rate: 1.1%; Rental vacancy rate: 9.7%

Newspapers: Mendocino County Observer (weekly circulation 3000)

LEGGETT (CDP). Covers a land area of 2.704 square miles and a water area of 0 square miles. Located at 39.86° N. Lat; 123.73° W. Long. Elevation is 984 feet.

Population: 122; Growth (since 2000): n/a; Density: 45.1 persons per square mile; Race: 82.8% White, 0.0% Black/African American, 0.0% Asian, 2.5% American Indian/Alaska Native, 0.0% Native Hawaiian/Other Pacific Islander, 14.8% Two or more races, 3.3% Hispanic of any race; Average household size: 2.22; Median age: 33.0; Age under 18: 23.8%; Age 65 and over: 9.8%; Males per 100 females: 106.8

School District(s)

Leggett Valley Unified (KG-12)
2012-13 Enrollment: 116. . . . . (707) 925-6285

Housing: Homeownership rate: 41.8%; Homeowner vacancy rate: 0.0%; Rental vacancy rate: 0.0%

LITTLE RIVER (CDP). Covers a land area of 1.672 square miles and a water area of 0 square miles. Located at 39.27° N. Lat; 123.78° W. Long. Elevation is 66 feet.

Population: 117; Growth (since 2000): n/a; Density: 70.0 persons per square mile; Race: 96.6% White, 0.0% Black/African American, 0.0% Asian, 0.9% American Indian/Alaska Native, 0.0% Native Hawaiian/Other Pacific Islander, 2.6% Two or more races, 1.7% Hispanic of any race; Average household size: 1.70; Median age: 54.7; Age under 18: 9.4%; Age 65 and over: 24.8%; Males per 100 females: 98.3

Housing: Homeownership rate: 58.0%; Homeowner vacancy rate: 7.0%; Rental vacancy rate: 6.5%

MANCHESTER (CDP). Covers a land area of 2.618 square miles and a water area of 0 square miles. Located at 38.97° N. Lat; 123.69° W. Long. Elevation is 85 feet.

Population: 195; Growth (since 2000): n/a; Density: 74.5 persons per square mile; Race: 77.4% White, 0.0% Black/African American, 0.5% Asian, 2.1% American Indian/Alaska Native, 0.0% Native Hawaiian/Other Pacific Islander, 5.1% Two or more races, 24.6% Hispanic of any race; Average household size: 2.47; Median age: 41.8; Age under 18: 25.6%; Age 65 and over: 15.9%; Males per 100 females: 101.0

School District(s)

Manchester Union Elementary (KG-08)
2012-13 Enrollment: 48. . . . . (707) 882-2374

Housing: Homeownership rate: 57.0%; Homeowner vacancy rate: 6.3%; Rental vacancy rate: 2.9%

MENDOCINO (CDP). Covers a land area of 2.257 square miles and a water area of 5.163 square miles. Located at 39.31° N. Lat; 123.81° W. Long. Elevation is 154 feet.

History: The town of Mendocino was named for Cape Mendocino, which Juan Cabrillo charted in 1542 and named for Don Antonio de Mendoza, first viceroy of New Spain (Mexico). A sawmill was built in 1852 by Harry Meiggs of San Francisco. Many of Mendocino's early residents were from New England, an influence seen in the architecture of its early buildings.

Population: 894; Growth (since 2000): 8.5%; Density: 396.0 persons per square mile; Race: 93.3% White, 0.6% Black/African American, 1.5% Asian, 0.9% American Indian/Alaska Native, 0.1% Native Hawaiian/Other Pacific Islander, 3.0% Two or more races, 4.7% Hispanic of any race; Average household size: 1.86; Median age: 56.1; Age under 18: 10.4%; Age 65 and over: 27.3%; Males per 100 females: 89.8

School District(s)

Mendocino Unified (KG-12)
2012-13 Enrollment: 548. . . . . (707) 937-5868

Housing: Homeownership rate: 60.7%; Homeowner vacancy rate: 3.9%; Rental vacancy rate: 9.2%

PHILO (CDP). Covers a land area of 2.037 square miles and a water area of 0 square miles. Located at 39.07° N. Lat; 123.45° W. Long. Elevation is 331 feet.

Population: 349; Growth (since 2000): n/a; Density: 171.4 persons per square mile; Race: 49.0% White, 0.6% Black/African American, 1.4% Asian, 1.1% American Indian/Alaska Native, 0.0% Native Hawaiian/Other Pacific Islander, 2.9% Two or more races, 58.5% Hispanic of any race; Average household size: 3.36; Median age: 30.4; Age under 18: 32.4%; Age 65 and over: 9.2%; Males per 100 females: 118.1

Housing: Homeownership rate: 35.7%; Homeowner vacancy rate: 0.0%; Rental vacancy rate: 1.5%

PIERCY (unincorporated postal area)

ZCTA: 95587

Covers a land area of 13.000 square miles and a water area of 0 square miles. Located at 39.96° N. Lat; 123.78° W. Long. Elevation is 794 feet.

Population: 201; Growth (since 2000): 4.1%; Density: 15.5 persons per square mile; Race: 88.6% White, 0.5% Black/African American, 1.5% Asian, 4.0% American Indian/Alaska Native, 0.0% Native Hawaiian/Other Pacific Islander, 5.0% Two or more races, 6.0% Hispanic of any race; Average household size: 2.16; Median age: 49.8; Age under 18: 14.9%; Age 65 and over: 20.9%; Males per 100 females: 118.5

Housing: Homeownership rate: 78.5%; Homeowner vacancy rate: 0.0%; Rental vacancy rate: 9.1%

POINT ARENA (city). Covers a land area of 1.350 square miles and a water area of 0 square miles. Located at 38.91° N. Lat; 123.70° W. Long. Elevation is 118 feet.

History: Point Arena began in 1859 when a store was opened here. The town developed as a center of lumbering operations, and was incorporated in 1908.

Population: 449; Growth (since 2000): -5.3%; Density: 332.6 persons per square mile; Race: 67.9% White, 0.4% Black/African American, 0.0% Asian, 0.2% American Indian/Alaska Native, 0.0% Native Hawaiian/Other Pacific Islander, 5.1% Two or more races, 33.4% Hispanic of any race; Average household size: 2.34; Median age: 40.0; Age under 18: 24.9%; Age 65 and over: 12.9%; Males per 100 females: 109.8

School District(s)

Arena Union Elementary (KG-12)
2012-13 Enrollment: 352. . . . . (707) 882-2803

Point Arena Joint Union High (09-12)
2012-13 Enrollment: 173. . . . . (707) 882-2803

Housing: Homeownership rate: 45.3%; Homeowner vacancy rate: 4.4%; Rental vacancy rate: 8.7%

Additional Information Contacts

City of Point Arena . . . . (707) 882-2122
http://www.cityofpointarena.com

POTTER VALLEY (CDP). Covers a land area of 4.030 square miles and a water area of 0.028 square miles. Located at 39.32° N. Lat; 123.11° W. Long. Elevation is 948 feet.

Population: 646; Growth (since 2000): n/a; Density: 160.3 persons per square mile; Race: 79.9% White, 0.3% Black/African American, 0.3% Asian, 2.0% American Indian/Alaska Native, 0.0% Native Hawaiian/Other Pacific Islander, 2.5% Two or more races, 23.8% Hispanic of any race; Average household size: 2.64; Median age: 41.6; Age under 18: 22.0%; Age 65 and over: 13.3%; Males per 100 females: 105.1

School District(s)

Potter Valley Community Unified (KG-12)
2012-13 Enrollment: 283. . . . . (707) 743-2101

Housing: Homeownership rate: 63.1%; Homeowner vacancy rate: 0.0%; Rental vacancy rate: 10.0%

REDWOOD VALLEY (CDP). Covers a land area of 2.736 square miles and a water area of 0.012 square miles. Located at 39.27° N. Lat; 123.20° W. Long. Elevation is 722 feet.

Population: 1,729; Growth (since 2000): n/a; Density: 631.9 persons per square mile; Race: 82.8% White, 0.4% Black/African American, 0.6% Asian, 3.6% American Indian/Alaska Native, 0.1% Native Hawaiian/Other Pacific Islander, 3.5% Two or more races, 17.6% Hispanic of any race; Average household size: 2.69; Median age: 41.2; Age under 18: 23.8%; Age 65 and over: 12.8%; Males per 100 females: 96.3

School District(s)

Ukiah Unified (KG-12)
2012-13 Enrollment: 6,163 . . . . (707) 472-5000

Housing: Homeownership rate: 74.3%; Homeowner vacancy rate: 1.2%; Rental vacancy rate: 3.5%

TALMAGE (CDP). Covers a land area of 1.590 square miles and a water area of 0.002 square miles. Located at 39.13° N. Lat; 123.16° W. Long. Elevation is 627 feet.

Population: 1,130; Growth (since 2000): -1.0%; Density: 710.8 persons per square mile; Race: 44.5% White, 0.3% Black/African American, 24.2% Asian, 2.4% American Indian/Alaska Native, 0.4% Native Hawaiian/Other Pacific Islander, 3.7% Two or more races, 32.4% Hispanic of any race; Average household size: 2.76; Median age: 37.0; Age under 18: 24.0%; Age 65 and over: 10.1%; Males per 100 females: 82.0

Housing: Homeownership rate: 47.0%; Homeowner vacancy rate: 1.3%; Rental vacancy rate: 11.2%

UKIAH (city). County seat. Covers a land area of 4.670 square miles and a water area of 0.052 square miles. Located at 39.15° N. Lat; 123.21° W. Long. Elevation is 633 feet.

History: The first settler in Ukiah was Samuel Lowry, who built a cabin here in 1856. Ukiah became the seat of Mendocino County in 1859.

Population: 16,075; Growth (since 2000): 3.7%; Density: 3,441.9 persons per square mile; Race: 72.1% White, 1.1% Black/African American, 2.6%

Asian, 3.7% American Indian/Alaska Native, 0.2% Native Hawaiian/Other Pacific Islander, 5.5% Two or more races, 27.7% Hispanic of any race; Average household size: 2.48; Median age: 35.9; Age under 18: 24.8%; Age 65 and over: 14.5%; Males per 100 females: 92.8; Marriage status: 33.9% never married, 42.9% now married, 3.1% separated, 6.4% widowed, 16.9% divorced; Foreign born: 11.7%; Speak English only: 73.7%; With disability: 15.6%; Veterans: 8.8%; Ancestry: 12.0% German, 9.6% Irish, 9.0% English, 6.1% Italian, 5.9% American

Employment: 6.6% management, business, and financial, 2.7% computer, engineering, and science, 11.6% education, legal, community service, arts, and media, 6.2% healthcare practitioners, 20.1% service, 28.4% sales and office, 14.3% natural resources, construction, and maintenance, 10.0% production, transportation, and material moving

Income: Per capita: $22,568; Median household: $42,609; Average household: $58,358; Households with income of $100,000 or more: 13.0%; Poverty rate: 22.4%

Educational Attainment: High school diploma or higher: 84.3%; Bachelor's degree or higher: 18.9%; Graduate/professional degree or higher: 7.6%

School District(s)

Mendocino County Office of Education (KG-12)
2012-13 Enrollment: 124. . . . . (707) 467-5000
Mendocino County Roc/rop
2012-13 Enrollment: n/a . . . . (707) 467-5123
Ukiah Unified (KG-12)
2012-13 Enrollment: 6,163 . . . . (707) 472-5000

Two-year College(s)

Mendocino College (Public)
Fall 2013 Enrollment: 3,729 . . . . (707) 468-3000
2013-14 Tuition: In-state $1,423; Out-of-state $7,123

Vocational/Technical School(s)

Ukiah Adult School (Public)
Fall 2013 Enrollment: 59 . . . . (707) 463-5217
2013-14 Tuition: $6,500

Housing: Homeownership rate: 43.4%; Median home value: $274,700; Median year structure built: 1969; Homeowner vacancy rate: 2.6%; Median gross rent: $926 per month; Rental vacancy rate: 3.7%

Health Insurance: 84.1% have insurance; 50.9% have private insurance; 44.2% have public insurance; 15.9% do not have insurance; 12.6% of children under 18 do not have insurance

Hospitals: Ukiah Valley Medical Center (101 beds)

Safety: Violent crime rate: 73.1 per 10,000 population; Property crime rate: 355.3 per 10,000 population

Newspapers: Ukiah Daily Journal (daily circulation 7000)

Transportation: Commute: 86.6% car, 0.3% public transportation, 4.2% walk, 4.2% work from home; Median travel time to work: 13.9 minutes; Amtrak: Bus service available.

Airports: Ukiah Municipal (general aviation)

Additional Information Contacts

City of Ukiah . . . . (707) 463-6217
http://www.cityofukiah.com

WESTPORT (unincorporated postal area)

ZCTA: 95488

Covers a land area of 88.718 square miles and a water area of 3.623 square miles. Located at 39.68° N. Lat; 123.74° W. Long. Elevation is 125 feet.

Population: 280; Growth (since 2000): -6.4%; Density: 3.2 persons per square mile; Race: 88.2% White, 0.4% Black/African American, 1.1% Asian, 1.1% American Indian/Alaska Native, 0.0% Native Hawaiian/Other Pacific Islander, 7.5% Two or more races, 1.4% Hispanic of any race; Average household size: 2.19; Median age: 50.2; Age under 18: 15.4%; Age 65 and over: 19.3%; Males per 100 females: 113.7

Housing: Homeownership rate: 61.7%; Homeowner vacancy rate: 9.2%; Rental vacancy rate: 2.0%

WILLITS (city). Covers a land area of 2.798 square miles and a water area of 0.005 square miles. Located at 39.41° N. Lat; 123.35° W. Long. Elevation is 1,391 feet.

History: Willits was once called Willitsville, named for Hiram Willits who purchased a store that had opened here in 1865. The town developed as a division point on the Northwestern Pacific Railroad, and the center of a hay, stock, and poultry raising region.

Population: 4,888; Growth (since 2000): -3.6%; Density: 1,746.8 persons per square mile; Race: 79.0% White, 0.7% Black/African American, 1.4% Asian, 4.4% American Indian/Alaska Native, 0.1% Native Hawaiian/Other Pacific Islander, 4.6% Two or more races, 20.6% Hispanic of any race; Average household size: 2.50; Median age: 37.8; Age under 18: 26.0%; Age 65 and over: 15.2%; Males per 100 females: 90.9; Marriage status: 28.8% never married, 44.3% now married, 3.6% separated, 12.6% widowed, 14.3% divorced; Foreign born: 5.7%; Speak English only: 90.5%; With disability: 18.4%; Veterans: 14.5%; Ancestry: 14.9% German, 14.8% Irish, 13.1% English, 8.7% Italian, 4.8% American

Employment: 17.4% management, business, and financial, 1.7% computer, engineering, and science, 15.0% education, legal, community service, arts, and media, 1.9% healthcare practitioners, 21.6% service, 26.5% sales and office, 6.8% natural resources, construction, and maintenance, 9.2% production, transportation, and material moving

Income: Per capita: $18,484; Median household: $31,147; Average household: $39,754; Households with income of $100,000 or more: 4.7%; Poverty rate: 30.2%

Educational Attainment: High school diploma or higher: 82.2%; Bachelor's degree or higher: 13.9%; Graduate/professional degree or higher: 4.5%

School District(s)

Willits Unified (KG-12)
2012-13 Enrollment: 1,992 . . . . (707) 459-5314

Housing: Homeownership rate: 44.1%; Median home value: $203,400; Median year structure built: 1970; Homeowner vacancy rate: 2.5%; Median gross rent: $913 per month; Rental vacancy rate: 4.3%

Health Insurance: 75.1% have insurance; 42.9% have private insurance; 42.0% have public insurance; 24.9% do not have insurance; 20.7% of children under 18 do not have insurance

Hospitals: Frank R Howard Memorial Hospital (38 beds)

Safety: Violent crime rate: 62.1 per 10,000 population; Property crime rate: 126.2 per 10,000 population

Newspapers: Willits News (weekly circulation 3100)

Transportation: Commute: 77.6% car, 0.8% public transportation, 14.9% walk, 3.1% work from home; Median travel time to work: 13.6 minutes; Amtrak: Bus service available.

Additional Information Contacts

City of Willits . . . . (707) 459-4601
http://thecityofwillits.com

YORKVILLE (unincorporated postal area)

ZCTA: 95494

Covers a land area of 102.943 square miles and a water area of 0 square miles. Located at 38.89° N. Lat; 123.34° W. Long. Elevation is 922 feet.

Population: 139; Growth (since 2000): -56.2%; Density: 1.4 persons per square mile; Race: 75.5% White, 1.4% Black/African American, 0.0% Asian, 0.0% American Indian/Alaska Native, 0.0% Native Hawaiian/Other Pacific Islander, 4.3% Two or more races, 27.3% Hispanic of any race; Average household size: 2.36; Median age: 49.5; Age under 18: 16.5%; Age 65 and over: 12.9%; Males per 100 females: 104.4

Housing: Homeownership rate: 54.2%; Homeowner vacancy rate: 0.0%; Rental vacancy rate: 0.0%

Merced County

Located in central California, in the San Joaquin Valley; includes the Diablo Range in the west and southwest, and the foothills of the Sierra Nevada in the east and northeast; watered by the Merced, San Joaquin, and Chowchilla Rivers. Covers a land area of 1,934.972 square miles, a water area of 43.537 square miles, and is located in the Pacific Time Zone at 37.19° N. Lat., 120.72° W. Long. The county was founded in 1855. County seat is Merced.

Merced County is part of the Merced, CA Metropolitan Statistical Area. The entire metro area includes: Merced County, CA

Weather Station: Los Banos — Elevation: 120 feet

	Jan	Feb	Mar	Apr	May	Jun	Jul	Aug	Sep	Oct	Nov	Dec
High	56	63	68	75	83	89	95	94	90	80	66	56
Low	37	41	45	48	54	58	62	61	58	51	43	36
Precip	2.0	1.9	1.5	0.6	0.5	0.1	0.0	0.0	0.2	0.5	1.0	1.5
Snow	0.0	0.0	0.0	0.0	0.0	0.0	0.0	0.0	0.0	0.0	0.0	0.0

High and Low temperatures in degrees Fahrenheit; Precipitation and Snow in inches

Weather Station: Los Banos Det Resv Elevation: 407 feet

	Jan	Feb	Mar	Apr	May	Jun	Jul	Aug	Sep	Oct	Nov	Dec
High	54	61	66	73	80	88	95	93	88	78	64	54
Low	39	43	46	50	55	60	65	63	61	54	46	39
Precip	1.7	1.7	1.4	0.5	0.4	0.0	0.0	0.0	0.2	0.4	0.9	1.3
Snow	0.0	0.0	0.0	0.0	0.0	0.0	0.0	0.0	0.0	0.0	0.0	0.0

High and Low temperatures in degrees Fahrenheit; Precipitation and Snow in inches

Weather Station: San Luis Dam Elevation: 276 feet

	Jan	Feb	Mar	Apr	May	Jun	Jul	Aug	Sep	Oct	Nov	Dec
High	55	61	66	72	79	86	92	91	87	79	65	56
Low	38	42	46	50	55	60	64	64	61	54	45	38
Precip	2.1	2.2	1.7	0.5	0.5	0.1	0.0	0.1	0.2	0.5	1.2	1.6
Snow	tr	0.0	0.0	0.0	0.0	0.0	0.0	0.0	0.0	0.0	0.0	0.0

High and Low temperatures in degrees Fahrenheit; Precipitation and Snow in inches

Population: 255,793; Growth (since 2000): 21.5%; Density: 132.2 persons per square mile; Race: 58.0% White, 3.9% Black/African American, 7.4% Asian, 1.4% American Indian/Alaska Native, 0.2% Native Hawaiian/Other Pacific Islander, 4.7% two or more races, 54.9% Hispanic of any race; Average household size: 3.32; Median age: 29.6; Age under 18: 31.5%; Age 65 and over: 9.4%; Males per 100 females: 101.3; Marriage status: 37.0% never married, 49.3% now married, 2.4% separated, 4.8% widowed, 8.9% divorced; Foreign born: 25.6%; Speak English only: 47.5%; With disability: 15.5%; Veterans: 6.2%; Ancestry: 5.8% Portuguese, 4.9% German, 3.9% Irish, 3.6% English, 2.3% American

Religion: Six largest groups: 39.9% Catholicism, 4.5% Non-denominational Protestant, 2.5% Baptist, 1.7% Pentecostal, 1.7% Latter-day Saints, 1.0% Methodist/Pietist

Economy: Unemployment rate: 10.4%; Leading industries: 18.4% retail trade; 14.9% health care and social assistance; 10.4% accommodation and food services; Farms: 2,486 totaling 978,667 acres; Company size: 3 employ 1,000 or more persons, 3 employ 500 to 999 persons, 46 employ 100 to 499 persons, 2,802 employ less than 100 persons; Business ownership: 3,821 women-owned, 323 Black-owned, 3,134 Hispanic-owned, 1,150 Asian-owned

Employment: 8.1% management, business, and financial, 1.7% computer, engineering, and science, 8.6% education, legal, community service, arts, and media, 3.5% healthcare practitioners, 18.2% service, 22.5% sales and office, 19.6% natural resources, construction, and maintenance, 17.9% production, transportation, and material moving

Income: Per capita: $18,177; Median household: $42,591; Average household: $59,420; Households with income of $100,000 or more: 14.8%; Poverty rate: 25.4%

Educational Attainment: High school diploma or higher: 66.7%; Bachelor's degree or higher: 12.6%; Graduate/professional degree or higher: 4.2%

Housing: Homeownership rate: 54.5%; Median home value: $146,400; Median year structure built: 1982; Homeowner vacancy rate: 3.2%; Median gross rent: $860 per month; Rental vacancy rate: 8.1%

Vital Statistics: Birth rate: 162.1 per 10,000 population; Death rate: 61.1 per 10,000 population; Age-adjusted cancer mortality rate: 164.2 deaths per 100,000 population

Health Insurance: 80.8% have insurance; 48.5% have private insurance; 40.4% have public insurance; 19.2% do not have insurance; 6.8% of children under 18 do not have insurance

Health Care: Physicians: 10.0 per 10,000 population; Hospital beds: 8.9 per 10,000 population; Hospital admissions: 527.5 per 10,000 population

Air Quality Index: 46.3% good, 44.4% moderate, 8.2% unhealthy for sensitive individuals, 1.1% unhealthy (percent of days)

Transportation: Commute: 89.8% car, 0.4% public transportation, 2.5% walk, 4.0% work from home; Median travel time to work: 26.3 minutes

Presidential Election: 51.7% Obama, 46.3% Romney (2012)

National and State Parks: Canal Farm State Historic Landmark; George J. Hatfield State Recreation Area; Great Valley Grasslands State Park; Kesterson National Wildlife Refuge; Los Banos State Waterfowl Area; McConnell State Recreation Area; Merced National Wildlife Refuge; San Luis National Wildlife Refuge; San Luis Reservoir State Recreation Area; Volta State Wildlife Area

Additional Information Contacts

Merced Government . . . . (209) 385-7366
http://www.co.merced.ca.us

Merced County Communities

ATWATER (city). Covers a land area of 6.087 square miles and a water area of 0.009 square miles. Located at 37.35° N. Lat; 120.60° W. Long. Elevation is 151 feet.

History: Incorporated 1922.

Population: 28,168; Growth (since 2000): 21.9%; Density: 4,627.3 persons per square mile; Race: 65.4% White, 4.3% Black/African American, 5.0% Asian, 1.3% American Indian/Alaska Native, 0.3% Native Hawaiian/Other Pacific Islander, 4.9% Two or more races, 52.6% Hispanic of any race; Average household size: 3.18; Median age: 30.0; Age under 18: 32.0%; Age 65 and over: 10.4%; Males per 100 females: 95.7; Marriage status: 35.3% never married, 48.1% now married, 2.4% separated, 4.7% widowed, 11.9% divorced; Foreign born: 21.6%; Speak English only: 53.2%; With disability: 16.3%; Veterans: 9.2%; Ancestry: 5.5% German, 4.7% Irish, 4.5% English, 3.7% American, 3.2% Portuguese

Employment: 6.9% management, business, and financial, 0.7% computer, engineering, and science, 8.3% education, legal, community service, arts, and media, 4.4% healthcare practitioners, 18.6% service, 27.2% sales and office, 15.6% natural resources, construction, and maintenance, 18.3% production, transportation, and material moving

Income: Per capita: $18,566; Median household: $42,162; Average household: $59,868; Households with income of $100,000 or more: 12.2%; Poverty rate: 24.4%

Educational Attainment: High school diploma or higher: 71.1%; Bachelor's degree or higher: 13.6%; Graduate/professional degree or higher: 4.7%

School District(s)

Atwater Elementary (KG-08)
2012-13 Enrollment: 4,710 . . . . (209) 357-6100
Merced County Office of Education (KG-12)
2012-13 Enrollment: 1,465 . . . . (209) 381-6600
Merced Union High (09-12)
2012-13 Enrollment: 10,078 . . . . (209) 385-6412

Housing: Homeownership rate: 55.4%; Median home value: $129,600; Median year structure built: 1978; Homeowner vacancy rate: 3.3%; Median gross rent: $906 per month; Rental vacancy rate: 10.9%

Health Insurance: 79.5% have insurance; 50.0% have private insurance; 38.2% have public insurance; 20.5% do not have insurance; 8.4% of children under 18 do not have insurance

Safety: Violent crime rate: 63.0 per 10,000 population; Property crime rate: 457.7 per 10,000 population

Transportation: Commute: 92.5% car, 0.4% public transportation, 1.2% walk, 3.8% work from home; Median travel time to work: 22.3 minutes

Airports: Castle (general aviation)

Additional Information Contacts

City of Atwater. . . . . (209) 357-6300
http://www.atwater.org

BALLICO (CDP). Covers a land area of 3.022 square miles and a water area of 0 square miles. Located at 37.45° N. Lat; 120.70° W. Long. Elevation is 151 feet.

Population: 406; Growth (since 2000): n/a; Density: 134.3 persons per square mile; Race: 58.4% White, 0.5% Black/African American, 2.7% Asian, 0.7% American Indian/Alaska Native, 0.5% Native Hawaiian/Other Pacific Islander, 5.7% Two or more races, 51.7% Hispanic of any race; Average household size: 3.36; Median age: 31.1; Age under 18: 29.6%; Age 65 and over: 9.1%; Males per 100 females: 113.7

School District(s)

Ballico-Cressey Elementary (KG-08)
2012-13 Enrollment: 312. . . . . (209) 632-5371

Housing: Homeownership rate: 63.7%; Homeowner vacancy rate: 1.3%; Rental vacancy rate: 4.3%

BEAR CREEK (CDP). Covers a land area of 0.057 square miles and a water area of 0 square miles. Located at 37.30° N. Lat; 120.42° W. Long. Elevation is 190 feet.

Population: 290; Growth (since 2000): n/a; Density: 5,060.9 persons per square mile; Race: 53.8% White, 1.4% Black/African American, 4.8% Asian, 0.7% American Indian/Alaska Native, 0.0% Native Hawaiian/Other Pacific Islander, 7.2% Two or more races, 58.6% Hispanic of any race; Average household size: 3.54; Median age: 27.0; Age under 18: 30.7%; Age 65 and over: 6.9%; Males per 100 females: 132.0

Housing: Homeownership rate: 31.7%; Homeowner vacancy rate: 0.0%; Rental vacancy rate: 6.6%

CRESSEY (CDP). Covers a land area of 1.758 square miles and a water area of 0 square miles. Located at 37.42° N. Lat; 120.66° W. Long. Elevation is 167 feet.

Population: 394; Growth (since 2000): n/a; Density: 224.1 persons per square mile; Race: 64.2% White, 0.3% Black/African American, 3.8% Asian, 0.8% American Indian/Alaska Native, 0.3% Native Hawaiian/Other Pacific Islander, 6.6% Two or more races, 49.5% Hispanic of any race; Average household size: 3.46; Median age: 35.8; Age under 18: 27.7%; Age 65 and over: 14.2%; Males per 100 females: 98.0

Housing: Homeownership rate: 77.2%; Homeowner vacancy rate: 0.0%; Rental vacancy rate: 10.3%

DELHI (CDP). Covers a land area of 3.510 square miles and a water area of 0 square miles. Located at 37.43° N. Lat; 120.78° W. Long. Elevation is 118 feet.

Population: 10,755; Growth (since 2000): 34.1%; Density: 3,063.7 persons per square mile; Race: 52.6% White, 1.1% Black/African American, 3.8% Asian, 1.5% American Indian/Alaska Native, 0.3% Native Hawaiian/Other Pacific Islander, 4.3% Two or more races, 71.7% Hispanic of any race; Average household size: 4.00; Median age: 27.5; Age under 18: 35.3%; Age 65 and over: 6.4%; Males per 100 females: 102.3; Marriage status: 33.0% never married, 59.4% now married, 1.5% separated, 3.8% widowed, 3.8% divorced; Foreign born: 37.6%; Speak English only: 24.8%; With disability: 15.7%; Veterans: 3.7%; Ancestry: 3.2% German, 2.6% Portuguese, 2.2% English, 2.0% Italian, 1.4% Irish

Employment: 4.6% management, business, and financial, 0.8% computer, engineering, and science, 8.9% education, legal, community service, arts, and media, 1.4% healthcare practitioners, 19.3% service, 17.5% sales and office, 20.2% natural resources, construction, and maintenance, 27.3% production, transportation, and material moving

Income: Per capita: $14,911; Median household: $48,053; Average household: $54,477; Households with income of $100,000 or more: 12.6%; Poverty rate: 14.4%

Educational Attainment: High school diploma or higher: 54.2%; Bachelor's degree or higher: 9.3%; Graduate/professional degree or higher: 2.0%

School District(s)

Delhi Unified (KG-12)
2012-13 Enrollment: 2,720 . . . . (209) 656-2000

Housing: Homeownership rate: 68.3%; Median home value: $134,300; Median year structure built: 1994; Homeowner vacancy rate: 2.9%; Median gross rent: $955 per month; Rental vacancy rate: 3.2%

Health Insurance: 81.8% have insurance; 57.5% have private insurance; 31.6% have public insurance; 18.2% do not have insurance; 6.3% of children under 18 do not have insurance

Transportation: Commute: 94.0% car, 0.0% public transportation, 0.9% walk, 3.1% work from home; Median travel time to work: 24.1 minutes

DOS PALOS (city). Covers a land area of 1.350 square miles and a water area of 0 square miles. Located at 36.99° N. Lat; 120.63° W. Long. Elevation is 118 feet.

History: Incorporated 1935.

Population: 4,950; Growth (since 2000): 8.1%; Density: 3,667.3 persons per square mile; Race: 68.2% White, 3.4% Black/African American, 0.7% Asian, 1.3% American Indian/Alaska Native, 0.1% Native Hawaiian/Other Pacific Islander, 4.6% Two or more races, 62.1% Hispanic of any race; Average household size: 3.28; Median age: 31.3; Age under 18: 31.7%; Age 65 and over: 10.8%; Males per 100 females: 96.1; Marriage status: 35.6% never married, 51.0% now married, 0.0% separated, 5.6% widowed, 7.8% divorced; Foreign born: 22.5%; Speak English only: 50.4%; With disability: 9.7%; Veterans: 5.7%; Ancestry: 5.6% Irish, 5.3% English, 4.9% Italian, 4.8% American, 3.7% German

Employment: 4.8% management, business, and financial, 0.7% computer, engineering, and science, 7.3% education, legal, community service, arts, and media, 0.0% healthcare practitioners, 9.6% service, 25.2% sales and office, 32.2% natural resources, construction, and maintenance, 20.2% production, transportation, and material moving

Income: Per capita: $12,831; Median household: $33,898; Average household: $40,410; Households with income of $100,000 or more: 3.1%; Poverty rate: 33.6%

Educational Attainment: High school diploma or higher: 62.6%; Bachelor's degree or higher: 7.3%; Graduate/professional degree or higher: 1.8%

School District(s)

Dos Palos Oro Loma Joint Unified (KG-12)
2012-13 Enrollment: 2,265 . . . . (209) 392-0200

Housing: Homeownership rate: 61.9%; Median home value: $87,700; Median year structure built: 1980; Homeowner vacancy rate: 3.2%; Median gross rent: $748 per month; Rental vacancy rate: 8.9%

Health Insurance: 81.0% have insurance; 41.2% have private insurance; 49.6% have public insurance; 19.0% do not have insurance; 4.5% of children under 18 do not have insurance

Safety: Violent crime rate: 175.5 per 10,000 population; Property crime rate: 414.1 per 10,000 population

Newspapers: Dos Palos Sun (weekly circulation 1000)

Transportation: Commute: 90.7% car, 0.0% public transportation, 2.5% walk, 6.8% work from home; Median travel time to work: 35.9 minutes

Additional Information Contacts

City of Dos Palos. . . . . (209) 392-2174

DOS PALOS Y (CDP). Covers a land area of 1.572 square miles and a water area of 0 square miles. Located at 37.05° N. Lat; 120.64° W. Long. Elevation is 112 feet.

Population: 323; Growth (since 2000): n/a; Density: 205.4 persons per square mile; Race: 69.7% White, 0.3% Black/African American, 0.3% Asian, 2.5% American Indian/Alaska Native, 0.0% Native Hawaiian/Other Pacific Islander, 1.9% Two or more races, 61.0% Hispanic of any race; Average household size: 3.23; Median age: 35.2; Age under 18: 30.3%; Age 65 and over: 15.2%; Males per 100 females: 107.1

Housing: Homeownership rate: 49.0%; Homeowner vacancy rate: 2.0%; Rental vacancy rate: 12.1%

EL NIDO (CDP). Covers a land area of 3.292 square miles and a water area of 0 square miles. Located at 37.13° N. Lat; 120.50° W. Long. Elevation is 141 feet.

Population: 330; Growth (since 2000): n/a; Density: 100.2 persons per square mile; Race: 49.1% White, 0.0% Black/African American, 2.7% Asian, 2.1% American Indian/Alaska Native, 0.0% Native Hawaiian/Other Pacific Islander, 1.5% Two or more races, 74.2% Hispanic of any race; Average household size: 3.51; Median age: 27.7; Age under 18: 34.5%; Age 65 and over: 7.9%; Males per 100 females: 121.5

School District(s)

El Nido Elementary (KG-08)
2012-13 Enrollment: 192. . . . . (209) 385-8420

Housing: Homeownership rate: 51.1%; Homeowner vacancy rate: 4.0%; Rental vacancy rate: 2.0%

FRANKLIN (CDP). Covers a land area of 2.010 square miles and a water area of 0 square miles. Located at 37.33° N. Lat; 120.53° W. Long.

Population: 6,149; Growth (since 2000): n/a; Density: 3,059.6 persons per square mile; Race: 56.2% White, 4.4% Black/African American, 15.1% Asian, 1.3% American Indian/Alaska Native, 0.2% Native Hawaiian/Other Pacific Islander, 5.4% Two or more races, 52.9% Hispanic of any race; Average household size: 3.66; Median age: 27.0; Age under 18: 35.2%; Age 65 and over: 7.2%; Males per 100 females: 100.2; Marriage status: 39.1% never married, 48.6% now married, 2.3% separated, 4.3% widowed, 7.9% divorced; Foreign born: 25.0%; Speak English only: 52.7%; With disability: 16.4%; Veterans: 4.9%; Ancestry: 5.7% German, 4.8% Portuguese, 3.4% Irish, 2.2% Arab, 2.1% American

Employment: 6.8% management, business, and financial, 0.8% computer, engineering, and science, 6.2% education, legal, community service, arts, and media, 3.1% healthcare practitioners, 12.8% service, 24.3% sales and office, 19.7% natural resources, construction, and maintenance, 26.2% production, transportation, and material moving

Income: Per capita: $15,587; Median household: $41,442; Average household: $51,913; Households with income of $100,000 or more: 13.7%; Poverty rate: 30.2%

Educational Attainment: High school diploma or higher: 61.4%; Bachelor's degree or higher: 5.6%; Graduate/professional degree or higher: 1.0%

Housing: Homeownership rate: 61.5%; Median home value: $109,200; Median year structure built: 1984; Homeowner vacancy rate: 4.8%; Median gross rent: $961 per month; Rental vacancy rate: 6.9%

Health Insurance: 81.1% have insurance; 44.0% have private insurance; 42.5% have public insurance; 18.9% do not have insurance; 7.8% of children under 18 do not have insurance

Transportation: Commute: 94.0% car, 0.0% public transportation, 0.0% walk, 5.1% work from home; Median travel time to work: 21.3 minutes

GUSTINE (city). Covers a land area of 1.551 square miles and a water area of 0 square miles. Located at 37.25° N. Lat; 120.99° W. Long. Elevation is 98 feet.

History: Incorporated 1915.

Population: 5,520; Growth (since 2000): 17.5%; Density: 3,559.1 persons per square mile; Race: 70.2% White, 1.3% Black/African American, 1.7% Asian, 1.0% American Indian/Alaska Native, 0.1% Native Hawaiian/Other Pacific Islander, 4.1% Two or more races, 50.2% Hispanic of any race; Average household size: 2.94; Median age: 35.3; Age under 18: 28.6%; Age 65 and over: 14.3%; Males per 100 females: 98.3; Marriage status: 27.6% never married, 53.1% now married, 0.3% separated, 7.0% widowed, 12.3% divorced; Foreign born: 26.2%; Speak English only: 49.5%; With disability: 16.3%; Veterans: 9.2%; Ancestry: 21.3% Portuguese, 10.8% German, 3.3% Italian, 2.8% Irish, 2.1% English

Employment: 7.2% management, business, and financial, 1.5% computer, engineering, and science, 2.5% education, legal, community service, arts, and media, 2.2% healthcare practitioners, 20.1% service, 32.4% sales and office, 15.7% natural resources, construction, and maintenance, 18.4% production, transportation, and material moving

Income: Per capita: $19,615; Median household: $33,947; Average household: $52,691; Households with income of $100,000 or more: 13.5%; Poverty rate: 22.0%

Educational Attainment: High school diploma or higher: 68.2%; Bachelor's degree or higher: 6.3%; Graduate/professional degree or higher: 3.2%

School District(s)

Gustine Unified (KG-12)
2012-13 Enrollment: 1,759 . . . . (209) 854-3784

Housing: Homeownership rate: 63.7%; Median home value: $103,600; Median year structure built: 1970; Homeowner vacancy rate: 3.4%; Median gross rent: $925 per month; Rental vacancy rate: 12.2%

Health Insurance: 78.5% have insurance; 46.1% have private insurance; 43.0% have public insurance; 21.5% do not have insurance; 11.5% of children under 18 do not have insurance

Safety: Violent crime rate: 69.0 per 10,000 population; Property crime rate: 221.0 per 10,000 population

Transportation: Commute: 96.5% car, 0.0% public transportation, 2.8% walk, 0.7% work from home; Median travel time to work: 28.4 minutes

Additional Information Contacts

City of Gustine. . . . . (209) 854-6471
http://www.cityofgustine.com

HILMAR-IRWIN (CDP). Covers a land area of 3.928 square miles and a water area of 0 square miles. Located at 37.40° N. Lat; 120.85° W. Long. Elevation is 92 feet.

Population: 5,197; Growth (since 2000): 8.1%; Density: 1,323.1 persons per square mile; Race: 86.1% White, 0.3% Black/African American, 1.7% Asian, 0.4% American Indian/Alaska Native, 0.0% Native Hawaiian/Other Pacific Islander, 3.0% Two or more races, 17.6% Hispanic of any race; Average household size: 2.96; Median age: 36.2; Age under 18: 26.7%; Age 65 and over: 13.7%; Males per 100 females: 96.9; Marriage status: 30.1% never married, 56.9% now married, 0.3% separated, 4.5% widowed, 8.4% divorced; Foreign born: 26.4%; Speak English only: 52.2%; With disability: 14.1%; Veterans: 5.8%; Ancestry: 52.6% Portuguese, 5.9% German, 4.4% English, 3.8% Swedish, 2.9% American

Employment: 13.2% management, business, and financial, 0.6% computer, engineering, and science, 7.1% education, legal, community service, arts, and media, 2.1% healthcare practitioners, 19.9% service, 22.7% sales and office, 13.7% natural resources, construction, and maintenance, 20.7% production, transportation, and material moving

Income: Per capita: $26,354; Median household: $51,506; Average household: $74,778; Households with income of $100,000 or more: 27.3%; Poverty rate: 8.8%

Educational Attainment: High school diploma or higher: 73.0%; Bachelor's degree or higher: 11.5%; Graduate/professional degree or higher: 3.7%

School District(s)

Hilmar Unified (KG-12)
2012-13 Enrollment: 2,242 . . . . (209) 667-5701

Housing: Homeownership rate: 73.4%; Median home value: $185,400; Median year structure built: 1985; Homeowner vacancy rate: 0.9%; Median gross rent: $1,083 per month; Rental vacancy rate: 6.8%

Health Insurance: 86.9% have insurance; 71.9% have private insurance; 25.8% have public insurance; 13.1% do not have insurance; 6.8% of children under 18 do not have insurance

Transportation: Commute: 96.6% car, 0.0% public transportation, 0.6% walk, 2.8% work from home; Median travel time to work: 23.7 minutes

LE GRAND (CDP). Covers a land area of 1.140 square miles and a water area of 0 square miles. Located at 37.23° N. Lat; 120.25° W. Long. Elevation is 253 feet.

Population: 1,659; Growth (since 2000): -5.7%; Density: 1,455.0 persons per square mile; Race: 52.4% White, 1.1% Black/African American, 1.0% Asian, 2.1% American Indian/Alaska Native, 0.1% Native Hawaiian/Other Pacific Islander, 3.6% Two or more races, 81.8% Hispanic of any race; Average household size: 3.62; Median age: 31.5; Age under 18: 32.2%; Age 65 and over: 9.8%; Males per 100 females: 99.4

School District(s)

Le Grand Union Elementary (KG-08)
2012-13 Enrollment: 421. . . . . (209) 389-4515

Le Grand Union High (09-12)
2012-13 Enrollment: 513. . . . . (209) 389-9403

Housing: Homeownership rate: 68.8%; Homeowner vacancy rate: 1.9%; Rental vacancy rate: 10.0%

LIVINGSTON (city). Covers a land area of 3.715 square miles and a water area of 0 square miles. Located at 37.39° N. Lat; 120.73° W. Long. Elevation is 131 feet.

History: Livingston developed as the trading center of a sweet potato belt.

Population: 13,058; Growth (since 2000): 24.7%; Density: 3,514.7 persons per square mile; Race: 40.3% White, 0.8% Black/African American, 17.0% Asian, 2.7% American Indian/Alaska Native, 0.1% Native Hawaiian/Other Pacific Islander, 4.2% Two or more races, 73.1% Hispanic of any race; Average household size: 4.14; Median age: 27.4; Age under 18: 32.6%; Age 65 and over: 7.0%; Males per 100 females: 102.1; Marriage status: 42.4% never married, 47.0% now married, 2.0% separated, 4.8% widowed, 5.8% divorced; Foreign born: 44.1%; Speak English only: 14.6%; With disability: 16.7%; Veterans: 3.6%; Ancestry: 2.0% American, 1.8% Portuguese, 0.9% Irish, 0.5% English, 0.3% European

Employment: 4.4% management, business, and financial, 1.3% computer, engineering, and science, 4.4% education, legal, community service, arts, and media, 1.9% healthcare practitioners, 16.2% service, 14.2% sales and office, 23.6% natural resources, construction, and maintenance, 34.0% production, transportation, and material moving

Income: Per capita: $13,387; Median household: $49,634; Average household: $55,085; Households with income of $100,000 or more: 9.4%; Poverty rate: 20.0%

Educational Attainment: High school diploma or higher: 50.4%; Bachelor's degree or higher: 8.0%; Graduate/professional degree or higher: 3.0%

School District(s)

Livingston Union Elementary (KG-08)
2012-13 Enrollment: 2,578 . . . . (209) 394-5400

Merced County Office of Education (KG-12)
2012-13 Enrollment: 1,465 . . . . (209) 381-6600

Merced Union High (09-12)
2012-13 Enrollment: 10,078 . . . . (209) 385-6412

Housing: Homeownership rate: 60.9%; Median home value: $161,900; Median year structure built: 1991; Homeowner vacancy rate: 2.1%; Median gross rent: $989 per month; Rental vacancy rate: 3.7%

Health Insurance: 77.3% have insurance; 46.6% have private insurance; 36.3% have public insurance; 22.7% do not have insurance; 6.3% of children under 18 do not have insurance

Safety: Violent crime rate: 24.1 per 10,000 population; Property crime rate: 143.2 per 10,000 population

Transportation: Commute: 89.8% car, 0.2% public transportation, 1.6% walk, 4.4% work from home; Median travel time to work: 21.1 minutes

Additional Information Contacts

City of Livingston. . . . . (209) 394-8041
http://www.livingstoncity.com

LOS BANOS (city). Covers a land area of 9.993 square miles and a water area of 0.124 square miles. Located at 37.06° N. Lat; 120.84° W. Long. Elevation is 118 feet.

History: Los Banos is located 26 miles southwest of Merced and its original Spanish spelling was Los Baños, meaning "the baths" in reference to a natural water spring that feeds the wetlands of the western San Joaquín Valley.

Population: 35,972; Growth (since 2000): 39.1%; Density: 3,599.7 persons per square mile; Race: 58.0% White, 3.8% Black/African American, 3.2% Asian, 1.4% American Indian/Alaska Native, 0.4% Native Hawaiian/Other Pacific Islander, 5.1% Two or more races, 64.9% Hispanic of any race; Average household size: 3.49; Median age: 29.8; Age under 18: 33.6%; Age 65 and over: 8.6%; Males per 100 females: 99.2; Marriage status: 35.5% never married, 53.0% now married, 3.2% separated, 4.1% widowed, 7.3% divorced; Foreign born: 26.5%; Speak English only: 47.6%; With disability: 8.8%; Veterans: 5.4%; Ancestry: 5.4% Portuguese, 4.2% Irish, 4.2% German, 3.7% Italian, 3.3% English

Employment: 5.6% management, business, and financial, 3.3% computer, engineering, and science, 4.9% education, legal, community service, arts, and media, 3.2% healthcare practitioners, 19.2% service, 23.3% sales and office, 22.0% natural resources, construction, and maintenance, 18.5% production, transportation, and material moving

Income: Per capita: $17,495; Median household: $47,117; Average household: $59,689; Households with income of $100,000 or more: 15.3%; Poverty rate: 25.0%

Educational Attainment: High school diploma or higher: 65.6%; Bachelor's degree or higher: 9.4%; Graduate/professional degree or higher: 2.6%

School District(s)

Los Banos Unified (KG-12)
2012-13 Enrollment: 9,892 . . . . (209) 826-3801
Merced County Office of Education (KG-12)
2012-13 Enrollment: 1,465 . . . . (209) 381-6600

Housing: Homeownership rate: 60.4%; Median home value: $143,500; Median year structure built: 1992; Homeowner vacancy rate: 4.1%; Median gross rent: $1,062 per month; Rental vacancy rate: 8.4%

Health Insurance: 79.7% have insurance; 47.8% have private insurance; 38.7% have public insurance; 20.3% do not have insurance; 7.9% of children under 18 do not have insurance

Hospitals: Memorial Hospital Los Banos (48 beds)

Safety: Violent crime rate: 29.5 per 10,000 population; Property crime rate: 286.8 per 10,000 population

Newspapers: Los Banos Enterprise (weekly circulation 4500)

Transportation: Commute: 96.3% car, 0.2% public transportation, 0.9% walk, 1.3% work from home; Median travel time to work: 42.1 minutes

Additional Information Contacts

City of Los Banos . . . . (209) 827-7000
http://www.losbanos.org

MCSWAIN (CDP). Covers a land area of 6.038 square miles and a water area of 0 square miles. Located at 37.31° N. Lat; 120.59° W. Long.

Population: 4,171; Growth (since 2000): n/a; Density: 690.8 persons per square mile; Race: 76.6% White, 1.3% Black/African American, 6.8% Asian, 0.8% American Indian/Alaska Native, 0.2% Native Hawaiian/Other Pacific Islander, 4.1% Two or more races, 25.9% Hispanic of any race; Average household size: 3.12; Median age: 40.5; Age under 18: 27.5%; Age 65 and over: 12.9%; Males per 100 females: 105.6; Marriage status: 22.8% never married, 66.9% now married, 1.7% separated, 4.8% widowed, 5.5% divorced; Foreign born: 14.8%; Speak English only: 71.9%; With disability: 10.5%; Veterans: 11.9%; Ancestry: 10.4% German, 9.6% English, 7.9% Irish, 7.5% Portuguese, 5.6% European

Employment: 15.1% management, business, and financial, 1.1% computer, engineering, and science, 11.7% education, legal, community service, arts, and media, 6.8% healthcare practitioners, 24.5% service, 17.0% sales and office, 11.4% natural resources, construction, and maintenance, 12.2% production, transportation, and material moving

Income: Per capita: $33,139; Median household: $98,289; Average household: $106,803; Households with income of $100,000 or more: 48.1%; Poverty rate: 5.8%

Educational Attainment: High school diploma or higher: 89.2%; Bachelor's degree or higher: 26.4%; Graduate/professional degree or higher: 10.1%

Housing: Homeownership rate: 89.7%; Median home value: $353,200; Median year structure built: 1993; Homeowner vacancy rate: 2.0%; Median gross rent: $1,101 per month; Rental vacancy rate: 7.2%

Health Insurance: 91.4% have insurance; 76.0% have private insurance; 26.6% have public insurance; 8.6% do not have insurance; 2.4% of children under 18 do not have insurance

Transportation: Commute: 94.1% car, 0.0% public transportation, 0.6% walk, 4.3% work from home; Median travel time to work: 31.6 minutes

MERCED (city). County seat. Covers a land area of 23.316 square miles and a water area of 0 square miles. Located at 37.31° N. Lat; 120.48° W. Long. Elevation is 171 feet.

History: Merced developed as the gateway to Yosemite National Park, and as the seat of Merced County.

Population: 78,958; Growth (since 2000): 23.6%; Density: 3,386.4 persons per square mile; Race: 52.2% White, 6.3% Black/African American, 11.8% Asian, 1.5% American Indian/Alaska Native, 0.2% Native Hawaiian/Other Pacific Islander, 5.5% Two or more races, 49.6% Hispanic of any race; Average household size: 3.13; Median age: 28.1; Age under 18: 31.8%; Age 65 and over: 8.8%; Males per 100 females: 96.3; Marriage status: 39.7% never married, 44.3% now married, 2.8% separated, 5.4% widowed, 10.5% divorced; Foreign born: 21.3%; Speak English only: 53.5%; With disability: 19.5%; Veterans: 6.1%; Ancestry: 3.9% German, 3.7% Irish, 3.6% English, 2.4% American, 2.1% Portuguese

Employment: 7.6% management, business, and financial, 2.1% computer, engineering, and science, 12.0% education, legal, community service, arts, and media, 4.5% healthcare practitioners, 21.8% service, 23.8% sales and office, 13.8% natural resources, construction, and maintenance, 14.5% production, transportation, and material moving

Income: Per capita: $16,876; Median household: $37,822; Average household: $52,560; Households with income of $100,000 or more: 12.9%; Poverty rate: 30.0%

Educational Attainment: High school diploma or higher: 71.7%; Bachelor's degree or higher: 15.7%; Graduate/professional degree or higher: 5.4%

School District(s)

Mcswain Union Elementary (KG-08)
2012-13 Enrollment: 858. . . . . (209) 354-2700
Merced City Elementary (KG-08)
2012-13 Enrollment: 10,671 . . . . (209) 385-6600
Merced County Office of Education (KG-12)
2012-13 Enrollment: 1,465 . . . . (209) 381-6600
Merced County Rop
2012-13 Enrollment: n/a . . . . (209) 381-6600
Merced Union High (09-12)
2012-13 Enrollment: 10,078 . . . . (209) 385-6412
Plainsburg Union Elementary (KG-08)
2012-13 Enrollment: 133. . . . . (209) 389-4707
Weaver Union (KG-08)
2012-13 Enrollment: 2,630 . . . . (209) 723-7606

Four-year College(s)

University of California-Merced (Public)
Fall 2013 Enrollment: 6,195 . . . . (209) 228-4400
2013-14 Tuition: In-state $13,160; Out-of-state $36,038

Two-year College(s)

Merced College (Public)
Fall 2013 Enrollment: 10,205 . . . . (209) 384-6000
2013-14 Tuition: In-state $1,138; Out-of-state $5,890

Vocational/Technical School(s)

Milan Institute-Merced (Private, For-profit)
Fall 2013 Enrollment: 148 . . . . (209) 230-9420
2013-14 Tuition: $16,789
Sierra College of Beauty (Private, For-profit)
Fall 2013 Enrollment: 181 . . . . (209) 723-2989
2013-14 Tuition: $9,100

Housing: Homeownership rate: 42.7%; Median home value: $137,900; Median year structure built: 1981; Homeowner vacancy rate: 3.5%; Median gross rent: $819 per month; Rental vacancy rate: 8.5%

Health Insurance: 83.1% have insurance; 46.9% have private insurance; 44.7% have public insurance; 16.9% do not have insurance; 5.0% of children under 18 do not have insurance

Hospitals: Mercy Medical Center (174 beds)

Safety: Violent crime rate: 68.4 per 10,000 population; Property crime rate: 325.5 per 10,000 population

Newspapers: Merced Sun-Star (daily circulation 19400)

Transportation: Commute: 87.2% car, 0.9% public transportation, 2.2% walk, 3.7% work from home; Median travel time to work: 22.4 minutes; Amtrak: Train service available.

Airports: Merced Regional/Macready Field (commercial service–non-primary)

Additional Information Contacts

City of Merced . . . . (209) 385-6834
http://www.cityofmerced.org

PLANADA (CDP). Covers a land area of 1.577 square miles and a water area of 0 square miles. Located at 37.29° N. Lat; 120.32° W. Long. Elevation is 226 feet.

History: Planada was called Geneva when it was platted in 1912 as a model town.

Population: 4,584; Growth (since 2000): 4.9%; Density: 2,906.6 persons per square mile; Race: 36.7% White, 0.5% Black/African American, 1.0% Asian, 0.5% American Indian/Alaska Native, 0.0% Native Hawaiian/Other Pacific Islander, 1.9% Two or more races, 94.8% Hispanic of any race; Average household size: 4.11; Median age: 27.1; Age under 18: 33.9%; Age 65 and over: 8.0%; Males per 100 females: 108.0; Marriage status: 40.8% never married, 50.3% now married, 3.8% separated, 4.3% widowed, 4.6% divorced; Foreign born: 46.2%; Speak English only: 14.3%; With disability: 20.2%; Veterans: 3.6%; Ancestry: 0.9% English, 0.5% African, 0.4% German, 0.4% Irish, 0.3% Other Arab

Employment: 7.9% management, business, and financial, 1.0% computer, engineering, and science, 8.7% education, legal, community service, arts, and media, 1.4% healthcare practitioners, 16.1% service, 15.5% sales and office, 30.4% natural resources, construction, and maintenance, 19.0% production, transportation, and material moving

Income: Per capita: $12,928; Median household: $35,017; Average household: $46,226; Households with income of $100,000 or more: 11.3%; Poverty rate: 27.1%

Educational Attainment: High school diploma or higher: 44.3%; Bachelor's degree or higher: 10.0%; Graduate/professional degree or higher: 2.5%

School District(s)

Le Grand Union High (09-12)
2012-13 Enrollment: 513. . . . . (209) 389-9403
Planada Elementary (KG-08)
2012-13 Enrollment: 764. . . . . (209) 382-0756

Housing: Homeownership rate: 58.2%; Median home value: $94,700; Median year structure built: 1978; Homeowner vacancy rate: 3.4%; Median gross rent: $645 per month; Rental vacancy rate: 7.3%

Health Insurance: 74.2% have insurance; 27.7% have private insurance; 50.2% have public insurance; 25.8% do not have insurance; 6.9% of children under 18 do not have insurance

Transportation: Commute: 86.7% car, 0.0% public transportation, 2.4% walk, 1.2% work from home; Median travel time to work: 29.2 minutes

SANTA NELLA (CDP). Covers a land area of 4.561 square miles and a water area of 0 square miles. Located at 37.10° N. Lat; 121.02° W. Long. Elevation is 154 feet.

Population: 1,380; Growth (since 2000): n/a; Density: 302.6 persons per square mile; Race: 60.3% White, 1.6% Black/African American, 2.2% Asian, 1.8% American Indian/Alaska Native, 0.0% Native Hawaiian/Other Pacific Islander, 2.7% Two or more races, 70.1% Hispanic of any race; Average household size: 3.37; Median age: 30.4; Age under 18: 33.9%; Age 65 and over: 6.7%; Males per 100 females: 120.1

School District(s)

Gustine Unified (KG-12)
2012-13 Enrollment: 1,759 . . . . (209) 854-3784

Housing: Homeownership rate: 55.2%; Homeowner vacancy rate: 14.4%; Rental vacancy rate: 8.0%

SNELLING (CDP). Covers a land area of 0.540 square miles and a water area of 0 square miles. Located at 37.52° N. Lat; 120.44° W. Long. Elevation is 256 feet.

Population: 231; Growth (since 2000): n/a; Density: 427.5 persons per square mile; Race: 89.2% White, 0.0% Black/African American, 2.6% Asian, 1.3% American Indian/Alaska Native, 0.0% Native Hawaiian/Other Pacific Islander, 1.3% Two or more races, 14.3% Hispanic of any race; Average household size: 2.46; Median age: 40.3; Age under 18: 26.4%; Age 65 and over: 15.2%; Males per 100 females: 110.0

School District(s)

Merced River Union Elementary (KG-08)
2012-13 Enrollment: 172. . . . . (209) 358-5679
Snelling-Merced Falls Union Elementary (KG-08)
2012-13 Enrollment: 104. . . . . (209) 563-6414

Housing: Homeownership rate: 52.2%; Homeowner vacancy rate: 3.9%; Rental vacancy rate: 6.1%

SOUTH DOS PALOS (CDP). Covers a land area of 1.535 square miles and a water area of 0 square miles. Located at 36.97° N. Lat; 120.65° W. Long. Elevation is 118 feet.

Population: 1,620; Growth (since 2000): 17.0%; Density: 1,055.6 persons per square mile; Race: 49.9% White, 8.3% Black/African American, 2.2% Asian, 1.3% American Indian/Alaska Native, 0.6% Native Hawaiian/Other Pacific Islander, 3.5% Two or more races, 77.9% Hispanic of any race; Average household size: 3.80; Median age: 25.8; Age under 18: 37.1%; Age 65 and over: 6.4%; Males per 100 females: 100.5

School District(s)

Dos Palos Oro Loma Joint Unified (KG-12)
2012-13 Enrollment: 2,265 . . . . (209) 392-0200

Housing: Homeownership rate: 56.8%; Homeowner vacancy rate: 3.5%; Rental vacancy rate: 10.7%

STEVINSON (CDP). Covers a land area of 1.130 square miles and a water area of 0 square miles. Located at 37.32° N. Lat; 120.85° W. Long. Elevation is 85 feet.

Population: 313; Growth (since 2000): n/a; Density: 276.9 persons per square mile; Race: 72.8% White, 1.3% Black/African American, 0.0% Asian, 0.0% American Indian/Alaska Native, 0.0% Native Hawaiian/Other Pacific Islander, 2.6% Two or more races, 42.5% Hispanic of any race; Average household size: 3.40; Median age: 28.9; Age under 18: 30.4%; Age 65 and over: 8.3%; Males per 100 females: 118.9

School District(s)

Hilmar Unified (KG-12)
2012-13 Enrollment: 2,242 . . . . (209) 667-5701

Housing: Homeownership rate: 56.5%; Homeowner vacancy rate: 0.0%; Rental vacancy rate: 4.8%

TUTTLE (CDP). Covers a land area of 1.759 square miles and a water area of 0 square miles. Located at 37.30° N. Lat; 120.38° W. Long. Elevation is 207 feet.

Population: 103; Growth (since 2000): n/a; Density: 58.6 persons per square mile; Race: 74.8% White, 5.8% Black/African American, 5.8% Asian, 0.0% American Indian/Alaska Native, 0.0% Native Hawaiian/Other Pacific Islander, 4.9% Two or more races, 30.1% Hispanic of any race; Average household size: 2.94; Median age: 43.5; Age under 18: 20.4%; Age 65 and over: 17.5%; Males per 100 females: 128.9

Housing: Homeownership rate: 68.6%; Homeowner vacancy rate: 0.0%; Rental vacancy rate: 14.3%

VOLTA (CDP). Covers a land area of 4.370 square miles and a water area of 0.064 square miles. Located at 37.08° N. Lat; 120.91° W. Long. Elevation is 105 feet.

Population: 246; Growth (since 2000): n/a; Density: 56.3 persons per square mile; Race: 81.7% White, 2.8% Black/African American, 0.4% Asian, 0.0% American Indian/Alaska Native, 1.6% Native Hawaiian/Other Pacific Islander, 1.6% Two or more races, 53.7% Hispanic of any race; Average household size: 2.96; Median age: 36.6; Age under 18: 24.0%; Age 65 and over: 11.0%; Males per 100 females: 101.6

Housing: Homeownership rate: 51.8%; Homeowner vacancy rate: 2.2%; Rental vacancy rate: 11.1%

WINTON (CDP). Covers a land area of 3.041 square miles and a water area of 0 square miles. Located at 37.39° N. Lat; 120.62° W. Long. Elevation is 177 feet.

Population: 10,613; Growth (since 2000): 20.2%; Density: 3,490.1 persons per square mile; Race: 53.7% White, 1.6% Black/African American, 6.6% Asian, 1.3% American Indian/Alaska Native, 0.1% Native Hawaiian/Other Pacific Islander, 4.1% Two or more races, 71.3% Hispanic of any race; Average household size: 3.90; Median age: 25.6; Age under 18: 37.1%; Age 65 and over: 6.3%; Males per 100 females: 100.9; Marriage status: 39.0% never married, 50.7% now married, 3.8% separated, 2.7% widowed, 7.6% divorced; Foreign born: 33.4%; Speak English only: 27.3%; With disability: 16.2%; Veterans: 5.2%; Ancestry: 4.7% German, 1.8% English, 1.7% Irish, 1.3% American, 1.2% Portuguese

Employment: 3.6% management, business, and financial, 1.1% computer, engineering, and science, 4.7% education, legal, community service, arts, and media, 2.0% healthcare practitioners, 17.2% service, 19.0% sales and office, 26.5% natural resources, construction, and maintenance, 25.8% production, transportation, and material moving

Income: Per capita: $13,005; Median household: $39,718; Average household: $47,734; Households with income of $100,000 or more: 8.7%; Poverty rate: 25.5%

Educational Attainment: High school diploma or higher: 48.7%; Bachelor's degree or higher: 5.0%; Graduate/professional degree or higher: 1.3%

School District(s)

Merced River Union Elementary (KG-08)
2012-13 Enrollment: 172. . . . . (209) 358-5679

Winton Elementary (KG-08)
2012-13 Enrollment: 1,870 . . . . (209) 357-6175

Housing: Homeownership rate: 53.4%; Median home value: $99,700; Median year structure built: 1983; Homeowner vacancy rate: 4.3%; Median gross rent: $860 per month; Rental vacancy rate: 10.4%

Health Insurance: 76.7% have insurance; 37.4% have private insurance; 46.0% have public insurance; 23.3% do not have insurance; 9.2% of children under 18 do not have insurance

Newspapers: Mid-Valley Publications (weekly circulation 35000)

Transportation: Commute: 90.1% car, 0.0% public transportation, 0.5% walk, 2.8% work from home; Median travel time to work: 27.1 minutes

Modoc County

Located in northeastern California; bounded on the north by Oregon, and on the east by Nevada; high plateau area, rising to Eagle Peak in the Warner Mountains on the east; drained by the Pit River; includes part of Goose Lake, Surprise Valley, and pa rt of Modoc National Forest. Covers a land area of 3,917.770 square miles, a water area of 285.629 square miles, and is located in the Pacific Time Zone at 41.59° N. Lat., 120.72° W. Long. The county was founded in 1874. County seat is Alturas.

Weather Station: Alturas — Elevation: 4,399 feet

	Jan	Feb	Mar	Apr	May	Jun	Jul	Aug	Sep	Oct	Nov	Dec
High	44	47	53	60	69	78	89	88	79	67	51	42
Low	18	20	25	28	34	40	44	42	35	27	22	18
Precip	1.3	1.3	1.5	1.2	1.4	0.8	0.3	0.3	0.5	0.9	1.6	1.4
Snow	4.5	2.8	2.4	0.6	0.5	tr	tr	0.0	0.0	0.1	3.2	3.3

High and Low temperatures in degrees Fahrenheit; Precipitation and Snow in inches

Weather Station: Cedarville — Elevation: 4,669 feet

	Jan	Feb	Mar	Apr	May	Jun	Jul	Aug	Sep	Oct	Nov	Dec
High	41	44	51	57	67	76	87	86	78	65	49	40
Low	21	24	29	33	41	47	54	52	43	34	26	20
Precip	1.6	1.3	1.4	1.2	1.2	0.7	0.2	0.3	0.4	0.8	1.8	1.7
Snow	3.4	2.4	1.1	0.7	tr	tr	0.0	0.0	tr	0.1	1.8	3.7

High and Low temperatures in degrees Fahrenheit; Precipitation and Snow in inches

Weather Station: Fort Bidwell — Elevation: 4,500 feet

	Jan	Feb	Mar	Apr	May	Jun	Jul	Aug	Sep	Oct	Nov	Dec
High	40	45	52	59	67	76	85	85	77	65	48	39
Low	22	24	29	33	39	45	51	49	43	34	27	21
Precip	2.5	2.2	2.0	1.7	1.3	0.9	0.3	0.3	0.5	1.1	2.5	2.9
Snow	13.6	9.5	6.9	3.5	0.4	tr	0.0	0.0	tr	0.6	7.2	13.1

High and Low temperatures in degrees Fahrenheit; Precipitation and Snow in inches

Weather Station: Jess Valley — Elevation: 5,399 feet

	Jan	Feb	Mar	Apr	May	Jun	Jul	Aug	Sep	Oct	Nov	Dec
High	42	44	49	55	64	73	83	83	76	64	49	41
Low	21	22	25	28	35	41	47	46	40	32	25	20
Precip	1.9	1.6	2.0	2.1	2.6	1.5	0.5	0.5	0.8	1.2	2.2	2.1
Snow	12.0	10.0	11.9	10.1	4.2	0.4	0.1	0.0	0.2	2.5	10.8	13.1

High and Low temperatures in degrees Fahrenheit; Precipitation and Snow in inches

Population: 9,686; Growth (since 2000): 2.5%; Density: 2.5 persons per square mile; Race: 83.5% White, 0.8% Black/African American, 0.8% Asian, 3.8% American Indian/Alaska Native, 0.2% Native Hawaiian/Other Pacific Islander, 3.8% two or more races, 13.9% Hispanic of any race; Average household size: 2.30; Median age: 46.1; Age under 18: 21.9%; Age 65 and over: 19.7%; Males per 100 females: 101.5; Marriage status: 24.2% never married, 55.2% now married, 1.3% separated, 7.9% widowed, 12.8% divorced; Foreign born: 7.1%; Speak English only: 87.2%; With disability: 21.1%; Veterans: 13.5%; Ancestry: 25.7% German, 22.0% Irish, 13.7% English, 4.9% French, 4.4% American

Religion: Six largest groups: 6.3% Catholicism, 3.6% Latter-day Saints, 2.4% Baptist, 1.1% Presbyterian-Reformed, 0.9% Adventist, 0.4% Pentecostal

Economy: Unemployment rate: 8.0%; Leading industries: 18.3% retail trade; 12.2% construction; 12.2% accommodation and food services; Farms: 437 totaling 523,522 acres; Company size: 0 employ 1,000 or more persons, 0 employ 500 to 999 persons, 1 employs 100 to 499 persons, 163 employ less than 100 persons; Business ownership: n/a women-owned, n/a Black-owned, n/a Hispanic-owned, n/a Asian-owned

Employment: 17.7% management, business, and financial, 3.6% computer, engineering, and science, 13.4% education, legal, community service, arts, and media, 3.5% healthcare practitioners, 22.3% service, 17.5% sales and office, 12.9% natural resources, construction, and maintenance, 9.1% production, transportation, and material moving

Income: Per capita: $21,200; Median household: $36,212; Average household: $48,765; Households with income of $100,000 or more: 11.0%; Poverty rate: 21.0%

Educational Attainment: High school diploma or higher: 84.8%; Bachelor's degree or higher: 18.7%; Graduate/professional degree or higher: 5.1%

Housing: Homeownership rate: 68.6%; Median home value: $164,100; Median year structure built: 1971; Homeowner vacancy rate: 2.8%; Median gross rent: $633 per month; Rental vacancy rate: 8.1%

Vital Statistics: Birth rate: 91.8 per 10,000 population; Death rate: 111.5 per 10,000 population; Age-adjusted cancer mortality rate: 168.9 deaths per 100,000 population

Health Insurance: 81.8% have insurance; 52.9% have private insurance; 45.9% have public insurance; 18.2% do not have insurance; 12.9% of children under 18 do not have insurance

Health Care: Physicians: 3.2 per 10,000 population; Hospital beds: 95.8 per 10,000 population; Hospital admissions: 525.4 per 10,000 population

Transportation: Commute: 75.9% car, 0.5% public transportation, 7.7% walk, 12.1% work from home; Median travel time to work: 16.9 minutes

Presidential Election: 27.9% Obama, 69.7% Romney (2012)

National and State Parks: Clear Lake National Wildlife Refuge; Long Bell State Game Refuge 1N; Modoc National Forest; Modoc National Wildlife Refuge; World War II Valor in the Pacific National Monument; Crane Mountain National Recreation Trail

Additional Information Contacts

Modoc Government. . . . . (530) 233-6426
http://www.co.modoc.ca.us

Modoc County Communities

ADIN (CDP). Covers a land area of 3.437 square miles and a water area of 0.006 square miles. Located at 41.20° N. Lat; 120.96° W. Long. Elevation is 4,203 feet.

Population: 272; Growth (since 2000): n/a; Density: 79.1 persons per square mile; Race: 88.2% White, 0.7% Black/African American, 0.0% Asian, 2.9% American Indian/Alaska Native, 0.0% Native Hawaiian/Other Pacific Islander, 4.8% Two or more races, 11.8% Hispanic of any race; Average household size: 2.17; Median age: 47.3; Age under 18: 21.0%; Age 65 and over: 18.8%; Males per 100 females: 91.5

Housing: Homeownership rate: 62.1%; Homeowner vacancy rate: 1.3%; Rental vacancy rate: 2.1%

ALTURAS (city). County seat. Covers a land area of 2.435 square miles and a water area of 0.014 square miles. Located at 41.49° N. Lat; 120.55° W. Long. Elevation is 4,370 feet.

History: Alturas began as a center for ranchers who raised stock, potatoes, and alfalfa. Until 1874 the town was called Dorris Bridge for its first settler, James Dorris, who built a wooden bridge across a creek in 1869. The citizens of Dorris Bridge forced the creation of Modoc County, and Alturas became the county seat.

Population: 2,827; Growth (since 2000): -2.2%; Density: 1,161.1 persons per square mile; Race: 86.0% White, 0.5% Black/African American, 1.6% Asian, 2.9% American Indian/Alaska Native, 0.2% Native Hawaiian/Other Pacific Islander, 4.6% Two or more races, 12.3% Hispanic of any race; Average household size: 2.27; Median age: 39.9; Age under 18: 24.8%; Age 65 and over: 15.3%; Males per 100 females: 92.7; Marriage status: 30.6% never married, 47.1% now married, 0.4% separated, 5.7% widowed, 16.5% divorced; Foreign born: 9.1%; Speak English only: 87.7%; With disability: 21.2%; Veterans: 14.9%; Ancestry: 30.6% German, 20.1% Irish, 15.3% English, 6.5% Dutch, 5.3% American

Employment: 6.4% management, business, and financial, 3.3% computer, engineering, and science, 10.9% education, legal, community service, arts, and media, 2.5% healthcare practitioners, 34.3% service, 26.4% sales and office, 11.6% natural resources, construction, and maintenance, 4.6% production, transportation, and material moving

Income: Per capita: $20,506; Median household: $27,500; Average household: $44,555; Households with income of $100,000 or more: 8.6%; Poverty rate: 29.3%

Educational Attainment: High school diploma or higher: 86.2%; Bachelor's degree or higher: 14.8%; Graduate/professional degree or higher: 2.2%

School District(s)

Modoc County Office of Education (PK-12)
2012-13 Enrollment: 54. . . . . (530) 233-7101
Modoc County Rop
2012-13 Enrollment: n/a . . . . (530) 233-7102
Modoc Joint Unified (KG-12)
2012-13 Enrollment: 793. . . . . (530) 233-7201

Housing: Homeownership rate: 55.8%; Median home value: $135,400; Median year structure built: 1959; Homeowner vacancy rate: 2.8%; Median gross rent: $631 per month; Rental vacancy rate: 7.8%

Health Insurance: 84.2% have insurance; 47.4% have private insurance; 51.1% have public insurance; 15.8% do not have insurance; 0.0% of children under 18 do not have insurance

Hospitals: Modoc Medical Center

Safety: Violent crime rate: 104.4 per 10,000 population; Property crime rate: 264.8 per 10,000 population

Newspapers: Modoc County Record (weekly circulation 4300)

Transportation: Commute: 75.8% car, 0.0% public transportation, 12.9% walk, 4.2% work from home; Median travel time to work: 9.3 minutes

Airports: California Pines (general aviation)

Additional Information Contacts

City of Alturas . . . . (530) 233-2512
http://www.cityofalturas.org

CALIFORNIA PINES (CDP). Covers a land area of 7.427 square miles and a water area of 0.141 square miles. Located at 41.41° N. Lat; 120.67° W. Long. Elevation is 4,406 feet.

Population: 520; Growth (since 2000): n/a; Density: 70.0 persons per square mile; Race: 80.0% White, 2.1% Black/African American, 1.2% Asian, 3.1% American Indian/Alaska Native, 0.4% Native Hawaiian/Other Pacific Islander, 6.9% Two or more races, 16.0% Hispanic of any race; Average household size: 2.41; Median age: 47.2; Age under 18: 24.8%; Age 65 and over: 20.2%; Males per 100 females: 108.8

Housing: Homeownership rate: 84.7%; Homeowner vacancy rate: 3.7%; Rental vacancy rate: 10.8%

CANBY (CDP). Covers a land area of 2.268 square miles and a water area of 0.041 square miles. Located at 41.45° N. Lat; 120.89° W. Long. Elevation is 4,314 feet.

Population: 315; Growth (since 2000): n/a; Density: 138.9 persons per square mile; Race: 92.7% White, 0.6% Black/African American, 0.3% Asian, 2.2% American Indian/Alaska Native, 0.0% Native Hawaiian/Other Pacific Islander, 1.3% Two or more races, 7.6% Hispanic of any race; Average household size: 2.48; Median age: 36.2; Age under 18: 27.6%; Age 65 and over: 15.9%; Males per 100 females: 85.3

School District(s)

Modoc County Office of Education (PK-12)
2012-13 Enrollment: 54. . . . . (530) 233-7101

Housing: Homeownership rate: 54.9%; Homeowner vacancy rate: 2.9%; Rental vacancy rate: 12.5%

CEDARVILLE (CDP). Covers a land area of 5.441 square miles and a water area of 0.004 square miles. Located at 41.53° N. Lat; 120.17° W. Long. Elevation is 4,652 feet.

Population: 514; Growth (since 2000): n/a; Density: 94.5 persons per square mile; Race: 82.1% White, 0.2% Black/African American, 0.0% Asian, 2.9% American Indian/Alaska Native, 0.0% Native Hawaiian/Other Pacific Islander, 3.3% Two or more races, 16.7% Hispanic of any race; Average household size: 2.07; Median age: 49.5; Age under 18: 18.3%; Age 65 and over: 26.5%; Males per 100 females: 89.0

School District(s)

Surprise Valley Joint Unified (KG-12)
2012-13 Enrollment: 127. . . . . (530) 279-6141

Housing: Homeownership rate: 61.6%; Homeowner vacancy rate: 1.3%; Rental vacancy rate: 12.5%

Hospitals: Surprise Valley Community Hospital (26 beds)

DAPHNEDALE PARK (CDP). Covers a land area of 1.331 square miles and a water area of 0.002 square miles. Located at 41.51° N. Lat; 120.55° W. Long. Elevation is 4,449 feet.

Population: 184; Growth (since 2000): n/a; Density: 138.3 persons per square mile; Race: 90.2% White, 1.1% Black/African American, 0.0% Asian, 3.3% American Indian/Alaska Native, 2.2% Native Hawaiian/Other Pacific Islander, 2.2% Two or more races, 9.8% Hispanic of any race; Average household size: 2.42; Median age: 45.8; Age under 18: 21.7%; Age 65 and over: 12.5%; Males per 100 females: 121.7

Housing: Homeownership rate: 72.3%; Homeowner vacancy rate: 1.8%; Rental vacancy rate: 4.5%

DAVIS CREEK (unincorporated postal area)

ZCTA: 96108

Covers a land area of 198.034 square miles and a water area of 1.489 square miles. Located at 41.77° N. Lat; 120.43° W. Long. Elevation is 4,846 feet.

Population: 122; Growth (since 2000): 34.1%; Density: 0.6 persons per square mile; Race: 91.8% White, 0.0% Black/African American, 0.0% Asian, 3.3% American Indian/Alaska Native, 0.0% Native Hawaiian/Other Pacific Islander, 2.5% Two or more races, 2.5% Hispanic of any race; Average household size: 2.14; Median age: 57.5; Age under 18: 13.9%; Age 65 and over: 33.6%; Males per 100 females: 110.3

Housing: Homeownership rate: 77.2%; Homeowner vacancy rate: 8.2%; Rental vacancy rate: 13.3%

EAGLEVILLE (CDP). Covers a land area of 0.970 square miles and a water area of 0 square miles. Located at 41.32° N. Lat; 120.11° W. Long. Elevation is 4,642 feet.

Population: 59; Growth (since 2000): n/a; Density: 60.8 persons per square mile; Race: 98.3% White, 0.0% Black/African American, 0.0% Asian, 0.0% American Indian/Alaska Native, 0.0% Native Hawaiian/Other Pacific Islander, 0.0% Two or more races, 3.4% Hispanic of any race; Average household size: 2.03; Median age: 56.6; Age under 18: 13.6%; Age 65 and over: 25.4%; Males per 100 females: 126.9

Housing: Homeownership rate: 72.4%; Homeowner vacancy rate: 0.0%; Rental vacancy rate: 0.0%

FORT BIDWELL (CDP). Covers a land area of 3.200 square miles and a water area of 0.017 square miles. Located at 41.86° N. Lat; 120.16° W. Long. Elevation is 4,564 feet.

Population: 173; Growth (since 2000): n/a; Density: 54.1 persons per square mile; Race: 43.4% White, 1.2% Black/African American, 0.0% Asian, 43.9% American Indian/Alaska Native, 0.0% Native Hawaiian/Other Pacific Islander, 5.8% Two or more races, 13.3% Hispanic of any race; Average household size: 2.19; Median age: 41.5; Age under 18: 20.2%; Age 65 and over: 18.5%; Males per 100 females: 80.2

Housing: Homeownership rate: 56.9%; Homeowner vacancy rate: 14.5%; Rental vacancy rate: 12.8%

LAKE CITY (CDP). Covers a land area of 5.817 square miles and a water area of 0.003 square miles. Located at 41.65° N. Lat; 120.22° W. Long. Elevation is 4,626 feet.

Population: 61; Growth (since 2000): n/a; Density: 10.5 persons per square mile; Race: 95.1% White, 0.0% Black/African American, 0.0% Asian, 0.0% American Indian/Alaska Native, 0.0% Native Hawaiian/Other Pacific Islander, 4.9% Two or more races, 0.0% Hispanic of any race; Average household size: 1.79; Median age: 62.2; Age under 18: 13.1%; Age 65 and over: 32.8%; Males per 100 females: 90.6

Housing: Homeownership rate: 91.2%; Homeowner vacancy rate: 2.9%; Rental vacancy rate: 25.0%

LIKELY (CDP). Covers a land area of 1.329 square miles and a water area of 0.005 square miles. Located at 41.23° N. Lat; 120.50° W. Long. Elevation is 4,449 feet.

Population: 63; Growth (since 2000): n/a; Density: 47.4 persons per square mile; Race: 90.5% White, 0.0% Black/African American, 0.0% Asian, 7.9% American Indian/Alaska Native, 0.0% Native Hawaiian/Other Pacific Islander, 1.6% Two or more races, 9.5% Hispanic of any race; Average household size: 1.85; Median age: 59.1; Age under 18: 7.9%; Age 65 and over: 39.7%; Males per 100 females: 103.2

School District(s)

Modoc Joint Unified (KG-12)
2012-13 Enrollment: 793. . . . . (530) 233-7201

Housing: Homeownership rate: 85.3%; Homeowner vacancy rate: 0.0%; Rental vacancy rate: 37.5%

NEW PINE CREEK (CDP). Covers a land area of 2.285 square miles and a water area of 0 square miles. Located at 41.99° N. Lat; 120.30° W. Long. Elevation is 4,849 feet.
Population: 98; Growth (since 2000): n/a; Density: 42.9 persons per square mile; Race: 90.8% White, 0.0% Black/African American, 0.0% Asian, 0.0% American Indian/Alaska Native, 1.0% Native Hawaiian/Other Pacific Islander, 8.2% Two or more races, 4.1% Hispanic of any race; Average household size: 1.85; Median age: 55.5; Age under 18: 10.2%; Age 65 and over: 31.6%; Males per 100 females: 122.7

School District(s)

Modoc Joint Unified (KG-12)
2012-13 Enrollment: 793. . . . . (530) 233-7201
Housing: Homeownership rate: 67.9%; Homeowner vacancy rate: 2.7%; Rental vacancy rate: 10.5%

NEWELL (CDP). Covers a land area of 2.407 square miles and a water area of 0.006 square miles. Located at 41.89° N. Lat; 121.36° W. Long. Elevation is 4,045 feet.
Population: 449; Growth (since 2000): n/a; Density: 186.5 persons per square mile; Race: 44.3% White, 0.4% Black/African American, 0.2% Asian, 5.1% American Indian/Alaska Native, 1.1% Native Hawaiian/Other Pacific Islander, 5.8% Two or more races, 60.4% Hispanic of any race; Average household size: 3.30; Median age: 29.4; Age under 18: 37.2%; Age 65 and over: 8.9%; Males per 100 females: 110.8
Housing: Homeownership rate: 61.0%; Homeowner vacancy rate: 1.2%; Rental vacancy rate: 8.6%

Mono County

Located in eastern California, in the Sierra Nevada; bounded on the east by Nevada; drained by the Owens, East Walker, and West Walker Rivers; includes the Sweetwater and White Mountains, and parts of Mono and Inyo National Forests; includes Mono Lak e, Mammoth Lakes, and other lakes. Covers a land area of 3,048.982 square miles, a water area of 82.894 square miles, and is located in the Pacific Time Zone at 37.92° N. Lat., 118.88° W. Long. The county was founded in 1861. County seat is Bridgeport.

Weather Station: Bodie — Elevation: 8,370 feet

	Jan	Feb	Mar	Apr	May	Jun	Jul	Aug	Sep	Oct	Nov	Dec
High	40	41	45	51	62	70	78	77	70	60	49	41
Low	6	8	12	19	25	31	35	33	27	19	13	7
Precip	1.7	1.7	1.4	0.9	0.8	0.7	0.6	0.5	0.5	0.6	1.1	1.4
Snow	13.0	13.8	14.8	5.7	3.0	0.5	tr	tr	0.4	2.2	9.3	13.2

High and Low temperatures in degrees Fahrenheit; Precipitation and Snow in inches

Weather Station: Bridgeport — Elevation: 6,470 feet

	Jan	Feb	Mar	Apr	May	Jun	Jul	Aug	Sep	Oct	Nov	Dec
High	43	46	53	61	68	77	84	83	76	67	54	43
Low	10	13	20	25	31	37	42	40	33	24	18	10
Precip	1.5	1.5	1.0	0.5	0.5	0.5	0.4	0.5	0.5	0.3	0.9	1.1
Snow	9.2	10.3	4.5	1.6	0.4	0.1	0.0	0.0	0.3	0.4	2.2	7.9

High and Low temperatures in degrees Fahrenheit; Precipitation and Snow in inches

Population: 14,202; Growth (since 2000): 10.5%; Density: 4.7 persons per square mile; Race: 82.4% White, 0.3% Black/African American, 1.4% Asian, 2.1% American Indian/Alaska Native, 0.1% Native Hawaiian/Other Pacific Islander, 2.9% two or more races, 26.5% Hispanic of any race; Average household size: 2.42; Median age: 37.2; Age under 18: 21.0%; Age 65 and over: 9.7%; Males per 100 females: 113.4; Marriage status: 34.7% never married, 49.4% now married, 1.9% separated, 3.4% widowed, 12.5% divorced; Foreign born: 17.0%; Speak English only: 77.6%; With disability: 7.8%; Veterans: 7.6%; Ancestry: 18.5% German, 13.4% Irish, 9.8% English, 5.8% Italian, 4.4% French
Religion: Six largest groups: 90.5% Catholicism, 2.4% Latter-day Saints, 1.0% Methodist/Pietist, 0.9% Non-denominational Protestant, 0.8% Baptist, 0.4% Lutheran
Economy: Unemployment rate: 7.8%; Leading industries: 25.0% accommodation and food services; 13.6% construction; 12.7% retail trade; Farms: 72 totaling 56,386 acres; Company size: 1 employs 1,000 or more persons, 0 employ 500 to 999 persons, 3 employ 100 to 499 persons, 556 employ less than 100 persons; Business ownership: 455 women-owned, n/a Black-owned, n/a Hispanic-owned, n/a Asian-owned
Employment: 15.2% management, business, and financial, 1.7% computer, engineering, and science, 13.0% education, legal, community service, arts, and media, 4.9% healthcare practitioners, 28.3% service, 22.8% sales and office, 10.5% natural resources, construction, and maintenance, 3.5% production, transportation, and material moving
Income: Per capita: $28,046; Median household: $61,757; Average household: $68,616; Households with income of $100,000 or more: 19.1%; Poverty rate: 8.5%
Educational Attainment: High school diploma or higher: 83.8%; Bachelor's degree or higher: 29.8%; Graduate/professional degree or higher: 10.4%
Housing: Homeownership rate: 56.0%; Median home value: $344,500; Median year structure built: 1978; Homeowner vacancy rate: 3.5%; Median gross rent: $1,118 per month; Rental vacancy rate: 28.5%
Vital Statistics: Birth rate: 102.3 per 10,000 population; Death rate: 28.4 per 10,000 population; Age-adjusted cancer mortality rate: Unreliable deaths per 100,000 population
Health Insurance: 79.3% have insurance; 61.7% have private insurance; 27.4% have public insurance; 20.7% do not have insurance; 7.8% of children under 18 do not have insurance
Health Care: Physicians: 18.1 per 10,000 population; Hospital beds: 11.8 per 10,000 population; Hospital admissions: 448.1 per 10,000 population
Air Quality Index: 86.3% good, 10.7% moderate, 1.6% unhealthy for sensitive individuals, 0.3% unhealthy, 1.1% very unhealthy (% of days)
Transportation: Commute: 66.6% car, 5.0% public transportation, 13.9% walk, 9.9% work from home; Median travel time to work: 16.2 minutes
Presidential Election: 52.3% Obama, 44.8% Romney (2012)
National and State Parks: Bodie State Historic Park; Inyo National Forest; Mono Basin National Forest Scenic Area; Mono Lake Tufa State Natural Reserve

Additional Information Contacts

Mono Government. . . . . (760) 932-5531
http://www.monocounty.ca.gov

Mono County Communities

ASPEN SPRINGS (CDP). Covers a land area of 3.569 square miles and a water area of <.001 square miles. Located at 37.55° N. Lat; 118.70° W. Long. Elevation is 7,109 feet.
Population: 65; Growth (since 2000): n/a; Density: 18.2 persons per square mile; Race: 95.4% White, 0.0% Black/African American, 3.1% Asian, 0.0% American Indian/Alaska Native, 0.0% Native Hawaiian/Other Pacific Islander, 1.5% Two or more races, 1.5% Hispanic of any race; Average household size: 2.60; Median age: 47.8; Age under 18: 21.5%; Age 65 and over: 10.8%; Males per 100 females: 85.7
Housing: Homeownership rate: 84.0%; Homeowner vacancy rate: 0.0%; Rental vacancy rate: 0.0%

BENTON (CDP). Covers a land area of 28.483 square miles and a water area of 0.020 square miles. Located at 37.85° N. Lat; 118.49° W. Long. Elevation is 5,387 feet.
Population: 280; Growth (since 2000): n/a; Density: 9.8 persons per square mile; Race: 71.1% White, 0.4% Black/African American, 0.4% Asian, 21.1% American Indian/Alaska Native, 0.0% Native Hawaiian/Other Pacific Islander, 1.8% Two or more races, 13.6% Hispanic of any race; Average household size: 2.30; Median age: 48.8; Age under 18: 19.3%; Age 65 and over: 12.5%; Males per 100 females: 105.9

School District(s)

Eastern Sierra Unified (KG-12)
2012-13 Enrollment: 458. . . . . (760) 932-7443
Housing: Homeownership rate: 70.4%; Homeowner vacancy rate: 1.1%; Rental vacancy rate: 15.6%

BRIDGEPORT (CDP). County seat. Covers a land area of 21.740 square miles and a water area of 0.008 square miles. Located at 38.26° N. Lat; 119.21° W. Long. Elevation is 6,463 feet.
Population: 575; Growth (since 2000): n/a; Density: 26.4 persons per square mile; Race: 84.2% White, 0.2% Black/African American, 0.2% Asian, 7.5% American Indian/Alaska Native, 0.0% Native Hawaiian/Other Pacific Islander, 3.7% Two or more races, 25.7% Hispanic of any race; Average household size: 2.18; Median age: 45.5; Age under 18: 20.7%; Age 65 and over: 17.2%; Males per 100 females: 103.2

School District(s)

Eastern Sierra Unified (KG-12)
2012-13 Enrollment: 458. . . . . (760) 932-7443

Mono County Office of Education (KG-12)
2012-13 Enrollment: 429. . . . . (760) 932-7311
Mono County Roc/p
2012-13 Enrollment: n/a . . . . (760) 932-7311

Housing: Homeownership rate: 62.3%; Homeowner vacancy rate: 5.3%; Rental vacancy rate: 19.0%

CHALFANT (CDP). Covers a land area of 28.022 square miles and a water area of 0.028 square miles. Located at 37.49° N. Lat; 118.39° W. Long.

Population: 651; Growth (since 2000): n/a; Density: 23.2 persons per square mile; Race: 91.2% White, 0.0% Black/African American, 0.8% Asian, 2.0% American Indian/Alaska Native, 0.0% Native Hawaiian/Other Pacific Islander, 3.5% Two or more races, 10.3% Hispanic of any race; Average household size: 2.47; Median age: 47.1; Age under 18: 20.1%; Age 65 and over: 16.1%; Males per 100 females: 100.3

Housing: Homeownership rate: 87.5%; Homeowner vacancy rate: 2.5%; Rental vacancy rate: 8.3%

COLEVILLE (CDP). Covers a land area of 13.757 square miles and a water area of 0 square miles. Located at 38.58° N. Lat; 119.52° W. Long. Elevation is 5,141 feet.

Population: 495; Growth (since 2000): n/a; Density: 36.0 persons per square mile; Race: 78.0% White, 1.2% Black/African American, 1.6% Asian, 2.0% American Indian/Alaska Native, 0.0% Native Hawaiian/Other Pacific Islander, 4.6% Two or more races, 22.2% Hispanic of any race; Average household size: 2.89; Median age: 25.7; Age under 18: 33.7%; Age 65 and over: 6.5%; Males per 100 females: 93.4

School District(s)

Eastern Sierra Unified (KG-12)
2012-13 Enrollment: 458. . . . . (760) 932-7443

Housing: Homeownership rate: 28.1%; Homeowner vacancy rate: 2.0%; Rental vacancy rate: 4.7%

CROWLEY LAKE (CDP). Covers a land area of 2.807 square miles and a water area of 0.015 square miles. Located at 37.57° N. Lat; 118.75° W. Long.

Population: 875; Growth (since 2000): n/a; Density: 311.7 persons per square mile; Race: 87.9% White, 0.5% Black/African American, 1.3% Asian, 0.7% American Indian/Alaska Native, 0.0% Native Hawaiian/Other Pacific Islander, 2.9% Two or more races, 14.6% Hispanic of any race; Average household size: 2.37; Median age: 45.1; Age under 18: 24.0%; Age 65 and over: 5.8%; Males per 100 females: 108.3

Housing: Homeownership rate: 78.2%; Homeowner vacancy rate: 3.0%; Rental vacancy rate: 12.0%

JUNE LAKE (CDP). Covers a land area of 7.988 square miles and a water area of 0.791 square miles. Located at 37.77° N. Lat; 119.11° W. Long. Elevation is 7,654 feet.

Population: 629; Growth (since 2000): n/a; Density: 78.7 persons per square mile; Race: 84.9% White, 0.0% Black/African American, 0.3% Asian, 1.1% American Indian/Alaska Native, 0.0% Native Hawaiian/Other Pacific Islander, 1.3% Two or more races, 21.8% Hispanic of any race; Average household size: 2.16; Median age: 41.7; Age under 18: 18.4%; Age 65 and over: 11.1%; Males per 100 females: 119.2

Housing: Homeownership rate: 54.2%; Homeowner vacancy rate: 8.1%; Rental vacancy rate: 11.7%

LEE VINING (CDP). Covers a land area of 5.218 square miles and a water area of 0.002 square miles. Located at 37.96° N. Lat; 119.13° W. Long. Elevation is 6,781 feet.

Population: 222; Growth (since 2000): n/a; Density: 42.5 persons per square mile; Race: 56.8% White, 0.0% Black/African American, 0.0% Asian, 11.3% American Indian/Alaska Native, 0.0% Native Hawaiian/Other Pacific Islander, 3.2% Two or more races, 43.2% Hispanic of any race; Average household size: 2.51; Median age: 30.4; Age under 18: 25.2%; Age 65 and over: 7.7%; Males per 100 females: 107.5

School District(s)

Eastern Sierra Unified (KG-12)
2012-13 Enrollment: 458. . . . . (760) 932-7443

Housing: Homeownership rate: 50.6%; Homeowner vacancy rate: 2.3%; Rental vacancy rate: 10.6%

MAMMOTH LAKES (town). Covers a land area of 24.866 square miles and a water area of 0.440 square miles. Located at 37.61° N. Lat; 118.97° W. Long. Elevation is 7,880 feet.

History: Devil Postpile National Monument is five miles west. Scene of small-scale gold rush, 1879—1880.

Population: 8,234; Growth (since 2000): 16.1%; Density: 331.1 persons per square mile; Race: 80.7% White, 0.4% Black/African American, 1.6% Asian, 0.6% American Indian/Alaska Native, 0.1% Native Hawaiian/Other Pacific Islander, 2.8% Two or more races, 33.7% Hispanic of any race; Average household size: 2.50; Median age: 32.6; Age under 18: 20.9%; Age 65 and over: 6.5%; Males per 100 females: 121.4; Marriage status: 43.9% never married, 45.6% now married, 2.3% separated, 1.7% widowed, 8.8% divorced; Foreign born: 23.0%; Speak English only: 70.5%; With disability: 4.4%; Veterans: 5.5%; Ancestry: 15.5% Irish, 15.2% German, 9.5% English, 4.5% Italian, 3.1% Scottish

Employment: 13.3% management, business, and financial, 0.9% computer, engineering, and science, 14.3% education, legal, community service, arts, and media, 5.8% healthcare practitioners, 35.2% service, 19.6% sales and office, 6.9% natural resources, construction, and maintenance, 4.0% production, transportation, and material moving

Income: Per capita: $25,466; Median household: $60,208; Average household: $67,304; Households with income of $100,000 or more: 17.5%; Poverty rate: 9.9%

Educational Attainment: High school diploma or higher: 78.3%; Bachelor's degree or higher: 32.4%; Graduate/professional degree or higher: 13.2%

School District(s)

Mammoth Unified (KG-12)
2012-13 Enrollment: 1,151 . . . . (760) 934-6802
Mono County Office of Education (KG-12)
2012-13 Enrollment: 429. . . . . (760) 932-7311

Housing: Homeownership rate: 46.5%; Median home value: $519,300; Median year structure built: 1978; Homeowner vacancy rate: 3.4%; Median gross rent: $1,197 per month; Rental vacancy rate: 33.6%

Health Insurance: 73.0% have insurance; 52.7% have private insurance; 26.1% have public insurance; 27.0% do not have insurance; 12.4% of children under 18 do not have insurance

Hospitals: Mammoth Hospital

Safety: Violent crime rate: 21.8 per 10,000 population; Property crime rate: 184.1 per 10,000 population

Newspapers: Mammoth Times (weekly circulation 4200)

Transportation: Commute: 56.8% car, 8.0% public transportation, 16.0% walk, 12.2% work from home; Median travel time to work: 12.1 minutes; Amtrak: Bus service available.

Airports: Mammoth Yosemite (primary service/non-hub)

Additional Information Contacts

Town of Mammoth Lakes . . . . (760) 934-8989
http://www.ci.mammoth-lakes.ca.us

MCGEE CREEK (CDP). Covers a land area of 4.012 square miles and a water area of 0 square miles. Located at 37.57° N. Lat; 118.79° W. Long.

Population: 41; Growth (since 2000): n/a; Density: 10.2 persons per square mile; Race: 95.1% White, 0.0% Black/African American, 0.0% Asian, 0.0% American Indian/Alaska Native, 0.0% Native Hawaiian/Other Pacific Islander, 4.9% Two or more races, 4.9% Hispanic of any race; Average household size: 1.95; Median age: 54.8; Age under 18: 17.1%; Age 65 and over: 34.1%; Males per 100 females: 105.0

Housing: Homeownership rate: 95.2%; Homeowner vacancy rate: 0.0%; Rental vacancy rate: 0.0%

MONO CITY (CDP). Covers a land area of 5.424 square miles and a water area of 0 square miles. Located at 38.04° N. Lat; 119.15° W. Long. Elevation is 6,768 feet.

Population: 172; Growth (since 2000): n/a; Density: 31.7 persons per square mile; Race: 90.7% White, 0.0% Black/African American, 1.2% Asian, 0.6% American Indian/Alaska Native, 0.0% Native Hawaiian/Other Pacific Islander, 6.4% Two or more races, 21.5% Hispanic of any race; Average household size: 2.73; Median age: 41.0; Age under 18: 23.8%; Age 65 and over: 8.7%; Males per 100 females: 91.1

Housing: Homeownership rate: 71.4%; Homeowner vacancy rate: 0.0%; Rental vacancy rate: 0.0%

PARADISE (CDP). Covers a land area of 4.352 square miles and a water area of 0 square miles. Located at 37.48° N. Lat; 118.60° W. Long.

Population: 153; Growth (since 2000): n/a; Density: 35.2 persons per square mile; Race: 85.0% White, 0.0% Black/African American, 3.9% Asian, 1.3% American Indian/Alaska Native, 0.0% Native Hawaiian/Other Pacific Islander, 6.5% Two or more races, 9.2% Hispanic of any race; Average household size: 2.07; Median age: 52.9; Age under 18: 12.4%; Age 65 and over: 21.6%; Males per 100 females: 104.0

Housing: Homeownership rate: 95.9%; Homeowner vacancy rate: 1.4%; Rental vacancy rate: 25.0%

SUNNY SLOPES (CDP). Covers a land area of 1.884 square miles and a water area of 0 square miles. Located at 37.57° N. Lat; 118.68° W. Long.

Population: 182; Growth (since 2000): n/a; Density: 96.6 persons per square mile; Race: 87.4% White, 0.0% Black/African American, 3.8% Asian, 1.1% American Indian/Alaska Native, 2.2% Native Hawaiian/Other Pacific Islander, 5.5% Two or more races, 1.6% Hispanic of any race; Average household size: 2.14; Median age: 47.2; Age under 18: 15.4%; Age 65 and over: 11.0%; Males per 100 females: 91.6

Housing: Homeownership rate: 69.5%; Homeowner vacancy rate: 0.0%; Rental vacancy rate: 0.0%

SWALL MEADOWS (CDP). Covers a land area of 4.462 square miles and a water area of 0 square miles. Located at 37.51° N. Lat; 118.64° W. Long.

Population: 220; Growth (since 2000): n/a; Density: 49.3 persons per square mile; Race: 91.4% White, 0.0% Black/African American, 2.3% Asian, 1.4% American Indian/Alaska Native, 0.0% Native Hawaiian/Other Pacific Islander, 4.1% Two or more races, 2.7% Hispanic of any race; Average household size: 2.24; Median age: 53.8; Age under 18: 16.4%; Age 65 and over: 19.1%; Males per 100 females: 89.7

Housing: Homeownership rate: 91.8%; Homeowner vacancy rate: 0.0%; Rental vacancy rate: 0.0%

TOPAZ (CDP). Covers a land area of 3.071 square miles and a water area of 1.297 square miles. Located at 38.65° N. Lat; 119.52° W. Long. Elevation is 5,046 feet.

Population: 50; Growth (since 2000): n/a; Density: 16.3 persons per square mile; Race: 88.0% White, 0.0% Black/African American, 0.0% Asian, 2.0% American Indian/Alaska Native, 0.0% Native Hawaiian/Other Pacific Islander, 0.0% Two or more races, 48.0% Hispanic of any race; Average household size: 2.38; Median age: 45.7; Age under 18: 22.0%; Age 65 and over: 28.0%; Males per 100 females: 78.6

Housing: Homeownership rate: 61.9%; Homeowner vacancy rate: 7.1%; Rental vacancy rate: 33.3%

WALKER (CDP). Covers a land area of 18.439 square miles and a water area of 0 square miles. Located at 38.53° N. Lat; 119.46° W. Long. Elevation is 5,403 feet.

Population: 721; Growth (since 2000): n/a; Density: 39.1 persons per square mile; Race: 87.2% White, 0.4% Black/African American, 0.4% Asian, 7.9% American Indian/Alaska Native, 0.1% Native Hawaiian/Other Pacific Islander, 2.1% Two or more races, 9.7% Hispanic of any race; Average household size: 2.15; Median age: 51.1; Age under 18: 17.2%; Age 65 and over: 27.2%; Males per 100 females: 95.4

Housing: Homeownership rate: 69.0%; Homeowner vacancy rate: 4.5%; Rental vacancy rate: 16.0%

Monterey County

Located in western California; bounded on the west by the Pacific Ocean and Monterey Bay, and on the north by the Pajaro River valley; crossed by the Salinas River valley, and the Gabilan, Diablo, and Santa Lucia Ranges; includes part of Los Padres N ational Forest. Covers a land area of 3,280.595 square miles, a water area of 490.626 square miles, and is located in the Pacific Time Zone at 36.24° N. Lat., 121.32° W. Long. The county was founded in 1850. County seat is Salinas.

Monterey County is part of the Salinas, CA Metropolitan Statistical Area. The entire metro area includes: Monterey County, CA

Weather Station: King City Elevation: 319 feet

	Jan	Feb	Mar	Apr	May	Jun	Jul	Aug	Sep	Oct	Nov	Dec
High	63	66	69	74	79	83	85	85	85	79	69	62
Low	37	40	42	43	47	50	53	53	51	45	40	36
Precip	2.3	2.6	2.2	0.8	0.3	0.1	0.0	0.0	0.2	0.6	1.1	1.9
Snow	0.0	0.0	0.0	0.0	0.0	0.0	0.0	0.0	0.0	0.0	0.0	tr

High and Low temperatures in degrees Fahrenheit; Precipitation and Snow in inches

Weather Station: Monterey Elevation: 384 feet

	Jan	Feb	Mar	Apr	May	Jun	Jul	Aug	Sep	Oct	Nov	Dec
High	60	61	62	64	64	67	68	69	71	70	64	60
Low	44	45	46	47	49	51	53	53	53	51	47	44
Precip	4.3	4.0	3.3	1.4	0.6	0.2	0.1	0.1	0.2	1.0	2.3	3.3
Snow	tr	tr	0.2	0.0	0.0	0.0	0.0	0.0	0.0	0.0	0.0	tr

High and Low temperatures in degrees Fahrenheit; Precipitation and Snow in inches

Weather Station: Priest Valley Elevation: 2,299 feet

	Jan	Feb	Mar	Apr	May	Jun	Jul	Aug	Sep	Oct	Nov	Dec
High	58	60	64	70	79	88	95	94	89	78	65	58
Low	30	32	34	35	40	45	51	50	46	38	32	29
Precip	4.7	4.3	3.8	1.2	0.6	0.1	0.1	0.0	0.2	1.0	1.8	3.3
Snow	0.2	0.1	tr	tr	0.0	0.0	0.0	0.0	0.0	0.0	0.0	0.1

High and Low temperatures in degrees Fahrenheit; Precipitation and Snow in inches

Weather Station: Salinas Municipal Arpt Elevation: 68 feet

	Jan	Feb	Mar	Apr	May	Jun	Jul	Aug	Sep	Oct	Nov	Dec
High	61	63	65	67	68	70	71	72	74	73	67	61
Low	41	43	44	46	50	53	55	55	54	50	44	40
Precip	2.4	2.4	2.3	0.9	0.3	0.1	0.0	0.0	0.2	0.6	1.2	1.7
Snow	na	na	na	na	na	na	na	na	na	na	na	na

High and Low temperatures in degrees Fahrenheit; Precipitation and Snow in inches

Weather Station: Salinas No 2 Elevation: 44 feet

	Jan	Feb	Mar	Apr	May	Jun	Jul	Aug	Sep	Oct	Nov	Dec
High	63	64	66	68	69	71	72	73	75	74	68	63
Low	41	43	45	46	50	52	55	55	54	50	45	41
Precip	3.0	3.0	2.6	1.0	0.4	0.1	0.0	0.0	0.1	0.7	1.7	2.3
Snow	0.0	0.0	0.0	0.0	0.0	0.0	0.0	0.0	0.0	0.0	0.0	0.0

High and Low temperatures in degrees Fahrenheit; Precipitation and Snow in inches

Population: 415,057; Growth (since 2000): 3.3%; Density: 126.5 persons per square mile; Race: 55.6% White, 3.1% Black/African American, 6.1% Asian, 1.3% American Indian/Alaska Native, 0.5% Native Hawaiian/Other Pacific Islander, 5.1% two or more races, 55.4% Hispanic of any race; Average household size: 3.15; Median age: 32.9; Age under 18: 26.7%; Age 65 and over: 10.7%; Males per 100 females: 105.9; Marriage status: 36.8% never married, 50.4% now married, 2.2% separated, 4.5% widowed, 8.3% divorced; Foreign born: 29.9%; Speak English only: 47.4%; With disability: 8.4%; Veterans: 7.1%; Ancestry: 7.4% German, 5.7% Irish, 5.6% English, 3.9% Italian, 1.9% French

Religion: Six largest groups: 36.2% Catholicism, 2.9% Non-denominational Protestant, 1.6% Buddhism, 1.5% Baptist, 1.5% Latter-day Saints, 1.1% Presbyterian-Reformed

Economy: Unemployment rate: 6.7%; Leading industries: 15.8% retail trade; 12.0% health care and social assistance; 11.8% accommodation and food services; Farms: 1,179 totaling 1,268,144 acres; Company size: 3 employ 1,000 or more persons, 3 employ 500 to 999 persons, 112 employ 100 to 499 persons, 8,187 employ less than 100 persons; Business ownership: 10,299 women-owned, 751 Black-owned, 6,925 Hispanic-owned, 2,368 Asian-owned

Employment: 11.4% management, business, and financial, 2.9% computer, engineering, and science, 9.5% education, legal, community service, arts, and media, 3.8% healthcare practitioners, 20.6% service, 21.6% sales and office, 19.0% natural resources, construction, and maintenance, 11.2% production, transportation, and material moving

Income: Per capita: $24,775; Median household: $59,168; Average household: $79,378; Households with income of $100,000 or more: 25.9%; Poverty rate: 17.0%

Educational Attainment: High school diploma or higher: 71.0%; Bachelor's degree or higher: 23.0%; Graduate/professional degree or higher: 8.8%

Housing: Homeownership rate: 50.8%; Median home value: $362,400; Median year structure built: 1973; Homeowner vacancy rate: 2.5%; Median gross rent: $1,209 per month; Rental vacancy rate: 4.9%

Vital Statistics: Birth rate: 159.1 per 10,000 population; Death rate: 55.9 per 10,000 population; Age-adjusted cancer mortality rate: 152.0 deaths per 100,000 population

Health Insurance: 78.4% have insurance; 57.0% have private insurance; 31.0% have public insurance; 21.6% do not have insurance; 9.2% of children under 18 do not have insurance
Health Care: Physicians: 17.7 per 10,000 population; Hospital beds: 17.0 per 10,000 population; Hospital admissions: 797.8 per 10,000 population
Air Quality Index: 88.5% good, 11.5% moderate, 0.0% unhealthy for sensitive individuals, 0.0% unhealthy (percent of days)
Transportation: Commute: 84.0% car, 1.9% public transportation, 2.9% walk, 5.2% work from home; Median travel time to work: 22.5 minutes
Presidential Election: 65.9% Obama, 31.9% Romney (2012)
National and State Parks: Andrew Molera State Park; Asilomar State Beach; Battle of Natividad State Historic Landmark; Carmel River State Beach; Elkhorn Slough National Estuarine Research Reserve; Fort Ord Dunes State Park; Garrapata State Park; Hastings Natural History State Reservation; Hilltown Ferry State Historic Landmark; John Little State Natural Reserve; Julia Pfeiffer Burns State Park; Limekiln State Park; Limekiln State Wilderness; Marina State Beach; Monterey State Beach; Monterey State Historic Park; Moss Landing State Beach; Moss Landing State Wildlife Area; Pfeiffer Big Sur State Park; Point Lobos State Natural Reserve; Point Sur State Historic Park; Salinas River National Wildlife Refuge; Salinas River State Beach; The California Sea Otter State Game Refuge; The Glass House State Historic Landmark; Zmudowski State Beach
Additional Information Contacts
Monterey Government. . . . . (831) 755-6900
http://www.co.monterey.ca.us

Monterey County Communities

AROMAS (CDP). Covers a land area of 4.736 square miles and a water area of 0.011 square miles. Located at 36.87° N. Lat; 121.63° W. Long. Elevation is 131 feet.
Population: 2,650; Growth (since 2000): -5.3%; Density: 559.5 persons per square mile; Race: 75.0% White, 0.6% Black/African American, 1.8% Asian, 1.4% American Indian/Alaska Native, 0.2% Native Hawaiian/Other Pacific Islander, 5.9% Two or more races, 34.9% Hispanic of any race; Average household size: 3.00; Median age: 42.2; Age under 18: 23.4%; Age 65 and over: 10.5%; Males per 100 females: 102.0; Marriage status: 26.6% never married, 59.4% now married, 1.8% separated, 6.2% widowed, 7.8% divorced; Foreign born: 15.6%; Speak English only: 71.3%; With disability: 12.7%; Veterans: 10.4%; Ancestry: 11.3% English, 11.1% German, 10.7% Irish, 7.1% French, 4.9% Italian
Employment: 11.6% management, business, and financial, 5.4% computer, engineering, and science, 7.8% education, legal, community service, arts, and media, 4.5% healthcare practitioners, 24.8% service, 18.9% sales and office, 10.5% natural resources, construction, and maintenance, 16.3% production, transportation, and material moving
Income: Per capita: $31,951; Median household: $73,500; Average household: $93,855; Households with income of $100,000 or more: 39.0%; Poverty rate: 9.6%
Educational Attainment: High school diploma or higher: 92.7%; Bachelor's degree or higher: 29.3%; Graduate/professional degree or higher: 7.0%
School District(s)
Aromas/san Juan Unified (KG-12)
2012-13 Enrollment: 1,170 . . . . (831) 623-4500
Housing: Homeownership rate: 76.9%; Median home value: $378,500; Median year structure built: 1974; Homeowner vacancy rate: 1.2%; Median gross rent: $1,438 per month; Rental vacancy rate: 2.3%
Health Insurance: 83.3% have insurance; 69.1% have private insurance; 22.6% have public insurance; 16.7% do not have insurance; 10.8% of children under 18 do not have insurance
Transportation: Commute: 88.9% car, 0.0% public transportation, 0.9% walk, 9.0% work from home; Median travel time to work: 28.3 minutes

BIG SUR (unincorporated postal area)
ZCTA: 93920
Covers a land area of 368.880 square miles and a water area of 8.099 square miles. Located at 36.09° N. Lat; 121.55° W. Long. Elevation is 144 feet.
Population: 1,369; Growth (since 2000): 37.4%; Density: 3.7 persons per square mile; Race: 85.5% White, 0.4% Black/African American, 1.1% Asian, 0.7% American Indian/Alaska Native, 0.1% Native Hawaiian/Other Pacific Islander, 2.3% Two or more races, 26.2% Hispanic of any race; Average household size: 2.04; Median age: 44.5; Age under 18: 15.7%; Age 65 and over: 12.1%; Males per 100 females: 114.9
School District(s)
Big Sur Unified (KG-12)
2012-13 Enrollment: 77. . . . . (805) 927-4507
Carmel Unified (KG-12)
2012-13 Enrollment: 2,358 . . . . (831) 624-1546
Housing: Homeownership rate: 32.9%; Homeowner vacancy rate: 1.4%; Rental vacancy rate: 1.2%

BORONDA (CDP). Covers a land area of 0.550 square miles and a water area of 0 square miles. Located at 36.69° N. Lat; 121.67° W. Long. Elevation is 62 feet.
Population: 1,710; Growth (since 2000): 29.1%; Density: 3,106.5 persons per square mile; Race: 38.7% White, 0.6% Black/African American, 6.8% Asian, 1.5% American Indian/Alaska Native, 0.4% Native Hawaiian/Other Pacific Islander, 6.8% Two or more races, 85.2% Hispanic of any race; Average household size: 4.34; Median age: 27.2; Age under 18: 32.6%; Age 65 and over: 6.9%; Males per 100 females: 102.4
Housing: Homeownership rate: 46.5%; Homeowner vacancy rate: 4.7%; Rental vacancy rate: 3.2%

BRADLEY (CDP). Covers a land area of 0.086 square miles and a water area of 0 square miles. Located at 35.86° N. Lat; 120.80° W. Long. Elevation is 548 feet.
Population: 93; Growth (since 2000): -22.5%; Density: 1,081.4 persons per square mile; Race: 91.4% White, 0.0% Black/African American, 0.0% Asian, 2.2% American Indian/Alaska Native, 0.0% Native Hawaiian/Other Pacific Islander, 1.1% Two or more races, 11.8% Hispanic of any race; Average household size: 2.51; Median age: 39.8; Age under 18: 23.7%; Age 65 and over: 9.7%; Males per 100 females: 111.4
School District(s)
Bradley Union Elementary (KG-08)
2012-13 Enrollment: 79. . . . . (805) 472-2310
Housing: Homeownership rate: 43.2%; Homeowner vacancy rate: 0.0%; Rental vacancy rate: 4.5%

CARMEL VALLEY VILLAGE (CDP). Covers a land area of 18.983 square miles and a water area of 0.196 square miles. Located at 36.50° N. Lat; 121.73° W. Long. Elevation is 846 feet.
History: Carmel Valley Village is located in the Santa Lucia range, known for its wine production and luxury hotels.
Population: 4,407; Growth (since 2000): -6.2%; Density: 232.2 persons per square mile; Race: 91.8% White, 0.5% Black/African American, 1.6% Asian, 0.5% American Indian/Alaska Native, 0.2% Native Hawaiian/Other Pacific Islander, 2.7% Two or more races, 7.4% Hispanic of any race; Average household size: 2.32; Median age: 51.7; Age under 18: 17.3%; Age 65 and over: 20.6%; Males per 100 females: 93.8; Marriage status: 23.8% never married, 59.4% now married, 0.4% separated, 3.5% widowed, 13.3% divorced; Foreign born: 9.8%; Speak English only: 86.6%; With disability: 12.2%; Veterans: 12.0%; Ancestry: 17.6% English, 16.9% German, 11.5% Irish, 8.7% Italian, 6.7% American
Employment: 16.9% management, business, and financial, 3.5% computer, engineering, and science, 13.5% education, legal, community service, arts, and media, 10.8% healthcare practitioners, 12.3% service, 30.5% sales and office, 9.1% natural resources, construction, and maintenance, 3.3% production, transportation, and material moving
Income: Per capita: $52,776; Median household: $92,500; Average household: $130,213; Households with income of $100,000 or more: 46.7%; Poverty rate: 7.1%
Educational Attainment: High school diploma or higher: 98.0%; Bachelor's degree or higher: 47.7%; Graduate/professional degree or higher: 19.7%
School District(s)
Carmel Unified (KG-12)
2012-13 Enrollment: 2,358 . . . . (831) 624-1546
Housing: Homeownership rate: 70.0%; Median home value: $738,000; Median year structure built: 1964; Homeowner vacancy rate: 2.4%; Median gross rent: $1,863 per month; Rental vacancy rate: 5.6%
Health Insurance: 91.8% have insurance; 82.2% have private insurance; 22.7% have public insurance; 8.2% do not have insurance; 6.1% of children under 18 do not have insurance
Transportation: Commute: 80.3% car, 0.9% public transportation, 0.6% walk, 16.9% work from home; Median travel time to work: 27.6 minutes

CARMEL-BY-THE-SEA (city). Covers a land area of 1.080 square miles and a water area of 0 square miles. Located at 36.55° N. Lat; 121.92° W. Long. Elevation is 223 feet.

History: Commonly called Carmel, the village dates from about 1904 when a group of writers and artists built small dwellings here. Carmel continued to attract artists, who struggled with non-artists to keep the village from becoming a "modern" city.

Population: 3,722; Growth (since 2000): -8.8%; Density: 3,445.5 persons per square mile; Race: 93.1% White, 0.3% Black/African American, 3.0% Asian, 0.2% American Indian/Alaska Native, 0.2% Native Hawaiian/Other Pacific Islander, 2.1% Two or more races, 4.7% Hispanic of any race; Average household size: 1.78; Median age: 59.2; Age under 18: 10.2%; Age 65 and over: 35.7%; Males per 100 females: 77.6; Marriage status: 18.9% never married, 62.3% now married, 3.2% separated, 6.7% widowed, 12.0% divorced; Foreign born: 7.8%; Speak English only: 93.4%; With disability: 6.6%; Veterans: 11.1%; Ancestry: 24.6% English, 16.6% German, 15.3% Irish, 9.4% French, 8.7% Scotch-Irish

Employment: 17.4% management, business, and financial, 5.6% computer, engineering, and science, 23.1% education, legal, community service, arts, and media, 10.8% healthcare practitioners, 14.2% service, 21.1% sales and office, 5.4% natural resources, construction, and maintenance, 2.4% production, transportation, and material moving

Income: Per capita: $46,391; Median household: $71,719; Average household: $100,727; Households with income of $100,000 or more: 40.9%; Poverty rate: 6.4%

Educational Attainment: High school diploma or higher: 96.6%; Bachelor's degree or higher: 60.8%; Graduate/professional degree or higher: 28.7%

School District(s)

Carmel Unified (KG-12)
2012-13 Enrollment: 2,358 . . . . (831) 624-1546

Housing: Homeownership rate: 56.5%; Median home value: 1 million+; Median year structure built: 1953; Homeowner vacancy rate: 5.3%; Median gross rent: $1,559 per month; Rental vacancy rate: 8.8%

Health Insurance: 86.6% have insurance; 80.8% have private insurance; 31.9% have public insurance; 13.4% do not have insurance; 14.4% of children under 18 do not have insurance

Safety: Violent crime rate: 23.5 per 10,000 population; Property crime rate: 273.9 per 10,000 population

Newspapers: Carmel Pine Cone (weekly circulation 22000)

Transportation: Commute: 74.4% car, 1.8% public transportation, 7.5% walk, 14.8% work from home; Median travel time to work: 21.7 minutes; Amtrak: Bus service available.

Additional Information Contacts

City of Carmel-by-the-Sea. . . . . (831) 620-2000
http://ci.carmel.ca.us

CASTROVILLE (CDP). Covers a land area of 1.057 square miles and a water area of 0 square miles. Located at 36.77° N. Lat; 121.75° W. Long. Elevation is 23 feet.

History: Castroville was founded in 1864 by Juan B. Castro on his father's rancho, which was called Bolsa Nueva y Morro Coyo (New Pocket and Lame Moor).

Population: 6,481; Growth (since 2000): -3.6%; Density: 6,133.7 persons per square mile; Race: 43.3% White, 1.5% Black/African American, 2.6% Asian, 1.5% American Indian/Alaska Native, 0.1% Native Hawaiian/Other Pacific Islander, 5.4% Two or more races, 90.1% Hispanic of any race; Average household size: 4.40; Median age: 26.7; Age under 18: 33.5%; Age 65 and over: 6.4%; Males per 100 females: 105.8; Marriage status: 46.7% never married, 47.6% now married, 2.2% separated, 3.4% widowed, 2.4% divorced; Foreign born: 43.2%; Speak English only: 14.5%; With disability: 6.8%; Veterans: 1.5%; Ancestry: 1.7% English, 1.6% Welsh, 1.3% Irish, 0.8% Arab, 0.4% Polish

Employment: 5.9% management, business, and financial, 0.4% computer, engineering, and science, 4.5% education, legal, community service, arts, and media, 0.1% healthcare practitioners, 14.7% service, 20.6% sales and office, 30.2% natural resources, construction, and maintenance, 23.6% production, transportation, and material moving

Income: Per capita: $13,525; Median household: $53,580; Average household: $54,996; Households with income of $100,000 or more: 9.8%; Poverty rate: 25.0%

Educational Attainment: High school diploma or higher: 39.5%; Bachelor's degree or higher: 5.0%; Graduate/professional degree or higher: 1.8%

School District(s)

North Monterey County Unified (KG-12)
2012-13 Enrollment: 4,284 . . . . (831) 633-3343

Housing: Homeownership rate: 40.9%; Median home value: $259,300; Median year structure built: 1972; Homeowner vacancy rate: 2.4%; Median gross rent: $972 per month; Rental vacancy rate: 2.0%

Health Insurance: 73.6% have insurance; 40.0% have private insurance; 39.7% have public insurance; 26.4% do not have insurance; 12.1% of children under 18 do not have insurance

Transportation: Commute: 87.6% car, 0.9% public transportation, 1.7% walk, 0.7% work from home; Median travel time to work: 21.7 minutes

CHUALAR (CDP). Covers a land area of 0.626 square miles and a water area of 0 square miles. Located at 36.57° N. Lat; 121.51° W. Long. Elevation is 115 feet.

History: The name of Chualar means "a place abounding in wild pigweed." The town grew as the center of a lettuce-producing area.

Population: 1,190; Growth (since 2000): -17.6%; Density: 1,900.5 persons per square mile; Race: 28.3% White, 0.1% Black/African American, 0.9% Asian, 0.2% American Indian/Alaska Native, 0.0% Native Hawaiian/Other Pacific Islander, 1.0% Two or more races, 96.7% Hispanic of any race; Average household size: 4.86; Median age: 26.6; Age under 18: 36.1%; Age 65 and over: 5.0%; Males per 100 females: 103.1

School District(s)

Chualar Union (KG-08)
2012-13 Enrollment: 341. . . . . (831) 679-2504

Housing: Homeownership rate: 45.7%; Homeowner vacancy rate: 0.0%; Rental vacancy rate: 1.5%

DEL MONTE FOREST (CDP). Covers a land area of 8.034 square miles and a water area of 2.612 square miles. Located at 36.58° N. Lat; 121.95° W. Long. Elevation is 207 feet.

History: The Del Monte Forest Property Owners was founded in 1951, as the Del Monte Forest Property Homeowners' Association. The name was later changed to be inclusive of the broader constituency of all property owners. In 1979 Del Monte Forest Property Owners incorporated under the California not-for-profit corporation law in order to gain the legal benefit of a more formal structure.

Population: 4,514; Growth (since 2000): -0.4%; Density: 561.9 persons per square mile; Race: 86.9% White, 1.0% Black/African American, 8.6% Asian, 0.2% American Indian/Alaska Native, 0.1% Native Hawaiian/Other Pacific Islander, 2.0% Two or more races, 3.7% Hispanic of any race; Average household size: 2.17; Median age: 57.8; Age under 18: 16.6%; Age 65 and over: 34.6%; Males per 100 females: 92.6; Marriage status: 37.7% never married, 53.4% now married, 0.4% separated, 5.5% widowed, 3.4% divorced; Foreign born: 9.1%; Speak English only: 84.1%; With disability: 10.2%; Veterans: 16.8%; Ancestry: 21.6% German, 16.6% English, 14.1% Irish, 6.5% Italian, 6.3% Scottish

Employment: 32.8% management, business, and financial, 5.2% computer, engineering, and science, 20.7% education, legal, community service, arts, and media, 6.3% healthcare practitioners, 8.9% service, 18.8% sales and office, 4.0% natural resources, construction, and maintenance, 3.2% production, transportation, and material moving

Income: Per capita: $48,786; Median household: $100,268; Average household: $146,361; Households with income of $100,000 or more: 50.3%; Poverty rate: 9.9%

Educational Attainment: High school diploma or higher: 98.8%; Bachelor's degree or higher: 62.5%; Graduate/professional degree or higher: 25.6%

Housing: Homeownership rate: 83.1%; Median home value: $945,200; Median year structure built: 1972; Homeowner vacancy rate: 4.0%; Median gross rent: $2,000+ per month; Rental vacancy rate: 5.4%

Health Insurance: 93.4% have insurance; 84.6% have private insurance; 37.3% have public insurance; 6.6% do not have insurance; 17.0% of children under 18 do not have insurance

Transportation: Commute: 40.2% car, 11.3% public transportation, 33.7% walk, 13.2% work from home; Median travel time to work: 14.8 minutes

DEL REY OAKS (city). Covers a land area of 0.481 square miles and a water area of 0.002 square miles. Located at 36.58° N. Lat; 121.83° W. Long. Elevation is 82 feet.

Population: 1,624; Growth (since 2000): -1.6%; Density: 3,376.3 persons per square mile; Race: 81.7% White, 1.0% Black/African American, 7.9% Asian, 0.7% American Indian/Alaska Native, 0.2% Native Hawaiian/Other Pacific Islander, 5.3% Two or more races, 10.4% Hispanic of any race;

Average household size: 2.32; Median age: 46.2; Age under 18: 17.5%; Age 65 and over: 19.0%; Males per 100 females: 91.1
Housing: Homeownership rate: 73.8%; Homeowner vacancy rate: 1.9%; Rental vacancy rate: 2.6%
Safety: Violent crime rate: 29.9 per 10,000 population; Property crime rate: 233.1 per 10,000 population
Additional Information Contacts
City of Del Rey Oaks . . . . (831) 394-8511
http://www.delreyoaks.org

ELKHORN (CDP). Covers a land area of 4.808 square miles and a water area of 0.022 square miles. Located at 36.81° N. Lat; 121.72° W. Long. Elevation is 10 feet.
Population: 1,565; Growth (since 2000): -1.6%; Density: 325.5 persons per square mile; Race: 71.7% White, 0.6% Black/African American, 4.0% Asian, 0.4% American Indian/Alaska Native, 0.2% Native Hawaiian/Other Pacific Islander, 4.8% Two or more races, 37.6% Hispanic of any race; Average household size: 2.94; Median age: 41.5; Age under 18: 23.3%; Age 65 and over: 11.8%; Males per 100 females: 97.4
Housing: Homeownership rate: 71.4%; Homeowner vacancy rate: 1.3%; Rental vacancy rate: 0.6%

GONZALES (city). Covers a land area of 1.921 square miles and a water area of 0.038 square miles. Located at 36.51° N. Lat; 121.44° W. Long. Elevation is 135 feet.
History: Gonzales developed around a milk-condensing plant serving the surrounding dairy farms.
Population: 8,187; Growth (since 2000): 8.8%; Density: 4,260.9 persons per square mile; Race: 42.3% White, 1.0% Black/African American, 2.3% Asian, 1.5% American Indian/Alaska Native, 0.2% Native Hawaiian/Other Pacific Islander, 4.3% Two or more races, 88.9% Hispanic of any race; Average household size: 4.29; Median age: 27.0; Age under 18: 34.9%; Age 65 and over: 6.0%; Males per 100 females: 104.7; Marriage status: 35.3% never married, 56.4% now married, 1.2% separated, 4.7% widowed, 3.6% divorced; Foreign born: 37.5%; Speak English only: 27.8%; With disability: 3.8%; Veterans: 0.6%; Ancestry: 2.5% German, 1.9% Portuguese, 1.3% Irish, 0.6% Scottish, 0.5% Italian
Employment: 3.4% management, business, and financial, 2.4% computer, engineering, and science, 7.1% education, legal, community service, arts, and media, 1.5% healthcare practitioners, 16.3% service, 15.5% sales and office, 35.1% natural resources, construction, and maintenance, 18.7% production, transportation, and material moving
Income: Per capita: $15,812; Median household: $50,168; Average household: $59,536; Households with income of $100,000 or more: 14.2%; Poverty rate: 23.9%
Educational Attainment: High school diploma or higher: 55.0%; Bachelor's degree or higher: 5.0%; Graduate/professional degree or higher: 1.3%

School District(s)

Gonzales Unified (KG-12)
2012-13 Enrollment: 2,443 . . . . (831) 675-0100
Housing: Homeownership rate: 53.5%; Median home value: $203,700; Median year structure built: 1986; Homeowner vacancy rate: 2.7%; Median gross rent: $1,222 per month; Rental vacancy rate: 2.1%
Health Insurance: 75.1% have insurance; 50.4% have private insurance; 28.8% have public insurance; 24.9% do not have insurance; 12.7% of children under 18 do not have insurance
Safety: Violent crime rate: 28.5 per 10,000 population; Property crime rate: 129.3 per 10,000 population
Transportation: Commute: 90.3% car, 0.8% public transportation, 2.3% walk, 2.5% work from home; Median travel time to work: 23.4 minutes
Additional Information Contacts
City of Gonzales . . . . (831) 675-5000
http://www.ci.gonzales.ca.us

GREENFIELD (city). Covers a land area of 2.135 square miles and a water area of <.001 square miles. Located at 36.32° N. Lat; 121.24° W. Long. Elevation is 289 feet.
History: Greenfield was named for the alfalfa fields, green the year round, which surrounded it.
Population: 16,330; Growth (since 2000): 29.8%; Density: 7,648.1 persons per square mile; Race: 36.6% White, 1.1% Black/African American, 1.1% Asian, 5.4% American Indian/Alaska Native, 0.1% Native Hawaiian/Other Pacific Islander, 4.0% Two or more races, 91.3% Hispanic of any race; Average household size: 4.71; Median age: 25.5; Age under 18: 35.8%; Age 65 and over: 4.7%; Males per 100 females: 109.8; Marriage status: 39.8% never married, 55.0% now married, 2.2% separated, 2.1% widowed, 3.0% divorced; Foreign born: 45.8%; Speak English only: 12.7%; With disability: 7.7%; Veterans: 2.9%; Ancestry: 1.2% German, 1.0% English, 0.4% European, 0.3% Italian, 0.3% Scotch-Irish
Employment: 3.0% management, business, and financial, 0.9% computer, engineering, and science, 9.2% education, legal, community service, arts, and media, 3.4% healthcare practitioners, 15.1% service, 18.7% sales and office, 35.1% natural resources, construction, and maintenance, 14.6% production, transportation, and material moving
Income: Per capita: $13,757; Median household: $53,805; Average household: $61,514; Households with income of $100,000 or more: 13.5%; Poverty rate: 24.5%
Educational Attainment: High school diploma or higher: 45.8%; Bachelor's degree or higher: 8.8%; Graduate/professional degree or higher: 1.2%

School District(s)

Greenfield Union Elementary (KG-08)
2012-13 Enrollment: 3,129 . . . . (831) 674-2840
South Monterey County Joint Union High (KG-12)
2012-13 Enrollment: 1,971 . . . . (831) 385-0606
Housing: Homeownership rate: 52.9%; Median home value: $166,300; Median year structure built: 1993; Homeowner vacancy rate: 3.4%; Median gross rent: $1,141 per month; Rental vacancy rate: 5.9%
Health Insurance: 70.9% have insurance; 38.8% have private insurance; 36.2% have public insurance; 29.1% do not have insurance; 10.4% of children under 18 do not have insurance
Safety: Violent crime rate: 52.6 per 10,000 population; Property crime rate: 153.1 per 10,000 population
Transportation: Commute: 91.3% car, 1.0% public transportation, 4.0% walk, 1.6% work from home; Median travel time to work: 26.2 minutes
Additional Information Contacts
City of Greenfield. . . . . (831) 674-5591
http://ci.greenfield.ca.us

JOLON (unincorporated postal area)
ZCTA: 93928
Covers a land area of 19.102 square miles and a water area of 0.019 square miles. Located at 36.04° N. Lat; 121.24° W. Long. Elevation is 971 feet.
Population: 506; Growth (since 2000): 102.4%; Density: 26.5 persons per square mile; Race: 70.4% White, 11.5% Black/African American, 7.3% Asian, 1.0% American Indian/Alaska Native, 0.6% Native Hawaiian/Other Pacific Islander, 3.0% Two or more races, 16.4% Hispanic of any race; Average household size: 3.09; Median age: 32.3; Age under 18: 15.2%; Age 65 and over: 2.8%; Males per 100 females: 266.7
Housing: Homeownership rate: n/a; Homeowner vacancy rate: 0.0%; Rental vacancy rate: 14.1%
Airports: Tusi AHP (Hunter Liggett) (general aviation)

KING CITY (city). Covers a land area of 3.845 square miles and a water area of 0.139 square miles. Located at 36.22° N. Lat; 121.13° W. Long. Elevation is 335 feet.
History: King City, named for one of its first settlers, was founded in 1868 and developed as the chief marketing center of the southern Salinas Valley.
Population: 12,874; Growth (since 2000): 16.0%; Density: 3,348.6 persons per square mile; Race: 47.9% White, 1.2% Black/African American, 1.3% Asian, 2.7% American Indian/Alaska Native, 0.1% Native Hawaiian/Other Pacific Islander, 4.5% Two or more races, 87.5% Hispanic of any race; Average household size: 4.26; Median age: 25.9; Age under 18: 34.0%; Age 65 and over: 5.9%; Males per 100 females: 115.7; Marriage status: 41.4% never married, 49.7% now married, 2.6% separated, 4.6% widowed, 4.3% divorced; Foreign born: 48.9%; Speak English only: 13.9%; With disability: 7.0%; Veterans: 1.9%; Ancestry: 3.5% German, 1.4% English, 0.8% American, 0.8% Irish, 0.7% Italian
Employment: 3.7% management, business, and financial, 0.7% computer, engineering, and science, 7.0% education, legal, community service, arts, and media, 0.7% healthcare practitioners, 12.5% service, 15.7% sales and office, 47.7% natural resources, construction, and maintenance, 11.9% production, transportation, and material moving
Income: Per capita: $13,344; Median household: $45,905; Average household: $57,476; Households with income of $100,000 or more: 14.9%; Poverty rate: 20.5%

Educational Attainment: High school diploma or higher: 42.4%; Bachelor's degree or higher: 5.2%; Graduate/professional degree or higher: 2.3%

School District(s)

Bitterwater-Tully Elementary (KG-08)
2012-13 Enrollment: 28. . . . . (831) 385-5339
King City Union (KG-08)
2012-13 Enrollment: 2,577 . . . . (831) 385-2940
South Monterey County Joint Union High (KG-12)
2012-13 Enrollment: 1,971 . . . . (831) 385-0606

Housing: Homeownership rate: 46.4%; Median home value: $159,400; Median year structure built: 1982; Homeowner vacancy rate: 3.2%; Median gross rent: $973 per month; Rental vacancy rate: 3.4%
Health Insurance: 66.6% have insurance; 40.0% have private insurance; 31.9% have public insurance; 33.4% do not have insurance; 12.3% of children under 18 do not have insurance
Hospitals: George L Mee Memorial Hospital (123 beds)
Safety: Violent crime rate: 51.3 per 10,000 population; Property crime rate: 151.6 per 10,000 population
Newspapers: South County Newspapers (weekly circulation 5600)
Transportation: Commute: 91.0% car, 0.6% public transportation, 2.0% walk, 1.3% work from home; Median travel time to work: 22.3 minutes; Amtrak: Bus service available.

Additional Information Contacts

City of King . . . . (831) 385-3281
http://www.kingcity.com

LAS LOMAS (CDP). Covers a land area of 1.037 square miles and a water area of 0 square miles. Located at 36.87° N. Lat; 121.73° W. Long. Elevation is 43 feet.
Population: 3,024; Growth (since 2000): -1.8%; Density: 2,916.3 persons per square mile; Race: 38.6% White, 1.2% Black/African American, 1.8% Asian, 3.1% American Indian/Alaska Native, 0.8% Native Hawaiian/Other Pacific Islander, 5.3% Two or more races, 89.2% Hispanic of any race; Average household size: 5.06; Median age: 27.7; Age under 18: 33.1%; Age 65 and over: 6.4%; Males per 100 females: 111.2; Marriage status: 39.2% never married, 54.5% now married, 3.3% separated, 2.0% widowed, 4.3% divorced; Foreign born: 43.1%; Speak English only: 14.4%; With disability: 5.9%; Veterans: 1.7%; Ancestry: 1.4% Portuguese, 0.7% German, 0.7% American, 0.6% Irish, 0.5% Danish
Employment: 3.1% management, business, and financial, 0.0% computer, engineering, and science, 10.6% education, legal, community service, arts, and media, 1.7% healthcare practitioners, 14.8% service, 19.8% sales and office, 30.8% natural resources, construction, and maintenance, 19.1% production, transportation, and material moving
Income: Per capita: $14,345; Median household: $66,204; Average household: $67,463; Households with income of $100,000 or more: 18.8%; Poverty rate: 12.8%
Educational Attainment: High school diploma or higher: 39.1%; Bachelor's degree or higher: 7.3%; Graduate/professional degree or higher: n/a
Housing: Homeownership rate: 61.5%; Median home value: $319,800; Median year structure built: 1977; Homeowner vacancy rate: 1.1%; Median gross rent: $1,521 per month; Rental vacancy rate: 2.5%
Health Insurance: 72.7% have insurance; 45.8% have private insurance; 29.3% have public insurance; 27.3% do not have insurance; 3.8% of children under 18 do not have insurance
Transportation: Commute: 92.0% car, 0.0% public transportation, 0.0% walk, 7.6% work from home; Median travel time to work: 26.6 minutes

LOCKWOOD (CDP). Covers a land area of 10.873 square miles and a water area of 0.034 square miles. Located at 35.94° N. Lat; 121.08° W. Long. Elevation is 971 feet.
Population: 379; Growth (since 2000): n/a; Density: 34.9 persons per square mile; Race: 78.4% White, 1.1% Black/African American, 0.5% Asian, 1.6% American Indian/Alaska Native, 0.0% Native Hawaiian/Other Pacific Islander, 3.7% Two or more races, 26.4% Hispanic of any race; Average household size: 2.33; Median age: 44.5; Age under 18: 25.9%; Age 65 and over: 12.4%; Males per 100 females: 101.6

School District(s)

San Antonio Union Elementary (KG-08)
2012-13 Enrollment: 161. . . . . (831) 385-3051

Housing: Homeownership rate: 59.5%; Homeowner vacancy rate: 1.0%; Rental vacancy rate: 13.0%

MARINA (city). Covers a land area of 8.883 square miles and a water area of 0.880 square miles. Located at 36.68° N. Lat; 121.79° W. Long. Elevation is 43 feet.
Population: 19,718; Growth (since 2000): -21.4%; Density: 2,219.8 persons per square mile; Race: 45.2% White, 7.5% Black/African American, 19.9% Asian, 0.7% American Indian/Alaska Native, 2.8% Native Hawaiian/Other Pacific Islander, 10.0% Two or more races, 27.2% Hispanic of any race; Average household size: 2.75; Median age: 34.0; Age under 18: 24.2%; Age 65 and over: 11.4%; Males per 100 females: 92.8; Marriage status: 37.7% never married, 45.6% now married, 2.5% separated, 5.0% widowed, 11.7% divorced; Foreign born: 21.5%; Speak English only: 64.1%; With disability: 11.4%; Veterans: 11.9%; Ancestry: 9.7% German, 8.3% Irish, 6.1% English, 4.7% Italian, 2.1% Polish
Employment: 11.9% management, business, and financial, 4.6% computer, engineering, and science, 10.4% education, legal, community service, arts, and media, 2.9% healthcare practitioners, 29.5% service, 26.5% sales and office, 5.2% natural resources, construction, and maintenance, 8.9% production, transportation, and material moving
Income: Per capita: $25,101; Median household: $51,847; Average household: $68,087; Households with income of $100,000 or more: 21.6%; Poverty rate: 19.2%
Educational Attainment: High school diploma or higher: 81.4%; Bachelor's degree or higher: 22.9%; Graduate/professional degree or higher: 8.2%

School District(s)

Monterey Peninsula Unified (KG-12)
2012-13 Enrollment: 10,729 . . . . (831) 645-1200

Housing: Homeownership rate: 43.3%; Median home value: $364,400; Median year structure built: 1974; Homeowner vacancy rate: 2.4%; Median gross rent: $1,137 per month; Rental vacancy rate: 3.6%
Health Insurance: 82.7% have insurance; 64.4% have private insurance; 31.6% have public insurance; 17.3% do not have insurance; 7.7% of children under 18 do not have insurance
Safety: Violent crime rate: 24.5 per 10,000 population; Property crime rate: 274.2 per 10,000 population
Transportation: Commute: 88.7% car, 3.8% public transportation, 2.3% walk, 3.4% work from home; Median travel time to work: 23.3 minutes

Additional Information Contacts

City of Marina . . . . (831) 884-1278
http://www.ci.marina.ca.us

MONTEREY (city). Covers a land area of 8.466 square miles and a water area of 3.298 square miles. Located at 36.60° N. Lat; 121.88° W. Long. Elevation is 26 feet.
History: Monterey was founded by the Spanish Crown and was the capital of old California for most of the time between 1775 and 1846, when it came under American rule. Monterey Bay was named in 1542 by Sebastian Vizcaino for the Count of Monte-Rey, Viceroy of Mexico. The Presidio and Mission San Carlos de Monterey were founded by Father Junipero Serra and Father Crespi in 1770. It was in Monterey that the first legislature met to form California's first constitution.
Population: 27,810; Growth (since 2000): -6.3%; Density: 3,284.9 persons per square mile; Race: 78.3% White, 2.8% Black/African American, 7.9% Asian, 0.5% American Indian/Alaska Native, 0.3% Native Hawaiian/Other Pacific Islander, 5.1% Two or more races, 13.7% Hispanic of any race; Average household size: 2.08; Median age: 36.9; Age under 18: 15.3%; Age 65 and over: 15.5%; Males per 100 females: 101.2; Marriage status: 31.3% never married, 49.1% now married, 1.7% separated, 6.2% widowed, 13.4% divorced; Foreign born: 19.9%; Speak English only: 73.5%; With disability: 10.2%; Veterans: 12.9%; Ancestry: 15.5% German, 11.0% Italian, 10.6% Irish, 10.4% English, 4.0% French
Employment: 19.7% management, business, and financial, 7.0% computer, engineering, and science, 16.1% education, legal, community service, arts, and media, 5.7% healthcare practitioners, 20.0% service, 21.5% sales and office, 5.3% natural resources, construction, and maintenance, 4.7% production, transportation, and material moving
Income: Per capita: $37,128; Median household: $63,958; Average household: $77,486; Households with income of $100,000 or more: 26.4%; Poverty rate: 10.4%
Educational Attainment: High school diploma or higher: 93.3%; Bachelor's degree or higher: 47.5%; Graduate/professional degree or higher: 23.1%

School District(s)

Monterey County Office of Education (KG-12)
2012-13 Enrollment: 1,606 . . . . (831) 755-0300

Monterey Peninsula Unified (KG-12)
2012-13 Enrollment: 10,729 . . . . (831) 645-1200

Four-year College(s)

Monterey Institute of International Studies (Private, Not-for-profit)
Fall 2013 Enrollment: 731 . . . . (831) 647-4100
Naval Postgraduate School (Public)
Fall 2013 Enrollment: 2,870 . . . . (831) 656-2511

Two-year College(s)

Monterey Peninsula College (Public)
Fall 2013 Enrollment: 9,519 . . . . (831) 646-4000
2013-14 Tuition: In-state $1,170; Out-of-state $5,466

Housing: Homeownership rate: 35.8%; Median home value: $617,300; Median year structure built: 1968; Homeowner vacancy rate: 2.0%; Median gross rent: $1,377 per month; Rental vacancy rate: 6.5%

Health Insurance: 83.9% have insurance; 72.9% have private insurance; 27.0% have public insurance; 16.1% do not have insurance; 4.3% of children under 18 do not have insurance

Hospitals: Community Hospital of the Monterey Peninsula (205 beds)

Safety: Violent crime rate: 40.9 per 10,000 population; Property crime rate: 377.7 per 10,000 population

Newspapers: Monterey County Herald (daily circulation 29600)

Transportation: Commute: 80.3% car, 2.1% public transportation, 6.7% walk, 6.7% work from home; Median travel time to work: 15.9 minutes; Amtrak: Bus service available.

Airports: Monterey Regional (primary service/non-hub)

Additional Information Contacts

City of Monterey . . . . (831) 646-3760
http://www.monterey.org

MOSS LANDING (CDP). Covers a land area of 0.398 square miles and a water area of 0.205 square miles. Located at 36.81° N. Lat; 121.79° W. Long. Elevation is 10 feet.

Population: 204; Growth (since 2000): -32.0%; Density: 513.0 persons per square mile; Race: 73.0% White, 3.4% Black/African American, 1.0% Asian, 0.5% American Indian/Alaska Native, 0.5% Native Hawaiian/Other Pacific Islander, 6.9% Two or more races, 22.5% Hispanic of any race; Average household size: 2.04; Median age: 46.5; Age under 18: 15.7%; Age 65 and over: 12.7%; Males per 100 females: 108.2

Housing: Homeownership rate: 55.0%; Homeowner vacancy rate: 0.0%; Rental vacancy rate: 8.2%

PACIFIC GROVE (city). Covers a land area of 2.865 square miles and a water area of 1.138 square miles. Located at 36.62° N. Lat; 121.93° W. Long. Elevation is 151 feet.

History: Pacific Grove, the site of the first Chautauqua in the west, was founded by Methodist Episcopal Church members in 1874 as a conference center, and developed as a family recreation and residential community.

Population: 15,041; Growth (since 2000): -3.1%; Density: 5,250.5 persons per square mile; Race: 84.5% White, 1.3% Black/African American, 5.8% Asian, 0.5% American Indian/Alaska Native, 0.3% Native Hawaiian/Other Pacific Islander, 4.4% Two or more races, 10.7% Hispanic of any race; Average household size: 2.09; Median age: 48.1; Age under 18: 16.5%; Age 65 and over: 21.6%; Males per 100 females: 85.2; Marriage status: 32.2% never married, 48.8% now married, 1.4% separated, 6.4% widowed, 12.6% divorced; Foreign born: 12.0%; Speak English only: 86.5%; With disability: 11.9%; Veterans: 12.6%; Ancestry: 17.7% German, 14.8% Irish, 13.1% English, 8.2% Italian, 4.8% American

Employment: 17.8% management, business, and financial, 5.9% computer, engineering, and science, 17.5% education, legal, community service, arts, and media, 4.6% healthcare practitioners, 21.3% service, 24.5% sales and office, 4.6% natural resources, construction, and maintenance, 3.9% production, transportation, and material moving

Income: Per capita: $44,343; Median household: $71,969; Average household: $96,987; Households with income of $100,000 or more: 34.1%; Poverty rate: 8.8%

Educational Attainment: High school diploma or higher: 95.5%; Bachelor's degree or higher: 50.4%; Graduate/professional degree or higher: 21.4%

School District(s)

Monterey County Office of Education (KG-12)
2012-13 Enrollment: 1,606 . . . . (831) 755-0300
Pacific Grove Unified (KG-12)
2012-13 Enrollment: 2,046 . . . . (831) 646-6520

Housing: Homeownership rate: 45.6%; Median home value: $667,000; Median year structure built: 1955; Homeowner vacancy rate: 3.8%; Median gross rent: $1,445 per month; Rental vacancy rate: 4.4%

Health Insurance: 87.9% have insurance; 78.5% have private insurance; 30.2% have public insurance; 12.1% do not have insurance; 5.2% of children under 18 do not have insurance

Safety: Violent crime rate: 14.2 per 10,000 population; Property crime rate: 198.5 per 10,000 population

Newspapers: Hometown Bulletin (weekly circulation 6500)

Transportation: Commute: 85.4% car, 1.4% public transportation, 2.9% walk, 6.5% work from home; Median travel time to work: 18.5 minutes

Additional Information Contacts

City of Pacific Grove . . . . (831) 648-3106
http://www.ci.pg.ca.us

PAJARO (CDP). Covers a land area of 0.927 square miles and a water area of 0 square miles. Located at 36.90° N. Lat; 121.74° W. Long. Elevation is 26 feet.

Population: 3,070; Growth (since 2000): -9.3%; Density: 3,312.2 persons per square mile; Race: 47.3% White, 0.5% Black/African American, 1.7% Asian, 2.5% American Indian/Alaska Native, 0.0% Native Hawaiian/Other Pacific Islander, 6.3% Two or more races, 94.1% Hispanic of any race; Average household size: 4.80; Median age: 25.6; Age under 18: 34.8%; Age 65 and over: 4.2%; Males per 100 females: 124.1; Marriage status: 42.2% never married, 53.9% now married, 2.4% separated, 2.3% widowed, 1.7% divorced; Foreign born: 55.4%; Speak English only: 3.5%; With disability: 5.9%; Veterans: 2.3%; Ancestry: 1.7% German, 0.5% Irish, 0.4% American, 0.2% Italian, 0.1% English

Employment: 0.0% management, business, and financial, 0.8% computer, engineering, and science, 2.3% education, legal, community service, arts, and media, 0.0% healthcare practitioners, 22.5% service, 9.3% sales and office, 50.8% natural resources, construction, and maintenance, 14.3% production, transportation, and material moving

Income: Per capita: $9,403; Median household: $37,975; Average household: $44,894; Households with income of $100,000 or more: 4.6%; Poverty rate: 33.6%

Educational Attainment: High school diploma or higher: 26.0%; Bachelor's degree or higher: 2.3%; Graduate/professional degree or higher: 2.3%

Housing: Homeownership rate: 22.7%; Median home value: $312,100; Median year structure built: 1970; Homeowner vacancy rate: 1.4%; Median gross rent: $1,130 per month; Rental vacancy rate: 3.2%

Health Insurance: 66.4% have insurance; 24.7% have private insurance; 45.5% have public insurance; 33.6% do not have insurance; 6.3% of children under 18 do not have insurance

Transportation: Commute: 83.0% car, 2.3% public transportation, 3.5% walk, 0.6% work from home; Median travel time to work: 22.8 minutes

PEBBLE BEACH (unincorporated postal area)

ZCTA: 93953

Covers a land area of 8.040 square miles and a water area of 1.191 square miles. Located at 36.59° N. Lat; 121.95° W. Long..

Population: 4,509; Growth (since 2000): -1.8%; Density: 560.8 persons per square mile; Race: 86.9% White, 1.0% Black/African American, 8.6% Asian, 0.2% American Indian/Alaska Native, 0.1% Native Hawaiian/Other Pacific Islander, 2.0% Two or more races, 3.7% Hispanic of any race; Average household size: 2.17; Median age: 57.8; Age under 18: 16.5%; Age 65 and over: 34.7%; Males per 100 females: 92.5; Marriage status: 15.7% never married, 71.7% now married, 0.3% separated, 7.9% widowed, 4.7% divorced; Foreign born: 11.6%; Speak English only: 81.5%; With disability: 10.2%; Veterans: 16.8%; Ancestry: 18.8% German, 17.9% English, 11.0% Irish, 6.4% Italian, 5.9% French

Employment: 32.8% management, business, and financial, 5.2% computer, engineering, and science, 20.7% education, legal, community service, arts, and media, 6.3% healthcare practitioners, 8.9% service, 18.8% sales and office, 4.0% natural resources, construction, and maintenance, 3.2% production, transportation, and material moving

Income: Per capita: $59,833; Median household: $100,268; Average household: $146,361; Households with income of $100,000 or more: 50.3%; Poverty rate: 9.9%

Educational Attainment: High school diploma or higher: 98.6%; Bachelor's degree or higher: 64.4%; Graduate/professional degree or higher: 27.7%

Housing: Homeownership rate: 83.2%; Median home value: $945,200; Median year structure built: 1972; Homeowner vacancy rate: 4.0%; Median gross rent: $2,000+ per month; Rental vacancy rate: 5.4%
Health Insurance: 93.4% have insurance; 84.6% have private insurance; 37.3% have public insurance; 6.6% do not have insurance; 17.0% of children under 18 do not have insurance
Transportation: Commute: 82.5% car, 0.0% public transportation, 3.8% walk, 10.0% work from home; Median travel time to work: 20.9 minutes

PINE CANYON (CDP). Covers a land area of 3.336 square miles and a water area of <.001 square miles. Located at 36.17° N. Lat; 121.14° W. Long.
Population: 1,822; Growth (since 2000): n/a; Density: 546.2 persons per square mile; Race: 64.4% White, 1.6% Black/African American, 1.0% Asian, 0.8% American Indian/Alaska Native, 0.0% Native Hawaiian/Other Pacific Islander, 5.3% Two or more races, 54.0% Hispanic of any race; Average household size: 3.28; Median age: 34.4; Age under 18: 30.5%; Age 65 and over: 9.9%; Males per 100 females: 104.0
Housing: Homeownership rate: 81.0%; Homeowner vacancy rate: 2.8%; Rental vacancy rate: 1.9%

PRUNEDALE (CDP). Covers a land area of 46.054 square miles and a water area of 0.146 square miles. Located at 36.81° N. Lat; 121.65° W. Long. Elevation is 92 feet.
History: Prunedale is located about 10 miles north of Salinas. Early settler and banker Charles Langley operated the post office. It's been suggested that Prunedale was named for the prune tree orchards that were once unsuccessfully grown there.
Population: 17,560; Growth (since 2000): 6.9%; Density: 381.3 persons per square mile; Race: 67.0% White, 1.0% Black/African American, 3.8% Asian, 1.1% American Indian/Alaska Native, 0.3% Native Hawaiian/Other Pacific Islander, 5.9% Two or more races, 41.7% Hispanic of any race; Average household size: 3.08; Median age: 40.1; Age under 18: 24.8%; Age 65 and over: 11.7%; Males per 100 females: 101.7; Marriage status: 32.4% never married, 56.7% now married, 1.9% separated, 4.2% widowed, 6.7% divorced; Foreign born: 24.3%; Speak English only: 59.0%; With disability: 11.2%; Veterans: 9.4%; Ancestry: 9.1% German, 8.8% Irish, 8.0% English, 4.8% Italian, 3.0% French
Employment: 13.3% management, business, and financial, 3.2% computer, engineering, and science, 7.6% education, legal, community service, arts, and media, 4.1% healthcare practitioners, 16.7% service, 26.1% sales and office, 15.1% natural resources, construction, and maintenance, 13.9% production, transportation, and material moving
Income: Per capita: $28,590; Median household: $75,186; Average household: $90,407; Households with income of $100,000 or more: 34.5%; Poverty rate: 9.7%
Educational Attainment: High school diploma or higher: 76.5%; Bachelor's degree or higher: 18.1%; Graduate/professional degree or higher: 6.5%
Housing: Homeownership rate: 76.3%; Median home value: $368,900; Median year structure built: 1976; Homeowner vacancy rate: 1.9%; Median gross rent: $1,382 per month; Rental vacancy rate: 3.8%
Health Insurance: 80.8% have insurance; 65.2% have private insurance; 27.6% have public insurance; 19.2% do not have insurance; 11.9% of children under 18 do not have insurance
Transportation: Commute: 93.6% car, 0.9% public transportation, 0.2% walk, 2.7% work from home; Median travel time to work: 27.1 minutes; Amtrak: Bus service available.

SALINAS (city). County seat. Covers a land area of 23.179 square miles and a water area of 0.038 square miles. Located at 36.69° N. Lat; 121.63° W. Long. Elevation is 52 feet.
History: Salinas began as Ranchos del Rey, a stock center for the mission at Carmel and the Monterey presidio. The town dates from 1856 when Deacon Elias Howe erected the Half-Way House, an inn, store, and county meeting hall. The town grew as the center for a cattle, dairy, and truck gardening area, with lettuce as a principal crop.
Population: 150,441; Growth (since 2000): -0.4%; Density: 6,490.5 persons per square mile; Race: 45.8% White, 2.0% Black/African American, 6.3% Asian, 1.3% American Indian/Alaska Native, 0.3% Native Hawaiian/Other Pacific Islander, 5.1% Two or more races, 75.0% Hispanic of any race; Average household size: 3.66; Median age: 28.8; Age under 18: 31.4%; Age 65 and over: 7.5%; Males per 100 females: 102.1; Marriage status: 41.4% never married, 48.5% now married, 2.5% separated, 3.7% widowed, 6.5% divorced; Foreign born: 36.9%; Speak English only: 31.5%; With disability: 7.2%; Veterans: 4.2%; Ancestry: 3.5% German, 2.4% Irish, 2.1% Italian, 2.0% English, 1.1% American
Employment: 7.6% management, business, and financial, 1.9% computer, engineering, and science, 6.1% education, legal, community service, arts, and media, 2.9% healthcare practitioners, 21.2% service, 21.0% sales and office, 24.5% natural resources, construction, and maintenance, 14.9% production, transportation, and material moving
Income: Per capita: $17,396; Median household: $49,264; Average household: $62,112; Households with income of $100,000 or more: 17.1%; Poverty rate: 21.0%
Educational Attainment: High school diploma or higher: 60.6%; Bachelor's degree or higher: 12.4%; Graduate/professional degree or higher: 3.8%

School District(s)

Alisal Union (KG-08)
2012-13 Enrollment: 8,748 . . . . (831) 753-5700
Graves Elementary (KG-08)
2012-13 Enrollment: 41. . . . . (831) 422-6392
Lagunita Elementary (KG-08)
2012-13 Enrollment: 100. . . . . (831) 449-2800
Mission Trails Rop
2012-13 Enrollment: n/a . . . . (831) 753-4209
Monterey County Office of Education (KG-12)
2012-13 Enrollment: 1,606 . . . . (831) 755-0300
North Monterey County Unified (KG-12)
2012-13 Enrollment: 4,284 . . . . (831) 633-3343
Salinas City Elementary (KG-06)
2012-13 Enrollment: 8,807 . . . . (831) 753-5600
Salinas Union High (07-12)
2012-13 Enrollment: 13,879 . . . . (831) 796-7000
Santa Rita Union Elementary (KG-08)
2012-13 Enrollment: 3,136 . . . . (831) 443-7200
Spreckels Union Elementary (KG-08)
2012-13 Enrollment: 987. . . . . (831) 455-2550
Washington Union Elementary (KG-08)
2012-13 Enrollment: 954. . . . . (831) 484-2166

Two-year College(s)

Hartnell College (Public)
Fall 2013 Enrollment: 9,439 . . . . (831) 755-6700
2013-14 Tuition: In-state $1,340; Out-of-state $6,704
Heald College-Salinas (Private, For-profit)
Fall 2013 Enrollment: 1,076 . . . . (831) 443-1700
2013-14 Tuition: In-state $13,620; Out-of-state $13,620

Vocational/Technical School(s)

CET-Salinas (Private, Not-for-profit)
Fall 2013 Enrollment: 65. . . . . (408) 287-7924
2013-14 Tuition: $9,958
Central Coast College (Private, For-profit)
Fall 2013 Enrollment: 233. . . . . (831) 424-6767
2013-14 Tuition: $14,457
Salinas Beauty College Inc (Private, For-profit)
Fall 2013 Enrollment: 66. . . . . (831) 753-9356
2013-14 Tuition: $13,050
Waynes College of Beauty (Private, For-profit)
Fall 2013 Enrollment: 42. . . . . (831) 443-4077
2013-14 Tuition: $13,032

Housing: Homeownership rate: 45.1%; Median home value: $254,900; Median year structure built: 1975; Homeowner vacancy rate: 2.5%; Median gross rent: $1,120 per month; Rental vacancy rate: 4.6%
Health Insurance: 75.0% have insurance; 48.3% have private insurance; 32.2% have public insurance; 25.0% do not have insurance; 8.7% of children under 18 do not have insurance
Hospitals: Natividad Medical Center (172 beds); Salinas Valley Memorial Hospital (266 beds)
Safety: Violent crime rate: 64.3 per 10,000 population; Property crime rate: 343.9 per 10,000 population
Newspapers: The Salinas Californian (daily circulation 19300)
Transportation: Commute: 83.5% car, 0.9% public transportation, 1.1% walk, 3.5% work from home; Median travel time to work: 23.2 minutes; Amtrak: Train service available.
Airports: Salinas Municipal (general aviation)
Additional Information Contacts
City of Salinas . . . . (831) 758-7381
http://www.ci.salinas.ca.us

SAN ARDO (CDP). Covers a land area of 0.449 square miles and a water area of 0 square miles. Located at 36.02° N. Lat; 120.91° W. Long. Elevation is 449 feet.

Population: 517; Growth (since 2000): 3.2%; Density: 1,150.7 persons per square mile; Race: 48.7% White, 0.2% Black/African American, 1.0% Asian, 0.6% American Indian/Alaska Native, 0.0% Native Hawaiian/Other Pacific Islander, 2.1% Two or more races, 70.2% Hispanic of any race; Average household size: 3.69; Median age: 26.6; Age under 18: 35.8%; Age 65 and over: 8.5%; Males per 100 females: 112.8

School District(s)

San Ardo Union Elementary (KG-08)
2012-13 Enrollment: 101 . . . . (831) 627-2520

Housing: Homeownership rate: 33.6%; Homeowner vacancy rate: 4.1%; Rental vacancy rate: 9.6%

SAN LUCAS (CDP). Covers a land area of 0.394 square miles and a water area of 0 square miles. Located at 36.13° N. Lat; 121.02° W. Long. Elevation is 410 feet.

Population: 269; Growth (since 2000): -35.8%; Density: 682.5 persons per square mile; Race: 42.0% White, 0.0% Black/African American, 2.2% Asian, 1.5% American Indian/Alaska Native, 0.0% Native Hawaiian/Other Pacific Islander, 7.1% Two or more races, 83.3% Hispanic of any race; Average household size: 4.01; Median age: 26.3; Age under 18: 32.3%; Age 65 and over: 4.5%; Males per 100 females: 110.2

School District(s)

San Lucas Union Elementary (KG-08)
2012-13 Enrollment: 74 . . . . (831) 382-4426

Housing: Homeownership rate: 53.7%; Homeowner vacancy rate: 0.0%; Rental vacancy rate: 11.4%

SAND CITY (city). Covers a land area of 0.562 square miles and a water area of 2.362 square miles. Located at 36.62° N. Lat; 121.85° W. Long. Elevation is 72 feet.

Population: 334; Growth (since 2000): 28.0%; Density: 593.9 persons per square mile; Race: 66.8% White, 3.9% Black/African American, 4.8% Asian, 0.9% American Indian/Alaska Native, 0.3% Native Hawaiian/Other Pacific Islander, 5.1% Two or more races, 36.8% Hispanic of any race; Average household size: 2.27; Median age: 34.1; Age under 18: 17.7%; Age 65 and over: 2.7%; Males per 100 females: 124.2

Housing: Homeownership rate: 14.0%; Homeowner vacancy rate: 10.0%; Rental vacancy rate: 7.4%

Safety: Violent crime rate: 87.2 per 10,000 population; Property crime rate: 2,877.9 per 10,000 population

Additional Information Contacts

City of Sand . . . . (831) 394-3054
http://www.sandcity.org

SEASIDE (city). Covers a land area of 9.237 square miles and a water area of 0.139 square miles. Located at 36.63° N. Lat; 121.82° W. Long. Elevation is 33 feet.

History: Founded 1887, incorporated 1954.

Population: 33,025; Growth (since 2000): 4.2%; Density: 3,575.3 persons per square mile; Race: 48.4% White, 8.4% Black/African American, 9.7% Asian, 1.1% American Indian/Alaska Native, 1.6% Native Hawaiian/Other Pacific Islander, 7.9% Two or more races, 43.4% Hispanic of any race; Average household size: 3.16; Median age: 30.6; Age under 18: 27.0%; Age 65 and over: 8.6%; Males per 100 females: 100.5; Marriage status: 38.0% never married, 46.6% now married, 2.3% separated, 5.5% widowed, 10.0% divorced; Foreign born: 29.6%; Speak English only: 55.7%; With disability: 8.7%; Veterans: 8.7%; Ancestry: 10.1% German, 6.7% Irish, 6.6% English, 4.8% Italian, 1.9% French

Employment: 10.3% management, business, and financial, 3.2% computer, engineering, and science, 9.4% education, legal, community service, arts, and media, 3.3% healthcare practitioners, 38.1% service, 21.8% sales and office, 7.2% natural resources, construction, and maintenance, 6.7% production, transportation, and material moving

Income: Per capita: $22,574; Median household: $55,871; Average household: $69,521; Households with income of $100,000 or more: 22.3%; Poverty rate: 16.4%

Educational Attainment: High school diploma or higher: 74.2%; Bachelor's degree or higher: 22.5%; Graduate/professional degree or higher: 8.0%

School District(s)

Monterey Peninsula Unified (KG-12)
2012-13 Enrollment: 10,729 . . . . (831) 645-1200

Four-year College(s)

California State University-Monterey Bay (Public)
Fall 2013 Enrollment: 5,732 . . . . (831) 582-3000
2013-14 Tuition: In-state $5,963; Out-of-state $17,123

Housing: Homeownership rate: 41.4%; Median home value: $367,400; Median year structure built: 1965; Homeowner vacancy rate: 2.2%; Median gross rent: $1,503 per month; Rental vacancy rate: 4.9%

Health Insurance: 73.5% have insurance; 56.8% have private insurance; 26.6% have public insurance; 26.5% do not have insurance; 14.1% of children under 18 do not have insurance

Safety: Violent crime rate: 35.1 per 10,000 population; Property crime rate: 173.1 per 10,000 population

Newspapers: Monterey Co. Weekly (weekly circulation 43000)

Transportation: Commute: 80.3% car, 6.4% public transportation, 3.2% walk, 6.5% work from home; Median travel time to work: 18.9 minutes; Amtrak: Bus service available.

Additional Information Contacts

City of Seaside . . . . (831) 899-6700
http://www.ci.seaside.ca.us

SOLEDAD (city). Covers a land area of 4.414 square miles and a water area of 0.152 square miles. Located at 36.44° N. Lat; 121.31° W. Long. Elevation is 190 feet.

History: Soledad, whose name means solitude, grew up around the Franciscan Mission of Nuestra Senora de la Soledad, founded in 1791 by Father Fermin de Lasuen.

Population: 25,738; Growth (since 2000): 128.5%; Density: 5,831.1 persons per square mile; Race: 49.1% White, 11.4% Black/African American, 2.9% Asian, 1.4% American Indian/Alaska Native, 0.4% Native Hawaiian/Other Pacific Islander, 2.9% Two or more races, 71.1% Hispanic of any race; Average household size: 4.27; Median age: 34.9; Age under 18: 22.0%; Age 65 and over: 4.6%; Males per 100 females: 235.5; Marriage status: 43.0% never married, 39.5% now married, 3.5% separated, 4.3% widowed, 13.1% divorced; Foreign born: 32.8%; Speak English only: 36.9%; With disability: 7.1%; Veterans: 5.3%; Ancestry: 3.3% Irish, 2.9% German, 1.8% African, 1.5% English, 1.5% Italian

Employment: 6.4% management, business, and financial, 0.7% computer, engineering, and science, 5.0% education, legal, community service, arts, and media, 1.8% healthcare practitioners, 18.5% service, 19.2% sales and office, 32.6% natural resources, construction, and maintenance, 15.9% production, transportation, and material moving

Income: Per capita: $10,098; Median household: $49,570; Average household: $63,406; Households with income of $100,000 or more: 19.9%; Poverty rate: 21.3%

Educational Attainment: High school diploma or higher: 51.7%; Bachelor's degree or higher: 3.2%; Graduate/professional degree or higher: 0.8%

School District(s)

Mission Union Elementary (KG-08)
2012-13 Enrollment: 123 . . . . (831) 678-3524
Soledad Unified (PK-12)
2012-13 Enrollment: 4,708 . . . . (831) 678-3987

Vocational/Technical School(s)

CET-Soledad (Private, Not-for-profit)
Fall 2013 Enrollment: 97 . . . . (408) 287-7924
2013-14 Tuition: $9,958

Housing: Homeownership rate: 57.1%; Median home value: $203,700; Median year structure built: 1992; Homeowner vacancy rate: 2.4%; Median gross rent: $1,049 per month; Rental vacancy rate: 4.1%

Health Insurance: 75.0% have insurance; 44.8% have private insurance; 34.1% have public insurance; 25.0% do not have insurance; 9.6% of children under 18 do not have insurance

Safety: Violent crime rate: 27.4 per 10,000 population; Property crime rate: 94.6 per 10,000 population

Transportation: Commute: 90.3% car, 0.8% public transportation, 1.2% walk, 2.6% work from home; Median travel time to work: 25.3 minutes

Additional Information Contacts

City of Soledad . . . . (831) 223-5000
http://www.ci.soledad.ca.us

SPRECKELS (CDP). Covers a land area of 0.122 square miles and a water area of 0 square miles. Located at 36.62° N. Lat; 121.65° W. Long. Elevation is 75 feet.

Population: 673; Growth (since 2000): 38.8%; Density: 5,509.4 persons per square mile; Race: 71.8% White, 0.0% Black/African American, 3.9%

Asian, 1.9% American Indian/Alaska Native, 0.0% Native Hawaiian/Other Pacific Islander, 3.1% Two or more races, 28.7% Hispanic of any race; Average household size: 2.94; Median age: 39.4; Age under 18: 25.6%; Age 65 and over: 11.3%; Males per 100 females: 93.9

School District(s)

Spreckels Union Elementary (KG-08)
2012-13 Enrollment: 987. . . . . (831) 455-2550

Housing: Homeownership rate: 69.9%; Homeowner vacancy rate: 3.6%; Rental vacancy rate: 2.8%

Napa County

Located in western California; bounded on the south by San Pablo Bay; a mountainous area in the Coast Ranges, crossed by the Napa River. Covers a land area of 748.361 square miles, a water area of 40.220 square miles, and is located in the Pacific Time Zone at 38.51° N. Lat., 122.33° W. Long. The county was founded in 1850. County seat is Napa.

Napa County is part of the Napa, CA Metropolitan Statistical Area. The entire metro area includes: Napa County, CA

Weather Station: Angwin Pac Union Col — Elevation: 1,714 feet

	Jan	Feb	Mar	Apr	May	Jun	Jul	Aug	Sep	Oct	Nov	Dec
High	53	56	60	66	74	80	86	85	82	72	59	53
Low	39	40	41	43	47	51	55	54	54	50	43	38
Precip	7.4	8.3	5.6	2.3	1.5	0.3	0.0	0.1	0.4	2.0	5.1	8.0
Snow	tr	tr	tr	tr	tr	0.0	0.0	0.0	0.0	0.0	0.0	0.1

High and Low temperatures in degrees Fahrenheit; Precipitation and Snow in inches

Weather Station: Calistoga — Elevation: 370 feet

	Jan	Feb	Mar	Apr	May	Jun	Jul	Aug	Sep	Oct	Nov	Dec
High	60	64	68	73	80	86	92	91	88	80	67	59
Low	37	39	41	42	47	50	53	52	50	45	40	37
Precip	7.5	8.0	5.7	2.0	1.3	0.3	0.0	0.1	0.3	2.0	4.6	8.1
Snow	tr	tr	0.0	0.0	0.0	0.0	0.0	0.0	0.0	0.0	0.0	0.0

High and Low temperatures in degrees Fahrenheit; Precipitation and Snow in inches

Weather Station: Markley Cove — Elevation: 479 feet

	Jan	Feb	Mar	Apr	May	Jun	Jul	Aug	Sep	Oct	Nov	Dec
High	56	60	66	71	79	87	94	93	89	79	65	56
Low	36	38	41	44	49	54	57	56	54	48	41	37
Precip	5.6	6.3	4.3	1.6	0.9	0.1	0.0	0.1	0.3	1.3	3.1	5.4
Snow	0.0	0.0	0.0	0.0	0.0	0.0	0.0	0.0	0.0	0.0	0.0	0.0

High and Low temperatures in degrees Fahrenheit; Precipitation and Snow in inches

Weather Station: Napa State Hospital — Elevation: 35 feet

	Jan	Feb	Mar	Apr	May	Jun	Jul	Aug	Sep	Oct	Nov	Dec
High	58	62	67	71	76	81	83	83	83	77	65	57
Low	40	42	43	45	50	53	55	55	53	49	44	39
Precip	5.0	5.6	3.8	1.5	1.0	0.2	0.0	0.1	0.3	1.4	3.4	5.1
Snow	0.0	0.0	tr	0.0	0.0	0.0	0.0	0.0	0.0	0.0	0.0	0.0

High and Low temperatures in degrees Fahrenheit; Precipitation and Snow in inches

Weather Station: Saint Helena — Elevation: 225 feet

	Jan	Feb	Mar	Apr	May	Jun	Jul	Aug	Sep	Oct	Nov	Dec
High	58	62	66	72	79	85	89	89	86	78	65	58
Low	38	41	43	45	50	53	55	55	52	48	43	38
Precip	6.7	7.6	5.2	1.9	1.1	0.2	0.0	0.1	0.3	1.8	4.2	7.6
Snow	0.0	0.0	0.0	0.0	0.0	0.0	0.0	0.0	0.0	0.0	0.0	0.0

High and Low temperatures in degrees Fahrenheit; Precipitation and Snow in inches

Population: 136,484; Growth (since 2000): 9.8%; Density: 182.4 persons per square mile; Race: 71.5% White, 2.0% Black/African American, 6.8% Asian, 0.8% American Indian/Alaska Native, 0.3% Native Hawaiian/Other Pacific Islander, 4.1% two or more races, 32.2% Hispanic of any race; Average household size: 2.69; Median age: 39.7; Age under 18: 23.1%; Age 65 and over: 15.1%; Males per 100 females: 99.8; Marriage status: 29.5% never married, 53.2% now married, 1.9% separated, 6.2% widowed, 11.0% divorced; Foreign born: 22.4%; Speak English only: 65.0%; With disability: 10.8%; Veterans: 8.8%; Ancestry: 12.6% German, 9.9% Irish, 9.3% English, 6.6% Italian, 3.2% French

Religion: Six largest groups: 35.1% Catholicism, 3.8% Adventist, 2.4% Muslim Estimate, 2.0% Non-denominational Protestant, 1.9% Baptist, 1.6% Latter-day Saints

Economy: Unemployment rate: 4.5%; Leading industries: 13.3% retail trade; 10.9% manufacturing; 10.3% construction; Farms: 1,685 totaling 253,370 acres; Company size: 3 employ 1,000 or more persons, 4 employ 500 to 999 persons, 67 employ 100 to 499 persons, 3,885 employ less than 100 persons; Business ownership: 3,983 women-owned, n/a Black-owned, 1,319 Hispanic-owned, 689 Asian-owned

Employment: 16.7% management, business, and financial, 3.5% computer, engineering, and science, 9.2% education, legal, community service, arts, and media, 5.9% healthcare practitioners, 20.6% service, 21.5% sales and office, 10.9% natural resources, construction, and maintenance, 11.8% production, transportation, and material moving

Income: Per capita: $34,795; Median household: $70,443; Average household: $94,451; Households with income of $100,000 or more: 33.6%; Poverty rate: 10.1%

Educational Attainment: High school diploma or higher: 83.1%; Bachelor's degree or higher: 31.3%; Graduate/professional degree or higher: 10.6%

Housing: Homeownership rate: 62.6%; Median home value: $428,600; Median year structure built: 1974; Homeowner vacancy rate: 2.4%; Median gross rent: $1,350 per month; Rental vacancy rate: 7.1%

Vital Statistics: Birth rate: 112.7 per 10,000 population; Death rate: 87.8 per 10,000 population; Age-adjusted cancer mortality rate: 174.3 deaths per 100,000 population

Health Insurance: 85.5% have insurance; 72.1% have private insurance; 26.9% have public insurance; 14.5% do not have insurance; 9.4% of children under 18 do not have insurance

Health Care: Physicians: 30.1 per 10,000 population; Hospital beds: 110.2 per 10,000 population; Hospital admissions: 1,057.6 per 10,000 population

Air Quality Index: 60.3% good, 39.2% moderate, 0.5% unhealthy for sensitive individuals, 0.0% unhealthy (percent of days)

Transportation: Commute: 87.8% car, 1.0% public transportation, 4.3% walk, 5.5% work from home; Median travel time to work: 23.6 minutes

Presidential Election: 61.7% Obama, 36.0% Romney (2012)

National and State Parks: Bale Grist Mill State Historic Park; Bothe-Napa Valley State Park; Las Posadas State Forest; Robert Louis Stevenson State Park

Additional Information Contacts

Napa Government. . . . . (707) 253-4421
http://www.countyofnapa.org

Napa County Communities

AMERICAN CANYON (city). Covers a land area of 4.837 square miles and a water area of 0.008 square miles. Located at 38.18° N. Lat; 122.26° W. Long. Elevation is 46 feet.

History: American Canyon was formerly known as Napa Junction and is part of the San Francisco Bay Area. It became incorporated on January 1, 1992.

Population: 19,454; Growth (since 2000): 99.0%; Density: 4,022.1 persons per square mile; Race: 38.9% White, 7.9% Black/African American, 32.9% Asian, 0.7% American Indian/Alaska Native, 0.9% Native Hawaiian/Other Pacific Islander, 6.6% Two or more races, 25.7% Hispanic of any race; Average household size: 3.43; Median age: 35.5; Age under 18: 28.3%; Age 65 and over: 9.6%; Males per 100 females: 96.0; Marriage status: 29.7% never married, 57.6% now married, 1.7% separated, 5.0% widowed, 7.7% divorced; Foreign born: 34.6%; Speak English only: 50.4%; With disability: 7.8%; Veterans: 7.3%; Ancestry: 5.8% Irish, 5.7% German, 4.3% English, 2.7% Italian, 2.0% Dutch

Employment: 13.5% management, business, and financial, 5.9% computer, engineering, and science, 8.1% education, legal, community service, arts, and media, 11.3% healthcare practitioners, 18.4% service, 21.3% sales and office, 7.4% natural resources, construction, and maintenance, 14.2% production, transportation, and material moving

Income: Per capita: $28,683; Median household: $83,230; Average household: $99,286; Households with income of $100,000 or more: 40.6%; Poverty rate: 8.6%

Educational Attainment: High school diploma or higher: 84.9%; Bachelor's degree or higher: 32.3%; Graduate/professional degree or higher: 10.8%

School District(s)

Napa Valley Unified (PK-12)
2012-13 Enrollment: 18,326 . . . . (707) 253-3715

Housing: Homeownership rate: 78.6%; Median home value: $330,200; Median year structure built: 1997; Homeowner vacancy rate: 2.6%; Median gross rent: $1,622 per month; Rental vacancy rate: 3.8%

Health Insurance: 88.1% have insurance; 72.4% have private insurance; 24.0% have public insurance; 11.9% do not have insurance; 3.1% of children under 18 do not have insurance

Safety: Violent crime rate: 26.9 per 10,000 population; Property crime rate: 254.1 per 10,000 population

Newspapers: American Canyon Eagle (weekly circulation 5000)

Transportation: Commute: 93.9% car, 0.9% public transportation, 1.3% walk, 3.4% work from home; Median travel time to work: 31.7 minutes

Additional Information Contacts

City of American Canyon. . . . . (707) 647-4360
http://cityofamericancanyon.org

ANGWIN (CDP). Covers a land area of 4.829 square miles and a water area of 0.042 square miles. Located at 38.58° N. Lat; 122.45° W. Long. Elevation is 1,752 feet.

Population: 3,051; Growth (since 2000): -3.1%; Density: 631.8 persons per square mile; Race: 69.6% White, 4.6% Black/African American, 11.1% Asian, 0.7% American Indian/Alaska Native, 0.2% Native Hawaiian/Other Pacific Islander, 6.2% Two or more races, 20.5% Hispanic of any race; Average household size: 2.50; Median age: 24.4; Age under 18: 13.5%; Age 65 and over: 8.4%; Males per 100 females: 102.3; Marriage status: 54.5% never married, 35.8% now married, 0.9% separated, 3.2% widowed, 6.5% divorced; Foreign born: 14.2%; Speak English only: 70.0%; With disability: 11.4%; Veterans: 3.1%; Ancestry: 18.0% German, 10.2% English, 4.5% Irish, 4.1% Scottish, 3.7% Dutch

Employment: 11.0% management, business, and financial, 1.0% computer, engineering, and science, 20.9% education, legal, community service, arts, and media, 6.5% healthcare practitioners, 23.0% service, 24.6% sales and office, 9.1% natural resources, construction, and maintenance, 3.8% production, transportation, and material moving

Income: Per capita: $19,517; Median household: $56,895; Average household: $74,276; Households with income of $100,000 or more: 22.2%; Poverty rate: 12.0%

Educational Attainment: High school diploma or higher: 91.5%; Bachelor's degree or higher: 43.4%; Graduate/professional degree or higher: 14.5%

School District(s)

Howell Mountain Elementary (KG-08)
2012-13 Enrollment: 105. . . . . (707) 965-2423

Four-year College(s)

Pacific Union College (Private, Not-for-profit, Seventh Day Adventists)
Fall 2013 Enrollment: 1,647 . . . . (707) 965-6313
2013-14 Tuition: In-state $27,480; Out-of-state $27,480

Housing: Homeownership rate: 52.0%; Median home value: $581,000; Median year structure built: 1967; Homeowner vacancy rate: 0.2%; Median gross rent: $1,072 per month; Rental vacancy rate: 5.9%

Health Insurance: 89.5% have insurance; 81.2% have private insurance; 19.8% have public insurance; 10.5% do not have insurance; 1.8% of children under 18 do not have insurance

Transportation: Commute: 60.6% car, 0.7% public transportation, 28.0% walk, 8.8% work from home; Median travel time to work: 13.5 minutes

---

CALISTOGA (city). Covers a land area of 2.595 square miles and a water area of 0.018 square miles. Located at 38.58° N. Lat; 122.58° W. Long. Elevation is 348 feet.

History: Calistoga was laid out by Samuel Brannan in 1859 as a health spa utilizing the hot springs here. He devised the name from California and Saratoga, the famous springs in New York State.

Population: 5,155; Growth (since 2000): -0.7%; Density: 1,986.2 persons per square mile; Race: 72.5% White, 0.5% Black/African American, 0.9% Asian, 0.4% American Indian/Alaska Native, 0.2% Native Hawaiian/Other Pacific Islander, 6.7% Two or more races, 49.4% Hispanic of any race; Average household size: 2.53; Median age: 40.0; Age under 18: 22.6%; Age 65 and over: 18.7%; Males per 100 females: 96.5; Marriage status: 28.2% never married, 53.5% now married, 2.4% separated, 5.8% widowed, 12.5% divorced; Foreign born: 27.3%; Speak English only: 56.3%; With disability: 13.4%; Veterans: 7.8%; Ancestry: 13.0% German, 9.2% English, 8.0% Irish, 6.8% Italian, 3.9% French

Employment: 23.6% management, business, and financial, 0.9% computer, engineering, and science, 5.6% education, legal, community service, arts, and media, 2.8% healthcare practitioners, 22.3% service, 8.6% sales and office, 22.3% natural resources, construction, and maintenance, 13.9% production, transportation, and material moving

Income: Per capita: $33,548; Median household: $55,895; Average household: $80,360; Households with income of $100,000 or more: 27.8%; Poverty rate: 12.7%

Educational Attainment: High school diploma or higher: 77.7%; Bachelor's degree or higher: 28.0%; Graduate/professional degree or higher: 8.9%

School District(s)

Calistoga Joint Unified (KG-12)
2012-13 Enrollment: 809. . . . . (707) 942-4703

Housing: Homeownership rate: 57.7%; Median home value: $358,100; Median year structure built: 1976; Homeowner vacancy rate: 3.4%; Median gross rent: $1,081 per month; Rental vacancy rate: 5.0%

Health Insurance: 79.6% have insurance; 65.0% have private insurance; 27.4% have public insurance; 20.4% do not have insurance; 11.7% of children under 18 do not have insurance

Safety: Violent crime rate: 17.2 per 10,000 population; Property crime rate: 143.6 per 10,000 population

Newspapers: Weekly Calistogan (weekly circulation 2500)

Transportation: Commute: 83.4% car, 2.4% public transportation, 6.5% walk, 2.1% work from home; Median travel time to work: 22.9 minutes

Additional Information Contacts

City of Calistoga . . . . (707) 942-2800
http://www.ci.calistoga.ca.us

DEER PARK (CDP). Covers a land area of 5.578 square miles and a water area of 0.004 square miles. Located at 38.54° N. Lat; 122.47° W. Long. Elevation is 568 feet.

History: Bale Grist Mill State Historic Park to Northwest.

Population: 1,267; Growth (since 2000): -11.6%; Density: 227.1 persons per square mile; Race: 87.5% White, 1.0% Black/African American, 4.0% Asian, 0.7% American Indian/Alaska Native, 0.0% Native Hawaiian/Other Pacific Islander, 2.0% Two or more races, 11.6% Hispanic of any race; Average household size: 2.21; Median age: 51.9; Age under 18: 15.1%; Age 65 and over: 21.7%; Males per 100 females: 91.1

Housing: Homeownership rate: 56.4%; Homeowner vacancy rate: 2.2%; Rental vacancy rate: 6.0%

MOSKOWITE CORNER (CDP). Covers a land area of 2.811 square miles and a water area of 0.005 square miles. Located at 38.44° N. Lat; 122.19° W. Long.

Population: 211; Growth (since 2000): n/a; Density: 75.1 persons per square mile; Race: 86.7% White, 0.5% Black/African American, 0.5% Asian, 6.6% American Indian/Alaska Native, 0.0% Native Hawaiian/Other Pacific Islander, 1.9% Two or more races, 11.8% Hispanic of any race; Average household size: 2.45; Median age: 49.4; Age under 18: 19.4%; Age 65 and over: 16.1%; Males per 100 females: 104.9

Housing: Homeownership rate: 90.6%; Homeowner vacancy rate: 1.3%; Rental vacancy rate: 18.2%

NAPA (city). County seat. Covers a land area of 17.839 square miles and a water area of 0.308 square miles. Located at 38.30° N. Lat; 122.30° W. Long. Elevation is 20 feet.

History: Settlers arrived in Napa in 1832. The town was founded in 1848 when Nathan Coombs erected a saloon here, and grew as a service center for ranchers and grape-growers in the valley.

Population: 76,915; Growth (since 2000): 6.0%; Density: 4,311.6 persons per square mile; Race: 75.1% White, 0.6% Black/African American, 2.3% Asian, 0.8% American Indian/Alaska Native, 0.2% Native Hawaiian/Other Pacific Islander, 3.7% Two or more races, 37.6% Hispanic of any race; Average household size: 2.69; Median age: 37.4; Age under 18: 24.5%; Age 65 and over: 13.6%; Males per 100 females: 97.4; Marriage status: 30.3% never married, 51.6% now married, 2.3% separated, 5.6% widowed, 12.5% divorced; Foreign born: 22.8%; Speak English only: 64.1%; With disability: 10.6%; Veterans: 8.7%; Ancestry: 12.4% German, 10.4% Irish, 8.9% English, 6.7% Italian, 3.0% French

Employment: 14.1% management, business, and financial, 3.4% computer, engineering, and science, 9.3% education, legal, community service, arts, and media, 4.7% healthcare practitioners, 22.1% service, 21.8% sales and office, 11.9% natural resources, construction, and maintenance, 12.6% production, transportation, and material moving

Income: Per capita: $30,668; Median household: $63,274; Average household: $81,216; Households with income of $100,000 or more: 29.1%; Poverty rate: 11.1%

Educational Attainment: High school diploma or higher: 80.2%; Bachelor's degree or higher: 27.1%; Graduate/professional degree or higher: 9.2%

School District(s)

Napa County Office of Education (PK-12)
2012-13 Enrollment: 137. . . . . (707) 253-6810
Napa County Rop
2012-13 Enrollment: n/a . . . . (707) 253-6831
Napa Valley Unified (PK-12)
2012-13 Enrollment: 18,326 . . . . (707) 253-3715

Two-year College(s)

Napa Valley College (Public)
Fall 2013 Enrollment: 6,308 . . . . (707) 253-3000
2013-14 Tuition: In-state $1,142; Out-of-state $5,942

Vocational/Technical School(s)

LeMelange Academy of Hair (Private, For-profit)
Fall 2013 Enrollment: 48 . . . . (707) 257-7767
2013-14 Tuition: $19,485

Housing: Homeownership rate: 57.4%; Median home value: $403,000; Median year structure built: 1973; Homeowner vacancy rate: 2.3%; Median gross rent: $1,320 per month; Rental vacancy rate: 5.7%

Health Insurance: 83.5% have insurance; 69.5% have private insurance; 26.7% have public insurance; 16.5% do not have insurance; 11.5% of children under 18 do not have insurance

Hospitals: Queen of the Valley Medical Center (166 beds)

Safety: Violent crime rate: 32.4 per 10,000 population; Property crime rate: 178.9 per 10,000 population

Newspapers: Napa Sentinel (weekly circulation 15000); Napa Valley Register (daily circulation 15000)

Transportation: Commute: 90.0% car, 1.1% public transportation, 3.2% walk, 4.1% work from home; Median travel time to work: 21.5 minutes; Amtrak: Bus service available.

Airports: Napa County (general aviation)

Additional Information Contacts

City of Napa. . . . . (707) 257-9500
http://www.cityofnapa.org

POPE VALLEY (unincorporated postal area)

ZCTA: 94567

Covers a land area of 131.413 square miles and a water area of 2.416 square miles. Located at 38.71° N. Lat; 122.39° W. Long. Elevation is 715 feet.

Population: 623; Growth (since 2000): 27.7%; Density: 4.7 persons per square mile; Race: 83.3% White, 0.2% Black/African American, 1.4% Asian, 1.3% American Indian/Alaska Native, 0.2% Native Hawaiian/Other Pacific Islander, 6.6% Two or more races, 25.2% Hispanic of any race; Average household size: 2.69; Median age: 39.8; Age under 18: 23.1%; Age 65 and over: 10.6%; Males per 100 females: 94.1

School District(s)

Pope Valley Union Elementary (KG-08)
2012-13 Enrollment: 53. . . . . (707) 965-2402

Housing: Homeownership rate: 75.6%; Homeowner vacancy rate: 3.2%; Rental vacancy rate: 9.5%

RUTHERFORD (CDP).

Covers a land area of 1.680 square miles and a water area of 0.004 square miles. Located at 38.46° N. Lat; 122.43° W. Long. Elevation is 174 feet.

Population: 164; Growth (since 2000): n/a; Density: 97.6 persons per square mile; Race: 75.0% White, 0.0% Black/African American, 0.0% Asian, 0.0% American Indian/Alaska Native, 0.0% Native Hawaiian/Other Pacific Islander, 6.7% Two or more races, 42.7% Hispanic of any race; Average household size: 2.31; Median age: 45.7; Age under 18: 22.6%; Age 65 and over: 17.7%; Males per 100 females: 105.0

Housing: Homeownership rate: 45.1%; Homeowner vacancy rate: 0.0%; Rental vacancy rate: 2.4%

SAINT HELENA (city).

Covers a land area of 4.986 square miles and a water area of 0.041 square miles. Located at 38.50° N. Lat; 122.47° W. Long. Elevation is 253 feet.

History: Many early residents of St. Helena came from the vineyard areas of Switzerland, Germany, and Italy, and continued the tradition of growing grapes for wine.

Population: 5,814; Growth (since 2000): -2.3%; Density: 1,166.1 persons per square mile; Race: 77.8% White, 0.4% Black/African American, 1.7% Asian, 0.6% American Indian/Alaska Native, 0.2% Native Hawaiian/Other Pacific Islander, 2.5% Two or more races, 32.9% Hispanic of any race; Average household size: 2.38; Median age: 42.9; Age under 18: 22.0%; Age 65 and over: 19.3%; Males per 100 females: 88.2; Marriage status: 24.8% never married, 56.3% now married, 0.4% separated, 9.2% widowed, 9.8% divorced; Foreign born: 16.8%; Speak English only: 72.5%; With disability: 11.1%; Veterans: 8.8%; Ancestry: 18.4% German, 16.6% English, 12.7% Italian, 12.0% Irish, 5.1% French

Employment: 23.9% management, business, and financial, 3.3% computer, engineering, and science, 10.5% education, legal, community service, arts, and media, 3.3% healthcare practitioners, 17.0% service, 26.1% sales and office, 8.6% natural resources, construction, and maintenance, 7.4% production, transportation, and material moving

Income: Per capita: $48,817; Median household: $77,786; Average household: $106,745; Households with income of $100,000 or more: 39.4%; Poverty rate: 6.8%

Educational Attainment: High school diploma or higher: 89.8%; Bachelor's degree or higher: 46.7%; Graduate/professional degree or higher: 15.3%

School District(s)

Saint Helena Unified (KG-12)
2012-13 Enrollment: 1,295 . . . . (707) 967-2708

Housing: Homeownership rate: 55.4%; Median home value: $870,200; Median year structure built: 1974; Homeowner vacancy rate: 2.7%; Median gross rent: $1,634 per month; Rental vacancy rate: 5.8%

Health Insurance: 89.7% have insurance; 79.4% have private insurance; 30.3% have public insurance; 10.3% do not have insurance; 6.3% of children under 18 do not have insurance

Hospitals: Saint Helena Hospital (181 beds)

Safety: Violent crime rate: 10.1 per 10,000 population; Property crime rate: 121.3 per 10,000 population

Newspapers: St. Helena Star (weekly circulation 4500)

Transportation: Commute: 75.4% car, 0.0% public transportation, 11.3% walk, 13.3% work from home; Median travel time to work: 21.6 minutes

Additional Information Contacts

City of Saint Helena. . . . . (707) 967-2792
http://www.ci.st-helena.ca.us

SILVERADO RESORT (CDP).

Covers a land area of 1.891 square miles and a water area of 0.010 square miles. Located at 38.36° N. Lat; 122.26° W. Long.

Population: 1,095; Growth (since 2000): n/a; Density: 579.1 persons per square mile; Race: 92.2% White, 0.1% Black/African American, 3.3% Asian, 0.1% American Indian/Alaska Native, 0.4% Native Hawaiian/Other Pacific Islander, 1.4% Two or more races, 5.4% Hispanic of any race; Average household size: 2.03; Median age: 61.8; Age under 18: 10.7%; Age 65 and over: 40.6%; Males per 100 females: 91.1

Housing: Homeownership rate: 91.1%; Homeowner vacancy rate: 2.0%; Rental vacancy rate: 87.0%

YOUNTVILLE (city).

Covers a land area of 1.531 square miles and a water area of 0 square miles. Located at 38.40° N. Lat; 122.37° W. Long. Elevation is 98 feet.

History: Yountville stands on what was once a section of Rancho Caymus, granted in 1836 to George C. Yount who came to California from North Carolina with the Wolfskill party.

Population: 2,933; Growth (since 2000): 0.6%; Density: 1,915.3 persons per square mile; Race: 89.4% White, 1.3% Black/African American, 1.7% Asian, 1.0% American Indian/Alaska Native, 0.0% Native Hawaiian/Other Pacific Islander, 3.4% Two or more races, 9.9% Hispanic of any race; Average household size: 1.85; Median age: 64.0; Age under 18: 8.1%; Age 65 and over: 48.7%; Males per 100 females: 136.3; Marriage status: 21.3% never married, 41.6% now married, 0.6% separated, 19.5% widowed, 17.6% divorced; Foreign born: 8.4%; Speak English only: 89.9%; With disability: 15.6%; Veterans: 15.4%; Ancestry: 23.3% German, 18.2% Irish, 14.3% English, 11.2% Italian, 4.8% French

Employment: 27.5% management, business, and financial, 2.9% computer, engineering, and science, 12.6% education, legal, community service, arts, and media, 3.3% healthcare practitioners, 17.9% service, 25.8% sales and office, 0.5% natural resources, construction, and maintenance, 9.4% production, transportation, and material moving

Income: Per capita: $50,607; Median household: $70,231; Average household: $108,896; Households with income of $100,000 or more: 34.7%; Poverty rate: 5.4%

Educational Attainment: High school diploma or higher: 90.8%; Bachelor's degree or higher: 44.6%; Graduate/professional degree or higher: 17.4%

School District(s)

Napa Valley Unified (PK-12)
2012-13 Enrollment: 18,326 . . . . (707) 253-3715

Housing: Homeownership rate: 65.5%; Median home value: $541,000; Median year structure built: 1979; Homeowner vacancy rate: 4.2%; Median gross rent: $1,834 per month; Rental vacancy rate: 5.2%

Health Insurance: 92.6% have insurance; 79.9% have private insurance; 40.6% have public insurance; 7.4% do not have insurance; 1.0% of children under 18 do not have insurance

Safety: Violent crime rate: 3.4 per 10,000 population; Property crime rate: 192.0 per 10,000 population

Transportation: Commute: 66.5% car, 0.6% public transportation, 12.9% walk, 16.4% work from home; Median travel time to work: 16.3 minutes

Additional Information Contacts

Town of Yountville. . . . . (707) 944-8851
http://www.townofyountville.com

Nevada County

Located in eastern California; mountainous area, extending from the foothills to the crest of the Sierra Nevada; partly in Tahoe National Forest; includes Donner Lake and other lakes. Covers a land area of 957.772 square miles, a water area of 16.029 square miles, and is located in the Pacific Time Zone at 39.30° N. Lat., 120.77° W. Long. The county was founded in 1851. County seat is Nevada City.

Nevada County is part of the Truckee-Grass Valley, CA Micropolitan Statistical Area. The entire metro area includes: Nevada County, CA

Weather Station: Boca — Elevation: 5,575 feet

	Jan	Feb	Mar	Apr	May	Jun	Jul	Aug	Sep	Oct	Nov	Dec
High	43	46	51	58	67	76	85	84	77	66	52	43
Low	11	14	20	24	30	34	38	36	30	25	19	14
Precip	3.5	3.4	2.9	1.2	1.0	0.6	0.5	0.4	0.8	1.4	2.7	3.9
Snow	19.5	19.8	15.9	5.6	1.1	0.1	0.0	0.0	0.2	1.0	8.9	20.8

High and Low temperatures in degrees Fahrenheit; Precipitation and Snow in inches

Weather Station: Donner Memorial St Pk — Elevation: 5,937 feet

	Jan	Feb	Mar	Apr	May	Jun	Jul	Aug	Sep	Oct	Nov	Dec
High	40	43	48	54	64	72	81	81	74	63	49	39
Low	16	17	21	26	32	37	42	41	36	29	23	16
Precip	6.8	6.5	5.6	2.5	1.7	0.7	0.3	0.4	1.0	2.0	5.0	6.7
Snow	39.6	40.9	33.5	15.5	2.9	0.5	0.0	0.0	0.2	2.6	14.3	35.4

High and Low temperatures in degrees Fahrenheit; Precipitation and Snow in inches

Weather Station: Grass Valley No 2 — Elevation: 2,399 feet

	Jan	Feb	Mar	Apr	May	Jun	Jul	Aug	Sep	Oct	Nov	Dec
High	54	55	58	63	71	79	87	87	82	72	59	53
Low	32	34	36	39	46	51	56	55	50	43	36	32
Precip	9.0	9.3	8.3	3.9	2.4	0.7	0.0	0.2	0.9	2.5	6.5	9.9
Snow	0.7	2.8	2.5	0.4	0.0	0.0	0.0	0.0	0.0	0.0	0.3	1.6

High and Low temperatures in degrees Fahrenheit; Precipitation and Snow in inches

Weather Station: Nevada City — Elevation: 2,780 feet

	Jan	Feb	Mar	Apr	May	Jun	Jul	Aug	Sep	Oct	Nov	Dec
High	51	53	57	63	71	79	87	86	81	70	57	49
Low	34	35	37	40	46	53	59	58	53	46	38	34
Precip	10.4	10.9	9.2	4.6	2.7	0.7	0.1	0.2	0.9	2.8	7.0	11.5
Snow	3.1	5.9	4.1	0.7	tr	0.0	0.0	0.0	0.0	0.0	0.7	3.7

High and Low temperatures in degrees Fahrenheit; Precipitation and Snow in inches

Weather Station: Sagehen Creek — Elevation: 6,336 feet

	Jan	Feb	Mar	Apr	May	Jun	Jul	Aug	Sep	Oct	Nov	Dec
High	40	42	48	53	62	71	79	78	72	60	46	39
Low	14	15	20	24	29	33	37	36	32	26	20	15
Precip	4.7	5.5	5.2	2.1	1.4	0.6	0.4	0.4	1.1	2.0	4.6	5.4
Snow	na	na	na	na	na	0.3	0.0	tr	0.4	2.1	na	na

High and Low temperatures in degrees Fahrenheit; Precipitation and Snow in inches

Weather Station: Truckee Rs — Elevation: 6,020 feet

	Jan	Feb	Mar	Apr	May	Jun	Jul	Aug	Sep	Oct	Nov	Dec
High	41	44	49	55	65	74	83	82	75	64	49	41
Low	16	18	23	27	33	38	43	42	36	29	22	17
Precip	5.3	5.3	4.3	2.1	1.3	0.6	0.3	0.5	0.9	1.6	3.7	5.0
Snow	42.8	43.4	34.0	16.1	3.6	0.8	0.0	0.0	0.7	3.4	18.0	36.8

High and Low temperatures in degrees Fahrenheit; Precipitation and Snow in inches

Population: 98,764; Growth (since 2000): 7.3%; Density: 103.1 persons per square mile; Race: 91.4% White, 0.4% Black/African American, 1.2% Asian, 1.1% American Indian/Alaska Native, 0.1% Native Hawaiian/Other Pacific Islander, 3.2% two or more races, 8.5% Hispanic of any race; Average household size: 2.35; Median age: 47.6; Age under 18: 19.3%; Age 65 and over: 19.4%; Males per 100 females: 97.8; Marriage status: 24.9% never married, 55.0% now married, 2.2% separated, 6.5% widowed, 13.6% divorced; Foreign born: 6.0%; Speak English only: 92.3%; With disability: 13.4%; Veterans: 12.6%; Ancestry: 20.3% German, 17.7% English, 16.2% Irish, 6.8% Italian, 4.8% American

Religion: Six largest groups: 12.7% Non-denominational Protestant, 8.1% Catholicism, 2.2% Baptist, 1.7% Latter-day Saints, 1.3% Methodist/Pietist, 0.8% Adventist

Economy: Unemployment rate: 5.8%; Leading industries: 16.6% construction; 13.5% retail trade; 11.7% professional, scientific, and technical services; Farms: 742 totaling 42,114 acres; Company size: 1 employs 1,000 or more persons, 2 employ 500 to 999 persons, 24 employ 100 to 499 persons, 2,926 employ less than 100 persons; Business ownership: 4,158 women-owned, n/a Black-owned, n/a Hispanic-owned, n/a Asian-owned

Employment: 16.5% management, business, and financial, 5.8% computer, engineering, and science, 11.3% education, legal, community service, arts, and media, 5.9% healthcare practitioners, 19.7% service, 24.7% sales and office, 10.0% natural resources, construction, and maintenance, 6.1% production, transportation, and material moving

Income: Per capita: $32,346; Median household: $57,353; Average household: $75,824; Households with income of $100,000 or more: 24.8%; Poverty rate: 12.0%

Educational Attainment: High school diploma or higher: 94.3%; Bachelor's degree or higher: 32.3%; Graduate/professional degree or higher: 11.1%

Housing: Homeownership rate: 72.0%; Median home value: $357,300; Median year structure built: 1982; Homeowner vacancy rate: 2.6%; Median gross rent: $1,217 per month; Rental vacancy rate: 6.2%

Vital Statistics: Birth rate: 77.1 per 10,000 population; Death rate: 87.6 per 10,000 population; Age-adjusted cancer mortality rate: 160.8 deaths per 100,000 population

Health Insurance: 85.2% have insurance; 68.8% have private insurance; 34.7% have public insurance; 14.8% do not have insurance; 9.2% of children under 18 do not have insurance

Health Care: Physicians: 23.1 per 10,000 population; Hospital beds: 14.8 per 10,000 population; Hospital admissions: 708.8 per 10,000 population

Air Quality Index: 65.8% good, 32.8% moderate, 1.4% unhealthy for sensitive individuals, 0.0% unhealthy (percent of days)

Transportation: Commute: 83.7% car, 0.8% public transportation, 2.0% walk, 11.9% work from home; Median travel time to work: 24.6 minutes

Presidential Election: 47.8% Obama, 48.8% Romney (2012)

National and State Parks: Donner Memorial State Park; Empire Mine State Historic Park; Malakoff Diggins State Historic Park; South Yuba River State Park; Tahoe National Forest

Additional Information Contacts

Nevada Government. . . . . (530) 265-1480
http://www.mynevadacounty.com

Nevada County Communities

ALTA SIERRA (CDP). Covers a land area of 8.317 square miles and a water area of 0.021 square miles. Located at 39.13° N. Lat; 121.05° W. Long. Elevation is 2,310 feet.

Population: 6,911; Growth (since 2000): 6.0%; Density: 830.9 persons per square mile; Race: 93.1% White, 0.3% Black/African American, 1.1% Asian, 0.8% American Indian/Alaska Native, 0.1% Native Hawaiian/Other Pacific Islander, 2.9% Two or more races, 7.1% Hispanic of any race; Average household size: 2.43; Median age: 49.8; Age under 18: 19.5%; Age 65 and over: 23.4%; Males per 100 females: 97.5; Marriage status: 20.8% never married, 62.4% now married, 0.7% separated, 7.5% widowed, 9.3% divorced; Foreign born: 3.8%; Speak English only: 96.5%; With disability: 14.2%; Veterans: 15.2%; Ancestry: 24.0% German, 18.2% English, 16.1% Irish, 8.2% Italian, 5.4% Danish

Employment: 12.4% management, business, and financial, 8.6% computer, engineering, and science, 13.4% education, legal, community service, arts, and media, 7.1% healthcare practitioners, 18.3% service, 27.9% sales and office, 4.3% natural resources, construction, and maintenance, 8.1% production, transportation, and material moving

Income: Per capita: $33,835; Median household: $67,097; Average household: $82,260; Households with income of $100,000 or more: 31.4%; Poverty rate: 2.1%

Educational Attainment: High school diploma or higher: 96.8%; Bachelor's degree or higher: 28.7%; Graduate/professional degree or higher: 11.7%

Housing: Homeownership rate: 84.9%; Median home value: $312,700; Median year structure built: 1984; Homeowner vacancy rate: 2.4%; Median gross rent: $1,413 per month; Rental vacancy rate: 5.1%

Health Insurance: 91.4% have insurance; 79.1% have private insurance; 33.7% have public insurance; 8.6% do not have insurance; 5.9% of children under 18 do not have insurance

Transportation: Commute: 82.0% car, 1.6% public transportation, 0.0% walk, 15.3% work from home; Median travel time to work: 26.9 minutes

FLORISTON (CDP). Covers a land area of 0.950 square miles and a water area of 0 square miles. Located at 39.39° N. Lat; 120.02° W. Long. Elevation is 5,426 feet.

Population: 73; Growth (since 2000): n/a; Density: 76.8 persons per square mile; Race: 91.8% White, 0.0% Black/African American, 0.0% Asian, 5.5% American Indian/Alaska Native, 0.0% Native Hawaiian/Other Pacific Islander, 2.7% Two or more races, 0.0% Hispanic of any race; Average household size: 1.92; Median age: 49.1; Age under 18: 12.3%; Age 65 and over: 11.0%; Males per 100 females: 92.1

Housing: Homeownership rate: 76.3%; Homeowner vacancy rate: 0.0%; Rental vacancy rate: 18.2%

GRASS VALLEY (city). Covers a land area of 4.743 square miles and a water area of 0 square miles. Located at 39.22° N. Lat; 121.06° W. Long. Elevation is 2,411 feet.

History: The rich quartz mines which were to make Grass Valley one of the outstanding gold towns were tapped in 1850. Between 1850 and 1857 the Gold Hill Mine alone produced four million dollars. Early residents of Grass Valley were Lola Montez, who lived here in retirement from 1852-1854, and Lotta Crabtree, Lola's protegee.

Population: 12,860; Growth (since 2000): 17.7%; Density: 2,711.3 persons per square mile; Race: 89.4% White, 0.4% Black/African American, 1.5% Asian, 1.6% American Indian/Alaska Native, 0.1% Native Hawaiian/Other Pacific Islander, 3.9% Two or more races, 10.4% Hispanic of any race; Average household size: 2.04; Median age: 43.2; Age under 18: 20.4%; Age 65 and over: 23.5%; Males per 100 females: 78.9; Marriage status: 27.6% never married, 40.4% now married, 5.4% separated, 12.7% widowed, 19.3% divorced; Foreign born: 7.6%; Speak English only: 89.1%; With disability: 22.2%; Veterans: 11.1%; Ancestry: 17.3% German, 15.8% English, 14.5% Irish, 7.8% Italian, 6.2% Scottish

Employment: 12.7% management, business, and financial, 7.8% computer, engineering, and science, 9.9% education, legal, community service, arts, and media, 6.9% healthcare practitioners, 27.7% service, 23.4% sales and office, 6.6% natural resources, construction, and maintenance, 5.0% production, transportation, and material moving

Income: Per capita: $27,019; Median household: $36,203; Average household: $55,183; Households with income of $100,000 or more: 9.7%; Poverty rate: 24.6%

Educational Attainment: High school diploma or higher: 88.3%; Bachelor's degree or higher: 26.6%; Graduate/professional degree or higher: 9.7%

School District(s)

Chicago Park Elementary (KG-08)
2012-13 Enrollment: 140. . . . . (530) 346-2153

Clear Creek Elementary (KG-08)
2012-13 Enrollment: 166. . . . . (530) 273-3664

Grass Valley Elementary (KG-08)
2012-13 Enrollment: 1,682 . . . . (530) 273-4483

Nevada County Office of Education (KG-12)
2012-13 Enrollment: 3,418 . . . . (530) 478-6400

Nevada Joint Union High (09-12)
2012-13 Enrollment: 3,300 . . . . (530) 273-3351

Pleasant Ridge Union Elementary (KG-08)
2012-13 Enrollment: 1,424 . . . . (530) 268-2800

Union Hill Elementary (KG-08)
2012-13 Enrollment: 662. . . . . (530) 273-0647

Housing: Homeownership rate: 39.4%; Median home value: $266,400; Median year structure built: 1976; Homeowner vacancy rate: 4.0%; Median gross rent: $925 per month; Rental vacancy rate: 6.7%

Health Insurance: 83.5% have insurance; 49.9% have private insurance; 51.5% have public insurance; 16.5% do not have insurance; 8.7% of children under 18 do not have insurance

Hospitals: Sierra Nevada Memorial Hospital (75 beds)

Safety: Violent crime rate: 89.9 per 10,000 population; Property crime rate: 587.1 per 10,000 population

Newspapers: The Union (daily circulation 15900)

Transportation: Commute: 85.9% car, 0.6% public transportation, 3.9% walk, 8.3% work from home; Median travel time to work: 13.3 minutes

Airports: Nevada County Air Park (general aviation)

Additional Information Contacts

City of Grass Valley. . . . . (530) 274-4312
http://www.cityofgrassvalley.com

KINGVALE (CDP). Covers a land area of 0.962 square miles and a water area of 0.009 square miles. Located at 39.32° N. Lat; 120.44° W. Long. Elevation is 6,132 feet.

Population: 143; Growth (since 2000): n/a; Density: 148.7 persons per square mile; Race: 94.4% White, 0.7% Black/African American, 0.0% Asian, 0.7% American Indian/Alaska Native, 0.7% Native Hawaiian/Other Pacific Islander, 2.1% Two or more races, 4.2% Hispanic of any race; Average household size: 2.07; Median age: 46.9; Age under 18: 13.3%; Age 65 and over: 9.8%; Males per 100 females: 127.0

School District(s)

Tahoe-Truckee Joint Unified (KG-12)
2012-13 Enrollment: 3,917 . . . . (530) 582-2500

Housing: Homeownership rate: 82.6%; Homeowner vacancy rate: 9.5%; Rental vacancy rate: 0.0%

LAKE OF THE PINES (CDP). Covers a land area of 1.495 square miles and a water area of 0.351 square miles. Located at 39.04° N. Lat; 121.06° W. Long. Elevation is 1,516 feet.

Population: 3,917; Growth (since 2000): -1.0%; Density: 2,620.0 persons per square mile; Race: 93.7% White, 0.1% Black/African American, 1.7% Asian, 0.5% American Indian/Alaska Native, 0.2% Native Hawaiian/Other Pacific Islander, 3.2% Two or more races, 6.3% Hispanic of any race; Average household size: 2.50; Median age: 49.5; Age under 18: 22.2%; Age 65 and over: 24.4%; Males per 100 females: 90.4; Marriage status: 22.3% never married, 57.0% now married, 1.2% separated, 10.1% widowed, 10.7% divorced; Foreign born: 5.7%; Speak English only: 90.4%; With disability: 12.9%; Veterans: 15.3%; Ancestry: 26.5% German, 19.6% Irish, 18.9% English, 9.1% American, 8.3% Swedish

Employment: 24.3% management, business, and financial, 2.9% computer, engineering, and science, 18.4% education, legal, community service, arts, and media, 6.2% healthcare practitioners, 9.1% service, 27.2% sales and office, 4.3% natural resources, construction, and maintenance, 7.7% production, transportation, and material moving

Income: Per capita: $42,333; Median household: $87,330; Average household: $94,996; Households with income of $100,000 or more: 43.0%; Poverty rate: 4.6%

Educational Attainment: High school diploma or higher: 96.3%; Bachelor's degree or higher: 30.4%; Graduate/professional degree or higher: 8.2%

Housing: Homeownership rate: 78.8%; Median home value: $335,500; Median year structure built: 1977; Homeowner vacancy rate: 3.2%; Median gross rent: $1,939 per month; Rental vacancy rate: 2.3%

Health Insurance: 93.8% have insurance; 87.3% have private insurance; 33.6% have public insurance; 6.3% do not have insurance; 2.7% of children under 18 do not have insurance

Transportation: Commute: 86.5% car, 1.3% public transportation, 2.3% walk, 9.9% work from home; Median travel time to work: 35.8 minutes

LAKE WILDWOOD (CDP). Covers a land area of 3.059 square miles and a water area of 0.453 square miles. Located at 39.23° N. Lat; 121.20° W. Long. Elevation is 1,529 feet.

Population: 4,991; Growth (since 2000): 2.5%; Density: 1,631.6 persons per square mile; Race: 94.7% White, 0.3% Black/African American, 1.1% Asian, 0.9% American Indian/Alaska Native, 0.2% Native Hawaiian/Other Pacific Islander, 2.1% Two or more races, 5.4% Hispanic of any race; Average household size: 2.24; Median age: 58.4; Age under 18: 16.9%; Age 65 and over: 36.9%; Males per 100 females: 92.6; Marriage status: 16.9% never married, 63.1% now married, 1.6% separated, 10.0% widowed, 10.0% divorced; Foreign born: 6.7%; Speak English only: 90.7%; With disability: 13.8%; Veterans: 19.5%; Ancestry: 21.7% German, 14.9% English, 14.8% Irish, 6.2% American, 6.0% Italian

Employment: 22.6% management, business, and financial, 2.2% computer, engineering, and science, 21.9% education, legal, community service, arts, and media, 3.5% healthcare practitioners, 13.6% service, 24.3% sales and office, 7.7% natural resources, construction, and maintenance, 4.4% production, transportation, and material moving

Income: Per capita: $37,174; Median household: $66,114; Average household: $80,172; Households with income of $100,000 or more: 24.5%; Poverty rate: 5.0%

Educational Attainment: High school diploma or higher: 95.5%; Bachelor's degree or higher: 40.6%; Graduate/professional degree or higher: 14.2%

Housing: Homeownership rate: 83.4%; Median home value: $363,800; Median year structure built: 1985; Homeowner vacancy rate: 3.2%; Median gross rent: $1,767 per month; Rental vacancy rate: 6.8%

Health Insurance: 90.5% have insurance; 82.0% have private insurance; 43.1% have public insurance; 9.5% do not have insurance; 9.8% of children under 18 do not have insurance

Transportation: Commute: 85.2% car, 0.8% public transportation, 0.0% walk, 11.6% work from home; Median travel time to work: 34.2 minutes

NEVADA CITY (city). County seat. Covers a land area of 2.188 square miles and a water area of 0.004 square miles. Located at 39.26° N. Lat; 121.03° W. Long. Elevation is 2,477 feet.

History: Nevada City drew its early wealth from gold mines—the rich placer diggings of the 1850's and 1860's, the hydraulic excavations of the 1870's, and the deep quartz mines of the early 1900's. The forerunner of Nevada City was Beer Creek Diggings or Caldwell's Upper Store, named for a log cabin store kept by Dr. A.B. Caldwell. The National Hotel in Nevada City was a stopping place in the 1860's and 1870's for five or six stagecoaches a day. It was in Nevada City that the first samples of ore from the Comstock Lode in Nevada were assayed in 1858.

Population: 3,068; Growth (since 2000): 2.2%; Density: 1,402.0 persons per square mile; Race: 92.5% White, 0.8% Black/African American, 1.5% Asian, 0.9% American Indian/Alaska Native, 0.0% Native Hawaiian/Other Pacific Islander, 3.0% Two or more races, 6.7% Hispanic of any race; Average household size: 2.09; Median age: 47.5; Age under 18: 16.9%; Age 65 and over: 18.2%; Males per 100 females: 100.4; Marriage status: 35.4% never married, 45.0% now married, 3.3% separated, 3.0% widowed, 16.5% divorced; Foreign born: 10.4%; Speak English only: 93.0%; With disability: 8.2%; Veterans: 6.8%; Ancestry: 24.0% German, 21.5% Irish, 13.6% English, 8.0% Scottish, 7.3% European

Employment: 15.2% management, business, and financial, 8.2% computer, engineering, and science, 12.8% education, legal, community service, arts, and media, 7.1% healthcare practitioners, 12.4% service, 31.2% sales and office, 8.2% natural resources, construction, and maintenance, 5.0% production, transportation, and material moving

Income: Per capita: $34,524; Median household: $62,386; Average household: $86,215; Households with income of $100,000 or more: 24.8%; Poverty rate: 6.6%

Educational Attainment: High school diploma or higher: 96.2%; Bachelor's degree or higher: 44.8%; Graduate/professional degree or higher: 15.6%

School District(s)

Nevada City Elementary (KG-08)
2012-13 Enrollment: 896. . . . . (530) 265-1820
Nevada County Office of Education (KG-12)
2012-13 Enrollment: 3,418 . . . . (530) 478-6400
Twin Ridges Elementary (KG-08)
2012-13 Enrollment: 97. . . . . (530) 265-9052

Housing: Homeownership rate: 57.9%; Median home value: $421,700; Median year structure built: 1944; Homeowner vacancy rate: 3.8%; Median gross rent: $1,111 per month; Rental vacancy rate: 4.8%

Health Insurance: 81.3% have insurance; 68.8% have private insurance; 26.8% have public insurance; 18.7% do not have insurance; 2.8% of children under 18 do not have insurance

Safety: Violent crime rate: 85.6 per 10,000 population; Property crime rate: 424.5 per 10,000 population

Transportation: Commute: 74.7% car, 3.4% public transportation, 4.1% walk, 8.4% work from home; Median travel time to work: 24.3 minutes

Additional Information Contacts

City of Nevada City . . . . (530) 265-2496
http://www.nevadacityca.gov

NORTH SAN JUAN (CDP). Covers a land area of 2.422 square miles and a water area of 0 square miles. Located at 39.37° N. Lat; 121.11° W. Long. Elevation is 2,113 feet.

Population: 269; Growth (since 2000): n/a; Density: 111.1 persons per square mile; Race: 83.3% White, 0.4% Black/African American, 4.1% Asian, 4.5% American Indian/Alaska Native, 0.0% Native Hawaiian/Other Pacific Islander, 7.8% Two or more races, 3.3% Hispanic of any race; Average household size: 2.07; Median age: 49.8; Age under 18: 16.0%; Age 65 and over: 14.1%; Males per 100 females: 124.2

Housing: Homeownership rate: 47.7%; Homeowner vacancy rate: 1.6%; Rental vacancy rate: 0.0%

PENN VALLEY (CDP). Covers a land area of 2.121 square miles and a water area of 0 square miles. Located at 39.20° N. Lat; 121.19° W. Long. Elevation is 1,401 feet.

Population: 1,621; Growth (since 2000): 16.9%; Density: 764.1 persons per square mile; Race: 88.5% White, 0.6% Black/African American, 1.4% Asian, 2.1% American Indian/Alaska Native, 0.0% Native Hawaiian/Other Pacific Islander, 5.6% Two or more races, 8.8% Hispanic of any race; Average household size: 2.57; Median age: 44.5; Age under 18: 22.4%; Age 65 and over: 18.2%; Males per 100 females: 93.7

School District(s)

Pleasant Valley Elementary (KG-08)
2012-13 Enrollment: 477. . . . . (530) 432-7311
Ready Springs Union Elementary (KG-12)
2012-13 Enrollment: 254. . . . . (530) 432-7311

Housing: Homeownership rate: 77.2%; Homeowner vacancy rate: 2.6%; Rental vacancy rate: 3.3%

ROUGH AND READY (CDP). Covers a land area of 3.170 square miles and a water area of 0 square miles. Located at 39.23° N. Lat; 121.14° W. Long. Elevation is 1,890 feet.

Population: 963; Growth (since 2000): n/a; Density: 303.8 persons per square mile; Race: 92.0% White, 0.3% Black/African American, 1.7% Asian, 0.6% American Indian/Alaska Native, 0.6% Native Hawaiian/Other Pacific Islander, 3.6% Two or more races, 5.8% Hispanic of any race; Average household size: 2.25; Median age: 49.5; Age under 18: 16.6%; Age 65 and over: 18.1%; Males per 100 females: 108.0

Housing: Homeownership rate: 77.6%; Homeowner vacancy rate: 1.2%; Rental vacancy rate: 10.2%

SODA SPRINGS (CDP). Covers a land area of 0.339 square miles and a water area of 0 square miles. Located at 39.32° N. Lat; 120.38° W. Long. Elevation is 6,768 feet.

Population: 81; Growth (since 2000): n/a; Density: 238.6 persons per square mile; Race: 97.5% White, 0.0% Black/African American, 0.0% Asian, 2.5% American Indian/Alaska Native, 0.0% Native Hawaiian/Other Pacific Islander, 0.0% Two or more races, 8.6% Hispanic of any race; Average household size: 1.98; Median age: 35.8; Age under 18: 11.1%; Age 65 and over: 9.9%; Males per 100 females: 211.5

Housing: Homeownership rate: 51.2%; Homeowner vacancy rate: 4.5%; Rental vacancy rate: 4.8%

TRUCKEE (town). Covers a land area of 32.322 square miles and a water area of 1.332 square miles. Located at 39.35° N. Lat; 120.19° W. Long. Elevation is 5,817 feet.

History: Truckee, once a lumber camp, grew as a railroad and stock-raising supply center.

Population: 16,180; Growth (since 2000): 16.7%; Density: 500.6 persons per square mile; Race: 86.5% White, 0.4% Black/African American, 1.5% Asian, 0.6% American Indian/Alaska Native, 0.1% Native Hawaiian/Other Pacific Islander, 2.1% Two or more races, 18.6% Hispanic of any race; Average household size: 2.54; Median age: 38.0; Age under 18: 23.3%; Age 65 and over: 7.8%; Males per 100 females: 108.9; Marriage status: 30.5% never married, 56.3% now married, 2.0% separated, 3.1% widowed, 10.1% divorced; Foreign born: 11.6%; Speak English only: 84.3%; With disability: 4.8%; Veterans: 6.3%; Ancestry: 20.5% German, 17.3% English, 16.7% Irish, 6.1% Italian, 4.8% French

Employment: 18.4% management, business, and financial, 5.2% computer, engineering, and science, 12.0% education, legal, community service, arts, and media, 3.8% healthcare practitioners, 25.7% service, 21.7% sales and office, 10.6% natural resources, construction, and maintenance, 2.7% production, transportation, and material moving

Income: Per capita: $37,058; Median household: $66,810; Average household: $93,029; Households with income of $100,000 or more: 31.8%; Poverty rate: 9.6%

Educational Attainment: High school diploma or higher: 93.8%; Bachelor's degree or higher: 41.9%; Graduate/professional degree or higher: 12.8%

School District(s)

Tahoe-Truckee Joint Unified (KG-12)
2012-13 Enrollment: 3,917 . . . . (530) 582-2500

Housing: Homeownership rate: 68.2%; Median home value: $443,400; Median year structure built: 1988; Homeowner vacancy rate: 3.3%; Median gross rent: $1,380 per month; Rental vacancy rate: 7.8%

Health Insurance: 81.4% have insurance; 70.3% have private insurance; 19.8% have public insurance; 18.6% do not have insurance; 13.2% of children under 18 do not have insurance

Hospitals: Tahoe Forest Hospital (25 beds)

Safety: Violent crime rate: 11.1 per 10,000 population; Property crime rate: 107.1 per 10,000 population

Newspapers: Sierra Sun (weekly circulation 6500)

Transportation: Commute: 87.6% car, 0.6% public transportation, 0.9% walk, 10.1% work from home; Median travel time to work: 21.5 minutes; Amtrak: Train service available.

Airports: Truckee-Tahoe (general aviation)

Additional Information Contacts

City of Truckee . . . . (530) 582-7700
http://www.townoftruckee.com

WASHINGTON (CDP). Covers a land area of 1.899 square miles and a water area of 0 square miles. Located at 39.36° N. Lat; 120.79° W. Long. Elevation is 2,641 feet.

Population: 185; Growth (since 2000): n/a; Density: 97.4 persons per square mile; Race: 89.7% White, 0.5% Black/African American, 0.0% Asian, 2.2% American Indian/Alaska Native, 0.0% Native Hawaiian/Other Pacific Islander, 5.4% Two or more races, 5.9% Hispanic of any race; Average household size: 1.88; Median age: 51.7; Age under 18: 13.5%; Age 65 and over: 16.8%; Males per 100 females: 160.6

School District(s)

Twin Ridges Elementary (KG-08)
2012-13 Enrollment: 97. . . . . (530) 265-9052

Housing: Homeownership rate: 61.1%; Homeowner vacancy rate: 0.0%; Rental vacancy rate: 2.8%

Orange County

Located in southern California; coastal plains and foothills area, drained by the Santa Ana River; bounded on the southwest by the Pacific Ocean; includes part of Cleveland National Forest. Covers a land area of 790.568 square miles, a water area of 157.498 square miles, and is located in the Pacific Time Zone at 33.68° N. Lat., 117.78° W. Long. The county was founded in 1889. County seat is Santa Ana.

Orange County is part of the Los Angeles-Long Beach-Anaheim, CA Metropolitan Statistical Area. The entire metro area includes: Anaheim-Santa Ana-Irvine, CA Metropolitan Division (Orange County, CA); Los Angeles-Long Beach-Glendale, CA Metropolitan Division (Los Angeles County, CA)

Weather Station: Laguna Beach — Elevation: 35 feet

	Jan	Feb	Mar	Apr	May	Jun	Jul	Aug	Sep	Oct	Nov	Dec
High	67	68	69	71	73	75	79	80	79	76	71	67
Low	43	45	47	49	54	57	60	60	58	54	47	43
Precip	2.6	3.5	2.1	0.9	0.2	0.1	0.1	0.0	0.3	0.6	1.2	2.0
Snow	0.0	0.0	0.0	0.0	0.0	0.0	0.0	0.0	0.0	0.0	0.0	0.0

High and Low temperatures in degrees Fahrenheit; Precipitation and Snow in inches

Weather Station: Newport Beach — Elevation: 9 feet

	Jan	Feb	Mar	Apr	May	Jun	Jul	Aug	Sep	Oct	Nov	Dec
High	64	64	64	65	67	69	72	73	73	71	68	64
Low	50	51	52	54	58	61	64	65	63	60	54	49
Precip	2.2	2.7	1.8	0.7	0.1	0.1	0.0	0.0	0.2	0.4	0.9	1.5
Snow	0.0	0.0	0.0	0.0	0.0	0.0	0.0	0.0	0.0	0.0	0.0	0.0

High and Low temperatures in degrees Fahrenheit; Precipitation and Snow in inches

Weather Station: Santa Ana Fire Station — Elevation: 134 feet

	Jan	Feb	Mar	Apr	May	Jun	Jul	Aug	Sep	Oct	Nov	Dec
High	70	70	72	74	75	78	83	85	84	80	74	69
Low	47	48	50	53	57	60	63	64	63	58	51	46
Precip	2.9	3.5	2.3	0.9	0.2	0.1	0.0	0.0	0.2	0.5	1.1	1.8
Snow	0.0	0.0	0.0	0.0	0.0	0.0	0.0	0.0	0.0	0.0	0.0	0.0

High and Low temperatures in degrees Fahrenheit; Precipitation and Snow in inches

Population: 3,010,232; Growth (since 2000): 5.8%; Density: 3,807.7 persons per square mile; Race: 60.8% White, 1.7% Black/African American, 17.9% Asian, 0.6% American Indian/Alaska Native, 0.3% Native Hawaiian/Other Pacific Islander, 4.2% two or more races, 33.7% Hispanic of any race; Average household size: 2.99; Median age: 36.2; Age under 18: 24.5%; Age 65 and over: 11.6%; Males per 100 females: 97.9; Marriage status: 33.7% never married, 52.3% now married, 2.1% separated, 4.9% widowed, 9.1% divorced; Foreign born: 30.4%; Speak English only: 54.5%; With disability: 7.8%; Veterans: 5.7%; Ancestry: 10.0% German, 7.6% Irish, 7.2% English, 4.2% Italian, 3.7% American

Religion: Six largest groups: 26.5% Catholicism, 4.1% Non-denominational Protestant, 3.4% Baptist, 2.2% Latter-day Saints, 1.7% Pentecostal, 1.3% Presbyterian-Reformed

Economy: Unemployment rate: 5.0%; Leading industries: 16.1% professional, scientific, and technical services; 12.3% health care and social assistance; 10.6% retail trade; Farms: 312 totaling 60,497 acres; Company size: 83 employ 1,000 or more persons, 122 employ 500 to 999 persons, 1,849 employ 100 to 499 persons, 86,328 employ less than 100 persons; Business ownership: 93,419 women-owned, 4,362 Black-owned, 40,865 Hispanic-owned, 63,394 Asian-owned

Employment: 18.0% management, business, and financial, 6.5% computer, engineering, and science, 10.5% education, legal, community service, arts, and media, 4.7% healthcare practitioners, 17.2% service, 26.3% sales and office, 6.9% natural resources, construction, and maintenance, 10.0% production, transportation, and material moving

Income: Per capita: $34,057; Median household: $75,422; Average household: $101,134; Households with income of $100,000 or more: 36.9%; Poverty rate: 12.4%

Educational Attainment: High school diploma or higher: 83.8%; Bachelor's degree or higher: 36.8%; Graduate/professional degree or higher: 12.9%

Housing: Homeownership rate: 59.2%; Median home value: $519,600; Median year structure built: 1975; Homeowner vacancy rate: 1.4%; Median gross rent: $1,498 per month; Rental vacancy rate: 5.9%

Vital Statistics: Birth rate: 122.5 per 10,000 population; Death rate: 59.9 per 10,000 population; Age-adjusted cancer mortality rate: 146.8 deaths per 100,000 population

Health Insurance: 82.7% have insurance; 65.2% have private insurance; 24.8% have public insurance; 17.3% do not have insurance; 8.6% of children under 18 do not have insurance

Health Care: Physicians: 29.8 per 10,000 population; Hospital beds: 19.5 per 10,000 population; Hospital admissions: 886.4 per 10,000 population

Air Quality Index: 41.4% good, 56.7% moderate, 1.9% unhealthy for sensitive individuals, 0.0% unhealthy (percent of days)

Transportation: Commute: 88.1% car, 2.8% public transportation, 2.0% walk, 5.0% work from home; Median travel time to work: 26.3 minutes

Presidential Election: 45.4% Obama, 52.4% Romney (2012)

National and State Parks: Bolsa Chica State Beach; Corona del Mar State Beach; Crystal Cove State Park; Doheny State Beach; Huntington State Beach; San Clemente State Beach; Seal Beach National Wildlife Refuge

Additional Information Contacts

Orange Government . . . . (714) 834-3100
http://www.ocgov.com

Orange County Communities

ALISO VIEJO (city). Covers a land area of 7.472 square miles and a water area of 0 square miles. Located at 33.58° N. Lat; 117.73° W. Long. Elevation is 469 feet.

History: Aliso Viejo was incorporated on July 1, 2001. Its name comes from the Spanish words for "old alder" or "old sycamore."

Population: 47,823; Growth (since 2000): 19.1%; Density: 6,400.4 persons per square mile; Race: 72.0% White, 2.0% Black/African American, 14.6% Asian, 0.3% American Indian/Alaska Native, 0.2% Native Hawaiian/Other Pacific Islander, 5.7% Two or more races, 17.1% Hispanic of any race; Average household size: 2.60; Median age: 35.1; Age under

18: 25.9%; Age 65 and over: 5.3%; Males per 100 females: 92.8; Marriage status: 30.3% never married, 56.4% now married, 1.9% separated, 3.1% widowed, 10.2% divorced; Foreign born: 23.1%; Speak English only: 69.4%; With disability: 4.3%; Veterans: 3.9%; Ancestry: 13.4% German, 12.0% Irish, 9.2% English, 6.8% Italian, 4.3% Iranian

Employment: 26.3% management, business, and financial, 10.7% computer, engineering, and science, 13.6% education, legal, community service, arts, and media, 5.1% healthcare practitioners, 11.1% service, 26.8% sales and office, 2.7% natural resources, construction, and maintenance, 3.5% production, transportation, and material moving

Income: Per capita: $44,699; Median household: $99,394; Average household: $115,756; Households with income of $100,000 or more: 49.7%; Poverty rate: 5.1%

Educational Attainment: High school diploma or higher: 95.2%; Bachelor's degree or higher: 57.4%; Graduate/professional degree or higher: 17.0%

School District(s)

Capistrano Unified (KG-12)
2012-13 Enrollment: 53,785 . . . . (949) 234-9200

Four-year College(s)

Soka University of America (Private, Not-for-profit)
Fall 2013 Enrollment: 412 . . . . (949) 480-4000
2013-14 Tuition: In-state $29,144; Out-of-state $29,144

Housing: Homeownership rate: 60.7%; Median home value: $462,800; Median year structure built: 1994; Homeowner vacancy rate: 1.2%; Median gross rent: $1,846 per month; Rental vacancy rate: 3.6%

Health Insurance: 90.1% have insurance; 83.2% have private insurance; 11.3% have public insurance; 9.9% do not have insurance; 4.3% of children under 18 do not have insurance

Safety: Violent crime rate: 5.0 per 10,000 population; Property crime rate: 63.0 per 10,000 population

Transportation: Commute: 88.5% car, 1.0% public transportation, 1.6% walk, 8.2% work from home; Median travel time to work: 25.4 minutes

Additional Information Contacts

City of Aliso Viejo . . . . (949) 425-2500
http://www.cityofalisoviejo.com

ANAHEIM (city). Covers a land area of 49.835 square miles and a water area of 0.976 square miles. Located at 33.86° N. Lat; 117.76° W. Long. Elevation is 157 feet.

History: Named for the Santa Ana River, and the German translation of home.

Population: 336,265; Growth (since 2000): 2.5%; Density: 6,747.5 persons per square mile; Race: 52.7% White, 2.8% Black/African American, 14.8% Asian, 0.8% American Indian/Alaska Native, 0.5% Native Hawaiian/Other Pacific Islander, 4.4% Two or more races, 52.8% Hispanic of any race; Average household size: 3.38; Median age: 32.4; Age under 18: 27.3%; Age 65 and over: 9.3%; Males per 100 females: 99.0; Marriage status: 36.1% never married, 51.2% now married, 3.4% separated, 4.5% widowed, 8.2% divorced; Foreign born: 37.1%; Speak English only: 39.0%; With disability: 7.7%; Veterans: 4.7%; Ancestry: 5.9% German, 4.2% American, 4.2% English, 4.1% Irish, 2.5% Italian

Employment: 12.3% management, business, and financial, 4.3% computer, engineering, and science, 7.7% education, legal, community service, arts, and media, 4.3% healthcare practitioners, 20.8% service, 25.7% sales and office, 9.4% natural resources, construction, and maintenance, 15.6% production, transportation, and material moving

Income: Per capita: $23,400; Median household: $59,165; Average household: $76,565; Households with income of $100,000 or more: 25.7%; Poverty rate: 16.1%

Educational Attainment: High school diploma or higher: 74.7%; Bachelor's degree or higher: 24.2%; Graduate/professional degree or higher: 7.2%

School District(s)

Anaheim City (KG-06)
2012-13 Enrollment: 19,126 . . . . (714) 517-7500
Anaheim Union High (07-12)
2012-13 Enrollment: 32,085 . . . . (714) 999-3511
Centralia Elementary (KG-06)
2012-13 Enrollment: 4,501 . . . . (714) 228-3100
Magnolia Elementary (KG-06)
2012-13 Enrollment: 6,353 . . . . (714) 761-5533
North Orange County Rop
2012-13 Enrollment: n/a . . . . (714) 502-5800
Orange Unified (PK-12)
2012-13 Enrollment: 29,854 . . . . (714) 628-4000
Placentia-Yorba Linda Unified (KG-12)
2012-13 Enrollment: 25,622 . . . . (714) 986-7000
Savanna Elementary (KG-06)
2012-13 Enrollment: 2,398 . . . . (714) 236-3800

Four-year College(s)

Bethesda University of California (Private, Not-for-profit, Other (none of the above))
Fall 2013 Enrollment: 353 . . . . (714) 517-1945
2013-14 Tuition: In-state $7,620; Out-of-state $7,620
Bristol University (Private, For-profit)
Fall 2013 Enrollment: 82 . . . . (714) 542-8086
California University of Management and Sciences (Private, Not-for-profit)
Fall 2013 Enrollment: 405 . . . . (714) 533-3946
2013-14 Tuition: In-state $10,745; Out-of-state $10,745
South Baylo University (Private, Not-for-profit)
Fall 2013 Enrollment: 647 . . . . (714) 533-1495
Southern California Institute of Technology (Private, For-profit)
Fall 2013 Enrollment: 496 . . . . (714) 300-0300
2013-14 Tuition: In-state $17,130; Out-of-state $17,130
West Coast University-Orange County (Private, For-profit)
Fall 2013 Enrollment: 1,528 . . . . (714) 782-1700
2013-14 Tuition: In-state $33,600; Out-of-state $33,600
Westwood College-Anaheim (Private, For-profit)
Fall 2013 Enrollment: 772 . . . . (714) 704-2720
2013-14 Tuition: In-state $15,148; Out-of-state $15,148

Two-year College(s)

American Career College-Anaheim (Private, For-profit)
Fall 2013 Enrollment: 1,565 . . . . (949) 783-4800
Everest College-Anaheim (Private, For-profit)
Fall 2013 Enrollment: 574 . . . . (714) 953-6500
2013-14 Tuition: In-state $13,896; Out-of-state $13,896

Vocational/Technical School(s)

Brownson Technical School (Private, For-profit)
Fall 2013 Enrollment: 45 . . . . (714) 774-9443
2013-14 Tuition: $14,038
California Career School (Private, For-profit)
Fall 2013 Enrollment: 212 . . . . (714) 635-6585
2013-14 Tuition: $6,290
Real Barbers College (Private, For-profit)
Fall 2013 Enrollment: 116 . . . . (714) 772-4423
2013-14 Tuition: $17,825

Housing: Homeownership rate: 48.5%; Median home value: $399,100; Median year structure built: 1972; Homeowner vacancy rate: 1.7%; Median gross rent: $1,344 per month; Rental vacancy rate: 7.2%

Health Insurance: 77.4% have insurance; 53.2% have private insurance; 29.2% have public insurance; 22.6% do not have insurance; 9.7% of children under 18 do not have insurance

Hospitals: Ahmc Anaheim Regional Medical Center (223 beds); Kaiser Foundation Hospital - Orange Co-Anaheim (200 beds); West Anaheim Medical Center (219 beds); Western Medical Center Hospital Anaheim (188 beds)

Safety: Violent crime rate: 32.7 per 10,000 population; Property crime rate: 278.3 per 10,000 population

Newspapers: OC Register Papers North (weekly circulation 135000)

Transportation: Commute: 88.8% car, 4.4% public transportation, 1.7% walk, 3.1% work from home; Median travel time to work: 27.0 minutes; Amtrak: Train service available.

Additional Information Contacts

City of Anaheim . . . . (714) 765-5166
http://www.anaheim.net

BREA (city). Covers a land area of 12.078 square miles and a water area of 0.031 square miles. Located at 33.92° N. Lat; 117.87° W. Long. Elevation is 361 feet.

History: Named for the Spanish translation of "asphaltum," used in local tar pits. Developed during an oil boom in the early 1900s. Of note is the campsite of Spanish explorer Don Gaspar de Portola, the first European to visit the area. Incorporated 1917.

Population: 39,282; Growth (since 2000): 10.9%; Density: 3,252.3 persons per square mile; Race: 67.1% White, 1.4% Black/African American, 18.2% Asian, 0.5% American Indian/Alaska Native, 0.2% Native Hawaiian/Other Pacific Islander, 4.4% Two or more races, 25.0% Hispanic of any race; Average household size: 2.75; Median age: 38.7; Age under

18: 23.1%; Age 65 and over: 12.6%; Males per 100 females: 95.2; Marriage status: 29.9% never married, 56.1% now married, 2.0% separated, 5.0% widowed, 9.0% divorced; Foreign born: 23.1%; Speak English only: 67.9%; With disability: 8.3%; Veterans: 6.5%; Ancestry: 16.3% German, 9.9% English, 8.9% Irish, 4.7% Italian, 3.7% American

Employment: 21.5% management, business, and financial, 7.8% computer, engineering, and science, 14.0% education, legal, community service, arts, and media, 5.1% healthcare practitioners, 13.7% service, 26.7% sales and office, 5.2% natural resources, construction, and maintenance, 6.1% production, transportation, and material moving

Income: Per capita: $34,788; Median household: $79,124; Average household: $95,888; Households with income of $100,000 or more: 39.1%; Poverty rate: 6.6%

Educational Attainment: High school diploma or higher: 91.2%; Bachelor's degree or higher: 40.9%; Graduate/professional degree or higher: 14.6%

School District(s)

Brea-Olinda Unified (KG-12)
2012-13 Enrollment: 5,972 . . . . (714) 990-7800

Housing: Homeownership rate: 64.9%; Median home value: $522,000; Median year structure built: 1975; Homeowner vacancy rate: 1.3%; Median gross rent: $1,464 per month; Rental vacancy rate: 5.3%

Health Insurance: 87.7% have insurance; 75.0% have private insurance; 21.7% have public insurance; 12.3% do not have insurance; 4.3% of children under 18 do not have insurance

Safety: Violent crime rate: 15.8 per 10,000 population; Property crime rate: 298.0 per 10,000 population

Transportation: Commute: 90.9% car, 1.5% public transportation, 1.7% walk, 4.9% work from home; Median travel time to work: 29.7 minutes

Additional Information Contacts

City of Brea . . . . (714) 990-7600
http://www.ci.brea.ca.us

BUENA PARK (city). Covers a land area of 10.524 square miles and a water area of 0.029 square miles. Located at 33.86° N. Lat; 118.00° W. Long. Elevation is 75 feet.

History: Named for the Spanish translation of "good". Knott's Berry Farm, a re-created gold rush town theme park; Movieland Wax Museum; a civic light opera and community playhouse; a Japanese village surrounding a deer compound; and a transportation Museum are here. Incorporated 1953.

Population: 80,530; Growth (since 2000): 2.9%; Density: 7,652.1 persons per square mile; Race: 45.3% White, 3.8% Black/African American, 26.7% Asian, 1.1% American Indian/Alaska Native, 0.6% Native Hawaiian/Other Pacific Islander, 5.1% Two or more races, 39.3% Hispanic of any race; Average household size: 3.37; Median age: 35.1; Age under 18: 25.3%; Age 65 and over: 10.6%; Males per 100 females: 97.4; Marriage status: 36.3% never married, 48.5% now married, 2.2% separated, 5.7% widowed, 9.5% divorced; Foreign born: 37.7%; Speak English only: 45.2%; With disability: 9.4%; Veterans: 5.1%; Ancestry: 6.4% German, 5.6% Irish, 3.7% English, 3.1% Italian, 2.7% American

Employment: 14.0% management, business, and financial, 5.1% computer, engineering, and science, 7.3% education, legal, community service, arts, and media, 5.7% healthcare practitioners, 18.7% service, 29.7% sales and office, 6.6% natural resources, construction, and maintenance, 12.8% production, transportation, and material moving

Income: Per capita: $23,623; Median household: $66,371; Average household: $79,637; Households with income of $100,000 or more: 28.6%; Poverty rate: 12.0%

Educational Attainment: High school diploma or higher: 82.3%; Bachelor's degree or higher: 27.9%; Graduate/professional degree or higher: 6.8%

School District(s)

Anaheim Union High (07-12)
2012-13 Enrollment: 32,085 . . . . (714) 999-3511
Buena Park Elementary (KG-08)
2012-13 Enrollment: 5,349 . . . . (714) 522-8412
Centralia Elementary (KG-06)
2012-13 Enrollment: 4,501 . . . . (714) 228-3100
Cypress Elementary (KG-06)
2012-13 Enrollment: 3,879 . . . . (714) 220-6900
Fullerton Joint Union High (09-12)
2012-13 Enrollment: 14,608 . . . . (714) 870-2800
Savanna Elementary (KG-06)
2012-13 Enrollment: 2,398 . . . . (714) 236-3800

Housing: Homeownership rate: 56.7%; Median home value: $393,900; Median year structure built: 1962; Homeowner vacancy rate: 1.1%; Median gross rent: $1,375 per month; Rental vacancy rate: 5.0%

Health Insurance: 80.4% have insurance; 60.0% have private insurance; 27.4% have public insurance; 19.6% do not have insurance; 7.8% of children under 18 do not have insurance

Safety: Violent crime rate: 26.7 per 10,000 population; Property crime rate: 262.0 per 10,000 population

Transportation: Commute: 86.4% car, 4.0% public transportation, 3.0% walk, 3.0% work from home; Median travel time to work: 29.2 minutes

Additional Information Contacts

City of Buena Park . . . . (714) 562-3500
http://www.buenapark.com

CAPISTRANO BEACH (unincorporated postal area)
ZCTA: 92624

Covers a land area of 1.373 square miles and a water area of 1.213 square miles. Located at 33.45° N. Lat; 117.66° W. Long. Elevation is 167 feet.

Population: 7,248; Growth (since 2000): -2.6%; Density: 5,277.1 persons per square mile; Race: 83.8% White, 0.7% Black/African American, 2.9% Asian, 0.8% American Indian/Alaska Native, 0.1% Native Hawaiian/Other Pacific Islander, 3.7% Two or more races, 19.6% Hispanic of any race; Average household size: 2.54; Median age: 43.1; Age under 18: 19.7%; Age 65 and over: 15.3%; Males per 100 females: 101.6; Marriage status: 29.6% never married, 54.8% now married, 0.5% separated, 3.7% widowed, 11.9% divorced; Foreign born: 9.9%; Speak English only: 86.9%; With disability: 5.8%; Veterans: 8.9%; Ancestry: 16.0% German, 14.2% English, 9.7% Irish, 8.2% Italian, 5.3% American

Employment: 26.3% management, business, and financial, 4.5% computer, engineering, and science, 6.6% education, legal, community service, arts, and media, 2.4% healthcare practitioners, 23.0% service, 24.9% sales and office, 9.0% natural resources, construction, and maintenance, 3.3% production, transportation, and material moving

Income: Per capita: $40,179; Median household: $68,066; Average household: $93,663; Households with income of $100,000 or more: 32.7%; Poverty rate: 11.4%

Educational Attainment: High school diploma or higher: 93.8%; Bachelor's degree or higher: 38.3%; Graduate/professional degree or higher: 9.6%

School District(s)

Capistrano Unified (KG-12)
2012-13 Enrollment: 53,785 . . . . (949) 234-9200

Housing: Homeownership rate: 61.1%; Median home value: $678,800; Median year structure built: 1973; Homeowner vacancy rate: 2.5%; Median gross rent: $1,753 per month; Rental vacancy rate: 7.2%

Health Insurance: 80.8% have insurance; 70.8% have private insurance; 20.7% have public insurance; 19.2% do not have insurance; 6.1% of children under 18 do not have insurance

Newspapers: San Clemente Times (weekly circulation 20000)

Transportation: Commute: 82.1% car, 0.5% public transportation, 1.9% walk, 14.3% work from home; Median travel time to work: 26.4 minutes

CORONA DEL MAR (unincorporated postal area)
ZCTA: 92625

Covers a land area of 2.553 square miles and a water area of 0.335 square miles. Located at 33.60° N. Lat; 117.86° W. Long. Elevation is 85 feet.

Population: 12,478; Growth (since 2000): -6.9%; Density: 4,887.6 persons per square mile; Race: 91.6% White, 0.4% Black/African American, 4.8% Asian, 0.2% American Indian/Alaska Native, 0.1% Native Hawaiian/Other Pacific Islander, 2.2% Two or more races, 4.9% Hispanic of any race; Average household size: 2.05; Median age: 50.2; Age under 18: 14.3%; Age 65 and over: 25.8%; Males per 100 females: 87.3; Marriage status: 24.2% never married, 56.6% now married, 1.4% separated, 7.8% widowed, 11.5% divorced; Foreign born: 10.6%; Speak English only: 87.5%; With disability: 7.7%; Veterans: 8.4%; Ancestry: 21.0% German, 18.1% English, 16.9% Irish, 9.3% Italian, 5.5% American

Employment: 33.9% management, business, and financial, 4.3% computer, engineering, and science, 16.9% education, legal, community service, arts, and media, 6.3% healthcare practitioners, 7.7% service, 27.2% sales and office, 2.6% natural resources, construction, and maintenance, 1.2% production, transportation, and material moving

Income: Per capita: $100,232; Median household: $116,270; Average household: $200,768; Households with income of $100,000 or more: 57.9%; Poverty rate: 8.6%
Educational Attainment: High school diploma or higher: 97.1%; Bachelor's degree or higher: 65.9%; Graduate/professional degree or higher: 28.8%

School District(s)

Newport-Mesa Unified (KG-12)
2012-13 Enrollment: 22,003 . . . . (714) 424-5000

Housing: Homeownership rate: 63.6%; Median home value: 1 million+; Median year structure built: 1968; Homeowner vacancy rate: 1.7%; Median gross rent: $1,975 per month; Rental vacancy rate: 5.6%
Health Insurance: 94.5% have insurance; 85.0% have private insurance; 27.3% have public insurance; 5.5% do not have insurance; 3.8% of children under 18 do not have insurance
Transportation: Commute: 83.7% car, 1.1% public transportation, 0.2% walk, 13.5% work from home; Median travel time to work: 22.6 minutes

---

COSTA MESA (city). Covers a land area of 15.654 square miles and a water area of 0.046 square miles. Located at 33.67° N. Lat; 117.91° W. Long. Elevation is 98 feet.
History: Museum featuring innovative cars is here. The city was named for its coastal location. Incorporated 1953.
Population: 109,960; Growth (since 2000): 1.1%; Density: 7,024.6 persons per square mile; Race: 68.5% White, 1.5% Black/African American, 7.9% Asian, 0.6% American Indian/Alaska Native, 0.5% Native Hawaiian/Other Pacific Islander, 4.7% Two or more races, 35.8% Hispanic of any race; Average household size: 2.68; Median age: 33.6; Age under 18: 21.5%; Age 65 and over: 9.2%; Males per 100 females: 103.7; Marriage status: 39.8% never married, 44.6% now married, 2.2% separated, 4.1% widowed, 11.5% divorced; Foreign born: 24.5%; Speak English only: 62.1%; With disability: 7.4%; Veterans: 4.9%; Ancestry: 13.6% German, 10.0% Irish, 9.4% English, 5.3% Italian, 3.4% American
Employment: 19.6% management, business, and financial, 5.2% computer, engineering, and science, 10.5% education, legal, community service, arts, and media, 3.7% healthcare practitioners, 20.7% service, 25.8% sales and office, 6.4% natural resources, construction, and maintenance, 8.0% production, transportation, and material moving
Income: Per capita: $34,100; Median household: $65,830; Average household: $89,278; Households with income of $100,000 or more: 31.1%; Poverty rate: 15.1%
Educational Attainment: High school diploma or higher: 85.4%; Bachelor's degree or higher: 35.7%; Graduate/professional degree or higher: 10.9%

School District(s)

Coastline Rop
2012-13 Enrollment: n/a . . . . (714) 979-1955
Newport-Mesa Unified (KG-12)
2012-13 Enrollment: 22,003 . . . . (714) 424-5000
Orange County Department of Education (KG-12)
2012-13 Enrollment: 7,184 . . . . (714) 966-4000
Sbc - Pacific Technology (06-12)
2012-13 Enrollment: 283. . . . . (714) 892-5066

Four-year College(s)

Pacific College (Private, For-profit)
Fall 2013 Enrollment: 277. . . . . (714) 662-4402
University of Phoenix-Southern California Campus (Private, For-profit)
Fall 2013 Enrollment: 9,954 . . . . (866) 766-0766
2013-14 Tuition: In-state $11,320; Out-of-state $11,320
Vanguard University of Southern California (Private, Not-for-profit, Assemblies of God Church)
Fall 2013 Enrollment: 2,415 . . . . (714) 556-3610
2013-14 Tuition: In-state $29,250; Out-of-state $29,250

Two-year College(s)

Orange Coast College (Public)
Fall 2013 Enrollment: 21,886 . . . . (714) 432-5072
2013-14 Tuition: In-state $1,184; Out-of-state $6,320

Vocational/Technical School(s)

Paul Mitchell the School-Costa Mesa (Private, For-profit)
Fall 2013 Enrollment: 188. . . . . (866) 500-5966
2013-14 Tuition: $18,925

Housing: Homeownership rate: 39.6%; Median home value: $580,700; Median year structure built: 1969; Homeowner vacancy rate: 1.2%; Median gross rent: $1,524 per month; Rental vacancy rate: 5.9%
Health Insurance: 78.1% have insurance; 62.3% have private insurance; 21.4% have public insurance; 21.9% do not have insurance; 10.3% of children under 18 do not have insurance
Hospitals: College Hospital Costa Mesa (125 beds)
Safety: Violent crime rate: 22.4 per 10,000 population; Property crime rate: 316.0 per 10,000 population
Newspapers: Daily Pilot (daily circulation 24500); Huntington Beach Independent (weekly circulation 31000); Independent (weekly circulation 65000); OC Weekly (weekly circulation 68000)
Transportation: Commute: 85.4% car, 3.0% public transportation, 2.5% walk, 5.5% work from home; Median travel time to work: 21.9 minutes

Additional Information Contacts

City of Costa Mesa . . . . (714) 754-5000
http://www.costamesaca.gov

COTO DE CAZA (CDP). Covers a land area of 7.951 square miles and a water area of 0.023 square miles. Located at 33.60° N. Lat; 117.59° W. Long. Elevation is 709 feet.
History: While some residents believe that "Coto de Caza" means "Preserve of the Hunt" in Portuguese, this is erroneous. Actually, "Coto de Caza" is Spanish for "Hunt Reserve" and implies that the reserve is private.
Population: 14,866; Growth (since 2000): 13.9%; Density: 1,869.7 persons per square mile; Race: 88.1% White, 0.9% Black/African American, 5.9% Asian, 0.2% American Indian/Alaska Native, 0.1% Native Hawaiian/Other Pacific Islander, 3.6% Two or more races, 7.9% Hispanic of any race; Average household size: 3.14; Median age: 42.2; Age under 18: 30.6%; Age 65 and over: 7.9%; Males per 100 females: 96.8; Marriage status: 23.2% never married, 71.3% now married, 1.1% separated, 1.6% widowed, 3.9% divorced; Foreign born: 10.5%; Speak English only: 87.9%; With disability: 4.3%; Veterans: 6.2%; Ancestry: 17.5% German, 15.2% Irish, 11.6% Italian, 11.1% English, 6.1% American
Employment: 32.3% management, business, and financial, 5.3% computer, engineering, and science, 11.3% education, legal, community service, arts, and media, 4.8% healthcare practitioners, 5.8% service, 35.2% sales and office, 2.9% natural resources, construction, and maintenance, 2.4% production, transportation, and material moving
Income: Per capita: $67,590; Median household: $163,657; Average household: $207,268; Households with income of $100,000 or more: 70.8%; Poverty rate: 2.7%
Educational Attainment: High school diploma or higher: 98.7%; Bachelor's degree or higher: 62.1%; Graduate/professional degree or higher: 20.3%

School District(s)

Capistrano Unified (KG-12)
2012-13 Enrollment: 53,785 . . . . (949) 234-9200

Housing: Homeownership rate: 91.7%; Median home value: $874,500; Median year structure built: 1994; Homeowner vacancy rate: 1.0%; Median gross rent: $2,000+ per month; Rental vacancy rate: 1.5%
Health Insurance: 97.2% have insurance; 93.4% have private insurance; 11.9% have public insurance; 2.8% do not have insurance; 1.0% of children under 18 do not have insurance
Newspapers: Mission News Group (weekly circulation 21500)
Transportation: Commute: 86.2% car, 0.0% public transportation, 0.0% walk, 13.1% work from home; Median travel time to work: 31.8 minutes

---

CYPRESS (city). Covers a land area of 6.581 square miles and a water area of 0.009 square miles. Located at 33.82° N. Lat; 118.04° W. Long. Elevation is 39 feet.
History: Named for the cypress tree, local to the California coast. The city's population has grown with the development of the area. Incorporated 1956.
Population: 47,802; Growth (since 2000): 3.4%; Density: 7,263.6 persons per square mile; Race: 54.4% White, 3.0% Black/African American, 31.3% Asian, 0.6% American Indian/Alaska Native, 0.5% Native Hawaiian/Other Pacific Islander, 4.9% Two or more races, 18.4% Hispanic of any race; Average household size: 3.02; Median age: 39.9; Age under 18: 23.7%; Age 65 and over: 12.9%; Males per 100 females: 94.2; Marriage status: 31.8% never married, 53.3% now married, 1.2% separated, 4.7% widowed, 10.2% divorced; Foreign born: 28.6%; Speak English only: 59.9%; With disability: 8.2%; Veterans: 6.9%; Ancestry: 9.5% Irish, 9.3% German, 7.1% English, 4.2% Italian, 2.6% French
Employment: 18.4% management, business, and financial, 7.0% computer, engineering, and science, 13.1% education, legal, community service, arts, and media, 6.1% healthcare practitioners, 12.0% service,

29.3% sales and office, 6.1% natural resources, construction, and maintenance, 7.9% production, transportation, and material moving
Income: Per capita: $32,444; Median household: $78,364; Average household: $96,227; Households with income of $100,000 or more: 38.3%; Poverty rate: 6.7%
Educational Attainment: High school diploma or higher: 92.0%; Bachelor's degree or higher: 39.8%; Graduate/professional degree or higher: 12.7%

School District(s)

Anaheim Union High (07-12)
2012-13 Enrollment: 32,085 . . . . (714) 999-3511
Cypress Elementary (KG-06)
2012-13 Enrollment: 3,879 . . . . (714) 220-6900

Four-year College(s)

Trident University International (Private, For-profit)
Fall 2013 Enrollment: 7,093 . . . . (800) 375-9878
2013-14 Tuition: In-state $6,600; Out-of-state $6,600

Two-year College(s)

Cypress College (Public)
Fall 2013 Enrollment: 15,881 . . . . (714) 484-7000
2013-14 Tuition: In-state $1,136; Out-of-state $6,152

Housing: Homeownership rate: 70.1%; Median home value: $496,600; Median year structure built: 1971; Homeowner vacancy rate: 0.9%; Median gross rent: $1,541 per month; Rental vacancy rate: 3.5%
Health Insurance: 85.8% have insurance; 73.6% have private insurance; 22.3% have public insurance; 14.2% do not have insurance; 8.9% of children under 18 do not have insurance
Safety: Violent crime rate: 10.2 per 10,000 population; Property crime rate: 190.4 per 10,000 population
Newspapers: Event News (weekly circulation 28000)
Transportation: Commute: 91.6% car, 1.1% public transportation, 1.5% walk, 2.9% work from home; Median travel time to work: 28.9 minutes
Additional Information Contacts
City of Cypress . . . . (714) 229-6700
http://www.ci.cypress.ca.us

DANA POINT (city). Covers a land area of 6.497 square miles and a water area of 22.987 square miles. Located at 33.46° N. Lat; 117.71° W. Long. Elevation is 144 feet.
History: Named for Richard Henry Dana, author of "Two Years Before the Mast". The cliffs at Dana Point were described by Dana in 1853 as "twice as high as our royal-mast-head" when his ship anchored here.
Population: 33,351; Growth (since 2000): -5.0%; Density: 5,133.1 persons per square mile; Race: 86.1% White, 0.9% Black/African American, 3.2% Asian, 0.7% American Indian/Alaska Native, 0.1% Native Hawaiian/Other Pacific Islander, 3.2% Two or more races, 17.0% Hispanic of any race; Average household size: 2.33; Median age: 44.8; Age under 18: 17.9%; Age 65 and over: 17.0%; Males per 100 females: 98.2; Marriage status: 27.7% never married, 52.7% now married, 1.6% separated, 5.6% widowed, 14.0% divorced; Foreign born: 12.9%; Speak English only: 84.3%; With disability: 7.9%; Veterans: 9.7%; Ancestry: 17.6% German, 15.2% English, 14.5% Irish, 8.9% Italian, 5.0% French
Employment: 23.0% management, business, and financial, 5.2% computer, engineering, and science, 11.5% education, legal, community service, arts, and media, 5.3% healthcare practitioners, 19.1% service, 25.0% sales and office, 5.9% natural resources, construction, and maintenance, 5.0% production, transportation, and material moving
Income: Per capita: $49,000; Median household: $80,133; Average household: $111,438; Households with income of $100,000 or more: 40.7%; Poverty rate: 8.3%
Educational Attainment: High school diploma or higher: 95.2%; Bachelor's degree or higher: 46.7%; Graduate/professional degree or higher: 17.0%

School District(s)

Capistrano Unified (KG-12)
2012-13 Enrollment: 53,785 . . . . (949) 234-9200

Housing: Homeownership rate: 58.6%; Median home value: $707,600; Median year structure built: 1979; Homeowner vacancy rate: 2.0%; Median gross rent: $1,787 per month; Rental vacancy rate: 7.0%
Health Insurance: 87.2% have insurance; 75.6% have private insurance; 23.6% have public insurance; 12.8% do not have insurance; 4.6% of children under 18 do not have insurance
Safety: Violent crime rate: 20.4 per 10,000 population; Property crime rate: 171.0 per 10,000 population
Transportation: Commute: 84.6% car, 1.4% public transportation, 2.9% walk, 9.4% work from home; Median travel time to work: 28.2 minutes
Additional Information Contacts
City of Dana Point . . . . (949) 248-3500
http://www.danapoint.org

FOOTHILL RANCH (unincorporated postal area)
ZCTA: 92610
Covers a land area of 9.804 square miles and a water area of 0 square miles. Located at 33.70° N. Lat; 117.68° W. Long. Elevation is 886 feet.
Population: 11,248; Growth (since 2000): 2.9%; Density: 1,147.3 persons per square mile; Race: 69.5% White, 1.7% Black/African American, 19.6% Asian, 0.3% American Indian/Alaska Native, 0.1% Native Hawaiian/Other Pacific Islander, 5.8% Two or more races, 13.5% Hispanic of any race; Average household size: 2.99; Median age: 35.7; Age under 18: 30.7%; Age 65 and over: 3.5%; Males per 100 females: 100.0; Marriage status: 26.0% never married, 65.5% now married, 1.9% separated, 1.7% widowed, 6.8% divorced; Foreign born: 20.2%; Speak English only: 77.4%; With disability: 4.6%; Veterans: 4.9%; Ancestry: 17.7% German, 10.8% English, 9.8% Irish, 6.7% Italian, 4.5% French
Employment: 28.0% management, business, and financial, 11.0% computer, engineering, and science, 11.5% education, legal, community service, arts, and media, 3.1% healthcare practitioners, 8.5% service, 30.1% sales and office, 1.5% natural resources, construction, and maintenance, 6.4% production, transportation, and material moving
Income: Per capita: $46,909; Median household: $124,471; Average household: $136,161; Households with income of $100,000 or more: 65.4%; Poverty rate: 2.0%
Educational Attainment: High school diploma or higher: 98.5%; Bachelor's degree or higher: 62.1%; Graduate/professional degree or higher: 18.9%

School District(s)

Saddleback Valley Unified (PK-12)
2012-13 Enrollment: 30,355 . . . . (949) 580-3200

Housing: Homeownership rate: 75.7%; Median home value: $580,800; Median year structure built: 1994; Homeowner vacancy rate: 1.8%; Median gross rent: $1,757 per month; Rental vacancy rate: 3.2%
Health Insurance: 96.4% have insurance; 92.1% have private insurance; 7.3% have public insurance; 3.6% do not have insurance; 0.9% of children under 18 do not have insurance
Transportation: Commute: 88.9% car, 0.7% public transportation, 1.3% walk, 7.1% work from home; Median travel time to work: 26.0 minutes

FOUNTAIN VALLEY (city). Covers a land area of 9.018 square miles and a water area of 0.013 square miles. Located at 33.71° N. Lat; 117.95° W. Long. Elevation is 33 feet.
History: Named for the artesian wells that were once located under the city. Incorporated 1957.
Population: 55,313; Growth (since 2000): 0.6%; Density: 6,133.5 persons per square mile; Race: 56.5% White, 0.9% Black/African American, 33.3% Asian, 0.4% American Indian/Alaska Native, 0.3% Native Hawaiian/Other Pacific Islander, 4.2% Two or more races, 13.1% Hispanic of any race; Average household size: 2.94; Median age: 42.6; Age under 18: 21.0%; Age 65 and over: 17.6%; Males per 100 females: 94.9; Marriage status: 29.5% never married, 54.0% now married, 1.2% separated, 5.7% widowed, 10.8% divorced; Foreign born: 30.2%; Speak English only: 59.2%; With disability: 9.5%; Veterans: 6.9%; Ancestry: 10.4% German, 8.9% Irish, 7.0% English, 4.6% Italian, 3.3% American
Employment: 18.2% management, business, and financial, 8.3% computer, engineering, and science, 10.7% education, legal, community service, arts, and media, 6.6% healthcare practitioners, 11.7% service, 30.8% sales and office, 5.3% natural resources, construction, and maintenance, 8.2% production, transportation, and material moving
Income: Per capita: $34,053; Median household: $80,870; Average household: $98,311; Households with income of $100,000 or more: 39.5%; Poverty rate: 8.0%
Educational Attainment: High school diploma or higher: 90.2%; Bachelor's degree or higher: 37.8%; Graduate/professional degree or higher: 12.2%

School District(s)

Fountain Valley Elementary (KG-08)
2012-13 Enrollment: 6,344 . . . . (714) 843-3200
Garden Grove Unified (KG-12)
2012-13 Enrollment: 47,599 . . . . (714) 663-6000

Huntington Beach Union High (09-12)
2012-13 Enrollment: 16,400 . . . . (714) 903-7000
Ocean View (KG-08)
2012-13 Enrollment: 9,418 . . . . (714) 847-2551

Two-year College(s)

Coastline Community College (Public)
Fall 2013 Enrollment: 10,378 . . . . (714) 546-7600
2013-14 Tuition: In-state $1,136; Out-of-state $5,288
Modern Technology School (Private, For-profit)
Fall 2013 Enrollment: 83 . . . . (714) 418-9100

Vocational/Technical School(s)

Coastline Beauty College (Private, For-profit)
Fall 2013 Enrollment: 197 . . . . (714) 531-1267
2013-14 Tuition: $9,200

Housing: Homeownership rate: 72.1%; Median home value: $604,100; Median year structure built: 1972; Homeowner vacancy rate: 0.8%; Median gross rent: $1,578 per month; Rental vacancy rate: 3.8%

Health Insurance: 89.5% have insurance; 73.8% have private insurance; 26.8% have public insurance; 10.5% do not have insurance; 1.9% of children under 18 do not have insurance

Hospitals: Fountain Valley Regional Hospital & Medical Center (413 beds); Orange Coast Memorial Medical Center (230 beds)

Safety: Violent crime rate: 16.2 per 10,000 population; Property crime rate: 206.0 per 10,000 population

Newspapers: OC Register Papers West (weekly circulation 113000)

Transportation: Commute: 91.6% car, 1.0% public transportation, 0.9% walk, 5.0% work from home; Median travel time to work: 25.0 minutes

Additional Information Contacts

City of Fountain Valley . . . . (714) 593-4400
http://www.fountainvalley.org

FULLERTON (city). Covers a land area of 22.353 square miles and a water area of 0.011 square miles. Located at 33.89° N. Lat; 117.93° W. Long. Elevation is 164 feet.

History: Named for George H. Fullerton, Land Company president who routed the railroad through the new town. Fullerton developed around citrus and walnut orchards with packing plants, and later became a large oil-producing center.

Population: 135,161; Growth (since 2000): 7.3%; Density: 6,046.7 persons per square mile; Race: 53.9% White, 2.3% Black/African American, 22.8% Asian, 0.6% American Indian/Alaska Native, 0.2% Native Hawaiian/Other Pacific Islander, 4.3% Two or more races, 34.4% Hispanic of any race; Average household size: 2.91; Median age: 34.8; Age under 18: 23.3%; Age 65 and over: 11.7%; Males per 100 females: 96.6; Marriage status: 37.8% never married, 49.4% now married, 2.1% separated, 4.7% widowed, 8.2% divorced; Foreign born: 31.1%; Speak English only: 53.2%; With disability: 8.2%; Veterans: 5.1%; Ancestry: 9.2% German, 6.7% English, 6.2% Irish, 3.5% Italian, 2.7% American

Employment: 17.0% management, business, and financial, 5.9% computer, engineering, and science, 12.0% education, legal, community service, arts, and media, 4.5% healthcare practitioners, 16.6% service, 27.5% sales and office, 6.4% natural resources, construction, and maintenance, 9.9% production, transportation, and material moving

Income: Per capita: $29,913; Median household: $67,384; Average household: $89,242; Households with income of $100,000 or more: 31.6%; Poverty rate: 16.0%

Educational Attainment: High school diploma or higher: 86.1%; Bachelor's degree or higher: 37.1%; Graduate/professional degree or higher: 12.6%

School District(s)

Fullerton Elementary (KG-08)
2012-13 Enrollment: 13,830 . . . . (714) 447-7400
Fullerton Joint Union High (09-12)
2012-13 Enrollment: 14,608 . . . . (714) 870-2800
Placentia-Yorba Linda Unified (KG-12)
2012-13 Enrollment: 25,622 . . . . (714) 986-7000

Four-year College(s)

California State University-Fullerton (Public)
Fall 2013 Enrollment: 38,325 . . . . (657) 278-2011
2013-14 Tuition: In-state $6,186; Out-of-state $17,346
Grace Mission University (Private, Not-for-profit, Presbyterian Church (USA))
Fall 2013 Enrollment: 136 . . . . (714) 525-0088
2013-14 Tuition: In-state $2,690; Out-of-state $2,690
Hope International University (Private, Not-for-profit, Christian Churches and Churches of Christ)
Fall 2013 Enrollment: 1,356 . . . . (714) 879-3901
2013-14 Tuition: In-state $26,050; Out-of-state $26,050
Marshall B Ketchum University (Private, Not-for-profit)
Fall 2013 Enrollment: 397 . . . . (714) 870-7226
Western State College of Law at Argosy University (Private, For-profit)
Fall 2013 Enrollment: 431 . . . . (714) 738-1000

Two-year College(s)

Fullerton College (Public)
Fall 2013 Enrollment: 24,301 . . . . (714) 992-7033
2013-14 Tuition: In-state $1,138; Out-of-state $6,010

Housing: Homeownership rate: 54.2%; Median home value: $478,900; Median year structure built: 1969; Homeowner vacancy rate: 1.1%; Median gross rent: $1,341 per month; Rental vacancy rate: 7.0%

Health Insurance: 79.7% have insurance; 62.4% have private insurance; 24.2% have public insurance; 20.3% do not have insurance; 13.0% of children under 18 do not have insurance

Hospitals: Saint Jude Medical Center (347 beds)

Safety: Violent crime rate: 26.6 per 10,000 population; Property crime rate: 276.3 per 10,000 population

Newspapers: Fullerton Observer (weekly circulation 9000)

Transportation: Commute: 87.9% car, 3.6% public transportation, 3.4% walk, 3.7% work from home; Median travel time to work: 28.1 minutes; Amtrak: Train service available.

Additional Information Contacts

City of Fullerton . . . . (714) 738-6310
http://www.ci.fullerton.ca.us

GARDEN GROVE (city). Covers a land area of 17.941 square miles and a water area of 0.018 square miles. Located at 33.78° N. Lat; 117.96° W. Long. Elevation is 89 feet.

History: Named for its abundance of citrus groves. Site of The Crystal Cathedral constructed of over 10,000 panes of glass. Founded 1877. Incorporated 1956.

Population: 170,883; Growth (since 2000): 3.4%; Density: 9,524.6 persons per square mile; Race: 39.9% White, 1.3% Black/African American, 37.1% Asian, 0.6% American Indian/Alaska Native, 0.6% Native Hawaiian/Other Pacific Islander, 3.6% Two or more races, 36.9% Hispanic of any race; Average household size: 3.67; Median age: 35.6; Age under 18: 25.6%; Age 65 and over: 10.8%; Males per 100 females: 99.6; Marriage status: 35.9% never married, 50.2% now married, 2.3% separated, 5.8% widowed, 8.1% divorced; Foreign born: 43.8%; Speak English only: 32.8%; With disability: 8.8%; Veterans: 4.5%; Ancestry: 5.0% German, 3.9% English, 3.9% Irish, 2.2% American, 1.6% Italian

Employment: 10.4% management, business, and financial, 5.0% computer, engineering, and science, 6.8% education, legal, community service, arts, and media, 3.5% healthcare practitioners, 22.0% service, 25.3% sales and office, 9.5% natural resources, construction, and maintenance, 17.4% production, transportation, and material moving

Income: Per capita: $20,849; Median household: $59,648; Average household: $73,625; Households with income of $100,000 or more: 25.2%; Poverty rate: 16.6%

Educational Attainment: High school diploma or higher: 72.5%; Bachelor's degree or higher: 18.6%; Graduate/professional degree or higher: 4.4%

School District(s)

Garden Grove Unified (KG-12)
2012-13 Enrollment: 47,599 . . . . (714) 663-6000
Orange Unified (PK-12)
2012-13 Enrollment: 29,854 . . . . (714) 628-4000
Westminster Elementary (KG-08)
2012-13 Enrollment: 9,619 . . . . (714) 894-7311

Two-year College(s)

Concorde Career College-Garden Grove (Private, For-profit)
Fall 2013 Enrollment: 898 . . . . (714) 703-1900

Vocational/Technical School(s)

Advance Beauty College (Private, For-profit)
Fall 2013 Enrollment: 506 . . . . (714) 530-2131
2013-14 Tuition: $501
CRU Institute (Private, For-profit)
Fall 2013 Enrollment: 55 . . . . (714) 894-3366
2013-14 Tuition: $15,500

California Career Institute (Private, For-profit)
Fall 2013 Enrollment: 45 . . . . (714) 539-5959
2013-14 Tuition: $25,500
Career Academy of Beauty (Private, For-profit)
Fall 2013 Enrollment: 167 . . . . (714) 897-3010
2013-14 Tuition: $16,935
Thanh Le College School of Cosmetology (Private, For-profit)
Fall 2013 Enrollment: 40 . . . . (714) 740-2755
2013-14 Tuition: $10,400

Housing: Homeownership rate: 57.0%; Median home value: $393,900; Median year structure built: 1964; Homeowner vacancy rate: 1.2%; Median gross rent: $1,322 per month; Rental vacancy rate: 4.6%

Health Insurance: 78.8% have insurance; 51.1% have private insurance; 33.2% have public insurance; 21.2% do not have insurance; 8.8% of children under 18 do not have insurance

Hospitals: Garden Grove Hospital & Medical Center (167 beds)

Safety: Violent crime rate: 25.9 per 10,000 population; Property crime rate: 193.6 per 10,000 population

Newspapers: Garden Grove Journal (weekly circulation 8400); Westminster Journal (weekly circulation 4500)

Transportation: Commute: 91.7% car, 3.3% public transportation, 1.5% walk, 1.9% work from home; Median travel time to work: 26.4 minutes

Additional Information Contacts

City of Garden Grove . . . . (714) 741-5000
http://www.ci.garden-grove.ca.us

HUNTINGTON BEACH (city). Covers a land area of 26.748 square miles and a water area of 5.134 square miles. Located at 33.69° N. Lat; 118.01° W. Long. Elevation is 39 feet.

History: Named for Henry E. Huntington, promoter of electric railroads in southern California. Huntington Beach was developing as a recreational resort when oil was discovered about 1920.

Population: 189,992; Growth (since 2000): 0.2%; Density: 7,102.9 persons per square mile; Race: 76.7% White, 1.0% Black/African American, 11.1% Asian, 0.5% American Indian/Alaska Native, 0.3% Native Hawaiian/Other Pacific Islander, 4.5% Two or more races, 17.1% Hispanic of any race; Average household size: 2.55; Median age: 40.2; Age under 18: 20.6%; Age 65 and over: 14.2%; Males per 100 females: 98.5; Marriage status: 31.8% never married, 51.5% now married, 1.7% separated, 5.4% widowed, 11.3% divorced; Foreign born: 16.6%; Speak English only: 77.0%; With disability: 8.3%; Veterans: 7.7%; Ancestry: 15.4% German, 12.5% Irish, 10.1% English, 7.4% Italian, 4.1% American

Employment: 20.1% management, business, and financial, 6.3% computer, engineering, and science, 12.1% education, legal, community service, arts, and media, 5.8% healthcare practitioners, 14.9% service, 27.3% sales and office, 6.8% natural resources, construction, and maintenance, 6.7% production, transportation, and material moving

Income: Per capita: $42,196; Median household: $81,389; Average household: $107,267; Households with income of $100,000 or more: 40.5%; Poverty rate: 8.9%

Educational Attainment: High school diploma or higher: 92.5%; Bachelor's degree or higher: 40.2%; Graduate/professional degree or higher: 14.2%

School District(s)

Fountain Valley Elementary (KG-08)
2012-13 Enrollment: 6,344 . . . . (714) 843-3200
Huntington Beach City Elementary (KG-08)
2012-13 Enrollment: 7,056 . . . . (714) 964-8888
Huntington Beach Union High (09-12)
2012-13 Enrollment: 16,400 . . . . (714) 903-7000
Ocean View (KG-08)
2012-13 Enrollment: 9,418 . . . . (714) 847-2551
Westminster Elementary (KG-08)
2012-13 Enrollment: 9,619 . . . . (714) 894-7311

Two-year College(s)

Golden West College (Public)
Fall 2013 Enrollment: 12,717 . . . . (714) 892-7711
2013-14 Tuition: In-state $1,176; Out-of-state $5,208

Vocational/Technical School(s)

The Academy of Radio and TV Broadcasting (Private, For-profit)
Fall 2013 Enrollment: 44 . . . . (714) 842-0100
2013-14 Tuition: $14,000

Housing: Homeownership rate: 60.4%; Median home value: $624,400; Median year structure built: 1972; Homeowner vacancy rate: 1.1%; Median gross rent: $1,559 per month; Rental vacancy rate: 5.4%

Health Insurance: 88.0% have insurance; 75.2% have private insurance; 22.8% have public insurance; 12.0% do not have insurance; 4.6% of children under 18 do not have insurance

Hospitals: Huntington Beach Hospital (135 beds)

Safety: Violent crime rate: 18.5 per 10,000 population; Property crime rate: 251.9 per 10,000 population

Newspapers: The Local News (weekly circulation 25000)

Transportation: Commute: 89.0% car, 1.0% public transportation, 1.7% walk, 5.8% work from home; Median travel time to work: 27.1 minutes

Additional Information Contacts

City of Huntington Beach. . . . . (714) 536-5202
http://www.ci.huntington-beach.ca.us

IRVINE (city). Covers a land area of 66.106 square miles and a water area of 0.348 square miles. Located at 33.68° N. Lat; 117.77° W. Long. Elevation is 56 feet.

History: Named for James Irvine of San Francisco, who purchased land here in 1870. Was built in the 1970s as a planned community on farmland that was part of the Irvine Ranch (which had been carved out of three Spanish and Mexican land grants in 1876). Incorporated 1971.

Population: 212,375; Growth (since 2000): 48.4%; Density: 3,212.6 persons per square mile; Race: 50.5% White, 1.8% Black/African American, 39.2% Asian, 0.2% American Indian/Alaska Native, 0.2% Native Hawaiian/Other Pacific Islander, 5.5% Two or more races, 9.2% Hispanic of any race; Average household size: 2.61; Median age: 33.9; Age under 18: 21.5%; Age 65 and over: 8.7%; Males per 100 females: 94.9; Marriage status: 37.0% never married, 52.0% now married, 1.0% separated, 3.0% widowed, 8.0% divorced; Foreign born: 36.0%; Speak English only: 55.2%; With disability: 5.4%; Veterans: 4.0%; Ancestry: 7.9% German, 6.3% English, 6.1% Irish, 4.5% Iranian, 3.8% Italian

Employment: 25.5% management, business, and financial, 15.1% computer, engineering, and science, 15.2% education, legal, community service, arts, and media, 6.3% healthcare practitioners, 8.6% service, 23.6% sales and office, 2.5% natural resources, construction, and maintenance, 3.4% production, transportation, and material moving

Income: Per capita: $43,096; Median household: $90,585; Average household: $115,296; Households with income of $100,000 or more: 45.5%; Poverty rate: 12.2%

Educational Attainment: High school diploma or higher: 96.3%; Bachelor's degree or higher: 64.9%; Graduate/professional degree or higher: 27.9%

School District(s)

Irvine Unified (KG-12)
2012-13 Enrollment: 29,072 . . . . (949) 936-5000
Tustin Unified (KG-12)
2012-13 Enrollment: 23,771 . . . . (714) 730-7301

Four-year College(s)

Brandman University (Private, Not-for-profit)
Fall 2013 Enrollment: 7,746 . . . . (949) 341-9800
2013-14 Tuition: In-state $8,800; Out-of-state $8,800
Concordia University-Irvine (Private, Not-for-profit, Lutheran Church - Missouri Synod)
Fall 2013 Enrollment: 4,046 . . . . (949) 854-8002
2013-14 Tuition: In-state $29,630; Out-of-state $29,630
Stanbridge College (Private, For-profit)
Fall 2013 Enrollment: 963 . . . . (949) 794-9090
The Chicago School of Professional Psychology at Irvine (Private, Not-for-profit)
Fall 2013 Enrollment: 273 . . . . (949) 737-5460
University of California-Irvine (Public)
Fall 2013 Enrollment: 28,895 . . . . (949) 824-5011
2013-14 Tuition: In-state $13,149; Out-of-state $36,027

Two-year College(s)

Fashion Institute of Design & Merchandising-Orange County (Private, For-profit)
Fall 2013 Enrollment: 214 . . . . (949) 851-6200
2013-14 Tuition: In-state $28,920; Out-of-state $28,920
Irvine Valley College (Public)
Fall 2013 Enrollment: 13,362 . . . . (949) 451-5100
2013-14 Tuition: In-state $1,453; Out-of-state $7,615

Housing: Homeownership rate: 50.2%; Median home value: $643,200; Median year structure built: 1991; Homeowner vacancy rate: 2.2%; Median gross rent: $1,846 per month; Rental vacancy rate: 6.2%

Health Insurance: 90.7% have insurance; 81.9% have private insurance; 14.3% have public insurance; 9.3% do not have insurance; 5.3% of children under 18 do not have insurance
Hospitals: Hoag Orthopedic Institute
Safety: Violent crime rate: 4.8 per 10,000 population; Property crime rate: 139.3 per 10,000 population
Newspapers: Irvine World News (weekly circulation 55000)
Transportation: Commute: 85.6% car, 1.5% public transportation, 3.7% walk, 6.9% work from home; Median travel time to work: 23.6 minutes; Amtrak: Train service available.
Additional Information Contacts
City of Irvine . . . . (949) 724-6000
http://www.ci.irvine.ca.us

LA HABRA (city). Covers a land area of 7.370 square miles and a water area of 0.006 square miles. Located at 33.93° N. Lat; 117.95° W. Long. Elevation is 299 feet.
History: Named for the Spanish translation of "pass," and its through the Puente Hills. La Habra was settled in the 1860s by Basque sheepherders. The city has grown along with the surrounding Los Angeles metropolitan area. Incorporated 1925.
Population: 60,239; Growth (since 2000): 2.1%; Density: 8,173.6 persons per square mile; Race: 58.3% White, 1.7% Black/African American, 9.4% Asian, 0.9% American Indian/Alaska Native, 0.2% Native Hawaiian/Other Pacific Islander, 4.2% Two or more races, 57.2% Hispanic of any race; Average household size: 3.16; Median age: 33.6; Age under 18: 26.7%; Age 65 and over: 10.9%; Males per 100 females: 97.0; Marriage status: 37.1% never married, 49.4% now married, 1.8% separated, 4.8% widowed, 8.7% divorced; Foreign born: 26.9%; Speak English only: 49.2%; With disability: 8.3%; Veterans: 5.5%; Ancestry: 7.0% German, 5.4% Irish, 5.3% English, 2.9% American, 2.7% Italian
Employment: 11.0% management, business, and financial, 3.5% computer, engineering, and science, 8.1% education, legal, community service, arts, and media, 3.0% healthcare practitioners, 23.7% service, 28.7% sales and office, 8.8% natural resources, construction, and maintenance, 13.3% production, transportation, and material moving
Income: Per capita: $24,647; Median household: $61,702; Average household: $77,258; Households with income of $100,000 or more: 25.7%; Poverty rate: 13.4%
Educational Attainment: High school diploma or higher: 79.3%; Bachelor's degree or higher: 21.1%; Graduate/professional degree or higher: 6.9%

School District(s)

Fullerton Joint Union High (09-12)
2012-13 Enrollment: 14,608 . . . . (714) 870-2800
La Habra City Elementary (KG-08)
2012-13 Enrollment: 5,251 . . . . (562) 690-2305
Lowell Joint (KG-08)
2012-13 Enrollment: 3,169 . . . . (562) 943-0211

Housing: Homeownership rate: 57.6%; Median home value: $376,500; Median year structure built: 1967; Homeowner vacancy rate: 1.5%; Median gross rent: $1,298 per month; Rental vacancy rate: 6.2%
Health Insurance: 77.9% have insurance; 56.8% have private insurance; 28.1% have public insurance; 22.1% do not have insurance; 12.6% of children under 18 do not have insurance
Safety: Violent crime rate: 14.3 per 10,000 population; Property crime rate: 187.1 per 10,000 population
Newspapers: La Habra Journal (weekly circulation 10000)
Transportation: Commute: 89.3% car, 4.0% public transportation, 2.3% walk, 2.3% work from home; Median travel time to work: 27.7 minutes
Additional Information Contacts
City of La Habra . . . . (562) 905-9700
http://www.ci.la-habra.ca.us

LA PALMA (city). Covers a land area of 1.808 square miles and a water area of 0.024 square miles. Located at 33.85° N. Lat; 118.04° W. Long. Elevation is 46 feet.
Population: 15,568; Growth (since 2000): 1.0%; Density: 8,612.6 persons per square mile; Race: 37.0% White, 5.2% Black/African American, 48.1% Asian, 0.4% American Indian/Alaska Native, 0.3% Native Hawaiian/Other Pacific Islander, 4.3% Two or more races, 16.0% Hispanic of any race; Average household size: 3.06; Median age: 41.2; Age under 18: 22.0%; Age 65 and over: 15.9%; Males per 100 females: 93.5; Marriage status: 30.2% never married, 54.8% now married, 1.3% separated, 5.6% widowed, 9.4% divorced; Foreign born: 32.5%; Speak English only: 56.5%; With disability: 8.4%; Veterans: 7.6%; Ancestry: 7.4% German, 6.8% English, 5.8% Irish, 3.5% Italian, 2.9% American
Employment: 16.1% management, business, and financial, 7.0% computer, engineering, and science, 12.8% education, legal, community service, arts, and media, 9.6% healthcare practitioners, 12.9% service, 26.1% sales and office, 5.3% natural resources, construction, and maintenance, 10.2% production, transportation, and material moving
Income: Per capita: $34,885; Median household: $85,759; Average household: $106,123; Households with income of $100,000 or more: 41.3%; Poverty rate: 9.0%
Educational Attainment: High school diploma or higher: 92.8%; Bachelor's degree or higher: 40.4%; Graduate/professional degree or higher: 12.8%

School District(s)

Anaheim Union High (07-12)
2012-13 Enrollment: 32,085 . . . . (714) 999-3511
Centralia Elementary (KG-06)
2012-13 Enrollment: 4,501 . . . . (714) 228-3100
Cypress Elementary (KG-06)
2012-13 Enrollment: 3,879 . . . . (714) 220-6900

Housing: Homeownership rate: 71.9%; Median home value: $568,300; Median year structure built: 1971; Homeowner vacancy rate: 0.3%; Median gross rent: $1,481 per month; Rental vacancy rate: 6.0%
Health Insurance: 84.0% have insurance; 71.4% have private insurance; 26.1% have public insurance; 16.0% do not have insurance; 9.1% of children under 18 do not have insurance
Hospitals: La Palma Intercommunity Hospital (139 beds)
Safety: Violent crime rate: 6.3 per 10,000 population; Property crime rate: 204.4 per 10,000 population
Transportation: Commute: 92.5% car, 1.5% public transportation, 2.1% walk, 2.7% work from home; Median travel time to work: 29.8 minutes
Additional Information Contacts
City of La Palma . . . . (714) 690-3300
http://www.cityoflapalma.org

LADERA RANCH (CDP). Covers a land area of 4.905 square miles and a water area of 0 square miles. Located at 33.55° N. Lat; 117.64° W. Long. Elevation is 551 feet.
Population: 22,980; Growth (since 2000): n/a; Density: 4,685.2 persons per square mile; Race: 77.9% White, 1.5% Black/African American, 12.1% Asian, 0.2% American Indian/Alaska Native, 0.1% Native Hawaiian/Other Pacific Islander, 5.5% Two or more races, 12.8% Hispanic of any race; Average household size: 3.23; Median age: 32.4; Age under 18: 38.3%; Age 65 and over: 3.6%; Males per 100 females: 96.3; Marriage status: 20.4% never married, 71.1% now married, 1.7% separated, 2.4% widowed, 6.2% divorced; Foreign born: 16.9%; Speak English only: 77.0%; With disability: 3.7%; Veterans: 6.7%; Ancestry: 20.2% German, 13.0% Irish, 12.4% English, 7.2% Italian, 4.7% Swedish
Employment: 31.7% management, business, and financial, 7.0% computer, engineering, and science, 13.5% education, legal, community service, arts, and media, 6.2% healthcare practitioners, 10.9% service, 27.6% sales and office, 1.0% natural resources, construction, and maintenance, 2.1% production, transportation, and material moving
Income: Per capita: $47,514; Median household: $124,047; Average household: $152,358; Households with income of $100,000 or more: 64.5%; Poverty rate: 4.0%
Educational Attainment: High school diploma or higher: 98.8%; Bachelor's degree or higher: 64.9%; Graduate/professional degree or higher: 24.4%

School District(s)

Capistrano Unified (KG-12)
2012-13 Enrollment: 53,785 . . . . (949) 234-9200

Housing: Homeownership rate: 73.1%; Median home value: $612,600; Median year structure built: 2005; Homeowner vacancy rate: 1.9%; Median gross rent: $1,896 per month; Rental vacancy rate: 4.7%
Health Insurance: 96.0% have insurance; 90.9% have private insurance; 8.4% have public insurance; 4.0% do not have insurance; 3.5% of children under 18 do not have insurance
Transportation: Commute: 88.5% car, 0.1% public transportation, 0.9% walk, 9.5% work from home; Median travel time to work: 29.7 minutes

LAGUNA BEACH (city). Covers a land area of 8.850 square miles and a water area of 0.971 square miles. Located at 33.54° N. Lat; 117.76° W. Long. Elevation is 20 feet.

History: Named for the Spanish translation of "small lake". Has profited from the rapid growth and prosperity of Orange County. Founded 1887. Incorporated 1927.

Population: 22,723; Growth (since 2000): -4.2%; Density: 2,567.6 persons per square mile; Race: 90.9% White, 0.8% Black/African American, 3.6% Asian, 0.3% American Indian/Alaska Native, 0.1% Native Hawaiian/Other Pacific Islander, 2.9% Two or more races, 7.3% Hispanic of any race; Average household size: 2.09; Median age: 48.3; Age under 18: 16.1%; Age 65 and over: 18.3%; Males per 100 females: 100.6; Marriage status: 27.9% never married, 52.8% now married, 2.6% separated, 4.0% widowed, 15.3% divorced; Foreign born: 11.9%; Speak English only: 85.4%; With disability: 6.6%; Veterans: 7.5%; Ancestry: 20.4% German, 16.3% English, 11.9% Irish, 7.4% Italian, 4.8% Scottish

Employment: 27.7% management, business, and financial, 4.9% computer, engineering, and science, 19.8% education, legal, community service, arts, and media, 6.1% healthcare practitioners, 7.3% service, 28.2% sales and office, 2.8% natural resources, construction, and maintenance, 3.1% production, transportation, and material moving

Income: Per capita: $75,460; Median household: $94,325; Average household: $155,606; Households with income of $100,000 or more: 47.8%; Poverty rate: 6.3%

Educational Attainment: High school diploma or higher: 97.4%; Bachelor's degree or higher: 65.0%; Graduate/professional degree or higher: 28.9%

School District(s)

Laguna Beach Unified (KG-12)
2012-13 Enrollment: 3,045 . . . . (949) 497-7700

Four-year College(s)

Laguna College of Art and Design (Private, Not-for-profit)
Fall 2013 Enrollment: 544 . . . . (949) 376-6000
2013-14 Tuition: In-state $26,500; Out-of-state $26,500

Housing: Homeownership rate: 60.0%; Median home value: 1 million+; Median year structure built: 1962; Homeowner vacancy rate: 1.7%; Median gross rent: $1,887 per month; Rental vacancy rate: 7.7%

Health Insurance: 92.3% have insurance; 82.7% have private insurance; 23.5% have public insurance; 7.7% do not have insurance; 3.0% of children under 18 do not have insurance

Safety: Violent crime rate: 17.6 per 10,000 population; Property crime rate: 201.2 per 10,000 population

Newspapers: Coastline Pilot (weekly circulation 12500); Laguna Beach Independent (weekly circulation 15000)

Transportation: Commute: 83.5% car, 0.5% public transportation, 2.3% walk, 12.6% work from home; Median travel time to work: 26.9 minutes

Additional Information Contacts

City of Laguna Beach . . . . (949) 497-0308
http://www.lagunabeachcity.net

LAGUNA HILLS (city). Covers a land area of 6.670 square miles and a water area of 0.025 square miles. Located at 33.59° N. Lat; 117.70° W. Long. Elevation is 371 feet.

History: This city was incorporated on December 20, 1991 and is located between Los Angeles and San Diego. Its name refers to its it proximity to Laguna Canyon and Laguna Beach.

Population: 30,344; Growth (since 2000): -2.7%; Density: 4,549.0 persons per square mile; Race: 72.7% White, 1.4% Black/African American, 12.6% Asian, 0.3% American Indian/Alaska Native, 0.2% Native Hawaiian/Other Pacific Islander, 4.7% Two or more races, 20.6% Hispanic of any race; Average household size: 2.86; Median age: 40.8; Age under 18: 22.3%; Age 65 and over: 12.8%; Males per 100 females: 95.5; Marriage status: 29.0% never married, 57.4% now married, 1.4% separated, 5.4% widowed, 8.2% divorced; Foreign born: 25.0%; Speak English only: 68.9%; With disability: 8.3%; Veterans: 6.6%; Ancestry: 15.6% German, 12.2% Irish, 9.7% English, 6.1% Italian, 4.1% Iranian

Employment: 21.7% management, business, and financial, 6.3% computer, engineering, and science, 10.8% education, legal, community service, arts, and media, 5.4% healthcare practitioners, 15.8% service, 27.2% sales and office, 6.8% natural resources, construction, and maintenance, 6.0% production, transportation, and material moving

Income: Per capita: $43,736; Median household: $90,704; Average household: $124,199; Households with income of $100,000 or more: 44.9%; Poverty rate: 6.7%

Educational Attainment: High school diploma or higher: 91.6%; Bachelor's degree or higher: 45.3%; Graduate/professional degree or higher: 16.8%

School District(s)

Saddleback Valley Unified (PK-12)
2012-13 Enrollment: 30,355 . . . . (949) 580-3200

Four-year College(s)

Allied American University (Private, For-profit)
Fall 2013 Enrollment: 2,628 . . . . (888) 384-0849

Housing: Homeownership rate: 74.7%; Median home value: $562,900; Median year structure built: 1979; Homeowner vacancy rate: 1.4%; Median gross rent: $1,782 per month; Rental vacancy rate: 11.2%

Health Insurance: 87.1% have insurance; 75.1% have private insurance; 18.8% have public insurance; 12.9% do not have insurance; 9.0% of children under 18 do not have insurance

Hospitals: Saddleback Memorial Medical Center (325 beds)

Safety: Violent crime rate: 17.0 per 10,000 population; Property crime rate: 163.2 per 10,000 population

Transportation: Commute: 86.1% car, 2.3% public transportation, 1.0% walk, 8.6% work from home; Median travel time to work: 26.0 minutes

Additional Information Contacts

City of Laguna Hills . . . . (949) 707-2600
http://www.ci.laguna-hills.ca.us

LAGUNA NIGUEL (city). Covers a land area of 14.833 square miles and a water area of 0.052 square miles. Located at 33.53° N. Lat; 117.70° W. Long. Elevation is 397 feet.

History: This city was incorporated on December 1, 1989. Its name originates from the Spanish word "Laguna," meaning lagoon and "Nigueli," the name of a Juaneño Indian village once located on Aliso Creek.

Population: 62,979; Growth (since 2000): 1.8%; Density: 4,245.8 persons per square mile; Race: 80.4% White, 1.2% Black/African American, 8.7% Asian, 0.3% American Indian/Alaska Native, 0.1% Native Hawaiian/Other Pacific Islander, 4.4% Two or more races, 13.9% Hispanic of any race; Average household size: 2.59; Median age: 42.8; Age under 18: 22.6%; Age 65 and over: 13.0%; Males per 100 females: 94.0; Marriage status: 26.3% never married, 58.9% now married, 1.4% separated, 4.6% widowed, 10.2% divorced; Foreign born: 21.1%; Speak English only: 75.1%; With disability: 6.4%; Veterans: 7.0%; Ancestry: 13.9% German, 13.1% Irish, 11.5% English, 8.0% Italian, 4.8% Iranian

Employment: 24.8% management, business, and financial, 8.7% computer, engineering, and science, 12.4% education, legal, community service, arts, and media, 6.8% healthcare practitioners, 11.2% service, 27.3% sales and office, 4.3% natural resources, construction, and maintenance, 4.4% production, transportation, and material moving

Income: Per capita: $50,477; Median household: $99,771; Average household: $129,796; Households with income of $100,000 or more: 50.0%; Poverty rate: 6.3%

Educational Attainment: High school diploma or higher: 96.3%; Bachelor's degree or higher: 54.6%; Graduate/professional degree or higher: 20.4%

School District(s)

Capistrano Unified (KG-12)
2012-13 Enrollment: 53,785 . . . . (949) 234-9200

Housing: Homeownership rate: 72.0%; Median home value: $662,200; Median year structure built: 1985; Homeowner vacancy rate: 0.9%; Median gross rent: $1,808 per month; Rental vacancy rate: 5.4%

Health Insurance: 90.5% have insurance; 81.1% have private insurance; 18.5% have public insurance; 9.5% do not have insurance; 7.7% of children under 18 do not have insurance

Safety: Violent crime rate: 8.8 per 10,000 population; Property crime rate: 96.2 per 10,000 population

Transportation: Commute: 87.7% car, 1.2% public transportation, 0.9% walk, 9.1% work from home; Median travel time to work: 28.5 minutes

Additional Information Contacts

City of Laguna Niguel . . . . (949) 362-4300
http://www.cityoflagunaniguel.org

LAGUNA WOODS (city). Covers a land area of 3.115 square miles and a water area of <.001 square miles. Located at 33.61° N. Lat; 117.73° W. Long. Elevation is 381 feet.

Population: 16,192; Growth (since 2000): -1.9%; Density: 5,197.3 persons per square mile; Race: 87.3% White, 0.7% Black/African American, 10.0% Asian, 0.1% American Indian/Alaska Native, 0.1% Native Hawaiian/Other Pacific Islander, 1.2% Two or more races, 4.0% Hispanic of any race;

Average household size: 1.42; Median age: 77.0; Age under 18: 0.3%; Age 65 and over: 79.5%; Males per 100 females: 55.1; Marriage status: 7.9% never married, 43.2% now married, 0.8% separated, 27.7% widowed, 21.2% divorced; Foreign born: 23.7%; Speak English only: 81.2%; With disability: 29.0%; Veterans: 18.1%; Ancestry: 14.5% German, 14.5% English, 9.8% Irish, 7.6% American, 6.2% Italian

Employment: 21.4% management, business, and financial, 6.0% computer, engineering, and science, 11.2% education, legal, community service, arts, and media, 7.3% healthcare practitioners, 19.0% service, 31.0% sales and office, 1.8% natural resources, construction, and maintenance, 2.3% production, transportation, and material moving

Income: Per capita: $39,312; Median household: $36,652; Average household: $55,523; Households with income of $100,000 or more: 11.2%; Poverty rate: 9.7%

Educational Attainment: High school diploma or higher: 94.1%; Bachelor's degree or higher: 40.3%; Graduate/professional degree or higher: 16.9%

Housing: Homeownership rate: 77.2%; Median home value: $198,300; Median year structure built: 1968; Homeowner vacancy rate: 4.1%; Median gross rent: $1,413 per month; Rental vacancy rate: 10.2%

Health Insurance: 96.1% have insurance; 59.5% have private insurance; 79.8% have public insurance; 3.9% do not have insurance; 0.0% of children under 18 do not have insurance

Safety: Violent crime rate: 3.0 per 10,000 population; Property crime rate: 79.6 per 10,000 population

Transportation: Commute: 82.8% car, 3.1% public transportation, 2.2% walk, 10.0% work from home; Median travel time to work: 26.2 minutes

Additional Information Contacts

City of Laguna Woods . . . . (949) 639-0500
http://www.lagunawoodscity.org

LAKE FOREST (city). Covers a land area of 17.816 square miles and a water area of 0.086 square miles. Located at 33.67° N. Lat; 117.67° W. Long. Elevation is 486 feet.

Population: 77,264; Growth (since 2000): 31.6%; Density: 4,336.8 persons per square mile; Race: 70.3% White, 1.7% Black/African American, 13.1% Asian, 0.5% American Indian/Alaska Native, 0.2% Native Hawaiian/Other Pacific Islander, 4.8% Two or more races, 24.6% Hispanic of any race; Average household size: 2.93; Median age: 37.2; Age under 18: 24.7%; Age 65 and over: 9.2%; Males per 100 females: 98.7; Marriage status: 28.2% never married, 58.6% now married, 1.4% separated, 3.8% widowed, 9.4% divorced; Foreign born: 23.9%; Speak English only: 68.2%; With disability: 6.6%; Veterans: 7.1%; Ancestry: 14.4% German, 9.7% Irish, 9.5% English, 6.1% Italian, 3.7% American

Employment: 20.8% management, business, and financial, 9.8% computer, engineering, and science, 10.1% education, legal, community service, arts, and media, 4.1% healthcare practitioners, 14.9% service, 27.9% sales and office, 5.9% natural resources, construction, and maintenance, 6.4% production, transportation, and material moving

Income: Per capita: $39,860; Median household: $93,631; Average household: $112,987; Households with income of $100,000 or more: 47.3%; Poverty rate: 6.0%

Educational Attainment: High school diploma or higher: 92.1%; Bachelor's degree or higher: 43.2%; Graduate/professional degree or higher: 13.5%

School District(s)

Saddleback Valley Unified (PK-12)
2012-13 Enrollment: 30,355 . . . . (949) 580-3200

Vocational/Technical School(s)

Marinello Schools of Beauty-Lake Forest (Private, For-profit)
Fall 2013 Enrollment: 567 . . . . (562) 945-2211
2013-14 Tuition: $18,511

Housing: Homeownership rate: 70.8%; Median home value: $490,800; Median year structure built: 1981; Homeowner vacancy rate: 1.3%; Median gross rent: $1,680 per month; Rental vacancy rate: 4.3%

Health Insurance: 87.6% have insurance; 77.1% have private insurance; 16.7% have public insurance; 12.4% do not have insurance; 7.2% of children under 18 do not have insurance

Safety: Violent crime rate: 13.2 per 10,000 population; Property crime rate: 102.5 per 10,000 population

Transportation: Commute: 90.4% car, 0.7% public transportation, 1.4% walk, 5.8% work from home; Median travel time to work: 25.3 minutes

Additional Information Contacts

City of Lake Forest . . . . (949) 461-3400
http://www.lakeforestca.gov

LAS FLORES (CDP). Covers a land area of 2.028 square miles and a water area of 0 square miles. Located at 33.58° N. Lat; 117.62° W. Long. Elevation is 715 feet.

Population: 5,971; Growth (since 2000): 6.2%; Density: 2,943.7 persons per square mile; Race: 75.2% White, 1.5% Black/African American, 13.1% Asian, 0.4% American Indian/Alaska Native, 0.2% Native Hawaiian/Other Pacific Islander, 5.3% Two or more races, 16.5% Hispanic of any race; Average household size: 3.12; Median age: 33.2; Age under 18: 34.0%; Age 65 and over: 3.7%; Males per 100 females: 99.4; Marriage status: 27.1% never married, 61.6% now married, 1.4% separated, 2.6% widowed, 8.7% divorced; Foreign born: 12.0%; Speak English only: 80.1%; With disability: 3.5%; Veterans: 4.5%; Ancestry: 15.8% German, 12.7% English, 10.0% Irish, 6.3% Italian, 5.2% Greek

Employment: 31.8% management, business, and financial, 9.5% computer, engineering, and science, 9.9% education, legal, community service, arts, and media, 5.5% healthcare practitioners, 9.5% service, 28.2% sales and office, 3.4% natural resources, construction, and maintenance, 2.1% production, transportation, and material moving

Income: Per capita: $47,699; Median household: $128,264; Average household: $151,322; Households with income of $100,000 or more: 61.6%; Poverty rate: 4.6%

Educational Attainment: High school diploma or higher: 98.2%; Bachelor's degree or higher: 55.9%; Graduate/professional degree or higher: 15.9%

School District(s)

Capistrano Unified (KG-12)
2012-13 Enrollment: 53,785 . . . . (949) 234-9200

Housing: Homeownership rate: 69.2%; Median home value: $591,800; Median year structure built: 1996; Homeowner vacancy rate: 0.7%; Median gross rent: $1,636 per month; Rental vacancy rate: 5.6%

Health Insurance: 92.2% have insurance; 88.7% have private insurance; 6.3% have public insurance; 7.8% do not have insurance; 2.3% of children under 18 do not have insurance

Transportation: Commute: 89.6% car, 0.7% public transportation, 0.0% walk, 8.4% work from home; Median travel time to work: 28.9 minutes

LOS ALAMITOS (city). Covers a land area of 4.050 square miles and a water area of 0.066 square miles. Located at 33.80° N. Lat; 118.06° W. Long. Elevation is 23 feet.

History: Named for the Spanish translation of "little poplars" or "cottonwoods". Incorporated 1960.

Population: 11,449; Growth (since 2000): -0.8%; Density: 2,827.0 persons per square mile; Race: 71.0% White, 2.8% Black/African American, 12.8% Asian, 0.4% American Indian/Alaska Native, 0.4% Native Hawaiian/Other Pacific Islander, 6.1% Two or more races, 21.1% Hispanic of any race; Average household size: 2.66; Median age: 38.7; Age under 18: 23.9%; Age 65 and over: 13.9%; Males per 100 females: 89.5; Marriage status: 31.0% never married, 50.8% now married, 2.1% separated, 5.8% widowed, 12.3% divorced; Foreign born: 14.8%; Speak English only: 77.0%; With disability: 8.6%; Veterans: 7.7%; Ancestry: 14.8% German, 11.9% Irish, 9.4% English, 5.4% Italian, 3.8% French

Employment: 22.9% management, business, and financial, 4.5% computer, engineering, and science, 11.7% education, legal, community service, arts, and media, 5.9% healthcare practitioners, 12.0% service, 27.6% sales and office, 6.6% natural resources, construction, and maintenance, 8.8% production, transportation, and material moving

Income: Per capita: $37,930; Median household: $82,679; Average household: $105,160; Households with income of $100,000 or more: 40.3%; Poverty rate: 8.5%

Educational Attainment: High school diploma or higher: 92.7%; Bachelor's degree or higher: 39.2%; Graduate/professional degree or higher: 13.8%

School District(s)

Los Alamitos Unified (KG-12)
2012-13 Enrollment: 9,912 . . . . (562) 799-4700

Four-year College(s)

Touro University Worldwide (Private, Not-for-profit)
Fall 2013 Enrollment: 363 . . . . (818) 874-4115
2013-14 Tuition: In-state $15,640; Out-of-state $15,640

Housing: Homeownership rate: 46.7%; Median home value: $613,600; Median year structure built: 1969; Homeowner vacancy rate: 0.8%; Median gross rent: $1,478 per month; Rental vacancy rate: 3.1%

Health Insurance: 88.4% have insurance; 77.2% have private insurance; 20.7% have public insurance; 11.6% do not have insurance; 11.0% of children under 18 do not have insurance

Hospitals: Los Alamitos Medical Center (167 beds)
Safety: Violent crime rate: 20.5 per 10,000 population; Property crime rate: 306.8 per 10,000 population
Newspapers: News-Enterprise (weekly circulation 32000)
Transportation: Commute: 89.2% car, 1.2% public transportation, 2.3% walk, 4.8% work from home; Median travel time to work: 27.3 minutes
Additional Information Contacts
City of Los Alamitos. . . . . (562) 431-3538
http://cityoflosalamitos.org

MIDWAY CITY (CDP). Covers a land area of 0.632 square miles and a water area of 0 square miles. Located at 33.74° N. Lat; 117.99° W. Long. Elevation is 39 feet.
Population: 8,485; Growth (since 2000): n/a; Density: 13,422.0 persons per square mile; Race: 34.0% White, 0.8% Black/African American, 47.1% Asian, 0.8% American Indian/Alaska Native, 0.5% Native Hawaiian/Other Pacific Islander, 3.1% Two or more races, 29.1% Hispanic of any race; Average household size: 3.45; Median age: 37.1; Age under 18: 24.8%; Age 65 and over: 12.8%; Males per 100 females: 98.0; Marriage status: 36.6% never married, 46.2% now married, 1.8% separated, 7.9% widowed, 9.3% divorced; Foreign born: 51.5%; Speak English only: 33.2%; With disability: 12.1%; Veterans: 2.3%; Ancestry: 6.7% German, 3.3% American, 3.1% English, 1.7% Irish, 1.5% French
Employment: 7.1% management, business, and financial, 2.1% computer, engineering, and science, 8.0% education, legal, community service, arts, and media, 3.0% healthcare practitioners, 33.4% service, 23.1% sales and office, 9.9% natural resources, construction, and maintenance, 13.3% production, transportation, and material moving
Income: Per capita: $17,829; Median household: $45,224; Average household: $56,507; Households with income of $100,000 or more: 17.8%; Poverty rate: 19.8%
Educational Attainment: High school diploma or higher: 68.4%; Bachelor's degree or higher: 19.5%; Graduate/professional degree or higher: 2.7%

School District(s)

Ocean View (KG-08)
2012-13 Enrollment: 9,418 . . . . (714) 847-2551
Westminster Elementary (KG-08)
2012-13 Enrollment: 9,619 . . . . (714) 894-7311
Housing: Homeownership rate: 41.2%; Median home value: $364,300; Median year structure built: 1968; Homeowner vacancy rate: 0.6%; Median gross rent: $1,306 per month; Rental vacancy rate: 7.2%
Health Insurance: 75.9% have insurance; 42.5% have private insurance; 37.4% have public insurance; 24.1% do not have insurance; 14.7% of children under 18 do not have insurance
Transportation: Commute: 87.0% car, 5.5% public transportation, 1.1% walk, 2.3% work from home; Median travel time to work: 31.7 minutes

MISSION VIEJO (city). Covers a land area of 17.739 square miles and a water area of 0.384 square miles. Located at 33.61° N. Lat; 117.66° W. Long. Elevation is 397 feet.
History: Named for the Spanish translation of "old building". Historic Mission Viejo to southeast; Mission San Juan Capistrano to south, site of annual return of swallows March 19.
Population: 93,305; Growth (since 2000): 0.2%; Density: 5,259.8 persons per square mile; Race: 79.8% White, 1.3% Black/African American, 9.1% Asian, 0.4% American Indian/Alaska Native, 0.2% Native Hawaiian/Other Pacific Islander, 4.6% Two or more races, 17.0% Hispanic of any race; Average household size: 2.78; Median age: 42.2; Age under 18: 22.8%; Age 65 and over: 14.5%; Males per 100 females: 95.4; Marriage status: 26.4% never married, 58.3% now married, 1.0% separated, 6.0% widowed, 9.3% divorced; Foreign born: 19.1%; Speak English only: 77.9%; With disability: 7.8%; Veterans: 8.4%; Ancestry: 17.2% German, 13.3% Irish, 10.8% English, 6.5% Italian, 4.5% American
Employment: 21.6% management, business, and financial, 9.3% computer, engineering, and science, 12.4% education, legal, community service, arts, and media, 5.3% healthcare practitioners, 13.4% service, 28.6% sales and office, 4.2% natural resources, construction, and maintenance, 5.3% production, transportation, and material moving
Income: Per capita: $40,909; Median household: $96,210; Average household: $113,097; Households with income of $100,000 or more: 48.1%; Poverty rate: 5.3%
Educational Attainment: High school diploma or higher: 94.5%; Bachelor's degree or higher: 45.2%; Graduate/professional degree or higher: 16.2%

School District(s)

Capistrano Unified (KG-12)
2012-13 Enrollment: 53,785 . . . . (949) 234-9200
Saddleback Valley Unified (PK-12)
2012-13 Enrollment: 30,355 . . . . (949) 580-3200

Two-year College(s)

Saddleback College (Public)
Fall 2013 Enrollment: 20,871 . . . . (949) 582-4500
2013-14 Tuition: In-state $762; Out-of-state $4,694
Housing: Homeownership rate: 77.9%; Median home value: $542,800; Median year structure built: 1979; Homeowner vacancy rate: 0.9%; Median gross rent: $1,825 per month; Rental vacancy rate: 4.9%
Health Insurance: 91.9% have insurance; 80.9% have private insurance; 21.4% have public insurance; 8.1% do not have insurance; 3.2% of children under 18 do not have insurance
Hospitals: Mission Hospital Regional Medical Center (331 beds)
Safety: Violent crime rate: 6.5 per 10,000 population; Property crime rate: 104.1 per 10,000 population
Transportation: Commute: 88.4% car, 1.5% public transportation, 0.5% walk, 8.7% work from home; Median travel time to work: 26.6 minutes
Additional Information Contacts
City of Mission Viejo . . . . (949) 470-3000
http://cityofmissionviejo.org

NEWPORT BEACH (city). Covers a land area of 23.805 square miles and a water area of 29.173 square miles. Located at 33.60° N. Lat; 117.89° W. Long. Elevation is 10 feet.
History: Named for its location on the ocean, by the McFadden brothers of Delaware, who plotted the townsite. Newport Beach grew around the lagoon-like harbor that once sheltered smugglers, operated as a commercial port from 1872 to 1898, and later became a center for pleasure craft.
Population: 85,186; Growth (since 2000): 21.6%; Density: 3,578.5 persons per square mile; Race: 87.3% White, 0.7% Black/African American, 7.0% Asian, 0.3% American Indian/Alaska Native, 0.1% Native Hawaiian/Other Pacific Islander, 2.9% Two or more races, 7.2% Hispanic of any race; Average household size: 2.19; Median age: 44.0; Age under 18: 17.3%; Age 65 and over: 19.0%; Males per 100 females: 97.1; Marriage status: 30.5% never married, 51.6% now married, 1.5% separated, 5.7% widowed, 12.1% divorced; Foreign born: 14.2%; Speak English only: 82.8%; With disability: 7.0%; Veterans: 8.0%; Ancestry: 16.9% German, 16.6% English, 15.1% Irish, 7.8% Italian, 6.4% American
Employment: 33.7% management, business, and financial, 5.2% computer, engineering, and science, 15.5% education, legal, community service, arts, and media, 6.3% healthcare practitioners, 8.1% service, 25.3% sales and office, 2.4% natural resources, construction, and maintenance, 3.5% production, transportation, and material moving
Income: Per capita: $78,494; Median household: $106,333; Average household: $173,263; Households with income of $100,000 or more: 53.0%; Poverty rate: 7.9%
Educational Attainment: High school diploma or higher: 97.5%; Bachelor's degree or higher: 64.1%; Graduate/professional degree or higher: 25.8%

School District(s)

Corcoran Joint Unified (KG-12)
2012-13 Enrollment: 3,334 . . . . (559) 992-8888
Mountain Empire Unified (PK-12)
2012-13 Enrollment: 2,956 . . . . (619) 473-9022
Newport-Mesa Unified (KG-12)
2012-13 Enrollment: 22,003 . . . . (714) 424-5000

Four-year College(s)

Interior Designers Institute (Private, For-profit)
Fall 2013 Enrollment: 296 . . . . (949) 675-4451
Housing: Homeownership rate: 54.8%; Median home value: 1 million+; Median year structure built: 1974; Homeowner vacancy rate: 1.7%; Median gross rent: $1,924 per month; Rental vacancy rate: 7.8%
Health Insurance: 91.5% have insurance; 82.9% have private insurance; 22.3% have public insurance; 8.5% do not have insurance; 4.2% of children under 18 do not have insurance
Hospitals: Hoag Memorial Hospital Presbyterian
Safety: Violent crime rate: 8.3 per 10,000 population; Property crime rate: 246.2 per 10,000 population
Newspapers: Balboa Beacon (weekly circulation 6000)
Transportation: Commute: 85.0% car, 1.0% public transportation, 2.0% walk, 9.7% work from home; Median travel time to work: 23.3 minutes

Additional Information Contacts

City of Newport Beach. . . . . (949) 644-3309
http://www.newportbeachca.gov

NEWPORT COAST (unincorporated postal area)

ZCTA: 92657

Covers a land area of 7.372 square miles and a water area of 0.683 square miles. Located at 33.60° N. Lat; 117.83° W. Long. Elevation is 659 feet.

Population: 9,741; Growth (since 2000): 74.4%; Density: 1,321.3 persons per square mile; Race: 75.9% White, 0.5% Black/African American, 17.5% Asian, 0.1% American Indian/Alaska Native, 0.0% Native Hawaiian/Other Pacific Islander, 4.8% Two or more races, 5.2% Hispanic of any race; Average household size: 2.58; Median age: 43.8; Age under 18: 24.5%; Age 65 and over: 11.5%; Males per 100 females: 93.6; Marriage status: 22.0% never married, 65.4% now married, 0.6% separated, 2.3% widowed, 10.3% divorced; Foreign born: 25.5%; Speak English only: 69.8%; With disability: 4.8%; Veterans: 4.8%; Ancestry: 14.6% English, 13.0% German, 9.1% Irish, 7.7% Iranian, 6.5% Italian

Employment: 41.2% management, business, and financial, 5.2% computer, engineering, and science, 17.3% education, legal, community service, arts, and media, 6.5% healthcare practitioners, 3.1% service, 24.8% sales and office, 0.5% natural resources, construction, and maintenance, 1.5% production, transportation, and material moving

Income: Per capita: $103,549; Median household: $156,440; Average household: $267,154; Households with income of $100,000 or more: 72.2%; Poverty rate: 3.6%

Educational Attainment: High school diploma or higher: 98.4%; Bachelor's degree or higher: 71.3%; Graduate/professional degree or higher: 34.4%

Housing: Homeownership rate: 74.4%; Median home value: 1 million+; Median year structure built: 1999; Homeowner vacancy rate: 2.1%; Median gross rent: $2,000+ per month; Rental vacancy rate: 8.9%

Health Insurance: 94.3% have insurance; 90.1% have private insurance; 13.0% have public insurance; 5.7% do not have insurance; 1.5% of children under 18 do not have insurance

Transportation: Commute: 82.0% car, 0.5% public transportation, 0.9% walk, 15.1% work from home; Median travel time to work: 26.6 minutes

NORTH TUSTIN (CDP). Covers a land area of 6.673 square miles and a water area of 0 square miles. Located at 33.76° N. Lat; 117.79° W. Long. Elevation is 256 feet.

Population: 24,917; Growth (since 2000): n/a; Density: 3,733.7 persons per square mile; Race: 83.6% White, 0.6% Black/African American, 8.0% Asian, 0.4% American Indian/Alaska Native, 0.2% Native Hawaiian/Other Pacific Islander, 3.5% Two or more races, 13.1% Hispanic of any race; Average household size: 2.88; Median age: 45.6; Age under 18: 23.5%; Age 65 and over: 19.1%; Males per 100 females: 96.3; Marriage status: 24.1% never married, 63.8% now married, 0.6% separated, 6.1% widowed, 6.0% divorced; Foreign born: 12.9%; Speak English only: 82.7%; With disability: 9.9%; Veterans: 8.9%; Ancestry: 17.5% German, 15.1% English, 11.0% Irish, 7.2% American, 5.4% Italian

Employment: 25.8% management, business, and financial, 7.6% computer, engineering, and science, 15.9% education, legal, community service, arts, and media, 7.0% healthcare practitioners, 8.5% service, 27.5% sales and office, 3.6% natural resources, construction, and maintenance, 4.1% production, transportation, and material moving

Income: Per capita: $56,606; Median household: $122,662; Average household: $162,446; Households with income of $100,000 or more: 62.1%; Poverty rate: 2.7%

Educational Attainment: High school diploma or higher: 96.6%; Bachelor's degree or higher: 55.9%; Graduate/professional degree or higher: 21.8%

Housing: Homeownership rate: 89.4%; Median home value: $776,600; Median year structure built: 1964; Homeowner vacancy rate: 0.9%; Median gross rent: $1,817 per month; Rental vacancy rate: 3.4%

Health Insurance: 93.5% have insurance; 82.9% have private insurance; 23.8% have public insurance; 6.5% do not have insurance; 4.4% of children under 18 do not have insurance

Transportation: Commute: 85.8% car, 0.2% public transportation, 1.8% walk, 10.3% work from home; Median travel time to work: 23.3 minutes

ORANGE (city). Covers a land area of 24.797 square miles and a water area of 0.443 square miles. Located at 33.80° N. Lat; 117.82° W. Long. Elevation is 190 feet.

History: Named for the important orange-growing industry of southern California. The city of Orange owes its existence to the orange industry. It was founded as Richland in 1868 by A.B. Chapman on land that he owned. He changed the name in 1875. Oranges were first brought into California from Mexico by the Franciscan padres about 1805.

Population: 136,416; Growth (since 2000): 5.9%; Density: 5,501.3 persons per square mile; Race: 67.1% White, 1.6% Black/African American, 11.3% Asian, 0.7% American Indian/Alaska Native, 0.3% Native Hawaiian/Other Pacific Islander, 4.0% Two or more races, 38.1% Hispanic of any race; Average household size: 3.00; Median age: 34.8; Age under 18: 23.5%; Age 65 and over: 10.7%; Males per 100 females: 101.5; Marriage status: 37.1% never married, 49.1% now married, 2.0% separated, 4.5% widowed, 9.3% divorced; Foreign born: 26.0%; Speak English only: 58.2%; With disability: 7.4%; Veterans: 5.2%; Ancestry: 9.4% American, 9.1% German, 6.8% Irish, 6.2% English, 3.7% Italian

Employment: 16.7% management, business, and financial, 5.8% computer, engineering, and science, 11.3% education, legal, community service, arts, and media, 4.9% healthcare practitioners, 17.8% service, 26.7% sales and office, 8.8% natural resources, construction, and maintenance, 8.1% production, transportation, and material moving

Income: Per capita: $31,535; Median household: $78,838; Average household: $97,270; Households with income of $100,000 or more: 37.9%; Poverty rate: 11.8%

Educational Attainment: High school diploma or higher: 83.4%; Bachelor's degree or higher: 33.0%; Graduate/professional degree or higher: 11.9%

School District(s)

Orange Unified (PK-12)
2012-13 Enrollment: 29,854 . . . . (714) 628-4000

Four-year College(s)

Argosy University-Orange County (Private, For-profit)
Fall 2013 Enrollment: 673. . . . . (714) 620-3700
2013-14 Tuition: In-state $13,663; Out-of-state $13,663

Chapman University (Private, Not-for-profit, Christian Church (Disciples of Christ))
Fall 2013 Enrollment: 7,892 . . . . (714) 997-6815
2013-14 Tuition: In-state $43,573; Out-of-state $43,573

ITT Technical Institute-Orange (Private, For-profit)
Fall 2013 Enrollment: 823. . . . . (714) 941-2400
2013-14 Tuition: In-state $18,048; Out-of-state $18,048

Two-year College(s)

Career Networks Institute (Private, For-profit)
Fall 2013 Enrollment: 561 . . . . (714) 437-9697

InterCoast Colleges-Orange (Private, For-profit)
Fall 2013 Enrollment: 134. . . . . (714) 712-7900

Santiago Canyon College (Public)
Fall 2013 Enrollment: 10,939 . . . . (714) 628-4900
2013-14 Tuition: In-state $1,142; Out-of-state $5,174

South Coast College (Private, For-profit)
Fall 2013 Enrollment: 374. . . . . (714) 867-5009

Vocational/Technical School(s)

COBA Academy (Private, For-profit)
Fall 2013 Enrollment: 40. . . . . (714) 633-5950
2013-14 Tuition: $16,753

Hair California Beauty Academy (Private, For-profit)
Fall 2013 Enrollment: 47. . . . . (714) 633-7170
2013-14 Tuition: $10,885

Housing: Homeownership rate: 60.6%; Median home value: $498,700; Median year structure built: 1972; Homeowner vacancy rate: 1.1%; Median gross rent: $1,487 per month; Rental vacancy rate: 5.1%

Health Insurance: 81.9% have insurance; 65.7% have private insurance; 23.1% have public insurance; 18.1% do not have insurance; 6.8% of children under 18 do not have insurance

Hospitals: Chapman Medical Center (114 beds); Saint Joseph Hospital (412 beds); University of California Irvine Medical Center (453 beds)

Safety: Violent crime rate: 10.5 per 10,000 population; Property crime rate: 172.3 per 10,000 population

Transportation: Commute: 88.8% car, 2.9% public transportation, 2.1% walk, 4.2% work from home; Median travel time to work: 25.1 minutes

Additional Information Contacts

City of Orange . . . . (714) 744-2222
http://www.cityoforange.org

PLACENTIA (city). Covers a land area of 6.568 square miles and a water area of 0.014 square miles. Located at 33.88° N. Lat; 117.85° W. Long. Elevation is 272 feet.

History: Named for the school district, which had been named in 1884 after the town in Newfoundland. Once a rural farming community. The city's population doubled between 1970 and 1990. Abundant orange trees exist throughout the city. Incorporated 1926.

Population: 50,533; Growth (since 2000): 8.7%; Density: 7,693.9 persons per square mile; Race: 62.1% White, 1.8% Black/African American, 14.9% Asian, 0.8% American Indian/Alaska Native, 0.1% Native Hawaiian/Other Pacific Islander, 4.0% Two or more races, 36.4% Hispanic of any race; Average household size: 3.07; Median age: 36.0; Age under 18: 24.6%; Age 65 and over: 12.6%; Males per 100 females: 97.0; Marriage status: 32.3% never married, 53.5% now married, 1.9% separated, 6.0% widowed, 8.2% divorced; Foreign born: 26.2%; Speak English only: 59.2%; With disability: 8.7%; Veterans: 5.8%; Ancestry: 12.1% German, 8.7% Irish, 7.6% English, 4.7% Italian, 4.0% American

Employment: 18.0% management, business, and financial, 6.6% computer, engineering, and science, 12.1% education, legal, community service, arts, and media, 4.0% healthcare practitioners, 14.7% service, 28.3% sales and office, 6.0% natural resources, construction, and maintenance, 10.3% production, transportation, and material moving

Income: Per capita: $30,003; Median household: $78,233; Average household: $93,166; Households with income of $100,000 or more: 37.9%; Poverty rate: 11.9%

Educational Attainment: High school diploma or higher: 83.8%; Bachelor's degree or higher: 34.2%; Graduate/professional degree or higher: 11.5%

School District(s)

Placentia-Yorba Linda Unified (KG-12)
2012-13 Enrollment: 25,622 . . . . (714) 986-7000

Housing: Homeownership rate: 65.2%; Median home value: $493,200; Median year structure built: 1975; Homeowner vacancy rate: 0.8%; Median gross rent: $1,477 per month; Rental vacancy rate: 4.7%

Health Insurance: 84.2% have insurance; 66.3% have private insurance; 25.6% have public insurance; 15.8% do not have insurance; 6.6% of children under 18 do not have insurance

Hospitals: Placentia Linda Hospital (114 beds)

Safety: Violent crime rate: 12.7 per 10,000 population; Property crime rate: 150.8 per 10,000 population

Transportation: Commute: 90.2% car, 2.7% public transportation, 1.7% walk, 3.7% work from home; Median travel time to work: 27.5 minutes

Additional Information Contacts

City of Placentia . . . . (714) 993-8117
http://placentia.org

RANCHO SANTA MARGARITA (city). Covers a land area of 12.957 square miles and a water area of 0.035 square miles. Located at 33.63° N. Lat; 117.60° W. Long. Elevation is 948 feet.

History: Named for St. Margaret, the Mexican land-grant rancho. Rancho Santa Margarita was a hacienda built by Pio Pico, Mexican governor of California, in 1837 near the Santa Margarita River. The rancho was later acquired by a corporation engaged in farming and ranching.

Population: 47,853; Growth (since 2000): 1.4%; Density: 3,693.1 persons per square mile; Race: 78.2% White, 1.9% Black/African American, 9.1% Asian, 0.4% American Indian/Alaska Native, 0.2% Native Hawaiian/Other Pacific Islander, 4.7% Two or more races, 18.6% Hispanic of any race; Average household size: 2.87; Median age: 36.0; Age under 18: 29.0%; Age 65 and over: 5.7%; Males per 100 females: 95.6; Marriage status: 29.5% never married, 58.2% now married, 1.4% separated, 2.7% widowed, 9.7% divorced; Foreign born: 17.0%; Speak English only: 76.9%; With disability: 4.2%; Veterans: 4.6%; Ancestry: 18.1% German, 13.1% Irish, 10.8% English, 8.4% Italian, 3.9% Polish

Employment: 22.6% management, business, and financial, 7.0% computer, engineering, and science, 11.9% education, legal, community service, arts, and media, 6.1% healthcare practitioners, 12.7% service, 29.7% sales and office, 4.8% natural resources, construction, and maintenance, 5.3% production, transportation, and material moving

Income: Per capita: $41,883; Median household: $104,113; Average household: $121,098; Households with income of $100,000 or more: 52.9%; Poverty rate: 3.9%

Educational Attainment: High school diploma or higher: 95.5%; Bachelor's degree or higher: 48.1%; Graduate/professional degree or higher: 16.4%

School District(s)

Capistrano Unified (KG-12)
2012-13 Enrollment: 53,785 . . . . (949) 234-9200

Saddleback Valley Unified (PK-12)
2012-13 Enrollment: 30,355 . . . . (949) 580-3200

Housing: Homeownership rate: 71.5%; Median home value: $516,800; Median year structure built: 1992; Homeowner vacancy rate: 1.2%; Median gross rent: $1,688 per month; Rental vacancy rate: 5.6%

Health Insurance: 92.0% have insurance; 84.6% have private insurance; 12.7% have public insurance; 8.0% do not have insurance; 3.0% of children under 18 do not have insurance

Safety: Violent crime rate: 3.5 per 10,000 population; Property crime rate: 59.0 per 10,000 population

Transportation: Commute: 90.0% car, 0.8% public transportation, 1.2% walk, 6.8% work from home; Median travel time to work: 28.0 minutes

Additional Information Contacts

City of Rancho Santa Margarita . . . . (949) 635-1800
http://www.cityofrsm.org

ROSSMOOR (CDP). Covers a land area of 1.538 square miles and a water area of 0 square miles. Located at 33.79° N. Lat; 118.08° W. Long. Elevation is 13 feet.

History: The Rossmoor community was developed from 1955 to 1961 by Ross W. Cortese who also developed the gated Leisure World retirement community in the city of Seal Beach, south of Rossmoor.

Population: 10,244; Growth (since 2000): -0.5%; Density: 6,660.9 persons per square mile; Race: 84.8% White, 0.8% Black/African American, 8.2% Asian, 0.4% American Indian/Alaska Native, 0.3% Native Hawaiian/Other Pacific Islander, 3.9% Two or more races, 11.5% Hispanic of any race; Average household size: 2.82; Median age: 45.5; Age under 18: 24.9%; Age 65 and over: 17.3%; Males per 100 females: 92.4; Marriage status: 22.5% never married, 64.9% now married, 0.5% separated, 7.2% widowed, 5.4% divorced; Foreign born: 10.0%; Speak English only: 86.3%; With disability: 10.2%; Veterans: 9.7%; Ancestry: 18.2% German, 14.5% English, 14.3% Irish, 7.2% Italian, 3.9% Polish

Employment: 24.7% management, business, and financial, 9.5% computer, engineering, and science, 15.1% education, legal, community service, arts, and media, 8.3% healthcare practitioners, 10.9% service, 25.3% sales and office, 2.1% natural resources, construction, and maintenance, 4.3% production, transportation, and material moving

Income: Per capita: $49,757; Median household: $108,807; Average household: $139,159; Households with income of $100,000 or more: 52.8%; Poverty rate: 3.3%

Educational Attainment: High school diploma or higher: 97.8%; Bachelor's degree or higher: 57.3%; Graduate/professional degree or higher: 21.8%

Housing: Homeownership rate: 87.6%; Median home value: $820,100; Median year structure built: 1959; Homeowner vacancy rate: 0.4%; Median gross rent: $1,636 per month; Rental vacancy rate: 3.6%

Health Insurance: 93.5% have insurance; 86.2% have private insurance; 21.8% have public insurance; 6.5% do not have insurance; 4.7% of children under 18 do not have insurance

Transportation: Commute: 92.5% car, 2.0% public transportation, 0.7% walk, 4.3% work from home; Median travel time to work: 29.9 minutes

SAN CLEMENTE (city). Covers a land area of 18.711 square miles and a water area of 0.757 square miles. Located at 33.45° N. Lat; 117.61° W. Long. Elevation is 233 feet.

History: Named for St. Clement, which originated with the explorer Vizcaino in 1602. San Clemente was founded in 1925 by a Los Angeles realtor as a village of white stucco, red-roofed buildings.

Population: 63,522; Growth (since 2000): 27.2%; Density: 3,394.9 persons per square mile; Race: 86.0% White, 0.6% Black/African American, 3.7% Asian, 0.6% American Indian/Alaska Native, 0.1% Native Hawaiian/Other Pacific Islander, 3.6% Two or more races, 16.8% Hispanic of any race; Average household size: 2.65; Median age: 39.7; Age under 18: 24.4%; Age 65 and over: 13.2%; Males per 100 females: 100.9; Marriage status: 24.3% never married, 60.2% now married, 1.8% separated, 4.4% widowed, 11.2% divorced; Foreign born: 11.1%; Speak English only: 84.8%; With disability: 7.8%; Veterans: 9.1%; Ancestry: 19.1% German, 15.4% Irish, 14.6% English, 8.1% Italian, 4.2% French

Employment: 22.8% management, business, and financial, 5.4% computer, engineering, and science, 12.7% education, legal, community service, arts, and media, 4.7% healthcare practitioners, 15.0% service,

28.6% sales and office, 6.6% natural resources, construction, and maintenance, 4.2% production, transportation, and material moving

Income: Per capita: $46,662; Median household: $90,071; Average household: $121,323; Households with income of $100,000 or more: 44.8%; Poverty rate: 8.6%

Educational Attainment: High school diploma or higher: 94.7%; Bachelor's degree or higher: 45.9%; Graduate/professional degree or higher: 16.0%

School District(s)

Capistrano Unified (KG-12)
2012-13 Enrollment: 53,785 . . . . (949) 234-9200
Fallbrook Union Elementary (KG-08)
2012-13 Enrollment: 5,554 . . . . (760) 731-5400

Housing: Homeownership rate: 64.1%; Median home value: $713,600; Median year structure built: 1981; Homeowner vacancy rate: 1.3%; Median gross rent: $1,682 per month; Rental vacancy rate: 5.8%

Health Insurance: 88.9% have insurance; 78.2% have private insurance; 21.3% have public insurance; 11.1% do not have insurance; 5.5% of children under 18 do not have insurance

Safety: Violent crime rate: 8.6 per 10,000 population; Property crime rate: 129.3 per 10,000 population

Newspapers: Sun Post (weekly circulation 10000)

Transportation: Commute: 83.5% car, 1.5% public transportation, 2.1% walk, 10.9% work from home; Median travel time to work: 29.5 minutes; Amtrak: Train service available.

Additional Information Contacts

City of San Clemente . . . . (949) 361-8200
http://san-clemente.org

SAN JUAN CAPISTRANO (city). Covers a land area of 14.115 square miles and a water area of 0.180 square miles. Located at 33.50° N. Lat; 117.65° W. Long. Elevation is 121 feet.

History: Named for the Mission, which was named for St. John Capistrano (1385-1456). San Juan Capistrano grew up around Mission San Juan Capistrano, founded in 1776 by Father Junipero Serra. The town became known for the swallows returning each March 19 to the mission.

Population: 34,593; Growth (since 2000): 2.3%; Density: 2,450.7 persons per square mile; Race: 77.1% White, 0.6% Black/African American, 2.8% Asian, 0.8% American Indian/Alaska Native, 0.1% Native Hawaiian/Other Pacific Islander, 3.5% Two or more races, 38.7% Hispanic of any race; Average household size: 3.03; Median age: 40.2; Age under 18: 24.6%; Age 65 and over: 15.6%; Males per 100 females: 98.3; Marriage status: 28.5% never married, 56.0% now married, 2.2% separated, 6.1% widowed, 9.4% divorced; Foreign born: 26.8%; Speak English only: 60.7%; With disability: 9.4%; Veterans: 7.8%; Ancestry: 13.4% German, 11.6% English, 10.9% Irish, 5.5% Italian, 4.0% American

Employment: 18.9% management, business, and financial, 4.3% computer, engineering, and science, 10.1% education, legal, community service, arts, and media, 2.8% healthcare practitioners, 25.5% service, 25.1% sales and office, 7.5% natural resources, construction, and maintenance, 5.9% production, transportation, and material moving

Income: Per capita: $38,117; Median household: $75,600; Average household: $114,345; Households with income of $100,000 or more: 38.6%; Poverty rate: 14.2%

Educational Attainment: High school diploma or higher: 82.8%; Bachelor's degree or higher: 33.0%; Graduate/professional degree or higher: 11.3%

School District(s)

Capistrano Unified (KG-12)
2012-13 Enrollment: 53,785 . . . . (949) 234-9200
Capistrano-Laguna Beach Rop
2012-13 Enrollment: n/a . . . . (949) 496-3118

Housing: Homeownership rate: 74.2%; Median home value: $522,000; Median year structure built: 1977; Homeowner vacancy rate: 1.3%; Median gross rent: $1,734 per month; Rental vacancy rate: 4.7%

Health Insurance: 78.1% have insurance; 62.7% have private insurance; 26.4% have public insurance; 21.9% do not have insurance; 14.4% of children under 18 do not have insurance

Safety: Violent crime rate: 16.0 per 10,000 population; Property crime rate: 123.4 per 10,000 population

Transportation: Commute: 86.6% car, 1.4% public transportation, 2.2% walk, 6.7% work from home; Median travel time to work: 24.1 minutes; Amtrak: Train service available.

Additional Information Contacts

City of San Juan Capistrano . . . . (949) 493-1171
http://www.sanjuancapistrano.org

SANTA ANA (city). County seat. Covers a land area of 27.270 square miles and a water area of 0.248 square miles. Located at 33.74° N. Lat; 117.88° W. Long. Elevation is 115 feet.

History: Named for the Spanish translatio of St. Anne, mother of the Virgin Mary. Santa Ana was founded in 1869 and grew around a large sugar-beet refinery, and as the seat of Orange County.

Population: 324,528; Growth (since 2000): -4.0%; Density: 11,900.8 persons per square mile; Race: 45.9% White, 1.5% Black/African American, 10.5% Asian, 1.0% American Indian/Alaska Native, 0.3% Native Hawaiian/Other Pacific Islander, 3.6% Two or more races, 78.2% Hispanic of any race; Average household size: 4.37; Median age: 29.1; Age under 18: 30.7%; Age 65 and over: 6.8%; Males per 100 females: 104.4; Marriage status: 42.2% never married, 47.7% now married, 3.5% separated, 4.1% widowed, 6.0% divorced; Foreign born: 47.8%; Speak English only: 17.1%; With disability: 8.1%; Veterans: 2.3%; Ancestry: 2.2% American, 1.9% German, 1.5% Irish, 1.4% English, 0.8% Italian

Employment: 7.3% management, business, and financial, 2.7% computer, engineering, and science, 4.7% education, legal, community service, arts, and media, 1.7% healthcare practitioners, 27.9% service, 23.9% sales and office, 11.5% natural resources, construction, and maintenance, 20.3% production, transportation, and material moving

Income: Per capita: $16,374; Median household: $53,335; Average household: $68,083; Households with income of $100,000 or more: 19.7%; Poverty rate: 21.5%

Educational Attainment: High school diploma or higher: 53.6%; Bachelor's degree or higher: 11.8%; Graduate/professional degree or higher: 3.3%

School District(s)

Central County Rop
2012-13 Enrollment: n/a . . . . (714) 966-3528
Garden Grove Unified (KG-12)
2012-13 Enrollment: 47,599 . . . . (714) 663-6000
Orange Unified (PK-12)
2012-13 Enrollment: 29,854 . . . . (714) 628-4000
Santa Ana Unified (KG-12)
2012-13 Enrollment: 57,410 . . . . (714) 558-5501
Tustin Unified (KG-12)
2012-13 Enrollment: 23,771 . . . . (714) 730-7301

Four-year College(s)

Taft University System (Private, For-profit)
Fall 2013 Enrollment: 785. . . . . (714) 850-4800
2013-14 Tuition: In-state $3,626; Out-of-state $3,626
The Art Institute of California-Argosy University Orange County (Private, For-profit)
Fall 2013 Enrollment: 1,761 . . . . (714) 830-0200
2013-14 Tuition: In-state $18,748; Out-of-state $18,748
Trinity Law School (Private, Not-for-profit, Other Protestant)
Fall 2013 Enrollment: 216. . . . . (714) 796-7141

Two-year College(s)

Santa Ana College (Public)
Fall 2013 Enrollment: 28,598 . . . . (714) 564-6000
2013-14 Tuition: In-state $1,142; Out-of-state $5,174

Vocational/Technical School(s)

American Institute of Massage Therapy (Private, For-profit)
Fall 2013 Enrollment: 28. . . . . (714) 432-7879
2013-14 Tuition: $10,500
Career College of California (Private, For-profit)
Fall 2013 Enrollment: 206. . . . . (714) 586-5775
2013-14 Tuition: $17,009
Colleen O'Haras Beauty Academy (Private, For-profit)
Fall 2013 Enrollment: 155. . . . . (714) 568-5399
2013-14 Tuition: $18,450
Everest College-Santa Ana (Private, For-profit)
Fall 2013 Enrollment: 433. . . . . (714) 656-1000
2013-14 Tuition: $21,388
Santa Ana Beauty Academy (Private, For-profit)
Fall 2013 Enrollment: 43. . . . . (714) 547-5177
2013-14 Tuition: $9,875
Santa Ana Beauty College (Private, For-profit)
Fall 2013 Enrollment: 114. . . . . (714) 835-0278
2013-14 Tuition: $9,580

Housing: Homeownership rate: 47.5%; Median home value: $334,900; Median year structure built: 1967; Homeowner vacancy rate: 1.9%; Median gross rent: $1,294 per month; Rental vacancy rate: 4.9%
Health Insurance: 66.7% have insurance; 38.5% have private insurance; 31.4% have public insurance; 33.3% do not have insurance; 14.8% of children under 18 do not have insurance
Hospitals: Coastal Communities Hospital (178 beds); Western Medical Center Santa Ana (282 beds)
Safety: Violent crime rate: 33.7 per 10,000 population; Property crime rate: 193.0 per 10,000 population
Newspapers: Long Beach Register (daily circulation 287000); Orange County Register (daily circulation 287000)
Transportation: Commute: 86.3% car, 7.1% public transportation, 2.4% walk, 1.4% work from home; Median travel time to work: 24.9 minutes; Amtrak: Train service available.
Airports: John Wayne Airport-Orange County (primary service/medium hub)
Additional Information Contacts
City of Santa Ana . . . . (714) 647-5400
http://www.ci.santa-ana.ca.us

SEAL BEACH (city). Covers a land area of 11.286 square miles and a water area of 1.754 square miles. Located at 33.75° N. Lat; 118.07° W. Long. Elevation is 13 feet.
History: Named for the species of seal along the California coast. Incorporated 1915.
Population: 24,168; Growth (since 2000): 0.0%; Density: 2,141.4 persons per square mile; Race: 83.4% White, 1.2% Black/African American, 9.6% Asian, 0.3% American Indian/Alaska Native, 0.2% Native Hawaiian/Other Pacific Islander, 3.5% Two or more races, 9.6% Hispanic of any race; Average household size: 1.84; Median age: 57.3; Age under 18: 13.0%; Age 65 and over: 38.3%; Males per 100 females: 78.8; Marriage status: 22.1% never married, 50.3% now married, 1.4% separated, 14.4% widowed, 13.2% divorced; Foreign born: 12.8%; Speak English only: 84.8%; With disability: 17.8%; Veterans: 12.4%; Ancestry: 17.0% German, 14.5% Irish, 13.5% English, 8.4% Italian, 4.4% French
Employment: 23.4% management, business, and financial, 7.4% computer, engineering, and science, 16.8% education, legal, community service, arts, and media, 8.0% healthcare practitioners, 11.8% service, 22.7% sales and office, 4.7% natural resources, construction, and maintenance, 5.2% production, transportation, and material moving
Income: Per capita: $44,170; Median household: $51,242; Average household: $83,753; Households with income of $100,000 or more: 27.8%; Poverty rate: 9.9%
Educational Attainment: High school diploma or higher: 93.9%; Bachelor's degree or higher: 43.8%; Graduate/professional degree or higher: 18.8%

School District(s)

Los Alamitos Unified (KG-12)
2012-13 Enrollment: 9,912 . . . . (562) 799-4700
Housing: Homeownership rate: 74.6%; Median home value: $291,800; Median year structure built: 1965; Homeowner vacancy rate: 2.0%; Median gross rent: $1,575 per month; Rental vacancy rate: 4.4%
Health Insurance: 93.4% have insurance; 75.5% have private insurance; 40.5% have public insurance; 6.6% do not have insurance; 7.8% of children under 18 do not have insurance
Safety: Violent crime rate: 6.5 per 10,000 population; Property crime rate: 186.3 per 10,000 population
Newspapers: Leisure World Golden Rain News (weekly circulation 9000); Seal Beach Sun (weekly circulation 30000)
Transportation: Commute: 88.4% car, 0.6% public transportation, 3.5% walk, 5.9% work from home; Median travel time to work: 28.8 minutes
Additional Information Contacts
City of Seal Beach. . . . . (562) 431-2527
http://www.sealbeachca.gov

SILVERADO (unincorporated postal area)
ZCTA: 92676
Covers a land area of 66.343 square miles and a water area of 0.728 square miles. Located at 33.75° N. Lat; 117.61° W. Long. Elevation is 1,211 feet.
Population: 1,945; Growth (since 2000): 5.8%; Density: 29.3 persons per square mile; Race: 89.3% White, 0.2% Black/African American, 3.5% Asian, 0.8% American Indian/Alaska Native, 0.1% Native Hawaiian/Other Pacific Islander, 3.9% Two or more races, 8.4% Hispanic of any race; Average household size: 2.44; Median age: 47.8; Age under 18: 18.1%; Age 65 and over: 8.4%; Males per 100 females: 103.5
Housing: Homeownership rate: 76.0%; Homeowner vacancy rate: 1.3%; Rental vacancy rate: 3.5%

STANTON (city). Covers a land area of 3.150 square miles and a water area of 0 square miles. Located at 33.80° N. Lat; 117.99° W. Long. Elevation is 66 feet.
History: Named for Philip A. Stanton, town founder and assemblyman from Los Angeles. Incorporated 1956.
Population: 38,186; Growth (since 2000): 2.1%; Density: 12,122.8 persons per square mile; Race: 44.5% White, 2.2% Black/African American, 23.1% Asian, 1.1% American Indian/Alaska Native, 0.6% Native Hawaiian/Other Pacific Islander, 4.2% Two or more races, 50.8% Hispanic of any race; Average household size: 3.50; Median age: 33.0; Age under 18: 27.7%; Age 65 and over: 10.0%; Males per 100 females: 98.0; Marriage status: 38.2% never married, 46.8% now married, 2.9% separated, 4.9% widowed, 10.1% divorced; Foreign born: 43.2%; Speak English only: 34.1%; With disability: 8.4%; Veterans: 5.0%; Ancestry: 4.5% German, 4.3% Irish, 3.0% English, 2.3% American, 1.8% Italian
Employment: 10.8% management, business, and financial, 4.5% computer, engineering, and science, 7.2% education, legal, community service, arts, and media, 3.3% healthcare practitioners, 21.7% service, 25.8% sales and office, 9.9% natural resources, construction, and maintenance, 16.8% production, transportation, and material moving
Income: Per capita: $19,779; Median household: $47,923; Average household: $61,818; Households with income of $100,000 or more: 18.0%; Poverty rate: 19.6%
Educational Attainment: High school diploma or higher: 68.4%; Bachelor's degree or higher: 19.1%; Graduate/professional degree or higher: 4.6%

School District(s)

Garden Grove Unified (KG-12)
2012-13 Enrollment: 47,599 . . . . (714) 663-6000
Magnolia Elementary (KG-06)
2012-13 Enrollment: 6,353 . . . . (714) 761-5533
Housing: Homeownership rate: 50.0%; Median home value: $271,400; Median year structure built: 1971; Homeowner vacancy rate: 2.1%; Median gross rent: $1,283 per month; Rental vacancy rate: 4.3%
Health Insurance: 73.1% have insurance; 45.9% have private insurance; 31.6% have public insurance; 26.9% do not have insurance; 13.3% of children under 18 do not have insurance
Safety: Violent crime rate: 28.6 per 10,000 population; Property crime rate: 179.4 per 10,000 population
Transportation: Commute: 86.0% car, 5.2% public transportation, 3.3% walk, 1.8% work from home; Median travel time to work: 28.0 minutes
Additional Information Contacts
City of Stanton. . . . . (714) 379-9222
http://www.ci.stanton.ca.us

SURFSIDE (unincorporated postal area)
ZCTA: 90743
Covers a land area of 0.083 square miles and a water area of 0.436 square miles. Located at 33.73° N. Lat; 118.09° W. Long. Elevation is 13 feet.
Population: 456; Growth (since 2000): 168.2%; Density: 5,507.7 persons per square mile; Race: 89.5% White, 0.0% Black/African American, 3.7% Asian, 0.0% American Indian/Alaska Native, 0.7% Native Hawaiian/Other Pacific Islander, 3.3% Two or more races, 9.9% Hispanic of any race; Average household size: 2.44; Median age: 45.2; Age under 18: 19.1%; Age 65 and over: 15.6%; Males per 100 females: 109.2
Housing: Homeownership rate: 62.6%; Homeowner vacancy rate: 2.5%; Rental vacancy rate: 6.6%

TRABUCO CANYON (unincorporated postal area)
ZCTA: 92678
Covers a land area of 15.075 square miles and a water area of 0.002 square miles. Located at 33.68° N. Lat; 117.53° W. Long. Elevation is 1,040 feet.
Population: 494; Growth (since 2000): n/a; Density: 32.8 persons per square mile; Race: 89.3% White, 1.0% Black/African American, 0.8% Asian, 1.2% American Indian/Alaska Native, 0.0% Native Hawaiian/Other Pacific Islander, 3.6% Two or more races, 11.7% Hispanic of any race; Average household size: 2.50; Median age: 42.6; Age under 18: 23.3%; Age 65 and over: 7.3%; Males per 100 females: 100.0

School District(s)

Saddleback Valley Unified (PK-12)
2012-13 Enrollment: 30,355 . . . . (949) 580-3200

Housing: Homeownership rate: 74.6%; Homeowner vacancy rate: 0.0%; Rental vacancy rate: 2.1%

ZCTA: 92679

Covers a land area of 22.615 square miles and a water area of 0.025 square miles. Located at 33.61° N. Lat; 117.60° W. Long. Elevation is 1,040 feet.

Population: 32,611; Growth (since 2000): 1.1%; Density: 1,442.0 persons per square mile; Race: 85.5% White, 1.1% Black/African American, 6.8% Asian, 0.3% American Indian/Alaska Native, 0.1% Native Hawaiian/Other Pacific Islander, 4.1% Two or more races, 10.4% Hispanic of any race; Average household size: 3.09; Median age: 40.5; Age under 18: 29.7%; Age 65 and over: 6.2%; Males per 100 females: 98.3; Marriage status: 26.6% never married, 65.7% now married, 0.9% separated, 2.2% widowed, 5.5% divorced; Foreign born: 11.4%; Speak English only: 86.5%; With disability: 3.4%; Veterans: 6.3%; Ancestry: 19.8% German, 15.3% Irish, 14.5% English, 9.9% Italian, 5.3% American

Employment: 30.8% management, business, and financial, 6.4% computer, engineering, and science, 11.9% education, legal, community service, arts, and media, 5.5% healthcare practitioners, 8.8% service, 29.7% sales and office, 2.8% natural resources, construction, and maintenance, 3.9% production, transportation, and material moving

Income: Per capita: $58,284; Median household: $142,803; Average household: $180,348; Households with income of $100,000 or more: 69.1%; Poverty rate: 3.2%

Educational Attainment: High school diploma or higher: 98.2%; Bachelor's degree or higher: 58.4%; Graduate/professional degree or higher: 18.9%

Housing: Homeownership rate: 87.4%; Median home value: $730,800; Median year structure built: 1993; Homeowner vacancy rate: 0.8%; Median gross rent: $1,989 per month; Rental vacancy rate: 4.1%

Health Insurance: 95.2% have insurance; 91.5% have private insurance; 10.3% have public insurance; 4.8% do not have insurance; 1.6% of children under 18 do not have insurance

Transportation: Commute: 88.3% car, 0.1% public transportation, 0.5% walk, 10.1% work from home; Median travel time to work: 30.5 minutes

TUSTIN (city). Covers a land area of 11.082 square miles and a water area of 0 square miles. Located at 33.73° N. Lat; 117.81° W. Long. Elevation is 141 feet.

History: Named for Columbus Tustin, the town's founder and postmaster, in 1867. Tustin's population increased almost tenfold between 1960 and 1970, and it more than doubled between 1970 and 1990. Founded 1868. Incorporated 1927.

Population: 75,540; Growth (since 2000): 11.9%; Density: 6,816.7 persons per square mile; Race: 52.6% White, 2.3% Black/African American, 20.3% Asian, 0.6% American Indian/Alaska Native, 0.4% Native Hawaiian/Other Pacific Islander, 4.7% Two or more races, 39.7% Hispanic of any race; Average household size: 2.98; Median age: 33.4; Age under 18: 26.8%; Age 65 and over: 8.5%; Males per 100 females: 94.7; Marriage status: 34.3% never married, 52.8% now married, 2.7% separated, 3.4% widowed, 9.5% divorced; Foreign born: 35.8%; Speak English only: 45.4%; With disability: 6.1%; Veterans: 4.2%; Ancestry: 6.9% German, 5.2% Irish, 4.6% English, 2.6% Italian, 2.4% American

Employment: 18.5% management, business, and financial, 8.3% computer, engineering, and science, 9.4% education, legal, community service, arts, and media, 5.3% healthcare practitioners, 17.0% service, 25.1% sales and office, 6.0% natural resources, construction, and maintenance, 10.6% production, transportation, and material moving

Income: Per capita: $31,524; Median household: $73,194; Average household: $93,926; Households with income of $100,000 or more: 34.1%; Poverty rate: 12.2%

Educational Attainment: High school diploma or higher: 83.8%; Bachelor's degree or higher: 39.0%; Graduate/professional degree or higher: 14.3%

School District(s)

Tustin Unified (KG-12)
2012-13 Enrollment: 23,771 . . . . (714) 730-7301

Housing: Homeownership rate: 50.8%; Median home value: $491,600; Median year structure built: 1979; Homeowner vacancy rate: 1.3%; Median gross rent: $1,496 per month; Rental vacancy rate: 5.8%

Health Insurance: 81.3% have insurance; 65.2% have private insurance; 20.6% have public insurance; 18.7% do not have insurance; 10.9% of children under 18 do not have insurance

Safety: Violent crime rate: 12.7 per 10,000 population; Property crime rate: 186.8 per 10,000 population

Transportation: Commute: 89.6% car, 3.0% public transportation, 1.3% walk, 4.1% work from home; Median travel time to work: 24.0 minutes

Additional Information Contacts

City of Tustin . . . . (714) 573-3000
http://www.tustinca.org

VILLA PARK (city). Covers a land area of 2.078 square miles and a water area of 0 square miles. Located at 33.82° N. Lat; 117.81° W. Long. Elevation is 341 feet.

History: Villa Park is a city in northern Orange County, California near Orange and Anaheim Hills that incorporated in 1962. Villa Park includes about 2,000 homes and the land is nearly 99% built out. The city is zoned for single-family residences; most house occupy half-acre lots.

Population: 5,812; Growth (since 2000): -3.1%; Density: 2,796.6 persons per square mile; Race: 78.3% White, 0.7% Black/African American, 14.7% Asian, 0.6% American Indian/Alaska Native, 0.0% Native Hawaiian/Other Pacific Islander, 2.9% Two or more races, 10.3% Hispanic of any race; Average household size: 2.92; Median age: 49.6; Age under 18: 20.0%; Age 65 and over: 24.3%; Males per 100 females: 97.4; Marriage status: 24.1% never married, 66.5% now married, 1.0% separated, 3.0% widowed, 6.4% divorced; Foreign born: 16.3%; Speak English only: 79.6%; With disability: 10.9%; Veterans: 9.1%; Ancestry: 19.8% German, 12.5% English, 8.9% Irish, 7.3% Italian, 5.3% American

Employment: 29.9% management, business, and financial, 4.5% computer, engineering, and science, 12.8% education, legal, community service, arts, and media, 7.7% healthcare practitioners, 7.5% service, 29.7% sales and office, 4.2% natural resources, construction, and maintenance, 3.7% production, transportation, and material moving

Income: Per capita: $66,895; Median household: $155,525; Average household: $202,029; Households with income of $100,000 or more: 74.1%; Poverty rate: 1.9%

Educational Attainment: High school diploma or higher: 96.1%; Bachelor's degree or higher: 54.7%; Graduate/professional degree or higher: 24.8%

School District(s)

Orange Unified (PK-12)
2012-13 Enrollment: 29,854 . . . . (714) 628-4000

Housing: Homeownership rate: 95.4%; Median home value: $944,200; Median year structure built: 1973; Homeowner vacancy rate: 0.5%; Median gross rent: $2,000+ per month; Rental vacancy rate: 3.2%

Health Insurance: 93.1% have insurance; 82.3% have private insurance; 28.6% have public insurance; 6.9% do not have insurance; 5.6% of children under 18 do not have insurance

Safety: Violent crime rate: 10.1 per 10,000 population; Property crime rate: 144.3 per 10,000 population

Transportation: Commute: 88.7% car, 1.0% public transportation, 1.1% walk, 9.3% work from home; Median travel time to work: 22.6 minutes

Additional Information Contacts

City of Villa Park . . . . (714) 998-1500
http://www.villapark.org

WESTMINSTER (city). Covers a land area of 10.049 square miles and a water area of 0 square miles. Located at 33.75° N. Lat; 117.99° W. Long. Elevation is 39 feet.

History: Named by Reverend L.P. Weber, in the 1870s, who founded the town for Presbyterians. Has been marked by urban growth during 1970s along with most of Southern California. Very high concentration of Vietnamese-Americans (Little Saigon). Founded 1870. Incorporated 1957.

Population: 89,701; Growth (since 2000): 1.7%; Density: 8,926.5 persons per square mile; Race: 35.7% White, 0.9% Black/African American, 47.5% Asian, 0.4% American Indian/Alaska Native, 0.4% Native Hawaiian/Other Pacific Islander, 3.6% Two or more races, 23.6% Hispanic of any race; Average household size: 3.40; Median age: 38.7; Age under 18: 23.3%; Age 65 and over: 14.3%; Males per 100 females: 97.8; Marriage status: 33.3% never married, 52.5% now married, 2.2% separated, 6.1% widowed, 8.1% divorced; Foreign born: 45.7%; Speak English only: 34.1%; With disability: 9.9%; Veterans: 5.1%; Ancestry: 5.9% German, 4.3% Irish, 4.2% English, 2.2% Italian, 1.6% American

Employment: 12.2% management, business, and financial, 5.2% computer, engineering, and science, 7.3% education, legal, community

service, arts, and media, 4.8% healthcare practitioners, 21.6% service, 25.4% sales and office, 8.0% natural resources, construction, and maintenance, 15.5% production, transportation, and material moving
Income: Per capita: $22,950; Median household: $52,633; Average household: $72,963; Households with income of $100,000 or more: 24.8%; Poverty rate: 16.7%
Educational Attainment: High school diploma or higher: 74.6%; Bachelor's degree or higher: 21.0%; Graduate/professional degree or higher: 5.2%

School District(s)

Garden Grove Unified (KG-12)
2012-13 Enrollment: 47,599 . . . . (714) 663-6000
Huntington Beach Union High (09-12)
2012-13 Enrollment: 16,400 . . . . (714) 903-7000
Ocean View (KG-08)
2012-13 Enrollment: 9,418 . . . . (714) 847-2551
Westminster Elementary (KG-08)
2012-13 Enrollment: 9,619 . . . . (714) 894-7311

Vocational/Technical School(s)

Asian American International Beauty College (Private, For-profit)
Fall 2013 Enrollment: 142 . . . . (714) 891-0508
2013-14 Tuition: $900
Housing: Homeownership rate: 57.9%; Median home value: $448,400; Median year structure built: 1969; Homeowner vacancy rate: 1.5%; Median gross rent: $1,334 per month; Rental vacancy rate: 7.3%
Health Insurance: 81.3% have insurance; 50.7% have private insurance; 37.1% have public insurance; 18.7% do not have insurance; 9.4% of children under 18 do not have insurance
Safety: Violent crime rate: 30.8 per 10,000 population; Property crime rate: 269.5 per 10,000 population
Newspapers: Westminster Herald (weekly circulation 4000)
Transportation: Commute: 90.9% car, 2.4% public transportation, 1.8% walk, 2.8% work from home; Median travel time to work: 26.8 minutes
Additional Information Contacts
City of Westminster . . . . (714) 898-3311
http://www.westminster-ca.gov

YORBA LINDA (city). Covers a land area of 19.483 square miles and a water area of 0.535 square miles. Located at 33.89° N. Lat; 117.77° W. Long. Elevation is 381 feet.
History: Named for the Yorba family, pioneers who came to California in 1769 with Father Serra. The city has grown tremendously along with the Southern California area; its population increased five-fold between 1970 and 1990. Yorba Linda is the birthplace of former President Richard M. Nixon. Incorporated 1967.
Population: 64,234; Growth (since 2000): 9.0%; Density: 3,297.0 persons per square mile; Race: 75.1% White, 1.3% Black/African American, 15.6% Asian, 0.4% American Indian/Alaska Native, 0.1% Native Hawaiian/Other Pacific Islander, 4.0% Two or more races, 14.4% Hispanic of any race; Average household size: 2.97; Median age: 41.7; Age under 18: 24.6%; Age 65 and over: 11.8%; Males per 100 females: 94.8; Marriage status: 26.4% never married, 61.7% now married, 0.8% separated, 5.1% widowed, 6.8% divorced; Foreign born: 18.0%; Speak English only: 75.8%; With disability: 7.1%; Veterans: 6.2%; Ancestry: 16.7% German, 11.6% English, 10.7% Irish, 6.2% Italian, 5.1% American
Employment: 26.1% management, business, and financial, 7.8% computer, engineering, and science, 13.1% education, legal, community service, arts, and media, 6.1% healthcare practitioners, 11.7% service, 25.6% sales and office, 4.7% natural resources, construction, and maintenance, 4.8% production, transportation, and material moving
Income: Per capita: $48,279; Median household: $112,259; Average household: $141,834; Households with income of $100,000 or more: 56.9%; Poverty rate: 3.1%
Educational Attainment: High school diploma or higher: 95.6%; Bachelor's degree or higher: 48.6%; Graduate/professional degree or higher: 18.8%

School District(s)

Placentia-Yorba Linda Unified (KG-12)
2012-13 Enrollment: 25,622 . . . . (714) 986-7000
Housing: Homeownership rate: 83.9%; Median home value: $677,100; Median year structure built: 1983; Homeowner vacancy rate: 1.2%; Median gross rent: $1,744 per month; Rental vacancy rate: 4.0%
Health Insurance: 93.6% have insurance; 84.9% have private insurance; 16.9% have public insurance; 6.4% do not have insurance; 3.0% of children under 18 do not have insurance
Safety: Violent crime rate: 4.4 per 10,000 population; Property crime rate: 103.7 per 10,000 population
Transportation: Commute: 91.2% car, 1.1% public transportation, 0.7% walk, 5.7% work from home; Median travel time to work: 30.7 minutes
Additional Information Contacts
City of Yorba Linda . . . . (714) 961-7100
http://www.ci.yorba-linda.ca.us

Placer County

Located in central and eastern California, partly in the Sacramento Valley; bounded on the east by Lake Tahoe and the Nevada border; drained by the Bear, Rubicon, and Middle Fork of the American River; includes parts of Tahoe and El Dorado National F orests. Covers a land area of 1,407.009 square miles, a water area of 95.447 square miles, and is located in the Pacific Time Zone at 39.06° N. Lat., 120.72° W. Long. The county was founded in 1851. County seat is Auburn.

Placer County is part of the Sacramento—Roseville—Arden-Arcade, CA Metropolitan Statistical Area. The entire metro area includes: El Dorado County, CA; Placer County, CA; Sacramento County, CA; Yolo County, CA

Weather Station: Auburn Elevation: 1,291 feet

	Jan	Feb	Mar	Apr	May	Jun	Jul	Aug	Sep	Oct	Nov	Dec
High	55	59	62	68	76	85	92	91	85	76	62	55
Low	38	40	43	46	52	58	63	63	59	52	43	37
Precip	6.2	6.4	5.7	2.7	1.5	0.4	0.0	0.1	0.6	1.7	4.3	6.0
Snow	0.1	0.2	0.3	0.2	0.0	0.0	0.0	0.0	0.0	0.0	0.2	0.1

High and Low temperatures in degrees Fahrenheit; Precipitation and Snow in inches

Weather Station: Colfax Elevation: 2,399 feet

	Jan	Feb	Mar	Apr	May	Jun	Jul	Aug	Sep	Oct	Nov	Dec
High	55	57	60	66	75	83	91	90	85	74	60	54
Low	35	36	38	42	48	55	61	59	55	47	39	35
Precip	8.0	8.5	6.9	3.2	1.7	0.6	0.1	0.1	0.8	2.4	6.0	8.3
Snow	1.7	3.2	2.0	0.5	0.0	0.0	0.0	0.0	0.0	0.0	0.3	1.9

High and Low temperatures in degrees Fahrenheit; Precipitation and Snow in inches

Weather Station: Tahoe City Elevation: 6,229 feet

	Jan	Feb	Mar	Apr	May	Jun	Jul	Aug	Sep	Oct	Nov	Dec
High	41	42	46	52	61	70	78	78	71	60	48	41
Low	20	21	24	28	34	40	45	45	40	33	26	21
Precip	6.1	6.0	4.7	2.1	1.4	0.7	0.2	0.3	0.8	1.9	4.3	5.7
Snow	37.7	40.3	31.8	13.2	2.1	0.4	0.0	0.0	0.3	2.5	16.1	34.8

High and Low temperatures in degrees Fahrenheit; Precipitation and Snow in inches

Population: 348,432; Growth (since 2000): 40.3%; Density: 247.6 persons per square mile; Race: 83.5% White, 1.4% Black/African American, 5.9% Asian, 0.9% American Indian/Alaska Native, 0.2% Native Hawaiian/Other Pacific Islander, 4.3% two or more races, 12.8% Hispanic of any race; Average household size: 2.60; Median age: 40.3; Age under 18: 24.4%; Age 65 and over: 15.4%; Males per 100 females: 95.4; Marriage status: 25.1% never married, 58.6% now married, 1.8% separated, 5.7% widowed, 10.6% divorced; Foreign born: 10.6%; Speak English only: 85.0%; With disability: 10.7%; Veterans: 11.0%; Ancestry: 18.7% German, 13.8% Irish, 13.4% English, 7.5% Italian, 4.4% American
Religion: Six largest groups: 14.7% Catholicism, 5.7% Non-denominational Protestant, 4.6% Methodist/Pietist, 4.4% Latter-day Saints, 2.8% Baptist, 1.8% Pentecostal
Economy: Unemployment rate: 5.8%; Leading industries: 13.1% construction; 12.9% retail trade; 12.4% professional, scientific, and technical services; Farms: 1,355 totaling 91,403 acres; Company size: 8 employ 1,000 or more persons, 10 employ 500 to 999 persons, 154 employ 100 to 499 persons, 9,416 employ less than 100 persons; Business ownership: 10,433 women-owned, 455 Black-owned, 1,968 Hispanic-owned, 2,445 Asian-owned
Employment: 18.8% management, business, and financial, 6.0% computer, engineering, and science, 10.7% education, legal, community service, arts, and media, 6.1% healthcare practitioners, 16.5% service, 27.7% sales and office, 7.1% natural resources, construction, and maintenance, 7.3% production, transportation, and material moving
Income: Per capita: $34,886; Median household: $72,725; Average household: $91,628; Households with income of $100,000 or more: 35.0%; Poverty rate: 8.7%
Educational Attainment: High school diploma or higher: 93.6%; Bachelor's degree or higher: 35.1%; Graduate/professional degree or higher: 11.4%

Housing: Homeownership rate: 71.0%; Median home value: $342,000; Median year structure built: 1990; Homeowner vacancy rate: 2.4%; Median gross rent: $1,242 per month; Rental vacancy rate: 7.4%
Vital Statistics: Birth rate: 103.8 per 10,000 population; Death rate: 76.9 per 10,000 population; Age-adjusted cancer mortality rate: 151.7 deaths per 100,000 population
Health Insurance: 90.1% have insurance; 78.8% have private insurance; 25.2% have public insurance; 9.9% do not have insurance; 4.8% of children under 18 do not have insurance
Health Care: Physicians: 30.6 per 10,000 population; Hospital beds: 11.0 per 10,000 population; Hospital admissions: 539.7 per 10,000 population
Air Quality Index: 75.6% good, 21.9% moderate, 1.6% unhealthy for sensitive individuals, 0.8% unhealthy (percent of days)
Transportation: Commute: 87.4% car, 1.3% public transportation, 1.6% walk, 7.8% work from home; Median travel time to work: 26.9 minutes
Presidential Election: 38.9% Obama, 58.9% Romney (2012)
National and State Parks: Auburn State Recreation Area; Burton Creek State Park; Kings Beach State Recreation Area; Tahoe State Recreation Area
Additional Information Contacts
Placer Government . . . . (530) 889-4020
http://www.placer.ca.gov

Placer County Communities

ALTA (CDP). Covers a land area of 2.384 square miles and a water area of 0.007 square miles. Located at 39.22° N. Lat; 120.80° W. Long. Elevation is 3,606 feet.
Population: 610; Growth (since 2000): n/a; Density: 255.9 persons per square mile; Race: 97.0% White, 0.2% Black/African American, 0.8% Asian, 0.5% American Indian/Alaska Native, 0.2% Native Hawaiian/Other Pacific Islander, 1.0% Two or more races, 3.8% Hispanic of any race; Average household size: 2.45; Median age: 46.9; Age under 18: 20.8%; Age 65 and over: 14.3%; Males per 100 females: 112.5

School District(s)

Alta-Dutch Flat Union Elementary (KG-08)
2012-13 Enrollment: 92. . . . . (530) 389-8283
Housing: Homeownership rate: 79.8%; Homeowner vacancy rate: 1.5%; Rental vacancy rate: 7.5%

APPLEGATE (unincorporated postal area)
ZCTA: 95703
Covers a land area of 4.451 square miles and a water area of 0 square miles. Located at 38.99° N. Lat; 120.98° W. Long. Elevation is 2,005 feet.
Population: 897; Growth (since 2000): -40.7%; Density: 201.5 persons per square mile; Race: 92.3% White, 0.9% Black/African American, 1.2% Asian, 1.7% American Indian/Alaska Native, 0.3% Native Hawaiian/Other Pacific Islander, 3.0% Two or more races, 6.2% Hispanic of any race; Average household size: 2.36; Median age: 48.0; Age under 18: 20.3%; Age 65 and over: 15.5%; Males per 100 females: 111.6
Housing: Homeownership rate: 78.9%; Homeowner vacancy rate: 3.5%; Rental vacancy rate: 8.8%

AUBURN (city). County seat. Covers a land area of 7.138 square miles and a water area of 0.028 square miles. Located at 38.90° N. Lat; 121.08° W. Long. Elevation is 1,227 feet.
History: Named for Auburn, New York by New York native Samuel W. Holladay. Auburn was a mining camp in 1848, first called Wood's Dry Diggings and renamed later by miners who had come from the town of the same name in New York. When the gold gave out, the railroad moved in, and Auburn became the center of an orchard area and the seat of Placer County.
Population: 13,330; Growth (since 2000): 7.0%; Density: 1,867.4 persons per square mile; Race: 89.0% White, 0.8% Black/African American, 1.8% Asian, 1.0% American Indian/Alaska Native, 0.1% Native Hawaiian/Other Pacific Islander, 4.4% Two or more races, 10.0% Hispanic of any race; Average household size: 2.27; Median age: 45.4; Age under 18: 19.8%; Age 65 and over: 19.0%; Males per 100 females: 89.5; Marriage status: 25.2% never married, 53.1% now married, 0.8% separated, 8.1% widowed, 13.6% divorced; Foreign born: 5.4%; Speak English only: 92.4%; With disability: 14.6%; Veterans: 8.8%; Ancestry: 22.3% German, 16.7% Irish, 16.3% English, 8.2% Italian, 5.6% American
Employment: 18.8% management, business, and financial, 4.5% computer, engineering, and science, 14.0% education, legal, community service, arts, and media, 5.4% healthcare practitioners, 17.8% service, 24.1% sales and office, 6.6% natural resources, construction, and maintenance, 8.8% production, transportation, and material moving
Income: Per capita: $36,412; Median household: $58,678; Average household: $81,542; Households with income of $100,000 or more: 28.8%; Poverty rate: 11.1%
Educational Attainment: High school diploma or higher: 94.4%; Bachelor's degree or higher: 34.2%; Graduate/professional degree or higher: 11.8%

School District(s)

Ackerman Elementary (KG-08)
2012-13 Enrollment: 542. . . . . (530) 885-1974
Auburn Union Elementary (KG-08)
2012-13 Enrollment: 2,135 . . . . (530) 885-7242
Forty-Niner Rop
2012-13 Enrollment: n/a . . . . (530) 889-5940
Placer County Office of Education (KG-12)
2012-13 Enrollment: 526. . . . . (530) 889-8020
Placer Union High (09-12)
2012-13 Enrollment: 4,329 . . . . (530) 886-4400
Housing: Homeownership rate: 58.8%; Median home value: $361,600; Median year structure built: 1975; Homeowner vacancy rate: 2.0%; Median gross rent: $978 per month; Rental vacancy rate: 6.5%
Health Insurance: 92.1% have insurance; 78.0% have private insurance; 30.2% have public insurance; 7.9% do not have insurance; 1.0% of children under 18 do not have insurance
Hospitals: Sutter Auburn Faith Hospital (110 beds)
Safety: Violent crime rate: 35.6 per 10,000 population; Property crime rate: 219.2 per 10,000 population
Newspapers: Auburn Journal (daily circulation 10800); Placer Sentinel (weekly circulation 20000)
Transportation: Commute: 84.1% car, 0.9% public transportation, 4.7% walk, 9.3% work from home; Median travel time to work: 22.2 minutes; Amtrak: Train service available.
Additional Information Contacts
City of Auburn . . . . (530) 823-4211
http://www.auburn.ca.gov

CARNELIAN BAY (CDP). Covers a land area of 1.301 square miles and a water area of 0.002 square miles. Located at 39.24° N. Lat; 120.08° W. Long. Elevation is 6,234 feet.
Population: 524; Growth (since 2000): n/a; Density: 402.7 persons per square mile; Race: 94.1% White, 0.2% Black/African American, 2.7% Asian, 0.8% American Indian/Alaska Native, 0.0% Native Hawaiian/Other Pacific Islander, 2.1% Two or more races, 2.5% Hispanic of any race; Average household size: 2.05; Median age: 49.3; Age under 18: 11.5%; Age 65 and over: 21.8%; Males per 100 females: 126.8
Housing: Homeownership rate: 66.8%; Homeowner vacancy rate: 10.0%; Rental vacancy rate: 7.9%

COLFAX (city). Covers a land area of 1.407 square miles and a water area of 0 square miles. Located at 39.09° N. Lat; 120.95° W. Long. Elevation is 2,425 feet.
History: Colfax was called Alden Grove by its settlers in 1849, then renamed Illinoistown in the early 1850's, and Colfax about 1869. Colfax served as the point where goods were transferred to muleback for the journey to remote mining camps.
Population: 1,963; Growth (since 2000): 31.2%; Density: 1,394.7 persons per square mile; Race: 89.6% White, 0.2% Black/African American, 1.5% Asian, 1.3% American Indian/Alaska Native, 0.1% Native Hawaiian/Other Pacific Islander, 4.5% Two or more races, 9.1% Hispanic of any race; Average household size: 2.38; Median age: 37.9; Age under 18: 25.4%; Age 65 and over: 11.4%; Males per 100 females: 92.3

School District(s)

Colfax Elementary (KG-12)
2012-13 Enrollment: 614. . . . . (530) 346-2202
Placer Union High (09-12)
2012-13 Enrollment: 4,329 . . . . (530) 886-4400
Housing: Homeownership rate: 46.9%; Homeowner vacancy rate: 4.0%; Rental vacancy rate: 12.5%
Newspapers: Colfax Record (weekly circulation 1800)
Additional Information Contacts
City of Colfax. . . . . (530) 346-2313
http://www.colfax-ca.gov

DOLLAR POINT (CDP). Covers a land area of 1.634 square miles and a water area of 0 square miles. Located at 39.19° N. Lat; 120.11° W. Long. Elevation is 6,483 feet.

Population: 1,215; Growth (since 2000): -21.1%; Density: 743.6 persons per square mile; Race: 94.2% White, 0.3% Black/African American, 1.6% Asian, 0.5% American Indian/Alaska Native, 0.0% Native Hawaiian/Other Pacific Islander, 1.4% Two or more races, 6.8% Hispanic of any race; Average household size: 2.13; Median age: 45.4; Age under 18: 15.5%; Age 65 and over: 16.1%; Males per 100 females: 108.0

Housing: Homeownership rate: 63.6%; Homeowner vacancy rate: 5.4%; Rental vacancy rate: 14.3%

DUTCH FLAT (CDP). Covers a land area of 0.593 square miles and a water area of 0 square miles. Located at 39.21° N. Lat; 120.83° W. Long. Elevation is 3,136 feet.

Population: 160; Growth (since 2000): n/a; Density: 270.0 persons per square mile; Race: 96.9% White, 0.0% Black/African American, 0.6% Asian, 1.9% American Indian/Alaska Native, 0.0% Native Hawaiian/Other Pacific Islander, 0.6% Two or more races, 2.5% Hispanic of any race; Average household size: 1.88; Median age: 55.0; Age under 18: 11.9%; Age 65 and over: 26.9%; Males per 100 females: 122.2

Housing: Homeownership rate: 76.5%; Homeowner vacancy rate: 2.9%; Rental vacancy rate: 12.5%

EMIGRANT GAP (unincorporated postal area)

ZCTA: 95715

Covers a land area of 26.056 square miles and a water area of 1.078 square miles. Located at 39.27° N. Lat; 120.68° W. Long. Elevation is 5,190 feet.

Population: 115; Growth (since 2000): -36.1%; Density: 4.4 persons per square mile; Race: 83.5% White, 0.0% Black/African American, 0.0% Asian, 5.2% American Indian/Alaska Native, 0.0% Native Hawaiian/Other Pacific Islander, 11.3% Two or more races, 4.3% Hispanic of any race; Average household size: 2.21; Median age: 47.4; Age under 18: 18.3%; Age 65 and over: 8.7%; Males per 100 females: 130.0

School District(s)

Alta-Dutch Flat Union Elementary (KG-08)
2012-13 Enrollment: 92 . . . . (530) 389-8283

Housing: Homeownership rate: 71.2%; Homeowner vacancy rate: 5.1%; Rental vacancy rate: 11.8%

FORESTHILL (CDP). Covers a land area of 11.188 square miles and a water area of 0 square miles. Located at 39.01° N. Lat; 120.83° W. Long. Elevation is 3,228 feet.

Population: 1,483; Growth (since 2000): -17.2%; Density: 132.6 persons per square mile; Race: 92.4% White, 0.5% Black/African American, 0.4% Asian, 2.0% American Indian/Alaska Native, 0.1% Native Hawaiian/Other Pacific Islander, 3.4% Two or more races, 6.5% Hispanic of any race; Average household size: 2.37; Median age: 45.7; Age under 18: 20.3%; Age 65 and over: 14.8%; Males per 100 females: 99.1

School District(s)

Foresthill Union Elementary (KG-08)
2012-13 Enrollment: 410 . . . . (530) 367-2966

Placer Union High (09-12)
2012-13 Enrollment: 4,329 . . . . (530) 886-4400

Housing: Homeownership rate: 65.1%; Homeowner vacancy rate: 1.4%; Rental vacancy rate: 6.0%

GOLD RUN (unincorporated postal area)

ZCTA: 95717

Covers a land area of 10.219 square miles and a water area of 0 square miles. Located at 39.14° N. Lat; 120.85° W. Long. Elevation is 3,212 feet.

Population: 231; Growth (since 2000): -43.0%; Density: 22.6 persons per square mile; Race: 92.2% White, 0.0% Black/African American, 0.0% Asian, 1.7% American Indian/Alaska Native, 0.0% Native Hawaiian/Other Pacific Islander, 1.7% Two or more races, 8.7% Hispanic of any race; Average household size: 2.04; Median age: 53.6; Age under 18: 12.1%; Age 65 and over: 22.5%; Males per 100 females: 108.1

Housing: Homeownership rate: 70.8%; Homeowner vacancy rate: 2.4%; Rental vacancy rate: 13.2%

GRANITE BAY (CDP). Covers a land area of 21.528 square miles and a water area of 0.044 square miles. Located at 38.76° N. Lat; 121.17° W. Long. Elevation is 427 feet.

Population: 20,402; Growth (since 2000): 5.2%; Density: 947.7 persons per square mile; Race: 88.0% White, 0.7% Black/African American, 5.6% Asian, 0.7% American Indian/Alaska Native, 0.1% Native Hawaiian/Other Pacific Islander, 3.7% Two or more races, 6.2% Hispanic of any race; Average household size: 2.83; Median age: 46.0; Age under 18: 26.0%; Age 65 and over: 14.5%; Males per 100 females: 98.5; Marriage status: 22.5% never married, 65.0% now married, 0.5% separated, 4.9% widowed, 7.6% divorced; Foreign born: 7.6%; Speak English only: 90.6%; With disability: 8.0%; Veterans: 8.2%; Ancestry: 19.9% German, 16.0% Irish, 15.2% English, 10.4% Italian, 5.0% French

Employment: 26.4% management, business, and financial, 7.2% computer, engineering, and science, 9.9% education, legal, community service, arts, and media, 10.5% healthcare practitioners, 9.1% service, 28.0% sales and office, 4.1% natural resources, construction, and maintenance, 4.8% production, transportation, and material moving

Income: Per capita: $55,061; Median household: $127,149; Average household: $161,663; Households with income of $100,000 or more: 60.5%; Poverty rate: 3.6%

Educational Attainment: High school diploma or higher: 96.9%; Bachelor's degree or higher: 54.1%; Graduate/professional degree or higher: 22.7%

School District(s)

Eureka Union (PK-08)
2012-13 Enrollment: 3,422 . . . . (916) 791-4939

Roseville Joint Union High (09-12)
2012-13 Enrollment: 10,206 . . . . (916) 786-2051

Housing: Homeownership rate: 89.0%; Median home value: $610,700; Median year structure built: 1986; Homeowner vacancy rate: 1.3%; Median gross rent: $1,680 per month; Rental vacancy rate: 8.8%

Health Insurance: 93.3% have insurance; 87.1% have private insurance; 16.8% have public insurance; 6.7% do not have insurance; 4.2% of children under 18 do not have insurance

Transportation: Commute: 86.5% car, 1.2% public transportation, 0.3% walk, 10.9% work from home; Median travel time to work: 26.9 minutes

HOMEWOOD (unincorporated postal area)

ZCTA: 96141

Covers a land area of 11.993 square miles and a water area of 0.444 square miles. Located at 39.08° N. Lat; 120.18° W. Long. Elevation is 6,234 feet.

Population: 744; Growth (since 2000): -11.4%; Density: 62.0 persons per square mile; Race: 95.4% White, 1.5% Black/African American, 1.6% Asian, 0.4% American Indian/Alaska Native, 0.0% Native Hawaiian/Other Pacific Islander, 0.9% Two or more races, 3.6% Hispanic of any race; Average household size: 2.03; Median age: 48.7; Age under 18: 15.6%; Age 65 and over: 16.1%; Males per 100 females: 116.9

Housing: Homeownership rate: 72.8%; Homeowner vacancy rate: 3.3%; Rental vacancy rate: 15.3%

KINGS BEACH (CDP). Covers a land area of 3.439 square miles and a water area of 0 square miles. Located at 39.25° N. Lat; 120.02° W. Long. Elevation is 6,250 feet.

Population: 3,796; Growth (since 2000): -6.0%; Density: 1,103.7 persons per square mile; Race: 84.7% White, 0.4% Black/African American, 0.4% Asian, 0.5% American Indian/Alaska Native, 0.1% Native Hawaiian/Other Pacific Islander, 3.2% Two or more races, 55.7% Hispanic of any race; Average household size: 2.73; Median age: 31.6; Age under 18: 24.3%; Age 65 and over: 5.9%; Males per 100 females: 125.3; Marriage status: 41.2% never married, 48.7% now married, 0.7% separated, 2.0% widowed, 8.2% divorced; Foreign born: 52.1%; Speak English only: 32.9%; With disability: 6.0%; Veterans: 1.5%; Ancestry: 8.9% German, 8.1% Irish, 4.8% English, 2.9% Swedish, 2.3% French

Employment: 7.7% management, business, and financial, 0.5% computer, engineering, and science, 5.5% education, legal, community service, arts, and media, 1.6% healthcare practitioners, 44.4% service, 10.2% sales and office, 22.1% natural resources, construction, and maintenance, 8.1% production, transportation, and material moving

Income: Per capita: $18,868; Median household: $38,026; Average household: $54,349; Households with income of $100,000 or more: 13.8%; Poverty rate: 17.7%

Educational Attainment: High school diploma or higher: 61.0%; Bachelor's degree or higher: 18.9%; Graduate/professional degree or higher: 2.5%

School District(s)

Tahoe-Truckee Joint Unified (KG-12)
2012-13 Enrollment: 3,917 . . . . (530) 582-2500

Housing: Homeownership rate: 40.5%; Median home value: $348,300; Median year structure built: 1971; Homeowner vacancy rate: 5.3%; Median gross rent: $893 per month; Rental vacancy rate: 14.4%

Health Insurance: 42.9% have insurance; 24.9% have private insurance; 18.8% have public insurance; 57.1% do not have insurance; 18.9% of children under 18 do not have insurance

Transportation: Commute: 80.7% car, 5.4% public transportation, 8.9% walk, 2.9% work from home; Median travel time to work: 19.0 minutes

LINCOLN (city). Covers a land area of 20.106 square miles and a water area of 0.024 square miles. Located at 38.88° N. Lat; 121.29° W. Long. Elevation is 167 feet.

History: Named after Charles Lincoln Wilson who first purchased the land where the city was established. Lincoln developed after 1870 around a pottery and terra cotta works.

Population: 42,819; Growth (since 2000): 282.1%; Density: 2,129.7 persons per square mile; Race: 79.6% White, 1.5% Black/African American, 6.2% Asian, 0.9% American Indian/Alaska Native, 0.3% Native Hawaiian/Other Pacific Islander, 4.2% Two or more races, 17.7% Hispanic of any race; Average household size: 2.59; Median age: 40.5; Age under 18: 24.2%; Age 65 and over: 23.5%; Males per 100 females: 92.5; Marriage status: 18.3% never married, 64.9% now married, 1.9% separated, 5.9% widowed, 10.8% divorced; Foreign born: 12.2%; Speak English only: 82.1%; With disability: 12.1%; Veterans: 15.9%; Ancestry: 16.4% German, 13.4% English, 12.0% Irish, 5.7% Italian, 4.8% American

Employment: 17.0% management, business, and financial, 3.8% computer, engineering, and science, 11.7% education, legal, community service, arts, and media, 4.4% healthcare practitioners, 19.1% service, 28.6% sales and office, 7.6% natural resources, construction, and maintenance, 7.8% production, transportation, and material moving

Income: Per capita: $31,911; Median household: $72,459; Average household: $81,896; Households with income of $100,000 or more: 31.1%; Poverty rate: 9.5%

Educational Attainment: High school diploma or higher: 93.7%; Bachelor's degree or higher: 32.1%; Graduate/professional degree or higher: 11.2%

School District(s)

Western Placer Unified (KG-12)
2012-13 Enrollment: 9,447 . . . . (916) 645-6350

Housing: Homeownership rate: 79.5%; Median home value: $324,900; Median year structure built: 2003; Homeowner vacancy rate: 2.5%; Median gross rent: $1,549 per month; Rental vacancy rate: 4.7%

Health Insurance: 90.6% have insurance; 78.3% have private insurance; 36.0% have public insurance; 9.4% do not have insurance; 7.4% of children under 18 do not have insurance

Safety: Violent crime rate: 5.6 per 10,000 population; Property crime rate: 123.4 per 10,000 population

Newspapers: News-Messenger (weekly circulation 6300)

Transportation: Commute: 87.8% car, 1.3% public transportation, 0.8% walk, 7.9% work from home; Median travel time to work: 27.7 minutes

Airports: Lincoln Regional/Karl Harder Field (general aviation)

Additional Information Contacts

City of Lincoln . . . . (916) 434-2400
http://www.ci.lincoln.ca.us

LOOMIS (town). Covers a land area of 7.267 square miles and a water area of 0 square miles. Located at 38.81° N. Lat; 121.20° W. Long. Elevation is 404 feet.

History: Loomis is the successor of Pine, which took its name from Pine Grove in nearby Secret Ravine, where mining began in 1850.

Population: 6,430; Growth (since 2000): 2.7%; Density: 884.8 persons per square mile; Race: 89.2% White, 0.5% Black/African American, 2.6% Asian, 1.2% American Indian/Alaska Native, 0.2% Native Hawaiian/Other Pacific Islander, 4.0% Two or more races, 8.8% Hispanic of any race; Average household size: 2.72; Median age: 42.1; Age under 18: 24.7%; Age 65 and over: 13.0%; Males per 100 females: 97.8; Marriage status: 26.7% never married, 53.6% now married, 0.2% separated, 8.8% widowed, 11.0% divorced; Foreign born: 2.4%; Speak English only: 94.5%; With disability: 11.1%; Veterans: 10.6%; Ancestry: 24.2% German, 20.1% English, 13.9% Italian, 13.7% Irish, 3.8% Portuguese

Employment: 9.8% management, business, and financial, 4.9% computer, engineering, and science, 9.8% education, legal, community service, arts, and media, 8.0% healthcare practitioners, 11.3% service, 34.6% sales and office, 12.6% natural resources, construction, and maintenance, 8.9% production, transportation, and material moving

Income: Per capita: $31,844; Median household: $76,635; Average household: $89,003; Households with income of $100,000 or more: 33.8%; Poverty rate: 6.3%

Educational Attainment: High school diploma or higher: 95.7%; Bachelor's degree or higher: 26.3%; Graduate/professional degree or higher: 5.5%

School District(s)

Loomis Union Elementary (KG-12)
2012-13 Enrollment: 3,219 . . . . (916) 652-1800
Placer Union High (09-12)
2012-13 Enrollment: 4,329 . . . . (530) 886-4400

Housing: Homeownership rate: 77.7%; Median home value: $302,100; Median year structure built: 1981; Homeowner vacancy rate: 1.2%; Median gross rent: $1,282 per month; Rental vacancy rate: 4.9%

Health Insurance: 90.5% have insurance; 81.8% have private insurance; 22.9% have public insurance; 9.5% do not have insurance; 6.4% of children under 18 do not have insurance

Newspapers: Loomis News (weekly circulation 1100)

Transportation: Commute: 92.6% car, 0.0% public transportation, 0.0% walk, 6.9% work from home; Median travel time to work: 25.9 minutes

Additional Information Contacts

Town of Loomis . . . . (916) 652-1840
http://www.loomis.ca.gov

MEADOW VISTA (CDP). Covers a land area of 5.281 square miles and a water area of 0.155 square miles. Located at 39.00° N. Lat; 121.03° W. Long. Elevation is 1,713 feet.

Population: 3,217; Growth (since 2000): 3.9%; Density: 609.1 persons per square mile; Race: 93.8% White, 0.0% Black/African American, 1.1% Asian, 0.7% American Indian/Alaska Native, 0.2% Native Hawaiian/Other Pacific Islander, 3.2% Two or more races, 5.3% Hispanic of any race; Average household size: 2.57; Median age: 48.3; Age under 18: 20.5%; Age 65 and over: 18.9%; Males per 100 females: 101.2; Marriage status: 17.7% never married, 69.1% now married, 1.7% separated, 3.8% widowed, 9.3% divorced; Foreign born: 4.9%; Speak English only: 96.2%; With disability: 14.8%; Veterans: 14.0%; Ancestry: 22.7% German, 18.4% English, 15.7% Irish, 8.6% Italian, 6.8% Scottish

Employment: 21.6% management, business, and financial, 6.0% computer, engineering, and science, 11.2% education, legal, community service, arts, and media, 6.0% healthcare practitioners, 9.5% service, 17.6% sales and office, 12.9% natural resources, construction, and maintenance, 15.3% production, transportation, and material moving

Income: Per capita: $33,335; Median household: $66,130; Average household: $79,943; Households with income of $100,000 or more: 20.6%; Poverty rate: 2.5%

Educational Attainment: High school diploma or higher: 96.3%; Bachelor's degree or higher: 29.0%; Graduate/professional degree or higher: 10.3%

School District(s)

Placer County Office of Education (KG-12)
2012-13 Enrollment: 526. . . . . (530) 889-8020
Placer Hills Union Elementary (KG-08)
2012-13 Enrollment: 853. . . . . (530) 878-2606

Housing: Homeownership rate: 84.1%; Median home value: $338,200; Median year structure built: 1971; Homeowner vacancy rate: 1.5%; Median gross rent: $1,350 per month; Rental vacancy rate: 6.6%

Health Insurance: 96.3% have insurance; 86.2% have private insurance; 30.7% have public insurance; 3.7% do not have insurance; 0.0% of children under 18 do not have insurance

Transportation: Commute: 90.3% car, 1.8% public transportation, 0.0% walk, 6.9% work from home; Median travel time to work: 33.9 minutes

NEWCASTLE (CDP). Covers a land area of 2.392 square miles and a water area of 0.004 square miles. Located at 38.87° N. Lat; 121.13° W. Long. Elevation is 945 feet.

Population: 1,224; Growth (since 2000): n/a; Density: 511.7 persons per square mile; Race: 90.9% White, 0.6% Black/African American, 1.4% Asian, 1.6% American Indian/Alaska Native, 0.0% Native Hawaiian/Other

Pacific Islander, 2.7% Two or more races, 8.5% Hispanic of any race; Average household size: 2.23; Median age: 51.3; Age under 18: 18.0%; Age 65 and over: 25.7%; Males per 100 females: 91.3

School District(s)

Loomis Union Elementary (KG-12)
2012-13 Enrollment: 3,219 . . . . (916) 652-1800
Newcastle Elementary (KG-12)
2012-13 Enrollment: 592. . . . . (916) 663-3307
Placer County Office of Education (KG-12)
2012-13 Enrollment: 526. . . . . (530) 889-8020

Housing: Homeownership rate: 78.8%; Homeowner vacancy rate: 4.4%; Rental vacancy rate: 12.2%

NORTH AUBURN (CDP). Covers a land area of 7.798 square miles and a water area of 0.003 square miles. Located at 38.93° N. Lat; 121.08° W. Long. Elevation is 1,470 feet.

Population: 13,022; Growth (since 2000): 9.9%; Density: 1,669.8 persons per square mile; Race: 85.1% White, 0.9% Black/African American, 2.3% Asian, 1.3% American Indian/Alaska Native, 0.1% Native Hawaiian/Other Pacific Islander, 3.5% Two or more races, 16.2% Hispanic of any race; Average household size: 2.36; Median age: 42.5; Age under 18: 21.0%; Age 65 and over: 20.3%; Males per 100 females: 93.2; Marriage status: 25.6% never married, 50.4% now married, 3.0% separated, 8.9% widowed, 15.1% divorced; Foreign born: 13.4%; Speak English only: 82.5%; With disability: 14.7%; Veterans: 12.9%; Ancestry: 21.0% German, 14.7% Irish, 10.8% English, 5.1% Italian, 4.5% American

Employment: 11.6% management, business, and financial, 1.5% computer, engineering, and science, 11.6% education, legal, community service, arts, and media, 3.5% healthcare practitioners, 23.3% service, 28.0% sales and office, 12.1% natural resources, construction, and maintenance, 8.3% production, transportation, and material moving

Income: Per capita: $24,337; Median household: $46,939; Average household: $62,045; Households with income of $100,000 or more: 19.9%; Poverty rate: 13.4%

Educational Attainment: High school diploma or higher: 83.9%; Bachelor's degree or higher: 17.7%; Graduate/professional degree or higher: 5.5%

Housing: Homeownership rate: 60.9%; Median home value: $239,400; Median year structure built: 1978; Homeowner vacancy rate: 2.9%; Median gross rent: $992 per month; Rental vacancy rate: 10.1%

Health Insurance: 82.5% have insurance; 65.7% have private insurance; 35.0% have public insurance; 17.5% do not have insurance; 11.8% of children under 18 do not have insurance

Transportation: Commute: 85.9% car, 1.2% public transportation, 2.1% walk, 9.9% work from home; Median travel time to work: 23.7 minutes

OLYMPIC VALLEY (unincorporated postal area)

ZCTA: 96146

Covers a land area of 20.935 square miles and a water area of 0.023 square miles. Located at 39.20° N. Lat; 120.24° W. Long..

Population: 1,366; Growth (since 2000): 47.5%; Density: 65.3 persons per square mile; Race: 91.2% White, 0.4% Black/African American, 5.2% Asian, 0.4% American Indian/Alaska Native, 0.1% Native Hawaiian/Other Pacific Islander, 2.0% Two or more races, 2.9% Hispanic of any race; Average household size: 2.20; Median age: 39.7; Age under 18: 18.2%; Age 65 and over: 13.0%; Males per 100 females: 142.2

Housing: Homeownership rate: 62.3%; Homeowner vacancy rate: 6.1%; Rental vacancy rate: 12.1%

PENRYN (CDP). Covers a land area of 1.823 square miles and a water area of 0 square miles. Located at 38.85° N. Lat; 121.17° W. Long. Elevation is 627 feet.

Population: 831; Growth (since 2000): n/a; Density: 455.7 persons per square mile; Race: 86.4% White, 0.4% Black/African American, 3.9% Asian, 2.6% American Indian/Alaska Native, 0.4% Native Hawaiian/Other Pacific Islander, 3.1% Two or more races, 9.5% Hispanic of any race; Average household size: 2.68; Median age: 43.2; Age under 18: 22.5%; Age 65 and over: 15.6%; Males per 100 females: 97.4

School District(s)

Loomis Union Elementary (KG-12)
2012-13 Enrollment: 3,219 . . . . (916) 652-1800

Housing: Homeownership rate: 80.6%; Homeowner vacancy rate: 2.0%; Rental vacancy rate: 11.6%

ROCKLIN (city). Covers a land area of 19.541 square miles and a water area of 0.053 square miles. Located at 38.81° N. Lat; 121.25° W. Long. Elevation is 259 feet.

History: Named for its numerous rock quarries, and for the Celtic translation of "spring". Early residents of Rocklin were primarily of Finnish ancestry.

Population: 56,974; Growth (since 2000): 56.8%; Density: 2,915.7 persons per square mile; Race: 82.6% White, 1.5% Black/African American, 7.2% Asian, 0.7% American Indian/Alaska Native, 0.3% Native Hawaiian/Other Pacific Islander, 5.0% Two or more races, 11.5% Hispanic of any race; Average household size: 2.71; Median age: 36.7; Age under 18: 27.4%; Age 65 and over: 10.9%; Males per 100 females: 94.0; Marriage status: 27.0% never married, 57.9% now married, 2.0% separated, 4.7% widowed, 10.4% divorced; Foreign born: 10.1%; Speak English only: 85.7%; With disability: 8.6%; Veterans: 9.8%; Ancestry: 16.9% German, 14.4% Irish, 11.8% English, 8.5% Italian, 5.1% American

Employment: 20.4% management, business, and financial, 7.4% computer, engineering, and science, 12.2% education, legal, community service, arts, and media, 5.7% healthcare practitioners, 16.6% service, 27.8% sales and office, 3.8% natural resources, construction, and maintenance, 6.1% production, transportation, and material moving

Income: Per capita: $34,290; Median household: $77,031; Average household: $91,694; Households with income of $100,000 or more: 36.7%; Poverty rate: 8.0%

Educational Attainment: High school diploma or higher: 95.2%; Bachelor's degree or higher: 40.8%; Graduate/professional degree or higher: 12.1%

School District(s)

Rocklin Unified (KG-12)
2012-13 Enrollment: 12,155 . . . . (916) 624-2428
Sbe - Western Sierra Collegiate Academy (07-12)
2012-13 Enrollment: 541. . . . . (916) 778-4544

Four-year College(s)

William Jessup University (Private, Not-for-profit, Other Protestant)
Fall 2013 Enrollment: 1,095 . . . . (916) 577-2200
2013-14 Tuition: In-state $24,040; Out-of-state $24,040

Two-year College(s)

Sierra College (Public)
Fall 2013 Enrollment: 18,374 . . . . (916) 624-3333
2013-14 Tuition: In-state $1,150; Out-of-state $6,190

Housing: Homeownership rate: 66.3%; Median home value: $328,600; Median year structure built: 1995; Homeowner vacancy rate: 2.5%; Median gross rent: $1,311 per month; Rental vacancy rate: 7.3%

Health Insurance: 92.0% have insurance; 82.9% have private insurance; 19.3% have public insurance; 8.0% do not have insurance; 2.4% of children under 18 do not have insurance

Safety: Violent crime rate: 10.4 per 10,000 population; Property crime rate: 169.6 per 10,000 population

Newspapers: The Placer Herald (weekly circulation 15000)

Transportation: Commute: 89.7% car, 1.4% public transportation, 0.8% walk, 6.5% work from home; Median travel time to work: 27.0 minutes; Amtrak: Train service available.

Additional Information Contacts

City of Rocklin . . . . (916) 625-5000
http://www.rocklin.ca.gov

ROSEVILLE (city). Covers a land area of 36.222 square miles and a water area of 0.001 square miles. Located at 38.77° N. Lat; 121.30° W. Long. Elevation is 164 feet.

History: Roseville grew around the Southern Pacific shops and yards, as a shipping center for plums, berries, almonds, and grapes.

Population: 118,788; Growth (since 2000): 48.6%; Density: 3,279.5 persons per square mile; Race: 79.3% White, 2.0% Black/African American, 8.4% Asian, 0.7% American Indian/Alaska Native, 0.3% Native Hawaiian/Other Pacific Islander, 5.0% Two or more races, 14.6% Hispanic of any race; Average household size: 2.62; Median age: 36.8; Age under 18: 26.3%; Age 65 and over: 13.4%; Males per 100 females: 91.9; Marriage status: 27.6% never married, 56.3% now married, 2.1% separated, 5.6% widowed, 10.5% divorced; Foreign born: 13.3%; Speak English only: 81.2%; With disability: 9.5%; Veterans: 9.8%; Ancestry: 17.7% German, 13.0% Irish, 11.6% English, 7.2% Italian, 3.9% American

Employment: 18.7% management, business, and financial, 7.2% computer, engineering, and science, 10.5% education, legal, community service, arts, and media, 6.4% healthcare practitioners, 15.5% service,

28.9% sales and office, 5.9% natural resources, construction, and maintenance, 7.0% production, transportation, and material moving
Income: Per capita: $33,622; Median household: $74,114; Average household: $89,296; Households with income of $100,000 or more: 36.1%; Poverty rate: 8.3%
Educational Attainment: High school diploma or higher: 94.1%; Bachelor's degree or higher: 35.6%; Graduate/professional degree or higher: 11.2%

School District(s)

Center Joint Unified (KG-12)
2012-13 Enrollment: 4,791 . . . . (916) 338-6330
Dry Creek Joint Elementary (KG-08)
2012-13 Enrollment: 6,888 . . . . (916) 770-8800
Eureka Union (PK-08)
2012-13 Enrollment: 3,422 . . . . (916) 791-4939
Loomis Union Elementary (KG-12)
2012-13 Enrollment: 3,219 . . . . (916) 652-1800
Roseville City Elementary (KG-08)
2012-13 Enrollment: 9,943 . . . . (916) 771-1600
Roseville Joint Union High (09-12)
2012-13 Enrollment: 10,206 . . . . (916) 786-2051

Two-year College(s)

Heald College-Roseville (Private, For-profit)
Fall 2013 Enrollment: 1,256 . . . . (916) 789-8600
2013-14 Tuition: In-state $13,620; Out-of-state $13,620

Vocational/Technical School(s)

InterCoast Colleges-Roseville (Private, For-profit)
Fall 2013 Enrollment: 3 . . . . (916) 786-6300
2013-14 Tuition: $19,395
Housing: Homeownership rate: 65.5%; Median home value: $312,400; Median year structure built: 1994; Homeowner vacancy rate: 2.3%; Median gross rent: $1,252 per month; Rental vacancy rate: 6.8%
Health Insurance: 90.8% have insurance; 79.0% have private insurance; 22.8% have public insurance; 9.2% do not have insurance; 4.0% of children under 18 do not have insurance
Hospitals: Kaiser Foundation Hospital - Roseville; Sutter Roseville Medical Center (172 beds)
Safety: Violent crime rate: 20.7 per 10,000 population; Property crime rate: 264.8 per 10,000 population
Newspapers: Press Tribune (weekly circulation 7000)
Transportation: Commute: 88.4% car, 1.3% public transportation, 1.9% walk, 6.2% work from home; Median travel time to work: 26.3 minutes; Amtrak: Train service available.
Additional Information Contacts
City of Roseville. . . . . (916) 774-5200
http://www.roseville.ca.us

SHERIDAN (CDP). Covers a land area of 26.038 square miles and a water area of 0.006 square miles. Located at 38.97° N. Lat; 121.35° W. Long. Elevation is 112 feet.
Population: 1,238; Growth (since 2000): n/a; Density: 47.5 persons per square mile; Race: 82.9% White, 0.6% Black/African American, 1.1% Asian, 1.6% American Indian/Alaska Native, 0.2% Native Hawaiian/Other Pacific Islander, 4.5% Two or more races, 20.4% Hispanic of any race; Average household size: 2.99; Median age: 40.7; Age under 18: 24.4%; Age 65 and over: 12.5%; Males per 100 females: 101.3

School District(s)

Western Placer Unified (KG-12)
2012-13 Enrollment: 9,447 . . . . (916) 645-6350
Housing: Homeownership rate: 74.7%; Homeowner vacancy rate: 2.5%; Rental vacancy rate: 0.0%

SUNNYSIDE-TAHOE CITY (CDP). Covers a land area of 3.380 square miles and a water area of 0 square miles. Located at 39.15° N. Lat; 120.16° W. Long. Elevation is 6,496 feet.
Population: 1,557; Growth (since 2000): -11.6%; Density: 460.6 persons per square mile; Race: 95.1% White, 0.2% Black/African American, 1.0% Asian, 0.3% American Indian/Alaska Native, 0.1% Native Hawaiian/Other Pacific Islander, 1.4% Two or more races, 5.4% Hispanic of any race; Average household size: 2.08; Median age: 40.7; Age under 18: 12.3%; Age 65 and over: 10.5%; Males per 100 females: 120.5

School District(s)

Newcastle Elementary (KG-12)
2012-13 Enrollment: 592. . . . . (916) 663-3307
Tahoe-Truckee Joint Unified (KG-12)
2012-13 Enrollment: 3,917 . . . . (530) 582-2500
Housing: Homeownership rate: 54.0%; Homeowner vacancy rate: 4.3%; Rental vacancy rate: 21.2%

TAHOE VISTA (CDP). Covers a land area of 2.716 square miles and a water area of 0 square miles. Located at 39.25° N. Lat; 120.05° W. Long. Elevation is 6,234 feet.
Population: 1,433; Growth (since 2000): -14.1%; Density: 527.7 persons per square mile; Race: 89.3% White, 0.2% Black/African American, 1.5% Asian, 0.6% American Indian/Alaska Native, 0.1% Native Hawaiian/Other Pacific Islander, 2.7% Two or more races, 24.6% Hispanic of any race; Average household size: 2.28; Median age: 40.4; Age under 18: 18.3%; Age 65 and over: 9.6%; Males per 100 females: 113.6
Housing: Homeownership rate: 63.3%; Homeowner vacancy rate: 4.9%; Rental vacancy rate: 14.4%
Newspapers: Tahoe World (weekly circulation 4800)

WEIMAR (unincorporated postal area)
ZCTA: 95736
Covers a land area of 0.251 square miles and a water area of 0 square miles. Located at 39.04° N. Lat; 120.98° W. Long. Elevation is 2,257 feet.
Population: 240; Growth (since 2000): 727.6%; Density: 957.1 persons per square mile; Race: 70.8% White, 4.2% Black/African American, 9.6% Asian, 0.0% American Indian/Alaska Native, 3.8% Native Hawaiian/Other Pacific Islander, 4.6% Two or more races, 11.7% Hispanic of any race; Average household size: 2.25; Median age: 29.7; Age under 18: 15.0%; Age 65 and over: 7.1%; Males per 100 females: 116.2

School District(s)

Placer Hills Union Elementary (KG-08)
2012-13 Enrollment: 853. . . . . (530) 878-2606
Housing: Homeownership rate: 10.4%; Homeowner vacancy rate: 0.0%; Rental vacancy rate: 0.0%

Plumas County

Located in northeastern California, in the Sierra Nevada; drained by the Feather River; includes parts of Plumas and Tahoe National Forests. Covers a land area of 2,553.043 square miles, a water area of 60.385 square miles, and is located in the Pacific Time Zone at 40.00° N. Lat., 120.83° W. Long. The county was founded in 1854. County seat is Quincy.

Weather Station: Canyon Dam — Elevation: 4,560 feet

	Jan	Feb	Mar	Apr	May	Jun	Jul	Aug	Sep	Oct	Nov	Dec
High	40	44	50	57	68	76	84	83	77	64	49	40
Low	24	25	28	31	38	44	49	47	42	35	29	24
Precip	6.1	6.6	5.2	2.6	1.6	0.8	0.2	0.2	0.7	2.1	4.5	6.5
Snow	25.8	24.5	16.7	7.0	0.3	0.0	0.0	0.0	0.1	0.9	8.0	22.7

High and Low temperatures in degrees Fahrenheit; Precipitation and Snow in inches

Weather Station: Chester — Elevation: 4,524 feet

	Jan	Feb	Mar	Apr	May	Jun	Jul	Aug	Sep	Oct	Nov	Dec
High	41	45	51	58	67	76	85	84	78	66	50	41
Low	21	23	26	30	36	42	46	45	39	32	27	21
Precip	5.8	5.6	4.8	2.3	1.8	0.7	0.4	0.2	0.7	1.9	4.0	5.4
Snow	27.7	21.9	15.7	4.3	0.4	0.1	0.0	0.0	0.1	0.7	8.9	23.0

High and Low temperatures in degrees Fahrenheit; Precipitation and Snow in inches

Weather Station: Portola — Elevation: 4,850 feet

	Jan	Feb	Mar	Apr	May	Jun	Jul	Aug	Sep	Oct	Nov	Dec
High	42	45	51	58	67	76	85	85	77	66	51	42
Low	19	22	26	29	35	39	44	42	37	30	24	20
Precip	3.8	3.9	3.4	1.4	1.0	0.5	0.3	0.3	0.6	1.1	2.5	3.5
Snow	8.5	9.5	5.7	2.4	0.1	tr	0.0	0.0	tr	0.3	2.9	7.2

High and Low temperatures in degrees Fahrenheit; Precipitation and Snow in inches

Population: 20,007; Growth (since 2000): -3.9%; Density: 7.8 persons per square mile; Race: 89.0% White, 1.0% Black/African American, 0.7% Asian, 2.7% American Indian/Alaska Native, 0.1% Native Hawaiian/Other Pacific Islander, 3.6% two or more races, 8.0% Hispanic of any race; Average household size: 2.20; Median age: 49.6; Age under 18: 18.0%; Age 65 and over: 20.8%; Males per 100 females: 100.0; Marriage status: 22.1% never married, 53.9% now married, 1.6% separated, 8.6% widowed, 15.4% divorced; Foreign born: 5.1%; Speak English only: 90.3%; With disability: 19.4%; Veterans: 14.2%; Ancestry: 20.8% German, 18.1% Irish, 16.4% English, 6.9% Italian, 4.6% European

Religion: Six largest groups: 6.1% Catholicism, 3.8% Latter-day Saints, 3.2% Methodist/Pietist, 2.7% Baptist, 2.5% Non-denominational Protestant, 2.1% Pentecostal
Economy: Unemployment rate: 7.3%; Leading industries: 16.2% accommodation and food services; 14.2% construction; 14.2% retail trade; Farms: 141 totaling 174,210 acres; Company size: 0 employ 1,000 or more persons, 0 employ 500 to 999 persons, 5 employ 100 to 499 persons, 614 employ less than 100 persons; Business ownership: 523 women-owned, n/a Black-owned, n/a Hispanic-owned, n/a Asian-owned
Employment: 12.9% management, business, and financial, 6.3% computer, engineering, and science, 10.2% education, legal, community service, arts, and media, 6.6% healthcare practitioners, 20.4% service, 21.2% sales and office, 13.7% natural resources, construction, and maintenance, 8.8% production, transportation, and material moving
Income: Per capita: $29,806; Median household: $45,794; Average household: $62,345; Households with income of $100,000 or more: 14.9%; Poverty rate: 15.2%
Educational Attainment: High school diploma or higher: 89.9%; Bachelor's degree or higher: 22.6%; Graduate/professional degree or higher: 9.4%
Housing: Homeownership rate: 69.5%; Median home value: $243,700; Median year structure built: 1978; Homeowner vacancy rate: 4.7%; Median gross rent: $799 per month; Rental vacancy rate: 14.2%
Vital Statistics: Birth rate: 82.7 per 10,000 population; Death rate: 109.8 per 10,000 population; Age-adjusted cancer mortality rate: 195.4 deaths per 100,000 population
Health Insurance: 81.7% have insurance; 61.0% have private insurance; 39.9% have public insurance; 18.3% do not have insurance; 18.5% of children under 18 do not have insurance
Health Care: Physicians: 12.4 per 10,000 population; Hospital beds: 64.1 per 10,000 population; Hospital admissions: 642.8 per 10,000 population
Air Quality Index: 54.6% good, 32.8% moderate, 10.9% unhealthy for sensitive individuals, 1.7% unhealthy (percent of days)
Transportation: Commute: 87.1% car, 0.2% public transportation, 4.6% walk, 7.2% work from home; Median travel time to work: 22.9 minutes
Presidential Election: 40.2% Obama, 57.2% Romney (2012)
National and State Parks: Mount Hough State Game Refuge; Plumas National Forest; Plumas-Eureka State Park; State Game Refuge One-P; State Game Refuge One-V
Additional Information Contacts
Plumas Government . . . . (530) 283-6170
http://www.countyofplumas.com

Plumas County Communities

BECKWOURTH (CDP). Covers a land area of 11.680 square miles and a water area of 0.005 square miles. Located at 39.84° N. Lat; 120.40° W. Long. Elevation is 4,911 feet.
Population: 432; Growth (since 2000): 26.3%; Density: 37.0 persons per square mile; Race: 93.1% White, 0.0% Black/African American, 0.5% Asian, 2.5% American Indian/Alaska Native, 0.2% Native Hawaiian/Other Pacific Islander, 2.1% Two or more races, 6.7% Hispanic of any race; Average household size: 2.20; Median age: 53.9; Age under 18: 16.4%; Age 65 and over: 22.7%; Males per 100 females: 118.2
Housing: Homeownership rate: 86.2%; Homeowner vacancy rate: 8.6%; Rental vacancy rate: 0.0%
Airports: Nervino (general aviation)

BELDEN (CDP). Covers a land area of 0.610 square miles and a water area of 0.116 square miles. Located at 40.01° N. Lat; 121.25° W. Long. Elevation is 2,221 feet.
Population: 22; Growth (since 2000): -15.4%; Density: 36.1 persons per square mile; Race: 90.9% White, 0.0% Black/African American, 0.0% Asian, 0.0% American Indian/Alaska Native, 0.0% Native Hawaiian/Other Pacific Islander, 9.1% Two or more races, 0.0% Hispanic of any race; Average household size: 1.69; Median age: 46.0; Age under 18: 13.6%; Age 65 and over: 9.1%; Males per 100 females: 266.7
Housing: Homeownership rate: 46.2%; Homeowner vacancy rate: 0.0%; Rental vacancy rate: 50.0%

BLAIRSDEN (CDP). Covers a land area of 0.542 square miles and a water area of 0 square miles. Located at 39.78° N. Lat; 120.61° W. Long. Elevation is 4,396 feet.
History: Blairsden grew as a center for winter sports in the upper Feather River recreation area.
Population: 39; Growth (since 2000): -22.0%; Density: 72.0 persons per square mile; Race: 97.4% White, 0.0% Black/African American, 0.0% Asian, 0.0% American Indian/Alaska Native, 0.0% Native Hawaiian/Other Pacific Islander, 0.0% Two or more races, 5.1% Hispanic of any race; Average household size: 1.77; Median age: 55.8; Age under 18: 7.7%; Age 65 and over: 35.9%; Males per 100 females: 77.3
Housing: Homeownership rate: 40.9%; Homeowner vacancy rate: 0.0%; Rental vacancy rate: 13.3%

BLAIRSDEN GRAEAGLE (unincorporated postal area)
ZCTA: 96103
Covers a land area of 125.702 square miles and a water area of 0.373 square miles. Located at 39.81° N. Lat; 120.67° W. Long..
Population: 1,725; Growth (since 2000): -6.1%; Density: 13.7 persons per square mile; Race: 95.7% White, 0.1% Black/African American, 1.0% Asian, 0.7% American Indian/Alaska Native, 0.0% Native Hawaiian/Other Pacific Islander, 1.9% Two or more races, 4.3% Hispanic of any race; Average household size: 2.00; Median age: 58.8; Age under 18: 9.9%; Age 65 and over: 34.8%; Males per 100 females: 96.7
Housing: Homeownership rate: 81.6%; Homeowner vacancy rate: 7.2%; Rental vacancy rate: 30.2%

C-ROAD (CDP). Covers a land area of 2.664 square miles and a water area of 0 square miles. Located at 39.76° N. Lat; 120.58° W. Long.
Population: 150; Growth (since 2000): -1.3%; Density: 56.3 persons per square mile; Race: 93.3% White, 0.0% Black/African American, 1.3% Asian, 0.0% American Indian/Alaska Native, 0.0% Native Hawaiian/Other Pacific Islander, 5.3% Two or more races, 6.0% Hispanic of any race; Average household size: 2.05; Median age: 53.3; Age under 18: 11.3%; Age 65 and over: 19.3%; Males per 100 females: 117.4
Housing: Homeownership rate: 89.0%; Homeowner vacancy rate: 3.0%; Rental vacancy rate: 0.0%

CANYON DAM (unincorporated postal area)
ZCTA: 95923
Covers a land area of 9.933 square miles and a water area of 0 square miles. Located at 40.13° N. Lat; 121.09° W. Long..
Population: 58; Growth (since 2000): -13.4%; Density: 5.8 persons per square mile; Race: 96.6% White, 0.0% Black/African American, 3.4% Asian, 0.0% American Indian/Alaska Native, 0.0% Native Hawaiian/Other Pacific Islander, 0.0% Two or more races, 0.0% Hispanic of any race; Average household size: 2.07; Median age: 47.0; Age under 18: 20.7%; Age 65 and over: 22.4%; Males per 100 females: 176.2
Housing: Homeownership rate: 60.7%; Homeowner vacancy rate: 0.0%; Rental vacancy rate: 0.0%

CHESTER (CDP). Covers a land area of 7.288 square miles and a water area of 0.081 square miles. Located at 40.30° N. Lat; 121.23° W. Long. Elevation is 4,534 feet.
History: Chester developed as a lumber town on the northwestern shore of Lake Alamanor.
Population: 2,144; Growth (since 2000): -7.4%; Density: 294.2 persons per square mile; Race: 91.1% White, 0.5% Black/African American, 1.0% Asian, 2.1% American Indian/Alaska Native, 0.2% Native Hawaiian/Other Pacific Islander, 3.4% Two or more races, 8.3% Hispanic of any race; Average household size: 2.26; Median age: 44.9; Age under 18: 21.7%; Age 65 and over: 14.5%; Males per 100 females: 101.7

School District(s)

Plumas Unified (KG-12)
2012-13 Enrollment: 2,125 . . . . (530) 283-6500
Housing: Homeownership rate: 60.2%; Homeowner vacancy rate: 3.5%; Rental vacancy rate: 15.7%
Hospitals: Seneca District Hospital (26 beds)
Newspapers: Chester Progressive (weekly circulation 3100)
Airports: Rogers Field (general aviation)

CHILCOOT-VINTON (CDP). Covers a land area of 13.207 square miles and a water area of 0 square miles. Located at 39.81° N. Lat; 120.14° W. Long. Elevation is 5,013 feet.
Population: 454; Growth (since 2000): 17.3%; Density: 34.4 persons per square mile; Race: 92.1% White, 0.2% Black/African American, 0.2% Asian, 0.9% American Indian/Alaska Native, 0.0% Native Hawaiian/Other Pacific Islander, 4.6% Two or more races, 8.4% Hispanic of any race; Average household size: 2.32; Median age: 45.6; Age under 18: 20.0%; Age 65 and over: 14.8%; Males per 100 females: 113.1

Housing: Homeownership rate: 78.0%; Homeowner vacancy rate: 5.0%; Rental vacancy rate: 12.2%

CLIO (CDP). Covers a land area of 0.576 square miles and a water area of 0 square miles. Located at 39.75° N. Lat; 120.57° W. Long. Elevation is 4,416 feet.
History: Clio's name was taken from the tradename on a heating stove in the general store, when the townsfolk were having trouble deciding on what to call their town.
Population: 66; Growth (since 2000): -26.7%; Density: 114.7 persons per square mile; Race: 97.0% White, 0.0% Black/African American, 0.0% Asian, 0.0% American Indian/Alaska Native, 1.5% Native Hawaiian/Other Pacific Islander, 0.0% Two or more races, 1.5% Hispanic of any race; Average household size: 1.69; Median age: 56.0; Age under 18: 10.6%; Age 65 and over: 27.3%; Males per 100 females: 94.1
Housing: Homeownership rate: 84.7%; Homeowner vacancy rate: 8.3%; Rental vacancy rate: 0.0%

CRESCENT MILLS (CDP). Covers a land area of 4.240 square miles and a water area of 0 square miles. Located at 40.10° N. Lat; 120.92° W. Long. Elevation is 3,527 feet.
Population: 196; Growth (since 2000): -24.0%; Density: 46.2 persons per square mile; Race: 87.8% White, 0.5% Black/African American, 0.0% Asian, 7.7% American Indian/Alaska Native, 0.0% Native Hawaiian/Other Pacific Islander, 4.1% Two or more races, 13.3% Hispanic of any race; Average household size: 2.11; Median age: 52.6; Age under 18: 18.9%; Age 65 and over: 21.4%; Males per 100 females: 90.3
Housing: Homeownership rate: 68.8%; Homeowner vacancy rate: 5.9%; Rental vacancy rate: 9.1%

CROMBERG (CDP). Covers a land area of 9.014 square miles and a water area of 0 square miles. Located at 39.87° N. Lat; 120.69° W. Long. Elevation is 4,285 feet.
Population: 261; Growth (since 2000): -10.0%; Density: 29.0 persons per square mile; Race: 91.6% White, 0.0% Black/African American, 2.3% Asian, 1.9% American Indian/Alaska Native, 0.0% Native Hawaiian/Other Pacific Islander, 3.1% Two or more races, 6.9% Hispanic of any race; Average household size: 2.16; Median age: 53.3; Age under 18: 11.1%; Age 65 and over: 26.1%; Males per 100 females: 91.9
Housing: Homeownership rate: 79.3%; Homeowner vacancy rate: 5.0%; Rental vacancy rate: 19.4%

DELLEKER (CDP). Covers a land area of 2.769 square miles and a water area of 0.002 square miles. Located at 39.81° N. Lat; 120.49° W. Long. Elevation is 4,885 feet.
Population: 705; Growth (since 2000): 4.6%; Density: 254.6 persons per square mile; Race: 71.3% White, 1.0% Black/African American, 0.4% Asian, 3.3% American Indian/Alaska Native, 0.0% Native Hawaiian/Other Pacific Islander, 5.1% Two or more races, 26.4% Hispanic of any race; Average household size: 2.64; Median age: 37.3; Age under 18: 28.2%; Age 65 and over: 11.3%; Males per 100 females: 95.3
Housing: Homeownership rate: 70.4%; Homeowner vacancy rate: 5.5%; Rental vacancy rate: 6.9%

EAST QUINCY (CDP). Covers a land area of 12.107 square miles and a water area of 0 square miles. Located at 39.92° N. Lat; 120.92° W. Long. Elevation is 3,491 feet.
Population: 2,489; Growth (since 2000): 3.8%; Density: 205.6 persons per square mile; Race: 87.3% White, 3.2% Black/African American, 0.6% Asian, 1.7% American Indian/Alaska Native, 0.0% Native Hawaiian/Other Pacific Islander, 5.9% Two or more races, 6.5% Hispanic of any race; Average household size: 2.27; Median age: 42.1; Age under 18: 21.1%; Age 65 and over: 14.0%; Males per 100 females: 103.5
Housing: Homeownership rate: 61.6%; Homeowner vacancy rate: 1.9%; Rental vacancy rate: 4.8%

EAST SHORE (CDP). Covers a land area of 1.183 square miles and a water area of 0 square miles. Located at 40.25° N. Lat; 121.08° W. Long. Elevation is 4,518 feet.
Population: 156; Growth (since 2000): -11.9%; Density: 131.9 persons per square mile; Race: 91.7% White, 0.0% Black/African American, 0.6% Asian, 4.5% American Indian/Alaska Native, 0.0% Native Hawaiian/Other Pacific Islander, 0.0% Two or more races, 4.5% Hispanic of any race; Average household size: 2.00; Median age: 60.8; Age under 18: 5.1%; Age 65 and over: 34.0%; Males per 100 females: 88.0
Housing: Homeownership rate: 83.4%; Homeowner vacancy rate: 7.1%; Rental vacancy rate: 30.0%

GOLD MOUNTAIN (CDP). Covers a land area of 6.091 square miles and a water area of 0 square miles. Located at 39.76° N. Lat; 120.52° W. Long.
Population: 80; Growth (since 2000): n/a; Density: 13.1 persons per square mile; Race: 97.5% White, 0.0% Black/African American, 0.0% Asian, 1.3% American Indian/Alaska Native, 0.0% Native Hawaiian/Other Pacific Islander, 1.3% Two or more races, 0.0% Hispanic of any race; Average household size: 1.95; Median age: 63.7; Age under 18: 2.5%; Age 65 and over: 42.5%; Males per 100 females: 110.5
Housing: Homeownership rate: 95.2%; Homeowner vacancy rate: 4.9%; Rental vacancy rate: 33.3%

GRAEAGLE (CDP). Covers a land area of 11.067 square miles and a water area of 0.057 square miles. Located at 39.75° N. Lat; 120.65° W. Long. Elevation is 4,373 feet.
Population: 737; Growth (since 2000): -11.3%; Density: 66.6 persons per square mile; Race: 97.4% White, 0.1% Black/African American, 0.0% Asian, 0.7% American Indian/Alaska Native, 0.0% Native Hawaiian/Other Pacific Islander, 1.4% Two or more races, 3.7% Hispanic of any race; Average household size: 1.88; Median age: 62.4; Age under 18: 9.5%; Age 65 and over: 43.0%; Males per 100 females: 94.5
Housing: Homeownership rate: 84.2%; Homeowner vacancy rate: 6.8%; Rental vacancy rate: 28.1%

GREENHORN (CDP). Covers a land area of 6.711 square miles and a water area of 0 square miles. Located at 39.90° N. Lat; 120.76° W. Long. Elevation is 4,436 feet.
Population: 236; Growth (since 2000): 61.6%; Density: 35.2 persons per square mile; Race: 90.3% White, 0.4% Black/African American, 0.8% Asian, 3.0% American Indian/Alaska Native, 0.0% Native Hawaiian/Other Pacific Islander, 3.0% Two or more races, 9.3% Hispanic of any race; Average household size: 2.23; Median age: 46.9; Age under 18: 18.2%; Age 65 and over: 18.2%; Males per 100 females: 96.7
Housing: Homeownership rate: 89.6%; Homeowner vacancy rate: 6.9%; Rental vacancy rate: 8.3%

GREENVILLE (CDP). Covers a land area of 7.992 square miles and a water area of 0 square miles. Located at 40.13° N. Lat; 120.95° W. Long. Elevation is 3,586 feet.
Population: 1,129; Growth (since 2000): -2.7%; Density: 141.3 persons per square mile; Race: 79.5% White, 0.1% Black/African American, 1.0% Asian, 11.8% American Indian/Alaska Native, 0.0% Native Hawaiian/Other Pacific Islander, 6.2% Two or more races, 9.7% Hispanic of any race; Average household size: 2.28; Median age: 45.4; Age under 18: 22.7%; Age 65 and over: 16.8%; Males per 100 females: 97.4

School District(s)

Plumas Unified (KG-12)
2012-13 Enrollment: 2,125 . . . . (530) 283-6500
Housing: Homeownership rate: 50.6%; Homeowner vacancy rate: 4.9%; Rental vacancy rate: 9.2%
Newspapers: Indian Valley Record (weekly circulation 1300)

HAMILTON BRANCH (CDP). Covers a land area of 1.085 square miles and a water area of 0 square miles. Located at 40.28° N. Lat; 121.10° W. Long. Elevation is 4,626 feet.
Population: 537; Growth (since 2000): -8.5%; Density: 494.7 persons per square mile; Race: 95.7% White, 0.4% Black/African American, 0.6% Asian, 0.0% American Indian/Alaska Native, 0.0% Native Hawaiian/Other Pacific Islander, 2.8% Two or more races, 3.7% Hispanic of any race; Average household size: 2.29; Median age: 52.3; Age under 18: 19.6%; Age 65 and over: 26.1%; Males per 100 females: 106.5
Housing: Homeownership rate: 85.9%; Homeowner vacancy rate: 2.9%; Rental vacancy rate: 19.5%

INDIAN FALLS (CDP). Covers a land area of 1.842 square miles and a water area of 0 square miles. Located at 40.06° N. Lat; 120.98° W. Long. Elevation is 3,258 feet.
Population: 54; Growth (since 2000): 45.9%; Density: 29.3 persons per square mile; Race: 92.6% White, 0.0% Black/African American, 1.9% Asian, 0.0% American Indian/Alaska Native, 0.0% Native Hawaiian/Other Pacific Islander, 3.7% Two or more races, 7.4% Hispanic of any race;

Average household size: 2.25; Median age: 45.3; Age under 18: 22.2%; Age 65 and over: 3.7%; Males per 100 females: 134.8

Housing: Homeownership rate: 91.6%; Homeowner vacancy rate: 0.0%; Rental vacancy rate: 0.0%

IRON HORSE (CDP). Covers a land area of 7.747 square miles and a water area of 0 square miles. Located at 39.78° N. Lat; 120.48° W. Long. Elevation is 4,944 feet.

Population: 297; Growth (since 2000): -7.5%; Density: 38.3 persons per square mile; Race: 92.9% White, 0.0% Black/African American, 0.3% Asian, 0.0% American Indian/Alaska Native, 0.0% Native Hawaiian/Other Pacific Islander, 2.7% Two or more races, 5.7% Hispanic of any race; Average household size: 2.36; Median age: 49.0; Age under 18: 17.2%; Age 65 and over: 18.5%; Males per 100 females: 96.7

Housing: Homeownership rate: 80.2%; Homeowner vacancy rate: 7.3%; Rental vacancy rate: 16.7%

JOHNSVILLE (CDP). Covers a land area of 13.756 square miles and a water area of 0.052 square miles. Located at 39.77° N. Lat; 120.70° W. Long. Elevation is 5,180 feet.

Population: 20; Growth (since 2000): -4.8%; Density: 1.5 persons per square mile; Race: 100.0% White, 0.0% Black/African American, 0.0% Asian, 0.0% American Indian/Alaska Native, 0.0% Native Hawaiian/Other Pacific Islander, 0.0% Two or more races, 0.0% Hispanic of any race; Average household size: 1.82; Median age: 57.5; Age under 18: 0.0%; Age 65 and over: 25.0%; Males per 100 females: 122.2

Housing: Homeownership rate: 90.9%; Homeowner vacancy rate: 9.1%; Rental vacancy rate: 0.0%

KEDDIE (CDP). Covers a land area of 0.645 square miles and a water area of 0 square miles. Located at 40.01° N. Lat; 120.95° W. Long. Elevation is 3,264 feet.

Population: 66; Growth (since 2000): -31.3%; Density: 102.3 persons per square mile; Race: 93.9% White, 3.0% Black/African American, 0.0% Asian, 0.0% American Indian/Alaska Native, 0.0% Native Hawaiian/Other Pacific Islander, 3.0% Two or more races, 0.0% Hispanic of any race; Average household size: 2.06; Median age: 52.5; Age under 18: 10.6%; Age 65 and over: 28.8%; Males per 100 females: 100.0

Housing: Homeownership rate: 78.2%; Homeowner vacancy rate: 0.0%; Rental vacancy rate: 22.2%

LA PORTE (CDP). Covers a land area of 4.457 square miles and a water area of 0 square miles. Located at 39.67° N. Lat; 120.99° W. Long. Elevation is 4,980 feet.

Population: 26; Growth (since 2000): -39.5%; Density: 5.8 persons per square mile; Race: 92.3% White, 3.8% Black/African American, 0.0% Asian, 3.8% American Indian/Alaska Native, 0.0% Native Hawaiian/Other Pacific Islander, 0.0% Two or more races, 0.0% Hispanic of any race; Average household size: 1.73; Median age: 56.0; Age under 18: 15.4%; Age 65 and over: 23.1%; Males per 100 females: 100.0

Housing: Homeownership rate: 66.7%; Homeowner vacancy rate: 16.7%; Rental vacancy rate: 0.0%

LAKE ALMANOR COUNTRY CLUB (CDP). Covers a land area of 2.743 square miles and a water area of 0 square miles. Located at 40.26° N. Lat; 121.15° W. Long. Elevation is 4,636 feet.

Population: 419; Growth (since 2000): -50.5%; Density: 152.7 persons per square mile; Race: 96.9% White, 0.5% Black/African American, 0.2% Asian, 0.5% American Indian/Alaska Native, 0.0% Native Hawaiian/Other Pacific Islander, 1.4% Two or more races, 1.9% Hispanic of any race; Average household size: 1.93; Median age: 65.8; Age under 18: 5.0%; Age 65 and over: 51.8%; Males per 100 females: 103.4

Housing: Homeownership rate: 89.0%; Homeowner vacancy rate: 3.0%; Rental vacancy rate: 35.9%

LAKE ALMANOR PENINSULA (CDP). Covers a land area of 3.036 square miles and a water area of 0 square miles. Located at 40.28° N. Lat; 121.13° W. Long. Elevation is 4,701 feet.

Population: 356; Growth (since 2000): 6.0%; Density: 117.3 persons per square mile; Race: 94.7% White, 0.0% Black/African American, 0.0% Asian, 2.5% American Indian/Alaska Native, 0.0% Native Hawaiian/Other Pacific Islander, 1.7% Two or more races, 6.2% Hispanic of any race; Average household size: 2.16; Median age: 54.3; Age under 18: 18.8%; Age 65 and over: 23.6%; Males per 100 females: 110.7

Housing: Homeownership rate: 77.6%; Homeowner vacancy rate: 16.3%; Rental vacancy rate: 48.6%

LAKE ALMANOR WEST (CDP). Covers a land area of 2.286 square miles and a water area of 0 square miles. Located at 40.23° N. Lat; 121.20° W. Long. Elevation is 4,665 feet.

Population: 270; Growth (since 2000): -17.9%; Density: 118.1 persons per square mile; Race: 95.9% White, 0.4% Black/African American, 0.0% Asian, 0.4% American Indian/Alaska Native, 0.4% Native Hawaiian/Other Pacific Islander, 2.6% Two or more races, 4.1% Hispanic of any race; Average household size: 2.01; Median age: 65.4; Age under 18: 4.4%; Age 65 and over: 51.9%; Males per 100 females: 107.7

Housing: Homeownership rate: 96.2%; Homeowner vacancy rate: 7.2%; Rental vacancy rate: 40.0%

LAKE DAVIS (CDP). Covers a land area of 5.378 square miles and a water area of 0.004 square miles. Located at 39.85° N. Lat; 120.46° W. Long. Elevation is 5,886 feet.

Population: 45; Growth (since 2000): 95.7%; Density: 8.4 persons per square mile; Race: 100.0% White, 0.0% Black/African American, 0.0% Asian, 0.0% American Indian/Alaska Native, 0.0% Native Hawaiian/Other Pacific Islander, 0.0% Two or more races, 4.4% Hispanic of any race; Average household size: 1.96; Median age: 60.5; Age under 18: 8.9%; Age 65 and over: 26.7%; Males per 100 females: 104.5

Housing: Homeownership rate: 100.0%; Homeowner vacancy rate: 0.0%; Rental vacancy rate: 0.0%

LITTLE GRASS VALLEY (CDP). Covers a land area of 10.002 square miles and a water area of 0 square miles. Located at 39.73° N. Lat; 120.96° W. Long. Elevation is 5,121 feet.

Population: 2; Growth (since 2000): n/a; Density: 0.2 persons per square mile; Race: 100.0% White, 0.0% Black/African American, 0.0% Asian, 0.0% American Indian/Alaska Native, 0.0% Native Hawaiian/Other Pacific Islander, 0.0% Two or more races, 0.0% Hispanic of any race; Average household size: 2.00; Median age: 55.5; Age under 18: 0.0%; Age 65 and over: 0.0%; Males per 100 females: 100.0

Housing: Homeownership rate: 100.0%; Homeowner vacancy rate: 0.0%; Rental vacancy rate: 0.0%

MEADOW VALLEY (CDP). Covers a land area of 8.520 square miles and a water area of 0 square miles. Located at 39.93° N. Lat; 121.08° W. Long. Elevation is 3,776 feet.

Population: 464; Growth (since 2000): -19.3%; Density: 54.5 persons per square mile; Race: 93.8% White, 0.0% Black/African American, 0.0% Asian, 2.8% American Indian/Alaska Native, 0.0% Native Hawaiian/Other Pacific Islander, 2.6% Two or more races, 4.5% Hispanic of any race; Average household size: 2.01; Median age: 52.4; Age under 18: 13.4%; Age 65 and over: 19.8%; Males per 100 females: 106.2

Housing: Homeownership rate: 74.0%; Homeowner vacancy rate: 3.4%; Rental vacancy rate: 3.2%

MOHAWK VISTA (CDP). Covers a land area of 11.961 square miles and a water area of 0 square miles. Located at 39.80° N. Lat; 120.59° W. Long. Elevation is 4,944 feet.

Population: 159; Growth (since 2000): 31.4%; Density: 13.3 persons per square mile; Race: 91.8% White, 0.0% Black/African American, 4.4% Asian, 0.6% American Indian/Alaska Native, 0.0% Native Hawaiian/Other Pacific Islander, 2.5% Two or more races, 2.5% Hispanic of any race; Average household size: 2.15; Median age: 59.3; Age under 18: 10.1%; Age 65 and over: 32.1%; Males per 100 females: 96.3

Housing: Homeownership rate: 83.7%; Homeowner vacancy rate: 3.1%; Rental vacancy rate: 14.3%

PLUMAS EUREKA (CDP). Covers a land area of 3.980 square miles and a water area of 0 square miles. Located at 39.80° N. Lat; 120.66° W. Long. Elevation is 4,373 feet.

Population: 339; Growth (since 2000): 5.9%; Density: 85.2 persons per square mile; Race: 96.2% White, 0.0% Black/African American, 0.9% Asian, 0.3% American Indian/Alaska Native, 0.0% Native Hawaiian/Other Pacific Islander, 1.8% Two or more races, 5.0% Hispanic of any race; Average household size: 2.03; Median age: 59.0; Age under 18: 10.0%; Age 65 and over: 32.2%; Males per 100 females: 94.8

Housing: Homeownership rate: 81.4%; Homeowner vacancy rate: 13.8%; Rental vacancy rate: 50.0%

PORTOLA (city). Covers a land area of 5.407 square miles and a water area of 0 square miles. Located at 39.82° N. Lat; 120.47° W. Long. Elevation is 4,856 feet.

History: Portola was named for the Portola Fiesta in San Francisco in 1909 which commemorated Gaspar de Portola, California's first Spanish governor. Portola developed as a lumber and railroad center.

Population: 2,104; Growth (since 2000): -5.5%; Density: 389.1 persons per square mile; Race: 83.7% White, 0.6% Black/African American, 0.6% Asian, 2.6% American Indian/Alaska Native, 0.0% Native Hawaiian/Other Pacific Islander, 3.0% Two or more races, 16.3% Hispanic of any race; Average household size: 2.34; Median age: 39.8; Age under 18: 23.9%; Age 65 and over: 14.4%; Males per 100 females: 93.4

School District(s)

Plumas County Office of Education (KG-12)
2012-13 Enrollment: 32. . . . . (530) 283-6500
Plumas Unified (KG-12)
2012-13 Enrollment: 2,125 . . . . (530) 283-6500

Housing: Homeownership rate: 54.3%; Homeowner vacancy rate: 6.8%; Rental vacancy rate: 21.0%

Hospitals: Eastern Plumas Hospital - Portola Campus (24 beds)

Additional Information Contacts

City of Portola . . . . (530) 832-4216
http://www.ci.portola.ca.us

PRATTVILLE (CDP). Covers a land area of 0.603 square miles and a water area of 0 square miles. Located at 40.21° N. Lat; 121.16° W. Long. Elevation is 4,534 feet.

Population: 33; Growth (since 2000): 17.9%; Density: 54.7 persons per square mile; Race: 100.0% White, 0.0% Black/African American, 0.0% Asian, 0.0% American Indian/Alaska Native, 0.0% Native Hawaiian/Other Pacific Islander, 0.0% Two or more races, 0.0% Hispanic of any race; Average household size: 2.36; Median age: 58.5; Age under 18: 24.2%; Age 65 and over: 36.4%; Males per 100 females: 135.7

Housing: Homeownership rate: 85.7%; Homeowner vacancy rate: 0.0%; Rental vacancy rate: 0.0%

QUINCY (CDP). County seat. Covers a land area of 4.239 square miles and a water area of 0 square miles. Located at 39.93° N. Lat; 120.95° W. Long. Elevation is 3,432 feet.

Population: 1,728; Growth (since 2000): -8.0%; Density: 407.6 persons per square mile; Race: 86.8% White, 2.1% Black/African American, 1.1% Asian, 1.7% American Indian/Alaska Native, 0.1% Native Hawaiian/Other Pacific Islander, 4.3% Two or more races, 7.6% Hispanic of any race; Average household size: 2.10; Median age: 45.5; Age under 18: 19.7%; Age 65 and over: 18.4%; Males per 100 females: 84.2

School District(s)

Plumas County Office of Education (KG-12)
2012-13 Enrollment: 32. . . . . (530) 283-6500
Plumas County Rop
2012-13 Enrollment: n/a . . . . (530) 283-6500
Plumas Unified (KG-12)
2012-13 Enrollment: 2,125 . . . . (530) 283-6500

Two-year College(s)

Feather River Community College District (Public)
Fall 2013 Enrollment: 1,782 . . . . (530) 283-0202
2013-14 Tuition: In-state $1,446; Out-of-state $6,996

Housing: Homeownership rate: 48.6%; Homeowner vacancy rate: 2.7%; Rental vacancy rate: 5.5%

Hospitals: Plumas District Hospital (26 beds)

Newspapers: Feather River Bulletin (weekly circulation 3500)

TAYLORSVILLE (CDP). Covers a land area of 3.248 square miles and a water area of 0 square miles. Located at 40.06° N. Lat; 120.84° W. Long. Elevation is 3,547 feet.

Population: 140; Growth (since 2000): -9.1%; Density: 43.1 persons per square mile; Race: 93.6% White, 0.0% Black/African American, 0.0% Asian, 2.1% American Indian/Alaska Native, 0.0% Native Hawaiian/Other Pacific Islander, 4.3% Two or more races, 0.7% Hispanic of any race; Average household size: 1.97; Median age: 50.3; Age under 18: 17.9%; Age 65 and over: 19.3%; Males per 100 females: 105.9

School District(s)

Plumas Unified (KG-12)
2012-13 Enrollment: 2,125 . . . . (530) 283-6500

Housing: Homeownership rate: 70.5%; Homeowner vacancy rate: 0.0%; Rental vacancy rate: 4.5%

TOBIN (CDP). Covers a land area of 5.029 square miles and a water area of 0 square miles. Located at 39.94° N. Lat; 121.30° W. Long. Elevation is 2,064 feet.

Population: 12; Growth (since 2000): 9.1%; Density: 2.4 persons per square mile; Race: 100.0% White, 0.0% Black/African American, 0.0% Asian, 0.0% American Indian/Alaska Native, 0.0% Native Hawaiian/Other Pacific Islander, 0.0% Two or more races, 0.0% Hispanic of any race; Average household size: 1.50; Median age: 52.8; Age under 18: 0.0%; Age 65 and over: 8.3%; Males per 100 females: 71.4

Housing: Homeownership rate: 25.0%; Homeowner vacancy rate: 0.0%; Rental vacancy rate: 12.5%

TWAIN (CDP). Covers a land area of 7.191 square miles and a water area of 0 square miles. Located at 40.04° N. Lat; 121.04° W. Long. Elevation is 2,858 feet.

Population: 82; Growth (since 2000): -5.7%; Density: 11.4 persons per square mile; Race: 91.5% White, 0.0% Black/African American, 0.0% Asian, 2.4% American Indian/Alaska Native, 0.0% Native Hawaiian/Other Pacific Islander, 3.7% Two or more races, 17.1% Hispanic of any race; Average household size: 2.05; Median age: 55.3; Age under 18: 12.2%; Age 65 and over: 20.7%; Males per 100 females: 82.2

Housing: Homeownership rate: 57.5%; Homeowner vacancy rate: 4.2%; Rental vacancy rate: 0.0%

VALLEY RANCH (CDP). Covers a land area of 1.137 square miles and a water area of 0 square miles. Located at 39.74° N. Lat; 120.56° W. Long. Elevation is 4,436 feet.

Population: 109; Growth (since 2000): 18.5%; Density: 95.8 persons per square mile; Race: 98.2% White, 0.0% Black/African American, 0.0% Asian, 0.0% American Indian/Alaska Native, 0.0% Native Hawaiian/Other Pacific Islander, 0.9% Two or more races, 1.8% Hispanic of any race; Average household size: 1.88; Median age: 63.8; Age under 18: 4.6%; Age 65 and over: 45.0%; Males per 100 females: 101.9

Housing: Homeownership rate: 93.1%; Homeowner vacancy rate: 0.0%; Rental vacancy rate: 33.3%

WARNER VALLEY (CDP). Covers a land area of 17.497 square miles and a water area of 0.029 square miles. Located at 40.40° N. Lat; 121.34° W. Long.

Population: 2; Growth (since 2000): n/a; Density: 0.1 persons per square mile; Race: 100.0% White, 0.0% Black/African American, 0.0% Asian, 0.0% American Indian/Alaska Native, 0.0% Native Hawaiian/Other Pacific Islander, 0.0% Two or more races, 0.0% Hispanic of any race; Average household size: 2.00; Median age: 30.5; Age under 18: 50.0%; Age 65 and over: 0.0%; Males per 100 females: All males

Housing: Homeownership rate: 100.0%; Homeowner vacancy rate: 0.0%; Rental vacancy rate: 0.0%

WHITEHAWK (CDP). Covers a land area of 2.530 square miles and a water area of 0 square miles. Located at 39.72° N. Lat; 120.55° W. Long. Elevation is 4,501 feet.

Population: 113; Growth (since 2000): 17.7%; Density: 44.7 persons per square mile; Race: 94.7% White, 0.0% Black/African American, 0.9% Asian, 0.0% American Indian/Alaska Native, 0.0% Native Hawaiian/Other Pacific Islander, 3.5% Two or more races, 1.8% Hispanic of any race; Average household size: 1.92; Median age: 65.3; Age under 18: 8.0%; Age 65 and over: 51.3%; Males per 100 females: 85.2

Housing: Homeownership rate: 88.1%; Homeowner vacancy rate: 15.9%; Rental vacancy rate: 30.0%

Riverside County

Located in southern California; bounded on the east by the Colorado River and the Arizona border; includes several mountain ranges, part of the Colorado Desert and Salton Sea, and parts of Cleveland and San Bernardino National Forests. Covers a land area of 7,206.480 square miles, a water area of 96.940 square miles, and is located in the Pacific Time Zone at 33.73° N. Lat., 116.00° W. Long. The county was founded in 1893. County seat is Riverside.

Riverside County is part of the Riverside-San Bernardino-Ontario, CA Metropolitan Statistical Area. The entire metro area includes: Riverside County, CA; San Bernardino County, CA

Weather Station: Blythe Elevation: 268 feet

	Jan	Feb	Mar	Apr	May	Jun	Jul	Aug	Sep	Oct	Nov	Dec
High	68	73	80	88	97	105	109	107	102	90	75	66
Low	40	44	49	55	63	70	77	77	69	57	45	39
Precip	0.5	0.6	0.3	0.1	0.1	tr	0.2	0.5	0.5	0.2	0.2	0.5
Snow	0.0	0.0	0.0	0.0	0.0	0.0	0.0	0.0	0.0	0.0	0.0	0.0

High and Low temperatures in degrees Fahrenheit; Precipitation and Snow in inches

Weather Station: Blythe Riverside Co Arpt Elevation: 390 feet

	Jan	Feb	Mar	Apr	May	Jun	Jul	Aug	Sep	Oct	Nov	Dec
High	68	72	80	87	96	105	109	107	101	90	76	67
Low	43	46	51	57	65	73	81	80	73	60	49	42
Precip	0.4	0.6	0.5	0.1	0.0	0.0	0.3	0.6	0.4	0.2	0.2	0.5
Snow	na	na	na	na	na	na	na	na	na	na	na	na

High and Low temperatures in degrees Fahrenheit; Precipitation and Snow in inches

Weather Station: Eagle Mountain Elevation: 973 feet

	Jan	Feb	Mar	Apr	May	Jun	Jul	Aug	Sep	Oct	Nov	Dec
High	65	69	75	83	91	100	104	103	97	86	73	64
Low	46	49	54	60	69	77	83	82	75	65	53	45
Precip	0.5	0.7	0.5	0.1	0.1	0.0	0.3	0.7	0.4	0.2	0.2	0.6
Snow	tr	0.0	0.0	0.0	0.0	0.0	0.0	0.0	0.0	0.0	0.0	0.0

High and Low temperatures in degrees Fahrenheit; Precipitation and Snow in inches

Weather Station: Elsinore Elevation: 1,285 feet

	Jan	Feb	Mar	Apr	May	Jun	Jul	Aug	Sep	Oct	Nov	Dec
High	66	68	72	78	84	91	98	99	93	83	72	66
Low	39	41	44	47	53	57	61	62	59	52	43	38
Precip	2.5	3.2	1.8	0.6	0.2	0.0	0.2	0.0	0.2	0.6	0.8	1.6
Snow	0.0	0.0	0.0	0.0	0.0	0.0	0.0	0.0	0.0	0.0	tr	0.0

High and Low temperatures in degrees Fahrenheit; Precipitation and Snow in inches

Weather Station: Hayfield Pumping Plant Elevation: 1,370 feet

	Jan	Feb	Mar	Apr	May	Jun	Jul	Aug	Sep	Oct	Nov	Dec
High	67	70	76	83	91	100	105	104	99	87	75	66
Low	40	42	46	52	60	67	75	74	67	55	45	38
Precip	0.8	0.8	0.6	0.1	0.1	tr	0.3	0.7	0.3	0.2	0.3	0.6
Snow	tr	0.0	0.0	0.0	0.0	0.0	0.0	0.0	0.0	0.0	0.0	0.0

High and Low temperatures in degrees Fahrenheit; Precipitation and Snow in inches

Weather Station: Idyllwild Fire Dept Elevation: 5,379 feet

	Jan	Feb	Mar	Apr	May	Jun	Jul	Aug	Sep	Oct	Nov	Dec
High	54	54	58	63	71	79	85	84	79	71	61	54
Low	29	29	31	34	40	46	53	54	48	40	33	29
Precip	5.3	5.6	4.1	1.8	0.5	0.2	0.7	0.8	0.9	1.2	2.4	3.2
Snow	8.9	7.8	7.3	3.1	0.5	tr	0.0	0.0	0.0	0.1	1.8	5.1

High and Low temperatures in degrees Fahrenheit; Precipitation and Snow in inches

Weather Station: Mecca Fire Station Elevation: -180 feet

	Jan	Feb	Mar	Apr	May	Jun	Jul	Aug	Sep	Oct	Nov	Dec
High	72	76	83	89	97	105	109	108	103	93	80	71
Low	40	43	49	55	62	68	75	76	69	57	46	38
Precip	0.5	0.6	0.4	0.1	0.0	tr	0.1	0.2	0.2	0.3	0.3	0.4
Snow	0.0	0.0	0.0	0.0	0.0	0.0	0.0	0.0	0.0	0.0	0.0	0.0

High and Low temperatures in degrees Fahrenheit; Precipitation and Snow in inches

Weather Station: Riverside Citrus Exp Stn Elevation: 985 feet

	Jan	Feb	Mar	Apr	May	Jun	Jul	Aug	Sep	Oct	Nov	Dec
High	67	68	71	76	80	87	94	95	91	83	74	67
Low	43	44	46	49	54	57	62	62	60	54	46	42
Precip	2.3	2.5	1.8	0.7	0.2	0.1	0.0	0.1	0.2	0.4	0.8	1.2
Snow	0.0	0.0	0.0	tr	0.0	0.0	0.0	0.0	0.0	0.0	0.0	tr

High and Low temperatures in degrees Fahrenheit; Precipitation and Snow in inches

Weather Station: Riverside Fire Sta 3 Elevation: 839 feet

	Jan	Feb	Mar	Apr	May	Jun	Jul	Aug	Sep	Oct	Nov	Dec
High	69	70	73	78	82	88	95	96	92	83	75	69
Low	43	44	47	50	55	59	64	64	61	54	46	41
Precip	2.0	2.7	1.7	0.7	0.2	0.1	0.0	0.1	0.1	0.5	0.8	1.1
Snow	0.0	0.0	0.0	0.0	0.0	0.0	0.0	0.0	0.0	0.0	0.0	0.0

High and Low temperatures in degrees Fahrenheit; Precipitation and Snow in inches

Weather Station: San Jacinto R S Elevation: 1,560 feet

	Jan	Feb	Mar	Apr	May	Jun	Jul	Aug	Sep	Oct	Nov	Dec
High	67	68	71	77	84	91	98	98	93	84	74	67
Low	38	40	43	46	51	55	61	62	57	50	42	36
Precip	2.7	2.9	2.0	0.8	0.4	0.1	0.2	0.2	0.3	0.6	0.9	1.6
Snow	0.0	0.0	0.0	0.0	0.0	0.0	0.0	0.0	0.0	0.0	tr	0.0

High and Low temperatures in degrees Fahrenheit; Precipitation and Snow in inches

Population: 2,189,641; Growth (since 2000): 41.7%; Density: 303.8 persons per square mile; Race: 61.0% White, 6.4% Black/African American, 6.0% Asian, 1.1% American Indian/Alaska Native, 0.3% Native Hawaiian/Other Pacific Islander, 4.8% two or more races, 45.5% Hispanic of any race; Average household size: 3.14; Median age: 33.7; Age under 18: 28.3%; Age 65 and over: 11.8%; Males per 100 females: 99.0; Marriage status: 33.0% never married, 51.6% now married, 2.4% separated, 5.1% widowed, 10.3% divorced; Foreign born: 21.9%; Speak English only: 60.1%; With disability: 10.7%; Veterans: 8.4%; Ancestry: 9.6% German, 6.9% Irish, 6.4% English, 3.7% Italian, 3.6% American

Religion: Six largest groups: 27.5% Catholicism, 5.8% Non-denominational Protestant, 2.4% Latter-day Saints, 1.9% Pentecostal, 1.9% Baptist, 0.9% Adventist

Economy: Unemployment rate: 8.4%; Leading industries: 14.5% retail trade; 12.2% health care and social assistance; 11.2% construction; Farms: 2,949 totaling 344,044 acres; Company size: 21 employs 1,000 or more persons, 42 employ 500 to 999 persons, 651 employs 100 to 499 persons, 33,706 employ less than 100 persons; Business ownership: 49,552 women-owned, 8,517 Black-owned, 39,177 Hispanic-owned, 13,068 Asian-owned

Employment: 12.1% management, business, and financial, 3.2% computer, engineering, and science, 9.1% education, legal, community service, arts, and media, 4.8% healthcare practitioners, 21.1% service, 25.7% sales and office, 11.2% natural resources, construction, and maintenance, 12.7% production, transportation, and material moving

Income: Per capita: $23,591; Median household: $56,529; Average household: $73,752; Households with income of $100,000 or more: 24.1%; Poverty rate: 16.2%

Educational Attainment: High school diploma or higher: 79.6%; Bachelor's degree or higher: 20.5%; Graduate/professional degree or higher: 7.3%

Housing: Homeownership rate: 67.4%; Median home value: $231,000; Median year structure built: 1987; Homeowner vacancy rate: 3.8%; Median gross rent: $1,168 per month; Rental vacancy rate: 9.5%

Vital Statistics: Birth rate: 135.4 per 10,000 population; Death rate: 67.0 per 10,000 population; Age-adjusted cancer mortality rate: 158.0 deaths per 100,000 population

Health Insurance: 79.8% have insurance; 56.9% have private insurance; 31.2% have public insurance; 20.2% do not have insurance; 11.0% of children under 18 do not have insurance

Health Care: Physicians: 11.7 per 10,000 population; Hospital beds: 14.8 per 10,000 population; Hospital admissions: 736.3 per 10,000 population

Air Quality Index: 10.1% good, 61.6% moderate, 24.4% unhealthy for sensitive individuals, 3.3% unhealthy, 0.5% very unhealthy (% of days)

Transportation: Commute: 90.4% car, 1.4% public transportation, 1.5% walk, 5.0% work from home; Median travel time to work: 32.0 minutes

Presidential Election: 48.8% Obama, 49.2% Romney (2012)

National and State Parks: California Citrus State Historic Park; Hidden Palms State Ecological Reserve; Joshua Tree National Park; Lake Perris State Recreation Area; Mount San Jacinto State Park; Mount San Jacinto State Wilderness; Santa Rosa Mountains State Wilderness

Additional Information Contacts

Riverside Government. . . . . (951) 955-1100
http://www.countyofriverside.us

Riverside County Communities

AGUANGA (CDP). Covers a land area of 13.599 square miles and a water area of 0 square miles. Located at 33.45° N. Lat; 116.86° W. Long. Elevation is 1,955 feet.

Population: 1,128; Growth (since 2000): n/a; Density: 82.9 persons per square mile; Race: 82.4% White, 1.0% Black/African American, 2.1% Asian, 1.8% American Indian/Alaska Native, 0.0% Native Hawaiian/Other Pacific Islander, 3.1% Two or more races, 24.3% Hispanic of any race; Average household size: 2.40; Median age: 53.4; Age under 18: 15.3%; Age 65 and over: 30.1%; Males per 100 females: 102.5

School District(s)

Hemet Unified (KG-12)
2012-13 Enrollment: 21,689 . . . . (951) 765-5100

Housing: Homeownership rate: 81.1%; Homeowner vacancy rate: 1.3%; Rental vacancy rate: 8.2%

ANZA (CDP). Covers a land area of 27.594 square miles and a water area of 0.082 square miles. Located at 33.57° N. Lat; 116.70° W. Long. Elevation is 3,921 feet.

Population: 3,014; Growth (since 2000): n/a; Density: 109.2 persons per square mile; Race: 80.0% White, 1.1% Black/African American, 1.2% Asian, 1.9% American Indian/Alaska Native, 0.1% Native Hawaiian/Other Pacific Islander, 4.2% Two or more races, 26.2% Hispanic of any race; Average household size: 2.60; Median age: 44.8; Age under 18: 22.5%; Age 65 and over: 16.5%; Males per 100 females: 102.8; Marriage status: 19.1% never married, 55.3% now married, 1.8% separated, 10.9% widowed, 14.7% divorced; Foreign born: 8.0%; Speak English only: 84.0%; With disability: 14.4%; Veterans: 12.3%; Ancestry: 16.2% French, 14.6% Irish, 12.0% German, 7.6% English, 6.7% Italian

Employment: 1.7% management, business, and financial, 0.0% computer, engineering, and science, 6.1% education, legal, community service, arts, and media, 2.9% healthcare practitioners, 23.1% service, 35.4% sales and office, 16.4% natural resources, construction, and maintenance, 14.3% production, transportation, and material moving

Income: Per capita: $20,315; Median household: $39,637; Average household: $50,517; Households with income of $100,000 or more: 11.6%; Poverty rate: 11.5%

Educational Attainment: High school diploma or higher: 82.7%; Bachelor's degree or higher: 3.0%; Graduate/professional degree or higher: 0.8%

School District(s)

Hemet Unified (KG-12)
2012-13 Enrollment: 21,689 . . . . (951) 765-5100

Housing: Homeownership rate: 71.6%; Median home value: $163,600; Median year structure built: 1983; Homeowner vacancy rate: 3.7%; Median gross rent: $893 per month; Rental vacancy rate: 8.8%

Health Insurance: 76.4% have insurance; 47.8% have private insurance; 50.2% have public insurance; 23.6% do not have insurance; 35.9% of children under 18 do not have insurance

Transportation: Commute: 94.6% car, 0.0% public transportation, 0.0% walk, 5.4% work from home; Median travel time to work: 40.6 minutes

BANNING (city). Covers a land area of 23.099 square miles and a water area of 0 square miles. Located at 33.95° N. Lat; 116.90° W. Long. Elevation is 2,349 feet.

History: Named for Phineas Banning, who operated a local stage line in the 1850s. Banning was laid out in 1883 by Phineas Banning, and grew as the center of a fruit-producing area.

Population: 29,603; Growth (since 2000): 25.6%; Density: 1,281.6 persons per square mile; Race: 64.7% White, 7.3% Black/African American, 5.2% Asian, 2.2% American Indian/Alaska Native, 0.1% Native Hawaiian/Other Pacific Islander, 4.9% Two or more races, 41.1% Hispanic of any race; Average household size: 2.61; Median age: 42.3; Age under 18: 22.9%; Age 65 and over: 25.9%; Males per 100 females: 93.4; Marriage status: 26.4% never married, 51.3% now married, 2.9% separated, 10.0% widowed, 12.4% divorced; Foreign born: 17.9%; Speak English only: 68.9%; With disability: 19.8%; Veterans: 12.8%; Ancestry: 9.8% German, 8.2% Irish, 6.7% English, 4.3% American, 3.9% Italian

Employment: 7.1% management, business, and financial, 1.1% computer, engineering, and science, 7.9% education, legal, community service, arts, and media, 4.1% healthcare practitioners, 26.6% service, 29.3% sales and office, 8.8% natural resources, construction, and maintenance, 15.1% production, transportation, and material moving

Income: Per capita: $20,650; Median household: $38,825; Average household: $48,566; Households with income of $100,000 or more: 8.8%; Poverty rate: 18.0%

Educational Attainment: High school diploma or higher: 80.3%; Bachelor's degree or higher: 15.8%; Graduate/professional degree or higher: 6.0%

School District(s)

Banning Unified (KG-12)
2012-13 Enrollment: 4,524 . . . . (951) 922-0200

Housing: Homeownership rate: 68.4%; Median home value: $159,300; Median year structure built: 1983; Homeowner vacancy rate: 4.1%; Median gross rent: $900 per month; Rental vacancy rate: 10.9%

Health Insurance: 80.8% have insurance; 48.1% have private insurance; 51.5% have public insurance; 19.2% do not have insurance; 18.9% of children under 18 do not have insurance

Hospitals: San Gorgonio Memorial Hospital (77 beds)

Safety: Violent crime rate: 42.3 per 10,000 population; Property crime rate: 264.9 per 10,000 population

Newspapers: Record Gazette (weekly circulation 2600)

Transportation: Commute: 92.3% car, 1.3% public transportation, 1.0% walk, 4.2% work from home; Median travel time to work: 23.9 minutes

Additional Information Contacts

City of Banning . . . . (951) 922-3105
http://www.ci.banning.ca.us

BEAUMONT (city). Covers a land area of 30.912 square miles and a water area of 0.014 square miles. Located at 33.86° N. Lat; 116.95° W. Long. Elevation is 2,612 feet.

History: Named for the French translation of "beautiful mountain". Beaumont, called San Gorgonio from 1884 to 1887, was settled after I.W. Smith followed some straying cattle to the summit of the pass here. The town grew when a developer promoted the region's fruit-growing potential.

Population: 36,877; Growth (since 2000): 223.9%; Density: 1,193.0 persons per square mile; Race: 62.8% White, 6.2% Black/African American, 7.7% Asian, 1.5% American Indian/Alaska Native, 0.2% Native Hawaiian/Other Pacific Islander, 5.2% Two or more races, 40.3% Hispanic of any race; Average household size: 3.08; Median age: 32.5; Age under 18: 30.2%; Age 65 and over: 10.5%; Males per 100 females: 95.2; Marriage status: 27.1% never married, 58.4% now married, 1.4% separated, 4.8% widowed, 9.7% divorced; Foreign born: 16.9%; Speak English only: 69.1%; With disability: 7.9%; Veterans: 8.0%; Ancestry: 10.7% German, 7.7% Irish, 5.5% English, 4.2% Italian, 3.5% American

Employment: 15.5% management, business, and financial, 2.7% computer, engineering, and science, 10.5% education, legal, community service, arts, and media, 10.7% healthcare practitioners, 18.8% service, 23.3% sales and office, 9.5% natural resources, construction, and maintenance, 9.0% production, transportation, and material moving

Income: Per capita: $26,404; Median household: $69,302; Average household: $79,975; Households with income of $100,000 or more: 32.1%; Poverty rate: 11.8%

Educational Attainment: High school diploma or higher: 86.0%; Bachelor's degree or higher: 25.2%; Graduate/professional degree or higher: 11.1%

School District(s)

Beaumont Unified (KG-12)
2012-13 Enrollment: 8,834 . . . . (951) 845-1631

Vocational/Technical School(s)

Beaumont Adult School (Public)
Fall 2013 Enrollment: 118 . . . . (951) 845-6012
2013-14 Tuition: $21,020

Housing: Homeownership rate: 75.0%; Median home value: $211,200; Median year structure built: 2002; Homeowner vacancy rate: 4.3%; Median gross rent: $1,076 per month; Rental vacancy rate: 5.9%

Health Insurance: 87.5% have insurance; 70.5% have private insurance; 24.8% have public insurance; 12.5% do not have insurance; 5.1% of children under 18 do not have insurance

Safety: Violent crime rate: 21.1 per 10,000 population; Property crime rate: 322.8 per 10,000 population

Transportation: Commute: 93.2% car, 0.4% public transportation, 1.3% walk, 3.9% work from home; Median travel time to work: 32.0 minutes

Additional Information Contacts

City of Beaumont. . . . . (951) 769-8520
http://www.ci.beaumont.ca.us

BERMUDA DUNES (CDP). Covers a land area of 2.946 square miles and a water area of 0 square miles. Located at 33.74° N. Lat; 116.29° W. Long. Elevation is 95 feet.

Population: 7,282; Growth (since 2000): 16.9%; Density: 2,471.7 persons per square mile; Race: 74.6% White, 2.5% Black/African American, 3.3% Asian, 0.9% American Indian/Alaska Native, 0.2% Native Hawaiian/Other Pacific Islander, 3.1% Two or more races, 32.6% Hispanic of any race; Average household size: 2.47; Median age: 39.1; Age under 18: 22.5%; Age 65 and over: 15.1%; Males per 100 females: 98.1; Marriage status: 29.0% never married, 55.5% now married, 3.2% separated, 2.7% widowed, 12.9% divorced; Foreign born: 14.7%; Speak English only: 75.5%; With disability: 8.3%; Veterans: 9.2%; Ancestry: 17.0% German, 12.4% Irish, 7.3% English, 7.2% Dutch, 4.7% Italian

Employment: 17.9% management, business, and financial, 1.4% computer, engineering, and science, 15.7% education, legal, community service, arts, and media, 2.5% healthcare practitioners, 17.1% service, 34.6% sales and office, 5.7% natural resources, construction, and maintenance, 5.1% production, transportation, and material moving
Income: Per capita: $35,317; Median household: $61,519; Average household: $91,237; Households with income of $100,000 or more: 27.5%; Poverty rate: 9.4%
Educational Attainment: High school diploma or higher: 91.1%; Bachelor's degree or higher: 33.2%; Graduate/professional degree or higher: 12.3%

School District(s)

Desert Sands Unified (KG-12)
2012-13 Enrollment: 29,159 . . . . (760) 777-4200

Housing: Homeownership rate: 59.2%; Median home value: $304,500; Median year structure built: 1987; Homeowner vacancy rate: 4.4%; Median gross rent: $1,124 per month; Rental vacancy rate: 19.8%
Health Insurance: 80.6% have insurance; 64.6% have private insurance; 23.3% have public insurance; 19.4% do not have insurance; 6.0% of children under 18 do not have insurance
Transportation: Commute: 93.7% car, 0.9% public transportation, 0.3% walk, 4.4% work from home; Median travel time to work: 21.3 minutes

BLYTHE (city). Covers a land area of 26.189 square miles and a water area of 0.783 square miles. Located at 33.65° N. Lat; 114.62° W. Long. Elevation is 272 feet.
History: Named for Thomas H. Blythe, landowner. Blythe was platted in 1910 by a syndicate who purchased the land from Englishman Blythe. The building of Boulder Dam on the Colorado River allowed for the controlled irrigation of the surrounding farmlands.
Population: 20,817; Growth (since 2000): 71.3%; Density: 794.9 persons per square mile; Race: 59.5% White, 15.0% Black/African American, 1.5% Asian, 1.2% American Indian/Alaska Native, 0.2% Native Hawaiian/Other Pacific Islander, 3.2% Two or more races, 53.2% Hispanic of any race; Average household size: 2.87; Median age: 38.0; Age under 18: 20.0%; Age 65 and over: 8.6%; Males per 100 females: 218.1; Marriage status: 40.9% never married, 41.3% now married, 3.1% separated, 3.5% widowed, 14.3% divorced; Foreign born: 17.4%; Speak English only: 55.1%; With disability: 13.8%; Veterans: 7.4%; Ancestry: 6.1% German, 5.0% Irish, 4.2% English, 2.3% American, 1.8% Italian
Employment: 12.8% management, business, and financial, 0.4% computer, engineering, and science, 8.3% education, legal, community service, arts, and media, 2.4% healthcare practitioners, 32.6% service, 20.6% sales and office, 9.6% natural resources, construction, and maintenance, 13.3% production, transportation, and material moving
Income: Per capita: $16,329; Median household: $46,856; Average household: $62,169; Households with income of $100,000 or more: 21.1%; Poverty rate: 19.2%
Educational Attainment: High school diploma or higher: 68.0%; Bachelor's degree or higher: 8.6%; Graduate/professional degree or higher: 2.7%

School District(s)

Palo Verde Unified (KG-12)
2012-13 Enrollment: 3,448 . . . . (760) 922-4164

Two-year College(s)

Palo Verde College (Public)
Fall 2013 Enrollment: 3,253 . . . . (760) 921-5500
2013-14 Tuition: In-state $1,288; Out-of-state $1,288

Housing: Homeownership rate: 52.3%; Median home value: $131,200; Median year structure built: 1975; Homeowner vacancy rate: 4.0%; Median gross rent: $753 per month; Rental vacancy rate: 10.3%
Health Insurance: 83.6% have insurance; 55.7% have private insurance; 34.3% have public insurance; 16.4% do not have insurance; 8.6% of children under 18 do not have insurance
Hospitals: Palo Verde Hospital (51 beds)
Safety: Violent crime rate: 31.5 per 10,000 population; Property crime rate: 335.9 per 10,000 population
Newspapers: Palo Verde Valley Times (weekly circulation 4000)
Transportation: Commute: 90.8% car, 1.0% public transportation, 2.5% walk, 4.0% work from home; Median travel time to work: 14.8 minutes
Airports: Blythe (general aviation)
Additional Information Contacts
City of Blythe . . . . (760) 922-6161
http://www.cityofblythe.ca.gov

CABAZON (CDP). Covers a land area of 4.868 square miles and a water area of 0.025 square miles. Located at 33.91° N. Lat; 116.78° W. Long. Elevation is 1,834 feet.
History: Cabazon grew up around the Southern Pacific Railway roundhouse.
Population: 2,535; Growth (since 2000): 13.7%; Density: 520.7 persons per square mile; Race: 69.1% White, 5.3% Black/African American, 1.5% Asian, 3.6% American Indian/Alaska Native, 0.6% Native Hawaiian/Other Pacific Islander, 5.9% Two or more races, 44.8% Hispanic of any race; Average household size: 3.19; Median age: 31.4; Age under 18: 31.5%; Age 65 and over: 8.3%; Males per 100 females: 101.0; Marriage status: 37.1% never married, 37.0% now married, 0.6% separated, 11.4% widowed, 14.5% divorced; Foreign born: 11.2%; Speak English only: 63.1%; With disability: 10.7%; Veterans: 4.3%; Ancestry: 9.9% Polish, 7.3% German, 3.0% Irish, 3.0% American, 2.8% Albanian
Employment: 2.4% management, business, and financial, 0.0% computer, engineering, and science, 16.2% education, legal, community service, arts, and media, 0.0% healthcare practitioners, 23.2% service, 24.1% sales and office, 27.6% natural resources, construction, and maintenance, 6.6% production, transportation, and material moving
Income: Per capita: $10,792; Median household: $33,333; Average household: $33,528; Households with income of $100,000 or more: n/a; Poverty rate: 22.1%
Educational Attainment: High school diploma or higher: 68.2%; Bachelor's degree or higher: 6.2%; Graduate/professional degree or higher: n/a

School District(s)

Banning Unified (KG-12)
2012-13 Enrollment: 4,524 . . . . (951) 922-0200

Housing: Homeownership rate: 58.0%; Median home value: $62,800; Median year structure built: 1973; Homeowner vacancy rate: 2.5%; Median gross rent: $1,079 per month; Rental vacancy rate: 5.6%
Health Insurance: 73.4% have insurance; 36.6% have private insurance; 41.9% have public insurance; 26.6% do not have insurance; 16.6% of children under 18 do not have insurance
Transportation: Commute: 88.3% car, 0.0% public transportation, 0.0% walk, 11.7% work from home; Median travel time to work: 21.5 minutes; Amtrak: Bus service available.

CALIMESA (city). Covers a land area of 14.847 square miles and a water area of 0 square miles. Located at 33.99° N. Lat; 117.05° W. Long. Elevation is 2,392 feet.
Population: 7,879; Growth (since 2000): 10.4%; Density: 530.7 persons per square mile; Race: 86.0% White, 1.1% Black/African American, 1.3% Asian, 1.3% American Indian/Alaska Native, 0.1% Native Hawaiian/Other Pacific Islander, 3.0% Two or more races, 22.4% Hispanic of any race; Average household size: 2.36; Median age: 48.8; Age under 18: 17.9%; Age 65 and over: 25.9%; Males per 100 females: 92.4; Marriage status: 19.8% never married, 58.6% now married, 1.7% separated, 8.3% widowed, 13.4% divorced; Foreign born: 10.5%; Speak English only: 82.9%; With disability: 20.3%; Veterans: 14.5%; Ancestry: 24.4% German, 13.7% English, 10.1% Irish, 5.0% American, 4.9% Italian
Employment: 15.6% management, business, and financial, 2.8% computer, engineering, and science, 8.9% education, legal, community service, arts, and media, 5.8% healthcare practitioners, 16.0% service, 29.8% sales and office, 9.5% natural resources, construction, and maintenance, 11.6% production, transportation, and material moving
Income: Per capita: $24,243; Median household: $44,034; Average household: $57,486; Households with income of $100,000 or more: 13.4%; Poverty rate: 13.4%
Educational Attainment: High school diploma or higher: 89.5%; Bachelor's degree or higher: 14.7%; Graduate/professional degree or higher: 4.1%

School District(s)

Yucaipa-Calimesa Joint Unified (KG-12)
2012-13 Enrollment: 9,663 . . . . (909) 797-0174

Housing: Homeownership rate: 80.7%; Median home value: $161,800; Median year structure built: 1976; Homeowner vacancy rate: 5.9%; Median gross rent: $1,141 per month; Rental vacancy rate: 10.3%
Health Insurance: 85.1% have insurance; 61.5% have private insurance; 39.9% have public insurance; 14.9% do not have insurance; 15.2% of children under 18 do not have insurance
Safety: Violent crime rate: 17.2 per 10,000 population; Property crime rate: 203.3 per 10,000 population

Transportation: Commute: 89.4% car, 0.0% public transportation, 0.0% walk, 8.1% work from home; Median travel time to work: 31.7 minutes
Additional Information Contacts
City of Calimesa . . . . (909) 795-9801
http://www.cityofcalimesa.net

CANYON LAKE (city). Covers a land area of 3.928 square miles and a water area of 0.743 square miles. Located at 33.69° N. Lat; 117.26° W. Long. Elevation is 1,384 feet.
Population: 10,561; Growth (since 2000): 6.1%; Density: 2,688.8 persons per square mile; Race: 89.9% White, 1.2% Black/African American, 1.8% Asian, 0.6% American Indian/Alaska Native, 0.3% Native Hawaiian/Other Pacific Islander, 3.2% Two or more races, 12.3% Hispanic of any race; Average household size: 2.68; Median age: 44.0; Age under 18: 21.7%; Age 65 and over: 17.1%; Males per 100 females: 99.5; Marriage status: 19.8% never married, 65.4% now married, 2.1% separated, 7.0% widowed, 7.8% divorced; Foreign born: 4.7%; Speak English only: 93.8%; With disability: 8.0%; Veterans: 11.3%; Ancestry: 22.3% German, 17.0% Irish, 10.6% American, 9.5% English, 6.4% Italian
Employment: 15.4% management, business, and financial, 1.4% computer, engineering, and science, 9.2% education, legal, community service, arts, and media, 7.5% healthcare practitioners, 16.3% service, 29.0% sales and office, 13.3% natural resources, construction, and maintenance, 7.8% production, transportation, and material moving
Income: Per capita: $34,333; Median household: $72,956; Average household: $91,193; Households with income of $100,000 or more: 33.4%; Poverty rate: 6.2%
Educational Attainment: High school diploma or higher: 95.6%; Bachelor's degree or higher: 23.6%; Graduate/professional degree or higher: 6.6%
Housing: Homeownership rate: 82.5%; Median home value: $304,900; Median year structure built: 1984; Homeowner vacancy rate: 2.9%; Median gross rent: $1,880 per month; Rental vacancy rate: 6.1%
Health Insurance: 88.8% have insurance; 77.2% have private insurance; 22.7% have public insurance; 11.2% do not have insurance; 7.5% of children under 18 do not have insurance
Safety: Violent crime rate: 2.7 per 10,000 population; Property crime rate: 143.5 per 10,000 population
Newspapers: The Friday Flyer (weekly circulation 6000)
Transportation: Commute: 91.0% car, 1.2% public transportation, 0.0% walk, 7.6% work from home; Median travel time to work: 43.4 minutes
Additional Information Contacts
City of Canyon Lake . . . . (951) 244-2955
http://www.cityofcanyonlake.com

CATHEDRAL CITY (city). Covers a land area of 21.499 square miles and a water area of 0.257 square miles. Located at 33.84° N. Lat; 116.46° W. Long. Elevation is 328 feet.
History: This city was incorporated in 1981 and is located in the Coachella Valley of Riverside County. This resort community shares a border with Palm Springs.
Population: 51,200; Growth (since 2000): 20.1%; Density: 2,381.5 persons per square mile; Race: 63.5% White, 2.6% Black/African American, 5.0% Asian, 1.1% American Indian/Alaska Native, 0.1% Native Hawaiian/Other Pacific Islander, 4.2% Two or more races, 58.8% Hispanic of any race; Average household size: 2.99; Median age: 36.0; Age under 18: 27.1%; Age 65 and over: 14.4%; Males per 100 females: 105.9; Marriage status: 36.1% never married, 46.4% now married, 2.3% separated, 4.9% widowed, 12.6% divorced; Foreign born: 34.3%; Speak English only: 44.9%; With disability: 12.3%; Veterans: 6.5%; Ancestry: 6.5% German, 4.6% Irish, 4.4% English, 3.9% American, 2.6% Italian
Employment: 8.0% management, business, and financial, 2.1% computer, engineering, and science, 6.1% education, legal, community service, arts, and media, 3.2% healthcare practitioners, 38.8% service, 22.7% sales and office, 11.4% natural resources, construction, and maintenance, 7.6% production, transportation, and material moving
Income: Per capita: $19,815; Median household: $44,406; Average household: $59,285; Households with income of $100,000 or more: 15.2%; Poverty rate: 20.5%
Educational Attainment: High school diploma or higher: 73.4%; Bachelor's degree or higher: 15.0%; Graduate/professional degree or higher: 5.8%

School District(s)

Palm Springs Unified (KG-12)
2012-13 Enrollment: 23,581 . . . . (760) 416-6000

Two-year College(s)

Mayfield College (Private, For-profit)
Fall 2013 Enrollment: 329 . . . . (760) 328-5554
2013-14 Tuition: In-state $12,750; Out-of-state $12,750
Housing: Homeownership rate: 63.1%; Median home value: $179,500; Median year structure built: 1987; Homeowner vacancy rate: 4.2%; Median gross rent: $1,124 per month; Rental vacancy rate: 11.0%
Health Insurance: 71.0% have insurance; 44.2% have private insurance; 35.5% have public insurance; 29.0% do not have insurance; 14.1% of children under 18 do not have insurance
Safety: Violent crime rate: 28.1 per 10,000 population; Property crime rate: 210.7 per 10,000 population
Transportation: Commute: 88.8% car, 2.3% public transportation, 1.1% walk, 6.1% work from home; Median travel time to work: 20.4 minutes
Additional Information Contacts
City of Cathedral . . . . (760) 770-0340
http://www.cathedralcity.gov

CHERRY VALLEY (CDP). Covers a land area of 8.087 square miles and a water area of 0 square miles. Located at 33.98° N. Lat; 116.97° W. Long. Elevation is 2,821 feet.
History: Edward Dean Museum of Decorative Arts is here.
Population: 6,362; Growth (since 2000): 8.0%; Density: 786.7 persons per square mile; Race: 85.7% White, 1.0% Black/African American, 1.4% Asian, 1.6% American Indian/Alaska Native, 0.1% Native Hawaiian/Other Pacific Islander, 3.2% Two or more races, 21.2% Hispanic of any race; Average household size: 2.37; Median age: 51.9; Age under 18: 16.6%; Age 65 and over: 29.1%; Males per 100 females: 90.7; Marriage status: 20.2% never married, 56.8% now married, 1.5% separated, 10.5% widowed, 12.5% divorced; Foreign born: 10.7%; Speak English only: 83.5%; With disability: 17.7%; Veterans: 13.1%; Ancestry: 14.8% German, 12.4% Irish, 9.8% English, 6.9% American, 5.7% Scottish
Employment: 13.5% management, business, and financial, 1.0% computer, engineering, and science, 11.1% education, legal, community service, arts, and media, 7.7% healthcare practitioners, 13.9% service, 26.6% sales and office, 12.6% natural resources, construction, and maintenance, 13.4% production, transportation, and material moving
Income: Per capita: $29,852; Median household: $54,929; Average household: $69,226; Households with income of $100,000 or more: 19.3%; Poverty rate: 7.2%
Educational Attainment: High school diploma or higher: 88.1%; Bachelor's degree or higher: 18.7%; Graduate/professional degree or higher: 8.9%
Housing: Homeownership rate: 80.3%; Median home value: $170,500; Median year structure built: 1976; Homeowner vacancy rate: 4.4%; Median gross rent: $976 per month; Rental vacancy rate: 5.5%
Health Insurance: 82.6% have insurance; 58.4% have private insurance; 42.7% have public insurance; 17.4% do not have insurance; 24.0% of children under 18 do not have insurance
Transportation: Commute: 92.5% car, 1.1% public transportation, 1.3% walk, 3.7% work from home; Median travel time to work: 30.7 minutes

COACHELLA (city). Covers a land area of 28.950 square miles and a water area of 0 square miles. Located at 33.69° N. Lat; 116.15° W. Long. Elevation is -69 feet.
History: Named for the Spanish translation of "shell," for the many local shells. Coachella developed in the heart of the Coachella Valley as a center for an agricultural area producing dates, grapefruit, cotton, and alfalfa.
Population: 40,704; Growth (since 2000): 79.1%; Density: 1,406.0 persons per square mile; Race: 48.1% White, 0.8% Black/African American, 0.7% Asian, 0.7% American Indian/Alaska Native, 0.1% Native Hawaiian/Other Pacific Islander, 2.6% Two or more races, 96.4% Hispanic of any race; Average household size: 4.52; Median age: 24.5; Age under 18: 38.8%; Age 65 and over: 4.5%; Males per 100 females: 99.3; Marriage status: 40.0% never married, 51.0% now married, 3.1% separated, 3.2% widowed, 5.8% divorced; Foreign born: 41.6%; Speak English only: 10.7%; With disability: 9.0%; Veterans: 1.2%; Ancestry: 0.4% American, 0.3% Irish, 0.2% German, 0.1% Norwegian, 0.1% Swedish
Employment: 4.0% management, business, and financial, 1.2% computer, engineering, and science, 5.1% education, legal, community service, arts, and media, 1.6% healthcare practitioners, 34.8% service, 19.5% sales and office, 23.1% natural resources, construction, and maintenance, 10.9% production, transportation, and material moving

Income: Per capita: $11,874; Median household: $40,965; Average household: $49,085; Households with income of $100,000 or more: 8.5%; Poverty rate: 30.9%
Educational Attainment: High school diploma or higher: 49.6%; Bachelor's degree or higher: 4.7%; Graduate/professional degree or higher: 0.9%

School District(s)

Coachella Valley Unified (KG-12)
2012-13 Enrollment: 18,720 . . . . (760) 399-5137

Vocational/Technical School(s)

CET-Coachella (Private, Not-for-profit)
Fall 2013 Enrollment: 187 . . . . (408) 287-7924
2013-14 Tuition: $10,165

Housing: Homeownership rate: 62.1%; Median home value: $137,600; Median year structure built: 1999; Homeowner vacancy rate: 6.4%; Median gross rent: $878 per month; Rental vacancy rate: 5.4%
Health Insurance: 64.9% have insurance; 30.3% have private insurance; 36.4% have public insurance; 35.1% do not have insurance; 16.7% of children under 18 do not have insurance
Safety: Violent crime rate: 27.2 per 10,000 population; Property crime rate: 316.6 per 10,000 population
Transportation: Commute: 93.8% car, 1.2% public transportation, 1.1% walk, 3.0% work from home; Median travel time to work: 21.5 minutes
Additional Information Contacts
City of Coachella . . . . (760) 398-3502
http://www.coachella.org

CORONA (city). Covers a land area of 38.825 square miles and a water area of 0.105 square miles. Located at 33.86° N. Lat; 117.56° W. Long. Elevation is 679 feet.
History: The city developed as a primary citrus-fruit producer and shipping center. The name Corona (circle) was derived from the three-mile circular drive around the city that was once used for car racing. Incorporated 1896.
Population: 152,374; Growth (since 2000): 21.9%; Density: 3,924.6 persons per square mile; Race: 59.7% White, 5.9% Black/African American, 9.9% Asian, 0.8% American Indian/Alaska Native, 0.4% Native Hawaiian/Other Pacific Islander, 5.1% Two or more races, 43.6% Hispanic of any race; Average household size: 3.38; Median age: 32.5; Age under 18: 30.0%; Age 65 and over: 7.3%; Males per 100 females: 97.0; Marriage status: 33.5% never married, 54.0% now married, 2.3% separated, 4.1% widowed, 8.5% divorced; Foreign born: 25.1%; Speak English only: 58.8%; With disability: 7.3%; Veterans: 6.3%; Ancestry: 8.7% German, 6.7% American, 6.1% Irish, 5.5% English, 3.3% Italian
Employment: 16.6% management, business, and financial, 5.0% computer, engineering, and science, 9.2% education, legal, community service, arts, and media, 4.9% healthcare practitioners, 14.7% service, 27.2% sales and office, 9.7% natural resources, construction, and maintenance, 13.0% production, transportation, and material moving
Income: Per capita: $26,832; Median household: $77,123; Average household: $90,460; Households with income of $100,000 or more: 36.0%; Poverty rate: 10.8%
Educational Attainment: High school diploma or higher: 83.3%; Bachelor's degree or higher: 25.8%; Graduate/professional degree or higher: 8.1%

School District(s)

Alvord Unified (KG-12)
2012-13 Enrollment: 19,634 . . . . (951) 509-5070
Corona-Norco Unified (KG-12)
2012-13 Enrollment: 53,437 . . . . (951) 736-5000
Lake Elsinore Unified (KG-12)
2012-13 Enrollment: 22,137 . . . . (951) 253-7000

Four-year College(s)

ITT Technical Institute-Corona (Private, For-profit)
Fall 2013 Enrollment: 479 . . . . (951) 277-5400
2013-14 Tuition: In-state $18,048; Out-of-state $18,048

Vocational/Technical School(s)

Salon Success Academy-Corona (Private, For-profit)
Fall 2013 Enrollment: 129 . . . . (909) 982-4200
2013-14 Tuition: $18,400

Housing: Homeownership rate: 67.2%; Median home value: $324,600; Median year structure built: 1989; Homeowner vacancy rate: 2.3%; Median gross rent: $1,329 per month; Rental vacancy rate: 5.3%
Health Insurance: 83.3% have insurance; 67.0% have private insurance; 21.5% have public insurance; 16.7% do not have insurance; 7.5% of children under 18 do not have insurance
Hospitals: Corona Regional Medical Center (228 beds)
Safety: Violent crime rate: 10.1 per 10,000 population; Property crime rate: 214.7 per 10,000 population
Newspapers: Sentinel Weekly News (weekly circulation 11000)
Transportation: Commute: 90.8% car, 1.8% public transportation, 1.2% walk, 4.8% work from home; Median travel time to work: 35.2 minutes
Additional Information Contacts
City of Corona . . . . (951) 279-3710
http://www.discovercorona.com

CORONITA (CDP). Covers a land area of 0.695 square miles and a water area of 0 square miles. Located at 33.88° N. Lat; 117.61° W. Long.
Population: 2,608; Growth (since 2000): n/a; Density: 3,753.8 persons per square mile; Race: 63.2% White, 1.5% Black/African American, 4.1% Asian, 1.2% American Indian/Alaska Native, 0.5% Native Hawaiian/Other Pacific Islander, 3.1% Two or more races, 51.7% Hispanic of any race; Average household size: 3.68; Median age: 33.8; Age under 18: 28.3%; Age 65 and over: 11.0%; Males per 100 females: 101.4; Marriage status: 37.9% never married, 45.2% now married, 2.1% separated, 7.6% widowed, 9.4% divorced; Foreign born: 23.4%; Speak English only: 52.8%; With disability: 10.6%; Veterans: 4.2%; Ancestry: 7.4% English, 7.0% Irish, 4.6% American, 4.5% German, 3.7% French
Employment: 10.7% management, business, and financial, 3.0% computer, engineering, and science, 9.4% education, legal, community service, arts, and media, 5.1% healthcare practitioners, 14.4% service, 27.8% sales and office, 13.1% natural resources, construction, and maintenance, 16.5% production, transportation, and material moving
Income: Per capita: $26,445; Median household: $76,713; Average household: $89,413; Households with income of $100,000 or more: 33.1%; Poverty rate: 12.8%
Educational Attainment: High school diploma or higher: 77.9%; Bachelor's degree or higher: 14.6%; Graduate/professional degree or higher: 5.1%
Housing: Homeownership rate: 83.8%; Median home value: $293,400; Median year structure built: 1965; Homeowner vacancy rate: 1.7%; Median gross rent: $2,000+ per month; Rental vacancy rate: 7.3%
Health Insurance: 85.0% have insurance; 67.7% have private insurance; 24.1% have public insurance; 15.0% do not have insurance; 3.9% of children under 18 do not have insurance
Transportation: Commute: 92.6% car, 0.0% public transportation, 0.0% walk, 7.4% work from home; Median travel time to work: 36.1 minutes

DESERT CENTER (CDP). Covers a land area of 30.425 square miles and a water area of 0 square miles. Located at 33.74° N. Lat; 115.37° W. Long. Elevation is 906 feet.
Population: 204; Growth (since 2000): n/a; Density: 6.7 persons per square mile; Race: 80.4% White, 0.5% Black/African American, 1.0% Asian, 1.5% American Indian/Alaska Native, 0.0% Native Hawaiian/Other Pacific Islander, 4.4% Two or more races, 18.6% Hispanic of any race; Average household size: 2.39; Median age: 47.5; Age under 18: 19.6%; Age 65 and over: 22.1%; Males per 100 females: 106.1

School District(s)

Desert Center Unified (KG-08)
2012-13 Enrollment: 15. . . . . (760) 392-4217

Housing: Homeownership rate: 71.7%; Homeowner vacancy rate: 8.8%; Rental vacancy rate: 33.3%

DESERT EDGE (CDP). Covers a land area of 2.268 square miles and a water area of 0 square miles. Located at 33.92° N. Lat; 116.44° W. Long. Elevation is 981 feet.
Population: 3,822; Growth (since 2000): n/a; Density: 1,685.5 persons per square mile; Race: 79.8% White, 0.4% Black/African American, 0.7% Asian, 0.9% American Indian/Alaska Native, 0.0% Native Hawaiian/Other Pacific Islander, 1.8% Two or more races, 31.9% Hispanic of any race; Average household size: 1.94; Median age: 63.8; Age under 18: 13.4%; Age 65 and over: 47.7%; Males per 100 females: 92.0; Marriage status: 16.9% never married, 55.2% now married, 4.5% separated, 12.3% widowed, 15.6% divorced; Foreign born: 23.5%; Speak English only: 72.8%; With disability: 26.5%; Veterans: 19.9%; Ancestry: 17.2% German, 12.8% English, 10.3% Irish, 7.1% American, 5.3% Scotch-Irish
Employment: 2.1% management, business, and financial, 0.0% computer, engineering, and science, 2.1% education, legal, community service, arts, and media, 0.0% healthcare practitioners, 33.9% service, 22.1% sales and office, 30.9% natural resources, construction, and maintenance, 8.8% production, transportation, and material moving

Income: Per capita: $19,928; Median household: $35,089; Average household: $37,799; Households with income of $100,000 or more: 5.7%; Poverty rate: 22.4%

Educational Attainment: High school diploma or higher: 80.0%; Bachelor's degree or higher: 13.2%; Graduate/professional degree or higher: 7.2%

Housing: Homeownership rate: 86.7%; Median home value: $35,500; Median year structure built: 1981; Homeowner vacancy rate: 5.5%; Median gross rent: $638 per month; Rental vacancy rate: 21.3%

Health Insurance: 79.5% have insurance; 46.9% have private insurance; 62.0% have public insurance; 20.5% do not have insurance; 23.6% of children under 18 do not have insurance

Transportation: Commute: 94.6% car, 0.0% public transportation, 2.7% walk, 0.0% work from home; Median travel time to work: 32.5 minutes

DESERT HOT SPRINGS (city). Covers a land area of 23.615 square miles and a water area of 0.027 square miles. Located at 33.97° N. Lat; 116.55° W. Long. Elevation is 1,076 feet.

History: Named for its desert location. Colorado River Aqueduct passes to North. Joshua Tree National Monument to East.

Population: 25,938; Growth (since 2000): 56.4%; Density: 1,098.4 persons per square mile; Race: 58.0% White, 8.2% Black/African American, 2.6% Asian, 1.4% American Indian/Alaska Native, 0.3% Native Hawaiian/Other Pacific Islander, 5.0% Two or more races, 52.6% Hispanic of any race; Average household size: 2.98; Median age: 31.0; Age under 18: 31.1%; Age 65 and over: 9.6%; Males per 100 females: 100.3; Marriage status: 33.8% never married, 46.1% now married, 3.0% separated, 6.1% widowed, 14.0% divorced; Foreign born: 24.8%; Speak English only: 51.3%; With disability: 12.6%; Veterans: 7.0%; Ancestry: 8.1% German, 6.7% Irish, 5.1% English, 3.6% European, 2.8% Italian

Employment: 8.3% management, business, and financial, 1.5% computer, engineering, and science, 7.0% education, legal, community service, arts, and media, 2.9% healthcare practitioners, 38.0% service, 21.1% sales and office, 12.1% natural resources, construction, and maintenance, 9.1% production, transportation, and material moving

Income: Per capita: $14,745; Median household: $32,473; Average household: $42,361; Households with income of $100,000 or more: 8.0%; Poverty rate: 32.0%

Educational Attainment: High school diploma or higher: 67.9%; Bachelor's degree or higher: 12.5%; Graduate/professional degree or higher: 5.1%

School District(s)

Palm Springs Unified (KG-12)
2012-13 Enrollment: 23,581 . . . . (760) 416-6000

Housing: Homeownership rate: 48.2%; Median home value: $121,600; Median year structure built: 1988; Homeowner vacancy rate: 8.6%; Median gross rent: $896 per month; Rental vacancy rate: 16.6%

Health Insurance: 69.9% have insurance; 34.7% have private insurance; 41.7% have public insurance; 30.1% do not have insurance; 15.4% of children under 18 do not have insurance

Safety: Violent crime rate: 99.2 per 10,000 population; Property crime rate: 394.8 per 10,000 population

Transportation: Commute: 87.8% car, 2.3% public transportation, 2.4% walk, 6.2% work from home; Median travel time to work: 32.9 minutes

Additional Information Contacts

City of Desert Hot Springs. . . . . (760) 329-6411
http://www.cityofdhs.org

DESERT PALMS (CDP). Covers a land area of 2.670 square miles and a water area of <.001 square miles. Located at 33.78° N. Lat; 116.30° W. Long.

Population: 6,957; Growth (since 2000): n/a; Density: 2,605.4 persons per square mile; Race: 96.7% White, 0.8% Black/African American, 1.4% Asian, 0.2% American Indian/Alaska Native, 0.1% Native Hawaiian/Other Pacific Islander, 0.6% Two or more races, 2.5% Hispanic of any race; Average household size: 1.70; Median age: 74.1; Age under 18: 0.2%; Age 65 and over: 83.1%; Males per 100 females: 79.2; Marriage status: 4.0% never married, 69.2% now married, 0.3% separated, 16.5% widowed, 10.3% divorced; Foreign born: 10.9%; Speak English only: 92.0%; With disability: 22.4%; Veterans: 23.8%; Ancestry: 18.7% English, 17.5% German, 9.7% Irish, 7.2% Russian, 5.7% American

Employment: 8.1% management, business, and financial, 0.0% computer, engineering, and science, 21.2% education, legal, community service, arts, and media, 9.5% healthcare practitioners, 21.7% service, 32.3% sales and office, 3.5% natural resources, construction, and maintenance, 3.7% production, transportation, and material moving

Income: Per capita: $46,098; Median household: $56,979; Average household: $75,725; Households with income of $100,000 or more: 24.1%; Poverty rate: 5.9%

Educational Attainment: High school diploma or higher: 96.8%; Bachelor's degree or higher: 41.4%; Graduate/professional degree or higher: 16.4%

Housing: Homeownership rate: 91.3%; Median home value: $364,600; Median year structure built: 2000; Homeowner vacancy rate: 2.4%; Median gross rent: $1,800 per month; Rental vacancy rate: 17.7%

Health Insurance: 99.4% have insurance; 78.8% have private insurance; 87.8% have public insurance; 0.6% do not have insurance; 0.0% of children under 18 do not have insurance

Transportation: Commute: 77.5% car, 0.0% public transportation, 3.0% walk, 16.4% work from home; Median travel time to work: 17.9 minutes

EAST HEMET (CDP). Covers a land area of 5.213 square miles and a water area of 0 square miles. Located at 33.73° N. Lat; 116.94° W. Long. Elevation is 1,690 feet.

Population: 17,418; Growth (since 2000): 17.5%; Density: 3,341.2 persons per square mile; Race: 70.4% White, 3.9% Black/African American, 1.6% Asian, 1.9% American Indian/Alaska Native, 0.2% Native Hawaiian/Other Pacific Islander, 4.9% Two or more races, 38.9% Hispanic of any race; Average household size: 3.26; Median age: 32.2; Age under 18: 30.0%; Age 65 and over: 10.4%; Males per 100 females: 98.1; Marriage status: 32.0% never married, 52.4% now married, 1.8% separated, 4.8% widowed, 10.8% divorced; Foreign born: 13.3%; Speak English only: 73.4%; With disability: 16.8%; Veterans: 9.6%; Ancestry: 14.8% German, 9.6% English, 9.0% Irish, 4.4% American, 4.0% French

Employment: 9.1% management, business, and financial, 2.0% computer, engineering, and science, 11.4% education, legal, community service, arts, and media, 6.1% healthcare practitioners, 22.5% service, 22.0% sales and office, 16.2% natural resources, construction, and maintenance, 10.5% production, transportation, and material moving

Income: Per capita: $20,747; Median household: $51,266; Average household: $66,892; Households with income of $100,000 or more: 19.5%; Poverty rate: 18.0%

Educational Attainment: High school diploma or higher: 78.8%; Bachelor's degree or higher: 14.5%; Graduate/professional degree or higher: 6.7%

Housing: Homeownership rate: 65.9%; Median home value: $153,500; Median year structure built: 1974; Homeowner vacancy rate: 3.5%; Median gross rent: $1,058 per month; Rental vacancy rate: 10.1%

Health Insurance: 79.8% have insurance; 51.2% have private insurance; 37.8% have public insurance; 20.2% do not have insurance; 9.4% of children under 18 do not have insurance

Transportation: Commute: 89.9% car, 0.7% public transportation, 2.5% walk, 5.4% work from home; Median travel time to work: 32.7 minutes

EASTVALE (city). Covers a land area of 11.405 square miles and a water area of 0.040 square miles. Located at 33.96° N. Lat; 117.58° W. Long. Elevation is 627 feet.

Population: 53,668; Growth (since 2000): n/a; Density: 4,705.5 persons per square mile; Race: 42.9% White, 9.7% Black/African American, 24.2% Asian, 0.5% American Indian/Alaska Native, 0.4% Native Hawaiian/Other Pacific Islander, 5.2% Two or more races, 40.0% Hispanic of any race; Average household size: 3.93; Median age: 30.9; Age under 18: 33.1%; Age 65 and over: 4.7%; Males per 100 females: 98.1; Marriage status: 30.0% never married, 61.6% now married, 1.6% separated, 2.6% widowed, 5.8% divorced; Foreign born: 30.2%; Speak English only: 50.6%; With disability: 5.6%; Veterans: 5.2%; Ancestry: 6.2% German, 4.2% Irish, 4.1% American, 3.0% English, 2.1% European

Employment: 18.6% management, business, and financial, 6.4% computer, engineering, and science, 10.2% education, legal, community service, arts, and media, 7.5% healthcare practitioners, 15.9% service, 25.3% sales and office, 7.0% natural resources, construction, and maintenance, 9.1% production, transportation, and material moving

Income: Per capita: $29,067; Median household: $107,445; Average household: $117,000; Households with income of $100,000 or more: 54.3%; Poverty rate: 4.7%

Educational Attainment: High school diploma or higher: 87.4%; Bachelor's degree or higher: 35.1%; Graduate/professional degree or higher: 12.3%

School District(s)

Corona-Norco Unified (KG-12)
2012-13 Enrollment: 53,437 . . . . (951) 736-5000

Housing: Homeownership rate: 82.7%; Median home value: $388,100; Median year structure built: 2005; Homeowner vacancy rate: 3.1%; Median gross rent: $2,000+ per month; Rental vacancy rate: 3.1%

Health Insurance: 86.2% have insurance; 73.6% have private insurance; 15.7% have public insurance; 13.8% do not have insurance; 6.2% of children under 18 do not have insurance

Safety: Violent crime rate: 11.5 per 10,000 population; Property crime rate: 183.1 per 10,000 population

Transportation: Commute: 92.1% car, 1.0% public transportation, 0.3% walk, 5.6% work from home; Median travel time to work: 41.4 minutes

---

EL CERRITO (CDP). Covers a land area of 2.553 square miles and a water area of 0.225 square miles. Located at 33.84° N. Lat; 117.52° W. Long. Elevation is 876 feet.

Population: 5,100; Growth (since 2000): 11.1%; Density: 1,997.7 persons per square mile; Race: 69.5% White, 1.8% Black/African American, 1.9% Asian, 1.1% American Indian/Alaska Native, 0.2% Native Hawaiian/Other Pacific Islander, 3.6% Two or more races, 52.1% Hispanic of any race; Average household size: 3.67; Median age: 35.7; Age under 18: 27.1%; Age 65 and over: 10.0%; Males per 100 females: 109.0; Marriage status: 33.7% never married, 55.4% now married, 2.2% separated, 2.1% widowed, 8.8% divorced; Foreign born: 21.6%; Speak English only: 59.6%; With disability: 10.6%; Veterans: 6.5%; Ancestry: 11.9% German, 9.7% American, 6.7% English, 6.4% Irish, 3.0% Italian

Employment: 8.5% management, business, and financial, 1.4% computer, engineering, and science, 11.0% education, legal, community service, arts, and media, 7.8% healthcare practitioners, 13.0% service, 32.2% sales and office, 9.7% natural resources, construction, and maintenance, 16.5% production, transportation, and material moving

Income: Per capita: $22,430; Median household: $60,917; Average household: $79,407; Households with income of $100,000 or more: 28.2%; Poverty rate: 8.7%

Educational Attainment: High school diploma or higher: 72.7%; Bachelor's degree or higher: 12.5%; Graduate/professional degree or higher: 6.3%

Housing: Homeownership rate: 79.3%; Median home value: $329,100; Median year structure built: 1975; Homeowner vacancy rate: 1.2%; Median gross rent: $1,352 per month; Rental vacancy rate: 4.0%

Health Insurance: 75.0% have insurance; 63.0% have private insurance; 22.0% have public insurance; 25.0% do not have insurance; 19.9% of children under 18 do not have insurance

Transportation: Commute: 89.3% car, 0.6% public transportation, 1.3% walk, 8.6% work from home; Median travel time to work: 35.0 minutes

---

EL SOBRANTE (CDP). Covers a land area of 7.211 square miles and a water area of 0 square miles. Located at 33.87° N. Lat; 117.46° W. Long.

History: El Sobrante, meaning "excess," "remainder," or "surplus land," was once inhabited by an indigenous tribe called the Huichin who were part of the Native American Ohlone people.

Population: 12,723; Growth (since 2000): n/a; Density: 1,764.4 persons per square mile; Race: 58.4% White, 7.9% Black/African American, 17.6% Asian, 0.6% American Indian/Alaska Native, 0.3% Native Hawaiian/Other Pacific Islander, 4.8% Two or more races, 28.5% Hispanic of any race; Average household size: 3.45; Median age: 35.8; Age under 18: 28.8%; Age 65 and over: 6.6%; Males per 100 females: 96.4; Marriage status: 27.3% never married, 66.7% now married, 1.0% separated, 1.0% widowed, 5.0% divorced; Foreign born: 20.9%; Speak English only: 64.6%; With disability: 3.6%; Veterans: 5.5%; Ancestry: 13.2% German, 10.1% English, 8.6% Irish, 5.6% American, 3.3% Italian

Employment: 20.5% management, business, and financial, 5.2% computer, engineering, and science, 16.0% education, legal, community service, arts, and media, 7.8% healthcare practitioners, 10.5% service, 27.4% sales and office, 5.0% natural resources, construction, and maintenance, 7.5% production, transportation, and material moving

Income: Per capita: $30,496; Median household: $105,133; Average household: $113,992; Households with income of $100,000 or more: 52.6%; Poverty rate: 6.8%

Educational Attainment: High school diploma or higher: 92.4%; Bachelor's degree or higher: 40.7%; Graduate/professional degree or higher: 17.4%

Housing: Homeownership rate: 91.4%; Median home value: $386,700; Median year structure built: 2002; Homeowner vacancy rate: 1.7%; Median gross rent: $2,000+ per month; Rental vacancy rate: 3.7%

Health Insurance: 83.0% have insurance; 76.6% have private insurance; 10.3% have public insurance; 17.0% do not have insurance; 12.5% of children under 18 do not have insurance

Transportation: Commute: 92.8% car, 1.9% public transportation, 0.5% walk, 4.3% work from home; Median travel time to work: 35.8 minutes

---

FRENCH VALLEY (CDP). Covers a land area of 10.867 square miles and a water area of 0.030 square miles. Located at 33.60° N. Lat; 117.11° W. Long. Elevation is 1,365 feet.

Population: 23,067; Growth (since 2000): n/a; Density: 2,122.6 persons per square mile; Race: 64.3% White, 7.9% Black/African American, 11.6% Asian, 1.0% American Indian/Alaska Native, 0.6% Native Hawaiian/Other Pacific Islander, 6.5% Two or more races, 27.4% Hispanic of any race; Average household size: 3.59; Median age: 30.5; Age under 18: 33.7%; Age 65 and over: 5.2%; Males per 100 females: 107.9; Marriage status: 27.4% never married, 60.4% now married, 1.5% separated, 3.3% widowed, 8.9% divorced; Foreign born: 15.3%; Speak English only: 71.2%; With disability: 7.8%; Veterans: 12.7%; Ancestry: 15.3% German, 11.0% Irish, 7.6% Italian, 6.9% English, 4.3% American

Employment: 14.7% management, business, and financial, 4.2% computer, engineering, and science, 6.9% education, legal, community service, arts, and media, 4.2% healthcare practitioners, 20.6% service, 29.4% sales and office, 7.9% natural resources, construction, and maintenance, 12.0% production, transportation, and material moving

Income: Per capita: $25,217; Median household: $85,055; Average household: $90,941; Households with income of $100,000 or more: 38.1%; Poverty rate: 4.1%

Educational Attainment: High school diploma or higher: 88.4%; Bachelor's degree or higher: 23.5%; Graduate/professional degree or higher: 7.1%

Housing: Homeownership rate: 82.8%; Median home value: $271,500; Median year structure built: 2005; Homeowner vacancy rate: 4.0%; Median gross rent: $1,879 per month; Rental vacancy rate: 7.2%

Health Insurance: 88.5% have insurance; 80.6% have private insurance; 15.8% have public insurance; 11.5% do not have insurance; 4.8% of children under 18 do not have insurance

Transportation: Commute: 92.0% car, 0.5% public transportation, 0.2% walk, 6.8% work from home; Median travel time to work: 42.4 minutes

---

GARNET (CDP). Covers a land area of 11.290 square miles and a water area of 0.135 square miles. Located at 33.92° N. Lat; 116.49° W. Long. Elevation is 712 feet.

Population: 7,543; Growth (since 2000): n/a; Density: 668.1 persons per square mile; Race: 56.3% White, 2.7% Black/African American, 0.8% Asian, 1.3% American Indian/Alaska Native, 0.1% Native Hawaiian/Other Pacific Islander, 3.8% Two or more races, 74.0% Hispanic of any race; Average household size: 3.47; Median age: 29.3; Age under 18: 33.5%; Age 65 and over: 8.9%; Males per 100 females: 103.2; Marriage status: 35.3% never married, 51.5% now married, 1.1% separated, 4.3% widowed, 8.9% divorced; Foreign born: 34.0%; Speak English only: 35.8%; With disability: 11.5%; Veterans: 6.3%; Ancestry: 5.0% Irish, 2.9% American, 2.8% English, 2.8% French, 2.5% German

Employment: 4.8% management, business, and financial, 0.2% computer, engineering, and science, 3.9% education, legal, community service, arts, and media, 2.7% healthcare practitioners, 40.0% service, 15.8% sales and office, 21.5% natural resources, construction, and maintenance, 11.1% production, transportation, and material moving

Income: Per capita: $13,884; Median household: $38,695; Average household: $45,781; Households with income of $100,000 or more: 4.0%; Poverty rate: 15.4%

Educational Attainment: High school diploma or higher: 68.8%; Bachelor's degree or higher: 10.6%; Graduate/professional degree or higher: 3.4%

Housing: Homeownership rate: 69.6%; Median home value: $103,700; Median year structure built: 1991; Homeowner vacancy rate: 5.0%; Median gross rent: $1,101 per month; Rental vacancy rate: 10.3%

Health Insurance: 63.7% have insurance; 39.2% have private insurance; 29.6% have public insurance; 36.3% do not have insurance; 31.7% of children under 18 do not have insurance

Transportation: Commute: 86.7% car, 0.0% public transportation, 0.6% walk, 11.6% work from home; Median travel time to work: 24.2 minutes

GOOD HOPE (CDP). Covers a land area of 11.233 square miles and a water area of 0 square miles. Located at 33.77° N. Lat; 117.28° W. Long. Elevation is 1,552 feet.

Population: 9,192; Growth (since 2000): n/a; Density: 818.3 persons per square mile; Race: 45.2% White, 7.3% Black/African American, 0.7% Asian, 1.1% American Indian/Alaska Native, 0.0% Native Hawaiian/Other Pacific Islander, 3.4% Two or more races, 79.6% Hispanic of any race; Average household size: 4.37; Median age: 27.2; Age under 18: 34.6%; Age 65 and over: 7.6%; Males per 100 females: 108.6; Marriage status: 48.3% never married, 40.8% now married, 3.8% separated, 3.3% widowed, 7.6% divorced; Foreign born: 33.2%; Speak English only: 27.0%; With disability: 13.6%; Veterans: 3.8%; Ancestry: 2.3% Italian, 1.8% American, 1.6% German, 1.5% Irish, 0.6% Norwegian

Employment: 4.6% management, business, and financial, 0.0% computer, engineering, and science, 2.2% education, legal, community service, arts, and media, 1.7% healthcare practitioners, 24.0% service, 30.0% sales and office, 23.5% natural resources, construction, and maintenance, 14.0% production, transportation, and material moving

Income: Per capita: $11,216; Median household: $32,490; Average household: $42,286; Households with income of $100,000 or more: 4.3%; Poverty rate: 40.6%

Educational Attainment: High school diploma or higher: 54.0%; Bachelor's degree or higher: 6.0%; Graduate/professional degree or higher: 0.8%

Housing: Homeownership rate: 59.8%; Median home value: $141,000; Median year structure built: 1979; Homeowner vacancy rate: 2.8%; Median gross rent: $961 per month; Rental vacancy rate: 5.8%

Health Insurance: 57.5% have insurance; 24.4% have private insurance; 37.6% have public insurance; 42.5% do not have insurance; 23.0% of children under 18 do not have insurance

Transportation: Commute: 91.1% car, 3.4% public transportation, 0.1% walk, 3.1% work from home; Median travel time to work: 37.3 minutes

GREEN ACRES (CDP). Covers a land area of 1.400 square miles and a water area of 0 square miles. Located at 33.73° N. Lat; 117.08° W. Long. Elevation is 1,581 feet.

Population: 1,805; Growth (since 2000): n/a; Density: 1,289.0 persons per square mile; Race: 66.0% White, 1.9% Black/African American, 1.4% Asian, 2.3% American Indian/Alaska Native, 0.1% Native Hawaiian/Other Pacific Islander, 6.4% Two or more races, 47.4% Hispanic of any race; Average household size: 3.22; Median age: 34.7; Age under 18: 28.7%; Age 65 and over: 11.2%; Males per 100 females: 108.2

Housing: Homeownership rate: 65.2%; Homeowner vacancy rate: 5.6%; Rental vacancy rate: 9.3%

HEMET (city). Covers a land area of 27.847 square miles and a water area of 0 square miles. Located at 33.74° N. Lat; 116.99° W. Long. Elevation is 1,594 feet.

History: Name may be from the Indian name for the valley, or from the Swedish "hemmet," meaning "in the home". Marked by fast growth during the 1970s and 1980s as a result of increased local agribusiness and the development of the aircraft industry in the area. Incorporated 1910.

Population: 78,657; Growth (since 2000): 33.7%; Density: 2,824.6 persons per square mile; Race: 67.7% White, 6.4% Black/African American, 3.0% Asian, 1.6% American Indian/Alaska Native, 0.4% Native Hawaiian/Other Pacific Islander, 5.2% Two or more races, 35.8% Hispanic of any race; Average household size: 2.59; Median age: 39.0; Age under 18: 25.9%; Age 65 and over: 22.1%; Males per 100 females: 88.9; Marriage status: 27.1% never married, 47.6% now married, 3.1% separated, 10.5% widowed, 14.7% divorced; Foreign born: 14.6%; Speak English only: 72.3%; With disability: 19.6%; Veterans: 12.1%; Ancestry: 14.5% German, 10.2% English, 9.5% Irish, 4.0% American, 3.6% Italian

Employment: 6.9% management, business, and financial, 2.1% computer, engineering, and science, 8.5% education, legal, community service, arts, and media, 3.4% healthcare practitioners, 26.2% service, 25.6% sales and office, 12.4% natural resources, construction, and maintenance, 14.9% production, transportation, and material moving

Income: Per capita: $17,917; Median household: $32,774; Average household: $45,077; Households with income of $100,000 or more: 8.6%; Poverty rate: 23.3%

Educational Attainment: High school diploma or higher: 79.7%; Bachelor's degree or higher: 11.9%; Graduate/professional degree or higher: 4.4%

School District(s)

Hemet Unified (KG-12)
2012-13 Enrollment: 21,689 . . . . (951) 765-5100

Vocational/Technical School(s)

Marinello Schools of Beauty-Hemet (Private, For-profit)
Fall 2013 Enrollment: 1,330 . . . . (562) 945-2211
2013-14 Tuition: $18,510

Housing: Homeownership rate: 61.7%; Median home value: $114,200; Median year structure built: 1982; Homeowner vacancy rate: 5.0%; Median gross rent: $948 per month; Rental vacancy rate: 17.5%

Health Insurance: 80.9% have insurance; 45.1% have private insurance; 49.2% have public insurance; 19.1% do not have insurance; 10.6% of children under 18 do not have insurance

Hospitals: Hemet Valley Medical Center (240 beds)

Safety: Violent crime rate: 54.7 per 10,000 population; Property crime rate: 485.1 per 10,000 population

Newspapers: Valley Chronicle (weekly circulation 40000)

Transportation: Commute: 90.7% car, 1.6% public transportation, 1.6% walk, 4.7% work from home; Median travel time to work: 30.9 minutes; Amtrak: Bus service available.

Additional Information Contacts

City of Hemet. . . . . (951) 765-2300
http://www.cityofhemet.org

HIGHGROVE (CDP). Covers a land area of 3.219 square miles and a water area of 0 square miles. Located at 34.01° N. Lat; 117.31° W. Long. Elevation is 951 feet.

History: Highgrove developed as a trading post for the surrounding citrus ranches.

Population: 3,988; Growth (since 2000): 15.8%; Density: 1,239.0 persons per square mile; Race: 52.8% White, 4.1% Black/African American, 2.8% Asian, 1.0% American Indian/Alaska Native, 0.3% Native Hawaiian/Other Pacific Islander, 4.2% Two or more races, 65.3% Hispanic of any race; Average household size: 3.51; Median age: 30.2; Age under 18: 31.2%; Age 65 and over: 7.2%; Males per 100 females: 102.8; Marriage status: 48.8% never married, 38.3% now married, 1.8% separated, 2.1% widowed, 10.8% divorced; Foreign born: 29.9%; Speak English only: 45.7%; With disability: 6.0%; Veterans: 3.4%; Ancestry: 5.5% Irish, 4.3% English, 4.2% German, 2.6% Swedish, 2.2% American

Employment: 4.9% management, business, and financial, 1.5% computer, engineering, and science, 6.2% education, legal, community service, arts, and media, 6.0% healthcare practitioners, 10.0% service, 17.2% sales and office, 13.8% natural resources, construction, and maintenance, 40.4% production, transportation, and material moving

Income: Per capita: $18,368; Median household: $42,138; Average household: $59,282; Households with income of $100,000 or more: 19.4%; Poverty rate: 25.4%

Educational Attainment: High school diploma or higher: 59.4%; Bachelor's degree or higher: 9.8%; Graduate/professional degree or higher: 3.9%

Housing: Homeownership rate: 55.7%; Median home value: $247,400; Median year structure built: 1976; Homeowner vacancy rate: 2.8%; Median gross rent: $948 per month; Rental vacancy rate: 7.5%

Health Insurance: 67.6% have insurance; 39.0% have private insurance; 33.2% have public insurance; 32.4% do not have insurance; 14.8% of children under 18 do not have insurance

Transportation: Commute: 96.4% car, 0.0% public transportation, 0.0% walk, 3.6% work from home; Median travel time to work: 21.2 minutes

HOME GARDENS (CDP). Covers a land area of 1.556 square miles and a water area of 0 square miles. Located at 33.88° N. Lat; 117.51° W. Long. Elevation is 669 feet.

Population: 11,570; Growth (since 2000): 22.3%; Density: 7,435.7 persons per square mile; Race: 45.6% White, 3.1% Black/African American, 5.8% Asian, 1.1% American Indian/Alaska Native, 0.4% Native Hawaiian/Other Pacific Islander, 5.1% Two or more races, 73.7% Hispanic of any race; Average household size: 4.19; Median age: 29.3; Age under 18: 31.3%; Age 65 and over: 7.5%; Males per 100 females: 107.6; Marriage status: 41.0% never married, 49.3% now married, 1.6% separated, 3.9% widowed, 5.8% divorced; Foreign born: 37.1%; Speak English only: 32.5%; With disability: 9.4%; Veterans: 2.9%; Ancestry: 3.8% German, 3.4% American, 2.3% Irish, 2.0% English, 1.2% Arab

Employment: 5.8% management, business, and financial, 4.6% computer, engineering, and science, 5.7% education, legal, community service, arts, and media, 0.8% healthcare practitioners, 16.4% service, 25.8% sales and office, 16.2% natural resources, construction, and maintenance, 24.7% production, transportation, and material moving

Income: Per capita: $15,362; Median household: $56,135; Average household: $59,478; Households with income of $100,000 or more: 14.7%; Poverty rate: 24.4%

Educational Attainment: High school diploma or higher: 61.2%; Bachelor's degree or higher: 10.3%; Graduate/professional degree or higher: 1.8%

Housing: Homeownership rate: 70.7%; Median home value: $207,000; Median year structure built: 1981; Homeowner vacancy rate: 2.3%; Median gross rent: $1,159 per month; Rental vacancy rate: 2.5%

Health Insurance: 71.5% have insurance; 42.8% have private insurance; 31.9% have public insurance; 28.5% do not have insurance; 12.1% of children under 18 do not have insurance

Transportation: Commute: 89.9% car, 2.5% public transportation, 1.7% walk, 2.4% work from home; Median travel time to work: 35.6 minutes

HOMELAND (CDP). Covers a land area of 4.270 square miles and a water area of 0 square miles. Located at 33.75° N. Lat; 117.11° W. Long. Elevation is 1,604 feet.

Population: 5,969; Growth (since 2000): 60.9%; Density: 1,398.0 persons per square mile; Race: 62.4% White, 2.2% Black/African American, 0.8% Asian, 1.4% American Indian/Alaska Native, 0.3% Native Hawaiian/Other Pacific Islander, 4.9% Two or more races, 52.1% Hispanic of any race; Average household size: 3.03; Median age: 36.1; Age under 18: 27.7%; Age 65 and over: 17.6%; Males per 100 females: 102.0; Marriage status: 31.1% never married, 51.9% now married, 0.4% separated, 6.4% widowed, 10.6% divorced; Foreign born: 23.8%; Speak English only: 52.8%; With disability: 15.2%; Veterans: 10.6%; Ancestry: 11.1% German, 7.0% Irish, 6.9% English, 5.3% American, 3.3% Italian

Employment: 8.9% management, business, and financial, 5.0% computer, engineering, and science, 2.9% education, legal, community service, arts, and media, 0.0% healthcare practitioners, 18.1% service, 23.1% sales and office, 11.9% natural resources, construction, and maintenance, 30.1% production, transportation, and material moving

Income: Per capita: $15,944; Median household: $38,526; Average household: $46,327; Households with income of $100,000 or more: 9.4%; Poverty rate: 17.1%

Educational Attainment: High school diploma or higher: 68.0%; Bachelor's degree or higher: 8.1%; Graduate/professional degree or higher: 3.2%

Housing: Homeownership rate: 67.7%; Median home value: $90,200; Median year structure built: 1980; Homeowner vacancy rate: 5.0%; Median gross rent: $1,050 per month; Rental vacancy rate: 5.5%

Health Insurance: 65.8% have insurance; 34.7% have private insurance; 41.2% have public insurance; 34.2% do not have insurance; 23.4% of children under 18 do not have insurance

Transportation: Commute: 86.1% car, 0.1% public transportation, 4.7% walk, 4.1% work from home; Median travel time to work: 36.7 minutes

IDYLLWILD-PINE COVE (CDP). Covers a land area of 13.723 square miles and a water area of 0.010 square miles. Located at 33.74° N. Lat; 116.73° W. Long.

Population: 3,874; Growth (since 2000): 10.6%; Density: 282.3 persons per square mile; Race: 88.6% White, 0.8% Black/African American, 3.5% Asian, 0.8% American Indian/Alaska Native, 0.2% Native Hawaiian/Other Pacific Islander, 3.8% Two or more races, 12.4% Hispanic of any race; Average household size: 2.10; Median age: 49.8; Age under 18: 19.1%; Age 65 and over: 20.0%; Males per 100 females: 99.2; Marriage status: 24.1% never married, 55.0% now married, 0.9% separated, 4.6% widowed, 16.3% divorced; Foreign born: 10.0%; Speak English only: 88.2%; With disability: 14.4%; Veterans: 10.3%; Ancestry: 25.3% German, 19.0% Irish, 17.9% English, 7.5% Scottish, 4.5% Italian

Employment: 12.8% management, business, and financial, 1.3% computer, engineering, and science, 21.3% education, legal, community service, arts, and media, 0.1% healthcare practitioners, 15.4% service, 31.3% sales and office, 13.7% natural resources, construction, and maintenance, 4.1% production, transportation, and material moving

Income: Per capita: $33,602; Median household: $58,403; Average household: $68,552; Households with income of $100,000 or more: 17.1%; Poverty rate: 16.7%

Educational Attainment: High school diploma or higher: 97.7%; Bachelor's degree or higher: 36.4%; Graduate/professional degree or higher: 13.6%

School District(s)

Hemet Unified (KG-12)
2012-13 Enrollment: 21,689 . . . . (951) 765-5100

Housing: Homeownership rate: 69.8%; Median home value: $265,000; Median year structure built: 1970; Homeowner vacancy rate: 8.5%; Median gross rent: $1,145 per month; Rental vacancy rate: 18.2%

Health Insurance: 86.3% have insurance; 64.9% have private insurance; 38.4% have public insurance; 13.7% do not have insurance; 7.1% of children under 18 do not have insurance

Newspapers: Idyllwild Town Crier (weekly circulation 3700)

Transportation: Commute: 83.8% car, 0.0% public transportation, 0.2% walk, 15.4% work from home; Median travel time to work: 24.3 minutes

INDIAN WELLS (city). Covers a land area of 14.321 square miles and a water area of 0.270 square miles. Located at 33.69° N. Lat; 116.34° W. Long. Elevation is 89 feet.

History: Indian Wells is located in the Coachella Valley between Palm Desert and La Quinta. It was incorporated on July 14, 1967 and named after a Cahuilla Indian water hole that was a major water source for local tribes.

Population: 4,958; Growth (since 2000): 29.9%; Density: 346.2 persons per square mile; Race: 95.2% White, 0.6% Black/African American, 1.7% Asian, 0.4% American Indian/Alaska Native, 0.0% Native Hawaiian/Other Pacific Islander, 1.0% Two or more races, 4.2% Hispanic of any race; Average household size: 1.80; Median age: 66.7; Age under 18: 6.3%; Age 65 and over: 55.1%; Males per 100 females: 84.6; Marriage status: 7.4% never married, 70.5% now married, 0.9% separated, 11.4% widowed, 10.7% divorced; Foreign born: 13.9%; Speak English only: 86.2%; With disability: 16.8%; Veterans: 18.5%; Ancestry: 18.2% English, 15.8% Irish, 14.5% German, 8.2% American, 5.3% Italian

Employment: 30.6% management, business, and financial, 3.6% computer, engineering, and science, 13.9% education, legal, community service, arts, and media, 8.7% healthcare practitioners, 12.0% service, 26.4% sales and office, 2.7% natural resources, construction, and maintenance, 2.1% production, transportation, and material moving

Income: Per capita: $88,238; Median household: $83,884; Average household: $162,165; Households with income of $100,000 or more: 45.6%; Poverty rate: 5.2%

Educational Attainment: High school diploma or higher: 96.3%; Bachelor's degree or higher: 53.0%; Graduate/professional degree or higher: 20.2%

School District(s)

Desert Sands Unified (KG-12)
2012-13 Enrollment: 29,159 . . . . (760) 777-4200

Housing: Homeownership rate: 83.3%; Median home value: $604,600; Median year structure built: 1985; Homeowner vacancy rate: 5.1%; Median gross rent: $828 per month; Rental vacancy rate: 15.4%

Health Insurance: 95.5% have insurance; 77.5% have private insurance; 60.5% have public insurance; 4.5% do not have insurance; 0.0% of children under 18 do not have insurance

Safety: Violent crime rate: 13.5 per 10,000 population; Property crime rate: 332.4 per 10,000 population

Transportation: Commute: 86.5% car, 0.3% public transportation, 1.5% walk, 10.1% work from home; Median travel time to work: 26.8 minutes

Additional Information Contacts

City of Indian Wells . . . . (760) 346-2489
http://www.cityofindianwells.org

INDIO (city). Covers a land area of 29.181 square miles and a water area of 0.008 square miles. Located at 33.73° N. Lat; 116.24° W. Long. Elevation is -13 feet.

History: Named for the Spanish translation of "Indian". Indio was established in 1876 as a distribution point for railroad freight, and developed as a trading center for the surrounding date, cotton, and alfalfa growers.

Population: 76,036; Growth (since 2000): 54.8%; Density: 2,605.7 persons per square mile; Race: 61.5% White, 2.4% Black/African American, 2.2% Asian, 1.0% American Indian/Alaska Native, 0.1% Native Hawaiian/Other Pacific Islander, 3.4% Two or more races, 67.8% Hispanic of any race; Average household size: 3.21; Median age: 32.2; Age under 18: 30.1%; Age 65 and over: 12.4%; Males per 100 females: 97.3; Marriage status: 32.3% never married, 53.3% now married, 3.2% separated, 4.9% widowed, 9.5% divorced; Foreign born: 26.5%; Speak English only: 44.1%; With disability: 11.2%; Veterans: 6.6%; Ancestry: 5.4% German, 4.1% Irish, 3.8% English, 2.6% Italian, 1.8% American

Employment: 10.6% management, business, and financial, 1.3% computer, engineering, and science, 8.3% education, legal, community service, arts, and media, 3.1% healthcare practitioners, 31.5% service, 24.5% sales and office, 12.7% natural resources, construction, and maintenance, 8.0% production, transportation, and material moving
Income: Per capita: $20,607; Median household: $50,068; Average household: $64,824; Households with income of $100,000 or more: 20.7%; Poverty rate: 21.9%
Educational Attainment: High school diploma or higher: 73.1%; Bachelor's degree or higher: 17.1%; Graduate/professional degree or higher: 6.3%

School District(s)

Coachella Valley Unified (KG-12)
2012-13 Enrollment: 18,720 . . . . (760) 399-5137
Desert Sands Unified (KG-12)
2012-13 Enrollment: 29,159 . . . . (760) 777-4200

Housing: Homeownership rate: 65.3%; Median home value: $192,600; Median year structure built: 1995; Homeowner vacancy rate: 5.0%; Median gross rent: $978 per month; Rental vacancy rate: 12.5%
Health Insurance: 76.2% have insurance; 47.2% have private insurance; 37.4% have public insurance; 23.8% do not have insurance; 11.2% of children under 18 do not have insurance
Hospitals: John F Kennedy Memorial Hospital (145 beds)
Safety: Violent crime rate: 58.3 per 10,000 population; Property crime rate: 336.4 per 10,000 population
Transportation: Commute: 92.2% car, 1.5% public transportation, 1.5% walk, 3.7% work from home; Median travel time to work: 22.9 minutes; Amtrak: Bus service available.
Additional Information Contacts
City of Indio . . . . (760) 391-4015
http://www.indio.org

INDIO HILLS (CDP). Covers a land area of 21.512 square miles and a water area of 0 square miles. Located at 33.84° N. Lat; 116.25° W. Long. Elevation is 1,135 feet.
Population: 972; Growth (since 2000): n/a; Density: 45.2 persons per square mile; Race: 55.8% White, 0.6% Black/African American, 0.5% Asian, 1.5% American Indian/Alaska Native, 0.1% Native Hawaiian/Other Pacific Islander, 1.2% Two or more races, 67.6% Hispanic of any race; Average household size: 3.20; Median age: 34.4; Age under 18: 26.4%; Age 65 and over: 8.7%; Males per 100 females: 114.6
Housing: Homeownership rate: 81.0%; Homeowner vacancy rate: 3.5%; Rental vacancy rate: 14.7%

JURUPA VALLEY (city).
Note: Statistics that would complete this profile are not available because the city was incorporated after the 2010 Census was released.

LA QUINTA (city). Covers a land area of 35.117 square miles and a water area of 0.434 square miles. Located at 33.64° N. Lat; 116.27° W. Long. Elevation is 135 feet.
Population: 37,467; Growth (since 2000): 58.1%; Density: 1,066.9 persons per square mile; Race: 78.7% White, 1.9% Black/African American, 3.1% Asian, 0.6% American Indian/Alaska Native, 0.1% Native Hawaiian/Other Pacific Islander, 3.3% Two or more races, 30.3% Hispanic of any race; Average household size: 2.52; Median age: 45.6; Age under 18: 21.9%; Age 65 and over: 20.9%; Males per 100 females: 93.5; Marriage status: 22.7% never married, 61.9% now married, 1.4% separated, 4.2% widowed, 11.2% divorced; Foreign born: 14.7%; Speak English only: 74.2%; With disability: 10.8%; Veterans: 11.6%; Ancestry: 16.3% German, 10.7% English, 10.2% Irish, 7.0% Italian, 3.4% American
Employment: 17.1% management, business, and financial, 2.9% computer, engineering, and science, 10.8% education, legal, community service, arts, and media, 6.2% healthcare practitioners, 22.8% service, 26.7% sales and office, 7.6% natural resources, construction, and maintenance, 5.9% production, transportation, and material moving
Income: Per capita: $38,447; Median household: $67,723; Average household: $96,431; Households with income of $100,000 or more: 32.4%; Poverty rate: 9.7%
Educational Attainment: High school diploma or higher: 89.6%; Bachelor's degree or higher: 33.7%; Graduate/professional degree or higher: 12.0%

School District(s)

Desert Sands Unified (KG-12)
2012-13 Enrollment: 29,159 . . . . (760) 777-4200

Vocational/Technical School(s)

Coachella Valley Beauty College (Private, For-profit)
Fall 2013 Enrollment: 129 . . . . (760) 772-5950
2013-14 Tuition: $10,675
Milan Institute of Cosmetology-La Quinta (Private, For-profit)
Fall 2013 Enrollment: 162 . . . . (707) 771-5520
2013-14 Tuition: $16,184

Housing: Homeownership rate: 75.3%; Median home value: $348,400; Median year structure built: 1998; Homeowner vacancy rate: 6.5%; Median gross rent: $1,373 per month; Rental vacancy rate: 16.5%
Health Insurance: 86.7% have insurance; 68.7% have private insurance; 35.1% have public insurance; 13.3% do not have insurance; 10.1% of children under 18 do not have insurance
Safety: Violent crime rate: 17.4 per 10,000 population; Property crime rate: 381.6 per 10,000 population
Transportation: Commute: 89.2% car, 0.7% public transportation, 0.8% walk, 7.1% work from home; Median travel time to work: 23.8 minutes; Amtrak: Bus service available.
Additional Information Contacts
City of La Quinta . . . . (760) 777-7000
http://www.la-quinta.org

LAKE ELSINORE (city). Covers a land area of 36.208 square miles and a water area of 5.479 square miles. Located at 33.68° N. Lat; 117.33° W. Long. Elevation is 1,296 feet.
History: Named for the Danish castle in Shakespeare's Hamlet. Incorporated 1888.
Population: 51,821; Growth (since 2000): 79.1%; Density: 1,431.2 persons per square mile; Race: 60.0% White, 5.3% Black/African American, 5.8% Asian, 0.9% American Indian/Alaska Native, 0.3% Native Hawaiian/Other Pacific Islander, 6.2% Two or more races, 48.4% Hispanic of any race; Average household size: 3.48; Median age: 29.8; Age under 18: 32.8%; Age 65 and over: 5.7%; Males per 100 females: 100.4; Marriage status: 34.5% never married, 54.0% now married, 2.8% separated, 2.9% widowed, 8.5% divorced; Foreign born: 21.6%; Speak English only: 61.6%; With disability: 8.5%; Veterans: 7.2%; Ancestry: 8.4% German, 7.6% Irish, 6.4% English, 3.8% Italian, 2.9% American
Employment: 13.6% management, business, and financial, 3.6% computer, engineering, and science, 6.4% education, legal, community service, arts, and media, 4.0% healthcare practitioners, 20.0% service, 26.8% sales and office, 10.6% natural resources, construction, and maintenance, 14.9% production, transportation, and material moving
Income: Per capita: $19,997; Median household: $61,472; Average household: $71,849; Households with income of $100,000 or more: 25.0%; Poverty rate: 14.2%
Educational Attainment: High school diploma or higher: 76.6%; Bachelor's degree or higher: 15.5%; Graduate/professional degree or higher: 4.5%

School District(s)

Lake Elsinore Unified (KG-12)
2012-13 Enrollment: 22,137 . . . . (951) 253-7000

Housing: Homeownership rate: 66.0%; Median home value: $209,000; Median year structure built: 1996; Homeowner vacancy rate: 4.6%; Median gross rent: $1,218 per month; Rental vacancy rate: 6.8%
Health Insurance: 78.9% have insurance; 56.4% have private insurance; 27.1% have public insurance; 21.1% do not have insurance; 9.8% of children under 18 do not have insurance
Safety: Violent crime rate: 18.3 per 10,000 population; Property crime rate: 265.7 per 10,000 population
Transportation: Commute: 90.1% car, 1.4% public transportation, 1.0% walk, 4.5% work from home; Median travel time to work: 43.2 minutes
Additional Information Contacts
City of Lake Elsinore . . . . (951) 674-3124
http://www.lake-elsinore.org

LAKE MATHEWS (CDP). Covers a land area of 15.927 square miles and a water area of 0 square miles. Located at 33.82° N. Lat; 117.37° W. Long.
Population: 5,890; Growth (since 2000): n/a; Density: 369.8 persons per square mile; Race: 72.0% White, 4.3% Black/African American, 3.3% Asian, 1.0% American Indian/Alaska Native, 0.1% Native Hawaiian/Other Pacific Islander, 4.3% Two or more races, 30.7% Hispanic of any race; Average household size: 3.18; Median age: 41.0; Age under 18: 24.0%; Age 65 and over: 12.3%; Males per 100 females: 105.7; Marriage status: 31.4% never married, 52.2% now married, 0.9% separated, 4.3%

widowed, 12.1% divorced; Foreign born: 12.2%; Speak English only: 70.6%; With disability: 10.7%; Veterans: 12.0%; Ancestry: 14.5% German, 12.8% Irish, 7.3% English, 5.0% American, 2.3% French
Employment: 17.6% management, business, and financial, 1.1% computer, engineering, and science, 8.3% education, legal, community service, arts, and media, 1.4% healthcare practitioners, 16.0% service, 25.3% sales and office, 10.4% natural resources, construction, and maintenance, 19.8% production, transportation, and material moving
Income: Per capita: $30,378; Median household: $69,883; Average household: $94,328; Households with income of $100,000 or more: 34.0%; Poverty rate: 10.0%
Educational Attainment: High school diploma or higher: 81.2%; Bachelor's degree or higher: 19.0%; Graduate/professional degree or higher: 8.9%
Housing: Homeownership rate: 85.2%; Median home value: $352,800; Median year structure built: 1982; Homeowner vacancy rate: 2.3%; Median gross rent: $1,337 per month; Rental vacancy rate: 3.5%
Health Insurance: 83.6% have insurance; 63.0% have private insurance; 29.4% have public insurance; 16.4% do not have insurance; 4.2% of children under 18 do not have insurance
Transportation: Commute: 96.8% car, 0.0% public transportation, 0.5% walk, 2.7% work from home; Median travel time to work: 40.6 minutes

LAKE RIVERSIDE (CDP). Covers a land area of 7.193 square miles and a water area of 0.084 square miles. Located at 33.52° N. Lat; 116.81° W. Long.
Population: 1,173; Growth (since 2000): n/a; Density: 163.1 persons per square mile; Race: 88.8% White, 1.8% Black/African American, 0.2% Asian, 1.4% American Indian/Alaska Native, 0.7% Native Hawaiian/Other Pacific Islander, 3.2% Two or more races, 15.9% Hispanic of any race; Average household size: 2.64; Median age: 45.5; Age under 18: 22.8%; Age 65 and over: 16.0%; Males per 100 females: 106.9
Housing: Homeownership rate: 86.0%; Homeowner vacancy rate: 5.7%; Rental vacancy rate: 8.8%

LAKELAND VILLAGE (CDP). Covers a land area of 8.676 square miles and a water area of 0.063 square miles. Located at 33.65° N. Lat; 117.37° W. Long. Elevation is 1,283 feet.
Population: 11,541; Growth (since 2000): 105.1%; Density: 1,330.2 persons per square mile; Race: 67.3% White, 2.5% Black/African American, 1.5% Asian, 1.1% American Indian/Alaska Native, 0.2% Native Hawaiian/Other Pacific Islander, 5.2% Two or more races, 44.3% Hispanic of any race; Average household size: 3.22; Median age: 33.0; Age under 18: 28.3%; Age 65 and over: 7.9%; Males per 100 females: 103.3; Marriage status: 32.3% never married, 47.5% now married, 2.2% separated, 5.3% widowed, 15.0% divorced; Foreign born: 19.3%; Speak English only: 67.2%; With disability: 13.1%; Veterans: 8.8%; Ancestry: 9.8% German, 9.0% Irish, 6.6% English, 5.7% American, 3.3% Italian
Employment: 8.5% management, business, and financial, 3.9% computer, engineering, and science, 5.1% education, legal, community service, arts, and media, 4.2% healthcare practitioners, 22.9% service, 24.8% sales and office, 14.7% natural resources, construction, and maintenance, 15.9% production, transportation, and material moving
Income: Per capita: $19,610; Median household: $43,071; Average household: $59,336; Households with income of $100,000 or more: 17.6%; Poverty rate: 23.9%
Educational Attainment: High school diploma or higher: 76.6%; Bachelor's degree or higher: 6.6%; Graduate/professional degree or higher: 2.3%
Housing: Homeownership rate: 64.6%; Median home value: $167,800; Median year structure built: 1981; Homeowner vacancy rate: 3.8%; Median gross rent: $1,144 per month; Rental vacancy rate: 9.3%
Health Insurance: 71.1% have insurance; 48.7% have private insurance; 29.6% have public insurance; 28.9% do not have insurance; 17.6% of children under 18 do not have insurance
Transportation: Commute: 91.4% car, 0.8% public transportation, 0.7% walk, 5.5% work from home; Median travel time to work: 40.5 minutes

LAKEVIEW (CDP). Covers a land area of 3.260 square miles and a water area of 0 square miles. Located at 33.83° N. Lat; 117.12° W. Long. Elevation is 1,450 feet.
Population: 2,104; Growth (since 2000): 30.0%; Density: 645.4 persons per square mile; Race: 53.1% White, 0.7% Black/African American, 0.3% Asian, 2.3% American Indian/Alaska Native, 0.1% Native Hawaiian/Other Pacific Islander, 3.5% Two or more races, 64.2% Hispanic of any race; Average household size: 3.88; Median age: 30.9; Age under 18: 32.4%; Age 65 and over: 8.8%; Males per 100 females: 98.1
Housing: Homeownership rate: 72.5%; Homeowner vacancy rate: 1.0%; Rental vacancy rate: 4.5%

MARCH ARB (CDP). Covers a land area of 11.953 square miles and a water area of <.001 square miles. Located at 33.89° N. Lat; 117.28° W. Long. Elevation is 1,549 feet.
Population: 1,159; Growth (since 2000): 213.2%; Density: 97.0 persons per square mile; Race: 70.0% White, 14.8% Black/African American, 3.0% Asian, 0.9% American Indian/Alaska Native, 0.2% Native Hawaiian/Other Pacific Islander, 3.2% Two or more races, 14.8% Hispanic of any race; Average household size: 1.80; Median age: 63.0; Age under 18: 13.5%; Age 65 and over: 48.8%; Males per 100 females: 106.2
Housing: Homeownership rate: 14.4%; Homeowner vacancy rate: 2.4%; Rental vacancy rate: 17.4%

MEAD VALLEY (CDP). Covers a land area of 19.169 square miles and a water area of 0 square miles. Located at 33.83° N. Lat; 117.29° W. Long. Elevation is 1,657 feet.
Population: 18,510; Growth (since 2000): n/a; Density: 965.6 persons per square mile; Race: 45.3% White, 8.2% Black/African American, 1.4% Asian, 1.0% American Indian/Alaska Native, 0.1% Native Hawaiian/Other Pacific Islander, 3.6% Two or more races, 72.4% Hispanic of any race; Average household size: 4.39; Median age: 28.3; Age under 18: 33.6%; Age 65 and over: 7.4%; Males per 100 females: 106.1; Marriage status: 41.3% never married, 46.8% now married, 2.2% separated, 4.6% widowed, 7.3% divorced; Foreign born: 29.1%; Speak English only: 34.3%; With disability: 10.9%; Veterans: 4.6%; Ancestry: 2.9% German, 1.6% Italian, 1.6% Irish, 1.5% English, 1.4% American
Employment: 3.9% management, business, and financial, 1.7% computer, engineering, and science, 4.6% education, legal, community service, arts, and media, 1.4% healthcare practitioners, 24.3% service, 17.3% sales and office, 20.7% natural resources, construction, and maintenance, 26.0% production, transportation, and material moving
Income: Per capita: $13,691; Median household: $43,367; Average household: $54,686; Households with income of $100,000 or more: 17.7%; Poverty rate: 31.2%
Educational Attainment: High school diploma or higher: 55.0%; Bachelor's degree or higher: 5.3%; Graduate/professional degree or higher: 1.0%
Housing: Homeownership rate: 68.2%; Median home value: $167,400; Median year structure built: 1982; Homeowner vacancy rate: 2.7%; Median gross rent: $1,057 per month; Rental vacancy rate: 4.5%
Health Insurance: 60.4% have insurance; 26.2% have private insurance; 36.8% have public insurance; 39.6% do not have insurance; 24.6% of children under 18 do not have insurance
Transportation: Commute: 93.3% car, 1.5% public transportation, 0.6% walk, 3.5% work from home; Median travel time to work: 37.0 minutes

MEADOWBROOK (CDP). Covers a land area of 6.856 square miles and a water area of 0.023 square miles. Located at 33.73° N. Lat; 117.29° W. Long.
Population: 3,185; Growth (since 2000): n/a; Density: 464.6 persons per square mile; Race: 63.9% White, 4.1% Black/African American, 1.6% Asian, 0.6% American Indian/Alaska Native, 0.1% Native Hawaiian/Other Pacific Islander, 4.7% Two or more races, 55.4% Hispanic of any race; Average household size: 3.24; Median age: 37.1; Age under 18: 25.8%; Age 65 and over: 13.7%; Males per 100 females: 105.2; Marriage status: 36.7% never married, 44.7% now married, 3.6% separated, 5.8% widowed, 12.8% divorced; Foreign born: 26.6%; Speak English only: 32.6%; With disability: 10.0%; Veterans: 6.3%; Ancestry: 5.2% Irish, 4.7% Italian, 4.5% English, 4.3% American, 4.1% German
Employment: 6.0% management, business, and financial, 5.0% computer, engineering, and science, 5.4% education, legal, community service, arts, and media, 2.2% healthcare practitioners, 18.0% service, 22.5% sales and office, 21.7% natural resources, construction, and maintenance, 19.1% production, transportation, and material moving
Income: Per capita: $11,966; Median household: $24,766; Average household: $39,089; Households with income of $100,000 or more: 3.4%; Poverty rate: 52.1%
Educational Attainment: High school diploma or higher: 55.4%; Bachelor's degree or higher: 8.3%; Graduate/professional degree or higher: 1.4%

Housing: Homeownership rate: 66.8%; Median home value: $135,200; Median year structure built: 1984; Homeowner vacancy rate: 2.5%; Median gross rent: $1,138 per month; Rental vacancy rate: 9.7%

Health Insurance: 57.8% have insurance; 28.7% have private insurance; 35.0% have public insurance; 42.2% do not have insurance; 45.6% of children under 18 do not have insurance

Transportation: Commute: 85.8% car, 0.7% public transportation, 0.0% walk, 3.9% work from home; Median travel time to work: 39.3 minutes

MECCA (CDP). Covers a land area of 6.959 square miles and a water area of 0 square miles. Located at 33.58° N. Lat; 116.06° W. Long. Elevation is -187 feet.

History: Mecca, a town of date gardens, was named because of its association with dates and the desert.

Population: 8,577; Growth (since 2000): 58.8%; Density: 1,232.5 persons per square mile; Race: 31.3% White, 0.5% Black/African American, 0.2% Asian, 0.5% American Indian/Alaska Native, 0.1% Native Hawaiian/Other Pacific Islander, 2.8% Two or more races, 98.7% Hispanic of any race; Average household size: 4.63; Median age: 23.7; Age under 18: 39.3%; Age 65 and over: 4.0%; Males per 100 females: 111.2; Marriage status: 43.6% never married, 47.2% now married, 5.7% separated, 4.3% widowed, 5.0% divorced; Foreign born: 49.3%; Speak English only: 7.1%; With disability: 9.4%; Veterans: 0.0%; Ancestry: 1.2% American, 0.5% British, 0.5% Scottish, 0.3% English, 0.2% Russian

Employment: 1.3% management, business, and financial, 0.0% computer, engineering, and science, 2.2% education, legal, community service, arts, and media, 0.0% healthcare practitioners, 28.3% service, 16.1% sales and office, 44.4% natural resources, construction, and maintenance, 7.8% production, transportation, and material moving

Income: Per capita: $7,778; Median household: $26,908; Average household: $31,627; Households with income of $100,000 or more: 1.6%; Poverty rate: 47.1%

Educational Attainment: High school diploma or higher: 29.3%; Bachelor's degree or higher: 1.4%; Graduate/professional degree or higher: n/a

School District(s)

Coachella Valley Unified (KG-12)
2012-13 Enrollment: 18,720 . . . . (760) 399-5137

Housing: Homeownership rate: 44.0%; Median home value: $96,700; Median year structure built: 1996; Homeowner vacancy rate: 1.1%; Median gross rent: $652 per month; Rental vacancy rate: 8.7%

Health Insurance: 62.4% have insurance; 16.1% have private insurance; 48.1% have public insurance; 37.6% do not have insurance; 15.6% of children under 18 do not have insurance

Transportation: Commute: 91.2% car, 1.6% public transportation, 2.1% walk, 4.4% work from home; Median travel time to work: 24.6 minutes

MENIFEE (city). Covers a land area of 46.466 square miles and a water area of 0.141 square miles. Located at 33.69° N. Lat; 117.18° W. Long. Elevation is 1,483 feet.

Population: 77,519; Growth (since 2000): n/a; Density: 1,668.3 persons per square mile; Race: 71.5% White, 5.0% Black/African American, 4.9% Asian, 0.8% American Indian/Alaska Native, 0.4% Native Hawaiian/Other Pacific Islander, 4.9% Two or more races, 33.0% Hispanic of any race; Average household size: 2.82; Median age: 38.1; Age under 18: 25.9%; Age 65 and over: 18.9%; Males per 100 females: 92.8; Marriage status: 27.1% never married, 52.8% now married, 2.0% separated, 7.3% widowed, 12.8% divorced; Foreign born: 13.8%; Speak English only: 78.0%; With disability: 13.5%; Veterans: 13.1%; Ancestry: 14.3% German, 11.4% Irish, 9.1% English, 5.5% Italian, 4.3% French

Employment: 11.5% management, business, and financial, 3.5% computer, engineering, and science, 7.9% education, legal, community service, arts, and media, 5.6% healthcare practitioners, 21.9% service, 27.7% sales and office, 11.0% natural resources, construction, and maintenance, 11.0% production, transportation, and material moving

Income: Per capita: $23,478; Median household: $54,903; Average household: $67,018; Households with income of $100,000 or more: 19.2%; Poverty rate: 10.3%

Educational Attainment: High school diploma or higher: 85.7%; Bachelor's degree or higher: 16.5%; Graduate/professional degree or higher: 5.3%

School District(s)

Menifee Union Elementary (KG-12)
2012-13 Enrollment: 9,955 . . . . (951) 672-1851
Perris Union High (07-12)
2012-13 Enrollment: 10,567 . . . . (951) 943-6369

Housing: Homeownership rate: 76.9%; Median home value: $193,100; Median year structure built: 1995; Homeowner vacancy rate: 4.1%; Median gross rent: $1,335 per month; Rental vacancy rate: 6.8%

Health Insurance: 84.5% have insurance; 62.9% have private insurance; 34.0% have public insurance; 15.5% do not have insurance; 7.9% of children under 18 do not have insurance

Safety: Violent crime rate: 12.0 per 10,000 population; Property crime rate: 203.3 per 10,000 population

Transportation: Commute: 90.8% car, 0.6% public transportation, 0.8% walk, 6.2% work from home; Median travel time to work: 38.0 minutes

Additional Information Contacts

City of Menifee . . . . (951) 672-6777
https://www.cityofmenifee.us

MESA VERDE (CDP). Covers a land area of 4.342 square miles and a water area of 0 square miles. Located at 33.60° N. Lat; 114.73° W. Long. Elevation is 390 feet.

Population: 1,023; Growth (since 2000): n/a; Density: 235.6 persons per square mile; Race: 57.6% White, 0.8% Black/African American, 0.4% Asian, 0.9% American Indian/Alaska Native, 0.1% Native Hawaiian/Other Pacific Islander, 3.8% Two or more races, 69.9% Hispanic of any race; Average household size: 3.28; Median age: 29.8; Age under 18: 32.7%; Age 65 and over: 10.0%; Males per 100 females: 110.9

Housing: Homeownership rate: 64.4%; Homeowner vacancy rate: 2.4%; Rental vacancy rate: 22.9%

MORENO VALLEY (city). Covers a land area of 51.275 square miles and a water area of 0.200 square miles. Located at 33.92° N. Lat; 117.21° W. Long. Elevation is 1,631 feet.

History: Named for the Spanish translation of "brownish" or "swarthy". As of 1990, Moreno Valley was California's fastest growing city. March Air Force Base in southwest is the oldest base in the Western United States. Incorporated 1984.

Population: 193,365; Growth (since 2000): 35.8%; Density: 3,771.2 persons per square mile; Race: 41.9% White, 18.0% Black/African American, 6.1% Asian, 0.9% American Indian/Alaska Native, 0.6% Native Hawaiian/Other Pacific Islander, 5.7% Two or more races, 54.4% Hispanic of any race; Average household size: 3.74; Median age: 28.6; Age under 18: 32.3%; Age 65 and over: 6.3%; Males per 100 females: 95.1; Marriage status: 38.2% never married, 48.7% now married, 3.6% separated, 3.8% widowed, 9.3% divorced; Foreign born: 24.7%; Speak English only: 49.3%; With disability: 9.4%; Veterans: 6.8%; Ancestry: 4.7% German, 3.4% American, 3.2% Irish, 2.9% English, 2.0% Italian

Employment: 9.4% management, business, and financial, 2.6% computer, engineering, and science, 7.5% education, legal, community service, arts, and media, 4.5% healthcare practitioners, 19.4% service, 28.5% sales and office, 10.5% natural resources, construction, and maintenance, 17.6% production, transportation, and material moving

Income: Per capita: $18,186; Median household: $54,918; Average household: $65,705; Households with income of $100,000 or more: 19.2%; Poverty rate: 19.5%

Educational Attainment: High school diploma or higher: 75.0%; Bachelor's degree or higher: 14.8%; Graduate/professional degree or higher: 4.3%

School District(s)

Moreno Valley Unified (KG-12)
2012-13 Enrollment: 34,922 . . . . (951) 571-7572
Riverside County Office of Education (KG-12)
2012-13 Enrollment: 7,864 . . . . (951) 826-6530
Val Verde Unified (KG-12)
2012-13 Enrollment: 19,832 . . . . (951) 940-6100

Two-year College(s)

Moreno Valley College (Public)
Fall 2013 Enrollment: 8,420 . . . . (951) 571-6100
2013-14 Tuition: In-state $1,416; Out-of-state $7,116
Sage College (Private, For-profit)
Fall 2013 Enrollment: 447 . . . . (951) 781-2727
2013-14 Tuition: In-state $12,460; Out-of-state $12,460

Vocational/Technical School(s)

Marinello Schools of Beauty-Moreno Valley (Private, For-profit)
Fall 2013 Enrollment: 254 . . . . (562) 945-2211
2013-14 Tuition: $18,511

Housing: Homeownership rate: 64.8%; Median home value: $178,400; Median year structure built: 1987; Homeowner vacancy rate: 3.4%; Median gross rent: $1,272 per month; Rental vacancy rate: 7.5%
Health Insurance: 75.9% have insurance; 48.8% have private insurance; 31.7% have public insurance; 24.1% do not have insurance; 13.5% of children under 18 do not have insurance
Hospitals: Kaiser Foundation Hospital - Moreno Valley; Riverside County Regional Medical Center (362 beds)
Safety: Violent crime rate: 31.7 per 10,000 population; Property crime rate: 291.7 per 10,000 population
Transportation: Commute: 92.0% car, 1.6% public transportation, 1.0% walk, 2.5% work from home; Median travel time to work: 34.2 minutes
Additional Information Contacts
City of Moreno Valley . . . . (951) 413-3000
http://www.moval.org

MOUNTAIN CENTER (CDP). Covers a land area of 1.884 square miles and a water area of 0.002 square miles. Located at 33.71° N. Lat; 116.73° W. Long. Elevation is 4,518 feet.
Population: 63; Growth (since 2000): n/a; Density: 33.4 persons per square mile; Race: 95.2% White, 0.0% Black/African American, 1.6% Asian, 1.6% American Indian/Alaska Native, 0.0% Native Hawaiian/Other Pacific Islander, 1.6% Two or more races, 23.8% Hispanic of any race; Average household size: 1.75; Median age: 53.5; Age under 18: 19.0%; Age 65 and over: 20.6%; Males per 100 females: 75.0
Housing: Homeownership rate: 69.5%; Homeowner vacancy rate: 28.6%; Rental vacancy rate: 26.7%

MURRIETA (city). Covers a land area of 33.577 square miles and a water area of 0.036 square miles. Located at 33.57° N. Lat; 117.19° W. Long. Elevation is 1,096 feet.
History: Named for Don Juan Murrieta, a sheep rancher who purchased 52,000 acres of land in the area in 1873. Unincorporated village. Has grown rapidly from 1980 to mid-1990s and is projected to continue to grow in 21st century.
Population: 103,466; Growth (since 2000): 133.7%; Density: 3,081.4 persons per square mile; Race: 69.7% White, 5.4% Black/African American, 9.2% Asian, 0.7% American Indian/Alaska Native, 0.4% Native Hawaiian/Other Pacific Islander, 6.1% Two or more races, 25.9% Hispanic of any race; Average household size: 3.15; Median age: 33.4; Age under 18: 30.4%; Age 65 and over: 10.1%; Males per 100 females: 95.2; Marriage status: 28.5% never married, 57.3% now married, 2.6% separated, 5.0% widowed, 9.2% divorced; Foreign born: 13.6%; Speak English only: 77.4%; With disability: 7.8%; Veterans: 10.3%; Ancestry: 13.6% German, 10.4% Irish, 9.9% English, 5.7% Italian, 4.9% American
Employment: 17.0% management, business, and financial, 5.2% computer, engineering, and science, 9.7% education, legal, community service, arts, and media, 5.7% healthcare practitioners, 21.0% service, 26.1% sales and office, 7.5% natural resources, construction, and maintenance, 7.7% production, transportation, and material moving
Income: Per capita: $28,452; Median household: $74,496; Average household: $88,971; Households with income of $100,000 or more: 33.9%; Poverty rate: 7.0%
Educational Attainment: High school diploma or higher: 92.0%; Bachelor's degree or higher: 29.0%; Graduate/professional degree or higher: 9.5%

School District(s)
Menifee Union Elementary (KG-12)
2012-13 Enrollment: 9,955 . . . . (951) 672-1851
Murrieta Valley Unified (KG-12)
2012-13 Enrollment: 22,929 . . . . (951) 696-1600
Temecula Valley Unified (KG-12)
2012-13 Enrollment: 30,337 . . . . (951) 676-2661

Four-year College(s)
The University of America (Private, Not-for-profit, Baptist)
Fall 2013 Enrollment: n/a . . . . (951) 200-3320
Housing: Homeownership rate: 70.5%; Median home value: $278,400; Median year structure built: 2000; Homeowner vacancy rate: 3.1%; Median gross rent: $1,502 per month; Rental vacancy rate: 7.8%
Health Insurance: 87.0% have insurance; 74.8% have private insurance; 20.7% have public insurance; 13.0% do not have insurance; 9.7% of children under 18 do not have insurance
Hospitals: Loma Linda University Medical Center - Murrieta; Southwest Healthcare System (96 beds)
Safety: Violent crime rate: 6.5 per 10,000 population; Property crime rate: 152.2 per 10,000 population
Transportation: Commute: 90.9% car, 0.2% public transportation, 0.9% walk, 6.2% work from home; Median travel time to work: 34.7 minutes
Airports: French Valley (general aviation)
Additional Information Contacts
City of Murrieta . . . . (951) 304-2489
http://www.murrieta.org

NORCO (city). Covers a land area of 13.962 square miles and a water area of 0.316 square miles. Located at 33.93° N. Lat; 117.55° W. Long. Elevation is 640 feet.
History: Named for the North Corona Land Company in 1922. Incorporated 1964.
Population: 27,063; Growth (since 2000): 12.0%; Density: 1,938.4 persons per square mile; Race: 76.3% White, 7.0% Black/African American, 3.1% Asian, 0.9% American Indian/Alaska Native, 0.2% Native Hawaiian/Other Pacific Islander, 3.2% Two or more races, 31.1% Hispanic of any race; Average household size: 3.23; Median age: 39.5; Age under 18: 20.3%; Age 65 and over: 9.7%; Males per 100 females: 136.8; Marriage status: 31.1% never married, 52.9% now married, 2.7% separated, 5.3% widowed, 10.7% divorced; Foreign born: 13.7%; Speak English only: 73.7%; With disability: 9.7%; Veterans: 7.7%; Ancestry: 14.9% German, 8.6% English, 7.6% Irish, 5.0% Italian, 4.5% European
Employment: 17.5% management, business, and financial, 3.6% computer, engineering, and science, 6.8% education, legal, community service, arts, and media, 4.6% healthcare practitioners, 15.4% service, 30.1% sales and office, 12.2% natural resources, construction, and maintenance, 9.7% production, transportation, and material moving
Income: Per capita: $27,032; Median household: $85,020; Average household: $98,114; Households with income of $100,000 or more: 40.7%; Poverty rate: 8.8%
Educational Attainment: High school diploma or higher: 81.3%; Bachelor's degree or higher: 17.8%; Graduate/professional degree or higher: 6.0%

School District(s)
Corona-Norco Unified (KG-12)
2012-13 Enrollment: 53,437 . . . . (951) 736-5000

Two-year College(s)
Norco College (Public)
Fall 2013 Enrollment: 9,648 . . . . (951) 372-7000
2013-14 Tuition: In-state $1,416; Out-of-state $7,116
Housing: Homeownership rate: 81.2%; Median home value: $383,200; Median year structure built: 1974; Homeowner vacancy rate: 1.9%; Median gross rent: $1,732 per month; Rental vacancy rate: 3.8%
Health Insurance: 88.2% have insurance; 69.1% have private insurance; 27.0% have public insurance; 11.8% do not have insurance; 4.0% of children under 18 do not have insurance
Safety: Violent crime rate: 15.3 per 10,000 population; Property crime rate: 216.0 per 10,000 population
Transportation: Commute: 89.7% car, 1.5% public transportation, 0.5% walk, 7.2% work from home; Median travel time to work: 35.5 minutes
Additional Information Contacts
City of Norco . . . . (951) 735-3900
http://www.ci.norco.ca.us

NORTH PALM SPRINGS (unincorporated postal area)
ZCTA: 92258
Covers a land area of 10.574 square miles and a water area of 0 square miles. Located at 33.92° N. Lat; 116.56° W. Long. Elevation is 863 feet.
Population: 861; Growth (since 2000): 20.1%; Density: 81.4 persons per square mile; Race: 46.2% White, 7.2% Black/African American, 0.8% Asian, 2.0% American Indian/Alaska Native, 0.1% Native Hawaiian/Other Pacific Islander, 2.9% Two or more races, 71.4% Hispanic of any race; Average household size: 3.24; Median age: 31.0; Age under 18: 29.2%; Age 65 and over: 8.4%; Males per 100 females: 120.8
Housing: Homeownership rate: 50.6%; Homeowner vacancy rate: 2.3%; Rental vacancy rate: 29.9%

NORTH SHORE (CDP). Covers a land area of 11.177 square miles and a water area of 0 square miles. Located at 33.52° N. Lat; 115.91° W. Long.
Population: 3,477; Growth (since 2000): n/a; Density: 311.1 persons per square mile; Race: 40.1% White, 0.9% Black/African American, 0.5% Asian, 0.7% American Indian/Alaska Native, 0.1% Native Hawaiian/Other

Pacific Islander, 3.4% Two or more races, 95.3% Hispanic of any race; Average household size: 4.64; Median age: 23.6; Age under 18: 39.9%; Age 65 and over: 3.8%; Males per 100 females: 110.6; Marriage status: 33.8% never married, 59.9% now married, 2.0% separated, 0.6% widowed, 5.7% divorced; Foreign born: 52.5%; Speak English only: 8.4%; With disability: 11.7%; Veterans: 0.7%; Ancestry: 1.9% American, 0.5% German, 0.5% Irish, 0.4% English

Employment: 6.5% management, business, and financial, 0.0% computer, engineering, and science, 2.8% education, legal, community service, arts, and media, 0.0% healthcare practitioners, 16.4% service, 3.2% sales and office, 59.1% natural resources, construction, and maintenance, 12.0% production, transportation, and material moving

Income: Per capita: $9,482; Median household: $25,833; Average household: $37,321; Households with income of $100,000 or more: 6.7%; Poverty rate: 38.7%

Educational Attainment: High school diploma or higher: 27.0%; Bachelor's degree or higher: 3.9%; Graduate/professional degree or higher: 3.9%

Housing: Homeownership rate: 80.8%; Median home value: $71,300; Median year structure built: 1991; Homeowner vacancy rate: 3.0%; Median gross rent: $913 per month; Rental vacancy rate: 12.5%

Health Insurance: 73.9% have insurance; 29.8% have private insurance; 52.5% have public insurance; 26.1% do not have insurance; 4.2% of children under 18 do not have insurance

Transportation: Commute: 98.1% car, 1.9% public transportation, 0.0% walk, 0.0% work from home; Median travel time to work: 30.9 minutes

NUEVO (CDP). Covers a land area of 6.771 square miles and a water area of 0 square miles. Located at 33.80° N. Lat; 117.14° W. Long. Elevation is 1,489 feet.

Population: 6,447; Growth (since 2000): 55.9%; Density: 952.1 persons per square mile; Race: 62.2% White, 1.8% Black/African American, 1.3% Asian, 1.4% American Indian/Alaska Native, 0.2% Native Hawaiian/Other Pacific Islander, 5.0% Two or more races, 54.5% Hispanic of any race; Average household size: 3.59; Median age: 32.9; Age under 18: 30.0%; Age 65 and over: 9.5%; Males per 100 females: 100.6; Marriage status: 36.8% never married, 52.1% now married, 0.8% separated, 3.1% widowed, 7.9% divorced; Foreign born: 22.1%; Speak English only: 50.4%; With disability: 7.8%; Veterans: 6.0%; Ancestry: 13.4% Irish, 8.6% German, 7.4% English, 2.8% American, 2.6% French

Employment: 9.5% management, business, and financial, 1.3% computer, engineering, and science, 13.8% education, legal, community service, arts, and media, 3.9% healthcare practitioners, 16.5% service, 25.3% sales and office, 16.0% natural resources, construction, and maintenance, 13.5% production, transportation, and material moving

Income: Per capita: $18,846; Median household: $56,590; Average household: $67,913; Households with income of $100,000 or more: 22.2%; Poverty rate: 19.0%

Educational Attainment: High school diploma or higher: 76.5%; Bachelor's degree or higher: 14.4%; Graduate/professional degree or higher: 3.1%

School District(s)

Nuview Union (KG-12)
2012-13 Enrollment: 2,345 . . . . (951) 928-0066

Housing: Homeownership rate: 78.0%; Median home value: $213,300; Median year structure built: 1985; Homeowner vacancy rate: 2.6%; Median gross rent: $1,135 per month; Rental vacancy rate: 4.1%

Health Insurance: 82.8% have insurance; 56.6% have private insurance; 31.2% have public insurance; 17.2% do not have insurance; 5.7% of children under 18 do not have insurance

Transportation: Commute: 92.9% car, 0.3% public transportation, 3.3% walk, 0.2% work from home; Median travel time to work: 33.6 minutes

OASIS (CDP). Covers a land area of 19.631 square miles and a water area of 0 square miles. Located at 33.53° N. Lat; 116.13° W. Long. Elevation is -144 feet.

Population: 6,890; Growth (since 2000): n/a; Density: 351.0 persons per square mile; Race: 24.6% White, 0.3% Black/African American, 0.6% Asian, 1.4% American Indian/Alaska Native, 0.0% Native Hawaiian/Other Pacific Islander, 1.6% Two or more races, 97.7% Hispanic of any race; Average household size: 4.67; Median age: 22.1; Age under 18: 42.1%; Age 65 and over: 2.9%; Males per 100 females: 115.9; Marriage status: 37.5% never married, 56.0% now married, 1.8% separated, 4.3% widowed, 2.1% divorced; Foreign born: 61.5%; Speak English only: 3.6%; With disability: 10.0%; Veterans: 0.2%; Ancestry: 0.8% Scotch-Irish, 0.8% Welsh, 0.8% Danish, 0.8% African, 0.5% German

Employment: 3.0% management, business, and financial, 0.0% computer, engineering, and science, 3.1% education, legal, community service, arts, and media, 0.0% healthcare practitioners, 17.4% service, 6.9% sales and office, 60.6% natural resources, construction, and maintenance, 8.9% production, transportation, and material moving

Income: Per capita: $7,474; Median household: $23,291; Average household: $31,241; Households with income of $100,000 or more: 1.2%; Poverty rate: 51.4%

Educational Attainment: High school diploma or higher: 19.6%; Bachelor's degree or higher: 0.8%; Graduate/professional degree or higher: 0.2%

Housing: Homeownership rate: 23.5%; Median home value: $11,200; Median year structure built: 1981; Homeowner vacancy rate: 1.1%; Median gross rent: $542 per month; Rental vacancy rate: 1.4%

Health Insurance: 58.6% have insurance; 16.5% have private insurance; 43.3% have public insurance; 41.4% do not have insurance; 17.9% of children under 18 do not have insurance

Transportation: Commute: 89.2% car, 1.5% public transportation, 5.6% walk, 3.2% work from home; Median travel time to work: 22.3 minutes

PALM DESERT (city). Covers a land area of 26.810 square miles and a water area of 0.204 square miles. Located at 33.74° N. Lat; 116.36° W. Long. Elevation is 220 feet.

History: Palm Desert was incorporated in 1973 and was initially known as "Old MacDonald Ranch," but became Palm Village in the 1920s when numerous date palm trees were planted.

Population: 48,445; Growth (since 2000): 17.7%; Density: 1,807.0 persons per square mile; Race: 82.5% White, 1.8% Black/African American, 3.4% Asian, 0.5% American Indian/Alaska Native, 0.1% Native Hawaiian/Other Pacific Islander, 2.5% Two or more races, 22.8% Hispanic of any race; Average household size: 2.08; Median age: 53.0; Age under 18: 15.6%; Age 65 and over: 32.9%; Males per 100 females: 88.7; Marriage status: 22.6% never married, 53.4% now married, 2.5% separated, 10.1% widowed, 13.9% divorced; Foreign born: 17.7%; Speak English only: 75.4%; With disability: 14.0%; Veterans: 13.1%; Ancestry: 15.2% German, 13.1% English, 9.7% Irish, 5.7% American, 4.3% Italian

Employment: 14.2% management, business, and financial, 2.2% computer, engineering, and science, 12.0% education, legal, community service, arts, and media, 8.2% healthcare practitioners, 24.9% service, 24.9% sales and office, 7.2% natural resources, construction, and maintenance, 6.4% production, transportation, and material moving

Income: Per capita: $40,266; Median household: $51,188; Average household: $81,445; Households with income of $100,000 or more: 23.4%; Poverty rate: 9.8%

Educational Attainment: High school diploma or higher: 91.3%; Bachelor's degree or higher: 34.6%; Graduate/professional degree or higher: 12.5%

School District(s)

Desert Sands Unified (KG-12)
2012-13 Enrollment: 29,159 . . . . (760) 777-4200

Two-year College(s)

College of the Desert (Public)
Fall 2013 Enrollment: 9,259 . . . . (760) 346-8041
2013-14 Tuition: In-state $1,316; Out-of-state $6,636

Vocational/Technical School(s)

International School of Beauty Inc (Private, For-profit)
Fall 2013 Enrollment: 229 . . . . (760) 674-1624
2013-14 Tuition: $16,000

Milan Institute-Palm Desert (Private, For-profit)
Fall 2013 Enrollment: 272 . . . . (760) 469-4545
2013-14 Tuition: $11,477

Housing: Homeownership rate: 65.6%; Median home value: $308,000; Median year structure built: 1984; Homeowner vacancy rate: 5.0%; Median gross rent: $1,103 per month; Rental vacancy rate: 16.8%

Health Insurance: 86.7% have insurance; 68.8% have private insurance; 42.2% have public insurance; 13.3% do not have insurance; 7.2% of children under 18 do not have insurance

Safety: Violent crime rate: 21.8 per 10,000 population; Property crime rate: 439.0 per 10,000 population

Newspapers: Desert Mobile Home News (weekly circulation 12000)

Transportation: Commute: 86.3% car, 2.3% public transportation, 1.6% walk, 7.7% work from home; Median travel time to work: 19.8 minutes; Amtrak: Bus service available.

Additional Information Contacts

City of Palm Desert . . . . (760) 346-0611
http://www.cityofpalmdesert.org

PALM SPRINGS (city). Covers a land area of 94.116 square miles and a water area of 0.859 square miles. Located at 33.80° N. Lat; 116.54° W. Long. Elevation is 479 feet.

History: Named for the palm trees and the warm water springs in the area. First known as Agua Caliente (hot water) because of its hot springs, settlement at Palm Springs dates from 1876 when the Southern Pacific laid tracks through Coachella Valley. Promoters in the 1930s brought about the development of the town as a winter resort.

Population: 44,552; Growth (since 2000): 4.1%; Density: 473.4 persons per square mile; Race: 75.7% White, 4.4% Black/African American, 4.4% Asian, 1.0% American Indian/Alaska Native, 0.2% Native Hawaiian/Other Pacific Islander, 3.1% Two or more races, 25.3% Hispanic of any race; Average household size: 1.93; Median age: 51.6; Age under 18: 13.7%; Age 65 and over: 26.5%; Males per 100 females: 129.3; Marriage status: 39.7% never married, 35.3% now married, 1.9% separated, 8.3% widowed, 16.7% divorced; Foreign born: 20.6%; Speak English only: 71.2%; With disability: 17.2%; Veterans: 12.0%; Ancestry: 13.5% German, 11.7% English, 10.3% Irish, 5.4% Italian, 3.4% French

Employment: 15.3% management, business, and financial, 3.1% computer, engineering, and science, 11.4% education, legal, community service, arts, and media, 7.1% healthcare practitioners, 26.1% service, 23.1% sales and office, 8.6% natural resources, construction, and maintenance, 5.3% production, transportation, and material moving

Income: Per capita: $35,578; Median household: $45,198; Average household: $68,904; Households with income of $100,000 or more: 19.9%; Poverty rate: 18.2%

Educational Attainment: High school diploma or higher: 87.9%; Bachelor's degree or higher: 34.1%; Graduate/professional degree or higher: 13.6%

School District(s)

Palm Springs Unified (KG-12)
2012-13 Enrollment: 23,581 . . . . (760) 416-6000

Two-year College(s)

Kaplan College-Palm Springs (Private, For-profit)
Fall 2013 Enrollment: 362 . . . . (760) 778-3540

Vocational/Technical School(s)

California Nurses Educational Institute (Private, For-profit)
Fall 2013 Enrollment: 223 . . . . (760) 416-5955
2013-14 Tuition: $29,000

Champion Institute of Cosmetology (Private, For-profit)
Fall 2013 Enrollment: 74 . . . . (760) 322-2227
2013-14 Tuition: $13,858

Housing: Homeownership rate: 58.7%; Median home value: $267,800; Median year structure built: 1975; Homeowner vacancy rate: 6.7%; Median gross rent: $950 per month; Rental vacancy rate: 15.5%

Health Insurance: 79.8% have insurance; 54.0% have private insurance; 41.5% have public insurance; 20.2% do not have insurance; 15.7% of children under 18 do not have insurance

Hospitals: Desert Regional Medical Center (398 beds)

Safety: Violent crime rate: 55.1 per 10,000 population; Property crime rate: 507.8 per 10,000 population

Newspapers: Desert Sun (daily circulation 45000); The Desert Sun (weekly circulation 20000)

Transportation: Commute: 80.7% car, 1.9% public transportation, 2.9% walk, 11.9% work from home; Median travel time to work: 21.6 minutes; Amtrak: Train and bus service available.

Airports: Bermuda Dunes (general aviation); Jacqueline Cochran Regional (general aviation); Palm Springs International (primary service/small hub)

Additional Information Contacts

City of Palm Springs . . . . (760) 323-8299
http://www.ci.palm-springs.ca.us

PERRIS (city). Covers a land area of 31.393 square miles and a water area of 0.110 square miles. Located at 33.79° N. Lat; 117.22° W. Long. Elevation is 1,453 feet.

History: Named for Fred T. Perris, town founder and chief engineer for the California Southern Railroad. Perris was platted in 1885 and incorporated in 1911, succeeding an older settlement known as Pinecate, just south along the Santa Fe Railway line.

Population: 68,386; Growth (since 2000): 89.0%; Density: 2,178.4 persons per square mile; Race: 42.3% White, 12.1% Black/African American, 3.6% Asian, 0.9% American Indian/Alaska Native, 0.4% Native Hawaiian/Other Pacific Islander, 5.1% Two or more races, 71.8% Hispanic of any race; Average household size: 4.16; Median age: 25.9; Age under 18: 37.0%; Age 65 and over: 4.9%; Males per 100 females: 98.3; Marriage status: 39.0% never married, 49.2% now married, 3.2% separated, 3.9% widowed, 7.9% divorced; Foreign born: 28.6%; Speak English only: 38.1%; With disability: 9.5%; Veterans: 4.3%; Ancestry: 2.9% German, 2.7% Irish, 1.3% English, 1.0% American, 0.8% Italian

Employment: 6.0% management, business, and financial, 1.4% computer, engineering, and science, 6.9% education, legal, community service, arts, and media, 3.4% healthcare practitioners, 21.5% service, 25.2% sales and office, 12.1% natural resources, construction, and maintenance, 23.5% production, transportation, and material moving

Income: Per capita: $13,666; Median household: $48,311; Average household: $54,663; Households with income of $100,000 or more: 11.6%; Poverty rate: 25.9%

Educational Attainment: High school diploma or higher: 62.0%; Bachelor's degree or higher: 8.4%; Graduate/professional degree or higher: 2.4%

School District(s)

Perris Elementary (KG-07)
2012-13 Enrollment: 5,837 . . . . (951) 657-3118

Perris Union High (07-12)
2012-13 Enrollment: 10,567 . . . . (951) 943-6369

Val Verde Unified (KG-12)
2012-13 Enrollment: 19,832 . . . . (951) 940-6100

Housing: Homeownership rate: 66.3%; Median home value: $155,600; Median year structure built: 1996; Homeowner vacancy rate: 5.5%; Median gross rent: $1,211 per month; Rental vacancy rate: 6.8%

Health Insurance: 72.7% have insurance; 39.9% have private insurance; 35.9% have public insurance; 27.3% do not have insurance; 12.0% of children under 18 do not have insurance

Safety: Violent crime rate: 33.4 per 10,000 population; Property crime rate: 282.4 per 10,000 population

Newspapers: Perris Progress/Perris City News (weekly circulation 3500)

Transportation: Commute: 93.8% car, 1.8% public transportation, 1.2% walk, 1.9% work from home; Median travel time to work: 37.0 minutes; Amtrak: Bus service available.

Additional Information Contacts

City of Perris . . . . (951) 943-6100
http://www.cityofperris.org

QUAIL VALLEY (unincorporated postal area)

ZCTA: 92587

Covers a land area of 7.903 square miles and a water area of 0.745 square miles. Located at 33.69° N. Lat; 117.25° W. Long. Elevation is 1,545 feet.

Population: 16,675; Growth (since 2000): 27.0%; Density: 2,110.0 persons per square mile; Race: 82.4% White, 1.8% Black/African American, 1.7% Asian, 0.9% American Indian/Alaska Native, 0.3% Native Hawaiian/Other Pacific Islander, 4.0% Two or more races, 27.8% Hispanic of any race; Average household size: 2.94; Median age: 38.1; Age under 18: 26.1%; Age 65 and over: 12.7%; Males per 100 females: 100.4; Marriage status: 26.0% never married, 59.8% now married, 2.5% separated, 6.1% widowed, 8.0% divorced; Foreign born: 9.8%; Speak English only: 81.4%; With disability: 8.8%; Veterans: 9.7%; Ancestry: 18.3% German, 14.0% Irish, 8.5% English, 7.4% American, 5.6% Italian

Employment: 13.9% management, business, and financial, 2.6% computer, engineering, and science, 7.8% education, legal, community service, arts, and media, 6.6% healthcare practitioners, 21.6% service, 24.6% sales and office, 13.1% natural resources, construction, and maintenance, 9.7% production, transportation, and material moving

Income: Per capita: $28,573; Median household: $67,321; Average household: $81,487; Households with income of $100,000 or more: 26.9%; Poverty rate: 11.5%

Educational Attainment: High school diploma or higher: 89.1%; Bachelor's degree or higher: 20.1%; Graduate/professional degree or higher: 5.7%

School District(s)

Menifee Union Elementary (KG-12)
2012-13 Enrollment: 9,955 . . . . (951) 672-1851

Housing: Homeownership rate: 79.0%; Median home value: $255,100; Median year structure built: 1985; Homeowner vacancy rate: 3.6%; Median gross rent: $1,752 per month; Rental vacancy rate: 6.6%

Health Insurance: 85.8% have insurance; 70.2% have private insurance; 25.6% have public insurance; 14.2% do not have insurance; 7.5% of children under 18 do not have insurance

Transportation: Commute: 89.7% car, 1.1% public transportation, 0.0% walk, 7.3% work from home; Median travel time to work: 42.4 minutes

RANCHO MIRAGE (city). Covers a land area of 24.447 square miles and a water area of 0.389 square miles. Located at 33.76° N. Lat; 116.43° W. Long. Elevation is 272 feet.

History: Rancho Mirage is a resort city in Palm Springs Valley and was incorporated on August 3, 1973. Rancho Mirage increased in popularity after World War II when its first resort, Thunderbird Guest Ranch, opened in 1946.

Population: 17,218; Growth (since 2000): 30.0%; Density: 704.3 persons per square mile; Race: 88.7% White, 1.5% Black/African American, 3.8% Asian, 0.5% American Indian/Alaska Native, 0.1% Native Hawaiian/Other Pacific Islander, 2.0% Two or more races, 11.4% Hispanic of any race; Average household size: 1.94; Median age: 62.3; Age under 18: 10.6%; Age 65 and over: 44.0%; Males per 100 females: 97.7; Marriage status: 23.0% never married, 55.1% now married, 1.0% separated, 10.3% widowed, 11.6% divorced; Foreign born: 13.6%; Speak English only: 82.1%; With disability: 15.6%; Veterans: 18.1%; Ancestry: 13.9% German, 11.7% English, 9.7% Irish, 7.8% Italian, 5.5% American

Employment: 20.3% management, business, and financial, 2.5% computer, engineering, and science, 8.5% education, legal, community service, arts, and media, 12.0% healthcare practitioners, 13.4% service, 32.8% sales and office, 6.7% natural resources, construction, and maintenance, 3.8% production, transportation, and material moving

Income: Per capita: $61,620; Median household: $77,526; Average household: $123,757; Households with income of $100,000 or more: 40.0%; Poverty rate: 13.6%

Educational Attainment: High school diploma or higher: 95.3%; Bachelor's degree or higher: 40.0%; Graduate/professional degree or higher: 17.7%

School District(s)

Palm Springs Unified (KG-12)
2012-13 Enrollment: 23,581 . . . . (760) 416-6000

Housing: Homeownership rate: 80.3%; Median home value: $518,000; Median year structure built: 1984; Homeowner vacancy rate: 5.0%; Median gross rent: $1,338 per month; Rental vacancy rate: 17.2%

Health Insurance: 90.1% have insurance; 71.2% have private insurance; 50.4% have public insurance; 9.9% do not have insurance; 7.1% of children under 18 do not have insurance

Hospitals: Eisenhower Medical Center (253 beds)

Safety: Violent crime rate: 14.6 per 10,000 population; Property crime rate: 357.0 per 10,000 population

Transportation: Commute: 80.3% car, 1.2% public transportation, 1.4% walk, 15.9% work from home; Median travel time to work: 22.3 minutes

Additional Information Contacts

City of Rancho Mirage. . . . . (760) 324-4511
http://www.ranchomirageca.gov

RIPLEY (CDP). Covers a land area of 1.701 square miles and a water area of 0 square miles. Located at 33.52° N. Lat; 114.65° W. Long. Elevation is 249 feet.

Population: 692; Growth (since 2000): n/a; Density: 406.9 persons per square mile; Race: 56.8% White, 14.9% Black/African American, 0.1% Asian, 0.3% American Indian/Alaska Native, 0.6% Native Hawaiian/Other Pacific Islander, 3.5% Two or more races, 77.6% Hispanic of any race; Average household size: 3.17; Median age: 24.8; Age under 18: 38.2%; Age 65 and over: 9.2%; Males per 100 females: 98.3

Housing: Homeownership rate: 35.8%; Homeowner vacancy rate: 2.5%; Rental vacancy rate: 25.8%

RIVERSIDE (city). County seat. Covers a land area of 81.140 square miles and a water area of 0.304 square miles. Located at 33.94° N. Lat; 117.39° W. Long. Elevation is 827 feet.

History: Named for its location on the upper canal of the Santa Ana River, in 1871. Riverside was established on the Jurupa Rancho of Don Juan Bandini, purchased in 1870 by the Southern California Colony Association, who surveyed the townsite. In 1873 a Riverside woman obtained from the Department of Agriculture two cuttings of a variety of orange that became the popular navel orange.

Population: 303,871; Growth (since 2000): 19.1%; Density: 3,745.0 persons per square mile; Race: 56.5% White, 7.0% Black/African American, 7.4% Asian, 1.1% American Indian/Alaska Native, 0.4% Native Hawaiian/Other Pacific Islander, 5.1% Two or more races, 49.0% Hispanic of any race; Average household size: 3.18; Median age: 30.0; Age under 18: 26.8%; Age 65 and over: 8.6%; Males per 100 females: 97.6; Marriage status: 39.5% never married, 46.1% now married, 2.5% separated, 4.6% widowed, 9.8% divorced; Foreign born: 23.0%; Speak English only: 57.4%; With disability: 9.2%; Veterans: 6.5%; Ancestry: 8.6% German, 6.4% Irish, 5.5% English, 3.6% Italian, 3.0% American

Employment: 10.1% management, business, and financial, 3.3% computer, engineering, and science, 12.1% education, legal, community service, arts, and media, 4.3% healthcare practitioners, 18.0% service, 25.8% sales and office, 10.7% natural resources, construction, and maintenance, 15.6% production, transportation, and material moving

Income: Per capita: $22,182; Median household: $55,636; Average household: $71,905; Households with income of $100,000 or more: 22.6%; Poverty rate: 19.1%

Educational Attainment: High school diploma or higher: 77.7%; Bachelor's degree or higher: 22.2%; Graduate/professional degree or higher: 9.5%

School District(s)

Alvord Unified (KG-12)
2012-13 Enrollment: 19,634 . . . . (951) 509-5070

California School for the Deaf-Riverside (State Sp (KG-12)
2012-13 Enrollment: 385. . . . . (951) 782-6500

Riverside County Office of Education (KG-12)
2012-13 Enrollment: 7,864 . . . . (951) 826-6530

Riverside County Office of Education Rop
2012-13 Enrollment: n/a . . . . (909) 826-6797

Riverside Unified (KG-12)
2012-13 Enrollment: 42,560 . . . . (951) 788-7131

Four-year College(s)

California Baptist University (Private, Not-for-profit, Southern Baptist)
Fall 2013 Enrollment: 7,144 . . . . (951) 689-5771
2013-14 Tuition: In-state $28,122; Out-of-state $28,122

La Sierra University (Private, Not-for-profit, Seventh Day Adventists)
Fall 2013 Enrollment: 2,440 . . . . (951) 785-2000
2013-14 Tuition: In-state $29,103; Out-of-state $29,103

Platt College-Riverside (Private, For-profit)
Fall 2013 Enrollment: 334 . . . . (951) 572-4300
2013-14 Tuition: In-state $14,572; Out-of-state $14,572

University of California-Riverside (Public)
Fall 2013 Enrollment: 21,207 . . . . (951) 827-1012
2013-14 Tuition: In-state $12,960; Out-of-state $35,838

Two-year College(s)

American College of Healthcare (Private, For-profit)
Fall 2013 Enrollment: 290 . . . . (951) 729-5320

Kaplan College-Riverside (Private, For-profit)
Fall 2013 Enrollment: 234 . . . . (951) 276-1704

Riverside City College (Public)
Fall 2013 Enrollment: 18,165 . . . . (951) 222-8000
2013-14 Tuition: In-state $1,426; Out-of-state $7,126

Vocational/Technical School(s)

InterCoast Colleges-Riverside (Private, For-profit)
Fall 2013 Enrollment: 84 . . . . (951) 779-0700
2013-14 Tuition: $15,223

North-West College-Riverside (Private, For-profit)
Fall 2013 Enrollment: 392 . . . . (951) 351-7750
2013-14 Tuition: $28,525

Riverside County Office of Education (Public)
Fall 2013 Enrollment: 386 . . . . (951) 826-4723
2013-14 Tuition: $1,900

Housing: Homeownership rate: 55.7%; Median home value: $235,900; Median year structure built: 1975; Homeowner vacancy rate: 2.4%; Median gross rent: $1,135 per month; Rental vacancy rate: 7.4%

Health Insurance: 79.1% have insurance; 56.1% have private insurance; 29.0% have public insurance; 20.9% do not have insurance; 10.8% of children under 18 do not have insurance

Hospitals: Kaiser Foundation Hospital - Riverside (215 beds); Parkview Community Hospital Medical Center (193 beds); Riverside Community Hospital

Safety: Violent crime rate: 42.0 per 10,000 population; Property crime rate: 335.2 per 10,000 population

Newspapers: Press-Enterprise (daily circulation 171000); Riverside County Record (weekly circulation 3000)

Transportation: Commute: 89.0% car, 2.6% public transportation, 2.8% walk, 3.8% work from home; Median travel time to work: 28.5 minutes; Amtrak: Train and bus service available.

Airports: March ARB (general aviation); Riverside Municipal (general aviation)

Additional Information Contacts

City of Riverside . . . . (951) 826-5311
http://www.riverside-ca.org

ROMOLAND (CDP). Covers a land area of 2.644 square miles and a water area of 0 square miles. Located at 33.76° N. Lat; 117.16° W. Long. Elevation is 1,444 feet.

Population: 1,684; Growth (since 2000): -39.1%; Density: 636.8 persons per square mile; Race: 56.9% White, 3.9% Black/African American, 2.1% Asian, 0.5% American Indian/Alaska Native, 0.7% Native Hawaiian/Other Pacific Islander, 5.5% Two or more races, 51.4% Hispanic of any race; Average household size: 3.70; Median age: 32.0; Age under 18: 29.8%; Age 65 and over: 7.8%; Males per 100 females: 100.0

School District(s)

Perris Union High (07-12)
2012-13 Enrollment: 10,567 . . . . (951) 943-6369
Romoland Elementary (KG-08)
2012-13 Enrollment: 3,233 . . . . (951) 926-9244

Housing: Homeownership rate: 77.1%; Homeowner vacancy rate: 3.3%; Rental vacancy rate: 3.7%

SAN JACINTO (city). Covers a land area of 25.716 square miles and a water area of 0.415 square miles. Located at 33.80° N. Lat; 116.99° W. Long. Elevation is 1,565 feet.

History: Named for the Spanish translation of "St. Hyacinth". San Jacinto was founded by Procco Akimo, a Russian exiled from his native land during the Tsarist terrors of the 1870s.

Population: 44,199; Growth (since 2000): 85.9%; Density: 1,718.7 persons per square mile; Race: 57.2% White, 6.6% Black/African American, 3.0% Asian, 1.8% American Indian/Alaska Native, 0.3% Native Hawaiian/Other Pacific Islander, 5.7% Two or more races, 52.3% Hispanic of any race; Average household size: 3.34; Median age: 30.3; Age under 18: 32.8%; Age 65 and over: 10.6%; Males per 100 females: 95.6; Marriage status: 33.6% never married, 48.9% now married, 2.0% separated, 5.7% widowed, 11.8% divorced; Foreign born: 20.4%; Speak English only: 61.4%; With disability: 14.3%; Veterans: 9.1%; Ancestry: 10.2% German, 6.9% English, 6.5% Irish, 3.4% American, 3.0% Italian

Employment: 7.7% management, business, and financial, 2.0% computer, engineering, and science, 8.7% education, legal, community service, arts, and media, 4.9% healthcare practitioners, 25.8% service, 26.1% sales and office, 11.8% natural resources, construction, and maintenance, 13.0% production, transportation, and material moving

Income: Per capita: $17,787; Median household: $46,769; Average household: $56,701; Households with income of $100,000 or more: 14.1%; Poverty rate: 17.4%

Educational Attainment: High school diploma or higher: 75.0%; Bachelor's degree or higher: 13.3%; Graduate/professional degree or higher: 4.5%

School District(s)

Nuview Union (KG-12)
2012-13 Enrollment: 2,345 . . . . (951) 928-0066
San Jacinto Unified (KG-12)
2012-13 Enrollment: 10,041 . . . . (951) 929-7700

Two-year College(s)

Mt San Jacinto Community College District (Public)
Fall 2013 Enrollment: 14,170 . . . . (951) 487-6752
2013-14 Tuition: In-state $1,386; Out-of-state $6,936

Vocational/Technical School(s)

Advance Beauty Techs Academy (Private, For-profit)
Fall 2013 Enrollment: 61 . . . . (951) 487-8751
2013-14 Tuition: $16,885

Housing: Homeownership rate: 68.0%; Median home value: $138,300; Median year structure built: 1991; Homeowner vacancy rate: 5.7%; Median gross rent: $1,064 per month; Rental vacancy rate: 10.3%

Health Insurance: 80.5% have insurance; 50.4% have private insurance; 39.0% have public insurance; 19.5% do not have insurance; 7.2% of children under 18 do not have insurance

Safety: Violent crime rate: 27.1 per 10,000 population; Property crime rate: 394.8 per 10,000 population

Transportation: Commute: 93.5% car, 0.1% public transportation, 2.4% walk, 2.9% work from home; Median travel time to work: 35.9 minutes

Additional Information Contacts

City of San Jacinto . . . . (951) 487-7330
http://www.ci.san-jacinto.ca.us

SKY VALLEY (CDP). Covers a land area of 24.269 square miles and a water area of 0 square miles. Located at 33.89° N. Lat; 116.35° W. Long. Elevation is 1,060 feet.

Population: 2,406; Growth (since 2000): n/a; Density: 99.1 persons per square mile; Race: 81.5% White, 1.5% Black/African American, 0.9% Asian, 1.4% American Indian/Alaska Native, 0.1% Native Hawaiian/Other Pacific Islander, 2.9% Two or more races, 28.3% Hispanic of any race; Average household size: 2.25; Median age: 53.5; Age under 18: 15.3%; Age 65 and over: 30.6%; Males per 100 females: 114.6

Housing: Homeownership rate: 80.2%; Homeowner vacancy rate: 5.0%; Rental vacancy rate: 23.2%

SUN CITY (unincorporated postal area)

ZCTA: 92585

Covers a land area of 20.303 square miles and a water area of 0 square miles. Located at 33.75° N. Lat; 117.17° W. Long. Elevation is 1,424 feet.

Population: 17,797; Growth (since 2000): 105.2%; Density: 876.6 persons per square mile; Race: 62.3% White, 4.8% Black/African American, 4.3% Asian, 0.9% American Indian/Alaska Native, 0.4% Native Hawaiian/Other Pacific Islander, 5.1% Two or more races, 45.6% Hispanic of any race; Average household size: 3.28; Median age: 32.6; Age under 18: 29.9%; Age 65 and over: 11.4%; Males per 100 females: 98.8; Marriage status: 33.5% never married, 52.1% now married, 1.7% separated, 4.8% widowed, 9.7% divorced; Foreign born: 17.1%; Speak English only: 67.8%; With disability: 10.9%; Veterans: 8.5%; Ancestry: 11.4% German, 8.4% English, 6.8% Irish, 5.1% Italian, 4.4% French

Employment: 8.7% management, business, and financial, 0.9% computer, engineering, and science, 6.7% education, legal, community service, arts, and media, 6.2% healthcare practitioners, 20.5% service, 29.9% sales and office, 12.9% natural resources, construction, and maintenance, 14.2% production, transportation, and material moving

Income: Per capita: $21,108; Median household: $61,782; Average household: $69,867; Households with income of $100,000 or more: 19.3%; Poverty rate: 14.1%

Educational Attainment: High school diploma or higher: 80.3%; Bachelor's degree or higher: 17.3%; Graduate/professional degree or higher: 4.9%

School District(s)

Menifee Union Elementary (KG-12)
2012-13 Enrollment: 9,955 . . . . (951) 672-1851

Housing: Homeownership rate: 79.2%; Median home value: $195,900; Median year structure built: 1999; Homeowner vacancy rate: 4.9%; Median gross rent: $1,404 per month; Rental vacancy rate: 3.6%

Health Insurance: 79.0% have insurance; 55.6% have private insurance; 31.6% have public insurance; 21.0% do not have insurance; 9.5% of children under 18 do not have insurance

Hospitals: Menifee Valley Medical Center (84 beds)

Transportation: Commute: 89.4% car, 0.5% public transportation, 2.0% walk, 7.1% work from home; Median travel time to work: 37.6 minutes

ZCTA: 92586

Covers a land area of 7.062 square miles and a water area of 0 square miles. Located at 33.71° N. Lat; 117.20° W. Long. Elevation is 1,424 feet.

Population: 19,815; Growth (since 2000): 9.2%; Density: 2,805.8 persons per square mile; Race: 80.1% White, 5.0% Black/African American, 3.0% Asian, 0.9% American Indian/Alaska Native, 0.3% Native Hawaiian/Other Pacific Islander, 3.3% Two or more races, 22.9% Hispanic of any race; Average household size: 2.05; Median age: 60.6; Age under 18: 13.8%; Age 65 and over: 42.4%; Males per 100 females: 79.1; Marriage status: 15.6% never married, 50.1% now married, 1.1% separated, 15.7% widowed, 18.5% divorced; Foreign born: 13.2%; Speak English only: 83.2%; With disability: 23.8%; Veterans: 17.7%; Ancestry: 17.3% German, 12.2% Irish, 11.5% English, 6.4% American, 4.6% Italian

Employment: 9.4% management, business, and financial, 2.5% computer, engineering, and science, 8.8% education, legal, community service, arts,

and media, 5.4% healthcare practitioners, 24.4% service, 30.0% sales and office, 10.0% natural resources, construction, and maintenance, 9.4% production, transportation, and material moving
Income: Per capita: $24,051; Median household: $35,935; Average household: $48,510; Households with income of $100,000 or more: 9.0%; Poverty rate: 12.5%
Educational Attainment: High school diploma or higher: 85.4%; Bachelor's degree or higher: 11.8%; Graduate/professional degree or higher: 4.2%
Housing: Homeownership rate: 73.0%; Median home value: $139,100; Median year structure built: 1980; Homeowner vacancy rate: 3.2%; Median gross rent: $1,043 per month; Rental vacancy rate: 8.8%
Health Insurance: 87.0% have insurance; 56.3% have private insurance; 56.2% have public insurance; 13.0% do not have insurance; 6.2% of children under 18 do not have insurance
Transportation: Commute: 87.6% car, 2.2% public transportation, 0.7% walk, 7.1% work from home; Median travel time to work: 37.4 minutes

TEMECULA (city). Covers a land area of 30.151 square miles and a water area of 0.016 square miles. Located at 33.50° N. Lat; 117.12° W. Long. Elevation is 1,017 feet.
History: Named for a local rancho belonging to Mission San Luis Rey. Temecula was founded in 1882 when the railroad connected San Bernardino with San Diego. In 1892 the railroad tracks were destroyed by torrential rains. Early residents of Temecula claimed that the wind blew here every afternoon.
Population: 100,097; Growth (since 2000): 73.4%; Density: 3,319.8 persons per square mile; Race: 70.8% White, 4.1% Black/African American, 9.8% Asian, 1.1% American Indian/Alaska Native, 0.4% Native Hawaiian/Other Pacific Islander, 5.9% Two or more races, 24.7% Hispanic of any race; Average household size: 3.15; Median age: 33.4; Age under 18: 30.7%; Age 65 and over: 7.8%; Males per 100 females: 95.9; Marriage status: 31.4% never married, 55.4% now married, 1.7% separated, 3.4% widowed, 9.8% divorced; Foreign born: 15.2%; Speak English only: 78.7%; With disability: 8.0%; Veterans: 10.1%; Ancestry: 12.6% German, 11.0% Irish, 8.1% English, 7.2% Italian, 3.2% Polish
Employment: 16.1% management, business, and financial, 5.4% computer, engineering, and science, 10.3% education, legal, community service, arts, and media, 6.1% healthcare practitioners, 20.3% service, 25.3% sales and office, 8.2% natural resources, construction, and maintenance, 8.4% production, transportation, and material moving
Income: Per capita: $28,018; Median household: $78,356; Average household: $88,867; Households with income of $100,000 or more: 36.5%; Poverty rate: 8.5%
Educational Attainment: High school diploma or higher: 91.5%; Bachelor's degree or higher: 29.8%; Graduate/professional degree or higher: 9.4%

School District(s)

Riverside County Office of Education (KG-12)
2012-13 Enrollment: 7,864 . . . . (951) 826-6530
Temecula Valley Unified (KG-12)
2012-13 Enrollment: 30,337 . . . . (951) 676-2661

Two-year College(s)

Professional Golfers Career College (Private, For-profit)
Fall 2013 Enrollment: 265 . . . . (800) 877-4380
2013-14 Tuition: In-state $15,400; Out-of-state $15,400
San Joaquin Valley College-Temecula (Private, For-profit)
Fall 2013 Enrollment: 393 . . . . (951) 296-6015
2013-14 Tuition: In-state $17,384; Out-of-state $17,384

Vocational/Technical School(s)

CET-Rancho Temecula (Private, Not-for-profit)
Fall 2013 Enrollment: 72 . . . . (408) 287-7924
2013-14 Tuition: $8,624
Paul Mitchell the School-Temecula (Private, For-profit)
Fall 2013 Enrollment: 275 . . . . (951) 694-4323
2013-14 Tuition: $18,110
Royale College of Beauty (Private, For-profit)
Fall 2013 Enrollment: 54 . . . . (951) 676-0833
2013-14 Tuition: $15,213

Housing: Homeownership rate: 69.2%; Median home value: $298,200; Median year structure built: 1996; Homeowner vacancy rate: 2.7%; Median gross rent: $1,509 per month; Rental vacancy rate: 7.1%
Health Insurance: 85.6% have insurance; 73.8% have private insurance; 19.4% have public insurance; 14.4% do not have insurance; 8.0% of children under 18 do not have insurance
Safety: Violent crime rate: 8.5 per 10,000 population; Property crime rate: 267.0 per 10,000 population
Transportation: Commute: 88.4% car, 0.7% public transportation, 1.3% walk, 6.9% work from home; Median travel time to work: 33.7 minutes
Airports: French Valley (general aviation)
Additional Information Contacts
City of Temecula . . . . (951) 694-6444
http://www.cityoftemecula.org

TEMESCAL VALLEY (CDP).
Note: Statistics that would complete this profile are not available because the CDP was created after the 2010 Census was released.

THERMAL (CDP). Covers a land area of 9.451 square miles and a water area of 0 square miles. Located at 33.63° N. Lat; 116.13° W. Long. Elevation is -118 feet.
Population: 2,865; Growth (since 2000): n/a; Density: 303.1 persons per square mile; Race: 36.1% White, 1.0% Black/African American, 1.1% Asian, 1.0% American Indian/Alaska Native, 0.0% Native Hawaiian/Other Pacific Islander, 1.9% Two or more races, 95.3% Hispanic of any race; Average household size: 4.19; Median age: 25.9; Age under 18: 37.3%; Age 65 and over: 6.8%; Males per 100 females: 111.6; Marriage status: 42.4% never married, 44.4% now married, 8.1% separated, 0.7% widowed, 12.5% divorced; Foreign born: 43.4%; Speak English only: 12.6%; With disability: 9.7%; Veterans: 1.4%; Ancestry: 2.3% French, 1.0% American, 0.2% Australian
Employment: 0.0% management, business, and financial, 0.0% computer, engineering, and science, 1.3% education, legal, community service, arts, and media, 4.8% healthcare practitioners, 41.5% service, 9.7% sales and office, 38.6% natural resources, construction, and maintenance, 4.1% production, transportation, and material moving
Income: Per capita: $9,801; Median household: $27,524; Average household: $37,054; Households with income of $100,000 or more: 3.1%; Poverty rate: 45.0%
Educational Attainment: High school diploma or higher: 49.1%; Bachelor's degree or higher: n/a; Graduate/professional degree or higher: n/a

School District(s)

Coachella Valley Unified (KG-12)
2012-13 Enrollment: 18,720 . . . . (760) 399-5137

Housing: Homeownership rate: 39.4%; Median home value: $23,400; Median year structure built: 1976; Homeowner vacancy rate: 0.7%; Median gross rent: $767 per month; Rental vacancy rate: 6.7%
Health Insurance: 61.7% have insurance; 18.0% have private insurance; 44.0% have public insurance; 38.3% do not have insurance; 4.2% of children under 18 do not have insurance
Transportation: Commute: 96.6% car, 1.4% public transportation, 2.0% walk, 0.0% work from home; Median travel time to work: 16.7 minutes

THOUSAND PALMS (CDP). Covers a land area of 23.636 square miles and a water area of 0 square miles. Located at 33.81° N. Lat; 116.35° W. Long. Elevation is 246 feet.
History: Joshua Tree National Monument to Northeast.
Population: 7,715; Growth (since 2000): 50.7%; Density: 326.4 persons per square mile; Race: 74.7% White, 1.4% Black/African American, 1.7% Asian, 1.0% American Indian/Alaska Native, 0.1% Native Hawaiian/Other Pacific Islander, 2.7% Two or more races, 52.5% Hispanic of any race; Average household size: 2.70; Median age: 43.3; Age under 18: 22.7%; Age 65 and over: 25.0%; Males per 100 females: 100.2; Marriage status: 36.7% never married, 44.0% now married, 0.2% separated, 8.2% widowed, 11.1% divorced; Foreign born: 29.8%; Speak English only: 53.3%; With disability: 19.3%; Veterans: 11.5%; Ancestry: 7.4% English, 6.1% German, 5.4% Irish, 3.8% Canadian, 2.9% French
Employment: 9.2% management, business, and financial, 2.2% computer, engineering, and science, 13.1% education, legal, community service, arts, and media, 1.7% healthcare practitioners, 35.0% service, 21.6% sales and office, 13.3% natural resources, construction, and maintenance, 3.9% production, transportation, and material moving
Income: Per capita: $19,477; Median household: $42,651; Average household: $51,024; Households with income of $100,000 or more: 12.2%; Poverty rate: 14.4%
Educational Attainment: High school diploma or higher: 78.7%; Bachelor's degree or higher: 15.1%; Graduate/professional degree or higher: 5.9%

School District(s)

Palm Springs Unified (KG-12)
2012-13 Enrollment: 23,581 . . . . (760) 416-6000

Housing: Homeownership rate: 78.2%; Median home value: $140,900; Median year structure built: 1985; Homeowner vacancy rate: 4.4%; Median gross rent: $1,228 per month; Rental vacancy rate: 11.9%

Health Insurance: 74.9% have insurance; 50.0% have private insurance; 41.8% have public insurance; 25.1% do not have insurance; 21.4% of children under 18 do not have insurance

Transportation: Commute: 90.9% car, 0.0% public transportation, 0.8% walk, 6.9% work from home; Median travel time to work: 24.9 minutes

VALLE VISTA (CDP). Covers a land area of 6.868 square miles and a water area of 0.208 square miles. Located at 33.74° N. Lat; 116.89° W. Long. Elevation is 1,775 feet.

Population: 14,578; Growth (since 2000): 39.0%; Density: 2,122.5 persons per square mile; Race: 79.2% White, 3.0% Black/African American, 1.9% Asian, 1.7% American Indian/Alaska Native, 0.3% Native Hawaiian/Other Pacific Islander, 4.6% Two or more races, 27.6% Hispanic of any race; Average household size: 2.67; Median age: 41.4; Age under 18: 24.9%; Age 65 and over: 19.4%; Males per 100 females: 91.9; Marriage status: 27.3% never married, 51.1% now married, 3.0% separated, 6.4% widowed, 15.3% divorced; Foreign born: 9.1%; Speak English only: 82.9%; With disability: 17.5%; Veterans: 10.3%; Ancestry: 13.1% English, 10.4% German, 9.9% Irish, 4.9% American, 4.8% French

Employment: 12.4% management, business, and financial, 3.0% computer, engineering, and science, 8.9% education, legal, community service, arts, and media, 5.1% healthcare practitioners, 23.4% service, 23.8% sales and office, 10.3% natural resources, construction, and maintenance, 13.1% production, transportation, and material moving

Income: Per capita: $21,273; Median household: $41,556; Average household: $58,127; Households with income of $100,000 or more: 14.7%; Poverty rate: 21.6%

Educational Attainment: High school diploma or higher: 83.7%; Bachelor's degree or higher: 15.5%; Graduate/professional degree or higher: 7.0%

Housing: Homeownership rate: 75.6%; Median home value: $127,000; Median year structure built: 1982; Homeowner vacancy rate: 4.4%; Median gross rent: $946 per month; Rental vacancy rate: 9.8%

Health Insurance: 82.5% have insurance; 54.1% have private insurance; 40.2% have public insurance; 17.5% do not have insurance; 6.5% of children under 18 do not have insurance

Transportation: Commute: 93.4% car, 0.5% public transportation, 0.3% walk, 3.9% work from home; Median travel time to work: 33.3 minutes

VISTA SANTA ROSA (CDP). Covers a land area of 16.121 square miles and a water area of 0.012 square miles. Located at 33.62° N. Lat; 116.21° W. Long. Elevation is -69 feet.

Population: 2,926; Growth (since 2000): n/a; Density: 181.5 persons per square mile; Race: 58.1% White, 0.3% Black/African American, 0.2% Asian, 4.8% American Indian/Alaska Native, 0.0% Native Hawaiian/Other Pacific Islander, 4.5% Two or more races, 85.0% Hispanic of any race; Average household size: 3.93; Median age: 29.8; Age under 18: 32.4%; Age 65 and over: 8.2%; Males per 100 females: 110.8; Marriage status: 43.6% never married, 48.5% now married, 2.0% separated, 2.1% widowed, 5.8% divorced; Foreign born: 27.8%; Speak English only: 23.3%; With disability: 5.9%; Veterans: 3.1%; Ancestry: 5.1% Italian, 3.3% German, 1.9% Scotch-Irish, 1.4% Irish, 0.7% English

Employment: 5.2% management, business, and financial, 0.0% computer, engineering, and science, 11.1% education, legal, community service, arts, and media, 4.1% healthcare practitioners, 31.2% service, 14.0% sales and office, 22.5% natural resources, construction, and maintenance, 11.9% production, transportation, and material moving

Income: Per capita: $14,883; Median household: $35,965; Average household: $51,440; Households with income of $100,000 or more: 9.9%; Poverty rate: 31.1%

Educational Attainment: High school diploma or higher: 59.6%; Bachelor's degree or higher: 8.0%; Graduate/professional degree or higher: 1.1%

Housing: Homeownership rate: 60.4%; Median home value: $207,600; Median year structure built: 1980; Homeowner vacancy rate: 4.8%; Median gross rent: $932 per month; Rental vacancy rate: 5.1%

Health Insurance: 82.2% have insurance; 45.5% have private insurance; 39.0% have public insurance; 17.8% do not have insurance; 2.7% of children under 18 do not have insurance

Transportation: Commute: 87.8% car, 0.2% public transportation, 5.5% walk, 6.5% work from home; Median travel time to work: 31.4 minutes

WARM SPRINGS (CDP). Covers a land area of 2.026 square miles and a water area of 0 square miles. Located at 33.70° N. Lat; 117.33° W. Long.

Population: 2,676; Growth (since 2000): n/a; Density: 1,320.6 persons per square mile; Race: 62.5% White, 4.4% Black/African American, 3.8% Asian, 0.9% American Indian/Alaska Native, 0.5% Native Hawaiian/Other Pacific Islander, 5.2% Two or more races, 46.0% Hispanic of any race; Average household size: 2.97; Median age: 31.1; Age under 18: 26.1%; Age 65 and over: 9.2%; Males per 100 females: 103.7; Marriage status: 30.7% never married, 49.2% now married, 6.1% separated, 1.3% widowed, 18.8% divorced; Foreign born: 15.3%; Speak English only: 81.3%; With disability: 9.0%; Veterans: 8.4%; Ancestry: 15.6% English, 10.0% Irish, 9.9% Hungarian, 8.0% German, 5.6% Italian

Employment: 9.9% management, business, and financial, 1.3% computer, engineering, and science, 6.8% education, legal, community service, arts, and media, 0.0% healthcare practitioners, 19.6% service, 41.2% sales and office, 8.0% natural resources, construction, and maintenance, 13.2% production, transportation, and material moving

Income: Per capita: $17,877; Median household: $69,666; Average household: $73,764; Households with income of $100,000 or more: 27.8%; Poverty rate: 7.6%

Educational Attainment: High school diploma or higher: 63.2%; Bachelor's degree or higher: 10.0%; Graduate/professional degree or higher: 3.3%

Housing: Homeownership rate: 45.9%; Median home value: $172,200; Median year structure built: 2001; Homeowner vacancy rate: 1.9%; Median gross rent: $1,319 per month; Rental vacancy rate: 11.1%

Health Insurance: 80.8% have insurance; 68.0% have private insurance; 21.2% have public insurance; 19.2% do not have insurance; 11.0% of children under 18 do not have insurance

Transportation: Commute: 90.4% car, 0.0% public transportation, 3.4% walk, 1.9% work from home; Median travel time to work: 41.0 minutes

WHITEWATER (CDP).

Note: Statistics that would complete this profile are not available because the CDP was created after the 2010 Census was released.

WILDOMAR (city). Covers a land area of 23.688 square miles and a water area of 0 square miles. Located at 33.62° N. Lat; 117.26° W. Long. Elevation is 1,270 feet.

Population: 32,176; Growth (since 2000): 128.8%; Density: 1,358.3 persons per square mile; Race: 69.5% White, 3.3% Black/African American, 4.5% Asian, 1.2% American Indian/Alaska Native, 0.2% Native Hawaiian/Other Pacific Islander, 5.3% Two or more races, 35.3% Hispanic of any race; Average household size: 3.22; Median age: 34.6; Age under 18: 27.9%; Age 65 and over: 10.6%; Males per 100 females: 97.6; Marriage status: 30.0% never married, 55.4% now married, 1.9% separated, 4.1% widowed, 10.5% divorced; Foreign born: 16.8%; Speak English only: 74.2%; With disability: 10.0%; Veterans: 10.3%; Ancestry: 14.8% German, 11.7% Irish, 6.9% English, 5.0% American, 4.8% Italian

Employment: 12.7% management, business, and financial, 3.1% computer, engineering, and science, 9.6% education, legal, community service, arts, and media, 2.9% healthcare practitioners, 23.7% service, 22.9% sales and office, 13.9% natural resources, construction, and maintenance, 11.2% production, transportation, and material moving

Income: Per capita: $23,360; Median household: $60,924; Average household: $73,520; Households with income of $100,000 or more: 24.5%; Poverty rate: 13.9%

Educational Attainment: High school diploma or higher: 84.3%; Bachelor's degree or higher: 16.3%; Graduate/professional degree or higher: 4.9%

School District(s)

Lake Elsinore Unified (KG-12)
2012-13 Enrollment: 22,137 . . . . (951) 253-7000
Nuview Union (KG-12)
2012-13 Enrollment: 2,345 . . . . (951) 928-0066

Housing: Homeownership rate: 73.4%; Median home value: $220,500; Median year structure built: 1991; Homeowner vacancy rate: 2.7%; Median gross rent: $1,403 per month; Rental vacancy rate: 5.1%

Health Insurance: 80.7% have insurance; 62.8% have private insurance; 25.3% have public insurance; 19.3% do not have insurance; 12.1% of children under 18 do not have insurance

Safety: Violent crime rate: 12.0 per 10,000 population; Property crime rate: 160.2 per 10,000 population

Transportation: Commute: 92.3% car, 0.0% public transportation, 0.2% walk, 6.0% work from home; Median travel time to work: 35.1 minutes

Additional Information Contacts

City of Wildomar . . . . (951) 677-7751
http://www.cityofwildomar.org

WINCHESTER (CDP). Covers a land area of 7.732 square miles and a water area of 0 square miles. Located at 33.71° N. Lat; 117.08° W. Long. Elevation is 1,473 feet.

Population: 2,534; Growth (since 2000): 17.6%; Density: 327.7 persons per square mile; Race: 62.2% White, 1.5% Black/African American, 1.8% Asian, 0.7% American Indian/Alaska Native, 0.1% Native Hawaiian/Other Pacific Islander, 5.0% Two or more races, 48.7% Hispanic of any race; Average household size: 3.30; Median age: 34.6; Age under 18: 30.1%; Age 65 and over: 11.5%; Males per 100 females: 102.6; Marriage status: 35.5% never married, 45.6% now married, 1.3% separated, 11.7% widowed, 7.3% divorced; Foreign born: 7.9%; Speak English only: 83.8%; With disability: 22.7%; Veterans: 10.7%; Ancestry: 21.2% German, 7.0% American, 5.7% Dutch, 5.0% English, 4.8% Irish

Employment: 29.0% management, business, and financial, 4.0% computer, engineering, and science, 7.2% education, legal, community service, arts, and media, 1.0% healthcare practitioners, 14.5% service, 27.2% sales and office, 6.2% natural resources, construction, and maintenance, 10.8% production, transportation, and material moving

Income: Per capita: $26,888; Median household: $53,798; Average household: $82,768; Households with income of $100,000 or more: 28.4%; Poverty rate: 18.3%

Educational Attainment: High school diploma or higher: 72.9%; Bachelor's degree or higher: 17.0%; Graduate/professional degree or higher: 3.7%

School District(s)

Hemet Unified (KG-12)
2012-13 Enrollment: 21,689 . . . . (951) 765-5100
Temecula Valley Unified (KG-12)
2012-13 Enrollment: 30,337 . . . . (951) 676-2661

Housing: Homeownership rate: 63.9%; Median home value: $160,200; Median year structure built: 1977; Homeowner vacancy rate: 4.3%; Median gross rent: $1,191 per month; Rental vacancy rate: 5.4%

Health Insurance: 76.3% have insurance; 52.1% have private insurance; 28.7% have public insurance; 23.7% do not have insurance; 21.7% of children under 18 do not have insurance

Transportation: Commute: 89.1% car, 0.0% public transportation, 3.9% walk, 7.0% work from home; Median travel time to work: 41.6 minutes

WOODCREST (CDP). Covers a land area of 11.410 square miles and a water area of 0 square miles. Located at 33.88° N. Lat; 117.37° W. Long. Elevation is 1,535 feet.

Population: 14,347; Growth (since 2000): 72.0%; Density: 1,257.4 persons per square mile; Race: 72.6% White, 5.0% Black/African American, 5.0% Asian, 0.5% American Indian/Alaska Native, 0.3% Native Hawaiian/Other Pacific Islander, 4.7% Two or more races, 28.7% Hispanic of any race; Average household size: 3.23; Median age: 39.9; Age under 18: 24.0%; Age 65 and over: 12.3%; Males per 100 females: 99.6; Marriage status: 33.1% never married, 56.9% now married, 1.3% separated, 2.8% widowed, 7.2% divorced; Foreign born: 13.5%; Speak English only: 75.4%; With disability: 8.4%; Veterans: 7.6%; Ancestry: 11.2% German, 10.3% English, 9.8% Irish, 5.0% Scottish, 3.3% Italian

Employment: 17.5% management, business, and financial, 5.6% computer, engineering, and science, 8.4% education, legal, community service, arts, and media, 4.7% healthcare practitioners, 15.0% service, 26.2% sales and office, 12.4% natural resources, construction, and maintenance, 10.0% production, transportation, and material moving

Income: Per capita: $29,877; Median household: $92,332; Average household: $106,906; Households with income of $100,000 or more: 46.3%; Poverty rate: 6.9%

Educational Attainment: High school diploma or higher: 88.4%; Bachelor's degree or higher: 23.7%; Graduate/professional degree or higher: 8.4%

Housing: Homeownership rate: 88.9%; Median home value: $341,400; Median year structure built: 1983; Homeowner vacancy rate: 2.1%; Median gross rent: $1,033 per month; Rental vacancy rate: 3.7%

Health Insurance: 85.0% have insurance; 68.8% have private insurance; 23.2% have public insurance; 15.0% do not have insurance; 7.4% of children under 18 do not have insurance

Transportation: Commute: 88.7% car, 1.5% public transportation, 1.5% walk, 6.9% work from home; Median travel time to work: 36.4 minutes

Sacramento County

Located in central California, in the Central Valley; bounded on the west by the Sacramento River; crossed by the American and Cosumnes Rivers. Covers a land area of 964.644 square miles, a water area of 29.374 square miles, and is located in the Pacific Time Zone at 38.45° N. Lat., 121.34° W. Long. The county was founded in 1850. County seat is Sacramento.

Sacramento County is part of the Sacramento—Roseville—Arden-Arcade, CA Metropolitan Statistical Area. The entire metro area includes: El Dorado County, CA; Placer County, CA; Sacramento County, CA; Yolo County, CA

Weather Station: Sacramento Executive Arpt — Elevation: 15 feet

	Jan	Feb	Mar	Apr	May	Jun	Jul	Aug	Sep	Oct	Nov	Dec
High	54	60	65	72	80	87	92	91	87	78	64	54
Low	39	42	44	47	51	56	59	58	56	50	43	38
Precip	3.7	3.6	2.7	1.1	0.7	0.2	0.0	0.1	0.3	0.9	2.0	3.1
Snow	na	na	na	na	na	na	na	na	na	na	na	na

High and Low temperatures in degrees Fahrenheit; Precipitation and Snow in inches

Weather Station: Sacramento Wso City — Elevation: 24 feet

	Jan	Feb	Mar	Apr	May	Jun	Jul	Aug	Sep	Oct	Nov	Dec
High	56	62	68	74	82	89	94	93	89	79	65	55
Low	41	44	47	50	54	59	61	61	59	53	46	41
Precip	3.8	4.0	3.0	1.2	0.8	0.2	0.0	0.0	0.4	1.0	2.3	3.4
Snow	na	na	na	na	na	na	na	na	na	na	na	na

High and Low temperatures in degrees Fahrenheit; Precipitation and Snow in inches

Population: 1,418,788; Growth (since 2000): 16.0%; Density: 1,470.8 persons per square mile; Race: 57.5% White, 10.4% Black/African American, 14.3% Asian, 1.0% American Indian/Alaska Native, 1.0% Native Hawaiian/Other Pacific Islander, 6.6% two or more races, 21.6% Hispanic of any race; Average household size: 2.71; Median age: 34.8; Age under 18: 25.6%; Age 65 and over: 11.2%; Males per 100 females: 96.0; Marriage status: 34.6% never married, 47.6% now married, 2.5% separated, 5.5% widowed, 12.2% divorced; Foreign born: 19.9%; Speak English only: 68.8%; With disability: 12.7%; Veterans: 8.8%; Ancestry: 11.4% German, 8.9% Irish, 7.6% English, 4.8% Italian, 3.0% American

Religion: Six largest groups: 16.2% Catholicism, 3.8% Non-denominational Protestant, 3.7% Baptist, 3.2% Latter-day Saints, 2.5% Pentecostal, 1.2% Methodist/Pietist

Economy: Unemployment rate: 6.8%; Leading industries: 13.7% professional, scientific, and technical services; 12.8% retail trade; 12.0% health care and social assistance; Farms: 1,352 totaling 246,840 acres; Company size: 17 employ 1,000 or more persons, 26 employ 500 to 999 persons, 617 employ 100 to 499 persons, 26,810 employ less than 100 persons; Business ownership: 35,001 women-owned, 6,972 Black-owned, 9,307 Hispanic-owned, 16,203 Asian-owned

Employment: 15.3% management, business, and financial, 7.1% computer, engineering, and science, 10.1% education, legal, community service, arts, and media, 5.0% healthcare practitioners, 19.3% service, 26.8% sales and office, 7.8% natural resources, construction, and maintenance, 8.6% production, transportation, and material moving

Income: Per capita: $26,739; Median household: $55,064; Average household: $72,200; Households with income of $100,000 or more: 23.1%; Poverty rate: 17.6%

Educational Attainment: High school diploma or higher: 85.9%; Bachelor's degree or higher: 28.0%; Graduate/professional degree or higher: 9.3%

Housing: Homeownership rate: 57.5%; Median home value: $234,200; Median year structure built: 1978; Homeowner vacancy rate: 2.5%; Median gross rent: $1,024 per month; Rental vacancy rate: 8.3%

Vital Statistics: Birth rate: 137.3 per 10,000 population; Death rate: 73.2 per 10,000 population; Age-adjusted cancer mortality rate: 175.1 deaths per 100,000 population

Health Insurance: 85.4% have insurance; 63.2% have private insurance; 32.5% have public insurance; 14.6% do not have insurance; 5.8% of children under 18 do not have insurance

Health Care: Physicians: 27.0 per 10,000 population; Hospital beds: 21.8 per 10,000 population; Hospital admissions: 1,066.2 per 10,000 population
Air Quality Index: 53.4% good, 40.3% moderate, 6.0% unhealthy for sensitive individuals, 0.3% unhealthy (percent of days)
Transportation: Commute: 87.7% car, 3.1% public transportation, 2.0% walk, 4.9% work from home; Median travel time to work: 25.7 minutes
Presidential Election: 57.5% Obama, 40.0% Romney (2012)
National and State Parks: Brannon Island State Recreational Area; Folsom Powerhouse State Historic Park; Governor's Mansion State Historic Park; Leland Stanford Mansion State Historic Park; Mormon Island Wetlands State Park; Nimbus Dam State Historical Landmark; Old Sacramento State Historic Park; Prairie City State Vehicular Recreation Area; Sutter's Fort State Historic Park
Additional Information Contacts
Sacramento Government . . . . (916) 874-5411
http://www.saccounty.net

Sacramento County Communities

ANTELOPE (CDP). Covers a land area of 6.837 square miles and a water area of 0 square miles. Located at 38.72° N. Lat; 121.36° W. Long. Elevation is 164 feet.
Population: 45,770; Growth (since 2000): n/a; Density: 6,694.2 persons per square mile; Race: 63.8% White, 8.8% Black/African American, 13.3% Asian, 0.9% American Indian/Alaska Native, 0.9% Native Hawaiian/Other Pacific Islander, 7.3% Two or more races, 14.5% Hispanic of any race; Average household size: 3.23; Median age: 31.4; Age under 18: 31.1%; Age 65 and over: 6.2%; Males per 100 females: 94.3; Marriage status: 33.5% never married, 54.4% now married, 2.8% separated, 3.7% widowed, 8.3% divorced; Foreign born: 25.6%; Speak English only: 64.1%; With disability: 9.6%; Veterans: 8.5%; Ancestry: 9.8% German, 7.9% Irish, 7.4% Ukrainian, 4.6% English, 4.0% Russian
Employment: 13.1% management, business, and financial, 6.2% computer, engineering, and science, 7.3% education, legal, community service, arts, and media, 5.0% healthcare practitioners, 18.7% service, 28.6% sales and office, 11.2% natural resources, construction, and maintenance, 9.9% production, transportation, and material moving
Income: Per capita: $23,925; Median household: $65,352; Average household: $77,673; Households with income of $100,000 or more: 24.9%; Poverty rate: 12.5%
Educational Attainment: High school diploma or higher: 90.3%; Bachelor's degree or higher: 21.2%; Graduate/professional degree or higher: 5.2%

School District(s)

Center Joint Unified (KG-12)
2012-13 Enrollment: 4,791 . . . . (916) 338-6330
Dry Creek Joint Elementary (KG-08)
2012-13 Enrollment: 6,888 . . . . (916) 770-8800
Roseville Joint Union High (09-12)
2012-13 Enrollment: 10,206 . . . . (916) 786-2051

Housing: Homeownership rate: 68.3%; Median home value: $210,400; Median year structure built: 1993; Homeowner vacancy rate: 2.7%; Median gross rent: $1,357 per month; Rental vacancy rate: 3.9%
Health Insurance: 84.5% have insurance; 65.2% have private insurance; 26.6% have public insurance; 15.5% do not have insurance; 8.2% of children under 18 do not have insurance
Transportation: Commute: 91.1% car, 1.2% public transportation, 0.4% walk, 6.1% work from home; Median travel time to work: 29.7 minutes

ARDEN-ARCADE (CDP). Covers a land area of 17.829 square miles and a water area of 0.090 square miles. Located at 38.60° N. Lat; 121.38° W. Long. Elevation is 56 feet.
Population: 92,186; Growth (since 2000): -4.0%; Density: 5,170.5 persons per square mile; Race: 70.2% White, 8.7% Black/African American, 5.6% Asian, 1.0% American Indian/Alaska Native, 0.6% Native Hawaiian/Other Pacific Islander, 5.9% Two or more races, 18.6% Hispanic of any race; Average household size: 2.24; Median age: 39.0; Age under 18: 20.9%; Age 65 and over: 15.7%; Males per 100 females: 90.1; Marriage status: 35.0% never married, 43.5% now married, 2.5% separated, 7.1% widowed, 14.5% divorced; Foreign born: 13.8%; Speak English only: 78.4%; With disability: 14.2%; Veterans: 9.3%; Ancestry: 15.0% German, 12.9% Irish, 11.1% English, 6.1% Italian, 4.2% American
Employment: 15.2% management, business, and financial, 5.8% computer, engineering, and science, 12.1% education, legal, community service, arts, and media, 5.5% healthcare practitioners, 20.0% service, 29.1% sales and office, 6.3% natural resources, construction, and maintenance, 6.1% production, transportation, and material moving
Income: Per capita: $30,862; Median household: $44,107; Average household: $68,545; Households with income of $100,000 or more: 20.1%; Poverty rate: 19.8%
Educational Attainment: High school diploma or higher: 89.2%; Bachelor's degree or higher: 33.8%; Graduate/professional degree or higher: 12.8%
Housing: Homeownership rate: 46.1%; Median home value: $277,000; Median year structure built: 1965; Homeowner vacancy rate: 2.4%; Median gross rent: $876 per month; Rental vacancy rate: 11.7%
Health Insurance: 83.8% have insurance; 61.2% have private insurance; 36.0% have public insurance; 16.2% do not have insurance; 5.5% of children under 18 do not have insurance
Transportation: Commute: 85.3% car, 3.8% public transportation, 3.0% walk, 5.8% work from home; Median travel time to work: 22.7 minutes

CARMICHAEL (CDP). Covers a land area of 13.528 square miles and a water area of 0.265 square miles. Located at 38.63° N. Lat; 121.32° W. Long. Elevation is 121 feet.
Population: 61,762; Growth (since 2000): 24.2%; Density: 4,565.4 persons per square mile; Race: 80.6% White, 4.8% Black/African American, 4.3% Asian, 0.9% American Indian/Alaska Native, 0.5% Native Hawaiian/Other Pacific Islander, 5.7% Two or more races, 11.7% Hispanic of any race; Average household size: 2.33; Median age: 42.4; Age under 18: 21.1%; Age 65 and over: 17.6%; Males per 100 females: 89.6; Marriage status: 30.0% never married, 47.2% now married, 2.1% separated, 8.4% widowed, 14.4% divorced; Foreign born: 11.2%; Speak English only: 84.2%; With disability: 15.0%; Veterans: 11.0%; Ancestry: 18.6% German, 14.6% English, 13.9% Irish, 7.7% Italian, 3.4% American
Employment: 17.2% management, business, and financial, 5.1% computer, engineering, and science, 11.1% education, legal, community service, arts, and media, 6.1% healthcare practitioners, 16.1% service, 29.9% sales and office, 8.5% natural resources, construction, and maintenance, 6.0% production, transportation, and material moving
Income: Per capita: $33,011; Median household: $54,101; Average household: $77,450; Households with income of $100,000 or more: 22.6%; Poverty rate: 13.9%
Educational Attainment: High school diploma or higher: 91.9%; Bachelor's degree or higher: 32.7%; Graduate/professional degree or higher: 13.3%

School District(s)

Sacramento City Unified (KG-12)
2012-13 Enrollment: 47,616 . . . . (916) 643-9000
San Juan Unified (KG-12)
2012-13 Enrollment: 47,752 . . . . (916) 971-7700

Housing: Homeownership rate: 55.6%; Median home value: $281,000; Median year structure built: 1971; Homeowner vacancy rate: 2.3%; Median gross rent: $945 per month; Rental vacancy rate: 9.8%
Health Insurance: 87.0% have insurance; 68.0% have private insurance; 33.8% have public insurance; 13.0% do not have insurance; 7.3% of children under 18 do not have insurance
Hospitals: Mercy San Juan Medical Center (260 beds)
Newspapers: Carmichael Times (weekly circulation 10000)
Transportation: Commute: 87.9% car, 2.8% public transportation, 2.2% walk, 5.4% work from home; Median travel time to work: 25.2 minutes

CITRUS HEIGHTS (city). Covers a land area of 14.228 square miles and a water area of 0 square miles. Located at 38.69° N. Lat; 121.29° W. Long. Elevation is 164 feet.
Population: 83,301; Growth (since 2000): -2.1%; Density: 5,854.6 persons per square mile; Race: 80.3% White, 3.3% Black/African American, 3.3% Asian, 0.9% American Indian/Alaska Native, 0.4% Native Hawaiian/Other Pacific Islander, 5.4% Two or more races, 16.5% Hispanic of any race; Average household size: 2.53; Median age: 36.2; Age under 18: 23.1%; Age 65 and over: 13.3%; Males per 100 females: 94.1; Marriage status: 31.9% never married, 48.4% now married, 3.0% separated, 5.3% widowed, 14.4% divorced; Foreign born: 13.6%; Speak English only: 80.5%; With disability: 13.7%; Veterans: 11.4%; Ancestry: 16.5% German, 12.3% Irish, 10.8% English, 6.6% Italian, 4.1% American
Employment: 13.3% management, business, and financial, 5.3% computer, engineering, and science, 7.5% education, legal, community service, arts, and media, 4.1% healthcare practitioners, 20.3% service, 30.7% sales and office, 10.6% natural resources, construction, and maintenance, 8.1% production, transportation, and material moving

Income: Per capita: $25,023; Median household: $52,183; Average household: $62,919; Households with income of $100,000 or more: 15.6%; Poverty rate: 14.7%

Educational Attainment: High school diploma or higher: 89.2%; Bachelor's degree or higher: 18.9%; Graduate/professional degree or higher: 4.9%

School District(s)

San Juan Unified (KG-12)
2012-13 Enrollment: 47,752 . . . . (916) 971-7700

Two-year College(s)

Carrington College California-Citrus Heights (Private, For-profit)
Fall 2013 Enrollment: 451 . . . . (916) 722-8200

Vocational/Technical School(s)

Citrus Heights Beauty College (Private, For-profit)
Fall 2013 Enrollment: 96 . . . . (916) 725-6861
2013-14 Tuition: $10,000

Housing: Homeownership rate: 57.6%; Median home value: $190,200; Median year structure built: 1976; Homeowner vacancy rate: 2.7%; Median gross rent: <$100 per month; Rental vacancy rate: 7.8%

Health Insurance: 84.0% have insurance; 65.2% have private insurance; 31.8% have public insurance; 16.0% do not have insurance; 6.7% of children under 18 do not have insurance

Safety: Violent crime rate: 37.5 per 10,000 population; Property crime rate: 310.9 per 10,000 population

Transportation: Commute: 91.3% car, 1.8% public transportation, 2.0% walk, 3.5% work from home; Median travel time to work: 25.5 minutes

Additional Information Contacts

City of Citrus Heights. . . . . (916) 725-2448
http://www.citrusheights.net/home/index.asp

CLAY (CDP). Covers a land area of 6.756 square miles and a water area of 0 square miles. Located at 38.31° N. Lat; 121.16° W. Long. Elevation is 105 feet.

Population: 1,195; Growth (since 2000): n/a; Density: 176.9 persons per square mile; Race: 82.1% White, 0.5% Black/African American, 0.7% Asian, 2.0% American Indian/Alaska Native, 0.0% Native Hawaiian/Other Pacific Islander, 5.7% Two or more races, 20.3% Hispanic of any race; Average household size: 2.97; Median age: 43.5; Age under 18: 24.6%; Age 65 and over: 12.7%; Males per 100 females: 95.9

Housing: Homeownership rate: 85.6%; Homeowner vacancy rate: 1.1%; Rental vacancy rate: 3.3%

COURTLAND (CDP). Covers a land area of 1.800 square miles and a water area of 0 square miles. Located at 38.33° N. Lat; 121.56° W. Long. Elevation is 13 feet.

Population: 355; Growth (since 2000): n/a; Density: 197.2 persons per square mile; Race: 69.6% White, 0.0% Black/African American, 1.1% Asian, 1.7% American Indian/Alaska Native, 0.0% Native Hawaiian/Other Pacific Islander, 6.5% Two or more races, 56.3% Hispanic of any race; Average household size: 2.41; Median age: 41.1; Age under 18: 21.7%; Age 65 and over: 18.6%; Males per 100 females: 102.9

School District(s)

River Delta Joint Unified (KG-12)
2012-13 Enrollment: 2,323 . . . . (707) 374-1700

Housing: Homeownership rate: 67.0%; Homeowner vacancy rate: 0.0%; Rental vacancy rate: 0.0%

ELK GROVE (city). Covers a land area of 42.190 square miles and a water area of 0.049 square miles. Located at 38.41° N. Lat; 121.38° W. Long. Elevation is 46 feet.

History: Named for the Elk Grove House hotel, opened by James Hall in 1850, and the numerous local elk. Old Elk Grove was founded in 1850 by Hall, who built the hotel. The new town of Elk Grove sprang up nearby after the Old Elk Grove hotel burned in 1857.

Population: 153,015; Growth (since 2000): 155.1%; Density: 3,626.8 persons per square mile; Race: 46.1% White, 11.2% Black/African American, 26.3% Asian, 0.6% American Indian/Alaska Native, 1.2% Native Hawaiian/Other Pacific Islander, 7.9% Two or more races, 18.0% Hispanic of any race; Average household size: 3.18; Median age: 34.3; Age under 18: 30.1%; Age 65 and over: 8.3%; Males per 100 females: 93.9; Marriage status: 30.1% never married, 56.0% now married, 2.1% separated, 4.6% widowed, 9.4% divorced; Foreign born: 22.6%; Speak English only: 66.4%; With disability: 10.4%; Veterans: 8.4%; Ancestry: 10.3% German, 7.3% Irish, 7.0% English, 4.5% Italian, 2.1% American

Employment: 17.3% management, business, and financial, 8.1% computer, engineering, and science, 11.8% education, legal, community service, arts, and media, 7.0% healthcare practitioners, 17.8% service, 25.3% sales and office, 5.4% natural resources, construction, and maintenance, 7.4% production, transportation, and material moving

Income: Per capita: $28,898; Median household: $77,791; Average household: $92,181; Households with income of $100,000 or more: 36.2%; Poverty rate: 9.5%

Educational Attainment: High school diploma or higher: 90.4%; Bachelor's degree or higher: 35.2%; Graduate/professional degree or higher: 9.8%

School District(s)

Elk Grove Unified (KG-12)
2012-13 Enrollment: 62,137 . . . . (916) 686-5085

Vocational/Technical School(s)

InterCoast Colleges-Elk Grove (Private, For-profit)
Fall 2013 Enrollment: 28 . . . . (916) 714-5400
2013-14 Tuition: $19,395

Housing: Homeownership rate: 74.6%; Median home value: $263,400; Median year structure built: 1998; Homeowner vacancy rate: 2.4%; Median gross rent: $1,447 per month; Rental vacancy rate: 5.6%

Health Insurance: 90.6% have insurance; 77.1% have private insurance; 21.8% have public insurance; 9.4% do not have insurance; 4.3% of children under 18 do not have insurance

Safety: Violent crime rate: 29.1 per 10,000 population; Property crime rate: 184.1 per 10,000 population

Newspapers: Elk Grove Citizen (weekly circulation 12000)

Transportation: Commute: 90.6% car, 2.6% public transportation, 0.8% walk, 4.6% work from home; Median travel time to work: 30.2 minutes; Amtrak: Bus service available.

Additional Information Contacts

City of Elk Grove . . . . (916) 691-2489
http://www.elkgrovecity.org

ELVERTA (CDP). Covers a land area of 8.842 square miles and a water area of 0 square miles. Located at 38.72° N. Lat; 121.45° W. Long. Elevation is 52 feet.

Population: 5,492; Growth (since 2000): n/a; Density: 621.1 persons per square mile; Race: 81.1% White, 2.1% Black/African American, 3.8% Asian, 1.4% American Indian/Alaska Native, 0.9% Native Hawaiian/Other Pacific Islander, 5.2% Two or more races, 15.6% Hispanic of any race; Average household size: 3.15; Median age: 38.6; Age under 18: 25.3%; Age 65 and over: 10.6%; Males per 100 females: 101.0; Marriage status: 28.6% never married, 57.1% now married, 3.0% separated, 4.0% widowed, 10.4% divorced; Foreign born: 17.1%; Speak English only: 71.3%; With disability: 11.5%; Veterans: 9.3%; Ancestry: 13.4% Irish, 12.9% German, 9.6% English, 9.0% Russian, 6.9% Ukrainian

Employment: 9.8% management, business, and financial, 7.2% computer, engineering, and science, 5.7% education, legal, community service, arts, and media, 2.2% healthcare practitioners, 14.6% service, 26.5% sales and office, 19.8% natural resources, construction, and maintenance, 14.3% production, transportation, and material moving

Income: Per capita: $21,550; Median household: $59,659; Average household: $67,051; Households with income of $100,000 or more: 18.7%; Poverty rate: 9.4%

Educational Attainment: High school diploma or higher: 85.0%; Bachelor's degree or higher: 11.4%; Graduate/professional degree or higher: 3.1%

School District(s)

Elverta Joint Elementary (KG-08)
2012-13 Enrollment: 306. . . . . (916) 991-2244

Housing: Homeownership rate: 79.8%; Median home value: $174,100; Median year structure built: 1978; Homeowner vacancy rate: 2.3%; Median gross rent: $1,439 per month; Rental vacancy rate: 3.6%

Health Insurance: 82.5% have insurance; 61.6% have private insurance; 30.0% have public insurance; 17.5% do not have insurance; 7.5% of children under 18 do not have insurance

Transportation: Commute: 92.9% car, 1.1% public transportation, 0.4% walk, 4.4% work from home; Median travel time to work: 30.6 minutes

---

FAIR OAKS (CDP). Covers a land area of 10.793 square miles and a water area of 0.452 square miles. Located at 38.65° N. Lat; 121.25° W. Long. Elevation is 174 feet.

Population: 30,912; Growth (since 2000): 10.4%; Density: 2,864.0 persons per square mile; Race: 85.7% White, 2.4% Black/African

American, 4.2% Asian, 0.8% American Indian/Alaska Native, 0.2% Native Hawaiian/Other Pacific Islander, 4.4% Two or more races, 9.6% Hispanic of any race; Average household size: 2.37; Median age: 45.8; Age under 18: 19.6%; Age 65 and over: 18.5%; Males per 100 females: 95.3; Marriage status: 27.8% never married, 52.8% now married, 1.5% separated, 6.1% widowed, 13.2% divorced; Foreign born: 11.7%; Speak English only: 84.4%; With disability: 10.6%; Veterans: 10.5%; Ancestry: 17.5% German, 14.6% Irish, 12.8% English, 7.2% Italian, 4.4% American
Employment: 19.5% management, business, and financial, 8.0% computer, engineering, and science, 11.4% education, legal, community service, arts, and media, 8.0% healthcare practitioners, 16.1% service, 24.3% sales and office, 6.1% natural resources, construction, and maintenance, 6.6% production, transportation, and material moving
Income: Per capita: $40,749; Median household: $73,995; Average household: $97,762; Households with income of $100,000 or more: 36.9%; Poverty rate: 11.1%
Educational Attainment: High school diploma or higher: 93.9%; Bachelor's degree or higher: 41.3%; Graduate/professional degree or higher: 15.5%

School District(s)

San Juan Unified (KG-12)
2012-13 Enrollment: 47,752 . . . . (916) 971-7700
Housing: Homeownership rate: 67.0%; Median home value: $364,500; Median year structure built: 1976; Homeowner vacancy rate: 1.4%; Median gross rent: $1,053 per month; Rental vacancy rate: 6.7%
Health Insurance: 90.4% have insurance; 76.9% have private insurance; 28.8% have public insurance; 9.6% do not have insurance; 1.6% of children under 18 do not have insurance
Transportation: Commute: 87.6% car, 2.0% public transportation, 0.9% walk, 7.5% work from home; Median travel time to work: 26.3 minutes

FLORIN (CDP). Covers a land area of 8.703 square miles and a water area of 0 square miles. Located at 38.48° N. Lat; 121.40° W. Long. Elevation is 33 feet.
Population: 47,513; Growth (since 2000): 71.8%; Density: 5,459.7 persons per square mile; Race: 31.6% White, 15.8% Black/African American, 28.6% Asian, 1.1% American Indian/Alaska Native, 1.7% Native Hawaiian/Other Pacific Islander, 6.8% Two or more races, 27.5% Hispanic of any race; Average household size: 3.19; Median age: 32.1; Age under 18: 29.0%; Age 65 and over: 11.3%; Males per 100 females: 96.2; Marriage status: 37.8% never married, 44.7% now married, 3.8% separated, 5.9% widowed, 11.6% divorced; Foreign born: 30.2%; Speak English only: 48.9%; With disability: 15.7%; Veterans: 6.5%; Ancestry: 5.8% German, 3.8% Irish, 3.3% English, 2.0% Italian, 1.7% American
Employment: 7.2% management, business, and financial, 3.6% computer, engineering, and science, 7.5% education, legal, community service, arts, and media, 2.6% healthcare practitioners, 25.7% service, 28.4% sales and office, 10.1% natural resources, construction, and maintenance, 14.8% production, transportation, and material moving
Income: Per capita: $16,211; Median household: $41,343; Average household: $51,361; Households with income of $100,000 or more: 10.5%; Poverty rate: 25.6%
Educational Attainment: High school diploma or higher: 70.7%; Bachelor's degree or higher: 10.0%; Graduate/professional degree or higher: 2.4%
Housing: Homeownership rate: 55.2%; Median home value: $142,300; Median year structure built: 1982; Homeowner vacancy rate: 2.3%; Median gross rent: $991 per month; Rental vacancy rate: 8.9%
Health Insurance: 80.0% have insurance; 46.1% have private insurance; 43.0% have public insurance; 20.0% do not have insurance; 9.3% of children under 18 do not have insurance
Transportation: Commute: 90.3% car, 2.9% public transportation, 1.0% walk, 4.2% work from home; Median travel time to work: 26.1 minutes

FOLSOM (city). Covers a land area of 21.945 square miles and a water area of 2.356 square miles. Located at 38.68° N. Lat; 121.15° W. Long. Elevation is 220 feet.
History: Named for Captain Joseph L. Folsom, who owned land on which the first railroad station was built. Folsom began as a camp laid out on the Mexican rancho, Rio de los Americanos, along the Coloma Road. A trail in 1847 when traced by Captain Sutter from his fort to his sawmill, the Coloma Road became the first route to the gold fields after Marshall 's discovery in 1848. In 1848 Captain Joseph L. Folsom purchased the land. The town was surveyed in 1855, and in 1856 it became the temporary terminus of the Sacramento Valley Railroad.
Population: 72,203; Growth (since 2000): 39.2%; Density: 3,290.1 persons per square mile; Race: 74.3% White, 5.7% Black/African American, 12.5% Asian, 0.6% American Indian/Alaska Native, 0.2% Native Hawaiian/Other Pacific Islander, 4.2% Two or more races, 11.2% Hispanic of any race; Average household size: 2.61; Median age: 37.6; Age under 18: 24.3%; Age 65 and over: 9.6%; Males per 100 females: 114.1; Marriage status: 28.6% never married, 56.0% now married, 1.6% separated, 4.0% widowed, 11.3% divorced; Foreign born: 15.2%; Speak English only: 78.7%; With disability: 7.9%; Veterans: 8.0%; Ancestry: 15.5% German, 11.0% Irish, 10.0% English, 7.5% Italian, 4.5% American
Employment: 22.8% management, business, and financial, 17.2% computer, engineering, and science, 10.1% education, legal, community service, arts, and media, 6.2% healthcare practitioners, 12.5% service, 22.3% sales and office, 3.8% natural resources, construction, and maintenance, 5.2% production, transportation, and material moving
Income: Per capita: $37,821; Median household: $98,359; Average household: $109,340; Households with income of $100,000 or more: 49.1%; Poverty rate: 4.6%
Educational Attainment: High school diploma or higher: 92.5%; Bachelor's degree or higher: 44.7%; Graduate/professional degree or higher: 16.9%

School District(s)

Folsom-Cordova Unified (PK-12)
2012-13 Enrollment: 19,117 . . . . (916) 294-9000

Two-year College(s)

Folsom Lake College (Public)
Fall 2013 Enrollment: 8,034 . . . . (916) 608-6572
2013-14 Tuition: In-state $1,104; Out-of-state $7,200
Housing: Homeownership rate: 69.9%; Median home value: $385,000; Median year structure built: 1994; Homeowner vacancy rate: 1.9%; Median gross rent: $1,372 per month; Rental vacancy rate: 5.2%
Health Insurance: 93.5% have insurance; 87.0% have private insurance; 15.6% have public insurance; 6.5% do not have insurance; 1.8% of children under 18 do not have insurance
Hospitals: Mercy Hospital of Folsom (85 beds)
Safety: Violent crime rate: 13.3 per 10,000 population; Property crime rate: 181.1 per 10,000 population
Newspapers: The Telegraph (weekly circulation 15000)
Transportation: Commute: 88.2% car, 2.5% public transportation, 1.2% walk, 6.5% work from home; Median travel time to work: 24.4 minutes
Additional Information Contacts
City of Folsom . . . . (916) 355-7201
http://www.folsom.ca.us

FOOTHILL FARMS (CDP). Covers a land area of 4.198 square miles and a water area of 0 square miles. Located at 38.69° N. Lat; 121.35° W. Long. Elevation is 141 feet.
Population: 33,121; Growth (since 2000): 90.1%; Density: 7,889.8 persons per square mile; Race: 64.2% White, 11.0% Black/African American, 5.2% Asian, 1.1% American Indian/Alaska Native, 0.6% Native Hawaiian/Other Pacific Islander, 7.8% Two or more races, 22.9% Hispanic of any race; Average household size: 2.82; Median age: 31.1; Age under 18: 27.8%; Age 65 and over: 8.7%; Males per 100 females: 95.3; Marriage status: 34.9% never married, 46.1% now married, 3.0% separated, 4.4% widowed, 14.6% divorced; Foreign born: 18.2%; Speak English only: 70.7%; With disability: 11.8%; Veterans: 8.6%; Ancestry: 13.9% German, 10.3% Irish, 7.3% English, 4.7% Ukrainian, 3.8% American
Employment: 9.8% management, business, and financial, 2.9% computer, engineering, and science, 7.4% education, legal, community service, arts, and media, 3.8% healthcare practitioners, 22.9% service, 28.5% sales and office, 12.0% natural resources, construction, and maintenance, 12.7% production, transportation, and material moving
Income: Per capita: $19,577; Median household: $45,432; Average household: $53,185; Households with income of $100,000 or more: 12.3%; Poverty rate: 24.0%
Educational Attainment: High school diploma or higher: 84.0%; Bachelor's degree or higher: 14.2%; Graduate/professional degree or higher: 3.3%
Housing: Homeownership rate: 53.7%; Median home value: $161,400; Median year structure built: 1976; Homeowner vacancy rate: 2.6%; Median gross rent: $1,018 per month; Rental vacancy rate: 7.2%
Health Insurance: 82.4% have insurance; 50.0% have private insurance; 42.1% have public insurance; 17.6% do not have insurance; 5.0% of children under 18 do not have insurance

Transportation: Commute: 90.3% car, 2.5% public transportation, 0.9% walk, 4.1% work from home; Median travel time to work: 27.6 minutes

FRANKLIN (CDP). Covers a land area of 2.106 square miles and a water area of 0 square miles. Located at 38.37° N. Lat; 121.46° W. Long. Elevation is 20 feet.

Population: 155; Growth (since 2000): n/a; Density: 73.6 persons per square mile; Race: 76.8% White, 0.0% Black/African American, 3.2% Asian, 0.0% American Indian/Alaska Native, 0.0% Native Hawaiian/Other Pacific Islander, 7.1% Two or more races, 27.1% Hispanic of any race; Average household size: 2.50; Median age: 42.8; Age under 18: 19.4%; Age 65 and over: 13.5%; Males per 100 females: 86.7

Housing: Homeownership rate: 71.0%; Homeowner vacancy rate: 0.0%; Rental vacancy rate: 18.2%

FREEPORT (CDP). Covers a land area of 0.044 square miles and a water area of 0 square miles. Located at 38.46° N. Lat; 121.50° W. Long. Elevation is 16 feet.

Population: 38; Growth (since 2000): n/a; Density: 855.4 persons per square mile; Race: 89.5% White, 0.0% Black/African American, 5.3% Asian, 0.0% American Indian/Alaska Native, 0.0% Native Hawaiian/Other Pacific Islander, 2.6% Two or more races, 15.8% Hispanic of any race; Average household size: 1.81; Median age: 56.5; Age under 18: 5.3%; Age 65 and over: 26.3%; Males per 100 females: 216.7

Housing: Homeownership rate: 42.8%; Homeowner vacancy rate: 0.0%; Rental vacancy rate: 14.3%

FRUITRIDGE POCKET (CDP). Covers a land area of 0.608 square miles and a water area of 0 square miles. Located at 38.53° N. Lat; 121.46° W. Long.

Population: 5,800; Growth (since 2000): n/a; Density: 9,536.4 persons per square mile; Race: 29.4% White, 18.1% Black/African American, 19.2% Asian, 1.8% American Indian/Alaska Native, 1.2% Native Hawaiian/Other Pacific Islander, 7.7% Two or more races, 40.4% Hispanic of any race; Average household size: 3.35; Median age: 29.7; Age under 18: 31.5%; Age 65 and over: 8.6%; Males per 100 females: 98.4; Marriage status: 47.9% never married, 38.5% now married, 4.5% separated, 6.5% widowed, 7.1% divorced; Foreign born: 26.4%; Speak English only: 48.9%; With disability: 23.7%; Veterans: 5.7%; Ancestry: 4.4% Italian, 3.5% German, 3.2% Irish, 2.7% Portuguese, 1.7% English

Employment: 7.7% management, business, and financial, 3.6% computer, engineering, and science, 5.2% education, legal, community service, arts, and media, 1.0% healthcare practitioners, 29.7% service, 25.4% sales and office, 18.0% natural resources, construction, and maintenance, 9.4% production, transportation, and material moving

Income: Per capita: $11,092; Median household: $26,607; Average household: $35,181; Households with income of $100,000 or more: 3.8%; Poverty rate: 46.2%

Educational Attainment: High school diploma or higher: 55.1%; Bachelor's degree or higher: 5.5%; Graduate/professional degree or higher: 2.2%

Housing: Homeownership rate: 42.4%; Median home value: $117,100; Median year structure built: 1958; Homeowner vacancy rate: 3.6%; Median gross rent: $859 per month; Rental vacancy rate: 7.6%

Health Insurance: 80.7% have insurance; 31.8% have private insurance; 57.2% have public insurance; 19.3% do not have insurance; 7.7% of children under 18 do not have insurance

Transportation: Commute: 87.9% car, 4.9% public transportation, 0.0% walk, 5.6% work from home; Median travel time to work: 24.3 minutes

GALT (city). Covers a land area of 5.931 square miles and a water area of 0.013 square miles. Located at 38.27° N. Lat; 121.30° W. Long. Elevation is 52 feet.

History: Named for the homestead of John McFarland in Canada, which was named for Scottish novelist John Galt. Galt was laid out in 1869 and developed as a center for the production of poultry and dairy products, figs and grain.

Population: 23,647; Growth (since 2000): 21.4%; Density: 3,986.8 persons per square mile; Race: 66.1% White, 1.8% Black/African American, 3.4% Asian, 1.5% American Indian/Alaska Native, 0.5% Native Hawaiian/Other Pacific Islander, 6.2% Two or more races, 42.8% Hispanic of any race; Average household size: 3.24; Median age: 32.4; Age under 18: 31.1%; Age 65 and over: 9.6%; Males per 100 females: 97.4; Marriage status: 28.4% never married, 53.5% now married, 1.8% separated, 5.4% widowed, 12.7% divorced; Foreign born: 17.7%; Speak English only: 66.8%; With disability: 13.3%; Veterans: 9.0%; Ancestry: 12.4% German, 7.6% Irish, 7.5% English, 6.7% Italian, 4.2% Portuguese

Employment: 10.3% management, business, and financial, 3.3% computer, engineering, and science, 7.8% education, legal, community service, arts, and media, 2.8% healthcare practitioners, 16.3% service, 26.6% sales and office, 17.6% natural resources, construction, and maintenance, 15.3% production, transportation, and material moving

Income: Per capita: $21,789; Median household: $57,100; Average household: $66,923; Households with income of $100,000 or more: 17.9%; Poverty rate: 19.5%

Educational Attainment: High school diploma or higher: 80.2%; Bachelor's degree or higher: 14.8%; Graduate/professional degree or higher: 3.5%

School District(s)

Galt Joint Union Elementary (KG-08)
2012-13 Enrollment: 3,792 . . . . (209) 744-4545

Galt Joint Union High (09-12)
2012-13 Enrollment: 2,306 . . . . (209) 745-0249

Housing: Homeownership rate: 73.6%; Median home value: $191,600; Median year structure built: 1993; Homeowner vacancy rate: 2.3%; Median gross rent: $1,067 per month; Rental vacancy rate: 5.2%

Health Insurance: 83.4% have insurance; 62.3% have private insurance; 33.9% have public insurance; 16.6% do not have insurance; 6.9% of children under 18 do not have insurance

Safety: Violent crime rate: 25.7 per 10,000 population; Property crime rate: 210.6 per 10,000 population

Newspapers: Galt Herald (weekly circulation 12000); Grapevine Independent (weekly circulation 11000)

Transportation: Commute: 94.4% car, 0.4% public transportation, 1.7% walk, 2.7% work from home; Median travel time to work: 28.5 minutes

Additional Information Contacts

City of Galt. . . . . (209) 366-7130
http://www.ci.galt.ca.us

GOLD RIVER (CDP). Covers a land area of 2.637 square miles and a water area of 0.084 square miles. Located at 38.63° N. Lat; 121.25° W. Long. Elevation is 118 feet.

Population: 7,912; Growth (since 2000): -1.4%; Density: 3,000.4 persons per square mile; Race: 73.8% White, 2.5% Black/African American, 18.0% Asian, 0.3% American Indian/Alaska Native, 0.4% Native Hawaiian/Other Pacific Islander, 3.9% Two or more races, 6.5% Hispanic of any race; Average household size: 2.37; Median age: 49.7; Age under 18: 20.0%; Age 65 and over: 19.7%; Males per 100 females: 90.9; Marriage status: 17.8% never married, 65.3% now married, 2.0% separated, 8.9% widowed, 8.0% divorced; Foreign born: 17.9%; Speak English only: 74.0%; With disability: 9.1%; Veterans: 14.0%; Ancestry: 12.6% German, 12.2% English, 10.9% Irish, 6.3% American, 4.9% Italian

Employment: 32.1% management, business, and financial, 12.0% computer, engineering, and science, 16.5% education, legal, community service, arts, and media, 7.7% healthcare practitioners, 10.2% service, 17.4% sales and office, 1.1% natural resources, construction, and maintenance, 2.9% production, transportation, and material moving

Income: Per capita: $59,760; Median household: $108,673; Average household: $141,343; Households with income of $100,000 or more: 52.9%; Poverty rate: 2.3%

Educational Attainment: High school diploma or higher: 98.0%; Bachelor's degree or higher: 60.6%; Graduate/professional degree or higher: 24.2%

School District(s)

San Juan Unified (KG-12)
2012-13 Enrollment: 47,752 . . . . (916) 971-7700

Two-year College(s)

Bryan College-Gold River (Private, For-profit)
Fall 2013 Enrollment: 326 . . . . (916) 649-2400

Housing: Homeownership rate: 83.6%; Median home value: $379,500; Median year structure built: 1991; Homeowner vacancy rate: 1.4%; Median gross rent: $1,398 per month; Rental vacancy rate: 10.7%

Health Insurance: 92.4% have insurance; 87.7% have private insurance; 20.5% have public insurance; 7.6% do not have insurance; 12.7% of children under 18 do not have insurance

Transportation: Commute: 85.0% car, 4.1% public transportation, 3.0% walk, 6.5% work from home; Median travel time to work: 22.6 minutes

HERALD (CDP). Covers a land area of 7.879 square miles and a water area of 0.022 square miles. Located at 38.29° N. Lat; 121.23° W. Long. Elevation is 72 feet.

Population: 1,184; Growth (since 2000): n/a; Density: 150.3 persons per square mile; Race: 78.9% White, 1.7% Black/African American, 5.4% Asian, 1.1% American Indian/Alaska Native, 0.6% Native Hawaiian/Other Pacific Islander, 3.5% Two or more races, 21.5% Hispanic of any race; Average household size: 3.16; Median age: 43.4; Age under 18: 22.7%; Age 65 and over: 13.4%; Males per 100 females: 114.9

School District(s)

Arcohe Union Elementary (KG-08)
2012-13 Enrollment: 414 . . . . (209) 748-2313

Housing: Homeownership rate: 84.3%; Homeowner vacancy rate: 2.3%; Rental vacancy rate: 3.5%

HOOD (CDP). Covers a land area of 0.315 square miles and a water area of 0 square miles. Located at 38.37° N. Lat; 121.52° W. Long. Elevation is 7 feet.

Population: 271; Growth (since 2000): n/a; Density: 859.9 persons per square mile; Race: 49.8% White, 0.0% Black/African American, 5.5% Asian, 5.5% American Indian/Alaska Native, 0.4% Native Hawaiian/Other Pacific Islander, 12.9% Two or more races, 50.6% Hispanic of any race; Average household size: 2.61; Median age: 44.1; Age under 18: 23.2%; Age 65 and over: 12.9%; Males per 100 females: 96.4

Housing: Homeownership rate: 66.4%; Homeowner vacancy rate: 0.0%; Rental vacancy rate: 5.3%

ISLETON (city). Covers a land area of 0.440 square miles and a water area of 0.052 square miles. Located at 38.16° N. Lat; 121.60° W. Long. Elevation is 10 feet.

History: Isleton grew as a farm trading and canning town in the midst of an asparagus-growing area.

Population: 804; Growth (since 2000): -2.9%; Density: 1,828.9 persons per square mile; Race: 67.4% White, 1.2% Black/African American, 5.1% Asian, 1.2% American Indian/Alaska Native, 0.5% Native Hawaiian/Other Pacific Islander, 7.2% Two or more races, 39.3% Hispanic of any race; Average household size: 2.43; Median age: 42.1; Age under 18: 23.8%; Age 65 and over: 16.8%; Males per 100 females: 107.2

School District(s)

River Delta Joint Unified (KG-12)
2012-13 Enrollment: 2,323 . . . . (707) 374-1700

Housing: Homeownership rate: 55.6%; Homeowner vacancy rate: 11.9%; Rental vacancy rate: 19.7%

Safety: Violent crime rate: 110.2 per 10,000 population; Property crime rate: 563.0 per 10,000 population

LA RIVIERA (CDP). Covers a land area of 1.850 square miles and a water area of 0.242 square miles. Located at 38.57° N. Lat; 121.35° W. Long. Elevation is 52 feet.

History: Sacramento State University to West.

Population: 10,802; Growth (since 2000): 5.1%; Density: 5,839.9 persons per square mile; Race: 67.7% White, 10.0% Black/African American, 7.1% Asian, 0.7% American Indian/Alaska Native, 0.8% Native Hawaiian/Other Pacific Islander, 7.4% Two or more races, 16.3% Hispanic of any race; Average household size: 2.39; Median age: 35.1; Age under 18: 19.6%; Age 65 and over: 12.7%; Males per 100 females: 100.4; Marriage status: 37.3% never married, 42.7% now married, 1.9% separated, 5.2% widowed, 14.9% divorced; Foreign born: 10.2%; Speak English only: 83.3%; With disability: 11.7%; Veterans: 11.7%; Ancestry: 10.5% German, 9.7% Irish, 8.0% English, 7.0% Italian, 3.8% Norwegian

Employment: 22.1% management, business, and financial, 8.7% computer, engineering, and science, 11.6% education, legal, community service, arts, and media, 6.3% healthcare practitioners, 17.5% service, 24.0% sales and office, 4.0% natural resources, construction, and maintenance, 5.8% production, transportation, and material moving

Income: Per capita: $28,560; Median household: $54,291; Average household: $67,205; Households with income of $100,000 or more: 21.0%; Poverty rate: 25.4%

Educational Attainment: High school diploma or higher: 94.6%; Bachelor's degree or higher: 35.7%; Graduate/professional degree or higher: 9.4%

Housing: Homeownership rate: 55.0%; Median home value: $210,500; Median year structure built: 1974; Homeowner vacancy rate: 1.8%; Median gross rent: $1,035 per month; Rental vacancy rate: 7.6%

Health Insurance: 89.5% have insurance; 68.4% have private insurance; 34.5% have public insurance; 10.5% do not have insurance; 1.9% of children under 18 do not have insurance

Transportation: Commute: 86.8% car, 4.9% public transportation, 1.8% walk, 3.2% work from home; Median travel time to work: 24.6 minutes

LEMON HILL (CDP). Covers a land area of 1.627 square miles and a water area of 0 square miles. Located at 38.52° N. Lat; 121.46° W. Long.

Population: 13,729; Growth (since 2000): n/a; Density: 8,440.4 persons per square mile; Race: 37.1% White, 10.9% Black/African American, 17.4% Asian, 1.8% American Indian/Alaska Native, 1.4% Native Hawaiian/Other Pacific Islander, 6.0% Two or more races, 49.5% Hispanic of any race; Average household size: 3.39; Median age: 28.5; Age under 18: 32.8%; Age 65 and over: 7.8%; Males per 100 females: 101.9; Marriage status: 40.0% never married, 41.5% now married, 4.5% separated, 6.6% widowed, 11.9% divorced; Foreign born: 35.8%; Speak English only: 45.2%; With disability: 17.0%; Veterans: 4.3%; Ancestry: 6.0% German, 5.1% Irish, 3.4% English, 2.4% Russian, 1.6% Italian

Employment: 3.7% management, business, and financial, 1.9% computer, engineering, and science, 5.0% education, legal, community service, arts, and media, 0.8% healthcare practitioners, 37.4% service, 23.5% sales and office, 10.8% natural resources, construction, and maintenance, 17.1% production, transportation, and material moving

Income: Per capita: $12,234; Median household: $27,204; Average household: $36,563; Households with income of $100,000 or more: 5.7%; Poverty rate: 38.6%

Educational Attainment: High school diploma or higher: 59.0%; Bachelor's degree or higher: 5.4%; Graduate/professional degree or higher: 0.3%

Housing: Homeownership rate: 38.8%; Median home value: $95,900; Median year structure built: 1962; Homeowner vacancy rate: 5.1%; Median gross rent: $846 per month; Rental vacancy rate: 10.0%

Health Insurance: 74.5% have insurance; 28.9% have private insurance; 52.9% have public insurance; 25.5% do not have insurance; 7.4% of children under 18 do not have insurance

Transportation: Commute: 89.3% car, 1.4% public transportation, 2.4% walk, 4.4% work from home; Median travel time to work: 26.8 minutes

MATHER (CDP). Covers a land area of 10.001 square miles and a water area of 0.025 square miles. Located at 38.55° N. Lat; 121.28° W. Long.

Population: 4,451; Growth (since 2000): n/a; Density: 445.1 persons per square mile; Race: 55.7% White, 8.8% Black/African American, 19.1% Asian, 0.9% American Indian/Alaska Native, 1.9% Native Hawaiian/Other Pacific Islander, 7.6% Two or more races, 15.8% Hispanic of any race; Average household size: 3.10; Median age: 31.6; Age under 18: 30.5%; Age 65 and over: 4.9%; Males per 100 females: 100.1; Marriage status: 27.0% never married, 56.1% now married, 4.6% separated, 3.1% widowed, 13.7% divorced; Foreign born: 23.7%; Speak English only: 63.0%; With disability: 7.7%; Veterans: 7.2%; Ancestry: 14.4% German, 8.1% Irish, 5.8% English, 3.6% American, 3.5% Ukrainian

Employment: 24.1% management, business, and financial, 7.7% computer, engineering, and science, 9.5% education, legal, community service, arts, and media, 5.6% healthcare practitioners, 9.1% service, 28.4% sales and office, 10.0% natural resources, construction, and maintenance, 5.6% production, transportation, and material moving

Income: Per capita: $31,139; Median household: $82,844; Average household: $94,494; Households with income of $100,000 or more: 37.0%; Poverty rate: 8.6%

Educational Attainment: High school diploma or higher: 95.1%; Bachelor's degree or higher: 36.3%; Graduate/professional degree or higher: 13.5%

School District(s)

Folsom-Cordova Unified (PK-12)
2012-13 Enrollment: 19,117 . . . . (916) 294-9000

Sacramento County Office of Education (KG-12)
2012-13 Enrollment: 1,148 . . . . (916) 228-2500

Housing: Homeownership rate: 73.9%; Median home value: $264,400; Median year structure built: 2003; Homeowner vacancy rate: 2.7%; Median gross rent: $1,187 per month; Rental vacancy rate: 5.1%

Health Insurance: 86.8% have insurance; 73.4% have private insurance; 18.2% have public insurance; 13.2% do not have insurance; 8.8% of children under 18 do not have insurance

Hospitals: VA Northern California Healthcare System

Transportation: Commute: 91.6% car, 1.8% public transportation, 1.0% walk, 3.0% work from home; Median travel time to work: 25.1 minutes

MCCLELLAN PARK (CDP). Covers a land area of 4.050 square miles and a water area of 0 square miles. Located at 38.66° N. Lat; 121.40° W. Long.

Population: 743; Growth (since 2000): n/a; Density: 183.4 persons per square mile; Race: 62.9% White, 13.3% Black/African American, 3.6% Asian, 1.7% American Indian/Alaska Native, 2.8% Native Hawaiian/Other Pacific Islander, 11.4% Two or more races, 14.8% Hispanic of any race; Average household size: 2.79; Median age: 22.6; Age under 18: 32.3%; Age 65 and over: 3.0%; Males per 100 females: 86.2

School District(s)

Twin Rivers Unified (KG-12)
2012-13 Enrollment: 31,420 . . . . (916) 566-1600

Housing: Homeownership rate: 0.5%; Homeowner vacancy rate: 0.0%; Rental vacancy rate: 12.6%

NORTH HIGHLANDS (CDP). Covers a land area of 8.831 square miles and a water area of 0 square miles. Located at 38.67° N. Lat; 121.37° W. Long. Elevation is 92 feet.

History: Grew dramatically 1970s-1990s.

Population: 42,694; Growth (since 2000): -3.4%; Density: 4,834.4 persons per square mile; Race: 63.2% White, 11.4% Black/African American, 4.8% Asian, 1.4% American Indian/Alaska Native, 0.7% Native Hawaiian/Other Pacific Islander, 7.3% Two or more races, 23.6% Hispanic of any race; Average household size: 2.92; Median age: 32.1; Age under 18: 27.7%; Age 65 and over: 11.1%; Males per 100 females: 96.0; Marriage status: 32.9% never married, 46.2% now married, 2.1% separated, 6.3% widowed, 14.6% divorced; Foreign born: 24.0%; Speak English only: 63.6%; With disability: 14.5%; Veterans: 10.8%; Ancestry: 9.4% German, 7.5% Ukrainian, 7.2% Irish, 6.0% English, 4.2% Russian

Employment: 7.0% management, business, and financial, 3.0% computer, engineering, and science, 7.3% education, legal, community service, arts, and media, 3.4% healthcare practitioners, 24.5% service, 31.8% sales and office, 12.5% natural resources, construction, and maintenance, 10.5% production, transportation, and material moving

Income: Per capita: $17,132; Median household: $39,633; Average household: $48,658; Households with income of $100,000 or more: 9.7%; Poverty rate: 25.3%

Educational Attainment: High school diploma or higher: 83.0%; Bachelor's degree or higher: 12.6%; Graduate/professional degree or higher: 2.6%

School District(s)

Twin Rivers Unified (KG-12)
2012-13 Enrollment: 31,420 . . . . (916) 566-1600

Vocational/Technical School(s)

Twin Rivers Adult School (Public)
Fall 2013 Enrollment: 51 . . . . (916) 566-2785
2013-14 Tuition: $22,000

Housing: Homeownership rate: 48.9%; Median home value: $143,300; Median year structure built: 1967; Homeowner vacancy rate: 3.5%; Median gross rent: $956 per month; Rental vacancy rate: 10.6%

Health Insurance: 79.8% have insurance; 42.3% have private insurance; 45.7% have public insurance; 20.2% do not have insurance; 8.6% of children under 18 do not have insurance

Transportation: Commute: 86.6% car, 2.3% public transportation, 1.4% walk, 7.0% work from home; Median travel time to work: 25.7 minutes

ORANGEVALE (CDP). Covers a land area of 11.515 square miles and a water area of 0.131 square miles. Located at 38.69° N. Lat; 121.22° W. Long. Elevation is 239 feet.

Population: 33,960; Growth (since 2000): 27.2%; Density: 2,949.1 persons per square mile; Race: 87.4% White, 1.4% Black/African American, 3.1% Asian, 0.9% American Indian/Alaska Native, 0.2% Native Hawaiian/Other Pacific Islander, 4.4% Two or more races, 10.2% Hispanic of any race; Average household size: 2.63; Median age: 40.7; Age under 18: 22.9%; Age 65 and over: 13.3%; Males per 100 females: 97.4; Marriage status: 28.0% never married, 52.5% now married, 2.4% separated, 5.2% widowed, 14.2% divorced; Foreign born: 8.5%; Speak English only: 87.2%; With disability: 11.3%; Veterans: 11.2%; Ancestry: 19.8% German, 14.7% English, 14.5% Irish, 7.3% Italian, 4.4% French

Employment: 17.2% management, business, and financial, 9.4% computer, engineering, and science, 6.9% education, legal, community service, arts, and media, 5.0% healthcare practitioners, 17.6% service, 25.0% sales and office, 11.3% natural resources, construction, and maintenance, 7.8% production, transportation, and material moving

Income: Per capita: $31,008; Median household: $65,717; Average household: $79,930; Households with income of $100,000 or more: 28.7%; Poverty rate: 7.7%

Educational Attainment: High school diploma or higher: 91.8%; Bachelor's degree or higher: 25.4%; Graduate/professional degree or higher: 7.8%

School District(s)

San Juan Unified (KG-12)
2012-13 Enrollment: 47,752 . . . . (916) 971-7700
Sbc - Pacific Technology (06-12)
2012-13 Enrollment: 283. . . . . (714) 892-5066

Housing: Homeownership rate: 73.5%; Median home value: $250,700; Median year structure built: 1974; Homeowner vacancy rate: 1.8%; Median gross rent: $1,187 per month; Rental vacancy rate: 7.9%

Health Insurance: 87.6% have insurance; 74.0% have private insurance; 26.8% have public insurance; 12.4% do not have insurance; 5.4% of children under 18 do not have insurance

Transportation: Commute: 89.0% car, 3.0% public transportation, 1.3% walk, 4.4% work from home; Median travel time to work: 26.6 minutes

PARKWAY (CDP). Covers a land area of 2.418 square miles and a water area of 0 square miles. Located at 38.50° N. Lat; 121.45° W. Long. Elevation is 20 feet.

Population: 14,670; Growth (since 2000): n/a; Density: 6,067.0 persons per square mile; Race: 35.6% White, 18.4% Black/African American, 13.6% Asian, 1.2% American Indian/Alaska Native, 2.0% Native Hawaiian/Other Pacific Islander, 7.6% Two or more races, 42.2% Hispanic of any race; Average household size: 3.19; Median age: 29.7; Age under 18: 31.5%; Age 65 and over: 9.8%; Males per 100 females: 96.8; Marriage status: 41.3% never married, 39.0% now married, 4.6% separated, 5.9% widowed, 13.9% divorced; Foreign born: 28.9%; Speak English only: 52.1%; With disability: 16.1%; Veterans: 6.4%; Ancestry: 5.5% German, 4.5% English, 3.0% Irish, 2.9% Portuguese, 2.5% Italian

Employment: 7.8% management, business, and financial, 2.1% computer, engineering, and science, 6.1% education, legal, community service, arts, and media, 1.3% healthcare practitioners, 26.7% service, 23.5% sales and office, 12.6% natural resources, construction, and maintenance, 19.9% production, transportation, and material moving

Income: Per capita: $16,068; Median household: $36,256; Average household: $49,812; Households with income of $100,000 or more: 11.9%; Poverty rate: 30.6%

Educational Attainment: High school diploma or higher: 72.9%; Bachelor's degree or higher: 11.0%; Graduate/professional degree or higher: 3.1%

Housing: Homeownership rate: 46.1%; Median home value: $148,200; Median year structure built: 1965; Homeowner vacancy rate: 3.9%; Median gross rent: $934 per month; Rental vacancy rate: 9.7%

Health Insurance: 80.7% have insurance; 38.6% have private insurance; 51.2% have public insurance; 19.3% do not have insurance; 7.7% of children under 18 do not have insurance

Transportation: Commute: 91.7% car, 2.8% public transportation, 1.1% walk, 2.9% work from home; Median travel time to work: 24.5 minutes

RANCHO CORDOVA (city). Covers a land area of 33.507 square miles and a water area of 0.367 square miles. Located at 38.58° N. Lat; 121.25° W. Long. Elevation is 89 feet.

History: Named for the location of the Cordova Vineyards in the center of a Mexican rancho. The town experienced rapid growth in the 1970s-1990s.

Population: 64,776; Growth (since 2000): 17.6%; Density: 1,933.2 persons per square mile; Race: 60.4% White, 10.1% Black/African American, 12.1% Asian, 1.0% American Indian/Alaska Native, 0.9% Native Hawaiian/Other Pacific Islander, 7.0% Two or more races, 19.7% Hispanic of any race; Average household size: 2.75; Median age: 33.1; Age under 18: 26.3%; Age 65 and over: 10.2%; Males per 100 females: 95.8; Marriage status: 35.1% never married, 47.2% now married, 2.7% separated, 5.5% widowed, 12.1% divorced; Foreign born: 24.8%; Speak English only: 64.6%; With disability: 13.0%; Veterans: 10.4%; Ancestry: 11.2% German, 8.4% Irish, 5.8% English, 4.3% Italian, 4.3% American

Employment: 13.7% management, business, and financial, 8.3% computer, engineering, and science, 7.9% education, legal, community service, arts, and media, 4.5% healthcare practitioners, 20.9% service, 26.5% sales and office, 8.9% natural resources, construction, and maintenance, 9.3% production, transportation, and material moving

Income: Per capita: $23,727; Median household: $52,152; Average household: $64,294; Households with income of $100,000 or more: 19.6%; Poverty rate: 17.8%
Educational Attainment: High school diploma or higher: 87.7%; Bachelor's degree or higher: 25.4%; Graduate/professional degree or higher: 7.5%

School District(s)

Elk Grove Unified (KG-12)
2012-13 Enrollment: 62,137 . . . . (916) 686-5085
Folsom-Cordova Unified (PK-12)
2012-13 Enrollment: 19,117 . . . . (916) 294-9000

Four-year College(s)

ITT Technical Institute-Rancho Cordova (Private, For-profit)
Fall 2013 Enrollment: 510 . . . . (916) 851-3900
2013-14 Tuition: In-state $18,048; Out-of-state $18,048

Two-year College(s)

Heald College-Rancho Cordova (Private, For-profit)
Fall 2013 Enrollment: 1,150 . . . . (916) 414-1700
2013-14 Tuition: In-state $13,620; Out-of-state $13,620
San Joaquin Valley College-Rancho Cordova (Private, For-profit)
Fall 2013 Enrollment: 144 . . . . (916) 638-7582
2013-14 Tuition: In-state $20,450; Out-of-state $20,450

Vocational/Technical School(s)

National Career Education (Private, For-profit)
Fall 2013 Enrollment: 51 . . . . (916) 969-4900
2013-14 Tuition: $11,984

Housing: Homeownership rate: 55.2%; Median home value: $191,300; Median year structure built: 1976; Homeowner vacancy rate: 3.3%; Median gross rent: $961 per month; Rental vacancy rate: 8.9%
Health Insurance: 84.2% have insurance; 59.8% have private insurance; 35.4% have public insurance; 15.8% do not have insurance; 5.3% of children under 18 do not have insurance
Safety: Violent crime rate: 52.0 per 10,000 population; Property crime rate: 325.6 per 10,000 population
Transportation: Commute: 87.9% car, 4.2% public transportation, 1.9% walk, 4.0% work from home; Median travel time to work: 24.4 minutes
Additional Information Contacts
City of Rancho Cordova . . . . (916) 851-8700
http://www.cityofranchocordova.org

RANCHO MURIETA (CDP). Covers a land area of 11.887 square miles and a water area of 0.181 square miles. Located at 38.50° N. Lat; 121.07° W. Long. Elevation is 167 feet.
History: Rancho Murieta is a gated community located in the foothills of the Sierra Nevada range, about 25 miles east of Sacramento.
Population: 5,488; Growth (since 2000): 30.9%; Density: 461.7 persons per square mile; Race: 88.8% White, 2.4% Black/African American, 2.9% Asian, 0.6% American Indian/Alaska Native, 0.1% Native Hawaiian/Other Pacific Islander, 3.8% Two or more races, 7.7% Hispanic of any race; Average household size: 2.39; Median age: 50.8; Age under 18: 20.7%; Age 65 and over: 24.2%; Males per 100 females: 93.9; Marriage status: 12.6% never married, 71.0% now married, 1.3% separated, 6.1% widowed, 10.3% divorced; Foreign born: 8.5%; Speak English only: 94.3%; With disability: 11.7%; Veterans: 19.4%; Ancestry: 21.2% Irish, 16.9% German, 15.0% English, 8.1% Italian, 5.8% Polish
Employment: 21.2% management, business, and financial, 11.4% computer, engineering, and science, 15.0% education, legal, community service, arts, and media, 9.6% healthcare practitioners, 6.5% service, 32.9% sales and office, 1.6% natural resources, construction, and maintenance, 1.9% production, transportation, and material moving
Income: Per capita: $51,130; Median household: $97,566; Average household: $120,443; Households with income of $100,000 or more: 49.2%; Poverty rate: 4.4%
Educational Attainment: High school diploma or higher: 97.4%; Bachelor's degree or higher: 45.5%; Graduate/professional degree or higher: 15.7%
Housing: Homeownership rate: 89.1%; Median home value: $397,600; Median year structure built: 1992; Homeowner vacancy rate: 2.7%; Median gross rent: $1,426 per month; Rental vacancy rate: 6.0%
Health Insurance: 94.4% have insurance; 88.7% have private insurance; 29.0% have public insurance; 5.6% do not have insurance; 5.9% of children under 18 do not have insurance
Transportation: Commute: 89.4% car, 0.5% public transportation, 0.0% walk, 9.3% work from home; Median travel time to work: 36.1 minutes

RIO LINDA (CDP). Covers a land area of 9.904 square miles and a water area of 0 square miles. Located at 38.69° N. Lat; 121.44° W. Long. Elevation is 56 feet.
Population: 15,106; Growth (since 2000): 44.3%; Density: 1,525.3 persons per square mile; Race: 77.1% White, 2.4% Black/African American, 4.4% Asian, 1.6% American Indian/Alaska Native, 0.4% Native Hawaiian/Other Pacific Islander, 5.4% Two or more races, 20.1% Hispanic of any race; Average household size: 3.14; Median age: 35.9; Age under 18: 27.1%; Age 65 and over: 10.4%; Males per 100 females: 101.0; Marriage status: 30.5% never married, 49.0% now married, 2.8% separated, 5.8% widowed, 14.7% divorced; Foreign born: 10.4%; Speak English only: 80.6%; With disability: 15.1%; Veterans: 12.0%; Ancestry: 14.2% German, 11.1% Irish, 7.3% English, 5.9% American, 5.4% Italian
Employment: 9.6% management, business, and financial, 5.4% computer, engineering, and science, 7.3% education, legal, community service, arts, and media, 2.8% healthcare practitioners, 21.1% service, 26.0% sales and office, 15.4% natural resources, construction, and maintenance, 12.4% production, transportation, and material moving
Income: Per capita: $21,884; Median household: $53,643; Average household: $67,615; Households with income of $100,000 or more: 20.3%; Poverty rate: 14.9%
Educational Attainment: High school diploma or higher: 80.3%; Bachelor's degree or higher: 12.7%; Graduate/professional degree or higher: 2.4%

School District(s)

Twin Rivers Unified (KG-12)
2012-13 Enrollment: 31,420 . . . . (916) 566-1600

Housing: Homeownership rate: 72.6%; Median home value: $179,300; Median year structure built: 1974; Homeowner vacancy rate: 2.8%; Median gross rent: $1,127 per month; Rental vacancy rate: 4.3%
Health Insurance: 84.4% have insurance; 63.4% have private insurance; 30.2% have public insurance; 15.6% do not have insurance; 5.4% of children under 18 do not have insurance
Transportation: Commute: 87.7% car, 1.4% public transportation, 1.9% walk, 6.3% work from home; Median travel time to work: 26.7 minutes

ROSEMONT (CDP). Covers a land area of 4.349 square miles and a water area of 0 square miles. Located at 38.55° N. Lat; 121.36° W. Long. Elevation is 49 feet.
Population: 22,681; Growth (since 2000): -1.0%; Density: 5,215.0 persons per square mile; Race: 59.5% White, 12.0% Black/African American, 10.7% Asian, 1.4% American Indian/Alaska Native, 0.6% Native Hawaiian/Other Pacific Islander, 8.1% Two or more races, 20.2% Hispanic of any race; Average household size: 2.68; Median age: 33.9; Age under 18: 24.4%; Age 65 and over: 9.9%; Males per 100 females: 96.7; Marriage status: 38.0% never married, 42.0% now married, 2.3% separated, 6.2% widowed, 13.8% divorced; Foreign born: 18.5%; Speak English only: 71.0%; With disability: 12.4%; Veterans: 9.8%; Ancestry: 12.2% German, 8.7% Irish, 5.5% Italian, 5.3% English, 3.3% American
Employment: 14.3% management, business, and financial, 9.6% computer, engineering, and science, 12.1% education, legal, community service, arts, and media, 3.7% healthcare practitioners, 18.5% service, 25.9% sales and office, 6.8% natural resources, construction, and maintenance, 9.1% production, transportation, and material moving
Income: Per capita: $24,659; Median household: $56,779; Average household: $62,730; Households with income of $100,000 or more: 17.5%; Poverty rate: 16.8%
Educational Attainment: High school diploma or higher: 89.7%; Bachelor's degree or higher: 26.8%; Graduate/professional degree or higher: 8.4%
Housing: Homeownership rate: 58.6%; Median home value: $185,300; Median year structure built: 1975; Homeowner vacancy rate: 1.9%; Median gross rent: $1,075 per month; Rental vacancy rate: 8.2%
Health Insurance: 84.4% have insurance; 67.1% have private insurance; 27.3% have public insurance; 15.6% do not have insurance; 6.5% of children under 18 do not have insurance
Transportation: Commute: 90.1% car, 5.4% public transportation, 0.8% walk, 2.6% work from home; Median travel time to work: 24.6 minutes

RYDE (unincorporated postal area)
ZCTA: 95680
Covers a land area of 2.010 square miles and a water area of 0.055 square miles. Located at 38.24° N. Lat; 121.59° W. Long..
Population: 146; Growth (since 2000): n/a; Density: 72.6 persons per square mile; Race: 60.3% White, 0.0% Black/African American, 2.1%

Asian, 2.1% American Indian/Alaska Native, 0.0% Native Hawaiian/Other Pacific Islander, 4.1% Two or more races, 55.5% Hispanic of any race; Average household size: 3.17; Median age: 33.7; Age under 18: 35.6%; Age 65 and over: 11.0%; Males per 100 females: 111.6

Housing: Homeownership rate: 54.3%; Homeowner vacancy rate: 0.0%; Rental vacancy rate: 4.5%

SACRAMENTO (city). State capital. County seat. Covers a land area of 97.915 square miles and a water area of 2.190 square miles. Located at 38.57° N. Lat; 121.47° W. Long. Elevation is 30 feet.

History: The town of Sacramento was laid out in 1848 on land belonging to Captain John Augustus Sutter, a Swiss ex-army officer who had developed a Mexican land grant and built a fort. The river on which Sutter settled had been named the Sacramento by Jose Moraga, comandante of the presidio of San Jose, in honor of the sacrament. James W. Marshall, a carpenter working on a mill for Sutter on the South Fork of the American River, found the gold flakes that led to the 1849 gold rush and eventually to California's admission to the Union. It spelled ruin for Sutter, whose lands were overrun by gold-seekers, but brought growth to the town of Sacramento as it became the supply center for the mines. In 1854 Sacramento became the official capital of the State of California.

Population: 466,488; Growth (since 2000): 14.6%; Density: 4,764.2 persons per square mile; Race: 45.0% White, 14.6% Black/African American, 18.3% Asian, 1.1% American Indian/Alaska Native, 1.4% Native Hawaiian/Other Pacific Islander, 7.1% Two or more races, 26.9% Hispanic of any race; Average household size: 2.62; Median age: 33.0; Age under 18: 24.9%; Age 65 and over: 10.6%; Males per 100 females: 94.9; Marriage status: 39.7% never married, 42.6% now married, 2.7% separated, 5.5% widowed, 12.2% divorced; Foreign born: 21.9%; Speak English only: 63.5%; With disability: 13.3%; Veterans: 7.6%; Ancestry: 8.5% German, 7.1% Irish, 5.7% English, 4.1% Italian, 2.1% American

Employment: 15.4% management, business, and financial, 6.9% computer, engineering, and science, 11.4% education, legal, community service, arts, and media, 4.6% healthcare practitioners, 20.1% service, 26.4% sales and office, 6.4% natural resources, construction, and maintenance, 8.8% production, transportation, and material moving

Income: Per capita: $25,508; Median household: $49,753; Average household: $65,908; Households with income of $100,000 or more: 19.6%; Poverty rate: 21.9%

Educational Attainment: High school diploma or higher: 82.4%; Bachelor's degree or higher: 29.3%; Graduate/professional degree or higher: 10.4%

School District(s)

Dry Creek Joint Elementary (KG-08)
2012-13 Enrollment: 6,888 . . . . (916) 770-8800
Elk Grove Unified (KG-12)
2012-13 Enrollment: 62,137 . . . . (916) 686-5085
Natomas Unified (KG-12)
2012-13 Enrollment: 12,454 . . . . (916) 567-5400
Nevada County Office of Education (KG-12)
2012-13 Enrollment: 3,418 . . . . (530) 478-6400
Robla Elementary (KG-06)
2012-13 Enrollment: 2,119 . . . . (916) 991-1728
Sacramento City Unified (KG-12)
2012-13 Enrollment: 47,616 . . . . (916) 643-9000
Sacramento County Office of Education (KG-12)
2012-13 Enrollment: 1,148 . . . . (916) 228-2500
Sacramento County Rop
2012-13 Enrollment: n/a . . . . (916) 228-2463
San Juan Unified (KG-12)
2012-13 Enrollment: 47,752 . . . . (916) 971-7700
Sbc - Aspire Public Schools (KG-12)
2012-13 Enrollment: 1,972 . . . . (510) 434-5000
Twin Rivers Unified (KG-12)
2012-13 Enrollment: 31,420 . . . . (916) 566-1600

Four-year College(s)

California State University-Sacramento (Public)
Fall 2013 Enrollment: 28,811 . . . . (916) 278-6011
2013-14 Tuition: In-state $6,628; Out-of-state $17,788
Epic Bible College (Private, Not-for-profit, Assemblies of God Church)
Fall 2013 Enrollment: 265 . . . . (916) 348-4689
2013-14 Tuition: In-state $9,690; Out-of-state $9,690
International Academy of Design and Technology-Sacramento (Private, For-profit)
Fall 2013 Enrollment: 194 . . . . (916) 285-9468
2013-14 Tuition: In-state $15,508; Out-of-state $15,508
The Art Institute of California-Argosy University Sacramento (Private, For-profit)
Fall 2013 Enrollment: 1,185 . . . . (916) 830-6320
2013-14 Tuition: In-state $18,748; Out-of-state $18,748
University of Phoenix-Sacramento Valley Campus (Private, For-profit)
Fall 2013 Enrollment: 3,421 . . . . (866) 766-0766
2013-14 Tuition: In-state $11,303; Out-of-state $11,303

Two-year College(s)

American River College (Public)
Fall 2013 Enrollment: 29,701 . . . . (916) 484-8011
2013-14 Tuition: In-state $1,104; Out-of-state $7,200
Asher College (Private, For-profit)
Fall 2013 Enrollment: 686 . . . . (916) 649-9600
Carrington College California-Sacramento (Private, For-profit)
Fall 2013 Enrollment: 1,267 . . . . (916) 361-1660
Charles A Jones Career and Education Center (Public)
Fall 2013 Enrollment: 1,032 . . . . (916) 433-2600
Cosumnes River College (Public)
Fall 2013 Enrollment: 13,949 . . . . (916) 688-7344
2013-14 Tuition: In-state $1,104; Out-of-state $7,200
Kaplan College-Sacramento (Private, For-profit)
Fall 2013 Enrollment: 547 . . . . (916) 649-8168
MTI College (Private, For-profit)
Fall 2013 Enrollment: 594 . . . . (916) 339-1500
Sacramento City College (Public)
Fall 2013 Enrollment: 23,509 . . . . (916) 558-2111
2013-14 Tuition: In-state $1,104; Out-of-state $7,200
Universal Technical Institute of Northern California Inc (Private, For-profit)
Fall 2013 Enrollment: 1,916 . . . . (916) 263-9100

Vocational/Technical School(s)

Anthem College-Sacramento (Private, For-profit)
Fall 2013 Enrollment: 257 . . . . (954) 400-2000
2013-14 Tuition: In-state $15,537; Out-of-state $15,537
CET-Sacramento (Private, Not-for-profit)
Fall 2013 Enrollment: 145 . . . . (408) 287-7924
2013-14 Tuition: $9,958
Cosmo Beauty Academy (Private, For-profit)
Fall 2013 Enrollment: 64 . . . . (916) 779-0143
2013-14 Tuition: $12,460
Federico Beauty Institute (Private, For-profit)
Fall 2013 Enrollment: 246 . . . . (916) 929-4242
2013-14 Tuition: $15,322
Le Cordon Bleu College of Culinary Arts-Sacramento (Private, For-profit)
Fall 2013 Enrollment: 375 . . . . (916) 830-6220
2013-14 Tuition: $17,200
Marinello Schools of Beauty-Sacramento (Private, For-profit)
Fall 2013 Enrollment: 561 . . . . (562) 945-2211
2013-14 Tuition: $18,510
My Le's Beauty College (Private, For-profit)
Fall 2013 Enrollment: 33 . . . . (916) 422-0223
2013-14 Tuition: $10,881
Paul Mitchell The School-Sacramento (Private, For-profit)
Fall 2013 Enrollment: 348 . . . . (916) 646-3523
2013-14 Tuition: $18,000

Housing: Homeownership rate: 49.4%; Median home value: $225,900; Median year structure built: 1972; Homeowner vacancy rate: 2.8%; Median gross rent: $999 per month; Rental vacancy rate: 8.3%

Health Insurance: 84.3% have insurance; 58.3% have private insurance; 35.2% have public insurance; 15.7% do not have insurance; 5.6% of children under 18 do not have insurance

Hospitals: Kaiser Foundation Hospital - Sacramento (340 beds); Kaiser Foundation Hospital South Sacramento (161 beds); Mercy General Hospital (399 beds); Methodist Hospital of Sacramento (355 beds); Sutter General Hospital (306 beds); University of California Davis Medical Center (528 beds)

Safety: Violent crime rate: 65.6 per 10,000 population; Property crime rate: 376.0 per 10,000 population

Newspapers: Sacramento Bee (daily circulation 274000); Sacramento Gazette (weekly circulation 1700); Sacramento News & Review (weekly circulation 85000); Valley Community Newspapers (weekly circulation 15000)

Transportation: Commute: 84.8% car, 4.0% public transportation, 3.1% walk, 4.5% work from home; Median travel time to work: 24.0 minutes; Amtrak: Train and bus service available.

Airports: McClellan Airfield (general aviation); Sacramento Executive (general aviation); Sacramento International (primary service/medium hub); Sacramento Mather (general aviation)

Additional Information Contacts

City of Sacramento . . . . (916) 264-5011
http://www.cityofsacramento.org

SLOUGHHOUSE (unincorporated postal area)

ZCTA: 95683

Covers a land area of 90.773 square miles and a water area of 0.416 square miles. Located at 38.51° N. Lat; 121.10° W. Long. Elevation is 102 feet.

Population: 6,180; Growth (since 2000): 31.2%; Density: 68.1 persons per square mile; Race: 87.1% White, 2.7% Black/African American, 3.0% Asian, 0.7% American Indian/Alaska Native, 0.2% Native Hawaiian/Other Pacific Islander, 3.7% Two or more races, 9.3% Hispanic of any race; Average household size: 2.43; Median age: 49.4; Age under 18: 21.7%; Age 65 and over: 22.7%; Males per 100 females: 97.3; Marriage status: 14.4% never married, 70.0% now married, 1.2% separated, 5.9% widowed, 9.7% divorced; Foreign born: 10.6%; Speak English only: 91.4%; With disability: 11.6%; Veterans: 18.0%; Ancestry: 19.6% Irish, 15.9% German, 13.8% English, 7.7% Italian, 6.9% American

Employment: 19.1% management, business, and financial, 10.2% computer, engineering, and science, 15.6% education, legal, community service, arts, and media, 8.7% healthcare practitioners, 6.6% service, 32.8% sales and office, 4.5% natural resources, construction, and maintenance, 2.4% production, transportation, and material moving

Income: Per capita: $49,089; Median household: $96,165; Average household: $117,363; Households with income of $100,000 or more: 47.4%; Poverty rate: 4.4%

Educational Attainment: High school diploma or higher: 95.4%; Bachelor's degree or higher: 43.5%; Graduate/professional degree or higher: 14.6%

School District(s)

Elk Grove Unified (KG-12)
2012-13 Enrollment: 62,137 . . . . (916) 686-5085

Housing: Homeownership rate: 87.6%; Median home value: $405,200; Median year structure built: 1991; Homeowner vacancy rate: 2.8%; Median gross rent: $1,384 per month; Rental vacancy rate: 6.0%

Health Insurance: 94.8% have insurance; 89.0% have private insurance; 27.4% have public insurance; 5.2% do not have insurance; 5.7% of children under 18 do not have insurance

Transportation: Commute: 84.5% car, 0.5% public transportation, 0.8% walk, 13.5% work from home; Median travel time to work: 39.3 minutes

VINEYARD (CDP).

Covers a land area of 17.206 square miles and a water area of 0 square miles. Located at 38.47° N. Lat; 121.32° W. Long. Elevation is 89 feet.

Population: 24,836; Growth (since 2000): 145.7%; Density: 1,443.4 persons per square mile; Race: 45.5% White, 9.8% Black/African American, 29.4% Asian, 0.7% American Indian/Alaska Native, 1.0% Native Hawaiian/Other Pacific Islander, 6.9% Two or more races, 17.8% Hispanic of any race; Average household size: 3.35; Median age: 33.8; Age under 18: 30.4%; Age 65 and over: 7.2%; Males per 100 females: 96.9; Marriage status: 30.3% never married, 56.7% now married, 1.3% separated, 4.4% widowed, 8.6% divorced; Foreign born: 25.4%; Speak English only: 64.0%; With disability: 9.8%; Veterans: 6.4%; Ancestry: 8.2% German, 6.5% English, 6.4% Irish, 2.8% Italian, 2.8% Norwegian

Employment: 14.3% management, business, and financial, 8.6% computer, engineering, and science, 7.7% education, legal, community service, arts, and media, 6.5% healthcare practitioners, 20.9% service, 26.1% sales and office, 6.5% natural resources, construction, and maintenance, 9.4% production, transportation, and material moving

Income: Per capita: $26,858; Median household: $75,633; Average household: $88,326; Households with income of $100,000 or more: 36.6%; Poverty rate: 12.9%

Educational Attainment: High school diploma or higher: 87.0%; Bachelor's degree or higher: 27.7%; Graduate/professional degree or higher: 7.1%

Housing: Homeownership rate: 77.8%; Median home value: $266,300; Median year structure built: 2001; Homeowner vacancy rate: 2.2%; Median gross rent: $1,570 per month; Rental vacancy rate: 3.9%

Health Insurance: 87.4% have insurance; 70.2% have private insurance; 24.8% have public insurance; 12.6% do not have insurance; 5.9% of children under 18 do not have insurance

Transportation: Commute: 90.5% car, 1.0% public transportation, 0.6% walk, 5.1% work from home; Median travel time to work: 28.6 minutes

WALNUT GROVE (CDP).

Covers a land area of 10.201 square miles and a water area of 0.723 square miles. Located at 38.25° N. Lat; 121.54° W. Long. Elevation is 10 feet.

Population: 1,542; Growth (since 2000): 130.5%; Density: 151.2 persons per square mile; Race: 61.2% White, 1.0% Black/African American, 7.1% Asian, 1.6% American Indian/Alaska Native, 0.0% Native Hawaiian/Other Pacific Islander, 3.1% Two or more races, 43.6% Hispanic of any race; Average household size: 2.62; Median age: 40.6; Age under 18: 23.2%; Age 65 and over: 15.6%; Males per 100 females: 112.1

School District(s)

River Delta Joint Unified (KG-12)
2012-13 Enrollment: 2,323 . . . . (707) 374-1700

Housing: Homeownership rate: 52.8%; Homeowner vacancy rate: 1.6%; Rental vacancy rate: 6.7%

WILTON (CDP).

Covers a land area of 29.002 square miles and a water area of 0 square miles. Located at 38.41° N. Lat; 121.21° W. Long. Elevation is 79 feet.

Population: 5,363; Growth (since 2000): 17.8%; Density: 184.9 persons per square mile; Race: 78.9% White, 3.2% Black/African American, 5.4% Asian, 0.8% American Indian/Alaska Native, 0.2% Native Hawaiian/Other Pacific Islander, 5.0% Two or more races, 12.7% Hispanic of any race; Average household size: 2.86; Median age: 45.5; Age under 18: 23.1%; Age 65 and over: 15.9%; Males per 100 females: 98.9; Marriage status: 21.8% never married, 61.6% now married, 3.7% separated, 9.8% widowed, 6.9% divorced; Foreign born: 8.3%; Speak English only: 86.5%; With disability: 13.5%; Veterans: 14.5%; Ancestry: 19.8% German, 13.1% Irish, 10.8% English, 5.6% Italian, 4.0% Norwegian

Employment: 23.4% management, business, and financial, 6.4% computer, engineering, and science, 10.1% education, legal, community service, arts, and media, 8.7% healthcare practitioners, 20.6% service, 21.7% sales and office, 6.3% natural resources, construction, and maintenance, 2.8% production, transportation, and material moving

Income: Per capita: $35,873; Median household: $78,148; Average household: $93,043; Households with income of $100,000 or more: 38.2%; Poverty rate: 15.3%

Educational Attainment: High school diploma or higher: 91.4%; Bachelor's degree or higher: 30.5%; Graduate/professional degree or higher: 10.4%

School District(s)

Elk Grove Unified (KG-12)
2012-13 Enrollment: 62,137 . . . . (916) 686-5085

Housing: Homeownership rate: 86.8%; Median home value: $393,200; Median year structure built: 1980; Homeowner vacancy rate: 2.2%; Median gross rent: $1,043 per month; Rental vacancy rate: 5.0%

Health Insurance: 90.5% have insurance; 81.9% have private insurance; 30.4% have public insurance; 9.5% do not have insurance; 5.8% of children under 18 do not have insurance

Newspapers: River Valley Times (weekly circulation 5500)

Transportation: Commute: 86.2% car, 0.0% public transportation, 1.5% walk, 10.7% work from home; Median travel time to work: 33.6 minutes

San Benito County

Located in western California, between the Santa Cruz Mountains and Gabilan Range on the west and the Diablo Range on the east; crossed by the San Benito River. Covers a land area of 1,388.710 square miles, a water area of 1.759 square miles, and is located in the Pacific Time Zone at 36.61° N. Lat., 121.09° W. Long. The county was founded in 1874. County seat is Hollister.

San Benito County is part of the San Jose-Sunnyvale-Santa Clara, CA Metropolitan Statistical Area. The entire metro area includes: San Benito County, CA; Santa Clara County, CA

Weather Station: Hollister 2 Elevation: 274 feet

	Jan	Feb	Mar	Apr	May	Jun	Jul	Aug	Sep	Oct	Nov	Dec
High	60	63	66	70	74	78	81	81	81	77	67	60
Low	38	41	43	44	48	51	53	54	52	48	42	37
Precip	2.9	2.9	2.2	0.9	0.4	0.1	0.0	0.0	0.2	0.7	1.6	2.1
Snow	0.0	0.0	0.0	0.0	0.0	0.0	0.0	0.0	0.0	0.0	0.0	0.0

High and Low temperatures in degrees Fahrenheit; Precipitation and Snow in inches

Weather Station: Pinnacles Natl Monument Elevation: 1,307 feet

	Jan	Feb	Mar	Apr	May	Jun	Jul	Aug	Sep	Oct	Nov	Dec
High	62	64	67	72	80	88	95	95	90	81	69	62
Low	32	35	37	38	42	46	50	49	47	41	36	32
Precip	3.4	3.4	3.1	1.0	0.5	0.1	0.1	0.0	0.2	0.9	1.5	2.5
Snow	0.1	tr	0.0	tr	0.0	0.0	0.0	0.0	0.0	0.0	0.0	tr

High and Low temperatures in degrees Fahrenheit; Precipitation and Snow in inches

Population: 55,269; Growth (since 2000): 3.8%; Density: 39.8 persons per square mile; Race: 63.7% White, 0.9% Black/African American, 2.6% Asian, 1.6% American Indian/Alaska Native, 0.2% Native Hawaiian/Other Pacific Islander, 4.9% two or more races, 56.4% Hispanic of any race; Average household size: 3.27; Median age: 34.3; Age under 18: 29.1%; Age 65 and over: 9.7%; Males per 100 females: 100.0; Marriage status: 30.1% never married, 55.0% now married, 2.5% separated, 4.5% widowed, 10.5% divorced; Foreign born: 20.1%; Speak English only: 61.4%; With disability: 8.7%; Veterans: 6.7%; Ancestry: 9.6% German, 9.2% Irish, 7.5% Italian, 5.8% English, 3.0% Portuguese

Religion: Six largest groups: 56.3% Catholicism, 2.1% Latter-day Saints, 2.0% Non-denominational Protestant, 1.2% Pentecostal, 1.0% Baptist, 0.6% Presbyterian-Reformed

Economy: Unemployment rate: 7.4%; Leading industries: 15.1% construction; 11.6% retail trade; 10.6% health care and social assistance; Farms: 628 totaling 604,319 acres; Company size: 0 employ 1,000 or more persons, 1 employs 500 to 999 persons, 13 employ 100 to 499 persons, 894 employ less than 100 persons; Business ownership: 1,106 women-owned, n/a Black-owned, n/a Hispanic-owned, n/a Asian-owned

Employment: 13.7% management, business, and financial, 3.3% computer, engineering, and science, 7.5% education, legal, community service, arts, and media, 3.1% healthcare practitioners, 18.4% service, 26.8% sales and office, 15.4% natural resources, construction, and maintenance, 11.8% production, transportation, and material moving

Income: Per capita: $25,914; Median household: $66,237; Average household: $80,980; Households with income of $100,000 or more: 29.9%; Poverty rate: 11.9%

Educational Attainment: High school diploma or higher: 76.9%; Bachelor's degree or higher: 18.2%; Graduate/professional degree or higher: 4.7%

Housing: Homeownership rate: 65.0%; Median home value: $343,000; Median year structure built: 1984; Homeowner vacancy rate: 2.0%; Median gross rent: $1,233 per month; Rental vacancy rate: 5.1%

Vital Statistics: Birth rate: 136.8 per 10,000 population; Death rate: 49.5 per 10,000 population; Age-adjusted cancer mortality rate: 153.0 deaths per 100,000 population

Health Insurance: 84.2% have insurance; 63.0% have private insurance; 29.7% have public insurance; 15.8% do not have insurance; 9.5% of children under 18 do not have insurance

Health Care: Physicians: 8.3 per 10,000 population; Hospital beds: 20.1 per 10,000 population; Hospital admissions: 540.9 per 10,000 population

Air Quality Index: 87.1% good, 12.9% moderate, 0.0% unhealthy for sensitive individuals, 0.0% unhealthy (percent of days)

Transportation: Commute: 92.6% car, 0.6% public transportation, 1.6% walk, 3.8% work from home; Median travel time to work: 30.2 minutes

Presidential Election: 58.8% Obama, 39.1% Romney (2012)

National and State Parks: Fremont Peak State Park; Hollister Hills State Vehicular Recreation Area; Pinnacles National Park; San Juan Bautista State Historic Park

Additional Information Contacts

San Benito Government . . . . (831) 636-4000
http://www.san-benito.ca.us

San Benito County Communities

HOLLISTER (city). County seat. Covers a land area of 7.290 square miles and a water area of 0 square miles. Located at 36.86° N. Lat; 121.40° W. Long. Elevation is 289 feet.

History: Named for Colonel W.W. Hollister, who drove the first flock of sheep across the continent. San Juan Bautista State Historical Park to west. Settled 1868. Incorporated 1874.

Population: 34,928; Growth (since 2000): 1.5%; Density: 4,791.4 persons per square mile; Race: 59.4% White, 1.0% Black/African American, 2.7% Asian, 1.8% American Indian/Alaska Native, 0.2% Native Hawaiian/Other Pacific Islander, 5.1% Two or more races, 65.7% Hispanic of any race; Average household size: 3.53; Median age: 30.8; Age under 18: 31.7%; Age 65 and over: 7.4%; Males per 100 females: 98.7; Marriage status: 32.2% never married, 53.2% now married, 2.6% separated, 4.1% widowed, 10.5% divorced; Foreign born: 23.4%; Speak English only: 53.8%; With disability: 8.0%; Veterans: 6.2%; Ancestry: 6.9% Irish, 6.1% German, 5.0% Italian, 3.7% English, 2.4% Portuguese

Employment: 10.3% management, business, and financial, 2.8% computer, engineering, and science, 6.1% education, legal, community service, arts, and media, 3.6% healthcare practitioners, 20.0% service, 27.7% sales and office, 16.6% natural resources, construction, and maintenance, 13.0% production, transportation, and material moving

Income: Per capita: $22,306; Median household: $62,412; Average household: $72,441; Households with income of $100,000 or more: 24.5%; Poverty rate: 13.3%

Educational Attainment: High school diploma or higher: 71.1%; Bachelor's degree or higher: 14.4%; Graduate/professional degree or higher: 2.7%

School District(s)

Cienega Union Elementary (KG-08)
2012-13 Enrollment: 30. . . . . (831) 637-3821
Hollister (KG-08)
2012-13 Enrollment: 5,623 . . . . (831) 630-6300
North County Joint Union Elementary (KG-08)
2012-13 Enrollment: 779. . . . . (831) 637-5574
San Benito County Office of Education (KG-12)
2012-13 Enrollment: 114. . . . . (831) 637-5393
San Benito High (09-12)
2012-13 Enrollment: 3,069 . . . . (831) 637-5831
Southside Elementary (KG-08)
2012-13 Enrollment: 251. . . . . (831) 637-4439

Housing: Homeownership rate: 61.1%; Median home value: $284,300; Median year structure built: 1987; Homeowner vacancy rate: 2.3%; Median gross rent: $1,217 per month; Rental vacancy rate: 5.0%

Health Insurance: 83.7% have insurance; 59.1% have private insurance; 31.9% have public insurance; 16.3% do not have insurance; 9.0% of children under 18 do not have insurance

Hospitals: Hazel Hawkins Memorial Hospital (101 beds)

Safety: Violent crime rate: 53.6 per 10,000 population; Property crime rate: 156.5 per 10,000 population

Newspapers: Free Lance (daily circulation 3000); The Pinnacle (weekly circulation 19000)

Transportation: Commute: 92.8% car, 0.8% public transportation, 1.7% walk, 3.0% work from home; Median travel time to work: 30.3 minutes

Airports: Hollister Municipal (general aviation)

Additional Information Contacts

City of Hollister . . . . (831) 636-4300
http://www.hollister.ca.gov/site/index.asp

PAICINES (unincorporated postal area)

ZCTA: 95043

Covers a land area of 858.553 square miles and a water area of 1.077 square miles. Located at 36.53° N. Lat; 120.95° W. Long. Elevation is 682 feet.

Population: 639; Growth (since 2000): -20.7%; Density: 0.7 persons per square mile; Race: 85.9% White, 0.3% Black/African American, 0.3% Asian, 0.9% American Indian/Alaska Native, 0.2% Native Hawaiian/Other Pacific Islander, 2.7% Two or more races, 26.8% Hispanic of any race; Average household size: 2.28; Median age: 48.4; Age under 18: 18.2%; Age 65 and over: 15.3%; Males per 100 females: 100.9

School District(s)

Jefferson Elementary (KG-08)
2012-13 Enrollment: 18. . . . . (831) 389-4593

Panoche Elementary (KG-08)
2012-13 Enrollment: 6. . . . . (831) 628-3438
Willow Grove Union Elementary (KG-08)
2012-13 Enrollment: 12. . . . . (831) 628-3256

Housing: Homeownership rate: 58.9%; Homeowner vacancy rate: 4.1%; Rental vacancy rate: 11.0%

RIDGEMARK (CDP). Covers a land area of 2.570 square miles and a water area of 0 square miles. Located at 36.81° N. Lat; 121.36° W. Long. Elevation is 489 feet.

Population: 3,016; Growth (since 2000): 10.0%; Density: 1,173.5 persons per square mile; Race: 83.6% White, 0.8% Black/African American, 3.5% Asian, 0.5% American Indian/Alaska Native, 0.1% Native Hawaiian/Other Pacific Islander, 3.4% Two or more races, 20.7% Hispanic of any race; Average household size: 2.47; Median age: 49.1; Age under 18: 20.6%; Age 65 and over: 24.7%; Males per 100 females: 93.1; Marriage status: 24.1% never married, 61.1% now married, 3.3% separated, 5.3% widowed, 9.5% divorced; Foreign born: 7.1%; Speak English only: 84.9%; With disability: 10.1%; Veterans: 11.8%; Ancestry: 20.0% German, 19.8% Irish, 13.3% Italian, 11.0% English, 4.0% Dutch

Employment: 24.9% management, business, and financial, 3.4% computer, engineering, and science, 15.9% education, legal, community service, arts, and media, 3.3% healthcare practitioners, 15.2% service, 25.2% sales and office, 4.9% natural resources, construction, and maintenance, 7.1% production, transportation, and material moving

Income: Per capita: $41,405; Median household: $99,913; Average household: $108,831; Households with income of $100,000 or more: 49.9%; Poverty rate: 6.2%

Educational Attainment: High school diploma or higher: 95.3%; Bachelor's degree or higher: 38.3%; Graduate/professional degree or higher: 11.7%

Housing: Homeownership rate: 83.5%; Median home value: $520,600; Median year structure built: 1986; Homeowner vacancy rate: 1.7%; Median gross rent: $1,773 per month; Rental vacancy rate: 6.1%

Health Insurance: 90.2% have insurance; 80.9% have private insurance; 25.8% have public insurance; 9.8% do not have insurance; 11.7% of children under 18 do not have insurance

Transportation: Commute: 92.7% car, 0.0% public transportation, 1.2% walk, 5.5% work from home; Median travel time to work: 30.0 minutes

SAN JUAN BAUTISTA (city). Covers a land area of 0.711 square miles and a water area of <.001 square miles. Located at 36.85° N. Lat; 121.54° W. Long. Elevation is 217 feet.

History: San Juan Bautista began with the founding of a Franciscan mission in 1797, the largest of the California missions. An adobe building erected about 1792 became a hotel in 1856 and a stopping place for as many as 11 stage lines on the San Francisco-Los Angeles route.

Population: 1,862; Growth (since 2000): 20.2%; Density: 2,618.1 persons per square mile; Race: 60.4% White, 0.6% Black/African American, 2.8% Asian, 3.1% American Indian/Alaska Native, 0.1% Native Hawaiian/Other Pacific Islander, 6.4% Two or more races, 48.7% Hispanic of any race; Average household size: 2.73; Median age: 38.7; Age under 18: 23.1%; Age 65 and over: 11.9%; Males per 100 females: 92.4

School District(s)

Aromas/san Juan Unified (KG-12)
2012-13 Enrollment: 1,170 . . . . (831) 623-4500

Housing: Homeownership rate: 50.6%; Homeowner vacancy rate: 3.6%; Rental vacancy rate: 5.1%

Additional Information Contacts

City of San Juan Bautista . . . . (831) 623-4661
http://www.san-juan-bautista.ca.us

TRES PINOS (CDP). Covers a land area of 3.597 square miles and a water area of 0 square miles. Located at 36.79° N. Lat; 121.31° W. Long. Elevation is 531 feet.

Population: 476; Growth (since 2000): n/a; Density: 132.3 persons per square mile; Race: 81.9% White, 0.6% Black/African American, 1.3% Asian, 1.7% American Indian/Alaska Native, 0.0% Native Hawaiian/Other Pacific Islander, 2.5% Two or more races, 23.5% Hispanic of any race; Average household size: 2.87; Median age: 44.5; Age under 18: 24.2%; Age 65 and over: 10.9%; Males per 100 females: 107.0

School District(s)

Tres Pinos Union Elementary (KG-08)
2012-13 Enrollment: 133. . . . . (831) 637-0503

Housing: Homeownership rate: 76.6%; Homeowner vacancy rate: 3.0%; Rental vacancy rate: 4.9%

San Bernardino County

Located in southern California; bounded on the northwest by Nevada, and on the west by the Colorado River and the Arizona border; includes parts of the Mojave and Colorado Deserts, several mountain ranges, and San Bernardino National Forest. Covers a land area of 20,056.937 square miles, a water area of 47.888 square miles, and is located in the Pacific Time Zone at 34.86° N. Lat., 116.18° W. Long. The county was founded in 1853. County seat is San Bernardino.

San Bernardino County is part of the Riverside-San Bernardino-Ontario, CA Metropolitan Statistical Area. The entire metro area includes: Riverside County, CA; San Bernardino County, CA

Weather Station: Barstow Fire Station — Elevation: 2,319 feet

	Jan	Feb	Mar	Apr	May	Jun	Jul	Aug	Sep	Oct	Nov	Dec
High	61	65	71	78	87	96	102	101	94	82	69	59
Low	35	38	43	48	55	63	69	68	61	51	41	33
Precip	0.9	1.0	0.7	0.2	0.1	0.1	0.3	0.2	0.3	0.3	0.5	0.6
Snow	0.0	0.0	tr	0.0	0.0	0.0	0.0	0.0	0.0	0.0	0.0	0.3

High and Low temperatures in degrees Fahrenheit; Precipitation and Snow in inches

Weather Station: Big Bear Lake — Elevation: 6,790 feet

	Jan	Feb	Mar	Apr	May	Jun	Jul	Aug	Sep	Oct	Nov	Dec
High	47	48	52	59	68	76	81	80	74	65	55	48
Low	22	23	25	29	36	42	48	47	42	33	26	21
Precip	4.4	4.3	2.8	1.0	0.4	0.2	0.7	1.0	0.4	0.9	1.4	2.6
Snow	15.2	15.8	15.3	3.9	0.6	tr	0.0	0.0	0.1	1.2	4.5	10.3

High and Low temperatures in degrees Fahrenheit; Precipitation and Snow in inches

Weather Station: Daggett Barstow-Daggett Arpt — Elevation: 1,921 feet

	Jan	Feb	Mar	Apr	May	Jun	Jul	Aug	Sep	Oct	Nov	Dec
High	61	65	72	80	89	99	105	103	95	83	70	60
Low	37	41	46	51	60	67	74	73	66	55	43	36
Precip	0.6	0.7	0.5	0.2	0.1	0.1	0.5	0.3	0.2	0.2	0.3	0.5
Snow	na	0.1	na	tr	0.0	na	0.0	na	na	na	na	na

High and Low temperatures in degrees Fahrenheit; Precipitation and Snow in inches

Weather Station: El Mirage — Elevation: 2,950 feet

	Jan	Feb	Mar	Apr	May	Jun	Jul	Aug	Sep	Oct	Nov	Dec
High	57	60	66	73	82	91	98	97	90	78	65	56
Low	30	33	37	41	49	55	61	60	54	45	35	29
Precip	1.0	1.2	0.9	0.3	0.2	0.1	0.2	0.3	0.2	0.3	0.3	0.8
Snow	0.2	0.2	0.2	tr	0.0	0.0	0.0	0.0	0.0	0.0	tr	0.8

High and Low temperatures in degrees Fahrenheit; Precipitation and Snow in inches

Weather Station: Iron Mountain — Elevation: 921 feet

	Jan	Feb	Mar	Apr	May	Jun	Jul	Aug	Sep	Oct	Nov	Dec
High	67	71	78	86	95	104	109	108	101	89	76	65
Low	44	48	52	59	68	76	81	80	73	61	51	43
Precip	0.5	0.7	0.5	0.1	0.1	tr	0.3	0.5	0.3	0.2	0.2	0.5
Snow	0.0	0.0	0.0	0.0	0.0	0.0	0.0	0.0	0.0	0.0	0.0	0.0

High and Low temperatures in degrees Fahrenheit; Precipitation and Snow in inches

Weather Station: Lake Arrowhead — Elevation: 5,205 feet

	Jan	Feb	Mar	Apr	May	Jun	Jul	Aug	Sep	Oct	Nov	Dec
High	45	48	53	60	69	78	83	82	76	64	53	45
Low	30	30	32	36	42	49	57	57	51	42	35	30
Precip	8.9	8.9	6.4	2.5	1.0	0.3	0.1	0.2	0.7	2.3	3.3	4.5
Snow	6.5	6.1	8.4	2.0	0.5	0.0	0.0	0.0	0.0	tr	0.5	3.7

High and Low temperatures in degrees Fahrenheit; Precipitation and Snow in inches

Weather Station: Mitchell Caverns — Elevation: 4,350 feet

	Jan	Feb	Mar	Apr	May	Jun	Jul	Aug	Sep	Oct	Nov	Dec
High	55	57	62	70	79	88	93	91	85	74	62	54
Low	39	40	43	48	57	66	71	70	64	55	45	38
Precip	1.5	1.9	1.5	0.6	0.2	0.1	1.0	1.4	1.0	0.8	0.6	1.2
Snow	0.3	0.3	0.6	0.1	tr	0.0	0.0	0.0	0.0	tr	0.1	0.8

High and Low temperatures in degrees Fahrenheit; Precipitation and Snow in inches

Weather Station: Needles Airport Elevation: 914 feet

	Jan	Feb	Mar	Apr	May	Jun	Jul	Aug	Sep	Oct	Nov	Dec
High	66	70	78	86	95	105	109	107	101	89	74	64
Low	44	47	52	59	68	77	84	83	75	62	50	43
Precip	0.7	0.8	0.6	0.2	0.1	0.0	0.2	0.6	0.4	0.2	0.4	0.5
Snow	0.0	na	na	na	na	na	na	na	na	na	na	na

High and Low temperatures in degrees Fahrenheit; Precipitation and Snow in inches

Weather Station: Parker Reservoir Elevation: 737 feet

	Jan	Feb	Mar	Apr	May	Jun	Jul	Aug	Sep	Oct	Nov	Dec
High	66	70	77	85	95	103	108	106	100	89	75	65
Low	44	47	53	60	69	77	83	82	75	63	51	43
Precip	1.1	1.1	0.8	0.2	0.1	0.0	0.5	0.6	0.6	0.4	0.4	0.6
Snow	0.0	0.0	0.0	0.0	0.0	0.0	0.0	0.0	0.0	0.0	0.0	0.0

High and Low temperatures in degrees Fahrenheit; Precipitation and Snow in inches

Weather Station: Redlands Elevation: 1,317 feet

	Jan	Feb	Mar	Apr	May	Jun	Jul	Aug	Sep	Oct	Nov	Dec
High	67	68	71	76	81	88	95	96	92	82	74	67
Low	41	43	45	48	53	57	62	63	60	53	45	40
Precip	2.7	3.3	2.1	1.0	0.3	0.1	0.1	0.1	0.3	0.6	1.0	1.6
Snow	0.0	0.0	0.0	0.0	0.0	0.0	0.0	0.0	0.0	0.0	0.0	0.0

High and Low temperatures in degrees Fahrenheit; Precipitation and Snow in inches

Weather Station: Trona Elevation: 1,694 feet

	Jan	Feb	Mar	Apr	May	Jun	Jul	Aug	Sep	Oct	Nov	Dec
High	58	63	70	78	87	98	105	102	95	83	68	57
Low	37	42	48	53	62	70	77	76	68	57	45	36
Precip	0.8	1.0	0.5	0.1	0.1	0.1	0.1	0.3	0.1	0.1	0.4	0.4
Snow	0.0	tr	0.0	0.0	0.0	0.0	0.0	0.0	0.0	0.0	0.0	tr

High and Low temperatures in degrees Fahrenheit; Precipitation and Snow in inches

Weather Station: Twentynine Palms Elevation: 1,975 feet

	Jan	Feb	Mar	Apr	May	Jun	Jul	Aug	Sep	Oct	Nov	Dec
High	64	68	76	83	92	101	106	104	97	86	72	63
Low	37	40	45	50	59	66	72	71	64	53	42	36
Precip	0.5	0.7	0.5	0.1	0.1	0.0	0.6	0.8	0.5	0.2	0.2	0.6
Snow	0.0	tr	0.0	0.0	0.0	0.0	0.0	0.0	0.0	0.0	0.0	0.2

High and Low temperatures in degrees Fahrenheit; Precipitation and Snow in inches

Weather Station: Victorville Pump Plant Elevation: 2,857 feet

	Jan	Feb	Mar	Apr	May	Jun	Jul	Aug	Sep	Oct	Nov	Dec
High	60	63	68	75	84	93	98	98	92	81	68	59
Low	32	35	38	43	49	56	62	62	56	46	36	31
Precip	1.0	1.3	1.0	0.4	0.2	0.1	0.2	0.2	0.2	0.4	0.5	0.9
Snow	tr	tr	0.0	0.0	0.0	0.0	0.0	0.0	0.0	0.0	0.0	0.0

High and Low temperatures in degrees Fahrenheit; Precipitation and Snow in inches

Population: 2,035,210; Growth (since 2000): 19.1%; Density: 101.5 persons per square mile; Race: 56.7% White, 8.9% Black/African American, 6.3% Asian, 1.1% American Indian/Alaska Native, 0.3% Native Hawaiian/Other Pacific Islander, 5.0% two or more races, 49.2% Hispanic of any race; Average household size: 3.26; Median age: 31.7; Age under 18: 29.2%; Age 65 and over: 8.9%; Males per 100 females: 98.8; Marriage status: 36.0% never married, 49.2% now married, 2.9% separated, 4.8% widowed, 10.1% divorced; Foreign born: 21.1%; Speak English only: 58.9%; With disability: 10.9%; Veterans: 7.2%; Ancestry: 8.3% German, 5.9% Irish, 5.2% English, 3.5% American, 3.3% Italian

Religion: Six largest groups: 21.9% Catholicism, 5.2% Non-denominational Protestant, 3.4% Baptist, 2.6% Latter-day Saints, 1.6% Adventist, 1.2% Pentecostal

Economy: Unemployment rate: 7.7%; Leading industries: 14.7% retail trade; 11.8% health care and social assistance; 9.7% accommodation and food services; Farms: 1,249 totaling 77,199 acres; Company size: 27 employ 1,000 or more persons, 35 employ 500 to 999 persons, 734 employ 100 to 499 persons, 31,360 employ less than 100 persons; Business ownership: 46,480 women-owned, 11,927 Black-owned, 42,016 Hispanic-owned, 17,531 Asian-owned

Employment: 10.9% management, business, and financial, 3.1% computer, engineering, and science, 9.2% education, legal, community service, arts, and media, 5.2% healthcare practitioners, 18.8% service, 26.1% sales and office, 10.6% natural resources, construction, and maintenance, 16.0% production, transportation, and material moving

Income: Per capita: $21,332; Median household: $54,090; Average household: $69,091; Households with income of $100,000 or more: 21.8%; Poverty rate: 18.7%

Educational Attainment: High school diploma or higher: 78.2%; Bachelor's degree or higher: 18.7%; Graduate/professional degree or higher: 6.5%

Housing: Homeownership rate: 62.8%; Median home value: $222,300; Median year structure built: 1981; Homeowner vacancy rate: 3.0%; Median gross rent: $1,102 per month; Rental vacancy rate: 8.7%

Vital Statistics: Birth rate: 146.9 per 10,000 population; Death rate: 62.9 per 10,000 population; Age-adjusted cancer mortality rate: 173.0 deaths per 100,000 population

Health Insurance: 79.8% have insurance; 54.5% have private insurance; 31.7% have public insurance; 20.2% do not have insurance; 9.9% of children under 18 do not have insurance

Health Care: Physicians: 17.9 per 10,000 population; Hospital beds: 26.5 per 10,000 population; Hospital admissions: 980.9 per 10,000 population

Air Quality Index: 19.5% good, 52.1% moderate, 23.0% unhealthy for sensitive individuals, 5.2% unhealthy, 0.3% very unhealthy (% of days)

Transportation: Commute: 91.0% car, 1.8% public transportation, 1.9% walk, 3.9% work from home; Median travel time to work: 29.9 minutes

Presidential Election: 51.4% Obama, 46.4% Romney (2012)

National and State Parks: Chino Hills State Park; Heart Bar State Park; Hulaville State Historic Landmark; Mitchell Caverns State Park; Mojave National Preserve; National Childreaus Forest; Providence Mountains State Recreation Area; San Bernardino National Forest; Secombe Lake State Urban Recreation Area; Silverwood Lake State Recreation Area

Additional Information Contacts

San Bernardino Government. . . . . (909) 387-3841
http://www.sbcounty.gov

San Bernardino County Communities

ADELANTO (city). Covers a land area of 56.009 square miles and a water area of 0.018 square miles. Located at 34.59° N. Lat; 117.44° W. Long. Elevation is 2,871 feet.

History: Named for the Spanish translation of "advance" or "progress". Aelanto developed as the center of an alfalfa-growing and poultry-raising area, reclaimed by irrigation from the Mojave River.

Population: 31,765; Growth (since 2000): 75.2%; Density: 567.1 persons per square mile; Race: 43.8% White, 20.5% Black/African American, 1.9% Asian, 1.3% American Indian/Alaska Native, 0.6% Native Hawaiian/Other Pacific Islander, 5.6% Two or more races, 58.3% Hispanic of any race; Average household size: 3.84; Median age: 25.3; Age under 18: 37.2%; Age 65 and over: 4.4%; Males per 100 females: 105.6; Marriage status: 43.2% never married, 45.6% now married, 3.1% separated, 3.4% widowed, 7.7% divorced; Foreign born: 18.4%; Speak English only: 56.9%; With disability: 10.1%; Veterans: 6.2%; Ancestry: 4.9% German, 3.0% Irish, 2.9% American, 2.8% Italian, 2.5% Polish

Employment: 7.5% management, business, and financial, 1.7% computer, engineering, and science, 7.2% education, legal, community service, arts, and media, 6.8% healthcare practitioners, 16.1% service, 25.3% sales and office, 12.1% natural resources, construction, and maintenance, 23.3% production, transportation, and material moving

Income: Per capita: $11,049; Median household: $38,768; Average household: $43,971; Households with income of $100,000 or more: 6.9%; Poverty rate: 33.7%

Educational Attainment: High school diploma or higher: 69.8%; Bachelor's degree or higher: 7.4%; Graduate/professional degree or higher: 1.6%

School District(s)

Adelanto Elementary (KG-12)
2012-13 Enrollment: 9,054 . . . . (760) 246-8691
Victor Valley Union High (07-12)
2012-13 Enrollment: 14,781 . . . . (760) 955-3201

Housing: Homeownership rate: 57.8%; Median home value: $95,900; Median year structure built: 1997; Homeowner vacancy rate: 6.6%; Median gross rent: $986 per month; Rental vacancy rate: 12.3%

Health Insurance: 81.0% have insurance; 39.0% have private insurance; 46.7% have public insurance; 19.0% do not have insurance; 5.0% of children under 18 do not have insurance

Safety: Violent crime rate: 63.5 per 10,000 population; Property crime rate: 284.3 per 10,000 population

Transportation: Commute: 91.0% car, 1.5% public transportation, 0.8% walk, 4.6% work from home; Median travel time to work: 36.9 minutes

Additional Information Contacts

City of Adelanto. . . . . (760) 246-2300
http://www.ci.adelanto.ca.us

AMBOY (unincorporated postal area)

ZCTA: 92304

Covers a land area of 41.167 square miles and a water area of 0 square miles. Located at 34.54° N. Lat; 115.64° W. Long. Elevation is 630 feet.

Population: 17; Growth (since 2000): -26.1%; Density: 0.4 persons per square mile; Race: 29.4% White, 0.0% Black/African American, 0.0% Asian, 0.0% American Indian/Alaska Native, 0.0% Native Hawaiian/Other Pacific Islander, 41.2% Two or more races, 58.8% Hispanic of any race; Average household size: 1.71; Median age: 46.5; Age under 18: 0.0%; Age 65 and over: 11.8%; Males per 100 females: 325.0

Housing: Homeownership rate: 28.6%; Homeowner vacancy rate: 0.0%; Rental vacancy rate: 0.0%

ANGELUS OAKS (unincorporated postal area)

ZCTA: 92305

Covers a land area of 99.976 square miles and a water area of 0.014 square miles. Located at 34.14° N. Lat; 116.82° W. Long. Elevation is 5,758 feet.

Population: 535; Growth (since 2000): 85.1%; Density: 5.4 persons per square mile; Race: 86.0% White, 0.2% Black/African American, 0.9% Asian, 0.7% American Indian/Alaska Native, 0.2% Native Hawaiian/Other Pacific Islander, 3.4% Two or more races, 16.6% Hispanic of any race; Average household size: 2.29; Median age: 48.2; Age under 18: 17.4%; Age 65 and over: 15.0%; Males per 100 females: 97.4

Housing: Homeownership rate: 76.0%; Homeowner vacancy rate: 4.7%; Rental vacancy rate: 10.6%

APPLE VALLEY (town). Covers a land area of 73.193 square miles and a water area of 0.330 square miles. Located at 34.53° N. Lat; 117.21° W. Long. Elevation is 2,946 feet.

History: Apple Valley was incorporated on November 14, 1988 and is located near the southern edge of the Mojave Desert. Its name originates from the Appleton Land Company which was based there in the early 1900s.

Population: 69,135; Growth (since 2000): 27.5%; Density: 944.6 persons per square mile; Race: 69.1% White, 9.1% Black/African American, 2.9% Asian, 1.1% American Indian/Alaska Native, 0.4% Native Hawaiian/Other Pacific Islander, 5.2% Two or more races, 29.2% Hispanic of any race; Average household size: 2.91; Median age: 37.0; Age under 18: 27.9%; Age 65 and over: 15.4%; Males per 100 females: 96.0; Marriage status: 28.2% never married, 53.5% now married, 2.1% separated, 7.0% widowed, 11.3% divorced; Foreign born: 7.6%; Speak English only: 84.0%; With disability: 15.4%; Veterans: 12.6%; Ancestry: 13.7% German, 11.1% English, 10.4% Irish, 5.7% Italian, 4.0% American

Employment: 8.6% management, business, and financial, 2.2% computer, engineering, and science, 12.5% education, legal, community service, arts, and media, 5.4% healthcare practitioners, 21.2% service, 26.1% sales and office, 12.1% natural resources, construction, and maintenance, 11.8% production, transportation, and material moving

Income: Per capita: $22,941; Median household: $48,432; Average household: $66,743; Households with income of $100,000 or more: 22.1%; Poverty rate: 20.2%

Educational Attainment: High school diploma or higher: 85.4%; Bachelor's degree or higher: 15.8%; Graduate/professional degree or higher: 7.1%

School District(s)

Apple Valley Unified (KG-12)
2012-13 Enrollment: 14,701 . . . . (760) 247-8001
San Bernardino County Office of Education (KG-12)
2012-13 Enrollment: 3,173 . . . . (909) 888-3228

Housing: Homeownership rate: 69.1%; Median home value: $171,600; Median year structure built: 1986; Homeowner vacancy rate: 4.0%; Median gross rent: $970 per month; Rental vacancy rate: 10.0%

Health Insurance: 83.9% have insurance; 55.1% have private insurance; 39.7% have public insurance; 16.1% do not have insurance; 9.4% of children under 18 do not have insurance

Hospitals: Saint Mary Medical Center (186 beds)

Safety: Violent crime rate: 26.0 per 10,000 population; Property crime rate: 224.0 per 10,000 population

Transportation: Commute: 89.8% car, 1.7% public transportation, 0.9% walk, 5.7% work from home; Median travel time to work: 29.2 minutes

Airports: Apple Valley (general aviation)

Additional Information Contacts

Town of Apple Valley. . . . . (760) 240-7000
http://www.applevalley.org

BAKER (CDP). Covers a land area of 2.688 square miles and a water area of 0 square miles. Located at 35.28° N. Lat; 116.07° W. Long. Elevation is 935 feet.

Population: 735; Growth (since 2000): n/a; Density: 273.5 persons per square mile; Race: 41.1% White, 0.1% Black/African American, 1.4% Asian, 0.7% American Indian/Alaska Native, 1.9% Native Hawaiian/Other Pacific Islander, 3.1% Two or more races, 68.3% Hispanic of any race; Average household size: 3.40; Median age: 26.1; Age under 18: 37.7%; Age 65 and over: 2.9%; Males per 100 females: 113.7

School District(s)

Baker Valley Unified (KG-12)
2012-13 Enrollment: 187. . . . . (760) 733-4567

Housing: Homeownership rate: 53.9%; Homeowner vacancy rate: 1.7%; Rental vacancy rate: 20.8%

BARSTOW (city). Covers a land area of 41.385 square miles and a water area of 0.009 square miles. Located at 34.87° N. Lat; 117.04° W. Long. Elevation is 2,175 feet.

History: Named for William Barstow Strong, president of the Santa Fe Railroad Company. Barstow, once a desert junction for overland wagon trains and an outfitting point for Death Valley expeditions, was a center for gold and silver mining in the 1890s. Later the town became a division point and shops for the Santa Fe Railway.

Population: 22,639; Growth (since 2000): 7.2%; Density: 547.0 persons per square mile; Race: 52.3% White, 14.6% Black/African American, 3.2% Asian, 2.1% American Indian/Alaska Native, 1.2% Native Hawaiian/Other Pacific Islander, 7.8% Two or more races, 42.8% Hispanic of any race; Average household size: 2.75; Median age: 31.1; Age under 18: 29.8%; Age 65 and over: 10.7%; Males per 100 females: 99.6; Marriage status: 34.9% never married, 46.5% now married, 2.7% separated, 6.5% widowed, 12.2% divorced; Foreign born: 11.0%; Speak English only: 74.8%; With disability: 17.9%; Veterans: 15.6%; Ancestry: 6.9% German, 5.9% Irish, 5.7% American, 5.2% English, 2.6% French

Employment: 10.9% management, business, and financial, 2.8% computer, engineering, and science, 10.4% education, legal, community service, arts, and media, 1.1% healthcare practitioners, 22.5% service, 24.8% sales and office, 14.4% natural resources, construction, and maintenance, 13.0% production, transportation, and material moving

Income: Per capita: $19,873; Median household: $42,354; Average household: $53,694; Households with income of $100,000 or more: 14.1%; Poverty rate: 26.2%

Educational Attainment: High school diploma or higher: 82.4%; Bachelor's degree or higher: 10.6%; Graduate/professional degree or higher: 4.2%

School District(s)

Barstow Unified (KG-12)
2012-13 Enrollment: 5,929 . . . . (760) 255-6000

Two-year College(s)

Barstow Community College (Public)
Fall 2013 Enrollment: 3,211 . . . . (760) 252-2411
2013-14 Tuition: In-state $1,104; Out-of-state $5,400

Housing: Homeownership rate: 49.0%; Median home value: $97,400; Median year structure built: 1968; Homeowner vacancy rate: 5.0%; Median gross rent: $776 per month; Rental vacancy rate: 16.0%

Health Insurance: 85.6% have insurance; 53.9% have private insurance; 42.1% have public insurance; 14.4% do not have insurance; 8.1% of children under 18 do not have insurance

Hospitals: Barstow Community Hospital (56 beds)

Safety: Violent crime rate: 98.9 per 10,000 population; Property crime rate: 339.2 per 10,000 population

Newspapers: Desert Dispatch (daily circulation 4500)

Transportation: Commute: 87.8% car, 3.3% public transportation, 6.2% walk, 1.8% work from home; Median travel time to work: 24.3 minutes; Amtrak: Train and bus service available.

Additional Information Contacts

City of Barstow . . . . (760) 256-3531
http://www.barstowca.org

BIG BEAR CITY (CDP). Covers a land area of 31.954 square miles and a water area of 0.017 square miles. Located at 34.25° N. Lat; 116.80° W. Long. Elevation is 6,772 feet.

History: Big Bear City is located 27 miles northeast of San Bernardino and east of the city of Big Bear Lake.

Population: 12,304; Growth (since 2000): 112.9%; Density: 385.1 persons per square mile; Race: 83.3% White, 0.7% Black/African American, 0.8% Asian, 1.6% American Indian/Alaska Native, 0.3% Native Hawaiian/Other Pacific Islander, 4.4% Two or more races, 18.9% Hispanic of any race; Average household size: 2.45; Median age: 42.9; Age under 18: 23.3%; Age 65 and over: 14.4%; Males per 100 females: 102.7; Marriage status: 29.6% never married, 48.2% now married, 3.5% separated, 5.9% widowed, 16.3% divorced; Foreign born: 11.3%; Speak English only: 83.2%; With disability: 15.4%; Veterans: 11.0%; Ancestry: 19.7% German, 15.1% Irish, 12.7% English, 7.6% Italian, 4.7% Swedish

Employment: 9.8% management, business, and financial, 2.7% computer, engineering, and science, 11.4% education, legal, community service, arts, and media, 1.8% healthcare practitioners, 20.1% service, 28.7% sales and office, 14.7% natural resources, construction, and maintenance, 10.8% production, transportation, and material moving

Income: Per capita: $21,647; Median household: $42,158; Average household: $52,424; Households with income of $100,000 or more: 12.7%; Poverty rate: 20.1%

Educational Attainment: High school diploma or higher: 84.5%; Bachelor's degree or higher: 15.7%; Graduate/professional degree or higher: 4.4%

School District(s)

Bear Valley Unified (KG-12)
2012-13 Enrollment: 2,606 . . . . (909) 866-4631

Housing: Homeownership rate: 68.1%; Median home value: $191,800; Median year structure built: 1976; Homeowner vacancy rate: 9.0%; Median gross rent: $979 per month; Rental vacancy rate: 14.0%

Health Insurance: 71.3% have insurance; 50.3% have private insurance; 33.5% have public insurance; 28.7% do not have insurance; 22.2% of children under 18 do not have insurance

Transportation: Commute: 87.4% car, 0.0% public transportation, 0.5% walk, 9.6% work from home; Median travel time to work: 25.9 minutes

BIG BEAR LAKE (city). Covers a land area of 6.346 square miles and a water area of 0.188 square miles. Located at 34.24° N. Lat; 116.90° W. Long. Elevation is 6,752 feet.

History: Big Bear Lake, formerly known as Yuhaviat or "Pine Place," is located in the San Bernardino Mountains west of Big Bear City. Once inhabited by the Serrano Native Americans, explorer Benjamin Davis Wilson changed its name upon discovering a dense population of grizzly bears.

Population: 5,019; Growth (since 2000): -7.7%; Density: 790.9 persons per square mile; Race: 83.8% White, 0.4% Black/African American, 1.6% Asian, 1.0% American Indian/Alaska Native, 0.2% Native Hawaiian/Other Pacific Islander, 3.3% Two or more races, 21.4% Hispanic of any race; Average household size: 2.28; Median age: 46.1; Age under 18: 19.8%; Age 65 and over: 20.4%; Males per 100 females: 104.7; Marriage status: 18.5% never married, 54.0% now married, 3.7% separated, 6.8% widowed, 20.7% divorced; Foreign born: 14.8%; Speak English only: 78.6%; With disability: 14.9%; Veterans: 10.9%; Ancestry: 19.6% German, 13.2% English, 8.4% Irish, 6.3% Italian, 5.9% American

Employment: 12.9% management, business, and financial, 1.4% computer, engineering, and science, 15.1% education, legal, community service, arts, and media, 1.2% healthcare practitioners, 23.7% service, 23.0% sales and office, 14.7% natural resources, construction, and maintenance, 8.1% production, transportation, and material moving

Income: Per capita: $24,957; Median household: $33,036; Average household: $56,351; Households with income of $100,000 or more: 15.5%; Poverty rate: 19.4%

Educational Attainment: High school diploma or higher: 83.7%; Bachelor's degree or higher: 22.1%; Graduate/professional degree or higher: 10.8%

School District(s)

Bear Valley Unified (KG-12)
2012-13 Enrollment: 2,606 . . . . (909) 866-4631

Housing: Homeownership rate: 58.1%; Median home value: $330,800; Median year structure built: 1976; Homeowner vacancy rate: 14.0%; Median gross rent: $936 per month; Rental vacancy rate: 45.2%

Health Insurance: 68.1% have insurance; 43.0% have private insurance; 40.6% have public insurance; 31.9% do not have insurance; 29.2% of children under 18 do not have insurance

Hospitals: Bear Valley Community Hospital (30 beds)

Safety: Violent crime rate: 108.9 per 10,000 population; Property crime rate: 418.0 per 10,000 population

Newspapers: Grizzly & Life (weekly circulation 9000)

Transportation: Commute: 80.2% car, 0.1% public transportation, 8.5% walk, 8.9% work from home; Median travel time to work: 15.9 minutes

Additional Information Contacts

City of Big Bear Lake. . . . . (909) 866-5831
http://www.citybigbearlake.com

BIG RIVER (CDP). Covers a land area of 10.827 square miles and a water area of 0.523 square miles. Located at 34.14° N. Lat; 114.36° W. Long. Elevation is 440 feet.

Population: 1,327; Growth (since 2000): 4.8%; Density: 122.6 persons per square mile; Race: 85.7% White, 1.1% Black/African American, 0.2% Asian, 3.8% American Indian/Alaska Native, 0.0% Native Hawaiian/Other Pacific Islander, 5.3% Two or more races, 12.1% Hispanic of any race; Average household size: 2.07; Median age: 54.9; Age under 18: 14.5%; Age 65 and over: 35.0%; Males per 100 females: 100.8

Housing: Homeownership rate: 79.6%; Homeowner vacancy rate: 3.8%; Rental vacancy rate: 34.1%

BLOOMINGTON (CDP). Covers a land area of 5.987 square miles and a water area of 0 square miles. Located at 34.06° N. Lat; 117.40° W. Long. Elevation is 1,099 feet.

Population: 23,851; Growth (since 2000): 23.5%; Density: 3,983.8 persons per square mile; Race: 54.5% White, 2.7% Black/African American, 1.4% Asian, 1.3% American Indian/Alaska Native, 0.2% Native Hawaiian/Other Pacific Islander, 3.9% Two or more races, 81.0% Hispanic of any race; Average household size: 4.36; Median age: 27.8; Age under 18: 33.6%; Age 65 and over: 6.6%; Males per 100 females: 103.3; Marriage status: 39.0% never married, 49.5% now married, 4.6% separated, 3.4% widowed, 8.0% divorced; Foreign born: 33.4%; Speak English only: 32.9%; With disability: 10.0%; Veterans: 3.8%; Ancestry: 4.5% German, 2.2% Irish, 1.5% English, 0.9% American, 0.9% Romanian

Employment: 5.5% management, business, and financial, 0.6% computer, engineering, and science, 5.1% education, legal, community service, arts, and media, 0.5% healthcare practitioners, 18.7% service, 23.9% sales and office, 18.5% natural resources, construction, and maintenance, 27.0% production, transportation, and material moving

Income: Per capita: $13,937; Median household: $47,888; Average household: $57,075; Households with income of $100,000 or more: 11.1%; Poverty rate: 20.4%

Educational Attainment: High school diploma or higher: 60.0%; Bachelor's degree or higher: 7.4%; Graduate/professional degree or higher: 1.2%

School District(s)

Colton Joint Unified (KG-12)
2012-13 Enrollment: 23,172 . . . . (909) 580-5000

Housing: Homeownership rate: 68.9%; Median home value: $169,300; Median year structure built: 1971; Homeowner vacancy rate: 2.6%; Median gross rent: $1,149 per month; Rental vacancy rate: 5.1%

Health Insurance: 69.2% have insurance; 40.8% have private insurance; 33.5% have public insurance; 30.8% do not have insurance; 14.5% of children under 18 do not have insurance

Transportation: Commute: 90.8% car, 2.9% public transportation, 1.2% walk, 4.2% work from home; Median travel time to work: 30.7 minutes

BLUEWATER (CDP). Covers a land area of 0.892 square miles and a water area of 0.451 square miles. Located at 34.18° N. Lat; 114.27° W. Long. Elevation is 367 feet.

Population: 172; Growth (since 2000): -35.1%; Density: 192.8 persons per square mile; Race: 90.7% White, 1.2% Black/African American, 0.0% Asian, 0.6% American Indian/Alaska Native, 0.6% Native Hawaiian/Other Pacific Islander, 1.7% Two or more races, 6.4% Hispanic of any race; Average household size: 1.54; Median age: 70.4; Age under 18: 4.7%; Age 65 and over: 62.2%; Males per 100 females: 107.2

Housing: Homeownership rate: 92.9%; Homeowner vacancy rate: 9.6%; Rental vacancy rate: 42.9%

CEDAR GLEN (unincorporated postal area)

ZCTA: 92321

Covers a land area of 6.505 square miles and a water area of 0.048 square miles. Located at 34.25° N. Lat; 117.15° W. Long. Elevation is 5,403 feet.

Population: 1,522; Growth (since 2000): 246.7%; Density: 234.0 persons per square mile; Race: 85.5% White, 0.2% Black/African American, 0.9% Asian, 0.3% American Indian/Alaska Native, 0.5% Native Hawaiian/Other Pacific Islander, 4.5% Two or more races, 32.3% Hispanic of any race; Average household size: 2.72; Median age: 37.5; Age under 18: 24.6%; Age 65 and over: 12.4%; Males per 100 females: 111.7

Housing: Homeownership rate: 65.3%; Homeowner vacancy rate: 8.8%; Rental vacancy rate: 12.5%

CEDARPINES PARK (unincorporated postal area)

ZCTA: 92322

Covers a land area of 2.992 square miles and a water area of 0 square miles. Located at 34.25° N. Lat; 117.33° W. Long. Elevation is 4,734 feet.

Population: 1,257; Growth (since 2000): n/a; Density: 420.2 persons per square mile; Race: 87.4% White, 0.3% Black/African American, 1.0% Asian, 1.0% American Indian/Alaska Native, 0.2% Native Hawaiian/Other Pacific Islander, 6.6% Two or more races, 13.8% Hispanic of any race; Average household size: 2.45; Median age: 45.2; Age under 18: 22.0%; Age 65 and over: 14.3%; Males per 100 females: 102.4

Housing: Homeownership rate: 80.0%; Homeowner vacancy rate: 6.3%; Rental vacancy rate: 10.4%

CHINO (city). Covers a land area of 29.639 square miles and a water area of 0.013 square miles. Located at 33.98° N. Lat; 117.66° W. Long. Elevation is 728 feet.

History: Named for the Santa Ana del Chino land grant of 1841. Chino was founded in 1887 when Richard Gird subdivided his Rancho del Chino and laid out a townsite in the center.

Population: 77,983; Growth (since 2000): 16.1%; Density: 2,631.1 persons per square mile; Race: 56.4% White, 6.2% Black/African American, 10.5% Asian, 1.0% American Indian/Alaska Native, 0.2% Native Hawaiian/Other Pacific Islander, 4.6% Two or more races, 53.8% Hispanic of any race; Average household size: 3.41; Median age: 33.2; Age under 18: 25.3%; Age 65 and over: 7.3%; Males per 100 females: 105.7; Marriage status: 35.4% never married, 50.4% now married, 2.7% separated, 4.3% widowed, 9.8% divorced; Foreign born: 22.6%; Speak English only: 55.1%; With disability: 8.8%; Veterans: 6.0%; Ancestry: 6.4% German, 5.0% Irish, 4.3% American, 3.2% English, 3.1% Italian

Employment: 14.3% management, business, and financial, 4.3% computer, engineering, and science, 8.9% education, legal, community service, arts, and media, 4.0% healthcare practitioners, 18.1% service, 26.1% sales and office, 9.3% natural resources, construction, and maintenance, 15.1% production, transportation, and material moving

Income: Per capita: $23,866; Median household: $71,466; Average household: $85,324; Households with income of $100,000 or more: 31.2%; Poverty rate: 10.0%

Educational Attainment: High school diploma or higher: 78.9%; Bachelor's degree or higher: 21.9%; Graduate/professional degree or higher: 5.6%

School District(s)

Chino Valley Unified (KG-12)
2012-13 Enrollment: 30,705 . . . . (909) 628-1201

Housing: Homeownership rate: 68.9%; Median home value: $330,900; Median year structure built: 1981; Homeowner vacancy rate: 2.1%; Median gross rent: $1,310 per month; Rental vacancy rate: 6.4%

Health Insurance: 82.5% have insurance; 66.3% have private insurance; 21.2% have public insurance; 17.5% do not have insurance; 8.7% of children under 18 do not have insurance

Hospitals: Chino Valley Medical Center (126 beds)

Safety: Violent crime rate: 32.0 per 10,000 population; Property crime rate: 253.3 per 10,000 population

Newspapers: Champion Newspapers (weekly circulation 42000)

Transportation: Commute: 92.8% car, 1.7% public transportation, 1.4% walk, 2.9% work from home; Median travel time to work: 33.7 minutes

Airports: Chino (general aviation)

Additional Information Contacts

City of Chino . . . . (909) 334-3250
http://www.cityofchino.org

CHINO HILLS (city). Covers a land area of 44.681 square miles and a water area of 0.068 square miles. Located at 33.94° N. Lat; 117.73° W. Long. Elevation is 860 feet.

History: This city was established by Richard Gird and incorporated in 1991. It's located in southern California, about 46 miles from Los Angeles.

Population: 74,799; Growth (since 2000): 12.0%; Density: 1,674.1 persons per square mile; Race: 50.8% White, 4.6% Black/African American, 30.3% Asian, 0.5% American Indian/Alaska Native, 0.2% Native Hawaiian/Other Pacific Islander, 4.9% Two or more races, 29.1% Hispanic of any race; Average household size: 3.25; Median age: 36.6; Age under 18: 27.1%; Age 65 and over: 7.0%; Males per 100 females: 97.7; Marriage status: 31.4% never married, 57.9% now married, 1.7% separated, 3.9% widowed, 6.9% divorced; Foreign born: 28.4%; Speak English only: 56.6%; With disability: 6.5%; Veterans: 4.9%; Ancestry: 7.8% German, 5.7% English, 4.7% Irish, 4.5% Italian, 3.1% American

Employment: 19.5% management, business, and financial, 7.6% computer, engineering, and science, 10.5% education, legal, community service, arts, and media, 8.5% healthcare practitioners, 12.8% service, 28.3% sales and office, 6.0% natural resources, construction, and maintenance, 6.9% production, transportation, and material moving

Income: Per capita: $34,955; Median household: $96,497; Average household: $112,878; Households with income of $100,000 or more: 48.1%; Poverty rate: 6.1%

Educational Attainment: High school diploma or higher: 92.0%; Bachelor's degree or higher: 43.3%; Graduate/professional degree or higher: 14.4%

School District(s)

Chino Valley Unified (KG-12)
2012-13 Enrollment: 30,705 . . . . (909) 628-1201

Housing: Homeownership rate: 80.3%; Median home value: $476,200; Median year structure built: 1989; Homeowner vacancy rate: 1.0%; Median gross rent: $1,783 per month; Rental vacancy rate: 5.4%

Health Insurance: 86.6% have insurance; 77.1% have private insurance; 14.2% have public insurance; 13.4% do not have insurance; 6.2% of children under 18 do not have insurance

Safety: Violent crime rate: 8.2 per 10,000 population; Property crime rate: 132.2 per 10,000 population

Transportation: Commute: 92.2% car, 1.4% public transportation, 0.7% walk, 4.5% work from home; Median travel time to work: 37.1 minutes

Additional Information Contacts

City of Chino Hills . . . . (909) 364-2600
http://www.chinohills.org

COLTON (city). Covers a land area of 15.324 square miles and a water area of 0.715 square miles. Located at 34.05° N. Lat; 117.33° W. Long. Elevation is 1,004 feet.

History: Named for David D. Colton, financial director of the Central Pacific Railroad. Colton began near the site of Rancho Jumuba, a Mission San Gabriel stock ranch established in the early 1800s. Fort Benson was erected here in the late 1850s by Jerome Benson, and trains of pack mules and horses stopped on their journey from Santa Fe. In 1875 Colton was a Southern Pacific Railroad terminus.

Population: 52,154; Growth (since 2000): 9.4%; Density: 3,403.4 persons per square mile; Race: 43.4% White, 9.7% Black/African American, 5.0% Asian, 1.3% American Indian/Alaska Native, 0.3% Native Hawaiian/Other Pacific Islander, 5.1% Two or more races, 71.0% Hispanic of any race; Average household size: 3.46; Median age: 28.4; Age under 18: 32.0%; Age 65 and over: 7.0%; Males per 100 females: 96.0; Marriage status: 43.1% never married, 45.5% now married, 3.7% separated, 3.7% widowed, 7.7% divorced; Foreign born: 25.6%; Speak English only: 48.0%; With disability: 8.9%; Veterans: 4.9%; Ancestry: 2.9% German, 2.3% English, 2.3% Irish, 2.1% Italian, 1.5% American

Employment: 7.0% management, business, and financial, 2.1% computer, engineering, and science, 6.1% education, legal, community service, arts, and media, 5.1% healthcare practitioners, 19.8% service, 26.3% sales and office, 11.6% natural resources, construction, and maintenance, 22.0% production, transportation, and material moving

Income: Per capita: $15,540; Median household: $39,604; Average household: $52,012; Households with income of $100,000 or more: 12.2%; Poverty rate: 24.5%

Educational Attainment: High school diploma or higher: 68.8%; Bachelor's degree or higher: 11.4%; Graduate/professional degree or higher: 4.5%

School District(s)

Colton Joint Unified (KG-12)
2012-13 Enrollment: 23,172 . . . . (909) 580-5000
Rialto Unified (KG-12)
2012-13 Enrollment: 26,596 . . . . (909) 820-7700
San Bernardino County Office of Education (KG-12)
2012-13 Enrollment: 3,173 . . . . (909) 888-3228

Two-year College(s)

Coast Career Institute (Private, For-profit)
Fall 2013 Enrollment: 92 . . . . (213) 747-6289
Four-D College (Private, For-profit)
Fall 2013 Enrollment: 641 . . . . (909) 783-9331

Vocational/Technical School(s)

Summit College (Private, For-profit)
Fall 2013 Enrollment: 947 . . . . (909) 422-8950
2013-14 Tuition: $29,400

Housing: Homeownership rate: 51.8%; Median home value: $158,700; Median year structure built: 1981; Homeowner vacancy rate: 2.6%; Median gross rent: $977 per month; Rental vacancy rate: 9.2%

Health Insurance: 73.5% have insurance; 42.1% have private insurance; 36.2% have public insurance; 26.5% do not have insurance; 14.7% of children under 18 do not have insurance

Hospitals: Arrowhead Regional Medical Center (373 beds)

Safety: Violent crime rate: 30.1 per 10,000 population; Property crime rate: 362.5 per 10,000 population

Newspapers: Inland Empire Newspapers (weekly circulation 20000)

Transportation: Commute: 93.4% car, 2.4% public transportation, 0.6% walk, 2.0% work from home; Median travel time to work: 27.3 minutes

Additional Information Contacts

City of Colton . . . . (909) 370-5099
http://www.ci.colton.ca.us

CRESTLINE (CDP). Covers a land area of 13.839 square miles and a water area of 0.140 square miles. Located at 34.25° N. Lat; 117.29° W. Long. Elevation is 4,613 feet.

Population: 10,770; Growth (since 2000): 5.4%; Density: 778.2 persons per square mile; Race: 86.2% White, 1.0% Black/African American, 0.9% Asian, 1.3% American Indian/Alaska Native, 0.2% Native Hawaiian/Other Pacific Islander, 5.5% Two or more races, 16.5% Hispanic of any race; Average household size: 2.46; Median age: 43.3; Age under 18: 22.1%; Age 65 and over: 12.1%; Males per 100 females: 103.2; Marriage status: 25.3% never married, 54.9% now married, 1.6% separated, 4.9% widowed, 15.0% divorced; Foreign born: 5.2%; Speak English only: 92.5%; With disability: 13.2%; Veterans: 11.5%; Ancestry: 25.3% German, 15.4% Irish, 13.6% English, 5.6% Italian, 5.1% Dutch

Employment: 18.0% management, business, and financial, 4.5% computer, engineering, and science, 9.5% education, legal, community service, arts, and media, 4.5% healthcare practitioners, 16.1% service, 24.9% sales and office, 13.0% natural resources, construction, and maintenance, 9.5% production, transportation, and material moving

Income: Per capita: $24,969; Median household: $48,050; Average household: $60,166; Households with income of $100,000 or more: 15.9%; Poverty rate: 19.1%

Educational Attainment: High school diploma or higher: 91.4%; Bachelor's degree or higher: 20.9%; Graduate/professional degree or higher: 9.1%

School District(s)

Rim of the World Unified (KG-12)
2012-13 Enrollment: 4,013 . . . . (909) 336-2031

Housing: Homeownership rate: 71.6%; Median home value: $194,600; Median year structure built: 1963; Homeowner vacancy rate: 6.7%; Median gross rent: $1,069 per month; Rental vacancy rate: 13.8%

Health Insurance: 85.2% have insurance; 59.4% have private insurance; 39.4% have public insurance; 14.8% do not have insurance; 9.8% of children under 18 do not have insurance

Newspapers: The Alpenhorn News (weekly circulation 2800)

Transportation: Commute: 85.3% car, 1.3% public transportation, 3.8% walk, 6.4% work from home; Median travel time to work: 34.4 minutes

DAGGETT (unincorporated postal area)

ZCTA: 92327

Covers a land area of 28.224 square miles and a water area of 0.241 square miles. Located at 34.86° N. Lat; 116.86° W. Long. Elevation is 2,014 feet.

Population: 632; Growth (since 2000): -4.0%; Density: 22.4 persons per square mile; Race: 75.2% White, 1.3% Black/African American, 0.5% Asian, 8.7% American Indian/Alaska Native, 0.6% Native Hawaiian/Other Pacific Islander, 3.6% Two or more races, 21.4% Hispanic of any race; Average household size: 2.32; Median age: 44.9; Age under 18: 21.2%; Age 65 and over: 15.3%; Males per 100 females: 113.5

School District(s)

Silver Valley Unified (PK-12)
2012-13 Enrollment: 2,395 . . . . (760) 254-2916

Housing: Homeownership rate: 51.7%; Homeowner vacancy rate: 2.7%; Rental vacancy rate: 28.9%

Airports: Barstow-Daggett (general aviation)

EARP (unincorporated postal area)

ZCTA: 92242

Covers a land area of 31.305 square miles and a water area of 1.151 square miles. Located at 34.16° N. Lat; 114.32° W. Long. Elevation is 397 feet.

Population: 1,539; Growth (since 2000): -0.4%; Density: 49.2 persons per square mile; Race: 86.1% White, 1.2% Black/African American, 0.1% Asian, 3.4% American Indian/Alaska Native, 0.1% Native Hawaiian/Other Pacific Islander, 5.0% Two or more races, 11.9% Hispanic of any race; Average household size: 2.00; Median age: 57.3; Age under 18: 13.5%; Age 65 and over: 37.6%; Males per 100 females: 102.5

Housing: Homeownership rate: 82.0%; Homeowner vacancy rate: 4.6%; Rental vacancy rate: 34.7%

ESSEX (unincorporated postal area)

ZCTA: 92332

Covers a land area of 894.748 square miles and a water area of 0 square miles. Located at 34.91° N. Lat; 115.34° W. Long. Elevation is 1,732 feet.

Population: 65; Growth (since 2000): -41.4%; Density: 0.1 persons per square mile; Race: 64.6% White, 3.1% Black/African American, 0.0% Asian, 12.3% American Indian/Alaska Native, 0.0% Native Hawaiian/Other Pacific Islander, 3.1% Two or more races, 29.2% Hispanic of any race; Average household size: 1.81; Median age: 51.5; Age under 18: 18.5%; Age 65 and over: 13.8%; Males per 100 females: 261.1

Housing: Homeownership rate: 52.7%; Homeowner vacancy rate: 0.0%; Rental vacancy rate: 0.0%

FAWNSKIN (unincorporated postal area)

ZCTA: 92333

Covers a land area of 4.173 square miles and a water area of 0 square miles. Located at 34.27° N. Lat; 116.95° W. Long. Elevation is 6,827 feet.

Population: 472; Growth (since 2000): 15.4%; Density: 113.1 persons per square mile; Race: 95.8% White, 0.0% Black/African American, 1.1% Asian, 0.0% American Indian/Alaska Native, 0.6% Native Hawaiian/Other Pacific Islander, 1.9% Two or more races, 7.2% Hispanic of any race; Average household size: 2.01; Median age: 54.6; Age under 18: 13.1%; Age 65 and over: 27.3%; Males per 100 females: 99.2

Housing: Homeownership rate: 71.9%; Homeowner vacancy rate: 9.0%; Rental vacancy rate: 24.1%

FONTANA (city). Covers a land area of 42.432 square miles and a water area of 0 square miles. Located at 34.11° N. Lat; 117.46° W. Long. Elevation is 1,237 feet.

History: Named for the Fontana Development Company, which was probably named for the Spanish translation of "fountain". Mormons farmed on the site in the 1850s; in the early 20th century extensive citrus orchards were planted. During World War II the Kaiser (steel) mill was built (closed 1982 and mainsection shipped to China, 1994) and Fontana began its transformation from an Agriculture to an industrial community. Incorporated 1952.

Population: 196,069; Growth (since 2000): 52.1%; Density: 4,620.8 persons per square mile; Race: 47.4% White, 10.0% Black/African American, 6.6% Asian, 1.0% American Indian/Alaska Native, 0.3% Native Hawaiian/Other Pacific Islander, 4.9% Two or more races, 66.8% Hispanic of any race; Average household size: 3.98; Median age: 28.7; Age under 18: 32.9%; Age 65 and over: 5.7%; Males per 100 females: 98.7; Marriage status: 37.9% never married, 51.3% now married, 2.5% separated, 3.5% widowed, 7.4% divorced; Foreign born: 30.3%; Speak English only: 41.6%; With disability: 9.1%; Veterans: 4.5%; Ancestry: 3.6% German, 3.2% Irish, 2.4% American, 2.4% Italian, 2.0% English

Employment: 10.4% management, business, and financial, 2.6% computer, engineering, and science, 7.0% education, legal, community

service, arts, and media, 4.1% healthcare practitioners, 17.0% service, 26.8% sales and office, 10.8% natural resources, construction, and maintenance, 21.4% production, transportation, and material moving
Income: Per capita: $19,299; Median household: $64,354; Average household: $75,136; Households with income of $100,000 or more: 25.1%; Poverty rate: 15.5%
Educational Attainment: High school diploma or higher: 71.8%; Bachelor's degree or higher: 15.8%; Graduate/professional degree or higher: 4.3%

School District(s)

Colton Joint Unified (KG-12)
2012-13 Enrollment: 23,172 . . . . (909) 580-5000
Etiwanda Elementary (KG-08)
2012-13 Enrollment: 13,163 . . . . (909) 899-2451
Fontana Unified (KG-12)
2012-13 Enrollment: 40,374 . . . . (909) 357-5600
Rialto Unified (KG-12)
2012-13 Enrollment: 26,596 . . . . (909) 820-7700

Vocational/Technical School(s)

Salon Success Academy-Fontana (Private, For-profit)
Fall 2013 Enrollment: 54 . . . . (909) 982-4200
2013-14 Tuition: $18,400
Westech College (Private, For-profit)
Fall 2013 Enrollment: 484 . . . . (909) 980-4474
2013-14 Tuition: $14,293

Housing: Homeownership rate: 68.9%; Median home value: $243,900; Median year structure built: 1987; Homeowner vacancy rate: 2.6%; Median gross rent: $1,112 per month; Rental vacancy rate: 6.0%
Health Insurance: 75.1% have insurance; 51.7% have private insurance; 27.8% have public insurance; 24.9% do not have insurance; 12.4% of children under 18 do not have insurance
Hospitals: Kaiser Foundation Hospital - Fontana (444 beds)
Safety: Violent crime rate: 35.6 per 10,000 population; Property crime rate: 201.0 per 10,000 population
Newspapers: Herald News (weekly circulation 11500)
Transportation: Commute: 93.2% car, 2.1% public transportation, 0.8% walk, 3.2% work from home; Median travel time to work: 32.1 minutes
Additional Information Contacts
City of Fontana . . . . (909) 350-7600
http://www.fontana.org

FOREST FALLS (unincorporated postal area)

ZCTA: 92339

Covers a land area of 10.571 square miles and a water area of 0 square miles. Located at 34.09° N. Lat; 116.94° W. Long. Elevation is 5,341 feet.
Population: 885; Growth (since 2000): -6.2%; Density: 83.7 persons per square mile; Race: 87.5% White, 0.6% Black/African American, 1.4% Asian, 0.9% American Indian/Alaska Native, 0.0% Native Hawaiian/Other Pacific Islander, 6.8% Two or more races, 12.1% Hispanic of any race; Average household size: 2.28; Median age: 45.0; Age under 18: 19.2%; Age 65 and over: 9.4%; Males per 100 females: 101.1

School District(s)

Bear Valley Unified (KG-12)
2012-13 Enrollment: 2,606 . . . . (909) 866-4631

Housing: Homeownership rate: 71.7%; Homeowner vacancy rate: 4.7%; Rental vacancy rate: 12.7%

FORT IRWIN (CDP).

Covers a land area of 7.053 square miles and a water area of 0 square miles. Located at 35.25° N. Lat; 116.68° W. Long. Elevation is 2,487 feet.
Population: 8,845; Growth (since 2000): n/a; Density: 1,254.1 persons per square mile; Race: 62.0% White, 12.3% Black/African American, 4.5% Asian, 1.2% American Indian/Alaska Native, 1.4% Native Hawaiian/Other Pacific Islander, 8.3% Two or more races, 25.6% Hispanic of any race; Average household size: 3.17; Median age: 23.9; Age under 18: 33.8%; Age 65 and over: 0.2%; Males per 100 females: 132.1; Marriage status: 30.1% never married, 67.8% now married, 0.2% separated, 0.2% widowed, 1.9% divorced; Foreign born: 11.0%; Speak English only: 77.0%; With disability: 4.2%; Veterans: 28.5%; Ancestry: 15.1% German, 8.5% Irish, 5.5% Italian, 3.9% European, 3.5% English
Employment: 6.0% management, business, and financial, 3.2% computer, engineering, and science, 10.5% education, legal, community service, arts, and media, 6.0% healthcare practitioners, 21.0% service, 33.5% sales and office, 6.4% natural resources, construction, and maintenance, 13.4% production, transportation, and material moving
Income: Per capita: $19,066; Median household: $49,778; Average household: $59,067; Households with income of $100,000 or more: 10.8%; Poverty rate: 9.4%
Educational Attainment: High school diploma or higher: 99.0%; Bachelor's degree or higher: 26.0%; Graduate/professional degree or higher: 7.9%

School District(s)

Silver Valley Unified (PK-12)
2012-13 Enrollment: 2,395 . . . . (760) 254-2916

Housing: Homeownership rate: 0.8%; Median home value: n/a; Median year structure built: 2001; Homeowner vacancy rate: 0.0%; Median gross rent: $1,195 per month; Rental vacancy rate: 4.3%
Health Insurance: 99.3% have insurance; 98.8% have private insurance; 2.5% have public insurance; 0.7% do not have insurance; 0.0% of children under 18 do not have insurance
Transportation: Commute: 73.0% car, 0.0% public transportation, 18.7% walk, 5.8% work from home; Median travel time to work: 5.9 minutes

GRAND TERRACE (city).

Covers a land area of 3.502 square miles and a water area of 0 square miles. Located at 34.03° N. Lat; 117.31° W. Long. Elevation is 1,063 feet.
Population: 12,040; Growth (since 2000): 3.6%; Density: 3,438.0 persons per square mile; Race: 65.7% White, 5.6% Black/African American, 6.5% Asian, 1.0% American Indian/Alaska Native, 0.3% Native Hawaiian/Other Pacific Islander, 5.2% Two or more races, 39.1% Hispanic of any race; Average household size: 2.71; Median age: 36.1; Age under 18: 23.1%; Age 65 and over: 12.5%; Males per 100 females: 92.9; Marriage status: 34.7% never married, 49.1% now married, 2.5% separated, 5.8% widowed, 10.4% divorced; Foreign born: 15.2%; Speak English only: 74.3%; With disability: 10.2%; Veterans: 9.0%; Ancestry: 8.2% German, 6.5% Irish, 6.5% English, 4.7% Italian, 4.0% American
Employment: 11.3% management, business, and financial, 4.9% computer, engineering, and science, 12.1% education, legal, community service, arts, and media, 8.6% healthcare practitioners, 13.3% service, 29.3% sales and office, 9.2% natural resources, construction, and maintenance, 11.4% production, transportation, and material moving
Income: Per capita: $30,446; Median household: $64,129; Average household: $81,204; Households with income of $100,000 or more: 28.8%; Poverty rate: 8.8%
Educational Attainment: High school diploma or higher: 87.8%; Bachelor's degree or higher: 24.4%; Graduate/professional degree or higher: 10.0%

School District(s)

Colton Joint Unified (KG-12)
2012-13 Enrollment: 23,172 . . . . (909) 580-5000

Housing: Homeownership rate: 63.4%; Median home value: $232,300; Median year structure built: 1978; Homeowner vacancy rate: 1.7%; Median gross rent: $1,177 per month; Rental vacancy rate: 7.0%
Health Insurance: 86.7% have insurance; 73.4% have private insurance; 20.5% have public insurance; 13.3% do not have insurance; 6.1% of children under 18 do not have insurance
Safety: Violent crime rate: 30.7 per 10,000 population; Property crime rate: 225.7 per 10,000 population
Transportation: Commute: 95.4% car, 0.8% public transportation, 0.0% walk, 2.6% work from home; Median travel time to work: 24.3 minutes
Additional Information Contacts
City of Grand Terrace . . . . (909) 824-6621
http://www.cityofgrandterrace.org/index.aspx

GREEN VALLEY LAKE (unincorporated postal area)

ZCTA: 92341

Covers a land area of 7.067 square miles and a water area of 0.016 square miles. Located at 34.24° N. Lat; 117.06° W. Long. Elevation is 6,939 feet.
Population: 410; Growth (since 2000): 34.4%; Density: 58.0 persons per square mile; Race: 93.4% White, 0.0% Black/African American, 1.0% Asian, 0.5% American Indian/Alaska Native, 0.0% Native Hawaiian/Other Pacific Islander, 2.9% Two or more races, 12.2% Hispanic of any race; Average household size: 2.32; Median age: 48.9; Age under 18: 16.6%; Age 65 and over: 15.6%; Males per 100 females: 121.6
Housing: Homeownership rate: 74.0%; Homeowner vacancy rate: 25.6%; Rental vacancy rate: 55.2%

HELENDALE (unincorporated postal area)

ZCTA: 92342

Covers a land area of 105.472 square miles and a water area of 0.740 square miles. Located at 34.76° N. Lat; 117.35° W. Long. Elevation is 2,434 feet.

Population: 6,379; Growth (since 2000): 29.2%; Density: 60.5 persons per square mile; Race: 79.6% White, 5.4% Black/African American, 3.3% Asian, 0.8% American Indian/Alaska Native, 0.3% Native Hawaiian/Other Pacific Islander, 4.0% Two or more races, 19.4% Hispanic of any race; Average household size: 2.53; Median age: 45.7; Age under 18: 22.3%; Age 65 and over: 21.6%; Males per 100 females: 100.0; Marriage status: 22.0% never married, 66.3% now married, 1.4% separated, 3.5% widowed, 8.1% divorced; Foreign born: 7.0%; Speak English only: 84.5%; With disability: 10.9%; Veterans: 17.4%; Ancestry: 14.7% German, 11.9% Italian, 9.9% English, 9.5% Irish, 7.7% American

Employment: 12.2% management, business, and financial, 2.4% computer, engineering, and science, 17.2% education, legal, community service, arts, and media, 4.8% healthcare practitioners, 15.2% service, 26.3% sales and office, 14.5% natural resources, construction, and maintenance, 7.3% production, transportation, and material moving

Income: Per capita: $25,062; Median household: $65,794; Average household: $71,917; Households with income of $100,000 or more: 24.1%; Poverty rate: 18.2%

Educational Attainment: High school diploma or higher: 87.6%; Bachelor's degree or higher: 23.7%; Graduate/professional degree or higher: 8.2%

School District(s)

Helendale Elementary (KG-12)
2012-13 Enrollment: 736. . . . . (760) 952-1180

Housing: Homeownership rate: 74.1%; Median home value: $201,400; Median year structure built: 1989; Homeowner vacancy rate: 7.5%; Median gross rent: $1,373 per month; Rental vacancy rate: 11.4%

Health Insurance: 89.0% have insurance; 64.8% have private insurance; 34.9% have public insurance; 11.0% do not have insurance; 2.2% of children under 18 do not have insurance

Transportation: Commute: 95.7% car, 0.0% public transportation, 2.2% walk, 2.1% work from home; Median travel time to work: 29.0 minutes

HESPERIA (city). Covers a land area of 73.096 square miles and a water area of 0.113 square miles. Located at 34.40° N. Lat; 117.32° W. Long. Elevation is 3,186 feet.

Population: 90,173; Growth (since 2000): 44.1%; Density: 1,233.6 persons per square mile; Race: 61.1% White, 5.8% Black/African American, 2.1% Asian, 1.2% American Indian/Alaska Native, 0.3% Native Hawaiian/Other Pacific Islander, 4.9% Two or more races, 48.9% Hispanic of any race; Average household size: 3.41; Median age: 30.5; Age under 18: 32.3%; Age 65 and over: 9.0%; Males per 100 females: 98.5; Marriage status: 34.8% never married, 49.5% now married, 2.1% separated, 5.1% widowed, 10.6% divorced; Foreign born: 13.6%; Speak English only: 67.7%; With disability: 12.9%; Veterans: 7.7%; Ancestry: 9.7% German, 7.7% Irish, 6.6% English, 3.5% Italian, 3.1% American

Employment: 7.8% management, business, and financial, 2.1% computer, engineering, and science, 8.4% education, legal, community service, arts, and media, 4.5% healthcare practitioners, 19.5% service, 24.5% sales and office, 14.2% natural resources, construction, and maintenance, 19.1% production, transportation, and material moving

Income: Per capita: $16,239; Median household: $44,158; Average household: $54,543; Households with income of $100,000 or more: 13.7%; Poverty rate: 25.3%

Educational Attainment: High school diploma or higher: 75.9%; Bachelor's degree or higher: 9.4%; Graduate/professional degree or higher: 3.1%

School District(s)

Adelanto Elementary (KG-12)
2012-13 Enrollment: 9,054 . . . . (760) 246-8691

Hesperia Unified (KG-12)
2012-13 Enrollment: 23,448 . . . . (760) 244-4411

Two-year College(s)

San Joaquin Valley College-Hesperia (Private, For-profit)
Fall 2013 Enrollment: 578 . . . . (760) 948-1947
2013-14 Tuition: In-state $16,658; Out-of-state $16,658

Housing: Homeownership rate: 66.9%; Median home value: $146,200; Median year structure built: 1985; Homeowner vacancy rate: 3.6%; Median gross rent: $1,052 per month; Rental vacancy rate: 8.4%

Health Insurance: 78.9% have insurance; 47.6% have private insurance; 38.0% have public insurance; 21.1% do not have insurance; 11.0% of children under 18 do not have insurance

Safety: Violent crime rate: 40.1 per 10,000 population; Property crime rate: 251.6 per 10,000 population

Newspapers: Hesperia Star (weekly circulation 19000); Valley Wide Newspapers (weekly circulation 20000)

Transportation: Commute: 90.4% car, 1.2% public transportation, 1.3% walk, 5.4% work from home; Median travel time to work: 37.1 minutes

Additional Information Contacts

City of Hesperia. . . . . (760) 947-1025
http://www.cityofhesperia.us

HIGHLAND (city). Covers a land area of 18.755 square miles and a water area of 0.135 square miles. Located at 34.11° N. Lat; 117.16° W. Long. Elevation is 1,309 feet.

History: Named for a Santa Fe Railroad station which was actually in a lowland area. Developed along with the Southern California area in the growth of agribusiness and aircraft industries.

Population: 53,104; Growth (since 2000): 19.1%; Density: 2,831.5 persons per square mile; Race: 52.4% White, 11.1% Black/African American, 7.4% Asian, 1.0% American Indian/Alaska Native, 0.3% Native Hawaiian/Other Pacific Islander, 5.4% Two or more races, 48.1% Hispanic of any race; Average household size: 3.42; Median age: 30.6; Age under 18: 31.9%; Age 65 and over: 7.7%; Males per 100 females: 95.1; Marriage status: 36.8% never married, 50.6% now married, 2.8% separated, 3.8% widowed, 8.8% divorced; Foreign born: 20.6%; Speak English only: 57.5%; With disability: 10.1%; Veterans: 6.5%; Ancestry: 8.4% German, 6.0% Irish, 4.2% English, 2.4% American, 2.3% Italian

Employment: 8.6% management, business, and financial, 3.2% computer, engineering, and science, 10.6% education, legal, community service, arts, and media, 6.3% healthcare practitioners, 22.7% service, 24.5% sales and office, 8.8% natural resources, construction, and maintenance, 15.3% production, transportation, and material moving

Income: Per capita: $21,188; Median household: $54,433; Average household: $73,468; Households with income of $100,000 or more: 25.7%; Poverty rate: 21.2%

Educational Attainment: High school diploma or higher: 73.5%; Bachelor's degree or higher: 19.8%; Graduate/professional degree or higher: 8.2%

School District(s)

Redlands Unified (KG-12)
2012-13 Enrollment: 21,379 . . . . (909) 307-5300

San Bernardino City Unified (KG-12)
2012-13 Enrollment: 54,102 . . . . (909) 381-1100

Housing: Homeownership rate: 65.3%; Median home value: $250,700; Median year structure built: 1982; Homeowner vacancy rate: 2.2%; Median gross rent: $977 per month; Rental vacancy rate: 8.7%

Health Insurance: 81.9% have insurance; 51.9% have private insurance; 36.4% have public insurance; 18.1% do not have insurance; 8.9% of children under 18 do not have insurance

Safety: Violent crime rate: 35.1 per 10,000 population; Property crime rate: 250.1 per 10,000 population

Newspapers: Highland Community News (weekly circulation 14600)

Transportation: Commute: 91.9% car, 1.4% public transportation, 0.9% walk, 4.6% work from home; Median travel time to work: 24.5 minutes

Additional Information Contacts

City of Highland. . . . . (909) 864-6861
http://www.ci.highland.ca.us

HINKLEY (unincorporated postal area)

ZCTA: 92347

Covers a land area of 146.597 square miles and a water area of 0.366 square miles. Located at 34.96° N. Lat; 117.22° W. Long. Elevation is 2,165 feet.

Population: 1,692; Growth (since 2000): -11.6%; Density: 11.5 persons per square mile; Race: 68.4% White, 2.9% Black/African American, 0.9% Asian, 1.4% American Indian/Alaska Native, 0.1% Native Hawaiian/Other Pacific Islander, 3.8% Two or more races, 40.1% Hispanic of any race; Average household size: 2.88; Median age: 38.9; Age under 18: 28.0%; Age 65 and over: 14.1%; Males per 100 females: 102.6

School District(s)

Barstow Unified (KG-12)
2012-13 Enrollment: 5,929 . . . . (760) 255-6000

Housing: Homeownership rate: 66.2%; Homeowner vacancy rate: 3.3%; Rental vacancy rate: 11.9%

HOMESTEAD VALLEY (CDP). Covers a land area of 33.881 square miles and a water area of 0 square miles. Located at 34.27° N. Lat; 116.41° W. Long.

Population: 3,032; Growth (since 2000): n/a; Density: 89.5 persons per square mile; Race: 85.6% White, 1.1% Black/African American, 1.0% Asian, 1.9% American Indian/Alaska Native, 0.3% Native Hawaiian/Other Pacific Islander, 3.7% Two or more races, 17.1% Hispanic of any race; Average household size: 2.18; Median age: 50.3; Age under 18: 17.3%; Age 65 and over: 21.2%; Males per 100 females: 109.1; Marriage status: 22.4% never married, 42.7% now married, 2.3% separated, 12.6% widowed, 22.4% divorced; Foreign born: 9.3%; Speak English only: 90.1%; With disability: 20.1%; Veterans: 18.1%; Ancestry: 24.7% German, 15.7% English, 9.4% Irish, 7.7% European, 5.5% American

Employment: 5.3% management, business, and financial, 3.0% computer, engineering, and science, 12.5% education, legal, community service, arts, and media, 8.5% healthcare practitioners, 17.6% service, 14.9% sales and office, 21.0% natural resources, construction, and maintenance, 17.1% production, transportation, and material moving

Income: Per capita: $17,201; Median household: $29,940; Average household: $37,368; Households with income of $100,000 or more: 4.9%; Poverty rate: 27.1%

Educational Attainment: High school diploma or higher: 79.6%; Bachelor's degree or higher: 7.9%; Graduate/professional degree or higher: 1.8%

Housing: Homeownership rate: 74.6%; Median home value: $64,500; Median year structure built: 1963; Homeowner vacancy rate: 5.6%; Median gross rent: $1,049 per month; Rental vacancy rate: 5.1%

Health Insurance: 78.7% have insurance; 35.9% have private insurance; 54.0% have public insurance; 21.3% do not have insurance; 0.0% of children under 18 do not have insurance

Transportation: Commute: 84.8% car, 0.0% public transportation, 0.0% walk, 13.1% work from home; Median travel time to work: 33.1 minutes

JOSHUA TREE (CDP). Covers a land area of 37.044 square miles and a water area of 0 square miles. Located at 34.12° N. Lat; 116.31° W. Long. Elevation is 2,736 feet.

History: Main entrance to East Joshua Tree National Monument to Southeast.

Population: 7,414; Growth (since 2000): 76.2%; Density: 200.1 persons per square mile; Race: 83.3% White, 3.2% Black/African American, 1.4% Asian, 1.1% American Indian/Alaska Native, 0.2% Native Hawaiian/Other Pacific Islander, 5.8% Two or more races, 17.6% Hispanic of any race; Average household size: 2.35; Median age: 38.8; Age under 18: 21.9%; Age 65 and over: 15.7%; Males per 100 females: 96.9; Marriage status: 30.9% never married, 43.4% now married, 3.9% separated, 6.3% widowed, 19.4% divorced; Foreign born: 4.1%; Speak English only: 88.2%; With disability: 20.8%; Veterans: 17.8%; Ancestry: 15.5% German, 10.5% English, 10.5% Irish, 8.1% European, 7.6% Italian

Employment: 5.5% management, business, and financial, 6.2% computer, engineering, and science, 17.0% education, legal, community service, arts, and media, 7.3% healthcare practitioners, 20.5% service, 23.3% sales and office, 12.4% natural resources, construction, and maintenance, 7.7% production, transportation, and material moving

Income: Per capita: $23,106; Median household: $40,326; Average household: $54,165; Households with income of $100,000 or more: 14.5%; Poverty rate: 20.7%

Educational Attainment: High school diploma or higher: 86.9%; Bachelor's degree or higher: 23.2%; Graduate/professional degree or higher: 8.5%

School District(s)

Morongo Unified (KG-12)
2012-13 Enrollment: 8,905 . . . . (760) 367-9191

Two-year College(s)

Copper Mountain Community College (Public)
Fall 2013 Enrollment: 1,783 . . . . (760) 366-3791
2013-14 Tuition: In-state $1,105; Out-of-state $5,689

Housing: Homeownership rate: 60.6%; Median home value: $118,600; Median year structure built: 1976; Homeowner vacancy rate: 3.9%; Median gross rent: $822 per month; Rental vacancy rate: 9.8%

Health Insurance: 82.5% have insurance; 48.8% have private insurance; 43.6% have public insurance; 17.5% do not have insurance; 4.0% of children under 18 do not have insurance

Hospitals: Hi - Desert Medical Center (181 beds)

Transportation: Commute: 83.4% car, 1.9% public transportation, 3.1% walk, 9.8% work from home; Median travel time to work: 32.7 minutes

LAKE ARROWHEAD (CDP). Covers a land area of 17.727 square miles and a water area of 1.224 square miles. Located at 34.25° N. Lat; 117.18° W. Long. Elevation is 5,174 feet.

History: Lake Arrowhead, formerly known as Little Bear Valley, is located in San Bernardino National Forest. The name was changed to Lake Arrowhead when the Arrowhead Lake Company bought the lake and surrounding land in 1920. There is a rock formation in the form of an arrowhead on the face of the San Bernardino Mountain.

Population: 12,424; Growth (since 2000): 39.1%; Density: 700.9 persons per square mile; Race: 86.4% White, 0.8% Black/African American, 1.2% Asian, 0.7% American Indian/Alaska Native, 0.3% Native Hawaiian/Other Pacific Islander, 3.8% Two or more races, 21.8% Hispanic of any race; Average household size: 2.65; Median age: 43.0; Age under 18: 24.5%; Age 65 and over: 14.0%; Males per 100 females: 103.8; Marriage status: 21.4% never married, 62.8% now married, 2.4% separated, 6.5% widowed, 9.2% divorced; Foreign born: 9.8%; Speak English only: 85.2%; With disability: 10.7%; Veterans: 12.5%; Ancestry: 18.2% German, 16.0% Irish, 12.2% English, 7.3% Italian, 5.3% Scottish

Employment: 12.4% management, business, and financial, 3.4% computer, engineering, and science, 16.7% education, legal, community service, arts, and media, 8.4% healthcare practitioners, 24.4% service, 20.5% sales and office, 9.7% natural resources, construction, and maintenance, 4.6% production, transportation, and material moving

Income: Per capita: $27,531; Median household: $60,795; Average household: $71,895; Households with income of $100,000 or more: 28.2%; Poverty rate: 11.2%

Educational Attainment: High school diploma or higher: 90.7%; Bachelor's degree or higher: 34.4%; Graduate/professional degree or higher: 13.6%

School District(s)

Rim of the World Unified (KG-12)
2012-13 Enrollment: 4,013 . . . . (909) 336-2031

Housing: Homeownership rate: 73.4%; Median home value: $278,800; Median year structure built: 1975; Homeowner vacancy rate: 7.9%; Median gross rent: $1,090 per month; Rental vacancy rate: 12.4%

Health Insurance: 85.1% have insurance; 70.1% have private insurance; 25.3% have public insurance; 14.9% do not have insurance; 5.8% of children under 18 do not have insurance

Hospitals: Mountains Community Hospital (37 beds)

Newspapers: Crestline Courier News (weekly circulation 3500); Mountain News (weekly circulation 7500)

Transportation: Commute: 87.3% car, 0.4% public transportation, 4.1% walk, 5.8% work from home; Median travel time to work: 28.6 minutes

LANDERS (unincorporated postal area)

ZCTA: 92285

Covers a land area of 171.020 square miles and a water area of 0 square miles. Located at 34.34° N. Lat; 116.54° W. Long. Elevation is 3,084 feet.

Population: 2,632; Growth (since 2000): 20.7%; Density: 15.4 persons per square mile; Race: 88.0% White, 0.9% Black/African American, 0.9% Asian, 2.1% American Indian/Alaska Native, 0.0% Native Hawaiian/Other Pacific Islander, 3.0% Two or more races, 16.1% Hispanic of any race; Average household size: 2.11; Median age: 51.3; Age under 18: 16.7%; Age 65 and over: 24.1%; Males per 100 females: 111.6; Marriage status: 28.1% never married, 33.1% now married, 2.7% separated, 15.8% widowed, 23.0% divorced; Foreign born: 9.8%; Speak English only: 92.8%; With disability: 24.6%; Veterans: 15.8%; Ancestry: 21.8% German, 14.8% English, 9.7% European, 9.6% American, 9.1% Irish

Employment: 2.7% management, business, and financial, 0.0% computer, engineering, and science, 11.8% education, legal, community service, arts, and media, 11.8% healthcare practitioners, 16.6% service, 18.1% sales and office, 22.9% natural resources, construction, and maintenance, 16.2% production, transportation, and material moving

Income: Per capita: $17,840; Median household: $22,917; Average household: $38,473; Households with income of $100,000 or more: 3.1%; Poverty rate: 37.6%

Educational Attainment: High school diploma or higher: 78.3%; Bachelor's degree or higher: 5.3%; Graduate/professional degree or higher: 0.9%

School District(s)

Morongo Unified (KG-12)
2012-13 Enrollment: 8,905 . . . . (760) 367-9191

Housing: Homeownership rate: 77.9%; Median home value: $66,000; Median year structure built: 1959; Homeowner vacancy rate: 5.7%; Median gross rent: $886 per month; Rental vacancy rate: 7.4%

Health Insurance: 71.5% have insurance; 26.3% have private insurance; 55.1% have public insurance; 28.5% do not have insurance; 15.0% of children under 18 do not have insurance

Transportation: Commute: 92.2% car, 0.0% public transportation, 0.0% walk, 4.3% work from home; Median travel time to work: 37.0 minutes

LENWOOD (CDP). Covers a land area of 2.214 square miles and a water area of 0 square miles. Located at 34.89° N. Lat; 117.11° W. Long. Elevation is 2,280 feet.

Population: 3,543; Growth (since 2000): 10.0%; Density: 1,600.6 persons per square mile; Race: 60.2% White, 6.2% Black/African American, 1.0% Asian, 2.7% American Indian/Alaska Native, 0.7% Native Hawaiian/Other Pacific Islander, 6.3% Two or more races, 47.3% Hispanic of any race; Average household size: 3.13; Median age: 29.4; Age under 18: 32.7%; Age 65 and over: 8.7%; Males per 100 females: 99.9; Marriage status: 31.3% never married, 51.3% now married, 0.6% separated, 4.0% widowed, 13.4% divorced; Foreign born: 7.8%; Speak English only: 79.7%; With disability: 6.3%; Veterans: 9.6%; Ancestry: 7.7% American, 6.2% German, 5.6% Irish, 1.9% Polish, 1.5% Italian

Employment: 4.4% management, business, and financial, 0.0% computer, engineering, and science, 5.5% education, legal, community service, arts, and media, 0.0% healthcare practitioners, 20.2% service, 24.0% sales and office, 21.0% natural resources, construction, and maintenance, 24.9% production, transportation, and material moving

Income: Per capita: $15,429; Median household: $43,667; Average household: $46,871; Households with income of $100,000 or more: 4.7%; Poverty rate: 28.7%

Educational Attainment: High school diploma or higher: 77.1%; Bachelor's degree or higher: 3.5%; Graduate/professional degree or higher: n/a

School District(s)

Barstow Unified (KG-12)
2012-13 Enrollment: 5,929 . . . . (760) 255-6000

Housing: Homeownership rate: 56.2%; Median home value: $84,300; Median year structure built: 1963; Homeowner vacancy rate: 3.5%; Median gross rent: $841 per month; Rental vacancy rate: 8.3%

Health Insurance: 87.4% have insurance; 57.8% have private insurance; 34.1% have public insurance; 12.6% do not have insurance; 0.6% of children under 18 do not have insurance

Transportation: Commute: 94.5% car, 3.1% public transportation, 0.0% walk, 2.4% work from home; Median travel time to work: 24.8 minutes

LOMA LINDA (city). Covers a land area of 7.516 square miles and a water area of <.001 square miles. Located at 34.04° N. Lat; 117.25° W. Long. Elevation is 1,165 feet.

History: Loma Linda, formerly known as Mound City, Mound Station, was incorporated on September 29, 1970. Its name means "beautiful hill."

Population: 23,261; Growth (since 2000): 24.5%; Density: 3,094.7 persons per square mile; Race: 47.8% White, 8.7% Black/African American, 28.3% Asian, 0.4% American Indian/Alaska Native, 0.7% Native Hawaiian/Other Pacific Islander, 5.4% Two or more races, 22.2% Hispanic of any race; Average household size: 2.56; Median age: 33.2; Age under 18: 20.9%; Age 65 and over: 13.9%; Males per 100 females: 88.0; Marriage status: 36.6% never married, 47.3% now married, 2.6% separated, 7.1% widowed, 8.9% divorced; Foreign born: 33.6%; Speak English only: 60.9%; With disability: 10.1%; Veterans: 5.5%; Ancestry: 8.3% German, 4.5% African, 4.4% Irish, 3.4% English, 2.8% Italian

Employment: 8.8% management, business, and financial, 3.5% computer, engineering, and science, 13.1% education, legal, community service, arts, and media, 24.8% healthcare practitioners, 15.7% service, 21.2% sales and office, 4.8% natural resources, construction, and maintenance, 8.0% production, transportation, and material moving

Income: Per capita: $30,621; Median household: $54,720; Average household: $77,960; Households with income of $100,000 or more: 26.3%; Poverty rate: 17.0%

Educational Attainment: High school diploma or higher: 89.0%; Bachelor's degree or higher: 50.1%; Graduate/professional degree or higher: 21.3%

School District(s)

Redlands Unified (KG-12)
2012-13 Enrollment: 21,379 . . . . (909) 307-5300

Four-year College(s)

Loma Linda University (Private, Not-for-profit, Seventh Day Adventists)
Fall 2013 Enrollment: 4,693 . . . . (909) 558-1000

Housing: Homeownership rate: 39.2%; Median home value: $281,400; Median year structure built: 1982; Homeowner vacancy rate: 2.5%; Median gross rent: $1,081 per month; Rental vacancy rate: 9.9%

Health Insurance: 84.6% have insurance; 67.2% have private insurance; 26.6% have public insurance; 15.4% do not have insurance; 14.7% of children under 18 do not have insurance

Hospitals: Loma Linda University Medical Center (724 beds); Loma Linda VA Medical Center (203 beds)

Safety: Violent crime rate: 25.7 per 10,000 population; Property crime rate: 304.2 per 10,000 population

Transportation: Commute: 87.8% car, 0.7% public transportation, 5.6% walk, 4.6% work from home; Median travel time to work: 19.2 minutes

Additional Information Contacts

City of Loma Linda . . . . (909) 799-2800
http://www.lomalinda-ca.gov

LUCERNE VALLEY (CDP). Covers a land area of 105.590 square miles and a water area of 0 square miles. Located at 34.44° N. Lat; 116.90° W. Long. Elevation is 2,953 feet.

Population: 5,811; Growth (since 2000): n/a; Density: 55.0 persons per square mile; Race: 77.6% White, 2.9% Black/African American, 1.5% Asian, 1.8% American Indian/Alaska Native, 0.0% Native Hawaiian/Other Pacific Islander, 4.5% Two or more races, 24.9% Hispanic of any race; Average household size: 2.66; Median age: 42.7; Age under 18: 24.5%; Age 65 and over: 16.2%; Males per 100 females: 106.1; Marriage status: 31.8% never married, 40.8% now married, 3.5% separated, 4.4% widowed, 22.9% divorced; Foreign born: 8.1%; Speak English only: 86.9%; With disability: 15.6%; Veterans: 18.0%; Ancestry: 18.1% German, 8.5% English, 7.9% Irish, 6.9% American, 5.3% Italian

Employment: 6.3% management, business, and financial, 5.6% computer, engineering, and science, 6.1% education, legal, community service, arts, and media, 0.6% healthcare practitioners, 16.2% service, 24.1% sales and office, 15.5% natural resources, construction, and maintenance, 25.6% production, transportation, and material moving

Income: Per capita: $16,796; Median household: $32,202; Average household: $46,343; Households with income of $100,000 or more: 8.5%; Poverty rate: 22.5%

Educational Attainment: High school diploma or higher: 83.7%; Bachelor's degree or higher: 10.1%; Graduate/professional degree or higher: 5.9%

School District(s)

Lucerne Valley Unified (KG-12)
2012-13 Enrollment: 2,668 . . . . (760) 248-6108

Housing: Homeownership rate: 66.8%; Median home value: $101,700; Median year structure built: 1974; Homeowner vacancy rate: 4.3%; Median gross rent: $749 per month; Rental vacancy rate: 9.0%

Health Insurance: 77.1% have insurance; 46.1% have private insurance; 40.7% have public insurance; 22.9% do not have insurance; 7.2% of children under 18 do not have insurance

Newspapers: The Leader (weekly circulation 2800)

Transportation: Commute: 90.5% car, 0.9% public transportation, 0.0% walk, 8.6% work from home; Median travel time to work: 40.6 minutes

LYTLE CREEK (CDP). Covers a land area of 6.018 square miles and a water area of 0 square miles. Located at 34.25° N. Lat; 117.50° W. Long. Elevation is 3,419 feet.

Population: 701; Growth (since 2000): n/a; Density: 116.5 persons per square mile; Race: 86.4% White, 0.9% Black/African American, 3.3% Asian, 1.0% American Indian/Alaska Native, 0.0% Native Hawaiian/Other Pacific Islander, 4.9% Two or more races, 14.0% Hispanic of any race; Average household size: 2.09; Median age: 52.0; Age under 18: 14.6%; Age 65 and over: 19.8%; Males per 100 females: 106.2

Housing: Homeownership rate: 72.9%; Homeowner vacancy rate: 2.8%; Rental vacancy rate: 15.0%

MENTONE (CDP). Covers a land area of 6.222 square miles and a water area of 0.012 square miles. Located at 34.06° N. Lat; 117.12° W. Long. Elevation is 1,650 feet.

Population: 8,720; Growth (since 2000): 11.8%; Density: 1,401.4 persons per square mile; Race: 70.1% White, 5.0% Black/African American, 4.0% Asian, 1.4% American Indian/Alaska Native, 0.4% Native Hawaiian/Other Pacific Islander, 4.9% Two or more races, 35.4% Hispanic of any race; Average household size: 2.84; Median age: 33.7; Age under 18: 26.8%; Age 65 and over: 9.2%; Males per 100 females: 97.3; Marriage status: 33.1% never married, 50.8% now married, 4.1% separated, 5.2% widowed, 10.9% divorced; Foreign born: 15.8%; Speak English only: 74.0%; With disability: 11.3%; Veterans: 6.9%; Ancestry: 16.7% German, 12.1% Irish, 8.2% English, 4.2% French, 3.9% American

Employment: 9.7% management, business, and financial, 3.7% computer, engineering, and science, 12.4% education, legal, community service, arts, and media, 9.3% healthcare practitioners, 23.4% service, 16.5% sales and office, 12.9% natural resources, construction, and maintenance, 12.2% production, transportation, and material moving

Income: Per capita: $23,618; Median household: $58,178; Average household: $69,127; Households with income of $100,000 or more: 21.3%; Poverty rate: 10.8%

Educational Attainment: High school diploma or higher: 85.8%; Bachelor's degree or higher: 19.8%; Graduate/professional degree or higher: 10.7%

School District(s)

Redlands Unified (KG-12)
2012-13 Enrollment: 21,379 . . . . (909) 307-5300

Housing: Homeownership rate: 61.0%; Median home value: $224,500; Median year structure built: 1979; Homeowner vacancy rate: 2.7%; Median gross rent: $893 per month; Rental vacancy rate: 8.3%

Health Insurance: 86.0% have insurance; 61.0% have private insurance; 29.5% have public insurance; 14.0% do not have insurance; 4.6% of children under 18 do not have insurance

Transportation: Commute: 94.2% car, 0.8% public transportation, 1.3% walk, 3.7% work from home; Median travel time to work: 25.2 minutes

MONTCLAIR (city). Covers a land area of 5.517 square miles and a water area of 0 square miles. Located at 34.07° N. Lat; 117.70° W. Long. Elevation is 1,066 feet.

History: Named for the French translation of "clear view of mountain". Incorporated 1956.

Population: 36,664; Growth (since 2000): 10.9%; Density: 6,645.4 persons per square mile; Race: 52.7% White, 5.2% Black/African American, 9.3% Asian, 1.2% American Indian/Alaska Native, 0.2% Native Hawaiian/Other Pacific Islander, 4.4% Two or more races, 70.2% Hispanic of any race; Average household size: 3.81; Median age: 30.7; Age under 18: 29.3%; Age 65 and over: 8.4%; Males per 100 females: 99.1; Marriage status: 39.2% never married, 47.6% now married, 3.9% separated, 4.6% widowed, 8.7% divorced; Foreign born: 36.3%; Speak English only: 34.6%; With disability: 9.2%; Veterans: 3.6%; Ancestry: 6.9% American, 4.0% German, 2.5% English, 2.5% Irish, 1.6% Italian

Employment: 6.4% management, business, and financial, 1.9% computer, engineering, and science, 5.5% education, legal, community service, arts, and media, 3.3% healthcare practitioners, 23.1% service, 25.4% sales and office, 12.1% natural resources, construction, and maintenance, 22.1% production, transportation, and material moving

Income: Per capita: $17,324; Median household: $50,220; Average household: $59,988; Households with income of $100,000 or more: 15.8%; Poverty rate: 18.1%

Educational Attainment: High school diploma or higher: 69.8%; Bachelor's degree or higher: 12.2%; Graduate/professional degree or higher: 2.3%

School District(s)

Chaffey Joint Union High (09-12)
2012-13 Enrollment: 25,020 . . . . (909) 988-8511
Ontario-Montclair Elementary (PK-08)
2012-13 Enrollment: 22,735 . . . . (909) 459-2500

Housing: Homeownership rate: 59.7%; Median home value: $250,400; Median year structure built: 1969; Homeowner vacancy rate: 2.0%; Median gross rent: $1,128 per month; Rental vacancy rate: 4.6%

Health Insurance: 73.7% have insurance; 47.6% have private insurance; 30.3% have public insurance; 26.3% do not have insurance; 14.6% of children under 18 do not have insurance

Hospitals: Montclair Hospital Medical Center (102 beds)

Safety: Violent crime rate: 49.5 per 10,000 population; Property crime rate: 429.5 per 10,000 population

Transportation: Commute: 91.3% car, 3.5% public transportation, 2.2% walk, 1.8% work from home; Median travel time to work: 30.9 minutes

Additional Information Contacts

City of Montclair. . . . . (909) 626-8571
http://www.cityofmontclair.org

MORONGO VALLEY (CDP). Covers a land area of 25.219 square miles and a water area of 0 square miles. Located at 34.07° N. Lat; 116.56° W. Long. Elevation is 2,582 feet.

Population: 3,552; Growth (since 2000): 84.1%; Density: 140.8 persons per square mile; Race: 86.6% White, 1.1% Black/African American, 0.9% Asian, 2.1% American Indian/Alaska Native, 0.1% Native Hawaiian/Other Pacific Islander, 4.0% Two or more races, 14.9% Hispanic of any race; Average household size: 2.21; Median age: 47.2; Age under 18: 18.2%; Age 65 and over: 15.5%; Males per 100 females: 105.6; Marriage status: 21.5% never married, 48.7% now married, 6.7% separated, 10.9% widowed, 18.9% divorced; Foreign born: 9.8%; Speak English only: 83.0%; With disability: 17.7%; Veterans: 15.0%; Ancestry: 15.1% Irish, 12.6% German, 11.4% English, 9.1% Italian, 9.0% Scotch-Irish

Employment: 7.0% management, business, and financial, 0.9% computer, engineering, and science, 16.6% education, legal, community service, arts, and media, 2.4% healthcare practitioners, 23.8% service, 24.1% sales and office, 17.9% natural resources, construction, and maintenance, 7.2% production, transportation, and material moving

Income: Per capita: $19,909; Median household: $30,383; Average household: $45,154; Households with income of $100,000 or more: 7.6%; Poverty rate: 26.9%

Educational Attainment: High school diploma or higher: 84.9%; Bachelor's degree or higher: 15.1%; Graduate/professional degree or higher: 7.2%

School District(s)

Morongo Unified (KG-12)
2012-13 Enrollment: 8,905 . . . . (760) 367-9191

Housing: Homeownership rate: 72.3%; Median home value: $118,000; Median year structure built: 1972; Homeowner vacancy rate: 4.7%; Median gross rent: $862 per month; Rental vacancy rate: 7.9%

Health Insurance: 72.9% have insurance; 37.6% have private insurance; 45.2% have public insurance; 27.1% do not have insurance; 23.7% of children under 18 do not have insurance

Transportation: Commute: 91.6% car, 0.0% public transportation, 3.8% walk, 4.6% work from home; Median travel time to work: 32.5 minutes

MOUNTAIN VIEW ACRES (CDP). Covers a land area of 1.571 square miles and a water area of 0 square miles. Located at 34.50° N. Lat; 117.35° W. Long. Elevation is 3,074 feet.

History: Roy Rogers Dale Evans Museum to Northeast.

Population: 3,130; Growth (since 2000): 24.2%; Density: 1,992.3 persons per square mile; Race: 55.8% White, 6.9% Black/African American, 3.1% Asian, 1.5% American Indian/Alaska Native, 0.5% Native Hawaiian/Other Pacific Islander, 4.6% Two or more races, 52.6% Hispanic of any race; Average household size: 3.42; Median age: 34.3; Age under 18: 28.3%; Age 65 and over: 11.3%; Males per 100 females: 102.9; Marriage status: 36.2% never married, 42.9% now married, 0.0% separated, 6.2% widowed, 14.7% divorced; Foreign born: 8.4%; Speak English only: 67.7%; With disability: 15.1%; Veterans: 14.0%; Ancestry: 11.5% German, 4.4% English, 3.9% Irish, 3.1% American, 3.0% Scottish

Employment: 5.4% management, business, and financial, 0.0% computer, engineering, and science, 9.6% education, legal, community service, arts, and media, 0.0% healthcare practitioners, 30.3% service, 18.5% sales and office, 23.9% natural resources, construction, and maintenance, 12.3% production, transportation, and material moving

Income: Per capita: $18,483; Median household: $56,198; Average household: $61,387; Households with income of $100,000 or more: 20.2%; Poverty rate: 11.4%

Educational Attainment: High school diploma or higher: 77.9%; Bachelor's degree or higher: 3.3%; Graduate/professional degree or higher: 1.4%

Housing: Homeownership rate: 72.9%; Median home value: $119,100; Median year structure built: 1983; Homeowner vacancy rate: 3.3%; Median gross rent: $1,138 per month; Rental vacancy rate: 4.7%

Health Insurance: 77.9% have insurance; 50.8% have private insurance; 37.5% have public insurance; 22.1% do not have insurance; 9.8% of children under 18 do not have insurance

Transportation: Commute: 89.5% car, 1.2% public transportation, 0.0% walk, 9.3% work from home; Median travel time to work: 37.5 minutes

MUSCOY (CDP). Covers a land area of 3.143 square miles and a water area of 0.004 square miles. Located at 34.16° N. Lat; 117.35° W. Long. Elevation is 1,388 feet.

History: California State University San Bernardino to Northwest.

Population: 10,644; Growth (since 2000): 19.3%; Density: 3,386.6 persons per square mile; Race: 41.9% White, 4.3% Black/African American, 0.9% Asian, 1.2% American Indian/Alaska Native, 0.2% Native Hawaiian/Other Pacific Islander, 4.7% Two or more races, 82.9% Hispanic of any race; Average household size: 4.64; Median age: 24.9; Age under 18: 35.5%; Age 65 and over: 5.6%; Males per 100 females: 102.8; Marriage status: 47.3% never married, 42.1% now married, 4.6% separated, 5.0% widowed, 5.5% divorced; Foreign born: 33.1%; Speak English only: 24.9%; With disability: 10.6%; Veterans: 3.4%; Ancestry: 2.1% German, 1.3% Irish, 1.2% English, 0.6% French, 0.6% Dutch

Employment: 2.8% management, business, and financial, 0.0% computer, engineering, and science, 5.7% education, legal, community service, arts, and media, 1.1% healthcare practitioners, 21.0% service, 18.2% sales and office, 20.2% natural resources, construction, and maintenance, 31.1% production, transportation, and material moving

Income: Per capita: $9,768; Median household: $38,438; Average household: $42,429; Households with income of $100,000 or more: 3.8%; Poverty rate: 32.2%

Educational Attainment: High school diploma or higher: 45.6%; Bachelor's degree or higher: 4.0%; Graduate/professional degree or higher: 0.7%

Housing: Homeownership rate: 56.8%; Median home value: $141,700; Median year structure built: 1960; Homeowner vacancy rate: 3.7%; Median gross rent: $1,041 per month; Rental vacancy rate: 8.2%

Health Insurance: 65.7% have insurance; 21.8% have private insurance; 47.2% have public insurance; 34.3% do not have insurance; 9.5% of children under 18 do not have insurance

Transportation: Commute: 90.8% car, 0.5% public transportation, 2.4% walk, 4.5% work from home; Median travel time to work: 33.1 minutes

NEEDLES (city). Covers a land area of 30.808 square miles and a water area of 0.467 square miles. Located at 34.82° N. Lat; 114.61° W. Long. Elevation is 495 feet.

History: Needles was founded as a way station after the Santa Fe tracks were laid in 1883, and was named for an isolated group of needle-like spires visible to the southeast in Arizona.

Population: 4,844; Growth (since 2000): 0.3%; Density: 157.2 persons per square mile; Race: 75.7% White, 2.0% Black/African American, 0.7% Asian, 8.2% American Indian/Alaska Native, 0.2% Native Hawaiian/Other Pacific Islander, 6.5% Two or more races, 22.4% Hispanic of any race; Average household size: 2.52; Median age: 39.3; Age under 18: 26.5%; Age 65 and over: 15.8%; Males per 100 females: 101.6; Marriage status: 29.4% never married, 43.0% now married, 5.9% separated, 7.6% widowed, 20.1% divorced; Foreign born: 4.4%; Speak English only: 92.4%; With disability: 20.4%; Veterans: 12.0%; Ancestry: 12.8% Irish, 8.1% English, 6.8% American, 6.4% German, 5.1% Italian

Employment: 5.3% management, business, and financial, 2.6% computer, engineering, and science, 4.1% education, legal, community service, arts, and media, 3.5% healthcare practitioners, 28.2% service, 27.1% sales and office, 12.3% natural resources, construction, and maintenance, 16.8% production, transportation, and material moving

Income: Per capita: $17,906; Median household: $30,051; Average household: $43,607; Households with income of $100,000 or more: 9.6%; Poverty rate: 30.8%

Educational Attainment: High school diploma or higher: 80.8%; Bachelor's degree or higher: 6.9%; Graduate/professional degree or higher: 2.6%

School District(s)

Needles Unified (KG-12)
2012-13 Enrollment: 862. . . . . (760) 326-3891

Housing: Homeownership rate: 52.9%; Median home value: $96,700; Median year structure built: 1973; Homeowner vacancy rate: 4.9%; Median gross rent: $595 per month; Rental vacancy rate: 17.2%

Health Insurance: 79.1% have insurance; 44.5% have private insurance; 46.9% have public insurance; 20.9% do not have insurance; 21.5% of children under 18 do not have insurance

Hospitals: Colorado River Medical Center (49 beds)

Safety: Violent crime rate: 30.4 per 10,000 population; Property crime rate: 421.7 per 10,000 population

Newspapers: Needles Desert Star (weekly circulation 4000)

Transportation: Commute: 82.9% car, 0.0% public transportation, 13.5% walk, 3.1% work from home; Median travel time to work: 26.5 minutes; Amtrak: Train service available.

Additional Information Contacts

City of Needles . . . . (760) 326-2113
http://www.cityofneedles.com

NEWBERRY SPRINGS (unincorporated postal area)

ZCTA: 92365

Covers a land area of 172.625 square miles and a water area of 0.968 square miles. Located at 34.90° N. Lat; 116.66° W. Long. Elevation is 1,860 feet.

Population: 2,637; Growth (since 2000): -8.9%; Density: 15.3 persons per square mile; Race: 78.0% White, 3.0% Black/African American, 1.4% Asian, 1.1% American Indian/Alaska Native, 0.7% Native Hawaiian/Other Pacific Islander, 4.5% Two or more races, 24.6% Hispanic of any race; Average household size: 2.61; Median age: 45.2; Age under 18: 22.0%; Age 65 and over: 16.8%; Males per 100 females: 103.2; Marriage status: 25.8% never married, 51.7% now married, 0.0% separated, 9.3% widowed, 13.2% divorced; Foreign born: 12.0%; Speak English only: 78.8%; With disability: 17.3%; Veterans: 18.5%; Ancestry: 18.6% German, 11.0% Irish, 10.9% English, 3.4% American, 3.3% European

Employment: 10.0% management, business, and financial, 1.3% computer, engineering, and science, 3.7% education, legal, community service, arts, and media, 10.0% healthcare practitioners, 34.7% service, 24.9% sales and office, 2.8% natural resources, construction, and maintenance, 12.5% production, transportation, and material moving

Income: Per capita: $18,711; Median household: $39,504; Average household: $47,810; Households with income of $100,000 or more: 4.9%; Poverty rate: 20.1%

Educational Attainment: High school diploma or higher: 77.8%; Bachelor's degree or higher: 11.4%; Graduate/professional degree or higher: 4.3%

School District(s)

Silver Valley Unified (PK-12)
2012-13 Enrollment: 2,395 . . . . (760) 254-2916

Housing: Homeownership rate: 71.2%; Median home value: $156,400; Median year structure built: 1984; Homeowner vacancy rate: 4.0%; Median gross rent: $714 per month; Rental vacancy rate: 10.9%

Health Insurance: 83.5% have insurance; 61.4% have private insurance; 38.5% have public insurance; 16.5% do not have insurance; 0.0% of children under 18 do not have insurance

Transportation: Commute: 91.6% car, 0.0% public transportation, 3.8% walk, 4.6% work from home; Median travel time to work: 29.0 minutes

NIPTON (unincorporated postal area)

ZCTA: 92364

Covers a land area of 514.166 square miles and a water area of 0 square miles. Located at 35.34° N. Lat; 115.43° W. Long. Elevation is 3,031 feet.

Population: 90; Growth (since 2000): -43.0%; Density: 0.2 persons per square mile; Race: 75.6% White, 2.2% Black/African American, 1.1% Asian, 3.3% American Indian/Alaska Native, 0.0% Native Hawaiian/Other Pacific Islander, 4.4% Two or more races, 24.4% Hispanic of any race; Average household size: 2.37; Median age: 43.3; Age under 18: 22.2%; Age 65 and over: 14.4%; Males per 100 females: 109.3

Housing: Homeownership rate: 52.6%; Homeowner vacancy rate: 4.8%; Rental vacancy rate: 14.3%

OAK GLEN (CDP). Covers a land area of 15.117 square miles and a water area of 0.004 square miles. Located at 34.05° N. Lat; 116.95° W. Long. Elevation is 4,806 feet.

Population: 638; Growth (since 2000): n/a; Density: 42.2 persons per square mile; Race: 85.4% White, 7.8% Black/African American, 0.3% Asian, 2.0% American Indian/Alaska Native, 0.2% Native Hawaiian/Other Pacific Islander, 2.0% Two or more races, 19.3% Hispanic of any race; Average household size: 2.54; Median age: 45.4; Age under 18: 11.3%; Age 65 and over: 13.6%; Males per 100 females: 171.5

Housing: Homeownership rate: 74.7%; Homeowner vacancy rate: 3.4%; Rental vacancy rate: 4.0%

OAK HILLS (CDP). Covers a land area of 24.390 square miles and a water area of 0 square miles. Located at 34.39° N. Lat; 117.40° W. Long. Elevation is 3,720 feet.

Population: 8,879; Growth (since 2000): n/a; Density: 364.0 persons per square mile; Race: 76.5% White, 3.0% Black/African American, 2.5% Asian, 1.1% American Indian/Alaska Native, 0.3% Native Hawaiian/Other Pacific Islander, 3.3% Two or more races, 30.6% Hispanic of any race; Average household size: 3.28; Median age: 39.1; Age under 18: 27.4%; Age 65 and over: 9.6%; Males per 100 females: 102.4; Marriage status: 28.9% never married, 60.2% now married, 2.5% separated, 3.4% widowed, 7.5% divorced; Foreign born: 10.7%; Speak English only: 72.9%; With disability: 9.3%; Veterans: 11.0%; Ancestry: 11.6% English, 10.9% German, 6.2% Irish, 3.6% Italian, 3.5% French

Employment: 12.6% management, business, and financial, 3.2% computer, engineering, and science, 7.6% education, legal, community service, arts, and media, 5.8% healthcare practitioners, 16.1% service, 26.6% sales and office, 17.1% natural resources, construction, and maintenance, 11.0% production, transportation, and material moving

Income: Per capita: $27,077; Median household: $74,801; Average household: $87,878; Households with income of $100,000 or more: 32.3%; Poverty rate: 8.7%

Educational Attainment: High school diploma or higher: 84.1%; Bachelor's degree or higher: 16.0%; Graduate/professional degree or higher: 7.5%

School District(s)

Hesperia Unified (KG-12)
2012-13 Enrollment: 23,448 . . . . (760) 244-4411

Housing: Homeownership rate: 88.7%; Median home value: $249,700; Median year structure built: 1993; Homeowner vacancy rate: 2.3%; Median gross rent: $1,611 per month; Rental vacancy rate: 6.1%

Health Insurance: 86.6% have insurance; 63.9% have private insurance; 30.2% have public insurance; 13.4% do not have insurance; 4.1% of children under 18 do not have insurance

Transportation: Commute: 95.9% car, 0.1% public transportation, 0.0% walk, 3.0% work from home; Median travel time to work: 39.1 minutes

ONTARIO (city). Covers a land area of 49.941 square miles and a water area of 0.065 square miles. Located at 34.04° N. Lat; 117.61° W. Long. Elevation is 1,004 feet.

History: Named for Ontario, Canada, home of town founder George B. Chaffey. Ontario was founded in 1882. It developed as a residential town surrounded by orange groves and ranches.

Population: 163,924; Growth (since 2000): 3.7%; Density: 3,282.4 persons per square mile; Race: 51.0% White, 6.4% Black/African American, 5.2% Asian, 1.0% American Indian/Alaska Native, 0.3% Native Hawaiian/Other Pacific Islander, 4.7% Two or more races, 69.0% Hispanic of any race; Average household size: 3.63; Median age: 29.9; Age under 18: 30.2%; Age 65 and over: 6.7%; Males per 100 females: 99.0; Marriage status: 39.0% never married, 47.3% now married, 3.4% separated, 4.2% widowed, 9.5% divorced; Foreign born: 30.3%; Speak English only: 41.3%; With disability: 8.9%; Veterans: 4.2%; Ancestry: 6.6% American, 4.0% German, 3.3% English, 2.9% Irish, 1.7% Italian

Employment: 8.7% management, business, and financial, 2.5% computer, engineering, and science, 6.9% education, legal, community service, arts, and media, 3.1% healthcare practitioners, 18.7% service, 27.0% sales and office, 10.1% natural resources, construction, and maintenance, 22.9% production, transportation, and material moving

Income: Per capita: $18,522; Median household: $54,249; Average household: $63,733; Households with income of $100,000 or more: 18.5%; Poverty rate: 18.1%

Educational Attainment: High school diploma or higher: 69.6%; Bachelor's degree or higher: 13.0%; Graduate/professional degree or higher: 3.3%

School District(s)

Chaffey Joint Union High (09-12)
2012-13 Enrollment: 25,020 . . . . (909) 988-8511
Chino Valley Unified (KG-12)
2012-13 Enrollment: 30,705 . . . . (909) 628-1201
Cucamonga Elementary (KG-08)
2012-13 Enrollment: 2,530 . . . . (909) 987-8942
Mountain View Elementary (KG-08)
2012-13 Enrollment: 2,733 . . . . (909) 947-2992
Ontario-Montclair Elementary (PK-08)
2012-13 Enrollment: 22,735 . . . . (909) 459-2500

Four-year College(s)

Argosy University-Inland Empire (Private, For-profit)
Fall 2013 Enrollment: 704 . . . . (909) 915-3800
2013-14 Tuition: In-state $13,663; Out-of-state $13,663
Everest College-Ontario Metro (Private, For-profit)
Fall 2013 Enrollment: 962 . . . . (909) 484-4311
2013-14 Tuition: In-state $14,238; Out-of-state $14,238
Platt College-Ontario (Private, For-profit)
Fall 2013 Enrollment: 467 . . . . (909) 941-9410
2013-14 Tuition: In-state $14,572; Out-of-state $14,572
West Coast University-Ontario (Private, For-profit)
Fall 2013 Enrollment: 1,103 . . . . (909) 467-6100
2013-14 Tuition: In-state $32,525; Out-of-state $32,525

Two-year College(s)

American Career College-Ontario (Private, For-profit)
Fall 2013 Enrollment: 1,634 . . . . (949) 783-4800
San Joaquin Valley College-Ontario (Private, For-profit)
Fall 2013 Enrollment: 698 . . . . (909) 948-7582
2013-14 Tuition: In-state $17,724; Out-of-state $17,724

Vocational/Technical School(s)

Everest College-Ontario (Private, For-profit)
Fall 2013 Enrollment: 782 . . . . (909) 984-5027
2013-14 Tuition: $21,388
Franklin Career College (Private, For-profit)
Fall 2013 Enrollment: n/a . . . . (909) 937-9007

Housing: Homeownership rate: 55.3%; Median home value: $250,900; Median year structure built: 1976; Homeowner vacancy rate: 2.0%; Median gross rent: $1,242 per month; Rental vacancy rate: 5.8%

Health Insurance: 75.0% have insurance; 50.9% have private insurance; 28.9% have public insurance; 25.0% do not have insurance; 11.7% of children under 18 do not have insurance

Safety: Violent crime rate: 26.9 per 10,000 population; Property crime rate: 268.0 per 10,000 population

Newspapers: Inland Valley Daily Bulletin (daily circulation 55000)

Transportation: Commute: 93.0% car, 1.5% public transportation, 1.6% walk, 2.2% work from home; Median travel time to work: 28.4 minutes; Amtrak: Train service available.

Airports: Ontario International (primary service/medium hub)

Additional Information Contacts

City of Ontario . . . . (909) 395-2000
http://www.ci.ontario.ca.us

ORO GRANDE (unincorporated postal area)

ZCTA: 92368

Covers a land area of 27.918 square miles and a water area of 0.447 square miles. Located at 34.65° N. Lat; 117.32° W. Long. Elevation is 2,661 feet.

Population: 1,113; Growth (since 2000): 24.4%; Density: 39.9 persons per square mile; Race: 65.4% White, 2.2% Black/African American, 1.3% Asian, 3.1% American Indian/Alaska Native, 0.0% Native Hawaiian/Other Pacific Islander, 5.3% Two or more races, 53.0% Hispanic of any race; Average household size: 3.21; Median age: 33.1; Age under 18: 31.4%; Age 65 and over: 12.6%; Males per 100 females: 113.6

School District(s)

Oro Grande Elementary (KG-12)
2012-13 Enrollment: 3,594 . . . . (760) 243-5884

Housing: Homeownership rate: 56.5%; Homeowner vacancy rate: 6.0%; Rental vacancy rate: 10.6%

PHELAN (CDP). Covers a land area of 60.097 square miles and a water area of 0 square miles. Located at 34.44° N. Lat; 117.52° W. Long. Elevation is 4,121 feet.

Population: 14,304; Growth (since 2000): n/a; Density: 238.0 persons per square mile; Race: 75.6% White, 1.9% Black/African American, 3.1% Asian, 1.0% American Indian/Alaska Native, 0.1% Native Hawaiian/Other Pacific Islander, 4.4% Two or more races, 28.9% Hispanic of any race; Average household size: 3.11; Median age: 37.9; Age under 18: 27.4%; Age 65 and over: 10.8%; Males per 100 females: 104.1; Marriage status: 27.3% never married, 54.0% now married, 3.3% separated, 4.7% widowed, 14.0% divorced; Foreign born: 8.3%; Speak English only: 80.9%; With disability: 17.8%; Veterans: 10.0%; Ancestry: 22.6% German, 11.1% Irish, 11.0% English, 4.4% American, 3.4% Dutch

Employment: 10.0% management, business, and financial, 1.6% computer, engineering, and science, 7.4% education, legal, community service, arts, and media, 4.1% healthcare practitioners, 15.3% service,

20.7% sales and office, 25.1% natural resources, construction, and maintenance, 16.0% production, transportation, and material moving
Income: Per capita: $22,500; Median household: $50,743; Average household: $62,206; Households with income of $100,000 or more: 19.7%; Poverty rate: 13.7%
Educational Attainment: High school diploma or higher: 84.0%; Bachelor's degree or higher: 10.8%; Graduate/professional degree or higher: 3.0%

School District(s)

Snowline Joint Unified (KG-12)
2012-13 Enrollment: 8,071 . . . . (760) 868-5817
Housing: Homeownership rate: 78.3%; Median home value: $129,300; Median year structure built: 1988; Homeowner vacancy rate: 2.9%; Median gross rent: $939 per month; Rental vacancy rate: 4.9%
Health Insurance: 85.6% have insurance; 60.0% have private insurance; 34.3% have public insurance; 14.4% do not have insurance; 2.5% of children under 18 do not have insurance
Transportation: Commute: 93.3% car, 0.2% public transportation, 0.0% walk, 5.9% work from home; Median travel time to work: 43.4 minutes

PINON HILLS (unincorporated postal area)

ZCTA: 92372

Covers a land area of 27.878 square miles and a water area of 0.003 square miles. Located at 34.45° N. Lat; 117.62° W. Long..
Population: 6,220; Growth (since 2000): 45.9%; Density: 223.1 persons per square mile; Race: 82.7% White, 0.9% Black/African American, 2.8% Asian, 0.8% American Indian/Alaska Native, 0.0% Native Hawaiian/Other Pacific Islander, 4.6% Two or more races, 23.5% Hispanic of any race; Average household size: 2.83; Median age: 41.8; Age under 18: 24.7%; Age 65 and over: 12.9%; Males per 100 females: 101.7; Marriage status: 25.5% never married, 48.7% now married, 2.2% separated, 11.4% widowed, 14.3% divorced; Foreign born: 10.8%; Speak English only: 85.3%; With disability: 18.8%; Veterans: 9.9%; Ancestry: 19.1% German, 15.0% English, 12.4% Irish, 9.6% American, 6.0% Italian
Employment: 16.4% management, business, and financial, 1.9% computer, engineering, and science, 5.6% education, legal, community service, arts, and media, 6.7% healthcare practitioners, 14.2% service, 21.7% sales and office, 14.8% natural resources, construction, and maintenance, 18.7% production, transportation, and material moving
Income: Per capita: $27,885; Median household: $35,896; Average household: $66,800; Households with income of $100,000 or more: 16.2%; Poverty rate: 16.2%
Educational Attainment: High school diploma or higher: 83.6%; Bachelor's degree or higher: 11.3%; Graduate/professional degree or higher: 2.8%

School District(s)

Snowline Joint Unified (KG-12)
2012-13 Enrollment: 8,071 . . . . (760) 868-5817
Housing: Homeownership rate: 77.9%; Median home value: $144,500; Median year structure built: 1985; Homeowner vacancy rate: 2.7%; Median gross rent: $1,291 per month; Rental vacancy rate: 9.3%
Health Insurance: 83.6% have insurance; 61.5% have private insurance; 34.0% have public insurance; 16.4% do not have insurance; 0.5% of children under 18 do not have insurance
Transportation: Commute: 90.9% car, 2.7% public transportation, 1.5% walk, 0.0% work from home; Median travel time to work: 51.8 minutes

PIONEERTOWN (unincorporated postal area)

ZCTA: 92268

Covers a land area of 80.840 square miles and a water area of 0 square miles. Located at 34.22° N. Lat; 116.56° W. Long. Elevation is 4,055 feet.
Population: 574; Growth (since 2000): 68.3%; Density: 7.1 persons per square mile; Race: 93.9% White, 1.4% Black/African American, 0.5% Asian, 0.5% American Indian/Alaska Native, 0.0% Native Hawaiian/Other Pacific Islander, 3.1% Two or more races, 3.7% Hispanic of any race; Average household size: 1.95; Median age: 56.4; Age under 18: 10.1%; Age 65 and over: 24.7%; Males per 100 females: 105.0
Housing: Homeownership rate: 86.7%; Homeowner vacancy rate: 1.9%; Rental vacancy rate: 4.9%

PIÑON HILLS (CDP). Covers a land area of 32.115 square miles and a water area of 0.003 square miles. Located at 34.44° N. Lat; 117.62° W. Long.
Population: 7,272; Growth (since 2000): n/a; Density: 226.4 persons per square mile; Race: 82.0% White, 0.8% Black/African American, 2.6% Asian, 0.9% American Indian/Alaska Native, 0.1% Native Hawaiian/Other Pacific Islander, 4.6% Two or more races, 23.9% Hispanic of any race; Average household size: 2.83; Median age: 41.4; Age under 18: 24.8%; Age 65 and over: 12.6%; Males per 100 females: 102.4; Marriage status: 23.8% never married, 50.7% now married, 1.9% separated, 11.8% widowed, 13.7% divorced; Foreign born: 10.6%; Speak English only: 85.8%; With disability: 20.9%; Veterans: 12.5%; Ancestry: 19.0% German, 14.2% English, 12.5% Irish, 8.4% American, 5.2% French
Employment: 15.0% management, business, and financial, 2.3% computer, engineering, and science, 5.1% education, legal, community service, arts, and media, 6.1% healthcare practitioners, 14.9% service, 20.9% sales and office, 13.5% natural resources, construction, and maintenance, 22.1% production, transportation, and material moving
Income: Per capita: $26,752; Median household: $35,236; Average household: $62,401; Households with income of $100,000 or more: 14.6%; Poverty rate: 15.8%
Educational Attainment: High school diploma or higher: 83.5%; Bachelor's degree or higher: 9.9%; Graduate/professional degree or higher: 2.4%
Housing: Homeownership rate: 77.4%; Median home value: $148,600; Median year structure built: 1985; Homeowner vacancy rate: 2.8%; Median gross rent: $1,273 per month; Rental vacancy rate: 8.9%
Health Insurance: 83.9% have insurance; 61.6% have private insurance; 35.5% have public insurance; 16.1% do not have insurance; 0.5% of children under 18 do not have insurance
Transportation: Commute: 91.7% car, 2.5% public transportation, 1.4% walk, 0.0% work from home; Median travel time to work: 52.0 minutes

RANCHO CUCAMONGA (city). Covers a land area of 39.851 square miles and a water area of 0.020 square miles. Located at 34.12° N. Lat; 117.56° W. Long. Elevation is 1,207 feet.
History: This city was incorporated in 1977 and is located east of Los Angeles. Its name originates from the Kucamongan people who were part of the largest groups of indigenous people in North America.
Population: 165,269; Growth (since 2000): 29.4%; Density: 4,147.2 persons per square mile; Race: 62.0% White, 9.2% Black/African American, 10.4% Asian, 0.7% American Indian/Alaska Native, 0.3% Native Hawaiian/Other Pacific Islander, 5.4% Two or more races, 34.9% Hispanic of any race; Average household size: 2.98; Median age: 34.5; Age under 18: 25.7%; Age 65 and over: 7.9%; Males per 100 females: 97.6; Marriage status: 33.7% never married, 52.0% now married, 2.3% separated, 4.1% widowed, 10.2% divorced; Foreign born: 19.3%; Speak English only: 66.5%; With disability: 8.1%; Veterans: 6.5%; Ancestry: 11.0% German, 7.1% Irish, 6.8% English, 6.3% Italian, 3.1% American
Employment: 17.1% management, business, and financial, 5.0% computer, engineering, and science, 11.4% education, legal, community service, arts, and media, 7.4% healthcare practitioners, 14.5% service, 29.0% sales and office, 7.0% natural resources, construction, and maintenance, 8.8% production, transportation, and material moving
Income: Per capita: $32,209; Median household: $77,835; Average household: $96,152; Households with income of $100,000 or more: 37.6%; Poverty rate: 6.9%
Educational Attainment: High school diploma or higher: 90.9%; Bachelor's degree or higher: 31.8%; Graduate/professional degree or higher: 11.4%

School District(s)

Alta Loma Elementary (KG-08)
2012-13 Enrollment: 6,062 . . . . (909) 484-5151
Baldy View Rop
2012-13 Enrollment: n/a . . . . (909) 980-6490
Central Elementary (KG-08)
2012-13 Enrollment: 4,692 . . . . (909) 989-8541
Chaffey Joint Union High (09-12)
2012-13 Enrollment: 25,020 . . . . (909) 988-8511
Cucamonga Elementary (KG-08)
2012-13 Enrollment: 2,530 . . . . (909) 987-8942
Etiwanda Elementary (KG-08)
2012-13 Enrollment: 13,163 . . . . (909) 899-2451
San Bernardino County Office of Education (KG-12)
2012-13 Enrollment: 3,173 . . . . (909) 888-3228

Two-year College(s)

Chaffey College (Public)
Fall 2013 Enrollment: 19,211 . . . . (909) 652-6000
2013-14 Tuition: In-state $1,153; Out-of-state $6,145

Universal Technical Institute of California Inc (Private, For-profit)
Fall 2013 Enrollment: 2,466 . . . . (909) 484-1929

Housing: Homeownership rate: 64.8%; Median home value: $358,800; Median year structure built: 1987; Homeowner vacancy rate: 1.6%; Median gross rent: $1,442 per month; Rental vacancy rate: 5.2%

Health Insurance: 87.4% have insurance; 74.9% have private insurance; 18.3% have public insurance; 12.6% do not have insurance; 5.9% of children under 18 do not have insurance

Safety: Violent crime rate: 19.2 per 10,000 population; Property crime rate: 222.0 per 10,000 population

Transportation: Commute: 92.0% car, 1.8% public transportation, 1.3% walk, 3.5% work from home; Median travel time to work: 30.4 minutes

Additional Information Contacts

City of Rancho Cucamonga . . . . (909) 477-2700
http://www.cityofrc.us

REDLANDS (city). Covers a land area of 36.126 square miles and a water area of 0.301 square miles. Located at 34.05° N. Lat; 117.17° W. Long. Elevation is 1,358 feet.

History: Named for the color of its soil, by E.G. Judson and Frank E. Brown, who plotted the town in 1887. Redlands developed as a residential community and a distribution center for the surrounding citrus farms. The University of Redlands was founded here in 1907 by the Southern California Baptist Convention.

Population: 68,747; Growth (since 2000): 8.1%; Density: 1,903.0 persons per square mile; Race: 69.0% White, 5.2% Black/African American, 7.6% Asian, 0.9% American Indian/Alaska Native, 0.3% Native Hawaiian/Other Pacific Islander, 4.9% Two or more races, 30.3% Hispanic of any race; Average household size: 2.68; Median age: 36.2; Age under 18: 23.7%; Age 65 and over: 13.1%; Males per 100 females: 90.9; Marriage status: 33.2% never married, 50.0% now married, 1.6% separated, 5.4% widowed, 11.4% divorced; Foreign born: 14.0%; Speak English only: 75.1%; With disability: 10.1%; Veterans: 8.5%; Ancestry: 14.7% German, 9.3% Irish, 8.8% English, 4.3% Italian, 3.3% Dutch

Employment: 14.0% management, business, and financial, 5.8% computer, engineering, and science, 16.2% education, legal, community service, arts, and media, 10.7% healthcare practitioners, 15.4% service, 23.4% sales and office, 6.3% natural resources, construction, and maintenance, 8.2% production, transportation, and material moving

Income: Per capita: $32,389; Median household: $66,835; Average household: $87,922; Households with income of $100,000 or more: 31.4%; Poverty rate: 12.5%

Educational Attainment: High school diploma or higher: 90.1%; Bachelor's degree or higher: 38.2%; Graduate/professional degree or higher: 17.1%

School District(s)

Colton-Redlands-Yucaipa Rop
2012-13 Enrollment: n/a . . . . (909) 793-3115

Gorman Elementary (KG-12)
2012-13 Enrollment: 1,740 . . . . (661) 248-6441

Redlands Unified (KG-12)
2012-13 Enrollment: 21,379 . . . . (909) 307-5300

Four-year College(s)

University of Redlands (Private, Not-for-profit)
Fall 2013 Enrollment: 5,147 . . . . (909) 793-2121
2013-14 Tuition: In-state $41,290; Out-of-state $41,290

Two-year College(s)

Ashdown College of Health Sciences (Private, For-profit)
Fall 2013 Enrollment: 41 . . . . (909) 793-4263
2013-14 Tuition: In-state $11,845; Out-of-state $11,845

Community Christian College (Private, Not-for-profit)
Fall 2013 Enrollment: 60 . . . . (909) 335-8863
2013-14 Tuition: In-state $11,148; Out-of-state $11,148

Vocational/Technical School(s)

Colton-Redlands-Yucaipa Regional Occupational Program (Public)
Fall 2013 Enrollment: 101 . . . . (909) 793-3115
2013-14 Tuition: $18,043

Salon Success Academy-Redlands (Private, For-profit)
Fall 2013 Enrollment: 93 . . . . (909) 982-4200
2013-14 Tuition: $18,400

Housing: Homeownership rate: 60.8%; Median home value: $285,500; Median year structure built: 1975; Homeowner vacancy rate: 2.2%; Median gross rent: $1,113 per month; Rental vacancy rate: 7.9%

Health Insurance: 87.6% have insurance; 69.8% have private insurance; 26.9% have public insurance; 12.4% do not have insurance; 7.4% of children under 18 do not have insurance

Hospitals: Redlands Community Hospital (172 beds)

Safety: Violent crime rate: 30.6 per 10,000 population; Property crime rate: 429.7 per 10,000 population

Newspapers: Redlands Daily Facts (daily circulation 6500)

Transportation: Commute: 89.1% car, 1.6% public transportation, 3.5% walk, 3.9% work from home; Median travel time to work: 22.7 minutes

Additional Information Contacts

City of Redlands . . . . (909) 798-7510
http://www.cityofredlands.org

RIALTO (city). Covers a land area of 22.351 square miles and a water area of 0.014 square miles. Located at 34.11° N. Lat; 117.39° W. Long. Elevation is 1,257 feet.

History: Named for Rivus Altus, the grand canal of Venice, in 1887. Rialto developed around several orange-packing plants in an area of citrus groves and vineyards.

Population: 99,171; Growth (since 2000): 7.9%; Density: 4,437.0 persons per square mile; Race: 44.0% White, 16.4% Black/African American, 2.3% Asian, 1.1% American Indian/Alaska Native, 0.4% Native Hawaiian/Other Pacific Islander, 4.7% Two or more races, 67.6% Hispanic of any race; Average household size: 3.92; Median age: 28.3; Age under 18: 32.9%; Age 65 and over: 7.0%; Males per 100 females: 94.7; Marriage status: 39.4% never married, 47.3% now married, 3.3% separated, 4.9% widowed, 8.4% divorced; Foreign born: 26.4%; Speak English only: 43.1%; With disability: 10.7%; Veterans: 5.2%; Ancestry: 3.6% German, 2.1% Irish, 2.0% American, 1.8% English, 1.7% Italian

Employment: 5.4% management, business, and financial, 1.8% computer, engineering, and science, 6.7% education, legal, community service, arts, and media, 2.3% healthcare practitioners, 21.1% service, 26.8% sales and office, 11.4% natural resources, construction, and maintenance, 24.6% production, transportation, and material moving

Income: Per capita: $15,948; Median household: $49,593; Average household: $59,804; Households with income of $100,000 or more: 15.0%; Poverty rate: 19.1%

Educational Attainment: High school diploma or higher: 68.5%; Bachelor's degree or higher: 9.9%; Graduate/professional degree or higher: 3.4%

School District(s)

Rialto Unified (KG-12)
2012-13 Enrollment: 26,596 . . . . (909) 820-7700

San Bernardino County Office of Education (KG-12)
2012-13 Enrollment: 3,173 . . . . (909) 888-3228

Housing: Homeownership rate: 64.6%; Median home value: $180,500; Median year structure built: 1981; Homeowner vacancy rate: 3.1%; Median gross rent: $1,081 per month; Rental vacancy rate: 9.7%

Health Insurance: 74.8% have insurance; 43.5% have private insurance; 36.0% have public insurance; 25.2% do not have insurance; 11.8% of children under 18 do not have insurance

Safety: Violent crime rate: 42.3 per 10,000 population; Property crime rate: 265.0 per 10,000 population

Transportation: Commute: 92.4% car, 2.9% public transportation, 0.7% walk, 3.1% work from home; Median travel time to work: 32.3 minutes

Additional Information Contacts

City of Rialto . . . . (909) 820-2525
http://www.ci.rialto.ca.us

RIMFOREST (unincorporated postal area)

ZCTA: 92378

Covers a land area of 0.829 square miles and a water area of 0 square miles. Located at 34.23° N. Lat; 117.23° W. Long. Elevation is 5,659 feet.

Population: 183; Growth (since 2000): n/a; Density: 220.8 persons per square mile; Race: 78.7% White, 1.1% Black/African American, 2.2% Asian, 2.2% American Indian/Alaska Native, 0.5% Native Hawaiian/Other Pacific Islander, 3.3% Two or more races, 25.1% Hispanic of any race; Average household size: 2.73; Median age: 38.5; Age under 18: 25.7%; Age 65 and over: 7.7%; Males per 100 females: 94.7

Housing: Homeownership rate: 71.6%; Homeowner vacancy rate: 0.0%; Rental vacancy rate: 4.8%

RUNNING SPRINGS (CDP). Covers a land area of 4.204 square miles and a water area of 0.009 square miles. Located at 34.21° N. Lat; 117.10° W. Long. Elevation is 6,109 feet.

Population: 4,862; Growth (since 2000): -5.1%; Density: 1,156.5 persons per square mile; Race: 89.0% White, 0.5% Black/African American, 1.0% Asian, 1.0% American Indian/Alaska Native, 0.1% Native Hawaiian/Other Pacific Islander, 5.5% Two or more races, 14.3% Hispanic of any race; Average household size: 2.50; Median age: 41.7; Age under 18: 23.0%; Age 65 and over: 11.1%; Males per 100 females: 105.5; Marriage status: 27.6% never married, 56.5% now married, 0.6% separated, 3.0% widowed, 12.9% divorced; Foreign born: 4.9%; Speak English only: 88.6%; With disability: 7.0%; Veterans: 10.9%; Ancestry: 23.3% German, 19.1% Irish, 14.4% English, 5.5% American, 4.2% Italian

Employment: 17.3% management, business, and financial, 4.8% computer, engineering, and science, 9.5% education, legal, community service, arts, and media, 7.8% healthcare practitioners, 19.7% service, 19.8% sales and office, 9.8% natural resources, construction, and maintenance, 11.2% production, transportation, and material moving

Income: Per capita: $26,338; Median household: $59,712; Average household: $68,360; Households with income of $100,000 or more: 22.6%; Poverty rate: 10.9%

Educational Attainment: High school diploma or higher: 94.0%; Bachelor's degree or higher: 21.7%; Graduate/professional degree or higher: 7.3%

School District(s)

Rim of the World Unified (KG-12)
2012-13 Enrollment: 4,013 . . . . (909) 336-2031

Housing: Homeownership rate: 73.0%; Median home value: $209,600; Median year structure built: 1972; Homeowner vacancy rate: 5.3%; Median gross rent: $1,155 per month; Rental vacancy rate: 12.6%

Health Insurance: 83.4% have insurance; 71.1% have private insurance; 24.0% have public insurance; 16.6% do not have insurance; 6.1% of children under 18 do not have insurance

Transportation: Commute: 88.6% car, 0.7% public transportation, 2.0% walk, 8.5% work from home; Median travel time to work: 36.1 minutes

SAN ANTONIO HEIGHTS (CDP). Covers a land area of 2.458 square miles and a water area of 0.161 square miles. Located at 34.16° N. Lat; 117.66° W. Long. Elevation is 2,103 feet.

Population: 3,371; Growth (since 2000): 8.0%; Density: 1,371.7 persons per square mile; Race: 82.0% White, 2.0% Black/African American, 8.4% Asian, 0.7% American Indian/Alaska Native, 0.4% Native Hawaiian/Other Pacific Islander, 3.0% Two or more races, 18.2% Hispanic of any race; Average household size: 2.80; Median age: 46.3; Age under 18: 20.8%; Age 65 and over: 16.9%; Males per 100 females: 101.1; Marriage status: 29.6% never married, 57.9% now married, 0.8% separated, 4.3% widowed, 8.1% divorced; Foreign born: 16.3%; Speak English only: 77.1%; With disability: 9.4%; Veterans: 10.6%; Ancestry: 24.0% German, 14.6% English, 9.6% Irish, 7.3% American, 5.2% French

Employment: 22.9% management, business, and financial, 2.9% computer, engineering, and science, 18.6% education, legal, community service, arts, and media, 11.2% healthcare practitioners, 9.5% service, 25.0% sales and office, 3.8% natural resources, construction, and maintenance, 6.1% production, transportation, and material moving

Income: Per capita: $53,915; Median household: $94,875; Average household: $151,560; Households with income of $100,000 or more: 46.8%; Poverty rate: 2.9%

Educational Attainment: High school diploma or higher: 92.9%; Bachelor's degree or higher: 46.0%; Graduate/professional degree or higher: 19.9%

Housing: Homeownership rate: 83.9%; Median home value: $486,900; Median year structure built: 1970; Homeowner vacancy rate: 0.8%; Median gross rent: $1,351 per month; Rental vacancy rate: 5.4%

Health Insurance: 89.4% have insurance; 80.1% have private insurance; 20.8% have public insurance; 10.6% do not have insurance; 16.8% of children under 18 do not have insurance

Transportation: Commute: 82.1% car, 3.0% public transportation, 2.5% walk, 4.7% work from home; Median travel time to work: 30.5 minutes

SAN BERNARDINO (city). County seat. Covers a land area of 59.201 square miles and a water area of 0.444 square miles. Located at 34.14° N. Lat; 117.30° W. Long. Elevation is 1,053 feet.

History: Named in 1810 for St. Bernardino of Siena, Italy, a 15th-century Franciscan by a group from San Gabriel Mission, who visited here on the feast day of Saint Bernardine of Siena. In 1851 Captain Jefferson Hunt and a group of Mormons purchased Rancho San Bernardino and laid out a city.

Population: 209,924; Growth (since 2000): 13.2%; Density: 3,546.0 persons per square mile; Race: 45.6% White, 15.0% Black/African American, 4.0% Asian, 1.3% American Indian/Alaska Native, 0.4% Native Hawaiian/Other Pacific Islander, 5.1% Two or more races, 60.0% Hispanic of any race; Average household size: 3.42; Median age: 28.5; Age under 18: 32.0%; Age 65 and over: 7.9%; Males per 100 females: 97.2; Marriage status: 43.7% never married, 40.6% now married, 3.9% separated, 5.0% widowed, 10.7% divorced; Foreign born: 22.7%; Speak English only: 53.3%; With disability: 13.2%; Veterans: 5.8%; Ancestry: 4.9% German, 3.0% Irish, 2.6% English, 2.3% American, 1.3% Italian

Employment: 7.2% management, business, and financial, 1.6% computer, engineering, and science, 7.9% education, legal, community service, arts, and media, 3.8% healthcare practitioners, 23.3% service, 25.0% sales and office, 12.1% natural resources, construction, and maintenance, 19.0% production, transportation, and material moving

Income: Per capita: $14,879; Median household: $38,385; Average household: $50,025; Households with income of $100,000 or more: 11.6%; Poverty rate: 32.4%

Educational Attainment: High school diploma or higher: 67.7%; Bachelor's degree or higher: 11.2%; Graduate/professional degree or higher: 3.6%

School District(s)

Redlands Unified (KG-12)
2012-13 Enrollment: 21,379 . . . . (909) 307-5300
San Bernardino City Unified (KG-12)
2012-13 Enrollment: 54,102 . . . . (909) 381-1100
San Bernardino County Office of Education (KG-12)
2012-13 Enrollment: 3,173 . . . . (909) 888-3228
San Bernardino County Rop
2012-13 Enrollment: n/a . . . . (909) 252-4559

Four-year College(s)

California State University-San Bernardino (Public)
Fall 2013 Enrollment: 18,398 . . . . (909) 537-5000
2013-14 Tuition: In-state $6,550; Out-of-state $17,710
ITT Technical Institute-San Bernardino (Private, For-profit)
Fall 2013 Enrollment: 730 . . . . (909) 806-4600
2013-14 Tuition: In-state $18,048; Out-of-state $18,048
The Art Institute of California-Argosy University Inland Empire (Private, For-profit)
Fall 2013 Enrollment: 2,307 . . . . (909) 915-2100
2013-14 Tuition: In-state $18,748; Out-of-state $18,748

Two-year College(s)

Concorde Career College-San Bernardino (Private, For-profit)
Fall 2013 Enrollment: 753 . . . . (909) 884-8891
Everest College-San Bernardino (Private, For-profit)
Fall 2013 Enrollment: 747 . . . . (909) 777-3300
2013-14 Tuition: In-state $13,572; Out-of-state $13,572
San Bernardino Valley College (Public)
Fall 2013 Enrollment: 12,329 . . . . (909) 384-4400
2013-14 Tuition: In-state $1,238; Out-of-state $4,420

Vocational/Technical School(s)

CET-San Bernardino (Private, Not-for-profit)
Fall 2013 Enrollment: 103 . . . . (408) 287-7924
2013-14 Tuition: $10,165
Salon Success Academy-San Bernardino (Private, For-profit)
Fall 2013 Enrollment: 30 . . . . (909) 982-4200
2013-14 Tuition: $18,400

Housing: Homeownership rate: 50.3%; Median home value: $152,800; Median year structure built: 1969; Homeowner vacancy rate: 3.2%; Median gross rent: $930 per month; Rental vacancy rate: 9.5%

Health Insurance: 75.3% have insurance; 39.4% have private insurance; 41.4% have public insurance; 24.7% do not have insurance; 10.1% of children under 18 do not have insurance

Hospitals: Community Hospital of San Bernardino (374 beds); Saint Bernardine Medical Center (463 beds)

Safety: Violent crime rate: 90.9 per 10,000 population; Property crime rate: 438.1 per 10,000 population

Newspapers: Precinct Reporter Group (weekly circulation 80000); San Bernardino Sun (daily circulation 62300)

Transportation: Commute: 89.6% car, 3.0% public transportation, 2.2% walk, 3.8% work from home; Median travel time to work: 27.0 minutes; Amtrak: Train service available.

Airports: San Bernardino International (general aviation)

Additional Information Contacts
City of San Bernardino .... (909) 384-7272
http://www.ci.san-bernardino.ca.us

SEARLES VALLEY (CDP). Covers a land area of 10.494 square miles and a water area of 0 square miles. Located at 35.77° N. Lat; 117.40° W. Long. Elevation is 2,090 feet.
Population: 1,739; Growth (since 2000): -7.7%; Density: 165.7 persons per square mile; Race: 80.8% White, 4.0% Black/African American, 0.9% Asian, 3.2% American Indian/Alaska Native, 0.3% Native Hawaiian/Other Pacific Islander, 6.0% Two or more races, 16.8% Hispanic of any race; Average household size: 2.41; Median age: 40.7; Age under 18: 25.1%; Age 65 and over: 15.8%; Males per 100 females: 104.1
Housing: Homeownership rate: 60.8%; Homeowner vacancy rate: 1.5%; Rental vacancy rate: 8.4%

SILVER LAKES (CDP). Covers a land area of 5.172 square miles and a water area of 0.398 square miles. Located at 34.75° N. Lat; 117.35° W. Long. Elevation is 2,444 feet.
Population: 5,623; Growth (since 2000): n/a; Density: 1,087.2 persons per square mile; Race: 81.2% White, 5.6% Black/African American, 3.5% Asian, 0.7% American Indian/Alaska Native, 0.3% Native Hawaiian/Other Pacific Islander, 3.9% Two or more races, 16.1% Hispanic of any race; Average household size: 2.51; Median age: 46.5; Age under 18: 22.5%; Age 65 and over: 23.0%; Males per 100 females: 96.7; Marriage status: 19.1% never married, 68.1% now married, 1.5% separated, 4.0% widowed, 8.8% divorced; Foreign born: 7.2%; Speak English only: 92.1%; With disability: 11.2%; Veterans: 18.6%; Ancestry: 15.8% German, 13.3% Italian, 11.9% English, 10.5% Irish, 5.2% Scottish
Employment: 5.2% management, business, and financial, 3.0% computer, engineering, and science, 21.1% education, legal, community service, arts, and media, 5.9% healthcare practitioners, 16.8% service, 29.8% sales and office, 10.3% natural resources, construction, and maintenance, 7.9% production, transportation, and material moving
Income: Per capita: $25,460; Median household: $64,771; Average household: $67,585; Households with income of $100,000 or more: 20.7%; Poverty rate: 16.9%
Educational Attainment: High school diploma or higher: 91.6%; Bachelor's degree or higher: 25.8%; Graduate/professional degree or higher: 8.6%
Housing: Homeownership rate: 75.9%; Median home value: $189,300; Median year structure built: 1989; Homeowner vacancy rate: 7.3%; Median gross rent: $1,377 per month; Rental vacancy rate: 12.0%
Health Insurance: 90.6% have insurance; 65.1% have private insurance; 37.4% have public insurance; 9.4% do not have insurance; 0.0% of children under 18 do not have insurance
Transportation: Commute: 95.8% car, 0.0% public transportation, 2.2% walk, 1.9% work from home; Median travel time to work: 31.6 minutes

SKYFOREST (unincorporated postal area)
ZCTA: 92385
Covers a land area of 8.414 square miles and a water area of 0 square miles. Located at 34.21° N. Lat; 117.19° W. Long. Elevation is 5,741 feet.
Population: 313; Growth (since 2000): n/a; Density: 37.2 persons per square mile; Race: 87.5% White, 2.9% Black/African American, 1.6% Asian, 0.3% American Indian/Alaska Native, 1.3% Native Hawaiian/Other Pacific Islander, 2.6% Two or more races, 7.0% Hispanic of any race; Average household size: 2.37; Median age: 50.1; Age under 18: 19.2%; Age 65 and over: 15.3%; Males per 100 females: 92.0
Housing: Homeownership rate: 80.3%; Homeowner vacancy rate: 6.1%; Rental vacancy rate: 17.6%

SPRING VALLEY LAKE (CDP). Covers a land area of 2.969 square miles and a water area of 0.564 square miles. Located at 34.50° N. Lat; 117.27° W. Long. Elevation is 2,779 feet.
Population: 8,220; Growth (since 2000): n/a; Density: 2,768.8 persons per square mile; Race: 78.5% White, 4.9% Black/African American, 4.6% Asian, 0.7% American Indian/Alaska Native, 0.3% Native Hawaiian/Other Pacific Islander, 5.2% Two or more races, 18.6% Hispanic of any race; Average household size: 2.68; Median age: 41.3; Age under 18: 23.5%; Age 65 and over: 16.5%; Males per 100 females: 95.2; Marriage status: 24.5% never married, 55.3% now married, 2.1% separated, 8.0% widowed, 12.2% divorced; Foreign born: 8.6%; Speak English only: 89.6%; With disability: 11.3%; Veterans: 9.8%; Ancestry: 15.6% English, 15.1% German, 12.5% Irish, 8.1% Italian, 5.6% French
Employment: 14.7% management, business, and financial, 2.5% computer, engineering, and science, 15.3% education, legal, community service, arts, and media, 6.0% healthcare practitioners, 19.7% service, 28.4% sales and office, 6.1% natural resources, construction, and maintenance, 7.3% production, transportation, and material moving
Income: Per capita: $22,947; Median household: $53,862; Average household: $65,282; Households with income of $100,000 or more: 21.1%; Poverty rate: 11.2%
Educational Attainment: High school diploma or higher: 95.2%; Bachelor's degree or higher: 16.6%; Graduate/professional degree or higher: 7.3%
Housing: Homeownership rate: 74.0%; Median home value: $194,600; Median year structure built: 1986; Homeowner vacancy rate: 3.2%; Median gross rent: $1,453 per month; Rental vacancy rate: 7.7%
Health Insurance: 89.0% have insurance; 70.0% have private insurance; 26.0% have public insurance; 11.0% do not have insurance; 3.9% of children under 18 do not have insurance
Transportation: Commute: 95.2% car, 0.0% public transportation, 0.9% walk, 3.0% work from home; Median travel time to work: 23.8 minutes

SUGARLOAF (unincorporated postal area)
ZCTA: 92386
Covers a land area of 1.917 square miles and a water area of 0 square miles. Located at 34.24° N. Lat; 116.83° W. Long. Elevation is 7,093 feet.
Population: 2,270; Growth (since 2000): 25.0%; Density: 1,183.9 persons per square mile; Race: 85.2% White, 0.5% Black/African American, 0.8% Asian, 2.6% American Indian/Alaska Native, 0.2% Native Hawaiian/Other Pacific Islander, 5.8% Two or more races, 17.5% Hispanic of any race; Average household size: 2.33; Median age: 41.7; Age under 18: 23.2%; Age 65 and over: 13.9%; Males per 100 females: 105.1
Housing: Homeownership rate: 61.6%; Homeowner vacancy rate: 11.5%; Rental vacancy rate: 8.2%

TWENTYNINE PALMS (city). Covers a land area of 59.143 square miles and a water area of 0 square miles. Located at 34.15° N. Lat; 116.07° W. Long. Elevation is 1,988 feet.
History: Named for the area's 29 Washingtonia palm trees, counted by the surveyor, in 1852. Headquarters for Joshua Tree National Monument.
Population: 25,048; Growth (since 2000): 69.7%; Density: 423.5 persons per square mile; Race: 71.6% White, 8.2% Black/African American, 3.9% Asian, 1.3% American Indian/Alaska Native, 1.4% Native Hawaiian/Other Pacific Islander, 6.9% Two or more races, 20.8% Hispanic of any race; Average household size: 2.68; Median age: 23.5; Age under 18: 25.6%; Age 65 and over: 5.8%; Males per 100 females: 129.0; Marriage status: 35.5% never married, 51.9% now married, 3.5% separated, 2.4% widowed, 10.2% divorced; Foreign born: 5.5%; Speak English only: 86.6%; With disability: 13.6%; Veterans: 21.4%; Ancestry: 18.2% German, 15.4% Irish, 7.7% English, 6.1% European, 5.2% Italian
Employment: 8.9% management, business, and financial, 3.8% computer, engineering, and science, 9.1% education, legal, community service, arts, and media, 3.8% healthcare practitioners, 27.3% service, 27.1% sales and office, 11.1% natural resources, construction, and maintenance, 8.9% production, transportation, and material moving
Income: Per capita: $20,615; Median household: $41,485; Average household: $52,547; Households with income of $100,000 or more: 10.8%; Poverty rate: 16.6%
Educational Attainment: High school diploma or higher: 90.1%; Bachelor's degree or higher: 20.0%; Graduate/professional degree or higher: 6.2%

School District(s)
Morongo Unified (KG-12)
2012-13 Enrollment: 8,905 .... (760) 367-9191
Housing: Homeownership rate: 33.8%; Median home value: $138,000; Median year structure built: 1980; Homeowner vacancy rate: 3.6%; Median gross rent: $929 per month; Rental vacancy rate: 9.2%
Health Insurance: 90.9% have insurance; 67.5% have private insurance; 33.5% have public insurance; 9.1% do not have insurance; 1.8% of children under 18 do not have insurance
Safety: Violent crime rate: 28.6 per 10,000 population; Property crime rate: 136.2 per 10,000 population
Newspapers: The Desert Trail (weekly circulation 3500)
Transportation: Commute: 77.0% car, 0.6% public transportation, 12.7% walk, 6.6% work from home; Median travel time to work: 14.9 minutes
Airports: Twentynine Palms (general aviation)
Additional Information Contacts

City of Twentynine Palms . . . . (760) 367-6799
http://www.ci.twentynine-palms.ca.us

TWIN PEAKS (unincorporated postal area)

ZCTA: 92391

Covers a land area of 2.334 square miles and a water area of 0 square miles. Located at 34.24° N. Lat; 117.23° W. Long. Elevation is 5,777 feet.

Population: 2,534; Growth (since 2000): n/a; Density: 1,085.5 persons per square mile; Race: 83.4% White, 0.7% Black/African American, 1.1% Asian, 1.5% American Indian/Alaska Native, 0.2% Native Hawaiian/Other Pacific Islander, 4.8% Two or more races, 29.9% Hispanic of any race; Average household size: 2.77; Median age: 35.8; Age under 18: 28.8%; Age 65 and over: 9.8%; Males per 100 females: 108.2; Marriage status: 34.5% never married, 46.4% now married, 3.7% separated, 9.8% widowed, 9.3% divorced; Foreign born: 15.0%; Speak English only: 73.6%; With disability: 8.9%; Veterans: 6.6%; Ancestry: 15.3% Irish, 12.4% German, 10.6% English, 9.4% Scottish, 7.0% French

Employment: 7.7% management, business, and financial, 0.0% computer, engineering, and science, 10.2% education, legal, community service, arts, and media, 7.9% healthcare practitioners, 46.7% service, 16.6% sales and office, 10.6% natural resources, construction, and maintenance, 0.4% production, transportation, and material moving

Income: Per capita: $19,620; Median household: $41,042; Average household: $57,162; Households with income of $100,000 or more: 27.2%; Poverty rate: 14.6%

Educational Attainment: High school diploma or higher: 81.8%; Bachelor's degree or higher: 17.4%; Graduate/professional degree or higher: 8.1%

School District(s)

Rim of the World Unified (KG-12)
2012-13 Enrollment: 4,013 . . . . (909) 336-2031

Housing: Homeownership rate: 62.0%; Median home value: $211,900; Median year structure built: 1966; Homeowner vacancy rate: 8.0%; Median gross rent: $1,315 per month; Rental vacancy rate: 8.7%

Health Insurance: 73.5% have insurance; 57.5% have private insurance; 20.8% have public insurance; 26.5% do not have insurance; 11.0% of children under 18 do not have insurance

Transportation: Commute: 89.5% car, 0.0% public transportation, 3.3% walk, 5.8% work from home; Median travel time to work: 30.3 minutes

UPLAND (city). Covers a land area of 15.617 square miles and a water area of 0.034 square miles. Located at 34.12° N. Lat; 117.66° W. Long. Elevation is 1,237 feet.

History: Named for its location at a higher elevation than nearby towns, in 1902. Upland developed around fruit-packing plants serving the surrounding area of orange and lemon orchards.

Population: 73,732; Growth (since 2000): 7.8%; Density: 4,721.3 persons per square mile; Race: 65.6% White, 7.3% Black/African American, 8.4% Asian, 0.7% American Indian/Alaska Native, 0.2% Native Hawaiian/Other Pacific Islander, 4.8% Two or more races, 38.0% Hispanic of any race; Average household size: 2.83; Median age: 36.1; Age under 18: 24.5%; Age 65 and over: 12.1%; Males per 100 females: 93.1; Marriage status: 34.5% never married, 49.8% now married, 2.3% separated, 5.1% widowed, 10.6% divorced; Foreign born: 18.5%; Speak English only: 66.2%; With disability: 9.6%; Veterans: 7.5%; Ancestry: 9.3% American, 9.0% German, 6.7% Irish, 6.3% English, 5.9% European

Employment: 15.8% management, business, and financial, 4.2% computer, engineering, and science, 11.5% education, legal, community service, arts, and media, 5.1% healthcare practitioners, 19.0% service, 27.7% sales and office, 6.4% natural resources, construction, and maintenance, 10.4% production, transportation, and material moving

Income: Per capita: $28,604; Median household: $62,667; Average household: $78,679; Households with income of $100,000 or more: 27.7%; Poverty rate: 13.5%

Educational Attainment: High school diploma or higher: 87.3%; Bachelor's degree or higher: 29.9%; Graduate/professional degree or higher: 10.8%

School District(s)

Upland Unified (KG-12)
2012-13 Enrollment: 11,908 . . . . (909) 985-1864

Four-year College(s)

Westwood College-Inland Empire (Private, For-profit)
Fall 2013 Enrollment: 979 . . . . (909) 931-7550
2013-14 Tuition: In-state $15,134; Out-of-state $15,134

Vocational/Technical School(s)

Salon Success Academy-Upland (Private, For-profit)
Fall 2013 Enrollment: 228 . . . . (909) 982-4200
2013-14 Tuition: $18,400

Housing: Homeownership rate: 57.9%; Median home value: $410,800; Median year structure built: 1976; Homeowner vacancy rate: 1.6%; Median gross rent: $1,174 per month; Rental vacancy rate: 8.3%

Health Insurance: 83.5% have insurance; 62.6% have private insurance; 29.0% have public insurance; 16.5% do not have insurance; 10.8% of children under 18 do not have insurance

Hospitals: San Antonio Community Hospital (329 beds)

Safety: Violent crime rate: 21.5 per 10,000 population; Property crime rate: 295.3 per 10,000 population

Transportation: Commute: 91.6% car, 2.6% public transportation, 1.2% walk, 3.0% work from home; Median travel time to work: 29.8 minutes

Additional Information Contacts

City of Upland . . . . (909) 931-4100
http://www.ci.upland.ca.us

VICTORVILLE (city). Covers a land area of 73.178 square miles and a water area of 0.563 square miles. Located at 34.53° N. Lat; 117.35° W. Long. Elevation is 2,726 feet.

History: Named for J.N. Victor, construction superintendent of the California Southern Railroad in the 1880s. First called Mormon Crossing from 1878 to 1885, the name was changed to Victor when mining commenced. By 1914 mining had been replaced by filming, with Victorville used as the locale for several hundred of Hollywood's "wild-west" movies.

Population: 115,903; Growth (since 2000): 81.0%; Density: 1,583.9 persons per square mile; Race: 48.5% White, 16.8% Black/African American, 4.0% Asian, 1.4% American Indian/Alaska Native, 0.4% Native Hawaiian/Other Pacific Islander, 6.3% Two or more races, 47.8% Hispanic of any race; Average household size: 3.40; Median age: 29.5; Age under 18: 32.8%; Age 65 and over: 8.1%; Males per 100 females: 100.4; Marriage status: 36.2% never married, 47.3% now married, 3.7% separated, 4.7% widowed, 11.8% divorced; Foreign born: 17.0%; Speak English only: 62.6%; With disability: 10.7%; Veterans: 7.4%; Ancestry: 7.4% German, 6.3% Irish, 5.6% English, 3.0% Italian, 1.8% American

Employment: 9.2% management, business, and financial, 2.3% computer, engineering, and science, 8.6% education, legal, community service, arts, and media, 3.6% healthcare practitioners, 22.6% service, 26.5% sales and office, 12.8% natural resources, construction, and maintenance, 14.5% production, transportation, and material moving

Income: Per capita: $16,477; Median household: $50,034; Average household: $58,269; Households with income of $100,000 or more: 16.5%; Poverty rate: 25.3%

Educational Attainment: High school diploma or higher: 77.7%; Bachelor's degree or higher: 10.8%; Graduate/professional degree or higher: 3.9%

School District(s)

Adelanto Elementary (KG-12)
2012-13 Enrollment: 9,054 . . . . (760) 246-8691

Hesperia Unified (KG-12)
2012-13 Enrollment: 23,448 . . . . (760) 244-4411

Oro Grande Elementary (KG-12)
2012-13 Enrollment: 3,594 . . . . (760) 243-5884

Snowline Joint Unified (KG-12)
2012-13 Enrollment: 8,071 . . . . (760) 868-5817

Victor Elementary (KG-06)
2012-13 Enrollment: 11,813 . . . . (760) 245-1691

Victor Valley Union High (07-12)
2012-13 Enrollment: 14,781 . . . . (760) 955-3201

Two-year College(s)

Victor Valley College (Public)
Fall 2013 Enrollment: 11,504 . . . . (760) 245-4271
2013-14 Tuition: In-state $1,114; Out-of-state $4,444

Vocational/Technical School(s)

Mojave Barber College (Private, For-profit)
Fall 2013 Enrollment: n/a . . . . (760) 955-2934

Victor Valley Beauty College Inc (Private, For-profit)
Fall 2013 Enrollment: 105 . . . . (760) 245-2522
2013-14 Tuition: $16,884

Housing: Homeownership rate: 61.9%; Median home value: $137,700; Median year structure built: 1993; Homeowner vacancy rate: 4.9%; Median gross rent: $1,098 per month; Rental vacancy rate: 11.1%

Health Insurance: 81.6% have insurance; 50.6% have private insurance; 37.3% have public insurance; 18.4% do not have insurance; 7.0% of children under 18 do not have insurance
Hospitals: Desert Valley Hospital (83 beds); Victor Valley Global Medical Center (119 beds)
Safety: Violent crime rate: 53.5 per 10,000 population; Property crime rate: 342.2 per 10,000 population
Newspapers: Daily Press (daily circulation 30400)
Transportation: Commute: 91.8% car, 1.1% public transportation, 0.9% walk, 5.2% work from home; Median travel time to work: 35.6 minutes; Amtrak: Train and bus service available.
Airports: Southern California Logistics (general aviation)
Additional Information Contacts
City of Victorville . . . . (760) 955-5000
http://ci.victorville.ca.us

WRIGHTWOOD (CDP). Covers a land area of 5.926 square miles and a water area of 0.003 square miles. Located at 34.35° N. Lat; 117.63° W. Long. Elevation is 5,935 feet.
Population: 4,525; Growth (since 2000): 17.9%; Density: 763.6 persons per square mile; Race: 91.2% White, 0.8% Black/African American, 1.1% Asian, 0.6% American Indian/Alaska Native, 0.2% Native Hawaiian/Other Pacific Islander, 3.6% Two or more races, 11.9% Hispanic of any race; Average household size: 2.44; Median age: 44.3; Age under 18: 23.1%; Age 65 and over: 13.5%; Males per 100 females: 105.5; Marriage status: 22.1% never married, 55.3% now married, 0.7% separated, 3.0% widowed, 19.6% divorced; Foreign born: 2.5%; Speak English only: 94.5%; With disability: 12.0%; Veterans: 16.0%; Ancestry: 18.9% German, 13.7% Irish, 12.8% English, 9.6% Italian, 6.9% Scottish
Employment: 9.8% management, business, and financial, 6.0% computer, engineering, and science, 19.7% education, legal, community service, arts, and media, 5.5% healthcare practitioners, 6.2% service, 31.4% sales and office, 13.4% natural resources, construction, and maintenance, 7.9% production, transportation, and material moving
Income: Per capita: $31,632; Median household: $70,938; Average household: $75,629; Households with income of $100,000 or more: 27.5%; Poverty rate: 4.6%
Educational Attainment: High school diploma or higher: 98.0%; Bachelor's degree or higher: 36.5%; Graduate/professional degree or higher: 14.4%

School District(s)

Snowline Joint Unified (KG-12)
2012-13 Enrollment: 8,071 . . . . (760) 868-5817
Housing: Homeownership rate: 74.8%; Median home value: $253,000; Median year structure built: 1974; Homeowner vacancy rate: 2.8%; Median gross rent: $1,085 per month; Rental vacancy rate: 10.6%
Health Insurance: 87.9% have insurance; 76.3% have private insurance; 23.1% have public insurance; 12.1% do not have insurance; 6.7% of children under 18 do not have insurance
Newspapers: Mountaineer Progress (weekly circulation 4300)
Transportation: Commute: 94.6% car, 0.0% public transportation, 0.0% walk, 4.8% work from home; Median travel time to work: 40.6 minutes

YERMO (unincorporated postal area)

ZCTA: 92398

Covers a land area of 28.019 square miles and a water area of 0.168 square miles. Located at 34.91° N. Lat; 116.85° W. Long. Elevation is 1,929 feet.
Population: 1,379; Growth (since 2000): 15.8%; Density: 49.2 persons per square mile; Race: 75.3% White, 2.8% Black/African American, 2.2% Asian, 2.1% American Indian/Alaska Native, 0.1% Native Hawaiian/Other Pacific Islander, 4.8% Two or more races, 25.2% Hispanic of any race; Average household size: 2.65; Median age: 40.3; Age under 18: 25.2%; Age 65 and over: 13.0%; Males per 100 females: 105.2

School District(s)

Silver Valley Unified (PK-12)
2012-13 Enrollment: 2,395 . . . . (760) 254-2916
Housing: Homeownership rate: 62.3%; Homeowner vacancy rate: 2.4%; Rental vacancy rate: 24.0%

YUCAIPA (city). Covers a land area of 27.888 square miles and a water area of 0.005 square miles. Located at 34.03° N. Lat; 117.04° W. Long. Elevation is 2,618 feet.
Population: 51,367; Growth (since 2000): 24.7%; Density: 1,841.9 persons per square mile; Race: 79.5% White, 1.6% Black/African American, 2.8% Asian, 0.9% American Indian/Alaska Native, 0.1% Native Hawaiian/Other Pacific Islander, 4.1% Two or more races, 27.1% Hispanic of any race; Average household size: 2.79; Median age: 37.8; Age under 18: 26.2%; Age 65 and over: 13.3%; Males per 100 females: 96.8; Marriage status: 28.4% never married, 55.1% now married, 1.8% separated, 5.3% widowed, 11.2% divorced; Foreign born: 9.7%; Speak English only: 81.5%; With disability: 12.3%; Veterans: 9.9%; Ancestry: 19.7% German, 14.0% Irish, 8.4% English, 5.0% Italian, 4.2% American
Employment: 13.9% management, business, and financial, 3.1% computer, engineering, and science, 11.5% education, legal, community service, arts, and media, 7.5% healthcare practitioners, 17.0% service, 26.4% sales and office, 11.4% natural resources, construction, and maintenance, 9.3% production, transportation, and material moving
Income: Per capita: $26,113; Median household: $57,674; Average household: $74,338; Households with income of $100,000 or more: 26.4%; Poverty rate: 13.8%
Educational Attainment: High school diploma or higher: 88.6%; Bachelor's degree or higher: 21.1%; Graduate/professional degree or higher: 7.9%

School District(s)

Yucaipa-Calimesa Joint Unified (KG-12)
2012-13 Enrollment: 9,663 . . . . (909) 797-0174

Two-year College(s)

Crafton Hills College (Public)
Fall 2013 Enrollment: 5,697 . . . . (909) 794-2161
2013-14 Tuition: In-state $1,134; Out-of-state $3,918
Housing: Homeownership rate: 74.1%; Median home value: $218,900; Median year structure built: 1975; Homeowner vacancy rate: 3.0%; Median gross rent: $1,061 per month; Rental vacancy rate: 9.0%
Health Insurance: 83.6% have insurance; 63.4% have private insurance; 28.4% have public insurance; 16.4% do not have insurance; 11.4% of children under 18 do not have insurance
Safety: Violent crime rate: 20.4 per 10,000 population; Property crime rate: 176.3 per 10,000 population
Newspapers: Yucaipa News-Mirror (weekly circulation 20300)
Transportation: Commute: 91.3% car, 1.3% public transportation, 1.2% walk, 4.8% work from home; Median travel time to work: 28.2 minutes
Additional Information Contacts
City of Yucaipa . . . . (909) 797-2489
http://www.yucaipa.org

YUCCA VALLEY (town). Covers a land area of 40.015 square miles and a water area of 0 square miles. Located at 34.12° N. Lat; 116.42° W. Long. Elevation is 3,369 feet.
History: Named for its abundance of Yucca brevifolia (Joshua trees). Joshua Tree National Monument to Southeast.
Population: 20,700; Growth (since 2000): 22.7%; Density: 517.3 persons per square mile; Race: 83.5% White, 3.2% Black/African American, 2.3% Asian, 1.1% American Indian/Alaska Native, 0.2% Native Hawaiian/Other Pacific Islander, 4.0% Two or more races, 17.8% Hispanic of any race; Average household size: 2.48; Median age: 40.6; Age under 18: 23.9%; Age 65 and over: 18.5%; Males per 100 females: 94.7; Marriage status: 28.4% never married, 46.7% now married, 1.6% separated, 10.6% widowed, 14.3% divorced; Foreign born: 7.1%; Speak English only: 88.7%; With disability: 14.9%; Veterans: 17.5%; Ancestry: 18.7% German, 12.3% English, 12.0% Irish, 8.2% European, 6.0% Italian
Employment: 13.1% management, business, and financial, 2.0% computer, engineering, and science, 10.1% education, legal, community service, arts, and media, 6.1% healthcare practitioners, 21.6% service, 26.0% sales and office, 14.9% natural resources, construction, and maintenance, 6.1% production, transportation, and material moving
Income: Per capita: $20,121; Median household: $41,804; Average household: $51,587; Households with income of $100,000 or more: 10.9%; Poverty rate: 20.5%
Educational Attainment: High school diploma or higher: 85.5%; Bachelor's degree or higher: 13.6%; Graduate/professional degree or higher: 4.4%

School District(s)

Morongo Unified (KG-12)
2012-13 Enrollment: 8,905 . . . . (760) 367-9191

Vocational/Technical School(s)

Elite Cosmetology School (Private, For-profit)
Fall 2013 Enrollment: 90 . . . . (760) 365-8222
2013-14 Tuition: $13,507

Housing: Homeownership rate: 63.5%; Median home value: $147,900; Median year structure built: 1977; Homeowner vacancy rate: 4.6%; Median gross rent: $919 per month; Rental vacancy rate: 9.6%
Health Insurance: 81.5% have insurance; 50.7% have private insurance; 42.0% have public insurance; 18.5% do not have insurance; 11.6% of children under 18 do not have insurance
Safety: Violent crime rate: 40.5 per 10,000 population; Property crime rate: 202.2 per 10,000 population
Newspapers: Hi-Desert Star (weekly circulation 11000)
Transportation: Commute: 85.6% car, 0.4% public transportation, 3.7% walk, 8.0% work from home; Median travel time to work: 25.4 minutes
Additional Information Contacts
City of Yucca Valley . . . . (760) 369-7207
http://www.yucca-valley.org

San Diego County

Located in southern California; bounded on the west by the Pacific Ocean, and on the south by the Mexican border; drained by the Santa Margarita, San Luis Rey, Sweetwater, Otay, and San Diego Rivers; includes part of Cleveland National Forest, and pa rt of the Colorado Desert. Covers a land area of 4,206.630 square miles, a water area of 319.055 square miles, and is located in the Pacific Time Zone at 33.02° N. Lat., 116.78° W. Long. The county was founded in 1850. County seat is San Diego.

San Diego County is part of the San Diego-Carlsbad, CA Metropolitan Statistical Area. The entire metro area includes: San Diego County, CA

Weather Station: Borrego Desert Park Elevation: 805 feet

	Jan	Feb	Mar	Apr	May	Jun	Jul	Aug	Sep	Oct	Nov	Dec
High	70	72	78	85	94	103	108	106	101	90	78	69
Low	45	47	50	54	61	68	76	76	70	61	51	44
Precip	1.2	1.5	0.8	0.2	0.1	0.0	0.3	0.5	0.3	0.3	0.4	0.8
Snow	0.0	tr	0.0	0.0	0.0	0.0	0.0	0.0	0.0	0.0	0.0	0.0

High and Low temperatures in degrees Fahrenheit; Precipitation and Snow in inches

Weather Station: Campo Elevation: 2,629 feet

	Jan	Feb	Mar	Apr	May	Jun	Jul	Aug	Sep	Oct	Nov	Dec
High	63	64	68	73	79	87	94	94	90	80	70	63
Low	34	35	36	38	42	45	52	53	49	42	36	33
Precip	3.2	3.4	2.4	1.0	0.2	0.1	0.3	0.7	0.4	0.8	1.1	2.0
Snow	0.1	0.2	tr	0.0	0.0	0.0	0.0	0.0	0.0	0.0	0.0	0.1

High and Low temperatures in degrees Fahrenheit; Precipitation and Snow in inches

Weather Station: Chula Vista Elevation: 56 feet

	Jan	Feb	Mar	Apr	May	Jun	Jul	Aug	Sep	Oct	Nov	Dec
High	68	68	68	70	70	72	76	78	78	76	71	68
Low	46	48	50	53	58	61	64	66	64	58	50	45
Precip	1.9	2.3	1.8	0.7	0.1	0.1	0.0	0.0	0.1	0.4	1.0	1.2
Snow	tr	0.0	0.0	0.0	0.0	0.0	0.0	0.0	tr	0.0	0.0	0.2

High and Low temperatures in degrees Fahrenheit; Precipitation and Snow in inches

Weather Station: Cuyamaca Elevation: 4,640 feet

	Jan	Feb	Mar	Apr	May	Jun	Jul	Aug	Sep	Oct	Nov	Dec
High	52	53	56	61	69	77	85	85	80	70	60	52
Low	31	31	34	37	42	48	56	55	49	40	34	29
Precip	6.0	6.6	5.8	2.5	0.8	0.2	0.4	0.9	0.7	1.1	3.1	4.6
Snow	4.6	6.7	6.5	2.8	0.1	0.0	0.0	0.0	0.0	tr	0.9	2.3

High and Low temperatures in degrees Fahrenheit; Precipitation and Snow in inches

Weather Station: El Cajon Elevation: 404 feet

	Jan	Feb	Mar	Apr	May	Jun	Jul	Aug	Sep	Oct	Nov	Dec
High	70	70	72	75	77	82	88	89	88	82	75	69
Low	42	44	47	50	55	59	63	64	62	55	46	41
Precip	2.4	2.7	2.4	0.8	0.2	0.1	0.1	0.0	0.2	0.6	1.3	1.6
Snow	0.0	0.0	0.0	0.0	0.0	0.0	0.0	0.0	0.0	0.0	tr	0.0

High and Low temperatures in degrees Fahrenheit; Precipitation and Snow in inches

Weather Station: Escondido No 2 Elevation: 600 feet

	Jan	Feb	Mar	Apr	May	Jun	Jul	Aug	Sep	Oct	Nov	Dec
High	69	69	70	75	77	82	87	89	86	80	73	69
Low	43	45	47	50	55	58	62	63	61	55	47	42
Precip	3.2	3.5	2.7	1.1	0.2	0.1	0.1	0.1	0.2	0.6	1.3	1.7
Snow	0.0	0.0	0.0	0.0	0.0	0.0	0.0	0.0	0.0	0.0	0.0	0.0

High and Low temperatures in degrees Fahrenheit; Precipitation and Snow in inches

Weather Station: Henshaw Dam Elevation: 2,700 feet

	Jan	Feb	Mar	Apr	May	Jun	Jul	Aug	Sep	Oct	Nov	Dec
High	61	62	65	70	77	85	93	94	89	79	69	61
Low	30	32	34	37	42	45	52	52	47	39	32	28
Precip	5.7	6.1	4.9	1.8	0.5	0.1	0.3	0.5	0.6	1.0	2.1	3.4
Snow	0.0	0.6	tr	0.0	0.0	0.0	0.0	0.0	0.0	0.0	tr	0.1

High and Low temperatures in degrees Fahrenheit; Precipitation and Snow in inches

Weather Station: Oceanside Marina Elevation: 9 feet

	Jan	Feb	Mar	Apr	May	Jun	Jul	Aug	Sep	Oct	Nov	Dec
High	64	63	63	64	65	67	71	72	72	70	67	64
Low	45	47	49	52	56	59	63	64	62	56	49	45
Precip	2.2	2.5	1.6	0.9	0.2	0.1	0.0	0.0	0.2	0.6	0.9	1.4
Snow	0.0	0.0	0.0	0.0	0.0	0.0	0.0	0.0	0.0	0.0	tr	0.0

High and Low temperatures in degrees Fahrenheit; Precipitation and Snow in inches

Weather Station: Palomar Mountain Observatory Elevation: 5,549 feet

	Jan	Feb	Mar	Apr	May	Jun	Jul	Aug	Sep	Oct	Nov	Dec
High	51	51	56	62	69	78	84	84	79	68	58	50
Low	35	35	38	41	48	56	62	63	58	49	41	35
Precip	5.7	6.7	4.8	1.7	0.6	0.1	0.4	0.8	0.5	1.1	2.4	3.3
Snow	2.9	5.0	7.6	1.9	tr	tr	0.0	0.0	0.0	tr	0.8	3.9

High and Low temperatures in degrees Fahrenheit; Precipitation and Snow in inches

Weather Station: Ramona Fire Dept Elevation: 1,470 feet

	Jan	Feb	Mar	Apr	May	Jun	Jul	Aug	Sep	Oct	Nov	Dec
High	67	67	69	73	77	84	90	91	88	80	73	67
Low	38	39	41	44	49	52	57	59	55	49	42	37
Precip	3.2	3.7	3.1	1.2	0.4	0.1	0.1	0.1	0.2	0.7	1.3	1.7
Snow	0.0	tr	tr	0.0	0.0	0.0	0.0	0.0	0.0	0.0	0.0	0.0

High and Low temperatures in degrees Fahrenheit; Precipitation and Snow in inches

Weather Station: San Diego Lindbergh Field Elevation: 13 feet

	Jan	Feb	Mar	Apr	May	Jun	Jul	Aug	Sep	Oct	Nov	Dec
High	66	66	66	68	69	72	75	77	76	73	70	65
Low	50	51	54	57	60	63	66	67	66	61	54	49
Precip	2.1	2.3	1.9	0.8	0.1	0.1	0.0	0.0	0.2	0.5	1.0	1.4
Snow	na	na	na	na	na	na	na	na	na	na	na	na

High and Low temperatures in degrees Fahrenheit; Precipitation and Snow in inches

Weather Station: San Pasqual Animal Pk Elevation: 419 feet

	Jan	Feb	Mar	Apr	May	Jun	Jul	Aug	Sep	Oct	Nov	Dec
High	71	71	73	77	79	84	90	92	90	84	77	71
Low	40	42	45	47	52	56	59	60	58	51	43	38
Precip	2.8	3.3	2.5	1.0	0.3	0.1	0.1	0.1	0.2	0.6	1.2	1.8
Snow	0.0	0.0	0.0	0.0	0.0	0.0	0.0	0.0	0.0	0.0	0.0	0.0

High and Low temperatures in degrees Fahrenheit; Precipitation and Snow in inches

Weather Station: Vista 2 NNE Elevation: 509 feet

	Jan	Feb	Mar	Apr	May	Jun	Jul	Aug	Sep	Oct	Nov	Dec
High	68	68	69	72	74	77	82	84	83	78	73	68
Low	45	46	48	50	55	58	61	62	61	56	49	45
Precip	2.9	2.9	2.3	0.9	0.2	0.1	0.1	0.1	0.2	0.6	1.2	1.6
Snow	0.0	0.0	0.0	0.0	0.0	0.0	0.0	0.0	0.0	0.0	0.0	0.0

High and Low temperatures in degrees Fahrenheit; Precipitation and Snow in inches

Population: 3,095,313; Growth (since 2000): 10.0%; Density: 735.8 persons per square mile; Race: 64.0% White, 5.1% Black/African American, 10.9% Asian, 0.9% American Indian/Alaska Native, 0.5% Native Hawaiian/Other Pacific Islander, 5.1% two or more races, 32.0% Hispanic of any race; Average household size: 2.75; Median age: 34.6; Age under 18: 23.4%; Age 65 and over: 11.4%; Males per 100 females: 100.8; Marriage status: 35.4% never married, 49.4% now married, 1.9% separated, 4.9% widowed, 10.3% divorced; Foreign born: 23.4%; Speak English only: 62.6%; With disability: 9.4%; Veterans: 10.0%; Ancestry: 11.2% German, 8.6% Irish, 8.5% English, 4.5% Italian, 2.9% American
Religion: Six largest groups: 25.9% Catholicism, 4.8% Non-denominational Protestant, 2.3% Latter-day Saints, 2.0% Baptist, 1.2% Buddhism, 1.1% Methodist/Pietist
Economy: Unemployment rate: 5.8%; Leading industries: 16.3% professional, scientific, and technical services; 11.9% retail trade; 11.0% health care and social assistance; Farms: 5,732 totaling 221,538 acres; Company size: 68 employ 1,000 or more persons, 96 employ 500 to 999 persons, 1,514 employ 100 to 499 persons, 75,648 employ less than 100 persons; Business ownership: 86,960 women-owned, 8,481 Black-owned, 44,157 Hispanic-owned, 29,239 Asian-owned
Employment: 15.8% management, business, and financial, 8.1% computer, engineering, and science, 11.0% education, legal, community

service, arts, and media, 5.2% healthcare practitioners, 19.4% service, 24.5% sales and office, 7.9% natural resources, construction, and maintenance, 8.1% production, transportation, and material moving

Income: Per capita: $30,668; Median household: $62,962; Average household: $84,889; Households with income of $100,000 or more: 29.4%; Poverty rate: 14.4%

Educational Attainment: High school diploma or higher: 85.5%; Bachelor's degree or higher: 34.6%; Graduate/professional degree or higher: 13.1%

Housing: Homeownership rate: 54.4%; Median home value: $402,100; Median year structure built: 1978; Homeowner vacancy rate: 1.9%; Median gross rent: $1,300 per month; Rental vacancy rate: 5.5%

Vital Statistics: Birth rate: 136.7 per 10,000 population; Death rate: 64.5 per 10,000 population; Age-adjusted cancer mortality rate: 159.5 deaths per 100,000 population

Health Insurance: 83.2% have insurance; 66.4% have private insurance; 25.7% have public insurance; 16.8% do not have insurance; 9.0% of children under 18 do not have insurance

Health Care: Physicians: 27.7 per 10,000 population; Hospital beds: 21.7 per 10,000 population; Hospital admissions: 1,054.0 per 10,000 population

Air Quality Index: 18.9% good, 75.9% moderate, 4.7% unhealthy for sensitive individuals, 0.3% unhealthy, 0.3% very unhealthy (% of days)

Transportation: Commute: 85.9% car, 3.1% public transportation, 2.8% walk, 6.4% work from home; Median travel time to work: 24.4 minutes

Presidential Election: 51.7% Obama, 46.2% Romney (2012)

National and State Parks: Anza-Borrego Desert State Park; Anza-Borrego Desert State Wilderness; Border Field State Park; Cabrillo National Monument; Cardiff State Beach; Carlsbad State Beach; Cleveland National Forest; Cuyamaca Mountain State Wilderness; Cuyamaca Rancho State Park; Leucadia State Beach; Moonlight State Beach; Ocotillo Wells State Vehicular Recreation Area; Old Town San Diego State Historic Park; Palomar Mountain State Park; San Elijo State Beach; San Onofre State Beach; San Pasqual Battlefield State Historic Park; Silver Strand State Beach; South Carlsbad State Beach; Sweetwater Marsh National Wildlife Refuge; Tijuana River National Estuarine Research Reserve; Torrey Pines State Beach; Torrey Pines State Natural Reserve; Pacific Crest National Scenic Trail; Inaja Nature National Recreation Trail

Additional Information Contacts

San Diego Government. . . . . (619) 531-5600
http://www.sdcounty.ca.gov

San Diego County Communities

ALPINE (CDP). Covers a land area of 26.781 square miles and a water area of 0.004 square miles. Located at 32.84° N. Lat; 116.76° W. Long. Elevation is 1,834 feet.

Population: 14,236; Growth (since 2000): 8.3%; Density: 531.6 persons per square mile; Race: 87.3% White, 1.2% Black/African American, 2.2% Asian, 1.6% American Indian/Alaska Native, 0.3% Native Hawaiian/Other Pacific Islander, 3.4% Two or more races, 14.6% Hispanic of any race; Average household size: 2.69; Median age: 41.9; Age under 18: 23.9%; Age 65 and over: 13.7%; Males per 100 females: 97.8; Marriage status: 26.3% never married, 56.9% now married, 1.9% separated, 7.0% widowed, 9.8% divorced; Foreign born: 9.3%; Speak English only: 84.5%; With disability: 13.3%; Veterans: 14.3%; Ancestry: 23.0% German, 12.1% Irish, 11.2% English, 6.9% Italian, 5.7% American

Employment: 17.4% management, business, and financial, 6.6% computer, engineering, and science, 11.5% education, legal, community service, arts, and media, 6.5% healthcare practitioners, 15.9% service, 25.9% sales and office, 8.4% natural resources, construction, and maintenance, 7.9% production, transportation, and material moving

Income: Per capita: $40,856; Median household: $76,833; Average household: $104,976; Households with income of $100,000 or more: 39.3%; Poverty rate: 8.1%

Educational Attainment: High school diploma or higher: 90.9%; Bachelor's degree or higher: 28.6%; Graduate/professional degree or higher: 11.1%

School District(s)

Alpine Union Elementary (PK-08)
2012-13 Enrollment: 1,863 . . . . (619) 445-3236

Housing: Homeownership rate: 68.5%; Median home value: $483,500; Median year structure built: 1985; Homeowner vacancy rate: 2.0%; Median gross rent: $1,247 per month; Rental vacancy rate: 6.3%

Health Insurance: 89.8% have insurance; 75.2% have private insurance; 28.2% have public insurance; 10.2% do not have insurance; 6.8% of children under 18 do not have insurance

Newspapers: Alpine Sun (weekly circulation 2300)

Transportation: Commute: 90.7% car, 1.2% public transportation, 1.1% walk, 6.9% work from home; Median travel time to work: 31.2 minutes

BONITA (CDP). Covers a land area of 4.996 square miles and a water area of 0.139 square miles. Located at 32.67° N. Lat; 117.01° W. Long. Elevation is 118 feet.

Population: 12,538; Growth (since 2000): 1.1%; Density: 2,509.4 persons per square mile; Race: 66.9% White, 3.7% Black/African American, 9.6% Asian, 0.9% American Indian/Alaska Native, 0.6% Native Hawaiian/Other Pacific Islander, 4.9% Two or more races, 40.7% Hispanic of any race; Average household size: 2.92; Median age: 43.9; Age under 18: 20.8%; Age 65 and over: 18.7%; Males per 100 females: 94.9; Marriage status: 26.8% never married, 57.0% now married, 1.6% separated, 6.0% widowed, 10.1% divorced; Foreign born: 22.5%; Speak English only: 57.4%; With disability: 9.3%; Veterans: 11.9%; Ancestry: 7.6% German, 7.2% English, 5.2% Irish, 4.3% Italian, 3.2% French

Employment: 15.5% management, business, and financial, 5.6% computer, engineering, and science, 12.1% education, legal, community service, arts, and media, 5.1% healthcare practitioners, 12.2% service, 30.1% sales and office, 8.8% natural resources, construction, and maintenance, 10.7% production, transportation, and material moving

Income: Per capita: $35,158; Median household: $82,208; Average household: $101,665; Households with income of $100,000 or more: 38.3%; Poverty rate: 11.4%

Educational Attainment: High school diploma or higher: 89.2%; Bachelor's degree or higher: 38.7%; Graduate/professional degree or higher: 17.7%

School District(s)

Chula Vista Elementary (KG-08)
2012-13 Enrollment: 28,524 . . . . (619) 425-9600

Housing: Homeownership rate: 73.1%; Median home value: $499,000; Median year structure built: 1974; Homeowner vacancy rate: 1.1%; Median gross rent: $1,622 per month; Rental vacancy rate: 5.5%

Health Insurance: 81.3% have insurance; 70.5% have private insurance; 26.7% have public insurance; 18.7% do not have insurance; 10.8% of children under 18 do not have insurance

Transportation: Commute: 89.0% car, 1.1% public transportation, 2.2% walk, 5.1% work from home; Median travel time to work: 23.9 minutes

BONSALL (CDP). Covers a land area of 13.395 square miles and a water area of 0.174 square miles. Located at 33.27° N. Lat; 117.19° W. Long. Elevation is 180 feet.

History: Bonsall was established as a trading center for a dairying and farming region.

Population: 3,982; Growth (since 2000): 17.1%; Density: 297.3 persons per square mile; Race: 80.2% White, 1.7% Black/African American, 3.5% Asian, 0.7% American Indian/Alaska Native, 0.3% Native Hawaiian/Other Pacific Islander, 4.2% Two or more races, 22.4% Hispanic of any race; Average household size: 2.57; Median age: 44.1; Age under 18: 21.2%; Age 65 and over: 17.2%; Males per 100 females: 96.7; Marriage status: 23.0% never married, 70.7% now married, 1.7% separated, 2.6% widowed, 3.7% divorced; Foreign born: 13.3%; Speak English only: 82.1%; With disability: 9.5%; Veterans: 10.9%; Ancestry: 20.1% English, 14.7% German, 11.9% Irish, 5.3% Italian, 2.5% Danish

Employment: 14.8% management, business, and financial, 4.3% computer, engineering, and science, 8.7% education, legal, community service, arts, and media, 0.4% healthcare practitioners, 7.3% service, 41.2% sales and office, 8.8% natural resources, construction, and maintenance, 14.5% production, transportation, and material moving

Income: Per capita: $39,426; Median household: $72,563; Average household: $104,360; Households with income of $100,000 or more: 34.2%; Poverty rate: 6.1%

Educational Attainment: High school diploma or higher: 91.6%; Bachelor's degree or higher: 40.3%; Graduate/professional degree or higher: 10.0%

School District(s)

Bonsall Union Elementary (KG-08)
2012-13 Enrollment: 2,087 . . . . (760) 631-5200

Housing: Homeownership rate: 72.1%; Median home value: $585,500; Median year structure built: 1983; Homeowner vacancy rate: 2.6%; Median gross rent: $1,143 per month; Rental vacancy rate: 4.2%

Health Insurance: 91.3% have insurance; 77.3% have private insurance; 29.6% have public insurance; 8.7% do not have insurance; 1.4% of children under 18 do not have insurance

Transportation: Commute: 82.9% car, 0.3% public transportation, 0.4% walk, 14.7% work from home; Median travel time to work: 27.3 minutes

BORREGO SPRINGS (CDP). Covers a land area of 43.071 square miles and a water area of 0.338 square miles. Located at 33.24° N. Lat; 116.36° W. Long. Elevation is 597 feet.

Population: 3,429; Growth (since 2000): 35.3%; Density: 79.6 persons per square mile; Race: 80.7% White, 0.6% Black/African American, 0.6% Asian, 1.0% American Indian/Alaska Native, 0.1% Native Hawaiian/Other Pacific Islander, 2.4% Two or more races, 35.5% Hispanic of any race; Average household size: 2.18; Median age: 56.6; Age under 18: 17.3%; Age 65 and over: 33.6%; Males per 100 females: 99.5; Marriage status: 20.2% never married, 56.5% now married, 1.2% separated, 14.2% widowed, 9.1% divorced; Foreign born: 27.5%; Speak English only: 64.4%; With disability: 15.4%; Veterans: 14.2%; Ancestry: 14.2% Irish, 13.3% German, 6.9% English, 5.4% American, 5.2% Welsh

Employment: 14.4% management, business, and financial, 2.8% computer, engineering, and science, 3.1% education, legal, community service, arts, and media, 1.1% healthcare practitioners, 30.7% service, 16.1% sales and office, 26.3% natural resources, construction, and maintenance, 5.5% production, transportation, and material moving

Income: Per capita: $22,278; Median household: $42,230; Average household: $47,284; Households with income of $100,000 or more: 6.4%; Poverty rate: 15.5%

Educational Attainment: High school diploma or higher: 77.5%; Bachelor's degree or higher: 26.0%; Graduate/professional degree or higher: 8.8%

School District(s)

Borrego Springs Unified (PK-12)
2012-13 Enrollment: 513. . . . . (760) 767-5357

Housing: Homeownership rate: 78.6%; Median home value: $195,700; Median year structure built: 1980; Homeowner vacancy rate: 8.0%; Median gross rent: <$100 per month; Rental vacancy rate: 12.1%

Health Insurance: 84.6% have insurance; 53.1% have private insurance; 55.4% have public insurance; 15.4% do not have insurance; 0.0% of children under 18 do not have insurance

Newspapers: Borrego Sun (weekly circulation 4000)

Transportation: Commute: 76.4% car, 0.0% public transportation, 8.7% walk, 6.6% work from home; Median travel time to work: 33.8 minutes

Airports: Borrego Valley (general aviation)

BOSTONIA (CDP). Covers a land area of 1.929 square miles and a water area of 0 square miles. Located at 32.82° N. Lat; 116.94° W. Long. Elevation is 486 feet.

Population: 15,379; Growth (since 2000): 1.4%; Density: 7,973.4 persons per square mile; Race: 70.8% White, 6.6% Black/African American, 2.4% Asian, 0.7% American Indian/Alaska Native, 0.6% Native Hawaiian/Other Pacific Islander, 7.3% Two or more races, 25.6% Hispanic of any race; Average household size: 2.74; Median age: 33.8; Age under 18: 24.8%; Age 65 and over: 11.4%; Males per 100 females: 94.6; Marriage status: 33.5% never married, 47.2% now married, 1.5% separated, 5.6% widowed, 13.6% divorced; Foreign born: 16.4%; Speak English only: 67.3%; With disability: 13.6%; Veterans: 10.4%; Ancestry: 11.4% German, 10.2% Irish, 7.5% English, 3.5% Italian, 2.6% Iraqi

Employment: 7.1% management, business, and financial, 2.1% computer, engineering, and science, 5.2% education, legal, community service, arts, and media, 3.7% healthcare practitioners, 23.8% service, 34.8% sales and office, 11.8% natural resources, construction, and maintenance, 11.5% production, transportation, and material moving

Income: Per capita: $19,491; Median household: $41,353; Average household: $54,534; Households with income of $100,000 or more: 13.2%; Poverty rate: 20.9%

Educational Attainment: High school diploma or higher: 83.0%; Bachelor's degree or higher: 12.3%; Graduate/professional degree or higher: 2.1%

Housing: Homeownership rate: 42.0%; Median home value: $249,300; Median year structure built: 1975; Homeowner vacancy rate: 2.9%; Median gross rent: $1,210 per month; Rental vacancy rate: 5.5%

Health Insurance: 82.7% have insurance; 55.5% have private insurance; 35.9% have public insurance; 17.3% do not have insurance; 10.0% of children under 18 do not have insurance

Transportation: Commute: 87.1% car, 4.6% public transportation, 2.2% walk, 5.0% work from home; Median travel time to work: 24.8 minutes

BOULEVARD (CDP). Covers a land area of 3.904 square miles and a water area of 0 square miles. Located at 32.66° N. Lat; 116.29° W. Long. Elevation is 3,353 feet.

Population: 315; Growth (since 2000): n/a; Density: 80.7 persons per square mile; Race: 86.3% White, 0.6% Black/African American, 1.0% Asian, 2.2% American Indian/Alaska Native, 0.0% Native Hawaiian/Other Pacific Islander, 5.4% Two or more races, 14.0% Hispanic of any race; Average household size: 2.33; Median age: 49.2; Age under 18: 22.5%; Age 65 and over: 16.8%; Males per 100 females: 114.3

School District(s)

Mountain Empire Unified (PK-12)
2012-13 Enrollment: 2,956 . . . . (619) 473-9022

Housing: Homeownership rate: 61.4%; Homeowner vacancy rate: 2.3%; Rental vacancy rate: 17.5%

CAMP PENDLETON NORTH (CDP). Covers a land area of 8.854 square miles and a water area of 0.203 square miles. Located at 33.32° N. Lat; 117.32° W. Long.

History: Camp Pendleton North is located at the southeast corner of the Marine Corps Base Camp Pendleton, north of Camp Pendleton South.

Population: 5,200; Growth (since 2000): -36.6%; Density: 587.3 persons per square mile; Race: 71.7% White, 9.6% Black/African American, 2.9% Asian, 1.6% American Indian/Alaska Native, 1.5% Native Hawaiian/Other Pacific Islander, 6.7% Two or more races, 22.3% Hispanic of any race; Average household size: 3.33; Median age: 21.3; Age under 18: 28.9%; Age 65 and over: 0.2%; Males per 100 females: 177.6; Marriage status: 43.6% never married, 54.9% now married, 0.5% separated, 0.1% widowed, 1.5% divorced; Foreign born: 8.0%; Speak English only: 81.8%; With disability: 3.6%; Veterans: 22.7%; Ancestry: 21.4% German, 19.2% Irish, 4.2% English, 4.0% Italian, 3.5% Scottish

Employment: 16.5% management, business, and financial, 0.0% computer, engineering, and science, 27.0% education, legal, community service, arts, and media, 5.1% healthcare practitioners, 22.6% service, 5.5% sales and office, 10.1% natural resources, construction, and maintenance, 13.3% production, transportation, and material moving

Income: Per capita: $19,486; Median household: $41,329; Average household: $51,237; Households with income of $100,000 or more: 10.6%; Poverty rate: 18.7%

Educational Attainment: High school diploma or higher: 98.9%; Bachelor's degree or higher: 38.0%; Graduate/professional degree or higher: 7.7%

Housing: Homeownership rate: 1.4%; Median home value: n/a; Median year structure built: 1990; Homeowner vacancy rate: 0.0%; Median gross rent: $1,791 per month; Rental vacancy rate: 15.2%

Health Insurance: 100.0% have insurance; 97.9% have private insurance; 3.2% have public insurance; 0.0% do not have insurance; 0.0% of children under 18 do not have insurance

Transportation: Commute: 64.5% car, 0.4% public transportation, 23.6% walk, 8.8% work from home; Median travel time to work: 13.2 minutes

CAMP PENDLETON SOUTH (CDP). Covers a land area of 3.907 square miles and a water area of 0.096 square miles. Located at 33.23° N. Lat; 117.38° W. Long. Elevation is 62 feet.

History: Camp Pendleton South is located at the southwest corner of the Marine Corps Base Camp Pendleton.

Population: 10,616; Growth (since 2000): 19.9%; Density: 2,717.2 persons per square mile; Race: 70.9% White, 9.3% Black/African American, 2.8% Asian, 1.4% American Indian/Alaska Native, 0.4% Native Hawaiian/Other Pacific Islander, 8.3% Two or more races, 24.4% Hispanic of any race; Average household size: 3.63; Median age: 21.7; Age under 18: 40.1%; Age 65 and over: 0.1%; Males per 100 females: 119.6; Marriage status: 23.1% never married, 75.8% now married, 0.1% separated, 0.1% widowed, 1.0% divorced; Foreign born: 5.1%; Speak English only: 85.8%; With disability: 5.1%; Veterans: 19.2%; Ancestry: 22.9% German, 15.3% Irish, 11.0% Italian, 7.4% English, 4.1% European

Employment: 18.1% management, business, and financial, 5.1% computer, engineering, and science, 7.6% education, legal, community service, arts, and media, 11.5% healthcare practitioners, 23.3% service, 28.8% sales and office, 5.7% natural resources, construction, and maintenance, 0.0% production, transportation, and material moving

Income: Per capita: $16,543; Median household: $49,950; Average household: $54,507; Households with income of $100,000 or more: 8.3%; Poverty rate: 8.8%
Educational Attainment: High school diploma or higher: 100.0%; Bachelor's degree or higher: 20.6%; Graduate/professional degree or higher: 5.3%
Housing: Homeownership rate: 0.4%; Median home value: n/a; Median year structure built: 2003; Homeowner vacancy rate: 0.0%; Median gross rent: $1,887 per month; Rental vacancy rate: 10.3%
Health Insurance: 99.0% have insurance; 98.0% have private insurance; 2.1% have public insurance; 1.0% do not have insurance; 1.6% of children under 18 do not have insurance
Transportation: Commute: 74.7% car, 0.3% public transportation, 13.7% walk, 7.7% work from home; Median travel time to work: 18.8 minutes

CAMPO (CDP). Covers a land area of 23.480 square miles and a water area of 0.007 square miles. Located at 32.64° N. Lat; 116.47° W. Long. Elevation is 2,615 feet.
Population: 2,684; Growth (since 2000): n/a; Density: 114.3 persons per square mile; Race: 77.6% White, 4.2% Black/African American, 1.2% Asian, 3.4% American Indian/Alaska Native, 0.2% Native Hawaiian/Other Pacific Islander, 4.2% Two or more races, 29.6% Hispanic of any race; Average household size: 2.77; Median age: 35.2; Age under 18: 30.2%; Age 65 and over: 10.7%; Males per 100 females: 119.6; Marriage status: 41.5% never married, 44.6% now married, 1.1% separated, 7.7% widowed, 6.2% divorced; Foreign born: 9.0%; Speak English only: 79.3%; With disability: 14.2%; Veterans: 11.0%; Ancestry: 36.2% Irish, 14.2% German, 10.2% Swedish, 7.2% English, 4.2% Polish
Employment: 7.0% management, business, and financial, 11.7% computer, engineering, and science, 3.9% education, legal, community service, arts, and media, 1.3% healthcare practitioners, 25.3% service, 24.8% sales and office, 9.7% natural resources, construction, and maintenance, 16.4% production, transportation, and material moving
Income: Per capita: $21,357; Median household: $50,245; Average household: $66,839; Households with income of $100,000 or more: 16.9%; Poverty rate: 38.8%
Educational Attainment: High school diploma or higher: 82.6%; Bachelor's degree or higher: 14.6%; Graduate/professional degree or higher: 4.9%

School District(s)

Mountain Empire Unified (PK-12)
2012-13 Enrollment: 2,956 . . . . (619) 473-9022
San Diego County Office of Education (PK-12)
2012-13 Enrollment: 4,151 . . . . (858) 292-3500

Housing: Homeownership rate: 75.0%; Median home value: $175,200; Median year structure built: 1976; Homeowner vacancy rate: 4.9%; Median gross rent: $1,199 per month; Rental vacancy rate: 13.4%
Health Insurance: 86.2% have insurance; 60.1% have private insurance; 34.0% have public insurance; 13.8% do not have insurance; 9.3% of children under 18 do not have insurance
Transportation: Commute: 94.4% car, 0.0% public transportation, 3.4% walk, 2.2% work from home; Median travel time to work: 35.1 minutes

CARDIFF BY THE SEA (unincorporated postal area)
ZCTA: 92007
Covers a land area of 2.444 square miles and a water area of 0.453 square miles. Located at 33.02° N. Lat; 117.27° W. Long..
Population: 10,429; Growth (since 2000): 0.6%; Density: 4,267.1 persons per square mile; Race: 87.4% White, 0.4% Black/African American, 3.1% Asian, 0.6% American Indian/Alaska Native, 0.2% Native Hawaiian/Other Pacific Islander, 3.4% Two or more races, 12.0% Hispanic of any race; Average household size: 2.34; Median age: 39.9; Age under 18: 18.1%; Age 65 and over: 11.7%; Males per 100 females: 100.9; Marriage status: 37.2% never married, 50.7% now married, 0.7% separated, 4.1% widowed, 8.0% divorced; Foreign born: 9.5%; Speak English only: 86.3%; With disability: 8.3%; Veterans: 6.4%; Ancestry: 13.4% English, 13.4% German, 11.7% Irish, 6.0% Italian, 4.2% European
Employment: 14.3% management, business, and financial, 8.8% computer, engineering, and science, 19.0% education, legal, community service, arts, and media, 7.8% healthcare practitioners, 10.7% service, 28.7% sales and office, 3.4% natural resources, construction, and maintenance, 7.3% production, transportation, and material moving
Income: Per capita: $49,587; Median household: $99,412; Average household: $127,617; Households with income of $100,000 or more: 49.8%; Poverty rate: 8.3%
Educational Attainment: High school diploma or higher: 93.4%; Bachelor's degree or higher: 55.2%; Graduate/professional degree or higher: 24.7%

School District(s)

Cardiff Elementary (KG-06)
2012-13 Enrollment: 763. . . . . (760) 632-5890

Housing: Homeownership rate: 59.1%; Median home value: $743,200; Median year structure built: 1977; Homeowner vacancy rate: 1.1%; Median gross rent: $1,769 per month; Rental vacancy rate: 5.9%
Health Insurance: 92.2% have insurance; 86.0% have private insurance; 15.4% have public insurance; 7.8% do not have insurance; 4.0% of children under 18 do not have insurance
Transportation: Commute: 84.3% car, 1.1% public transportation, 1.3% walk, 10.1% work from home; Median travel time to work: 23.6 minutes

CARLSBAD (city). Covers a land area of 37.722 square miles and a water area of 1.388 square miles. Located at 33.12° N. Lat; 117.28° W. Long. Elevation is 52 feet.
History: Named for Karlsbad, Bohemia, because of the similarity of their waters. Carlsbad's population more than tripled from 1970 to 1990. Settled in the 1880s. Incorporated 1952.
Population: 105,328; Growth (since 2000): 34.6%; Density: 2,792.2 persons per square mile; Race: 82.8% White, 1.3% Black/African American, 7.1% Asian, 0.5% American Indian/Alaska Native, 0.2% Native Hawaiian/Other Pacific Islander, 4.2% Two or more races, 13.3% Hispanic of any race; Average household size: 2.53; Median age: 40.4; Age under 18: 24.1%; Age 65 and over: 14.0%; Males per 100 females: 95.6; Marriage status: 26.5% never married, 56.8% now married, 1.2% separated, 4.9% widowed, 11.9% divorced; Foreign born: 13.9%; Speak English only: 82.4%; With disability: 7.4%; Veterans: 8.8%; Ancestry: 16.5% German, 16.4% English, 11.8% Irish, 7.8% Italian, 4.0% American
Employment: 23.7% management, business, and financial, 11.4% computer, engineering, and science, 13.9% education, legal, community service, arts, and media, 5.6% healthcare practitioners, 12.1% service, 24.1% sales and office, 4.4% natural resources, construction, and maintenance, 4.7% production, transportation, and material moving
Income: Per capita: $43,441; Median household: $83,908; Average household: $108,358; Households with income of $100,000 or more: 43.0%; Poverty rate: 10.6%
Educational Attainment: High school diploma or higher: 96.0%; Bachelor's degree or higher: 51.9%; Graduate/professional degree or higher: 21.0%

School District(s)

Carlsbad Unified (KG-12)
2012-13 Enrollment: 10,956 . . . . (760) 331-5000
Encinitas Union Elementary (KG-06)
2012-13 Enrollment: 5,448 . . . . (760) 944-4300
San Marcos Unified (KG-12)
2012-13 Enrollment: 19,617 . . . . (760) 752-1299

Two-year College(s)

Golf Academy of America-Carlsbad (Private, For-profit)
Fall 2013 Enrollment: 230 . . . . (800) 342-7342
2013-14 Tuition: In-state $16,670; Out-of-state $16,670

Vocational/Technical School(s)

Gemological Institute of America-Carlsbad (Private, Not-for-profit)
Fall 2013 Enrollment: 192. . . . . (760) 603-4000
2013-14 Tuition: $19,510

Housing: Homeownership rate: 64.8%; Median home value: $614,000; Median year structure built: 1986; Homeowner vacancy rate: 1.4%; Median gross rent: $1,631 per month; Rental vacancy rate: 4.6%
Health Insurance: 90.2% have insurance; 81.0% have private insurance; 19.9% have public insurance; 9.8% do not have insurance; 5.0% of children under 18 do not have insurance
Safety: Violent crime rate: 20.0 per 10,000 population; Property crime rate: 188.7 per 10,000 population
Transportation: Commute: 85.7% car, 2.2% public transportation, 1.1% walk, 9.4% work from home; Median travel time to work: 28.3 minutes
Airports: McClellan-Palomar (primary service/non-hub)

Additional Information Contacts

City of Carlsbad. . . . . (760) 434-2820
http://www.carlsbadca.gov

CASA DE ORO-MOUNT HELIX (CDP). Covers a land area of 6.853 square miles and a water area of 0 square miles. Located at 32.76° N. Lat; 116.97° W. Long.

Population: 18,762; Growth (since 2000): -0.6%; Density: 2,737.8 persons per square mile; Race: 79.3% White, 5.9% Black/African American, 3.2% Asian, 0.5% American Indian/Alaska Native, 0.5% Native Hawaiian/Other Pacific Islander, 5.3% Two or more races, 17.2% Hispanic of any race; Average household size: 2.67; Median age: 45.4; Age under 18: 21.0%; Age 65 and over: 18.6%; Males per 100 females: 95.8; Marriage status: 27.7% never married, 53.5% now married, 1.8% separated, 6.5% widowed, 12.4% divorced; Foreign born: 12.6%; Speak English only: 81.5%; With disability: 11.4%; Veterans: 11.5%; Ancestry: 18.0% German, 14.4% Irish, 10.5% English, 6.1% Italian, 3.4% Norwegian

Employment: 22.1% management, business, and financial, 6.2% computer, engineering, and science, 15.2% education, legal, community service, arts, and media, 6.7% healthcare practitioners, 13.2% service, 23.3% sales and office, 6.5% natural resources, construction, and maintenance, 6.9% production, transportation, and material moving

Income: Per capita: $37,903; Median household: $76,461; Average household: $101,921; Households with income of $100,000 or more: 38.8%; Poverty rate: 12.2%

Educational Attainment: High school diploma or higher: 93.1%; Bachelor's degree or higher: 41.3%; Graduate/professional degree or higher: 19.8%

Housing: Homeownership rate: 72.3%; Median home value: $555,900; Median year structure built: 1969; Homeowner vacancy rate: 1.4%; Median gross rent: $1,181 per month; Rental vacancy rate: 5.2%

Health Insurance: 89.9% have insurance; 72.1% have private insurance; 31.9% have public insurance; 10.1% do not have insurance; 4.0% of children under 18 do not have insurance

Transportation: Commute: 85.7% car, 1.9% public transportation, 1.1% walk, 9.9% work from home; Median travel time to work: 24.3 minutes

CHULA VISTA (city). Covers a land area of 49.631 square miles and a water area of 2.463 square miles. Located at 32.63° N. Lat; 117.02° W. Long. Elevation is 66 feet.

History: Named for the Spanish translation of "pretty view". Chula Vista grew around an agricultural district called the South Bay Region, with flowers and bulbs grown commercially.

Population: 243,916; Growth (since 2000): 40.5%; Density: 4,914.6 persons per square mile; Race: 53.7% White, 4.6% Black/African American, 14.4% Asian, 0.8% American Indian/Alaska Native, 0.6% Native Hawaiian/Other Pacific Islander, 5.8% Two or more races, 58.2% Hispanic of any race; Average household size: 3.21; Median age: 33.7; Age under 18: 27.9%; Age 65 and over: 10.0%; Males per 100 females: 93.9; Marriage status: 32.6% never married, 53.2% now married, 2.5% separated, 5.1% widowed, 9.1% divorced; Foreign born: 31.1%; Speak English only: 42.9%; With disability: 8.7%; Veterans: 10.4%; Ancestry: 4.9% German, 4.6% Irish, 2.9% English, 2.5% Italian, 1.5% American

Employment: 13.2% management, business, and financial, 4.9% computer, engineering, and science, 9.2% education, legal, community service, arts, and media, 6.5% healthcare practitioners, 20.3% service, 28.1% sales and office, 8.0% natural resources, construction, and maintenance, 9.8% production, transportation, and material moving

Income: Per capita: $25,104; Median household: $64,801; Average household: $78,558; Households with income of $100,000 or more: 28.9%; Poverty rate: 11.8%

Educational Attainment: High school diploma or higher: 81.3%; Bachelor's degree or higher: 26.9%; Graduate/professional degree or higher: 8.8%

School District(s)

Chula Vista Elementary (KG-08)
2012-13 Enrollment: 28,524 . . . . (619) 425-9600
Mountain Empire Unified (PK-12)
2012-13 Enrollment: 2,956 . . . . (619) 473-9022
San Diego County Office of Education (PK-12)
2012-13 Enrollment: 4,151 . . . . (858) 292-3500
Sbc - High Tech High (KG-12)
2012-13 Enrollment: 2,276 . . . . (619) 243-5014
Sweetwater Union High (07-12)
2012-13 Enrollment: 40,916 . . . . (619) 691-5500

Four-year College(s)

United States University (Private, For-profit)
Fall 2013 Enrollment: 282 . . . . (619) 477-6310
2013-14 Tuition: In-state $8,060; Out-of-state $8,060

Two-year College(s)

Kaplan College-Chula Vista (Private, For-profit)
Fall 2013 Enrollment: 299 . . . . (619) 498-4100
Pima Medical Institute-Chula Vista (Private, For-profit)
Fall 2013 Enrollment: 927 . . . . (619) 425-3200
San Joaquin Valley College-San Diego (Private, For-profit)
Fall 2013 Enrollment: 9 . . . . (619) 426-7582
2013-14 Tuition: In-state $28,825; Out-of-state $28,825
Southwestern College (Public)
Fall 2013 Enrollment: 19,591 . . . . (619) 421-6700
2013-14 Tuition: In-state $1,334; Out-of-state $5,366

Housing: Homeownership rate: 58.1%; Median home value: $351,500; Median year structure built: 1982; Homeowner vacancy rate: 2.4%; Median gross rent: $1,255 per month; Rental vacancy rate: 4.5%

Health Insurance: 82.3% have insurance; 65.0% have private insurance; 24.9% have public insurance; 17.7% do not have insurance; 9.9% of children under 18 do not have insurance

Hospitals: Sharp Chula Vista Medical Center (343 beds)

Safety: Violent crime rate: 23.3 per 10,000 population; Property crime rate: 207.2 per 10,000 population

Newspapers: The Star-News (weekly circulation 33500)

Transportation: Commute: 90.0% car, 3.3% public transportation, 1.3% walk, 3.8% work from home; Median travel time to work: 26.8 minutes

Additional Information Contacts

City of Chula Vista . . . . (619) 691-5041
http://www.chulavistaca.gov

CORONADO (city). Covers a land area of 7.931 square miles and a water area of 24.735 square miles. Located at 32.66° N. Lat; 117.16° W. Long. Elevation is 16 feet.

History: Named for the Los Coronados Islands, by the Coronado Beach Company. Coronado developed as a residential and resort community on the islands across San Diego Bay from the city of San Diego. The Hotel Del Coronado was designed by Stanford White.

Population: 18,912; Growth (since 2000): -21.5%; Density: 2,384.6 persons per square mile; Race: 88.1% White, 2.1% Black/African American, 3.0% Asian, 0.5% American Indian/Alaska Native, 0.3% Native Hawaiian/Other Pacific Islander, 3.5% Two or more races, 12.2% Hispanic of any race; Average household size: 2.31; Median age: 40.7; Age under 18: 20.4%; Age 65 and over: 18.4%; Males per 100 females: 107.4; Marriage status: 27.6% never married, 56.2% now married, 2.0% separated, 5.9% widowed, 10.3% divorced; Foreign born: 10.4%; Speak English only: 83.7%; With disability: 9.8%; Veterans: 20.7%; Ancestry: 19.3% German, 16.6% English, 14.6% Irish, 5.0% Italian, 4.4% French

Employment: 25.3% management, business, and financial, 7.8% computer, engineering, and science, 17.9% education, legal, community service, arts, and media, 11.9% healthcare practitioners, 9.5% service, 20.1% sales and office, 4.1% natural resources, construction, and maintenance, 3.4% production, transportation, and material moving

Income: Per capita: $49,771; Median household: $91,103; Average household: $121,335; Households with income of $100,000 or more: 46.2%; Poverty rate: 6.7%

Educational Attainment: High school diploma or higher: 98.4%; Bachelor's degree or higher: 58.3%; Graduate/professional degree or higher: 27.9%

School District(s)

Coronado Unified (KG-12)
2012-13 Enrollment: 3,174 . . . . (619) 522-8900

Housing: Homeownership rate: 48.8%; Median home value: 1 million+; Median year structure built: 1973; Homeowner vacancy rate: 2.4%; Median gross rent: $2,000+ per month; Rental vacancy rate: 4.8%

Health Insurance: 93.5% have insurance; 87.1% have private insurance; 25.7% have public insurance; 6.5% do not have insurance; 3.8% of children under 18 do not have insurance

Hospitals: Sharp Coronado Hospital & Healthcare Center (204 beds)

Safety: Violent crime rate: 4.7 per 10,000 population; Property crime rate: 239.4 per 10,000 population

Newspapers: Coronado Eagle & Journal (weekly circulation 12500)

Transportation: Commute: 69.8% car, 2.4% public transportation, 7.0% walk, 14.7% work from home; Median travel time to work: 19.8 minutes

Additional Information Contacts

City of Coronado . . . . (619) 522-7300
http://www.coronado.ca.us

CREST (CDP). Covers a land area of 6.531 square miles and a water area of 0 square miles. Located at 32.80° N. Lat; 116.87° W. Long. Elevation is 1,640 feet.

Population: 2,593; Growth (since 2000): -4.5%; Density: 397.0 persons per square mile; Race: 89.8% White, 0.9% Black/African American, 1.5% Asian, 0.8% American Indian/Alaska Native, 0.3% Native Hawaiian/Other Pacific Islander, 3.3% Two or more races, 12.3% Hispanic of any race; Average household size: 2.70; Median age: 44.8; Age under 18: 19.1%; Age 65 and over: 12.5%; Males per 100 females: 105.0; Marriage status: 24.4% never married, 55.9% now married, 2.3% separated, 4.3% widowed, 15.4% divorced; Foreign born: 8.5%; Speak English only: 86.1%; With disability: 20.0%; Veterans: 13.9%; Ancestry: 29.6% German, 21.2% Irish, 14.5% English, 4.5% French, 4.3% Italian

Employment: 11.6% management, business, and financial, 3.2% computer, engineering, and science, 10.2% education, legal, community service, arts, and media, 4.1% healthcare practitioners, 14.9% service, 20.8% sales and office, 29.0% natural resources, construction, and maintenance, 6.1% production, transportation, and material moving

Income: Per capita: $39,070; Median household: $75,429; Average household: $86,349; Households with income of $100,000 or more: 28.8%; Poverty rate: 6.1%

Educational Attainment: High school diploma or higher: 90.0%; Bachelor's degree or higher: 21.2%; Graduate/professional degree or higher: 6.7%

Housing: Homeownership rate: 84.0%; Median home value: $355,900; Median year structure built: 1975; Homeowner vacancy rate: 1.0%; Median gross rent: $1,196 per month; Rental vacancy rate: 4.9%

Health Insurance: 91.1% have insurance; 67.1% have private insurance; 34.0% have public insurance; 8.9% do not have insurance; 12.9% of children under 18 do not have insurance

Transportation: Commute: 89.0% car, 1.3% public transportation, 1.9% walk, 7.0% work from home; Median travel time to work: 32.7 minutes

DEL MAR (city). Covers a land area of 1.707 square miles and a water area of 0.070 square miles. Located at 32.96° N. Lat; 117.26° W. Long. Elevation is 112 feet.

History: Del Mar is Spanish for "of the sea" or "by the sea", because it is located near the Pacific Ocean. Colonel Jacob Taylor purchased 338 acres (1.37 sq. km.) from Enoch Talbert in 1885, with visions of building a seaside resort for the rich and famous.

Population: 4,161; Growth (since 2000): -5.2%; Density: 2,437.9 persons per square mile; Race: 94.0% White, 0.2% Black/African American, 2.8% Asian, 0.2% American Indian/Alaska Native, 0.1% Native Hawaiian/Other Pacific Islander, 2.0% Two or more races, 4.2% Hispanic of any race; Average household size: 2.02; Median age: 48.6; Age under 18: 13.6%; Age 65 and over: 20.8%; Males per 100 females: 102.1; Marriage status: 18.8% never married, 67.4% now married, 1.3% separated, 3.3% widowed, 10.5% divorced; Foreign born: 15.0%; Speak English only: 92.5%; With disability: 6.3%; Veterans: 12.5%; Ancestry: 17.7% German, 13.9% Irish, 13.2% English, 7.7% Italian, 5.9% Polish

Employment: 28.9% management, business, and financial, 7.2% computer, engineering, and science, 16.7% education, legal, community service, arts, and media, 13.7% healthcare practitioners, 5.0% service, 25.9% sales and office, 1.9% natural resources, construction, and maintenance, 0.7% production, transportation, and material moving

Income: Per capita: $100,753; Median household: $107,457; Average household: $203,213; Households with income of $100,000 or more: 55.9%; Poverty rate: 1.6%

Educational Attainment: High school diploma or higher: 98.7%; Bachelor's degree or higher: 77.7%; Graduate/professional degree or higher: 39.1%

School District(s)

Del Mar Union Elementary (KG-06)
2012-13 Enrollment: 4,384 . . . . (858) 755-9301

Housing: Homeownership rate: 53.9%; Median home value: 1 million+; Median year structure built: 1973; Homeowner vacancy rate: 2.6%; Median gross rent: $1,904 per month; Rental vacancy rate: 7.9%

Health Insurance: 92.2% have insurance; 86.5% have private insurance; 23.1% have public insurance; 7.8% do not have insurance; 8.0% of children under 18 do not have insurance

Safety: Violent crime rate: 37.3 per 10,000 population; Property crime rate: 417.2 per 10,000 population

Newspapers: Del Mar Times (weekly circulation 17000)

Transportation: Commute: 71.4% car, 1.3% public transportation, 2.7% walk, 23.6% work from home; Median travel time to work: 20.0 minutes

Additional Information Contacts

City of Del Mar. . . . . (858) 755-9313
http://www.delmar.ca.us

DESCANSO (CDP). Covers a land area of 19.216 square miles and a water area of 0 square miles. Located at 32.87° N. Lat; 116.63° W. Long. Elevation is 3,392 feet.

Population: 1,423; Growth (since 2000): n/a; Density: 74.1 persons per square mile; Race: 90.7% White, 0.4% Black/African American, 1.1% Asian, 2.0% American Indian/Alaska Native, 0.6% Native Hawaiian/Other Pacific Islander, 2.0% Two or more races, 10.5% Hispanic of any race; Average household size: 2.43; Median age: 49.0; Age under 18: 18.0%; Age 65 and over: 13.7%; Males per 100 females: 101.8

School District(s)

Mountain Empire Unified (PK-12)
2012-13 Enrollment: 2,956 . . . . (619) 473-9022

Housing: Homeownership rate: 75.2%; Homeowner vacancy rate: 3.3%; Rental vacancy rate: 9.4%

DULZURA (unincorporated postal area)

ZCTA: 91917

Covers a land area of 36.216 square miles and a water area of 0 square miles. Located at 32.61° N. Lat; 116.72° W. Long. Elevation is 1,053 feet.

Population: 992; Growth (since 2000): 40.1%; Density: 27.4 persons per square mile; Race: 71.6% White, 1.2% Black/African American, 1.4% Asian, 1.2% American Indian/Alaska Native, 0.5% Native Hawaiian/Other Pacific Islander, 3.8% Two or more races, 55.7% Hispanic of any race; Average household size: 3.26; Median age: 39.8; Age under 18: 24.7%; Age 65 and over: 12.8%; Males per 100 females: 107.1

Housing: Homeownership rate: 63.4%; Homeowner vacancy rate: 1.6%; Rental vacancy rate: 9.4%

EL CAJON (city). Covers a land area of 14.433 square miles and a water area of 0 square miles. Located at 32.80° N. Lat; 116.96° W. Long. Elevation is 433 feet.

History: El Cajon has been nicknamed "The Big Box Valley" and "The Corners" and was initially the agrarian and communications center of San Diego County.

Population: 99,478; Growth (since 2000): 4.9%; Density: 6,892.5 persons per square mile; Race: 69.3% White, 6.3% Black/African American, 3.6% Asian, 0.8% American Indian/Alaska Native, 0.5% Native Hawaiian/Other Pacific Islander, 6.9% Two or more races, 28.2% Hispanic of any race; Average household size: 2.84; Median age: 33.7; Age under 18: 25.7%; Age 65 and over: 11.0%; Males per 100 females: 95.6; Marriage status: 36.2% never married, 45.6% now married, 2.4% separated, 6.2% widowed, 12.0% divorced; Foreign born: 29.7%; Speak English only: 57.9%; With disability: 12.6%; Veterans: 9.3%; Ancestry: 11.0% German, 8.3% Assyrian/Chaldean/Syriac, 7.8% Irish, 5.8% English, 5.3% Iraqi

Employment: 11.2% management, business, and financial, 3.0% computer, engineering, and science, 8.7% education, legal, community service, arts, and media, 3.0% healthcare practitioners, 25.5% service, 29.2% sales and office, 9.3% natural resources, construction, and maintenance, 10.0% production, transportation, and material moving

Income: Per capita: $19,803; Median household: $44,112; Average household: $57,907; Households with income of $100,000 or more: 15.8%; Poverty rate: 26.4%

Educational Attainment: High school diploma or higher: 78.4%; Bachelor's degree or higher: 17.5%; Graduate/professional degree or higher: 5.5%

School District(s)

Cajon Valley Union (KG-08)
2012-13 Enrollment: 16,231 . . . . (619) 588-3005
Dehesa Elementary (KG-12)
2012-13 Enrollment: 2,122 . . . . (619) 444-2161
Grossmont Union High (KG-12)
2012-13 Enrollment: 22,965 . . . . (619) 644-8000
Julian Union Elementary (KG-12)
2012-13 Enrollment: 2,979 . . . . (760) 765-0661
La Mesa-Spring Valley (KG-08)
2012-13 Enrollment: 12,070 . . . . (619) 668-5700
San Diego County Office of Education (PK-12)
2012-13 Enrollment: 4,151 . . . . (858) 292-3500
Santee Elementary (KG-08)
2012-13 Enrollment: 6,418 . . . . (619) 258-2300

Four-year College(s)

San Diego Christian College (Private, Not-for-profit, Undenominational)
Fall 2013 Enrollment: 914 . . . . (619) 201-8700
2013-14 Tuition: In-state $25,888; Out-of-state $25,888
Southern California Seminary (Private, Not-for-profit, Baptist)
Fall 2013 Enrollment: 189 . . . . (619) 201-8999
2013-14 Tuition: In-state $13,692; Out-of-state $13,692

Two-year College(s)

Advanced Training Associates (Private, For-profit)
Fall 2013 Enrollment: 103 . . . . (619) 596-2766
Bellus Academy-El Cajon (Private, For-profit)
Fall 2013 Enrollment: 184 . . . . (619) 442-3407
Cuyamaca College (Public)
Fall 2013 Enrollment: 8,859 . . . . (619) 660-4000
2013-14 Tuition: In-state $1,386; Out-of-state $6,896
Grossmont College (Public)
Fall 2013 Enrollment: 18,618 . . . . (619) 644-7000
2013-14 Tuition: In-state $1,387; Out-of-state $6,897

Housing: Homeownership rate: 41.2%; Median home value: $314,800; Median year structure built: 1972; Homeowner vacancy rate: 1.9%; Median gross rent: $1,087 per month; Rental vacancy rate: 4.8%

Health Insurance: 79.6% have insurance; 48.1% have private insurance; 38.8% have public insurance; 20.4% do not have insurance; 11.0% of children under 18 do not have insurance

Safety: Violent crime rate: 37.8 per 10,000 population; Property crime rate: 267.6 per 10,000 population

Newspapers: East Co. Californian (weekly circulation 32000); East Co. Gazette (weekly circulation 15000)

Transportation: Commute: 87.4% car, 3.5% public transportation, 2.2% walk, 5.2% work from home; Median travel time to work: 24.0 minutes

Additional Information Contacts

City of El Cajon . . . . (619) 441-1716
http://www.ci.el-cajon.ca.us

ENCINITAS (city). Covers a land area of 18.812 square miles and a water area of 1.178 square miles. Located at 33.05° N. Lat; 117.26° W. Long. Elevation is 82 feet.

History: Named for the Spanish translation of "little oaks," first used by the Portola expedition in 1769. Encinitas was settled in 1854 by a group of Germans from Chicago, and developed around the growing of blossoms and bulbs.

Population: 59,518; Growth (since 2000): 2.6%; Density: 3,163.9 persons per square mile; Race: 85.8% White, 0.6% Black/African American, 3.9% Asian, 0.5% American Indian/Alaska Native, 0.2% Native Hawaiian/Other Pacific Islander, 3.4% Two or more races, 13.7% Hispanic of any race; Average household size: 2.45; Median age: 41.5; Age under 18: 20.6%; Age 65 and over: 12.8%; Males per 100 females: 97.9; Marriage status: 31.1% never married, 54.2% now married, 0.7% separated, 3.8% widowed, 10.9% divorced; Foreign born: 12.8%; Speak English only: 82.9%; With disability: 7.0%; Veterans: 7.6%; Ancestry: 15.3% German, 14.2% English, 12.6% Irish, 6.2% Italian, 4.6% American

Employment: 20.0% management, business, and financial, 9.7% computer, engineering, and science, 16.3% education, legal, community service, arts, and media, 6.1% healthcare practitioners, 14.0% service, 24.4% sales and office, 4.7% natural resources, construction, and maintenance, 4.6% production, transportation, and material moving

Income: Per capita: $46,797; Median household: $91,795; Average household: $119,220; Households with income of $100,000 or more: 46.3%; Poverty rate: 9.3%

Educational Attainment: High school diploma or higher: 93.6%; Bachelor's degree or higher: 55.4%; Graduate/professional degree or higher: 23.5%

School District(s)

Encinitas Union Elementary (KG-06)
2012-13 Enrollment: 5,448 . . . . (760) 944-4300
San Dieguito Union High (07-12)
2012-13 Enrollment: 12,365 . . . . (760) 753-6491

Housing: Homeownership rate: 63.0%; Median home value: $695,200; Median year structure built: 1978; Homeowner vacancy rate: 1.0%; Median gross rent: $1,720 per month; Rental vacancy rate: 5.3%

Health Insurance: 87.9% have insurance; 80.7% have private insurance; 17.2% have public insurance; 12.1% do not have insurance; 7.7% of children under 18 do not have insurance

Hospitals: Scripps Memorial Hospital - Encinitas (140 beds)

Safety: Violent crime rate: 20.7 per 10,000 population; Property crime rate: 176.0 per 10,000 population

Newspapers: Coast News Group (weekly circulation 88000)

Transportation: Commute: 82.6% car, 1.8% public transportation, 1.8% walk, 11.1% work from home; Median travel time to work: 24.5 minutes

Additional Information Contacts

City of Encinitas. . . . . (760) 633-2600
http://www.ci.encinitas.ca.us

ESCONDIDO (city). Covers a land area of 36.813 square miles and a water area of 0.176 square miles. Located at 33.13° N. Lat; 117.07° W. Long. Elevation is 646 feet.

History: Named for the Spanish translation of "hidden," first used by the Anza expedition in 1776. Escondido was laid out in 1885 when part of the Wolfskill Ranch (originally on the Rancho Rincon del Diablo) was purchased by a syndicate. The town became a center of a grape-growing industry.

Population: 143,911; Growth (since 2000): 7.8%; Density: 3,909.3 persons per square mile; Race: 60.4% White, 2.5% Black/African American, 6.1% Asian, 1.0% American Indian/Alaska Native, 0.2% Native Hawaiian/Other Pacific Islander, 4.4% Two or more races, 48.9% Hispanic of any race; Average household size: 3.12; Median age: 32.5; Age under 18: 27.6%; Age 65 and over: 10.5%; Males per 100 females: 98.2; Marriage status: 34.0% never married, 51.3% now married, 2.0% separated, 5.4% widowed, 9.3% divorced; Foreign born: 28.0%; Speak English only: 52.0%; With disability: 9.4%; Veterans: 7.5%; Ancestry: 10.2% English, 9.2% German, 6.8% Irish, 3.2% Italian, 2.4% American

Employment: 11.0% management, business, and financial, 4.5% computer, engineering, and science, 7.8% education, legal, community service, arts, and media, 3.7% healthcare practitioners, 24.8% service, 23.3% sales and office, 13.2% natural resources, construction, and maintenance, 11.8% production, transportation, and material moving

Income: Per capita: $21,653; Median household: $49,362; Average household: $67,053; Households with income of $100,000 or more: 20.2%; Poverty rate: 18.7%

Educational Attainment: High school diploma or higher: 72.1%; Bachelor's degree or higher: 21.0%; Graduate/professional degree or higher: 6.1%

School District(s)

Dehesa Elementary (KG-12)
2012-13 Enrollment: 2,122 . . . . (619) 444-2161
Escondido Union (KG-08)
2012-13 Enrollment: 19,365 . . . . (760) 432-2400
Escondido Union High (09-12)
2012-13 Enrollment: 9,196 . . . . (760) 291-3200
San Diego County Office of Education (PK-12)
2012-13 Enrollment: 4,151 . . . . (858) 292-3500
San Pasqual Union Elementary (KG-08)
2012-13 Enrollment: 556. . . . . (760) 745-4931

Four-year College(s)

John Paul the Great Catholic University (Private, Not-for-profit, Roman Catholic)
Fall 2013 Enrollment: 263 . . . . (858) 653-6740
2013-14 Tuition: In-state $24,900; Out-of-state $24,900
Westminster Theological Seminary in California (Private, Not-for-profit)
Fall 2013 Enrollment: 143 . . . . (760) 480-8474

Vocational/Technical School(s)

Healing Hands School of Holistic Health (Private, For-profit)
Fall 2013 Enrollment: 228 . . . . (760) 746-9364
2013-14 Tuition: $9,900

Housing: Homeownership rate: 52.2%; Median home value: $324,600; Median year structure built: 1979; Homeowner vacancy rate: 2.2%; Median gross rent: $1,182 per month; Rental vacancy rate: 6.0%

Health Insurance: 74.4% have insurance; 53.4% have private insurance; 27.6% have public insurance; 25.6% do not have insurance; 13.8% of children under 18 do not have insurance

Hospitals: Palomar Health Downtown Campus (332 beds)

Safety: Violent crime rate: 40.1 per 10,000 population; Property crime rate: 266.7 per 10,000 population

Newspapers: North County Spectrum (weekly circulation 2000); North County Times (daily circulation 87000)

Transportation: Commute: 92.4% car, 1.6% public transportation, 1.6% walk, 3.0% work from home; Median travel time to work: 25.8 minutes

Additional Information Contacts

City of Escondido . . . . (760) 839-4880
http://www.escondido.org

EUCALYPTUS HILLS (CDP). Covers a land area of 4.759 square miles and a water area of 0.015 square miles. Located at 32.88° N. Lat; 116.94° W. Long. Elevation is 666 feet.

Population: 5,313; Growth (since 2000): n/a; Density: 1,116.4 persons per square mile; Race: 85.9% White, 3.7% Black/African American, 1.6% Asian, 1.1% American Indian/Alaska Native, 0.1% Native Hawaiian/Other Pacific Islander, 4.0% Two or more races, 14.7% Hispanic of any race; Average household size: 2.94; Median age: 37.5; Age under 18: 26.0%; Age 65 and over: 12.7%; Males per 100 females: 102.7; Marriage status: 17.0% never married, 72.2% now married, 1.7% separated, 3.5% widowed, 7.3% divorced; Foreign born: 6.2%; Speak English only: 88.4%; With disability: 11.1%; Veterans: 19.8%; Ancestry: 17.3% English, 13.4% German, 12.8% Irish, 8.6% French, 4.7% Italian

Employment: 17.8% management, business, and financial, 9.1% computer, engineering, and science, 7.9% education, legal, community service, arts, and media, 6.9% healthcare practitioners, 11.6% service, 25.0% sales and office, 16.3% natural resources, construction, and maintenance, 5.4% production, transportation, and material moving

Income: Per capita: $32,085; Median household: $75,432; Average household: $96,445; Households with income of $100,000 or more: 34.8%; Poverty rate: 4.8%

Educational Attainment: High school diploma or higher: 93.2%; Bachelor's degree or higher: 33.3%; Graduate/professional degree or higher: 10.1%

Housing: Homeownership rate: 72.0%; Median home value: $380,300; Median year structure built: 1973; Homeowner vacancy rate: 0.8%; Median gross rent: $1,848 per month; Rental vacancy rate: 6.1%

Health Insurance: 88.7% have insurance; 80.6% have private insurance; 23.1% have public insurance; 11.3% do not have insurance; 11.4% of children under 18 do not have insurance

Transportation: Commute: 89.3% car, 0.0% public transportation, 0.0% walk, 10.7% work from home; Median travel time to work: 28.0 minutes

FAIRBANKS RANCH (CDP). Covers a land area of 5.074 square miles and a water area of 0.005 square miles. Located at 32.99° N. Lat; 117.19° W. Long.

History: The entire population is contained within two gated communities, divided into North and South sections by the formerly private San Dieguito Road. It is commonly considered to be part of the Rancho Santa Fe area within San Diego County, and is even included within the proposed boundaries for the city of Rancho Santa Fe.

Population: 3,148; Growth (since 2000): 40.3%; Density: 620.4 persons per square mile; Race: 88.3% White, 0.8% Black/African American, 6.6% Asian, 0.2% American Indian/Alaska Native, 0.1% Native Hawaiian/Other Pacific Islander, 2.9% Two or more races, 7.1% Hispanic of any race; Average household size: 2.86; Median age: 49.4; Age under 18: 24.1%; Age 65 and over: 17.7%; Males per 100 females: 94.7; Marriage status: 10.5% never married, 78.1% now married, 0.0% separated, 5.4% widowed, 6.0% divorced; Foreign born: 19.1%; Speak English only: 78.2%; With disability: 4.8%; Veterans: 8.6%; Ancestry: 19.3% English, 18.9% German, 10.0% Iranian, 8.8% Russian, 8.6% American

Employment: 35.0% management, business, and financial, 12.0% computer, engineering, and science, 12.4% education, legal, community service, arts, and media, 13.3% healthcare practitioners, 0.0% service, 21.6% sales and office, 5.8% natural resources, construction, and maintenance, 0.0% production, transportation, and material moving

Income: Per capita: $54,127; Median household: $115,885; Average household: $156,994; Households with income of $100,000 or more: 59.7%; Poverty rate: 3.0%

Educational Attainment: High school diploma or higher: 98.4%; Bachelor's degree or higher: 76.9%; Graduate/professional degree or higher: 47.3%

Housing: Homeownership rate: 93.8%; Median home value: 1 million+; Median year structure built: 1993; Homeowner vacancy rate: 2.1%; Median gross rent: n/a per month; Rental vacancy rate: 4.1%

Health Insurance: 100.0% have insurance; 94.0% have private insurance; 19.8% have public insurance; 0.0% do not have insurance; 0.0% of children under 18 do not have insurance

Transportation: Commute: 69.7% car, 0.0% public transportation, 0.0% walk, 30.3% work from home; Median travel time to work: 25.7 minutes

FALLBROOK (CDP). Covers a land area of 17.528 square miles and a water area of 0.033 square miles. Located at 33.37° N. Lat; 117.23° W. Long. Elevation is 682 feet.

History: Named for Fallbrook, Pennsylvania, home of early settler and first postmaster Charles V. Reche. Fallbrook was settled in the 1880s and became a citrus-growing region, with avocado orchards added later.

Population: 30,534; Growth (since 2000): 4.9%; Density: 1,742.0 persons per square mile; Race: 67.0% White, 1.6% Black/African American, 1.9% Asian, 0.8% American Indian/Alaska Native, 0.2% Native Hawaiian/Other Pacific Islander, 4.3% Two or more races, 45.2% Hispanic of any race; Average household size: 3.04; Median age: 34.7; Age under 18: 26.3%; Age 65 and over: 13.9%; Males per 100 females: 99.5; Marriage status: 28.0% never married, 58.6% now married, 2.2% separated, 5.7% widowed, 7.8% divorced; Foreign born: 22.9%; Speak English only: 61.8%; With disability: 12.9%; Veterans: 12.5%; Ancestry: 12.6% German, 12.4% English, 9.1% Irish, 3.8% American, 3.5% Italian

Employment: 14.0% management, business, and financial, 4.6% computer, engineering, and science, 7.9% education, legal, community service, arts, and media, 4.6% healthcare practitioners, 23.3% service, 20.9% sales and office, 16.3% natural resources, construction, and maintenance, 8.5% production, transportation, and material moving

Income: Per capita: $26,711; Median household: $55,396; Average household: $74,810; Households with income of $100,000 or more: 22.2%; Poverty rate: 15.6%

Educational Attainment: High school diploma or higher: 78.5%; Bachelor's degree or higher: 21.5%; Graduate/professional degree or higher: 7.6%

School District(s)

Fallbrook Union Elementary (KG-08)
2012-13 Enrollment: 5,554 . . . . (760) 731-5400
Fallbrook Union High (09-12)
2012-13 Enrollment: 2,760 . . . . (760) 723-6332

Housing: Homeownership rate: 59.2%; Median home value: $371,000; Median year structure built: 1979; Homeowner vacancy rate: 2.4%; Median gross rent: $1,057 per month; Rental vacancy rate: 8.5%

Health Insurance: 81.4% have insurance; 60.1% have private insurance; 33.1% have public insurance; 18.6% do not have insurance; 7.1% of children under 18 do not have insurance

Hospitals: Fallbrook Hospital (146 beds)

Newspapers: Anza Valley Outlook (weekly circulation 2200); Fallbrook Village News (weekly circulation 13000)

Transportation: Commute: 87.8% car, 0.7% public transportation, 4.4% walk, 5.9% work from home; Median travel time to work: 27.2 minutes

GRANITE HILLS (CDP). Covers a land area of 2.849 square miles and a water area of 0 square miles. Located at 32.80° N. Lat; 116.91° W. Long. Elevation is 659 feet.

Population: 3,035; Growth (since 2000): -6.5%; Density: 1,065.4 persons per square mile; Race: 86.2% White, 1.4% Black/African American, 1.5% Asian, 0.9% American Indian/Alaska Native, 0.3% Native Hawaiian/Other Pacific Islander, 4.5% Two or more races, 13.2% Hispanic of any race; Average household size: 2.93; Median age: 47.0; Age under 18: 17.7%; Age 65 and over: 18.6%; Males per 100 females: 102.1; Marriage status: 25.5% never married, 58.2% now married, 1.2% separated, 7.1% widowed, 9.2% divorced; Foreign born: 9.9%; Speak English only: 81.4%; With disability: 14.4%; Veterans: 14.9%; Ancestry: 20.2% German, 14.6% Irish, 9.7% English, 6.4% Scottish, 5.2% American

Employment: 19.6% management, business, and financial, 13.6% computer, engineering, and science, 7.3% education, legal, community service, arts, and media, 2.2% healthcare practitioners, 20.4% service, 19.8% sales and office, 12.3% natural resources, construction, and maintenance, 4.8% production, transportation, and material moving

Income: Per capita: $50,637; Median household: $94,625; Average household: $144,860; Households with income of $100,000 or more: 48.2%; Poverty rate: 8.3%

Educational Attainment: High school diploma or higher: 95.2%; Bachelor's degree or higher: 33.2%; Graduate/professional degree or higher: 7.7%

Housing: Homeownership rate: 88.6%; Median home value: $507,600; Median year structure built: 1965; Homeowner vacancy rate: 1.8%; Median gross rent: $1,883 per month; Rental vacancy rate: 4.0%

Health Insurance: 91.6% have insurance; 74.8% have private insurance; 34.5% have public insurance; 8.4% do not have insurance; 3.2% of children under 18 do not have insurance

Transportation: Commute: 90.1% car, 0.0% public transportation, 2.5% walk, 4.2% work from home; Median travel time to work: 21.7 minutes

GUATAY (unincorporated postal area)

ZCTA: 91931

Covers a land area of 14.466 square miles and a water area of 0 square miles. Located at 32.85° N. Lat; 116.56° W. Long. Elevation is 3,999 feet.

Population: 592; Growth (since 2000): -24.3%; Density: 40.9 persons per square mile; Race: 87.3% White, 0.0% Black/African American, 0.5% Asian, 1.4% American Indian/Alaska Native, 0.0% Native Hawaiian/Other Pacific Islander, 3.0% Two or more races, 21.1% Hispanic of any race; Average household size: 2.39; Median age: 43.7; Age under 18: 24.0%; Age 65 and over: 12.2%; Males per 100 females: 106.3

Housing: Homeownership rate: 66.1%; Homeowner vacancy rate: 4.0%; Rental vacancy rate: 7.7%

HARBISON CANYON (CDP).

Covers a land area of 10.059 square miles and a water area of 0 square miles. Located at 32.83° N. Lat; 116.84° W. Long. Elevation is 906 feet.

Population: 3,841; Growth (since 2000): 5.4%; Density: 381.9 persons per square mile; Race: 88.6% White, 0.3% Black/African American, 1.8% Asian, 1.9% American Indian/Alaska Native, 0.2% Native Hawaiian/Other Pacific Islander, 3.4% Two or more races, 16.2% Hispanic of any race; Average household size: 2.86; Median age: 42.4; Age under 18: 22.3%; Age 65 and over: 10.8%; Males per 100 females: 103.9; Marriage status: 25.4% never married, 59.0% now married, 2.2% separated, 4.7% widowed, 10.9% divorced; Foreign born: 8.3%; Speak English only: 86.4%; With disability: 11.0%; Veterans: 13.7%; Ancestry: 16.2% German, 10.7% Irish, 10.5% English, 6.0% Italian, 4.0% Swedish

Employment: 13.2% management, business, and financial, 5.3% computer, engineering, and science, 9.6% education, legal, community service, arts, and media, 5.9% healthcare practitioners, 19.8% service, 22.4% sales and office, 13.2% natural resources, construction, and maintenance, 10.4% production, transportation, and material moving

Income: Per capita: $28,928; Median household: $79,893; Average household: $87,337; Households with income of $100,000 or more: 32.7%; Poverty rate: 9.2%

Educational Attainment: High school diploma or higher: 89.7%; Bachelor's degree or higher: 22.0%; Graduate/professional degree or higher: 8.6%

Housing: Homeownership rate: 86.4%; Median home value: $340,400; Median year structure built: 1992; Homeowner vacancy rate: 2.3%; Median gross rent: $1,230 per month; Rental vacancy rate: 1.6%

Health Insurance: 85.7% have insurance; 69.7% have private insurance; 25.6% have public insurance; 14.3% do not have insurance; 15.4% of children under 18 do not have insurance

Transportation: Commute: 95.5% car, 0.0% public transportation, 1.1% walk, 2.3% work from home; Median travel time to work: 26.3 minutes

HIDDEN MEADOWS (CDP).

Covers a land area of 6.583 square miles and a water area of 0 square miles. Located at 33.22° N. Lat; 117.12° W. Long. Elevation is 1,496 feet.

Population: 3,485; Growth (since 2000): 0.6%; Density: 529.4 persons per square mile; Race: 82.2% White, 1.9% Black/African American, 9.1% Asian, 0.3% American Indian/Alaska Native, 0.2% Native Hawaiian/Other Pacific Islander, 3.6% Two or more races, 9.4% Hispanic of any race; Average household size: 2.48; Median age: 52.7; Age under 18: 15.0%; Age 65 and over: 25.1%; Males per 100 females: 97.5; Marriage status: 13.9% never married, 70.5% now married, 0.4% separated, 6.1% widowed, 9.4% divorced; Foreign born: 13.6%; Speak English only: 85.9%; With disability: 10.5%; Veterans: 18.5%; Ancestry: 21.5% German, 18.4% English, 7.6% Irish, 7.2% French, 5.2% Polish

Employment: 32.8% management, business, and financial, 13.3% computer, engineering, and science, 14.0% education, legal, community service, arts, and media, 4.0% healthcare practitioners, 7.5% service, 22.0% sales and office, 5.5% natural resources, construction, and maintenance, 0.9% production, transportation, and material moving

Income: Per capita: $47,804; Median household: $95,625; Average household: $109,093; Households with income of $100,000 or more: 45.8%; Poverty rate: 7.4%

Educational Attainment: High school diploma or higher: 94.3%; Bachelor's degree or higher: 45.3%; Graduate/professional degree or higher: 17.1%

Housing: Homeownership rate: 88.3%; Median home value: $520,500; Median year structure built: 1986; Homeowner vacancy rate: 2.6%; Median gross rent: $1,222 per month; Rental vacancy rate: 7.9%

Health Insurance: 97.9% have insurance; 84.9% have private insurance; 36.5% have public insurance; 2.1% do not have insurance; 0.0% of children under 18 do not have insurance

Transportation: Commute: 92.5% car, 0.0% public transportation, 0.0% walk, 6.6% work from home; Median travel time to work: 29.9 minutes

IMPERIAL BEACH (city).

Covers a land area of 4.161 square miles and a water area of 0.324 square miles. Located at 32.57° N. Lat; 117.11° W. Long. Elevation is 20 feet.

History: Named for the hope that purchasers would be attracted to the development. Incorporated 1956.

Population: 26,324; Growth (since 2000): -2.5%; Density: 6,325.9 persons per square mile; Race: 62.6% White, 4.4% Black/African American, 6.6% Asian, 1.0% American Indian/Alaska Native, 0.7% Native Hawaiian/Other Pacific Islander, 6.6% Two or more races, 49.0% Hispanic of any race; Average household size: 2.82; Median age: 31.0; Age under 18: 25.4%; Age 65 and over: 9.0%; Males per 100 females: 101.1; Marriage status: 37.6% never married, 45.9% now married, 3.6% separated, 4.9% widowed, 11.7% divorced; Foreign born: 19.5%; Speak English only: 55.2%; With disability: 11.4%; Veterans: 12.0%; Ancestry: 9.7% German, 8.9% Irish, 4.8% English, 3.2% Italian, 2.1% American

Employment: 11.9% management, business, and financial, 4.2% computer, engineering, and science, 8.1% education, legal, community service, arts, and media, 3.3% healthcare practitioners, 25.0% service, 28.5% sales and office, 7.6% natural resources, construction, and maintenance, 11.3% production, transportation, and material moving

Income: Per capita: $20,183; Median household: $49,268; Average household: $58,025; Households with income of $100,000 or more: 13.5%; Poverty rate: 18.6%

Educational Attainment: High school diploma or higher: 80.8%; Bachelor's degree or higher: 17.3%; Graduate/professional degree or higher: 5.3%

School District(s)

South Bay Union Elementary (KG-08)
2012-13 Enrollment: 7,773 . . . . (619) 628-1600
Sweetwater Union High (07-12)
2012-13 Enrollment: 40,916 . . . . (619) 691-5500

Housing: Homeownership rate: 30.2%; Median home value: $340,900; Median year structure built: 1969; Homeowner vacancy rate: 2.3%; Median gross rent: $1,171 per month; Rental vacancy rate: 5.4%

Health Insurance: 80.4% have insurance; 55.2% have private insurance; 33.1% have public insurance; 19.6% do not have insurance; 13.2% of children under 18 do not have insurance

Safety: Violent crime rate: 49.3 per 10,000 population; Property crime rate: 168.2 per 10,000 population

Newspapers: Eagle & Times (weekly circulation 6500)

Transportation: Commute: 85.5% car, 5.7% public transportation, 2.5% walk, 3.3% work from home; Median travel time to work: 25.5 minutes

Additional Information Contacts

City of Imperial Beach . . . . (619) 423-8303
http://www.imperialbeachca.gov

JACUMBA (CDP).

Covers a land area of 6.119 square miles and a water area of 0.007 square miles. Located at 32.64° N. Lat; 116.19° W. Long.

Population: 561; Growth (since 2000): n/a; Density: 91.7 persons per square mile; Race: 69.3% White, 0.7% Black/African American, 1.1% Asian, 2.7% American Indian/Alaska Native, 0.0% Native Hawaiian/Other Pacific Islander, 5.9% Two or more races, 36.9% Hispanic of any race; Average household size: 2.60; Median age: 39.9; Age under 18: 25.1%; Age 65 and over: 14.1%; Males per 100 females: 101.8

School District(s)

Mountain Empire Unified (PK-12)
2012-13 Enrollment: 2,956 . . . . (619) 473-9022

Housing: Homeownership rate: 57.0%; Homeowner vacancy rate: 7.4%; Rental vacancy rate: 7.9%

JAMUL (CDP).

Covers a land area of 16.583 square miles and a water area of 0.250 square miles. Located at 32.72° N. Lat; 116.87° W. Long. Elevation is 997 feet.

Population: 6,163; Growth (since 2000): 4.1%; Density: 371.6 persons per square mile; Race: 86.0% White, 2.1% Black/African American, 2.4%

Asian, 0.5% American Indian/Alaska Native, 0.2% Native Hawaiian/Other Pacific Islander, 4.2% Two or more races, 19.3% Hispanic of any race; Average household size: 3.20; Median age: 44.4; Age under 18: 22.7%; Age 65 and over: 13.4%; Males per 100 females: 101.0; Marriage status: 27.2% never married, 58.0% now married, 0.3% separated, 5.3% widowed, 9.5% divorced; Foreign born: 15.3%; Speak English only: 71.6%; With disability: 8.3%; Veterans: 9.0%; Ancestry: 17.2% German, 12.9% Irish, 11.5% English, 7.2% Assyrian/Chaldean/Syriac, 6.4% Italian

Employment: 15.5% management, business, and financial, 5.3% computer, engineering, and science, 13.3% education, legal, community service, arts, and media, 3.4% healthcare practitioners, 14.1% service, 29.8% sales and office, 11.4% natural resources, construction, and maintenance, 7.2% production, transportation, and material moving

Income: Per capita: $37,216; Median household: $100,804; Average household: $113,741; Households with income of $100,000 or more: 50.5%; Poverty rate: 5.7%

Educational Attainment: High school diploma or higher: 90.7%; Bachelor's degree or higher: 30.1%; Graduate/professional degree or higher: 15.6%

School District(s)

Jamul-Dulzura Union Elementary (KG-12)
2012-13 Enrollment: 1,114 . . . . (619) 669-7700

Housing: Homeownership rate: 88.8%; Median home value: $562,100; Median year structure built: 1982; Homeowner vacancy rate: 0.9%; Median gross rent: $1,872 per month; Rental vacancy rate: 2.7%

Health Insurance: 89.1% have insurance; 80.7% have private insurance; 19.0% have public insurance; 10.9% do not have insurance; 9.7% of children under 18 do not have insurance

Transportation: Commute: 91.0% car, 0.0% public transportation, 0.9% walk, 6.8% work from home; Median travel time to work: 27.5 minutes

JULIAN (CDP). Covers a land area of 7.839 square miles and a water area of 0 square miles. Located at 33.07° N. Lat; 116.59° W. Long. Elevation is 4,222 feet.

History: Julian was established by the Bailey brothers and their cousins, the Julian brothers, who moved into the region in 1869, shortly after placer gold was discovered near the site of the town. The 1870's was a boom time for Julian, which settled into being a farmers' trading center when the gold was gone.

Population: 1,502; Growth (since 2000): -7.3%; Density: 191.6 persons per square mile; Race: 89.3% White, 0.3% Black/African American, 0.8% Asian, 1.8% American Indian/Alaska Native, 0.0% Native Hawaiian/Other Pacific Islander, 2.4% Two or more races, 13.0% Hispanic of any race; Average household size: 2.24; Median age: 50.8; Age under 18: 18.8%; Age 65 and over: 19.8%; Males per 100 females: 96.1

School District(s)

Julian Union Elementary (KG-12)
2012-13 Enrollment: 2,979 . . . . (760) 765-0661
Julian Union High (09-12)
2012-13 Enrollment: 178. . . . . (760) 765-0606

Housing: Homeownership rate: 73.0%; Homeowner vacancy rate: 3.0%; Rental vacancy rate: 9.5%

Newspapers: Julian News (weekly circulation 2500)

LA JOLLA (unincorporated postal area)

ZCTA: 92037

Covers a land area of 13.078 square miles and a water area of 2.018 square miles. Located at 32.86° N. Lat; 117.25° W. Long. Elevation is 105 feet.

Population: 46,781; Growth (since 2000): 9.8%; Density: 3,577.1 persons per square mile; Race: 76.3% White, 1.2% Black/African American, 16.1% Asian, 0.2% American Indian/Alaska Native, 0.1% Native Hawaiian/Other Pacific Islander, 3.9% Two or more races, 9.2% Hispanic of any race; Average household size: 2.16; Median age: 34.7; Age under 18: 13.3%; Age 65 and over: 18.4%; Males per 100 females: 94.1; Marriage status: 37.3% never married, 47.7% now married, 0.6% separated, 4.9% widowed, 10.0% divorced; Foreign born: 19.7%; Speak English only: 75.1%; With disability: 6.7%; Veterans: 7.1%; Ancestry: 13.7% German, 11.6% Irish, 11.4% English, 6.5% Italian, 4.5% American

Employment: 24.9% management, business, and financial, 16.7% computer, engineering, and science, 18.2% education, legal, community service, arts, and media, 7.9% healthcare practitioners, 10.8% service, 17.8% sales and office, 1.7% natural resources, construction, and maintenance, 1.9% production, transportation, and material moving

Income: Per capita: $64,476; Median household: $99,367; Average household: $151,265; Households with income of $100,000 or more: 49.9%; Poverty rate: 12.2%

Educational Attainment: High school diploma or higher: 98.9%; Bachelor's degree or higher: 76.4%; Graduate/professional degree or higher: 40.7%

School District(s)

San Diego Unified (KG-12)
2012-13 Enrollment: 130,271 . . . . (619) 725-8000

Four-year College(s)

National University (Private, Not-for-profit)
Fall 2013 Enrollment: 18,207 . . . . (800) 628-8648
2013-14 Tuition: In-state $12,096; Out-of-state $12,096
Sanford-Burnham Medical Research Institute (Private, Not-for-profit)
Fall 2013 Enrollment: 32 . . . . (858) 646-3100
University of California-San Diego (Public)
Fall 2013 Enrollment: 29,517 . . . . (858) 534-2230
2013-14 Tuition: In-state $13,271; Out-of-state $36,149

Two-year College(s)

National University (Private, Not-for-profit)
Fall 2013 Enrollment: 18,207 . . . . (800) 628-8648
2013-14 Tuition: In-state $12,096; Out-of-state $12,096
Sanford-Burnham Medical Research Institute (Private, Not-for-profit)
Fall 2013 Enrollment: 32 . . . . (858) 646-3100
University of California-San Diego (Public)
Fall 2013 Enrollment: 29,517 . . . . (858) 534-2230
2013-14 Tuition: In-state $13,271; Out-of-state $36,149

Vocational/Technical School(s)

National University (Private, Not-for-profit)
Fall 2013 Enrollment: 18,207 . . . . (800) 628-8648
2013-14 Tuition: In-state $12,096; Out-of-state $12,096
Sanford-Burnham Medical Research Institute (Private, Not-for-profit)
Fall 2013 Enrollment: 32 . . . . (858) 646-3100
University of California-San Diego (Public)
Fall 2013 Enrollment: 29,517 . . . . (858) 534-2230
2013-14 Tuition: In-state $13,271; Out-of-state $36,149

Housing: Homeownership rate: 58.9%; Median home value: 1 million+; Median year structure built: 1972; Homeowner vacancy rate: 1.6%; Median gross rent: $1,727 per month; Rental vacancy rate: 6.5%

Health Insurance: 94.1% have insurance; 87.4% have private insurance; 22.1% have public insurance; 5.9% do not have insurance; 1.0% of children under 18 do not have insurance

Hospitals: Scripps Green Hospital (173 beds); Scripps Memorial Hospital La Jolla (293 beds)

Newspapers: La Jolla Light (weekly circulation 18000)

Transportation: Commute: 72.2% car, 5.1% public transportation, 5.5% walk, 12.4% work from home; Median travel time to work: 19.5 minutes

LA MESA (city). Covers a land area of 9.076 square miles and a water area of 0.040 square miles. Located at 32.77° N. Lat; 117.02° W. Long. Elevation is 528 feet.

History: Named for the Spanish translation of "flat-topped hill". La Mesa developed as a residential community on land formerly called Allison's Springs, used for grazing sheep.

Population: 57,065; Growth (since 2000): 4.2%; Density: 6,287.3 persons per square mile; Race: 71.8% White, 7.7% Black/African American, 5.8% Asian, 0.8% American Indian/Alaska Native, 0.6% Native Hawaiian/Other Pacific Islander, 5.8% Two or more races, 20.5% Hispanic of any race; Average household size: 2.30; Median age: 37.1; Age under 18: 19.6%; Age 65 and over: 14.2%; Males per 100 females: 90.8; Marriage status: 33.3% never married, 44.6% now married, 1.3% separated, 6.7% widowed, 15.4% divorced; Foreign born: 13.9%; Speak English only: 78.2%; With disability: 12.0%; Veterans: 13.9%; Ancestry: 16.3% German, 12.1% Irish, 9.1% English, 5.6% Italian, 3.4% American

Employment: 16.1% management, business, and financial, 6.7% computer, engineering, and science, 13.2% education, legal, community service, arts, and media, 6.1% healthcare practitioners, 19.3% service, 24.1% sales and office, 8.4% natural resources, construction, and maintenance, 6.2% production, transportation, and material moving

Income: Per capita: $30,570; Median household: $53,605; Average household: $71,138; Households with income of $100,000 or more: 22.3%; Poverty rate: 12.7%

Educational Attainment: High school diploma or higher: 91.8%; Bachelor's degree or higher: 35.0%; Graduate/professional degree or higher: 11.6%

School District(s)

Cajon Valley Union (KG-08)
2012-13 Enrollment: 16,231 . . . . (619) 588-3005
Grossmont Union High (KG-12)
2012-13 Enrollment: 22,965 . . . . (619) 644-8000
La Mesa-Spring Valley (KG-08)
2012-13 Enrollment: 12,070 . . . . (619) 668-5700
Lemon Grove (PK-08)
2012-13 Enrollment: 3,901 . . . . (619) 825-5600
Mountain Empire Unified (PK-12)
2012-13 Enrollment: 2,956 . . . . (619) 473-9022
San Diego County Office of Education (PK-12)
2012-13 Enrollment: 4,151 . . . . (858) 292-3500
San Diego Unified (KG-12)
2012-13 Enrollment: 130,271 . . . . (619) 725-8000

Vocational/Technical School(s)

California Hair Design Academy (Private, For-profit)
Fall 2013 Enrollment: 219 . . . . (619) 461-8600
2013-14 Tuition: $15,125

Housing: Homeownership rate: 45.8%; Median home value: $365,000; Median year structure built: 1967; Homeowner vacancy rate: 1.4%; Median gross rent: $1,208 per month; Rental vacancy rate: 7.2%

Health Insurance: 84.9% have insurance; 68.6% have private insurance; 27.6% have public insurance; 15.1% do not have insurance; 7.7% of children under 18 do not have insurance

Hospitals: Grossmont Hospital (536 beds)

Safety: Violent crime rate: 31.0 per 10,000 population; Property crime rate: 336.5 per 10,000 population

Transportation: Commute: 87.6% car, 3.0% public transportation, 1.7% walk, 6.2% work from home; Median travel time to work: 23.3 minutes

Additional Information Contacts

City of La Mesa . . . . (619) 463-6611
http://www.cityoflamesa.org

LA PRESA (CDP). Covers a land area of 5.496 square miles and a water area of 0.522 square miles. Located at 32.71° N. Lat; 117.00° W. Long. Elevation is 354 feet.

Population: 34,169; Growth (since 2000): 4.4%; Density: 6,217.4 persons per square mile; Race: 44.1% White, 13.0% Black/African American, 9.4% Asian, 0.8% American Indian/Alaska Native, 1.2% Native Hawaiian/Other Pacific Islander, 7.4% Two or more races, 47.3% Hispanic of any race; Average household size: 3.33; Median age: 32.7; Age under 18: 28.0%; Age 65 and over: 10.5%; Males per 100 females: 95.9; Marriage status: 36.5% never married, 47.5% now married, 2.1% separated, 5.2% widowed, 10.8% divorced; Foreign born: 27.7%; Speak English only: 47.6%; With disability: 11.9%; Veterans: 11.8%; Ancestry: 7.3% German, 6.6% Irish, 3.4% English, 3.1% Italian, 1.3% French

Employment: 9.6% management, business, and financial, 5.4% computer, engineering, and science, 7.6% education, legal, community service, arts, and media, 3.5% healthcare practitioners, 24.3% service, 25.6% sales and office, 13.6% natural resources, construction, and maintenance, 10.4% production, transportation, and material moving

Income: Per capita: $22,319; Median household: $60,542; Average household: $71,393; Households with income of $100,000 or more: 20.0%; Poverty rate: 13.0%

Educational Attainment: High school diploma or higher: 79.0%; Bachelor's degree or higher: 16.7%; Graduate/professional degree or higher: 4.7%

Housing: Homeownership rate: 62.3%; Median home value: $268,800; Median year structure built: 1973; Homeowner vacancy rate: 2.2%; Median gross rent: $1,179 per month; Rental vacancy rate: 5.7%

Health Insurance: 80.3% have insurance; 59.0% have private insurance; 29.2% have public insurance; 19.7% do not have insurance; 12.8% of children under 18 do not have insurance

Transportation: Commute: 89.8% car, 2.6% public transportation, 1.4% walk, 4.8% work from home; Median travel time to work: 27.0 minutes

LAKE SAN MARCOS (CDP). Covers a land area of 1.721 square miles and a water area of 0.086 square miles. Located at 33.12° N. Lat; 117.21° W. Long. Elevation is 525 feet.

Population: 4,437; Growth (since 2000): 7.2%; Density: 2,578.6 persons per square mile; Race: 89.7% White, 0.8% Black/African American, 3.0% Asian, 0.5% American Indian/Alaska Native, 0.1% Native Hawaiian/Other Pacific Islander, 1.8% Two or more races, 10.5% Hispanic of any race; Average household size: 1.91; Median age: 63.3; Age under 18: 8.2%; Age 65 and over: 46.8%; Males per 100 females: 79.3; Marriage status: 17.6% never married, 47.3% now married, 0.2% separated, 19.6% widowed, 15.5% divorced; Foreign born: 11.5%; Speak English only: 83.7%; With disability: 25.2%; Veterans: 20.7%; Ancestry: 30.6% English, 13.8% German, 8.5% Irish, 5.8% Italian, 4.6% European

Employment: 19.6% management, business, and financial, 8.7% computer, engineering, and science, 17.0% education, legal, community service, arts, and media, 4.1% healthcare practitioners, 25.0% service, 18.4% sales and office, 2.8% natural resources, construction, and maintenance, 4.4% production, transportation, and material moving

Income: Per capita: $37,427; Median household: $45,302; Average household: $65,762; Households with income of $100,000 or more: 13.7%; Poverty rate: 15.4%

Educational Attainment: High school diploma or higher: 95.9%; Bachelor's degree or higher: 38.5%; Graduate/professional degree or higher: 11.5%

Housing: Homeownership rate: 78.9%; Median home value: $399,100; Median year structure built: 1980; Homeowner vacancy rate: 2.3%; Median gross rent: $1,741 per month; Rental vacancy rate: 5.3%

Health Insurance: 89.6% have insurance; 69.6% have private insurance; 51.2% have public insurance; 10.4% do not have insurance; 0.0% of children under 18 do not have insurance

Transportation: Commute: 86.5% car, 0.0% public transportation, 0.0% walk, 13.5% work from home; Median travel time to work: 24.9 minutes

LAKESIDE (CDP). Covers a land area of 6.900 square miles and a water area of 0.380 square miles. Located at 32.86° N. Lat; 116.90° W. Long. Elevation is 413 feet.

Population: 20,648; Growth (since 2000): 5.6%; Density: 2,992.3 persons per square mile; Race: 85.0% White, 1.1% Black/African American, 1.7% Asian, 0.9% American Indian/Alaska Native, 0.3% Native Hawaiian/Other Pacific Islander, 4.6% Two or more races, 17.6% Hispanic of any race; Average household size: 2.79; Median age: 39.1; Age under 18: 24.5%; Age 65 and over: 12.9%; Males per 100 females: 96.6; Marriage status: 27.3% never married, 57.1% now married, 1.8% separated, 4.8% widowed, 10.7% divorced; Foreign born: 9.2%; Speak English only: 83.3%; With disability: 14.1%; Veterans: 13.7%; Ancestry: 19.9% German, 16.1% Irish, 11.8% English, 5.5% Italian, 4.6% French

Employment: 12.5% management, business, and financial, 6.1% computer, engineering, and science, 10.7% education, legal, community service, arts, and media, 3.4% healthcare practitioners, 15.7% service, 28.7% sales and office, 14.9% natural resources, construction, and maintenance, 8.0% production, transportation, and material moving

Income: Per capita: $26,300; Median household: $57,439; Average household: $74,446; Households with income of $100,000 or more: 29.0%; Poverty rate: 12.3%

Educational Attainment: High school diploma or higher: 88.8%; Bachelor's degree or higher: 20.6%; Graduate/professional degree or higher: 6.6%

School District(s)

Grossmont Union High (KG-12)
2012-13 Enrollment: 22,965 . . . . (619) 644-8000
Lakeside Union Elementary (KG-12)
2012-13 Enrollment: 5,475 . . . . (619) 390-2600

Housing: Homeownership rate: 69.0%; Median home value: $325,000; Median year structure built: 1978; Homeowner vacancy rate: 2.9%; Median gross rent: $1,071 per month; Rental vacancy rate: 6.6%

Health Insurance: 87.6% have insurance; 70.0% have private insurance; 28.3% have public insurance; 12.4% do not have insurance; 7.8% of children under 18 do not have insurance

Transportation: Commute: 90.7% car, 0.9% public transportation, 1.4% walk, 5.4% work from home; Median travel time to work: 26.5 minutes

LEMON GROVE (city). Covers a land area of 3.880 square miles and a water area of 0 square miles. Located at 32.73° N. Lat; 117.03° W. Long. Elevation is 446 feet.

Population: 25,320; Growth (since 2000): 1.6%; Density: 6,525.3 persons per square mile; Race: 51.6% White, 13.8% Black/African American, 6.4% Asian, 0.9% American Indian/Alaska Native, 1.1% Native Hawaiian/Other Pacific Islander, 7.1% Two or more races, 41.2% Hispanic of any race; Average household size: 2.96; Median age: 35.0; Age under 18: 25.5%; Age 65 and over: 11.2%; Males per 100 females: 95.3; Marriage status: 40.7% never married, 41.9% now married, 2.7% separated, 5.3% widowed, 12.1% divorced; Foreign born: 18.9%; Speak English only:

60.4%; With disability: 12.1%; Veterans: 12.1%; Ancestry: 7.0% Irish, 6.5% German, 5.1% English, 3.8% American, 3.4% Italian
Employment: 12.3% management, business, and financial, 3.1% computer, engineering, and science, 7.8% education, legal, community service, arts, and media, 3.1% healthcare practitioners, 24.4% service, 26.4% sales and office, 11.3% natural resources, construction, and maintenance, 11.7% production, transportation, and material moving
Income: Per capita: $22,310; Median household: $51,496; Average household: $62,090; Households with income of $100,000 or more: 17.0%; Poverty rate: 18.5%
Educational Attainment: High school diploma or higher: 81.5%; Bachelor's degree or higher: 14.9%; Graduate/professional degree or higher: 4.2%

School District(s)

Lemon Grove (PK-08)
2012-13 Enrollment: 3,901 . . . . (619) 825-5600
Housing: Homeownership rate: 54.6%; Median home value: $287,600; Median year structure built: 1964; Homeowner vacancy rate: 2.0%; Median gross rent: $1,154 per month; Rental vacancy rate: 5.0%
Health Insurance: 80.3% have insurance; 57.7% have private insurance; 30.1% have public insurance; 19.7% do not have insurance; 12.4% of children under 18 do not have insurance
Safety: Violent crime rate: 55.4 per 10,000 population; Property crime rate: 194.6 per 10,000 population
Transportation: Commute: 89.5% car, 4.0% public transportation, 1.4% walk, 4.2% work from home; Median travel time to work: 25.7 minutes
Additional Information Contacts
City of Lemon Grove . . . . (619) 825-3800
http://www.ci.lemon-grove.ca.us

MOUNT LAGUNA (CDP). Covers a land area of 1.697 square miles and a water area of 0 square miles. Located at 32.87° N. Lat; 116.42° W. Long. Elevation is 5,987 feet.
Population: 57; Growth (since 2000): n/a; Density: 33.6 persons per square mile; Race: 96.5% White, 0.0% Black/African American, 1.8% Asian, 0.0% American Indian/Alaska Native, 0.0% Native Hawaiian/Other Pacific Islander, 0.0% Two or more races, 1.8% Hispanic of any race; Average household size: 1.78; Median age: 61.5; Age under 18: 7.0%; Age 65 and over: 43.9%; Males per 100 females: 90.0
Housing: Homeownership rate: 78.2%; Homeowner vacancy rate: 0.0%; Rental vacancy rate: 12.5%

NATIONAL CITY (city). Covers a land area of 7.277 square miles and a water area of 1.839 square miles. Located at 32.67° N. Lat; 117.10° W. Long. Elevation is 66 feet.
History: Named for the Rancho de la Nacion, on which the town was laid out. Incorporated 1887.
Population: 58,582; Growth (since 2000): 8.0%; Density: 8,050.4 persons per square mile; Race: 42.2% White, 5.2% Black/African American, 18.3% Asian, 1.1% American Indian/Alaska Native, 0.8% Native Hawaiian/Other Pacific Islander, 4.8% Two or more races, 63.0% Hispanic of any race; Average household size: 3.41; Median age: 30.2; Age under 18: 25.5%; Age 65 and over: 10.6%; Males per 100 females: 105.5; Marriage status: 39.0% never married, 46.5% now married, 3.1% separated, 6.0% widowed, 8.5% divorced; Foreign born: 41.2%; Speak English only: 27.1%; With disability: 8.8%; Veterans: 6.0%; Ancestry: 2.5% German, 2.3% Irish, 1.3% Italian, 1.3% English, 1.1% American
Employment: 6.3% management, business, and financial, 1.6% computer, engineering, and science, 5.1% education, legal, community service, arts, and media, 3.7% healthcare practitioners, 29.7% service, 25.2% sales and office, 13.0% natural resources, construction, and maintenance, 15.4% production, transportation, and material moving
Income: Per capita: $16,563; Median household: $37,933; Average household: $49,660; Households with income of $100,000 or more: 10.6%; Poverty rate: 25.3%
Educational Attainment: High school diploma or higher: 69.8%; Bachelor's degree or higher: 12.5%; Graduate/professional degree or higher: 2.6%

School District(s)

National Elementary (KG-08)
2012-13 Enrollment: 5,947 . . . . (619) 336-7500
San Diego County Office of Education (PK-12)
2012-13 Enrollment: 4,151 . . . . (858) 292-3500
Sweetwater Union High (07-12)
2012-13 Enrollment: 40,916 . . . . (619) 691-5500

Four-year College(s)

California College San Diego (Private, Not-for-profit)
Fall 2013 Enrollment: 203 . . . . (619) 680-4430
2013-14 Tuition: In-state $18,480; Out-of-state $18,480
ITT Technical Institute-National City (Private, For-profit)
Fall 2013 Enrollment: 1,209 . . . . (619) 327-1800
2013-14 Tuition: In-state $18,048; Out-of-state $18,048

Two-year College(s)

Bellus Academy-National City (Private, For-profit)
Fall 2013 Enrollment: 185 . . . . (619) 474-6607
Housing: Homeownership rate: 33.5%; Median home value: $262,300; Median year structure built: 1968; Homeowner vacancy rate: 2.1%; Median gross rent: $968 per month; Rental vacancy rate: 5.6%
Health Insurance: 69.5% have insurance; 39.8% have private insurance; 36.2% have public insurance; 30.5% do not have insurance; 17.6% of children under 18 do not have insurance
Hospitals: Paradise Valley Hospital (301 beds)
Safety: Violent crime rate: 52.7 per 10,000 population; Property crime rate: 316.9 per 10,000 population
Transportation: Commute: 81.6% car, 7.3% public transportation, 3.3% walk, 6.2% work from home; Median travel time to work: 24.6 minutes
Additional Information Contacts
City of National City. . . . . (619) 336-4241
http://www.ci.national-city.ca.us

OCEANSIDE (city). Covers a land area of 41.235 square miles and a water area of 0.939 square miles. Located at 33.22° N. Lat; 117.31° W. Long. Elevation is 66 feet.
History: Named for its location on the Pacific Ocean by J.C. Hayes, in 1883. Oceanside was settled by a group of English gentry who moved down from the San Luis Rey Valley to the ocean-front site. The town grew as a beach resort and residential area.
Population: 167,086; Growth (since 2000): 3.8%; Density: 4,052.1 persons per square mile; Race: 65.2% White, 4.7% Black/African American, 6.6% Asian, 0.8% American Indian/Alaska Native, 1.3% Native Hawaiian/Other Pacific Islander, 5.8% Two or more races, 35.9% Hispanic of any race; Average household size: 2.80; Median age: 35.2; Age under 18: 23.8%; Age 65 and over: 12.9%; Males per 100 females: 97.4; Marriage status: 31.7% never married, 51.9% now married, 1.8% separated, 5.2% widowed, 11.1% divorced; Foreign born: 20.7%; Speak English only: 65.4%; With disability: 10.3%; Veterans: 12.9%; Ancestry: 12.0% German, 10.6% English, 8.5% Irish, 4.5% Italian, 2.5% American
Employment: 13.4% management, business, and financial, 5.8% computer, engineering, and science, 8.3% education, legal, community service, arts, and media, 4.5% healthcare practitioners, 21.5% service, 26.2% sales and office, 10.6% natural resources, construction, and maintenance, 9.7% production, transportation, and material moving
Income: Per capita: $26,863; Median household: $58,153; Average household: $74,030; Households with income of $100,000 or more: 24.1%; Poverty rate: 13.3%
Educational Attainment: High school diploma or higher: 83.4%; Bachelor's degree or higher: 24.8%; Graduate/professional degree or higher: 8.3%

School District(s)

Bonsall Union Elementary (KG-08)
2012-13 Enrollment: 2,087 . . . . (760) 631-5200
Fallbrook Union Elementary (KG-08)
2012-13 Enrollment: 5,554 . . . . (760) 731-5400
Mountain Empire Unified (PK-12)
2012-13 Enrollment: 2,956 . . . . (619) 473-9022
Oceanside Unified (KG-12)
2012-13 Enrollment: 21,215 . . . . (760) 966-4000
Vista Unified (KG-12)
2012-13 Enrollment: 25,642 . . . . (760) 726-2170

Two-year College(s)

MiraCosta College (Public)
Fall 2013 Enrollment: 14,537 . . . . (760) 757-2121
2013-14 Tuition: In-state $1,148; Out-of-state $5,588

Vocational/Technical School(s)

MediaTech Institute-Oceanside (Private, For-profit)
Fall 2013 Enrollment: 51 . . . . (760) 231-5368
2013-14 Tuition: $24,000
Oceanside College of Beauty (Private, For-profit)
Fall 2013 Enrollment: 70 . . . . (760) 757-6161
2013-14 Tuition: $14,603

Housing: Homeownership rate: 59.1%; Median home value: $347,000; Median year structure built: 1982; Homeowner vacancy rate: 2.2%; Median gross rent: $1,373 per month; Rental vacancy rate: 6.2%
Health Insurance: 81.8% have insurance; 64.5% have private insurance; 28.0% have public insurance; 18.2% do not have insurance; 8.9% of children under 18 do not have insurance
Hospitals: Tri - City Medical Center (397 beds)
Safety: Violent crime rate: 36.7 per 10,000 population; Property crime rate: 260.5 per 10,000 population
Transportation: Commute: 89.1% car, 2.7% public transportation, 1.4% walk, 4.9% work from home; Median travel time to work: 27.5 minutes; Amtrak: Train service available.
Additional Information Contacts
City of Oceanside .... (760) 435-4500
http://www.ci.oceanside.ca.us

PALA (unincorporated postal area)
ZCTA: 92059
Covers a land area of 27.855 square miles and a water area of 0 square miles. Located at 33.38° N. Lat; 117.07° W. Long. Elevation is 397 feet.
Population: 1,618; Growth (since 2000): -11.1%; Density: 58.1 persons per square mile; Race: 26.1% White, 1.5% Black/African American, 0.6% Asian, 38.8% American Indian/Alaska Native, 0.2% Native Hawaiian/Other Pacific Islander, 10.2% Two or more races, 42.2% Hispanic of any race; Average household size: 3.23; Median age: 30.9; Age under 18: 30.5%; Age 65 and over: 9.7%; Males per 100 females: 96.8
School District(s)
Bonsall Union Elementary (KG-08)
2012-13 Enrollment: 2,087 .... (760) 631-5200
Housing: Homeownership rate: 66.2%; Homeowner vacancy rate: 0.6%; Rental vacancy rate: 4.0%

PALOMAR MOUNTAIN (unincorporated postal area)
ZCTA: 92060
Covers a land area of 69.623 square miles and a water area of 2.070 square miles. Located at 33.35° N. Lat; 116.85° W. Long. Elevation is 5,325 feet.
Population: 218; Growth (since 2000): -3.1%; Density: 3.1 persons per square mile; Race: 92.2% White, 0.0% Black/African American, 0.0% Asian, 1.8% American Indian/Alaska Native, 0.9% Native Hawaiian/Other Pacific Islander, 4.1% Two or more races, 3.2% Hispanic of any race; Average household size: 1.88; Median age: 55.2; Age under 18: 9.6%; Age 65 and over: 17.0%; Males per 100 females: 120.2
Housing: Homeownership rate: 73.3%; Homeowner vacancy rate: 2.3%; Rental vacancy rate: 8.8%

PAUMA VALLEY (unincorporated postal area)
ZCTA: 92061
Covers a land area of 39.707 square miles and a water area of 0 square miles. Located at 33.30° N. Lat; 116.92° W. Long. Elevation is 807 feet.
Population: 2,499; Growth (since 2000): -4.1%; Density: 62.9 persons per square mile; Race: 47.1% White, 0.5% Black/African American, 1.2% Asian, 22.7% American Indian/Alaska Native, 0.1% Native Hawaiian/Other Pacific Islander, 3.1% Two or more races, 36.6% Hispanic of any race; Average household size: 2.80; Median age: 42.0; Age under 18: 23.8%; Age 65 and over: 17.9%; Males per 100 females: 106.7
School District(s)
Valley Center-Pauma Unified (KG-12)
2012-13 Enrollment: 4,154 .... (760) 749-0464
Housing: Homeownership rate: 73.6%; Homeowner vacancy rate: 2.8%; Rental vacancy rate: 5.2%

PINE VALLEY (CDP). Covers a land area of 7.146 square miles and a water area of 0 square miles. Located at 32.84° N. Lat; 116.51° W. Long. Elevation is 3,743 feet.
History: Pine Valley was settled in 1869 by Major William H. Emory, who is said to have acquired the land in exchange for two horses. The community became a resort area.
Population: 1,510; Growth (since 2000): 0.6%; Density: 211.3 persons per square mile; Race: 93.2% White, 0.4% Black/African American, 1.1% Asian, 0.4% American Indian/Alaska Native, 0.1% Native Hawaiian/Other Pacific Islander, 3.5% Two or more races, 10.2% Hispanic of any race; Average household size: 2.48; Median age: 48.3; Age under 18: 18.5%; Age 65 and over: 13.4%; Males per 100 females: 100.3
School District(s)
Mountain Empire Unified (PK-12)
2012-13 Enrollment: 2,956 .... (619) 473-9022
Housing: Homeownership rate: 81.7%; Homeowner vacancy rate: 1.4%; Rental vacancy rate: 5.9%

POTRERO (CDP). Covers a land area of 3.149 square miles and a water area of 0 square miles. Located at 32.61° N. Lat; 116.61° W. Long. Elevation is 2,336 feet.
Population: 656; Growth (since 2000): n/a; Density: 208.3 persons per square mile; Race: 51.5% White, 0.0% Black/African American, 0.0% Asian, 1.2% American Indian/Alaska Native, 0.5% Native Hawaiian/Other Pacific Islander, 4.0% Two or more races, 76.1% Hispanic of any race; Average household size: 3.47; Median age: 32.4; Age under 18: 33.1%; Age 65 and over: 10.4%; Males per 100 females: 103.1
School District(s)
Mountain Empire Unified (PK-12)
2012-13 Enrollment: 2,956 .... (619) 473-9022
Housing: Homeownership rate: 59.7%; Homeowner vacancy rate: 5.0%; Rental vacancy rate: 1.3%

POWAY (city). Covers a land area of 39.079 square miles and a water area of 0.086 square miles. Located at 32.99° N. Lat; 117.02° W. Long. Elevation is 515 feet.
History: This city was incorporated on December 1, 1980 and is located north of the city of San Diego and south of the city of Escondido. Its name originates from the language of the Diegueño Indians.
Population: 47,811; Growth (since 2000): -0.5%; Density: 1,223.4 persons per square mile; Race: 76.9% White, 1.6% Black/African American, 10.2% Asian, 0.6% American Indian/Alaska Native, 0.2% Native Hawaiian/Other Pacific Islander, 4.3% Two or more races, 15.7% Hispanic of any race; Average household size: 2.93; Median age: 41.3; Age under 18: 25.0%; Age 65 and over: 12.3%; Males per 100 females: 97.1; Marriage status: 26.2% never married, 59.4% now married, 1.3% separated, 4.8% widowed, 9.7% divorced; Foreign born: 16.2%; Speak English only: 78.7%; With disability: 8.1%; Veterans: 12.7%; Ancestry: 19.0% German, 13.0% Irish, 10.9% English, 6.6% Italian, 4.6% French
Employment: 21.0% management, business, and financial, 12.1% computer, engineering, and science, 11.0% education, legal, community service, arts, and media, 5.2% healthcare practitioners, 15.7% service, 23.8% sales and office, 6.0% natural resources, construction, and maintenance, 5.2% production, transportation, and material moving
Income: Per capita: $40,375; Median household: $93,856; Average household: $119,071; Households with income of $100,000 or more: 47.0%; Poverty rate: 5.3%
Educational Attainment: High school diploma or higher: 93.8%; Bachelor's degree or higher: 45.7%; Graduate/professional degree or higher: 16.6%
School District(s)
Poway Unified (KG-12)
2012-13 Enrollment: 35,196 .... (858) 521-2703
Two-year College(s)
Bellus Academy-Poway (Private, For-profit)
Fall 2013 Enrollment: 372 .... (858) 748-1490
Housing: Homeownership rate: 74.4%; Median home value: $495,100; Median year structure built: 1977; Homeowner vacancy rate: 1.1%; Median gross rent: $1,479 per month; Rental vacancy rate: 5.5%
Health Insurance: 91.8% have insurance; 82.2% have private insurance; 19.9% have public insurance; 8.2% do not have insurance; 4.9% of children under 18 do not have insurance
Hospitals: Pomerado Hospital (107 beds)
Safety: Violent crime rate: 18.2 per 10,000 population; Property crime rate: 116.3 per 10,000 population
Newspapers: Pomerado Newspapers (weekly circulation 43000)
Transportation: Commute: 90.3% car, 1.2% public transportation, 1.5% walk, 5.4% work from home; Median travel time to work: 24.0 minutes
Additional Information Contacts
City of Poway .... (858) 668-4400
http://www.poway.org

RAINBOW (CDP). Covers a land area of 11.042 square miles and a water area of 0 square miles. Located at 33.41° N. Lat; 117.14° W. Long. Elevation is 1,043 feet.
Population: 1,832; Growth (since 2000): -9.6%; Density: 165.9 persons per square mile; Race: 72.3% White, 1.0% Black/African American, 2.3%

Asian, 0.7% American Indian/Alaska Native, 0.7% Native Hawaiian/Other Pacific Islander, 2.8% Two or more races, 36.3% Hispanic of any race; Average household size: 2.71; Median age: 45.3; Age under 18: 18.7%; Age 65 and over: 20.1%; Males per 100 females: 97.2

School District(s)

Vallecitos Elementary (KG-12)
2012-13 Enrollment: 369. . . . . (760) 451-8200

Housing: Homeownership rate: 73.8%; Homeowner vacancy rate: 2.6%; Rental vacancy rate: 6.1%

RAMONA (CDP). Covers a land area of 38.412 square miles and a water area of 0.021 square miles. Located at 33.05° N. Lat; 116.88° W. Long. Elevation is 1,427 feet.

History: Named for the novel of the same name by Helen Hunt Jackson. The village of Ramona was founded in 1886 in a region of poultry farms.

Population: 20,292; Growth (since 2000): 29.3%; Density: 528.3 persons per square mile; Race: 78.3% White, 0.7% Black/African American, 1.4% Asian, 1.1% American Indian/Alaska Native, 0.3% Native Hawaiian/Other Pacific Islander, 3.6% Two or more races, 31.2% Hispanic of any race; Average household size: 3.04; Median age: 36.7; Age under 18: 25.9%; Age 65 and over: 10.1%; Males per 100 females: 101.0; Marriage status: 32.0% never married, 53.7% now married, 1.7% separated, 3.9% widowed, 10.5% divorced; Foreign born: 20.6%; Speak English only: 67.9%; With disability: 10.8%; Veterans: 10.1%; Ancestry: 17.8% German, 14.5% Irish, 9.8% English, 4.7% Italian, 3.4% American

Employment: 12.1% management, business, and financial, 4.6% computer, engineering, and science, 7.0% education, legal, community service, arts, and media, 2.1% healthcare practitioners, 26.3% service, 20.3% sales and office, 16.1% natural resources, construction, and maintenance, 11.5% production, transportation, and material moving

Income: Per capita: $24,109; Median household: $64,882; Average household: $78,339; Households with income of $100,000 or more: 26.6%; Poverty rate: 11.7%

Educational Attainment: High school diploma or higher: 75.4%; Bachelor's degree or higher: 15.4%; Graduate/professional degree or higher: 4.1%

School District(s)

Ramona City Unified (KG-12)
2012-13 Enrollment: 5,868 . . . . (760) 787-2000

Housing: Homeownership rate: 63.2%; Median home value: $366,200; Median year structure built: 1979; Homeowner vacancy rate: 1.8%; Median gross rent: $1,134 per month; Rental vacancy rate: 6.1%

Health Insurance: 79.8% have insurance; 58.6% have private insurance; 28.8% have public insurance; 20.2% do not have insurance; 9.3% of children under 18 do not have insurance

Newspapers: Ramona Sentinel (weekly circulation 5500)

Transportation: Commute: 89.3% car, 0.2% public transportation, 2.0% walk, 6.9% work from home; Median travel time to work: 30.3 minutes

Airports: Ramona (general aviation)

RANCHITA (unincorporated postal area)

ZCTA: 92066

Covers a land area of 19.837 square miles and a water area of 0 square miles. Located at 33.22° N. Lat; 116.54° W. Long. Elevation is 4,065 feet.

Population: 378; Growth (since 2000): 11.8%; Density: 19.1 persons per square mile; Race: 86.2% White, 2.6% Black/African American, 1.9% Asian, 0.5% American Indian/Alaska Native, 0.0% Native Hawaiian/Other Pacific Islander, 4.8% Two or more races, 14.3% Hispanic of any race; Average household size: 2.25; Median age: 51.4; Age under 18: 16.4%; Age 65 and over: 16.9%; Males per 100 females: 106.6

Housing: Homeownership rate: 76.8%; Homeowner vacancy rate: 0.8%; Rental vacancy rate: 7.1%

RANCHO SAN DIEGO (CDP). Covers a land area of 8.701 square miles and a water area of 0 square miles. Located at 32.76° N. Lat; 116.92° W. Long. Elevation is 361 feet.

Population: 21,208; Growth (since 2000): 5.2%; Density: 2,437.4 persons per square mile; Race: 82.7% White, 3.9% Black/African American, 4.4% Asian, 0.5% American Indian/Alaska Native, 0.3% Native Hawaiian/Other Pacific Islander, 4.8% Two or more races, 14.7% Hispanic of any race; Average household size: 2.70; Median age: 41.2; Age under 18: 22.1%; Age 65 and over: 13.4%; Males per 100 females: 94.1; Marriage status: 28.1% never married, 55.5% now married, 2.0% separated, 5.5% widowed, 10.9% divorced; Foreign born: 17.4%; Speak English only: 73.2%; With disability: 9.1%; Veterans: 13.4%; Ancestry: 15.9% German, 10.5% English, 10.4% Assyrian/Chaldean/Syriac, 10.3% Irish, 6.0% Italian

Employment: 20.7% management, business, and financial, 4.0% computer, engineering, and science, 13.1% education, legal, community service, arts, and media, 5.7% healthcare practitioners, 16.2% service, 27.4% sales and office, 6.0% natural resources, construction, and maintenance, 6.9% production, transportation, and material moving

Income: Per capita: $38,315; Median household: $81,631; Average household: $103,024; Households with income of $100,000 or more: 36.8%; Poverty rate: 5.7%

Educational Attainment: High school diploma or higher: 91.8%; Bachelor's degree or higher: 38.0%; Graduate/professional degree or higher: 13.5%

Housing: Homeownership rate: 71.2%; Median home value: $470,200; Median year structure built: 1985; Homeowner vacancy rate: 0.8%; Median gross rent: $1,643 per month; Rental vacancy rate: 6.5%

Health Insurance: 89.4% have insurance; 76.9% have private insurance; 23.6% have public insurance; 10.6% do not have insurance; 6.1% of children under 18 do not have insurance

Transportation: Commute: 91.8% car, 1.2% public transportation, 1.3% walk, 4.5% work from home; Median travel time to work: 25.0 minutes

RANCHO SANTA FE (CDP). Covers a land area of 6.715 square miles and a water area of 0.073 square miles. Located at 33.02° N. Lat; 117.20° W. Long. Elevation is 246 feet.

History: Rancho Santa Fe has its origins as Rancho San Dieguito, a Mexican land grant made during 1836-1845 to Juan Mar_a Osuna (the first mayor or alcalde of the San Diego area). In 1906 it was sold to the Atchison, Topeka and Santa Fe Railway Company, which renamed it after the second transcontinental railroad to reach California.

Population: 3,117; Growth (since 2000): -4.2%; Density: 464.2 persons per square mile; Race: 93.4% White, 0.3% Black/African American, 2.8% Asian, 0.0% American Indian/Alaska Native, 0.1% Native Hawaiian/Other Pacific Islander, 1.9% Two or more races, 5.6% Hispanic of any race; Average household size: 2.61; Median age: 51.3; Age under 18: 23.2%; Age 65 and over: 23.8%; Males per 100 females: 96.4; Marriage status: 18.4% never married, 68.3% now married, 1.4% separated, 6.7% widowed, 6.5% divorced; Foreign born: 13.0%; Speak English only: 84.1%; With disability: 6.9%; Veterans: 12.0%; Ancestry: 18.9% English, 15.0% German, 13.4% Irish, 8.9% Scottish, 5.9% American

Employment: 42.7% management, business, and financial, 6.7% computer, engineering, and science, 13.0% education, legal, community service, arts, and media, 4.1% healthcare practitioners, 3.7% service, 20.9% sales and office, 1.9% natural resources, construction, and maintenance, 7.0% production, transportation, and material moving

Income: Per capita: $69,062; Median household: $107,227; Average household: $186,819; Households with income of $100,000 or more: 52.9%; Poverty rate: 12.0%

Educational Attainment: High school diploma or higher: 100.0%; Bachelor's degree or higher: 81.9%; Graduate/professional degree or higher: 39.4%

School District(s)

Rancho Santa Fe Elementary (KG-08)
2012-13 Enrollment: 670. . . . . (858) 756-1141
Solana Beach Elementary (KG-06)
2012-13 Enrollment: 2,989 . . . . (858) 794-7100

Housing: Homeownership rate: 84.5%; Median home value: 1 million+; Median year structure built: 1976; Homeowner vacancy rate: 2.4%; Median gross rent: $2,000+ per month; Rental vacancy rate: 12.3%

Health Insurance: 94.7% have insurance; 87.3% have private insurance; 22.5% have public insurance; 5.3% do not have insurance; 3.4% of children under 18 do not have insurance

Newspapers: Ranch Coast Newspapers (weekly circulation 7000)

Transportation: Commute: 80.7% car, 0.0% public transportation, 0.0% walk, 19.3% work from home; Median travel time to work: 24.3 minutes

SAN DIEGO (city). County seat. Covers a land area of 325.188 square miles and a water area of 47.210 square miles. Located at 32.82° N. Lat; 117.13° W. Long. Elevation is 62 feet.

History: In 1769 Governor Portola and Franciscan friar Junipero Serra established a mission and presidio on the site of San Diego, and named them for the bay which had been charted in 1602 by Sebastian Vizcaino of Spain. San Diego became the center of the coastal hide trade, and was organized in 1834 as a pueblo. For a time after 1838 San Diego was a department of Los Angeles, but by 1850 the present Old Town was incorporated as a city. Next to it was New Town, or Davis's Folly, named for William Heath Davis, who first built there. Later this part of town was called Horton's Addition for Alonzo E. Horton, who developed the waterfront land. San Diego became the transcontinental terminus of the Santa Fe Railroad in 1885.

Population: 1,307,402; Growth (since 2000): 6.9%; Density: 4,020.4 persons per square mile; Race: 58.9% White, 6.7% Black/African American, 15.9% Asian, 0.6% American Indian/Alaska Native, 0.5% Native Hawaiian/Other Pacific Islander, 5.1% Two or more races, 28.8% Hispanic of any race; Average household size: 2.60; Median age: 33.6; Age under 18: 21.4%; Age 65 and over: 10.7%; Males per 100 females: 102.1; Marriage status: 40.3% never married, 45.2% now married, 2.0% separated, 4.6% widowed, 10.0% divorced; Foreign born: 26.2%; Speak English only: 60.2%; With disability: 8.7%; Veterans: 9.3%; Ancestry: 9.8% German, 7.9% Irish, 6.4% English, 4.4% Italian, 2.9% American

Employment: 16.6% management, business, and financial, 10.5% computer, engineering, and science, 12.3% education, legal, community service, arts, and media, 5.7% healthcare practitioners, 19.0% service, 23.2% sales and office, 5.8% natural resources, construction, and maintenance, 7.0% production, transportation, and material moving

Income: Per capita: $33,152; Median household: $64,058; Average household: $87,395; Households with income of $100,000 or more: 30.5%; Poverty rate: 15.6%

Educational Attainment: High school diploma or higher: 87.0%; Bachelor's degree or higher: 41.7%; Graduate/professional degree or higher: 16.7%

School District(s)

Chula Vista Elementary (KG-08)
2012-13 Enrollment: 28,524 . . . . (619) 425-9600
Dehesa Elementary (KG-12)
2012-13 Enrollment: 2,122 . . . . (619) 444-2161
Del Mar Union Elementary (KG-06)
2012-13 Enrollment: 4,384 . . . . (858) 755-9301
Mono County Office of Education (KG-12)
2012-13 Enrollment: 429. . . . . (760) 932-7311
Poway Unified (KG-12)
2012-13 Enrollment: 35,196 . . . . (858) 521-2703
San Diego County Office of Education (PK-12)
2012-13 Enrollment: 4,151 . . . . (858) 292-3500
San Diego County Rop
2012-13 Enrollment: n/a . . . . (858) 292-3514
San Diego Unified (KG-12)
2012-13 Enrollment: 130,271 . . . . (619) 725-8000
San Dieguito Union High (07-12)
2012-13 Enrollment: 12,365 . . . . (760) 753-6491
San Ysidro Elementary (PK-08)
2012-13 Enrollment: 5,235 . . . . (619) 428-4476
Solana Beach Elementary (KG-06)
2012-13 Enrollment: 2,989 . . . . (858) 794-7100
South Bay Union Elementary (KG-08)
2012-13 Enrollment: 7,773 . . . . (619) 628-1600
Sweetwater Union High (07-12)
2012-13 Enrollment: 40,916 . . . . (619) 691-5500

Four-year College(s)

Alliant International University (Private, Not-for-profit)
Fall 2013 Enrollment: 4,201 . . . . (866) 825-5426
2013-14 Tuition: In-state $15,816; Out-of-state $15,816
Argosy University-San Diego (Private, For-profit)
Fall 2013 Enrollment: 487 . . . . (619) 321-3000
2013-14 Tuition: In-state $13,663; Out-of-state $13,663
Bethel Seminary-San Diego (Private, Not-for-profit, Baptist)
Fall 2013 Enrollment: 178 . . . . (619) 325-5200
California College San Diego (Private, Not-for-profit)
Fall 2013 Enrollment: 762 . . . . (619) 680-4430
2013-14 Tuition: In-state $18,480; Out-of-state $18,480
California Miramar University (Private, For-profit)
Fall 2013 Enrollment: 317 . . . . (858) 653-3000
2013-14 Tuition: In-state $7,990; Out-of-state $7,990
California Western School of Law (Private, Not-for-profit)
Fall 2013 Enrollment: 704 . . . . (619) 525-7073
Coleman University (Private, Not-for-profit)
Fall 2013 Enrollment: 833 . . . . (858) 499-0202
2013-14 Tuition: In-state $20,200; Out-of-state $20,200
Design Institute of San Diego (Private, For-profit)
Fall 2013 Enrollment: 181 . . . . (858) 566-1200
2013-14 Tuition: In-state $20,470; Out-of-state $20,470
Horizon University (Private, Not-for-profit, Other (none of the above))
Fall 2013 Enrollment: 58 . . . . (858) 695-8587
2013-14 Tuition: In-state $9,250; Out-of-state $9,250
Newschool of Architecture and Design (Private, For-profit)
Fall 2013 Enrollment: 514 . . . . (800) 490-7081
2013-14 Tuition: In-state $24,536; Out-of-state $24,536
Pacific College of Oriental Medicine-San Diego (Private, For-profit)
Fall 2013 Enrollment: 510 . . . . (619) 574-6909
2013-14 Tuition: In-state $8,088; Out-of-state $8,088
Platt College-San Diego (Private, For-profit)
Fall 2013 Enrollment: 370 . . . . (619) 265-0107
2013-14 Tuition: In-state $23,250; Out-of-state $23,250
Point Loma Nazarene University (Private, Not-for-profit, Church of the Nazarene)
Fall 2013 Enrollment: 3,359 . . . . (619) 849-2200
2013-14 Tuition: In-state $30,356; Out-of-state $30,356
San Diego State University (Public)
Fall 2013 Enrollment: 31,899 . . . . (619) 594-5200
2013-14 Tuition: In-state $6,766; Out-of-state $17,926
The Art Institute of California-Argosy University San Diego (Private, For-profit)
Fall 2013 Enrollment: 1,869 . . . . (858) 598-1200
2013-14 Tuition: In-state $18,748; Out-of-state $18,748
Thomas Jefferson School of Law (Private, Not-for-profit)
Fall 2013 Enrollment: 1,036 . . . . (619) 961-4325
University of Phoenix-San Diego Campus (Private, For-profit)
Fall 2013 Enrollment: 6,122 . . . . (866) 766-0766
2013-14 Tuition: In-state $11,275; Out-of-state $11,275
University of San Diego (Private, Not-for-profit, Roman Catholic)
Fall 2013 Enrollment: 8,321 . . . . (619) 260-4600
2013-14 Tuition: In-state $41,392; Out-of-state $41,392

Two-year College(s)

Concorde Career College-San Diego (Private, For-profit)
Fall 2013 Enrollment: 895 . . . . (619) 688-0800
Fashion Institute of Design & Merchandising-San Diego (Private, For-profit)
Fall 2013 Enrollment: 169 . . . . (619) 235-2049
2013-14 Tuition: In-state $28,920; Out-of-state $28,920
International Professional School of Bodywork (Private, For-profit)
Fall 2013 Enrollment: 215 . . . . (858) 505-1100
2013-14 Tuition: In-state $6,659; Out-of-state $6,659
Kaplan College-San Diego (Private, For-profit)
Fall 2013 Enrollment: 1,354 . . . . (858) 279-4500
San Diego City College (Public)
Fall 2013 Enrollment: 16,310 . . . . (619) 388-3400
2013-14 Tuition: In-state $1,142; Out-of-state $5,702
San Diego Mesa College (Public)
Fall 2013 Enrollment: 24,251 . . . . (619) 388-2604
2013-14 Tuition: In-state $1,142; Out-of-state $5,702
San Diego Miramar College (Public)
Fall 2013 Enrollment: 11,891 . . . . (619) 388-7800
2013-14 Tuition: In-state $1,142; Out-of-state $5,702

Vocational/Technical School(s)

Associated Technical College-San Diego (Private, For-profit)
Fall 2013 Enrollment: 110 . . . . (619) 234-2181
2013-14 Tuition: $17,008
Avance Beauty College (Private, For-profit)
Fall 2013 Enrollment: 54 . . . . (619) 575-1511
2013-14 Tuition: $14,964
CET-San Diego (Private, Not-for-profit)
Fall 2013 Enrollment: 267 . . . . (408) 287-7924
2013-14 Tuition: $10,165
Mueller College (Private, For-profit)
Fall 2013 Enrollment: 105 . . . . (619) 291-9811
2013-14 Tuition: In-state $19,152; Out-of-state $19,152
Paul Mitchell the School-San Diego (Private, For-profit)
Fall 2013 Enrollment: 301 . . . . (619) 398-1590
2013-14 Tuition: $18,925
San Diego College (Private, For-profit)
Fall 2013 Enrollment: 278 . . . . (619) 338-0813
2013-14 Tuition: $16,283

San Diego Continuing Education (Public)
Fall 2013 Enrollment: n/a . . . . (619) 388-4881
San Diego Culinary Institute (Private, For-profit)
Fall 2013 Enrollment: 54 . . . . (619) 644-2100
2013-14 Tuition: $21,660
Tramy Beauty School (Private, For-profit)
Fall 2013 Enrollment: 270 . . . . (619) 229-8188
2013-14 Tuition: $10,106

Housing: Homeownership rate: 48.3%; Median home value: $437,400; Median year structure built: 1975; Homeowner vacancy rate: 1.9%; Median gross rent: $1,329 per month; Rental vacancy rate: 5.2%

Health Insurance: 83.4% have insurance; 67.2% have private insurance; 24.6% have public insurance; 16.6% do not have insurance; 8.5% of children under 18 do not have insurance

Hospitals: Alvarado Hospital Medical Center (231 beds); Kaiser Foundation Hospital - San Diego (392 beds); Scripps Mercy Hospital (700 beds); Sharp Memorial Hospital (464 beds); University of California San Diego Medical Center (558 beds); VA San Diego Healthcare System (238 beds)

Safety: Violent crime rate: 39.3 per 10,000 population; Property crime rate: 235.1 per 10,000 population

Newspapers: Community Newspaper Group (weekly circulation 80000); San Diego Reader (weekly circulation 169000); San Diego Union-Tribune (daily circulation 261000)

Transportation: Commute: 84.1% car, 4.0% public transportation, 3.1% walk, 6.7% work from home; Median travel time to work: 22.5 minutes; Amtrak: Train service available.

Airports: Brown Field Municipal (general aviation); Gillespie Field (general aviation); Miramar MCAS/Mitscher Field (general aviation); Montgomery Field (general aviation); North Island NAS /Halsey Field/ (general aviation); San Diego International (primary service/large hub)

Additional Information Contacts

City of San Diego . . . . (619) 236-5555
http://www.sandiego.gov

SAN DIEGO COUNTRY ESTATES (CDP). Covers a land area of 16.850 square miles and a water area of 0 square miles. Located at 33.01° N. Lat; 116.79° W. Long. Elevation is 1,509 feet.

Population: 10,109; Growth (since 2000): 9.1%; Density: 599.9 persons per square mile; Race: 90.1% White, 0.9% Black/African American, 1.5% Asian, 0.9% American Indian/Alaska Native, 0.3% Native Hawaiian/Other Pacific Islander, 3.6% Two or more races, 11.1% Hispanic of any race; Average household size: 2.93; Median age: 41.1; Age under 18: 25.3%; Age 65 and over: 11.2%; Males per 100 females: 101.1; Marriage status: 26.5% never married, 57.8% now married, 0.6% separated, 6.0% widowed, 9.8% divorced; Foreign born: 5.2%; Speak English only: 93.5%; With disability: 8.3%; Veterans: 13.4%; Ancestry: 20.7% German, 19.0% English, 13.1% Irish, 5.8% Italian, 4.7% French

Employment: 15.4% management, business, and financial, 9.0% computer, engineering, and science, 7.2% education, legal, community service, arts, and media, 5.6% healthcare practitioners, 15.9% service, 29.1% sales and office, 8.2% natural resources, construction, and maintenance, 9.5% production, transportation, and material moving

Income: Per capita: $33,705; Median household: $92,566; Average household: $99,734; Households with income of $100,000 or more: 44.2%; Poverty rate: 4.9%

Educational Attainment: High school diploma or higher: 96.6%; Bachelor's degree or higher: 31.6%; Graduate/professional degree or higher: 9.6%

Housing: Homeownership rate: 88.8%; Median home value: $364,800; Median year structure built: 1987; Homeowner vacancy rate: 1.5%; Median gross rent: $2,000+ per month; Rental vacancy rate: 4.0%

Health Insurance: 94.9% have insurance; 87.7% have private insurance; 18.2% have public insurance; 5.1% do not have insurance; 0.7% of children under 18 do not have insurance

Transportation: Commute: 90.9% car, 0.0% public transportation, 0.6% walk, 7.0% work from home; Median travel time to work: 39.4 minutes

SAN MARCOS (city). Covers a land area of 24.370 square miles and a water area of 0.020 square miles. Located at 33.13° N. Lat; 117.17° W. Long. Elevation is 581 feet.

History: Named for a rancho of Mission San Luis Rey, which was named for St. Mark the Evangelist. San Marcos, established at the confluence of three valleys, is on the former Rancho Los Vallecitos de San Marcos. The Mulberry Grove and Silk Factory was established near San Marcos in the late 1920s in an attempt to build a silkworm culture in southern California.

Population: 83,781; Growth (since 2000): 52.4%; Density: 3,437.9 persons per square mile; Race: 63.5% White, 2.3% Black/African American, 9.0% Asian, 0.7% American Indian/Alaska Native, 0.4% Native Hawaiian/Other Pacific Islander, 5.1% Two or more races, 36.6% Hispanic of any race; Average household size: 3.05; Median age: 32.9; Age under 18: 27.8%; Age 65 and over: 10.2%; Males per 100 females: 95.6; Marriage status: 31.6% never married, 53.9% now married, 1.1% separated, 5.3% widowed, 9.2% divorced; Foreign born: 23.5%; Speak English only: 61.8%; With disability: 8.2%; Veterans: 7.2%; Ancestry: 17.1% English, 9.9% German, 7.6% Irish, 5.9% Italian, 3.1% American

Employment: 14.1% management, business, and financial, 8.0% computer, engineering, and science, 9.2% education, legal, community service, arts, and media, 3.9% healthcare practitioners, 19.5% service, 26.5% sales and office, 8.7% natural resources, construction, and maintenance, 10.1% production, transportation, and material moving

Income: Per capita: $24,484; Median household: $53,657; Average household: $71,631; Households with income of $100,000 or more: 23.7%; Poverty rate: 14.6%

Educational Attainment: High school diploma or higher: 80.6%; Bachelor's degree or higher: 28.3%; Graduate/professional degree or higher: 8.1%

School District(s)

Mountain Empire Unified (PK-12)
2012-13 Enrollment: 2,956 . . . . (619) 473-9022
San Diego County Office of Education (PK-12)
2012-13 Enrollment: 4,151 . . . . (858) 292-3500
San Marcos Unified (KG-12)
2012-13 Enrollment: 19,617 . . . . (760) 752-1299
Sbc - High Tech High (KG-12)
2012-13 Enrollment: 2,276 . . . . (619) 243-5014

Four-year College(s)

California College San Diego (Private, Not-for-profit)
Fall 2013 Enrollment: 269 . . . . (619) 680-4430
2013-14 Tuition: In-state $18,480; Out-of-state $18,480
California State University-San Marcos (Public)
Fall 2013 Enrollment: 11,300 . . . . (760) 750-4000
2013-14 Tuition: In-state $6,649; Out-of-state $17,809
University of St Augustine for Health Sciences (Private, For-profit)
Fall 2013 Enrollment: 1,705 . . . . (904) 826-0084

Two-year College(s)

Palomar College (Public)
Fall 2013 Enrollment: 24,665 . . . . (760) 744-1150
2013-14 Tuition: In-state $1,328; Out-of-state $5,472

Vocational/Technical School(s)

Palomar Institute of Cosmetology (Private, For-profit)
Fall 2013 Enrollment: 136 . . . . (760) 744-7900
2013-14 Tuition: $17,005

Housing: Homeownership rate: 62.8%; Median home value: $362,000; Median year structure built: 1988; Homeowner vacancy rate: 2.1%; Median gross rent: $1,314 per month; Rental vacancy rate: 5.7%

Health Insurance: 82.5% have insurance; 66.5% have private insurance; 22.1% have public insurance; 17.5% do not have insurance; 6.9% of children under 18 do not have insurance

Safety: Violent crime rate: 24.4 per 10,000 population; Property crime rate: 159.6 per 10,000 population

Newspapers: Sun Newspapers (weekly circulation 8000)

Transportation: Commute: 92.0% car, 1.6% public transportation, 1.3% walk, 4.3% work from home; Median travel time to work: 24.7 minutes

Additional Information Contacts

City of San Marcos . . . . (760) 744-1050
http://www.ci.san-marcos.ca.us

SAN YSIDRO (unincorporated postal area)

ZCTA: 92173

Covers a land area of 5.059 square miles and a water area of 0.205 square miles. Located at 32.55° N. Lat; 117.04° W. Long. Elevation is 62 feet.

Population: 29,429; Growth (since 2000): 3.3%; Density: 5,817.3 persons per square mile; Race: 58.3% White, 1.5% Black/African American, 2.3% Asian, 0.8% American Indian/Alaska Native, 0.3% Native Hawaiian/Other Pacific Islander, 3.5% Two or more races, 93.2% Hispanic of any race; Average household size: 3.88; Median age: 29.2; Age under 18: 31.6%; Age 65 and over: 9.1%; Males per 100 females: 89.6; Marriage status:

37.5% never married, 49.2% now married, 4.8% separated, 4.8% widowed, 8.5% divorced; Foreign born: 45.3%; Speak English only: 8.5%; With disability: 12.7%; Veterans: 3.2%; Ancestry: 0.7% English, 0.6% German, 0.6% Irish, 0.4% Ethiopian, 0.3% Italian

Employment: 7.2% management, business, and financial, 1.6% computer, engineering, and science, 5.6% education, legal, community service, arts, and media, 1.7% healthcare practitioners, 25.7% service, 29.6% sales and office, 12.0% natural resources, construction, and maintenance, 16.6% production, transportation, and material moving

Income: Per capita: $12,673; Median household: $36,621; Average household: $46,345; Households with income of $100,000 or more: 9.8%; Poverty rate: 28.4%

Educational Attainment: High school diploma or higher: 54.3%; Bachelor's degree or higher: 9.8%; Graduate/professional degree or higher: 2.1%

Housing: Homeownership rate: 35.1%; Median home value: $254,300; Median year structure built: 1977; Homeowner vacancy rate: 1.8%; Median gross rent: $917 per month; Rental vacancy rate: 3.8%

Health Insurance: 71.1% have insurance; 36.4% have private insurance; 40.1% have public insurance; 28.9% do not have insurance; 15.2% of children under 18 do not have insurance

Transportation: Commute: 83.6% car, 7.3% public transportation, 4.6% walk, 3.1% work from home; Median travel time to work: 27.2 minutes

SANTA YSABEL (unincorporated postal area)

ZCTA: 92070

Covers a land area of 133.174 square miles and a water area of 3.308 square miles. Located at 33.15° N. Lat; 116.73° W. Long. Elevation is 2,989 feet.

Population: 1,245; Growth (since 2000): 9.1%; Density: 9.3 persons per square mile; Race: 59.3% White, 0.6% Black/African American, 0.9% Asian, 31.9% American Indian/Alaska Native, 0.0% Native Hawaiian/Other Pacific Islander, 2.5% Two or more races, 12.4% Hispanic of any race; Average household size: 2.43; Median age: 44.2; Age under 18: 22.7%; Age 65 and over: 17.3%; Males per 100 females: 101.1

School District(s)

Spencer Valley Elementary (KG-12)
2012-13 Enrollment: 3,215 . . . . (760) 765-0336

Housing: Homeownership rate: 66.8%; Homeowner vacancy rate: 2.3%; Rental vacancy rate: 4.5%

SANTEE (city). Covers a land area of 16.235 square miles and a water area of 0.293 square miles. Located at 32.85° N. Lat; 116.99° W. Long. Elevation is 351 feet.

History: This city was incorporated on December 1, 1980 and is located in eastern San Diego County. Santee is the eleventh largest of San Diego County's 18 cities and has one of the lowest crime rates.

Population: 53,413; Growth (since 2000): 0.8%; Density: 3,289.9 persons per square mile; Race: 82.5% White, 2.0% Black/African American, 3.8% Asian, 0.8% American Indian/Alaska Native, 0.5% Native Hawaiian/Other Pacific Islander, 5.4% Two or more races, 16.3% Hispanic of any race; Average household size: 2.72; Median age: 37.2; Age under 18: 23.8%; Age 65 and over: 10.7%; Males per 100 females: 93.6; Marriage status: 30.9% never married, 49.8% now married, 1.5% separated, 5.2% widowed, 14.1% divorced; Foreign born: 8.3%; Speak English only: 85.0%; With disability: 11.1%; Veterans: 12.3%; Ancestry: 22.2% German, 15.6% Irish, 10.8% English, 8.1% Italian, 4.2% American

Employment: 16.1% management, business, and financial, 6.1% computer, engineering, and science, 10.3% education, legal, community service, arts, and media, 4.6% healthcare practitioners, 15.6% service, 29.8% sales and office, 8.8% natural resources, construction, and maintenance, 8.7% production, transportation, and material moving

Income: Per capita: $29,324; Median household: $70,899; Average household: $82,446; Households with income of $100,000 or more: 31.4%; Poverty rate: 7.7%

Educational Attainment: High school diploma or higher: 91.0%; Bachelor's degree or higher: 22.5%; Graduate/professional degree or higher: 7.2%

School District(s)

Grossmont Union High (KG-12)
2012-13 Enrollment: 22,965 . . . . (619) 644-8000
Santee Elementary (KG-08)
2012-13 Enrollment: 6,418 . . . . (619) 258-2300

Housing: Homeownership rate: 70.4%; Median home value: $323,500; Median year structure built: 1977; Homeowner vacancy rate: 1.5%; Median gross rent: $1,315 per month; Rental vacancy rate: 4.0%

Health Insurance: 89.0% have insurance; 76.1% have private insurance; 22.2% have public insurance; 11.0% do not have insurance; 7.0% of children under 18 do not have insurance

Safety: Violent crime rate: 27.9 per 10,000 population; Property crime rate: 208.3 per 10,000 population

Transportation: Commute: 92.1% car, 1.2% public transportation, 0.8% walk, 3.9% work from home; Median travel time to work: 23.9 minutes

Additional Information Contacts

City of Santee . . . . (619) 258-4100
http://www.ci.santee.ca.us

SOLANA BEACH (city). Covers a land area of 3.520 square miles and a water area of 0.104 square miles. Located at 32.99° N. Lat; 117.26° W. Long. Elevation is 72 feet.

History: Until 1923, the main area known as Solana Beach was originally called Lockwood Mesa. The area first settled by the George H. Jones family in 1886. In 1986 the community officially incorporated as the city of Solana Beach.

Population: 12,867; Growth (since 2000): -0.9%; Density: 3,655.9 persons per square mile; Race: 85.8% White, 0.5% Black/African American, 4.0% Asian, 0.5% American Indian/Alaska Native, 0.1% Native Hawaiian/Other Pacific Islander, 3.4% Two or more races, 15.9% Hispanic of any race; Average household size: 2.28; Median age: 43.7; Age under 18: 18.5%; Age 65 and over: 18.7%; Males per 100 females: 97.5; Marriage status: 30.8% never married, 51.3% now married, 1.6% separated, 5.5% widowed, 12.4% divorced; Foreign born: 17.6%; Speak English only: 77.5%; With disability: 6.6%; Veterans: 9.2%; Ancestry: 17.8% German, 13.4% Irish, 10.7% English, 9.4% Italian, 4.7% Swedish

Employment: 23.7% management, business, and financial, 10.2% computer, engineering, and science, 15.7% education, legal, community service, arts, and media, 6.0% healthcare practitioners, 17.4% service, 23.3% sales and office, 1.6% natural resources, construction, and maintenance, 2.1% production, transportation, and material moving

Income: Per capita: $56,156; Median household: $86,451; Average household: $127,290; Households with income of $100,000 or more: 44.3%; Poverty rate: 8.9%

Educational Attainment: High school diploma or higher: 91.9%; Bachelor's degree or higher: 61.7%; Graduate/professional degree or higher: 28.1%

School District(s)

San Dieguito Union High (07-12)
2012-13 Enrollment: 12,365 . . . . (760) 753-6491
Solana Beach Elementary (KG-06)
2012-13 Enrollment: 2,989 . . . . (858) 794-7100

Housing: Homeownership rate: 60.2%; Median home value: $954,900; Median year structure built: 1975; Homeowner vacancy rate: 1.4%; Median gross rent: $1,899 per month; Rental vacancy rate: 6.3%

Health Insurance: 86.6% have insurance; 76.6% have private insurance; 24.1% have public insurance; 13.4% do not have insurance; 13.9% of children under 18 do not have insurance

Safety: Violent crime rate: 20.4 per 10,000 population; Property crime rate: 222.1 per 10,000 population

Transportation: Commute: 74.3% car, 2.4% public transportation, 4.3% walk, 16.0% work from home; Median travel time to work: 21.6 minutes; Amtrak: Train service available.

Additional Information Contacts

City of Solana Beach. . . . . (858) 720-2400
http://www.ci.solana-beach.ca.us

SPRING VALLEY (CDP). Covers a land area of 7.165 square miles and a water area of 0.209 square miles. Located at 32.73° N. Lat; 116.98° W. Long. Elevation is 390 feet.

History: Named for a spring in the area. The Bancroft Ranch House Museum (1856) is a national historic landmark.

Population: 28,205; Growth (since 2000): 5.8%; Density: 3,936.4 persons per square mile; Race: 59.5% White, 11.1% Black/African American, 5.9% Asian, 0.8% American Indian/Alaska Native, 0.8% Native Hawaiian/Other Pacific Islander, 6.5% Two or more races, 32.6% Hispanic of any race; Average household size: 3.01; Median age: 35.0; Age under 18: 26.5%; Age 65 and over: 10.5%; Males per 100 females: 95.2; Marriage status: 32.7% never married, 49.0% now married, 2.9% separated, 4.9% widowed, 13.4% divorced; Foreign born: 15.8%; Speak English only:

67.3%; With disability: 13.1%; Veterans: 13.9%; Ancestry: 13.3% German, 11.5% Irish, 9.4% English, 5.6% Italian, 3.1% American
Employment: 16.9% management, business, and financial, 4.3% computer, engineering, and science, 11.3% education, legal, community service, arts, and media, 2.6% healthcare practitioners, 19.7% service, 26.9% sales and office, 8.9% natural resources, construction, and maintenance, 9.4% production, transportation, and material moving
Income: Per capita: $27,529; Median household: $66,002; Average household: $80,691; Households with income of $100,000 or more: 29.8%; Poverty rate: 11.5%
Educational Attainment: High school diploma or higher: 87.2%; Bachelor's degree or higher: 23.7%; Graduate/professional degree or higher: 7.5%

School District(s)

Grossmont Union High (KG-12)
2012-13 Enrollment: 22,965 . . . . (619) 644-8000
La Mesa-Spring Valley (KG-08)
2012-13 Enrollment: 12,070 . . . . (619) 668-5700

Housing: Homeownership rate: 63.6%; Median home value: $336,900; Median year structure built: 1976; Homeowner vacancy rate: 1.9%; Median gross rent: $1,411 per month; Rental vacancy rate: 4.9%
Health Insurance: 83.9% have insurance; 62.9% have private insurance; 30.4% have public insurance; 16.1% do not have insurance; 8.2% of children under 18 do not have insurance
Transportation: Commute: 92.5% car, 1.9% public transportation, 0.7% walk, 4.0% work from home; Median travel time to work: 25.9 minutes

---

TECATE (unincorporated postal area)

ZCTA: 91980

Covers a land area of 3.581 square miles and a water area of 0 square miles. Located at 32.59° N. Lat; 116.62° W. Long. Elevation is 1,795 feet.
Population: 165; Growth (since 2000): 89.7%; Density: 46.1 persons per square mile; Race: 52.7% White, 0.0% Black/African American, 3.0% Asian, 0.6% American Indian/Alaska Native, 0.0% Native Hawaiian/Other Pacific Islander, 1.2% Two or more races, 80.0% Hispanic of any race; Average household size: 4.02; Median age: 35.5; Age under 18: 30.3%; Age 65 and over: 14.5%; Males per 100 females: 91.9
Housing: Homeownership rate: 43.9%; Homeowner vacancy rate: 0.0%; Rental vacancy rate: 7.7%

VALLEY CENTER (CDP). Covers a land area of 27.426 square miles and a water area of 0 square miles. Located at 33.23° N. Lat; 117.02° W. Long. Elevation is 1,312 feet.
Population: 9,277; Growth (since 2000): 26.7%; Density: 338.3 persons per square mile; Race: 73.1% White, 0.9% Black/African American, 3.2% Asian, 2.0% American Indian/Alaska Native, 0.2% Native Hawaiian/Other Pacific Islander, 4.6% Two or more races, 27.8% Hispanic of any race; Average household size: 3.08; Median age: 42.1; Age under 18: 24.3%; Age 65 and over: 12.5%; Males per 100 females: 100.0; Marriage status: 28.2% never married, 60.1% now married, 2.4% separated, 3.8% widowed, 8.0% divorced; Foreign born: 17.7%; Speak English only: 73.4%; With disability: 9.4%; Veterans: 8.0%; Ancestry: 13.3% English, 9.9% Irish, 7.8% German, 3.9% Italian, 3.1% American
Employment: 13.2% management, business, and financial, 6.0% computer, engineering, and science, 11.0% education, legal, community service, arts, and media, 1.5% healthcare practitioners, 16.3% service, 26.0% sales and office, 12.2% natural resources, construction, and maintenance, 13.8% production, transportation, and material moving
Income: Per capita: $30,438; Median household: $85,146; Average household: $101,023; Households with income of $100,000 or more: 41.2%; Poverty rate: 5.9%
Educational Attainment: High school diploma or higher: 82.7%; Bachelor's degree or higher: 26.8%; Graduate/professional degree or higher: 7.7%

School District(s)

Valley Center-Pauma Unified (KG-12)
2012-13 Enrollment: 4,154 . . . . (760) 749-0464
Warner Unified (KG-12)
2012-13 Enrollment: 284. . . . . (760) 782-3517

Housing: Homeownership rate: 80.6%; Median home value: $440,600; Median year structure built: 1986; Homeowner vacancy rate: 1.7%; Median gross rent: $1,542 per month; Rental vacancy rate: 2.8%
Health Insurance: 75.1% have insurance; 64.5% have private insurance; 18.8% have public insurance; 24.9% do not have insurance; 18.6% of children under 18 do not have insurance
Newspapers: Valley Roadrunner (weekly circulation 3500)
Transportation: Commute: 93.8% car, 0.8% public transportation, 0.1% walk, 5.4% work from home; Median travel time to work: 33.9 minutes

---

VISTA (city). Covers a land area of 18.678 square miles and a water area of 0 square miles. Located at 33.19° N. Lat; 117.24° W. Long. Elevation is 325 feet.
History: Named for the Spanish translation of "view". The post office at Vista was established in 1890 when the Oceanside-Escondido branch of the Santa Fe Railway was completed. Development of the town began in 1926 when water was brought from Lake Henshaw.
Population: 93,834; Growth (since 2000): 4.4%; Density: 5,023.7 persons per square mile; Race: 63.5% White, 3.3% Black/African American, 4.2% Asian, 1.2% American Indian/Alaska Native, 0.7% Native Hawaiian/Other Pacific Islander, 5.3% Two or more races, 48.4% Hispanic of any race; Average household size: 3.13; Median age: 31.1; Age under 18: 26.7%; Age 65 and over: 9.2%; Males per 100 females: 100.7; Marriage status: 35.8% never married, 49.0% now married, 1.4% separated, 4.5% widowed, 10.8% divorced; Foreign born: 26.3%; Speak English only: 55.5%; With disability: 9.6%; Veterans: 7.8%; Ancestry: 14.4% English, 9.0% German, 6.6% Irish, 2.6% Italian, 2.4% French
Employment: 10.8% management, business, and financial, 5.1% computer, engineering, and science, 7.0% education, legal, community service, arts, and media, 3.5% healthcare practitioners, 24.0% service, 24.0% sales and office, 12.4% natural resources, construction, and maintenance, 13.2% production, transportation, and material moving
Income: Per capita: $21,114; Median household: $47,346; Average household: $61,576; Households with income of $100,000 or more: 16.3%; Poverty rate: 16.0%
Educational Attainment: High school diploma or higher: 74.6%; Bachelor's degree or higher: 19.1%; Graduate/professional degree or higher: 5.3%

School District(s)

Armona Union Elementary (KG-12)
2012-13 Enrollment: 2,060 . . . . (559) 583-5000
Lakeside Union Elementary (KG-12)
2012-13 Enrollment: 5,475 . . . . (619) 390-2600
Mountain Empire Unified (PK-12)
2012-13 Enrollment: 2,956 . . . . (619) 473-9022
San Diego County Office of Education (PK-12)
2012-13 Enrollment: 4,151 . . . . (858) 292-3500
San Marcos Unified (KG-12)
2012-13 Enrollment: 19,617 . . . . (760) 752-1299
Vista Unified (KG-12)
2012-13 Enrollment: 25,642 . . . . (760) 726-2170

Two-year College(s)

Kaplan College-Vista (Private, For-profit)
Fall 2013 Enrollment: 896. . . . . (760) 630-1555

Housing: Homeownership rate: 51.8%; Median home value: $340,200; Median year structure built: 1981; Homeowner vacancy rate: 2.2%; Median gross rent: $1,221 per month; Rental vacancy rate: 5.9%
Health Insurance: 75.4% have insurance; 56.6% have private insurance; 25.3% have public insurance; 24.6% do not have insurance; 10.4% of children under 18 do not have insurance
Safety: Violent crime rate: 46.0 per 10,000 population; Property crime rate: 211.5 per 10,000 population
Transportation: Commute: 91.3% car, 2.5% public transportation, 1.4% walk, 3.6% work from home; Median travel time to work: 23.9 minutes

Additional Information Contacts

City of Vista . . . . (760) 726-1340
http://www.cityofvista.com

WARNER SPRINGS (unincorporated postal area)

ZCTA: 92086

Covers a land area of 220.425 square miles and a water area of 0.448 square miles. Located at 33.33° N. Lat; 116.66° W. Long. Elevation is 3,130 feet.
Population: 1,573; Growth (since 2000): 32.7%; Density: 7.1 persons per square mile; Race: 80.7% White, 1.6% Black/African American, 2.3% Asian, 7.9% American Indian/Alaska Native, 0.0% Native Hawaiian/Other Pacific Islander, 3.1% Two or more races, 17.7% Hispanic of any race; Average household size: 2.15; Median age: 54.7; Age under 18: 11.7%; Age 65 and over: 28.2%; Males per 100 females: 88.2

School District(s)

Warner Unified (KG-12)
2012-13 Enrollment: 284. . . . . (760) 782-3517

Housing: Homeownership rate: 77.7%; Homeowner vacancy rate: 4.4%; Rental vacancy rate: 4.5%

WINTER GARDENS (CDP). Covers a land area of 4.430 square miles and a water area of 0.001 square miles. Located at 32.84° N. Lat; 116.93° W. Long. Elevation is 676 feet.

Population: 20,631; Growth (since 2000): 4.3%; Density: 4,657.6 persons per square mile; Race: 81.6% White, 2.0% Black/African American, 1.7% Asian, 1.1% American Indian/Alaska Native, 0.5% Native Hawaiian/Other Pacific Islander, 5.3% Two or more races, 20.8% Hispanic of any race; Average household size: 2.75; Median age: 36.8; Age under 18: 24.3%; Age 65 and over: 10.3%; Males per 100 females: 97.4; Marriage status: 28.9% never married, 52.3% now married, 1.6% separated, 5.4% widowed, 13.4% divorced; Foreign born: 10.7%; Speak English only: 80.3%; With disability: 12.0%; Veterans: 13.3%; Ancestry: 16.2% German, 13.2% Irish, 10.0% English, 6.0% Italian, 5.4% American

Employment: 14.0% management, business, and financial, 4.0% computer, engineering, and science, 7.3% education, legal, community service, arts, and media, 3.5% healthcare practitioners, 20.4% service, 28.8% sales and office, 14.7% natural resources, construction, and maintenance, 7.3% production, transportation, and material moving

Income: Per capita: $26,268; Median household: $60,352; Average household: $72,817; Households with income of $100,000 or more: 21.1%; Poverty rate: 11.7%

Educational Attainment: High school diploma or higher: 87.7%; Bachelor's degree or higher: 15.5%; Graduate/professional degree or higher: 5.9%

Housing: Homeownership rate: 57.1%; Median home value: $296,300; Median year structure built: 1976; Homeowner vacancy rate: 3.0%; Median gross rent: $1,141 per month; Rental vacancy rate: 5.5%

Health Insurance: 86.6% have insurance; 68.8% have private insurance; 28.0% have public insurance; 13.4% do not have insurance; 10.7% of children under 18 do not have insurance

Transportation: Commute: 91.4% car, 1.5% public transportation, 0.6% walk, 4.8% work from home; Median travel time to work: 27.1 minutes

San Francisco County and City

Located in western California; coextensive with the city of San Francisco; bounded on the west by the Pacific Ocean, on the north by the Golden Gate, and on the east by San Francisco Bay. Covers a land area of 46.873 square miles, a water area of 185.016 square miles, and is located in the Pacific Time Zone at 37.73° N. Lat., 123.03° W. Long. The city was founded in 1850. Consolidated city-county government. Elevation is 52 feet. County seat is San Francisco.

San Francisco County and City is part of the San Francisco-Oakland-Hayward, CA Metropolitan Statistical Area. The entire metro area includes: Oakland-Hayward-Berkeley, CA Metropolitan Division (Alameda County, CA; Contra Costa County, CA); San Francisco-Redwood City-South San Francisco, CA Metropolitan Division (San Francisco County, CA; San Mateo County, CA); San Rafael, CA Metropolitan Division (Marin County, CA)

Weather Station: San Francisco — Elevation: 174 feet

	Jan	Feb	Mar	Apr	May	Jun	Jul	Aug	Sep	Oct	Nov	Dec
High	58	61	63	64	66	68	68	69	71	70	64	58
Low	46	48	49	50	52	53	55	56	56	54	51	47
Precip	4.4	4.5	3.2	1.4	0.7	0.2	0.0	0.1	0.2	1.1	3.1	4.4
Snow	na	na	na	na	na	na	na	na	na	na	na	na

High and Low temperatures in degrees Fahrenheit; Precipitation and Snow in inches

Weather Station: San Francisco Oceanside — Elevation: 35 feet

	Jan	Feb	Mar	Apr	May	Jun	Jul	Aug	Sep	Oct	Nov	Dec
High	58	60	60	60	61	62	63	64	65	65	62	58
Low	45	46	47	48	50	52	54	55	54	53	49	45
Precip	3.9	4.2	2.8	1.1	0.7	0.1	0.0	0.1	0.1	0.9	2.5	4.0
Snow	0.0	0.0	0.0	0.0	0.0	0.0	0.0	0.0	0.0	0.0	0.0	0.0

High and Low temperatures in degrees Fahrenheit; Precipitation and Snow in inches

Economy: Unemployment rate: 4.3%; Leading industries: 19.9% professional, scientific, and technical services; 12.8% accommodation and food services; 11.3% retail trade; Farms: 6 totaling 12 acres; Company size: 41 employs 1,000 or more persons, 52 employ 500 to 999 persons, 681 employs 100 to 499 persons, 30,939 employ less than 100 persons; Business ownership: 31,639 women-owned, 2,786 Black-owned, 6,914 Hispanic-owned, 25,236 Asian-owned

Vital Statistics: Birth rate: 107.4 per 10,000 population; Death rate: 71.0 per 10,000 population; Age-adjusted cancer mortality rate: 154.6 deaths per 100,000 population

Health Care: Physicians: 66.1 per 10,000 population; Hospital beds: 47.8 per 10,000 population; Hospital admissions: 1,331.4 per 10,000 population

Religion: Six largest groups: 15.0% Catholicism, 5.2% Methodist/Pietist, 2.8% Baptist, 2.2% Buddhism, 1.6% Judaism, 1.6% Eastern Liturgical (Orthodox)

Air Quality Index: 69.6% good, 29.9% moderate, 0.5% unhealthy for sensitive individuals, 0.0% unhealthy (percent of days)

Presidential Election: 83.4% Obama, 13.3% Romney (2012)

National and State Parks: Baker Beach State Park; Candlestick Point State Recreation Area; Farallon Islands State Game Refuge; Farallon National Wildlife Refuge; Fort Point National Historic Site; James D Phelan Beach State Park; San Francisco Maritime National Historical Park

History: San Francisco Bay was discovered by the Spanish in 1769. Spanish settlement began in 1776 when Don Juan Bautista de Anza and a group of soldiers brought 200 colonists overland from Mexico. A presidio was built to protect the new pueblo, and Mission San Francisco de Asis was established by Father Junipero Serra. The pueblo, called Yerba Buena, was a town of tents and adobe huts until Captain William A. Richardson built the first house in 1835, followed by Jacob Primer Leese 's store in 1836. In 1846 Captain John B. Montgomery took possession of the town for the United States, and the name was changed to San Francisco. The discovery of gold on the American River brought thousands of fortune-seekers through San Francisco. Many of them stayed to establish the multiethnic neighborhoods of the city. The first cable cars appeared in 1873, as the population continued to grow. On April 18, 1906, the devastating earthquake on the San Andreas fault destroyed some 30,000 buildings in San Francisco, but the city rose immediately from the ashes as reconstruction started.

Population: 805,235; Growth (since 2000): 3.7%; Density: 17,179.2 persons per square mile; Race: 48.5% White, 6.1% Black/African American, 33.3% Asian, 0.5% American Indian/Alaska Native, 0.4% Native Hawaiian/Other Pacific Islander, 4.7% Two or more races, 15.1% Hispanic of any race; Average household size: 2.26; Median age: 38.5; Age under 18: 13.4%; Age 65 and over: 13.6%; Males per 100 females: 102.9; Marriage status: 46.7% never married, 39.7% now married, 1.5% separated, 5.2% widowed, 8.4% divorced; Foreign born: 35.6%; Speak English only: 55.0%; With disability: 10.6%; Veterans: 4.2%; Ancestry: 8.2% German, 8.0% Irish, 5.1% English, 4.9% Italian, 2.5% Russian

Employment: 21.7% management, business, and financial, 10.4% computer, engineering, and science, 14.8% education, legal, community service, arts, and media, 4.8% healthcare practitioners, 17.3% service, 21.7% sales and office, 4.1% natural resources, construction, and maintenance, 5.2% production, transportation, and material moving

Income: Per capita: $48,486; Median household: $75,604; Average household: $110,208; Households with income of $100,000 or more: 39.4%; Poverty rate: 13.5%

Educational Attainment: High school diploma or higher: 86.3%; Bachelor's degree or higher: 52.4%; Graduate/professional degree or higher: 20.7%

School District(s)

San Francisco County Office of Education (KG-12)
2012-13 Enrollment: 638. . . . . (415) 241-6000

San Francisco County Rop
2012-13 Enrollment: n/a . . . . (415) 379-7751

San Francisco Unified (KG-12)
2012-13 Enrollment: 56,970 . . . . (415) 241-6000

Sbe - Mission Preparatory (KG-08)
2012-13 Enrollment: 102. . . . . (415) 508-9626

Sbe - San Francisco Flex Academy (09-12)
2012-13 Enrollment: 150. . . . . (415) 710-6759

Four-year College(s)

Academy of Art University (Private, For-profit)
Fall 2013 Enrollment: 16,001 . . . . (415) 274-2200
2013-14 Tuition: In-state $19,130; Out-of-state $19,130

American College of Traditional Chinese Medicine (Private, Not-for-profit)
Fall 2013 Enrollment: 268 . . . . (415) 282-7600

American Conservatory Theater (Private, Not-for-profit)
Fall 2013 Enrollment: 31 . . . . (415) 834-3200

California College of the Arts (Private, Not-for-profit)
Fall 2013 Enrollment: 1,949 . . . . (510) 594-3600
2013-14 Tuition: In-state $40,334; Out-of-state $40,334
California Institute of Integral Studies (Private, Not-for-profit)
Fall 2013 Enrollment: 1,271 . . . . (415) 575-6100
Fashion Institute of Design & Merchandising-San Francisco (Private, For-profit)
Fall 2013 Enrollment: 637 . . . . (415) 675-5200
2013-14 Tuition: In-state $28,920; Out-of-state $28,920
Golden Gate University-San Francisco (Private, Not-for-profit)
Fall 2013 Enrollment: 3,227 . . . . (415) 442-7800
2013-14 Tuition: In-state $14,400; Out-of-state $14,400
San Francisco Art Institute (Private, Not-for-profit)
Fall 2013 Enrollment: 680 . . . . (415) 771-7020
2013-14 Tuition: In-state $38,406; Out-of-state $38,406
San Francisco Conservatory of Music (Private, Not-for-profit)
Fall 2013 Enrollment: 399 . . . . (415) 864-7326
2013-14 Tuition: In-state $39,580; Out-of-state $39,580
San Francisco State University (Public)
Fall 2013 Enrollment: 29,905 . . . . (415) 338-1111
2013-14 Tuition: In-state $6,450; Out-of-state $17,610
Saybrook University (Private, Not-for-profit)
Fall 2013 Enrollment: 589 . . . . (415) 433-9200
The Art Institute of California-Argosy University San Francisco (Private, For-profit)
Fall 2013 Enrollment: 1,317 . . . . (415) 865-0198
2013-14 Tuition: In-state $18,748; Out-of-state $18,748
University of California-Hastings College of Law (Public)
Fall 2013 Enrollment: 1,088 . . . . (415) 565-4600
University of California-San Francisco (Public)
Fall 2013 Enrollment: 3,079 . . . . (415) 476-9000
University of San Francisco (Private, Not-for-profit, Roman Catholic)
Fall 2013 Enrollment: 10,112 . . . . (415) 422-5555
2013-14 Tuition: In-state $40,294; Out-of-state $40,294

Two-year College(s)

City College of San Francisco (Public)
Fall 2013 Enrollment: 26,706 . . . . (415) 239-3000
2013-14 Tuition: In-state $1,274; Out-of-state $6,748
Heald College-San Francisco (Private, For-profit)
Fall 2013 Enrollment: 1,074 . . . . (415) 808-3000
2013-14 Tuition: In-state $13,620; Out-of-state $13,620
Le Cordon Bleu College of Culinary Arts-San Francisco (Private, For-profit)
Fall 2013 Enrollment: 489 . . . . (415) 216-4416
2013-14 Tuition: In-state $13,761; Out-of-state $13,761
Miami Ad School-San Francisco (Private, For-profit)
Fall 2013 Enrollment: 131 . . . . (415) 837-0966
2013-14 Tuition: In-state $17,400; Out-of-state $17,400

Vocational/Technical School(s)

Cinta Aveda Institute (Private, For-profit)
Fall 2013 Enrollment: 221 . . . . (415) 989-4400
2013-14 Tuition: $22,575
Everest College-San Francisco (Private, For-profit)
Fall 2013 Enrollment: 267 . . . . (415) 777-2500
2013-14 Tuition: $15,009
Marinello Schools of Beauty-San Francisco (Private, For-profit)
Fall 2013 Enrollment: 616 . . . . (562) 945-2211
2013-14 Tuition: $18,511
San Francisco Institute of Esthetics and Cosmetology (Private, For-profit)
Fall 2013 Enrollment: 204 . . . . (415) 355-1734
2013-14 Tuition: $20,000

Housing: Homeownership rate: 35.7%; Median home value: $744,600; Median year structure built: 1941; Homeowner vacancy rate: 2.3%; Median gross rent: $1,488 per month; Rental vacancy rate: 5.4%

Health Insurance: 88.9% have insurance; 71.0% have private insurance; 26.4% have public insurance; 11.1% do not have insurance; 4.1% of children under 18 do not have insurance

Hospitals: California Pacific Medical Center - Davies Campus Hospital (341 beds); California Pacific Medical Center - Pacific Campus Hospital (341 beds); California Pacific Medical Center - Saint Luke's Campus (260 beds); Chinese Hospital (54 beds); Kaiser Foundation Hospital - San Francisco (620 beds); Laguna Honda Hospital & Rehabilitation Center (1147 beds); Saint Francis Memorial Hospital (356 beds); Saint Mary's Medical Center (531 beds); San Francisco General Hospital (639 beds); San Francisco VA Medical Center (244 beds); UCSF Medical Center (688 beds)

Safety: Violent crime rate: 84.7 per 10,000 population; Property crime rate: 579.5 per 10,000 population

Newspapers: Bay Guardian (weekly circulation 153000); SF Weekly (weekly circulation 116000); San Francisco Chronicle (daily circulation 312000); San Francisco Examiner (daily circulation 165000)

Transportation: Commute: 44.5% car, 32.6% public transportation, 10.1% walk, 7.0% work from home; Median travel time to work: 30.5 minutes; Amtrak: Train and bus service available.

Airports: San Francisco International (primary service/large hub)

Additional Information Contacts

City of San Francisco . . . . (415) 554-4851
http://www.sfgov.org

San Joaquin County

Located in central California, in the San Joaquin Valley; touches the Coast Ranges in the southwest, and the foothills of the Sierra Nevada in the east; watered by the San Joaquin, Mokelumne, Stanislaus, and Calaveras Rivers. Covers a land area of 1,391.321 square miles, a water area of 35.177 square miles, and is located in the Pacific Time Zone at 37.94° N. Lat., 121.27° W. Long. The county was founded in 1850. County seat is Stockton.

San Joaquin County is part of the Stockton-Lodi, CA Metropolitan Statistical Area. The entire metro area includes: San Joaquin County, CA

Weather Station: Lodi — Elevation: 40 feet

	Jan	Feb	Mar	Apr	May	Jun	Jul	Aug	Sep	Oct	Nov	Dec
High	55	62	68	74	81	87	91	91	87	78	65	55
Low	38	40	43	46	51	55	57	56	54	48	41	37
Precip	3.6	3.4	2.9	1.3	0.6	0.1	0.0	0.0	0.3	1.1	2.2	3.2
Snow	0.0	0.0	0.0	0.0	0.0	0.0	0.0	0.0	0.0	0.0	0.0	0.0

High and Low temperatures in degrees Fahrenheit; Precipitation and Snow in inches

Weather Station: Stockton Fire Stn #4 — Elevation: 12 feet

	Jan	Feb	Mar	Apr	May	Jun	Jul	Aug	Sep	Oct	Nov	Dec
High	56	63	68	74	82	88	93	93	89	81	66	56
Low	37	40	43	46	51	55	57	56	53	47	41	36
Precip	3.4	3.2	2.6	1.4	0.6	0.1	0.0	0.0	0.3	1.0	2.1	2.9
Snow	0.0	0.0	0.0	0.0	0.0	0.0	0.0	0.0	0.0	0.0	0.0	0.0

High and Low temperatures in degrees Fahrenheit; Precipitation and Snow in inches

Weather Station: Stockton Metropolitan Arpt — Elevation: 21 feet

	Jan	Feb	Mar	Apr	May	Jun	Jul	Aug	Sep	Oct	Nov	Dec
High	55	61	67	73	82	89	94	93	88	79	65	54
Low	38	41	44	47	52	57	61	60	57	50	43	38
Precip	2.7	2.5	2.1	0.9	0.5	0.1	0.0	0.0	0.3	0.8	1.6	2.1
Snow	na	na	na	na	na	na	na	na	na	na	na	na

High and Low temperatures in degrees Fahrenheit; Precipitation and Snow in inches

Population: 685,306; Growth (since 2000): 21.6%; Density: 492.6 persons per square mile; Race: 51.0% White, 7.6% Black/African American, 14.4% Asian, 1.1% American Indian/Alaska Native, 0.5% Native Hawaiian/Other Pacific Islander, 6.4% two or more races, 38.9% Hispanic of any race; Average household size: 3.12; Median age: 32.7; Age under 18: 29.3%; Age 65 and over: 10.4%; Males per 100 females: 99.2; Marriage status: 33.7% never married, 50.8% now married, 2.5% separated, 5.5% widowed, 10.0% divorced; Foreign born: 23.1%; Speak English only: 60.1%; With disability: 11.7%; Veterans: 7.2%; Ancestry: 9.3% German, 6.7% Irish, 4.9% Italian, 4.5% English, 2.6% Portuguese

Religion: Six largest groups: 26.8% Catholicism, 3.7% Non-denominational Protestant, 2.7% Baptist, 2.3% Latter-day Saints, 1.7% Pentecostal, 1.5% Muslim Estimate

Economy: Unemployment rate: 9.9%; Leading industries: 15.0% retail trade; 12.8% health care and social assistance; 10.0% other services (except public administration); Farms: 3,580 totaling 787,015 acres; Company size: 7 employ 1,000 or more persons, 12 employ 500 to 999 persons, 222 employ 100 to 499 persons, 10,486 employ less than 100 persons; Business ownership: 12,735 women-owned, 2,329 Black-owned, 7,173 Hispanic-owned, 6,650 Asian-owned

Employment: 11.2% management, business, and financial, 3.4% computer, engineering, and science, 8.9% education, legal, community service, arts, and media, 4.7% healthcare practitioners, 18.2% service, 24.7% sales and office, 13.0% natural resources, construction, and maintenance, 15.9% production, transportation, and material moving

Income: Per capita: $22,589; Median household: $53,380; Average household: $70,435; Households with income of $100,000 or more: 22.6%; Poverty rate: 18.2%
Educational Attainment: High school diploma or higher: 77.3%; Bachelor's degree or higher: 18.1%; Graduate/professional degree or higher: 5.7%
Housing: Homeownership rate: 59.2%; Median home value: $208,000; Median year structure built: 1980; Homeowner vacancy rate: 2.8%; Median gross rent: $1,026 per month; Rental vacancy rate: 8.1%
Vital Statistics: Birth rate: 148.0 per 10,000 population; Death rate: 70.7 per 10,000 population; Age-adjusted cancer mortality rate: 179.2 deaths per 100,000 population
Health Insurance: 82.9% have insurance; 57.8% have private insurance; 33.9% have public insurance; 17.1% do not have insurance; 7.0% of children under 18 do not have insurance
Health Care: Physicians: 15.5 per 10,000 population; Hospital beds: 16.6 per 10,000 population; Hospital admissions: 907.6 per 10,000 population
Air Quality Index: 35.1% good, 56.7% moderate, 5.8% unhealthy for sensitive individuals, 2.5% unhealthy (percent of days)
Transportation: Commute: 91.1% car, 1.4% public transportation, 1.9% walk, 4.2% work from home; Median travel time to work: 29.4 minutes
Presidential Election: 54.7% Obama, 43.4% Romney (2012)
Additional Information Contacts
San Joaquin Government . . . . (209) 468-3211
http://www.sjgov.org

San Joaquin County Communities

ACAMPO (CDP). Covers a land area of 0.938 square miles and a water area of 0 square miles. Located at 38.17° N. Lat; 121.28° W. Long. Elevation is 52 feet.
Population: 341; Growth (since 2000): n/a; Density: 363.7 persons per square mile; Race: 49.6% White, 0.0% Black/African American, 0.9% Asian, 0.3% American Indian/Alaska Native, 2.3% Native Hawaiian/Other Pacific Islander, 7.0% Two or more races, 58.4% Hispanic of any race; Average household size: 3.63; Median age: 30.6; Age under 18: 30.8%; Age 65 and over: 10.9%; Males per 100 females: 114.5

School District(s)

Lodi Unified (KG-12)
2012-13 Enrollment: 30,222 . . . . (209) 331-7000
Oak View Union Elementary (KG-08)
2012-13 Enrollment: 402. . . . . (209) 368-0636
Housing: Homeownership rate: 59.6%; Homeowner vacancy rate: 0.0%; Rental vacancy rate: 2.6%

AUGUST (CDP). Covers a land area of 1.251 square miles and a water area of 0 square miles. Located at 37.98° N. Lat; 121.26° W. Long. Elevation is 26 feet.
Population: 8,390; Growth (since 2000): 7.5%; Density: 6,705.8 persons per square mile; Race: 46.7% White, 2.7% Black/African American, 4.3% Asian, 2.2% American Indian/Alaska Native, 0.2% Native Hawaiian/Other Pacific Islander, 6.9% Two or more races, 70.3% Hispanic of any race; Average household size: 3.61; Median age: 28.0; Age under 18: 34.0%; Age 65 and over: 7.0%; Males per 100 females: 107.1; Marriage status: 37.9% never married, 48.0% now married, 4.9% separated, 3.8% widowed, 10.3% divorced; Foreign born: 38.0%; Speak English only: 37.1%; With disability: 14.5%; Veterans: 5.6%; Ancestry: 7.6% German, 5.0% Irish, 2.1% English, 1.5% Norwegian, 1.1% Italian
Employment: 0.6% management, business, and financial, 0.7% computer, engineering, and science, 3.4% education, legal, community service, arts, and media, 0.8% healthcare practitioners, 22.4% service, 21.0% sales and office, 31.9% natural resources, construction, and maintenance, 19.2% production, transportation, and material moving
Income: Per capita: $11,925; Median household: $28,780; Average household: $40,175; Households with income of $100,000 or more: 4.8%; Poverty rate: 40.9%
Educational Attainment: High school diploma or higher: 48.8%; Bachelor's degree or higher: 2.7%; Graduate/professional degree or higher: 0.4%
Housing: Homeownership rate: 50.0%; Median home value: $72,000; Median year structure built: 1964; Homeowner vacancy rate: 3.6%; Median gross rent: $880 per month; Rental vacancy rate: 10.7%
Health Insurance: 71.4% have insurance; 26.9% have private insurance; 49.3% have public insurance; 28.6% do not have insurance; 11.4% of children under 18 do not have insurance
Transportation: Commute: 96.0% car, 0.2% public transportation, 1.2% walk, 1.5% work from home; Median travel time to work: 25.3 minutes

CLEMENTS (unincorporated postal area)
ZCTA: 95227
Covers a land area of 37.123 square miles and a water area of 2.894 square miles. Located at 38.21° N. Lat; 121.05° W. Long. Elevation is 138 feet.
Population: 941; Growth (since 2000): 31.2%; Density: 25.3 persons per square mile; Race: 88.3% White, 0.5% Black/African American, 0.9% Asian, 0.7% American Indian/Alaska Native, 0.7% Native Hawaiian/Other Pacific Islander, 4.8% Two or more races, 13.2% Hispanic of any race; Average household size: 2.54; Median age: 47.7; Age under 18: 19.9%; Age 65 and over: 19.6%; Males per 100 females: 102.8
Housing: Homeownership rate: 72.7%; Homeowner vacancy rate: 2.5%; Rental vacancy rate: 3.8%

COLLIERVILLE (CDP). Covers a land area of 6.595 square miles and a water area of 0.010 square miles. Located at 38.21° N. Lat; 121.27° W. Long. Elevation is 62 feet.
Population: 1,934; Growth (since 2000): n/a; Density: 293.3 persons per square mile; Race: 80.2% White, 0.7% Black/African American, 2.5% Asian, 1.1% American Indian/Alaska Native, 0.1% Native Hawaiian/Other Pacific Islander, 3.5% Two or more races, 26.8% Hispanic of any race; Average household size: 2.87; Median age: 43.3; Age under 18: 23.7%; Age 65 and over: 16.6%; Males per 100 females: 100.0
Housing: Homeownership rate: 77.8%; Homeowner vacancy rate: 3.0%; Rental vacancy rate: 5.1%

COUNTRY CLUB (CDP). Covers a land area of 1.827 square miles and a water area of 0.151 square miles. Located at 37.97° N. Lat; 121.34° W. Long. Elevation is 13 feet.
Population: 9,379; Growth (since 2000): -0.9%; Density: 5,134.1 persons per square mile; Race: 61.2% White, 5.0% Black/African American, 6.7% Asian, 1.7% American Indian/Alaska Native, 0.4% Native Hawaiian/Other Pacific Islander, 8.5% Two or more races, 40.4% Hispanic of any race; Average household size: 2.70; Median age: 36.9; Age under 18: 25.8%; Age 65 and over: 14.4%; Males per 100 females: 92.7; Marriage status: 34.1% never married, 42.0% now married, 2.7% separated, 9.0% widowed, 14.9% divorced; Foreign born: 9.6%; Speak English only: 78.0%; With disability: 20.2%; Veterans: 10.9%; Ancestry: 10.8% German, 7.1% Irish, 4.5% English, 4.3% Italian, 3.4% Dutch
Employment: 9.9% management, business, and financial, 1.5% computer, engineering, and science, 10.7% education, legal, community service, arts, and media, 5.8% healthcare practitioners, 21.8% service, 28.3% sales and office, 9.6% natural resources, construction, and maintenance, 12.5% production, transportation, and material moving
Income: Per capita: $20,659; Median household: $44,519; Average household: $54,251; Households with income of $100,000 or more: 7.2%; Poverty rate: 16.8%
Educational Attainment: High school diploma or higher: 79.3%; Bachelor's degree or higher: 12.4%; Graduate/professional degree or higher: 4.6%
Housing: Homeownership rate: 66.5%; Median home value: $128,400; Median year structure built: 1955; Homeowner vacancy rate: 2.7%; Median gross rent: $997 per month; Rental vacancy rate: 8.5%
Health Insurance: 80.8% have insurance; 49.3% have private insurance; 43.6% have public insurance; 19.2% do not have insurance; 13.2% of children under 18 do not have insurance
Transportation: Commute: 95.5% car, 1.0% public transportation, 0.8% walk, 1.1% work from home; Median travel time to work: 18.7 minutes

DOGTOWN (CDP). Covers a land area of 12.967 square miles and a water area of 0.022 square miles. Located at 38.21° N. Lat; 121.15° W. Long. Elevation is 151 feet.
Population: 2,506; Growth (since 2000): n/a; Density: 193.3 persons per square mile; Race: 81.4% White, 0.6% Black/African American, 2.3% Asian, 0.9% American Indian/Alaska Native, 0.1% Native Hawaiian/Other Pacific Islander, 4.6% Two or more races, 25.5% Hispanic of any race; Average household size: 2.95; Median age: 42.9; Age under 18: 24.7%; Age 65 and over: 14.2%; Males per 100 females: 102.9; Marriage status: 25.3% never married, 57.0% now married, 2.0% separated, 5.6% widowed, 12.2% divorced; Foreign born: 22.7%; Speak English only: 60.4%; With disability: 12.7%; Veterans: 10.6%; Ancestry: 15.1% German, 11.7% Irish, 9.6% English, 4.9% Italian, 4.3% American

Employment: 16.9% management, business, and financial, 1.3% computer, engineering, and science, 7.2% education, legal, community service, arts, and media, 7.4% healthcare practitioners, 17.8% service, 21.9% sales and office, 20.4% natural resources, construction, and maintenance, 7.2% production, transportation, and material moving
Income: Per capita: $30,120; Median household: $61,909; Average household: $87,331; Households with income of $100,000 or more: 36.7%; Poverty rate: 11.7%
Educational Attainment: High school diploma or higher: 77.0%; Bachelor's degree or higher: 21.6%; Graduate/professional degree or higher: 9.6%
Housing: Homeownership rate: 80.3%; Median home value: $415,000; Median year structure built: 1984; Homeowner vacancy rate: 2.0%; Median gross rent: $1,411 per month; Rental vacancy rate: 5.6%
Health Insurance: 86.5% have insurance; 74.0% have private insurance; 30.8% have public insurance; 13.5% do not have insurance; 3.7% of children under 18 do not have insurance
Transportation: Commute: 80.4% car, 0.0% public transportation, 4.9% walk, 14.4% work from home; Median travel time to work: 36.4 minutes

ESCALON (city). Covers a land area of 2.301 square miles and a water area of 0.067 square miles. Located at 37.79° N. Lat; 121.00° W. Long. Elevation is 118 feet.
Population: 7,132; Growth (since 2000): 19.6%; Density: 3,099.7 persons per square mile; Race: 81.6% White, 0.4% Black/African American, 1.3% Asian, 1.1% American Indian/Alaska Native, 0.3% Native Hawaiian/Other Pacific Islander, 3.6% Two or more races, 27.0% Hispanic of any race; Average household size: 2.87; Median age: 36.0; Age under 18: 27.1%; Age 65 and over: 12.5%; Males per 100 females: 96.0; Marriage status: 27.3% never married, 55.1% now married, 1.6% separated, 5.5% widowed, 12.1% divorced; Foreign born: 13.3%; Speak English only: 80.3%; With disability: 10.1%; Veterans: 6.1%; Ancestry: 14.7% German, 14.3% Irish, 9.3% American, 8.2% Italian, 7.5% Portuguese
Employment: 15.2% management, business, and financial, 1.2% computer, engineering, and science, 10.9% education, legal, community service, arts, and media, 5.4% healthcare practitioners, 16.4% service, 26.8% sales and office, 9.8% natural resources, construction, and maintenance, 14.4% production, transportation, and material moving
Income: Per capita: $26,235; Median household: $55,875; Average household: $70,871; Households with income of $100,000 or more: 29.3%; Poverty rate: 13.2%
Educational Attainment: High school diploma or higher: 86.3%; Bachelor's degree or higher: 19.3%; Graduate/professional degree or higher: 5.1%

School District(s)

Escalon Unified (KG-12)
2012-13 Enrollment: 2,815 . . . . (209) 838-3591
Housing: Homeownership rate: 72.3%; Median home value: $219,400; Median year structure built: 1985; Homeowner vacancy rate: 2.5%; Median gross rent: $951 per month; Rental vacancy rate: 5.9%
Health Insurance: 92.9% have insurance; 84.7% have private insurance; 18.4% have public insurance; 7.1% do not have insurance; 5.4% of children under 18 do not have insurance
Safety: Violent crime rate: 13.7 per 10,000 population; Property crime rate: 261.5 per 10,000 population
Transportation: Commute: 91.7% car, 1.7% public transportation, 1.8% walk, 3.1% work from home; Median travel time to work: 24.4 minutes
Additional Information Contacts
City of Escalon . . . . (209) 691-7400
http://www.cityofescalon.org

FARMINGTON (CDP). Covers a land area of 2.542 square miles and a water area of 0 square miles. Located at 37.93° N. Lat; 121.00° W. Long. Elevation is 112 feet.
Population: 207; Growth (since 2000): -21.0%; Density: 81.4 persons per square mile; Race: 79.2% White, 3.4% Black/African American, 2.9% Asian, 0.5% American Indian/Alaska Native, 0.0% Native Hawaiian/Other Pacific Islander, 5.3% Two or more races, 20.3% Hispanic of any race; Average household size: 2.62; Median age: 43.9; Age under 18: 21.7%; Age 65 and over: 13.0%; Males per 100 females: 102.9

School District(s)

Escalon Unified (KG-12)
2012-13 Enrollment: 2,815 . . . . (209) 838-3591
Housing: Homeownership rate: 68.3%; Homeowner vacancy rate: 11.5%; Rental vacancy rate: 10.7%

FRENCH CAMP (CDP). Covers a land area of 3.142 square miles and a water area of <.001 square miles. Located at 37.87° N. Lat; 121.27° W. Long. Elevation is 20 feet.
History: French Camp was named for the Hudson's Bay Company trappers, many of them French-Canadians, who camped in this area from 1830 to 1845, hunting beaver along the river.
Population: 3,376; Growth (since 2000): -17.8%; Density: 1,074.5 persons per square mile; Race: 49.7% White, 12.1% Black/African American, 4.8% Asian, 0.9% American Indian/Alaska Native, 0.3% Native Hawaiian/Other Pacific Islander, 4.8% Two or more races, 51.8% Hispanic of any race; Average household size: 3.19; Median age: 30.1; Age under 18: 21.7%; Age 65 and over: 7.0%; Males per 100 females: 193.1; Marriage status: 49.4% never married, 37.9% now married, 3.7% separated, 3.4% widowed, 9.3% divorced; Foreign born: 26.5%; Speak English only: 52.8%; With disability: 12.4%; Veterans: 5.2%; Ancestry: 6.0% German, 4.6% Irish, 3.6% Italian, 3.1% English, 2.3% American
Employment: 3.9% management, business, and financial, 0.8% computer, engineering, and science, 10.6% education, legal, community service, arts, and media, 3.5% healthcare practitioners, 15.0% service, 14.4% sales and office, 33.8% natural resources, construction, and maintenance, 18.1% production, transportation, and material moving
Income: Per capita: $10,597; Median household: $42,768; Average household: $49,086; Households with income of $100,000 or more: 5.2%; Poverty rate: 36.5%
Educational Attainment: High school diploma or higher: 58.0%; Bachelor's degree or higher: 4.8%; Graduate/professional degree or higher: 2.2%

School District(s)

Manteca Unified (KG-12)
2012-13 Enrollment: 23,235 . . . . (209) 825-3200
Housing: Homeownership rate: 54.2%; Median home value: $119,800; Median year structure built: 1964; Homeowner vacancy rate: 3.5%; Median gross rent: $1,085 per month; Rental vacancy rate: 13.4%
Health Insurance: 64.3% have insurance; 34.1% have private insurance; 35.2% have public insurance; 35.7% do not have insurance; 14.6% of children under 18 do not have insurance
Hospitals: San Joaquin General Hospital (234 beds)
Transportation: Commute: 84.9% car, 0.8% public transportation, 3.2% walk, 8.1% work from home; Median travel time to work: 24.1 minutes

GARDEN ACRES (CDP). Covers a land area of 2.589 square miles and a water area of 0 square miles. Located at 37.96° N. Lat; 121.23° W. Long. Elevation is 33 feet.
Population: 10,648; Growth (since 2000): 9.2%; Density: 4,113.4 persons per square mile; Race: 49.2% White, 2.2% Black/African American, 3.4% Asian, 1.6% American Indian/Alaska Native, 0.4% Native Hawaiian/Other Pacific Islander, 6.5% Two or more races, 68.9% Hispanic of any race; Average household size: 3.76; Median age: 28.7; Age under 18: 33.0%; Age 65 and over: 8.0%; Males per 100 females: 105.4; Marriage status: 33.9% never married, 51.4% now married, 4.6% separated, 3.4% widowed, 11.3% divorced; Foreign born: 32.3%; Speak English only: 39.4%; With disability: 12.0%; Veterans: 3.7%; Ancestry: 6.4% German, 4.8% Irish, 3.5% French, 3.3% Italian, 2.0% English
Employment: 2.3% management, business, and financial, 0.0% computer, engineering, and science, 5.4% education, legal, community service, arts, and media, 1.1% healthcare practitioners, 24.9% service, 20.4% sales and office, 21.8% natural resources, construction, and maintenance, 24.0% production, transportation, and material moving
Income: Per capita: $12,988; Median household: $40,739; Average household: $48,173; Households with income of $100,000 or more: 8.1%; Poverty rate: 22.5%
Educational Attainment: High school diploma or higher: 51.7%; Bachelor's degree or higher: 5.3%; Graduate/professional degree or higher: 1.2%
Housing: Homeownership rate: 56.7%; Median home value: $103,300; Median year structure built: 1962; Homeowner vacancy rate: 2.2%; Median gross rent: $932 per month; Rental vacancy rate: 7.0%
Health Insurance: 71.7% have insurance; 35.2% have private insurance; 43.0% have public insurance; 28.3% do not have insurance; 6.0% of children under 18 do not have insurance
Transportation: Commute: 92.2% car, 1.8% public transportation, 0.0% walk, 4.7% work from home; Median travel time to work: 24.5 minutes

HOLT (unincorporated postal area)

ZCTA: 95234

Covers a land area of 33.586 square miles and a water area of 2.118 square miles. Located at 37.93° N. Lat; 121.53° W. Long..

Population: 70; Growth (since 2000): n/a; Density: 2.1 persons per square mile; Race: 44.3% White, 1.4% Black/African American, 0.0% Asian, 0.0% American Indian/Alaska Native, 0.0% Native Hawaiian/Other Pacific Islander, 1.4% Two or more races, 90.0% Hispanic of any race; Average household size: 3.33; Median age: 25.5; Age under 18: 35.7%; Age 65 and over: 2.9%; Males per 100 females: 133.3

Housing: Homeownership rate: 4.8%; Homeowner vacancy rate: 0.0%; Rental vacancy rate: 4.8%

KENNEDY (CDP). Covers a land area of 1.175 square miles and a water area of 0 square miles. Located at 37.93° N. Lat; 121.25° W. Long. Elevation is 23 feet.

Population: 3,254; Growth (since 2000): -0.6%; Density: 2,769.3 persons per square mile; Race: 15.9% White, 6.1% Black/African American, 7.9% Asian, 0.7% American Indian/Alaska Native, 0.1% Native Hawaiian/Other Pacific Islander, 4.4% Two or more races, 77.2% Hispanic of any race; Average household size: 4.21; Median age: 26.8; Age under 18: 36.2%; Age 65 and over: 8.5%; Males per 100 females: 102.0; Marriage status: 39.0% never married, 46.9% now married, 1.7% separated, 5.6% widowed, 8.5% divorced; Foreign born: 44.2%; Speak English only: 24.2%; With disability: 13.2%; Veterans: 3.7%; Ancestry: 3.0% American, 0.9% English, 0.9% Swiss, 0.7% German, 0.4% Russian

Employment: 5.1% management, business, and financial, 0.8% computer, engineering, and science, 1.9% education, legal, community service, arts, and media, 1.2% healthcare practitioners, 26.2% service, 20.1% sales and office, 19.3% natural resources, construction, and maintenance, 25.3% production, transportation, and material moving

Income: Per capita: $11,240; Median household: $38,428; Average household: $43,001; Households with income of $100,000 or more: 1.1%; Poverty rate: 33.8%

Educational Attainment: High school diploma or higher: 49.2%; Bachelor's degree or higher: 3.8%; Graduate/professional degree or higher: 2.2%

Housing: Homeownership rate: 59.0%; Median home value: $106,300; Median year structure built: 1965; Homeowner vacancy rate: 1.9%; Median gross rent: $1,037 per month; Rental vacancy rate: 7.3%

Health Insurance: 63.8% have insurance; 30.2% have private insurance; 39.0% have public insurance; 36.2% do not have insurance; 16.2% of children under 18 do not have insurance

Transportation: Commute: 87.3% car, 2.3% public transportation, 0.0% walk, 9.7% work from home; Median travel time to work: 33.1 minutes

LATHROP (city). Covers a land area of 21.931 square miles and a water area of 1.102 square miles. Located at 37.82° N. Lat; 121.31° W. Long. Elevation is 23 feet.

Population: 18,023; Growth (since 2000): 72.6%; Density: 821.8 persons per square mile; Race: 41.1% White, 7.2% Black/African American, 22.0% Asian, 1.3% American Indian/Alaska Native, 0.8% Native Hawaiian/Other Pacific Islander, 6.9% Two or more races, 42.6% Hispanic of any race; Average household size: 3.77; Median age: 30.5; Age under 18: 32.3%; Age 65 and over: 6.5%; Males per 100 females: 99.7; Marriage status: 36.2% never married, 50.7% now married, 2.6% separated, 4.6% widowed, 8.5% divorced; Foreign born: 27.7%; Speak English only: 50.6%; With disability: 8.8%; Veterans: 6.0%; Ancestry: 6.8% German, 3.8% Irish, 2.8% Italian, 2.4% English, 2.2% American

Employment: 8.9% management, business, and financial, 3.0% computer, engineering, and science, 6.2% education, legal, community service, arts, and media, 5.3% healthcare practitioners, 17.6% service, 25.6% sales and office, 12.3% natural resources, construction, and maintenance, 21.1% production, transportation, and material moving

Income: Per capita: $17,595; Median household: $60,843; Average household: $68,467; Households with income of $100,000 or more: 18.5%; Poverty rate: 10.5%

Educational Attainment: High school diploma or higher: 76.0%; Bachelor's degree or higher: 12.9%; Graduate/professional degree or higher: 1.9%

School District(s)

Manteca Unified (KG-12)
2012-13 Enrollment: 23,235 . . . . (209) 825-3200

Four-year College(s)

ITT Technical Institute-Lathrop (Private, For-profit)
Fall 2013 Enrollment: 492 . . . . (209) 858-0077
2013-14 Tuition: In-state $18,048; Out-of-state $18,048

Housing: Homeownership rate: 75.3%; Median home value: $191,200; Median year structure built: 1997; Homeowner vacancy rate: 3.7%; Median gross rent: $1,514 per month; Rental vacancy rate: 5.5%

Health Insurance: 78.9% have insurance; 60.0% have private insurance; 24.6% have public insurance; 21.1% do not have insurance; 11.9% of children under 18 do not have insurance

Transportation: Commute: 94.1% car, 2.4% public transportation, 0.1% walk, 2.4% work from home; Median travel time to work: 38.2 minutes

Additional Information Contacts

City of Lathrop . . . . (209) 941-7220
http://www.ci.lathrop.ca.us

LINCOLN VILLAGE (CDP). Covers a land area of 0.736 square miles and a water area of 0 square miles. Located at 38.01° N. Lat; 121.33° W. Long. Elevation is 13 feet.

Population: 4,381; Growth (since 2000): 3.9%; Density: 5,952.8 persons per square mile; Race: 67.8% White, 3.5% Black/African American, 6.1% Asian, 1.3% American Indian/Alaska Native, 0.3% Native Hawaiian/Other Pacific Islander, 8.7% Two or more races, 32.5% Hispanic of any race; Average household size: 2.79; Median age: 36.2; Age under 18: 27.9%; Age 65 and over: 13.9%; Males per 100 females: 90.9; Marriage status: 37.6% never married, 47.8% now married, 2.2% separated, 5.4% widowed, 9.1% divorced; Foreign born: 13.1%; Speak English only: 76.2%; With disability: 10.5%; Veterans: 9.1%; Ancestry: 14.4% German, 8.1% Irish, 8.0% European, 7.3% Italian, 6.1% English

Employment: 8.9% management, business, and financial, 2.8% computer, engineering, and science, 19.7% education, legal, community service, arts, and media, 0.0% healthcare practitioners, 19.0% service, 24.5% sales and office, 13.8% natural resources, construction, and maintenance, 11.3% production, transportation, and material moving

Income: Per capita: $22,723; Median household: $51,571; Average household: $58,916; Households with income of $100,000 or more: 13.7%; Poverty rate: 9.2%

Educational Attainment: High school diploma or higher: 90.3%; Bachelor's degree or higher: 25.2%; Graduate/professional degree or higher: 8.0%

Housing: Homeownership rate: 70.0%; Median home value: $174,900; Median year structure built: 1957; Homeowner vacancy rate: 2.1%; Median gross rent: $1,084 per month; Rental vacancy rate: 10.6%

Health Insurance: 80.3% have insurance; 57.9% have private insurance; 36.6% have public insurance; 19.7% do not have insurance; 3.1% of children under 18 do not have insurance

Transportation: Commute: 93.3% car, 0.0% public transportation, 0.0% walk, 4.8% work from home; Median travel time to work: 22.6 minutes

LINDEN (CDP). Covers a land area of 7.409 square miles and a water area of 0.052 square miles. Located at 38.02° N. Lat; 121.10° W. Long. Elevation is 92 feet.

Population: 1,784; Growth (since 2000): 61.7%; Density: 240.8 persons per square mile; Race: 86.4% White, 0.3% Black/African American, 1.4% Asian, 0.6% American Indian/Alaska Native, 0.1% Native Hawaiian/Other Pacific Islander, 4.1% Two or more races, 21.6% Hispanic of any race; Average household size: 2.83; Median age: 36.9; Age under 18: 28.9%; Age 65 and over: 12.4%; Males per 100 females: 98.2

School District(s)

Linden Unified (KG-12)
2012-13 Enrollment: 2,321 . . . . (209) 887-3894

Housing: Homeownership rate: 77.6%; Homeowner vacancy rate: 2.0%; Rental vacancy rate: 6.0%

Newspapers: Linden Herald (weekly circulation 1200)

LOCKEFORD (CDP). Covers a land area of 8.341 square miles and a water area of 0.046 square miles. Located at 38.15° N. Lat; 121.15° W. Long. Elevation is 102 feet.

Population: 3,233; Growth (since 2000): 1.7%; Density: 387.6 persons per square mile; Race: 78.1% White, 0.3% Black/African American, 2.0% Asian, 0.7% American Indian/Alaska Native, 0.4% Native Hawaiian/Other Pacific Islander, 5.7% Two or more races, 29.6% Hispanic of any race; Average household size: 2.82; Median age: 39.2; Age under 18: 25.6%; Age 65 and over: 14.5%; Males per 100 females: 108.2; Marriage status: 27.8% never married, 56.3% now married, 1.9% separated, 9.6%

widowed, 6.3% divorced; Foreign born: 16.1%; Speak English only: 75.0%; With disability: 15.5%; Veterans: 8.0%; Ancestry: 25.7% German, 11.1% English, 10.7% Irish, 5.8% French, 5.2% Italian

Employment: 16.0% management, business, and financial, 0.0% computer, engineering, and science, 5.7% education, legal, community service, arts, and media, 2.4% healthcare practitioners, 13.0% service, 24.3% sales and office, 25.4% natural resources, construction, and maintenance, 13.2% production, transportation, and material moving

Income: Per capita: $22,821; Median household: $43,847; Average household: $56,657; Households with income of $100,000 or more: 12.4%; Poverty rate: 18.6%

Educational Attainment: High school diploma or higher: 75.4%; Bachelor's degree or higher: 11.0%; Graduate/professional degree or higher: 3.2%

School District(s)

Lodi Unified (KG-12)
2012-13 Enrollment: 30,222 . . . . (209) 331-7000

Housing: Homeownership rate: 75.5%; Median home value: $266,200; Median year structure built: 1977; Homeowner vacancy rate: 2.3%; Median gross rent: $1,143 per month; Rental vacancy rate: 11.1%

Health Insurance: 76.5% have insurance; 49.6% have private insurance; 39.0% have public insurance; 23.5% do not have insurance; 12.8% of children under 18 do not have insurance

Transportation: Commute: 90.6% car, 0.0% public transportation, 3.7% walk, 4.0% work from home; Median travel time to work: 27.6 minutes

LODI (city). Covers a land area of 13.611 square miles and a water area of 0.214 square miles. Located at 38.12° N. Lat; 121.29° W. Long. Elevation is 49 feet.

History: San Joaquin County Historical Museum to South. Founded in 1869 and settled by wheat farmers from the Dakotas, mostly of German descent. Incorporated 1906.

Population: 62,134; Growth (since 2000): 9.0%; Density: 4,565.1 persons per square mile; Race: 68.7% White, 0.8% Black/African American, 6.9% Asian, 0.9% American Indian/Alaska Native, 0.2% Native Hawaiian/Other Pacific Islander, 4.6% Two or more races, 36.4% Hispanic of any race; Average household size: 2.78; Median age: 34.3; Age under 18: 27.8%; Age 65 and over: 13.5%; Males per 100 females: 95.5; Marriage status: 31.0% never married, 50.6% now married, 2.2% separated, 7.1% widowed, 11.3% divorced; Foreign born: 20.4%; Speak English only: 65.3%; With disability: 11.7%; Veterans: 7.7%; Ancestry: 17.4% German, 9.3% Irish, 6.7% Italian, 6.4% English, 2.8% American

Employment: 10.3% management, business, and financial, 2.3% computer, engineering, and science, 10.4% education, legal, community service, arts, and media, 4.5% healthcare practitioners, 18.6% service, 23.5% sales and office, 15.2% natural resources, construction, and maintenance, 15.2% production, transportation, and material moving

Income: Per capita: $24,149; Median household: $48,701; Average household: $67,351; Households with income of $100,000 or more: 20.4%; Poverty rate: 18.1%

Educational Attainment: High school diploma or higher: 77.2%; Bachelor's degree or higher: 19.3%; Graduate/professional degree or higher: 6.2%

School District(s)

Lodi Unified (KG-12)
2012-13 Enrollment: 30,222 . . . . (209) 331-7000

Housing: Homeownership rate: 54.7%; Median home value: $228,600; Median year structure built: 1974; Homeowner vacancy rate: 2.3%; Median gross rent: $998 per month; Rental vacancy rate: 8.2%

Health Insurance: 81.6% have insurance; 55.8% have private insurance; 36.3% have public insurance; 18.4% do not have insurance; 7.3% of children under 18 do not have insurance

Hospitals: Lodi Memorial Hospital (181 beds)

Safety: Violent crime rate: 45.1 per 10,000 population; Property crime rate: 361.6 per 10,000 population

Newspapers: Lodi News-Sentinel (daily circulation 16400)

Transportation: Commute: 91.9% car, 0.8% public transportation, 2.1% walk, 3.9% work from home; Median travel time to work: 22.4 minutes; Amtrak: Train service available.

Additional Information Contacts

City of Lodi . . . . (209) 333-6800
http://www.lodi.gov

MANTECA (city). Covers a land area of 17.733 square miles and a water area of 0.024 square miles. Located at 37.80° N. Lat; 121.23° W. Long. Elevation is 36 feet.

History: Manteca began in 1870 as Cowell's Station, a stop on the Central Pacific Railroad. It became a shipping center for dairy products.

Population: 67,096; Growth (since 2000): 36.2%; Density: 3,783.6 persons per square mile; Race: 62.4% White, 4.3% Black/African American, 7.1% Asian, 1.1% American Indian/Alaska Native, 0.6% Native Hawaiian/Other Pacific Islander, 7.2% Two or more races, 37.7% Hispanic of any race; Average household size: 3.08; Median age: 33.6; Age under 18: 29.0%; Age 65 and over: 9.9%; Males per 100 females: 96.8; Marriage status: 30.9% never married, 54.3% now married, 2.7% separated, 4.5% widowed, 10.3% divorced; Foreign born: 15.5%; Speak English only: 70.8%; With disability: 11.1%; Veterans: 8.8%; Ancestry: 12.3% German, 10.0% Irish, 6.1% Portuguese, 6.0% Italian, 5.3% English

Employment: 11.3% management, business, and financial, 3.0% computer, engineering, and science, 7.4% education, legal, community service, arts, and media, 4.5% healthcare practitioners, 16.3% service, 28.0% sales and office, 11.3% natural resources, construction, and maintenance, 18.1% production, transportation, and material moving

Income: Per capita: $23,511; Median household: $61,458; Average household: $71,328; Households with income of $100,000 or more: 22.4%; Poverty rate: 10.8%

Educational Attainment: High school diploma or higher: 82.4%; Bachelor's degree or higher: 15.4%; Graduate/professional degree or higher: 4.5%

School District(s)

Manteca Unified (KG-12)
2012-13 Enrollment: 23,235 . . . . (209) 825-3200
New Jerusalem Elementary (KG-12)
2012-13 Enrollment: 3,117 . . . . (209) 830-6363

Vocational/Technical School(s)

Toni & Guy Hairdressing Academy-Manteca (Private, For-profit)
Fall 2013 Enrollment: 54 . . . . (209) 824-8000
2013-14 Tuition: $16,000

Housing: Homeownership rate: 62.6%; Median home value: $212,900; Median year structure built: 1985; Homeowner vacancy rate: 2.7%; Median gross rent: $1,150 per month; Rental vacancy rate: 6.5%

Health Insurance: 85.3% have insurance; 67.8% have private insurance; 27.7% have public insurance; 14.7% do not have insurance; 7.4% of children under 18 do not have insurance

Hospitals: Doctors Hospital of Manteca (73 beds); Kaiser Foundation Hospital - Manteca (61 beds)

Safety: Violent crime rate: 29.3 per 10,000 population; Property crime rate: 373.5 per 10,000 population

Newspapers: Manteca Bulletin (daily circulation 7000)

Transportation: Commute: 93.6% car, 1.3% public transportation, 1.3% walk, 2.7% work from home; Median travel time to work: 31.7 minutes

Additional Information Contacts

City of Manteca . . . . (209) 456-8000
http://www.ci.manteca.ca.us

MORADA (CDP). Covers a land area of 2.981 square miles and a water area of 0.007 square miles. Located at 38.04° N. Lat; 121.25° W. Long. Elevation is 39 feet.

History: San Joaquin County Historic Museum to North.

Population: 3,828; Growth (since 2000): 2.7%; Density: 1,284.1 persons per square mile; Race: 74.4% White, 1.2% Black/African American, 10.8% Asian, 0.7% American Indian/Alaska Native, 0.8% Native Hawaiian/Other Pacific Islander, 5.2% Two or more races, 17.7% Hispanic of any race; Average household size: 2.67; Median age: 48.4; Age under 18: 21.1%; Age 65 and over: 20.9%; Males per 100 females: 101.4; Marriage status: 28.6% never married, 45.5% now married, 1.6% separated, 12.3% widowed, 13.6% divorced; Foreign born: 8.6%; Speak English only: 86.7%; With disability: 20.7%; Veterans: 9.6%; Ancestry: 14.9% Italian, 10.3% Irish, 9.8% English, 6.6% German, 5.8% French

Employment: 22.8% management, business, and financial, 8.4% computer, engineering, and science, 14.5% education, legal, community service, arts, and media, 13.2% healthcare practitioners, 8.7% service, 21.1% sales and office, 5.6% natural resources, construction, and maintenance, 5.6% production, transportation, and material moving

Income: Per capita: $47,270; Median household: $60,847; Average household: $111,979; Households with income of $100,000 or more: 35.3%; Poverty rate: 4.0%

Educational Attainment: High school diploma or higher: 89.3%; Bachelor's degree or higher: 39.7%; Graduate/professional degree or higher: 19.8%

Housing: Homeownership rate: 89.1%; Median home value: $353,100; Median year structure built: 1966; Homeowner vacancy rate: 2.3%; Median gross rent: n/a per month; Rental vacancy rate: 8.2%

Health Insurance: 90.9% have insurance; 71.9% have private insurance; 49.4% have public insurance; 9.1% do not have insurance; 1.9% of children under 18 do not have insurance

Transportation: Commute: 92.3% car, 0.0% public transportation, 0.0% walk, 7.7% work from home; Median travel time to work: 27.9 minutes

MOUNTAIN HOUSE (CDP). Covers a land area of 3.192 square miles and a water area of 0 square miles. Located at 37.77° N. Lat; 121.55° W. Long. Elevation is 59 feet.

Population: 9,675; Growth (since 2000): n/a; Density: 3,030.8 persons per square mile; Race: 35.8% White, 9.3% Black/African American, 39.6% Asian, 0.5% American Indian/Alaska Native, 0.7% Native Hawaiian/Other Pacific Islander, 7.2% Two or more races, 16.9% Hispanic of any race; Average household size: 3.45; Median age: 31.4; Age under 18: 34.6%; Age 65 and over: 3.8%; Males per 100 females: 98.9; Marriage status: 28.4% never married, 57.1% now married, 2.5% separated, 4.5% widowed, 10.0% divorced; Foreign born: 33.5%; Speak English only: 55.1%; With disability: 4.5%; Veterans: 2.6%; Ancestry: 5.9% German, 4.6% Afghan, 3.5% Irish, 2.6% Italian, 2.5% Norwegian

Employment: 12.4% management, business, and financial, 10.8% computer, engineering, and science, 2.0% education, legal, community service, arts, and media, 7.2% healthcare practitioners, 8.6% service, 36.1% sales and office, 6.9% natural resources, construction, and maintenance, 16.0% production, transportation, and material moving

Income: Per capita: $28,175; Median household: $96,607; Average household: $100,160; Households with income of $100,000 or more: 48.7%; Poverty rate: 6.2%

Educational Attainment: High school diploma or higher: 92.7%; Bachelor's degree or higher: 37.4%; Graduate/professional degree or higher: 11.4%

School District(s)

Lammersville Joint Unified (KG-08)
2012-13 Enrollment: 2,360 . . . . (209) 836-7400

Housing: Homeownership rate: 78.6%; Median home value: $346,700; Median year structure built: 2005; Homeowner vacancy rate: 4.9%; Median gross rent: $2,000+ per month; Rental vacancy rate: 5.6%

Health Insurance: 93.7% have insurance; 85.1% have private insurance; 13.1% have public insurance; 6.3% do not have insurance; 2.3% of children under 18 do not have insurance

Transportation: Commute: 89.8% car, 2.0% public transportation, 0.0% walk, 7.7% work from home; Median travel time to work: 50.6 minutes

PETERS (CDP). Covers a land area of 2.527 square miles and a water area of 0.006 square miles. Located at 37.98° N. Lat; 121.04° W. Long. Elevation is 102 feet.

Population: 672; Growth (since 2000): n/a; Density: 265.9 persons per square mile; Race: 79.2% White, 1.0% Black/African American, 3.0% Asian, 2.2% American Indian/Alaska Native, 0.0% Native Hawaiian/Other Pacific Islander, 5.7% Two or more races, 22.8% Hispanic of any race; Average household size: 3.25; Median age: 41.5; Age under 18: 25.3%; Age 65 and over: 11.0%; Males per 100 females: 92.0

Housing: Homeownership rate: 89.8%; Homeowner vacancy rate: 1.6%; Rental vacancy rate: 4.5%

RIPON (city). Covers a land area of 5.305 square miles and a water area of 0.190 square miles. Located at 37.74° N. Lat; 121.13° W. Long. Elevation is 69 feet.

History: Ripon developed around the Schenley Distillery, at one time claimed by the residents to be the "World's Largest Exclusive Brandy Distillery."

Population: 14,297; Growth (since 2000): 40.9%; Density: 2,695.2 persons per square mile; Race: 79.7% White, 1.5% Black/African American, 4.2% Asian, 0.9% American Indian/Alaska Native, 0.3% Native Hawaiian/Other Pacific Islander, 5.0% Two or more races, 22.2% Hispanic of any race; Average household size: 2.93; Median age: 37.1; Age under 18: 28.8%; Age 65 and over: 11.8%; Males per 100 females: 95.8; Marriage status: 25.7% never married, 60.9% now married, 2.1% separated, 5.4% widowed, 8.1% divorced; Foreign born: 7.7%; Speak English only: 83.8%; With disability: 9.0%; Veterans: 9.3%; Ancestry: 13.5% German, 9.9% English, 9.9% Dutch, 8.6% Italian, 8.5% American

Employment: 15.0% management, business, and financial, 3.8% computer, engineering, and science, 13.1% education, legal, community service, arts, and media, 7.8% healthcare practitioners, 15.5% service, 23.0% sales and office, 10.5% natural resources, construction, and maintenance, 11.5% production, transportation, and material moving

Income: Per capita: $32,730; Median household: $72,637; Average household: $94,769; Households with income of $100,000 or more: 37.4%; Poverty rate: 9.7%

Educational Attainment: High school diploma or higher: 90.4%; Bachelor's degree or higher: 27.4%; Graduate/professional degree or higher: 8.7%

School District(s)

Ripon Unified (KG-12)
2012-13 Enrollment: 3,238 . . . . (209) 599-2131

Housing: Homeownership rate: 72.7%; Median home value: $288,700; Median year structure built: 1990; Homeowner vacancy rate: 1.6%; Median gross rent: $1,123 per month; Rental vacancy rate: 7.4%

Health Insurance: 93.0% have insurance; 77.4% have private insurance; 24.8% have public insurance; 7.0% do not have insurance; 1.8% of children under 18 do not have insurance

Safety: Violent crime rate: 10.1 per 10,000 population; Property crime rate: 231.1 per 10,000 population

Newspapers: Ripon Record (weekly circulation 3000)

Transportation: Commute: 94.9% car, 0.7% public transportation, 1.0% walk, 3.0% work from home; Median travel time to work: 25.5 minutes

Additional Information Contacts

City of Ripon . . . . (209) 599-2108
http://www.cityofripon.org

STOCKTON (city). County seat. Covers a land area of 61.670 square miles and a water area of 3.083 square miles. Located at 37.98° N. Lat; 121.31° W. Long. Elevation is 13 feet.

History: Stockton was founded by Captain Charles M. Weber, a German who came to California in 1841 and first settled in San Jose. In 1847 Weber founded the town of Tuleburg where he built corrals, planted wheat, and set up houses for ranchers. He moved there himself in 1848, and in 1849 renamed the town Stockton for his friend, Commodore Robert Stockton. The gold rush brought activity to the new town, which became the seat of San Joaquin County in 1850. Stockton developed as an inland port on the San Joaquin River, shipping the agricultural produce of the valley on ocean-going freighters to San Francisco.

Population: 291,707; Growth (since 2000): 19.7%; Density: 4,730.2 persons per square mile; Race: 37.0% White, 12.2% Black/African American, 21.5% Asian, 1.1% American Indian/Alaska Native, 0.6% Native Hawaiian/Other Pacific Islander, 6.9% Two or more races, 40.3% Hispanic of any race; Average household size: 3.16; Median age: 30.8; Age under 18: 29.9%; Age 65 and over: 10.0%; Males per 100 females: 96.1; Marriage status: 37.7% never married, 46.6% now married, 2.7% separated, 5.6% widowed, 10.1% divorced; Foreign born: 26.2%; Speak English only: 54.0%; With disability: 12.4%; Veterans: 6.3%; Ancestry: 5.7% German, 4.5% Irish, 3.4% Italian, 3.1% English, 1.5% American

Employment: 8.8% management, business, and financial, 2.7% computer, engineering, and science, 9.7% education, legal, community service, arts, and media, 5.1% healthcare practitioners, 21.5% service, 24.6% sales and office, 11.4% natural resources, construction, and maintenance, 16.2% production, transportation, and material moving

Income: Per capita: $19,896; Median household: $46,831; Average household: $62,710; Households with income of $100,000 or more: 18.6%; Poverty rate: 24.3%

Educational Attainment: High school diploma or higher: 74.4%; Bachelor's degree or higher: 17.7%; Graduate/professional degree or higher: 5.8%

School District(s)

Escalon Unified (KG-12)
2012-13 Enrollment: 2,815 . . . . (209) 838-3591
Lincoln Unified (KG-12)
2012-13 Enrollment: 9,132 . . . . (209) 953-8700
Linden Unified (KG-12)
2012-13 Enrollment: 2,321 . . . . (209) 887-3894
Lodi Unified (KG-12)
2012-13 Enrollment: 30,222 . . . . (209) 331-7000
Manteca Unified (KG-12)
2012-13 Enrollment: 23,235 . . . . (209) 825-3200

San Joaquin County Office of Education (KG-12)
2012-13 Enrollment: 3,452 . . . . (209) 468-4800
San Joaquin County Rop
2012-13 Enrollment: n/a . . . . (209) 468-9005
Sbc - Aspire Public Schools (KG-12)
2012-13 Enrollment: 1,972 . . . . (510) 434-5000
Stockton Unified (KG-12)
2012-13 Enrollment: 38,435 . . . . (209) 933-7000

Four-year College(s)

Humphreys College-Stockton and Modesto Campuses (Private, Not-for-profit)
Fall 2013 Enrollment: 990 . . . . (209) 478-0800
2013-14 Tuition: In-state $11,277; Out-of-state $11,277
University of the Pacific (Private, Not-for-profit)
Fall 2013 Enrollment: 6,421 . . . . (209) 946-2011
2013-14 Tuition: In-state $39,810; Out-of-state $39,810

Two-year College(s)

Carrington College California-Stockton (Private, For-profit)
Fall 2013 Enrollment: 465 . . . . (209) 956-1240
Heald College-Stockton (Private, For-profit)
Fall 2013 Enrollment: 1,418 . . . . (209) 473-5200
2013-14 Tuition: In-state $13,620; Out-of-state $13,620
San Joaquin Delta College (Public)
Fall 2013 Enrollment: 17,629 . . . . (209) 954-5151
2013-14 Tuition: In-state $1,104; Out-of-state $6,432

Vocational/Technical School(s)

Hollywood Beauty College (Private, For-profit)
Fall 2013 Enrollment: 115 . . . . (209) 951-7572
2013-14 Tuition: $16,040
MTI Business College Inc (Private, For-profit)
Fall 2013 Enrollment: 138 . . . . (209) 957-3030
2013-14 Tuition: $8,200
Xavier College School of Nursing (Private, For-profit)
Fall 2013 Enrollment: 52 . . . . (209) 941-0968
2013-14 Tuition: $25,000

Housing: Homeownership rate: 51.6%; Median home value: $166,500; Median year structure built: 1978; Homeowner vacancy rate: 3.2%; Median gross rent: $959 per month; Rental vacancy rate: 9.4%

Health Insurance: 82.0% have insurance; 50.8% have private insurance; 39.1% have public insurance; 18.0% do not have insurance; 7.0% of children under 18 do not have insurance

Hospitals: Dameron Hospital (188 beds); Saint Joseph's Medical Center of Stockton (294 beds)

Safety: Violent crime rate: 120.8 per 10,000 population; Property crime rate: 503.0 per 10,000 population

Newspapers: The Record (daily circulation 58300); The Record (weekly circulation 35000)

Transportation: Commute: 91.7% car, 1.3% public transportation, 1.6% walk, 3.6% work from home; Median travel time to work: 27.0 minutes; Amtrak: Train service available.

Airports: Stockton Metropolitan (primary service/non-hub)

Additional Information Contacts

City of Stockton . . . . (209) 937-8212
http://www.stocktongov.com

TAFT MOSSWOOD (CDP). Covers a land area of 0.473 square miles and a water area of 0.013 square miles. Located at 37.91° N. Lat; 121.28° W. Long.

Population: 1,530; Growth (since 2000): 10.2%; Density: 3,236.8 persons per square mile; Race: 29.0% White, 12.5% Black/African American, 12.0% Asian, 0.7% American Indian/Alaska Native, 0.1% Native Hawaiian/Other Pacific Islander, 5.5% Two or more races, 71.8% Hispanic of any race; Average household size: 4.17; Median age: 27.9; Age under 18: 33.6%; Age 65 and over: 9.7%; Males per 100 females: 104.3

Housing: Homeownership rate: 58.2%; Homeowner vacancy rate: 5.8%; Rental vacancy rate: 12.1%

TERMINOUS (CDP). Covers a land area of 0.977 square miles and a water area of <.001 square miles. Located at 38.12° N. Lat; 121.49° W. Long. Elevation is -7 feet.

Population: 381; Growth (since 2000): n/a; Density: 389.8 persons per square mile; Race: 88.7% White, 0.5% Black/African American, 1.8% Asian, 1.6% American Indian/Alaska Native, 0.0% Native Hawaiian/Other Pacific Islander, 3.9% Two or more races, 10.5% Hispanic of any race; Average household size: 2.09; Median age: 60.3; Age under 18: 8.9%; Age 65 and over: 39.9%; Males per 100 females: 100.5

Housing: Homeownership rate: 85.2%; Homeowner vacancy rate: 3.7%; Rental vacancy rate: 22.9%

THORNTON (CDP). Covers a land area of 2.127 square miles and a water area of 0.028 square miles. Located at 38.23° N. Lat; 121.43° W. Long. Elevation is 13 feet.

Population: 1,131; Growth (since 2000): n/a; Density: 531.8 persons per square mile; Race: 49.0% White, 3.8% Black/African American, 4.0% Asian, 0.3% American Indian/Alaska Native, 0.1% Native Hawaiian/Other Pacific Islander, 3.7% Two or more races, 68.1% Hispanic of any race; Average household size: 3.65; Median age: 28.6; Age under 18: 35.7%; Age 65 and over: 8.6%; Males per 100 females: 95.0

School District(s)

New Hope Elementary (KG-08)
2012-13 Enrollment: 216 . . . . (209) 794-2376

Housing: Homeownership rate: 43.2%; Homeowner vacancy rate: 0.7%; Rental vacancy rate: 3.8%

TRACY (city). Covers a land area of 22.003 square miles and a water area of 0.136 square miles. Located at 37.72° N. Lat; 121.45° W. Long. Elevation is 52 feet.

History: Tracy was a stopping place of travelers from the time it was laid out on the Southern Pacific Railroad in the early 1870's.

Population: 82,922; Growth (since 2000): 45.7%; Density: 3,768.7 persons per square mile; Race: 52.7% White, 7.2% Black/African American, 14.7% Asian, 0.9% American Indian/Alaska Native, 0.9% Native Hawaiian/Other Pacific Islander, 7.7% Two or more races, 36.9% Hispanic of any race; Average household size: 3.40; Median age: 32.3; Age under 18: 32.2%; Age 65 and over: 6.9%; Males per 100 females: 98.3; Marriage status: 29.7% never married, 57.6% now married, 2.5% separated, 4.2% widowed, 8.5% divorced; Foreign born: 25.6%; Speak English only: 59.0%; With disability: 8.3%; Veterans: 6.9%; Ancestry: 8.8% German, 7.2% Irish, 5.8% Italian, 4.4% Portuguese, 4.2% English

Employment: 14.8% management, business, and financial, 7.3% computer, engineering, and science, 6.2% education, legal, community service, arts, and media, 3.8% healthcare practitioners, 14.9% service, 26.4% sales and office, 11.8% natural resources, construction, and maintenance, 14.8% production, transportation, and material moving

Income: Per capita: $26,652; Median household: $76,098; Average household: $89,151; Households with income of $100,000 or more: 35.9%; Poverty rate: 8.2%

Educational Attainment: High school diploma or higher: 82.6%; Bachelor's degree or higher: 20.9%; Graduate/professional degree or higher: 4.5%

School District(s)

Banta Elementary (KG-08)
2012-13 Enrollment: 319 . . . . (209) 835-0843
Jefferson Elementary (KG-08)
2012-13 Enrollment: 2,477 . . . . (209) 836-3388
Lammersville Joint Unified (KG-08)
2012-13 Enrollment: 2,360 . . . . (209) 836-7400
New Jerusalem Elementary (KG-12)
2012-13 Enrollment: 3,117 . . . . (209) 830-6363
Tracy Joint Unified (KG-12)
2012-13 Enrollment: 17,405 . . . . (209) 830-3200

Housing: Homeownership rate: 66.4%; Median home value: $257,400; Median year structure built: 1993; Homeowner vacancy rate: 2.5%; Median gross rent: $1,389 per month; Rental vacancy rate: 5.9%

Health Insurance: 86.7% have insurance; 70.8% have private insurance; 22.7% have public insurance; 13.3% do not have insurance; 4.9% of children under 18 do not have insurance

Hospitals: Sutter Tracy Community Hospital (79 beds)

Safety: Violent crime rate: 17.8 per 10,000 population; Property crime rate: 262.5 per 10,000 population

Newspapers: Tracy Press (daily circulation 7700)

Transportation: Commute: 90.6% car, 2.4% public transportation, 1.4% walk, 4.3% work from home; Median travel time to work: 40.8 minutes; Amtrak: Train and bus service available.

Additional Information Contacts

City of Tracy . . . . (209) 831-6000
http://www.ci.tracy.ca.us

VICTOR (CDP). Covers a land area of 1.255 square miles and a water area of 0 square miles. Located at 38.14° N. Lat; 121.20° W. Long. Elevation is 79 feet.

Population: 293; Growth (since 2000): n/a; Density: 233.4 persons per square mile; Race: 60.4% White, 0.0% Black/African American, 6.5% Asian, 2.4% American Indian/Alaska Native, 0.0% Native Hawaiian/Other Pacific Islander, 3.8% Two or more races, 51.2% Hispanic of any race; Average household size: 2.99; Median age: 32.5; Age under 18: 30.0%; Age 65 and over: 14.3%; Males per 100 females: 92.8

School District(s)

Lodi Unified (KG-12)
2012-13 Enrollment: 30,222 . . . . (209) 331-7000

Housing: Homeownership rate: 65.3%; Homeowner vacancy rate: 3.0%; Rental vacancy rate: 10.5%

WATERLOO (CDP). Covers a land area of 5.435 square miles and a water area of 0 square miles. Located at 38.04° N. Lat; 121.18° W. Long. Elevation is 59 feet.

Population: 572; Growth (since 2000): n/a; Density: 105.2 persons per square mile; Race: 78.7% White, 0.0% Black/African American, 3.7% Asian, 0.9% American Indian/Alaska Native, 0.2% Native Hawaiian/Other Pacific Islander, 3.1% Two or more races, 26.6% Hispanic of any race; Average household size: 2.72; Median age: 47.1; Age under 18: 20.5%; Age 65 and over: 17.7%; Males per 100 females: 105.0

Housing: Homeownership rate: 76.2%; Homeowner vacancy rate: 0.6%; Rental vacancy rate: 3.8%

WOODBRIDGE (CDP). Covers a land area of 3.013 square miles and a water area of 0.107 square miles. Located at 38.17° N. Lat; 121.31° W. Long. Elevation is 43 feet.

Population: 3,984; Growth (since 2000): n/a; Density: 1,322.4 persons per square mile; Race: 75.2% White, 0.4% Black/African American, 5.0% Asian, 1.2% American Indian/Alaska Native, 0.2% Native Hawaiian/Other Pacific Islander, 3.4% Two or more races, 31.0% Hispanic of any race; Average household size: 2.78; Median age: 42.6; Age under 18: 24.2%; Age 65 and over: 13.9%; Males per 100 females: 97.2; Marriage status: 25.6% never married, 60.4% now married, 1.1% separated, 5.0% widowed, 9.0% divorced; Foreign born: 11.2%; Speak English only: 75.4%; With disability: 12.5%; Veterans: 13.8%; Ancestry: 21.4% German, 9.7% Italian, 9.2% Irish, 7.4% English, 7.2% French

Employment: 19.7% management, business, and financial, 4.0% computer, engineering, and science, 12.8% education, legal, community service, arts, and media, 7.4% healthcare practitioners, 12.3% service, 22.1% sales and office, 8.5% natural resources, construction, and maintenance, 13.3% production, transportation, and material moving

Income: Per capita: $32,401; Median household: $67,672; Average household: $82,619; Households with income of $100,000 or more: 27.0%; Poverty rate: 15.1%

Educational Attainment: High school diploma or higher: 91.4%; Bachelor's degree or higher: 31.9%; Graduate/professional degree or higher: 12.9%

Housing: Homeownership rate: 75.6%; Median home value: $268,900; Median year structure built: 1983; Homeowner vacancy rate: 1.2%; Median gross rent: <$100 per month; Rental vacancy rate: 4.1%

Health Insurance: 88.1% have insurance; 72.9% have private insurance; 27.9% have public insurance; 11.9% do not have insurance; 4.7% of children under 18 do not have insurance

Transportation: Commute: 91.9% car, 0.8% public transportation, 0.5% walk, 6.8% work from home; Median travel time to work: 30.4 minutes

San Luis Obispo County

Located in southwestern California; bounded on the west by the Pacific Ocean; drained by the Salinas and Santa Maria Rivers; includes the Santa Lucia, Temblor, and La Panza Ranges. Covers a land area of 3,298.567 square miles, a water area of 316.980 square miles, and is located in the Pacific Time Zone at 35.39° N. Lat., 120.45° W. Long. The county was founded in 1850. County seat is San Luis Obispo.

San Luis Obispo County is part of the San Luis Obispo-Paso Robles-Arroyo Grande, CA Metropolitan Statistical Area. The entire metro area includes: San Luis Obispo County, CA

Weather Station: Morro Bay Fire Dept — Elevation: 115 feet

	Jan	Feb	Mar	Apr	May	Jun	Jul	Aug	Sep	Oct	Nov	Dec
High	62	63	64	64	64	64	66	66	67	68	67	62
Low	42	44	45	46	48	50	53	53	52	50	46	42
Precip	3.4	3.9	3.3	1.1	0.4	0.1	0.0	0.1	0.2	0.8	1.4	2.5
Snow	0.0	tr	0.0	0.0	0.0	0.0	0.0	0.0	0.0	0.0	0.0	0.0

High and Low temperatures in degrees Fahrenheit; Precipitation and Snow in inches

Weather Station: Paso Robles — Elevation: 700 feet

	Jan	Feb	Mar	Apr	May	Jun	Jul	Aug	Sep	Oct	Nov	Dec
High	62	64	68	74	81	87	91	92	89	80	68	61
Low	34	37	40	41	46	49	53	52	49	43	37	32
Precip	3.2	3.3	2.8	0.8	0.3	0.0	0.0	0.0	0.2	0.8	1.2	2.2
Snow	0.0	tr	tr	0.0	0.0	0.0	0.0	0.0	0.0	0.0	0.0	0.1

High and Low temperatures in degrees Fahrenheit; Precipitation and Snow in inches

Weather Station: Paso Robles Caa Arpt — Elevation: 813 feet

	Jan	Feb	Mar	Apr	May	Jun	Jul	Aug	Sep	Oct	Nov	Dec
High	60	63	67	73	81	88	94	94	89	80	68	60
Low	35	38	40	41	46	50	54	54	51	44	38	34
Precip	2.7	2.7	2.5	0.7	0.3	0.0	0.0	0.0	0.2	0.6	1.0	1.8
Snow	na	na	na	na	na	na	na	na	na	na	na	na

High and Low temperatures in degrees Fahrenheit; Precipitation and Snow in inches

Weather Station: San Luis Obispo Polytech — Elevation: 314 feet

	Jan	Feb	Mar	Apr	May	Jun	Jul	Aug	Sep	Oct	Nov	Dec
High	65	65	67	70	72	76	79	80	81	77	71	65
Low	42	44	45	46	48	51	53	54	53	50	46	42
Precip	4.8	5.7	4.0	1.2	0.5	0.1	0.0	0.1	0.3	0.9	2.1	3.6
Snow	0.0	0.0	0.0	0.0	0.0	0.0	0.0	0.0	0.0	0.0	0.0	0.0

High and Low temperatures in degrees Fahrenheit; Precipitation and Snow in inches

Population: 269,637; Growth (since 2000): 9.3%; Density: 81.7 persons per square mile; Race: 82.6% White, 2.1% Black/African American, 3.2% Asian, 0.9% American Indian/Alaska Native, 0.1% Native Hawaiian/Other Pacific Islander, 3.8% two or more races, 20.8% Hispanic of any race; Average household size: 2.48; Median age: 39.4; Age under 18: 18.9%; Age 65 and over: 15.2%; Males per 100 females: 104.8; Marriage status: 33.6% never married, 50.4% now married, 2.2% separated, 5.8% widowed, 10.3% divorced; Foreign born: 10.4%; Speak English only: 82.0%; With disability: 10.8%; Veterans: 9.6%; Ancestry: 16.9% German, 12.5% English, 11.7% Irish, 6.6% Italian, 5.1% American

Religion: Six largest groups: 33.0% Catholicism, 4.2% Lutheran, 3.6% Non-denominational Protestant, 2.4% Latter-day Saints, 1.9% Pentecostal, 1.8% Holiness

Economy: Unemployment rate: 5.3%; Leading industries: 14.9% retail trade; 12.8% health care and social assistance; 11.4% construction; Farms: 2,666 totaling 1,338,874 acres; Company size: 3 employ 1,000 or more persons, 7 employ 500 to 999 persons, 65 employ 100 to 499 persons, 7,811 employs less than 100 persons; Business ownership: 8,285 women-owned, n/a Black-owned, 2,369 Hispanic-owned, 1,082 Asian-owned

Employment: 13.5% management, business, and financial, 5.5% computer, engineering, and science, 11.1% education, legal, community service, arts, and media, 5.6% healthcare practitioners, 20.7% service, 25.4% sales and office, 10.3% natural resources, construction, and maintenance, 8.1% production, transportation, and material moving

Income: Per capita: $29,954; Median household: $58,697; Average household: $77,043; Households with income of $100,000 or more: 26.2%; Poverty rate: 14.3%

Educational Attainment: High school diploma or higher: 89.6%; Bachelor's degree or higher: 31.5%; Graduate/professional degree or higher: 11.7%

Housing: Homeownership rate: 59.7%; Median home value: $426,600; Median year structure built: 1981; Homeowner vacancy rate: 2.1%; Median gross rent: $1,211 per month; Rental vacancy rate: 5.5%

Vital Statistics: Birth rate: 96.3 per 10,000 population; Death rate: 78.6 per 10,000 population; Age-adjusted cancer mortality rate: 145.4 deaths per 100,000 population

Health Insurance: 86.2% have insurance; 72.1% have private insurance; 28.3% have public insurance; 13.8% do not have insurance; 8.2% of children under 18 do not have insurance

Health Care: Physicians: 26.1 per 10,000 population; Hospital beds: 65.6 per 10,000 population; Hospital admissions: 766.5 per 10,000 population

Air Quality Index: 35.3% good, 62.2% moderate, 2.2% unhealthy for sensitive individuals, 0.0% unhealthy, 0.3% very unhealthy (% of days)

Transportation: Commute: 84.7% car, 1.4% public transportation, 4.0% walk, 6.9% work from home; Median travel time to work: 21.1 minutes
Presidential Election: 49.0% Obama, 48.1% Romney (2012)
National and State Parks: Atascadero State Beach; Avila State Beach; Cayucos State Beach; Estero Bluffs State Park; Harmony Headlands State Park; Hearst San Simeon State Historical Monument; Hearst San Simeon State Park; Los Osos Oaks State Natural Reserve; MontaA±a de Oro State Park; Morro Bay State Park; Morro Strand State Beach; Oceano Dunes State Vehicular Recreation Area; Pismo State Beach
Additional Information Contacts
San Luis Obispo Government . . . . (805) 781-5450
http://www.slocounty.ca.gov

San Luis Obispo County Communities

ARROYO GRANDE (city). Covers a land area of 5.835 square miles and a water area of 0 square miles. Located at 35.12° N. Lat; 120.58° W. Long. Elevation is 118 feet.
History: Arroyo Grande, once a stagecoach station, grew in 1877 when a land rush brought cattle and grain ranchers.
Population: 17,252; Growth (since 2000): 8.8%; Density: 2,956.5 persons per square mile; Race: 85.3% White, 0.9% Black/African American, 3.4% Asian, 0.7% American Indian/Alaska Native, 0.1% Native Hawaiian/Other Pacific Islander, 4.6% Two or more races, 15.7% Hispanic of any race; Average household size: 2.41; Median age: 45.4; Age under 18: 21.1%; Age 65 and over: 20.2%; Males per 100 females: 92.6; Marriage status: 24.4% never married, 55.4% now married, 1.6% separated, 8.3% widowed, 11.8% divorced; Foreign born: 9.2%; Speak English only: 84.3%; With disability: 11.9%; Veterans: 12.2%; Ancestry: 15.6% German, 14.4% English, 12.3% Irish, 6.5% Italian, 5.2% American
Employment: 16.0% management, business, and financial, 5.2% computer, engineering, and science, 12.6% education, legal, community service, arts, and media, 4.4% healthcare practitioners, 19.8% service, 26.2% sales and office, 8.0% natural resources, construction, and maintenance, 7.7% production, transportation, and material moving
Income: Per capita: $33,347; Median household: $63,802; Average household: $80,168; Households with income of $100,000 or more: 30.9%; Poverty rate: 7.4%
Educational Attainment: High school diploma or higher: 93.2%; Bachelor's degree or higher: 35.2%; Graduate/professional degree or higher: 12.2%

School District(s)

Lucia Mar Unified (KG-12)
2012-13 Enrollment: 10,566 . . . . (805) 474-3000
Santa Lucia Rop
2012-13 Enrollment: n/a . . . . (805) 474-3000
Housing: Homeownership rate: 66.2%; Median home value: $448,500; Median year structure built: 1978; Homeowner vacancy rate: 1.9%; Median gross rent: $1,139 per month; Rental vacancy rate: 4.0%
Health Insurance: 89.8% have insurance; 77.0% have private insurance; 29.7% have public insurance; 10.2% do not have insurance; 6.3% of children under 18 do not have insurance
Safety: Violent crime rate: 17.6 per 10,000 population; Property crime rate: 258.0 per 10,000 population
Transportation: Commute: 88.6% car, 0.7% public transportation, 3.1% walk, 5.0% work from home; Median travel time to work: 19.1 minutes
Additional Information Contacts
City of Arroyo Grande . . . . (805) 473-5400
http://www.arroyogrande.org

ATASCADERO (city). Covers a land area of 25.641 square miles and a water area of 0.489 square miles. Located at 35.49° N. Lat; 120.69° W. Long. Elevation is 879 feet.
History: Atascadero was laid out in 1913 as a model community. The plan failed to materialize, and the community grew as a center for the surrounding farms raising chickens and turkeys.
Population: 28,310; Growth (since 2000): 7.2%; Density: 1,104.1 persons per square mile; Race: 86.4% White, 2.1% Black/African American, 2.4% Asian, 1.0% American Indian/Alaska Native, 0.2% Native Hawaiian/Other Pacific Islander, 3.6% Two or more races, 15.6% Hispanic of any race; Average household size: 2.51; Median age: 41.0; Age under 18: 21.4%; Age 65 and over: 13.0%; Males per 100 females: 103.2; Marriage status: 27.1% never married, 56.3% now married, 1.9% separated, 5.3% widowed, 11.3% divorced; Foreign born: 6.7%; Speak English only: 89.0%; With disability: 11.6%; Veterans: 11.2%; Ancestry: 20.3% German, 14.6% English, 10.8% Irish, 6.5% Italian, 6.3% American
Employment: 13.4% management, business, and financial, 5.7% computer, engineering, and science, 11.0% education, legal, community service, arts, and media, 10.3% healthcare practitioners, 17.8% service, 24.1% sales and office, 10.0% natural resources, construction, and maintenance, 7.7% production, transportation, and material moving
Income: Per capita: $31,434; Median household: $65,344; Average household: $78,917; Households with income of $100,000 or more: 26.8%; Poverty rate: 10.5%
Educational Attainment: High school diploma or higher: 92.1%; Bachelor's degree or higher: 28.2%; Graduate/professional degree or higher: 9.0%

School District(s)

Atascadero Unified (KG-12)
2012-13 Enrollment: 4,784 . . . . (805) 462-4200
Housing: Homeownership rate: 63.5%; Median home value: $381,600; Median year structure built: 1980; Homeowner vacancy rate: 2.2%; Median gross rent: $1,146 per month; Rental vacancy rate: 5.8%
Health Insurance: 88.1% have insurance; 75.7% have private insurance; 26.2% have public insurance; 11.9% do not have insurance; 9.2% of children under 18 do not have insurance
Safety: Violent crime rate: 33.5 per 10,000 population; Property crime rate: 188.0 per 10,000 population
Newspapers: Atascadero News (weekly circulation 7200)
Transportation: Commute: 88.4% car, 1.3% public transportation, 0.6% walk, 8.1% work from home; Median travel time to work: 22.4 minutes; Amtrak: Bus service available.
Additional Information Contacts
City of Atascadero . . . . (805) 461-5000
http://www.atascadero.org

AVILA BEACH (unincorporated postal area)
ZCTA: 93424
Covers a land area of 2.633 square miles and a water area of 0.616 square miles. Located at 35.19° N. Lat; 120.73° W. Long. Elevation is 69 feet.
Population: 1,261; Growth (since 2000): 58.2%; Density: 478.9 persons per square mile; Race: 93.6% White, 0.5% Black/African American, 1.5% Asian, 0.4% American Indian/Alaska Native, 0.0% Native Hawaiian/Other Pacific Islander, 1.8% Two or more races, 7.2% Hispanic of any race; Average household size: 1.85; Median age: 59.3; Age under 18: 9.5%; Age 65 and over: 35.3%; Males per 100 females: 88.2
Housing: Homeownership rate: 62.9%; Homeowner vacancy rate: 3.8%; Rental vacancy rate: 8.6%

AVILLA BEACH (CDP). Covers a land area of 6.011 square miles and a water area of 0.017 square miles. Located at 35.20° N. Lat; 120.72° W. Long.
Population: 1,627; Growth (since 2000): n/a; Density: 270.7 persons per square mile; Race: 92.6% White, 0.8% Black/African American, 2.0% Asian, 0.4% American Indian/Alaska Native, 0.0% Native Hawaiian/Other Pacific Islander, 2.0% Two or more races, 6.8% Hispanic of any race; Average household size: 1.93; Median age: 56.9; Age under 18: 11.2%; Age 65 and over: 31.3%; Males per 100 females: 91.4
Housing: Homeownership rate: 62.8%; Homeowner vacancy rate: 3.1%; Rental vacancy rate: 7.4%

BLACKLAKE (CDP). Covers a land area of 1.045 square miles and a water area of 0 square miles. Located at 35.05° N. Lat; 120.54° W. Long.
Population: 930; Growth (since 2000): n/a; Density: 889.5 persons per square mile; Race: 93.0% White, 0.9% Black/African American, 2.6% Asian, 0.8% American Indian/Alaska Native, 0.0% Native Hawaiian/Other Pacific Islander, 1.3% Two or more races, 7.5% Hispanic of any race; Average household size: 1.97; Median age: 66.9; Age under 18: 7.5%; Age 65 and over: 56.7%; Males per 100 females: 94.2
Housing: Homeownership rate: 86.0%; Homeowner vacancy rate: 2.6%; Rental vacancy rate: 23.6%

CALLENDER (CDP). Covers a land area of 2.286 square miles and a water area of 0 square miles. Located at 35.05° N. Lat; 120.58° W. Long. Elevation is 102 feet.
Population: 1,262; Growth (since 2000): n/a; Density: 552.2 persons per square mile; Race: 79.5% White, 0.6% Black/African American, 3.8% Asian, 1.7% American Indian/Alaska Native, 0.0% Native Hawaiian/Other

Pacific Islander, 4.3% Two or more races, 28.1% Hispanic of any race; Average household size: 2.87; Median age: 41.8; Age under 18: 23.1%; Age 65 and over: 12.8%; Males per 100 females: 106.5

Housing: Homeownership rate: 65.9%; Homeowner vacancy rate: 2.3%; Rental vacancy rate: 1.3%

CAMBRIA (CDP). Covers a land area of 8.508 square miles and a water area of 0 square miles. Located at 35.55° N. Lat; 121.08° W. Long. Elevation is 43 feet.

History: Cambria, formerly known as "Slabtown" because its buildings were made from rough slabs of wood, is a seaside village located midway between San Francisco and Los Angeles.

Population: 6,032; Growth (since 2000): -3.2%; Density: 708.9 persons per square mile; Race: 85.6% White, 0.3% Black/African American, 1.3% Asian, 0.8% American Indian/Alaska Native, 0.2% Native Hawaiian/Other Pacific Islander, 2.5% Two or more races, 19.7% Hispanic of any race; Average household size: 2.18; Median age: 57.1; Age under 18: 14.2%; Age 65 and over: 31.7%; Males per 100 females: 90.6; Marriage status: 17.0% never married, 66.0% now married, 0.4% separated, 8.3% widowed, 8.8% divorced; Foreign born: 13.3%; Speak English only: 81.3%; With disability: 14.8%; Veterans: 15.4%; Ancestry: 18.8% German, 15.9% English, 11.0% Irish, 7.3% Italian, 6.8% American

Employment: 16.5% management, business, and financial, 4.5% computer, engineering, and science, 14.8% education, legal, community service, arts, and media, 5.6% healthcare practitioners, 28.4% service, 17.7% sales and office, 5.4% natural resources, construction, and maintenance, 7.1% production, transportation, and material moving

Income: Per capita: $41,504; Median household: $60,581; Average household: $89,636; Households with income of $100,000 or more: 31.4%; Poverty rate: 7.9%

Educational Attainment: High school diploma or higher: 91.1%; Bachelor's degree or higher: 46.2%; Graduate/professional degree or higher: 19.7%

School District(s)

Coast Unified (KG-12)
2012-13 Enrollment: 762. . . . . (805) 927-3880

Housing: Homeownership rate: 71.9%; Median home value: $646,400; Median year structure built: 1983; Homeowner vacancy rate: 3.4%; Median gross rent: $1,313 per month; Rental vacancy rate: 10.1%

Health Insurance: 87.9% have insurance; 69.7% have private insurance; 45.8% have public insurance; 12.1% do not have insurance; 2.3% of children under 18 do not have insurance

Newspapers: The Cambrian (weekly circulation 4200)

Transportation: Commute: 83.2% car, 0.0% public transportation, 1.8% walk, 12.4% work from home; Median travel time to work: 23.3 minutes

CAYUCOS (CDP). Covers a land area of 3.100 square miles and a water area of 0.377 square miles. Located at 35.44° N. Lat; 120.89° W. Long. Elevation is 75 feet.

History: Cayucos was named for the canoes of the Native Americans who lived here when Juan Rodriguez Cabrillo named the bay in 1542. The town was laid out in 1875 by James Cass, who had built a wharf here five years earlier.

Population: 2,592; Growth (since 2000): -11.9%; Density: 836.1 persons per square mile; Race: 91.3% White, 0.2% Black/African American, 2.1% Asian, 0.5% American Indian/Alaska Native, 0.3% Native Hawaiian/Other Pacific Islander, 3.4% Two or more races, 8.0% Hispanic of any race; Average household size: 1.97; Median age: 53.0; Age under 18: 13.0%; Age 65 and over: 25.2%; Males per 100 females: 91.9; Marriage status: 16.4% never married, 59.7% now married, 3.9% separated, 10.0% widowed, 13.8% divorced; Foreign born: 11.6%; Speak English only: 89.0%; With disability: 16.8%; Veterans: 9.8%; Ancestry: 25.7% German, 18.0% English, 11.1% Irish, 5.4% Norwegian, 4.1% French

Employment: 14.5% management, business, and financial, 12.2% computer, engineering, and science, 9.6% education, legal, community service, arts, and media, 1.2% healthcare practitioners, 21.9% service, 28.4% sales and office, 5.5% natural resources, construction, and maintenance, 6.7% production, transportation, and material moving

Income: Per capita: $41,938; Median household: $58,971; Average household: $78,706; Households with income of $100,000 or more: 28.7%; Poverty rate: 12.0%

Educational Attainment: High school diploma or higher: 92.3%; Bachelor's degree or higher: 39.5%; Graduate/professional degree or higher: 17.5%

School District(s)

Cayucos Elementary (KG-08)
2012-13 Enrollment: 217. . . . . (805) 995-3694

Housing: Homeownership rate: 59.5%; Median home value: $650,000; Median year structure built: 1974; Homeowner vacancy rate: 4.6%; Median gross rent: $1,238 per month; Rental vacancy rate: 12.8%

Health Insurance: 84.9% have insurance; 71.3% have private insurance; 41.7% have public insurance; 15.1% do not have insurance; 0.0% of children under 18 do not have insurance

Transportation: Commute: 86.3% car, 4.1% public transportation, 1.3% walk, 8.2% work from home; Median travel time to work: 20.0 minutes

CRESTON (CDP). Covers a land area of 0.564 square miles and a water area of 0.005 square miles. Located at 35.52° N. Lat; 120.52° W. Long. Elevation is 1,119 feet.

Population: 94; Growth (since 2000): n/a; Density: 166.7 persons per square mile; Race: 94.7% White, 0.0% Black/African American, 1.1% Asian, 2.1% American Indian/Alaska Native, 0.0% Native Hawaiian/Other Pacific Islander, 2.1% Two or more races, 6.4% Hispanic of any race; Average household size: 2.61; Median age: 39.0; Age under 18: 23.4%; Age 65 and over: 13.8%; Males per 100 females: 80.8

School District(s)

Atascadero Unified (KG-12)
2012-13 Enrollment: 4,784 . . . . (805) 462-4200

Housing: Homeownership rate: 75.0%; Homeowner vacancy rate: 0.0%; Rental vacancy rate: 0.0%

EDNA (CDP). Covers a land area of 1.219 square miles and a water area of 0 square miles. Located at 35.21° N. Lat; 120.61° W. Long. Elevation is 243 feet.

Population: 193; Growth (since 2000): n/a; Density: 158.3 persons per square mile; Race: 95.9% White, 0.0% Black/African American, 0.0% Asian, 1.6% American Indian/Alaska Native, 0.0% Native Hawaiian/Other Pacific Islander, 0.0% Two or more races, 11.4% Hispanic of any race; Average household size: 2.80; Median age: 45.4; Age under 18: 21.8%; Age 65 and over: 15.5%; Males per 100 females: 119.3

Housing: Homeownership rate: 72.4%; Homeowner vacancy rate: 0.0%; Rental vacancy rate: 5.0%

EL PASO DE ROBLES (PASO ROBLES) (city). Covers a land area of 19.120 square miles and a water area of 0.305 square miles. Located at 35.64° N. Lat; 120.65° W. Long.

Population: 29,793; Growth (since 2000): 22.6%; Density: 1,558.2 persons per square mile; Race: 77.7% White, 2.1% Black/African American, 2.0% Asian, 1.0% American Indian/Alaska Native, 0.2% Native Hawaiian/Other Pacific Islander, 3.9% Two or more races, 34.5% Hispanic of any race; Average household size: 2.73; Median age: 35.3; Age under 18: 26.3%; Age 65 and over: 13.4%; Males per 100 females: 94.9; Marriage status: 28.6% never married, 56.2% now married, 3.6% separated, 6.3% widowed, 9.0% divorced; Foreign born: 17.1%; Speak English only: 72.9%; With disability: 9.6%; Veterans: 11.0%; Ancestry: 13.5% German, 9.8% Irish, 9.4% English, 5.1% American, 4.5% Italian

Employment: 10.8% management, business, and financial, 4.3% computer, engineering, and science, 7.7% education, legal, community service, arts, and media, 4.7% healthcare practitioners, 21.3% service, 26.2% sales and office, 12.9% natural resources, construction, and maintenance, 12.3% production, transportation, and material moving

Income: Per capita: $27,967; Median household: $58,976; Average household: $74,879; Households with income of $100,000 or more: 25.4%; Poverty rate: 12.1%

Educational Attainment: High school diploma or higher: 85.2%; Bachelor's degree or higher: 21.4%; Graduate/professional degree or higher: 7.5%

School District(s)

Paso Robles Joint Unified (KG-12)
2012-13 Enrollment: 6,601 . . . . (805) 769-1000
San Miguel Joint Union (KG-08)
2012-13 Enrollment: 746. . . . . (805) 467-3216

Vocational/Technical School(s)

Design's School of Cosmetology (Private, For-profit)
Fall 2013 Enrollment: 61 . . . . (805) 237-8575
2013-14 Tuition: $14,075

Housing: Homeownership rate: 59.1%; Median home value: $347,200; Median year structure built: 1988; Homeowner vacancy rate: 1.9%; Median gross rent: $1,116 per month; Rental vacancy rate: 3.8%

Health Insurance: 84.7% have insurance; 64.4% have private insurance; 33.2% have public insurance; 15.3% do not have insurance; 8.2% of children under 18 do not have insurance
Safety: Violent crime rate: 33.4 per 10,000 population; Property crime rate: 275.4 per 10,000 population
Newspapers: Paso Robles Press (weekly circulation 7500)
Transportation: Commute: 89.4% car, 2.0% public transportation, 1.4% walk, 5.4% work from home; Median travel time to work: 22.4 minutes
Additional Information Contacts
City of Paso Robles . . . . (805) 227-7276
http://www.prcity.com

GARDEN FARMS (CDP). Covers a land area of 1.093 square miles and a water area of 0 square miles. Located at 35.42° N. Lat; 120.61° W. Long. Elevation is 955 feet.
Population: 386; Growth (since 2000): n/a; Density: 353.0 persons per square mile; Race: 90.2% White, 0.5% Black/African American, 1.3% Asian, 0.5% American Indian/Alaska Native, 0.0% Native Hawaiian/Other Pacific Islander, 2.1% Two or more races, 10.4% Hispanic of any race; Average household size: 2.43; Median age: 45.7; Age under 18: 20.7%; Age 65 and over: 11.9%; Males per 100 females: 88.3
Housing: Homeownership rate: 69.8%; Homeowner vacancy rate: 0.0%; Rental vacancy rate: 2.0%

GROVER BEACH (city). Covers a land area of 2.310 square miles and a water area of 0.004 square miles. Located at 35.12° N. Lat; 120.62° W. Long. Elevation is 59 feet.
Population: 13,156; Growth (since 2000): 0.7%; Density: 5,695.1 persons per square mile; Race: 75.7% White, 1.1% Black/African American, 4.1% Asian, 1.4% American Indian/Alaska Native, 0.3% Native Hawaiian/Other Pacific Islander, 5.3% Two or more races, 29.2% Hispanic of any race; Average household size: 2.54; Median age: 36.9; Age under 18: 22.3%; Age 65 and over: 11.8%; Males per 100 females: 95.7; Marriage status: 31.7% never married, 49.3% now married, 4.3% separated, 5.9% widowed, 13.1% divorced; Foreign born: 11.7%; Speak English only: 82.2%; With disability: 13.8%; Veterans: 8.4%; Ancestry: 11.8% German, 11.1% English, 10.1% Irish, 7.4% American, 6.3% Italian
Employment: 6.9% management, business, and financial, 3.4% computer, engineering, and science, 9.0% education, legal, community service, arts, and media, 3.1% healthcare practitioners, 27.2% service, 30.5% sales and office, 10.3% natural resources, construction, and maintenance, 9.6% production, transportation, and material moving
Income: Per capita: $25,861; Median household: $47,207; Average household: $62,338; Households with income of $100,000 or more: 18.2%; Poverty rate: 12.4%
Educational Attainment: High school diploma or higher: 84.6%; Bachelor's degree or higher: 20.4%; Graduate/professional degree or higher: 6.1%

School District(s)

Lucia Mar Unified (KG-12)
2012-13 Enrollment: 10,566 . . . . (805) 474-3000
Housing: Homeownership rate: 46.7%; Median home value: $388,300; Median year structure built: 1980; Homeowner vacancy rate: 2.0%; Median gross rent: $1,186 per month; Rental vacancy rate: 3.7%
Health Insurance: 80.4% have insurance; 60.1% have private insurance; 30.2% have public insurance; 19.6% do not have insurance; 5.5% of children under 18 do not have insurance
Safety: Violent crime rate: 29.1 per 10,000 population; Property crime rate: 226.2 per 10,000 population
Transportation: Commute: 87.2% car, 1.4% public transportation, 2.9% walk, 6.2% work from home; Median travel time to work: 19.5 minutes; Amtrak: Train service available.
Additional Information Contacts
City of Grover Beach . . . . (805) 489-9657
http://www.grover.org

LAKE NACIMIENTO (CDP). Covers a land area of 10.268 square miles and a water area of 0.023 square miles. Located at 35.73° N. Lat; 120.87° W. Long. Elevation is 984 feet.
Population: 2,411; Growth (since 2000): 10.8%; Density: 234.8 persons per square mile; Race: 89.3% White, 0.5% Black/African American, 1.0% Asian, 1.8% American Indian/Alaska Native, 0.2% Native Hawaiian/Other Pacific Islander, 4.1% Two or more races, 10.6% Hispanic of any race; Average household size: 2.40; Median age: 45.1; Age under 18: 20.3%; Age 65 and over: 14.3%; Males per 100 females: 104.0
Housing: Homeownership rate: 76.6%; Homeowner vacancy rate: 3.8%; Rental vacancy rate: 6.0%

LOS BERROS (CDP). Covers a land area of 2.512 square miles and a water area of 0 square miles. Located at 35.08° N. Lat; 120.55° W. Long. Elevation is 207 feet.
Population: 641; Growth (since 2000): n/a; Density: 255.2 persons per square mile; Race: 82.2% White, 0.6% Black/African American, 1.9% Asian, 0.2% American Indian/Alaska Native, 0.2% Native Hawaiian/Other Pacific Islander, 8.0% Two or more races, 23.9% Hispanic of any race; Average household size: 3.02; Median age: 40.8; Age under 18: 27.1%; Age 65 and over: 17.8%; Males per 100 females: 90.2
Housing: Homeownership rate: 68.2%; Homeowner vacancy rate: 0.7%; Rental vacancy rate: 5.6%

LOS OSOS (CDP). Covers a land area of 12.763 square miles and a water area of 0.020 square miles. Located at 35.31° N. Lat; 120.82° W. Long. Elevation is 131 feet.
Population: 14,276; Growth (since 2000): n/a; Density: 1,118.5 persons per square mile; Race: 86.2% White, 0.6% Black/African American, 5.2% Asian, 0.7% American Indian/Alaska Native, 0.1% Native Hawaiian/Other Pacific Islander, 3.3% Two or more races, 13.8% Hispanic of any race; Average household size: 2.38; Median age: 47.2; Age under 18: 17.9%; Age 65 and over: 18.7%; Males per 100 females: 95.5; Marriage status: 26.6% never married, 54.5% now married, 1.4% separated, 7.9% widowed, 11.0% divorced; Foreign born: 7.2%; Speak English only: 90.0%; With disability: 14.2%; Veterans: 11.3%; Ancestry: 17.5% German, 16.2% English, 12.2% Irish, 6.9% American, 6.0% Italian
Employment: 10.4% management, business, and financial, 6.7% computer, engineering, and science, 12.3% education, legal, community service, arts, and media, 6.2% healthcare practitioners, 17.6% service, 28.5% sales and office, 12.0% natural resources, construction, and maintenance, 6.4% production, transportation, and material moving
Income: Per capita: $32,328; Median household: $57,813; Average household: $70,980; Households with income of $100,000 or more: 21.3%; Poverty rate: 9.0%
Educational Attainment: High school diploma or higher: 94.9%; Bachelor's degree or higher: 37.7%; Graduate/professional degree or higher: 13.8%

School District(s)

San Luis Coastal Unified (PK-12)
2012-13 Enrollment: 7,535 . . . . (805) 549-1200
Housing: Homeownership rate: 67.7%; Median home value: $371,300; Median year structure built: 1975; Homeowner vacancy rate: 1.3%; Median gross rent: $1,348 per month; Rental vacancy rate: 4.7%
Health Insurance: 86.5% have insurance; 74.3% have private insurance; 27.8% have public insurance; 13.5% do not have insurance; 7.6% of children under 18 do not have insurance
Transportation: Commute: 87.9% car, 0.4% public transportation, 2.5% walk, 8.6% work from home; Median travel time to work: 20.2 minutes

LOS RANCHOS (CDP). Covers a land area of 2.829 square miles and a water area of 0.003 square miles. Located at 35.21° N. Lat; 120.63° W. Long.
Population: 1,477; Growth (since 2000): n/a; Density: 522.0 persons per square mile; Race: 94.0% White, 0.1% Black/African American, 2.1% Asian, 0.1% American Indian/Alaska Native, 0.0% Native Hawaiian/Other Pacific Islander, 2.4% Two or more races, 3.9% Hispanic of any race; Average household size: 2.53; Median age: 51.9; Age under 18: 21.2%; Age 65 and over: 24.1%; Males per 100 females: 101.8
Housing: Homeownership rate: 89.9%; Homeowner vacancy rate: 1.1%; Rental vacancy rate: 0.0%

MORRO BAY (city). Covers a land area of 5.303 square miles and a water area of 5.019 square miles. Located at 35.37° N. Lat; 120.87° W. Long. Elevation is 62 feet.
History: Morro Bay is named for a large rock, sometimes called the Gilbraltar of the Pacific, which rises 576 feet above a lagoon behind sand dunes. Morro is Spanish for "headland."
Population: 10,234; Growth (since 2000): -1.1%; Density: 1,930.0 persons per square mile; Race: 87.1% White, 0.4% Black/African American, 2.5% Asian, 0.9% American Indian/Alaska Native, 0.1% Native Hawaiian/Other Pacific Islander, 3.0% Two or more races, 14.9% Hispanic of any race; Average household size: 2.08; Median age: 48.9; Age under 18: 15.0%; Age 65 and over: 23.7%; Males per 100 females: 95.8; Marriage status:

23.2% never married, 53.7% now married, 4.2% separated, 8.1% widowed, 15.0% divorced; Foreign born: 11.0%; Speak English only: 81.2%; With disability: 10.1%; Veterans: 10.6%; Ancestry: 19.0% German, 17.4% English, 13.3% Irish, 8.3% Italian, 4.0% French

Employment: 15.2% management, business, and financial, 7.2% computer, engineering, and science, 14.0% education, legal, community service, arts, and media, 4.4% healthcare practitioners, 20.6% service, 26.8% sales and office, 7.0% natural resources, construction, and maintenance, 4.6% production, transportation, and material moving

Income: Per capita: $31,899; Median household: $49,470; Average household: $63,942; Households with income of $100,000 or more: 19.7%; Poverty rate: 13.8%

Educational Attainment: High school diploma or higher: 91.9%; Bachelor's degree or higher: 36.2%; Graduate/professional degree or higher: 14.5%

School District(s)

San Luis Coastal Unified (PK-12)
2012-13 Enrollment: 7,535 . . . . (805) 549-1200

Housing: Homeownership rate: 53.3%; Median home value: $484,800; Median year structure built: 1972; Homeowner vacancy rate: 3.3%; Median gross rent: $1,270 per month; Rental vacancy rate: 6.3%

Health Insurance: 82.3% have insurance; 62.5% have private insurance; 37.3% have public insurance; 17.7% do not have insurance; 8.6% of children under 18 do not have insurance

Safety: Violent crime rate: 29.8 per 10,000 population; Property crime rate: 164.2 per 10,000 population

Transportation: Commute: 83.5% car, 1.1% public transportation, 5.5% walk, 7.0% work from home; Median travel time to work: 19.7 minutes

Additional Information Contacts

City of Morro Bay. . . . . (805) 772-6200
http://www.morro-bay.ca.us

NIPOMO (CDP). Covers a land area of 14.852 square miles and a water area of <.001 square miles. Located at 35.03° N. Lat; 120.50° W. Long. Elevation is 331 feet.

History: Nipomo grew on an early land grant that remained in the hands of the founding family.

Population: 16,714; Growth (since 2000): 32.4%; Density: 1,125.4 persons per square mile; Race: 73.5% White, 1.1% Black/African American, 2.5% Asian, 1.2% American Indian/Alaska Native, 0.2% Native Hawaiian/Other Pacific Islander, 4.7% Two or more races, 39.8% Hispanic of any race; Average household size: 3.05; Median age: 37.0; Age under 18: 26.5%; Age 65 and over: 12.6%; Males per 100 females: 97.8; Marriage status: 25.6% never married, 59.3% now married, 2.6% separated, 4.3% widowed, 10.8% divorced; Foreign born: 10.8%; Speak English only: 75.9%; With disability: 9.5%; Veterans: 6.0%; Ancestry: 15.2% German, 11.5% Irish, 9.8% English, 7.4% Italian, 4.0% American

Employment: 12.2% management, business, and financial, 2.6% computer, engineering, and science, 12.5% education, legal, community service, arts, and media, 3.4% healthcare practitioners, 23.1% service, 22.5% sales and office, 13.1% natural resources, construction, and maintenance, 10.5% production, transportation, and material moving

Income: Per capita: $26,052; Median household: $60,226; Average household: $76,224; Households with income of $100,000 or more: 24.4%; Poverty rate: 11.5%

Educational Attainment: High school diploma or higher: 84.9%; Bachelor's degree or higher: 24.9%; Graduate/professional degree or higher: 8.7%

School District(s)

Lucia Mar Unified (KG-12)
2012-13 Enrollment: 10,566 . . . . (805) 474-3000

Housing: Homeownership rate: 71.2%; Median home value: $369,600; Median year structure built: 1988; Homeowner vacancy rate: 1.7%; Median gross rent: $1,380 per month; Rental vacancy rate: 3.1%

Health Insurance: 85.4% have insurance; 66.4% have private insurance; 30.9% have public insurance; 14.6% do not have insurance; 8.3% of children under 18 do not have insurance

Transportation: Commute: 92.3% car, 1.5% public transportation, 0.8% walk, 4.2% work from home; Median travel time to work: 24.0 minutes

---

OAK SHORES (CDP). Covers a land area of 5.065 square miles and a water area of <.001 square miles. Located at 35.77° N. Lat; 120.98° W. Long.

Population: 337; Growth (since 2000): n/a; Density: 66.5 persons per square mile; Race: 94.4% White, 0.9% Black/African American, 1.2% Asian, 0.6% American Indian/Alaska Native, 0.0% Native Hawaiian/Other Pacific Islander, 1.8% Two or more races, 9.2% Hispanic of any race; Average household size: 2.15; Median age: 50.6; Age under 18: 15.1%; Age 65 and over: 24.0%; Males per 100 females: 106.7

Housing: Homeownership rate: 77.0%; Homeowner vacancy rate: 4.7%; Rental vacancy rate: 2.7%

OCEANO (CDP). Covers a land area of 1.532 square miles and a water area of 0.015 square miles. Located at 35.10° N. Lat; 120.61° W. Long. Elevation is 30 feet.

Population: 7,286; Growth (since 2000): 0.4%; Density: 4,756.8 persons per square mile; Race: 70.1% White, 0.9% Black/African American, 2.3% Asian, 1.6% American Indian/Alaska Native, 0.1% Native Hawaiian/Other Pacific Islander, 4.4% Two or more races, 47.8% Hispanic of any race; Average household size: 2.80; Median age: 35.4; Age under 18: 23.9%; Age 65 and over: 12.4%; Males per 100 females: 101.9; Marriage status: 36.7% never married, 44.6% now married, 1.8% separated, 8.4% widowed, 10.3% divorced; Foreign born: 18.3%; Speak English only: 61.7%; With disability: 15.3%; Veterans: 9.8%; Ancestry: 10.4% German, 8.9% English, 4.3% Irish, 3.0% Portuguese, 2.8% American

Employment: 6.5% management, business, and financial, 1.8% computer, engineering, and science, 7.6% education, legal, community service, arts, and media, 2.1% healthcare practitioners, 31.7% service, 25.2% sales and office, 14.5% natural resources, construction, and maintenance, 10.6% production, transportation, and material moving

Income: Per capita: $19,314; Median household: $43,567; Average household: $51,231; Households with income of $100,000 or more: 9.9%; Poverty rate: 18.9%

Educational Attainment: High school diploma or higher: 71.3%; Bachelor's degree or higher: 13.4%; Graduate/professional degree or higher: 5.0%

School District(s)

Lucia Mar Unified (KG-12)
2012-13 Enrollment: 10,566 . . . . (805) 474-3000

Housing: Homeownership rate: 52.0%; Median home value: $222,200; Median year structure built: 1976; Homeowner vacancy rate: 3.7%; Median gross rent: <$100 per month; Rental vacancy rate: 5.9%

Health Insurance: 69.9% have insurance; 38.4% have private insurance; 43.2% have public insurance; 30.1% do not have insurance; 20.4% of children under 18 do not have insurance

Transportation: Commute: 92.8% car, 0.4% public transportation, 3.1% walk, 1.4% work from home; Median travel time to work: 19.8 minutes

---

PISMO BEACH (city). Covers a land area of 3.599 square miles and a water area of 9.877 square miles. Located at 35.15° N. Lat; 120.67° W. Long. Elevation is 56 feet.

History: Pismo Beach grew as a seaside resort, known for its Pismo clams.

Population: 7,655; Growth (since 2000): -10.5%; Density: 2,126.9 persons per square mile; Race: 91.1% White, 0.7% Black/African American, 2.7% Asian, 0.5% American Indian/Alaska Native, 0.1% Native Hawaiian/Other Pacific Islander, 2.7% Two or more races, 9.3% Hispanic of any race; Average household size: 1.99; Median age: 51.8; Age under 18: 13.3%; Age 65 and over: 26.0%; Males per 100 females: 93.5; Marriage status: 20.3% never married, 58.0% now married, 4.5% separated, 5.5% widowed, 16.1% divorced; Foreign born: 5.8%; Speak English only: 89.5%; With disability: 14.6%; Veterans: 13.7%; Ancestry: 23.3% German, 21.8% English, 14.5% Irish, 9.4% Italian, 8.5% American

Employment: 17.2% management, business, and financial, 4.5% computer, engineering, and science, 11.6% education, legal, community service, arts, and media, 6.8% healthcare practitioners, 19.9% service, 28.3% sales and office, 5.3% natural resources, construction, and maintenance, 6.5% production, transportation, and material moving

Income: Per capita: $39,375; Median household: $65,859; Average household: $78,767; Households with income of $100,000 or more: 25.7%; Poverty rate: 7.2%

Educational Attainment: High school diploma or higher: 95.6%; Bachelor's degree or higher: 36.9%; Graduate/professional degree or higher: 14.8%

School District(s)

Lucia Mar Unified (KG-12)
2012-13 Enrollment: 10,566 . . . . (805) 474-3000

Housing: Homeownership rate: 61.0%; Median home value: $589,400; Median year structure built: 1979; Homeowner vacancy rate: 2.5%; Median gross rent: $1,355 per month; Rental vacancy rate: 9.6%

Health Insurance: 91.3% have insurance; 75.7% have private insurance; 36.8% have public insurance; 8.7% do not have insurance; 0.0% of children under 18 do not have insurance
Safety: Violent crime rate: 28.1 per 10,000 population; Property crime rate: 405.2 per 10,000 population
Transportation: Commute: 78.6% car, 2.7% public transportation, 2.9% walk, 12.1% work from home; Median travel time to work: 19.9 minutes
Additional Information Contacts
City of Pismo Beach . . . . (805) 773-4657
http://www.pismobeach.org

SAN LUIS OBISPO (city). County seat. Covers a land area of 12.777 square miles and a water area of 0.153 square miles. Located at 35.27° N. Lat; 120.67° W. Long. Elevation is 233 feet.
History: The town of San Luis Obispo grew up around Mission San Luis Obispo de Tolosa, founded by Father Junipero Serra in 1772 and named for St. Louis, Bishop of Toulouse, perhaps because two volcanic peaks in the area looked like a bishop's mitre.
Population: 45,119; Growth (since 2000): 2.1%; Density: 3,531.2 persons per square mile; Race: 84.5% White, 1.2% Black/African American, 5.2% Asian, 0.6% American Indian/Alaska Native, 0.1% Native Hawaiian/Other Pacific Islander, 4.0% Two or more races, 14.7% Hispanic of any race; Average household size: 2.29; Median age: 26.5; Age under 18: 12.2%; Age 65 and over: 12.0%; Males per 100 females: 109.1; Marriage status: 58.1% never married, 30.6% now married, 1.4% separated, 4.3% widowed, 7.0% divorced; Foreign born: 9.3%; Speak English only: 82.5%; With disability: 8.9%; Veterans: 6.0%; Ancestry: 18.2% German, 12.4% Irish, 10.9% English, 7.6% Italian, 4.0% French
Employment: 14.1% management, business, and financial, 9.3% computer, engineering, and science, 13.5% education, legal, community service, arts, and media, 3.9% healthcare practitioners, 20.7% service, 27.8% sales and office, 4.1% natural resources, construction, and maintenance, 6.6% production, transportation, and material moving
Income: Per capita: $26,129; Median household: $45,032; Average household: $63,853; Households with income of $100,000 or more: 20.8%; Poverty rate: 32.4%
Educational Attainment: High school diploma or higher: 93.3%; Bachelor's degree or higher: 47.4%; Graduate/professional degree or higher: 18.7%

School District(s)

San Luis Coastal Unified (PK-12)
2012-13 Enrollment: 7,535 . . . . (805) 549-1200
San Luis Obispo County Office of Education (KG-12)
2012-13 Enrollment: 665. . . . . (805) 543-7732

Four-year College(s)

California Polytechnic State University-San Luis Obispo (Public)
Fall 2013 Enrollment: 19,703 . . . . (805) 756-1111
2013-14 Tuition: In-state $8,724; Out-of-state $19,884

Two-year College(s)

Central California School (Private, For-profit)
Fall 2013 Enrollment: 412 . . . . (805) 543-9123
2013-14 Tuition: In-state $9,535; Out-of-state $9,535
Cuesta College (Public)
Fall 2013 Enrollment: 9,256 . . . . (805) 546-3100
2013-14 Tuition: In-state $1,230; Out-of-state $6,404

Vocational/Technical School(s)

Laurus College (Private, For-profit)
Fall 2013 Enrollment: 856 . . . . (805) 267-1690
2013-14 Tuition: $10,400
Housing: Homeownership rate: 39.3%; Median home value: $519,500; Median year structure built: 1974; Homeowner vacancy rate: 1.6%; Median gross rent: $1,233 per month; Rental vacancy rate: 5.7%
Health Insurance: 88.5% have insurance; 79.6% have private insurance; 19.4% have public insurance; 11.5% do not have insurance; 6.4% of children under 18 do not have insurance
Hospitals: French Hospital Medical Center (112 beds); Sierra Vista Regional Medical Center (201 beds)
Safety: Violent crime rate: 34.9 per 10,000 population; Property crime rate: 385.1 per 10,000 population
Newspapers: The Bay News (weekly circulation 18500); The Coast News (weekly circulation 25000); The New Times (weekly circulation 42000); The Tribune (daily circulation 37400)
Transportation: Commute: 76.6% car, 2.7% public transportation, 7.4% walk, 5.1% work from home; Median travel time to work: 14.8 minutes; Amtrak: Train and bus service available.
Airports: San Luis County Regional (primary service/non-hub)
Additional Information Contacts
City of San Luis Obispo. . . . . (805) 781-7100
http://www.slocity.org

SAN MIGUEL (CDP). Covers a land area of 1.705 square miles and a water area of 0 square miles. Located at 35.75° N. Lat; 120.69° W. Long. Elevation is 633 feet.
History: The village of San Miguel grew around the Mission San Miguel Arcangel, founded in 1797. Almond growing was an early industry.
Population: 2,336; Growth (since 2000): 63.7%; Density: 1,369.9 persons per square mile; Race: 70.1% White, 2.8% Black/African American, 0.8% Asian, 2.5% American Indian/Alaska Native, 0.0% Native Hawaiian/Other Pacific Islander, 3.5% Two or more races, 51.2% Hispanic of any race; Average household size: 3.33; Median age: 28.3; Age under 18: 33.1%; Age 65 and over: 4.6%; Males per 100 females: 103.8

School District(s)

Pleasant Valley Joint Union Elementary (KG-08)
2012-13 Enrollment: 126. . . . . (805) 467-3453
San Miguel Joint Union (KG-08)
2012-13 Enrollment: 746. . . . . (805) 467-3216
Shandon Joint Unified (KG-12)
2012-13 Enrollment: 308. . . . . (805) 238-0286
Housing: Homeownership rate: 62.3%; Homeowner vacancy rate: 3.7%; Rental vacancy rate: 8.0%

SAN SIMEON (CDP). Covers a land area of 0.797 square miles and a water area of 0 square miles. Located at 35.62° N. Lat; 121.14° W. Long. Elevation is 20 feet.
Population: 462; Growth (since 2000): n/a; Density: 579.9 persons per square mile; Race: 58.4% White, 0.9% Black/African American, 1.9% Asian, 1.1% American Indian/Alaska Native, 0.4% Native Hawaiian/Other Pacific Islander, 2.6% Two or more races, 55.8% Hispanic of any race; Average household size: 2.34; Median age: 40.7; Age under 18: 22.9%; Age 65 and over: 18.0%; Males per 100 females: 105.3
Housing: Homeownership rate: 44.2%; Homeowner vacancy rate: 2.2%; Rental vacancy rate: 11.3%

SANTA MARGARITA (CDP). Covers a land area of 0.518 square miles and a water area of 0 square miles. Located at 35.39° N. Lat; 120.61° W. Long. Elevation is 1,010 feet.
Population: 1,259; Growth (since 2000): n/a; Density: 2,432.4 persons per square mile; Race: 85.5% White, 0.6% Black/African American, 2.7% Asian, 2.2% American Indian/Alaska Native, 0.0% Native Hawaiian/Other Pacific Islander, 5.6% Two or more races, 16.4% Hispanic of any race; Average household size: 2.48; Median age: 41.1; Age under 18: 20.4%; Age 65 and over: 8.6%; Males per 100 females: 101.8

School District(s)

Atascadero Unified (KG-12)
2012-13 Enrollment: 4,784 . . . . (805) 462-4200
Housing: Homeownership rate: 65.8%; Homeowner vacancy rate: 1.5%; Rental vacancy rate: 2.3%

SHANDON (CDP). Covers a land area of 2.946 square miles and a water area of 0.043 square miles. Located at 35.65° N. Lat; 120.38° W. Long. Elevation is 1,040 feet.
Population: 1,295; Growth (since 2000): 31.3%; Density: 439.6 persons per square mile; Race: 64.9% White, 2.6% Black/African American, 0.5% Asian, 1.4% American Indian/Alaska Native, 0.2% Native Hawaiian/Other Pacific Islander, 3.2% Two or more races, 53.5% Hispanic of any race; Average household size: 3.49; Median age: 30.6; Age under 18: 32.3%; Age 65 and over: 7.2%; Males per 100 females: 103.6

School District(s)

Shandon Joint Unified (KG-12)
2012-13 Enrollment: 308. . . . . (805) 238-0286
Housing: Homeownership rate: 64.5%; Homeowner vacancy rate: 5.5%; Rental vacancy rate: 8.3%

TEMPLETON (CDP). Covers a land area of 7.717 square miles and a water area of 0.049 square miles. Located at 35.56° N. Lat; 120.72° W. Long. Elevation is 807 feet.
Population: 7,674; Growth (since 2000): 63.7%; Density: 994.4 persons per square mile; Race: 89.0% White, 0.8% Black/African American, 1.6% Asian, 1.0% American Indian/Alaska Native, 0.1% Native Hawaiian/Other Pacific Islander, 3.0% Two or more races, 15.3% Hispanic of any race;

Average household size: 2.68; Median age: 40.8; Age under 18: 26.7%; Age 65 and over: 14.5%; Males per 100 females: 89.1; Marriage status: 19.7% never married, 61.2% now married, 2.6% separated, 7.9% widowed, 11.3% divorced; Foreign born: 9.3%; Speak English only: 87.6%; With disability: 13.9%; Veterans: 10.4%; Ancestry: 15.2% German, 13.7% English, 9.4% Irish, 9.2% Italian, 7.1% American

Employment: 13.2% management, business, and financial, 3.9% computer, engineering, and science, 9.2% education, legal, community service, arts, and media, 7.4% healthcare practitioners, 24.0% service, 25.7% sales and office, 9.8% natural resources, construction, and maintenance, 6.8% production, transportation, and material moving

Income: Per capita: $33,873; Median household: $68,833; Average household: $87,758; Households with income of $100,000 or more: 32.4%; Poverty rate: 6.2%

Educational Attainment: High school diploma or higher: 93.4%; Bachelor's degree or higher: 28.9%; Graduate/professional degree or higher: 9.8%

School District(s)

Templeton Unified (KG-12)
2012-13 Enrollment: 2,360 . . . . (805) 434-5800

Housing: Homeownership rate: 70.7%; Median home value: $378,500; Median year structure built: 1989; Homeowner vacancy rate: 1.2%; Median gross rent: $1,106 per month; Rental vacancy rate: 6.9%

Health Insurance: 88.6% have insurance; 77.6% have private insurance; 25.3% have public insurance; 11.4% do not have insurance; 4.2% of children under 18 do not have insurance

Hospitals: Twin Cities Community Hospital (84 beds)

Transportation: Commute: 92.5% car, 0.4% public transportation, 0.9% walk, 4.6% work from home; Median travel time to work: 25.1 minutes

WHITLEY GARDENS (CDP). Covers a land area of 1.377 square miles and a water area of 0.011 square miles. Located at 35.66° N. Lat; 120.51° W. Long. Elevation is 906 feet.

Population: 285; Growth (since 2000): n/a; Density: 206.9 persons per square mile; Race: 91.2% White, 0.4% Black/African American, 0.4% Asian, 2.1% American Indian/Alaska Native, 0.0% Native Hawaiian/Other Pacific Islander, 1.4% Two or more races, 15.1% Hispanic of any race; Average household size: 2.59; Median age: 45.1; Age under 18: 20.0%; Age 65 and over: 12.6%; Males per 100 females: 111.1

Housing: Homeownership rate: 60.0%; Homeowner vacancy rate: 0.0%; Rental vacancy rate: 6.3%

WOODLANDS (CDP). Covers a land area of 1.654 square miles and a water area of 0 square miles. Located at 35.03° N. Lat; 120.55° W. Long.

Population: 576; Growth (since 2000): n/a; Density: 348.3 persons per square mile; Race: 93.9% White, 1.2% Black/African American, 3.1% Asian, 0.0% American Indian/Alaska Native, 0.2% Native Hawaiian/Other Pacific Islander, 1.0% Two or more races, 4.7% Hispanic of any race; Average household size: 2.13; Median age: 59.2; Age under 18: 6.6%; Age 65 and over: 26.4%; Males per 100 females: 93.9

Housing: Homeownership rate: 94.5%; Homeowner vacancy rate: 15.8%; Rental vacancy rate: 0.0%

San Mateo County

Located in western California, on the San Francisco-San Mateo peninsula; bounded on the west by the Pacific Ocean, and on the east by San Francisco Bay; includes part of the Santa Cruz Mountains. Covers a land area of 448.408 square miles, a water area of 292.551 square miles, and is located in the Pacific Time Zone at 37.41° N. Lat., 122.37° W. Long. The county was founded in 1856. County seat is Redwood City.

San Mateo County is part of the San Francisco-Oakland-Hayward, CA Metropolitan Statistical Area. The entire metro area includes: Oakland-Hayward-Berkeley, CA Metropolitan Division (Alameda County, CA; Contra Costa County, CA); San Francisco-Redwood City-South San Francisco, CA Metropolitan Division (San Francisco County, CA; San Mateo County, CA); San Rafael, CA Metropolitan Division (Marin County, CA)

Weather Station: Half Moon Bay Elevation: 16 feet

	Jan	Feb	Mar	Apr	May	Jun	Jul	Aug	Sep	Oct	Nov	Dec
High	59	60	60	61	62	64	65	66	67	66	63	59
Low	43	44	44	45	48	50	52	53	51	48	45	43
Precip	5.5	5.4	4.1	1.8	0.9	0.3	0.1	0.2	0.4	1.6	3.0	4.8
Snow	0.0	0.0	0.0	0.0	0.0	0.0	0.0	0.0	0.0	0.0	tr	0.0

High and Low temperatures in degrees Fahrenheit; Precipitation and Snow in inches

Weather Station: Pacifica 4 SSE Elevation: 475 feet

	Jan	Feb	Mar	Apr	May	Jun	Jul	Aug	Sep	Oct	Nov	Dec
High	57	59	61	64	66	69	71	71	72	69	62	57
Low	46	47	47	48	50	52	53	54	54	53	50	46
Precip	5.6	6.1	4.0	1.8	1.1	0.2	0.0	0.1	0.3	1.4	3.3	5.9
Snow	0.0	0.0	0.0	0.0	0.0	0.0	0.0	0.0	0.0	0.0	0.0	0.0

High and Low temperatures in degrees Fahrenheit; Precipitation and Snow in inches

Weather Station: Redwood City Elevation: 30 feet

	Jan	Feb	Mar	Apr	May	Jun	Jul	Aug	Sep	Oct	Nov	Dec
High	58	62	66	70	74	79	82	82	80	75	65	58
Low	40	43	45	46	50	53	56	56	54	50	44	40
Precip	3.9	4.1	3.0	1.1	0.5	0.1	0.0	0.1	0.2	1.1	2.3	3.6
Snow	tr	0.0	tr	0.0	0.0	0.0	0.0	0.0	0.0	0.0	0.0	0.0

High and Low temperatures in degrees Fahrenheit; Precipitation and Snow in inches

Weather Station: San Francisco Int'l Arpt Elevation: 7 feet

	Jan	Feb	Mar	Apr	May	Jun	Jul	Aug	Sep	Oct	Nov	Dec
High	56	60	62	65	68	71	72	73	74	71	63	57
Low	44	46	47	49	51	53	55	56	55	53	48	44
Precip	4.2	4.2	3.0	1.2	0.5	0.1	0.0	0.0	0.2	0.9	2.3	3.9
Snow	na	na	na	na	na	na	na	na	na	na	na	na

High and Low temperatures in degrees Fahrenheit; Precipitation and Snow in inches

Weather Station: San Gregorio 2 SE Elevation: 274 feet

	Jan	Feb	Mar	Apr	May	Jun	Jul	Aug	Sep	Oct	Nov	Dec
High	59	60	61	63	65	68	70	70	71	68	63	59
Low	40	41	42	43	46	48	51	51	49	45	42	40
Precip	5.7	5.8	4.7	2.2	1.0	0.3	0.1	0.2	0.3	1.4	3.6	5.6
Snow	0.0	0.0	0.0	0.0	0.0	0.0	0.0	0.0	0.0	0.0	0.0	0.0

High and Low temperatures in degrees Fahrenheit; Precipitation and Snow in inches

Weather Station: Woodside Fire Stn 1 Elevation: 379 feet

	Jan	Feb	Mar	Apr	May	Jun	Jul	Aug	Sep	Oct	Nov	Dec
High	60	64	68	73	78	84	89	89	86	79	67	60
Low	37	39	41	43	46	49	52	51	50	46	40	37
Precip	6.1	6.0	4.4	1.8	0.8	0.2	0.0	0.1	0.2	1.3	3.7	5.7
Snow	0.0	0.0	0.0	0.0	0.0	0.0	0.0	0.0	0.0	0.0	0.0	0.0

High and Low temperatures in degrees Fahrenheit; Precipitation and Snow in inches

Population: 718,451; Growth (since 2000): 1.6%; Density: 1,602.2 persons per square mile; Race: 53.4% White, 2.8% Black/African American, 24.8% Asian, 0.5% American Indian/Alaska Native, 1.4% Native Hawaiian/Other Pacific Islander, 5.3% two or more races, 25.4% Hispanic of any race; Average household size: 2.75; Median age: 39.3; Age under 18: 22.2%; Age 65 and over: 13.4%; Males per 100 females: 96.7; Marriage status: 31.7% never married, 53.5% now married, 1.7% separated, 5.4% widowed, 9.3% divorced; Foreign born: 34.0%; Speak English only: 54.0%; With disability: 7.8%; Veterans: 5.7%; Ancestry: 8.3% German, 8.2% Irish, 6.8% Italian, 6.3% English, 2.3% American

Religion: Six largest groups: 33.9% Catholicism, 1.9% Latter-day Saints, 1.5% Presbyterian-Reformed, 1.2% Non-denominational Protestant, 1.1% Baptist, 0.9% Buddhism

Economy: Unemployment rate: 4.1%; Leading industries: 15.0% professional, scientific, and technical services; 11.3% health care and social assistance; 10.3% retail trade; Farms: 334 totaling 48,160 acres; Company size: 31 employs 1,000 or more persons, 33 employ 500 to 999 persons, 397 employ 100 to 499 persons, 19,632 employ less than 100 persons; Business ownership: 22,312 women-owned, 1,184 Black-owned, 8,743 Hispanic-owned, 13,882 Asian-owned

Employment: 19.5% management, business, and financial, 9.3% computer, engineering, and science, 10.1% education, legal, community service, arts, and media, 5.6% healthcare practitioners, 18.4% service, 23.2% sales and office, 6.5% natural resources, construction, and maintenance, 7.4% production, transportation, and material moving

Income: Per capita: $45,732; Median household: $88,202; Average household: $126,129; Households with income of $100,000 or more: 44.8%; Poverty rate: 7.6%

Educational Attainment: High school diploma or higher: 88.6%; Bachelor's degree or higher: 44.4%; Graduate/professional degree or higher: 17.6%

Housing: Homeownership rate: 59.4%; Median home value: $722,200; Median year structure built: 1963; Homeowner vacancy rate: 1.3%; Median gross rent: $1,602 per month; Rental vacancy rate: 4.6%

Vital Statistics: Birth rate: 122.2 per 10,000 population; Death rate: 64.8 per 10,000 population; Age-adjusted cancer mortality rate: 143.8 deaths per 100,000 population

Health Insurance: 89.3% have insurance; 76.1% have private insurance; 23.6% have public insurance; 10.7% do not have insurance; 4.6% of children under 18 do not have insurance

Health Care: Physicians: 37.5 per 10,000 population; Hospital beds: 22.3 per 10,000 population; Hospital admissions: 688.6 per 10,000 population

Air Quality Index: 71.5% good, 27.7% moderate, 0.8% unhealthy for sensitive individuals, 0.0% unhealthy (percent of days)

Transportation: Commute: 81.2% car, 8.7% public transportation, 2.6% walk, 5.2% work from home; Median travel time to work: 25.7 minutes

Presidential Election: 72.1% Obama, 25.7% Romney (2012)

National and State Parks: Año Nuevo State Park; Bean Hollow State Beach; Burleigh Murray Ranch State Park; Butano State Park; Casa De Tableta State Historic Landmark; Gray Whale Cove State Beach; Half Moon Bay State Beach; La Honda Store State Historic Landmark; Mateo Coast State Beaches; Montara State Beach; Pescadero State Beach; Pigeon Point Light Station State Historic Park; Pomponio State Beach; Portola Redwoods State Park; San Bruno Mountain State Park; San Francisco State Fish and Game Refuge; San Gregorio State Beach; Thornton State Beach

Additional Information Contacts

San Mateo Government . . . . (650) 363-4000
http://www.co.sanmateo.ca.us

San Mateo County Communities

ATHERTON (town). Covers a land area of 5.017 square miles and a water area of 0.032 square miles. Located at 37.45° N. Lat; 122.20° W. Long. Elevation is 59 feet.

History: The first estate in Atherton was Faxon Dean Atherton's Valparaiso Park, laid out in 1860. When James L. Flood, a former San Francisco saloonkeeper who gained his wealth in the Virginia City mines, built the extravagant Linden Towers, his aristocratic neighbors debated as to whether or not to accept him in the community.

Population: 6,914; Growth (since 2000): -3.9%; Density: 1,378.2 persons per square mile; Race: 80.5% White, 1.1% Black/African American, 13.2% Asian, 0.1% American Indian/Alaska Native, 0.7% Native Hawaiian/Other Pacific Islander, 3.1% Two or more races, 3.9% Hispanic of any race; Average household size: 2.80; Median age: 48.2; Age under 18: 22.3%; Age 65 and over: 22.6%; Males per 100 females: 96.6; Marriage status: 24.7% never married, 65.9% now married, 0.7% separated, 4.7% widowed, 4.8% divorced; Foreign born: 14.6%; Speak English only: 84.4%; With disability: 6.8%; Veterans: 10.0%; Ancestry: 15.3% German, 15.0% English, 11.3% Irish, 7.8% Italian, 7.7% European

Employment: 47.7% management, business, and financial, 8.3% computer, engineering, and science, 11.3% education, legal, community service, arts, and media, 7.4% healthcare practitioners, 8.4% service, 15.0% sales and office, 0.8% natural resources, construction, and maintenance, 1.0% production, transportation, and material moving

Income: Per capita: $134,691; Median household: $239,886; Average household: $408,404; Households with income of $100,000 or more: 77.0%; Poverty rate: 3.6%

Educational Attainment: High school diploma or higher: 98.0%; Bachelor's degree or higher: 84.1%; Graduate/professional degree or higher: 41.5%

School District(s)

Las Lomitas Elementary (KG-08)
2012-13 Enrollment: 1,419 . . . . (650) 854-2880
Menlo Park City Elementary (KG-08)
2012-13 Enrollment: 2,799 . . . . (650) 321-7140
Redwood City Elementary (KG-08)
2012-13 Enrollment: 9,210 . . . . (650) 423-2200
Sequoia Union High (09-12)
2012-13 Enrollment: 9,247 . . . . (650) 369-1411

Four-year College(s)

Menlo College (Private, Not-for-profit)
Fall 2013 Enrollment: 745. . . . . (800) 556-3656
2013-14 Tuition: In-state $37,100; Out-of-state $37,100

Housing: Homeownership rate: 90.8%; Median home value: 1 million+; Median year structure built: 1958; Homeowner vacancy rate: 1.6%; Median gross rent: $2,000+ per month; Rental vacancy rate: 3.9%

Health Insurance: 97.9% have insurance; 91.9% have private insurance; 20.8% have public insurance; 2.1% do not have insurance; 0.0% of children under 18 do not have insurance

Safety: Violent crime rate: 13.7 per 10,000 population; Property crime rate: 158.0 per 10,000 population

Transportation: Commute: 81.4% car, 4.1% public transportation, 3.0% walk, 10.7% work from home; Median travel time to work: 23.4 minutes

Additional Information Contacts

Town of Atherton. . . . . (650) 752-0500
http://www.ci.atherton.ca.us

BELMONT (city). Covers a land area of 4.621 square miles and a water area of 0.009 square miles. Located at 37.51° N. Lat; 122.29° W. Long. Elevation is 43 feet.

History: Named for a variation of the French translation of "beautiful mountain". The site of Belmont was visited by Captain George Vancouver in 1792, who reported that it was an enchanting spot. William Chapman Ralston, one of the founders of the Bank of California, poured his Comstock mining millions into an estate that he built here in the 1860s, where he entertained influential guests from around the world.

Population: 25,835; Growth (since 2000): 2.8%; Density: 5,590.2 persons per square mile; Race: 67.6% White, 1.6% Black/African American, 19.9% Asian, 0.3% American Indian/Alaska Native, 0.8% Native Hawaiian/Other Pacific Islander, 6.1% Two or more races, 11.5% Hispanic of any race; Average household size: 2.39; Median age: 40.9; Age under 18: 20.9%; Age 65 and over: 14.9%; Males per 100 females: 95.4; Marriage status: 27.2% never married, 57.1% now married, 0.4% separated, 5.8% widowed, 9.9% divorced; Foreign born: 27.7%; Speak English only: 65.6%; With disability: 7.9%; Veterans: 6.7%; Ancestry: 12.6% German, 10.6% Irish, 9.1% English, 8.2% Italian, 4.1% French

Employment: 25.6% management, business, and financial, 15.8% computer, engineering, and science, 10.7% education, legal, community service, arts, and media, 6.3% healthcare practitioners, 12.4% service, 20.6% sales and office, 4.9% natural resources, construction, and maintenance, 3.6% production, transportation, and material moving

Income: Per capita: $53,968; Median household: $102,895; Average household: $133,513; Households with income of $100,000 or more: 50.8%; Poverty rate: 5.5%

Educational Attainment: High school diploma or higher: 95.4%; Bachelor's degree or higher: 55.5%; Graduate/professional degree or higher: 25.0%

School District(s)

Belmont-Redwood Shores Elementary (KG-08)
2012-13 Enrollment: 3,607 . . . . (650) 637-4800
Sequoia Union High (09-12)
2012-13 Enrollment: 9,247 . . . . (650) 369-1411

Four-year College(s)

Notre Dame de Namur University (Private, Not-for-profit, Roman Catholic)
Fall 2013 Enrollment: 2,030 . . . . (650) 508-3500
2013-14 Tuition: In-state $31,126; Out-of-state $31,126

Housing: Homeownership rate: 59.4%; Median home value: $882,400; Median year structure built: 1962; Homeowner vacancy rate: 0.7%; Median gross rent: $1,564 per month; Rental vacancy rate: 5.2%

Health Insurance: 93.6% have insurance; 84.4% have private insurance; 21.7% have public insurance; 6.4% do not have insurance; 1.2% of children under 18 do not have insurance

Safety: Violent crime rate: 10.1 per 10,000 population; Property crime rate: 163.7 per 10,000 population

Transportation: Commute: 82.4% car, 5.0% public transportation, 1.6% walk, 9.0% work from home; Median travel time to work: 25.6 minutes

Additional Information Contacts

City of Belmont . . . . (650) 595-7413
http://www.belmont.gov

BRISBANE (city). Covers a land area of 3.096 square miles and a water area of 16.981 square miles. Located at 37.68° N. Lat; 122.38° W. Long. Elevation is 115 feet.

History: Cow Palace Arena (Daly City) and Candlestick Park baseball stadium (San Francisco) to North.

Population: 4,282; Growth (since 2000): 19.0%; Density: 1,383.3 persons per square mile; Race: 60.2% White, 1.9% Black/African American, 25.3% Asian, 0.5% American Indian/Alaska Native, 1.0% Native Hawaiian/Other Pacific Islander, 6.9% Two or more races, 16.6% Hispanic of any race; Average household size: 2.34; Median age: 41.7; Age under 18: 19.3%; Age 65 and over: 10.0%; Males per 100 females: 100.7; Marriage status: 35.0% never married, 47.1% now married, 2.0% separated, 4.5% widowed, 13.4% divorced; Foreign born: 26.3%; Speak English only: 63.9%; With disability: 10.0%; Veterans: 6.7%; Ancestry: 13.0% German, 11.0% Irish, 6.5% English, 4.3% Italian, 3.8% Scottish

Employment: 17.8% management, business, and financial, 9.0% computer, engineering, and science, 16.1% education, legal, community service, arts, and media, 3.3% healthcare practitioners, 14.6% service, 26.2% sales and office, 5.8% natural resources, construction, and maintenance, 7.3% production, transportation, and material moving

Income: Per capita: $46,843; Median household: $78,542; Average household: $102,640; Households with income of $100,000 or more: 37.5%; Poverty rate: 3.6%

Educational Attainment: High school diploma or higher: 92.8%; Bachelor's degree or higher: 52.0%; Graduate/professional degree or higher: 16.1%

School District(s)

Brisbane Elementary (KG-08)
2012-13 Enrollment: 519 . . . . (415) 467-0550

Housing: Homeownership rate: 64.1%; Median home value: $603,000; Median year structure built: 1970; Homeowner vacancy rate: 1.3%; Median gross rent: $1,367 per month; Rental vacancy rate: 5.5%

Health Insurance: 87.8% have insurance; 78.5% have private insurance; 18.3% have public insurance; 12.2% do not have insurance; 8.7% of children under 18 do not have insurance

Safety: Violent crime rate: 11.3 per 10,000 population; Property crime rate: 221.3 per 10,000 population

Transportation: Commute: 79.8% car, 8.9% public transportation, 5.0% walk, 2.6% work from home; Median travel time to work: 24.6 minutes

Additional Information Contacts

City of Brisbane . . . . (415) 508-2113
http://www.ci.brisbane.ca.us

BROADMOOR (CDP). Covers a land area of 0.450 square miles and a water area of 0 square miles. Located at 37.69° N. Lat; 122.48° W. Long. Elevation is 344 feet.

Population: 4,176; Growth (since 2000): 3.7%; Density: 9,277.0 persons per square mile; Race: 40.8% White, 2.4% Black/African American, 40.1% Asian, 0.7% American Indian/Alaska Native, 1.1% Native Hawaiian/Other Pacific Islander, 6.3% Two or more races, 23.5% Hispanic of any race; Average household size: 3.02; Median age: 41.7; Age under 18: 20.5%; Age 65 and over: 15.7%; Males per 100 females: 95.9; Marriage status: 25.9% never married, 53.9% now married, 0.0% separated, 6.5% widowed, 13.7% divorced; Foreign born: 36.9%; Speak English only: 53.9%; With disability: 9.6%; Veterans: 5.6%; Ancestry: 8.3% Irish, 6.0% Italian, 3.3% English, 2.9% American, 2.7% African

Employment: 14.4% management, business, and financial, 6.7% computer, engineering, and science, 9.9% education, legal, community service, arts, and media, 7.5% healthcare practitioners, 19.2% service, 25.3% sales and office, 8.8% natural resources, construction, and maintenance, 8.1% production, transportation, and material moving

Income: Per capita: $31,092; Median household: $76,250; Average household: $87,824; Households with income of $100,000 or more: 36.8%; Poverty rate: 10.6%

Educational Attainment: High school diploma or higher: 86.9%; Bachelor's degree or higher: 24.7%; Graduate/professional degree or higher: 7.2%

Housing: Homeownership rate: 76.9%; Median home value: $547,900; Median year structure built: 1950; Homeowner vacancy rate: 0.7%; Median gross rent: $1,728 per month; Rental vacancy rate: 1.9%

Health Insurance: 87.9% have insurance; 73.3% have private insurance; 22.9% have public insurance; 12.1% do not have insurance; 0.0% of children under 18 do not have insurance

Safety: Violent crime rate: 32.6 per 10,000 population; Property crime rate: 127.9 per 10,000 population

Transportation: Commute: 81.2% car, 10.5% public transportation, 2.0% walk, 4.3% work from home; Median travel time to work: 23.7 minutes

BURLINGAME (city). Covers a land area of 4.406 square miles and a water area of 1.651 square miles. Located at 37.59° N. Lat; 122.36° W. Long. Elevation is 39 feet.

History: Burlingame was the product of banker William C. Ralston's dream of a colony where San Franciscans could have summer homes. Ralston named the place for His Excellency, the Honourable Anson Burlingame, High Minister Plenipotentiary and Envoy Extraordinary to the Court of Pekin, who visited him here. Ralston was one of the founders of the Bank of California.

Population: 28,806; Growth (since 2000): 2.3%; Density: 6,538.1 persons per square mile; Race: 67.7% White, 1.2% Black/African American, 20.3% Asian, 0.3% American Indian/Alaska Native, 0.5% Native Hawaiian/Other Pacific Islander, 5.0% Two or more races, 13.8% Hispanic of any race; Average household size: 2.29; Median age: 40.5; Age under 18: 21.7%; Age 65 and over: 14.0%; Males per 100 females: 90.4; Marriage status: 33.2% never married, 50.9% now married, 1.8% separated, 5.6% widowed, 10.3% divorced; Foreign born: 24.5%; Speak English only: 68.1%; With disability: 5.5%; Veterans: 5.1%; Ancestry: 14.4% Irish, 11.4% German, 10.4% Italian, 7.7% English, 3.0% American

Employment: 27.2% management, business, and financial, 9.0% computer, engineering, and science, 12.2% education, legal, community service, arts, and media, 6.1% healthcare practitioners, 11.2% service, 22.0% sales and office, 6.2% natural resources, construction, and maintenance, 6.0% production, transportation, and material moving

Income: Per capita: $57,038; Median household: $84,854; Average household: $134,812; Households with income of $100,000 or more: 42.6%; Poverty rate: 7.5%

Educational Attainment: High school diploma or higher: 95.5%; Bachelor's degree or higher: 58.3%; Graduate/professional degree or higher: 25.6%

School District(s)

Burlingame Elementary (KG-08)
2012-13 Enrollment: 3,037 . . . . (650) 259-3800
San Mateo County Rop
2012-13 Enrollment: n/a . . . . (650) 802-5400
San Mateo Union High (09-12)
2012-13 Enrollment: 8,244 . . . . (650) 558-2299

Housing: Homeownership rate: 47.1%; Median home value: 1 million+; Median year structure built: 1956; Homeowner vacancy rate: 1.3%; Median gross rent: $1,521 per month; Rental vacancy rate: 4.5%

Health Insurance: 93.1% have insurance; 85.6% have private insurance; 17.4% have public insurance; 6.9% do not have insurance; 3.0% of children under 18 do not have insurance

Hospitals: Mills - Peninsula Medical Center

Safety: Violent crime rate: 12.4 per 10,000 population; Property crime rate: 222.1 per 10,000 population

Transportation: Commute: 77.8% car, 12.3% public transportation, 3.0% walk, 5.7% work from home; Median travel time to work: 27.2 minutes

Additional Information Contacts

City of Burlingame . . . . (650) 558-7200
http://www.burlingame.org

COLMA (town). Covers a land area of 1.909 square miles and a water area of 0 square miles. Located at 37.68° N. Lat; 122.45° W. Long. Elevation is 115 feet.

History: Much of land in cemetaries known as City of Souls. Formerly Lawndale, it took (1941) name of former town of Colma, which had been absorbed (1936) by Daly City.

Population: 1,792; Growth (since 2000): 50.5%; Density: 938.6 persons per square mile; Race: 34.6% White, 3.3% Black/African American, 34.5% Asian, 0.4% American Indian/Alaska Native, 0.5% Native Hawaiian/Other Pacific Islander, 6.3% Two or more races, 39.5% Hispanic of any race; Average household size: 3.13; Median age: 36.4; Age under 18: 21.8%; Age 65 and over: 11.4%; Males per 100 females: 92.7

School District(s)

Jefferson Elementary (KG-12)
2012-13 Enrollment: 7,027 . . . . (650) 991-1000

Housing: Homeownership rate: 39.7%; Homeowner vacancy rate: 1.7%; Rental vacancy rate: 2.3%

Safety: Violent crime rate: 33.8 per 10,000 population; Property crime rate: 1,843.3 per 10,000 population

Additional Information Contacts

Town of Colma . . . . (650) 997-8300
http://www.colma.ca.gov

DALY CITY (city). Covers a land area of 7.664 square miles and a water area of 0 square miles. Located at 37.70° N. Lat; 122.46° W. Long. Elevation is 407 feet.

History: Named for John D. Daly, owner of a local dairy ranch. A fort was built here in 1859 by settlers who wanted to protect their land from speculators. Unsuccessful in defending it, the owners were later upheld by an 1866 Supreme Court decision.

Population: 101,123; Growth (since 2000): -2.4%; Density: 13,195.0 persons per square mile; Race: 23.6% White, 3.6% Black/African American, 55.6% Asian, 0.4% American Indian/Alaska Native, 0.8% Native Hawaiian/Other Pacific Islander, 4.9% Two or more races, 23.7% Hispanic of any race; Average household size: 3.23; Median age: 38.3; Age under 18: 19.4%; Age 65 and over: 13.5%; Males per 100 females: 97.5; Marriage status: 36.9% never married, 50.0% now married, 1.8% separated, 5.6% widowed, 7.5% divorced; Foreign born: 52.1%; Speak English only: 31.4%; With disability: 8.1%; Veterans: 4.3%; Ancestry: 2.4% Irish, 2.3% Italian, 2.1% German, 1.5% English, 1.3% European

Employment: 11.8% management, business, and financial, 5.7% computer, engineering, and science, 5.7% education, legal, community service, arts, and media, 5.9% healthcare practitioners, 26.3% service, 29.0% sales and office, 5.0% natural resources, construction, and maintenance, 10.6% production, transportation, and material moving

Income: Per capita: $28,827; Median household: $74,436; Average household: $89,180; Households with income of $100,000 or more: 35.2%; Poverty rate: 8.6%

Educational Attainment: High school diploma or higher: 86.1%; Bachelor's degree or higher: 33.2%; Graduate/professional degree or higher: 6.0%

School District(s)

Bayshore Elementary (KG-12)
2012-13 Enrollment: 389. . . . . (415) 467-5443
Brisbane Elementary (KG-08)
2012-13 Enrollment: 519. . . . . (415) 467-0550
Jefferson Elementary (KG-12)
2012-13 Enrollment: 7,027 . . . . (650) 991-1000
Jefferson Union High (09-12)
2012-13 Enrollment: 4,870 . . . . (650) 550-7900
South San Francisco Unified (KG-12)
2012-13 Enrollment: 9,265 . . . . (650) 877-8700

Vocational/Technical School(s)

Hilltop Beauty School (Private, For-profit)
Fall 2013 Enrollment: 126 . . . . (650) 992-4949
2013-14 Tuition: $11,860

Housing: Homeownership rate: 56.5%; Median home value: $552,700; Median year structure built: 1966; Homeowner vacancy rate: 1.9%; Median gross rent: $1,542 per month; Rental vacancy rate: 4.2%

Health Insurance: 86.0% have insurance; 70.4% have private insurance; 24.8% have public insurance; 14.0% do not have insurance; 6.1% of children under 18 do not have insurance

Hospitals: Seton Medical Center (357 beds)

Safety: Violent crime rate: 21.3 per 10,000 population; Property crime rate: 175.3 per 10,000 population

Transportation: Commute: 74.5% car, 20.1% public transportation, 2.5% walk, 1.9% work from home; Median travel time to work: 28.6 minutes

Additional Information Contacts

City of Daly City. . . . . (650) 991-8000
http://www.dalycity.org

EAST PALO ALTO (city). Covers a land area of 2.505 square miles and a water area of 0.107 square miles. Located at 37.47° N. Lat; 122.13° W. Long. Elevation is 16 feet.

History: East Palo Alto was once inhabited by the Ohlone/Costanoan tribe of Native Americans. It was incorporated on July 1, 1983.

Population: 28,155; Growth (since 2000): -4.6%; Density: 11,238.8 persons per square mile; Race: 28.8% White, 16.7% Black/African American, 3.8% Asian, 0.4% American Indian/Alaska Native, 7.5% Native Hawaiian/Other Pacific Islander, 4.8% Two or more races, 64.5% Hispanic of any race; Average household size: 4.03; Median age: 28.1; Age under 18: 31.9%; Age 65 and over: 5.9%; Males per 100 females: 102.7; Marriage status: 43.6% never married, 45.1% now married, 2.9% separated, 3.7% widowed, 7.7% divorced; Foreign born: 40.2%; Speak English only: 29.9%; With disability: 7.4%; Veterans: 3.2%; Ancestry: 3.2% American, 1.5% German, 1.2% French, 1.2% English, 0.9% Italian

Employment: 8.0% management, business, and financial, 3.7% computer, engineering, and science, 6.3% education, legal, community service, arts, and media, 2.1% healthcare practitioners, 41.6% service, 20.5% sales and office, 8.4% natural resources, construction, and maintenance, 9.4% production, transportation, and material moving

Income: Per capita: $18,385; Median household: $50,142; Average household: $69,136; Households with income of $100,000 or more: 21.4%; Poverty rate: 18.4%

Educational Attainment: High school diploma or higher: 67.1%; Bachelor's degree or higher: 16.3%; Graduate/professional degree or higher: 6.7%

School District(s)

Ravenswood City Elementary (KG-12)
2012-13 Enrollment: 4,077 . . . . (650) 329-2800
San Mateo County Office of Education (KG-12)
2012-13 Enrollment: 441. . . . . (650) 802-5550
Sequoia Union High (09-12)
2012-13 Enrollment: 9,247 . . . . (650) 369-1411

Housing: Homeownership rate: 42.8%; Median home value: $378,800; Median year structure built: 1964; Homeowner vacancy rate: 2.1%; Median gross rent: $1,244 per month; Rental vacancy rate: 13.3%

Health Insurance: 76.0% have insurance; 45.8% have private insurance; 34.2% have public insurance; 24.0% do not have insurance; 11.1% of children under 18 do not have insurance

Safety: Violent crime rate: 119.3 per 10,000 population; Property crime rate: 205.3 per 10,000 population

Transportation: Commute: 85.8% car, 4.7% public transportation, 3.3% walk, 2.8% work from home; Median travel time to work: 23.9 minutes

Additional Information Contacts

City of East Palo Alto. . . . . (650) 853-3100
http://www.ci.east-palo-alto.ca.us

EL GRANADA (CDP). Covers a land area of 4.822 square miles and a water area of 0 square miles. Located at 37.51° N. Lat; 122.47° W. Long. Elevation is 33 feet.

Population: 5,467; Growth (since 2000): -4.5%; Density: 1,133.7 persons per square mile; Race: 84.3% White, 0.8% Black/African American, 3.5% Asian, 0.7% American Indian/Alaska Native, 0.1% Native Hawaiian/Other Pacific Islander, 4.5% Two or more races, 14.9% Hispanic of any race; Average household size: 2.60; Median age: 44.5; Age under 18: 21.9%; Age 65 and over: 10.6%; Males per 100 females: 96.4; Marriage status: 26.2% never married, 58.5% now married, 1.7% separated, 2.7% widowed, 12.5% divorced; Foreign born: 16.7%; Speak English only: 81.8%; With disability: 7.0%; Veterans: 10.4%; Ancestry: 20.8% German, 16.6% Irish, 16.3% English, 10.1% Italian, 4.6% French

Employment: 22.3% management, business, and financial, 11.4% computer, engineering, and science, 16.8% education, legal, community service, arts, and media, 6.2% healthcare practitioners, 12.2% service, 21.3% sales and office, 6.5% natural resources, construction, and maintenance, 3.3% production, transportation, and material moving

Income: Per capita: $56,758; Median household: $109,914; Average household: $154,015; Households with income of $100,000 or more: 56.5%; Poverty rate: 5.1%

Educational Attainment: High school diploma or higher: 92.3%; Bachelor's degree or higher: 58.4%; Graduate/professional degree or higher: 29.2%

Housing: Homeownership rate: 75.9%; Median home value: $810,500; Median year structure built: 1976; Homeowner vacancy rate: 0.7%; Median gross rent: $1,690 per month; Rental vacancy rate: 4.0%

Health Insurance: 90.8% have insurance; 83.3% have private insurance; 18.9% have public insurance; 9.2% do not have insurance; 0.0% of children under 18 do not have insurance

Transportation: Commute: 89.1% car, 1.1% public transportation, 2.1% walk, 7.1% work from home; Median travel time to work: 30.9 minutes

EMERALD LAKE HILLS (CDP). Covers a land area of 1.196 square miles and a water area of 0.007 square miles. Located at 37.47° N. Lat; 122.27° W. Long. Elevation is 531 feet.

History: Emerald Lake Hills was originally conceived as a resort community for city-weary San Franciscans during World War I. Emerald Lake Hills actually consists of two large subdivisions created around 1920: Emerald Lake (even though there are two lakes) and Emerald Hills.

Population: 4,278; Growth (since 2000): 9.7%; Density: 3,577.2 persons per square mile; Race: 85.4% White, 0.9% Black/African American, 7.5% Asian, 0.1% American Indian/Alaska Native, 0.4% Native Hawaiian/Other Pacific Islander, 4.3% Two or more races, 6.7% Hispanic of any race; Average household size: 2.74; Median age: 46.0; Age under 18: 22.8%; Age 65 and over: 12.9%; Males per 100 females: 99.1; Marriage status: 21.2% never married, 68.0% now married, 0.7% separated, 2.2% widowed, 8.5% divorced; Foreign born: 12.0%; Speak English only: 88.1%; With disability: 4.9%; Veterans: 7.4%; Ancestry: 15.1% English, 14.5% German, 12.5% Irish, 12.2% Italian, 7.4% Greek
Employment: 33.0% management, business, and financial, 12.0% computer, engineering, and science, 17.8% education, legal, community service, arts, and media, 5.4% healthcare practitioners, 6.6% service, 21.9% sales and office, 1.5% natural resources, construction, and maintenance, 1.8% production, transportation, and material moving
Income: Per capita: $71,841; Median household: $159,663; Average household: $208,009; Households with income of $100,000 or more: 70.1%; Poverty rate: 3.6%
Educational Attainment: High school diploma or higher: 96.5%; Bachelor's degree or higher: 65.3%; Graduate/professional degree or higher: 31.9%
Housing: Homeownership rate: 90.4%; Median home value: 1 million+; Median year structure built: 1973; Homeowner vacancy rate: 1.1%; Median gross rent: $2,000+ per month; Rental vacancy rate: 7.4%
Health Insurance: 98.2% have insurance; 93.3% have private insurance; 16.2% have public insurance; 1.8% do not have insurance; 0.0% of children under 18 do not have insurance
Transportation: Commute: 82.1% car, 1.1% public transportation, 3.0% walk, 13.7% work from home; Median travel time to work: 27.3 minutes

FOSTER CITY (city). Covers a land area of 3.756 square miles and a water area of 16.085 square miles. Located at 37.56° N. Lat; 122.25° W. Long. Elevation is 7 feet.
History: This city was incorporated on April 27, 1971 and named after T. Jack Foster who owned much of the land encompassing the city and was influential in its original design.
Population: 30,567; Growth (since 2000): 6.1%; Density: 8,137.6 persons per square mile; Race: 45.5% White, 1.9% Black/African American, 45.0% Asian, 0.1% American Indian/Alaska Native, 0.6% Native Hawaiian/Other Pacific Islander, 5.0% Two or more races, 6.5% Hispanic of any race; Average household size: 2.53; Median age: 39.3; Age under 18: 22.6%; Age 65 and over: 13.4%; Males per 100 females: 93.5; Marriage status: 23.3% never married, 62.9% now married, 1.3% separated, 5.9% widowed, 7.9% divorced; Foreign born: 41.5%; Speak English only: 50.0%; With disability: 5.9%; Veterans: 4.7%; Ancestry: 8.3% German, 5.3% Irish, 5.3% English, 4.7% Russian, 4.0% Italian
Employment: 25.4% management, business, and financial, 22.4% computer, engineering, and science, 9.4% education, legal, community service, arts, and media, 6.9% healthcare practitioners, 8.1% service, 21.1% sales and office, 2.5% natural resources, construction, and maintenance, 4.2% production, transportation, and material moving
Income: Per capita: $52,638; Median household: $114,260; Average household: $135,725; Households with income of $100,000 or more: 57.6%; Poverty rate: 4.6%
Educational Attainment: High school diploma or higher: 96.3%; Bachelor's degree or higher: 62.3%; Graduate/professional degree or higher: 28.6%

School District(s)

San Mateo-Foster City (KG-08)
2012-13 Enrollment: 11,456 . . . . (650) 312-7700
Housing: Homeownership rate: 57.9%; Median home value: $847,400; Median year structure built: 1976; Homeowner vacancy rate: 0.8%; Median gross rent: $2,000+ per month; Rental vacancy rate: 3.5%
Health Insurance: 95.9% have insurance; 87.5% have private insurance; 18.6% have public insurance; 4.1% do not have insurance; 1.6% of children under 18 do not have insurance
Safety: Violent crime rate: 4.6 per 10,000 population; Property crime rate: 93.4 per 10,000 population
Newspapers: Islander (weekly circulation 6000)
Transportation: Commute: 87.0% car, 3.7% public transportation, 1.0% walk, 6.5% work from home; Median travel time to work: 26.0 minutes
Additional Information Contacts
City of Foster City . . . . (650) 286-3200
http://www.fostercity.org

HALF MOON BAY (city). Covers a land area of 6.424 square miles and a water area of 0.020 square miles. Located at 37.47° N. Lat; 122.44° W. Long. Elevation is 75 feet.
History: Named for its semi-circle location on the bay. Two rancheros were built on opposite sides of Pilarcitos Creek, which runs into Half Moon Bay, in the 1840's. Around these houses a settlement grew, called Spanishtown when it was platted in 1863. About 1900 the name of the town was changed to Half Moon Bay.
Population: 11,324; Growth (since 2000): -4.4%; Density: 1,762.6 persons per square mile; Race: 75.8% White, 0.7% Black/African American, 4.3% Asian, 0.6% American Indian/Alaska Native, 0.1% Native Hawaiian/Other Pacific Islander, 3.4% Two or more races, 31.5% Hispanic of any race; Average household size: 2.72; Median age: 43.2; Age under 18: 22.4%; Age 65 and over: 15.6%; Males per 100 females: 95.1; Marriage status: 24.1% never married, 61.9% now married, 2.2% separated, 4.0% widowed, 10.0% divorced; Foreign born: 25.8%; Speak English only: 64.8%; With disability: 8.6%; Veterans: 8.1%; Ancestry: 12.0% German, 11.7% English, 10.8% Italian, 8.1% Irish, 4.2% Portuguese
Employment: 23.7% management, business, and financial, 7.7% computer, engineering, and science, 13.0% education, legal, community service, arts, and media, 4.1% healthcare practitioners, 20.2% service, 14.9% sales and office, 9.8% natural resources, construction, and maintenance, 6.7% production, transportation, and material moving
Income: Per capita: $51,932; Median household: $99,715; Average household: $134,755; Households with income of $100,000 or more: 49.7%; Poverty rate: 7.4%
Educational Attainment: High school diploma or higher: 82.4%; Bachelor's degree or higher: 45.3%; Graduate/professional degree or higher: 19.8%

School District(s)

Cabrillo Unified (KG-12)
2012-13 Enrollment: 3,324 . . . . (650) 712-7100
Housing: Homeownership rate: 70.9%; Median home value: $699,600; Median year structure built: 1977; Homeowner vacancy rate: 1.0%; Median gross rent: $1,682 per month; Rental vacancy rate: 1.9%
Health Insurance: 89.4% have insurance; 76.7% have private insurance; 25.9% have public insurance; 10.6% do not have insurance; 5.4% of children under 18 do not have insurance
Newspapers: The Review (weekly circulation 7000)
Transportation: Commute: 86.7% car, 1.8% public transportation, 2.3% walk, 7.0% work from home; Median travel time to work: 28.9 minutes
Additional Information Contacts
City of Half Moon Bay . . . . (650) 726-8270
http://ci.half-moon-bay.ca.us

HIGHLANDS-BAYWOOD PARK (CDP). Covers a land area of 1.807 square miles and a water area of 0 square miles. Located at 37.52° N. Lat; 122.34° W. Long. Elevation is 518 feet.
History: In the state legislature Baywood Park is located in the 8th Senate District, represented by Democrat Leland Yee, and in the 19th Assembly District, represented by Democrat Gene Mullin.
Population: 4,027; Growth (since 2000): -4.3%; Density: 2,228.0 persons per square mile; Race: 66.0% White, 1.3% Black/African American, 25.3% Asian, 0.2% American Indian/Alaska Native, 0.4% Native Hawaiian/Other Pacific Islander, 5.6% Two or more races, 7.6% Hispanic of any race; Average household size: 2.69; Median age: 44.6; Age under 18: 26.3%; Age 65 and over: 20.0%; Males per 100 females: 102.1; Marriage status: 23.7% never married, 61.6% now married, 0.7% separated, 7.2% widowed, 7.5% divorced; Foreign born: 27.0%; Speak English only: 68.5%; With disability: 8.9%; Veterans: 8.5%; Ancestry: 15.5% Irish, 12.0% English, 8.9% German, 7.3% Italian, 5.7% Iranian
Employment: 34.0% management, business, and financial, 13.1% computer, engineering, and science, 16.5% education, legal, community service, arts, and media, 5.6% healthcare practitioners, 8.3% service, 18.6% sales and office, 2.1% natural resources, construction, and maintenance, 1.8% production, transportation, and material moving
Income: Per capita: $58,089; Median household: $131,765; Average household: $161,299; Households with income of $100,000 or more: 65.7%; Poverty rate: 5.2%
Educational Attainment: High school diploma or higher: 97.2%; Bachelor's degree or higher: 64.2%; Graduate/professional degree or higher: 31.7%
Housing: Homeownership rate: 88.0%; Median home value: 1 million+; Median year structure built: 1959; Homeowner vacancy rate: 0.5%; Median gross rent: $1,900 per month; Rental vacancy rate: 7.6%

Health Insurance: 97.8% have insurance; 87.8% have private insurance; 24.1% have public insurance; 2.2% do not have insurance; 2.5% of children under 18 do not have insurance
Transportation: Commute: 87.7% car, 4.2% public transportation, 1.7% walk, 5.8% work from home; Median travel time to work: 25.1 minutes

HILLSBOROUGH (town). Covers a land area of 6.190 square miles and a water area of 0 square miles. Located at 37.56° N. Lat; 122.36° W. Long. Elevation is 322 feet.
History: Named for Hillsborough, New Hampshire, the ancestral home of W.D.M. Howard, former owner of the site. The founders of Hillsborough planned it as a community of estates for the wealthy, and decreed that it should have no post office, no telegraph or express office, no stores, saloons, hotels, boarding houses, newspapers, and no sidewalks.
Population: 10,825; Growth (since 2000): 0.0%; Density: 1,748.9 persons per square mile; Race: 66.3% White, 0.4% Black/African American, 28.1% Asian, 0.1% American Indian/Alaska Native, 0.2% Native Hawaiian/Other Pacific Islander, 3.9% Two or more races, 3.4% Hispanic of any race; Average household size: 2.93; Median age: 47.5; Age under 18: 26.6%; Age 65 and over: 20.5%; Males per 100 females: 94.8; Marriage status: 22.7% never married, 71.4% now married, 0.4% separated, 3.7% widowed, 2.3% divorced; Foreign born: 22.6%; Speak English only: 72.8%; With disability: 6.0%; Veterans: 5.8%; Ancestry: 13.6% German, 12.0% Irish, 10.2% English, 6.5% Italian, 4.0% European
Employment: 40.2% management, business, and financial, 6.7% computer, engineering, and science, 13.7% education, legal, community service, arts, and media, 13.6% healthcare practitioners, 4.7% service, 16.0% sales and office, 2.4% natural resources, construction, and maintenance, 2.6% production, transportation, and material moving
Income: Per capita: $118,953; Median household: $236,528; Average household: $361,882; Households with income of $100,000 or more: 83.2%; Poverty rate: 3.1%
Educational Attainment: High school diploma or higher: 96.1%; Bachelor's degree or higher: 76.0%; Graduate/professional degree or higher: 43.2%

School District(s)

Hillsborough City Elementary (KG-08)
2012-13 Enrollment: 1,523 . . . . (650) 342-5193
Housing: Homeownership rate: 94.5%; Median home value: 1 million+; Median year structure built: 1961; Homeowner vacancy rate: 1.3%; Median gross rent: $2,000+ per month; Rental vacancy rate: 4.2%
Health Insurance: 98.9% have insurance; 92.2% have private insurance; 19.8% have public insurance; 1.1% do not have insurance; 0.0% of children under 18 do not have insurance
Safety: Violent crime rate: 0.0 per 10,000 population; Property crime rate: 50.7 per 10,000 population
Transportation: Commute: 86.6% car, 3.7% public transportation, 1.3% walk, 7.6% work from home; Median travel time to work: 24.7 minutes
Additional Information Contacts
Town of Hillsborough. . . . . (650) 375-7400
http://www.hillsborough.net

LA HONDA (CDP). Covers a land area of 4.247 square miles and a water area of 0.015 square miles. Located at 37.32° N. Lat; 122.26° W. Long. Elevation is 390 feet.
Population: 928; Growth (since 2000): n/a; Density: 218.5 persons per square mile; Race: 87.4% White, 1.4% Black/African American, 1.7% Asian, 0.0% American Indian/Alaska Native, 0.2% Native Hawaiian/Other Pacific Islander, 7.3% Two or more races, 7.4% Hispanic of any race; Average household size: 2.23; Median age: 47.6; Age under 18: 16.5%; Age 65 and over: 8.7%; Males per 100 females: 113.8

School District(s)

La Honda-Pescadero Unified (KG-12)
2012-13 Enrollment: 343. . . . . (650) 879-0286
San Mateo County Office of Education (KG-12)
2012-13 Enrollment: 441. . . . . (650) 802-5550
Housing: Homeownership rate: 71.3%; Homeowner vacancy rate: 2.3%; Rental vacancy rate: 3.3%

LADERA (CDP). Covers a land area of 0.443 square miles and a water area of 0 square miles. Located at 37.40° N. Lat; 122.20° W. Long. Elevation is 305 feet.
Population: 1,426; Growth (since 2000): n/a; Density: 3,221.9 persons per square mile; Race: 89.0% White, 0.2% Black/African American, 6.9% Asian, 0.1% American Indian/Alaska Native, 0.0% Native Hawaiian/Other Pacific Islander, 3.5% Two or more races, 2.3% Hispanic of any race; Average household size: 2.72; Median age: 46.0; Age under 18: 28.4%; Age 65 and over: 20.5%; Males per 100 females: 94.5
Housing: Homeownership rate: 91.7%; Homeowner vacancy rate: 0.2%; Rental vacancy rate: 2.2%

LOMA MAR (CDP). Covers a land area of 1.735 square miles and a water area of 0 square miles. Located at 37.27° N. Lat; 122.30° W. Long. Elevation is 243 feet.
Population: 113; Growth (since 2000): n/a; Density: 65.1 persons per square mile; Race: 89.4% White, 1.8% Black/African American, 2.7% Asian, 0.0% American Indian/Alaska Native, 0.0% Native Hawaiian/Other Pacific Islander, 6.2% Two or more races, 10.6% Hispanic of any race; Average household size: 2.09; Median age: 44.8; Age under 18: 19.5%; Age 65 and over: 8.0%; Males per 100 females: 117.3
Housing: Homeownership rate: 57.4%; Homeowner vacancy rate: 0.0%; Rental vacancy rate: 0.0%

MENLO PARK (city). Covers a land area of 9.790 square miles and a water area of 7.625 square miles. Located at 37.48° N. Lat; 122.15° W. Long. Elevation is 72 feet.
History: Named for Menlough in County Galway, Ireland, former home of two ranchers. Menlo Park developed with the advent of the railroad in 1863 around the estate of the two Irishmen. In 1871 Milton S. Latham, governor and U.S. Senator, built a mansion here.
Population: 32,026; Growth (since 2000): 4.0%; Density: 3,271.4 persons per square mile; Race: 70.2% White, 4.8% Black/African American, 9.9% Asian, 0.5% American Indian/Alaska Native, 1.4% Native Hawaiian/Other Pacific Islander, 4.5% Two or more races, 18.4% Hispanic of any race; Average household size: 2.53; Median age: 38.7; Age under 18: 24.4%; Age 65 and over: 14.3%; Males per 100 females: 93.7; Marriage status: 30.7% never married, 53.9% now married, 1.4% separated, 4.6% widowed, 10.7% divorced; Foreign born: 23.7%; Speak English only: 69.6%; With disability: 6.3%; Veterans: 6.2%; Ancestry: 12.9% English, 12.7% German, 10.3% Irish, 7.2% Italian, 3.1% Scottish
Employment: 26.1% management, business, and financial, 14.9% computer, engineering, and science, 17.6% education, legal, community service, arts, and media, 7.0% healthcare practitioners, 11.8% service, 16.1% sales and office, 2.5% natural resources, construction, and maintenance, 4.0% production, transportation, and material moving
Income: Per capita: $67,898; Median household: $112,262; Average household: $173,663; Households with income of $100,000 or more: 56.1%; Poverty rate: 6.1%
Educational Attainment: High school diploma or higher: 92.8%; Bachelor's degree or higher: 70.4%; Graduate/professional degree or higher: 39.8%

School District(s)

Las Lomitas Elementary (KG-08)
2012-13 Enrollment: 1,419 . . . . (650) 854-2880
Menlo Park City Elementary (KG-08)
2012-13 Enrollment: 2,799 . . . . (650) 321-7140
Ravenswood City Elementary (KG-12)
2012-13 Enrollment: 4,077 . . . . (650) 329-2800
Redwood City Elementary (KG-08)
2012-13 Enrollment: 9,210 . . . . (650) 423-2200

Four-year College(s)

Saint Patrick's Seminary and University (Private, Not-for-profit, Roman Catholic)
Fall 2013 Enrollment: 92 . . . . (650) 325-5621
Housing: Homeownership rate: 56.1%; Median home value: 1 million+; Median year structure built: 1959; Homeowner vacancy rate: 1.1%; Median gross rent: $1,800 per month; Rental vacancy rate: 5.2%
Health Insurance: 93.4% have insurance; 83.5% have private insurance; 19.2% have public insurance; 6.6% do not have insurance; 2.8% of children under 18 do not have insurance
Hospitals: Menlo Park Surgical Hospital (16 beds)
Safety: Violent crime rate: 16.0 per 10,000 population; Property crime rate: 194.3 per 10,000 population
Newspapers: Palo Alto Daily News (daily circulation 30000)
Transportation: Commute: 77.0% car, 4.3% public transportation, 2.7% walk, 8.7% work from home; Median travel time to work: 22.1 minutes
Additional Information Contacts
City of Menlo Park . . . . (650) 330-6620
http://www.ci.menlo-park.ca.us

MILLBRAE (city). Covers a land area of 3.247 square miles and a water area of 0.012 square miles. Located at 37.60° N. Lat; 122.40° W. Long. Elevation is 33 feet.

History: Named for Darius Ogden Mills, a San Francisco banker and promoter. Millbrae was established on the former estate of Mills who built a house here in 1866. Mills had a herd of dairy cattle, a dairy, and a glass-domed conservatory, all built with the fortune he made from supplying miners with grubstakes, which lead to the founding of the Bank of California.

Population: 21,532; Growth (since 2000): 3.9%; Density: 6,632.1 persons per square mile; Race: 47.3% White, 0.8% Black/African American, 42.8% Asian, 0.2% American Indian/Alaska Native, 1.0% Native Hawaiian/Other Pacific Islander, 4.4% Two or more races, 11.9% Hispanic of any race; Average household size: 2.65; Median age: 44.8; Age under 18: 20.1%; Age 65 and over: 19.7%; Males per 100 females: 90.0; Marriage status: 26.7% never married, 55.4% now married, 1.3% separated, 9.1% widowed, 8.8% divorced; Foreign born: 38.0%; Speak English only: 49.5%; With disability: 8.8%; Veterans: 6.9%; Ancestry: 9.5% Italian, 8.7% Irish, 7.6% German, 4.4% English, 2.6% American

Employment: 20.9% management, business, and financial, 6.6% computer, engineering, and science, 8.7% education, legal, community service, arts, and media, 7.7% healthcare practitioners, 14.2% service, 26.2% sales and office, 8.7% natural resources, construction, and maintenance, 6.9% production, transportation, and material moving

Income: Per capita: $42,042; Median household: $88,451; Average household: $111,261; Households with income of $100,000 or more: 43.0%; Poverty rate: 5.7%

Educational Attainment: High school diploma or higher: 91.6%; Bachelor's degree or higher: 41.1%; Graduate/professional degree or higher: 14.6%

School District(s)

Millbrae Elementary (KG-08)
2012-13 Enrollment: 2,374 . . . . (650) 697-5693

San Mateo Union High (09-12)
2012-13 Enrollment: 8,244 . . . . (650) 558-2299

Housing: Homeownership rate: 63.5%; Median home value: $901,700; Median year structure built: 1961; Homeowner vacancy rate: 0.7%; Median gross rent: $1,724 per month; Rental vacancy rate: 4.8%

Health Insurance: 90.7% have insurance; 81.1% have private insurance; 25.1% have public insurance; 9.3% do not have insurance; 4.9% of children under 18 do not have insurance

Transportation: Commute: 81.8% car, 9.3% public transportation, 2.4% walk, 4.1% work from home; Median travel time to work: 27.5 minutes

Additional Information Contacts

City of Millbrae. . . . . (650) 259-2334
http://www.ci.millbrae.ca.us

MONTARA (CDP). Covers a land area of 3.878 square miles and a water area of 0 square miles. Located at 37.55° N. Lat; 122.49° W. Long. Elevation is 102 feet.

History: Nearby Montara Point has lighthouse and radio compass station.

Population: 2,909; Growth (since 2000): -1.4%; Density: 750.1 persons per square mile; Race: 85.6% White, 0.6% Black/African American, 4.9% Asian, 0.7% American Indian/Alaska Native, 0.0% Native Hawaiian/Other Pacific Islander, 4.8% Two or more races, 11.1% Hispanic of any race; Average household size: 2.62; Median age: 46.0; Age under 18: 21.2%; Age 65 and over: 12.2%; Males per 100 females: 92.5; Marriage status: 26.4% never married, 57.1% now married, 0.6% separated, 4.5% widowed, 11.9% divorced; Foreign born: 11.8%; Speak English only: 89.6%; With disability: 5.6%; Veterans: 7.9%; Ancestry: 23.9% German, 21.9% Irish, 20.8% European, 17.5% English, 9.3% Italian

Employment: 23.2% management, business, and financial, 9.3% computer, engineering, and science, 17.8% education, legal, community service, arts, and media, 5.9% healthcare practitioners, 9.8% service, 16.0% sales and office, 10.0% natural resources, construction, and maintenance, 8.1% production, transportation, and material moving

Income: Per capita: $47,892; Median household: $150,071; Average household: $150,289; Households with income of $100,000 or more: 72.3%; Poverty rate: 0.1%

Educational Attainment: High school diploma or higher: 95.8%; Bachelor's degree or higher: 58.7%; Graduate/professional degree or higher: 21.6%

School District(s)

Cabrillo Unified (KG-12)
2012-13 Enrollment: 3,324 . . . . (650) 712-7100

Housing: Homeownership rate: 81.0%; Median home value: $743,000; Median year structure built: 1968; Homeowner vacancy rate: 0.9%; Median gross rent: $1,973 per month; Rental vacancy rate: 5.3%

Health Insurance: 99.2% have insurance; 91.0% have private insurance; 18.0% have public insurance; 0.8% do not have insurance; 1.5% of children under 18 do not have insurance

Transportation: Commute: 69.8% car, 2.5% public transportation, 4.7% walk, 20.0% work from home; Median travel time to work: 27.5 minutes

MOSS BEACH (CDP). Covers a land area of 2.254 square miles and a water area of 0 square miles. Located at 37.52° N. Lat; 122.50° W. Long. Elevation is 66 feet.

Population: 3,103; Growth (since 2000): 58.9%; Density: 1,377.0 persons per square mile; Race: 73.5% White, 0.8% Black/African American, 3.8% Asian, 1.4% American Indian/Alaska Native, 0.3% Native Hawaiian/Other Pacific Islander, 4.3% Two or more races, 29.1% Hispanic of any race; Average household size: 2.81; Median age: 43.2; Age under 18: 22.9%; Age 65 and over: 11.7%; Males per 100 females: 99.9; Marriage status: 21.3% never married, 64.1% now married, 5.9% separated, 6.6% widowed, 8.1% divorced; Foreign born: 10.0%; Speak English only: 78.3%; With disability: 6.0%; Veterans: 10.9%; Ancestry: 15.6% European, 15.4% German, 14.2% Irish, 12.2% English, 9.5% Italian

Employment: 32.7% management, business, and financial, 3.9% computer, engineering, and science, 14.7% education, legal, community service, arts, and media, 5.8% healthcare practitioners, 14.1% service, 9.6% sales and office, 5.3% natural resources, construction, and maintenance, 13.9% production, transportation, and material moving

Income: Per capita: $50,898; Median household: $106,429; Average household: $129,951; Households with income of $100,000 or more: 50.4%; Poverty rate: 9.2%

Educational Attainment: High school diploma or higher: 88.5%; Bachelor's degree or higher: 42.4%; Graduate/professional degree or higher: 17.6%

Housing: Homeownership rate: 81.8%; Median home value: $680,300; Median year structure built: 1975; Homeowner vacancy rate: 1.2%; Median gross rent: $2,000+ per month; Rental vacancy rate: 6.3%

Health Insurance: 93.3% have insurance; 83.2% have private insurance; 23.8% have public insurance; 6.7% do not have insurance; 2.8% of children under 18 do not have insurance

Transportation: Commute: 69.6% car, 14.3% public transportation, 0.0% walk, 16.1% work from home; Median travel time to work: 31.0 minutes

NORTH FAIR OAKS (CDP). Covers a land area of 1.200 square miles and a water area of 0 square miles. Located at 37.48° N. Lat; 122.20° W. Long. Elevation is 26 feet.

Population: 14,687; Growth (since 2000): -4.9%; Density: 12,236.5 persons per square mile; Race: 48.1% White, 1.6% Black/African American, 3.7% Asian, 1.0% American Indian/Alaska Native, 1.5% Native Hawaiian/Other Pacific Islander, 5.1% Two or more races, 73.1% Hispanic of any race; Average household size: 3.67; Median age: 31.0; Age under 18: 27.7%; Age 65 and over: 6.6%; Males per 100 females: 113.0; Marriage status: 45.6% never married, 41.2% now married, 3.0% separated, 3.4% widowed, 9.8% divorced; Foreign born: 53.9%; Speak English only: 27.3%; With disability: 7.0%; Veterans: 3.0%; Ancestry: 4.2% English, 4.2% German, 3.4% Irish, 2.7% Italian, 1.8% European

Employment: 9.4% management, business, and financial, 3.6% computer, engineering, and science, 6.4% education, legal, community service, arts, and media, 2.2% healthcare practitioners, 31.6% service, 19.8% sales and office, 14.4% natural resources, construction, and maintenance, 12.7% production, transportation, and material moving

Income: Per capita: $24,560; Median household: $60,459; Average household: $84,537; Households with income of $100,000 or more: 30.8%; Poverty rate: 25.1%

Educational Attainment: High school diploma or higher: 60.3%; Bachelor's degree or higher: 21.6%; Graduate/professional degree or higher: 10.7%

Housing: Homeownership rate: 46.9%; Median home value: $538,600; Median year structure built: 1958; Homeowner vacancy rate: 1.0%; Median gross rent: $1,313 per month; Rental vacancy rate: 5.1%

Health Insurance: 76.1% have insurance; 45.1% have private insurance; 37.8% have public insurance; 23.9% do not have insurance; 4.3% of children under 18 do not have insurance

Transportation: Commute: 79.2% car, 8.3% public transportation, 5.1% walk, 3.6% work from home; Median travel time to work: 23.4 minutes

PACIFICA (city). Covers a land area of 12.658 square miles and a water area of 0.002 square miles. Located at 37.61° N. Lat; 122.48° W. Long. Elevation is 82 feet.

History: Named for its location on the Pacific Ocean, in 1957 by vote of the inhabitants. Formed by the consolidation of several communities in 1957. City sits almost directly astride San Andreas Fault. Incorporated 1957.

Population: 37,234; Growth (since 2000): -3.0%; Density: 2,941.5 persons per square mile; Race: 64.9% White, 2.6% Black/African American, 19.4% Asian, 0.6% American Indian/Alaska Native, 0.8% Native Hawaiian/Other Pacific Islander, 7.1% Two or more races, 16.8% Hispanic of any race; Average household size: 2.65; Median age: 41.5; Age under 18: 20.7%; Age 65 and over: 12.1%; Males per 100 females: 95.6; Marriage status: 31.8% never married, 52.3% now married, 1.4% separated, 4.9% widowed, 11.0% divorced; Foreign born: 20.6%; Speak English only: 72.1%; With disability: 7.7%; Veterans: 6.8%; Ancestry: 13.9% Irish, 11.2% German, 8.6% Italian, 8.3% English, 2.8% European

Employment: 18.6% management, business, and financial, 7.9% computer, engineering, and science, 12.2% education, legal, community service, arts, and media, 7.3% healthcare practitioners, 16.1% service, 24.0% sales and office, 7.1% natural resources, construction, and maintenance, 6.7% production, transportation, and material moving

Income: Per capita: $43,953; Median household: $94,707; Average household: $114,991; Households with income of $100,000 or more: 47.4%; Poverty rate: 4.8%

Educational Attainment: High school diploma or higher: 94.6%; Bachelor's degree or higher: 40.1%; Graduate/professional degree or higher: 13.4%

School District(s)

Jefferson Union High (09-12)
2012-13 Enrollment: 4,870 . . . . (650) 550-7900
Pacifica (KG-08)
2012-13 Enrollment: 3,234 . . . . (650) 738-6600

Housing: Homeownership rate: 68.3%; Median home value: $610,000; Median year structure built: 1965; Homeowner vacancy rate: 0.9%; Median gross rent: $1,739 per month; Rental vacancy rate: 4.8%

Health Insurance: 92.4% have insurance; 85.6% have private insurance; 18.0% have public insurance; 7.6% do not have insurance; 5.4% of children under 18 do not have insurance

Safety: Violent crime rate: 17.1 per 10,000 population; Property crime rate: 141.8 per 10,000 population

Newspapers: Pacifica Tribune (weekly circulation 7000)

Transportation: Commute: 83.9% car, 7.0% public transportation, 0.9% walk, 6.7% work from home; Median travel time to work: 27.7 minutes

Additional Information Contacts

City of Pacifica. . . . . (650) 738-7300
http://www.cityofpacifica.org

PESCADERO (CDP). Covers a land area of 4.026 square miles and a water area of 0.009 square miles. Located at 37.24° N. Lat; 122.38° W. Long. Elevation is 39 feet.

Population: 643; Growth (since 2000): n/a; Density: 159.7 persons per square mile; Race: 48.8% White, 0.3% Black/African American, 0.8% Asian, 0.3% American Indian/Alaska Native, 0.2% Native Hawaiian/Other Pacific Islander, 3.9% Two or more races, 62.5% Hispanic of any race; Average household size: 3.20; Median age: 33.5; Age under 18: 27.8%; Age 65 and over: 12.3%; Males per 100 females: 110.1

School District(s)

La Honda-Pescadero Unified (KG-12)
2012-13 Enrollment: 343. . . . . (650) 879-0286

Housing: Homeownership rate: 44.1%; Homeowner vacancy rate: 2.3%; Rental vacancy rate: 4.4%

PORTOLA VALLEY (town). Covers a land area of 9.092 square miles and a water area of 0.001 square miles. Located at 37.37° N. Lat; 122.22° W. Long. Elevation is 459 feet.

History: Incorporated in 1964, it was named for Spanish explorer Gaspar de Portola, who led the first party of Europeans to explore the San Francisco Peninsula, in 1769.

Population: 4,353; Growth (since 2000): -2.4%; Density: 478.8 persons per square mile; Race: 91.0% White, 0.3% Black/African American, 5.6% Asian, 0.1% American Indian/Alaska Native, 0.0% Native Hawaiian/Other Pacific Islander, 2.4% Two or more races, 4.0% Hispanic of any race; Average household size: 2.47; Median age: 51.3; Age under 18: 23.0%; Age 65 and over: 26.9%; Males per 100 females: 98.4; Marriage status: 17.7% never married, 68.0% now married, 0.5% separated, 5.8% widowed, 8.5% divorced; Foreign born: 11.1%; Speak English only: 87.8%; With disability: 9.8%; Veterans: 13.8%; Ancestry: 20.5% German, 19.7% English, 15.6% Irish, 6.6% European, 5.9% American

Employment: 34.6% management, business, and financial, 18.5% computer, engineering, and science, 15.7% education, legal, community service, arts, and media, 6.8% healthcare practitioners, 6.0% service, 13.3% sales and office, 2.9% natural resources, construction, and maintenance, 2.2% production, transportation, and material moving

Income: Per capita: $143,529; Median household: $163,384; Average household: $347,278; Households with income of $100,000 or more: 65.5%; Poverty rate: 2.8%

Educational Attainment: High school diploma or higher: 95.6%; Bachelor's degree or higher: 80.5%; Graduate/professional degree or higher: 44.5%

School District(s)

Portola Valley Elementary (KG-08)
2012-13 Enrollment: 671. . . . . (650) 851-1777

Housing: Homeownership rate: 79.8%; Median home value: 1 million+; Median year structure built: 1966; Homeowner vacancy rate: 1.0%; Median gross rent: $2,000+ per month; Rental vacancy rate: 9.8%

Health Insurance: 94.7% have insurance; 88.9% have private insurance; 31.8% have public insurance; 5.3% do not have insurance; 6.1% of children under 18 do not have insurance

Transportation: Commute: 76.5% car, 2.8% public transportation, 0.2% walk, 17.1% work from home; Median travel time to work: 29.6 minutes

Additional Information Contacts

Town of Portola Valley . . . . (650) 851-1701
http://www.portolavalley.net

REDWOOD CITY (city). County seat. Covers a land area of 19.420 square miles and a water area of 15.205 square miles. Located at 37.52° N. Lat; 122.21° W. Long. Elevation is 20 feet.

History: Named for the commercial use of the redwood trees in the area. Mexican rancheros began in 1850 to ship redwood lumber from the Embarcadero de las Pulgas on Redwood Creek, and the community became a busy shipbuilding, wagonmaking, and blacksmithing center. The town was renamed Redwood City in 1858.

Population: 76,815; Growth (since 2000): 1.9%; Density: 3,955.5 persons per square mile; Race: 60.2% White, 2.4% Black/African American, 10.7% Asian, 0.7% American Indian/Alaska Native, 1.0% Native Hawaiian/Other Pacific Islander, 5.5% Two or more races, 38.8% Hispanic of any race; Average household size: 2.69; Median age: 36.7; Age under 18: 23.7%; Age 65 and over: 10.6%; Males per 100 females: 99.2; Marriage status: 32.7% never married, 51.0% now married, 1.7% separated, 4.8% widowed, 11.5% divorced; Foreign born: 31.5%; Speak English only: 54.5%; With disability: 7.6%; Veterans: 5.6%; Ancestry: 9.2% German, 8.4% Irish, 7.5% Italian, 5.6% English, 2.6% French

Employment: 17.8% management, business, and financial, 10.4% computer, engineering, and science, 9.9% education, legal, community service, arts, and media, 4.4% healthcare practitioners, 19.7% service, 22.4% sales and office, 8.1% natural resources, construction, and maintenance, 7.4% production, transportation, and material moving

Income: Per capita: $40,562; Median household: $79,419; Average household: $110,750; Households with income of $100,000 or more: 40.9%; Poverty rate: 9.0%

Educational Attainment: High school diploma or higher: 84.3%; Bachelor's degree or higher: 40.2%; Graduate/professional degree or higher: 16.2%

School District(s)

Belmont-Redwood Shores Elementary (KG-08)
2012-13 Enrollment: 3,607 . . . . (650) 637-4800
Redwood City Elementary (KG-08)
2012-13 Enrollment: 9,210 . . . . (650) 423-2200
San Mateo County Office of Education (KG-12)
2012-13 Enrollment: 441. . . . . (650) 802-5550
Sbe - Everest Public High (09-12)
2012-13 Enrollment: 383. . . . . (650) 366-1050
Sequoia Union High (09-12)
2012-13 Enrollment: 9,247 . . . . (650) 369-1411

Two-year College(s)

Canada College (Public)
Fall 2013 Enrollment: 6,620 . . . . (650) 306-3100
2013-14 Tuition: In-state $1,344; Out-of-state $8,420

Housing: Homeownership rate: 50.6%; Median home value: $765,400; Median year structure built: 1963; Homeowner vacancy rate: 1.3%; Median gross rent: $1,486 per month; Rental vacancy rate: 3.9%

Health Insurance: 85.4% have insurance; 67.9% have private insurance; 26.5% have public insurance; 14.6% do not have insurance; 5.3% of children under 18 do not have insurance

Hospitals: Kaiser Foundation Hospital - Redwood City (171 beds); Sequoia Hospital

Safety: Violent crime rate: 23.8 per 10,000 population; Property crime rate: 234.7 per 10,000 population

Transportation: Commute: 84.2% car, 4.5% public transportation, 3.0% walk, 5.4% work from home; Median travel time to work: 23.2 minutes

Additional Information Contacts

City of Redwood . . . . (650) 780-7220
http://www.redwoodcity.org

SAN BRUNO (city). Covers a land area of 5.478 square miles and a water area of 0 square miles. Located at 37.63° N. Lat; 122.43° W. Long. Elevation is 20 feet.

History: Named for St. Bruno, a German saint of the 11th century, founder of the Carthusian Order. San Bruno began as a roadhouse where travelers on the stagecoach from San Francisco changed horses. The community developed around vegetable and poultry farms.

Population: 41,114; Growth (since 2000): 2.4%; Density: 7,505.0 persons per square mile; Race: 49.5% White, 2.3% Black/African American, 25.4% Asian, 0.6% American Indian/Alaska Native, 3.3% Native Hawaiian/Other Pacific Islander, 6.6% Two or more races, 29.2% Hispanic of any race; Average household size: 2.77; Median age: 38.8; Age under 18: 21.0%; Age 65 and over: 12.7%; Males per 100 females: 97.1; Marriage status: 35.2% never married, 49.7% now married, 2.0% separated, 6.1% widowed, 8.9% divorced; Foreign born: 35.1%; Speak English only: 50.1%; With disability: 8.4%; Veterans: 4.9%; Ancestry: 9.9% Irish, 9.7% Italian, 5.9% German, 3.8% English, 2.0% Russian

Employment: 15.5% management, business, and financial, 7.6% computer, engineering, and science, 9.7% education, legal, community service, arts, and media, 4.7% healthcare practitioners, 17.8% service, 26.3% sales and office, 9.0% natural resources, construction, and maintenance, 9.5% production, transportation, and material moving

Income: Per capita: $35,371; Median household: $78,911; Average household: $95,721; Households with income of $100,000 or more: 37.5%; Poverty rate: 6.6%

Educational Attainment: High school diploma or higher: 90.3%; Bachelor's degree or higher: 35.0%; Graduate/professional degree or higher: 9.5%

School District(s)

Millbrae Elementary (KG-08)
2012-13 Enrollment: 2,374 . . . . (650) 697-5693
San Bruno Park Elementary (KG-08)
2012-13 Enrollment: 2,686 . . . . (650) 624-3100
San Francisco Unified (KG-12)
2012-13 Enrollment: 56,970 . . . . (415) 241-6000
San Mateo Union High (09-12)
2012-13 Enrollment: 8,244 . . . . (650) 558-2299
South San Francisco Unified (KG-12)
2012-13 Enrollment: 9,265 . . . . (650) 877-8700

Two-year College(s)

Skyline College (Public)
Fall 2013 Enrollment: 10,067 . . . . (650) 738-4100
2013-14 Tuition: In-state $1,447; Out-of-state $1,447

Housing: Homeownership rate: 60.8%; Median home value: $597,900; Median year structure built: 1961; Homeowner vacancy rate: 1.1%; Median gross rent: $1,643 per month; Rental vacancy rate: 3.9%

Health Insurance: 89.3% have insurance; 77.8% have private insurance; 21.4% have public insurance; 10.7% do not have insurance; 7.1% of children under 18 do not have insurance

Safety: Violent crime rate: 24.0 per 10,000 population; Property crime rate: 235.8 per 10,000 population

Transportation: Commute: 83.0% car, 11.3% public transportation, 1.1% walk, 3.2% work from home; Median travel time to work: 25.4 minutes

Additional Information Contacts

City of San Bruno . . . . (650) 616-7056
http://sanbruno.ca.gov

SAN CARLOS (city). Covers a land area of 5.538 square miles and a water area of 0.003 square miles. Located at 37.50° N. Lat; 122.27° W. Long. Elevation is 30 feet.

History: San Carlos was named for Lieutenant Juan Manuel de Ayala's ship the San Carlos, first vessel to enter the Golden Gate. This was the site of Rancho Las Pulgas (Land of the Fleas).

Population: 28,406; Growth (since 2000): 2.5%; Density: 5,129.3 persons per square mile; Race: 79.2% White, 0.8% Black/African American, 11.5% Asian, 0.2% American Indian/Alaska Native, 0.2% Native Hawaiian/Other Pacific Islander, 5.1% Two or more races, 10.1% Hispanic of any race; Average household size: 2.46; Median age: 42.6; Age under 18: 23.6%; Age 65 and over: 14.2%; Males per 100 females: 93.6; Marriage status: 24.1% never married, 61.2% now married, 1.4% separated, 5.2% widowed, 9.5% divorced; Foreign born: 19.2%; Speak English only: 78.3%; With disability: 6.0%; Veterans: 7.2%; Ancestry: 16.0% German, 14.0% English, 13.9% Irish, 10.4% Italian, 4.5% European

Employment: 26.1% management, business, and financial, 11.8% computer, engineering, and science, 15.1% education, legal, community service, arts, and media, 6.6% healthcare practitioners, 8.3% service, 24.3% sales and office, 4.3% natural resources, construction, and maintenance, 3.6% production, transportation, and material moving

Income: Per capita: $59,677; Median household: $118,021; Average household: $150,820; Households with income of $100,000 or more: 54.9%; Poverty rate: 4.4%

Educational Attainment: High school diploma or higher: 96.6%; Bachelor's degree or higher: 60.0%; Graduate/professional degree or higher: 27.3%

School District(s)

San Carlos Elementary (KG-08)
2012-13 Enrollment: 3,333 . . . . (650) 508-7333

Housing: Homeownership rate: 71.8%; Median home value: $918,800; Median year structure built: 1958; Homeowner vacancy rate: 1.4%; Median gross rent: $1,538 per month; Rental vacancy rate: 5.3%

Health Insurance: 93.7% have insurance; 86.0% have private insurance; 19.2% have public insurance; 6.3% do not have insurance; 4.1% of children under 18 do not have insurance

Transportation: Commute: 85.7% car, 4.7% public transportation, 1.3% walk, 6.5% work from home; Median travel time to work: 26.3 minutes

Additional Information Contacts

City of San Carlos . . . . (650) 802-4219
http://www.cityofsancarlos.org

SAN GREGORIO (unincorporated postal area)

ZCTA: 94074

Covers a land area of 18.541 square miles and a water area of 0.025 square miles. Located at 37.33° N. Lat; 122.34° W. Long. Elevation is 66 feet.

Population: 214; Growth (since 2000): -25.4%; Density: 11.5 persons per square mile; Race: 87.9% White, 0.5% Black/African American, 5.6% Asian, 0.5% American Indian/Alaska Native, 0.0% Native Hawaiian/Other Pacific Islander, 1.9% Two or more races, 9.3% Hispanic of any race; Average household size: 2.64; Median age: 43.0; Age under 18: 17.3%; Age 65 and over: 12.1%; Males per 100 females: 130.1

Housing: Homeownership rate: 61.7%; Homeowner vacancy rate: 0.0%; Rental vacancy rate: 3.1%

SAN MATEO (city). Covers a land area of 12.130 square miles and a water area of 3.754 square miles. Located at 37.56° N. Lat; 122.31° W. Long. Elevation is 46 feet.

History: Named by Spanish explorers for the apostle St. Matthew. San Mateo was founded on Cayetano Arenas' Rancho San Mateo. John B. Cooper, a deserter from the British Navy, took up residence here in 1851 in a hut made of brush. The town was platted in 1863.

Population: 97,207; Growth (since 2000): 5.1%; Density: 8,014.0 persons per square mile; Race: 57.8% White, 2.4% Black/African American, 18.9% Asian, 0.5% American Indian/Alaska Native, 2.1% Native Hawaiian/Other Pacific Islander, 5.7% Two or more races, 26.6% Hispanic of any race; Average household size: 2.51; Median age: 38.9; Age under 18: 20.8%; Age 65 and over: 14.4%; Males per 100 females: 95.4; Marriage status: 31.9% never married, 51.4% now married, 1.8% separated, 5.7% widowed, 11.0% divorced; Foreign born: 32.9%; Speak English only: 55.8%; With disability: 9.0%; Veterans: 5.8%; Ancestry: 9.0% German, 8.6% Irish, 8.5% Italian, 6.1% English, 2.2% American

Employment: 19.2% management, business, and financial, 9.7% computer, engineering, and science, 10.5% education, legal, community

service, arts, and media, 4.5% healthcare practitioners, 20.2% service, 23.1% sales and office, 6.3% natural resources, construction, and maintenance, 6.5% production, transportation, and material moving
Income: Per capita: $45,202; Median household: $85,669; Average household: $114,444; Households with income of $100,000 or more: 42.5%; Poverty rate: 7.1%
Educational Attainment: High school diploma or higher: 88.4%; Bachelor's degree or higher: 44.4%; Graduate/professional degree or higher: 17.5%

School District(s)

San Mateo County Office of Education (KG-12)
2012-13 Enrollment: 441 . . . . (650) 802-5550
San Mateo Union High (09-12)
2012-13 Enrollment: 8,244 . . . . (650) 558-2299
San Mateo-Foster City (KG-08)
2012-13 Enrollment: 11,456 . . . . (650) 312-7700

Two-year College(s)

College of San Mateo (Public)
Fall 2013 Enrollment: 9,377 . . . . (650) 574-6161
2013-14 Tuition: In-state $1,418; Out-of-state $6,150
Gurnick Academy of Medical Arts (Private, For-profit)
Fall 2013 Enrollment: 843 . . . . (650) 685-6616

Housing: Homeownership rate: 52.3%; Median home value: $710,700; Median year structure built: 1960; Homeowner vacancy rate: 1.5%; Median gross rent: $1,660 per month; Rental vacancy rate: 3.7%
Health Insurance: 88.3% have insurance; 75.2% have private insurance; 24.4% have public insurance; 11.7% do not have insurance; 3.6% of children under 18 do not have insurance
Hospitals: San Mateo Medical Center (509 beds)
Safety: Violent crime rate: 23.8 per 10,000 population; Property crime rate: 205.6 per 10,000 population
Newspapers: San Mateo County Times (daily circulation 29400); San Mateo Daily Journal (daily circulation 14800)
Transportation: Commute: 82.1% car, 7.6% public transportation, 3.5% walk, 4.2% work from home; Median travel time to work: 24.9 minutes
Additional Information Contacts
City of San Mateo . . . . (650) 522-7000
http://www.cityofsanmateo.org

SOUTH SAN FRANCISCO (city). Covers a land area of 9.141 square miles and a water area of 21.017 square miles. Located at 37.66° N. Lat; 122.38° W. Long. Elevation is 16 feet.
History: Named for its location south of San Francisco. South San Francisco developed as an industrial city of steel mills, foundries, smelters and refineries on the southern outskirts of San Francisco.
Population: 63,632; Growth (since 2000): 5.1%; Density: 6,961.4 persons per square mile; Race: 37.3% White, 2.6% Black/African American, 36.6% Asian, 0.6% American Indian/Alaska Native, 1.7% Native Hawaiian/Other Pacific Islander, 6.1% Two or more races, 34.0% Hispanic of any race; Average household size: 3.01; Median age: 38.1; Age under 18: 21.7%; Age 65 and over: 13.1%; Males per 100 females: 97.6; Marriage status: 31.3% never married, 54.7% now married, 1.9% separated, 6.2% widowed, 7.7% divorced; Foreign born: 42.0%; Speak English only: 40.4%; With disability: 9.2%; Veterans: 5.3%; Ancestry: 5.7% Italian, 4.8% Irish, 3.6% German, 2.7% English, 1.1% American
Employment: 15.6% management, business, and financial, 6.6% computer, engineering, and science, 7.4% education, legal, community service, arts, and media, 5.7% healthcare practitioners, 19.6% service, 26.0% sales and office, 7.0% natural resources, construction, and maintenance, 12.1% production, transportation, and material moving
Income: Per capita: $31,459; Median household: $76,785; Average household: $92,977; Households with income of $100,000 or more: 36.7%; Poverty rate: 7.1%
Educational Attainment: High school diploma or higher: 84.7%; Bachelor's degree or higher: 29.8%; Graduate/professional degree or higher: 7.8%

School District(s)

San Mateo County Office of Education (KG-12)
2012-13 Enrollment: 441 . . . . (650) 802-5550
South San Francisco Unified (KG-12)
2012-13 Enrollment: 9,265 . . . . (650) 877-8700

Vocational/Technical School(s)

NCP College of Nursing-South San Francisco (Private, For-profit)
Fall 2013 Enrollment: 73 . . . . (650) 871-0701

Housing: Homeownership rate: 60.2%; Median home value: $585,000; Median year structure built: 1964; Homeowner vacancy rate: 1.3%; Median gross rent: $1,477 per month; Rental vacancy rate: 4.0%
Health Insurance: 89.8% have insurance; 75.3% have private insurance; 24.4% have public insurance; 10.2% do not have insurance; 5.1% of children under 18 do not have insurance
Hospitals: Kaiser Foundation Hospital - South San Francisco (127 beds)
Safety: Violent crime rate: 17.8 per 10,000 population; Property crime rate: 179.6 per 10,000 population
Transportation: Commute: 82.0% car, 10.2% public transportation, 3.8% walk, 2.5% work from home; Median travel time to work: 23.8 minutes
Additional Information Contacts
City of South San Francisco . . . . (650) 877-8500
http://www.ssf.net

WEST MENLO PARK (CDP). Covers a land area of 0.486 square miles and a water area of 0 square miles. Located at 37.43° N. Lat; 122.20° W. Long. Elevation is 115 feet.
History: The name Menlo comes from the 1850s when two Irish immigrants erected a gate with a wooden arch bearing the inscription "Menlo Park" at the entrance to their property. The word "Menlo" derived from the owners' former home of Menlough in County Galway, Ireland.
Population: 3,659; Growth (since 2000): 0.8%; Density: 7,526.9 persons per square mile; Race: 81.5% White, 0.8% Black/African American, 11.4% Asian, 0.1% American Indian/Alaska Native, 0.1% Native Hawaiian/Other Pacific Islander, 4.8% Two or more races, 5.5% Hispanic of any race; Average household size: 2.69; Median age: 40.4; Age under 18: 29.2%; Age 65 and over: 13.3%; Males per 100 females: 95.7; Marriage status: 26.4% never married, 60.8% now married, 1.5% separated, 3.4% widowed, 9.4% divorced; Foreign born: 17.7%; Speak English only: 79.8%; With disability: 7.0%; Veterans: 6.9%; Ancestry: 16.1% English, 15.2% German, 9.2% Irish, 7.5% European, 6.4% Italian
Employment: 28.1% management, business, and financial, 18.3% computer, engineering, and science, 17.5% education, legal, community service, arts, and media, 6.6% healthcare practitioners, 6.2% service, 20.8% sales and office, 0.5% natural resources, construction, and maintenance, 2.1% production, transportation, and material moving
Income: Per capita: $84,467; Median household: $164,432; Average household: $235,441; Households with income of $100,000 or more: 71.2%; Poverty rate: 3.3%
Educational Attainment: High school diploma or higher: 98.0%; Bachelor's degree or higher: 77.1%; Graduate/professional degree or higher: 44.0%
Housing: Homeownership rate: 80.5%; Median home value: 1 million+; Median year structure built: 1957; Homeowner vacancy rate: 0.9%; Median gross rent: $2,000+ per month; Rental vacancy rate: 5.3%
Health Insurance: 97.8% have insurance; 94.0% have private insurance; 14.9% have public insurance; 2.2% do not have insurance; 0.0% of children under 18 do not have insurance
Transportation: Commute: 81.8% car, 2.5% public transportation, 1.0% walk, 10.5% work from home; Median travel time to work: 24.6 minutes

WOODSIDE (town). Covers a land area of 11.732 square miles and a water area of 0 square miles. Located at 37.42° N. Lat; 122.26° W. Long. Elevation is 387 feet.
History: In 1849, during the California Gold Rush, 20-year-old Mathias Alfred Parkhurst purchased 127 acres (0.5 sq. km.) of timberland and named it "Woodside"; of course, this name was kept. By the late 19th century, Woodside was home to country estates.
Population: 5,287; Growth (since 2000): -1.2%; Density: 450.6 persons per square mile; Race: 89.2% White, 0.4% Black/African American, 6.3% Asian, 0.1% American Indian/Alaska Native, 0.1% Native Hawaiian/Other Pacific Islander, 2.7% Two or more races, 4.6% Hispanic of any race; Average household size: 2.67; Median age: 48.8; Age under 18: 23.5%; Age 65 and over: 20.2%; Males per 100 females: 95.4; Marriage status: 25.7% never married, 60.7% now married, 0.9% separated, 6.5% widowed, 7.1% divorced; Foreign born: 13.8%; Speak English only: 88.9%; With disability: 5.2%; Veterans: 9.2%; Ancestry: 16.5% Italian, 15.0% English, 14.5% German, 11.8% Irish, 7.3% European
Employment: 32.7% management, business, and financial, 10.0% computer, engineering, and science, 10.5% education, legal, community service, arts, and media, 3.5% healthcare practitioners, 13.0% service, 22.2% sales and office, 5.6% natural resources, construction, and maintenance, 2.4% production, transportation, and material moving

Income: Per capita: $117,760; Median household: $212,917; Average household: $336,953; Households with income of $100,000 or more: 71.1%; Poverty rate: 4.6%

Educational Attainment: High school diploma or higher: 96.5%; Bachelor's degree or higher: 66.5%; Graduate/professional degree or higher: 35.5%

School District(s)

Sequoia Union High (09-12)
2012-13 Enrollment: 9,247 . . . . (650) 369-1411

Woodside Elementary (KG-08)
2012-13 Enrollment: 453. . . . . (650) 851-1571

Housing: Homeownership rate: 87.1%; Median home value: 1 million+; Median year structure built: 1962; Homeowner vacancy rate: 0.9%; Median gross rent: $1,212 per month; Rental vacancy rate: 3.7%

Health Insurance: 96.5% have insurance; 86.0% have private insurance; 24.5% have public insurance; 3.5% do not have insurance; 1.0% of children under 18 do not have insurance

Transportation: Commute: 75.6% car, 5.9% public transportation, 1.7% walk, 14.1% work from home; Median travel time to work: 25.7 minutes

Additional Information Contacts

Town of Woodside . . . . (650) 851-6790
http://www.woodsidetown.org

Santa Barbara County

Located in southwestern California; bounded on the west by the Santa Barbara Channel of the Pacific Ocean; includes several islands, and the Santa Ynez and San Rafael Mountains; includes part of Los Padres National Forest. Covers a land area of 2,735.085 square miles, a water area of 1,053.993 square miles, and is located in the Pacific Time Zone at 34.54° N. Lat., 120.04° W. Long. The county was founded in 1850. County seat is Santa Barbara.

Santa Barbara County is part of the Santa Maria-Santa Barbara, CA Metropolitan Statistical Area. The entire metro area includes: Santa Barbara County, CA

Weather Station: Cachuma Lake — Elevation: 780 feet

	Jan	Feb	Mar	Apr	May	Jun	Jul	Aug	Sep	Oct	Nov	Dec
High	66	67	70	75	79	85	91	92	89	83	74	66
Low	39	41	43	44	48	50	53	53	52	48	43	39
Precip	4.8	5.4	3.9	1.3	0.5	0.1	0.0	0.0	0.1	0.9	1.6	3.2
Snow	0.0	0.0	0.0	0.0	0.0	0.0	0.0	0.0	0.0	0.0	0.0	0.0

High and Low temperatures in degrees Fahrenheit; Precipitation and Snow in inches

Weather Station: Lompoc — Elevation: 95 feet

	Jan	Feb	Mar	Apr	May	Jun	Jul	Aug	Sep	Oct	Nov	Dec
High	66	67	68	70	71	73	74	75	76	75	70	66
Low	42	44	45	46	50	52	55	55	54	50	45	41
Precip	3.2	3.7	2.9	0.9	0.3	0.0	0.0	0.0	0.1	0.7	1.4	2.3
Snow	0.0	0.0	0.0	0.0	0.0	0.0	0.0	0.0	0.0	0.0	0.0	0.0

High and Low temperatures in degrees Fahrenheit; Precipitation and Snow in inches

Weather Station: New Cuyama Fire Stn — Elevation: 2,160 feet

	Jan	Feb	Mar	Apr	May	Jun	Jul	Aug	Sep	Oct	Nov	Dec
High	61	62	66	72	80	88	94	93	88	78	67	61
Low	33	35	37	39	45	50	56	55	51	43	36	32
Precip	1.5	1.8	1.6	0.5	0.3	0.0	0.1	0.1	0.2	0.3	0.6	1.0
Snow	tr	tr	0.1	0.1	0.0	tr	0.0	0.0	0.0	0.0	tr	tr

High and Low temperatures in degrees Fahrenheit; Precipitation and Snow in inches

Weather Station: Santa Barbara — Elevation: 4 feet

	Jan	Feb	Mar	Apr	May	Jun	Jul	Aug	Sep	Oct	Nov	Dec
High	65	65	67	70	70	72	75	77	76	73	69	65
Low	46	47	49	51	54	57	59	60	59	55	50	46
Precip	4.3	4.8	3.2	1.0	0.3	0.1	0.0	0.0	0.1	0.8	1.5	2.6
Snow	0.0	0.0	0.0	0.0	0.0	0.0	0.0	0.0	0.0	0.0	0.0	0.0

High and Low temperatures in degrees Fahrenheit; Precipitation and Snow in inches

Weather Station: Santa Barbara Municipal Arpt — Elevation: 8 feet

	Jan	Feb	Mar	Apr	May	Jun	Jul	Aug	Sep	Oct	Nov	Dec
High	64	65	66	68	70	72	75	75	75	73	69	65
Low	40	43	46	47	51	54	57	57	55	51	44	39
Precip	3.7	3.6	3.5	0.9	0.3	0.1	0.0	0.1	0.3	0.8	1.5	2.5
Snow	na	na	na	na	na	na	na	na	na	na	na	na

High and Low temperatures in degrees Fahrenheit; Precipitation and Snow in inches

Weather Station: Santa Maria Hancock Field — Elevation: 232 feet

	Jan	Feb	Mar	Apr	May	Jun	Jul	Aug	Sep	Oct	Nov	Dec
High	64	65	66	68	69	71	74	74	75	74	69	64
Low	40	42	43	44	48	51	54	54	53	49	43	39
Precip	2.7	3.1	2.7	0.9	0.3	0.1	0.0	0.0	0.1	0.5	1.3	1.8
Snow	na	na	na	na	na	na	na	na	na	na	na	na

High and Low temperatures in degrees Fahrenheit; Precipitation and Snow in inches

Population: 423,895; Growth (since 2000): 6.1%; Density: 155.0 persons per square mile; Race: 69.6% White, 2.0% Black/African American, 4.9% Asian, 1.3% American Indian/Alaska Native, 0.2% Native Hawaiian/Other Pacific Islander, 4.6% two or more races, 42.9% Hispanic of any race; Average household size: 2.86; Median age: 33.6; Age under 18: 23.1%; Age 65 and over: 12.8%; Males per 100 females: 100.8; Marriage status: 38.3% never married, 47.5% now married, 2.2% separated, 5.2% widowed, 8.9% divorced; Foreign born: 23.4%; Speak English only: 59.8%; With disability: 10.0%; Veterans: 8.0%; Ancestry: 11.2% German, 8.5% Irish, 8.5% English, 4.3% Italian, 3.0% American

Religion: Six largest groups: 34.7% Catholicism, 2.0% Pentecostal, 1.7% Latter-day Saints, 1.6% Baptist, 1.1% Methodist/Pietist, 0.9% Lutheran

Economy: Unemployment rate: 5.4%; Leading industries: 13.4% retail trade; 12.2% health care and social assistance; 12.0% professional, scientific, and technical services; Farms: 1,597 totaling 701,039 acres; Company size: 3 employ 1,000 or more persons, 12 employ 500 to 999 persons, 154 employ 100 to 499 persons, 11,060 employ less than 100 persons; Business ownership: 11,281 women-owned, n/a Black-owned, 5,518 Hispanic-owned, 2,335 Asian-owned

Employment: 13.5% management, business, and financial, 6.2% computer, engineering, and science, 11.5% education, legal, community service, arts, and media, 3.9% healthcare practitioners, 21.6% service, 21.2% sales and office, 13.8% natural resources, construction, and maintenance, 8.2% production, transportation, and material moving

Income: Per capita: $30,352; Median household: $62,779; Average household: $88,230; Households with income of $100,000 or more: 29.5%; Poverty rate: 16.0%

Educational Attainment: High school diploma or higher: 79.1%; Bachelor's degree or higher: 31.3%; Graduate/professional degree or higher: 12.9%

Housing: Homeownership rate: 52.7%; Median home value: $453,000; Median year structure built: 1972; Homeowner vacancy rate: 1.7%; Median gross rent: $1,340 per month; Rental vacancy rate: 4.5%

Vital Statistics: Birth rate: 133.2 per 10,000 population; Death rate: 68.0 per 10,000 population; Age-adjusted cancer mortality rate: 139.5 deaths per 100,000 population

Health Insurance: 81.6% have insurance; 62.5% have private insurance; 29.8% have public insurance; 18.4% do not have insurance; 10.5% of children under 18 do not have insurance

Health Care: Physicians: 24.2 per 10,000 population; Hospital beds: 17.6 per 10,000 population; Hospital admissions: 770.0 per 10,000 population

Air Quality Index: 72.6% good, 26.8% moderate, 0.5% unhealthy for sensitive individuals, 0.0% unhealthy (percent of days)

Transportation: Commute: 81.0% car, 3.7% public transportation, 4.6% walk, 5.3% work from home; Median travel time to work: 19.4 minutes

Presidential Election: 57.1% Obama, 40.3% Romney (2012)

National and State Parks: Carpinteria State Beach; Channel Islands National Park; Chumash Painted Cave State Historic Park; El CapitA¡n State Beach; El Presidio de Santa Barbara State Historic Park; Gaviota State Park; La Purisima Mission State Historic Park; Point Sal State Beach; Refugio State Beach

Additional Information Contacts

Santa Barbara Government . . . . (805) 568-2190
http://www.countyofsb.org

Santa Barbara County Communities

BALLARD (CDP). Covers a land area of 1.180 square miles and a water area of <.001 square miles. Located at 34.63° N. Lat; 120.12° W. Long. Elevation is 669 feet.

Population: 467; Growth (since 2000): n/a; Density: 395.8 persons per square mile; Race: 92.5% White, 0.6% Black/African American, 0.4% Asian, 0.2% American Indian/Alaska Native, 0.0% Native Hawaiian/Other Pacific Islander, 3.6% Two or more races, 9.9% Hispanic of any race; Average household size: 2.83; Median age: 45.7; Age under 18: 24.2%; Age 65 and over: 13.9%; Males per 100 females: 89.1

Housing: Homeownership rate: 81.2%; Homeowner vacancy rate: 2.2%; Rental vacancy rate: 3.1%

BUELLTON (city). Covers a land area of 1.582 square miles and a water area of <.001 square miles. Located at 34.62° N. Lat; 120.19° W. Long. Elevation is 358 feet.

History: Buellton grew up at the crossroads between two Spanish missions, Mission Santa Ynez and Mission La Purisima.

Population: 4,828; Growth (since 2000): 26.1%; Density: 3,051.5 persons per square mile; Race: 81.0% White, 0.8% Black/African American, 2.8% Asian, 1.6% American Indian/Alaska Native, 0.1% Native Hawaiian/Other Pacific Islander, 4.9% Two or more races, 30.1% Hispanic of any race; Average household size: 2.74; Median age: 39.1; Age under 18: 25.4%; Age 65 and over: 13.2%; Males per 100 females: 95.5; Marriage status: 29.3% never married, 56.3% now married, 3.7% separated, 4.4% widowed, 10.0% divorced; Foreign born: 23.8%; Speak English only: 62.2%; With disability: 7.4%; Veterans: 10.3%; Ancestry: 11.3% English, 8.6% Italian, 8.3% German, 7.6% Irish, 6.1% Danish

Employment: 15.0% management, business, and financial, 4.0% computer, engineering, and science, 5.7% education, legal, community service, arts, and media, 2.7% healthcare practitioners, 32.6% service, 23.4% sales and office, 9.0% natural resources, construction, and maintenance, 7.7% production, transportation, and material moving

Income: Per capita: $30,047; Median household: $66,076; Average household: $81,092; Households with income of $100,000 or more: 37.3%; Poverty rate: 9.8%

Educational Attainment: High school diploma or higher: 78.1%; Bachelor's degree or higher: 23.4%; Graduate/professional degree or higher: 8.2%

School District(s)

Buellton Union Elementary (KG-08)
2012-13 Enrollment: 652. . . . . (805) 686-2767

Housing: Homeownership rate: 69.6%; Median home value: $407,800; Median year structure built: 1981; Homeowner vacancy rate: 2.5%; Median gross rent: $1,027 per month; Rental vacancy rate: 4.4%

Health Insurance: 80.1% have insurance; 68.6% have private insurance; 19.4% have public insurance; 19.9% do not have insurance; 6.1% of children under 18 do not have insurance

Safety: Violent crime rate: 14.2 per 10,000 population; Property crime rate: 125.8 per 10,000 population

Transportation: Commute: 82.8% car, 5.0% public transportation, 5.1% walk, 3.7% work from home; Median travel time to work: 27.3 minutes; Amtrak: Bus service available.

Additional Information Contacts

City of Buellton . . . . (805) 688-5177
http://www.cityofbuellton.com

CARPINTERIA (city). Covers a land area of 2.586 square miles and a water area of 6.686 square miles. Located at 34.39° N. Lat; 119.50° W. Long. Elevation is 33 feet.

History: Established 1863 on site of Indian village visited by Portola in 1769.

Population: 13,040; Growth (since 2000): -8.1%; Density: 5,043.4 persons per square mile; Race: 71.7% White, 0.8% Black/African American, 2.3% Asian, 1.1% American Indian/Alaska Native, 0.1% Native Hawaiian/Other Pacific Islander, 4.1% Two or more races, 48.7% Hispanic of any race; Average household size: 2.74; Median age: 39.5; Age under 18: 21.4%; Age 65 and over: 13.8%; Males per 100 females: 97.2; Marriage status: 34.8% never married, 49.1% now married, 3.0% separated, 5.8% widowed, 10.2% divorced; Foreign born: 25.7%; Speak English only: 60.0%; With disability: 11.7%; Veterans: 7.1%; Ancestry: 11.4% German, 9.3% English, 8.8% Irish, 3.9% French, 3.8% Italian

Employment: 11.2% management, business, and financial, 6.0% computer, engineering, and science, 11.8% education, legal, community service, arts, and media, 3.0% healthcare practitioners, 22.9% service, 25.3% sales and office, 12.8% natural resources, construction, and maintenance, 6.8% production, transportation, and material moving

Income: Per capita: $35,850; Median household: $68,375; Average household: $89,504; Households with income of $100,000 or more: 32.9%; Poverty rate: 7.5%

Educational Attainment: High school diploma or higher: 80.8%; Bachelor's degree or higher: 31.8%; Graduate/professional degree or higher: 11.4%

School District(s)

Carpinteria Unified (KG-12)
2012-13 Enrollment: 2,308 . . . . (805) 684-4511

Four-year College(s)

Pacifica Graduate Institute (Private, For-profit)
Fall 2013 Enrollment: 1,060 . . . . (805) 969-3626

Vocational/Technical School(s)

International Sports Sciences Association (Private, For-profit)
Fall 2013 Enrollment: n/a . . . . (800) 892-4772

Housing: Homeownership rate: 49.3%; Median home value: $537,900; Median year structure built: 1975; Homeowner vacancy rate: 1.8%; Median gross rent: $1,402 per month; Rental vacancy rate: 6.5%

Health Insurance: 78.6% have insurance; 63.6% have private insurance; 28.2% have public insurance; 21.4% do not have insurance; 19.9% of children under 18 do not have insurance

Safety: Violent crime rate: 15.8 per 10,000 population; Property crime rate: 196.4 per 10,000 population

Newspapers: Coastal View (weekly circulation 6800)

Transportation: Commute: 78.0% car, 4.4% public transportation, 5.2% walk, 4.9% work from home; Median travel time to work: 22.2 minutes; Amtrak: Train service available.

Additional Information Contacts

City of Carpinteria . . . . (805) 684-5405
http://www.ci.carpinteria.ca.us

CASMALIA (CDP). Covers a land area of 0.188 square miles and a water area of 0 square miles. Located at 34.84° N. Lat; 120.53° W. Long. Elevation is 266 feet.

Population: 138; Growth (since 2000): n/a; Density: 732.2 persons per square mile; Race: 65.9% White, 2.2% Black/African American, 0.7% Asian, 0.0% American Indian/Alaska Native, 0.0% Native Hawaiian/Other Pacific Islander, 9.4% Two or more races, 42.0% Hispanic of any race; Average household size: 2.42; Median age: 43.0; Age under 18: 21.0%; Age 65 and over: 14.5%; Males per 100 females: 102.9

Housing: Homeownership rate: 50.9%; Homeowner vacancy rate: 0.0%; Rental vacancy rate: 6.7%

CUYAMA (CDP). Covers a land area of 0.453 square miles and a water area of 0.004 square miles. Located at 34.93° N. Lat; 119.61° W. Long. Elevation is 2,274 feet.

Population: 57; Growth (since 2000): n/a; Density: 125.7 persons per square mile; Race: 70.2% White, 0.0% Black/African American, 0.0% Asian, 3.5% American Indian/Alaska Native, 0.0% Native Hawaiian/Other Pacific Islander, 1.8% Two or more races, 70.2% Hispanic of any race; Average household size: 2.85; Median age: 34.2; Age under 18: 24.6%; Age 65 and over: 8.8%; Males per 100 females: 137.5

Housing: Homeownership rate: 50.0%; Homeowner vacancy rate: 0.0%; Rental vacancy rate: 23.1%

GAREY (CDP). Covers a land area of 1.265 square miles and a water area of 0.004 square miles. Located at 34.89° N. Lat; 120.31° W. Long. Elevation is 381 feet.

Population: 68; Growth (since 2000): n/a; Density: 53.8 persons per square mile; Race: 77.9% White, 0.0% Black/African American, 0.0% Asian, 1.5% American Indian/Alaska Native, 0.0% Native Hawaiian/Other Pacific Islander, 13.2% Two or more races, 30.9% Hispanic of any race; Average household size: 2.43; Median age: 45.0; Age under 18: 19.1%; Age 65 and over: 13.2%; Males per 100 females: 112.5

Housing: Homeownership rate: 71.4%; Homeowner vacancy rate: 0.0%; Rental vacancy rate: 0.0%

GOLETA (city). Covers a land area of 7.903 square miles and a water area of 0.072 square miles. Located at 34.43° N. Lat; 119.86° W. Long. Elevation is 20 feet.

History: Goleta was named for a schooner built by Captain William G. Dana of Nipomo in 1828.

Population: 29,888; Growth (since 2000): -45.9%; Density: 3,782.1 persons per square mile; Race: 69.7% White, 1.6% Black/African American, 9.1% Asian, 0.9% American Indian/Alaska Native, 0.1% Native Hawaiian/Other Pacific Islander, 4.6% Two or more races, 32.9% Hispanic of any race; Average household size: 2.72; Median age: 36.5; Age under 18: 21.2%; Age 65 and over: 13.5%; Males per 100 females: 101.3; Marriage status: 37.6% never married, 46.8% now married, 1.9% separated, 6.2% widowed, 9.4% divorced; Foreign born: 23.2%; Speak

English only: 61.5%; With disability: 8.0%; Veterans: 6.9%; Ancestry: 11.9% German, 11.2% Irish, 9.4% English, 4.1% Italian, 2.4% Polish
Employment: 14.2% management, business, and financial, 12.0% computer, engineering, and science, 15.9% education, legal, community service, arts, and media, 4.2% healthcare practitioners, 16.4% service, 23.3% sales and office, 6.0% natural resources, construction, and maintenance, 8.0% production, transportation, and material moving
Income: Per capita: $33,069; Median household: $73,691; Average household: $91,283; Households with income of $100,000 or more: 34.7%; Poverty rate: 6.9%
Educational Attainment: High school diploma or higher: 88.1%; Bachelor's degree or higher: 44.3%; Graduate/professional degree or higher: 21.4%

School District(s)

Goleta Union Elementary (KG-06)
2012-13 Enrollment: 3,611 . . . . (805) 681-1200
Santa Barbara Unified (KG-12)
2012-13 Enrollment: 15,489 . . . . (805) 963-4338
Housing: Homeownership rate: 53.6%; Median home value: $613,200; Median year structure built: 1970; Homeowner vacancy rate: 1.2%; Median gross rent: $1,607 per month; Rental vacancy rate: 4.5%
Health Insurance: 90.9% have insurance; 81.8% have private insurance; 20.6% have public insurance; 9.1% do not have insurance; 5.4% of children under 18 do not have insurance
Safety: Violent crime rate: 14.1 per 10,000 population; Property crime rate: 148.4 per 10,000 population
Transportation: Commute: 79.6% car, 3.2% public transportation, 4.4% walk, 5.1% work from home; Median travel time to work: 16.2 minutes; Amtrak: Train service available.
Additional Information Contacts
City of Goleta. . . . . (805) 961-7500
http://www.cityofgoleta.org

GUADALUPE (city). Covers a land area of 1.309 square miles and a water area of 0.005 square miles. Located at 34.96° N. Lat; 120.57° W. Long. Elevation is 85 feet.
History: Guadalupe developed as a shipping center for an area of farms and ranches.
Population: 7,080; Growth (since 2000): 25.1%; Density: 5,406.9 persons per square mile; Race: 48.0% White, 1.0% Black/African American, 3.9% Asian, 1.5% American Indian/Alaska Native, 0.1% Native Hawaiian/Other Pacific Islander, 6.2% Two or more races, 86.2% Hispanic of any race; Average household size: 3.91; Median age: 28.2; Age under 18: 34.2%; Age 65 and over: 8.0%; Males per 100 females: 101.3; Marriage status: 33.5% never married, 55.1% now married, 1.5% separated, 3.6% widowed, 7.7% divorced; Foreign born: 36.1%; Speak English only: 26.0%; With disability: 9.6%; Veterans: 3.4%; Ancestry: 1.5% English, 1.4% Irish, 0.7% German, 0.5% American, 0.5% French
Employment: 2.8% management, business, and financial, 1.1% computer, engineering, and science, 8.3% education, legal, community service, arts, and media, 1.3% healthcare practitioners, 23.3% service, 13.6% sales and office, 33.8% natural resources, construction, and maintenance, 15.7% production, transportation, and material moving
Income: Per capita: $14,899; Median household: $47,923; Average household: $55,088; Households with income of $100,000 or more: 10.7%; Poverty rate: 19.7%
Educational Attainment: High school diploma or higher: 47.0%; Bachelor's degree or higher: 5.9%; Graduate/professional degree or higher: 1.1%

School District(s)

Guadalupe Union Elementary (KG-08)
2012-13 Enrollment: 1,182 . . . . (805) 343-2114
Housing: Homeownership rate: 51.8%; Median home value: $190,300; Median year structure built: 1980; Homeowner vacancy rate: 0.4%; Median gross rent: $1,012 per month; Rental vacancy rate: 3.3%
Health Insurance: 77.1% have insurance; 38.0% have private insurance; 44.9% have public insurance; 22.9% do not have insurance; 6.0% of children under 18 do not have insurance
Safety: Violent crime rate: 13.9 per 10,000 population; Property crime rate: 72.2 per 10,000 population
Transportation: Commute: 88.3% car, 6.7% public transportation, 3.1% walk, 1.6% work from home; Median travel time to work: 21.7 minutes; Amtrak: Train service available.
Additional Information Contacts
City of Guadalupe . . . . (805) 356-3891
http://www.ci.guadalupe.ca.us.

ISLA VISTA (CDP). Covers a land area of 1.849 square miles and a water area of 0.017 square miles. Located at 34.41° N. Lat; 119.86° W. Long. Elevation is 46 feet.
History: University of California (Santa Barbara) to East.
Population: 23,096; Growth (since 2000): 25.9%; Density: 12,492.0 persons per square mile; Race: 64.4% White, 2.6% Black/African American, 14.7% Asian, 0.5% American Indian/Alaska Native, 0.2% Native Hawaiian/Other Pacific Islander, 6.1% Two or more races, 22.8% Hispanic of any race; Average household size: 3.08; Median age: 20.7; Age under 18: 3.0%; Age 65 and over: 1.3%; Males per 100 females: 97.1; Marriage status: 92.7% never married, 5.4% now married, 0.5% separated, 0.9% widowed, 1.0% divorced; Foreign born: 14.7%; Speak English only: 65.3%; With disability: 4.2%; Veterans: 0.7%; Ancestry: 11.2% German, 9.4% Irish, 6.9% Italian, 5.8% English, 4.0% Polish
Employment: 6.0% management, business, and financial, 6.1% computer, engineering, and science, 17.9% education, legal, community service, arts, and media, 2.4% healthcare practitioners, 34.3% service, 26.6% sales and office, 1.8% natural resources, construction, and maintenance, 4.8% production, transportation, and material moving
Income: Per capita: $9,245; Median household: $22,332; Average household: $34,846; Households with income of $100,000 or more: 6.7%; Poverty rate: 62.8%
Educational Attainment: High school diploma or higher: 79.4%; Bachelor's degree or higher: 50.4%; Graduate/professional degree or higher: 31.4%
Housing: Homeownership rate: 2.6%; Median home value: $391,900; Median year structure built: 1975; Homeowner vacancy rate: 1.5%; Median gross rent: $1,392 per month; Rental vacancy rate: 1.9%
Health Insurance: 92.9% have insurance; 88.3% have private insurance; 7.9% have public insurance; 7.1% do not have insurance; 8.0% of children under 18 do not have insurance
Transportation: Commute: 39.0% car, 6.2% public transportation, 14.7% walk, 5.5% work from home; Median travel time to work: 13.8 minutes

LOMPOC (city). Covers a land area of 11.597 square miles and a water area of 0.078 square miles. Located at 34.66° N. Lat; 120.47° W. Long. Elevation is 105 feet.
History: Lompoc originated as a land colonization project in 1874 when the California Immigrant Union purchased and subdivided Ranchos Lompoc and Mission Vieja. The name of Lompoc is of Indian origin meaning "shell mounds."
Population: 42,434; Growth (since 2000): 3.2%; Density: 3,659.0 persons per square mile; Race: 61.2% White, 5.7% Black/African American, 3.8% Asian, 1.8% American Indian/Alaska Native, 0.4% Native Hawaiian/Other Pacific Islander, 5.8% Two or more races, 50.8% Hispanic of any race; Average household size: 2.90; Median age: 33.9; Age under 18: 26.4%; Age 65 and over: 10.0%; Males per 100 females: 114.9; Marriage status: 34.4% never married, 48.8% now married, 3.6% separated, 4.1% widowed, 12.8% divorced; Foreign born: 22.5%; Speak English only: 56.5%; With disability: 11.6%; Veterans: 10.7%; Ancestry: 9.0% German, 8.2% Irish, 6.8% English, 4.2% American, 3.1% Italian
Employment: 10.1% management, business, and financial, 4.6% computer, engineering, and science, 7.3% education, legal, community service, arts, and media, 3.5% healthcare practitioners, 27.3% service, 21.5% sales and office, 15.5% natural resources, construction, and maintenance, 10.2% production, transportation, and material moving
Income: Per capita: $19,865; Median household: $45,818; Average household: $59,745; Households with income of $100,000 or more: 17.2%; Poverty rate: 23.7%
Educational Attainment: High school diploma or higher: 73.0%; Bachelor's degree or higher: 14.2%; Graduate/professional degree or higher: 4.7%

School District(s)

Lompoc Unified (KG-12)
2012-13 Enrollment: 9,811 . . . . (805) 742-3300
Housing: Homeownership rate: 48.6%; Median home value: $235,500; Median year structure built: 1971; Homeowner vacancy rate: 2.2%; Median gross rent: $969 per month; Rental vacancy rate: 7.1%
Health Insurance: 81.2% have insurance; 47.9% have private insurance; 42.3% have public insurance; 18.8% do not have insurance; 9.2% of children under 18 do not have insurance
Hospitals: Lompoc Valley Medical Center (170 beds)

Safety: Violent crime rate: 43.1 per 10,000 population; Property crime rate: 241.2 per 10,000 population

Transportation: Commute: 87.5% car, 4.8% public transportation, 3.6% walk, 2.3% work from home; Median travel time to work: 25.1 minutes; Amtrak: Bus service available.

Airports: Vandenberg AFB (general aviation)

Additional Information Contacts

City of Lompoc . . . . (805) 736-1261
http://www.ci.lompoc.ca.us

LOS ALAMOS (CDP). Covers a land area of 3.868 square miles and a water area of <.001 square miles. Located at 34.73° N. Lat; 120.27° W. Long. Elevation is 568 feet.

Population: 1,890; Growth (since 2000): 37.8%; Density: 488.6 persons per square mile; Race: 88.2% White, 0.3% Black/African American, 1.7% Asian, 0.5% American Indian/Alaska Native, 0.0% Native Hawaiian/Other Pacific Islander, 2.2% Two or more races, 40.9% Hispanic of any race; Average household size: 3.01; Median age: 38.2; Age under 18: 26.2%; Age 65 and over: 9.5%; Males per 100 females: 100.2

School District(s)

Orcutt Union Elementary (KG-12)
2012-13 Enrollment: 5,087 . . . . (805) 938-8900

Housing: Homeownership rate: 61.5%; Homeowner vacancy rate: 1.5%; Rental vacancy rate: 6.4%

LOS OLIVOS (CDP). Covers a land area of 2.459 square miles and a water area of <.001 square miles. Located at 34.66° N. Lat; 120.12° W. Long. Elevation is 837 feet.

Population: 1,132; Growth (since 2000): n/a; Density: 460.4 persons per square mile; Race: 92.7% White, 0.1% Black/African American, 1.1% Asian, 0.4% American Indian/Alaska Native, 0.4% Native Hawaiian/Other Pacific Islander, 1.9% Two or more races, 11.0% Hispanic of any race; Average household size: 2.46; Median age: 48.0; Age under 18: 21.8%; Age 65 and over: 15.4%; Males per 100 females: 97.9

School District(s)

Los Olivos Elementary (KG-12)
2012-13 Enrollment: 471. . . . . (805) 688-4025

Housing: Homeownership rate: 68.5%; Homeowner vacancy rate: 0.3%; Rental vacancy rate: 2.7%

MISSION CANYON (CDP). Covers a land area of 1.517 square miles and a water area of 0.030 square miles. Located at 34.46° N. Lat; 119.72° W. Long. Elevation is 633 feet.

Population: 2,381; Growth (since 2000): -8.8%; Density: 1,569.2 persons per square mile; Race: 92.1% White, 0.6% Black/African American, 1.7% Asian, 0.7% American Indian/Alaska Native, 0.5% Native Hawaiian/Other Pacific Islander, 3.0% Two or more races, 8.3% Hispanic of any race; Average household size: 2.33; Median age: 51.3; Age under 18: 15.5%; Age 65 and over: 20.2%; Males per 100 females: 95.5

Housing: Homeownership rate: 76.7%; Homeowner vacancy rate: 0.8%; Rental vacancy rate: 4.4%

MISSION HILLS (CDP). Covers a land area of 1.229 square miles and a water area of 0.008 square miles. Located at 34.69° N. Lat; 120.44° W. Long. Elevation is 325 feet.

Population: 3,576; Growth (since 2000): 13.8%; Density: 2,909.5 persons per square mile; Race: 75.2% White, 2.5% Black/African American, 3.5% Asian, 2.1% American Indian/Alaska Native, 0.3% Native Hawaiian/Other Pacific Islander, 5.6% Two or more races, 31.8% Hispanic of any race; Average household size: 3.03; Median age: 40.0; Age under 18: 26.7%; Age 65 and over: 14.7%; Males per 100 females: 99.6; Marriage status: 28.9% never married, 58.3% now married, 1.2% separated, 5.6% widowed, 7.3% divorced; Foreign born: 10.5%; Speak English only: 73.0%; With disability: 9.7%; Veterans: 16.8%; Ancestry: 11.7% German, 9.2% English, 7.9% Irish, 6.1% European, 3.5% American

Employment: 15.6% management, business, and financial, 7.4% computer, engineering, and science, 7.7% education, legal, community service, arts, and media, 3.7% healthcare practitioners, 18.3% service, 16.8% sales and office, 11.4% natural resources, construction, and maintenance, 19.1% production, transportation, and material moving

Income: Per capita: $30,284; Median household: $73,368; Average household: $94,380; Households with income of $100,000 or more: 37.3%; Poverty rate: 4.0%

Educational Attainment: High school diploma or higher: 87.7%; Bachelor's degree or higher: 19.8%; Graduate/professional degree or higher: 7.7%

School District(s)

Los Angeles Unified (PK-12)
2012-13 Enrollment: 655,455 . . . . (213) 241-1000

Housing: Homeownership rate: 84.8%; Median home value: $244,600; Median year structure built: 1966; Homeowner vacancy rate: 0.7%; Median gross rent: $1,604 per month; Rental vacancy rate: 2.2%

Health Insurance: 83.6% have insurance; 68.2% have private insurance; 30.5% have public insurance; 16.4% do not have insurance; 12.4% of children under 18 do not have insurance

Transportation: Commute: 87.3% car, 4.2% public transportation, 0.0% walk, 7.4% work from home; Median travel time to work: 35.0 minutes

MONTECITO (CDP). Covers a land area of 9.259 square miles and a water area of 0.006 square miles. Located at 34.44° N. Lat; 119.63° W. Long. Elevation is 180 feet.

History: The site of present-day Montecito, along with the entire south coast of Santa Barbara County, was inhabited for over 10,000 years by the Chumash Indians. The Spanish arrived in the late 18th century, but left the region largely unsettled while they built the Presidio and Mission Santa Barbara farther west.

Population: 8,965; Growth (since 2000): -10.4%; Density: 968.3 persons per square mile; Race: 92.2% White, 0.6% Black/African American, 2.4% Asian, 0.4% American Indian/Alaska Native, 0.1% Native Hawaiian/Other Pacific Islander, 2.5% Two or more races, 6.7% Hispanic of any race; Average household size: 2.34; Median age: 50.0; Age under 18: 16.9%; Age 65 and over: 26.0%; Males per 100 females: 87.3; Marriage status: 30.1% never married, 55.8% now married, 2.5% separated, 6.1% widowed, 7.9% divorced; Foreign born: 9.6%; Speak English only: 91.8%; With disability: 8.4%; Veterans: 8.8%; Ancestry: 21.3% English, 18.1% German, 15.7% Irish, 7.4% Italian, 5.4% Scottish

Employment: 28.5% management, business, and financial, 6.4% computer, engineering, and science, 22.7% education, legal, community service, arts, and media, 5.7% healthcare practitioners, 11.4% service, 20.9% sales and office, 2.1% natural resources, construction, and maintenance, 2.2% production, transportation, and material moving

Income: Per capita: $81,148; Median household: $125,560; Average household: $222,795; Households with income of $100,000 or more: 57.0%; Poverty rate: 7.1%

Educational Attainment: High school diploma or higher: 97.8%; Bachelor's degree or higher: 69.4%; Graduate/professional degree or higher: 32.6%

Housing: Homeownership rate: 73.5%; Median home value: 1 million+; Median year structure built: 1966; Homeowner vacancy rate: 2.4%; Median gross rent: $2,000+ per month; Rental vacancy rate: 8.7%

Health Insurance: 93.9% have insurance; 84.5% have private insurance; 25.1% have public insurance; 6.1% do not have insurance; 3.3% of children under 18 do not have insurance

Newspapers: Montecito Journal (weekly circulation 20000)

Transportation: Commute: 63.4% car, 0.3% public transportation, 10.8% walk, 22.7% work from home; Median travel time to work: 19.1 minutes

NEW CUYAMA (CDP). Covers a land area of 0.706 square miles and a water area of 0 square miles. Located at 34.94° N. Lat; 119.68° W. Long. Elevation is 2,142 feet.

Population: 517; Growth (since 2000): n/a; Density: 732.7 persons per square mile; Race: 80.9% White, 0.6% Black/African American, 0.6% Asian, 2.7% American Indian/Alaska Native, 0.0% Native Hawaiian/Other Pacific Islander, 5.0% Two or more races, 45.3% Hispanic of any race; Average household size: 2.92; Median age: 35.1; Age under 18: 30.9%; Age 65 and over: 12.2%; Males per 100 females: 105.2

School District(s)

Cuyama Joint Unified (KG-12)
2012-13 Enrollment: 240. . . . . (661) 766-2482

Housing: Homeownership rate: 67.2%; Homeowner vacancy rate: 1.7%; Rental vacancy rate: 9.2%

ORCUTT (CDP). Covers a land area of 11.124 square miles and a water area of 0.005 square miles. Located at 34.87° N. Lat; 120.42° W. Long. Elevation is 358 feet.

Population: 28,905; Growth (since 2000): 0.3%; Density: 2,598.4 persons per square mile; Race: 81.9% White, 1.4% Black/African American, 3.9% Asian, 1.2% American Indian/Alaska Native, 0.2% Native Hawaiian/Other

Pacific Islander, 4.5% Two or more races, 23.8% Hispanic of any race; Average household size: 2.71; Median age: 42.3; Age under 18: 24.3%; Age 65 and over: 17.6%; Males per 100 females: 96.1; Marriage status: 23.3% never married, 58.1% now married, 1.1% separated, 7.9% widowed, 10.7% divorced; Foreign born: 9.6%; Speak English only: 85.7%; With disability: 12.4%; Veterans: 14.8%; Ancestry: 19.5% German, 13.5% Irish, 11.2% English, 6.0% American, 5.2% Italian

Employment: 15.9% management, business, and financial, 8.2% computer, engineering, and science, 10.6% education, legal, community service, arts, and media, 4.5% healthcare practitioners, 17.9% service, 23.1% sales and office, 13.5% natural resources, construction, and maintenance, 6.3% production, transportation, and material moving

Income: Per capita: $31,262; Median household: $69,179; Average household: $84,007; Households with income of $100,000 or more: 33.1%; Poverty rate: 6.5%

Educational Attainment: High school diploma or higher: 90.5%; Bachelor's degree or higher: 27.1%; Graduate/professional degree or higher: 9.7%

School District(s)

Orcutt Union Elementary (KG-12)
2012-13 Enrollment: 5,087 . . . . (805) 938-8900

Housing: Homeownership rate: 78.1%; Median home value: $325,400; Median year structure built: 1978; Homeowner vacancy rate: 1.9%; Median gross rent: $1,555 per month; Rental vacancy rate: 4.5%

Health Insurance: 86.2% have insurance; 73.1% have private insurance; 28.0% have public insurance; 13.8% do not have insurance; 11.1% of children under 18 do not have insurance

Transportation: Commute: 93.8% car, 1.1% public transportation, 0.3% walk, 3.8% work from home; Median travel time to work: 21.9 minutes

---

SANTA BARBARA (city). County seat. Covers a land area of 19.468 square miles and a water area of 22.500 square miles. Located at 34.40° N. Lat; 119.71° W. Long. Elevation is 49 feet.

History: Sebastian Vizcaino sailed into the bay here in 1602 and named it Santa Barbara for the saint of that name. The presidio of Santa Barbara was founded in 1782 by Captain Jose Francisco Ortega and Governor Neve, followed in 1786 by Mission Santa Barbara. Following secularization of the mission in 1834, Santa Barbara was the home of wealthy Spanish landowners. In 1846 John C. Fremont captured Santa Barbara and held it under the American flag. After years of cattle ranching and shipping, Santa Barbara began in the early 1900's to develop as a wealthy residential community and a tourist area.

Population: 88,410; Growth (since 2000): -4.2%; Density: 4,541.3 persons per square mile; Race: 75.1% White, 1.6% Black/African American, 3.5% Asian, 1.0% American Indian/Alaska Native, 0.1% Native Hawaiian/Other Pacific Islander, 3.9% Two or more races, 38.0% Hispanic of any race; Average household size: 2.45; Median age: 36.8; Age under 18: 18.6%; Age 65 and over: 14.2%; Males per 100 females: 98.5; Marriage status: 40.1% never married, 43.6% now married, 2.3% separated, 5.4% widowed, 10.9% divorced; Foreign born: 25.5%; Speak English only: 60.9%; With disability: 9.8%; Veterans: 5.8%; Ancestry: 11.4% German, 9.7% English, 8.6% Irish, 5.6% Italian, 3.0% French

Employment: 16.5% management, business, and financial, 6.6% computer, engineering, and science, 13.7% education, legal, community service, arts, and media, 4.6% healthcare practitioners, 24.6% service, 20.2% sales and office, 8.3% natural resources, construction, and maintenance, 5.6% production, transportation, and material moving

Income: Per capita: $37,225; Median household: $65,034; Average household: $93,370; Households with income of $100,000 or more: 31.2%; Poverty rate: 14.0%

Educational Attainment: High school diploma or higher: 83.3%; Bachelor's degree or higher: 41.7%; Graduate/professional degree or higher: 18.0%

School District(s)

Cold Spring Elementary (KG-06)
2012-13 Enrollment: 175. . . . . (805) 969-2678
Goleta Union Elementary (KG-06)
2012-13 Enrollment: 3,611 . . . . (805) 681-1200
Hope Elementary (KG-06)
2012-13 Enrollment: 986. . . . . (805) 682-2564
Montecito Union Elementary (KG-06)
2012-13 Enrollment: 471. . . . . (805) 969-3249
Santa Barbara County Office of Education (KG-12)
2012-13 Enrollment: 567. . . . . (805) 964-4711
Santa Barbara County Rop
2012-13 Enrollment: n/a . . . . (805) 937-8427
Santa Barbara Unified (KG-12)
2012-13 Enrollment: 15,489 . . . . (805) 963-4338

Four-year College(s)

Antioch University-Santa Barbara (Private, Not-for-profit)
Fall 2013 Enrollment: 375. . . . . (805) 962-8179
Brooks Institute (Private, For-profit)
Fall 2013 Enrollment: 518 . . . . (805) 966-3888
2013-14 Tuition: In-state $20,120; Out-of-state $20,120
Fielding Graduate University (Private, Not-for-profit)
Fall 2013 Enrollment: 1,190 . . . . (805) 687-1099
The Santa Barbara and Ventura Colleges of LawâÇ"Santa Barbara (Private, Not-for-profit)
Fall 2013 Enrollment: 107. . . . . (805) 979-9860
University of California-Santa Barbara (Public)
Fall 2013 Enrollment: 22,225 . . . . (805) 893-8000
2013-14 Tuition: In-state $13,746; Out-of-state $36,624
Westmont College (Private, Not-for-profit)
Fall 2013 Enrollment: 1,321 . . . . (805) 565-6000
2013-14 Tuition: In-state $38,510; Out-of-state $38,510

Two-year College(s)

Santa Barbara City College (Public)
Fall 2013 Enrollment: 19,331 . . . . (805) 965-0581
2013-14 Tuition: In-state $1,374; Out-of-state $7,254

Vocational/Technical School(s)

Paul Mitchell the School-Santa Barbara (Private, For-profit)
Fall 2013 Enrollment: 127. . . . . (805) 966-1931
2013-14 Tuition: $16,925

Housing: Homeownership rate: 38.9%; Median home value: $832,100; Median year structure built: 1963; Homeowner vacancy rate: 1.3%; Median gross rent: $1,484 per month; Rental vacancy rate: 4.1%

Health Insurance: 78.9% have insurance; 63.2% have private insurance; 26.4% have public insurance; 21.1% do not have insurance; 14.2% of children under 18 do not have insurance

Hospitals: Goleta Valley Cottage Hospital (122 beds); Santa Barbara Cottage Hospital (404 beds)

Safety: Violent crime rate: 40.2 per 10,000 population; Property crime rate: 296.6 per 10,000 population

Newspapers: Santa Barbara Independent (weekly circulation 40000); Santa Barbara News-Press (daily circulation 39300)

Transportation: Commute: 74.5% car, 6.1% public transportation, 6.8% walk, 5.8% work from home; Median travel time to work: 16.7 minutes; Amtrak: Train service available.

Airports: Santa Barbara Municipal (primary service/non-hub)

Additional Information Contacts

City of Santa Barbara . . . . (805) 963-0611
http://www.santabarbaraca.gov

SANTA MARIA (city). Covers a land area of 22.756 square miles and a water area of 0.639 square miles. Located at 34.93° N. Lat; 120.44° W. Long. Elevation is 217 feet.

History: The first building erected in Santa Maria in 1871 was a general store to accommodate farmers who had begun irrigating the land. Later, oil was discovered nearby.

Population: 99,553; Growth (since 2000): 28.6%; Density: 4,374.9 persons per square mile; Race: 56.2% White, 1.7% Black/African American, 5.1% Asian, 1.8% American Indian/Alaska Native, 0.2% Native Hawaiian/Other Pacific Islander, 5.1% Two or more races, 70.4% Hispanic of any race; Average household size: 3.66; Median age: 28.6; Age under 18: 31.4%; Age 65 and over: 9.4%; Males per 100 females: 102.2; Marriage status: 37.7% never married, 49.9% now married, 2.8% separated, 5.1% widowed, 7.3% divorced; Foreign born: 34.7%; Speak English only: 35.7%; With disability: 10.1%; Veterans: 6.3%; Ancestry: 5.7% German, 4.2% Irish, 3.5% English, 1.8% Italian, 1.8% American

Employment: 7.1% management, business, and financial, 3.3% computer, engineering, and science, 5.3% education, legal, community service, arts, and media, 2.8% healthcare practitioners, 18.2% service, 19.8% sales and office, 29.6% natural resources, construction, and maintenance, 13.9% production, transportation, and material moving

Income: Per capita: $18,560; Median household: $50,563; Average household: $65,046; Households with income of $100,000 or more: 18.3%; Poverty rate: 20.7%

Educational Attainment: High school diploma or higher: 60.3%; Bachelor's degree or higher: 12.9%; Graduate/professional degree or higher: 3.7%

School District(s)

Blochman Union Elementary (KG-12)
2012-13 Enrollment: 820 . . . . (805) 937-1148
Orcutt Union Elementary (KG-12)
2012-13 Enrollment: 5,087 . . . . (805) 938-8900
Santa Barbara County Rop
2012-13 Enrollment: n/a . . . . (805) 937-8427
Santa Maria Joint Union High (09-12)
2012-13 Enrollment: 7,636 . . . . (805) 922-4573
Santa Maria-Bonita (KG-08)
2012-13 Enrollment: 15,050 . . . . (805) 928-1783

Four-year College(s)

Santa Barbara Business College-Santa Maria (Private, For-profit)
Fall 2013 Enrollment: 188 . . . . (805) 922-8256
2013-14 Tuition: In-state $12,464; Out-of-state $12,464

Two-year College(s)

Allan Hancock College (Public)
Fall 2013 Enrollment: 10,885 . . . . (805) 922-6966
2013-14 Tuition: In-state $1,346; Out-of-state $6,666

Vocational/Technical School(s)

CET-Santa Maria (Private, Not-for-profit)
Fall 2013 Enrollment: 155 . . . . (408) 287-7924
2013-14 Tuition: $9,958

Housing: Homeownership rate: 51.6%; Median home value: $251,500; Median year structure built: 1979; Homeowner vacancy rate: 1.9%; Median gross rent: $1,138 per month; Rental vacancy rate: 3.8%

Health Insurance: 72.2% have insurance; 40.9% have private insurance; 38.2% have public insurance; 27.8% do not have insurance; 11.5% of children under 18 do not have insurance

Hospitals: Marian Regional Medical Center (227 beds)

Safety: Violent crime rate: 48.0 per 10,000 population; Property crime rate: 287.5 per 10,000 population

Newspapers: Adobe Press & Times Press Recorder (weekly circulation 7500); Lompoc Record (daily circulation 6600); Santa Maria Times (daily circulation 19300); The Sun (weekly circulation 20000)

Transportation: Commute: 92.9% car, 1.9% public transportation, 1.7% walk, 2.1% work from home; Median travel time to work: 21.1 minutes; Amtrak: Train service available.

Airports: Santa Maria Public/Capt G Allan Hancock Field (primary service/non-hub)

Additional Information Contacts

City of Santa Maria . . . . (805) 925-0951
http://www.cityofsantamaria.org/home.shtml

SANTA YNEZ (CDP). Covers a land area of 5.136 square miles and a water area of 0.007 square miles. Located at 34.62° N. Lat; 120.09° W. Long. Elevation is 607 feet.

History: Site of Mission Santa Ynez (established 1804), still in use as a church.

Population: 4,418; Growth (since 2000): -3.6%; Density: 860.2 persons per square mile; Race: 85.9% White, 0.3% Black/African American, 1.2% Asian, 5.3% American Indian/Alaska Native, 0.1% Native Hawaiian/Other Pacific Islander, 3.9% Two or more races, 14.5% Hispanic of any race; Average household size: 2.54; Median age: 47.8; Age under 18: 20.7%; Age 65 and over: 19.9%; Males per 100 females: 96.3; Marriage status: 27.5% never married, 63.5% now married, 4.5% separated, 6.0% widowed, 3.1% divorced; Foreign born: 11.8%; Speak English only: 85.0%; With disability: 10.4%; Veterans: 10.7%; Ancestry: 21.3% English, 20.8% German, 11.2% Irish, 6.2% Italian, 5.9% French

Employment: 21.7% management, business, and financial, 6.1% computer, engineering, and science, 11.0% education, legal, community service, arts, and media, 4.4% healthcare practitioners, 23.9% service, 22.9% sales and office, 6.0% natural resources, construction, and maintenance, 3.9% production, transportation, and material moving

Income: Per capita: $48,359; Median household: $104,728; Average household: $130,413; Households with income of $100,000 or more: 54.1%; Poverty rate: 6.3%

Educational Attainment: High school diploma or higher: 92.4%; Bachelor's degree or higher: 40.1%; Graduate/professional degree or higher: 9.7%

School District(s)

College Elementary (KG-08)
2012-13 Enrollment: 426 . . . . (805) 686-7300
Santa Ynez Valley Union High (09-12)
2012-13 Enrollment: 1,018 . . . . (805) 688-6487

Housing: Homeownership rate: 76.2%; Median home value: $728,200; Median year structure built: 1978; Homeowner vacancy rate: 1.3%; Median gross rent: $2,000+ per month; Rental vacancy rate: 11.3%

Health Insurance: 87.9% have insurance; 81.4% have private insurance; 24.3% have public insurance; 12.1% do not have insurance; 9.5% of children under 18 do not have insurance

Transportation: Commute: 82.6% car, 0.2% public transportation, 9.4% walk, 4.2% work from home; Median travel time to work: 18.6 minutes

---

SISQUOC (CDP). Covers a land area of 2.230 square miles and a water area of 0.004 square miles. Located at 34.86° N. Lat; 120.29° W. Long. Elevation is 436 feet.

Population: 183; Growth (since 2000): n/a; Density: 82.1 persons per square mile; Race: 79.8% White, 0.0% Black/African American, 1.6% Asian, 2.7% American Indian/Alaska Native, 0.0% Native Hawaiian/Other Pacific Islander, 10.9% Two or more races, 31.7% Hispanic of any race; Average household size: 2.65; Median age: 38.6; Age under 18: 26.8%; Age 65 and over: 9.3%; Males per 100 females: 108.0

Housing: Homeownership rate: 60.8%; Homeowner vacancy rate: 2.3%; Rental vacancy rate: 0.0%

SOLVANG (city). Covers a land area of 2.425 square miles and a water area of 0.001 square miles. Located at 34.59° N. Lat; 120.14° W. Long. Elevation is 505 feet.

History: Solvang was built near Mission Santa Ynez, founded in 1804 by Father Estevan Tapis. Many of Solvang's early residents were immigrants from Denmark.

Population: 5,245; Growth (since 2000): -1.6%; Density: 2,162.7 persons per square mile; Race: 82.5% White, 0.7% Black/African American, 1.4% Asian, 1.1% American Indian/Alaska Native, 0.0% Native Hawaiian/Other Pacific Islander, 2.6% Two or more races, 29.2% Hispanic of any race; Average household size: 2.39; Median age: 45.0; Age under 18: 20.9%; Age 65 and over: 20.9%; Males per 100 females: 93.0; Marriage status: 25.1% never married, 53.6% now married, 3.8% separated, 8.8% widowed, 12.6% divorced; Foreign born: 17.2%; Speak English only: 79.9%; With disability: 14.9%; Veterans: 13.4%; Ancestry: 15.9% English, 15.7% German, 11.9% Irish, 10.1% Danish, 5.0% American

Employment: 14.7% management, business, and financial, 6.8% computer, engineering, and science, 17.2% education, legal, community service, arts, and media, 2.2% healthcare practitioners, 24.3% service, 23.5% sales and office, 8.0% natural resources, construction, and maintenance, 3.4% production, transportation, and material moving

Income: Per capita: $39,816; Median household: $63,626; Average household: $82,987; Households with income of $100,000 or more: 25.9%; Poverty rate: 8.0%

Educational Attainment: High school diploma or higher: 88.6%; Bachelor's degree or higher: 39.1%; Graduate/professional degree or higher: 15.5%

School District(s)

Ballard Elementary (KG-06)
2012-13 Enrollment: 117 . . . . (805) 688-4812
Solvang Elementary (KG-08)
2012-13 Enrollment: 618 . . . . (805) 697-4453

Housing: Homeownership rate: 57.9%; Median home value: $621,800; Median year structure built: 1982; Homeowner vacancy rate: 3.8%; Median gross rent: $1,409 per month; Rental vacancy rate: 6.9%

Health Insurance: 86.8% have insurance; 71.1% have private insurance; 35.1% have public insurance; 13.2% do not have insurance; 9.4% of children under 18 do not have insurance

Hospitals: Santa Ynez Valley Cottage Hospital (20 beds)

Safety: Violent crime rate: 13.0 per 10,000 population; Property crime rate: 130.3 per 10,000 population

Newspapers: Santa Ynez Valley News (weekly circulation 7500)

Transportation: Commute: 82.8% car, 0.0% public transportation, 5.5% walk, 10.6% work from home; Median travel time to work: 25.2 minutes; Amtrak: Bus service available.

Additional Information Contacts

City of Solvang . . . . (805) 688-5575
http://www.cityofsolvang.com

SUMMERLAND (CDP). Covers a land area of 1.983 square miles and a water area of 0.007 square miles. Located at 34.43° N. Lat; 119.59° W. Long. Elevation is 121 feet.
History: Summerland was founded as a colony of spiritualists but soon became an oil town, with derricks rising from the ocean.
Population: 1,448; Growth (since 2000): -6.3%; Density: 730.3 persons per square mile; Race: 89.4% White, 0.2% Black/African American, 2.8% Asian, 0.5% American Indian/Alaska Native, 0.4% Native Hawaiian/Other Pacific Islander, 3.1% Two or more races, 13.3% Hispanic of any race; Average household size: 2.11; Median age: 49.2; Age under 18: 14.6%; Age 65 and over: 17.7%; Males per 100 females: 92.0

School District(s)

Carpinteria Unified (KG-12)
2012-13 Enrollment: 2,308 . . . . (805) 684-4511
Housing: Homeownership rate: 52.6%; Homeowner vacancy rate: 3.2%; Rental vacancy rate: 9.7%

TORO CANYON (CDP). Covers a land area of 3.570 square miles and a water area of 0.003 square miles. Located at 34.42° N. Lat; 119.56° W. Long. Elevation is 49 feet.
Population: 1,508; Growth (since 2000): -11.1%; Density: 422.4 persons per square mile; Race: 92.0% White, 0.5% Black/African American, 0.9% Asian, 0.5% American Indian/Alaska Native, 0.1% Native Hawaiian/Other Pacific Islander, 1.2% Two or more races, 19.4% Hispanic of any race; Average household size: 2.43; Median age: 50.2; Age under 18: 16.8%; Age 65 and over: 22.1%; Males per 100 females: 91.1
Housing: Homeownership rate: 71.0%; Homeowner vacancy rate: 1.6%; Rental vacancy rate: 6.6%

VANDENBERG AFB (CDP). Covers a land area of 22.034 square miles and a water area of 0.087 square miles. Located at 34.72° N. Lat; 120.49° W. Long.
Population: 3,338; Growth (since 2000): -45.7%; Density: 151.5 persons per square mile; Race: 69.4% White, 9.2% Black/African American, 6.2% Asian, 0.8% American Indian/Alaska Native, 0.7% Native Hawaiian/Other Pacific Islander, 9.5% Two or more races, 18.5% Hispanic of any race; Average household size: 3.44; Median age: 22.5; Age under 18: 38.6%; Age 65 and over: 0.2%; Males per 100 females: 118.0; Marriage status: 19.4% never married, 77.6% now married, 1.9% separated, 0.3% widowed, 2.6% divorced; Foreign born: 3.9%; Speak English only: 87.6%; With disability: 1.2%; Veterans: 43.8%; Ancestry: 20.0% German, 8.4% English, 8.1% Irish, 6.1% Italian, 5.8% American
Employment: 7.8% management, business, and financial, 11.0% computer, engineering, and science, 13.2% education, legal, community service, arts, and media, 6.2% healthcare practitioners, 30.2% service, 14.3% sales and office, 9.6% natural resources, construction, and maintenance, 7.8% production, transportation, and material moving
Income: Per capita: $20,830; Median household: $65,142; Average household: $67,386; Households with income of $100,000 or more: 16.6%; Poverty rate: 12.6%
Educational Attainment: High school diploma or higher: 96.0%; Bachelor's degree or higher: 26.4%; Graduate/professional degree or higher: 9.9%

School District(s)

Lompoc Unified (KG-12)
2012-13 Enrollment: 9,811 . . . . (805) 742-3300
Housing: Homeownership rate: 1.4%; Median home value: n/a; Median year structure built: 1997; Homeowner vacancy rate: 0.0%; Median gross rent: $1,597 per month; Rental vacancy rate: 2.2%
Health Insurance: 99.8% have insurance; 98.4% have private insurance; 4.6% have public insurance; 0.2% do not have insurance; 0.0% of children under 18 do not have insurance
Transportation: Commute: 83.9% car, 0.0% public transportation, 7.2% walk, 5.0% work from home; Median travel time to work: 8.9 minutes

VANDENBERG VILLAGE (CDP). Covers a land area of 5.247 square miles and a water area of <.001 square miles. Located at 34.71° N. Lat; 120.46° W. Long. Elevation is 371 feet.
History: Vandenberg Village is located in the Lompoc Valley at the westerly end of the Santa Ynez River Basin, in Santa Barbara County. It is known for its fertile agriculture and abundant flower crops.
Population: 6,497; Growth (since 2000): 12.0%; Density: 1,238.3 persons per square mile; Race: 77.4% White, 4.2% Black/African American, 5.0% Asian, 0.9% American Indian/Alaska Native, 0.9% Native Hawaiian/Other Pacific Islander, 5.0% Two or more races, 18.7% Hispanic of any race; Average household size: 2.54; Median age: 45.0; Age under 18: 22.6%; Age 65 and over: 20.6%; Males per 100 females: 96.0; Marriage status: 24.7% never married, 58.1% now married, 0.8% separated, 8.8% widowed, 8.4% divorced; Foreign born: 10.3%; Speak English only: 87.5%; With disability: 15.0%; Veterans: 25.2%; Ancestry: 24.9% German, 15.2% Irish, 13.9% English, 4.9% French, 3.9% Italian
Employment: 24.4% management, business, and financial, 7.0% computer, engineering, and science, 6.6% education, legal, community service, arts, and media, 7.4% healthcare practitioners, 24.5% service, 17.2% sales and office, 8.7% natural resources, construction, and maintenance, 4.3% production, transportation, and material moving
Income: Per capita: $36,167; Median household: $77,750; Average household: $89,220; Households with income of $100,000 or more: 36.2%; Poverty rate: 6.1%
Educational Attainment: High school diploma or higher: 92.5%; Bachelor's degree or higher: 29.1%; Graduate/professional degree or higher: 11.7%
Housing: Homeownership rate: 76.6%; Median home value: $292,700; Median year structure built: 1970; Homeowner vacancy rate: 2.1%; Median gross rent: $1,412 per month; Rental vacancy rate: 6.1%
Health Insurance: 89.3% have insurance; 78.3% have private insurance; 35.3% have public insurance; 10.7% do not have insurance; 11.3% of children under 18 do not have insurance
Transportation: Commute: 95.7% car, 1.7% public transportation, 0.3% walk, 1.7% work from home; Median travel time to work: 18.2 minutes

Santa Clara County

Located in western California, touching the southern end of San Francisco Bay; includes part of the Diablo Range on the east and the Santa Cruz Mountains on the west. Covers a land area of 1,290.100 square miles, a water area of 13.967 square miles, and is located in the Pacific Time Zone at 37.22° N. Lat., 121.69° W. Long. The county was founded in 1850. County seat is San Jose.

Santa Clara County is part of the San Jose-Sunnyvale-Santa Clara, CA Metropolitan Statistical Area. The entire metro area includes: San Benito County, CA; Santa Clara County, CA

Weather Station: Gilroy Elevation: 193 feet

	Jan	Feb	Mar	Apr	May	Jun	Jul	Aug	Sep	Oct	Nov	Dec
High	60	64	68	73	78	84	88	88	85	79	68	60
Low	39	41	44	46	50	53	55	55	53	49	43	38
Precip	4.4	4.1	3.3	1.2	0.5	0.1	0.0	0.0	0.3	1.0	2.2	3.6
Snow	0.0	0.0	0.0	0.0	0.0	0.0	0.0	0.0	0.0	0.0	0.0	0.0

High and Low temperatures in degrees Fahrenheit; Precipitation and Snow in inches

Weather Station: Los Gatos Elevation: 365 feet

	Jan	Feb	Mar	Apr	May	Jun	Jul	Aug	Sep	Oct	Nov	Dec
High	58	62	66	71	76	81	85	84	82	75	64	58
Low	39	41	43	45	49	52	56	55	53	49	43	39
Precip	4.7	5.0	3.8	1.4	0.6	0.1	0.0	0.0	0.2	1.0	2.3	4.0
Snow	0.0	tr	0.0	0.0	0.0	0.0	0.0	0.0	0.0	0.0	0.0	0.0

High and Low temperatures in degrees Fahrenheit; Precipitation and Snow in inches

Weather Station: Mount Hamilton Elevation: 4,205 feet

	Jan	Feb	Mar	Apr	May	Jun	Jul	Aug	Sep	Oct	Nov	Dec
High	49	49	51	56	63	71	78	78	74	65	54	49
Low	38	37	38	40	47	55	64	64	59	51	42	37
Precip	4.6	4.7	3.9	1.8	1.1	0.3	0.0	0.1	0.4	1.3	3.2	4.1
Snow	3.2	5.0	4.8	1.2	tr	tr	0.0	0.0	0.0	tr	0.2	1.8

High and Low temperatures in degrees Fahrenheit; Precipitation and Snow in inches

Weather Station: Palo Alto Elevation: 24 feet

	Jan	Feb	Mar	Apr	May	Jun	Jul	Aug	Sep	Oct	Nov	Dec
High	58	61	65	69	73	78	79	79	78	73	64	58
Low	39	41	43	45	49	52	55	55	53	48	43	38
Precip	3.1	3.5	2.5	0.9	0.4	0.1	0.0	0.0	0.2	0.7	1.6	2.9
Snow	0.0	0.0	0.0	0.0	0.0	0.0	0.0	0.0	0.0	0.0	0.0	0.0

High and Low temperatures in degrees Fahrenheit; Precipitation and Snow in inches

Weather Station: San Jose Elevation: 95 feet

	Jan	Feb	Mar	Apr	May	Jun	Jul	Aug	Sep	Oct	Nov	Dec
High	59	63	67	70	75	80	83	82	81	75	65	58
Low	42	45	47	49	53	56	58	59	57	53	47	42
Precip	3.0	3.2	2.4	1.1	0.5	0.1	0.0	0.0	0.2	0.8	1.6	2.6
Snow	0.0	tr	tr	tr	0.0	0.0	0.0	0.0	0.0	0.0	0.0	tr

High and Low temperatures in degrees Fahrenheit; Precipitation and Snow in inches

Population: 1,781,642; Growth (since 2000): 5.9%; Density: 1,381.0 persons per square mile; Race: 47.0% White, 2.6% Black/African American, 32.0% Asian, 0.7% American Indian/Alaska Native, 0.4% Native Hawaiian/Other Pacific Islander, 4.9% two or more races, 26.9% Hispanic of any race; Average household size: 2.90; Median age: 36.2; Age under 18: 24.1%; Age 65 and over: 11.1%; Males per 100 females: 100.7; Marriage status: 32.5% never married, 54.9% now married, 1.6% separated, 4.5% widowed, 8.0% divorced; Foreign born: 37.1%; Speak English only: 48.8%; With disability: 7.7%; Veterans: 4.8%; Ancestry: 7.5% German, 5.6% Irish, 5.5% English, 4.5% Italian, 1.8% American

Religion: Six largest groups: 25.1% Catholicism, 4.3% Non-denominational Protestant, 2.5% Hindu, 1.4% Baptist, 1.4% Latter-day Saints, 1.3% Buddhism

Economy: Unemployment rate: 5.1%; Leading industries: 18.5% professional, scientific, and technical services; 11.9% health care and social assistance; 10.8% retail trade; Farms: 1,003 totaling 229,927 acres; Company size: 74 employ 1,000 or more persons, 103 employ 500 to 999 persons, 1,060 employ 100 to 499 persons, 44,398 employ less than 100 persons; Business ownership: 46,414 women-owned, n/a Black-owned, 16,812 Hispanic-owned, 44,514 Asian-owned

Employment: 19.0% management, business, and financial, 16.8% computer, engineering, and science, 9.7% education, legal, community service, arts, and media, 4.3% healthcare practitioners, 14.8% service, 20.6% sales and office, 6.6% natural resources, construction, and maintenance, 8.2% production, transportation, and material moving

Income: Per capita: $41,513; Median household: $91,702; Average household: $120,718; Households with income of $100,000 or more: 46.3%; Poverty rate: 10.2%

Educational Attainment: High school diploma or higher: 86.5%; Bachelor's degree or higher: 46.5%; Graduate/professional degree or higher: 20.7%

Housing: Homeownership rate: 57.7%; Median home value: $645,600; Median year structure built: 1972; Homeowner vacancy rate: 1.4%; Median gross rent: $1,566 per month; Rental vacancy rate: 4.3%

Vital Statistics: Birth rate: 126.7 per 10,000 population; Death rate: 53.9 per 10,000 population; Age-adjusted cancer mortality rate: 140.3 deaths per 100,000 population

Health Insurance: 88.5% have insurance; 73.2% have private insurance; 23.2% have public insurance; 11.5% do not have insurance; 4.2% of children under 18 do not have insurance

Health Care: Physicians: 34.3 per 10,000 population; Hospital beds: 21.7 per 10,000 population; Hospital admissions: 905.2 per 10,000 population

Air Quality Index: 58.6% good, 39.2% moderate, 1.9% unhealthy for sensitive individuals, 0.3% unhealthy (percent of days)

Transportation: Commute: 86.9% car, 3.4% public transportation, 2.0% walk, 4.7% work from home; Median travel time to work: 25.0 minutes

Presidential Election: 69.9% Obama, 27.6% Romney (2012)

National and State Parks: Henry W. Coe State Park; Pacheco State Park

Additional Information Contacts

Santa Clara Government. . . . . (408) 299-5001
http://www.sccgov.org

Santa Clara County Communities

ALUM ROCK (CDP). Covers a land area of 1.204 square miles and a water area of 0 square miles. Located at 37.37° N. Lat; 121.83° W. Long. Elevation is 151 feet.

Population: 15,536; Growth (since 2000): 15.3%; Density: 12,899.0 persons per square mile; Race: 42.4% White, 1.3% Black/African American, 13.1% Asian, 1.9% American Indian/Alaska Native, 0.5% Native Hawaiian/Other Pacific Islander, 5.6% Two or more races, 70.7% Hispanic of any race; Average household size: 4.17; Median age: 31.7; Age under 18: 28.2%; Age 65 and over: 9.0%; Males per 100 females: 105.9; Marriage status: 38.4% never married, 50.3% now married, 1.7% separated, 4.7% widowed, 6.6% divorced; Foreign born: 34.4%; Speak English only: 36.2%; With disability: 10.3%; Veterans: 4.7%; Ancestry: 2.1% Italian, 2.0% Portuguese, 1.7% English, 1.5% German, 1.4% Irish

Employment: 6.0% management, business, and financial, 3.3% computer, engineering, and science, 8.0% education, legal, community service, arts, and media, 1.1% healthcare practitioners, 25.4% service, 24.1% sales and office, 15.2% natural resources, construction, and maintenance, 16.9% production, transportation, and material moving

Income: Per capita: $19,623; Median household: $69,692; Average household: $79,262; Households with income of $100,000 or more: 33.5%; Poverty rate: 11.7%

Educational Attainment: High school diploma or higher: 67.4%; Bachelor's degree or higher: 13.0%; Graduate/professional degree or higher: 3.1%

Housing: Homeownership rate: 64.9%; Median home value: $384,500; Median year structure built: 1956; Homeowner vacancy rate: 1.8%; Median gross rent: $1,429 per month; Rental vacancy rate: 3.2%

Health Insurance: 82.3% have insurance; 54.3% have private insurance; 33.6% have public insurance; 17.7% do not have insurance; 4.7% of children under 18 do not have insurance

Transportation: Commute: 90.3% car, 3.8% public transportation, 0.9% walk, 2.1% work from home; Median travel time to work: 26.6 minutes

ALVISO (unincorporated postal area)

ZCTA: 95002

Covers a land area of 11.972 square miles and a water area of 2.307 square miles. Located at 37.44° N. Lat; 122.01° W. Long. Elevation is 3 feet.

Population: 2,077; Growth (since 2000): -2.4%; Density: 173.5 persons per square mile; Race: 37.8% White, 2.1% Black/African American, 17.4% Asian, 1.3% American Indian/Alaska Native, 0.3% Native Hawaiian/Other Pacific Islander, 4.5% Two or more races, 61.1% Hispanic of any race; Average household size: 3.59; Median age: 35.4; Age under 18: 25.9%; Age 65 and over: 9.3%; Males per 100 females: 104.2

School District(s)

Santa Clara Unified (KG-12)
2012-13 Enrollment: 15,151 . . . . (408) 423-2000

Housing: Homeownership rate: 59.1%; Homeowner vacancy rate: 0.6%; Rental vacancy rate: 2.1%

BURBANK (CDP). Covers a land area of 0.403 square miles and a water area of 0 square miles. Located at 37.32° N. Lat; 121.93° W. Long. Elevation is 121 feet.

Population: 4,926; Growth (since 2000): -6.0%; Density: 12,218.4 persons per square mile; Race: 60.8% White, 2.7% Black/African American, 7.7% Asian, 1.3% American Indian/Alaska Native, 0.3% Native Hawaiian/Other Pacific Islander, 5.9% Two or more races, 50.9% Hispanic of any race; Average household size: 2.62; Median age: 34.5; Age under 18: 22.8%; Age 65 and over: 6.2%; Males per 100 females: 100.9; Marriage status: 45.1% never married, 33.7% now married, 1.6% separated, 2.7% widowed, 18.5% divorced; Foreign born: 29.7%; Speak English only: 54.7%; With disability: 9.4%; Veterans: 8.3%; Ancestry: 9.8% German, 5.0% Irish, 3.9% Italian, 3.4% English, 2.2% French

Employment: 9.1% management, business, and financial, 6.6% computer, engineering, and science, 7.7% education, legal, community service, arts, and media, 2.4% healthcare practitioners, 26.2% service, 28.8% sales and office, 9.5% natural resources, construction, and maintenance, 9.8% production, transportation, and material moving

Income: Per capita: $29,755; Median household: $61,883; Average household: $77,936; Households with income of $100,000 or more: 27.4%; Poverty rate: 15.2%

Educational Attainment: High school diploma or higher: 78.5%; Bachelor's degree or higher: 25.4%; Graduate/professional degree or higher: 7.0%

Housing: Homeownership rate: 43.9%; Median home value: $457,900; Median year structure built: 1947; Homeowner vacancy rate: 2.0%; Median gross rent: $1,129 per month; Rental vacancy rate: 3.3%

Health Insurance: 81.5% have insurance; 68.5% have private insurance; 17.7% have public insurance; 18.5% do not have insurance; 2.7% of children under 18 do not have insurance

Transportation: Commute: 85.7% car, 5.7% public transportation, 2.7% walk, 2.7% work from home; Median travel time to work: 22.7 minutes

CAMBRIAN PARK (CDP). Covers a land area of 0.596 square miles and a water area of 0 square miles. Located at 37.26° N. Lat; 121.93° W. Long. Elevation is 239 feet.

Population: 3,282; Growth (since 2000): 0.7%; Density: 5,503.8 persons per square mile; Race: 79.2% White, 0.8% Black/African American, 6.7% Asian, 0.9% American Indian/Alaska Native, 0.6% Native Hawaiian/Other Pacific Islander, 6.1% Two or more races, 18.0% Hispanic of any race; Average household size: 2.86; Median age: 42.4; Age under 18: 24.0%; Age 65 and over: 12.4%; Males per 100 females: 101.1; Marriage status: 27.5% never married, 54.7% now married, 0.8% separated, 7.2%

widowed, 10.6% divorced; Foreign born: 10.8%; Speak English only: 87.6%; With disability: 12.9%; Veterans: 7.0%; Ancestry: 17.8% English, 15.2% Irish, 13.4% Italian, 10.3% German, 5.3% Polish

Employment: 22.1% management, business, and financial, 3.1% computer, engineering, and science, 9.5% education, legal, community service, arts, and media, 4.8% healthcare practitioners, 15.7% service, 22.4% sales and office, 19.2% natural resources, construction, and maintenance, 3.1% production, transportation, and material moving

Income: Per capita: $42,579; Median household: $99,483; Average household: $115,572; Households with income of $100,000 or more: 49.4%; Poverty rate: 1.8%

Educational Attainment: High school diploma or higher: 93.2%; Bachelor's degree or higher: 34.4%; Graduate/professional degree or higher: 11.8%

Housing: Homeownership rate: 79.7%; Median home value: $682,800; Median year structure built: 1955; Homeowner vacancy rate: 0.8%; Median gross rent: $2,000+ per month; Rental vacancy rate: 4.1%

Health Insurance: 92.4% have insurance; 86.1% have private insurance; 19.4% have public insurance; 7.6% do not have insurance; 3.3% of children under 18 do not have insurance

Transportation: Commute: 93.8% car, 0.0% public transportation, 0.0% walk, 5.1% work from home; Median travel time to work: 20.1 minutes

CAMPBELL (city). Covers a land area of 5.798 square miles and a water area of 0.088 square miles. Located at 37.28° N. Lat; 121.95° W. Long. Elevation is 200 feet.

History: Named for William Campbell, pioneer sawmill operator, by his son Benjamin, who founded the town. Founded 1885. Incorporated 1952.

Population: 39,349; Growth (since 2000): 3.2%; Density: 6,786.5 persons per square mile; Race: 66.9% White, 2.9% Black/African American, 16.1% Asian, 0.7% American Indian/Alaska Native, 0.4% Native Hawaiian/Other Pacific Islander, 6.1% Two or more races, 18.4% Hispanic of any race; Average household size: 2.42; Median age: 38.3; Age under 18: 21.0%; Age 65 and over: 11.2%; Males per 100 females: 96.2; Marriage status: 35.9% never married, 47.2% now married, 1.7% separated, 4.8% widowed, 12.1% divorced; Foreign born: 22.3%; Speak English only: 71.1%; With disability: 8.5%; Veterans: 5.6%; Ancestry: 12.4% German, 11.1% Irish, 7.9% Italian, 7.8% English, 4.1% European

Employment: 21.0% management, business, and financial, 12.9% computer, engineering, and science, 11.1% education, legal, community service, arts, and media, 4.2% healthcare practitioners, 14.4% service, 24.0% sales and office, 6.8% natural resources, construction, and maintenance, 5.5% production, transportation, and material moving

Income: Per capita: $44,865; Median household: $88,300; Average household: $108,934; Households with income of $100,000 or more: 43.7%; Poverty rate: 7.2%

Educational Attainment: High school diploma or higher: 93.1%; Bachelor's degree or higher: 45.8%; Graduate/professional degree or higher: 16.4%

School District(s)

Campbell Union (KG-08)
2012-13 Enrollment: 7,701 . . . . (408) 364-4200
Campbell Union High (09-12)
2012-13 Enrollment: 7,373 . . . . (408) 371-0960

Vocational/Technical School(s)

International Culinary Center-California (Private, For-profit)
Fall 2013 Enrollment: 124 . . . . (408) 370-9190
2013-14 Tuition: $33,773

Housing: Homeownership rate: 50.1%; Median home value: $666,900; Median year structure built: 1970; Homeowner vacancy rate: 1.8%; Median gross rent: $1,494 per month; Rental vacancy rate: 4.6%

Health Insurance: 89.5% have insurance; 79.0% have private insurance; 19.7% have public insurance; 10.5% do not have insurance; 2.7% of children under 18 do not have insurance

Safety: Violent crime rate: 26.1 per 10,000 population; Property crime rate: 385.5 per 10,000 population

Newspapers: Campbell Express (weekly circulation 2700)

Transportation: Commute: 88.2% car, 2.5% public transportation, 1.7% walk, 4.8% work from home; Median travel time to work: 23.8 minutes

Additional Information Contacts

City of Campbell . . . . (408) 866-2125
http://www.ci.campbell.ca.us

COYOTE (unincorporated postal area)
ZCTA: 95013

Covers a land area of 1.527 square miles and a water area of 0 square miles. Located at 37.22° N. Lat; 121.74° W. Long. Elevation is 259 feet.

Population: 80; Growth (since 2000): n/a; Density: 52.4 persons per square mile; Race: 37.5% White, 0.0% Black/African American, 5.0% Asian, 0.0% American Indian/Alaska Native, 0.0% Native Hawaiian/Other Pacific Islander, 1.3% Two or more races, 60.0% Hispanic of any race; Average household size: 2.76; Median age: 38.6; Age under 18: 21.2%; Age 65 and over: 15.0%; Males per 100 females: 135.3

Housing: Homeownership rate: 31.0%; Homeowner vacancy rate: 0.0%; Rental vacancy rate: 4.8%

CUPERTINO (city). Covers a land area of 11.256 square miles and a water area of <.001 square miles. Located at 37.32° N. Lat; 122.04° W. Long. Elevation is 236 feet.

History: Named for Arroyo de San Jose Cupertino, which was named for a 17th-century Italian saint. Cupertino was settled in the 1850s by squatters who banded together when the owners of Rancho Quito tried to remove them from the land.

Population: 58,302; Growth (since 2000): 15.3%; Density: 5,179.5 persons per square mile; Race: 31.3% White, 0.6% Black/African American, 63.3% Asian, 0.2% American Indian/Alaska Native, 0.1% Native Hawaiian/Other Pacific Islander, 3.3% Two or more races, 3.6% Hispanic of any race; Average household size: 2.87; Median age: 39.9; Age under 18: 27.6%; Age 65 and over: 12.5%; Males per 100 females: 97.4; Marriage status: 23.0% never married, 66.3% now married, 0.6% separated, 5.5% widowed, 5.2% divorced; Foreign born: 49.9%; Speak English only: 37.0%; With disability: 6.0%; Veterans: 3.2%; Ancestry: 5.0% German, 4.1% Irish, 3.9% English, 2.7% Italian, 1.7% American

Employment: 26.5% management, business, and financial, 35.1% computer, engineering, and science, 9.7% education, legal, community service, arts, and media, 5.7% healthcare practitioners, 5.1% service, 13.3% sales and office, 1.7% natural resources, construction, and maintenance, 2.9% production, transportation, and material moving

Income: Per capita: $53,941; Median household: $129,976; Average household: $153,786; Households with income of $100,000 or more: 64.2%; Poverty rate: 4.3%

Educational Attainment: High school diploma or higher: 96.5%; Bachelor's degree or higher: 74.6%; Graduate/professional degree or higher: 41.1%

School District(s)

Cupertino Union (PK-08)
2012-13 Enrollment: 19,035 . . . . (408) 252-3000
Fremont Union High (09-12)
2012-13 Enrollment: 10,664 . . . . (408) 522-2200

Two-year College(s)

De Anza College (Public)
Fall 2013 Enrollment: 23,261 . . . . (408) 864-5678
2013-14 Tuition: In-state $1,542; Out-of-state $8,022

Housing: Homeownership rate: 62.5%; Median home value: 1 million+; Median year structure built: 1971; Homeowner vacancy rate: 0.8%; Median gross rent: $2,000+ per month; Rental vacancy rate: 4.7%

Health Insurance: 95.8% have insurance; 88.4% have private insurance; 16.0% have public insurance; 4.2% do not have insurance; 1.3% of children under 18 do not have insurance

Safety: Violent crime rate: 6.8 per 10,000 population; Property crime rate: 134.3 per 10,000 population

Transportation: Commute: 88.6% car, 2.5% public transportation, 1.2% walk, 5.9% work from home; Median travel time to work: 25.4 minutes

Additional Information Contacts

City of Cupertino . . . . (408) 777-3200
http://www.cupertino.org

EAST FOOTHILLS (CDP). Covers a land area of 2.283 square miles and a water area of 0 square miles. Located at 37.38° N. Lat; 121.82° W. Long. Elevation is 344 feet.

Population: 8,269; Growth (since 2000): 1.7%; Density: 3,622.1 persons per square mile; Race: 58.7% White, 2.5% Black/African American, 17.5% Asian, 0.9% American Indian/Alaska Native, 0.5% Native Hawaiian/Other Pacific Islander, 5.2% Two or more races, 37.7% Hispanic of any race; Average household size: 3.05; Median age: 42.0; Age under 18: 22.0%; Age 65 and over: 15.6%; Males per 100 females: 99.9; Marriage status: 24.4% never married, 61.6% now married, 0.8% separated, 5.5% widowed, 8.5% divorced; Foreign born: 24.8%; Speak English only: 59.9%;

With disability: 8.1%; Veterans: 8.0%; Ancestry: 10.9% Italian, 9.1% Irish, 7.7% German, 6.8% English, 3.2% Portuguese
Employment: 20.4% management, business, and financial, 7.9% computer, engineering, and science, 13.3% education, legal, community service, arts, and media, 4.5% healthcare practitioners, 14.3% service, 22.3% sales and office, 9.8% natural resources, construction, and maintenance, 7.6% production, transportation, and material moving
Income: Per capita: $46,467; Median household: $111,591; Average household: $131,100; Households with income of $100,000 or more: 52.4%; Poverty rate: 6.4%
Educational Attainment: High school diploma or higher: 91.7%; Bachelor's degree or higher: 38.7%; Graduate/professional degree or higher: 13.5%
Housing: Homeownership rate: 84.1%; Median home value: $616,600; Median year structure built: 1959; Homeowner vacancy rate: 1.3%; Median gross rent: $2,000+ per month; Rental vacancy rate: 5.3%
Health Insurance: 90.9% have insurance; 79.3% have private insurance; 24.5% have public insurance; 9.1% do not have insurance; 5.2% of children under 18 do not have insurance
Transportation: Commute: 86.7% car, 2.5% public transportation, 0.2% walk, 8.2% work from home; Median travel time to work: 25.7 minutes

FRUITDALE (CDP). Covers a land area of 0.269 square miles and a water area of 0 square miles. Located at 37.31° N. Lat; 121.94° W. Long. Elevation is 154 feet.
Population: 935; Growth (since 2000): 4.5%; Density: 3,475.3 persons per square mile; Race: 67.7% White, 3.3% Black/African American, 11.8% Asian, 1.2% American Indian/Alaska Native, 0.4% Native Hawaiian/Other Pacific Islander, 6.2% Two or more races, 26.1% Hispanic of any race; Average household size: 2.39; Median age: 41.7; Age under 18: 18.3%; Age 65 and over: 9.4%; Males per 100 females: 100.2
Housing: Homeownership rate: 54.0%; Homeowner vacancy rate: 1.0%; Rental vacancy rate: 2.9%

GILROY (city). Covers a land area of 16.146 square miles and a water area of 0.010 square miles. Located at 37.01° N. Lat; 121.59° W. Long. Elevation is 200 feet.
History: Gilroy was named by Scotchman John Cameron, an early settler who took the name Gilroy when he jumped ship at Monterey in 1814. He acquired Rancho San Ysidro by marrying Ygnacio Ortega's daughter.
Population: 48,821; Growth (since 2000): 17.7%; Density: 3,023.7 persons per square mile; Race: 58.7% White, 1.9% Black/African American, 7.1% Asian, 1.7% American Indian/Alaska Native, 0.2% Native Hawaiian/Other Pacific Islander, 5.1% Two or more races, 57.8% Hispanic of any race; Average household size: 3.39; Median age: 32.4; Age under 18: 30.7%; Age 65 and over: 8.4%; Males per 100 females: 98.5; Marriage status: 32.7% never married, 55.1% now married, 2.8% separated, 4.1% widowed, 8.1% divorced; Foreign born: 26.3%; Speak English only: 51.3%; With disability: 7.8%; Veterans: 4.9%; Ancestry: 7.6% German, 6.3% Italian, 6.1% Irish, 4.9% English, 2.0% French
Employment: 13.4% management, business, and financial, 5.2% computer, engineering, and science, 8.0% education, legal, community service, arts, and media, 3.5% healthcare practitioners, 18.9% service, 24.5% sales and office, 16.4% natural resources, construction, and maintenance, 10.1% production, transportation, and material moving
Income: Per capita: $28,852; Median household: $78,360; Average household: $95,897; Households with income of $100,000 or more: 38.0%; Poverty rate: 15.5%
Educational Attainment: High school diploma or higher: 75.7%; Bachelor's degree or higher: 24.8%; Graduate/professional degree or higher: 8.4%

School District(s)

Gilroy Unified (KG-12)
2012-13 Enrollment: 11,571 . . . . (408) 847-2700
Santa Clara County Rop
2012-13 Enrollment: n/a . . . . (408) 733-0881

Two-year College(s)

Gavilan College (Public)
Fall 2013 Enrollment: 5,834 . . . . (408) 848-4800
2013-14 Tuition: In-state $1,246; Out-of-state $6,654

Vocational/Technical School(s)

CET-Gilroy (Private, Not-for-profit)
Fall 2013 Enrollment: 104 . . . . (408) 287-7924
2013-14 Tuition: $9,394

Housing: Homeownership rate: 60.8%; Median home value: $433,600; Median year structure built: 1985; Homeowner vacancy rate: 1.7%; Median gross rent: $1,325 per month; Rental vacancy rate: 4.6%
Health Insurance: 83.9% have insurance; 61.7% have private insurance; 29.2% have public insurance; 16.1% do not have insurance; 5.4% of children under 18 do not have insurance
Hospitals: Saint Louise Regional Hospital (93 beds)
Safety: Violent crime rate: 35.1 per 10,000 population; Property crime rate: 339.6 per 10,000 population
Newspapers: The Dispatch (daily circulation 4300)
Transportation: Commute: 87.8% car, 2.7% public transportation, 1.4% walk, 3.3% work from home; Median travel time to work: 29.6 minutes; Amtrak: Bus service available.

Additional Information Contacts

City of Gilroy . . . . (408) 846-0400
http://www.cityofgilroy.org/cityofgilroy

LEXINGTON HILLS (CDP). Covers a land area of 4.686 square miles and a water area of 0.034 square miles. Located at 37.16° N. Lat; 121.99° W. Long. Elevation is 1,257 feet.
Population: 2,421; Growth (since 2000): -1.3%; Density: 516.7 persons per square mile; Race: 88.7% White, 0.4% Black/African American, 3.7% Asian, 0.2% American Indian/Alaska Native, 0.0% Native Hawaiian/Other Pacific Islander, 4.5% Two or more races, 8.0% Hispanic of any race; Average household size: 2.55; Median age: 44.8; Age under 18: 22.3%; Age 65 and over: 10.5%; Males per 100 females: 105.9
Housing: Homeownership rate: 80.4%; Homeowner vacancy rate: 1.3%; Rental vacancy rate: 2.6%

LOS ALTOS (city). Covers a land area of 6.487 square miles and a water area of 0 square miles. Located at 37.37° N. Lat; 122.10° W. Long. Elevation is 157 feet.
History: Named for the Spanish translation of "the heights". Incorporated 1952.
Population: 28,976; Growth (since 2000): 4.6%; Density: 4,467.0 persons per square mile; Race: 70.6% White, 0.5% Black/African American, 23.5% Asian, 0.2% American Indian/Alaska Native, 0.2% Native Hawaiian/Other Pacific Islander, 4.3% Two or more races, 3.9% Hispanic of any race; Average household size: 2.68; Median age: 46.2; Age under 18: 26.1%; Age 65 and over: 20.0%; Males per 100 females: 93.1; Marriage status: 17.9% never married, 69.5% now married, 0.9% separated, 6.9% widowed, 5.6% divorced; Foreign born: 23.4%; Speak English only: 72.7%; With disability: 6.5%; Veterans: 7.3%; Ancestry: 15.9% German, 13.8% English, 10.0% Irish, 6.6% Italian, 3.5% European
Employment: 33.9% management, business, and financial, 22.5% computer, engineering, and science, 14.2% education, legal, community service, arts, and media, 7.5% healthcare practitioners, 4.2% service, 15.0% sales and office, 1.0% natural resources, construction, and maintenance, 1.7% production, transportation, and material moving
Income: Per capita: $84,440; Median household: $157,907; Average household: $223,581; Households with income of $100,000 or more: 66.1%; Poverty rate: 2.1%
Educational Attainment: High school diploma or higher: 98.8%; Bachelor's degree or higher: 78.7%; Graduate/professional degree or higher: 45.6%

School District(s)

Cupertino Union (PK-08)
2012-13 Enrollment: 19,035 . . . . (408) 252-3000
Los Altos Elementary (KG-08)
2012-13 Enrollment: 4,505 . . . . (650) 947-1150
Mountain View-Los Altos Union High (09-12)
2012-13 Enrollment: 3,737 . . . . (650) 940-4650
Santa Clara County Office of Education (KG-12)
2012-13 Enrollment: 8,770 . . . . (408) 453-6500

Housing: Homeownership rate: 83.8%; Median home value: 1 million+; Median year structure built: 1960; Homeowner vacancy rate: 0.7%; Median gross rent: $2,000+ per month; Rental vacancy rate: 5.0%
Health Insurance: 97.5% have insurance; 91.4% have private insurance; 20.0% have public insurance; 2.5% do not have insurance; 1.3% of children under 18 do not have insurance
Safety: Violent crime rate: 7.6 per 10,000 population; Property crime rate: 118.4 per 10,000 population
Newspapers: Town Crier (weekly circulation 16000)
Transportation: Commute: 84.0% car, 2.0% public transportation, 2.2% walk, 9.0% work from home; Median travel time to work: 22.1 minutes

Additional Information Contacts
City of Los Altos . . . . (650) 947-2700
http://www.losaltosca.gov

LOS ALTOS HILLS (town). Covers a land area of 8.802 square miles and a water area of 0 square miles. Located at 37.37° N. Lat; 122.14° W. Long. Elevation is 289 feet.
History: Stanford University to North.
Population: 7,922; Growth (since 2000): 0.3%; Density: 900.0 persons per square mile; Race: 68.4% White, 0.5% Black/African American, 26.6% Asian, 0.1% American Indian/Alaska Native, 0.1% Native Hawaiian/Other Pacific Islander, 3.7% Two or more races, 2.7% Hispanic of any race; Average household size: 2.78; Median age: 50.2; Age under 18: 22.9%; Age 65 and over: 23.2%; Males per 100 females: 97.8; Marriage status: 20.3% never married, 72.0% now married, 0.9% separated, 3.0% widowed, 4.8% divorced; Foreign born: 31.2%; Speak English only: 65.7%; With disability: 7.0%; Veterans: 7.3%; Ancestry: 12.4% German, 10.7% English, 7.0% Irish, 5.7% Italian, 4.1% Iranian
Employment: 38.1% management, business, and financial, 16.6% computer, engineering, and science, 15.6% education, legal, community service, arts, and media, 8.6% healthcare practitioners, 4.0% service, 13.8% sales and office, 2.8% natural resources, construction, and maintenance, 0.5% production, transportation, and material moving
Income: Per capita: $114,480; Median household: $205,694; Average household: $316,771; Households with income of $100,000 or more: 76.8%; Poverty rate: 3.8%
Educational Attainment: High school diploma or higher: 97.9%; Bachelor's degree or higher: 84.7%; Graduate/professional degree or higher: 50.9%

School District(s)

Los Altos Elementary (KG-08)
2012-13 Enrollment: 4,505 . . . . (650) 947-1150

Two-year College(s)

Foothill College (Public)
Fall 2013 Enrollment: 14,814 . . . . (650) 949-7777
2013-14 Tuition: In-state $1,536; Out-of-state $8,016
Housing: Homeownership rate: 91.3%; Median home value: 1 million+; Median year structure built: 1970; Homeowner vacancy rate: 1.2%; Median gross rent: $2,000+ per month; Rental vacancy rate: 4.2%
Health Insurance: 95.3% have insurance; 87.0% have private insurance; 23.0% have public insurance; 4.7% do not have insurance; 3.0% of children under 18 do not have insurance
Safety: Violent crime rate: 2.4 per 10,000 population; Property crime rate: 100.0 per 10,000 population
Transportation: Commute: 89.1% car, 0.0% public transportation, 0.0% walk, 9.1% work from home; Median travel time to work: 22.6 minutes
Additional Information Contacts
Town of Los Altos Hills . . . . (650) 941-7222
http://www.losaltoshills.ca.gov

LOS GATOS (town). Covers a land area of 11.080 square miles and a water area of 0.080 square miles. Located at 37.23° N. Lat; 121.95° W. Long. Elevation is 344 feet.
History: Named for the Spanish tranlation of "the cats," referring to the region's wildcats. Los Gatos developed on the former Rancho Rinconada de los Gatos ("little corner of the cats"), named for the mountain lions and wildcats which once lived in the hills.
Population: 29,413; Growth (since 2000): 2.9%; Density: 2,654.6 persons per square mile; Race: 81.8% White, 0.9% Black/African American, 10.9% Asian, 0.3% American Indian/Alaska Native, 0.2% Native Hawaiian/Other Pacific Islander, 4.4% Two or more races, 7.2% Hispanic of any race; Average household size: 2.35; Median age: 45.0; Age under 18: 22.3%; Age 65 and over: 17.9%; Males per 100 females: 92.0; Marriage status: 23.6% never married, 60.4% now married, 1.4% separated, 5.4% widowed, 10.6% divorced; Foreign born: 17.1%; Speak English only: 80.4%; With disability: 7.4%; Veterans: 9.6%; Ancestry: 16.0% German, 15.7% Irish, 12.1% English, 8.5% Italian, 4.9% European
Employment: 30.3% management, business, and financial, 11.9% computer, engineering, and science, 13.8% education, legal, community service, arts, and media, 6.4% healthcare practitioners, 6.7% service, 23.9% sales and office, 3.4% natural resources, construction, and maintenance, 3.6% production, transportation, and material moving
Income: Per capita: $70,420; Median household: $122,476; Average household: $166,958; Households with income of $100,000 or more: 56.5%; Poverty rate: 4.6%
Educational Attainment: High school diploma or higher: 97.8%; Bachelor's degree or higher: 67.8%; Graduate/professional degree or higher: 30.3%

School District(s)

Campbell Union (KG-08)
2012-13 Enrollment: 7,701 . . . . (408) 364-4200
Lakeside Joint (KG-05)
2012-13 Enrollment: 92. . . . . (408) 354-2372
Loma Prieta Joint Union Elementary (KG-08)
2012-13 Enrollment: 453. . . . . (408) 353-1101
Los Gatos Union Elementary (KG-08)
2012-13 Enrollment: 3,188 . . . . (408) 335-2000
Los Gatos-Saratoga Joint Union High (09-12)
2012-13 Enrollment: 3,232 . . . . (408) 354-2520
Union Elementary (KG-08)
2012-13 Enrollment: 5,298 . . . . (408) 377-8010
Housing: Homeownership rate: 63.0%; Median home value: 1 million+; Median year structure built: 1968; Homeowner vacancy rate: 1.0%; Median gross rent: $1,728 per month; Rental vacancy rate: 4.5%
Health Insurance: 96.1% have insurance; 88.7% have private insurance; 22.8% have public insurance; 3.9% do not have insurance; 0.8% of children under 18 do not have insurance
Safety: Violent crime rate: 8.2 per 10,000 population; Property crime rate: 181.5 per 10,000 population
Newspapers: Los Gatos Weekly Times (weekly circulation 19000); Saratoga News (weekly circulation 9500)
Transportation: Commute: 86.7% car, 0.9% public transportation, 1.8% walk, 8.6% work from home; Median travel time to work: 24.8 minutes
Additional Information Contacts
Town of Los Gatos . . . . (408) 354-6834
http://www.town.los-gatos.ca.us

LOYOLA (CDP). Covers a land area of 1.468 square miles and a water area of 0 square miles. Located at 37.35° N. Lat; 122.10° W. Long. Elevation is 243 feet.
History: The name comes from a 1904 plan by the Jesuits of Santa Clara University to build a new university named for their founder, St. Ignatius of Loyola, in the area. If the plan had come to fruition, the university would have been located in the area of the present-day golf course on Country Club Drive.
Population: 3,261; Growth (since 2000): -6.2%; Density: 2,220.8 persons per square mile; Race: 70.3% White, 0.6% Black/African American, 23.3% Asian, 0.0% American Indian/Alaska Native, 0.1% Native Hawaiian/Other Pacific Islander, 4.6% Two or more races, 3.5% Hispanic of any race; Average household size: 2.80; Median age: 47.5; Age under 18: 24.9%; Age 65 and over: 19.9%; Males per 100 females: 97.4; Marriage status: 19.0% never married, 70.9% now married, 1.9% separated, 5.0% widowed, 5.0% divorced; Foreign born: 26.0%; Speak English only: 70.2%; With disability: 6.3%; Veterans: 5.3%; Ancestry: 18.9% English, 16.2% Irish, 13.7% German, 13.0% Italian, 6.7% French
Employment: 37.7% management, business, and financial, 15.8% computer, engineering, and science, 21.9% education, legal, community service, arts, and media, 6.7% healthcare practitioners, 2.7% service, 13.3% sales and office, 1.3% natural resources, construction, and maintenance, 0.5% production, transportation, and material moving
Income: Per capita: $97,292; Median household: $205,417; Average household: $284,850; Households with income of $100,000 or more: 79.6%; Poverty rate: 3.0%
Educational Attainment: High school diploma or higher: 99.1%; Bachelor's degree or higher: 83.7%; Graduate/professional degree or higher: 52.9%
Housing: Homeownership rate: 90.7%; Median home value: 1 million+; Median year structure built: 1959; Homeowner vacancy rate: 1.0%; Median gross rent: $2,000+ per month; Rental vacancy rate: 4.4%
Health Insurance: 98.7% have insurance; 94.7% have private insurance; 17.6% have public insurance; 1.3% do not have insurance; 0.0% of children under 18 do not have insurance
Transportation: Commute: 87.1% car, 0.7% public transportation, 0.9% walk, 10.7% work from home; Median travel time to work: 22.6 minutes

MILPITAS (city). Covers a land area of 13.591 square miles and a water area of 0.050 square miles. Located at 37.44° N. Lat; 121.89° W. Long. Elevation is 20 feet.
History: Named for the Spanish translation of "little cornfields," for the vegetable gardens in the area. Incorporated 1954.

Population: 66,790; Growth (since 2000): 6.5%; Density: 4,914.4 persons per square mile; Race: 20.5% White, 2.9% Black/African American, 62.2% Asian, 0.5% American Indian/Alaska Native, 0.5% Native Hawaiian/Other Pacific Islander, 4.6% Two or more races, 16.8% Hispanic of any race; Average household size: 3.34; Median age: 36.1; Age under 18: 22.9%; Age 65 and over: 9.5%; Males per 100 females: 104.5; Marriage status: 31.8% never married, 56.4% now married, 2.3% separated, 4.7% widowed, 7.1% divorced; Foreign born: 49.7%; Speak English only: 35.5%; With disability: 7.3%; Veterans: 3.7%; Ancestry: 4.1% German, 3.3% Irish, 2.9% English, 1.8% Italian, 1.5% French

Employment: 15.5% management, business, and financial, 22.4% computer, engineering, and science, 6.4% education, legal, community service, arts, and media, 3.8% healthcare practitioners, 14.9% service, 21.5% sales and office, 4.8% natural resources, construction, and maintenance, 10.8% production, transportation, and material moving

Income: Per capita: $33,789; Median household: $95,466; Average household: $112,679; Households with income of $100,000 or more: 48.1%; Poverty rate: 7.2%

Educational Attainment: High school diploma or higher: 85.8%; Bachelor's degree or higher: 40.8%; Graduate/professional degree or higher: 14.3%

School District(s)

Milpitas Unified (KG-12)
2012-13 Enrollment: 10,033 . . . . (408) 635-2600

Two-year College(s)

Heald College-San Jose (Private, For-profit)
Fall 2013 Enrollment: 1,671 . . . . (408) 934-4900
2013-14 Tuition: In-state $13,620; Out-of-state $13,620

Housing: Homeownership rate: 66.8%; Median home value: $513,300; Median year structure built: 1978; Homeowner vacancy rate: 1.2%; Median gross rent: $1,742 per month; Rental vacancy rate: 3.1%

Health Insurance: 90.0% have insurance; 74.9% have private insurance; 21.0% have public insurance; 10.0% do not have insurance; 3.6% of children under 18 do not have insurance

Safety: Violent crime rate: 13.4 per 10,000 population; Property crime rate: 297.3 per 10,000 population

Newspapers: Milpitas Post (weekly circulation 66000)

Transportation: Commute: 91.5% car, 2.5% public transportation, 0.8% walk, 3.8% work from home; Median travel time to work: 23.3 minutes

Additional Information Contacts

City of Milpitas. . . . . (408) 586-3000
http://www.ci.milpitas.ca.gov

MONTE SERENO (city). Covers a land area of 1.615 square miles and a water area of 0 square miles. Located at 37.24° N. Lat; 121.99° W. Long. Elevation is 502 feet.

History: The Monte Sereno area was part of the 1839 Alta California land grant of Rancho Rinconada de Los Gatos. The city incorporated on May 14, 1957 to protect its semi-rural atmosphere.

Population: 3,341; Growth (since 2000): -4.1%; Density: 2,068.4 persons per square mile; Race: 80.8% White, 0.4% Black/African American, 13.9% Asian, 0.4% American Indian/Alaska Native, 0.0% Native Hawaiian/Other Pacific Islander, 3.7% Two or more races, 4.8% Hispanic of any race; Average household size: 2.76; Median age: 48.3; Age under 18: 24.4%; Age 65 and over: 19.4%; Males per 100 females: 96.3; Marriage status: 15.1% never married, 74.2% now married, 1.0% separated, 6.1% widowed, 4.6% divorced; Foreign born: 12.2%; Speak English only: 88.8%; With disability: 9.9%; Veterans: 9.2%; Ancestry: 16.3% Irish, 15.1% German, 13.4% Italian, 11.3% English, 9.6% European

Employment: 39.1% management, business, and financial, 4.3% computer, engineering, and science, 14.3% education, legal, community service, arts, and media, 8.0% healthcare practitioners, 2.9% service, 25.9% sales and office, 1.4% natural resources, construction, and maintenance, 4.1% production, transportation, and material moving

Income: Per capita: $96,858; Median household: $182,417; Average household: $264,619; Households with income of $100,000 or more: 71.9%; Poverty rate: 2.4%

Educational Attainment: High school diploma or higher: 99.8%; Bachelor's degree or higher: 68.8%; Graduate/professional degree or higher: 29.2%

Housing: Homeownership rate: 90.0%; Median home value: 1 million+; Median year structure built: 1964; Homeowner vacancy rate: 1.3%; Median gross rent: $2,000+ per month; Rental vacancy rate: 5.4%

Health Insurance: 96.3% have insurance; 91.9% have private insurance; 22.7% have public insurance; 3.7% do not have insurance; 4.8% of children under 18 do not have insurance

Safety: Violent crime rate: 2.9 per 10,000 population; Property crime rate: 94.5 per 10,000 population

Transportation: Commute: 86.5% car, 0.0% public transportation, 0.3% walk, 12.8% work from home; Median travel time to work: 29.2 minutes

Additional Information Contacts

City of Monte Sereno. . . . . (408) 354-7635
http://www.montesereno.org

MORGAN HILL (city). Covers a land area of 12.882 square miles and a water area of 0 square miles. Located at 37.13° N. Lat; 121.64° W. Long. Elevation is 348 feet.

History: Named for Morgan Hill, who acquired a ranch here when he married Diana Murphy. The ranch was named Ojo de Agua de la Coche ("sight of water from the coach"). Murphy was an Irish immigrant who brought his family to California in 1844 with the first party to cross the Sierra Nevada through Truckee Pass. By 1883 the Murphy family owned three million acres of land in California, Nevada, and Arizona.

Population: 37,882; Growth (since 2000): 12.9%; Density: 2,940.8 persons per square mile; Race: 65.2% White, 2.0% Black/African American, 10.2% Asian, 0.9% American Indian/Alaska Native, 0.3% Native Hawaiian/Other Pacific Islander, 6.2% Two or more races, 34.0% Hispanic of any race; Average household size: 3.04; Median age: 36.8; Age under 18: 28.6%; Age 65 and over: 9.5%; Males per 100 females: 97.9; Marriage status: 29.8% never married, 57.6% now married, 1.7% separated, 4.0% widowed, 8.5% divorced; Foreign born: 18.9%; Speak English only: 69.1%; With disability: 7.8%; Veterans: 6.5%; Ancestry: 13.5% German, 9.2% English, 9.1% Irish, 7.7% Italian, 2.6% American

Employment: 20.5% management, business, and financial, 7.3% computer, engineering, and science, 11.0% education, legal, community service, arts, and media, 4.5% healthcare practitioners, 17.6% service, 25.0% sales and office, 7.1% natural resources, construction, and maintenance, 7.0% production, transportation, and material moving

Income: Per capita: $40,507; Median household: $95,531; Average household: $122,617; Households with income of $100,000 or more: 46.9%; Poverty rate: 9.9%

Educational Attainment: High school diploma or higher: 87.1%; Bachelor's degree or higher: 37.4%; Graduate/professional degree or higher: 14.1%

School District(s)

Morgan Hill Unified (KG-12)
2012-13 Enrollment: 9,248 . . . . (408) 201-6023
Santa Clara County Office of Education (KG-12)
2012-13 Enrollment: 8,770 . . . . (408) 453-6500

Housing: Homeownership rate: 71.4%; Median home value: $576,700; Median year structure built: 1984; Homeowner vacancy rate: 1.7%; Median gross rent: $1,607 per month; Rental vacancy rate: 2.6%

Health Insurance: 88.3% have insurance; 74.3% have private insurance; 21.8% have public insurance; 11.7% do not have insurance; 6.1% of children under 18 do not have insurance

Safety: Violent crime rate: 15.8 per 10,000 population; Property crime rate: 169.4 per 10,000 population

Newspapers: Times (weekly circulation 4000)

Transportation: Commute: 85.6% car, 3.0% public transportation, 1.7% walk, 6.9% work from home; Median travel time to work: 31.0 minutes; Amtrak: Train service available.

Additional Information Contacts

City of Morgan Hill. . . . . (408) 779-7271
http://www.morgan-hill.ca.gov

MOUNT HAMILTON (unincorporated postal area)

ZCTA: 95140

Covers a land area of 123.726 square miles and a water area of 0.079 square miles. Located at 37.39° N. Lat; 121.62° W. Long..

Population: 191; Growth (since 2000): 445.7%; Density: 1.5 persons per square mile; Race: 84.8% White, 1.0% Black/African American, 3.7% Asian, 0.0% American Indian/Alaska Native, 0.0% Native Hawaiian/Other Pacific Islander, 8.4% Two or more races, 4.7% Hispanic of any race; Average household size: 2.36; Median age: 47.3; Age under 18: 16.2%; Age 65 and over: 15.7%; Males per 100 females: 135.8

Housing: Homeownership rate: 51.9%; Homeowner vacancy rate: 0.0%; Rental vacancy rate: 6.8%

MOUNTAIN VIEW (city). Covers a land area of 11.995 square miles and a water area of 0.278 square miles. Located at 37.40° N. Lat; 122.08° W. Long. Elevation is 105 feet.

History: Named for the view of the Santa Cruz Mountains, Mt. Diablo, and Mt. Hamilton. Before the railroad arrived in 1864, Mountain View was a main stop for the four-horse Concord coaches on the San Francisco-San Jose line. The town grew up around packing houses and canneries serving the surrounding orchards and berry patches.

Population: 74,066; Growth (since 2000): 4.7%; Density: 6,174.6 persons per square mile; Race: 56.0% White, 2.2% Black/African American, 26.0% Asian, 0.5% American Indian/Alaska Native, 0.5% Native Hawaiian/Other Pacific Islander, 5.1% Two or more races, 21.7% Hispanic of any race; Average household size: 2.31; Median age: 35.9; Age under 18: 19.7%; Age 65 and over: 10.6%; Males per 100 females: 103.6; Marriage status: 34.7% never married, 51.6% now married, 1.5% separated, 4.1% widowed, 9.7% divorced; Foreign born: 37.8%; Speak English only: 55.1%; With disability: 6.3%; Veterans: 4.5%; Ancestry: 9.9% German, 7.6% English, 6.6% Irish, 4.3% Italian, 2.6% Russian

Employment: 18.9% management, business, and financial, 27.3% computer, engineering, and science, 12.9% education, legal, community service, arts, and media, 4.9% healthcare practitioners, 12.9% service, 14.4% sales and office, 4.1% natural resources, construction, and maintenance, 4.7% production, transportation, and material moving

Income: Per capita: $54,758; Median household: $97,338; Average household: $126,738; Households with income of $100,000 or more: 49.2%; Poverty rate: 8.1%

Educational Attainment: High school diploma or higher: 91.4%; Bachelor's degree or higher: 62.6%; Graduate/professional degree or higher: 34.2%

School District(s)

Los Altos Elementary (KG-08)
2012-13 Enrollment: 4,505 . . . . (650) 947-1150
Mountain View Whisman (KG-08)
2012-13 Enrollment: 5,010 . . . . (650) 526-3552
Mountain View-Los Altos Union High (09-12)
2012-13 Enrollment: 3,737 . . . . (650) 940-4650

Housing: Homeownership rate: 41.7%; Median home value: $788,700; Median year structure built: 1970; Homeowner vacancy rate: 1.3%; Median gross rent: $1,616 per month; Rental vacancy rate: 4.4%

Health Insurance: 89.4% have insurance; 79.0% have private insurance; 17.8% have public insurance; 10.6% do not have insurance; 2.1% of children under 18 do not have insurance

Hospitals: El Camino Hospital (395 beds)

Safety: Violent crime rate: 20.3 per 10,000 population; Property crime rate: 220.4 per 10,000 population

Transportation: Commute: 80.8% car, 5.2% public transportation, 2.7% walk, 4.7% work from home; Median travel time to work: 21.1 minutes

Additional Information Contacts

City of Mountain View . . . . (650) 903-6301
http://www.ci.mtnview.ca.us

PALO ALTO (city). Covers a land area of 23.884 square miles and a water area of 1.903 square miles. Located at 37.40° N. Lat; 122.14° W. Long. Elevation is 30 feet.

History: Named for the Spanish translation of "tall tree," one of which shaded the camp of the Gaspar de Portola expedition in 1769. The town of Palo Alto developed around Stanford University, founded in 1887 on the Palo Alto Stock Farm where Leland Stanford (railroad builder, financier, governor and U.S. senator) raised thoroughbred horses.

Population: 64,403; Growth (since 2000): 9.9%; Density: 2,696.5 persons per square mile; Race: 64.2% White, 1.9% Black/African American, 27.1% Asian, 0.2% American Indian/Alaska Native, 0.2% Native Hawaiian/Other Pacific Islander, 4.2% Two or more races, 6.2% Hispanic of any race; Average household size: 2.41; Median age: 41.9; Age under 18: 23.4%; Age 65 and over: 17.1%; Males per 100 females: 95.7; Marriage status: 26.9% never married, 59.4% now married, 1.4% separated, 5.1% widowed, 8.5% divorced; Foreign born: 31.0%; Speak English only: 61.7%; With disability: 7.1%; Veterans: 5.5%; Ancestry: 11.6% English, 10.6% German, 7.4% Irish, 4.8% Russian, 4.3% Italian

Employment: 28.5% management, business, and financial, 21.8% computer, engineering, and science, 18.8% education, legal, community service, arts, and media, 7.5% healthcare practitioners, 7.0% service, 12.1% sales and office, 2.0% natural resources, construction, and maintenance, 2.2% production, transportation, and material moving

Income: Per capita: $73,329; Median household: $121,465; Average household: $180,566; Households with income of $100,000 or more: 58.5%; Poverty rate: 5.7%

Educational Attainment: High school diploma or higher: 97.5%; Bachelor's degree or higher: 79.8%; Graduate/professional degree or higher: 51.3%

School District(s)

Palo Alto Unified (KG-12)
2012-13 Enrollment: 12,357 . . . . (650) 329-3700

Four-year College(s)

Palo Alto University (Private, Not-for-profit)
Fall 2013 Enrollment: 948 . . . . (800) 818-6136
Sofia University (Private, Not-for-profit)
Fall 2013 Enrollment: 453 . . . . (650) 493-4430

Housing: Homeownership rate: 55.7%; Median home value: 1 million+; Median year structure built: 1960; Homeowner vacancy rate: 1.5%; Median gross rent: $1,947 per month; Rental vacancy rate: 5.6%

Health Insurance: 94.6% have insurance; 88.0% have private insurance; 19.1% have public insurance; 5.4% do not have insurance; 2.2% of children under 18 do not have insurance

Hospitals: Lucile Salter Packard Children's Hospital at Stanford (264 beds); Palo Alto VA Medical Center (900 beds)

Safety: Violent crime rate: 8.1 per 10,000 population; Property crime rate: 221.5 per 10,000 population

Newspapers: Mountain View Voice (weekly circulation 18000); Palo Alto Weekly (weekly circulation 48000); The Almanac (weekly circulation 15000)

Transportation: Commute: 70.9% car, 5.3% public transportation, 5.8% walk, 8.6% work from home; Median travel time to work: 22.1 minutes

Airports: Palo Alto Airport of Santa Clara County (general aviation)

Additional Information Contacts

City of Palo Alto. . . . . (650) 329-2100
http://www.cityofpaloalto.org

SAN JOSE (city). County seat. Covers a land area of 176.526 square miles and a water area of 3.439 square miles. Located at 37.30° N. Lat; 121.82° W. Long. Elevation is 82 feet.

History: In 1777 the viceroy of Mexico ordered nine soldiers, five settlers with their families, and one cowboy to found the Pueblo de San Jose de Guadalupe, named in honor of St. Joseph. This was the first Spanish town established in California. San Jose began to grow in the 1840 's with immigration from the east on the overland route, and in 1846 Captain Thomas Fallon raised the United States flag over the town hall. When the gold rush started, San Jose became a supply station for prospectors and miners. The first California Legislature convened in San Jose in 1849 and the city was incorporated in 1850, but the capital was moved to Benicia in 1851.

Population: 945,942; Growth (since 2000): 5.7%; Density: 5,358.6 persons per square mile; Race: 42.8% White, 3.2% Black/African American, 32.0% Asian, 0.9% American Indian/Alaska Native, 0.4% Native Hawaiian/Other Pacific Islander, 5.0% Two or more races, 33.2% Hispanic of any race; Average household size: 3.09; Median age: 35.2; Age under 18: 24.8%; Age 65 and over: 10.1%; Males per 100 females: 101.1; Marriage status: 34.4% never married, 52.8% now married, 1.8% separated, 4.5% widowed, 8.2% divorced; Foreign born: 38.6%; Speak English only: 43.9%; With disability: 8.1%; Veterans: 4.5%; Ancestry: 6.2% German, 4.6% Irish, 4.3% Italian, 4.2% English, 1.6% American

Employment: 16.8% management, business, and financial, 12.8% computer, engineering, and science, 8.7% education, legal, community service, arts, and media, 4.0% healthcare practitioners, 17.3% service, 22.4% sales and office, 7.7% natural resources, construction, and maintenance, 10.2% production, transportation, and material moving

Income: Per capita: $34,025; Median household: $81,829; Average household: $104,448; Households with income of $100,000 or more: 40.8%; Poverty rate: 12.2%

Educational Attainment: High school diploma or higher: 82.3%; Bachelor's degree or higher: 37.4%; Graduate/professional degree or higher: 14.1%

School District(s)

Alum Rock Union Elementary (KG-08)
2012-13 Enrollment: 12,659 . . . . (408) 928-6800
Berryessa Union Elementary (KG-08)
2012-13 Enrollment: 7,980 . . . . (408) 923-1880
Cambrian (KG-08)
2012-13 Enrollment: 3,373 . . . . (408) 377-2103

Campbell Union (KG-08)
2012-13 Enrollment: 7,701 . . . . (408) 364-4200
Campbell Union High (09-12)
2012-13 Enrollment: 7,373 . . . . (408) 371-0960
Cupertino Union (PK-08)
2012-13 Enrollment: 19,035 . . . . (408) 252-3000
East Side Union High (KG-12)
2012-13 Enrollment: 26,297 . . . . (408) 347-5000
Evergreen Elementary (KG-08)
2012-13 Enrollment: 13,375 . . . . (408) 270-6800
Franklin-Mckinley Elementary (KG-08)
2012-13 Enrollment: 10,703 . . . . (408) 283-6006
Fremont Union High (09-12)
2012-13 Enrollment: 10,664 . . . . (408) 522-2200
Luther Burbank (KG-08)
2012-13 Enrollment: 561. . . . . (408) 295-2450
Metro Education
2012-13 Enrollment: n/a . . . . (408) 723-6414
Moreland Elementary (KG-08)
2012-13 Enrollment: 4,477 . . . . (408) 874-2901
Morgan Hill Unified (KG-12)
2012-13 Enrollment: 9,248 . . . . (408) 201-6023
Mt. Pleasant Elementary (KG-08)
2012-13 Enrollment: 2,540 . . . . (408) 223-3710
Oak Grove Elementary (KG-08)
2012-13 Enrollment: 11,372 . . . . (408) 227-8300
Orchard Elementary (KG-08)
2012-13 Enrollment: 878. . . . . (408) 944-0397
San Jose Unified (KG-12)
2012-13 Enrollment: 33,184 . . . . (408) 535-6000
Santa Clara County Office of Education (KG-12)
2012-13 Enrollment: 8,770 . . . . (408) 453-6500
Union Elementary (KG-08)
2012-13 Enrollment: 5,298 . . . . (408) 377-8010

Four-year College(s)

International Technological University (Private, Not-for-profit)
Fall 2013 Enrollment: 1,342 . . . . (888) 408-4968
San Jose State University (Public)
Fall 2013 Enrollment: 31,278 . . . . (408) 924-1000
2013-14 Tuition: In-state $7,343; Out-of-state $18,503
The National Hispanic University (Private, For-profit)
Fall 2013 Enrollment: 813. . . . . (408) 254-6900
2013-14 Tuition: In-state $8,196; Out-of-state $8,196
University of Phoenix-Bay Area Campus (Private, For-profit)
Fall 2013 Enrollment: 1,655 . . . . (866) 766-0766
2013-14 Tuition: In-state $11,308; Out-of-state $11,308

Two-year College(s)

Carrington College California-San Jose (Private, For-profit)
Fall 2013 Enrollment: 693 . . . . (408) 960-0162
Evergreen Valley College (Public)
Fall 2013 Enrollment: 9,211 . . . . (408) 274-7900
2013-14 Tuition: In-state $1,326; Out-of-state $7,010
San Jose City College (Public)
Fall 2013 Enrollment: 9,446 . . . . (408) 298-2181
2013-14 Tuition: In-state $1,324; Out-of-state $6,946

Vocational/Technical School(s)

BioHealth College (Private, For-profit)
Fall 2013 Enrollment: 123. . . . . (408) 428-0208
2013-14 Tuition: $13,395
CET-Sobrato (Private, Not-for-profit)
Fall 2013 Enrollment: 345. . . . . (408) 287-7924
2013-14 Tuition: $9,958
Everest College-San Jose (Private, For-profit)
Fall 2013 Enrollment: 172. . . . . (408) 246-4171
2013-14 Tuition: $15,009
WestMed College (Private, Not-for-profit)
Fall 2013 Enrollment: 356. . . . . (408) 236-1170
2013-14 Tuition: $31,616

Housing: Homeownership rate: 58.5%; Median home value: $560,400; Median year structure built: 1974; Homeowner vacancy rate: 1.6%; Median gross rent: $1,474 per month; Rental vacancy rate: 4.3%

Health Insurance: 86.2% have insurance; 67.4% have private insurance; 25.7% have public insurance; 13.8% do not have insurance; 4.9% of children under 18 do not have insurance

Hospitals: Good Samaritan Hospital (474 beds); Kaiser Foundation Hospital - San Jose (228 beds); O'Connor Hospital (358 beds); Regional Medical Center of San Jose (204 beds); Santa Clara Valley Medical Center (524 beds)

Safety: Violent crime rate: 32.4 per 10,000 population; Property crime rate: 257.1 per 10,000 population

Newspapers: Almaden Times (weekly circulation 21500); Metro Newspapers (weekly circulation 83000); San Jose Mercury-News (daily circulation 229000); Silicon Valley Community Newspapers (weekly circulation 126000)

Transportation: Commute: 88.8% car, 3.5% public transportation, 1.7% walk, 3.9% work from home; Median travel time to work: 25.9 minutes; Amtrak: Train service available.

Airports: Norman Y. Mineta San Jose International (primary service/medium hub)

Additional Information Contacts

City of San Jose . . . . (408) 535-3500
http://www.sanjoseca.gov

SAN MARTIN (CDP). Covers a land area of 11.596 square miles and a water area of 0 square miles. Located at 37.08° N. Lat; 121.60° W. Long. Elevation is 289 feet.

Population: 7,027; Growth (since 2000): 66.1%; Density: 606.0 persons per square mile; Race: 61.6% White, 0.4% Black/African American, 6.7% Asian, 1.0% American Indian/Alaska Native, 0.3% Native Hawaiian/Other Pacific Islander, 5.1% Two or more races, 46.2% Hispanic of any race; Average household size: 3.46; Median age: 38.5; Age under 18: 25.3%; Age 65 and over: 11.7%; Males per 100 females: 103.9; Marriage status: 29.2% never married, 56.2% now married, 1.9% separated, 5.2% widowed, 9.4% divorced; Foreign born: 22.2%; Speak English only: 58.3%; With disability: 10.6%; Veterans: 4.5%; Ancestry: 12.7% English, 9.3% German, 6.8% Irish, 6.5% Italian, 3.2% Swedish

Employment: 22.2% management, business, and financial, 6.1% computer, engineering, and science, 7.3% education, legal, community service, arts, and media, 2.4% healthcare practitioners, 16.6% service, 25.2% sales and office, 9.9% natural resources, construction, and maintenance, 10.4% production, transportation, and material moving

Income: Per capita: $36,527; Median household: $92,261; Average household: $120,008; Households with income of $100,000 or more: 48.2%; Poverty rate: 9.4%

Educational Attainment: High school diploma or higher: 77.1%; Bachelor's degree or higher: 23.2%; Graduate/professional degree or higher: 5.7%

School District(s)

Morgan Hill Unified (KG-12)
2012-13 Enrollment: 9,248 . . . . (408) 201-6023

Housing: Homeownership rate: 65.7%; Median home value: $690,200; Median year structure built: 1971; Homeowner vacancy rate: 1.9%; Median gross rent: $1,427 per month; Rental vacancy rate: 1.7%

Health Insurance: 85.0% have insurance; 66.5% have private insurance; 28.8% have public insurance; 15.0% do not have insurance; 1.2% of children under 18 do not have insurance

Transportation: Commute: 89.1% car, 1.2% public transportation, 0.4% walk, 8.7% work from home; Median travel time to work: 29.6 minutes

SANTA CLARA (city). Covers a land area of 18.407 square miles and a water area of 0 square miles. Located at 37.36° N. Lat; 121.97° W. Long. Elevation is 72 feet.

History: Named for the Mission de Santa Clara de Asis, which was named for St. Clare of Assisi. Santa Clara was settled by miners who invested their stakes in the valley's fertile farmlands. The first orchards were planted by padres at Mission Santa Clara de Asis, founded in 1777 on the Rio Guadalupe. Santa Clara College was chartered in 1855 on the site of the mission.

Population: 116,468; Growth (since 2000): 13.8%; Density: 6,327.3 persons per square mile; Race: 45.0% White, 2.7% Black/African American, 37.7% Asian, 0.5% American Indian/Alaska Native, 0.6% Native Hawaiian/Other Pacific Islander, 5.3% Two or more races, 19.4% Hispanic of any race; Average household size: 2.63; Median age: 34.1; Age under 18: 21.3%; Age 65 and over: 10.0%; Males per 100 females: 102.0; Marriage status: 34.1% never married, 54.2% now married, 1.6% separated, 3.9% widowed, 7.8% divorced; Foreign born: 39.6%; Speak English only: 49.2%; With disability: 7.7%; Veterans: 4.6%; Ancestry: 7.0% German, 5.3% Irish, 5.2% English, 3.9% Italian, 2.2% Portuguese

Employment: 19.9% management, business, and financial, 22.6% computer, engineering, and science, 8.2% education, legal, community service, arts, and media, 3.8% healthcare practitioners, 13.4% service, 19.9% sales and office, 5.0% natural resources, construction, and maintenance, 7.2% production, transportation, and material moving

Income: Per capita: $39,966; Median household: $91,583; Average household: $108,726; Households with income of $100,000 or more: 46.0%; Poverty rate: 9.0%

Educational Attainment: High school diploma or higher: 91.8%; Bachelor's degree or higher: 51.6%; Graduate/professional degree or higher: 23.0%

School District(s)

Cupertino Union (PK-08)
2012-13 Enrollment: 19,035 . . . . (408) 252-3000
Santa Clara Unified (KG-12)
2012-13 Enrollment: 15,151 . . . . (408) 423-2000

Four-year College(s)

Santa Clara University (Private, Not-for-profit, Roman Catholic)
Fall 2013 Enrollment: 8,770 . . . . (408) 554-4000
2013-14 Tuition: In-state $42,156; Out-of-state $42,156

Two-year College(s)

Mission College (Public)
Fall 2013 Enrollment: 9,130 . . . . (408) 988-2200
2013-14 Tuition: In-state $1,174; Out-of-state $6,070

Vocational/Technical School(s)

Academy for Salon Professionals (Private, For-profit)
Fall 2013 Enrollment: 228 . . . . (408) 261-9201
2013-14 Tuition: $18,500
Institute for Business and Technology (Private, For-profit)
Fall 2013 Enrollment: 173 . . . . (408) 727-1060
2013-14 Tuition: $13,661
Marinello Schools of Beauty-Santa Clara (Private, For-profit)
Fall 2013 Enrollment: 566 . . . . (562) 945-2211
2013-14 Tuition: $18,510

Housing: Homeownership rate: 46.0%; Median home value: $613,200; Median year structure built: 1969; Homeowner vacancy rate: 1.3%; Median gross rent: $1,609 per month; Rental vacancy rate: 4.6%

Health Insurance: 90.7% have insurance; 78.6% have private insurance; 19.9% have public insurance; 9.3% do not have insurance; 2.9% of children under 18 do not have insurance

Hospitals: Kaiser Foundation Hospital - Santa Clara (286 beds)

Safety: Violent crime rate: 14.3 per 10,000 population; Property crime rate: 251.6 per 10,000 population

Newspapers: Santa Clara Weekly (weekly circulation 15000)

Transportation: Commute: 87.1% car, 3.6% public transportation, 3.3% walk, 3.7% work from home; Median travel time to work: 21.8 minutes; Amtrak: Train service available.

Additional Information Contacts

City of Santa Clara . . . . (408) 615-2200
http://santaclaraca.gov

SARATOGA (city). Covers a land area of 12.382 square miles and a water area of 0 square miles. Located at 37.27° N. Lat; 122.03° W. Long. Elevation is 423 feet.

History: Saratoga began as McCarthysville, laid out by Martin McCarthy at the foot of a mountain toll road. It was renamed Saratoga in 1863 for the nearby springs which reminded residents of Saratoga Springs in New York.

Population: 29,926; Growth (since 2000): 0.3%; Density: 2,416.9 persons per square mile; Race: 53.9% White, 0.3% Black/African American, 41.4% Asian, 0.1% American Indian/Alaska Native, 0.1% Native Hawaiian/Other Pacific Islander, 3.6% Two or more races, 3.5% Hispanic of any race; Average household size: 2.77; Median age: 47.8; Age under 18: 24.0%; Age 65 and over: 20.3%; Males per 100 females: 95.7; Marriage status: 18.8% never married, 70.0% now married, 0.9% separated, 6.6% widowed, 4.6% divorced; Foreign born: 37.0%; Speak English only: 56.8%; With disability: 6.9%; Veterans: 6.5%; Ancestry: 9.9% German, 8.7% English, 7.4% Irish, 6.0% Italian, 2.6% Iranian

Employment: 36.3% management, business, and financial, 22.4% computer, engineering, and science, 10.2% education, legal, community service, arts, and media, 7.7% healthcare practitioners, 5.5% service, 15.4% sales and office, 1.2% natural resources, construction, and maintenance, 1.4% production, transportation, and material moving

Income: Per capita: $75,986; Median household: $159,212; Average household: $208,543; Households with income of $100,000 or more: 69.4%; Poverty rate: 3.7%

Educational Attainment: High school diploma or higher: 98.4%; Bachelor's degree or higher: 77.9%; Graduate/professional degree or higher: 41.8%

School District(s)

Campbell Union (KG-08)
2012-13 Enrollment: 7,701 . . . . (408) 364-4200
Campbell Union High (09-12)
2012-13 Enrollment: 7,373 . . . . (408) 371-0960
Cupertino Union (PK-08)
2012-13 Enrollment: 19,035 . . . . (408) 252-3000
Los Gatos-Saratoga Joint Union High (09-12)
2012-13 Enrollment: 3,232 . . . . (408) 354-2520
Saratoga Union Elementary (KG-08)
2012-13 Enrollment: 2,096 . . . . (408) 867-3424

Two-year College(s)

West Valley College (Public)
Fall 2013 Enrollment: 9,636 . . . . (408) 867-2200
2013-14 Tuition: In-state $1,178; Out-of-state $6,074

Housing: Homeownership rate: 86.2%; Median home value: 1 million+; Median year structure built: 1967; Homeowner vacancy rate: 0.7%; Median gross rent: $2,000+ per month; Rental vacancy rate: 4.3%

Health Insurance: 97.6% have insurance; 91.4% have private insurance; 20.4% have public insurance; 2.4% do not have insurance; 0.9% of children under 18 do not have insurance

Safety: Violent crime rate: 4.5 per 10,000 population; Property crime rate: 71.9 per 10,000 population

Transportation: Commute: 89.2% car, 0.6% public transportation, 0.3% walk, 9.2% work from home; Median travel time to work: 26.9 minutes

Additional Information Contacts

City of Saratoga. . . . . (408) 686-1200
http://www.saratoga.ca.us

STANFORD (CDP). Covers a land area of 2.731 square miles and a water area of 0.045 square miles. Located at 37.43° N. Lat; 122.17° W. Long. Elevation is 95 feet.

History: Named for Leland Stanford, Jr., whose father contributed funding to establish Stanford University. Stanford University in West part of city.

Population: 13,809; Growth (since 2000): 3.7%; Density: 5,057.2 persons per square mile; Race: 57.4% White, 4.7% Black/African American, 27.4% Asian, 0.6% American Indian/Alaska Native, 0.2% Native Hawaiian/Other Pacific Islander, 7.8% Two or more races, 10.4% Hispanic of any race; Average household size: 1.96; Median age: 22.6; Age under 18: 6.6%; Age 65 and over: 4.5%; Males per 100 females: 118.3; Marriage status: 77.0% never married, 21.0% now married, 0.4% separated, 1.1% widowed, 0.8% divorced; Foreign born: 24.0%; Speak English only: 66.8%; With disability: 3.7%; Veterans: 1.1%; Ancestry: 10.7% German, 9.6% Irish, 6.4% English, 5.3% Italian, 3.5% Polish

Employment: 9.4% management, business, and financial, 17.7% computer, engineering, and science, 40.9% education, legal, community service, arts, and media, 4.4% healthcare practitioners, 8.8% service, 16.5% sales and office, 1.4% natural resources, construction, and maintenance, 0.8% production, transportation, and material moving

Income: Per capita: $33,695; Median household: $64,280; Average household: $134,745; Households with income of $100,000 or more: 39.2%; Poverty rate: 17.3%

Educational Attainment: High school diploma or higher: 98.9%; Bachelor's degree or higher: 93.4%; Graduate/professional degree or higher: 63.3%

School District(s)

Palo Alto Unified (KG-12)
2012-13 Enrollment: 12,357 . . . . (650) 329-3700

Four-year College(s)

Stanford University (Private, Not-for-profit)
Fall 2013 Enrollment: 18,346 . . . . (650) 723-2300
2013-14 Tuition: In-state $43,683; Out-of-state $43,683

Housing: Homeownership rate: 20.2%; Median home value: 1 million+; Median year structure built: 1977; Homeowner vacancy rate: 0.9%; Median gross rent: $1,393 per month; Rental vacancy rate: 0.9%

Health Insurance: 97.4% have insurance; 95.3% have private insurance; 7.3% have public insurance; 2.6% do not have insurance; 0.0% of children under 18 do not have insurance

Hospitals: Stanford Hospital (613 beds)

Transportation: Commute: 24.1% car, 3.1% public transportation, 19.6% walk, 7.4% work from home; Median travel time to work: 12.5 minutes

SUNNYVALE (city). Covers a land area of 21.987 square miles and a water area of 0.702 square miles. Located at 37.39° N. Lat; 122.03° W. Long. Elevation is 125 feet.

History: Named for its sunny climate. Sunnyvale began as a ranchers' trading center on land purchased by Martin Murphy Jr. from Rancho Pastoria de las Borregas. The Murphy family settled here in 1849 and had their two-story house, framed in Boston, shipped round the Horn.

Population: 140,081; Growth (since 2000): 6.3%; Density: 6,370.9 persons per square mile; Race: 43.0% White, 2.0% Black/African American, 40.9% Asian, 0.5% American Indian/Alaska Native, 0.5% Native Hawaiian/Other Pacific Islander, 4.5% Two or more races, 18.9% Hispanic of any race; Average household size: 2.61; Median age: 35.6; Age under 18: 22.4%; Age 65 and over: 11.2%; Males per 100 females: 101.5; Marriage status: 29.5% never married, 58.9% now married, 1.0% separated, 4.2% widowed, 7.4% divorced; Foreign born: 44.2%; Speak English only: 45.9%; With disability: 6.7%; Veterans: 5.0%; Ancestry: 7.3% German, 4.9% English, 4.8% Irish, 2.9% Italian, 2.2% European

Employment: 18.7% management, business, and financial, 30.2% computer, engineering, and science, 8.4% education, legal, community service, arts, and media, 3.6% healthcare practitioners, 12.0% service, 16.4% sales and office, 4.6% natural resources, construction, and maintenance, 5.9% production, transportation, and material moving

Income: Per capita: $45,977; Median household: $100,043; Average household: $119,865; Households with income of $100,000 or more: 50.0%; Poverty rate: 8.1%

Educational Attainment: High school diploma or higher: 90.7%; Bachelor's degree or higher: 58.3%; Graduate/professional degree or higher: 28.2%

School District(s)

Cupertino Union (PK-08)
2012-13 Enrollment: 19,035 . . . . (408) 252-3000
Fremont Union High (09-12)
2012-13 Enrollment: 10,664 . . . . (408) 522-2200
North County Regional Occupational Center/program
2012-13 Enrollment: n/a . . . . (408) 522-2201
Santa Clara County Office of Education (KG-12)
2012-13 Enrollment: 8,770 . . . . (408) 453-6500
Santa Clara Unified (KG-12)
2012-13 Enrollment: 15,151 . . . . (408) 423-2000
Sunnyvale (KG-08)
2012-13 Enrollment: 6,751 . . . . (408) 522-8200

Four-year College(s)

Cogswell College (Private, For-profit)
Fall 2013 Enrollment: 472. . . . . (800) 264-7955
2013-14 Tuition: In-state $16,160; Out-of-state $16,160
The Art Institute of California-Argosy University-Silicon Valley (Private, For-profit)
Fall 2013 Enrollment: 570. . . . . (408) 962-6400
2013-14 Tuition: In-state $18,748; Out-of-state $18,748
University of East-West Medicine (Private, For-profit)
Fall 2013 Enrollment: 177. . . . . (408) 733-1878

Housing: Homeownership rate: 48.0%; Median home value: $710,700; Median year structure built: 1972; Homeowner vacancy rate: 1.1%; Median gross rent: $1,606 per month; Rental vacancy rate: 4.4%

Health Insurance: 89.9% have insurance; 78.8% have private insurance; 19.0% have public insurance; 10.1% do not have insurance; 4.6% of children under 18 do not have insurance

Safety: Violent crime rate: 9.7 per 10,000 population; Property crime rate: 164.3 per 10,000 population

Transportation: Commute: 87.0% car, 4.5% public transportation, 1.3% walk, 4.3% work from home; Median travel time to work: 23.0 minutes

Additional Information Contacts

City of Sunnyvale . . . . (408) 730-7500
http://www.sunnyvale.ca.gov

Santa Cruz County

Located in western California, at the base of the San Francisco-San Mateo Peninsula; bounded on the west by the Pacific Ocean and Monterey Bay, and on the south by the Pajaro River; also drained by the San Lorenzo River. Covers a land area of 445.170 square miles, a water area of 161.996 square miles, and is located in the Pacific Time Zone at 37.01° N. Lat., 122.01° W. Long. The county was founded in 1850. County seat is Santa Cruz.

Santa Cruz County is part of the Santa Cruz-Watsonville, CA Metropolitan Statistical Area. The entire metro area includes: Santa Cruz County, CA

Weather Station: Ben Lomond No 4 — Elevation: 419 feet

	Jan	Feb	Mar	Apr	May	Jun	Jul	Aug	Sep	Oct	Nov	Dec
High	62	64	67	72	77	82	85	86	84	78	68	61
Low	37	39	40	42	46	48	51	50	49	44	40	37
Precip	10.0	10.2	7.1	3.1	1.2	0.2	0.0	0.1	0.3	2.3	5.9	9.6
Snow	tr	0.1	tr	0.0	0.0	0.0	0.0	0.0	0.0	0.0	tr	0.1

High and Low temperatures in degrees Fahrenheit; Precipitation and Snow in inches

Weather Station: Santa Cruz — Elevation: 129 feet

	Jan	Feb	Mar	Apr	May	Jun	Jul	Aug	Sep	Oct	Nov	Dec
High	61	62	64	68	70	73	74	74	74	72	65	60
Low	41	43	44	46	49	51	54	54	53	49	44	41
Precip	6.5	6.3	4.6	1.9	0.9	0.2	0.0	0.0	0.3	1.3	3.6	5.5
Snow	0.0	0.0	0.0	0.0	tr	0.0	0.0	0.0	0.0	0.0	0.0	0.0

High and Low temperatures in degrees Fahrenheit; Precipitation and Snow in inches

Weather Station: Watsonville Waterworks — Elevation: 95 feet

	Jan	Feb	Mar	Apr	May	Jun	Jul	Aug	Sep	Oct	Nov	Dec
High	61	63	65	68	69	72	72	73	74	72	67	61
Low	39	42	44	45	49	52	54	54	52	48	43	39
Precip	4.6	4.7	3.6	1.6	0.6	0.1	0.0	0.0	0.2	1.1	2.7	4.0
Snow	0.0	0.0	0.0	0.0	0.0	0.0	0.0	0.0	0.0	0.0	0.0	0.0

High and Low temperatures in degrees Fahrenheit; Precipitation and Snow in inches

Population: 262,382; Growth (since 2000): 2.7%; Density: 589.4 persons per square mile; Race: 72.5% White, 1.1% Black/African American, 4.2% Asian, 0.9% American Indian/Alaska Native, 0.1% Native Hawaiian/Other Pacific Islander, 4.7% two or more races, 32.0% Hispanic of any race; Average household size: 2.66; Median age: 36.9; Age under 18: 21.1%; Age 65 and over: 11.1%; Males per 100 females: 99.6; Marriage status: 39.1% never married, 45.9% now married, 1.7% separated, 4.2% widowed, 10.8% divorced; Foreign born: 18.3%; Speak English only: 69.0%; With disability: 8.8%; Veterans: 6.0%; Ancestry: 13.6% German, 11.5% English, 10.8% Irish, 6.9% Italian, 3.9% European

Religion: Six largest groups: 19.2% Catholicism, 2.6% Non-denominational Protestant, 1.4% Latter-day Saints, 1.2% Buddhism, 1.2% Pentecostal, 0.6% Presbyterian-Reformed

Economy: Unemployment rate: 6.4%; Leading industries: 13.2% health care and social assistance; 13.0% retail trade; 13.0% professional, scientific, and technical services; Farms: 667 totaling 99,983 acres; Company size: 1 employs 1,000 or more persons, 4 employ 500 to 999 persons, 83 employ 100 to 499 persons, 6,697 employ less than 100 persons; Business ownership: 9,949 women-owned, n/a Black-owned, n/a Hispanic-owned, 1,390 Asian-owned

Employment: 15.8% management, business, and financial, 7.2% computer, engineering, and science, 12.6% education, legal, community service, arts, and media, 5.0% healthcare practitioners, 18.8% service, 21.4% sales and office, 11.8% natural resources, construction, and maintenance, 7.3% production, transportation, and material moving

Income: Per capita: $32,295; Median household: $66,519; Average household: $88,776; Households with income of $100,000 or more: 32.0%; Poverty rate: 14.6%

Educational Attainment: High school diploma or higher: 84.9%; Bachelor's degree or higher: 37.0%; Graduate/professional degree or higher: 14.3%

Housing: Homeownership rate: 57.5%; Median home value: $557,500; Median year structure built: 1971; Homeowner vacancy rate: 1.6%; Median gross rent: $1,385 per month; Rental vacancy rate: 3.5%

Vital Statistics: Birth rate: 118.8 per 10,000 population; Death rate: 65.0 per 10,000 population; Age-adjusted cancer mortality rate: 150.8 deaths per 100,000 population

Health Insurance: 85.1% have insurance; 68.1% have private insurance; 26.4% have public insurance; 14.9% do not have insurance; 5.1% of children under 18 do not have insurance

Health Care: Physicians: 25.2 per 10,000 population; Hospital beds: 15.5 per 10,000 population; Hospital admissions: 755.8 per 10,000 population

Air Quality Index: 78.9% good, 15.3% moderate, 5.8% unhealthy for sensitive individuals, 0.0% unhealthy (percent of days)

Transportation: Commute: 81.1% car, 2.6% public transportation, 4.3% walk, 6.7% work from home; Median travel time to work: 25.4 minutes

Presidential Election: 75.2% Obama, 21.1% Romney (2012)

National and State Parks: Big Basin Redwoods State Park; Castle Rock State Park; Ellicott Slough National Wildlife Refuge; Henry Cowell Redwoods State Park; Lighthouse Field State Beach; Manresa State Beach; Natural Bridges State Beach; New Brighton State Beach; Santa Cruz Mission State Historic Park; Seacliff State Beach; Sunset State Beach; The Forest of Nisene Marks State Park; Twin Lakes State Beach; Watsonville State Wildlife Area; West Waddell Creek State Wilderness; Wilder Ranch State Park

Additional Information Contacts

Santa Cruz Government . . . . (831) 454-2200
http://www.co.santa-cruz.ca.us

Santa Cruz County Communities

AMESTI (CDP). Covers a land area of 2.992 square miles and a water area of 0.064 square miles. Located at 36.96° N. Lat; 121.78° W. Long. Elevation is 148 feet.

Population: 3,478; Growth (since 2000): 42.8%; Density: 1,162.6 persons per square mile; Race: 54.3% White, 0.3% Black/African American, 2.6% Asian, 1.2% American Indian/Alaska Native, 0.0% Native Hawaiian/Other Pacific Islander, 3.9% Two or more races, 65.4% Hispanic of any race; Average household size: 3.53; Median age: 31.3; Age under 18: 31.6%; Age 65 and over: 9.6%; Males per 100 females: 95.3; Marriage status: 37.6% never married, 51.5% now married, 2.7% separated, 3.3% widowed, 7.5% divorced; Foreign born: 25.0%; Speak English only: 41.2%; With disability: 10.4%; Veterans: 7.5%; Ancestry: 11.6% German, 5.9% Irish, 5.7% English, 4.0% Scottish, 3.9% Russian

Employment: 8.7% management, business, and financial, 0.7% computer, engineering, and science, 15.6% education, legal, community service, arts, and media, 3.1% healthcare practitioners, 21.6% service, 29.6% sales and office, 18.2% natural resources, construction, and maintenance, 2.6% production, transportation, and material moving

Income: Per capita: $20,809; Median household: $49,841; Average household: $71,056; Households with income of $100,000 or more: 20.3%; Poverty rate: 9.3%

Educational Attainment: High school diploma or higher: 75.3%; Bachelor's degree or higher: 14.6%; Graduate/professional degree or higher: 4.9%

Housing: Homeownership rate: 61.5%; Median home value: $336,200; Median year structure built: 1976; Homeowner vacancy rate: 0.3%; Median gross rent: $1,183 per month; Rental vacancy rate: 1.3%

Health Insurance: 82.4% have insurance; 64.3% have private insurance; 40.4% have public insurance; 17.6% do not have insurance; 3.2% of children under 18 do not have insurance

Transportation: Commute: 92.3% car, 1.7% public transportation, 0.3% walk, 3.5% work from home; Median travel time to work: 23.6 minutes

APTOS (CDP). Covers a land area of 6.354 square miles and a water area of 0 square miles. Located at 36.99° N. Lat; 121.89° W. Long. Elevation is 108 feet.

History: Aptos has a history as a fashionable resort. In the late 1900's Claus Spreckels, founder of the sugar company, bought most of Don Rafael Castro's Rancho Aptos and built a lavish estate with a race track.

Population: 6,220; Growth (since 2000): -33.8%; Density: 978.9 persons per square mile; Race: 87.1% White, 0.9% Black/African American, 4.0% Asian, 0.7% American Indian/Alaska Native, 0.1% Native Hawaiian/Other Pacific Islander, 4.3% Two or more races, 9.8% Hispanic of any race; Average household size: 2.41; Median age: 46.9; Age under 18: 18.5%; Age 65 and over: 17.7%; Males per 100 females: 97.8; Marriage status: 32.7% never married, 49.7% now married, 1.4% separated, 3.5% widowed, 14.1% divorced; Foreign born: 7.4%; Speak English only: 87.1%; With disability: 5.8%; Veterans: 5.5%; Ancestry: 17.3% Irish, 13.0% English, 12.5% German, 8.2% Italian, 7.8% American

Employment: 25.0% management, business, and financial, 8.2% computer, engineering, and science, 12.8% education, legal, community service, arts, and media, 7.1% healthcare practitioners, 13.7% service, 20.9% sales and office, 8.8% natural resources, construction, and maintenance, 3.5% production, transportation, and material moving

Income: Per capita: $40,761; Median household: $75,845; Average household: $95,565; Households with income of $100,000 or more: 31.6%; Poverty rate: 12.3%

Educational Attainment: High school diploma or higher: 97.4%; Bachelor's degree or higher: 46.5%; Graduate/professional degree or higher: 14.2%

School District(s)

Pajaro Valley Unified (KG-12)
2012-13 Enrollment: 20,001 . . . . (831) 786-2100

Santa Cruz City High (KG-12)
2012-13 Enrollment: 4,716 . . . . (831) 429-3410

Two-year College(s)

Cabrillo College (Public)
Fall 2013 Enrollment: 13,666 . . . . (831) 479-6100
2013-14 Tuition: In-state $1,358; Out-of-state $5,698

Housing: Homeownership rate: 75.6%; Median home value: $630,100; Median year structure built: 1973; Homeowner vacancy rate: 1.5%; Median gross rent: $1,522 per month; Rental vacancy rate: 0.8%

Health Insurance: 91.5% have insurance; 84.7% have private insurance; 22.9% have public insurance; 8.5% do not have insurance; 8.1% of children under 18 do not have insurance

Transportation: Commute: 78.7% car, 0.8% public transportation, 0.3% walk, 15.8% work from home; Median travel time to work: 25.0 minutes

APTOS HILLS-LARKIN VALLEY (CDP). Covers a land area of 9.245 square miles and a water area of 0.033 square miles. Located at 36.95° N. Lat; 121.82° W. Long.

Population: 2,381; Growth (since 2000): 0.8%; Density: 257.5 persons per square mile; Race: 81.3% White, 0.5% Black/African American, 2.3% Asian, 0.2% American Indian/Alaska Native, 0.0% Native Hawaiian/Other Pacific Islander, 3.2% Two or more races, 22.7% Hispanic of any race; Average household size: 2.72; Median age: 46.9; Age under 18: 19.1%; Age 65 and over: 13.9%; Males per 100 females: 103.3

Housing: Homeownership rate: 78.7%; Homeowner vacancy rate: 0.6%; Rental vacancy rate: 3.6%

BEN LOMOND (CDP). Covers a land area of 8.360 square miles and a water area of 0 square miles. Located at 37.08° N. Lat; 122.09° W. Long. Elevation is 331 feet.

History: Ben Lomond developed in the 1880's at the base of Ben Lomond Mountain, named by a Scottish immigrant.

Population: 6,234; Growth (since 2000): 163.7%; Density: 745.7 persons per square mile; Race: 91.3% White, 0.5% Black/African American, 1.1% Asian, 0.8% American Indian/Alaska Native, 0.2% Native Hawaiian/Other Pacific Islander, 4.5% Two or more races, 8.3% Hispanic of any race; Average household size: 2.52; Median age: 44.1; Age under 18: 19.5%; Age 65 and over: 10.2%; Males per 100 females: 101.9; Marriage status: 27.8% never married, 56.4% now married, 1.0% separated, 3.6% widowed, 12.2% divorced; Foreign born: 3.4%; Speak English only: 94.1%; With disability: 7.0%; Veterans: 11.6%; Ancestry: 20.1% German, 17.4% English, 14.0% Irish, 8.6% Italian, 6.1% European

Employment: 18.9% management, business, and financial, 8.5% computer, engineering, and science, 14.1% education, legal, community service, arts, and media, 3.2% healthcare practitioners, 15.7% service, 27.7% sales and office, 7.1% natural resources, construction, and maintenance, 4.7% production, transportation, and material moving

Income: Per capita: $37,330; Median household: $74,301; Average household: $92,040; Households with income of $100,000 or more: 40.0%; Poverty rate: 8.1%

Educational Attainment: High school diploma or higher: 97.2%; Bachelor's degree or higher: 37.4%; Graduate/professional degree or higher: 11.1%

School District(s)

San Lorenzo Valley Unified (KG-12)
2012-13 Enrollment: 4,444 . . . . (831) 336-5194

Housing: Homeownership rate: 74.1%; Median home value: $542,200; Median year structure built: 1963; Homeowner vacancy rate: 0.7%; Median gross rent: $1,275 per month; Rental vacancy rate: 3.0%

Health Insurance: 86.7% have insurance; 71.7% have private insurance; 24.5% have public insurance; 13.3% do not have insurance; 2.2% of children under 18 do not have insurance

Transportation: Commute: 88.9% car, 0.2% public transportation, 1.1% walk, 8.5% work from home; Median travel time to work: 36.5 minutes

BONNY DOON (CDP). Covers a land area of 16.688 square miles and a water area of 0 square miles. Located at 37.04° N. Lat; 122.14° W. Long. Elevation is 1,253 feet.

Population: 2,678; Growth (since 2000): n/a; Density: 160.5 persons per square mile; Race: 92.4% White, 0.3% Black/African American, 1.9% Asian, 0.6% American Indian/Alaska Native, 0.2% Native Hawaiian/Other Pacific Islander, 2.8% Two or more races, 6.3% Hispanic of any race;

Average household size: 2.44; Median age: 47.5; Age under 18: 16.7%; Age 65 and over: 13.4%; Males per 100 females: 110.7; Marriage status: 29.6% never married, 52.3% now married, 1.7% separated, 2.8% widowed, 15.4% divorced; Foreign born: 6.1%; Speak English only: 89.9%; With disability: 8.5%; Veterans: 7.2%; Ancestry: 19.5% German, 17.7% English, 17.1% Irish, 7.9% Norwegian, 5.9% Scottish

Employment: 19.8% management, business, and financial, 7.3% computer, engineering, and science, 16.8% education, legal, community service, arts, and media, 3.8% healthcare practitioners, 13.9% service, 22.3% sales and office, 9.2% natural resources, construction, and maintenance, 6.8% production, transportation, and material moving

Income: Per capita: $44,013; Median household: $91,875; Average household: $114,592; Households with income of $100,000 or more: 46.0%; Poverty rate: 13.6%

Educational Attainment: High school diploma or higher: 93.7%; Bachelor's degree or higher: 50.3%; Graduate/professional degree or higher: 20.5%

Housing: Homeownership rate: 73.3%; Median home value: $676,700; Median year structure built: 1976; Homeowner vacancy rate: 1.2%; Median gross rent: $1,206 per month; Rental vacancy rate: 4.9%

Health Insurance: 84.1% have insurance; 75.0% have private insurance; 21.3% have public insurance; 15.9% do not have insurance; 1.6% of children under 18 do not have insurance

Transportation: Commute: 79.9% car, 0.0% public transportation, 1.7% walk, 16.1% work from home; Median travel time to work: 34.8 minutes

BOULDER CREEK (CDP). Covers a land area of 7.512 square miles and a water area of 0 square miles. Located at 37.13° N. Lat; 122.13° W. Long. Elevation is 479 feet.

History: Boulder Creek began as a redwood lumber camp at the junction of Bear Creek and the San Lorenzo River, and later developed as a colony of summer homes.

Population: 4,923; Growth (since 2000): 20.6%; Density: 655.4 persons per square mile; Race: 90.0% White, 1.1% Black/African American, 1.6% Asian, 0.6% American Indian/Alaska Native, 0.1% Native Hawaiian/Other Pacific Islander, 4.1% Two or more races, 7.4% Hispanic of any race; Average household size: 2.32; Median age: 45.4; Age under 18: 18.0%; Age 65 and over: 8.8%; Males per 100 females: 105.2; Marriage status: 30.6% never married, 50.5% now married, 0.6% separated, 4.1% widowed, 14.8% divorced; Foreign born: 2.2%; Speak English only: 96.6%; With disability: 13.0%; Veterans: 9.2%; Ancestry: 20.7% German, 17.2% English, 16.1% Irish, 11.5% Italian, 5.3% European

Employment: 14.4% management, business, and financial, 12.6% computer, engineering, and science, 5.9% education, legal, community service, arts, and media, 5.8% healthcare practitioners, 15.5% service, 28.3% sales and office, 12.9% natural resources, construction, and maintenance, 4.6% production, transportation, and material moving

Income: Per capita: $40,838; Median household: $77,114; Average household: $94,369; Households with income of $100,000 or more: 36.9%; Poverty rate: 10.1%

Educational Attainment: High school diploma or higher: 96.0%; Bachelor's degree or higher: 33.0%; Graduate/professional degree or higher: 8.9%

School District(s)

San Lorenzo Valley Unified (KG-12)
2012-13 Enrollment: 4,444 . . . . (831) 336-5194

Housing: Homeownership rate: 71.6%; Median home value: $416,400; Median year structure built: 1957; Homeowner vacancy rate: 2.1%; Median gross rent: $1,545 per month; Rental vacancy rate: 6.5%

Health Insurance: 89.6% have insurance; 74.6% have private insurance; 25.1% have public insurance; 10.4% do not have insurance; 4.9% of children under 18 do not have insurance

Transportation: Commute: 90.1% car, 0.3% public transportation, 1.0% walk, 6.4% work from home; Median travel time to work: 37.3 minutes

BROOKDALE (CDP). Covers a land area of 3.847 square miles and a water area of 0 square miles. Located at 37.11° N. Lat; 122.11° W. Long. Elevation is 443 feet.

Population: 1,991; Growth (since 2000): n/a; Density: 517.5 persons per square mile; Race: 89.9% White, 0.5% Black/African American, 1.0% Asian, 0.6% American Indian/Alaska Native, 0.4% Native Hawaiian/Other Pacific Islander, 4.4% Two or more races, 10.1% Hispanic of any race; Average household size: 2.47; Median age: 42.3; Age under 18: 21.3%; Age 65 and over: 8.3%; Males per 100 females: 104.8

Housing: Homeownership rate: 61.0%; Homeowner vacancy rate: 1.4%; Rental vacancy rate: 4.8%

CAPITOLA (city). Covers a land area of 1.593 square miles and a water area of 0.083 square miles. Located at 36.98° N. Lat; 121.95° W. Long. Elevation is 13 feet.

History: Incorporated 1949.

Population: 9,918; Growth (since 2000): -1.1%; Density: 6,225.6 persons per square mile; Race: 80.3% White, 1.2% Black/African American, 4.3% Asian, 0.6% American Indian/Alaska Native, 0.1% Native Hawaiian/Other Pacific Islander, 4.7% Two or more races, 19.7% Hispanic of any race; Average household size: 2.11; Median age: 41.9; Age under 18: 16.6%; Age 65 and over: 15.5%; Males per 100 females: 90.8; Marriage status: 35.3% never married, 43.6% now married, 2.9% separated, 6.2% widowed, 14.9% divorced; Foreign born: 11.9%; Speak English only: 79.6%; With disability: 10.2%; Veterans: 6.4%; Ancestry: 18.1% English, 15.7% German, 11.8% Irish, 8.7% Italian, 6.9% French

Employment: 15.0% management, business, and financial, 9.7% computer, engineering, and science, 13.2% education, legal, community service, arts, and media, 7.1% healthcare practitioners, 16.5% service, 26.3% sales and office, 4.6% natural resources, construction, and maintenance, 7.6% production, transportation, and material moving

Income: Per capita: $36,532; Median household: $54,064; Average household: $82,434; Households with income of $100,000 or more: 25.3%; Poverty rate: 8.0%

Educational Attainment: High school diploma or higher: 92.4%; Bachelor's degree or higher: 40.6%; Graduate/professional degree or higher: 15.1%

School District(s)

Santa Cruz County Rop
2012-13 Enrollment: n/a . . . . (831) 466-5766

Soquel Union Elementary (KG-08)
2012-13 Enrollment: 1,954 . . . . (831) 464-5639

Housing: Homeownership rate: 46.5%; Median home value: $455,900; Median year structure built: 1972; Homeowner vacancy rate: 2.3%; Median gross rent: $1,588 per month; Rental vacancy rate: 4.8%

Health Insurance: 80.6% have insurance; 66.4% have private insurance; 24.4% have public insurance; 19.4% do not have insurance; 8.4% of children under 18 do not have insurance

Safety: Violent crime rate: 37.9 per 10,000 population; Property crime rate: 597.7 per 10,000 population

Transportation: Commute: 80.8% car, 2.9% public transportation, 6.1% walk, 7.0% work from home; Median travel time to work: 26.6 minutes

Additional Information Contacts

City of Capitola . . . . (831) 475-7300
http://www.cityofcapitola.org

CORRALITOS (CDP). Covers a land area of 8.987 square miles and a water area of 0.014 square miles. Located at 36.98° N. Lat; 121.79° W. Long. Elevation is 269 feet.

Population: 2,326; Growth (since 2000): -4.3%; Density: 258.8 persons per square mile; Race: 85.1% White, 0.7% Black/African American, 2.1% Asian, 0.5% American Indian/Alaska Native, 0.0% Native Hawaiian/Other Pacific Islander, 3.4% Two or more races, 22.9% Hispanic of any race; Average household size: 2.80; Median age: 45.1; Age under 18: 21.7%; Age 65 and over: 14.5%; Males per 100 females: 98.5

Housing: Homeownership rate: 74.0%; Homeowner vacancy rate: 0.8%; Rental vacancy rate: 2.3%

DAVENPORT (CDP). Covers a land area of 2.834 square miles and a water area of 0.010 square miles. Located at 37.02° N. Lat; 122.20° W. Long. Elevation is 39 feet.

Population: 408; Growth (since 2000): n/a; Density: 143.9 persons per square mile; Race: 66.7% White, 1.5% Black/African American, 2.9% Asian, 1.2% American Indian/Alaska Native, 0.0% Native Hawaiian/Other Pacific Islander, 7.6% Two or more races, 42.2% Hispanic of any race; Average household size: 2.84; Median age: 40.3; Age under 18: 19.4%; Age 65 and over: 10.0%; Males per 100 females: 137.2

School District(s)

Pacific Elementary (KG-06)
2012-13 Enrollment: 104. . . . . (831) 425-7002

Housing: Homeownership rate: 56.1%; Homeowner vacancy rate: 1.4%; Rental vacancy rate: 1.8%

DAY VALLEY (CDP). Covers a land area of 18.807 square miles and a water area of 0 square miles. Located at 37.03° N. Lat; 121.86° W. Long. Elevation is 1,322 feet.

Population: 3,409; Growth (since 2000): -5.0%; Density: 181.3 persons per square mile; Race: 85.0% White, 0.6% Black/African American, 2.5% Asian, 0.7% American Indian/Alaska Native, 0.1% Native Hawaiian/Other Pacific Islander, 5.0% Two or more races, 13.8% Hispanic of any race; Average household size: 2.65; Median age: 48.0; Age under 18: 20.0%; Age 65 and over: 16.4%; Males per 100 females: 101.0; Marriage status: 28.2% never married, 61.2% now married, 0.6% separated, 4.9% widowed, 5.7% divorced; Foreign born: 14.8%; Speak English only: 75.5%; With disability: 5.6%; Veterans: 8.3%; Ancestry: 17.5% English, 14.1% German, 12.7% Irish, 8.3% Scottish, 7.3% Italian

Employment: 19.5% management, business, and financial, 7.0% computer, engineering, and science, 8.6% education, legal, community service, arts, and media, 9.2% healthcare practitioners, 18.5% service, 21.5% sales and office, 8.0% natural resources, construction, and maintenance, 7.8% production, transportation, and material moving

Income: Per capita: $38,029; Median household: $76,116; Average household: $109,153; Households with income of $100,000 or more: 43.6%; Poverty rate: 18.4%

Educational Attainment: High school diploma or higher: 81.6%; Bachelor's degree or higher: 42.7%; Graduate/professional degree or higher: 16.5%

Housing: Homeownership rate: 78.7%; Median home value: $800,800; Median year structure built: 1977; Homeowner vacancy rate: 1.3%; Median gross rent: $869 per month; Rental vacancy rate: 1.8%

Health Insurance: 86.2% have insurance; 67.4% have private insurance; 31.1% have public insurance; 13.8% do not have insurance; 8.4% of children under 18 do not have insurance

Transportation: Commute: 84.3% car, 1.7% public transportation, 1.3% walk, 11.0% work from home; Median travel time to work: 26.9 minutes

FELTON (CDP). Covers a land area of 4.552 square miles and a water area of 0 square miles. Located at 37.04° N. Lat; 122.08° W. Long. Elevation is 285 feet.

History: Felton was founded on the former Rancho Zayante, purchased by Isaac Graham in 1841.

Population: 4,057; Growth (since 2000): 286.0%; Density: 891.2 persons per square mile; Race: 91.0% White, 0.6% Black/African American, 1.7% Asian, 0.7% American Indian/Alaska Native, 0.3% Native Hawaiian/Other Pacific Islander, 4.2% Two or more races, 7.0% Hispanic of any race; Average household size: 2.37; Median age: 44.0; Age under 18: 18.2%; Age 65 and over: 10.1%; Males per 100 females: 101.1; Marriage status: 26.5% never married, 56.9% now married, 1.0% separated, 3.5% widowed, 13.2% divorced; Foreign born: 7.7%; Speak English only: 89.7%; With disability: 7.4%; Veterans: 9.0%; Ancestry: 28.4% German, 18.1% English, 10.3% French, 9.0% Italian, 6.9% Irish

Employment: 23.1% management, business, and financial, 14.4% computer, engineering, and science, 11.1% education, legal, community service, arts, and media, 6.1% healthcare practitioners, 11.7% service, 16.9% sales and office, 9.8% natural resources, construction, and maintenance, 7.0% production, transportation, and material moving

Income: Per capita: $39,659; Median household: $76,821; Average household: $99,139; Households with income of $100,000 or more: 37.6%; Poverty rate: 2.2%

Educational Attainment: High school diploma or higher: 94.5%; Bachelor's degree or higher: 42.2%; Graduate/professional degree or higher: 17.8%

School District(s)

San Lorenzo Valley Unified (KG-12)
2012-13 Enrollment: 4,444 . . . . (831) 336-5194

Housing: Homeownership rate: 69.5%; Median home value: $491,300; Median year structure built: 1958; Homeowner vacancy rate: 2.1%; Median gross rent: $1,109 per month; Rental vacancy rate: 3.0%

Health Insurance: 92.6% have insurance; 81.4% have private insurance; 17.7% have public insurance; 7.4% do not have insurance; 1.6% of children under 18 do not have insurance

Transportation: Commute: 92.1% car, 1.4% public transportation, 0.7% walk, 5.4% work from home; Median travel time to work: 30.9 minutes

FREEDOM (CDP). Covers a land area of 1.104 square miles and a water area of 0 square miles. Located at 36.94° N. Lat; 121.80° W. Long. Elevation is 125 feet.

History: When prohibition changed the lifestyle of its residents, the community of Whiskey Hill changed its name to Freedom.

Population: 3,070; Growth (since 2000): -48.8%; Density: 2,780.8 persons per square mile; Race: 47.3% White, 1.4% Black/African American, 3.3% Asian, 1.0% American Indian/Alaska Native, 0.0% Native Hawaiian/Other Pacific Islander, 5.1% Two or more races, 70.7% Hispanic of any race; Average household size: 3.95; Median age: 30.2; Age under 18: 29.4%; Age 65 and over: 8.9%; Males per 100 females: 103.0; Marriage status: 40.4% never married, 47.6% now married, 0.5% separated, 4.9% widowed, 7.1% divorced; Foreign born: 27.4%; Speak English only: 43.8%; With disability: 8.3%; Veterans: 3.6%; Ancestry: 7.6% American, 5.0% German, 4.7% Irish, 2.4% Portuguese, 1.4% Italian

Employment: 8.0% management, business, and financial, 0.3% computer, engineering, and science, 3.9% education, legal, community service, arts, and media, 6.2% healthcare practitioners, 28.3% service, 17.9% sales and office, 22.4% natural resources, construction, and maintenance, 13.0% production, transportation, and material moving

Income: Per capita: $17,488; Median household: $55,625; Average household: $69,011; Households with income of $100,000 or more: 20.2%; Poverty rate: 29.5%

Educational Attainment: High school diploma or higher: 65.2%; Bachelor's degree or higher: 12.0%; Graduate/professional degree or higher: 3.1%

School District(s)

Pajaro Valley Unified (KG-12)
2012-13 Enrollment: 20,001 . . . . (831) 786-2100

Housing: Homeownership rate: 65.6%; Median home value: $396,900; Median year structure built: 1956; Homeowner vacancy rate: 1.4%; Median gross rent: $1,629 per month; Rental vacancy rate: 2.2%

Health Insurance: 79.4% have insurance; 50.8% have private insurance; 35.2% have public insurance; 20.6% do not have insurance; 3.4% of children under 18 do not have insurance

Transportation: Commute: 82.7% car, 4.3% public transportation, 2.8% walk, 2.9% work from home; Median travel time to work: 23.6 minutes

INTERLAKEN (CDP). Covers a land area of 9.805 square miles and a water area of 0.397 square miles. Located at 36.95° N. Lat; 121.74° W. Long. Elevation is 128 feet.

Population: 7,321; Growth (since 2000): -0.1%; Density: 746.6 persons per square mile; Race: 52.7% White, 0.8% Black/African American, 4.1% Asian, 1.7% American Indian/Alaska Native, 0.0% Native Hawaiian/Other Pacific Islander, 5.5% Two or more races, 71.9% Hispanic of any race; Average household size: 4.27; Median age: 30.5; Age under 18: 29.2%; Age 65 and over: 8.6%; Males per 100 females: 109.6; Marriage status: 33.2% never married, 56.8% now married, 2.3% separated, 3.4% widowed, 6.5% divorced; Foreign born: 34.7%; Speak English only: 39.3%; With disability: 8.7%; Veterans: 4.2%; Ancestry: 5.4% German, 4.5% Italian, 3.7% Irish, 3.4% English, 1.7% African

Employment: 5.6% management, business, and financial, 1.6% computer, engineering, and science, 9.1% education, legal, community service, arts, and media, 2.9% healthcare practitioners, 24.2% service, 24.9% sales and office, 19.6% natural resources, construction, and maintenance, 12.1% production, transportation, and material moving

Income: Per capita: $21,473; Median household: $73,158; Average household: $83,712; Households with income of $100,000 or more: 31.5%; Poverty rate: 12.2%

Educational Attainment: High school diploma or higher: 60.6%; Bachelor's degree or higher: 13.9%; Graduate/professional degree or higher: 3.4%

Housing: Homeownership rate: 71.4%; Median home value: $330,400; Median year structure built: 1968; Homeowner vacancy rate: 0.7%; Median gross rent: $1,381 per month; Rental vacancy rate: 1.8%

Health Insurance: 75.4% have insurance; 49.4% have private insurance; 33.2% have public insurance; 24.6% do not have insurance; 7.6% of children under 18 do not have insurance

Transportation: Commute: 88.8% car, 1.1% public transportation, 2.6% walk, 3.3% work from home; Median travel time to work: 25.5 minutes

LA SELVA BEACH (CDP). Covers a land area of 5.297 square miles and a water area of 0 square miles. Located at 36.93° N. Lat; 121.84° W. Long. Elevation is 82 feet.

Population: 2,843; Growth (since 2000): n/a; Density: 536.8 persons per square mile; Race: 84.4% White, 0.9% Black/African American, 4.1% Asian, 0.8% American Indian/Alaska Native, 0.1% Native Hawaiian/Other Pacific Islander, 4.5% Two or more races, 13.1% Hispanic of any race; Average household size: 2.41; Median age: 46.5; Age under 18: 21.5%; Age 65 and over: 15.0%; Males per 100 females: 98.5; Marriage status: 22.9% never married, 60.9% now married, 2.3% separated, 7.3% widowed, 8.8% divorced; Foreign born: 6.1%; Speak English only: 92.5%; With disability: 9.6%; Veterans: 8.8%; Ancestry: 19.8% English, 18.7% German, 16.9% Irish, 10.3% American, 6.4% Norwegian

Employment: 27.9% management, business, and financial, 15.4% computer, engineering, and science, 11.8% education, legal, community service, arts, and media, 4.9% healthcare practitioners, 10.4% service, 18.0% sales and office, 6.9% natural resources, construction, and maintenance, 4.7% production, transportation, and material moving

Income: Per capita: $47,956; Median household: $79,591; Average household: $105,155; Households with income of $100,000 or more: 46.1%; Poverty rate: 9.9%

Educational Attainment: High school diploma or higher: 99.2%; Bachelor's degree or higher: 48.9%; Graduate/professional degree or higher: 18.9%

School District(s)

Pajaro Valley Unified (KG-12)
2012-13 Enrollment: 20,001 . . . . (831) 786-2100

Housing: Homeownership rate: 67.6%; Median home value: $841,100; Median year structure built: 1972; Homeowner vacancy rate: 0.4%; Median gross rent: $1,417 per month; Rental vacancy rate: 5.7%

Health Insurance: 92.1% have insurance; 78.4% have private insurance; 28.8% have public insurance; 7.9% do not have insurance; 0.0% of children under 18 do not have insurance

Transportation: Commute: 76.5% car, 0.0% public transportation, 4.0% walk, 13.8% work from home; Median travel time to work: 28.4 minutes

LIVE OAK (CDP). Covers a land area of 3.243 square miles and a water area of 0 square miles. Located at 36.99° N. Lat; 121.98° W. Long. Elevation is 105 feet.

Population: 17,158; Growth (since 2000): 3.2%; Density: 5,291.4 persons per square mile; Race: 73.6% White, 1.4% Black/African American, 4.5% Asian, 1.0% American Indian/Alaska Native, 0.2% Native Hawaiian/Other Pacific Islander, 5.0% Two or more races, 28.0% Hispanic of any race; Average household size: 2.59; Median age: 38.8; Age under 18: 21.4%; Age 65 and over: 12.7%; Males per 100 females: 96.0; Marriage status: 36.0% never married, 44.9% now married, 1.8% separated, 6.1% widowed, 13.1% divorced; Foreign born: 19.5%; Speak English only: 70.8%; With disability: 10.4%; Veterans: 5.0%; Ancestry: 14.4% English, 13.0% German, 11.8% Irish, 5.7% Italian, 3.7% French

Employment: 13.3% management, business, and financial, 6.3% computer, engineering, and science, 9.4% education, legal, community service, arts, and media, 6.4% healthcare practitioners, 24.4% service, 23.0% sales and office, 10.1% natural resources, construction, and maintenance, 7.2% production, transportation, and material moving

Income: Per capita: $30,904; Median household: $63,490; Average household: $81,027; Households with income of $100,000 or more: 29.5%; Poverty rate: 14.6%

Educational Attainment: High school diploma or higher: 85.2%; Bachelor's degree or higher: 35.3%; Graduate/professional degree or higher: 13.0%

Housing: Homeownership rate: 55.9%; Median home value: $540,200; Median year structure built: 1976; Homeowner vacancy rate: 1.8%; Median gross rent: $1,428 per month; Rental vacancy rate: 1.9%

Health Insurance: 84.0% have insurance; 66.8% have private insurance; 26.5% have public insurance; 16.0% do not have insurance; 5.9% of children under 18 do not have insurance

Transportation: Commute: 81.0% car, 3.4% public transportation, 5.1% walk, 5.9% work from home; Median travel time to work: 22.6 minutes

LOMPICO (CDP). Covers a land area of 3.374 square miles and a water area of <.001 square miles. Located at 37.11° N. Lat; 122.05° W. Long. Elevation is 666 feet.

Population: 1,137; Growth (since 2000): n/a; Density: 337.0 persons per square mile; Race: 88.4% White, 0.5% Black/African American, 1.8% Asian, 1.1% American Indian/Alaska Native, 0.4% Native Hawaiian/Other Pacific Islander, 5.6% Two or more races, 10.1% Hispanic of any race; Average household size: 2.34; Median age: 44.2; Age under 18: 17.6%; Age 65 and over: 6.3%; Males per 100 females: 106.4

Housing: Homeownership rate: 79.0%; Homeowner vacancy rate: 3.8%; Rental vacancy rate: 8.9%

MOUNT HERMON (CDP). Covers a land area of 0.889 square miles and a water area of 0 square miles. Located at 37.05° N. Lat; 122.05° W. Long. Elevation is 400 feet.

Population: 1,037; Growth (since 2000): n/a; Density: 1,166.3 persons per square mile; Race: 93.0% White, 0.6% Black/African American, 1.4% Asian, 0.3% American Indian/Alaska Native, 0.1% Native Hawaiian/Other Pacific Islander, 3.0% Two or more races, 8.0% Hispanic of any race; Average household size: 2.54; Median age: 39.0; Age under 18: 22.9%; Age 65 and over: 9.5%; Males per 100 females: 94.2

Housing: Homeownership rate: 51.5%; Homeowner vacancy rate: 0.0%; Rental vacancy rate: 5.3%

PAJARO DUNES (CDP). Covers a land area of 2.562 square miles and a water area of 0.026 square miles. Located at 36.87° N. Lat; 121.81° W. Long.

Population: 144; Growth (since 2000): n/a; Density: 56.2 persons per square mile; Race: 63.9% White, 0.0% Black/African American, 4.2% Asian, 0.0% American Indian/Alaska Native, 0.0% Native Hawaiian/Other Pacific Islander, 0.7% Two or more races, 37.5% Hispanic of any race; Average household size: 2.72; Median age: 45.0; Age under 18: 26.4%; Age 65 and over: 13.2%; Males per 100 females: 75.6

Housing: Homeownership rate: 69.8%; Homeowner vacancy rate: 0.0%; Rental vacancy rate: 46.7%

PARADISE PARK (CDP). Covers a land area of 0.279 square miles and a water area of 0 square miles. Located at 37.01° N. Lat; 122.04° W. Long. Elevation is 56 feet.

Population: 389; Growth (since 2000): n/a; Density: 1,396.2 persons per square mile; Race: 95.4% White, 0.5% Black/African American, 0.8% Asian, 0.8% American Indian/Alaska Native, 0.0% Native Hawaiian/Other Pacific Islander, 1.5% Two or more races, 3.9% Hispanic of any race; Average household size: 1.92; Median age: 57.1; Age under 18: 9.3%; Age 65 and over: 32.9%; Males per 100 females: 90.7

Housing: Homeownership rate: 91.6%; Homeowner vacancy rate: 3.1%; Rental vacancy rate: 0.0%

PASATIEMPO (CDP). Covers a land area of 0.884 square miles and a water area of 0 square miles. Located at 37.00° N. Lat; 122.03° W. Long. Elevation is 407 feet.

Population: 1,041; Growth (since 2000): n/a; Density: 1,178.1 persons per square mile; Race: 88.9% White, 0.5% Black/African American, 3.3% Asian, 0.6% American Indian/Alaska Native, 0.1% Native Hawaiian/Other Pacific Islander, 4.6% Two or more races, 8.2% Hispanic of any race; Average household size: 2.46; Median age: 53.7; Age under 18: 16.3%; Age 65 and over: 27.1%; Males per 100 females: 102.9

Housing: Homeownership rate: 90.8%; Homeowner vacancy rate: 1.5%; Rental vacancy rate: 4.9%

PLEASURE POINT (CDP).

Note: Statistics that would complete this profile are not available because the CDP was created after the 2010 Census was released.

RIO DEL MAR (CDP). Covers a land area of 3.001 square miles and a water area of 1.611 square miles. Located at 36.96° N. Lat; 121.88° W. Long. Elevation is 144 feet.

Population: 9,216; Growth (since 2000): 0.2%; Density: 3,071.2 persons per square mile; Race: 90.2% White, 0.7% Black/African American, 3.4% Asian, 0.5% American Indian/Alaska Native, 0.1% Native Hawaiian/Other Pacific Islander, 3.1% Two or more races, 9.8% Hispanic of any race; Average household size: 2.35; Median age: 47.0; Age under 18: 19.7%; Age 65 and over: 18.4%; Males per 100 females: 92.6; Marriage status: 21.5% never married, 58.8% now married, 0.6% separated, 7.2% widowed, 12.4% divorced; Foreign born: 9.3%; Speak English only: 90.0%; With disability: 8.9%; Veterans: 10.8%; Ancestry: 21.2% German, 18.2% English, 16.2% Irish, 14.7% Italian, 5.9% French

Employment: 24.4% management, business, and financial, 5.4% computer, engineering, and science, 14.8% education, legal, community service, arts, and media, 7.2% healthcare practitioners, 11.8% service,

23.9% sales and office, 6.7% natural resources, construction, and maintenance, 5.7% production, transportation, and material moving

Income: Per capita: $51,912; Median household: $93,909; Average household: $118,214; Households with income of $100,000 or more: 47.6%; Poverty rate: 6.4%

Educational Attainment: High school diploma or higher: 97.7%; Bachelor's degree or higher: 49.2%; Graduate/professional degree or higher: 20.6%

Housing: Homeownership rate: 72.7%; Median home value: $697,000; Median year structure built: 1974; Homeowner vacancy rate: 1.9%; Median gross rent: $1,812 per month; Rental vacancy rate: 8.4%

Health Insurance: 94.6% have insurance; 86.6% have private insurance; 25.3% have public insurance; 5.4% do not have insurance; 1.3% of children under 18 do not have insurance

Transportation: Commute: 89.8% car, 0.8% public transportation, 0.9% walk, 7.0% work from home; Median travel time to work: 28.3 minutes

SANTA CRUZ (city). County seat. Covers a land area of 12.740 square miles and a water area of 3.088 square miles. Located at 36.97° N. Lat; 122.04° W. Long. Elevation is 36 feet.

History: A Franciscan mission was founded in 1791 at Santa Cruz by Father Fermin de Lasuen. In 1797 a boatload of colonists established the Villa de Branciforte, with instructions from the Governor for an adobe house to be built for each settler. The colonists turned out to be vagabonds and ex-convicts, and conflicts with the mission priests abounded. By 1840 the mission had been abandoned but the town that took its name developed into a trading center for lumber from the redwood forests. A foundry was established in 1848 for making iron picks for the mines and plows for the farms. Santa Cruz was granted a city charter in 1866.

Population: 59,946; Growth (since 2000): 9.8%; Density: 4,705.2 persons per square mile; Race: 74.5% White, 1.8% Black/African American, 7.7% Asian, 0.7% American Indian/Alaska Native, 0.2% Native Hawaiian/Other Pacific Islander, 5.7% Two or more races, 19.4% Hispanic of any race; Average household size: 2.39; Median age: 29.9; Age under 18: 13.7%; Age 65 and over: 8.8%; Males per 100 females: 100.5; Marriage status: 56.1% never married, 30.3% now married, 1.6% separated, 3.0% widowed, 10.5% divorced; Foreign born: 13.3%; Speak English only: 77.0%; With disability: 8.0%; Veterans: 4.2%; Ancestry: 15.1% German, 12.0% Irish, 11.2% English, 7.7% Italian, 5.3% European

Employment: 14.2% management, business, and financial, 8.9% computer, engineering, and science, 19.5% education, legal, community service, arts, and media, 4.4% healthcare practitioners, 20.0% service, 21.0% sales and office, 6.9% natural resources, construction, and maintenance, 5.2% production, transportation, and material moving

Income: Per capita: $29,151; Median household: $61,600; Average household: $81,474; Households with income of $100,000 or more: 28.5%; Poverty rate: 21.9%

Educational Attainment: High school diploma or higher: 92.4%; Bachelor's degree or higher: 49.4%; Graduate/professional degree or higher: 21.4%

School District(s)

Bonny Doon Union Elementary (KG-06)
2012-13 Enrollment: 132. . . . . (831) 427-2300
Happy Valley Elementary (KG-06)
2012-13 Enrollment: 127. . . . . (831) 429-1456
Live Oak Elementary (KG-12)
2012-13 Enrollment: 2,118 . . . . (831) 475-6333
Santa Cruz City Elementary (KG-06)
2012-13 Enrollment: 2,360 . . . . (831) 429-3410
Santa Cruz City High (KG-12)
2012-13 Enrollment: 4,716 . . . . (831) 429-3410
Santa Cruz County Office of Education (KG-12)
2012-13 Enrollment: 1,393 . . . . (831) 466-5600
Scotts Valley Unified (PK-12)
2012-13 Enrollment: 2,479 . . . . (831) 438-1820
Soquel Union Elementary (KG-08)
2012-13 Enrollment: 1,954 . . . . (831) 464-5639

Four-year College(s)

Five Branches University (Private, For-profit)
Fall 2013 Enrollment: 402 . . . . (831) 476-9424
University of California-Santa Cruz (Public)
Fall 2013 Enrollment: 17,203 . . . . (831) 459-0111
2013-14 Tuition: In-state $13,397; Out-of-state $36,275

Vocational/Technical School(s)

Cosmo Factory Cosmetology Academy (Private, For-profit)
Fall 2013 Enrollment: 30 . . . . (831) 621-6161
2013-14 Tuition: $15,358
UEI College-Santa Cruz (Private, For-profit)
Fall 2013 Enrollment: 131 . . . . (949) 272-7200
2013-14 Tuition: $24,900

Housing: Homeownership rate: 43.3%; Median home value: $643,800; Median year structure built: 1964; Homeowner vacancy rate: 1.2%; Median gross rent: $1,490 per month; Rental vacancy rate: 3.4%

Health Insurance: 87.4% have insurance; 74.6% have private insurance; 19.7% have public insurance; 12.6% do not have insurance; 2.7% of children under 18 do not have insurance

Hospitals: Dominican Hospital (379 beds); Sutter Maternity & Surgery Center of Santa Cruz (30 beds)

Safety: Violent crime rate: 65.1 per 10,000 population; Property crime rate: 505.9 per 10,000 population

Newspapers: Good Times (weekly circulation 45000); Metro Santa Cruz (weekly circulation 34000)

Transportation: Commute: 67.8% car, 5.4% public transportation, 9.9% walk, 6.1% work from home; Median travel time to work: 22.0 minutes; Amtrak: Bus service available.

Additional Information Contacts

City of Santa Cruz . . . . (831) 420-5030
http://www.cityofsantacruz.com

SCOTTS VALLEY (city). Covers a land area of 4.595 square miles and a water area of 0 square miles. Located at 37.06° N. Lat; 122.01° W. Long. Elevation is 561 feet.

Population: 11,580; Growth (since 2000): 1.7%; Density: 2,520.4 persons per square mile; Race: 86.0% White, 0.9% Black/African American, 5.1% Asian, 0.5% American Indian/Alaska Native, 0.2% Native Hawaiian/Other Pacific Islander, 4.9% Two or more races, 10.0% Hispanic of any race; Average household size: 2.55; Median age: 41.7; Age under 18: 24.7%; Age 65 and over: 13.6%; Males per 100 females: 95.1; Marriage status: 33.3% never married, 51.0% now married, 0.6% separated, 5.7% widowed, 10.0% divorced; Foreign born: 10.5%; Speak English only: 88.2%; With disability: 8.0%; Veterans: 7.4%; Ancestry: 21.7% German, 14.7% English, 13.0% Irish, 10.4% Italian, 5.1% American

Employment: 24.1% management, business, and financial, 8.3% computer, engineering, and science, 10.9% education, legal, community service, arts, and media, 6.1% healthcare practitioners, 14.7% service, 25.3% sales and office, 7.7% natural resources, construction, and maintenance, 2.9% production, transportation, and material moving

Income: Per capita: $43,164; Median household: $101,837; Average household: $116,058; Households with income of $100,000 or more: 52.0%; Poverty rate: 3.2%

Educational Attainment: High school diploma or higher: 95.6%; Bachelor's degree or higher: 45.2%; Graduate/professional degree or higher: 16.5%

School District(s)

Scotts Valley Unified (PK-12)
2012-13 Enrollment: 2,479 . . . . (831) 438-1820

Housing: Homeownership rate: 73.4%; Median home value: $586,100; Median year structure built: 1982; Homeowner vacancy rate: 1.4%; Median gross rent: $1,948 per month; Rental vacancy rate: 3.2%

Health Insurance: 93.4% have insurance; 88.2% have private insurance; 15.7% have public insurance; 6.6% do not have insurance; 0.0% of children under 18 do not have insurance

Safety: Violent crime rate: 9.4 per 10,000 population; Property crime rate: 245.4 per 10,000 population

Newspapers: Press Banner (weekly circulation 20000); Santa Cruz Sentinel (daily circulation 24400)

Transportation: Commute: 90.5% car, 0.6% public transportation, 0.9% walk, 6.7% work from home; Median travel time to work: 25.1 minutes; Amtrak: Bus service available.

Additional Information Contacts

City of Scotts Valley . . . . (831) 440-5600
http://www.scottsvalley.org

SEACLIFF (CDP). Covers a land area of 0.767 square miles and a water area of <.001 square miles. Located at 36.98° N. Lat; 121.92° W. Long. Elevation is 108 feet.

Population: 3,267; Growth (since 2000): n/a; Density: 4,261.9 persons per square mile; Race: 84.4% White, 0.9% Black/African American, 3.1%

Asian, 1.2% American Indian/Alaska Native, 0.1% Native Hawaiian/Other Pacific Islander, 4.5% Two or more races, 14.8% Hispanic of any race; Average household size: 2.13; Median age: 43.8; Age under 18: 16.9%; Age 65 and over: 12.8%; Males per 100 females: 90.5; Marriage status: 38.0% never married, 43.8% now married, 0.6% separated, 4.7% widowed, 13.6% divorced; Foreign born: 6.7%; Speak English only: 86.8%; With disability: 11.6%; Veterans: 7.7%; Ancestry: 21.8% German, 13.7% Irish, 12.9% English, 8.3% Italian, 6.0% Polish

Employment: 18.2% management, business, and financial, 2.7% computer, engineering, and science, 13.4% education, legal, community service, arts, and media, 3.7% healthcare practitioners, 19.5% service, 24.9% sales and office, 8.6% natural resources, construction, and maintenance, 9.0% production, transportation, and material moving

Income: Per capita: $33,257; Median household: $60,424; Average household: $74,199; Households with income of $100,000 or more: 23.5%; Poverty rate: 15.2%

Educational Attainment: High school diploma or higher: 95.0%; Bachelor's degree or higher: 47.2%; Graduate/professional degree or higher: 19.9%

Housing: Homeownership rate: 51.8%; Median home value: $533,300; Median year structure built: 1969; Homeowner vacancy rate: 1.6%; Median gross rent: $1,336 per month; Rental vacancy rate: 2.5%

Health Insurance: 89.7% have insurance; 69.0% have private insurance; 32.9% have public insurance; 10.3% do not have insurance; 4.5% of children under 18 do not have insurance

Transportation: Commute: 83.9% car, 2.0% public transportation, 3.5% walk, 6.4% work from home; Median travel time to work: 24.3 minutes

SOQUEL (CDP). Covers a land area of 4.598 square miles and a water area of 0 square miles. Located at 37.00° N. Lat; 121.95° W. Long. Elevation is 33 feet.

History: Soquel developed as a lumber town. It was near Soquel Creek in 1769 that Portola and his men first mentioned the "high trees of a red color" and named them redwoods.

Population: 9,644; Growth (since 2000): 89.8%; Density: 2,097.4 persons per square mile; Race: 81.9% White, 0.9% Black/African American, 3.7% Asian, 0.7% American Indian/Alaska Native, 0.2% Native Hawaiian/Other Pacific Islander, 5.4% Two or more races, 16.7% Hispanic of any race; Average household size: 2.45; Median age: 43.2; Age under 18: 20.1%; Age 65 and over: 12.6%; Males per 100 females: 91.8; Marriage status: 31.2% never married, 49.1% now married, 2.8% separated, 4.1% widowed, 15.7% divorced; Foreign born: 11.0%; Speak English only: 85.2%; With disability: 10.5%; Veterans: 7.1%; Ancestry: 18.0% German, 13.6% Italian, 12.0% English, 10.7% Irish, 8.7% European

Employment: 21.1% management, business, and financial, 6.1% computer, engineering, and science, 11.7% education, legal, community service, arts, and media, 8.3% healthcare practitioners, 16.0% service, 21.2% sales and office, 10.1% natural resources, construction, and maintenance, 5.5% production, transportation, and material moving

Income: Per capita: $38,165; Median household: $74,803; Average household: $94,120; Households with income of $100,000 or more: 36.4%; Poverty rate: 5.8%

Educational Attainment: High school diploma or higher: 95.8%; Bachelor's degree or higher: 41.9%; Graduate/professional degree or higher: 13.8%

School District(s)

Mountain Elementary (KG-06)
2012-13 Enrollment: 132 . . . . (831) 475-6812

Santa Cruz City High (KG-12)
2012-13 Enrollment: 4,716 . . . . (831) 429-3410

Soquel Union Elementary (KG-08)
2012-13 Enrollment: 1,954 . . . . (831) 464-5639

Housing: Homeownership rate: 70.3%; Median home value: $505,200; Median year structure built: 1977; Homeowner vacancy rate: 1.4%; Median gross rent: $1,448 per month; Rental vacancy rate: 2.4%

Health Insurance: 89.3% have insurance; 77.2% have private insurance; 24.5% have public insurance; 10.7% do not have insurance; 3.9% of children under 18 do not have insurance

Transportation: Commute: 88.3% car, 0.8% public transportation, 1.9% walk, 6.8% work from home; Median travel time to work: 25.0 minutes

TWIN LAKES (CDP). Covers a land area of 0.690 square miles and a water area of 0.520 square miles. Located at 36.96° N. Lat; 121.99° W. Long. Elevation is 52 feet.

Population: 4,917; Growth (since 2000): -11.1%; Density: 7,122.2 persons per square mile; Race: 79.3% White, 1.4% Black/African American, 2.6% Asian, 1.2% American Indian/Alaska Native, 0.2% Native Hawaiian/Other Pacific Islander, 4.4% Two or more races, 22.6% Hispanic of any race; Average household size: 2.15; Median age: 36.8; Age under 18: 15.7%; Age 65 and over: 14.3%; Males per 100 females: 94.8; Marriage status: 44.4% never married, 34.2% now married, 0.3% separated, 5.0% widowed, 16.4% divorced; Foreign born: 6.6%; Speak English only: 85.0%; With disability: 10.0%; Veterans: 4.3%; Ancestry: 22.0% Irish, 17.2% German, 13.5% Italian, 12.1% English, 4.9% European

Employment: 11.0% management, business, and financial, 7.1% computer, engineering, and science, 24.8% education, legal, community service, arts, and media, 3.9% healthcare practitioners, 15.2% service, 28.8% sales and office, 5.1% natural resources, construction, and maintenance, 4.2% production, transportation, and material moving

Income: Per capita: $31,302; Median household: $48,686; Average household: $68,125; Households with income of $100,000 or more: 25.9%; Poverty rate: 19.7%

Educational Attainment: High school diploma or higher: 92.2%; Bachelor's degree or higher: 38.8%; Graduate/professional degree or higher: 16.6%

Housing: Homeownership rate: 36.9%; Median home value: $518,200; Median year structure built: 1972; Homeowner vacancy rate: 3.5%; Median gross rent: $1,412 per month; Rental vacancy rate: 3.9%

Health Insurance: 80.2% have insurance; 63.9% have private insurance; 27.8% have public insurance; 19.8% do not have insurance; 9.1% of children under 18 do not have insurance

Transportation: Commute: 83.2% car, 2.9% public transportation, 3.4% walk, 3.1% work from home; Median travel time to work: 23.6 minutes

WATSONVILLE (city). Covers a land area of 6.687 square miles and a water area of 0.096 square miles. Located at 36.92° N. Lat; 121.77° W. Long. Elevation is 33 feet.

History: Watsonville was laid out in 1852 by Judge John H. Watson and D.S. Gregory on land purchased from Don Sebastian Rodriguez' Rancho Bolsa del Pajaro. One man's success with an apple orchard in 1853 led others to plant fruit trees, and Watsonville became a major producer of apples, strawberries, apricots, and other garden crops, with packing houses and canneries.

Population: 51,199; Growth (since 2000): 15.7%; Density: 7,656.6 persons per square mile; Race: 43.7% White, 0.7% Black/African American, 3.3% Asian, 1.2% American Indian/Alaska Native, 0.1% Native Hawaiian/Other Pacific Islander, 4.4% Two or more races, 81.4% Hispanic of any race; Average household size: 3.75; Median age: 29.2; Age under 18: 31.5%; Age 65 and over: 8.3%; Males per 100 females: 99.2; Marriage status: 41.2% never married, 48.1% now married, 2.3% separated, 4.1% widowed, 6.6% divorced; Foreign born: 41.2%; Speak English only: 24.1%; With disability: 8.8%; Veterans: 3.2%; Ancestry: 3.3% German, 2.6% English, 2.5% Irish, 1.2% Portuguese, 1.1% Italian

Employment: 7.3% management, business, and financial, 2.2% computer, engineering, and science, 5.3% education, legal, community service, arts, and media, 1.9% healthcare practitioners, 23.7% service, 19.1% sales and office, 26.4% natural resources, construction, and maintenance, 14.0% production, transportation, and material moving

Income: Per capita: $16,263; Median household: $43,905; Average household: $57,817; Households with income of $100,000 or more: 14.6%; Poverty rate: 20.7%

Educational Attainment: High school diploma or higher: 54.2%; Bachelor's degree or higher: 9.3%; Graduate/professional degree or higher: 2.7%

School District(s)

Pajaro Valley Unified (KG-12)
2012-13 Enrollment: 20,001 . . . . (831) 786-2100

Vocational/Technical School(s)

CET-Watsonville (Private, Not-for-profit)
Fall 2013 Enrollment: 88 . . . . (408) 287-7924
2013-14 Tuition: $9,958

Housing: Homeownership rate: 44.0%; Median home value: $310,400; Median year structure built: 1975; Homeowner vacancy rate: 1.9%; Median gross rent: $1,133 per month; Rental vacancy rate: 2.5%

Health Insurance: 76.8% have insurance; 44.0% have private insurance; 39.5% have public insurance; 23.2% do not have insurance; 6.9% of children under 18 do not have insurance
Hospitals: Watsonville Community Hospital (106 beds)
Safety: Violent crime rate: 45.5 per 10,000 population; Property crime rate: 251.2 per 10,000 population
Newspapers: Register-Pajaronian (daily circulation 5200)
Transportation: Commute: 85.7% car, 2.1% public transportation, 3.4% walk, 2.8% work from home; Median travel time to work: 21.9 minutes
Airports: Watsonville Municipal (general aviation)
Additional Information Contacts
City of Watsonville . . . . (831) 768-3010
http://cityofwatsonville.org

ZAYANTE (CDP). Covers a land area of 2.725 square miles and a water area of 0 square miles. Located at 37.09° N. Lat; 122.04° W. Long. Elevation is 499 feet.
Population: 705; Growth (since 2000): n/a; Density: 258.7 persons per square mile; Race: 91.8% White, 1.4% Black/African American, 0.6% Asian, 0.9% American Indian/Alaska Native, 0.0% Native Hawaiian/Other Pacific Islander, 2.8% Two or more races, 8.1% Hispanic of any race; Average household size: 2.32; Median age: 40.7; Age under 18: 18.3%; Age 65 and over: 6.7%; Males per 100 females: 104.9
Housing: Homeownership rate: 70.8%; Homeowner vacancy rate: 1.8%; Rental vacancy rate: 6.3%

Shasta County

Located in northern California; mountainous area, with the Klamath Mountains on the west and the Cascade Range on the east; includes Shasta Lake, Lassen Peak, and Shasta and Lassen National Forests. Covers a land area of 3,775.402 square miles, a water area of 72.020 square miles, and is located in the Pacific Time Zone at 40.76° N. Lat., 122.04° W. Long. The county was founded in 1850. County seat is Redding.

Shasta County is part of the Redding, CA Metropolitan Statistical Area. The entire metro area includes: Shasta County, CA

Weather Station: Burney — Elevation: 3,158 feet

	Jan	Feb	Mar	Apr	May	Jun	Jul	Aug	Sep	Oct	Nov	Dec
High	44	49	55	62	72	80	89	88	81	69	52	43
Low	20	23	26	30	36	41	45	42	36	28	25	20
Precip	3.6	4.6	4.0	2.1	1.6	0.7	0.2	0.3	0.7	1.6	3.8	4.7
Snow	na	na	na	3.0	0.1	0.0	0.0	0.0	0.0	0.1	3.1	na

High and Low temperatures in degrees Fahrenheit; Precipitation and Snow in inches

Weather Station: Hat Creek — Elevation: 3,015 feet

	Jan	Feb	Mar	Apr	May	Jun	Jul	Aug	Sep	Oct	Nov	Dec
High	48	53	58	65	74	82	90	90	84	72	55	47
Low	23	25	29	33	39	44	48	45	39	31	27	23
Precip	2.6	2.9	2.7	1.6	1.4	0.7	0.2	0.2	0.6	1.2	2.5	2.6
Snow	3.4	2.5	1.3	0.5	tr	0.0	0.0	0.0	0.0	tr	1.3	4.5

High and Low temperatures in degrees Fahrenheit; Precipitation and Snow in inches

Weather Station: Manzanita Lake — Elevation: 5,749 feet

	Jan	Feb	Mar	Apr	May	Jun	Jul	Aug	Sep	Oct	Nov	Dec
High	43	43	47	53	62	70	79	78	72	61	47	42
Low	22	22	24	28	35	40	45	44	40	33	26	22
Precip	5.8	5.5	5.6	3.5	2.9	1.5	0.4	0.4	1.2	2.8	5.2	5.8
Snow	34.5	33.9	32.7	21.2	6.0	1.0	0.1	0.0	0.2	3.7	17.6	31.3

High and Low temperatures in degrees Fahrenheit; Precipitation and Snow in inches

Weather Station: Redding Municipal Arpt — Elevation: 501 feet

	Jan	Feb	Mar	Apr	May	Jun	Jul	Aug	Sep	Oct	Nov	Dec
High	55	60	65	71	81	90	99	97	91	79	64	55
Low	37	39	43	47	54	61	66	63	58	49	41	36
Precip	6.4	5.7	4.3	2.3	2.2	0.7	0.1	0.2	0.6	1.8	3.5	6.1
Snow	na	na	na	na	na	na	na	na	na	na	na	na

High and Low temperatures in degrees Fahrenheit; Precipitation and Snow in inches

Weather Station: Shasta Dam — Elevation: 1,075 feet

	Jan	Feb	Mar	Apr	May	Jun	Jul	Aug	Sep	Oct	Nov	Dec
High	53	57	62	69	78	86	95	94	88	76	61	53
Low	40	41	44	48	55	62	68	67	62	55	46	40
Precip	10.3	11.7	9.5	4.7	3.3	1.4	0.2	0.2	1.0	3.0	7.4	12.1
Snow	0.0	0.0	0.2	0.0	0.0	0.0	0.0	0.0	0.0	0.0	0.0	0.4

High and Low temperatures in degrees Fahrenheit; Precipitation and Snow in inches

Weather Station: Whiskeytown Reservoir — Elevation: 1,294 feet

	Jan	Feb	Mar	Apr	May	Jun	Jul	Aug	Sep	Oct	Nov	Dec
High	54	57	63	69	78	87	96	96	90	77	61	53
Low	36	38	41	45	53	59	64	62	58	50	41	36
Precip	10.4	11.5	9.8	4.4	3.3	1.3	0.3	0.1	0.9	3.0	8.2	11.6
Snow	0.8	0.0	0.0	0.0	0.0	0.0	0.0	0.0	0.0	0.0	0.0	0.1

High and Low temperatures in degrees Fahrenheit; Precipitation and Snow in inches

Population: 177,223; Growth (since 2000): 8.6%; Density: 46.9 persons per square mile; Race: 86.7% White, 0.9% Black/African American, 2.5% Asian, 2.8% American Indian/Alaska Native, 0.2% Native Hawaiian/Other Pacific Islander, 4.4% two or more races, 8.4% Hispanic of any race; Average household size: 2.48; Median age: 41.8; Age under 18: 22.4%; Age 65 and over: 16.9%; Males per 100 females: 96.7; Marriage status: 27.2% never married, 51.6% now married, 2.1% separated, 7.2% widowed, 14.1% divorced; Foreign born: 5.2%; Speak English only: 91.3%; With disability: 17.9%; Veterans: 12.8%; Ancestry: 17.4% German, 14.1% Irish, 11.4% English, 9.3% American, 5.5% Italian
Religion: Six largest groups: 8.6% Non-denominational Protestant, 4.9% Catholicism, 4.0% Latter-day Saints, 3.6% Holiness, 1.3% Pentecostal, 1.2% Baptist
Economy: Unemployment rate: 7.7%; Leading industries: 15.4% retail trade; 15.2% health care and social assistance; 10.7% construction; Farms: 1,544 totaling 376,306 acres; Company size: 1 employs 1,000 or more persons, 2 employ 500 to 999 persons, 53 employ 100 to 499 persons, 4,138 employ less than 100 persons; Business ownership: 3,873 women-owned, 25 Black-owned, 472 Hispanic-owned, n/a Asian-owned
Employment: 13.0% management, business, and financial, 3.7% computer, engineering, and science, 9.8% education, legal, community service, arts, and media, 6.0% healthcare practitioners, 21.2% service, 26.9% sales and office, 11.0% natural resources, construction, and maintenance, 8.5% production, transportation, and material moving
Income: Per capita: $23,670; Median household: $44,651; Average household: $59,066; Households with income of $100,000 or more: 15.2%; Poverty rate: 17.5%
Educational Attainment: High school diploma or higher: 88.4%; Bachelor's degree or higher: 18.8%; Graduate/professional degree or higher: 6.3%
Housing: Homeownership rate: 64.4%; Median home value: $220,000; Median year structure built: 1979; Homeowner vacancy rate: 2.2%; Median gross rent: $919 per month; Rental vacancy rate: 6.7%
Vital Statistics: Birth rate: 113.4 per 10,000 population; Death rate: 113.9 per 10,000 population; Age-adjusted cancer mortality rate: 194.0 deaths per 100,000 population
Health Insurance: 84.2% have insurance; 56.7% have private insurance; 42.0% have public insurance; 15.8% do not have insurance; 9.7% of children under 18 do not have insurance
Health Care: Physicians: 23.2 per 10,000 population; Hospital beds: 34.0 per 10,000 population; Hospital admissions: 1,373.1 per 10,000 population
Air Quality Index: 89.9% good, 10.1% moderate, 0.0% unhealthy for sensitive individuals, 0.0% unhealthy (percent of days)
Transportation: Commute: 89.3% car, 0.7% public transportation, 2.1% walk, 5.8% work from home; Median travel time to work: 20.1 minutes
Presidential Election: 33.9% Obama, 63.3% Romney (2012)
National and State Parks: Ahjumawi Lava Springs State Park; Castle Crags State Park; Cinder Flats State Wildlife Area; Lassen Volcanic National Park; Latour Demonstration State Forest; McArthur-Burney Falls Memorial State Park; Shasta National Forest; Shasta State Historic Park; Whiskeytown-Shasta-Trinity National Recreation Area
Additional Information Contacts
Shasta Government . . . . (530) 225-5557
http://www.co.shasta.ca.us

Shasta County Communities

ANDERSON (city). Covers a land area of 6.372 square miles and a water area of 0.248 square miles. Located at 40.45° N. Lat; 122.30° W. Long. Elevation is 433 feet.
History: The town of Anderson developed on the American Ranch bought in 1856 by Elias Anderson. It became a stopping place on the trail to the Trinity mines.
Population: 9,932; Growth (since 2000): 10.1%; Density: 1,558.7 persons per square mile; Race: 83.3% White, 0.7% Black/African American, 2.6% Asian, 4.3% American Indian/Alaska Native, 0.2% Native Hawaiian/Other

Pacific Islander, 5.4% Two or more races, 10.8% Hispanic of any race; Average household size: 2.52; Median age: 34.1; Age under 18: 27.6%; Age 65 and over: 12.8%; Males per 100 females: 87.6; Marriage status: 31.4% never married, 42.4% now married, 3.1% separated, 10.3% widowed, 15.9% divorced; Foreign born: 5.7%; Speak English only: 91.0%; With disability: 18.8%; Veterans: 9.1%; Ancestry: 15.7% Irish, 15.5% German, 9.1% American, 8.5% English, 6.2% Italian

Employment: 7.3% management, business, and financial, 1.8% computer, engineering, and science, 8.6% education, legal, community service, arts, and media, 4.1% healthcare practitioners, 24.5% service, 29.1% sales and office, 11.9% natural resources, construction, and maintenance, 12.7% production, transportation, and material moving

Income: Per capita: $17,060; Median household: $34,559; Average household: $42,558; Households with income of $100,000 or more: 5.4%; Poverty rate: 23.9%

Educational Attainment: High school diploma or higher: 80.8%; Bachelor's degree or higher: 7.8%; Graduate/professional degree or higher: 1.2%

School District(s)

Anderson Union High (09-12)
2012-13 Enrollment: 2,032 . . . . (530) 378-0568
Cascade Union Elementary (KG-08)
2012-13 Enrollment: 1,292 . . . . (530) 378-7000
Happy Valley Union Elementary (KG-08)
2012-13 Enrollment: 507. . . . . (530) 357-2134
Pacheco Union Elementary (KG-08)
2012-13 Enrollment: 559. . . . . (530) 224-4585

Housing: Homeownership rate: 47.9%; Median home value: $152,900; Median year structure built: 1976; Homeowner vacancy rate: 2.8%; Median gross rent: $790 per month; Rental vacancy rate: 4.6%

Health Insurance: 83.6% have insurance; 44.3% have private insurance; 51.7% have public insurance; 16.4% do not have insurance; 6.4% of children under 18 do not have insurance

Safety: Violent crime rate: 62.4 per 10,000 population; Property crime rate: 714.0 per 10,000 population

Transportation: Commute: 91.5% car, 0.0% public transportation, 2.1% walk, 4.1% work from home; Median travel time to work: 16.6 minutes

Additional Information Contacts

City of Anderson . . . . (530) 378-6626
http://www.ci.anderson.ca.us

BELLA VISTA (CDP). Covers a land area of 22.199 square miles and a water area of 0.142 square miles. Located at 40.65° N. Lat; 122.26° W. Long. Elevation is 561 feet.

Population: 2,781; Growth (since 2000): n/a; Density: 125.3 persons per square mile; Race: 92.0% White, 0.6% Black/African American, 1.1% Asian, 1.5% American Indian/Alaska Native, 0.2% Native Hawaiian/Other Pacific Islander, 3.1% Two or more races, 6.4% Hispanic of any race; Average household size: 2.67; Median age: 46.2; Age under 18: 21.4%; Age 65 and over: 17.9%; Males per 100 females: 97.4; Marriage status: 22.6% never married, 62.4% now married, 1.0% separated, 5.5% widowed, 9.5% divorced; Foreign born: 1.8%; Speak English only: 98.0%; With disability: 17.2%; Veterans: 16.4%; Ancestry: 34.0% Irish, 27.2% German, 15.7% English, 7.9% American, 6.1% Italian

Employment: 5.0% management, business, and financial, 3.3% computer, engineering, and science, 7.8% education, legal, community service, arts, and media, 4.5% healthcare practitioners, 21.9% service, 25.1% sales and office, 21.0% natural resources, construction, and maintenance, 11.5% production, transportation, and material moving

Income: Per capita: $22,812; Median household: $57,986; Average household: $64,368; Households with income of $100,000 or more: 17.8%; Poverty rate: 7.9%

Educational Attainment: High school diploma or higher: 81.9%; Bachelor's degree or higher: 10.4%; Graduate/professional degree or higher: 2.8%

School District(s)

Bella Vista Elementary (KG-08)
2012-13 Enrollment: 356. . . . . (530) 549-4415

Housing: Homeownership rate: 82.4%; Median home value: $257,600; Median year structure built: 1981; Homeowner vacancy rate: 2.2%; Median gross rent: $1,104 per month; Rental vacancy rate: 6.2%

Health Insurance: 91.0% have insurance; 59.0% have private insurance; 48.7% have public insurance; 9.0% do not have insurance; 0.0% of children under 18 do not have insurance

Transportation: Commute: 79.5% car, 0.0% public transportation, 1.4% walk, 15.6% work from home; Median travel time to work: 27.5 minutes

BIG BEND (CDP). Covers a land area of 5.735 square miles and a water area of 0.089 square miles. Located at 41.01° N. Lat; 121.93° W. Long. Elevation is 1,686 feet.

Population: 102; Growth (since 2000): -31.5%; Density: 17.8 persons per square mile; Race: 83.3% White, 0.0% Black/African American, 0.0% Asian, 9.8% American Indian/Alaska Native, 0.0% Native Hawaiian/Other Pacific Islander, 5.9% Two or more races, 2.0% Hispanic of any race; Average household size: 1.76; Median age: 50.3; Age under 18: 10.8%; Age 65 and over: 16.7%; Males per 100 females: 131.8

School District(s)

Indian Springs Elementary (KG-08)
2012-13 Enrollment: 12. . . . . (530) 337-6219

Housing: Homeownership rate: 56.9%; Homeowner vacancy rate: 0.0%; Rental vacancy rate: 0.0%

BURNEY (CDP). Covers a land area of 5.196 square miles and a water area of 0.005 square miles. Located at 40.89° N. Lat; 121.68° W. Long. Elevation is 3,123 feet.

History: The town of Burney was named for Samuel Burney, an early English settler. Burney grew as a trading center for a lumber, farming, and stock-raising area.

Population: 3,154; Growth (since 2000): -2.0%; Density: 607.0 persons per square mile; Race: 85.1% White, 0.4% Black/African American, 0.2% Asian, 7.4% American Indian/Alaska Native, 0.1% Native Hawaiian/Other Pacific Islander, 4.9% Two or more races, 8.4% Hispanic of any race; Average household size: 2.40; Median age: 42.5; Age under 18: 23.8%; Age 65 and over: 16.9%; Males per 100 females: 95.8; Marriage status: 31.5% never married, 37.4% now married, 0.8% separated, 13.2% widowed, 17.8% divorced; Foreign born: 2.3%; Speak English only: 97.4%; With disability: 19.6%; Veterans: 7.7%; Ancestry: 14.9% Irish, 13.9% German, 11.9% English, 11.7% American, 9.1% European

Employment: 2.6% management, business, and financial, 5.6% computer, engineering, and science, 10.2% education, legal, community service, arts, and media, 9.2% healthcare practitioners, 36.8% service, 16.5% sales and office, 7.6% natural resources, construction, and maintenance, 11.5% production, transportation, and material moving

Income: Per capita: $19,323; Median household: $37,069; Average household: $43,624; Households with income of $100,000 or more: 5.5%; Poverty rate: 17.4%

Educational Attainment: High school diploma or higher: 86.0%; Bachelor's degree or higher: 9.7%; Graduate/professional degree or higher: 1.5%

School District(s)

Fall River Joint Unified (KG-12)
2012-13 Enrollment: 1,168 . . . . (530) 335-4538

Housing: Homeownership rate: 63.1%; Median home value: $144,700; Median year structure built: 1974; Homeowner vacancy rate: 2.2%; Median gross rent: $546 per month; Rental vacancy rate: 7.4%

Health Insurance: 85.5% have insurance; 45.8% have private insurance; 56.4% have public insurance; 14.5% do not have insurance; 3.8% of children under 18 do not have insurance

Newspapers: Intermountain News (weekly circulation 3300)

Transportation: Commute: 80.6% car, 0.0% public transportation, 16.0% walk, 2.0% work from home; Median travel time to work: 20.4 minutes

CASSEL (CDP). Covers a land area of 2.026 square miles and a water area of 0.075 square miles. Located at 40.92° N. Lat; 121.55° W. Long. Elevation is 3,192 feet.

Population: 207; Growth (since 2000): n/a; Density: 102.2 persons per square mile; Race: 93.7% White, 0.0% Black/African American, 0.0% Asian, 1.4% American Indian/Alaska Native, 0.0% Native Hawaiian/Other Pacific Islander, 2.9% Two or more races, 2.9% Hispanic of any race; Average household size: 2.23; Median age: 57.7; Age under 18: 15.5%; Age 65 and over: 29.5%; Males per 100 females: 105.0

Housing: Homeownership rate: 87.1%; Homeowner vacancy rate: 5.7%; Rental vacancy rate: 20.0%

CASTELLA (unincorporated postal area)

ZCTA: 96017

Covers a land area of 146.103 square miles and a water area of 0.657 square miles. Located at 41.08° N. Lat; 122.23° W. Long. Elevation is 1,949 feet.

Population: 171; Growth (since 2000): -23.0%; Density: 1.2 persons per square mile; Race: 93.6% White, 0.0% Black/African American, 0.0% Asian, 1.2% American Indian/Alaska Native, 0.0% Native Hawaiian/Other Pacific Islander, 5.3% Two or more races, 7.0% Hispanic of any race; Average household size: 2.25; Median age: 51.3; Age under 18: 19.3%; Age 65 and over: 18.7%; Males per 100 females: 147.8

School District(s)

Castle Rock Union Elementary (KG-08)
2012-13 Enrollment: 76. . . . . (530) 235-0101

Housing: Homeownership rate: 64.4%; Homeowner vacancy rate: 3.9%; Rental vacancy rate: 3.4%

COTTONWOOD (CDP). Covers a land area of 2.314 square miles and a water area of 0 square miles. Located at 40.39° N. Lat; 122.29° W. Long. Elevation is 433 feet.

History: Cottonwood began as a trading center for miners.

Population: 3,316; Growth (since 2000): 12.0%; Density: 1,433.0 persons per square mile; Race: 85.8% White, 0.1% Black/African American, 3.3% Asian, 3.0% American Indian/Alaska Native, 0.1% Native Hawaiian/Other Pacific Islander, 4.2% Two or more races, 10.6% Hispanic of any race; Average household size: 2.76; Median age: 35.8; Age under 18: 28.6%; Age 65 and over: 10.6%; Males per 100 females: 94.1; Marriage status: 31.2% never married, 38.1% now married, 2.8% separated, 10.7% widowed, 20.0% divorced; Foreign born: 9.2%; Speak English only: 81.0%; With disability: 20.1%; Veterans: 11.0%; Ancestry: 18.9% German, 10.1% Irish, 8.7% English, 8.7% American, 7.8% Swedish

Employment: 7.5% management, business, and financial, 5.7% computer, engineering, and science, 3.8% education, legal, community service, arts, and media, 5.6% healthcare practitioners, 35.7% service, 9.8% sales and office, 20.0% natural resources, construction, and maintenance, 12.0% production, transportation, and material moving

Income: Per capita: $17,992; Median household: $45,241; Average household: $53,506; Households with income of $100,000 or more: 13.0%; Poverty rate: 32.3%

Educational Attainment: High school diploma or higher: 74.9%; Bachelor's degree or higher: 8.6%; Graduate/professional degree or higher: 4.2%

School District(s)

Anderson Union High (09-12)
2012-13 Enrollment: 2,032 . . . . (530) 378-0568
Cottonwood Union Elementary (KG-08)
2012-13 Enrollment: 1,109 . . . . (530) 347-3165
Evergreen Union (KG-08)
2012-13 Enrollment: 1,012 . . . . (530) 347-3411

Housing: Homeownership rate: 63.3%; Median home value: $148,200; Median year structure built: 1977; Homeowner vacancy rate: 4.3%; Median gross rent: $1,052 per month; Rental vacancy rate: 7.7%

Health Insurance: 83.1% have insurance; 50.2% have private insurance; 47.2% have public insurance; 16.9% do not have insurance; 4.1% of children under 18 do not have insurance

Transportation: Commute: 95.5% car, 0.0% public transportation, 0.0% walk, 1.9% work from home; Median travel time to work: 36.8 minutes

FALL RIVER MILLS (CDP). Covers a land area of 2.593 square miles and a water area of 0.159 square miles. Located at 41.01° N. Lat; 121.44° W. Long. Elevation is 3,327 feet.

History: Fall River Mills developed at the junction of the Pit and Fall Rivers as a lumber community.

Population: 573; Growth (since 2000): -11.6%; Density: 221.0 persons per square mile; Race: 78.5% White, 0.0% Black/African American, 0.5% Asian, 5.2% American Indian/Alaska Native, 0.3% Native Hawaiian/Other Pacific Islander, 5.6% Two or more races, 18.3% Hispanic of any race; Average household size: 2.35; Median age: 41.8; Age under 18: 24.4%; Age 65 and over: 21.5%; Males per 100 females: 96.2

School District(s)

Fall River Joint Unified (KG-12)
2012-13 Enrollment: 1,168 . . . . (530) 335-4538

Housing: Homeownership rate: 56.2%; Homeowner vacancy rate: 6.4%; Rental vacancy rate: 8.9%

Hospitals: Mayers Memorial Hospital (121 beds)

Newspapers: Mountain Echo (weekly circulation 3500)

FRENCH GULCH (CDP). Covers a land area of 12.332 square miles and a water area of 0.037 square miles. Located at 40.72° N. Lat; 122.63° W. Long. Elevation is 1,394 feet.

History: French Gulch was a depot on the Shasta-Yreka Turnpike, where a party of Frenchmen first did some mining about 1850.

Population: 346; Growth (since 2000): 36.2%; Density: 28.1 persons per square mile; Race: 85.5% White, 0.9% Black/African American, 0.9% Asian, 4.3% American Indian/Alaska Native, 0.3% Native Hawaiian/Other Pacific Islander, 5.8% Two or more races, 4.9% Hispanic of any race; Average household size: 2.35; Median age: 49.6; Age under 18: 18.5%; Age 65 and over: 18.5%; Males per 100 females: 104.7

School District(s)

French Gulch-Whiskeytown Elementary (KG-08)
2012-13 Enrollment: 23. . . . . (530) 359-2151

Housing: Homeownership rate: 81.0%; Homeowner vacancy rate: 3.2%; Rental vacancy rate: 6.7%

HAT CREEK (CDP). Covers a land area of 50.013 square miles and a water area of 0.171 square miles. Located at 40.79° N. Lat; 121.47° W. Long. Elevation is 3,314 feet.

Population: 309; Growth (since 2000): n/a; Density: 6.2 persons per square mile; Race: 77.3% White, 1.3% Black/African American, 0.6% Asian, 14.6% American Indian/Alaska Native, 1.3% Native Hawaiian/Other Pacific Islander, 1.9% Two or more races, 6.5% Hispanic of any race; Average household size: 2.26; Median age: 51.9; Age under 18: 19.1%; Age 65 and over: 20.7%; Males per 100 females: 96.8

Housing: Homeownership rate: 69.9%; Homeowner vacancy rate: 3.1%; Rental vacancy rate: 6.8%

IGO (unincorporated postal area)

ZCTA: 96047

Covers a land area of 205.910 square miles and a water area of 0.301 square miles. Located at 40.47° N. Lat; 122.66° W. Long. Elevation is 1,089 feet.

Population: 1,004; Growth (since 2000): 10.7%; Density: 4.9 persons per square mile; Race: 86.2% White, 0.6% Black/African American, 0.8% Asian, 4.9% American Indian/Alaska Native, 0.1% Native Hawaiian/Other Pacific Islander, 6.3% Two or more races, 7.7% Hispanic of any race; Average household size: 2.37; Median age: 48.9; Age under 18: 17.5%; Age 65 and over: 18.2%; Males per 100 females: 103.7

School District(s)

Igo Ono Platina Union Elementary (KG-08)
2012-13 Enrollment: 78. . . . . (530) 396-2841

Housing: Homeownership rate: 77.4%; Homeowner vacancy rate: 3.2%; Rental vacancy rate: 5.9%

KESWICK (CDP). Covers a land area of 3.378 square miles and a water area of 0.126 square miles. Located at 40.61° N. Lat; 122.46° W. Long. Elevation is 741 feet.

Population: 451; Growth (since 2000): n/a; Density: 133.5 persons per square mile; Race: 86.3% White, 0.0% Black/African American, 1.3% Asian, 5.1% American Indian/Alaska Native, 0.0% Native Hawaiian/Other Pacific Islander, 6.4% Two or more races, 3.1% Hispanic of any race; Average household size: 2.52; Median age: 46.1; Age under 18: 21.5%; Age 65 and over: 18.4%; Males per 100 females: 105.0

Housing: Homeownership rate: 83.2%; Homeowner vacancy rate: 1.9%; Rental vacancy rate: 6.3%

LAKEHEAD (CDP). Covers a land area of 4.695 square miles and a water area of 0.584 square miles. Located at 40.90° N. Lat; 122.40° W. Long. Elevation is 1,161 feet.

Population: 461; Growth (since 2000): n/a; Density: 98.2 persons per square mile; Race: 91.3% White, 0.0% Black/African American, 0.4% Asian, 2.8% American Indian/Alaska Native, 0.0% Native Hawaiian/Other Pacific Islander, 4.8% Two or more races, 2.4% Hispanic of any race; Average household size: 2.02; Median age: 57.7; Age under 18: 9.1%; Age 65 and over: 28.9%; Males per 100 females: 114.4

Housing: Homeownership rate: 80.2%; Homeowner vacancy rate: 5.6%; Rental vacancy rate: 13.0%

MCARTHUR (CDP). Covers a land area of 1.001 square miles and a water area of 0.015 square miles. Located at 41.04° N. Lat; 121.41° W. Long. Elevation is 3,310 feet.

Population: 338; Growth (since 2000): -7.4%; Density: 337.5 persons per square mile; Race: 64.2% White, 0.0% Black/African American, 0.0% Asian, 4.4% American Indian/Alaska Native, 0.0% Native Hawaiian/Other Pacific Islander, 2.4% Two or more races, 35.2% Hispanic of any race; Average household size: 2.66; Median age: 39.6; Age under 18: 26.9%; Age 65 and over: 16.6%; Males per 100 females: 103.6

School District(s)

Fall River Joint Unified (KG-12)
2012-13 Enrollment: 1,168 . . . . (530) 335-4538

Housing: Homeownership rate: 74.8%; Homeowner vacancy rate: 3.1%; Rental vacancy rate: 5.9%

MILLVILLE (CDP). Covers a land area of 8.046 square miles and a water area of 0.167 square miles. Located at 40.56° N. Lat; 122.18° W. Long. Elevation is 515 feet.

Population: 727; Growth (since 2000): 19.2%; Density: 90.4 persons per square mile; Race: 92.6% White, 0.0% Black/African American, 0.8% Asian, 0.8% American Indian/Alaska Native, 0.1% Native Hawaiian/Other Pacific Islander, 2.6% Two or more races, 6.9% Hispanic of any race; Average household size: 2.71; Median age: 47.4; Age under 18: 24.5%; Age 65 and over: 18.6%; Males per 100 females: 93.9

School District(s)

Millville Elementary (KG-08)
2012-13 Enrollment: 257. . . . . (530) 547-4471

Housing: Homeownership rate: 85.8%; Homeowner vacancy rate: 1.7%; Rental vacancy rate: 5.0%

MONTGOMERY CREEK (CDP). Covers a land area of 3.253 square miles and a water area of 0.048 square miles. Located at 40.84° N. Lat; 121.92° W. Long. Elevation is 2,133 feet.

Population: 163; Growth (since 2000): 69.8%; Density: 50.1 persons per square mile; Race: 71.8% White, 1.2% Black/African American, 0.0% Asian, 9.8% American Indian/Alaska Native, 0.0% Native Hawaiian/Other Pacific Islander, 11.7% Two or more races, 11.0% Hispanic of any race; Average household size: 2.48; Median age: 40.4; Age under 18: 29.4%; Age 65 and over: 15.3%; Males per 100 females: 109.0

School District(s)

Mountain Union Elementary (KG-08)
2012-13 Enrollment: 74. . . . . (530) 337-6214

Housing: Homeownership rate: 68.9%; Homeowner vacancy rate: 2.3%; Rental vacancy rate: 0.0%

MOUNTAIN GATE (CDP). Covers a land area of 1.979 square miles and a water area of 0 square miles. Located at 40.72° N. Lat; 122.33° W. Long. Elevation is 899 feet.

Population: 943; Growth (since 2000): n/a; Density: 476.6 persons per square mile; Race: 90.1% White, 0.7% Black/African American, 0.5% Asian, 2.9% American Indian/Alaska Native, 0.0% Native Hawaiian/Other Pacific Islander, 4.3% Two or more races, 5.2% Hispanic of any race; Average household size: 2.34; Median age: 46.4; Age under 18: 19.3%; Age 65 and over: 17.8%; Males per 100 females: 100.6

Housing: Homeownership rate: 65.5%; Homeowner vacancy rate: 1.8%; Rental vacancy rate: 9.6%

OAK RUN (unincorporated postal area)

ZCTA: 96069

Covers a land area of 88.608 square miles and a water area of 0.153 square miles. Located at 40.69° N. Lat; 122.02° W. Long. Elevation is 1,617 feet.

Population: 982; Growth (since 2000): 19.8%; Density: 11.1 persons per square mile; Race: 92.2% White, 0.7% Black/African American, 0.5% Asian, 1.8% American Indian/Alaska Native, 0.0% Native Hawaiian/Other Pacific Islander, 3.0% Two or more races, 3.9% Hispanic of any race; Average household size: 2.35; Median age: 49.7; Age under 18: 17.8%; Age 65 and over: 19.3%; Males per 100 females: 108.9

School District(s)

Oak Run Elementary (KG-08)
2012-13 Enrollment: 17. . . . . (530) 472-3241

Housing: Homeownership rate: 82.6%; Homeowner vacancy rate: 2.3%; Rental vacancy rate: 1.4%

OLD STATION (CDP). Covers a land area of 2.220 square miles and a water area of 0.001 square miles. Located at 40.67° N. Lat; 121.41° W. Long. Elevation is 4,383 feet.

Population: 51; Growth (since 2000): n/a; Density: 23.0 persons per square mile; Race: 96.1% White, 0.0% Black/African American, 0.0% Asian, 2.0% American Indian/Alaska Native, 0.0% Native Hawaiian/Other Pacific Islander, 2.0% Two or more races, 3.9% Hispanic of any race; Average household size: 1.76; Median age: 61.9; Age under 18: 2.0%; Age 65 and over: 37.3%; Males per 100 females: 131.8

Housing: Homeownership rate: 86.2%; Homeowner vacancy rate: 10.7%; Rental vacancy rate: 42.9%

PALO CEDRO (CDP). Covers a land area of 3.679 square miles and a water area of 0.075 square miles. Located at 40.55° N. Lat; 122.24° W. Long. Elevation is 469 feet.

Population: 1,269; Growth (since 2000): 1.8%; Density: 345.0 persons per square mile; Race: 91.7% White, 0.6% Black/African American, 0.5% Asian, 1.9% American Indian/Alaska Native, 0.1% Native Hawaiian/Other Pacific Islander, 3.5% Two or more races, 5.8% Hispanic of any race; Average household size: 2.66; Median age: 48.3; Age under 18: 22.8%; Age 65 and over: 22.5%; Males per 100 females: 96.4

School District(s)

Junction Elementary (KG-08)
2012-13 Enrollment: 282. . . . . (530) 547-3274
North Cow Creek Elementary (KG-08)
2012-13 Enrollment: 268. . . . . (530) 549-4488
Shasta County Office of Education (KG-12)
2012-13 Enrollment: 429. . . . . (530) 225-0200
Shasta Union High (06-12)
2012-13 Enrollment: 5,728 . . . . (530) 241-3261

Housing: Homeownership rate: 86.7%; Homeowner vacancy rate: 1.9%; Rental vacancy rate: 7.2%

REDDING (city). County seat. Covers a land area of 59.647 square miles and a water area of 1.528 square miles. Located at 40.57° N. Lat; 122.36° W. Long. Elevation is 564 feet.

History: Although Redding was founded on land once belonging to Pierson B. Reading's Rancho Buena Ventura, a Mexican land grant, the town was named for B.B. Redding, a Central Pacific Railroad land agent. Redding developed as a shipping center for the farming and mining district, and as the seat of Shasta County since 1888.

Population: 89,861; Growth (since 2000): 11.1%; Density: 1,506.5 persons per square mile; Race: 85.8% White, 1.2% Black/African American, 3.4% Asian, 2.3% American Indian/Alaska Native, 0.2% Native Hawaiian/Other Pacific Islander, 4.6% Two or more races, 8.7% Hispanic of any race; Average household size: 2.43; Median age: 38.5; Age under 18: 22.8%; Age 65 and over: 16.4%; Males per 100 females: 93.8; Marriage status: 29.5% never married, 48.3% now married, 1.9% separated, 6.9% widowed, 15.3% divorced; Foreign born: 5.3%; Speak English only: 90.6%; With disability: 16.6%; Veterans: 12.0%; Ancestry: 17.1% German, 12.7% Irish, 11.0% English, 9.7% American, 5.9% Italian

Employment: 14.6% management, business, and financial, 4.0% computer, engineering, and science, 10.5% education, legal, community service, arts, and media, 5.7% healthcare practitioners, 20.9% service, 27.1% sales and office, 9.8% natural resources, construction, and maintenance, 7.4% production, transportation, and material moving

Income: Per capita: $23,443; Median household: $44,236; Average household: $58,466; Households with income of $100,000 or more: 15.4%; Poverty rate: 18.2%

Educational Attainment: High school diploma or higher: 90.1%; Bachelor's degree or higher: 22.4%; Graduate/professional degree or higher: 7.8%

School District(s)

Columbia Elementary (KG-08)
2012-13 Enrollment: 880. . . . . (530) 223-1915
Enterprise Elementary (KG-08)
2012-13 Enrollment: 3,644 . . . . (530) 224-4100
Gateway Unified (KG-12)
2012-13 Enrollment: 4,029 . . . . (530) 245-7900
Grant Elementary (KG-08)
2012-13 Enrollment: 611. . . . . (530) 243-0561
Pacheco Union Elementary (KG-08)
2012-13 Enrollment: 559. . . . . (530) 224-4585
Redding Elementary (KG-12)
2012-13 Enrollment: 3,387 . . . . (530) 225-0011

Shasta County Office of Education (KG-12)
2012-13 Enrollment: 429 . . . . (530) 225-0200
Shasta Union High (06-12)
2012-13 Enrollment: 5,728 . . . . (530) 241-3261
Shasta-Trinity Rop
2012-13 Enrollment: n/a . . . . (530) 246-3302

Four-year College(s)

Shasta Bible College and Graduate School (Private, Not-for-profit, Baptist)
Fall 2013 Enrollment: 53 . . . . (530) 221-4275
2013-14 Tuition: In-state $10,360; Out-of-state $10,360
Simpson University (Private, Not-for-profit, Christ and Missionary Alliance Church)
Fall 2013 Enrollment: 1,255 . . . . (530) 224-5600
2013-14 Tuition: In-state $23,300; Out-of-state $23,300

Two-year College(s)

Shasta College (Public)
Fall 2013 Enrollment: 8,479 . . . . (530) 242-7500
2013-14 Tuition: In-state $1,183; Out-of-state $6,223

Vocational/Technical School(s)

Shasta School of Cosmetology (Private, For-profit)
Fall 2013 Enrollment: 71 . . . . (530) 243-7990
2013-14 Tuition: $11,050

Housing: Homeownership rate: 55.3%; Median home value: $228,000; Median year structure built: 1981; Homeowner vacancy rate: 2.3%; Median gross rent: $944 per month; Rental vacancy rate: 6.9%

Health Insurance: 84.0% have insurance; 57.8% have private insurance; 40.1% have public insurance; 16.0% do not have insurance; 10.3% of children under 18 do not have insurance

Hospitals: Mercy Medical Center - Redding (256 beds); Patients' Hospital of Redding; Shasta Regional Medical Center (246 beds)

Safety: Violent crime rate: 64.3 per 10,000 population; Property crime rate: 414.6 per 10,000 population

Newspapers: Anderson Valley Post (weekly circulation 15100); Record Searchlight (daily circulation 33500)

Transportation: Commute: 89.5% car, 1.2% public transportation, 2.2% walk, 4.8% work from home; Median travel time to work: 16.9 minutes; Amtrak: Train and bus service available.

Airports: Redding Municipal (primary service/non-hub)

Additional Information Contacts

City of Redding . . . . (530) 225-4060
http://www.ci.redding.ca.us

ROUND MOUNTAIN (CDP). Covers a land area of 1.677 square miles and a water area of 0.007 square miles. Located at 40.80° N. Lat; 121.94° W. Long. Elevation is 2,083 feet.

Population: 155; Growth (since 2000): 27.0%; Density: 92.4 persons per square mile; Race: 81.3% White, 0.6% Black/African American, 1.9% Asian, 7.7% American Indian/Alaska Native, 0.6% Native Hawaiian/Other Pacific Islander, 7.1% Two or more races, 7.7% Hispanic of any race; Average household size: 2.09; Median age: 47.8; Age under 18: 17.4%; Age 65 and over: 20.0%; Males per 100 females: 98.7

Housing: Homeownership rate: 77.0%; Homeowner vacancy rate: 1.7%; Rental vacancy rate: 5.3%

SHASTA (CDP). Covers a land area of 10.978 square miles and a water area of 0.004 square miles. Located at 40.59° N. Lat; 122.48° W. Long. Elevation is 1,047 feet.

Population: 1,771; Growth (since 2000): n/a; Density: 161.3 persons per square mile; Race: 91.0% White, 0.6% Black/African American, 1.3% Asian, 2.1% American Indian/Alaska Native, 0.1% Native Hawaiian/Other Pacific Islander, 4.5% Two or more races, 3.2% Hispanic of any race; Average household size: 2.45; Median age: 50.6; Age under 18: 19.1%; Age 65 and over: 18.6%; Males per 100 females: 106.7

School District(s)

Shasta Union Elementary (KG-08)
2012-13 Enrollment: 119 . . . . (530) 243-1110

Housing: Homeownership rate: 85.9%; Homeowner vacancy rate: 1.7%; Rental vacancy rate: 5.5%

SHASTA LAKE (city). Covers a land area of 10.921 square miles and a water area of 0.008 square miles. Located at 40.68° N. Lat; 122.38° W. Long. Elevation is 807 feet.

History: Shasta Lake began as five small communities formerly known as Central Valley before it became incorporated on July 2, 1993. It is the closest city to Lake Shasta and the Shasta Dam, popular tourist attractions.

Population: 10,164; Growth (since 2000): 12.8%; Density: 930.7 persons per square mile; Race: 86.1% White, 0.7% Black/African American, 2.3% Asian, 3.8% American Indian/Alaska Native, 0.1% Native Hawaiian/Other Pacific Islander, 5.0% Two or more races, 8.5% Hispanic of any race; Average household size: 2.57; Median age: 38.8; Age under 18: 24.3%; Age 65 and over: 14.4%; Males per 100 females: 99.5; Marriage status: 21.8% never married, 56.6% now married, 3.1% separated, 7.8% widowed, 13.8% divorced; Foreign born: 7.4%; Speak English only: 90.7%; With disability: 19.7%; Veterans: 15.2%; Ancestry: 18.2% German, 16.4% Irish, 9.7% English, 8.3% American, 4.9% Italian

Employment: 6.3% management, business, and financial, 4.8% computer, engineering, and science, 9.6% education, legal, community service, arts, and media, 4.6% healthcare practitioners, 22.5% service, 30.7% sales and office, 11.8% natural resources, construction, and maintenance, 9.7% production, transportation, and material moving

Income: Per capita: $19,773; Median household: $38,724; Average household: $48,398; Households with income of $100,000 or more: 11.8%; Poverty rate: 21.2%

Educational Attainment: High school diploma or higher: 85.7%; Bachelor's degree or higher: 11.7%; Graduate/professional degree or higher: 2.6%

School District(s)

Gateway Unified (KG-12)
2012-13 Enrollment: 4,029 . . . . (530) 245-7900

Housing: Homeownership rate: 66.5%; Median home value: $167,300; Median year structure built: 1978; Homeowner vacancy rate: 2.0%; Median gross rent: $984 per month; Rental vacancy rate: 5.2%

Health Insurance: 84.9% have insurance; 50.5% have private insurance; 48.2% have public insurance; 15.1% do not have insurance; 6.6% of children under 18 do not have insurance

Newspapers: Shasta Lake Bulletin (weekly circulation 1400)

Transportation: Commute: 92.4% car, 0.6% public transportation, 0.7% walk, 5.4% work from home; Median travel time to work: 19.5 minutes

Additional Information Contacts

City of Shasta Lake . . . . (530) 275-7400
http://www.ci.shasta-lake.ca.us

SHINGLETOWN (CDP). Covers a land area of 24.650 square miles and a water area of 0.069 square miles. Located at 40.51° N. Lat; 121.86° W. Long. Elevation is 3,491 feet.

Population: 2,283; Growth (since 2000): 2.7%; Density: 92.6 persons per square mile; Race: 93.0% White, 0.2% Black/African American, 0.4% Asian, 2.1% American Indian/Alaska Native, 0.0% Native Hawaiian/Other Pacific Islander, 3.6% Two or more races, 3.8% Hispanic of any race; Average household size: 2.27; Median age: 53.2; Age under 18: 15.7%; Age 65 and over: 24.6%; Males per 100 females: 101.7

School District(s)

Black Butte Union Elementary (KG-08)
2012-13 Enrollment: 208 . . . . (530) 474-3125

Housing: Homeownership rate: 83.3%; Homeowner vacancy rate: 4.1%; Rental vacancy rate: 13.3%

Newspapers: Ridge Rider News (weekly circulation 1200)

WHITMORE (unincorporated postal area)

ZCTA: 96096

Covers a land area of 113.879 square miles and a water area of 0.138 square miles. Located at 40.65° N. Lat; 121.82° W. Long. Elevation is 2,247 feet.

Population: 695; Growth (since 2000): -15.7%; Density: 6.1 persons per square mile; Race: 92.5% White, 0.3% Black/African American, 0.3% Asian, 2.0% American Indian/Alaska Native, 0.0% Native Hawaiian/Other Pacific Islander, 4.2% Two or more races, 4.6% Hispanic of any race; Average household size: 2.39; Median age: 52.0; Age under 18: 15.7%; Age 65 and over: 20.1%; Males per 100 females: 101.4

School District(s)

Whitmore Union Elementary (KG-08)
2012-13 Enrollment: 32 . . . . (530) 472-3243

Housing: Homeownership rate: 83.9%; Homeowner vacancy rate: 2.4%; Rental vacancy rate: 9.4%

Sierra County

Located in northeastern California, in the Sierra Nevada Mountains; bounded on the east by Nevada; drained by the Yuba River and its tributaries; includes parts of Tahoe and Plumas National Forests. Covers a land area of 953.214 square miles, a water area of 8.996 square miles, and is located in the Pacific Time Zone at 39.58° N. Lat., 120.52° W. Long. The county was founded in 1852. County seat is Downieville.

Weather Station: Downieville Elevation: 2,914 feet

	Jan	Feb	Mar	Apr	May	Jun	Jul	Aug	Sep	Oct	Nov	Dec
High	49	53	59	66	74	82	90	90	84	73	56	47
Low	29	30	33	36	42	46	50	49	45	39	33	29
Precip	10.8	10.9	9.3	4.9	3.4	0.9	0.2	0.2	1.1	3.6	7.8	11.5
Snow	7.0	8.8	7.2	1.2	0.1	0.0	0.0	0.0	0.0	0.2	1.6	7.0

High and Low temperatures in degrees Fahrenheit; Precipitation and Snow in inches

Population: 3,240; Growth (since 2000): -8.9%; Density: 3.4 persons per square mile; Race: 93.3% White, 0.2% Black/African American, 0.4% Asian, 1.4% American Indian/Alaska Native, 0.1% Native Hawaiian/Other Pacific Islander, 2.4% two or more races, 8.3% Hispanic of any race; Average household size: 2.16; Median age: 50.9; Age under 18: 17.0%; Age 65 and over: 20.9%; Males per 100 females: 103.3; Marriage status: 25.5% never married, 54.3% now married, 3.1% separated, 7.3% widowed, 12.9% divorced; Foreign born: 7.1%; Speak English only: 90.6%; With disability: 20.3%; Veterans: 16.8%; Ancestry: 22.6% English, 17.1% German, 13.3% Irish, 7.3% Polish, 6.5% European

Religion: Six largest groups: 5.0% Pentecostal, 3.8% Catholicism, 3.1% Latter-day Saints, 2.0% Methodist/Pietist, 1.2% Non-denominational Protestant, 0.1% Other Groups

Economy: Unemployment rate: 7.8%; Leading industries: 20.6% accommodation and food services; 17.6% construction; 13.2% retail trade; Farms: 48 totaling 39,141 acres; Company size: 0 employ 1,000 or more persons, 0 employ 500 to 999 persons, 0 employ 100 to 499 persons, 68 employ less than 100 persons; Business ownership: n/a women-owned, n/a Black-owned, n/a Hispanic-owned, n/a Asian-owned

Employment: 15.9% management, business, and financial, 1.0% computer, engineering, and science, 7.8% education, legal, community service, arts, and media, 5.1% healthcare practitioners, 18.7% service, 21.3% sales and office, 18.6% natural resources, construction, and maintenance, 11.7% production, transportation, and material moving

Income: Per capita: $24,996; Median household: $39,009; Average household: $55,972; Households with income of $100,000 or more: 13.9%; Poverty rate: 19.4%

Educational Attainment: High school diploma or higher: 89.4%; Bachelor's degree or higher: 18.5%; Graduate/professional degree or higher: 2.1%

Housing: Homeownership rate: 71.9%; Median home value: $231,400; Median year structure built: 1973; Homeowner vacancy rate: 3.0%; Median gross rent: $1,040 per month; Rental vacancy rate: 10.7%

Vital Statistics: Birth rate: 85.3 per 10,000 population; Death rate: 131.3 per 10,000 population; Age-adjusted cancer mortality rate: Suppressed deaths per 100,000 population

Health Insurance: 79.4% have insurance; 56.1% have private insurance; 38.1% have public insurance; 20.6% do not have insurance; 30.5% of children under 18 do not have insurance

Health Care: Physicians: 6.5 per 10,000 population; Hospital beds: 0.0 per 10,000 population; Hospital admissions: 0.0 per 10,000 population

Transportation: Commute: 83.2% car, 0.9% public transportation, 5.9% walk, 6.9% work from home; Median travel time to work: 27.5 minutes

Presidential Election: 36.6% Obama, 59.4% Romney (2012)

Additional Information Contacts

Sierra Government . . . . (530) 289-3295
http://www.sierracounty.ca.gov

Sierra County Communities

ALLEGHANY (CDP). Covers a land area of 0.349 square miles and a water area of 0 square miles. Located at 39.47° N. Lat; 120.84° W. Long. Elevation is 4,426 feet.

Population: 58; Growth (since 2000): n/a; Density: 166.2 persons per square mile; Race: 100.0% White, 0.0% Black/African American, 0.0% Asian, 0.0% American Indian/Alaska Native, 0.0% Native Hawaiian/Other Pacific Islander, 0.0% Two or more races, 1.7% Hispanic of any race; Average household size: 2.15; Median age: 53.0; Age under 18: 13.8%; Age 65 and over: 12.1%; Males per 100 females: 123.1

Housing: Homeownership rate: 59.2%; Homeowner vacancy rate: 5.9%; Rental vacancy rate: 0.0%

CALPINE (CDP). Covers a land area of 0.710 square miles and a water area of 0.002 square miles. Located at 39.66° N. Lat; 120.44° W. Long. Elevation is 4,977 feet.

Population: 205; Growth (since 2000): n/a; Density: 288.8 persons per square mile; Race: 89.8% White, 0.0% Black/African American, 0.0% Asian, 0.0% American Indian/Alaska Native, 0.5% Native Hawaiian/Other Pacific Islander, 4.9% Two or more races, 12.7% Hispanic of any race; Average household size: 2.14; Median age: 49.8; Age under 18: 18.0%; Age 65 and over: 14.1%; Males per 100 females: 97.1

Housing: Homeownership rate: 77.1%; Homeowner vacancy rate: 3.8%; Rental vacancy rate: 15.4%

DOWNIEVILLE (CDP). County seat. Covers a land area of 3.181 square miles and a water area of 0.006 square miles. Located at 39.58° N. Lat; 120.82° W. Long. Elevation is 2,930 feet.

Population: 282; Growth (since 2000): n/a; Density: 88.7 persons per square mile; Race: 95.4% White, 0.0% Black/African American, 0.7% Asian, 1.4% American Indian/Alaska Native, 0.0% Native Hawaiian/Other Pacific Islander, 2.5% Two or more races, 4.3% Hispanic of any race; Average household size: 1.92; Median age: 56.5; Age under 18: 14.2%; Age 65 and over: 27.0%; Males per 100 females: 104.3

School District(s)

Sierra-Plumas Joint Unified (KG-12)
2012-13 Enrollment: 379. . . . . (530) 994-1044

Housing: Homeownership rate: 69.4%; Homeowner vacancy rate: 3.8%; Rental vacancy rate: 14.8%

Newspapers: Mountain Messenger (weekly circulation 2400)

GOODYEARS BAR (CDP). Covers a land area of 2.050 square miles and a water area of 0.017 square miles. Located at 39.55° N. Lat; 120.89° W. Long. Elevation is 2,674 feet.

Population: 68; Growth (since 2000): n/a; Density: 33.2 persons per square mile; Race: 94.1% White, 0.0% Black/African American, 0.0% Asian, 5.9% American Indian/Alaska Native, 0.0% Native Hawaiian/Other Pacific Islander, 0.0% Two or more races, 1.5% Hispanic of any race; Average household size: 1.79; Median age: 56.0; Age under 18: 4.4%; Age 65 and over: 23.5%; Males per 100 females: 161.5

Housing: Homeownership rate: 57.9%; Homeowner vacancy rate: 0.0%; Rental vacancy rate: 11.1%

LOYALTON (city). Covers a land area of 0.355 square miles and a water area of 0 square miles. Located at 39.68° N. Lat; 120.24° W. Long. Elevation is 4,951 feet.

History: Loyalton, which began as a lumber town, was named during the Civil War by mountaineers who were loyal Unionmen.

Population: 769; Growth (since 2000): -10.8%; Density: 2,163.2 persons per square mile; Race: 91.2% White, 0.3% Black/African American, 0.0% Asian, 2.7% American Indian/Alaska Native, 0.0% Native Hawaiian/Other Pacific Islander, 3.3% Two or more races, 14.0% Hispanic of any race; Average household size: 2.40; Median age: 46.2; Age under 18: 20.3%; Age 65 and over: 19.6%; Males per 100 females: 101.3

School District(s)

Sierra-Plumas Joint Unified (KG-12)
2012-13 Enrollment: 379. . . . . (530) 994-1044

Housing: Homeownership rate: 73.1%; Homeowner vacancy rate: 3.4%; Rental vacancy rate: 8.8%

Newspapers: Sierra Booster (weekly circulation 3500)

PIKE (CDP). Covers a land area of 4.287 square miles and a water area of 0 square miles. Located at 39.43° N. Lat; 121.00° W. Long. Elevation is 3,445 feet.

Population: 134; Growth (since 2000): n/a; Density: 31.3 persons per square mile; Race: 97.0% White, 0.0% Black/African American, 1.5% Asian, 0.7% American Indian/Alaska Native, 0.0% Native Hawaiian/Other Pacific Islander, 0.7% Two or more races, 1.5% Hispanic of any race; Average household size: 2.03; Median age: 50.9; Age under 18: 11.9%; Age 65 and over: 20.9%; Males per 100 females: 100.0

Housing: Homeownership rate: 87.9%; Homeowner vacancy rate: 0.0%; Rental vacancy rate: 0.0%

SATTLEY (CDP). Covers a land area of 2.047 square miles and a water area of 0.002 square miles. Located at 39.63° N. Lat; 120.44° W. Long. Elevation is 4,947 feet.

Population: 49; Growth (since 2000): n/a; Density: 23.9 persons per square mile; Race: 98.0% White, 0.0% Black/African American, 0.0% Asian, 2.0% American Indian/Alaska Native, 0.0% Native Hawaiian/Other Pacific Islander, 0.0% Two or more races, 2.0% Hispanic of any race; Average household size: 1.96; Median age: 48.8; Age under 18: 18.4%; Age 65 and over: 10.2%; Males per 100 females: 88.5

Housing: Homeownership rate: 60.0%; Homeowner vacancy rate: 6.3%; Rental vacancy rate: 0.0%

SIERRA BROOKS (CDP). Covers a land area of 1.370 square miles and a water area of 0 square miles. Located at 39.64° N. Lat; 120.22° W. Long. Elevation is 5,177 feet.

Population: 478; Growth (since 2000): n/a; Density: 348.8 persons per square mile; Race: 97.5% White, 0.0% Black/African American, 0.2% Asian, 0.8% American Indian/Alaska Native, 0.2% Native Hawaiian/Other Pacific Islander, 1.3% Two or more races, 4.6% Hispanic of any race; Average household size: 2.57; Median age: 45.8; Age under 18: 27.2%; Age 65 and over: 17.4%; Males per 100 females: 98.3

Housing: Homeownership rate: 82.3%; Homeowner vacancy rate: 4.3%; Rental vacancy rate: 0.0%

SIERRA CITY (CDP). Covers a land area of 2.151 square miles and a water area of <.001 square miles. Located at 39.57° N. Lat; 120.63° W. Long. Elevation is 4,176 feet.

Population: 221; Growth (since 2000): n/a; Density: 102.8 persons per square mile; Race: 90.5% White, 0.0% Black/African American, 1.4% Asian, 0.9% American Indian/Alaska Native, 0.0% Native Hawaiian/Other Pacific Islander, 1.8% Two or more races, 9.5% Hispanic of any race; Average household size: 1.96; Median age: 56.6; Age under 18: 7.2%; Age 65 and over: 25.8%; Males per 100 females: 102.8

Housing: Homeownership rate: 77.0%; Homeowner vacancy rate: 1.1%; Rental vacancy rate: 21.2%

SIERRAVILLE (CDP). Covers a land area of 5.020 square miles and a water area of <.001 square miles. Located at 39.58° N. Lat; 120.36° W. Long. Elevation is 4,957 feet.

Population: 200; Growth (since 2000): n/a; Density: 39.8 persons per square mile; Race: 93.5% White, 1.0% Black/African American, 0.0% Asian, 0.0% American Indian/Alaska Native, 0.0% Native Hawaiian/Other Pacific Islander, 0.5% Two or more races, 8.0% Hispanic of any race; Average household size: 2.11; Median age: 52.6; Age under 18: 10.5%; Age 65 and over: 22.5%; Males per 100 females: 117.4

School District(s)

Sierra County Office of Education (KG-12)
2012-13 Enrollment: 2. . . . . (530) 994-1044

William (R) Rouse Rop
2012-13 Enrollment: n/a . . . . (530) 993-4991

Housing: Homeownership rate: 71.6%; Homeowner vacancy rate: 1.4%; Rental vacancy rate: 12.9%

VERDI (CDP). Covers a land area of 4.173 square miles and a water area of 0.013 square miles. Located at 39.53° N. Lat; 120.02° W. Long. Elevation is 5,134 feet.

Population: 162; Growth (since 2000): n/a; Density: 38.8 persons per square mile; Race: 94.4% White, 0.0% Black/African American, 0.6% Asian, 0.0% American Indian/Alaska Native, 0.0% Native Hawaiian/Other Pacific Islander, 1.9% Two or more races, 6.2% Hispanic of any race; Average household size: 2.08; Median age: 55.8; Age under 18: 8.6%; Age 65 and over: 24.7%; Males per 100 females: 116.0

Housing: Homeownership rate: 87.2%; Homeowner vacancy rate: 2.9%; Rental vacancy rate: 0.0%

Siskiyou County

Located in northern California; bounded on the north by Oregon; includes part of the Klamath Mountains in the west and the Cascade Range in the east, and the sources of the Sacramento and McCloud Rivers; includes Tule and Lower Klamath Lakes, and par ts of Klamath, Shasta, and Modoc National Forests. Covers a land area of 6,277.887 square miles, a water area of 69.456 square miles, and is located in the Pacific Time Zone at 41.59° N. Lat., 122.53° W. Long. The county was founded in 1852. County seat is Yreka.

Weather Station: Callahan Elevation: 3,185 feet

	Jan	Feb	Mar	Apr	May	Jun	Jul	Aug	Sep	Oct	Nov	Dec
High	45	51	57	63	71	79	87	86	79	68	51	44
Low	26	28	31	34	39	44	49	48	42	36	30	26
Precip	3.5	2.8	2.2	1.3	1.3	0.8	0.5	0.3	0.4	1.2	3.0	4.0
Snow	0.9	0.3	1.2	0.3	0.1	0.0	0.0	0.0	0.0	0.1	1.0	1.6

High and Low temperatures in degrees Fahrenheit; Precipitation and Snow in inches

Weather Station: Dunsmuir Treatment Plant Elevation: 2,169 feet

	Jan	Feb	Mar	Apr	May	Jun	Jul	Aug	Sep	Oct	Nov	Dec
High	50	54	59	66	74	82	90	90	84	72	57	50
Low	30	31	34	37	44	50	54	51	46	40	34	30
Precip	11.1	10.6	9.0	4.4	3.0	1.2	0.2	0.3	0.9	3.2	7.9	11.9
Snow	8.0	7.5	4.5	0.5	0.0	0.0	0.0	0.0	0.0	tr	1.7	8.1

High and Low temperatures in degrees Fahrenheit; Precipitation and Snow in inches

Weather Station: Lava Beds Nat Monument Elevation: 4,770 feet

	Jan	Feb	Mar	Apr	May	Jun	Jul	Aug	Sep	Oct	Nov	Dec
High	42	45	51	57	66	75	85	85	77	65	49	41
Low	23	25	28	32	39	44	52	51	45	36	28	23
Precip	1.7	1.9	1.9	1.1	1.2	0.9	0.6	0.4	0.5	1.0	1.6	1.7
Snow	10.1	7.7	7.5	3.3	1.1	0.1	tr	0.0	tr	0.3	4.5	8.6

High and Low temperatures in degrees Fahrenheit; Precipitation and Snow in inches

Weather Station: Mc Cloud Elevation: 3,279 feet

	Jan	Feb	Mar	Apr	May	Jun	Jul	Aug	Sep	Oct	Nov	Dec
High	47	50	55	62	71	80	88	88	82	70	54	47
Low	25	26	29	33	39	45	49	47	42	34	29	25
Precip	8.1	8.5	7.0	3.4	2.6	1.1	0.2	0.3	0.8	2.6	6.0	8.7
Snow	14.3	13.9	9.8	1.5	tr	0.0	0.0	0.0	0.0	0.2	4.9	16.0

High and Low temperatures in degrees Fahrenheit; Precipitation and Snow in inches

Weather Station: Mount Shasta Elevation: 3,535 feet

	Jan	Feb	Mar	Apr	May	Jun	Jul	Aug	Sep	Oct	Nov	Dec
High	44	48	53	60	68	76	85	84	77	65	51	44
Low	27	28	30	34	40	46	50	48	43	37	30	26
Precip	6.9	6.9	5.8	2.9	2.2	1.3	0.4	0.3	0.7	2.2	5.0	7.9
Snow	18.8	19.3	13.0	4.3	0.3	0.1	0.0	0.0	tr	0.2	7.3	23.8

High and Low temperatures in degrees Fahrenheit; Precipitation and Snow in inches

Weather Station: Tulelake Elevation: 4,035 feet

	Jan	Feb	Mar	Apr	May	Jun	Jul	Aug	Sep	Oct	Nov	Dec
High	41	46	52	60	68	76	84	84	77	65	48	39
Low	21	23	26	30	37	43	47	44	37	31	25	20
Precip	1.4	1.2	1.1	1.0	1.1	0.8	0.3	0.3	0.5	0.8	1.4	1.4
Snow	6.1	4.0	2.3	1.1	0.1	0.0	0.0	0.0	0.0	0.2	3.3	5.8

High and Low temperatures in degrees Fahrenheit; Precipitation and Snow in inches

Weather Station: Yreka Elevation: 2,625 feet

	Jan	Feb	Mar	Apr	May	Jun	Jul	Aug	Sep	Oct	Nov	Dec
High	46	51	58	64	73	82	92	91	83	70	53	45
Low	25	27	30	34	40	46	52	50	44	35	29	24
Precip	3.2	2.1	1.6	1.2	1.3	1.0	0.5	0.4	0.6	1.0	2.9	4.0
Snow	3.7	2.5	0.8	0.2	tr	0.0	0.0	0.0	0.0	0.1	1.2	3.8

High and Low temperatures in degrees Fahrenheit; Precipitation and Snow in inches

Population: 44,900; Growth (since 2000): 1.4%; Density: 7.2 persons per square mile; Race: 84.7% White, 1.3% Black/African American, 1.2% Asian, 4.0% American Indian/Alaska Native, 0.2% Native Hawaiian/Other Pacific Islander, 5.3% two or more races, 10.3% Hispanic of any race; Average household size: 2.28; Median age: 47.0; Age under 18: 20.8%; Age 65 and over: 19.6%; Males per 100 females: 99.5; Marriage status: 23.9% never married, 55.1% now married, 2.1% separated, 6.5% widowed, 14.5% divorced; Foreign born: 5.4%; Speak English only: 90.3%; With disability: 19.1%; Veterans: 13.4%; Ancestry: 18.4% German, 15.0% English, 14.5% Irish, 7.3% Italian, 4.2% American

Religion: Six largest groups: 9.1% Catholicism, 4.3% Baptist, 3.6% Latter-day Saints, 3.0% Non-denominational Protestant, 2.5% Methodist/Pietist, 2.0% Pentecostal

Economy: Unemployment rate: 8.4%; Leading industries: 16.1% retail trade; 12.0% accommodation and food services; 10.6% construction; Farms: 929 totaling 722,855 acres; Company size: 0 employ 1,000 or more persons, 0 employ 500 to 999 persons, 7 employ 100 to 499 persons, 1,112 employ less than 100 persons; Business ownership: 1,333 women-owned, n/a Black-owned, 235 Hispanic-owned, n/a Asian-owned

Employment: 12.8% management, business, and financial, 3.7% computer, engineering, and science, 13.0% education, legal, community service, arts, and media, 4.6% healthcare practitioners, 21.5% service, 24.9% sales and office, 10.5% natural resources, construction, and maintenance, 9.1% production, transportation, and material moving
Income: Per capita: $22,293; Median household: $37,709; Average household: $50,428; Households with income of $100,000 or more: 9.8%; Poverty rate: 21.0%
Educational Attainment: High school diploma or higher: 89.0%; Bachelor's degree or higher: 23.9%; Graduate/professional degree or higher: 7.6%
Housing: Homeownership rate: 64.7%; Median home value: $200,800; Median year structure built: 1974; Homeowner vacancy rate: 2.8%; Median gross rent: $802 per month; Rental vacancy rate: 8.4%
Vital Statistics: Birth rate: 106.6 per 10,000 population; Death rate: 120.3 per 10,000 population; Age-adjusted cancer mortality rate: 175.0 deaths per 100,000 population
Health Insurance: 85.1% have insurance; 55.6% have private insurance; 46.6% have public insurance; 14.9% do not have insurance; 9.4% of children under 18 do not have insurance
Health Care: Physicians: 14.0 per 10,000 population; Hospital beds: 13.0 per 10,000 population; Hospital admissions: 617.3 per 10,000 population
Air Quality Index: 95.1% good, 4.4% moderate, 0.5% unhealthy for sensitive individuals, 0.0% unhealthy (percent of days)
Transportation: Commute: 83.3% car, 0.7% public transportation, 5.2% walk, 9.2% work from home; Median travel time to work: 18.8 minutes
Presidential Election: 40.6% Obama, 56.2% Romney (2012)
National and State Parks: Klamath National Forest; Lava Beds National Monument; Lower Klamath National Wildlife Refuge; Tule Lake National Wildlife Refuge; Sisson Calahan National Recreation Trail; Clear Creek National Recreation Trail; Boundary National Recreation Trail
Additional Information Contacts
Siskiyou Government . . . . (530) 842-8081
http://www.co.siskiyou.ca.us

Siskiyou County Communities

CALLAHAN (unincorporated postal area)
ZCTA: 96014
Covers a land area of 132.729 square miles and a water area of 0.553 square miles. Located at 41.33° N. Lat; 122.77° W. Long. Elevation is 3,150 feet.
Population: 211; Growth (since 2000): -26.2%; Density: 1.6 persons per square mile; Race: 87.7% White, 0.0% Black/African American, 0.5% Asian, 3.3% American Indian/Alaska Native, 0.0% Native Hawaiian/Other Pacific Islander, 7.6% Two or more races, 4.3% Hispanic of any race; Average household size: 2.15; Median age: 52.4; Age under 18: 16.1%; Age 65 and over: 22.7%; Males per 100 females: 113.1
Housing: Homeownership rate: 75.6%; Homeowner vacancy rate: 1.3%; Rental vacancy rate: 11.1%

CARRICK (CDP). Covers a land area of 0.059 square miles and a water area of 0 square miles. Located at 41.45° N. Lat; 122.36° W. Long. Elevation is 3,474 feet.
Population: 131; Growth (since 2000): -16.0%; Density: 2,227.7 persons per square mile; Race: 84.0% White, 5.3% Black/African American, 1.5% Asian, 1.5% American Indian/Alaska Native, 0.0% Native Hawaiian/Other Pacific Islander, 6.9% Two or more races, 6.1% Hispanic of any race; Average household size: 2.52; Median age: 42.8; Age under 18: 27.5%; Age 65 and over: 9.2%; Males per 100 females: 98.5
Housing: Homeownership rate: 65.4%; Homeowner vacancy rate: 5.4%; Rental vacancy rate: 14.3%

DORRIS (city). Covers a land area of 0.702 square miles and a water area of 0.016 square miles. Located at 41.96° N. Lat; 121.92° W. Long. Elevation is 4,245 feet.
History: Dorris was settled by a religious group from Iowa called the Dunkards. It developed as a trading center for farmers and vacationers.
Population: 939; Growth (since 2000): 6.0%; Density: 1,336.7 persons per square mile; Race: 81.4% White, 2.0% Black/African American, 0.5% Asian, 1.9% American Indian/Alaska Native, 0.9% Native Hawaiian/Other Pacific Islander, 5.1% Two or more races, 21.0% Hispanic of any race; Average household size: 2.58; Median age: 38.2; Age under 18: 25.6%; Age 65 and over: 14.5%; Males per 100 females: 102.4

School District(s)
Butte Valley Unified (KG-12)
2012-13 Enrollment: 324. . . . . (530) 397-4000
Housing: Homeownership rate: 68.2%; Homeowner vacancy rate: 3.9%; Rental vacancy rate: 7.2%
Safety: Violent crime rate: 11.0 per 10,000 population; Property crime rate: 186.8 per 10,000 population

DUNSMUIR (city). Covers a land area of 1.698 square miles and a water area of 0.037 square miles. Located at 41.23° N. Lat; 122.27° W. Long. Elevation is 2,290 feet.
History: Dunsmuir developed as a Southern Pacific Railroad division point, and as a supply center for hunters and fishermen.
Population: 1,650; Growth (since 2000): -14.2%; Density: 971.8 persons per square mile; Race: 87.5% White, 1.9% Black/African American, 0.9% Asian, 1.0% American Indian/Alaska Native, 0.2% Native Hawaiian/Other Pacific Islander, 6.6% Two or more races, 10.1% Hispanic of any race; Average household size: 2.16; Median age: 47.0; Age under 18: 19.4%; Age 65 and over: 17.1%; Males per 100 females: 105.7
School District(s)
Dunsmuir Elementary (KG-08)
2012-13 Enrollment: 130. . . . . (530) 235-4828
Dunsmuir Joint Union High (09-12)
2012-13 Enrollment: 87. . . . . (530) 235-4835
Housing: Homeownership rate: 54.5%; Homeowner vacancy rate: 2.8%; Rental vacancy rate: 15.6%
Safety: Violent crime rate: 25.2 per 10,000 population; Property crime rate: 214.0 per 10,000 population
Additional Information Contacts
City of Dunsmuir . . . . (530) 235-4822
http://ci.dunsmuir.ca.us

EDGEWOOD (CDP). Covers a land area of 1.016 square miles and a water area of 0.005 square miles. Located at 41.46° N. Lat; 122.43° W. Long. Elevation is 2,956 feet.
Population: 43; Growth (since 2000): -35.8%; Density: 42.3 persons per square mile; Race: 95.3% White, 0.0% Black/African American, 0.0% Asian, 0.0% American Indian/Alaska Native, 0.0% Native Hawaiian/Other Pacific Islander, 2.3% Two or more races, 4.7% Hispanic of any race; Average household size: 2.39; Median age: 54.8; Age under 18: 20.9%; Age 65 and over: 14.0%; Males per 100 females: 79.2
School District(s)
Butteville Union Elementary (KG-08)
2012-13 Enrollment: 202. . . . . (530) 938-2255
Housing: Homeownership rate: 88.9%; Homeowner vacancy rate: 0.0%; Rental vacancy rate: 0.0%

ETNA (city). Covers a land area of 0.758 square miles and a water area of <.001 square miles. Located at 41.46° N. Lat; 122.90° W. Long. Elevation is 2,936 feet.
History: The town of Etna grew up around a flour mill, named the Rough and Ready, which began competition in 1856 with the neighboring Etna Mills. Rivalry between the settlements existed until the post office was shifted from Etna to Rough and Ready in 1863, and the winner took over the loser's name.
Population: 737; Growth (since 2000): -5.6%; Density: 972.8 persons per square mile; Race: 85.1% White, 0.0% Black/African American, 0.1% Asian, 3.8% American Indian/Alaska Native, 0.1% Native Hawaiian/Other Pacific Islander, 10.0% Two or more races, 3.5% Hispanic of any race; Average household size: 2.26; Median age: 48.5; Age under 18: 23.5%; Age 65 and over: 20.8%; Males per 100 females: 101.9
School District(s)
Scott Valley Unified (KG-12)
2012-13 Enrollment: 684. . . . . (530) 468-2727
Housing: Homeownership rate: 63.7%; Homeowner vacancy rate: 4.5%; Rental vacancy rate: 4.8%
Safety: Violent crime rate: 13.9 per 10,000 population; Property crime rate: 41.6 per 10,000 population

FORKS OF SALMON (unincorporated postal area)
ZCTA: 96031
Covers a land area of 354.410 square miles and a water area of 0.887 square miles. Located at 41.19° N. Lat; 123.18° W. Long..
Population: 158; Growth (since 2000): -6.0%; Density: 0.4 persons per square mile; Race: 70.9% White, 0.0% Black/African American, 0.6%

Asian, 23.4% American Indian/Alaska Native, 0.0% Native Hawaiian/Other Pacific Islander, 4.4% Two or more races, 0.6% Hispanic of any race; Average household size: 1.95; Median age: 54.0; Age under 18: 12.7%; Age 65 and over: 18.4%; Males per 100 females: 139.4

School District(s)

Forks of Salmon Elementary (KG-08)
2012-13 Enrollment: 11. . . . . (530) 462-4762

Housing: Homeownership rate: 65.4%; Homeowner vacancy rate: 0.0%; Rental vacancy rate: 0.0%

FORT JONES (city). Covers a land area of 0.602 square miles and a water area of 0 square miles. Located at 41.61° N. Lat; 122.84° W. Long. Elevation is 2,759 feet.

History: Fort Jones has been known by a variety of names: Wheelock, for the man who built a hotel here in the 1850's; Scottsburg, for the surrounding Scott Valley named for John Scott, who discovered gold; Ottiewa, for a group of Shasta Indians. The present name was given in 1852 when the First United States Dragoons built a camp here, which they occupied until 1858.

Population: 839; Growth (since 2000): 27.1%; Density: 1,393.1 persons per square mile; Race: 77.5% White, 3.9% Black/African American, 1.0% Asian, 7.3% American Indian/Alaska Native, 0.0% Native Hawaiian/Other Pacific Islander, 7.6% Two or more races, 12.3% Hispanic of any race; Average household size: 2.34; Median age: 39.1; Age under 18: 20.0%; Age 65 and over: 13.1%; Males per 100 females: 136.3

School District(s)

Scott Valley Unified (KG-12)
2012-13 Enrollment: 684. . . . . (530) 468-2727

Housing: Homeownership rate: 59.9%; Homeowner vacancy rate: 2.7%; Rental vacancy rate: 5.4%

Safety: Violent crime rate: 12.2 per 10,000 population; Property crime rate: 109.4 per 10,000 population

Newspapers: Pioneer Press Papers (weekly circulation 14000)

GAZELLE (CDP). Covers a land area of 0.580 square miles and a water area of <.001 square miles. Located at 41.51° N. Lat; 122.52° W. Long. Elevation is 2,772 feet.

Population: 70; Growth (since 2000): -48.5%; Density: 120.6 persons per square mile; Race: 92.9% White, 0.0% Black/African American, 0.0% Asian, 5.7% American Indian/Alaska Native, 0.0% Native Hawaiian/Other Pacific Islander, 0.0% Two or more races, 7.1% Hispanic of any race; Average household size: 1.89; Median age: 53.7; Age under 18: 11.4%; Age 65 and over: 25.7%; Males per 100 females: 112.1

School District(s)

Gazelle Union Elementary (KG-08)
2012-13 Enrollment: 41. . . . . (530) 435-2321

Housing: Homeownership rate: 73.0%; Homeowner vacancy rate: 3.6%; Rental vacancy rate: 35.3%

GREENVIEW (CDP). Covers a land area of 1.295 square miles and a water area of 0.084 square miles. Located at 41.54° N. Lat; 122.92° W. Long. Elevation is 2,812 feet.

Population: 201; Growth (since 2000): 0.5%; Density: 155.2 persons per square mile; Race: 80.1% White, 0.0% Black/African American, 0.5% Asian, 5.0% American Indian/Alaska Native, 0.0% Native Hawaiian/Other Pacific Islander, 10.4% Two or more races, 9.5% Hispanic of any race; Average household size: 2.28; Median age: 52.6; Age under 18: 15.9%; Age 65 and over: 19.4%; Males per 100 females: 97.1

Housing: Homeownership rate: 73.9%; Homeowner vacancy rate: 1.5%; Rental vacancy rate: 4.0%

GRENADA (CDP). Covers a land area of 0.516 square miles and a water area of 0.001 square miles. Located at 41.64° N. Lat; 122.53° W. Long. Elevation is 2,566 feet.

Population: 367; Growth (since 2000): 4.6%; Density: 711.5 persons per square mile; Race: 83.7% White, 0.5% Black/African American, 0.3% Asian, 9.5% American Indian/Alaska Native, 0.0% Native Hawaiian/Other Pacific Islander, 5.2% Two or more races, 3.3% Hispanic of any race; Average household size: 2.27; Median age: 44.5; Age under 18: 22.1%; Age 65 and over: 25.9%; Males per 100 females: 92.1

School District(s)

Grenada Elementary (KG-08)
2012-13 Enrollment: 177. . . . . (530) 436-2233

Housing: Homeownership rate: 49.3%; Homeowner vacancy rate: 2.4%; Rental vacancy rate: 23.4%

HAPPY CAMP (CDP). Covers a land area of 12.107 square miles and a water area of 0.239 square miles. Located at 41.82° N. Lat; 123.39° W. Long. Elevation is 1,070 feet.

Population: 1,190; Growth (since 2000): n/a; Density: 98.3 persons per square mile; Race: 68.4% White, 0.2% Black/African American, 0.6% Asian, 23.3% American Indian/Alaska Native, 0.1% Native Hawaiian/Other Pacific Islander, 6.0% Two or more races, 8.0% Hispanic of any race; Average household size: 2.27; Median age: 47.3; Age under 18: 20.0%; Age 65 and over: 16.3%; Males per 100 females: 107.0

School District(s)

Happy Camp Union Elementary (KG-08)
2012-13 Enrollment: 118. . . . . (530) 493-2267

Siskiyou Union High (07-12)
2012-13 Enrollment: 596. . . . . (530) 926-3006

Housing: Homeownership rate: 57.0%; Homeowner vacancy rate: 3.4%; Rental vacancy rate: 8.0%

HORNBROOK (CDP). Covers a land area of 1.165 square miles and a water area of 0.011 square miles. Located at 41.90° N. Lat; 122.56° W. Long. Elevation is 2,159 feet.

Population: 248; Growth (since 2000): -13.3%; Density: 212.9 persons per square mile; Race: 78.6% White, 0.0% Black/African American, 0.0% Asian, 6.0% American Indian/Alaska Native, 0.0% Native Hawaiian/Other Pacific Islander, 11.3% Two or more races, 7.7% Hispanic of any race; Average household size: 2.30; Median age: 46.7; Age under 18: 20.2%; Age 65 and over: 21.4%; Males per 100 females: 87.9

School District(s)

Hornbrook Elementary (KG-08)
2012-13 Enrollment: 31. . . . . (530) 475-3598

Housing: Homeownership rate: 66.7%; Homeowner vacancy rate: 6.3%; Rental vacancy rate: 11.9%

KLAMATH RIVER (unincorporated postal area)

ZCTA: 96050

Covers a land area of 285.745 square miles and a water area of 0.770 square miles. Located at 41.90° N. Lat; 122.89° W. Long. Elevation is 1,739 feet.

Population: 414; Growth (since 2000): -11.3%; Density: 1.4 persons per square mile; Race: 88.6% White, 0.0% Black/African American, 0.5% Asian, 5.1% American Indian/Alaska Native, 0.2% Native Hawaiian/Other Pacific Islander, 3.6% Two or more races, 3.1% Hispanic of any race; Average household size: 1.98; Median age: 55.6; Age under 18: 10.6%; Age 65 and over: 25.6%; Males per 100 females: 107.0

Housing: Homeownership rate: 68.9%; Homeowner vacancy rate: 2.7%; Rental vacancy rate: 3.0%

MACDOEL (CDP). Covers a land area of 0.148 square miles and a water area of 0 square miles. Located at 41.83° N. Lat; 122.01° W. Long. Elevation is 4,268 feet.

History: Macdoel was settled by a religious group from Iowa known as the Dunkards. It became a business center for the Butte Valley Irrigation District, and the location of sawmills.

Population: 133; Growth (since 2000): -5.0%; Density: 897.8 persons per square mile; Race: 42.9% White, 0.0% Black/African American, 0.0% Asian, 4.5% American Indian/Alaska Native, 0.0% Native Hawaiian/Other Pacific Islander, 0.8% Two or more races, 58.6% Hispanic of any race; Average household size: 3.24; Median age: 30.6; Age under 18: 33.1%; Age 65 and over: 9.0%; Males per 100 females: 129.3

School District(s)

Butte Valley Unified (KG-12)
2012-13 Enrollment: 324. . . . . (530) 397-4000

Housing: Homeownership rate: 43.9%; Homeowner vacancy rate: 0.0%; Rental vacancy rate: 0.0%

MCCLOUD (CDP). Covers a land area of 2.422 square miles and a water area of 0.066 square miles. Located at 41.25° N. Lat; 122.14° W. Long. Elevation is 3,271 feet.

History: McCloud preserves, under altered spelling, the name of the Scot, Alexander Roderick McLeod, who in 1827 led a band of Hudson's Bay Company trappers into northern California. McCloud developed as a lumber town with a sawmill.

Population: 1,101; Growth (since 2000): -18.0%; Density: 454.5 persons per square mile; Race: 94.4% White, 0.7% Black/African American, 0.5% Asian, 0.9% American Indian/Alaska Native, 0.0% Native Hawaiian/Other

Pacific Islander, 3.0% Two or more races, 5.9% Hispanic of any race; Average household size: 2.08; Median age: 51.8; Age under 18: 17.1%; Age 65 and over: 26.4%; Males per 100 females: 94.2

School District(s)

Mccloud Union Elementary (KG-08)
2012-13 Enrollment: 74. . . . . (530) 964-2133
Siskiyou Union High (07-12)
2012-13 Enrollment: 596. . . . . (530) 926-3006

Housing: Homeownership rate: 62.5%; Homeowner vacancy rate: 2.9%; Rental vacancy rate: 11.2%

MONTAGUE (city). Covers a land area of 1.778 square miles and a water area of 0.015 square miles. Located at 41.73° N. Lat; 122.53° W. Long. Elevation is 2,539 feet.

Population: 1,443; Growth (since 2000): -0.9%; Density: 811.7 persons per square mile; Race: 86.7% White, 0.3% Black/African American, 0.6% Asian, 4.6% American Indian/Alaska Native, 0.1% Native Hawaiian/Other Pacific Islander, 6.6% Two or more races, 7.4% Hispanic of any race; Average household size: 2.47; Median age: 37.9; Age under 18: 25.5%; Age 65 and over: 12.8%; Males per 100 females: 95.3

School District(s)

Big Springs Union Elementary (KG-08)
2012-13 Enrollment: 126. . . . . (530) 459-3189
Bogus Elementary (KG-06)
2012-13 Enrollment: 12. . . . . (530) 459-3163
Delphic Elementary (KG-08)
2012-13 Enrollment: 33. . . . . (530) 842-3653
Little Shasta Elementary (KG-06)
2012-13 Enrollment: 26. . . . . (530) 459-3269
Montague Elementary (KG-08)
2012-13 Enrollment: 167. . . . . (530) 459-3001
Willow Creek Elementary (KG-08)
2012-13 Enrollment: 50. . . . . (530) 459-3313

Housing: Homeownership rate: 64.4%; Homeowner vacancy rate: 2.4%; Rental vacancy rate: 10.4%

Safety: Violent crime rate: 14.2 per 10,000 population; Property crime rate: 113.4 per 10,000 population

Airports: Siskiyou County (general aviation)

Additional Information Contacts

City of Montague . . . . (530) 459-3030
http://ci.montague.ca.us

MOUNT HEBRON (CDP). Covers a land area of 0.713 square miles and a water area of 0 square miles. Located at 41.79° N. Lat; 122.01° W. Long. Elevation is 4,262 feet.

Population: 95; Growth (since 2000): 3.3%; Density: 133.2 persons per square mile; Race: 76.8% White, 0.0% Black/African American, 0.0% Asian, 1.1% American Indian/Alaska Native, 0.0% Native Hawaiian/Other Pacific Islander, 3.2% Two or more races, 43.2% Hispanic of any race; Average household size: 2.91; Median age: 42.3; Age under 18: 17.9%; Age 65 and over: 16.8%; Males per 100 females: 131.7

Housing: Homeownership rate: 75.0%; Homeowner vacancy rate: 0.0%; Rental vacancy rate: 27.3%

MOUNT SHASTA (city). Covers a land area of 3.766 square miles and a water area of 0.004 square miles. Located at 41.32° N. Lat; 122.32° W. Long. Elevation is 3,586 feet.

History: Mount Shasta was settled in the 1850's near the base of the snow-capped mountain. Early travelers knew the place as Sisson's for J.H. Sisson, pioneer postmaster and hotel keeper. In 1924 the town became Mount Shasta.

Population: 3,394; Growth (since 2000): -6.3%; Density: 901.2 persons per square mile; Race: 89.6% White, 1.8% Black/African American, 1.6% Asian, 0.6% American Indian/Alaska Native, 0.1% Native Hawaiian/Other Pacific Islander, 4.8% Two or more races, 8.2% Hispanic of any race; Average household size: 2.02; Median age: 45.7; Age under 18: 20.4%; Age 65 and over: 18.2%; Males per 100 females: 84.7; Marriage status: 26.6% never married, 44.6% now married, 6.2% separated, 7.2% widowed, 21.6% divorced; Foreign born: 5.4%; Speak English only: 91.3%; With disability: 12.6%; Veterans: 12.2%; Ancestry: 21.0% German, 19.1% Italian, 16.8% English, 11.2% Irish, 10.9% French

Employment: 11.0% management, business, and financial, 4.7% computer, engineering, and science, 17.0% education, legal, community service, arts, and media, 5.1% healthcare practitioners, 19.1% service, 31.9% sales and office, 7.3% natural resources, construction, and maintenance, 3.9% production, transportation, and material moving

Income: Per capita: $26,800; Median household: $43,193; Average household: $53,808; Households with income of $100,000 or more: 16.5%; Poverty rate: 13.0%

Educational Attainment: High school diploma or higher: 92.8%; Bachelor's degree or higher: 35.1%; Graduate/professional degree or higher: 8.8%

School District(s)

Mt. Shasta Union Elementary (KG-08)
2012-13 Enrollment: 518. . . . . (530) 926-6007
Siskiyou County Office of Education (KG-12)
2012-13 Enrollment: 435. . . . . (530) 842-8400
Siskiyou Union High (07-12)
2012-13 Enrollment: 596. . . . . (530) 926-3006

Housing: Homeownership rate: 47.0%; Median home value: $282,200; Median year structure built: 1977; Homeowner vacancy rate: 2.5%; Median gross rent: $922 per month; Rental vacancy rate: 5.8%

Health Insurance: 81.0% have insurance; 57.3% have private insurance; 32.3% have public insurance; 19.0% do not have insurance; 15.4% of children under 18 do not have insurance

Hospitals: Mercy Medical Center - Mount Shasta (80 beds)

Safety: Violent crime rate: 15.1 per 10,000 population; Property crime rate: 208.5 per 10,000 population

Newspapers: Mt. Shasta Newspapers (weekly circulation 9800)

Transportation: Commute: 74.5% car, 0.0% public transportation, 3.5% walk, 21.6% work from home; Median travel time to work: 15.1 minutes

Additional Information Contacts

City of Mount Shasta . . . . (530) 926-7510
http://ci.mt-shasta.ca.us

SCOTT BAR (unincorporated postal area)

ZCTA: 96085

Covers a land area of 74.638 square miles and a water area of 0.088 square miles. Located at 41.74° N. Lat; 123.08° W. Long. Elevation is 1,729 feet.

Population: 85; Growth (since 2000): 25.0%; Density: 1.1 persons per square mile; Race: 76.5% White, 7.1% Black/African American, 1.2% Asian, 4.7% American Indian/Alaska Native, 0.0% Native Hawaiian/Other Pacific Islander, 9.4% Two or more races, 2.4% Hispanic of any race; Average household size: 2.13; Median age: 45.3; Age under 18: 23.5%; Age 65 and over: 20.0%; Males per 100 females: 107.3

Housing: Homeownership rate: 70.0%; Homeowner vacancy rate: 3.4%; Rental vacancy rate: 0.0%

SEIAD VALLEY (unincorporated postal area)

ZCTA: 96086

Covers a land area of 256.742 square miles and a water area of 0.576 square miles. Located at 41.92° N. Lat; 123.26° W. Long. Elevation is 1,388 feet.

Population: 338; Growth (since 2000): 4.3%; Density: 1.3 persons per square mile; Race: 81.1% White, 0.0% Black/African American, 0.9% Asian, 8.9% American Indian/Alaska Native, 0.0% Native Hawaiian/Other Pacific Islander, 7.7% Two or more races, 7.4% Hispanic of any race; Average household size: 2.19; Median age: 51.8; Age under 18: 15.4%; Age 65 and over: 21.3%; Males per 100 females: 98.8

School District(s)

Seiad Elementary (KG-08)
2012-13 Enrollment: 31. . . . . (530) 496-3308

Housing: Homeownership rate: 71.4%; Homeowner vacancy rate: 3.3%; Rental vacancy rate: 2.2%

SOMES BAR (unincorporated postal area)

ZCTA: 95568

Covers a land area of 81.252 square miles and a water area of 1.155 square miles. Located at 41.45° N. Lat; 123.46° W. Long. Elevation is 692 feet.

Population: 136; Growth (since 2000): -31.0%; Density: 1.7 persons per square mile; Race: 55.1% White, 0.7% Black/African American, 1.5% Asian, 34.6% American Indian/Alaska Native, 0.0% Native Hawaiian/Other Pacific Islander, 7.4% Two or more races, 8.1% Hispanic of any race; Average household size: 2.11; Median age: 48.5; Age under 18: 25.0%; Age 65 and over: 19.1%; Males per 100 females: 100.0

School District(s)

Junction Elementary (KG-08)
2012-13 Enrollment: 24. . . . . (530) 469-3373

Housing: Homeownership rate: 57.8%; Homeowner vacancy rate: 2.6%; Rental vacancy rate: 3.6%

TENNANT (CDP). Covers a land area of 0.243 square miles and a water area of <.001 square miles. Located at 41.58° N. Lat; 121.92° W. Long. Elevation is 4,797 feet.

Population: 41; Growth (since 2000): -34.9%; Density: 169.1 persons per square mile; Race: 87.8% White, 0.0% Black/African American, 0.0% Asian, 4.9% American Indian/Alaska Native, 0.0% Native Hawaiian/Other Pacific Islander, 4.9% Two or more races, 9.8% Hispanic of any race; Average household size: 1.52; Median age: 59.5; Age under 18: 2.4%; Age 65 and over: 29.3%; Males per 100 females: 156.3

Housing: Homeownership rate: 74.0%; Homeowner vacancy rate: 0.0%; Rental vacancy rate: 0.0%

TULELAKE (city). Covers a land area of 0.410 square miles and a water area of 0.002 square miles. Located at 41.95° N. Lat; 121.47° W. Long. Elevation is 4,035 feet.

History: In World War II, a relocation camp for evacuated Japanese and Japanese-Americans was nearby. Lava Beds National Monument to south. Incorporated 1937.

Population: 1,010; Growth (since 2000): -1.0%; Density: 2,464.7 persons per square mile; Race: 55.7% White, 0.1% Black/African American, 0.1% Asian, 1.5% American Indian/Alaska Native, 0.0% Native Hawaiian/Other Pacific Islander, 6.4% Two or more races, 59.5% Hispanic of any race; Average household size: 2.91; Median age: 29.4; Age under 18: 33.7%; Age 65 and over: 10.1%; Males per 100 females: 102.4

School District(s)

Modoc County Office of Education (PK-12)
2012-13 Enrollment: 54. . . . . (530) 233-7101

Tulelake Basin Joint Unified (KG-12)
2012-13 Enrollment: 471. . . . . (530) 667-2295

Housing: Homeownership rate: 49.8%; Homeowner vacancy rate: 6.0%; Rental vacancy rate: 12.1%

Safety: Violent crime rate: 10.1 per 10,000 population; Property crime rate: 81.1 per 10,000 population

WEED (city). Covers a land area of 4.790 square miles and a water area of 0.005 square miles. Located at 41.41° N. Lat; 122.38° W. Long. Elevation is 3,428 feet.

History: Weed developed as a lumber town with mills along the railroad sidings.

Population: 2,967; Growth (since 2000): -0.4%; Density: 619.5 persons per square mile; Race: 74.9% White, 6.9% Black/African American, 4.1% Asian, 2.4% American Indian/Alaska Native, 0.9% Native Hawaiian/Other Pacific Islander, 6.4% Two or more races, 16.0% Hispanic of any race; Average household size: 2.49; Median age: 32.7; Age under 18: 24.8%; Age 65 and over: 14.0%; Males per 100 females: 100.7; Marriage status: 43.1% never married, 35.7% now married, 2.2% separated, 5.3% widowed, 15.8% divorced; Foreign born: 5.0%; Speak English only: 88.4%; With disability: 17.1%; Veterans: 7.8%; Ancestry: 19.5% German, 17.2% Irish, 10.2% Italian, 8.4% English, 5.7% Dutch

Employment: 13.4% management, business, and financial, 5.6% computer, engineering, and science, 4.4% education, legal, community service, arts, and media, 2.9% healthcare practitioners, 27.9% service, 21.7% sales and office, 9.7% natural resources, construction, and maintenance, 14.4% production, transportation, and material moving

Income: Per capita: $14,111; Median household: $28,170; Average household: $35,957; Households with income of $100,000 or more: 1.6%; Poverty rate: 34.5%

Educational Attainment: High school diploma or higher: 85.3%; Bachelor's degree or higher: 14.4%; Graduate/professional degree or higher: 4.7%

School District(s)

Siskiyou Union High (07-12)
2012-13 Enrollment: 596. . . . . (530) 926-3006

Weed Union Elementary (KG-08)
2012-13 Enrollment: 244. . . . . (530) 926-6007

Two-year College(s)

College of the Siskiyous (Public)
Fall 2013 Enrollment: 2,533 . . . . (530) 938-5555
2013-14 Tuition: In-state $1,146; Out-of-state $6,666

Housing: Homeownership rate: 48.0%; Median home value: $157,100; Median year structure built: 1973; Homeowner vacancy rate: 3.3%; Median gross rent: $740 per month; Rental vacancy rate: 8.8%

Health Insurance: 85.0% have insurance; 53.8% have private insurance; 42.5% have public insurance; 15.0% do not have insurance; 3.1% of children under 18 do not have insurance

Safety: Violent crime rate: 88.8 per 10,000 population; Property crime rate: 375.8 per 10,000 population

Transportation: Commute: 82.6% car, 0.0% public transportation, 10.1% walk, 5.0% work from home; Median travel time to work: 14.4 minutes

Airports: Weed (general aviation)

Additional Information Contacts

City of Weed . . . . (530) 938-5020
http://www.ci.weed.ca.us

YREKA (city). County seat. Covers a land area of 9.980 square miles and a water area of 0.073 square miles. Located at 41.72° N. Lat; 122.63° W. Long. Elevation is 2,589 feet.

History: After Abraham Thompson struck it rich at Black Gulch Camp in 1851, a community known as Thompson's Dry Diggings sprang up. A town laid out the same year was first called Shasta Butte City, but soon renamed Yreka. Yreka developed as the seat of Siskiyou County.

Population: 7,765; Growth (since 2000): 6.5%; Density: 778.1 persons per square mile; Race: 83.6% White, 0.7% Black/African American, 1.2% Asian, 6.3% American Indian/Alaska Native, 0.1% Native Hawaiian/Other Pacific Islander, 5.8% Two or more races, 9.7% Hispanic of any race; Average household size: 2.27; Median age: 41.7; Age under 18: 24.1%; Age 65 and over: 19.2%; Males per 100 females: 89.5; Marriage status: 27.5% never married, 47.0% now married, 1.8% separated, 8.8% widowed, 16.6% divorced; Foreign born: 3.8%; Speak English only: 91.1%; With disability: 21.2%; Veterans: 13.1%; Ancestry: 14.0% Irish, 12.6% German, 11.5% English, 6.2% Italian, 5.2% American

Employment: 14.1% management, business, and financial, 4.0% computer, engineering, and science, 10.5% education, legal, community service, arts, and media, 3.4% healthcare practitioners, 26.5% service, 28.7% sales and office, 3.3% natural resources, construction, and maintenance, 9.4% production, transportation, and material moving

Income: Per capita: $20,050; Median household: $27,500; Average household: $47,256; Households with income of $100,000 or more: 9.8%; Poverty rate: 32.2%

Educational Attainment: High school diploma or higher: 87.4%; Bachelor's degree or higher: 18.0%; Graduate/professional degree or higher: 7.2%

School District(s)

Siskiyou County Office of Education (KG-12)
2012-13 Enrollment: 435. . . . . (530) 842-8400

Siskiyou Rop
2012-13 Enrollment: n/a . . . . (530) 842-6151

Yreka Union Elementary (KG-08)
2012-13 Enrollment: 1,019 . . . . (530) 842-1168

Yreka Union High (09-12)
2012-13 Enrollment: 722. . . . . (530) 842-2521

Housing: Homeownership rate: 51.6%; Median home value: $170,500; Median year structure built: 1972; Homeowner vacancy rate: 2.4%; Median gross rent: $775 per month; Rental vacancy rate: 6.7%

Health Insurance: 89.2% have insurance; 50.7% have private insurance; 54.4% have public insurance; 10.8% do not have insurance; 3.2% of children under 18 do not have insurance

Hospitals: Fairchild Medical Center (25 beds)

Safety: Violent crime rate: 64.1 per 10,000 population; Property crime rate: 363.9 per 10,000 population

Newspapers: Siskiyou Daily News (daily circulation 5600)

Transportation: Commute: 84.3% car, 0.5% public transportation, 7.5% walk, 5.7% work from home; Median travel time to work: 14.1 minutes

Additional Information Contacts

City of Yreka . . . . (530) 841-2386
http://ci.yreka.ca.us

Solano County

Located in central and western California; bounded on the southwest by San Pablo Bay, on the south by Carquinez Strait and Suisun Bay, and on the southeast by the Sacramento River. Covers a land area of 821.765 square miles, a water area of 84.427 square miles, and is located in the

Pacific Time Zone at 38.27° N. Lat., 121.94° W. Long. The county was founded in 1850. County seat is Fairfield.

Solano County is part of the Vallejo-Fairfield, CA Metropolitan Statistical Area. The entire metro area includes: Solano County, CA

Weather Station: Fairfield Elevation: 40 feet

	Jan	Feb	Mar	Apr	May	Jun	Jul	Aug	Sep	Oct	Nov	Dec
High	55	62	67	72	79	86	90	90	87	78	65	56
Low	38	41	44	47	51	55	57	56	55	51	44	38
Precip	4.7	5.1	3.4	1.3	0.8	0.2	0.0	0.0	0.2	1.2	2.9	4.9
Snow	0.0	0.0	0.0	0.0	0.0	0.0	0.0	0.0	0.0	0.0	0.0	0.1

High and Low temperatures in degrees Fahrenheit; Precipitation and Snow in inches

Weather Station: Lake Solano Elevation: 189 feet

	Jan	Feb	Mar	Apr	May	Jun	Jul	Aug	Sep	Oct	Nov	Dec
High	55	61	67	73	81	89	96	94	89	79	65	56
Low	37	41	44	47	53	58	59	58	55	50	43	37
Precip	5.3	5.5	3.7	1.3	0.8	0.1	0.0	0.0	0.2	1.1	2.9	5.0
Snow	0.0	0.0	0.0	0.0	0.0	0.0	0.0	0.0	0.0	0.0	0.0	tr

High and Low temperatures in degrees Fahrenheit; Precipitation and Snow in inches

Weather Station: Vacaville Elevation: 109 feet

	Jan	Feb	Mar	Apr	May	Jun	Jul	Aug	Sep	Oct	Nov	Dec
High	56	62	68	74	82	90	96	94	90	80	66	56
Low	38	41	44	46	51	56	59	57	55	50	43	38
Precip	5.2	5.4	3.7	1.3	0.8	0.1	0.0	0.1	0.3	1.0	3.1	5.2
Snow	tr	0.0	0.0	0.0	0.0	0.0	0.0	0.0	0.0	0.0	0.0	0.1

High and Low temperatures in degrees Fahrenheit; Precipitation and Snow in inches

Population: 413,344; Growth (since 2000): 4.8%; Density: 503.0 persons per square mile; Race: 51.0% White, 14.7% Black/African American, 14.6% Asian, 0.8% American Indian/Alaska Native, 0.9% Native Hawaiian/Other Pacific Islander, 7.6% two or more races, 24.0% Hispanic of any race; Average household size: 2.83; Median age: 36.9; Age under 18: 24.6%; Age 65 and over: 11.3%; Males per 100 females: 99.5; Marriage status: 32.9% never married, 50.6% now married, 2.4% separated, 5.3% widowed, 11.2% divorced; Foreign born: 20.1%; Speak English only: 70.4%; With disability: 10.9%; Veterans: 11.2%; Ancestry: 9.2% German, 7.7% Irish, 6.4% English, 4.2% Italian, 3.8% European
Religion: Six largest groups: 19.6% Catholicism, 5.0% Baptist, 4.6% Non-denominational Protestant, 2.5% Latter-day Saints, 1.3% Pentecostal, 1.0% Methodist/Pietist
Economy: Unemployment rate: 6.3%; Leading industries: 15.9% retail trade; 12.9% health care and social assistance; 10.6% accommodation and food services; Farms: 860 totaling 407,101 acres; Company size: 5 employ 1,000 or more persons, 8 employ 500 to 999 persons, 130 employ 100 to 499 persons, 6,543 employ less than 100 persons; Business ownership: 8,475 women-owned, 2,448 Black-owned, 3,099 Hispanic-owned, 4,262 Asian-owned
Employment: 14.1% management, business, and financial, 4.4% computer, engineering, and science, 8.6% education, legal, community service, arts, and media, 6.3% healthcare practitioners, 19.9% service, 25.2% sales and office, 9.7% natural resources, construction, and maintenance, 11.6% production, transportation, and material moving
Income: Per capita: $28,929; Median household: $67,177; Average household: $82,971; Households with income of $100,000 or more: 30.0%; Poverty rate: 13.0%
Educational Attainment: High school diploma or higher: 87.2%; Bachelor's degree or higher: 24.3%; Graduate/professional degree or higher: 7.3%
Housing: Homeownership rate: 63.3%; Median home value: $262,400; Median year structure built: 1980; Homeowner vacancy rate: 2.5%; Median gross rent: $1,264 per month; Rental vacancy rate: 7.7%
Vital Statistics: Birth rate: 123.3 per 10,000 population; Death rate: 72.5 per 10,000 population; Age-adjusted cancer mortality rate: 173.0 deaths per 100,000 population
Health Insurance: 87.1% have insurance; 69.4% have private insurance; 29.2% have public insurance; 12.9% do not have insurance; 5.8% of children under 18 do not have insurance
Health Care: Physicians: 19.9 per 10,000 population; Hospital beds: 21.4 per 10,000 population; Hospital admissions: 782.1 per 10,000 population
Air Quality Index: 66.0% good, 31.5% moderate, 2.5% unhealthy for sensitive individuals, 0.0% unhealthy (percent of days)
Transportation: Commute: 90.0% car, 2.6% public transportation, 2.3% walk, 3.8% work from home; Median travel time to work: 28.9 minutes
Presidential Election: 62.8% Obama, 35.1% Romney (2012)
National and State Parks: Benicia Capitol State Historic Park; Benicia Capitol State Historical Monument; Benicia State Recreation Area; Putah Creek State Wildlife Area
Additional Information Contacts
Solano Government . . . . (707) 784-6100
http://www.solanocounty.com

Solano County Communities

ALLENDALE (CDP). Covers a land area of 6.136 square miles and a water area of 0.064 square miles. Located at 38.44° N. Lat; 121.98° W. Long. Elevation is 121 feet.
Population: 1,506; Growth (since 2000): n/a; Density: 245.4 persons per square mile; Race: 82.3% White, 3.3% Black/African American, 2.8% Asian, 1.5% American Indian/Alaska Native, 0.1% Native Hawaiian/Other Pacific Islander, 4.8% Two or more races, 15.6% Hispanic of any race; Average household size: 2.84; Median age: 47.3; Age under 18: 21.0%; Age 65 and over: 16.1%; Males per 100 females: 105.2
Housing: Homeownership rate: 89.2%; Homeowner vacancy rate: 0.0%; Rental vacancy rate: 5.0%

BENICIA (city). Covers a land area of 12.929 square miles and a water area of 2.791 square miles. Located at 38.07° N. Lat; 122.15° W. Long. Elevation is 26 feet.
History: Benicia began as Santa Francisca, named in honor of Vallejo's wife, and founded on Vallejo's Rancho Suscol which he deeded in 1846 to Dr. Robert Semple, editor of the "Californian," and Thomas O. Larkin, U.S. consul to Alta California. When Yerba Buena became San Francisco, Vallejo changed his town to his wife's second name, Benicia. In 1849 Benicia was a waypoint on a main road to the mines. In 1853-1854 it served as the state capital.
Population: 26,997; Growth (since 2000): 0.5%; Density: 2,088.1 persons per square mile; Race: 72.5% White, 5.6% Black/African American, 11.1% Asian, 0.5% American Indian/Alaska Native, 0.4% Native Hawaiian/Other Pacific Islander, 6.7% Two or more races, 12.0% Hispanic of any race; Average household size: 2.52; Median age: 42.9; Age under 18: 23.4%; Age 65 and over: 12.5%; Males per 100 females: 92.7; Marriage status: 28.8% never married, 53.7% now married, 1.7% separated, 4.3% widowed, 13.1% divorced; Foreign born: 10.4%; Speak English only: 85.0%; With disability: 8.9%; Veterans: 10.5%; Ancestry: 16.8% German, 13.5% Irish, 13.3% English, 5.9% Italian, 3.8% French
Employment: 21.2% management, business, and financial, 5.7% computer, engineering, and science, 12.6% education, legal, community service, arts, and media, 8.2% healthcare practitioners, 15.3% service, 23.2% sales and office, 6.6% natural resources, construction, and maintenance, 7.3% production, transportation, and material moving
Income: Per capita: $42,715; Median household: $88,502; Average household: $107,263; Households with income of $100,000 or more: 44.5%; Poverty rate: 5.7%
Educational Attainment: High school diploma or higher: 94.4%; Bachelor's degree or higher: 40.7%; Graduate/professional degree or higher: 14.8%

School District(s)

Benicia Unified (KG-12)
2012-13 Enrollment: 4,894 . . . . (707) 747-8300
Housing: Homeownership rate: 70.5%; Median home value: $422,700; Median year structure built: 1980; Homeowner vacancy rate: 2.0%; Median gross rent: $1,334 per month; Rental vacancy rate: 6.1%
Health Insurance: 91.3% have insurance; 81.1% have private insurance; 21.9% have public insurance; 8.7% do not have insurance; 5.5% of children under 18 do not have insurance
Safety: Violent crime rate: 10.9 per 10,000 population; Property crime rate: 139.0 per 10,000 population
Newspapers: Benicia Herald (daily circulation 3400)
Transportation: Commute: 86.1% car, 4.5% public transportation, 1.7% walk, 6.1% work from home; Median travel time to work: 29.8 minutes
Additional Information Contacts
City of Benicia . . . . (707) 746-4200
http://www.ci.benicia.ca.us

BIRDS LANDING (unincorporated postal area)
ZCTA: 94512
Covers a land area of 20.161 square miles and a water area of 0.011 square miles. Located at 38.13° N. Lat; 121.83° W. Long. Elevation is 52 feet.

Population: 108; Growth (since 2000): -16.9%; Density: 5.4 persons per square mile; Race: 73.1% White, 1.9% Black/African American, 3.7% Asian, 0.0% American Indian/Alaska Native, 2.8% Native Hawaiian/Other Pacific Islander, 0.9% Two or more races, 23.1% Hispanic of any race; Average household size: 2.70; Median age: 47.0; Age under 18: 13.9%; Age 65 and over: 15.7%; Males per 100 females: 125.0

Housing: Homeownership rate: 50.0%; Homeowner vacancy rate: 0.0%; Rental vacancy rate: 0.0%

DIXON (city). Covers a land area of 6.996 square miles and a water area of 0.096 square miles. Located at 38.45° N. Lat; 121.82° W. Long. Elevation is 62 feet.

History: Dixon developed as a farming and dairying center named for its founder, Thomas Dickson, though the spelling was changed. The town grew up soon after the advent of the first railroad.

Population: 18,351; Growth (since 2000): 14.0%; Density: 2,623.2 persons per square mile; Race: 71.0% White, 3.1% Black/African American, 3.7% Asian, 1.0% American Indian/Alaska Native, 0.3% Native Hawaiian/Other Pacific Islander, 5.5% Two or more races, 40.5% Hispanic of any race; Average household size: 3.13; Median age: 33.3; Age under 18: 29.1%; Age 65 and over: 8.5%; Males per 100 females: 97.8; Marriage status: 29.8% never married, 55.8% now married, 2.8% separated, 4.0% widowed, 10.3% divorced; Foreign born: 19.9%; Speak English only: 67.6%; With disability: 9.6%; Veterans: 8.1%; Ancestry: 15.0% Irish, 11.7% German, 9.9% English, 5.0% European, 4.6% Italian

Employment: 12.4% management, business, and financial, 4.6% computer, engineering, and science, 8.8% education, legal, community service, arts, and media, 4.9% healthcare practitioners, 19.1% service, 24.2% sales and office, 11.0% natural resources, construction, and maintenance, 15.0% production, transportation, and material moving

Income: Per capita: $27,650; Median household: $72,522; Average household: $84,515; Households with income of $100,000 or more: 32.1%; Poverty rate: 11.0%

Educational Attainment: High school diploma or higher: 80.8%; Bachelor's degree or higher: 22.1%; Graduate/professional degree or higher: 7.2%

School District(s)

Dixon Unified (KG-12)
2012-13 Enrollment: 3,537 . . . . (707) 693-6300
Sbe - Dixon Montessori Charter (KG-08)
2012-13 Enrollment: 362. . . . . (707) 678-8953

Housing: Homeownership rate: 66.6%; Median home value: $278,600; Median year structure built: 1985; Homeowner vacancy rate: 2.0%; Median gross rent: $1,157 per month; Rental vacancy rate: 5.2%

Health Insurance: 86.8% have insurance; 68.8% have private insurance; 26.0% have public insurance; 13.2% do not have insurance; 5.6% of children under 18 do not have insurance

Safety: Violent crime rate: 18.7 per 10,000 population; Property crime rate: 219.3 per 10,000 population

Newspapers: Dixon Tribune (weekly circulation 5600); Independent Voice (weekly circulation 4500)

Transportation: Commute: 94.1% car, 0.8% public transportation, 1.0% walk, 3.2% work from home; Median travel time to work: 22.1 minutes

Additional Information Contacts

City of Dixon . . . . (707) 678-7000
http://www.ci.dixon.ca.us

ELMIRA (CDP). Covers a land area of 0.531 square miles and a water area of 0 square miles. Located at 38.35° N. Lat; 121.91° W. Long. Elevation is 75 feet.

Population: 188; Growth (since 2000): -8.3%; Density: 353.9 persons per square mile; Race: 79.8% White, 0.5% Black/African American, 1.1% Asian, 5.3% American Indian/Alaska Native, 0.0% Native Hawaiian/Other Pacific Islander, 4.3% Two or more races, 25.0% Hispanic of any race; Average household size: 2.21; Median age: 43.4; Age under 18: 18.1%; Age 65 and over: 13.8%; Males per 100 females: 118.6

Housing: Homeownership rate: 53.0%; Homeowner vacancy rate: 0.0%; Rental vacancy rate: 7.0%

FAIRFIELD (city). County seat. Covers a land area of 37.390 square miles and a water area of 0.245 square miles. Located at 38.26° N. Lat; 122.04° W. Long. Elevation is 13 feet.

History: Fairfield was founded in 1859 by two sea captains, Robert H. Waterman and Archibald A. Ritchie, on a part of their rancho. They induced the transfer of the seat of Solano County from Benicia by their donation of land for a townsite.

Population: 105,321; Growth (since 2000): 9.5%; Density: 2,816.8 persons per square mile; Race: 46.0% White, 15.7% Black/African American, 14.9% Asian, 0.8% American Indian/Alaska Native, 1.1% Native Hawaiian/Other Pacific Islander, 8.8% Two or more races, 27.3% Hispanic of any race; Average household size: 2.98; Median age: 33.7; Age under 18: 27.1%; Age 65 and over: 10.2%; Males per 100 females: 97.0; Marriage status: 33.2% never married, 52.3% now married, 1.8% separated, 5.2% widowed, 9.3% divorced; Foreign born: 21.3%; Speak English only: 67.0%; With disability: 10.3%; Veterans: 11.2%; Ancestry: 7.3% German, 6.0% Irish, 4.5% English, 3.7% Italian, 3.2% American

Employment: 12.8% management, business, and financial, 4.3% computer, engineering, and science, 6.9% education, legal, community service, arts, and media, 6.0% healthcare practitioners, 20.0% service, 27.6% sales and office, 9.7% natural resources, construction, and maintenance, 12.6% production, transportation, and material moving

Income: Per capita: $26,611; Median household: $64,702; Average household: $79,786; Households with income of $100,000 or more: 29.2%; Poverty rate: 13.6%

Educational Attainment: High school diploma or higher: 86.4%; Bachelor's degree or higher: 23.4%; Graduate/professional degree or higher: 6.3%

School District(s)

Fairfield-Suisun Unified (KG-12)
2012-13 Enrollment: 21,400 . . . . (707) 399-5000
Solano County Office of Education (PK-12)
2012-13 Enrollment: 537. . . . . (707) 399-4400
Solano County Rop
2012-13 Enrollment: n/a . . . . (707) 399-4800
Travis Unified (KG-12)
2012-13 Enrollment: 5,466 . . . . (707) 437-4604

Two-year College(s)

InterCoast Colleges-Fairfield (Private, For-profit)
Fall 2013 Enrollment: 118. . . . . (707) 421-9700
Solano Community College (Public)
Fall 2013 Enrollment: 9,583 . . . . (707) 864-7000
2013-14 Tuition: In-state $1,416; Out-of-state $7,386

Vocational/Technical School(s)

Milan Institute of Cosmetology-Fairfield (Private, For-profit)
Fall 2013 Enrollment: 98 . . . . (707) 425-2288
2013-14 Tuition: $16,184

Housing: Homeownership rate: 60.4%; Median home value: $263,500; Median year structure built: 1983; Homeowner vacancy rate: 2.5%; Median gross rent: $1,271 per month; Rental vacancy rate: 7.1%

Health Insurance: 88.2% have insurance; 70.3% have private insurance; 28.8% have public insurance; 11.8% do not have insurance; 3.2% of children under 18 do not have insurance

Hospitals: Northbay Medical Center (132 beds)

Safety: Violent crime rate: 45.9 per 10,000 population; Property crime rate: 325.9 per 10,000 population

Newspapers: Daily Republic (daily circulation 17000)

Transportation: Commute: 89.7% car, 2.2% public transportation, 3.2% walk, 3.5% work from home; Median travel time to work: 27.7 minutes

Airports: Travis AFB (general aviation)

Additional Information Contacts

City of Fairfield . . . . (707) 428-7400
http://www.fairfield.ca.gov

GREEN VALLEY (CDP). Covers a land area of 8.308 square miles and a water area of 0.001 square miles. Located at 38.26° N. Lat; 122.16° W. Long. Elevation is 115 feet.

Population: 1,625; Growth (since 2000): -12.6%; Density: 195.6 persons per square mile; Race: 86.9% White, 2.5% Black/African American, 5.0% Asian, 0.4% American Indian/Alaska Native, 0.6% Native Hawaiian/Other Pacific Islander, 3.4% Two or more races, 7.4% Hispanic of any race; Average household size: 2.40; Median age: 55.5; Age under 18: 13.2%; Age 65 and over: 29.0%; Males per 100 females: 102.4

Housing: Homeownership rate: 91.5%; Homeowner vacancy rate: 2.2%; Rental vacancy rate: 9.4%

HARTLEY (CDP). Covers a land area of 6.477 square miles and a water area of 0.028 square miles. Located at 38.42° N. Lat; 121.95° W. Long. Elevation is 121 feet.

Population: 2,510; Growth (since 2000): n/a; Density: 387.5 persons per square mile; Race: 77.9% White, 2.8% Black/African American, 2.8% Asian, 1.0% American Indian/Alaska Native, 0.6% Native Hawaiian/Other Pacific Islander, 5.0% Two or more races, 20.3% Hispanic of any race; Average household size: 2.87; Median age: 44.8; Age under 18: 21.6%; Age 65 and over: 14.8%; Males per 100 females: 102.7; Marriage status: 26.5% never married, 59.2% now married, 1.4% separated, 3.3% widowed, 11.0% divorced; Foreign born: 6.1%; Speak English only: 91.4%; With disability: 13.6%; Veterans: 12.2%; Ancestry: 18.4% German, 13.5% Irish, 11.4% European, 10.4% English, 8.9% Italian

Employment: 13.4% management, business, and financial, 5.7% computer, engineering, and science, 9.5% education, legal, community service, arts, and media, 7.3% healthcare practitioners, 11.3% service, 19.7% sales and office, 17.3% natural resources, construction, and maintenance, 15.9% production, transportation, and material moving

Income: Per capita: $39,654; Median household: $95,132; Average household: $112,351; Households with income of $100,000 or more: 44.0%; Poverty rate: 4.7%

Educational Attainment: High school diploma or higher: 92.2%; Bachelor's degree or higher: 17.0%; Graduate/professional degree or higher: 6.4%

Housing: Homeownership rate: 80.5%; Median home value: $431,700; Median year structure built: 1980; Homeowner vacancy rate: 1.4%; Median gross rent: $1,493 per month; Rental vacancy rate: 6.0%

Health Insurance: 85.4% have insurance; 72.9% have private insurance; 23.2% have public insurance; 14.6% do not have insurance; 7.5% of children under 18 do not have insurance

Transportation: Commute: 92.6% car, 0.0% public transportation, 0.0% walk, 7.4% work from home; Median travel time to work: 29.2 minutes

RIO VISTA (city). Covers a land area of 6.691 square miles and a water area of 0.403 square miles. Located at 38.18° N. Lat; 121.71° W. Long. Elevation is 20 feet.

History: Rio Vista was laid out on the edge of the Sacramento River in 1857 by Colonel N.H. Davis, who called the settlement Brazos del Rio (arms of the river). The town, renamed Rio Vista in 1860, prospered around its wharf, but was completely washed away by floods in 1862. The residents rebuilt further back from the river.

Population: 7,360; Growth (since 2000): 61.0%; Density: 1,100.0 persons per square mile; Race: 81.6% White, 5.1% Black/African American, 4.9% Asian, 0.7% American Indian/Alaska Native, 0.2% Native Hawaiian/Other Pacific Islander, 3.7% Two or more races, 12.4% Hispanic of any race; Average household size: 2.13; Median age: 57.2; Age under 18: 15.6%; Age 65 and over: 32.3%; Males per 100 females: 92.6; Marriage status: 24.3% never married, 52.9% now married, 1.0% separated, 11.1% widowed, 11.7% divorced; Foreign born: 11.0%; Speak English only: 86.8%; With disability: 17.3%; Veterans: 15.0%; Ancestry: 14.4% Irish, 14.3% German, 11.5% English, 8.4% European, 8.4% Italian

Employment: 16.6% management, business, and financial, 3.2% computer, engineering, and science, 16.0% education, legal, community service, arts, and media, 3.3% healthcare practitioners, 17.2% service, 23.2% sales and office, 11.2% natural resources, construction, and maintenance, 9.3% production, transportation, and material moving

Income: Per capita: $35,024; Median household: $55,458; Average household: $71,512; Households with income of $100,000 or more: 22.4%; Poverty rate: 11.4%

Educational Attainment: High school diploma or higher: 90.2%; Bachelor's degree or higher: 24.5%; Graduate/professional degree or higher: 8.9%

School District(s)

River Delta Joint Unified (KG-12)
2012-13 Enrollment: 2,323 . . . . (707) 374-1700

Housing: Homeownership rate: 77.7%; Median home value: $216,100; Median year structure built: 2000; Homeowner vacancy rate: 2.7%; Median gross rent: $1,187 per month; Rental vacancy rate: 13.7%

Health Insurance: 80.8% have insurance; 64.9% have private insurance; 47.9% have public insurance; 19.2% do not have insurance; 13.8% of children under 18 do not have insurance

Safety: Violent crime rate: 42.0 per 10,000 population; Property crime rate: 321.4 per 10,000 population

Newspapers: River News-Herald (weekly circulation 4900)

Transportation: Commute: 88.5% car, 0.5% public transportation, 5.4% walk, 3.8% work from home; Median travel time to work: 38.1 minutes; Amtrak: Train service available.

Additional Information Contacts

City of Rio Vista. . . . . (707) 374-6451
http://riovistacity.com

SUISUN CITY (city). Covers a land area of 4.105 square miles and a water area of 0.058 square miles. Located at 38.25° N. Lat; 122.01° W. Long. Elevation is 7 feet.

History: In the 1850's boats sailed up Suisun Slough through salt-water marshes to a landing at Suisun City. The town was laid out by Captain Josiah Wing in 1854.

Population: 28,111; Growth (since 2000): 7.6%; Density: 6,847.6 persons per square mile; Race: 38.4% White, 20.3% Black/African American, 19.0% Asian, 0.7% American Indian/Alaska Native, 1.2% Native Hawaiian/Other Pacific Islander, 10.0% Two or more races, 24.0% Hispanic of any race; Average household size: 3.15; Median age: 33.0; Age under 18: 27.5%; Age 65 and over: 7.7%; Males per 100 females: 96.9; Marriage status: 34.6% never married, 51.6% now married, 2.4% separated, 3.9% widowed, 9.9% divorced; Foreign born: 21.3%; Speak English only: 69.5%; With disability: 9.6%; Veterans: 11.6%; Ancestry: 8.6% African, 5.0% Irish, 4.6% German, 4.2% English, 2.6% Italian

Employment: 12.9% management, business, and financial, 4.8% computer, engineering, and science, 5.1% education, legal, community service, arts, and media, 6.7% healthcare practitioners, 20.8% service, 26.5% sales and office, 9.4% natural resources, construction, and maintenance, 13.8% production, transportation, and material moving

Income: Per capita: $25,483; Median household: $70,311; Average household: $80,567; Households with income of $100,000 or more: 29.3%; Poverty rate: 13.5%

Educational Attainment: High school diploma or higher: 87.7%; Bachelor's degree or higher: 20.4%; Graduate/professional degree or higher: 4.1%

School District(s)

Fairfield-Suisun Unified (KG-12)
2012-13 Enrollment: 21,400 . . . . (707) 399-5000

Housing: Homeownership rate: 69.3%; Median home value: $215,300; Median year structure built: 1984; Homeowner vacancy rate: 3.0%; Median gross rent: $1,418 per month; Rental vacancy rate: 5.9%

Health Insurance: 88.4% have insurance; 67.3% have private insurance; 29.0% have public insurance; 11.6% do not have insurance; 6.1% of children under 18 do not have insurance

Safety: Violent crime rate: 22.2 per 10,000 population; Property crime rate: 218.7 per 10,000 population

Transportation: Commute: 90.5% car, 3.0% public transportation, 1.8% walk, 3.1% work from home; Median travel time to work: 31.6 minutes; Amtrak: Train service available.

Additional Information Contacts

City of Suisun City. . . . . (707) 421-7300
http://www.suisun.com

TRAVIS AFB (unincorporated postal area)

ZCTA: 94535

Covers a land area of 3.811 square miles and a water area of 0.007 square miles. Located at 38.28° N. Lat; 121.92° W. Long..

Population: 3,793; Growth (since 2000): -61.9%; Density: 995.2 persons per square mile; Race: 64.4% White, 12.2% Black/African American, 7.2% Asian, 0.5% American Indian/Alaska Native, 1.4% Native Hawaiian/Other Pacific Islander, 9.9% Two or more races, 15.6% Hispanic of any race; Average household size: 3.49; Median age: 22.1; Age under 18: 33.2%; Age 65 and over: 0.2%; Males per 100 females: 127.9; Marriage status: 44.7% never married, 52.0% now married, 0.9% separated, 1.2% widowed, 2.1% divorced; Foreign born: 6.3%; Speak English only: 88.1%; With disability: 2.9%; Veterans: 21.1%; Ancestry: 19.1% German, 11.7% Irish, 9.0% European, 6.7% American, 4.4% Polish

Employment: 14.1% management, business, and financial, 3.0% computer, engineering, and science, 5.7% education, legal, community service, arts, and media, 23.6% healthcare practitioners, 16.7% service, 26.4% sales and office, 6.1% natural resources, construction, and maintenance, 4.4% production, transportation, and material moving

Income: Per capita: $18,170; Median household: $50,970; Average household: $59,954; Households with income of $100,000 or more: 16.0%; Poverty rate: 12.7%

Educational Attainment: High school diploma or higher: 99.5%; Bachelor's degree or higher: 29.1%; Graduate/professional degree or higher: 5.6%

School District(s)

Travis Unified (KG-12)
2012-13 Enrollment: 5,466 . . . . (707) 437-4604

Housing: Homeownership rate: 1.1%; Median home value: n/a; Median year structure built: 2000; Homeowner vacancy rate: 0.0%; Median gross rent: $1,788 per month; Rental vacancy rate: 7.9%

Health Insurance: 99.1% have insurance; 98.2% have private insurance; 3.0% have public insurance; 0.9% do not have insurance; 0.0% of children under 18 do not have insurance

Transportation: Commute: 54.8% car, 9.1% public transportation, 22.5% walk, 11.5% work from home; Median travel time to work: 9.4 minutes

VACAVILLE (city). Covers a land area of 28.373 square miles and a water area of 0.212 square miles. Located at 38.36° N. Lat; 121.97° W. Long. Elevation is 174 feet.

History: Before 1850, when Vacaville was founded, the land here was the range for the cattle herds of Rancho de los Putos. In this region the poet Edwin Markham spent his youth.

Population: 92,428; Growth (since 2000): 4.3%; Density: 3,257.7 persons per square mile; Race: 66.3% White, 10.3% Black/African American, 6.1% Asian, 0.9% American Indian/Alaska Native, 0.6% Native Hawaiian/Other Pacific Islander, 7.0% Two or more races, 22.9% Hispanic of any race; Average household size: 2.71; Median age: 37.2; Age under 18: 23.3%; Age 65 and over: 10.5%; Males per 100 females: 112.5; Marriage status: 32.2% never married, 50.1% now married, 2.6% separated, 4.3% widowed, 13.5% divorced; Foreign born: 12.6%; Speak English only: 80.4%; With disability: 10.2%; Veterans: 13.6%; Ancestry: 13.4% German, 9.8% Irish, 8.3% European, 8.0% English, 5.7% Italian

Employment: 12.0% management, business, and financial, 3.6% computer, engineering, and science, 9.9% education, legal, community service, arts, and media, 6.7% healthcare practitioners, 21.4% service, 25.2% sales and office, 10.4% natural resources, construction, and maintenance, 11.0% production, transportation, and material moving

Income: Per capita: $29,681; Median household: $73,582; Average household: $87,736; Households with income of $100,000 or more: 31.7%; Poverty rate: 9.9%

Educational Attainment: High school diploma or higher: 87.4%; Bachelor's degree or higher: 22.2%; Graduate/professional degree or higher: 7.3%

School District(s)

Travis Unified (KG-12)
2012-13 Enrollment: 5,466 . . . . (707) 437-4604
Vacaville Unified (KG-12)
2012-13 Enrollment: 12,657 . . . . (707) 453-6117

Vocational/Technical School(s)

Blake Austin College (Private, For-profit)
Fall 2013 Enrollment: 321 . . . . (707) 455-0557
2013-14 Tuition: $33,372

Housing: Homeownership rate: 63.5%; Median home value: $269,500; Median year structure built: 1982; Homeowner vacancy rate: 2.1%; Median gross rent: $1,369 per month; Rental vacancy rate: 6.8%

Health Insurance: 90.4% have insurance; 76.3% have private insurance; 26.2% have public insurance; 9.6% do not have insurance; 3.8% of children under 18 do not have insurance

Hospitals: Kaiser Foundation Hospital - Vacaville

Safety: Violent crime rate: 21.3 per 10,000 population; Property crime rate: 222.2 per 10,000 population

Newspapers: The Reporter (daily circulation 17900)

Transportation: Commute: 93.7% car, 0.8% public transportation, 1.8% walk, 2.6% work from home; Median travel time to work: 25.8 minutes

Airports: Nut Tree (general aviation)

Additional Information Contacts

City of Vacaville. . . . . (707) 449-5100
http://www.ci.vacaville.ca.us

VALLEJO (city). Covers a land area of 30.671 square miles and a water area of 18.869 square miles. Located at 38.11° N. Lat; 122.26° W. Long. Elevation is 69 feet.

History: General Mariano Vallejo selected this site on which to found a city that would bear his name. The town was laid out when Vallejo offered the new State of California land for a capital plus endowment for a university, museum, church, schools, and parks. When Vallejo failed to provide the promised amenities, the capital was moved to Benecia. The town flourished in spite of this when nearby Mare Island was purchased in 1853 for a United States navy yard.

Population: 115,942; Growth (since 2000): -0.7%; Density: 3,780.1 persons per square mile; Race: 32.8% White, 22.1% Black/African American, 24.9% Asian, 0.7% American Indian/Alaska Native, 1.1% Native Hawaiian/Other Pacific Islander, 7.5% Two or more races, 22.6% Hispanic of any race; Average household size: 2.82; Median age: 37.9; Age under 18: 23.2%; Age 65 and over: 12.1%; Males per 100 females: 94.3; Marriage status: 36.0% never married, 46.0% now married, 2.8% separated, 6.6% widowed, 11.5% divorced; Foreign born: 28.2%; Speak English only: 61.3%; With disability: 12.3%; Veterans: 9.5%; Ancestry: 5.4% German, 4.7% Irish, 4.3% English, 2.9% Italian, 2.5% American

Employment: 14.7% management, business, and financial, 4.9% computer, engineering, and science, 8.4% education, legal, community service, arts, and media, 6.3% healthcare practitioners, 20.9% service, 24.5% sales and office, 8.9% natural resources, construction, and maintenance, 11.4% production, transportation, and material moving

Income: Per capita: $25,996; Median household: $58,371; Average household: $72,361; Households with income of $100,000 or more: 24.3%; Poverty rate: 17.5%

Educational Attainment: High school diploma or higher: 86.4%; Bachelor's degree or higher: 23.3%; Graduate/professional degree or higher: 6.3%

School District(s)

Vallejo City Unified (KG-12)
2012-13 Enrollment: 15,157 . . . . (707) 556-8921

Four-year College(s)

California Maritime Academy (Public)
Fall 2013 Enrollment: 1,045 . . . . (707) 654-1000
2013-14 Tuition: In-state $6,536; Out-of-state $17,696
Touro University California (Private, Not-for-profit, Jewish)
Fall 2013 Enrollment: 1,357 . . . . (707) 638-5276

Vocational/Technical School(s)

Hinton Barber College (Private, For-profit)
Fall 2013 Enrollment: 56 . . . . (707) 647-2800
2013-14 Tuition: $12,257

Housing: Homeownership rate: 59.7%; Median home value: $218,300; Median year structure built: 1970; Homeowner vacancy rate: 3.0%; Median gross rent: $1,192 per month; Rental vacancy rate: 9.4%

Health Insurance: 83.2% have insurance; 61.4% have private insurance; 32.3% have public insurance; 16.8% do not have insurance; 9.4% of children under 18 do not have insurance

Hospitals: Kaiser Foundation Hospital & Rehab Center (267 beds); Sutter Solano Medical Center (111 beds)

Safety: Violent crime rate: 86.1 per 10,000 population; Property crime rate: 484.6 per 10,000 population

Newspapers: Vallejo Times-Herald (daily circulation 17300)

Transportation: Commute: 87.8% car, 4.7% public transportation, 2.0% walk, 3.9% work from home; Median travel time to work: 33.0 minutes; Amtrak: Bus service available.

Additional Information Contacts

City of Vallejo . . . . (707) 648-4527
http://www.ci.vallejo.ca.us

Sonoma County

Located in western California, in the Coast Ranges; bounded on the west by the Pacific Ocean, and on the south by San Pablo Bay; drained by the Russian River. Covers a land area of 1,575.849 square miles, a water area of 192.098 square miles, and is located in the Pacific Time Zone at 38.53° N. Lat., 122.95° W. Long. The county was founded in 1850. County seat is Santa Rosa.

Sonoma County is part of the Santa Rosa, CA Metropolitan Statistical Area. The entire metro area includes: Sonoma County, CA

Weather Station: Cloverdale Elevation: 333 feet

	Jan	Feb	Mar	Apr	May	Jun	Jul	Aug	Sep	Oct	Nov	Dec
High	58	62	67	72	80	87	93	92	87	78	65	57
Low	39	41	44	46	51	56	56	57	55	50	44	39
Precip	8.2	7.9	5.7	2.6	1.4	0.2	0.0	0.1	0.4	1.9	5.6	8.6
Snow	0.0	0.0	0.0	0.0	0.0	0.0	0.0	0.0	0.0	0.0	0.0	0.0

High and Low temperatures in degrees Fahrenheit; Precipitation and Snow in inches

Weather Station: Graton Elevation: 200 feet

	Jan	Feb	Mar	Apr	May	Jun	Jul	Aug	Sep	Oct	Nov	Dec
High	57	62	66	71	76	82	84	84	83	78	66	57
Low	36	38	40	41	44	47	49	49	47	43	39	35
Precip	8.2	7.9	5.7	2.3	1.3	0.3	0.0	0.1	0.3	1.9	5.3	8.1
Snow	0.0	0.0	0.0	tr	0.0	0.0	0.0	0.0	0.0	0.0	0.0	0.0

High and Low temperatures in degrees Fahrenheit; Precipitation and Snow in inches

Weather Station: Healdsburg Elevation: 107 feet

	Jan	Feb	Mar	Apr	May	Jun	Jul	Aug	Sep	Oct	Nov	Dec
High	58	62	67	73	80	86	90	89	85	77	65	57
Low	40	42	44	46	50	54	55	54	53	49	43	39
Precip	8.3	8.4	6.3	2.5	1.5	0.2	0.0	0.1	0.3	2.1	5.3	8.6
Snow	tr	tr	0.0	0.0	0.0	0.0	0.0	0.0	0.0	0.0	0.0	0.0

High and Low temperatures in degrees Fahrenheit; Precipitation and Snow in inches

Weather Station: Petaluma Fire Station 2 Elevation: 30 feet

	Jan	Feb	Mar	Apr	May	Jun	Jul	Aug	Sep	Oct	Nov	Dec
High	57	62	65	69	73	79	82	82	81	76	65	57
Low	39	41	42	44	47	51	52	52	51	47	42	38
Precip	4.8	5.5	3.7	1.5	0.8	0.2	0.0	0.1	0.2	1.3	3.1	5.1
Snow	0.0	tr	0.0	tr	0.0	0.0	0.0	0.0	0.0	0.0	0.0	0.0

High and Low temperatures in degrees Fahrenheit; Precipitation and Snow in inches

Weather Station: Santa Rosa Elevation: 166 feet

	Jan	Feb	Mar	Apr	May	Jun	Jul	Aug	Sep	Oct	Nov	Dec
High	58	62	65	69	73	79	81	81	81	77	65	58
Low	39	42	43	45	48	52	53	53	52	49	43	39
Precip	5.9	6.1	4.5	1.8	1.2	0.2	0.0	0.1	0.3	1.6	4.0	6.1
Snow	0.0	0.0	0.0	0.0	0.0	0.0	0.0	0.0	0.0	0.0	0.0	0.0

High and Low temperatures in degrees Fahrenheit; Precipitation and Snow in inches

Weather Station: Sonoma Elevation: 97 feet

	Jan	Feb	Mar	Apr	May	Jun	Jul	Aug	Sep	Oct	Nov	Dec
High	58	63	67	71	77	84	89	88	86	79	66	58
Low	38	40	42	43	47	51	53	52	50	47	42	37
Precip	6.0	6.2	4.3	1.7	1.1	0.2	0.0	0.1	0.2	1.5	3.8	5.5
Snow	0.0	0.0	0.0	0.0	0.0	0.0	0.0	0.0	0.0	0.0	0.0	0.0

High and Low temperatures in degrees Fahrenheit; Precipitation and Snow in inches

Population: 483,878; Growth (since 2000): 5.5%; Density: 307.1 persons per square mile; Race: 76.8% White, 1.6% Black/African American, 3.8% Asian, 1.3% American Indian/Alaska Native, 0.3% Native Hawaiian/Other Pacific Islander, 4.4% two or more races, 24.9% Hispanic of any race; Average household size: 2.55; Median age: 39.9; Age under 18: 22.0%; Age 65 and over: 13.9%; Males per 100 females: 96.7; Marriage status: 31.8% never married, 49.4% now married, 1.9% separated, 5.4% widowed, 13.3% divorced; Foreign born: 16.6%; Speak English only: 74.5%; With disability: 10.7%; Veterans: 8.7%; Ancestry: 14.7% German, 12.6% Irish, 10.9% English, 9.3% Italian, 3.8% American

Religion: Six largest groups: 22.3% Catholicism, 1.9% Latter-day Saints, 1.9% Buddhism, 1.5% Non-denominational Protestant, 1.4% Baptist, 1.0% Lutheran

Economy: Unemployment rate: 5.0%; Leading industries: 13.3% retail trade; 12.8% construction; 11.5% professional, scientific, and technical services; Farms: 3,579 totaling 589,771 acres; Company size: 3 employ 1,000 or more persons, 8 employ 500 to 999 persons, 195 employ 100 to 499 persons, 13,039 employ less than 100 persons; Business ownership: 15,951 women-owned, n/a Black-owned, 4,096 Hispanic-owned, n/a Asian-owned

Employment: 15.9% management, business, and financial, 4.7% computer, engineering, and science, 10.2% education, legal, community service, arts, and media, 4.9% healthcare practitioners, 19.7% service, 24.6% sales and office, 10.2% natural resources, construction, and maintenance, 9.7% production, transportation, and material moving

Income: Per capita: $32,835; Median household: $63,356; Average household: $83,823; Households with income of $100,000 or more: 29.0%; Poverty rate: 11.9%

Educational Attainment: High school diploma or higher: 86.7%; Bachelor's degree or higher: 32.2%; Graduate/professional degree or higher: 11.4%

Housing: Homeownership rate: 60.5%; Median home value: $407,400; Median year structure built: 1977; Homeowner vacancy rate: 1.9%; Median gross rent: $1,265 per month; Rental vacancy rate: 5.1%

Vital Statistics: Birth rate: 104.2 per 10,000 population; Death rate: 81.0 per 10,000 population; Age-adjusted cancer mortality rate: 160.7 deaths per 100,000 population

Health Insurance: 85.9% have insurance; 69.2% have private insurance; 28.9% have public insurance; 14.1% do not have insurance; 6.8% of children under 18 do not have insurance

Health Care: Physicians: 24.6 per 10,000 population; Hospital beds: 24.9 per 10,000 population; Hospital admissions: 702.9 per 10,000 population

Air Quality Index: 81.1% good, 18.9% moderate, 0.0% unhealthy for sensitive individuals, 0.0% unhealthy (percent of days)

Transportation: Commute: 86.3% car, 1.8% public transportation, 3.0% walk, 6.8% work from home; Median travel time to work: 25.3 minutes

Presidential Election: 70.8% Obama, 26.0% Romney (2012)

National and State Parks: Annadel State Park; Armstrong Redwoods State Natural Reserve; Austin Creek State Recreation Area; Fort Ross State Historic Park; Jack London State Historic Park; Kruse Rhododendron State Natural Reserve; Petaluma Adobe State Historic Park; Salt Point State Park; San Pablo Bay National Wildlife Refuge; Sonoma Coast State Park; Sonoma State Historic Park; Sugarloaf Ridge State Park; Vallejo Home State Historical Monument

Additional Information Contacts

Sonoma Government . . . . (707) 565-2241
http://www.sonoma-county.org

Sonoma County Communities

ANNAPOLIS (unincorporated postal area)

ZCTA: 95412

Covers a land area of 85.685 square miles and a water area of 0 square miles. Located at 38.71° N. Lat; 123.35° W. Long. Elevation is 771 feet.

Population: 401; Growth (since 2000): -45.0%; Density: 4.7 persons per square mile; Race: 66.8% White, 0.0% Black/African American, 0.5% Asian, 21.2% American Indian/Alaska Native, 0.2% Native Hawaiian/Other Pacific Islander, 1.0% Two or more races, 26.7% Hispanic of any race; Average household size: 2.57; Median age: 44.1; Age under 18: 18.2%; Age 65 and over: 16.7%; Males per 100 females: 107.8

School District(s)

Horicon Elementary (KG-08)
2012-13 Enrollment: 60. . . . . (707) 886-5322

Housing: Homeownership rate: 66.9%; Homeowner vacancy rate: 1.9%; Rental vacancy rate: 7.1%

BLOOMFIELD (CDP). Covers a land area of 8.137 square miles and a water area of 0.007 square miles. Located at 38.32° N. Lat; 122.83° W. Long. Elevation is 56 feet.

Population: 345; Growth (since 2000): n/a; Density: 42.4 persons per square mile; Race: 81.7% White, 0.0% Black/African American, 1.2% Asian, 0.0% American Indian/Alaska Native, 0.0% Native Hawaiian/Other Pacific Islander, 2.0% Two or more races, 18.0% Hispanic of any race; Average household size: 2.56; Median age: 47.4; Age under 18: 16.2%; Age 65 and over: 18.0%; Males per 100 females: 84.5

Housing: Homeownership rate: 65.9%; Homeowner vacancy rate: 0.0%; Rental vacancy rate: 2.1%

BODEGA (CDP). Covers a land area of 2.902 square miles and a water area of 0 square miles. Located at 38.35° N. Lat; 122.97° W. Long. Elevation is 115 feet.

Population: 220; Growth (since 2000): n/a; Density: 75.8 persons per square mile; Race: 95.0% White, 0.0% Black/African American, 0.9% Asian, 0.9% American Indian/Alaska Native, 0.0% Native Hawaiian/Other Pacific Islander, 3.2% Two or more races, 4.1% Hispanic of any race; Average household size: 1.88; Median age: 54.5; Age under 18: 11.4%; Age 65 and over: 17.7%; Males per 100 females: 94.7

Housing: Homeownership rate: 56.4%; Homeowner vacancy rate: 1.5%; Rental vacancy rate: 0.0%

BODEGA BAY (CDP). Covers a land area of 8.345 square miles and a water area of 4.179 square miles. Located at 38.32° N. Lat; 123.03° W. Long. Elevation is 59 feet.

History: In 1811 the Russian-American Fur Company founded the settlement of Port Roumiantzoff on Bodega Bay, which had been named for its discoverer, Lieutenant Juan Francisco de la Bodega y Cuadra, who came this way in 1775. In 1835 General Mariano Vallejo granted land at Bodega Bay to three sailors, hoping that this would check Russian expansion along the coast. In 1848 Captain Stephen Smith erected a warehouse and later a hotel, and the town became a shipping center for the local potatoes known as Bodega Reds. Dairying later replaced potato farming, and the bay silted in.

Population: 1,077; Growth (since 2000): -24.3%; Density: 129.1 persons per square mile; Race: 88.3% White, 0.2% Black/African American, 3.1% Asian, 0.4% American Indian/Alaska Native, 0.4% Native Hawaiian/Other Pacific Islander, 3.2% Two or more races, 11.7% Hispanic of any race; Average household size: 2.00; Median age: 57.2; Age under 18: 12.2%; Age 65 and over: 29.1%; Males per 100 females: 105.9

School District(s)

Shoreline Unified (KG-12)
2012-13 Enrollment: 554 . . . . (707) 878-2266

Housing: Homeownership rate: 67.9%; Homeowner vacancy rate: 4.6%; Rental vacancy rate: 23.7%

BOYES HOT SPRINGS (CDP). Covers a land area of 1.059 square miles and a water area of 0 square miles. Located at 38.31° N. Lat; 122.49° W. Long. Elevation is 135 feet.

History: Boyes Hot Springs developed as a resort area around hot mineral springs.

Population: 6,656; Growth (since 2000): -0.1%; Density: 6,286.3 persons per square mile; Race: 67.7% White, 0.7% Black/African American, 1.3% Asian, 1.4% American Indian/Alaska Native, 0.1% Native Hawaiian/Other Pacific Islander, 3.7% Two or more races, 49.1% Hispanic of any race; Average household size: 2.86; Median age: 34.0; Age under 18: 26.5%; Age 65 and over: 9.3%; Males per 100 females: 103.3; Marriage status: 35.7% never married, 50.1% now married, 1.3% separated, 3.8% widowed, 10.4% divorced; Foreign born: 28.5%; Speak English only: 49.3%; With disability: 7.7%; Veterans: 5.7%; Ancestry: 8.8% Italian, 8.6% German, 8.0% Irish, 6.6% English, 2.4% American

Employment: 7.5% management, business, and financial, 1.3% computer, engineering, and science, 8.6% education, legal, community service, arts, and media, 2.5% healthcare practitioners, 38.7% service, 19.8% sales and office, 14.2% natural resources, construction, and maintenance, 7.3% production, transportation, and material moving

Income: Per capita: $26,325; Median household: $56,074; Average household: $79,845; Households with income of $100,000 or more: 23.2%; Poverty rate: 12.9%

Educational Attainment: High school diploma or higher: 70.2%; Bachelor's degree or higher: 24.9%; Graduate/professional degree or higher: 8.7%

Housing: Homeownership rate: 53.8%; Median home value: $394,900; Median year structure built: 1972; Homeowner vacancy rate: 1.6%; Median gross rent: $1,228 per month; Rental vacancy rate: 3.6%

Health Insurance: 72.5% have insurance; 52.1% have private insurance; 29.3% have public insurance; 27.5% do not have insurance; 15.0% of children under 18 do not have insurance

Transportation: Commute: 80.9% car, 4.7% public transportation, 4.8% walk, 3.8% work from home; Median travel time to work: 24.0 minutes

CARMET (CDP). Covers a land area of 0.287 square miles and a water area of 0 square miles. Located at 38.37° N. Lat; 123.07° W. Long. Elevation is 72 feet.

Population: 47; Growth (since 2000): n/a; Density: 164.0 persons per square mile; Race: 91.5% White, 0.0% Black/African American, 2.1% Asian, 0.0% American Indian/Alaska Native, 0.0% Native Hawaiian/Other Pacific Islander, 6.4% Two or more races, 0.0% Hispanic of any race; Average household size: 1.62; Median age: 59.3; Age under 18: 4.3%; Age 65 and over: 31.9%; Males per 100 females: 95.8

Housing: Homeownership rate: 82.7%; Homeowner vacancy rate: 7.7%; Rental vacancy rate: 16.7%

CAZADERO (CDP). Covers a land area of 7.116 square miles and a water area of 0.001 square miles. Located at 38.53° N. Lat; 123.11° W. Long. Elevation is 115 feet.

Population: 354; Growth (since 2000): n/a; Density: 49.7 persons per square mile; Race: 89.8% White, 0.3% Black/African American, 1.4% Asian, 2.0% American Indian/Alaska Native, 0.0% Native Hawaiian/Other Pacific Islander, 5.1% Two or more races, 6.5% Hispanic of any race; Average household size: 2.16; Median age: 46.7; Age under 18: 16.9%; Age 65 and over: 13.8%; Males per 100 females: 122.6

School District(s)

Fort Ross Elementary (KG-08)
2012-13 Enrollment: 29 . . . . (707) 847-3390
Montgomery Elementary (KG-08)
2012-13 Enrollment: 32 . . . . (707) 632-5221

Housing: Homeownership rate: 65.8%; Homeowner vacancy rate: 1.8%; Rental vacancy rate: 9.2%

CLOVERDALE (city). Covers a land area of 2.648 square miles and a water area of 0 square miles. Located at 38.80° N. Lat; 123.02° W. Long. Elevation is 335 feet.

History: Cloverdale developed as the center of an orange-growing area at the head of the Santa Rosa Valley.

Population: 8,618; Growth (since 2000): 26.2%; Density: 3,255.1 persons per square mile; Race: 74.9% White, 0.6% Black/African American, 1.1% Asian, 1.8% American Indian/Alaska Native, 0.1% Native Hawaiian/Other Pacific Islander, 3.7% Two or more races, 32.8% Hispanic of any race; Average household size: 2.68; Median age: 39.7; Age under 18: 23.8%; Age 65 and over: 16.0%; Males per 100 females: 99.5; Marriage status: 23.7% never married, 57.4% now married, 0.5% separated, 5.6% widowed, 13.3% divorced; Foreign born: 17.6%; Speak English only: 66.4%; With disability: 13.3%; Veterans: 9.0%; Ancestry: 17.1% German, 7.4% English, 7.2% Irish, 7.1% Italian, 5.3% Swedish

Employment: 13.6% management, business, and financial, 2.9% computer, engineering, and science, 6.6% education, legal, community service, arts, and media, 3.5% healthcare practitioners, 21.7% service, 22.1% sales and office, 18.1% natural resources, construction, and maintenance, 11.5% production, transportation, and material moving

Income: Per capita: $27,243; Median household: $58,294; Average household: $70,632; Households with income of $100,000 or more: 23.2%; Poverty rate: 5.0%

Educational Attainment: High school diploma or higher: 79.9%; Bachelor's degree or higher: 21.5%; Graduate/professional degree or higher: 8.4%

School District(s)

Cloverdale Unified (KG-12)
2012-13 Enrollment: 1,445 . . . . (707) 894-1920

Housing: Homeownership rate: 66.0%; Median home value: $328,800; Median year structure built: 1986; Homeowner vacancy rate: 4.1%; Median gross rent: $1,245 per month; Rental vacancy rate: 4.9%

Health Insurance: 88.3% have insurance; 70.6% have private insurance; 31.0% have public insurance; 11.7% do not have insurance; 8.3% of children under 18 do not have insurance

Safety: Violent crime rate: 5.7 per 10,000 population; Property crime rate: 181.2 per 10,000 population

Newspapers: Cloverdale Reveille (weekly circulation 2300)

Transportation: Commute: 90.1% car, 0.0% public transportation, 1.6% walk, 8.1% work from home; Median travel time to work: 25.2 minutes; Amtrak: Bus service available.

Additional Information Contacts

City of Cloverdale . . . . (707) 894-2521
http://www.cloverdale.net

COTATI (city). Covers a land area of 1.880 square miles and a water area of 0.003 square miles. Located at 38.33° N. Lat; 122.71° W. Long. Elevation is 108 feet.

History: Cotati developed on the former Rancho Cotati as a trading center of a poultry and farming area.

Population: 7,265; Growth (since 2000): 12.3%; Density: 3,864.5 persons per square mile; Race: 81.6% White, 1.7% Black/African American, 3.9% Asian, 1.0% American Indian/Alaska Native, 0.4% Native Hawaiian/Other Pacific Islander, 5.5% Two or more races, 17.3% Hispanic of any race; Average household size: 2.44; Median age: 36.2; Age under 18: 21.9%; Age 65 and over: 8.4%; Males per 100 females: 90.5; Marriage status: 34.3% never married, 47.4% now married, 3.3% separated, 4.2% widowed, 14.1% divorced; Foreign born: 12.1%; Speak English only: 83.9%; With disability: 8.9%; Veterans: 7.3%; Ancestry: 21.9% German, 15.7% Irish, 12.5% Italian, 11.1% English, 5.3% Scottish

Employment: 17.1% management, business, and financial, 5.6% computer, engineering, and science, 9.3% education, legal, community service, arts, and media, 6.9% healthcare practitioners, 16.7% service, 27.5% sales and office, 6.9% natural resources, construction, and maintenance, 9.8% production, transportation, and material moving

Income: Per capita: $34,109; Median household: $62,849; Average household: $80,825; Households with income of $100,000 or more: 27.2%; Poverty rate: 10.6%

Educational Attainment: High school diploma or higher: 87.6%; Bachelor's degree or higher: 33.3%; Graduate/professional degree or higher: 8.1%

School District(s)

Cotati-Rohnert Park Unified (KG-12)
2012-13 Enrollment: 5,855 . . . . (707) 792-4722

Housing: Homeownership rate: 59.1%; Median home value: $363,600; Median year structure built: 1983; Homeowner vacancy rate: 2.0%; Median gross rent: $1,228 per month; Rental vacancy rate: 5.6%

Health Insurance: 88.1% have insurance; 71.0% have private insurance; 25.4% have public insurance; 11.9% do not have insurance; 4.0% of children under 18 do not have insurance

Safety: Violent crime rate: 47.4 per 10,000 population; Property crime rate: 106.9 per 10,000 population

Transportation: Commute: 89.3% car, 1.6% public transportation, 1.4% walk, 4.3% work from home; Median travel time to work: 26.9 minutes

Additional Information Contacts

City of Cotati . . . . (707) 792-4600
http://www.ci.cotati.ca.us

EL VERANO (CDP). Covers a land area of 1.142 square miles and a water area of 0 square miles. Located at 38.30° N. Lat; 122.49° W. Long. Elevation is 108 feet.

History: Sonoma Mission State Historical Park to East.

Population: 4,123; Growth (since 2000): 4.3%; Density: 3,609.5 persons per square mile; Race: 74.1% White, 0.5% Black/African American, 2.4% Asian, 0.5% American Indian/Alaska Native, 0.3% Native Hawaiian/Other Pacific Islander, 4.7% Two or more races, 37.8% Hispanic of any race; Average household size: 2.80; Median age: 35.7; Age under 18: 26.4%; Age 65 and over: 9.6%; Males per 100 females: 98.3; Marriage status: 29.1% never married, 54.1% now married, 2.3% separated, 1.8% widowed, 14.9% divorced; Foreign born: 29.3%; Speak English only: 60.6%; With disability: 12.3%; Veterans: 6.2%; Ancestry: 14.6% German, 12.7% Irish, 11.2% Italian, 11.2% English, 3.7% Swedish

Employment: 15.4% management, business, and financial, 4.0% computer, engineering, and science, 16.2% education, legal, community service, arts, and media, 3.5% healthcare practitioners, 22.3% service, 19.9% sales and office, 9.3% natural resources, construction, and maintenance, 9.3% production, transportation, and material moving

Income: Per capita: $23,873; Median household: $45,906; Average household: $62,940; Households with income of $100,000 or more: 20.0%; Poverty rate: 15.5%

Educational Attainment: High school diploma or higher: 74.3%; Bachelor's degree or higher: 30.9%; Graduate/professional degree or higher: 5.6%

Housing: Homeownership rate: 53.6%; Median home value: $414,100; Median year structure built: 1976; Homeowner vacancy rate: 1.7%; Median gross rent: $1,287 per month; Rental vacancy rate: 4.1%

Health Insurance: 77.3% have insurance; 55.0% have private insurance; 28.6% have public insurance; 22.7% do not have insurance; 0.5% of children under 18 do not have insurance

Transportation: Commute: 84.7% car, 0.0% public transportation, 3.8% walk, 8.4% work from home; Median travel time to work: 20.9 minutes

ELDRIDGE (CDP). Covers a land area of 0.652 square miles and a water area of 0 square miles. Located at 38.33° N. Lat; 122.51° W. Long. Elevation is 177 feet.

History: Jack London State Historical Park to Northwest.

Population: 1,233; Growth (since 2000): -19.6%; Density: 1,891.1 persons per square mile; Race: 80.1% White, 0.8% Black/African American, 2.9% Asian, 0.2% American Indian/Alaska Native, 0.5% Native Hawaiian/Other Pacific Islander, 3.7% Two or more races, 26.4% Hispanic of any race; Average household size: 2.46; Median age: 39.8; Age under 18: 22.2%; Age 65 and over: 11.0%; Males per 100 females: 100.8

Housing: Homeownership rate: 53.4%; Homeowner vacancy rate: 2.2%; Rental vacancy rate: 12.4%

Hospitals: Sonoma Developmental Center (1421 beds)

FETTERS HOT SPRINGS-AGUA CALIENTE (CDP). Covers a land area of 1.472 square miles and a water area of 0 square miles. Located at 38.33° N. Lat; 122.49° W. Long. Elevation is 141 feet.

History: In 1908, George and Emma Fetters opened the Fetters Hot Springs resort. "Agua Caliente" means "hot water" and refers to the hot springs found in this region.

Population: 4,144; Growth (since 2000): 65.4%; Density: 2,815.6 persons per square mile; Race: 70.6% White, 0.6% Black/African American, 1.6% Asian, 0.9% American Indian/Alaska Native, 0.2% Native Hawaiian/Other Pacific Islander, 4.4% Two or more races, 46.5% Hispanic of any race; Average household size: 2.91; Median age: 34.8; Age under 18: 27.4%; Age 65 and over: 9.2%; Males per 100 females: 98.8; Marriage status: 34.1% never married, 51.5% now married, 1.5% separated, 2.4% widowed, 12.0% divorced; Foreign born: 36.2%; Speak English only: 54.9%; With disability: 5.0%; Veterans: 2.8%; Ancestry: 10.3% English, 8.3% German, 7.8% Irish, 6.4% French, 5.0% European

Employment: 14.2% management, business, and financial, 7.1% computer, engineering, and science, 11.9% education, legal, community service, arts, and media, 3.8% healthcare practitioners, 19.8% service, 17.6% sales and office, 8.4% natural resources, construction, and maintenance, 17.2% production, transportation, and material moving

Income: Per capita: $34,260; Median household: $60,795; Average household: $94,931; Households with income of $100,000 or more: 30.2%; Poverty rate: 18.3%

Educational Attainment: High school diploma or higher: 72.2%; Bachelor's degree or higher: 37.6%; Graduate/professional degree or higher: 14.1%

Housing: Homeownership rate: 58.0%; Median home value: $517,500; Median year structure built: 1975; Homeowner vacancy rate: 2.4%; Median gross rent: $1,227 per month; Rental vacancy rate: 8.0%

Health Insurance: 85.1% have insurance; 71.1% have private insurance; 23.6% have public insurance; 14.9% do not have insurance; 4.5% of children under 18 do not have insurance

Transportation: Commute: 85.1% car, 2.8% public transportation, 0.0% walk, 7.4% work from home; Median travel time to work: 26.6 minutes

FORESTVILLE (CDP). Covers a land area of 5.257 square miles and a water area of 0 square miles. Located at 38.48° N. Lat; 122.89° W. Long. Elevation is 171 feet.

Population: 3,293; Growth (since 2000): 38.9%; Density: 626.4 persons per square mile; Race: 88.5% White, 1.0% Black/African American, 1.6% Asian, 1.1% American Indian/Alaska Native, 0.2% Native Hawaiian/Other Pacific Islander, 3.0% Two or more races, 12.3% Hispanic of any race; Average household size: 2.28; Median age: 47.5; Age under 18: 17.6%; Age 65 and over: 14.1%; Males per 100 females: 101.3; Marriage status: 33.1% never married, 50.7% now married, 2.7% separated, 5.5% widowed, 10.7% divorced; Foreign born: 8.7%; Speak English only: 91.2%; With disability: 17.1%; Veterans: 12.0%; Ancestry: 19.6% German, 16.2% English, 14.1% Irish, 12.7% Italian, 4.9% American

Employment: 9.5% management, business, and financial, 3.7% computer, engineering, and science, 16.9% education, legal, community service, arts, and media, 5.4% healthcare practitioners, 15.6% service, 30.2% sales and office, 10.4% natural resources, construction, and maintenance, 8.2% production, transportation, and material moving

Income: Per capita: $29,236; Median household: $49,477; Average household: $62,547; Households with income of $100,000 or more: 17.0%; Poverty rate: 11.5%

Educational Attainment: High school diploma or higher: 91.0%; Bachelor's degree or higher: 30.3%; Graduate/professional degree or higher: 13.8%

School District(s)

Forestville Union Elementary (KG-08)
2012-13 Enrollment: 355. . . . . (707) 887-9767

West Sonoma County Union High (PK-12)
2012-13 Enrollment: 2,176 . . . . (707) 824-6403

Housing: Homeownership rate: 70.2%; Median home value: $411,000; Median year structure built: 1963; Homeowner vacancy rate: 1.2%; Median gross rent: $1,224 per month; Rental vacancy rate: 6.5%

Health Insurance: 84.2% have insurance; 72.6% have private insurance; 27.1% have public insurance; 15.8% do not have insurance; 0.0% of children under 18 do not have insurance

Transportation: Commute: 82.7% car, 0.5% public transportation, 3.4% walk, 12.2% work from home; Median travel time to work: 27.4 minutes

FULTON (CDP). Covers a land area of 1.949 square miles and a water area of 0 square miles. Located at 38.49° N. Lat; 122.77° W. Long. Elevation is 135 feet.

Population: 541; Growth (since 2000): n/a; Density: 277.6 persons per square mile; Race: 64.5% White, 0.6% Black/African American, 2.0% Asian, 2.2% American Indian/Alaska Native, 0.2% Native Hawaiian/Other Pacific Islander, 3.0% Two or more races, 34.4% Hispanic of any race; Average household size: 2.81; Median age: 37.8; Age under 18: 24.0%; Age 65 and over: 12.0%; Males per 100 females: 100.4

Housing: Homeownership rate: 56.6%; Homeowner vacancy rate: 1.8%; Rental vacancy rate: 4.7%

GEYSERVILLE (CDP). Covers a land area of 4.588 square miles and a water area of 0 square miles. Located at 38.72° N. Lat; 122.90° W. Long. Elevation is 213 feet.

Population: 862; Growth (since 2000): n/a; Density: 187.9 persons per square mile; Race: 70.6% White, 0.6% Black/African American, 1.6% Asian, 0.8% American Indian/Alaska Native, 0.0% Native Hawaiian/Other Pacific Islander, 4.1% Two or more races, 38.1% Hispanic of any race; Average household size: 2.85; Median age: 39.9; Age under 18: 23.3%; Age 65 and over: 9.7%; Males per 100 females: 116.0

School District(s)

Geyserville Unified (KG-12)
2012-13 Enrollment: 268 . . . . (707) 857-3592

Housing: Homeownership rate: 58.4%; Homeowner vacancy rate: 1.7%; Rental vacancy rate: 0.0%

GLEN ELLEN (CDP). Covers a land area of 2.102 square miles and a water area of 0.001 square miles. Located at 38.36° N. Lat; 122.54° W. Long. Elevation is 253 feet.

History: Near the community of Glen Ellen, author Jack London spent his last years running an experimental model farm while he continued his writing. At the time of his death in 1916, he had completed but never lived in the stone structure called Wolf House.

Population: 784; Growth (since 2000): -21.0%; Density: 372.9 persons per square mile; Race: 88.4% White, 0.4% Black/African American, 2.0% Asian, 1.1% American Indian/Alaska Native, 0.4% Native Hawaiian/Other Pacific Islander, 5.4% Two or more races, 8.5% Hispanic of any race; Average household size: 2.12; Median age: 51.4; Age under 18: 16.1%; Age 65 and over: 13.1%; Males per 100 females: 103.6

School District(s)

Sonoma Valley Unified (KG-12)
2012-13 Enrollment: 4,670 . . . . (707) 935-6000

Housing: Homeownership rate: 60.5%; Homeowner vacancy rate: 1.3%; Rental vacancy rate: 4.0%

GRATON (CDP). Covers a land area of 1.579 square miles and a water area of 0 square miles. Located at 38.44° N. Lat; 122.87° W. Long. Elevation is 108 feet.

Population: 1,707; Growth (since 2000): -6.0%; Density: 1,080.9 persons per square mile; Race: 82.1% White, 0.6% Black/African American, 1.5% Asian, 1.7% American Indian/Alaska Native, 0.2% Native Hawaiian/Other Pacific Islander, 5.5% Two or more races, 18.9% Hispanic of any race; Average household size: 2.49; Median age: 45.9; Age under 18: 20.1%; Age 65 and over: 13.9%; Males per 100 females: 90.7

Housing: Homeownership rate: 72.2%; Homeowner vacancy rate: 0.6%; Rental vacancy rate: 2.6%

GUERNEVILLE (CDP). Covers a land area of 9.709 square miles and a water area of 0.170 square miles. Located at 38.52° N. Lat; 122.99° W. Long. Elevation is 59 feet.

History: Guerneville was named for George Guerne, its founder, who built a large mill here in 1865. The area became noted for its apple industry.

Population: 4,534; Growth (since 2000): 85.7%; Density: 467.0 persons per square mile; Race: 86.6% White, 0.7% Black/African American, 1.0% Asian, 1.5% American Indian/Alaska Native, 0.3% Native Hawaiian/Other Pacific Islander, 4.9% Two or more races, 12.2% Hispanic of any race; Average household size: 1.95; Median age: 48.2; Age under 18: 14.2%; Age 65 and over: 13.5%; Males per 100 females: 119.8; Marriage status: 44.4% never married, 28.8% now married, 1.3% separated, 6.9% widowed, 20.0% divorced; Foreign born: 5.2%; Speak English only: 90.4%; With disability: 22.5%; Veterans: 8.4%; Ancestry: 20.4% German, 18.7% Irish, 16.5% English, 6.2% Italian, 5.9% American

Employment: 15.7% management, business, and financial, 4.6% computer, engineering, and science, 17.4% education, legal, community service, arts, and media, 2.0% healthcare practitioners, 24.4% service, 17.4% sales and office, 10.0% natural resources, construction, and maintenance, 8.4% production, transportation, and material moving

Income: Per capita: $31,820; Median household: $38,113; Average household: $57,191; Households with income of $100,000 or more: 17.1%; Poverty rate: 24.5%

Educational Attainment: High school diploma or higher: 91.3%; Bachelor's degree or higher: 35.3%; Graduate/professional degree or higher: 17.6%

School District(s)

Guerneville Elementary (KG-08)
2012-13 Enrollment: 281 . . . . (707) 887-7762

Housing: Homeownership rate: 56.2%; Median home value: $343,400; Median year structure built: 1949; Homeowner vacancy rate: 3.6%; Median gross rent: $962 per month; Rental vacancy rate: 7.7%

Health Insurance: 84.4% have insurance; 54.7% have private insurance; 43.6% have public insurance; 15.6% do not have insurance; 1.8% of children under 18 do not have insurance

Transportation: Commute: 80.8% car, 2.8% public transportation, 5.4% walk, 10.9% work from home; Median travel time to work: 32.7 minutes

HEALDSBURG (city). Covers a land area of 4.457 square miles and a water area of 0.007 square miles. Located at 38.62° N. Lat; 122.87° W. Long. Elevation is 105 feet.

History: Healdsburg was founded as a trading post in 1852 by Harmon G. Heald. Many of the early residents of Healdsburg were Italian grape-growers.

Population: 11,254; Growth (since 2000): 5.0%; Density: 2,525.1 persons per square mile; Race: 74.1% White, 0.5% Black/African American, 1.1% Asian, 1.8% American Indian/Alaska Native, 0.2% Native Hawaiian/Other Pacific Islander, 3.4% Two or more races, 33.9% Hispanic of any race; Average household size: 2.56; Median age: 40.8; Age under 18: 22.6%; Age 65 and over: 15.0%; Males per 100 females: 96.5; Marriage status: 30.8% never married, 49.2% now married, 2.1% separated, 7.3% widowed, 12.7% divorced; Foreign born: 21.9%; Speak English only: 69.1%; With disability: 11.3%; Veterans: 7.7%; Ancestry: 13.3% German, 11.4% Italian, 10.3% Irish, 10.2% English, 4.3% American

Employment: 21.0% management, business, and financial, 4.6% computer, engineering, and science, 8.7% education, legal, community service, arts, and media, 3.1% healthcare practitioners, 19.7% service, 21.4% sales and office, 12.5% natural resources, construction, and maintenance, 9.1% production, transportation, and material moving

Income: Per capita: $31,121; Median household: $56,969; Average household: $77,945; Households with income of $100,000 or more: 29.3%; Poverty rate: 14.5%

Educational Attainment: High school diploma or higher: 85.7%; Bachelor's degree or higher: 34.0%; Graduate/professional degree or higher: 14.4%

School District(s)

Alexander Valley Union Elementary (KG-06)
2012-13 Enrollment: 114 . . . . (707) 433-1375

Healdsburg Unified (KG-12)
2012-13 Enrollment: 1,813 . . . . (707) 431-3488

West Side Union Elementary (KG-06)
2012-13 Enrollment: 179 . . . . (707) 433-3923

Housing: Homeownership rate: 57.5%; Median home value: $473,300; Median year structure built: 1975; Homeowner vacancy rate: 2.7%; Median gross rent: $1,274 per month; Rental vacancy rate: 4.2%

Health Insurance: 81.3% have insurance; 65.4% have private insurance; 30.0% have public insurance; 18.7% do not have insurance; 9.8% of children under 18 do not have insurance

Hospitals: Healdsburg District Hospital (43 beds)

Safety: Violent crime rate: 21.8 per 10,000 population; Property crime rate: 205.5 per 10,000 population

Newspapers: Sonoma West Times & News/Healdsburg Trib (weekly circulation 6000)

Transportation: Commute: 79.8% car, 1.6% public transportation, 5.9% walk, 7.3% work from home; Median travel time to work: 20.6 minutes; Amtrak: Bus service available.

Additional Information Contacts

City of Healdsburg . . . . (707) 431-3300
http://www.ci.healdsburg.ca.us

JENNER (CDP). Covers a land area of 2.110 square miles and a water area of 0.288 square miles. Located at 38.45° N. Lat; 123.12° W. Long. Elevation is 16 feet.

Population: 136; Growth (since 2000): n/a; Density: 64.5 persons per square mile; Race: 91.9% White, 1.5% Black/African American, 1.5% Asian, 0.0% American Indian/Alaska Native, 0.0% Native Hawaiian/Other Pacific Islander, 5.1% Two or more races, 5.9% Hispanic of any race; Average household size: 1.70; Median age: 58.5; Age under 18: 5.1%; Age 65 and over: 22.1%; Males per 100 females: 106.1

Housing: Homeownership rate: 66.3%; Homeowner vacancy rate: 1.9%; Rental vacancy rate: 35.7%

KENWOOD (CDP). Covers a land area of 5.163 square miles and a water area of 0 square miles. Located at 38.42° N. Lat; 122.54° W. Long. Elevation is 423 feet.

Population: 1,028; Growth (since 2000): n/a; Density: 199.1 persons per square mile; Race: 90.5% White, 0.1% Black/African American, 2.2% Asian, 0.1% American Indian/Alaska Native, 0.2% Native Hawaiian/Other Pacific Islander, 2.5% Two or more races, 7.7% Hispanic of any race; Average household size: 2.16; Median age: 53.7; Age under 18: 14.4%; Age 65 and over: 23.4%; Males per 100 females: 94.0

School District(s)

Kenwood (KG-06)
2012-13 Enrollment: 163. . . . . (707) 833-2500

Housing: Homeownership rate: 73.0%; Homeowner vacancy rate: 0.6%; Rental vacancy rate: 2.3%

Newspapers: Kenwood Press (weekly circulation 8000)

LARKFIELD-WIKIUP (CDP). Covers a land area of 5.308 square miles and a water area of 0 square miles. Located at 38.51° N. Lat; 122.75° W. Long. Elevation is 197 feet.

Population: 8,884; Growth (since 2000): 18.8%; Density: 1,673.8 persons per square mile; Race: 79.3% White, 0.9% Black/African American, 3.3% Asian, 1.9% American Indian/Alaska Native, 0.2% Native Hawaiian/Other Pacific Islander, 4.5% Two or more races, 22.3% Hispanic of any race; Average household size: 2.57; Median age: 41.0; Age under 18: 24.2%; Age 65 and over: 14.3%; Males per 100 females: 97.2; Marriage status: 29.4% never married, 51.5% now married, 2.4% separated, 6.1% widowed, 13.0% divorced; Foreign born: 8.0%; Speak English only: 84.7%; With disability: 9.5%; Veterans: 10.4%; Ancestry: 16.9% German, 15.0% Irish, 12.6% English, 10.8% Italian, 5.4% American

Employment: 15.2% management, business, and financial, 7.2% computer, engineering, and science, 14.8% education, legal, community service, arts, and media, 3.4% healthcare practitioners, 16.9% service, 25.9% sales and office, 9.6% natural resources, construction, and maintenance, 7.1% production, transportation, and material moving

Income: Per capita: $37,156; Median household: $74,076; Average household: $88,562; Households with income of $100,000 or more: 38.0%; Poverty rate: 9.7%

Educational Attainment: High school diploma or higher: 93.4%; Bachelor's degree or higher: 37.3%; Graduate/professional degree or higher: 12.4%

Housing: Homeownership rate: 67.3%; Median home value: $414,500; Median year structure built: 1981; Homeowner vacancy rate: 1.1%; Median gross rent: $1,295 per month; Rental vacancy rate: 6.5%

Health Insurance: 89.6% have insurance; 72.7% have private insurance; 27.6% have public insurance; 10.4% do not have insurance; 3.5% of children under 18 do not have insurance

Transportation: Commute: 94.3% car, 0.3% public transportation, 0.0% walk, 5.0% work from home; Median travel time to work: 21.7 minutes

MONTE RIO (CDP). Covers a land area of 1.904 square miles and a water area of 0.073 square miles. Located at 38.47° N. Lat; 123.01° W. Long. Elevation is 43 feet.

History: Monte Rio grew up along the Russian River as a summer resort.

Population: 1,152; Growth (since 2000): 4.3%; Density: 605.2 persons per square mile; Race: 90.9% White, 0.9% Black/African American, 1.0% Asian, 0.5% American Indian/Alaska Native, 0.1% Native Hawaiian/Other Pacific Islander, 5.3% Two or more races, 6.9% Hispanic of any race; Average household size: 1.87; Median age: 50.7; Age under 18: 11.5%; Age 65 and over: 15.3%; Males per 100 females: 119.8

School District(s)

Monte Rio Union Elementary (KG-08)
2012-13 Enrollment: 91. . . . . (707) 865-2266

Housing: Homeownership rate: 56.9%; Homeowner vacancy rate: 3.7%; Rental vacancy rate: 9.1%

OCCIDENTAL (CDP). Covers a land area of 4.966 square miles and a water area of 0 square miles. Located at 38.40° N. Lat; 122.93° W. Long. Elevation is 594 feet.

Population: 1,115; Growth (since 2000): -12.3%; Density: 224.5 persons per square mile; Race: 89.0% White, 0.6% Black/African American, 2.8% Asian, 0.6% American Indian/Alaska Native, 0.0% Native Hawaiian/Other Pacific Islander, 4.9% Two or more races, 7.3% Hispanic of any race; Average household size: 2.10; Median age: 48.5; Age under 18: 17.2%; Age 65 and over: 13.0%; Males per 100 females: 103.8

School District(s)

Harmony Union Elementary (KG-12)
2012-13 Enrollment: 716. . . . . (707) 874-3280

Housing: Homeownership rate: 68.6%; Homeowner vacancy rate: 4.2%; Rental vacancy rate: 6.6%

PENNGROVE (CDP). Covers a land area of 4.024 square miles and a water area of 0 square miles. Located at 38.30° N. Lat; 122.67° W. Long. Elevation is 85 feet.

Population: 2,522; Growth (since 2000): n/a; Density: 626.7 persons per square mile; Race: 87.7% White, 0.8% Black/African American, 2.1% Asian, 1.0% American Indian/Alaska Native, 0.1% Native Hawaiian/Other Pacific Islander, 3.9% Two or more races, 11.6% Hispanic of any race; Average household size: 2.42; Median age: 44.8; Age under 18: 17.5%; Age 65 and over: 14.4%; Males per 100 females: 98.4; Marriage status: 22.3% never married, 58.3% now married, 0.0% separated, 6.0% widowed, 13.3% divorced; Foreign born: 10.6%; Speak English only: 79.8%; With disability: 7.6%; Veterans: 7.7%; Ancestry: 17.1% Irish, 14.8% German, 10.5% European, 9.7% English, 7.0% Norwegian

Employment: 28.1% management, business, and financial, 3.7% computer, engineering, and science, 5.0% education, legal, community service, arts, and media, 8.2% healthcare practitioners, 16.7% service, 22.6% sales and office, 10.6% natural resources, construction, and maintenance, 5.2% production, transportation, and material moving

Income: Per capita: $54,122; Median household: $73,583; Average household: $130,427; Households with income of $100,000 or more: 45.1%; Poverty rate: 5.7%

Educational Attainment: High school diploma or higher: 92.5%; Bachelor's degree or higher: 39.4%; Graduate/professional degree or higher: 10.0%

School District(s)

Petaluma City Elementary (KG-08)
2012-13 Enrollment: 2,413 . . . . (707) 778-4813

Housing: Homeownership rate: 61.5%; Median home value: $681,500; Median year structure built: 1976; Homeowner vacancy rate: 1.4%; Median gross rent: $1,334 per month; Rental vacancy rate: 3.1%

Health Insurance: 91.0% have insurance; 84.3% have private insurance; 23.8% have public insurance; 9.0% do not have insurance; 3.5% of children under 18 do not have insurance

Transportation: Commute: 89.4% car, 4.0% public transportation, 1.0% walk, 3.4% work from home; Median travel time to work: 31.8 minutes

PETALUMA (city). Covers a land area of 14.382 square miles and a water area of 0.107 square miles. Located at 38.24° N. Lat; 122.63° W. Long. Elevation is 30 feet.

History: A Mexican colony was established here in 1833, followed by an American settlement in 1852. In 1878 Canadian Lyman Ryce began poultry raising here, leading to the town's nickname of The World's Egg Basket, or Chickaluma. Ryce developed artificial incubators and brooders, and Petaluma flourished as a chicken and egg center.

Population: 57,941; Growth (since 2000): 6.2%; Density: 4,028.7 persons per square mile; Race: 80.4% White, 1.4% Black/African American, 4.5% Asian, 0.6% American Indian/Alaska Native, 0.2% Native Hawaiian/Other Pacific Islander, 4.1% Two or more races, 21.5% Hispanic of any race; Average household size: 2.63; Median age: 40.3; Age under 18: 23.2%; Age 65 and over: 13.1%; Males per 100 females: 96.3; Marriage status: 27.9% never married, 54.1% now married, 1.8% separated, 5.2% widowed, 12.8% divorced; Foreign born: 16.8%; Speak English only: 74.6%; With disability: 8.9%; Veterans: 8.5%; Ancestry: 15.9% German, 15.2% Irish, 12.0% English, 10.9% Italian, 3.9% American

Employment: 17.8% management, business, and financial, 4.3% computer, engineering, and science, 10.9% education, legal, community service, arts, and media, 5.2% healthcare practitioners, 18.5% service, 25.9% sales and office, 9.3% natural resources, construction, and maintenance, 8.1% production, transportation, and material moving

Income: Per capita: $35,088; Median household: $80,243; Average household: $93,319; Households with income of $100,000 or more: 37.4%; Poverty rate: 9.6%

Educational Attainment: High school diploma or higher: 89.5%; Bachelor's degree or higher: 36.8%; Graduate/professional degree or higher: 11.6%

School District(s)

Cinnabar Elementary (KG-06)
2012-13 Enrollment: 175. . . . . (707) 765-4345

Dunham Elementary (KG-06)
2012-13 Enrollment: 177. . . . . (707) 795-5050
Laguna Joint Elementary (KG-06)
2012-13 Enrollment: 15. . . . . (707) 762-6051
Liberty Elementary (KG-12)
2012-13 Enrollment: 1,062 . . . . (707) 795-4380
Lincoln Elementary (KG-06)
2012-13 Enrollment: 8. . . . . (707) 763-0045
Old Adobe Union (KG-06)
2012-13 Enrollment: 1,684 . . . . (707) 765-4322
Petaluma City Elementary (KG-08)
2012-13 Enrollment: 2,413 . . . . (707) 778-4813
Petaluma Joint Union High (KG-12)
2012-13 Enrollment: 5,380 . . . . (707) 778-4795
Sbe - River Montessori Elementary Charter (01-06)
2012-13 Enrollment: 166. . . . . (707) 778-6414
Two Rock Union (KG-06)
2012-13 Enrollment: 188. . . . . (707) 762-6617
Union Joint Elementary (KG-06)
2012-13 Enrollment: 10. . . . . (707) 762-2047
Waugh Elementary (KG-06)
2012-13 Enrollment: 924. . . . . (707) 765-3331
Wilmar Union Elementary (KG-06)
2012-13 Enrollment: 244. . . . . (707) 765-4340

Housing: Homeownership rate: 65.2%; Median home value: $428,800; Median year structure built: 1978; Homeowner vacancy rate: 1.3%; Median gross rent: $1,442 per month; Rental vacancy rate: 4.8%

Health Insurance: 88.8% have insurance; 76.4% have private insurance; 23.4% have public insurance; 11.2% do not have insurance; 4.4% of children under 18 do not have insurance

Hospitals: Petaluma Valley Hospital (80 beds)

Safety: Violent crime rate: 30.2 per 10,000 population; Property crime rate: 171.0 per 10,000 population

Newspapers: The Argus Courier (weekly circulation 10000)

Transportation: Commute: 86.3% car, 2.4% public transportation, 2.7% walk, 6.0% work from home; Median travel time to work: 29.3 minutes; Amtrak: Bus service available.

Additional Information Contacts
City of Petaluma . . . . (707) 778-4345
http://cityofpetaluma.net/index.html

RIO NIDO (unincorporated postal area)

ZCTA: 95471

Covers a land area of 1.442 square miles and a water area of 0 square miles. Located at 38.52° N. Lat; 122.97° W. Long. Elevation is 75 feet.

Population: 522; Growth (since 2000): 76.4%; Density: 362.0 persons per square mile; Race: 84.9% White, 0.8% Black/African American, 1.3% Asian, 1.5% American Indian/Alaska Native, 0.8% Native Hawaiian/Other Pacific Islander, 6.5% Two or more races, 10.9% Hispanic of any race; Average household size: 1.84; Median age: 47.6; Age under 18: 12.8%; Age 65 and over: 10.0%; Males per 100 females: 114.8

Housing: Homeownership rate: 59.9%; Homeowner vacancy rate: 4.5%; Rental vacancy rate: 7.2%

ROHNERT PARK (city). Covers a land area of 7.003 square miles and a water area of 0.005 square miles. Located at 38.35° N. Lat; 122.70° W. Long. Elevation is 105 feet.

History: Rohnert Park once belonged to the nation of the Miwok Indians and was incorporated on August 28, 1962. Rohnert Park is located approximately 50 miles north of San Francisco.

Population: 40,971; Growth (since 2000): -3.0%; Density: 5,850.9 persons per square mile; Race: 76.1% White, 1.9% Black/African American, 5.2% Asian, 1.0% American Indian/Alaska Native, 0.4% Native Hawaiian/Other Pacific Islander, 5.7% Two or more races, 22.1% Hispanic of any race; Average household size: 2.57; Median age: 33.0; Age under 18: 20.9%; Age 65 and over: 9.3%; Males per 100 females: 95.3; Marriage status: 41.3% never married, 40.3% now married, 2.0% separated, 5.1% widowed, 13.3% divorced; Foreign born: 16.2%; Speak English only: 75.0%; With disability: 10.2%; Veterans: 7.1%; Ancestry: 15.1% German, 12.8% Irish, 9.8% Italian, 8.4% English, 3.4% European

Employment: 13.5% management, business, and financial, 4.2% computer, engineering, and science, 9.3% education, legal, community service, arts, and media, 3.2% healthcare practitioners, 22.3% service, 29.6% sales and office, 8.1% natural resources, construction, and maintenance, 9.7% production, transportation, and material moving

Income: Per capita: $26,987; Median household: $56,621; Average household: $68,098; Households with income of $100,000 or more: 22.0%; Poverty rate: 13.9%

Educational Attainment: High school diploma or higher: 87.4%; Bachelor's degree or higher: 23.6%; Graduate/professional degree or higher: 6.2%

School District(s)

Cotati-Rohnert Park Unified (KG-12)
2012-13 Enrollment: 5,855 . . . . (707) 792-4722
Harmony Union Elementary (KG-12)
2012-13 Enrollment: 716. . . . . (707) 874-3280

Four-year College(s)

Sonoma State University (Public)
Fall 2013 Enrollment: 9,120 . . . . (707) 664-2880
2013-14 Tuition: In-state $7,234; Out-of-state $18,394

Housing: Homeownership rate: 54.0%; Median home value: $300,600; Median year structure built: 1980; Homeowner vacancy rate: 2.1%; Median gross rent: $1,238 per month; Rental vacancy rate: 4.8%

Health Insurance: 84.9% have insurance; 71.1% have private insurance; 23.1% have public insurance; 15.1% do not have insurance; 4.7% of children under 18 do not have insurance

Safety: Violent crime rate: 43.6 per 10,000 population; Property crime rate: 166.2 per 10,000 population

Newspapers: Community Voice (weekly circulation 13000)

Transportation: Commute: 89.5% car, 2.6% public transportation, 0.9% walk, 4.2% work from home; Median travel time to work: 27.7 minutes; Amtrak: Bus service available.

Additional Information Contacts
City of Rohnert Park . . . . (707) 588-2226
http://www.ci.rohnert-park.ca.us

ROSELAND (CDP). Covers a land area of 0.940 square miles and a water area of 0 square miles. Located at 38.42° N. Lat; 122.72° W. Long. Elevation is 135 feet.

Population: 6,325; Growth (since 2000): -0.7%; Density: 6,726.5 persons per square mile; Race: 51.1% White, 2.1% Black/African American, 4.4% Asian, 3.5% American Indian/Alaska Native, 0.2% Native Hawaiian/Other Pacific Islander, 5.8% Two or more races, 59.7% Hispanic of any race; Average household size: 3.63; Median age: 30.2; Age under 18: 28.9%; Age 65 and over: 6.8%; Males per 100 females: 111.4; Marriage status: 36.8% never married, 50.5% now married, 5.1% separated, 4.3% widowed, 8.4% divorced; Foreign born: 34.6%; Speak English only: 45.8%; With disability: 12.5%; Veterans: 4.3%; Ancestry: 7.5% German, 4.1% English, 4.1% Irish, 3.6% American, 2.6% Italian

Employment: 6.5% management, business, and financial, 3.3% computer, engineering, and science, 7.7% education, legal, community service, arts, and media, 2.6% healthcare practitioners, 19.7% service, 25.0% sales and office, 16.8% natural resources, construction, and maintenance, 18.4% production, transportation, and material moving

Income: Per capita: $20,321; Median household: $52,261; Average household: $66,380; Households with income of $100,000 or more: 23.3%; Poverty rate: 14.9%

Educational Attainment: High school diploma or higher: 63.0%; Bachelor's degree or higher: 13.1%; Graduate/professional degree or higher: 6.8%

Housing: Homeownership rate: 50.8%; Median home value: $267,700; Median year structure built: 1962; Homeowner vacancy rate: 1.4%; Median gross rent: $1,206 per month; Rental vacancy rate: 3.0%

Health Insurance: 76.1% have insurance; 48.5% have private insurance; 33.1% have public insurance; 23.9% do not have insurance; 10.7% of children under 18 do not have insurance

Transportation: Commute: 89.6% car, 1.3% public transportation, 3.2% walk, 3.9% work from home; Median travel time to work: 22.6 minutes

SALMON CREEK (CDP). Covers a land area of 1.114 square miles and a water area of 0 square miles. Located at 38.35° N. Lat; 123.06° W. Long. Elevation is 46 feet.

Population: 86; Growth (since 2000): n/a; Density: 77.2 persons per square mile; Race: 100.0% White, 0.0% Black/African American, 0.0% Asian, 0.0% American Indian/Alaska Native, 0.0% Native Hawaiian/Other Pacific Islander, 0.0% Two or more races, 1.2% Hispanic of any race; Average household size: 1.91; Median age: 59.0; Age under 18: 5.8%; Age 65 and over: 26.7%; Males per 100 females: 104.8

Housing: Homeownership rate: 75.6%; Homeowner vacancy rate: 10.3%; Rental vacancy rate: 0.0%

SANTA ROSA (city). County seat. Covers a land area of 41.294 square miles and a water area of 0.205 square miles. Located at 38.45° N. Lat; 122.71° W. Long. Elevation is 164 feet.

History: Santa Rosa was named by Padre Juan Amarosa of Mission San Rafael. The town developed as a distribution center for the ranches of the Sonoma Valley. Luther Burbank (1849-1926) chose this as the site for his experiments in plant breeding, and worked here for half a century developing new varieties of cultivated plants.

Population: 167,815; Growth (since 2000): 13.7%; Density: 4,063.9 persons per square mile; Race: 71.0% White, 2.4% Black/African American, 5.2% Asian, 1.7% American Indian/Alaska Native, 0.5% Native Hawaiian/Other Pacific Islander, 5.1% Two or more races, 28.6% Hispanic of any race; Average household size: 2.59; Median age: 36.7; Age under 18: 23.4%; Age 65 and over: 13.5%; Males per 100 females: 95.2; Marriage status: 34.3% never married, 46.7% now married, 2.1% separated, 5.6% widowed, 13.4% divorced; Foreign born: 19.3%; Speak English only: 70.0%; With disability: 11.3%; Veterans: 8.3%; Ancestry: 12.6% German, 10.8% Irish, 9.3% English, 8.0% Italian, 4.6% European

Employment: 14.1% management, business, and financial, 4.8% computer, engineering, and science, 9.5% education, legal, community service, arts, and media, 4.7% healthcare practitioners, 20.5% service, 25.6% sales and office, 9.6% natural resources, construction, and maintenance, 11.1% production, transportation, and material moving

Income: Per capita: $29,688; Median household: $60,354; Average household: $77,521; Households with income of $100,000 or more: 25.5%; Poverty rate: 13.5%

Educational Attainment: High school diploma or higher: 84.8%; Bachelor's degree or higher: 30.0%; Graduate/professional degree or higher: 11.0%

School District(s)

Bellevue Union Elementary (KG-06)
2012-13 Enrollment: 1,736 . . . . (707) 542-5197
Bennett Valley Union Elementary (KG-06)
2012-13 Enrollment: 1,011 . . . . (707) 542-2201
Mark West Union Elementary (KG-08)
2012-13 Enrollment: 1,444 . . . . (707) 524-2970
Oak Grove Union Elementary (KG-12)
2012-13 Enrollment: 899. . . . . (707) 545-0171
Piner-Olivet Union Elementary (KG-12)
2012-13 Enrollment: 1,491 . . . . (707) 522-3000
Rincon Valley Union Elementary (PK-08)
2012-13 Enrollment: 3,373 . . . . (707) 542-7375
Roseland Elementary (KG-12)
2012-13 Enrollment: 2,442 . . . . (707) 545-0102
Santa Rosa Elementary (KG-08)
2012-13 Enrollment: 5,197 . . . . (707) 528-5352
Santa Rosa High (05-12)
2012-13 Enrollment: 11,233 . . . . (707) 528-5181
Sonoma County Office of Education (PK-12)
2012-13 Enrollment: 946. . . . . (707) 524-2600
Sonoma County Rop
2012-13 Enrollment: n/a . . . . (707) 524-2720
Windsor Unified (KG-12)
2012-13 Enrollment: 5,617 . . . . (707) 837-7701
Wright Elementary (KG-08)
2012-13 Enrollment: 1,610 . . . . (707) 542-0550

Four-year College(s)

Bergin University of Canine Studies (Private, Not-for-profit)
Fall 2013 Enrollment: 50. . . . . (707) 545-3647

Two-year College(s)

Empire College School of Business (Private, For-profit)
Fall 2013 Enrollment: 419 . . . . (707) 546-4000
Santa Rosa Junior College (Public)
Fall 2013 Enrollment: 22,094 . . . . (707) 527-4011
2013-14 Tuition: In-state $1,280; Out-of-state $6,599

Vocational/Technical School(s)

Lytles Redwood Empire Beauty College Inc (Private, For-profit)
Fall 2013 Enrollment: 126 . . . . (707) 545-8490
2013-14 Tuition: $19,219

Housing: Homeownership rate: 54.2%; Median home value: $360,800; Median year structure built: 1978; Homeowner vacancy rate: 2.0%; Median gross rent: $1,244 per month; Rental vacancy rate: 5.0%

Health Insurance: 83.7% have insurance; 63.4% have private insurance; 31.5% have public insurance; 16.3% do not have insurance; 8.7% of children under 18 do not have insurance

Hospitals: Kaiser Foundation Hospital - Santa Rosa (117 beds); Santa Rosa Memorial Hospital (209 beds); Sutter Medical Center of Santa Rosa (175 beds)

Safety: Violent crime rate: 31.5 per 10,000 population; Property crime rate: 204.4 per 10,000 population

Newspapers: North Bay Bohemian (weekly circulation 25000); Press Democrat (daily circulation 82700)

Transportation: Commute: 88.6% car, 1.9% public transportation, 3.0% walk, 4.7% work from home; Median travel time to work: 22.8 minutes; Amtrak: Bus service available.

Airports: Charles M. Schulz - Sonoma County (primary service/non-hub)

Additional Information Contacts

City of Santa Rosa . . . . (707) 543-3010
http://ci.santa-rosa.ca.us

SEA RANCH (CDP). Covers a land area of 16.138 square miles and a water area of 0.042 square miles. Located at 38.74° N. Lat; 123.48° W. Long. Elevation is 112 feet.

Population: 1,305; Growth (since 2000): n/a; Density: 80.9 persons per square mile; Race: 93.5% White, 1.1% Black/African American, 0.8% Asian, 0.2% American Indian/Alaska Native, 0.0% Native Hawaiian/Other Pacific Islander, 1.5% Two or more races, 9.0% Hispanic of any race; Average household size: 1.89; Median age: 63.7; Age under 18: 8.0%; Age 65 and over: 45.6%; Males per 100 females: 91.6

Housing: Homeownership rate: 85.7%; Homeowner vacancy rate: 3.4%; Rental vacancy rate: 38.8%

SEBASTOPOL (city). Covers a land area of 1.853 square miles and a water area of 0 square miles. Located at 38.40° N. Lat; 122.83° W. Long. Elevation is 82 feet.

History: A fight between two residents in Sebastopol in 1855 led to the name for the town, in reference to the Crimean War siege then taking place. Sebastopol developed as a trading center for vineyard and orchard owners, famous for its Gravenstein apples.

Population: 7,379; Growth (since 2000): -5.1%; Density: 3,982.4 persons per square mile; Race: 88.2% White, 1.0% Black/African American, 1.6% Asian, 0.8% American Indian/Alaska Native, 0.3% Native Hawaiian/Other Pacific Islander, 4.1% Two or more races, 12.0% Hispanic of any race; Average household size: 2.21; Median age: 46.1; Age under 18: 20.5%; Age 65 and over: 17.4%; Males per 100 females: 79.9; Marriage status: 31.3% never married, 40.5% now married, 2.0% separated, 5.8% widowed, 22.5% divorced; Foreign born: 11.4%; Speak English only: 86.4%; With disability: 13.0%; Veterans: 9.6%; Ancestry: 19.1% German, 15.8% Irish, 13.5% English, 8.0% Italian, 4.8% French

Employment: 16.0% management, business, and financial, 7.6% computer, engineering, and science, 13.4% education, legal, community service, arts, and media, 8.5% healthcare practitioners, 19.1% service, 21.5% sales and office, 6.5% natural resources, construction, and maintenance, 7.3% production, transportation, and material moving

Income: Per capita: $34,807; Median household: $53,677; Average household: $69,614; Households with income of $100,000 or more: 23.2%; Poverty rate: 8.5%

Educational Attainment: High school diploma or higher: 94.9%; Bachelor's degree or higher: 39.2%; Graduate/professional degree or higher: 16.6%

School District(s)

Gravenstein Union Elementary (KG-08)
2012-13 Enrollment: 711. . . . . (707) 823-7008
Oak Grove Union Elementary (KG-12)
2012-13 Enrollment: 899. . . . . (707) 545-0171
Sebastopol Union Elementary (KG-08)
2012-13 Enrollment: 1,018 . . . . (707) 829-4570
Twin Hills Union Elementary (KG-12)
2012-13 Enrollment: 1,190 . . . . (707) 823-0871
West Sonoma County Union High (PK-12)
2012-13 Enrollment: 2,176 . . . . (707) 824-6403

Housing: Homeownership rate: 52.9%; Median home value: $492,500; Median year structure built: 1973; Homeowner vacancy rate: 0.7%; Median gross rent: $1,228 per month; Rental vacancy rate: 4.2%

Health Insurance: 87.7% have insurance; 74.0% have private insurance; 29.3% have public insurance; 12.3% do not have insurance; 11.8% of children under 18 do not have insurance

Hospitals: Palm Drive Hospital (37 beds)

Safety: Violent crime rate: 30.4 per 10,000 population; Property crime rate: 192.9 per 10,000 population

Transportation: Commute: 78.7% car, 1.1% public transportation, 9.0% walk, 8.9% work from home; Median travel time to work: 24.0 minutes

Additional Information Contacts

City of Sebastopol . . . . (707) 823-1153
http://www.ci.sebastopol.ca.us

SERENO DEL MAR (CDP). Covers a land area of 0.737 square miles and a water area of 0 square miles. Located at 38.38° N. Lat; 123.07° W. Long.

Population: 126; Growth (since 2000): n/a; Density: 170.9 persons per square mile; Race: 93.7% White, 0.8% Black/African American, 0.8% Asian, 0.0% American Indian/Alaska Native, 0.8% Native Hawaiian/Other Pacific Islander, 2.4% Two or more races, 6.3% Hispanic of any race; Average household size: 2.00; Median age: 59.3; Age under 18: 7.1%; Age 65 and over: 36.5%; Males per 100 females: 100.0

Housing: Homeownership rate: 85.7%; Homeowner vacancy rate: 3.6%; Rental vacancy rate: 18.2%

SONOMA (city). Covers a land area of 2.742 square miles and a water area of 0 square miles. Located at 38.29° N. Lat; 122.46° W. Long. Elevation is 85 feet.

History: Sonoma began when Mission San Francisco Solano was founded here in 1823 by Father Jose Altimira. When the missions were secularized in 1834, Governor Jose Figueroa ordered Alferez Mariano Vallejo to found the Pueblo de Sonoma on the site. Vallejo's pueblo was invaded on June 14, 1846, by a group of trappers and settlers led by Ezekiel Merritt, acting on orders from Captain John Fremont who was camped nearby, who proclaimed California a Republic. In the plaza the bear flag was raised, a hastily improvised strip of unbleached cotton and a smaller strip of red flannel, with a star and a brown bear painted on it by William L. Todd, nephew of Mrs. Abraham Lincoln. Vallejo stayed on as a resident of the American town, which soon became known as a center for wine making.

Population: 10,648; Growth (since 2000): 16.7%; Density: 3,883.3 persons per square mile; Race: 86.8% White, 0.5% Black/African American, 2.8% Asian, 0.5% American Indian/Alaska Native, 0.2% Native Hawaiian/Other Pacific Islander, 2.5% Two or more races, 15.3% Hispanic of any race; Average household size: 2.10; Median age: 49.2; Age under 18: 18.0%; Age 65 and over: 25.0%; Males per 100 females: 83.6; Marriage status: 21.3% never married, 50.2% now married, 1.6% separated, 9.9% widowed, 18.6% divorced; Foreign born: 8.8%; Speak English only: 86.5%; With disability: 12.3%; Veterans: 11.1%; Ancestry: 19.9% Irish, 18.4% German, 13.1% English, 11.4% Italian, 7.7% French

Employment: 21.2% management, business, and financial, 2.8% computer, engineering, and science, 14.7% education, legal, community service, arts, and media, 8.2% healthcare practitioners, 19.4% service, 20.8% sales and office, 6.7% natural resources, construction, and maintenance, 6.4% production, transportation, and material moving

Income: Per capita: $45,595; Median household: $63,729; Average household: $94,932; Households with income of $100,000 or more: 33.1%; Poverty rate: 6.6%

Educational Attainment: High school diploma or higher: 93.8%; Bachelor's degree or higher: 40.4%; Graduate/professional degree or higher: 14.0%

School District(s)

Sonoma Valley Unified (KG-12)
2012-13 Enrollment: 4,670 . . . . (707) 935-6000

Housing: Homeownership rate: 59.1%; Median home value: $532,200; Median year structure built: 1976; Homeowner vacancy rate: 2.6%; Median gross rent: $1,385 per month; Rental vacancy rate: 7.0%

Health Insurance: 91.7% have insurance; 80.3% have private insurance; 33.5% have public insurance; 8.3% do not have insurance; 11.1% of children under 18 do not have insurance

Hospitals: Sonoma Valley Hospital (49 beds)

Safety: Violent crime rate: 34.8 per 10,000 population; Property crime rate: 194.3 per 10,000 population

Newspapers: Sonoma Index Tribune (weekly circulation 10200); Sonoma Valley Sun (weekly circulation 15000)

Transportation: Commute: 80.4% car, 0.6% public transportation, 7.5% walk, 8.3% work from home; Median travel time to work: 25.5 minutes

Additional Information Contacts

City of Sonoma . . . . (707) 938-3681
http://www.sonomacity.org

TEMELEC (CDP). Covers a land area of 1.588 square miles and a water area of 0 square miles. Located at 38.26° N. Lat; 122.50° W. Long. Elevation is 98 feet.

Population: 1,441; Growth (since 2000): -7.4%; Density: 907.4 persons per square mile; Race: 95.5% White, 0.3% Black/African American, 2.2% Asian, 0.3% American Indian/Alaska Native, 0.3% Native Hawaiian/Other Pacific Islander, 1.1% Two or more races, 4.7% Hispanic of any race; Average household size: 1.50; Median age: 71.5; Age under 18: 0.8%; Age 65 and over: 68.8%; Males per 100 females: 63.9

Housing: Homeownership rate: 86.7%; Homeowner vacancy rate: 3.9%; Rental vacancy rate: 6.5%

THE SEA RANCH (unincorporated postal area)

ZCTA: 95497

Covers a land area of 16.155 square miles and a water area of 0.086 square miles. Located at 38.74° N. Lat; 123.48° W. Long..

Population: 1,305; Growth (since 2000): 73.8%; Density: 80.8 persons per square mile; Race: 93.5% White, 1.1% Black/African American, 0.8% Asian, 0.2% American Indian/Alaska Native, 0.0% Native Hawaiian/Other Pacific Islander, 1.5% Two or more races, 9.0% Hispanic of any race; Average household size: 1.89; Median age: 63.7; Age under 18: 8.0%; Age 65 and over: 45.6%; Males per 100 females: 91.6

Housing: Homeownership rate: 85.7%; Homeowner vacancy rate: 3.4%; Rental vacancy rate: 38.8%

TIMBER COVE (CDP). Covers a land area of 5.651 square miles and a water area of 0 square miles. Located at 38.54° N. Lat; 123.26° W. Long.

Population: 164; Growth (since 2000): n/a; Density: 29.0 persons per square mile; Race: 92.7% White, 0.6% Black/African American, 3.7% Asian, 0.6% American Indian/Alaska Native, 0.0% Native Hawaiian/Other Pacific Islander, 2.4% Two or more races, 5.5% Hispanic of any race; Average household size: 1.93; Median age: 55.4; Age under 18: 13.4%; Age 65 and over: 20.1%; Males per 100 females: 127.8

Housing: Homeownership rate: 61.2%; Homeowner vacancy rate: 5.4%; Rental vacancy rate: 19.5%

VALLEY FORD (CDP). Covers a land area of 2.642 square miles and a water area of 0 square miles. Located at 38.32° N. Lat; 122.91° W. Long. Elevation is 49 feet.

Population: 147; Growth (since 2000): n/a; Density: 55.6 persons per square mile; Race: 71.4% White, 0.7% Black/African American, 0.0% Asian, 0.0% American Indian/Alaska Native, 0.0% Native Hawaiian/Other Pacific Islander, 5.4% Two or more races, 35.4% Hispanic of any race; Average household size: 2.58; Median age: 39.5; Age under 18: 23.8%; Age 65 and over: 15.6%; Males per 100 females: 116.2

Housing: Homeownership rate: 47.3%; Homeowner vacancy rate: 0.0%; Rental vacancy rate: 3.1%

VILLA GRANDE (unincorporated postal area)

ZCTA: 95486

Covers a land area of 0.019 square miles and a water area of 0 square miles. Located at 38.47° N. Lat; 123.02° W. Long. Elevation is 52 feet.

Population: 62; Growth (since 2000): n/a; Density: 3,201.2 persons per square mile; Race: 90.3% White, 0.0% Black/African American, 1.6% Asian, 0.0% American Indian/Alaska Native, 0.0% Native Hawaiian/Other Pacific Islander, 8.1% Two or more races, 4.8% Hispanic of any race; Average household size: 1.59; Median age: 56.0; Age under 18: 1.6%; Age 65 and over: 22.6%; Males per 100 females: 67.6

Housing: Homeownership rate: 66.6%; Homeowner vacancy rate: 0.0%; Rental vacancy rate: 0.0%

WINDSOR (town). Covers a land area of 7.268 square miles and a water area of 0.025 square miles. Located at 38.54° N. Lat; 122.81° W. Long. Elevation is 118 feet.

Population: 26,801; Growth (since 2000): 17.8%; Density: 3,687.5 persons per square mile; Race: 73.9% White, 0.8% Black/African American, 3.0% Asian, 2.2% American Indian/Alaska Native, 0.2% Native Hawaiian/Other Pacific Islander, 4.7% Two or more races, 31.8% Hispanic of any race; Average household size: 2.98; Median age: 37.0; Age under 18: 28.0%; Age 65 and over: 10.9%; Males per 100 females: 96.6; Marriage status: 26.1% never married, 57.3% now married, 1.4% separated, 5.9% widowed, 10.7% divorced; Foreign born: 14.0%; Speak English only: 76.1%; With disability: 9.2%; Veterans: 9.2%; Ancestry: 15.2% German, 13.4% Irish, 11.6% English, 10.1% Italian, 4.4% American

Employment: 16.8% management, business, and financial, 5.7% computer, engineering, and science, 8.8% education, legal, community service, arts, and media, 6.2% healthcare practitioners, 19.2% service, 24.4% sales and office, 10.0% natural resources, construction, and maintenance, 8.8% production, transportation, and material moving
Income: Per capita: $31,921; Median household: $81,098; Average household: $92,683; Households with income of $100,000 or more: 37.5%; Poverty rate: 3.3%
Educational Attainment: High school diploma or higher: 87.5%; Bachelor's degree or higher: 28.6%; Graduate/professional degree or higher: 8.3%

School District(s)

Windsor Unified (KG-12)
2012-13 Enrollment: 5,617 . . . . (707) 837-7701
Housing: Homeownership rate: 75.8%; Median home value: $379,600; Median year structure built: 1990; Homeowner vacancy rate: 1.6%; Median gross rent: $1,681 per month; Rental vacancy rate: 2.7%
Health Insurance: 91.8% have insurance; 80.3% have private insurance; 20.9% have public insurance; 8.2% do not have insurance; 3.0% of children under 18 do not have insurance
Safety: Violent crime rate: 38.5 per 10,000 population; Property crime rate: 98.7 per 10,000 population
Transportation: Commute: 90.1% car, 1.0% public transportation, 2.0% walk, 5.9% work from home; Median travel time to work: 23.5 minutes
Additional Information Contacts
Town of Windsor . . . . (707) 838-1000
http://www.ci.windsor.ca.us

Stanislaus County

Located in central California, in the San Joaquin Valley; bounded on the west by the Coast Ranges; watered by the San Joaquin, Tuolumne, and Stanislaus Rivers. Covers a land area of 1,494.827 square miles, a water area of 19.860 square miles, and is located in the Pacific Time Zone at 37.56° N. Lat., 121.00° W. Long. The county was founded in 1854. County seat is Modesto.

Stanislaus County is part of the Modesto, CA Metropolitan Statistical Area. The entire metro area includes: Stanislaus County, CA

Weather Station: Modesto — Elevation: 90 feet

	Jan	Feb	Mar	Apr	May	Jun	Jul	Aug	Sep	Oct	Nov	Dec
High	55	62	68	74	82	89	94	93	88	78	65	55
Low	39	43	46	49	54	59	63	62	58	52	44	39
Precip	2.6	2.4	2.1	0.9	0.6	0.1	0.0	0.0	0.3	0.7	1.3	2.0
Snow	na	na	na	na	na	na	na	na	na	na	na	na

High and Low temperatures in degrees Fahrenheit; Precipitation and Snow in inches

Weather Station: Newman — Elevation: 89 feet

	Jan	Feb	Mar	Apr	May	Jun	Jul	Aug	Sep	Oct	Nov	Dec
High	56	63	70	77	85	93	97	95	91	82	67	57
Low	38	40	43	46	52	57	61	60	56	49	42	37
Precip	2.6	2.3	1.7	0.6	0.4	0.1	0.0	0.0	0.3	0.6	1.2	1.7
Snow	0.0	0.0	0.0	0.0	0.0	0.0	0.0	0.0	0.0	0.0	0.0	0.0

High and Low temperatures in degrees Fahrenheit; Precipitation and Snow in inches

Population: 514,453; Growth (since 2000): 15.1%; Density: 344.2 persons per square mile; Race: 65.6% White, 2.9% Black/African American, 5.1% Asian, 1.1% American Indian/Alaska Native, 0.7% Native Hawaiian/Other Pacific Islander, 5.4% two or more races, 41.9% Hispanic of any race; Average household size: 3.08; Median age: 32.9; Age under 18: 28.6%; Age 65 and over: 10.7%; Males per 100 females: 97.9; Marriage status: 33.0% never married, 51.4% now married, 2.2% separated, 5.1% widowed, 10.5% divorced; Foreign born: 20.5%; Speak English only: 59.3%; With disability: 13.1%; Veterans: 6.8%; Ancestry: 9.7% German, 7.6% Irish, 6.0% English, 4.5% Portuguese, 3.9% Italian
Religion: Six largest groups: 20.9% Catholicism, 3.9% Pentecostal, 3.6% Non-denominational Protestant, 2.9% Baptist, 2.7% Latter-day Saints, 1.2% Methodist/Pietist
Economy: Unemployment rate: 10.0%; Leading industries: 16.4% retail trade; 12.8% health care and social assistance; 9.7% accommodation and food services; Farms: 4,143 totaling 768,046 acres; Company size: 5 employ 1,000 or more persons, 11 employs 500 to 999 persons, 161 employs 100 to 499 persons, 8,230 employ less than 100 persons; Business ownership: 9,393 women-owned, 820 Black-owned, 5,082 Hispanic-owned, 2,707 Asian-owned
Employment: 10.3% management, business, and financial, 2.7% computer, engineering, and science, 9.3% education, legal, community service, arts, and media, 4.3% healthcare practitioners, 18.1% service, 24.4% sales and office, 13.9% natural resources, construction, and maintenance, 16.9% production, transportation, and material moving
Income: Per capita: $21,663; Median household: $49,297; Average household: $65,123; Households with income of $100,000 or more: 19.2%; Poverty rate: 20.3%
Educational Attainment: High school diploma or higher: 76.4%; Bachelor's degree or higher: 16.4%; Graduate/professional degree or higher: 5.3%
Housing: Homeownership rate: 60.2%; Median home value: $172,900; Median year structure built: 1980; Homeowner vacancy rate: 2.7%; Median gross rent: $992 per month; Rental vacancy rate: 8.4%
Vital Statistics: Birth rate: 147.7 per 10,000 population; Death rate: 70.0 per 10,000 population; Age-adjusted cancer mortality rate: 165.8 deaths per 100,000 population
Health Insurance: 82.2% have insurance; 55.5% have private insurance; 35.4% have public insurance; 17.8% do not have insurance; 6.5% of children under 18 do not have insurance
Health Care: Physicians: 16.5 per 10,000 population; Hospital beds: 26.7 per 10,000 population; Hospital admissions: 1,052.6 per 10,000 population
Air Quality Index: 44.9% good, 39.7% moderate, 12.3% unhealthy for sensitive individuals, 3.0% unhealthy (percent of days)
Transportation: Commute: 91.2% car, 1.0% public transportation, 1.8% walk, 4.2% work from home; Median travel time to work: 26.6 minutes
Presidential Election: 49.2% Obama, 48.4% Romney (2012)
National and State Parks: Adamsville State Historic Landmark; Caswell Memorial State Park; Henry W. Coe State Wilderness; Turlock Lake State Recreation Area
Additional Information Contacts
Stanislaus Government . . . . (209) 525-4494
http://www.co.stanislaus.ca.us

Stanislaus County Communities

AIRPORT (CDP). Covers a land area of 0.586 square miles and a water area of 0.011 square miles. Located at 37.63° N. Lat; 120.98° W. Long.
Population: 1,964; Growth (since 2000): n/a; Density: 3,351.8 persons per square mile; Race: 56.4% White, 2.1% Black/African American, 3.4% Asian, 2.4% American Indian/Alaska Native, 0.2% Native Hawaiian/Other Pacific Islander, 6.9% Two or more races, 63.6% Hispanic of any race; Average household size: 3.79; Median age: 29.7; Age under 18: 31.1%; Age 65 and over: 6.2%; Males per 100 females: 105.0
Housing: Homeownership rate: 33.7%; Homeowner vacancy rate: 1.1%; Rental vacancy rate: 12.1%

BRET HARTE (CDP). Covers a land area of 0.549 square miles and a water area of 0 square miles. Located at 37.60° N. Lat; 121.00° W. Long.
Population: 5,152; Growth (since 2000): -0.2%; Density: 9,388.7 persons per square mile; Race: 47.4% White, 1.0% Black/African American, 0.8% Asian, 1.0% American Indian/Alaska Native, 0.9% Native Hawaiian/Other Pacific Islander, 3.8% Two or more races, 82.9% Hispanic of any race; Average household size: 4.35; Median age: 25.5; Age under 18: 35.9%; Age 65 and over: 5.6%; Males per 100 females: 109.4; Marriage status: 39.6% never married, 53.5% now married, 1.5% separated, 2.7% widowed, 4.2% divorced; Foreign born: 48.7%; Speak English only: 10.1%; With disability: 14.8%; Veterans: 2.2%; Ancestry: 1.8% American, 1.5% Portuguese, 1.3% Arab, 1.0% German, 0.8% Irish
Employment: 2.8% management, business, and financial, 0.0% computer, engineering, and science, 1.1% education, legal, community service, arts, and media, 0.0% healthcare practitioners, 27.9% service, 12.8% sales and office, 31.7% natural resources, construction, and maintenance, 23.7% production, transportation, and material moving
Income: Per capita: $9,612; Median household: $29,750; Average household: $37,126; Households with income of $100,000 or more: 4.0%; Poverty rate: 34.3%
Educational Attainment: High school diploma or higher: 31.4%; Bachelor's degree or higher: 1.0%; Graduate/professional degree or higher: 0.4%
Housing: Homeownership rate: 46.8%; Median home value: $57,000; Median year structure built: 1958; Homeowner vacancy rate: 1.9%; Median gross rent: $996 per month; Rental vacancy rate: 6.9%

Health Insurance: 77.2% have insurance; 26.9% have private insurance; 52.7% have public insurance; 22.8% do not have insurance; 4.6% of children under 18 do not have insurance

Transportation: Commute: 92.1% car, 1.6% public transportation, 0.6% walk, 3.5% work from home; Median travel time to work: 28.7 minutes

BYSTROM (CDP). Covers a land area of 0.707 square miles and a water area of 0.020 square miles. Located at 37.62° N. Lat; 120.98° W. Long. Elevation is 89 feet.

Population: 4,008; Growth (since 2000): -11.3%; Density: 5,667.4 persons per square mile; Race: 50.0% White, 2.0% Black/African American, 2.3% Asian, 1.5% American Indian/Alaska Native, 0.4% Native Hawaiian/Other Pacific Islander, 4.3% Two or more races, 76.2% Hispanic of any race; Average household size: 3.71; Median age: 28.3; Age under 18: 33.3%; Age 65 and over: 6.9%; Males per 100 females: 110.0; Marriage status: 33.7% never married, 47.0% now married, 4.7% separated, 5.1% widowed, 14.2% divorced; Foreign born: 36.5%; Speak English only: 22.8%; With disability: 14.7%; Veterans: 4.5%; Ancestry: 2.9% German, 2.9% Portuguese, 2.2% Irish, 1.3% American, 0.7% Italian

Employment: 3.0% management, business, and financial, 0.0% computer, engineering, and science, 0.8% education, legal, community service, arts, and media, 2.3% healthcare practitioners, 15.4% service, 20.3% sales and office, 24.7% natural resources, construction, and maintenance, 33.5% production, transportation, and material moving

Income: Per capita: $10,940; Median household: $23,750; Average household: $32,735; Households with income of $100,000 or more: 2.2%; Poverty rate: 31.7%

Educational Attainment: High school diploma or higher: 40.3%; Bachelor's degree or higher: 2.4%; Graduate/professional degree or higher: 0.3%

Housing: Homeownership rate: 49.4%; Median home value: $74,000; Median year structure built: 1969; Homeowner vacancy rate: 0.2%; Median gross rent: $779 per month; Rental vacancy rate: 8.9%

Health Insurance: 73.3% have insurance; 33.0% have private insurance; 44.6% have public insurance; 26.7% do not have insurance; 8.7% of children under 18 do not have insurance

Transportation: Commute: 86.9% car, 0.0% public transportation, 2.4% walk, 10.7% work from home; Median travel time to work: 23.0 minutes

CERES (city). Covers a land area of 8.011 square miles and a water area of 0.008 square miles. Located at 37.60° N. Lat; 120.95° W. Long. Elevation is 92 feet.

History: Ceres grew as the center of an agricultural area producing dates, figs, peaches, apricots and pears.

Population: 45,417; Growth (since 2000): 31.2%; Density: 5,669.1 persons per square mile; Race: 57.7% White, 2.6% Black/African American, 6.8% Asian, 1.3% American Indian/Alaska Native, 0.8% Native Hawaiian/Other Pacific Islander, 5.5% Two or more races, 56.0% Hispanic of any race; Average household size: 3.55; Median age: 29.4; Age under 18: 32.2%; Age 65 and over: 7.7%; Males per 100 females: 97.9; Marriage status: 35.3% never married, 50.4% now married, 2.2% separated, 4.5% widowed, 9.8% divorced; Foreign born: 26.7%; Speak English only: 47.0%; With disability: 13.1%; Veterans: 5.8%; Ancestry: 7.4% German, 5.8% Irish, 4.4% English, 3.8% American, 2.7% Italian

Employment: 6.4% management, business, and financial, 1.8% computer, engineering, and science, 6.0% education, legal, community service, arts, and media, 2.8% healthcare practitioners, 20.0% service, 22.3% sales and office, 16.9% natural resources, construction, and maintenance, 23.8% production, transportation, and material moving

Income: Per capita: $19,051; Median household: $47,306; Average household: $62,927; Households with income of $100,000 or more: 14.4%; Poverty rate: 20.5%

Educational Attainment: High school diploma or higher: 66.9%; Bachelor's degree or higher: 10.3%; Graduate/professional degree or higher: 2.3%

School District(s)

Ceres Unified (KG-12)
2012-13 Enrollment: 12,839 . . . . (209) 556-1500

Housing: Homeownership rate: 63.1%; Median home value: $157,100; Median year structure built: 1985; Homeowner vacancy rate: 2.5%; Median gross rent: $954 per month; Rental vacancy rate: 8.2%

Health Insurance: 82.5% have insurance; 51.6% have private insurance; 38.2% have public insurance; 17.5% do not have insurance; 4.6% of children under 18 do not have insurance

Safety: Violent crime rate: 29.0 per 10,000 population; Property crime rate: 374.9 per 10,000 population

Newspapers: Ceres Courier (weekly circulation 19000)

Transportation: Commute: 91.9% car, 1.5% public transportation, 1.3% walk, 3.5% work from home; Median travel time to work: 27.7 minutes

Additional Information Contacts

City of Ceres . . . . (209) 538-5700
http://www.ci.ceres.ca.us

COWAN (CDP). Covers a land area of 0.156 square miles and a water area of 0 square miles. Located at 37.56° N. Lat; 120.99° W. Long.

Population: 318; Growth (since 2000): n/a; Density: 2,033.5 persons per square mile; Race: 86.2% White, 0.0% Black/African American, 0.0% Asian, 0.6% American Indian/Alaska Native, 0.0% Native Hawaiian/Other Pacific Islander, 3.1% Two or more races, 50.6% Hispanic of any race; Average household size: 3.38; Median age: 37.0; Age under 18: 27.0%; Age 65 and over: 11.6%; Males per 100 females: 105.2

Housing: Homeownership rate: 78.7%; Homeowner vacancy rate: 1.3%; Rental vacancy rate: 16.7%

CROWS LANDING (CDP). Covers a land area of 3.169 square miles and a water area of 0 square miles. Located at 37.39° N. Lat; 121.08° W. Long. Elevation is 115 feet.

Population: 355; Growth (since 2000): n/a; Density: 112.0 persons per square mile; Race: 45.6% White, 1.4% Black/African American, 0.0% Asian, 0.3% American Indian/Alaska Native, 0.0% Native Hawaiian/Other Pacific Islander, 1.4% Two or more races, 69.9% Hispanic of any race; Average household size: 2.93; Median age: 37.7; Age under 18: 27.9%; Age 65 and over: 15.8%; Males per 100 females: 107.6

School District(s)

Newman-Crows Landing Unified (KG-12)
2012-13 Enrollment: 2,867 . . . . (209) 862-2933

Housing: Homeownership rate: 63.7%; Homeowner vacancy rate: 2.5%; Rental vacancy rate: 6.4%

DEL RIO (CDP). Covers a land area of 1.823 square miles and a water area of 0.253 square miles. Located at 37.75° N. Lat; 121.01° W. Long. Elevation is 128 feet.

Population: 1,270; Growth (since 2000): 8.7%; Density: 696.5 persons per square mile; Race: 80.9% White, 2.0% Black/African American, 11.3% Asian, 0.4% American Indian/Alaska Native, 0.1% Native Hawaiian/Other Pacific Islander, 3.3% Two or more races, 8.4% Hispanic of any race; Average household size: 2.62; Median age: 50.6; Age under 18: 20.0%; Age 65 and over: 19.4%; Males per 100 females: 96.3

Housing: Homeownership rate: 93.6%; Homeowner vacancy rate: 3.0%; Rental vacancy rate: 5.9%

DENAIR (CDP). Covers a land area of 1.981 square miles and a water area of 0 square miles. Located at 37.53° N. Lat; 120.80° W. Long. Elevation is 125 feet.

Population: 4,404; Growth (since 2000): 27.8%; Density: 2,222.9 persons per square mile; Race: 77.8% White, 0.6% Black/African American, 1.0% Asian, 1.2% American Indian/Alaska Native, 0.1% Native Hawaiian/Other Pacific Islander, 3.5% Two or more races, 32.3% Hispanic of any race; Average household size: 3.04; Median age: 34.8; Age under 18: 28.0%; Age 65 and over: 10.9%; Males per 100 females: 96.8; Marriage status: 34.0% never married, 52.2% now married, 1.4% separated, 3.6% widowed, 10.2% divorced; Foreign born: 13.5%; Speak English only: 67.9%; With disability: 7.8%; Veterans: 7.8%; Ancestry: 19.0% German, 15.7% Irish, 13.8% Portuguese, 10.2% English, 4.3% French

Employment: 6.9% management, business, and financial, 3.5% computer, engineering, and science, 11.3% education, legal, community service, arts, and media, 4.8% healthcare practitioners, 17.1% service, 23.7% sales and office, 16.1% natural resources, construction, and maintenance, 16.6% production, transportation, and material moving

Income: Per capita: $24,239; Median household: $64,028; Average household: $75,454; Households with income of $100,000 or more: 24.8%; Poverty rate: 22.1%

Educational Attainment: High school diploma or higher: 76.6%; Bachelor's degree or higher: 22.4%; Graduate/professional degree or higher: 4.2%

School District(s)

Denair Unified (KG-12)
2012-13 Enrollment: 1,524 . . . . (209) 632-7514

Gratton Elementary (KG-08)
2012-13 Enrollment: 130 . . . . (209) 632-0505

Housing: Homeownership rate: 77.7%; Median home value: $171,000; Median year structure built: 1978; Homeowner vacancy rate: 2.1%; Median gross rent: $916 per month; Rental vacancy rate: 5.2%

Health Insurance: 83.0% have insurance; 63.3% have private insurance; 26.1% have public insurance; 17.0% do not have insurance; 2.4% of children under 18 do not have insurance

Transportation: Commute: 90.3% car, 0.0% public transportation, 1.9% walk, 5.9% work from home; Median travel time to work: 26.8 minutes; Amtrak: Train service available.

DIABLO GRANDE (CDP). Covers a land area of 5.113 square miles and a water area of <.001 square miles. Located at 37.40° N. Lat; 121.28° W. Long. Elevation is 1,020 feet.

Population: 826; Growth (since 2000): n/a; Density: 161.5 persons per square mile; Race: 61.7% White, 9.3% Black/African American, 8.5% Asian, 0.4% American Indian/Alaska Native, 0.7% Native Hawaiian/Other Pacific Islander, 10.0% Two or more races, 30.8% Hispanic of any race; Average household size: 2.69; Median age: 37.9; Age under 18: 26.3%; Age 65 and over: 7.7%; Males per 100 females: 110.7

Housing: Homeownership rate: 78.5%; Homeowner vacancy rate: 10.6%; Rental vacancy rate: 16.0%

EAST OAKDALE (CDP). Covers a land area of 4.771 square miles and a water area of 0.442 square miles. Located at 37.78° N. Lat; 120.81° W. Long. Elevation is 144 feet.

Population: 2,762; Growth (since 2000): 0.7%; Density: 578.9 persons per square mile; Race: 91.6% White, 0.3% Black/African American, 2.2% Asian, 0.7% American Indian/Alaska Native, 0.2% Native Hawaiian/Other Pacific Islander, 2.3% Two or more races, 10.3% Hispanic of any race; Average household size: 2.62; Median age: 50.0; Age under 18: 20.3%; Age 65 and over: 21.1%; Males per 100 females: 94.5; Marriage status: 19.3% never married, 68.2% now married, 0.7% separated, 4.8% widowed, 7.7% divorced; Foreign born: 6.4%; Speak English only: 80.5%; With disability: 9.3%; Veterans: 13.0%; Ancestry: 14.8% German, 12.3% Irish, 11.8% Italian, 9.6% English, 8.1% American

Employment: 20.1% management, business, and financial, 7.5% computer, engineering, and science, 8.9% education, legal, community service, arts, and media, 8.9% healthcare practitioners, 6.7% service, 24.6% sales and office, 9.7% natural resources, construction, and maintenance, 13.6% production, transportation, and material moving

Income: Per capita: $44,573; Median household: $94,226; Average household: $115,171; Households with income of $100,000 or more: 45.0%; Poverty rate: 1.8%

Educational Attainment: High school diploma or higher: 95.0%; Bachelor's degree or higher: 30.9%; Graduate/professional degree or higher: 14.4%

Housing: Homeownership rate: 93.2%; Median home value: $460,600; Median year structure built: 1992; Homeowner vacancy rate: 1.8%; Median gross rent: $890 per month; Rental vacancy rate: 5.3%

Health Insurance: 91.0% have insurance; 85.3% have private insurance; 22.6% have public insurance; 9.0% do not have insurance; 2.8% of children under 18 do not have insurance

Transportation: Commute: 93.0% car, 0.0% public transportation, 0.0% walk, 6.4% work from home; Median travel time to work: 31.7 minutes

---

EMPIRE (CDP). Covers a land area of 1.563 square miles and a water area of 0 square miles. Located at 37.64° N. Lat; 120.90° W. Long. Elevation is 118 feet.

Population: 4,189; Growth (since 2000): 7.3%; Density: 2,679.5 persons per square mile; Race: 54.3% White, 0.5% Black/African American, 1.4% Asian, 1.3% American Indian/Alaska Native, 0.2% Native Hawaiian/Other Pacific Islander, 6.4% Two or more races, 54.3% Hispanic of any race; Average household size: 3.32; Median age: 32.8; Age under 18: 29.3%; Age 65 and over: 9.9%; Males per 100 females: 100.7; Marriage status: 40.2% never married, 42.9% now married, 1.2% separated, 4.0% widowed, 12.9% divorced; Foreign born: 15.9%; Speak English only: 56.3%; With disability: 17.4%; Veterans: 6.6%; Ancestry: 11.8% Irish, 10.6% German, 5.7% American, 5.2% French, 3.1% English

Employment: 5.7% management, business, and financial, 1.5% computer, engineering, and science, 7.1% education, legal, community service, arts, and media, 2.4% healthcare practitioners, 24.9% service, 14.0% sales and office, 12.1% natural resources, construction, and maintenance, 32.3% production, transportation, and material moving

Income: Per capita: $11,770; Median household: $30,359; Average household: $36,253; Households with income of $100,000 or more: 1.5%; Poverty rate: 36.7%

Educational Attainment: High school diploma or higher: 66.1%; Bachelor's degree or higher: 5.0%; Graduate/professional degree or higher: 0.9%

School District(s)

Empire Union Elementary (KG-08)
2012-13 Enrollment: 2,894 . . . . (209) 521-2800

Sbe - Aspire Vanguard College Preparatory Academy (06-12)
2012-13 Enrollment: 329 . . . . (209) 521-3010

Housing: Homeownership rate: 59.6%; Median home value: $100,200; Median year structure built: 1968; Homeowner vacancy rate: 2.0%; Median gross rent: $996 per month; Rental vacancy rate: 10.5%

Health Insurance: 72.3% have insurance; 38.5% have private insurance; 41.5% have public insurance; 27.7% do not have insurance; 2.8% of children under 18 do not have insurance

Transportation: Commute: 86.1% car, 0.0% public transportation, 4.2% walk, 2.8% work from home; Median travel time to work: 18.8 minutes

---

GRAYSON (CDP). Covers a land area of 2.549 square miles and a water area of 0 square miles. Located at 37.58° N. Lat; 121.18° W. Long. Elevation is 52 feet.

Population: 952; Growth (since 2000): -11.6%; Density: 373.5 persons per square mile; Race: 47.8% White, 1.8% Black/African American, 0.3% Asian, 0.4% American Indian/Alaska Native, 0.0% Native Hawaiian/Other Pacific Islander, 5.9% Two or more races, 86.0% Hispanic of any race; Average household size: 3.81; Median age: 29.0; Age under 18: 33.4%; Age 65 and over: 6.9%; Males per 100 females: 114.4

Housing: Homeownership rate: 64.4%; Homeowner vacancy rate: 4.7%; Rental vacancy rate: 11.9%

HICKMAN (CDP). Covers a land area of 1.076 square miles and a water area of 0.009 square miles. Located at 37.63° N. Lat; 120.75° W. Long. Elevation is 174 feet.

Population: 641; Growth (since 2000): 40.3%; Density: 595.7 persons per square mile; Race: 78.5% White, 0.2% Black/African American, 0.6% Asian, 2.3% American Indian/Alaska Native, 0.0% Native Hawaiian/Other Pacific Islander, 3.1% Two or more races, 28.1% Hispanic of any race; Average household size: 3.32; Median age: 35.2; Age under 18: 27.5%; Age 65 and over: 10.8%; Males per 100 females: 104.1

School District(s)

Hickman Community Charter (KG-08)
2012-13 Enrollment: 1,126 . . . . (209) 874-1816

Housing: Homeownership rate: 73.0%; Homeowner vacancy rate: 2.7%; Rental vacancy rate: 3.7%

HUGHSON (city). Covers a land area of 1.815 square miles and a water area of 0 square miles. Located at 37.60° N. Lat; 120.87° W. Long. Elevation is 125 feet.

Population: 6,640; Growth (since 2000): 66.8%; Density: 3,658.0 persons per square mile; Race: 77.2% White, 0.8% Black/African American, 1.5% Asian, 1.1% American Indian/Alaska Native, 0.2% Native Hawaiian/Other Pacific Islander, 4.4% Two or more races, 43.2% Hispanic of any race; Average household size: 3.20; Median age: 32.8; Age under 18: 30.5%; Age 65 and over: 10.8%; Males per 100 females: 93.8; Marriage status: 32.3% never married, 47.3% now married, 0.9% separated, 8.3% widowed, 12.1% divorced; Foreign born: 18.9%; Speak English only: 63.3%; With disability: 17.3%; Veterans: 7.3%; Ancestry: 17.2% German, 14.2% Irish, 7.1% English, 3.6% Portuguese, 3.2% American

Employment: 7.7% management, business, and financial, 1.2% computer, engineering, and science, 12.5% education, legal, community service, arts, and media, 1.7% healthcare practitioners, 16.2% service, 32.8% sales and office, 11.0% natural resources, construction, and maintenance, 17.0% production, transportation, and material moving

Income: Per capita: $21,327; Median household: $49,209; Average household: $65,297; Households with income of $100,000 or more: 24.8%; Poverty rate: 18.6%

Educational Attainment: High school diploma or higher: 75.6%; Bachelor's degree or higher: 14.8%; Graduate/professional degree or higher: 5.5%

School District(s)

Hughson Unified (KG-12)
2012-13 Enrollment: 2,186 . . . . (209) 883-4428

Keyes Union (KG-12)
2012-13 Enrollment: 1,098 . . . . (209) 669-2921

Housing: Homeownership rate: 67.1%; Median home value: $195,000; Median year structure built: 1990; Homeowner vacancy rate: 1.5%; Median gross rent: $1,170 per month; Rental vacancy rate: 13.1%

Health Insurance: 84.8% have insurance; 60.1% have private insurance; 31.8% have public insurance; 15.2% do not have insurance; 5.7% of children under 18 do not have insurance

Safety: Violent crime rate: 10.1 per 10,000 population; Property crime rate: 213.1 per 10,000 population

Transportation: Commute: 92.9% car, 0.0% public transportation, 0.4% walk, 5.5% work from home; Median travel time to work: 28.5 minutes

Additional Information Contacts

City of Hughson. . . . . (209) 883-4054
http://www.hughson.org

KEYES (CDP). Covers a land area of 2.829 square miles and a water area of 0 square miles. Located at 37.56° N. Lat; 120.91° W. Long. Elevation is 92 feet.

Population: 5,601; Growth (since 2000): 22.4%; Density: 1,980.1 persons per square mile; Race: 55.5% White, 1.3% Black/African American, 3.6% Asian, 1.1% American Indian/Alaska Native, 0.6% Native Hawaiian/Other Pacific Islander, 3.7% Two or more races, 57.7% Hispanic of any race; Average household size: 3.51; Median age: 29.5; Age under 18: 33.5%; Age 65 and over: 8.0%; Males per 100 females: 99.9; Marriage status: 31.8% never married, 50.2% now married, 4.8% separated, 5.6% widowed, 12.4% divorced; Foreign born: 24.6%; Speak English only: 48.7%; With disability: 19.3%; Veterans: 2.3%; Ancestry: 11.0% German, 10.5% Irish, 3.9% Portuguese, 3.5% English, 3.4% Italian

Employment: 7.7% management, business, and financial, 1.0% computer, engineering, and science, 4.2% education, legal, community service, arts, and media, 0.6% healthcare practitioners, 18.0% service, 22.0% sales and office, 21.5% natural resources, construction, and maintenance, 25.0% production, transportation, and material moving

Income: Per capita: $12,229; Median household: $34,967; Average household: $42,611; Households with income of $100,000 or more: 5.9%; Poverty rate: 34.9%

Educational Attainment: High school diploma or higher: 64.8%; Bachelor's degree or higher: 4.5%; Graduate/professional degree or higher: 1.1%

School District(s)

Keyes Union (KG-12)
2012-13 Enrollment: 1,098 . . . . (209) 669-2921

Housing: Homeownership rate: 67.0%; Median home value: $115,700; Median year structure built: 1980; Homeowner vacancy rate: 3.4%; Median gross rent: $937 per month; Rental vacancy rate: 6.9%

Health Insurance: 78.2% have insurance; 36.4% have private insurance; 46.5% have public insurance; 21.8% do not have insurance; 7.6% of children under 18 do not have insurance

Transportation: Commute: 93.9% car, 0.5% public transportation, 0.5% walk, 2.9% work from home; Median travel time to work: 24.9 minutes

MODESTO (city). County seat. Covers a land area of 36.867 square miles and a water area of 0.225 square miles. Located at 37.66° N. Lat; 120.99° W. Long. Elevation is 89 feet.

History: Modesto was laid out by the Southern Pacific Railroad in 1870 and named Modesto by company officials who wanted to name the town for San Francisco banker W.C. Ralston but deferred to his modesty.

Population: 201,165; Growth (since 2000): 6.5%; Density: 5,456.5 persons per square mile; Race: 65.0% White, 4.2% Black/African American, 6.7% Asian, 1.2% American Indian/Alaska Native, 1.0% Native Hawaiian/Other Pacific Islander, 6.3% Two or more races, 35.5% Hispanic of any race; Average household size: 2.87; Median age: 34.2; Age under 18: 26.8%; Age 65 and over: 11.7%; Males per 100 females: 95.0; Marriage status: 33.9% never married, 48.8% now married, 2.5% separated, 5.6% widowed, 11.7% divorced; Foreign born: 16.8%; Speak English only: 64.8%; With disability: 14.5%; Veterans: 7.3%; Ancestry: 10.8% German, 7.8% Irish, 6.4% English, 4.3% Italian, 3.8% American

Employment: 10.1% management, business, and financial, 3.0% computer, engineering, and science, 10.5% education, legal, community service, arts, and media, 5.4% healthcare practitioners, 19.3% service, 26.4% sales and office, 11.3% natural resources, construction, and maintenance, 14.0% production, transportation, and material moving

Income: Per capita: $22,439; Median household: $47,060; Average household: $63,838; Households with income of $100,000 or more: 18.5%; Poverty rate: 20.8%

Educational Attainment: High school diploma or higher: 81.0%; Bachelor's degree or higher: 18.2%; Graduate/professional degree or higher: 6.4%

School District(s)

Ceres Unified (KG-12)
2012-13 Enrollment: 12,839 . . . . (209) 556-1500

Empire Union Elementary (KG-08)
2012-13 Enrollment: 2,894 . . . . (209) 521-2800

Hart-Ransom Union Elementary (KG-08)
2012-13 Enrollment: 1,041 . . . . (209) 523-9996

Modesto City Elementary (KG-08)
2012-13 Enrollment: 15,237 . . . . (209) 576-4011

Modesto City High (09-12)
2012-13 Enrollment: 14,741 . . . . (209) 576-4011

Paradise Elementary (KG-08)
2012-13 Enrollment: 199. . . . . (209) 524-0184

Salida Union Elementary (KG-08)
2012-13 Enrollment: 2,602 . . . . (209) 545-0339

Shiloh Elementary (KG-08)
2012-13 Enrollment: 143. . . . . (209) 522-2261

Stanislaus County Office of Education (KG-12)
2012-13 Enrollment: 2,193 . . . . (209) 238-1700

Stanislaus Union Elementary (KG-08)
2012-13 Enrollment: 3,140 . . . . (209) 529-9546

Sylvan Union Elementary (KG-08)
2012-13 Enrollment: 8,476 . . . . (209) 574-5000

Yosemite Rop
2012-13 Enrollment: n/a . . . . (209) 525-5093

Two-year College(s)

Modesto Junior College (Public)
Fall 2013 Enrollment: 17,084 . . . . (209) 575-6550
2013-14 Tuition: In-state $1,150; Out-of-state $6,046

Vocational/Technical School(s)

Adrian's College of Beauty Modesto (Private, For-profit)
Fall 2013 Enrollment: 275. . . . . (209) 526-2040
2013-14 Tuition: $15,085

California Beauty School (Private, For-profit)
Fall 2013 Enrollment: 114. . . . . (209) 524-5184
2013-14 Tuition: $15,180

Computer Tutor Business and Technical Institute (Private, For-profit)
Fall 2013 Enrollment: 121. . . . . (209) 545-5200
2013-14 Tuition: $8,280

SICE Paul Mitchell Partner School (Private, For-profit)
Fall 2013 Enrollment: 73. . . . . (209) 577-0644
2013-14 Tuition: $15,240

Toni & Guy Hairdressing Academy-Modesto (Private, For-profit)
Fall 2013 Enrollment: 47. . . . . (209) 521-1000
2013-14 Tuition: $16,000

Housing: Homeownership rate: 57.1%; Median home value: $167,100; Median year structure built: 1977; Homeowner vacancy rate: 2.8%; Median gross rent: $1,012 per month; Rental vacancy rate: 9.1%

Health Insurance: 82.5% have insurance; 54.9% have private insurance; 37.3% have public insurance; 17.5% do not have insurance; 7.9% of children under 18 do not have insurance

Hospitals: Doctors Medical Center (456 beds); Memorial Medical Center (112 beds); Stanislaus Surgical Hospital

Safety: Violent crime rate: 83.4 per 10,000 population; Property crime rate: 489.1 per 10,000 population

Newspapers: Modesto Bee (daily circulation 79600)

Transportation: Commute: 91.2% car, 1.7% public transportation, 1.4% walk, 3.6% work from home; Median travel time to work: 25.2 minutes; Amtrak: Train service available.

Airports: Modesto City County-Harry Sham Field (primary service/non-hub)

Additional Information Contacts

City of Modesto . . . . (209) 577-5200
http://www.ci.modesto.ca.us

MONTEREY PARK TRACT (CDP). Covers a land area of 0.047 square miles and a water area of 0 square miles. Located at 37.53° N. Lat; 121.01° W. Long.

Population: 133; Growth (since 2000): n/a; Density: 2,814.6 persons per square mile; Race: 57.9% White, 12.8% Black/African American, 0.0% Asian, 0.0% American Indian/Alaska Native, 0.0% Native Hawaiian/Other Pacific Islander, 0.8% Two or more races, 84.2% Hispanic of any race; Average household size: 3.80; Median age: 26.6; Age under 18: 34.6%; Age 65 and over: 9.8%; Males per 100 females: 90.0

Housing: Homeownership rate: 42.8%; Homeowner vacancy rate: 15.8%; Rental vacancy rate: 9.1%

NEWMAN (city). Covers a land area of 2.102 square miles and a water area of 0 square miles. Located at 37.32° N. Lat; 121.02° W. Long. Elevation is 89 feet.

History: Laid out 1887, incorporated 1908.

Population: 10,224; Growth (since 2000): 44.1%; Density: 4,864.2 persons per square mile; Race: 66.6% White, 2.3% Black/African American, 1.9% Asian, 1.0% American Indian/Alaska Native, 0.4% Native Hawaiian/Other Pacific Islander, 5.4% Two or more races, 61.6% Hispanic of any race; Average household size: 3.38; Median age: 30.7; Age under 18: 32.4%; Age 65 and over: 8.5%; Males per 100 females: 97.9; Marriage status: 34.1% never married, 54.4% now married, 3.3% separated, 2.3% widowed, 9.2% divorced; Foreign born: 23.4%; Speak English only: 46.6%; With disability: 9.6%; Veterans: 8.1%; Ancestry: 10.4% Irish, 9.1% Portuguese, 4.6% German, 3.0% English, 1.8% Italian

Employment: 3.8% management, business, and financial, 3.1% computer, engineering, and science, 4.4% education, legal, community service, arts, and media, 2.6% healthcare practitioners, 25.1% service, 22.5% sales and office, 12.5% natural resources, construction, and maintenance, 25.9% production, transportation, and material moving

Income: Per capita: $16,702; Median household: $48,121; Average household: $55,589; Households with income of $100,000 or more: 16.7%; Poverty rate: 22.5%

Educational Attainment: High school diploma or higher: 72.6%; Bachelor's degree or higher: 11.5%; Graduate/professional degree or higher: 2.2%

School District(s)

Newman-Crows Landing Unified (KG-12)
2012-13 Enrollment: 2,867 . . . . (209) 862-2933

Housing: Homeownership rate: 66.6%; Median home value: $133,600; Median year structure built: 1994; Homeowner vacancy rate: 5.9%; Median gross rent: $961 per month; Rental vacancy rate: 6.9%

Health Insurance: 74.0% have insurance; 47.6% have private insurance; 31.8% have public insurance; 26.0% do not have insurance; 10.0% of children under 18 do not have insurance

Safety: Violent crime rate: 33.7 per 10,000 population; Property crime rate: 185.2 per 10,000 population

Newspapers: Gustine Press Standard (weekly circulation 1500); West Side Index (weekly circulation 2100)

Transportation: Commute: 90.4% car, 0.0% public transportation, 4.7% walk, 4.3% work from home; Median travel time to work: 33.2 minutes

Additional Information Contacts

City of Newman . . . . (209) 862-3725
http://www.cityofnewman.com

OAKDALE (city). Covers a land area of 6.045 square miles and a water area of 0.050 square miles. Located at 37.76° N. Lat; 120.85° W. Long. Elevation is 157 feet.

History: Oakdale was founded in 1871 on a site covered with oak trees. Dairying became the principal industry.

Population: 20,675; Growth (since 2000): 33.4%; Density: 3,420.4 persons per square mile; Race: 80.1% White, 0.8% Black/African American, 2.2% Asian, 1.0% American Indian/Alaska Native, 0.2% Native Hawaiian/Other Pacific Islander, 4.1% Two or more races, 26.1% Hispanic of any race; Average household size: 2.81; Median age: 34.9; Age under 18: 27.9%; Age 65 and over: 12.3%; Males per 100 females: 95.4; Marriage status: 28.6% never married, 54.0% now married, 1.8% separated, 5.5% widowed, 11.9% divorced; Foreign born: 10.7%; Speak English only: 80.3%; With disability: 11.1%; Veterans: 9.4%; Ancestry: 12.7% German, 12.6% Irish, 9.0% English, 7.1% American, 5.9% Italian

Employment: 13.1% management, business, and financial, 4.2% computer, engineering, and science, 9.3% education, legal, community service, arts, and media, 3.2% healthcare practitioners, 16.4% service, 23.0% sales and office, 14.4% natural resources, construction, and maintenance, 16.4% production, transportation, and material moving

Income: Per capita: $25,213; Median household: $56,610; Average household: $71,325; Households with income of $100,000 or more: 24.2%; Poverty rate: 16.1%

Educational Attainment: High school diploma or higher: 84.7%; Bachelor's degree or higher: 14.6%; Graduate/professional degree or higher: 5.5%

School District(s)

Oakdale Joint Unified (KG-12)
2012-13 Enrollment: 5,295 . . . . (209) 848-4884

Housing: Homeownership rate: 61.1%; Median home value: $199,500; Median year structure built: 1986; Homeowner vacancy rate: 2.7%; Median gross rent: $1,083 per month; Rental vacancy rate: 7.7%

Health Insurance: 84.4% have insurance; 65.9% have private insurance; 30.6% have public insurance; 15.6% do not have insurance; 3.8% of children under 18 do not have insurance

Hospitals: Oak Valley District Hospital (141 beds)

Safety: Violent crime rate: 23.4 per 10,000 population; Property crime rate: 387.1 per 10,000 population

Newspapers: Escalon Times (weekly circulation 11000); Oakdale Leader (weekly circulation 6000)

Transportation: Commute: 89.9% car, 1.1% public transportation, 2.4% walk, 5.4% work from home; Median travel time to work: 25.3 minutes

Additional Information Contacts

City of Oakdale . . . . (209) 845-3570
http://www.ci.oakdale.ca.us

PARKLAWN (CDP). Covers a land area of 0.166 square miles and a water area of 0 square miles. Located at 37.61° N. Lat; 120.98° W. Long.

Population: 1,337; Growth (since 2000): n/a; Density: 8,045.1 persons per square mile; Race: 50.3% White, 1.8% Black/African American, 0.5% Asian, 1.6% American Indian/Alaska Native, 0.0% Native Hawaiian/Other Pacific Islander, 5.2% Two or more races, 81.5% Hispanic of any race; Average household size: 4.19; Median age: 26.4; Age under 18: 34.2%; Age 65 and over: 6.5%; Males per 100 females: 96.6

Housing: Homeownership rate: 48.9%; Homeowner vacancy rate: 1.3%; Rental vacancy rate: 6.9%

PATTERSON (city). Covers a land area of 5.954 square miles and a water area of 0 square miles. Located at 37.47° N. Lat; 121.14° W. Long. Elevation is 102 feet.

History: Incorporated 1919.

Population: 20,413; Growth (since 2000): 75.9%; Density: 3,428.5 persons per square mile; Race: 49.6% White, 6.3% Black/African American, 5.2% Asian, 1.1% American Indian/Alaska Native, 1.4% Native Hawaiian/Other Pacific Islander, 5.9% Two or more races, 58.6% Hispanic of any race; Average household size: 3.63; Median age: 29.1; Age under 18: 33.8%; Age 65 and over: 6.3%; Males per 100 females: 101.1; Marriage status: 30.0% never married, 57.2% now married, 2.8% separated, 3.4% widowed, 9.4% divorced; Foreign born: 27.0%; Speak English only: 45.0%; With disability: 9.6%; Veterans: 5.5%; Ancestry: 4.9% German, 4.1% Irish, 3.8% English, 3.5% Portuguese, 2.4% Italian

Employment: 12.4% management, business, and financial, 2.8% computer, engineering, and science, 6.8% education, legal, community service, arts, and media, 1.9% healthcare practitioners, 15.4% service, 20.7% sales and office, 20.2% natural resources, construction, and maintenance, 19.9% production, transportation, and material moving

Income: Per capita: $19,530; Median household: $55,016; Average household: $66,426; Households with income of $100,000 or more: 20.3%; Poverty rate: 16.0%

Educational Attainment: High school diploma or higher: 68.1%; Bachelor's degree or higher: 11.6%; Graduate/professional degree or higher: 2.9%

School District(s)

Patterson Joint Unified (KG-12)
2012-13 Enrollment: 5,888 . . . . (209) 895-7700

Housing: Homeownership rate: 67.5%; Median home value: $162,100; Median year structure built: 2000; Homeowner vacancy rate: 4.5%; Median gross rent: $1,246 per month; Rental vacancy rate: 5.7%

Health Insurance: 82.0% have insurance; 55.3% have private insurance; 32.7% have public insurance; 18.0% do not have insurance; 2.7% of children under 18 do not have insurance

Safety: Violent crime rate: 19.8 per 10,000 population; Property crime rate: 304.3 per 10,000 population

Newspapers: Patterson Irrigator (weekly circulation 7500)
Transportation: Commute: 94.5% car, 0.1% public transportation, 1.3% walk, 3.4% work from home; Median travel time to work: 41.0 minutes

Additional Information Contacts

City of Patterson . . . . (209) 895-8000
http://www.ci.patterson.ca.us

RIVERBANK (city). Covers a land area of 4.092 square miles and a water area of 0.024 square miles. Located at 37.73° N. Lat; 120.94° W. Long. Elevation is 141 feet.

History: Incorporated 1922.

Population: 22,678; Growth (since 2000): 43.3%; Density: 5,541.8 persons per square mile; Race: 65.9% White, 2.1% Black/African American, 3.4% Asian, 1.2% American Indian/Alaska Native, 0.4% Native Hawaiian/Other Pacific Islander, 5.2% Two or more races, 52.1% Hispanic of any race; Average household size: 3.42; Median age: 31.0; Age under 18: 31.1%; Age 65 and over: 8.3%; Males per 100 females: 99.3; Marriage status: 34.4% never married, 53.5% now married, 0.8% separated, 3.7% widowed, 8.4% divorced; Foreign born: 21.8%; Speak English only: 53.5%; With disability: 9.7%; Veterans: 6.1%; Ancestry: 7.2% Irish, 6.8% German, 4.6% American, 3.6% Italian, 3.1% English

Employment: 9.8% management, business, and financial, 1.1% computer, engineering, and science, 9.1% education, legal, community service, arts, and media, 4.2% healthcare practitioners, 18.4% service, 26.0% sales and office, 11.6% natural resources, construction, and maintenance, 19.8% production, transportation, and material moving

Income: Per capita: $20,101; Median household: $57,951; Average household: $67,212; Households with income of $100,000 or more: 23.1%; Poverty rate: 16.0%

Educational Attainment: High school diploma or higher: 76.3%; Bachelor's degree or higher: 14.3%; Graduate/professional degree or higher: 3.5%

School District(s)

Riverbank Unified (KG-12)
2012-13 Enrollment: 2,794 . . . . (209) 869-2538
Sylvan Union Elementary (KG-08)
2012-13 Enrollment: 8,476 . . . . (209) 574-5000

Housing: Homeownership rate: 72.3%; Median home value: $172,800; Median year structure built: 1994; Homeowner vacancy rate: 2.8%; Median gross rent: $1,055 per month; Rental vacancy rate: 7.0%

Health Insurance: 84.6% have insurance; 60.5% have private insurance; 31.1% have public insurance; 15.4% do not have insurance; 5.1% of children under 18 do not have insurance

Safety: Violent crime rate: 15.8 per 10,000 population; Property crime rate: 291.8 per 10,000 population

Transportation: Commute: 96.0% car, 0.1% public transportation, 1.3% walk, 1.9% work from home; Median travel time to work: 25.6 minutes

Additional Information Contacts

City of Riverbank . . . . (209) 863-7122
http://www.riverbank.org

RIVERDALE PARK (CDP). Covers a land area of 1.437 square miles and a water area of 0.046 square miles. Located at 37.60° N. Lat; 121.04° W. Long. Elevation is 69 feet.

Population: 1,128; Growth (since 2000): 3.1%; Density: 785.2 persons per square mile; Race: 51.0% White, 0.5% Black/African American, 2.6% Asian, 2.2% American Indian/Alaska Native, 0.0% Native Hawaiian/Other Pacific Islander, 7.0% Two or more races, 62.1% Hispanic of any race; Average household size: 3.78; Median age: 29.6; Age under 18: 32.9%; Age 65 and over: 7.1%; Males per 100 females: 108.5

Housing: Homeownership rate: 58.1%; Homeowner vacancy rate: 1.7%; Rental vacancy rate: 8.1%

ROUSE (CDP). Covers a land area of 0.238 square miles and a water area of 0 square miles. Located at 37.62° N. Lat; 121.01° W. Long.

Population: 2,005; Growth (since 2000): n/a; Density: 8,411.9 persons per square mile; Race: 44.7% White, 5.0% Black/African American, 9.9% Asian, 1.2% American Indian/Alaska Native, 0.6% Native Hawaiian/Other Pacific Islander, 5.7% Two or more races, 63.8% Hispanic of any race; Average household size: 4.15; Median age: 25.9; Age under 18: 34.9%; Age 65 and over: 6.5%; Males per 100 females: 109.7

Housing: Homeownership rate: 34.4%; Homeowner vacancy rate: 2.9%; Rental vacancy rate: 11.6%

SALIDA (CDP). Covers a land area of 5.320 square miles and a water area of 0.251 square miles. Located at 37.72° N. Lat; 121.09° W. Long. Elevation is 69 feet.

History: Salida developed as a shipping center for fruit, alfalfa and grain, and as a center for dove and quail hunting.

Population: 13,722; Growth (since 2000): 9.3%; Density: 2,579.1 persons per square mile; Race: 61.8% White, 3.2% Black/African American, 4.9% Asian, 0.8% American Indian/Alaska Native, 0.6% Native Hawaiian/Other Pacific Islander, 5.9% Two or more races, 46.8% Hispanic of any race; Average household size: 3.47; Median age: 31.2; Age under 18: 32.0%; Age 65 and over: 6.3%; Males per 100 females: 102.6; Marriage status: 34.5% never married, 53.8% now married, 1.3% separated, 3.3% widowed, 8.5% divorced; Foreign born: 19.3%; Speak English only: 64.5%; With disability: 9.8%; Veterans: 7.3%; Ancestry: 6.8% German, 6.6% Irish, 6.5% English, 5.2% Italian, 5.1% Portuguese

Employment: 9.3% management, business, and financial, 1.1% computer, engineering, and science, 8.6% education, legal, community service, arts, and media, 2.5% healthcare practitioners, 15.0% service, 29.8% sales and office, 14.6% natural resources, construction, and maintenance, 19.2% production, transportation, and material moving

Income: Per capita: $23,782; Median household: $70,763; Average household: $81,610; Households with income of $100,000 or more: 25.8%; Poverty rate: 7.3%

Educational Attainment: High school diploma or higher: 81.6%; Bachelor's degree or higher: 15.7%; Graduate/professional degree or higher: 3.0%

School District(s)

Salida Union Elementary (KG-08)
2012-13 Enrollment: 2,602 . . . . (209) 545-0339

Two-year College(s)

Heald College-Modesto (Private, For-profit)
Fall 2013 Enrollment: 1,091 . . . . (209) 416-3700
2013-14 Tuition: In-state $13,620; Out-of-state $13,620
Kaplan College-Modesto (Private, For-profit)
Fall 2013 Enrollment: 490 . . . . (209) 543-7000
San Joaquin Valley College-Modesto (Private, For-profit)
Fall 2013 Enrollment: 318 . . . . (209) 543-8800
2013-14 Tuition: In-state $15,528; Out-of-state $15,528

Housing: Homeownership rate: 78.2%; Median home value: $178,100; Median year structure built: 1993; Homeowner vacancy rate: 2.8%; Median gross rent: $1,442 per month; Rental vacancy rate: 6.0%

Health Insurance: 87.3% have insurance; 75.2% have private insurance; 16.8% have public insurance; 12.7% do not have insurance; 4.3% of children under 18 do not have insurance

Transportation: Commute: 97.3% car, 0.0% public transportation, 0.4% walk, 1.6% work from home; Median travel time to work: 30.5 minutes

SHACKELFORD (CDP). Covers a land area of 0.672 square miles and a water area of 0.010 square miles. Located at 37.61° N. Lat; 120.99° W. Long. Elevation is 82 feet.

Population: 3,371; Growth (since 2000): -34.8%; Density: 5,019.4 persons per square mile; Race: 46.3% White, 0.8% Black/African American, 1.8% Asian, 1.9% American Indian/Alaska Native, 0.0% Native Hawaiian/Other Pacific Islander, 4.9% Two or more races, 79.6% Hispanic of any race; Average household size: 3.75; Median age: 27.4; Age under 18: 34.9%; Age 65 and over: 6.5%; Males per 100 females: 103.9; Marriage status: 33.5% never married, 56.5% now married, 4.5% separated, 1.2% widowed, 8.9% divorced; Foreign born: 35.0%; Speak English only: 24.3%; With disability: 16.1%; Veterans: 2.7%; Ancestry: 6.2% American, 3.5% Irish, 2.5% German, 1.8% English, 1.4% Italian

Employment: 9.0% management, business, and financial, 0.0% computer, engineering, and science, 3.9% education, legal, community service, arts, and media, 0.0% healthcare practitioners, 29.9% service, 7.6% sales and office, 23.7% natural resources, construction, and maintenance, 25.9% production, transportation, and material moving

Income: Per capita: $6,812; Median household: $19,311; Average household: $23,508; Households with income of $100,000 or more: n/a; Poverty rate: 60.3%

Educational Attainment: High school diploma or higher: 36.0%; Bachelor's degree or higher: 1.6%; Graduate/professional degree or higher: 0.7%

Housing: Homeownership rate: 37.4%; Median home value: $78,500; Median year structure built: 1960; Homeowner vacancy rate: 2.0%; Median gross rent: $780 per month; Rental vacancy rate: 13.4%

Health Insurance: 72.6% have insurance; 17.2% have private insurance; 58.2% have public insurance; 27.4% do not have insurance; 2.2% of children under 18 do not have insurance
Transportation: Commute: 85.0% car, 2.9% public transportation, 5.3% walk, 2.4% work from home; Median travel time to work: 29.6 minutes

TURLOCK (city). Covers a land area of 16.928 square miles and a water area of 0 square miles. Located at 37.51° N. Lat; 120.86° W. Long. Elevation is 102 feet.
History: Turlock developed as a service center for farms dependent on the Turlock Irrigation District launched in 1887.
Population: 68,549; Growth (since 2000): 22.8%; Density: 4,049.4 persons per square mile; Race: 69.8% White, 1.7% Black/African American, 5.6% Asian, 0.9% American Indian/Alaska Native, 0.5% Native Hawaiian/Other Pacific Islander, 5.0% Two or more races, 36.4% Hispanic of any race; Average household size: 2.96; Median age: 32.5; Age under 18: 27.5%; Age 65 and over: 11.7%; Males per 100 females: 94.8; Marriage status: 33.0% never married, 51.7% now married, 1.9% separated, 5.8% widowed, 9.4% divorced; Foreign born: 24.8%; Speak English only: 55.7%; With disability: 11.8%; Veterans: 6.0%; Ancestry: 11.0% German, 7.1% Portuguese, 6.9% Assyrian/Chaldean/Syriac, 6.4% English, 6.1% Irish
Employment: 10.8% management, business, and financial, 3.3% computer, engineering, and science, 11.2% education, legal, community service, arts, and media, 5.3% healthcare practitioners, 16.9% service, 25.3% sales and office, 10.0% natural resources, construction, and maintenance, 17.2% production, transportation, and material moving
Income: Per capita: $23,199; Median household: $53,270; Average household: $66,925; Households with income of $100,000 or more: 21.1%; Poverty rate: 17.2%
Educational Attainment: High school diploma or higher: 80.7%; Bachelor's degree or higher: 22.9%; Graduate/professional degree or higher: 7.8%

School District(s)

Chatom Union (KG-08)
2012-13 Enrollment: 659. . . . . (209) 664-8505
Stanislaus County Office of Education (KG-12)
2012-13 Enrollment: 2,193 . . . . (209) 238-1700
Turlock Unified (KG-12)
2012-13 Enrollment: 13,956 . . . . (209) 667-0633

Four-year College(s)

California State University-Stanislaus (Public)
Fall 2013 Enrollment: 8,917 . . . . (209) 667-3122
2013-14 Tuition: In-state $6,491; Out-of-state $17,651

Vocational/Technical School(s)

Adrian's College of Beauty Turlock (Private, For-profit)
Fall 2013 Enrollment: 157 . . . . (209) 632-2233
2013-14 Tuition: $15,085

Housing: Homeownership rate: 55.4%; Median home value: $196,400; Median year structure built: 1984; Homeowner vacancy rate: 2.6%; Median gross rent: $960 per month; Rental vacancy rate: 9.0%
Health Insurance: 83.6% have insurance; 61.4% have private insurance; 30.6% have public insurance; 16.4% do not have insurance; 6.0% of children under 18 do not have insurance
Hospitals: Emanuel Medical Center (150 beds)
Safety: Violent crime rate: 44.2 per 10,000 population; Property crime rate: 375.3 per 10,000 population
Newspapers: Turlock Journal (weekly circulation 6000)
Transportation: Commute: 92.4% car, 0.4% public transportation, 1.8% walk, 4.1% work from home; Median travel time to work: 22.5 minutes; Amtrak: Train service available.

Additional Information Contacts

City of Turlock . . . . (209) 668-5540
http://www.ci.turlock.ca.us

VALLEY HOME (CDP). Covers a land area of 1.025 square miles and a water area of 0 square miles. Located at 37.83° N. Lat; 120.92° W. Long. Elevation is 154 feet.
Population: 228; Growth (since 2000): n/a; Density: 222.4 persons per square mile; Race: 81.6% White, 0.9% Black/African American, 0.0% Asian, 1.3% American Indian/Alaska Native, 0.0% Native Hawaiian/Other Pacific Islander, 4.4% Two or more races, 14.9% Hispanic of any race; Average household size: 2.92; Median age: 40.0; Age under 18: 22.4%; Age 65 and over: 10.1%; Males per 100 females: 90.0

School District(s)

Valley Home Joint Elementary (KG-08)
2012-13 Enrollment: 166. . . . . (209) 847-0117

Housing: Homeownership rate: 64.1%; Homeowner vacancy rate: 5.7%; Rental vacancy rate: 3.4%

VERNALIS (unincorporated postal area)

ZCTA: 95385

Covers a land area of 24.839 square miles and a water area of 0.119 square miles. Located at 37.61° N. Lat; 121.25° W. Long..
Population: 429; Growth (since 2000): 63.7%; Density: 17.3 persons per square mile; Race: 68.8% White, 0.7% Black/African American, 1.6% Asian, 0.9% American Indian/Alaska Native, 0.2% Native Hawaiian/Other Pacific Islander, 4.2% Two or more races, 38.9% Hispanic of any race; Average household size: 2.51; Median age: 44.1; Age under 18: 19.6%; Age 65 and over: 10.5%; Males per 100 females: 127.0
Housing: Homeownership rate: 50.3%; Homeowner vacancy rate: 1.1%; Rental vacancy rate: 3.4%

WATERFORD (city). Covers a land area of 2.328 square miles and a water area of 0.041 square miles. Located at 37.64° N. Lat; 120.75° W. Long. Elevation is 171 feet.
Population: 8,456; Growth (since 2000): 22.1%; Density: 3,632.1 persons per square mile; Race: 71.0% White, 0.9% Black/African American, 1.5% Asian, 1.3% American Indian/Alaska Native, 0.1% Native Hawaiian/Other Pacific Islander, 4.6% Two or more races, 42.3% Hispanic of any race; Average household size: 3.43; Median age: 29.6; Age under 18: 32.9%; Age 65 and over: 7.2%; Males per 100 females: 103.1; Marriage status: 32.4% never married, 51.2% now married, 1.2% separated, 4.1% widowed, 12.3% divorced; Foreign born: 19.0%; Speak English only: 66.0%; With disability: 14.8%; Veterans: 6.9%; Ancestry: 8.0% German, 6.9% Irish, 5.9% American, 4.9% English, 4.7% Italian
Employment: 7.6% management, business, and financial, 0.7% computer, engineering, and science, 7.6% education, legal, community service, arts, and media, 3.8% healthcare practitioners, 24.3% service, 25.3% sales and office, 21.0% natural resources, construction, and maintenance, 9.7% production, transportation, and material moving
Income: Per capita: $16,409; Median household: $52,808; Average household: $57,062; Households with income of $100,000 or more: 9.8%; Poverty rate: 23.3%
Educational Attainment: High school diploma or higher: 66.0%; Bachelor's degree or higher: 8.5%; Graduate/professional degree or higher: 2.7%

School District(s)

Roberts Ferry Union Elementary (KG-08)
2012-13 Enrollment: 159. . . . . (209) 874-2331
Waterford Unified (KG-12)
2012-13 Enrollment: 3,817 . . . . (209) 874-1809

Housing: Homeownership rate: 66.2%; Median home value: $138,700; Median year structure built: 1992; Homeowner vacancy rate: 2.5%; Median gross rent: $902 per month; Rental vacancy rate: 7.1%
Health Insurance: 83.3% have insurance; 56.4% have private insurance; 33.9% have public insurance; 16.7% do not have insurance; 3.9% of children under 18 do not have insurance
Safety: Violent crime rate: 33.8 per 10,000 population; Property crime rate: 260.8 per 10,000 population
Transportation: Commute: 92.8% car, 0.2% public transportation, 2.0% walk, 4.2% work from home; Median travel time to work: 31.2 minutes

Additional Information Contacts

City of Waterford . . . . (209) 874-2328
http://www.cityofwaterford.org

WEST MODESTO (CDP). Covers a land area of 1.986 square miles and a water area of 0.046 square miles. Located at 37.62° N. Lat; 121.04° W. Long.
Population: 5,682; Growth (since 2000): -6.8%; Density: 2,861.1 persons per square mile; Race: 53.2% White, 2.4% Black/African American, 4.6% Asian, 1.5% American Indian/Alaska Native, 0.1% Native Hawaiian/Other Pacific Islander, 5.0% Two or more races, 62.1% Hispanic of any race; Average household size: 3.55; Median age: 30.2; Age under 18: 30.9%; Age 65 and over: 8.1%; Males per 100 females: 103.4; Marriage status: 40.9% never married, 40.3% now married, 1.8% separated, 7.0% widowed, 11.9% divorced; Foreign born: 28.5%; Speak English only: 39.4%; With disability: 15.6%; Veterans: 3.7%; Ancestry: 6.6% Irish, 6.5% Portuguese, 5.6% German, 3.8% English, 2.8% American

Employment: 2.2% management, business, and financial, 0.0% computer, engineering, and science, 6.1% education, legal, community service, arts, and media, 0.1% healthcare practitioners, 28.6% service, 18.9% sales and office, 23.5% natural resources, construction, and maintenance, 20.7% production, transportation, and material moving

Income: Per capita: $13,705; Median household: $30,333; Average household: $46,853; Households with income of $100,000 or more: 12.1%; Poverty rate: 38.2%

Educational Attainment: High school diploma or higher: 48.2%; Bachelor's degree or higher: 5.8%; Graduate/professional degree or higher: 1.4%

Housing: Homeownership rate: 49.7%; Median home value: $87,500; Median year structure built: 1953; Homeowner vacancy rate: 3.5%; Median gross rent: $896 per month; Rental vacancy rate: 7.0%

Health Insurance: 74.7% have insurance; 22.8% have private insurance; 58.0% have public insurance; 25.3% do not have insurance; 8.6% of children under 18 do not have insurance

Transportation: Commute: 86.2% car, 2.6% public transportation, 3.0% walk, 1.9% work from home; Median travel time to work: 34.9 minutes

WESTLEY (CDP). Covers a land area of 1.743 square miles and a water area of 0 square miles. Located at 37.55° N. Lat; 121.21° W. Long. Elevation is 89 feet.

Population: 603; Growth (since 2000): -19.3%; Density: 345.9 persons per square mile; Race: 35.2% White, 0.0% Black/African American, 0.2% Asian, 0.8% American Indian/Alaska Native, 0.0% Native Hawaiian/Other Pacific Islander, 2.8% Two or more races, 96.0% Hispanic of any race; Average household size: 4.03; Median age: 25.9; Age under 18: 40.1%; Age 65 and over: 6.6%; Males per 100 females: 102.3

School District(s)

Patterson Joint Unified (KG-12)
2012-13 Enrollment: 5,888 . . . . (209) 895-7700

Housing: Homeownership rate: 21.5%; Homeowner vacancy rate: 0.0%; Rental vacancy rate: 4.9%

Sutter County

Located in north central California, in the Sacramento Valley; bounded on the west by the Sacramento River, and on the east by the Feather River. Covers a land area of 602.410 square miles, a water area of 6.080 square miles, and is located in the Pacific Time Zone at 39.04° N. Lat., 121.70° W. Long. The county was founded in 1850. County seat is Yuba City.

Sutter County is part of the Yuba City, CA Metropolitan Statistical Area. The entire metro area includes: Sutter County, CA; Yuba County, CA

Population: 94,737; Growth (since 2000): 20.0%; Density: 157.3 persons per square mile; Race: 61.0% White, 2.0% Black/African American, 14.4% Asian, 1.4% American Indian/Alaska Native, 0.3% Native Hawaiian/Other Pacific Islander, 5.6% two or more races, 28.8% Hispanic of any race; Average household size: 2.98; Median age: 34.5; Age under 18: 27.6%; Age 65 and over: 12.7%; Males per 100 females: 98.5; Marriage status: 28.2% never married, 55.6% now married, 2.3% separated, 6.1% widowed, 10.1% divorced; Foreign born: 22.7%; Speak English only: 63.0%; With disability: 13.6%; Veterans: 9.8%; Ancestry: 13.6% German, 9.7% Irish, 6.9% English, 4.7% American, 3.2% Italian

Religion: Six largest groups: 9.7% Catholicism, 6.9% Holiness, 3.5% Latter-day Saints, 2.7% Non-denominational Protestant, 2.4% Pentecostal, 1.7% Baptist

Economy: Unemployment rate: 10.9%; Leading industries: 16.8% retail trade; 14.5% health care and social assistance; 9.8% construction; Farms: 1,358 totaling 375,174 acres; Company size: 0 employ 1,000 or more persons, 2 employ 500 to 999 persons, 22 employ 100 to 499 persons, 1,682 employ less than 100 persons; Business ownership: 1,867 women-owned, n/a Black-owned, n/a Hispanic-owned, n/a Asian-owned

Employment: 12.0% management, business, and financial, 3.3% computer, engineering, and science, 8.2% education, legal, community service, arts, and media, 4.8% healthcare practitioners, 19.3% service, 24.6% sales and office, 17.0% natural resources, construction, and maintenance, 10.8% production, transportation, and material moving

Income: Per capita: $23,602; Median household: $50,408; Average household: $68,744; Households with income of $100,000 or more: 20.1%; Poverty rate: 16.7%

Educational Attainment: High school diploma or higher: 78.3%; Bachelor's degree or higher: 18.7%; Graduate/professional degree or higher: 5.4%

Housing: Homeownership rate: 61.1%; Median home value: $188,500; Median year structure built: 1978; Homeowner vacancy rate: 2.1%; Median gross rent: $889 per month; Rental vacancy rate: 6.8%

Vital Statistics: Birth rate: 137.5 per 10,000 population; Death rate: 74.1 per 10,000 population; Age-adjusted cancer mortality rate: 156.9 deaths per 100,000 population

Health Insurance: 81.1% have insurance; 53.6% have private insurance; 37.8% have public insurance; 18.9% do not have insurance; 9.4% of children under 18 do not have insurance

Health Care: Physicians: 20.0 per 10,000 population; Hospital beds: 0.0 per 10,000 population; Hospital admissions: 0.0 per 10,000 population

Air Quality Index: 71.8% good, 28.2% moderate, 0.0% unhealthy for sensitive individuals, 0.0% unhealthy (percent of days)

Transportation: Commute: 91.4% car, 1.3% public transportation, 1.8% walk, 3.9% work from home; Median travel time to work: 27.4 minutes

Presidential Election: 38.1% Obama, 59.9% Romney (2012)

National and State Parks: Sutter Buttes State Park; Sutter National Wildlife Refuge

Additional Information Contacts

Sutter Government . . . . (530) 822-7106
http://www.co.sutter.ca.us

Sutter County Communities

EAST NICOLAUS (CDP). Covers a land area of 4.589 square miles and a water area of 0 square miles. Located at 38.91° N. Lat; 121.54° W. Long. Elevation is 43 feet.

Population: 225; Growth (since 2000): n/a; Density: 49.0 persons per square mile; Race: 70.7% White, 0.0% Black/African American, 8.4% Asian, 0.4% American Indian/Alaska Native, 0.0% Native Hawaiian/Other Pacific Islander, 2.2% Two or more races, 21.8% Hispanic of any race; Average household size: 2.56; Median age: 47.4; Age under 18: 21.3%; Age 65 and over: 21.8%; Males per 100 females: 112.3

School District(s)

Marcum-Illinois Union Elementary (KG-12)
2012-13 Enrollment: 2,299 . . . . (530) 656-2407

Housing: Homeownership rate: 76.1%; Homeowner vacancy rate: 0.0%; Rental vacancy rate: 22.2%

LIVE OAK (city). Covers a land area of 1.869 square miles and a water area of 0 square miles. Located at 39.27° N. Lat; 121.67° W. Long. Elevation is 79 feet.

History: Incorporated 1947.

Population: 8,392; Growth (since 2000): 34.7%; Density: 4,491.3 persons per square mile; Race: 53.5% White, 1.6% Black/African American, 11.7% Asian, 1.5% American Indian/Alaska Native, 0.2% Native Hawaiian/Other Pacific Islander, 5.5% Two or more races, 48.8% Hispanic of any race; Average household size: 3.42; Median age: 31.7; Age under 18: 30.6%; Age 65 and over: 10.7%; Males per 100 females: 89.9; Marriage status: 32.2% never married, 52.0% now married, 3.0% separated, 7.4% widowed, 8.5% divorced; Foreign born: 33.0%; Speak English only: 45.3%; With disability: 14.9%; Veterans: 6.5%; Ancestry: 7.0% German, 5.2% American, 4.6% Irish, 2.9% English, 2.2% French

Employment: 7.6% management, business, and financial, 3.1% computer, engineering, and science, 8.1% education, legal, community service, arts, and media, 2.9% healthcare practitioners, 19.3% service, 14.4% sales and office, 26.7% natural resources, construction, and maintenance, 17.9% production, transportation, and material moving

Income: Per capita: $16,885; Median household: $43,717; Average household: $54,789; Households with income of $100,000 or more: 11.5%; Poverty rate: 19.2%

Educational Attainment: High school diploma or higher: 63.6%; Bachelor's degree or higher: 12.1%; Graduate/professional degree or higher: 2.8%

School District(s)

Live Oak Unified (KG-12)
2012-13 Enrollment: 1,740 . . . . (530) 695-5400
Nuestro Elementary (KG-12)
2012-13 Enrollment: 885. . . . . (530) 822-5100

Housing: Homeownership rate: 65.8%; Median home value: $154,500; Median year structure built: 1981; Homeowner vacancy rate: 2.6%; Median gross rent: $884 per month; Rental vacancy rate: 8.2%

Health Insurance: 67.8% have insurance; 39.1% have private insurance; 35.4% have public insurance; 32.2% do not have insurance; 23.0% of children under 18 do not have insurance

Transportation: Commute: 95.3% car, 0.8% public transportation, 1.1% walk, 2.5% work from home; Median travel time to work: 32.5 minutes

Additional Information Contacts

City of Live Oak . . . . (530) 695-2112
http://www.liveoakcity.org

MERIDIAN (CDP). Covers a land area of 5.296 square miles and a water area of 0 square miles. Located at 39.14° N. Lat; 121.91° W. Long. Elevation is 49 feet.

Population: 358; Growth (since 2000): n/a; Density: 67.6 persons per square mile; Race: 74.9% White, 0.6% Black/African American, 0.0% Asian, 2.0% American Indian/Alaska Native, 0.0% Native Hawaiian/Other Pacific Islander, 6.4% Two or more races, 23.7% Hispanic of any race; Average household size: 2.45; Median age: 45.7; Age under 18: 20.1%; Age 65 and over: 15.4%; Males per 100 females: 108.1

School District(s)

Meridian Elementary (KG-08)
2012-13 Enrollment: 76 . . . . (530) 696-2604
Winship-Robbins (KG-08)
2012-13 Enrollment: 170 . . . . (530) 696-2451

Housing: Homeownership rate: 67.8%; Homeowner vacancy rate: 2.9%; Rental vacancy rate: 2.1%

NICOLAUS (CDP). Covers a land area of 3.138 square miles and a water area of 0 square miles. Located at 38.90° N. Lat; 121.57° W. Long. Elevation is 36 feet.

Population: 211; Growth (since 2000): n/a; Density: 67.2 persons per square mile; Race: 88.2% White, 0.5% Black/African American, 2.4% Asian, 0.0% American Indian/Alaska Native, 0.0% Native Hawaiian/Other Pacific Islander, 4.3% Two or more races, 6.2% Hispanic of any race; Average household size: 2.25; Median age: 51.1; Age under 18: 16.6%; Age 65 and over: 29.9%; Males per 100 females: 104.9

School District(s)

East Nicolaus Joint Union High (09-12)
2012-13 Enrollment: 345 . . . . (530) 656-2255

Housing: Homeownership rate: 70.6%; Homeowner vacancy rate: 0.0%; Rental vacancy rate: 3.4%

PLEASANT GROVE (unincorporated postal area)

ZCTA: 95668

Covers a land area of 60.608 square miles and a water area of 0.140 square miles. Located at 38.83° N. Lat; 121.50° W. Long. Elevation is 49 feet.

Population: 815; Growth (since 2000): -8.6%; Density: 13.4 persons per square mile; Race: 82.5% White, 0.5% Black/African American, 4.7% Asian, 1.1% American Indian/Alaska Native, 0.0% Native Hawaiian/Other Pacific Islander, 3.8% Two or more races, 14.0% Hispanic of any race; Average household size: 2.78; Median age: 42.0; Age under 18: 24.0%; Age 65 and over: 16.3%; Males per 100 females: 117.3

School District(s)

Pleasant Grove Joint Union (KG-08)
2012-13 Enrollment: 175 . . . . (916) 655-3235

Housing: Homeownership rate: 71.3%; Homeowner vacancy rate: 0.5%; Rental vacancy rate: 2.3%

RIO OSO (CDP). Covers a land area of 6.533 square miles and a water area of 0 square miles. Located at 38.95° N. Lat; 121.53° W. Long. Elevation is 43 feet.

Population: 356; Growth (since 2000): n/a; Density: 54.5 persons per square mile; Race: 77.0% White, 1.4% Black/African American, 7.3% Asian, 2.0% American Indian/Alaska Native, 0.3% Native Hawaiian/Other Pacific Islander, 3.1% Two or more races, 14.9% Hispanic of any race; Average household size: 2.87; Median age: 42.2; Age under 18: 23.9%; Age 65 and over: 15.4%; Males per 100 females: 103.4

School District(s)

Browns Elementary (KG-08)
2012-13 Enrollment: 152 . . . . (530) 633-2523

Housing: Homeownership rate: 76.6%; Homeowner vacancy rate: 2.0%; Rental vacancy rate: 6.5%

ROBBINS (CDP). Covers a land area of 2.594 square miles and a water area of 0.009 square miles. Located at 38.87° N. Lat; 121.71° W. Long. Elevation is 23 feet.

Population: 323; Growth (since 2000): n/a; Density: 124.5 persons per square mile; Race: 64.4% White, 0.0% Black/African American, 1.5% Asian, 2.8% American Indian/Alaska Native, 0.0% Native Hawaiian/Other Pacific Islander, 2.2% Two or more races, 56.0% Hispanic of any race; Average household size: 3.02; Median age: 36.2; Age under 18: 26.6%; Age 65 and over: 8.4%; Males per 100 females: 113.9

School District(s)

Winship-Robbins (KG-08)
2012-13 Enrollment: 170 . . . . (530) 696-2451

Housing: Homeownership rate: 72.0%; Homeowner vacancy rate: 2.5%; Rental vacancy rate: 11.8%

SUTTER (CDP). Covers a land area of 3.036 square miles and a water area of 0 square miles. Located at 39.16° N. Lat; 121.75° W. Long. Elevation is 75 feet.

Population: 2,904; Growth (since 2000): 0.7%; Density: 956.7 persons per square mile; Race: 86.2% White, 0.6% Black/African American, 1.0% Asian, 1.9% American Indian/Alaska Native, 0.0% Native Hawaiian/Other Pacific Islander, 4.8% Two or more races, 14.1% Hispanic of any race; Average household size: 2.84; Median age: 39.1; Age under 18: 27.2%; Age 65 and over: 12.1%; Males per 100 females: 105.1; Marriage status: 24.0% never married, 61.7% now married, 3.5% separated, 5.1% widowed, 9.2% divorced; Foreign born: 3.9%; Speak English only: 95.2%; With disability: 14.4%; Veterans: 10.2%; Ancestry: 16.9% German, 11.8% Irish, 8.2% Italian, 6.4% English, 5.4% Portuguese

Employment: 13.7% management, business, and financial, 6.0% computer, engineering, and science, 10.2% education, legal, community service, arts, and media, 9.1% healthcare practitioners, 7.7% service, 29.4% sales and office, 10.8% natural resources, construction, and maintenance, 13.0% production, transportation, and material moving

Income: Per capita: $29,967; Median household: $62,736; Average household: $79,389; Households with income of $100,000 or more: 26.2%; Poverty rate: 10.6%

Educational Attainment: High school diploma or higher: 93.1%; Bachelor's degree or higher: 16.6%; Graduate/professional degree or higher: 3.0%

School District(s)

Brittan Elementary (KG-08)
2012-13 Enrollment: 455 . . . . (530) 822-5155
Sutter Union High (09-12)
2012-13 Enrollment: 681 . . . . (530) 822-5161

Housing: Homeownership rate: 76.1%; Median home value: $180,600; Median year structure built: 1975; Homeowner vacancy rate: 2.1%; Median gross rent: $928 per month; Rental vacancy rate: 3.9%

Health Insurance: 91.3% have insurance; 70.1% have private insurance; 30.8% have public insurance; 8.7% do not have insurance; 2.7% of children under 18 do not have insurance

Transportation: Commute: 93.7% car, 0.0% public transportation, 3.5% walk, 0.0% work from home; Median travel time to work: 25.3 minutes

TROWBRIDGE (CDP). Covers a land area of 6.747 square miles and a water area of 0 square miles. Located at 38.93° N. Lat; 121.51° W. Long. Elevation is 49 feet.

Population: 226; Growth (since 2000): n/a; Density: 33.5 persons per square mile; Race: 73.9% White, 1.3% Black/African American, 11.1% Asian, 2.2% American Indian/Alaska Native, 0.0% Native Hawaiian/Other Pacific Islander, 4.9% Two or more races, 16.8% Hispanic of any race; Average household size: 2.79; Median age: 43.0; Age under 18: 22.6%; Age 65 and over: 15.0%; Males per 100 females: 101.8

Housing: Homeownership rate: 79.1%; Homeowner vacancy rate: 0.0%; Rental vacancy rate: 0.0%

YUBA CITY (city). County seat. Covers a land area of 14.578 square miles and a water area of 0.078 square miles. Located at 39.13° N. Lat; 121.64° W. Long. Elevation is 59 feet.

History: Yuba City was laid out in 1849 by Samuel Brannan, Pierson B. Reading, and Henry Cheever. The town developed as the center of a peach-growing region, and as the seat of Sutter County.

Population: 64,925; Growth (since 2000): 76.6%; Density: 4,453.5 persons per square mile; Race: 57.6% White, 2.5% Black/African American, 17.2% Asian, 1.4% American Indian/Alaska Native, 0.4% Native Hawaiian/Other Pacific Islander, 5.9% Two or more races, 28.4% Hispanic

of any race; Average household size: 2.99; Median age: 33.0; Age under 18: 28.2%; Age 65 and over: 11.7%; Males per 100 females: 97.9; Marriage status: 28.9% never married, 55.0% now married, 2.1% separated, 5.8% widowed, 10.2% divorced; Foreign born: 24.9%; Speak English only: 59.5%; With disability: 13.1%; Veterans: 9.8%; Ancestry: 12.6% German, 8.9% Irish, 6.7% English, 4.6% American, 2.5% Italian
Employment: 11.6% management, business, and financial, 3.3% computer, engineering, and science, 7.2% education, legal, community service, arts, and media, 4.1% healthcare practitioners, 20.9% service, 27.0% sales and office, 15.0% natural resources, construction, and maintenance, 11.0% production, transportation, and material moving
Income: Per capita: $22,898; Median household: $48,871; Average household: $66,884; Households with income of $100,000 or more: 18.9%; Poverty rate: 17.5%
Educational Attainment: High school diploma or higher: 78.4%; Bachelor's degree or higher: 18.7%; Graduate/professional degree or higher: 5.2%

School District(s)

Franklin Elementary (KG-08)
2012-13 Enrollment: 491 . . . . (530) 822-5151
Sutter County Office of Education (KG-12)
2012-13 Enrollment: 403 . . . . (530) 822-2900
Tri-County Rop
2012-13 Enrollment: n/a . . . . (530) 822-2953
Yuba City Unified (KG-12)
2012-13 Enrollment: 13,298 . . . . (530) 822-5200

Two-year College(s)

Cambridge Junior College-Yuba City (Private, For-profit)
Fall 2013 Enrollment: 167 . . . . (530) 674-9199

Housing: Homeownership rate: 56.9%; Median home value: $185,100; Median year structure built: 1982; Homeowner vacancy rate: 2.3%; Median gross rent: $892 per month; Rental vacancy rate: 7.1%
Health Insurance: 81.1% have insurance; 52.6% have private insurance; 37.9% have public insurance; 18.9% do not have insurance; 8.0% of children under 18 do not have insurance
Hospitals: Sutter Surgical Hospital - North Valley
Safety: Violent crime rate: 26.7 per 10,000 population; Property crime rate: 304.0 per 10,000 population
Transportation: Commute: 92.4% car, 1.7% public transportation, 1.5% walk, 2.9% work from home; Median travel time to work: 26.9 minutes
Additional Information Contacts
City of Yuba City . . . . (530) 822-4609
http://www.yubacity.net

Tehama County

Located in northern California; drained by the Sacramento River; includes part of the Klamath, Coast Range, and Sierra Nevada Mountains. Covers a land area of 2,949.708 square miles, a water area of 12.462 square miles, and is located in the Pacific Time Zone at 40.13° N. Lat., 122.23° W. Long. The county was founded in 1856. County seat is Red Bluff.

Tehama County is part of the Red Bluff, CA Micropolitan Statistical Area. The entire metro area includes: Tehama County, CA

Weather Station: Mineral — Elevation: 4,874 feet

	Jan	Feb	Mar	Apr	May	Jun	Jul	Aug	Sep	Oct	Nov	Dec
High	42	44	48	53	63	72	81	81	74	63	48	41
Low	22	23	26	29	34	39	43	41	37	31	27	23
Precip	8.9	8.9	7.9	4.2	3.2	1.4	0.2	0.2	1.2	3.4	7.0	9.7
Snow	29.6	30.8	28.6	13.3	1.8	0.1	0.0	0.0	0.1	1.7	8.5	23.2

High and Low temperatures in degrees Fahrenheit; Precipitation and Snow in inches

Weather Station: Red Bluff Municipal Arpt — Elevation: 349 feet

	Jan	Feb	Mar	Apr	May	Jun	Jul	Aug	Sep	Oct	Nov	Dec
High	56	61	66	72	82	91	98	96	91	79	63	55
Low	38	41	44	47	54	61	65	63	59	51	42	38
Precip	4.4	4.0	3.2	1.5	1.1	0.5	0.1	0.1	0.6	1.3	2.9	4.3
Snow	na	na	na	na	na	na	na	na	na	na	na	na

High and Low temperatures in degrees Fahrenheit; Precipitation and Snow in inches

Population: 63,463; Growth (since 2000): 13.2%; Density: 21.5 persons per square mile; Race: 81.5% White, 0.6% Black/African American, 1.0% Asian, 2.6% American Indian/Alaska Native, 0.1% Native Hawaiian/Other Pacific Islander, 4.3% two or more races, 21.9% Hispanic of any race; Average household size: 2.63; Median age: 39.5; Age under 18: 25.5%; Age 65 and over: 15.9%; Males per 100 females: 99.2; Marriage status: 26.1% never married, 54.5% now married, 2.6% separated, 7.0% widowed, 12.4% divorced; Foreign born: 8.9%; Speak English only: 81.2%; With disability: 18.2%; Veterans: 11.8%; Ancestry: 17.1% German, 12.7% Irish, 10.4% English, 7.9% American, 3.8% Italian
Religion: Six largest groups: 17.7% Catholicism, 3.3% Latter-day Saints, 2.9% Pentecostal, 1.5% Baptist, 0.9% Holiness, 0.8% Methodist/Pietist
Economy: Unemployment rate: 8.0%; Leading industries: 15.7% retail trade; 14.4% health care and social assistance; 12.4% accommodation and food services; Farms: 1,743 totaling 616,521 acres; Company size: 0 employ 1,000 or more persons, 1 employs 500 to 999 persons, 11 employs 100 to 499 persons, 963 employ less than 100 persons; Business ownership: 1,368 women-owned, n/a Black-owned, n/a Hispanic-owned, n/a Asian-owned
Employment: 12.0% management, business, and financial, 1.5% computer, engineering, and science, 8.7% education, legal, community service, arts, and media, 2.6% healthcare practitioners, 22.5% service, 23.2% sales and office, 14.4% natural resources, construction, and maintenance, 15.0% production, transportation, and material moving
Income: Per capita: $20,439; Median household: $41,924; Average household: $54,024; Households with income of $100,000 or more: 13.3%; Poverty rate: 19.7%
Educational Attainment: High school diploma or higher: 81.1%; Bachelor's degree or higher: 13.5%; Graduate/professional degree or higher: 4.6%
Housing: Homeownership rate: 64.7%; Median home value: $177,100; Median year structure built: 1979; Homeowner vacancy rate: 2.9%; Median gross rent: $821 per month; Rental vacancy rate: 7.5%
Vital Statistics: Birth rate: 114.8 per 10,000 population; Death rate: 91.2 per 10,000 population; Age-adjusted cancer mortality rate: 158.4 deaths per 100,000 population
Health Insurance: 83.1% have insurance; 52.2% have private insurance; 45.5% have public insurance; 16.9% do not have insurance; 9.3% of children under 18 do not have insurance
Health Care: Physicians: 10.1 per 10,000 population; Hospital beds: 10.3 per 10,000 population; Hospital admissions: 518.3 per 10,000 population
Air Quality Index: 78.6% good, 20.9% moderate, 0.5% unhealthy for sensitive individuals, 0.0% unhealthy (percent of days)
Transportation: Commute: 89.0% car, 1.0% public transportation, 2.6% walk, 5.6% work from home; Median travel time to work: 23.3 minutes
Presidential Election: 34.5% Obama, 62.3% Romney (2012)
National and State Parks: Tehama State Wildlife Area; William B. Ide Adobe State Historic Park; Woodson Bridge State Recreation Area; Ides Cove National Recreation Trail
Additional Information Contacts
Tehama Government . . . . (530) 527-4655
http://www.co.tehama.ca.us

Tehama County Communities

BEND (CDP). Covers a land area of 2.918 square miles and a water area of 0.256 square miles. Located at 40.26° N. Lat; 122.21° W. Long. Elevation is 335 feet.
Population: 619; Growth (since 2000): n/a; Density: 212.1 persons per square mile; Race: 92.1% White, 0.6% Black/African American, 0.5% Asian, 2.4% American Indian/Alaska Native, 0.0% Native Hawaiian/Other Pacific Islander, 2.1% Two or more races, 7.8% Hispanic of any race; Average household size: 2.48; Median age: 48.3; Age under 18: 20.2%; Age 65 and over: 22.9%; Males per 100 females: 105.6
Housing: Homeownership rate: 82.4%; Homeowner vacancy rate: 1.4%; Rental vacancy rate: 6.4%

CORNING (city). Covers a land area of 3.550 square miles and a water area of 0 square miles. Located at 39.93° N. Lat; 122.18° W. Long. Elevation is 276 feet.
History: Corning grew as the center of an olive-producing area, with olive oil refining and olive canning as chief industries.
Population: 7,663; Growth (since 2000): 13.7%; Density: 2,158.8 persons per square mile; Race: 71.9% White, 0.6% Black/African American, 1.1% Asian, 2.6% American Indian/Alaska Native, 0.1% Native Hawaiian/Other Pacific Islander, 4.2% Two or more races, 42.7% Hispanic of any race; Average household size: 2.90; Median age: 29.2; Age under 18: 32.4%; Age 65 and over: 10.1%; Males per 100 females: 94.5; Marriage status: 33.0% never married, 48.7% now married, 3.2% separated, 6.1% widowed, 12.1% divorced; Foreign born: 13.4%; Speak English only:

68.4%; With disability: 15.6%; Veterans: 8.1%; Ancestry: 13.0% English, 10.4% German, 6.6% Irish, 6.4% American, 2.7% Scottish

Employment: 9.7% management, business, and financial, 0.4% computer, engineering, and science, 5.3% education, legal, community service, arts, and media, 2.1% healthcare practitioners, 24.4% service, 25.4% sales and office, 22.4% natural resources, construction, and maintenance, 10.2% production, transportation, and material moving

Income: Per capita: $15,496; Median household: $42,590; Average household: $47,718; Households with income of $100,000 or more: 8.4%; Poverty rate: 25.9%

Educational Attainment: High school diploma or higher: 81.1%; Bachelor's degree or higher: 12.4%; Graduate/professional degree or higher: 3.1%

School District(s)

Corning Union Elementary (KG-08)
2012-13 Enrollment: 1,900 . . . . (530) 824-7700
Corning Union High (09-12)
2012-13 Enrollment: 980. . . . . (530) 824-8000
Kirkwood Elementary (KG-08)
2012-13 Enrollment: 97. . . . . (530) 824-7773
Richfield Elementary (KG-08)
2012-13 Enrollment: 249. . . . . (530) 824-3354

Housing: Homeownership rate: 49.5%; Median home value: $157,100; Median year structure built: 1978; Homeowner vacancy rate: 3.1%; Median gross rent: $904 per month; Rental vacancy rate: 8.4%

Health Insurance: 83.3% have insurance; 43.5% have private insurance; 53.0% have public insurance; 16.7% do not have insurance; 8.7% of children under 18 do not have insurance

Safety: Violent crime rate: 61.6 per 10,000 population; Property crime rate: 393.1 per 10,000 population

Newspapers: Corning Observer (weekly circulation 6000)

Transportation: Commute: 87.1% car, 0.0% public transportation, 3.2% walk, 4.3% work from home; Median travel time to work: 18.6 minutes

Additional Information Contacts

City of Corning. . . . . (530) 824-7029
http://www.corning.org

FLOURNOY (CDP). Covers a land area of 5.796 square miles and a water area of 0 square miles. Located at 39.93° N. Lat; 122.45° W. Long. Elevation is 561 feet.

Population: 101; Growth (since 2000): n/a; Density: 17.4 persons per square mile; Race: 89.1% White, 0.0% Black/African American, 3.0% Asian, 1.0% American Indian/Alaska Native, 2.0% Native Hawaiian/Other Pacific Islander, 1.0% Two or more races, 8.9% Hispanic of any race; Average household size: 2.35; Median age: 48.9; Age under 18: 18.8%; Age 65 and over: 19.8%; Males per 100 females: 90.6

School District(s)

Flournoy Union Elementary (KG-08)
2012-13 Enrollment: 33. . . . . (530) 833-5331

Housing: Homeownership rate: 86.1%; Homeowner vacancy rate: 0.0%; Rental vacancy rate: 0.0%

GERBER (CDP). Covers a land area of 0.923 square miles and a water area of 0 square miles. Located at 40.06° N. Lat; 122.15° W. Long. Elevation is 230 feet.

Population: 1,060; Growth (since 2000): n/a; Density: 1,148.5 persons per square mile; Race: 54.2% White, 0.6% Black/African American, 0.8% Asian, 5.2% American Indian/Alaska Native, 0.0% Native Hawaiian/Other Pacific Islander, 4.2% Two or more races, 49.6% Hispanic of any race; Average household size: 2.89; Median age: 34.0; Age under 18: 28.6%; Age 65 and over: 11.1%; Males per 100 females: 105.0

School District(s)

Gerber Union Elementary (KG-08)
2012-13 Enrollment: 381. . . . . (530) 385-1041

Housing: Homeownership rate: 60.5%; Homeowner vacancy rate: 5.5%; Rental vacancy rate: 10.4%

LAKE CALIFORNIA (CDP). Covers a land area of 6.295 square miles and a water area of 0.333 square miles. Located at 40.36° N. Lat; 122.21° W. Long.

Population: 3,054; Growth (since 2000): n/a; Density: 485.1 persons per square mile; Race: 90.1% White, 0.4% Black/African American, 1.0% Asian, 2.7% American Indian/Alaska Native, 0.2% Native Hawaiian/Other Pacific Islander, 3.9% Two or more races, 8.2% Hispanic of any race; Average household size: 2.69; Median age: 36.9; Age under 18: 27.2%; Age 65 and over: 14.2%; Males per 100 females: 100.9; Marriage status: 20.8% never married, 62.1% now married, 5.6% separated, 4.4% widowed, 12.6% divorced; Foreign born: 4.5%; Speak English only: 96.2%; With disability: 19.5%; Veterans: 18.0%; Ancestry: 26.8% German, 13.1% English, 10.9% Irish, 8.7% French, 8.3% American

Employment: 16.1% management, business, and financial, 4.7% computer, engineering, and science, 8.2% education, legal, community service, arts, and media, 3.8% healthcare practitioners, 13.4% service, 45.0% sales and office, 3.7% natural resources, construction, and maintenance, 5.1% production, transportation, and material moving

Income: Per capita: $27,116; Median household: $54,914; Average household: $61,290; Households with income of $100,000 or more: 14.3%; Poverty rate: 8.1%

Educational Attainment: High school diploma or higher: 91.0%; Bachelor's degree or higher: 13.2%; Graduate/professional degree or higher: 3.0%

Housing: Homeownership rate: 72.3%; Median home value: $213,100; Median year structure built: 2001; Homeowner vacancy rate: 4.9%; Median gross rent: $1,138 per month; Rental vacancy rate: 8.1%

Health Insurance: 84.9% have insurance; 64.1% have private insurance; 39.3% have public insurance; 15.1% do not have insurance; 20.0% of children under 18 do not have insurance

Transportation: Commute: 94.0% car, 0.0% public transportation, 0.0% walk, 6.0% work from home; Median travel time to work: 22.5 minutes

---

LAS FLORES (CDP). Covers a land area of 0.358 square miles and a water area of 0 square miles. Located at 40.07° N. Lat; 122.16° W. Long. Elevation is 253 feet.

Population: 187; Growth (since 2000): n/a; Density: 523.0 persons per square mile; Race: 67.9% White, 0.0% Black/African American, 0.0% Asian, 2.7% American Indian/Alaska Native, 0.0% Native Hawaiian/Other Pacific Islander, 7.5% Two or more races, 38.5% Hispanic of any race; Average household size: 2.92; Median age: 33.9; Age under 18: 31.0%; Age 65 and over: 12.8%; Males per 100 females: 120.0

Housing: Homeownership rate: 75.1%; Homeowner vacancy rate: 4.0%; Rental vacancy rate: 5.9%

LOS MOLINOS (CDP). Covers a land area of 2.194 square miles and a water area of 0.023 square miles. Located at 40.03° N. Lat; 122.10° W. Long. Elevation is 223 feet.

History: Los Molinos (Spanish for "the mills") developed as headquarters for small dairy, poultry, and orchard tracts.

Population: 2,037; Growth (since 2000): 4.4%; Density: 928.4 persons per square mile; Race: 77.6% White, 0.0% Black/African American, 0.3% Asian, 1.9% American Indian/Alaska Native, 0.1% Native Hawaiian/Other Pacific Islander, 4.3% Two or more races, 26.4% Hispanic of any race; Average household size: 2.55; Median age: 41.7; Age under 18: 23.7%; Age 65 and over: 17.8%; Males per 100 females: 98.7

School District(s)

Lassen View Union Elementary (KG-08)
2012-13 Enrollment: 308. . . . . (530) 527-5162
Los Molinos Unified (KG-12)
2012-13 Enrollment: 583. . . . . (530) 384-7826

Housing: Homeownership rate: 62.0%; Homeowner vacancy rate: 3.7%; Rental vacancy rate: 17.6%

MANTON (CDP). Covers a land area of 17.696 square miles and a water area of 0.026 square miles. Located at 40.43° N. Lat; 121.85° W. Long. Elevation is 2,008 feet.

Population: 347; Growth (since 2000): -6.7%; Density: 19.6 persons per square mile; Race: 89.9% White, 0.0% Black/African American, 0.3% Asian, 5.8% American Indian/Alaska Native, 0.0% Native Hawaiian/Other Pacific Islander, 2.0% Two or more races, 10.1% Hispanic of any race; Average household size: 2.27; Median age: 53.9; Age under 18: 14.7%; Age 65 and over: 25.1%; Males per 100 females: 110.3

School District(s)

Manton Joint Union Elementary (KG-08)
2012-13 Enrollment: 37. . . . . (530) 474-3167

Housing: Homeownership rate: 84.2%; Homeowner vacancy rate: 0.0%; Rental vacancy rate: 7.4%

MILL CREEK (unincorporated postal area)

ZCTA: 96061

Covers a land area of 41.279 square miles and a water area of 0.105 square miles. Located at 40.34° N. Lat; 121.48° W. Long. Elevation is 4,737 feet.

Population: 36; Growth (since 2000): -53.2%; Density: 0.9 persons per square mile; Race: 94.4% White, 0.0% Black/African American, 0.0% Asian, 5.6% American Indian/Alaska Native, 0.0% Native Hawaiian/Other Pacific Islander, 0.0% Two or more races, 2.8% Hispanic of any race; Average household size: 2.00; Median age: 63.0; Age under 18: 2.8%; Age 65 and over: 47.2%; Males per 100 females: 125.0

Housing: Homeownership rate: 88.9%; Homeowner vacancy rate: 5.9%; Rental vacancy rate: 0.0%

MINERAL (CDP). Covers a land area of 44.365 square miles and a water area of 0.111 square miles. Located at 40.41° N. Lat; 121.58° W. Long. Elevation is 4,918 feet.

History: Mineral developed as a vacation town on the edge of a wide mountain meadow, and as the headquarters of Lassen Volcanic National Park.

Population: 123; Growth (since 2000): -14.0%; Density: 2.8 persons per square mile; Race: 93.5% White, 0.0% Black/African American, 0.8% Asian, 0.8% American Indian/Alaska Native, 0.0% Native Hawaiian/Other Pacific Islander, 4.1% Two or more races, 3.3% Hispanic of any race; Average household size: 1.92; Median age: 50.8; Age under 18: 15.4%; Age 65 and over: 22.8%; Males per 100 females: 105.0

School District(s)

Mineral Elementary (KG-12)
2012-13 Enrollment: 128. . . . . (530) 595-3322

Housing: Homeownership rate: 62.5%; Homeowner vacancy rate: 4.8%; Rental vacancy rate: 4.0%

PASKENTA (CDP). Covers a land area of 1.081 square miles and a water area of 0 square miles. Located at 39.88° N. Lat; 122.55° W. Long. Elevation is 755 feet.

Population: 112; Growth (since 2000): n/a; Density: 103.6 persons per square mile; Race: 84.8% White, 0.0% Black/African American, 0.0% Asian, 0.0% American Indian/Alaska Native, 0.0% Native Hawaiian/Other Pacific Islander, 8.0% Two or more races, 17.0% Hispanic of any race; Average household size: 2.43; Median age: 51.0; Age under 18: 17.0%; Age 65 and over: 21.4%; Males per 100 females: 103.6

School District(s)

Elkins Elementary (KG-08)
2012-13 Enrollment: 13. . . . . (530) 833-5582

Housing: Homeownership rate: 69.6%; Homeowner vacancy rate: 0.0%; Rental vacancy rate: 0.0%

PAYNES CREEK (CDP). Covers a land area of 3.429 square miles and a water area of 0.001 square miles. Located at 40.34° N. Lat; 121.92° W. Long. Elevation is 1,850 feet.

Population: 57; Growth (since 2000): n/a; Density: 16.6 persons per square mile; Race: 89.5% White, 0.0% Black/African American, 0.0% Asian, 3.5% American Indian/Alaska Native, 0.0% Native Hawaiian/Other Pacific Islander, 5.3% Two or more races, 12.3% Hispanic of any race; Average household size: 2.38; Median age: 45.8; Age under 18: 19.3%; Age 65 and over: 24.6%; Males per 100 females: 137.5

School District(s)

Plum Valley Elementary (KG-08)
2012-13 Enrollment: 17. . . . . (530) 597-2248

Housing: Homeownership rate: 75.0%; Homeowner vacancy rate: 0.0%; Rental vacancy rate: 33.3%

PROBERTA (CDP). Covers a land area of 1.431 square miles and a water area of 0 square miles. Located at 40.08° N. Lat; 122.18° W. Long. Elevation is 253 feet.

Population: 267; Growth (since 2000): n/a; Density: 186.5 persons per square mile; Race: 65.2% White, 0.0% Black/African American, 0.4% Asian, 2.6% American Indian/Alaska Native, 0.4% Native Hawaiian/Other Pacific Islander, 3.0% Two or more races, 34.1% Hispanic of any race; Average household size: 2.97; Median age: 33.1; Age under 18: 28.1%; Age 65 and over: 13.5%; Males per 100 females: 103.8

Housing: Homeownership rate: 66.7%; Homeowner vacancy rate: 3.2%; Rental vacancy rate: 11.8%

RANCHO TEHAMA RESERVE (CDP). Covers a land area of 11.639 square miles and a water area of 0.078 square miles. Located at 40.00° N. Lat; 122.43° W. Long. Elevation is 525 feet.

Population: 1,485; Growth (since 2000): 5.6%; Density: 127.6 persons per square mile; Race: 79.5% White, 1.4% Black/African American, 1.4% Asian, 3.5% American Indian/Alaska Native, 0.3% Native Hawaiian/Other Pacific Islander, 6.9% Two or more races, 14.4% Hispanic of any race; Average household size: 2.53; Median age: 48.5; Age under 18: 19.9%; Age 65 and over: 21.4%; Males per 100 females: 100.4

Housing: Homeownership rate: 81.1%; Homeowner vacancy rate: 6.5%; Rental vacancy rate: 6.7%

RED BLUFF (city). County seat. Covers a land area of 7.563 square miles and a water area of 0.114 square miles. Located at 40.17° N. Lat; 122.24° W. Long. Elevation is 305 feet.

History: Red Bluff was established near the old Rancho de la Barranca Colorado, named for the reddish sand and gravel cliff along the Sacramento River. The town was first called Leodocia by the gold-seekers who settled here, who found no gold but rather wealth from wheat fields and vineyards. Paddle wheel steamers from Sacramento visited Red Bluff in the 1850's, delivering supplies for the Trinity mines.

Population: 14,076; Growth (since 2000): 7.1%; Density: 1,861.3 persons per square mile; Race: 80.7% White, 0.9% Black/African American, 1.3% Asian, 3.1% American Indian/Alaska Native, 0.1% Native Hawaiian/Other Pacific Islander, 5.5% Two or more races, 21.6% Hispanic of any race; Average household size: 2.54; Median age: 32.2; Age under 18: 28.1%; Age 65 and over: 13.3%; Males per 100 females: 92.4; Marriage status: 30.6% never married, 47.9% now married, 4.4% separated, 6.4% widowed, 15.2% divorced; Foreign born: 7.3%; Speak English only: 81.4%; With disability: 20.2%; Veterans: 9.6%; Ancestry: 18.0% German, 12.1% Irish, 8.5% English, 6.7% American, 6.0% Italian

Employment: 7.7% management, business, and financial, 2.6% computer, engineering, and science, 9.7% education, legal, community service, arts, and media, 2.6% healthcare practitioners, 24.4% service, 26.2% sales and office, 9.5% natural resources, construction, and maintenance, 17.2% production, transportation, and material moving

Income: Per capita: $16,862; Median household: $32,705; Average household: $44,816; Households with income of $100,000 or more: 7.6%; Poverty rate: 26.5%

Educational Attainment: High school diploma or higher: 80.9%; Bachelor's degree or higher: 9.4%; Graduate/professional degree or higher: 3.6%

School District(s)

Antelope Elementary (KG-08)
2012-13 Enrollment: 607. . . . . (530) 527-1272
Mineral Elementary (KG-12)
2012-13 Enrollment: 128. . . . . (530) 595-3322
Red Bluff Joint Union High (07-12)
2012-13 Enrollment: 1,667 . . . . (530) 529-8700
Red Bluff Union Elementary (KG-08)
2012-13 Enrollment: 2,181 . . . . (530) 527-7200
Reeds Creek Elementary (KG-08)
2012-13 Enrollment: 118. . . . . (530) 527-6006
Tehama County Office of Education (PK-12)
2012-13 Enrollment: 184. . . . . (530) 527-5811
Tehama County Rop
2012-13 Enrollment: n/a . . . . (530) 528-7341

Housing: Homeownership rate: 42.3%; Median home value: $158,100; Median year structure built: 1976; Homeowner vacancy rate: 3.5%; Median gross rent: $737 per month; Rental vacancy rate: 7.3%

Health Insurance: 83.2% have insurance; 45.4% have private insurance; 53.3% have public insurance; 16.8% do not have insurance; 7.5% of children under 18 do not have insurance

Hospitals: Saint Elizabeth Community Hospital (83 beds)

Safety: Violent crime rate: 103.0 per 10,000 population; Property crime rate: 662.0 per 10,000 population

Newspapers: Red Bluff Daily News (daily circulation 6800)

Transportation: Commute: 89.1% car, 2.4% public transportation, 2.9% walk, 3.9% work from home; Median travel time to work: 21.4 minutes; Amtrak: Bus service available.

Airports: Red Bluff Municipal (general aviation)

Additional Information Contacts

City of Red Bluff . . . . (530) 527-2605
http://www.cityofredbluff.org

RICHFIELD (CDP). Covers a land area of 0.560 square miles and a water area of 0 square miles. Located at 39.97° N. Lat; 122.17° W. Long. Elevation is 272 feet.

Population: 306; Growth (since 2000): n/a; Density: 546.6 persons per square mile; Race: 86.3% White, 0.0% Black/African American, 0.0% Asian, 1.3% American Indian/Alaska Native, 0.0% Native Hawaiian/Other Pacific Islander, 1.0% Two or more races, 21.2% Hispanic of any race; Average household size: 2.71; Median age: 40.0; Age under 18: 25.5%; Age 65 and over: 14.7%; Males per 100 females: 117.0

Housing: Homeownership rate: 71.7%; Homeowner vacancy rate: 0.0%; Rental vacancy rate: 8.6%

TEHAMA (city). Covers a land area of 0.794 square miles and a water area of 0 square miles. Located at 40.02° N. Lat; 122.13° W. Long. Elevation is 210 feet.

History: Tehama was settled in 1847 when Robert H. Thomas built an adobe on his Rancho de los Saucos (ranch of the elder trees). Tehama became an early freighting and trading center, and served as the seat of Tehama County until 1857.

Population: 418; Growth (since 2000): -3.2%; Density: 526.3 persons per square mile; Race: 82.8% White, 1.4% Black/African American, 0.2% Asian, 5.5% American Indian/Alaska Native, 0.0% Native Hawaiian/Other Pacific Islander, 3.6% Two or more races, 13.6% Hispanic of any race; Average household size: 2.53; Median age: 44.1; Age under 18: 23.0%; Age 65 and over: 19.6%; Males per 100 females: 101.0

Housing: Homeownership rate: 71.6%; Homeowner vacancy rate: 4.8%; Rental vacancy rate: 11.3%

VINA (CDP). Covers a land area of 1.352 square miles and a water area of 0 square miles. Located at 39.93° N. Lat; 122.05° W. Long. Elevation is 210 feet.

Population: 237; Growth (since 2000): n/a; Density: 175.3 persons per square mile; Race: 82.3% White, 0.4% Black/African American, 0.8% Asian, 3.0% American Indian/Alaska Native, 0.0% Native Hawaiian/Other Pacific Islander, 5.1% Two or more races, 17.7% Hispanic of any race; Average household size: 2.90; Median age: 40.9; Age under 18: 20.7%; Age 65 and over: 21.5%; Males per 100 females: 125.7

School District(s)

Los Molinos Unified (KG-12)
2012-13 Enrollment: 583. . . . . (530) 384-7826

Housing: Homeownership rate: 72.9%; Homeowner vacancy rate: 3.8%; Rental vacancy rate: 9.5%

Trinity County

Located in northern California; drained by the Trinity, Eel, and Mad Rivers; includes parts of the Klamath Mountains, the Coast Ranges, and Trinity, Shasta, and Mendocino National Forests. Covers a land area of 3,179.254 square miles, a water area of 28.343 square miles, and is located in the Pacific Time Zone at 40.65° N. Lat., 123.11° W. Long. The county was founded in 1850. County seat is Weaverville.

Weather Station: Trinity River Hatchery Elevation: 1,859 feet

	Jan	Feb	Mar	Apr	May	Jun	Jul	Aug	Sep	Oct	Nov	Dec
High	48	54	60	66	76	84	93	92	86	74	56	47
Low	32	33	35	37	43	48	53	51	45	39	36	32
Precip	5.4	5.2	4.1	2.1	1.7	0.8	0.2	0.2	0.6	1.7	4.3	6.3
Snow	1.6	1.6	0.8	tr	0.0	0.0	0.0	0.0	0.0	0.0	0.4	1.8

High and Low temperatures in degrees Fahrenheit; Precipitation and Snow in inches

Population: 13,786; Growth (since 2000): 5.9%; Density: 4.3 persons per square mile; Race: 87.3% White, 0.4% Black/African American, 0.7% Asian, 4.8% American Indian/Alaska Native, 0.1% Native Hawaiian/Other Pacific Islander, 5.2% two or more races, 7.0% Hispanic of any race; Average household size: 2.20; Median age: 49.3; Age under 18: 18.3%; Age 65 and over: 20.1%; Males per 100 females: 106.6; Marriage status: 20.3% never married, 52.8% now married, 2.3% separated, 8.2% widowed, 18.7% divorced; Foreign born: 3.4%; Speak English only: 92.8%; With disability: 22.7%; Veterans: 14.8%; Ancestry: 23.7% German, 18.3% Irish, 15.1% English, 5.8% French, 5.1% Italian

Religion: Six largest groups: 2.8% Latter-day Saints, 2.5% Pentecostal, 2.0% Catholicism, 1.7% Non-denominational Protestant, 1.1% Holiness, 1.1% Adventist

Economy: Unemployment rate: 8.3%; Leading industries: 20.0% retail trade; 17.4% accommodation and food services; 14.0% construction; Farms: 247 totaling 175,948 acres; Company size: 0 employ 1,000 or more persons, 0 employ 500 to 999 persons, 2 employ 100 to 499 persons, 263 employ less than 100 persons; Business ownership: n/a women-owned, n/a Black-owned, n/a Hispanic-owned, n/a Asian-owned

Employment: 13.8% management, business, and financial, 3.0% computer, engineering, and science, 11.5% education, legal, community service, arts, and media, 3.5% healthcare practitioners, 24.6% service, 25.4% sales and office, 11.3% natural resources, construction, and maintenance, 6.9% production, transportation, and material moving

Income: Per capita: $22,905; Median household: $36,890; Average household: $51,299; Households with income of $100,000 or more: 12.1%; Poverty rate: 19.2%

Educational Attainment: High school diploma or higher: 91.3%; Bachelor's degree or higher: 21.3%; Graduate/professional degree or higher: 4.9%

Housing: Homeownership rate: 70.4%; Median home value: $257,400; Median year structure built: 1976; Homeowner vacancy rate: 2.6%; Median gross rent: $758 per month; Rental vacancy rate: 6.3%

Vital Statistics: Birth rate: 89.2 per 10,000 population; Death rate: 114.5 per 10,000 population; Age-adjusted cancer mortality rate: 166.3 deaths per 100,000 population

Health Insurance: 78.4% have insurance; 45.3% have private insurance; 47.4% have public insurance; 21.6% do not have insurance; 12.2% of children under 18 do not have insurance

Health Care: Physicians: 5.9 per 10,000 population; Hospital beds: 27.0 per 10,000 population; Hospital admissions: 368.1 per 10,000 population

Air Quality Index: 100.0% good, 0.0% moderate, 0.0% unhealthy for sensitive individuals, 0.0% unhealthy (percent of days)

Transportation: Commute: 84.2% car, 2.1% public transportation, 5.4% walk, 5.4% work from home; Median travel time to work: 18.3 minutes

Presidential Election: 47.1% Obama, 48.2% Romney (2012)

National and State Parks: Ellen Pickett State Forest; Trinity National Forest; Weaverville Joss House State Historic Park

Additional Information Contacts

Trinity Government . . . . (530) 623-1217
http://www.trinitycounty.org

Trinity County Communities

BIG BAR (unincorporated postal area)

ZCTA: 96010

Covers a land area of 402.101 square miles and a water area of 0.003 square miles. Located at 40.91° N. Lat; 123.31° W. Long. Elevation is 1,247 feet.

Population: 239; Growth (since 2000): -5.5%; Density: 0.6 persons per square mile; Race: 82.4% White, 0.8% Black/African American, 0.4% Asian, 5.9% American Indian/Alaska Native, 0.0% Native Hawaiian/Other Pacific Islander, 5.0% Two or more races, 7.9% Hispanic of any race; Average household size: 2.28; Median age: 50.3; Age under 18: 17.6%; Age 65 and over: 22.6%; Males per 100 females: 125.5

School District(s)

Cox Bar Elementary (KG-08)
2012-13 Enrollment: 10. . . . . (530) 623-6316

Housing: Homeownership rate: 72.8%; Homeowner vacancy rate: 0.0%; Rental vacancy rate: 3.4%

BURNT RANCH (CDP). Covers a land area of 13.380 square miles and a water area of 0.001 square miles. Located at 40.81° N. Lat; 123.51° W. Long. Elevation is 1,516 feet.

Population: 281; Growth (since 2000): n/a; Density: 21.0 persons per square mile; Race: 85.8% White, 0.0% Black/African American, 1.4% Asian, 5.3% American Indian/Alaska Native, 0.0% Native Hawaiian/Other Pacific Islander, 7.1% Two or more races, 6.8% Hispanic of any race; Average household size: 2.18; Median age: 52.1; Age under 18: 13.5%; Age 65 and over: 21.0%; Males per 100 females: 124.8

School District(s)

Burnt Ranch Elementary (KG-08)
2012-13 Enrollment: 97. . . . . (530) 629-2543

Housing: Homeownership rate: 82.1%; Homeowner vacancy rate: 0.0%; Rental vacancy rate: 8.0%

COFFEE CREEK (CDP). Covers a land area of 11.520 square miles and a water area of 0.019 square miles. Located at 41.08° N. Lat; 122.72° W. Long. Elevation is 2,520 feet.

Population: 217; Growth (since 2000): n/a; Density: 18.8 persons per square mile; Race: 91.2% White, 0.0% Black/African American, 2.3% Asian, 2.3% American Indian/Alaska Native, 0.0% Native Hawaiian/Other Pacific Islander, 2.8% Two or more races, 7.4% Hispanic of any race; Average household size: 2.19; Median age: 50.2; Age under 18: 14.7%; Age 65 and over: 24.9%; Males per 100 females: 102.8

Housing: Homeownership rate: 78.8%; Homeowner vacancy rate: 1.5%; Rental vacancy rate: 10.0%

DOUGLAS CITY (CDP). Covers a land area of 25.043 square miles and a water area of 0.013 square miles. Located at 40.68° N. Lat; 122.92° W. Long. Elevation is 1,673 feet.

Population: 713; Growth (since 2000): n/a; Density: 28.5 persons per square mile; Race: 89.6% White, 0.0% Black/African American, 1.1% Asian, 3.1% American Indian/Alaska Native, 0.3% Native Hawaiian/Other Pacific Islander, 4.1% Two or more races, 6.6% Hispanic of any race; Average household size: 2.17; Median age: 50.8; Age under 18: 15.3%; Age 65 and over: 21.3%; Males per 100 females: 110.9

School District(s)

Douglas City Elementary (KG-08)
2012-13 Enrollment: 165. . . . . (530) 623-6350

Housing: Homeownership rate: 77.6%; Homeowner vacancy rate: 1.6%; Rental vacancy rate: 15.7%

HAYFORK (CDP). Covers a land area of 72.098 square miles and a water area of 0.022 square miles. Located at 40.58° N. Lat; 123.12° W. Long. Elevation is 2,310 feet.

Population: 2,368; Growth (since 2000): 2.3%; Density: 32.8 persons per square mile; Race: 84.4% White, 0.2% Black/African American, 0.3% Asian, 6.8% American Indian/Alaska Native, 0.1% Native Hawaiian/Other Pacific Islander, 6.5% Two or more races, 8.0% Hispanic of any race; Average household size: 2.27; Median age: 46.9; Age under 18: 19.9%; Age 65 and over: 18.8%; Males per 100 females: 103.8

School District(s)

Mountain Valley Unified (KG-12)
2012-13 Enrollment: 340. . . . . (530) 628-5265

Housing: Homeownership rate: 64.8%; Homeowner vacancy rate: 1.3%; Rental vacancy rate: 3.2%

HYAMPOM (CDP). Covers a land area of 20.273 square miles and a water area of 0 square miles. Located at 40.63° N. Lat; 123.47° W. Long. Elevation is 1,322 feet.

Population: 241; Growth (since 2000): n/a; Density: 11.9 persons per square mile; Race: 82.6% White, 0.0% Black/African American, 0.0% Asian, 8.3% American Indian/Alaska Native, 0.0% Native Hawaiian/Other Pacific Islander, 6.2% Two or more races, 7.9% Hispanic of any race; Average household size: 1.96; Median age: 50.7; Age under 18: 11.2%; Age 65 and over: 17.8%; Males per 100 females: 136.3

School District(s)

Mountain Valley Unified (KG-12)
2012-13 Enrollment: 340. . . . . (530) 628-5265

Housing: Homeownership rate: 64.3%; Homeowner vacancy rate: 3.7%; Rental vacancy rate: 10.2%

JUNCTION CITY (CDP). Covers a land area of 27.904 square miles and a water area of 0.045 square miles. Located at 40.72° N. Lat; 123.05° W. Long. Elevation is 1,604 feet.

Population: 680; Growth (since 2000): n/a; Density: 24.4 persons per square mile; Race: 87.8% White, 0.1% Black/African American, 0.3% Asian, 4.3% American Indian/Alaska Native, 0.0% Native Hawaiian/Other Pacific Islander, 4.6% Two or more races, 7.2% Hispanic of any race; Average household size: 2.25; Median age: 52.3; Age under 18: 16.2%; Age 65 and over: 22.6%; Males per 100 females: 100.6

School District(s)

Junction City Elementary (KG-08)
2012-13 Enrollment: 80. . . . . (530) 623-6381

Housing: Homeownership rate: 80.6%; Homeowner vacancy rate: 2.5%; Rental vacancy rate: 4.6%

LEWISTON (CDP). Covers a land area of 20.009 square miles and a water area of 0 square miles. Located at 40.70° N. Lat; 122.82° W. Long. Elevation is 1,814 feet.

Population: 1,193; Growth (since 2000): -8.6%; Density: 59.6 persons per square mile; Race: 90.0% White, 0.7% Black/African American, 0.5% Asian, 3.1% American Indian/Alaska Native, 0.4% Native Hawaiian/Other Pacific Islander, 3.5% Two or more races, 6.5% Hispanic of any race; Average household size: 2.16; Median age: 51.4; Age under 18: 16.9%; Age 65 and over: 21.5%; Males per 100 females: 102.2

School District(s)

Lewiston Elementary (KG-08)
2012-13 Enrollment: 54. . . . . (530) 778-3984

Housing: Homeownership rate: 73.1%; Homeowner vacancy rate: 3.5%; Rental vacancy rate: 10.2%

MAD RIVER (CDP). Covers a land area of 34.653 square miles and a water area of 0 square miles. Located at 40.43° N. Lat; 123.49° W. Long. Elevation is 2,513 feet.

Population: 420; Growth (since 2000): n/a; Density: 12.1 persons per square mile; Race: 91.2% White, 0.2% Black/African American, 0.2% Asian, 2.6% American Indian/Alaska Native, 0.0% Native Hawaiian/Other Pacific Islander, 4.0% Two or more races, 5.0% Hispanic of any race; Average household size: 2.12; Median age: 50.0; Age under 18: 18.1%; Age 65 and over: 16.0%; Males per 100 females: 117.6

Housing: Homeownership rate: 64.1%; Homeowner vacancy rate: 1.6%; Rental vacancy rate: 10.0%

PLATINA (unincorporated postal area)

ZCTA: 96076

Covers a land area of 207.049 square miles and a water area of 0.024 square miles. Located at 40.39° N. Lat; 122.94° W. Long..

Population: 166; Growth (since 2000): -19.4%; Density: 0.8 persons per square mile; Race: 88.6% White, 0.6% Black/African American, 0.6% Asian, 3.6% American Indian/Alaska Native, 0.6% Native Hawaiian/Other Pacific Islander, 3.6% Two or more races, 9.0% Hispanic of any race; Average household size: 1.84; Median age: 55.3; Age under 18: 11.4%; Age 65 and over: 16.3%; Males per 100 females: 112.8

School District(s)

Igo Ono Platina Union Elementary (KG-08)
2012-13 Enrollment: 78. . . . . (530) 396-2841

Housing: Homeownership rate: 67.5%; Homeowner vacancy rate: 1.7%; Rental vacancy rate: 0.0%

RUTH (CDP). Covers a land area of 38.842 square miles and a water area of 1.678 square miles. Located at 40.29° N. Lat; 123.35° W. Long. Elevation is 2,726 feet.

Population: 195; Growth (since 2000): n/a; Density: 5.0 persons per square mile; Race: 87.2% White, 0.0% Black/African American, 0.5% Asian, 4.6% American Indian/Alaska Native, 0.0% Native Hawaiian/Other Pacific Islander, 7.2% Two or more races, 1.0% Hispanic of any race; Average household size: 1.94; Median age: 54.9; Age under 18: 12.3%; Age 65 and over: 24.1%; Males per 100 females: 97.0

Housing: Homeownership rate: 73.8%; Homeowner vacancy rate: 2.7%; Rental vacancy rate: 3.7%

SALYER (unincorporated postal area)

ZCTA: 95563

Covers a land area of 60.218 square miles and a water area of 0.065 square miles. Located at 40.88° N. Lat; 123.50° W. Long. Elevation is 620 feet.

Population: 652; Growth (since 2000): 0.8%; Density: 10.8 persons per square mile; Race: 81.3% White, 0.0% Black/African American, 0.0% Asian, 12.1% American Indian/Alaska Native, 0.0% Native Hawaiian/Other Pacific Islander, 5.4% Two or more races, 7.8% Hispanic of any race; Average household size: 2.31; Median age: 49.1; Age under 18: 16.6%; Age 65 and over: 17.5%; Males per 100 females: 109.0

Housing: Homeownership rate: 72.3%; Homeowner vacancy rate: 0.5%; Rental vacancy rate: 4.9%

TRINITY CENTER (CDP). Covers a land area of 5.231 square miles and a water area of 0 square miles. Located at 40.98° N. Lat; 122.71° W. Long. Elevation is 2,454 feet.

Population: 267; Growth (since 2000): n/a; Density: 51.0 persons per square mile; Race: 93.3% White, 0.0% Black/African American, 0.4%

Asian, 2.6% American Indian/Alaska Native, 1.1% Native Hawaiian/Other Pacific Islander, 1.9% Two or more races, 4.1% Hispanic of any race; Average household size: 1.95; Median age: 62.0; Age under 18: 9.0%; Age 65 and over: 40.8%; Males per 100 females: 97.8

School District(s)

Coffee Creek Elementary (KG-08)
2012-13 Enrollment: 14. . . . . (530) 266-3344
Trinity Center Elementary (KG-08)
2012-13 Enrollment: 12. . . . . (530) 266-3342

Housing: Homeownership rate: 80.3%; Homeowner vacancy rate: 8.9%; Rental vacancy rate: 0.0%

TRINITY VILLAGE (CDP). Covers a land area of 4.013 square miles and a water area of 0 square miles. Located at 40.88° N. Lat; 123.51° W. Long. Elevation is 689 feet.

Population: 297; Growth (since 2000): n/a; Density: 74.0 persons per square mile; Race: 90.6% White, 0.3% Black/African American, 0.0% Asian, 6.1% American Indian/Alaska Native, 0.0% Native Hawaiian/Other Pacific Islander, 3.0% Two or more races, 1.3% Hispanic of any race; Average household size: 2.17; Median age: 54.0; Age under 18: 12.5%; Age 65 and over: 23.2%; Males per 100 females: 109.2

Housing: Homeownership rate: 78.9%; Homeowner vacancy rate: 7.6%; Rental vacancy rate: 3.3%

WEAVERVILLE (CDP). County seat. Covers a land area of 10.424 square miles and a water area of 0 square miles. Located at 40.75° N. Lat; 122.93° W. Long. Elevation is 2,051 feet.

History: Weaverville, an early mining town, developed as the seat of Trinity County.

Population: 3,600; Growth (since 2000): 1.3%; Density: 345.4 persons per square mile; Race: 87.8% White, 0.3% Black/African American, 1.1% Asian, 4.2% American Indian/Alaska Native, 0.0% Native Hawaiian/Other Pacific Islander, 5.4% Two or more races, 7.1% Hispanic of any race; Average household size: 2.30; Median age: 44.4; Age under 18: 23.4%; Age 65 and over: 18.6%; Males per 100 females: 94.5; Marriage status: 19.0% never married, 42.7% now married, 4.1% separated, 12.0% widowed, 26.3% divorced; Foreign born: 3.7%; Speak English only: 92.1%; With disability: 20.4%; Veterans: 5.8%; Ancestry: 27.1% German, 17.4% English, 14.4% Irish, 7.9% Polish, 7.3% Norwegian

Employment: 10.1% management, business, and financial, 7.4% computer, engineering, and science, 11.1% education, legal, community service, arts, and media, 4.1% healthcare practitioners, 30.6% service, 30.5% sales and office, 1.0% natural resources, construction, and maintenance, 5.2% production, transportation, and material moving

Income: Per capita: $26,584; Median household: $37,898; Average household: $56,617; Households with income of $100,000 or more: 14.8%; Poverty rate: 13.8%

Educational Attainment: High school diploma or higher: 91.9%; Bachelor's degree or higher: 23.1%; Graduate/professional degree or higher: 6.4%

School District(s)

Trinity Alps Unified (KG-12)
2012-13 Enrollment: 732. . . . . (530) 623-6104
Trinity County Office of Education (KG-12)
2012-13 Enrollment: 21. . . . . (530) 623-2861

Housing: Homeownership rate: 60.0%; Median home value: $208,100; Median year structure built: 1975; Homeowner vacancy rate: 2.8%; Median gross rent: $736 per month; Rental vacancy rate: 6.8%

Health Insurance: 78.4% have insurance; 46.5% have private insurance; 44.4% have public insurance; 21.6% do not have insurance; 7.4% of children under 18 do not have insurance

Hospitals: Trinity Hospital

Newspapers: Trinity Journal (weekly circulation 4300)

Transportation: Commute: 81.9% car, 3.9% public transportation, 9.5% walk, 0.0% work from home; Median travel time to work: 10.5 minutes

ZENIA (unincorporated postal area)

ZCTA: 95595

Covers a land area of 244.802 square miles and a water area of 0.028 square miles. Located at 40.11° N. Lat; 123.43° W. Long. Elevation is 2,966 feet.

Population: 262; Growth (since 2000): 3.6%; Density: 1.1 persons per square mile; Race: 82.1% White, 0.0% Black/African American, 0.0% Asian, 7.3% American Indian/Alaska Native, 0.0% Native Hawaiian/Other Pacific Islander, 10.3% Two or more races, 5.0% Hispanic of any race; Average household size: 2.20; Median age: 45.6; Age under 18: 20.2%; Age 65 and over: 13.0%; Males per 100 females: 104.7

Housing: Homeownership rate: 74.0%; Homeowner vacancy rate: 3.3%; Rental vacancy rate: 3.1%

Tulare County

Located in central California, from the San Joaquin Valley to the crest of the Sierra Nevada; drained by the Kaweah, Saint Johns, Tule, and Kern Rivers; includes parts of Inyo and Sequoia National Forests. Covers a land area of 4,824.214 square miles, a water area of 14.437 square miles, and is located in the Pacific Time Zone at 36.23° N. Lat., 118.78° W. Long. The county was founded in 1852. County seat is Visalia.

Tulare County is part of the Visalia-Porterville, CA Metropolitan Statistical Area. The entire metro area includes: Tulare County, CA

Weather Station: Ash Mountain Elevation: 1,708 feet

	Jan	Feb	Mar	Apr	May	Jun	Jul	Aug	Sep	Oct	Nov	Dec
High	59	62	65	71	81	91	99	98	92	81	67	59
Low	37	40	42	46	53	61	67	67	61	52	43	37
Precip	5.1	4.8	4.7	2.2	1.1	0.4	0.1	0.1	0.5	1.4	2.8	3.6
Snow	0.3	0.1	0.1	tr	0.0	0.0	0.0	0.0	0.0	0.0	0.2	0.1

High and Low temperatures in degrees Fahrenheit; Precipitation and Snow in inches

Weather Station: Grant Grove Elevation: 6,599 feet

	Jan	Feb	Mar	Apr	May	Jun	Jul	Aug	Sep	Oct	Nov	Dec
High	44	44	45	50	58	68	76	76	69	60	50	44
Low	27	26	28	31	39	46	53	52	47	40	32	27
Precip	8.3	7.7	7.0	3.5	1.7	0.5	0.2	0.1	0.9	2.3	4.2	6.1
Snow	35.6	38.0	41.7	19.0	4.4	0.4	0.0	0.0	0.2	3.1	12.1	26.7

High and Low temperatures in degrees Fahrenheit; Precipitation and Snow in inches

Weather Station: Lemon Cove Elevation: 513 feet

	Jan	Feb	Mar	Apr	May	Jun	Jul	Aug	Sep	Oct	Nov	Dec
High	57	64	70	76	85	93	98	97	92	81	67	57
Low	38	42	45	48	53	59	64	62	58	50	42	37
Precip	2.9	2.5	2.6	1.3	0.6	0.2	0.0	0.0	0.2	0.7	1.5	1.9
Snow	0.0	0.0	0.0	0.0	0.0	0.0	0.0	0.0	0.0	0.0	0.0	0.0

High and Low temperatures in degrees Fahrenheit; Precipitation and Snow in inches

Weather Station: Lindsay Elevation: 419 feet

	Jan	Feb	Mar	Apr	May	Jun	Jul	Aug	Sep	Oct	Nov	Dec
High	59	65	71	77	86	92	98	97	92	81	67	58
Low	37	39	43	46	52	57	63	61	56	47	40	35
Precip	2.4	2.2	2.2	1.1	0.4	0.1	0.0	0.0	0.2	0.6	1.3	1.6
Snow	0.1	0.0	0.0	0.0	0.0	0.0	0.0	0.0	0.0	0.0	0.0	0.0

High and Low temperatures in degrees Fahrenheit; Precipitation and Snow in inches

Weather Station: Lodgepole Elevation: 6,734 feet

	Jan	Feb	Mar	Apr	May	Jun	Jul	Aug	Sep	Oct	Nov	Dec
High	39	41	45	50	58	68	76	75	69	58	46	38
Low	16	18	22	26	33	39	45	44	38	30	23	17
Precip	8.9	9.0	7.1	3.3	1.5	0.6	0.6	0.3	1.0	2.1	4.5	6.7
Snow	47.4	51.6	47.3	20.5	5.5	0.7	0.0	0.0	0.2	3.4	16.4	36.9

High and Low temperatures in degrees Fahrenheit; Precipitation and Snow in inches

Weather Station: Porterville Elevation: 393 feet

	Jan	Feb	Mar	Apr	May	Jun	Jul	Aug	Sep	Oct	Nov	Dec
High	58	65	71	77	85	93	98	97	92	83	68	59
Low	38	42	46	49	55	61	66	65	60	52	43	37
Precip	2.2	2.0	2.2	0.9	0.4	0.1	0.0	0.0	0.2	0.5	1.2	1.5
Snow	0.0	0.0	0.0	0.0	0.0	0.0	0.0	0.0	0.0	0.0	0.0	0.0

High and Low temperatures in degrees Fahrenheit; Precipitation and Snow in inches

Weather Station: Three Rivers Edison Ph 1 Elevation: 1,140 feet

	Jan	Feb	Mar	Apr	May	Jun	Jul	Aug	Sep	Oct	Nov	Dec
High	59	63	68	75	84	92	99	98	92	81	67	58
Low	36	38	41	45	51	58	65	64	58	49	40	35
Precip	4.8	4.4	4.3	2.0	1.0	0.3	0.1	0.0	0.5	1.1	2.6	3.6
Snow	0.0	0.0	0.0	0.0	0.0	0.0	0.0	0.0	0.0	0.0	0.0	0.0

High and Low temperatures in degrees Fahrenheit; Precipitation and Snow in inches

Weather Station: Visalia Elevation: 325 feet

	Jan	Feb	Mar	Apr	May	Jun	Jul	Aug	Sep	Oct	Nov	Dec
High	55	62	68	74	82	89	94	93	88	78	65	55
Low	39	42	46	49	56	61	66	65	60	52	44	38
Precip	2.1	1.9	1.9	1.0	0.4	0.1	0.0	0.0	0.2	0.6	1.1	1.6
Snow	0.1	0.0	0.0	0.0	0.0	0.0	0.0	0.0	0.0	0.0	0.0	0.0

High and Low temperatures in degrees Fahrenheit; Precipitation and Snow in inches

Population: 442,179; Growth (since 2000): 20.2%; Density: 91.7 persons per square mile; Race: 60.1% White, 1.6% Black/African American, 3.4% Asian, 1.6% American Indian/Alaska Native, 0.1% Native Hawaiian/Other Pacific Islander, 4.2% two or more races, 60.6% Hispanic of any race; Average household size: 3.36; Median age: 29.6; Age under 18: 32.6%; Age 65 and over: 9.4%; Males per 100 females: 100.3; Marriage status: 34.0% never married, 51.7% now married, 2.4% separated, 5.1% widowed, 9.3% divorced; Foreign born: 22.8%; Speak English only: 50.8%; With disability: 10.7%; Veterans: 6.0%; Ancestry: 5.2% German, 4.1% Irish, 3.6% English, 3.2% American, 2.4% Portuguese

Religion: Six largest groups: 23.2% Catholicism, 3.6% Pentecostal, 2.7% Baptist, 2.6% Non-denominational Protestant, 1.8% Latter-day Saints, 1.6% Holiness

Economy: Unemployment rate: 11.7%; Leading industries: 17.2% retail trade; 13.7% health care and social assistance; 9.5% construction; Farms: 4,931 totaling 1,239,000 acres; Company size: 3 employ 1,000 or more persons, 6 employ 500 to 999 persons, 121 employs 100 to 499 persons, 6,005 employ less than 100 persons; Business ownership: 6,765 women-owned, 339 Black-owned, 6,502 Hispanic-owned, n/a Asian-owned

Employment: 9.3% management, business, and financial, 1.7% computer, engineering, and science, 8.8% education, legal, community service, arts, and media, 3.8% healthcare practitioners, 19.2% service, 21.1% sales and office, 21.4% natural resources, construction, and maintenance, 14.7% production, transportation, and material moving

Income: Per capita: $17,894; Median household: $42,708; Average household: $58,700; Households with income of $100,000 or more: 15.7%; Poverty rate: 26.2%

Educational Attainment: High school diploma or higher: 68.0%; Bachelor's degree or higher: 13.3%; Graduate/professional degree or higher: 4.5%

Housing: Homeownership rate: 58.8%; Median home value: $163,100; Median year structure built: 1980; Homeowner vacancy rate: 2.4%; Median gross rent: $821 per month; Rental vacancy rate: 5.8%

Vital Statistics: Birth rate: 176.0 per 10,000 population; Death rate: 62.7 per 10,000 population; Age-adjusted cancer mortality rate: 160.9 deaths per 100,000 population

Health Insurance: 78.5% have insurance; 44.5% have private insurance; 41.4% have public insurance; 21.5% do not have insurance; 10.2% of children under 18 do not have insurance

Health Care: Physicians: 11.0 per 10,000 population; Hospital beds: 28.2 per 10,000 population; Hospital admissions: 839.3 per 10,000 population

Air Quality Index: 22.2% good, 50.1% moderate, 24.1% unhealthy for sensitive individuals, 3.6% unhealthy (percent of days)

Transportation: Commute: 91.3% car, 0.8% public transportation, 2.1% walk, 3.4% work from home; Median travel time to work: 21.3 minutes

Presidential Election: 39.9% Obama, 58.2% Romney (2012)

National and State Parks: Colonel Allensworth State Historic Park; Pixley National Wildlife Refuge; Sequoia National Forest; Sequoia National Park

Additional Information Contacts

Tulare Government . . . . (559) 636-5000
http://www.co.tulare.ca.us

Tulare County Communities

ALLENSWORTH (CDP). Covers a land area of 3.102 square miles and a water area of 0 square miles. Located at 35.85° N. Lat; 119.39° W. Long. Elevation is 210 feet.

Population: 471; Growth (since 2000): n/a; Density: 151.8 persons per square mile; Race: 33.5% White, 4.7% Black/African American, 1.7% Asian, 0.0% American Indian/Alaska Native, 0.0% Native Hawaiian/Other Pacific Islander, 0.8% Two or more races, 92.6% Hispanic of any race; Average household size: 4.10; Median age: 23.4; Age under 18: 39.7%; Age 65 and over: 5.3%; Males per 100 females: 97.1

School District(s)

Allensworth Elementary (KG-08)
2012-13 Enrollment: 79. . . . . (661) 849-2401

Housing: Homeownership rate: 48.7%; Homeowner vacancy rate: 0.0%; Rental vacancy rate: 11.8%

ALPAUGH (CDP). Covers a land area of 1.005 square miles and a water area of 0 square miles. Located at 35.89° N. Lat; 119.49° W. Long. Elevation is 213 feet.

Population: 1,026; Growth (since 2000): 34.8%; Density: 1,020.8 persons per square mile; Race: 37.1% White, 0.4% Black/African American, 0.4% Asian, 1.1% American Indian/Alaska Native, 0.0% Native Hawaiian/Other Pacific Islander, 2.8% Two or more races, 84.5% Hispanic of any race; Average household size: 4.54; Median age: 21.8; Age under 18: 42.3%; Age 65 and over: 6.0%; Males per 100 females: 107.3

School District(s)

Alpaugh Unified (KG-12)
2012-13 Enrollment: 577. . . . . (559) 949-8413

Housing: Homeownership rate: 53.1%; Homeowner vacancy rate: 1.6%; Rental vacancy rate: 0.9%

BADGER (unincorporated postal area)
ZCTA: 93603

Covers a land area of 43.516 square miles and a water area of 0.034 square miles. Located at 36.62° N. Lat; 118.96° W. Long. Elevation is 3,038 feet.

Population: 222; Growth (since 2000): -14.6%; Density: 5.1 persons per square mile; Race: 87.4% White, 1.8% Black/African American, 1.4% Asian, 2.7% American Indian/Alaska Native, 0.0% Native Hawaiian/Other Pacific Islander, 3.6% Two or more races, 7.7% Hispanic of any race; Average household size: 2.00; Median age: 51.8; Age under 18: 13.1%; Age 65 and over: 24.3%; Males per 100 females: 105.6

School District(s)

Cutler-Orosi Joint Unified (KG-12)
2012-13 Enrollment: 4,128 . . . . (559) 528-4763

Housing: Homeownership rate: 55.8%; Homeowner vacancy rate: 1.6%; Rental vacancy rate: 9.3%

CALIFORNIA HOT SPRINGS (CDP). Covers a land area of 0.748 square miles and a water area of 0 square miles. Located at 35.89° N. Lat; 118.66° W. Long. Elevation is 3,314 feet.

Population: 37; Growth (since 2000): n/a; Density: 49.5 persons per square mile; Race: 91.9% White, 0.0% Black/African American, 2.7% Asian, 0.0% American Indian/Alaska Native, 0.0% Native Hawaiian/Other Pacific Islander, 5.4% Two or more races, 8.1% Hispanic of any race; Average household size: 1.68; Median age: 60.5; Age under 18: 5.4%; Age 65 and over: 37.8%; Males per 100 females: 85.0

School District(s)

Hot Springs Elementary (KG-08)
2012-13 Enrollment: 14. . . . . (661) 548-6544

Housing: Homeownership rate: 72.7%; Homeowner vacancy rate: 5.9%; Rental vacancy rate: 0.0%

CAMP NELSON (CDP). Covers a land area of 1.238 square miles and a water area of 0 square miles. Located at 36.14° N. Lat; 118.61° W. Long. Elevation is 4,898 feet.

Population: 97; Growth (since 2000): n/a; Density: 78.3 persons per square mile; Race: 96.9% White, 0.0% Black/African American, 0.0% Asian, 0.0% American Indian/Alaska Native, 0.0% Native Hawaiian/Other Pacific Islander, 1.0% Two or more races, 6.2% Hispanic of any race; Average household size: 1.76; Median age: 60.2; Age under 18: 8.2%; Age 65 and over: 37.1%; Males per 100 females: 115.6

Housing: Homeownership rate: 80.0%; Homeowner vacancy rate: 17.0%; Rental vacancy rate: 25.0%

CUTLER (CDP). Covers a land area of 0.807 square miles and a water area of 0 square miles. Located at 36.53° N. Lat; 119.29° W. Long. Elevation is 361 feet.

Population: 5,000; Growth (since 2000): 11.3%; Density: 6,194.8 persons per square mile; Race: 48.4% White, 1.0% Black/African American, 1.3% Asian, 1.1% American Indian/Alaska Native, 0.0% Native Hawaiian/Other Pacific Islander, 3.4% Two or more races, 96.6% Hispanic of any race; Average household size: 4.61; Median age: 24.6; Age under 18: 37.2%; Age 65 and over: 5.2%; Males per 100 females: 113.9; Marriage status: 42.7% never married, 44.4% now married, 6.0% separated, 5.1% widowed, 7.8% divorced; Foreign born: 38.8%; Speak English only: 21.4%; With disability: 7.8%; Veterans: 0.3%; Ancestry: 1.5% Swedish

Employment: 4.1% management, business, and financial, 1.5% computer, engineering, and science, 5.5% education, legal, community service, arts, and media, 0.0% healthcare practitioners, 22.7% service, 11.5% sales and office, 30.4% natural resources, construction, and maintenance, 24.3% production, transportation, and material moving

Income: Per capita: $7,966; Median household: $26,019; Average household: $32,456; Households with income of $100,000 or more: 4.9%; Poverty rate: 52.6%

Educational Attainment: High school diploma or higher: 38.3%; Bachelor's degree or higher: 4.1%; Graduate/professional degree or higher: 0.7%

School District(s)

Cutler-Orosi Joint Unified (KG-12)
2012-13 Enrollment: 4,128 . . . . (559) 528-4763

Housing: Homeownership rate: 43.7%; Median home value: $127,900; Median year structure built: 1982; Homeowner vacancy rate: 1.0%; Median gross rent: $642 per month; Rental vacancy rate: 4.0%

Health Insurance: 74.7% have insurance; 21.4% have private insurance; 60.3% have public insurance; 25.3% do not have insurance; 2.8% of children under 18 do not have insurance

Transportation: Commute: 82.4% car, 0.0% public transportation, 9.7% walk, 1.2% work from home; Median travel time to work: 21.1 minutes

---

DELFT COLONY (CDP). Covers a land area of 0.066 square miles and a water area of 0 square miles. Located at 36.51° N. Lat; 119.45° W. Long. Elevation is 312 feet.

Population: 454; Growth (since 2000): n/a; Density: 6,916.9 persons per square mile; Race: 46.9% White, 2.9% Black/African American, 0.0% Asian, 0.0% American Indian/Alaska Native, 0.0% Native Hawaiian/Other Pacific Islander, 0.9% Two or more races, 94.3% Hispanic of any race; Average household size: 4.09; Median age: 26.0; Age under 18: 33.5%; Age 65 and over: 7.5%; Males per 100 females: 111.2

Housing: Homeownership rate: 49.5%; Homeowner vacancy rate: 1.8%; Rental vacancy rate: 13.8%

DINUBA (city). Covers a land area of 6.470 square miles and a water area of 0 square miles. Located at 36.55° N. Lat; 119.40° W. Long. Elevation is 335 feet.

History: Incorporated 1906.

Population: 21,453; Growth (since 2000): 27.4%; Density: 3,315.7 persons per square mile; Race: 52.0% White, 0.7% Black/African American, 2.1% Asian, 0.9% American Indian/Alaska Native, 0.1% Native Hawaiian/Other Pacific Islander, 4.0% Two or more races, 84.4% Hispanic of any race; Average household size: 3.81; Median age: 27.2; Age under 18: 34.9%; Age 65 and over: 7.8%; Males per 100 females: 103.3; Marriage status: 37.5% never married, 51.6% now married, 3.7% separated, 3.2% widowed, 7.7% divorced; Foreign born: 32.4%; Speak English only: 31.6%; With disability: 10.1%; Veterans: 4.2%; Ancestry: 2.3% German, 1.9% Irish, 1.2% American, 1.2% English, 1.0% French

Employment: 5.9% management, business, and financial, 1.2% computer, engineering, and science, 6.8% education, legal, community service, arts, and media, 2.5% healthcare practitioners, 14.6% service, 16.9% sales and office, 27.7% natural resources, construction, and maintenance, 24.4% production, transportation, and material moving

Income: Per capita: $13,259; Median household: $39,328; Average household: $48,935; Households with income of $100,000 or more: 6.8%; Poverty rate: 28.6%

Educational Attainment: High school diploma or higher: 56.5%; Bachelor's degree or higher: 6.8%; Graduate/professional degree or higher: 1.7%

School District(s)

Dinuba Unified (KG-12)
2012-13 Enrollment: 6,241 . . . . (559) 595-7200
Kings Canyon Joint Unified (KG-12)
2012-13 Enrollment: 9,954 . . . . (559) 305-7005

Housing: Homeownership rate: 56.7%; Median home value: $148,600; Median year structure built: 1977; Homeowner vacancy rate: 2.3%; Median gross rent: $835 per month; Rental vacancy rate: 4.2%

Health Insurance: 73.2% have insurance; 33.6% have private insurance; 44.3% have public insurance; 26.8% do not have insurance; 6.8% of children under 18 do not have insurance

Safety: Violent crime rate: 91.3 per 10,000 population; Property crime rate: 371.6 per 10,000 population

Newspapers: Dinuba Sentinel (weekly circulation 3000)

Transportation: Commute: 92.6% car, 0.3% public transportation, 1.7% walk, 1.8% work from home; Median travel time to work: 24.0 minutes

Additional Information Contacts

City of Dinuba . . . . (559) 591-5900
http://www.dinuba.org

DUCOR (CDP). Covers a land area of 0.610 square miles and a water area of 0 square miles. Located at 35.89° N. Lat; 119.05° W. Long. Elevation is 548 feet.

Population: 612; Growth (since 2000): 21.4%; Density: 1,002.9 persons per square mile; Race: 41.0% White, 0.0% Black/African American, 3.3% Asian, 2.5% American Indian/Alaska Native, 0.0% Native Hawaiian/Other Pacific Islander, 3.9% Two or more races, 82.0% Hispanic of any race; Average household size: 4.31; Median age: 27.6; Age under 18: 32.7%; Age 65 and over: 8.3%; Males per 100 females: 104.0

School District(s)

Ducor Union Elementary (KG-08)
2012-13 Enrollment: 179. . . . . (559) 534-2261

Housing: Homeownership rate: 73.9%; Homeowner vacancy rate: 0.9%; Rental vacancy rate: 11.9%

EARLIMART (CDP). Covers a land area of 2.106 square miles and a water area of 0 square miles. Located at 35.88° N. Lat; 119.27° W. Long. Elevation is 282 feet.

History: Earlimart grew up around a cotton-oil plant, cotton gin, and sheep and wool loading sheds along the railroad.

Population: 8,537; Growth (since 2000): 29.7%; Density: 4,052.8 persons per square mile; Race: 37.4% White, 0.8% Black/African American, 6.3% Asian, 0.5% American Indian/Alaska Native, 0.0% Native Hawaiian/Other Pacific Islander, 4.6% Two or more races, 91.4% Hispanic of any race; Average household size: 4.39; Median age: 23.5; Age under 18: 40.0%; Age 65 and over: 6.0%; Males per 100 females: 105.3; Marriage status: 37.7% never married, 52.4% now married, 4.4% separated, 5.5% widowed, 4.5% divorced; Foreign born: 41.2%; Speak English only: 9.7%; With disability: 7.6%; Veterans: 0.9%; Ancestry: 0.6% American, 0.6% English, 0.4% Barbadian, 0.3% German, 0.2% Scottish

Employment: 7.1% management, business, and financial, 0.3% computer, engineering, and science, 3.1% education, legal, community service, arts, and media, 1.1% healthcare practitioners, 14.9% service, 9.5% sales and office, 53.1% natural resources, construction, and maintenance, 10.9% production, transportation, and material moving

Income: Per capita: $8,547; Median household: $26,208; Average household: $32,917; Households with income of $100,000 or more: 3.1%; Poverty rate: 45.6%

Educational Attainment: High school diploma or higher: 33.4%; Bachelor's degree or higher: 2.0%; Graduate/professional degree or higher: 0.7%

School District(s)

Earlimart Elementary (KG-08)
2012-13 Enrollment: 1,881 . . . . (661) 849-4241

Housing: Homeownership rate: 51.9%; Median home value: $116,100; Median year structure built: 1987; Homeowner vacancy rate: 1.0%; Median gross rent: $580 per month; Rental vacancy rate: 2.1%

Health Insurance: 73.1% have insurance; 22.5% have private insurance; 54.1% have public insurance; 26.9% do not have insurance; 9.7% of children under 18 do not have insurance

Transportation: Commute: 87.8% car, 1.3% public transportation, 6.7% walk, 2.8% work from home; Median travel time to work: 23.2 minutes

---

EAST OROSI (CDP). Covers a land area of 0.248 square miles and a water area of 0 square miles. Located at 36.55° N. Lat; 119.26° W. Long. Elevation is 394 feet.

Population: 495; Growth (since 2000): 16.2%; Density: 1,996.2 persons per square mile; Race: 42.2% White, 0.0% Black/African American, 0.4% Asian, 1.0% American Indian/Alaska Native, 0.2% Native Hawaiian/Other Pacific Islander, 3.4% Two or more races, 94.1% Hispanic of any race; Average household size: 4.42; Median age: 24.2; Age under 18: 36.6%; Age 65 and over: 6.3%; Males per 100 females: 126.0

Housing: Homeownership rate: 41.1%; Homeowner vacancy rate: 2.1%; Rental vacancy rate: 1.5%

EAST PORTERVILLE (CDP). Covers a land area of 2.981 square miles and a water area of 0.018 square miles. Located at 36.06° N. Lat; 118.97° W. Long. Elevation is 486 feet.

Population: 6,767; Growth (since 2000): 0.5%; Density: 2,270.3 persons per square mile; Race: 54.1% White, 1.0% Black/African American, 1.5% Asian, 2.3% American Indian/Alaska Native, 0.9% Native Hawaiian/Other Pacific Islander, 4.4% Two or more races, 72.9% Hispanic of any race; Average household size: 4.13; Median age: 25.4; Age under 18: 36.6%; Age 65 and over: 6.3%; Males per 100 females: 106.0; Marriage status: 41.0% never married, 50.1% now married, 3.4% separated, 3.4% widowed, 5.6% divorced; Foreign born: 35.1%; Speak English only: 30.7%; With disability: 11.4%; Veterans: 5.2%; Ancestry: 4.5% German, 2.0% Irish, 1.6% English, 1.3% Dutch, 1.1% American

Employment: 2.0% management, business, and financial, 0.1% computer, engineering, and science, 3.9% education, legal, community service, arts, and media, 2.8% healthcare practitioners, 18.5% service, 14.5% sales and office, 41.5% natural resources, construction, and maintenance, 16.7% production, transportation, and material moving

Income: Per capita: $11,046; Median household: $30,336; Average household: $41,252; Households with income of $100,000 or more: 5.6%; Poverty rate: 35.9%

Educational Attainment: High school diploma or higher: 43.8%; Bachelor's degree or higher: 3.4%; Graduate/professional degree or higher: 0.8%

Housing: Homeownership rate: 47.4%; Median home value: $97,200; Median year structure built: 1972; Homeowner vacancy rate: 1.3%; Median gross rent: $694 per month; Rental vacancy rate: 4.7%

Health Insurance: 72.5% have insurance; 23.9% have private insurance; 52.5% have public insurance; 27.5% do not have insurance; 13.8% of children under 18 do not have insurance

Transportation: Commute: 94.0% car, 1.4% public transportation, 0.1% walk, 1.9% work from home; Median travel time to work: 31.6 minutes

EAST TULARE VILLA (CDP). Covers a land area of 0.482 square miles and a water area of 0 square miles. Located at 36.20° N. Lat; 119.28° W. Long.

Population: 778; Growth (since 2000): n/a; Density: 1,614.1 persons per square mile; Race: 63.1% White, 1.2% Black/African American, 1.3% Asian, 0.8% American Indian/Alaska Native, 0.0% Native Hawaiian/Other Pacific Islander, 4.6% Two or more races, 55.0% Hispanic of any race; Average household size: 3.74; Median age: 32.1; Age under 18: 33.2%; Age 65 and over: 7.5%; Males per 100 females: 102.1

Housing: Homeownership rate: 60.1%; Homeowner vacancy rate: 0.8%; Rental vacancy rate: 2.3%

EL RANCHO (CDP). Covers a land area of 0.072 square miles and a water area of 0 square miles. Located at 36.22° N. Lat; 119.07° W. Long.

Population: 124; Growth (since 2000): n/a; Density: 1,722.0 persons per square mile; Race: 57.3% White, 0.8% Black/African American, 0.0% Asian, 0.8% American Indian/Alaska Native, 0.0% Native Hawaiian/Other Pacific Islander, 1.6% Two or more races, 94.4% Hispanic of any race; Average household size: 4.28; Median age: 32.5; Age under 18: 28.2%; Age 65 and over: 16.9%; Males per 100 females: 134.0

Housing: Homeownership rate: 62.1%; Homeowner vacancy rate: 0.0%; Rental vacancy rate: 8.3%

EXETER (city). Covers a land area of 2.463 square miles and a water area of 0 square miles. Located at 36.29° N. Lat; 119.15° W. Long. Elevation is 390 feet.

History: Incorporated 1911.

Population: 10,334; Growth (since 2000): 12.7%; Density: 4,195.6 persons per square mile; Race: 69.2% White, 0.6% Black/African American, 1.3% Asian, 1.7% American Indian/Alaska Native, 0.1% Native Hawaiian/Other Pacific Islander, 3.7% Two or more races, 45.5% Hispanic of any race; Average household size: 3.04; Median age: 31.2; Age under 18: 31.8%; Age 65 and over: 11.5%; Males per 100 females: 94.5; Marriage status: 34.7% never married, 49.9% now married, 2.4% separated, 6.1% widowed, 9.3% divorced; Foreign born: 11.5%; Speak English only: 75.0%; With disability: 11.0%; Veterans: 6.5%; Ancestry: 7.1% English, 6.9% Irish, 4.1% German, 2.8% American, 2.0% Dutch

Employment: 11.3% management, business, and financial, 1.8% computer, engineering, and science, 10.6% education, legal, community service, arts, and media, 1.2% healthcare practitioners, 20.9% service, 19.4% sales and office, 15.3% natural resources, construction, and maintenance, 19.5% production, transportation, and material moving

Income: Per capita: $18,288; Median household: $39,063; Average household: $55,845; Households with income of $100,000 or more: 14.0%; Poverty rate: 29.9%

Educational Attainment: High school diploma or higher: 76.7%; Bachelor's degree or higher: 14.6%; Graduate/professional degree or higher: 4.0%

School District(s)

Exeter Union Elementary (KG-08)
2012-13 Enrollment: 1,870 . . . . (559) 592-9421

Exeter Union High (09-12)
2012-13 Enrollment: 1,093 . . . . (559) 592-9421

Housing: Homeownership rate: 60.2%; Median home value: $159,700; Median year structure built: 1978; Homeowner vacancy rate: 3.4%; Median gross rent: $848 per month; Rental vacancy rate: 6.3%

Health Insurance: 83.8% have insurance; 49.5% have private insurance; 42.4% have public insurance; 16.2% do not have insurance; 8.5% of children under 18 do not have insurance

Safety: Violent crime rate: 19.0 per 10,000 population; Property crime rate: 237.0 per 10,000 population

Newspapers: Foothills Sun-Gazette (weekly circulation 3000)

Transportation: Commute: 94.8% car, 0.4% public transportation, 1.5% walk, 2.5% work from home; Median travel time to work: 21.2 minutes

Additional Information Contacts

City of Exeter. . . . . (559) 592-3710
http://www.cityofexeter.com

FARMERSVILLE (city). Covers a land area of 2.258 square miles and a water area of 0 square miles. Located at 36.31° N. Lat; 119.21° W. Long. Elevation is 358 feet.

Population: 10,588; Growth (since 2000): 21.2%; Density: 4,688.2 persons per square mile; Race: 50.0% White, 0.6% Black/African American, 0.7% Asian, 2.0% American Indian/Alaska Native, 0.0% Native Hawaiian/Other Pacific Islander, 4.2% Two or more races, 83.8% Hispanic of any race; Average household size: 4.08; Median age: 26.2; Age under 18: 36.8%; Age 65 and over: 6.6%; Males per 100 females: 101.5; Marriage status: 40.0% never married, 48.8% now married, 2.8% separated, 4.6% widowed, 6.6% divorced; Foreign born: 30.9%; Speak English only: 27.7%; With disability: 11.4%; Veterans: 2.8%; Ancestry: 2.8% German, 1.6% English, 0.9% Irish, 0.8% American, 0.8% Italian

Employment: 3.3% management, business, and financial, 0.5% computer, engineering, and science, 4.8% education, legal, community service, arts, and media, 1.7% healthcare practitioners, 21.7% service, 22.8% sales and office, 23.2% natural resources, construction, and maintenance, 22.1% production, transportation, and material moving

Income: Per capita: $11,205; Median household: $32,384; Average household: $42,680; Households with income of $100,000 or more: 5.5%; Poverty rate: 32.9%

Educational Attainment: High school diploma or higher: 49.5%; Bachelor's degree or higher: 3.5%; Graduate/professional degree or higher: 1.5%

School District(s)

Farmersville Unified (KG-12)
2012-13 Enrollment: 2,646 . . . . (559) 592-2010

Housing: Homeownership rate: 61.3%; Median home value: $105,100; Median year structure built: 1980; Homeowner vacancy rate: 2.5%; Median gross rent: $728 per month; Rental vacancy rate: 4.2%

Health Insurance: 76.4% have insurance; 26.2% have private insurance; 53.1% have public insurance; 23.6% do not have insurance; 6.1% of children under 18 do not have insurance

Safety: Violent crime rate: 43.6 per 10,000 population; Property crime rate: 239.2 per 10,000 population

Transportation: Commute: 90.1% car, 2.4% public transportation, 1.0% walk, 4.2% work from home; Median travel time to work: 23.4 minutes

Additional Information Contacts

City of Farmersville . . . . (559) 747-0458
http://www.cityoffarmersville-ca.gov

GOSHEN (CDP). Covers a land area of 1.772 square miles and a water area of 0 square miles. Located at 36.35° N. Lat; 119.42° W. Long. Elevation is 285 feet.

Population: 3,006; Growth (since 2000): 25.6%; Density: 1,696.4 persons per square mile; Race: 39.5% White, 2.5% Black/African American, 0.4% Asian, 3.0% American Indian/Alaska Native, 0.0% Native Hawaiian/Other Pacific Islander, 4.9% Two or more races, 82.6% Hispanic of any race; Average household size: 3.89; Median age: 27.1; Age under 18: 35.7%;

Age 65 and over: 6.8%; Males per 100 females: 107.3; Marriage status: 41.1% never married, 50.1% now married, 2.2% separated, 3.0% widowed, 5.7% divorced; Foreign born: 24.1%; Speak English only: 32.1%; With disability: 9.4%; Veterans: 2.4%; Ancestry: 2.6% Irish, 2.2% German, 1.9% English, 1.9% Other Arab, 0.6% Portuguese

Employment: 5.5% management, business, and financial, 1.0% computer, engineering, and science, 6.1% education, legal, community service, arts, and media, 0.0% healthcare practitioners, 19.8% service, 23.0% sales and office, 19.9% natural resources, construction, and maintenance, 24.7% production, transportation, and material moving

Income: Per capita: $11,453; Median household: $41,583; Average household: $47,360; Households with income of $100,000 or more: 4.8%; Poverty rate: 19.9%

Educational Attainment: High school diploma or higher: 55.4%; Bachelor's degree or higher: 3.1%; Graduate/professional degree or higher: 1.2%

Housing: Homeownership rate: 52.3%; Median home value: $110,000; Median year structure built: 1976; Homeowner vacancy rate: 2.4%; Median gross rent: $828 per month; Rental vacancy rate: 10.0%

Health Insurance: 78.9% have insurance; 22.8% have private insurance; 57.6% have public insurance; 21.1% do not have insurance; 7.6% of children under 18 do not have insurance

Transportation: Commute: 84.8% car, 2.4% public transportation, 9.9% walk, 1.8% work from home; Median travel time to work: 19.3 minutes; Amtrak: Bus service available.

IDLEWILD (CDP). Covers a land area of 0.459 square miles and a water area of 0 square miles. Located at 35.81° N. Lat; 118.67° W. Long. Elevation is 3,714 feet.

Population: 43; Growth (since 2000): n/a; Density: 93.6 persons per square mile; Race: 100.0% White, 0.0% Black/African American, 0.0% Asian, 0.0% American Indian/Alaska Native, 0.0% Native Hawaiian/Other Pacific Islander, 0.0% Two or more races, 0.0% Hispanic of any race; Average household size: 2.53; Median age: 50.4; Age under 18: 14.0%; Age 65 and over: 16.3%; Males per 100 females: 87.0

Housing: Homeownership rate: 82.4%; Homeowner vacancy rate: 0.0%; Rental vacancy rate: 0.0%

IVANHOE (CDP). Covers a land area of 2.014 square miles and a water area of 0 square miles. Located at 36.39° N. Lat; 119.22° W. Long. Elevation is 364 feet.

Population: 4,495; Growth (since 2000): 0.5%; Density: 2,232.0 persons per square mile; Race: 44.5% White, 0.4% Black/African American, 0.6% Asian, 1.8% American Indian/Alaska Native, 0.0% Native Hawaiian/Other Pacific Islander, 3.2% Two or more races, 83.5% Hispanic of any race; Average household size: 3.94; Median age: 27.4; Age under 18: 34.8%; Age 65 and over: 7.2%; Males per 100 females: 104.9; Marriage status: 39.5% never married, 51.6% now married, 1.0% separated, 3.6% widowed, 5.3% divorced; Foreign born: 43.9%; Speak English only: 20.5%; With disability: 8.9%; Veterans: 4.6%; Ancestry: 3.2% English, 2.8% German, 0.4% Portuguese, 0.3% Canadian, 0.3% Irish

Employment: 5.4% management, business, and financial, 0.0% computer, engineering, and science, 0.0% education, legal, community service, arts, and media, 1.8% healthcare practitioners, 14.8% service, 25.8% sales and office, 35.7% natural resources, construction, and maintenance, 16.5% production, transportation, and material moving

Income: Per capita: $10,348; Median household: $29,688; Average household: $36,109; Households with income of $100,000 or more: 3.3%; Poverty rate: 34.0%

Educational Attainment: High school diploma or higher: 37.8%; Bachelor's degree or higher: 3.6%; Graduate/professional degree or higher: n/a

School District(s)

Visalia Unified (KG-12)
2012-13 Enrollment: 27,617 . . . . (559) 730-7300

Housing: Homeownership rate: 60.7%; Median home value: $105,300; Median year structure built: 1976; Homeowner vacancy rate: 1.1%; Median gross rent: $669 per month; Rental vacancy rate: 7.6%

Health Insurance: 62.4% have insurance; 34.7% have private insurance; 33.1% have public insurance; 37.6% do not have insurance; 18.8% of children under 18 do not have insurance

Transportation: Commute: 98.3% car, 0.0% public transportation, 1.7% walk, 0.0% work from home; Median travel time to work: 23.1 minutes

---

KENNEDY MEADOWS (CDP). Covers a land area of 5.823 square miles and a water area of 0 square miles. Located at 36.01° N. Lat; 118.11° W. Long.

Population: 28; Growth (since 2000): n/a; Density: 4.8 persons per square mile; Race: 89.3% White, 0.0% Black/African American, 0.0% Asian, 3.6% American Indian/Alaska Native, 0.0% Native Hawaiian/Other Pacific Islander, 0.0% Two or more races, 10.7% Hispanic of any race; Average household size: 1.87; Median age: 61.0; Age under 18: 10.7%; Age 65 and over: 42.9%; Males per 100 females: 115.4

Housing: Homeownership rate: 80.0%; Homeowner vacancy rate: 7.7%; Rental vacancy rate: 0.0%

LEMON COVE (CDP). Covers a land area of 0.834 square miles and a water area of 0 square miles. Located at 36.38° N. Lat; 119.03° W. Long.

Population: 308; Growth (since 2000): 3.4%; Density: 369.5 persons per square mile; Race: 84.7% White, 0.0% Black/African American, 1.0% Asian, 1.6% American Indian/Alaska Native, 0.6% Native Hawaiian/Other Pacific Islander, 8.1% Two or more races, 24.7% Hispanic of any race; Average household size: 2.57; Median age: 39.6; Age under 18: 26.6%; Age 65 and over: 14.3%; Males per 100 females: 106.7

School District(s)

Sequoia Union Elementary (KG-08)
2012-13 Enrollment: 306. . . . . (559) 564-2106

Housing: Homeownership rate: 64.2%; Homeowner vacancy rate: 0.0%; Rental vacancy rate: 6.0%

LINDCOVE (CDP). Covers a land area of 0.682 square miles and a water area of 0 square miles. Located at 36.36° N. Lat; 119.07° W. Long. Elevation is 453 feet.

Population: 406; Growth (since 2000): n/a; Density: 595.0 persons per square mile; Race: 70.0% White, 0.5% Black/African American, 0.0% Asian, 3.7% American Indian/Alaska Native, 0.0% Native Hawaiian/Other Pacific Islander, 2.2% Two or more races, 48.5% Hispanic of any race; Average household size: 3.17; Median age: 34.7; Age under 18: 26.1%; Age 65 and over: 15.5%; Males per 100 females: 106.1

Housing: Homeownership rate: 65.7%; Homeowner vacancy rate: 3.4%; Rental vacancy rate: 4.3%

LINDSAY (city). Covers a land area of 2.610 square miles and a water area of 0 square miles. Located at 36.21° N. Lat; 119.09° W. Long. Elevation is 387 feet.

History: Lindsay grew up around citrus and olive orchards, with citrus-packing houses, olive canneries, and olive oil plants.

Population: 11,768; Growth (since 2000): 14.3%; Density: 4,509.4 persons per square mile; Race: 55.1% White, 0.7% Black/African American, 2.3% Asian, 1.1% American Indian/Alaska Native, 0.0% Native Hawaiian/Other Pacific Islander, 3.7% Two or more races, 85.5% Hispanic of any race; Average household size: 3.87; Median age: 24.6; Age under 18: 38.4%; Age 65 and over: 7.5%; Males per 100 females: 101.3; Marriage status: 38.8% never married, 48.7% now married, 2.2% separated, 4.7% widowed, 7.8% divorced; Foreign born: 34.3%; Speak English only: 21.2%; With disability: 8.0%; Veterans: 2.6%; Ancestry: 2.1% German, 1.8% American, 1.2% Irish, 1.1% English, 1.0% Swiss

Employment: 4.5% management, business, and financial, 1.5% computer, engineering, and science, 5.5% education, legal, community service, arts, and media, 2.4% healthcare practitioners, 21.1% service, 14.4% sales and office, 29.9% natural resources, construction, and maintenance, 20.7% production, transportation, and material moving

Income: Per capita: $10,813; Median household: $31,425; Average household: $41,952; Households with income of $100,000 or more: 6.3%; Poverty rate: 42.5%

Educational Attainment: High school diploma or higher: 46.5%; Bachelor's degree or higher: 5.6%; Graduate/professional degree or higher: 1.9%

School District(s)

Lindsay Unified (KG-12)
2012-13 Enrollment: 4,130 . . . . (559) 562-5111

Housing: Homeownership rate: 50.6%; Median home value: $121,100; Median year structure built: 1973; Homeowner vacancy rate: 2.0%; Median gross rent: $729 per month; Rental vacancy rate: 6.2%

Health Insurance: 72.0% have insurance; 27.8% have private insurance; 47.3% have public insurance; 28.0% do not have insurance; 12.1% of children under 18 do not have insurance

Safety: Violent crime rate: 30.3 per 10,000 population; Property crime rate: 234.7 per 10,000 population

Transportation: Commute: 92.7% car, 0.2% public transportation, 3.1% walk, 1.9% work from home; Median travel time to work: 20.7 minutes

Additional Information Contacts

City of Lindsay. . . . . (559) 562-7103
http://www.lindsay.ca.us

LINNELL CAMP (CDP). Covers a land area of 0.117 square miles and a water area of 0 square miles. Located at 36.31° N. Lat; 119.22° W. Long.

Population: 849; Growth (since 2000): n/a; Density: 7,248.4 persons per square mile; Race: 46.8% White, 0.4% Black/African American, 0.9% Asian, 2.1% American Indian/Alaska Native, 0.0% Native Hawaiian/Other Pacific Islander, 3.5% Two or more races, 98.0% Hispanic of any race; Average household size: 4.40; Median age: 21.9; Age under 18: 41.8%; Age 65 and over: 2.1%; Males per 100 females: 96.1

Housing: Homeownership rate: 2.1%; Homeowner vacancy rate: 0.0%; Rental vacancy rate: 0.0%

LONDON (CDP). Covers a land area of 0.629 square miles and a water area of 0 square miles. Located at 36.48° N. Lat; 119.44° W. Long. Elevation is 299 feet.

Population: 1,869; Growth (since 2000): 1.1%; Density: 2,970.0 persons per square mile; Race: 40.7% White, 0.3% Black/African American, 0.0% Asian, 2.5% American Indian/Alaska Native, 0.0% Native Hawaiian/Other Pacific Islander, 4.3% Two or more races, 92.9% Hispanic of any race; Average household size: 4.76; Median age: 25.6; Age under 18: 36.2%; Age 65 and over: 4.7%; Males per 100 females: 123.3

Housing: Homeownership rate: 39.9%; Homeowner vacancy rate: 0.6%; Rental vacancy rate: 1.7%

MATHENY (CDP). Covers a land area of 0.430 square miles and a water area of 0 square miles. Located at 36.17° N. Lat; 119.35° W. Long.

Population: 1,212; Growth (since 2000): n/a; Density: 2,820.5 persons per square mile; Race: 53.7% White, 3.6% Black/African American, 0.3% Asian, 2.0% American Indian/Alaska Native, 0.0% Native Hawaiian/Other Pacific Islander, 4.4% Two or more races, 73.4% Hispanic of any race; Average household size: 3.79; Median age: 26.9; Age under 18: 37.9%; Age 65 and over: 8.2%; Males per 100 females: 106.8

Housing: Homeownership rate: 48.4%; Homeowner vacancy rate: 0.6%; Rental vacancy rate: 4.5%

MCCLENNEY TRACT (CDP). Covers a land area of 0.616 square miles and a water area of 0 square miles. Located at 35.82° N. Lat; 118.65° W. Long.

Population: 10; Growth (since 2000): n/a; Density: 16.2 persons per square mile; Race: 90.0% White, 0.0% Black/African American, 0.0% Asian, 0.0% American Indian/Alaska Native, 0.0% Native Hawaiian/Other Pacific Islander, 10.0% Two or more races, 0.0% Hispanic of any race; Average household size: 2.50; Median age: 55.0; Age under 18: 30.0%; Age 65 and over: 50.0%; Males per 100 females: 42.9

Housing: Homeownership rate: 75.0%; Homeowner vacancy rate: 0.0%; Rental vacancy rate: 0.0%

MONSON (CDP). Covers a land area of 0.492 square miles and a water area of 0 square miles. Located at 36.49° N. Lat; 119.34° W. Long. Elevation is 325 feet.

Population: 188; Growth (since 2000): n/a; Density: 382.3 persons per square mile; Race: 64.4% White, 0.5% Black/African American, 2.1% Asian, 2.7% American Indian/Alaska Native, 0.0% Native Hawaiian/Other Pacific Islander, 0.0% Two or more races, 78.2% Hispanic of any race; Average household size: 3.84; Median age: 27.2; Age under 18: 30.9%; Age 65 and over: 11.2%; Males per 100 females: 102.2

Housing: Homeownership rate: 55.1%; Homeowner vacancy rate: 3.4%; Rental vacancy rate: 4.3%

OROSI (CDP). Covers a land area of 2.446 square miles and a water area of 0 square miles. Located at 36.54° N. Lat; 119.29° W. Long. Elevation is 374 feet.

Population: 8,770; Growth (since 2000): n/a; Density: 3,586.2 persons per square mile; Race: 44.0% White, 0.7% Black/African American, 9.2% Asian, 0.6% American Indian/Alaska Native, 0.0% Native Hawaiian/Other Pacific Islander, 3.9% Two or more races, 86.7% Hispanic of any race; Average household size: 4.42; Median age: 26.4; Age under 18: 35.2%; Age 65 and over: 7.4%; Males per 100 females: 107.0; Marriage status: 37.8% never married, 53.8% now married, 3.9% separated, 3.2% widowed, 5.3% divorced; Foreign born: 49.9%; Speak English only: 15.1%; With disability: 9.1%; Veterans: 3.1%; Ancestry: 1.6% English, 1.1% American, 0.9% Portuguese, 0.2% German, 0.2% Irish

Employment: 3.3% management, business, and financial, 0.0% computer, engineering, and science, 3.3% education, legal, community service, arts, and media, 0.5% healthcare practitioners, 13.3% service, 10.5% sales and office, 50.4% natural resources, construction, and maintenance, 18.6% production, transportation, and material moving

Income: Per capita: $8,797; Median household: $33,319; Average household: $36,931; Households with income of $100,000 or more: 3.3%; Poverty rate: 32.9%

Educational Attainment: High school diploma or higher: 33.6%; Bachelor's degree or higher: 2.6%; Graduate/professional degree or higher: 0.2%

School District(s)

Cutler-Orosi Joint Unified (KG-12)
2012-13 Enrollment: 4,128 . . . . (559) 528-4763

Housing: Homeownership rate: 56.3%; Median home value: $121,600; Median year structure built: 1980; Homeowner vacancy rate: 2.6%; Median gross rent: $595 per month; Rental vacancy rate: 3.7%

Health Insurance: 68.3% have insurance; 19.7% have private insurance; 52.8% have public insurance; 31.7% do not have insurance; 19.1% of children under 18 do not have insurance

Transportation: Commute: 89.3% car, 0.4% public transportation, 0.5% walk, 1.9% work from home; Median travel time to work: 30.6 minutes

PANORAMA HEIGHTS (CDP). Covers a land area of 0.475 square miles and a water area of 0 square miles. Located at 35.81° N. Lat; 118.63° W. Long. Elevation is 4,938 feet.

Population: 41; Growth (since 2000): n/a; Density: 86.3 persons per square mile; Race: 85.4% White, 2.4% Black/African American, 0.0% Asian, 2.4% American Indian/Alaska Native, 0.0% Native Hawaiian/Other Pacific Islander, 0.0% Two or more races, 9.8% Hispanic of any race; Average household size: 1.86; Median age: 58.3; Age under 18: 4.9%; Age 65 and over: 34.1%; Males per 100 females: 115.8

Housing: Homeownership rate: 90.9%; Homeowner vacancy rate: 4.8%; Rental vacancy rate: 0.0%

PATTERSON TRACT (CDP). Covers a land area of 1.446 square miles and a water area of 0 square miles. Located at 36.38° N. Lat; 119.30° W. Long.

Population: 1,752; Growth (since 2000): n/a; Density: 1,211.5 persons per square mile; Race: 57.0% White, 0.0% Black/African American, 4.2% Asian, 1.9% American Indian/Alaska Native, 0.0% Native Hawaiian/Other Pacific Islander, 4.0% Two or more races, 64.7% Hispanic of any race; Average household size: 3.60; Median age: 30.4; Age under 18: 31.9%; Age 65 and over: 10.4%; Males per 100 females: 107.1

Housing: Homeownership rate: 61.4%; Homeowner vacancy rate: 2.6%; Rental vacancy rate: 3.6%

PIERPOINT (CDP). Covers a land area of 0.408 square miles and a water area of 0 square miles. Located at 36.14° N. Lat; 118.63° W. Long.

Population: 52; Growth (since 2000): n/a; Density: 127.5 persons per square mile; Race: 98.1% White, 0.0% Black/African American, 0.0% Asian, 0.0% American Indian/Alaska Native, 0.0% Native Hawaiian/Other Pacific Islander, 0.0% Two or more races, 1.9% Hispanic of any race; Average household size: 2.00; Median age: 56.5; Age under 18: 11.5%; Age 65 and over: 25.0%; Males per 100 females: 85.7

Housing: Homeownership rate: 77.0%; Homeowner vacancy rate: 4.8%; Rental vacancy rate: 14.3%

PINE FLAT (CDP). Covers a land area of 1.162 square miles and a water area of 0 square miles. Located at 35.87° N. Lat; 118.64° W. Long. Elevation is 3,717 feet.

Population: 166; Growth (since 2000): n/a; Density: 142.9 persons per square mile; Race: 95.2% White, 0.0% Black/African American, 1.8% Asian, 1.8% American Indian/Alaska Native, 0.0% Native Hawaiian/Other Pacific Islander, 1.2% Two or more races, 6.6% Hispanic of any race; Average household size: 2.05; Median age: 54.3; Age under 18: 19.3%; Age 65 and over: 30.1%; Males per 100 females: 104.9

Housing: Homeownership rate: 81.5%; Homeowner vacancy rate: 4.3%; Rental vacancy rate: 6.3%

PIXLEY (CDP). Covers a land area of 3.114 square miles and a water area of 0 square miles. Located at 35.98° N. Lat; 119.29° W. Long. Elevation is 272 feet.

History: Pixley, dating from the railroad building era, was named for Frank Pixley, founder and editor of the San Francisco weekly, "The Argonaut."

Population: 3,310; Growth (since 2000): 28.0%; Density: 1,062.8 persons per square mile; Race: 44.5% White, 2.7% Black/African American, 0.5% Asian, 0.8% American Indian/Alaska Native, 0.0% Native Hawaiian/Other Pacific Islander, 3.5% Two or more races, 80.8% Hispanic of any race; Average household size: 4.15; Median age: 24.7; Age under 18: 38.3%; Age 65 and over: 6.3%; Males per 100 females: 107.3; Marriage status: 36.2% never married, 54.9% now married, 2.2% separated, 5.5% widowed, 3.4% divorced; Foreign born: 39.6%; Speak English only: 23.4%; With disability: 10.5%; Veterans: 1.7%; Ancestry: 3.6% English, 0.5% Irish, 0.4% German, 0.2% American

Employment: 3.5% management, business, and financial, 2.5% computer, engineering, and science, 0.8% education, legal, community service, arts, and media, 2.2% healthcare practitioners, 15.3% service, 10.9% sales and office, 51.8% natural resources, construction, and maintenance, 13.0% production, transportation, and material moving

Income: Per capita: $11,741; Median household: $30,809; Average household: $48,194; Households with income of $100,000 or more: 2.6%; Poverty rate: 42.3%

Educational Attainment: High school diploma or higher: 42.7%; Bachelor's degree or higher: 3.4%; Graduate/professional degree or higher: n/a

School District(s)

Pixley Union Elementary (KG-08)
2012-13 Enrollment: 1,139 . . . . (559) 757-5207

Housing: Homeownership rate: 54.3%; Median home value: $121,300; Median year structure built: 1974; Homeowner vacancy rate: 1.6%; Median gross rent: $823 per month; Rental vacancy rate: 9.2%

Health Insurance: 70.4% have insurance; 16.8% have private insurance; 55.3% have public insurance; 29.6% do not have insurance; 4.4% of children under 18 do not have insurance

Transportation: Commute: 94.8% car, 1.9% public transportation, 2.1% walk, 1.2% work from home; Median travel time to work: 22.8 minutes

PLAINVIEW (CDP). Covers a land area of 0.309 square miles and a water area of 0 square miles. Located at 36.14° N. Lat; 119.14° W. Long. Elevation is 354 feet.

Population: 945; Growth (since 2000): n/a; Density: 3,057.1 persons per square mile; Race: 37.9% White, 0.8% Black/African American, 0.2% Asian, 2.1% American Indian/Alaska Native, 0.0% Native Hawaiian/Other Pacific Islander, 4.2% Two or more races, 91.5% Hispanic of any race; Average household size: 4.52; Median age: 23.1; Age under 18: 41.7%; Age 65 and over: 6.2%; Males per 100 females: 104.5

Housing: Homeownership rate: 51.2%; Homeowner vacancy rate: 2.7%; Rental vacancy rate: 3.7%

PONDEROSA (CDP). Covers a land area of 0.813 square miles and a water area of 0.001 square miles. Located at 36.10° N. Lat; 118.53° W. Long. Elevation is 7,188 feet.

Population: 16; Growth (since 2000): n/a; Density: 19.7 persons per square mile; Race: 81.3% White, 0.0% Black/African American, 0.0% Asian, 0.0% American Indian/Alaska Native, 0.0% Native Hawaiian/Other Pacific Islander, 12.5% Two or more races, 25.0% Hispanic of any race; Average household size: 1.78; Median age: 65.3; Age under 18: 12.5%; Age 65 and over: 56.3%; Males per 100 females: 100.0

Housing: Homeownership rate: 88.9%; Homeowner vacancy rate: 11.1%; Rental vacancy rate: 0.0%

POPLAR-COTTON CENTER (CDP). Covers a land area of 1.283 square miles and a water area of 0 square miles. Located at 36.06° N. Lat; 119.15° W. Long. Elevation is 377 feet.

Population: 2,470; Growth (since 2000): 65.1%; Density: 1,924.6 persons per square mile; Race: 70.0% White, 0.0% Black/African American, 14.4% Asian, 0.6% American Indian/Alaska Native, 0.0% Native Hawaiian/Other Pacific Islander, 1.7% Two or more races, 73.2% Hispanic of any race; Average household size: 4.29; Median age: 24.8; Age under 18: 38.8%; Age 65 and over: 8.1%; Males per 100 females: 104.3

Housing: Homeownership rate: 45.5%; Homeowner vacancy rate: 1.9%; Rental vacancy rate: 5.1%

PORTERVILLE (city). Covers a land area of 17.607 square miles and a water area of 0.072 square miles. Located at 36.06° N. Lat; 119.03° W. Long. Elevation is 459 feet.

History: Founded 1859 on the old Los Angeles—San Francisco stage route. Incorporated 1902.

Population: 54,165; Growth (since 2000): 36.7%; Density: 3,076.3 persons per square mile; Race: 58.8% White, 1.2% Black/African American, 4.7% Asian, 1.9% American Indian/Alaska Native, 0.1% Native Hawaiian/Other Pacific Islander, 4.7% Two or more races, 61.9% Hispanic of any race; Average household size: 3.39; Median age: 28.8; Age under 18: 33.5%; Age 65 and over: 9.4%; Males per 100 females: 97.9; Marriage status: 34.6% never married, 49.5% now married, 2.5% separated, 5.9% widowed, 10.0% divorced; Foreign born: 19.0%; Speak English only: 50.3%; With disability: 11.2%; Veterans: 7.4%; Ancestry: 5.4% German, 3.7% Irish, 3.4% English, 2.6% American, 2.0% Italian

Employment: 7.0% management, business, and financial, 0.9% computer, engineering, and science, 9.2% education, legal, community service, arts, and media, 4.6% healthcare practitioners, 24.4% service, 22.1% sales and office, 18.7% natural resources, construction, and maintenance, 13.0% production, transportation, and material moving

Income: Per capita: $17,248; Median household: $41,905; Average household: $55,020; Households with income of $100,000 or more: 13.1%; Poverty rate: 27.0%

Educational Attainment: High school diploma or higher: 68.9%; Bachelor's degree or higher: 10.5%; Graduate/professional degree or higher: 3.0%

School District(s)

Alta Vista Elementary (KG-08)
2012-13 Enrollment: 560. . . . . (559) 782-5700
Burton Elementary (KG-12)
2012-13 Enrollment: 4,228 . . . . (559) 781-8020
Citrus South Tule Elementary (KG-06)
2012-13 Enrollment: 53. . . . . (559) 784-6333
Hope Elementary (KG-08)
2012-13 Enrollment: 208. . . . . (559) 784-1064
Pleasant View Elementary (KG-08)
2012-13 Enrollment: 569. . . . . (559) 784-6769
Porterville Unified (KG-12)
2012-13 Enrollment: 13,835 . . . . (559) 793-2455
Rockford Elementary (KG-08)
2012-13 Enrollment: 406. . . . . (559) 784-5406
Tulare County Organization for Vocational Educatio
2012-13 Enrollment: n/a . . . . (559) 794-2406
Woodville Union Elementary (KG-08)
2012-13 Enrollment: 496. . . . . (559) 686-9712

Two-year College(s)

Porterville College (Public)
Fall 2013 Enrollment: 3,810 . . . . (559) 791-2200
2013-14 Tuition: In-state $1,322; Out-of-state $7,006

Housing: Homeownership rate: 57.3%; Median home value: $149,100; Median year structure built: 1982; Homeowner vacancy rate: 2.9%; Median gross rent: $772 per month; Rental vacancy rate: 6.3%

Health Insurance: 80.2% have insurance; 47.2% have private insurance; 41.3% have public insurance; 19.8% do not have insurance; 11.9% of children under 18 do not have insurance

Hospitals: Sierra View District Hospital (163 beds)

Safety: Violent crime rate: 35.1 per 10,000 population; Property crime rate: 272.5 per 10,000 population

Newspapers: Porterville Recorder (daily circulation 9100); Southern Sierra Messenger (weekly circulation 4000)

Transportation: Commute: 93.9% car, 1.0% public transportation, 1.1% walk, 2.2% work from home; Median travel time to work: 21.1 minutes

Airports: Porterville Municipal (general aviation)

Additional Information Contacts

City of Porterville . . . . (559) 782-7499
http://www.ci.porterville.ca.us

POSEY (CDP). Covers a land area of 0.357 square miles and a water area of 0 square miles. Located at 35.81° N. Lat; 118.68° W. Long. Elevation is 3,560 feet.

Population: 10; Growth (since 2000): n/a; Density: 28.0 persons per square mile; Race: 60.0% White, 0.0% Black/African American, 0.0% Asian, 30.0% American Indian/Alaska Native, 0.0% Native Hawaiian/Other Pacific Islander, 10.0% Two or more races, 30.0% Hispanic of any race;

Average household size: 2.00; Median age: 52.0; Age under 18: 0.0%; Age 65 and over: 30.0%; Males per 100 females: 66.7

Housing: Homeownership rate: 80.0%; Homeowner vacancy rate: 0.0%; Rental vacancy rate: 0.0%

POSO PARK (CDP). Covers a land area of 0.044 square miles and a water area of 0 square miles. Located at 35.81° N. Lat; 118.64° W. Long. Elevation is 4,665 feet.

Population: 9; Growth (since 2000): n/a; Density: 206.5 persons per square mile; Race: 100.0% White, 0.0% Black/African American, 0.0% Asian, 0.0% American Indian/Alaska Native, 0.0% Native Hawaiian/Other Pacific Islander, 0.0% Two or more races, 0.0% Hispanic of any race; Average household size: 2.25; Median age: 57.8; Age under 18: 0.0%; Age 65 and over: 44.4%; Males per 100 females: 350.0

Housing: Homeownership rate: 100.0%; Homeowner vacancy rate: 0.0%; Rental vacancy rate: 0.0%

RICHGROVE (CDP). Covers a land area of 0.452 square miles and a water area of 0 square miles. Located at 35.80° N. Lat; 119.11° W. Long. Elevation is 515 feet.

Population: 2,882; Growth (since 2000): 5.8%; Density: 6,376.2 persons per square mile; Race: 37.1% White, 0.7% Black/African American, 4.9% Asian, 1.3% American Indian/Alaska Native, 0.2% Native Hawaiian/Other Pacific Islander, 3.1% Two or more races, 93.9% Hispanic of any race; Average household size: 4.82; Median age: 22.9; Age under 18: 40.1%; Age 65 and over: 4.5%; Males per 100 females: 111.8; Marriage status: 48.3% never married, 46.8% now married, 2.2% separated, 2.1% widowed, 2.8% divorced; Foreign born: 45.5%; Speak English only: 5.1%; With disability: 8.4%; Veterans: 1.4%; Ancestry: 1.6% Polish, 0.5% Arab, 0.2% German

Employment: 0.9% management, business, and financial, 0.0% computer, engineering, and science, 7.1% education, legal, community service, arts, and media, 2.4% healthcare practitioners, 14.9% service, 12.2% sales and office, 52.4% natural resources, construction, and maintenance, 10.2% production, transportation, and material moving

Income: Per capita: $8,684; Median household: $30,200; Average household: $41,517; Households with income of $100,000 or more: 8.6%; Poverty rate: 42.1%

Educational Attainment: High school diploma or higher: 32.2%; Bachelor's degree or higher: 5.4%; Graduate/professional degree or higher: n/a

School District(s)

Richgrove Elementary (KG-08)
2012-13 Enrollment: 685. . . . . (661) 725-2424

Housing: Homeownership rate: 45.4%; Median home value: $121,600; Median year structure built: 1981; Homeowner vacancy rate: 0.0%; Median gross rent: $650 per month; Rental vacancy rate: 0.3%

Health Insurance: 69.1% have insurance; 23.5% have private insurance; 47.2% have public insurance; 30.9% do not have insurance; 9.6% of children under 18 do not have insurance

Transportation: Commute: 88.9% car, 1.5% public transportation, 3.2% walk, 1.5% work from home; Median travel time to work: 21.4 minutes

RODRIGUEZ CAMP (CDP). Covers a land area of 0.263 square miles and a water area of 0 square miles. Located at 35.81° N. Lat; 119.14° W. Long.

Population: 156; Growth (since 2000): n/a; Density: 592.3 persons per square mile; Race: 32.7% White, 0.0% Black/African American, 0.0% Asian, 0.0% American Indian/Alaska Native, 0.0% Native Hawaiian/Other Pacific Islander, 4.5% Two or more races, 96.8% Hispanic of any race; Average household size: 4.59; Median age: 19.1; Age under 18: 45.5%; Age 65 and over: 1.3%; Males per 100 females: 110.8

Housing: Homeownership rate: n/a; Homeowner vacancy rate: 0.0%; Rental vacancy rate: 0.0%

SEQUOIA CREST (CDP). Covers a land area of 1.022 square miles and a water area of 0 square miles. Located at 36.19° N. Lat; 118.63° W. Long.

Population: 10; Growth (since 2000): n/a; Density: 9.8 persons per square mile; Race: 100.0% White, 0.0% Black/African American, 0.0% Asian, 0.0% American Indian/Alaska Native, 0.0% Native Hawaiian/Other Pacific Islander, 0.0% Two or more races, 0.0% Hispanic of any race; Average household size: 1.67; Median age: 64.5; Age under 18: 20.0%; Age 65 and over: 40.0%; Males per 100 females: 150.0

Housing: Homeownership rate: 83.3%; Homeowner vacancy rate: 16.7%; Rental vacancy rate: 0.0%

SEQUOIA NATIONAL PARK (unincorporated postal area)
ZCTA: 93262

Covers a land area of 89.594 square miles and a water area of 0.325 square miles. Located at 36.62° N. Lat; 118.70° W. Long..

Population: 63; Growth (since 2000): 65.8%; Density: 0.7 persons per square mile; Race: 68.3% White, 3.2% Black/African American, 12.7% Asian, 1.6% American Indian/Alaska Native, 0.0% Native Hawaiian/Other Pacific Islander, 4.8% Two or more races, 28.6% Hispanic of any race; Average household size: 1.50; Median age: 26.5; Age under 18: 0.0%; Age 65 and over: 3.2%; Males per 100 females: 186.4

Housing: Homeownership rate: n/a; Homeowner vacancy rate: 0.0%; Rental vacancy rate: 0.0%

SEVILLE (CDP). Covers a land area of 0.636 square miles and a water area of 0 square miles. Located at 36.49° N. Lat; 119.22° W. Long. Elevation is 354 feet.

Population: 480; Growth (since 2000): n/a; Density: 754.5 persons per square mile; Race: 41.7% White, 0.0% Black/African American, 0.0% Asian, 1.0% American Indian/Alaska Native, 0.0% Native Hawaiian/Other Pacific Islander, 3.3% Two or more races, 95.4% Hispanic of any race; Average household size: 4.44; Median age: 24.0; Age under 18: 37.1%; Age 65 and over: 5.2%; Males per 100 females: 123.3

Housing: Homeownership rate: 51.0%; Homeowner vacancy rate: 1.8%; Rental vacancy rate: 1.8%

SPRINGVILLE (CDP). Covers a land area of 4.183 square miles and a water area of 0.017 square miles. Located at 36.11° N. Lat; 118.84° W. Long. Elevation is 1,024 feet.

Population: 934; Growth (since 2000): -15.8%; Density: 223.3 persons per square mile; Race: 89.5% White, 0.5% Black/African American, 0.7% Asian, 2.1% American Indian/Alaska Native, 0.0% Native Hawaiian/Other Pacific Islander, 4.4% Two or more races, 11.7% Hispanic of any race; Average household size: 2.19; Median age: 50.3; Age under 18: 18.5%; Age 65 and over: 20.9%; Males per 100 females: 95.0

School District(s)

Springville Union Elementary (KG-08)
2012-13 Enrollment: 317. . . . . (559) 539-2605

Housing: Homeownership rate: 61.8%; Homeowner vacancy rate: 3.3%; Rental vacancy rate: 15.1%

STRATHMORE (CDP). Covers a land area of 1.406 square miles and a water area of 0.013 square miles. Located at 36.14° N. Lat; 119.06° W. Long. Elevation is 400 feet.

Population: 2,819; Growth (since 2000): 9.1%; Density: 2,004.5 persons per square mile; Race: 52.9% White, 0.4% Black/African American, 0.2% Asian, 1.5% American Indian/Alaska Native, 0.0% Native Hawaiian/Other Pacific Islander, 3.8% Two or more races, 79.4% Hispanic of any race; Average household size: 4.00; Median age: 25.5; Age under 18: 37.3%; Age 65 and over: 7.1%; Males per 100 females: 99.6; Marriage status: 34.7% never married, 55.2% now married, 4.4% separated, 5.8% widowed, 4.3% divorced; Foreign born: 28.9%; Speak English only: 28.0%; With disability: 7.3%; Veterans: 3.1%; Ancestry: 7.5% English, 3.2% German, 2.9% Irish, 2.0% American, 0.4% Dutch

Employment: 2.2% management, business, and financial, 0.0% computer, engineering, and science, 2.3% education, legal, community service, arts, and media, 0.0% healthcare practitioners, 9.5% service, 21.9% sales and office, 42.5% natural resources, construction, and maintenance, 21.7% production, transportation, and material moving

Income: Per capita: $9,561; Median household: $26,047; Average household: $38,492; Households with income of $100,000 or more: 6.6%; Poverty rate: 36.9%

Educational Attainment: High school diploma or higher: 48.2%; Bachelor's degree or higher: 4.4%; Graduate/professional degree or higher: 1.1%

School District(s)

Porterville Unified (KG-12)
2012-13 Enrollment: 13,835 . . . . (559) 793-2455
Strathmore Union Elementary (KG-08)
2012-13 Enrollment: 832. . . . . (559) 568-1283
Sunnyside Union Elementary (KG-08)
2012-13 Enrollment: 363. . . . . (559) 568-1741

Housing: Homeownership rate: 51.9%; Median home value: $125,500; Median year structure built: 1976; Homeowner vacancy rate: 1.9%; Median gross rent: $741 per month; Rental vacancy rate: 6.4%

Health Insurance: 73.3% have insurance; 26.0% have private insurance; 51.1% have public insurance; 26.7% do not have insurance; 15.2% of children under 18 do not have insurance

Transportation: Commute: 100.0% car, 0.0% public transportation, 0.0% walk, 0.0% work from home; Median travel time to work: 17.9 minutes

SUGARLOAF VILLAGE (CDP). Covers a land area of 0.067 square miles and a water area of 0 square miles. Located at 35.83° N. Lat; 118.64° W. Long. Elevation is 5,203 feet.

Population: 10; Growth (since 2000): n/a; Density: 149.1 persons per square mile; Race: 90.0% White, 0.0% Black/African American, 0.0% Asian, 0.0% American Indian/Alaska Native, 0.0% Native Hawaiian/Other Pacific Islander, 10.0% Two or more races, 20.0% Hispanic of any race; Average household size: 2.00; Median age: 71.0; Age under 18: 10.0%; Age 65 and over: 70.0%; Males per 100 females: 66.7

Housing: Homeownership rate: 100.0%; Homeowner vacancy rate: 0.0%; Rental vacancy rate: 0.0%

SULTANA (CDP). Covers a land area of 0.444 square miles and a water area of 0 square miles. Located at 36.55° N. Lat; 119.34° W. Long. Elevation is 364 feet.

Population: 775; Growth (since 2000): n/a; Density: 1,746.4 persons per square mile; Race: 40.6% White, 0.0% Black/African American, 0.8% Asian, 0.4% American Indian/Alaska Native, 0.0% Native Hawaiian/Other Pacific Islander, 3.5% Two or more races, 89.7% Hispanic of any race; Average household size: 3.52; Median age: 27.1; Age under 18: 38.5%; Age 65 and over: 8.1%; Males per 100 females: 102.3

School District(s)

Monson-Sultana Joint Union Elementary (KG-08)
2012-13 Enrollment: 450. . . . . (559) 591-1634

Housing: Homeownership rate: 34.1%; Homeowner vacancy rate: 4.9%; Rental vacancy rate: 3.2%

TERRA BELLA (CDP). Covers a land area of 2.721 square miles and a water area of 0 square miles. Located at 35.96° N. Lat; 119.03° W. Long. Elevation is 486 feet.

Population: 3,310; Growth (since 2000): -4.5%; Density: 1,216.6 persons per square mile; Race: 43.1% White, 0.2% Black/African American, 2.3% Asian, 0.6% American Indian/Alaska Native, 0.1% Native Hawaiian/Other Pacific Islander, 1.5% Two or more races, 87.4% Hispanic of any race; Average household size: 4.19; Median age: 26.1; Age under 18: 37.9%; Age 65 and over: 6.6%; Males per 100 females: 104.6; Marriage status: 31.1% never married, 62.9% now married, 0.0% separated, 4.0% widowed, 2.0% divorced; Foreign born: 51.5%; Speak English only: 12.1%; With disability: 11.7%; Veterans: 1.7%; Ancestry: 1.7% Irish, 1.3% English, 1.0% Scotch-Irish, 0.8% German, 0.4% Scottish

Employment: 0.0% management, business, and financial, 2.8% computer, engineering, and science, 1.2% education, legal, community service, arts, and media, 0.0% healthcare practitioners, 9.0% service, 7.8% sales and office, 71.1% natural resources, construction, and maintenance, 8.0% production, transportation, and material moving

Income: Per capita: $9,680; Median household: $26,633; Average household: $38,171; Households with income of $100,000 or more: 2.8%; Poverty rate: 43.9%

Educational Attainment: High school diploma or higher: 28.5%; Bachelor's degree or higher: 5.6%; Graduate/professional degree or higher: n/a

School District(s)

Saucelito Elementary (KG-08)
2012-13 Enrollment: 82. . . . . (559) 784-2164

Terra Bella Union Elementary (KG-08)
2012-13 Enrollment: 936. . . . . (559) 535-4451

Housing: Homeownership rate: 48.4%; Median home value: $109,100; Median year structure built: 1975; Homeowner vacancy rate: 1.0%; Median gross rent: $602 per month; Rental vacancy rate: 3.8%

Health Insurance: 71.3% have insurance; 16.9% have private insurance; 62.1% have public insurance; 28.7% do not have insurance; 4.1% of children under 18 do not have insurance

Transportation: Commute: 93.2% car, 0.0% public transportation, 3.9% walk, 0.0% work from home; Median travel time to work: 28.6 minutes

TEVISTON (CDP). Covers a land area of 2.171 square miles and a water area of 0 square miles. Located at 35.93° N. Lat; 119.28° W. Long.

Population: 1,214; Growth (since 2000): n/a; Density: 559.2 persons per square mile; Race: 37.0% White, 4.1% Black/African American, 0.8% Asian, 0.7% American Indian/Alaska Native, 0.0% Native Hawaiian/Other Pacific Islander, 4.6% Two or more races, 85.6% Hispanic of any race; Average household size: 4.12; Median age: 24.0; Age under 18: 39.3%; Age 65 and over: 5.8%; Males per 100 females: 102.0

Housing: Homeownership rate: 43.7%; Homeowner vacancy rate: 7.2%; Rental vacancy rate: 5.1%

THREE RIVERS (CDP). Covers a land area of 44.505 square miles and a water area of 0 square miles. Located at 36.43° N. Lat; 118.88° W. Long. Elevation is 843 feet.

Population: 2,182; Growth (since 2000): -2.9%; Density: 49.0 persons per square mile; Race: 90.6% White, 0.3% Black/African American, 1.4% Asian, 1.2% American Indian/Alaska Native, 0.0% Native Hawaiian/Other Pacific Islander, 3.0% Two or more races, 9.7% Hispanic of any race; Average household size: 2.14; Median age: 52.3; Age under 18: 16.2%; Age 65 and over: 24.4%; Males per 100 females: 98.2

School District(s)

Three Rivers Union Elementary (KG-08)
2012-13 Enrollment: 142. . . . . (559) 561-4466

Housing: Homeownership rate: 72.7%; Homeowner vacancy rate: 3.1%; Rental vacancy rate: 7.6%

Newspapers: Kaweah Commonwealth (weekly circulation 3500)

TIPTON (CDP). Covers a land area of 1.010 square miles and a water area of 0 square miles. Located at 36.06° N. Lat; 119.31° W. Long. Elevation is 276 feet.

History: Tipton developed as a shipping center for cotton, milk, and poultry.

Population: 2,543; Growth (since 2000): 42.1%; Density: 2,518.5 persons per square mile; Race: 60.4% White, 0.1% Black/African American, 0.4% Asian, 0.6% American Indian/Alaska Native, 0.0% Native Hawaiian/Other Pacific Islander, 2.2% Two or more races, 84.4% Hispanic of any race; Average household size: 4.17; Median age: 24.0; Age under 18: 40.7%; Age 65 and over: 5.0%; Males per 100 females: 107.6; Marriage status: 41.2% never married, 51.7% now married, 0.5% separated, 3.7% widowed, 3.4% divorced; Foreign born: 45.1%; Speak English only: 21.3%; With disability: 10.9%; Veterans: 2.2%; Ancestry: 6.9% Portuguese, 3.0% Irish, 2.9% American, 2.6% English, 2.5% Arab

Employment: 3.6% management, business, and financial, 0.8% computer, engineering, and science, 2.3% education, legal, community service, arts, and media, 1.2% healthcare practitioners, 14.6% service, 15.6% sales and office, 43.9% natural resources, construction, and maintenance, 17.9% production, transportation, and material moving

Income: Per capita: $10,132; Median household: $34,158; Average household: $39,884; Households with income of $100,000 or more: 1.3%; Poverty rate: 14.7%

Educational Attainment: High school diploma or higher: 38.0%; Bachelor's degree or higher: 2.3%; Graduate/professional degree or higher: 1.1%

School District(s)

Tipton Elementary (KG-08)
2012-13 Enrollment: 607. . . . . (559) 752-4213

Housing: Homeownership rate: 47.5%; Median home value: $105,400; Median year structure built: 1983; Homeowner vacancy rate: 1.4%; Median gross rent: $859 per month; Rental vacancy rate: 7.5%

Health Insurance: 67.5% have insurance; 26.0% have private insurance; 44.6% have public insurance; 32.5% do not have insurance; 15.8% of children under 18 do not have insurance

Transportation: Commute: 96.5% car, 0.3% public transportation, 3.2% walk, 0.0% work from home; Median travel time to work: 18.1 minutes

TONYVILLE (CDP). Covers a land area of 0.050 square miles and a water area of 0 square miles. Located at 36.25° N. Lat; 119.09° W. Long. Elevation is 361 feet.

Population: 316; Growth (since 2000): n/a; Density: 6,257.9 persons per square mile; Race: 56.3% White, 0.0% Black/African American, 3.8% Asian, 0.0% American Indian/Alaska Native, 0.0% Native Hawaiian/Other Pacific Islander, 3.5% Two or more races, 90.5% Hispanic of any race; Average household size: 5.02; Median age: 27.3; Age under 18: 32.9%; Age 65 and over: 4.7%; Males per 100 females: 129.0

Housing: Homeownership rate: 36.5%; Homeowner vacancy rate: 0.0%; Rental vacancy rate: 4.8%

TOOLEVILLE (CDP). Covers a land area of 0.067 square miles and a water area of 0 square miles. Located at 36.29° N. Lat; 119.12° W. Long. Elevation is 397 feet.

Population: 339; Growth (since 2000): n/a; Density: 5,077.3 persons per square mile; Race: 42.8% White, 1.5% Black/African American, 2.4% Asian, 5.6% American Indian/Alaska Native, 0.6% Native Hawaiian/Other Pacific Islander, 3.5% Two or more races, 82.3% Hispanic of any race; Average household size: 4.35; Median age: 22.4; Age under 18: 36.6%; Age 65 and over: 5.6%; Males per 100 females: 100.6

Housing: Homeownership rate: 62.8%; Homeowner vacancy rate: 0.0%; Rental vacancy rate: 6.5%

TRAVER (CDP). Covers a land area of 0.843 square miles and a water area of 0 square miles. Located at 36.45° N. Lat; 119.48° W. Long. Elevation is 289 feet.

Population: 713; Growth (since 2000): -2.6%; Density: 845.4 persons per square mile; Race: 42.4% White, 0.1% Black/African American, 0.8% Asian, 3.1% American Indian/Alaska Native, 0.3% Native Hawaiian/Other Pacific Islander, 3.2% Two or more races, 77.3% Hispanic of any race; Average household size: 4.35; Median age: 29.7; Age under 18: 31.1%; Age 65 and over: 10.8%; Males per 100 females: 106.7

School District(s)

Traver Joint Elementary (KG-08)
2012-13 Enrollment: 227. . . . . (559) 897-2755

Housing: Homeownership rate: 57.9%; Homeowner vacancy rate: 4.0%; Rental vacancy rate: 2.8%

TULARE (city). Covers a land area of 20.931 square miles and a water area of 0.085 square miles. Located at 36.20° N. Lat; 119.34° W. Long. Elevation is 289 feet.

History: Tulare was founded in 1872 as division headquarters and a railroad repair center for the Southern Pacific Railroad. When the railroad shops were removed in 1891, the town turned to orchards and vineyards and became a shipping center.

Population: 59,278; Growth (since 2000): 34.7%; Density: 2,832.0 persons per square mile; Race: 61.3% White, 3.9% Black/African American, 2.2% Asian, 1.2% American Indian/Alaska Native, 0.1% Native Hawaiian/Other Pacific Islander, 4.8% Two or more races, 57.5% Hispanic of any race; Average household size: 3.33; Median age: 29.1; Age under 18: 33.3%; Age 65 and over: 9.0%; Males per 100 females: 96.6; Marriage status: 33.8% never married, 51.9% now married, 2.5% separated, 5.1% widowed, 9.3% divorced; Foreign born: 20.5%; Speak English only: 56.3%; With disability: 11.3%; Veterans: 5.9%; Ancestry: 7.5% Portuguese, 4.3% German, 3.4% American, 3.2% Irish, 3.2% English

Employment: 8.5% management, business, and financial, 2.2% computer, engineering, and science, 8.8% education, legal, community service, arts, and media, 3.4% healthcare practitioners, 19.5% service, 24.1% sales and office, 16.4% natural resources, construction, and maintenance, 17.1% production, transportation, and material moving

Income: Per capita: $18,260; Median household: $45,485; Average household: $58,691; Households with income of $100,000 or more: 14.6%; Poverty rate: 21.4%

Educational Attainment: High school diploma or higher: 73.2%; Bachelor's degree or higher: 11.4%; Graduate/professional degree or higher: 3.5%

School District(s)

Buena Vista Elementary (KG-08)
2012-13 Enrollment: 198. . . . . (559) 686-2015
Oak Valley Union Elementary (KG-08)
2012-13 Enrollment: 448. . . . . (559) 688-2908
Palo Verde Union Elementary (KG-08)
2012-13 Enrollment: 533. . . . . (559) 688-0648
Sundale Union Elementary (KG-08)
2012-13 Enrollment: 793. . . . . (559) 688-7451
Tulare City (KG-08)
2012-13 Enrollment: 9,434 . . . . (559) 685-7200
Tulare Joint Union High (09-12)
2012-13 Enrollment: 5,306 . . . . (559) 688-2021
Waukena Joint Union Elementary (KG-08)
2012-13 Enrollment: 281. . . . . (559) 686-3328

Vocational/Technical School(s)

Tulare Beauty College (Private, For-profit)
Fall 2013 Enrollment: 36. . . . . (559) 229-7480
2013-14 Tuition: $10,000

Housing: Homeownership rate: 58.7%; Median home value: $157,600; Median year structure built: 1984; Homeowner vacancy rate: 2.8%; Median gross rent: $919 per month; Rental vacancy rate: 5.5%

Health Insurance: 79.9% have insurance; 49.2% have private insurance; 37.7% have public insurance; 20.1% do not have insurance; 9.5% of children under 18 do not have insurance

Hospitals: Tulare Regional Medical Center (112 beds)

Safety: Violent crime rate: 70.0 per 10,000 population; Property crime rate: 425.4 per 10,000 population

Newspapers: Tulare Advance-Register (daily circulation 7000)

Transportation: Commute: 94.5% car, 0.8% public transportation, 1.3% walk, 2.1% work from home; Median travel time to work: 19.6 minutes

Additional Information Contacts

City of Tulare. . . . . (559) 684-4200
http://www.ci.tulare.ca.us

VISALIA (city). County seat. Covers a land area of 36.246 square miles and a water area of 0.020 square miles. Located at 36.33° N. Lat; 119.32° W. Long. Elevation is 331 feet.

History: Visalia was founded in 1852 by Nathaniel Vice, a bear hunter, who combined his own surname with his wife's given name, Sallie, to form Visalia. The early town of Visalia was a cattle town noted for the skill of its saddlemakers. The town became the seat of Tulare County.

Population: 124,442; Growth (since 2000): 35.9%; Density: 3,433.3 persons per square mile; Race: 64.5% White, 2.1% Black/African American, 5.4% Asian, 1.4% American Indian/Alaska Native, 0.1% Native Hawaiian/Other Pacific Islander, 4.6% Two or more races, 46.0% Hispanic of any race; Average household size: 2.98; Median age: 31.6; Age under 18: 30.1%; Age 65 and over: 10.3%; Males per 100 females: 95.2; Marriage status: 31.1% never married, 51.5% now married, 2.1% separated, 5.7% widowed, 11.8% divorced; Foreign born: 14.1%; Speak English only: 68.6%; With disability: 10.8%; Veterans: 7.3%; Ancestry: 7.1% German, 6.4% Irish, 5.7% American, 4.6% English, 2.7% Italian

Employment: 12.4% management, business, and financial, 2.6% computer, engineering, and science, 11.5% education, legal, community service, arts, and media, 5.7% healthcare practitioners, 21.0% service, 25.4% sales and office, 9.4% natural resources, construction, and maintenance, 12.0% production, transportation, and material moving

Income: Per capita: $23,144; Median household: $52,899; Average household: $68,924; Households with income of $100,000 or more: 22.6%; Poverty rate: 19.2%

Educational Attainment: High school diploma or higher: 81.8%; Bachelor's degree or higher: 21.6%; Graduate/professional degree or higher: 8.3%

School District(s)

Alpaugh Unified (KG-12)
2012-13 Enrollment: 577. . . . . (559) 949-8413
Liberty Elementary (KG-08)
2012-13 Enrollment: 323. . . . . (559) 686-1675
Outside Creek Elementary (KG-08)
2012-13 Enrollment: 114. . . . . (559) 747-0710
Stone Corral Elementary (KG-12)
2012-13 Enrollment: 484. . . . . (559) 528-4455
Tulare County Office of Education (KG-12)
2012-13 Enrollment: 2,246 . . . . (559) 733-6300
Visalia Unified (KG-12)
2012-13 Enrollment: 27,617 . . . . (559) 730-7300

Two-year College(s)

College of the Sequoias (Public)
Fall 2013 Enrollment: 10,720 . . . . (559) 730-3700
2013-14 Tuition: In-state $1,362; Out-of-state $5,922
San Joaquin Valley College-Visalia (Private, For-profit)
Fall 2013 Enrollment: 1,616 . . . . (559) 651-2500
2013-14 Tuition: In-state $16,606; Out-of-state $16,606

Vocational/Technical School(s)

Advanced Career Institute (Private, For-profit)
Fall 2013 Enrollment: 241. . . . . (559) 651-1978
2013-14 Tuition: $9,555
Estes Institute of Cosmetology Arts and Science (Private, For-profit)
Fall 2013 Enrollment: 89. . . . . (559) 733-3617
2013-14 Tuition: $12,575

Milan Institute of Cosmetology-Visalia (Private, For-profit)
Fall 2013 Enrollment: 276 . . . . (559) 730-5350
2013-14 Tuition: $16,184

Milan Institute-Visalia (Private, For-profit)
Fall 2013 Enrollment: 354 . . . . (559) 684-3900
2013-14 Tuition: $11,907

Housing: Homeownership rate: 61.4%; Median home value: $177,100; Median year structure built: 1983; Homeowner vacancy rate: 2.6%; Median gross rent: $956 per month; Rental vacancy rate: 6.7%

Health Insurance: 83.8% have insurance; 57.3% have private insurance; 34.9% have public insurance; 16.2% do not have insurance; 8.7% of children under 18 do not have insurance

Hospitals: Kaweah Delta Medical Center (495 beds)

Safety: Violent crime rate: 39.1 per 10,000 population; Property crime rate: 379.7 per 10,000 population

Newspapers: Visalia Times-Delta (daily circulation 19700)

Transportation: Commute: 90.9% car, 1.0% public transportation, 1.3% walk, 4.2% work from home; Median travel time to work: 19.9 minutes; Amtrak: Train service available.

Airports: Visalia Municipal (commercial service–non-primary)

Additional Information Contacts

City of Visalia. . . . . (559) 713-4300
http://www.ci.visalia.ca.us

WAUKENA (CDP). Covers a land area of 0.942 square miles and a water area of 0 square miles. Located at 36.14° N. Lat; 119.51° W. Long. Elevation is 226 feet.

Population: 108; Growth (since 2000): n/a; Density: 114.6 persons per square mile; Race: 79.6% White, 0.0% Black/African American, 0.0% Asian, 2.8% American Indian/Alaska Native, 0.0% Native Hawaiian/Other Pacific Islander, 0.0% Two or more races, 41.7% Hispanic of any race; Average household size: 2.92; Median age: 30.3; Age under 18: 31.5%; Age 65 and over: 6.5%; Males per 100 females: 125.0

Housing: Homeownership rate: 40.5%; Homeowner vacancy rate: 0.0%; Rental vacancy rate: 8.3%

WEST GOSHEN (CDP). Covers a land area of 1.178 square miles and a water area of 0 square miles. Located at 36.35° N. Lat; 119.45° W. Long.

Population: 511; Growth (since 2000): n/a; Density: 433.9 persons per square mile; Race: 54.0% White, 0.4% Black/African American, 1.4% Asian, 2.0% American Indian/Alaska Native, 0.0% Native Hawaiian/Other Pacific Islander, 4.1% Two or more races, 70.1% Hispanic of any race; Average household size: 3.68; Median age: 26.4; Age under 18: 32.9%; Age 65 and over: 7.2%; Males per 100 females: 115.6

Housing: Homeownership rate: 51.8%; Homeowner vacancy rate: 1.4%; Rental vacancy rate: 4.3%

WOODLAKE (city). Covers a land area of 2.248 square miles and a water area of 0.517 square miles. Located at 36.41° N. Lat; 119.10° W. Long. Elevation is 440 feet.

History: Settled 1914, incorporated 1939.

Population: 7,279; Growth (since 2000): 9.4%; Density: 3,238.7 persons per square mile; Race: 50.7% White, 0.5% Black/African American, 0.7% Asian, 1.5% American Indian/Alaska Native, 0.1% Native Hawaiian/Other Pacific Islander, 4.3% Two or more races, 87.7% Hispanic of any race; Average household size: 3.70; Median age: 26.4; Age under 18: 36.1%; Age 65 and over: 7.3%; Males per 100 females: 102.3; Marriage status: 34.6% never married, 51.1% now married, 2.3% separated, 4.2% widowed, 10.2% divorced; Foreign born: 28.3%; Speak English only: 30.4%; With disability: 9.5%; Veterans: 2.1%; Ancestry: 2.2% German, 1.5% Italian, 1.4% Irish, 1.4% Scotch-Irish, 1.3% English

Employment: 2.2% management, business, and financial, 0.3% computer, engineering, and science, 8.6% education, legal, community service, arts, and media, 2.0% healthcare practitioners, 25.4% service, 16.1% sales and office, 27.4% natural resources, construction, and maintenance, 18.1% production, transportation, and material moving

Income: Per capita: $12,505; Median household: $35,805; Average household: $46,160; Households with income of $100,000 or more: 7.6%; Poverty rate: 26.1%

Educational Attainment: High school diploma or higher: 54.4%; Bachelor's degree or higher: 7.2%; Graduate/professional degree or higher: 1.6%

Housing: Homeownership rate: 49.3%; Median home value: $111,500; Median year structure built: 1979; Homeowner vacancy rate: 2.0%; Median gross rent: $576 per month; Rental vacancy rate: 4.2%

Health Insurance: 77.0% have insurance; 29.5% have private insurance; 52.9% have public insurance; 23.0% do not have insurance; 4.9% of children under 18 do not have insurance

Safety: Violent crime rate: 13.5 per 10,000 population; Property crime rate: 180.7 per 10,000 population

Transportation: Commute: 92.9% car, 0.4% public transportation, 3.2% walk, 1.0% work from home; Median travel time to work: 21.5 minutes

Additional Information Contacts

City of Woodlake . . . . (559) 564-8055
http://www.cityofwoodlake.com/home.asp

WOODVILLE (CDP). Covers a land area of 4.352 square miles and a water area of 0 square miles. Located at 36.09° N. Lat; 119.20° W. Long. Elevation is 338 feet.

Population: 1,740; Growth (since 2000): 3.7%; Density: 399.9 persons per square mile; Race: 77.3% White, 0.1% Black/African American, 0.3% Asian, 1.8% American Indian/Alaska Native, 0.0% Native Hawaiian/Other Pacific Islander, 1.9% Two or more races, 88.8% Hispanic of any race; Average household size: 4.25; Median age: 26.5; Age under 18: 35.9%; Age 65 and over: 6.4%; Males per 100 females: 117.8

Housing: Homeownership rate: 54.7%; Homeowner vacancy rate: 0.0%; Rental vacancy rate: 3.1%

YETTEM (CDP). Covers a land area of 0.153 square miles and a water area of 0 square miles. Located at 36.49° N. Lat; 119.25° W. Long. Elevation is 344 feet.

Population: 211; Growth (since 2000): n/a; Density: 1,374.7 persons per square mile; Race: 22.7% White, 2.4% Black/African American, 0.0% Asian, 0.0% American Indian/Alaska Native, 0.0% Native Hawaiian/Other Pacific Islander, 4.7% Two or more races, 94.3% Hispanic of any race; Average household size: 4.14; Median age: 23.8; Age under 18: 37.0%; Age 65 and over: 4.7%; Males per 100 females: 119.8

School District(s)

Cutler-Orosi Joint Unified (KG-12)
2012-13 Enrollment: 4,128 . . . . (559) 528-4763

Housing: Homeownership rate: 25.5%; Homeowner vacancy rate: 23.5%; Rental vacancy rate: 11.6%

Tuolumne County

Located in central and eastern California, in the Sierra Nevada; drained by the Tuolumne and Stanislaus Rivers; includes part of the Stanislaus National Forest. Covers a land area of 2,220.884 square miles, a water area of 53.546 square miles, and is located in the Pacific Time Zone at 38.02° N. Lat., 119.96° W. Long. The county was founded in 1850. County seat is Sonora.

Tuolumne County is part of the Sonora, CA Micropolitan Statistical Area. The entire metro area includes: Tuolumne County, CA

Weather Station: Cherry Valley Dam — Elevation: 4,765 feet

	Jan	Feb	Mar	Apr	May	Jun	Jul	Aug	Sep	Oct	Nov	Dec
High	48	50	54	61	70	79	87	87	80	68	55	48
Low	30	30	32	36	44	50	57	56	51	43	35	30
Precip	9.6	8.8	7.2	3.6	2.1	0.8	0.2	0.1	0.9	2.9	5.6	7.3
Snow	24.4	24.4	23.2	8.1	0.8	0.1	0.0	0.0	tr	0.5	6.6	19.9

High and Low temperatures in degrees Fahrenheit; Precipitation and Snow in inches

Weather Station: Hetch Hetchy — Elevation: 3,870 feet

	Jan	Feb	Mar	Apr	May	Jun	Jul	Aug	Sep	Oct	Nov	Dec
High	48	52	57	62	70	78	86	86	80	70	56	47
Low	31	32	34	39	45	51	58	57	52	44	36	31
Precip	6.6	6.0	5.6	3.2	2.1	0.7	0.3	0.1	0.8	2.1	4.2	5.4
Snow	9.5	11.5	9.6	2.8	0.1	tr	0.0	0.0	0.0	0.0	1.8	9.9

High and Low temperatures in degrees Fahrenheit; Precipitation and Snow in inches

Population: 55,365; Growth (since 2000): 1.6%; Density: 24.9 persons per square mile; Race: 87.2% White, 2.1% Black/African American, 1.0% Asian, 1.9% American Indian/Alaska Native, 0.1% Native Hawaiian/Other Pacific Islander, 3.7% two or more races, 10.7% Hispanic of any race; Average household size: 2.30; Median age: 47.3; Age under 18: 17.5%; Age 65 and over: 20.4%; Males per 100 females: 112.0; Marriage status: 24.8% never married, 54.3% now married, 1.7% separated, 7.6%

widowed, 13.3% divorced; Foreign born: 4.8%; Speak English only: 92.4%; With disability: 18.4%; Veterans: 11.9%; Ancestry: 19.3% German, 15.5% Irish, 13.7% English, 8.1% Italian, 5.4% American

Religion: Six largest groups: 26.6% Catholicism, 6.3% Non-denominational Protestant, 3.1% Pentecostal, 2.6% Latter-day Saints, 1.9% Adventist, 1.6% Baptist

Economy: Unemployment rate: 7.1%; Leading industries: 13.7% construction; 13.3% retail trade; 12.9% health care and social assistance; Farms: 391 totaling 87,813 acres; Company size: 1 employs 1,000 or more persons, 1 employs 500 to 999 persons, 8 employ 100 to 499 persons, 1,301 employs less than 100 persons; Business ownership: n/a women-owned, n/a Black-owned, n/a Hispanic-owned, n/a Asian-owned

Employment: 13.4% management, business, and financial, 3.8% computer, engineering, and science, 10.1% education, legal, community service, arts, and media, 5.0% healthcare practitioners, 26.3% service, 21.5% sales and office, 10.1% natural resources, construction, and maintenance, 9.8% production, transportation, and material moving

Income: Per capita: $25,943; Median household: $48,426; Average household: $62,918; Households with income of $100,000 or more: 16.6%; Poverty rate: 14.5%

Educational Attainment: High school diploma or higher: 89.1%; Bachelor's degree or higher: 19.5%; Graduate/professional degree or higher: 6.5%

Housing: Homeownership rate: 69.8%; Median home value: $269,400; Median year structure built: 1978; Homeowner vacancy rate: 3.5%; Median gross rent: $919 per month; Rental vacancy rate: 9.5%

Vital Statistics: Birth rate: 80.0 per 10,000 population; Death rate: 100.2 per 10,000 population; Age-adjusted cancer mortality rate: 147.1 deaths per 100,000 population

Health Insurance: 88.1% have insurance; 64.8% have private insurance; 44.6% have public insurance; 11.9% do not have insurance; 6.7% of children under 18 do not have insurance

Health Care: Physicians: 20.9 per 10,000 population; Hospital beds: 27.8 per 10,000 population; Hospital admissions: 931.2 per 10,000 population

Air Quality Index: 90.7% good, 9.0% moderate, 0.3% unhealthy for sensitive individuals, 0.0% unhealthy (percent of days)

Transportation: Commute: 87.5% car, 0.4% public transportation, 4.2% walk, 6.3% work from home; Median travel time to work: 25.1 minutes

Presidential Election: 40.9% Obama, 56.5% Romney (2012)

National and State Parks: Columbia State Historic Park; Railtown 1897 State Historic Park; Stanislaus National Forest; Tuolumne State Game Refuge

Additional Information Contacts

Tuolumne Government . . . . (209) 533-5521
http://www.tuolumnecounty.ca.gov

Tuolumne County Communities

BIG OAK FLAT (unincorporated postal area)

ZCTA: 95305

Covers a land area of 14.262 square miles and a water area of 0.556 square miles. Located at 37.79° N. Lat; 120.27° W. Long. Elevation is 2,838 feet.

Population: 245; Growth (since 2000): 64.4%; Density: 17.2 persons per square mile; Race: 92.7% White, 0.0% Black/African American, 0.8% Asian, 2.0% American Indian/Alaska Native, 0.4% Native Hawaiian/Other Pacific Islander, 3.3% Two or more races, 4.1% Hispanic of any race; Average household size: 2.27; Median age: 49.1; Age under 18: 15.5%; Age 65 and over: 15.1%; Males per 100 females: 102.5

Housing: Homeownership rate: 63.9%; Homeowner vacancy rate: 2.8%; Rental vacancy rate: 17.0%

CEDAR RIDGE (CDP). Covers a land area of 7.789 square miles and a water area of 0.009 square miles. Located at 38.07° N. Lat; 120.27° W. Long. Elevation is 3,717 feet.

Population: 1,132; Growth (since 2000): n/a; Density: 145.3 persons per square mile; Race: 94.2% White, 0.3% Black/African American, 0.4% Asian, 0.5% American Indian/Alaska Native, 0.1% Native Hawaiian/Other Pacific Islander, 4.1% Two or more races, 6.3% Hispanic of any race; Average household size: 2.35; Median age: 52.2; Age under 18: 17.4%; Age 65 and over: 20.9%; Males per 100 females: 106.6

Housing: Homeownership rate: 84.6%; Homeowner vacancy rate: 4.9%; Rental vacancy rate: 10.1%

CHINESE CAMP (CDP). Covers a land area of 0.898 square miles and a water area of 0.003 square miles. Located at 37.87° N. Lat; 120.44° W. Long. Elevation is 1,273 feet.

History: At Chinese Camp some 5,000 Chinese miners searched for gold in the 1850's. Just west, on a plain at the foot of Table Mountain, the first tong war in California was waged in 1856.

Population: 126; Growth (since 2000): -13.7%; Density: 140.3 persons per square mile; Race: 73.0% White, 0.0% Black/African American, 0.0% Asian, 5.6% American Indian/Alaska Native, 0.0% Native Hawaiian/Other Pacific Islander, 8.7% Two or more races, 19.8% Hispanic of any race; Average household size: 2.52; Median age: 43.5; Age under 18: 23.8%; Age 65 and over: 11.9%; Males per 100 females: 106.6

School District(s)

Jamestown Elementary (KG-09)
2012-13 Enrollment: 534. . . . . (209) 984-4058

Housing: Homeownership rate: 72.0%; Homeowner vacancy rate: 2.6%; Rental vacancy rate: 0.0%

COLD SPRINGS (CDP). Covers a land area of 1.734 square miles and a water area of 0 square miles. Located at 38.16° N. Lat; 120.05° W. Long. Elevation is 5,669 feet.

Population: 181; Growth (since 2000): n/a; Density: 104.4 persons per square mile; Race: 96.7% White, 0.6% Black/African American, 0.6% Asian, 1.7% American Indian/Alaska Native, 0.0% Native Hawaiian/Other Pacific Islander, 0.6% Two or more races, 2.2% Hispanic of any race; Average household size: 1.93; Median age: 51.5; Age under 18: 15.5%; Age 65 and over: 23.8%; Males per 100 females: 112.9

Housing: Homeownership rate: 70.2%; Homeowner vacancy rate: 1.5%; Rental vacancy rate: 20.0%

COLUMBIA (CDP). Covers a land area of 5.961 square miles and a water area of 0.018 square miles. Located at 38.03° N. Lat; 120.42° W. Long. Elevation is 2,139 feet.

History: Columbia was once known as the Gem of the Southern Mines, the richest, noisiest, fastest-growing camp in the Mother Lode in 1850. Thaddeus Hildreth and his brother found gold here and within a month Hildreth's Diggings, as it was called, had 6,000 residents.

Population: 2,297; Growth (since 2000): -4.5%; Density: 385.3 persons per square mile; Race: 89.9% White, 1.2% Black/African American, 1.3% Asian, 1.1% American Indian/Alaska Native, 0.0% Native Hawaiian/Other Pacific Islander, 5.4% Two or more races, 7.4% Hispanic of any race; Average household size: 2.22; Median age: 47.8; Age under 18: 20.5%; Age 65 and over: 21.1%; Males per 100 females: 97.3

School District(s)

Columbia Union (KG-08)
2012-13 Enrollment: 584. . . . . (209) 532-0202

Housing: Homeownership rate: 65.9%; Homeowner vacancy rate: 2.1%; Rental vacancy rate: 8.1%

Airports: Columbia (general aviation)

EAST SONORA (CDP). Covers a land area of 2.476 square miles and a water area of 0.005 square miles. Located at 37.97° N. Lat; 120.34° W. Long. Elevation is 2,106 feet.

Population: 2,266; Growth (since 2000): 9.0%; Density: 915.3 persons per square mile; Race: 94.0% White, 0.3% Black/African American, 1.4% Asian, 0.7% American Indian/Alaska Native, 0.0% Native Hawaiian/Other Pacific Islander, 2.0% Two or more races, 6.7% Hispanic of any race; Average household size: 1.87; Median age: 60.4; Age under 18: 12.7%; Age 65 and over: 43.2%; Males per 100 females: 74.7

Housing: Homeownership rate: 60.3%; Homeowner vacancy rate: 5.3%; Rental vacancy rate: 11.1%

GROVELAND (CDP). Covers a land area of 9.561 square miles and a water area of 0.006 square miles. Located at 37.83° N. Lat; 120.24° W. Long. Elevation is 2,851 feet.

Population: 601; Growth (since 2000): n/a; Density: 62.9 persons per square mile; Race: 90.2% White, 0.3% Black/African American, 1.5% Asian, 1.5% American Indian/Alaska Native, 0.3% Native Hawaiian/Other Pacific Islander, 3.3% Two or more races, 8.2% Hispanic of any race; Average household size: 2.17; Median age: 49.6; Age under 18: 15.3%; Age 65 and over: 19.0%; Males per 100 females: 104.4

School District(s)

Big Oak Flat-Groveland Unified (KG-12)
2012-13 Enrollment: 360. . . . . (209) 962-5765

Housing: Homeownership rate: 65.7%; Homeowner vacancy rate: 2.2%; Rental vacancy rate: 10.4%

JAMESTOWN (CDP). Covers a land area of 2.994 square miles and a water area of 0.002 square miles. Located at 37.96° N. Lat; 120.41° W. Long. Elevation is 1,427 feet.
History: Called Jimtown by the miners, Jamestown was named for Colonel George F. James, a San Francisco lawyer who tried his luck at mining here in 1848. The Humbug Mine was the biggest producer in Jamestown.
Population: 3,433; Growth (since 2000): 13.8%; Density: 1,146.4 persons per square mile; Race: 85.9% White, 0.6% Black/African American, 0.8% Asian, 2.8% American Indian/Alaska Native, 0.1% Native Hawaiian/Other Pacific Islander, 5.9% Two or more races, 14.9% Hispanic of any race; Average household size: 2.28; Median age: 44.7; Age under 18: 21.9%; Age 65 and over: 22.4%; Males per 100 females: 90.2; Marriage status: 27.7% never married, 49.9% now married, 3.8% separated, 9.4% widowed, 13.0% divorced; Foreign born: 4.2%; Speak English only: 95.3%; With disability: 16.9%; Veterans: 8.3%; Ancestry: 20.8% German, 14.7% Irish, 14.3% English, 5.9% American, 5.3% Dutch
Employment: 8.7% management, business, and financial, 2.3% computer, engineering, and science, 3.2% education, legal, community service, arts, and media, 0.0% healthcare practitioners, 38.3% service, 22.0% sales and office, 16.0% natural resources, construction, and maintenance, 9.4% production, transportation, and material moving
Income: Per capita: $19,617; Median household: $29,123; Average household: $44,373; Households with income of $100,000 or more: 8.8%; Poverty rate: 32.2%
Educational Attainment: High school diploma or higher: 87.8%; Bachelor's degree or higher: 7.6%; Graduate/professional degree or higher: 0.7%

School District(s)

Jamestown Elementary (KG-09)
2012-13 Enrollment: 534. . . . . (209) 984-4058

Housing: Homeownership rate: 58.9%; Median home value: $161,500; Median year structure built: 1984; Homeowner vacancy rate: 3.4%; Median gross rent: $861 per month; Rental vacancy rate: 9.5%
Health Insurance: 88.8% have insurance; 44.7% have private insurance; 58.0% have public insurance; 11.2% do not have insurance; 5.1% of children under 18 do not have insurance
Transportation: Commute: 93.2% car, 1.4% public transportation, 2.7% walk, 0.0% work from home; Median travel time to work: 28.7 minutes

LA GRANGE (unincorporated postal area)
ZCTA: 95329
Covers a land area of 109.261 square miles and a water area of 7.866 square miles. Located at 37.67° N. Lat; 120.41° W. Long..
Population: 2,460; Growth (since 2000): 41.7%; Density: 22.5 persons per square mile; Race: 88.5% White, 0.9% Black/African American, 2.1% Asian, 1.7% American Indian/Alaska Native, 0.1% Native Hawaiian/Other Pacific Islander, 3.5% Two or more races, 11.7% Hispanic of any race; Average household size: 2.46; Median age: 49.9; Age under 18: 19.5%; Age 65 and over: 20.0%; Males per 100 females: 105.9

School District(s)

Big Oak Flat-Groveland Unified (KG-12)
2012-13 Enrollment: 360. . . . . (209) 962-5765
Tuolumne County Superintendent of Schools (PK-12)
2012-13 Enrollment: 127. . . . . (209) 536-2000

Housing: Homeownership rate: 81.0%; Homeowner vacancy rate: 6.7%; Rental vacancy rate: 7.4%

LONG BARN (CDP). Covers a land area of 2.877 square miles and a water area of 0.001 square miles. Located at 38.09° N. Lat; 120.13° W. Long. Elevation is 5,013 feet.
Population: 155; Growth (since 2000): n/a; Density: 53.9 persons per square mile; Race: 90.3% White, 0.6% Black/African American, 0.0% Asian, 1.9% American Indian/Alaska Native, 0.0% Native Hawaiian/Other Pacific Islander, 3.9% Two or more races, 8.4% Hispanic of any race; Average household size: 1.91; Median age: 54.3; Age under 18: 14.8%; Age 65 and over: 21.9%; Males per 100 females: 115.3

School District(s)

Summerville Union High (KG-12)
2012-13 Enrollment: 1,088 . . . . (209) 928-3498

Housing: Homeownership rate: 66.7%; Homeowner vacancy rate: 1.8%; Rental vacancy rate: 17.6%

MI-WUK VILLAGE (CDP). Covers a land area of 2.778 square miles and a water area of 0.006 square miles. Located at 38.06° N. Lat; 120.18° W. Long. Elevation is 4,678 feet.
Population: 941; Growth (since 2000): -36.6%; Density: 338.7 persons per square mile; Race: 92.6% White, 0.5% Black/African American, 0.3% Asian, 1.8% American Indian/Alaska Native, 0.0% Native Hawaiian/Other Pacific Islander, 3.6% Two or more races, 7.5% Hispanic of any race; Average household size: 2.26; Median age: 50.9; Age under 18: 17.0%; Age 65 and over: 21.5%; Males per 100 females: 104.1
Housing: Homeownership rate: 76.9%; Homeowner vacancy rate: 4.7%; Rental vacancy rate: 11.5%

MONO VISTA (CDP). Covers a land area of 2.836 square miles and a water area of 0.003 square miles. Located at 38.01° N. Lat; 120.27° W. Long. Elevation is 2,992 feet.
Population: 3,127; Growth (since 2000): 1.8%; Density: 1,102.7 persons per square mile; Race: 89.4% White, 0.2% Black/African American, 1.2% Asian, 1.9% American Indian/Alaska Native, 0.3% Native Hawaiian/Other Pacific Islander, 5.1% Two or more races, 9.6% Hispanic of any race; Average household size: 2.56; Median age: 40.5; Age under 18: 23.4%; Age 65 and over: 15.5%; Males per 100 females: 99.9; Marriage status: 30.5% never married, 49.5% now married, 2.3% separated, 6.8% widowed, 13.2% divorced; Foreign born: 5.1%; Speak English only: 92.5%; With disability: 26.4%; Veterans: 14.1%; Ancestry: 16.8% German, 8.1% English, 8.0% European, 7.3% Italian, 6.2% Swedish
Employment: 12.7% management, business, and financial, 2.1% computer, engineering, and science, 12.8% education, legal, community service, arts, and media, 5.0% healthcare practitioners, 24.9% service, 12.4% sales and office, 24.5% natural resources, construction, and maintenance, 5.6% production, transportation, and material moving
Income: Per capita: $21,027; Median household: $37,353; Average household: $50,552; Households with income of $100,000 or more: 11.4%; Poverty rate: 20.8%
Educational Attainment: High school diploma or higher: 91.4%; Bachelor's degree or higher: 15.4%; Graduate/professional degree or higher: 3.1%
Housing: Homeownership rate: 74.1%; Median home value: $222,400; Median year structure built: 1978; Homeowner vacancy rate: 5.3%; Median gross rent: $839 per month; Rental vacancy rate: 10.5%
Health Insurance: 91.9% have insurance; 56.3% have private insurance; 52.9% have public insurance; 8.1% do not have insurance; 0.0% of children under 18 do not have insurance
Transportation: Commute: 80.4% car, 0.0% public transportation, 2.9% walk, 16.6% work from home; Median travel time to work: 19.1 minutes

PHOENIX LAKE (CDP). Covers a land area of 11.010 square miles and a water area of 0.129 square miles. Located at 38.01° N. Lat; 120.31° W. Long. Elevation is 2,434 feet.
Population: 4,269; Growth (since 2000): n/a; Density: 387.7 persons per square mile; Race: 93.5% White, 0.4% Black/African American, 1.2% Asian, 0.9% American Indian/Alaska Native, 0.1% Native Hawaiian/Other Pacific Islander, 2.8% Two or more races, 7.1% Hispanic of any race; Average household size: 2.42; Median age: 52.9; Age under 18: 18.1%; Age 65 and over: 26.7%; Males per 100 females: 96.5; Marriage status: 13.8% never married, 66.4% now married, 1.0% separated, 11.5% widowed, 8.3% divorced; Foreign born: 4.5%; Speak English only: 93.0%; With disability: 20.4%; Veterans: 18.2%; Ancestry: 15.6% American, 14.3% English, 12.5% German, 11.6% Irish, 7.9% Italian
Employment: 13.4% management, business, and financial, 6.2% computer, engineering, and science, 15.9% education, legal, community service, arts, and media, 10.1% healthcare practitioners, 21.5% service, 22.5% sales and office, 4.4% natural resources, construction, and maintenance, 6.1% production, transportation, and material moving
Income: Per capita: $33,563; Median household: $69,904; Average household: $82,826; Households with income of $100,000 or more: 27.8%; Poverty rate: 5.3%
Educational Attainment: High school diploma or higher: 93.1%; Bachelor's degree or higher: 36.8%; Graduate/professional degree or higher: 12.0%
Housing: Homeownership rate: 87.0%; Median home value: $300,600; Median year structure built: 1980; Homeowner vacancy rate: 2.8%; Median gross rent: $1,415 per month; Rental vacancy rate: 5.7%
Health Insurance: 92.0% have insurance; 78.1% have private insurance; 45.9% have public insurance; 8.0% do not have insurance; 11.1% of children under 18 do not have insurance

Transportation: Commute: 91.9% car, 0.0% public transportation, 1.5% walk, 6.6% work from home; Median travel time to work: 20.8 minutes

PINE MOUNTAIN LAKE (CDP). Covers a land area of 18.972 square miles and a water area of 0.280 square miles. Located at 37.86° N. Lat; 120.18° W. Long.

Population: 2,796; Growth (since 2000): n/a; Density: 147.4 persons per square mile; Race: 92.8% White, 0.6% Black/African American, 0.9% Asian, 0.9% American Indian/Alaska Native, 0.3% Native Hawaiian/Other Pacific Islander, 3.8% Two or more races, 6.5% Hispanic of any race; Average household size: 2.08; Median age: 60.0; Age under 18: 13.3%; Age 65 and over: 36.3%; Males per 100 females: 94.6; Marriage status: 10.5% never married, 68.0% now married, 0.0% separated, 7.9% widowed, 13.6% divorced; Foreign born: 4.5%; Speak English only: 95.3%; With disability: 16.4%; Veterans: 21.8%; Ancestry: 24.2% English, 15.6% German, 9.9% American, 9.8% Irish, 6.5% Scottish

Employment: 11.8% management, business, and financial, 3.4% computer, engineering, and science, 7.0% education, legal, community service, arts, and media, 7.6% healthcare practitioners, 32.9% service, 27.9% sales and office, 5.7% natural resources, construction, and maintenance, 3.6% production, transportation, and material moving

Income: Per capita: $31,361; Median household: $49,893; Average household: $63,829; Households with income of $100,000 or more: 18.5%; Poverty rate: 11.5%

Educational Attainment: High school diploma or higher: 96.4%; Bachelor's degree or higher: 28.2%; Graduate/professional degree or higher: 6.5%

Housing: Homeownership rate: 83.0%; Median home value: $264,400; Median year structure built: 1984; Homeowner vacancy rate: 5.2%; Median gross rent: $791 per month; Rental vacancy rate: 20.7%

Health Insurance: 89.1% have insurance; 71.4% have private insurance; 45.1% have public insurance; 10.9% do not have insurance; 15.9% of children under 18 do not have insurance

Transportation: Commute: 90.0% car, 0.0% public transportation, 2.6% walk, 7.4% work from home; Median travel time to work: 28.9 minutes

SIERRA VILLAGE (CDP). Covers a land area of 2.525 square miles and a water area of 0.004 square miles. Located at 38.08° N. Lat; 120.16° W. Long. Elevation is 4,849 feet.

Population: 456; Growth (since 2000): n/a; Density: 180.6 persons per square mile; Race: 92.3% White, 0.7% Black/African American, 0.7% Asian, 1.5% American Indian/Alaska Native, 0.2% Native Hawaiian/Other Pacific Islander, 3.1% Two or more races, 7.9% Hispanic of any race; Average household size: 2.06; Median age: 53.4; Age under 18: 14.3%; Age 65 and over: 23.7%; Males per 100 females: 113.1

Housing: Homeownership rate: 69.7%; Homeowner vacancy rate: 4.9%; Rental vacancy rate: 11.8%

SONORA (city). County seat. Covers a land area of 3.064 square miles and a water area of 0.014 square miles. Located at 37.98° N. Lat; 120.38° W. Long. Elevation is 1,785 feet.

History: In 1848 Sonora was Sonorian Camp, settled by Mexicans from the state of Sonora. Men of several nationalities came during 1849, prompting the new California government to impose a tax on foreign-born miners. It was Chileans who in 1851 discovered the richest pocket mine in the Mother Lode, the Big Bonanza on Piety Hill.

Population: 4,903; Growth (since 2000): 10.9%; Density: 1,600.1 persons per square mile; Race: 89.8% White, 0.5% Black/African American, 1.6% Asian, 1.9% American Indian/Alaska Native, 0.2% Native Hawaiian/Other Pacific Islander, 4.2% Two or more races, 11.1% Hispanic of any race; Average household size: 2.10; Median age: 39.7; Age under 18: 19.9%; Age 65 and over: 16.6%; Males per 100 females: 93.0; Marriage status: 28.9% never married, 42.6% now married, 2.0% separated, 8.8% widowed, 19.8% divorced; Foreign born: 5.5%; Speak English only: 91.5%; With disability: 18.8%; Veterans: 12.3%; Ancestry: 18.7% German, 17.6% English, 16.6% Irish, 8.1% Italian, 4.9% Scottish

Employment: 14.5% management, business, and financial, 3.3% computer, engineering, and science, 15.1% education, legal, community service, arts, and media, 3.3% healthcare practitioners, 26.5% service, 20.0% sales and office, 6.3% natural resources, construction, and maintenance, 11.0% production, transportation, and material moving

Income: Per capita: $26,127; Median household: $31,386; Average household: $53,710; Households with income of $100,000 or more: 14.0%; Poverty rate: 24.3%

Educational Attainment: High school diploma or higher: 85.7%; Bachelor's degree or higher: 24.1%; Graduate/professional degree or higher: 7.8%

School District(s)

Belleview Elementary (KG-08)
2012-13 Enrollment: 128. . . . . (209) 586-5510

Curtis Creek Elementary (KG-08)
2012-13 Enrollment: 465. . . . . (209) 533-1083

Sonora Elementary (KG-08)
2012-13 Enrollment: 662. . . . . (209) 532-5491

Sonora Union High (09-12)
2012-13 Enrollment: 1,186 . . . . (209) 533-8510

Summerville Union High (KG-12)
2012-13 Enrollment: 1,088 . . . . (209) 928-3498

Tuolumne County Superintendent of Schools (PK-12)
2012-13 Enrollment: 127. . . . . (209) 536-2000

Two-year College(s)

Columbia College (Public)
Fall 2013 Enrollment: 2,626 . . . . (209) 588-5100
2013-14 Tuition: In-state $1,150; Out-of-state $6,046

Housing: Homeownership rate: 40.8%; Median home value: $296,800; Median year structure built: 1964; Homeowner vacancy rate: 4.6%; Median gross rent: $798 per month; Rental vacancy rate: 8.6%

Health Insurance: 81.5% have insurance; 54.5% have private insurance; 46.4% have public insurance; 18.5% do not have insurance; 9.5% of children under 18 do not have insurance

Hospitals: Sonora Regional Medical Center (152 beds)

Safety: Violent crime rate: 27.2 per 10,000 population; Property crime rate: 636.8 per 10,000 population

Newspapers: Union Democrat (daily circulation 11800)

Transportation: Commute: 81.1% car, 1.9% public transportation, 8.8% walk, 7.9% work from home; Median travel time to work: 23.6 minutes

Additional Information Contacts

City of Sonora . . . . (209) 532-4541
http://www.sonoraca.com

SOULSBYVILLE (CDP). Covers a land area of 3.010 square miles and a water area of 0.006 square miles. Located at 37.99° N. Lat; 120.26° W. Long. Elevation is 2,930 feet.

History: Soulsbyville developed as a mining town in 1856.

Population: 2,215; Growth (since 2000): 28.1%; Density: 735.8 persons per square mile; Race: 92.0% White, 0.1% Black/African American, 0.6% Asian, 1.9% American Indian/Alaska Native, 0.1% Native Hawaiian/Other Pacific Islander, 3.6% Two or more races, 9.3% Hispanic of any race; Average household size: 2.54; Median age: 42.9; Age under 18: 22.7%; Age 65 and over: 15.8%; Males per 100 females: 101.4

School District(s)

Soulsbyville Elementary (KG-08)
2012-13 Enrollment: 481. . . . . (209) 532-1419

Housing: Homeownership rate: 77.2%; Homeowner vacancy rate: 3.0%; Rental vacancy rate: 2.4%

STRAWBERRY (CDP). Covers a land area of 0.521 square miles and a water area of 0.008 square miles. Located at 38.20° N. Lat; 120.01° W. Long. Elevation is 5,325 feet.

Population: 86; Growth (since 2000): n/a; Density: 164.9 persons per square mile; Race: 95.3% White, 0.0% Black/African American, 0.0% Asian, 0.0% American Indian/Alaska Native, 0.0% Native Hawaiian/Other Pacific Islander, 3.5% Two or more races, 8.1% Hispanic of any race; Average household size: 1.79; Median age: 55.7; Age under 18: 12.8%; Age 65 and over: 26.7%; Males per 100 females: 120.5

Housing: Homeownership rate: 89.3%; Homeowner vacancy rate: 12.5%; Rental vacancy rate: 16.7%

TUOLUMNE CITY (CDP). Covers a land area of 2.332 square miles and a water area of 0.030 square miles. Located at 37.96° N. Lat; 120.24° W. Long. Elevation is 2,592 feet.

Population: 1,779; Growth (since 2000): -4.6%; Density: 762.9 persons per square mile; Race: 87.0% White, 0.7% Black/African American, 0.7% Asian, 4.7% American Indian/Alaska Native, 0.1% Native Hawaiian/Other Pacific Islander, 4.1% Two or more races, 11.6% Hispanic of any race; Average household size: 2.33; Median age: 41.4; Age under 18: 22.3%; Age 65 and over: 16.9%; Males per 100 females: 91.3

School District(s)

Summerville Elementary (KG-08)
2012-13 Enrollment: 348. . . . . (209) 928-4291
Summerville Union High (KG-12)
2012-13 Enrollment: 1,088 . . . . (209) 928-3498

Housing: Homeownership rate: 52.3%; Homeowner vacancy rate: 3.6%; Rental vacancy rate: 4.7%

TUTTLETOWN (CDP). Covers a land area of 7.350 square miles and a water area of 0.007 square miles. Located at 38.01° N. Lat; 120.45° W. Long. Elevation is 1,440 feet.
Population: 668; Growth (since 2000): n/a; Density: 90.9 persons per square mile; Race: 91.8% White, 0.7% Black/African American, 0.7% Asian, 2.1% American Indian/Alaska Native, 0.1% Native Hawaiian/Other Pacific Islander, 2.7% Two or more races, 7.2% Hispanic of any race; Average household size: 2.28; Median age: 51.7; Age under 18: 17.1%; Age 65 and over: 22.2%; Males per 100 females: 93.1
Housing: Homeownership rate: 77.5%; Homeowner vacancy rate: 2.6%; Rental vacancy rate: 13.2%

TWAIN HARTE (CDP). Covers a land area of 3.699 square miles and a water area of 0.019 square miles. Located at 38.04° N. Lat; 120.23° W. Long. Elevation is 3,648 feet.
History: 1849 California Gold Rush region. Named for authors Mark Twain and Bret Harte who lived, wrote, and traveled in Nevada and California during rush years.
Population: 2,226; Growth (since 2000): -13.9%; Density: 601.7 persons per square mile; Race: 91.0% White, 0.2% Black/African American, 1.4% Asian, 1.5% American Indian/Alaska Native, 0.2% Native Hawaiian/Other Pacific Islander, 3.6% Two or more races, 7.7% Hispanic of any race; Average household size: 2.20; Median age: 52.0; Age under 18: 15.9%; Age 65 and over: 25.8%; Males per 100 females: 105.9

School District(s)

Twain Harte-Long Barn Union Elementary (KG-08)
2012-13 Enrollment: 282. . . . . (209) 586-3772

Housing: Homeownership rate: 70.7%; Homeowner vacancy rate: 3.5%; Rental vacancy rate: 12.0%

Ventura County

Located in southern California; bounded on the south by the Pacific Ocean; drained by the Santa Clara, Ventura, and Cuyama Rivers; includes Mt. Pinos, some of the Santa Barbara Islands, and part of Los Padres National Forest. Covers a land area of 1,843.133 square miles, a water area of 365.249 square miles, and is located in the Pacific Time Zone at 34.36° N. Lat., 119.13° W. Long. The county was founded in 1873. County seat is San Buenaventura (aka Ventura).

Ventura County is part of the Oxnard-Thousand Oaks-Ventura, CA Metropolitan Statistical Area. The entire metro area includes: Ventura County, CA

Weather Station: Ojai — Elevation: 750 feet

	Jan	Feb	Mar	Apr	May	Jun	Jul	Aug	Sep	Oct	Nov	Dec
High	68	69	71	75	78	83	89	91	88	81	73	67
Low	37	39	41	44	48	52	56	56	53	47	41	36
Precip	4.7	5.6	3.7	1.2	0.4	0.1	0.0	0.1	0.2	0.9	1.6	2.7
Snow	0.0	0.0	0.0	0.0	0.0	0.0	0.0	0.0	0.0	0.0	0.0	0.0

High and Low temperatures in degrees Fahrenheit; Precipitation and Snow in inches

Weather Station: Oxnard — Elevation: 48 feet

	Jan	Feb	Mar	Apr	May	Jun	Jul	Aug	Sep	Oct	Nov	Dec
High	66	66	66	68	68	71	73	74	74	73	70	66
Low	46	47	49	51	54	57	60	60	59	55	50	46
Precip	3.5	4.2	3.0	0.8	0.2	0.1	0.0	0.1	0.2	0.4	1.5	2.2
Snow	0.0	0.0	0.0	0.0	0.0	0.0	0.0	0.0	0.0	0.0	0.0	0.0

High and Low temperatures in degrees Fahrenheit; Precipitation and Snow in inches

Population: 823,318; Growth (since 2000): 9.3%; Density: 446.7 persons per square mile; Race: 68.7% White, 1.8% Black/African American, 6.7% Asian, 1.0% American Indian/Alaska Native, 0.2% Native Hawaiian/Other Pacific Islander, 4.5% two or more races, 40.3% Hispanic of any race; Average household size: 3.04; Median age: 36.2; Age under 18: 25.7%; Age 65 and over: 11.7%; Males per 100 females: 98.7; Marriage status: 31.9% never married, 52.9% now married, 1.8% separated, 5.0% widowed, 10.2% divorced; Foreign born: 22.8%; Speak English only: 62.2%; With disability: 9.9%; Veterans: 7.8%; Ancestry: 11.6% German, 9.0% Irish, 8.6% English, 5.2% Italian, 3.2% American
Religion: Six largest groups: 28.2% Catholicism, 4.1% Non-denominational Protestant, 2.5% Latter-day Saints, 1.9% Baptist, 1.5% Lutheran, 1.3% Pentecostal
Economy: Unemployment rate: 6.3%; Leading industries: 13.4% professional, scientific, and technical services; 12.9% retail trade; 12.9% health care and social assistance; Farms: 2,150 totaling 281,046 acres; Company size: 7 employ 1,000 or more persons, 20 employ 500 to 999 persons, 279 employ 100 to 499 persons, 19,581 employs less than 100 persons; Business ownership: 23,059 women-owned, 1,038 Black-owned, 12,040 Hispanic-owned, 5,583 Asian-owned
Employment: 16.4% management, business, and financial, 6.1% computer, engineering, and science, 10.5% education, legal, community service, arts, and media, 4.6% healthcare practitioners, 17.2% service, 24.9% sales and office, 10.8% natural resources, construction, and maintenance, 9.7% production, transportation, and material moving
Income: Per capita: $32,930; Median household: $76,544; Average household: $98,869; Households with income of $100,000 or more: 37.2%; Poverty rate: 11.1%
Educational Attainment: High school diploma or higher: 82.8%; Bachelor's degree or higher: 31.4%; Graduate/professional degree or higher: 11.6%
Housing: Homeownership rate: 65.3%; Median home value: $442,200; Median year structure built: 1975; Homeowner vacancy rate: 1.4%; Median gross rent: $1,470 per month; Rental vacancy rate: 4.8%
Vital Statistics: Birth rate: 126.4 per 10,000 population; Death rate: 64.9 per 10,000 population; Age-adjusted cancer mortality rate: 142.8 deaths per 100,000 population
Health Insurance: 83.8% have insurance; 67.2% have private insurance; 26.0% have public insurance; 16.2% do not have insurance; 8.1% of children under 18 do not have insurance
Health Care: Physicians: 20.7 per 10,000 population; Hospital beds: 15.1 per 10,000 population; Hospital admissions: 847.0 per 10,000 population
Air Quality Index: 57.0% good, 41.6% moderate, 1.4% unhealthy for sensitive individuals, 0.0% unhealthy (percent of days)
Transportation: Commute: 89.4% car, 1.3% public transportation, 2.1% walk, 5.5% work from home; Median travel time to work: 24.6 minutes
Presidential Election: 51.7% Obama, 46.1% Romney (2012)
National and State Parks: Boney Mountain State Wilderness; Emma Wood State Beach; Hopper Mountain National Wildlife Refuge; Los Padres National Forest; Mandalay State Beach; McGrath State Beach; Point Mugu State Park; San Buenaventura State Beach; Piedra Blanca National Recreation Trail

Additional Information Contacts

Ventura Government. . . . . (805) 654-5000
http://www.countyofventura.org

Ventura County Communities

BELL CANYON (CDP). Covers a land area of 3.621 square miles and a water area of 0 square miles. Located at 34.21° N. Lat; 118.69° W. Long.
Population: 2,049; Growth (since 2000): n/a; Density: 565.8 persons per square mile; Race: 84.1% White, 2.8% Black/African American, 8.7% Asian, 0.2% American Indian/Alaska Native, 0.0% Native Hawaiian/Other Pacific Islander, 3.6% Two or more races, 5.0% Hispanic of any race; Average household size: 3.10; Median age: 46.5; Age under 18: 25.4%; Age 65 and over: 12.2%; Males per 100 females: 101.1
Housing: Homeownership rate: 95.2%; Homeowner vacancy rate: 1.7%; Rental vacancy rate: 5.7%

CAMARILLO (city). Covers a land area of 19.528 square miles and a water area of 0.015 square miles. Located at 34.22° N. Lat; 119.03° W. Long. Elevation is 177 feet.
History: Camarillo was named for an early ranchero.
Population: 65,201; Growth (since 2000): 14.2%; Density: 3,338.9 persons per square mile; Race: 75.1% White, 1.9% Black/African American, 10.2% Asian, 0.6% American Indian/Alaska Native, 0.2% Native Hawaiian/Other Pacific Islander, 4.8% Two or more races, 22.9% Hispanic of any race; Average household size: 2.64; Median age: 40.8; Age under 18: 23.2%; Age 65 and over: 17.2%; Males per 100 females: 93.7; Marriage status: 27.0% never married, 55.8% now married, 1.3% separated, 7.0% widowed, 10.2% divorced; Foreign born: 15.0%; Speak

English only: 76.3%; With disability: 11.0%; Veterans: 11.7%; Ancestry: 15.6% German, 10.9% English, 10.4% Irish, 6.3% Italian, 3.3% French
Employment: 18.2% management, business, and financial, 8.5% computer, engineering, and science, 12.5% education, legal, community service, arts, and media, 5.7% healthcare practitioners, 13.8% service, 26.9% sales and office, 7.3% natural resources, construction, and maintenance, 6.9% production, transportation, and material moving
Income: Per capita: $38,879; Median household: $86,287; Average household: $105,206; Households with income of $100,000 or more: 42.1%; Poverty rate: 5.8%
Educational Attainment: High school diploma or higher: 91.8%; Bachelor's degree or higher: 38.4%; Graduate/professional degree or higher: 14.4%

School District(s)

Oxnard Union High (KG-12)
2012-13 Enrollment: 16,780 . . . . (805) 385-2500
Pleasant Valley (KG-08)
2012-13 Enrollment: 7,277 . . . . (805) 482-2763
Somis Union (KG-12)
2012-13 Enrollment: 251. . . . . (805) 386-8258
Ventura County Office of Education (KG-12)
2012-13 Enrollment: 2,590 . . . . (805) 383-1902
Ventura County Rop
2012-13 Enrollment: n/a . . . . (805) 388-4423

Four-year College(s)

California State University-Channel Islands (Public)
Fall 2013 Enrollment: 5,140 . . . . (805) 437-8400
2013-14 Tuition: In-state $6,471; Out-of-state $17,631
St John's Seminary (Private, Not-for-profit, Roman Catholic)
Fall 2013 Enrollment: 108 . . . . (805) 482-2755

Housing: Homeownership rate: 69.6%; Median home value: $453,400; Median year structure built: 1978; Homeowner vacancy rate: 1.4%; Median gross rent: $1,646 per month; Rental vacancy rate: 5.2%
Health Insurance: 89.4% have insurance; 78.0% have private insurance; 25.1% have public insurance; 10.6% do not have insurance; 7.1% of children under 18 do not have insurance
Hospitals: Saint Johns Pleasant Valley Hospital (187 beds)
Safety: Violent crime rate: 11.0 per 10,000 population; Property crime rate: 170.8 per 10,000 population
Newspapers: Ventura County Star (daily circulation 78000)
Transportation: Commute: 91.7% car, 1.0% public transportation, 1.4% walk, 4.1% work from home; Median travel time to work: 22.3 minutes; Amtrak: Train service available.
Airports: Camarillo (general aviation)

Additional Information Contacts

City of Camarillo . . . . (805) 388-5300
http://www.ci.camarillo.ca.us

CASA CONEJO (CDP). Covers a land area of 0.475 square miles and a water area of 0 square miles. Located at 34.18° N. Lat; 118.94° W. Long. Elevation is 653 feet.

Population: 3,249; Growth (since 2000): 2.2%; Density: 6,836.5 persons per square mile; Race: 78.8% White, 0.8% Black/African American, 4.9% Asian, 0.6% American Indian/Alaska Native, 0.1% Native Hawaiian/Other Pacific Islander, 4.6% Two or more races, 26.2% Hispanic of any race; Average household size: 3.28; Median age: 38.4; Age under 18: 25.2%; Age 65 and over: 11.5%; Males per 100 females: 103.3; Marriage status: 33.6% never married, 51.2% now married, 0.4% separated, 4.2% widowed, 11.0% divorced; Foreign born: 21.4%; Speak English only: 75.3%; With disability: 10.4%; Veterans: 10.6%; Ancestry: 17.8% German, 10.7% French, 8.1% Irish, 6.0% English, 4.1% Italian
Employment: 16.7% management, business, and financial, 6.3% computer, engineering, and science, 4.1% education, legal, community service, arts, and media, 0.7% healthcare practitioners, 28.6% service, 23.1% sales and office, 15.8% natural resources, construction, and maintenance, 4.7% production, transportation, and material moving
Income: Per capita: $27,432; Median household: $87,500; Average household: $101,133; Households with income of $100,000 or more: 42.9%; Poverty rate: 13.7%
Educational Attainment: High school diploma or higher: 87.7%; Bachelor's degree or higher: 21.6%; Graduate/professional degree or higher: 7.3%
Housing: Homeownership rate: 82.6%; Median home value: $430,800; Median year structure built: 1965; Homeowner vacancy rate: 0.8%; Median gross rent: $2,000+ per month; Rental vacancy rate: 2.3%
Health Insurance: 77.9% have insurance; 58.7% have private insurance; 28.5% have public insurance; 22.1% do not have insurance; 5.8% of children under 18 do not have insurance
Transportation: Commute: 90.4% car, 0.0% public transportation, 2.4% walk, 5.4% work from home; Median travel time to work: 23.2 minutes

CHANNEL ISLANDS BEACH (CDP). Covers a land area of 0.404 square miles and a water area of 0.007 square miles. Located at 34.16° N. Lat; 119.23° W. Long. Elevation is 7 feet.

Population: 3,103; Growth (since 2000): -1.2%; Density: 7,684.0 persons per square mile; Race: 87.4% White, 0.9% Black/African American, 3.5% Asian, 0.5% American Indian/Alaska Native, 0.2% Native Hawaiian/Other Pacific Islander, 4.2% Two or more races, 13.0% Hispanic of any race; Average household size: 2.30; Median age: 44.8; Age under 18: 16.9%; Age 65 and over: 14.1%; Males per 100 females: 111.7; Marriage status: 31.2% never married, 47.3% now married, 0.9% separated, 2.3% widowed, 19.3% divorced; Foreign born: 7.2%; Speak English only: 88.9%; With disability: 8.8%; Veterans: 13.7%; Ancestry: 19.2% Irish, 18.1% German, 16.0% English, 11.8% Italian, 8.3% Swedish
Employment: 18.5% management, business, and financial, 6.2% computer, engineering, and science, 16.0% education, legal, community service, arts, and media, 3.9% healthcare practitioners, 3.0% service, 31.0% sales and office, 14.8% natural resources, construction, and maintenance, 6.8% production, transportation, and material moving
Income: Per capita: $56,512; Median household: $72,237; Average household: $124,060; Households with income of $100,000 or more: 43.0%; Poverty rate: 2.1%
Educational Attainment: High school diploma or higher: 99.2%; Bachelor's degree or higher: 43.1%; Graduate/professional degree or higher: 17.6%
Housing: Homeownership rate: 53.8%; Median home value: $768,500; Median year structure built: 1976; Homeowner vacancy rate: 3.4%; Median gross rent: $1,907 per month; Rental vacancy rate: 9.5%
Health Insurance: 82.2% have insurance; 71.3% have private insurance; 23.5% have public insurance; 17.8% do not have insurance; 4.9% of children under 18 do not have insurance
Transportation: Commute: 78.4% car, 1.1% public transportation, 7.0% walk, 12.8% work from home; Median travel time to work: 27.5 minutes

EL RIO (CDP). Covers a land area of 2.024 square miles and a water area of 0 square miles. Located at 34.25° N. Lat; 119.16° W. Long. Elevation is 92 feet.

History: El Rio was founded by Simon Cohn who opened a general store here called New Jerusalem.
Population: 7,198; Growth (since 2000): 16.2%; Density: 3,556.5 persons per square mile; Race: 48.6% White, 0.8% Black/African American, 1.0% Asian, 2.8% American Indian/Alaska Native, 0.3% Native Hawaiian/Other Pacific Islander, 4.4% Two or more races, 86.0% Hispanic of any race; Average household size: 4.41; Median age: 29.6; Age under 18: 30.0%; Age 65 and over: 9.2%; Males per 100 females: 106.9; Marriage status: 40.8% never married, 50.9% now married, 3.6% separated, 2.2% widowed, 6.2% divorced; Foreign born: 35.6%; Speak English only: 26.4%; With disability: 10.7%; Veterans: 3.7%; Ancestry: 3.8% English, 3.3% Irish, 2.8% German, 2.0% American, 0.9% Italian
Employment: 10.1% management, business, and financial, 0.0% computer, engineering, and science, 3.0% education, legal, community service, arts, and media, 3.8% healthcare practitioners, 14.6% service, 23.7% sales and office, 19.1% natural resources, construction, and maintenance, 25.8% production, transportation, and material moving
Income: Per capita: $16,958; Median household: $60,318; Average household: $64,783; Households with income of $100,000 or more: 17.9%; Poverty rate: 17.0%
Educational Attainment: High school diploma or higher: 57.7%; Bachelor's degree or higher: 5.2%; Graduate/professional degree or higher: 1.6%
Housing: Homeownership rate: 60.2%; Median home value: $275,900; Median year structure built: 1957; Homeowner vacancy rate: 1.4%; Median gross rent: $1,042 per month; Rental vacancy rate: 2.8%
Health Insurance: 63.8% have insurance; 38.9% have private insurance; 31.0% have public insurance; 36.2% do not have insurance; 17.8% of children under 18 do not have insurance
Transportation: Commute: 96.7% car, 0.0% public transportation, 0.8% walk, 1.6% work from home; Median travel time to work: 21.9 minutes

FILLMORE (city). Covers a land area of 3.364 square miles and a water area of 0.001 square miles. Located at 34.40° N. Lat; 118.92° W. Long. Elevation is 456 feet.

History: Fillmore grew as the center of a lemon and orange orchard area. Near Fillmore was the Moreno Rancho, the site of Helen Hunt Jackson 's novel "Ramona."

Population: 15,002; Growth (since 2000): 10.0%; Density: 4,460.1 persons per square mile; Race: 57.2% White, 0.5% Black/African American, 1.0% Asian, 1.2% American Indian/Alaska Native, 0.1% Native Hawaiian/Other Pacific Islander, 5.3% Two or more races, 74.7% Hispanic of any race; Average household size: 3.57; Median age: 31.9; Age under 18: 30.2%; Age 65 and over: 10.3%; Males per 100 females: 99.8; Marriage status: 34.3% never married, 51.3% now married, 0.8% separated, 5.6% widowed, 8.9% divorced; Foreign born: 24.1%; Speak English only: 43.3%; With disability: 9.8%; Veterans: 6.4%; Ancestry: 5.0% Irish, 4.3% German, 4.1% English, 1.9% American, 1.7% Scottish

Employment: 9.1% management, business, and financial, 2.3% computer, engineering, and science, 7.5% education, legal, community service, arts, and media, 3.1% healthcare practitioners, 21.5% service, 26.0% sales and office, 14.8% natural resources, construction, and maintenance, 15.6% production, transportation, and material moving

Income: Per capita: $20,064; Median household: $55,186; Average household: $70,133; Households with income of $100,000 or more: 23.7%; Poverty rate: 20.7%

Educational Attainment: High school diploma or higher: 66.1%; Bachelor's degree or higher: 13.9%; Graduate/professional degree or higher: 5.4%

School District(s)

Fillmore Unified (KG-12)
2012-13 Enrollment: 3,812 . . . . (805) 524-6000

Housing: Homeownership rate: 64.4%; Median home value: $305,000; Median year structure built: 1975; Homeowner vacancy rate: 3.0%; Median gross rent: $1,262 per month; Rental vacancy rate: 4.5%

Health Insurance: 81.5% have insurance; 55.9% have private insurance; 32.3% have public insurance; 18.5% do not have insurance; 11.9% of children under 18 do not have insurance

Safety: Violent crime rate: 17.1 per 10,000 population; Property crime rate: 100.0 per 10,000 population

Newspapers: Fillmore Gazette (weekly circulation 3000)

Transportation: Commute: 90.4% car, 1.7% public transportation, 3.5% walk, 2.8% work from home; Median travel time to work: 30.9 minutes; Amtrak: Bus service available.

Additional Information Contacts

City of Fillmore . . . . (805) 524-1500
http://www.fillmoreca.com

LAKE SHERWOOD (CDP). Covers a land area of 3.135 square miles and a water area of 0.188 square miles. Located at 34.13° N. Lat; 118.89° W. Long.

Population: 1,527; Growth (since 2000): n/a; Density: 487.0 persons per square mile; Race: 89.6% White, 0.3% Black/African American, 6.6% Asian, 0.1% American Indian/Alaska Native, 0.0% Native Hawaiian/Other Pacific Islander, 2.8% Two or more races, 3.4% Hispanic of any race; Average household size: 2.74; Median age: 49.0; Age under 18: 24.1%; Age 65 and over: 16.1%; Males per 100 females: 96.3

Housing: Homeownership rate: 93.2%; Homeowner vacancy rate: 2.4%; Rental vacancy rate: 7.3%

MEINERS OAKS (CDP). Covers a land area of 1.408 square miles and a water area of 0 square miles. Located at 34.45° N. Lat; 119.27° W. Long. Elevation is 741 feet.

Population: 3,571; Growth (since 2000): -4.8%; Density: 2,535.8 persons per square mile; Race: 78.1% White, 0.4% Black/African American, 1.4% Asian, 1.6% American Indian/Alaska Native, 0.0% Native Hawaiian/Other Pacific Islander, 3.1% Two or more races, 29.9% Hispanic of any race; Average household size: 2.78; Median age: 40.2; Age under 18: 23.8%; Age 65 and over: 12.9%; Males per 100 females: 92.4; Marriage status: 32.5% never married, 46.5% now married, 1.0% separated, 7.9% widowed, 13.1% divorced; Foreign born: 17.7%; Speak English only: 69.1%; With disability: 9.5%; Veterans: 7.8%; Ancestry: 11.7% Irish, 9.2% German, 8.0% English, 4.1% Norwegian, 3.9% Polish

Employment: 19.6% management, business, and financial, 2.2% computer, engineering, and science, 14.2% education, legal, community service, arts, and media, 4.4% healthcare practitioners, 39.0% service, 8.7% sales and office, 7.6% natural resources, construction, and maintenance, 4.3% production, transportation, and material moving

Income: Per capita: $29,748; Median household: $54,405; Average household: $76,359; Households with income of $100,000 or more: 27.6%; Poverty rate: 13.5%

Educational Attainment: High school diploma or higher: 78.7%; Bachelor's degree or higher: 30.6%; Graduate/professional degree or higher: 9.8%

Housing: Homeownership rate: 62.2%; Median home value: $445,700; Median year structure built: 1959; Homeowner vacancy rate: 1.1%; Median gross rent: $1,201 per month; Rental vacancy rate: 6.7%

Health Insurance: 77.8% have insurance; 59.6% have private insurance; 27.5% have public insurance; 22.2% do not have insurance; 0.0% of children under 18 do not have insurance

Transportation: Commute: 89.1% car, 0.0% public transportation, 0.4% walk, 6.8% work from home; Median travel time to work: 20.2 minutes

MIRA MONTE (CDP). Covers a land area of 4.570 square miles and a water area of 0.017 square miles. Located at 34.43° N. Lat; 119.28° W. Long. Elevation is 643 feet.

Population: 6,854; Growth (since 2000): -4.5%; Density: 1,499.7 persons per square mile; Race: 87.4% White, 0.6% Black/African American, 1.9% Asian, 0.9% American Indian/Alaska Native, 0.0% Native Hawaiian/Other Pacific Islander, 3.3% Two or more races, 18.3% Hispanic of any race; Average household size: 2.44; Median age: 48.0; Age under 18: 19.4%; Age 65 and over: 21.1%; Males per 100 females: 93.2; Marriage status: 24.2% never married, 56.4% now married, 1.9% separated, 6.9% widowed, 12.4% divorced; Foreign born: 8.3%; Speak English only: 90.9%; With disability: 16.6%; Veterans: 9.1%; Ancestry: 22.4% German, 19.8% English, 15.1% Irish, 5.6% Italian, 4.8% American

Employment: 18.0% management, business, and financial, 6.2% computer, engineering, and science, 13.4% education, legal, community service, arts, and media, 3.7% healthcare practitioners, 18.1% service, 23.0% sales and office, 9.9% natural resources, construction, and maintenance, 7.7% production, transportation, and material moving

Income: Per capita: $36,549; Median household: $73,079; Average household: $90,248; Households with income of $100,000 or more: 34.7%; Poverty rate: 11.9%

Educational Attainment: High school diploma or higher: 91.7%; Bachelor's degree or higher: 27.5%; Graduate/professional degree or higher: 10.3%

Housing: Homeownership rate: 79.5%; Median home value: $444,700; Median year structure built: 1967; Homeowner vacancy rate: 2.2%; Median gross rent: $1,464 per month; Rental vacancy rate: 4.0%

Health Insurance: 89.3% have insurance; 75.3% have private insurance; 33.4% have public insurance; 10.7% do not have insurance; 7.1% of children under 18 do not have insurance

Transportation: Commute: 85.5% car, 0.0% public transportation, 3.7% walk, 7.9% work from home; Median travel time to work: 28.5 minutes

MOORPARK (city). Covers a land area of 12.579 square miles and a water area of 0.220 square miles. Located at 34.29° N. Lat; 118.88° W. Long. Elevation is 515 feet.

History: Moorpark is located in Southern California and was incorporated as a city on July 1, 1983. It was named after the Moorpark apricot which grew throughout the valley.

Population: 34,421; Growth (since 2000): 9.6%; Density: 2,736.4 persons per square mile; Race: 75.1% White, 1.5% Black/African American, 6.8% Asian, 0.7% American Indian/Alaska Native, 0.1% Native Hawaiian/Other Pacific Islander, 4.8% Two or more races, 31.4% Hispanic of any race; Average household size: 3.28; Median age: 34.7; Age under 18: 27.5%; Age 65 and over: 7.1%; Males per 100 females: 98.6; Marriage status: 30.8% never married, 57.7% now married, 1.6% separated, 3.5% widowed, 8.0% divorced; Foreign born: 17.9%; Speak English only: 70.0%; With disability: 6.5%; Veterans: 5.1%; Ancestry: 14.2% German, 11.3% Irish, 10.7% English, 6.3% Italian, 4.8% American

Employment: 22.1% management, business, and financial, 6.3% computer, engineering, and science, 9.5% education, legal, community service, arts, and media, 3.6% healthcare practitioners, 18.4% service, 25.1% sales and office, 6.4% natural resources, construction, and maintenance, 8.5% production, transportation, and material moving

Income: Per capita: $35,224; Median household: $96,779; Average household: $113,976; Households with income of $100,000 or more: 48.2%; Poverty rate: 7.2%

Educational Attainment: High school diploma or higher: 87.9%; Bachelor's degree or higher: 37.4%; Graduate/professional degree or higher: 12.6%

School District(s)

Moorpark Unified (KG-12)
2012-13 Enrollment: 6,984 . . . . (805) 378-6300

Two-year College(s)

Moorpark College (Public)
Fall 2013 Enrollment: 14,206 . . . . (805) 378-1400
2013-14 Tuition: In-state $1,388; Out-of-state $7,050

Housing: Homeownership rate: 78.0%; Median home value: $520,300; Median year structure built: 1986; Homeowner vacancy rate: 1.0%; Median gross rent: $1,705 per month; Rental vacancy rate: 2.9%

Health Insurance: 88.1% have insurance; 79.8% have private insurance; 15.8% have public insurance; 11.9% do not have insurance; 8.4% of children under 18 do not have insurance

Safety: Violent crime rate: 10.5 per 10,000 population; Property crime rate: 116.0 per 10,000 population

Transportation: Commute: 89.8% car, 1.8% public transportation, 1.5% walk, 6.1% work from home; Median travel time to work: 25.0 minutes; Amtrak: Train service available.

Additional Information Contacts

City of Moorpark . . . . (805) 517-6212
http://ci.moorpark.ca.us

NEWBURY PARK (unincorporated postal area)

ZCTA: 91320

Covers a land area of 18.248 square miles and a water area of 0 square miles. Located at 34.18° N. Lat; 118.95° W. Long. Elevation is 623 feet.

Population: 44,274; Growth (since 2000): 17.2%; Density: 2,426.3 persons per square mile; Race: 77.4% White, 1.3% Black/African American, 10.5% Asian, 0.5% American Indian/Alaska Native, 0.1% Native Hawaiian/Other Pacific Islander, 4.2% Two or more races, 16.9% Hispanic of any race; Average household size: 2.93; Median age: 39.9; Age under 18: 26.6%; Age 65 and over: 11.6%; Males per 100 females: 98.3; Marriage status: 24.9% never married, 62.4% now married, 1.1% separated, 4.3% widowed, 8.4% divorced; Foreign born: 19.9%; Speak English only: 75.6%; With disability: 7.8%; Veterans: 8.3%; Ancestry: 14.3% German, 11.9% English, 9.8% Irish, 8.1% Italian, 4.1% French

Employment: 21.8% management, business, and financial, 10.4% computer, engineering, and science, 11.4% education, legal, community service, arts, and media, 6.2% healthcare practitioners, 14.7% service, 24.1% sales and office, 5.6% natural resources, construction, and maintenance, 5.8% production, transportation, and material moving

Income: Per capita: $43,615; Median household: $104,665; Average household: $130,134; Households with income of $100,000 or more: 53.2%; Poverty rate: 6.5%

Educational Attainment: High school diploma or higher: 92.4%; Bachelor's degree or higher: 47.6%; Graduate/professional degree or higher: 19.7%

Housing: Homeownership rate: 78.9%; Median home value: $576,600; Median year structure built: 1978; Homeowner vacancy rate: 0.8%; Median gross rent: $1,858 per month; Rental vacancy rate: 3.1%

Health Insurance: 89.4% have insurance; 81.4% have private insurance; 18.0% have public insurance; 10.6% do not have insurance; 8.2% of children under 18 do not have insurance

Transportation: Commute: 85.1% car, 1.2% public transportation, 2.3% walk, 8.5% work from home; Median travel time to work: 24.2 minutes

---

OAK PARK (CDP). Covers a land area of 5.290 square miles and a water area of 0 square miles. Located at 34.18° N. Lat; 118.77° W. Long. Elevation is 1,106 feet.

Population: 13,811; Growth (since 2000): 495.3%; Density: 2,610.6 persons per square mile; Race: 83.1% White, 1.0% Black/African American, 11.3% Asian, 0.2% American Indian/Alaska Native, 0.1% Native Hawaiian/Other Pacific Islander, 3.2% Two or more races, 6.0% Hispanic of any race; Average household size: 2.68; Median age: 41.7; Age under 18: 26.2%; Age 65 and over: 8.5%; Males per 100 females: 92.6; Marriage status: 25.4% never married, 59.8% now married, 0.4% separated, 3.5% widowed, 11.2% divorced; Foreign born: 15.4%; Speak English only: 80.4%; With disability: 4.7%; Veterans: 5.3%; Ancestry: 13.5% German, 13.3% Irish, 13.0% Italian, 9.8% English, 8.9% Russian

Employment: 27.2% management, business, and financial, 10.2% computer, engineering, and science, 18.6% education, legal, community service, arts, and media, 7.6% healthcare practitioners, 10.1% service, 22.3% sales and office, 2.2% natural resources, construction, and maintenance, 1.9% production, transportation, and material moving

Income: Per capita: $58,927; Median household: $128,218; Average household: $162,583; Households with income of $100,000 or more: 61.4%; Poverty rate: 4.7%

Educational Attainment: High school diploma or higher: 97.3%; Bachelor's degree or higher: 62.5%; Graduate/professional degree or higher: 25.9%

School District(s)

Oak Park Unified (KG-12)
2012-13 Enrollment: 4,510 . . . . (818) 735-3200

Housing: Homeownership rate: 74.5%; Median home value: $635,100; Median year structure built: 1986; Homeowner vacancy rate: 1.2%; Median gross rent: $1,996 per month; Rental vacancy rate: 3.5%

Health Insurance: 94.6% have insurance; 90.2% have private insurance; 11.5% have public insurance; 5.4% do not have insurance; 1.4% of children under 18 do not have insurance

Transportation: Commute: 88.8% car, 0.1% public transportation, 0.3% walk, 9.9% work from home; Median travel time to work: 27.8 minutes

---

OAK VIEW (CDP). Covers a land area of 1.962 square miles and a water area of 0 square miles. Located at 34.40° N. Lat; 119.30° W. Long. Elevation is 538 feet.

Population: 4,066; Growth (since 2000): -3.2%; Density: 2,072.4 persons per square mile; Race: 79.4% White, 0.3% Black/African American, 0.8% Asian, 1.5% American Indian/Alaska Native, 0.1% Native Hawaiian/Other Pacific Islander, 3.8% Two or more races, 29.9% Hispanic of any race; Average household size: 2.87; Median age: 39.6; Age under 18: 23.9%; Age 65 and over: 10.2%; Males per 100 females: 100.0; Marriage status: 34.7% never married, 44.6% now married, 2.1% separated, 4.6% widowed, 16.1% divorced; Foreign born: 9.2%; Speak English only: 85.1%; With disability: 13.3%; Veterans: 8.6%; Ancestry: 17.8% German, 16.6% Irish, 13.5% English, 5.7% American, 4.5% Scottish

Employment: 13.6% management, business, and financial, 4.8% computer, engineering, and science, 7.8% education, legal, community service, arts, and media, 5.7% healthcare practitioners, 21.8% service, 17.2% sales and office, 20.8% natural resources, construction, and maintenance, 8.3% production, transportation, and material moving

Income: Per capita: $32,761; Median household: $72,077; Average household: $90,869; Households with income of $100,000 or more: 35.9%; Poverty rate: 6.3%

Educational Attainment: High school diploma or higher: 87.5%; Bachelor's degree or higher: 20.6%; Graduate/professional degree or higher: 8.0%

School District(s)

Ventura Unified (KG-12)
2012-13 Enrollment: 17,402 . . . . (805) 641-5000

Housing: Homeownership rate: 71.5%; Median home value: $398,600; Median year structure built: 1966; Homeowner vacancy rate: 1.3%; Median gross rent: $1,313 per month; Rental vacancy rate: 5.8%

Health Insurance: 80.6% have insurance; 66.0% have private insurance; 25.4% have public insurance; 19.4% do not have insurance; 6.3% of children under 18 do not have insurance

Transportation: Commute: 87.7% car, 0.0% public transportation, 3.9% walk, 5.6% work from home; Median travel time to work: 24.3 minutes

---

OJAI (city). Covers a land area of 4.386 square miles and a water area of 0.015 square miles. Located at 34.45° N. Lat; 119.25° W. Long. Elevation is 745 feet.

History: Originally called Nordhoff in honor of writer Charles Nordhoff, the name was changed to Ojai in 1916 when E.D. Libbey persuaded the residents to remodel the town in a Spanish style and advertise itself as a resort. Thacher Preparatory School was opened here in 1888 by two yale men, S.D. and W.L. Thacher.

Population: 7,461; Growth (since 2000): -5.1%; Density: 1,701.3 persons per square mile; Race: 87.9% White, 0.6% Black/African American, 2.1% Asian, 0.6% American Indian/Alaska Native, 0.0% Native Hawaiian/Other Pacific Islander, 2.9% Two or more races, 17.9% Hispanic of any race; Average household size: 2.34; Median age: 47.1; Age under 18: 20.4%; Age 65 and over: 19.2%; Males per 100 females: 84.9; Marriage status: 23.8% never married, 54.2% now married, 2.0% separated, 6.6% widowed, 15.3% divorced; Foreign born: 10.4%; Speak English only: 83.9%; With disability: 11.9%; Veterans: 8.4%; Ancestry: 19.5% English, 16.6% German, 15.2% Irish, 6.4% Italian, 5.5% French

Employment: 22.0% management, business, and financial, 3.3% computer, engineering, and science, 18.3% education, legal, community service, arts, and media, 2.7% healthcare practitioners, 22.5% service, 19.0% sales and office, 8.4% natural resources, construction, and maintenance, 3.7% production, transportation, and material moving

Income: Per capita: $33,552; Median household: $59,520; Average household: $83,568; Households with income of $100,000 or more: 27.5%; Poverty rate: 11.5%

Educational Attainment: High school diploma or higher: 91.8%; Bachelor's degree or higher: 42.4%; Graduate/professional degree or higher: 18.7%

School District(s)

Ojai Unified (KG-12)
2012-13 Enrollment: 2,879 . . . . (805) 640-4300

Housing: Homeownership rate: 55.2%; Median home value: $566,400; Median year structure built: 1968; Homeowner vacancy rate: 1.7%; Median gross rent: $1,261 per month; Rental vacancy rate: 5.4%

Health Insurance: 82.3% have insurance; 64.6% have private insurance; 32.9% have public insurance; 17.7% do not have insurance; 9.8% of children under 18 do not have insurance

Hospitals: Ojai Valley Community Hospital (103 beds)

Safety: Violent crime rate: 18.5 per 10,000 population; Property crime rate: 135.8 per 10,000 population

Newspapers: Ojai Valley News (weekly circulation 11000)

Transportation: Commute: 77.6% car, 0.0% public transportation, 4.3% walk, 15.9% work from home; Median travel time to work: 22.9 minutes

Additional Information Contacts

City of Ojai. . . . . (805) 646-5581
http://ci.ojai.ca.us

OXNARD (city). Covers a land area of 26.894 square miles and a water area of 12.314 square miles. Located at 34.20° N. Lat; 119.20° W. Long. Elevation is 52 feet.

History: Oxnard was founded in 1898 with the establishment of the American Beet Sugar Company's converting plant, and named for the company's owners.

Population: 197,899; Growth (since 2000): 16.2%; Density: 7,358.4 persons per square mile; Race: 48.2% White, 2.9% Black/African American, 7.4% Asian, 1.5% American Indian/Alaska Native, 0.3% Native Hawaiian/Other Pacific Islander, 4.6% Two or more races, 73.5% Hispanic of any race; Average household size: 3.95; Median age: 29.9; Age under 18: 29.8%; Age 65 and over: 8.3%; Males per 100 females: 103.0; Marriage status: 38.2% never married, 48.7% now married, 2.7% separated, 4.4% widowed, 8.7% divorced; Foreign born: 37.0%; Speak English only: 32.1%; With disability: 10.1%; Veterans: 6.2%; Ancestry: 3.8% German, 3.6% Irish, 2.5% English, 1.6% Italian, 1.2% American

Employment: 8.7% management, business, and financial, 3.3% computer, engineering, and science, 6.1% education, legal, community service, arts, and media, 3.2% healthcare practitioners, 19.1% service, 23.5% sales and office, 19.6% natural resources, construction, and maintenance, 16.5% production, transportation, and material moving

Income: Per capita: $20,605; Median household: $60,784; Average household: $75,627; Households with income of $100,000 or more: 24.9%; Poverty rate: 16.7%

Educational Attainment: High school diploma or higher: 64.3%; Bachelor's degree or higher: 15.6%; Graduate/professional degree or higher: 4.5%

School District(s)

Hueneme Elementary (KG-08)
2012-13 Enrollment: 8,332 . . . . (805) 488-3588

Ocean View (KG-08)
2012-13 Enrollment: 2,550 . . . . (805) 488-4441

Oxnard (KG-08)
2012-13 Enrollment: 16,533 . . . . (805) 385-1501

Oxnard Union High (KG-12)
2012-13 Enrollment: 16,780 . . . . (805) 385-2500

Rio Elementary (KG-08)
2012-13 Enrollment: 4,692 . . . . (805) 485-3111

Ventura County Office of Education (KG-12)
2012-13 Enrollment: 2,590 . . . . (805) 383-1902

Four-year College(s)

ITT Technical Institute-Oxnard (Private, For-profit)
Fall 2013 Enrollment: 312. . . . . (805) 988-0143
2013-14 Tuition: In-state $18,048; Out-of-state $18,048

Two-year College(s)

Oxnard College (Public)
Fall 2013 Enrollment: 6,939 . . . . (805) 986-5800
2013-14 Tuition: In-state $1,388; Out-of-state $7,050

Vocational/Technical School(s)

CET-Oxnard (Private, Not-for-profit)
Fall 2013 Enrollment: 133 . . . . (408) 287-7924
2013-14 Tuition: $9,958

Modern Beauty Academy (Private, For-profit)
Fall 2013 Enrollment: 48 . . . . (805) 483-4994
2013-14 Tuition: $16,451

Pacific Coast Trade School (Private, For-profit)
Fall 2013 Enrollment: 401 . . . . (805) 487-9260
2013-14 Tuition: $10,975

Housing: Homeownership rate: 55.8%; Median home value: $323,700; Median year structure built: 1973; Homeowner vacancy rate: 1.8%; Median gross rent: $1,304 per month; Rental vacancy rate: 3.7%

Health Insurance: 74.6% have insurance; 48.4% have private insurance; 32.6% have public insurance; 25.4% do not have insurance; 12.0% of children under 18 do not have insurance

Hospitals: Saint Johns Regional Medical Center (230 beds)

Safety: Violent crime rate: 32.1 per 10,000 population; Property crime rate: 250.5 per 10,000 population

Transportation: Commute: 92.7% car, 1.6% public transportation, 1.5% walk, 2.6% work from home; Median travel time to work: 23.1 minutes; Amtrak: Train service available.

Airports: Oxnard (general aviation)

Additional Information Contacts

City of Oxnard . . . . (805) 385-7430
http://www.ci.oxnard.ca.us

PIRU (CDP). Covers a land area of 2.820 square miles and a water area of 0.016 square miles. Located at 34.41° N. Lat; 118.80° W. Long. Elevation is 709 feet.

Population: 2,063; Growth (since 2000): 72.5%; Density: 731.7 persons per square mile; Race: 51.5% White, 0.8% Black/African American, 0.5% Asian, 2.1% American Indian/Alaska Native, 0.0% Native Hawaiian/Other Pacific Islander, 4.8% Two or more races, 84.7% Hispanic of any race; Average household size: 3.94; Median age: 29.4; Age under 18: 32.8%; Age 65 and over: 7.5%; Males per 100 females: 106.5

School District(s)

Fillmore Unified (KG-12)
2012-13 Enrollment: 3,812 . . . . (805) 524-6000

Housing: Homeownership rate: 57.8%; Homeowner vacancy rate: 1.6%; Rental vacancy rate: 4.3%

POINT MUGU NAWC (unincorporated postal area)

ZCTA: 93042

Covers a land area of 22.639 square miles and a water area of 3.395 square miles. Located at 33.26° N. Lat; 119.50° W. Long..

Population: 56; Growth (since 2000): n/a; Density: 2.5 persons per square mile; Race: 78.6% White, 8.9% Black/African American, 3.6% Asian, 0.0% American Indian/Alaska Native, 1.8% Native Hawaiian/Other Pacific Islander, 0.0% Two or more races, 14.3% Hispanic of any race; Average household size: 0.00; Median age: 28.9; Age under 18: 0.0%; Age 65 and over: 0.0%; Males per 100 females: ***.*

Housing: Homeownership rate: n/a; Homeowner vacancy rate: 100.0%; Rental vacancy rate: 0.0%

PORT HUENEME (city). Covers a land area of 4.451 square miles and a water area of 0.220 square miles. Located at 34.16° N. Lat; 119.20° W. Long. Elevation is 13 feet.

History: Port Hueneme developed as a seaport around a natural harbor, with a citrus packing plant and fish cannery. The name Hueneme is of Indian origin meaning "place of security."

Population: 21,723; Growth (since 2000): -0.6%; Density: 4,880.7 persons per square mile; Race: 56.9% White, 5.1% Black/African American, 6.0% Asian, 1.4% American Indian/Alaska Native, 0.5% Native Hawaiian/Other Pacific Islander, 6.1% Two or more races, 52.3% Hispanic of any race; Average household size: 2.95; Median age: 31.3; Age under 18: 26.6%; Age 65 and over: 11.0%; Males per 100 females: 103.2; Marriage status: 34.9% never married, 45.7% now married, 2.5% separated, 6.0% widowed, 13.4% divorced; Foreign born: 21.6%; Speak English only: 55.4%; With disability: 13.8%; Veterans: 12.2%; Ancestry: 8.8% German, 7.6% Irish, 5.7% English, 2.3% American, 2.3% French

Employment: 14.3% management, business, and financial, 3.7% computer, engineering, and science, 6.8% education, legal, community service, arts, and media, 1.9% healthcare practitioners, 23.8% service, 27.5% sales and office, 10.4% natural resources, construction, and maintenance, 11.8% production, transportation, and material moving
Income: Per capita: $24,212; Median household: $52,720; Average household: $66,829; Households with income of $100,000 or more: 19.3%; Poverty rate: 17.5%
Educational Attainment: High school diploma or higher: 79.1%; Bachelor's degree or higher: 20.0%; Graduate/professional degree or higher: 7.7%

School District(s)

Hueneme Elementary (KG-08)
2012-13 Enrollment: 8,332 . . . . (805) 488-3588
Housing: Homeownership rate: 48.3%; Median home value: $303,500; Median year structure built: 1973; Homeowner vacancy rate: 2.7%; Median gross rent: $1,431 per month; Rental vacancy rate: 6.0%
Health Insurance: 78.6% have insurance; 55.9% have private insurance; 32.5% have public insurance; 21.4% do not have insurance; 6.8% of children under 18 do not have insurance
Safety: Violent crime rate: 26.0 per 10,000 population; Property crime rate: 184.8 per 10,000 population
Transportation: Commute: 84.5% car, 1.8% public transportation, 7.9% walk, 3.5% work from home; Median travel time to work: 24.0 minutes
Additional Information Contacts
City of Port Hueneme . . . . (805) 986-6500
http://www.ci.port-hueneme.ca.us

SAN BUENAVENTURA (VENTURA) (city). County seat. Covers a land area of 21.655 square miles and a water area of 10.440 square miles. Located at 34.27° N. Lat; 119.26° W. Long.
Population: 106,433; Growth (since 2000): 5.5%; Density: 4,915.0 persons per square mile; Race: 76.6% White, 1.6% Black/African American, 3.4% Asian, 1.2% American Indian/Alaska Native, 0.2% Native Hawaiian/Other Pacific Islander, 5.2% Two or more races, 31.8% Hispanic of any race; Average household size: 2.57; Median age: 39.0; Age under 18: 22.5%; Age 65 and over: 13.3%; Males per 100 females: 97.7; Marriage status: 31.8% never married, 48.8% now married, 2.1% separated, 5.7% widowed, 13.7% divorced; Foreign born: 14.9%; Speak English only: 74.0%; With disability: 11.1%; Veterans: 9.6%; Ancestry: 14.8% German, 11.2% Irish, 11.0% English, 5.3% Italian, 3.5% American
Employment: 15.1% management, business, and financial, 6.6% computer, engineering, and science, 13.2% education, legal, community service, arts, and media, 6.1% healthcare practitioners, 17.4% service, 25.1% sales and office, 8.2% natural resources, construction, and maintenance, 8.3% production, transportation, and material moving
Income: Per capita: $32,311; Median household: $65,137; Average household: $81,785; Households with income of $100,000 or more: 29.1%; Poverty rate: 10.7%
Educational Attainment: High school diploma or higher: 88.9%; Bachelor's degree or higher: 33.1%; Graduate/professional degree or higher: 12.9%

School District(s)

Mesa Union Elementary (KG-12)
2012-13 Enrollment: 1,387 . . . . (805) 485-1411
Ventura County Office of Education (KG-12)
2012-13 Enrollment: 2,590 . . . . (805) 383-1902
Ventura Unified (KG-12)
2012-13 Enrollment: 17,402 . . . . (805) 641-5000

Four-year College(s)

Santa Barbara Business College-Ventura (Private, For-profit)
Fall 2013 Enrollment: 349 . . . . (805) 339-2999
2013-14 Tuition: In-state $12,580; Out-of-state $12,580
The Santa Barbara and Ventura Colleges of Law-Ventura (Private, Not-for-profit)
Fall 2013 Enrollment: 107 . . . . (805) 765-9300

Two-year College(s)

Ventura College (Public)
Fall 2013 Enrollment: 12,908 . . . . (805) 654-6400
2013-14 Tuition: In-state $1,388; Out-of-state $7,050

Vocational/Technical School(s)

Lu Ross Academy (Private, For-profit)
Fall 2013 Enrollment: 186 . . . . (805) 643-5690
2013-14 Tuition: $17,700
Ventura Adult and Continuing Education (Public)
Fall 2013 Enrollment: 142 . . . . (805) 289-1744
2013-14 Tuition: $7,049
Housing: Homeownership rate: 55.9%; Median home value: $429,100; Median year structure built: 1970; Homeowner vacancy rate: 1.3%; Median gross rent: $1,353 per month; Rental vacancy rate: 5.5%
Health Insurance: 85.9% have insurance; 68.8% have private insurance; 28.2% have public insurance; 14.1% do not have insurance; 5.4% of children under 18 do not have insurance
Hospitals: Community Memorial Hospital San Buenaventura (240 beds); Ventura County Medical Center (208 beds)
Safety: Violent crime rate: 24.2 per 10,000 population; Property crime rate: 372.2 per 10,000 population
Newspapers: Ventura County Reporter (weekly circulation 35000)
Transportation: Commute: 88.3% car, 1.9% public transportation, 2.2% walk, 5.6% work from home; Median travel time to work: 22.5 minutes
Additional Information Contacts
City of Ventura. . . . . (805) 654-7800
http://www.ci.ventura.ca.us

SANTA PAULA (city). Covers a land area of 4.593 square miles and a water area of 0.114 square miles. Located at 34.35° N. Lat; 119.07° W. Long. Elevation is 279 feet.
History: Santa Paula was laid out in 1875 in an area of lemon orchards, and grew with the development of the oil industry. Pipelines carried oil from the Santa Paula refineries to the coast for shipping.
Population: 29,321; Growth (since 2000): 2.5%; Density: 6,384.3 persons per square mile; Race: 63.0% White, 0.5% Black/African American, 0.7% Asian, 1.6% American Indian/Alaska Native, 0.1% Native Hawaiian/Other Pacific Islander, 3.7% Two or more races, 79.5% Hispanic of any race; Average household size: 3.50; Median age: 31.1; Age under 18: 29.7%; Age 65 and over: 10.6%; Males per 100 females: 101.9; Marriage status: 34.7% never married, 50.6% now married, 1.9% separated, 5.9% widowed, 8.8% divorced; Foreign born: 31.2%; Speak English only: 40.2%; With disability: 10.5%; Veterans: 5.2%; Ancestry: 6.0% German, 5.4% English, 3.1% Irish, 1.6% French, 1.2% Italian
Employment: 7.3% management, business, and financial, 2.1% computer, engineering, and science, 5.8% education, legal, community service, arts, and media, 1.5% healthcare practitioners, 21.9% service, 22.8% sales and office, 23.9% natural resources, construction, and maintenance, 14.8% production, transportation, and material moving
Income: Per capita: $19,558; Median household: $53,496; Average household: $67,357; Households with income of $100,000 or more: 21.3%; Poverty rate: 19.4%
Educational Attainment: High school diploma or higher: 64.3%; Bachelor's degree or higher: 13.4%; Graduate/professional degree or higher: 4.7%

School District(s)

Briggs Elementary (PK-08)
2012-13 Enrollment: 563. . . . . (805) 525-7540
Mupu Elementary (KG-08)
2012-13 Enrollment: 209. . . . . (805) 525-0422
Santa Clara Elementary (KG-06)
2012-13 Enrollment: 56. . . . . (805) 525-4573
Santa Paula Elementary (KG-08)
2012-13 Enrollment: 3,757 . . . . (805) 933-8800
Santa Paula Union High (09-12)
2012-13 Enrollment: 1,667 . . . . (805) 525-0988

Four-year College(s)

Thomas Aquinas College (Private, Not-for-profit, Roman Catholic)
Fall 2013 Enrollment: 366 . . . . (805) 525-4417
2013-14 Tuition: In-state $24,500; Out-of-state $24,500
Housing: Homeownership rate: 56.2%; Median home value: $316,200; Median year structure built: 1968; Homeowner vacancy rate: 2.0%; Median gross rent: $1,139 per month; Rental vacancy rate: 4.1%
Health Insurance: 77.9% have insurance; 52.0% have private insurance; 32.7% have public insurance; 22.1% do not have insurance; 8.0% of children under 18 do not have insurance
Safety: Violent crime rate: 35.8 per 10,000 population; Property crime rate: 177.7 per 10,000 population
Newspapers: Santa Paula Times (weekly circulation 9000)
Transportation: Commute: 93.2% car, 1.5% public transportation, 1.8% walk, 1.8% work from home; Median travel time to work: 25.9 minutes; Amtrak: Bus service available.
Additional Information Contacts

City of Santa Paula . . . . (805) 525-4478
http://www.ci.santa-paula.ca.us

SANTA ROSA VALLEY (CDP). Covers a land area of 6.861 square miles and a water area of 0 square miles. Located at 34.25° N. Lat; 118.90° W. Long.

Population: 3,334; Growth (since 2000): n/a; Density: 486.0 persons per square mile; Race: 87.1% White, 0.7% Black/African American, 5.6% Asian, 0.4% American Indian/Alaska Native, 0.1% Native Hawaiian/Other Pacific Islander, 3.0% Two or more races, 10.6% Hispanic of any race; Average household size: 3.00; Median age: 48.9; Age under 18: 21.8%; Age 65 and over: 14.9%; Males per 100 females: 96.2; Marriage status: 22.2% never married, 65.3% now married, 1.6% separated, 4.2% widowed, 8.2% divorced; Foreign born: 10.8%; Speak English only: 91.6%; With disability: 4.8%; Veterans: 7.2%; Ancestry: 28.3% German, 18.8% English, 13.9% Irish, 6.5% Italian, 6.2% Norwegian

Employment: 30.5% management, business, and financial, 10.4% computer, engineering, and science, 5.6% education, legal, community service, arts, and media, 14.4% healthcare practitioners, 6.8% service, 24.9% sales and office, 3.1% natural resources, construction, and maintenance, 4.3% production, transportation, and material moving

Income: Per capita: $68,412; Median household: $160,968; Average household: $200,860; Households with income of $100,000 or more: 68.4%; Poverty rate: 4.8%

Educational Attainment: High school diploma or higher: 96.2%; Bachelor's degree or higher: 56.7%; Graduate/professional degree or higher: 23.9%

Housing: Homeownership rate: 93.2%; Median home value: 1 million+; Median year structure built: 1986; Homeowner vacancy rate: 0.5%; Median gross rent: $2,000+ per month; Rental vacancy rate: 2.6%

Health Insurance: 92.5% have insurance; 86.6% have private insurance; 15.4% have public insurance; 7.5% do not have insurance; 13.0% of children under 18 do not have insurance

Transportation: Commute: 90.6% car, 0.8% public transportation, 0.4% walk, 8.2% work from home; Median travel time to work: 30.2 minutes

SANTA SUSANA (CDP). Covers a land area of 1.113 square miles and a water area of 0 square miles. Located at 34.26° N. Lat; 118.67° W. Long. Elevation is 968 feet.

Population: 1,037; Growth (since 2000): n/a; Density: 931.5 persons per square mile; Race: 87.2% White, 1.6% Black/African American, 2.2% Asian, 0.2% American Indian/Alaska Native, 0.0% Native Hawaiian/Other Pacific Islander, 5.6% Two or more races, 15.0% Hispanic of any race; Average household size: 2.55; Median age: 44.4; Age under 18: 17.9%; Age 65 and over: 9.1%; Males per 100 females: 105.3

Housing: Homeownership rate: 75.8%; Homeowner vacancy rate: 2.8%; Rental vacancy rate: 4.8%

SATICOY (CDP). Covers a land area of 0.373 square miles and a water area of 0 square miles. Located at 34.28° N. Lat; 119.15° W. Long. Elevation is 154 feet.

Population: 1,029; Growth (since 2000): n/a; Density: 2,760.7 persons per square mile; Race: 40.1% White, 0.9% Black/African American, 0.2% Asian, 2.8% American Indian/Alaska Native, 0.0% Native Hawaiian/Other Pacific Islander, 6.6% Two or more races, 87.0% Hispanic of any race; Average household size: 3.93; Median age: 28.0; Age under 18: 32.2%; Age 65 and over: 8.8%; Males per 100 females: 109.1

School District(s)

Ventura Unified (KG-12)
2012-13 Enrollment: 17,402 . . . . (805) 641-5000

Housing: Homeownership rate: 35.9%; Homeowner vacancy rate: 2.1%; Rental vacancy rate: 5.1%

SIMI VALLEY (city). Covers a land area of 41.480 square miles and a water area of 0.767 square miles. Located at 34.27° N. Lat; 118.75° W. Long. Elevation is 768 feet.

History: The population doubled between 1970 and 1990 because of its close proximity to the burgeoning Los Angeles area, reflecting the boom in the city's metropolitan area and in Southern California in general. Laid out 1887, Incorporated 1969.

Population: 124,237; Growth (since 2000): 11.6%; Density: 2,995.1 persons per square mile; Race: 75.3% White, 1.4% Black/African American, 9.3% Asian, 0.6% American Indian/Alaska Native, 0.1% Native Hawaiian/Other Pacific Islander, 4.6% Two or more races, 23.3% Hispanic of any race; Average household size: 3.00; Median age: 37.8; Age under 18: 25.0%; Age 65 and over: 10.6%; Males per 100 females: 96.6; Marriage status: 29.2% never married, 55.5% now married, 1.3% separated, 4.6% widowed, 10.7% divorced; Foreign born: 18.9%; Speak English only: 74.2%; With disability: 9.1%; Veterans: 7.2%; Ancestry: 15.2% German, 11.9% Irish, 10.7% English, 8.1% Italian, 5.4% American

Employment: 19.8% management, business, and financial, 6.8% computer, engineering, and science, 10.4% education, legal, community service, arts, and media, 4.6% healthcare practitioners, 16.3% service, 27.6% sales and office, 7.1% natural resources, construction, and maintenance, 7.5% production, transportation, and material moving

Income: Per capita: $36,516; Median household: $87,269; Average household: $106,175; Households with income of $100,000 or more: 44.2%; Poverty rate: 6.6%

Educational Attainment: High school diploma or higher: 90.0%; Bachelor's degree or higher: 32.3%; Graduate/professional degree or higher: 10.3%

School District(s)

Armona Union Elementary (KG-12)
2012-13 Enrollment: 2,060 . . . . (559) 583-5000
Jamestown Elementary (KG-09)
2012-13 Enrollment: 534. . . . . (209) 984-4058
Jefferson Elementary (KG-12)
2012-13 Enrollment: 7,027 . . . . (650) 991-1000
Liberty Elementary (KG-12)
2012-13 Enrollment: 1,062 . . . . (707) 795-4380
Maricopa Unified (KG-12)
2012-13 Enrollment: 2,366 . . . . (661) 769-8231
Nuestro Elementary (KG-12)
2012-13 Enrollment: 885. . . . . (530) 822-5100
Simi Valley Unified (KG-12)
2012-13 Enrollment: 18,857 . . . . (805) 306-4500
Spencer Valley Elementary (KG-12)
2012-13 Enrollment: 3,215 . . . . (760) 765-0336
Stockton Unified (KG-12)
2012-13 Enrollment: 38,435 . . . . (209) 933-7000
West Covina Unified (KG-12)
2012-13 Enrollment: 14,460 . . . . (626) 939-4600

Vocational/Technical School(s)

EMS Training Institute (Private, For-profit)
Fall 2013 Enrollment: 103 . . . . (805) 582-2124

Housing: Homeownership rate: 74.1%; Median home value: $432,000; Median year structure built: 1978; Homeowner vacancy rate: 1.2%; Median gross rent: $1,675 per month; Rental vacancy rate: 4.6%

Health Insurance: 88.5% have insurance; 77.3% have private insurance; 19.9% have public insurance; 11.5% do not have insurance; 5.9% of children under 18 do not have insurance

Hospitals: Simi Valley Hospital & Health Care Services (185 beds)

Safety: Violent crime rate: 10.5 per 10,000 population; Property crime rate: 135.4 per 10,000 population

Transportation: Commute: 90.4% car, 1.3% public transportation, 1.0% walk, 5.8% work from home; Median travel time to work: 28.4 minutes; Amtrak: Train service available.

Additional Information Contacts

City of Simi Valley . . . . (805) 583-6700
http://www.ci.simi-valley.ca.us

SOMIS (unincorporated postal area)

ZCTA: 93066

Covers a land area of 41.575 square miles and a water area of <.001 square miles. Located at 34.30° N. Lat; 119.01° W. Long. Elevation is 305 feet.

Population: 3,102; Growth (since 2000): 5.3%; Density: 74.6 persons per square mile; Race: 78.6% White, 0.7% Black/African American, 2.7% Asian, 0.7% American Indian/Alaska Native, 0.3% Native Hawaiian/Other Pacific Islander, 2.7% Two or more races, 36.5% Hispanic of any race; Average household size: 3.04; Median age: 44.1; Age under 18: 21.6%; Age 65 and over: 17.2%; Males per 100 females: 104.6; Marriage status: 25.6% never married, 62.9% now married, 1.6% separated, 6.8% widowed, 4.7% divorced; Foreign born: 20.2%; Speak English only: 61.1%; With disability: 10.9%; Veterans: 11.2%; Ancestry: 14.5% German, 11.3% Irish, 7.5% English, 3.3% Italian, 2.8% Scottish

Employment: 20.0% management, business, and financial, 6.3% computer, engineering, and science, 11.1% education, legal, community service, arts, and media, 3.1% healthcare practitioners, 15.4% service,

27.5% sales and office, 8.5% natural resources, construction, and maintenance, 8.2% production, transportation, and material moving
Income: Per capita: $51,619; Median household: $85,363; Average household: $145,386; Households with income of $100,000 or more: 43.8%; Poverty rate: 12.5%
Educational Attainment: High school diploma or higher: 85.2%; Bachelor's degree or higher: 39.5%; Graduate/professional degree or higher: 13.6%

School District(s)

Mesa Union Elementary (KG-12)
2012-13 Enrollment: 1,387 . . . . (805) 485-1411
Somis Union (KG-12)
2012-13 Enrollment: 251. . . . . (805) 386-8258
Housing: Homeownership rate: 67.9%; Median home value: $882,400; Median year structure built: 1972; Homeowner vacancy rate: 1.0%; Median gross rent: $1,377 per month; Rental vacancy rate: 4.1%
Health Insurance: 80.4% have insurance; 63.8% have private insurance; 32.4% have public insurance; 19.6% do not have insurance; 11.0% of children under 18 do not have insurance
Transportation: Commute: 82.4% car, 1.4% public transportation, 3.6% walk, 10.3% work from home; Median travel time to work: 22.8 minutes

THOUSAND OAKS (city). Covers a land area of 55.031 square miles and a water area of 0.150 square miles. Located at 34.19° N. Lat; 118.87° W. Long. Elevation is 886 feet.
History: one of the fastest-growing U.S. cities, marked by a population increase of more than 35% between 1980 and 1990. Once known generally as the Conejo Valley, it became a stagecoach stop in 1874. California Lutheran University is there. Incorporated 1964.
Population: 126,683; Growth (since 2000): 8.3%; Density: 2,302.0 persons per square mile; Race: 80.3% White, 1.3% Black/African American, 8.7% Asian, 0.4% American Indian/Alaska Native, 0.1% Native Hawaiian/Other Pacific Islander, 3.8% Two or more races, 16.8% Hispanic of any race; Average household size: 2.73; Median age: 41.5; Age under 18: 23.7%; Age 65 and over: 14.7%; Males per 100 females: 95.8; Marriage status: 27.9% never married, 57.6% now married, 1.3% separated, 5.3% widowed, 9.2% divorced; Foreign born: 19.5%; Speak English only: 75.7%; With disability: 8.8%; Veterans: 7.3%; Ancestry: 15.1% German, 11.5% English, 11.3% Irish, 7.6% Italian, 3.5% American
Employment: 22.5% management, business, and financial, 9.3% computer, engineering, and science, 13.5% education, legal, community service, arts, and media, 5.7% healthcare practitioners, 14.7% service, 24.7% sales and office, 4.8% natural resources, construction, and maintenance, 4.8% production, transportation, and material moving
Income: Per capita: $45,522; Median household: $100,476; Average household: $125,321; Households with income of $100,000 or more: 50.3%; Poverty rate: 6.8%
Educational Attainment: High school diploma or higher: 92.5%; Bachelor's degree or higher: 48.5%; Graduate/professional degree or higher: 20.0%

School District(s)

Conejo Valley Unified (KG-12)
2012-13 Enrollment: 20,595 . . . . (805) 497-9511
Ventura County Office of Education (KG-12)
2012-13 Enrollment: 2,590 . . . . (805) 383-1902

Four-year College(s)

California Lutheran University (Private, Not-for-profit, Evangelical Lutheran Church)
Fall 2013 Enrollment: 4,282 . . . . (805) 492-2411
2013-14 Tuition: In-state $35,720; Out-of-state $35,720
Housing: Homeownership rate: 73.1%; Median home value: $593,900; Median year structure built: 1977; Homeowner vacancy rate: 0.8%; Median gross rent: $1,825 per month; Rental vacancy rate: 5.6%
Health Insurance: 89.3% have insurance; 80.2% have private insurance; 20.6% have public insurance; 10.7% do not have insurance; 6.9% of children under 18 do not have insurance
Hospitals: Los Robles Hospital & Medical Center (395 beds)
Safety: Violent crime rate: 10.8 per 10,000 population; Property crime rate: 124.5 per 10,000 population
Transportation: Commute: 86.8% car, 0.8% public transportation, 2.4% walk, 7.8% work from home; Median travel time to work: 24.3 minutes
Additional Information Contacts
City of Thousand Oaks . . . . (805) 449-2100
http://www.ci.thousand-oaks.ca.us/default.asp

Yolo County

Located in central California, in the Sacramento Valley; bounded on the east by the Sacramento River. Covers a land area of 1,014.689 square miles, a water area of 8.868 square miles, and is located in the Pacific Time Zone at 38.68° N. Lat., 121.90° W. Long. The county was founded in 1850. County seat is Woodland.

Yolo County is part of the Sacramento—Roseville—Arden-Arcade, CA Metropolitan Statistical Area. The entire metro area includes: El Dorado County, CA; Placer County, CA; Sacramento County, CA; Yolo County, CA

Weather Station: Davis 2 WSW Exp Farm Elevation: 60 feet

	Jan	Feb	Mar	Apr	May	Jun	Jul	Aug	Sep	Oct	Nov	Dec
High	54	60	66	73	81	88	93	92	89	79	65	54
Low	38	40	43	46	51	55	57	56	54	49	42	37
Precip	3.9	4.0	2.9	1.1	0.6	0.2	0.0	0.1	0.3	0.9	2.3	3.5
Snow	0.0	0.0	0.0	0.0	0.0	0.0	0.0	0.0	0.0	0.0	0.0	0.0

High and Low temperatures in degrees Fahrenheit; Precipitation and Snow in inches

Weather Station: Winters Elevation: 134 feet

	Jan	Feb	Mar	Apr	May	Jun	Jul	Aug	Sep	Oct	Nov	Dec
High	56	62	69	76	84	92	97	96	91	81	67	57
Low	38	42	45	49	54	59	61	60	57	51	44	38
Precip	4.9	5.1	3.4	1.2	0.8	0.1	0.0	0.0	0.2	1.0	2.8	4.5
Snow	tr	tr	0.0	0.0	0.0	0.0	0.0	0.0	0.0	0.0	0.0	tr

High and Low temperatures in degrees Fahrenheit; Precipitation and Snow in inches

Weather Station: Woodland 1 WNW Elevation: 68 feet

	Jan	Feb	Mar	Apr	May	Jun	Jul	Aug	Sep	Oct	Nov	Dec
High	55	60	67	74	82	90	95	94	90	79	64	55
Low	39	43	46	48	54	58	60	59	58	52	44	39
Precip	4.3	4.5	3.0	1.3	0.6	0.2	0.0	0.1	0.4	1.1	2.4	3.6
Snow	0.0	0.0	0.0	0.0	0.0	0.0	0.0	0.0	0.0	0.0	0.0	tr

High and Low temperatures in degrees Fahrenheit; Precipitation and Snow in inches

Population: 200,849; Growth (since 2000): 19.1%; Density: 197.9 persons per square mile; Race: 63.2% White, 2.6% Black/African American, 13.0% Asian, 1.1% American Indian/Alaska Native, 0.5% Native Hawaiian/Other Pacific Islander, 5.8% two or more races, 30.3% Hispanic of any race; Average household size: 2.74; Median age: 30.4; Age under 18: 22.7%; Age 65 and over: 9.8%; Males per 100 females: 95.2; Marriage status: 41.1% never married, 45.5% now married, 1.7% separated, 4.2% widowed, 9.2% divorced; Foreign born: 21.7%; Speak English only: 65.3%; With disability: 10.3%; Veterans: 6.6%; Ancestry: 12.1% German, 8.7% Irish, 8.7% English, 4.6% Italian, 3.1% European
Religion: Six largest groups: 21.6% Catholicism, 2.4% Latter-day Saints, 2.4% Baptist, 2.2% Muslim Estimate, 1.4% Methodist/Pietist, 1.4% Non-denominational Protestant
Economy: Unemployment rate: 6.7%; Leading industries: 11.8% retail trade; 10.8% professional, scientific, and technical services; 10.7% accommodation and food services; Farms: 1,011 totaling 460,824 acres; Company size: 2 employ 1,000 or more persons, 7 employ 500 to 999 persons, 78 employ 100 to 499 persons, 3,766 employ less than 100 persons; Business ownership: 4,423 women-owned, n/a Black-owned, 1,662 Hispanic-owned, 1,559 Asian-owned
Employment: 14.2% management, business, and financial, 9.6% computer, engineering, and science, 16.0% education, legal, community service, arts, and media, 5.3% healthcare practitioners, 16.6% service, 20.6% sales and office, 9.3% natural resources, construction, and maintenance, 8.5% production, transportation, and material moving
Income: Per capita: $27,730; Median household: $55,918; Average household: $77,162; Households with income of $100,000 or more: 26.8%; Poverty rate: 19.1%
Educational Attainment: High school diploma or higher: 84.3%; Bachelor's degree or higher: 37.9%; Graduate/professional degree or higher: 17.7%
Housing: Homeownership rate: 52.8%; Median home value: $314,300; Median year structure built: 1979; Homeowner vacancy rate: 1.9%; Median gross rent: $1,082 per month; Rental vacancy rate: 5.0%
Vital Statistics: Birth rate: 114.8 per 10,000 population; Death rate: 57.6 per 10,000 population; Age-adjusted cancer mortality rate: 155.4 deaths per 100,000 population
Health Insurance: 86.8% have insurance; 70.5% have private insurance; 24.9% have public insurance; 13.2% do not have insurance; 6.1% of children under 18 do not have insurance

Health Care: Physicians: 31.3 per 10,000 population; Hospital beds: 7.9 per 10,000 population; Hospital admissions: 359.2 per 10,000 population
Air Quality Index: 94.0% good, 6.0% moderate, 0.0% unhealthy for sensitive individuals, 0.0% unhealthy (percent of days)
Transportation: Commute: 79.3% car, 3.7% public transportation, 2.7% walk, 4.4% work from home; Median travel time to work: 21.6 minutes
Presidential Election: 65.2% Obama, 32.0% Romney (2012)
National and State Parks: Fremont Weir State Wildlife Area; Woodland Opera House State Historic Park
Additional Information Contacts
Yolo Government . . . . (530) 666-8195
http://www.yolocounty.org

Yolo County Communities

BROOKS (unincorporated postal area)
ZCTA: 95606
Covers a land area of 36.319 square miles and a water area of 0 square miles. Located at 38.76° N. Lat; 122.20° W. Long. Elevation is 341 feet.
Population: 196; Growth (since 2000): -47.7%; Density: 5.4 persons per square mile; Race: 69.4% White, 1.0% Black/African American, 1.5% Asian, 21.9% American Indian/Alaska Native, 0.0% Native Hawaiian/Other Pacific Islander, 1.5% Two or more races, 16.8% Hispanic of any race; Average household size: 2.51; Median age: 40.8; Age under 18: 26.0%; Age 65 and over: 12.8%; Males per 100 females: 110.8
Housing: Homeownership rate: 66.7%; Homeowner vacancy rate: 1.9%; Rental vacancy rate: 0.0%

CAPAY (unincorporated postal area)
ZCTA: 95607
Covers a land area of 134.250 square miles and a water area of 0.253 square miles. Located at 38.83° N. Lat; 122.13° W. Long. Elevation is 210 feet.
Population: 431; Growth (since 2000): 69.0%; Density: 3.2 persons per square mile; Race: 78.0% White, 1.2% Black/African American, 1.6% Asian, 1.9% American Indian/Alaska Native, 0.0% Native Hawaiian/Other Pacific Islander, 4.6% Two or more races, 16.9% Hispanic of any race; Average household size: 2.33; Median age: 49.5; Age under 18: 18.8%; Age 65 and over: 17.9%; Males per 100 females: 107.2
Housing: Homeownership rate: 69.8%; Homeowner vacancy rate: 0.0%; Rental vacancy rate: 0.0%

CLARKSBURG (CDP). Covers a land area of 2.029 square miles and a water area of 0 square miles. Located at 38.42° N. Lat; 121.54° W. Long. Elevation is 10 feet.
Population: 418; Growth (since 2000): n/a; Density: 206.0 persons per square mile; Race: 81.1% White, 0.5% Black/African American, 3.8% Asian, 0.5% American Indian/Alaska Native, 0.2% Native Hawaiian/Other Pacific Islander, 5.0% Two or more races, 26.1% Hispanic of any race; Average household size: 2.49; Median age: 48.7; Age under 18: 23.0%; Age 65 and over: 22.0%; Males per 100 females: 98.1

School District(s)

River Delta Joint Unified (KG-12)
2012-13 Enrollment: 2,323 . . . . (707) 374-1700
Housing: Homeownership rate: 68.5%; Homeowner vacancy rate: 0.0%; Rental vacancy rate: 10.0%

DAVIS (city). Covers a land area of 9.887 square miles and a water area of 0.032 square miles. Located at 38.56° N. Lat; 121.74° W. Long. Elevation is 52 feet.
History: Named for Jerome C. Davis, who settled here in the early 1850s. Davis owned wheat and barley fields, orchards and vineyards, and herds of livestock here. The community developed around the University of California branch.
Population: 65,622; Growth (since 2000): 8.8%; Density: 6,637.0 persons per square mile; Race: 64.9% White, 2.3% Black/African American, 21.9% Asian, 0.5% American Indian/Alaska Native, 0.2% Native Hawaiian/Other Pacific Islander, 5.4% Two or more races, 12.5% Hispanic of any race; Average household size: 2.55; Median age: 25.2; Age under 18: 16.4%; Age 65 and over: 8.5%; Males per 100 females: 90.5; Marriage status: 53.9% never married, 37.2% now married, 1.1% separated, 2.5% widowed, 6.4% divorced; Foreign born: 18.8%; Speak English only: 73.8%; With disability: 6.3%; Veterans: 4.2%; Ancestry: 13.4% German, 10.6% English, 10.5% Irish, 6.0% Italian, 4.6% European
Employment: 14.6% management, business, and financial, 15.2% computer, engineering, and science, 26.8% education, legal, community service, arts, and media, 7.9% healthcare practitioners, 13.3% service, 15.7% sales and office, 2.6% natural resources, construction, and maintenance, 3.9% production, transportation, and material moving
Income: Per capita: $32,455; Median household: $60,114; Average household: $87,002; Households with income of $100,000 or more: 32.7%; Poverty rate: 26.3%
Educational Attainment: High school diploma or higher: 95.8%; Bachelor's degree or higher: 70.2%; Graduate/professional degree or higher: 39.2%

School District(s)

Davis Joint Unified (KG-12)
2012-13 Enrollment: 8,599 . . . . (530) 757-5300

Four-year College(s)

University of California-Davis (Public)
Fall 2013 Enrollment: 33,307 . . . . (530) 752-1011
2013-14 Tuition: In-state $13,895; Out-of-state $36,773
Housing: Homeownership rate: 43.0%; Median home value: $529,300; Median year structure built: 1980; Homeowner vacancy rate: 0.9%; Median gross rent: $1,248 per month; Rental vacancy rate: 3.5%
Health Insurance: 92.0% have insurance; 85.3% have private insurance; 14.0% have public insurance; 8.0% do not have insurance; 3.8% of children under 18 do not have insurance
Hospitals: Sutter Davis Hospital (48 beds)
Safety: Violent crime rate: 15.6 per 10,000 population; Property crime rate: 268.7 per 10,000 population
Newspapers: Davis Enterprise (daily circulation 10300)
Transportation: Commute: 63.7% car, 6.5% public transportation, 3.4% walk, 5.2% work from home; Median travel time to work: 20.4 minutes; Amtrak: Train service available.
Airports: Yolo County (general aviation)
Additional Information Contacts
City of Davis . . . . (530) 757-5602
http://cityofdavis.org

DUNNIGAN (CDP). Covers a land area of 5.226 square miles and a water area of 0 square miles. Located at 38.89° N. Lat; 121.97° W. Long. Elevation is 69 feet.
Population: 1,416; Growth (since 2000): n/a; Density: 271.0 persons per square mile; Race: 59.0% White, 7.6% Black/African American, 1.3% Asian, 1.8% American Indian/Alaska Native, 0.1% Native Hawaiian/Other Pacific Islander, 6.3% Two or more races, 41.2% Hispanic of any race; Average household size: 2.81; Median age: 41.7; Age under 18: 25.6%; Age 65 and over: 19.8%; Males per 100 females: 91.1
Housing: Homeownership rate: 80.7%; Homeowner vacancy rate: 1.9%; Rental vacancy rate: 16.7%

ESPARTO (CDP). Covers a land area of 4.601 square miles and a water area of 0 square miles. Located at 38.69° N. Lat; 122.02° W. Long. Elevation is 190 feet.
Population: 3,108; Growth (since 2000): 67.3%; Density: 675.5 persons per square mile; Race: 59.7% White, 1.4% Black/African American, 4.2% Asian, 1.6% American Indian/Alaska Native, 0.2% Native Hawaiian/Other Pacific Islander, 3.8% Two or more races, 49.5% Hispanic of any race; Average household size: 3.19; Median age: 33.1; Age under 18: 28.6%; Age 65 and over: 10.2%; Males per 100 females: 100.5; Marriage status: 26.6% never married, 55.8% now married, 3.8% separated, 6.1% widowed, 11.6% divorced; Foreign born: 23.9%; Speak English only: 60.1%; With disability: 16.6%; Veterans: 6.9%; Ancestry: 16.9% Irish, 12.0% German, 8.8% English, 4.2% Italian, 2.8% Swedish
Employment: 11.3% management, business, and financial, 8.4% computer, engineering, and science, 7.4% education, legal, community service, arts, and media, 0.6% healthcare practitioners, 32.0% service, 14.2% sales and office, 14.3% natural resources, construction, and maintenance, 11.9% production, transportation, and material moving
Income: Per capita: $21,289; Median household: $64,000; Average household: $67,911; Households with income of $100,000 or more: 20.5%; Poverty rate: 13.5%
Educational Attainment: High school diploma or higher: 72.9%; Bachelor's degree or higher: 12.5%; Graduate/professional degree or higher: 5.3%

School District(s)

Esparto Unified (KG-12)
2012-13 Enrollment: 987. . . . . (530) 787-3446

Housing: Homeownership rate: 70.8%; Median home value: $209,800; Median year structure built: 1984; Homeowner vacancy rate: 2.3%; Median gross rent: $1,143 per month; Rental vacancy rate: 5.0%

Health Insurance: 87.0% have insurance; 70.2% have private insurance; 28.0% have public insurance; 13.0% do not have insurance; 4.4% of children under 18 do not have insurance

Transportation: Commute: 95.2% car, 0.0% public transportation, 1.3% walk, 1.6% work from home; Median travel time to work: 26.9 minutes

GUINDA (CDP). Covers a land area of 2.907 square miles and a water area of 0 square miles. Located at 38.83° N. Lat; 122.20° W. Long. Elevation is 361 feet.

Population: 254; Growth (since 2000): n/a; Density: 87.4 persons per square mile; Race: 68.9% White, 10.2% Black/African American, 0.4% Asian, 0.0% American Indian/Alaska Native, 0.4% Native Hawaiian/Other Pacific Islander, 3.1% Two or more races, 26.8% Hispanic of any race; Average household size: 2.44; Median age: 50.8; Age under 18: 18.1%; Age 65 and over: 20.9%; Males per 100 females: 103.2

Housing: Homeownership rate: 81.7%; Homeowner vacancy rate: 2.3%; Rental vacancy rate: 5.0%

KNIGHTS LANDING (CDP). Covers a land area of 0.501 square miles and a water area of 0 square miles. Located at 38.80° N. Lat; 121.72° W. Long. Elevation is 36 feet.

Population: 995; Growth (since 2000): n/a; Density: 1,985.7 persons per square mile; Race: 56.3% White, 0.4% Black/African American, 0.7% Asian, 1.0% American Indian/Alaska Native, 0.0% Native Hawaiian/Other Pacific Islander, 7.6% Two or more races, 64.7% Hispanic of any race; Average household size: 3.14; Median age: 34.3; Age under 18: 26.6%; Age 65 and over: 11.3%; Males per 100 females: 108.6

School District(s)

Woodland Joint Unified (KG-12)
2012-13 Enrollment: 10,126 . . . . (530) 662-0201

Housing: Homeownership rate: 67.2%; Homeowner vacancy rate: 2.7%; Rental vacancy rate: 9.6%

MADISON (CDP). Covers a land area of 1.547 square miles and a water area of 0 square miles. Located at 38.67° N. Lat; 121.97° W. Long. Elevation is 151 feet.

Population: 503; Growth (since 2000): n/a; Density: 325.1 persons per square mile; Race: 44.5% White, 0.2% Black/African American, 0.6% Asian, 1.6% American Indian/Alaska Native, 0.6% Native Hawaiian/Other Pacific Islander, 5.8% Two or more races, 76.3% Hispanic of any race; Average household size: 3.71; Median age: 28.6; Age under 18: 30.8%; Age 65 and over: 8.5%; Males per 100 females: 113.1

School District(s)

Esparto Unified (KG-12)
2012-13 Enrollment: 987. . . . . (530) 787-3446

Housing: Homeownership rate: 63.7%; Homeowner vacancy rate: 0.0%; Rental vacancy rate: 3.9%

MONUMENT HILLS (CDP). Covers a land area of 4.026 square miles and a water area of 0 square miles. Located at 38.66° N. Lat; 121.88° W. Long.

Population: 1,542; Growth (since 2000): n/a; Density: 383.1 persons per square mile; Race: 75.4% White, 1.3% Black/African American, 5.0% Asian, 2.1% American Indian/Alaska Native, 1.1% Native Hawaiian/Other Pacific Islander, 5.2% Two or more races, 26.1% Hispanic of any race; Average household size: 2.93; Median age: 42.9; Age under 18: 24.6%; Age 65 and over: 10.2%; Males per 100 females: 107.3

Housing: Homeownership rate: 85.7%; Homeowner vacancy rate: 3.0%; Rental vacancy rate: 10.7%

RUMSEY (unincorporated postal area)

ZCTA: 95679

Covers a land area of 45.900 square miles and a water area of 0.267 square miles. Located at 38.90° N. Lat; 122.35° W. Long. Elevation is 420 feet.

Population: 55; Growth (since 2000): n/a; Density: 1.2 persons per square mile; Race: 94.5% White, 0.0% Black/African American, 1.8% Asian, 0.0% American Indian/Alaska Native, 0.0% Native Hawaiian/Other Pacific Islander, 0.0% Two or more races, 10.9% Hispanic of any race; Average household size: 2.04; Median age: 47.1; Age under 18: 12.7%; Age 65 and over: 18.2%; Males per 100 females: 103.7

Housing: Homeownership rate: 62.9%; Homeowner vacancy rate: 0.0%; Rental vacancy rate: 9.1%

UNIVERSITY OF CALIFORNIA DAVIS (CDP). Covers a land area of 1.459 square miles and a water area of 0 square miles. Located at 38.54° N. Lat; 121.76° W. Long.

History: The Univeristy of California, Davis, also known as UCD or UC Davis, is a public research university located in Davis, California, just west of Sacramento and was established in 1908.

Population: 5,786; Growth (since 2000): n/a; Density: 3,966.8 persons per square mile; Race: 42.2% White, 2.5% Black/African American, 42.2% Asian, 0.4% American Indian/Alaska Native, 0.1% Native Hawaiian/Other Pacific Islander, 6.3% Two or more races, 12.6% Hispanic of any race; Average household size: 2.34; Median age: 19.6; Age under 18: 5.4%; Age 65 and over: 0.2%; Males per 100 females: 82.2; Marriage status: 90.2% never married, 9.4% now married, 0.0% separated, 0.1% widowed, 0.3% divorced; Foreign born: 23.3%; Speak English only: 53.5%; With disability: 2.8%; Veterans: 0.4%; Ancestry: 10.0% Irish, 9.6% German, 6.6% English, 3.6% Italian, 3.4% European

Employment: 7.2% management, business, and financial, 11.9% computer, engineering, and science, 39.3% education, legal, community service, arts, and media, 0.8% healthcare practitioners, 13.7% service, 22.5% sales and office, 0.4% natural resources, construction, and maintenance, 4.1% production, transportation, and material moving

Income: Per capita: $6,877; Median household: $26,940; Average household: $36,412; Households with income of $100,000 or more: 5.9%; Poverty rate: 41.1%

Educational Attainment: High school diploma or higher: 99.0%; Bachelor's degree or higher: 83.7%; Graduate/professional degree or higher: 50.3%

Housing: Homeownership rate: 0.1%; Median home value: n/a; Median year structure built: 1978; Homeowner vacancy rate: 0.0%; Median gross rent: $987 per month; Rental vacancy rate: 0.6%

Health Insurance: 95.6% have insurance; 86.2% have private insurance; 11.2% have public insurance; 4.4% do not have insurance; 2.5% of children under 18 do not have insurance

Transportation: Commute: 21.6% car, 3.3% public transportation, 13.8% walk, 8.9% work from home; Median travel time to work: 13.5 minutes

WEST SACRAMENTO (city). Covers a land area of 21.425 square miles and a water area of 1.421 square miles. Located at 38.55° N. Lat; 121.55° W. Long. Elevation is 20 feet.

Population: 48,744; Growth (since 2000): 54.2%; Density: 2,275.1 persons per square mile; Race: 60.6% White, 4.8% Black/African American, 10.5% Asian, 1.6% American Indian/Alaska Native, 1.1% Native Hawaiian/Other Pacific Islander, 7.7% Two or more races, 31.4% Hispanic of any race; Average household size: 2.78; Median age: 33.6; Age under 18: 26.7%; Age 65 and over: 9.8%; Males per 100 females: 97.7; Marriage status: 32.1% never married, 50.2% now married, 2.5% separated, 5.7% widowed, 12.0% divorced; Foreign born: 24.6%; Speak English only: 62.2%; With disability: 13.9%; Veterans: 7.9%; Ancestry: 10.3% German, 8.5% Irish, 6.7% English, 5.1% Russian, 3.8% Italian

Employment: 15.8% management, business, and financial, 7.4% computer, engineering, and science, 9.9% education, legal, community service, arts, and media, 4.4% healthcare practitioners, 19.6% service, 23.2% sales and office, 10.6% natural resources, construction, and maintenance, 9.1% production, transportation, and material moving

Income: Per capita: $24,827; Median household: $53,394; Average household: $68,475; Households with income of $100,000 or more: 23.2%; Poverty rate: 19.9%

Educational Attainment: High school diploma or higher: 81.1%; Bachelor's degree or higher: 24.2%; Graduate/professional degree or higher: 7.8%

School District(s)

Washington Unified (KG-12)
2012-13 Enrollment: 7,697 . . . . (916) 375-7600

Two-year College(s)

Wyotech-West Sacramento (Private, For-profit)
Fall 2013 Enrollment: 155 . . . . (916) 376-8888

Housing: Homeownership rate: 58.8%; Median home value: $241,000; Median year structure built: 1982; Homeowner vacancy rate: 3.0%; Median gross rent: $891 per month; Rental vacancy rate: 7.0%

Health Insurance: 83.9% have insurance; 61.2% have private insurance; 30.9% have public insurance; 16.1% do not have insurance; 6.8% of children under 18 do not have insurance

Safety: Violent crime rate: 41.2 per 10,000 population; Property crime rate: 298.1 per 10,000 population
Newspapers: The News Ledger (weekly circulation 2300); West Sacramento Press (weekly circulation 6000)
Transportation: Commute: 89.7% car, 2.1% public transportation, 1.2% walk, 4.7% work from home; Median travel time to work: 22.8 minutes
Additional Information Contacts
City of West Sacramento .... (916) 617-4500
http://www.cityofwestsacramento.org

WINTERS (city). Covers a land area of 2.912 square miles and a water area of 0.025 square miles. Located at 38.53° N. Lat; 121.98° W. Long. Elevation is 135 feet.
History: Incorporated 1898.
Population: 6,624; Growth (since 2000): 8.1%; Density: 2,274.5 persons per square mile; Race: 70.0% White, 0.6% Black/African American, 1.0% Asian, 0.8% American Indian/Alaska Native, 0.1% Native Hawaiian/Other Pacific Islander, 5.0% Two or more races, 52.4% Hispanic of any race; Average household size: 3.03; Median age: 35.9; Age under 18: 25.8%; Age 65 and over: 9.1%; Males per 100 females: 102.4; Marriage status: 27.7% never married, 58.3% now married, 2.0% separated, 4.1% widowed, 9.9% divorced; Foreign born: 20.3%; Speak English only: 66.1%; With disability: 13.1%; Veterans: 8.6%; Ancestry: 14.1% English, 9.5% Irish, 8.2% German, 5.2% European, 4.5% Italian
Employment: 10.5% management, business, and financial, 4.0% computer, engineering, and science, 14.5% education, legal, community service, arts, and media, 2.2% healthcare practitioners, 23.1% service, 19.2% sales and office, 12.2% natural resources, construction, and maintenance, 14.4% production, transportation, and material moving
Income: Per capita: $27,266; Median household: $55,887; Average household: $73,386; Households with income of $100,000 or more: 28.2%; Poverty rate: 4.3%
Educational Attainment: High school diploma or higher: 81.2%; Bachelor's degree or higher: 24.2%; Graduate/professional degree or higher: 7.0%

School District(s)

Winters Joint Unified (KG-12)
2012-13 Enrollment: 1,522 .... (530) 795-6100
Housing: Homeownership rate: 65.2%; Median home value: $267,100; Median year structure built: 1985; Homeowner vacancy rate: 1.7%; Median gross rent: $963 per month; Rental vacancy rate: 5.0%
Health Insurance: 86.7% have insurance; 71.6% have private insurance; 25.8% have public insurance; 13.3% do not have insurance; 5.7% of children under 18 do not have insurance
Safety: Violent crime rate: 11.4 per 10,000 population; Property crime rate: 164.5 per 10,000 population
Newspapers: Winters Express (weekly circulation 2600)
Transportation: Commute: 84.8% car, 0.9% public transportation, 3.5% walk, 5.7% work from home; Median travel time to work: 26.2 minutes
Additional Information Contacts
City of Winters.................................. (530) 795-4910
http://www.cityofwinters.org

WOODLAND (city). County seat. Covers a land area of 15.303 square miles and a water area of 0 square miles. Located at 38.67° N. Lat; 121.75° W. Long. Elevation is 69 feet.
History: Named by Major F.S. Freeman, store owner, in 1859. Woodland's first settler came in 1853. A blacksmith shop followed, and soon a town grew up around it. First named Yolo City, Woodland acquired its present name when the post office opened in 1859.
Population: 55,468; Growth (since 2000): 12.9%; Density: 3,624.7 persons per square mile; Race: 62.9% White, 1.5% Black/African American, 6.2% Asian, 1.3% American Indian/Alaska Native, 0.3% Native Hawaiian/Other Pacific Islander, 5.2% Two or more races, 47.4% Hispanic of any race; Average household size: 2.91; Median age: 33.7; Age under 18: 27.5%; Age 65 and over: 10.9%; Males per 100 females: 97.0; Marriage status: 31.2% never married, 51.8% now married, 2.0% separated, 5.5% widowed, 11.5% divorced; Foreign born: 22.5%; Speak English only: 59.9%; With disability: 11.5%; Veterans: 8.2%; Ancestry: 12.3% German, 8.0% English, 6.8% Irish, 4.1% Italian, 2.9% American
Employment: 13.1% management, business, and financial, 6.2% computer, engineering, and science, 7.9% education, legal, community service, arts, and media, 4.0% healthcare practitioners, 17.2% service, 24.9% sales and office, 14.1% natural resources, construction, and maintenance, 12.5% production, transportation, and material moving
Income: Per capita: $25,525; Median household: $55,147; Average household: $70,493; Households with income of $100,000 or more: 22.2%; Poverty rate: 12.7%
Educational Attainment: High school diploma or higher: 78.1%; Bachelor's degree or higher: 23.0%; Graduate/professional degree or higher: 8.8%

School District(s)

Woodland Joint Unified (KG-12)
2012-13 Enrollment: 10,126 .... (530) 662-0201
Yolo County Office of Education (KG-12)
2012-13 Enrollment: 319......................... (530) 668-6700
Yolo County Rop
2012-13 Enrollment: n/a .... (530) 668-3770

Two-year College(s)

Woodland Community College (Public)
Fall 2013 Enrollment: 2,641 .... (530) 661-5700
2013-14 Tuition: In-state $1,144; Out-of-state $6,184

Vocational/Technical School(s)

Cambridge Junior College-Woodland (Private, For-profit)
Fall 2013 Enrollment: 96 .... (530) 662-0100
2013-14 Tuition: $15,326
Housing: Homeownership rate: 55.9%; Median home value: $256,200; Median year structure built: 1977; Homeowner vacancy rate: 2.0%; Median gross rent: $922 per month; Rental vacancy rate: 6.1%
Health Insurance: 83.4% have insurance; 62.5% have private insurance; 30.6% have public insurance; 16.6% do not have insurance; 6.4% of children under 18 do not have insurance
Hospitals: Woodland Memorial Hospital (103 beds)
Safety: Violent crime rate: 48.1 per 10,000 population; Property crime rate: 343.6 per 10,000 population
Newspapers: Daily Democrat (daily circulation 9400)
Transportation: Commute: 89.4% car, 2.5% public transportation, 2.3% walk, 2.8% work from home; Median travel time to work: 20.9 minutes
Airports: Watts-Woodland (general aviation)
Additional Information Contacts
City of Woodland................................ (530) 661-5850
http://www.cityofwoodland.org

YOLO (CDP). Covers a land area of 1.380 square miles and a water area of 0 square miles. Located at 38.74° N. Lat; 121.81° W. Long. Elevation is 82 feet.
Population: 450; Growth (since 2000): n/a; Density: 326.1 persons per square mile; Race: 61.8% White, 0.0% Black/African American, 0.0% Asian, 2.0% American Indian/Alaska Native, 0.0% Native Hawaiian/Other Pacific Islander, 2.7% Two or more races, 65.1% Hispanic of any race; Average household size: 3.02; Median age: 35.9; Age under 18: 30.0%; Age 65 and over: 9.1%; Males per 100 females: 90.7

School District(s)

Woodland Joint Unified (KG-12)
2012-13 Enrollment: 10,126 .... (530) 662-0201
Housing: Homeownership rate: 47.6%; Homeowner vacancy rate: 2.7%; Rental vacancy rate: 4.9%

ZAMORA (unincorporated postal area)

ZCTA: 95698

Covers a land area of 42.989 square miles and a water area of 0.297 square miles. Located at 38.82° N. Lat; 121.91° W. Long. Elevation is 52 feet.
Population: 236; Growth (since 2000): n/a; Density: 5.5 persons per square mile; Race: 81.8% White, 0.8% Black/African American, 0.4% Asian, 0.4% American Indian/Alaska Native, 0.0% Native Hawaiian/Other Pacific Islander, 4.7% Two or more races, 35.2% Hispanic of any race; Average household size: 2.59; Median age: 45.5; Age under 18: 21.2%; Age 65 and over: 15.7%; Males per 100 females: 103.4
Housing: Homeownership rate: 74.8%; Homeowner vacancy rate: 1.4%; Rental vacancy rate: 0.0%

Yuba County

Located in north central California, in the Sacramento Valley; drained by the Yuba and Bear Rivers; includes parts of Plumas and Tahoe National Forests. Covers a land area of 631.838 square miles, a water area of 11.969 square miles, and is located in the Pacific Time Zone at 39.27° N.

Lat., 121.34° W. Long. The county was founded in 1850. County seat is Marysville.

Yuba County is part of the Yuba City, CA Metropolitan Statistical Area. The entire metro area includes: Sutter County, CA; Yuba County, CA

Weather Station: Marysville Elevation: 57 feet

	Jan	Feb	Mar	Apr	May	Jun	Jul	Aug	Sep	Oct	Nov	Dec
High	55	62	68	74	82	90	96	95	90	80	64	56
Low	39	43	46	49	55	60	63	62	59	52	44	39
Precip	4.0	3.8	3.4	1.7	0.9	0.2	tr	0.1	0.4	1.2	2.8	4.1
Snow	0.0	0.0	0.0	0.0	0.0	0.0	0.0	0.0	0.0	0.0	tr	0.0

High and Low temperatures in degrees Fahrenheit; Precipitation and Snow in inches

Weather Station: Strawberry Valley Elevation: 3,808 feet

	Jan	Feb	Mar	Apr	May	Jun	Jul	Aug	Sep	Oct	Nov	Dec
High	50	50	54	59	67	75	83	83	78	69	55	49
Low	30	30	32	35	41	47	52	51	47	41	34	30
Precip	13.8	14.3	11.8	6.2	3.9	1.1	0.1	0.2	1.2	4.2	9.7	15.6
Snow	17.6	22.5	21.3	8.6	0.6	tr	0.0	0.0	0.0	0.5	4.5	17.9

High and Low temperatures in degrees Fahrenheit; Precipitation and Snow in inches

Population: 72,155; Growth (since 2000): 19.8%; Density: 114.2 persons per square mile; Race: 68.4% White, 3.3% Black/African American, 6.7% Asian, 2.3% American Indian/Alaska Native, 0.4% Native Hawaiian/Other Pacific Islander, 7.1% two or more races, 25.0% Hispanic of any race; Average household size: 2.92; Median age: 32.1; Age under 18: 29.1%; Age 65 and over: 10.1%; Males per 100 females: 101.5; Marriage status: 28.9% never married, 52.6% now married, 2.9% separated, 5.3% widowed, 13.2% divorced; Foreign born: 12.3%; Speak English only: 75.3%; With disability: 16.5%; Veterans: 12.9%; Ancestry: 13.7% German, 11.7% Irish, 7.1% English, 4.2% Italian, 3.6% American

Religion: Six largest groups: 16.8% Catholicism, 4.3% Latter-day Saints, 2.4% Non-denominational Protestant, 1.8% Pentecostal, 1.8% Holiness, 1.7% Buddhism

Economy: Unemployment rate: 10.5%; Leading industries: 16.1% retail trade; 10.6% construction; 10.4% professional, scientific, and technical services; Farms: 795 totaling 187,638 acres; Company size: 1 employs 1,000 or more persons, 0 employ 500 to 999 persons, 8 employ 100 to 499 persons, 787 employ less than 100 persons; Business ownership: 1,712 women-owned, n/a Black-owned, 454 Hispanic-owned, n/a Asian-owned

Employment: 10.4% management, business, and financial, 3.7% computer, engineering, and science, 8.7% education, legal, community service, arts, and media, 4.5% healthcare practitioners, 21.0% service, 26.1% sales and office, 14.3% natural resources, construction, and maintenance, 11.3% production, transportation, and material moving

Income: Per capita: $19,244; Median household: $44,902; Average household: $55,847; Households with income of $100,000 or more: 12.8%; Poverty rate: 21.6%

Educational Attainment: High school diploma or higher: 79.0%; Bachelor's degree or higher: 13.7%; Graduate/professional degree or higher: 3.8%

Housing: Homeownership rate: 59.5%; Median home value: $171,000; Median year structure built: 1979; Homeowner vacancy rate: 3.6%; Median gross rent: $863 per month; Rental vacancy rate: 10.6%

Vital Statistics: Birth rate: 174.8 per 10,000 population; Death rate: 64.2 per 10,000 population; Age-adjusted cancer mortality rate: 196.8 deaths per 100,000 population

Health Insurance: 83.4% have insurance; 50.1% have private insurance; 43.8% have public insurance; 16.6% do not have insurance; 6.9% of children under 18 do not have insurance

Health Care: Physicians: 6.2 per 10,000 population; Hospital beds: 29.2 per 10,000 population; Hospital admissions: 1,630.8 per 10,000 population

Transportation: Commute: 89.1% car, 1.0% public transportation, 2.5% walk, 5.3% work from home; Median travel time to work: 29.5 minutes

Presidential Election: 38.8% Obama, 58.3% Romney (2012)

National and State Parks: Lake of the Woods State Wildlife Area

Additional Information Contacts

Yuba Government . . . . (530) 749-7510
http://www.co.yuba.ca.us

Yuba County Communities

BEALE AFB (CDP). Covers a land area of 10.048 square miles and a water area of 0.010 square miles. Located at 39.11° N. Lat; 121.35° W. Long.

Population: 1,319; Growth (since 2000): -74.2%; Density: 131.3 persons per square mile; Race: 71.9% White, 8.9% Black/African American, 3.4% Asian, 2.4% American Indian/Alaska Native, 0.6% Native Hawaiian/Other Pacific Islander, 8.9% Two or more races, 14.5% Hispanic of any race; Average household size: 3.45; Median age: 23.3; Age under 18: 43.7%; Age 65 and over: 0.2%; Males per 100 females: 98.9

School District(s)

Wheatland (KG-08)
2012-13 Enrollment: 1,236 . . . . (530) 633-3130

Housing: Homeownership rate: 0.6%; Homeowner vacancy rate: 0.0%; Rental vacancy rate: 44.8%

BROWNS VALLEY (unincorporated postal area)

ZCTA: 95918

Covers a land area of 69.095 square miles and a water area of 2.001 square miles. Located at 39.30° N. Lat; 121.34° W. Long. Elevation is 269 feet.

Population: 2,339; Growth (since 2000): 59.4%; Density: 33.9 persons per square mile; Race: 86.1% White, 0.6% Black/African American, 2.9% Asian, 2.1% American Indian/Alaska Native, 0.0% Native Hawaiian/Other Pacific Islander, 6.0% Two or more races, 8.4% Hispanic of any race; Average household size: 2.59; Median age: 47.9; Age under 18: 20.7%; Age 65 and over: 17.9%; Males per 100 females: 103.7

School District(s)

Marysville Joint Unified (KG-12)
2012-13 Enrollment: 9,815 . . . . (530) 741-6000

Housing: Homeownership rate: 83.3%; Homeowner vacancy rate: 2.1%; Rental vacancy rate: 6.2%

CAMPTONVILLE (CDP). Covers a land area of 0.874 square miles and a water area of 0 square miles. Located at 39.45° N. Lat; 121.05° W. Long. Elevation is 2,825 feet.

Population: 158; Growth (since 2000): n/a; Density: 180.8 persons per square mile; Race: 74.1% White, 0.0% Black/African American, 1.3% Asian, 9.5% American Indian/Alaska Native, 0.0% Native Hawaiian/Other Pacific Islander, 12.7% Two or more races, 3.2% Hispanic of any race; Average household size: 2.26; Median age: 44.3; Age under 18: 22.8%; Age 65 and over: 14.6%; Males per 100 females: 102.6

School District(s)

Camptonville Elementary (KG-12)
2012-13 Enrollment: 425. . . . . (530) 288-3277

Housing: Homeownership rate: 55.7%; Homeowner vacancy rate: 0.0%; Rental vacancy rate: 8.8%

CHALLENGE-BROWNSVILLE (CDP). Covers a land area of 9.662 square miles and a water area of 0 square miles. Located at 39.46° N. Lat; 121.26° W. Long. Elevation is 2,313 feet.

Population: 1,148; Growth (since 2000): 7.4%; Density: 118.8 persons per square mile; Race: 87.6% White, 0.9% Black/African American, 0.4% Asian, 2.7% American Indian/Alaska Native, 0.3% Native Hawaiian/Other Pacific Islander, 7.2% Two or more races, 7.8% Hispanic of any race; Average household size: 2.40; Median age: 47.7; Age under 18: 19.9%; Age 65 and over: 21.7%; Males per 100 females: 100.3

School District(s)

Marysville Joint Unified (KG-12)
2012-13 Enrollment: 9,815 . . . . (530) 741-6000

Housing: Homeownership rate: 71.2%; Homeowner vacancy rate: 5.2%; Rental vacancy rate: 10.3%

DOBBINS (CDP). Covers a land area of 7.749 square miles and a water area of 0.072 square miles. Located at 39.36° N. Lat; 121.21° W. Long. Elevation is 1,742 feet.

Population: 624; Growth (since 2000): n/a; Density: 80.5 persons per square mile; Race: 82.9% White, 0.8% Black/African American, 1.0% Asian, 8.3% American Indian/Alaska Native, 0.0% Native Hawaiian/Other Pacific Islander, 5.6% Two or more races, 4.5% Hispanic of any race; Average household size: 2.43; Median age: 47.8; Age under 18: 21.2%; Age 65 and over: 15.7%; Males per 100 females: 118.2

School District(s)

Marysville Joint Unified (KG-12)
2012-13 Enrollment: 9,815 . . . . (530) 741-6000

Housing: Homeownership rate: 67.7%; Homeowner vacancy rate: 0.6%; Rental vacancy rate: 16.0%

LINDA (CDP). Covers a land area of 8.546 square miles and a water area of 0 square miles. Located at 39.12° N. Lat; 121.54° W. Long. Elevation is 69 feet.

History: Seat of Yuba College.

Population: 17,773; Growth (since 2000): 31.9%; Density: 2,079.7 persons per square mile; Race: 56.1% White, 4.1% Black/African American, 13.0% Asian, 2.0% American Indian/Alaska Native, 0.5% Native Hawaiian/Other Pacific Islander, 7.3% Two or more races, 32.5% Hispanic of any race; Average household size: 3.26; Median age: 27.9; Age under 18: 33.4%; Age 65 and over: 7.3%; Males per 100 females: 100.1; Marriage status: 36.8% never married, 45.8% now married, 4.0% separated, 5.2% widowed, 12.3% divorced; Foreign born: 16.4%; Speak English only: 64.1%; With disability: 16.9%; Veterans: 10.7%; Ancestry: 8.4% Irish, 8.2% German, 5.5% English, 3.5% Italian, 3.0% American

Employment: 7.3% management, business, and financial, 3.3% computer, engineering, and science, 3.4% education, legal, community service, arts, and media, 3.8% healthcare practitioners, 26.4% service, 27.1% sales and office, 15.3% natural resources, construction, and maintenance, 13.4% production, transportation, and material moving

Income: Per capita: $13,898; Median household: $34,734; Average household: $43,667; Households with income of $100,000 or more: 7.9%; Poverty rate: 29.5%

Educational Attainment: High school diploma or higher: 72.4%; Bachelor's degree or higher: 7.1%; Graduate/professional degree or higher: 1.3%

Housing: Homeownership rate: 49.1%; Median home value: $132,100; Median year structure built: 1979; Homeowner vacancy rate: 4.3%; Median gross rent: $855 per month; Rental vacancy rate: 9.5%

Health Insurance: 78.4% have insurance; 35.4% have private insurance; 51.3% have public insurance; 21.6% do not have insurance; 8.0% of children under 18 do not have insurance

Transportation: Commute: 91.5% car, 0.8% public transportation, 0.8% walk, 4.7% work from home; Median travel time to work: 25.7 minutes

LOMA RICA (CDP). Covers a land area of 18.483 square miles and a water area of 0 square miles. Located at 39.32° N. Lat; 121.40° W. Long. Elevation is 410 feet.

Population: 2,368; Growth (since 2000): 14.1%; Density: 128.1 persons per square mile; Race: 88.0% White, 0.8% Black/African American, 0.8% Asian, 2.5% American Indian/Alaska Native, 0.1% Native Hawaiian/Other Pacific Islander, 5.4% Two or more races, 8.9% Hispanic of any race; Average household size: 2.68; Median age: 47.4; Age under 18: 21.5%; Age 65 and over: 17.7%; Males per 100 females: 98.7

Housing: Homeownership rate: 85.6%; Homeowner vacancy rate: 3.1%; Rental vacancy rate: 11.8%

MARYSVILLE (city). County seat. Covers a land area of 3.464 square miles and a water area of 0.121 square miles. Located at 39.15° N. Lat; 121.58° W. Long. Elevation is 62 feet.

History: Here in 1842 Theodore Cordua built a trading post that became a way station on the Oregon-California Trail. The townsite was laid out in 1848 and named in 1849 for Mary Murphy Covillaud, a survivor of the Donner party and wife of one of the owners of the townsite. At one time Marysville was the head of navigation on the Feather River, but mining changed the face of the countryside and raised the bed of the river.

Population: 12,072; Growth (since 2000): -1.6%; Density: 3,485.1 persons per square mile; Race: 71.0% White, 4.3% Black/African American, 4.1% Asian, 2.5% American Indian/Alaska Native, 0.3% Native Hawaiian/Other Pacific Islander, 7.4% Two or more races, 24.2% Hispanic of any race; Average household size: 2.44; Median age: 32.5; Age under 18: 25.1%; Age 65 and over: 12.0%; Males per 100 females: 99.6; Marriage status: 30.9% never married, 44.1% now married, 2.1% separated, 6.9% widowed, 18.1% divorced; Foreign born: 8.6%; Speak English only: 85.0%; With disability: 19.8%; Veterans: 12.4%; Ancestry: 12.9% Irish, 11.4% German, 7.5% English, 5.2% American, 3.3% Italian

Employment: 7.6% management, business, and financial, 2.0% computer, engineering, and science, 12.1% education, legal, community service, arts, and media, 4.3% healthcare practitioners, 26.8% service, 23.5% sales and office, 14.2% natural resources, construction, and maintenance, 9.5% production, transportation, and material moving

Income: Per capita: $18,049; Median household: $33,777; Average household: $47,048; Households with income of $100,000 or more: 6.3%; Poverty rate: 32.3%

Educational Attainment: High school diploma or higher: 78.3%; Bachelor's degree or higher: 11.2%; Graduate/professional degree or higher: 3.1%

School District(s)

Camptonville Elementary (KG-12)
2012-13 Enrollment: 425. . . . . (530) 288-3277

Marysville Joint Unified (KG-12)
2012-13 Enrollment: 9,815 . . . . (530) 741-6000

Yuba County Office of Education (KG-12)
2012-13 Enrollment: 536. . . . . (530) 749-4900

Two-year College(s)

Yuba College (Public)
Fall 2013 Enrollment: 6,874 . . . . (530) 741-6700
2013-14 Tuition: In-state $1,144; Out-of-state $6,184

Housing: Homeownership rate: 39.1%; Median home value: $125,300; Median year structure built: 1962; Homeowner vacancy rate: 2.7%; Median gross rent: $835 per month; Rental vacancy rate: 10.2%

Health Insurance: 86.5% have insurance; 43.4% have private insurance; 52.5% have public insurance; 13.5% do not have insurance; 7.7% of children under 18 do not have insurance

Hospitals: Rideout Memorial Hospital (164 beds)

Safety: Violent crime rate: 71.5 per 10,000 population; Property crime rate: 443.0 per 10,000 population

Newspapers: Appeal-Democrat (daily circulation 20000)

Transportation: Commute: 86.2% car, 0.9% public transportation, 5.0% walk, 5.9% work from home; Median travel time to work: 25.2 minutes; Amtrak: Bus service available.

Airports: Yuba County (general aviation)

Additional Information Contacts

City of Marysville . . . . (530) 749-3901
http://www.marysville.ca.us

OLIVEHURST (CDP). Covers a land area of 7.473 square miles and a water area of 0 square miles. Located at 39.08° N. Lat; 121.55° W. Long. Elevation is 66 feet.

Population: 13,656; Growth (since 2000): 23.5%; Density: 1,827.5 persons per square mile; Race: 62.5% White, 2.4% Black/African American, 5.7% Asian, 2.9% American Indian/Alaska Native, 0.4% Native Hawaiian/Other Pacific Islander, 6.9% Two or more races, 36.6% Hispanic of any race; Average household size: 3.30; Median age: 29.9; Age under 18: 31.8%; Age 65 and over: 8.4%; Males per 100 females: 100.5; Marriage status: 32.6% never married, 50.0% now married, 3.2% separated, 5.2% widowed, 12.2% divorced; Foreign born: 18.5%; Speak English only: 62.5%; With disability: 16.3%; Veterans: 10.0%; Ancestry: 10.4% Irish, 10.2% German, 5.0% Romanian, 4.9% English, 3.1% American

Employment: 9.1% management, business, and financial, 1.4% computer, engineering, and science, 5.8% education, legal, community service, arts, and media, 1.9% healthcare practitioners, 21.5% service, 28.8% sales and office, 15.8% natural resources, construction, and maintenance, 15.7% production, transportation, and material moving

Income: Per capita: $15,322; Median household: $42,915; Average household: $49,732; Households with income of $100,000 or more: 6.3%; Poverty rate: 19.5%

Educational Attainment: High school diploma or higher: 64.7%; Bachelor's degree or higher: 6.1%; Graduate/professional degree or higher: 2.2%

School District(s)

Marysville Joint Unified (KG-12)
2012-13 Enrollment: 9,815 . . . . (530) 741-6000

Housing: Homeownership rate: 61.6%; Median home value: $144,000; Median year structure built: 1976; Homeowner vacancy rate: 3.8%; Median gross rent: $822 per month; Rental vacancy rate: 5.0%

Health Insurance: 81.0% have insurance; 43.2% have private insurance; 47.5% have public insurance; 19.0% do not have insurance; 6.7% of children under 18 do not have insurance

Transportation: Commute: 91.8% car, 1.0% public transportation, 1.3% walk, 3.6% work from home; Median travel time to work: 27.4 minutes

OREGON HOUSE (unincorporated postal area)

ZCTA: 95962

Covers a land area of 29.710 square miles and a water area of 0.162 square miles. Located at 39.34° N. Lat; 121.26° W. Long. Elevation is 1,526 feet.

Population: 1,567; Growth (since 2000): 3.6%; Density: 52.7 persons per square mile; Race: 90.7% White, 0.5% Black/African American, 2.0% Asian, 1.5% American Indian/Alaska Native, 0.0% Native Hawaiian/Other Pacific Islander, 4.0% Two or more races, 6.2% Hispanic of any race; Average household size: 2.31; Median age: 49.9; Age under 18: 18.6%; Age 65 and over: 15.2%; Males per 100 females: 104.0

School District(s)

Marysville Joint Unified (KG-12)
2012-13 Enrollment: 9,815 . . . . (530) 741-6000

Housing: Homeownership rate: 69.8%; Homeowner vacancy rate: 2.7%; Rental vacancy rate: 5.5%

PLUMAS LAKE (CDP). Covers a land area of 8.382 square miles and a water area of 0 square miles. Located at 38.99° N. Lat; 121.56° W. Long. Elevation is 46 feet.

Population: 5,853; Growth (since 2000): n/a; Density: 698.3 persons per square mile; Race: 67.0% White, 6.4% Black/African American, 8.1% Asian, 1.2% American Indian/Alaska Native, 0.8% Native Hawaiian/Other Pacific Islander, 8.8% Two or more races, 22.4% Hispanic of any race; Average household size: 3.35; Median age: 29.1; Age under 18: 36.6%; Age 65 and over: 3.4%; Males per 100 females: 104.6; Marriage status: 16.9% never married, 72.9% now married, 1.4% separated, 2.8% widowed, 7.4% divorced; Foreign born: 8.3%; Speak English only: 82.8%; With disability: 9.2%; Veterans: 15.6%; Ancestry: 18.4% German, 13.0% Irish, 7.9% English, 6.1% Italian, 4.5% Swedish

Employment: 14.0% management, business, and financial, 9.8% computer, engineering, and science, 9.6% education, legal, community service, arts, and media, 5.6% healthcare practitioners, 18.8% service, 25.2% sales and office, 9.6% natural resources, construction, and maintenance, 7.3% production, transportation, and material moving

Income: Per capita: $25,529; Median household: $80,605; Average household: $85,437; Households with income of $100,000 or more: 31.2%; Poverty rate: 3.9%

Educational Attainment: High school diploma or higher: 91.3%; Bachelor's degree or higher: 25.9%; Graduate/professional degree or higher: 6.7%

School District(s)

Plumas Lake Elementary (KG-08)
2012-13 Enrollment: 1,077 . . . . (530) 743-4428

Housing: Homeownership rate: 84.9%; Median home value: $197,100; Median year structure built: n/a; Homeowner vacancy rate: 6.2%; Median gross rent: $1,647 per month; Rental vacancy rate: 6.0%

Health Insurance: 93.1% have insurance; 81.2% have private insurance; 19.3% have public insurance; 6.9% do not have insurance; 1.3% of children under 18 do not have insurance

Transportation: Commute: 93.6% car, 0.5% public transportation, 0.8% walk, 2.7% work from home; Median travel time to work: 35.5 minutes

SMARTSVILLE (CDP). Covers a land area of 0.717 square miles and a water area of 0 square miles. Located at 39.21° N. Lat; 121.29° W. Long. Elevation is 669 feet.

Population: 177; Growth (since 2000): n/a; Density: 246.9 persons per square mile; Race: 88.7% White, 0.0% Black/African American, 0.0% Asian, 2.8% American Indian/Alaska Native, 0.0% Native Hawaiian/Other Pacific Islander, 3.4% Two or more races, 10.2% Hispanic of any race; Average household size: 3.00; Median age: 38.3; Age under 18: 28.2%; Age 65 and over: 15.8%; Males per 100 females: 101.1

Housing: Homeownership rate: 71.1%; Homeowner vacancy rate: 0.0%; Rental vacancy rate: 5.6%

STRAWBERRY VALLEY (unincorporated postal area)

ZCTA: 95981

Covers a land area of 41.091 square miles and a water area of 0.253 square miles. Located at 39.69° N. Lat; 121.00° W. Long. Elevation is 3,757 feet.

Population: 97; Growth (since 2000): -1.0%; Density: 2.4 persons per square mile; Race: 80.4% White, 1.0% Black/African American, 0.0% Asian, 13.4% American Indian/Alaska Native, 0.0% Native Hawaiian/Other Pacific Islander, 3.1% Two or more races, 10.3% Hispanic of any race; Average household size: 2.06; Median age: 50.8; Age under 18: 22.7%; Age 65 and over: 20.6%; Males per 100 females: 98.0

Housing: Homeownership rate: 59.6%; Homeowner vacancy rate: 12.5%; Rental vacancy rate: 13.6%

WHEATLAND (city). Covers a land area of 1.479 square miles and a water area of 0.007 square miles. Located at 39.01° N. Lat; 121.43° W. Long. Elevation is 92 feet.

History: Wheatland was settled in 1844 by William Johnson, whose ranch was visited in 1847 by members of the Donner party seeking help for those still snowbound at Donner Lake. The town developed as the center of a hop-growing area, and was the site in 1913 of California's first strike by field workers for better living conditions.

Population: 3,456; Growth (since 2000): 51.9%; Density: 2,336.6 persons per square mile; Race: 76.2% White, 1.2% Black/African American, 5.9% Asian, 1.7% American Indian/Alaska Native, 0.1% Native Hawaiian/Other Pacific Islander, 6.9% Two or more races, 17.9% Hispanic of any race; Average household size: 2.84; Median age: 33.2; Age under 18: 29.6%; Age 65 and over: 10.4%; Males per 100 females: 93.0; Marriage status: 27.4% never married, 60.8% now married, 1.6% separated, 4.8% widowed, 7.0% divorced; Foreign born: 15.7%; Speak English only: 75.4%; With disability: 12.4%; Veterans: 14.1%; Ancestry: 19.0% German, 12.8% Irish, 8.0% English, 6.1% Italian, 4.8% American

Employment: 7.5% management, business, and financial, 6.2% computer, engineering, and science, 9.5% education, legal, community service, arts, and media, 4.3% healthcare practitioners, 25.7% service, 27.1% sales and office, 6.6% natural resources, construction, and maintenance, 13.1% production, transportation, and material moving

Income: Per capita: $22,242; Median household: $61,409; Average household: $64,788; Households with income of $100,000 or more: 13.6%; Poverty rate: 19.3%

Educational Attainment: High school diploma or higher: 83.6%; Bachelor's degree or higher: 15.2%; Graduate/professional degree or higher: 4.7%

School District(s)

Wheatland (KG-08)
2012-13 Enrollment: 1,236 . . . . (530) 633-3130
Wheatland Union High (07-12)
2012-13 Enrollment: 713. . . . . (530) 633-3100

Housing: Homeownership rate: 62.8%; Median home value: $166,700; Median year structure built: 1984; Homeowner vacancy rate: 3.3%; Median gross rent: $769 per month; Rental vacancy rate: 5.4%

Health Insurance: 85.8% have insurance; 64.5% have private insurance; 30.9% have public insurance; 14.2% do not have insurance; 8.2% of children under 18 do not have insurance

Safety: Violent crime rate: 0.0 per 10,000 population; Property crime rate: 139.1 per 10,000 population

Transportation: Commute: 94.0% car, 0.6% public transportation, 1.5% walk, 0.9% work from home; Median travel time to work: 34.7 minutes

Additional Information Contacts

City of Wheatland . . . . (530) 633-2761
http://www.wheatland.ca.gov

CDP = Census Designated Place

CDP = Census Designated Place

Comparative Statistics

This section compares the 100 largest cities by population in the state, by the following data points:

Population

Place	2000 Census	2010 Census	Growth 2000–2010 (%)
Alhambra	85,804	83,089	-3.1
Anaheim	328,014	336,265	2.5
Antioch	90,532	102,372	13.0
Arden-Arcade	96,025	92,186	-4.0
Bakersfield	247,057	347,483	40.6
Berkeley	102,743	112,580	9.5
Buena Park	78,282	80,530	2.8
Burbank	100,316	103,340	3.0
Carlsbad	78,247	105,328	34.6
Carson	89,730	91,714	2.2
Chico	59,954	86,187	43.7
Chino	67,168	77,983	16.1
Chula Vista	173,556	243,916	40.5
Citrus Heights	85,071	83,301	-2.0
Clovis	68,468	95,631	39.6
Compton	93,493	96,455	3.1
Concord	121,780	122,067	0.2
Corona	124,966	152,374	21.9
Costa Mesa	108,724	109,960	1.1
Daly City	103,621	101,123	-2.4
Downey	107,323	111,772	4.1
East Los Angeles	124,283	126,496	1.7
El Cajon	94,869	99,478	4.8
El Monte	115,965	113,475	-2.1
Elk Grove	59,984	153,015	155.0
Escondido	133,559	143,911	7.7
Fairfield	96,178	105,321	9.5
Fontana	128,929	196,069	52.0
Fremont	203,413	214,089	5.2
Fresno	427,652	494,665	15.6
Fullerton	126,003	135,161	7.2
Garden Grove	165,196	170,883	3.4
Glendale	194,973	191,719	-1.6
Hawthorne	84,112	84,293	0.2
Hayward	140,030	144,186	2.9
Hemet	58,812	78,657	33.7
Hesperia	62,582	90,173	44.0
Huntington Beach	189,594	189,992	0.2
Inglewood	112,580	109,673	-2.5
Irvine	143,072	212,375	48.4
Lakewood	79,345	80,048	0.8
Lancaster	118,718	156,633	31.9
Livermore	73,345	80,968	10.3
Long Beach	461,522	462,257	0.1
Los Angeles	3,694,820	3,792,621	2.6
Menifee	n/a	77,519	n/a
Merced	63,893	78,958	23.5
Mission Viejo	93,102	93,305	0.2
Modesto	188,856	201,165	6.5
Moreno Valley	142,381	193,365	35.8

Place	2000 Census	2010 Census	Growth 2000–2010 (%)
Murrieta	44,282	103,466	133.6
Newport Beach	70,032	85,186	21.6
Norwalk	103,298	105,549	2.1
Oakland	399,484	390,724	-2.1
Oceanside	161,029	167,086	3.7
Ontario	158,007	163,924	3.7
Orange	128,821	136,416	5.9
Oxnard	170,358	197,899	16.1
Palmdale	116,670	152,750	30.9
Pasadena	133,936	137,122	2.3
Pomona	149,473	149,058	-0.2
Rancho Cucamonga	127,743	165,269	29.3
Redding	80,865	89,861	11.1
Rialto	91,873	99,171	7.9
Richmond	99,216	103,701	4.5
Riverside	255,166	303,871	19.0
Roseville	79,921	118,788	48.6
Sacramento	407,018	466,488	14.6
Salinas	151,060	150,441	-0.4
San Bernardino	185,401	209,924	13.2
San Buenaventura (Ventura)	100,916	106,433	5.4
San Diego	1,223,400	1,307,402	6.8
San Francisco	776,733	805,235	3.6
San Jose	894,943	945,942	5.7
San Leandro	79,452	84,950	6.9
San Marcos	54,977	83,781	52.3
San Mateo	92,482	97,207	5.1
Santa Ana	337,977	324,528	-3.9
Santa Barbara	92,325	88,410	-4.2
Santa Clara	102,361	116,468	13.7
Santa Clarita	151,088	176,320	16.7
Santa Maria	77,423	99,553	28.5
Santa Monica	84,084	89,736	6.7
Santa Rosa	147,595	167,815	13.7
Simi Valley	111,351	124,237	11.5
South Gate	96,375	94,396	-2.0
Stockton	243,771	291,707	19.6
Sunnyvale	131,760	140,081	6.3
Temecula	57,716	100,097	73.4
Thousand Oaks	117,005	126,683	8.2
Torrance	137,946	145,438	5.4
Tracy	56,929	82,922	45.6
Vacaville	88,625	92,428	4.2
Vallejo	116,760	115,942	-0.7
Victorville	64,029	115,903	81.0
Visalia	91,565	124,442	35.9
Vista	89,857	93,834	4.4
West Covina	105,080	106,098	0.9
Westminster	88,207	89,701	1.6
Whittier	83,680	85,331	1.9

NOTE: Louisville merged with Jefferson County in 2003.
SOURCE: U.S. Census Bureau, Census 2010, Census 2000

Physical Characteristics

Place	Density (persons per square mile)	Land Area (square miles)	Water Area (square miles)	Elevation (feet)
Alhambra	10,889.0	7.63	0.00	492
Anaheim	6,747.5	49.84	0.98	157
Antioch	3,611.2	28.35	0.73	43
Arden-Arcade	5,170.5	17.83	0.09	56
Bakersfield	2,444.2	142.16	1.44	404
Berkeley	10,752.4	10.47	7.23	171
Buena Park	7,652.1	10.52	0.03	75
Burbank	5,959.3	17.34	0.04	607
Carlsbad	2,792.2	37.72	1.39	52
Carson	4,898.2	18.72	0.24	39
Chico	2,617.8	32.92	0.17	197
Chino	2,631.1	29.64	0.01	728
Chula Vista	4,914.6	49.63	2.46	66
Citrus Heights	5,854.6	14.23	0.00	164
Clovis	4,108.2	23.28	0.00	361
Compton	9,633.7	10.01	0.10	69
Concord	3,996.2	30.55	0.00	75
Corona	3,924.6	38.83	0.10	679
Costa Mesa	7,024.6	15.65	0.05	98
Daly City	13,195.0	7.66	0.00	407
Downey	9,008.0	12.41	0.16	118
East Los Angeles	16,983.2	7.45	0.00	200
El Cajon	6,892.5	14.43	0.00	433
El Monte	11,866.9	9.56	0.09	299
Elk Grove	3,626.8	42.19	0.05	46
Escondido	3,909.3	36.81	0.18	646
Fairfield	2,816.8	37.39	0.25	13
Fontana	4,620.8	42.43	0.00	1,237
Fremont	2,763.9	77.46	10.15	56
Fresno	4,418.4	111.96	0.35	308
Fullerton	6,046.7	22.35	0.01	164
Garden Grove	9,524.6	17.94	0.02	89
Glendale	6,295.5	30.45	0.13	522
Hawthorne	13,861.2	6.08	0.01	72
Hayward	3,181.3	45.32	18.43	105
Hemet	2,824.6	27.85	0.00	1,594
Hesperia	1,233.6	73.10	0.11	3,186
Huntington Beach	7,102.9	26.75	5.13	39
Inglewood	12,094.7	9.07	0.02	131
Irvine	3,212.6	66.11	0.35	56
Lakewood	8,502.4	9.41	0.05	46
Lancaster	1,661.4	94.28	0.27	2,359
Livermore	3,216.5	25.17	0.00	492
Long Beach	9,191.2	50.29	1.14	30
Los Angeles	8,092.3	468.67	34.02	292
Menifee	1,668.3	46.47	0.14	1,483
Merced	3,386.4	23.32	0.00	171
Mission Viejo	5,259.8	17.74	0.38	397
Modesto	5,456.5	36.87	0.23	89
Moreno Valley	3,771.2	51.27	0.20	1,631

Place	Density (persons per square mile)	Land Area (square miles)	Water Area (square miles)	Elevation (feet)
Murrieta	3,081.4	33.58	0.04	1,096
Newport Beach	3,578.5	23.80	29.17	10
Norwalk	10,873.5	9.71	0.04	92
Oakland	7,004.0	55.79	22.22	43
Oceanside	4,052.1	41.23	0.94	66
Ontario	3,282.4	49.94	0.07	1,004
Orange	5,501.3	24.80	0.44	190
Oxnard	7,358.4	26.89	12.31	52
Palmdale	1,441.6	105.96	0.25	2,657
Pasadena	5,969.6	22.97	0.16	863
Pomona	6,494.5	22.95	0.01	850
Rancho Cucamonga	4,147.2	39.85	0.02	1,207
Redding	1,506.5	59.65	1.53	564
Rialto	4,437.0	22.35	0.01	1,257
Richmond	3,448.9	30.07	22.41	46
Riverside	3,745.0	81.14	0.30	827
Roseville	3,279.5	36.22	0.00	164
Sacramento	4,764.2	97.92	2.19	30
Salinas	6,490.5	23.18	0.04	52
San Bernardino	3,546.0	59.20	0.44	1,053
San Buenaventura (Ventura)	4,915.0	21.65	10.44	n/a
San Diego	4,020.4	325.19	47.21	62
San Francisco	17,179.2	46.87	185.02	52
San Jose	5,358.6	176.53	3.44	82
San Leandro	6,366.8	13.34	2.32	56
San Marcos	3,437.9	24.37	0.02	581
San Mateo	8,014.0	12.13	3.75	46
Santa Ana	11,900.8	27.27	0.25	115
Santa Barbara	4,541.3	19.47	22.50	49
Santa Clara	6,327.3	18.41	0.00	72
Santa Clarita	3,344.7	52.72	0.06	1,207
Santa Maria	4,374.9	22.76	0.64	217
Santa Monica	10,664.1	8.41	0.00	105
Santa Rosa	4,063.9	41.29	0.21	164
Simi Valley	2,995.1	41.48	0.77	768
South Gate	13,045.0	7.24	0.12	115
Stockton	4,730.2	61.67	3.08	13
Sunnyvale	6,370.9	21.99	0.70	125
Temecula	3,319.8	30.15	0.02	1,017
Thousand Oaks	2,302.0	55.03	0.15	886
Torrance	7,102.2	20.48	0.08	89
Tracy	3,768.7	22.00	0.14	52
Vacaville	3,257.7	28.37	0.21	174
Vallejo	3,780.1	30.67	18.87	69
Victorville	1,583.9	73.18	0.56	2,726
Visalia	3,433.3	36.25	0.02	331
Vista	5,023.7	18.68	0.00	325
West Covina	6,614.3	16.04	0.05	384
Westminster	8,926.5	10.05	0.00	39
Whittier	5,824.9	14.65	0.02	367

SOURCE: U.S. Census Bureau, Census 2010

Population by Race/Hispanic Origin

Place	White[1] (%)	Black[1] (%)	Asian[1] (%)	AIAN[1,2] (%)	NHOPI[1,3] (%)	Two or More Races (%)	Hispanic[4] (%)
Alhambra	28.3	1.5	52.9	0.6	0.1	3.5	34.4
Anaheim	52.7	2.8	14.8	0.8	0.5	4.4	52.8
Antioch	48.9	17.3	10.5	0.9	0.8	7.7	31.7
Arden-Arcade	70.2	8.7	5.6	1.0	0.6	5.9	18.6
Bakersfield	56.8	8.2	6.2	1.5	0.1	4.9	45.5
Berkeley	59.5	10.0	19.3	0.4	0.2	6.2	10.8
Buena Park	45.3	3.8	26.7	1.1	0.6	5.1	39.3
Burbank	72.7	2.5	11.6	0.5	0.1	4.8	24.5
Carlsbad	82.8	1.3	7.1	0.5	0.2	4.2	13.3
Carson	23.8	23.8	25.6	0.6	2.6	4.8	38.6
Chico	80.8	2.1	4.2	1.4	0.2	5.0	15.4
Chino	56.4	6.2	10.5	1.0	0.2	4.6	53.8
Chula Vista	53.7	4.6	14.4	0.8	0.6	5.8	58.2
Citrus Heights	80.3	3.3	3.3	0.9	0.4	5.4	16.5
Clovis	70.9	2.7	10.7	1.4	0.2	4.8	25.6
Compton	25.9	32.9	0.3	0.7	0.7	3.4	65.0
Concord	64.5	3.6	11.1	0.7	0.7	6.4	30.6
Corona	59.7	5.9	9.9	0.8	0.4	5.1	43.6
Costa Mesa	68.5	1.5	7.9	0.6	0.5	4.7	35.8
Daly City	23.6	3.6	55.6	0.4	0.8	4.9	23.7
Downey	56.6	3.9	7.0	0.7	0.2	4.1	70.7
East Los Angeles	50.5	0.6	0.9	1.2	0.0	3.3	97.1
El Cajon	69.3	6.3	3.6	0.8	0.5	6.9	28.2
El Monte	38.8	0.8	25.1	1.0	0.1	3.2	69.0
Elk Grove	46.1	11.2	26.3	0.6	1.2	7.9	18.0
Escondido	60.4	2.5	6.1	1.0	0.2	4.4	48.9
Fairfield	46.0	15.7	14.9	0.8	1.1	8.8	27.3
Fontana	47.4	10.0	6.6	1.0	0.3	4.9	66.8
Fremont	32.8	3.3	50.6	0.5	0.5	5.9	14.8
Fresno	49.6	8.3	12.6	1.7	0.2	5.0	46.9
Fullerton	53.9	2.3	22.8	0.6	0.2	4.3	34.4
Garden Grove	39.9	1.3	37.1	0.6	0.6	3.6	36.9
Glendale	71.1	1.3	16.4	0.3	0.1	4.5	17.4
Hawthorne	32.8	27.7	6.7	0.7	1.2	4.7	52.9
Hayward	34.2	11.9	22.0	1.0	3.1	7.1	40.7
Hemet	67.7	6.4	3.0	1.6	0.4	5.2	35.8
Hesperia	61.1	5.8	2.1	1.2	0.3	4.9	48.9
Huntington Beach	76.7	1.0	11.1	0.5	0.3	4.5	17.1
Inglewood	23.3	43.9	1.4	0.7	0.3	4.1	50.6
Irvine	50.5	1.8	39.2	0.2	0.2	5.5	9.2
Lakewood	56.0	8.7	16.4	0.7	0.9	5.7	30.1
Lancaster	49.6	20.5	4.3	1.0	0.2	5.4	38.0
Livermore	74.6	2.1	8.4	0.6	0.3	5.4	20.9
Long Beach	46.1	13.5	12.9	0.7	1.1	5.3	40.8
Los Angeles	49.8	9.6	11.3	0.7	0.1	4.6	48.5
Menifee	71.5	5.0	4.9	0.8	0.4	4.9	33.0
Merced	52.2	6.3	11.8	1.5	0.2	5.5	49.6
Mission Viejo	79.8	1.3	9.1	0.4	0.2	4.6	17.0
Modesto	65.0	4.2	6.7	1.2	1.0	6.3	35.5
Moreno Valley	41.9	18.0	6.1	0.9	0.6	5.7	54.4

Place	White[1] (%)	Black[1] (%)	Asian[1] (%)	AIAN[1,2] (%)	NHOPI[1,3] (%)	Two or More Races (%)	Hispanic[4] (%)
Murrieta	69.7	5.4	9.2	0.7	0.4	6.1	25.9
Newport Beach	87.3	0.7	7.0	0.3	0.1	2.9	7.2
Norwalk	49.4	4.4	12.0	1.1	0.4	4.3	70.1
Oakland	34.5	28.0	16.8	0.8	0.6	5.6	25.4
Oceanside	65.2	4.7	6.6	0.8	1.3	5.8	35.9
Ontario	51.0	6.4	5.2	1.0	0.3	4.7	69.0
Orange	67.1	1.6	11.3	0.7	0.3	4.0	38.1
Oxnard	48.2	2.9	7.4	1.5	0.3	4.6	73.5
Palmdale	49.0	14.8	4.3	0.9	0.2	5.4	54.4
Pasadena	55.8	10.7	14.3	0.6	0.1	4.9	33.7
Pomona	48.0	7.3	8.5	1.2	0.2	4.5	70.5
Rancho Cucamonga	62.0	9.2	10.4	0.7	0.3	5.4	34.9
Redding	85.8	1.2	3.4	2.3	0.2	4.6	8.7
Rialto	44.0	16.4	2.3	1.1	0.4	4.7	67.6
Richmond	31.4	26.6	13.5	0.6	0.5	5.6	39.5
Riverside	56.5	7.0	7.4	1.1	0.4	5.1	49.0
Roseville	79.3	2.0	8.4	0.7	0.3	5.0	14.6
Sacramento	45.0	14.6	18.3	1.1	1.4	7.1	26.9
Salinas	45.8	2.0	6.3	1.3	0.3	5.1	75.0
San Bernardino	45.6	15.0	4.0	1.3	0.4	5.1	60.0
San Buenaventura (Ventura)	76.6	1.6	3.4	1.2	0.2	5.2	31.8
San Diego	58.9	6.7	15.9	0.6	0.5	5.1	28.8
San Francisco	48.5	6.1	33.3	0.5	0.4	4.7	15.1
San Jose	42.8	3.2	32.0	0.9	0.4	5.0	33.2
San Leandro	37.6	12.3	29.7	0.8	0.8	5.6	27.4
San Marcos	63.5	2.3	9.0	0.7	0.4	5.1	36.6
San Mateo	57.8	2.4	18.9	0.5	2.1	5.7	26.6
Santa Ana	45.9	1.5	10.5	1.0	0.3	3.6	78.2
Santa Barbara	75.1	1.6	3.5	1.0	0.1	3.9	38.0
Santa Clara	45.0	2.7	37.7	0.5	0.6	5.3	19.4
Santa Clarita	70.9	3.2	8.5	0.6	0.2	4.7	29.5
Santa Maria	56.2	1.7	5.1	1.8	0.2	5.1	70.4
Santa Monica	77.6	3.9	9.0	0.4	0.1	4.4	13.1
Santa Rosa	71.0	2.4	5.2	1.7	0.5	5.1	28.6
Simi Valley	75.3	1.4	9.3	0.6	0.1	4.6	23.3
South Gate	50.5	0.9	0.8	0.9	0.1	3.7	94.8
Stockton	37.0	12.2	21.5	1.1	0.6	6.9	40.3
Sunnyvale	43.0	2.0	40.9	0.5	0.5	4.5	18.9
Temecula	70.8	4.1	9.8	1.1	0.4	5.9	24.7
Thousand Oaks	80.3	1.3	8.7	0.4	0.1	3.8	16.8
Torrance	51.1	2.7	34.5	0.4	0.4	5.5	16.1
Tracy	52.7	7.2	14.7	0.9	0.9	7.7	36.9
Vacaville	66.3	10.3	6.1	0.9	0.6	7.0	22.9
Vallejo	32.8	22.1	24.9	0.7	1.1	7.5	22.6
Victorville	48.5	16.8	4.0	1.4	0.4	6.3	47.8
Visalia	64.5	2.1	5.4	1.4	0.1	4.6	46.0
Vista	63.5	3.3	4.2	1.2	0.7	5.3	48.4
West Covina	42.8	4.5	25.8	1.0	0.2	4.4	53.2
Westminster	35.7	0.9	47.5	0.4	0.4	3.6	23.6
Whittier	64.6	1.3	3.8	1.3	0.1	4.4	65.7

NOTE: (1) Exclude multiple race combinations; (2) American Indian/Alaska Native; (3) Native Hawaiian/Other Pacific Islander; (4) May be of any race
SOURCE: U.S. Census Bureau, Census 2010

Average Household Size, Age, and Male/Female Ratio

Place	Average Household Size (persons)	Median Age (years)	Age Under 18 (%)	Age 65 and Over (%)	Males per 100 Females
Alhambra	2.82	39.3	18.9	14.3	89.9
Anaheim	3.38	32.4	27.3	9.3	99.0
Antioch	3.15	33.8	28.1	8.8	94.8
Arden-Arcade	2.24	39.0	20.9	15.7	90.1
Bakersfield	3.10	30.0	31.5	8.4	96.0
Berkeley	2.17	31.0	12.3	11.7	95.6
Buena Park	3.37	35.1	25.3	10.6	97.4
Burbank	2.45	38.9	19.8	13.3	93.6
Carlsbad	2.53	40.4	24.1	14.0	95.6
Carson	3.56	37.6	24.0	13.8	91.9
Chico	2.38	28.6	19.5	10.6	98.2
Chino	3.41	33.2	25.3	7.3	105.7
Chula Vista	3.21	33.7	27.9	10.0	93.9
Citrus Heights	2.53	36.2	23.1	13.3	94.1
Clovis	2.85	34.1	28.1	10.6	93.2
Compton	4.15	28.0	33.1	7.5	94.8
Concord	2.73	37.0	22.9	11.8	98.8
Corona	3.38	32.5	30.0	7.3	97.0
Costa Mesa	2.68	33.6	21.5	9.2	103.7
Daly City	3.23	38.3	19.4	13.5	97.5
Downey	3.27	33.3	26.8	10.4	94.1
East Los Angeles	4.09	29.1	31.5	8.6	98.9
El Cajon	2.84	33.7	25.7	11.0	95.6
El Monte	4.04	31.6	28.4	9.3	100.9
Elk Grove	3.18	34.3	30.1	8.3	93.9
Escondido	3.12	32.5	27.6	10.5	98.2
Fairfield	2.98	33.7	27.1	10.2	97.0
Fontana	3.98	28.7	32.9	5.7	98.7
Fremont	2.99	36.8	24.9	10.2	98.9
Fresno	3.07	29.3	30.1	9.3	96.7
Fullerton	2.91	34.8	23.3	11.7	96.6
Garden Grove	3.67	35.6	25.6	10.8	99.6
Glendale	2.63	41.0	18.6	15.6	91.1
Hawthorne	2.94	31.5	27.5	7.4	93.2
Hayward	3.12	33.5	24.5	10.2	97.4
Hemet	2.59	39.0	25.9	22.1	88.9
Hesperia	3.41	30.5	32.3	9.0	98.5
Huntington Beach	2.55	40.2	20.6	14.2	98.5
Inglewood	2.97	33.4	26.7	9.4	90.6
Irvine	2.61	33.9	21.5	8.7	94.9
Lakewood	3.01	37.5	24.3	11.4	94.3
Lancaster	3.16	30.4	30.1	8.1	100.6
Livermore	2.76	38.3	25.5	10.3	98.6
Long Beach	2.78	33.2	24.9	9.3	96.1
Los Angeles	2.81	34.1	23.1	10.5	99.2
Menifee	2.82	38.1	25.9	18.9	92.8
Merced	3.13	28.1	31.8	8.8	96.3
Mission Viejo	2.78	42.2	22.8	14.5	95.4
Modesto	2.87	34.2	26.8	11.7	95.0
Moreno Valley	3.74	28.6	32.3	6.3	95.1

Place	Average Household Size (persons)	Median Age (years)	Age Under 18 (%)	Age 65 and Over (%)	Males per 100 Females
Murrieta	3.15	33.4	30.4	10.1	95.2
Newport Beach	2.19	44.0	17.3	19.0	97.1
Norwalk	3.83	32.5	27.6	9.9	98.5
Oakland	2.49	36.2	21.3	11.1	94.2
Oceanside	2.80	35.2	23.8	12.9	97.4
Ontario	3.63	29.9	30.2	6.7	99.0
Orange	3.00	34.8	23.5	10.7	101.5
Oxnard	3.95	29.9	29.8	8.3	103.0
Palmdale	3.55	29.7	33.1	6.6	95.3
Pasadena	2.42	37.2	19.3	13.5	95.1
Pomona	3.77	29.5	29.4	7.6	100.0
Rancho Cucamonga	2.98	34.5	25.7	7.9	97.6
Redding	2.43	38.5	22.8	16.4	93.8
Rialto	3.92	28.3	32.9	7.0	94.7
Richmond	2.83	34.8	24.9	10.2	94.8
Riverside	3.18	30.0	26.8	8.6	97.6
Roseville	2.62	36.8	26.3	13.4	91.9
Sacramento	2.62	33.0	24.9	10.6	94.9
Salinas	3.66	28.8	31.4	7.5	102.1
San Bernardino	3.42	28.5	32.0	7.9	97.2
San Buenaventura (Ventura)	2.57	39.0	22.5	13.3	97.7
San Diego	2.60	33.6	21.4	10.7	102.1
San Francisco	2.26	38.5	13.4	13.6	102.9
San Jose	3.09	35.2	24.8	10.1	101.1
San Leandro	2.74	39.3	22.3	13.8	92.3
San Marcos	3.05	32.9	27.8	10.2	95.6
San Mateo	2.51	38.9	20.8	14.4	95.4
Santa Ana	4.37	29.1	30.7	6.8	104.4
Santa Barbara	2.45	36.8	18.6	14.2	98.5
Santa Clara	2.63	34.1	21.3	10.0	102.0
Santa Clarita	2.94	36.2	26.2	9.6	97.1
Santa Maria	3.66	28.6	31.4	9.4	102.2
Santa Monica	1.87	40.4	14.0	15.0	93.2
Santa Rosa	2.59	36.7	23.4	13.5	95.2
Simi Valley	3.00	37.8	25.0	10.6	96.6
South Gate	4.05	29.4	31.1	7.0	96.4
Stockton	3.16	30.8	29.9	10.0	96.1
Sunnyvale	2.61	35.6	22.4	11.2	101.5
Temecula	3.15	33.4	30.7	7.8	95.9
Thousand Oaks	2.73	41.5	23.7	14.7	95.8
Torrance	2.58	41.3	21.9	14.9	94.7
Tracy	3.40	32.3	32.2	6.9	98.3
Vacaville	2.71	37.2	23.3	10.5	112.5
Vallejo	2.82	37.9	23.2	12.1	94.3
Victorville	3.40	29.5	32.8	8.1	100.4
Visalia	2.98	31.6	30.1	10.3	95.2
Vista	3.13	31.1	26.7	9.2	100.7
West Covina	3.34	36.0	24.6	12.1	93.1
Westminster	3.40	38.7	23.3	14.3	97.8
Whittier	2.96	35.4	25.4	11.7	94.0

SOURCE: U.S. Census Bureau, Census 2010

Foreign Born, Language Spoken, Disabled Persons, and Veterans

Place	Foreign Born (%)	Speak English Only at Home (%)	With a Disability (%)	Veterans (%)
Alhambra	50.50	25.5	8.4	3.1
Anaheim	37.10	39.0	7.7	4.7
Antioch	20.40	66.4	12.8	7.0
Arden-Arcade	13.80	78.4	14.2	9.3
Bakersfield	18.70	62.1	10.9	6.5
Berkeley	21.20	73.9	7.9	3.9
Buena Park	37.70	45.2	9.4	5.1
Burbank	35.20	52.0	9.9	5.0
Carlsbad	13.90	82.4	7.4	8.8
Carson	35.00	46.0	10.4	6.0
Chico	7.70	86.1	12.4	7.3
Chino	22.60	55.1	8.8	6.0
Chula Vista	31.10	42.9	8.7	10.4
Citrus Heights	13.60	80.5	13.7	11.4
Clovis	11.20	76.9	10.7	8.9
Compton	30.20	36.8	12.3	3.7
Concord	25.60	65.0	10.8	7.7
Corona	25.10	58.8	7.3	6.3
Costa Mesa	24.50	62.1	7.4	4.9
Daly City	52.10	31.4	8.1	4.3
Downey	35.30	30.9	8.7	4.4
East Los Angeles	42.90	12.4	8.8	1.8
El Cajon	29.70	57.9	12.6	9.3
El Monte	51.40	13.9	8.7	2.3
Elk Grove	22.60	66.4	10.4	8.4
Escondido	28.00	52.0	9.4	7.5
Fairfield	21.30	67.0	10.3	11.2
Fontana	30.30	41.6	9.1	4.5
Fremont	43.70	41.6	7.2	4.5
Fresno	20.90	58.3	12.3	6.2
Fullerton	31.10	53.2	8.2	5.1
Garden Grove	43.80	32.8	8.8	4.5
Glendale	54.80	30.1	12.9	3.2
Hawthorne	33.20	43.6	7.9	3.8
Hayward	38.10	42.8	9.8	5.3
Hemet	14.60	72.3	19.6	12.1
Hesperia	13.60	67.7	12.9	7.7
Huntington Beach	16.60	77.0	8.3	7.7
Inglewood	27.80	48.7	10.9	5.6
Irvine	36.00	55.2	5.4	4.0
Lakewood	21.10	65.7	10.1	6.7
Lancaster	14.60	74.4	9.9	8.1
Livermore	16.60	78.3	7.8	8.7
Long Beach	26.00	55.2	9.9	6.0
Los Angeles	38.80	39.8	9.5	3.6
Menifee	13.80	78.0	13.5	13.1
Merced	21.30	53.5	19.5	6.1
Mission Viejo	19.10	77.9	7.8	8.4
Modesto	16.80	64.8	14.5	7.3
Moreno Valley	24.70	49.3	9.4	6.8

Place	Foreign Born (%)	Speak English Only at Home (%)	With a Disability (%)	Veterans (%)
Murrieta	13.60	77.4	7.8	10.3
Newport Beach	14.20	82.8	7.0	8.0
Norwalk	35.50	32.0	9.5	4.4
Oakland	27.00	60.1	11.4	4.8
Oceanside	20.70	65.4	10.3	12.9
Ontario	30.30	41.3	8.9	4.2
Orange	26.00	58.2	7.4	5.2
Oxnard	37.00	32.1	10.1	6.2
Palmdale	25.10	58.2	10.6	6.8
Pasadena	30.50	55.4	9.7	5.1
Pomona	34.50	35.3	8.1	3.5
Rancho Cucamonga	19.30	66.5	8.1	6.5
Redding	5.30	90.6	16.6	12.0
Rialto	26.40	43.1	10.7	5.2
Richmond	32.70	50.6	10.5	5.0
Riverside	23.00	57.4	9.2	6.5
Roseville	13.30	81.2	9.5	9.8
Sacramento	21.90	63.5	13.3	7.6
Salinas	36.90	31.5	7.2	4.2
San Bernardino	22.70	53.3	13.2	5.8
San Buenaventura (Ventura)	14.90	74.0	11.1	9.6
San Diego	26.20	60.2	8.7	9.3
San Francisco	35.60	55.0	10.6	4.2
San Jose	38.60	43.9	8.1	4.5
San Leandro	34.50	50.9	9.8	5.8
San Marcos	23.50	61.8	8.2	7.2
San Mateo	32.90	55.8	9.0	5.8
Santa Ana	47.80	17.1	8.1	2.3
Santa Barbara	25.50	60.9	9.8	5.8
Santa Clara	39.60	49.2	7.7	4.6
Santa Clarita	20.50	69.5	9.1	6.4
Santa Maria	34.70	35.7	10.1	6.3
Santa Monica	23.30	72.3	9.9	4.7
Santa Rosa	19.30	70.0	11.3	8.3
Simi Valley	18.90	74.2	9.1	7.2
South Gate	43.30	9.7	8.5	1.6
Stockton	26.20	54.0	12.4	6.3
Sunnyvale	44.20	45.9	6.7	5.0
Temecula	15.20	78.7	8.0	10.1
Thousand Oaks	19.50	75.7	8.8	7.3
Torrance	29.50	61.5	9.1	6.9
Tracy	25.60	59.0	8.3	6.9
Vacaville	12.60	80.4	10.2	13.6
Vallejo	28.20	61.3	12.3	9.5
Victorville	17.00	62.6	10.7	7.4
Visalia	14.10	68.6	10.8	7.3
Vista	26.30	55.5	9.6	7.8
West Covina	34.30	44.5	10.4	5.5
Westminster	45.70	34.1	9.9	5.1
Whittier	19.00	55.9	9.7	5.9

SOURCE: U.S. Census Bureau, American Community Survey, 2009-2013 Five-Year Estimates

Five Largest Ancestry Groups

Place	Group 1	Group 2	Group 3	Group 4	Group 5
Alhambra	American (4.4%)	Irish (2.1%)	German (2.1%)	Italian (1.8%)	English (1.4%)
Anaheim	German (5.9%)	American (4.2%)	English (4.2%)	Irish (4.1%)	Italian (2.5%)
Antioch	Irish (7.8%)	German (7.5%)	Italian (5.5%)	English (4.5%)	American (2.9%)
Arden-Arcade	German (15.0%)	Irish (12.9%)	English (11.1%)	Italian (6.1%)	American (4.2%)
Bakersfield	German (8.2%)	Irish (6.9%)	English (5.6%)	American (3.6%)	Italian (2.8%)
Berkeley	German (9.6%)	English (8.5%)	Irish (8.1%)	Italian (4.5%)	Russian (3.3%)
Buena Park	German (6.4%)	Irish (5.6%)	English (3.7%)	Italian (3.1%)	American (2.7%)
Burbank	Armenian (13.3%)	German (9.1%)	Irish (7.9%)	Italian (6.2%)	English (6.2%)
Carlsbad	German (16.5%)	English (16.4%)	Irish (11.8%)	Italian (7.8%)	American (4.0%)
Carson	African (4.2%)	German (2.3%)	English (1.9%)	Irish (1.5%)	Nigerian (1.3%)
Chico	German (17.4%)	Irish (13.5%)	English (11.2%)	Italian (7.9%)	American (6.2%)
Chino	German (6.4%)	Irish (5.0%)	American (4.3%)	English (3.2%)	Italian (3.1%)
Chula Vista	German (4.9%)	Irish (4.6%)	English (2.9%)	Italian (2.5%)	American (1.5%)
Citrus Heights	German (16.5%)	Irish (12.3%)	English (10.8%)	Italian (6.6%)	American (4.1%)
Clovis	German (14.9%)	Irish (10.3%)	English (9.4%)	Italian (6.1%)	American (2.6%)
Compton	African (2.3%)	American (1.5%)	Belizean (0.3%)	Irish (0.3%)	English (0.3%)
Concord	German (11.5%)	Irish (10.2%)	English (8.8%)	Italian (6.5%)	American (3.5%)
Corona	German (8.7%)	American (6.7%)	Irish (6.1%)	English (5.5%)	Italian (3.3%)
Costa Mesa	German (13.6%)	Irish (10.0%)	English (9.4%)	Italian (5.3%)	American (3.4%)
Daly City	Irish (2.4%)	Italian (2.3%)	German (2.1%)	English (1.5%)	European (1.3%)
Downey	German (3.4%)	American (2.4%)	Irish (2.3%)	English (2.2%)	Italian (1.4%)
East Los Angeles	American (1.1%)	German (0.4%)	Italian (0.3%)	French (0.2%)	Irish (0.2%)
El Cajon	German (11.0%)	Assyrian[1] (8.3%)	Irish (7.8%)	English (5.8%)	Iraqi (5.3%)
El Monte	American (1.3%)	German (1.2%)	Irish (0.8%)	English (0.7%)	Italian (0.4%)
Elk Grove	German (10.3%)	Irish (7.3%)	English (7.0%)	Italian (4.5%)	American (2.1%)
Escondido	English (10.2%)	German (9.2%)	Irish (6.8%)	Italian (3.2%)	American (2.4%)
Fairfield	German (7.3%)	Irish (6.0%)	English (4.5%)	Italian (3.7%)	American (3.2%)
Fontana	German (3.6%)	Irish (3.2%)	American (2.4%)	Italian (2.4%)	English (2.0%)
Fremont	German (6.6%)	Irish (5.3%)	English (4.0%)	Italian (3.0%)	Portuguese (2.3%)
Fresno	German (7.8%)	Irish (5.1%)	English (4.3%)	Italian (3.2%)	American (1.5%)
Fullerton	German (9.2%)	English (6.7%)	Irish (6.2%)	Italian (3.5%)	American (2.7%)
Garden Grove	German (5.0%)	English (3.9%)	Irish (3.9%)	American (2.2%)	Italian (1.6%)
Glendale	Armenian (37.3%)	German (5.0%)	Iranian (4.9%)	English (4.1%)	Irish (4.0%)
Hawthorne	American (13.9%)	German (2.1%)	Irish (1.6%)	African (1.4%)	English (1.2%)
Hayward	German (4.5%)	Irish (3.5%)	Portuguese (2.8%)	English (2.7%)	Italian (1.8%)
Hemet	German (14.5%)	English (10.2%)	Irish (9.5%)	American (4.0%)	Italian (3.6%)
Hesperia	German (9.7%)	Irish (7.7%)	English (6.6%)	Italian (3.5%)	American (3.1%)
Huntington Beach	German (15.4%)	Irish (12.5%)	English (10.1%)	Italian (7.4%)	American (4.1%)
Inglewood	American (1.8%)	African (1.6%)	Belizean (0.9%)	French (0.6%)	Irish (0.5%)
Irvine	German (7.9%)	English (6.3%)	Irish (6.1%)	Iranian (4.5%)	Italian (3.8%)
Lakewood	German (9.3%)	Irish (6.5%)	English (6.4%)	American (3.4%)	Italian (3.1%)
Lancaster	German (6.7%)	English (4.7%)	Irish (4.6%)	Italian (2.7%)	American (2.2%)
Livermore	German (15.5%)	Irish (12.7%)	English (10.7%)	Italian (7.8%)	Portuguese (3.9%)
Long Beach	German (6.9%)	Irish (6.0%)	English (4.8%)	Italian (2.7%)	American (2.3%)
Los Angeles	German (4.5%)	Irish (3.8%)	English (3.2%)	Italian (2.7%)	Russian (2.4%)
Menifee	German (14.3%)	Irish (11.4%)	English (9.1%)	Italian (5.5%)	French (4.3%)
Merced	German (3.9%)	Irish (3.7%)	English (3.6%)	American (2.4%)	Portuguese (2.1%)
Mission Viejo	German (17.2%)	Irish (13.3%)	English (10.8%)	Italian (6.5%)	American (4.5%)
Modesto	German (10.8%)	Irish (7.8%)	English (6.4%)	Italian (4.3%)	American (3.8%)
Moreno Valley	German (4.7%)	American (3.4%)	Irish (3.2%)	English (2.9%)	Italian (2.0%)

Place	Group 1	Group 2	Group 3	Group 4	Group 5
Murrieta	German (13.6%)	Irish (10.4%)	English (9.9%)	Italian (5.7%)	American (4.9%)
Newport Beach	German (16.9%)	English (16.6%)	Irish (15.1%)	Italian (7.8%)	American (6.4%)
Norwalk	German (2.0%)	American (2.0%)	English (1.9%)	Irish (1.9%)	Italian (1.1%)
Oakland	German (5.4%)	Irish (4.7%)	English (4.1%)	Italian (2.8%)	European (1.9%)
Oceanside	German (12.0%)	English (10.6%)	Irish (8.5%)	Italian (4.5%)	American (2.5%)
Ontario	American (6.6%)	German (4.0%)	English (3.3%)	Irish (2.9%)	Italian (1.7%)
Orange	American (9.4%)	German (9.1%)	Irish (6.8%)	English (6.2%)	Italian (3.7%)
Oxnard	German (3.8%)	Irish (3.6%)	English (2.5%)	Italian (1.6%)	American (1.2%)
Palmdale	German (6.1%)	Irish (5.3%)	English (4.1%)	Italian (2.6%)	American (1.8%)
Pasadena	German (7.3%)	Irish (6.2%)	English (6.1%)	Armenian (3.8%)	Italian (3.3%)
Pomona	German (3.3%)	Irish (2.8%)	English (1.8%)	Italian (1.7%)	American (1.5%)
Rancho Cucamonga	German (11.0%)	Irish (7.1%)	English (6.8%)	Italian (6.3%)	American (3.1%)
Redding	German (17.1%)	Irish (12.7%)	English (11.0%)	American (9.7%)	Italian (5.9%)
Rialto	German (3.6%)	Irish (2.1%)	American (2.0%)	English (1.8%)	Italian (1.7%)
Richmond	German (3.8%)	Irish (3.0%)	English (2.7%)	Italian (2.2%)	African (1.9%)
Riverside	German (8.6%)	Irish (6.4%)	English (5.5%)	Italian (3.6%)	American (3.0%)
Roseville	German (17.7%)	Irish (13.0%)	English (11.6%)	Italian (7.2%)	American (3.9%)
Sacramento	German (8.5%)	Irish (7.1%)	English (5.7%)	Italian (4.1%)	American (2.1%)
Salinas	German (3.5%)	Irish (2.4%)	Italian (2.1%)	English (2.0%)	American (1.1%)
San Bernardino	German (4.9%)	Irish (3.0%)	English (2.6%)	American (2.3%)	Italian (1.3%)
San Buenaventura (Ventura)	German (14.8%)	Irish (11.2%)	English (11.0%)	Italian (5.3%)	American (3.5%)
San Diego	German (9.8%)	Irish (7.9%)	English (6.4%)	Italian (4.4%)	American (2.9%)
San Francisco	German (8.2%)	Irish (8.0%)	English (5.1%)	Italian (4.9%)	Russian (2.5%)
San Jose	German (6.2%)	Irish (4.6%)	Italian (4.3%)	English (4.2%)	American (1.6%)
San Leandro	German (5.0%)	Irish (4.4%)	English (4.3%)	Portuguese (3.4%)	Italian (3.4%)
San Marcos	English (17.1%)	German (9.9%)	Irish (7.6%)	Italian (5.9%)	American (3.1%)
San Mateo	German (9.0%)	Irish (8.6%)	Italian (8.5%)	English (6.1%)	American (2.2%)
Santa Ana	American (2.2%)	German (1.9%)	Irish (1.5%)	English (1.4%)	Italian (0.8%)
Santa Barbara	German (11.4%)	English (9.7%)	Irish (8.6%)	Italian (5.6%)	French (3.0%)
Santa Clara	German (7.0%)	Irish (5.3%)	English (5.2%)	Italian (3.9%)	Portuguese (2.2%)
Santa Clarita	German (12.8%)	Irish (10.7%)	English (8.8%)	Italian (7.0%)	American (4.0%)
Santa Maria	German (5.7%)	Irish (4.2%)	English (3.5%)	Italian (1.8%)	American (1.8%)
Santa Monica	German (12.4%)	Irish (11.7%)	English (9.3%)	Italian (7.3%)	Russian (5.8%)
Santa Rosa	German (12.6%)	Irish (10.8%)	English (9.3%)	Italian (8.0%)	European (4.6%)
Simi Valley	German (15.2%)	Irish (11.9%)	English (10.7%)	Italian (8.1%)	American (5.4%)
South Gate	American (0.9%)	Irish (0.7%)	English (0.5%)	Italian (0.5%)	German (0.4%)
Stockton	German (5.7%)	Irish (4.5%)	Italian (3.4%)	English (3.1%)	American (1.5%)
Sunnyvale	German (7.3%)	English (4.9%)	Irish (4.8%)	Italian (2.9%)	European (2.2%)
Temecula	German (12.6%)	Irish (11.0%)	English (8.1%)	Italian (7.2%)	Polish (3.2%)
Thousand Oaks	German (15.1%)	English (11.5%)	Irish (11.3%)	Italian (7.6%)	American (3.5%)
Torrance	German (10.4%)	Irish (8.3%)	English (7.4%)	Italian (4.6%)	American (3.9%)
Tracy	German (8.8%)	Irish (7.2%)	Italian (5.8%)	Portuguese (4.4%)	English (4.2%)
Vacaville	German (13.4%)	Irish (9.8%)	European (8.3%)	English (8.0%)	Italian (5.7%)
Vallejo	German (5.4%)	Irish (4.7%)	English (4.3%)	Italian (2.9%)	American (2.5%)
Victorville	German (7.4%)	Irish (6.3%)	English (5.6%)	Italian (3.0%)	American (1.8%)
Visalia	German (7.1%)	Irish (6.4%)	American (5.7%)	English (4.6%)	Italian (2.7%)
Vista	English (14.4%)	German (9.0%)	Irish (6.6%)	Italian (2.6%)	French (2.4%)
West Covina	German (4.0%)	Irish (3.1%)	English (2.7%)	Italian (1.8%)	American (1.2%)
Westminster	German (5.9%)	Irish (4.3%)	English (4.2%)	Italian (2.2%)	American (1.6%)
Whittier	German (6.5%)	English (4.9%)	Irish (4.7%)	Italian (2.9%)	American (1.7%)

NOTE: (1) Assyrian/Chaldean/Syriac; "French" excludes Basque; Please refer to the User Guide for more information.
SOURCE: U.S. Census Bureau, American Community Survey, 2009-2013 Five-Year Estimates

Marriage Status

Place	Never Married (%)	Now Married[1] (%)	Separated (%)	Widowed (%)	Divorced (%)
Alhambra	36.7	49.3	1.9	6.1	7.9
Anaheim	36.1	51.2	3.4	4.5	8.2
Antioch	35.5	49.4	2.5	5.1	10.1
Arden-Arcade	35.0	43.5	2.5	7.1	14.5
Bakersfield	35.4	50.2	3.1	4.7	9.7
Berkeley	55.0	33.7	1.3	3.4	7.8
Buena Park	36.3	48.5	2.2	5.7	9.5
Burbank	34.4	49.8	1.9	6.2	9.5
Carlsbad	26.5	56.8	1.2	4.9	11.9
Carson	38.7	46.7	2.3	6.3	8.3
Chico	45.7	37.7	1.8	4.9	11.7
Chino	35.4	50.4	2.7	4.3	9.8
Chula Vista	32.6	53.2	2.5	5.1	9.1
Citrus Heights	31.9	48.4	3.0	5.3	14.4
Clovis	31.4	52.5	2.4	5.2	10.9
Compton	46.8	40.8	3.0	4.9	7.4
Concord	32.2	52.2	2.2	4.9	10.7
Corona	33.5	54.0	2.3	4.1	8.5
Costa Mesa	39.8	44.6	2.2	4.1	11.5
Daly City	36.9	50.0	1.8	5.6	7.5
Downey	38.6	47.6	2.6	5.2	8.6
East Los Angeles	47.8	41.6	3.3	5.1	5.4
El Cajon	36.2	45.6	2.4	6.2	12.0
El Monte	40.3	48.1	3.0	5.5	6.1
Elk Grove	30.1	56.0	2.1	4.6	9.4
Escondido	34.0	51.3	2.0	5.4	9.3
Fairfield	33.2	52.3	1.8	5.2	9.3
Fontana	37.9	51.3	2.5	3.5	7.4
Fremont	26.4	62.0	1.6	4.7	6.9
Fresno	39.7	44.7	3.0	5.1	10.5
Fullerton	37.8	49.4	2.1	4.7	8.2
Garden Grove	35.9	50.2	2.3	5.8	8.1
Glendale	32.4	53.2	2.1	6.7	7.7
Hawthorne	45.7	40.5	3.4	4.1	9.7
Hayward	37.4	48.6	2.8	5.6	8.3
Hemet	27.1	47.6	3.1	10.5	14.7
Hesperia	34.8	49.5	2.1	5.1	10.6
Huntington Beach	31.8	51.5	1.7	5.4	11.3
Inglewood	45.0	39.7	4.1	4.9	10.4
Irvine	37.0	52.0	1.0	3.0	8.0
Lakewood	32.9	50.7	1.7	5.8	10.6
Lancaster	37.6	47.6	3.0	4.9	10.0
Livermore	27.7	57.8	2.0	4.2	10.3
Long Beach	44.1	40.7	3.2	4.7	10.4
Los Angeles	45.1	41.8	2.9	4.7	8.4
Menifee	27.1	52.8	2.0	7.3	12.8
Merced	39.7	44.3	2.8	5.4	10.5
Mission Viejo	26.4	58.3	1.0	6.0	9.3
Modesto	33.9	48.8	2.5	5.6	11.7
Moreno Valley	38.2	48.7	3.6	3.8	9.3

Place	Never Married (%)	Now Married[1] (%)	Separated (%)	Widowed (%)	Divorced (%)
Murrieta	28.5	57.3	2.6	5.0	9.2
Newport Beach	30.5	51.6	1.5	5.7	12.1
Norwalk	39.6	46.9	2.8	5.7	7.7
Oakland	44.2	39.8	2.9	5.7	10.4
Oceanside	31.7	51.9	1.8	5.2	11.1
Ontario	39.0	47.3	3.4	4.2	9.5
Orange	37.1	49.1	2.0	4.5	9.3
Oxnard	38.2	48.7	2.7	4.4	8.7
Palmdale	39.0	48.4	2.8	3.6	9.0
Pasadena	39.5	45.2	2.6	6.1	9.2
Pomona	42.9	44.9	3.1	4.5	7.7
Rancho Cucamonga	33.7	52.0	2.3	4.1	10.2
Redding	29.5	48.3	1.9	6.9	15.3
Rialto	39.4	47.3	3.3	4.9	8.4
Richmond	39.4	44.6	3.8	5.1	10.9
Riverside	39.5	46.1	2.5	4.6	9.8
Roseville	27.6	56.3	2.1	5.6	10.5
Sacramento	39.7	42.6	2.7	5.5	12.2
Salinas	41.4	48.5	2.5	3.7	6.5
San Bernardino	43.7	40.6	3.9	5.0	10.7
San Buenaventura (Ventura)	31.8	48.8	2.1	5.7	13.7
San Diego	40.3	45.2	2.0	4.6	10.0
San Francisco	46.7	39.7	1.5	5.2	8.4
San Jose	34.4	52.8	1.8	4.5	8.2
San Leandro	34.1	50.5	1.7	6.0	9.4
San Marcos	31.6	53.9	1.1	5.3	9.2
San Mateo	31.9	51.4	1.8	5.7	11.0
Santa Ana	42.2	47.7	3.5	4.1	6.0
Santa Barbara	40.1	43.6	2.3	5.4	10.9
Santa Clara	34.1	54.2	1.6	3.9	7.8
Santa Clarita	32.3	53.2	1.8	4.3	10.2
Santa Maria	37.7	49.9	2.8	5.1	7.3
Santa Monica	44.5	37.9	2.0	5.4	12.3
Santa Rosa	34.3	46.7	2.1	5.6	13.4
Simi Valley	29.2	55.5	1.3	4.6	10.7
South Gate	44.1	46.3	3.7	3.7	5.9
Stockton	37.7	46.6	2.7	5.6	10.1
Sunnyvale	29.5	58.9	1.0	4.2	7.4
Temecula	31.4	55.4	1.7	3.4	9.8
Thousand Oaks	27.9	57.6	1.3	5.3	9.2
Torrance	28.7	54.8	1.7	6.3	10.2
Tracy	29.7	57.6	2.5	4.2	8.5
Vacaville	32.2	50.1	2.6	4.3	13.5
Vallejo	36.0	46.0	2.8	6.6	11.5
Victorville	36.2	47.3	3.7	4.7	11.8
Visalia	31.1	51.5	2.1	5.7	11.8
Vista	35.8	49.0	1.4	4.5	10.8
West Covina	35.5	50.4	2.3	5.9	8.2
Westminster	33.3	52.5	2.2	6.1	8.1
Whittier	38.1	46.7	2.5	5.4	9.8

NOTE: (1) Includes separated.
SOURCE: U.S. Census Bureau, American Community Survey, 2009-2013 Five-Year Estimates

Employment by Occupation

Place	MBF[1] (%)	CES[2] (%)	ELCAM[3] (%)	HPT[4] (%)	S[5] (%)	SO[6] (%)	NRCM[7] (%)	PTMM[8] (%)
Alhambra	14.3	6.1	11.5	5.1	19.4	29.5	5.1	9.0
Anaheim	12.3	4.3	7.7	4.3	20.8	25.7	9.4	15.6
Antioch	12.1	3.8	8.2	4.7	22.6	27.9	9.9	10.8
Arden-Arcade	15.2	5.8	12.1	5.5	20.0	29.1	6.3	6.1
Bakersfield	11.5	3.6	10.4	5.4	19.2	23.6	13.1	13.1
Berkeley	18.5	15.2	27.5	4.4	11.0	16.7	3.2	3.5
Buena Park	14.0	5.1	7.3	5.7	18.7	29.7	6.6	12.8
Burbank	18.8	6.3	17.9	6.1	12.4	25.5	4.9	8.0
Carlsbad	23.7	11.4	13.9	5.6	12.1	24.1	4.4	4.7
Carson	11.4	3.8	7.6	7.7	18.1	26.8	7.7	16.9
Chico	13.6	5.3	12.2	6.2	23.4	25.0	6.5	7.9
Chino	14.3	4.3	8.9	4.0	18.1	26.1	9.3	15.1
Chula Vista	13.2	4.9	9.2	6.5	20.3	28.1	8.0	9.8
Citrus Heights	13.3	5.3	7.5	4.1	20.3	30.7	10.6	8.1
Clovis	13.2	4.9	13.3	8.3	17.7	27.3	7.9	7.5
Compton	6.0	1.0	5.5	2.7	21.4	26.9	10.8	25.7
Concord	15.8	6.2	8.7	5.0	21.2	24.6	9.8	8.7
Corona	16.6	5.0	9.2	4.9	14.7	27.2	9.7	13.0
Costa Mesa	19.6	5.2	10.5	3.7	20.7	25.8	6.4	8.0
Daly City	11.8	5.7	5.7	5.9	26.3	29.0	5.0	10.6
Downey	13.2	2.8	9.7	4.7	16.9	29.7	8.4	14.5
East Los Angeles	5.0	1.4	5.7	1.3	21.1	25.6	14.1	25.9
El Cajon	11.2	3.0	8.7	3.0	25.5	29.2	9.3	10.0
El Monte	6.9	3.2	5.0	2.2	24.0	22.6	11.5	24.5
Elk Grove	17.3	8.1	11.8	7.0	17.8	25.3	5.4	7.4
Escondido	11.0	4.5	7.8	3.7	24.8	23.3	13.2	11.8
Fairfield	12.8	4.3	6.9	6.0	20.0	27.6	9.7	12.6
Fontana	10.4	2.6	7.0	4.1	17.0	26.8	10.8	21.4
Fremont	20.1	23.1	8.1	4.9	10.9	20.5	4.8	7.7
Fresno	10.6	2.7	10.3	5.7	20.9	25.7	11.4	12.7
Fullerton	17.0	5.9	12.0	4.5	16.6	27.5	6.4	9.9
Garden Grove	10.4	5.0	6.8	3.5	22.0	25.3	9.5	17.4
Glendale	15.9	5.4	14.7	6.3	16.1	26.7	5.4	9.4
Hawthorne	10.2	2.6	7.5	3.2	26.6	26.6	8.9	14.3
Hayward	11.9	5.5	6.8	3.9	18.2	26.9	10.7	16.1
Hemet	6.9	2.1	8.5	3.4	26.2	25.6	12.4	14.9
Hesperia	7.8	2.1	8.4	4.5	19.5	24.5	14.2	19.1
Huntington Beach	20.1	6.3	12.1	5.8	14.9	27.3	6.8	6.7
Inglewood	10.5	1.8	8.6	3.3	25.9	27.8	8.8	13.4
Irvine	25.5	15.1	15.2	6.3	8.6	23.6	2.5	3.4
Lakewood	15.2	5.4	10.2	6.1	16.0	27.2	7.5	12.4
Lancaster	10.5	4.6	10.5	5.9	20.0	26.9	10.5	11.1
Livermore	18.9	11.9	9.7	4.4	15.8	23.8	7.7	7.7
Long Beach	14.0	4.4	12.3	4.3	19.6	25.8	7.1	12.4
Los Angeles	13.3	3.9	14.2	4.0	21.0	23.3	8.2	12.1
Menifee	11.5	3.5	7.9	5.6	21.9	27.7	11.0	11.0
Merced	7.6	2.1	12.0	4.5	21.8	23.8	13.8	14.5
Mission Viejo	21.6	9.3	12.4	5.3	13.4	28.6	4.2	5.3
Modesto	10.1	3.0	10.5	5.4	19.3	26.4	11.3	14.0
Moreno Valley	9.4	2.6	7.5	4.5	19.4	28.5	10.5	17.6

Place	MBF[1] (%)	CES[2] (%)	ELCAM[3] (%)	HPT[4] (%)	S[5] (%)	SO[6] (%)	NRCM[7] (%)	PTMM[8] (%)
Murrieta	17.0	5.2	9.7	5.7	21.0	26.1	7.5	7.7
Newport Beach	33.7	5.2	15.5	6.3	8.1	25.3	2.4	3.5
Norwalk	8.5	2.5	7.8	3.6	18.9	28.2	10.7	19.7
Oakland	16.1	6.9	15.4	3.6	20.2	20.8	7.2	9.7
Oceanside	13.4	5.8	8.3	4.5	21.5	26.2	10.6	9.7
Ontario	8.7	2.5	6.9	3.1	18.7	27.0	10.1	22.9
Orange	16.7	5.8	11.3	4.9	17.8	26.7	8.8	8.1
Oxnard	8.7	3.3	6.1	3.2	19.1	23.5	19.6	16.5
Palmdale	9.8	4.2	7.6	4.3	20.5	27.2	11.4	15.0
Pasadena	18.3	8.7	19.2	6.5	15.4	20.6	5.2	6.0
Pomona	8.7	2.9	7.8	2.7	21.7	25.8	11.0	19.5
Rancho Cucamonga	17.1	5.0	11.4	7.4	14.5	29.0	7.0	8.8
Redding	14.6	4.0	10.5	5.7	20.9	27.1	9.8	7.4
Rialto	5.4	1.8	6.7	2.3	21.1	26.8	11.4	24.6
Richmond	11.7	4.5	10.7	3.7	25.2	21.7	11.2	11.3
Riverside	10.1	3.3	12.1	4.3	18.0	25.8	10.7	15.6
Roseville	18.7	7.2	10.5	6.4	15.5	28.9	5.9	7.0
Sacramento	15.4	6.9	11.4	4.6	20.1	26.4	6.4	8.8
Salinas	7.6	1.9	6.1	2.9	21.2	21.0	24.5	14.9
San Bernardino	7.2	1.6	7.9	3.8	23.3	25.0	12.1	19.0
San Buenaventura (Ventura)	15.1	6.6	13.2	6.1	17.4	25.1	8.2	8.3
San Diego	16.6	10.5	12.3	5.7	19.0	23.2	5.8	7.0
San Francisco	21.7	10.4	14.8	4.8	17.3	21.7	4.1	5.2
San Jose	16.8	12.8	8.7	4.0	17.3	22.4	7.7	10.2
San Leandro	13.1	6.9	8.7	3.8	18.5	26.3	8.7	13.9
San Marcos	14.1	8.0	9.2	3.9	19.5	26.5	8.7	10.1
San Mateo	19.2	9.7	10.5	4.5	20.2	23.1	6.3	6.5
Santa Ana	7.3	2.7	4.7	1.7	27.9	23.9	11.5	20.3
Santa Barbara	16.5	6.6	13.7	4.6	24.6	20.2	8.3	5.6
Santa Clara	19.9	22.6	8.2	3.8	13.4	19.9	5.0	7.2
Santa Clarita	17.2	5.4	12.1	5.7	16.3	27.0	8.0	8.3
Santa Maria	7.1	3.3	5.3	2.8	18.2	19.8	29.6	13.9
Santa Monica	25.1	7.2	27.1	5.9	10.3	20.0	1.9	2.6
Santa Rosa	14.1	4.8	9.5	4.7	20.5	25.6	9.6	11.1
Simi Valley	19.8	6.8	10.4	4.6	16.3	27.6	7.1	7.5
South Gate	6.2	1.1	6.7	1.9	17.3	28.8	10.8	27.2
Stockton	8.8	2.7	9.7	5.1	21.5	24.6	11.4	16.2
Sunnyvale	18.7	30.2	8.4	3.6	12.0	16.4	4.6	5.9
Temecula	16.1	5.4	10.3	6.1	20.3	25.3	8.2	8.4
Thousand Oaks	22.5	9.3	13.5	5.7	14.7	24.7	4.8	4.8
Torrance	20.2	10.8	12.0	6.3	12.0	25.9	5.3	7.5
Tracy	14.8	7.3	6.2	3.8	14.9	26.4	11.8	14.8
Vacaville	12.0	3.6	9.9	6.7	21.4	25.2	10.4	11.0
Vallejo	14.7	4.9	8.4	6.3	20.9	24.5	8.9	11.4
Victorville	9.2	2.3	8.6	3.6	22.6	26.5	12.8	14.5
Visalia	12.4	2.6	11.5	5.7	21.0	25.4	9.4	12.0
Vista	10.8	5.1	7.0	3.5	24.0	24.0	12.4	13.2
West Covina	14.3	4.1	8.3	6.2	16.4	30.4	7.5	12.9
Westminster	12.2	5.2	7.3	4.8	21.6	25.4	8.0	15.5
Whittier	13.3	3.9	13.6	4.3	16.3	29.8	6.4	12.3

NOTES: (1) Management, business, and financial occupations; (2) Computer, engineering, and science occupations; (3) Education, legal, community service, arts, and media occupations; (4) Healthcare practitioners and technical occupations; (5) Service occupations; (6) Sales and office occupations; (7) Natural resources, construction, and maintenance occupations; (8) Production, transportation, and material moving occupations

SOURCE: U.S. Census Bureau, American Community Survey, 2009-2013 Five-Year Estimates

Educational Attainment

Place	Percent of Population 25 Years and Over with:		
	High School Diploma or Higher[1]	Bachelor's Degree or Higher	Graduate/Professional Degree or Higher
Alhambra	80.4	32.8	10.9
Anaheim	74.7	24.2	7.2
Antioch	87.2	19.9	4.6
Arden-Arcade	89.2	33.8	12.8
Bakersfield	78.5	20.0	6.7
Berkeley	94.9	69.7	37.4
Buena Park	82.3	27.9	6.8
Burbank	88.0	37.5	10.8
Carlsbad	96.0	51.9	21.0
Carson	80.1	24.0	5.6
Chico	91.2	33.8	11.9
Chino	78.9	21.9	5.6
Chula Vista	81.3	26.9	8.8
Citrus Heights	89.2	18.9	4.9
Clovis	89.0	30.2	10.3
Compton	59.2	6.7	1.8
Concord	87.6	30.5	9.4
Corona	83.3	25.8	8.1
Costa Mesa	85.4	35.7	10.9
Daly City	86.1	33.2	6.0
Downey	77.0	20.6	6.1
East Los Angeles	45.6	5.5	1.3
El Cajon	78.4	17.5	5.5
El Monte	56.8	12.0	2.1
Elk Grove	90.4	35.2	9.8
Escondido	72.1	21.0	6.1
Fairfield	86.4	23.4	6.3
Fontana	71.8	15.8	4.3
Fremont	91.0	50.9	23.0
Fresno	75.0	20.3	6.5
Fullerton	86.1	37.1	12.6
Garden Grove	72.5	18.6	4.4
Glendale	84.4	38.2	12.1
Hawthorne	74.4	18.0	4.4
Hayward	79.5	24.2	6.1
Hemet	79.7	11.9	4.4
Hesperia	75.9	9.4	3.1
Huntington Beach	92.5	40.2	14.2
Inglewood	71.8	17.4	6.1
Irvine	96.3	64.9	27.9
Lakewood	87.4	27.5	7.7
Lancaster	79.8	15.7	5.4
Livermore	92.0	38.9	13.2
Long Beach	79.3	28.5	10.1
Los Angeles	74.5	31.1	10.4
Menifee	85.7	16.5	5.3
Merced	71.7	15.7	5.4
Mission Viejo	94.5	45.2	16.2
Modesto	81.0	18.2	6.4
Moreno Valley	75.0	14.8	4.3

Place	Percent of Population 25 Years and Over with: High School Diploma or Higher[1]	Bachelor's Degree or Higher	Graduate/Professional Degree or Higher
Murrieta	92.0	29.0	9.5
Newport Beach	97.5	64.1	25.8
Norwalk	72.4	14.8	4.5
Oakland	80.2	38.1	16.6
Oceanside	83.4	24.8	8.3
Ontario	69.6	13.0	3.3
Orange	83.4	33.0	11.9
Oxnard	64.3	15.6	4.5
Palmdale	74.2	15.3	4.9
Pasadena	85.8	48.7	21.9
Pomona	66.3	16.5	4.9
Rancho Cucamonga	90.9	31.8	11.4
Redding	90.1	22.4	7.8
Rialto	68.5	9.9	3.4
Richmond	77.4	26.2	9.4
Riverside	77.7	22.2	9.5
Roseville	94.1	35.6	11.2
Sacramento	82.4	29.3	10.4
Salinas	60.6	12.4	3.8
San Bernardino	67.7	11.2	3.6
San Buenaventura (Ventura)	88.9	33.1	12.9
San Diego	87.0	41.7	16.7
San Francisco	86.3	52.4	20.7
San Jose	82.3	37.4	14.1
San Leandro	82.0	27.3	8.1
San Marcos	80.6	28.3	8.1
San Mateo	88.4	44.4	17.5
Santa Ana	53.6	11.8	3.3
Santa Barbara	83.3	41.7	18.0
Santa Clara	91.8	51.6	23.0
Santa Clarita	88.1	31.9	10.0
Santa Maria	60.3	12.9	3.7
Santa Monica	95.1	64.7	28.8
Santa Rosa	84.8	30.0	11.0
Simi Valley	90.0	32.3	10.3
South Gate	52.5	6.2	1.4
Stockton	74.4	17.7	5.8
Sunnyvale	90.7	58.3	28.2
Temecula	91.5	29.8	9.4
Thousand Oaks	92.5	48.5	20.0
Torrance	93.0	44.7	15.0
Tracy	82.6	20.9	4.5
Vacaville	87.4	22.2	7.3
Vallejo	86.4	23.3	6.3
Victorville	77.7	10.8	3.9
Visalia	81.8	21.6	8.3
Vista	74.6	19.1	5.3
West Covina	83.1	27.3	6.7
Westminster	74.6	21.0	5.2
Whittier	83.6	24.5	9.1

NOTE: (1) Includes General Equivalency Diploma (GED)
SOURCE: U.S. Census Bureau, American Community Survey, 2009-2013 Five-Year Estimates

Health Insurance

Place	Percent of Total Population with: Any Insurance	Private Insurance	Public Insurance	No Insurance	Percent of Population[1] Under Age 18 without Health Insurance
Alhambra	81.1	60.7	27.3	18.9	6.4
Anaheim	77.4	53.2	29.2	22.6	9.7
Antioch	85.8	64.9	30.1	14.2	7.7
Arden-Arcade	83.8	61.2	36.0	16.2	5.5
Bakersfield	81.8	57.5	31.8	18.2	9.0
Berkeley	91.4	81.6	19.6	8.6	3.0
Buena Park	80.4	60.0	27.4	19.6	7.8
Burbank	84.9	69.9	22.1	15.1	5.7
Carlsbad	90.2	81.0	19.9	9.8	5.0
Carson	83.3	62.2	29.3	16.7	7.9
Chico	83.5	64.5	28.3	16.5	7.7
Chino	82.5	66.3	21.2	17.5	8.7
Chula Vista	82.3	65.0	24.9	17.7	9.9
Citrus Heights	84.0	65.2	31.8	16.0	6.7
Clovis	86.9	70.6	26.8	13.1	5.6
Compton	73.2	34.8	43.0	26.8	9.7
Concord	85.2	69.4	26.1	14.8	7.0
Corona	83.3	67.0	21.5	16.7	7.5
Costa Mesa	78.1	62.3	21.4	21.9	10.3
Daly City	86.0	70.4	24.8	14.0	6.1
Downey	78.3	56.6	26.8	21.7	9.2
East Los Angeles	63.8	31.3	35.4	36.2	17.9
El Cajon	79.6	48.1	38.8	20.4	11.0
El Monte	69.6	32.6	40.0	30.4	8.8
Elk Grove	90.6	77.1	21.8	9.4	4.3
Escondido	74.4	53.4	27.6	25.6	13.8
Fairfield	88.2	70.3	28.8	11.8	3.2
Fontana	75.1	51.7	27.8	24.9	12.4
Fremont	91.5	78.7	19.4	8.5	2.9
Fresno	80.4	47.0	41.5	19.6	6.9
Fullerton	79.7	62.4	24.2	20.3	13.0
Garden Grove	78.8	51.1	33.2	21.2	8.8
Glendale	80.4	53.6	32.7	19.6	9.1
Hawthorne	74.4	49.1	30.5	25.6	11.6
Hayward	81.8	60.3	29.6	18.2	7.0
Hemet	80.9	45.1	49.2	19.1	10.6
Hesperia	78.9	47.6	38.0	21.1	11.0
Huntington Beach	88.0	75.2	22.8	12.0	4.6
Inglewood	73.9	49.2	30.8	26.1	13.3
Irvine	90.7	81.9	14.3	9.3	5.3
Lakewood	87.7	73.2	22.3	12.3	5.5
Lancaster	83.9	59.8	30.9	16.1	10.2
Livermore	91.2	82.7	18.3	8.8	5.0
Long Beach	80.4	55.4	31.8	19.6	7.6
Los Angeles	74.4	49.3	30.9	25.6	10.6
Menifee	84.5	62.9	34.0	15.5	7.9
Merced	83.1	46.9	44.7	16.9	5.0
Mission Viejo	91.9	80.9	21.4	8.1	3.2
Modesto	82.5	54.9	37.3	17.5	7.9
Moreno Valley	75.9	48.8	31.7	24.1	13.5

Place	Percent of Total Population with: Any Insurance	Private Insurance	Public Insurance	No Insurance	Percent of Population[1] Under Age 18 without Health Insurance
Murrieta	87.0	74.8	20.7	13.0	9.7
Newport Beach	91.5	82.9	22.3	8.5	4.2
Norwalk	75.8	51.5	29.1	24.2	9.7
Oakland	82.7	57.1	33.6	17.3	7.1
Oceanside	81.8	64.5	28.0	18.2	8.9
Ontario	75.0	50.9	28.9	25.0	11.7
Orange	81.9	65.7	23.1	18.1	6.8
Oxnard	74.6	48.4	32.6	25.4	12.0
Palmdale	81.2	50.1	36.6	18.8	8.0
Pasadena	82.9	65.6	25.1	17.1	9.3
Pomona	74.0	44.4	33.4	26.0	10.0
Rancho Cucamonga	87.4	74.9	18.3	12.6	5.9
Redding	84.0	57.8	40.1	16.0	10.3
Rialto	74.8	43.5	36.0	25.2	11.8
Richmond	79.3	55.4	33.2	20.7	11.6
Riverside	79.1	56.1	29.0	20.9	10.8
Roseville	90.8	79.0	22.8	9.2	4.0
Sacramento	84.3	58.3	35.2	15.7	5.6
Salinas	75.0	48.3	32.2	25.0	8.7
San Bernardino	75.3	39.4	41.4	24.7	10.1
San Buenaventura (Ventura)	85.9	68.8	28.2	14.1	5.4
San Diego	83.4	67.2	24.6	16.6	8.5
San Francisco	88.9	71.0	26.4	11.1	4.1
San Jose	86.2	67.4	25.7	13.8	4.9
San Leandro	86.0	67.0	28.5	14.0	5.2
San Marcos	82.5	66.5	22.1	17.5	6.9
San Mateo	88.3	75.2	24.4	11.7	3.6
Santa Ana	66.7	38.5	31.4	33.3	14.8
Santa Barbara	78.9	63.2	26.4	21.1	14.2
Santa Clara	90.7	78.6	19.9	9.3	2.9
Santa Clarita	86.8	74.4	20.2	13.2	6.9
Santa Maria	72.2	40.9	38.2	27.8	11.5
Santa Monica	88.9	76.3	21.3	11.1	5.6
Santa Rosa	83.7	63.4	31.5	16.3	8.7
Simi Valley	88.5	77.3	19.9	11.5	5.9
South Gate	69.1	39.1	33.1	30.9	11.8
Stockton	82.0	50.8	39.1	18.0	7.0
Sunnyvale	89.9	78.8	19.0	10.1	4.6
Temecula	85.6	73.8	19.4	14.4	8.0
Thousand Oaks	89.3	80.2	20.6	10.7	6.9
Torrance	88.0	75.0	23.0	12.0	7.4
Tracy	86.7	70.8	22.7	13.3	4.9
Vacaville	90.4	76.3	26.2	9.6	3.8
Vallejo	83.2	61.4	32.3	16.8	9.4
Victorville	81.6	50.6	37.3	18.4	7.0
Visalia	83.8	57.3	34.9	16.2	8.7
Vista	75.4	56.6	25.3	24.6	10.4
West Covina	82.1	62.1	26.1	17.9	7.7
Westminster	81.3	50.7	37.1	18.7	9.4
Whittier	84.9	66.8	25.5	15.1	8.0

NOTE: (1) Civilian noninstitutionalized population.
SOURCE: U.S. Census Bureau, American Community Survey, 2009-2013 Five-Year Estimates

Income and Poverty

Place	Average Household Income ($)	Median Household Income ($)	Per Capita Income ($)	Households w/$100,000+ Income (%)	Poverty Rate (%)
Alhambra	70,002	54,148	25,703	22.9	13.9
Anaheim	76,565	59,165	23,400	25.7	16.1
Antioch	77,188	65,254	24,678	28.2	14.9
Arden-Arcade	68,545	44,107	30,862	20.1	19.8
Bakersfield	72,299	56,204	23,316	23.3	20.4
Berkeley	97,635	63,312	41,308	33.6	18.7
Buena Park	79,637	66,371	23,623	28.6	12.0
Burbank	82,531	66,240	33,663	29.9	9.4
Carlsbad	108,358	83,908	43,441	43.0	10.6
Carson	82,086	72,235	23,762	30.9	10.0
Chico	58,659	43,372	24,221	16.6	23.2
Chino	85,324	71,466	23,866	31.2	10.0
Chula Vista	78,558	64,801	25,104	28.9	11.8
Citrus Heights	62,919	52,183	25,023	15.6	14.7
Clovis	80,267	65,260	27,906	27.9	13.2
Compton	52,123	42,953	13,548	11.5	26.3
Concord	84,220	65,798	31,359	31.4	12.1
Corona	90,460	77,123	26,832	36.0	10.8
Costa Mesa	89,278	65,830	34,100	31.1	15.1
Daly City	89,180	74,436	28,827	35.2	8.6
Downey	75,200	60,939	23,055	24.2	11.8
East Los Angeles	46,658	37,982	12,511	8.4	26.9
El Cajon	57,907	44,112	19,803	15.8	26.4
El Monte	52,809	39,535	14,735	12.1	24.3
Elk Grove	92,181	77,791	28,898	36.2	9.5
Escondido	67,053	49,362	21,653	20.2	18.7
Fairfield	79,786	64,702	26,611	29.2	13.6
Fontana	75,136	64,354	19,299	25.1	15.5
Fremont	119,720	101,535	40,190	50.9	6.0
Fresno	58,850	42,015	19,455	15.7	28.9
Fullerton	89,242	67,384	29,913	31.6	16.0
Garden Grove	73,625	59,648	20,849	25.2	16.6
Glendale	77,174	53,020	29,290	25.5	14.2
Hawthorne	57,114	44,649	20,162	12.9	19.2
Hayward	77,320	62,013	25,208	26.8	14.4
Hemet	45,077	32,774	17,917	8.6	23.3
Hesperia	54,543	44,158	16,239	13.7	25.3
Huntington Beach	107,267	81,389	42,196	40.5	8.9
Inglewood	57,780	43,394	20,150	14.1	22.4
Irvine	115,296	90,585	43,096	45.5	12.2
Lakewood	86,509	77,786	29,354	35.1	8.1
Lancaster	63,569	50,193	20,156	18.0	21.5
Livermore	116,498	99,161	42,213	49.6	5.7
Long Beach	73,779	52,711	27,040	23.3	20.2
Los Angeles	77,102	49,497	27,829	22.9	22.0
Menifee	67,018	54,903	23,478	19.2	10.3
Merced	52,560	37,822	16,876	12.9	30.0
Mission Viejo	113,097	96,210	40,909	48.1	5.3
Modesto	63,838	47,060	22,439	18.5	20.8
Moreno Valley	65,705	54,918	18,186	19.2	19.5

Place	Average Household Income ($)	Median Household Income ($)	Per Capita Income ($)	Households w/$100,000+ Income (%)	Poverty Rate (%)
Murrieta	88,971	74,496	28,452	33.9	7.0
Newport Beach	173,263	106,333	78,494	53.0	7.9
Norwalk	70,938	60,770	19,449	22.7	12.9
Oakland	78,684	52,583	31,971	25.2	20.5
Oceanside	74,030	58,153	26,863	24.1	13.3
Ontario	63,733	54,249	18,522	18.5	18.1
Orange	97,270	78,838	31,535	37.9	11.8
Oxnard	75,627	60,784	20,605	24.9	16.7
Palmdale	67,093	53,922	18,797	21.5	21.2
Pasadena	99,695	69,302	41,152	34.9	13.2
Pomona	61,755	49,474	17,035	16.2	21.6
Rancho Cucamonga	96,152	77,835	32,209	37.6	6.9
Redding	58,466	44,236	23,443	15.4	18.2
Rialto	59,804	49,593	15,948	15.0	19.1
Richmond	71,818	54,589	25,722	22.8	18.5
Riverside	71,905	55,636	22,182	22.6	19.1
Roseville	89,296	74,114	33,622	36.1	8.3
Sacramento	65,908	49,753	25,508	19.6	21.9
Salinas	62,112	49,264	17,396	17.1	21.0
San Bernardino	50,025	38,385	14,879	11.6	32.4
San Buenaventura (Ventura)	81,785	65,137	32,311	29.1	10.7
San Diego	87,395	64,058	33,152	30.5	15.6
San Francisco	110,208	75,604	48,486	39.4	13.5
San Jose	104,448	81,829	34,025	40.8	12.2
San Leandro	77,090	63,055	28,801	27.8	10.0
San Marcos	71,631	53,657	24,484	23.7	14.6
San Mateo	114,444	85,669	45,202	42.5	7.1
Santa Ana	68,083	53,335	16,374	19.7	21.5
Santa Barbara	93,370	65,034	37,225	31.2	14.0
Santa Clara	108,726	91,583	39,966	46.0	9.0
Santa Clarita	99,137	82,607	33,818	38.5	9.5
Santa Maria	65,046	50,563	18,560	18.3	20.7
Santa Monica	109,645	73,649	57,390	38.1	11.2
Santa Rosa	77,521	60,354	29,688	25.5	13.5
Simi Valley	106,175	87,269	36,516	44.2	6.6
South Gate	53,366	42,776	14,259	11.4	21.1
Stockton	62,710	46,831	19,896	18.6	24.3
Sunnyvale	119,865	100,043	45,977	50.0	8.1
Temecula	88,867	78,356	28,018	36.5	8.5
Thousand Oaks	125,321	100,476	45,522	50.3	6.8
Torrance	92,415	77,061	36,234	36.2	7.4
Tracy	89,151	76,098	26,652	35.9	8.2
Vacaville	87,736	73,582	29,681	31.7	9.9
Vallejo	72,361	58,371	25,996	24.3	17.5
Victorville	58,269	50,034	16,477	16.5	25.3
Visalia	68,924	52,899	23,144	22.6	19.2
Vista	61,576	47,346	21,114	16.3	16.0
West Covina	80,897	67,088	24,859	28.6	10.0
Westminster	72,963	52,633	22,950	24.8	16.7
Whittier	85,281	68,522	28,149	31.7	12.4

SOURCE: U.S. Census Bureau, American Community Survey, 2009-2013 Five-Year Estimates

Housing

Place	Homeownership Rate (%)	Median Home Value ($)	Median Year Structure Built	Homeowner Vacancy Rate (%)	Median Gross Rent ($/month)	Rental Vacancy Rate (%)
Alhambra	40.8	$478,500	1956	1.3	$1,211	5.3
Anaheim	48.5	$399,100	1972	1.7	$1,344	7.2
Antioch	64.3	$233,600	1983	2.7	$1,315	8.2
Arden-Arcade	46.1	$277,000	1965	2.4	$876	11.7
Bakersfield	59.7	$179,700	1986	3.2	$979	9.0
Berkeley	41.0	$698,600	Before 1940	1.0	$1,298	4.5
Buena Park	56.7	$393,900	1962	1.1	$1,375	5.0
Burbank	44.0	$554,700	1957	1.6	$1,365	5.3
Carlsbad	64.8	$614,000	1986	1.4	$1,631	4.6
Carson	76.8	$340,900	1965	1.3	$1,347	3.7
Chico	42.7	$266,500	1979	2.0	$907	5.8
Chino	68.9	$330,900	1981	2.1	$1,310	6.4
Chula Vista	58.1	$351,500	1982	2.4	$1,255	4.5
Citrus Heights	57.6	$190,200	1976	2.7	<$101	7.8
Clovis	62.2	$247,000	1989	2.3	$1,039	6.4
Compton	55.2	$237,800	1954	2.9	$1,043	5.9
Concord	61.1	$356,500	1970	1.9	$1,282	7.0
Corona	67.2	$324,600	1989	2.3	$1,329	5.3
Costa Mesa	39.6	$580,700	1969	1.2	$1,524	5.9
Daly City	56.5	$552,700	1966	1.9	$1,542	4.2
Downey	50.5	$409,800	1958	1.4	$1,214	4.9
East Los Angeles	35.7	$288,900	1950	1.2	$968	3.2
El Cajon	41.2	$314,800	1972	1.9	$1,087	4.8
El Monte	42.2	$345,200	1962	1.4	$1,071	4.6
Elk Grove	74.6	$263,400	1998	2.4	$1,447	5.6
Escondido	52.2	$324,600	1979	2.2	$1,182	6.0
Fairfield	60.4	$263,500	1983	2.5	$1,271	7.1
Fontana	68.9	$243,900	1987	2.6	$1,112	6.0
Fremont	62.6	$600,300	1976	1.3	$1,566	4.5
Fresno	49.1	$180,100	1977	2.6	$884	7.6
Fullerton	54.2	$478,900	1969	1.1	$1,341	7.0
Garden Grove	57.0	$393,900	1964	1.2	$1,322	4.6
Glendale	38.1	$587,800	1962	1.3	$1,294	5.5
Hawthorne	26.7	$386,500	1967	1.5	$1,021	4.6
Hayward	52.7	$321,500	1971	2.3	$1,292	6.6
Hemet	61.7	$114,200	1982	5.0	$948	17.5
Hesperia	66.9	$146,200	1985	3.6	$1,052	8.4
Huntington Beach	60.4	$624,400	1972	1.1	$1,559	5.4
Inglewood	36.9	$328,200	1959	1.5	$1,076	5.5
Irvine	50.2	$643,200	1991	2.2	$1,846	6.2
Lakewood	72.1	$413,000	1957	1.1	$1,537	5.7
Lancaster	60.4	$159,200	1985	3.8	$1,069	9.4
Livermore	70.1	$476,400	1977	1.5	$1,448	4.8
Long Beach	41.6	$417,600	1956	2.0	$1,106	7.2
Los Angeles	38.2	$446,100	1960	2.1	$1,175	6.1
Menifee	76.9	$193,100	1995	4.1	$1,335	6.8
Merced	42.7	$137,900	1981	3.5	$819	8.5
Mission Viejo	77.9	$542,800	1979	0.9	$1,825	4.9
Modesto	57.1	$167,100	1977	2.8	$1,012	9.1
Moreno Valley	64.8	$178,400	1987	3.4	$1,272	7.5

Place	Homeownership Rate (%)	Median Home Value ($)	Median Year Structure Built	Homeowner Vacancy Rate (%)	Median Gross Rent ($/month)	Rental Vacancy Rate (%)
Murrieta	70.5	$278,400	2000	3.1	$1,502	7.8
Newport Beach	54.8	1 million+	1974	1.7	$1,924	7.8
Norwalk	65.1	$315,500	1957	1.4	$1,306	3.8
Oakland	41.0	$428,900	1949	3.0	$1,087	8.5
Oceanside	59.1	$347,000	1982	2.2	$1,373	6.2
Ontario	55.3	$250,900	1976	2.0	$1,242	5.8
Orange	60.6	$498,700	1972	1.1	$1,487	5.1
Oxnard	55.8	$323,700	1973	1.8	$1,304	3.7
Palmdale	67.9	$172,000	1989	3.2	$1,155	9.4
Pasadena	45.0	$601,500	1957	2.3	$1,348	6.6
Pomona	55.1	$258,700	1965	2.0	$1,104	5.9
Rancho Cucamonga	64.8	$358,800	1987	1.6	$1,442	5.2
Redding	55.3	$228,000	1981	2.3	$944	6.9
Rialto	64.6	$180,500	1981	3.1	$1,081	9.7
Richmond	51.7	$270,200	1962	2.5	$1,172	8.1
Riverside	55.7	$235,900	1975	2.4	$1,135	7.4
Roseville	65.5	$312,400	1994	2.3	$1,252	6.8
Sacramento	49.4	$225,900	1972	2.8	$999	8.3
Salinas	45.1	$254,900	1975	2.5	$1,120	4.6
San Bernardino	50.3	$152,800	1969	3.2	$930	9.5
San Buenaventura (Ventura)	55.9	$429,100	1970	1.3	$1,353	5.5
San Diego	48.3	$437,400	1975	1.9	$1,329	5.2
San Francisco	35.7	$744,600	1941	2.3	$1,488	5.4
San Jose	58.5	$560,400	1974	1.6	$1,474	4.3
San Leandro	57.5	$367,300	1958	1.4	$1,213	5.8
San Marcos	62.8	$362,000	1988	2.1	$1,314	5.7
San Mateo	52.3	$710,700	1960	1.5	$1,660	3.7
Santa Ana	47.5	$334,900	1967	1.9	$1,294	4.9
Santa Barbara	38.9	$832,100	1963	1.3	$1,484	4.1
Santa Clara	46.0	$613,200	1969	1.3	$1,609	4.6
Santa Clarita	71.2	$373,700	1983	1.4	$1,509	6.0
Santa Maria	51.6	$251,500	1979	1.9	$1,138	3.8
Santa Monica	28.4	$999,900	1964	1.1	$1,533	5.1
Santa Rosa	54.2	$360,800	1978	2.0	$1,244	5.0
Simi Valley	74.1	$432,000	1978	1.2	$1,675	4.6
South Gate	45.8	$292,100	1950	1.5	$984	3.6
Stockton	51.6	$166,500	1978	3.2	$959	9.4
Sunnyvale	48.0	$710,700	1972	1.1	$1,606	4.4
Temecula	69.2	$298,200	1996	2.7	$1,509	7.1
Thousand Oaks	73.1	$593,900	1977	0.8	$1,825	5.6
Torrance	56.4	$613,600	1963	0.8	$1,432	5.3
Tracy	66.4	$257,400	1993	2.5	$1,389	5.9
Vacaville	63.5	$269,500	1982	2.1	$1,369	6.8
Vallejo	59.7	$218,300	1970	3.0	$1,192	9.4
Victorville	61.9	$137,700	1993	4.9	$1,098	11.1
Visalia	61.4	$177,100	1983	2.6	$956	6.7
Vista	51.8	$340,200	1981	2.2	$1,221	5.9
West Covina	65.5	$378,200	1965	1.1	$1,375	4.8
Westminster	57.9	$448,400	1969	1.5	$1,334	7.3
Whittier	57.3	$418,800	1956	1.3	$1,180	5.1

SOURCE: U.S. Census Bureau, Census 2010; U.S. Census Bureau, American Community Survey, 2009-2013 Five-Year Estimates

Commute to Work

Place	Automobile (%)	Public Trans-portation (%)	Walk (%)	Work from Home (%)	Median Travel Time to Work (minutes)
Alhambra	89.5	4.1	1.5	3.9	29.3
Anaheim	88.8	4.4	1.7	3.1	27.0
Antioch	87.6	5.8	1.3	4.0	40.0
Arden-Arcade	85.3	3.8	3.0	5.8	22.7
Bakersfield	92.9	1.2	1.4	2.8	22.9
Berkeley	43.5	20.2	15.4	10.9	26.9
Buena Park	86.4	4.0	3.0	3.0	29.2
Burbank	86.7	2.9	2.9	5.0	24.8
Carlsbad	85.7	2.2	1.1	9.4	28.3
Carson	90.9	3.1	1.5	3.6	26.4
Chico	81.7	1.3	5.4	5.0	17.3
Chino	92.8	1.7	1.4	2.9	33.7
Chula Vista	90.0	3.3	1.3	3.8	26.8
Citrus Heights	91.3	1.8	2.0	3.5	25.5
Clovis	93.6	0.3	1.3	3.1	20.5
Compton	87.5	6.2	1.6	3.0	27.6
Concord	82.4	9.8	1.8	3.6	30.0
Corona	90.8	1.8	1.2	4.8	35.2
Costa Mesa	85.4	3.0	2.5	5.5	21.9
Daly City	74.5	20.1	2.5	1.9	28.6
Downey	92.1	2.9	1.8	2.4	27.7
East Los Angeles	78.8	12.7	4.0	2.3	29.0
El Cajon	87.4	3.5	2.2	5.2	24.0
El Monte	86.1	6.2	2.6	3.5	30.3
Elk Grove	90.6	2.6	0.8	4.6	30.2
Escondido	92.4	1.6	1.6	3.0	25.8
Fairfield	89.7	2.2	3.2	3.5	27.7
Fontana	93.2	2.1	0.8	3.2	32.1
Fremont	85.9	7.4	1.4	3.8	29.7
Fresno	89.3	2.0	1.8	3.7	21.7
Fullerton	87.9	3.6	3.4	3.7	28.1
Garden Grove	91.7	3.3	1.5	1.9	26.4
Glendale	84.4	4.5	3.8	5.8	26.5
Hawthorne	85.8	7.3	1.8	2.7	27.6
Hayward	85.9	8.1	2.2	2.4	29.1
Hemet	90.7	1.6	1.6	4.7	30.9
Hesperia	90.4	1.2	1.3	5.4	37.1
Huntington Beach	89.0	1.0	1.7	5.8	27.1
Inglewood	84.1	7.6	2.0	4.2	28.5
Irvine	85.6	1.5	3.7	6.9	23.6
Lakewood	92.0	2.1	1.5	3.1	27.7
Lancaster	94.1	1.6	1.1	2.4	30.6
Livermore	88.5	3.3	1.2	5.1	29.1
Long Beach	82.7	7.7	2.6	4.7	28.7
Los Angeles	77.2	11.0	3.7	5.6	29.2
Menifee	90.8	0.6	0.8	6.2	38.0
Merced	87.2	0.9	2.2	3.7	22.4
Mission Viejo	88.4	1.5	0.5	8.7	26.6
Modesto	91.2	1.7	1.4	3.6	25.2
Moreno Valley	92.0	1.6	1.0	2.5	34.2

Place	Automobile (%)	Public Transportation (%)	Walk (%)	Work from Home (%)	Median Travel Time to Work (minutes)
Murrieta	90.9	0.2	0.9	6.2	34.7
Newport Beach	85.0	1.0	2.0	9.7	23.3
Norwalk	91.1	3.9	1.8	1.9	28.2
Oakland	66.4	18.3	4.2	6.7	28.3
Oceanside	89.1	2.7	1.4	4.9	27.5
Ontario	93.0	1.5	1.6	2.2	28.4
Orange	88.8	2.9	2.1	4.2	25.1
Oxnard	92.7	1.6	1.5	2.6	23.1
Palmdale	91.0	2.8	0.8	4.6	40.5
Pasadena	80.4	6.4	4.6	5.6	26.1
Pomona	88.6	3.4	2.5	3.6	29.1
Rancho Cucamonga	92.0	1.8	1.3	3.5	30.4
Redding	89.5	1.2	2.2	4.8	16.9
Rialto	92.4	2.9	0.7	3.1	32.3
Richmond	79.9	13.2	2.0	3.1	31.4
Riverside	89.0	2.6	2.8	3.8	28.5
Roseville	88.4	1.3	1.9	6.2	26.3
Sacramento	84.8	4.0	3.1	4.5	24.0
Salinas	83.5	0.9	1.1	3.5	23.2
San Bernardino	89.6	3.0	2.2	3.8	27.0
San Buenaventura (Ventura)	88.3	1.9	2.2	5.6	22.5
San Diego	84.1	4.0	3.1	6.7	22.5
San Francisco	44.5	32.6	10.1	7.0	30.5
San Jose	88.8	3.5	1.7	3.9	25.9
San Leandro	81.9	11.2	1.8	3.0	28.4
San Marcos	92.0	1.6	1.3	4.3	24.7
San Mateo	82.1	7.6	3.5	4.2	24.9
Santa Ana	86.3	7.1	2.4	1.4	24.9
Santa Barbara	74.5	6.1	6.8	5.8	16.7
Santa Clara	87.1	3.6	3.3	3.7	21.8
Santa Clarita	88.4	3.2	1.5	5.7	32.2
Santa Maria	92.9	1.9	1.7	2.1	21.1
Santa Monica	76.0	3.8	5.6	9.5	26.2
Santa Rosa	88.6	1.9	3.0	4.7	22.8
Simi Valley	90.4	1.3	1.0	5.8	28.4
South Gate	87.2	6.9	2.3	2.3	29.0
Stockton	91.7	1.3	1.6	3.6	27.0
Sunnyvale	87.0	4.5	1.3	4.3	23.0
Temecula	88.4	0.7	1.3	6.9	33.7
Thousand Oaks	86.8	0.8	2.4	7.8	24.3
Torrance	89.4	2.5	1.8	4.5	25.8
Tracy	90.6	2.4	1.4	4.3	40.8
Vacaville	93.7	0.8	1.8	2.6	25.8
Vallejo	87.8	4.7	2.0	3.9	33.0
Victorville	91.8	1.1	0.9	5.2	35.6
Visalia	90.9	1.0	1.3	4.2	19.9
Vista	91.3	2.5	1.4	3.6	23.9
West Covina	91.0	3.4	0.6	3.5	33.2
Westminster	90.9	2.4	1.8	2.8	26.8
Whittier	90.0	2.7	2.2	2.8	29.8

SOURCE: U.S. Census Bureau, American Community Survey, 2009-2013 Five-Year Estimates

Crime

Place	Violent Crime Rate (crimes per 10,000 population)	Property Crime Rate (crimes per 10,000 population)
Alhambra	19.2	209.4
Anaheim	32.7	278.3
Antioch	88.9	417.1
Arden-Arcade	n/a	n/a
Bakersfield	51.3	464.7
Berkeley	48.4	462.7
Buena Park	26.7	262.0
Burbank	16.3	232.0
Carlsbad	20.0	188.7
Carson	42.8	241.0
Chico	33.9	291.5
Chino	32.0	253.3
Chula Vista	23.3	207.2
Citrus Heights	37.5	310.9
Clovis	18.2	342.2
Compton	126.9	259.2
Concord	32.4	347.3
Corona	10.1	214.7
Costa Mesa	22.4	316.0
Daly City	21.3	175.3
Downey	28.8	290.8
East Los Angeles	n/a	n/a
El Cajon	37.8	267.6
El Monte	29.4	188.8
Elk Grove	29.1	184.1
Escondido	40.1	266.7
Fairfield	45.9	325.9
Fontana	35.6	201.0
Fremont	12.2	182.5
Fresno	50.2	443.8
Fullerton	26.6	276.3
Garden Grove	25.9	193.6
Glendale	9.3	163.7
Hawthorne	67.3	260.3
Hayward	39.0	320.9
Hemet	54.7	485.1
Hesperia	40.1	251.6
Huntington Beach	18.5	251.9
Inglewood	66.2	243.4
Irvine	4.8	139.3
Lakewood	27.7	254.3
Lancaster	52.1	218.7
Livermore	32.0	217.0
Long Beach	50.0	276.8
Los Angeles	42.6	221.3
Menifee	12.0	203.3
Merced	68.4	325.5
Mission Viejo	6.5	104.1
Modesto	83.4	489.1
Moreno Valley	31.7	291.7

Place	Violent Crime Rate (crimes per 10,000 population)	Property Crime Rate (crimes per 10,000 population)
Murrieta	6.5	152.2
Newport Beach	8.3	246.2
Norwalk	38.2	210.9
Oakland	197.7	623.3
Oceanside	36.7	260.5
Ontario	26.9	268.0
Orange	10.5	172.3
Oxnard	32.1	250.5
Palmdale	48.5	213.6
Pasadena	31.2	271.9
Pomona	53.4	290.3
Rancho Cucamonga	19.2	222.0
Redding	64.3	414.6
Rialto	42.3	265.0
Richmond	103.6	449.6
Riverside	42.0	335.2
Roseville	20.7	264.8
Sacramento	65.6	376.0
Salinas	64.3	343.9
San Bernardino	90.9	438.1
San Buenaventura (Ventura)	24.2	372.2
San Diego	39.3	235.1
San Francisco	84.7	579.5
San Jose	32.4	257.1
San Leandro	45.0	452.6
San Marcos	24.4	159.6
San Mateo	23.8	205.6
Santa Ana	33.7	193.0
Santa Barbara	40.2	296.6
Santa Clara	14.3	251.6
Santa Clarita	13.5	132.4
Santa Maria	48.0	287.5
Santa Monica	35.0	383.2
Santa Rosa	31.5	204.4
Simi Valley	10.5	135.4
South Gate	51.9	282.2
Stockton	120.8	503.0
Sunnyvale	9.7	164.3
Temecula	8.5	267.0
Thousand Oaks	10.8	124.5
Torrance	12.7	188.8
Tracy	17.8	262.5
Vacaville	21.3	222.2
Vallejo	86.1	484.6
Victorville	53.5	342.2
Visalia	39.1	379.7
Vista	46.0	211.5
West Covina	21.4	312.4
Westminster	30.8	269.5
Whittier	25.8	275.7

NOTE: n/a not available.
SOURCE: Federal Bureau of Investigation, Uniform Crime Reports, 2013

Community Rankings

This section ranks incorporated places and CDPs (Census Designated Places) with populations of 10,000 or more. Unincorporated postal areas were not considered. For each topic below, you will find two tables, one in Descending Order—highest to lowest, and one in Ascending Order—lowest to highest. Four topics are exceptions to this rule, and only include Descending Order—Water Area, Ancestry (five tables), Native Hawaiian/Other Pacific Islander, and Commute to Work: Public Transportation. This is because there are an extraordinarily large number of places that place at the bottom of these topics with zero numbers.

Land Area

Top 150 Places Ranked in *Descending* Order

State Rank	Nat'l Rank	Sq. Miles	Place
1	9	468.670	**Los Angeles** (city) Los Angeles County
2	18	325.188	**San Diego** (city) San Diego County
3	37	203.523	**California City** (city) Kern County
4	45	176.526	**San Jose** (city) Santa Clara County
5	59	142.164	**Bakersfield** (city) Kern County
6	85	111.957	**Fresno** (city) Fresno County
7	98	105.961	**Palmdale** (city) Los Angeles County
8	121	97.915	**Sacramento** (city) Sacramento County
9	130	94.276	**Lancaster** (city) Los Angeles County
10	132	94.116	**Palm Springs** (city) Riverside County
11	152	81.140	**Riverside** (city) Riverside County
12	164	77.459	**Fremont** (city) Alameda County
13	176	73.193	**Apple Valley** (town) San Bernardino County
14	178	73.178	**Victorville** (city) San Bernardino County
15	180	73.096	**Hesperia** (city) San Bernardino County
16	207	66.106	**Irvine** (city) Orange County
17	236	61.670	**Stockton** (city) San Joaquin County
18	254	60.097	**Phelan** (CDP) San Bernardino County
19	260	59.647	**Redding** (city) Shasta County
20	268	59.201	**San Bernardino** (city) San Bernardino County
21	269	59.143	**Twentynine Palms** (city) San Bernardino County
22	291	56.009	**Adelanto** (city) San Bernardino County
23	295	55.786	**Oakland** (city) Alameda County
24	311	55.031	**Thousand Oaks** (city) Ventura County
25	336	52.716	**Santa Clarita** (city) Los Angeles County
26	341	52.121	**Rosamond** (CDP) Kern County
27	352	51.275	**Moreno Valley** (city) Riverside County
28	360	50.293	**Long Beach** (city) Los Angeles County
29	362	49.941	**Ontario** (city) San Bernardino County
30	366	49.835	**Anaheim** (city) Orange County
31	370	49.631	**Chula Vista** (city) San Diego County
32	385	48.454	**El Dorado Hills** (CDP) El Dorado County
33	411	46.873	**San Francisco** (city) San Francisco County
34	419	46.466	**Menifee** (city) Riverside County
35	429	46.054	**Prunedale** (CDP) Monterey County
36	441	45.323	**Hayward** (city) Alameda County
37	450	44.681	**Chino Hills** (city) San Bernardino County
38	490	42.432	**Fontana** (city) San Bernardino County
39	499	42.190	**Elk Grove** (city) Sacramento County
40	521	41.480	**Simi Valley** (city) Ventura County
41	526	41.385	**Barstow** (city) San Bernardino County
42	531	41.294	**Santa Rosa** (city) Sonoma County
43	533	41.235	**Oceanside** (city) San Diego County
44	557	40.015	**Yucca Valley** (town) San Bernardino County
45	562	39.851	**Rancho Cucamonga** (city) San Bernardino County
46	579	39.079	**Poway** (city) San Diego County
47	587	38.825	**Corona** (city) Riverside County
48	601	38.412	**Ramona** (CDP) San Diego County
49	611	37.722	**Carlsbad** (city) San Diego County
50	620	37.390	**Fairfield** (city) Solano County
51	633	36.867	**Modesto** (city) Stanislaus County
52	637	36.813	**Escondido** (city) San Diego County
53	656	36.246	**Visalia** (city) Tulare County
54	658	36.222	**Roseville** (city) Placer County
55	660	36.208	**Lake Elsinore** (city) Riverside County
56	663	36.126	**Redlands** (city) San Bernardino County
57	724	35.117	**La Quinta** (city) Riverside County
58	787	33.964	**Rosedale** (CDP) Kern County
59	810	33.577	**Murrieta** (city) Riverside County
60	814	33.507	**Rancho Cordova** (city) Sacramento County
61	845	32.923	**Chico** (city) Butte County
62	872	32.322	**Truckee** (town) Nevada County
63	892	31.954	**Big Bear City** (CDP) San Bernardino County
64	916	31.393	**Perris** (city) Riverside County
65	936	30.912	**Beaumont** (city) Riverside County
66	948	30.671	**Vallejo** (city) Solano County
67	956	30.546	**Concord** (city) Contra Costa County
68	960	30.453	**Glendale** (city) Los Angeles County
69	971	30.151	**Temecula** (city) Riverside County
70	974	30.068	**Richmond** (city) Contra Costa County
71	989	29.639	**Chino** (city) San Bernardino County
72	1017	29.181	**Indio** (city) Riverside County
73	1026	28.950	**Coachella** (city) Riverside County
74	1062	28.373	**Vacaville** (city) Solano County
75	1064	28.349	**Antioch** (city) Contra Costa County
76	1084	27.945	**Shafter** (city) Kern County
77	1088	27.888	**Yucaipa** (city) San Bernardino County
78	1089	27.847	**Hemet** (city) Riverside County
79	1110	27.440	**Novato** (city) Marin County
80	1121	27.270	**Santa Ana** (city) Orange County
81	1148	26.894	**Oxnard** (city) Ventura County
82	1152	26.810	**Palm Desert** (city) Riverside County
83	1159	26.781	**Alpine** (CDP) San Diego County
84	1161	26.748	**Huntington Beach** (city) Orange County
85	1194	26.189	**Blythe** (city) Riverside County
86	1209	25.716	**San Jacinto** (city) Riverside County
87	1214	25.641	**Atascadero** (city) San Luis Obispo County
88	1239	25.173	**Livermore** (city) Alameda County
89	1258	24.797	**Orange** (city) Orange County
90	1279	24.447	**Rancho Mirage** (city) Riverside County
91	1284	24.370	**San Marcos** (city) San Diego County
92	1301	24.113	**Pleasanton** (city) Alameda County
93	1318	23.884	**Palo Alto** (city) Santa Clara County
94	1321	23.805	**Newport Beach** (city) Orange County
95	1329	23.688	**Wildomar** (city) Riverside County
96	1334	23.615	**Desert Hot Springs** (city) Riverside County
97	1351	23.316	**Merced** (city) Merced County
98	1355	23.278	**Clovis** (city) Fresno County
99	1367	23.179	**Salinas** (city) Monterey County
100	1374	23.099	**Banning** (city) Riverside County
101	1383	22.970	**Pasadena** (city) Los Angeles County
102	1385	22.952	**Pomona** (city) Los Angeles County
103	1401	22.756	**Santa Maria** (city) Santa Barbara County
104	1428	22.353	**Fullerton** (city) Orange County
105	1429	22.351	**Rialto** (city) San Bernardino County
106	1457	22.003	**Tracy** (city) San Joaquin County
107	1461	21.987	**Sunnyvale** (city) Santa Clara County
108	1462	21.945	**Folsom** (city) Sacramento County
109	1464	21.931	**Lathrop** (city) San Joaquin County
110	1485	21.655	**San Buenaventura (Ventura)** (city) Ventura County
111	1492	21.528	**Granite Bay** (CDP) Placer County
112	1493	21.499	**Cathedral City** (city) Riverside County
113	1499	21.425	**West Sacramento** (city) Yolo County
114	1523	20.931	**Tulare** (city) Tulare County
115	1540	20.796	**McKinleyville** (CDP) Humboldt County
116	1544	20.766	**Ridgecrest** (city) Kern County
117	1565	20.478	**Torrance** (city) Los Angeles County
118	1594	20.106	**Lincoln** (city) Placer County
119	1625	19.785	**Malibu** (city) Los Angeles County
120	1632	19.757	**Walnut Creek** (city) Contra Costa County
121	1646	19.541	**Rocklin** (city) Placer County
122	1647	19.528	**Camarillo** (city) Ventura County
123	1650	19.483	**Yorba Linda** (city) Orange County
124	1651	19.469	**Union City** (city) Alameda County
125	1652	19.468	**Santa Barbara** (city) Santa Barbara County
126	1657	19.422	**Avenal** (city) Kings County
127	1658	19.420	**Redwood City** (city) San Mateo County
128	1660	19.393	**Glendora** (city) Los Angeles County
129	1670	19.169	**Mead Valley** (CDP) Riverside County
130	1675	19.120	**El Paso de Robles (Paso Robles)** (city) San Luis Obispo County
131	1699	18.812	**Encinitas** (city) San Diego County
132	1706	18.755	**Highland** (city) San Bernardino County
133	1709	18.724	**Carson** (city) Los Angeles County
134	1710	18.711	**San Clemente** (city) Orange County
135	1714	18.678	**Vista** (city) San Diego County
136	1736	18.407	**Santa Clara** (city) Santa Clara County
137	1751	18.308	**Paradise** (town) Butte County
138	1764	18.061	**San Ramon** (city) Contra Costa County
139	1767	18.028	**Danville** (town) Contra Costa County
140	1774	17.941	**Garden Grove** (city) Orange County
141	1783	17.839	**Napa** (city) Napa County
142	1785	17.829	**Arden-Arcade** (CDP) Sacramento County
143	1787	17.816	**Lake Forest** (city) Orange County
144	1793	17.739	**Mission Viejo** (city) Orange County
145	1795	17.733	**Manteca** (city) San Joaquin County
146	1796	17.727	**Lake Arrowhead** (CDP) San Bernardino County
147	1805	17.607	**Porterville** (city) Tulare County
148	1810	17.528	**Fallbrook** (CDP) San Diego County
149	1823	17.341	**Burbank** (city) Los Angeles County
150	1835	17.218	**Pittsburg** (city) Contra Costa County

Note: *The state column ranks the top/bottom 150 places from all places in the state with population of 10,000 or more. The national column ranks the top/bottom 150 places from all places in the country with population of 10,000 or more. Places that are unincorporated were not considered in the rankings. Please refer to the User Guide for additional information.*

Land Area

Top 150 Places Ranked in *Ascending* Order

State Rank	Nat'l Rank	Sq. Miles	Place
1	2	0.748	**Walnut Park** (CDP) Los Angeles County
2	5	0.822	**East Rancho Dominguez** (CDP) Los Angeles County
3	8	0.887	**Citrus** (CDP) Los Angeles County
4	10	0.946	**Hawaiian Gardens** (city) Los Angeles County
5	15	1.014	**Del Aire** (CDP) Los Angeles County
6	19	1.093	**Lennox** (CDP) Los Angeles County
7	21	1.175	**Cudahy** (city) Los Angeles County
8	22	1.178	**Maywood** (city) Los Angeles County
9	24	1.197	**Cherryland** (CDP) Alameda County
10	26	1.200	**North Fair Oaks** (CDP) San Mateo County
11	28	1.204	**Alum Rock** (CDP) Santa Clara County
12	32	1.246	**Emeryville** (city) Alameda County
13	41	1.427	**Hermosa Beach** (city) Los Angeles County
14	47	1.508	**South San Jose Hills** (CDP) Los Angeles County
15	50	1.538	**Rossmoor** (CDP) Orange County
16	51	1.556	**Home Gardens** (CDP) Riverside County
17	52	1.561	**East San Gabriel** (CDP) Los Angeles County
18	57	1.621	**Artesia** (city) Los Angeles County
19	58	1.627	**Lemon Hill** (CDP) Sacramento County
20	62	1.678	**Piedmont** (city) Alameda County
21	69	1.761	**West Puente Valley** (CDP) Los Angeles County
22	72	1.788	**Albany** (city) Alameda County
23	73	1.808	**La Palma** (city) Orange County
24	80	1.838	**Ashland** (CDP) Alameda County
25	81	1.841	**View Park-Windsor Hills** (CDP) Los Angeles County
26	84	1.848	**Westmont** (CDP) Los Angeles County
27	85	1.849	**Isla Vista** (CDP) Santa Barbara County
28	86	1.850	**La Riviera** (CDP) Sacramento County
29	91	1.887	**West Hollywood** (city) Los Angeles County
30	94	1.911	**Lomita** (city) Los Angeles County
31	96	1.929	**Bostonia** (CDP) San Diego County
32	103	1.974	**Lawndale** (city) Los Angeles County
33	113	2.014	**Valinda** (CDP) Los Angeles County
34	125	2.102	**Newman** (city) Stanislaus County
35	129	2.135	**Greenfield** (city) Monterey County
36	135	2.189	**Signal Hill** (city) Los Angeles County
37	137	2.194	**Parlier** (city) Fresno County
38	149	2.258	**Farmersville** (city) Tulare County
39	152	2.266	**West Carson** (CDP) Los Angeles County
40	161	2.310	**Grover Beach** (city) San Luis Obispo County
41	172	2.374	**San Fernando** (city) Los Angeles County
42	178	2.418	**Parkway** (CDP) Sacramento County
43	183	2.459	**Bell Gardens** (city) Los Angeles County
44	184	2.463	**Exeter** (city) Tulare County
45	189	2.501	**Bell** (city) Los Angeles County
46	192	2.505	**East Palo Alto** (city) San Mateo County
47	194	2.519	**West Whittier-Los Nietos** (CDP) Los Angeles County
48	210	2.586	**Carpinteria** (city) Santa Barbara County
49	211	2.589	**Garden Acres** (CDP) San Joaquin County
50	215	2.610	**Lindsay** (city) Tulare County
51	221	2.634	**San Pablo** (city) Contra Costa County
52	231	2.668	**McFarland** (city) Kern County
53	232	2.677	**San Anselmo** (town) Marin County
54	242	2.706	**Avocado Heights** (CDP) Los Angeles County
55	251	2.731	**Stanford** (CDP) Santa Clara County
56	254	2.742	**Sonoma** (city) Sonoma County
57	259	2.763	**San Lorenzo** (CDP) Alameda County
58	261	2.765	**Fairview** (CDP) Alameda County
59	262	2.765	**El Sobrante** (CDP) Contra Costa County
60	281	2.828	**Kingsburg** (city) Fresno County
61	284	2.843	**South El Monte** (city) Los Angeles County
62	290	2.865	**Pacific Grove** (city) Monterey County
63	310	2.953	**Sierra Madre** (city) Los Angeles County
64	323	3.013	**Huntington Park** (city) Los Angeles County
65	327	3.027	**Larkspur** (city) Marin County
66	330	3.041	**Winton** (CDP) Merced County
67	340	3.115	**Laguna Woods** (city) Orange County
68	344	3.143	**Muscoy** (CDP) San Bernardino County
69	348	3.150	**Stanton** (city) Orange County
70	364	3.233	**Kerman** (city) Fresno County
71	365	3.243	**Live Oak** (CDP) Santa Cruz County
72	367	3.247	**Millbrae** (city) San Mateo County
73	373	3.278	**Mendota** (city) Fresno County
74	384	3.364	**Fillmore** (city) Ventura County
75	393	3.405	**South Pasadena** (city) Los Angeles County
76	400	3.426	**La Crescenta-Montrose** (CDP) Los Angeles County
77	405	3.464	**Marysville** (city) Yuba County
78	408	3.479	**La Puente** (city) Los Angeles County
79	415	3.502	**Grand Terrace** (city) San Bernardino County
80	419	3.510	**Delhi** (CDP) Merced County
81	423	3.520	**Solana Beach** (city) San Diego County
82	433	3.580	**Florence-Graham** (CDP) Los Angeles County
83	453	3.688	**El Cerrito** (city) Contra Costa County
84	462	3.715	**Livingston** (city) Merced County
85	469	3.756	**Foster City** (city) San Mateo County
86	471	3.762	**Quartz Hill** (CDP) Los Angeles County
87	472	3.762	**Willowbrook** (CDP) Los Angeles County
88	473	3.767	**San Marino** (city) Los Angeles County
89	492	3.836	**Clayton** (city) Contra Costa County
90	494	3.845	**King City** (city) Monterey County
91	503	3.880	**Lemon Grove** (city) San Diego County
92	512	3.907	**Camp Pendleton South** (CDP) San Diego County
93	517	3.928	**Canyon Lake** (city) Riverside County
94	521	3.937	**Manhattan Beach** (city) Los Angeles County
95	537	4.006	**Temple City** (city) Los Angeles County
96	547	4.050	**Los Alamitos** (city) Orange County
97	558	4.092	**Riverbank** (city) Stanislaus County
98	559	4.105	**Suisun City** (city) Solano County
99	569	4.145	**San Gabriel** (city) Los Angeles County
100	572	4.161	**Imperial Beach** (city) San Diego County
101	585	4.198	**Foothill Farms** (CDP) Sacramento County
102	624	4.349	**Rosemont** (CDP) Sacramento County
103	642	4.406	**Burlingame** (city) San Mateo County
104	643	4.414	**Soledad** (city) Monterey County
105	647	4.430	**Winter Gardens** (CDP) San Diego County
106	653	4.451	**Port Hueneme** (city) Ventura County
107	654	4.457	**Healdsburg** (city) Sonoma County
108	682	4.590	**Lamont** (CDP) Kern County
109	683	4.593	**Santa Paula** (city) Ventura County
110	685	4.595	**Scotts Valley** (city) Santa Cruz County
111	696	4.621	**Belmont** (city) San Mateo County
112	700	4.637	**Tamalpais-Homestead Valley** (CDP) Marin County
113	711	4.670	**Ukiah** (city) Mendocino County
114	722	4.729	**Paramount** (city) Los Angeles County
115	726	4.743	**Grass Valley** (city) Nevada County
116	733	4.763	**Mill Valley** (city) Marin County
117	736	4.774	**Palos Verdes Estates** (city) Los Angeles County
118	744	4.819	**Arvin** (city) Kern County
119	751	4.837	**American Canyon** (city) Napa County
120	754	4.840	**Lynwood** (city) Los Angeles County
121	755	4.845	**Fortuna** (city) Humboldt County
122	767	4.905	**Ladera Ranch** (CDP) Orange County
123	789	4.996	**Bonita** (CDP) San Diego County
124	811	5.084	**Reedley** (city) Fresno County
125	816	5.111	**Culver City** (city) Los Angeles County
126	820	5.136	**Selma** (city) Fresno County
127	828	5.162	**Rosemead** (city) Los Angeles County
128	841	5.213	**East Hemet** (CDP) Riverside County
129	855	5.290	**Oak Park** (CDP) Ventura County
130	857	5.303	**Morro Bay** (city) San Luis Obispo County
131	860	5.305	**Ripon** (city) San Joaquin County
132	864	5.320	**Salida** (CDP) Stanislaus County
133	865	5.323	**Pinole** (city) Contra Costa County
134	869	5.337	**South Whittier** (CDP) Los Angeles County
135	895	5.463	**El Segundo** (city) Los Angeles County
136	899	5.478	**San Bruno** (city) San Mateo County
137	903	5.496	**La Presa** (CDP) San Diego County
138	907	5.517	**Montclair** (city) San Bernardino County
139	912	5.524	**Sanger** (city) Fresno County
140	915	5.538	**San Carlos** (city) San Mateo County
141	950	5.708	**Beverly Hills** (city) Los Angeles County
142	973	5.798	**Campbell** (city) Santa Clara County
143	976	5.812	**Placerville** (city) El Dorado County
144	983	5.829	**Gardena** (city) Los Angeles County
145	984	5.835	**Arroyo Grande** (city) San Luis Obispo County
146	993	5.856	**Imperial** (city) Imperial County
147	1019	5.931	**Galt** (city) Sacramento County
148	1025	5.954	**Patterson** (city) Stanislaus County
149	1030	5.987	**Bloomington** (CDP) San Bernardino County
150	1045	6.045	**Oakdale** (city) Stanislaus County

Note: *The state column ranks the top/bottom 150 places from all places in the state with population of 10,000 or more. The national column ranks the top/bottom 150 places from all places in the country with population of 10,000 or more. Places that are unincorporated were not considered in the rankings. Please refer to the User Guide for additional information.*

Water Area

Top 150 Places Ranked in *Descending* Order

State Rank	Nat'l Rank	Sq. Miles	Place
1	8	185.016	**San Francisco** (city) San Francisco County
2	33	47.210	**San Diego** (city) San Diego County
3	46	34.023	**Los Angeles** (city) Los Angeles County
4	48	29.173	**Newport Beach** (city) Orange County
5	57	24.735	**Coronado** (city) San Diego County
6	64	22.987	**Dana Point** (city) Orange County
7	65	22.500	**Santa Barbara** (city) Santa Barbara County
8	66	22.412	**Richmond** (city) Contra Costa County
9	69	22.216	**Oakland** (city) Alameda County
10	71	21.017	**South San Francisco** (city) San Mateo County
11	76	18.869	**Vallejo** (city) Solano County
12	79	18.425	**Hayward** (city) Alameda County
13	86	16.085	**Foster City** (city) San Mateo County
14	95	15.205	**Redwood City** (city) San Mateo County
15	124	12.349	**Alameda** (city) Alameda County
16	125	12.314	**Oxnard** (city) Ventura County
17	131	11.974	**Hercules** (city) Contra Costa County
18	147	10.440	**San Buenaventura (Ventura)** (city) Ventura County
19	154	10.151	**Fremont** (city) Alameda County
20	180	8.252	**Pinole** (city) Contra Costa County
21	192	7.625	**Menlo Park** (city) San Mateo County
22	205	7.226	**Berkeley** (city) Alameda County
23	217	6.686	**Carpinteria** (city) Santa Barbara County
24	227	6.442	**South Lake Tahoe** (city) El Dorado County
25	243	5.952	**San Rafael** (city) Marin County
26	254	5.479	**Lake Elsinore** (city) Riverside County
27	269	5.134	**Huntington Beach** (city) Orange County
28	270	5.070	**Eureka** (city) Humboldt County
29	272	5.019	**Morro Bay** (city) San Luis Obispo County
30	337	3.754	**San Mateo** (city) San Mateo County
31	351	3.677	**Albany** (city) Alameda County
32	372	3.439	**San Jose** (city) Santa Clara County
33	388	3.298	**Monterey** (city) Monterey County
34	412	3.088	**Santa Cruz** (city) Santa Cruz County
35	414	3.083	**Stockton** (city) San Joaquin County
36	438	2.791	**Benicia** (city) Solano County
37	487	2.463	**Chula Vista** (city) San Diego County
38	507	2.356	**Folsom** (city) Sacramento County
39	514	2.320	**San Leandro** (city) Alameda County
40	542	2.190	**Sacramento** (city) Sacramento County
41	589	1.936	**Pittsburg** (city) Contra Costa County
42	598	1.903	**Palo Alto** (city) Santa Clara County
43	603	1.897	**Arcata** (city) Humboldt County
44	615	1.839	**National City** (city) San Diego County
45	643	1.754	**Seal Beach** (city) Orange County
46	668	1.651	**Burlingame** (city) San Mateo County
47	702	1.528	**Redding** (city) Shasta County
48	739	1.445	**Bakersfield** (city) Kern County
49	749	1.421	**West Sacramento** (city) Yolo County
50	765	1.388	**Carlsbad** (city) San Diego County
51	791	1.332	**Truckee** (town) Nevada County
52	854	1.224	**Lake Arrowhead** (CDP) San Bernardino County
53	876	1.178	**Encinitas** (city) San Diego County
54	885	1.144	**Long Beach** (city) Los Angeles County
55	891	1.138	**Pacific Grove** (city) Monterey County
56	901	1.102	**Lathrop** (city) San Joaquin County
57	971	1.004	**Martinez** (city) Contra Costa County
58	983	0.976	**Anaheim** (city) Orange County
59	986	0.971	**Laguna Beach** (city) Orange County
60	1004	0.939	**Oceanside** (city) San Diego County
61	1044	0.880	**Marina** (city) Monterey County
62	1062	0.859	**Palm Springs** (city) Riverside County
63	1092	0.821	**Discovery Bay** (CDP) Contra Costa County
64	1094	0.817	**Bay Point** (CDP) Contra Costa County
65	1127	0.783	**Blythe** (city) Riverside County
66	1140	0.767	**Simi Valley** (city) Ventura County
67	1141	0.764	**Emeryville** (city) Alameda County
68	1149	0.757	**San Clemente** (city) Orange County
69	1160	0.743	**Canyon Lake** (city) Riverside County
70	1168	0.734	**Antioch** (city) Contra Costa County
71	1186	0.715	**Colton** (city) San Bernardino County
72	1196	0.702	**Sunnyvale** (city) Santa Clara County
73	1251	0.651	**Ridgecrest** (city) Kern County
74	1258	0.639	**Santa Maria** (city) Santa Barbara County
75	1306	0.586	**Pico Rivera** (city) Los Angeles County
76	1338	0.563	**Victorville** (city) San Bernardino County
77	1376	0.535	**Yorba Linda** (city) Orange County
78	1395	0.522	**La Presa** (CDP) San Diego County
79	1401	0.517	**Novato** (city) Marin County
80	1440	0.489	**Atascadero** (city) San Luis Obispo County
81	1490	0.452	**Fair Oaks** (CDP) Sacramento County
82	1492	0.452	**Clearlake** (city) Lake County
83	1497	0.444	**San Bernardino** (city) San Bernardino County
84	1499	0.443	**Orange** (city) Orange County
85	1515	0.434	**La Quinta** (city) Riverside County
86	1554	0.415	**San Jacinto** (city) Riverside County
87	1587	0.390	**San Dimas** (city) Los Angeles County
88	1588	0.389	**Rancho Mirage** (city) Riverside County
89	1597	0.384	**Mission Viejo** (city) Orange County
90	1605	0.380	**Lakeside** (CDP) San Diego County
91	1629	0.367	**Rancho Cordova** (city) Sacramento County
92	1660	0.351	**Fresno** (city) Fresno County
93	1669	0.348	**Irvine** (city) Orange County
94	1715	0.330	**Apple Valley** (town) San Bernardino County
95	1745	0.324	**Imperial Beach** (city) San Diego County
96	1760	0.316	**Norco** (city) Riverside County
97	1782	0.308	**Napa** (city) Napa County
98	1785	0.305	**El Paso de Robles (Paso Robles)** (city) San Luis Obispo County
99	1787	0.304	**Riverside** (city) Riverside County
100	1795	0.302	**Oakley** (city) Contra Costa County
101	1799	0.301	**Redlands** (city) San Bernardino County
102	1823	0.293	**Santee** (city) San Diego County
103	1853	0.284	**Castro Valley** (CDP) Alameda County
104	1865	0.278	**Mountain View** (city) Santa Clara County
105	1884	0.271	**Lancaster** (city) Los Angeles County
106	1894	0.265	**Carmichael** (CDP) Sacramento County
107	1918	0.257	**Cathedral City** (city) Riverside County
108	1930	0.255	**Palmdale** (city) Los Angeles County
109	1946	0.251	**Salida** (CDP) Stanislaus County
110	1958	0.248	**Santa Ana** (city) Orange County
111	1970	0.245	**Fairfield** (city) Solano County
112	1977	0.244	**Carson** (city) Los Angeles County
113	1981	0.242	**La Riviera** (CDP) Sacramento County
114	2039	0.225	**Modesto** (city) Stanislaus County
115	2053	0.220	**Moorpark** (city) Ventura County
116	2054	0.220	**Port Hueneme** (city) Ventura County
117	2068	0.218	**McKinleyville** (CDP) Humboldt County
118	2074	0.216	**Larkspur** (city) Marin County
119	2077	0.215	**Rosamond** (CDP) Kern County
120	2079	0.214	**Lodi** (city) San Joaquin County
121	2082	0.212	**Vacaville** (city) Solano County
122	2094	0.209	**Spring Valley** (CDP) San Diego County
123	2100	0.208	**Arcadia** (city) Los Angeles County
124	2102	0.208	**Valle Vista** (CDP) Riverside County
125	2115	0.205	**Santa Rosa** (city) Sonoma County
126	2118	0.204	**Palm Desert** (city) Riverside County
127	2137	0.200	**Moreno Valley** (city) Riverside County
128	2176	0.190	**Ripon** (city) San Joaquin County
129	2206	0.180	**San Juan Capistrano** (city) Orange County
130	2223	0.176	**Escondido** (city) San Diego County
131	2247	0.172	**Chico** (city) Butte County
132	2283	0.166	**Lafayette** (city) Contra Costa County
133	2292	0.165	**Glendora** (city) Los Angeles County
134	2318	0.160	**Downey** (city) Los Angeles County
135	2328	0.158	**Pasadena** (city) Los Angeles County
136	2337	0.155	**Baldwin Park** (city) Los Angeles County
137	2343	0.153	**San Luis Obispo** (city) San Luis Obispo County
138	2346	0.153	**Pleasanton** (city) Alameda County
139	2350	0.152	**El Dorado Hills** (CDP) El Dorado County
140	2352	0.152	**Soledad** (city) Monterey County
141	2362	0.150	**Thousand Oaks** (city) Ventura County
142	2378	0.146	**Prunedale** (CDP) Monterey County
143	2400	0.141	**Menifee** (city) Riverside County
144	2408	0.140	**Crestline** (CDP) San Bernardino County
145	2415	0.139	**King City** (city) Monterey County
146	2416	0.139	**Bonita** (CDP) San Diego County
147	2418	0.139	**Seaside** (city) Monterey County
148	2421	0.138	**Claremont** (city) Los Angeles County
149	2442	0.136	**Tracy** (city) San Joaquin County
150	2446	0.136	**Avocado Heights** (CDP) Los Angeles County

Note: *The state column ranks the top/bottom 150 places from all places in the state with population of 10,000 or more. The national column ranks the top/bottom 150 places from all places in the country with population of 10,000 or more. Places that are unincorporated were not considered in the rankings. Please refer to the User Guide for additional information.*

Elevation

Top 150 Places Ranked in *Descending* Order

State Rank	Nat'l Rank	Feet	Place
1	7	6,772	**Big Bear City** (CDP) San Bernardino County
2	17	6,237	**South Lake Tahoe** (city) El Dorado County
3	28	5,817	**Truckee** (town) Nevada County
4	64	5,174	**Lake Arrowhead** (CDP) San Bernardino County
5	105	4,613	**Crestline** (CDP) San Bernardino County
6	156	4,186	**Susanville** (city) Lassen County
7	160	4,121	**Phelan** (CDP) San Bernardino County
8	166	3,970	**Tehachapi** (city) Kern County
9	191	3,369	**Yucca Valley** (town) San Bernardino County
10	204	3,186	**Hesperia** (city) San Bernardino County
11	215	2,946	**Apple Valley** (town) San Bernardino County
12	218	2,871	**Adelanto** (city) San Bernardino County
13	225	2,726	**Victorville** (city) San Bernardino County
14	233	2,661	**Lake Los Angeles** (CDP) Los Angeles County
15	234	2,657	**Palmdale** (city) Los Angeles County
16	236	2,618	**Yucaipa** (city) San Bernardino County
17	237	2,612	**Beaumont** (city) Riverside County
18	248	2,497	**Quartz Hill** (CDP) Los Angeles County
19	253	2,411	**Grass Valley** (city) Nevada County
20	256	2,405	**California City** (city) Kern County
21	260	2,359	**Lancaster** (city) Los Angeles County
22	263	2,349	**Banning** (city) Riverside County
23	264	2,342	**Rosamond** (CDP) Kern County
24	265	2,333	**Magalia** (CDP) Butte County
25	267	2,290	**Ridgecrest** (city) Kern County
26	274	2,175	**Barstow** (city) San Bernardino County
27	288	1,988	**Twentynine Palms** (city) San Bernardino County
28	297	1,867	**Placerville** (city) El Dorado County
29	306	1,834	**Alpine** (CDP) San Diego County
30	308	1,791	**Diamond Springs** (CDP) El Dorado County
31	309	1,778	**Paradise** (town) Butte County
32	310	1,775	**Valle Vista** (CDP) Riverside County
33	316	1,690	**East Hemet** (CDP) Riverside County
34	317	1,683	**Agoura Hills** (city) Los Angeles County
35	321	1,657	**Mead Valley** (CDP) Riverside County
36	327	1,631	**Moreno Valley** (city) Riverside County
37	332	1,594	**Hemet** (city) Riverside County
38	334	1,572	**La Crescenta-Montrose** (CDP) Los Angeles County
39	336	1,565	**San Jacinto** (city) Riverside County
40	338	1,535	**Woodcrest** (CDP) Riverside County
41	345	1,509	**San Diego Country Estates** (CDP) San Diego County
42	350	1,483	**Menifee** (city) Riverside County
43	353	1,470	**North Auburn** (CDP) Placer County
44	354	1,453	**Perris** (city) Riverside County
45	358	1,427	**Ramona** (CDP) San Diego County
46	362	1,417	**Clearlake** (city) Lake County
47	371	1,388	**Muscoy** (CDP) San Bernardino County
48	372	1,384	**Canyon Lake** (city) Riverside County
49	377	1,365	**French Valley** (CDP) Riverside County
50	379	1,358	**Altadena** (CDP) Los Angeles County
50	379	1,358	**Redlands** (city) San Bernardino County
52	390	1,309	**Highland** (city) San Bernardino County
53	400	1,296	**Lake Elsinore** (city) Riverside County
54	410	1,283	**Lakeland Village** (CDP) Riverside County
55	416	1,270	**Wildomar** (city) Riverside County
56	419	1,257	**Rialto** (city) San Bernardino County
57	431	1,237	**Fontana** (city) San Bernardino County
57	431	1,237	**Upland** (city) San Bernardino County
59	438	1,227	**Auburn** (city) Placer County
59	438	1,227	**Castaic** (CDP) Los Angeles County
61	446	1,207	**Rancho Cucamonga** (city) San Bernardino County
61	446	1,207	**Santa Clarita** (city) Los Angeles County
63	451	1,204	**Cameron Park** (CDP) El Dorado County
64	467	1,188	**La Cañada Flintridge** (city) Los Angeles County
65	484	1,168	**Claremont** (city) Los Angeles County
66	488	1,165	**Loma Linda** (city) San Bernardino County
67	540	1,106	**Oak Park** (CDP) Ventura County
68	545	1,099	**Bloomington** (CDP) San Bernardino County
69	548	1,096	**Murrieta** (city) Riverside County
70	568	1,076	**Desert Hot Springs** (city) Riverside County
71	572	1,070	**San Fernando** (city) Los Angeles County
72	580	1,066	**Montclair** (city) San Bernardino County
73	587	1,063	**Grand Terrace** (city) San Bernardino County
74	591	1,060	**La Verne** (city) Los Angeles County
75	606	1,053	**San Bernardino** (city) San Bernardino County
76	664	1,017	**Temecula** (city) Riverside County
77	680	1,004	**Colton** (city) San Bernardino County
77	680	1,004	**Ontario** (city) San Bernardino County
79	770	955	**San Dimas** (city) Los Angeles County
80	780	948	**Rancho Santa Margarita** (city) Orange County
81	824	928	**Calabasas** (city) Los Angeles County
82	924	886	**Thousand Oaks** (city) Ventura County
83	940	879	**Atascadero** (city) San Luis Obispo County
84	990	863	**Pasadena** (city) Los Angeles County
85	999	860	**Chino Hills** (city) San Bernardino County
86	1021	850	**Pomona** (city) Los Angeles County
87	1073	827	**Riverside** (city) Riverside County
87	1073	827	**Sierra Madre** (city) Los Angeles County
89	1114	807	**Avenal** (city) Kings County
89	1114	807	**Shasta Lake** (city) Shasta County
91	1195	774	**Glendora** (city) Los Angeles County
92	1211	768	**El Dorado Hills** (CDP) El Dorado County
92	1211	768	**Simi Valley** (city) Ventura County
94	1330	728	**Chino** (city) San Bernardino County
95	1391	709	**Coto de Caza** (CDP) Orange County
96	1435	696	**Diamond Bar** (city) Los Angeles County
97	1466	682	**Fallbrook** (CDP) San Diego County
98	1479	679	**Corona** (city) Riverside County
99	1491	676	**Winter Gardens** (CDP) San Diego County
100	1503	673	**Coalinga** (city) Fresno County
101	1511	669	**Home Gardens** (CDP) Riverside County
102	1546	659	**South Pasadena** (city) Los Angeles County
103	1593	646	**Escondido** (city) San Diego County
104	1618	640	**Norco** (city) Riverside County
105	1642	633	**Ukiah** (city) Mendocino County
106	1671	627	**Eastvale** (city) Riverside County
107	1749	610	**Azusa** (city) Los Angeles County
108	1770	607	**Burbank** (city) Los Angeles County
109	1833	597	**Fairview** (CDP) Alameda County
110	1884	584	**Citrus** (CDP) Los Angeles County
111	1891	581	**San Marcos** (city) San Diego County
112	1918	571	**Monrovia** (city) Los Angeles County
113	1929	564	**Redding** (city) Shasta County
113	1929	564	**San Marino** (city) Los Angeles County
115	1936	561	**Scotts Valley** (city) Santa Cruz County
115	1936	561	**Walnut** (city) Los Angeles County
117	1946	558	**Covina** (city) Los Angeles County
118	1959	551	**Ladera Ranch** (CDP) Orange County
119	2001	528	**La Mesa** (city) San Diego County
120	2011	525	**Rowland Heights** (CDP) Los Angeles County
121	2014	522	**Glendale** (city) Los Angeles County
122	2026	515	**Moorpark** (city) Ventura County
122	2026	515	**Poway** (city) San Diego County
124	2036	512	**Duarte** (city) Los Angeles County
125	2070	499	**Moraga** (town) Contra Costa County
126	2079	495	**Orinda** (city) Contra Costa County
127	2085	492	**Alhambra** (city) Los Angeles County
127	2085	492	**Livermore** (city) Alameda County
129	2098	486	**Bostonia** (CDP) San Diego County
129	2098	486	**Lake Forest** (city) Orange County
129	2098	486	**San Ramon** (city) Contra Costa County
132	2104	482	**Arcadia** (city) Los Angeles County
133	2115	479	**Palm Springs** (city) Riverside County
134	2133	469	**Aliso Viejo** (city) Orange County
134	2133	469	**Oildale** (CDP) Kern County
136	2154	459	**Porterville** (city) Tulare County
137	2166	456	**Fillmore** (city) Ventura County
138	2174	453	**Hacienda Heights** (CDP) Los Angeles County
139	2178	449	**Arvin** (city) Kern County
140	2184	446	**Lemon Grove** (city) San Diego County
141	2211	433	**El Cajon** (city) San Diego County
142	2223	427	**Granite Bay** (CDP) Placer County
143	2226	423	**Saratoga** (city) Santa Clara County
144	2234	420	**San Gabriel** (city) Los Angeles County
145	2240	417	**South San Jose Hills** (CDP) Los Angeles County
146	2250	413	**Lakeside** (CDP) San Diego County
147	2268	407	**Daly City** (city) San Mateo County
148	2280	404	**Bakersfield** (city) Kern County
148	2280	404	**Lamont** (CDP) Kern County
150	2283	400	**Temple City** (city) Los Angeles County

Note: *The state column ranks the top/bottom 150 places from all places in the state with population of 10,000 or more. The national column ranks the top/bottom 150 places from all places in the country with population of 10,000 or more. Places that are unincorporated were not considered in the rankings. Please refer to the User Guide for additional information.*

Elevation

Top 150 Places Ranked in *Ascending* Order

State Rank	Nat'l Rank	Feet	Place
1	1	-112	**Brawley** (city) Imperial County
2	2	-69	**Coachella** (city) Riverside County
3	3	-59	**Imperial** (city) Imperial County
4	4	-39	**El Centro** (city) Imperial County
5	5	-13	**Indio** (city) Riverside County
6	8	3	**Calexico** (city) Imperial County
7	62	7	**Discovery Bay** (CDP) Contra Costa County
7	62	7	**Foster City** (city) San Mateo County
7	62	7	**Suisun City** (city) Solano County
10	139	10	**Newport Beach** (city) Orange County
11	217	13	**Fairfield** (city) Solano County
11	217	13	**Port Hueneme** (city) Ventura County
11	217	13	**Rossmoor** (CDP) Orange County
11	217	13	**Seal Beach** (city) Orange County
11	217	13	**Stockton** (city) San Joaquin County
16	272	16	**Coronado** (city) San Diego County
16	272	16	**East Palo Alto** (city) San Mateo County
16	272	16	**South San Francisco** (city) San Mateo County
19	318	20	**Goleta** (city) Santa Barbara County
19	318	20	**Imperial Beach** (city) San Diego County
19	318	20	**Laguna Beach** (city) Orange County
19	318	20	**Milpitas** (city) Santa Clara County
19	318	20	**Napa** (city) Napa County
19	318	20	**Newark** (city) Alameda County
19	318	20	**Novato** (city) Marin County
19	318	20	**Oakley** (city) Contra Costa County
19	318	20	**Parkway** (CDP) Sacramento County
19	318	20	**Redwood City** (city) San Mateo County
19	318	20	**San Bruno** (city) San Mateo County
19	318	20	**West Sacramento** (city) Yolo County
31	390	23	**Arcata** (city) Humboldt County
31	390	23	**Emeryville** (city) Alameda County
31	390	23	**Lathrop** (city) San Joaquin County
31	390	23	**Los Alamitos** (city) Orange County
31	390	23	**Martinez** (city) Contra Costa County
36	436	26	**Benicia** (city) Solano County
36	436	26	**Hermosa Beach** (city) Los Angeles County
36	436	26	**Monterey** (city) Monterey County
36	436	26	**North Fair Oaks** (CDP) San Mateo County
36	436	26	**Pittsburg** (city) Contra Costa County
41	466	30	**Long Beach** (city) Los Angeles County
41	466	30	**Palo Alto** (city) Santa Clara County
41	466	30	**Petaluma** (city) Sonoma County
41	466	30	**Sacramento** (city) Sacramento County
41	466	30	**San Carlos** (city) San Mateo County
46	513	33	**Alameda** (city) Alameda County
46	513	33	**Carpinteria** (city) Santa Barbara County
46	513	33	**Florin** (CDP) Sacramento County
46	513	33	**Fountain Valley** (city) Orange County
46	513	33	**Garden Acres** (CDP) San Joaquin County
46	513	33	**Hawaiian Gardens** (city) Los Angeles County
46	513	33	**Larkspur** (city) Marin County
46	513	33	**Millbrae** (city) San Mateo County
46	513	33	**Seaside** (city) Monterey County
46	513	33	**Watsonville** (city) Santa Cruz County
56	553	36	**Manteca** (city) San Joaquin County
56	553	36	**San Lorenzo** (CDP) Alameda County
56	553	36	**Santa Cruz** (city) Santa Cruz County
59	584	39	**Burlingame** (city) San Mateo County
59	584	39	**Carson** (city) Los Angeles County
59	584	39	**Cypress** (city) Orange County
59	584	39	**Eureka** (city) Humboldt County
59	584	39	**Huntington Beach** (city) Orange County
59	584	39	**Westminster** (city) Orange County
65	619	43	**Albany** (city) Alameda County
65	619	43	**Antioch** (city) Contra Costa County
65	619	43	**Ashland** (CDP) Alameda County
65	619	43	**Belmont** (city) San Mateo County
65	619	43	**Marina** (city) Monterey County
65	619	43	**Oakland** (city) Alameda County
65	619	43	**San Rafael** (city) Marin County
65	619	43	**West Carson** (CDP) Los Angeles County
73	655	46	**American Canyon** (city) Napa County
73	655	46	**Cerritos** (city) Los Angeles County
73	655	46	**Elk Grove** (city) Sacramento County
73	655	46	**Isla Vista** (CDP) Santa Barbara County
73	655	46	**La Palma** (city) Orange County
73	655	46	**Lakewood** (city) Los Angeles County
73	655	46	**Richmond** (city) Contra Costa County
73	655	46	**San Anselmo** (town) Marin County
73	655	46	**San Mateo** (city) San Mateo County
82	689	49	**Gardena** (city) Los Angeles County
82	689	49	**Lodi** (city) San Joaquin County
82	689	49	**Rosemont** (CDP) Sacramento County
82	689	49	**Santa Barbara** (city) Santa Barbara County
86	717	52	**Artesia** (city) Los Angeles County
86	717	52	**Carlsbad** (city) San Diego County
86	717	52	**Davis** (city) Yolo County
86	717	52	**Galt** (city) Sacramento County
86	717	52	**La Riviera** (CDP) Sacramento County
86	717	52	**Oxnard** (city) Ventura County
86	717	52	**Pleasant Hill** (city) Contra Costa County
86	717	52	**Salinas** (city) Monterey County
86	717	52	**San Francisco** (city) San Francisco County
86	717	52	**San Pablo** (city) Contra Costa County
86	717	52	**Tracy** (city) San Joaquin County
97	745	56	**Arden-Arcade** (CDP) Sacramento County
97	745	56	**Fremont** (city) Alameda County
97	745	56	**Irvine** (city) Orange County
97	745	56	**Rio Linda** (CDP) Sacramento County
97	745	56	**San Leandro** (city) Alameda County
102	770	59	**Grover Beach** (city) San Luis Obispo County
102	770	59	**Lawndale** (city) Los Angeles County
102	770	59	**Yuba City** (city) Sutter County
105	800	62	**Bay Point** (CDP) Contra Costa County
105	800	62	**Camp Pendleton South** (CDP) San Diego County
105	800	62	**Dixon** (city) Solano County
105	800	62	**Marysville** (city) Yuba County
105	800	62	**Morro Bay** (city) San Luis Obispo County
105	800	62	**Redondo Beach** (city) Los Angeles County
105	800	62	**San Diego** (city) San Diego County
112	825	66	**Cherryland** (CDP) Alameda County
112	825	66	**Chula Vista** (city) San Diego County
112	825	66	**Fortuna** (city) Humboldt County
112	825	66	**Manhattan Beach** (city) Los Angeles County
112	825	66	**National City** (city) San Diego County
112	825	66	**Oceanside** (city) San Diego County
112	825	66	**Olivehurst** (CDP) Yuba County
112	825	66	**Stanton** (city) Orange County
112	825	66	**Union City** (city) Alameda County
121	854	69	**Compton** (city) Los Angeles County
121	854	69	**El Cerrito** (city) Contra Costa County
121	854	69	**Linda** (CDP) Yuba County
121	854	69	**Paramount** (city) Los Angeles County
121	854	69	**Ripon** (city) San Joaquin County
121	854	69	**Salida** (CDP) Stanislaus County
121	854	69	**Vallejo** (city) Solano County
121	854	69	**Woodland** (city) Yolo County
129	880	72	**Bellflower** (city) Los Angeles County
129	880	72	**East Rancho Dominguez** (CDP) Los Angeles County
129	880	72	**Hawthorne** (city) Los Angeles County
129	880	72	**Lennox** (CDP) Los Angeles County
129	880	72	**Menlo Park** (city) San Mateo County
129	880	72	**Santa Clara** (city) Santa Clara County
129	880	72	**Solana Beach** (city) San Diego County
136	908	75	**Buena Park** (city) Orange County
136	908	75	**Concord** (city) Contra Costa County
136	908	75	**Half Moon Bay** (city) San Mateo County
139	932	79	**Brentwood** (city) Contra Costa County
139	932	79	**Hercules** (city) Contra Costa County
141	955	82	**Encinitas** (city) San Diego County
141	955	82	**Mill Valley** (city) Marin County
141	955	82	**Pacifica** (city) San Mateo County
141	955	82	**San Jose** (city) Santa Clara County
145	975	85	**Sonoma** (city) Sonoma County
146	999	89	**Garden Grove** (city) Orange County
146	999	89	**Modesto** (city) Stanislaus County
146	999	89	**Newman** (city) Stanislaus County
146	999	89	**Rancho Cordova** (city) Sacramento County
146	999	89	**Torrance** (city) Los Angeles County

Note: *The state column ranks the top/bottom 150 places from all places in the state with population of 10,000 or more. The national column ranks the top/bottom 150 places from all places in the country with population of 10,000 or more. Places that are unincorporated were not considered in the rankings. Please refer to the User Guide for additional information.*

Population

Top 150 Places Ranked in *Descending* Order

State Rank	Nat'l Rank	Number	Place
1	2	3,792,621	**Los Angeles** (city) Los Angeles County
2	12	1,307,402	**San Diego** (city) San Diego County
3	14	945,942	**San Jose** (city) Santa Clara County
4	17	805,235	**San Francisco** (city) San Francisco County
5	39	494,665	**Fresno** (city) Fresno County
6	42	466,488	**Sacramento** (city) Sacramento County
7	43	462,257	**Long Beach** (city) Los Angeles County
8	54	390,724	**Oakland** (city) Alameda County
9	58	347,483	**Bakersfield** (city) Kern County
10	61	336,265	**Anaheim** (city) Orange County
11	65	324,528	**Santa Ana** (city) Orange County
12	69	303,871	**Riverside** (city) Riverside County
13	74	291,707	**Stockton** (city) San Joaquin County
14	86	243,916	**Chula Vista** (city) San Diego County
15	106	214,089	**Fremont** (city) Alameda County
16	108	212,375	**Irvine** (city) Orange County
17	111	209,924	**San Bernardino** (city) San Bernardino County
18	120	201,165	**Modesto** (city) Stanislaus County
19	125	197,899	**Oxnard** (city) Ventura County
20	127	196,069	**Fontana** (city) San Bernardino County
21	132	193,365	**Moreno Valley** (city) Riverside County
22	133	191,719	**Glendale** (city) Los Angeles County
23	135	189,992	**Huntington Beach** (city) Orange County
24	147	176,320	**Santa Clarita** (city) Los Angeles County
25	152	170,883	**Garden Grove** (city) Orange County
26	153	167,815	**Santa Rosa** (city) Sonoma County
27	155	167,086	**Oceanside** (city) San Diego County
28	157	165,269	**Rancho Cucamonga** (city) San Bernardino County
29	159	163,924	**Ontario** (city) San Bernardino County
30	163	156,633	**Lancaster** (city) Los Angeles County
31	171	153,015	**Elk Grove** (city) Sacramento County
32	173	152,750	**Palmdale** (city) Los Angeles County
33	174	152,374	**Corona** (city) Riverside County
34	175	150,441	**Salinas** (city) Monterey County
35	176	149,058	**Pomona** (city) Los Angeles County
36	181	145,438	**Torrance** (city) Los Angeles County
37	184	144,186	**Hayward** (city) Alameda County
38	186	143,911	**Escondido** (city) San Diego County
39	191	140,081	**Sunnyvale** (city) Santa Clara County
40	196	137,122	**Pasadena** (city) Los Angeles County
41	197	136,416	**Orange** (city) Orange County
42	200	135,161	**Fullerton** (city) Orange County
43	211	126,683	**Thousand Oaks** (city) Ventura County
44	213	126,496	**East Los Angeles** (CDP) Los Angeles County
45	219	124,442	**Visalia** (city) Tulare County
46	221	124,237	**Simi Valley** (city) Ventura County
47	225	122,067	**Concord** (city) Contra Costa County
48	231	118,788	**Roseville** (city) Placer County
49	241	116,468	**Santa Clara** (city) Santa Clara County
50	243	115,942	**Vallejo** (city) Solano County
51	244	115,903	**Victorville** (city) San Bernardino County
52	249	113,475	**El Monte** (city) Los Angeles County
53	251	112,580	**Berkeley** (city) Alameda County
54	253	111,772	**Downey** (city) Los Angeles County
55	257	109,960	**Costa Mesa** (city) Orange County
56	258	109,673	**Inglewood** (city) Los Angeles County
57	270	106,433	**San Buenaventura (Ventura)** (city) Ventura County
58	273	106,098	**West Covina** (city) Los Angeles County
59	275	105,549	**Norwalk** (city) Los Angeles County
60	277	105,328	**Carlsbad** (city) San Diego County
61	278	105,321	**Fairfield** (city) Solano County
62	285	103,701	**Richmond** (city) Contra Costa County
63	287	103,466	**Murrieta** (city) Riverside County
64	288	103,340	**Burbank** (city) Los Angeles County
65	292	102,372	**Antioch** (city) Contra Costa County
66	295	101,123	**Daly City** (city) San Mateo County
67	297	100,097	**Temecula** (city) Riverside County
68	306	99,553	**Santa Maria** (city) Santa Barbara County
69	307	99,478	**El Cajon** (city) San Diego County
70	310	99,171	**Rialto** (city) San Bernardino County
71	319	97,207	**San Mateo** (city) San Mateo County
72	326	96,455	**Compton** (city) Los Angeles County
73	328	95,631	**Clovis** (city) Fresno County
74	332	94,396	**South Gate** (city) Los Angeles County
75	336	93,834	**Vista** (city) San Diego County
76	338	93,305	**Mission Viejo** (city) Orange County
77	343	92,428	**Vacaville** (city) Solano County
78	346	92,186	**Arden-Arcade** (CDP) Sacramento County
79	348	91,714	**Carson** (city) Los Angeles County
80	359	90,173	**Hesperia** (city) San Bernardino County
81	361	89,861	**Redding** (city) Shasta County
82	364	89,736	**Santa Monica** (city) Los Angeles County
83	365	89,701	**Westminster** (city) Orange County
84	371	88,410	**Santa Barbara** (city) Santa Barbara County
85	387	86,187	**Chico** (city) Butte County
86	389	85,331	**Whittier** (city) Los Angeles County
87	390	85,186	**Newport Beach** (city) Orange County
88	394	84,950	**San Leandro** (city) Alameda County
89	400	84,293	**Hawthorne** (city) Los Angeles County
90	406	83,781	**San Marcos** (city) San Diego County
91	409	83,301	**Citrus Heights** (city) Sacramento County
92	410	83,089	**Alhambra** (city) Los Angeles County
93	411	82,922	**Tracy** (city) San Joaquin County
94	425	80,968	**Livermore** (city) Alameda County
95	429	80,530	**Buena Park** (city) Orange County
96	434	80,048	**Lakewood** (city) Los Angeles County
97	440	78,958	**Merced** (city) Merced County
98	443	78,657	**Hemet** (city) Riverside County
99	446	77,983	**Chino** (city) San Bernardino County
100	448	77,519	**Menifee** (city) Riverside County
101	451	77,264	**Lake Forest** (city) Orange County
102	455	76,915	**Napa** (city) Napa County
103	456	76,815	**Redwood City** (city) San Mateo County
104	461	76,616	**Bellflower** (city) Los Angeles County
105	469	76,036	**Indio** (city) Riverside County
106	473	75,540	**Tustin** (city) Orange County
107	474	75,390	**Baldwin Park** (city) Los Angeles County
108	484	74,799	**Chino Hills** (city) San Bernardino County
109	488	74,066	**Mountain View** (city) Santa Clara County
110	490	73,812	**Alameda** (city) Alameda County
111	492	73,732	**Upland** (city) San Bernardino County
112	500	72,203	**Folsom** (city) Sacramento County
113	501	72,148	**San Ramon** (city) Contra Costa County
114	518	70,285	**Pleasanton** (city) Alameda County
115	524	69,772	**Lynwood** (city) Los Angeles County
116	525	69,516	**Union City** (city) Alameda County
117	526	69,135	**Apple Valley** (town) San Bernardino County
118	527	68,747	**Redlands** (city) San Bernardino County
119	529	68,549	**Turlock** (city) Stanislaus County
120	531	68,386	**Perris** (city) Riverside County
121	546	67,096	**Manteca** (city) San Joaquin County
122	551	66,790	**Milpitas** (city) Santa Clara County
123	553	66,748	**Redondo Beach** (city) Los Angeles County
124	570	65,622	**Davis** (city) Yolo County
125	577	65,201	**Camarillo** (city) Ventura County
126	578	64,925	**Yuba City** (city) Sutter County
127	581	64,776	**Rancho Cordova** (city) Sacramento County
128	585	64,403	**Palo Alto** (city) Santa Clara County
129	587	64,234	**Yorba Linda** (city) Orange County
130	589	64,173	**Walnut Creek** (city) Contra Costa County
131	591	63,632	**South San Francisco** (city) San Mateo County
132	594	63,522	**San Clemente** (city) Orange County
133	595	63,387	**Florence-Graham** (CDP) Los Angeles County
134	598	63,264	**Pittsburg** (city) Contra Costa County
135	602	62,979	**Laguna Niguel** (city) Orange County
136	603	62,942	**Pico Rivera** (city) Los Angeles County
137	605	62,500	**Montebello** (city) Los Angeles County
138	615	62,134	**Lodi** (city) San Joaquin County
139	617	61,762	**Carmichael** (CDP) Sacramento County
140	620	61,416	**Madera** (city) Madera County
141	621	61,388	**Castro Valley** (CDP) Alameda County
142	645	60,269	**Monterey Park** (city) Los Angeles County
143	646	60,239	**La Habra** (city) Orange County
144	649	59,946	**Santa Cruz** (city) Santa Cruz County
145	655	59,518	**Encinitas** (city) San Diego County
146	662	59,278	**Tulare** (city) Tulare County
147	665	58,829	**Gardena** (city) Los Angeles County
148	669	58,582	**National City** (city) San Diego County
149	675	58,302	**Cupertino** (city) Santa Clara County
150	680	58,114	**Huntington Park** (city) Los Angeles County

***Note:** The state column ranks the top/bottom 150 places from all places in the state with population of 10,000 or more. The national column ranks the top/bottom 150 places from all places in the country with population of 10,000 or more. Places that are unincorporated were not considered in the rankings. Please refer to the User Guide for additional information.*

Population

Top 150 Places Ranked in *Ascending* Order

State Rank	Nat'l Rank	Number	Place
1	1	10,001	**Del Aire** (CDP) Los Angeles County
2	2	10,003	**Fairview** (CDP) Alameda County
3	21	10,080	**Emeryville** (city) Alameda County
4	33	10,109	**San Diego Country Estates** (CDP) San Diego County
5	54	10,164	**Shasta Lake** (city) Shasta County
6	77	10,224	**Newman** (city) Stanislaus County
7	86	10,234	**Morro Bay** (city) San Luis Obispo County
8	90	10,244	**Rossmoor** (CDP) Orange County
9	121	10,334	**Exeter** (city) Tulare County
10	141	10,389	**Placerville** (city) El Dorado County
11	203	10,561	**Canyon Lake** (city) Riverside County
12	212	10,588	**Farmersville** (city) Tulare County
13	221	10,613	**Winton** (CDP) Merced County
14	223	10,616	**Camp Pendleton South** (CDP) San Diego County
15	233	10,644	**Muscoy** (CDP) San Bernardino County
16	235	10,648	**Garden Acres** (CDP) San Joaquin County
16	235	10,648	**Sonoma** (city) Sonoma County
18	247	10,667	**Piedmont** (city) Alameda County
19	268	10,735	**Tamalpais-Homestead Valley** (CDP) Marin County
20	275	10,755	**Delhi** (CDP) Merced County
21	280	10,770	**Crestline** (CDP) San Bernardino County
22	291	10,802	**La Riviera** (CDP) Sacramento County
23	300	10,825	**Hillsborough** (town) San Mateo County
24	315	10,866	**Citrus** (CDP) Los Angeles County
25	325	10,897	**Clayton** (city) Contra Costa County
26	332	10,912	**Quartz Hill** (CDP) Los Angeles County
27	333	10,917	**Sierra Madre** (city) Los Angeles County
28	363	11,014	**Mendota** (city) Fresno County
29	364	11,016	**Signal Hill** (city) Los Angeles County
30	369	11,037	**Diamond Springs** (CDP) El Dorado County
31	383	11,075	**View Park-Windsor Hills** (CDP) Los Angeles County
32	443	11,254	**Healdsburg** (city) Sonoma County
33	463	11,310	**Magalia** (CDP) Butte County
34	470	11,324	**Half Moon Bay** (city) San Mateo County
35	488	11,382	**Kingsburg** (city) Fresno County
36	512	11,449	**Los Alamitos** (city) Orange County
37	544	11,541	**Lakeland Village** (CDP) Riverside County
38	556	11,565	**Sun Village** (CDP) Los Angeles County
39	559	11,570	**Home Gardens** (CDP) Riverside County
40	562	11,580	**Scotts Valley** (city) Santa Cruz County
41	603	11,768	**Lindsay** (city) Tulare County
42	647	11,926	**Fortuna** (city) Humboldt County
42	647	11,926	**Larkspur** (city) Marin County
44	682	12,040	**Grand Terrace** (city) San Bernardino County
45	692	12,072	**Marysville** (city) Yuba County
46	749	12,304	**Big Bear City** (CDP) San Bernardino County
47	758	12,328	**Lake Los Angeles** (CDP) Los Angeles County
48	764	12,336	**San Anselmo** (town) Marin County
49	790	12,424	**Lake Arrowhead** (CDP) San Bernardino County
50	813	12,538	**Bonita** (CDP) San Diego County
51	836	12,645	**Malibu** (city) Los Angeles County
52	845	12,669	**El Sobrante** (CDP) Contra Costa County
53	854	12,707	**McFarland** (city) Kern County
54	860	12,723	**El Sobrante** (CDP) Riverside County
55	882	12,823	**Commerce** (city) Los Angeles County
56	888	12,860	**Grass Valley** (city) Nevada County
57	890	12,867	**Solana Beach** (city) San Diego County
58	893	12,874	**King City** (city) Monterey County
59	926	13,022	**North Auburn** (CDP) Placer County
60	928	13,040	**Carpinteria** (city) Santa Barbara County
61	933	13,058	**Livingston** (city) Merced County
62	959	13,147	**San Marino** (city) Los Angeles County
63	962	13,156	**Grover Beach** (city) San Luis Obispo County
64	1001	13,330	**Auburn** (city) Placer County
65	1009	13,352	**Discovery Bay** (CDP) Contra Costa County
66	1015	13,380	**Coalinga** (city) Fresno County
67	1031	13,438	**Palos Verdes Estates** (city) Los Angeles County
68	1060	13,544	**Kerman** (city) Fresno County
69	1092	13,656	**Olivehurst** (CDP) Yuba County
70	1112	13,722	**Salida** (CDP) Stanislaus County
71	1114	13,729	**Lemon Hill** (CDP) Sacramento County
72	1132	13,809	**Stanford** (CDP) Santa Clara County
73	1134	13,811	**Oak Park** (CDP) Ventura County
74	1151	13,903	**Mill Valley** (city) Marin County
75	1193	14,058	**Rosedale** (CDP) Kern County
76	1197	14,076	**Red Bluff** (city) Tehama County
77	1207	14,120	**California City** (city) Kern County
78	1236	14,236	**Alpine** (CDP) San Diego County
79	1239	14,254	**Hawaiian Gardens** (city) Los Angeles County
80	1245	14,276	**Los Osos** (CDP) San Luis Obispo County
81	1249	14,297	**Ripon** (city) San Joaquin County
82	1252	14,304	**Phelan** (CDP) San Bernardino County
83	1260	14,347	**Woodcrest** (CDP) Riverside County
84	1272	14,414	**Tehachapi** (city) Kern County
85	1290	14,494	**Parlier** (city) Fresno County
86	1313	14,570	**Alamo** (CDP) Contra Costa County
87	1317	14,578	**Valle Vista** (CDP) Riverside County
88	1333	14,670	**Parkway** (CDP) Sacramento County
89	1336	14,687	**North Fair Oaks** (CDP) San Mateo County
90	1347	14,728	**Cherryland** (CDP) Alameda County
91	1352	14,758	**Imperial** (city) Imperial County
92	1377	14,866	**Coto de Caza** (CDP) Orange County
93	1379	14,874	**East San Gabriel** (CDP) Los Angeles County
94	1403	15,002	**Fillmore** (city) Ventura County
95	1410	15,041	**Pacific Grove** (city) Monterey County
96	1423	15,106	**Rio Linda** (CDP) Sacramento County
97	1425	15,120	**Lamont** (CDP) Kern County
98	1431	15,135	**East Rancho Dominguez** (CDP) Los Angeles County
99	1444	15,177	**McKinleyville** (CDP) Humboldt County
100	1461	15,250	**Clearlake** (city) Lake County
101	1492	15,379	**Bostonia** (CDP) San Diego County
102	1497	15,411	**Avocado Heights** (CDP) Los Angeles County
103	1513	15,505	**Avenal** (city) Kings County
104	1519	15,536	**Alum Rock** (CDP) Santa Clara County
105	1522	15,546	**Oroville** (city) Butte County
106	1530	15,568	**La Palma** (city) Orange County
107	1614	15,966	**Walnut Park** (CDP) Los Angeles County
108	1624	16,016	**Moraga** (town) Contra Costa County
109	1632	16,075	**Ukiah** (city) Mendocino County
110	1650	16,180	**Truckee** (town) Nevada County
111	1652	16,192	**Laguna Woods** (city) Orange County
112	1660	16,223	**Santa Fe Springs** (city) Los Angeles County
113	1678	16,330	**Greenfield** (city) Monterey County
114	1712	16,522	**Artesia** (city) Los Angeles County
115	1731	16,654	**El Segundo** (city) Los Angeles County
116	1740	16,714	**Nipomo** (CDP) San Luis Obispo County
117	1779	16,988	**Shafter** (city) Kern County
118	1801	17,158	**Live Oak** (CDP) Santa Cruz County
119	1807	17,218	**Rancho Mirage** (city) Riverside County
120	1809	17,231	**Arcata** (city) Humboldt County
121	1816	17,252	**Arroyo Grande** (city) San Luis Obispo County
122	1845	17,418	**East Hemet** (CDP) Riverside County
123	1868	17,557	**Stevenson Ranch** (CDP) Los Angeles County
124	1870	17,560	**Prunedale** (CDP) Monterey County
125	1883	17,643	**Orinda** (city) Contra Costa County
126	1899	17,773	**Linda** (CDP) Yuba County
127	1925	17,947	**Susanville** (city) Lassen County
128	1933	18,023	**Lathrop** (city) San Joaquin County
129	1955	18,150	**Rosamond** (CDP) Kern County
130	1970	18,228	**Cameron Park** (CDP) El Dorado County
131	1994	18,351	**Dixon** (city) Solano County
132	2004	18,390	**Pinole** (city) Contra Costa County
133	2019	18,510	**Mead Valley** (CDP) Riverside County
134	2025	18,539	**Albany** (city) Alameda County
135	2055	18,720	**Chowchilla** (city) Madera County
136	2060	18,762	**Casa de Oro-Mount Helix** (CDP) San Diego County
137	2082	18,912	**Coronado** (city) San Diego County
138	2096	19,015	**Castaic** (CDP) Los Angeles County
139	2147	19,304	**Arvin** (city) Kern County
140	2165	19,454	**American Canyon** (city) Napa County
141	2173	19,506	**Hermosa Beach** (city) Los Angeles County
142	2197	19,653	**La Crescenta-Montrose** (CDP) Los Angeles County
143	2201	19,718	**Marina** (city) Monterey County
144	2250	20,116	**South El Monte** (city) Los Angeles County
145	2265	20,246	**La Cañada Flintridge** (city) Los Angeles County
146	2268	20,256	**Lomita** (city) Los Angeles County
147	2273	20,292	**Ramona** (CDP) San Diego County
148	2281	20,330	**Agoura Hills** (city) Los Angeles County
149	2290	20,402	**Granite Bay** (CDP) Placer County
150	2292	20,413	**Patterson** (city) Stanislaus County

Note: *The state column ranks the top/bottom 150 places from all places in the state with population of 10,000 or more. The national column ranks the top/bottom 150 places from all places in the country with population of 10,000 or more. Places that are unincorporated were not considered in the rankings. Please refer to the User Guide for additional information.*

Population Growth

Top 150 Places Ranked in *Descending* Order

State Rank	Nat'l Rank	Percent	Place
1	23	495.3	**Oak Park** (CDP) Ventura County
2	43	282.1	**Lincoln** (city) Placer County
3	57	223.9	**Beaumont** (city) Riverside County
4	94	155.1	**Elk Grove** (city) Sacramento County
5	101	145.7	**Vineyard** (CDP) Sacramento County
6	115	133.7	**El Dorado Hills** (CDP) El Dorado County
6	115	133.7	**Murrieta** (city) Riverside County
8	122	128.8	**Wildomar** (city) Riverside County
9	123	128.5	**Soledad** (city) Monterey County
10	130	125.8	**Diamond Springs** (CDP) El Dorado County
11	133	120.9	**Brentwood** (city) Contra Costa County
12	139	112.9	**Big Bear City** (CDP) San Bernardino County
13	155	105.1	**Lakeland Village** (CDP) Riverside County
14	165	99.0	**American Canyon** (city) Napa County
15	169	95.2	**Imperial** (city) Imperial County
16	182	90.1	**Foothill Farms** (CDP) Sacramento County
17	186	89.0	**Perris** (city) Riverside County
18	199	85.9	**San Jacinto** (city) Riverside County
19	215	81.0	**Victorville** (city) San Bernardino County
20	222	79.1	**Coachella** (city) Riverside County
20	222	79.1	**Lake Elsinore** (city) Riverside County
22	228	76.6	**Yuba City** (city) Sutter County
23	233	75.9	**Patterson** (city) Stanislaus County
24	237	75.2	**Adelanto** (city) San Bernardino County
25	249	73.4	**Temecula** (city) Riverside County
26	253	72.6	**Lathrop** (city) San Joaquin County
27	255	72.0	**Woodcrest** (CDP) Riverside County
28	258	71.8	**Florin** (CDP) Sacramento County
29	260	71.6	**Corcoran** (city) Kings County
30	261	71.3	**Blythe** (city) Riverside County
31	271	69.7	**Twentynine Palms** (city) San Bernardino County
32	278	68.4	**California City** (city) Kern County
33	280	68.2	**Chowchilla** (city) Madera County
34	289	66.5	**Rosedale** (CDP) Kern County
35	321	61.3	**San Ramon** (city) Contra Costa County
36	337	58.4	**Kerman** (city) Fresno County
37	342	58.1	**La Quinta** (city) Riverside County
38	350	56.8	**Rocklin** (city) Placer County
39	353	56.4	**Desert Hot Springs** (city) Riverside County
40	369	54.8	**Indio** (city) Riverside County
41	374	54.2	**West Sacramento** (city) Yolo County
42	379	53.6	**Dublin** (city) Alameda County
43	389	52.4	**San Marcos** (city) San Diego County
44	393	52.1	**Fontana** (city) San Bernardino County
45	420	49.0	**Arvin** (city) Kern County
46	423	48.7	**Discovery Bay** (CDP) Contra Costa County
47	424	48.6	**Roseville** (city) Placer County
48	427	48.4	**Irvine** (city) Orange County
49	446	46.5	**Emeryville** (city) Alameda County
50	455	45.7	**Tracy** (city) San Joaquin County
51	468	44.3	**Rio Linda** (CDP) Sacramento County
52	472	44.1	**Hesperia** (city) San Bernardino County
52	472	44.1	**Newman** (city) Stanislaus County
54	479	43.8	**Chico** (city) Butte County
55	485	43.3	**Riverbank** (city) Stanislaus County
56	500	42.3	**Calexico** (city) Imperial County
57	503	42.1	**Madera** (city) Madera County
58	517	40.9	**Ripon** (city) San Joaquin County
59	521	40.6	**Bakersfield** (city) Kern County
60	526	40.5	**Chula Vista** (city) San Diego County
61	540	39.7	**Clovis** (city) Fresno County
62	543	39.6	**Mendota** (city) Fresno County
63	552	39.2	**Folsom** (city) Sacramento County
64	555	39.1	**Lake Arrowhead** (CDP) San Bernardino County
64	555	39.1	**Los Banos** (city) Merced County
66	559	39.0	**Valle Vista** (CDP) Riverside County
67	571	38.3	**Oakley** (city) Contra Costa County
68	604	36.7	**Porterville** (city) Tulare County
69	606	36.6	**Delano** (city) Kern County
70	612	36.2	**Manteca** (city) San Joaquin County
71	619	35.9	**Visalia** (city) Tulare County
72	621	35.8	**Moreno Valley** (city) Riverside County
73	644	34.7	**Tulare** (city) Tulare County
74	649	34.6	**Carlsbad** (city) San Diego County
75	656	34.1	**Delhi** (CDP) Merced County
76	664	33.7	**Hemet** (city) Riverside County
77	670	33.4	**Oakdale** (city) Stanislaus County
77	670	33.4	**Shafter** (city) Kern County
79	690	32.5	**Susanville** (city) Lassen County
80	692	32.4	**Nipomo** (CDP) San Luis Obispo County
81	698	32.1	**McFarland** (city) Kern County
82	704	31.9	**Lancaster** (city) Los Angeles County
82	704	31.9	**Linda** (CDP) Yuba County
84	711	31.6	**Lake Forest** (city) Orange County
84	711	31.6	**Tehachapi** (city) Kern County
86	720	31.2	**Ceres** (city) Stanislaus County
87	724	30.9	**Palmdale** (city) Los Angeles County
88	741	30.0	**Parlier** (city) Fresno County
88	741	30.0	**Rancho Mirage** (city) Riverside County
90	744	29.8	**Greenfield** (city) Monterey County
91	752	29.5	**Hanford** (city) Kings County
92	754	29.4	**Rancho Cucamonga** (city) San Bernardino County
93	757	29.3	**Ramona** (CDP) San Diego County
94	773	28.6	**Santa Maria** (city) Santa Barbara County
95	784	28.2	**Sanger** (city) Fresno County
96	803	27.5	**Apple Valley** (town) San Bernardino County
97	809	27.4	**Dinuba** (city) Tulare County
98	821	27.2	**Orangevale** (CDP) Sacramento County
98	821	27.2	**San Clemente** (city) Orange County
100	841	26.5	**Rosamond** (CDP) Kern County
101	856	25.9	**Isla Vista** (CDP) Santa Barbara County
102	866	25.6	**Banning** (city) Riverside County
103	872	25.3	**Cameron Park** (CDP) El Dorado County
104	891	24.7	**Livingston** (city) Merced County
104	891	24.7	**Yucaipa** (city) San Bernardino County
106	900	24.5	**Loma Linda** (city) San Bernardino County
107	904	24.4	**Lemoore** (city) Kings County
108	916	24.2	**Carmichael** (CDP) Sacramento County
109	933	23.7	**Kingsburg** (city) Fresno County
110	940	23.6	**Merced** (city) Merced County
111	945	23.5	**Bloomington** (CDP) San Bernardino County
111	945	23.5	**Hercules** (city) Contra Costa County
111	945	23.5	**Olivehurst** (CDP) Yuba County
114	970	22.8	**Turlock** (city) Stanislaus County
115	973	22.7	**Yucca Valley** (town) San Bernardino County
116	979	22.6	**El Paso de Robles (Paso Robles)** (city) San Luis Obispo County
117	991	22.3	**Home Gardens** (CDP) Riverside County
118	1007	21.9	**Atwater** (city) Merced County
118	1007	21.9	**Corona** (city) Riverside County
120	1019	21.6	**Newport Beach** (city) Orange County
121	1027	21.4	**Galt** (city) Sacramento County
122	1041	21.2	**Farmersville** (city) Tulare County
123	1075	20.2	**Winton** (CDP) Merced County
124	1081	20.1	**Cathedral City** (city) Riverside County
124	1081	20.1	**Wasco** (city) Kern County
126	1092	19.9	**Camp Pendleton South** (CDP) San Diego County
127	1101	19.7	**Stockton** (city) San Joaquin County
128	1106	19.5	**Oroville** (city) Butte County
129	1111	19.4	**Selma** (city) Fresno County
130	1114	19.3	**Muscoy** (CDP) San Bernardino County
131	1124	19.1	**Aliso Viejo** (city) Orange County
131	1124	19.1	**Highland** (city) San Bernardino County
131	1124	19.1	**Riverside** (city) Riverside County
134	1169	18.0	**Signal Hill** (city) Los Angeles County
135	1177	17.8	**Windsor** (town) Sonoma County
136	1182	17.7	**Gilroy** (city) Santa Clara County
136	1182	17.7	**Grass Valley** (city) Nevada County
136	1182	17.7	**Palm Desert** (city) Riverside County
139	1190	17.6	**Rancho Cordova** (city) Sacramento County
140	1197	17.5	**East Hemet** (CDP) Riverside County
141	1212	17.2	**Oildale** (CDP) Kern County
142	1234	16.7	**Santa Clarita** (city) Los Angeles County
142	1234	16.7	**Sonoma** (city) Sonoma County
142	1234	16.7	**Truckee** (town) Nevada County
145	1242	16.6	**Reedley** (city) Fresno County
146	1264	16.2	**Oxnard** (city) Ventura County
147	1276	16.1	**Chino** (city) San Bernardino County
148	1283	16.0	**Clearlake** (city) Lake County
148	1283	16.0	**King City** (city) Monterey County
150	1308	15.7	**Fresno** (city) Fresno County

Note: *The state column ranks the top/bottom 150 places from all places in the state with population of 10,000 or more. The national column ranks the top/bottom 150 places from all places in the country with population of 10,000 or more. Places that are unincorporated were not considered in the rankings. Please refer to the User Guide for additional information.*

Population Growth

Top 150 Places Ranked in *Ascending* Order

State Rank	Nat'l Rank	Percent	Place
1	4	-45.9	**Goleta** (city) Santa Barbara County
2	28	-21.5	**Coronado** (city) San Diego County
3	29	-21.4	**Marina** (city) Monterey County
4	137	-9.3	**South Lake Tahoe** (city) El Dorado County
5	172	-8.1	**Carpinteria** (city) Santa Barbara County
6	220	-7.0	**Santa Fe Springs** (city) Los Angeles County
7	233	-6.8	**Alamo** (CDP) Contra Costa County
8	257	-6.3	**Monterey** (city) Monterey County
9	331	-5.3	**Huntington Park** (city) Los Angeles County
10	348	-5.0	**Dana Point** (city) Orange County
11	354	-4.9	**North Fair Oaks** (CDP) San Mateo County
11	354	-4.9	**South El Monte** (city) Los Angeles County
13	370	-4.8	**Cerritos** (city) Los Angeles County
14	393	-4.6	**East Palo Alto** (city) San Mateo County
14	393	-4.6	**San Dimas** (city) Los Angeles County
16	407	-4.5	**Bell Gardens** (city) Los Angeles County
17	421	-4.4	**Half Moon Bay** (city) San Mateo County
18	442	-4.2	**Laguna Beach** (city) Orange County
18	442	-4.2	**Santa Barbara** (city) Santa Barbara County
20	466	-4.0	**Arden-Arcade** (CDP) Sacramento County
20	466	-4.0	**Santa Ana** (city) Orange County
22	493	-3.7	**West Hollywood** (city) Los Angeles County
23	508	-3.6	**Hawaiian Gardens** (city) Los Angeles County
23	508	-3.6	**San Pablo** (city) Contra Costa County
25	529	-3.4	**North Highlands** (CDP) Sacramento County
25	529	-3.4	**Pinole** (city) Contra Costa County
27	558	-3.2	**Alhambra** (city) Los Angeles County
27	558	-3.2	**Bell** (city) Los Angeles County
29	565	-3.1	**Pacific Grove** (city) Monterey County
30	578	-3.0	**La Puente** (city) Los Angeles County
30	578	-3.0	**Pacifica** (city) San Mateo County
30	578	-3.0	**Rohnert Park** (city) Sonoma County
33	604	-2.8	**Walnut** (city) Los Angeles County
34	616	-2.7	**Laguna Hills** (city) Orange County
35	629	-2.6	**Inglewood** (city) Los Angeles County
35	629	-2.6	**Piedmont** (city) Alameda County
37	642	-2.5	**Imperial Beach** (city) San Diego County
38	653	-2.4	**Daly City** (city) San Mateo County
38	653	-2.4	**Maywood** (city) Los Angeles County
40	680	-2.2	**Oakland** (city) Alameda County
41	692	-2.1	**Citrus Heights** (city) Sacramento County
41	692	-2.1	**El Monte** (city) Los Angeles County
41	692	-2.1	**Paramount** (city) Los Angeles County
41	692	-2.1	**South Gate** (city) Los Angeles County
45	724	-1.9	**Laguna Woods** (city) Orange County
46	744	-1.8	**La Verne** (city) Los Angeles County
47	760	-1.7	**Cudahy** (city) Los Angeles County
47	760	-1.7	**Glendale** (city) Los Angeles County
49	773	-1.6	**Marysville** (city) Yuba County
50	821	-1.3	**Diamond Bar** (city) Los Angeles County
50	821	-1.3	**Walnut Park** (CDP) Los Angeles County
52	851	-1.1	**Morro Bay** (city) San Luis Obispo County
53	863	-1.0	**Agoura Hills** (city) Los Angeles County
53	863	-1.0	**Rosemont** (CDP) Sacramento County
55	886	-0.9	**Bay Point** (CDP) Contra Costa County
55	886	-0.9	**Lennox** (CDP) Los Angeles County
55	886	-0.9	**Monrovia** (city) Los Angeles County
55	886	-0.9	**Solana Beach** (city) San Diego County
59	905	-0.8	**Duarte** (city) Los Angeles County
59	905	-0.8	**Los Alamitos** (city) Orange County
59	905	-0.8	**Pico Rivera** (city) Los Angeles County
62	924	-0.7	**Larkspur** (city) Marin County
62	924	-0.7	**Paradise** (town) Butte County
62	924	-0.7	**Vallejo** (city) Solano County
65	943	-0.6	**Baldwin Park** (city) Los Angeles County
65	943	-0.6	**Casa de Oro-Mount Helix** (CDP) San Diego County
65	943	-0.6	**Port Hueneme** (city) Ventura County
68	962	-0.5	**Poway** (city) San Diego County
68	962	-0.5	**Rossmoor** (CDP) Orange County
70	986	-0.4	**La Cañada Flintridge** (city) Los Angeles County
70	986	-0.4	**Salinas** (city) Monterey County
72	1006	-0.3	**Pomona** (city) Los Angeles County
72	1006	-0.3	**San Anselmo** (town) Marin County
74	1025	-0.2	**San Gabriel** (city) Los Angeles County
74	1025	-0.2	**Walnut Creek** (city) Contra Costa County
76	1041	-0.1	**Lafayette** (city) Contra Costa County
76	1041	-0.1	**Lynwood** (city) Los Angeles County
76	1041	-0.1	**Martinez** (city) Contra Costa County
79	1065	0.0	**Hillsborough** (town) San Mateo County
79	1065	0.0	**Seal Beach** (city) Orange County
81	1104	0.2	**Concord** (city) Contra Costa County
81	1104	0.2	**Culver City** (city) Los Angeles County
81	1104	0.2	**Hawthorne** (city) Los Angeles County
81	1104	0.2	**Huntington Beach** (city) Orange County
81	1104	0.2	**Long Beach** (city) Los Angeles County
81	1104	0.2	**Mission Viejo** (city) Orange County
81	1104	0.2	**Newark** (city) Alameda County
81	1104	0.2	**West Puente Valley** (CDP) Los Angeles County
89	1126	0.3	**Orcutt** (CDP) Santa Barbara County
89	1126	0.3	**Orinda** (city) Contra Costa County
89	1126	0.3	**San Fernando** (city) Los Angeles County
89	1126	0.3	**Saratoga** (city) Santa Clara County
93	1151	0.4	**Altadena** (CDP) Los Angeles County
93	1151	0.4	**Monterey Park** (city) Los Angeles County
93	1151	0.4	**Tamalpais-Homestead Valley** (CDP) Marin County
96	1175	0.5	**Benicia** (city) Solano County
96	1175	0.5	**Rosemead** (city) Los Angeles County
98	1197	0.6	**Fountain Valley** (city) Orange County
98	1197	0.6	**Malibu** (city) Los Angeles County
98	1197	0.6	**Montebello** (city) Los Angeles County
101	1212	0.7	**Grover Beach** (city) San Luis Obispo County
101	1212	0.7	**Palos Verdes Estates** (city) Los Angeles County
101	1212	0.7	**Westmont** (CDP) Los Angeles County
104	1237	0.8	**Danville** (town) Contra Costa County
104	1237	0.8	**Santee** (city) San Diego County
106	1256	0.9	**Artesia** (city) Los Angeles County
106	1256	0.9	**Lakewood** (city) Los Angeles County
106	1256	0.9	**Rowland Heights** (CDP) Los Angeles County
109	1282	1.0	**Beverly Hills** (city) Los Angeles County
109	1282	1.0	**La Palma** (city) Orange County
109	1282	1.0	**Lomita** (city) Los Angeles County
109	1282	1.0	**Pleasant Hill** (city) Contra Costa County
109	1282	1.0	**West Covina** (city) Los Angeles County
114	1303	1.1	**Bonita** (CDP) San Diego County
114	1303	1.1	**Costa Mesa** (city) Orange County
114	1303	1.1	**View Park-Windsor Hills** (CDP) Los Angeles County
117	1318	1.2	**Rancho Palos Verdes** (city) Los Angeles County
118	1337	1.3	**Clayton** (city) Contra Costa County
118	1337	1.3	**Glendora** (city) Los Angeles County
120	1360	1.4	**Bostonia** (CDP) San Diego County
120	1360	1.4	**Rancho Santa Margarita** (city) Orange County
122	1381	1.5	**Hollister** (city) San Benito County
123	1401	1.6	**El Cerrito** (city) Contra Costa County
123	1401	1.6	**Lemon Grove** (city) San Diego County
123	1401	1.6	**San Marino** (city) Los Angeles County
123	1401	1.6	**South San Jose Hills** (CDP) Los Angeles County
123	1401	1.6	**West Whittier-Los Nietos** (CDP) Los Angeles County
128	1422	1.7	**Avocado Heights** (CDP) Los Angeles County
128	1422	1.7	**Hacienda Heights** (CDP) Los Angeles County
128	1422	1.7	**Scotts Valley** (city) Santa Cruz County
128	1422	1.7	**Westminster** (city) Orange County
132	1438	1.8	**East Los Angeles** (CDP) Los Angeles County
132	1438	1.8	**Laguna Niguel** (city) Orange County
134	1463	1.9	**Gardena** (city) Los Angeles County
134	1463	1.9	**Redwood City** (city) San Mateo County
136	1480	2.0	**Commerce** (city) Los Angeles County
136	1480	2.0	**Covina** (city) Los Angeles County
136	1480	2.0	**Whittier** (city) Los Angeles County
139	1500	2.1	**Alameda** (city) Alameda County
139	1500	2.1	**La Habra** (city) Orange County
139	1500	2.1	**San Luis Obispo** (city) San Luis Obispo County
139	1500	2.1	**Stanton** (city) Orange County
143	1529	2.2	**Carson** (city) Los Angeles County
143	1529	2.2	**Mill Valley** (city) Marin County
143	1529	2.2	**Norwalk** (city) Los Angeles County
146	1545	2.3	**Burlingame** (city) San Mateo County
146	1545	2.3	**San Juan Capistrano** (city) Orange County
148	1570	2.4	**Pasadena** (city) Los Angeles County
148	1570	2.4	**San Bruno** (city) San Mateo County
150	1596	2.5	**Anaheim** (city) Orange County

Note: *The state column ranks the top/bottom 150 places from all places in the state with population of 10,000 or more. The national column ranks the top/bottom 150 places from all places in the country with population of 10,000 or more. Places that are unincorporated were not considered in the rankings. Please refer to the User Guide for additional information.*

Population Density

Top 150 Places Ranked in *Descending* Order

State Rank	Nat'l Rank	Pop./ Sq. Mi.	Place
1	10	23,247.5	**Maywood** (city) Los Angeles County
2	12	21,352.0	**Walnut Park** (CDP) Los Angeles County
3	13	20,809.4	**Lennox** (CDP) Los Angeles County
4	16	20,259.3	**Cudahy** (city) Los Angeles County
5	17	19,290.7	**Huntington Park** (city) Los Angeles County
6	20	18,412.3	**East Rancho Dominguez** (CDP) Los Angeles County
7	22	18,225.6	**West Hollywood** (city) Los Angeles County
8	24	17,704.2	**Florence-Graham** (CDP) Los Angeles County
9	26	17,239.9	**Westmont** (CDP) Los Angeles County
10	27	17,179.2	**San Francisco** (city) San Francisco County
11	28	17,112.4	**Bell Gardens** (city) Los Angeles County
12	30	16,983.2	**East Los Angeles** (CDP) Los Angeles County
13	32	16,599.0	**Lawndale** (city) Los Angeles County
14	42	15,069.5	**Hawaiian Gardens** (city) Los Angeles County
15	47	14,415.7	**Lynwood** (city) Los Angeles County
16	49	14,188.0	**Bell** (city) Los Angeles County
17	52	13,861.2	**Hawthorne** (city) Los Angeles County
18	54	13,673.6	**Hermosa Beach** (city) Los Angeles County
19	56	13,628.8	**South San Jose Hills** (CDP) Los Angeles County
20	58	13,195.0	**Daly City** (city) San Mateo County
21	61	13,045.0	**South Gate** (city) Los Angeles County
22	62	12,899.0	**Alum Rock** (CDP) Santa Clara County
23	63	12,851.8	**West Puente Valley** (CDP) Los Angeles County
24	66	12,525.0	**Bellflower** (city) Los Angeles County
25	67	12,492.0	**Isla Vista** (CDP) Santa Barbara County
26	71	12,301.9	**Cherryland** (CDP) Alameda County
27	72	12,251.8	**Citrus** (CDP) Los Angeles County
28	73	12,236.5	**North Fair Oaks** (CDP) San Mateo County
29	75	12,122.8	**Stanton** (city) Orange County
30	76	12,094.7	**Inglewood** (city) Los Angeles County
31	77	11,926.7	**Ashland** (CDP) Alameda County
32	78	11,900.8	**Santa Ana** (city) Orange County
33	79	11,866.9	**El Monte** (city) Los Angeles County
34	87	11,445.4	**La Puente** (city) Los Angeles County
35	88	11,438.4	**Paramount** (city) Los Angeles County
36	91	11,369.2	**Baldwin Park** (city) Los Angeles County
37	92	11,330.9	**Valinda** (CDP) Los Angeles County
38	95	11,238.8	**East Palo Alto** (city) San Mateo County
39	99	11,063.4	**San Pablo** (city) Contra Costa County
40	102	10,889.0	**Alhambra** (city) Los Angeles County
41	104	10,873.5	**Norwalk** (city) Los Angeles County
42	109	10,768.7	**Redondo Beach** (city) Los Angeles County
43	111	10,752.4	**Berkeley** (city) Alameda County
44	114	10,708.9	**South Whittier** (CDP) Los Angeles County
45	115	10,664.1	**Santa Monica** (city) Los Angeles County
46	117	10,601.3	**Lomita** (city) Los Angeles County
47	121	10,414.9	**Rosemead** (city) Los Angeles County
48	124	10,367.2	**Albany** (city) Alameda County
49	126	10,194.7	**Artesia** (city) Los Angeles County
50	129	10,138.5	**West Whittier-Los Nietos** (CDP) Los Angeles County
51	130	10,092.2	**Gardena** (city) Los Angeles County
52	134	9,959.9	**San Fernando** (city) Los Angeles County
53	135	9,864.4	**Del Aire** (CDP) Los Angeles County
54	142	9,633.7	**Compton** (city) Los Angeles County
55	143	9,583.1	**San Gabriel** (city) Los Angeles County
56	145	9,576.0	**West Carson** (CDP) Los Angeles County
57	147	9,564.6	**Willowbrook** (CDP) Los Angeles County
58	148	9,526.6	**East San Gabriel** (CDP) Los Angeles County
59	149	9,524.6	**Garden Grove** (city) Orange County
60	160	9,191.2	**Long Beach** (city) Los Angeles County
61	167	9,008.0	**Downey** (city) Los Angeles County
62	170	8,926.5	**Westminster** (city) Orange County
63	171	8,923.8	**Manhattan Beach** (city) Los Angeles County
64	175	8,877.2	**Temple City** (city) Los Angeles County
65	185	8,612.6	**La Palma** (city) Orange County
66	188	8,502.4	**Lakewood** (city) Los Angeles County
67	189	8,486.6	**San Lorenzo** (CDP) Alameda County
68	190	8,440.4	**Lemon Hill** (CDP) Sacramento County
69	199	8,173.6	**La Habra** (city) Orange County
70	200	8,137.6	**Foster City** (city) San Mateo County
71	203	8,092.3	**Los Angeles** (city) Los Angeles County
72	204	8,091.7	**Emeryville** (city) Alameda County
73	205	8,050.4	**National City** (city) San Diego County
74	210	8,014.0	**San Mateo** (city) San Mateo County
75	213	7,973.4	**Bostonia** (CDP) San Diego County
76	219	7,889.8	**Foothill Farms** (CDP) Sacramento County
77	221	7,855.8	**Monterey Park** (city) Los Angeles County
78	231	7,693.9	**Placentia** (city) Orange County
79	235	7,656.6	**Watsonville** (city) Santa Cruz County
80	236	7,652.1	**Buena Park** (city) Orange County
81	237	7,648.1	**Greenfield** (city) Monterey County
82	242	7,607.2	**Culver City** (city) Los Angeles County
83	246	7,587.5	**Pico Rivera** (city) Los Angeles County
84	251	7,523.0	**South Pasadena** (city) Los Angeles County
85	252	7,505.0	**San Bruno** (city) San Mateo County
86	253	7,500.7	**Montebello** (city) Los Angeles County
87	259	7,435.7	**Home Gardens** (CDP) Riverside County
88	263	7,358.4	**Oxnard** (city) Ventura County
89	267	7,263.6	**Cypress** (city) Orange County
90	281	7,102.9	**Huntington Beach** (city) Orange County
91	283	7,102.2	**Torrance** (city) Los Angeles County
92	286	7,075.0	**South El Monte** (city) Los Angeles County
93	287	7,024.6	**Costa Mesa** (city) Orange County
94	291	7,004.0	**Oakland** (city) Alameda County
95	295	6,961.4	**South San Francisco** (city) San Mateo County
96	296	6,956.3	**Alameda** (city) Alameda County
97	303	6,892.5	**El Cajon** (city) San Diego County
98	305	6,847.6	**Suisun City** (city) Solano County
99	307	6,816.7	**Tustin** (city) Orange County
100	310	6,803.0	**Covina** (city) Los Angeles County
101	313	6,786.5	**Campbell** (city) Santa Clara County
102	315	6,747.5	**Anaheim** (city) Orange County
103	320	6,694.2	**Antelope** (CDP) Sacramento County
104	325	6,660.9	**Rossmoor** (CDP) Orange County
105	327	6,645.4	**Montclair** (city) San Bernardino County
106	331	6,637.0	**Davis** (city) Yolo County
107	332	6,632.1	**Millbrae** (city) San Mateo County
108	335	6,614.3	**West Covina** (city) Los Angeles County
109	336	6,606.9	**Parlier** (city) Fresno County
110	341	6,538.1	**Burlingame** (city) San Mateo County
111	343	6,525.3	**Lemon Grove** (city) San Diego County
112	346	6,494.5	**Pomona** (city) Los Angeles County
113	347	6,490.5	**Salinas** (city) Monterey County
114	361	6,400.4	**Aliso Viejo** (city) Orange County
115	362	6,385.8	**El Cerrito** (city) Contra Costa County
116	363	6,384.3	**Santa Paula** (city) Ventura County
117	365	6,370.9	**Sunnyvale** (city) Santa Clara County
118	367	6,366.8	**San Leandro** (city) Alameda County
119	369	6,358.5	**Piedmont** (city) Alameda County
120	373	6,327.3	**Santa Clara** (city) Santa Clara County
121	374	6,325.9	**Imperial Beach** (city) San Diego County
122	378	6,295.5	**Glendale** (city) Los Angeles County
123	380	6,287.3	**La Mesa** (city) San Diego County
124	387	6,217.4	**La Presa** (CDP) San Diego County
125	391	6,189.4	**La Mirada** (city) Los Angeles County
126	394	6,174.6	**Mountain View** (city) Santa Clara County
127	400	6,133.5	**Fountain Valley** (city) Orange County
128	410	6,067.0	**Parkway** (CDP) Sacramento County
129	412	6,046.7	**Fullerton** (city) Orange County
130	418	6,015.1	**View Park-Windsor Hills** (CDP) Los Angeles County
131	425	5,975.5	**Beverly Hills** (city) Los Angeles County
132	430	5,969.6	**Pasadena** (city) Los Angeles County
133	433	5,959.3	**Burbank** (city) Los Angeles County
134	449	5,854.6	**Citrus Heights** (city) Sacramento County
135	450	5,850.9	**Rohnert Park** (city) Sonoma County
136	452	5,839.9	**La Riviera** (CDP) Sacramento County
137	454	5,831.1	**Soledad** (city) Monterey County
138	457	5,824.9	**Whittier** (city) Los Angeles County
139	467	5,736.4	**La Crescenta-Montrose** (CDP) Los Angeles County
140	475	5,695.6	**Avocado Heights** (CDP) Los Angeles County
141	476	5,695.1	**Grover Beach** (city) San Luis Obispo County
142	482	5,669.1	**Ceres** (city) Stanislaus County
143	487	5,620.7	**Cerritos** (city) Los Angeles County
144	490	5,590.2	**Belmont** (city) San Mateo County
145	501	5,541.8	**Riverbank** (city) Stanislaus County
146	508	5,501.3	**Orange** (city) Orange County
147	514	5,459.7	**Florin** (CDP) Sacramento County
148	516	5,456.5	**Modesto** (city) Stanislaus County
149	528	5,358.6	**San Jose** (city) Santa Clara County
150	538	5,291.4	**Live Oak** (CDP) Santa Cruz County

Note: *The state column ranks the top/bottom 150 places from all places in the state with population of 10,000 or more. The national column ranks the top/bottom 150 places from all places in the country with population of 10,000 or more. Places that are unincorporated were not considered in the rankings. Please refer to the User Guide for additional information.*

Population Density

Top 150 Places Ranked in *Ascending* Order

State Rank	Nat'l Rank	Pop./ Sq. Mi.	Place
1	4	69.4	**California City** (city) Kern County
2	58	238.0	**Phelan** (CDP) San Bernardino County
3	165	348.2	**Rosamond** (CDP) Kern County
4	211	381.3	**Prunedale** (CDP) Monterey County
5	215	385.1	**Big Bear City** (CDP) San Bernardino County
6	244	413.9	**Rosedale** (CDP) Kern County
7	252	423.5	**Twentynine Palms** (city) San Bernardino County
8	303	473.4	**Palm Springs** (city) Riverside County
9	340	500.6	**Truckee** (town) Nevada County
10	370	517.3	**Yucca Valley** (town) San Bernardino County
11	382	528.3	**Ramona** (CDP) San Diego County
12	388	531.6	**Alpine** (CDP) San Diego County
13	406	547.0	**Barstow** (city) San Bernardino County
14	430	567.1	**Adelanto** (city) San Bernardino County
15	470	599.9	**San Diego Country Estates** (CDP) San Diego County
16	480	607.9	**Shafter** (city) Kern County
17	505	639.1	**Malibu** (city) Los Angeles County
18	539	663.2	**Diamond Springs** (CDP) El Dorado County
19	599	700.9	**Lake Arrowhead** (CDP) San Bernardino County
20	602	704.3	**Rancho Mirage** (city) Riverside County
21	633	729.8	**McKinleyville** (CDP) Humboldt County
22	692	778.2	**Crestline** (CDP) San Bernardino County
23	713	794.9	**Blythe** (city) Riverside County
24	719	798.3	**Avenal** (city) Kings County
25	734	807.0	**Magalia** (CDP) Butte County
26	750	821.8	**Lathrop** (city) San Joaquin County
27	806	869.0	**El Dorado Hills** (CDP) El Dorado County
28	881	930.7	**Shasta Lake** (city) Shasta County
29	904	944.6	**Apple Valley** (town) San Bernardino County
30	907	947.7	**Granite Bay** (CDP) Placer County
31	935	965.6	**Mead Valley** (CDP) Riverside County
32	1071	1,066.9	**La Quinta** (city) Riverside County
33	1091	1,082.3	**Sun Village** (CDP) Los Angeles County
34	1108	1,098.4	**Desert Hot Springs** (city) Riverside County
35	1123	1,104.1	**Atascadero** (city) San Luis Obispo County
36	1141	1,118.5	**Los Osos** (CDP) San Luis Obispo County
37	1151	1,125.4	**Nipomo** (CDP) San Luis Obispo County
38	1251	1,193.0	**Beaumont** (city) Riverside County
39	1257	1,196.5	**Oroville** (city) Butte County
40	1297	1,223.4	**Poway** (city) San Diego County
41	1314	1,233.6	**Hesperia** (city) San Bernardino County
42	1346	1,257.4	**Woodcrest** (CDP) Riverside County
43	1357	1,265.6	**Lake Los Angeles** (CDP) Los Angeles County
44	1379	1,281.6	**Banning** (city) Riverside County
45	1442	1,329.9	**Ridgecrest** (city) Kern County
46	1443	1,330.2	**Lakeland Village** (CDP) Riverside County
47	1476	1,358.3	**Wildomar** (city) Riverside County
48	1523	1,391.1	**Orinda** (city) Contra Costa County
49	1547	1,406.0	**Coachella** (city) Riverside County
50	1586	1,431.2	**Lake Elsinore** (city) Riverside County
51	1587	1,432.0	**Paradise** (town) Butte County
52	1600	1,441.6	**Palmdale** (city) Los Angeles County
53	1605	1,443.4	**Vineyard** (CDP) Sacramento County
54	1631	1,459.8	**Tehachapi** (city) Kern County
55	1683	1,505.6	**Clearlake** (city) Lake County
56	1685	1,506.5	**Redding** (city) Shasta County
57	1687	1,507.2	**Alamo** (CDP) Contra Costa County
58	1718	1,525.3	**Rio Linda** (CDP) Sacramento County
59	1757	1,558.2	**El Paso de Robles (Paso Robles)** (city) San Luis Obispo County
60	1770	1,569.8	**Lafayette** (city) Contra Costa County
61	1787	1,583.9	**Victorville** (city) San Bernardino County
62	1851	1,641.2	**Cameron Park** (CDP) El Dorado County
63	1876	1,661.4	**Lancaster** (city) Los Angeles County
64	1889	1,668.3	**Menifee** (city) Riverside County
65	1893	1,669.8	**North Auburn** (CDP) Placer County
66	1901	1,674.1	**Chino Hills** (city) San Bernardino County
67	1933	1,697.8	**Moraga** (town) Contra Costa County
68	1960	1,718.7	**San Jacinto** (city) Riverside County
69	1994	1,742.0	**Fallbrook** (CDP) San Diego County
70	2003	1,748.9	**Hillsborough** (town) San Mateo County
71	2019	1,762.6	**Half Moon Bay** (city) San Mateo County
72	2021	1,764.4	**El Sobrante** (CDP) Riverside County
73	2051	1,787.2	**Calabasas** (city) Los Angeles County
74	2052	1,787.6	**Placerville** (city) El Dorado County
75	2079	1,807.0	**Palm Desert** (city) Riverside County
76	2105	1,827.5	**Olivehurst** (CDP) Yuba County
77	2107	1,828.1	**Santa Fe Springs** (city) Los Angeles County
78	2121	1,841.9	**Yucaipa** (city) San Bernardino County
79	2148	1,861.3	**Red Bluff** (city) Tehama County
80	2150	1,867.4	**Auburn** (city) Placer County
81	2155	1,869.7	**Coto de Caza** (CDP) Orange County
82	2178	1,891.6	**Novato** (city) Marin County
83	2183	1,894.2	**Arcata** (city) Humboldt County
84	2195	1,903.0	**Redlands** (city) San Bernardino County
85	2222	1,930.0	**Morro Bay** (city) San Luis Obispo County
86	2227	1,933.2	**Rancho Cordova** (city) Sacramento County
87	2233	1,938.4	**Norco** (city) Riverside County
88	2265	1,961.7	**Commerce** (city) Los Angeles County
89	2375	2,079.7	**Linda** (CDP) Yuba County
90	2387	2,088.1	**Benicia** (city) Solano County
91	2409	2,106.3	**South Lake Tahoe** (city) El Dorado County
92	2426	2,122.5	**Valle Vista** (CDP) Riverside County
93	2427	2,122.6	**French Valley** (CDP) Riverside County
94	2436	2,129.7	**Lincoln** (city) Placer County
95	2449	2,141.4	**Seal Beach** (city) Orange County
96	2456	2,147.0	**Discovery Bay** (CDP) Contra Costa County
97	2487	2,178.4	**Perris** (city) Riverside County
98	2497	2,186.7	**Coalinga** (city) Fresno County
99	2520	2,219.2	**San Dimas** (city) Los Angeles County
100	2521	2,219.8	**Marina** (city) Monterey County
101	2528	2,235.0	**Oakley** (city) Contra Costa County
102	2560	2,262.9	**Susanville** (city) Lassen County
103	2576	2,275.1	**West Sacramento** (city) Yolo County
104	2604	2,302.0	**Thousand Oaks** (city) Ventura County
105	2615	2,315.0	**Tamalpais-Homestead Valley** (CDP) Marin County
106	2636	2,331.9	**Danville** (town) Contra Costa County
107	2666	2,346.5	**La Cañada Flintridge** (city) Los Angeles County
108	2693	2,381.5	**Cathedral City** (city) Riverside County
109	2696	2,384.6	**Coronado** (city) San Diego County
110	2721	2,416.9	**Saratoga** (city) Santa Clara County
111	2745	2,437.4	**Rancho San Diego** (CDP) San Diego County
112	2757	2,443.5	**Chowchilla** (city) Madera County
113	2758	2,444.2	**Bakersfield** (city) Kern County
114	2765	2,450.7	**San Juan Capistrano** (city) Orange County
115	2776	2,461.4	**Fortuna** (city) Humboldt County
116	2811	2,509.4	**Bonita** (CDP) San Diego County
117	2819	2,519.9	**Imperial** (city) Imperial County
118	2820	2,520.4	**Scotts Valley** (city) Santa Cruz County
119	2823	2,525.1	**Healdsburg** (city) Sonoma County
120	2850	2,567.6	**Laguna Beach** (city) Orange County
121	2857	2,579.1	**Salida** (CDP) Stanislaus County
122	2860	2,582.0	**Glendora** (city) Los Angeles County
123	2878	2,598.4	**Orcutt** (CDP) Santa Barbara County
124	2885	2,605.7	**Indio** (city) Riverside County
125	2890	2,608.7	**Agoura Hills** (city) Los Angeles County
126	2893	2,610.6	**Oak Park** (CDP) Ventura County
127	2898	2,616.5	**Claremont** (city) Los Angeles County
128	2901	2,617.8	**Chico** (city) Butte County
129	2904	2,618.8	**Castaic** (CDP) Los Angeles County
130	2908	2,623.2	**Dixon** (city) Solano County
131	2914	2,631.1	**Chino** (city) San Bernardino County
132	2929	2,654.6	**Los Gatos** (town) Santa Clara County
133	2961	2,688.8	**Canyon Lake** (city) Riverside County
134	2962	2,689.5	**Monrovia** (city) Los Angeles County
135	2966	2,695.2	**Ripon** (city) San Joaquin County
136	2968	2,696.5	**Palo Alto** (city) Santa Clara County
137	2976	2,710.1	**Wasco** (city) Kern County
138	2977	2,711.3	**Grass Valley** (city) Nevada County
139	2984	2,717.2	**Camp Pendleton South** (CDP) San Diego County
140	2995	2,736.4	**Moorpark** (city) Ventura County
141	2996	2,737.8	**Casa de Oro-Mount Helix** (CDP) San Diego County
142	3009	2,760.0	**Stevenson Ranch** (CDP) Los Angeles County
143	3012	2,763.9	**Fremont** (city) Alameda County
144	3029	2,792.2	**Carlsbad** (city) San Diego County
145	3046	2,815.0	**Palos Verdes Estates** (city) Los Angeles County
146	3048	2,816.8	**Fairfield** (city) Solano County
147	3051	2,824.6	**Hemet** (city) Riverside County
148	3058	2,827.0	**Los Alamitos** (city) Orange County
149	3062	2,831.5	**Highland** (city) San Bernardino County
150	3063	2,832.0	**Tulare** (city) Tulare County

Note: *The state column ranks the top/bottom 150 places from all places in the state with population of 10,000 or more. The national column ranks the top/bottom 150 places from all places in the country with population of 10,000 or more. Places that are unincorporated were not considered in the rankings. Please refer to the User Guide for additional information.*

White Population

Top 150 Places Ranked in *Descending* Order

State Rank	Nat'l Rank	Percent	Place
1	896	92.0	**Paradise** (town) Butte County
2	919	91.9	**Magalia** (CDP) Butte County
3	994	91.5	**Malibu** (city) Los Angeles County
4	1087	90.9	**Laguna Beach** (city) Orange County
5	1188	90.3	**San Anselmo** (town) Marin County
6	1218	90.1	**San Diego Country Estates** (CDP) San Diego County
7	1250	89.9	**Canyon Lake** (city) Riverside County
8	1329	89.4	**Grass Valley** (city) Nevada County
9	1371	89.1	**Cameron Park** (CDP) El Dorado County
10	1385	89.0	**Auburn** (city) Placer County
11	1415	88.8	**Mill Valley** (city) Marin County
12	1435	88.7	**Rancho Mirage** (city) Riverside County
13	1494	88.3	**Diamond Springs** (CDP) El Dorado County
14	1520	88.1	**Coronado** (city) San Diego County
14	1520	88.1	**Coto de Caza** (CDP) Orange County
16	1541	88.0	**Granite Bay** (CDP) Placer County
16	1541	88.0	**Tamalpais-Homestead Valley** (CDP) Marin County
18	1626	87.4	**Orangevale** (CDP) Sacramento County
19	1636	87.3	**Alpine** (CDP) San Diego County
19	1636	87.3	**Laguna Woods** (city) Orange County
19	1636	87.3	**Newport Beach** (city) Orange County
22	1663	87.1	**Morro Bay** (city) San Luis Obispo County
23	1693	86.9	**Alamo** (CDP) Contra Costa County
24	1707	86.8	**Hermosa Beach** (city) Los Angeles County
24	1707	86.8	**Sonoma** (city) Sonoma County
26	1757	86.5	**Larkspur** (city) Marin County
26	1757	86.5	**Truckee** (town) Nevada County
28	1768	86.4	**Atascadero** (city) San Luis Obispo County
28	1768	86.4	**Lake Arrowhead** (CDP) San Bernardino County
30	1798	86.2	**Crestline** (CDP) San Bernardino County
30	1798	86.2	**Los Osos** (CDP) San Luis Obispo County
32	1811	86.1	**Dana Point** (city) Orange County
32	1811	86.1	**Shasta Lake** (city) Shasta County
34	1831	86.0	**San Clemente** (city) Orange County
34	1831	86.0	**Scotts Valley** (city) Santa Cruz County
36	1853	85.8	**Encinitas** (city) San Diego County
36	1853	85.8	**Redding** (city) Shasta County
36	1853	85.8	**Solana Beach** (city) San Diego County
39	1869	85.7	**Fair Oaks** (CDP) Sacramento County
39	1869	85.7	**McKinleyville** (CDP) Humboldt County
41	1912	85.3	**Arroyo Grande** (city) San Luis Obispo County
42	1932	85.1	**Clayton** (city) Contra Costa County
42	1932	85.1	**North Auburn** (CDP) Placer County
44	1953	85.0	**Lakeside** (CDP) San Diego County
45	1971	84.8	**Rossmoor** (CDP) Orange County
46	1982	84.7	**Lafayette** (city) Contra Costa County
47	1996	84.5	**Manhattan Beach** (city) Los Angeles County
47	1996	84.5	**Pacific Grove** (city) Monterey County
47	1996	84.5	**San Luis Obispo** (city) San Luis Obispo County
50	2023	84.3	**Agoura Hills** (city) Los Angeles County
51	2037	84.2	**West Hollywood** (city) Los Angeles County
52	2064	84.0	**Oildale** (CDP) Kern County
53	2077	83.9	**Calabasas** (city) Los Angeles County
53	2077	83.9	**Placerville** (city) El Dorado County
55	2107	83.6	**North Tustin** (CDP) Orange County
56	2118	83.5	**Yucca Valley** (town) San Bernardino County
57	2129	83.4	**Seal Beach** (city) Orange County
58	2140	83.3	**Big Bear City** (CDP) San Bernardino County
58	2140	83.3	**El Dorado Hills** (CDP) El Dorado County
60	2152	83.2	**Rosedale** (CDP) Kern County
61	2165	83.1	**Danville** (town) Contra Costa County
61	2165	83.1	**Oak Park** (CDP) Ventura County
63	2198	82.8	**Carlsbad** (city) San Diego County
64	2208	82.7	**Rancho San Diego** (CDP) San Diego County
65	2214	82.6	**Rocklin** (city) Placer County
66	2223	82.5	**Palm Desert** (city) Riverside County
66	2223	82.5	**Santee** (city) San Diego County
68	2238	82.4	**Beverly Hills** (city) Los Angeles County
68	2238	82.4	**Orinda** (city) Contra Costa County
70	2275	82.1	**Sierra Madre** (city) Los Angeles County
71	2294	81.9	**Orcutt** (CDP) Santa Barbara County
72	2304	81.8	**Arcata** (city) Humboldt County
72	2304	81.8	**Los Gatos** (town) Santa Clara County
74	2314	81.7	**Discovery Bay** (CDP) Contra Costa County
75	2323	81.6	**Winter Gardens** (CDP) San Diego County
76	2357	81.2	**Fortuna** (city) Humboldt County
77	2397	80.8	**Chico** (city) Butte County
78	2408	80.7	**Red Bluff** (city) Tehama County
79	2418	80.6	**Carmichael** (CDP) Sacramento County
80	2436	80.4	**Laguna Niguel** (city) Orange County
80	2436	80.4	**Petaluma** (city) Sonoma County
82	2453	80.3	**Citrus Heights** (city) Sacramento County
82	2453	80.3	**Thousand Oaks** (city) Ventura County
84	2466	80.1	**Oakdale** (city) Stanislaus County
85	2497	79.8	**Mission Viejo** (city) Orange County
86	2506	79.7	**Ripon** (city) San Joaquin County
87	2517	79.6	**Lincoln** (city) Placer County
88	2523	79.5	**Yucaipa** (city) San Bernardino County
89	2539	79.3	**Casa de Oro-Mount Helix** (CDP) San Diego County
89	2539	79.3	**Eureka** (city) Humboldt County
89	2539	79.3	**Roseville** (city) Placer County
92	2554	79.2	**San Carlos** (city) San Mateo County
92	2554	79.2	**Valle Vista** (CDP) Riverside County
94	2594	78.7	**La Quinta** (city) Riverside County
94	2594	78.7	**Walnut Creek** (city) Contra Costa County
96	2634	78.3	**Monterey** (city) Monterey County
96	2634	78.3	**Ramona** (CDP) San Diego County
98	2641	78.2	**Rancho Santa Margarita** (city) Orange County
99	2653	78.0	**El Segundo** (city) Los Angeles County
100	2663	77.9	**Ladera Ranch** (CDP) Orange County
101	2672	77.7	**El Paso de Robles (Paso Robles)** (city) San Luis Obispo County
102	2682	77.6	**Santa Monica** (city) Los Angeles County
103	2703	77.4	**Ridgecrest** (city) Kern County
104	2730	77.1	**Martinez** (city) Contra Costa County
104	2730	77.1	**Rio Linda** (CDP) Sacramento County
104	2730	77.1	**San Juan Capistrano** (city) Orange County
107	2743	77.0	**Palos Verdes Estates** (city) Los Angeles County
108	2751	76.9	**Poway** (city) San Diego County
109	2761	76.7	**Huntington Beach** (city) Orange County
110	2769	76.6	**San Buenaventura (Ventura)** (city) Ventura County
111	2790	76.3	**Norco** (city) Riverside County
112	2793	76.2	**Moraga** (town) Contra Costa County
113	2802	76.1	**Rohnert Park** (city) Sonoma County
114	2810	76.0	**Novato** (city) Marin County
115	2825	75.8	**Half Moon Bay** (city) San Mateo County
116	2842	75.7	**Grover Beach** (city) San Luis Obispo County
116	2842	75.7	**Palm Springs** (city) Riverside County
118	2851	75.6	**Phelan** (CDP) San Bernardino County
119	2874	75.3	**Kingsburg** (city) Fresno County
119	2874	75.3	**Quartz Hill** (CDP) Los Angeles County
119	2874	75.3	**Simi Valley** (city) Ventura County
122	2885	75.2	**Oroville** (city) Butte County
123	2892	75.1	**Camarillo** (city) Ventura County
123	2892	75.1	**Glendora** (city) Los Angeles County
123	2892	75.1	**Moorpark** (city) Ventura County
123	2892	75.1	**Napa** (city) Napa County
123	2892	75.1	**Santa Barbara** (city) Santa Barbara County
123	2892	75.1	**Yorba Linda** (city) Orange County
129	2912	74.9	**Pleasant Hill** (city) Contra Costa County
130	2936	74.6	**Livermore** (city) Alameda County
130	2936	74.6	**Redondo Beach** (city) Los Angeles County
132	2941	74.5	**Santa Cruz** (city) Santa Cruz County
133	2957	74.3	**Folsom** (city) Sacramento County
134	2960	74.2	**La Verne** (city) Los Angeles County
134	2960	74.2	**Piedmont** (city) Alameda County
136	2973	74.1	**Healdsburg** (city) Sonoma County
137	2986	73.9	**Windsor** (town) Sonoma County
138	2990	73.8	**Clearlake** (city) Lake County
139	3000	73.6	**Live Oak** (CDP) Santa Cruz County
140	3004	73.5	**Nipomo** (CDP) San Luis Obispo County
140	3004	73.5	**South Lake Tahoe** (city) El Dorado County
142	3057	72.7	**Burbank** (city) Los Angeles County
142	3057	72.7	**Laguna Hills** (city) Orange County
144	3063	72.6	**Woodcrest** (CDP) Riverside County
145	3071	72.5	**Benicia** (city) Solano County
146	3090	72.1	**Ukiah** (city) Mendocino County
147	3097	72.0	**Aliso Viejo** (city) Orange County
147	3097	72.0	**San Dimas** (city) Los Angeles County
149	3108	71.8	**La Mesa** (city) San Diego County
150	3117	71.7	**Carpinteria** (city) Santa Barbara County

Note: *The state column ranks the top/bottom 150 places from all places in the state with population of 10,000 or more. The national column ranks the top/bottom 150 places from all places in the country with population of 10,000 or more. Places that are unincorporated were not considered in the rankings. Please refer to the User Guide for additional information.*

White Population

Top 150 Places Ranked in *Ascending* Order

State Rank	Nat'l Rank	Percent	Place
1	21	6.0	**View Park-Windsor Hills** (CDP) Los Angeles County
2	65	15.8	**Westmont** (CDP) Los Angeles County
3	96	19.4	**Monterey Park** (city) Los Angeles County
4	106	20.5	**Milpitas** (city) Santa Clara County
5	112	21.1	**Rosemead** (city) Los Angeles County
6	117	22.0	**Hercules** (city) Contra Costa County
7	121	22.9	**Willowbrook** (CDP) Los Angeles County
8	122	23.1	**Cerritos** (city) Los Angeles County
9	125	23.3	**Inglewood** (city) Los Angeles County
10	128	23.5	**Rowland Heights** (CDP) Los Angeles County
11	130	23.6	**Daly City** (city) San Mateo County
12	131	23.7	**Walnut** (city) Los Angeles County
13	132	23.8	**Carson** (city) Los Angeles County
14	134	23.9	**Union City** (city) Alameda County
15	142	24.6	**Gardena** (city) Los Angeles County
16	148	25.4	**San Gabriel** (city) Los Angeles County
17	153	25.9	**Compton** (city) Los Angeles County
18	171	28.3	**Alhambra** (city) Los Angeles County
19	177	28.8	**East Palo Alto** (city) San Mateo County
20	196	30.6	**Ashland** (CDP) Alameda County
21	203	31.3	**Cupertino** (city) Santa Clara County
22	206	31.4	**Richmond** (city) Contra Costa County
23	208	31.5	**East Rancho Dominguez** (CDP) Los Angeles County
24	209	31.6	**Florin** (CDP) Sacramento County
25	212	32.2	**San Pablo** (city) Contra Costa County
26	213	32.3	**Arcadia** (city) Los Angeles County
27	221	32.8	**Fremont** (city) Alameda County
27	221	32.8	**Hawthorne** (city) Los Angeles County
27	221	32.8	**Vallejo** (city) Solano County
30	228	33.2	**Diamond Bar** (city) Los Angeles County
31	233	33.6	**Temple City** (city) Los Angeles County
32	236	33.9	**East San Gabriel** (CDP) Los Angeles County
33	237	34.2	**Hayward** (city) Alameda County
34	242	34.5	**Oakland** (city) Alameda County
35	247	35.2	**West Carson** (CDP) Los Angeles County
36	252	35.6	**Parkway** (CDP) Sacramento County
37	253	35.7	**Westminster** (city) Orange County
38	256	36.0	**Corcoran** (city) Kings County
39	262	36.4	**Delano** (city) Kern County
40	265	36.5	**Pittsburg** (city) Contra Costa County
41	267	36.6	**Greenfield** (city) Monterey County
42	270	37.0	**La Palma** (city) Orange County
42	270	37.0	**Stockton** (city) San Joaquin County
44	272	37.1	**Lemon Hill** (CDP) Sacramento County
45	274	37.3	**South San Francisco** (city) San Mateo County
46	280	37.6	**San Leandro** (city) Alameda County
47	282	37.7	**Florence-Graham** (CDP) Los Angeles County
48	283	37.9	**Lennox** (CDP) Los Angeles County
49	290	38.4	**Suisun City** (city) Solano County
50	295	38.8	**El Monte** (city) Los Angeles County
51	297	38.9	**American Canyon** (city) Napa County
52	299	39.0	**Artesia** (city) Los Angeles County
52	299	39.0	**Avenal** (city) Kings County
54	309	39.3	**Lynwood** (city) Los Angeles County
55	319	39.9	**Garden Grove** (city) Orange County
56	322	40.3	**Livingston** (city) Merced County
57	325	40.5	**Hacienda Heights** (CDP) Los Angeles County
58	332	41.0	**Cherryland** (CDP) Alameda County
59	335	41.1	**Lathrop** (city) San Joaquin County
60	340	41.3	**Newark** (city) Alameda County
60	340	41.3	**San Marino** (city) Los Angeles County
62	343	41.4	**Bay Point** (CDP) Contra Costa County
63	351	41.9	**Moreno Valley** (city) Riverside County
63	351	41.9	**Muscoy** (CDP) San Bernardino County
65	357	42.2	**Bellflower** (city) Los Angeles County
65	357	42.2	**National City** (city) San Diego County
65	357	42.2	**Signal Hill** (city) Los Angeles County
68	361	42.3	**Perris** (city) Riverside County
69	362	42.4	**Alum Rock** (CDP) Santa Clara County
70	363	42.5	**Paramount** (city) Los Angeles County
71	369	42.8	**McFarland** (city) Kern County
71	369	42.8	**San Jose** (city) Santa Clara County
71	369	42.8	**West Covina** (city) Los Angeles County
74	375	42.9	**Eastvale** (city) Riverside County
75	377	43.0	**Sunnyvale** (city) Santa Clara County
76	383	43.4	**Colton** (city) San Bernardino County
77	387	43.6	**Lawndale** (city) Los Angeles County
78	390	43.7	**Watsonville** (city) Santa Cruz County
79	392	43.8	**Adelanto** (city) San Bernardino County
80	395	43.9	**Baldwin Park** (city) Los Angeles County
81	398	44.0	**Rialto** (city) San Bernardino County
82	401	44.1	**La Presa** (CDP) San Diego County
83	404	44.2	**Lamont** (CDP) Kern County
84	405	44.5	**Emeryville** (city) Alameda County
84	405	44.5	**Stanton** (city) Orange County
86	415	45.0	**Fairview** (CDP) Alameda County
86	415	45.0	**Sacramento** (city) Sacramento County
86	415	45.0	**Santa Clara** (city) Santa Clara County
89	423	45.2	**Marina** (city) Monterey County
90	425	45.3	**Buena Park** (city) Orange County
90	425	45.3	**Mead Valley** (CDP) Riverside County
90	425	45.3	**South San Jose Hills** (CDP) Los Angeles County
93	431	45.4	**Hawaiian Gardens** (city) Los Angeles County
94	435	45.5	**Foster City** (city) San Mateo County
94	435	45.5	**Vineyard** (CDP) Sacramento County
96	437	45.6	**Home Gardens** (CDP) Riverside County
96	437	45.6	**San Bernardino** (city) San Bernardino County
98	446	45.8	**Salinas** (city) Monterey County
99	448	45.9	**Santa Ana** (city) Orange County
100	452	46.0	**Fairfield** (city) Solano County
101	453	46.1	**Elk Grove** (city) Sacramento County
101	453	46.1	**Long Beach** (city) Los Angeles County
103	455	46.2	**Pinole** (city) Contra Costa County
104	476	47.3	**Millbrae** (city) San Mateo County
105	477	47.4	**Fontana** (city) San Bernardino County
105	477	47.4	**San Lorenzo** (CDP) Alameda County
107	488	47.8	**Loma Linda** (city) San Bernardino County
108	491	47.9	**King City** (city) Monterey County
109	495	48.0	**Pomona** (city) Los Angeles County
109	495	48.0	**Shafter** (city) Kern County
111	499	48.1	**Coachella** (city) Riverside County
111	499	48.1	**North Fair Oaks** (CDP) San Mateo County
113	502	48.2	**Oxnard** (city) Ventura County
114	504	48.4	**Seaside** (city) Monterey County
115	509	48.5	**San Francisco** (city) San Francisco County
115	509	48.5	**Valinda** (CDP) Los Angeles County
115	509	48.5	**Victorville** (city) San Bernardino County
118	519	48.9	**Antioch** (city) Contra Costa County
119	523	49.0	**Palmdale** (city) Los Angeles County
120	526	49.1	**Soledad** (city) Monterey County
121	528	49.2	**Cudahy** (city) Los Angeles County
121	528	49.2	**Garden Acres** (CDP) San Joaquin County
121	528	49.2	**Wasco** (city) Kern County
124	533	49.4	**La Puente** (city) Los Angeles County
124	533	49.4	**Norwalk** (city) Los Angeles County
126	535	49.5	**Bell Gardens** (city) Los Angeles County
126	535	49.5	**San Bruno** (city) San Mateo County
128	537	49.6	**Fresno** (city) Fresno County
128	537	49.6	**Lancaster** (city) Los Angeles County
128	537	49.6	**Patterson** (city) Stanislaus County
131	542	49.8	**Los Angeles** (city) Los Angeles County
132	546	49.9	**Madera** (city) Madera County
133	549	50.0	**Farmersville** (city) Tulare County
133	549	50.0	**Parlier** (city) Fresno County
135	557	50.3	**West Puente Valley** (CDP) Los Angeles County
136	559	50.4	**South El Monte** (city) Los Angeles County
137	563	50.5	**East Los Angeles** (CDP) Los Angeles County
137	563	50.5	**Irvine** (city) Orange County
137	563	50.5	**South Gate** (city) Los Angeles County
140	570	50.6	**El Sobrante** (CDP) Contra Costa County
140	570	50.6	**Kerman** (city) Fresno County
142	580	50.8	**Alameda** (city) Alameda County
142	580	50.8	**Chino Hills** (city) San Bernardino County
144	585	51.0	**Ontario** (city) San Bernardino County
144	585	51.0	**San Fernando** (city) Los Angeles County
146	588	51.1	**Torrance** (city) Los Angeles County
147	589	51.2	**Huntington Park** (city) Los Angeles County
148	593	51.3	**Dublin** (city) Alameda County
149	597	51.6	**Lemon Grove** (city) San Diego County
150	604	51.9	**Duarte** (city) Los Angeles County

Note: *The state column ranks the top/bottom 150 places from all places in the state with population of 10,000 or more. The national column ranks the top/bottom 150 places from all places in the country with population of 10,000 or more. Places that are unincorporated were not considered in the rankings. Please refer to the User Guide for additional information.*

Black/African American Population

Top 150 Places Ranked in *Descending* Order

State Rank	Nat'l Rank	Percent	Place
1	28	84.8	**View Park-Windsor Hills** (CDP) Los Angeles County
2	201	51.1	**Westmont** (CDP) Los Angeles County
3	268	43.9	**Inglewood** (city) Los Angeles County
4	383	34.4	**Willowbrook** (CDP) Los Angeles County
5	406	32.9	**Compton** (city) Los Angeles County
6	513	28.0	**Oakland** (city) Alameda County
7	526	27.7	**Hawthorne** (city) Los Angeles County
8	552	26.6	**Richmond** (city) Contra Costa County
9	606	24.4	**Gardena** (city) Los Angeles County
10	619	23.8	**Carson** (city) Los Angeles County
11	623	23.7	**Altadena** (CDP) Los Angeles County
12	677	22.1	**Vallejo** (city) Solano County
13	710	21.0	**Fairview** (CDP) Alameda County
14	724	20.5	**Adelanto** (city) San Bernardino County
14	724	20.5	**Lancaster** (city) Los Angeles County
16	733	20.3	**Suisun City** (city) Solano County
17	761	19.5	**Ashland** (CDP) Alameda County
18	782	18.9	**Hercules** (city) Contra Costa County
19	813	18.4	**Parkway** (CDP) Sacramento County
20	836	18.0	**Moreno Valley** (city) Riverside County
21	846	17.7	**Pittsburg** (city) Contra Costa County
22	851	17.5	**Emeryville** (city) Alameda County
23	861	17.3	**Antioch** (city) Contra Costa County
24	882	16.8	**Victorville** (city) San Bernardino County
25	890	16.7	**East Palo Alto** (city) San Mateo County
26	907	16.4	**Rialto** (city) San Bernardino County
27	940	15.9	**East Rancho Dominguez** (CDP) Los Angeles County
28	946	15.8	**Florin** (CDP) Sacramento County
28	946	15.8	**San Pablo** (city) Contra Costa County
30	951	15.7	**Fairfield** (city) Solano County
31	984	15.2	**California City** (city) Kern County
32	997	15.0	**Blythe** (city) Riverside County
32	997	15.0	**Corcoran** (city) Kings County
32	997	15.0	**San Bernardino** (city) San Bernardino County
35	1008	14.8	**Palmdale** (city) Los Angeles County
36	1021	14.6	**Barstow** (city) San Bernardino County
36	1021	14.6	**Sacramento** (city) Sacramento County
38	1057	14.0	**Bellflower** (city) Los Angeles County
39	1070	13.8	**Lemon Grove** (city) San Diego County
40	1085	13.6	**Signal Hill** (city) Los Angeles County
41	1088	13.5	**Long Beach** (city) Los Angeles County
42	1097	13.4	**Pinole** (city) Contra Costa County
43	1111	13.2	**El Sobrante** (CDP) Contra Costa County
44	1121	13.0	**La Presa** (CDP) San Diego County
45	1154	12.6	**Chowchilla** (city) Madera County
46	1163	12.5	**Susanville** (city) Lassen County
47	1174	12.3	**San Leandro** (city) Alameda County
48	1180	12.2	**Stockton** (city) San Joaquin County
49	1194	12.1	**Perris** (city) Riverside County
50	1201	12.0	**Rosemont** (CDP) Sacramento County
51	1210	11.9	**Hayward** (city) Alameda County
52	1221	11.7	**Paramount** (city) Los Angeles County
53	1229	11.6	**Bay Point** (CDP) Contra Costa County
54	1238	11.5	**Cherryland** (CDP) Alameda County
55	1244	11.4	**North Highlands** (CDP) Sacramento County
55	1244	11.4	**Soledad** (city) Monterey County
57	1256	11.3	**Lake Los Angeles** (CDP) Los Angeles County
58	1263	11.2	**Elk Grove** (city) Sacramento County
59	1273	11.1	**Highland** (city) San Bernardino County
59	1273	11.1	**Spring Valley** (CDP) San Diego County
61	1284	11.0	**Foothill Farms** (CDP) Sacramento County
62	1289	10.9	**Lemon Hill** (CDP) Sacramento County
63	1312	10.7	**Pasadena** (city) Los Angeles County
63	1312	10.7	**West Carson** (CDP) Los Angeles County
65	1333	10.5	**Avenal** (city) Kings County
66	1352	10.3	**Lynwood** (city) Los Angeles County
66	1352	10.3	**Vacaville** (city) Solano County
68	1381	10.1	**Lawndale** (city) Los Angeles County
68	1381	10.1	**Rancho Cordova** (city) Sacramento County
70	1392	10.0	**Berkeley** (city) Alameda County
70	1392	10.0	**Fontana** (city) San Bernardino County
70	1392	10.0	**La Riviera** (CDP) Sacramento County
73	1415	9.8	**Vineyard** (CDP) Sacramento County
74	1422	9.7	**Colton** (city) San Bernardino County
74	1422	9.7	**Eastvale** (city) Riverside County
76	1436	9.6	**Los Angeles** (city) Los Angeles County
77	1449	9.5	**Culver City** (city) Los Angeles County
78	1457	9.4	**Dublin** (city) Alameda County
79	1464	9.3	**Camp Pendleton South** (CDP) San Diego County
80	1471	9.2	**Florence-Graham** (CDP) Los Angeles County
80	1471	9.2	**Rancho Cucamonga** (city) San Bernardino County
82	1482	9.1	**Apple Valley** (town) San Bernardino County
83	1489	9.0	**Tehachapi** (city) Kern County
84	1510	8.8	**Antelope** (CDP) Sacramento County
85	1517	8.7	**Arden-Arcade** (CDP) Sacramento County
85	1517	8.7	**Lakewood** (city) Los Angeles County
85	1517	8.7	**Loma Linda** (city) San Bernardino County
88	1556	8.4	**Seaside** (city) Monterey County
89	1563	8.3	**Fresno** (city) Fresno County
90	1573	8.2	**Bakersfield** (city) Kern County
90	1573	8.2	**Desert Hot Springs** (city) Riverside County
90	1573	8.2	**Mead Valley** (CDP) Riverside County
90	1573	8.2	**Twentynine Palms** (city) San Bernardino County
94	1586	8.1	**Rosamond** (CDP) Kern County
95	1613	7.9	**American Canyon** (city) Napa County
95	1613	7.9	**Delano** (city) Kern County
95	1613	7.9	**El Sobrante** (CDP) Riverside County
95	1613	7.9	**French Valley** (CDP) Riverside County
99	1640	7.7	**El Cerrito** (city) Contra Costa County
99	1640	7.7	**La Mesa** (city) San Diego County
101	1653	7.6	**Wasco** (city) Kern County
102	1669	7.5	**Marina** (city) Monterey County
103	1684	7.4	**Duarte** (city) Los Angeles County
104	1696	7.3	**Banning** (city) Riverside County
104	1696	7.3	**Oakley** (city) Contra Costa County
104	1696	7.3	**Pomona** (city) Los Angeles County
104	1696	7.3	**Quartz Hill** (CDP) Los Angeles County
104	1696	7.3	**Upland** (city) San Bernardino County
109	1712	7.2	**Lathrop** (city) San Joaquin County
109	1712	7.2	**Tracy** (city) San Joaquin County
111	1744	7.0	**Norco** (city) Riverside County
111	1744	7.0	**Riverside** (city) Riverside County
111	1744	7.0	**Sun Village** (CDP) Los Angeles County
114	1764	6.9	**Castro Valley** (CDP) Alameda County
114	1764	6.9	**Cerritos** (city) Los Angeles County
116	1780	6.8	**Monrovia** (city) Los Angeles County
117	1793	6.7	**San Diego** (city) San Diego County
118	1808	6.6	**Bostonia** (CDP) San Diego County
118	1808	6.6	**Brentwood** (city) Contra Costa County
118	1808	6.6	**San Jacinto** (city) Riverside County
121	1840	6.4	**Alameda** (city) Alameda County
121	1840	6.4	**Hemet** (city) Riverside County
121	1840	6.4	**Lemoore** (city) Kings County
121	1840	6.4	**Ontario** (city) San Bernardino County
125	1873	6.3	**El Cajon** (city) San Diego County
125	1873	6.3	**Merced** (city) Merced County
125	1873	6.3	**Patterson** (city) Stanislaus County
125	1873	6.3	**Union City** (city) Alameda County
129	1890	6.2	**Beaumont** (city) Riverside County
129	1890	6.2	**Chino** (city) San Bernardino County
131	1911	6.1	**San Francisco** (city) San Francisco County
132	1947	5.9	**Casa de Oro-Mount Helix** (CDP) San Diego County
132	1947	5.9	**Corona** (city) Riverside County
134	1971	5.8	**Hesperia** (city) San Bernardino County
135	1983	5.7	**Folsom** (city) Sacramento County
135	1983	5.7	**Lompoc** (city) Santa Barbara County
137	2001	5.6	**Benicia** (city) Solano County
137	2001	5.6	**Grand Terrace** (city) San Bernardino County
139	2050	5.4	**Murrieta** (city) Riverside County
140	2066	5.3	**Lake Elsinore** (city) Riverside County
140	2066	5.3	**Lomita** (city) Los Angeles County
142	2090	5.2	**La Palma** (city) Orange County
142	2090	5.2	**Montclair** (city) San Bernardino County
142	2090	5.2	**National City** (city) San Diego County
142	2090	5.2	**Redlands** (city) San Bernardino County
146	2116	5.1	**Port Hueneme** (city) Ventura County
147	2139	5.0	**Menifee** (city) Riverside County
147	2139	5.0	**Woodcrest** (CDP) Riverside County
149	2156	4.9	**Hanford** (city) Kings County
150	2182	4.8	**Carmichael** (CDP) Sacramento County

Note: *The state column ranks the top/bottom 150 places from all places in the state with population of 10,000 or more. The national column ranks the top/bottom 150 places from all places in the country with population of 10,000 or more. Places that are unincorporated were not considered in the rankings. Please refer to the User Guide for additional information.*

Black/African American Population

Top 150 Places Ranked in *Ascending* Order

State Rank	Nat'l Rank	Percent	Place
1	15	0.3	**Calexico** (city) Imperial County
1	15	0.3	**Saratoga** (city) Santa Clara County
3	56	0.4	**Diamond Springs** (CDP) El Dorado County
3	56	0.4	**Grass Valley** (city) Nevada County
3	56	0.4	**Hillsborough** (town) San Mateo County
3	56	0.4	**Magalia** (CDP) Butte County
3	56	0.4	**Monterey Park** (city) Los Angeles County
3	56	0.4	**Morro Bay** (city) San Luis Obispo County
3	56	0.4	**Paradise** (town) Butte County
3	56	0.4	**San Marino** (city) Los Angeles County
3	56	0.4	**Truckee** (town) Nevada County
3	56	0.4	**Walnut Park** (CDP) Los Angeles County
13	131	0.5	**Alamo** (CDP) Contra Costa County
13	131	0.5	**Fillmore** (city) Ventura County
13	131	0.5	**Healdsburg** (city) Sonoma County
13	131	0.5	**Kerman** (city) Fresno County
13	131	0.5	**Kingsburg** (city) Fresno County
13	131	0.5	**La Cañada Flintridge** (city) Los Angeles County
13	131	0.5	**Los Altos** (city) Santa Clara County
13	131	0.5	**Rosemead** (city) Los Angeles County
13	131	0.5	**Santa Paula** (city) Ventura County
13	131	0.5	**Solana Beach** (city) San Diego County
13	131	0.5	**Sonoma** (city) Sonoma County
13	131	0.5	**South El Monte** (city) Los Angeles County
25	234	0.6	**Cupertino** (city) Santa Clara County
25	234	0.6	**East Los Angeles** (CDP) Los Angeles County
25	234	0.6	**Encinitas** (city) San Diego County
25	234	0.6	**Exeter** (city) Tulare County
25	234	0.6	**Farmersville** (city) Tulare County
25	234	0.6	**Fortuna** (city) Humboldt County
25	234	0.6	**Los Osos** (CDP) San Luis Obispo County
25	234	0.6	**Maywood** (city) Los Angeles County
25	234	0.6	**Napa** (city) Napa County
25	234	0.6	**North Tustin** (CDP) Orange County
25	234	0.6	**Parlier** (city) Fresno County
25	234	0.6	**San Clemente** (city) Orange County
25	234	0.6	**San Juan Capistrano** (city) Orange County
38	327	0.7	**Big Bear City** (CDP) San Bernardino County
38	327	0.7	**Commerce** (city) Los Angeles County
38	327	0.7	**Dinuba** (city) Tulare County
38	327	0.7	**Granite Bay** (CDP) Placer County
38	327	0.7	**Half Moon Bay** (city) San Mateo County
38	327	0.7	**La Crescenta-Montrose** (CDP) Los Angeles County
38	327	0.7	**Lafayette** (city) Contra Costa County
38	327	0.7	**Laguna Woods** (city) Orange County
38	327	0.7	**Lindsay** (city) Tulare County
38	327	0.7	**McKinleyville** (CDP) Humboldt County
38	327	0.7	**Newport Beach** (city) Orange County
38	327	0.7	**Ramona** (CDP) San Diego County
38	327	0.7	**Reedley** (city) Fresno County
38	327	0.7	**Shasta Lake** (city) Shasta County
38	327	0.7	**Watsonville** (city) Santa Cruz County
53	424	0.8	**Auburn** (city) Placer County
53	424	0.8	**Cameron Park** (CDP) El Dorado County
53	424	0.8	**Carpinteria** (city) Santa Barbara County
53	424	0.8	**Coachella** (city) Riverside County
53	424	0.8	**El Monte** (city) Los Angeles County
53	424	0.8	**Huntington Park** (city) Los Angeles County
53	424	0.8	**Laguna Beach** (city) Orange County
53	424	0.8	**Lake Arrowhead** (CDP) San Bernardino County
53	424	0.8	**Livingston** (city) Merced County
53	424	0.8	**Lodi** (city) San Joaquin County
53	424	0.8	**Manhattan Beach** (city) Los Angeles County
53	424	0.8	**Mill Valley** (city) Marin County
53	424	0.8	**Millbrae** (city) San Mateo County
53	424	0.8	**Oakdale** (city) Stanislaus County
53	424	0.8	**Oildale** (CDP) Kern County
53	424	0.8	**Orinda** (city) Contra Costa County
53	424	0.8	**Placerville** (city) El Dorado County
53	424	0.8	**Rossmoor** (CDP) Orange County
53	424	0.8	**San Carlos** (city) San Mateo County
53	424	0.8	**Tamalpais-Homestead Valley** (CDP) Marin County
53	424	0.8	**Temple City** (city) Los Angeles County
53	424	0.8	**Windsor** (town) Sonoma County
75	548	0.9	**Arroyo Grande** (city) San Luis Obispo County
75	548	0.9	**Avocado Heights** (CDP) Los Angeles County
75	548	0.9	**Bell** (city) Los Angeles County
75	548	0.9	**Bell Gardens** (city) Los Angeles County
75	548	0.9	**Coto de Caza** (CDP) Orange County
75	548	0.9	**Dana Point** (city) Orange County
75	548	0.9	**Danville** (town) Contra Costa County
75	548	0.9	**Fountain Valley** (city) Orange County
75	548	0.9	**Lamont** (CDP) Kern County
75	548	0.9	**Los Gatos** (town) Santa Clara County
75	548	0.9	**Montebello** (city) Los Angeles County
75	548	0.9	**North Auburn** (CDP) Placer County
75	548	0.9	**Red Bluff** (city) Tehama County
75	548	0.9	**San Anselmo** (town) Marin County
75	548	0.9	**San Diego Country Estates** (CDP) San Diego County
75	548	0.9	**San Fernando** (city) Los Angeles County
75	548	0.9	**Sanger** (city) Fresno County
75	548	0.9	**Scotts Valley** (city) Santa Cruz County
75	548	0.9	**South Gate** (city) Los Angeles County
75	548	0.9	**South Lake Tahoe** (city) El Dorado County
75	548	0.9	**Westminster** (city) Orange County
96	640	1.0	**Arvin** (city) Kern County
96	640	1.0	**Crestline** (CDP) San Bernardino County
96	640	1.0	**Hollister** (city) San Benito County
96	640	1.0	**Huntington Beach** (city) Orange County
96	640	1.0	**Mendota** (city) Fresno County
96	640	1.0	**Oak Park** (CDP) Ventura County
96	640	1.0	**Pico Rivera** (city) Los Angeles County
96	640	1.0	**Prunedale** (CDP) Monterey County
96	640	1.0	**San Gabriel** (city) Los Angeles County
96	640	1.0	**West Whittier-Los Nietos** (CDP) Los Angeles County
106	745	1.1	**Delhi** (CDP) Merced County
106	745	1.1	**Greenfield** (city) Monterey County
106	745	1.1	**Grover Beach** (city) San Luis Obispo County
106	745	1.1	**Lakeside** (CDP) San Diego County
106	745	1.1	**Nipomo** (CDP) San Luis Obispo County
106	745	1.1	**Ukiah** (city) Mendocino County
112	830	1.2	**Alpine** (CDP) San Diego County
112	830	1.2	**Arcadia** (city) Los Angeles County
112	830	1.2	**Baldwin Park** (city) Los Angeles County
112	830	1.2	**Burlingame** (city) San Mateo County
112	830	1.2	**Canyon Lake** (city) Riverside County
112	830	1.2	**Hermosa Beach** (city) Los Angeles County
112	830	1.2	**King City** (city) Monterey County
112	830	1.2	**Laguna Niguel** (city) Orange County
112	830	1.2	**Malibu** (city) Los Angeles County
112	830	1.2	**Palos Verdes Estates** (city) Los Angeles County
112	830	1.2	**Porterville** (city) Tulare County
112	830	1.2	**Redding** (city) Shasta County
112	830	1.2	**San Luis Obispo** (city) San Luis Obispo County
112	830	1.2	**Seal Beach** (city) Orange County
112	830	1.2	**Selma** (city) Fresno County
127	919	1.3	**Agoura Hills** (city) Los Angeles County
127	919	1.3	**Alum Rock** (CDP) Santa Clara County
127	919	1.3	**Carlsbad** (city) San Diego County
127	919	1.3	**Clayton** (city) Contra Costa County
127	919	1.3	**Garden Grove** (city) Orange County
127	919	1.3	**Glendale** (city) Los Angeles County
127	919	1.3	**Mission Viejo** (city) Orange County
127	919	1.3	**Pacific Grove** (city) Monterey County
127	919	1.3	**Piedmont** (city) Alameda County
127	919	1.3	**Shafter** (city) Kern County
127	919	1.3	**Thousand Oaks** (city) Ventura County
127	919	1.3	**Whittier** (city) Los Angeles County
127	919	1.3	**Yorba Linda** (city) Orange County
140	994	1.4	**Brea** (city) Orange County
140	994	1.4	**Cudahy** (city) Los Angeles County
140	994	1.4	**Hacienda Heights** (CDP) Los Angeles County
140	994	1.4	**La Puente** (city) Los Angeles County
140	994	1.4	**Laguna Hills** (city) Orange County
140	994	1.4	**Live Oak** (CDP) Santa Cruz County
140	994	1.4	**Orangevale** (CDP) Sacramento County
140	994	1.4	**Orcutt** (CDP) Santa Barbara County
140	994	1.4	**Petaluma** (city) Sonoma County
140	994	1.4	**Simi Valley** (city) Ventura County
150	1071	1.5	**Alhambra** (city) Los Angeles County

Note: *The state column ranks the top/bottom 150 places from all places in the state with population of 10,000 or more. The national column ranks the top/bottom 150 places from all places in the country with population of 10,000 or more. Places that are unincorporated were not considered in the rankings. Please refer to the User Guide for additional information.*

Asian Population

Top 150 Places Ranked in *Descending* Order

State Rank	Nat'l Rank	Percent	Place
1	2	66.9	**Monterey Park** (city) Los Angeles County
2	3	63.6	**Walnut** (city) Los Angeles County
3	4	63.3	**Cupertino** (city) Santa Clara County
4	5	62.2	**Milpitas** (city) Santa Clara County
5	6	61.9	**Cerritos** (city) Los Angeles County
6	7	60.7	**Rosemead** (city) Los Angeles County
6	7	60.7	**San Gabriel** (city) Los Angeles County
8	9	59.8	**Rowland Heights** (CDP) Los Angeles County
9	10	59.2	**Arcadia** (city) Los Angeles County
10	14	55.7	**Temple City** (city) Los Angeles County
11	15	55.6	**Daly City** (city) San Mateo County
12	17	53.5	**San Marino** (city) Los Angeles County
13	20	52.9	**Alhambra** (city) Los Angeles County
14	21	52.5	**Diamond Bar** (city) Los Angeles County
15	23	50.9	**Union City** (city) Alameda County
16	24	50.6	**Fremont** (city) Alameda County
17	27	49.9	**East San Gabriel** (CDP) Los Angeles County
18	30	48.1	**La Palma** (city) Orange County
19	31	47.5	**Westminster** (city) Orange County
20	36	45.5	**Hercules** (city) Contra Costa County
21	37	45.0	**Foster City** (city) San Mateo County
22	40	42.8	**Millbrae** (city) San Mateo County
23	41	41.4	**Saratoga** (city) Santa Clara County
24	42	40.9	**Sunnyvale** (city) Santa Clara County
25	47	39.2	**Irvine** (city) Orange County
26	49	37.7	**Santa Clara** (city) Santa Clara County
27	52	37.1	**Artesia** (city) Los Angeles County
27	52	37.1	**Garden Grove** (city) Orange County
27	52	37.1	**Hacienda Heights** (CDP) Los Angeles County
30	56	36.6	**South San Francisco** (city) San Mateo County
31	58	35.6	**San Ramon** (city) Contra Costa County
32	63	34.5	**Torrance** (city) Los Angeles County
33	70	33.3	**Fountain Valley** (city) Orange County
33	70	33.3	**San Francisco** (city) San Francisco County
35	72	32.9	**American Canyon** (city) Napa County
36	73	32.0	**San Jose** (city) Santa Clara County
37	76	31.3	**Cypress** (city) Orange County
38	77	31.2	**Alameda** (city) Alameda County
38	77	31.2	**Albany** (city) Alameda County
40	79	31.1	**South Pasadena** (city) Los Angeles County
41	80	31.0	**West Carson** (CDP) Los Angeles County
42	82	30.3	**Chino Hills** (city) San Bernardino County
43	83	29.7	**San Leandro** (city) Alameda County
44	85	29.4	**Vineyard** (CDP) Sacramento County
45	89	29.0	**Rancho Palos Verdes** (city) Los Angeles County
46	91	28.6	**Florin** (CDP) Sacramento County
47	92	28.3	**Loma Linda** (city) San Bernardino County
48	93	28.1	**Hillsborough** (town) San Mateo County
49	96	27.5	**Emeryville** (city) Alameda County
50	98	27.4	**Stanford** (CDP) Santa Clara County
51	99	27.3	**El Cerrito** (city) Contra Costa County
51	99	27.3	**La Crescenta-Montrose** (CDP) Los Angeles County
53	101	27.2	**Newark** (city) Alameda County
54	104	27.1	**Palo Alto** (city) Santa Clara County
55	106	26.8	**Dublin** (city) Alameda County
56	107	26.7	**Buena Park** (city) Orange County
57	109	26.3	**Elk Grove** (city) Sacramento County
58	110	26.2	**Gardena** (city) Los Angeles County
59	112	26.0	**Mountain View** (city) Santa Clara County
60	114	25.8	**La Cañada Flintridge** (city) Los Angeles County
60	114	25.8	**West Covina** (city) Los Angeles County
62	117	25.6	**Carson** (city) Los Angeles County
63	121	25.4	**San Bruno** (city) San Mateo County
64	125	25.1	**El Monte** (city) Los Angeles County
65	126	24.9	**Vallejo** (city) Solano County
66	131	24.2	**Eastvale** (city) Riverside County
67	135	23.5	**Los Altos** (city) Santa Clara County
68	138	23.2	**Pleasanton** (city) Alameda County
69	139	23.1	**Stanton** (city) Orange County
70	142	22.9	**Pinole** (city) Contra Costa County
70	142	22.9	**Stevenson Ranch** (CDP) Los Angeles County
72	148	22.8	**Fullerton** (city) Orange County
73	158	22.0	**Hayward** (city) Alameda County
73	158	22.0	**Lathrop** (city) San Joaquin County
75	160	21.9	**Davis** (city) Yolo County
76	162	21.6	**San Lorenzo** (CDP) Alameda County
77	163	21.5	**Stockton** (city) San Joaquin County
78	165	21.4	**Castro Valley** (CDP) Alameda County
79	172	20.4	**Signal Hill** (city) Los Angeles County
80	175	20.3	**Burlingame** (city) San Mateo County
80	175	20.3	**Tustin** (city) Orange County
82	181	19.9	**Belmont** (city) San Mateo County
82	181	19.9	**Marina** (city) Monterey County
84	190	19.4	**Pacifica** (city) San Mateo County
85	192	19.3	**Berkeley** (city) Alameda County
86	199	19.0	**Suisun City** (city) Solano County
87	202	18.9	**San Mateo** (city) San Mateo County
88	206	18.4	**Ashland** (CDP) Alameda County
89	207	18.3	**National City** (city) San Diego County
89	207	18.3	**Sacramento** (city) Sacramento County
91	209	18.2	**Brea** (city) Orange County
91	209	18.2	**Piedmont** (city) Alameda County
93	217	17.8	**La Mirada** (city) Los Angeles County
94	222	17.6	**El Sobrante** (CDP) Riverside County
95	226	17.4	**Lemon Hill** (CDP) Sacramento County
96	230	17.3	**Palos Verdes Estates** (city) Los Angeles County
97	235	17.2	**Yuba City** (city) Sutter County
98	238	17.0	**Livingston** (city) Merced County
99	243	16.8	**Oakland** (city) Alameda County
100	249	16.4	**Glendale** (city) Los Angeles County
100	249	16.4	**Lakewood** (city) Los Angeles County
102	255	16.1	**Campbell** (city) Santa Clara County
103	260	15.9	**San Diego** (city) San Diego County
104	266	15.8	**Duarte** (city) Los Angeles County
105	269	15.7	**El Sobrante** (CDP) Contra Costa County
106	271	15.6	**Pittsburg** (city) Contra Costa County
106	271	15.6	**Yorba Linda** (city) Orange County
108	286	15.2	**Fairview** (CDP) Alameda County
109	301	14.9	**Fairfield** (city) Solano County
109	301	14.9	**Moraga** (town) Contra Costa County
109	301	14.9	**Placentia** (city) Orange County
109	301	14.9	**San Pablo** (city) Contra Costa County
113	308	14.8	**Anaheim** (city) Orange County
113	308	14.8	**Culver City** (city) Los Angeles County
115	312	14.7	**Isla Vista** (CDP) Santa Barbara County
115	312	14.7	**Tracy** (city) San Joaquin County
117	318	14.6	**Aliso Viejo** (city) Orange County
118	325	14.4	**Chula Vista** (city) San Diego County
118	325	14.4	**Lomita** (city) Los Angeles County
120	332	14.3	**Pasadena** (city) Los Angeles County
121	336	14.2	**Baldwin Park** (city) Los Angeles County
122	351	13.6	**Parkway** (CDP) Sacramento County
122	351	13.6	**Pleasant Hill** (city) Contra Costa County
124	354	13.5	**Richmond** (city) Contra Costa County
125	361	13.3	**Antelope** (CDP) Sacramento County
126	364	13.1	**Alum Rock** (CDP) Santa Clara County
126	364	13.1	**Claremont** (city) Los Angeles County
126	364	13.1	**Lake Forest** (city) Orange County
129	369	13.0	**Linda** (CDP) Yuba County
130	376	12.9	**Long Beach** (city) Los Angeles County
131	382	12.8	**Los Alamitos** (city) Orange County
132	385	12.7	**Delano** (city) Kern County
133	392	12.6	**Fresno** (city) Fresno County
133	392	12.6	**Laguna Hills** (city) Orange County
135	398	12.5	**Folsom** (city) Sacramento County
135	398	12.5	**Walnut Creek** (city) Contra Costa County
137	410	12.1	**Ladera Ranch** (CDP) Orange County
137	410	12.1	**Rancho Cordova** (city) Sacramento County
139	414	12.0	**Norwalk** (city) Los Angeles County
139	414	12.0	**Redondo Beach** (city) Los Angeles County
141	418	11.9	**Covina** (city) Los Angeles County
141	418	11.9	**Valinda** (CDP) Los Angeles County
143	424	11.8	**Merced** (city) Merced County
144	432	11.6	**Bellflower** (city) Los Angeles County
144	432	11.6	**Burbank** (city) Los Angeles County
144	432	11.6	**French Valley** (CDP) Riverside County
147	438	11.5	**San Carlos** (city) San Mateo County
148	441	11.4	**Castaic** (CDP) Los Angeles County
148	441	11.4	**Orinda** (city) Contra Costa County
150	452	11.3	**Los Angeles** (city) Los Angeles County

Note: *The state column ranks the top/bottom 150 places from all places in the state with population of 10,000 or more. The national column ranks the top/bottom 150 places from all places in the country with population of 10,000 or more. Places that are unincorporated were not considered in the rankings. Please refer to the User Guide for additional information.*

Asian Population

Top 150 Places Ranked in *Ascending* Order

State Rank	Nat'l Rank	Percent	Place
1	20	0.2	**East Rancho Dominguez** (CDP) Los Angeles County
1	20	0.2	**Florence-Graham** (CDP) Los Angeles County
3	61	0.3	**Compton** (city) Los Angeles County
3	61	0.3	**Maywood** (city) Los Angeles County
3	61	0.3	**Willowbrook** (CDP) Los Angeles County
6	108	0.4	**Westmont** (CDP) Los Angeles County
7	198	0.5	**Lamont** (CDP) Kern County
7	198	0.5	**Parlier** (city) Fresno County
9	321	0.6	**Bell Gardens** (city) Los Angeles County
9	321	0.6	**Cudahy** (city) Los Angeles County
9	321	0.6	**Walnut Park** (CDP) Los Angeles County
12	452	0.7	**Avenal** (city) Kings County
12	452	0.7	**Bell** (city) Los Angeles County
12	452	0.7	**Coachella** (city) Riverside County
12	452	0.7	**Farmersville** (city) Tulare County
12	452	0.7	**Huntington Park** (city) Los Angeles County
12	452	0.7	**Lynwood** (city) Los Angeles County
12	452	0.7	**McFarland** (city) Kern County
12	452	0.7	**Mendota** (city) Fresno County
12	452	0.7	**Santa Paula** (city) Ventura County
12	452	0.7	**Shafter** (city) Kern County
12	452	0.7	**Wasco** (city) Kern County
23	629	0.8	**Arvin** (city) Kern County
23	629	0.8	**Big Bear City** (CDP) San Bernardino County
23	629	0.8	**Corcoran** (city) Kings County
23	629	0.8	**Lennox** (CDP) Los Angeles County
23	629	0.8	**Magalia** (CDP) Butte County
23	629	0.8	**South Gate** (city) Los Angeles County
29	801	0.9	**Crestline** (CDP) San Bernardino County
29	801	0.9	**East Los Angeles** (CDP) Los Angeles County
29	801	0.9	**Fortuna** (city) Humboldt County
29	801	0.9	**Lake Los Angeles** (CDP) Los Angeles County
29	801	0.9	**Muscoy** (CDP) San Bernardino County
29	801	0.9	**Placerville** (city) El Dorado County
35	963	1.0	**Diamond Springs** (CDP) El Dorado County
35	963	1.0	**Fillmore** (city) Ventura County
35	963	1.0	**Oildale** (CDP) Kern County
35	963	1.0	**San Fernando** (city) Los Angeles County
39	1097	1.1	**Clearlake** (city) Lake County
39	1097	1.1	**Commerce** (city) Los Angeles County
39	1097	1.1	**Greenfield** (city) Monterey County
39	1097	1.1	**Healdsburg** (city) Sonoma County
39	1097	1.1	**Sun Village** (CDP) Los Angeles County
39	1097	1.1	**Susanville** (city) Lassen County
45	1214	1.2	**Lake Arrowhead** (CDP) San Bernardino County
46	1330	1.3	**Calexico** (city) Imperial County
46	1330	1.3	**Exeter** (city) Tulare County
46	1330	1.3	**King City** (city) Monterey County
46	1330	1.3	**Paradise** (town) Butte County
46	1330	1.3	**Red Bluff** (city) Tehama County
46	1330	1.3	**View Park-Windsor Hills** (CDP) Los Angeles County
52	1428	1.4	**Bloomington** (CDP) San Bernardino County
52	1428	1.4	**Brawley** (city) Imperial County
52	1428	1.4	**Inglewood** (city) Los Angeles County
52	1428	1.4	**McKinleyville** (CDP) Humboldt County
52	1428	1.4	**Mead Valley** (CDP) Riverside County
52	1428	1.4	**Ramona** (CDP) San Diego County
58	1546	1.5	**Blythe** (city) Riverside County
58	1546	1.5	**Grass Valley** (city) Nevada County
58	1546	1.5	**Lakeland Village** (CDP) Riverside County
58	1546	1.5	**San Diego Country Estates** (CDP) San Diego County
58	1546	1.5	**Truckee** (town) Nevada County
58	1546	1.5	**West Whittier-Los Nietos** (CDP) Los Angeles County
64	1648	1.6	**East Hemet** (CDP) Riverside County
65	1759	1.7	**Lakeside** (CDP) San Diego County
65	1759	1.7	**Tehachapi** (city) Kern County
65	1759	1.7	**Winter Gardens** (CDP) San Diego County
68	1856	1.8	**Auburn** (city) Placer County
68	1856	1.8	**Canyon Lake** (city) Riverside County
70	1969	1.9	**Adelanto** (city) San Bernardino County
70	1969	1.9	**Fallbrook** (CDP) San Diego County
70	1969	1.9	**Newman** (city) Stanislaus County
70	1969	1.9	**Valle Vista** (CDP) Riverside County
74	2059	2.0	**El Paso de Robles (Paso Robles)** (city) San Luis Obispo County
75	2130	2.1	**Chowchilla** (city) Madera County
75	2130	2.1	**Dinuba** (city) Tulare County
75	2130	2.1	**Hesperia** (city) San Bernardino County
78	2192	2.2	**Alpine** (CDP) San Diego County
78	2192	2.2	**Indio** (city) Riverside County
78	2192	2.2	**Madera** (city) Madera County
78	2192	2.2	**Oakdale** (city) Stanislaus County
78	2192	2.2	**Tulare** (city) Tulare County
83	2273	2.3	**Cameron Park** (CDP) El Dorado County
83	2273	2.3	**Carpinteria** (city) Santa Barbara County
83	2273	2.3	**El Centro** (city) Imperial County
83	2273	2.3	**Lindsay** (city) Tulare County
83	2273	2.3	**Napa** (city) Napa County
83	2273	2.3	**North Auburn** (CDP) Placer County
83	2273	2.3	**Rialto** (city) San Bernardino County
83	2273	2.3	**Shasta Lake** (city) Shasta County
83	2273	2.3	**Yucca Valley** (town) San Bernardino County
92	2343	2.4	**Atascadero** (city) San Luis Obispo County
92	2343	2.4	**Bostonia** (CDP) San Diego County
94	2420	2.5	**Imperial** (city) Imperial County
94	2420	2.5	**Morro Bay** (city) San Luis Obispo County
94	2420	2.5	**Nipomo** (CDP) San Luis Obispo County
97	2484	2.6	**Arcata** (city) Humboldt County
97	2484	2.6	**California City** (city) Kern County
97	2484	2.6	**Desert Hot Springs** (city) Riverside County
97	2484	2.6	**Malibu** (city) Los Angeles County
97	2484	2.6	**Pico Rivera** (city) Los Angeles County
97	2484	2.6	**Ukiah** (city) Mendocino County
103	2543	2.7	**Hollister** (city) San Benito County
104	2593	2.8	**Camp Pendleton South** (CDP) San Diego County
104	2593	2.8	**Quartz Hill** (CDP) Los Angeles County
104	2593	2.8	**Rosedale** (CDP) Kern County
104	2593	2.8	**San Juan Capistrano** (city) Orange County
104	2593	2.8	**Sonoma** (city) Sonoma County
104	2593	2.8	**Yucaipa** (city) San Bernardino County
110	2647	2.9	**Apple Valley** (town) San Bernardino County
110	2647	2.9	**Soledad** (city) Monterey County
112	2704	3.0	**Coalinga** (city) Fresno County
112	2704	3.0	**Coronado** (city) San Diego County
112	2704	3.0	**Hemet** (city) Riverside County
112	2704	3.0	**Paramount** (city) Los Angeles County
112	2704	3.0	**San Jacinto** (city) Riverside County
112	2704	3.0	**Windsor** (town) Sonoma County
118	2755	3.1	**La Quinta** (city) Riverside County
118	2755	3.1	**Norco** (city) Riverside County
118	2755	3.1	**Orangevale** (CDP) Sacramento County
118	2755	3.1	**Phelan** (CDP) San Bernardino County
118	2755	3.1	**Sanger** (city) Fresno County
123	2807	3.2	**Barstow** (city) San Bernardino County
123	2807	3.2	**Casa de Oro-Mount Helix** (CDP) San Diego County
123	2807	3.2	**Dana Point** (city) Orange County
123	2807	3.2	**Los Banos** (city) Merced County
127	2870	3.3	**Citrus Heights** (city) Sacramento County
127	2870	3.3	**Reedley** (city) Fresno County
127	2870	3.3	**Watsonville** (city) Santa Cruz County
130	2912	3.4	**Arroyo Grande** (city) San Luis Obispo County
130	2912	3.4	**Galt** (city) Sacramento County
130	2912	3.4	**Garden Acres** (CDP) San Joaquin County
130	2912	3.4	**Kingsburg** (city) Fresno County
130	2912	3.4	**Palm Desert** (city) Riverside County
130	2912	3.4	**Redding** (city) Shasta County
130	2912	3.4	**Riverbank** (city) Stanislaus County
130	2912	3.4	**San Buenaventura (Ventura)** (city) Ventura County
138	2957	3.5	**San Anselmo** (town) Marin County
138	2957	3.5	**Santa Barbara** (city) Santa Barbara County
140	2998	3.6	**El Cajon** (city) San Diego County
140	2998	3.6	**Laguna Beach** (city) Orange County
140	2998	3.6	**Perris** (city) Riverside County
140	2998	3.6	**Rosamond** (CDP) Kern County
144	3039	3.7	**Dixon** (city) Solano County
144	3039	3.7	**North Fair Oaks** (CDP) San Mateo County
144	3039	3.7	**San Clemente** (city) Orange County
147	3088	3.8	**Delhi** (CDP) Merced County
147	3088	3.8	**East Palo Alto** (city) San Mateo County
147	3088	3.8	**Lompoc** (city) Santa Barbara County
147	3088	3.8	**Prunedale** (CDP) Monterey County

Note: *The state column ranks the top/bottom 150 places from all places in the state with population of 10,000 or more. The national column ranks the top/bottom 150 places from all places in the country with population of 10,000 or more. Places that are unincorporated were not considered in the rankings. Please refer to the User Guide for additional information.*

American Indian/Alaska Native Population

Top 150 Places Ranked in *Descending* Order

State Rank	Nat'l Rank	Percent	Place
1	42	5.4	**Greenfield** (city) Monterey County
2	56	4.6	**McKinleyville** (CDP) Humboldt County
3	71	3.8	**Shasta Lake** (city) Shasta County
4	74	3.7	**Eureka** (city) Humboldt County
4	74	3.7	**Fortuna** (city) Humboldt County
4	74	3.7	**Oroville** (city) Butte County
4	74	3.7	**Ukiah** (city) Mendocino County
8	86	3.4	**Susanville** (city) Lassen County
9	97	3.1	**Madera** (city) Madera County
9	97	3.1	**Red Bluff** (city) Tehama County
11	107	2.9	**Olivehurst** (CDP) Yuba County
12	115	2.7	**King City** (city) Monterey County
12	115	2.7	**Livingston** (city) Merced County
14	121	2.6	**Clearlake** (city) Lake County
15	131	2.5	**Marysville** (city) Yuba County
16	140	2.3	**Arcata** (city) Humboldt County
16	140	2.3	**Redding** (city) Shasta County
18	148	2.2	**Banning** (city) Riverside County
18	148	2.2	**Windsor** (town) Sonoma County
20	154	2.1	**Barstow** (city) San Bernardino County
20	154	2.1	**Selma** (city) Fresno County
22	164	2.0	**Chowchilla** (city) Madera County
22	164	2.0	**Farmersville** (city) Tulare County
22	164	2.0	**Linda** (CDP) Yuba County
25	178	1.9	**Alum Rock** (CDP) Santa Clara County
25	178	1.9	**East Hemet** (CDP) Riverside County
25	178	1.9	**Porterville** (city) Tulare County
28	187	1.8	**Healdsburg** (city) Sonoma County
28	187	1.8	**Hollister** (city) San Benito County
28	187	1.8	**Lemon Hill** (CDP) Sacramento County
28	187	1.8	**Lompoc** (city) Santa Barbara County
28	187	1.8	**Oildale** (CDP) Kern County
28	187	1.8	**San Jacinto** (city) Riverside County
28	187	1.8	**Santa Maria** (city) Santa Barbara County
35	208	1.7	**Exeter** (city) Tulare County
35	208	1.7	**Fresno** (city) Fresno County
35	208	1.7	**Gilroy** (city) Santa Clara County
35	208	1.7	**Santa Rosa** (city) Sonoma County
35	208	1.7	**Valle Vista** (CDP) Riverside County
35	208	1.7	**Walnut Park** (CDP) Los Angeles County
41	228	1.6	**Alpine** (CDP) San Diego County
41	228	1.6	**Big Bear City** (CDP) San Bernardino County
41	228	1.6	**Diamond Springs** (CDP) El Dorado County
41	228	1.6	**Garden Acres** (CDP) San Joaquin County
41	228	1.6	**Grass Valley** (city) Nevada County
41	228	1.6	**Hemet** (city) Riverside County
41	228	1.6	**Placerville** (city) El Dorado County
41	228	1.6	**Rio Linda** (CDP) Sacramento County
41	228	1.6	**Santa Paula** (city) Ventura County
41	228	1.6	**West Sacramento** (city) Yolo County
51	251	1.5	**Bakersfield** (city) Kern County
51	251	1.5	**Beaumont** (city) Riverside County
51	251	1.5	**Delhi** (CDP) Merced County
51	251	1.5	**Galt** (city) Sacramento County
51	251	1.5	**Lamont** (CDP) Kern County
51	251	1.5	**Merced** (city) Merced County
51	251	1.5	**Oxnard** (city) Ventura County
51	251	1.5	**West Whittier-Los Nietos** (CDP) Los Angeles County
59	280	1.4	**Camp Pendleton South** (CDP) San Diego County
59	280	1.4	**Cherryland** (CDP) Alameda County
59	280	1.4	**Chico** (city) Butte County
59	280	1.4	**Clovis** (city) Fresno County
59	280	1.4	**Corcoran** (city) Kings County
59	280	1.4	**Desert Hot Springs** (city) Riverside County
59	280	1.4	**Grover Beach** (city) San Luis Obispo County
59	280	1.4	**Lake Los Angeles** (CDP) Los Angeles County
59	280	1.4	**Lemoore** (city) Kings County
59	280	1.4	**Los Banos** (city) Merced County
59	280	1.4	**Mendota** (city) Fresno County
59	280	1.4	**North Highlands** (CDP) Sacramento County
59	280	1.4	**Pico Rivera** (city) Los Angeles County
59	280	1.4	**Port Hueneme** (city) Ventura County
59	280	1.4	**Rosemont** (CDP) Sacramento County
59	280	1.4	**Santa Fe Springs** (city) Los Angeles County
59	280	1.4	**Soledad** (city) Monterey County
59	280	1.4	**Sun Village** (CDP) Los Angeles County
59	280	1.4	**Tehachapi** (city) Kern County
59	280	1.4	**Victorville** (city) San Bernardino County
59	280	1.4	**Visalia** (city) Tulare County
59	280	1.4	**Yuba City** (city) Sutter County
81	332	1.3	**Adelanto** (city) San Bernardino County
81	332	1.3	**Atwater** (city) Merced County
81	332	1.3	**Bloomington** (CDP) San Bernardino County
81	332	1.3	**Ceres** (city) Stanislaus County
81	332	1.3	**Coalinga** (city) Fresno County
81	332	1.3	**Colton** (city) San Bernardino County
81	332	1.3	**Commerce** (city) Los Angeles County
81	332	1.3	**Crestline** (CDP) San Bernardino County
81	332	1.3	**El Centro** (city) Imperial County
81	332	1.3	**Hanford** (city) Kings County
81	332	1.3	**Huntington Park** (city) Los Angeles County
81	332	1.3	**Kerman** (city) Fresno County
81	332	1.3	**Kingsburg** (city) Fresno County
81	332	1.3	**Lathrop** (city) San Joaquin County
81	332	1.3	**McFarland** (city) Kern County
81	332	1.3	**North Auburn** (CDP) Placer County
81	332	1.3	**Quartz Hill** (CDP) Los Angeles County
81	332	1.3	**Salinas** (city) Monterey County
81	332	1.3	**San Bernardino** (city) San Bernardino County
81	332	1.3	**San Fernando** (city) Los Angeles County
81	332	1.3	**Sanger** (city) Fresno County
81	332	1.3	**South Whittier** (CDP) Los Angeles County
81	332	1.3	**Twentynine Palms** (city) San Bernardino County
81	332	1.3	**Whittier** (city) Los Angeles County
81	332	1.3	**Winton** (CDP) Merced County
81	332	1.3	**Woodland** (city) Yolo County
107	390	1.2	**Arvin** (city) Kern County
107	390	1.2	**Avenal** (city) Kings County
107	390	1.2	**Azusa** (city) Los Angeles County
107	390	1.2	**Blythe** (city) Riverside County
107	390	1.2	**East Los Angeles** (CDP) Los Angeles County
107	390	1.2	**Fillmore** (city) Ventura County
107	390	1.2	**Hawaiian Gardens** (city) Los Angeles County
107	390	1.2	**Hesperia** (city) San Bernardino County
107	390	1.2	**Magalia** (CDP) Butte County
107	390	1.2	**Modesto** (city) Stanislaus County
107	390	1.2	**Montclair** (city) San Bernardino County
107	390	1.2	**Muscoy** (CDP) San Bernardino County
107	390	1.2	**Nipomo** (CDP) San Luis Obispo County
107	390	1.2	**Orcutt** (CDP) Santa Barbara County
107	390	1.2	**Parkway** (CDP) Sacramento County
107	390	1.2	**Parlier** (city) Fresno County
107	390	1.2	**Pomona** (city) Los Angeles County
107	390	1.2	**Ridgecrest** (city) Kern County
107	390	1.2	**Riverbank** (city) Stanislaus County
107	390	1.2	**Rosamond** (CDP) Kern County
107	390	1.2	**San Buenaventura (Ventura)** (city) Ventura County
107	390	1.2	**San Rafael** (city) Marin County
107	390	1.2	**Shafter** (city) Kern County
107	390	1.2	**South El Monte** (city) Los Angeles County
107	390	1.2	**Tulare** (city) Tulare County
107	390	1.2	**Vista** (city) San Diego County
107	390	1.2	**Watsonville** (city) Santa Cruz County
107	390	1.2	**Wildomar** (city) Riverside County
135	474	1.1	**Apple Valley** (town) San Bernardino County
135	474	1.1	**Ashland** (CDP) Alameda County
135	474	1.1	**Bay Point** (CDP) Contra Costa County
135	474	1.1	**Bell Gardens** (city) Los Angeles County
135	474	1.1	**Buena Park** (city) Orange County
135	474	1.1	**Cameron Park** (CDP) El Dorado County
135	474	1.1	**Carpinteria** (city) Santa Barbara County
135	474	1.1	**Cathedral City** (city) Riverside County
135	474	1.1	**Citrus** (CDP) Los Angeles County
135	474	1.1	**Covina** (city) Los Angeles County
135	474	1.1	**Florin** (CDP) Sacramento County
135	474	1.1	**Foothill Farms** (CDP) Sacramento County
135	474	1.1	**Home Gardens** (CDP) Riverside County
135	474	1.1	**La Puente** (city) Los Angeles County
135	474	1.1	**Lakeland Village** (CDP) Riverside County
135	474	1.1	**Lindsay** (city) Tulare County

Note: *The state column ranks the top/bottom 150 places from all places in the state with population of 10,000 or more. The national column ranks the top/bottom 150 places from all places in the country with population of 10,000 or more. Places that are unincorporated were not considered in the rankings. Please refer to the User Guide for additional information.*

American Indian/Alaska Native Population

Top 150 Places Ranked in *Ascending* Order

State Rank	Nat'l Rank	Percent	Place
1	1	0.0	**San Marino** (city) Los Angeles County
2	61	0.1	**Alamo** (CDP) Contra Costa County
2	61	0.1	**Beverly Hills** (city) Los Angeles County
2	61	0.1	**Foster City** (city) San Mateo County
2	61	0.1	**Hillsborough** (town) San Mateo County
2	61	0.1	**La Cañada Flintridge** (city) Los Angeles County
2	61	0.1	**Laguna Woods** (city) Orange County
2	61	0.1	**Orinda** (city) Contra Costa County
2	61	0.1	**Piedmont** (city) Alameda County
2	61	0.1	**Saratoga** (city) Santa Clara County
11	722	0.2	**Calabasas** (city) Los Angeles County
11	722	0.2	**Coto de Caza** (CDP) Orange County
11	722	0.2	**Cupertino** (city) Santa Clara County
11	722	0.2	**Danville** (town) Contra Costa County
11	722	0.2	**Irvine** (city) Orange County
11	722	0.2	**Ladera Ranch** (CDP) Orange County
11	722	0.2	**Larkspur** (city) Marin County
11	722	0.2	**Los Altos** (city) Santa Clara County
11	722	0.2	**Malibu** (city) Los Angeles County
11	722	0.2	**Manhattan Beach** (city) Los Angeles County
11	722	0.2	**Mill Valley** (city) Marin County
11	722	0.2	**Millbrae** (city) San Mateo County
11	722	0.2	**Moraga** (town) Contra Costa County
11	722	0.2	**Oak Park** (CDP) Ventura County
11	722	0.2	**Palo Alto** (city) Santa Clara County
11	722	0.2	**Palos Verdes Estates** (city) Los Angeles County
11	722	0.2	**Rancho Palos Verdes** (city) Los Angeles County
11	722	0.2	**San Carlos** (city) San Mateo County
11	722	0.2	**Tamalpais-Homestead Valley** (CDP) Marin County
11	722	0.2	**Walnut** (city) Los Angeles County
11	722	0.2	**Walnut Creek** (city) Contra Costa County
32	1626	0.3	**Agoura Hills** (city) Los Angeles County
32	1626	0.3	**Aliso Viejo** (city) Orange County
32	1626	0.3	**Arcadia** (city) Los Angeles County
32	1626	0.3	**Belmont** (city) San Mateo County
32	1626	0.3	**Burlingame** (city) San Mateo County
32	1626	0.3	**Cerritos** (city) Los Angeles County
32	1626	0.3	**Clayton** (city) Contra Costa County
32	1626	0.3	**Diamond Bar** (city) Los Angeles County
32	1626	0.3	**Glendale** (city) Los Angeles County
32	1626	0.3	**Hermosa Beach** (city) Los Angeles County
32	1626	0.3	**Lafayette** (city) Contra Costa County
32	1626	0.3	**Laguna Beach** (city) Orange County
32	1626	0.3	**Laguna Hills** (city) Orange County
32	1626	0.3	**Laguna Niguel** (city) Orange County
32	1626	0.3	**Los Gatos** (town) Santa Clara County
32	1626	0.3	**Newport Beach** (city) Orange County
32	1626	0.3	**Pleasanton** (city) Alameda County
32	1626	0.3	**San Anselmo** (town) Marin County
32	1626	0.3	**San Ramon** (city) Contra Costa County
32	1626	0.3	**Seal Beach** (city) Orange County
32	1626	0.3	**West Hollywood** (city) Los Angeles County
53	2369	0.4	**Berkeley** (city) Alameda County
53	2369	0.4	**Daly City** (city) San Mateo County
53	2369	0.4	**East Palo Alto** (city) San Mateo County
53	2369	0.4	**East San Gabriel** (CDP) Los Angeles County
53	2369	0.4	**El Segundo** (city) Los Angeles County
53	2369	0.4	**Emeryville** (city) Alameda County
53	2369	0.4	**Fountain Valley** (city) Orange County
53	2369	0.4	**Hercules** (city) Contra Costa County
53	2369	0.4	**La Crescenta-Montrose** (CDP) Los Angeles County
53	2369	0.4	**La Palma** (city) Orange County
53	2369	0.4	**Loma Linda** (city) San Bernardino County
53	2369	0.4	**Los Alamitos** (city) Orange County
53	2369	0.4	**Mission Viejo** (city) Orange County
53	2369	0.4	**Monterey Park** (city) Los Angeles County
53	2369	0.4	**North Tustin** (CDP) Orange County
53	2369	0.4	**Pleasant Hill** (city) Contra Costa County
53	2369	0.4	**Rancho Santa Margarita** (city) Orange County
53	2369	0.4	**Redondo Beach** (city) Los Angeles County
53	2369	0.4	**Rossmoor** (CDP) Orange County
53	2369	0.4	**Rowland Heights** (CDP) Los Angeles County
53	2369	0.4	**Santa Monica** (city) Los Angeles County
53	2369	0.4	**Sierra Madre** (city) Los Angeles County
53	2369	0.4	**South Pasadena** (city) Los Angeles County
53	2369	0.4	**Stevenson Ranch** (CDP) Los Angeles County
53	2369	0.4	**Temple City** (city) Los Angeles County
53	2369	0.4	**Thousand Oaks** (city) Ventura County
53	2369	0.4	**Torrance** (city) Los Angeles County
53	2369	0.4	**View Park-Windsor Hills** (CDP) Los Angeles County
53	2369	0.4	**Westminster** (city) Orange County
53	2369	0.4	**Yorba Linda** (city) Orange County
83	2874	0.5	**Albany** (city) Alameda County
83	2874	0.5	**Benicia** (city) Solano County
83	2874	0.5	**Brea** (city) Orange County
83	2874	0.5	**Burbank** (city) Los Angeles County
83	2874	0.5	**Calexico** (city) Imperial County
83	2874	0.5	**Carlsbad** (city) San Diego County
83	2874	0.5	**Casa de Oro-Mount Helix** (CDP) San Diego County
83	2874	0.5	**Castro Valley** (CDP) Alameda County
83	2874	0.5	**Chino Hills** (city) San Bernardino County
83	2874	0.5	**Claremont** (city) Los Angeles County
83	2874	0.5	**Coronado** (city) San Diego County
83	2874	0.5	**Culver City** (city) Los Angeles County
83	2874	0.5	**Davis** (city) Yolo County
83	2874	0.5	**Dublin** (city) Alameda County
83	2874	0.5	**Eastvale** (city) Riverside County
83	2874	0.5	**El Cerrito** (city) Contra Costa County
83	2874	0.5	**El Dorado Hills** (CDP) El Dorado County
83	2874	0.5	**Encinitas** (city) San Diego County
83	2874	0.5	**Fremont** (city) Alameda County
83	2874	0.5	**Huntington Beach** (city) Orange County
83	2874	0.5	**Isla Vista** (CDP) Santa Barbara County
83	2874	0.5	**Lake Forest** (city) Orange County
83	2874	0.5	**Menlo Park** (city) San Mateo County
83	2874	0.5	**Milpitas** (city) Santa Clara County
83	2874	0.5	**Monterey** (city) Monterey County
83	2874	0.5	**Mountain View** (city) Santa Clara County
83	2874	0.5	**Pacific Grove** (city) Monterey County
83	2874	0.5	**Palm Desert** (city) Riverside County
83	2874	0.5	**Rancho Mirage** (city) Riverside County
83	2874	0.5	**Rancho San Diego** (CDP) San Diego County
83	2874	0.5	**San Francisco** (city) San Francisco County
83	2874	0.5	**San Mateo** (city) San Mateo County
83	2874	0.5	**Santa Clara** (city) Santa Clara County
83	2874	0.5	**Scotts Valley** (city) Santa Cruz County
83	2874	0.5	**Solana Beach** (city) San Diego County
83	2874	0.5	**Sonoma** (city) Sonoma County
83	2874	0.5	**Sunnyvale** (city) Santa Clara County
83	2874	0.5	**Union City** (city) Alameda County
83	2874	0.5	**Woodcrest** (CDP) Riverside County
122	3244	0.6	**Alameda** (city) Alameda County
122	3244	0.6	**Alhambra** (city) Los Angeles County
122	3244	0.6	**Artesia** (city) Los Angeles County
122	3244	0.6	**Brentwood** (city) Contra Costa County
122	3244	0.6	**Camarillo** (city) Ventura County
122	3244	0.6	**Canyon Lake** (city) Riverside County
122	3244	0.6	**Carson** (city) Los Angeles County
122	3244	0.6	**Castaic** (CDP) Los Angeles County
122	3244	0.6	**Costa Mesa** (city) Orange County
122	3244	0.6	**Cypress** (city) Orange County
122	3244	0.6	**Del Aire** (CDP) Los Angeles County
122	3244	0.6	**Discovery Bay** (CDP) Contra Costa County
122	3244	0.6	**El Sobrante** (CDP) Riverside County
122	3244	0.6	**Elk Grove** (city) Sacramento County
122	3244	0.6	**Folsom** (city) Sacramento County
122	3244	0.6	**Fullerton** (city) Orange County
122	3244	0.6	**Garden Grove** (city) Orange County
122	3244	0.6	**Gardena** (city) Los Angeles County
122	3244	0.6	**Hacienda Heights** (CDP) Los Angeles County
122	3244	0.6	**Half Moon Bay** (city) San Mateo County
122	3244	0.6	**La Quinta** (city) Riverside County
122	3244	0.6	**Livermore** (city) Alameda County
122	3244	0.6	**Novato** (city) Marin County
122	3244	0.6	**Pacifica** (city) San Mateo County
122	3244	0.6	**Pasadena** (city) Los Angeles County
122	3244	0.6	**Petaluma** (city) Sonoma County
122	3244	0.6	**Poway** (city) San Diego County
122	3244	0.6	**Richmond** (city) Contra Costa County
122	3244	0.6	**San Bruno** (city) San Mateo County

***Note:** The state column ranks the top/bottom 150 places from all places in the state with population of 10,000 or more. The national column ranks the top/bottom 150 places from all places in the country with population of 10,000 or more. Places that are unincorporated were not considered in the rankings. Please refer to the User Guide for additional information.*

Native Hawaiian/Other Pacific Islander Population

Top 150 Places Ranked in *Descending* Order

State Rank	Nat'l Rank	Percent	Place
1	19	7.5	**East Palo Alto** (city) San Mateo County
2	33	3.3	**San Bruno** (city) San Mateo County
3	34	3.1	**Hayward** (city) Alameda County
4	37	2.8	**Marina** (city) Monterey County
5	41	2.6	**Carson** (city) Los Angeles County
6	51	2.1	**Cherryland** (CDP) Alameda County
6	51	2.1	**San Mateo** (city) San Mateo County
8	54	2.0	**Parkway** (CDP) Sacramento County
9	63	1.7	**Florin** (CDP) Sacramento County
9	63	1.7	**South San Francisco** (city) San Mateo County
11	68	1.6	**Seaside** (city) Monterey County
12	71	1.5	**Newark** (city) Alameda County
12	71	1.5	**North Fair Oaks** (CDP) San Mateo County
14	75	1.4	**Lemon Hill** (CDP) Sacramento County
14	75	1.4	**Menlo Park** (city) San Mateo County
14	75	1.4	**Patterson** (city) Stanislaus County
14	75	1.4	**Sacramento** (city) Sacramento County
14	75	1.4	**Twentynine Palms** (city) San Bernardino County
14	75	1.4	**West Carson** (CDP) Los Angeles County
20	86	1.3	**Del Aire** (CDP) Los Angeles County
20	86	1.3	**Fairview** (CDP) Alameda County
20	86	1.3	**Oceanside** (city) San Diego County
20	86	1.3	**Union City** (city) Alameda County
24	92	1.2	**Ashland** (CDP) Alameda County
24	92	1.2	**Barstow** (city) San Bernardino County
24	92	1.2	**Elk Grove** (city) Sacramento County
24	92	1.2	**Hawthorne** (city) Los Angeles County
24	92	1.2	**La Presa** (CDP) San Diego County
24	92	1.2	**Signal Hill** (city) Los Angeles County
24	92	1.2	**Suisun City** (city) Solano County
31	103	1.1	**Fairfield** (city) Solano County
31	103	1.1	**Lawndale** (city) Los Angeles County
31	103	1.1	**Lemon Grove** (city) San Diego County
31	103	1.1	**Long Beach** (city) Los Angeles County
31	103	1.1	**Vallejo** (city) Solano County
31	103	1.1	**West Sacramento** (city) Yolo County
37	113	1.0	**Millbrae** (city) San Mateo County
37	113	1.0	**Modesto** (city) Stanislaus County
37	113	1.0	**Pittsburg** (city) Contra Costa County
37	113	1.0	**Redwood City** (city) San Mateo County
37	113	1.0	**Vineyard** (CDP) Sacramento County
42	128	0.9	**American Canyon** (city) Napa County
42	128	0.9	**Antelope** (CDP) Sacramento County
42	128	0.9	**El Sobrante** (CDP) Contra Costa County
42	128	0.9	**Lakewood** (city) Los Angeles County
42	128	0.9	**Rancho Cordova** (city) Sacramento County
42	128	0.9	**Tracy** (city) San Joaquin County
48	145	0.8	**Antioch** (city) Contra Costa County
48	145	0.8	**Bellflower** (city) Los Angeles County
48	145	0.8	**Belmont** (city) San Mateo County
48	145	0.8	**Ceres** (city) Stanislaus County
48	145	0.8	**Daly City** (city) San Mateo County
48	145	0.8	**La Riviera** (CDP) Sacramento County
48	145	0.8	**Lathrop** (city) San Joaquin County
48	145	0.8	**Lennox** (CDP) Los Angeles County
48	145	0.8	**National City** (city) San Diego County
48	145	0.8	**Pacifica** (city) San Mateo County
48	145	0.8	**Paramount** (city) Los Angeles County
48	145	0.8	**San Leandro** (city) Alameda County
48	145	0.8	**San Lorenzo** (CDP) Alameda County
48	145	0.8	**Spring Valley** (CDP) San Diego County
62	176	0.7	**Bay Point** (CDP) Contra Costa County
62	176	0.7	**Castro Valley** (CDP) Alameda County
62	176	0.7	**Compton** (city) Los Angeles County
62	176	0.7	**Concord** (city) Contra Costa County
62	176	0.7	**East Rancho Dominguez** (CDP) Los Angeles County
62	176	0.7	**Gardena** (city) Los Angeles County
62	176	0.7	**Imperial Beach** (city) San Diego County
62	176	0.7	**Loma Linda** (city) San Bernardino County
62	176	0.7	**Lomita** (city) Los Angeles County
62	176	0.7	**North Highlands** (CDP) Sacramento County
62	176	0.7	**Vista** (city) San Diego County
73	202	0.6	**Adelanto** (city) San Bernardino County
73	202	0.6	**Arden-Arcade** (CDP) Sacramento County
73	202	0.6	**Bonita** (CDP) San Diego County
73	202	0.6	**Bostonia** (CDP) San Diego County
73	202	0.6	**Buena Park** (city) Orange County
73	202	0.6	**Chula Vista** (city) San Diego County
73	202	0.6	**Dublin** (city) Alameda County
73	202	0.6	**Eureka** (city) Humboldt County
73	202	0.6	**Foothill Farms** (CDP) Sacramento County
73	202	0.6	**Foster City** (city) San Mateo County
73	202	0.6	**French Valley** (CDP) Riverside County
73	202	0.6	**Garden Grove** (city) Orange County
73	202	0.6	**La Mesa** (city) San Diego County
73	202	0.6	**Manteca** (city) San Joaquin County
73	202	0.6	**Moreno Valley** (city) Riverside County
73	202	0.6	**Oakland** (city) Alameda County
73	202	0.6	**Rosemont** (CDP) Sacramento County
73	202	0.6	**Salida** (CDP) Stanislaus County
73	202	0.6	**San Pablo** (city) Contra Costa County
73	202	0.6	**Santa Clara** (city) Santa Clara County
73	202	0.6	**Stanton** (city) Orange County
73	202	0.6	**Stockton** (city) San Joaquin County
73	202	0.6	**Susanville** (city) Lassen County
73	202	0.6	**Vacaville** (city) Solano County
97	251	0.5	**Alameda** (city) Alameda County
97	251	0.5	**Alum Rock** (CDP) Santa Clara County
97	251	0.5	**Anaheim** (city) Orange County
97	251	0.5	**Burlingame** (city) San Mateo County
97	251	0.5	**Carmichael** (CDP) Sacramento County
97	251	0.5	**Casa de Oro-Mount Helix** (CDP) San Diego County
97	251	0.5	**Costa Mesa** (city) Orange County
97	251	0.5	**Cypress** (city) Orange County
97	251	0.5	**El Cajon** (city) San Diego County
97	251	0.5	**Fremont** (city) Alameda County
97	251	0.5	**Galt** (city) Sacramento County
97	251	0.5	**Linda** (CDP) Yuba County
97	251	0.5	**Milpitas** (city) Santa Clara County
97	251	0.5	**Mountain View** (city) Santa Clara County
97	251	0.5	**Port Hueneme** (city) Ventura County
97	251	0.5	**Richmond** (city) Contra Costa County
97	251	0.5	**Ridgecrest** (city) Kern County
97	251	0.5	**San Diego** (city) San Diego County
97	251	0.5	**Santa Rosa** (city) Sonoma County
97	251	0.5	**Santee** (city) San Diego County
97	251	0.5	**Sunnyvale** (city) Santa Clara County
97	251	0.5	**Turlock** (city) Stanislaus County
97	251	0.5	**Winter Gardens** (CDP) San Diego County
120	288	0.4	**Apple Valley** (town) San Bernardino County
120	288	0.4	**Benicia** (city) Solano County
120	288	0.4	**Brentwood** (city) Contra Costa County
120	288	0.4	**California City** (city) Kern County
120	288	0.4	**Camp Pendleton South** (CDP) San Diego County
120	288	0.4	**Campbell** (city) Santa Clara County
120	288	0.4	**Citrus Heights** (city) Sacramento County
120	288	0.4	**Corona** (city) Riverside County
120	288	0.4	**Discovery Bay** (CDP) Contra Costa County
120	288	0.4	**Eastvale** (city) Riverside County
120	288	0.4	**Garden Acres** (CDP) San Joaquin County
120	288	0.4	**Hawaiian Gardens** (city) Los Angeles County
120	288	0.4	**Hemet** (city) Riverside County
120	288	0.4	**Hercules** (city) Contra Costa County
120	288	0.4	**Home Gardens** (CDP) Riverside County
120	288	0.4	**Lemoore** (city) Kings County
120	288	0.4	**Lompoc** (city) Santa Barbara County
120	288	0.4	**Los Alamitos** (city) Orange County
120	288	0.4	**Los Banos** (city) Merced County
120	288	0.4	**Menifee** (city) Riverside County
120	288	0.4	**Murrieta** (city) Riverside County
120	288	0.4	**Newman** (city) Stanislaus County
120	288	0.4	**Norwalk** (city) Los Angeles County
120	288	0.4	**Oakley** (city) Contra Costa County
120	288	0.4	**Olivehurst** (CDP) Yuba County
120	288	0.4	**Oroville** (city) Butte County
120	288	0.4	**Perris** (city) Riverside County
120	288	0.4	**Rialto** (city) San Bernardino County
120	288	0.4	**Rio Linda** (CDP) Sacramento County
120	288	0.4	**Riverbank** (city) Stanislaus County
120	288	0.4	**Riverside** (city) Riverside County

Note: *The state column ranks the top/bottom 150 places from all places in the state with population of 10,000 or more. The national column ranks the top/bottom 150 places from all places in the country with population of 10,000 or more. Places that are unincorporated were not considered in the rankings. Please refer to the User Guide for additional information.*

Two or More Races

Top 150 Places Ranked in *Descending* Order

State Rank	Nat'l Rank	Percent	Place
1	29	10.0	**Marina** (city) Monterey County
1	29	10.0	**Suisun City** (city) Solano County
3	34	8.8	**Fairfield** (city) Solano County
4	41	8.3	**Camp Pendleton South** (CDP) San Diego County
5	43	8.1	**Rosemont** (CDP) Sacramento County
6	50	7.9	**Elk Grove** (city) Sacramento County
6	50	7.9	**Seaside** (city) Monterey County
8	54	7.8	**Barstow** (city) San Bernardino County
8	54	7.8	**Foothill Farms** (CDP) Sacramento County
8	54	7.8	**Stanford** (CDP) Santa Clara County
11	58	7.7	**Antioch** (city) Contra Costa County
11	58	7.7	**El Sobrante** (CDP) Contra Costa County
11	58	7.7	**Tracy** (city) San Joaquin County
11	58	7.7	**West Sacramento** (city) Yolo County
15	62	7.6	**Fairview** (CDP) Alameda County
15	62	7.6	**Parkway** (CDP) Sacramento County
17	67	7.5	**Vallejo** (city) Solano County
18	69	7.4	**La Presa** (CDP) San Diego County
18	69	7.4	**La Riviera** (CDP) Sacramento County
18	69	7.4	**Marysville** (city) Yuba County
21	73	7.3	**Antelope** (CDP) Sacramento County
21	73	7.3	**Bostonia** (CDP) San Diego County
21	73	7.3	**Linda** (CDP) Yuba County
21	73	7.3	**North Highlands** (CDP) Sacramento County
21	73	7.3	**Pittsburg** (city) Contra Costa County
26	80	7.2	**Cherryland** (CDP) Alameda County
26	80	7.2	**Manteca** (city) San Joaquin County
28	84	7.1	**Alameda** (city) Alameda County
28	84	7.1	**Hayward** (city) Alameda County
28	84	7.1	**Lemon Grove** (city) San Diego County
28	84	7.1	**Oakley** (city) Contra Costa County
28	84	7.1	**Pacifica** (city) San Mateo County
28	84	7.1	**Sacramento** (city) Sacramento County
34	91	7.0	**Rancho Cordova** (city) Sacramento County
34	91	7.0	**Vacaville** (city) Solano County
36	95	6.9	**Brentwood** (city) Contra Costa County
36	95	6.9	**El Cajon** (city) San Diego County
36	95	6.9	**Lathrop** (city) San Joaquin County
36	95	6.9	**Olivehurst** (CDP) Yuba County
36	95	6.9	**Pinole** (city) Contra Costa County
36	95	6.9	**Stockton** (city) San Joaquin County
36	95	6.9	**Twentynine Palms** (city) San Bernardino County
36	95	6.9	**Vineyard** (CDP) Sacramento County
44	107	6.8	**Florin** (CDP) Sacramento County
44	107	6.8	**Lemoore** (city) Kings County
46	111	6.7	**Albany** (city) Alameda County
46	111	6.7	**Benicia** (city) Solano County
46	111	6.7	**Union City** (city) Alameda County
49	120	6.6	**American Canyon** (city) Napa County
49	120	6.6	**Arcata** (city) Humboldt County
49	120	6.6	**Imperial Beach** (city) San Diego County
49	120	6.6	**Newark** (city) Alameda County
49	120	6.6	**San Bruno** (city) San Mateo County
54	128	6.5	**Bay Point** (CDP) Contra Costa County
54	128	6.5	**El Cerrito** (city) Contra Costa County
54	128	6.5	**French Valley** (CDP) Riverside County
54	128	6.5	**Garden Acres** (CDP) San Joaquin County
54	128	6.5	**Rosamond** (CDP) Kern County
54	128	6.5	**San Lorenzo** (CDP) Alameda County
54	128	6.5	**Spring Valley** (CDP) San Diego County
61	140	6.4	**Clearlake** (city) Lake County
61	140	6.4	**Concord** (city) Contra Costa County
61	140	6.4	**Emeryville** (city) Alameda County
64	147	6.3	**Castro Valley** (CDP) Alameda County
64	147	6.3	**Lomita** (city) Los Angeles County
64	147	6.3	**Martinez** (city) Contra Costa County
64	147	6.3	**Modesto** (city) Stanislaus County
64	147	6.3	**Oroville** (city) Butte County
64	147	6.3	**Victorville** (city) San Bernardino County
70	157	6.2	**Berkeley** (city) Alameda County
70	157	6.2	**Galt** (city) Sacramento County
70	157	6.2	**Hercules** (city) Contra Costa County
70	157	6.2	**Lake Elsinore** (city) Riverside County
70	157	6.2	**Morgan Hill** (city) Santa Clara County
75	168	6.1	**Belmont** (city) San Mateo County
75	168	6.1	**Campbell** (city) Santa Clara County
75	168	6.1	**Culver City** (city) Los Angeles County
75	168	6.1	**Isla Vista** (CDP) Santa Barbara County
75	168	6.1	**Los Alamitos** (city) Orange County
75	168	6.1	**Murrieta** (city) Riverside County
75	168	6.1	**Port Hueneme** (city) Ventura County
75	168	6.1	**South San Francisco** (city) San Mateo County
83	183	6.0	**Dublin** (city) Alameda County
83	183	6.0	**Lemon Hill** (CDP) Sacramento County
85	192	5.9	**Altadena** (CDP) Los Angeles County
85	192	5.9	**Arden-Arcade** (CDP) Sacramento County
85	192	5.9	**Ashland** (CDP) Alameda County
85	192	5.9	**Eureka** (city) Humboldt County
85	192	5.9	**Fremont** (city) Alameda County
85	192	5.9	**Patterson** (city) Stanislaus County
85	192	5.9	**Prunedale** (CDP) Monterey County
85	192	5.9	**Salida** (CDP) Stanislaus County
85	192	5.9	**Temecula** (city) Riverside County
85	192	5.9	**Yuba City** (city) Sutter County
95	207	5.8	**Chula Vista** (city) San Diego County
95	207	5.8	**La Mesa** (city) San Diego County
95	207	5.8	**Lompoc** (city) Santa Barbara County
95	207	5.8	**Oceanside** (city) San Diego County
95	207	5.8	**Redondo Beach** (city) Los Angeles County
100	222	5.7	**Aliso Viejo** (city) Orange County
100	222	5.7	**Carmichael** (CDP) Sacramento County
100	222	5.7	**Discovery Bay** (CDP) Contra Costa County
100	222	5.7	**El Segundo** (city) Los Angeles County
100	222	5.7	**Lakewood** (city) Los Angeles County
100	222	5.7	**Lawndale** (city) Los Angeles County
100	222	5.7	**Moreno Valley** (city) Riverside County
100	222	5.7	**Ridgecrest** (city) Kern County
100	222	5.7	**Rohnert Park** (city) Sonoma County
100	222	5.7	**San Jacinto** (city) Riverside County
100	222	5.7	**San Mateo** (city) San Mateo County
100	222	5.7	**Santa Cruz** (city) Santa Cruz County
100	222	5.7	**Signal Hill** (city) Los Angeles County
113	243	5.6	**Adelanto** (city) San Bernardino County
113	243	5.6	**Alum Rock** (CDP) Santa Clara County
113	243	5.6	**California City** (city) Kern County
113	243	5.6	**Del Aire** (CDP) Los Angeles County
113	243	5.6	**Lake Los Angeles** (CDP) Los Angeles County
113	243	5.6	**Oakland** (city) Alameda County
113	243	5.6	**Richmond** (city) Contra Costa County
113	243	5.6	**San Leandro** (city) Alameda County
121	259	5.5	**Ceres** (city) Stanislaus County
121	259	5.5	**Crestline** (CDP) San Bernardino County
121	259	5.5	**Dixon** (city) Solano County
121	259	5.5	**Imperial** (city) Imperial County
121	259	5.5	**Irvine** (city) Orange County
121	259	5.5	**Ladera Ranch** (CDP) Orange County
121	259	5.5	**Merced** (city) Merced County
121	259	5.5	**Pleasant Hill** (city) Contra Costa County
121	259	5.5	**Red Bluff** (city) Tehama County
121	259	5.5	**Redwood City** (city) San Mateo County
121	259	5.5	**South Pasadena** (city) Los Angeles County
121	259	5.5	**Torrance** (city) Los Angeles County
121	259	5.5	**Ukiah** (city) Mendocino County
134	281	5.4	**Citrus Heights** (city) Sacramento County
134	281	5.4	**Davis** (city) Yolo County
134	281	5.4	**Hanford** (city) Kings County
134	281	5.4	**Highland** (city) San Bernardino County
134	281	5.4	**Lancaster** (city) Los Angeles County
134	281	5.4	**Livermore** (city) Alameda County
134	281	5.4	**Loma Linda** (city) San Bernardino County
134	281	5.4	**Newman** (city) Stanislaus County
134	281	5.4	**Palmdale** (city) Los Angeles County
134	281	5.4	**Rancho Cucamonga** (city) San Bernardino County
134	281	5.4	**Rio Linda** (CDP) Sacramento County
134	281	5.4	**San Pablo** (city) Contra Costa County
134	281	5.4	**Santee** (city) San Diego County
147	302	5.3	**Casa de Oro-Mount Helix** (CDP) San Diego County
147	302	5.3	**Castaic** (CDP) Los Angeles County
147	302	5.3	**Fillmore** (city) Ventura County
147	302	5.3	**Grover Beach** (city) San Luis Obispo County

Note: *The state column ranks the top/bottom 150 places from all places in the state with population of 10,000 or more. The national column ranks the top/bottom 150 places from all places in the country with population of 10,000 or more. Places that are unincorporated were not considered in the rankings. Please refer to the User Guide for additional information.*

Two or More Races

Top 150 Places Ranked in *Ascending* Order

State Rank	Nat'l Rank	Percent	Place
1	295	1.2	**Laguna Woods** (city) Orange County
2	1559	2.0	**Rancho Mirage** (city) Riverside County
3	1707	2.1	**Truckee** (town) Nevada County
4	1866	2.2	**Avenal** (city) Kings County
4	1866	2.2	**Rosemead** (city) Los Angeles County
6	2300	2.5	**Corcoran** (city) Kings County
6	2300	2.5	**Palm Desert** (city) Riverside County
6	2300	2.5	**Sonoma** (city) Sonoma County
9	2448	2.6	**Coachella** (city) Riverside County
10	2722	2.8	**Arcadia** (city) Los Angeles County
11	2829	2.9	**Laguna Beach** (city) Orange County
11	2829	2.9	**Monterey Park** (city) Los Angeles County
11	2829	2.9	**Newport Beach** (city) Orange County
11	2829	2.9	**San Gabriel** (city) Los Angeles County
11	2829	2.9	**Soledad** (city) Monterey County
11	2829	2.9	**Temple City** (city) Los Angeles County
11	2829	2.9	**Willowbrook** (CDP) Los Angeles County
18	2940	3.0	**Morro Bay** (city) San Luis Obispo County
18	2940	3.0	**South San Jose Hills** (CDP) Los Angeles County
20	3047	3.1	**Bell Gardens** (city) Los Angeles County
20	3047	3.1	**Malibu** (city) Los Angeles County
20	3047	3.1	**Palm Springs** (city) Riverside County
20	3047	3.1	**Rowland Heights** (CDP) Los Angeles County
20	3047	3.1	**San Marino** (city) Los Angeles County
25	3140	3.2	**Blythe** (city) Riverside County
25	3140	3.2	**Canyon Lake** (city) Riverside County
25	3140	3.2	**Dana Point** (city) Orange County
25	3140	3.2	**El Monte** (city) Los Angeles County
25	3140	3.2	**Hacienda Heights** (CDP) Los Angeles County
25	3140	3.2	**Norco** (city) Riverside County
25	3140	3.2	**Oak Park** (CDP) Ventura County
25	3140	3.2	**Susanville** (city) Lassen County
25	3140	3.2	**Wasco** (city) Kern County
25	3140	3.2	**Westmont** (CDP) Los Angeles County
35	3218	3.3	**Alamo** (CDP) Contra Costa County
35	3218	3.3	**Avocado Heights** (CDP) Los Angeles County
35	3218	3.3	**Cupertino** (city) Santa Clara County
35	3218	3.3	**East Los Angeles** (CDP) Los Angeles County
35	3218	3.3	**La Quinta** (city) Riverside County
35	3218	3.3	**Los Osos** (CDP) San Luis Obispo County
35	3218	3.3	**Walnut Park** (CDP) Los Angeles County
42	3303	3.4	**Alpine** (CDP) San Diego County
42	3303	3.4	**Compton** (city) Los Angeles County
42	3303	3.4	**East San Gabriel** (CDP) Los Angeles County
42	3303	3.4	**Encinitas** (city) San Diego County
42	3303	3.4	**Half Moon Bay** (city) San Mateo County
42	3303	3.4	**Healdsburg** (city) Sonoma County
42	3303	3.4	**Indio** (city) Riverside County
42	3303	3.4	**La Cañada Flintridge** (city) Los Angeles County
42	3303	3.4	**Lynwood** (city) Los Angeles County
42	3303	3.4	**Mendota** (city) Fresno County
42	3303	3.4	**Solana Beach** (city) San Diego County
42	3303	3.4	**South El Monte** (city) Los Angeles County
54	3385	3.5	**Alhambra** (city) Los Angeles County
54	3385	3.5	**Coronado** (city) San Diego County
54	3385	3.5	**East Rancho Dominguez** (CDP) Los Angeles County
54	3385	3.5	**McFarland** (city) Kern County
54	3385	3.5	**North Auburn** (CDP) Placer County
54	3385	3.5	**North Tustin** (CDP) Orange County
54	3385	3.5	**Paradise** (town) Butte County
54	3385	3.5	**Parlier** (city) Fresno County
54	3385	3.5	**San Anselmo** (town) Marin County
54	3385	3.5	**San Juan Capistrano** (city) Orange County
54	3385	3.5	**Sanger** (city) Fresno County
54	3385	3.5	**Seal Beach** (city) Orange County
54	3385	3.5	**Tehachapi** (city) Kern County
54	3385	3.5	**Valinda** (CDP) Los Angeles County
54	3385	3.5	**Walnut** (city) Los Angeles County
54	3385	3.5	**West Whittier-Los Nietos** (CDP) Los Angeles County
70	3466	3.6	**Agoura Hills** (city) Los Angeles County
70	3466	3.6	**Artesia** (city) Los Angeles County
70	3466	3.6	**Atascadero** (city) San Luis Obispo County
70	3466	3.6	**Coto de Caza** (CDP) Orange County
70	3466	3.6	**Florence-Graham** (CDP) Los Angeles County
70	3466	3.6	**Garden Grove** (city) Orange County
70	3466	3.6	**La Crescenta-Montrose** (CDP) Los Angeles County
70	3466	3.6	**Mead Valley** (CDP) Riverside County
70	3466	3.6	**Mill Valley** (city) Marin County
70	3466	3.6	**Palos Verdes Estates** (city) Los Angeles County
70	3466	3.6	**Ramona** (CDP) San Diego County
70	3466	3.6	**San Clemente** (city) Orange County
70	3466	3.6	**San Diego Country Estates** (CDP) San Diego County
70	3466	3.6	**Santa Ana** (city) Orange County
70	3466	3.6	**Saratoga** (city) Santa Clara County
70	3466	3.6	**West Hollywood** (city) Los Angeles County
70	3466	3.6	**Westminster** (city) Orange County
87	3548	3.7	**Baldwin Park** (city) Los Angeles County
87	3548	3.7	**Delano** (city) Kern County
87	3548	3.7	**Exeter** (city) Tulare County
87	3548	3.7	**Granite Bay** (CDP) Placer County
87	3548	3.7	**La Puente** (city) Los Angeles County
87	3548	3.7	**Lindsay** (city) Tulare County
87	3548	3.7	**Montebello** (city) Los Angeles County
87	3548	3.7	**Napa** (city) Napa County
87	3548	3.7	**Pico Rivera** (city) Los Angeles County
87	3548	3.7	**San Fernando** (city) Los Angeles County
87	3548	3.7	**Santa Paula** (city) Ventura County
87	3548	3.7	**South Gate** (city) Los Angeles County
87	3548	3.7	**South Lake Tahoe** (city) El Dorado County
100	3627	3.8	**Cerritos** (city) Los Angeles County
100	3627	3.8	**Chowchilla** (city) Madera County
100	3627	3.8	**Huntington Park** (city) Los Angeles County
100	3627	3.8	**Lake Arrowhead** (CDP) San Bernardino County
100	3627	3.8	**Selma** (city) Fresno County
100	3627	3.8	**Shafter** (city) Kern County
100	3627	3.8	**Thousand Oaks** (city) Ventura County
107	3685	3.9	**Bloomington** (CDP) San Bernardino County
107	3685	3.9	**Diamond Bar** (city) Los Angeles County
107	3685	3.9	**El Paso de Robles (Paso Robles)** (city) San Luis Obispo County
107	3685	3.9	**Grass Valley** (city) Nevada County
107	3685	3.9	**Hawaiian Gardens** (city) Los Angeles County
107	3685	3.9	**Hillsborough** (town) San Mateo County
107	3685	3.9	**Rossmoor** (CDP) Orange County
107	3685	3.9	**Santa Barbara** (city) Santa Barbara County
115	3742	4.0	**Brawley** (city) Imperial County
115	3742	4.0	**Calabasas** (city) Los Angeles County
115	3742	4.0	**Cameron Park** (CDP) El Dorado County
115	3742	4.0	**Danville** (town) Contra Costa County
115	3742	4.0	**Diamond Springs** (CDP) El Dorado County
115	3742	4.0	**Dinuba** (city) Tulare County
115	3742	4.0	**Greenfield** (city) Monterey County
115	3742	4.0	**Orange** (city) Orange County
115	3742	4.0	**Placentia** (city) Orange County
115	3742	4.0	**San Luis Obispo** (city) San Luis Obispo County
115	3742	4.0	**Tamalpais-Homestead Valley** (CDP) Marin County
115	3742	4.0	**West Puente Valley** (CDP) Los Angeles County
115	3742	4.0	**Yorba Linda** (city) Orange County
115	3742	4.0	**Yucca Valley** (town) San Bernardino County
129	3803	4.1	**Carpinteria** (city) Santa Barbara County
129	3803	4.1	**Citrus** (CDP) Los Angeles County
129	3803	4.1	**Coalinga** (city) Fresno County
129	3803	4.1	**Downey** (city) Los Angeles County
129	3803	4.1	**Inglewood** (city) Los Angeles County
129	3803	4.1	**Larkspur** (city) Marin County
129	3803	4.1	**Oakdale** (city) Stanislaus County
129	3803	4.1	**Petaluma** (city) Sonoma County
129	3803	4.1	**Reedley** (city) Fresno County
129	3803	4.1	**South Whittier** (CDP) Los Angeles County
129	3803	4.1	**Winton** (CDP) Merced County
129	3803	4.1	**Yucaipa** (city) San Bernardino County
141	3867	4.2	**Arvin** (city) Kern County
141	3867	4.2	**Calexico** (city) Imperial County
141	3867	4.2	**Carlsbad** (city) San Diego County
141	3867	4.2	**Cathedral City** (city) Riverside County
141	3867	4.2	**Farmersville** (city) Tulare County
141	3867	4.2	**Folsom** (city) Sacramento County
141	3867	4.2	**Fountain Valley** (city) Orange County
141	3867	4.2	**Hermosa Beach** (city) Los Angeles County
141	3867	4.2	**La Habra** (city) Orange County
141	3867	4.2	**Lafayette** (city) Contra Costa County

Note: *The state column ranks the top/bottom 150 places from all places in the state with population of 10,000 or more. The national column ranks the top/bottom 150 places from all places in the country with population of 10,000 or more. Places that are unincorporated were not considered in the rankings. Please refer to the User Guide for additional information.*

Hispanic Population

Top 150 Places Ranked in *Descending* Order

State Rank	Nat'l Rank	Percent	Place
1	4	97.5	**Parlier** (city) Fresno County
2	5	97.4	**Maywood** (city) Los Angeles County
2	5	97.4	**Walnut Park** (CDP) Los Angeles County
4	7	97.1	**East Los Angeles** (CDP) Los Angeles County
4	7	97.1	**Huntington Park** (city) Los Angeles County
6	10	96.8	**Calexico** (city) Imperial County
7	13	96.6	**Mendota** (city) Fresno County
8	14	96.4	**Coachella** (city) Riverside County
9	15	96.0	**Cudahy** (city) Los Angeles County
10	17	95.7	**Bell Gardens** (city) Los Angeles County
11	24	94.8	**South Gate** (city) Los Angeles County
12	26	94.5	**Commerce** (city) Los Angeles County
12	26	94.5	**Lamont** (CDP) Kern County
14	32	93.1	**Bell** (city) Los Angeles County
15	33	93.0	**Lennox** (CDP) Los Angeles County
16	35	92.7	**Arvin** (city) Kern County
17	37	92.5	**San Fernando** (city) Los Angeles County
18	41	91.5	**McFarland** (city) Kern County
19	42	91.3	**Greenfield** (city) Monterey County
20	43	91.2	**Pico Rivera** (city) Los Angeles County
21	46	90.0	**Florence-Graham** (CDP) Los Angeles County
22	51	87.6	**West Whittier-Los Nietos** (CDP) Los Angeles County
23	52	87.5	**King City** (city) Monterey County
24	55	86.6	**Lynwood** (city) Los Angeles County
25	58	86.2	**South San Jose Hills** (CDP) Los Angeles County
26	62	85.5	**Lindsay** (city) Tulare County
26	62	85.5	**West Puente Valley** (CDP) Los Angeles County
28	66	85.1	**La Puente** (city) Los Angeles County
29	70	84.9	**South El Monte** (city) Los Angeles County
30	74	84.4	**Dinuba** (city) Tulare County
31	78	83.8	**Farmersville** (city) Tulare County
32	79	82.9	**Muscoy** (CDP) San Bernardino County
33	82	82.1	**Avocado Heights** (CDP) Los Angeles County
34	84	82.0	**East Rancho Dominguez** (CDP) Los Angeles County
35	85	81.6	**El Centro** (city) Imperial County
36	86	81.5	**Brawley** (city) Imperial County
37	87	81.4	**Watsonville** (city) Santa Cruz County
38	90	81.0	**Bloomington** (CDP) San Bernardino County
38	90	81.0	**Santa Fe Springs** (city) Los Angeles County
40	93	80.5	**Sanger** (city) Fresno County
41	95	80.3	**Shafter** (city) Kern County
42	98	80.1	**Baldwin Park** (city) Los Angeles County
43	100	79.5	**Santa Paula** (city) Ventura County
44	103	79.3	**Montebello** (city) Los Angeles County
45	104	78.8	**Valinda** (CDP) Los Angeles County
46	106	78.6	**Paramount** (city) Los Angeles County
47	109	78.2	**Santa Ana** (city) Orange County
48	112	77.6	**Selma** (city) Fresno County
49	113	77.2	**Hawaiian Gardens** (city) Los Angeles County
50	114	77.1	**South Whittier** (CDP) Los Angeles County
51	116	76.7	**Madera** (city) Madera County
51	116	76.7	**Wasco** (city) Kern County
53	119	76.3	**Reedley** (city) Fresno County
54	121	75.0	**Salinas** (city) Monterey County
55	123	74.8	**Imperial** (city) Imperial County
56	124	74.7	**Fillmore** (city) Ventura County
57	126	73.7	**Home Gardens** (CDP) Riverside County
58	127	73.5	**Oxnard** (city) Ventura County
59	128	73.1	**Livingston** (city) Merced County
59	128	73.1	**North Fair Oaks** (CDP) San Mateo County
61	130	72.8	**Citrus** (CDP) Los Angeles County
62	131	72.4	**Mead Valley** (CDP) Riverside County
63	133	71.8	**Avenal** (city) Kings County
63	133	71.8	**Perris** (city) Riverside County
65	135	71.7	**Delhi** (CDP) Merced County
65	135	71.7	**Kerman** (city) Fresno County
67	138	71.5	**Delano** (city) Kern County
68	140	71.3	**Winton** (CDP) Merced County
69	142	71.1	**Soledad** (city) Monterey County
70	143	71.0	**Colton** (city) San Bernardino County
71	145	70.7	**Alum Rock** (CDP) Santa Clara County
71	145	70.7	**Downey** (city) Los Angeles County
73	148	70.5	**Pomona** (city) Los Angeles County
74	149	70.4	**Santa Maria** (city) Santa Barbara County
75	150	70.2	**Montclair** (city) San Bernardino County
76	152	70.1	**Norwalk** (city) Los Angeles County
77	158	69.0	**El Monte** (city) Los Angeles County
77	158	69.0	**Ontario** (city) San Bernardino County
79	160	68.9	**Garden Acres** (CDP) San Joaquin County
80	166	67.8	**Indio** (city) Riverside County
81	167	67.6	**Azusa** (city) Los Angeles County
81	167	67.6	**Rialto** (city) San Bernardino County
83	171	66.8	**Fontana** (city) San Bernardino County
84	173	65.7	**Hollister** (city) San Benito County
84	173	65.7	**Whittier** (city) Los Angeles County
86	176	65.0	**Compton** (city) Los Angeles County
87	178	64.9	**Los Banos** (city) Merced County
88	180	64.5	**East Palo Alto** (city) San Mateo County
89	182	63.9	**Willowbrook** (CDP) Los Angeles County
90	185	63.2	**Sun Village** (CDP) Los Angeles County
91	187	63.0	**National City** (city) San Diego County
92	189	62.6	**Corcoran** (city) Kings County
93	192	61.9	**Porterville** (city) Tulare County
94	194	61.6	**Newman** (city) Stanislaus County
95	196	61.0	**Lawndale** (city) Los Angeles County
96	202	60.0	**San Bernardino** (city) San Bernardino County
97	215	58.8	**Cathedral City** (city) Riverside County
98	217	58.6	**Patterson** (city) Stanislaus County
99	219	58.3	**Adelanto** (city) San Bernardino County
100	220	58.2	**Chula Vista** (city) San Diego County
101	224	57.8	**Gilroy** (city) Santa Clara County
102	226	57.5	**Tulare** (city) Tulare County
103	228	57.2	**La Habra** (city) Orange County
104	231	56.5	**San Pablo** (city) Contra Costa County
105	233	56.0	**Ceres** (city) Stanislaus County
106	238	54.9	**Bay Point** (CDP) Contra Costa County
107	243	54.4	**Moreno Valley** (city) Riverside County
107	243	54.4	**Palmdale** (city) Los Angeles County
109	245	54.0	**Cherryland** (CDP) Alameda County
110	247	53.8	**Chino** (city) San Bernardino County
111	249	53.6	**Lake Los Angeles** (CDP) Los Angeles County
112	252	53.5	**Coalinga** (city) Fresno County
113	257	53.2	**Blythe** (city) Riverside County
113	257	53.2	**West Covina** (city) Los Angeles County
115	260	52.9	**Hawthorne** (city) Los Angeles County
116	262	52.8	**Anaheim** (city) Orange County
117	263	52.6	**Atwater** (city) Merced County
117	263	52.6	**Desert Hot Springs** (city) Riverside County
119	265	52.4	**Covina** (city) Los Angeles County
120	267	52.3	**Bellflower** (city) Los Angeles County
120	267	52.3	**Port Hueneme** (city) Ventura County
120	267	52.3	**San Jacinto** (city) Riverside County
123	270	52.1	**Riverbank** (city) Stanislaus County
124	279	50.8	**Lompoc** (city) Santa Barbara County
124	279	50.8	**Stanton** (city) Orange County
126	281	50.6	**Inglewood** (city) Los Angeles County
127	292	49.6	**Merced** (city) Merced County
128	293	49.5	**Lemon Hill** (CDP) Sacramento County
129	294	49.0	**Imperial Beach** (city) San Diego County
129	294	49.0	**Riverside** (city) Riverside County
131	296	48.9	**Escondido** (city) San Diego County
131	296	48.9	**Hesperia** (city) San Bernardino County
133	298	48.7	**Carpinteria** (city) Santa Barbara County
134	304	48.5	**Los Angeles** (city) Los Angeles County
135	306	48.4	**Lake Elsinore** (city) Riverside County
135	306	48.4	**Vista** (city) San Diego County
137	311	48.1	**Highland** (city) San Bernardino County
138	315	47.8	**Duarte** (city) Los Angeles County
138	315	47.8	**Victorville** (city) San Bernardino County
140	320	47.4	**Woodland** (city) Yolo County
141	321	47.3	**La Presa** (CDP) San Diego County
142	322	47.2	**Del Aire** (CDP) Los Angeles County
143	323	47.1	**Hanford** (city) Kings County
144	327	46.9	**Fresno** (city) Fresno County
145	328	46.8	**Salida** (CDP) Stanislaus County
146	330	46.7	**Westmont** (CDP) Los Angeles County
147	333	46.0	**Visalia** (city) Tulare County
148	335	45.5	**Bakersfield** (city) Kern County
148	335	45.5	**Exeter** (city) Tulare County
148	335	45.5	**Hacienda Heights** (CDP) Los Angeles County

Note: *The state column ranks the top/bottom 150 places from all places in the state with population of 10,000 or more. The national column ranks the top/bottom 150 places from all places in the country with population of 10,000 or more. Places that are unincorporated were not considered in the rankings. Please refer to the User Guide for additional information.*

Hispanic Population

Top 150 Places Ranked in *Ascending* Order

State Rank	Nat'l Rank	Percent	Place
1	1236	3.4	**Hillsborough** (town) San Mateo County
2	1280	3.5	**Saratoga** (city) Santa Clara County
3	1323	3.6	**Cupertino** (city) Santa Clara County
4	1428	3.9	**Los Altos** (city) Santa Clara County
4	1428	3.9	**Piedmont** (city) Alameda County
6	1459	4.0	**Laguna Woods** (city) Orange County
7	1626	4.5	**Mill Valley** (city) Marin County
8	1662	4.6	**Orinda** (city) Contra Costa County
8	1662	4.6	**Tamalpais-Homestead Valley** (CDP) Marin County
10	1696	4.7	**Palos Verdes Estates** (city) Los Angeles County
11	1996	5.7	**Beverly Hills** (city) Los Angeles County
12	2017	5.8	**Alamo** (CDP) Contra Costa County
12	2017	5.8	**Lafayette** (city) Contra Costa County
12	2017	5.8	**San Anselmo** (town) Marin County
15	2071	6.0	**Oak Park** (CDP) Ventura County
16	2093	6.1	**Malibu** (city) Los Angeles County
17	2113	6.2	**Granite Bay** (CDP) Placer County
17	2113	6.2	**Palo Alto** (city) Santa Clara County
19	2135	6.3	**La Cañada Flintridge** (city) Los Angeles County
20	2162	6.4	**Calabasas** (city) Los Angeles County
21	2195	6.5	**Foster City** (city) San Mateo County
21	2195	6.5	**San Marino** (city) Los Angeles County
21	2195	6.5	**View Park-Windsor Hills** (CDP) Los Angeles County
24	2275	6.8	**Danville** (town) Contra Costa County
24	2275	6.8	**Magalia** (CDP) Butte County
26	2300	6.9	**Manhattan Beach** (city) Los Angeles County
27	2323	7.0	**Moraga** (town) Contra Costa County
27	2323	7.0	**Paradise** (town) Butte County
29	2345	7.1	**McKinleyville** (CDP) Humboldt County
30	2369	7.2	**Los Gatos** (town) Santa Clara County
30	2369	7.2	**Newport Beach** (city) Orange County
32	2388	7.3	**Laguna Beach** (city) Orange County
33	2472	7.7	**Larkspur** (city) Marin County
34	2512	7.9	**Coto de Caza** (CDP) Orange County
35	2590	8.4	**Hermosa Beach** (city) Los Angeles County
36	2605	8.5	**Rancho Palos Verdes** (city) Los Angeles County
36	2605	8.5	**Shasta Lake** (city) Shasta County
38	2623	8.6	**Walnut Creek** (city) Contra Costa County
39	2636	8.7	**Redding** (city) Shasta County
39	2636	8.7	**San Ramon** (city) Contra Costa County
41	2683	9.0	**Clayton** (city) Contra Costa County
41	2683	9.0	**El Dorado Hills** (CDP) El Dorado County
43	2715	9.2	**Emeryville** (city) Alameda County
43	2715	9.2	**Irvine** (city) Orange County
45	2744	9.5	**Agoura Hills** (city) Los Angeles County
46	2760	9.6	**Fair Oaks** (CDP) Sacramento County
46	2760	9.6	**Seal Beach** (city) Orange County
48	2811	10.0	**Auburn** (city) Placer County
48	2811	10.0	**Scotts Valley** (city) Santa Cruz County
50	2828	10.1	**San Carlos** (city) San Mateo County
51	2835	10.2	**Albany** (city) Alameda County
51	2835	10.2	**Orangevale** (CDP) Sacramento County
53	2850	10.3	**Pleasanton** (city) Alameda County
54	2861	10.4	**Grass Valley** (city) Nevada County
54	2861	10.4	**Stanford** (CDP) Santa Clara County
56	2871	10.5	**West Hollywood** (city) Los Angeles County
57	2895	10.7	**Pacific Grove** (city) Monterey County
58	2911	10.8	**Berkeley** (city) Alameda County
59	2932	11.0	**Alameda** (city) Alameda County
60	2944	11.1	**El Cerrito** (city) Contra Costa County
60	2944	11.1	**San Diego Country Estates** (CDP) San Diego County
62	2952	11.2	**Folsom** (city) Sacramento County
63	2967	11.3	**Cameron Park** (CDP) El Dorado County
64	2980	11.4	**La Crescenta-Montrose** (CDP) Los Angeles County
64	2980	11.4	**Rancho Mirage** (city) Riverside County
66	2992	11.5	**Belmont** (city) San Mateo County
66	2992	11.5	**Rocklin** (city) Placer County
66	2992	11.5	**Rossmoor** (CDP) Orange County
69	3005	11.6	**Arcata** (city) Humboldt County
69	3005	11.6	**Eureka** (city) Humboldt County
71	3014	11.7	**Carmichael** (CDP) Sacramento County
72	3034	11.9	**Millbrae** (city) San Mateo County
73	3046	12.0	**Benicia** (city) Solano County
73	3046	12.0	**Cerritos** (city) Los Angeles County
75	3055	12.1	**Arcadia** (city) Los Angeles County
75	3055	12.1	**Pleasant Hill** (city) Contra Costa County
77	3070	12.2	**Coronado** (city) San Diego County
78	3078	12.3	**Canyon Lake** (city) Riverside County
79	3096	12.5	**Davis** (city) Yolo County
79	3096	12.5	**Diamond Springs** (CDP) El Dorado County
79	3096	12.5	**Oroville** (city) Butte County
82	3124	12.8	**Ladera Ranch** (CDP) Orange County
83	3166	13.1	**Fountain Valley** (city) Orange County
83	3166	13.1	**North Tustin** (CDP) Orange County
83	3166	13.1	**Santa Monica** (city) Los Angeles County
86	3182	13.3	**Carlsbad** (city) San Diego County
87	3221	13.7	**Encinitas** (city) San Diego County
87	3221	13.7	**Monterey** (city) Monterey County
89	3228	13.8	**Burlingame** (city) San Mateo County
89	3228	13.8	**Los Osos** (CDP) San Luis Obispo County
91	3239	13.9	**Laguna Niguel** (city) Orange County
92	3289	14.4	**Yorba Linda** (city) Orange County
93	3296	14.5	**Antelope** (CDP) Sacramento County
93	3296	14.5	**Dublin** (city) Alameda County
95	3308	14.6	**Alpine** (CDP) San Diego County
95	3308	14.6	**Hercules** (city) Contra Costa County
95	3308	14.6	**Roseville** (city) Placer County
98	3316	14.7	**Martinez** (city) Contra Costa County
98	3316	14.7	**Rancho San Diego** (CDP) San Diego County
98	3316	14.7	**San Luis Obispo** (city) San Luis Obispo County
101	3329	14.8	**Fremont** (city) Alameda County
102	3333	14.9	**Morro Bay** (city) San Luis Obispo County
102	3333	14.9	**Sierra Madre** (city) Los Angeles County
104	3354	15.1	**San Francisco** (city) San Francisco County
105	3357	15.2	**Redondo Beach** (city) Los Angeles County
106	3365	15.3	**Sonoma** (city) Sonoma County
107	3370	15.4	**Chico** (city) Butte County
108	3380	15.5	**Discovery Bay** (CDP) Contra Costa County
109	3389	15.6	**Atascadero** (city) San Luis Obispo County
110	3398	15.7	**Arroyo Grande** (city) San Luis Obispo County
110	3398	15.7	**El Segundo** (city) Los Angeles County
110	3398	15.7	**Poway** (city) San Diego County
113	3414	15.9	**Solana Beach** (city) San Diego County
114	3418	16.0	**La Palma** (city) Orange County
115	3423	16.1	**Stevenson Ranch** (CDP) Los Angeles County
115	3423	16.1	**Torrance** (city) Los Angeles County
117	3431	16.2	**North Auburn** (CDP) Placer County
118	3437	16.3	**La Riviera** (CDP) Sacramento County
118	3437	16.3	**Santee** (city) San Diego County
120	3459	16.5	**Citrus Heights** (city) Sacramento County
120	3459	16.5	**Crestline** (CDP) San Bernardino County
122	3477	16.8	**Milpitas** (city) Santa Clara County
122	3477	16.8	**Pacifica** (city) San Mateo County
122	3477	16.8	**San Clemente** (city) Orange County
122	3477	16.8	**Thousand Oaks** (city) Ventura County
126	3485	17.0	**Dana Point** (city) Orange County
126	3485	17.0	**Fortuna** (city) Humboldt County
126	3485	17.0	**Mission Viejo** (city) Orange County
129	3494	17.1	**Aliso Viejo** (city) Orange County
129	3494	17.1	**Huntington Beach** (city) Orange County
131	3499	17.2	**Casa de Oro-Mount Helix** (CDP) San Diego County
132	3516	17.4	**Castro Valley** (CDP) Alameda County
132	3516	17.4	**Glendale** (city) Los Angeles County
134	3526	17.6	**Lakeside** (CDP) San Diego County
135	3531	17.7	**Lincoln** (city) Placer County
135	3531	17.7	**Rosedale** (CDP) Kern County
137	3537	17.8	**Vineyard** (CDP) Sacramento County
137	3537	17.8	**Yucca Valley** (town) San Bernardino County
139	3545	17.9	**Placerville** (city) El Dorado County
139	3545	17.9	**Ridgecrest** (city) Kern County
141	3551	18.0	**Elk Grove** (city) Sacramento County
142	3571	18.4	**Campbell** (city) Santa Clara County
142	3571	18.4	**Cypress** (city) Orange County
142	3571	18.4	**Menlo Park** (city) San Mateo County
145	3586	18.6	**Arden-Arcade** (CDP) Sacramento County
145	3586	18.6	**Rancho Santa Margarita** (city) Orange County
145	3586	18.6	**South Pasadena** (city) Los Angeles County
145	3586	18.6	**Truckee** (town) Nevada County
149	3601	18.9	**Big Bear City** (CDP) San Bernardino County
149	3601	18.9	**Sunnyvale** (city) Santa Clara County

***Note:** The state column ranks the top/bottom 150 places from all places in the state with population of 10,000 or more. The national column ranks the top/bottom 150 places from all places in the country with population of 10,000 or more. Places that are unincorporated were not considered in the rankings. Please refer to the User Guide for additional information.*

Average Household Size

Top 150 Places Ranked in *Descending* Order

State Rank	Nat'l Rank	Persons	Place
1	3	4.9	**East Rancho Dominguez** (CDP) Los Angeles County
1	3	4.9	**South San Jose Hills** (CDP) Los Angeles County
3	7	4.7	**Greenfield** (city) Monterey County
3	7	4.7	**West Puente Valley** (CDP) Los Angeles County
5	10	4.6	**Muscoy** (CDP) San Bernardino County
6	11	4.6	**Valinda** (CDP) Los Angeles County
7	12	4.5	**Lynwood** (city) Los Angeles County
8	13	4.5	**Florence-Graham** (CDP) Los Angeles County
9	14	4.5	**Mendota** (city) Fresno County
10	15	4.5	**Coachella** (city) Riverside County
11	17	4.4	**Arvin** (city) Kern County
12	19	4.4	**Lamont** (CDP) Kern County
13	20	4.4	**McFarland** (city) Kern County
13	20	4.4	**Walnut Park** (CDP) Los Angeles County
15	22	4.4	**Parlier** (city) Fresno County
16	23	4.3	**Mead Valley** (CDP) Riverside County
16	23	4.3	**South El Monte** (city) Los Angeles County
18	26	4.3	**Santa Ana** (city) Orange County
19	27	4.3	**Baldwin Park** (city) Los Angeles County
19	27	4.3	**Bloomington** (CDP) San Bernardino County
21	31	4.3	**Lennox** (CDP) Los Angeles County
22	32	4.3	**Bell Gardens** (city) Los Angeles County
23	34	4.2	**Soledad** (city) Monterey County
24	35	4.2	**King City** (city) Monterey County
25	37	4.2	**Cudahy** (city) Los Angeles County
26	38	4.2	**La Puente** (city) Los Angeles County
27	40	4.1	**Home Gardens** (CDP) Riverside County
28	42	4.1	**Alum Rock** (CDP) Santa Clara County
29	43	4.1	**Maywood** (city) Los Angeles County
29	43	4.1	**Perris** (city) Riverside County
31	45	4.1	**Citrus** (CDP) Los Angeles County
31	45	4.1	**Compton** (city) Los Angeles County
33	47	4.1	**Livingston** (city) Merced County
34	48	4.1	**Delano** (city) Kern County
35	49	4.0	**Avenal** (city) Kings County
35	49	4.0	**East Los Angeles** (CDP) Los Angeles County
37	51	4.0	**Farmersville** (city) Tulare County
37	51	4.0	**Willowbrook** (CDP) Los Angeles County
39	53	4.0	**South Gate** (city) Los Angeles County
40	55	4.0	**El Monte** (city) Los Angeles County
41	56	4.0	**East Palo Alto** (city) San Mateo County
42	57	4.0	**Avocado Heights** (CDP) Los Angeles County
43	59	4.0	**Delhi** (CDP) Merced County
43	59	4.0	**Hawaiian Gardens** (city) Los Angeles County
45	63	3.9	**Fontana** (city) San Bernardino County
46	65	3.9	**Huntington Park** (city) Los Angeles County
47	68	3.9	**Oxnard** (city) Ventura County
48	70	3.9	**San Fernando** (city) Los Angeles County
49	71	3.9	**Bell** (city) Los Angeles County
49	71	3.9	**Eastvale** (city) Riverside County
51	76	3.9	**Rialto** (city) San Bernardino County
52	77	3.9	**Winton** (CDP) Merced County
53	79	3.8	**Lindsay** (city) Tulare County
53	79	3.8	**Paramount** (city) Los Angeles County
55	81	3.8	**Shafter** (city) Kern County
55	81	3.8	**Wasco** (city) Kern County
57	84	3.8	**Sun Village** (CDP) Los Angeles County
58	85	3.8	**Adelanto** (city) San Bernardino County
59	87	3.8	**Norwalk** (city) Los Angeles County
60	88	3.8	**Madera** (city) Madera County
61	89	3.8	**Dinuba** (city) Tulare County
61	89	3.8	**Montclair** (city) San Bernardino County
63	93	3.8	**Calexico** (city) Imperial County
63	93	3.8	**West Whittier-Los Nietos** (CDP) Los Angeles County
65	97	3.7	**Commerce** (city) Los Angeles County
65	97	3.7	**Lathrop** (city) San Joaquin County
65	97	3.7	**Pico Rivera** (city) Los Angeles County
65	97	3.7	**Pomona** (city) Los Angeles County
65	97	3.7	**South Whittier** (CDP) Los Angeles County
70	103	3.7	**Garden Acres** (CDP) San Joaquin County
70	103	3.7	**Lake Los Angeles** (CDP) Los Angeles County
72	105	3.7	**Watsonville** (city) Santa Cruz County
73	106	3.7	**Moreno Valley** (city) Riverside County
73	106	3.7	**Rosemead** (city) Los Angeles County
75	112	3.6	**Garden Grove** (city) Orange County
75	112	3.6	**Kerman** (city) Fresno County
75	112	3.6	**North Fair Oaks** (CDP) San Mateo County
78	116	3.6	**Salinas** (city) Monterey County
78	116	3.6	**Santa Maria** (city) Santa Barbara County
80	121	3.6	**Reedley** (city) Fresno County
81	127	3.6	**Camp Pendleton South** (CDP) San Diego County
81	127	3.6	**Ontario** (city) San Bernardino County
81	127	3.6	**Patterson** (city) Stanislaus County
84	134	3.6	**Sanger** (city) Fresno County
85	139	3.5	**French Valley** (CDP) Riverside County
85	139	3.5	**Selma** (city) Fresno County
87	142	3.5	**Fillmore** (city) Ventura County
88	148	3.5	**Carson** (city) Los Angeles County
89	150	3.5	**Ceres** (city) Stanislaus County
89	150	3.5	**Palmdale** (city) Los Angeles County
91	155	3.5	**Hollister** (city) San Benito County
92	157	3.5	**Artesia** (city) Los Angeles County
93	160	3.5	**Corcoran** (city) Kings County
93	160	3.5	**Santa Paula** (city) Ventura County
93	160	3.5	**Stanton** (city) Orange County
96	163	3.4	**Los Banos** (city) Merced County
97	166	3.4	**Lake Elsinore** (city) Riverside County
98	171	3.4	**Salida** (CDP) Stanislaus County
99	174	3.4	**Colton** (city) San Bernardino County
100	179	3.4	**El Sobrante** (CDP) Riverside County
101	184	3.4	**American Canyon** (city) Napa County
101	184	3.4	**Azusa** (city) Los Angeles County
103	190	3.4	**Highland** (city) San Bernardino County
103	190	3.4	**Riverbank** (city) Stanislaus County
103	190	3.4	**San Bernardino** (city) San Bernardino County
106	196	3.4	**Bay Point** (CDP) Contra Costa County
106	196	3.4	**Chino** (city) San Bernardino County
106	196	3.4	**Hesperia** (city) San Bernardino County
106	196	3.4	**National City** (city) San Diego County
106	196	3.4	**Walnut** (city) Los Angeles County
111	206	3.4	**Tracy** (city) San Joaquin County
111	206	3.4	**Victorville** (city) San Bernardino County
111	206	3.4	**Westminster** (city) Orange County
114	209	3.3	**Gilroy** (city) Santa Clara County
114	209	3.3	**Lemon Hill** (CDP) Sacramento County
114	209	3.3	**Porterville** (city) Tulare County
117	213	3.3	**Anaheim** (city) Orange County
117	213	3.3	**Corona** (city) Riverside County
117	213	3.3	**Newman** (city) Stanislaus County
117	213	3.3	**Santa Fe Springs** (city) Los Angeles County
117	213	3.3	**Union City** (city) Alameda County
122	223	3.3	**Buena Park** (city) Orange County
122	223	3.3	**Lawndale** (city) Los Angeles County
124	231	3.3	**Rowland Heights** (CDP) Los Angeles County
125	236	3.3	**Vineyard** (CDP) Sacramento County
126	241	3.3	**Imperial** (city) Imperial County
126	241	3.3	**Milpitas** (city) Santa Clara County
126	241	3.3	**San Jacinto** (city) Riverside County
126	241	3.3	**West Covina** (city) Los Angeles County
130	247	3.3	**Hacienda Heights** (CDP) Los Angeles County
130	247	3.3	**La Presa** (CDP) San Diego County
130	247	3.3	**Tulare** (city) Tulare County
133	258	3.3	**Olivehurst** (CDP) Yuba County
134	265	3.2	**Castaic** (CDP) Los Angeles County
134	265	3.2	**Oakley** (city) Contra Costa County
136	271	3.2	**Moorpark** (city) Ventura County
136	271	3.2	**San Pablo** (city) Contra Costa County
138	276	3.2	**Downey** (city) Los Angeles County
138	276	3.2	**Montebello** (city) Los Angeles County
138	276	3.2	**Newark** (city) Alameda County
138	276	3.2	**Westmont** (CDP) Los Angeles County
142	286	3.2	**East Hemet** (CDP) Riverside County
142	286	3.2	**Linda** (CDP) Yuba County
144	294	3.2	**Brawley** (city) Imperial County
144	294	3.2	**Chino Hills** (city) San Bernardino County
146	299	3.2	**Galt** (city) Sacramento County
147	308	3.2	**Antelope** (CDP) Sacramento County
147	308	3.2	**Daly City** (city) San Mateo County
147	308	3.2	**Ladera Ranch** (CDP) Orange County
147	308	3.2	**Norco** (city) Riverside County

Note: *The state column ranks the top/bottom 150 places from all places in the state with population of 10,000 or more. The national column ranks the top/bottom 150 places from all places in the country with population of 10,000 or more. Places that are unincorporated were not considered in the rankings. Please refer to the User Guide for additional information.*

Average Household Size

Top 150 Places Ranked in *Ascending* Order

State Rank	Nat'l Rank	Persons	Place
1	1	1.4	**Laguna Woods** (city) Orange County
2	2	1.5	**West Hollywood** (city) Los Angeles County
3	10	1.7	**Emeryville** (city) Alameda County
4	15	1.8	**Seal Beach** (city) Orange County
5	19	1.8	**Santa Monica** (city) Los Angeles County
6	28	1.9	**Palm Springs** (city) Riverside County
7	33	1.9	**Rancho Mirage** (city) Riverside County
8	38	1.9	**Stanford** (CDP) Santa Clara County
9	50	2.0	**Larkspur** (city) Marin County
10	72	2.0	**Grass Valley** (city) Nevada County
10	72	2.0	**Hermosa Beach** (city) Los Angeles County
12	102	2.0	**Monterey** (city) Monterey County
12	102	2.0	**Morro Bay** (city) San Luis Obispo County
12	102	2.0	**Palm Desert** (city) Riverside County
12	102	2.0	**Walnut Creek** (city) Contra Costa County
16	114	2.0	**Laguna Beach** (city) Orange County
16	114	2.0	**Pacific Grove** (city) Monterey County
18	129	2.1	**Arcata** (city) Humboldt County
18	129	2.1	**Sonoma** (city) Sonoma County
20	244	2.1	**Berkeley** (city) Alameda County
20	244	2.1	**Paradise** (town) Butte County
22	312	2.1	**Newport Beach** (city) Orange County
23	493	2.2	**Arden-Arcade** (CDP) Sacramento County
24	573	2.2	**San Francisco** (city) San Francisco County
24	573	2.2	**Sierra Madre** (city) Los Angeles County
26	623	2.2	**Auburn** (city) Placer County
26	623	2.2	**Eureka** (city) Humboldt County
26	623	2.2	**Mill Valley** (city) Marin County
29	673	2.2	**Solana Beach** (city) San Diego County
30	720	2.2	**Beverly Hills** (city) Los Angeles County
30	720	2.2	**Burlingame** (city) San Mateo County
30	720	2.2	**Redondo Beach** (city) Los Angeles County
30	720	2.2	**San Luis Obispo** (city) San Luis Obispo County
34	778	2.3	**Culver City** (city) Los Angeles County
34	778	2.3	**La Mesa** (city) San Diego County
36	837	2.3	**Coronado** (city) San Diego County
36	837	2.3	**El Cerrito** (city) Contra Costa County
36	837	2.3	**Mountain View** (city) Santa Clara County
39	944	2.3	**Carmichael** (CDP) Sacramento County
39	944	2.3	**Dana Point** (city) Orange County
41	997	2.3	**El Segundo** (city) Los Angeles County
41	997	2.3	**Magalia** (CDP) Butte County
41	997	2.3	**San Anselmo** (town) Marin County
44	1049	2.3	**Los Gatos** (town) Santa Clara County
45	1107	2.3	**North Auburn** (CDP) Placer County
45	1107	2.3	**South Lake Tahoe** (city) El Dorado County
47	1172	2.3	**Fair Oaks** (CDP) Sacramento County
47	1172	2.3	**Malibu** (city) Los Angeles County
47	1172	2.3	**Placerville** (city) El Dorado County
50	1234	2.3	**Chico** (city) Butte County
50	1234	2.3	**Diamond Springs** (CDP) El Dorado County
50	1234	2.3	**Los Osos** (CDP) San Luis Obispo County
50	1234	2.3	**Pleasant Hill** (city) Contra Costa County
54	1310	2.3	**Belmont** (city) San Mateo County
54	1310	2.3	**La Riviera** (CDP) Sacramento County
54	1310	2.3	**Santa Cruz** (city) Santa Cruz County
57	1361	2.4	**Alameda** (city) Alameda County
57	1361	2.4	**McKinleyville** (CDP) Humboldt County
59	1416	2.4	**Arroyo Grande** (city) San Luis Obispo County
59	1416	2.4	**Palo Alto** (city) Santa Clara County
59	1416	2.4	**Tamalpais-Homestead Valley** (CDP) Marin County
62	1478	2.4	**Campbell** (city) Santa Clara County
62	1478	2.4	**Martinez** (city) Contra Costa County
62	1478	2.4	**Pasadena** (city) Los Angeles County
65	1550	2.4	**Redding** (city) Shasta County
65	1550	2.4	**South Pasadena** (city) Los Angeles County
65	1550	2.4	**View Park-Windsor Hills** (CDP) Los Angeles County
68	1625	2.4	**Marysville** (city) Yuba County
68	1625	2.4	**San Rafael** (city) Marin County
70	1689	2.4	**Big Bear City** (CDP) San Bernardino County
70	1689	2.4	**Burbank** (city) Los Angeles County
70	1689	2.4	**Encinitas** (city) San Diego County
70	1689	2.4	**Santa Barbara** (city) Santa Barbara County
74	1764	2.4	**Crestline** (CDP) San Bernardino County
74	1764	2.4	**San Carlos** (city) San Mateo County
74	1764	2.4	**Susanville** (city) Lassen County
77	1889	2.4	**Clearlake** (city) Lake County
77	1889	2.4	**Ukiah** (city) Mendocino County
77	1889	2.4	**Yucca Valley** (town) San Bernardino County
80	1959	2.4	**Albany** (city) Alameda County
80	1959	2.4	**Fortuna** (city) Humboldt County
80	1959	2.4	**Lomita** (city) Los Angeles County
80	1959	2.4	**Oakland** (city) Alameda County
84	2027	2.5	**Manhattan Beach** (city) Los Angeles County
85	2089	2.5	**Atascadero** (city) San Luis Obispo County
85	2089	2.5	**San Mateo** (city) San Mateo County
87	2139	2.5	**Benicia** (city) Solano County
87	2139	2.5	**La Quinta** (city) Riverside County
89	2193	2.5	**Carlsbad** (city) San Diego County
89	2193	2.5	**Citrus Heights** (city) Sacramento County
89	2193	2.5	**Foster City** (city) San Mateo County
89	2193	2.5	**Menlo Park** (city) San Mateo County
89	2193	2.5	**Novato** (city) Marin County
94	2259	2.5	**Grover Beach** (city) San Luis Obispo County
94	2259	2.5	**Red Bluff** (city) Tehama County
94	2259	2.5	**Ridgecrest** (city) Kern County
94	2259	2.5	**Truckee** (town) Nevada County
98	2323	2.5	**Davis** (city) Yolo County
98	2323	2.5	**Huntington Beach** (city) Orange County
98	2323	2.5	**Scotts Valley** (city) Santa Cruz County
101	2375	2.5	**Healdsburg** (city) Sonoma County
101	2375	2.5	**Loma Linda** (city) San Bernardino County
103	2423	2.5	**Claremont** (city) Los Angeles County
103	2423	2.5	**Moraga** (town) Contra Costa County
103	2423	2.5	**Rohnert Park** (city) Sonoma County
103	2423	2.5	**San Buenaventura (Ventura)** (city) Ventura County
103	2423	2.5	**Shasta Lake** (city) Shasta County
108	2469	2.5	**Lafayette** (city) Contra Costa County
108	2469	2.5	**Torrance** (city) Los Angeles County
110	2521	2.5	**Hemet** (city) Riverside County
110	2521	2.5	**Laguna Niguel** (city) Orange County
110	2521	2.5	**Lincoln** (city) Placer County
110	2521	2.5	**Live Oak** (CDP) Santa Cruz County
110	2521	2.5	**Santa Rosa** (city) Sonoma County
115	2564	2.6	**Aliso Viejo** (city) Orange County
115	2564	2.6	**Oroville** (city) Butte County
115	2564	2.6	**San Diego** (city) San Diego County
118	2608	2.6	**Banning** (city) Riverside County
118	2608	2.6	**Cameron Park** (CDP) El Dorado County
118	2608	2.6	**Folsom** (city) Sacramento County
118	2608	2.6	**Irvine** (city) Orange County
118	2608	2.6	**Sunnyvale** (city) Santa Clara County
123	2656	2.6	**Roseville** (city) Placer County
123	2656	2.6	**Sacramento** (city) Sacramento County
125	2696	2.6	**Glendale** (city) Los Angeles County
125	2696	2.6	**Orangevale** (CDP) Sacramento County
125	2696	2.6	**Petaluma** (city) Sonoma County
125	2696	2.6	**Santa Clara** (city) Santa Clara County
129	2757	2.6	**Camarillo** (city) Ventura County
129	2757	2.6	**Signal Hill** (city) Los Angeles County
131	2824	2.6	**El Sobrante** (CDP) Contra Costa County
131	2824	2.6	**Lake Arrowhead** (CDP) San Bernardino County
131	2824	2.6	**Millbrae** (city) San Mateo County
131	2824	2.6	**Monrovia** (city) Los Angeles County
131	2824	2.6	**Pacifica** (city) San Mateo County
131	2824	2.6	**Palos Verdes Estates** (city) Los Angeles County
131	2824	2.6	**Rancho Palos Verdes** (city) Los Angeles County
131	2824	2.6	**San Clemente** (city) Orange County
139	2869	2.6	**Los Alamitos** (city) Orange County
140	2919	2.6	**Casa de Oro-Mount Helix** (CDP) San Diego County
140	2919	2.6	**Valle Vista** (CDP) Riverside County
142	2975	2.6	**Canyon Lake** (city) Riverside County
142	2975	2.6	**Costa Mesa** (city) Orange County
142	2975	2.6	**Los Altos** (city) Santa Clara County
142	2975	2.6	**Oak Park** (CDP) Ventura County
142	2975	2.6	**Redlands** (city) San Bernardino County
142	2975	2.6	**Rosemont** (CDP) Sacramento County
142	2975	2.6	**Twentynine Palms** (city) San Bernardino County
149	3040	2.6	**Alpine** (CDP) San Diego County
149	3040	2.6	**Castro Valley** (CDP) Alameda County

Note: *The state column ranks the top/bottom 150 places from all places in the state with population of 10,000 or more. The national column ranks the top/bottom 150 places from all places in the country with population of 10,000 or more. Places that are unincorporated were not considered in the rankings. Please refer to the User Guide for additional information.*

Median Age

Top 150 Places Ranked in *Descending* Order

State Rank	Nat'l Rank	Years	Place
1	1	77.0	**Laguna Woods** (city) Orange County
2	18	62.3	**Rancho Mirage** (city) Riverside County
3	26	57.3	**Seal Beach** (city) Orange County
4	42	53.0	**Palm Desert** (city) Riverside County
5	51	51.6	**Palm Springs** (city) Riverside County
6	68	50.2	**Paradise** (town) Butte County
7	78	49.9	**Palos Verdes Estates** (city) Los Angeles County
8	89	49.2	**Sonoma** (city) Sonoma County
9	92	49.0	**Magalia** (CDP) Butte County
10	97	48.9	**Morro Bay** (city) San Luis Obispo County
11	108	48.5	**Larkspur** (city) Marin County
12	110	48.3	**Laguna Beach** (city) Orange County
13	121	48.1	**Pacific Grove** (city) Monterey County
14	123	47.9	**Walnut Creek** (city) Contra Costa County
15	129	47.8	**Malibu** (city) Los Angeles County
15	129	47.8	**Orinda** (city) Contra Costa County
15	129	47.8	**Rancho Palos Verdes** (city) Los Angeles County
15	129	47.8	**Saratoga** (city) Santa Clara County
19	135	47.7	**Alamo** (CDP) Contra Costa County
20	142	47.5	**Hillsborough** (town) San Mateo County
21	158	47.2	**Los Osos** (CDP) San Luis Obispo County
22	161	47.1	**Diamond Springs** (CDP) El Dorado County
22	161	47.1	**View Park-Windsor Hills** (CDP) Los Angeles County
24	194	46.6	**Mill Valley** (city) Marin County
24	194	46.6	**Sierra Madre** (city) Los Angeles County
26	216	46.2	**Los Altos** (city) Santa Clara County
26	216	46.2	**Piedmont** (city) Alameda County
28	229	46.0	**Granite Bay** (CDP) Placer County
29	236	45.9	**La Cañada Flintridge** (city) Los Angeles County
30	247	45.8	**Fair Oaks** (CDP) Sacramento County
31	262	45.6	**La Quinta** (city) Riverside County
31	262	45.6	**North Tustin** (CDP) Orange County
33	274	45.5	**Rossmoor** (CDP) Orange County
33	274	45.5	**Tamalpais-Homestead Valley** (CDP) Marin County
35	291	45.4	**Arroyo Grande** (city) San Luis Obispo County
35	291	45.4	**Auburn** (city) Placer County
35	291	45.4	**Casa de Oro-Mount Helix** (CDP) San Diego County
38	309	45.3	**San Marino** (city) Los Angeles County
39	323	45.2	**Lafayette** (city) Contra Costa County
40	351	45.0	**Clayton** (city) Contra Costa County
40	351	45.0	**Los Gatos** (town) Santa Clara County
40	351	45.0	**Moraga** (town) Contra Costa County
43	367	44.9	**San Anselmo** (town) Marin County
44	380	44.8	**Dana Point** (city) Orange County
44	380	44.8	**Millbrae** (city) San Mateo County
46	429	44.5	**Danville** (town) Contra Costa County
47	494	44.0	**Canyon Lake** (city) Riverside County
47	494	44.0	**Cerritos** (city) Los Angeles County
47	494	44.0	**Newport Beach** (city) Orange County
50	514	43.9	**Bonita** (CDP) San Diego County
51	552	43.7	**Solana Beach** (city) San Diego County
52	569	43.6	**Beverly Hills** (city) Los Angeles County
53	588	43.5	**El Cerrito** (city) Contra Costa County
54	632	43.3	**Crestline** (CDP) San Bernardino County
55	659	43.2	**Grass Valley** (city) Nevada County
55	659	43.2	**Half Moon Bay** (city) San Mateo County
57	677	43.1	**Arcadia** (city) Los Angeles County
57	677	43.1	**Monterey Park** (city) Los Angeles County
57	677	43.1	**Walnut** (city) Los Angeles County
60	699	43.0	**Lake Arrowhead** (CDP) San Bernardino County
61	720	42.9	**Benicia** (city) Solano County
61	720	42.9	**Big Bear City** (CDP) San Bernardino County
61	720	42.9	**La Verne** (city) Los Angeles County
64	755	42.8	**Laguna Niguel** (city) Orange County
65	810	42.6	**Fountain Valley** (city) Orange County
65	810	42.6	**Novato** (city) Marin County
65	810	42.6	**Pinole** (city) Contra Costa County
65	810	42.6	**San Carlos** (city) San Mateo County
65	810	42.6	**San Dimas** (city) Los Angeles County
70	843	42.5	**North Auburn** (CDP) Placer County
71	876	42.4	**Agoura Hills** (city) Los Angeles County
71	876	42.4	**Carmichael** (CDP) Sacramento County
73	905	42.3	**Banning** (city) Riverside County
73	905	42.3	**Orcutt** (CDP) Santa Barbara County
75	932	42.2	**Coto de Caza** (CDP) Orange County
75	932	42.2	**Martinez** (city) Contra Costa County
75	932	42.2	**Mission Viejo** (city) Orange County
78	955	42.1	**West Carson** (CDP) Los Angeles County
79	980	42.0	**Temple City** (city) Los Angeles County
80	1008	41.9	**Alpine** (CDP) San Diego County
80	1008	41.9	**Palo Alto** (city) Santa Clara County
82	1043	41.8	**Altadena** (CDP) Los Angeles County
83	1073	41.7	**Oak Park** (CDP) Ventura County
83	1073	41.7	**Scotts Valley** (city) Santa Cruz County
83	1073	41.7	**Yorba Linda** (city) Orange County
86	1100	41.6	**Calabasas** (city) Los Angeles County
86	1100	41.6	**La Crescenta-Montrose** (CDP) Los Angeles County
88	1132	41.5	**Encinitas** (city) San Diego County
88	1132	41.5	**Pacifica** (city) San Mateo County
88	1132	41.5	**Thousand Oaks** (city) Ventura County
91	1167	41.4	**Valle Vista** (CDP) Riverside County
92	1204	41.3	**Poway** (city) San Diego County
92	1204	41.3	**Torrance** (city) Los Angeles County
94	1244	41.2	**Castro Valley** (CDP) Alameda County
94	1244	41.2	**La Palma** (city) Orange County
94	1244	41.2	**Rancho San Diego** (CDP) San Diego County
97	1274	41.1	**Fairview** (CDP) Alameda County
97	1274	41.1	**San Diego Country Estates** (CDP) San Diego County
99	1296	41.0	**Atascadero** (city) San Luis Obispo County
99	1296	41.0	**Diamond Bar** (city) Los Angeles County
99	1296	41.0	**Glendale** (city) Los Angeles County
102	1321	40.9	**Belmont** (city) San Mateo County
102	1321	40.9	**Manhattan Beach** (city) Los Angeles County
104	1349	40.8	**Camarillo** (city) Ventura County
104	1349	40.8	**Healdsburg** (city) Sonoma County
104	1349	40.8	**Laguna Hills** (city) Orange County
107	1373	40.7	**Alameda** (city) Alameda County
107	1373	40.7	**Coronado** (city) San Diego County
107	1373	40.7	**Orangevale** (CDP) Sacramento County
107	1373	40.7	**Pleasant Hill** (city) Contra Costa County
111	1404	40.6	**Cameron Park** (CDP) El Dorado County
111	1404	40.6	**El Dorado Hills** (CDP) El Dorado County
111	1404	40.6	**El Sobrante** (CDP) Contra Costa County
111	1404	40.6	**Yucca Valley** (town) San Bernardino County
115	1437	40.5	**Burlingame** (city) San Mateo County
115	1437	40.5	**Culver City** (city) Los Angeles County
115	1437	40.5	**Lincoln** (city) Placer County
115	1437	40.5	**Pleasanton** (city) Alameda County
119	1472	40.4	**Carlsbad** (city) San Diego County
119	1472	40.4	**Placerville** (city) El Dorado County
119	1472	40.4	**Santa Monica** (city) Los Angeles County
119	1472	40.4	**West Hollywood** (city) Los Angeles County
123	1505	40.3	**Petaluma** (city) Sonoma County
123	1505	40.3	**San Gabriel** (city) Los Angeles County
125	1538	40.2	**East San Gabriel** (CDP) Los Angeles County
125	1538	40.2	**Glendora** (city) Los Angeles County
125	1538	40.2	**Huntington Beach** (city) Orange County
125	1538	40.2	**Rowland Heights** (CDP) Los Angeles County
125	1538	40.2	**San Juan Capistrano** (city) Orange County
125	1538	40.2	**San Rafael** (city) Marin County
131	1576	40.1	**Hacienda Heights** (CDP) Los Angeles County
131	1576	40.1	**Prunedale** (CDP) Monterey County
131	1576	40.1	**Rosedale** (CDP) Kern County
131	1576	40.1	**South Pasadena** (city) Los Angeles County
135	1635	39.9	**Clearlake** (city) Lake County
135	1635	39.9	**Cupertino** (city) Santa Clara County
135	1635	39.9	**Cypress** (city) Orange County
135	1635	39.9	**Duarte** (city) Los Angeles County
135	1635	39.9	**Woodcrest** (CDP) Riverside County
140	1710	39.7	**San Clemente** (city) Orange County
141	1736	39.6	**Discovery Bay** (CDP) Contra Costa County
141	1736	39.6	**Lomita** (city) Los Angeles County
143	1770	39.5	**Carpinteria** (city) Santa Barbara County
143	1770	39.5	**Norco** (city) Riverside County
145	1839	39.3	**Alhambra** (city) Los Angeles County
145	1839	39.3	**Foster City** (city) San Mateo County
145	1839	39.3	**Redondo Beach** (city) Los Angeles County
145	1839	39.3	**San Leandro** (city) Alameda County
149	1872	39.2	**El Segundo** (city) Los Angeles County
150	1904	39.1	**Lakeside** (CDP) San Diego County

Note: *The state column ranks the top/bottom 150 places from all places in the state with population of 10,000 or more. The national column ranks the top/bottom 150 places from all places in the country with population of 10,000 or more. Places that are unincorporated were not considered in the rankings. Please refer to the User Guide for additional information.*

Median Age

Top 150 Places Ranked in *Ascending* Order

State Rank	Nat'l Rank	Years	Place
1	9	20.7	**Isla Vista** (CDP) Santa Barbara County
2	26	21.7	**Camp Pendleton South** (CDP) San Diego County
3	51	22.6	**Stanford** (CDP) Santa Clara County
4	77	23.5	**Twentynine Palms** (city) San Bernardino County
5	95	24.0	**Arvin** (city) Kern County
6	104	24.5	**Coachella** (city) Riverside County
7	106	24.6	**Lindsay** (city) Tulare County
8	107	24.7	**Lamont** (CDP) Kern County
9	112	24.9	**Muscoy** (CDP) San Bernardino County
10	122	25.1	**Parlier** (city) Fresno County
11	124	25.2	**Davis** (city) Yolo County
12	125	25.3	**Adelanto** (city) San Bernardino County
13	136	25.5	**Greenfield** (city) Monterey County
14	142	25.6	**Winton** (CDP) Merced County
15	146	25.7	**McFarland** (city) Kern County
16	150	25.9	**King City** (city) Monterey County
16	150	25.9	**Perris** (city) Riverside County
16	150	25.9	**Shafter** (city) Kern County
19	157	26.1	**Arcata** (city) Humboldt County
19	157	26.1	**East Rancho Dominguez** (CDP) Los Angeles County
21	160	26.2	**Farmersville** (city) Tulare County
21	160	26.2	**Mendota** (city) Fresno County
23	167	26.3	**Florence-Graham** (CDP) Los Angeles County
24	172	26.5	**San Luis Obispo** (city) San Luis Obispo County
25	178	26.6	**Madera** (city) Madera County
26	192	27.0	**Cudahy** (city) Los Angeles County
27	200	27.2	**Dinuba** (city) Tulare County
28	203	27.3	**Bell Gardens** (city) Los Angeles County
29	208	27.4	**Livingston** (city) Merced County
30	210	27.5	**Delhi** (CDP) Merced County
31	219	27.7	**Lennox** (CDP) Los Angeles County
32	221	27.8	**Bloomington** (CDP) San Bernardino County
32	221	27.8	**Lynwood** (city) Los Angeles County
34	229	27.9	**Linda** (CDP) Yuba County
34	229	27.9	**Maywood** (city) Los Angeles County
36	235	28.0	**Compton** (city) Los Angeles County
37	238	28.1	**East Palo Alto** (city) San Mateo County
37	238	28.1	**Merced** (city) Merced County
39	247	28.2	**Kerman** (city) Fresno County
39	247	28.2	**Willowbrook** (CDP) Los Angeles County
41	254	28.3	**Mead Valley** (CDP) Riverside County
41	254	28.3	**Rialto** (city) San Bernardino County
41	254	28.3	**Wasco** (city) Kern County
44	260	28.4	**Colton** (city) San Bernardino County
44	260	28.4	**Hawaiian Gardens** (city) Los Angeles County
46	267	28.5	**Delano** (city) Kern County
46	267	28.5	**Lemon Hill** (CDP) Sacramento County
46	267	28.5	**San Bernardino** (city) San Bernardino County
49	275	28.6	**Chico** (city) Butte County
49	275	28.6	**Lemoore** (city) Kings County
49	275	28.6	**Moreno Valley** (city) Riverside County
49	275	28.6	**Paramount** (city) Los Angeles County
49	275	28.6	**Santa Maria** (city) Santa Barbara County
54	286	28.7	**Fontana** (city) San Bernardino County
54	286	28.7	**Garden Acres** (CDP) San Joaquin County
56	292	28.8	**Porterville** (city) Tulare County
56	292	28.8	**Salinas** (city) Monterey County
58	307	28.9	**Bell** (city) Los Angeles County
58	307	28.9	**Huntington Park** (city) Los Angeles County
60	322	29.1	**East Los Angeles** (CDP) Los Angeles County
60	322	29.1	**Patterson** (city) Stanislaus County
60	322	29.1	**Reedley** (city) Fresno County
60	322	29.1	**Santa Ana** (city) Orange County
60	322	29.1	**Tulare** (city) Tulare County
65	331	29.2	**Sanger** (city) Fresno County
65	331	29.2	**Watsonville** (city) Santa Cruz County
67	342	29.3	**Azusa** (city) Los Angeles County
67	342	29.3	**Fresno** (city) Fresno County
67	342	29.3	**Home Gardens** (CDP) Riverside County
70	349	29.4	**Ceres** (city) Stanislaus County
70	349	29.4	**South Gate** (city) Los Angeles County
72	359	29.5	**Pomona** (city) Los Angeles County
72	359	29.5	**Selma** (city) Fresno County
72	359	29.5	**Victorville** (city) San Bernardino County
75	372	29.7	**Palmdale** (city) Los Angeles County
75	372	29.7	**Parkway** (CDP) Sacramento County
75	372	29.7	**South San Jose Hills** (CDP) Los Angeles County
78	383	29.8	**Lake Elsinore** (city) Riverside County
78	383	29.8	**Los Banos** (city) Merced County
80	394	29.9	**Imperial** (city) Imperial County
80	394	29.9	**Lake Los Angeles** (CDP) Los Angeles County
80	394	29.9	**Olivehurst** (CDP) Yuba County
80	394	29.9	**Ontario** (city) San Bernardino County
80	394	29.9	**Oxnard** (city) Ventura County
80	394	29.9	**Santa Cruz** (city) Santa Cruz County
80	394	29.9	**Westmont** (CDP) Los Angeles County
87	411	30.0	**Atwater** (city) Merced County
87	411	30.0	**Bakersfield** (city) Kern County
87	411	30.0	**Riverside** (city) Riverside County
90	421	30.1	**Bay Point** (CDP) Contra Costa County
91	430	30.2	**Brawley** (city) Imperial County
91	430	30.2	**National City** (city) San Diego County
91	430	30.2	**Walnut Park** (CDP) Los Angeles County
94	446	30.3	**San Jacinto** (city) Riverside County
95	460	30.4	**Lancaster** (city) Los Angeles County
95	460	30.4	**South El Monte** (city) Los Angeles County
97	468	30.5	**Baldwin Park** (city) Los Angeles County
97	468	30.5	**French Valley** (CDP) Riverside County
97	468	30.5	**Hesperia** (city) San Bernardino County
97	468	30.5	**Lathrop** (city) San Joaquin County
101	483	30.6	**Highland** (city) San Bernardino County
101	483	30.6	**Seaside** (city) Monterey County
103	493	30.7	**Citrus** (CDP) Los Angeles County
103	493	30.7	**Montclair** (city) San Bernardino County
103	493	30.7	**Newman** (city) Stanislaus County
103	493	30.7	**San Fernando** (city) Los Angeles County
107	513	30.8	**Hollister** (city) San Benito County
107	513	30.8	**Stockton** (city) San Joaquin County
109	530	30.9	**Eastvale** (city) Riverside County
109	530	30.9	**Hanford** (city) Kings County
111	548	31.0	**Berkeley** (city) Alameda County
111	548	31.0	**Desert Hot Springs** (city) Riverside County
111	548	31.0	**Imperial Beach** (city) San Diego County
111	548	31.0	**North Fair Oaks** (CDP) San Mateo County
111	548	31.0	**Riverbank** (city) Stanislaus County
116	565	31.1	**Barstow** (city) San Bernardino County
116	565	31.1	**Foothill Farms** (CDP) Sacramento County
116	565	31.1	**Santa Paula** (city) Ventura County
116	565	31.1	**Vista** (city) San Diego County
120	572	31.2	**Commerce** (city) Los Angeles County
120	572	31.2	**Exeter** (city) Tulare County
120	572	31.2	**Salida** (CDP) Stanislaus County
123	590	31.3	**Port Hueneme** (city) Ventura County
124	608	31.4	**Antelope** (CDP) Sacramento County
124	608	31.4	**Ashland** (CDP) Alameda County
124	608	31.4	**Oildale** (CDP) Kern County
124	608	31.4	**Sun Village** (CDP) Los Angeles County
128	628	31.5	**Hawthorne** (city) Los Angeles County
128	628	31.5	**La Puente** (city) Los Angeles County
128	628	31.5	**Oroville** (city) Butte County
131	640	31.6	**El Monte** (city) Los Angeles County
131	640	31.6	**San Pablo** (city) Contra Costa County
131	640	31.6	**Visalia** (city) Tulare County
134	658	31.7	**Alum Rock** (CDP) Santa Clara County
134	658	31.7	**Valinda** (CDP) Los Angeles County
136	678	31.8	**Calexico** (city) Imperial County
136	678	31.8	**El Centro** (city) Imperial County
138	687	31.9	**Bellflower** (city) Los Angeles County
138	687	31.9	**Coalinga** (city) Fresno County
138	687	31.9	**Fillmore** (city) Ventura County
138	687	31.9	**Lawndale** (city) Los Angeles County
142	715	32.0	**Oakley** (city) Contra Costa County
142	715	32.0	**Rosamond** (CDP) Kern County
142	715	32.0	**South Whittier** (CDP) Los Angeles County
145	733	32.1	**Florin** (CDP) Sacramento County
145	733	32.1	**North Highlands** (CDP) Sacramento County
147	755	32.2	**East Hemet** (CDP) Riverside County
147	755	32.2	**Indio** (city) Riverside County
147	755	32.2	**Red Bluff** (city) Tehama County
150	777	32.3	**Cherryland** (CDP) Alameda County

Note: *The state column ranks the top/bottom 150 places from all places in the state with population of 10,000 or more. The national column ranks the top/bottom 150 places from all places in the country with population of 10,000 or more. Places that are unincorporated were not considered in the rankings. Please refer to the User Guide for additional information.*

Population Under Age 18

Top 150 Places Ranked in *Descending* Order

State Rank	Nat'l Rank	Percent	Place
1	14	40.1	**Camp Pendleton South** (CDP) San Diego County
2	18	38.8	**Coachella** (city) Riverside County
3	21	38.4	**Arvin** (city) Kern County
3	21	38.4	**Lindsay** (city) Tulare County
5	24	38.3	**Ladera Ranch** (CDP) Orange County
6	37	37.2	**Adelanto** (city) San Bernardino County
7	38	37.1	**Parlier** (city) Fresno County
7	38	37.1	**Winton** (CDP) Merced County
9	41	37.0	**Perris** (city) Riverside County
10	47	36.8	**Farmersville** (city) Tulare County
11	54	36.0	**Shafter** (city) Kern County
12	56	35.8	**Greenfield** (city) Monterey County
12	56	35.8	**Lamont** (CDP) Kern County
14	63	35.5	**Muscoy** (CDP) San Bernardino County
15	70	35.3	**Delhi** (CDP) Merced County
16	75	35.2	**McFarland** (city) Kern County
17	79	35.1	**East Rancho Dominguez** (CDP) Los Angeles County
18	83	35.0	**Cudahy** (city) Los Angeles County
18	83	35.0	**Florence-Graham** (CDP) Los Angeles County
20	87	34.9	**Dinuba** (city) Tulare County
21	93	34.7	**Madera** (city) Madera County
22	102	34.3	**Kerman** (city) Fresno County
23	113	34.0	**Bell Gardens** (city) Los Angeles County
23	113	34.0	**King City** (city) Monterey County
25	118	33.9	**Mendota** (city) Fresno County
26	120	33.8	**Patterson** (city) Stanislaus County
27	123	33.7	**French Valley** (CDP) Riverside County
28	131	33.6	**Bloomington** (CDP) San Bernardino County
28	131	33.6	**Los Banos** (city) Merced County
28	131	33.6	**Mead Valley** (CDP) Riverside County
28	131	33.6	**Sanger** (city) Fresno County
32	138	33.5	**Porterville** (city) Tulare County
33	146	33.4	**Imperial** (city) Imperial County
33	146	33.4	**Linda** (CDP) Yuba County
35	149	33.3	**Tulare** (city) Tulare County
36	158	33.2	**Lake Los Angeles** (CDP) Los Angeles County
36	158	33.2	**Lennox** (CDP) Los Angeles County
38	163	33.1	**Compton** (city) Los Angeles County
38	163	33.1	**Eastvale** (city) Riverside County
38	163	33.1	**Palmdale** (city) Los Angeles County
41	169	33.0	**Garden Acres** (CDP) San Joaquin County
42	178	32.9	**Fontana** (city) San Bernardino County
42	178	32.9	**Lynwood** (city) Los Angeles County
42	178	32.9	**Rialto** (city) San Bernardino County
45	186	32.8	**Lake Elsinore** (city) Riverside County
45	186	32.8	**Lemon Hill** (CDP) Sacramento County
45	186	32.8	**San Jacinto** (city) Riverside County
45	186	32.8	**Victorville** (city) San Bernardino County
45	186	32.8	**Willowbrook** (CDP) Los Angeles County
50	196	32.6	**Brawley** (city) Imperial County
50	196	32.6	**Livingston** (city) Merced County
50	196	32.6	**Maywood** (city) Los Angeles County
50	196	32.6	**Paramount** (city) Los Angeles County
54	206	32.5	**Reedley** (city) Fresno County
55	216	32.4	**Newman** (city) Stanislaus County
56	222	32.3	**Hesperia** (city) San Bernardino County
56	222	32.3	**Lathrop** (city) San Joaquin County
56	222	32.3	**Moreno Valley** (city) Riverside County
59	233	32.2	**Ceres** (city) Stanislaus County
59	233	32.2	**Stevenson Ranch** (CDP) Los Angeles County
59	233	32.2	**Tracy** (city) San Joaquin County
62	239	32.1	**Hawaiian Gardens** (city) Los Angeles County
62	239	32.1	**Selma** (city) Fresno County
64	251	32.0	**Atwater** (city) Merced County
64	251	32.0	**Bell** (city) Los Angeles County
64	251	32.0	**Colton** (city) San Bernardino County
64	251	32.0	**Salida** (CDP) Stanislaus County
64	251	32.0	**San Bernardino** (city) San Bernardino County
69	262	31.9	**East Palo Alto** (city) San Mateo County
69	262	31.9	**Highland** (city) San Bernardino County
71	268	31.8	**Exeter** (city) Tulare County
71	268	31.8	**Merced** (city) Merced County
71	268	31.8	**Olivehurst** (CDP) Yuba County
74	279	31.7	**Hollister** (city) San Benito County
74	279	31.7	**Huntington Park** (city) Los Angeles County
76	295	31.5	**Bakersfield** (city) Kern County
76	295	31.5	**East Los Angeles** (CDP) Los Angeles County
76	295	31.5	**Parkway** (CDP) Sacramento County
76	295	31.5	**Watsonville** (city) Santa Cruz County
80	309	31.4	**Salinas** (city) Monterey County
80	309	31.4	**Santa Maria** (city) Santa Barbara County
82	318	31.3	**Home Gardens** (CDP) Riverside County
83	327	31.2	**Brentwood** (city) Contra Costa County
84	335	31.1	**Antelope** (CDP) Sacramento County
84	335	31.1	**Calexico** (city) Imperial County
84	335	31.1	**Desert Hot Springs** (city) Riverside County
84	335	31.1	**Galt** (city) Sacramento County
84	335	31.1	**Riverbank** (city) Stanislaus County
84	335	31.1	**South Gate** (city) Los Angeles County
90	347	31.0	**Hanford** (city) Kings County
90	347	31.0	**Sun Village** (CDP) Los Angeles County
90	347	31.0	**Westmont** (CDP) Los Angeles County
93	368	30.8	**Lemoore** (city) Kings County
94	383	30.7	**Gilroy** (city) Santa Clara County
94	383	30.7	**Santa Ana** (city) Orange County
94	383	30.7	**Temecula** (city) Riverside County
97	396	30.6	**Coto de Caza** (CDP) Orange County
98	408	30.5	**Bay Point** (CDP) Contra Costa County
98	408	30.5	**Oakley** (city) Contra Costa County
100	424	30.4	**Murrieta** (city) Riverside County
100	424	30.4	**South San Jose Hills** (CDP) Los Angeles County
100	424	30.4	**Vineyard** (CDP) Sacramento County
103	443	30.3	**Castaic** (CDP) Los Angeles County
104	451	30.2	**Beaumont** (city) Riverside County
104	451	30.2	**Fillmore** (city) Ventura County
104	451	30.2	**Ontario** (city) San Bernardino County
107	468	30.1	**Elk Grove** (city) Sacramento County
107	468	30.1	**Fresno** (city) Fresno County
107	468	30.1	**Indio** (city) Riverside County
107	468	30.1	**Lancaster** (city) Los Angeles County
107	468	30.1	**Visalia** (city) Tulare County
112	485	30.0	**Corona** (city) Riverside County
112	485	30.0	**East Hemet** (CDP) Riverside County
112	485	30.0	**South El Monte** (city) Los Angeles County
115	509	29.9	**Baldwin Park** (city) Los Angeles County
115	509	29.9	**Stockton** (city) San Joaquin County
117	522	29.8	**Barstow** (city) San Bernardino County
117	522	29.8	**Commerce** (city) Los Angeles County
117	522	29.8	**Oxnard** (city) Ventura County
120	539	29.7	**El Centro** (city) Imperial County
120	539	29.7	**Santa Paula** (city) Ventura County
120	539	29.7	**Walnut Park** (CDP) Los Angeles County
123	554	29.6	**Kingsburg** (city) Fresno County
123	554	29.6	**San Ramon** (city) Contra Costa County
125	572	29.5	**El Dorado Hills** (CDP) El Dorado County
126	583	29.4	**Pomona** (city) Los Angeles County
126	583	29.4	**San Fernando** (city) Los Angeles County
128	602	29.3	**Montclair** (city) San Bernardino County
129	618	29.2	**Valinda** (CDP) Los Angeles County
130	632	29.1	**Dixon** (city) Solano County
130	632	29.1	**Rosamond** (CDP) Kern County
132	646	29.0	**Florin** (CDP) Sacramento County
132	646	29.0	**Manteca** (city) San Joaquin County
132	646	29.0	**Rancho Santa Margarita** (city) Orange County
135	674	28.8	**El Sobrante** (CDP) Riverside County
135	674	28.8	**Oildale** (CDP) Kern County
135	674	28.8	**Ripon** (city) San Joaquin County
135	674	28.8	**Wasco** (city) Kern County
139	697	28.7	**La Puente** (city) Los Angeles County
140	717	28.6	**Morgan Hill** (city) Santa Clara County
141	737	28.5	**South Whittier** (CDP) Los Angeles County
142	760	28.4	**Bellflower** (city) Los Angeles County
142	760	28.4	**Citrus** (CDP) Los Angeles County
142	760	28.4	**Delano** (city) Kern County
142	760	28.4	**El Monte** (city) Los Angeles County
146	784	28.3	**American Canyon** (city) Napa County
146	784	28.3	**Lakeland Village** (CDP) Riverside County
146	784	28.3	**Piedmont** (city) Alameda County
146	784	28.3	**San Pablo** (city) Contra Costa County
150	812	28.2	**Alum Rock** (CDP) Santa Clara County

Note: *The state column ranks the top/bottom 150 places from all places in the state with population of 10,000 or more. The national column ranks the top/bottom 150 places from all places in the country with population of 10,000 or more. Places that are unincorporated were not considered in the rankings. Please refer to the User Guide for additional information.*

Population Under Age 18

Top 150 Places Ranked in *Ascending* Order

State Rank	Nat'l Rank	Percent	Place
1	3	0.3	**Laguna Woods** (city) Orange County
2	11	3.0	**Isla Vista** (CDP) Santa Barbara County
3	12	4.6	**West Hollywood** (city) Los Angeles County
4	19	6.6	**Stanford** (CDP) Santa Clara County
5	41	10.2	**Emeryville** (city) Alameda County
6	46	10.6	**Rancho Mirage** (city) Riverside County
7	67	12.2	**San Luis Obispo** (city) San Luis Obispo County
8	70	12.3	**Berkeley** (city) Alameda County
9	74	12.6	**Arcata** (city) Humboldt County
10	80	13.0	**Seal Beach** (city) Orange County
11	86	13.4	**San Francisco** (city) San Francisco County
12	94	13.7	**Palm Springs** (city) Riverside County
12	94	13.7	**Santa Cruz** (city) Santa Cruz County
14	108	14.0	**Santa Monica** (city) Los Angeles County
15	118	14.3	**Susanville** (city) Lassen County
16	148	15.0	**Morro Bay** (city) San Luis Obispo County
17	155	15.3	**Monterey** (city) Monterey County
18	163	15.6	**Palm Desert** (city) Riverside County
19	177	15.9	**Hermosa Beach** (city) Los Angeles County
20	185	16.1	**Laguna Beach** (city) Orange County
21	209	16.4	**Davis** (city) Yolo County
22	216	16.5	**Pacific Grove** (city) Monterey County
23	226	16.7	**Walnut Creek** (city) Contra Costa County
24	257	17.2	**Paradise** (town) Butte County
25	270	17.3	**Newport Beach** (city) Orange County
26	276	17.4	**El Cerrito** (city) Contra Costa County
27	318	17.9	**Corcoran** (city) Kings County
27	318	17.9	**Dana Point** (city) Orange County
27	318	17.9	**Los Osos** (CDP) San Luis Obispo County
30	334	18.0	**Sonoma** (city) Sonoma County
30	334	18.0	**Tehachapi** (city) Kern County
32	345	18.1	**Monterey Park** (city) Los Angeles County
33	348	18.2	**Larkspur** (city) Marin County
34	383	18.5	**Claremont** (city) Los Angeles County
34	383	18.5	**Solana Beach** (city) San Diego County
36	398	18.6	**Glendale** (city) Los Angeles County
36	398	18.6	**Santa Barbara** (city) Santa Barbara County
38	419	18.7	**Malibu** (city) Los Angeles County
38	419	18.7	**West Carson** (CDP) Los Angeles County
40	437	18.8	**Culver City** (city) Los Angeles County
41	453	18.9	**Alhambra** (city) Los Angeles County
41	453	18.9	**View Park-Windsor Hills** (CDP) Los Angeles County
43	487	19.1	**Chowchilla** (city) Madera County
43	487	19.1	**Magalia** (CDP) Butte County
45	514	19.2	**Sierra Madre** (city) Los Angeles County
46	533	19.3	**Pasadena** (city) Los Angeles County
46	533	19.3	**Redondo Beach** (city) Los Angeles County
46	533	19.3	**San Rafael** (city) Marin County
49	555	19.4	**Beverly Hills** (city) Los Angeles County
49	555	19.4	**Daly City** (city) San Mateo County
51	583	19.5	**Chico** (city) Butte County
52	605	19.6	**Fair Oaks** (CDP) Sacramento County
52	605	19.6	**La Mesa** (city) San Diego County
52	605	19.6	**La Riviera** (CDP) Sacramento County
55	631	19.7	**Mountain View** (city) Santa Clara County
56	658	19.8	**Auburn** (city) Placer County
56	658	19.8	**Burbank** (city) Los Angeles County
56	658	19.8	**Pleasant Hill** (city) Contra Costa County
56	658	19.8	**San Gabriel** (city) Los Angeles County
60	696	20.0	**Blythe** (city) Riverside County
60	696	20.0	**Eureka** (city) Humboldt County
62	719	20.1	**Millbrae** (city) San Mateo County
63	776	20.3	**Norco** (city) Riverside County
63	776	20.3	**Rowland Heights** (CDP) Los Angeles County
65	807	20.4	**Cerritos** (city) Los Angeles County
65	807	20.4	**Coronado** (city) San Diego County
65	807	20.4	**Diamond Springs** (CDP) El Dorado County
65	807	20.4	**Grass Valley** (city) Nevada County
69	840	20.5	**Martinez** (city) Contra Costa County
69	840	20.5	**Pinole** (city) Contra Costa County
71	867	20.6	**Encinitas** (city) San Diego County
71	867	20.6	**Huntington Beach** (city) Orange County
71	867	20.6	**South Lake Tahoe** (city) El Dorado County
74	891	20.7	**Alameda** (city) Alameda County
74	891	20.7	**Fairview** (CDP) Alameda County
74	891	20.7	**Pacifica** (city) San Mateo County
77	928	20.8	**Bonita** (CDP) San Diego County
77	928	20.8	**San Mateo** (city) San Mateo County
79	967	20.9	**Arden-Arcade** (CDP) Sacramento County
79	967	20.9	**Belmont** (city) San Mateo County
79	967	20.9	**Loma Linda** (city) San Bernardino County
79	967	20.9	**Rohnert Park** (city) Sonoma County
79	967	20.9	**San Dimas** (city) Los Angeles County
79	967	20.9	**Walnut** (city) Los Angeles County
85	1007	21.0	**Campbell** (city) Santa Clara County
85	1007	21.0	**Casa de Oro-Mount Helix** (CDP) San Diego County
85	1007	21.0	**Fountain Valley** (city) Orange County
85	1007	21.0	**North Auburn** (CDP) Placer County
85	1007	21.0	**San Bruno** (city) San Mateo County
90	1051	21.1	**Arroyo Grande** (city) San Luis Obispo County
90	1051	21.1	**Carmichael** (CDP) Sacramento County
90	1051	21.1	**La Mirada** (city) Los Angeles County
93	1087	21.2	**Goleta** (city) Santa Barbara County
93	1087	21.2	**Temple City** (city) Los Angeles County
95	1121	21.3	**El Sobrante** (CDP) Contra Costa County
95	1121	21.3	**La Verne** (city) Los Angeles County
95	1121	21.3	**Oakland** (city) Alameda County
95	1121	21.3	**Santa Clara** (city) Santa Clara County
99	1158	21.4	**Atascadero** (city) San Luis Obispo County
99	1158	21.4	**Avenal** (city) Kings County
99	1158	21.4	**Carpinteria** (city) Santa Barbara County
99	1158	21.4	**Diamond Bar** (city) Los Angeles County
99	1158	21.4	**Live Oak** (CDP) Santa Cruz County
99	1158	21.4	**San Diego** (city) San Diego County
105	1195	21.5	**Costa Mesa** (city) Orange County
105	1195	21.5	**Irvine** (city) Orange County
107	1235	21.6	**Lomita** (city) Los Angeles County
108	1271	21.7	**Burlingame** (city) San Mateo County
108	1271	21.7	**Canyon Lake** (city) Riverside County
108	1271	21.7	**Moraga** (town) Contra Costa County
108	1271	21.7	**South San Francisco** (city) San Mateo County
112	1315	21.8	**Arcadia** (city) Los Angeles County
113	1349	21.9	**East San Gabriel** (CDP) Los Angeles County
113	1349	21.9	**La Quinta** (city) Riverside County
113	1349	21.9	**Placerville** (city) El Dorado County
113	1349	21.9	**Torrance** (city) Los Angeles County
117	1390	22.0	**Hacienda Heights** (CDP) Los Angeles County
117	1390	22.0	**La Palma** (city) Orange County
117	1390	22.0	**Soledad** (city) Monterey County
120	1435	22.1	**Crestline** (CDP) San Bernardino County
120	1435	22.1	**Rancho San Diego** (CDP) San Diego County
122	1472	22.2	**Altadena** (CDP) Los Angeles County
122	1472	22.2	**Duarte** (city) Los Angeles County
122	1472	22.2	**Rancho Palos Verdes** (city) Los Angeles County
125	1516	22.3	**El Segundo** (city) Los Angeles County
125	1516	22.3	**Grover Beach** (city) San Luis Obispo County
125	1516	22.3	**Laguna Hills** (city) Orange County
125	1516	22.3	**Los Gatos** (town) Santa Clara County
125	1516	22.3	**San Leandro** (city) Alameda County
130	1565	22.4	**Dublin** (city) Alameda County
130	1565	22.4	**Half Moon Bay** (city) San Mateo County
130	1565	22.4	**Sunnyvale** (city) Santa Clara County
133	1610	22.5	**Artesia** (city) Los Angeles County
133	1610	22.5	**San Buenaventura (Ventura)** (city) Ventura County
135	1650	22.6	**Foster City** (city) San Mateo County
135	1650	22.6	**Healdsburg** (city) Sonoma County
135	1650	22.6	**Laguna Niguel** (city) Orange County
138	1700	22.7	**McKinleyville** (CDP) Humboldt County
138	1700	22.7	**Novato** (city) Marin County
138	1700	22.7	**Rosemead** (city) Los Angeles County
141	1744	22.8	**Gardena** (city) Los Angeles County
141	1744	22.8	**Hercules** (city) Contra Costa County
141	1744	22.8	**Mission Viejo** (city) Orange County
141	1744	22.8	**Redding** (city) Shasta County
145	1787	22.9	**Banning** (city) Riverside County
145	1787	22.9	**Concord** (city) Contra Costa County
145	1787	22.9	**Milpitas** (city) Santa Clara County
145	1787	22.9	**Orangevale** (CDP) Sacramento County
149	1881	23.1	**Brea** (city) Orange County
149	1881	23.1	**Citrus Heights** (city) Sacramento County

Note: *The state column ranks the top/bottom 150 places from all places in the state with population of 10,000 or more. The national column ranks the top/bottom 150 places from all places in the country with population of 10,000 or more. Places that are unincorporated were not considered in the rankings. Please refer to the User Guide for additional information.*

Population Age 65 and Over

Top 150 Places Ranked in *Descending* Order

State Rank	Nat'l Rank	Percent	Place
1	2	79.5	**Laguna Woods** (city) Orange County
2	18	44.0	**Rancho Mirage** (city) Riverside County
3	23	38.3	**Seal Beach** (city) Orange County
4	32	32.9	**Palm Desert** (city) Riverside County
5	79	26.6	**Walnut Creek** (city) Contra Costa County
6	82	26.5	**Palm Springs** (city) Riverside County
7	94	25.9	**Banning** (city) Riverside County
8	106	25.1	**Paradise** (town) Butte County
9	109	25.0	**Sonoma** (city) Sonoma County
10	124	24.2	**Palos Verdes Estates** (city) Los Angeles County
11	133	23.7	**Magalia** (CDP) Butte County
11	133	23.7	**Morro Bay** (city) San Luis Obispo County
13	138	23.5	**Grass Valley** (city) Nevada County
13	138	23.5	**Lincoln** (city) Placer County
15	144	23.2	**Rancho Palos Verdes** (city) Los Angeles County
16	186	22.1	**Diamond Springs** (CDP) El Dorado County
16	186	22.1	**Hemet** (city) Riverside County
18	206	21.6	**Pacific Grove** (city) Monterey County
19	209	21.5	**Larkspur** (city) Marin County
20	218	21.3	**View Park-Windsor Hills** (CDP) Los Angeles County
21	236	20.9	**La Quinta** (city) Riverside County
22	260	20.5	**Hillsborough** (town) San Mateo County
23	279	20.3	**North Auburn** (CDP) Placer County
23	279	20.3	**Saratoga** (city) Santa Clara County
25	288	20.2	**Arroyo Grande** (city) San Luis Obispo County
26	296	20.1	**Orinda** (city) Contra Costa County
27	307	20.0	**Los Altos** (city) Santa Clara County
28	341	19.7	**Millbrae** (city) San Mateo County
29	373	19.4	**Valle Vista** (CDP) Riverside County
30	381	19.3	**Monterey Park** (city) Los Angeles County
31	404	19.1	**Beverly Hills** (city) Los Angeles County
31	404	19.1	**Moraga** (town) Contra Costa County
31	404	19.1	**North Tustin** (CDP) Orange County
34	435	19.0	**Auburn** (city) Placer County
34	435	19.0	**Newport Beach** (city) Orange County
36	453	18.9	**Menifee** (city) Riverside County
36	453	18.9	**Mill Valley** (city) Marin County
38	484	18.7	**Bonita** (CDP) San Diego County
38	484	18.7	**Los Osos** (CDP) San Luis Obispo County
38	484	18.7	**Solana Beach** (city) San Diego County
41	495	18.6	**Casa de Oro-Mount Helix** (CDP) San Diego County
42	508	18.5	**Fair Oaks** (CDP) Sacramento County
42	508	18.5	**Yucca Valley** (town) San Bernardino County
44	525	18.4	**Coronado** (city) San Diego County
44	525	18.4	**Malibu** (city) Los Angeles County
46	544	18.3	**Laguna Beach** (city) Orange County
47	595	18.0	**West Carson** (CDP) Los Angeles County
48	616	17.9	**El Cerrito** (city) Contra Costa County
48	616	17.9	**Los Gatos** (town) Santa Clara County
50	659	17.7	**Cerritos** (city) Los Angeles County
50	659	17.7	**Placerville** (city) El Dorado County
52	688	17.6	**Alamo** (CDP) Contra Costa County
52	688	17.6	**Carmichael** (CDP) Sacramento County
52	688	17.6	**Fountain Valley** (city) Orange County
52	688	17.6	**Orcutt** (CDP) Santa Barbara County
52	688	17.6	**San Marino** (city) Los Angeles County
57	741	17.4	**Sierra Madre** (city) Los Angeles County
58	762	17.3	**Fortuna** (city) Humboldt County
58	762	17.3	**Rossmoor** (CDP) Orange County
60	786	17.2	**Camarillo** (city) Ventura County
61	820	17.1	**Canyon Lake** (city) Riverside County
61	820	17.1	**Palo Alto** (city) Santa Clara County
63	848	17.0	**Dana Point** (city) Orange County
64	874	16.9	**La Verne** (city) Los Angeles County
65	939	16.6	**Lafayette** (city) Contra Costa County
66	971	16.5	**Claremont** (city) Los Angeles County
67	1004	16.4	**Redding** (city) Shasta County
68	1033	16.3	**Arcadia** (city) Los Angeles County
69	1150	15.9	**La Palma** (city) Orange County
70	1180	15.8	**Duarte** (city) Los Angeles County
70	1180	15.8	**San Rafael** (city) Marin County
72	1222	15.7	**Arden-Arcade** (CDP) Sacramento County
72	1222	15.7	**La Cañada Flintridge** (city) Los Angeles County
72	1222	15.7	**Novato** (city) Marin County
75	1258	15.6	**Glendale** (city) Los Angeles County
75	1258	15.6	**Half Moon Bay** (city) San Mateo County
75	1258	15.6	**San Juan Capistrano** (city) Orange County
78	1295	15.5	**Monterey** (city) Monterey County
78	1295	15.5	**Pinole** (city) Contra Costa County
78	1295	15.5	**San Dimas** (city) Los Angeles County
81	1326	15.4	**Apple Valley** (town) San Bernardino County
81	1326	15.4	**Hacienda Heights** (CDP) Los Angeles County
81	1326	15.4	**Piedmont** (city) Alameda County
84	1386	15.2	**La Mirada** (city) Los Angeles County
85	1433	15.1	**Temple City** (city) Los Angeles County
86	1466	15.0	**Clearlake** (city) Lake County
86	1466	15.0	**Healdsburg** (city) Sonoma County
86	1466	15.0	**Santa Monica** (city) Los Angeles County
89	1502	14.9	**Belmont** (city) San Mateo County
89	1502	14.9	**Culver City** (city) Los Angeles County
89	1502	14.9	**Torrance** (city) Los Angeles County
89	1502	14.9	**West Hollywood** (city) Los Angeles County
93	1574	14.7	**Clayton** (city) Contra Costa County
93	1574	14.7	**Thousand Oaks** (city) Ventura County
95	1653	14.5	**Granite Bay** (CDP) Placer County
95	1653	14.5	**Mission Viejo** (city) Orange County
95	1653	14.5	**Ukiah** (city) Mendocino County
98	1691	14.4	**Big Bear City** (CDP) San Bernardino County
98	1691	14.4	**Cameron Park** (CDP) El Dorado County
98	1691	14.4	**Cathedral City** (city) Riverside County
98	1691	14.4	**Danville** (town) Contra Costa County
98	1691	14.4	**San Mateo** (city) San Mateo County
98	1691	14.4	**Shasta Lake** (city) Shasta County
104	1740	14.3	**Alhambra** (city) Los Angeles County
104	1740	14.3	**Menlo Park** (city) San Mateo County
104	1740	14.3	**Westminster** (city) Orange County
107	1781	14.2	**Altadena** (CDP) Los Angeles County
107	1781	14.2	**Huntington Beach** (city) Orange County
107	1781	14.2	**La Mesa** (city) San Diego County
107	1781	14.2	**San Carlos** (city) San Mateo County
107	1781	14.2	**Santa Barbara** (city) Santa Barbara County
112	1832	14.1	**Gardena** (city) Los Angeles County
112	1832	14.1	**Glendora** (city) Los Angeles County
112	1832	14.1	**Tamalpais-Homestead Valley** (CDP) Marin County
115	1865	14.0	**Burlingame** (city) San Mateo County
115	1865	14.0	**Carlsbad** (city) San Diego County
115	1865	14.0	**Lake Arrowhead** (CDP) San Bernardino County
115	1865	14.0	**San Gabriel** (city) Los Angeles County
119	1911	13.9	**Fallbrook** (CDP) San Diego County
119	1911	13.9	**Loma Linda** (city) San Bernardino County
119	1911	13.9	**Los Alamitos** (city) Orange County
119	1911	13.9	**Pleasant Hill** (city) Contra Costa County
123	1964	13.8	**Carpinteria** (city) Santa Barbara County
123	1964	13.8	**Carson** (city) Los Angeles County
123	1964	13.8	**San Leandro** (city) Alameda County
126	2011	13.7	**Alpine** (CDP) San Diego County
127	2052	13.6	**Artesia** (city) Los Angeles County
127	2052	13.6	**East San Gabriel** (CDP) Los Angeles County
127	2052	13.6	**Montebello** (city) Los Angeles County
127	2052	13.6	**Napa** (city) Napa County
127	2052	13.6	**San Francisco** (city) San Francisco County
127	2052	13.6	**Scotts Valley** (city) Santa Cruz County
133	2095	13.5	**Alameda** (city) Alameda County
133	2095	13.5	**Daly City** (city) San Mateo County
133	2095	13.5	**Goleta** (city) Santa Barbara County
133	2095	13.5	**Lodi** (city) San Joaquin County
133	2095	13.5	**Pasadena** (city) Los Angeles County
133	2095	13.5	**San Anselmo** (town) Marin County
133	2095	13.5	**Santa Rosa** (city) Sonoma County
140	2143	13.4	**Castro Valley** (CDP) Alameda County
140	2143	13.4	**El Paso de Robles (Paso Robles)** (city) San Luis Obispo County
140	2143	13.4	**Foster City** (city) San Mateo County
140	2143	13.4	**Rancho San Diego** (CDP) San Diego County
140	2143	13.4	**Roseville** (city) Placer County
145	2183	13.3	**Burbank** (city) Los Angeles County
145	2183	13.3	**Citrus Heights** (city) Sacramento County
145	2183	13.3	**Orangevale** (CDP) Sacramento County
145	2183	13.3	**Red Bluff** (city) Tehama County
145	2183	13.3	**San Buenaventura (Ventura)** (city) Ventura County
145	2183	13.3	**Santa Fe Springs** (city) Los Angeles County

Note: *The state column ranks the top/bottom 150 places from all places in the state with population of 10,000 or more. The national column ranks the top/bottom 150 places from all places in the country with population of 10,000 or more. Places that are unincorporated were not considered in the rankings. Please refer to the User Guide for additional information.*

Population Age 65 and Over

Top 150 Places Ranked in *Ascending* Order

State Rank	Nat'l Rank	Percent	Place
1	3	0.1	**Camp Pendleton South** (CDP) San Diego County
2	12	1.3	**Isla Vista** (CDP) Santa Barbara County
3	27	3.6	**Ladera Ranch** (CDP) Orange County
4	36	4.0	**Avenal** (city) Kings County
5	51	4.4	**Adelanto** (city) San Bernardino County
6	53	4.5	**Coachella** (city) Riverside County
6	53	4.5	**Stanford** (CDP) Santa Clara County
8	59	4.6	**McFarland** (city) Kern County
8	59	4.6	**Soledad** (city) Monterey County
10	63	4.7	**Eastvale** (city) Riverside County
10	63	4.7	**Greenfield** (city) Monterey County
10	63	4.7	**Mendota** (city) Fresno County
13	77	4.9	**Perris** (city) Riverside County
14	86	5.1	**Arvin** (city) Kern County
14	86	5.1	**Cudahy** (city) Los Angeles County
14	86	5.1	**Wasco** (city) Kern County
17	97	5.2	**Bell Gardens** (city) Los Angeles County
17	97	5.2	**French Valley** (CDP) Riverside County
19	112	5.3	**Aliso Viejo** (city) Orange County
19	112	5.3	**Corcoran** (city) Kings County
19	112	5.3	**East Rancho Dominguez** (CDP) Los Angeles County
22	128	5.4	**Florence-Graham** (CDP) Los Angeles County
22	128	5.4	**Lamont** (CDP) Kern County
22	128	5.4	**Lennox** (CDP) Los Angeles County
22	128	5.4	**Lynwood** (city) Los Angeles County
26	145	5.5	**Parlier** (city) Fresno County
27	157	5.6	**Muscoy** (CDP) San Bernardino County
28	164	5.7	**Castaic** (CDP) Los Angeles County
28	164	5.7	**Fontana** (city) San Bernardino County
28	164	5.7	**Lake Elsinore** (city) Riverside County
28	164	5.7	**Rancho Santa Margarita** (city) Orange County
32	175	5.8	**Twentynine Palms** (city) San Bernardino County
33	187	5.9	**East Palo Alto** (city) San Mateo County
33	187	5.9	**King City** (city) Monterey County
35	198	6.0	**Maywood** (city) Los Angeles County
36	205	6.1	**Delano** (city) Kern County
37	213	6.2	**Antelope** (CDP) Sacramento County
38	222	6.3	**Moreno Valley** (city) Riverside County
38	222	6.3	**Paramount** (city) Los Angeles County
38	222	6.3	**Patterson** (city) Stanislaus County
38	222	6.3	**Salida** (CDP) Stanislaus County
38	222	6.3	**Stevenson Ranch** (CDP) Los Angeles County
38	222	6.3	**Winton** (CDP) Merced County
44	242	6.4	**Delhi** (CDP) Merced County
45	258	6.5	**Bay Point** (CDP) Contra Costa County
45	258	6.5	**Imperial** (city) Imperial County
45	258	6.5	**Lathrop** (city) San Joaquin County
48	276	6.6	**Bloomington** (CDP) San Bernardino County
48	276	6.6	**El Sobrante** (CDP) Riverside County
48	276	6.6	**Farmersville** (city) Tulare County
48	276	6.6	**Huntington Park** (city) Los Angeles County
48	276	6.6	**North Fair Oaks** (CDP) San Mateo County
48	276	6.6	**Palmdale** (city) Los Angeles County
48	276	6.6	**Shafter** (city) Kern County
48	276	6.6	**Susanville** (city) Lassen County
56	292	6.7	**Oakley** (city) Contra Costa County
56	292	6.7	**Ontario** (city) San Bernardino County
58	312	6.8	**Bell** (city) Los Angeles County
58	312	6.8	**Santa Ana** (city) Orange County
60	331	6.9	**Lawndale** (city) Los Angeles County
60	331	6.9	**Tracy** (city) San Joaquin County
62	348	7.0	**Chino Hills** (city) San Bernardino County
62	348	7.0	**Chowchilla** (city) Madera County
62	348	7.0	**Colton** (city) San Bernardino County
62	348	7.0	**Livingston** (city) Merced County
62	348	7.0	**Rialto** (city) San Bernardino County
62	348	7.0	**South Gate** (city) Los Angeles County
68	367	7.1	**Moorpark** (city) Ventura County
69	383	7.2	**Kerman** (city) Fresno County
69	383	7.2	**Vineyard** (CDP) Sacramento County
71	408	7.3	**Chino** (city) San Bernardino County
71	408	7.3	**Corona** (city) Riverside County
71	408	7.3	**Dublin** (city) Alameda County
71	408	7.3	**Lemoore** (city) Kings County
71	408	7.3	**Linda** (CDP) Yuba County
76	425	7.4	**Hawthorne** (city) Los Angeles County
76	425	7.4	**Hollister** (city) San Benito County
76	425	7.4	**Mead Valley** (CDP) Riverside County
79	447	7.5	**Compton** (city) Los Angeles County
79	447	7.5	**Home Gardens** (CDP) Riverside County
79	447	7.5	**Lindsay** (city) Tulare County
79	447	7.5	**Salinas** (city) Monterey County
83	462	7.6	**Ashland** (CDP) Alameda County
83	462	7.6	**Lake Los Angeles** (CDP) Los Angeles County
83	462	7.6	**Madera** (city) Madera County
83	462	7.6	**Pomona** (city) Los Angeles County
87	481	7.7	**Azusa** (city) Los Angeles County
87	481	7.7	**Ceres** (city) Stanislaus County
87	481	7.7	**Highland** (city) San Bernardino County
87	481	7.7	**Suisun City** (city) Solano County
91	506	7.8	**Citrus** (CDP) Los Angeles County
91	506	7.8	**Dinuba** (city) Tulare County
91	506	7.8	**Lemon Hill** (CDP) Sacramento County
91	506	7.8	**San Ramon** (city) Contra Costa County
91	506	7.8	**Temecula** (city) Riverside County
91	506	7.8	**Truckee** (town) Nevada County
97	525	7.9	**Coalinga** (city) Fresno County
97	525	7.9	**Coto de Caza** (CDP) Orange County
97	525	7.9	**Hawaiian Gardens** (city) Los Angeles County
97	525	7.9	**Lakeland Village** (CDP) Riverside County
97	525	7.9	**Rancho Cucamonga** (city) San Bernardino County
97	525	7.9	**San Bernardino** (city) San Bernardino County
103	546	8.0	**Baldwin Park** (city) Los Angeles County
103	546	8.0	**Garden Acres** (CDP) San Joaquin County
103	546	8.0	**South San Jose Hills** (CDP) Los Angeles County
106	570	8.1	**Lancaster** (city) Los Angeles County
106	570	8.1	**Victorville** (city) San Bernardino County
106	570	8.1	**Walnut Park** (CDP) Los Angeles County
106	570	8.1	**Willowbrook** (CDP) Los Angeles County
110	592	8.2	**Arcata** (city) Humboldt County
110	592	8.2	**Rosamond** (CDP) Kern County
112	614	8.3	**Elk Grove** (city) Sacramento County
112	614	8.3	**Oxnard** (city) Ventura County
112	614	8.3	**Riverbank** (city) Stanislaus County
112	614	8.3	**Signal Hill** (city) Los Angeles County
112	614	8.3	**Watsonville** (city) Santa Cruz County
117	644	8.4	**Bakersfield** (city) Kern County
117	644	8.4	**California City** (city) Kern County
117	644	8.4	**Gilroy** (city) Santa Clara County
117	644	8.4	**Montclair** (city) San Bernardino County
117	644	8.4	**Olivehurst** (CDP) Yuba County
117	644	8.4	**San Fernando** (city) Los Angeles County
117	644	8.4	**Westmont** (CDP) Los Angeles County
124	671	8.5	**Cherryland** (CDP) Alameda County
124	671	8.5	**Davis** (city) Yolo County
124	671	8.5	**Dixon** (city) Solano County
124	671	8.5	**Newman** (city) Stanislaus County
124	671	8.5	**Oak Park** (CDP) Ventura County
124	671	8.5	**Tustin** (city) Orange County
130	699	8.6	**Bellflower** (city) Los Angeles County
130	699	8.6	**Blythe** (city) Riverside County
130	699	8.6	**East Los Angeles** (CDP) Los Angeles County
130	699	8.6	**Los Banos** (city) Merced County
130	699	8.6	**Pittsburg** (city) Contra Costa County
130	699	8.6	**Riverside** (city) Riverside County
130	699	8.6	**Seaside** (city) Monterey County
130	699	8.6	**Sun Village** (CDP) Los Angeles County
138	733	8.7	**Foothill Farms** (CDP) Sacramento County
138	733	8.7	**Irvine** (city) Orange County
138	733	8.7	**South Whittier** (CDP) Los Angeles County
138	733	8.7	**Valinda** (CDP) Los Angeles County
142	767	8.8	**Antioch** (city) Contra Costa County
142	767	8.8	**Merced** (city) Merced County
142	767	8.8	**San Pablo** (city) Contra Costa County
142	767	8.8	**Santa Cruz** (city) Santa Cruz County
142	767	8.8	**Tehachapi** (city) Kern County
147	801	8.9	**Rosedale** (CDP) Kern County
147	801	8.9	**South El Monte** (city) Los Angeles County
149	835	9.0	**Alum Rock** (CDP) Santa Clara County
149	835	9.0	**Hermosa Beach** (city) Los Angeles County

Note: *The state column ranks the top/bottom 150 places from all places in the state with population of 10,000 or more. The national column ranks the top/bottom 150 places from all places in the country with population of 10,000 or more. Places that are unincorporated were not considered in the rankings. Please refer to the User Guide for additional information.*

Males per 100 Females

Top 150 Places Ranked in *Descending* Order

State Rank	Nat'l Rank	Ratio	Place
1	2	294.8	**Corcoran** (city) Kings County
2	3	273.7	**Susanville** (city) Lassen County
3	4	262.5	**Avenal** (city) Kings County
4	7	235.5	**Soledad** (city) Monterey County
5	8	234.8	**Tehachapi** (city) Kern County
6	10	218.1	**Blythe** (city) Riverside County
7	19	160.3	**Wasco** (city) Kern County
8	29	149.1	**Delano** (city) Kern County
9	36	144.0	**California City** (city) Kern County
10	43	136.8	**Norco** (city) Riverside County
11	53	129.3	**Palm Springs** (city) Riverside County
12	54	129.0	**Twentynine Palms** (city) San Bernardino County
13	58	128.4	**West Hollywood** (city) Los Angeles County
14	59	128.3	**McFarland** (city) Kern County
15	66	123.6	**Mendota** (city) Fresno County
16	71	123.1	**Coalinga** (city) Fresno County
17	84	119.6	**Camp Pendleton South** (CDP) San Diego County
18	87	118.3	**Stanford** (CDP) Santa Clara County
19	98	115.7	**King City** (city) Monterey County
20	102	114.9	**Lompoc** (city) Santa Barbara County
21	106	114.1	**Folsom** (city) Sacramento County
22	109	113.6	**South Lake Tahoe** (city) El Dorado County
23	112	113.0	**North Fair Oaks** (CDP) San Mateo County
24	118	112.5	**Vacaville** (city) Solano County
25	125	111.7	**Lamont** (CDP) Kern County
26	131	111.3	**Hermosa Beach** (city) Los Angeles County
27	146	109.8	**Greenfield** (city) Monterey County
28	155	109.1	**San Luis Obispo** (city) San Luis Obispo County
29	159	108.9	**Truckee** (town) Nevada County
30	161	108.8	**Dublin** (city) Alameda County
31	167	108.2	**Arvin** (city) Kern County
32	175	107.9	**French Valley** (CDP) Riverside County
33	180	107.6	**Home Gardens** (CDP) Riverside County
34	186	107.4	**Coronado** (city) San Diego County
35	204	106.6	**Sun Village** (CDP) Los Angeles County
36	217	106.1	**Mead Valley** (CDP) Riverside County
37	218	106.0	**Eureka** (city) Humboldt County
38	223	105.9	**Alum Rock** (CDP) Santa Clara County
38	223	105.9	**Cathedral City** (city) Riverside County
40	231	105.7	**Chino** (city) San Bernardino County
41	235	105.6	**Adelanto** (city) San Bernardino County
41	235	105.6	**Lennox** (CDP) Los Angeles County
41	235	105.6	**Shafter** (city) Kern County
44	241	105.5	**National City** (city) San Diego County
45	243	105.4	**Garden Acres** (CDP) San Joaquin County
46	258	104.9	**Parlier** (city) Fresno County
47	266	104.5	**Maywood** (city) Los Angeles County
47	266	104.5	**Milpitas** (city) Santa Clara County
49	273	104.4	**Santa Ana** (city) Orange County
50	286	104.1	**Phelan** (CDP) San Bernardino County
51	290	104.0	**Madera** (city) Madera County
51	290	104.0	**Reedley** (city) Fresno County
53	297	103.8	**Lake Arrowhead** (CDP) San Bernardino County
54	301	103.7	**Costa Mesa** (city) Orange County
55	308	103.6	**Mountain View** (city) Santa Clara County
56	329	103.3	**Bloomington** (CDP) San Bernardino County
56	329	103.3	**Dinuba** (city) Tulare County
56	329	103.3	**Lakeland Village** (CDP) Riverside County
59	338	103.2	**Atascadero** (city) San Luis Obispo County
59	338	103.2	**Crestline** (CDP) San Bernardino County
59	338	103.2	**Port Hueneme** (city) Ventura County
62	350	103.0	**Oxnard** (city) Ventura County
63	354	102.9	**San Francisco** (city) San Francisco County
64	367	102.8	**Muscoy** (CDP) San Bernardino County
65	376	102.7	**Big Bear City** (CDP) San Bernardino County
65	376	102.7	**East Palo Alto** (city) San Mateo County
67	380	102.6	**Salida** (CDP) Stanislaus County
68	398	102.3	**Delhi** (CDP) Merced County
69	404	102.2	**Citrus** (CDP) Los Angeles County
69	404	102.2	**Santa Maria** (city) Santa Barbara County
71	413	102.1	**Livingston** (city) Merced County
71	413	102.1	**Salinas** (city) Monterey County
71	413	102.1	**San Diego** (city) San Diego County
74	425	102.0	**Santa Clara** (city) Santa Clara County
75	435	101.9	**Cherryland** (CDP) Alameda County
75	435	101.9	**Lemon Hill** (CDP) Sacramento County
75	435	101.9	**Santa Paula** (city) Ventura County
75	435	101.9	**South El Monte** (city) Los Angeles County
79	450	101.7	**Bell** (city) Los Angeles County
79	450	101.7	**Prunedale** (CDP) Monterey County
81	462	101.5	**Farmersville** (city) Tulare County
81	462	101.5	**Orange** (city) Orange County
81	462	101.5	**Sunnyvale** (city) Santa Clara County
81	462	101.5	**Walnut Park** (CDP) Los Angeles County
85	474	101.4	**South San Jose Hills** (CDP) Los Angeles County
86	481	101.3	**Goleta** (city) Santa Barbara County
86	481	101.3	**Lawndale** (city) Los Angeles County
86	481	101.3	**Lindsay** (city) Tulare County
89	490	101.2	**Castaic** (CDP) Los Angeles County
89	490	101.2	**Monterey** (city) Monterey County
91	501	101.1	**Imperial Beach** (city) San Diego County
91	501	101.1	**Patterson** (city) Stanislaus County
91	501	101.1	**San Diego Country Estates** (CDP) San Diego County
91	501	101.1	**San Jose** (city) Santa Clara County
95	516	101.0	**Discovery Bay** (CDP) Contra Costa County
95	516	101.0	**Ramona** (CDP) San Diego County
95	516	101.0	**Rio Linda** (CDP) Sacramento County
98	526	100.9	**El Monte** (city) Los Angeles County
98	526	100.9	**San Clemente** (city) Orange County
98	526	100.9	**Winton** (CDP) Merced County
101	538	100.8	**Lake Los Angeles** (CDP) Los Angeles County
102	548	100.7	**San Fernando** (city) Los Angeles County
102	548	100.7	**Vista** (city) San Diego County
104	560	100.6	**Laguna Beach** (city) Orange County
104	560	100.6	**Lancaster** (city) Los Angeles County
104	560	100.6	**Malibu** (city) Los Angeles County
104	560	100.6	**Rosamond** (CDP) Kern County
108	578	100.5	**Del Aire** (CDP) Los Angeles County
108	578	100.5	**Olivehurst** (CDP) Yuba County
108	578	100.5	**Santa Cruz** (city) Santa Cruz County
108	578	100.5	**Seaside** (city) Monterey County
108	578	100.5	**Valinda** (CDP) Los Angeles County
113	595	100.4	**La Riviera** (CDP) Sacramento County
113	595	100.4	**Lake Elsinore** (city) Riverside County
113	595	100.4	**Manhattan Beach** (city) Los Angeles County
113	595	100.4	**Victorville** (city) San Bernardino County
117	613	100.3	**Desert Hot Springs** (city) Riverside County
117	613	100.3	**Ridgecrest** (city) Kern County
117	613	100.3	**Selma** (city) Fresno County
120	629	100.2	**Florence-Graham** (CDP) Los Angeles County
121	638	100.1	**Linda** (CDP) Yuba County
122	653	100.0	**Pomona** (city) Los Angeles County
123	671	99.9	**Clearlake** (city) Lake County
124	683	99.8	**Fillmore** (city) Ventura County
125	697	99.7	**Bay Point** (CDP) Contra Costa County
125	697	99.7	**Bell Gardens** (city) Los Angeles County
125	697	99.7	**La Puente** (city) Los Angeles County
125	697	99.7	**Lathrop** (city) San Joaquin County
125	697	99.7	**San Rafael** (city) Marin County
130	715	99.6	**Barstow** (city) San Bernardino County
130	715	99.6	**Garden Grove** (city) Orange County
130	715	99.6	**Huntington Park** (city) Los Angeles County
130	715	99.6	**Kerman** (city) Fresno County
130	715	99.6	**Marysville** (city) Yuba County
130	715	99.6	**Woodcrest** (CDP) Riverside County
136	736	99.5	**Canyon Lake** (city) Riverside County
136	736	99.5	**Fallbrook** (CDP) San Diego County
136	736	99.5	**Shasta Lake** (city) Shasta County
139	753	99.4	**El Segundo** (city) Los Angeles County
139	753	99.4	**Hawaiian Gardens** (city) Los Angeles County
141	776	99.3	**Coachella** (city) Riverside County
141	776	99.3	**Newark** (city) Alameda County
141	776	99.3	**Riverbank** (city) Stanislaus County
144	789	99.2	**Arcata** (city) Humboldt County
144	789	99.2	**Los Angeles** (city) Los Angeles County
144	789	99.2	**Los Banos** (city) Merced County
144	789	99.2	**Redwood City** (city) San Mateo County
144	789	99.2	**Watsonville** (city) Santa Cruz County
149	813	99.1	**Lemoore** (city) Kings County
149	813	99.1	**Montclair** (city) San Bernardino County

Note: *The state column ranks the top/bottom 150 places from all places in the state with population of 10,000 or more. The national column ranks the top/bottom 150 places from all places in the country with population of 10,000 or more. Places that are unincorporated were not considered in the rankings. Please refer to the User Guide for additional information.*

Males per 100 Females

Top 150 Places Ranked in *Ascending* Order

State Rank	Nat'l Rank	Ratio	Place
1	1	42.7	**Chowchilla** (city) Madera County
2	2	55.1	**Laguna Woods** (city) Orange County
3	18	78.8	**Seal Beach** (city) Orange County
4	21	78.9	**Grass Valley** (city) Nevada County
5	39	80.6	**View Park-Windsor Hills** (CDP) Los Angeles County
6	63	81.9	**Larkspur** (city) Marin County
7	105	83.6	**Sonoma** (city) Sonoma County
8	131	84.3	**Beverly Hills** (city) Los Angeles County
9	186	85.2	**Pacific Grove** (city) Monterey County
10	197	85.3	**Mill Valley** (city) Marin County
11	277	86.4	**Walnut Creek** (city) Contra Costa County
12	313	86.8	**Westmont** (CDP) Los Angeles County
13	371	87.4	**San Anselmo** (town) Marin County
14	435	88.0	**Loma Linda** (city) San Bernardino County
15	494	88.4	**Claremont** (city) Los Angeles County
16	532	88.7	**Palm Desert** (city) Riverside County
17	568	88.9	**Diamond Springs** (CDP) El Dorado County
17	568	88.9	**Hemet** (city) Riverside County
19	606	89.1	**Culver City** (city) Los Angeles County
20	631	89.2	**Moraga** (town) Contra Costa County
21	671	89.5	**Auburn** (city) Placer County
21	671	89.5	**Los Alamitos** (city) Orange County
23	689	89.6	**Calexico** (city) Imperial County
23	689	89.6	**Carmichael** (CDP) Sacramento County
23	689	89.6	**Duarte** (city) Los Angeles County
26	734	89.8	**Sierra Madre** (city) Los Angeles County
27	754	89.9	**Alhambra** (city) Los Angeles County
27	754	89.9	**La Verne** (city) Los Angeles County
29	774	90.0	**Millbrae** (city) San Mateo County
30	798	90.1	**Arden-Arcade** (CDP) Sacramento County
30	798	90.1	**Hercules** (city) Contra Costa County
32	838	90.3	**Placerville** (city) El Dorado County
32	838	90.3	**South Pasadena** (city) Los Angeles County
34	869	90.4	**Burlingame** (city) San Mateo County
35	893	90.5	**Davis** (city) Yolo County
35	893	90.5	**Paradise** (town) Butte County
35	893	90.5	**San Dimas** (city) Los Angeles County
35	893	90.5	**Temple City** (city) Los Angeles County
39	921	90.6	**Inglewood** (city) Los Angeles County
39	921	90.6	**Pinole** (city) Contra Costa County
41	975	90.8	**Albany** (city) Alameda County
41	975	90.8	**La Mesa** (city) San Diego County
43	999	90.9	**Redlands** (city) San Bernardino County
44	1059	91.1	**Glendale** (city) Los Angeles County
45	1091	91.2	**Arcadia** (city) Los Angeles County
46	1206	91.6	**Monrovia** (city) Los Angeles County
47	1233	91.7	**Alameda** (city) Alameda County
48	1300	91.9	**Carson** (city) Los Angeles County
48	1300	91.9	**Roseville** (city) Placer County
48	1300	91.9	**Valle Vista** (CDP) Riverside County
51	1343	92.0	**Los Gatos** (town) Santa Clara County
52	1381	92.1	**Willowbrook** (CDP) Los Angeles County
53	1414	92.2	**La Mirada** (city) Los Angeles County
53	1414	92.2	**Monterey Park** (city) Los Angeles County
55	1458	92.3	**El Cerrito** (city) Contra Costa County
55	1458	92.3	**San Leandro** (city) Alameda County
57	1487	92.4	**Red Bluff** (city) Tehama County
57	1487	92.4	**Rossmoor** (CDP) Orange County
57	1487	92.4	**San Marino** (city) Los Angeles County
60	1513	92.5	**Lincoln** (city) Placer County
61	1546	92.6	**Arroyo Grande** (city) San Luis Obispo County
61	1546	92.6	**Cerritos** (city) Los Angeles County
61	1546	92.6	**Gardena** (city) Los Angeles County
61	1546	92.6	**Oak Park** (CDP) Ventura County
65	1581	92.7	**Benicia** (city) Solano County
66	1629	92.8	**Aliso Viejo** (city) Orange County
66	1629	92.8	**Marina** (city) Monterey County
66	1629	92.8	**Menifee** (city) Riverside County
66	1629	92.8	**Ukiah** (city) Mendocino County
70	1668	92.9	**Grand Terrace** (city) San Bernardino County
70	1668	92.9	**Kingsburg** (city) Fresno County
70	1668	92.9	**La Crescenta-Montrose** (CDP) Los Angeles County
73	1695	93.0	**Santa Fe Springs** (city) Los Angeles County
74	1728	93.1	**Altadena** (CDP) Los Angeles County
74	1728	93.1	**Fortuna** (city) Humboldt County
74	1728	93.1	**Los Altos** (city) Santa Clara County
74	1728	93.1	**Upland** (city) San Bernardino County
74	1728	93.1	**West Covina** (city) Los Angeles County
79	1763	93.2	**Clovis** (city) Fresno County
79	1763	93.2	**Hawthorne** (city) Los Angeles County
79	1763	93.2	**North Auburn** (CDP) Placer County
79	1763	93.2	**San Gabriel** (city) Los Angeles County
79	1763	93.2	**Santa Monica** (city) Los Angeles County
84	1811	93.3	**Covina** (city) Los Angeles County
84	1811	93.3	**Lomita** (city) Los Angeles County
84	1811	93.3	**Montebello** (city) Los Angeles County
87	1851	93.4	**Banning** (city) Riverside County
87	1851	93.4	**Clayton** (city) Contra Costa County
89	1897	93.5	**Danville** (town) Contra Costa County
89	1897	93.5	**Foster City** (city) San Mateo County
89	1897	93.5	**La Palma** (city) Orange County
89	1897	93.5	**La Quinta** (city) Riverside County
93	1940	93.6	**Burbank** (city) Los Angeles County
93	1940	93.6	**Calabasas** (city) Los Angeles County
93	1940	93.6	**Novato** (city) Marin County
93	1940	93.6	**San Carlos** (city) San Mateo County
93	1940	93.6	**Santee** (city) San Diego County
98	1985	93.7	**Camarillo** (city) Ventura County
98	1985	93.7	**Glendora** (city) Los Angeles County
98	1985	93.7	**Menlo Park** (city) San Mateo County
98	1985	93.7	**Oroville** (city) Butte County
102	2037	93.8	**Redding** (city) Shasta County
103	2082	93.9	**Chula Vista** (city) San Diego County
103	2082	93.9	**Elk Grove** (city) Sacramento County
105	2131	94.0	**East San Gabriel** (CDP) Los Angeles County
105	2131	94.0	**Laguna Niguel** (city) Orange County
105	2131	94.0	**Rocklin** (city) Placer County
105	2131	94.0	**Whittier** (city) Los Angeles County
109	2182	94.1	**Citrus Heights** (city) Sacramento County
109	2182	94.1	**Downey** (city) Los Angeles County
109	2182	94.1	**Pleasant Hill** (city) Contra Costa County
109	2182	94.1	**Rancho San Diego** (CDP) San Diego County
113	2226	94.2	**Brentwood** (city) Contra Costa County
113	2226	94.2	**Cypress** (city) Orange County
113	2226	94.2	**Oakland** (city) Alameda County
116	2258	94.3	**Antelope** (CDP) Sacramento County
116	2258	94.3	**Brawley** (city) Imperial County
116	2258	94.3	**Cameron Park** (CDP) El Dorado County
116	2258	94.3	**Lakewood** (city) Los Angeles County
116	2258	94.3	**Rancho Palos Verdes** (city) Los Angeles County
116	2258	94.3	**Vallejo** (city) Solano County
122	2294	94.4	**Bellflower** (city) Los Angeles County
122	2294	94.4	**Orinda** (city) Contra Costa County
122	2294	94.4	**Tamalpais-Homestead Valley** (CDP) Marin County
125	2327	94.5	**Castro Valley** (CDP) Alameda County
125	2327	94.5	**Exeter** (city) Tulare County
125	2327	94.5	**Lafayette** (city) Contra Costa County
128	2358	94.6	**Bostonia** (CDP) San Diego County
129	2403	94.7	**El Centro** (city) Imperial County
129	2403	94.7	**La Cañada Flintridge** (city) Los Angeles County
129	2403	94.7	**Lynwood** (city) Los Angeles County
129	2403	94.7	**Paramount** (city) Los Angeles County
129	2403	94.7	**Piedmont** (city) Alameda County
129	2403	94.7	**Rialto** (city) San Bernardino County
129	2403	94.7	**Torrance** (city) Los Angeles County
129	2403	94.7	**Tustin** (city) Orange County
129	2403	94.7	**Yucca Valley** (town) San Bernardino County
138	2450	94.8	**Antioch** (city) Contra Costa County
138	2450	94.8	**Compton** (city) Los Angeles County
138	2450	94.8	**Hacienda Heights** (CDP) Los Angeles County
138	2450	94.8	**Hillsborough** (town) San Mateo County
138	2450	94.8	**Richmond** (city) Contra Costa County
138	2450	94.8	**Turlock** (city) Stanislaus County
138	2450	94.8	**Yorba Linda** (city) Orange County
145	2486	94.9	**Bonita** (CDP) San Diego County
145	2486	94.9	**El Paso de Robles (Paso Robles)** (city) San Luis Obispo County
145	2486	94.9	**Fountain Valley** (city) Orange County
145	2486	94.9	**Irvine** (city) Orange County
145	2486	94.9	**Oildale** (CDP) Kern County
145	2486	94.9	**Pittsburg** (city) Contra Costa County

Note: *The state column ranks the top/bottom 150 places from all places in the state with population of 10,000 or more. The national column ranks the top/bottom 150 places from all places in the country with population of 10,000 or more. Places that are unincorporated were not considered in the rankings. Please refer to the User Guide for additional information.*

Marriage Status: Never Married

Top 150 Places Ranked in *Descending* Order

State Rank	Nat'l Rank	Percent	Place
1	1	92.7	**Isla Vista** (CDP) Santa Barbara County
2	10	77.0	**Stanford** (CDP) Santa Clara County
3	45	61.4	**West Hollywood** (city) Los Angeles County
4	52	60.1	**Arcata** (city) Humboldt County
5	66	58.1	**San Luis Obispo** (city) San Luis Obispo County
6	86	56.1	**Santa Cruz** (city) Santa Cruz County
7	102	55.0	**Berkeley** (city) Alameda County
8	119	53.9	**Davis** (city) Yolo County
9	133	52.8	**Mendota** (city) Fresno County
10	140	52.6	**Westmont** (CDP) Los Angeles County
11	153	52.0	**Cudahy** (city) Los Angeles County
12	176	50.5	**East Rancho Dominguez** (CDP) Los Angeles County
13	195	49.6	**Maywood** (city) Los Angeles County
14	199	49.2	**Willowbrook** (CDP) Los Angeles County
15	206	49.1	**Florence-Graham** (CDP) Los Angeles County
16	211	48.8	**Bell Gardens** (city) Los Angeles County
17	217	48.6	**Azusa** (city) Los Angeles County
18	220	48.5	**Emeryville** (city) Alameda County
19	228	48.1	**Lynwood** (city) Los Angeles County
20	239	47.8	**East Los Angeles** (CDP) Los Angeles County
21	244	47.7	**Huntington Park** (city) Los Angeles County
22	261	47.3	**Muscoy** (CDP) San Bernardino County
23	265	47.2	**Wasco** (city) Kern County
24	272	46.8	**Compton** (city) Los Angeles County
25	275	46.7	**San Francisco** (city) San Francisco County
26	292	46.1	**Bell** (city) Los Angeles County
27	306	45.7	**Chico** (city) Butte County
27	306	45.7	**Hawthorne** (city) Los Angeles County
29	311	45.6	**North Fair Oaks** (CDP) San Mateo County
29	311	45.6	**Parlier** (city) Fresno County
31	318	45.3	**Lennox** (CDP) Los Angeles County
32	324	45.1	**Los Angeles** (city) Los Angeles County
33	328	45.0	**Inglewood** (city) Los Angeles County
34	329	44.9	**Corcoran** (city) Kings County
35	335	44.8	**Hermosa Beach** (city) Los Angeles County
35	335	44.8	**Signal Hill** (city) Los Angeles County
37	343	44.5	**Santa Monica** (city) Los Angeles County
38	354	44.4	**Delano** (city) Kern County
38	354	44.4	**Paramount** (city) Los Angeles County
40	364	44.2	**Oakland** (city) Alameda County
41	368	44.1	**Long Beach** (city) Los Angeles County
41	368	44.1	**South Gate** (city) Los Angeles County
43	385	43.7	**San Bernardino** (city) San Bernardino County
44	394	43.6	**Cherryland** (CDP) Alameda County
44	394	43.6	**East Palo Alto** (city) San Mateo County
46	406	43.4	**Lawndale** (city) Los Angeles County
46	406	43.4	**San Fernando** (city) Los Angeles County
48	416	43.2	**Adelanto** (city) San Bernardino County
49	427	43.1	**Colton** (city) San Bernardino County
50	431	43.0	**Soledad** (city) Monterey County
51	439	42.9	**Pomona** (city) Los Angeles County
52	451	42.8	**Madera** (city) Madera County
53	457	42.7	**Commerce** (city) Los Angeles County
53	457	42.7	**La Puente** (city) Los Angeles County
53	457	42.7	**South San Jose Hills** (CDP) Los Angeles County
56	464	42.6	**Coalinga** (city) Fresno County
57	471	42.5	**San Pablo** (city) Contra Costa County
57	471	42.5	**Walnut Park** (CDP) Los Angeles County
59	476	42.4	**Livingston** (city) Merced County
60	484	42.2	**Santa Ana** (city) Orange County
61	495	42.0	**Baldwin Park** (city) Los Angeles County
61	495	42.0	**Citrus** (CDP) Los Angeles County
61	495	42.0	**Susanville** (city) Lassen County
64	500	41.9	**Lamont** (CDP) Kern County
65	511	41.6	**Ashland** (CDP) Alameda County
66	520	41.5	**West Puente Valley** (CDP) Los Angeles County
67	528	41.4	**King City** (city) Monterey County
67	528	41.4	**Salinas** (city) Monterey County
69	532	41.3	**Mead Valley** (CDP) Riverside County
69	532	41.3	**Parkway** (CDP) Sacramento County
69	532	41.3	**Rohnert Park** (city) Sonoma County
72	540	41.2	**Watsonville** (city) Santa Cruz County
73	553	41.0	**Eureka** (city) Humboldt County
73	553	41.0	**Home Gardens** (CDP) Riverside County
73	553	41.0	**Lake Los Angeles** (CDP) Los Angeles County
76	566	40.9	**Arvin** (city) Kern County
76	566	40.9	**Blythe** (city) Riverside County
78	576	40.8	**McFarland** (city) Kern County
79	583	40.7	**Lemon Grove** (city) San Diego County
80	597	40.5	**Bay Point** (CDP) Contra Costa County
80	597	40.5	**South El Monte** (city) Los Angeles County
82	612	40.4	**Hawaiian Gardens** (city) Los Angeles County
83	614	40.3	**El Monte** (city) Los Angeles County
83	614	40.3	**San Diego** (city) San Diego County
85	633	40.1	**Santa Barbara** (city) Santa Barbara County
86	640	40.0	**Coachella** (city) Riverside County
86	640	40.0	**Farmersville** (city) Tulare County
86	640	40.0	**Lemon Hill** (CDP) Sacramento County
89	654	39.8	**Costa Mesa** (city) Orange County
89	654	39.8	**Greenfield** (city) Monterey County
91	660	39.7	**Fresno** (city) Fresno County
91	660	39.7	**Merced** (city) Merced County
91	660	39.7	**Palm Springs** (city) Riverside County
91	660	39.7	**Sacramento** (city) Sacramento County
95	666	39.6	**Norwalk** (city) Los Angeles County
95	666	39.6	**Pico Rivera** (city) Los Angeles County
97	676	39.5	**Pasadena** (city) Los Angeles County
97	676	39.5	**Riverside** (city) Riverside County
99	682	39.4	**Rialto** (city) San Bernardino County
99	682	39.4	**Richmond** (city) Contra Costa County
101	697	39.2	**Avocado Heights** (CDP) Los Angeles County
101	697	39.2	**Montclair** (city) San Bernardino County
103	714	39.0	**Avenal** (city) Kings County
103	714	39.0	**Bellflower** (city) Los Angeles County
103	714	39.0	**Bloomington** (CDP) San Bernardino County
103	714	39.0	**National City** (city) San Diego County
103	714	39.0	**Ontario** (city) San Bernardino County
103	714	39.0	**Palmdale** (city) Los Angeles County
103	714	39.0	**Perris** (city) Riverside County
103	714	39.0	**Tehachapi** (city) Kern County
103	714	39.0	**Winton** (CDP) Merced County
112	730	38.9	**Montebello** (city) Los Angeles County
112	730	38.9	**West Whittier-Los Nietos** (CDP) Los Angeles County
114	743	38.8	**Lindsay** (city) Tulare County
115	754	38.7	**Carson** (city) Los Angeles County
116	767	38.6	**Downey** (city) Los Angeles County
116	767	38.6	**Valinda** (CDP) Los Angeles County
118	777	38.5	**Pittsburg** (city) Contra Costa County
119	783	38.4	**Alum Rock** (CDP) Santa Clara County
120	802	38.2	**Moreno Valley** (city) Riverside County
120	802	38.2	**Oxnard** (city) Ventura County
120	802	38.2	**Stanton** (city) Orange County
123	810	38.1	**South Whittier** (CDP) Los Angeles County
123	810	38.1	**Whittier** (city) Los Angeles County
125	820	38.0	**Claremont** (city) Los Angeles County
125	820	38.0	**Rosemont** (CDP) Sacramento County
125	820	38.0	**Seaside** (city) Monterey County
128	829	37.9	**Fontana** (city) San Bernardino County
129	839	37.8	**Florin** (CDP) Sacramento County
129	839	37.8	**Fullerton** (city) Orange County
129	839	37.8	**Gardena** (city) Los Angeles County
132	847	37.7	**Chowchilla** (city) Madera County
132	847	37.7	**Marina** (city) Monterey County
132	847	37.7	**Santa Maria** (city) Santa Barbara County
132	847	37.7	**Stockton** (city) San Joaquin County
136	866	37.6	**Goleta** (city) Santa Barbara County
136	866	37.6	**Imperial Beach** (city) San Diego County
136	866	37.6	**Lancaster** (city) Los Angeles County
139	881	37.5	**Dinuba** (city) Tulare County
140	894	37.4	**Hayward** (city) Alameda County
141	900	37.3	**La Riviera** (CDP) Sacramento County
142	924	37.1	**La Habra** (city) Orange County
142	924	37.1	**Orange** (city) Orange County
144	936	37.0	**Irvine** (city) Orange County
145	947	36.9	**Daly City** (city) San Mateo County
145	947	36.9	**Santa Fe Springs** (city) Los Angeles County
145	947	36.9	**Sun Village** (CDP) Los Angeles County
148	966	36.8	**Highland** (city) San Bernardino County
148	966	36.8	**Linda** (CDP) Yuba County
150	976	36.7	**Alhambra** (city) Los Angeles County

***Note:** The state column ranks the top/bottom 150 places from all places in the state with population of 10,000 or more. The national column ranks the top/bottom 150 places from all places in the country with population of 10,000 or more. Places that are unincorporated were not considered in the rankings. Please refer to the User Guide for additional information.*

Marriage Status: Never Married

Top 150 Places Ranked in *Ascending* Order

State Rank	Nat'l Rank	Percent	Place
1	8	7.9	**Laguna Woods** (city) Orange County
2	49	17.9	**Los Altos** (city) Santa Clara County
3	65	18.3	**Discovery Bay** (CDP) Contra Costa County
3	65	18.3	**Lincoln** (city) Placer County
5	80	18.8	**Saratoga** (city) Santa Clara County
6	93	19.1	**Palos Verdes Estates** (city) Los Angeles County
7	132	19.8	**Canyon Lake** (city) Riverside County
8	136	19.9	**Danville** (town) Contra Costa County
9	158	20.2	**Alamo** (CDP) Contra Costa County
10	172	20.4	**Ladera Ranch** (CDP) Orange County
11	203	20.8	**Rancho Palos Verdes** (city) Los Angeles County
12	226	21.0	**Orinda** (city) Contra Costa County
13	253	21.3	**Sonoma** (city) Sonoma County
14	262	21.4	**Lake Arrowhead** (CDP) San Bernardino County
14	262	21.4	**San Marino** (city) Los Angeles County
16	296	21.6	**Lafayette** (city) Contra Costa County
17	313	21.8	**Shasta Lake** (city) Shasta County
18	347	22.1	**Seal Beach** (city) Orange County
19	385	22.3	**Rosedale** (CDP) Kern County
20	401	22.4	**El Dorado Hills** (CDP) El Dorado County
20	401	22.4	**Piedmont** (city) Alameda County
22	423	22.5	**Granite Bay** (CDP) Placer County
22	423	22.5	**Mill Valley** (city) Marin County
22	423	22.5	**Rossmoor** (CDP) Orange County
25	440	22.6	**Palm Desert** (city) Riverside County
26	459	22.7	**Hillsborough** (town) San Mateo County
26	459	22.7	**La Quinta** (city) Riverside County
28	520	23.0	**Cupertino** (city) Santa Clara County
28	520	23.0	**Rancho Mirage** (city) Riverside County
30	540	23.1	**Camp Pendleton South** (CDP) San Diego County
31	565	23.2	**Coto de Caza** (CDP) Orange County
31	565	23.2	**Morro Bay** (city) San Luis Obispo County
33	593	23.3	**Foster City** (city) San Mateo County
33	593	23.3	**Orcutt** (CDP) Santa Barbara County
35	613	23.4	**Cameron Park** (CDP) El Dorado County
35	613	23.4	**Larkspur** (city) Marin County
37	648	23.5	**Clayton** (city) Contra Costa County
38	671	23.6	**Los Gatos** (town) Santa Clara County
38	671	23.6	**Magalia** (CDP) Butte County
40	713	23.8	**San Ramon** (city) Contra Costa County
41	766	24.1	**Half Moon Bay** (city) San Mateo County
41	766	24.1	**North Tustin** (CDP) Orange County
41	766	24.1	**San Carlos** (city) San Mateo County
44	808	24.3	**San Clemente** (city) Orange County
45	831	24.4	**Arroyo Grande** (city) San Luis Obispo County
45	831	24.4	**Diamond Springs** (CDP) El Dorado County
47	862	24.5	**Tamalpais-Homestead Valley** (CDP) Marin County
48	884	24.6	**Novato** (city) Marin County
49	1007	25.2	**Auburn** (city) Placer County
50	1025	25.3	**Crestline** (CDP) San Bernardino County
50	1025	25.3	**Paradise** (town) Butte County
52	1055	25.4	**Oak Park** (CDP) Ventura County
52	1055	25.4	**Pleasanton** (city) Alameda County
54	1106	25.6	**Nipomo** (CDP) San Luis Obispo County
54	1106	25.6	**North Auburn** (CDP) Placer County
56	1141	25.7	**Ripon** (city) San Joaquin County
56	1141	25.7	**Walnut Creek** (city) Contra Costa County
58	1188	25.9	**Sierra Madre** (city) Los Angeles County
59	1203	26.0	**San Anselmo** (town) Marin County
60	1227	26.1	**Calabasas** (city) Los Angeles County
60	1227	26.1	**Windsor** (town) Sonoma County
62	1254	26.2	**La Cañada Flintridge** (city) Los Angeles County
62	1254	26.2	**Poway** (city) San Diego County
64	1281	26.3	**Alpine** (CDP) San Diego County
64	1281	26.3	**Laguna Niguel** (city) Orange County
66	1298	26.4	**Banning** (city) Riverside County
66	1298	26.4	**Fremont** (city) Alameda County
66	1298	26.4	**Mission Viejo** (city) Orange County
66	1298	26.4	**Yorba Linda** (city) Orange County
70	1327	26.5	**Albany** (city) Alameda County
70	1327	26.5	**Carlsbad** (city) San Diego County
70	1327	26.5	**San Diego Country Estates** (CDP) San Diego County
73	1355	26.6	**Los Osos** (CDP) San Luis Obispo County
74	1392	26.7	**Millbrae** (city) San Mateo County
75	1419	26.8	**Bonita** (CDP) San Diego County
76	1456	26.9	**Palo Alto** (city) Santa Clara County
77	1483	27.0	**Camarillo** (city) Ventura County
77	1483	27.0	**Rocklin** (city) Placer County
79	1502	27.1	**Atascadero** (city) San Luis Obispo County
79	1502	27.1	**Beaumont** (city) Riverside County
79	1502	27.1	**Hemet** (city) Riverside County
79	1502	27.1	**Menifee** (city) Riverside County
83	1523	27.2	**Belmont** (city) San Mateo County
84	1557	27.3	**Brentwood** (city) Contra Costa County
84	1557	27.3	**El Sobrante** (CDP) Riverside County
84	1557	27.3	**Lakeside** (CDP) San Diego County
84	1557	27.3	**Phelan** (CDP) San Bernardino County
84	1557	27.3	**Valle Vista** (CDP) Riverside County
89	1589	27.4	**French Valley** (CDP) Riverside County
90	1635	27.6	**Coronado** (city) San Diego County
90	1635	27.6	**Grass Valley** (city) Nevada County
90	1635	27.6	**Roseville** (city) Placer County
93	1673	27.7	**Casa de Oro-Mount Helix** (CDP) San Diego County
93	1673	27.7	**Dana Point** (city) Orange County
93	1673	27.7	**Livermore** (city) Alameda County
96	1703	27.8	**Fair Oaks** (CDP) Sacramento County
97	1728	27.9	**Laguna Beach** (city) Orange County
97	1728	27.9	**Petaluma** (city) Sonoma County
97	1728	27.9	**Thousand Oaks** (city) Ventura County
100	1756	28.0	**Fallbrook** (CDP) San Diego County
100	1756	28.0	**Orangevale** (CDP) Sacramento County
102	1791	28.1	**Agoura Hills** (city) Los Angeles County
102	1791	28.1	**Rancho San Diego** (CDP) San Diego County
104	1823	28.2	**Apple Valley** (town) San Bernardino County
104	1823	28.2	**East San Gabriel** (CDP) Los Angeles County
104	1823	28.2	**Lake Forest** (city) Orange County
107	1881	28.4	**Galt** (city) Sacramento County
107	1881	28.4	**Yucaipa** (city) San Bernardino County
107	1881	28.4	**Yucca Valley** (town) San Bernardino County
110	1911	28.5	**Murrieta** (city) Riverside County
110	1911	28.5	**San Juan Capistrano** (city) Orange County
112	1944	28.6	**El Paso de Robles (Paso Robles)** (city) San Luis Obispo County
112	1944	28.6	**Folsom** (city) Sacramento County
112	1944	28.6	**Oakdale** (city) Stanislaus County
115	1976	28.7	**Torrance** (city) Los Angeles County
116	2011	28.8	**Benicia** (city) Solano County
117	2039	28.9	**Imperial** (city) Imperial County
117	2039	28.9	**Ridgecrest** (city) Kern County
117	2039	28.9	**Winter Gardens** (CDP) San Diego County
117	2039	28.9	**Yuba City** (city) Sutter County
121	2070	29.0	**Laguna Hills** (city) Orange County
122	2090	29.1	**Arcadia** (city) Los Angeles County
122	2090	29.1	**Stevenson Ranch** (CDP) Los Angeles County
124	2116	29.2	**Simi Valley** (city) Ventura County
125	2145	29.3	**Temple City** (city) Los Angeles County
126	2166	29.4	**Castro Valley** (CDP) Alameda County
127	2198	29.5	**Cerritos** (city) Los Angeles County
127	2198	29.5	**Fountain Valley** (city) Orange County
127	2198	29.5	**Rancho Santa Margarita** (city) Orange County
127	2198	29.5	**Redding** (city) Shasta County
127	2198	29.5	**Sunnyvale** (city) Santa Clara County
132	2234	29.6	**Big Bear City** (CDP) San Bernardino County
132	2234	29.6	**Pleasant Hill** (city) Contra Costa County
134	2258	29.7	**American Canyon** (city) Napa County
134	2258	29.7	**Tracy** (city) San Joaquin County
136	2277	29.8	**Dixon** (city) Solano County
136	2277	29.8	**El Cerrito** (city) Contra Costa County
136	2277	29.8	**Morgan Hill** (city) Santa Clara County
139	2300	29.9	**Brea** (city) Orange County
140	2320	30.0	**Carmichael** (CDP) Sacramento County
140	2320	30.0	**Eastvale** (city) Riverside County
140	2320	30.0	**Fortuna** (city) Humboldt County
140	2320	30.0	**Hanford** (city) Kings County
140	2320	30.0	**Patterson** (city) Stanislaus County
140	2320	30.0	**Wildomar** (city) Riverside County
146	2350	30.1	**Elk Grove** (city) Sacramento County
146	2350	30.1	**Kingsburg** (city) Fresno County
146	2350	30.1	**Malibu** (city) Los Angeles County
146	2350	30.1	**Manhattan Beach** (city) Los Angeles County
150	2380	30.2	**La Palma** (city) Orange County

Note: *The state column ranks the top/bottom 150 places from all places in the state with population of 10,000 or more. The national column ranks the top/bottom 150 places from all places in the country with population of 10,000 or more. Places that are unincorporated were not considered in the rankings. Please refer to the User Guide for additional information.*

Marriage Status: Now Married

Top 150 Places Ranked in *Descending* Order

State Rank	Nat'l Rank	Percent	Place
1	6	75.8	**Camp Pendleton South** (CDP) San Diego County
2	37	71.4	**Hillsborough** (town) San Mateo County
3	42	71.3	**Coto de Caza** (CDP) Orange County
4	43	71.1	**Ladera Ranch** (CDP) Orange County
5	45	70.7	**Alamo** (CDP) Contra Costa County
6	48	70.3	**Piedmont** (city) Alameda County
7	54	70.0	**Saratoga** (city) Santa Clara County
8	63	69.5	**Los Altos** (city) Santa Clara County
8	63	69.5	**Palos Verdes Estates** (city) Los Angeles County
10	111	68.1	**Orinda** (city) Contra Costa County
11	122	67.9	**San Marino** (city) Los Angeles County
12	171	66.9	**Discovery Bay** (CDP) Contra Costa County
13	181	66.7	**El Sobrante** (CDP) Riverside County
14	186	66.6	**El Dorado Hills** (CDP) El Dorado County
15	199	66.3	**Cupertino** (city) Santa Clara County
16	216	66.0	**San Ramon** (city) Contra Costa County
17	227	65.9	**Danville** (town) Contra Costa County
18	256	65.4	**Canyon Lake** (city) Riverside County
19	278	65.1	**La Cañada Flintridge** (city) Los Angeles County
20	285	65.0	**Granite Bay** (CDP) Placer County
20	285	65.0	**Lafayette** (city) Contra Costa County
22	295	64.9	**Lincoln** (city) Placer County
22	295	64.9	**Rossmoor** (CDP) Orange County
24	329	64.5	**Rosedale** (CDP) Kern County
25	347	64.3	**Rancho Palos Verdes** (city) Los Angeles County
26	399	63.8	**North Tustin** (CDP) Orange County
27	466	62.9	**Clayton** (city) Contra Costa County
27	466	62.9	**Foster City** (city) San Mateo County
29	479	62.8	**Lake Arrowhead** (CDP) San Bernardino County
30	548	62.1	**Pleasanton** (city) Alameda County
31	565	62.0	**Fremont** (city) Alameda County
32	581	61.9	**Half Moon Bay** (city) San Mateo County
32	581	61.9	**La Quinta** (city) Riverside County
34	604	61.7	**Albany** (city) Alameda County
34	604	61.7	**Yorba Linda** (city) Orange County
36	621	61.6	**Eastvale** (city) Riverside County
37	664	61.2	**San Carlos** (city) San Mateo County
38	715	60.9	**Ripon** (city) San Joaquin County
39	783	60.4	**French Valley** (CDP) Riverside County
39	783	60.4	**Los Gatos** (town) Santa Clara County
41	813	60.2	**Calabasas** (city) Los Angeles County
41	813	60.2	**Mill Valley** (city) Marin County
41	813	60.2	**San Clemente** (city) Orange County
44	829	60.1	**Cameron Park** (CDP) El Dorado County
45	854	59.9	**Stevenson Ranch** (CDP) Los Angeles County
46	871	59.8	**Oak Park** (CDP) Ventura County
47	885	59.7	**Tamalpais-Homestead Valley** (CDP) Marin County
48	930	59.4	**Delhi** (CDP) Merced County
48	930	59.4	**Palo Alto** (city) Santa Clara County
48	930	59.4	**Poway** (city) San Diego County
51	948	59.3	**Nipomo** (CDP) San Luis Obispo County
52	977	59.1	**Brentwood** (city) Contra Costa County
53	1006	58.9	**East San Gabriel** (CDP) Los Angeles County
53	1006	58.9	**Laguna Niguel** (city) Orange County
53	1006	58.9	**Sunnyvale** (city) Santa Clara County
56	1025	58.8	**Arcadia** (city) Los Angeles County
57	1060	58.6	**Fallbrook** (CDP) San Diego County
57	1060	58.6	**Lake Forest** (city) Orange County
59	1089	58.4	**Beaumont** (city) Riverside County
60	1103	58.3	**Imperial** (city) Imperial County
60	1103	58.3	**Mission Viejo** (city) Orange County
62	1121	58.2	**Rancho Santa Margarita** (city) Orange County
62	1121	58.2	**Walnut** (city) Los Angeles County
64	1129	58.1	**Castaic** (CDP) Los Angeles County
64	1129	58.1	**Orcutt** (CDP) Santa Barbara County
66	1145	58.0	**La Crescenta-Montrose** (CDP) Los Angeles County
66	1145	58.0	**Manhattan Beach** (city) Los Angeles County
68	1166	57.9	**Chino Hills** (city) San Bernardino County
68	1166	57.9	**Rocklin** (city) Placer County
70	1180	57.8	**Livermore** (city) Alameda County
70	1180	57.8	**San Diego Country Estates** (CDP) San Diego County
72	1195	57.7	**Cerritos** (city) Los Angeles County
72	1195	57.7	**Moorpark** (city) Ventura County
74	1211	57.6	**American Canyon** (city) Napa County
74	1211	57.6	**Morgan Hill** (city) Santa Clara County
74	1211	57.6	**Thousand Oaks** (city) Ventura County
74	1211	57.6	**Tracy** (city) San Joaquin County
78	1245	57.4	**Laguna Hills** (city) Orange County
79	1260	57.3	**Murrieta** (city) Riverside County
79	1260	57.3	**Windsor** (town) Sonoma County
81	1276	57.2	**Patterson** (city) Stanislaus County
82	1297	57.1	**Belmont** (city) San Mateo County
82	1297	57.1	**Lakeside** (CDP) San Diego County
84	1311	57.0	**Bonita** (CDP) San Diego County
85	1323	56.9	**Alpine** (CDP) San Diego County
85	1323	56.9	**Union City** (city) Alameda County
85	1323	56.9	**Woodcrest** (CDP) Riverside County
88	1339	56.8	**Carlsbad** (city) San Diego County
89	1352	56.7	**Agoura Hills** (city) Los Angeles County
89	1352	56.7	**Novato** (city) Marin County
89	1352	56.7	**Prunedale** (CDP) Monterey County
89	1352	56.7	**Vineyard** (CDP) Sacramento County
93	1376	56.6	**Diamond Bar** (city) Los Angeles County
93	1376	56.6	**Kingsburg** (city) Fresno County
93	1376	56.6	**Shasta Lake** (city) Shasta County
96	1424	56.4	**Aliso Viejo** (city) Orange County
96	1424	56.4	**Milpitas** (city) Santa Clara County
98	1443	56.3	**Atascadero** (city) San Luis Obispo County
98	1443	56.3	**Roseville** (city) Placer County
98	1443	56.3	**Sierra Madre** (city) Los Angeles County
98	1443	56.3	**Truckee** (town) Nevada County
102	1464	56.2	**Coronado** (city) San Diego County
102	1464	56.2	**El Paso de Robles (Paso Robles)** (city) San Luis Obispo County
104	1476	56.1	**Brea** (city) Orange County
104	1476	56.1	**Shafter** (city) Kern County
106	1495	56.0	**Dublin** (city) Alameda County
106	1495	56.0	**Elk Grove** (city) Sacramento County
106	1495	56.0	**Folsom** (city) Sacramento County
106	1495	56.0	**San Juan Capistrano** (city) Orange County
110	1512	55.9	**Moraga** (town) Contra Costa County
110	1512	55.9	**San Anselmo** (town) Marin County
110	1512	55.9	**Temple City** (city) Los Angeles County
113	1531	55.8	**Camarillo** (city) Ventura County
113	1531	55.8	**Dixon** (city) Solano County
115	1595	55.5	**Rancho San Diego** (CDP) San Diego County
115	1595	55.5	**Simi Valley** (city) Ventura County
117	1618	55.4	**Arroyo Grande** (city) San Luis Obispo County
117	1618	55.4	**Millbrae** (city) San Mateo County
117	1618	55.4	**Temecula** (city) Riverside County
117	1618	55.4	**Wildomar** (city) Riverside County
121	1650	55.2	**Hercules** (city) Contra Costa County
122	1671	55.1	**Gilroy** (city) Santa Clara County
122	1671	55.1	**Rancho Mirage** (city) Riverside County
122	1671	55.1	**Yucaipa** (city) San Bernardino County
125	1697	55.0	**Greenfield** (city) Monterey County
125	1697	55.0	**Hacienda Heights** (CDP) Los Angeles County
125	1697	55.0	**Yuba City** (city) Sutter County
128	1711	54.9	**Crestline** (CDP) San Bernardino County
129	1733	54.8	**Castro Valley** (CDP) Alameda County
129	1733	54.8	**La Palma** (city) Orange County
129	1733	54.8	**Torrance** (city) Los Angeles County
132	1756	54.7	**Rowland Heights** (CDP) Los Angeles County
132	1756	54.7	**South San Francisco** (city) San Mateo County
134	1773	54.6	**Hanford** (city) Kings County
134	1773	54.6	**Reedley** (city) Fresno County
136	1792	54.5	**Los Osos** (CDP) San Luis Obispo County
137	1809	54.4	**Antelope** (CDP) Sacramento County
137	1809	54.4	**Newman** (city) Stanislaus County
139	1829	54.3	**Manteca** (city) San Joaquin County
140	1847	54.2	**El Cerrito** (city) Contra Costa County
140	1847	54.2	**Encinitas** (city) San Diego County
140	1847	54.2	**Santa Clara** (city) Santa Clara County
143	1871	54.1	**Petaluma** (city) Sonoma County
144	1895	54.0	**Corona** (city) Riverside County
144	1895	54.0	**Fountain Valley** (city) Orange County
144	1895	54.0	**Lake Elsinore** (city) Riverside County
144	1895	54.0	**Oakdale** (city) Stanislaus County
144	1895	54.0	**Phelan** (CDP) San Bernardino County
149	1916	53.9	**Menlo Park** (city) San Mateo County
149	1916	53.9	**San Marcos** (city) San Diego County

Note: *The state column ranks the top/bottom 150 places from all places in the state with population of 10,000 or more. The national column ranks the top/bottom 150 places from all places in the country with population of 10,000 or more. Places that are unincorporated were not considered in the rankings. Please refer to the User Guide for additional information.*

Marriage Status: Now Married

Top 150 Places Ranked in *Ascending* Order

State Rank	Nat'l Rank	Percent	Place
1	1	5.4	**Isla Vista** (CDP) Santa Barbara County
2	20	21.0	**Stanford** (CDP) Santa Clara County
3	21	21.2	**West Hollywood** (city) Los Angeles County
4	41	25.5	**Arcata** (city) Humboldt County
5	95	30.3	**Santa Cruz** (city) Santa Cruz County
6	105	30.6	**San Luis Obispo** (city) San Luis Obispo County
7	162	33.1	**Emeryville** (city) Alameda County
8	179	33.7	**Berkeley** (city) Alameda County
9	183	33.8	**Westmont** (CDP) Los Angeles County
10	244	35.3	**Palm Springs** (city) Riverside County
11	289	36.6	**Corcoran** (city) Kings County
12	296	36.8	**Susanville** (city) Lassen County
13	322	37.2	**Davis** (city) Yolo County
14	344	37.7	**Chico** (city) Butte County
15	353	37.9	**Santa Monica** (city) Los Angeles County
16	390	38.4	**East Rancho Dominguez** (CDP) Los Angeles County
17	427	39.0	**Parkway** (CDP) Sacramento County
18	442	39.3	**Oroville** (city) Butte County
19	447	39.4	**Eureka** (city) Humboldt County
20	454	39.5	**Soledad** (city) Monterey County
21	466	39.7	**Inglewood** (city) Los Angeles County
21	466	39.7	**San Francisco** (city) San Francisco County
23	474	39.8	**Clearlake** (city) Lake County
23	474	39.8	**Oakland** (city) Alameda County
25	511	40.3	**Rohnert Park** (city) Sonoma County
26	526	40.4	**Grass Valley** (city) Nevada County
27	535	40.5	**Hawthorne** (city) Los Angeles County
28	542	40.6	**Hermosa Beach** (city) Los Angeles County
28	542	40.6	**San Bernardino** (city) San Bernardino County
30	546	40.7	**Azusa** (city) Los Angeles County
30	546	40.7	**Long Beach** (city) Los Angeles County
30	546	40.7	**Willowbrook** (CDP) Los Angeles County
33	558	40.8	**Compton** (city) Los Angeles County
34	571	41.0	**Wasco** (city) Kern County
35	577	41.1	**Mendota** (city) Fresno County
36	581	41.2	**North Fair Oaks** (CDP) San Mateo County
37	588	41.3	**Blythe** (city) Riverside County
38	612	41.5	**Lemon Hill** (CDP) Sacramento County
39	618	41.6	**East Los Angeles** (CDP) Los Angeles County
39	618	41.6	**Oildale** (CDP) Kern County
41	632	41.8	**Los Angeles** (city) Los Angeles County
42	638	41.9	**Cherryland** (CDP) Alameda County
42	638	41.9	**Lemon Grove** (city) San Diego County
44	648	42.0	**Rosemont** (CDP) Sacramento County
45	658	42.1	**Chowchilla** (city) Madera County
45	658	42.1	**Muscoy** (CDP) San Bernardino County
47	666	42.2	**Signal Hill** (city) Los Angeles County
48	676	42.3	**Tehachapi** (city) Kern County
49	712	42.6	**Lynwood** (city) Los Angeles County
49	712	42.6	**Sacramento** (city) Sacramento County
51	727	42.7	**Cudahy** (city) Los Angeles County
51	727	42.7	**La Riviera** (CDP) Sacramento County
53	746	42.9	**Florence-Graham** (CDP) Los Angeles County
53	746	42.9	**Ukiah** (city) Mendocino County
55	777	43.2	**Ashland** (CDP) Alameda County
55	777	43.2	**Laguna Woods** (city) Orange County
57	788	43.3	**Coalinga** (city) Fresno County
57	788	43.3	**Huntington Park** (city) Los Angeles County
59	804	43.4	**Lawndale** (city) Los Angeles County
60	818	43.5	**Arden-Arcade** (CDP) Sacramento County
61	830	43.6	**Santa Barbara** (city) Santa Barbara County
62	848	43.7	**Maywood** (city) Los Angeles County
63	871	43.9	**Delano** (city) Kern County
64	883	44.0	**Bell Gardens** (city) Los Angeles County
65	896	44.1	**Bell** (city) Los Angeles County
65	896	44.1	**Marysville** (city) Yuba County
67	910	44.2	**San Pablo** (city) Contra Costa County
68	919	44.3	**Bay Point** (CDP) Contra Costa County
68	919	44.3	**Merced** (city) Merced County
70	956	44.6	**Costa Mesa** (city) Orange County
70	956	44.6	**La Mesa** (city) San Diego County
70	956	44.6	**Paramount** (city) Los Angeles County
70	956	44.6	**Richmond** (city) Contra Costa County
74	975	44.7	**Florin** (CDP) Sacramento County
74	975	44.7	**Fresno** (city) Fresno County
76	998	44.8	**San Fernando** (city) Los Angeles County
76	998	44.8	**Santa Fe Springs** (city) Los Angeles County
78	1006	44.9	**Live Oak** (CDP) Santa Cruz County
78	1006	44.9	**Pomona** (city) Los Angeles County
80	1019	45.0	**Commerce** (city) Los Angeles County
81	1031	45.1	**East Palo Alto** (city) San Mateo County
82	1043	45.2	**Pasadena** (city) Los Angeles County
82	1043	45.2	**San Diego** (city) San Diego County
84	1078	45.5	**Colton** (city) San Bernardino County
84	1078	45.5	**Madera** (city) Madera County
84	1078	45.5	**South Lake Tahoe** (city) El Dorado County
84	1078	45.5	**South San Jose Hills** (CDP) Los Angeles County
88	1099	45.6	**Adelanto** (city) San Bernardino County
88	1099	45.6	**El Cajon** (city) San Diego County
88	1099	45.6	**Marina** (city) Monterey County
91	1119	45.7	**Montebello** (city) Los Angeles County
91	1119	45.7	**Port Hueneme** (city) Ventura County
93	1137	45.8	**Linda** (CDP) Yuba County
94	1149	45.9	**Gardena** (city) Los Angeles County
94	1149	45.9	**Imperial Beach** (city) San Diego County
94	1149	45.9	**Pittsburg** (city) Contra Costa County
94	1149	45.9	**View Park-Windsor Hills** (CDP) Los Angeles County
98	1167	46.0	**Bellflower** (city) Los Angeles County
98	1167	46.0	**Vallejo** (city) Solano County
98	1167	46.0	**West Whittier-Los Nietos** (CDP) Los Angeles County
101	1179	46.1	**Desert Hot Springs** (city) Riverside County
101	1179	46.1	**Foothill Farms** (CDP) Sacramento County
101	1179	46.1	**Riverside** (city) Riverside County
104	1198	46.2	**North Highlands** (CDP) Sacramento County
105	1213	46.3	**South Gate** (city) Los Angeles County
106	1231	46.4	**Avenal** (city) Kings County
106	1231	46.4	**Cathedral City** (city) Riverside County
106	1231	46.4	**West Puente Valley** (CDP) Los Angeles County
109	1249	46.5	**Baldwin Park** (city) Los Angeles County
109	1249	46.5	**Barstow** (city) San Bernardino County
109	1249	46.5	**National City** (city) San Diego County
112	1264	46.6	**Hawaiian Gardens** (city) Los Angeles County
112	1264	46.6	**Pico Rivera** (city) Los Angeles County
112	1264	46.6	**Seaside** (city) Monterey County
112	1264	46.6	**Stockton** (city) San Joaquin County
116	1287	46.7	**Carson** (city) Los Angeles County
116	1287	46.7	**Santa Rosa** (city) Sonoma County
116	1287	46.7	**Sun Village** (CDP) Los Angeles County
116	1287	46.7	**Whittier** (city) Los Angeles County
116	1287	46.7	**Yucca Valley** (town) San Bernardino County
121	1307	46.8	**Goleta** (city) Santa Barbara County
121	1307	46.8	**Lennox** (CDP) Los Angeles County
121	1307	46.8	**Mead Valley** (CDP) Riverside County
121	1307	46.8	**Stanton** (city) Orange County
125	1327	46.9	**Norwalk** (city) Los Angeles County
126	1346	47.0	**Livingston** (city) Merced County
127	1371	47.2	**Bostonia** (CDP) San Diego County
127	1371	47.2	**Brawley** (city) Imperial County
127	1371	47.2	**Campbell** (city) Santa Clara County
127	1371	47.2	**Carmichael** (CDP) Sacramento County
127	1371	47.2	**Rancho Cordova** (city) Sacramento County
132	1389	47.3	**Citrus** (CDP) Los Angeles County
132	1389	47.3	**Loma Linda** (city) San Bernardino County
132	1389	47.3	**Ontario** (city) San Bernardino County
132	1389	47.3	**Rialto** (city) San Bernardino County
132	1389	47.3	**Victorville** (city) San Bernardino County
137	1404	47.4	**McKinleyville** (CDP) Humboldt County
138	1420	47.5	**Avocado Heights** (CDP) Los Angeles County
138	1420	47.5	**La Presa** (CDP) San Diego County
138	1420	47.5	**Lake Los Angeles** (CDP) Los Angeles County
138	1420	47.5	**Lakeland Village** (CDP) Riverside County
142	1437	47.6	**Downey** (city) Los Angeles County
142	1437	47.6	**Hemet** (city) Riverside County
142	1437	47.6	**Lancaster** (city) Los Angeles County
142	1437	47.6	**Montclair** (city) San Bernardino County
146	1458	47.7	**La Puente** (city) Los Angeles County
146	1458	47.7	**Santa Ana** (city) Orange County
148	1485	47.8	**Parlier** (city) Fresno County
149	1504	47.9	**Red Bluff** (city) Tehama County
150	1519	48.0	**Placerville** (city) El Dorado County

Note: *The state column ranks the top/bottom 150 places from all places in the state with population of 10,000 or more. The national column ranks the top/bottom 150 places from all places in the country with population of 10,000 or more. Places that are unincorporated were not considered in the rankings. Please refer to the User Guide for additional information.*

Marriage Status: Separated

Top 150 Places Ranked in *Descending* Order

State Rank	Nat'l Rank	Percent	Place
1	44	5.4	**Grass Valley** (city) Nevada County
2	47	5.3	**Calexico** (city) Imperial County
2	47	5.3	**Willowbrook** (CDP) Los Angeles County
4	75	5.0	**Avenal** (city) Kings County
4	75	5.0	**Walnut Park** (CDP) Los Angeles County
6	112	4.7	**South San Jose Hills** (CDP) Los Angeles County
7	126	4.6	**Bloomington** (CDP) San Bernardino County
7	126	4.6	**Corcoran** (city) Kings County
7	126	4.6	**Garden Acres** (CDP) San Joaquin County
7	126	4.6	**Muscoy** (CDP) San Bernardino County
7	126	4.6	**Parkway** (CDP) Sacramento County
12	149	4.5	**Kingsburg** (city) Fresno County
12	149	4.5	**Lemon Hill** (CDP) Sacramento County
14	165	4.4	**Chowchilla** (city) Madera County
14	165	4.4	**Huntington Park** (city) Los Angeles County
14	165	4.4	**Lake Los Angeles** (CDP) Los Angeles County
14	165	4.4	**Red Bluff** (city) Tehama County
18	185	4.3	**Eureka** (city) Humboldt County
18	185	4.3	**Grover Beach** (city) San Luis Obispo County
18	185	4.3	**Hawaiian Gardens** (city) Los Angeles County
18	185	4.3	**South El Monte** (city) Los Angeles County
22	212	4.2	**Bay Point** (CDP) Contra Costa County
22	212	4.2	**Cudahy** (city) Los Angeles County
22	212	4.2	**Morro Bay** (city) San Luis Obispo County
25	236	4.1	**Inglewood** (city) Los Angeles County
26	267	4.0	**Linda** (CDP) Yuba County
27	305	3.9	**Florence-Graham** (CDP) Los Angeles County
27	305	3.9	**Montclair** (city) San Bernardino County
27	305	3.9	**Oroville** (city) Butte County
27	305	3.9	**San Bernardino** (city) San Bernardino County
31	342	3.8	**Florin** (CDP) Sacramento County
31	342	3.8	**Gardena** (city) Los Angeles County
31	342	3.8	**McFarland** (city) Kern County
31	342	3.8	**Oildale** (CDP) Kern County
31	342	3.8	**Richmond** (city) Contra Costa County
31	342	3.8	**Westmont** (CDP) Los Angeles County
31	342	3.8	**Winton** (CDP) Merced County
38	387	3.7	**Bell Gardens** (city) Los Angeles County
38	387	3.7	**Colton** (city) San Bernardino County
38	387	3.7	**Dinuba** (city) Tulare County
38	387	3.7	**Lennox** (CDP) Los Angeles County
38	387	3.7	**South Gate** (city) Los Angeles County
38	387	3.7	**Victorville** (city) San Bernardino County
44	438	3.6	**El Centro** (city) Imperial County
44	438	3.6	**El Paso de Robles (Paso Robles)** (city) San Luis Obispo County
44	438	3.6	**Imperial Beach** (city) San Diego County
44	438	3.6	**La Puente** (city) Los Angeles County
44	438	3.6	**Lompoc** (city) Santa Barbara County
44	438	3.6	**Montebello** (city) Los Angeles County
44	438	3.6	**Moreno Valley** (city) Riverside County
44	438	3.6	**Selma** (city) Fresno County
44	438	3.6	**Shafter** (city) Kern County
53	487	3.5	**Big Bear City** (CDP) San Bernardino County
53	487	3.5	**Santa Ana** (city) Orange County
53	487	3.5	**Soledad** (city) Monterey County
53	487	3.5	**Tehachapi** (city) Kern County
53	487	3.5	**Twentynine Palms** (city) San Bernardino County
58	554	3.4	**Anaheim** (city) Orange County
58	554	3.4	**Bellflower** (city) Los Angeles County
58	554	3.4	**Hawthorne** (city) Los Angeles County
58	554	3.4	**Ontario** (city) San Bernardino County
58	554	3.4	**Placerville** (city) El Dorado County
58	554	3.4	**Wasco** (city) Kern County
64	615	3.3	**Bell** (city) Los Angeles County
64	615	3.3	**East Los Angeles** (CDP) Los Angeles County
64	615	3.3	**East Rancho Dominguez** (CDP) Los Angeles County
64	615	3.3	**Lynwood** (city) Los Angeles County
64	615	3.3	**Maywood** (city) Los Angeles County
64	615	3.3	**Newman** (city) Stanislaus County
64	615	3.3	**Parlier** (city) Fresno County
64	615	3.3	**Phelan** (CDP) San Bernardino County
64	615	3.3	**Rialto** (city) San Bernardino County
64	615	3.3	**San Anselmo** (town) Marin County
74	686	3.2	**Coalinga** (city) Fresno County
74	686	3.2	**Indio** (city) Riverside County
74	686	3.2	**Long Beach** (city) Los Angeles County
74	686	3.2	**Los Banos** (city) Merced County
74	686	3.2	**Olivehurst** (CDP) Yuba County
74	686	3.2	**Perris** (city) Riverside County
74	686	3.2	**Sanger** (city) Fresno County
81	747	3.1	**Adelanto** (city) San Bernardino County
81	747	3.1	**Artesia** (city) Los Angeles County
81	747	3.1	**Bakersfield** (city) Kern County
81	747	3.1	**Blythe** (city) Riverside County
81	747	3.1	**Coachella** (city) Riverside County
81	747	3.1	**Hanford** (city) Kings County
81	747	3.1	**Hemet** (city) Riverside County
81	747	3.1	**National City** (city) San Diego County
81	747	3.1	**Pico Rivera** (city) Los Angeles County
81	747	3.1	**Pomona** (city) Los Angeles County
81	747	3.1	**Shasta Lake** (city) Shasta County
81	747	3.1	**Ukiah** (city) Mendocino County
93	815	3.0	**Carpinteria** (city) Santa Barbara County
93	815	3.0	**Cherryland** (CDP) Alameda County
93	815	3.0	**Citrus Heights** (city) Sacramento County
93	815	3.0	**Compton** (city) Los Angeles County
93	815	3.0	**Desert Hot Springs** (city) Riverside County
93	815	3.0	**El Monte** (city) Los Angeles County
93	815	3.0	**El Sobrante** (CDP) Contra Costa County
93	815	3.0	**Foothill Farms** (CDP) Sacramento County
93	815	3.0	**Fresno** (city) Fresno County
93	815	3.0	**Lancaster** (city) Los Angeles County
93	815	3.0	**North Auburn** (CDP) Placer County
93	815	3.0	**North Fair Oaks** (CDP) San Mateo County
93	815	3.0	**Susanville** (city) Lassen County
93	815	3.0	**Valle Vista** (CDP) Riverside County
107	906	2.9	**Baldwin Park** (city) Los Angeles County
107	906	2.9	**Banning** (city) Riverside County
107	906	2.9	**Delano** (city) Kern County
107	906	2.9	**East Palo Alto** (city) San Mateo County
107	906	2.9	**Hercules** (city) Contra Costa County
107	906	2.9	**Lamont** (CDP) Kern County
107	906	2.9	**Los Angeles** (city) Los Angeles County
107	906	2.9	**Oakland** (city) Alameda County
107	906	2.9	**Ridgecrest** (city) Kern County
107	906	2.9	**Spring Valley** (CDP) San Diego County
107	906	2.9	**Stanton** (city) Orange County
118	1005	2.8	**Antelope** (CDP) Sacramento County
118	1005	2.8	**Covina** (city) Los Angeles County
118	1005	2.8	**Dixon** (city) Solano County
118	1005	2.8	**Farmersville** (city) Tulare County
118	1005	2.8	**Gilroy** (city) Santa Clara County
118	1005	2.8	**Hayward** (city) Alameda County
118	1005	2.8	**Highland** (city) San Bernardino County
118	1005	2.8	**Lake Elsinore** (city) Riverside County
118	1005	2.8	**Merced** (city) Merced County
118	1005	2.8	**Norwalk** (city) Los Angeles County
118	1005	2.8	**Palmdale** (city) Los Angeles County
118	1005	2.8	**Patterson** (city) Stanislaus County
118	1005	2.8	**Pinole** (city) Contra Costa County
118	1005	2.8	**Rio Linda** (CDP) Sacramento County
118	1005	2.8	**Santa Maria** (city) Santa Barbara County
118	1005	2.8	**Vallejo** (city) Solano County
118	1005	2.8	**West Puente Valley** (CDP) Los Angeles County
135	1100	2.7	**Barstow** (city) San Bernardino County
135	1100	2.7	**Chino** (city) San Bernardino County
135	1100	2.7	**Lemon Grove** (city) San Diego County
135	1100	2.7	**Malibu** (city) Los Angeles County
135	1100	2.7	**Manteca** (city) San Joaquin County
135	1100	2.7	**Norco** (city) Riverside County
135	1100	2.7	**Oxnard** (city) Ventura County
135	1100	2.7	**Paramount** (city) Los Angeles County
135	1100	2.7	**Rancho Cordova** (city) Sacramento County
135	1100	2.7	**Sacramento** (city) Sacramento County
135	1100	2.7	**South Whittier** (CDP) Los Angeles County
135	1100	2.7	**Stockton** (city) San Joaquin County
135	1100	2.7	**Sun Village** (CDP) Los Angeles County
135	1100	2.7	**Tustin** (city) Orange County
149	1195	2.6	**Arvin** (city) Kern County
149	1195	2.6	**Avocado Heights** (CDP) Los Angeles County

Note: *The state column ranks the top/bottom 150 places from all places in the state with population of 10,000 or more. The national column ranks the top/bottom 150 places from all places in the country with population of 10,000 or more. Places that are unincorporated were not considered in the rankings. Please refer to the User Guide for additional information.*

Marriage Status: Separated

Top 150 Places Ranked in *Ascending* Order

State Rank	Nat'l Rank	Percent	Place
1	6	0.1	**Camp Pendleton South** (CDP) San Diego County
2	50	0.3	**Alamo** (CDP) Contra Costa County
3	80	0.4	**Belmont** (city) San Mateo County
3	80	0.4	**Hillsborough** (town) San Mateo County
3	80	0.4	**Oak Park** (CDP) Ventura County
3	80	0.4	**Stanford** (CDP) Santa Clara County
7	133	0.5	**Granite Bay** (CDP) Placer County
7	133	0.5	**Isla Vista** (CDP) Santa Barbara County
7	133	0.5	**Orinda** (city) Contra Costa County
7	133	0.5	**Rossmoor** (CDP) Orange County
11	212	0.6	**Cupertino** (city) Santa Clara County
11	212	0.6	**Hermosa Beach** (city) Los Angeles County
11	212	0.6	**North Tustin** (CDP) Orange County
11	212	0.6	**Palos Verdes Estates** (city) Los Angeles County
11	212	0.6	**San Diego Country Estates** (CDP) San Diego County
11	212	0.6	**Scotts Valley** (city) Santa Cruz County
17	344	0.7	**Encinitas** (city) San Diego County
17	344	0.7	**La Cañada Flintridge** (city) Los Angeles County
17	344	0.7	**San Marino** (city) Los Angeles County
20	467	0.8	**Auburn** (city) Placer County
20	467	0.8	**Clayton** (city) Contra Costa County
20	467	0.8	**Fillmore** (city) Ventura County
20	467	0.8	**Laguna Woods** (city) Orange County
20	467	0.8	**Riverbank** (city) Stanislaus County
20	467	0.8	**Walnut** (city) Los Angeles County
20	467	0.8	**Yorba Linda** (city) Orange County
27	620	0.9	**Citrus** (CDP) Los Angeles County
27	620	0.9	**Los Altos** (city) Santa Clara County
27	620	0.9	**Manhattan Beach** (city) Los Angeles County
27	620	0.9	**Moraga** (town) Contra Costa County
27	620	0.9	**Saratoga** (city) Santa Clara County
32	763	1.0	**Agoura Hills** (city) Los Angeles County
32	763	1.0	**Discovery Bay** (CDP) Contra Costa County
32	763	1.0	**El Dorado Hills** (CDP) El Dorado County
32	763	1.0	**El Sobrante** (CDP) Riverside County
32	763	1.0	**Irvine** (city) Orange County
32	763	1.0	**Mission Viejo** (city) Orange County
32	763	1.0	**Rancho Mirage** (city) Riverside County
32	763	1.0	**Sierra Madre** (city) Los Angeles County
32	763	1.0	**Sunnyvale** (city) Santa Clara County
32	763	1.0	**Walnut Creek** (city) Contra Costa County
42	923	1.1	**Cameron Park** (CDP) El Dorado County
42	923	1.1	**Coto de Caza** (CDP) Orange County
42	923	1.1	**Danville** (town) Contra Costa County
42	923	1.1	**Davis** (city) Yolo County
42	923	1.1	**El Cerrito** (city) Contra Costa County
42	923	1.1	**El Segundo** (city) Los Angeles County
42	923	1.1	**Lafayette** (city) Contra Costa County
42	923	1.1	**Mill Valley** (city) Marin County
42	923	1.1	**Orcutt** (CDP) Santa Barbara County
42	923	1.1	**San Marcos** (city) San Diego County
52	1096	1.2	**Carlsbad** (city) San Diego County
52	1096	1.2	**Cerritos** (city) Los Angeles County
52	1096	1.2	**Cypress** (city) Orange County
52	1096	1.2	**Diamond Bar** (city) Los Angeles County
52	1096	1.2	**Fountain Valley** (city) Orange County
52	1096	1.2	**Rancho Palos Verdes** (city) Los Angeles County
52	1096	1.2	**Tamalpais-Homestead Valley** (CDP) Marin County
52	1096	1.2	**Temple City** (city) Los Angeles County
60	1281	1.3	**Berkeley** (city) Alameda County
60	1281	1.3	**Camarillo** (city) Ventura County
60	1281	1.3	**East San Gabriel** (CDP) Los Angeles County
60	1281	1.3	**Foster City** (city) San Mateo County
60	1281	1.3	**La Mesa** (city) San Diego County
60	1281	1.3	**La Palma** (city) Orange County
60	1281	1.3	**McKinleyville** (CDP) Humboldt County
60	1281	1.3	**Millbrae** (city) San Mateo County
60	1281	1.3	**Poway** (city) San Diego County
60	1281	1.3	**Salida** (CDP) Stanislaus County
60	1281	1.3	**San Gabriel** (city) Los Angeles County
60	1281	1.3	**Simi Valley** (city) Ventura County
60	1281	1.3	**Thousand Oaks** (city) Ventura County
60	1281	1.3	**Union City** (city) Alameda County
60	1281	1.3	**Vineyard** (CDP) Sacramento County
60	1281	1.3	**Woodcrest** (CDP) Riverside County
76	1490	1.4	**Beaumont** (city) Riverside County
76	1490	1.4	**Castro Valley** (CDP) Alameda County
76	1490	1.4	**La Quinta** (city) Riverside County
76	1490	1.4	**Laguna Hills** (city) Orange County
76	1490	1.4	**Laguna Niguel** (city) Orange County
76	1490	1.4	**Lake Forest** (city) Orange County
76	1490	1.4	**Los Gatos** (town) Santa Clara County
76	1490	1.4	**Los Osos** (CDP) San Luis Obispo County
76	1490	1.4	**Menlo Park** (city) San Mateo County
76	1490	1.4	**Novato** (city) Marin County
76	1490	1.4	**Pacific Grove** (city) Monterey County
76	1490	1.4	**Pacifica** (city) San Mateo County
76	1490	1.4	**Palo Alto** (city) Santa Clara County
76	1490	1.4	**Piedmont** (city) Alameda County
76	1490	1.4	**Rancho Santa Margarita** (city) Orange County
76	1490	1.4	**Rowland Heights** (CDP) Los Angeles County
76	1490	1.4	**San Carlos** (city) San Mateo County
76	1490	1.4	**San Luis Obispo** (city) San Luis Obispo County
76	1490	1.4	**San Ramon** (city) Contra Costa County
76	1490	1.4	**Seal Beach** (city) Orange County
76	1490	1.4	**Vista** (city) San Diego County
76	1490	1.4	**West Hollywood** (city) Los Angeles County
76	1490	1.4	**Windsor** (town) Sonoma County
99	1674	1.5	**Altadena** (CDP) Los Angeles County
99	1674	1.5	**Bostonia** (CDP) San Diego County
99	1674	1.5	**Delhi** (CDP) Merced County
99	1674	1.5	**Fair Oaks** (CDP) Sacramento County
99	1674	1.5	**French Valley** (CDP) Riverside County
99	1674	1.5	**Kerman** (city) Fresno County
99	1674	1.5	**La Mirada** (city) Los Angeles County
99	1674	1.5	**Mountain View** (city) Santa Clara County
99	1674	1.5	**Newport Beach** (city) Orange County
99	1674	1.5	**Rosedale** (CDP) Kern County
99	1674	1.5	**San Francisco** (city) San Francisco County
99	1674	1.5	**Santee** (city) San Diego County
99	1674	1.5	**Signal Hill** (city) Los Angeles County
112	1866	1.6	**Arroyo Grande** (city) San Luis Obispo County
112	1866	1.6	**Bonita** (CDP) San Diego County
112	1866	1.6	**Crestline** (CDP) San Bernardino County
112	1866	1.6	**Dana Point** (city) Orange County
112	1866	1.6	**Eastvale** (city) Riverside County
112	1866	1.6	**Folsom** (city) Sacramento County
112	1866	1.6	**Fremont** (city) Alameda County
112	1866	1.6	**Home Gardens** (CDP) Riverside County
112	1866	1.6	**Moorpark** (city) Ventura County
112	1866	1.6	**Oakley** (city) Contra Costa County
112	1866	1.6	**Paradise** (town) Butte County
112	1866	1.6	**Pleasant Hill** (city) Contra Costa County
112	1866	1.6	**Pleasanton** (city) Alameda County
112	1866	1.6	**Redlands** (city) San Bernardino County
112	1866	1.6	**Santa Clara** (city) Santa Clara County
112	1866	1.6	**Santa Cruz** (city) Santa Cruz County
112	1866	1.6	**Solana Beach** (city) San Diego County
112	1866	1.6	**Sonoma** (city) Sonoma County
112	1866	1.6	**Winter Gardens** (CDP) San Diego County
112	1866	1.6	**Yucca Valley** (town) San Bernardino County
132	2054	1.7	**Alum Rock** (CDP) Santa Clara County
132	2054	1.7	**American Canyon** (city) Napa County
132	2054	1.7	**Benicia** (city) Solano County
132	2054	1.7	**Brentwood** (city) Contra Costa County
132	2054	1.7	**Campbell** (city) Santa Clara County
132	2054	1.7	**Chino Hills** (city) San Bernardino County
132	2054	1.7	**Claremont** (city) Los Angeles County
132	2054	1.7	**Glendora** (city) Los Angeles County
132	2054	1.7	**Huntington Beach** (city) Orange County
132	2054	1.7	**Ladera Ranch** (CDP) Orange County
132	2054	1.7	**Lakewood** (city) Los Angeles County
132	2054	1.7	**Monterey** (city) Monterey County
132	2054	1.7	**Morgan Hill** (city) Santa Clara County
132	2054	1.7	**Ramona** (CDP) San Diego County
132	2054	1.7	**Redwood City** (city) San Mateo County
132	2054	1.7	**Reedley** (city) Fresno County
132	2054	1.7	**San Leandro** (city) Alameda County
132	2054	1.7	**San Lorenzo** (CDP) Alameda County
132	2054	1.7	**Temecula** (city) Riverside County

Note: *The state column ranks the top/bottom 150 places from all places in the state with population of 10,000 or more. The national column ranks the top/bottom 150 places from all places in the country with population of 10,000 or more. Places that are unincorporated were not considered in the rankings. Please refer to the User Guide for additional information.*

Marriage Status: Widowed

Top 150 Places Ranked in *Descending* Order

State Rank	Nat'l Rank	Percent	Place
1	2	27.7	**Laguna Woods** (city) Orange County
2	20	14.4	**Seal Beach** (city) Orange County
3	34	12.7	**Grass Valley** (city) Nevada County
4	113	10.6	**Yucca Valley** (town) San Bernardino County
5	122	10.5	**Hemet** (city) Riverside County
6	144	10.3	**Diamond Springs** (CDP) El Dorado County
6	144	10.3	**Rancho Mirage** (city) Riverside County
8	160	10.2	**Duarte** (city) Los Angeles County
8	160	10.2	**Paradise** (town) Butte County
8	160	10.2	**Walnut Creek** (city) Contra Costa County
11	179	10.1	**Palm Desert** (city) Riverside County
12	197	10.0	**Banning** (city) Riverside County
13	217	9.9	**Sonoma** (city) Sonoma County
14	348	9.3	**Magalia** (CDP) Butte County
15	403	9.1	**Millbrae** (city) San Mateo County
16	452	8.9	**North Auburn** (CDP) Placer County
17	602	8.5	**West Carson** (CDP) Los Angeles County
18	648	8.4	**Carmichael** (CDP) Sacramento County
18	648	8.4	**Clearlake** (city) Lake County
20	696	8.3	**Arroyo Grande** (city) San Luis Obispo County
20	696	8.3	**Palm Springs** (city) Riverside County
22	786	8.1	**Auburn** (city) Placer County
22	786	8.1	**Morro Bay** (city) San Luis Obispo County
24	833	8.0	**Santa Fe Springs** (city) Los Angeles County
25	881	7.9	**Los Osos** (CDP) San Luis Obispo County
25	881	7.9	**Orcutt** (CDP) Santa Barbara County
25	881	7.9	**Placerville** (city) El Dorado County
28	942	7.8	**Shasta Lake** (city) Shasta County
29	986	7.7	**Fortuna** (city) Humboldt County
29	986	7.7	**Monterey Park** (city) Los Angeles County
31	1110	7.5	**Rancho Palos Verdes** (city) Los Angeles County
31	1110	7.5	**Temple City** (city) Los Angeles County
33	1177	7.4	**View Park-Windsor Hills** (CDP) Los Angeles County
34	1250	7.3	**Healdsburg** (city) Sonoma County
34	1250	7.3	**La Verne** (city) Los Angeles County
34	1250	7.3	**Larkspur** (city) Marin County
34	1250	7.3	**Menifee** (city) Riverside County
38	1323	7.2	**Pleasant Hill** (city) Contra Costa County
38	1323	7.2	**Rossmoor** (CDP) Orange County
40	1398	7.1	**Arden-Arcade** (CDP) Sacramento County
40	1398	7.1	**Lodi** (city) San Joaquin County
40	1398	7.1	**Loma Linda** (city) San Bernardino County
40	1398	7.1	**Pinole** (city) Contra Costa County
40	1398	7.1	**Ridgecrest** (city) Kern County
40	1398	7.1	**San Lorenzo** (CDP) Alameda County
46	1478	7.0	**Alpine** (CDP) San Diego County
46	1478	7.0	**Apple Valley** (town) San Bernardino County
46	1478	7.0	**Camarillo** (city) Ventura County
46	1478	7.0	**Canyon Lake** (city) Riverside County
50	1553	6.9	**El Cerrito** (city) Contra Costa County
50	1553	6.9	**Los Altos** (city) Santa Clara County
50	1553	6.9	**Marysville** (city) Yuba County
50	1553	6.9	**Redding** (city) Shasta County
54	1628	6.8	**Montebello** (city) Los Angeles County
55	1706	6.7	**Gardena** (city) Los Angeles County
55	1706	6.7	**Glendale** (city) Los Angeles County
55	1706	6.7	**La Mesa** (city) San Diego County
58	1779	6.6	**Kerman** (city) Fresno County
58	1779	6.6	**Lemon Hill** (CDP) Sacramento County
58	1779	6.6	**Sanger** (city) Fresno County
58	1779	6.6	**Saratoga** (city) Santa Clara County
58	1779	6.6	**Vallejo** (city) Solano County
63	1858	6.5	**Barstow** (city) San Bernardino County
63	1858	6.5	**Casa de Oro-Mount Helix** (CDP) San Diego County
63	1858	6.5	**Cerritos** (city) Los Angeles County
63	1858	6.5	**Lake Arrowhead** (CDP) San Bernardino County
67	1936	6.4	**Arcadia** (city) Los Angeles County
67	1936	6.4	**Beverly Hills** (city) Los Angeles County
67	1936	6.4	**Calexico** (city) Imperial County
67	1936	6.4	**Oroville** (city) Butte County
67	1936	6.4	**Pacific Grove** (city) Monterey County
67	1936	6.4	**Red Bluff** (city) Tehama County
67	1936	6.4	**Ukiah** (city) Mendocino County
67	1936	6.4	**Valle Vista** (CDP) Riverside County
67	1936	6.4	**West Whittier-Los Nietos** (CDP) Los Angeles County
76	2038	6.3	**Carson** (city) Los Angeles County
76	2038	6.3	**El Paso de Robles (Paso Robles)** (city) San Luis Obispo County
76	2038	6.3	**Glendora** (city) Los Angeles County
76	2038	6.3	**North Highlands** (CDP) Sacramento County
76	2038	6.3	**Torrance** (city) Los Angeles County
81	2119	6.2	**Burbank** (city) Los Angeles County
81	2119	6.2	**Cameron Park** (CDP) El Dorado County
81	2119	6.2	**El Cajon** (city) San Diego County
81	2119	6.2	**Goleta** (city) Santa Barbara County
81	2119	6.2	**Hacienda Heights** (CDP) Los Angeles County
81	2119	6.2	**Monterey** (city) Monterey County
81	2119	6.2	**Rosemont** (CDP) Sacramento County
81	2119	6.2	**South San Francisco** (city) San Mateo County
89	2198	6.1	**Alhambra** (city) Los Angeles County
89	2198	6.1	**Castro Valley** (CDP) Alameda County
89	2198	6.1	**Desert Hot Springs** (city) Riverside County
89	2198	6.1	**Exeter** (city) Tulare County
89	2198	6.1	**Fair Oaks** (CDP) Sacramento County
89	2198	6.1	**Live Oak** (CDP) Santa Cruz County
89	2198	6.1	**North Tustin** (CDP) Orange County
89	2198	6.1	**Pasadena** (city) Los Angeles County
89	2198	6.1	**San Bruno** (city) San Mateo County
89	2198	6.1	**San Juan Capistrano** (city) Orange County
89	2198	6.1	**West Puente Valley** (CDP) Los Angeles County
89	2198	6.1	**Westminster** (city) Orange County
101	2296	6.0	**Bonita** (CDP) San Diego County
101	2296	6.0	**Brawley** (city) Imperial County
101	2296	6.0	**Mission Viejo** (city) Orange County
101	2296	6.0	**National City** (city) San Diego County
101	2296	6.0	**Placentia** (city) Orange County
101	2296	6.0	**Port Hueneme** (city) Ventura County
101	2296	6.0	**Quartz Hill** (CDP) Los Angeles County
101	2296	6.0	**San Diego Country Estates** (CDP) San Diego County
101	2296	6.0	**San Leandro** (city) Alameda County
110	2383	5.9	**Ashland** (CDP) Alameda County
110	2383	5.9	**Big Bear City** (CDP) San Bernardino County
110	2383	5.9	**Citrus** (CDP) Los Angeles County
110	2383	5.9	**Coronado** (city) San Diego County
110	2383	5.9	**Culver City** (city) Los Angeles County
110	2383	5.9	**Del Aire** (CDP) Los Angeles County
110	2383	5.9	**Emeryville** (city) Alameda County
110	2383	5.9	**Florin** (CDP) Sacramento County
110	2383	5.9	**Foster City** (city) San Mateo County
110	2383	5.9	**Grover Beach** (city) San Luis Obispo County
110	2383	5.9	**Kingsburg** (city) Fresno County
110	2383	5.9	**Lincoln** (city) Placer County
110	2383	5.9	**Malibu** (city) Los Angeles County
110	2383	5.9	**Moraga** (town) Contra Costa County
110	2383	5.9	**Parkway** (CDP) Sacramento County
110	2383	5.9	**Porterville** (city) Tulare County
110	2383	5.9	**Rosemead** (city) Los Angeles County
110	2383	5.9	**San Dimas** (city) Los Angeles County
110	2383	5.9	**Santa Paula** (city) Ventura County
110	2383	5.9	**Sun Village** (CDP) Los Angeles County
110	2383	5.9	**West Covina** (city) Los Angeles County
110	2383	5.9	**Windsor** (town) Sonoma County
132	2479	5.8	**Belmont** (city) San Mateo County
132	2479	5.8	**Carpinteria** (city) Santa Barbara County
132	2479	5.8	**Garden Grove** (city) Orange County
132	2479	5.8	**Grand Terrace** (city) San Bernardino County
132	2479	5.8	**Lafayette** (city) Contra Costa County
132	2479	5.8	**Lakewood** (city) Los Angeles County
132	2479	5.8	**Los Alamitos** (city) Orange County
132	2479	5.8	**Rio Linda** (CDP) Sacramento County
132	2479	5.8	**San Gabriel** (city) Los Angeles County
132	2479	5.8	**Turlock** (city) Stanislaus County
132	2479	5.8	**Yuba City** (city) Sutter County
143	2574	5.7	**Buena Park** (city) Orange County
143	2574	5.7	**Chowchilla** (city) Madera County
143	2574	5.7	**Commerce** (city) Los Angeles County
143	2574	5.7	**Fallbrook** (CDP) San Diego County
143	2574	5.7	**Fountain Valley** (city) Orange County
143	2574	5.7	**Newport Beach** (city) Orange County
143	2574	5.7	**Norwalk** (city) Los Angeles County
143	2574	5.7	**Novato** (city) Marin County

Note: *The state column ranks the top/bottom 150 places from all places in the state with population of 10,000 or more. The national column ranks the top/bottom 150 places from all places in the country with population of 10,000 or more. Places that are unincorporated were not considered in the rankings. Please refer to the User Guide for additional information.*

Marriage Status: Widowed

Top 150 Places Ranked in *Ascending* Order

State Rank	Nat'l Rank	Percent	Place
1	4	0.1	**Camp Pendleton South** (CDP) San Diego County
2	11	0.9	**Isla Vista** (CDP) Santa Barbara County
3	13	1.0	**El Sobrante** (CDP) Riverside County
4	16	1.1	**Stanford** (CDP) Santa Clara County
5	28	1.6	**Coto de Caza** (CDP) Orange County
6	67	2.1	**Greenfield** (city) Monterey County
7	82	2.3	**Cudahy** (city) Los Angeles County
7	82	2.3	**Newman** (city) Stanislaus County
9	92	2.4	**Ladera Ranch** (CDP) Orange County
9	92	2.4	**Lake Los Angeles** (CDP) Los Angeles County
9	92	2.4	**Maywood** (city) Los Angeles County
9	92	2.4	**Parlier** (city) Fresno County
9	92	2.4	**Twentynine Palms** (city) San Bernardino County
14	117	2.5	**Davis** (city) Yolo County
15	138	2.6	**Albany** (city) Alameda County
15	138	2.6	**Eastvale** (city) Riverside County
17	156	2.7	**Rancho Santa Margarita** (city) Orange County
17	156	2.7	**Winton** (CDP) Merced County
19	187	2.8	**Woodcrest** (CDP) Riverside County
20	220	2.9	**Castaic** (CDP) Los Angeles County
20	220	2.9	**Lake Elsinore** (city) Riverside County
20	220	2.9	**Lennox** (CDP) Los Angeles County
23	246	3.0	**Irvine** (city) Orange County
23	246	3.0	**Santa Cruz** (city) Santa Cruz County
23	246	3.0	**Shafter** (city) Kern County
26	281	3.1	**Agoura Hills** (city) Los Angeles County
26	281	3.1	**Aliso Viejo** (city) Orange County
26	281	3.1	**Mendota** (city) Fresno County
26	281	3.1	**Truckee** (town) Nevada County
30	307	3.2	**Arvin** (city) Kern County
30	307	3.2	**Coachella** (city) Riverside County
30	307	3.2	**Dinuba** (city) Tulare County
30	307	3.2	**El Dorado Hills** (CDP) El Dorado County
30	307	3.2	**Hermosa Beach** (city) Los Angeles County
30	307	3.2	**Reedley** (city) Fresno County
30	307	3.2	**Signal Hill** (city) Los Angeles County
30	307	3.2	**Stevenson Ranch** (CDP) Los Angeles County
38	347	3.3	**Alamo** (CDP) Contra Costa County
38	347	3.3	**French Valley** (CDP) Riverside County
38	347	3.3	**Rosedale** (CDP) Kern County
38	347	3.3	**Salida** (CDP) Stanislaus County
42	382	3.4	**Adelanto** (city) San Bernardino County
42	382	3.4	**Berkeley** (city) Alameda County
42	382	3.4	**Bloomington** (CDP) San Bernardino County
42	382	3.4	**Dublin** (city) Alameda County
42	382	3.4	**Garden Acres** (CDP) San Joaquin County
42	382	3.4	**North Fair Oaks** (CDP) San Mateo County
42	382	3.4	**Patterson** (city) Stanislaus County
42	382	3.4	**San Ramon** (city) Contra Costa County
42	382	3.4	**Temecula** (city) Riverside County
42	382	3.4	**Tustin** (city) Orange County
52	424	3.5	**Blythe** (city) Riverside County
52	424	3.5	**Florence-Graham** (CDP) Los Angeles County
52	424	3.5	**Fontana** (city) San Bernardino County
52	424	3.5	**Moorpark** (city) Ventura County
52	424	3.5	**Oak Park** (CDP) Ventura County
52	424	3.5	**Piedmont** (city) Alameda County
52	424	3.5	**South Pasadena** (city) Los Angeles County
52	424	3.5	**Tamalpais-Homestead Valley** (CDP) Marin County
60	478	3.6	**Bell Gardens** (city) Los Angeles County
60	478	3.6	**Palmdale** (city) Los Angeles County
60	478	3.6	**Wasco** (city) Kern County
63	519	3.7	**Antelope** (CDP) Sacramento County
63	519	3.7	**Coalinga** (city) Fresno County
63	519	3.7	**Colton** (city) San Bernardino County
63	519	3.7	**East Palo Alto** (city) San Mateo County
63	519	3.7	**Hillsborough** (town) San Mateo County
63	519	3.7	**Riverbank** (city) Stanislaus County
63	519	3.7	**Salinas** (city) Monterey County
63	519	3.7	**South Gate** (city) Los Angeles County
71	571	3.8	**Arcata** (city) Humboldt County
71	571	3.8	**Delhi** (CDP) Merced County
71	571	3.8	**Encinitas** (city) San Diego County
71	571	3.8	**Highland** (city) San Bernardino County
71	571	3.8	**La Cañada Flintridge** (city) Los Angeles County
71	571	3.8	**Lake Forest** (city) Orange County
71	571	3.8	**Moreno Valley** (city) Riverside County
71	571	3.8	**Paramount** (city) Los Angeles County
71	571	3.8	**Walnut Park** (CDP) Los Angeles County
80	629	3.9	**Avenal** (city) Kings County
80	629	3.9	**Chino Hills** (city) San Bernardino County
80	629	3.9	**Corcoran** (city) Kings County
80	629	3.9	**El Segundo** (city) Los Angeles County
80	629	3.9	**Home Gardens** (CDP) Riverside County
80	629	3.9	**Perris** (city) Riverside County
80	629	3.9	**Ramona** (CDP) San Diego County
80	629	3.9	**Santa Clara** (city) Santa Clara County
80	629	3.9	**Suisun City** (city) Solano County
89	676	4.0	**Dixon** (city) Solano County
89	676	4.0	**East Rancho Dominguez** (CDP) Los Angeles County
89	676	4.0	**Folsom** (city) Sacramento County
89	676	4.0	**Half Moon Bay** (city) San Mateo County
89	676	4.0	**Laguna Beach** (city) Orange County
89	676	4.0	**Lamont** (CDP) Kern County
89	676	4.0	**Lynwood** (city) Los Angeles County
89	676	4.0	**Manhattan Beach** (city) Los Angeles County
89	676	4.0	**Morgan Hill** (city) Santa Clara County
98	718	4.1	**Azusa** (city) Los Angeles County
98	718	4.1	**Brentwood** (city) Contra Costa County
98	718	4.1	**California City** (city) Kern County
98	718	4.1	**Corona** (city) Riverside County
98	718	4.1	**Costa Mesa** (city) Orange County
98	718	4.1	**Gilroy** (city) Santa Clara County
98	718	4.1	**Hawthorne** (city) Los Angeles County
98	718	4.1	**Hollister** (city) San Benito County
98	718	4.1	**Huntington Park** (city) Los Angeles County
98	718	4.1	**Lompoc** (city) Santa Barbara County
98	718	4.1	**Los Banos** (city) Merced County
98	718	4.1	**McFarland** (city) Kern County
98	718	4.1	**Mountain View** (city) Santa Clara County
98	718	4.1	**Rancho Cucamonga** (city) San Bernardino County
98	718	4.1	**Santa Ana** (city) Orange County
98	718	4.1	**Watsonville** (city) Santa Cruz County
98	718	4.1	**Wildomar** (city) Riverside County
115	768	4.2	**La Crescenta-Montrose** (CDP) Los Angeles County
115	768	4.2	**La Quinta** (city) Riverside County
115	768	4.2	**Livermore** (city) Alameda County
115	768	4.2	**Madera** (city) Madera County
115	768	4.2	**Ontario** (city) San Bernardino County
115	768	4.2	**Pleasanton** (city) Alameda County
115	768	4.2	**Prunedale** (CDP) Monterey County
115	768	4.2	**Redondo Beach** (city) Los Angeles County
115	768	4.2	**San Fernando** (city) Los Angeles County
115	768	4.2	**Sunnyvale** (city) Santa Clara County
115	768	4.2	**Tracy** (city) San Joaquin County
126	840	4.3	**Benicia** (city) Solano County
126	840	4.3	**Calabasas** (city) Los Angeles County
126	840	4.3	**Chino** (city) San Bernardino County
126	840	4.3	**Delano** (city) Kern County
126	840	4.3	**Nipomo** (CDP) San Luis Obispo County
126	840	4.3	**San Luis Obispo** (city) San Luis Obispo County
126	840	4.3	**Santa Clarita** (city) Los Angeles County
126	840	4.3	**Soledad** (city) Monterey County
126	840	4.3	**Vacaville** (city) Solano County
126	840	4.3	**Valinda** (CDP) Los Angeles County
136	904	4.4	**Foothill Farms** (CDP) Sacramento County
136	904	4.4	**Hercules** (city) Contra Costa County
136	904	4.4	**Imperial** (city) Imperial County
136	904	4.4	**Lemoore** (city) Kings County
136	904	4.4	**Oxnard** (city) Ventura County
136	904	4.4	**Rosamond** (CDP) Kern County
136	904	4.4	**San Anselmo** (town) Marin County
136	904	4.4	**San Clemente** (city) Orange County
136	904	4.4	**Vineyard** (CDP) Sacramento County
136	904	4.4	**Willowbrook** (CDP) Los Angeles County
146	965	4.5	**Anaheim** (city) Orange County
146	965	4.5	**Bell** (city) Los Angeles County
146	965	4.5	**Ceres** (city) Stanislaus County
146	965	4.5	**Manteca** (city) San Joaquin County
146	965	4.5	**Orange** (city) Orange County

Note: *The state column ranks the top/bottom 150 places from all places in the state with population of 10,000 or more. The national column ranks the top/bottom 150 places from all places in the country with population of 10,000 or more. Places that are unincorporated were not considered in the rankings. Please refer to the User Guide for additional information.*

Marriage Status: Divorced

Top 150 Places Ranked in *Descending* Order

State Rank	Nat'l Rank	Percent	Place
1	6	21.2	**Laguna Woods** (city) Orange County
2	23	19.3	**Grass Valley** (city) Nevada County
3	35	18.6	**Sonoma** (city) Sonoma County
4	46	18.1	**Marysville** (city) Yuba County
5	64	17.8	**Oroville** (city) Butte County
6	127	16.9	**Ukiah** (city) Mendocino County
7	149	16.7	**Palm Springs** (city) Riverside County
8	159	16.6	**Clearlake** (city) Lake County
8	159	16.6	**Oildale** (CDP) Kern County
10	172	16.5	**Susanville** (city) Lassen County
11	194	16.3	**Big Bear City** (CDP) San Bernardino County
12	222	16.1	**Larkspur** (city) Marin County
13	241	16.0	**Paradise** (town) Butte County
14	339	15.4	**La Mesa** (city) San Diego County
15	366	15.3	**Laguna Beach** (city) Orange County
15	366	15.3	**Redding** (city) Shasta County
15	366	15.3	**Valle Vista** (CDP) Riverside County
18	386	15.2	**Magalia** (CDP) Butte County
18	386	15.2	**Red Bluff** (city) Tehama County
20	413	15.1	**North Auburn** (CDP) Placer County
21	437	15.0	**Crestline** (CDP) San Bernardino County
21	437	15.0	**Lakeland Village** (CDP) Riverside County
21	437	15.0	**Morro Bay** (city) San Luis Obispo County
24	464	14.9	**La Riviera** (CDP) Sacramento County
25	514	14.7	**Hemet** (city) Riverside County
25	514	14.7	**Rio Linda** (CDP) Sacramento County
27	543	14.6	**Corcoran** (city) Kings County
27	543	14.6	**Diamond Springs** (CDP) El Dorado County
27	543	14.6	**Foothill Farms** (CDP) Sacramento County
27	543	14.6	**North Highlands** (CDP) Sacramento County
31	573	14.5	**Arden-Arcade** (CDP) Sacramento County
31	573	14.5	**Chowchilla** (city) Madera County
31	573	14.5	**View Park-Windsor Hills** (CDP) Los Angeles County
34	613	14.4	**Carmichael** (CDP) Sacramento County
34	613	14.4	**Citrus Heights** (city) Sacramento County
36	637	14.3	**Blythe** (city) Riverside County
36	637	14.3	**Yucca Valley** (town) San Bernardino County
38	667	14.2	**Eureka** (city) Humboldt County
38	667	14.2	**Orangevale** (CDP) Sacramento County
40	698	14.1	**Santee** (city) San Diego County
41	738	14.0	**Dana Point** (city) Orange County
41	738	14.0	**Desert Hot Springs** (city) Riverside County
41	738	14.0	**Phelan** (CDP) San Bernardino County
44	766	13.9	**Palm Desert** (city) Riverside County
44	766	13.9	**Parkway** (CDP) Sacramento County
46	809	13.8	**Rosemont** (CDP) Sacramento County
46	809	13.8	**San Anselmo** (town) Marin County
46	809	13.8	**Shasta Lake** (city) Shasta County
49	850	13.7	**Martinez** (city) Contra Costa County
49	850	13.7	**San Buenaventura (Ventura)** (city) Ventura County
51	889	13.6	**Auburn** (city) Placer County
51	889	13.6	**Bostonia** (CDP) San Diego County
51	889	13.6	**South Lake Tahoe** (city) El Dorado County
54	920	13.5	**Placerville** (city) El Dorado County
54	920	13.5	**Vacaville** (city) Solano County
56	969	13.4	**Monterey** (city) Monterey County
56	969	13.4	**Port Hueneme** (city) Ventura County
56	969	13.4	**Santa Rosa** (city) Sonoma County
56	969	13.4	**Spring Valley** (CDP) San Diego County
56	969	13.4	**Winter Gardens** (CDP) San Diego County
61	1025	13.3	**Rohnert Park** (city) Sonoma County
62	1051	13.2	**Fair Oaks** (CDP) Sacramento County
62	1051	13.2	**Seal Beach** (city) Orange County
64	1090	13.1	**Benicia** (city) Solano County
64	1090	13.1	**Grover Beach** (city) San Luis Obispo County
64	1090	13.1	**Live Oak** (CDP) Santa Cruz County
64	1090	13.1	**Pleasant Hill** (city) Contra Costa County
64	1090	13.1	**Soledad** (city) Monterey County
69	1134	13.0	**Novato** (city) Marin County
70	1186	12.9	**Tehachapi** (city) Kern County
71	1223	12.8	**Lompoc** (city) Santa Barbara County
71	1223	12.8	**Menifee** (city) Riverside County
71	1223	12.8	**Petaluma** (city) Sonoma County
74	1270	12.7	**El Segundo** (city) Los Angeles County
74	1270	12.7	**Galt** (city) Sacramento County
74	1270	12.7	**Healdsburg** (city) Sonoma County
77	1312	12.6	**Cathedral City** (city) Riverside County
77	1312	12.6	**Pacific Grove** (city) Monterey County
79	1361	12.5	**Emeryville** (city) Alameda County
79	1361	12.5	**Napa** (city) Napa County
81	1398	12.4	**Banning** (city) Riverside County
81	1398	12.4	**Casa de Oro-Mount Helix** (CDP) San Diego County
81	1398	12.4	**El Sobrante** (CDP) Contra Costa County
81	1398	12.4	**Solana Beach** (city) San Diego County
85	1444	12.3	**Linda** (CDP) Yuba County
85	1444	12.3	**Los Alamitos** (city) Orange County
85	1444	12.3	**Santa Monica** (city) Los Angeles County
85	1444	12.3	**Tamalpais-Homestead Valley** (CDP) Marin County
85	1444	12.3	**West Carson** (CDP) Los Angeles County
90	1497	12.2	**Barstow** (city) San Bernardino County
90	1497	12.2	**Lomita** (city) Los Angeles County
90	1497	12.2	**McKinleyville** (CDP) Humboldt County
90	1497	12.2	**Mill Valley** (city) Marin County
90	1497	12.2	**Olivehurst** (CDP) Yuba County
90	1497	12.2	**Ridgecrest** (city) Kern County
90	1497	12.2	**Sacramento** (city) Sacramento County
97	1545	12.1	**Agoura Hills** (city) Los Angeles County
97	1545	12.1	**Campbell** (city) Santa Clara County
97	1545	12.1	**Lemon Grove** (city) San Diego County
97	1545	12.1	**Newport Beach** (city) Orange County
97	1545	12.1	**Rancho Cordova** (city) Sacramento County
97	1545	12.1	**Sierra Madre** (city) Los Angeles County
103	1604	12.0	**El Cajon** (city) San Diego County
103	1604	12.0	**West Sacramento** (city) Yolo County
105	1646	11.9	**Atwater** (city) Merced County
105	1646	11.9	**Carlsbad** (city) San Diego County
105	1646	11.9	**Fortuna** (city) Humboldt County
105	1646	11.9	**Lemon Hill** (CDP) Sacramento County
105	1646	11.9	**Oakdale** (city) Stanislaus County
105	1646	11.9	**West Hollywood** (city) Los Angeles County
111	1695	11.8	**Arroyo Grande** (city) San Luis Obispo County
111	1695	11.8	**Redondo Beach** (city) Los Angeles County
111	1695	11.8	**San Jacinto** (city) Riverside County
111	1695	11.8	**San Rafael** (city) Marin County
111	1695	11.8	**Victorville** (city) San Bernardino County
111	1695	11.8	**Visalia** (city) Tulare County
117	1750	11.7	**Chico** (city) Butte County
117	1750	11.7	**Imperial Beach** (city) San Diego County
117	1750	11.7	**Marina** (city) Monterey County
117	1750	11.7	**Modesto** (city) Stanislaus County
121	1804	11.6	**Florin** (CDP) Sacramento County
121	1804	11.6	**Rancho Mirage** (city) Riverside County
123	1859	11.5	**Costa Mesa** (city) Orange County
123	1859	11.5	**Redwood City** (city) San Mateo County
123	1859	11.5	**Vallejo** (city) Solano County
123	1859	11.5	**Woodland** (city) Yolo County
127	1910	11.4	**Hermosa Beach** (city) Los Angeles County
127	1910	11.4	**Redlands** (city) San Bernardino County
129	1954	11.3	**Apple Valley** (town) San Bernardino County
129	1954	11.3	**Atascadero** (city) San Luis Obispo County
129	1954	11.3	**Folsom** (city) Sacramento County
129	1954	11.3	**Garden Acres** (CDP) San Joaquin County
129	1954	11.3	**Huntington Beach** (city) Orange County
129	1954	11.3	**Lodi** (city) San Joaquin County
135	2009	11.2	**Alameda** (city) Alameda County
135	2009	11.2	**La Quinta** (city) Riverside County
135	2009	11.2	**Oak Park** (CDP) Ventura County
135	2009	11.2	**San Clemente** (city) Orange County
135	2009	11.2	**Yucaipa** (city) San Bernardino County
140	2066	11.1	**Brawley** (city) Imperial County
140	2066	11.1	**Oceanside** (city) San Diego County
140	2066	11.1	**Quartz Hill** (CDP) Los Angeles County
140	2066	11.1	**Walnut Creek** (city) Contra Costa County
144	2111	11.0	**California City** (city) Kern County
144	2111	11.0	**Los Osos** (CDP) San Luis Obispo County
144	2111	11.0	**Pacifica** (city) San Mateo County
144	2111	11.0	**San Mateo** (city) San Mateo County
148	2168	10.9	**Clovis** (city) Fresno County
148	2168	10.9	**Culver City** (city) Los Angeles County
148	2168	10.9	**Encinitas** (city) San Diego County

Note: *The state column ranks the top/bottom 150 places from all places in the state with population of 10,000 or more. The national column ranks the top/bottom 150 places from all places in the country with population of 10,000 or more. Places that are unincorporated were not considered in the rankings. Please refer to the User Guide for additional information.*

Marriage Status: Divorced

Top 150 Places Ranked in *Ascending* Order

State Rank	Nat'l Rank	Percent	Place
1	2	0.8	**Stanford** (CDP) Santa Clara County
2	4	1.0	**Camp Pendleton South** (CDP) San Diego County
2	4	1.0	**Isla Vista** (CDP) Santa Barbara County
4	13	2.3	**Hillsborough** (town) San Mateo County
5	21	3.0	**Cudahy** (city) Los Angeles County
5	21	3.0	**Greenfield** (city) Monterey County
5	21	3.0	**Mendota** (city) Fresno County
8	40	3.7	**Bell Gardens** (city) Los Angeles County
9	43	3.8	**Delhi** (CDP) Merced County
9	43	3.8	**Piedmont** (city) Alameda County
11	49	3.9	**Coto de Caza** (CDP) Orange County
11	49	3.9	**Walnut** (city) Los Angeles County
13	57	4.1	**Parlier** (city) Fresno County
14	67	4.3	**King City** (city) Monterey County
14	67	4.3	**Maywood** (city) Los Angeles County
16	73	4.4	**Florence-Graham** (CDP) Los Angeles County
16	73	4.4	**Lamont** (CDP) Kern County
18	92	4.6	**Saratoga** (city) Santa Clara County
18	92	4.6	**Walnut Park** (CDP) Los Angeles County
20	99	4.7	**La Puente** (city) Los Angeles County
21	108	4.8	**McFarland** (city) Kern County
22	116	4.9	**Citrus** (CDP) Los Angeles County
22	116	4.9	**Huntington Park** (city) Los Angeles County
22	116	4.9	**La Cañada Flintridge** (city) Los Angeles County
22	116	4.9	**Lennox** (CDP) Los Angeles County
26	125	5.0	**Arvin** (city) Kern County
26	125	5.0	**El Sobrante** (CDP) Riverside County
28	156	5.2	**Cupertino** (city) Santa Clara County
29	173	5.3	**Bell** (city) Los Angeles County
29	173	5.3	**Lynwood** (city) Los Angeles County
31	186	5.4	**Calexico** (city) Imperial County
31	186	5.4	**East Los Angeles** (CDP) Los Angeles County
31	186	5.4	**Rossmoor** (CDP) Orange County
31	186	5.4	**San Marino** (city) Los Angeles County
35	199	5.5	**Kerman** (city) Fresno County
35	199	5.5	**Muscoy** (CDP) San Bernardino County
35	199	5.5	**Orinda** (city) Contra Costa County
38	218	5.6	**Los Altos** (city) Santa Clara County
39	231	5.7	**Arcadia** (city) Los Angeles County
39	231	5.7	**Willowbrook** (CDP) Los Angeles County
41	251	5.8	**Alamo** (CDP) Contra Costa County
41	251	5.8	**Coachella** (city) Riverside County
41	251	5.8	**Eastvale** (city) Riverside County
41	251	5.8	**Home Gardens** (CDP) Riverside County
41	251	5.8	**Livingston** (city) Merced County
46	277	5.9	**Artesia** (city) Los Angeles County
46	277	5.9	**South Gate** (city) Los Angeles County
48	294	6.0	**North Tustin** (CDP) Orange County
48	294	6.0	**Santa Ana** (city) Orange County
48	294	6.0	**South El Monte** (city) Los Angeles County
51	321	6.1	**El Monte** (city) Los Angeles County
51	321	6.1	**West Puente Valley** (CDP) Los Angeles County
53	348	6.2	**Ladera Ranch** (CDP) Orange County
54	368	6.3	**Baldwin Park** (city) Los Angeles County
54	368	6.3	**Cerritos** (city) Los Angeles County
56	395	6.4	**Davis** (city) Yolo County
56	395	6.4	**Diamond Bar** (city) Los Angeles County
56	395	6.4	**Rosemead** (city) Los Angeles County
59	420	6.5	**Azusa** (city) Los Angeles County
59	420	6.5	**Palos Verdes Estates** (city) Los Angeles County
59	420	6.5	**Salinas** (city) Monterey County
62	442	6.6	**Alum Rock** (CDP) Santa Clara County
62	442	6.6	**Commerce** (city) Los Angeles County
62	442	6.6	**Farmersville** (city) Tulare County
62	442	6.6	**Watsonville** (city) Santa Cruz County
66	466	6.7	**Monterey Park** (city) Los Angeles County
66	466	6.7	**Pinole** (city) Contra Costa County
66	466	6.7	**Prunedale** (CDP) Monterey County
66	466	6.7	**South San Jose Hills** (CDP) Los Angeles County
66	466	6.7	**Union City** (city) Alameda County
71	493	6.8	**Yorba Linda** (city) Orange County
72	525	6.9	**Chino Hills** (city) San Bernardino County
72	525	6.9	**Fremont** (city) Alameda County
72	525	6.9	**Rowland Heights** (CDP) Los Angeles County
72	525	6.9	**San Ramon** (city) Contra Costa County
76	554	7.0	**Claremont** (city) Los Angeles County
76	554	7.0	**San Luis Obispo** (city) San Luis Obispo County
76	554	7.0	**Shafter** (city) Kern County
79	587	7.1	**East Rancho Dominguez** (CDP) Los Angeles County
79	587	7.1	**Milpitas** (city) Santa Clara County
81	620	7.2	**Paramount** (city) Los Angeles County
81	620	7.2	**San Gabriel** (city) Los Angeles County
81	620	7.2	**Woodcrest** (CDP) Riverside County
84	655	7.3	**Delano** (city) Kern County
84	655	7.3	**East San Gabriel** (CDP) Los Angeles County
84	655	7.3	**Hacienda Heights** (CDP) Los Angeles County
84	655	7.3	**Los Banos** (city) Merced County
84	655	7.3	**Mead Valley** (CDP) Riverside County
84	655	7.3	**Santa Maria** (city) Santa Barbara County
84	655	7.3	**Temple City** (city) Los Angeles County
91	689	7.4	**Compton** (city) Los Angeles County
91	689	7.4	**Fontana** (city) San Bernardino County
91	689	7.4	**Kingsburg** (city) Fresno County
91	689	7.4	**La Mirada** (city) Los Angeles County
91	689	7.4	**Rancho Palos Verdes** (city) Los Angeles County
91	689	7.4	**Sunnyvale** (city) Santa Clara County
97	729	7.5	**Daly City** (city) San Mateo County
97	729	7.5	**La Crescenta-Montrose** (CDP) Los Angeles County
97	729	7.5	**Madera** (city) Madera County
97	729	7.5	**San Fernando** (city) Los Angeles County
97	729	7.5	**Valinda** (CDP) Los Angeles County
102	770	7.6	**Granite Bay** (CDP) Placer County
102	770	7.6	**Hawaiian Gardens** (city) Los Angeles County
102	770	7.6	**Lafayette** (city) Contra Costa County
102	770	7.6	**Winton** (CDP) Merced County
106	808	7.7	**Adelanto** (city) San Bernardino County
106	808	7.7	**American Canyon** (city) Napa County
106	808	7.7	**Colton** (city) San Bernardino County
106	808	7.7	**Dinuba** (city) Tulare County
106	808	7.7	**East Palo Alto** (city) San Mateo County
106	808	7.7	**El Dorado Hills** (CDP) El Dorado County
106	808	7.7	**Glendale** (city) Los Angeles County
106	808	7.7	**Moraga** (town) Contra Costa County
106	808	7.7	**Norwalk** (city) Los Angeles County
106	808	7.7	**Pomona** (city) Los Angeles County
106	808	7.7	**South San Francisco** (city) San Mateo County
106	808	7.7	**Stevenson Ranch** (CDP) Los Angeles County
118	849	7.8	**Berkeley** (city) Alameda County
118	849	7.8	**Canyon Lake** (city) Riverside County
118	849	7.8	**Castaic** (CDP) Los Angeles County
118	849	7.8	**Fallbrook** (CDP) San Diego County
118	849	7.8	**Lindsay** (city) Tulare County
118	849	7.8	**Reedley** (city) Fresno County
118	849	7.8	**Santa Clara** (city) Santa Clara County
125	902	7.9	**Alhambra** (city) Los Angeles County
125	902	7.9	**Avocado Heights** (CDP) Los Angeles County
125	902	7.9	**Foster City** (city) San Mateo County
125	902	7.9	**Manhattan Beach** (city) Los Angeles County
125	902	7.9	**Perris** (city) Riverside County
130	949	8.0	**Bloomington** (CDP) San Bernardino County
130	949	8.0	**Irvine** (city) Orange County
130	949	8.0	**Moorpark** (city) Ventura County
133	1000	8.1	**Garden Grove** (city) Orange County
133	1000	8.1	**Gilroy** (city) Santa Clara County
133	1000	8.1	**Ripon** (city) San Joaquin County
133	1000	8.1	**Wasco** (city) Kern County
133	1000	8.1	**Westminster** (city) Orange County
138	1044	8.2	**Anaheim** (city) Orange County
138	1044	8.2	**El Centro** (city) Imperial County
138	1044	8.2	**Fullerton** (city) Orange County
138	1044	8.2	**Laguna Hills** (city) Orange County
138	1044	8.2	**Placentia** (city) Orange County
138	1044	8.2	**San Jose** (city) Santa Clara County
138	1044	8.2	**West Covina** (city) Los Angeles County
145	1092	8.3	**Antelope** (CDP) Sacramento County
145	1092	8.3	**Carson** (city) Los Angeles County
145	1092	8.3	**Hayward** (city) Alameda County
145	1092	8.3	**Pico Rivera** (city) Los Angeles County
145	1092	8.3	**Pleasanton** (city) Alameda County
150	1135	8.4	**Imperial** (city) Imperial County

Note: *The state column ranks the top/bottom 150 places from all places in the state with population of 10,000 or more. The national column ranks the top/bottom 150 places from all places in the country with population of 10,000 or more. Places that are unincorporated were not considered in the rankings. Please refer to the User Guide for additional information.*

Foreign Born

Top 150 Places Ranked in *Descending* Order

State Rank	Nat'l Rank	Percent	Place
1	21	57.0	**Rowland Heights** (CDP) Los Angeles County
2	22	56.9	**Rosemead** (city) Los Angeles County
3	23	56.1	**San Gabriel** (city) Los Angeles County
4	24	55.1	**Mendota** (city) Fresno County
5	25	54.8	**Glendale** (city) Los Angeles County
6	26	54.4	**Monterey Park** (city) Los Angeles County
7	28	53.9	**North Fair Oaks** (CDP) San Mateo County
8	32	52.1	**Daly City** (city) San Mateo County
9	33	51.4	**El Monte** (city) Los Angeles County
10	40	50.5	**Alhambra** (city) Los Angeles County
10	40	50.5	**Huntington Park** (city) Los Angeles County
12	42	49.9	**Cupertino** (city) Santa Clara County
13	45	49.7	**Milpitas** (city) Santa Clara County
14	49	48.9	**King City** (city) Monterey County
15	50	48.8	**Arcadia** (city) Los Angeles County
16	54	48.1	**Artesia** (city) Los Angeles County
16	54	48.1	**Lennox** (CDP) Los Angeles County
18	58	47.9	**Cudahy** (city) Los Angeles County
19	59	47.8	**Santa Ana** (city) Orange County
19	59	47.8	**Walnut** (city) Los Angeles County
21	62	47.7	**Calexico** (city) Imperial County
22	65	47.3	**Walnut Park** (CDP) Los Angeles County
23	70	46.6	**Temple City** (city) Los Angeles County
24	71	46.3	**Maywood** (city) Los Angeles County
25	74	46.0	**South El Monte** (city) Los Angeles County
25	74	46.0	**Union City** (city) Alameda County
27	77	45.8	**Arvin** (city) Kern County
27	77	45.8	**Greenfield** (city) Monterey County
29	79	45.7	**Westminster** (city) Orange County
30	80	45.6	**Baldwin Park** (city) Los Angeles County
31	82	45.1	**Cerritos** (city) Los Angeles County
32	84	44.7	**Hawaiian Gardens** (city) Los Angeles County
33	86	44.5	**Bell Gardens** (city) Los Angeles County
34	91	44.4	**Bell** (city) Los Angeles County
34	91	44.4	**East San Gabriel** (CDP) Los Angeles County
36	98	44.2	**Sunnyvale** (city) Santa Clara County
37	99	44.1	**Livingston** (city) Merced County
38	104	43.8	**Florence-Graham** (CDP) Los Angeles County
38	104	43.8	**Garden Grove** (city) Orange County
40	107	43.7	**Fremont** (city) Alameda County
41	113	43.3	**South Gate** (city) Los Angeles County
42	116	43.2	**Stanton** (city) Orange County
43	120	43.0	**Lamont** (CDP) Kern County
44	122	42.9	**East Los Angeles** (CDP) Los Angeles County
44	122	42.9	**McFarland** (city) Kern County
46	126	42.7	**Hacienda Heights** (CDP) Los Angeles County
47	128	42.4	**Diamond Bar** (city) Los Angeles County
48	131	42.3	**San Pablo** (city) Contra Costa County
49	135	42.0	**South San Francisco** (city) San Mateo County
50	140	41.6	**Coachella** (city) Riverside County
51	141	41.5	**Foster City** (city) San Mateo County
52	145	41.3	**La Puente** (city) Los Angeles County
53	147	41.2	**National City** (city) San Diego County
53	147	41.2	**South San Jose Hills** (CDP) Los Angeles County
53	147	41.2	**Watsonville** (city) Santa Cruz County
56	155	40.6	**Parlier** (city) Fresno County
57	159	40.2	**East Palo Alto** (city) San Mateo County
57	159	40.2	**Lawndale** (city) Los Angeles County
59	161	40.1	**Avenal** (city) Kings County
60	164	39.7	**East Rancho Dominguez** (CDP) Los Angeles County
61	166	39.6	**Santa Clara** (city) Santa Clara County
62	170	39.3	**Lynwood** (city) Los Angeles County
63	172	39.2	**West Puente Valley** (CDP) Los Angeles County
64	173	39.1	**Valinda** (CDP) Los Angeles County
65	179	38.8	**Los Angeles** (city) Los Angeles County
66	182	38.6	**San Jose** (city) Santa Clara County
67	186	38.4	**San Marino** (city) Los Angeles County
68	190	38.1	**Delano** (city) Kern County
68	190	38.1	**Hayward** (city) Alameda County
70	192	38.0	**Millbrae** (city) San Mateo County
71	196	37.8	**Mountain View** (city) Santa Clara County
71	196	37.8	**Paramount** (city) Los Angeles County
73	203	37.7	**Buena Park** (city) Orange County
74	206	37.6	**Delhi** (CDP) Merced County
75	211	37.4	**Beverly Hills** (city) Los Angeles County
76	212	37.3	**Montebello** (city) Los Angeles County
77	215	37.1	**Anaheim** (city) Orange County
77	215	37.1	**Home Gardens** (CDP) Riverside County
79	219	37.0	**Oxnard** (city) Ventura County
79	219	37.0	**Saratoga** (city) Santa Clara County
81	223	36.9	**Salinas** (city) Monterey County
81	223	36.9	**West Carson** (CDP) Los Angeles County
83	233	36.4	**Citrus** (CDP) Los Angeles County
83	233	36.4	**Commerce** (city) Los Angeles County
85	238	36.3	**Montclair** (city) San Bernardino County
86	241	36.0	**Irvine** (city) Orange County
87	246	35.8	**Lemon Hill** (CDP) Sacramento County
87	246	35.8	**Tustin** (city) Orange County
89	254	35.6	**San Francisco** (city) San Francisco County
90	257	35.5	**Norwalk** (city) Los Angeles County
91	263	35.3	**Downey** (city) Los Angeles County
92	265	35.2	**Burbank** (city) Los Angeles County
92	265	35.2	**San Fernando** (city) Los Angeles County
94	269	35.1	**Bay Point** (CDP) Contra Costa County
94	269	35.1	**San Bruno** (city) San Mateo County
96	271	35.0	**Carson** (city) Los Angeles County
97	277	34.9	**Duarte** (city) Los Angeles County
98	282	34.7	**Kerman** (city) Fresno County
98	282	34.7	**Santa Maria** (city) Santa Barbara County
100	287	34.6	**American Canyon** (city) Napa County
101	289	34.5	**Pomona** (city) Los Angeles County
101	289	34.5	**San Leandro** (city) Alameda County
103	293	34.4	**Alum Rock** (CDP) Santa Clara County
104	296	34.3	**Cathedral City** (city) Riverside County
104	296	34.3	**Lindsay** (city) Tulare County
104	296	34.3	**West Covina** (city) Los Angeles County
107	303	34.1	**La Crescenta-Montrose** (CDP) Los Angeles County
108	306	34.0	**Ashland** (CDP) Alameda County
109	312	33.8	**Avocado Heights** (CDP) Los Angeles County
109	312	33.8	**Gardena** (city) Los Angeles County
111	315	33.7	**Cherryland** (CDP) Alameda County
111	315	33.7	**Willowbrook** (CDP) Los Angeles County
113	320	33.6	**Loma Linda** (city) San Bernardino County
114	322	33.5	**Newark** (city) Alameda County
115	327	33.4	**Bloomington** (CDP) San Bernardino County
115	327	33.4	**Winton** (CDP) Merced County
117	333	33.2	**Hawthorne** (city) Los Angeles County
117	333	33.2	**Pico Rivera** (city) Los Angeles County
117	333	33.2	**Reedley** (city) Fresno County
120	338	33.1	**Muscoy** (CDP) San Bernardino County
121	342	32.9	**San Mateo** (city) San Mateo County
122	344	32.8	**Soledad** (city) Monterey County
123	348	32.7	**Richmond** (city) Contra Costa County
124	350	32.6	**Hercules** (city) Contra Costa County
125	353	32.5	**La Palma** (city) Orange County
126	355	32.4	**Dinuba** (city) Tulare County
127	356	32.3	**Garden Acres** (CDP) San Joaquin County
127	356	32.3	**Signal Hill** (city) Los Angeles County
129	366	31.9	**Azusa** (city) Los Angeles County
129	366	31.9	**El Centro** (city) Imperial County
131	371	31.8	**San Lorenzo** (CDP) Alameda County
132	376	31.6	**Albany** (city) Alameda County
132	376	31.6	**San Ramon** (city) Contra Costa County
134	380	31.5	**Redwood City** (city) San Mateo County
135	385	31.3	**Pittsburg** (city) Contra Costa County
136	389	31.2	**Madera** (city) Madera County
136	389	31.2	**Santa Paula** (city) Ventura County
138	392	31.1	**Chula Vista** (city) San Diego County
138	392	31.1	**Fullerton** (city) Orange County
140	394	31.0	**Palo Alto** (city) Santa Clara County
141	398	30.9	**Farmersville** (city) Tulare County
142	406	30.5	**Pasadena** (city) Los Angeles County
143	410	30.3	**Fontana** (city) San Bernardino County
143	410	30.3	**Ontario** (city) San Bernardino County
145	413	30.2	**Compton** (city) Los Angeles County
145	413	30.2	**Eastvale** (city) Riverside County
145	413	30.2	**Florin** (CDP) Sacramento County
145	413	30.2	**Fountain Valley** (city) Orange County
149	431	29.7	**El Cajon** (city) San Diego County
150	434	29.6	**Seaside** (city) Monterey County

Note: *The state column ranks the top/bottom 150 places from all places in the state with population of 10,000 or more. The national column ranks the top/bottom 150 places from all places in the country with population of 10,000 or more. Places that are unincorporated were not considered in the rankings. Please refer to the User Guide for additional information.*

Foreign Born

Top 150 Places Ranked in *Ascending* Order

State Rank	Nat'l Rank	Percent	Place
1	538	2.7	**Magalia** (CDP) Butte County
2	1032	4.1	**McKinleyville** (CDP) Humboldt County
3	1168	4.5	**Paradise** (town) Butte County
4	1224	4.7	**Canyon Lake** (city) Riverside County
5	1294	4.9	**Oildale** (CDP) Kern County
6	1362	5.1	**Camp Pendleton South** (CDP) San Diego County
7	1400	5.2	**Crestline** (CDP) San Bernardino County
7	1400	5.2	**San Diego Country Estates** (CDP) San Diego County
9	1432	5.3	**Redding** (city) Shasta County
10	1466	5.4	**Auburn** (city) Placer County
11	1492	5.5	**Twentynine Palms** (city) San Bernardino County
12	1564	5.7	**Diamond Springs** (CDP) El Dorado County
13	1587	5.8	**Rosedale** (CDP) Kern County
14	1646	6.0	**Cameron Park** (CDP) El Dorado County
15	1702	6.2	**Arcata** (city) Humboldt County
16	1851	6.7	**Atascadero** (city) San Luis Obispo County
17	1961	7.1	**Yucca Valley** (town) San Bernardino County
18	1988	7.2	**Los Osos** (CDP) San Luis Obispo County
18	1988	7.2	**View Park-Windsor Hills** (CDP) Los Angeles County
20	2009	7.3	**Red Bluff** (city) Tehama County
21	2042	7.4	**Shasta Lake** (city) Shasta County
21	2042	7.4	**Susanville** (city) Lassen County
23	2069	7.5	**Oroville** (city) Butte County
24	2092	7.6	**Apple Valley** (town) San Bernardino County
24	2092	7.6	**Granite Bay** (CDP) Placer County
24	2092	7.6	**Grass Valley** (city) Nevada County
27	2129	7.7	**Chico** (city) Butte County
27	2129	7.7	**Discovery Bay** (CDP) Contra Costa County
27	2129	7.7	**Ripon** (city) San Joaquin County
30	2202	8.0	**Eureka** (city) Humboldt County
30	2202	8.0	**Quartz Hill** (CDP) Los Angeles County
32	2273	8.3	**Phelan** (CDP) San Bernardino County
32	2273	8.3	**Santee** (city) San Diego County
34	2311	8.5	**Orangevale** (CDP) Sacramento County
35	2333	8.6	**Fortuna** (city) Humboldt County
35	2333	8.6	**Marysville** (city) Yuba County
37	2374	8.8	**Ridgecrest** (city) Kern County
37	2374	8.8	**Sonoma** (city) Sonoma County
39	2439	9.1	**Valle Vista** (CDP) Riverside County
40	2456	9.2	**Arroyo Grande** (city) San Luis Obispo County
40	2456	9.2	**Clearlake** (city) Lake County
40	2456	9.2	**Lakeside** (CDP) San Diego County
40	2456	9.2	**San Anselmo** (town) Marin County
44	2479	9.3	**Alpine** (CDP) San Diego County
44	2479	9.3	**San Luis Obispo** (city) San Luis Obispo County
46	2519	9.5	**Placerville** (city) El Dorado County
47	2535	9.6	**Orcutt** (CDP) Santa Barbara County
48	2558	9.7	**Yucaipa** (city) San Bernardino County
49	2574	9.8	**Lake Arrowhead** (CDP) San Bernardino County
50	2626	10.0	**Rossmoor** (CDP) Orange County
51	2648	10.1	**Rocklin** (city) Placer County
52	2670	10.2	**La Riviera** (CDP) Sacramento County
53	2709	10.4	**Benicia** (city) Solano County
53	2709	10.4	**Coronado** (city) San Diego County
53	2709	10.4	**Rio Linda** (CDP) Sacramento County
56	2726	10.5	**Coto de Caza** (CDP) Orange County
56	2726	10.5	**Hermosa Beach** (city) Los Angeles County
56	2726	10.5	**Scotts Valley** (city) Santa Cruz County
59	2750	10.6	**Clayton** (city) Contra Costa County
60	2765	10.7	**Alamo** (CDP) Contra Costa County
60	2765	10.7	**Oakdale** (city) Stanislaus County
60	2765	10.7	**Winter Gardens** (CDP) San Diego County
63	2786	10.8	**Nipomo** (CDP) San Luis Obispo County
63	2786	10.8	**Tehachapi** (city) Kern County
65	2801	10.9	**Manhattan Beach** (city) Los Angeles County
66	2815	11.0	**Barstow** (city) San Bernardino County
66	2815	11.0	**Morro Bay** (city) San Luis Obispo County
68	2838	11.1	**San Clemente** (city) Orange County
69	2858	11.2	**Carmichael** (CDP) Sacramento County
69	2858	11.2	**Clovis** (city) Fresno County
69	2858	11.2	**Tamalpais-Homestead Valley** (CDP) Marin County
72	2881	11.3	**Big Bear City** (CDP) San Bernardino County
73	2893	11.4	**Martinez** (city) Contra Costa County
74	2907	11.5	**Exeter** (city) Tulare County
75	2917	11.6	**Truckee** (town) Nevada County
76	2933	11.7	**California City** (city) Kern County
76	2933	11.7	**Fair Oaks** (CDP) Sacramento County
76	2933	11.7	**Grover Beach** (city) San Luis Obispo County
76	2933	11.7	**Ukiah** (city) Mendocino County
80	2950	11.8	**Danville** (town) Contra Costa County
81	2967	11.9	**Laguna Beach** (city) Orange County
82	2984	12.0	**El Dorado Hills** (CDP) El Dorado County
82	2984	12.0	**Pacific Grove** (city) Monterey County
84	3012	12.2	**Lincoln** (city) Placer County
85	3057	12.5	**Rosamond** (CDP) Kern County
86	3068	12.6	**Casa de Oro-Mount Helix** (CDP) San Diego County
86	3068	12.6	**Vacaville** (city) Solano County
88	3085	12.8	**Encinitas** (city) San Diego County
88	3085	12.8	**Seal Beach** (city) Orange County
90	3097	12.9	**Dana Point** (city) Orange County
90	3097	12.9	**North Tustin** (CDP) Orange County
92	3137	13.3	**East Hemet** (CDP) Riverside County
92	3137	13.3	**Roseville** (city) Placer County
92	3137	13.3	**Santa Cruz** (city) Santa Cruz County
95	3154	13.4	**El Segundo** (city) Los Angeles County
95	3154	13.4	**Lafayette** (city) Contra Costa County
95	3154	13.4	**North Auburn** (CDP) Placer County
98	3168	13.5	**Woodcrest** (CDP) Riverside County
99	3178	13.6	**Chowchilla** (city) Madera County
99	3178	13.6	**Citrus Heights** (city) Sacramento County
99	3178	13.6	**Hesperia** (city) San Bernardino County
99	3178	13.6	**Murrieta** (city) Riverside County
99	3178	13.6	**Rancho Mirage** (city) Riverside County
104	3196	13.7	**Norco** (city) Riverside County
105	3202	13.8	**Arden-Arcade** (CDP) Sacramento County
105	3202	13.8	**Menifee** (city) Riverside County
107	3219	13.9	**Carlsbad** (city) San Diego County
107	3219	13.9	**La Mesa** (city) San Diego County
107	3219	13.9	**Moraga** (town) Contra Costa County
110	3227	14.0	**Redlands** (city) San Bernardino County
110	3227	14.0	**Windsor** (town) Sonoma County
112	3241	14.1	**Visalia** (city) Tulare County
113	3247	14.2	**Newport Beach** (city) Orange County
113	3247	14.2	**Orinda** (city) Contra Costa County
115	3265	14.4	**Piedmont** (city) Alameda County
116	3283	14.6	**Brentwood** (city) Contra Costa County
116	3283	14.6	**Hemet** (city) Riverside County
116	3283	14.6	**Lancaster** (city) Los Angeles County
119	3294	14.7	**Isla Vista** (CDP) Santa Barbara County
119	3294	14.7	**La Quinta** (city) Riverside County
121	3308	14.8	**Lake Los Angeles** (CDP) Los Angeles County
121	3308	14.8	**Los Alamitos** (city) Orange County
123	3323	14.9	**Mill Valley** (city) Marin County
123	3323	14.9	**San Buenaventura (Ventura)** (city) Ventura County
125	3334	15.0	**Camarillo** (city) Ventura County
126	3361	15.2	**Folsom** (city) Sacramento County
126	3361	15.2	**Grand Terrace** (city) San Bernardino County
126	3361	15.2	**La Verne** (city) Los Angeles County
126	3361	15.2	**Temecula** (city) Riverside County
130	3375	15.3	**French Valley** (CDP) Riverside County
131	3387	15.4	**Oak Park** (CDP) Ventura County
132	3394	15.5	**Manteca** (city) San Joaquin County
133	3426	15.8	**Spring Valley** (CDP) San Diego County
134	3442	16.0	**Glendora** (city) Los Angeles County
135	3448	16.1	**Hanford** (city) Kings County
135	3448	16.1	**Sierra Madre** (city) Los Angeles County
137	3457	16.2	**Lemoore** (city) Kings County
137	3457	16.2	**Poway** (city) San Diego County
137	3457	16.2	**Rohnert Park** (city) Sonoma County
140	3466	16.3	**Malibu** (city) Los Angeles County
141	3473	16.4	**Bostonia** (CDP) San Diego County
141	3473	16.4	**Linda** (CDP) Yuba County
143	3486	16.6	**Huntington Beach** (city) Orange County
143	3486	16.6	**Livermore** (city) Alameda County
145	3499	16.8	**Modesto** (city) Stanislaus County
145	3499	16.8	**Petaluma** (city) Sonoma County
145	3499	16.8	**Wildomar** (city) Riverside County
148	3509	16.9	**Beaumont** (city) Riverside County
148	3509	16.9	**Ladera Ranch** (CDP) Orange County
150	3520	17.0	**Rancho Santa Margarita** (city) Orange County

Note: *The state column ranks the top/bottom 150 places from all places in the state with population of 10,000 or more. The national column ranks the top/bottom 150 places from all places in the country with population of 10,000 or more. Places that are unincorporated were not considered in the rankings. Please refer to the User Guide for additional information.*

Speak English Only at Home

Top 150 Places Ranked in *Descending* Order

State Rank	Nat'l Rank	Percent	Place
1	363	96.2	**Magalia** (CDP) Butte County
2	975	93.8	**Canyon Lake** (city) Riverside County
3	1047	93.5	**San Diego Country Estates** (CDP) San Diego County
4	1097	93.3	**Paradise** (town) Butte County
5	1296	92.5	**Crestline** (CDP) San Bernardino County
6	1325	92.4	**Auburn** (city) Placer County
7	1674	90.7	**McKinleyville** (CDP) Humboldt County
7	1674	90.7	**Shasta Lake** (city) Shasta County
9	1694	90.6	**Granite Bay** (CDP) Placer County
9	1694	90.6	**Redding** (city) Shasta County
11	1780	90.2	**Diamond Springs** (CDP) El Dorado County
11	1780	90.2	**View Park-Windsor Hills** (CDP) Los Angeles County
13	1828	90.0	**Los Osos** (CDP) San Luis Obispo County
14	1848	89.9	**Alamo** (CDP) Contra Costa County
15	1931	89.4	**Cameron Park** (CDP) El Dorado County
15	1931	89.4	**Clayton** (city) Contra Costa County
17	1968	89.2	**Discovery Bay** (CDP) Contra Costa County
18	1980	89.1	**Grass Valley** (city) Nevada County
18	1980	89.1	**Hermosa Beach** (city) Los Angeles County
20	2000	89.0	**Arcata** (city) Humboldt County
20	2000	89.0	**Atascadero** (city) San Luis Obispo County
20	2000	89.0	**Oildale** (CDP) Kern County
23	2024	88.9	**Eureka** (city) Humboldt County
23	2024	88.9	**San Anselmo** (town) Marin County
25	2059	88.7	**Yucca Valley** (town) San Bernardino County
26	2146	88.2	**Scotts Valley** (city) Santa Cruz County
27	2198	87.9	**Coto de Caza** (CDP) Orange County
28	2297	87.2	**Orangevale** (CDP) Sacramento County
29	2337	86.9	**Ridgecrest** (city) Kern County
29	2337	86.9	**Rosedale** (CDP) Kern County
31	2375	86.6	**Twentynine Palms** (city) San Bernardino County
32	2391	86.5	**Pacific Grove** (city) Monterey County
32	2391	86.5	**Sonoma** (city) Sonoma County
34	2419	86.3	**Rossmoor** (CDP) Orange County
35	2432	86.2	**Tamalpais-Homestead Valley** (CDP) Marin County
36	2444	86.1	**Chico** (city) Butte County
36	2444	86.1	**Lafayette** (city) Contra Costa County
38	2464	86.0	**El Dorado Hills** (CDP) El Dorado County
39	2485	85.9	**Quartz Hill** (CDP) Los Angeles County
40	2500	85.8	**Camp Pendleton South** (CDP) San Diego County
41	2514	85.7	**Danville** (town) Contra Costa County
41	2514	85.7	**Manhattan Beach** (city) Los Angeles County
41	2514	85.7	**Orcutt** (CDP) Santa Barbara County
41	2514	85.7	**Rocklin** (city) Placer County
45	2549	85.4	**Laguna Beach** (city) Orange County
46	2571	85.2	**Fortuna** (city) Humboldt County
46	2571	85.2	**Lake Arrowhead** (CDP) San Bernardino County
46	2571	85.2	**Placerville** (city) El Dorado County
49	2605	85.0	**Benicia** (city) Solano County
49	2605	85.0	**Malibu** (city) Los Angeles County
49	2605	85.0	**Marysville** (city) Yuba County
49	2605	85.0	**Santee** (city) San Diego County
53	2636	84.8	**San Clemente** (city) Orange County
53	2636	84.8	**Seal Beach** (city) Orange County
55	2674	84.5	**Alpine** (CDP) San Diego County
56	2684	84.4	**Fair Oaks** (CDP) Sacramento County
57	2692	84.3	**Arroyo Grande** (city) San Luis Obispo County
57	2692	84.3	**Dana Point** (city) Orange County
57	2692	84.3	**Truckee** (town) Nevada County
60	2708	84.2	**Carmichael** (CDP) Sacramento County
61	2722	84.1	**Mill Valley** (city) Marin County
62	2733	84.0	**Apple Valley** (town) San Bernardino County
63	2751	83.8	**Martinez** (city) Contra Costa County
63	2751	83.8	**Ripon** (city) San Joaquin County
65	2760	83.7	**Coronado** (city) San Diego County
66	2804	83.3	**La Riviera** (CDP) Sacramento County
66	2804	83.3	**Lakeside** (CDP) San Diego County
68	2816	83.2	**Big Bear City** (CDP) San Bernardino County
69	2840	82.9	**Encinitas** (city) San Diego County
69	2840	82.9	**Oroville** (city) Butte County
69	2840	82.9	**Valle Vista** (CDP) Riverside County
72	2858	82.8	**Newport Beach** (city) Orange County
73	2870	82.7	**North Tustin** (CDP) Orange County
74	2892	82.5	**North Auburn** (CDP) Placer County
74	2892	82.5	**San Luis Obispo** (city) San Luis Obispo County
76	2909	82.4	**Carlsbad** (city) San Diego County
77	2918	82.3	**Piedmont** (city) Alameda County
78	2933	82.2	**Grover Beach** (city) San Luis Obispo County
79	2944	82.1	**Lincoln** (city) Placer County
79	2944	82.1	**Rancho Mirage** (city) Riverside County
81	2978	81.7	**Clearlake** (city) Lake County
82	2999	81.5	**Casa de Oro-Mount Helix** (CDP) San Diego County
82	2999	81.5	**Yucaipa** (city) San Bernardino County
84	3009	81.4	**Red Bluff** (city) Tehama County
85	3026	81.2	**Laguna Woods** (city) Orange County
85	3026	81.2	**Moraga** (town) Contra Costa County
85	3026	81.2	**Morro Bay** (city) San Luis Obispo County
85	3026	81.2	**Roseville** (city) Placer County
89	3048	80.9	**Phelan** (CDP) San Bernardino County
90	3058	80.8	**Larkspur** (city) Marin County
91	3082	80.6	**Orinda** (city) Contra Costa County
91	3082	80.6	**Rio Linda** (CDP) Sacramento County
93	3093	80.5	**California City** (city) Kern County
93	3093	80.5	**Citrus Heights** (city) Sacramento County
95	3106	80.4	**Los Gatos** (town) Santa Clara County
95	3106	80.4	**Oak Park** (CDP) Ventura County
95	3106	80.4	**Vacaville** (city) Solano County
98	3118	80.3	**Oakdale** (city) Stanislaus County
98	3118	80.3	**Winter Gardens** (CDP) San Diego County
100	3142	80.0	**Sierra Madre** (city) Los Angeles County
101	3234	78.7	**Folsom** (city) Sacramento County
101	3234	78.7	**Poway** (city) San Diego County
101	3234	78.7	**Temecula** (city) Riverside County
104	3246	78.6	**Agoura Hills** (city) Los Angeles County
105	3259	78.4	**Arden-Arcade** (CDP) Sacramento County
106	3264	78.3	**Livermore** (city) Alameda County
106	3264	78.3	**San Carlos** (city) San Mateo County
108	3276	78.2	**La Mesa** (city) San Diego County
109	3289	78.0	**El Segundo** (city) Los Angeles County
109	3289	78.0	**Menifee** (city) Riverside County
109	3289	78.0	**Susanville** (city) Lassen County
112	3297	77.9	**Mission Viejo** (city) Orange County
113	3316	77.5	**Solana Beach** (city) San Diego County
114	3325	77.4	**Brentwood** (city) Contra Costa County
114	3325	77.4	**Murrieta** (city) Riverside County
116	3335	77.2	**Pleasant Hill** (city) Contra Costa County
117	3348	77.0	**Huntington Beach** (city) Orange County
117	3348	77.0	**Ladera Ranch** (CDP) Orange County
117	3348	77.0	**Los Alamitos** (city) Orange County
117	3348	77.0	**Santa Cruz** (city) Santa Cruz County
121	3360	76.9	**Clovis** (city) Fresno County
121	3360	76.9	**Rancho Santa Margarita** (city) Orange County
121	3360	76.9	**Walnut Creek** (city) Contra Costa County
124	3390	76.5	**La Verne** (city) Los Angeles County
125	3401	76.3	**Camarillo** (city) Ventura County
126	3415	76.1	**Windsor** (town) Sonoma County
127	3425	75.9	**Nipomo** (CDP) San Luis Obispo County
127	3425	75.9	**Palos Verdes Estates** (city) Los Angeles County
129	3439	75.8	**Yorba Linda** (city) Orange County
130	3443	75.7	**Thousand Oaks** (city) Ventura County
131	3450	75.6	**Novato** (city) Marin County
132	3456	75.4	**Palm Desert** (city) Riverside County
132	3456	75.4	**Woodcrest** (CDP) Riverside County
134	3472	75.1	**Laguna Niguel** (city) Orange County
134	3472	75.1	**Redlands** (city) San Bernardino County
136	3480	75.0	**Exeter** (city) Tulare County
136	3480	75.0	**Redondo Beach** (city) Los Angeles County
136	3480	75.0	**Rohnert Park** (city) Sonoma County
139	3497	74.8	**Barstow** (city) San Bernardino County
140	3507	74.6	**Petaluma** (city) Sonoma County
141	3520	74.4	**Lancaster** (city) Los Angeles County
142	3526	74.3	**Grand Terrace** (city) San Bernardino County
143	3529	74.2	**La Quinta** (city) Riverside County
143	3529	74.2	**Simi Valley** (city) Ventura County
143	3529	74.2	**Wildomar** (city) Riverside County
146	3538	74.1	**Glendora** (city) Los Angeles County
147	3545	74.0	**San Buenaventura (Ventura)** (city) Ventura County
148	3551	73.9	**Berkeley** (city) Alameda County
149	3560	73.8	**Davis** (city) Yolo County
150	3563	73.7	**Norco** (city) Riverside County

***Note:** The state column ranks the top/bottom 150 places from all places in the state with population of 10,000 or more. The national column ranks the top/bottom 150 places from all places in the country with population of 10,000 or more. Places that are unincorporated were not considered in the rankings. Please refer to the User Guide for additional information.*

Speak English Only at Home

Top 150 Places Ranked in *Ascending* Order

State Rank	Nat'l Rank	Percent	Place
1	3	3.5	**Calexico** (city) Imperial County
2	5	4.8	**Huntington Park** (city) Los Angeles County
3	13	7.3	**Cudahy** (city) Los Angeles County
4	15	8.2	**Bell Gardens** (city) Los Angeles County
4	15	8.2	**Maywood** (city) Los Angeles County
6	20	8.7	**Walnut Park** (CDP) Los Angeles County
7	24	9.7	**South Gate** (city) Los Angeles County
8	27	10.7	**Coachella** (city) Riverside County
9	28	11.1	**Lennox** (CDP) Los Angeles County
10	29	11.5	**Bell** (city) Los Angeles County
10	29	11.5	**Mendota** (city) Fresno County
12	35	11.9	**Florence-Graham** (CDP) Los Angeles County
13	37	12.3	**Arvin** (city) Kern County
14	38	12.4	**East Los Angeles** (CDP) Los Angeles County
15	40	12.7	**Greenfield** (city) Monterey County
16	41	12.8	**South El Monte** (city) Los Angeles County
17	43	13.3	**Lamont** (CDP) Kern County
18	46	13.9	**El Monte** (city) Los Angeles County
18	46	13.9	**King City** (city) Monterey County
20	50	14.6	**Livingston** (city) Merced County
21	51	14.8	**McFarland** (city) Kern County
22	55	16.2	**South San Jose Hills** (CDP) Los Angeles County
23	57	16.4	**Baldwin Park** (city) Los Angeles County
23	57	16.4	**Lynwood** (city) Los Angeles County
25	60	17.1	**Santa Ana** (city) Orange County
26	61	17.4	**Parlier** (city) Fresno County
27	63	18.2	**Rosemead** (city) Los Angeles County
28	76	20.9	**Hawaiian Gardens** (city) Los Angeles County
29	78	21.2	**Lindsay** (city) Tulare County
30	80	21.7	**La Puente** (city) Los Angeles County
30	80	21.7	**Monterey Park** (city) Los Angeles County
32	83	22.3	**West Puente Valley** (CDP) Los Angeles County
33	85	23.0	**East Rancho Dominguez** (CDP) Los Angeles County
34	86	23.1	**Commerce** (city) Los Angeles County
35	87	23.6	**San Fernando** (city) Los Angeles County
36	89	23.9	**El Centro** (city) Imperial County
37	91	24.0	**Paramount** (city) Los Angeles County
38	92	24.1	**Watsonville** (city) Santa Cruz County
39	93	24.4	**Delano** (city) Kern County
40	96	24.8	**Delhi** (CDP) Merced County
41	97	24.9	**Muscoy** (CDP) San Bernardino County
42	101	25.5	**Alhambra** (city) Los Angeles County
42	101	25.5	**Valinda** (CDP) Los Angeles County
44	104	26.0	**Pico Rivera** (city) Los Angeles County
45	108	26.6	**Rowland Heights** (CDP) Los Angeles County
46	110	26.8	**San Gabriel** (city) Los Angeles County
47	112	27.1	**National City** (city) San Diego County
48	115	27.3	**North Fair Oaks** (CDP) San Mateo County
48	115	27.3	**Winton** (CDP) Merced County
50	117	27.5	**Montebello** (city) Los Angeles County
51	119	27.6	**Avocado Heights** (CDP) Los Angeles County
52	120	27.7	**Farmersville** (city) Tulare County
53	122	28.0	**Avenal** (city) Kings County
54	125	28.7	**Kerman** (city) Fresno County
54	125	28.7	**Shafter** (city) Kern County
56	134	29.9	**East Palo Alto** (city) San Mateo County
57	136	30.1	**Glendale** (city) Los Angeles County
58	138	30.2	**Willowbrook** (CDP) Los Angeles County
59	140	30.8	**Wasco** (city) Kern County
60	143	30.9	**Downey** (city) Los Angeles County
61	144	31.4	**Daly City** (city) San Mateo County
62	146	31.5	**Salinas** (city) Monterey County
63	147	31.6	**Dinuba** (city) Tulare County
64	150	32.0	**Norwalk** (city) Los Angeles County
65	151	32.1	**Oxnard** (city) Ventura County
66	156	32.5	**Home Gardens** (CDP) Riverside County
67	159	32.8	**Garden Grove** (city) Orange County
68	161	32.9	**Artesia** (city) Los Angeles County
68	161	32.9	**Bloomington** (CDP) San Bernardino County
68	161	32.9	**San Pablo** (city) Contra Costa County
71	165	33.3	**Hacienda Heights** (CDP) Los Angeles County
72	166	33.7	**Brawley** (city) Imperial County
73	168	34.1	**Stanton** (city) Orange County
73	168	34.1	**Westminster** (city) Orange County
75	172	34.3	**Mead Valley** (CDP) Riverside County
76	174	34.4	**Citrus** (CDP) Los Angeles County
77	175	34.5	**Lawndale** (city) Los Angeles County
78	177	34.6	**Montclair** (city) San Bernardino County
78	177	34.6	**Temple City** (city) Los Angeles County
80	181	35.3	**Pomona** (city) Los Angeles County
81	183	35.5	**Milpitas** (city) Santa Clara County
82	184	35.6	**West Whittier-Los Nietos** (CDP) Los Angeles County
83	185	35.7	**Santa Maria** (city) Santa Barbara County
84	188	36.2	**Alum Rock** (CDP) Santa Clara County
85	191	36.6	**Imperial** (city) Imperial County
86	192	36.7	**Reedley** (city) Fresno County
87	193	36.8	**Compton** (city) Los Angeles County
87	193	36.8	**Walnut** (city) Los Angeles County
89	195	36.9	**Soledad** (city) Monterey County
90	196	37.0	**Cupertino** (city) Santa Clara County
90	196	37.0	**Madera** (city) Madera County
92	200	37.3	**Union City** (city) Alameda County
93	201	37.4	**Arcadia** (city) Los Angeles County
94	205	38.1	**Perris** (city) Riverside County
95	206	38.3	**East San Gabriel** (CDP) Los Angeles County
96	207	39.0	**Anaheim** (city) Orange County
97	210	39.4	**Garden Acres** (CDP) San Joaquin County
98	211	39.5	**Cerritos** (city) Los Angeles County
99	212	39.8	**Los Angeles** (city) Los Angeles County
100	218	40.2	**Santa Paula** (city) Ventura County
101	220	40.4	**South San Francisco** (city) San Mateo County
102	223	40.8	**South Whittier** (CDP) Los Angeles County
103	225	40.9	**Santa Fe Springs** (city) Los Angeles County
104	226	41.3	**Ontario** (city) San Bernardino County
105	229	41.6	**Fontana** (city) San Bernardino County
105	229	41.6	**Fremont** (city) Alameda County
107	231	41.8	**Sanger** (city) Fresno County
108	232	41.9	**Azusa** (city) Los Angeles County
108	232	41.9	**Cherryland** (CDP) Alameda County
110	236	42.1	**Selma** (city) Fresno County
111	242	42.8	**Hayward** (city) Alameda County
112	245	42.9	**Bay Point** (CDP) Contra Costa County
112	245	42.9	**Chula Vista** (city) San Diego County
114	250	43.1	**Rialto** (city) San Bernardino County
115	252	43.3	**Fillmore** (city) Ventura County
116	254	43.6	**Hawthorne** (city) Los Angeles County
117	258	43.9	**Diamond Bar** (city) Los Angeles County
117	258	43.9	**San Jose** (city) Santa Clara County
119	261	44.1	**Indio** (city) Riverside County
120	266	44.5	**West Covina** (city) Los Angeles County
121	271	44.9	**Cathedral City** (city) Riverside County
122	273	45.0	**Patterson** (city) Stanislaus County
123	276	45.2	**Buena Park** (city) Orange County
123	276	45.2	**Lemon Hill** (CDP) Sacramento County
125	281	45.4	**Tustin** (city) Orange County
126	286	45.9	**Sunnyvale** (city) Santa Clara County
127	287	46.0	**Carson** (city) Los Angeles County
128	296	46.2	**Ashland** (CDP) Alameda County
129	300	46.4	**Duarte** (city) Los Angeles County
130	303	46.6	**Newman** (city) Stanislaus County
131	308	47.0	**Bellflower** (city) Los Angeles County
131	308	47.0	**Ceres** (city) Stanislaus County
133	311	47.1	**San Marino** (city) Los Angeles County
134	319	47.6	**Del Aire** (CDP) Los Angeles County
134	319	47.6	**La Presa** (CDP) San Diego County
134	319	47.6	**Los Banos** (city) Merced County
137	328	47.9	**Gardena** (city) Los Angeles County
138	331	48.0	**Colton** (city) San Bernardino County
139	333	48.1	**West Carson** (CDP) Los Angeles County
140	337	48.4	**Beverly Hills** (city) Los Angeles County
141	339	48.6	**San Lorenzo** (CDP) Alameda County
142	342	48.7	**Inglewood** (city) Los Angeles County
143	344	48.9	**Florin** (CDP) Sacramento County
144	348	49.2	**La Habra** (city) Orange County
144	348	49.2	**Santa Clara** (city) Santa Clara County
146	350	49.3	**Moreno Valley** (city) Riverside County
147	352	49.4	**Corcoran** (city) Kings County
148	354	49.5	**Millbrae** (city) San Mateo County
148	354	49.5	**Newark** (city) Alameda County
150	357	50.0	**Foster City** (city) San Mateo County

Note: *The state column ranks the top/bottom 150 places from all places in the state with population of 10,000 or more. The national column ranks the top/bottom 150 places from all places in the country with population of 10,000 or more. Places that are unincorporated were not considered in the rankings. Please refer to the User Guide for additional information.*

Population with a Disability

Top 150 Places Ranked in *Descending* Order

State Rank	Nat'l Rank	Percent	Place
1	3	29.0	**Laguna Woods** (city) Orange County
2	7	26.4	**Clearlake** (city) Lake County
3	32	23.3	**Magalia** (CDP) Butte County
4	40	22.7	**Paradise** (town) Butte County
5	49	22.2	**Grass Valley** (city) Nevada County
6	61	21.8	**Oroville** (city) Butte County
7	135	20.2	**Red Bluff** (city) Tehama County
8	165	19.8	**Banning** (city) Riverside County
8	165	19.8	**Marysville** (city) Yuba County
10	176	19.7	**Shasta Lake** (city) Shasta County
11	188	19.6	**Hemet** (city) Riverside County
12	195	19.5	**Merced** (city) Merced County
13	318	18.2	**Oildale** (CDP) Kern County
14	349	17.9	**Barstow** (city) San Bernardino County
15	357	17.8	**Phelan** (CDP) San Bernardino County
15	357	17.8	**Seal Beach** (city) Orange County
17	377	17.7	**Susanville** (city) Lassen County
18	384	17.6	**Diamond Springs** (CDP) El Dorado County
18	384	17.6	**Eureka** (city) Humboldt County
20	399	17.5	**Valle Vista** (CDP) Riverside County
21	436	17.2	**Palm Springs** (city) Riverside County
22	466	17.0	**Fortuna** (city) Humboldt County
22	466	17.0	**Lemon Hill** (CDP) Sacramento County
24	481	16.9	**Linda** (CDP) Yuba County
25	499	16.8	**East Hemet** (CDP) Riverside County
26	515	16.7	**Livingston** (city) Merced County
26	515	16.7	**Placerville** (city) El Dorado County
28	536	16.6	**Redding** (city) Shasta County
29	593	16.3	**Atwater** (city) Merced County
29	593	16.3	**Olivehurst** (CDP) Yuba County
31	610	16.2	**Winton** (CDP) Merced County
32	632	16.1	**Parkway** (CDP) Sacramento County
33	717	15.7	**Delhi** (CDP) Merced County
33	717	15.7	**Florin** (CDP) Sacramento County
35	740	15.6	**Rancho Mirage** (city) Riverside County
35	740	15.6	**Ukiah** (city) Mendocino County
37	791	15.4	**Apple Valley** (town) San Bernardino County
37	791	15.4	**Big Bear City** (CDP) San Bernardino County
39	869	15.1	**Chowchilla** (city) Madera County
39	869	15.1	**Rio Linda** (CDP) Sacramento County
41	899	15.0	**California City** (city) Kern County
41	899	15.0	**Carmichael** (CDP) Sacramento County
43	920	14.9	**Yucca Valley** (town) San Bernardino County
44	957	14.7	**North Auburn** (CDP) Placer County
45	979	14.6	**Auburn** (city) Placer County
46	1007	14.5	**Modesto** (city) Stanislaus County
46	1007	14.5	**North Highlands** (CDP) Sacramento County
48	1058	14.3	**Montebello** (city) Los Angeles County
48	1058	14.3	**San Jacinto** (city) Riverside County
50	1086	14.2	**Arden-Arcade** (CDP) Sacramento County
50	1086	14.2	**Los Osos** (CDP) San Luis Obispo County
52	1119	14.1	**Lakeside** (CDP) San Diego County
53	1145	14.0	**Palm Desert** (city) Riverside County
53	1145	14.0	**West Hollywood** (city) Los Angeles County
55	1177	13.9	**McKinleyville** (CDP) Humboldt County
55	1177	13.9	**Tehachapi** (city) Kern County
55	1177	13.9	**West Sacramento** (city) Yolo County
58	1201	13.8	**Blythe** (city) Riverside County
58	1201	13.8	**Grover Beach** (city) San Luis Obispo County
58	1201	13.8	**Port Hueneme** (city) Ventura County
61	1228	13.7	**Citrus Heights** (city) Sacramento County
62	1258	13.6	**Bostonia** (CDP) San Diego County
62	1258	13.6	**Calexico** (city) Imperial County
62	1258	13.6	**Fairview** (CDP) Alameda County
62	1258	13.6	**Pittsburg** (city) Contra Costa County
62	1258	13.6	**Twentynine Palms** (city) San Bernardino County
67	1298	13.5	**Menifee** (city) Riverside County
68	1324	13.4	**Ridgecrest** (city) Kern County
69	1347	13.3	**Alpine** (CDP) San Diego County
69	1347	13.3	**Galt** (city) Sacramento County
69	1347	13.3	**Sacramento** (city) Sacramento County
72	1393	13.2	**Brawley** (city) Imperial County
72	1393	13.2	**Crestline** (CDP) San Bernardino County
72	1393	13.2	**San Bernardino** (city) San Bernardino County
75	1426	13.1	**Ceres** (city) Stanislaus County
75	1426	13.1	**Lakeland Village** (CDP) Riverside County
75	1426	13.1	**Pinole** (city) Contra Costa County
75	1426	13.1	**Spring Valley** (CDP) San Diego County
75	1426	13.1	**Yuba City** (city) Sutter County
80	1458	13.0	**Rancho Cordova** (city) Sacramento County
81	1489	12.9	**Fallbrook** (CDP) San Diego County
81	1489	12.9	**Glendale** (city) Los Angeles County
81	1489	12.9	**Hesperia** (city) San Bernardino County
84	1522	12.8	**Antioch** (city) Contra Costa County
85	1554	12.7	**Lake Los Angeles** (CDP) Los Angeles County
86	1580	12.6	**Desert Hot Springs** (city) Riverside County
86	1580	12.6	**El Cajon** (city) San Diego County
88	1618	12.5	**El Centro** (city) Imperial County
88	1618	12.5	**West Puente Valley** (CDP) Los Angeles County
90	1655	12.4	**Chico** (city) Butte County
90	1655	12.4	**Orcutt** (CDP) Santa Barbara County
90	1655	12.4	**Pleasant Hill** (city) Contra Costa County
90	1655	12.4	**Rosemont** (CDP) Sacramento County
90	1655	12.4	**South Lake Tahoe** (city) El Dorado County
90	1655	12.4	**Stockton** (city) San Joaquin County
90	1655	12.4	**View Park-Windsor Hills** (CDP) Los Angeles County
90	1655	12.4	**West Whittier-Los Nietos** (CDP) Los Angeles County
98	1705	12.3	**Cathedral City** (city) Riverside County
98	1705	12.3	**Compton** (city) Los Angeles County
98	1705	12.3	**Fresno** (city) Fresno County
98	1705	12.3	**Sonoma** (city) Sonoma County
98	1705	12.3	**Vallejo** (city) Solano County
98	1705	12.3	**Westmont** (CDP) Los Angeles County
98	1705	12.3	**Yucaipa** (city) San Bernardino County
105	1744	12.2	**South El Monte** (city) Los Angeles County
106	1788	12.1	**Lemon Grove** (city) San Diego County
106	1788	12.1	**Lincoln** (city) Placer County
108	1824	12.0	**Corcoran** (city) Kings County
108	1824	12.0	**El Sobrante** (CDP) Contra Costa County
108	1824	12.0	**Garden Acres** (CDP) San Joaquin County
108	1824	12.0	**La Mesa** (city) San Diego County
108	1824	12.0	**San Lorenzo** (CDP) Alameda County
108	1824	12.0	**Winter Gardens** (CDP) San Diego County
114	1872	11.9	**Arroyo Grande** (city) San Luis Obispo County
114	1872	11.9	**Cherryland** (CDP) Alameda County
114	1872	11.9	**La Presa** (CDP) San Diego County
114	1872	11.9	**Pacific Grove** (city) Monterey County
114	1872	11.9	**Walnut Creek** (city) Contra Costa County
114	1872	11.9	**West Carson** (CDP) Los Angeles County
120	1912	11.8	**East Rancho Dominguez** (CDP) Los Angeles County
120	1912	11.8	**Foothill Farms** (CDP) Sacramento County
120	1912	11.8	**Turlock** (city) Stanislaus County
123	1952	11.7	**Carpinteria** (city) Santa Barbara County
123	1952	11.7	**La Riviera** (CDP) Sacramento County
123	1952	11.7	**Lodi** (city) San Joaquin County
123	1952	11.7	**Rosamond** (CDP) Kern County
123	1952	11.7	**Santa Fe Springs** (city) Los Angeles County
128	1996	11.6	**Atascadero** (city) San Luis Obispo County
128	1996	11.6	**Lompoc** (city) Santa Barbara County
128	1996	11.6	**San Pablo** (city) Contra Costa County
131	2049	11.5	**Woodland** (city) Yolo County
132	2082	11.4	**Artesia** (city) Los Angeles County
132	2082	11.4	**Casa de Oro-Mount Helix** (CDP) San Diego County
132	2082	11.4	**Farmersville** (city) Tulare County
132	2082	11.4	**Hanford** (city) Kings County
132	2082	11.4	**Imperial Beach** (city) San Diego County
132	2082	11.4	**Marina** (city) Monterey County
132	2082	11.4	**Oakland** (city) Alameda County
139	2134	11.3	**Bay Point** (CDP) Contra Costa County
139	2134	11.3	**Cameron Park** (CDP) El Dorado County
139	2134	11.3	**Healdsburg** (city) Sonoma County
139	2134	11.3	**Orangevale** (CDP) Sacramento County
139	2134	11.3	**Santa Rosa** (city) Sonoma County
139	2134	11.3	**Shafter** (city) Kern County
139	2134	11.3	**Tulare** (city) Tulare County
146	2178	11.2	**Emeryville** (city) Alameda County
146	2178	11.2	**Indio** (city) Riverside County
146	2178	11.2	**Porterville** (city) Tulare County
146	2178	11.2	**Prunedale** (CDP) Monterey County
146	2178	11.2	**San Fernando** (city) Los Angeles County

***Note:** The state column ranks the top/bottom 150 places from all places in the state with population of 10,000 or more. The national column ranks the top/bottom 150 places from all places in the country with population of 10,000 or more. Places that are unincorporated were not considered in the rankings. Please refer to the User Guide for additional information.*

Population with a Disability

Top 150 Places Ranked in *Ascending* Order

State Rank	Nat'l Rank	Percent	Place
1	13	3.6	**El Sobrante** (CDP) Riverside County
2	16	3.7	**Ladera Ranch** (CDP) Orange County
2	16	3.7	**Stanford** (CDP) Santa Clara County
4	30	4.2	**Isla Vista** (CDP) Santa Barbara County
4	30	4.2	**Rancho Santa Margarita** (city) Orange County
6	34	4.3	**Aliso Viejo** (city) Orange County
6	34	4.3	**Coto de Caza** (CDP) Orange County
8	42	4.4	**Piedmont** (city) Alameda County
9	64	4.7	**Oak Park** (CDP) Ventura County
10	71	4.8	**Truckee** (town) Nevada County
11	80	4.9	**San Ramon** (city) Contra Costa County
12	104	5.1	**Camp Pendleton South** (CDP) San Diego County
13	119	5.2	**Manhattan Beach** (city) Los Angeles County
14	128	5.3	**Hermosa Beach** (city) Los Angeles County
15	138	5.4	**Irvine** (city) Orange County
16	159	5.5	**Alamo** (CDP) Contra Costa County
16	159	5.5	**Burlingame** (city) San Mateo County
16	159	5.5	**Dublin** (city) Alameda County
19	179	5.6	**Eastvale** (city) Riverside County
19	179	5.6	**La Cañada Flintridge** (city) Los Angeles County
21	199	5.7	**El Segundo** (city) Los Angeles County
22	237	5.9	**Foster City** (city) San Mateo County
22	237	5.9	**Lennox** (CDP) Los Angeles County
24	258	6.0	**Cupertino** (city) Santa Clara County
24	258	6.0	**Hillsborough** (town) San Mateo County
24	258	6.0	**San Carlos** (city) San Mateo County
27	272	6.1	**Stevenson Ranch** (CDP) Los Angeles County
27	272	6.1	**Tustin** (city) Orange County
27	272	6.1	**Walnut** (city) Los Angeles County
30	305	6.3	**Davis** (city) Yolo County
30	305	6.3	**Menlo Park** (city) San Mateo County
30	305	6.3	**Mountain View** (city) Santa Clara County
33	333	6.4	**Calabasas** (city) Los Angeles County
33	333	6.4	**El Dorado Hills** (CDP) El Dorado County
33	333	6.4	**Lafayette** (city) Contra Costa County
33	333	6.4	**Laguna Niguel** (city) Orange County
33	333	6.4	**Palos Verdes Estates** (city) Los Angeles County
38	358	6.5	**Chino Hills** (city) San Bernardino County
38	358	6.5	**Los Altos** (city) Santa Clara County
38	358	6.5	**Maywood** (city) Los Angeles County
38	358	6.5	**Moorpark** (city) Ventura County
38	358	6.5	**San Marino** (city) Los Angeles County
43	386	6.6	**Agoura Hills** (city) Los Angeles County
43	386	6.6	**Laguna Beach** (city) Orange County
43	386	6.6	**Lake Forest** (city) Orange County
43	386	6.6	**Pleasanton** (city) Alameda County
43	386	6.6	**Solana Beach** (city) San Diego County
48	408	6.7	**Arcadia** (city) Los Angeles County
48	408	6.7	**Azusa** (city) Los Angeles County
48	408	6.7	**Redondo Beach** (city) Los Angeles County
48	408	6.7	**Sunnyvale** (city) Santa Clara County
52	435	6.8	**Albany** (city) Alameda County
52	435	6.8	**La Crescenta-Montrose** (CDP) Los Angeles County
54	465	6.9	**Clayton** (city) Contra Costa County
54	465	6.9	**East San Gabriel** (CDP) Los Angeles County
54	465	6.9	**Saratoga** (city) Santa Clara County
54	465	6.9	**Tamalpais-Homestead Valley** (CDP) Marin County
58	486	7.0	**Castaic** (CDP) Los Angeles County
58	486	7.0	**Encinitas** (city) San Diego County
58	486	7.0	**King City** (city) Monterey County
58	486	7.0	**Newport Beach** (city) Orange County
58	486	7.0	**North Fair Oaks** (CDP) San Mateo County
63	520	7.1	**Imperial** (city) Imperial County
63	520	7.1	**Mendota** (city) Fresno County
63	520	7.1	**Orinda** (city) Contra Costa County
63	520	7.1	**Palo Alto** (city) Santa Clara County
63	520	7.1	**Sierra Madre** (city) Los Angeles County
63	520	7.1	**Soledad** (city) Monterey County
63	520	7.1	**South Pasadena** (city) Los Angeles County
63	520	7.1	**Yorba Linda** (city) Orange County
71	550	7.2	**Bell Gardens** (city) Los Angeles County
71	550	7.2	**Diamond Bar** (city) Los Angeles County
71	550	7.2	**Fremont** (city) Alameda County
71	550	7.2	**Salinas** (city) Monterey County
75	589	7.3	**Corona** (city) Riverside County
75	589	7.3	**Danville** (town) Contra Costa County
75	589	7.3	**Milpitas** (city) Santa Clara County
78	624	7.4	**Carlsbad** (city) San Diego County
78	624	7.4	**Costa Mesa** (city) Orange County
78	624	7.4	**East Palo Alto** (city) San Mateo County
78	624	7.4	**Los Gatos** (town) Santa Clara County
78	624	7.4	**Orange** (city) Orange County
83	669	7.5	**Moraga** (town) Contra Costa County
84	703	7.6	**Florence-Graham** (CDP) Los Angeles County
84	703	7.6	**Redwood City** (city) San Mateo County
86	749	7.7	**Anaheim** (city) Orange County
86	749	7.7	**Greenfield** (city) Monterey County
86	749	7.7	**Hercules** (city) Contra Costa County
86	749	7.7	**Monrovia** (city) Los Angeles County
86	749	7.7	**Pacifica** (city) San Mateo County
86	749	7.7	**Parlier** (city) Fresno County
86	749	7.7	**Rowland Heights** (CDP) Los Angeles County
86	749	7.7	**Santa Clara** (city) Santa Clara County
94	797	7.8	**American Canyon** (city) Napa County
94	797	7.8	**French Valley** (CDP) Riverside County
94	797	7.8	**Gilroy** (city) Santa Clara County
94	797	7.8	**Huntington Park** (city) Los Angeles County
94	797	7.8	**Livermore** (city) Alameda County
94	797	7.8	**McFarland** (city) Kern County
94	797	7.8	**Mission Viejo** (city) Orange County
94	797	7.8	**Morgan Hill** (city) Santa Clara County
94	797	7.8	**Murrieta** (city) Riverside County
94	797	7.8	**Newark** (city) Alameda County
94	797	7.8	**San Clemente** (city) Orange County
105	853	7.9	**Arvin** (city) Kern County
105	853	7.9	**Beaumont** (city) Riverside County
105	853	7.9	**Belmont** (city) San Mateo County
105	853	7.9	**Berkeley** (city) Alameda County
105	853	7.9	**Dana Point** (city) Orange County
105	853	7.9	**Delano** (city) Kern County
105	853	7.9	**Discovery Bay** (CDP) Contra Costa County
105	853	7.9	**Folsom** (city) Sacramento County
105	853	7.9	**Hawthorne** (city) Los Angeles County
105	853	7.9	**San Gabriel** (city) Los Angeles County
115	903	8.0	**Canyon Lake** (city) Riverside County
115	903	8.0	**Cerritos** (city) Los Angeles County
115	903	8.0	**Citrus** (CDP) Los Angeles County
115	903	8.0	**Goleta** (city) Santa Barbara County
115	903	8.0	**Granite Bay** (CDP) Placer County
115	903	8.0	**Hollister** (city) San Benito County
115	903	8.0	**Lindsay** (city) Tulare County
115	903	8.0	**San Anselmo** (town) Marin County
115	903	8.0	**Santa Cruz** (city) Santa Cruz County
115	903	8.0	**Scotts Valley** (city) Santa Cruz County
115	903	8.0	**Temecula** (city) Riverside County
126	953	8.1	**Avenal** (city) Kings County
126	953	8.1	**Daly City** (city) San Mateo County
126	953	8.1	**Pomona** (city) Los Angeles County
126	953	8.1	**Poway** (city) San Diego County
126	953	8.1	**Rancho Cucamonga** (city) San Bernardino County
126	953	8.1	**Rosemead** (city) Los Angeles County
126	953	8.1	**San Jose** (city) Santa Clara County
126	953	8.1	**Santa Ana** (city) Orange County
126	953	8.1	**Signal Hill** (city) Los Angeles County
126	953	8.1	**Wasco** (city) Kern County
136	997	8.2	**Culver City** (city) Los Angeles County
136	997	8.2	**Cypress** (city) Orange County
136	997	8.2	**Fullerton** (city) Orange County
136	997	8.2	**San Marcos** (city) San Diego County
136	997	8.2	**Union City** (city) Alameda County
141	1041	8.3	**Brea** (city) Orange County
141	1041	8.3	**Hacienda Heights** (CDP) Los Angeles County
141	1041	8.3	**Huntington Beach** (city) Orange County
141	1041	8.3	**La Habra** (city) Orange County
141	1041	8.3	**Laguna Hills** (city) Orange County
141	1041	8.3	**Lynwood** (city) Los Angeles County
141	1041	8.3	**San Diego Country Estates** (CDP) San Diego County
141	1041	8.3	**Tracy** (city) San Joaquin County
149	1092	8.4	**Alhambra** (city) Los Angeles County
149	1092	8.4	**Brentwood** (city) Contra Costa County

Note: *The state column ranks the top/bottom 150 places from all places in the state with population of 10,000 or more. The national column ranks the top/bottom 150 places from all places in the country with population of 10,000 or more. Places that are unincorporated were not considered in the rankings. Please refer to the User Guide for additional information.*

Veterans

Top 150 Places Ranked in *Descending* Order

State Rank	Nat'l Rank	Percent	Place
1	53	21.4	**Twentynine Palms** (city) San Bernardino County
2	60	20.7	**Coronado** (city) San Diego County
3	78	19.4	**California City** (city) Kern County
4	84	19.2	**Camp Pendleton South** (CDP) San Diego County
5	94	18.6	**Ridgecrest** (city) Kern County
6	106	18.1	**Laguna Woods** (city) Orange County
6	106	18.1	**Rancho Mirage** (city) Riverside County
8	129	17.5	**Yucca Valley** (town) San Bernardino County
9	162	16.5	**Magalia** (CDP) Butte County
10	186	16.0	**Lemoore** (city) Kings County
11	194	15.9	**Lincoln** (city) Placer County
12	207	15.6	**Barstow** (city) San Bernardino County
13	234	15.2	**Shasta Lake** (city) Shasta County
14	257	14.8	**Orcutt** (CDP) Santa Barbara County
14	257	14.8	**Rosamond** (CDP) Kern County
16	299	14.3	**Alpine** (CDP) San Diego County
16	299	14.3	**Clearlake** (city) Lake County
18	317	14.1	**Cameron Park** (CDP) El Dorado County
19	339	13.9	**La Mesa** (city) San Diego County
19	339	13.9	**Spring Valley** (CDP) San Diego County
21	351	13.7	**Lakeside** (CDP) San Diego County
22	358	13.6	**Diamond Springs** (CDP) El Dorado County
22	358	13.6	**Paradise** (town) Butte County
22	358	13.6	**Vacaville** (city) Solano County
25	388	13.4	**Rancho San Diego** (CDP) San Diego County
25	388	13.4	**San Diego Country Estates** (CDP) San Diego County
27	401	13.3	**Winter Gardens** (CDP) San Diego County
28	429	13.1	**Menifee** (city) Riverside County
28	429	13.1	**Palm Desert** (city) Riverside County
30	461	12.9	**Monterey** (city) Monterey County
30	461	12.9	**North Auburn** (CDP) Placer County
30	461	12.9	**Oceanside** (city) San Diego County
33	482	12.8	**Banning** (city) Riverside County
34	499	12.7	**French Valley** (CDP) Riverside County
34	499	12.7	**Poway** (city) San Diego County
36	518	12.6	**Apple Valley** (town) San Bernardino County
36	518	12.6	**Pacific Grove** (city) Monterey County
38	542	12.5	**Fallbrook** (CDP) San Diego County
38	542	12.5	**Lake Arrowhead** (CDP) San Bernardino County
40	566	12.4	**Marysville** (city) Yuba County
40	566	12.4	**Seal Beach** (city) Orange County
42	586	12.3	**Quartz Hill** (CDP) Los Angeles County
42	586	12.3	**Santee** (city) San Diego County
44	603	12.2	**Arroyo Grande** (city) San Luis Obispo County
44	603	12.2	**Port Hueneme** (city) Ventura County
46	629	12.1	**Eureka** (city) Humboldt County
46	629	12.1	**Hemet** (city) Riverside County
46	629	12.1	**Lemon Grove** (city) San Diego County
49	652	12.0	**Imperial Beach** (city) San Diego County
49	652	12.0	**Palm Springs** (city) Riverside County
49	652	12.0	**Redding** (city) Shasta County
49	652	12.0	**Rio Linda** (CDP) Sacramento County
53	675	11.9	**Bonita** (CDP) San Diego County
53	675	11.9	**Marina** (city) Monterey County
55	697	11.8	**La Presa** (CDP) San Diego County
56	720	11.7	**Camarillo** (city) Ventura County
56	720	11.7	**La Riviera** (CDP) Sacramento County
58	756	11.6	**La Quinta** (city) Riverside County
58	756	11.6	**Suisun City** (city) Solano County
60	796	11.5	**Casa de Oro-Mount Helix** (CDP) San Diego County
60	796	11.5	**Crestline** (CDP) San Bernardino County
62	831	11.4	**Citrus Heights** (city) Sacramento County
63	858	11.3	**Canyon Lake** (city) Riverside County
63	858	11.3	**Los Osos** (CDP) San Luis Obispo County
63	858	11.3	**Oroville** (city) Butte County
66	900	11.2	**Atascadero** (city) San Luis Obispo County
66	900	11.2	**Fairfield** (city) Solano County
66	900	11.2	**Orangevale** (CDP) Sacramento County
69	933	11.1	**Grass Valley** (city) Nevada County
69	933	11.1	**Sonoma** (city) Sonoma County
71	976	11.0	**Big Bear City** (CDP) San Bernardino County
71	976	11.0	**Carmichael** (CDP) Sacramento County
71	976	11.0	**El Paso de Robles (Paso Robles)** (city) San Luis Obispo County
74	1065	10.8	**Hanford** (city) Kings County
74	1065	10.8	**North Highlands** (CDP) Sacramento County
76	1118	10.7	**Fortuna** (city) Humboldt County
76	1118	10.7	**Linda** (CDP) Yuba County
76	1118	10.7	**Lompoc** (city) Santa Barbara County
79	1169	10.6	**McKinleyville** (CDP) Humboldt County
79	1169	10.6	**Morro Bay** (city) San Luis Obispo County
81	1222	10.5	**Benicia** (city) Solano County
81	1222	10.5	**Discovery Bay** (CDP) Contra Costa County
81	1222	10.5	**Fair Oaks** (CDP) Sacramento County
84	1272	10.4	**Bostonia** (CDP) San Diego County
84	1272	10.4	**Chula Vista** (city) San Diego County
84	1272	10.4	**Rancho Cordova** (city) Sacramento County
87	1328	10.3	**Murrieta** (city) Riverside County
87	1328	10.3	**Valle Vista** (CDP) Riverside County
87	1328	10.3	**Wildomar** (city) Riverside County
90	1386	10.2	**Clayton** (city) Contra Costa County
91	1445	10.1	**Imperial** (city) Imperial County
91	1445	10.1	**Ramona** (CDP) San Diego County
91	1445	10.1	**Temecula** (city) Riverside County
94	1492	10.0	**Olivehurst** (CDP) Yuba County
94	1492	10.0	**Phelan** (CDP) San Bernardino County
96	1565	9.9	**View Park-Windsor Hills** (CDP) Los Angeles County
96	1565	9.9	**Yucaipa** (city) San Bernardino County
98	1640	9.8	**El Dorado Hills** (CDP) El Dorado County
98	1640	9.8	**Rocklin** (city) Placer County
98	1640	9.8	**Rosemont** (CDP) Sacramento County
98	1640	9.8	**Roseville** (city) Placer County
98	1640	9.8	**Yuba City** (city) Sutter County
103	1706	9.7	**Dana Point** (city) Orange County
103	1706	9.7	**Martinez** (city) Contra Costa County
103	1706	9.7	**Rossmoor** (CDP) Orange County
106	1770	9.6	**East Hemet** (CDP) Riverside County
106	1770	9.6	**Los Gatos** (town) Santa Clara County
106	1770	9.6	**Red Bluff** (city) Tehama County
106	1770	9.6	**San Buenaventura (Ventura)** (city) Ventura County
110	1832	9.5	**Placerville** (city) El Dorado County
110	1832	9.5	**Vallejo** (city) Solano County
112	1897	9.4	**Oakdale** (city) Stanislaus County
112	1897	9.4	**Prunedale** (CDP) Monterey County
112	1897	9.4	**Rosedale** (CDP) Kern County
115	1977	9.3	**Arden-Arcade** (CDP) Sacramento County
115	1977	9.3	**El Cajon** (city) San Diego County
115	1977	9.3	**Rancho Palos Verdes** (city) Los Angeles County
115	1977	9.3	**Ripon** (city) San Joaquin County
115	1977	9.3	**San Diego** (city) San Diego County
120	2042	9.2	**Atwater** (city) Merced County
120	2042	9.2	**Oildale** (CDP) Kern County
120	2042	9.2	**Solana Beach** (city) San Diego County
120	2042	9.2	**Windsor** (town) Sonoma County
124	2103	9.1	**San Clemente** (city) Orange County
124	2103	9.1	**San Jacinto** (city) Riverside County
126	2178	9.0	**Galt** (city) Sacramento County
126	2178	9.0	**Grand Terrace** (city) San Bernardino County
126	2178	9.0	**San Dimas** (city) Los Angeles County
129	2253	8.9	**Brentwood** (city) Contra Costa County
129	2253	8.9	**Clovis** (city) Fresno County
129	2253	8.9	**Larkspur** (city) Marin County
129	2253	8.9	**North Tustin** (CDP) Orange County
133	2312	8.8	**Auburn** (city) Placer County
133	2312	8.8	**Carlsbad** (city) San Diego County
133	2312	8.8	**Lakeland Village** (CDP) Riverside County
133	2312	8.8	**Manteca** (city) San Joaquin County
133	2312	8.8	**Susanville** (city) Lassen County
133	2312	8.8	**Tehachapi** (city) Kern County
133	2312	8.8	**Ukiah** (city) Mendocino County
133	2312	8.8	**Walnut Creek** (city) Contra Costa County
141	2383	8.7	**Danville** (town) Contra Costa County
141	2383	8.7	**La Verne** (city) Los Angeles County
141	2383	8.7	**Lafayette** (city) Contra Costa County
141	2383	8.7	**Livermore** (city) Alameda County
141	2383	8.7	**Napa** (city) Napa County
141	2383	8.7	**Seaside** (city) Monterey County
147	2468	8.6	**Foothill Farms** (CDP) Sacramento County
147	2468	8.6	**Lake Los Angeles** (CDP) Los Angeles County
149	2535	8.5	**Antelope** (CDP) Sacramento County
149	2535	8.5	**Petaluma** (city) Sonoma County

***Note:** The state column ranks the top/bottom 150 places from all places in the state with population of 10,000 or more. The national column ranks the top/bottom 150 places from all places in the country with population of 10,000 or more. Places that are unincorporated were not considered in the rankings. Please refer to the User Guide for additional information.*

Veterans

Top 150 Places Ranked in *Ascending* Order

State Rank	Nat'l Rank	Percent	Place
1	2	0.6	**Mendota** (city) Fresno County
2	5	0.7	**Isla Vista** (CDP) Santa Barbara County
3	8	0.9	**Bell Gardens** (city) Los Angeles County
3	8	0.9	**Lennox** (CDP) Los Angeles County
3	8	0.9	**Maywood** (city) Los Angeles County
3	8	0.9	**McFarland** (city) Kern County
7	13	1.1	**Stanford** (CDP) Santa Clara County
8	15	1.2	**Arvin** (city) Kern County
8	15	1.2	**Coachella** (city) Riverside County
8	15	1.2	**Cudahy** (city) Los Angeles County
8	15	1.2	**Florence-Graham** (CDP) Los Angeles County
8	15	1.2	**Lamont** (CDP) Kern County
13	20	1.3	**Huntington Park** (city) Los Angeles County
14	28	1.6	**South Gate** (city) Los Angeles County
15	34	1.8	**Calexico** (city) Imperial County
15	34	1.8	**East Los Angeles** (CDP) Los Angeles County
15	34	1.8	**Lynwood** (city) Los Angeles County
15	34	1.8	**Walnut Park** (CDP) Los Angeles County
19	42	1.9	**King City** (city) Monterey County
20	52	2.1	**Bell** (city) Los Angeles County
20	52	2.1	**Willowbrook** (CDP) Los Angeles County
22	60	2.3	**Baldwin Park** (city) Los Angeles County
22	60	2.3	**El Monte** (city) Los Angeles County
22	60	2.3	**Santa Ana** (city) Orange County
25	70	2.4	**Kerman** (city) Fresno County
25	70	2.4	**Parlier** (city) Fresno County
27	76	2.5	**Rosemead** (city) Los Angeles County
28	80	2.6	**Lindsay** (city) Tulare County
28	80	2.6	**South El Monte** (city) Los Angeles County
30	85	2.7	**Artesia** (city) Los Angeles County
30	85	2.7	**South San Jose Hills** (CDP) Los Angeles County
32	92	2.8	**Delano** (city) Kern County
32	92	2.8	**Farmersville** (city) Tulare County
32	92	2.8	**Hawaiian Gardens** (city) Los Angeles County
32	92	2.8	**Paramount** (city) Los Angeles County
36	101	2.9	**Greenfield** (city) Monterey County
36	101	2.9	**Home Gardens** (CDP) Riverside County
36	101	2.9	**West Hollywood** (city) Los Angeles County
39	111	3.0	**Azusa** (city) Los Angeles County
39	111	3.0	**Commerce** (city) Los Angeles County
39	111	3.0	**North Fair Oaks** (CDP) San Mateo County
42	118	3.1	**Alhambra** (city) Los Angeles County
42	118	3.1	**La Puente** (city) Los Angeles County
42	118	3.1	**San Fernando** (city) Los Angeles County
42	118	3.1	**San Gabriel** (city) Los Angeles County
46	133	3.2	**Cupertino** (city) Santa Clara County
46	133	3.2	**East Palo Alto** (city) San Mateo County
46	133	3.2	**East Rancho Dominguez** (CDP) Los Angeles County
46	133	3.2	**Glendale** (city) Los Angeles County
46	133	3.2	**Watsonville** (city) Santa Cruz County
51	152	3.4	**Citrus** (CDP) Los Angeles County
51	152	3.4	**Muscoy** (CDP) San Bernardino County
53	162	3.5	**Ashland** (CDP) Alameda County
53	162	3.5	**Lawndale** (city) Los Angeles County
53	162	3.5	**Pomona** (city) Los Angeles County
53	162	3.5	**Valinda** (CDP) Los Angeles County
57	175	3.6	**Livingston** (city) Merced County
57	175	3.6	**Los Angeles** (city) Los Angeles County
57	175	3.6	**Montclair** (city) San Bernardino County
60	184	3.7	**Compton** (city) Los Angeles County
60	184	3.7	**Delhi** (CDP) Merced County
60	184	3.7	**Garden Acres** (CDP) San Joaquin County
60	184	3.7	**Milpitas** (city) Santa Clara County
60	184	3.7	**Walnut** (city) Los Angeles County
60	184	3.7	**West Puente Valley** (CDP) Los Angeles County
66	200	3.8	**Bloomington** (CDP) San Bernardino County
66	200	3.8	**Hawthorne** (city) Los Angeles County
66	200	3.8	**Monterey Park** (city) Los Angeles County
66	200	3.8	**Shafter** (city) Kern County
66	200	3.8	**Wasco** (city) Kern County
71	214	3.9	**Aliso Viejo** (city) Orange County
71	214	3.9	**Berkeley** (city) Alameda County
71	214	3.9	**Duarte** (city) Los Angeles County
71	214	3.9	**Rowland Heights** (CDP) Los Angeles County
75	229	4.0	**Irvine** (city) Orange County
76	243	4.1	**Beverly Hills** (city) Los Angeles County
76	243	4.1	**Montebello** (city) Los Angeles County
76	243	4.1	**Temple City** (city) Los Angeles County
79	256	4.2	**Avocado Heights** (CDP) Los Angeles County
79	256	4.2	**Davis** (city) Yolo County
79	256	4.2	**Del Aire** (CDP) Los Angeles County
79	256	4.2	**Dinuba** (city) Tulare County
79	256	4.2	**Ontario** (city) San Bernardino County
79	256	4.2	**Salinas** (city) Monterey County
79	256	4.2	**San Francisco** (city) San Francisco County
79	256	4.2	**Santa Cruz** (city) Santa Cruz County
79	256	4.2	**Tustin** (city) Orange County
88	279	4.3	**Daly City** (city) San Mateo County
88	279	4.3	**East San Gabriel** (CDP) Los Angeles County
88	279	4.3	**Lemon Hill** (CDP) Sacramento County
88	279	4.3	**Perris** (city) Riverside County
92	298	4.4	**Arcadia** (city) Los Angeles County
92	298	4.4	**Downey** (city) Los Angeles County
92	298	4.4	**Norwalk** (city) Los Angeles County
92	298	4.4	**Reedley** (city) Fresno County
92	298	4.4	**South Pasadena** (city) Los Angeles County
97	312	4.5	**Diamond Bar** (city) Los Angeles County
97	312	4.5	**Fontana** (city) San Bernardino County
97	312	4.5	**Fremont** (city) Alameda County
97	312	4.5	**Garden Grove** (city) Orange County
97	312	4.5	**Mountain View** (city) Santa Clara County
97	312	4.5	**San Jose** (city) Santa Clara County
103	337	4.6	**Avenal** (city) Kings County
103	337	4.6	**Chowchilla** (city) Madera County
103	337	4.6	**Mead Valley** (CDP) Riverside County
103	337	4.6	**Rancho Santa Margarita** (city) Orange County
103	337	4.6	**Sanger** (city) Fresno County
103	337	4.6	**Santa Clara** (city) Santa Clara County
103	337	4.6	**Union City** (city) Alameda County
110	360	4.7	**Albany** (city) Alameda County
110	360	4.7	**Alum Rock** (CDP) Santa Clara County
110	360	4.7	**Anaheim** (city) Orange County
110	360	4.7	**Cherryland** (CDP) Alameda County
110	360	4.7	**Foster City** (city) San Mateo County
110	360	4.7	**La Crescenta-Montrose** (CDP) Los Angeles County
110	360	4.7	**Madera** (city) Madera County
110	360	4.7	**Santa Monica** (city) Los Angeles County
118	382	4.8	**Culver City** (city) Los Angeles County
118	382	4.8	**Oakland** (city) Alameda County
118	382	4.8	**Sun Village** (CDP) Los Angeles County
121	399	4.9	**Chino Hills** (city) San Bernardino County
121	399	4.9	**Colton** (city) San Bernardino County
121	399	4.9	**Costa Mesa** (city) Orange County
121	399	4.9	**Emeryville** (city) Alameda County
121	399	4.9	**Gilroy** (city) Santa Clara County
121	399	4.9	**Pico Rivera** (city) Los Angeles County
121	399	4.9	**San Bruno** (city) San Mateo County
121	399	4.9	**Selma** (city) Fresno County
129	429	5.0	**Brawley** (city) Imperial County
129	429	5.0	**Burbank** (city) Los Angeles County
129	429	5.0	**Live Oak** (CDP) Santa Cruz County
129	429	5.0	**Richmond** (city) Contra Costa County
129	429	5.0	**San Ramon** (city) Contra Costa County
129	429	5.0	**Stanton** (city) Orange County
129	429	5.0	**Sunnyvale** (city) Santa Clara County
136	458	5.1	**Buena Park** (city) Orange County
136	458	5.1	**Burlingame** (city) San Mateo County
136	458	5.1	**El Centro** (city) Imperial County
136	458	5.1	**Fullerton** (city) Orange County
136	458	5.1	**Hacienda Heights** (CDP) Los Angeles County
136	458	5.1	**Moorpark** (city) Ventura County
136	458	5.1	**Pasadena** (city) Los Angeles County
136	458	5.1	**San Marino** (city) Los Angeles County
136	458	5.1	**Stevenson Ranch** (CDP) Los Angeles County
136	458	5.1	**Westminster** (city) Orange County
146	482	5.2	**Dublin** (city) Alameda County
146	482	5.2	**Eastvale** (city) Riverside County
146	482	5.2	**Newark** (city) Alameda County
146	482	5.2	**Orange** (city) Orange County
146	482	5.2	**Rialto** (city) San Bernardino County

Note: *The state column ranks the top/bottom 150 places from all places in the state with population of 10,000 or more. The national column ranks the top/bottom 150 places from all places in the country with population of 10,000 or more. Places that are unincorporated were not considered in the rankings. Please refer to the User Guide for additional information.*

Ancestry: German

Top 150 Places Ranked in *Descending* Order

State Rank	Nat'l Rank	Percent	Place
1	1	76.8	**Chilton** (city) Calumet County
2	2	73.3	**Barton** (town) Washington County
3	3	73.0	**Addison** (town) Washington County
4	4	72.6	**Dyersville** (city) Dubuque County
5	5	70.9	**Jackson** (town) Washington County
6	6	70.5	**Howards Grove** (village) Sheboygan County
7	7	70.3	**Mayville** (city) Dodge County
8	8	69.9	**Minster** (village) Auglaize County
9	9	69.1	**Hartford** (town) Washington County
9	9	69.1	**Polk** (town) Washington County
11	11	68.4	**Medford** (town) Taylor County
12	12	68.1	**Brillion** (city) Calumet County
13	13	67.8	**Kiel** (city) Manitowoc County
14	14	67.7	**Hortonville** (village) Outagamie County
15	15	66.9	**Wakefield** (township) Stearns County
16	16	66.1	**Center** (town) Outagamie County
17	17	66.0	**Plymouth** (town) Sheboygan County
17	17	66.0	**Sheboygan** (town) Sheboygan County
17	17	66.0	**Trenton** (town) Washington County
20	20	65.8	**Fayette** (township) Juniata County
20	20	65.8	**Wheatland** (town) Kenosha County
22	22	65.5	**Kewaskum** (village) Washington County
23	23	65.4	**Springfield** (town) Dane County
24	24	65.2	**Empire** (town) Fond du Lac County
25	25	64.8	**Mukwa** (town) Waupaca County
26	26	64.2	**Albany** (city) Stearns County
27	27	64.0	**Jackson** (village) Washington County
28	28	63.9	**New Bremen** (village) Auglaize County
29	29	63.8	**New Ulm** (city) Brown County
30	30	63.0	**Coldwater** (village) Mercer County
30	30	63.0	**West Bend** (town) Washington County
32	32	62.3	**Breese** (city) Clinton County
33	33	61.9	**Taycheedah** (town) Fond du Lac County
34	34	61.4	**Merrill** (town) Lincoln County
34	34	61.4	**New Holstein** (city) Calumet County
36	36	60.9	**Beaver Dam** (town) Dodge County
36	36	60.9	**Friendship** (town) Fond du Lac County
36	36	60.9	**Mandan** (city) Morton County
39	39	60.8	**Miami Heights** (CDP) Hamilton County
40	40	60.6	**Plymouth** (city) Sheboygan County
40	40	60.6	**Sheboygan Falls** (city) Sheboygan County
42	42	60.4	**Medford** (city) Taylor County
43	43	60.3	**Merrill** (city) Lincoln County
43	43	60.3	**Saint Marys** (city) Elk County
45	45	60.2	**Elizabeth** (township) Lancaster County
46	46	59.7	**Stettin** (town) Marathon County
47	47	59.6	**Merton** (village) Waukesha County
48	48	59.5	**Wales** (village) Waukesha County
49	49	59.4	**Dale** (town) Outagamie County
49	49	59.4	**Germantown** (village) Washington County
49	49	59.4	**Grundy Center** (city) Grundy County
49	49	59.4	**Saint Augusta** (city) Stearns County
53	53	59.3	**Columbus** (city) Columbia County
53	53	59.3	**Farmington** (town) Washington County
55	55	59.2	**Fond du Lac** (town) Fond du Lac County
55	55	59.2	**Wayne** (city) Wayne County
57	57	59.1	**Caledonia** (city) Houston County
58	58	58.9	**Ixonia** (town) Jefferson County
58	58	58.9	**Lodi** (town) Columbia County
60	60	58.3	**Horicon** (city) Dodge County
61	61	58.2	**Johnson Creek** (village) Jefferson County
62	62	58.0	**Oakland** (town) Jefferson County
62	62	58.0	**Sauk Centre** (city) Stearns County
64	64	57.8	**Richfield** (village) Washington County
65	65	57.7	**Harrison** (town) Calumet County
65	65	57.7	**Sebewaing** (township) Huron County
67	67	57.6	**Fox** (township) Elk County
67	67	57.6	**West Bend** (city) Washington County
69	69	57.4	**Grafton** (town) Ozaukee County
69	69	57.4	**Ripon** (city) Fond du Lac County
71	71	57.3	**Harrison** (city) Hamilton County
72	72	57.2	**Carroll** (city) Carroll County
72	72	57.2	**Washington** (township) Schuylkill County
74	74	57.1	**Kronenwetter** (village) Marathon County
75	75	56.9	**Ellington** (town) Outagamie County
76	76	56.8	**Norwood Young America** (city) Carver County
76	76	56.8	**Saukville** (village) Ozaukee County
78	78	56.5	**Sherwood** (village) Calumet County
78	78	56.5	**Slinger** (village) Washington County
80	80	56.4	**Delphos** (city) Allen County
80	80	56.4	**Oregon** (town) Dane County
80	80	56.4	**Shelby** (town) La Crosse County
83	83	56.3	**Lisbon** (town) Waukesha County
83	83	56.3	**Sussex** (village) Waukesha County
85	85	56.2	**Bismarck** (city) Burleigh County
85	85	56.2	**Poynette** (village) Columbia County
87	87	56.0	**Alsace** (township) Berks County
87	87	56.0	**Jordan** (city) Scott County
89	89	55.9	**Eagle** (town) Waukesha County
90	90	55.8	**Waukesha** (town) Waukesha County
91	91	55.7	**Clayton** (town) Winnebago County
91	91	55.7	**Pine Grove** (township) Schuylkill County
93	93	55.6	**Ashippun** (town) Dodge County
93	93	55.6	**Rockland** (township) Berks County
95	95	55.5	**Clintonville** (city) Waupaca County
95	95	55.5	**Pewaukee** (city) Waukesha County
95	95	55.5	**Sevastopol** (town) Door County
98	98	55.3	**Lake Crystal** (city) Blue Earth County
98	98	55.3	**Plainview** (city) Wabasha County
98	98	55.3	**Rock Rapids** (city) Lyon County
101	101	55.2	**De Witt** (city) Clinton County
101	101	55.2	**Merton** (town) Waukesha County
101	101	55.2	**Watertown** (city) Jefferson County
104	104	55.1	**Hartford** (city) Washington County
105	105	55.0	**Upper Augusta** (township) Northumberland County
106	106	54.9	**Delhi Hills** (CDP) Hamilton County
107	107	54.8	**Aberdeen** (city) Brown County
107	107	54.8	**Delafield** (town) Waukesha County
109	109	54.7	**Jamestown** (city) Stutsman County
110	110	54.6	**Cottage Grove** (town) Dane County
110	110	54.6	**Hallam** (borough) York County
110	110	54.6	**Vernon** (town) Waukesha County
113	113	54.5	**Monticello** (city) Jones County
113	113	54.5	**Mukwonago** (town) Waukesha County
115	115	54.4	**Milbank** (city) Grant County
116	116	54.3	**Beulah** (city) Mercer County
116	116	54.3	**Cross Plains** (village) Dane County
116	116	54.3	**Lima** (town) Sheboygan County
119	119	54.2	**Algoma** (city) Kewaunee County
119	119	54.2	**Cold Spring** (city) Stearns County
119	119	54.2	**Lodi** (city) Columbia County
119	119	54.2	**Monfort Heights** (CDP) Hamilton County
123	123	54.1	**Mack** (CDP) Hamilton County
123	123	54.1	**North Mankato** (city) Nicollet County
125	125	54.0	**Menasha** (town) Winnebago County
125	125	54.0	**Rome** (town) Adams County
127	127	53.9	**Hays** (city) Ellis County
128	128	53.8	**Brockway** (township) Stearns County
128	128	53.8	**Dent** (CDP) Hamilton County
128	128	53.8	**Lake Wazeecha** (CDP) Wood County
128	128	53.8	**Sleepy Eye** (city) Brown County
132	132	53.7	**Zumbrota** (city) Goodhue County
133	133	53.6	**Dickinson** (city) Stark County
134	134	53.5	**Beaver Dam** (city) Dodge County
134	134	53.5	**Fond du Lac** (city) Fond du Lac County
134	134	53.5	**Wescott** (town) Shawano County
137	137	53.4	**Eagle Point** (town) Chippewa County
137	137	53.4	**Grafton** (village) Ozaukee County
139	139	53.3	**Freeburg** (village) Saint Clair County
140	140	53.2	**Lake Wisconsin** (CDP) Columbia County
140	140	53.2	**Marshfield** (city) Wood County
142	142	53.1	**Dell Rapids** (city) Minnehaha County
142	142	53.1	**Lake Mills** (city) Jefferson County
142	142	53.1	**Muskego** (city) Waukesha County
142	142	53.1	**Oregon** (village) Dane County
142	142	53.1	**Portage** (city) Columbia County
147	147	53.0	**Hereford** (township) Berks County
147	147	53.0	**Marysville** (city) Marshall County
147	147	53.0	**North Fond du Lac** (village) Fond du Lac County
150	150	52.9	**Blackhawk** (CDP) Meade County

Note: *The state column ranks the top/bottom 150 places from all places in the state with population of 10,000 or more. The national column ranks the top/bottom 150 places from all places in the country with population of 10,000 or more. Places that are unincorporated were not considered in the rankings. Please refer to the User Guide for additional information.*

Ancestry: English

Top 150 Places Ranked in *Descending* Order

State Rank	Nat'l Rank	Percent	Place
1	1	84.4	**Hildale** (city) Washington County
2	2	66.2	**Colorado City** (town) Mohave County
3	3	42.2	**Alpine** (city) Utah County
4	4	41.5	**Fruit Heights** (city) Davis County
4	4	41.5	**Manti** (city) Sanpete County
6	6	40.8	**Highland** (city) Utah County
7	7	40.5	**Mapleton** (city) Utah County
8	8	39.1	**Beaver** (city) Beaver County
9	9	38.4	**Centerville** (city) Davis County
10	10	38.2	**Hooper** (city) Weber County
10	10	38.2	**Hopkinton** (town) Merrimack County
12	12	37.8	**Sheridan** (city) Grant County
13	13	36.9	**Santa Clara** (city) Washington County
14	14	36.0	**Saint George** (town) Knox County
15	15	35.9	**Farmingdale** (town) Kennebec County
16	16	35.7	**Bountiful** (city) Davis County
17	17	35.6	**Rockport** (town) Knox County
18	18	35.4	**Kanab** (city) Kane County
18	18	35.4	**McCall** (city) Valley County
20	20	35.0	**Wolfeboro** (CDP) Carroll County
21	21	34.8	**Farr West** (city) Weber County
21	21	34.8	**Providence** (city) Cache County
23	23	34.6	**Bristol** (town) Lincoln County
23	23	34.6	**Rexburg** (city) Madison County
25	25	34.5	**North Logan** (city) Cache County
26	26	34.3	**Boothbay** (town) Lincoln County
26	26	34.3	**Parowan** (city) Iron County
28	28	34.2	**Pleasant View** (city) Weber County
29	29	33.8	**Wellsville** (city) Cache County
30	30	33.6	**Monmouth** (town) Kennebec County
31	31	33.5	**Holladay** (city) Salt Lake County
32	32	33.4	**Hyde Park** (city) Cache County
32	32	33.4	**Trent Woods** (town) Craven County
34	34	33.0	**Salem** (city) Utah County
35	35	32.9	**Delta** (city) Millard County
36	36	32.8	**Freeport** (town) Cumberland County
36	36	32.8	**Midway** (city) Wasatch County
36	36	32.8	**West Bountiful** (city) Davis County
39	39	32.6	**Farmington** (city) Davis County
39	39	32.6	**Kaysville** (city) Davis County
41	41	32.5	**Kennebunkport** (town) York County
42	42	32.4	**Wolfeboro** (town) Carroll County
43	43	32.2	**Woodstock** (town) Windsor County
44	44	32.0	**Santaquin** (city) Utah County
45	45	31.9	**Chichester** (town) Merrimack County
46	46	31.8	**American Fork** (city) Utah County
46	46	31.8	**Anson** (town) Somerset County
46	46	31.8	**Camden** (town) Knox County
46	46	31.8	**Hyrum** (city) Cache County
50	50	31.6	**Spring Arbor** (township) Jackson County
51	51	31.5	**Poland** (town) Androscoggin County
52	52	31.4	**Herriman** (city) Salt Lake County
53	53	31.3	**Morgan** (city) Morgan County
54	54	31.1	**Alamo** (town) Wheeler County
54	54	31.1	**Charlestown** (town) Sullivan County
56	56	31.0	**Spanish Fork** (city) Utah County
56	56	31.0	**Waldoboro** (town) Lincoln County
58	58	30.9	**Ivins** (city) Washington County
59	59	30.8	**Yarmouth** (town) Cumberland County
60	60	30.7	**Cedar Hills** (city) Utah County
61	61	30.6	**Bethel** (town) Oxford County
61	61	30.6	**Bridgton** (town) Cumberland County
61	61	30.6	**Lake San Marcos** (CDP) San Diego County
61	61	30.6	**Rockland** (city) Knox County
61	61	30.6	**Saint George** (city) Washington County
61	61	30.6	**Woods Cross** (city) Davis County
67	67	30.5	**Cedar City** (city) Iron County
68	68	30.3	**North Salt Lake** (city) Davis County
68	68	30.3	**South Jordan** (city) Salt Lake County
70	70	30.2	**Eagle Mountain** (city) Utah County
71	71	30.1	**Preston** (city) Franklin County
72	72	29.9	**Camden** (CDP) Knox County
73	73	29.8	**South Beach** (CDP) Indian River County
74	74	29.7	**Harpswell** (town) Cumberland County
74	74	29.7	**Indian River Shores** (town) Indian River County
76	76	29.5	**Helena** (city) Telfair County
76	76	29.5	**Manchester** (town) Kennebec County
76	76	29.5	**Nephi** (city) Juab County
76	76	29.5	**Washington Terrace** (city) Weber County
80	80	29.4	**Yarmouth** (CDP) Cumberland County
81	81	29.3	**Springville** (city) Utah County
82	82	29.2	**Clinton** (town) Kennebec County
82	82	29.2	**Grantsville** (city) Tooele County
84	84	29.1	**Little Compton** (town) Newport County
84	84	29.1	**Plain City** (city) Weber County
86	86	29.0	**Cottonwood Heights** (city) Salt Lake County
86	86	29.0	**Warren** (town) Knox County
88	88	28.9	**Madison** (town) Carroll County
88	88	28.9	**Washington** (city) Washington County
90	90	28.8	**Lindon** (city) Utah County
90	90	28.8	**Livermore Falls** (town) Androscoggin County
90	90	28.8	**Nibley** (city) Cache County
93	93	28.7	**Orem** (city) Utah County
93	93	28.7	**Woolwich** (town) Sagadahoc County
95	95	28.6	**Pleasant Grove** (city) Utah County
96	96	28.5	**Arundel** (town) York County
96	96	28.5	**China** (town) Kennebec County
98	98	28.4	**Lehi** (city) Utah County
98	98	28.4	**Tamworth** (town) Carroll County
100	100	28.3	**Bradford** (town) Orange County
100	100	28.3	**Enoch** (city) Iron County
102	102	28.2	**Oneida** (town) Scott County
102	102	28.2	**Oxford** (town) Oxford County
102	102	28.2	**South Weber** (city) Davis County
105	105	28.1	**Maeser** (CDP) Uintah County
105	105	28.1	**Walpole** (town) Cheshire County
107	107	28.0	**Hampden** (CDP) Penobscot County
107	107	28.0	**Sandy** (city) Salt Lake County
109	109	27.9	**Northfield** (town) Franklin County
109	109	27.9	**Perry** (city) Box Elder County
111	111	27.8	**Limerick** (town) York County
111	111	27.8	**Orleans** (town) Barnstable County
111	111	27.8	**Riverton** (city) Salt Lake County
114	114	27.7	**Draper** (city) Salt Lake County
114	114	27.7	**Hartland** (town) Windsor County
114	114	27.7	**Otisco** (town) Onondaga County
114	114	27.7	**Saratoga Springs** (city) Utah County
114	114	27.7	**Smithfield** (city) Cache County
119	119	27.6	**Bluffdale** (city) Salt Lake County
119	119	27.6	**Bowdoin** (town) Sagadahoc County
119	119	27.6	**East Bloomfield** (town) Ontario County
119	119	27.6	**North Yarmouth** (town) Cumberland County
119	119	27.6	**Syracuse** (city) Davis County
124	124	27.5	**Harrison** (town) Cumberland County
124	124	27.5	**Highland Park** (town) Dallas County
124	124	27.5	**South Eliot** (CDP) York County
127	127	27.4	**Hampden** (town) Penobscot County
127	127	27.4	**Montpelier** (city) Bear Lake County
127	127	27.4	**Winston** (city) Douglas County
130	130	27.3	**Buxton** (town) York County
130	130	27.3	**North Ogden** (city) Weber County
130	130	27.3	**White Hall** (city) Jefferson County
133	133	27.2	**Thetford** (town) Orange County
134	134	27.1	**Greene** (town) Chenango County
134	134	27.1	**Wakefield** (town) Carroll County
136	136	26.9	**New Durham** (town) Strafford County
136	136	26.9	**Stansbury Park** (CDP) Tooele County
136	136	26.9	**Surfside Beach** (town) Horry County
139	139	26.8	**Stratham** (town) Rockingham County
140	140	26.6	**Concord** (township) Jackson County
140	140	26.6	**Millcreek** (CDP) Salt Lake County
140	140	26.6	**Peterborough** (CDP) Hillsborough County
140	140	26.6	**Turner** (town) Androscoggin County
144	144	26.5	**Foster** (town) Providence County
144	144	26.5	**Hope** (township) Barry County
144	144	26.5	**Norwich** (town) Windsor County
147	147	26.4	**Belle Meade** (city) Davidson County
148	148	26.3	**Belfast** (city) Waldo County
149	149	26.2	**Richfield** (city) Sevier County
149	149	26.2	**South Duxbury** (CDP) Plymouth County

Note: *The state column ranks the top/bottom 150 places from all places in the state with population of 10,000 or more. The national column ranks the top/bottom 150 places from all places in the country with population of 10,000 or more. Places that are unincorporated were not considered in the rankings. Please refer to the User Guide for additional information.*

Ancestry: American

Top 150 Places Ranked in *Descending* Order

State Rank	Nat'l Rank	Percent	Place
1	1	66.4	**La Follette** (city) Campbell County
2	2	60.0	**Gloverville** (CDP) Aiken County
3	3	54.6	**Clearwater** (CDP) Aiken County
4	4	54.4	**Treasure Lake** (CDP) Clearfield County
5	5	51.7	**Healdton** (city) Carter County
6	6	45.9	**Bonifay** (city) Holmes County
7	7	45.8	**Harlem** (CDP) Hendry County
8	8	45.5	**Bean Station** (city) Grainger County
8	8	45.5	**Stanford** (city) Lincoln County
10	10	44.5	**Pell City** (city) Saint Clair County
11	11	44.3	**New Tazewell** (town) Claiborne County
12	12	43.9	**Dresden** (town) Weakley County
13	13	43.6	**Hartford** (city) Ohio County
14	14	43.2	**Blue Hill** (town) Hancock County
15	15	43.1	**Eaton** (town) Madison County
16	16	43.0	**Church Hill** (city) Hawkins County
17	17	42.6	**Middlesborough** (city) Bell County
18	18	42.1	**Temple** (city) Carroll County
19	19	41.1	**Georgetown** (city) Vermilion County
20	20	40.9	**Grantville** (city) Coweta County
20	20	40.9	**Summerville** (city) Chattooga County
22	22	40.6	**Morehead** (city) Rowan County
23	23	40.5	**Bayou Vista** (CDP) Saint Mary Parish
24	24	40.4	**Lone Grove** (city) Carter County
24	24	40.4	**Wilkesboro** (town) Wilkes County
26	26	39.9	**Chincoteague** (town) Accomack County
27	27	39.8	**Bremen** (city) Haralson County
28	28	39.7	**Cullowhee** (CDP) Jackson County
29	29	39.4	**Nassau Village-Ratliff** (CDP) Nassau County
30	30	38.8	**Crab Orchard** (CDP) Raleigh County
31	31	38.7	**Stanton** (city) Powell County
32	32	38.4	**Rogersville** (town) Hawkins County
33	33	38.2	**Cookeville** (city) Putnam County
34	34	38.0	**Livingston** (town) Overton County
35	35	37.6	**Gray Summit** (CDP) Franklin County
35	35	37.6	**Harrogate** (city) Claiborne County
37	37	37.4	**North Terre Haute** (CDP) Vigo County
38	38	37.3	**Mount Carmel** (CDP) Clermont County
39	39	36.9	**Atkins** (city) Pope County
39	39	36.9	**Burnettown** (town) Aiken County
39	39	36.9	**De Funiak Springs** (city) Walton County
42	42	36.8	**Lake of the Woods** (CDP) Champaign County
42	42	36.8	**Suncoast Estates** (CDP) Lee County
44	44	36.7	**Lancaster** (city) Garrard County
44	44	36.7	**Sandy** (township) Clearfield County
46	46	36.6	**Donalsonville** (city) Seminole County
47	47	36.3	**Bradford** (township) Clearfield County
47	47	36.3	**Broadway** (town) Rockingham County
47	47	36.3	**Jena** (town) La Salle Parish
50	50	36.2	**Algood** (city) Putnam County
50	50	36.2	**Sylva** (town) Jackson County
52	52	36.0	**Unicoi** (town) Unicoi County
53	53	35.6	**Bloomingdale** (CDP) Sullivan County
53	53	35.6	**Somerset** (city) Pulaski County
53	53	35.6	**Timberville** (town) Rockingham County
56	56	35.5	**Beaver Dam** (city) Ohio County
56	56	35.5	**Oliver Springs** (town) Anderson County
58	58	35.4	**Bucksport** (CDP) Hancock County
59	59	35.1	**England** (city) Lonoke County
59	59	35.1	**Fairview** (CDP) Walker County
59	59	35.1	**LaFayette** (city) Walker County
62	62	34.9	**Bucksport** (town) Hancock County
62	62	34.9	**Mountain City** (town) Johnson County
62	62	34.9	**Shepherdsville** (city) Bullitt County
65	65	34.8	**Blennerhassett** (CDP) Wood County
66	66	34.7	**South Lebanon** (village) Warren County
67	67	34.5	**Mount Carmel** (town) Hawkins County
68	68	34.3	**Hannahs Mill** (CDP) Upson County
69	69	34.2	**Mills** (town) Natrona County
69	69	34.2	**Rockwood** (city) Roane County
71	71	33.5	**North Wilkesboro** (town) Wilkes County
71	71	33.5	**Odenville** (town) Saint Clair County
73	73	33.3	**Ward** (city) Lonoke County
74	74	33.2	**Bawcomville** (CDP) Ouachita Parish
75	75	33.1	**Bethel** (village) Clermont County
75	75	33.1	**Grottoes** (town) Rockingham County
77	77	33.0	**Shelbyville** (city) Bedford County
78	78	32.7	**Dawson Springs** (city) Hopkins County
78	78	32.7	**Galena** (city) Cherokee County
78	78	32.7	**Pike Road** (town) Montgomery County
81	81	32.6	**Erwin** (town) Unicoi County
81	81	32.6	**Honea Path** (town) Anderson County
83	83	32.5	**West Tisbury** (town) Dukes County
84	84	32.3	**Pearisburg** (town) Giles County
85	85	32.2	**Evansville** (town) Natrona County
86	86	32.0	**Moody** (city) Saint Clair County
86	86	32.0	**Pittsburg** (city) Crawford County
88	88	31.9	**Woodbury** (town) Cannon County
89	89	31.8	**Dandridge** (town) Jefferson County
90	90	31.7	**Withamsville** (CDP) Clermont County
91	91	31.5	**Margaret** (town) Saint Clair County
92	92	31.4	**Pigeon Forge** (city) Sevier County
93	93	31.3	**Alva** (CDP) Lee County
94	94	31.1	**Hilliard** (town) Nassau County
95	95	30.8	**Monterey** (town) Putnam County
96	96	30.7	**Icard** (CDP) Burke County
97	97	30.5	**Flemingsburg** (city) Fleming County
97	97	30.5	**Shady Spring** (CDP) Raleigh County
99	99	30.4	**Irvine** (city) Estill County
100	100	30.3	**Cloverdale** (CDP) Botetourt County
100	100	30.3	**Hamilton** (town) Madison County
100	100	30.3	**Sylacauga** (city) Talladega County
100	100	30.3	**Underwood-Petersville** (CDP) Lauderdale County
104	104	30.2	**Central City** (city) Muhlenberg County
104	104	30.2	**Harriman** (city) Roane County
104	104	30.2	**Prestonsburg** (city) Floyd County
107	107	30.1	**Stuarts Draft** (CDP) Augusta County
108	108	30.0	**Madison** (town) Madison County
108	108	30.0	**Verona** (CDP) Augusta County
108	108	30.0	**Waynesville** (town) Haywood County
111	111	29.8	**Granville** (town) Washington County
111	111	29.8	**Paris** (city) Bourbon County
111	111	29.8	**Winchester** (city) Clark County
114	114	29.7	**Byron** (city) Peach County
114	114	29.7	**Emmett** (city) Gem County
114	114	29.7	**Hillview** (city) Bullitt County
114	114	29.7	**Oak Grove** (CDP) Washington County
114	114	29.7	**Sunnyvale** (town) Dallas County
114	114	29.7	**Wickenburg** (town) Maricopa County
120	120	29.6	**Jefferson City** (city) Jefferson County
121	121	29.5	**Ball** (town) Rapides Parish
121	121	29.5	**Corinth** (town) Penobscot County
121	121	29.5	**Lincoln** (city) Talladega County
124	124	29.4	**Manchester** (city) Coffee County
124	124	29.4	**Owensboro** (city) Daviess County
126	126	29.3	**Kings Mountain** (city) Cleveland County
127	127	29.2	**Buckner** (CDP) Oldham County
127	127	29.2	**Malabar** (town) Brevard County
129	129	29.1	**Baxter Springs** (city) Cherokee County
130	130	28.9	**Kingston** (city) Roane County
130	130	28.9	**Morristown** (city) Hamblen County
132	132	28.8	**Bayshore** (CDP) New Hanover County
132	132	28.8	**Buena Vista** (independent city)
134	134	28.7	**Grissom AFB** (CDP) Miami County
134	134	28.7	**Hodgenville** (city) Larue County
136	136	28.5	**Claiborne** (CDP) Ouachita Parish
136	136	28.5	**Inwood** (CDP) Polk County
136	136	28.5	**Moyock** (CDP) Currituck County
136	136	28.5	**Richlands** (town) Tazewell County
136	136	28.5	**Tabor City** (town) Columbus County
141	141	28.4	**Dundee** (town) Polk County
141	141	28.4	**Jan Phyl Village** (CDP) Polk County
141	141	28.4	**Morgan** (city) Morgan County
144	144	28.3	**West Liberty** (city) Morgan County
145	145	28.2	**Bicknell** (city) Knox County
145	145	28.2	**Fort Scott** (city) Bourbon County
145	145	28.2	**Putney** (CDP) Dougherty County
148	148	28.1	**Berwick** (town) Saint Mary Parish
148	148	28.1	**Corinth** (town) Saratoga County
148	148	28.1	**Middleton** (city) Canyon County

***Note:** The state column ranks the top/bottom 150 places from all places in the state with population of 10,000 or more. The national column ranks the top/bottom 150 places from all places in the country with population of 10,000 or more. Places that are unincorporated were not considered in the rankings. Please refer to the User Guide for additional information.*

Ancestry: Irish

Top 150 Places Ranked in *Descending* Order

State Rank	Nat'l Rank	Percent	Place
1	1	52.0	**Pearl River** (CDP) Rockland County
2	2	51.7	**Ocean Bluff-Brant Rock** (CDP) Plymouth County
3	3	50.6	**Green Harbor-Cedar Crest** (CDP) Plymouth County
4	4	49.4	**Rockledge** (borough) Montgomery County
5	5	48.3	**Walpole** (CDP) Norfolk County
6	6	47.4	**North Scituate** (CDP) Plymouth County
7	7	47.0	**Scituate** (CDP) Plymouth County
8	8	46.9	**Marshfield** (town) Plymouth County
9	9	46.2	**Scituate** (town) Plymouth County
10	10	45.8	**Ridley Park** (borough) Delaware County
11	11	45.5	**Spring Lake Heights** (borough) Monmouth County
12	12	45.3	**Oak Valley** (CDP) Gloucester County
13	13	45.2	**Hanover** (town) Plymouth County
14	14	44.7	**Norwell** (town) Plymouth County
15	15	44.2	**Glenside** (CDP) Montgomery County
15	15	44.2	**Manasquan** (borough) Monmouth County
17	17	43.8	**Norwood** (borough) Delaware County
18	18	42.9	**Walpole** (town) Norfolk County
18	18	42.9	**Wynantskill** (CDP) Rensselaer County
20	20	42.8	**Springfield** (township) Delaware County
21	21	42.6	**Folsom** (CDP) Delaware County
21	21	42.6	**Glenolden** (borough) Delaware County
21	21	42.6	**Highlands** (borough) Monmouth County
24	24	42.2	**Marshfield** (CDP) Plymouth County
25	25	41.7	**North Middletown** (CDP) Monmouth County
26	26	41.6	**Braintree Town** (city) Norfolk County
27	27	41.4	**Weymouth Town** (city) Norfolk County
28	28	41.1	**Littleton Common** (CDP) Middlesex County
28	28	41.1	**North Wildwood** (city) Cape May County
30	30	41.0	**Bridgewater** (CDP) Plymouth County
31	31	40.9	**Abington** (cdp/town) Plymouth County
31	31	40.9	**Nahant** (cdp/town) Essex County
31	31	40.9	**Spring Lake** (borough) Monmouth County
34	34	40.6	**Whitman** (town) Plymouth County
35	35	40.5	**Cohasset** (town) Norfolk County
35	35	40.5	**Hopedale** (CDP) Worcester County
35	35	40.5	**Sayville** (CDP) Suffolk County
38	38	40.4	**Brielle** (borough) Monmouth County
39	39	40.3	**Hull** (cdp/town) Plymouth County
40	40	40.2	**Gloucester City** (city) Camden County
41	41	39.9	**Churchville** (CDP) Bucks County
42	42	39.7	**Haddon Heights** (borough) Camden County
43	43	39.6	**Notre Dame** (CDP) Saint Joseph County
44	44	39.5	**Ashland** (borough) Schuylkill County
44	44	39.5	**Hingham** (town) Plymouth County
46	46	39.4	**Avon** (town) Norfolk County
47	47	39.3	**Garden City** (village) Nassau County
47	47	39.3	**Tinicum** (township) Delaware County
49	49	39.2	**Milton** (cdp/town) Norfolk County
49	49	39.2	**Ramtown** (CDP) Monmouth County
51	51	39.1	**Ridley** (township) Delaware County
52	52	38.8	**Bridgewater** (town) Plymouth County
53	53	38.5	**Hanson** (town) Plymouth County
53	53	38.5	**North Reading** (town) Middlesex County
53	53	38.5	**Prospect Park** (borough) Delaware County
53	53	38.5	**Rockland** (town) Plymouth County
57	57	38.4	**Hingham** (CDP) Plymouth County
58	58	38.3	**Foxborough** (town) Norfolk County
59	59	38.1	**Foxborough** (CDP) Norfolk County
60	60	38.0	**Barrington** (borough) Camden County
61	61	37.9	**Aldan** (borough) Delaware County
61	61	37.9	**Mansfield Center** (CDP) Bristol County
61	61	37.9	**National Park** (borough) Gloucester County
64	64	37.8	**East Sandwich** (CDP) Barnstable County
65	65	37.6	**Haverford** (township) Delaware County
65	65	37.6	**West Brandywine** (township) Chester County
67	67	37.5	**East Bridgewater** (town) Plymouth County
68	68	37.4	**Buzzards Bay** (CDP) Barnstable County
69	69	37.3	**Blauvelt** (CDP) Rockland County
69	69	37.3	**East Quogue** (CDP) Suffolk County
71	71	37.2	**Canton** (town) Norfolk County
71	71	37.2	**North Falmouth** (CDP) Barnstable County
73	73	37.1	**Pembroke** (town) Plymouth County
73	73	37.1	**Upton** (CDP) Worcester County
73	73	37.1	**Woodbury Heights** (borough) Gloucester County
76	76	36.9	**Fair Haven** (borough) Monmouth County
77	77	36.8	**Clementon** (borough) Camden County
77	77	36.8	**Duxbury** (town) Plymouth County
79	79	36.7	**Fairview** (CDP) Monmouth County
79	79	36.7	**Folcroft** (borough) Delaware County
79	79	36.7	**Newtown** (township) Delaware County
82	82	36.6	**Rockville Centre** (village) Nassau County
83	83	36.5	**Oceanport** (borough) Monmouth County
83	83	36.5	**West Bridgewater** (town) Plymouth County
85	85	36.2	**Audubon** (borough) Camden County
85	85	36.2	**Campo** (CDP) San Diego County
87	87	36.0	**Orleans** (town) Jefferson County
87	87	36.0	**Shark River Hills** (CDP) Monmouth County
89	89	35.8	**Drexel Hill** (CDP) Delaware County
89	89	35.8	**Trappe** (borough) Montgomery County
89	89	35.8	**West Sayville** (CDP) Suffolk County
92	92	35.5	**Leonardo** (CDP) Monmouth County
92	92	35.5	**Little Silver** (borough) Monmouth County
94	94	35.3	**Bethlehem** (township) Hunterdon County
95	95	35.2	**East Islip** (CDP) Suffolk County
95	95	35.2	**Kingston** (town) Plymouth County
97	97	35.1	**Dedham** (cdp/town) Norfolk County
97	97	35.1	**Hopedale** (town) Worcester County
97	97	35.1	**Wilmington** (cdp/town) Middlesex County
100	100	35.0	**Green Island** (town/village) Albany County
100	100	35.0	**Medford Lakes** (borough) Burlington County
102	102	34.9	**Holbrook** (cdp/town) Norfolk County
102	102	34.9	**Mansfield** (town) Bristol County
104	104	34.8	**LaFayette** (town) Onondaga County
104	104	34.8	**North Plymouth** (CDP) Plymouth County
104	104	34.8	**Norton** (town) Bristol County
104	104	34.8	**Tuckerton** (borough) Ocean County
104	104	34.8	**Wakefield** (cdp/town) Middlesex County
109	109	34.7	**Cape Neddick** (CDP) York County
109	109	34.7	**Tewksbury** (town) Middlesex County
109	109	34.7	**Woodlyn** (CDP) Delaware County
109	109	34.7	**Woolwich** (township) Gloucester County
113	113	34.6	**Wanamassa** (CDP) Monmouth County
114	114	34.5	**East Shoreham** (CDP) Suffolk County
114	114	34.5	**Horsham** (CDP) Montgomery County
114	114	34.5	**Skippack** (CDP) Montgomery County
117	117	34.4	**Plymouth** (town) Plymouth County
117	117	34.4	**Western Springs** (village) Cook County
119	119	34.3	**Bethel** (township) Delaware County
119	119	34.3	**Melrose** (city) Middlesex County
119	119	34.3	**Point Pleasant** (borough) Ocean County
122	122	34.2	**Aston** (township) Delaware County
122	122	34.2	**North Seekonk** (CDP) Bristol County
122	122	34.2	**Wanakah** (CDP) Erie County
122	122	34.2	**Westvale** (CDP) Onondaga County
126	126	34.1	**Reading** (cdp/town) Middlesex County
126	126	34.1	**Winthrop Town** (city) Suffolk County
128	128	34.0	**Atkinson** (town) Rockingham County
128	128	34.0	**Bella Vista** (CDP) Shasta County
128	128	34.0	**Hopkinton** (CDP) Middlesex County
128	128	34.0	**Plymouth** (CDP) Plymouth County
128	128	34.0	**Washington** (town) Dutchess County
128	128	34.0	**Williston Park** (village) Nassau County
134	134	33.9	**Norwood** (cdp/town) Norfolk County
135	135	33.8	**Clinton** (town) Worcester County
135	135	33.8	**Halifax** (town) Plymouth County
135	135	33.8	**Mystic Island** (CDP) Ocean County
135	135	33.8	**Wall** (township) Monmouth County
139	139	33.7	**Massapequa Park** (village) Nassau County
140	140	33.6	**Cold Spring Harbor** (CDP) Suffolk County
140	140	33.6	**Dalton** (town) Berkshire County
142	142	33.5	**Colonie** (village) Albany County
142	142	33.5	**Middletown** (township) Monmouth County
142	142	33.5	**Seabrook** (town) Rockingham County
142	142	33.5	**Waterford** (township) Camden County
146	146	33.4	**Medfield** (CDP) Norfolk County
146	146	33.4	**Montgomery** (village) Orange County
146	146	33.4	**Mount Ephraim** (borough) Camden County
149	149	33.3	**Dover** (town) Dutchess County
149	149	33.3	**Fort Salonga** (CDP) Suffolk County

Note: *The state column ranks the top/bottom 150 places from all places in the state with population of 10,000 or more. The national column ranks the top/bottom 150 places from all places in the country with population of 10,000 or more. Places that are unincorporated were not considered in the rankings. Please refer to the User Guide for additional information.*

Ancestry: Italian

Top 150 Places Ranked in *Descending* Order

State Rank	Nat'l Rank	Percent	Place
1	1	51.2	**Johnston** (town) Providence County
2	2	50.9	**Fairfield** (township) Essex County
3	3	49.0	**North Massapequa** (CDP) Nassau County
4	4	47.7	**East Haven** (cdp/town) New Haven County
5	5	47.3	**Watertown** (CDP) Litchfield County
6	6	46.3	**Massapequa** (CDP) Nassau County
7	7	45.4	**Eastchester** (CDP) Westchester County
8	8	45.3	**Thornwood** (CDP) Westchester County
9	9	44.4	**Glendora** (CDP) Camden County
10	10	44.0	**Frankfort** (village) Herkimer County
11	11	43.5	**Hawthorne** (CDP) Westchester County
12	12	43.4	**Hammonton** (town) Atlantic County
13	13	43.3	**North Branford** (town) New Haven County
13	13	43.3	**Turnersville** (CDP) Gloucester County
15	15	42.8	**West Islip** (CDP) Suffolk County
16	16	42.6	**Massapequa Park** (village) Nassau County
17	17	42.1	**Franklin Square** (CDP) Nassau County
18	18	41.9	**Islip Terrace** (CDP) Suffolk County
19	19	41.6	**Watertown** (town) Litchfield County
20	20	41.4	**Nesconset** (CDP) Suffolk County
21	21	41.1	**Lake Grove** (village) Suffolk County
22	22	40.4	**North Haven** (cdp/town) New Haven County
23	23	40.3	**Gibbstown** (CDP) Gloucester County
24	24	40.2	**Saint James** (CDP) Suffolk County
24	24	40.2	**Seaford** (CDP) Nassau County
26	26	40.1	**East Hanover** (township) Morris County
26	26	40.1	**Saugus** (cdp/town) Essex County
28	28	39.9	**Marlboro** (CDP) Ulster County
29	29	39.7	**Beach Haven West** (CDP) Ocean County
30	30	39.5	**East Islip** (CDP) Suffolk County
30	30	39.5	**Smithtown** (CDP) Suffolk County
32	32	39.3	**Jefferson Valley-Yorktown** (CDP) Westchester County
33	33	39.2	**Jessup** (borough) Lackawanna County
33	33	39.2	**Monmouth Beach** (borough) Monmouth County
35	35	39.0	**Brightwaters** (village) Suffolk County
36	36	38.7	**South Farmingdale** (CDP) Nassau County
37	37	38.1	**Frankfort** (town) Herkimer County
37	37	38.1	**Richwood** (CDP) Gloucester County
39	39	38.0	**Bayville** (village) Nassau County
39	39	38.0	**Malverne** (village) Nassau County
39	39	38.0	**North Providence** (town) Providence County
42	42	37.9	**Cedar Grove** (township) Essex County
43	43	37.8	**Plainedge** (CDP) Nassau County
44	44	37.7	**Holtsville** (CDP) Suffolk County
44	44	37.7	**Oakville** (CDP) Litchfield County
46	46	37.6	**Blackwood** (CDP) Camden County
46	46	37.6	**Holbrook** (CDP) Suffolk County
48	48	37.4	**Center Moriches** (CDP) Suffolk County
48	48	37.4	**Dunmore** (borough) Lackawanna County
48	48	37.4	**Smithtown** (town) Suffolk County
51	51	37.2	**North Great River** (CDP) Suffolk County
52	52	37.1	**Blue Point** (CDP) Suffolk County
52	52	37.1	**East Norwich** (CDP) Nassau County
52	52	37.1	**Ronkonkoma** (CDP) Suffolk County
52	52	37.1	**West Pittston** (borough) Luzerne County
56	56	36.9	**Hauppauge** (CDP) Suffolk County
57	57	36.8	**Bohemia** (CDP) Suffolk County
57	57	36.8	**Farmingville** (CDP) Suffolk County
57	57	36.8	**Old Forge** (borough) Lackawanna County
57	57	36.8	**Pemberwick** (CDP) Fairfield County
61	61	36.7	**Mechanicville** (city) Saratoga County
61	61	36.7	**Miller Place** (CDP) Suffolk County
61	61	36.7	**Nutley** (township) Essex County
61	61	36.7	**Selden** (CDP) Suffolk County
61	61	36.7	**Wood-Ridge** (borough) Bergen County
66	66	36.6	**Glen Head** (CDP) Nassau County
67	67	36.5	**Pittston** (city) Luzerne County
68	68	36.4	**Centerport** (CDP) Suffolk County
69	69	36.2	**Barnegat** (CDP) Ocean County
70	70	36.1	**Mahopac** (CDP) Putnam County
70	70	36.1	**Ocean Acres** (CDP) Ocean County
72	72	36.0	**Lindenhurst** (village) Suffolk County
72	72	36.0	**Lyncourt** (CDP) Onondaga County
72	72	36.0	**Union Vale** (town) Dutchess County
72	72	36.0	**Washington** (township) Gloucester County
76	76	35.9	**Eastchester** (town) Westchester County
77	77	35.8	**Garden City South** (CDP) Nassau County
77	77	35.8	**Greenwich** (township) Gloucester County
77	77	35.8	**Manorville** (CDP) Suffolk County
80	80	35.7	**Lake Pocotopaug** (CDP) Middlesex County
80	80	35.7	**Moonachie** (borough) Bergen County
80	80	35.7	**Oyster Bay** (CDP) Nassau County
83	83	35.6	**East Freehold** (CDP) Monmouth County
83	83	35.6	**Oakdale** (CDP) Suffolk County
83	83	35.6	**Ramtown** (CDP) Monmouth County
86	86	35.5	**Kensington** (CDP) Hartford County
86	86	35.5	**Pelham Manor** (village) Westchester County
88	88	35.4	**Holiday City-Berkeley** (CDP) Ocean County
88	88	35.4	**Yaphank** (CDP) Suffolk County
90	90	35.2	**Carmel** (town) Putnam County
91	91	35.1	**Commack** (CDP) Suffolk County
92	92	34.9	**Hazlet** (township) Monmouth County
92	92	34.9	**Somers** (town) Westchester County
94	94	34.5	**Bethpage** (CDP) Nassau County
94	94	34.5	**Middle Island** (CDP) Suffolk County
94	94	34.5	**Port Jefferson Station** (CDP) Suffolk County
97	97	34.4	**Lynnfield** (cdp/town) Essex County
98	98	34.3	**Kings Park** (CDP) Suffolk County
98	98	34.3	**North Babylon** (CDP) Suffolk County
98	98	34.3	**West Babylon** (CDP) Suffolk County
101	101	34.2	**Totowa** (borough) Passaic County
102	102	34.1	**Ellwood City** (borough) Lawrence County
102	102	34.1	**Stoneham** (cdp/town) Middlesex County
104	104	34.0	**Cranston** (city) Providence County
104	104	34.0	**Shirley** (CDP) Suffolk County
106	106	33.9	**Pequannock** (township) Morris County
106	106	33.9	**Pine Lake Park** (CDP) Ocean County
108	108	33.8	**East Fishkill** (town) Dutchess County
108	108	33.8	**Montrose** (CDP) Westchester County
110	110	33.7	**Locust Valley** (CDP) Nassau County
110	110	33.7	**Neshannock** (township) Lawrence County
110	110	33.7	**West Bay Shore** (CDP) Suffolk County
110	110	33.7	**Yorktown** (town) Westchester County
114	114	33.6	**Holiday City South** (CDP) Ocean County
114	114	33.6	**Kenmore** (village) Erie County
114	114	33.6	**Lacey** (township) Ocean County
114	114	33.6	**Prospect** (town) New Haven County
114	114	33.6	**Roseland** (borough) Essex County
114	114	33.6	**Wantagh** (CDP) Nassau County
120	120	33.5	**Waldwick** (borough) Bergen County
120	120	33.5	**Wolcott** (town) New Haven County
122	122	33.4	**East Shoreham** (CDP) Suffolk County
122	122	33.4	**South Huntington** (CDP) Suffolk County
122	122	33.4	**West Sayville** (CDP) Suffolk County
125	125	33.3	**Exeter** (borough) Luzerne County
125	125	33.3	**Toms River** (township) Ocean County
127	127	33.2	**East Williston** (village) Nassau County
127	127	33.2	**Lyndhurst** (township) Bergen County
129	129	33.1	**Lake Ronkonkoma** (CDP) Suffolk County
129	129	33.1	**Toms River** (CDP) Ocean County
129	129	33.1	**Westerly** (CDP) Washington County
132	132	33.0	**Cold Spring Harbor** (CDP) Suffolk County
132	132	33.0	**Mount Sinai** (CDP) Suffolk County
134	134	32.9	**Hasbrouck Heights** (borough) Bergen County
134	134	32.9	**Stafford** (township) Ocean County
136	136	32.8	**Berlin** (town) Hartford County
136	136	32.8	**Galeville** (CDP) Onondaga County
136	136	32.8	**West Caldwell** (township) Essex County
139	139	32.7	**Putnam Valley** (town) Putnam County
139	139	32.7	**Sound Beach** (CDP) Suffolk County
141	141	32.6	**Babylon** (village) Suffolk County
141	141	32.6	**Centereach** (CDP) Suffolk County
141	141	32.6	**Elwood** (CDP) Suffolk County
141	141	32.6	**Middletown** (township) Monmouth County
141	141	32.6	**North Patchogue** (CDP) Suffolk County
146	146	32.5	**Lincroft** (CDP) Monmouth County
147	147	32.4	**Barnegat** (township) Ocean County
147	147	32.4	**Caldwell** (borough) Essex County
147	147	32.4	**Levittown** (CDP) Nassau County
147	147	32.4	**Oceanport** (borough) Monmouth County

Note: *The state column ranks the top/bottom 150 places from all places in the state with population of 10,000 or more. The national column ranks the top/bottom 150 places from all places in the country with population of 10,000 or more. Places that are unincorporated were not considered in the rankings. Please refer to the User Guide for additional information.*

Employment: Management, Business, and Financial Occupations

Top 150 Places Ranked in *Descending* Order

State Rank	Nat'l Rank	Percent	Place
1	4	40.2	**Hillsborough** (town) San Mateo County
2	5	38.7	**Alamo** (CDP) Contra Costa County
3	11	36.6	**Danville** (town) Contra Costa County
4	12	36.3	**Saratoga** (city) Santa Clara County
5	15	35.8	**Piedmont** (city) Alameda County
6	19	35.2	**Orinda** (city) Contra Costa County
7	25	34.5	**Hermosa Beach** (city) Los Angeles County
7	25	34.5	**La Cañada Flintridge** (city) Los Angeles County
9	33	33.9	**Los Altos** (city) Santa Clara County
10	35	33.7	**Newport Beach** (city) Orange County
11	39	32.9	**Calabasas** (city) Los Angeles County
12	42	32.6	**Manhattan Beach** (city) Los Angeles County
13	45	32.3	**Coto de Caza** (CDP) Orange County
14	55	31.8	**Clayton** (city) Contra Costa County
15	58	31.7	**Ladera Ranch** (CDP) Orange County
16	68	31.3	**Tamalpais-Homestead Valley** (CDP) Marin County
17	72	31.2	**Lafayette** (city) Contra Costa County
18	77	30.7	**San Marino** (city) Los Angeles County
19	87	30.3	**Los Gatos** (town) Santa Clara County
20	112	29.2	**Moraga** (town) Contra Costa County
21	125	28.8	**San Ramon** (city) Contra Costa County
22	133	28.7	**Stevenson Ranch** (CDP) Los Angeles County
23	138	28.5	**Palo Alto** (city) Santa Clara County
24	144	28.4	**Palos Verdes Estates** (city) Los Angeles County
25	172	27.7	**Laguna Beach** (city) Orange County
25	172	27.7	**Rancho Palos Verdes** (city) Los Angeles County
27	181	27.5	**Mill Valley** (city) Marin County
28	188	27.3	**Beverly Hills** (city) Los Angeles County
29	194	27.2	**Burlingame** (city) San Mateo County
29	194	27.2	**Oak Park** (CDP) Ventura County
31	210	26.8	**San Anselmo** (town) Marin County
32	220	26.7	**Malibu** (city) Los Angeles County
32	220	26.7	**Redondo Beach** (city) Los Angeles County
34	239	26.5	**Cupertino** (city) Santa Clara County
35	244	26.4	**Granite Bay** (CDP) Placer County
36	251	26.3	**Aliso Viejo** (city) Orange County
36	251	26.3	**El Dorado Hills** (CDP) El Dorado County
38	257	26.1	**Menlo Park** (city) San Mateo County
38	257	26.1	**San Carlos** (city) San Mateo County
38	257	26.1	**Yorba Linda** (city) Orange County
41	276	25.8	**North Tustin** (CDP) Orange County
41	276	25.8	**Walnut Creek** (city) Contra Costa County
43	288	25.6	**Belmont** (city) San Mateo County
44	295	25.5	**Irvine** (city) Orange County
44	295	25.5	**Larkspur** (city) Marin County
46	307	25.4	**Foster City** (city) San Mateo County
46	307	25.4	**Pleasanton** (city) Alameda County
48	316	25.3	**Agoura Hills** (city) Los Angeles County
48	316	25.3	**Coronado** (city) San Diego County
50	330	25.1	**Santa Monica** (city) Los Angeles County
51	347	24.8	**Laguna Niguel** (city) Orange County
52	354	24.7	**Rossmoor** (CDP) Orange County
53	405	24.1	**Scotts Valley** (city) Santa Cruz County
54	441	23.7	**Carlsbad** (city) San Diego County
54	441	23.7	**Diamond Bar** (city) Los Angeles County
54	441	23.7	**Half Moon Bay** (city) San Mateo County
54	441	23.7	**Solana Beach** (city) San Diego County
58	460	23.5	**Dublin** (city) Alameda County
59	466	23.4	**Seal Beach** (city) Orange County
60	477	23.3	**Arcadia** (city) Los Angeles County
60	477	23.3	**Emeryville** (city) Alameda County
62	506	23.0	**Dana Point** (city) Orange County
63	515	22.9	**Discovery Bay** (CDP) Contra Costa County
63	515	22.9	**Los Alamitos** (city) Orange County
65	528	22.8	**Folsom** (city) Sacramento County
65	528	22.8	**San Clemente** (city) Orange County
65	528	22.8	**West Hollywood** (city) Los Angeles County
68	555	22.6	**Rancho Santa Margarita** (city) Orange County
69	566	22.5	**South Pasadena** (city) Los Angeles County
69	566	22.5	**Thousand Oaks** (city) Ventura County
71	580	22.3	**Novato** (city) Marin County
71	580	22.3	**Pleasant Hill** (city) Contra Costa County
73	597	22.1	**Casa de Oro-Mount Helix** (CDP) San Diego County
73	597	22.1	**La Riviera** (CDP) Sacramento County
73	597	22.1	**Moorpark** (city) Ventura County
76	619	21.9	**El Segundo** (city) Los Angeles County
77	646	21.7	**Laguna Hills** (city) Orange County
77	646	21.7	**San Francisco** (city) San Francisco County
79	661	21.6	**East San Gabriel** (CDP) Los Angeles County
79	661	21.6	**Fairview** (CDP) Alameda County
79	661	21.6	**La Crescenta-Montrose** (CDP) Los Angeles County
79	661	21.6	**Mission Viejo** (city) Orange County
83	671	21.5	**Brea** (city) Orange County
84	683	21.4	**Laguna Woods** (city) Orange County
85	701	21.2	**Benicia** (city) Solano County
85	701	21.2	**Castro Valley** (CDP) Alameda County
85	701	21.2	**Sonoma** (city) Sonoma County
88	725	21.0	**Campbell** (city) Santa Clara County
88	725	21.0	**Healdsburg** (city) Sonoma County
88	725	21.0	**Poway** (city) San Diego County
91	740	20.9	**Millbrae** (city) San Mateo County
92	754	20.8	**Lake Forest** (city) Orange County
92	754	20.8	**Sierra Madre** (city) Los Angeles County
94	767	20.7	**Rancho San Diego** (CDP) San Diego County
95	800	20.5	**Castaic** (CDP) Los Angeles County
95	800	20.5	**El Sobrante** (CDP) Riverside County
95	800	20.5	**Monrovia** (city) Los Angeles County
95	800	20.5	**Morgan Hill** (city) Santa Clara County
99	818	20.4	**Rocklin** (city) Placer County
99	818	20.4	**Rosedale** (CDP) Kern County
101	831	20.3	**Rancho Mirage** (city) Riverside County
102	843	20.2	**Torrance** (city) Los Angeles County
103	852	20.1	**Fremont** (city) Alameda County
103	852	20.1	**Huntington Beach** (city) Orange County
103	852	20.1	**San Dimas** (city) Los Angeles County
103	852	20.1	**Walnut** (city) Los Angeles County
107	869	20.0	**Encinitas** (city) San Diego County
108	881	19.9	**Santa Clara** (city) Santa Clara County
109	888	19.8	**Culver City** (city) Los Angeles County
109	888	19.8	**Martinez** (city) Contra Costa County
109	888	19.8	**Simi Valley** (city) Ventura County
112	914	19.7	**El Cerrito** (city) Contra Costa County
112	914	19.7	**Monterey** (city) Monterey County
114	929	19.6	**Alameda** (city) Alameda County
114	929	19.6	**Costa Mesa** (city) Orange County
116	940	19.5	**Chino Hills** (city) San Bernardino County
116	940	19.5	**Claremont** (city) Los Angeles County
116	940	19.5	**Fair Oaks** (CDP) Sacramento County
119	976	19.3	**Hercules** (city) Contra Costa County
120	993	19.2	**San Mateo** (city) San Mateo County
120	993	19.2	**View Park-Windsor Hills** (CDP) Los Angeles County
122	1004	19.1	**Hacienda Heights** (CDP) Los Angeles County
123	1036	18.9	**Cerritos** (city) Los Angeles County
123	1036	18.9	**Livermore** (city) Alameda County
123	1036	18.9	**Mountain View** (city) Santa Clara County
123	1036	18.9	**San Juan Capistrano** (city) Orange County
127	1058	18.8	**Auburn** (city) Placer County
127	1058	18.8	**Burbank** (city) Los Angeles County
129	1072	18.7	**Roseville** (city) Placer County
129	1072	18.7	**Sunnyvale** (city) Santa Clara County
131	1098	18.6	**Eastvale** (city) Riverside County
131	1098	18.6	**Pacifica** (city) San Mateo County
133	1115	18.5	**Berkeley** (city) Alameda County
133	1115	18.5	**Del Aire** (CDP) Los Angeles County
133	1115	18.5	**La Verne** (city) Los Angeles County
133	1115	18.5	**Tustin** (city) Orange County
137	1141	18.4	**Cypress** (city) Orange County
137	1141	18.4	**Truckee** (town) Nevada County
139	1156	18.3	**Pasadena** (city) Los Angeles County
140	1176	18.2	**Camarillo** (city) Ventura County
140	1176	18.2	**Fountain Valley** (city) Orange County
142	1194	18.1	**Camp Pendleton South** (CDP) San Diego County
143	1214	18.0	**Crestline** (CDP) San Bernardino County
143	1214	18.0	**Placentia** (city) Orange County
145	1231	17.9	**Glendora** (city) Los Angeles County
145	1231	17.9	**San Rafael** (city) Marin County
147	1256	17.8	**Pacific Grove** (city) Monterey County
147	1256	17.8	**Petaluma** (city) Sonoma County
147	1256	17.8	**Redwood City** (city) San Mateo County
150	1311	17.5	**Norco** (city) Riverside County

Note: *The state column ranks the top/bottom 150 places from all places in the state with population of 10,000 or more. The national column ranks the top/bottom 150 places from all places in the country with population of 10,000 or more. Places that are unincorporated were not considered in the rankings. Please refer to the User Guide for additional information.*

Employment: Management, Business, and Financial Occupations

Top 150 Places Ranked in *Ascending* Order

State Rank	Nat'l Rank	Percent	Place
1	1	0.9	**Avenal** (city) Kings County
2	3	1.6	**Parlier** (city) Fresno County
3	4	1.7	**Arvin** (city) Kern County
4	7	2.3	**Garden Acres** (CDP) San Joaquin County
5	8	2.4	**East Rancho Dominguez** (CDP) Los Angeles County
5	8	2.4	**Lamont** (CDP) Kern County
7	11	2.8	**Muscoy** (CDP) San Bernardino County
8	12	2.9	**Wasco** (city) Kern County
9	15	3.0	**Greenfield** (city) Monterey County
9	15	3.0	**Walnut Park** (CDP) Los Angeles County
11	17	3.1	**Maywood** (city) Los Angeles County
12	20	3.3	**Farmersville** (city) Tulare County
12	20	3.3	**Lennox** (CDP) Los Angeles County
14	25	3.5	**Mendota** (city) Fresno County
15	27	3.6	**Bell Gardens** (city) Los Angeles County
15	27	3.6	**Cudahy** (city) Los Angeles County
15	27	3.6	**Winton** (CDP) Merced County
18	30	3.7	**King City** (city) Monterey County
18	30	3.7	**Lemon Hill** (CDP) Sacramento County
20	34	3.8	**Newman** (city) Stanislaus County
21	35	3.9	**Florence-Graham** (CDP) Los Angeles County
21	35	3.9	**Lynwood** (city) Los Angeles County
21	35	3.9	**Mead Valley** (CDP) Riverside County
24	41	4.0	**Coachella** (city) Riverside County
24	41	4.0	**Corcoran** (city) Kings County
24	41	4.0	**Delano** (city) Kern County
27	47	4.4	**Bell** (city) Los Angeles County
27	47	4.4	**Livingston** (city) Merced County
29	54	4.5	**Lindsay** (city) Tulare County
30	57	4.6	**Delhi** (CDP) Merced County
31	59	4.7	**South El Monte** (city) Los Angeles County
32	62	4.8	**McFarland** (city) Kern County
33	70	5.0	**East Los Angeles** (CDP) Los Angeles County
34	85	5.2	**South San Jose Hills** (CDP) Los Angeles County
35	91	5.3	**Huntington Park** (city) Los Angeles County
36	96	5.4	**Rialto** (city) San Bernardino County
37	103	5.5	**Bloomington** (CDP) San Bernardino County
38	110	5.6	**Clearlake** (city) Lake County
38	110	5.6	**Commerce** (city) Los Angeles County
38	110	5.6	**Los Banos** (city) Merced County
41	122	5.7	**Westmont** (CDP) Los Angeles County
42	131	5.8	**Home Gardens** (CDP) Riverside County
43	139	5.9	**Dinuba** (city) Tulare County
44	147	6.0	**Alum Rock** (CDP) Santa Clara County
44	147	6.0	**Compton** (city) Los Angeles County
44	147	6.0	**Isla Vista** (CDP) Santa Barbara County
44	147	6.0	**Perris** (city) Riverside County
44	147	6.0	**Selma** (city) Fresno County
49	166	6.2	**La Puente** (city) Los Angeles County
49	166	6.2	**South Gate** (city) Los Angeles County
49	166	6.2	**Sun Village** (CDP) Los Angeles County
52	184	6.3	**National City** (city) San Diego County
52	184	6.3	**Shasta Lake** (city) Shasta County
54	193	6.4	**Ceres** (city) Stanislaus County
54	193	6.4	**Montclair** (city) San Bernardino County
54	193	6.4	**Soledad** (city) Monterey County
57	205	6.5	**Baldwin Park** (city) Los Angeles County
58	216	6.6	**Shafter** (city) Kern County
58	216	6.6	**Ukiah** (city) Mendocino County
60	248	6.9	**Atwater** (city) Merced County
60	248	6.9	**El Monte** (city) Los Angeles County
60	248	6.9	**Grover Beach** (city) San Luis Obispo County
60	248	6.9	**Hemet** (city) Riverside County
60	248	6.9	**West Puente Valley** (CDP) Los Angeles County
65	268	7.0	**Bay Point** (CDP) Contra Costa County
65	268	7.0	**Colton** (city) San Bernardino County
65	268	7.0	**North Highlands** (CDP) Sacramento County
65	268	7.0	**Porterville** (city) Tulare County
65	268	7.0	**Tehachapi** (city) Kern County
70	288	7.1	**Banning** (city) Riverside County
70	288	7.1	**Bostonia** (CDP) San Diego County
70	288	7.1	**San Pablo** (city) Contra Costa County
70	288	7.1	**Santa Maria** (city) Santa Barbara County
74	311	7.2	**Florin** (CDP) Sacramento County
74	311	7.2	**San Bernardino** (city) San Bernardino County
76	328	7.3	**Citrus** (CDP) Los Angeles County
76	328	7.3	**Linda** (CDP) Yuba County
76	328	7.3	**Santa Ana** (city) Orange County
76	328	7.3	**Santa Paula** (city) Ventura County
76	328	7.3	**Watsonville** (city) Santa Cruz County
81	357	7.5	**Adelanto** (city) San Bernardino County
82	380	7.6	**Hawaiian Gardens** (city) Los Angeles County
82	380	7.6	**Marysville** (city) Yuba County
82	380	7.6	**Merced** (city) Merced County
82	380	7.6	**Reedley** (city) Fresno County
82	380	7.6	**Salinas** (city) Monterey County
87	406	7.7	**Lake Los Angeles** (CDP) Los Angeles County
87	406	7.7	**Red Bluff** (city) Tehama County
87	406	7.7	**San Jacinto** (city) Riverside County
87	406	7.7	**Valinda** (CDP) Los Angeles County
91	419	7.8	**Hesperia** (city) San Bernardino County
91	419	7.8	**Paramount** (city) Los Angeles County
91	419	7.8	**Parkway** (CDP) Sacramento County
94	456	8.0	**Cathedral City** (city) Riverside County
94	456	8.0	**East Palo Alto** (city) San Mateo County
94	456	8.0	**Willowbrook** (CDP) Los Angeles County
97	519	8.3	**Desert Hot Springs** (city) Riverside County
97	519	8.3	**Oildale** (CDP) Kern County
97	519	8.3	**Sanger** (city) Fresno County
100	546	8.4	**Calexico** (city) Imperial County
100	546	8.4	**Madera** (city) Madera County
102	569	8.5	**Lakeland Village** (CDP) Riverside County
102	569	8.5	**Norwalk** (city) Los Angeles County
102	569	8.5	**Tulare** (city) Tulare County
105	602	8.6	**Apple Valley** (town) San Bernardino County
105	602	8.6	**Highland** (city) San Bernardino County
107	627	8.7	**Lemoore** (city) Kings County
107	627	8.7	**Ontario** (city) San Bernardino County
107	627	8.7	**Oxnard** (city) Ventura County
107	627	8.7	**Pomona** (city) Los Angeles County
111	653	8.8	**Loma Linda** (city) San Bernardino County
111	653	8.8	**Pico Rivera** (city) Los Angeles County
111	653	8.8	**Rosamond** (CDP) Kern County
111	653	8.8	**Stockton** (city) San Joaquin County
115	684	8.9	**Eureka** (city) Humboldt County
115	684	8.9	**Lathrop** (city) San Joaquin County
115	684	8.9	**South Lake Tahoe** (city) El Dorado County
115	684	8.9	**Twentynine Palms** (city) San Bernardino County
119	757	9.1	**Azusa** (city) Los Angeles County
119	757	9.1	**East Hemet** (CDP) Riverside County
119	757	9.1	**Fillmore** (city) Ventura County
119	757	9.1	**Olivehurst** (CDP) Yuba County
123	789	9.2	**Hanford** (city) Kings County
123	789	9.2	**Susanville** (city) Lassen County
123	789	9.2	**Victorville** (city) San Bernardino County
126	832	9.3	**Salida** (CDP) Stanislaus County
127	863	9.4	**Lawndale** (city) Los Angeles County
127	863	9.4	**Moreno Valley** (city) Riverside County
127	863	9.4	**North Fair Oaks** (CDP) San Mateo County
127	863	9.4	**San Fernando** (city) Los Angeles County
127	863	9.4	**Stanford** (CDP) Santa Clara County
132	940	9.6	**La Presa** (CDP) San Diego County
132	940	9.6	**Rio Linda** (CDP) Sacramento County
134	977	9.7	**Placerville** (city) El Dorado County
135	1004	9.8	**Big Bear City** (CDP) San Bernardino County
135	1004	9.8	**Foothill Farms** (CDP) Sacramento County
135	1004	9.8	**Palmdale** (city) Los Angeles County
135	1004	9.8	**Riverbank** (city) Stanislaus County
139	1067	10.0	**Cherryland** (CDP) Alameda County
139	1067	10.0	**Phelan** (CDP) San Bernardino County
141	1108	10.1	**Arcata** (city) Humboldt County
141	1108	10.1	**Lompoc** (city) Santa Barbara County
141	1108	10.1	**Modesto** (city) Stanislaus County
141	1108	10.1	**Riverside** (city) Riverside County
145	1145	10.2	**Bellflower** (city) Los Angeles County
145	1145	10.2	**Gardena** (city) Los Angeles County
145	1145	10.2	**Hawthorne** (city) Los Angeles County
148	1177	10.3	**El Centro** (city) Imperial County
148	1177	10.3	**Galt** (city) Sacramento County
148	1177	10.3	**Hollister** (city) San Benito County

Note: *The state column ranks the top/bottom 150 places from all places in the state with population of 10,000 or more. The national column ranks the top/bottom 150 places from all places in the country with population of 10,000 or more. Places that are unincorporated were not considered in the rankings. Please refer to the User Guide for additional information.*

Employment: Computer, Engineering, and Science Occupations

Top 150 Places Ranked in *Descending* Order

State Rank	Nat'l Rank	Percent	Place
1	2	35.1	**Cupertino** (city) Santa Clara County
2	5	30.2	**Sunnyvale** (city) Santa Clara County
3	6	27.3	**Mountain View** (city) Santa Clara County
4	12	23.1	**Fremont** (city) Alameda County
5	14	22.6	**Santa Clara** (city) Santa Clara County
6	15	22.5	**Los Altos** (city) Santa Clara County
7	16	22.4	**Foster City** (city) San Mateo County
7	16	22.4	**Milpitas** (city) Santa Clara County
7	16	22.4	**Saratoga** (city) Santa Clara County
10	22	21.8	**Palo Alto** (city) Santa Clara County
11	32	20.3	**Albany** (city) Alameda County
12	38	18.8	**San Ramon** (city) Contra Costa County
13	52	17.7	**Stanford** (CDP) Santa Clara County
14	60	17.2	**Folsom** (city) Sacramento County
15	68	16.5	**Pleasanton** (city) Alameda County
16	79	15.8	**Belmont** (city) San Mateo County
17	86	15.4	**Dublin** (city) Alameda County
17	86	15.4	**Ridgecrest** (city) Kern County
19	95	15.2	**Berkeley** (city) Alameda County
19	95	15.2	**Davis** (city) Yolo County
21	100	15.1	**Irvine** (city) Orange County
22	108	14.9	**Menlo Park** (city) San Mateo County
23	110	14.8	**El Cerrito** (city) Contra Costa County
24	137	13.8	**Emeryville** (city) Alameda County
25	184	12.9	**Campbell** (city) Santa Clara County
26	190	12.8	**San Jose** (city) Santa Clara County
27	229	12.2	**Union City** (city) Alameda County
28	239	12.1	**Poway** (city) San Diego County
29	246	12.0	**Goleta** (city) Santa Barbara County
30	255	11.9	**Livermore** (city) Alameda County
30	255	11.9	**Los Gatos** (town) Santa Clara County
32	262	11.8	**San Carlos** (city) San Mateo County
33	293	11.4	**Carlsbad** (city) San Diego County
33	293	11.4	**Walnut Creek** (city) Contra Costa County
35	299	11.3	**Cerritos** (city) Los Angeles County
36	318	11.1	**Hercules** (city) Contra Costa County
37	333	10.9	**Clayton** (city) Contra Costa County
38	342	10.8	**Torrance** (city) Los Angeles County
39	353	10.7	**Aliso Viejo** (city) Orange County
40	363	10.6	**Newark** (city) Alameda County
41	374	10.5	**Rancho Palos Verdes** (city) Los Angeles County
41	374	10.5	**San Diego** (city) San Diego County
43	393	10.4	**Hermosa Beach** (city) Los Angeles County
43	393	10.4	**Lafayette** (city) Contra Costa County
43	393	10.4	**Redwood City** (city) San Mateo County
43	393	10.4	**San Francisco** (city) San Francisco County
47	407	10.3	**East San Gabriel** (CDP) Los Angeles County
48	424	10.2	**California City** (city) Kern County
48	424	10.2	**Oak Park** (CDP) Ventura County
48	424	10.2	**Redondo Beach** (city) Los Angeles County
48	424	10.2	**Solana Beach** (city) San Diego County
52	439	10.1	**Sierra Madre** (city) Los Angeles County
53	465	9.9	**El Segundo** (city) Los Angeles County
53	465	9.9	**Piedmont** (city) Alameda County
55	478	9.8	**Cameron Park** (CDP) El Dorado County
55	478	9.8	**Lake Forest** (city) Orange County
55	478	9.8	**Stevenson Ranch** (CDP) Los Angeles County
58	490	9.7	**Encinitas** (city) San Diego County
58	490	9.7	**San Mateo** (city) San Mateo County
60	514	9.6	**Rosemont** (CDP) Sacramento County
61	524	9.5	**Rossmoor** (CDP) Orange County
62	537	9.4	**Orangevale** (CDP) Sacramento County
63	550	9.3	**Arcadia** (city) Los Angeles County
63	550	9.3	**Mill Valley** (city) Marin County
63	550	9.3	**Mission Viejo** (city) Orange County
63	550	9.3	**San Luis Obispo** (city) San Luis Obispo County
63	550	9.3	**Thousand Oaks** (city) Ventura County
68	581	9.1	**Pinole** (city) Contra Costa County
69	595	9.0	**Burlingame** (city) San Mateo County
69	595	9.0	**Orinda** (city) Contra Costa County
69	595	9.0	**San Diego Country Estates** (CDP) San Diego County
69	595	9.0	**Walnut** (city) Los Angeles County
73	622	8.9	**Pleasant Hill** (city) Contra Costa County
73	622	8.9	**Santa Cruz** (city) Santa Cruz County
75	642	8.8	**El Dorado Hills** (CDP) El Dorado County
76	667	8.7	**La Riviera** (CDP) Sacramento County
76	667	8.7	**Laguna Niguel** (city) Orange County
76	667	8.7	**Pasadena** (city) Los Angeles County
76	667	8.7	**South Pasadena** (city) Los Angeles County
80	695	8.6	**Palos Verdes Estates** (city) Los Angeles County
80	695	8.6	**San Marino** (city) Los Angeles County
80	695	8.6	**Vineyard** (CDP) Sacramento County
83	715	8.5	**Camarillo** (city) Ventura County
83	715	8.5	**Moraga** (town) Contra Costa County
85	744	8.4	**Diamond Bar** (city) Los Angeles County
86	767	8.3	**Alameda** (city) Alameda County
86	767	8.3	**Fountain Valley** (city) Orange County
86	767	8.3	**Manhattan Beach** (city) Los Angeles County
86	767	8.3	**Rancho Cordova** (city) Sacramento County
86	767	8.3	**Scotts Valley** (city) Santa Cruz County
86	767	8.3	**Tustin** (city) Orange County
92	794	8.2	**Danville** (town) Contra Costa County
92	794	8.2	**La Cañada Flintridge** (city) Los Angeles County
92	794	8.2	**Larkspur** (city) Marin County
92	794	8.2	**Martinez** (city) Contra Costa County
92	794	8.2	**Orcutt** (CDP) Santa Barbara County
97	821	8.1	**Elk Grove** (city) Sacramento County
97	821	8.1	**Temple City** (city) Los Angeles County
99	848	8.0	**Fair Oaks** (CDP) Sacramento County
99	848	8.0	**San Marcos** (city) San Diego County
101	874	7.9	**Pacifica** (city) San Mateo County
102	901	7.8	**Brea** (city) Orange County
102	901	7.8	**Coronado** (city) San Diego County
102	901	7.8	**Grass Valley** (city) Nevada County
102	901	7.8	**Yorba Linda** (city) Orange County
106	924	7.7	**Agoura Hills** (city) Los Angeles County
106	924	7.7	**El Sobrante** (CDP) Contra Costa County
106	924	7.7	**Half Moon Bay** (city) San Mateo County
106	924	7.7	**Malibu** (city) Los Angeles County
110	957	7.6	**Chino Hills** (city) San Bernardino County
110	957	7.6	**North Tustin** (CDP) Orange County
110	957	7.6	**San Bruno** (city) San Mateo County
113	992	7.5	**Culver City** (city) Los Angeles County
113	992	7.5	**Rosamond** (CDP) Kern County
115	1022	7.4	**Rocklin** (city) Placer County
115	1022	7.4	**Seal Beach** (city) Orange County
115	1022	7.4	**West Sacramento** (city) Yolo County
118	1061	7.3	**Morgan Hill** (city) Santa Clara County
118	1061	7.3	**Tracy** (city) San Joaquin County
120	1097	7.2	**Castro Valley** (CDP) Alameda County
120	1097	7.2	**Granite Bay** (CDP) Placer County
120	1097	7.2	**Morro Bay** (city) San Luis Obispo County
120	1097	7.2	**Roseville** (city) Placer County
120	1097	7.2	**Santa Monica** (city) Los Angeles County
125	1137	7.1	**Calabasas** (city) Los Angeles County
126	1190	7.0	**Cypress** (city) Orange County
126	1190	7.0	**La Palma** (city) Orange County
126	1190	7.0	**Ladera Ranch** (CDP) Orange County
126	1190	7.0	**Monterey** (city) Monterey County
126	1190	7.0	**Rancho Santa Margarita** (city) Orange County
126	1190	7.0	**West Carson** (CDP) Los Angeles County
132	1224	6.9	**Oakland** (city) Alameda County
132	1224	6.9	**Sacramento** (city) Sacramento County
132	1224	6.9	**San Leandro** (city) Alameda County
135	1267	6.8	**Simi Valley** (city) Ventura County
136	1303	6.7	**Hillsborough** (town) San Mateo County
136	1303	6.7	**La Mesa** (city) San Diego County
136	1303	6.7	**Los Osos** (CDP) San Luis Obispo County
136	1303	6.7	**San Dimas** (city) Los Angeles County
140	1354	6.6	**Alpine** (CDP) San Diego County
140	1354	6.6	**Millbrae** (city) San Mateo County
140	1354	6.6	**Placentia** (city) Orange County
140	1354	6.6	**San Buenaventura (Ventura)** (city) Ventura County
140	1354	6.6	**Santa Barbara** (city) Santa Barbara County
140	1354	6.6	**South San Francisco** (city) San Mateo County
146	1402	6.5	**Signal Hill** (city) Los Angeles County
147	1445	6.4	**Castaic** (CDP) Los Angeles County
147	1445	6.4	**Del Aire** (CDP) Los Angeles County
147	1445	6.4	**Eastvale** (city) Riverside County
150	1484	6.3	**Burbank** (city) Los Angeles County

Note: *The state column ranks the top/bottom 150 places from all places in the state with population of 10,000 or more. The national column ranks the top/bottom 150 places from all places in the country with population of 10,000 or more. Places that are unincorporated were not considered in the rankings. Please refer to the User Guide for additional information.*

Employment: Computer, Engineering, and Science Occupations

Top 150 Places Ranked in *Ascending* Order

State Rank	Nat'l Rank	Percent	Place
1	1	0.0	**Avenal** (city) Kings County
1	1	0.0	**Garden Acres** (CDP) San Joaquin County
1	1	0.0	**Kerman** (city) Fresno County
1	1	0.0	**McFarland** (city) Kern County
1	1	0.0	**Muscoy** (CDP) San Bernardino County
6	13	0.3	**Delano** (city) Kern County
6	13	0.3	**Maywood** (city) Los Angeles County
6	13	0.3	**Mendota** (city) Fresno County
9	21	0.4	**Blythe** (city) Riverside County
9	21	0.4	**Florence-Graham** (CDP) Los Angeles County
9	21	0.4	**Walnut Park** (CDP) Los Angeles County
12	29	0.5	**Cudahy** (city) Los Angeles County
12	29	0.5	**Farmersville** (city) Tulare County
12	29	0.5	**Lamont** (CDP) Kern County
12	29	0.5	**Lennox** (CDP) Los Angeles County
12	29	0.5	**Willowbrook** (CDP) Los Angeles County
17	37	0.6	**Bloomington** (CDP) San Bernardino County
18	46	0.7	**Arvin** (city) Kern County
18	46	0.7	**Atwater** (city) Merced County
18	46	0.7	**Bell Gardens** (city) Los Angeles County
18	46	0.7	**Clearlake** (city) Lake County
18	46	0.7	**Commerce** (city) Los Angeles County
18	46	0.7	**Corcoran** (city) Kings County
18	46	0.7	**King City** (city) Monterey County
18	46	0.7	**Soledad** (city) Monterey County
18	46	0.7	**Wasco** (city) Kern County
27	65	0.8	**Delhi** (CDP) Merced County
27	65	0.8	**Huntington Park** (city) Los Angeles County
29	80	0.9	**Greenfield** (city) Monterey County
29	80	0.9	**Oroville** (city) Butte County
29	80	0.9	**Porterville** (city) Tulare County
29	80	0.9	**Reedley** (city) Fresno County
33	101	1.0	**Compton** (city) Los Angeles County
33	101	1.0	**Lynwood** (city) Los Angeles County
35	120	1.1	**Banning** (city) Riverside County
35	120	1.1	**Bell** (city) Los Angeles County
35	120	1.1	**Riverbank** (city) Stanislaus County
35	120	1.1	**Salida** (CDP) Stanislaus County
35	120	1.1	**Shafter** (city) Kern County
35	120	1.1	**South Gate** (city) Los Angeles County
35	120	1.1	**Winton** (CDP) Merced County
42	150	1.2	**Calexico** (city) Imperial County
42	150	1.2	**Coachella** (city) Riverside County
42	150	1.2	**Dinuba** (city) Tulare County
42	150	1.2	**El Centro** (city) Imperial County
46	172	1.3	**East Rancho Dominguez** (CDP) Los Angeles County
46	172	1.3	**Indio** (city) Riverside County
46	172	1.3	**Livingston** (city) Merced County
46	172	1.3	**San Fernando** (city) Los Angeles County
50	202	1.4	**Brawley** (city) Imperial County
50	202	1.4	**Canyon Lake** (city) Riverside County
50	202	1.4	**Chowchilla** (city) Madera County
50	202	1.4	**East Los Angeles** (CDP) Los Angeles County
50	202	1.4	**Hawaiian Gardens** (city) Los Angeles County
50	202	1.4	**Olivehurst** (CDP) Yuba County
50	202	1.4	**Perris** (city) Riverside County
57	239	1.5	**Coalinga** (city) Fresno County
57	239	1.5	**Desert Hot Springs** (city) Riverside County
57	239	1.5	**Lindsay** (city) Tulare County
57	239	1.5	**North Auburn** (CDP) Placer County
57	239	1.5	**Pico Rivera** (city) Los Angeles County
57	239	1.5	**South El Monte** (city) Los Angeles County
57	239	1.5	**Valinda** (CDP) Los Angeles County
57	239	1.5	**West Whittier-Los Nietos** (CDP) Los Angeles County
65	283	1.6	**National City** (city) San Diego County
65	283	1.6	**Phelan** (CDP) San Bernardino County
65	283	1.6	**San Bernardino** (city) San Bernardino County
65	283	1.6	**Susanville** (city) Lassen County
65	283	1.6	**West Puente Valley** (CDP) Los Angeles County
70	325	1.7	**Adelanto** (city) San Bernardino County
70	325	1.7	**Mead Valley** (CDP) Riverside County
70	325	1.7	**Sanger** (city) Fresno County
73	360	1.8	**Ceres** (city) Stanislaus County
73	360	1.8	**Exeter** (city) Tulare County
73	360	1.8	**Inglewood** (city) Los Angeles County
73	360	1.8	**La Puente** (city) Los Angeles County
73	360	1.8	**Madera** (city) Madera County
73	360	1.8	**Magalia** (CDP) Butte County
73	360	1.8	**Oildale** (CDP) Kern County
73	360	1.8	**Paramount** (city) Los Angeles County
73	360	1.8	**Rialto** (city) San Bernardino County
73	360	1.8	**Westmont** (CDP) Los Angeles County
83	425	1.9	**Lemon Hill** (CDP) Sacramento County
83	425	1.9	**Montclair** (city) San Bernardino County
83	425	1.9	**Parlier** (city) Fresno County
83	425	1.9	**Salinas** (city) Monterey County
83	425	1.9	**South San Jose Hills** (CDP) Los Angeles County
88	479	2.0	**East Hemet** (CDP) Riverside County
88	479	2.0	**Marysville** (city) Yuba County
88	479	2.0	**San Jacinto** (city) Riverside County
88	479	2.0	**Yucca Valley** (town) San Bernardino County
92	536	2.1	**Bostonia** (CDP) San Diego County
92	536	2.1	**Cathedral City** (city) Riverside County
92	536	2.1	**Colton** (city) San Bernardino County
92	536	2.1	**Hemet** (city) Riverside County
92	536	2.1	**Hesperia** (city) San Bernardino County
92	536	2.1	**Merced** (city) Merced County
92	536	2.1	**Parkway** (CDP) Sacramento County
92	536	2.1	**Santa Paula** (city) Ventura County
92	536	2.1	**Selma** (city) Fresno County
101	586	2.2	**Apple Valley** (town) San Bernardino County
101	586	2.2	**Baldwin Park** (city) Los Angeles County
101	586	2.2	**Palm Desert** (city) Riverside County
101	586	2.2	**Tulare** (city) Tulare County
101	586	2.2	**Watsonville** (city) Santa Cruz County
106	649	2.3	**Fillmore** (city) Ventura County
106	649	2.3	**Lodi** (city) San Joaquin County
106	649	2.3	**Victorville** (city) San Bernardino County
109	704	2.4	**Bellflower** (city) Los Angeles County
110	754	2.5	**Norwalk** (city) Los Angeles County
110	754	2.5	**Ontario** (city) San Bernardino County
110	754	2.5	**Rancho Mirage** (city) Riverside County
113	820	2.6	**Cherryland** (CDP) Alameda County
113	820	2.6	**Fontana** (city) San Bernardino County
113	820	2.6	**Hanford** (city) Kings County
113	820	2.6	**Hawthorne** (city) Los Angeles County
113	820	2.6	**Lemoore** (city) Kings County
113	820	2.6	**Moreno Valley** (city) Riverside County
113	820	2.6	**Nipomo** (CDP) San Luis Obispo County
113	820	2.6	**Red Bluff** (city) Tehama County
113	820	2.6	**San Pablo** (city) Contra Costa County
113	820	2.6	**Visalia** (city) Tulare County
123	893	2.7	**Beaumont** (city) Riverside County
123	893	2.7	**Big Bear City** (CDP) San Bernardino County
123	893	2.7	**Fresno** (city) Fresno County
123	893	2.7	**Santa Ana** (city) Orange County
123	893	2.7	**Stockton** (city) San Joaquin County
123	893	2.7	**Ukiah** (city) Mendocino County
129	952	2.8	**Barstow** (city) San Bernardino County
129	952	2.8	**Bay Point** (CDP) Contra Costa County
129	952	2.8	**Downey** (city) Los Angeles County
129	952	2.8	**Fortuna** (city) Humboldt County
129	952	2.8	**Hollister** (city) San Benito County
129	952	2.8	**Patterson** (city) Stanislaus County
129	952	2.8	**Sonoma** (city) Sonoma County
136	1025	2.9	**Foothill Farms** (CDP) Sacramento County
136	1025	2.9	**La Quinta** (city) Riverside County
136	1025	2.9	**Placerville** (city) El Dorado County
136	1025	2.9	**Pomona** (city) Los Angeles County
140	1089	3.0	**Azusa** (city) Los Angeles County
140	1089	3.0	**El Cajon** (city) San Diego County
140	1089	3.0	**Kingsburg** (city) Fresno County
140	1089	3.0	**Lake Los Angeles** (CDP) Los Angeles County
140	1089	3.0	**Lathrop** (city) San Joaquin County
140	1089	3.0	**Manteca** (city) San Joaquin County
140	1089	3.0	**Modesto** (city) Stanislaus County
140	1089	3.0	**North Highlands** (CDP) Sacramento County
140	1089	3.0	**Valle Vista** (CDP) Riverside County
149	1168	3.1	**Eureka** (city) Humboldt County
149	1168	3.1	**Lawndale** (city) Los Angeles County

Note: *The state column ranks the top/bottom 150 places from all places in the state with population of 10,000 or more. The national column ranks the top/bottom 150 places from all places in the country with population of 10,000 or more. Places that are unincorporated were not considered in the rankings. Please refer to the User Guide for additional information.*

Employment: Education, Legal, Community Service, Arts, and Media Occupations

Top 150 Places Ranked in *Descending* Order

State Rank	Nat'l Rank	Percent	Place
1	1	40.9	**Stanford** (CDP) Santa Clara County
2	8	31.3	**View Park-Windsor Hills** (CDP) Los Angeles County
3	15	27.5	**Berkeley** (city) Alameda County
4	17	27.1	**Santa Monica** (city) Los Angeles County
5	18	26.9	**Claremont** (city) Los Angeles County
6	20	26.8	**Davis** (city) Yolo County
7	40	24.8	**South Pasadena** (city) Los Angeles County
8	47	24.4	**Albany** (city) Alameda County
8	47	24.4	**Malibu** (city) Los Angeles County
10	69	23.1	**Altadena** (CDP) Los Angeles County
10	69	23.1	**Culver City** (city) Los Angeles County
10	69	23.1	**Emeryville** (city) Alameda County
10	69	23.1	**West Hollywood** (city) Los Angeles County
14	92	22.1	**Tamalpais-Homestead Valley** (CDP) Marin County
15	97	21.9	**Piedmont** (city) Alameda County
16	105	21.6	**Sierra Madre** (city) Los Angeles County
17	114	21.4	**La Cañada Flintridge** (city) Los Angeles County
18	150	20.2	**La Crescenta-Montrose** (CDP) Los Angeles County
19	155	20.1	**Beverly Hills** (city) Los Angeles County
20	158	20.0	**San Anselmo** (town) Marin County
21	167	19.8	**Lafayette** (city) Contra Costa County
21	167	19.8	**Laguna Beach** (city) Orange County
23	180	19.5	**Santa Cruz** (city) Santa Cruz County
24	205	19.2	**Pasadena** (city) Los Angeles County
25	227	18.8	**Palo Alto** (city) Santa Clara County
26	239	18.6	**Calabasas** (city) Los Angeles County
26	239	18.6	**Oak Park** (CDP) Ventura County
28	245	18.5	**Susanville** (city) Lassen County
29	251	18.4	**El Cerrito** (city) Contra Costa County
30	274	18.1	**Mill Valley** (city) Marin County
30	274	18.1	**Moraga** (town) Contra Costa County
32	277	18.0	**Manhattan Beach** (city) Los Angeles County
33	281	17.9	**Burbank** (city) Los Angeles County
33	281	17.9	**Coronado** (city) San Diego County
33	281	17.9	**Isla Vista** (CDP) Santa Barbara County
36	294	17.7	**Palos Verdes Estates** (city) Los Angeles County
37	302	17.6	**Agoura Hills** (city) Los Angeles County
37	302	17.6	**Menlo Park** (city) San Mateo County
39	312	17.5	**Pacific Grove** (city) Monterey County
40	366	16.8	**Seal Beach** (city) Orange County
41	376	16.7	**Arcata** (city) Humboldt County
41	376	16.7	**Lake Arrowhead** (CDP) San Bernardino County
43	418	16.3	**Encinitas** (city) San Diego County
43	418	16.3	**Larkspur** (city) Marin County
45	435	16.2	**Redlands** (city) San Bernardino County
46	447	16.1	**Lemoore** (city) Kings County
46	447	16.1	**Monterey** (city) Monterey County
48	462	16.0	**El Sobrante** (CDP) Riverside County
49	471	15.9	**Goleta** (city) Santa Barbara County
49	471	15.9	**North Tustin** (CDP) Orange County
51	500	15.7	**El Segundo** (city) Los Angeles County
51	500	15.7	**Solana Beach** (city) San Diego County
53	521	15.6	**Orinda** (city) Contra Costa County
54	537	15.5	**Newport Beach** (city) Orange County
55	550	15.4	**Oakland** (city) Alameda County
56	583	15.2	**Casa de Oro-Mount Helix** (CDP) San Diego County
56	583	15.2	**Irvine** (city) Orange County
58	604	15.1	**Rossmoor** (CDP) Orange County
58	604	15.1	**San Carlos** (city) San Mateo County
58	604	15.1	**Walnut Creek** (city) Contra Costa County
61	656	14.8	**Placerville** (city) El Dorado County
61	656	14.8	**Rancho Palos Verdes** (city) Los Angeles County
61	656	14.8	**San Francisco** (city) San Francisco County
64	680	14.7	**Glendale** (city) Los Angeles County
64	680	14.7	**Sonoma** (city) Sonoma County
66	744	14.4	**Alameda** (city) Alameda County
66	744	14.4	**Stevenson Ranch** (CDP) Los Angeles County
68	771	14.3	**San Marino** (city) Los Angeles County
69	795	14.2	**Hermosa Beach** (city) Los Angeles County
69	795	14.2	**Los Altos** (city) Santa Clara County
69	795	14.2	**Los Angeles** (city) Los Angeles County
72	851	14.0	**Auburn** (city) Placer County
72	851	14.0	**Brea** (city) Orange County
72	851	14.0	**Morro Bay** (city) San Luis Obispo County
75	878	13.9	**Carlsbad** (city) San Diego County
76	904	13.8	**Arcadia** (city) Los Angeles County
76	904	13.8	**Los Gatos** (town) Santa Clara County
78	931	13.7	**Hillsborough** (town) San Mateo County
78	931	13.7	**La Mirada** (city) Los Angeles County
78	931	13.7	**La Verne** (city) Los Angeles County
78	931	13.7	**Redondo Beach** (city) Los Angeles County
78	931	13.7	**Santa Barbara** (city) Santa Barbara County
83	969	13.6	**Aliso Viejo** (city) Orange County
83	969	13.6	**Whittier** (city) Los Angeles County
85	993	13.5	**Ladera Ranch** (CDP) Orange County
85	993	13.5	**San Luis Obispo** (city) San Luis Obispo County
85	993	13.5	**Thousand Oaks** (city) Ventura County
88	1021	13.4	**Glendora** (city) Los Angeles County
89	1045	13.3	**Clovis** (city) Fresno County
89	1045	13.3	**East San Gabriel** (CDP) Los Angeles County
91	1079	13.2	**La Mesa** (city) San Diego County
91	1079	13.2	**San Buenaventura (Ventura)** (city) Ventura County
93	1117	13.1	**Cypress** (city) Orange County
93	1117	13.1	**Loma Linda** (city) San Bernardino County
93	1117	13.1	**Rancho San Diego** (CDP) San Diego County
93	1117	13.1	**Ripon** (city) San Joaquin County
93	1117	13.1	**San Rafael** (city) Marin County
93	1117	13.1	**Yorba Linda** (city) Orange County
99	1147	13.0	**Half Moon Bay** (city) San Mateo County
100	1188	12.9	**Cameron Park** (CDP) El Dorado County
100	1188	12.9	**Mountain View** (city) Santa Clara County
102	1228	12.8	**La Palma** (city) Orange County
102	1228	12.8	**Signal Hill** (city) Los Angeles County
104	1263	12.7	**San Clemente** (city) Orange County
104	1263	12.7	**Temple City** (city) Los Angeles County
106	1307	12.6	**Arroyo Grande** (city) San Luis Obispo County
106	1307	12.6	**Benicia** (city) Solano County
106	1307	12.6	**Pleasant Hill** (city) Contra Costa County
106	1307	12.6	**Quartz Hill** (CDP) Los Angeles County
110	1346	12.5	**Apple Valley** (town) San Bernardino County
110	1346	12.5	**Camarillo** (city) Ventura County
110	1346	12.5	**Duarte** (city) Los Angeles County
110	1346	12.5	**Nipomo** (CDP) San Luis Obispo County
110	1346	12.5	**Novato** (city) Marin County
115	1380	12.4	**Laguna Niguel** (city) Orange County
115	1380	12.4	**McKinleyville** (CDP) Humboldt County
115	1380	12.4	**Mission Viejo** (city) Orange County
115	1380	12.4	**Monrovia** (city) Los Angeles County
115	1380	12.4	**San Dimas** (city) Los Angeles County
115	1380	12.4	**Sun Village** (CDP) Los Angeles County
121	1421	12.3	**Castaic** (CDP) Los Angeles County
121	1421	12.3	**Long Beach** (city) Los Angeles County
121	1421	12.3	**Los Osos** (CDP) San Luis Obispo County
121	1421	12.3	**San Diego** (city) San Diego County
125	1460	12.2	**Burlingame** (city) San Mateo County
125	1460	12.2	**Chico** (city) Butte County
125	1460	12.2	**El Centro** (city) Imperial County
125	1460	12.2	**Pacifica** (city) San Mateo County
125	1460	12.2	**Rocklin** (city) Placer County
130	1505	12.1	**Arden-Arcade** (CDP) Sacramento County
130	1505	12.1	**Bonita** (CDP) San Diego County
130	1505	12.1	**Grand Terrace** (city) San Bernardino County
130	1505	12.1	**Huntington Beach** (city) Orange County
130	1505	12.1	**Marysville** (city) Yuba County
130	1505	12.1	**Placentia** (city) Orange County
130	1505	12.1	**Riverside** (city) Riverside County
130	1505	12.1	**Rosemont** (CDP) Sacramento County
130	1505	12.1	**Santa Clarita** (city) Los Angeles County
139	1552	12.0	**Fullerton** (city) Orange County
139	1552	12.0	**Merced** (city) Merced County
139	1552	12.0	**Palm Desert** (city) Riverside County
139	1552	12.0	**Torrance** (city) Los Angeles County
139	1552	12.0	**Truckee** (town) Nevada County
144	1586	11.9	**Alamo** (CDP) Contra Costa County
144	1586	11.9	**Rancho Santa Margarita** (city) Orange County
146	1642	11.8	**Carpinteria** (city) Santa Barbara County
146	1642	11.8	**Elk Grove** (city) Sacramento County
148	1698	11.7	**Lincoln** (city) Placer County
148	1698	11.7	**Los Alamitos** (city) Orange County
148	1698	11.7	**Pinole** (city) Contra Costa County

Note: *The state column ranks the top/bottom 150 places from all places in the state with population of 10,000 or more. The national column ranks the top/bottom 150 places from all places in the country with population of 10,000 or more. Places that are unincorporated were not considered in the rankings. Please refer to the User Guide for additional information.*

Employment: Education, Legal, Community Service, Arts, and Media Occupations

Top 150 Places Ranked in *Ascending* Order

State Rank	Nat'l Rank	Percent	Place
1	2	1.8	**Mendota** (city) Fresno County
2	3	1.9	**Avenal** (city) Kings County
3	9	2.9	**Cudahy** (city) Los Angeles County
4	13	3.3	**Arvin** (city) Kern County
5	14	3.4	**Lamont** (CDP) Kern County
5	14	3.4	**Linda** (CDP) Yuba County
7	22	3.6	**Tehachapi** (city) Kern County
8	26	3.7	**Oakley** (city) Contra Costa County
9	28	3.8	**Florence-Graham** (CDP) Los Angeles County
9	28	3.8	**McFarland** (city) Kern County
9	28	3.8	**Willowbrook** (CDP) Los Angeles County
12	34	3.9	**Hawaiian Gardens** (city) Los Angeles County
13	35	4.0	**South San Jose Hills** (CDP) Los Angeles County
14	40	4.1	**Wasco** (city) Kern County
15	45	4.2	**Parlier** (city) Fresno County
16	55	4.4	**Corcoran** (city) Kings County
16	55	4.4	**Diamond Springs** (CDP) El Dorado County
16	55	4.4	**Livingston** (city) Merced County
16	55	4.4	**Newman** (city) Stanislaus County
20	62	4.5	**Huntington Park** (city) Los Angeles County
21	67	4.6	**Mead Valley** (CDP) Riverside County
22	73	4.7	**Santa Ana** (city) Orange County
22	73	4.7	**Winton** (CDP) Merced County
24	81	4.8	**Farmersville** (city) Tulare County
25	87	4.9	**Bay Point** (CDP) Contra Costa County
25	87	4.9	**Delano** (city) Kern County
25	87	4.9	**Los Banos** (city) Merced County
28	97	5.0	**El Monte** (city) Los Angeles County
28	97	5.0	**Lemon Hill** (CDP) Sacramento County
28	97	5.0	**Soledad** (city) Monterey County
31	110	5.1	**Bloomington** (CDP) San Bernardino County
31	110	5.1	**Coachella** (city) Riverside County
31	110	5.1	**Lakeland Village** (CDP) Riverside County
31	110	5.1	**National City** (city) San Diego County
31	110	5.1	**Suisun City** (city) Solano County
36	122	5.2	**Artesia** (city) Los Angeles County
36	122	5.2	**Bostonia** (CDP) San Diego County
36	122	5.2	**East Rancho Dominguez** (CDP) Los Angeles County
36	122	5.2	**South El Monte** (city) Los Angeles County
36	122	5.2	**Westmont** (CDP) Los Angeles County
41	136	5.3	**Lynwood** (city) Los Angeles County
41	136	5.3	**Santa Maria** (city) Santa Barbara County
41	136	5.3	**Watsonville** (city) Santa Cruz County
44	147	5.4	**Garden Acres** (CDP) San Joaquin County
44	147	5.4	**South Lake Tahoe** (city) El Dorado County
46	159	5.5	**Compton** (city) Los Angeles County
46	159	5.5	**Lindsay** (city) Tulare County
46	159	5.5	**Montclair** (city) San Bernardino County
46	159	5.5	**Rosemead** (city) Los Angeles County
50	192	5.7	**Bell Gardens** (city) Los Angeles County
50	192	5.7	**Daly City** (city) San Mateo County
50	192	5.7	**East Los Angeles** (CDP) Los Angeles County
50	192	5.7	**Home Gardens** (CDP) Riverside County
50	192	5.7	**Muscoy** (CDP) San Bernardino County
55	203	5.8	**Olivehurst** (CDP) Yuba County
55	203	5.8	**Santa Paula** (city) Ventura County
55	203	5.8	**Valinda** (CDP) Los Angeles County
58	220	5.9	**Ashland** (CDP) Alameda County
58	220	5.9	**Pittsburg** (city) Contra Costa County
60	235	6.0	**Baldwin Park** (city) Los Angeles County
60	235	6.0	**Ceres** (city) Stanislaus County
60	235	6.0	**Lawndale** (city) Los Angeles County
60	235	6.0	**Madera** (city) Madera County
60	235	6.0	**Paramount** (city) Los Angeles County
65	257	6.1	**Cathedral City** (city) Riverside County
65	257	6.1	**Colton** (city) San Bernardino County
65	257	6.1	**Hollister** (city) San Benito County
65	257	6.1	**Oxnard** (city) Ventura County
65	257	6.1	**Parkway** (CDP) Sacramento County
65	257	6.1	**Salinas** (city) Monterey County
65	257	6.1	**Walnut Park** (CDP) Los Angeles County
72	292	6.2	**Lathrop** (city) San Joaquin County
72	292	6.2	**Tracy** (city) San Joaquin County
74	312	6.3	**East Palo Alto** (city) San Mateo County
74	312	6.3	**Maywood** (city) Los Angeles County
76	331	6.4	**Lake Elsinore** (city) Riverside County
76	331	6.4	**Milpitas** (city) Santa Clara County
76	331	6.4	**North Fair Oaks** (CDP) San Mateo County
76	331	6.4	**San Pablo** (city) Contra Costa County
80	353	6.5	**California City** (city) Kern County
80	353	6.5	**Cherryland** (CDP) Alameda County
82	384	6.6	**Rosamond** (CDP) Kern County
83	409	6.7	**Commerce** (city) Los Angeles County
83	409	6.7	**Rialto** (city) San Bernardino County
83	409	6.7	**South Gate** (city) Los Angeles County
86	433	6.8	**Dinuba** (city) Tulare County
86	433	6.8	**Garden Grove** (city) Orange County
86	433	6.8	**Hayward** (city) Alameda County
86	433	6.8	**Newark** (city) Alameda County
86	433	6.8	**Norco** (city) Riverside County
86	433	6.8	**Oildale** (CDP) Kern County
86	433	6.8	**Patterson** (city) Stanislaus County
86	433	6.8	**Port Hueneme** (city) Ventura County
86	433	6.8	**Rowland Heights** (CDP) Los Angeles County
86	433	6.8	**Union City** (city) Alameda County
96	461	6.9	**Avocado Heights** (CDP) Los Angeles County
96	461	6.9	**Citrus** (CDP) Los Angeles County
96	461	6.9	**Fairfield** (city) Solano County
96	461	6.9	**French Valley** (CDP) Riverside County
96	461	6.9	**Ontario** (city) San Bernardino County
96	461	6.9	**Orangevale** (CDP) Sacramento County
96	461	6.9	**Perris** (city) Riverside County
103	507	7.0	**Desert Hot Springs** (city) Riverside County
103	507	7.0	**Fontana** (city) San Bernardino County
103	507	7.0	**King City** (city) Monterey County
103	507	7.0	**Lennox** (CDP) Los Angeles County
103	507	7.0	**Ramona** (CDP) San Diego County
103	507	7.0	**San Lorenzo** (CDP) Alameda County
103	507	7.0	**Vista** (city) San Diego County
110	547	7.1	**La Puente** (city) Los Angeles County
110	547	7.1	**Lake Los Angeles** (CDP) Los Angeles County
110	547	7.1	**Shafter** (city) Kern County
113	573	7.2	**Adelanto** (city) San Bernardino County
113	573	7.2	**Bell** (city) Los Angeles County
113	573	7.2	**Kerman** (city) Fresno County
113	573	7.2	**San Diego Country Estates** (CDP) San Diego County
113	573	7.2	**Selma** (city) Fresno County
113	573	7.2	**Stanton** (city) Orange County
113	573	7.2	**Yuba City** (city) Sutter County
120	606	7.3	**Antelope** (CDP) Sacramento County
120	606	7.3	**Buena Park** (city) Orange County
120	606	7.3	**Lompoc** (city) Santa Barbara County
120	606	7.3	**North Highlands** (CDP) Sacramento County
120	606	7.3	**Rio Linda** (CDP) Sacramento County
120	606	7.3	**Westminster** (city) Orange County
120	606	7.3	**Winter Gardens** (CDP) San Diego County
127	646	7.4	**Brawley** (city) Imperial County
127	646	7.4	**Foothill Farms** (CDP) Sacramento County
127	646	7.4	**Manteca** (city) San Joaquin County
127	646	7.4	**Phelan** (CDP) San Bernardino County
127	646	7.4	**South San Francisco** (city) San Mateo County
132	682	7.5	**Citrus Heights** (city) Sacramento County
132	682	7.5	**Fillmore** (city) Ventura County
132	682	7.5	**Florin** (CDP) Sacramento County
132	682	7.5	**Hawthorne** (city) Los Angeles County
132	682	7.5	**Moreno Valley** (city) Riverside County
137	716	7.6	**Bellflower** (city) Los Angeles County
137	716	7.6	**Camp Pendleton South** (CDP) San Diego County
137	716	7.6	**Carson** (city) Los Angeles County
137	716	7.6	**Del Aire** (CDP) Los Angeles County
137	716	7.6	**La Presa** (CDP) San Diego County
137	716	7.6	**Palmdale** (city) Los Angeles County
137	716	7.6	**Pico Rivera** (city) Los Angeles County
137	716	7.6	**Prunedale** (CDP) Monterey County
137	716	7.6	**West Puente Valley** (CDP) Los Angeles County
146	759	7.7	**Anaheim** (city) Orange County
146	759	7.7	**El Paso de Robles (Paso Robles)** (city) San Luis Obispo County
146	759	7.7	**Vineyard** (CDP) Sacramento County
149	794	7.8	**Escondido** (city) San Diego County
149	794	7.8	**Galt** (city) Sacramento County

Note: *The state column ranks the top/bottom 150 places from all places in the state with population of 10,000 or more. The national column ranks the top/bottom 150 places from all places in the country with population of 10,000 or more. Places that are unincorporated were not considered in the rankings. Please refer to the User Guide for additional information.*

Employment: Healthcare Practitioners

Top 150 Places Ranked in *Descending* Order

State Rank	Nat'l Rank	Percent	Place
1	1	24.8	**Loma Linda** (city) San Bernardino County
2	6	15.7	**San Marino** (city) Los Angeles County
3	16	13.6	**Hillsborough** (town) San Mateo County
4	30	12.9	**Cerritos** (city) Los Angeles County
5	55	12.0	**Rancho Mirage** (city) Riverside County
6	56	11.9	**Coronado** (city) San Diego County
7	73	11.5	**Camp Pendleton South** (CDP) San Diego County
8	79	11.4	**Walnut** (city) Los Angeles County
9	89	11.3	**American Canyon** (city) Napa County
10	118	10.7	**Beaumont** (city) Riverside County
10	118	10.7	**Redlands** (city) San Bernardino County
12	129	10.6	**Larkspur** (city) Marin County
13	141	10.5	**Granite Bay** (CDP) Placer County
14	152	10.3	**Atascadero** (city) San Luis Obispo County
15	231	9.6	**La Palma** (city) Orange County
15	231	9.6	**Mill Valley** (city) Marin County
17	253	9.5	**Rancho Palos Verdes** (city) Los Angeles County
18	294	9.3	**South Pasadena** (city) Los Angeles County
19	336	9.1	**Piedmont** (city) Alameda County
20	377	8.9	**Palos Verdes Estates** (city) Los Angeles County
21	441	8.6	**Grand Terrace** (city) San Bernardino County
22	465	8.5	**Chino Hills** (city) San Bernardino County
22	465	8.5	**Paradise** (town) Butte County
24	491	8.4	**Lake Arrowhead** (CDP) San Bernardino County
25	519	8.3	**Clovis** (city) Fresno County
25	519	8.3	**Orinda** (city) Contra Costa County
25	519	8.3	**Rossmoor** (CDP) Orange County
28	559	8.2	**Benicia** (city) Solano County
28	559	8.2	**Palm Desert** (city) Riverside County
28	559	8.2	**Sonoma** (city) Sonoma County
31	597	8.1	**Diamond Bar** (city) Los Angeles County
31	597	8.1	**Lafayette** (city) Contra Costa County
33	636	8.0	**Beverly Hills** (city) Los Angeles County
33	636	8.0	**Emeryville** (city) Alameda County
33	636	8.0	**Fair Oaks** (CDP) Sacramento County
33	636	8.0	**Moraga** (town) Contra Costa County
33	636	8.0	**Seal Beach** (city) Orange County
38	668	7.9	**Davis** (city) Yolo County
38	668	7.9	**San Anselmo** (town) Marin County
40	718	7.8	**Albany** (city) Alameda County
40	718	7.8	**El Sobrante** (CDP) Riverside County
40	718	7.8	**Ripon** (city) San Joaquin County
40	718	7.8	**Rosedale** (CDP) Kern County
44	755	7.7	**Alamo** (CDP) Contra Costa County
44	755	7.7	**Carson** (city) Los Angeles County
44	755	7.7	**Millbrae** (city) San Mateo County
44	755	7.7	**Saratoga** (city) Santa Clara County
48	804	7.6	**Coalinga** (city) Fresno County
48	804	7.6	**Fairview** (CDP) Alameda County
48	804	7.6	**Oak Park** (CDP) Ventura County
48	804	7.6	**West Carson** (CDP) Los Angeles County
52	848	7.5	**Canyon Lake** (city) Riverside County
52	848	7.5	**Danville** (town) Contra Costa County
52	848	7.5	**Eastvale** (city) Riverside County
52	848	7.5	**Los Altos** (city) Santa Clara County
52	848	7.5	**Palo Alto** (city) Santa Clara County
52	848	7.5	**Susanville** (city) Lassen County
52	848	7.5	**Yucaipa** (city) San Bernardino County
59	903	7.4	**Rancho Cucamonga** (city) San Bernardino County
60	954	7.3	**Laguna Woods** (city) Orange County
60	954	7.3	**Manhattan Beach** (city) Los Angeles County
60	954	7.3	**Pacifica** (city) San Mateo County
63	1083	7.1	**Calabasas** (city) Los Angeles County
63	1083	7.1	**Palm Springs** (city) Riverside County
63	1083	7.1	**Walnut Creek** (city) Contra Costa County
66	1138	7.0	**Clayton** (city) Contra Costa County
66	1138	7.0	**Elk Grove** (city) Sacramento County
66	1138	7.0	**Menlo Park** (city) San Mateo County
66	1138	7.0	**North Tustin** (CDP) Orange County
70	1192	6.9	**Arcadia** (city) Los Angeles County
70	1192	6.9	**Foster City** (city) San Mateo County
70	1192	6.9	**Grass Valley** (city) Nevada County
70	1192	6.9	**Hercules** (city) Contra Costa County
74	1253	6.8	**Adelanto** (city) San Bernardino County
74	1253	6.8	**Artesia** (city) Los Angeles County
74	1253	6.8	**Laguna Niguel** (city) Orange County
74	1253	6.8	**Malibu** (city) Los Angeles County
78	1339	6.7	**Casa de Oro-Mount Helix** (CDP) San Diego County
78	1339	6.7	**San Ramon** (city) Contra Costa County
78	1339	6.7	**Stevenson Ranch** (CDP) Los Angeles County
78	1339	6.7	**Suisun City** (city) Solano County
78	1339	6.7	**Vacaville** (city) Solano County
83	1404	6.6	**Fountain Valley** (city) Orange County
83	1404	6.6	**San Carlos** (city) San Mateo County
83	1404	6.6	**Union City** (city) Alameda County
86	1488	6.5	**Alpine** (CDP) San Diego County
86	1488	6.5	**Chula Vista** (city) San Diego County
86	1488	6.5	**Pasadena** (city) Los Angeles County
86	1488	6.5	**Vineyard** (CDP) Sacramento County
90	1560	6.4	**Discovery Bay** (CDP) Contra Costa County
90	1560	6.4	**Live Oak** (CDP) Santa Cruz County
90	1560	6.4	**Los Gatos** (town) Santa Clara County
90	1560	6.4	**Roseville** (city) Placer County
94	1625	6.3	**Arcata** (city) Humboldt County
94	1625	6.3	**Belmont** (city) San Mateo County
94	1625	6.3	**El Dorado Hills** (CDP) El Dorado County
94	1625	6.3	**Glendale** (city) Los Angeles County
94	1625	6.3	**Highland** (city) San Bernardino County
94	1625	6.3	**Irvine** (city) Orange County
94	1625	6.3	**La Riviera** (CDP) Sacramento County
94	1625	6.3	**McKinleyville** (CDP) Humboldt County
94	1625	6.3	**Newport Beach** (city) Orange County
94	1625	6.3	**Sierra Madre** (city) Los Angeles County
94	1625	6.3	**Torrance** (city) Los Angeles County
94	1625	6.3	**Vallejo** (city) Solano County
106	1723	6.2	**Chico** (city) Butte County
106	1723	6.2	**Folsom** (city) Sacramento County
106	1723	6.2	**La Cañada Flintridge** (city) Los Angeles County
106	1723	6.2	**La Crescenta-Montrose** (CDP) Los Angeles County
106	1723	6.2	**La Quinta** (city) Riverside County
106	1723	6.2	**Ladera Ranch** (CDP) Orange County
106	1723	6.2	**Los Osos** (CDP) San Luis Obispo County
106	1723	6.2	**Ukiah** (city) Mendocino County
106	1723	6.2	**West Covina** (city) Los Angeles County
106	1723	6.2	**Windsor** (town) Sonoma County
116	1812	6.1	**Burbank** (city) Los Angeles County
116	1812	6.1	**Burlingame** (city) San Mateo County
116	1812	6.1	**Carmichael** (CDP) Sacramento County
116	1812	6.1	**Cypress** (city) Orange County
116	1812	6.1	**East Hemet** (CDP) Riverside County
116	1812	6.1	**Encinitas** (city) San Diego County
116	1812	6.1	**La Mesa** (city) San Diego County
116	1812	6.1	**La Verne** (city) Los Angeles County
116	1812	6.1	**Laguna Beach** (city) Orange County
116	1812	6.1	**Lakewood** (city) Los Angeles County
116	1812	6.1	**Monrovia** (city) Los Angeles County
116	1812	6.1	**Rancho Santa Margarita** (city) Orange County
116	1812	6.1	**San Buenaventura (Ventura)** (city) Ventura County
116	1812	6.1	**Scotts Valley** (city) Santa Cruz County
116	1812	6.1	**Temecula** (city) Riverside County
116	1812	6.1	**Yorba Linda** (city) Orange County
116	1812	6.1	**Yucca Valley** (town) San Bernardino County
133	1919	6.0	**Culver City** (city) Los Angeles County
133	1919	6.0	**Fairfield** (city) Solano County
133	1919	6.0	**Hanford** (city) Kings County
133	1919	6.0	**Oakley** (city) Contra Costa County
133	1919	6.0	**Solana Beach** (city) San Diego County
133	1919	6.0	**Tehachapi** (city) Kern County
133	1919	6.0	**Valinda** (CDP) Los Angeles County
140	2017	5.9	**Castro Valley** (CDP) Alameda County
140	2017	5.9	**Daly City** (city) San Mateo County
140	2017	5.9	**Lancaster** (city) Los Angeles County
140	2017	5.9	**Lemoore** (city) Kings County
140	2017	5.9	**Los Alamitos** (city) Orange County
140	2017	5.9	**Placerville** (city) El Dorado County
140	2017	5.9	**Santa Monica** (city) Los Angeles County
147	2114	5.8	**Agoura Hills** (city) Los Angeles County
147	2114	5.8	**Brentwood** (city) Contra Costa County
147	2114	5.8	**El Cerrito** (city) Contra Costa County
147	2114	5.8	**Huntington Beach** (city) Orange County

Note: *The state column ranks the top/bottom 150 places from all places in the state with population of 10,000 or more. The national column ranks the top/bottom 150 places from all places in the country with population of 10,000 or more. Places that are unincorporated were not considered in the rankings. Please refer to the User Guide for additional information.*

Employment: Healthcare Practitioners

Top 150 Places Ranked in *Ascending* Order

State Rank	Nat'l Rank	Percent	Place
1	1	0.0	**Avenal** (city) Kings County
1	1	0.0	**McFarland** (city) Kern County
3	4	0.3	**Parlier** (city) Fresno County
4	6	0.5	**Bloomington** (CDP) San Bernardino County
4	6	0.5	**Wasco** (city) Kern County
6	8	0.6	**Bell** (city) Los Angeles County
7	9	0.7	**King City** (city) Monterey County
7	9	0.7	**Lamont** (CDP) Kern County
9	11	0.8	**Cudahy** (city) Los Angeles County
9	11	0.8	**Home Gardens** (CDP) Riverside County
9	11	0.8	**Lemon Hill** (CDP) Sacramento County
9	11	0.8	**Maywood** (city) Los Angeles County
9	11	0.8	**Shafter** (city) Kern County
9	11	0.8	**Walnut Park** (CDP) Los Angeles County
15	20	1.0	**Willowbrook** (CDP) Los Angeles County
16	23	1.1	**Alum Rock** (CDP) Santa Clara County
16	23	1.1	**Arvin** (city) Kern County
16	23	1.1	**Barstow** (city) San Bernardino County
16	23	1.1	**Bell Gardens** (city) Los Angeles County
16	23	1.1	**Garden Acres** (CDP) San Joaquin County
16	23	1.1	**Muscoy** (CDP) San Bernardino County
22	30	1.2	**Exeter** (city) Tulare County
22	30	1.2	**Florence-Graham** (CDP) Los Angeles County
22	30	1.2	**Huntington Park** (city) Los Angeles County
25	37	1.3	**East Los Angeles** (CDP) Los Angeles County
25	37	1.3	**East Rancho Dominguez** (CDP) Los Angeles County
25	37	1.3	**Parkway** (CDP) Sacramento County
28	41	1.4	**Delhi** (CDP) Merced County
28	41	1.4	**Mead Valley** (CDP) Riverside County
30	49	1.5	**Cherryland** (CDP) Alameda County
30	49	1.5	**Santa Paula** (city) Ventura County
32	56	1.6	**Chowchilla** (city) Madera County
32	56	1.6	**Coachella** (city) Riverside County
34	71	1.7	**Calexico** (city) Imperial County
34	71	1.7	**Farmersville** (city) Tulare County
34	71	1.7	**Lennox** (CDP) Los Angeles County
34	71	1.7	**Santa Ana** (city) Orange County
38	80	1.8	**Big Bear City** (CDP) San Bernardino County
38	80	1.8	**Soledad** (city) Monterey County
40	95	1.9	**Livingston** (city) Merced County
40	95	1.9	**Olivehurst** (CDP) Yuba County
40	95	1.9	**Oroville** (city) Butte County
40	95	1.9	**Patterson** (city) Stanislaus County
40	95	1.9	**Port Hueneme** (city) Ventura County
40	95	1.9	**South Gate** (city) Los Angeles County
40	95	1.9	**Watsonville** (city) Santa Cruz County
47	114	2.0	**Mendota** (city) Fresno County
47	114	2.0	**Sanger** (city) Fresno County
47	114	2.0	**Winton** (CDP) Merced County
50	122	2.1	**Avocado Heights** (CDP) Los Angeles County
50	122	2.1	**East Palo Alto** (city) San Mateo County
50	122	2.1	**Lawndale** (city) Los Angeles County
50	122	2.1	**Lynwood** (city) Los Angeles County
50	122	2.1	**Ramona** (CDP) San Diego County
50	122	2.1	**South El Monte** (city) Los Angeles County
56	140	2.2	**Bay Point** (CDP) Contra Costa County
56	140	2.2	**Clearlake** (city) Lake County
56	140	2.2	**El Monte** (city) Los Angeles County
56	140	2.2	**Hawaiian Gardens** (city) Los Angeles County
56	140	2.2	**North Fair Oaks** (CDP) San Mateo County
61	156	2.3	**California City** (city) Kern County
61	156	2.3	**Commerce** (city) Los Angeles County
61	156	2.3	**Rialto** (city) San Bernardino County
61	156	2.3	**South San Jose Hills** (CDP) Los Angeles County
61	156	2.3	**Sun Village** (CDP) Los Angeles County
66	177	2.4	**Ashland** (CDP) Alameda County
66	177	2.4	**Blythe** (city) Riverside County
66	177	2.4	**Isla Vista** (CDP) Santa Barbara County
66	177	2.4	**Lindsay** (city) Tulare County
66	177	2.4	**Paramount** (city) Los Angeles County
66	177	2.4	**Pico Rivera** (city) Los Angeles County
72	198	2.5	**Dinuba** (city) Tulare County
72	198	2.5	**Salida** (CDP) Stanislaus County
72	198	2.5	**South Whittier** (CDP) Los Angeles County
75	217	2.6	**Baldwin Park** (city) Los Angeles County

State Rank	Nat'l Rank	Percent	Place
75	217	2.6	**Florin** (CDP) Sacramento County
75	217	2.6	**Newman** (city) Stanislaus County
75	217	2.6	**Red Bluff** (city) Tehama County
75	217	2.6	**Spring Valley** (CDP) San Diego County
75	217	2.6	**West Puente Valley** (CDP) Los Angeles County
81	253	2.7	**Compton** (city) Los Angeles County
81	253	2.7	**Corcoran** (city) Kings County
81	253	2.7	**Pomona** (city) Los Angeles County
81	253	2.7	**Reedley** (city) Fresno County
81	253	2.7	**San Pablo** (city) Contra Costa County
86	280	2.8	**Ceres** (city) Stanislaus County
86	280	2.8	**Citrus** (CDP) Los Angeles County
86	280	2.8	**Galt** (city) Sacramento County
86	280	2.8	**Rio Linda** (CDP) Sacramento County
86	280	2.8	**San Juan Capistrano** (city) Orange County
86	280	2.8	**Santa Maria** (city) Santa Barbara County
92	320	2.9	**Brawley** (city) Imperial County
92	320	2.9	**Delano** (city) Kern County
92	320	2.9	**Desert Hot Springs** (city) Riverside County
92	320	2.9	**El Sobrante** (CDP) Contra Costa County
92	320	2.9	**Kerman** (city) Fresno County
92	320	2.9	**Marina** (city) Monterey County
92	320	2.9	**Salinas** (city) Monterey County
92	320	2.9	**Westmont** (CDP) Los Angeles County
92	320	2.9	**Wildomar** (city) Riverside County
101	370	3.0	**Carpinteria** (city) Santa Barbara County
101	370	3.0	**El Cajon** (city) San Diego County
101	370	3.0	**La Habra** (city) Orange County
104	396	3.1	**Azusa** (city) Los Angeles County
104	396	3.1	**Fillmore** (city) Ventura County
104	396	3.1	**Grover Beach** (city) San Luis Obispo County
104	396	3.1	**Healdsburg** (city) Sonoma County
104	396	3.1	**Indio** (city) Riverside County
104	396	3.1	**Lemon Grove** (city) San Diego County
104	396	3.1	**Ontario** (city) San Bernardino County
104	396	3.1	**Selma** (city) Fresno County
112	437	3.2	**Cathedral City** (city) Riverside County
112	437	3.2	**Hawthorne** (city) Los Angeles County
112	437	3.2	**Los Banos** (city) Merced County
112	437	3.2	**Oakdale** (city) Stanislaus County
112	437	3.2	**Oxnard** (city) Ventura County
112	437	3.2	**Rohnert Park** (city) Sonoma County
112	437	3.2	**San Fernando** (city) Los Angeles County
119	480	3.3	**Imperial Beach** (city) San Diego County
119	480	3.3	**Inglewood** (city) Los Angeles County
119	480	3.3	**Montclair** (city) San Bernardino County
119	480	3.3	**Santa Fe Springs** (city) Los Angeles County
119	480	3.3	**Seaside** (city) Monterey County
119	480	3.3	**Stanton** (city) Orange County
125	529	3.4	**Fortuna** (city) Humboldt County
125	529	3.4	**Greenfield** (city) Monterey County
125	529	3.4	**Hemet** (city) Riverside County
125	529	3.4	**Lakeside** (CDP) San Diego County
125	529	3.4	**Nipomo** (CDP) San Luis Obispo County
125	529	3.4	**North Highlands** (CDP) Sacramento County
125	529	3.4	**Perris** (city) Riverside County
125	529	3.4	**Rosemead** (city) Los Angeles County
125	529	3.4	**Tulare** (city) Tulare County
134	595	3.5	**Garden Grove** (city) Orange County
134	595	3.5	**Gilroy** (city) Santa Clara County
134	595	3.5	**La Presa** (CDP) San Diego County
134	595	3.5	**Lompoc** (city) Santa Barbara County
134	595	3.5	**Montebello** (city) Los Angeles County
134	595	3.5	**North Auburn** (CDP) Placer County
134	595	3.5	**Vista** (city) San Diego County
134	595	3.5	**Winter Gardens** (CDP) San Diego County
142	655	3.6	**Hollister** (city) San Benito County
142	655	3.6	**Lomita** (city) Los Angeles County
142	655	3.6	**Madera** (city) Madera County
142	655	3.6	**Moorpark** (city) Ventura County
142	655	3.6	**Norwalk** (city) Los Angeles County
142	655	3.6	**Oakland** (city) Alameda County
142	655	3.6	**San Dimas** (city) Los Angeles County
142	655	3.6	**Sunnyvale** (city) Santa Clara County
142	655	3.6	**Victorville** (city) San Bernardino County

Note: *The state column ranks the top/bottom 150 places from all places in the state with population of 10,000 or more. The national column ranks the top/bottom 150 places from all places in the country with population of 10,000 or more. Places that are unincorporated were not considered in the rankings. Please refer to the User Guide for additional information.*

Employment: Service Occupations

Top 150 Places Ranked in *Descending* Order

State Rank	Nat'l Rank	Percent	Place
1	5	41.6	**East Palo Alto** (city) San Mateo County
2	15	38.8	**Cathedral City** (city) Riverside County
3	18	38.1	**Seaside** (city) Monterey County
4	19	38.0	**Desert Hot Springs** (city) Riverside County
5	22	37.4	**Lemon Hill** (CDP) Sacramento County
6	23	37.2	**South Lake Tahoe** (city) El Dorado County
6	23	37.2	**Susanville** (city) Lassen County
8	25	36.5	**Tehachapi** (city) Kern County
9	34	34.8	**Coachella** (city) Riverside County
10	37	34.3	**Isla Vista** (CDP) Santa Barbara County
11	53	33.3	**Bay Point** (CDP) Contra Costa County
12	57	33.2	**Lennox** (CDP) Los Angeles County
13	67	32.6	**Blythe** (city) Riverside County
14	73	32.2	**Lawndale** (city) Los Angeles County
15	85	31.6	**North Fair Oaks** (CDP) San Mateo County
16	86	31.5	**Indio** (city) Riverside County
16	86	31.5	**San Pablo** (city) Contra Costa County
18	114	30.2	**Clearlake** (city) Lake County
19	132	29.7	**National City** (city) San Diego County
20	143	29.5	**Marina** (city) Monterey County
21	201	28.2	**Oroville** (city) Butte County
22	215	27.9	**Santa Ana** (city) Orange County
23	220	27.8	**Eureka** (city) Humboldt County
24	224	27.7	**Grass Valley** (city) Nevada County
25	229	27.6	**Westmont** (CDP) Los Angeles County
26	241	27.4	**Hawaiian Gardens** (city) Los Angeles County
27	248	27.3	**Lompoc** (city) Santa Barbara County
27	248	27.3	**Twentynine Palms** (city) San Bernardino County
29	257	27.2	**Grover Beach** (city) San Luis Obispo County
29	257	27.2	**Pittsburg** (city) Contra Costa County
31	270	26.8	**Marysville** (city) Yuba County
32	277	26.7	**Parkway** (CDP) Sacramento County
33	285	26.6	**Banning** (city) Riverside County
33	285	26.6	**Hawthorne** (city) Los Angeles County
35	299	26.4	**Linda** (CDP) Yuba County
36	309	26.3	**Ashland** (CDP) Alameda County
36	309	26.3	**Daly City** (city) San Mateo County
36	309	26.3	**Ramona** (CDP) San Diego County
39	319	26.2	**Hemet** (city) Riverside County
40	325	26.1	**Palm Springs** (city) Riverside County
41	347	25.9	**Inglewood** (city) Los Angeles County
42	355	25.8	**San Jacinto** (city) Riverside County
43	367	25.7	**Brawley** (city) Imperial County
43	367	25.7	**Florin** (CDP) Sacramento County
43	367	25.7	**Truckee** (town) Nevada County
46	384	25.5	**Azusa** (city) Los Angeles County
46	384	25.5	**El Cajon** (city) San Diego County
46	384	25.5	**San Juan Capistrano** (city) Orange County
49	395	25.4	**Alum Rock** (CDP) Santa Clara County
50	421	25.2	**Richmond** (city) Contra Costa County
51	432	25.1	**Diamond Springs** (CDP) El Dorado County
51	432	25.1	**Hanford** (city) Kings County
51	432	25.1	**Newman** (city) Stanislaus County
54	446	25.0	**Imperial** (city) Imperial County
54	446	25.0	**Imperial Beach** (city) San Diego County
54	446	25.0	**Rosemead** (city) Los Angeles County
57	460	24.9	**Avocado Heights** (CDP) Los Angeles County
57	460	24.9	**Garden Acres** (CDP) San Joaquin County
57	460	24.9	**Palm Desert** (city) Riverside County
60	476	24.8	**Artesia** (city) Los Angeles County
60	476	24.8	**Escondido** (city) San Diego County
62	505	24.6	**Placerville** (city) El Dorado County
62	505	24.6	**Santa Barbara** (city) Santa Barbara County
64	522	24.5	**Citrus** (CDP) Los Angeles County
64	522	24.5	**North Highlands** (CDP) Sacramento County
66	536	24.4	**El Centro** (city) Imperial County
66	536	24.4	**Fortuna** (city) Humboldt County
66	536	24.4	**Lake Arrowhead** (CDP) San Bernardino County
66	536	24.4	**Lemon Grove** (city) San Diego County
66	536	24.4	**Live Oak** (CDP) Santa Cruz County
66	536	24.4	**Porterville** (city) Tulare County
66	536	24.4	**Red Bluff** (city) Tehama County
73	553	24.3	**La Presa** (CDP) San Diego County
73	553	24.3	**Lake Los Angeles** (CDP) Los Angeles County
73	553	24.3	**Mead Valley** (CDP) Riverside County
76	572	24.2	**San Rafael** (city) Marin County
77	590	24.1	**Cherryland** (CDP) Alameda County
78	601	24.0	**El Monte** (city) Los Angeles County
78	601	24.0	**Vista** (city) San Diego County
80	617	23.9	**Avenal** (city) Kings County
80	617	23.9	**Quartz Hill** (CDP) Los Angeles County
82	634	23.8	**Bostonia** (CDP) San Diego County
82	634	23.8	**Port Hueneme** (city) Ventura County
82	634	23.8	**South El Monte** (city) Los Angeles County
85	651	23.7	**La Habra** (city) Orange County
85	651	23.7	**Watsonville** (city) Santa Cruz County
85	651	23.7	**Wildomar** (city) Riverside County
88	693	23.4	**Arcata** (city) Humboldt County
88	693	23.4	**Chico** (city) Butte County
88	693	23.4	**Valle Vista** (CDP) Riverside County
91	710	23.3	**Camp Pendleton South** (CDP) San Diego County
91	710	23.3	**Fallbrook** (CDP) San Diego County
91	710	23.3	**North Auburn** (CDP) Placer County
91	710	23.3	**San Bernardino** (city) San Bernardino County
95	752	23.1	**Montclair** (city) San Bernardino County
95	752	23.1	**Nipomo** (CDP) San Luis Obispo County
97	778	23.0	**Calexico** (city) Imperial County
98	794	22.9	**Carpinteria** (city) Santa Barbara County
98	794	22.9	**Foothill Farms** (CDP) Sacramento County
98	794	22.9	**Lakeland Village** (CDP) Riverside County
98	794	22.9	**Paradise** (town) Butte County
102	822	22.8	**La Quinta** (city) Riverside County
103	841	22.7	**Highland** (city) San Bernardino County
104	859	22.6	**Antioch** (city) Contra Costa County
104	859	22.6	**Victorville** (city) San Bernardino County
106	879	22.5	**Barstow** (city) San Bernardino County
106	879	22.5	**East Hemet** (CDP) Riverside County
106	879	22.5	**Lemoore** (city) Kings County
106	879	22.5	**Shasta Lake** (city) Shasta County
110	915	22.3	**Del Aire** (CDP) Los Angeles County
110	915	22.3	**Rohnert Park** (city) Sonoma County
112	963	22.1	**Napa** (city) Napa County
112	963	22.1	**Sanger** (city) Fresno County
114	983	22.0	**Garden Grove** (city) Orange County
114	983	22.0	**McKinleyville** (CDP) Humboldt County
116	1007	21.9	**Menifee** (city) Riverside County
116	1007	21.9	**Santa Paula** (city) Ventura County
118	1035	21.8	**California City** (city) Kern County
118	1035	21.8	**Huntington Park** (city) Los Angeles County
118	1035	21.8	**Merced** (city) Merced County
118	1035	21.8	**San Gabriel** (city) Los Angeles County
122	1060	21.7	**Farmersville** (city) Tulare County
122	1060	21.7	**Pomona** (city) Los Angeles County
122	1060	21.7	**Stanton** (city) Orange County
125	1083	21.6	**Paramount** (city) Los Angeles County
125	1083	21.6	**Westminster** (city) Orange County
125	1083	21.6	**Yucca Valley** (town) San Bernardino County
128	1108	21.5	**Fillmore** (city) Ventura County
128	1108	21.5	**Oceanside** (city) San Diego County
128	1108	21.5	**Olivehurst** (CDP) Yuba County
128	1108	21.5	**Perris** (city) Riverside County
128	1108	21.5	**Stockton** (city) San Joaquin County
133	1138	21.4	**Compton** (city) Los Angeles County
133	1138	21.4	**Florence-Graham** (CDP) Los Angeles County
133	1138	21.4	**Vacaville** (city) Solano County
136	1162	21.3	**Baldwin Park** (city) Los Angeles County
136	1162	21.3	**El Paso de Robles (Paso Robles)** (city) San Luis Obispo County
136	1162	21.3	**Magalia** (CDP) Butte County
136	1162	21.3	**Oakley** (city) Contra Costa County
136	1162	21.3	**Oildale** (CDP) Kern County
136	1162	21.3	**Pacific Grove** (city) Monterey County
142	1192	21.2	**Apple Valley** (town) San Bernardino County
142	1192	21.2	**Concord** (city) Contra Costa County
142	1192	21.2	**Salinas** (city) Monterey County
142	1192	21.2	**South San Jose Hills** (CDP) Los Angeles County
146	1222	21.1	**East Los Angeles** (CDP) Los Angeles County
146	1222	21.1	**Lindsay** (city) Tulare County
146	1222	21.1	**Rialto** (city) San Bernardino County
146	1222	21.1	**Rio Linda** (CDP) Sacramento County
146	1222	21.1	**Walnut Park** (CDP) Los Angeles County

Note: *The state column ranks the top/bottom 150 places from all places in the state with population of 10,000 or more. The national column ranks the top/bottom 150 places from all places in the country with population of 10,000 or more. Places that are unincorporated were not considered in the rankings. Please refer to the User Guide for additional information.*

Employment: Service Occupations

Top 150 Places Ranked in *Ascending* Order

State Rank	Nat'l Rank	Percent	Place
1	4	4.0	**Piedmont** (city) Alameda County
2	6	4.2	**Los Altos** (city) Santa Clara County
3	9	4.7	**Hillsborough** (town) San Mateo County
4	12	4.9	**San Marino** (city) Los Angeles County
5	16	5.1	**Cupertino** (city) Santa Clara County
6	20	5.5	**Saratoga** (city) Santa Clara County
7	23	5.6	**Alamo** (CDP) Contra Costa County
8	27	5.8	**Coto de Caza** (CDP) Orange County
9	31	5.9	**Palos Verdes Estates** (city) Los Angeles County
10	37	6.2	**La Cañada Flintridge** (city) Los Angeles County
11	43	6.4	**Rancho Palos Verdes** (city) Los Angeles County
12	56	6.7	**Calabasas** (city) Los Angeles County
12	56	6.7	**Los Gatos** (town) Santa Clara County
14	66	7.0	**Manhattan Beach** (city) Los Angeles County
14	66	7.0	**Palo Alto** (city) Santa Clara County
16	80	7.2	**Lafayette** (city) Contra Costa County
17	85	7.3	**Laguna Beach** (city) Orange County
18	107	7.7	**Orinda** (city) Contra Costa County
19	120	7.9	**Danville** (town) Contra Costa County
20	129	8.1	**Foster City** (city) San Mateo County
20	129	8.1	**Newport Beach** (city) Orange County
20	129	8.1	**Sierra Madre** (city) Los Angeles County
23	143	8.3	**San Carlos** (city) San Mateo County
24	158	8.5	**North Tustin** (CDP) Orange County
25	168	8.6	**Irvine** (city) Orange County
25	168	8.6	**Mill Valley** (city) Marin County
27	187	8.8	**San Ramon** (city) Contra Costa County
27	187	8.8	**South Pasadena** (city) Los Angeles County
27	187	8.8	**Stanford** (CDP) Santa Clara County
30	211	9.0	**Tamalpais-Homestead Valley** (CDP) Marin County
31	223	9.1	**Granite Bay** (CDP) Placer County
31	223	9.1	**Stevenson Ranch** (CDP) Los Angeles County
33	246	9.3	**Beverly Hills** (city) Los Angeles County
34	256	9.4	**Mendota** (city) Fresno County
35	269	9.5	**Coronado** (city) San Diego County
36	290	9.7	**Albany** (city) Alameda County
37	295	9.8	**Emeryville** (city) Alameda County
37	295	9.8	**La Crescenta-Montrose** (CDP) Los Angeles County
39	322	10.0	**Larkspur** (city) Marin County
40	338	10.1	**Oak Park** (CDP) Ventura County
41	360	10.3	**Arcadia** (city) Los Angeles County
41	360	10.3	**Cerritos** (city) Los Angeles County
41	360	10.3	**Santa Monica** (city) Los Angeles County
44	378	10.4	**Malibu** (city) Los Angeles County
44	378	10.4	**San Anselmo** (town) Marin County
46	396	10.5	**El Sobrante** (CDP) Riverside County
46	396	10.5	**Walnut** (city) Los Angeles County
48	408	10.6	**Hermosa Beach** (city) Los Angeles County
49	450	10.9	**Fremont** (city) Alameda County
49	450	10.9	**Ladera Ranch** (CDP) Orange County
49	450	10.9	**Rossmoor** (CDP) Orange County
52	468	11.0	**Berkeley** (city) Alameda County
53	485	11.1	**Aliso Viejo** (city) Orange County
53	485	11.1	**Redondo Beach** (city) Los Angeles County
55	509	11.2	**Burlingame** (city) San Mateo County
55	509	11.2	**Laguna Niguel** (city) Orange County
57	535	11.3	**Moraga** (town) Contra Costa County
58	571	11.5	**Walnut Creek** (city) Contra Costa County
59	618	11.7	**Fountain Valley** (city) Orange County
59	618	11.7	**Yorba Linda** (city) Orange County
61	634	11.8	**Menlo Park** (city) San Mateo County
61	634	11.8	**Seal Beach** (city) Orange County
63	651	11.9	**Agoura Hills** (city) Los Angeles County
63	651	11.9	**View Park-Windsor Hills** (CDP) Los Angeles County
65	680	12.0	**Clayton** (city) Contra Costa County
65	680	12.0	**Cypress** (city) Orange County
65	680	12.0	**Los Alamitos** (city) Orange County
65	680	12.0	**Sunnyvale** (city) Santa Clara County
65	680	12.0	**Torrance** (city) Los Angeles County
70	701	12.1	**Carlsbad** (city) San Diego County
70	701	12.1	**Claremont** (city) Los Angeles County
72	722	12.2	**Bonita** (CDP) San Diego County
72	722	12.2	**Dublin** (city) Alameda County
74	738	12.3	**El Dorado Hills** (CDP) El Dorado County
75	756	12.4	**Belmont** (city) San Mateo County
75	756	12.4	**Burbank** (city) Los Angeles County
75	756	12.4	**Pleasanton** (city) Alameda County
78	775	12.5	**Folsom** (city) Sacramento County
78	775	12.5	**King City** (city) Monterey County
80	796	12.6	**Diamond Bar** (city) Los Angeles County
81	822	12.7	**Rancho Santa Margarita** (city) Orange County
82	846	12.8	**Chino Hills** (city) San Bernardino County
83	864	12.9	**La Palma** (city) Orange County
83	864	12.9	**Mountain View** (city) Santa Clara County
85	895	13.0	**Arvin** (city) Kern County
85	895	13.0	**El Segundo** (city) Los Angeles County
87	924	13.1	**El Cerrito** (city) Contra Costa County
87	924	13.1	**Fairview** (CDP) Alameda County
89	947	13.2	**Casa de Oro-Mount Helix** (CDP) San Diego County
89	947	13.2	**McFarland** (city) Kern County
91	970	13.3	**Davis** (city) Yolo County
91	970	13.3	**Grand Terrace** (city) San Bernardino County
91	970	13.3	**La Mirada** (city) Los Angeles County
94	983	13.4	**Mission Viejo** (city) Orange County
94	983	13.4	**Rancho Mirage** (city) Riverside County
94	983	13.4	**Santa Clara** (city) Santa Clara County
97	1061	13.7	**Brea** (city) Orange County
97	1061	13.7	**Lamont** (CDP) Kern County
99	1085	13.8	**Camarillo** (city) Ventura County
100	1143	14.0	**Encinitas** (city) San Diego County
100	1143	14.0	**Glendora** (city) Los Angeles County
100	1143	14.0	**Pleasant Hill** (city) Contra Costa County
103	1167	14.1	**Castro Valley** (CDP) Alameda County
104	1199	14.2	**Millbrae** (city) San Mateo County
105	1223	14.3	**San Dimas** (city) Los Angeles County
106	1246	14.4	**Campbell** (city) Santa Clara County
106	1246	14.4	**Shafter** (city) Kern County
108	1281	14.5	**Rancho Cucamonga** (city) San Bernardino County
108	1281	14.5	**Reedley** (city) Fresno County
108	1281	14.5	**Ridgecrest** (city) Kern County
108	1281	14.5	**Union City** (city) Alameda County
112	1312	14.6	**Culver City** (city) Los Angeles County
112	1312	14.6	**Dinuba** (city) Tulare County
112	1312	14.6	**Kingsburg** (city) Fresno County
112	1312	14.6	**Madera** (city) Madera County
116	1345	14.7	**Corona** (city) Riverside County
116	1345	14.7	**Newark** (city) Alameda County
116	1345	14.7	**Placentia** (city) Orange County
116	1345	14.7	**Scotts Valley** (city) Santa Cruz County
116	1345	14.7	**Thousand Oaks** (city) Ventura County
121	1375	14.8	**Temple City** (city) Los Angeles County
122	1407	14.9	**Huntington Beach** (city) Orange County
122	1407	14.9	**Lake Forest** (city) Orange County
122	1407	14.9	**Milpitas** (city) Santa Clara County
122	1407	14.9	**Rosedale** (CDP) Kern County
122	1407	14.9	**Tracy** (city) San Joaquin County
127	1442	15.0	**Brentwood** (city) Contra Costa County
127	1442	15.0	**Salida** (CDP) Stanislaus County
127	1442	15.0	**San Clemente** (city) Orange County
127	1442	15.0	**Woodcrest** (CDP) Riverside County
131	1475	15.1	**Castaic** (CDP) Los Angeles County
131	1475	15.1	**Greenfield** (city) Monterey County
133	1506	15.2	**Martinez** (city) Contra Costa County
134	1529	15.3	**Benicia** (city) Solano County
134	1529	15.3	**Phelan** (CDP) San Bernardino County
136	1567	15.4	**Norco** (city) Riverside County
136	1567	15.4	**Pasadena** (city) Los Angeles County
136	1567	15.4	**Patterson** (city) Stanislaus County
136	1567	15.4	**Redlands** (city) San Bernardino County
140	1592	15.5	**Ripon** (city) San Joaquin County
140	1592	15.5	**Roseville** (city) Placer County
142	1625	15.6	**Santee** (city) San Diego County
143	1657	15.7	**Hacienda Heights** (CDP) Los Angeles County
143	1657	15.7	**Hercules** (city) Contra Costa County
143	1657	15.7	**Lakeside** (CDP) San Diego County
143	1657	15.7	**Loma Linda** (city) San Bernardino County
143	1657	15.7	**Poway** (city) San Diego County
148	1695	15.8	**Alameda** (city) Alameda County
148	1695	15.8	**Laguna Hills** (city) Orange County
148	1695	15.8	**Livermore** (city) Alameda County

Note: *The state column ranks the top/bottom 150 places from all places in the state with population of 10,000 or more. The national column ranks the top/bottom 150 places from all places in the country with population of 10,000 or more. Places that are unincorporated were not considered in the rankings. Please refer to the User Guide for additional information.*

Employment: Sales and Office Occupations

Top 150 Places Ranked in *Descending* Order

State Rank	Nat'l Rank	Percent	Place
1	20	35.2	**Coto de Caza** (CDP) Orange County
2	29	34.8	**Bostonia** (CDP) San Diego County
3	76	32.8	**Artesia** (city) Los Angeles County
3	76	32.8	**Rancho Mirage** (city) Riverside County
5	141	31.8	**North Highlands** (CDP) Sacramento County
6	169	31.5	**Citrus** (CDP) Los Angeles County
7	182	31.4	**Rowland Heights** (CDP) Los Angeles County
8	209	31.1	**Covina** (city) Los Angeles County
9	229	31.0	**Laguna Woods** (city) Orange County
10	252	30.8	**Fountain Valley** (city) Orange County
11	262	30.7	**Citrus Heights** (city) Sacramento County
11	262	30.7	**Shasta Lake** (city) Shasta County
13	294	30.5	**Grover Beach** (city) San Luis Obispo County
13	294	30.5	**Imperial** (city) Imperial County
13	294	30.5	**Temple City** (city) Los Angeles County
16	312	30.4	**West Covina** (city) Los Angeles County
17	329	30.2	**Oildale** (CDP) Kern County
18	344	30.1	**Bonita** (CDP) San Diego County
18	344	30.1	**Norco** (city) Riverside County
18	344	30.1	**Westmont** (CDP) Los Angeles County
21	376	29.9	**Carmichael** (CDP) Sacramento County
22	395	29.8	**Gardena** (city) Los Angeles County
22	395	29.8	**Salida** (CDP) Stanislaus County
22	395	29.8	**Santee** (city) San Diego County
22	395	29.8	**Whittier** (city) Los Angeles County
26	422	29.7	**Buena Park** (city) Orange County
26	422	29.7	**Downey** (city) Los Angeles County
26	422	29.7	**Magalia** (CDP) Butte County
26	422	29.7	**Rancho Santa Margarita** (city) Orange County
26	422	29.7	**Walnut** (city) Los Angeles County
31	448	29.6	**Rohnert Park** (city) Sonoma County
31	448	29.6	**Rosedale** (CDP) Kern County
31	448	29.6	**San Dimas** (city) Los Angeles County
34	469	29.5	**Alhambra** (city) Los Angeles County
35	492	29.4	**French Valley** (CDP) Riverside County
35	492	29.4	**Santa Fe Springs** (city) Los Angeles County
37	524	29.3	**Banning** (city) Riverside County
37	524	29.3	**Cypress** (city) Orange County
37	524	29.3	**Grand Terrace** (city) San Bernardino County
37	524	29.3	**Hacienda Heights** (CDP) Los Angeles County
37	524	29.3	**Lomita** (city) Los Angeles County
42	558	29.2	**El Cajon** (city) San Diego County
42	558	29.2	**Glendora** (city) Los Angeles County
44	583	29.1	**Arden-Arcade** (CDP) Sacramento County
44	583	29.1	**San Diego Country Estates** (CDP) San Diego County
46	604	29.0	**Canyon Lake** (city) Riverside County
46	604	29.0	**Daly City** (city) San Mateo County
46	604	29.0	**Rancho Cucamonga** (city) San Bernardino County
49	624	28.9	**Roseville** (city) Placer County
50	651	28.8	**Arcadia** (city) Los Angeles County
50	651	28.8	**Camp Pendleton South** (CDP) San Diego County
50	651	28.8	**Olivehurst** (CDP) Yuba County
50	651	28.8	**South Gate** (city) Los Angeles County
50	651	28.8	**Winter Gardens** (CDP) San Diego County
55	674	28.7	**Bellflower** (city) Los Angeles County
55	674	28.7	**Big Bear City** (CDP) San Bernardino County
55	674	28.7	**Brentwood** (city) Contra Costa County
55	674	28.7	**Calexico** (city) Imperial County
55	674	28.7	**La Habra** (city) Orange County
55	674	28.7	**Lakeside** (CDP) San Diego County
61	701	28.6	**Antelope** (CDP) Sacramento County
61	701	28.6	**Lincoln** (city) Placer County
61	701	28.6	**Mission Viejo** (city) Orange County
61	701	28.6	**Pico Rivera** (city) Los Angeles County
61	701	28.6	**San Clemente** (city) Orange County
61	701	28.6	**San Fernando** (city) Los Angeles County
61	701	28.6	**Valinda** (CDP) Los Angeles County
68	733	28.5	**Foothill Farms** (CDP) Sacramento County
68	733	28.5	**Imperial Beach** (city) San Diego County
68	733	28.5	**Los Osos** (CDP) San Luis Obispo County
68	733	28.5	**Moreno Valley** (city) Riverside County
72	771	28.4	**Florin** (CDP) Sacramento County
72	771	28.4	**Fortuna** (city) Humboldt County
72	771	28.4	**San Gabriel** (city) Los Angeles County
72	771	28.4	**Ukiah** (city) Mendocino County
76	800	28.3	**Chino Hills** (city) San Bernardino County
76	800	28.3	**Placentia** (city) Orange County
76	800	28.3	**Rosemead** (city) Los Angeles County
79	827	28.2	**Laguna Beach** (city) Orange County
79	827	28.2	**Norwalk** (city) Los Angeles County
79	827	28.2	**West Whittier-Los Nietos** (CDP) Los Angeles County
82	860	28.1	**Cerritos** (city) Los Angeles County
82	860	28.1	**Chula Vista** (city) San Diego County
82	860	28.1	**Diamond Springs** (CDP) El Dorado County
82	860	28.1	**San Lorenzo** (CDP) Alameda County
86	904	28.0	**Granite Bay** (CDP) Placer County
86	904	28.0	**Manteca** (city) San Joaquin County
86	904	28.0	**North Auburn** (CDP) Placer County
86	904	28.0	**Oakley** (city) Contra Costa County
90	939	27.9	**Antioch** (city) Contra Costa County
90	939	27.9	**Lake Forest** (city) Orange County
92	972	27.8	**Inglewood** (city) Los Angeles County
92	972	27.8	**La Mirada** (city) Los Angeles County
92	972	27.8	**Rocklin** (city) Placer County
92	972	27.8	**San Luis Obispo** (city) San Luis Obispo County
92	972	27.8	**South Whittier** (CDP) Los Angeles County
97	1015	27.7	**Duarte** (city) Los Angeles County
97	1015	27.7	**Hollister** (city) San Benito County
97	1015	27.7	**Menifee** (city) Riverside County
97	1015	27.7	**Upland** (city) San Bernardino County
101	1062	27.6	**Fairfield** (city) Solano County
101	1062	27.6	**Ladera Ranch** (CDP) Orange County
101	1062	27.6	**Los Alamitos** (city) Orange County
101	1062	27.6	**Montebello** (city) Los Angeles County
101	1062	27.6	**Monterey Park** (city) Los Angeles County
101	1062	27.6	**Simi Valley** (city) Ventura County
107	1110	27.5	**El Sobrante** (CDP) Contra Costa County
107	1110	27.5	**Fullerton** (city) Orange County
107	1110	27.5	**North Tustin** (CDP) Orange County
107	1110	27.5	**Port Hueneme** (city) Ventura County
111	1156	27.4	**El Sobrante** (CDP) Riverside County
111	1156	27.4	**Rancho San Diego** (CDP) San Diego County
113	1198	27.3	**Clovis** (city) Fresno County
113	1198	27.3	**Huntington Beach** (city) Orange County
113	1198	27.3	**Laguna Niguel** (city) Orange County
116	1236	27.2	**Atwater** (city) Merced County
116	1236	27.2	**Corona** (city) Riverside County
116	1236	27.2	**Laguna Hills** (city) Orange County
116	1236	27.2	**Lakewood** (city) Los Angeles County
116	1236	27.2	**Palmdale** (city) Los Angeles County
121	1286	27.1	**Dublin** (city) Alameda County
121	1286	27.1	**Eureka** (city) Humboldt County
121	1286	27.1	**Hercules** (city) Contra Costa County
121	1286	27.1	**Linda** (CDP) Yuba County
121	1286	27.1	**Redding** (city) Shasta County
121	1286	27.1	**Twentynine Palms** (city) San Bernardino County
127	1337	27.0	**La Verne** (city) Los Angeles County
127	1337	27.0	**Ontario** (city) San Bernardino County
127	1337	27.0	**Santa Clarita** (city) Los Angeles County
127	1337	27.0	**West Puente Valley** (CDP) Los Angeles County
127	1337	27.0	**Yuba City** (city) Sutter County
132	1394	26.9	**Camarillo** (city) Ventura County
132	1394	26.9	**Compton** (city) Los Angeles County
132	1394	26.9	**Hayward** (city) Alameda County
132	1394	26.9	**Kingsburg** (city) Fresno County
132	1394	26.9	**Lancaster** (city) Los Angeles County
132	1394	26.9	**Pinole** (city) Contra Costa County
132	1394	26.9	**Spring Valley** (CDP) San Diego County
139	1464	26.8	**Aliso Viejo** (city) Orange County
139	1464	26.8	**Carson** (city) Los Angeles County
139	1464	26.8	**Commerce** (city) Los Angeles County
139	1464	26.8	**Fontana** (city) San Bernardino County
139	1464	26.8	**Lake Elsinore** (city) Riverside County
139	1464	26.8	**Morro Bay** (city) San Luis Obispo County
139	1464	26.8	**Rialto** (city) San Bernardino County
146	1515	26.7	**Brea** (city) Orange County
146	1515	26.7	**Glendale** (city) Los Angeles County
146	1515	26.7	**La Quinta** (city) Riverside County
146	1515	26.7	**Orange** (city) Orange County
150	1565	26.6	**Galt** (city) Sacramento County

Note: *The state column ranks the top/bottom 150 places from all places in the state with population of 10,000 or more. The national column ranks the top/bottom 150 places from all places in the country with population of 10,000 or more. Places that are unincorporated were not considered in the rankings. Please refer to the User Guide for additional information.*

Employment: Sales and Office Occupations

Top 150 Places Ranked in *Ascending* Order

State Rank	Nat'l Rank	Percent	Place
1	1	7.2	**Mendota** (city) Fresno County
2	3	11.4	**Arvin** (city) Kern County
3	5	11.7	**McFarland** (city) Kern County
4	6	12.1	**Palo Alto** (city) Santa Clara County
5	13	13.3	**Cupertino** (city) Santa Clara County
5	13	13.3	**Parlier** (city) Fresno County
7	19	13.5	**Avenal** (city) Kings County
8	24	14.2	**Livingston** (city) Merced County
9	27	14.4	**Lindsay** (city) Tulare County
9	27	14.4	**Mountain View** (city) Santa Clara County
11	32	14.7	**Lamont** (CDP) Kern County
12	34	14.9	**Half Moon Bay** (city) San Mateo County
13	37	15.0	**Los Altos** (city) Santa Clara County
14	39	15.1	**Wasco** (city) Kern County
15	44	15.4	**Saratoga** (city) Santa Clara County
16	48	15.7	**Davis** (city) Yolo County
16	48	15.7	**King City** (city) Monterey County
18	54	16.0	**Hillsborough** (town) San Mateo County
19	55	16.1	**Albany** (city) Alameda County
19	55	16.1	**Menlo Park** (city) San Mateo County
21	63	16.4	**Sunnyvale** (city) Santa Clara County
22	67	16.5	**Piedmont** (city) Alameda County
22	67	16.5	**Stanford** (CDP) Santa Clara County
24	71	16.7	**Berkeley** (city) Alameda County
25	73	16.8	**Kerman** (city) Fresno County
26	76	16.9	**Dinuba** (city) Tulare County
27	86	17.1	**Delano** (city) Kern County
27	86	17.1	**Lemoore** (city) Kings County
29	92	17.2	**Emeryville** (city) Alameda County
29	92	17.2	**Reedley** (city) Fresno County
31	98	17.3	**Mead Valley** (CDP) Riverside County
32	105	17.5	**Delhi** (CDP) Merced County
33	115	17.7	**Selma** (city) Fresno County
33	115	17.7	**Tehachapi** (city) Kern County
35	126	17.8	**Lafayette** (city) Contra Costa County
35	126	17.8	**San Anselmo** (town) Marin County
37	134	17.9	**South Pasadena** (city) Los Angeles County
38	151	18.2	**Muscoy** (CDP) San Bernardino County
38	151	18.2	**Susanville** (city) Lassen County
40	186	18.7	**Greenfield** (city) Monterey County
40	186	18.7	**Madera** (city) Madera County
42	212	19.0	**Winton** (CDP) Merced County
43	222	19.1	**Lake Los Angeles** (CDP) Los Angeles County
43	222	19.1	**Watsonville** (city) Santa Cruz County
45	231	19.2	**Corcoran** (city) Kings County
45	231	19.2	**El Cerrito** (city) Contra Costa County
45	231	19.2	**Soledad** (city) Monterey County
48	257	19.4	**Exeter** (city) Tulare County
49	270	19.5	**Coachella** (city) Riverside County
49	270	19.5	**Ridgecrest** (city) Kern County
51	287	19.6	**Malibu** (city) Los Angeles County
52	309	19.8	**North Fair Oaks** (CDP) San Mateo County
52	309	19.8	**Santa Maria** (city) Santa Barbara County
54	321	19.9	**Orinda** (city) Contra Costa County
54	321	19.9	**Santa Clara** (city) Santa Clara County
56	340	20.0	**Santa Monica** (city) Los Angeles County
57	354	20.1	**Coronado** (city) San Diego County
58	363	20.2	**Santa Barbara** (city) Santa Barbara County
58	363	20.2	**Shafter** (city) Kern County
60	380	20.3	**Placerville** (city) El Dorado County
60	380	20.3	**Ramona** (CDP) San Diego County
62	401	20.4	**Altadena** (CDP) Los Angeles County
62	401	20.4	**Garden Acres** (CDP) San Joaquin County
64	418	20.5	**East Palo Alto** (city) San Mateo County
64	418	20.5	**Fremont** (city) Alameda County
64	418	20.5	**La Cañada Flintridge** (city) Los Angeles County
64	418	20.5	**Lake Arrowhead** (CDP) San Bernardino County
68	438	20.6	**Belmont** (city) San Mateo County
68	438	20.6	**Blythe** (city) Riverside County
68	438	20.6	**Pasadena** (city) Los Angeles County
71	464	20.7	**Patterson** (city) Stanislaus County
71	464	20.7	**Phelan** (CDP) San Bernardino County
71	464	20.7	**View Park-Windsor Hills** (CDP) Los Angeles County
74	482	20.8	**Hermosa Beach** (city) Los Angeles County
74	482	20.8	**Oakland** (city) Alameda County
74	482	20.8	**Sonoma** (city) Sonoma County
77	507	20.9	**Fallbrook** (CDP) San Diego County
77	507	20.9	**Moraga** (town) Contra Costa County
79	527	21.0	**Culver City** (city) Los Angeles County
79	527	21.0	**Maywood** (city) Los Angeles County
79	527	21.0	**Salinas** (city) Monterey County
79	527	21.0	**Santa Cruz** (city) Santa Cruz County
83	545	21.1	**Desert Hot Springs** (city) Riverside County
83	545	21.1	**Foster City** (city) San Mateo County
83	545	21.1	**San Pablo** (city) Contra Costa County
83	545	21.1	**South El Monte** (city) Los Angeles County
87	571	21.2	**Loma Linda** (city) San Bernardino County
88	594	21.3	**American Canyon** (city) Napa County
88	594	21.3	**Clayton** (city) Contra Costa County
90	618	21.4	**Ashland** (CDP) Alameda County
90	618	21.4	**Healdsburg** (city) Sonoma County
92	643	21.5	**Lompoc** (city) Santa Barbara County
92	643	21.5	**Milpitas** (city) Santa Clara County
92	643	21.5	**Monterey** (city) Monterey County
95	675	21.6	**Walnut Creek** (city) Contra Costa County
96	707	21.7	**Richmond** (city) Contra Costa County
96	707	21.7	**San Francisco** (city) San Francisco County
96	707	21.7	**Truckee** (town) Nevada County
99	729	21.8	**Coalinga** (city) Fresno County
99	729	21.8	**Hanford** (city) Kings County
99	729	21.8	**Napa** (city) Napa County
99	729	21.8	**Seaside** (city) Monterey County
103	762	21.9	**Manhattan Beach** (city) Los Angeles County
104	787	22.0	**Burlingame** (city) San Mateo County
104	787	22.0	**East Hemet** (CDP) Riverside County
104	787	22.0	**Newark** (city) Alameda County
104	787	22.0	**San Ramon** (city) Contra Costa County
108	812	22.1	**Cherryland** (CDP) Alameda County
108	812	22.1	**McKinleyville** (CDP) Humboldt County
108	812	22.1	**Porterville** (city) Tulare County
108	812	22.1	**Sanger** (city) Fresno County
112	836	22.2	**Lennox** (CDP) Los Angeles County
113	881	22.3	**Ceres** (city) Stanislaus County
113	881	22.3	**Folsom** (city) Sacramento County
113	881	22.3	**Oak Park** (CDP) Ventura County
113	881	22.3	**Pleasanton** (city) Alameda County
117	906	22.4	**Cudahy** (city) Los Angeles County
117	906	22.4	**Redwood City** (city) San Mateo County
117	906	22.4	**San Jose** (city) Santa Clara County
117	906	22.4	**South San Jose Hills** (CDP) Los Angeles County
121	940	22.5	**Cameron Park** (CDP) El Dorado County
121	940	22.5	**Newman** (city) Stanislaus County
121	940	22.5	**Nipomo** (CDP) San Luis Obispo County
121	940	22.5	**San Rafael** (city) Marin County
121	940	22.5	**South Lake Tahoe** (city) El Dorado County
126	974	22.6	**El Monte** (city) Los Angeles County
127	1004	22.7	**Cathedral City** (city) Riverside County
127	1004	22.7	**East Rancho Dominguez** (CDP) Los Angeles County
127	1004	22.7	**Larkspur** (city) Marin County
127	1004	22.7	**Mill Valley** (city) Marin County
127	1004	22.7	**San Marino** (city) Los Angeles County
127	1004	22.7	**Seal Beach** (city) Orange County
127	1004	22.7	**Sun Village** (CDP) Los Angeles County
134	1041	22.8	**Fairview** (CDP) Alameda County
134	1041	22.8	**Farmersville** (city) Tulare County
134	1041	22.8	**Quartz Hill** (CDP) Los Angeles County
134	1041	22.8	**Santa Paula** (city) Ventura County
138	1080	22.9	**Calabasas** (city) Los Angeles County
138	1080	22.9	**California City** (city) Kern County
138	1080	22.9	**East San Gabriel** (CDP) Los Angeles County
138	1080	22.9	**Wildomar** (city) Riverside County
142	1126	23.0	**Baldwin Park** (city) Los Angeles County
142	1126	23.0	**Bell Gardens** (city) Los Angeles County
142	1126	23.0	**Live Oak** (CDP) Santa Cruz County
142	1126	23.0	**Oakdale** (city) Stanislaus County
142	1126	23.0	**Ripon** (city) San Joaquin County
147	1162	23.1	**Discovery Bay** (CDP) Contra Costa County
147	1162	23.1	**Orcutt** (CDP) Santa Barbara County
147	1162	23.1	**Palm Springs** (city) Riverside County
147	1162	23.1	**Paradise** (town) Butte County

Note: *The state column ranks the top/bottom 150 places from all places in the state with population of 10,000 or more. The national column ranks the top/bottom 150 places from all places in the country with population of 10,000 or more. Places that are unincorporated were not considered in the rankings. Please refer to the User Guide for additional information.*

Employment: Natural Resources, Construction, and Maintenance Occupations

Top 150 Places Ranked in *Descending* Order

State Rank	Nat'l Rank	Percent	Place
1	1	61.8	**Mendota** (city) Fresno County
2	2	54.6	**McFarland** (city) Kern County
3	3	50.6	**Arvin** (city) Kern County
4	4	48.5	**Avenal** (city) Kings County
5	5	47.7	**King City** (city) Monterey County
6	6	47.1	**Lamont** (CDP) Kern County
7	9	38.3	**Delano** (city) Kern County
8	10	36.7	**Wasco** (city) Kern County
9	11	35.1	**Greenfield** (city) Monterey County
10	12	33.3	**Shafter** (city) Kern County
11	13	32.9	**Reedley** (city) Fresno County
12	14	32.6	**Corcoran** (city) Kings County
12	14	32.6	**Soledad** (city) Monterey County
14	17	32.0	**Madera** (city) Madera County
15	19	29.9	**Lindsay** (city) Tulare County
16	20	29.6	**Santa Maria** (city) Santa Barbara County
17	21	28.6	**Parlier** (city) Fresno County
18	23	27.7	**Dinuba** (city) Tulare County
19	25	26.5	**Winton** (CDP) Merced County
20	26	26.4	**Watsonville** (city) Santa Cruz County
21	30	25.3	**Selma** (city) Fresno County
22	31	25.1	**Phelan** (CDP) San Bernardino County
23	34	24.5	**Salinas** (city) Monterey County
24	37	23.9	**Santa Paula** (city) Ventura County
25	39	23.6	**Livingston** (city) Merced County
26	43	23.2	**Farmersville** (city) Tulare County
27	44	23.1	**Coachella** (city) Riverside County
28	51	22.0	**Los Banos** (city) Merced County
29	55	21.8	**Garden Acres** (CDP) San Joaquin County
30	66	20.8	**Kerman** (city) Fresno County
30	66	20.8	**Rosamond** (CDP) Kern County
32	68	20.7	**Mead Valley** (CDP) Riverside County
32	68	20.7	**Sun Village** (CDP) Los Angeles County
34	73	20.2	**Delhi** (CDP) Merced County
34	73	20.2	**Muscoy** (CDP) San Bernardino County
34	73	20.2	**Patterson** (city) Stanislaus County
37	81	19.6	**Oxnard** (city) Ventura County
38	95	18.7	**Porterville** (city) Tulare County
39	97	18.6	**Coalinga** (city) Fresno County
40	99	18.5	**Bloomington** (CDP) San Bernardino County
41	108	18.1	**Sanger** (city) Fresno County
42	122	17.6	**Galt** (city) Sacramento County
43	132	17.1	**Cudahy** (city) Los Angeles County
44	135	16.9	**Ceres** (city) Stanislaus County
45	138	16.8	**Lake Los Angeles** (CDP) Los Angeles County
46	144	16.6	**Clearlake** (city) Lake County
46	144	16.6	**Hollister** (city) San Benito County
48	156	16.4	**East Rancho Dominguez** (CDP) Los Angeles County
48	156	16.4	**Gilroy** (city) Santa Clara County
48	156	16.4	**Tulare** (city) Tulare County
51	162	16.3	**Fallbrook** (CDP) San Diego County
52	168	16.2	**East Hemet** (CDP) Riverside County
52	168	16.2	**Home Gardens** (CDP) Riverside County
54	173	16.1	**Ramona** (CDP) San Diego County
55	190	15.8	**Olivehurst** (CDP) Yuba County
56	200	15.6	**Atwater** (city) Merced County
57	204	15.5	**Lompoc** (city) Santa Barbara County
58	206	15.4	**Rio Linda** (CDP) Sacramento County
59	210	15.3	**Exeter** (city) Tulare County
59	210	15.3	**Linda** (CDP) Yuba County
61	217	15.2	**Alum Rock** (CDP) Santa Clara County
61	217	15.2	**Bell Gardens** (city) Los Angeles County
61	217	15.2	**Lodi** (city) San Joaquin County
61	217	15.2	**Maywood** (city) Los Angeles County
65	224	15.1	**Prunedale** (CDP) Monterey County
66	228	15.0	**Yuba City** (city) Sutter County
67	232	14.9	**Lakeside** (CDP) San Diego County
67	232	14.9	**Yucca Valley** (town) San Bernardino County
69	238	14.8	**Fillmore** (city) Ventura County
70	241	14.7	**Big Bear City** (CDP) San Bernardino County
70	241	14.7	**Lakeland Village** (CDP) Riverside County
70	241	14.7	**San Fernando** (city) Los Angeles County
70	241	14.7	**Winter Gardens** (CDP) San Diego County
74	247	14.6	**Salida** (CDP) Stanislaus County
75	264	14.4	**Barstow** (city) San Bernardino County
75	264	14.4	**Calexico** (city) Imperial County
75	264	14.4	**North Fair Oaks** (CDP) San Mateo County
75	264	14.4	**Oakdale** (city) Stanislaus County
79	275	14.3	**Ukiah** (city) Mendocino County
80	282	14.2	**Hesperia** (city) San Bernardino County
80	282	14.2	**Marysville** (city) Yuba County
82	295	14.1	**East Los Angeles** (CDP) Los Angeles County
82	295	14.1	**South El Monte** (city) Los Angeles County
82	295	14.1	**Woodland** (city) Yolo County
85	305	14.0	**Kingsburg** (city) Fresno County
86	317	13.9	**Bay Point** (CDP) Contra Costa County
86	317	13.9	**Florence-Graham** (CDP) Los Angeles County
86	317	13.9	**San Pablo** (city) Contra Costa County
86	317	13.9	**Wildomar** (city) Riverside County
90	325	13.8	**Merced** (city) Merced County
90	325	13.8	**Quartz Hill** (CDP) Los Angeles County
92	340	13.6	**La Presa** (CDP) San Diego County
93	347	13.5	**Oakley** (city) Contra Costa County
93	347	13.5	**Orcutt** (CDP) Santa Barbara County
95	355	13.4	**Tehachapi** (city) Kern County
96	371	13.3	**Brawley** (city) Imperial County
96	371	13.3	**Canyon Lake** (city) Riverside County
96	371	13.3	**Hanford** (city) Kings County
96	371	13.3	**Hawaiian Gardens** (city) Los Angeles County
96	371	13.3	**Lennox** (CDP) Los Angeles County
96	371	13.3	**South San Jose Hills** (CDP) Los Angeles County
102	383	13.2	**Escondido** (city) San Diego County
102	383	13.2	**La Puente** (city) Los Angeles County
104	392	13.1	**Bakersfield** (city) Kern County
104	392	13.1	**Nipomo** (CDP) San Luis Obispo County
106	403	13.0	**Crestline** (CDP) San Bernardino County
106	403	13.0	**National City** (city) San Diego County
108	413	12.9	**Bell** (city) Los Angeles County
108	413	12.9	**Chowchilla** (city) Madera County
108	413	12.9	**El Paso de Robles (Paso Robles)** (city) San Luis Obispo County
111	427	12.8	**Carpinteria** (city) Santa Barbara County
111	427	12.8	**Pittsburg** (city) Contra Costa County
111	427	12.8	**Victorville** (city) San Bernardino County
114	444	12.7	**Commerce** (city) Los Angeles County
114	444	12.7	**Indio** (city) Riverside County
116	458	12.6	**Parkway** (CDP) Sacramento County
116	458	12.6	**Willowbrook** (CDP) Los Angeles County
118	475	12.5	**Healdsburg** (city) Sonoma County
118	475	12.5	**Lemoore** (city) Kings County
118	475	12.5	**Newman** (city) Stanislaus County
118	475	12.5	**North Highlands** (CDP) Sacramento County
122	494	12.4	**California City** (city) Kern County
122	494	12.4	**Hemet** (city) Riverside County
122	494	12.4	**Oildale** (CDP) Kern County
122	494	12.4	**Vista** (city) San Diego County
122	494	12.4	**Woodcrest** (CDP) Riverside County
127	513	12.3	**Lathrop** (city) San Joaquin County
128	524	12.2	**Baldwin Park** (city) Los Angeles County
128	524	12.2	**Norco** (city) Riverside County
130	549	12.1	**Adelanto** (city) San Bernardino County
130	549	12.1	**Apple Valley** (town) San Bernardino County
130	549	12.1	**Desert Hot Springs** (city) Riverside County
130	549	12.1	**Montclair** (city) San Bernardino County
130	549	12.1	**North Auburn** (CDP) Placer County
130	549	12.1	**Perris** (city) Riverside County
130	549	12.1	**San Bernardino** (city) San Bernardino County
137	572	12.0	**Foothill Farms** (CDP) Sacramento County
137	572	12.0	**Los Osos** (CDP) San Luis Obispo County
139	586	11.9	**El Centro** (city) Imperial County
139	586	11.9	**Napa** (city) Napa County
141	607	11.8	**Bostonia** (CDP) San Diego County
141	607	11.8	**San Jacinto** (city) Riverside County
141	607	11.8	**Shasta Lake** (city) Shasta County
141	607	11.8	**Tracy** (city) San Joaquin County
145	630	11.7	**Cherryland** (CDP) Alameda County
146	647	11.6	**Brentwood** (city) Contra Costa County
146	647	11.6	**Colton** (city) San Bernardino County
146	647	11.6	**Ridgecrest** (city) Kern County
146	647	11.6	**Riverbank** (city) Stanislaus County
150	678	11.5	**El Monte** (city) Los Angeles County

Note: *The state column ranks the top/bottom 150 places from all places in the state with population of 10,000 or more. The national column ranks the top/bottom 150 places from all places in the country with population of 10,000 or more. Places that are unincorporated were not considered in the rankings. Please refer to the User Guide for additional information.*

Employment: Natural Resources, Construction, and Maintenance Occupations

Top 150 Places Ranked in *Ascending* Order

State Rank	Nat'l Rank	Percent	Place
1	2	0.3	**San Marino** (city) Los Angeles County
2	10	0.9	**Piedmont** (city) Alameda County
3	12	1.0	**Ladera Ranch** (CDP) Orange County
3	12	1.0	**Los Altos** (city) Santa Clara County
5	20	1.2	**Hermosa Beach** (city) Los Angeles County
5	20	1.2	**Saratoga** (city) Santa Clara County
7	29	1.4	**La Cañada Flintridge** (city) Los Angeles County
7	29	1.4	**Stanford** (CDP) Santa Clara County
9	42	1.6	**Clayton** (city) Contra Costa County
9	42	1.6	**Solana Beach** (city) San Diego County
11	56	1.7	**Beverly Hills** (city) Los Angeles County
11	56	1.7	**Cupertino** (city) Santa Clara County
11	56	1.7	**Moraga** (town) Contra Costa County
11	56	1.7	**West Hollywood** (city) Los Angeles County
15	62	1.8	**Isla Vista** (CDP) Santa Barbara County
15	62	1.8	**Laguna Woods** (city) Orange County
15	62	1.8	**Orinda** (city) Contra Costa County
18	71	1.9	**Calabasas** (city) Los Angeles County
18	71	1.9	**Manhattan Beach** (city) Los Angeles County
18	71	1.9	**Santa Monica** (city) Los Angeles County
21	83	2.0	**Alamo** (CDP) Contra Costa County
21	83	2.0	**Emeryville** (city) Alameda County
21	83	2.0	**Palo Alto** (city) Santa Clara County
24	99	2.1	**Rossmoor** (CDP) Orange County
25	112	2.2	**Oak Park** (CDP) Ventura County
26	138	2.4	**Hillsborough** (town) San Mateo County
26	138	2.4	**Lafayette** (city) Contra Costa County
26	138	2.4	**Newport Beach** (city) Orange County
26	138	2.4	**Rancho Palos Verdes** (city) Los Angeles County
30	151	2.5	**Foster City** (city) San Mateo County
30	151	2.5	**Irvine** (city) Orange County
30	151	2.5	**Menlo Park** (city) San Mateo County
33	169	2.6	**Davis** (city) Yolo County
33	169	2.6	**Mill Valley** (city) Marin County
35	187	2.7	**Aliso Viejo** (city) Orange County
35	187	2.7	**Palos Verdes Estates** (city) Los Angeles County
35	187	2.7	**Tamalpais-Homestead Valley** (CDP) Marin County
38	203	2.8	**Laguna Beach** (city) Orange County
39	219	2.9	**Albany** (city) Alameda County
39	219	2.9	**Coto de Caza** (CDP) Orange County
39	219	2.9	**Danville** (town) Contra Costa County
39	219	2.9	**Malibu** (city) Los Angeles County
43	236	3.0	**Cerritos** (city) Los Angeles County
44	257	3.1	**Agoura Hills** (city) Los Angeles County
45	281	3.2	**Arcadia** (city) Los Angeles County
45	281	3.2	**Berkeley** (city) Alameda County
45	281	3.2	**Stevenson Ranch** (CDP) Los Angeles County
48	308	3.3	**Dublin** (city) Alameda County
48	308	3.3	**Walnut Creek** (city) Contra Costa County
50	324	3.4	**Los Gatos** (town) Santa Clara County
50	324	3.4	**View Park-Windsor Hills** (CDP) Los Angeles County
52	355	3.5	**Diamond Bar** (city) Los Angeles County
53	377	3.6	**North Tustin** (CDP) Orange County
53	377	3.6	**San Ramon** (city) Contra Costa County
53	377	3.6	**Susanville** (city) Lassen County
53	377	3.6	**Walnut** (city) Los Angeles County
57	407	3.7	**Claremont** (city) Los Angeles County
57	407	3.7	**South Pasadena** (city) Los Angeles County
59	442	3.8	**Folsom** (city) Sacramento County
59	442	3.8	**Hercules** (city) Contra Costa County
59	442	3.8	**Larkspur** (city) Marin County
59	442	3.8	**Rocklin** (city) Placer County
63	466	3.9	**El Dorado Hills** (CDP) El Dorado County
63	466	3.9	**Redondo Beach** (city) Los Angeles County
65	500	4.0	**Culver City** (city) Los Angeles County
65	500	4.0	**La Riviera** (CDP) Sacramento County
67	518	4.1	**Coronado** (city) San Diego County
67	518	4.1	**Granite Bay** (CDP) Placer County
67	518	4.1	**Mountain View** (city) Santa Clara County
67	518	4.1	**San Francisco** (city) San Francisco County
67	518	4.1	**San Luis Obispo** (city) San Luis Obispo County
72	553	4.2	**Mission Viejo** (city) Orange County
73	584	4.3	**Laguna Niguel** (city) Orange County
73	584	4.3	**San Carlos** (city) San Mateo County
75	608	4.4	**Carlsbad** (city) San Diego County
75	608	4.4	**El Segundo** (city) Los Angeles County
75	608	4.4	**Pleasanton** (city) Alameda County
78	641	4.5	**Alameda** (city) Alameda County
79	692	4.6	**Pacific Grove** (city) Monterey County
79	692	4.6	**Sunnyvale** (city) Santa Clara County
81	729	4.7	**Encinitas** (city) San Diego County
81	729	4.7	**Rowland Heights** (CDP) Los Angeles County
81	729	4.7	**Seal Beach** (city) Orange County
81	729	4.7	**Yorba Linda** (city) Orange County
85	765	4.8	**Artesia** (city) Los Angeles County
85	765	4.8	**Fremont** (city) Alameda County
85	765	4.8	**Loma Linda** (city) San Bernardino County
85	765	4.8	**Milpitas** (city) Santa Clara County
85	765	4.8	**Rancho Santa Margarita** (city) Orange County
85	765	4.8	**Thousand Oaks** (city) Ventura County
91	813	4.9	**Belmont** (city) San Mateo County
91	813	4.9	**Burbank** (city) Los Angeles County
91	813	4.9	**La Crescenta-Montrose** (CDP) Los Angeles County
91	813	4.9	**Sierra Madre** (city) Los Angeles County
95	846	5.0	**Daly City** (city) San Mateo County
95	846	5.0	**El Sobrante** (CDP) Riverside County
95	846	5.0	**Santa Clara** (city) Santa Clara County
98	891	5.1	**Alhambra** (city) Los Angeles County
99	947	5.2	**Brea** (city) Orange County
99	947	5.2	**El Cerrito** (city) Contra Costa County
99	947	5.2	**Marina** (city) Monterey County
99	947	5.2	**Pasadena** (city) Los Angeles County
99	947	5.2	**West Carson** (CDP) Los Angeles County
104	987	5.3	**Fountain Valley** (city) Orange County
104	987	5.3	**Hacienda Heights** (CDP) Los Angeles County
104	987	5.3	**La Palma** (city) Orange County
104	987	5.3	**Monterey** (city) Monterey County
104	987	5.3	**Torrance** (city) Los Angeles County
109	1023	5.4	**Elk Grove** (city) Sacramento County
109	1023	5.4	**Glendale** (city) Los Angeles County
109	1023	5.4	**Signal Hill** (city) Los Angeles County
112	1073	5.5	**Monterey Park** (city) Los Angeles County
113	1109	5.6	**Monrovia** (city) Los Angeles County
114	1149	5.7	**Arcata** (city) Humboldt County
114	1149	5.7	**Camp Pendleton South** (CDP) San Diego County
116	1199	5.8	**San Diego** (city) San Diego County
116	1199	5.8	**Temple City** (city) Los Angeles County
118	1246	5.9	**Dana Point** (city) Orange County
118	1246	5.9	**Lake Forest** (city) Orange County
118	1246	5.9	**Roseville** (city) Placer County
118	1246	5.9	**San Anselmo** (town) Marin County
122	1316	6.0	**Chino Hills** (city) San Bernardino County
122	1316	6.0	**Goleta** (city) Santa Barbara County
122	1316	6.0	**La Verne** (city) Los Angeles County
122	1316	6.0	**Placentia** (city) Orange County
122	1316	6.0	**Poway** (city) San Diego County
122	1316	6.0	**Rancho San Diego** (CDP) San Diego County
122	1316	6.0	**Tustin** (city) Orange County
129	1381	6.1	**Cypress** (city) Orange County
129	1381	6.1	**Fair Oaks** (CDP) Sacramento County
129	1381	6.1	**Pinole** (city) Contra Costa County
132	1450	6.2	**Burlingame** (city) San Mateo County
133	1499	6.3	**Arden-Arcade** (CDP) Sacramento County
133	1499	6.3	**East San Gabriel** (CDP) Los Angeles County
133	1499	6.3	**Redlands** (city) San Bernardino County
133	1499	6.3	**San Mateo** (city) San Mateo County
133	1499	6.3	**Union City** (city) Alameda County
138	1545	6.4	**Costa Mesa** (city) Orange County
138	1545	6.4	**Fullerton** (city) Orange County
138	1545	6.4	**Moorpark** (city) Ventura County
138	1545	6.4	**Novato** (city) Marin County
138	1545	6.4	**Sacramento** (city) Sacramento County
138	1545	6.4	**Upland** (city) San Bernardino County
138	1545	6.4	**Whittier** (city) Los Angeles County
145	1622	6.5	**Altadena** (CDP) Los Angeles County
145	1622	6.5	**Casa de Oro-Mount Helix** (CDP) San Diego County
145	1622	6.5	**Chico** (city) Butte County
145	1622	6.5	**Fairview** (CDP) Alameda County
145	1622	6.5	**Vineyard** (CDP) Sacramento County
150	1683	6.6	**Auburn** (city) Placer County

Note: *The state column ranks the top/bottom 150 places from all places in the state with population of 10,000 or more. The national column ranks the top/bottom 150 places from all places in the country with population of 10,000 or more. Places that are unincorporated were not considered in the rankings. Please refer to the User Guide for additional information.*

Employment: Production, Transportation, and Material Moving Occupations

Top 150 Places Ranked in *Descending* Order

State Rank	Nat'l Rank	Percent	Place
1	7	34.5	**Maywood** (city) Los Angeles County
2	11	34.0	**Livingston** (city) Merced County
3	12	33.9	**Walnut Park** (CDP) Los Angeles County
4	17	33.1	**Parlier** (city) Fresno County
5	22	32.1	**Cudahy** (city) Los Angeles County
6	23	31.9	**Bell Gardens** (city) Los Angeles County
7	28	31.4	**Lynwood** (city) Los Angeles County
8	29	31.1	**Muscoy** (CDP) San Bernardino County
9	30	31.0	**Florence-Graham** (CDP) Los Angeles County
9	30	31.0	**Huntington Park** (city) Los Angeles County
11	37	30.1	**East Rancho Dominguez** (CDP) Los Angeles County
12	43	29.7	**Willowbrook** (CDP) Los Angeles County
13	46	29.6	**South San Jose Hills** (CDP) Los Angeles County
14	51	29.4	**Bell** (city) Los Angeles County
15	77	27.4	**South El Monte** (city) Los Angeles County
16	79	27.3	**Delhi** (CDP) Merced County
17	81	27.2	**South Gate** (city) Los Angeles County
18	86	27.0	**Bloomington** (CDP) San Bernardino County
19	104	26.1	**Baldwin Park** (city) Los Angeles County
20	107	26.0	**Mead Valley** (CDP) Riverside County
20	107	26.0	**Paramount** (city) Los Angeles County
22	111	25.9	**East Los Angeles** (CDP) Los Angeles County
22	111	25.9	**Newman** (city) Stanislaus County
24	114	25.8	**Winton** (CDP) Merced County
25	116	25.7	**Compton** (city) Los Angeles County
26	119	25.6	**West Puente Valley** (CDP) Los Angeles County
27	134	24.7	**Home Gardens** (CDP) Riverside County
28	137	24.6	**Rialto** (city) San Bernardino County
29	147	24.5	**El Monte** (city) Los Angeles County
30	152	24.4	**Dinuba** (city) Tulare County
31	158	24.3	**Commerce** (city) Los Angeles County
32	168	24.0	**Garden Acres** (CDP) San Joaquin County
33	177	23.8	**Ceres** (city) Stanislaus County
34	184	23.5	**Perris** (city) Riverside County
35	189	23.3	**Adelanto** (city) San Bernardino County
36	208	22.9	**Ontario** (city) San Bernardino County
37	230	22.3	**La Puente** (city) Los Angeles County
37	230	22.3	**Valinda** (CDP) Los Angeles County
39	240	22.1	**Farmersville** (city) Tulare County
39	240	22.1	**Montclair** (city) San Bernardino County
41	246	22.0	**Colton** (city) San Bernardino County
42	256	21.8	**Wasco** (city) Kern County
43	270	21.5	**Cherryland** (CDP) Alameda County
44	278	21.4	**Fontana** (city) San Bernardino County
45	296	21.2	**Pico Rivera** (city) Los Angeles County
46	301	21.1	**Lathrop** (city) San Joaquin County
47	318	20.9	**West Whittier-Los Nietos** (CDP) Los Angeles County
48	324	20.8	**Selma** (city) Fresno County
49	332	20.7	**Kerman** (city) Fresno County
49	332	20.7	**Lindsay** (city) Tulare County
51	346	20.6	**Hawaiian Gardens** (city) Los Angeles County
52	377	20.3	**Santa Ana** (city) Orange County
53	408	19.9	**Parkway** (CDP) Sacramento County
53	408	19.9	**Patterson** (city) Stanislaus County
55	415	19.8	**Riverbank** (city) Stanislaus County
56	423	19.7	**Norwalk** (city) Los Angeles County
57	438	19.5	**Exeter** (city) Tulare County
57	438	19.5	**Pomona** (city) Los Angeles County
59	468	19.2	**Salida** (CDP) Stanislaus County
60	476	19.1	**Hesperia** (city) San Bernardino County
61	488	19.0	**San Bernardino** (city) San Bernardino County
62	498	18.9	**Lennox** (CDP) Los Angeles County
63	512	18.7	**Avocado Heights** (CDP) Los Angeles County
63	512	18.7	**South Whittier** (CDP) Los Angeles County
65	541	18.5	**Los Banos** (city) Merced County
66	556	18.3	**Atwater** (city) Merced County
67	591	18.1	**Arvin** (city) Kern County
67	591	18.1	**Manteca** (city) San Joaquin County
69	610	18.0	**Lake Los Angeles** (CDP) Los Angeles County
70	668	17.6	**Moreno Valley** (city) Riverside County
71	676	17.5	**Lamont** (CDP) Kern County
71	676	17.5	**Santa Fe Springs** (city) Los Angeles County
73	691	17.4	**Garden Grove** (city) Orange County
74	718	17.2	**Red Bluff** (city) Tehama County
74	718	17.2	**Turlock** (city) Stanislaus County
76	739	17.1	**Lemon Hill** (CDP) Sacramento County
76	739	17.1	**Montebello** (city) Los Angeles County
76	739	17.1	**Tulare** (city) Tulare County
79	770	16.9	**Alum Rock** (CDP) Santa Clara County
79	770	16.9	**Ashland** (CDP) Alameda County
79	770	16.9	**Bellflower** (city) Los Angeles County
79	770	16.9	**Carson** (city) Los Angeles County
79	770	16.9	**Sanger** (city) Fresno County
84	787	16.8	**Stanton** (city) Orange County
85	797	16.7	**Westmont** (CDP) Los Angeles County
86	825	16.5	**Oxnard** (city) Ventura County
86	825	16.5	**San Fernando** (city) Los Angeles County
88	839	16.4	**Oakdale** (city) Stanislaus County
88	839	16.4	**Shafter** (city) Kern County
90	876	16.2	**Stockton** (city) San Joaquin County
91	890	16.1	**Hayward** (city) Alameda County
92	909	16.0	**Gardena** (city) Los Angeles County
92	909	16.0	**Phelan** (CDP) San Bernardino County
92	909	16.0	**Rosemead** (city) Los Angeles County
95	929	15.9	**Lakeland Village** (CDP) Riverside County
95	929	15.9	**Newark** (city) Alameda County
95	929	15.9	**Soledad** (city) Monterey County
98	972	15.7	**Olivehurst** (CDP) Yuba County
99	996	15.6	**Anaheim** (city) Orange County
99	996	15.6	**Corcoran** (city) Kings County
99	996	15.6	**Fillmore** (city) Ventura County
99	996	15.6	**Riverside** (city) Riverside County
103	1017	15.5	**Oildale** (CDP) Kern County
103	1017	15.5	**Westminster** (city) Orange County
105	1035	15.4	**National City** (city) San Diego County
106	1050	15.3	**Galt** (city) Sacramento County
106	1050	15.3	**Highland** (city) San Bernardino County
108	1068	15.2	**Delano** (city) Kern County
108	1068	15.2	**Lodi** (city) San Joaquin County
110	1083	15.1	**Banning** (city) Riverside County
110	1083	15.1	**Chino** (city) San Bernardino County
112	1107	15.0	**Dixon** (city) Solano County
112	1107	15.0	**Palmdale** (city) Los Angeles County
114	1128	14.9	**Hemet** (city) Riverside County
114	1128	14.9	**Lake Elsinore** (city) Riverside County
114	1128	14.9	**Madera** (city) Madera County
114	1128	14.9	**Salinas** (city) Monterey County
114	1128	14.9	**San Pablo** (city) Contra Costa County
119	1152	14.8	**Florin** (CDP) Sacramento County
119	1152	14.8	**Santa Paula** (city) Ventura County
119	1152	14.8	**Tracy** (city) San Joaquin County
122	1163	14.7	**Lemoore** (city) Kings County
123	1184	14.6	**Greenfield** (city) Monterey County
124	1203	14.5	**Downey** (city) Los Angeles County
124	1203	14.5	**Merced** (city) Merced County
124	1203	14.5	**San Lorenzo** (CDP) Alameda County
124	1203	14.5	**Victorville** (city) San Bernardino County
128	1224	14.4	**Azusa** (city) Los Angeles County
129	1249	14.3	**Hawthorne** (city) Los Angeles County
129	1249	14.3	**Reedley** (city) Fresno County
131	1269	14.2	**American Canyon** (city) Napa County
131	1269	14.2	**Brawley** (city) Imperial County
131	1269	14.2	**Kingsburg** (city) Fresno County
134	1316	14.0	**Calexico** (city) Imperial County
134	1316	14.0	**Mendota** (city) Fresno County
134	1316	14.0	**Modesto** (city) Stanislaus County
134	1316	14.0	**Watsonville** (city) Santa Cruz County
138	1337	13.9	**Coalinga** (city) Fresno County
138	1337	13.9	**Oroville** (city) Butte County
138	1337	13.9	**Prunedale** (CDP) Monterey County
138	1337	13.9	**San Leandro** (city) Alameda County
138	1337	13.9	**Santa Maria** (city) Santa Barbara County
138	1337	13.9	**Sun Village** (CDP) Los Angeles County
144	1363	13.8	**Suisun City** (city) Solano County
145	1392	13.7	**Magalia** (CDP) Butte County
146	1457	13.4	**Inglewood** (city) Los Angeles County
146	1457	13.4	**Linda** (CDP) Yuba County
148	1483	13.3	**Blythe** (city) Riverside County
148	1483	13.3	**La Habra** (city) Orange County
150	1508	13.2	**Citrus** (CDP) Los Angeles County

***Note:** The state column ranks the top/bottom 150 places from all places in the state with population of 10,000 or more. The national column ranks the top/bottom 150 places from all places in the country with population of 10,000 or more. Places that are unincorporated were not considered in the rankings. Please refer to the User Guide for additional information.*

Employment: Production, Transportation, and Material Moving Occupations

Top 150 Places Ranked in *Ascending* Order

State Rank	Nat'l Rank	Percent	Place
1	1	0.0	**Camp Pendleton South** (CDP) San Diego County
2	3	0.8	**Stanford** (CDP) Santa Clara County
3	15	1.4	**Malibu** (city) Los Angeles County
3	15	1.4	**Saratoga** (city) Santa Clara County
5	21	1.5	**La Cañada Flintridge** (city) Los Angeles County
6	25	1.6	**Mill Valley** (city) Marin County
7	26	1.7	**Los Altos** (city) Santa Clara County
8	38	1.9	**Oak Park** (CDP) Ventura County
9	41	2.0	**Piedmont** (city) Alameda County
10	45	2.1	**Agoura Hills** (city) Los Angeles County
10	45	2.1	**Ladera Ranch** (CDP) Orange County
10	45	2.1	**Solana Beach** (city) San Diego County
13	54	2.2	**Palo Alto** (city) Santa Clara County
13	54	2.2	**Sierra Madre** (city) Los Angeles County
15	61	2.3	**Laguna Woods** (city) Orange County
15	61	2.3	**Moraga** (town) Contra Costa County
17	74	2.4	**Coto de Caza** (CDP) Orange County
17	74	2.4	**Orinda** (city) Contra Costa County
19	81	2.5	**Alamo** (CDP) Contra Costa County
20	92	2.6	**Beverly Hills** (city) Los Angeles County
20	92	2.6	**Hillsborough** (town) San Mateo County
20	92	2.6	**Palos Verdes Estates** (city) Los Angeles County
20	92	2.6	**Santa Monica** (city) Los Angeles County
20	92	2.6	**Tamalpais-Homestead Valley** (CDP) Marin County
25	101	2.7	**Emeryville** (city) Alameda County
25	101	2.7	**San Marino** (city) Los Angeles County
25	101	2.7	**Truckee** (town) Nevada County
28	115	2.8	**Calabasas** (city) Los Angeles County
28	115	2.8	**Danville** (town) Contra Costa County
30	125	2.9	**Cupertino** (city) Santa Clara County
30	125	2.9	**Larkspur** (city) Marin County
30	125	2.9	**Scotts Valley** (city) Santa Cruz County
30	125	2.9	**West Hollywood** (city) Los Angeles County
34	137	3.0	**Albany** (city) Alameda County
34	137	3.0	**Manhattan Beach** (city) Los Angeles County
36	151	3.1	**Lafayette** (city) Contra Costa County
36	151	3.1	**Laguna Beach** (city) Orange County
38	188	3.3	**Pleasant Hill** (city) Contra Costa County
39	197	3.4	**Coronado** (city) San Diego County
39	197	3.4	**Irvine** (city) Orange County
39	197	3.4	**San Ramon** (city) Contra Costa County
42	214	3.5	**Aliso Viejo** (city) Orange County
42	214	3.5	**Berkeley** (city) Alameda County
42	214	3.5	**Newport Beach** (city) Orange County
45	235	3.6	**Belmont** (city) San Mateo County
45	235	3.6	**Los Gatos** (town) Santa Clara County
45	235	3.6	**San Carlos** (city) San Mateo County
48	269	3.8	**El Cerrito** (city) Contra Costa County
48	269	3.8	**Rancho Mirage** (city) Riverside County
50	289	3.9	**Davis** (city) Yolo County
50	289	3.9	**Pacific Grove** (city) Monterey County
50	289	3.9	**Stevenson Ranch** (CDP) Los Angeles County
53	311	4.0	**Culver City** (city) Los Angeles County
53	311	4.0	**Menlo Park** (city) San Mateo County
55	331	4.1	**North Tustin** (CDP) Orange County
55	331	4.1	**Walnut Creek** (city) Contra Costa County
57	352	4.2	**Foster City** (city) San Mateo County
57	352	4.2	**Pleasanton** (city) Alameda County
57	352	4.2	**San Clemente** (city) Orange County
57	352	4.2	**Susanville** (city) Lassen County
61	373	4.3	**Arcadia** (city) Los Angeles County
61	373	4.3	**Hermosa Beach** (city) Los Angeles County
61	373	4.3	**Rossmoor** (CDP) Orange County
64	398	4.4	**Claremont** (city) Los Angeles County
64	398	4.4	**Dublin** (city) Alameda County
64	398	4.4	**Laguna Niguel** (city) Orange County
64	398	4.4	**South Pasadena** (city) Los Angeles County
68	424	4.5	**Redondo Beach** (city) Los Angeles County
69	450	4.6	**Encinitas** (city) San Diego County
69	450	4.6	**Lake Arrowhead** (CDP) San Bernardino County
69	450	4.6	**Morro Bay** (city) San Luis Obispo County
72	470	4.7	**Carlsbad** (city) San Diego County
72	470	4.7	**Monterey** (city) Monterey County
72	470	4.7	**Mountain View** (city) Santa Clara County
75	491	4.8	**Granite Bay** (CDP) Placer County

State Rank	Nat'l Rank	Percent	Place
75	491	4.8	**Isla Vista** (CDP) Santa Barbara County
75	491	4.8	**San Anselmo** (town) Marin County
75	491	4.8	**Thousand Oaks** (city) Ventura County
75	491	4.8	**Yorba Linda** (city) Orange County
80	524	4.9	**East San Gabriel** (CDP) Los Angeles County
80	524	4.9	**View Park-Windsor Hills** (CDP) Los Angeles County
82	548	5.0	**Dana Point** (city) Orange County
82	548	5.0	**Grass Valley** (city) Nevada County
84	569	5.1	**Rancho Palos Verdes** (city) Los Angeles County
85	602	5.2	**Folsom** (city) Sacramento County
85	602	5.2	**Poway** (city) San Diego County
85	602	5.2	**San Francisco** (city) San Francisco County
85	602	5.2	**Santa Cruz** (city) Santa Cruz County
85	602	5.2	**Seal Beach** (city) Orange County
90	633	5.3	**Mission Viejo** (city) Orange County
90	633	5.3	**Novato** (city) Marin County
90	633	5.3	**Palm Springs** (city) Riverside County
90	633	5.3	**Rancho Santa Margarita** (city) Orange County
90	633	5.3	**Rosedale** (CDP) Kern County
95	664	5.4	**El Dorado Hills** (CDP) El Dorado County
95	664	5.4	**San Rafael** (city) Marin County
97	691	5.5	**Campbell** (city) Santa Clara County
98	712	5.6	**La Crescenta-Montrose** (CDP) Los Angeles County
98	712	5.6	**Martinez** (city) Contra Costa County
98	712	5.6	**Santa Barbara** (city) Santa Barbara County
101	741	5.7	**Walnut** (city) Los Angeles County
102	764	5.8	**La Riviera** (CDP) Sacramento County
103	792	5.9	**La Quinta** (city) Riverside County
103	792	5.9	**San Juan Capistrano** (city) Orange County
103	792	5.9	**Sunnyvale** (city) Santa Clara County
106	817	6.0	**Burlingame** (city) San Mateo County
106	817	6.0	**Carmichael** (CDP) Sacramento County
106	817	6.0	**Cerritos** (city) Los Angeles County
106	817	6.0	**Imperial** (city) Imperial County
106	817	6.0	**Laguna Hills** (city) Orange County
106	817	6.0	**Pasadena** (city) Los Angeles County
106	817	6.0	**Quartz Hill** (CDP) Los Angeles County
113	853	6.1	**Arden-Arcade** (CDP) Sacramento County
113	853	6.1	**Brea** (city) Orange County
113	853	6.1	**Clayton** (city) Contra Costa County
113	853	6.1	**Rocklin** (city) Placer County
113	853	6.1	**Yucca Valley** (town) San Bernardino County
118	886	6.2	**Altadena** (CDP) Los Angeles County
118	886	6.2	**La Mesa** (city) San Diego County
120	916	6.3	**Orcutt** (CDP) Santa Barbara County
121	942	6.4	**Lake Forest** (city) Orange County
121	942	6.4	**Los Osos** (CDP) San Luis Obispo County
121	942	6.4	**Palm Desert** (city) Riverside County
121	942	6.4	**Sonoma** (city) Sonoma County
125	970	6.5	**San Mateo** (city) San Mateo County
126	993	6.6	**Fair Oaks** (CDP) Sacramento County
126	993	6.6	**San Luis Obispo** (city) San Luis Obispo County
128	1020	6.7	**Half Moon Bay** (city) San Mateo County
128	1020	6.7	**Huntington Beach** (city) Orange County
128	1020	6.7	**Pacifica** (city) San Mateo County
128	1020	6.7	**San Dimas** (city) Los Angeles County
128	1020	6.7	**Seaside** (city) Monterey County
133	1049	6.8	**Arcata** (city) Humboldt County
133	1049	6.8	**Carpinteria** (city) Santa Barbara County
133	1049	6.8	**El Segundo** (city) Los Angeles County
133	1049	6.8	**Temple City** (city) Los Angeles County
137	1081	6.9	**Camarillo** (city) Ventura County
137	1081	6.9	**Casa de Oro-Mount Helix** (CDP) San Diego County
137	1081	6.9	**Chino Hills** (city) San Bernardino County
137	1081	6.9	**Diamond Bar** (city) Los Angeles County
137	1081	6.9	**Diamond Springs** (CDP) El Dorado County
137	1081	6.9	**Millbrae** (city) San Mateo County
137	1081	6.9	**Rancho San Diego** (CDP) San Diego County
144	1123	7.0	**Morgan Hill** (city) Santa Clara County
144	1123	7.0	**Roseville** (city) Placer County
144	1123	7.0	**San Diego** (city) San Diego County
147	1168	7.2	**Live Oak** (CDP) Santa Cruz County
147	1168	7.2	**Santa Clara** (city) Santa Clara County
149	1193	7.3	**Benicia** (city) Solano County
149	1193	7.3	**Brentwood** (city) Contra Costa County

Note: *The state column ranks the top/bottom 150 places from all places in the state with population of 10,000 or more. The national column ranks the top/bottom 150 places from all places in the country with population of 10,000 or more. Places that are unincorporated were not considered in the rankings. Please refer to the User Guide for additional information.*

Per Capita Income

Top 150 Places Ranked in *Descending* Order

State Rank	Nat'l Rank	Dollars	Place
1	1	118,953	**Hillsborough** (town) San Mateo County
2	7	99,276	**Malibu** (city) Los Angeles County
3	8	98,949	**Piedmont** (city) Alameda County
4	18	89,351	**Palos Verdes Estates** (city) Los Angeles County
5	27	84,440	**Los Altos** (city) Santa Clara County
6	31	82,019	**Mill Valley** (city) Marin County
7	32	81,090	**Manhattan Beach** (city) Los Angeles County
8	38	78,494	**Newport Beach** (city) Orange County
9	43	77,530	**Orinda** (city) Contra Costa County
10	47	76,656	**La Cañada Flintridge** (city) Los Angeles County
11	49	76,240	**San Marino** (city) Los Angeles County
12	50	75,986	**Saratoga** (city) Santa Clara County
13	51	75,890	**Beverly Hills** (city) Los Angeles County
14	53	75,460	**Laguna Beach** (city) Orange County
15	57	73,329	**Palo Alto** (city) Santa Clara County
16	60	72,984	**Alamo** (CDP) Contra Costa County
17	67	70,420	**Los Gatos** (town) Santa Clara County
18	70	69,756	**Larkspur** (city) Marin County
19	71	69,606	**Hermosa Beach** (city) Los Angeles County
20	77	67,902	**Lafayette** (city) Contra Costa County
21	78	67,898	**Menlo Park** (city) San Mateo County
22	80	67,590	**Coto de Caza** (CDP) Orange County
23	87	66,731	**Calabasas** (city) Los Angeles County
24	100	64,289	**Tamalpais-Homestead Valley** (CDP) Marin County
25	117	61,916	**Danville** (town) Contra Costa County
26	120	61,620	**Rancho Mirage** (city) Riverside County
27	130	59,677	**San Carlos** (city) San Mateo County
28	142	58,927	**Oak Park** (CDP) Ventura County
29	155	57,733	**Rancho Palos Verdes** (city) Los Angeles County
30	160	57,390	**Santa Monica** (city) Los Angeles County
31	165	57,132	**Moraga** (town) Contra Costa County
32	169	57,038	**Burlingame** (city) San Mateo County
33	180	56,606	**North Tustin** (CDP) Orange County
34	186	56,156	**Solana Beach** (city) San Diego County
35	193	55,595	**San Anselmo** (town) Marin County
36	200	55,061	**Granite Bay** (CDP) Placer County
37	205	54,758	**Mountain View** (city) Santa Clara County
38	214	54,193	**West Hollywood** (city) Los Angeles County
39	219	53,968	**Belmont** (city) San Mateo County
40	221	53,941	**Cupertino** (city) Santa Clara County
41	229	53,689	**Redondo Beach** (city) Los Angeles County
42	248	52,638	**Foster City** (city) San Mateo County
43	258	52,174	**Clayton** (city) Contra Costa County
44	265	51,932	**Half Moon Bay** (city) San Mateo County
45	277	51,314	**Walnut Creek** (city) Contra Costa County
46	282	51,091	**San Ramon** (city) Contra Costa County
47	292	50,540	**Pleasanton** (city) Alameda County
48	294	50,492	**Agoura Hills** (city) Los Angeles County
49	295	50,477	**Laguna Niguel** (city) Orange County
50	309	49,771	**Coronado** (city) San Diego County
51	310	49,757	**Rossmoor** (CDP) Orange County
52	313	49,626	**Sierra Madre** (city) Los Angeles County
53	326	49,000	**Dana Point** (city) Orange County
54	332	48,800	**Emeryville** (city) Alameda County
55	343	48,486	**San Francisco** (city) San Francisco County
56	350	48,279	**Yorba Linda** (city) Orange County
57	370	47,909	**Stevenson Ranch** (CDP) Los Angeles County
58	382	47,514	**Ladera Ranch** (CDP) Orange County
59	403	47,043	**South Pasadena** (city) Los Angeles County
60	410	46,797	**Encinitas** (city) San Diego County
61	416	46,662	**San Clemente** (city) Orange County
62	420	46,627	**El Dorado Hills** (CDP) El Dorado County
63	422	46,563	**Discovery Bay** (CDP) Contra Costa County
64	427	46,215	**View Park-Windsor Hills** (CDP) Los Angeles County
65	443	45,977	**Sunnyvale** (city) Santa Clara County
66	453	45,595	**Sonoma** (city) Sonoma County
67	455	45,522	**Thousand Oaks** (city) Ventura County
68	467	45,202	**San Mateo** (city) San Mateo County
69	474	45,069	**San Rafael** (city) Marin County
70	482	45,003	**Culver City** (city) Los Angeles County
71	487	44,865	**Campbell** (city) Santa Clara County
72	498	44,699	**Aliso Viejo** (city) Orange County
73	514	44,343	**Pacific Grove** (city) Monterey County
74	524	44,170	**Seal Beach** (city) Orange County
75	527	44,153	**El Cerrito** (city) Contra Costa County
76	535	44,000	**Novato** (city) Marin County
77	539	43,953	**Pacifica** (city) San Mateo County
78	554	43,736	**Laguna Hills** (city) Orange County
79	570	43,441	**Carlsbad** (city) San Diego County
80	580	43,218	**El Segundo** (city) Los Angeles County
81	583	43,164	**Scotts Valley** (city) Santa Cruz County
82	589	43,096	**Irvine** (city) Orange County
83	595	43,031	**Pleasant Hill** (city) Contra Costa County
84	616	42,715	**Benicia** (city) Solano County
85	619	42,660	**Dublin** (city) Alameda County
86	643	42,213	**Livermore** (city) Alameda County
87	645	42,196	**Huntington Beach** (city) Orange County
88	652	42,042	**Millbrae** (city) San Mateo County
89	658	41,883	**Rancho Santa Margarita** (city) Orange County
90	677	41,612	**Altadena** (CDP) Los Angeles County
91	690	41,340	**Alameda** (city) Alameda County
92	693	41,308	**Berkeley** (city) Alameda County
93	706	41,152	**Pasadena** (city) Los Angeles County
94	718	40,909	**Mission Viejo** (city) Orange County
95	721	40,856	**Alpine** (CDP) San Diego County
96	729	40,749	**Fair Oaks** (CDP) Sacramento County
97	737	40,562	**Redwood City** (city) San Mateo County
98	745	40,507	**Morgan Hill** (city) Santa Clara County
99	753	40,375	**Poway** (city) San Diego County
100	760	40,266	**Palm Desert** (city) Riverside County
101	763	40,190	**Fremont** (city) Alameda County
102	783	39,976	**Rosedale** (CDP) Kern County
103	784	39,967	**Albany** (city) Alameda County
104	785	39,966	**Santa Clara** (city) Santa Clara County
105	795	39,860	**Lake Forest** (city) Orange County
106	829	39,440	**La Crescenta-Montrose** (CDP) Los Angeles County
107	835	39,312	**Laguna Woods** (city) Orange County
108	847	39,169	**Fairview** (CDP) Alameda County
109	848	39,164	**Martinez** (city) Contra Costa County
110	850	39,137	**Arcadia** (city) Los Angeles County
111	872	38,879	**Camarillo** (city) Ventura County
112	883	38,681	**Castro Valley** (CDP) Alameda County
113	905	38,447	**La Quinta** (city) Riverside County
114	912	38,315	**Rancho San Diego** (CDP) San Diego County
115	925	38,117	**San Juan Capistrano** (city) Orange County
116	946	37,930	**Los Alamitos** (city) Orange County
117	948	37,903	**Casa de Oro-Mount Helix** (CDP) San Diego County
118	959	37,821	**Folsom** (city) Sacramento County
119	1015	37,225	**Santa Barbara** (city) Santa Barbara County
120	1020	37,128	**Monterey** (city) Monterey County
121	1027	37,058	**Truckee** (town) Nevada County
122	1043	36,822	**Claremont** (city) Los Angeles County
123	1047	36,793	**Hercules** (city) Contra Costa County
124	1057	36,657	**Castaic** (CDP) Los Angeles County
125	1070	36,516	**Simi Valley** (city) Ventura County
126	1080	36,412	**Auburn** (city) Placer County
127	1095	36,234	**Torrance** (city) Los Angeles County
128	1141	35,850	**Carpinteria** (city) Santa Barbara County
129	1171	35,578	**Palm Springs** (city) Riverside County
130	1197	35,371	**San Bruno** (city) San Mateo County
131	1210	35,232	**San Dimas** (city) Los Angeles County
132	1212	35,224	**Moorpark** (city) Ventura County
133	1215	35,205	**Walnut** (city) Los Angeles County
134	1222	35,158	**Bonita** (CDP) San Diego County
135	1226	35,088	**Petaluma** (city) Sonoma County
136	1244	34,955	**Chino Hills** (city) San Bernardino County
137	1253	34,885	**La Palma** (city) Orange County
138	1263	34,788	**Brea** (city) Orange County
139	1271	34,689	**Pinole** (city) Contra Costa County
140	1275	34,658	**East San Gabriel** (CDP) Los Angeles County
141	1276	34,653	**Cameron Park** (CDP) El Dorado County
142	1328	34,333	**Canyon Lake** (city) Riverside County
143	1331	34,313	**Diamond Bar** (city) Los Angeles County
144	1333	34,290	**Rocklin** (city) Placer County
145	1338	34,238	**Cerritos** (city) Los Angeles County
146	1358	34,100	**Costa Mesa** (city) Orange County
147	1361	34,053	**Fountain Valley** (city) Orange County
148	1364	34,025	**San Jose** (city) Santa Clara County
149	1389	33,818	**Santa Clarita** (city) Los Angeles County
150	1391	33,789	**Milpitas** (city) Santa Clara County

Note: *The state column ranks the top/bottom 150 places from all places in the state with population of 10,000 or more. The national column ranks the top/bottom 150 places from all places in the country with population of 10,000 or more. Places that are unincorporated were not considered in the rankings. Please refer to the User Guide for additional information.*

Per Capita Income

Top 150 Places Ranked in *Ascending* Order

State Rank	Nat'l Rank	Dollars	Place
1	5	8,013	**Avenal** (city) Kings County
2	6	8,182	**Corcoran** (city) Kings County
3	8	8,781	**Mendota** (city) Fresno County
4	9	8,903	**McFarland** (city) Kern County
5	11	9,245	**Isla Vista** (CDP) Santa Barbara County
6	14	9,768	**Muscoy** (CDP) San Bernardino County
7	17	10,098	**Soledad** (city) Monterey County
8	18	10,304	**Arvin** (city) Kern County
9	19	10,453	**Delano** (city) Kern County
10	20	10,501	**Wasco** (city) Kern County
11	22	10,735	**Lamont** (CDP) Kern County
12	24	10,813	**Lindsay** (city) Tulare County
13	27	11,049	**Adelanto** (city) San Bernardino County
14	28	11,060	**Willowbrook** (CDP) Los Angeles County
15	29	11,092	**Parlier** (city) Fresno County
16	31	11,136	**Florence-Graham** (CDP) Los Angeles County
17	32	11,205	**Farmersville** (city) Tulare County
18	34	11,298	**Cudahy** (city) Los Angeles County
19	45	11,632	**Bell Gardens** (city) Los Angeles County
20	47	11,793	**Lennox** (CDP) Los Angeles County
21	50	11,874	**Coachella** (city) Riverside County
22	52	11,890	**Maywood** (city) Los Angeles County
23	56	12,064	**Huntington Park** (city) Los Angeles County
24	57	12,076	**Bell** (city) Los Angeles County
25	58	12,187	**Lynwood** (city) Los Angeles County
26	60	12,234	**Lemon Hill** (CDP) Sacramento County
27	68	12,511	**East Los Angeles** (CDP) Los Angeles County
28	70	12,637	**Walnut Park** (CDP) Los Angeles County
29	75	12,878	**East Rancho Dominguez** (CDP) Los Angeles County
30	80	12,988	**Garden Acres** (CDP) San Joaquin County
31	81	13,005	**Winton** (CDP) Merced County
32	84	13,135	**Chowchilla** (city) Madera County
33	85	13,137	**Calexico** (city) Imperial County
34	86	13,259	**Dinuba** (city) Tulare County
35	90	13,344	**King City** (city) Monterey County
36	92	13,387	**Livingston** (city) Merced County
37	94	13,406	**South San Jose Hills** (CDP) Los Angeles County
38	99	13,548	**Compton** (city) Los Angeles County
39	101	13,666	**Perris** (city) Riverside County
40	102	13,691	**Mead Valley** (CDP) Riverside County
41	106	13,757	**Greenfield** (city) Monterey County
42	110	13,898	**Linda** (CDP) Yuba County
43	112	13,937	**Bloomington** (CDP) San Bernardino County
44	122	14,259	**South Gate** (city) Los Angeles County
45	124	14,291	**South El Monte** (city) Los Angeles County
46	132	14,459	**Madera** (city) Madera County
47	133	14,476	**Paramount** (city) Los Angeles County
48	135	14,520	**Hawaiian Gardens** (city) Los Angeles County
49	139	14,635	**Westmont** (CDP) Los Angeles County
50	147	14,735	**El Monte** (city) Los Angeles County
51	148	14,745	**Desert Hot Springs** (city) Riverside County
52	159	14,879	**San Bernardino** (city) San Bernardino County
53	163	14,911	**Delhi** (CDP) Merced County
54	179	15,314	**Baldwin Park** (city) Los Angeles County
55	181	15,322	**Olivehurst** (CDP) Yuba County
56	185	15,362	**Home Gardens** (CDP) Riverside County
57	188	15,471	**Shafter** (city) Kern County
58	189	15,540	**Colton** (city) San Bernardino County
59	190	15,541	**La Puente** (city) Los Angeles County
60	200	15,724	**Selma** (city) Fresno County
61	221	15,944	**Reedley** (city) Fresno County
62	223	15,948	**Rialto** (city) San Bernardino County
63	225	15,963	**Commerce** (city) Los Angeles County
64	226	15,978	**Sanger** (city) Fresno County
65	228	15,986	**Tehachapi** (city) Kern County
66	232	16,068	**Parkway** (CDP) Sacramento County
67	239	16,177	**Clearlake** (city) Lake County
68	245	16,211	**Florin** (CDP) Sacramento County
69	249	16,239	**Hesperia** (city) San Bernardino County
70	250	16,263	**Watsonville** (city) Santa Cruz County
71	254	16,329	**Blythe** (city) Riverside County
72	261	16,374	**Santa Ana** (city) Orange County
73	267	16,444	**Sun Village** (CDP) Los Angeles County
74	270	16,477	**Victorville** (city) San Bernardino County
75	271	16,494	**Kerman** (city) Fresno County
76	276	16,530	**Susanville** (city) Lassen County
77	279	16,543	**Camp Pendleton South** (CDP) San Diego County
78	282	16,563	**National City** (city) San Diego County
79	293	16,702	**Newman** (city) Stanislaus County
80	299	16,778	**West Puente Valley** (CDP) Los Angeles County
81	310	16,862	**Red Bluff** (city) Tehama County
82	311	16,876	**Merced** (city) Merced County
83	314	16,919	**Lake Los Angeles** (CDP) Los Angeles County
84	329	17,035	**Pomona** (city) Los Angeles County
85	346	17,132	**North Highlands** (CDP) Sacramento County
86	358	17,248	**Porterville** (city) Tulare County
87	363	17,324	**Montclair** (city) San Bernardino County
88	370	17,396	**Salinas** (city) Monterey County
89	379	17,488	**Oildale** (CDP) Kern County
90	380	17,495	**Los Banos** (city) Merced County
91	385	17,541	**Valinda** (CDP) Los Angeles County
92	393	17,581	**Bay Point** (CDP) Contra Costa County
93	394	17,582	**San Pablo** (city) Contra Costa County
94	396	17,595	**Lathrop** (city) San Joaquin County
95	400	17,621	**San Fernando** (city) Los Angeles County
96	410	17,669	**Rosemead** (city) Los Angeles County
97	432	17,787	**San Jacinto** (city) Riverside County
98	437	17,814	**Lawndale** (city) Los Angeles County
99	445	17,852	**Oroville** (city) Butte County
100	456	17,917	**Hemet** (city) Riverside County
101	480	18,047	**Azusa** (city) Los Angeles County
102	482	18,049	**Marysville** (city) Yuba County
103	500	18,186	**Moreno Valley** (city) Riverside County
104	516	18,260	**Tulare** (city) Tulare County
105	520	18,288	**Exeter** (city) Tulare County
106	531	18,385	**East Palo Alto** (city) San Mateo County
107	538	18,467	**Brawley** (city) Imperial County
108	548	18,522	**Ontario** (city) San Bernardino County
109	558	18,560	**Santa Maria** (city) Santa Barbara County
110	559	18,566	**Atwater** (city) Merced County
111	562	18,578	**Citrus** (CDP) Los Angeles County
112	593	18,737	**Coalinga** (city) Fresno County
113	601	18,797	**Palmdale** (city) Los Angeles County
114	611	18,829	**Arcata** (city) Humboldt County
115	619	18,877	**El Centro** (city) Imperial County
116	635	18,971	**Pico Rivera** (city) Los Angeles County
117	644	19,051	**Ceres** (city) Stanislaus County
118	686	19,299	**Fontana** (city) San Bernardino County
119	691	19,331	**Ashland** (CDP) Alameda County
120	711	19,449	**Norwalk** (city) Los Angeles County
121	714	19,455	**Fresno** (city) Fresno County
122	720	19,491	**Bostonia** (CDP) San Diego County
123	729	19,530	**Patterson** (city) Stanislaus County
124	733	19,558	**Santa Paula** (city) Ventura County
125	737	19,577	**Foothill Farms** (CDP) Sacramento County
126	745	19,610	**Lakeland Village** (CDP) Riverside County
127	750	19,623	**Alum Rock** (CDP) Santa Clara County
128	771	19,773	**Shasta Lake** (city) Shasta County
129	773	19,776	**West Whittier-Los Nietos** (CDP) Los Angeles County
130	774	19,779	**Stanton** (city) Orange County
131	782	19,803	**El Cajon** (city) San Diego County
132	784	19,815	**Cathedral City** (city) Riverside County
133	792	19,865	**Lompoc** (city) Santa Barbara County
134	793	19,873	**Barstow** (city) San Bernardino County
135	802	19,896	**South Whittier** (CDP) Los Angeles County
135	802	19,896	**Stockton** (city) San Joaquin County
137	821	19,997	**Lake Elsinore** (city) Riverside County
138	830	20,064	**Fillmore** (city) Ventura County
139	842	20,101	**Riverbank** (city) Stanislaus County
140	846	20,115	**Cherryland** (CDP) Alameda County
141	848	20,121	**Yucca Valley** (town) San Bernardino County
142	855	20,150	**Inglewood** (city) Los Angeles County
143	857	20,156	**Lancaster** (city) Los Angeles County
144	859	20,162	**Hawthorne** (city) Los Angeles County
145	861	20,183	**Imperial Beach** (city) San Diego County
146	902	20,397	**Bellflower** (city) Los Angeles County
147	945	20,605	**Oxnard** (city) Ventura County
148	946	20,607	**Indio** (city) Riverside County
149	948	20,615	**Twentynine Palms** (city) San Bernardino County
150	955	20,650	**Banning** (city) Riverside County

Note: *The state column ranks the top/bottom 150 places from all places in the state with population of 10,000 or more. The national column ranks the top/bottom 150 places from all places in the country with population of 10,000 or more. Places that are unincorporated were not considered in the rankings. Please refer to the User Guide for additional information.*

Median Household Income

Top 150 Places Ranked in *Descending* Order

State Rank	Nat'l Rank	Dollars	Place
1	1	236,528	**Hillsborough** (town) San Mateo County
2	7	207,222	**Piedmont** (city) Alameda County
3	24	164,437	**Orinda** (city) Contra Costa County
4	25	163,889	**Palos Verdes Estates** (city) Los Angeles County
5	26	163,657	**Coto de Caza** (CDP) Orange County
6	33	160,220	**Alamo** (CDP) Contra Costa County
7	35	159,212	**Saratoga** (city) Santa Clara County
8	39	157,907	**Los Altos** (city) Santa Clara County
9	41	156,952	**La Cañada Flintridge** (city) Los Angeles County
10	67	139,259	**Manhattan Beach** (city) Los Angeles County
11	74	136,207	**Lafayette** (city) Contra Costa County
12	75	136,116	**Danville** (town) Contra Costa County
13	89	133,869	**Malibu** (city) Los Angeles County
14	96	131,758	**San Marino** (city) Los Angeles County
15	105	129,976	**Cupertino** (city) Santa Clara County
16	115	128,218	**Oak Park** (CDP) Ventura County
17	119	127,313	**San Ramon** (city) Contra Costa County
18	121	127,159	**Clayton** (city) Contra Costa County
19	122	127,149	**Granite Bay** (CDP) Placer County
20	138	124,583	**Calabasas** (city) Los Angeles County
21	142	124,047	**Ladera Ranch** (CDP) Orange County
22	150	122,662	**North Tustin** (CDP) Orange County
23	152	122,476	**Los Gatos** (town) Santa Clara County
24	156	121,921	**Mill Valley** (city) Marin County
25	159	121,465	**Palo Alto** (city) Santa Clara County
26	169	120,353	**Moraga** (town) Contra Costa County
27	178	119,025	**El Dorado Hills** (CDP) El Dorado County
28	181	118,893	**Rancho Palos Verdes** (city) Los Angeles County
29	183	118,317	**Pleasanton** (city) Alameda County
30	188	118,021	**San Carlos** (city) San Mateo County
31	202	116,655	**Stevenson Ranch** (CDP) Los Angeles County
32	204	115,840	**Tamalpais-Homestead Valley** (CDP) Marin County
33	209	115,236	**Dublin** (city) Alameda County
34	217	114,260	**Foster City** (city) San Mateo County
35	246	112,262	**Menlo Park** (city) San Mateo County
36	247	112,259	**Yorba Linda** (city) Orange County
37	256	111,508	**Discovery Bay** (CDP) Contra Costa County
38	292	108,807	**Rossmoor** (CDP) Orange County
39	309	107,885	**Agoura Hills** (city) Los Angeles County
40	321	107,445	**Eastvale** (city) Riverside County
41	339	106,333	**Newport Beach** (city) Orange County
42	357	105,133	**El Sobrante** (CDP) Riverside County
43	370	104,113	**Rancho Santa Margarita** (city) Orange County
44	376	103,811	**Castaic** (CDP) Los Angeles County
45	402	102,895	**Belmont** (city) San Mateo County
46	415	101,837	**Scotts Valley** (city) Santa Cruz County
47	418	101,655	**Hermosa Beach** (city) Los Angeles County
48	420	101,535	**Fremont** (city) Alameda County
49	422	101,250	**Walnut** (city) Los Angeles County
50	434	100,476	**Thousand Oaks** (city) Ventura County
51	435	100,379	**San Anselmo** (town) Marin County
52	441	100,043	**Sunnyvale** (city) Santa Clara County
53	442	99,958	**Rosedale** (CDP) Kern County
54	445	99,771	**Laguna Niguel** (city) Orange County
55	448	99,715	**Half Moon Bay** (city) San Mateo County
56	455	99,496	**Redondo Beach** (city) Los Angeles County
57	458	99,394	**Aliso Viejo** (city) Orange County
58	467	99,161	**Livermore** (city) Alameda County
59	482	98,359	**Folsom** (city) Sacramento County
60	495	97,338	**Mountain View** (city) Santa Clara County
61	509	96,779	**Moorpark** (city) Ventura County
62	512	96,750	**Hercules** (city) Contra Costa County
63	520	96,497	**Chino Hills** (city) San Bernardino County
64	527	96,210	**Mission Viejo** (city) Orange County
65	546	95,531	**Morgan Hill** (city) Santa Clara County
66	548	95,466	**Milpitas** (city) Santa Clara County
67	567	94,707	**Pacifica** (city) San Mateo County
68	575	94,325	**Laguna Beach** (city) Orange County
69	585	93,856	**Poway** (city) San Diego County
70	591	93,631	**Lake Forest** (city) Orange County
71	614	92,566	**San Diego Country Estates** (CDP) San Diego County
72	624	92,332	**Woodcrest** (CDP) Riverside County
73	643	91,795	**Encinitas** (city) San Diego County
74	646	91,583	**Santa Clara** (city) Santa Clara County
75	648	91,475	**Brentwood** (city) Contra Costa County
76	653	91,220	**Fairview** (CDP) Alameda County
77	658	91,103	**Coronado** (city) San Diego County
78	668	90,704	**Laguna Hills** (city) Orange County
79	673	90,585	**Irvine** (city) Orange County
80	688	90,071	**San Clemente** (city) Orange County
81	698	89,594	**Cerritos** (city) Los Angeles County
82	707	89,375	**La Crescenta-Montrose** (CDP) Los Angeles County
83	717	89,137	**Larkspur** (city) Marin County
84	724	88,837	**Sierra Madre** (city) Los Angeles County
85	735	88,502	**Benicia** (city) Solano County
86	738	88,451	**Millbrae** (city) San Mateo County
87	739	88,422	**Diamond Bar** (city) Los Angeles County
88	743	88,300	**Campbell** (city) Santa Clara County
89	769	87,324	**Claremont** (city) Los Angeles County
90	773	87,269	**Simi Valley** (city) Ventura County
91	802	86,451	**Solana Beach** (city) San Diego County
92	807	86,287	**Camarillo** (city) Ventura County
93	816	86,141	**Beverly Hills** (city) Los Angeles County
94	828	85,847	**Newark** (city) Alameda County
95	833	85,759	**La Palma** (city) Orange County
96	840	85,669	**San Mateo** (city) San Mateo County
97	845	85,481	**El Cerrito** (city) Contra Costa County
98	854	85,058	**South Pasadena** (city) Los Angeles County
99	855	85,055	**French Valley** (CDP) Riverside County
100	857	85,020	**Norco** (city) Riverside County
101	862	84,854	**Burlingame** (city) San Mateo County
102	883	84,341	**El Segundo** (city) Los Angeles County
103	897	83,908	**Carlsbad** (city) San Diego County
104	909	83,230	**American Canyon** (city) Napa County
105	911	83,211	**Castro Valley** (CDP) Alameda County
106	912	83,112	**Martinez** (city) Contra Costa County
107	916	82,895	**Altadena** (CDP) Los Angeles County
108	921	82,679	**Los Alamitos** (city) Orange County
109	928	82,607	**Santa Clarita** (city) Los Angeles County
110	939	82,208	**Bonita** (CDP) San Diego County
111	944	82,083	**Union City** (city) Alameda County
112	949	81,961	**La Mirada** (city) Los Angeles County
113	954	81,829	**San Jose** (city) Santa Clara County
114	964	81,631	**Rancho San Diego** (CDP) San Diego County
115	968	81,593	**Walnut Creek** (city) Contra Costa County
116	975	81,389	**Huntington Beach** (city) Orange County
117	983	81,098	**Windsor** (town) Sonoma County
118	997	80,870	**Fountain Valley** (city) Orange County
119	999	80,833	**Del Aire** (CDP) Los Angeles County
120	1034	80,243	**Petaluma** (city) Sonoma County
121	1039	80,133	**Dana Point** (city) Orange County
122	1050	79,926	**Albany** (city) Alameda County
123	1051	79,896	**View Park-Windsor Hills** (CDP) Los Angeles County
124	1070	79,419	**Redwood City** (city) San Mateo County
125	1083	79,124	**Brea** (city) Orange County
126	1091	78,911	**San Bruno** (city) San Mateo County
127	1094	78,838	**Orange** (city) Orange County
128	1097	78,685	**San Dimas** (city) Los Angeles County
129	1104	78,364	**Cypress** (city) Orange County
130	1105	78,360	**Gilroy** (city) Santa Clara County
131	1106	78,356	**Temecula** (city) Riverside County
132	1109	78,233	**Placentia** (city) Orange County
133	1128	77,835	**Rancho Cucamonga** (city) San Bernardino County
134	1131	77,791	**Elk Grove** (city) Sacramento County
135	1132	77,786	**Lakewood** (city) Los Angeles County
136	1135	77,704	**Arcadia** (city) Los Angeles County
137	1136	77,702	**Novato** (city) Marin County
138	1142	77,526	**Rancho Mirage** (city) Riverside County
139	1154	77,333	**Culver City** (city) Los Angeles County
140	1155	77,326	**Pleasant Hill** (city) Contra Costa County
141	1157	77,315	**Pinole** (city) Contra Costa County
142	1164	77,123	**Corona** (city) Riverside County
143	1168	77,061	**Torrance** (city) Los Angeles County
144	1169	77,043	**Oakley** (city) Contra Costa County
145	1170	77,040	**La Verne** (city) Los Angeles County
146	1171	77,031	**Rocklin** (city) Placer County
147	1178	76,839	**Hacienda Heights** (CDP) Los Angeles County
148	1179	76,833	**Alpine** (CDP) San Diego County
149	1180	76,785	**South San Francisco** (city) San Mateo County
150	1193	76,461	**Casa de Oro-Mount Helix** (CDP) San Diego County

Note: *The state column ranks the top/bottom 150 places from all places in the state with population of 10,000 or more. The national column ranks the top/bottom 150 places from all places in the country with population of 10,000 or more. Places that are unincorporated were not considered in the rankings. Please refer to the User Guide for additional information.*

Median Household Income

Top 150 Places Ranked in *Ascending* Order

State Rank	Nat'l Rank	Dollars	Place
1	19	22,332	**Isla Vista** (CDP) Santa Barbara County
2	26	24,264	**Mendota** (city) Fresno County
3	42	25,061	**Clearlake** (city) Lake County
4	91	27,204	**Lemon Hill** (CDP) Sacramento County
5	150	28,794	**Avenal** (city) Kings County
6	212	30,654	**Westmont** (CDP) Los Angeles County
7	249	31,336	**Arcata** (city) Humboldt County
8	258	31,425	**Lindsay** (city) Tulare County
9	315	32,384	**Farmersville** (city) Tulare County
10	317	32,473	**Desert Hot Springs** (city) Riverside County
11	330	32,705	**Red Bluff** (city) Tehama County
12	336	32,774	**Hemet** (city) Riverside County
13	345	32,914	**Corcoran** (city) Kings County
14	352	32,999	**Arvin** (city) Kern County
15	371	33,305	**Oildale** (CDP) Kern County
16	404	33,777	**Marysville** (city) Yuba County
17	457	34,672	**Lamont** (CDP) Kern County
18	465	34,734	**Linda** (CDP) Yuba County
19	489	35,122	**Delano** (city) Kern County
20	504	35,327	**Parlier** (city) Fresno County
21	509	35,433	**McFarland** (city) Kern County
22	525	35,543	**Florence-Graham** (CDP) Los Angeles County
23	551	35,985	**Bell** (city) Los Angeles County
24	568	36,203	**Grass Valley** (city) Nevada County
25	571	36,236	**Calexico** (city) Imperial County
26	573	36,256	**Parkway** (CDP) Sacramento County
27	584	36,332	**Willowbrook** (CDP) Los Angeles County
28	587	36,397	**Huntington Park** (city) Los Angeles County
29	597	36,618	**Eureka** (city) Humboldt County
30	601	36,652	**Laguna Woods** (city) Orange County
31	612	36,857	**Oroville** (city) Butte County
32	636	37,114	**Maywood** (city) Los Angeles County
33	660	37,466	**Chowchilla** (city) Madera County
34	678	37,659	**Lennox** (CDP) Los Angeles County
35	695	37,822	**Merced** (city) Merced County
36	706	37,933	**National City** (city) San Diego County
37	710	37,982	**East Los Angeles** (CDP) Los Angeles County
38	726	38,170	**Bell Gardens** (city) Los Angeles County
39	730	38,267	**Cudahy** (city) Los Angeles County
40	747	38,385	**San Bernardino** (city) San Bernardino County
41	753	38,438	**Muscoy** (CDP) San Bernardino County
42	766	38,612	**Magalia** (CDP) Butte County
43	774	38,724	**Shasta Lake** (city) Shasta County
44	777	38,768	**Adelanto** (city) San Bernardino County
45	781	38,825	**Banning** (city) Riverside County
46	803	39,061	**Wasco** (city) Kern County
47	804	39,063	**Exeter** (city) Tulare County
48	829	39,328	**Dinuba** (city) Tulare County
49	850	39,535	**El Monte** (city) Los Angeles County
50	858	39,604	**Colton** (city) San Bernardino County
51	861	39,633	**North Highlands** (CDP) Sacramento County
52	870	39,718	**Winton** (CDP) Merced County
53	950	40,739	**Garden Acres** (CDP) San Joaquin County
54	951	40,740	**Lynwood** (city) Los Angeles County
55	964	40,837	**Paradise** (town) Butte County
56	980	40,965	**Coachella** (city) Riverside County
57	982	41,004	**South Lake Tahoe** (city) El Dorado County
58	985	41,026	**Fortuna** (city) Humboldt County
59	1020	41,343	**Florin** (CDP) Sacramento County
60	1022	41,353	**Bostonia** (CDP) San Diego County
61	1032	41,485	**Twentynine Palms** (city) San Bernardino County
62	1034	41,556	**Valle Vista** (CDP) Riverside County
63	1060	41,784	**Brawley** (city) Imperial County
64	1061	41,804	**Yucca Valley** (town) San Bernardino County
65	1064	41,845	**Madera** (city) Madera County
66	1069	41,905	**Porterville** (city) Tulare County
67	1078	41,974	**Shafter** (city) Kern County
68	1081	42,015	**Fresno** (city) Fresno County
69	1083	42,017	**Hawaiian Gardens** (city) Los Angeles County
70	1097	42,158	**Big Bear City** (CDP) San Bernardino County
71	1099	42,162	**Atwater** (city) Merced County
72	1100	42,166	**El Centro** (city) Imperial County
73	1108	42,270	**Walnut Park** (CDP) Los Angeles County
74	1112	42,354	**Barstow** (city) San Bernardino County
75	1120	42,415	**Sanger** (city) Fresno County
76	1140	42,609	**Ukiah** (city) Mendocino County
77	1156	42,776	**South Gate** (city) Los Angeles County
78	1169	42,915	**Olivehurst** (CDP) Yuba County
79	1173	42,953	**Compton** (city) Los Angeles County
80	1182	43,071	**Lakeland Village** (CDP) Riverside County
81	1216	43,324	**Selma** (city) Fresno County
82	1222	43,367	**Mead Valley** (CDP) Riverside County
83	1223	43,372	**Chico** (city) Butte County
84	1226	43,394	**Inglewood** (city) Los Angeles County
85	1231	43,441	**Bay Point** (CDP) Contra Costa County
86	1259	43,750	**Lake Los Angeles** (CDP) Los Angeles County
87	1268	43,905	**Watsonville** (city) Santa Cruz County
88	1271	43,949	**Tehachapi** (city) Kern County
89	1282	44,096	**Placerville** (city) El Dorado County
90	1283	44,104	**South El Monte** (city) Los Angeles County
91	1285	44,107	**Arden-Arcade** (CDP) Sacramento County
92	1287	44,112	**El Cajon** (city) San Diego County
93	1295	44,158	**Hesperia** (city) San Bernardino County
94	1304	44,236	**Redding** (city) Shasta County
95	1318	44,406	**Cathedral City** (city) Riverside County
96	1342	44,649	**Hawthorne** (city) Los Angeles County
97	1349	44,727	**East Rancho Dominguez** (CDP) Los Angeles County
98	1365	44,934	**Paramount** (city) Los Angeles County
99	1371	44,983	**San Pablo** (city) Contra Costa County
100	1375	45,032	**San Luis Obispo** (city) San Luis Obispo County
101	1386	45,198	**Palm Springs** (city) Riverside County
102	1400	45,432	**Foothill Farms** (CDP) Sacramento County
103	1405	45,485	**Tulare** (city) Tulare County
104	1423	45,760	**Rosemead** (city) Los Angeles County
105	1428	45,818	**Lompoc** (city) Santa Barbara County
106	1438	45,905	**King City** (city) Monterey County
107	1481	46,500	**Coalinga** (city) Fresno County
108	1498	46,769	**San Jacinto** (city) Riverside County
109	1505	46,831	**Stockton** (city) San Joaquin County
110	1509	46,856	**Blythe** (city) Riverside County
111	1514	46,939	**North Auburn** (CDP) Placer County
112	1527	47,060	**Modesto** (city) Stanislaus County
113	1535	47,117	**Los Banos** (city) Merced County
114	1538	47,145	**Reedley** (city) Fresno County
115	1545	47,207	**Grover Beach** (city) San Luis Obispo County
116	1551	47,306	**Ceres** (city) Stanislaus County
117	1554	47,346	**Vista** (city) San Diego County
118	1565	47,488	**Montebello** (city) Los Angeles County
119	1586	47,769	**Lawndale** (city) Los Angeles County
120	1597	47,888	**Bloomington** (CDP) San Bernardino County
121	1603	47,923	**Stanton** (city) Orange County
122	1613	48,050	**Crestline** (CDP) San Bernardino County
123	1616	48,053	**Delhi** (CDP) Merced County
124	1620	48,085	**Ashland** (CDP) Alameda County
125	1624	48,121	**Newman** (city) Stanislaus County
126	1634	48,251	**Gardena** (city) Los Angeles County
127	1638	48,311	**Perris** (city) Riverside County
128	1647	48,432	**Apple Valley** (town) San Bernardino County
129	1675	48,701	**Lodi** (city) San Joaquin County
130	1677	48,729	**Commerce** (city) Los Angeles County
131	1691	48,871	**Yuba City** (city) Sutter County
132	1702	49,001	**McKinleyville** (CDP) Humboldt County
133	1726	49,264	**Salinas** (city) Monterey County
134	1727	49,265	**Cherryland** (CDP) Alameda County
135	1728	49,268	**Imperial Beach** (city) San Diego County
136	1735	49,362	**Escondido** (city) San Diego County
137	1742	49,470	**Morro Bay** (city) San Luis Obispo County
138	1743	49,474	**Pomona** (city) Los Angeles County
139	1745	49,497	**Los Angeles** (city) Los Angeles County
140	1749	49,570	**Soledad** (city) Monterey County
141	1751	49,593	**Rialto** (city) San Bernardino County
142	1754	49,634	**Livingston** (city) Merced County
143	1755	49,637	**Bellflower** (city) Los Angeles County
144	1760	49,748	**Kerman** (city) Fresno County
145	1761	49,753	**Sacramento** (city) Sacramento County
146	1778	49,950	**Camp Pendleton South** (CDP) San Diego County
147	1785	50,034	**Victorville** (city) San Bernardino County
148	1789	50,068	**Indio** (city) Riverside County
149	1798	50,142	**East Palo Alto** (city) San Mateo County
150	1804	50,193	**Lancaster** (city) Los Angeles County

Note: *The state column ranks the top/bottom 150 places from all places in the state with population of 10,000 or more. The national column ranks the top/bottom 150 places from all places in the country with population of 10,000 or more. Places that are unincorporated were not considered in the rankings. Please refer to the User Guide for additional information.*

Average Household Income

Top 150 Places Ranked in *Descending* Order

State Rank	Nat'l Rank	Dollars	Place
1	1	361,882	**Hillsborough** (town) San Mateo County
2	9	293,923	**Piedmont** (city) Alameda County
3	22	247,171	**Palos Verdes Estates** (city) Los Angeles County
4	23	245,202	**Malibu** (city) Los Angeles County
5	31	232,943	**La Cañada Flintridge** (city) Los Angeles County
6	36	225,497	**San Marino** (city) Los Angeles County
7	37	223,581	**Los Altos** (city) Santa Clara County
8	44	215,668	**Orinda** (city) Contra Costa County
9	48	209,620	**Alamo** (CDP) Contra Costa County
10	50	208,543	**Saratoga** (city) Santa Clara County
11	54	207,268	**Coto de Caza** (CDP) Orange County
12	60	200,982	**Manhattan Beach** (city) Los Angeles County
13	82	184,635	**Mill Valley** (city) Marin County
14	87	180,566	**Palo Alto** (city) Santa Clara County
15	91	179,752	**Lafayette** (city) Contra Costa County
16	92	179,670	**Calabasas** (city) Los Angeles County
17	97	177,485	**Beverly Hills** (city) Los Angeles County
18	108	173,663	**Menlo Park** (city) San Mateo County
19	109	173,263	**Newport Beach** (city) Orange County
20	119	168,952	**Danville** (town) Contra Costa County
21	127	166,958	**Los Gatos** (town) Santa Clara County
22	134	162,583	**Oak Park** (CDP) Ventura County
23	135	162,446	**North Tustin** (CDP) Orange County
24	140	161,686	**Moraga** (town) Contra Costa County
25	141	161,663	**Granite Bay** (CDP) Placer County
26	146	159,264	**Tamalpais-Homestead Valley** (CDP) Marin County
27	159	155,606	**Laguna Beach** (city) Orange County
28	172	154,268	**Rancho Palos Verdes** (city) Los Angeles County
29	176	153,786	**Cupertino** (city) Santa Clara County
30	183	152,358	**Ladera Ranch** (CDP) Orange County
31	191	150,820	**San Carlos** (city) San Mateo County
32	213	147,573	**San Ramon** (city) Contra Costa County
33	217	146,933	**Stevenson Ranch** (CDP) Los Angeles County
34	227	145,622	**Clayton** (city) Contra Costa County
35	241	142,891	**Pleasanton** (city) Alameda County
36	245	142,705	**Hermosa Beach** (city) Los Angeles County
37	246	142,660	**Larkspur** (city) Marin County
38	255	141,834	**Yorba Linda** (city) Orange County
39	272	139,613	**Agoura Hills** (city) Los Angeles County
40	275	139,159	**Rossmoor** (CDP) Orange County
41	286	137,935	**El Dorado Hills** (CDP) El Dorado County
42	307	135,725	**Foster City** (city) San Mateo County
43	314	134,812	**Burlingame** (city) San Mateo County
44	317	134,755	**Half Moon Bay** (city) San Mateo County
45	318	134,745	**Stanford** (CDP) Santa Clara County
46	327	133,513	**Belmont** (city) San Mateo County
47	366	130,238	**San Anselmo** (town) Marin County
48	370	129,796	**Laguna Niguel** (city) Orange County
49	395	127,290	**Solana Beach** (city) San Diego County
50	396	127,116	**Dublin** (city) Alameda County
51	402	126,738	**Mountain View** (city) Santa Clara County
52	409	126,361	**Discovery Bay** (CDP) Contra Costa County
53	421	125,321	**Thousand Oaks** (city) Ventura County
54	439	124,292	**Redondo Beach** (city) Los Angeles County
55	441	124,199	**Laguna Hills** (city) Orange County
56	448	123,757	**Rancho Mirage** (city) Riverside County
57	459	122,617	**Morgan Hill** (city) Santa Clara County
58	461	122,481	**Rosedale** (CDP) Kern County
59	472	121,335	**Coronado** (city) San Diego County
60	473	121,323	**San Clemente** (city) Orange County
61	476	121,098	**Rancho Santa Margarita** (city) Orange County
62	497	119,865	**Sunnyvale** (city) Santa Clara County
63	502	119,720	**Fremont** (city) Alameda County
64	510	119,220	**Encinitas** (city) San Diego County
65	511	119,071	**Poway** (city) San Diego County
66	524	118,053	**Walnut** (city) Los Angeles County
67	528	117,826	**Sierra Madre** (city) Los Angeles County
68	539	117,000	**Eastvale** (city) Riverside County
69	541	116,857	**Altadena** (CDP) Los Angeles County
70	549	116,498	**Livermore** (city) Alameda County
71	556	116,058	**Scotts Valley** (city) Santa Cruz County
72	560	115,756	**Aliso Viejo** (city) Orange County
73	565	115,518	**South Pasadena** (city) Los Angeles County
74	570	115,296	**Irvine** (city) Orange County
75	572	115,256	**Castaic** (CDP) Los Angeles County
76	575	114,991	**Pacifica** (city) San Mateo County
77	590	114,444	**San Mateo** (city) San Mateo County
78	592	114,345	**San Juan Capistrano** (city) Orange County
79	595	113,992	**El Sobrante** (CDP) Riverside County
80	596	113,976	**Moorpark** (city) Ventura County
81	624	113,097	**Mission Viejo** (city) Orange County
82	632	112,987	**Lake Forest** (city) Orange County
83	634	112,878	**Chino Hills** (city) San Bernardino County
84	638	112,790	**Fairview** (CDP) Alameda County
85	639	112,679	**Milpitas** (city) Santa Clara County
86	667	111,438	**Dana Point** (city) Orange County
87	668	111,422	**San Rafael** (city) Marin County
88	671	111,261	**Millbrae** (city) San Mateo County
89	679	110,750	**Redwood City** (city) San Mateo County
90	689	110,208	**San Francisco** (city) San Francisco County
91	694	110,030	**Arcadia** (city) Los Angeles County
92	696	109,950	**Walnut Creek** (city) Contra Costa County
93	703	109,645	**Santa Monica** (city) Los Angeles County
94	708	109,342	**Claremont** (city) Los Angeles County
95	709	109,340	**Folsom** (city) Sacramento County
96	711	109,266	**La Crescenta-Montrose** (CDP) Los Angeles County
97	714	109,213	**Novato** (city) Marin County
98	720	108,934	**Campbell** (city) Santa Clara County
99	726	108,726	**Santa Clara** (city) Santa Clara County
100	733	108,358	**Carlsbad** (city) San Diego County
101	739	108,016	**Cerritos** (city) Los Angeles County
102	746	107,718	**View Park-Windsor Hills** (CDP) Los Angeles County
103	754	107,267	**Huntington Beach** (city) Orange County
104	755	107,263	**Benicia** (city) Solano County
105	760	107,025	**Hercules** (city) Contra Costa County
106	763	106,906	**Woodcrest** (CDP) Riverside County
107	778	106,175	**Simi Valley** (city) Ventura County
108	780	106,123	**La Palma** (city) Orange County
109	792	105,652	**Diamond Bar** (city) Los Angeles County
110	796	105,466	**El Segundo** (city) Los Angeles County
111	804	105,206	**Camarillo** (city) Ventura County
112	805	105,160	**Los Alamitos** (city) Orange County
113	808	104,976	**Alpine** (CDP) San Diego County
114	812	104,850	**Brentwood** (city) Contra Costa County
115	821	104,618	**Castro Valley** (CDP) Alameda County
116	824	104,448	**San Jose** (city) Santa Clara County
117	869	103,034	**Culver City** (city) Los Angeles County
118	870	103,024	**Rancho San Diego** (CDP) San Diego County
119	890	102,381	**El Cerrito** (city) Contra Costa County
120	900	101,921	**Casa de Oro-Mount Helix** (CDP) San Diego County
121	909	101,665	**Bonita** (CDP) San Diego County
122	911	101,587	**Pleasant Hill** (city) Contra Costa County
123	925	101,241	**Albany** (city) Alameda County
124	927	101,202	**East San Gabriel** (CDP) Los Angeles County
125	951	100,605	**Alameda** (city) Alameda County
126	979	99,734	**San Diego Country Estates** (CDP) San Diego County
127	980	99,695	**Pasadena** (city) Los Angeles County
128	996	99,286	**American Canyon** (city) Napa County
129	1005	99,137	**Santa Clarita** (city) Los Angeles County
130	1032	98,311	**Fountain Valley** (city) Orange County
131	1039	98,114	**Norco** (city) Riverside County
132	1050	97,762	**Fair Oaks** (CDP) Sacramento County
133	1051	97,756	**San Dimas** (city) Los Angeles County
134	1054	97,662	**Martinez** (city) Contra Costa County
135	1055	97,635	**Berkeley** (city) Alameda County
136	1063	97,434	**Union City** (city) Alameda County
137	1068	97,270	**Orange** (city) Orange County
138	1077	96,987	**Pacific Grove** (city) Monterey County
139	1095	96,493	**Newark** (city) Alameda County
140	1100	96,431	**La Quinta** (city) Riverside County
141	1105	96,227	**Cypress** (city) Orange County
142	1107	96,152	**Rancho Cucamonga** (city) San Bernardino County
143	1115	95,897	**Gilroy** (city) Santa Clara County
144	1116	95,888	**Brea** (city) Orange County
145	1127	95,721	**San Bruno** (city) San Mateo County
146	1136	95,373	**Pinole** (city) Contra Costa County
147	1150	94,977	**La Mirada** (city) Los Angeles County
148	1151	94,932	**Sonoma** (city) Sonoma County
149	1154	94,769	**Ripon** (city) San Joaquin County
150	1156	94,754	**La Verne** (city) Los Angeles County

Note: *The state column ranks the top/bottom 150 places from all places in the state with population of 10,000 or more. The national column ranks the top/bottom 150 places from all places in the country with population of 10,000 or more. Places that are unincorporated were not considered in the rankings. Please refer to the User Guide for additional information.*

Average Household Income

Top 150 Places Ranked in *Ascending* Order

State Rank	Nat'l Rank	Dollars	Place
1	13	32,067	**Mendota** (city) Fresno County
2	27	34,846	**Isla Vista** (CDP) Santa Barbara County
3	32	35,392	**Clearlake** (city) Lake County
4	38	36,247	**Avenal** (city) Kings County
5	39	36,563	**Lemon Hill** (CDP) Sacramento County
6	100	39,697	**McFarland** (city) Kern County
7	171	41,952	**Lindsay** (city) Tulare County
8	182	42,272	**Arvin** (city) Kern County
9	187	42,361	**Desert Hot Springs** (city) Riverside County
10	192	42,429	**Muscoy** (CDP) San Bernardino County
11	202	42,680	**Farmersville** (city) Tulare County
12	208	42,864	**Willowbrook** (CDP) Los Angeles County
13	223	43,256	**Westmont** (CDP) Los Angeles County
14	231	43,447	**Bell** (city) Los Angeles County
15	235	43,598	**Parlier** (city) Fresno County
16	237	43,667	**Linda** (CDP) Yuba County
17	246	43,907	**Corcoran** (city) Kings County
18	253	43,971	**Adelanto** (city) San Bernardino County
19	284	44,605	**Cudahy** (city) Los Angeles County
20	300	44,816	**Red Bluff** (city) Tehama County
21	301	44,818	**Florence-Graham** (CDP) Los Angeles County
22	312	44,986	**Huntington Park** (city) Los Angeles County
23	318	45,041	**Lamont** (CDP) Kern County
24	320	45,077	**Hemet** (city) Riverside County
25	363	45,732	**Oildale** (CDP) Kern County
26	388	46,187	**Arcata** (city) Humboldt County
27	396	46,273	**Lennox** (CDP) Los Angeles County
28	410	46,419	**Bell Gardens** (city) Los Angeles County
29	422	46,608	**Wasco** (city) Kern County
30	431	46,658	**East Los Angeles** (CDP) Los Angeles County
31	439	46,755	**Delano** (city) Kern County
32	463	47,048	**Marysville** (city) Yuba County
33	469	47,121	**Maywood** (city) Los Angeles County
34	499	47,527	**Eureka** (city) Humboldt County
35	514	47,734	**Winton** (CDP) Merced County
36	536	48,173	**Garden Acres** (CDP) San Joaquin County
37	555	48,388	**Magalia** (CDP) Butte County
38	557	48,398	**Shasta Lake** (city) Shasta County
39	562	48,436	**Oroville** (city) Butte County
40	571	48,566	**Banning** (city) Riverside County
41	579	48,658	**North Highlands** (CDP) Sacramento County
42	614	48,935	**Dinuba** (city) Tulare County
43	626	49,085	**Coachella** (city) Riverside County
44	654	49,473	**Calexico** (city) Imperial County
45	664	49,660	**National City** (city) San Diego County
46	670	49,732	**Olivehurst** (CDP) Yuba County
47	679	49,812	**Parkway** (CDP) Sacramento County
48	696	50,025	**San Bernardino** (city) San Bernardino County
49	743	50,676	**Lynwood** (city) Los Angeles County
50	790	51,352	**Madera** (city) Madera County
51	792	51,361	**Florin** (CDP) Sacramento County
52	809	51,587	**Yucca Valley** (town) San Bernardino County
53	834	52,012	**Colton** (city) San Bernardino County
54	840	52,035	**Walnut Park** (CDP) Los Angeles County
55	851	52,123	**Compton** (city) Los Angeles County
56	857	52,173	**Hawaiian Gardens** (city) Los Angeles County
57	876	52,424	**Big Bear City** (CDP) San Bernardino County
58	883	52,547	**Twentynine Palms** (city) San Bernardino County
59	884	52,560	**Merced** (city) Merced County
60	903	52,809	**El Monte** (city) Los Angeles County
61	937	53,114	**Paradise** (town) Butte County
62	939	53,169	**Paramount** (city) Los Angeles County
63	941	53,185	**Foothill Farms** (CDP) Sacramento County
64	958	53,366	**South Gate** (city) Los Angeles County
65	978	53,694	**Barstow** (city) San Bernardino County
66	980	53,767	**Chowchilla** (city) Madera County
67	1047	54,475	**Selma** (city) Fresno County
68	1048	54,477	**Delhi** (CDP) Merced County
69	1051	54,507	**Camp Pendleton South** (CDP) San Diego County
70	1058	54,534	**Bostonia** (CDP) San Diego County
71	1061	54,543	**Hesperia** (city) San Bernardino County
72	1066	54,607	**East Rancho Dominguez** (CDP) Los Angeles County
73	1073	54,663	**Perris** (city) Riverside County
74	1077	54,686	**Mead Valley** (CDP) Riverside County
75	1095	54,970	**Tehachapi** (city) Kern County
76	1098	55,020	**Porterville** (city) Tulare County
77	1103	55,085	**Livingston** (city) Merced County
78	1109	55,151	**Shafter** (city) Kern County
79	1112	55,183	**Grass Valley** (city) Nevada County
80	1125	55,348	**San Pablo** (city) Contra Costa County
81	1130	55,395	**South Lake Tahoe** (city) El Dorado County
82	1138	55,523	**Laguna Woods** (city) Orange County
83	1145	55,589	**Newman** (city) Stanislaus County
84	1172	55,845	**Exeter** (city) Tulare County
85	1192	56,062	**South El Monte** (city) Los Angeles County
86	1196	56,087	**Sanger** (city) Fresno County
87	1243	56,701	**San Jacinto** (city) Riverside County
88	1261	56,923	**Bay Point** (CDP) Contra Costa County
89	1262	56,932	**Ashland** (CDP) Alameda County
90	1274	57,075	**Bloomington** (CDP) San Bernardino County
91	1277	57,114	**Hawthorne** (city) Los Angeles County
92	1299	57,350	**Commerce** (city) Los Angeles County
93	1313	57,476	**King City** (city) Monterey County
94	1324	57,581	**Lawndale** (city) Los Angeles County
95	1339	57,780	**Inglewood** (city) Los Angeles County
96	1344	57,817	**Watsonville** (city) Santa Cruz County
97	1351	57,907	**El Cajon** (city) San Diego County
98	1366	58,025	**Imperial Beach** (city) San Diego County
99	1375	58,127	**Valle Vista** (CDP) Riverside County
100	1384	58,269	**Victorville** (city) San Bernardino County
101	1393	58,358	**Ukiah** (city) Mendocino County
102	1400	58,466	**Redding** (city) Shasta County
103	1420	58,659	**Chico** (city) Butte County
104	1421	58,691	**Tulare** (city) Tulare County
105	1433	58,850	**Fresno** (city) Fresno County
106	1434	58,853	**Fortuna** (city) Humboldt County
107	1465	59,280	**Lake Los Angeles** (CDP) Los Angeles County
108	1468	59,285	**Cathedral City** (city) Riverside County
109	1469	59,291	**Brawley** (city) Imperial County
110	1473	59,336	**Lakeland Village** (CDP) Riverside County
111	1484	59,478	**Home Gardens** (CDP) Riverside County
112	1496	59,689	**Los Banos** (city) Merced County
113	1501	59,745	**Lompoc** (city) Santa Barbara County
114	1504	59,753	**Reedley** (city) Fresno County
115	1505	59,783	**Sun Village** (CDP) Los Angeles County
116	1506	59,804	**Rialto** (city) San Bernardino County
117	1510	59,868	**Atwater** (city) Merced County
118	1515	59,975	**Susanville** (city) Lassen County
119	1516	59,988	**Montclair** (city) San Bernardino County
120	1527	60,166	**Crestline** (CDP) San Bernardino County
121	1543	60,391	**El Centro** (city) Imperial County
122	1562	60,752	**South San Jose Hills** (CDP) Los Angeles County
123	1564	60,768	**California City** (city) Kern County
124	1620	61,340	**Rosemead** (city) Los Angeles County
125	1631	61,514	**Greenfield** (city) Monterey County
126	1634	61,549	**Placerville** (city) El Dorado County
127	1637	61,576	**Vista** (city) San Diego County
128	1643	61,649	**Baldwin Park** (city) Los Angeles County
129	1647	61,755	**Pomona** (city) Los Angeles County
130	1654	61,818	**Stanton** (city) Orange County
131	1659	61,911	**McKinleyville** (CDP) Humboldt County
132	1670	62,045	**North Auburn** (CDP) Placer County
133	1671	62,083	**La Puente** (city) Los Angeles County
134	1674	62,090	**Lemon Grove** (city) San Diego County
135	1676	62,112	**Salinas** (city) Monterey County
136	1681	62,169	**Blythe** (city) Riverside County
137	1687	62,206	**Phelan** (CDP) San Bernardino County
138	1698	62,338	**Grover Beach** (city) San Luis Obispo County
139	1703	62,366	**Cherryland** (CDP) Alameda County
140	1737	62,710	**Stockton** (city) San Joaquin County
141	1740	62,730	**Rosemont** (CDP) Sacramento County
142	1743	62,775	**Kerman** (city) Fresno County
143	1746	62,822	**Gardena** (city) Los Angeles County
144	1752	62,919	**Citrus Heights** (city) Sacramento County
145	1754	62,927	**Ceres** (city) Stanislaus County
146	1773	63,244	**Coalinga** (city) Fresno County
147	1774	63,272	**San Fernando** (city) Los Angeles County
148	1787	63,406	**Soledad** (city) Monterey County
149	1796	63,549	**Bellflower** (city) Los Angeles County
150	1797	63,569	**Lancaster** (city) Los Angeles County

Note: *The state column ranks the top/bottom 150 places from all places in the state with population of 10,000 or more. The national column ranks the top/bottom 150 places from all places in the country with population of 10,000 or more. Places that are unincorporated were not considered in the rankings. Please refer to the User Guide for additional information.*

Households with Income of $100,000 or More

Top 150 Places Ranked in *Descending* Order

State Rank	Nat'l Rank	Percent	Place
1	2	83.2	**Hillsborough** (town) San Mateo County
2	9	77.9	**Piedmont** (city) Alameda County
3	28	71.6	**Orinda** (city) Contra Costa County
4	31	71.2	**La Cañada Flintridge** (city) Los Angeles County
5	37	70.8	**Coto de Caza** (CDP) Orange County
6	39	70.4	**Alamo** (CDP) Contra Costa County
7	43	69.4	**Saratoga** (city) Santa Clara County
8	61	67.0	**Palos Verdes Estates** (city) Los Angeles County
9	72	66.1	**Los Altos** (city) Santa Clara County
10	78	65.4	**Manhattan Beach** (city) Los Angeles County
11	85	64.7	**San Ramon** (city) Contra Costa County
12	88	64.5	**Ladera Ranch** (CDP) Orange County
13	92	64.2	**Cupertino** (city) Santa Clara County
14	95	64.1	**Clayton** (city) Contra Costa County
15	98	64.0	**Danville** (town) Contra Costa County
16	117	62.7	**Malibu** (city) Los Angeles County
17	122	62.1	**North Tustin** (CDP) Orange County
17	122	62.1	**San Marino** (city) Los Angeles County
19	132	61.4	**Lafayette** (city) Contra Costa County
19	132	61.4	**Oak Park** (CDP) Ventura County
21	146	60.5	**Granite Bay** (CDP) Placer County
22	153	59.9	**Calabasas** (city) Los Angeles County
23	171	59.0	**Tamalpais-Homestead Valley** (CDP) Marin County
24	178	58.8	**Stevenson Ranch** (CDP) Los Angeles County
25	179	58.7	**Dublin** (city) Alameda County
26	182	58.6	**El Dorado Hills** (CDP) El Dorado County
27	186	58.5	**Moraga** (town) Contra Costa County
27	186	58.5	**Palo Alto** (city) Santa Clara County
29	189	58.3	**Rancho Palos Verdes** (city) Los Angeles County
30	193	58.2	**Pleasanton** (city) Alameda County
31	197	57.9	**Mill Valley** (city) Marin County
32	203	57.6	**Foster City** (city) San Mateo County
33	221	56.9	**Yorba Linda** (city) Orange County
34	229	56.5	**Los Gatos** (town) Santa Clara County
35	237	56.2	**Discovery Bay** (CDP) Contra Costa County
36	238	56.1	**Menlo Park** (city) San Mateo County
37	283	54.9	**San Carlos** (city) San Mateo County
38	286	54.7	**Agoura Hills** (city) Los Angeles County
39	301	54.3	**Eastvale** (city) Riverside County
40	320	53.9	**Castaic** (CDP) Los Angeles County
41	343	53.0	**Newport Beach** (city) Orange County
42	348	52.9	**Rancho Santa Margarita** (city) Orange County
43	349	52.8	**Rossmoor** (CDP) Orange County
44	358	52.6	**El Sobrante** (CDP) Riverside County
45	387	52.0	**Scotts Valley** (city) Santa Cruz County
46	413	51.0	**Hermosa Beach** (city) Los Angeles County
47	414	50.9	**Fremont** (city) Alameda County
48	418	50.8	**Belmont** (city) San Mateo County
49	425	50.5	**Walnut** (city) Los Angeles County
50	430	50.3	**Thousand Oaks** (city) Ventura County
51	436	50.1	**San Anselmo** (town) Marin County
52	440	50.0	**Laguna Niguel** (city) Orange County
52	440	50.0	**Rosedale** (CDP) Kern County
52	440	50.0	**Sunnyvale** (city) Santa Clara County
55	455	49.7	**Aliso Viejo** (city) Orange County
55	455	49.7	**Half Moon Bay** (city) San Mateo County
55	455	49.7	**Redondo Beach** (city) Los Angeles County
58	463	49.6	**Livermore** (city) Alameda County
59	477	49.2	**Mountain View** (city) Santa Clara County
60	482	49.1	**Folsom** (city) Sacramento County
61	521	48.2	**Moorpark** (city) Ventura County
62	526	48.1	**Chino Hills** (city) San Bernardino County
62	526	48.1	**Hercules** (city) Contra Costa County
62	526	48.1	**Milpitas** (city) Santa Clara County
62	526	48.1	**Mission Viejo** (city) Orange County
66	545	47.8	**Laguna Beach** (city) Orange County
67	561	47.4	**Pacifica** (city) San Mateo County
68	564	47.3	**Lake Forest** (city) Orange County
69	574	47.0	**Fairview** (CDP) Alameda County
69	574	47.0	**Poway** (city) San Diego County
71	580	46.9	**Morgan Hill** (city) Santa Clara County
72	584	46.7	**Brentwood** (city) Contra Costa County
73	599	46.3	**Encinitas** (city) San Diego County
73	599	46.3	**Woodcrest** (CDP) Riverside County
75	606	46.2	**Coronado** (city) San Diego County
76	619	46.0	**Santa Clara** (city) Santa Clara County
77	637	45.5	**Irvine** (city) Orange County
78	644	45.3	**Beverly Hills** (city) Los Angeles County
79	657	44.9	**Laguna Hills** (city) Orange County
80	660	44.8	**San Clemente** (city) Orange County
81	668	44.6	**Cerritos** (city) Los Angeles County
82	674	44.5	**Benicia** (city) Solano County
83	680	44.3	**Solana Beach** (city) San Diego County
84	685	44.2	**Claremont** (city) Los Angeles County
84	685	44.2	**San Diego Country Estates** (CDP) San Diego County
84	685	44.2	**Simi Valley** (city) Ventura County
87	693	44.1	**La Crescenta-Montrose** (CDP) Los Angeles County
87	693	44.1	**Larkspur** (city) Marin County
87	693	44.1	**Sierra Madre** (city) Los Angeles County
90	717	43.7	**Campbell** (city) Santa Clara County
91	730	43.5	**Diamond Bar** (city) Los Angeles County
92	747	43.0	**Carlsbad** (city) San Diego County
92	747	43.0	**Millbrae** (city) San Mateo County
94	775	42.6	**Burlingame** (city) San Mateo County
95	782	42.5	**San Mateo** (city) San Mateo County
96	794	42.3	**El Segundo** (city) Los Angeles County
97	805	42.1	**Camarillo** (city) Ventura County
98	815	42.0	**South Pasadena** (city) Los Angeles County
99	827	41.9	**Castro Valley** (CDP) Alameda County
100	846	41.4	**Altadena** (CDP) Los Angeles County
100	846	41.4	**Union City** (city) Alameda County
102	849	41.3	**La Palma** (city) Orange County
103	861	41.1	**El Cerrito** (city) Contra Costa County
103	861	41.1	**Newark** (city) Alameda County
105	874	40.9	**Redwood City** (city) San Mateo County
106	879	40.8	**San Jose** (city) Santa Clara County
106	879	40.8	**View Park-Windsor Hills** (CDP) Los Angeles County
108	885	40.7	**Dana Point** (city) Orange County
108	885	40.7	**Martinez** (city) Contra Costa County
108	885	40.7	**Norco** (city) Riverside County
111	891	40.6	**American Canyon** (city) Napa County
111	891	40.6	**Walnut Creek** (city) Contra Costa County
113	898	40.5	**Huntington Beach** (city) Orange County
114	902	40.4	**Albany** (city) Alameda County
115	910	40.3	**Los Alamitos** (city) Orange County
116	920	40.1	**Novato** (city) Marin County
117	923	40.0	**Rancho Mirage** (city) Riverside County
118	950	39.5	**Fountain Valley** (city) Orange County
119	956	39.4	**Arcadia** (city) Los Angeles County
119	956	39.4	**San Francisco** (city) San Francisco County
121	963	39.3	**Alpine** (CDP) San Diego County
121	963	39.3	**Pleasant Hill** (city) Contra Costa County
123	970	39.2	**Stanford** (CDP) Santa Clara County
124	977	39.1	**Brea** (city) Orange County
125	987	39.0	**Culver City** (city) Los Angeles County
125	987	39.0	**La Mirada** (city) Los Angeles County
127	1000	38.8	**Casa de Oro-Mount Helix** (CDP) San Diego County
128	1010	38.6	**San Juan Capistrano** (city) Orange County
129	1018	38.5	**Santa Clarita** (city) Los Angeles County
130	1029	38.3	**Bonita** (CDP) San Diego County
130	1029	38.3	**Cypress** (city) Orange County
132	1040	38.1	**French Valley** (CDP) Riverside County
132	1040	38.1	**Santa Monica** (city) Los Angeles County
134	1049	38.0	**Gilroy** (city) Santa Clara County
134	1049	38.0	**San Dimas** (city) Los Angeles County
136	1056	37.9	**Orange** (city) Orange County
136	1056	37.9	**Placentia** (city) Orange County
138	1077	37.6	**La Verne** (city) Los Angeles County
138	1077	37.6	**Rancho Cucamonga** (city) San Bernardino County
140	1084	37.5	**San Bruno** (city) San Mateo County
140	1084	37.5	**Windsor** (town) Sonoma County
142	1092	37.4	**Petaluma** (city) Sonoma County
142	1092	37.4	**Ripon** (city) San Joaquin County
144	1114	37.2	**San Rafael** (city) Marin County
145	1121	37.0	**Oakley** (city) Contra Costa County
146	1124	36.9	**Fair Oaks** (CDP) Sacramento County
147	1131	36.8	**Rancho San Diego** (CDP) San Diego County
148	1139	36.7	**Rocklin** (city) Placer County
148	1139	36.7	**South San Francisco** (city) San Mateo County
150	1148	36.6	**Vineyard** (CDP) Sacramento County

Note: *The state column ranks the top/bottom 150 places from all places in the state with population of 10,000 or more. The national column ranks the top/bottom 150 places from all places in the country with population of 10,000 or more. Places that are unincorporated were not considered in the rankings. Please refer to the User Guide for additional information.*

Households with Income of $100,000 or More

Top 150 Places Ranked in *Ascending* Order

State Rank	Nat'l Rank	Percent	Place
1	5	1.8	**Mendota** (city) Fresno County
2	35	3.8	**Muscoy** (CDP) San Bernardino County
3	37	3.9	**McFarland** (city) Kern County
4	54	4.6	**Clearlake** (city) Lake County
5	99	5.5	**Cudahy** (city) Los Angeles County
5	99	5.5	**Farmersville** (city) Tulare County
7	105	5.6	**Avenal** (city) Kings County
8	117	5.7	**Lemon Hill** (CDP) Sacramento County
9	154	6.3	**Lindsay** (city) Tulare County
9	154	6.3	**Marysville** (city) Yuba County
9	154	6.3	**Olivehurst** (CDP) Yuba County
12	188	6.7	**Huntington Park** (city) Los Angeles County
12	188	6.7	**Isla Vista** (CDP) Santa Barbara County
14	199	6.8	**Dinuba** (city) Tulare County
15	206	6.9	**Adelanto** (city) San Bernardino County
15	206	6.9	**Bell** (city) Los Angeles County
17	213	7.0	**Corcoran** (city) Kings County
18	227	7.1	**Parlier** (city) Fresno County
19	238	7.2	**Bell Gardens** (city) Los Angeles County
20	245	7.3	**Arvin** (city) Kern County
21	257	7.4	**Florence-Graham** (CDP) Los Angeles County
21	257	7.4	**Oildale** (CDP) Kern County
23	270	7.5	**Willowbrook** (CDP) Los Angeles County
24	281	7.6	**Red Bluff** (city) Tehama County
25	317	7.9	**Linda** (CDP) Yuba County
26	334	8.0	**Desert Hot Springs** (city) Riverside County
27	344	8.1	**Garden Acres** (CDP) San Joaquin County
27	344	8.1	**Lennox** (CDP) Los Angeles County
29	375	8.3	**Camp Pendleton South** (CDP) San Diego County
30	386	8.4	**East Los Angeles** (CDP) Los Angeles County
31	401	8.5	**Coachella** (city) Riverside County
32	414	8.6	**Hemet** (city) Riverside County
32	414	8.6	**Maywood** (city) Los Angeles County
34	431	8.7	**Oroville** (city) Butte County
34	431	8.7	**Wasco** (city) Kern County
34	431	8.7	**Winton** (CDP) Merced County
37	449	8.8	**Banning** (city) Riverside County
37	449	8.8	**Magalia** (CDP) Butte County
39	488	9.1	**Westmont** (CDP) Los Angeles County
40	519	9.3	**Delano** (city) Kern County
41	538	9.4	**Eureka** (city) Humboldt County
41	538	9.4	**Livingston** (city) Merced County
43	586	9.7	**Grass Valley** (city) Nevada County
43	586	9.7	**North Highlands** (CDP) Sacramento County
45	621	9.9	**Lynwood** (city) Los Angeles County
46	633	10.0	**Lamont** (CDP) Kern County
47	719	10.5	**Florin** (CDP) Sacramento County
48	741	10.6	**National City** (city) San Diego County
49	764	10.7	**Calexico** (city) Imperial County
50	779	10.8	**Twentynine Palms** (city) San Bernardino County
51	803	10.9	**Yucca Valley** (town) San Bernardino County
52	826	11.1	**Arcata** (city) Humboldt County
52	826	11.1	**Bloomington** (CDP) San Bernardino County
52	826	11.1	**Paramount** (city) Los Angeles County
52	826	11.1	**Shafter** (city) Kern County
56	847	11.2	**Laguna Woods** (city) Orange County
57	862	11.3	**Hawaiian Gardens** (city) Los Angeles County
58	878	11.4	**South Gate** (city) Los Angeles County
59	894	11.5	**Compton** (city) Los Angeles County
60	919	11.6	**Perris** (city) Riverside County
60	919	11.6	**San Bernardino** (city) San Bernardino County
62	951	11.8	**Shasta Lake** (city) Shasta County
63	966	11.9	**Madera** (city) Madera County
63	966	11.9	**Parkway** (CDP) Sacramento County
65	986	12.0	**Selma** (city) Fresno County
66	1004	12.1	**El Monte** (city) Los Angeles County
67	1025	12.2	**Atwater** (city) Merced County
67	1025	12.2	**Colton** (city) San Bernardino County
67	1025	12.2	**East Rancho Dominguez** (CDP) Los Angeles County
70	1055	12.3	**Foothill Farms** (CDP) Sacramento County
70	1055	12.3	**Sun Village** (CDP) Los Angeles County
72	1076	12.4	**Fortuna** (city) Humboldt County
73	1105	12.6	**Delhi** (CDP) Merced County
73	1105	12.6	**Lawndale** (city) Los Angeles County
75	1126	12.7	**Big Bear City** (CDP) San Bernardino County
76	1149	12.9	**Hawthorne** (city) Los Angeles County
76	1149	12.9	**Merced** (city) Merced County
76	1149	12.9	**South El Monte** (city) Los Angeles County
79	1163	13.0	**Ukiah** (city) Mendocino County
79	1163	13.0	**Walnut Park** (CDP) Los Angeles County
81	1179	13.1	**Porterville** (city) Tulare County
82	1194	13.2	**Bostonia** (CDP) San Diego County
83	1209	13.3	**Paradise** (town) Butte County
84	1243	13.5	**Chowchilla** (city) Madera County
84	1243	13.5	**Greenfield** (city) Monterey County
84	1243	13.5	**Imperial Beach** (city) San Diego County
87	1265	13.6	**South Lake Tahoe** (city) El Dorado County
88	1275	13.7	**Bay Point** (CDP) Contra Costa County
88	1275	13.7	**Hesperia** (city) San Bernardino County
88	1275	13.7	**San Pablo** (city) Contra Costa County
91	1310	14.0	**Ashland** (CDP) Alameda County
91	1310	14.0	**Exeter** (city) Tulare County
93	1324	14.1	**Barstow** (city) San Bernardino County
93	1324	14.1	**Inglewood** (city) Los Angeles County
93	1324	14.1	**San Jacinto** (city) Riverside County
96	1340	14.2	**Brawley** (city) Imperial County
97	1354	14.3	**Reedley** (city) Fresno County
98	1362	14.4	**Ceres** (city) Stanislaus County
99	1389	14.6	**Tulare** (city) Tulare County
99	1389	14.6	**Watsonville** (city) Santa Cruz County
101	1403	14.7	**Home Gardens** (CDP) Riverside County
101	1403	14.7	**Lake Los Angeles** (CDP) Los Angeles County
101	1403	14.7	**Susanville** (city) Lassen County
101	1403	14.7	**Valle Vista** (CDP) Riverside County
105	1423	14.8	**Baldwin Park** (city) Los Angeles County
105	1423	14.8	**South San Jose Hills** (CDP) Los Angeles County
107	1437	14.9	**King City** (city) Monterey County
108	1452	15.0	**Cherryland** (CDP) Alameda County
108	1452	15.0	**Rialto** (city) San Bernardino County
110	1479	15.2	**Cathedral City** (city) Riverside County
111	1490	15.3	**Los Banos** (city) Merced County
112	1504	15.4	**Commerce** (city) Los Angeles County
112	1504	15.4	**Redding** (city) Shasta County
114	1531	15.6	**Citrus Heights** (city) Sacramento County
114	1531	15.6	**Sanger** (city) Fresno County
116	1545	15.7	**Fresno** (city) Fresno County
117	1554	15.8	**El Cajon** (city) San Diego County
117	1554	15.8	**Montclair** (city) San Bernardino County
117	1554	15.8	**Rosemead** (city) Los Angeles County
120	1568	15.9	**Crestline** (CDP) San Bernardino County
121	1610	16.2	**La Puente** (city) Los Angeles County
121	1610	16.2	**Pomona** (city) Los Angeles County
123	1626	16.3	**Vista** (city) San Diego County
124	1643	16.5	**Placerville** (city) El Dorado County
124	1643	16.5	**Victorville** (city) San Bernardino County
126	1661	16.6	**Chico** (city) Butte County
126	1661	16.6	**San Fernando** (city) Los Angeles County
126	1661	16.6	**Tehachapi** (city) Kern County
129	1673	16.7	**Newman** (city) Stanislaus County
130	1707	17.0	**Lemon Grove** (city) San Diego County
131	1719	17.1	**Salinas** (city) Monterey County
132	1728	17.2	**Lompoc** (city) Santa Barbara County
132	1728	17.2	**McKinleyville** (CDP) Humboldt County
134	1769	17.5	**Rosemont** (CDP) Sacramento County
135	1781	17.6	**Lakeland Village** (CDP) Riverside County
136	1792	17.7	**Mead Valley** (CDP) Riverside County
137	1815	17.9	**Galt** (city) Sacramento County
138	1834	18.0	**Lancaster** (city) Los Angeles County
138	1834	18.0	**Stanton** (city) Orange County
140	1856	18.2	**Grover Beach** (city) San Luis Obispo County
141	1873	18.3	**Santa Maria** (city) Santa Barbara County
142	1885	18.4	**Kerman** (city) Fresno County
143	1897	18.5	**Lathrop** (city) San Joaquin County
143	1897	18.5	**Modesto** (city) Stanislaus County
143	1897	18.5	**Ontario** (city) San Bernardino County
146	1909	18.6	**Gardena** (city) Los Angeles County
146	1909	18.6	**Stockton** (city) San Joaquin County
148	1927	18.7	**El Centro** (city) Imperial County
149	1935	18.8	**Bellflower** (city) Los Angeles County
150	1947	18.9	**Azusa** (city) Los Angeles County

Note: *The state column ranks the top/bottom 150 places from all places in the state with population of 10,000 or more. The national column ranks the top/bottom 150 places from all places in the country with population of 10,000 or more. Places that are unincorporated were not considered in the rankings. Please refer to the User Guide for additional information.*

Poverty Rate

Top 150 Places Ranked in *Descending* Order

State Rank	Nat'l Rank	Percent	Place
1	1	62.8	**Isla Vista** (CDP) Santa Barbara County
2	13	47.4	**Mendota** (city) Fresno County
3	35	42.5	**Lindsay** (city) Tulare County
4	49	40.4	**Avenal** (city) Kings County
5	62	38.6	**Lemon Hill** (CDP) Sacramento County
6	95	36.3	**Clearlake** (city) Lake County
7	111	35.5	**Parlier** (city) Fresno County
8	133	34.4	**Westmont** (CDP) Los Angeles County
9	145	34.1	**Arcata** (city) Humboldt County
10	156	33.7	**Adelanto** (city) San Bernardino County
11	168	33.1	**Willowbrook** (CDP) Los Angeles County
12	171	32.9	**Farmersville** (city) Tulare County
12	171	32.9	**McFarland** (city) Kern County
14	179	32.7	**Arvin** (city) Kern County
15	191	32.4	**San Bernardino** (city) San Bernardino County
15	191	32.4	**San Luis Obispo** (city) San Luis Obispo County
15	191	32.4	**Wasco** (city) Kern County
18	194	32.3	**Lennox** (CDP) Los Angeles County
18	194	32.3	**Marysville** (city) Yuba County
20	200	32.2	**Muscoy** (CDP) San Bernardino County
21	208	32.0	**Desert Hot Springs** (city) Riverside County
22	214	31.8	**Cudahy** (city) Los Angeles County
23	229	31.2	**Mead Valley** (CDP) Riverside County
24	235	30.9	**Coachella** (city) Riverside County
25	237	30.8	**Oildale** (CDP) Kern County
26	241	30.7	**Florence-Graham** (CDP) Los Angeles County
27	246	30.6	**Parkway** (CDP) Sacramento County
28	266	30.2	**Bell** (city) Los Angeles County
29	276	30.0	**Merced** (city) Merced County
30	279	29.9	**Delano** (city) Kern County
30	279	29.9	**Exeter** (city) Tulare County
32	298	29.5	**Linda** (CDP) Yuba County
33	312	29.1	**Bay Point** (CDP) Contra Costa County
34	328	28.9	**Fresno** (city) Fresno County
35	336	28.8	**Lamont** (CDP) Kern County
36	338	28.7	**Corcoran** (city) Kings County
36	338	28.7	**Huntington Park** (city) Los Angeles County
38	341	28.6	**Dinuba** (city) Tulare County
39	354	28.3	**Maywood** (city) Los Angeles County
40	378	27.7	**Chowchilla** (city) Madera County
40	378	27.7	**Madera** (city) Madera County
42	386	27.6	**Bell Gardens** (city) Los Angeles County
43	423	27.0	**Porterville** (city) Tulare County
44	427	26.9	**East Los Angeles** (CDP) Los Angeles County
45	443	26.6	**Lake Los Angeles** (CDP) Los Angeles County
46	450	26.5	**Red Bluff** (city) Tehama County
47	459	26.4	**El Cajon** (city) San Diego County
48	466	26.3	**Compton** (city) Los Angeles County
48	466	26.3	**Davis** (city) Yolo County
50	476	26.2	**Barstow** (city) San Bernardino County
51	498	25.9	**Cherryland** (CDP) Alameda County
51	498	25.9	**Perris** (city) Riverside County
53	514	25.6	**Florin** (CDP) Sacramento County
54	523	25.5	**Winton** (CDP) Merced County
55	534	25.4	**Calexico** (city) Imperial County
55	534	25.4	**La Riviera** (CDP) Sacramento County
57	541	25.3	**Hesperia** (city) San Bernardino County
57	541	25.3	**Lynwood** (city) Los Angeles County
57	541	25.3	**National City** (city) San Diego County
57	541	25.3	**North Highlands** (CDP) Sacramento County
57	541	25.3	**Victorville** (city) San Bernardino County
62	556	25.1	**North Fair Oaks** (CDP) San Mateo County
63	563	25.0	**Los Banos** (city) Merced County
64	568	24.9	**El Centro** (city) Imperial County
65	583	24.6	**Grass Valley** (city) Nevada County
66	589	24.5	**Colton** (city) San Bernardino County
66	589	24.5	**Greenfield** (city) Monterey County
68	601	24.4	**Atwater** (city) Merced County
68	601	24.4	**Hawaiian Gardens** (city) Los Angeles County
68	601	24.4	**Home Gardens** (CDP) Riverside County
71	614	24.3	**El Monte** (city) Los Angeles County
71	614	24.3	**Stockton** (city) San Joaquin County
73	626	24.2	**Reedley** (city) Fresno County
74	638	24.1	**Brawley** (city) Imperial County
75	646	24.0	**California City** (city) Kern County
75	646	24.0	**Foothill Farms** (CDP) Sacramento County
77	655	23.9	**Lakeland Village** (CDP) Riverside County
78	662	23.8	**Eureka** (city) Humboldt County
79	671	23.7	**Lompoc** (city) Santa Barbara County
80	700	23.4	**Kerman** (city) Fresno County
81	710	23.3	**Hemet** (city) Riverside County
81	710	23.3	**Oroville** (city) Butte County
81	710	23.3	**Selma** (city) Fresno County
84	721	23.2	**Chico** (city) Butte County
85	762	22.8	**Coalinga** (city) Fresno County
86	775	22.7	**Sanger** (city) Fresno County
87	789	22.5	**Garden Acres** (CDP) San Joaquin County
87	789	22.5	**Newman** (city) Stanislaus County
89	797	22.4	**Inglewood** (city) Los Angeles County
89	797	22.4	**Ukiah** (city) Mendocino County
91	832	22.1	**Paramount** (city) Los Angeles County
91	832	22.1	**Susanville** (city) Lassen County
93	844	22.0	**Los Angeles** (city) Los Angeles County
94	853	21.9	**Indio** (city) Riverside County
94	853	21.9	**Sacramento** (city) Sacramento County
94	853	21.9	**Santa Cruz** (city) Santa Cruz County
97	872	21.7	**Walnut Park** (CDP) Los Angeles County
98	881	21.6	**Pomona** (city) Los Angeles County
98	881	21.6	**Valle Vista** (CDP) Riverside County
100	892	21.5	**Lancaster** (city) Los Angeles County
100	892	21.5	**Santa Ana** (city) Orange County
102	905	21.4	**Tulare** (city) Tulare County
103	918	21.3	**Soledad** (city) Monterey County
104	924	21.2	**Highland** (city) San Bernardino County
104	924	21.2	**Palmdale** (city) Los Angeles County
104	924	21.2	**Shasta Lake** (city) Shasta County
107	935	21.1	**South Gate** (city) Los Angeles County
108	947	21.0	**Salinas** (city) Monterey County
109	955	20.9	**Bostonia** (CDP) San Diego County
110	964	20.8	**Modesto** (city) Stanislaus County
110	964	20.8	**San Pablo** (city) Contra Costa County
112	975	20.7	**Fillmore** (city) Ventura County
112	975	20.7	**Santa Maria** (city) Santa Barbara County
112	975	20.7	**Watsonville** (city) Santa Cruz County
115	993	20.5	**Cathedral City** (city) Riverside County
115	993	20.5	**Ceres** (city) Stanislaus County
115	993	20.5	**King City** (city) Monterey County
115	993	20.5	**Oakland** (city) Alameda County
115	993	20.5	**Yucca Valley** (town) San Bernardino County
120	1014	20.4	**Bakersfield** (city) Kern County
120	1014	20.4	**Bloomington** (CDP) San Bernardino County
122	1021	20.3	**Fortuna** (city) Humboldt County
123	1028	20.2	**Apple Valley** (town) San Bernardino County
123	1028	20.2	**Long Beach** (city) Los Angeles County
125	1041	20.1	**Azusa** (city) Los Angeles County
125	1041	20.1	**Big Bear City** (CDP) San Bernardino County
127	1052	20.0	**East Rancho Dominguez** (CDP) Los Angeles County
127	1052	20.0	**Livingston** (city) Merced County
129	1065	19.9	**West Sacramento** (city) Yolo County
130	1081	19.8	**Arden-Arcade** (CDP) Sacramento County
131	1100	19.6	**Stanton** (city) Orange County
132	1115	19.5	**Galt** (city) Sacramento County
132	1115	19.5	**Hanford** (city) Kings County
132	1115	19.5	**Moreno Valley** (city) Riverside County
132	1115	19.5	**Olivehurst** (CDP) Yuba County
136	1131	19.4	**Santa Paula** (city) Ventura County
136	1131	19.4	**South El Monte** (city) Los Angeles County
138	1157	19.2	**Blythe** (city) Riverside County
138	1157	19.2	**Hawthorne** (city) Los Angeles County
138	1157	19.2	**Marina** (city) Monterey County
138	1157	19.2	**Visalia** (city) Tulare County
142	1175	19.1	**Crestline** (CDP) San Bernardino County
142	1175	19.1	**Quartz Hill** (CDP) Los Angeles County
142	1175	19.1	**Rialto** (city) San Bernardino County
142	1175	19.1	**Riverside** (city) Riverside County
142	1175	19.1	**Shafter** (city) Kern County
147	1215	18.8	**Rosemead** (city) Los Angeles County
148	1222	18.7	**Berkeley** (city) Alameda County
148	1222	18.7	**Escondido** (city) San Diego County
150	1230	18.6	**Imperial Beach** (city) San Diego County

Note: *The state column ranks the top/bottom 150 places from all places in the state with population of 10,000 or more. The national column ranks the top/bottom 150 places from all places in the country with population of 10,000 or more. Places that are unincorporated were not considered in the rankings. Please refer to the User Guide for additional information.*

Poverty Rate

Top 150 Places Ranked in *Ascending* Order

State Rank	Nat'l Rank	Percent	Place
1	12	1.5	**Orinda** (city) Contra Costa County
2	41	1.8	**La Cañada Flintridge** (city) Los Angeles County
3	65	2.1	**Los Altos** (city) Santa Clara County
4	83	2.3	**Alamo** (CDP) Contra Costa County
5	123	2.6	**Mill Valley** (city) Marin County
6	144	2.7	**Coto de Caza** (CDP) Orange County
6	144	2.7	**North Tustin** (CDP) Orange County
8	220	3.1	**Hillsborough** (town) San Mateo County
8	220	3.1	**Yorba Linda** (city) Orange County
10	247	3.2	**Palos Verdes Estates** (city) Los Angeles County
10	247	3.2	**Scotts Valley** (city) Santa Cruz County
12	278	3.3	**Rossmoor** (CDP) Orange County
12	278	3.3	**Windsor** (town) Sonoma County
14	303	3.4	**Hermosa Beach** (city) Los Angeles County
14	303	3.4	**Lafayette** (city) Contra Costa County
14	303	3.4	**Manhattan Beach** (city) Los Angeles County
17	365	3.6	**Granite Bay** (CDP) Placer County
18	391	3.7	**Clayton** (city) Contra Costa County
18	391	3.7	**Saratoga** (city) Santa Clara County
20	428	3.8	**Dublin** (city) Alameda County
20	428	3.8	**El Dorado Hills** (CDP) El Dorado County
20	428	3.8	**San Ramon** (city) Contra Costa County
23	453	3.9	**Rancho Santa Margarita** (city) Orange County
24	478	4.0	**Ladera Ranch** (CDP) Orange County
24	478	4.0	**Larkspur** (city) Marin County
26	520	4.1	**French Valley** (CDP) Riverside County
26	520	4.1	**Piedmont** (city) Alameda County
28	546	4.2	**Stevenson Ranch** (CDP) Los Angeles County
29	578	4.3	**Cupertino** (city) Santa Clara County
30	618	4.4	**Moraga** (town) Contra Costa County
30	618	4.4	**San Carlos** (city) San Mateo County
32	656	4.5	**Rancho Palos Verdes** (city) Los Angeles County
33	680	4.6	**Danville** (town) Contra Costa County
33	680	4.6	**Folsom** (city) Sacramento County
33	680	4.6	**Foster City** (city) San Mateo County
33	680	4.6	**Los Gatos** (town) Santa Clara County
37	710	4.7	**Eastvale** (city) Riverside County
37	710	4.7	**Oak Park** (CDP) Ventura County
39	745	4.8	**El Segundo** (city) Los Angeles County
39	745	4.8	**Pacifica** (city) San Mateo County
39	745	4.8	**Pleasanton** (city) Alameda County
42	773	4.9	**San Diego Country Estates** (CDP) San Diego County
43	800	5.0	**Discovery Bay** (CDP) Contra Costa County
44	821	5.1	**Aliso Viejo** (city) Orange County
45	855	5.2	**Cameron Park** (CDP) El Dorado County
45	855	5.2	**Tamalpais-Homestead Valley** (CDP) Marin County
47	883	5.3	**Mission Viejo** (city) Orange County
47	883	5.3	**Poway** (city) San Diego County
47	883	5.3	**Walnut Creek** (city) Contra Costa County
50	909	5.4	**Redondo Beach** (city) Los Angeles County
50	909	5.4	**San Marino** (city) Los Angeles County
52	937	5.5	**Belmont** (city) San Mateo County
52	937	5.5	**Cerritos** (city) Los Angeles County
54	988	5.7	**Benicia** (city) Solano County
54	988	5.7	**Brentwood** (city) Contra Costa County
54	988	5.7	**Livermore** (city) Alameda County
54	988	5.7	**Millbrae** (city) San Mateo County
54	988	5.7	**Palo Alto** (city) Santa Clara County
54	988	5.7	**Rancho San Diego** (CDP) San Diego County
60	1020	5.8	**Camarillo** (city) Ventura County
61	1048	5.9	**Diamond Bar** (city) Los Angeles County
62	1071	6.0	**Fremont** (city) Alameda County
62	1071	6.0	**Hercules** (city) Contra Costa County
62	1071	6.0	**Lake Forest** (city) Orange County
65	1095	6.1	**Chino Hills** (city) San Bernardino County
65	1095	6.1	**Menlo Park** (city) San Mateo County
67	1134	6.2	**Canyon Lake** (city) Riverside County
67	1134	6.2	**Walnut** (city) Los Angeles County
69	1157	6.3	**Laguna Beach** (city) Orange County
69	1157	6.3	**Laguna Niguel** (city) Orange County
69	1157	6.3	**Martinez** (city) Contra Costa County
72	1212	6.5	**Orcutt** (CDP) Santa Barbara County
73	1235	6.6	**Brea** (city) Orange County
73	1235	6.6	**Calabasas** (city) Los Angeles County
73	1235	6.6	**San Bruno** (city) San Mateo County
73	1235	6.6	**San Dimas** (city) Los Angeles County
73	1235	6.6	**Simi Valley** (city) Ventura County
73	1235	6.6	**Sonoma** (city) Sonoma County
79	1275	6.7	**Coronado** (city) San Diego County
79	1275	6.7	**Cypress** (city) Orange County
79	1275	6.7	**Laguna Hills** (city) Orange County
79	1275	6.7	**South Pasadena** (city) Los Angeles County
83	1303	6.8	**El Sobrante** (CDP) Riverside County
83	1303	6.8	**Thousand Oaks** (city) Ventura County
85	1329	6.9	**Goleta** (city) Santa Barbara County
85	1329	6.9	**Rancho Cucamonga** (city) San Bernardino County
85	1329	6.9	**Woodcrest** (CDP) Riverside County
88	1355	7.0	**La Mirada** (city) Los Angeles County
88	1355	7.0	**Murrieta** (city) Riverside County
88	1355	7.0	**San Anselmo** (town) Marin County
91	1383	7.1	**Agoura Hills** (city) Los Angeles County
91	1383	7.1	**Culver City** (city) Los Angeles County
91	1383	7.1	**San Mateo** (city) San Mateo County
91	1383	7.1	**South San Francisco** (city) San Mateo County
95	1407	7.2	**Campbell** (city) Santa Clara County
95	1407	7.2	**Claremont** (city) Los Angeles County
95	1407	7.2	**Fairview** (CDP) Alameda County
95	1407	7.2	**Milpitas** (city) Santa Clara County
95	1407	7.2	**Moorpark** (city) Ventura County
95	1407	7.2	**Novato** (city) Marin County
101	1432	7.3	**Salida** (CDP) Stanislaus County
102	1453	7.4	**Arroyo Grande** (city) San Luis Obispo County
102	1453	7.4	**Half Moon Bay** (city) San Mateo County
102	1453	7.4	**La Crescenta-Montrose** (CDP) Los Angeles County
102	1453	7.4	**Torrance** (city) Los Angeles County
106	1482	7.5	**Burlingame** (city) San Mateo County
106	1482	7.5	**Carpinteria** (city) Santa Barbara County
108	1509	7.6	**Rosedale** (CDP) Kern County
109	1533	7.7	**Newark** (city) Alameda County
109	1533	7.7	**Orangevale** (CDP) Sacramento County
109	1533	7.7	**Santee** (city) San Diego County
112	1572	7.8	**Castro Valley** (CDP) Alameda County
112	1572	7.8	**East San Gabriel** (CDP) Los Angeles County
112	1572	7.8	**Glendora** (city) Los Angeles County
115	1601	7.9	**La Verne** (city) Los Angeles County
115	1601	7.9	**Newport Beach** (city) Orange County
117	1629	8.0	**Fountain Valley** (city) Orange County
117	1629	8.0	**Rocklin** (city) Placer County
119	1651	8.1	**Alpine** (CDP) San Diego County
119	1651	8.1	**Hacienda Heights** (CDP) Los Angeles County
119	1651	8.1	**Lakewood** (city) Los Angeles County
119	1651	8.1	**Mountain View** (city) Santa Clara County
119	1651	8.1	**Sunnyvale** (city) Santa Clara County
124	1684	8.2	**Tracy** (city) San Joaquin County
125	1705	8.3	**Dana Point** (city) Orange County
125	1705	8.3	**Roseville** (city) Placer County
125	1705	8.3	**Sierra Madre** (city) Los Angeles County
125	1705	8.3	**View Park-Windsor Hills** (CDP) Los Angeles County
129	1730	8.4	**Union City** (city) Alameda County
130	1754	8.5	**El Cerrito** (city) Contra Costa County
130	1754	8.5	**Los Alamitos** (city) Orange County
130	1754	8.5	**Temecula** (city) Riverside County
133	1782	8.6	**American Canyon** (city) Napa County
133	1782	8.6	**Castaic** (CDP) Los Angeles County
133	1782	8.6	**Daly City** (city) San Mateo County
133	1782	8.6	**San Clemente** (city) Orange County
137	1823	8.8	**Beverly Hills** (city) Los Angeles County
137	1823	8.8	**Camp Pendleton South** (CDP) San Diego County
137	1823	8.8	**Grand Terrace** (city) San Bernardino County
137	1823	8.8	**Norco** (city) Riverside County
137	1823	8.8	**Pacific Grove** (city) Monterey County
142	1841	8.9	**Huntington Beach** (city) Orange County
142	1841	8.9	**Solana Beach** (city) San Diego County
144	1865	9.0	**La Palma** (city) Orange County
144	1865	9.0	**Los Osos** (CDP) San Luis Obispo County
144	1865	9.0	**Redwood City** (city) San Mateo County
144	1865	9.0	**San Lorenzo** (CDP) Alameda County
144	1865	9.0	**Santa Clara** (city) Santa Clara County
149	1889	9.1	**Del Aire** (CDP) Los Angeles County
149	1889	9.1	**Pleasant Hill** (city) Contra Costa County

Note: *The state column ranks the top/bottom 150 places from all places in the state with population of 10,000 or more. The national column ranks the top/bottom 150 places from all places in the country with population of 10,000 or more. Places that are unincorporated were not considered in the rankings. Please refer to the User Guide for additional information.*

Educational Attainment: High School Diploma or Higher

Top 150 Places Ranked in *Descending* Order

State Rank	Nat'l Rank	Percent	Place
1	1	100.0	**Camp Pendleton South** (CDP) San Diego County
2	9	99.0	**Hermosa Beach** (city) Los Angeles County
3	13	98.9	**Stanford** (CDP) Santa Clara County
4	17	98.8	**Ladera Ranch** (CDP) Orange County
4	17	98.8	**Los Altos** (city) Santa Clara County
6	25	98.7	**Alamo** (CDP) Contra Costa County
6	25	98.7	**Clayton** (city) Contra Costa County
6	25	98.7	**Coto de Caza** (CDP) Orange County
9	43	98.4	**Coronado** (city) San Diego County
9	43	98.4	**Saratoga** (city) Santa Clara County
11	52	98.3	**Malibu** (city) Los Angeles County
12	61	98.2	**Manhattan Beach** (city) Los Angeles County
13	78	98.1	**La Cañada Flintridge** (city) Los Angeles County
13	78	98.1	**Tamalpais-Homestead Valley** (CDP) Marin County
15	100	97.9	**Moraga** (town) Contra Costa County
15	100	97.9	**Palos Verdes Estates** (city) Los Angeles County
15	100	97.9	**Piedmont** (city) Alameda County
18	116	97.8	**Danville** (town) Contra Costa County
18	116	97.8	**Los Gatos** (town) Santa Clara County
18	116	97.8	**Orinda** (city) Contra Costa County
18	116	97.8	**Rossmoor** (CDP) Orange County
22	131	97.7	**Rancho Palos Verdes** (city) Los Angeles County
23	148	97.6	**El Dorado Hills** (CDP) El Dorado County
23	148	97.6	**Lafayette** (city) Contra Costa County
25	163	97.5	**Larkspur** (city) Marin County
25	163	97.5	**Newport Beach** (city) Orange County
25	163	97.5	**Palo Alto** (city) Santa Clara County
28	184	97.4	**Calabasas** (city) Los Angeles County
28	184	97.4	**Laguna Beach** (city) Orange County
30	202	97.3	**Mill Valley** (city) Marin County
30	202	97.3	**Oak Park** (CDP) Ventura County
30	202	97.3	**San Ramon** (city) Contra Costa County
30	202	97.3	**Walnut Creek** (city) Contra Costa County
34	287	96.9	**Granite Bay** (CDP) Placer County
35	306	96.8	**Sierra Madre** (city) Los Angeles County
36	346	96.6	**North Tustin** (CDP) Orange County
36	346	96.6	**San Carlos** (city) San Mateo County
36	346	96.6	**San Diego Country Estates** (CDP) San Diego County
39	372	96.5	**Cupertino** (city) Santa Clara County
40	423	96.3	**Albany** (city) Alameda County
40	423	96.3	**Foster City** (city) San Mateo County
40	423	96.3	**Irvine** (city) Orange County
40	423	96.3	**Laguna Niguel** (city) Orange County
40	423	96.3	**South Pasadena** (city) Los Angeles County
45	453	96.2	**Emeryville** (city) Alameda County
45	453	96.2	**San Anselmo** (town) Marin County
47	474	96.1	**Hillsborough** (town) San Mateo County
48	501	96.0	**Carlsbad** (city) San Diego County
48	501	96.0	**El Segundo** (city) Los Angeles County
50	558	95.8	**Davis** (city) Yolo County
50	558	95.8	**Pleasant Hill** (city) Contra Costa County
52	580	95.7	**Agoura Hills** (city) Los Angeles County
52	580	95.7	**Redondo Beach** (city) Los Angeles County
52	580	95.7	**View Park-Windsor Hills** (CDP) Los Angeles County
55	615	95.6	**Canyon Lake** (city) Riverside County
55	615	95.6	**Scotts Valley** (city) Santa Cruz County
55	615	95.6	**Yorba Linda** (city) Orange County
58	644	95.5	**Burlingame** (city) San Mateo County
58	644	95.5	**Pacific Grove** (city) Monterey County
58	644	95.5	**Rancho Santa Margarita** (city) Orange County
61	668	95.4	**Belmont** (city) San Mateo County
62	696	95.3	**Rancho Mirage** (city) Riverside County
63	732	95.2	**Aliso Viejo** (city) Orange County
63	732	95.2	**Dana Point** (city) Orange County
63	732	95.2	**Rocklin** (city) Placer County
63	732	95.2	**West Hollywood** (city) Los Angeles County
67	766	95.1	**Santa Monica** (city) Los Angeles County
68	790	95.0	**Pleasanton** (city) Alameda County
68	790	95.0	**Stevenson Ranch** (CDP) Los Angeles County
70	823	94.9	**Berkeley** (city) Alameda County
70	823	94.9	**Los Osos** (CDP) San Luis Obispo County
72	852	94.8	**Discovery Bay** (CDP) Contra Costa County
72	852	94.8	**La Crescenta-Montrose** (CDP) Los Angeles County
72	852	94.8	**San Marino** (city) Los Angeles County
75	881	94.7	**Beverly Hills** (city) Los Angeles County
75	881	94.7	**San Clemente** (city) Orange County
77	910	94.6	**La Riviera** (CDP) Sacramento County
77	910	94.6	**Pacifica** (city) San Mateo County
79	937	94.5	**Mission Viejo** (city) Orange County
80	970	94.4	**Auburn** (city) Placer County
80	970	94.4	**Benicia** (city) Solano County
80	970	94.4	**Cameron Park** (CDP) El Dorado County
83	1077	94.1	**Laguna Woods** (city) Orange County
83	1077	94.1	**Roseville** (city) Placer County
85	1160	93.9	**Fair Oaks** (CDP) Sacramento County
85	1160	93.9	**Seal Beach** (city) Orange County
87	1192	93.8	**Poway** (city) San Diego County
87	1192	93.8	**Sonoma** (city) Sonoma County
87	1192	93.8	**Truckee** (town) Nevada County
90	1224	93.7	**Lincoln** (city) Placer County
90	1224	93.7	**Martinez** (city) Contra Costa County
92	1264	93.6	**Encinitas** (city) San Diego County
93	1369	93.3	**Monterey** (city) Monterey County
93	1369	93.3	**San Luis Obispo** (city) San Luis Obispo County
95	1399	93.2	**Arroyo Grande** (city) San Luis Obispo County
95	1399	93.2	**Walnut** (city) Los Angeles County
97	1431	93.1	**Campbell** (city) Santa Clara County
97	1431	93.1	**Casa de Oro-Mount Helix** (CDP) San Diego County
97	1431	93.1	**Cerritos** (city) Los Angeles County
100	1468	93.0	**El Cerrito** (city) Contra Costa County
100	1468	93.0	**Torrance** (city) Los Angeles County
102	1494	92.9	**Diamond Springs** (CDP) El Dorado County
103	1532	92.8	**La Palma** (city) Orange County
103	1532	92.8	**Menlo Park** (city) San Mateo County
105	1569	92.7	**Claremont** (city) Los Angeles County
105	1569	92.7	**Los Alamitos** (city) Orange County
107	1595	92.6	**Culver City** (city) Los Angeles County
108	1629	92.5	**Folsom** (city) Sacramento County
108	1629	92.5	**Huntington Beach** (city) Orange County
108	1629	92.5	**Thousand Oaks** (city) Ventura County
111	1670	92.4	**El Sobrante** (CDP) Riverside County
111	1670	92.4	**Santa Cruz** (city) Santa Cruz County
113	1702	92.3	**Novato** (city) Marin County
113	1702	92.3	**San Dimas** (city) Los Angeles County
115	1734	92.2	**Arcata** (city) Humboldt County
115	1734	92.2	**Fairview** (CDP) Alameda County
115	1734	92.2	**Hercules** (city) Contra Costa County
118	1768	92.1	**Atascadero** (city) San Luis Obispo County
118	1768	92.1	**Castro Valley** (CDP) Alameda County
118	1768	92.1	**Lake Forest** (city) Orange County
121	1799	92.0	**Chino Hills** (city) San Bernardino County
121	1799	92.0	**Cypress** (city) Orange County
121	1799	92.0	**Diamond Bar** (city) Los Angeles County
121	1799	92.0	**Livermore** (city) Alameda County
121	1799	92.0	**Murrieta** (city) Riverside County
126	1830	91.9	**Carmichael** (CDP) Sacramento County
126	1830	91.9	**Morro Bay** (city) San Luis Obispo County
126	1830	91.9	**Solana Beach** (city) San Diego County
129	1856	91.8	**Camarillo** (city) Ventura County
129	1856	91.8	**La Mesa** (city) San Diego County
129	1856	91.8	**Orangevale** (CDP) Sacramento County
129	1856	91.8	**Rancho San Diego** (CDP) San Diego County
129	1856	91.8	**Santa Clara** (city) Santa Clara County
134	1906	91.6	**Laguna Hills** (city) Orange County
134	1906	91.6	**Millbrae** (city) San Mateo County
136	1944	91.5	**Dublin** (city) Alameda County
136	1944	91.5	**La Verne** (city) Los Angeles County
136	1944	91.5	**Temecula** (city) Riverside County
139	1965	91.4	**Crestline** (CDP) San Bernardino County
139	1965	91.4	**Mountain View** (city) Santa Clara County
141	1992	91.3	**Arcadia** (city) Los Angeles County
141	1992	91.3	**Palm Desert** (city) Riverside County
143	2024	91.2	**Brea** (city) Orange County
143	2024	91.2	**Castaic** (CDP) Los Angeles County
143	2024	91.2	**Chico** (city) Butte County
146	2050	91.1	**Paradise** (town) Butte County
147	2071	91.0	**Fremont** (city) Alameda County
147	2071	91.0	**Santee** (city) San Diego County
149	2102	90.9	**Alpine** (CDP) San Diego County
149	2102	90.9	**Magalia** (CDP) Butte County

Note: *The state column ranks the top/bottom 150 places from all places in the state with population of 10,000 or more. The national column ranks the top/bottom 150 places from all places in the country with population of 10,000 or more. Places that are unincorporated were not considered in the rankings. Please refer to the User Guide for additional information.*

Educational Attainment: High School Diploma or Higher

Top 150 Places Ranked in *Ascending* Order

State Rank	Nat'l Rank	Percent	Place
1	1	29.0	**Mendota** (city) Fresno County
2	3	36.7	**Lamont** (CDP) Kern County
3	4	36.8	**Arvin** (city) Kern County
4	6	39.0	**Maywood** (city) Los Angeles County
5	7	40.0	**Huntington Park** (city) Los Angeles County
6	8	40.9	**Florence-Graham** (CDP) Los Angeles County
7	9	41.0	**McFarland** (city) Kern County
8	11	41.6	**Bell Gardens** (city) Los Angeles County
9	12	41.8	**Parlier** (city) Fresno County
10	13	42.4	**King City** (city) Monterey County
11	14	42.8	**Cudahy** (city) Los Angeles County
12	15	44.5	**Avenal** (city) Kings County
13	17	45.3	**Bell** (city) Los Angeles County
14	18	45.5	**Walnut Park** (CDP) Los Angeles County
15	20	45.6	**East Los Angeles** (CDP) Los Angeles County
15	20	45.6	**Muscoy** (CDP) San Bernardino County
17	22	45.8	**Greenfield** (city) Monterey County
18	25	46.5	**Lindsay** (city) Tulare County
19	26	47.1	**Lennox** (CDP) Los Angeles County
20	28	48.7	**Winton** (CDP) Merced County
21	29	49.0	**South El Monte** (city) Los Angeles County
22	30	49.5	**Farmersville** (city) Tulare County
23	31	49.6	**Coachella** (city) Riverside County
24	33	50.4	**Livingston** (city) Merced County
25	34	51.0	**Lynwood** (city) Los Angeles County
26	35	51.7	**East Rancho Dominguez** (CDP) Los Angeles County
26	35	51.7	**Garden Acres** (CDP) San Joaquin County
26	35	51.7	**Soledad** (city) Monterey County
29	40	52.4	**South San Jose Hills** (CDP) Los Angeles County
30	41	52.5	**South Gate** (city) Los Angeles County
31	42	53.4	**Delano** (city) Kern County
32	44	53.6	**Commerce** (city) Los Angeles County
32	44	53.6	**Santa Ana** (city) Orange County
32	44	53.6	**Wasco** (city) Kern County
35	47	53.7	**Willowbrook** (CDP) Los Angeles County
36	49	54.2	**Delhi** (CDP) Merced County
36	49	54.2	**Watsonville** (city) Santa Cruz County
38	52	55.0	**Mead Valley** (CDP) Riverside County
39	56	55.4	**Calexico** (city) Imperial County
40	57	55.8	**Corcoran** (city) Kings County
41	59	56.1	**Hawaiian Gardens** (city) Los Angeles County
42	60	56.5	**Dinuba** (city) Tulare County
43	61	56.7	**Madera** (city) Madera County
44	62	56.8	**El Monte** (city) Los Angeles County
45	64	57.0	**Paramount** (city) Los Angeles County
46	65	57.4	**Kerman** (city) Fresno County
47	66	57.8	**San Fernando** (city) Los Angeles County
48	67	58.3	**Baldwin Park** (city) Los Angeles County
49	68	58.5	**Selma** (city) Fresno County
50	70	58.8	**Shafter** (city) Kern County
51	71	59.0	**Lemon Hill** (CDP) Sacramento County
52	73	59.2	**Compton** (city) Los Angeles County
53	77	60.0	**Bloomington** (CDP) San Bernardino County
53	77	60.0	**La Puente** (city) Los Angeles County
55	80	60.3	**North Fair Oaks** (CDP) San Mateo County
55	80	60.3	**Santa Maria** (city) Santa Barbara County
57	82	60.4	**Sanger** (city) Fresno County
58	85	60.6	**Salinas** (city) Monterey County
59	88	61.1	**Reedley** (city) Fresno County
60	91	61.2	**Home Gardens** (CDP) Riverside County
61	94	62.0	**Perris** (city) Riverside County
61	94	62.0	**West Puente Valley** (CDP) Los Angeles County
63	103	62.9	**Rosemead** (city) Los Angeles County
63	103	62.9	**Sun Village** (CDP) Los Angeles County
65	107	63.5	**San Pablo** (city) Contra Costa County
66	114	64.3	**Oxnard** (city) Ventura County
66	114	64.3	**Santa Paula** (city) Ventura County
68	121	64.7	**Olivehurst** (CDP) Yuba County
69	128	65.6	**Los Banos** (city) Merced County
70	132	66.1	**Fillmore** (city) Ventura County
71	137	66.3	**Pomona** (city) Los Angeles County
72	143	66.9	**Ceres** (city) Stanislaus County
73	146	67.1	**East Palo Alto** (city) San Mateo County
74	147	67.2	**Bay Point** (CDP) Contra Costa County
74	147	67.2	**El Centro** (city) Imperial County
76	150	67.4	**Alum Rock** (CDP) Santa Clara County
77	151	67.5	**Pico Rivera** (city) Los Angeles County
77	151	67.5	**Valinda** (CDP) Los Angeles County
79	155	67.7	**San Bernardino** (city) San Bernardino County
80	157	67.9	**Desert Hot Springs** (city) Riverside County
81	158	68.0	**Blythe** (city) Riverside County
82	163	68.1	**Patterson** (city) Stanislaus County
83	164	68.2	**West Whittier-Los Nietos** (CDP) Los Angeles County
84	165	68.3	**Westmont** (CDP) Los Angeles County
85	167	68.4	**Stanton** (city) Orange County
86	168	68.5	**Rialto** (city) San Bernardino County
87	173	68.8	**Colton** (city) San Bernardino County
88	176	68.9	**Brawley** (city) Imperial County
88	176	68.9	**Chowchilla** (city) Madera County
88	176	68.9	**Porterville** (city) Tulare County
91	188	69.4	**Cherryland** (CDP) Alameda County
92	193	69.6	**Ontario** (city) San Bernardino County
93	198	69.8	**Adelanto** (city) San Bernardino County
93	198	69.8	**Lake Los Angeles** (CDP) Los Angeles County
93	198	69.8	**Montclair** (city) San Bernardino County
93	198	69.8	**Montebello** (city) Los Angeles County
93	198	69.8	**National City** (city) San Diego County
98	222	70.7	**Florin** (CDP) Sacramento County
99	233	71.1	**Atwater** (city) Merced County
99	233	71.1	**Hollister** (city) San Benito County
101	241	71.4	**Lawndale** (city) Los Angeles County
102	243	71.7	**Merced** (city) Merced County
103	246	71.8	**Fontana** (city) San Bernardino County
103	246	71.8	**Inglewood** (city) Los Angeles County
105	255	72.1	**Escondido** (city) San Diego County
106	261	72.4	**Linda** (CDP) Yuba County
106	261	72.4	**Norwalk** (city) Los Angeles County
108	265	72.5	**Garden Grove** (city) Orange County
108	265	72.5	**South Whittier** (CDP) Los Angeles County
110	271	72.6	**Newman** (city) Stanislaus County
111	281	72.9	**Parkway** (CDP) Sacramento County
112	285	73.0	**Lompoc** (city) Santa Barbara County
113	287	73.1	**Indio** (city) Riverside County
113	287	73.1	**Santa Fe Springs** (city) Los Angeles County
115	291	73.2	**Tulare** (city) Tulare County
116	293	73.3	**Coalinga** (city) Fresno County
117	296	73.4	**Cathedral City** (city) Riverside County
118	299	73.5	**Highland** (city) San Bernardino County
119	306	73.7	**Avocado Heights** (CDP) Los Angeles County
120	311	73.8	**Tehachapi** (city) Kern County
121	329	74.2	**Palmdale** (city) Los Angeles County
121	329	74.2	**Seaside** (city) Monterey County
123	340	74.4	**Hawthorne** (city) Los Angeles County
123	340	74.4	**Stockton** (city) San Joaquin County
125	346	74.5	**Los Angeles** (city) Los Angeles County
126	348	74.6	**Vista** (city) San Diego County
126	348	74.6	**Westminster** (city) Orange County
128	354	74.7	**Anaheim** (city) Orange County
129	359	74.8	**Susanville** (city) Lassen County
130	361	74.9	**Ashland** (CDP) Alameda County
131	365	75.0	**Fresno** (city) Fresno County
131	365	75.0	**Moreno Valley** (city) Riverside County
131	365	75.0	**San Jacinto** (city) Riverside County
134	375	75.2	**Azusa** (city) Los Angeles County
135	381	75.4	**Ramona** (CDP) San Diego County
136	395	75.7	**Gilroy** (city) Santa Clara County
137	407	75.9	**Hesperia** (city) San Bernardino County
138	415	76.0	**Lathrop** (city) San Joaquin County
139	417	76.1	**Citrus** (CDP) Los Angeles County
140	424	76.3	**Riverbank** (city) Stanislaus County
141	431	76.5	**Prunedale** (CDP) Monterey County
142	438	76.6	**Lake Elsinore** (city) Riverside County
142	438	76.6	**Lakeland Village** (CDP) Riverside County
144	440	76.7	**Exeter** (city) Tulare County
145	446	76.8	**Monterey Park** (city) Los Angeles County
145	446	76.8	**San Gabriel** (city) Los Angeles County
147	460	77.0	**Downey** (city) Los Angeles County
148	475	77.2	**Lodi** (city) San Joaquin County
149	486	77.4	**Richmond** (city) Contra Costa County
150	504	77.7	**Riverside** (city) Riverside County

Note: *The state column ranks the top/bottom 150 places from all places in the state with population of 10,000 or more. The national column ranks the top/bottom 150 places from all places in the country with population of 10,000 or more. Places that are unincorporated were not considered in the rankings. Please refer to the User Guide for additional information.*

Educational Attainment: Bachelor's Degree or Higher

Top 150 Places Ranked in *Descending* Order

State Rank	Nat'l Rank	Percent	Place
1	1	93.4	**Stanford** (CDP) Santa Clara County
2	9	82.7	**Piedmont** (city) Alameda County
3	22	79.8	**Palo Alto** (city) Santa Clara County
4	27	78.7	**Los Altos** (city) Santa Clara County
5	30	77.9	**Orinda** (city) Contra Costa County
5	30	77.9	**Saratoga** (city) Santa Clara County
7	43	76.4	**Palos Verdes Estates** (city) Los Angeles County
8	49	76.0	**Hillsborough** (town) San Mateo County
9	57	75.2	**La Cañada Flintridge** (city) Los Angeles County
10	63	74.7	**Mill Valley** (city) Marin County
11	66	74.6	**Cupertino** (city) Santa Clara County
12	70	74.3	**Moraga** (town) Contra Costa County
13	72	74.0	**Manhattan Beach** (city) Los Angeles County
14	85	72.9	**Lafayette** (city) Contra Costa County
15	87	72.8	**Tamalpais-Homestead Valley** (CDP) Marin County
16	88	72.7	**San Marino** (city) Los Angeles County
17	92	72.4	**Alamo** (CDP) Contra Costa County
18	102	71.5	**Albany** (city) Alameda County
18	102	71.5	**Emeryville** (city) Alameda County
20	108	70.9	**Hermosa Beach** (city) Los Angeles County
21	117	70.4	**Menlo Park** (city) San Mateo County
22	119	70.2	**Davis** (city) Yolo County
23	126	69.7	**Berkeley** (city) Alameda County
24	149	67.8	**Los Gatos** (town) Santa Clara County
25	208	65.0	**Laguna Beach** (city) Orange County
26	209	64.9	**Irvine** (city) Orange County
26	209	64.9	**Ladera Ranch** (CDP) Orange County
26	209	64.9	**Rancho Palos Verdes** (city) Los Angeles County
29	215	64.7	**Santa Monica** (city) Los Angeles County
30	221	64.5	**San Ramon** (city) Contra Costa County
31	230	64.1	**Newport Beach** (city) Orange County
32	253	63.3	**Danville** (town) Contra Costa County
33	260	63.0	**South Pasadena** (city) Los Angeles County
34	264	62.8	**San Anselmo** (town) Marin County
35	268	62.6	**Larkspur** (city) Marin County
35	268	62.6	**Mountain View** (city) Santa Clara County
37	270	62.5	**Oak Park** (CDP) Ventura County
38	274	62.3	**Foster City** (city) San Mateo County
39	278	62.1	**Coto de Caza** (CDP) Orange County
40	286	62.0	**Calabasas** (city) Los Angeles County
41	298	61.7	**Solana Beach** (city) San Diego County
42	305	61.2	**Malibu** (city) Los Angeles County
43	311	61.0	**Walnut Creek** (city) Contra Costa County
44	332	60.0	**San Carlos** (city) San Mateo County
45	353	59.1	**Sierra Madre** (city) Los Angeles County
46	361	58.7	**El Cerrito** (city) Contra Costa County
47	366	58.6	**Beverly Hills** (city) Los Angeles County
47	366	58.6	**West Hollywood** (city) Los Angeles County
49	371	58.3	**Burlingame** (city) San Mateo County
49	371	58.3	**Coronado** (city) San Diego County
49	371	58.3	**Sunnyvale** (city) Santa Clara County
52	376	58.0	**Redondo Beach** (city) Los Angeles County
53	394	57.4	**Aliso Viejo** (city) Orange County
54	399	57.3	**Rossmoor** (CDP) Orange County
55	423	56.5	**Pleasanton** (city) Alameda County
56	453	55.9	**North Tustin** (CDP) Orange County
57	474	55.5	**Belmont** (city) San Mateo County
58	477	55.4	**Encinitas** (city) San Diego County
59	492	55.0	**Claremont** (city) Los Angeles County
60	509	54.6	**Laguna Niguel** (city) Orange County
61	515	54.4	**Agoura Hills** (city) Los Angeles County
62	530	54.1	**Granite Bay** (CDP) Placer County
63	534	54.0	**Stevenson Ranch** (CDP) Los Angeles County
64	583	52.5	**Arcadia** (city) Los Angeles County
65	585	52.4	**El Dorado Hills** (CDP) El Dorado County
65	585	52.4	**San Francisco** (city) San Francisco County
67	593	52.3	**Walnut** (city) Los Angeles County
68	606	51.9	**Carlsbad** (city) San Diego County
69	611	51.8	**La Crescenta-Montrose** (CDP) Los Angeles County
70	625	51.6	**Santa Clara** (city) Santa Clara County
71	651	50.9	**Fremont** (city) Alameda County
72	661	50.6	**Culver City** (city) Los Angeles County
73	665	50.4	**Dublin** (city) Alameda County
73	665	50.4	**Isla Vista** (CDP) Santa Barbara County
73	665	50.4	**Pacific Grove** (city) Monterey County
76	683	50.1	**Loma Linda** (city) San Bernardino County
77	690	50.0	**View Park-Windsor Hills** (CDP) Los Angeles County
78	697	49.9	**Clayton** (city) Contra Costa County
79	716	49.4	**Santa Cruz** (city) Santa Cruz County
80	745	48.8	**Pleasant Hill** (city) Contra Costa County
81	752	48.7	**Pasadena** (city) Los Angeles County
82	758	48.6	**Cerritos** (city) Los Angeles County
82	758	48.6	**Yorba Linda** (city) Orange County
84	767	48.5	**El Segundo** (city) Los Angeles County
84	767	48.5	**Thousand Oaks** (city) Ventura County
86	774	48.4	**Diamond Bar** (city) Los Angeles County
87	784	48.1	**Alameda** (city) Alameda County
87	784	48.1	**Rancho Santa Margarita** (city) Orange County
89	807	47.5	**Monterey** (city) Monterey County
90	814	47.4	**San Luis Obispo** (city) San Luis Obispo County
91	847	46.7	**Dana Point** (city) Orange County
92	888	45.9	**San Clemente** (city) Orange County
93	894	45.8	**Campbell** (city) Santa Clara County
94	898	45.7	**Poway** (city) San Diego County
95	922	45.3	**Half Moon Bay** (city) San Mateo County
95	922	45.3	**Laguna Hills** (city) Orange County
97	928	45.2	**Mission Viejo** (city) Orange County
97	928	45.2	**Scotts Valley** (city) Santa Cruz County
99	936	45.1	**San Rafael** (city) Marin County
100	946	44.9	**East San Gabriel** (CDP) Los Angeles County
101	958	44.7	**Folsom** (city) Sacramento County
101	958	44.7	**Torrance** (city) Los Angeles County
103	972	44.4	**Altadena** (CDP) Los Angeles County
103	972	44.4	**San Mateo** (city) San Mateo County
105	977	44.3	**Goleta** (city) Santa Barbara County
106	984	44.2	**Arcata** (city) Humboldt County
107	1002	43.9	**Novato** (city) Marin County
108	1010	43.8	**Seal Beach** (city) Orange County
109	1035	43.3	**Chino Hills** (city) San Bernardino County
110	1042	43.2	**Lake Forest** (city) Orange County
111	1117	41.9	**Truckee** (town) Nevada County
112	1125	41.7	**San Diego** (city) San Diego County
112	1125	41.7	**Santa Barbara** (city) Santa Barbara County
114	1150	41.3	**Casa de Oro-Mount Helix** (CDP) San Diego County
114	1150	41.3	**Fair Oaks** (CDP) Sacramento County
116	1161	41.1	**Millbrae** (city) San Mateo County
117	1163	41.0	**Hercules** (city) Contra Costa County
118	1174	40.9	**Brea** (city) Orange County
119	1180	40.8	**Milpitas** (city) Santa Clara County
119	1180	40.8	**Rocklin** (city) Placer County
121	1187	40.7	**Benicia** (city) Solano County
121	1187	40.7	**El Sobrante** (CDP) Riverside County
123	1209	40.4	**La Palma** (city) Orange County
123	1209	40.4	**Sonoma** (city) Sonoma County
125	1219	40.3	**Laguna Woods** (city) Orange County
126	1229	40.2	**Huntington Beach** (city) Orange County
126	1229	40.2	**Redwood City** (city) San Mateo County
128	1238	40.1	**Pacifica** (city) San Mateo County
129	1245	40.0	**Rancho Mirage** (city) Riverside County
130	1258	39.8	**Cypress** (city) Orange County
131	1302	39.2	**Los Alamitos** (city) Orange County
132	1314	39.0	**Tustin** (city) Orange County
133	1323	38.9	**Livermore** (city) Alameda County
134	1337	38.7	**Bonita** (CDP) San Diego County
135	1361	38.4	**Camarillo** (city) Ventura County
136	1374	38.2	**Fairview** (CDP) Alameda County
136	1374	38.2	**Glendale** (city) Los Angeles County
136	1374	38.2	**Redlands** (city) San Bernardino County
139	1383	38.1	**Oakland** (city) Alameda County
140	1390	38.0	**Rancho San Diego** (CDP) San Diego County
141	1408	37.8	**Fountain Valley** (city) Orange County
142	1418	37.7	**Los Osos** (CDP) San Luis Obispo County
143	1431	37.5	**Burbank** (city) Los Angeles County
144	1437	37.4	**Moorpark** (city) Ventura County
144	1437	37.4	**Morgan Hill** (city) Santa Clara County
144	1437	37.4	**San Jose** (city) Santa Clara County
147	1457	37.1	**Fullerton** (city) Orange County
148	1464	37.0	**Temple City** (city) Los Angeles County
149	1473	36.9	**Castro Valley** (CDP) Alameda County
149	1473	36.9	**Rowland Heights** (CDP) Los Angeles County

Note: *The state column ranks the top/bottom 150 places from all places in the state with population of 10,000 or more. The national column ranks the top/bottom 150 places from all places in the country with population of 10,000 or more. Places that are unincorporated were not considered in the rankings. Please refer to the User Guide for additional information.*

Educational Attainment: Bachelor's Degree or Higher

Top 150 Places Ranked in *Ascending* Order

State Rank	Nat'l Rank	Percent	Place
1	1	1.6	**Mendota** (city) Fresno County
2	2	2.0	**Lamont** (CDP) Kern County
3	3	3.1	**Corcoran** (city) Kings County
4	4	3.2	**Soledad** (city) Monterey County
5	5	3.3	**Arvin** (city) Kern County
5	5	3.3	**Florence-Graham** (CDP) Los Angeles County
7	7	3.5	**Cudahy** (city) Los Angeles County
7	7	3.5	**Farmersville** (city) Tulare County
9	12	3.9	**McFarland** (city) Kern County
9	12	3.9	**Parlier** (city) Fresno County
11	14	4.0	**Avenal** (city) Kings County
11	14	4.0	**Muscoy** (CDP) San Bernardino County
11	14	4.0	**Wasco** (city) Kern County
14	18	4.4	**Maywood** (city) Los Angeles County
15	20	4.6	**Walnut Park** (CDP) Los Angeles County
16	23	4.7	**Coachella** (city) Riverside County
17	25	4.9	**East Rancho Dominguez** (CDP) Los Angeles County
18	27	5.0	**Winton** (CDP) Merced County
19	29	5.2	**Bell Gardens** (city) Los Angeles County
19	29	5.2	**King City** (city) Monterey County
19	29	5.2	**Willowbrook** (CDP) Los Angeles County
22	32	5.3	**Garden Acres** (CDP) San Joaquin County
22	32	5.3	**Lennox** (CDP) Los Angeles County
22	32	5.3	**Mead Valley** (CDP) Riverside County
25	35	5.4	**Lemon Hill** (CDP) Sacramento County
26	36	5.5	**East Los Angeles** (CDP) Los Angeles County
27	37	5.6	**Lindsay** (city) Tulare County
27	37	5.6	**Lynwood** (city) Los Angeles County
29	40	5.8	**Huntington Park** (city) Los Angeles County
30	41	5.9	**Bell** (city) Los Angeles County
30	41	5.9	**Commerce** (city) Los Angeles County
32	46	6.1	**Olivehurst** (CDP) Yuba County
33	48	6.2	**South Gate** (city) Los Angeles County
34	51	6.5	**Clearlake** (city) Lake County
35	52	6.6	**Lakeland Village** (CDP) Riverside County
36	56	6.7	**Compton** (city) Los Angeles County
37	57	6.8	**Delano** (city) Kern County
37	57	6.8	**Dinuba** (city) Tulare County
39	67	7.1	**Linda** (CDP) Yuba County
40	69	7.4	**Adelanto** (city) San Bernardino County
40	69	7.4	**Bloomington** (CDP) San Bernardino County
42	73	7.5	**Shafter** (city) Kern County
43	80	7.8	**South San Jose Hills** (CDP) Los Angeles County
44	81	7.9	**Paramount** (city) Los Angeles County
45	87	8.0	**Livingston** (city) Merced County
45	87	8.0	**South El Monte** (city) Los Angeles County
47	94	8.4	**Perris** (city) Riverside County
48	97	8.6	**Blythe** (city) Riverside County
49	101	8.8	**Greenfield** (city) Monterey County
49	101	8.8	**West Puente Valley** (CDP) Los Angeles County
51	112	9.1	**Sun Village** (CDP) Los Angeles County
52	114	9.2	**Lake Los Angeles** (CDP) Los Angeles County
52	114	9.2	**Tehachapi** (city) Kern County
54	118	9.3	**Chowchilla** (city) Madera County
54	118	9.3	**Delhi** (CDP) Merced County
54	118	9.3	**Oildale** (CDP) Kern County
54	118	9.3	**Watsonville** (city) Santa Cruz County
58	128	9.4	**Hesperia** (city) San Bernardino County
58	128	9.4	**La Puente** (city) Los Angeles County
58	128	9.4	**Los Banos** (city) Merced County
58	128	9.4	**Madera** (city) Madera County
58	128	9.4	**Red Bluff** (city) Tehama County
63	135	9.5	**Westmont** (CDP) Los Angeles County
64	149	9.9	**Rialto** (city) San Bernardino County
65	161	10.0	**Florin** (CDP) Sacramento County
66	176	10.2	**West Whittier-Los Nietos** (CDP) Los Angeles County
67	184	10.3	**Ceres** (city) Stanislaus County
67	184	10.3	**Home Gardens** (CDP) Riverside County
69	193	10.4	**Selma** (city) Fresno County
69	193	10.4	**Susanville** (city) Lassen County
71	200	10.5	**Porterville** (city) Tulare County
72	208	10.6	**Barstow** (city) San Bernardino County
72	208	10.6	**Brawley** (city) Imperial County
72	208	10.6	**Kerman** (city) Fresno County
75	218	10.8	**Phelan** (CDP) San Bernardino County
75	218	10.8	**Sanger** (city) Fresno County
75	218	10.8	**Victorville** (city) San Bernardino County
78	225	10.9	**Pico Rivera** (city) Los Angeles County
79	231	11.0	**Parkway** (CDP) Sacramento County
80	247	11.2	**Marysville** (city) Yuba County
80	247	11.2	**San Bernardino** (city) San Bernardino County
82	254	11.3	**Baldwin Park** (city) Los Angeles County
82	254	11.3	**Hawaiian Gardens** (city) Los Angeles County
84	260	11.4	**Colton** (city) San Bernardino County
84	260	11.4	**San Fernando** (city) Los Angeles County
84	260	11.4	**Tulare** (city) Tulare County
87	269	11.5	**Newman** (city) Stanislaus County
88	276	11.6	**Patterson** (city) Stanislaus County
89	286	11.7	**Santa Fe Springs** (city) Los Angeles County
89	286	11.7	**Shasta Lake** (city) Shasta County
91	295	11.8	**Santa Ana** (city) Orange County
92	302	11.9	**Hemet** (city) Riverside County
92	302	11.9	**Rosamond** (CDP) Kern County
94	308	12.0	**California City** (city) Kern County
94	308	12.0	**El Monte** (city) Los Angeles County
96	322	12.2	**Montclair** (city) San Bernardino County
97	328	12.3	**Bostonia** (CDP) San Diego County
97	328	12.3	**Oroville** (city) Butte County
99	340	12.4	**Salinas** (city) Monterey County
100	348	12.5	**Desert Hot Springs** (city) Riverside County
100	348	12.5	**National City** (city) San Diego County
102	356	12.6	**North Highlands** (CDP) Sacramento County
103	366	12.7	**Rio Linda** (CDP) Sacramento County
103	366	12.7	**San Pablo** (city) Contra Costa County
105	387	12.9	**Coalinga** (city) Fresno County
105	387	12.9	**Lathrop** (city) San Joaquin County
105	387	12.9	**Santa Maria** (city) Santa Barbara County
108	394	13.0	**Alum Rock** (CDP) Santa Clara County
108	394	13.0	**Ontario** (city) San Bernardino County
110	426	13.3	**San Jacinto** (city) Riverside County
111	430	13.4	**Calexico** (city) Imperial County
111	430	13.4	**Citrus** (CDP) Los Angeles County
111	430	13.4	**Santa Paula** (city) Ventura County
111	430	13.4	**Valinda** (CDP) Los Angeles County
115	448	13.6	**Atwater** (city) Merced County
115	448	13.6	**Yucca Valley** (town) San Bernardino County
117	470	13.9	**Fillmore** (city) Ventura County
118	499	14.2	**Foothill Farms** (CDP) Sacramento County
118	499	14.2	**Lompoc** (city) Santa Barbara County
118	499	14.2	**Oakley** (city) Contra Costa County
121	510	14.3	**Cherryland** (CDP) Alameda County
121	510	14.3	**Riverbank** (city) Stanislaus County
121	510	14.3	**South Whittier** (CDP) Los Angeles County
124	517	14.4	**Hollister** (city) San Benito County
124	517	14.4	**Rosemead** (city) Los Angeles County
126	525	14.5	**East Hemet** (CDP) Riverside County
126	525	14.5	**Reedley** (city) Fresno County
128	536	14.6	**Exeter** (city) Tulare County
128	536	14.6	**Oakdale** (city) Stanislaus County
130	549	14.7	**Bay Point** (CDP) Contra Costa County
131	564	14.8	**Galt** (city) Sacramento County
131	564	14.8	**Moreno Valley** (city) Riverside County
131	564	14.8	**Norwalk** (city) Los Angeles County
134	582	14.9	**Lemon Grove** (city) San Diego County
135	603	15.0	**Cathedral City** (city) Riverside County
136	636	15.3	**Palmdale** (city) Los Angeles County
137	649	15.4	**Manteca** (city) San Joaquin County
137	649	15.4	**Ramona** (CDP) San Diego County
139	668	15.5	**Lake Elsinore** (city) Riverside County
139	668	15.5	**Valle Vista** (CDP) Riverside County
139	668	15.5	**Winter Gardens** (CDP) San Diego County
142	680	15.6	**Magalia** (CDP) Butte County
142	680	15.6	**Oxnard** (city) Ventura County
144	694	15.7	**Big Bear City** (CDP) San Bernardino County
144	694	15.7	**Lancaster** (city) Los Angeles County
144	694	15.7	**Merced** (city) Merced County
144	694	15.7	**Salida** (CDP) Stanislaus County
148	703	15.8	**Apple Valley** (town) San Bernardino County
148	703	15.8	**Banning** (city) Riverside County
148	703	15.8	**Fontana** (city) San Bernardino County

Note: *The state column ranks the top/bottom 150 places from all places in the state with population of 10,000 or more. The national column ranks the top/bottom 150 places from all places in the country with population of 10,000 or more. Places that are unincorporated were not considered in the rankings. Please refer to the User Guide for additional information.*

Educational Attainment: Graduate/Professional Degree or Higher

Top 150 Places Ranked in *Descending* Order

State Rank	Nat'l Rank	Percent	Place
1	1	63.3	**Stanford** (CDP) Santa Clara County
2	8	51.3	**Palo Alto** (city) Santa Clara County
3	24	45.6	**Los Altos** (city) Santa Clara County
4	27	45.1	**Piedmont** (city) Alameda County
5	40	43.2	**Hillsborough** (town) San Mateo County
6	49	41.8	**Saratoga** (city) Santa Clara County
7	54	41.1	**Cupertino** (city) Santa Clara County
8	56	40.5	**Albany** (city) Alameda County
9	60	39.8	**Menlo Park** (city) San Mateo County
10	63	39.2	**Davis** (city) Yolo County
11	74	38.1	**Mill Valley** (city) Marin County
12	85	37.4	**Berkeley** (city) Alameda County
13	93	37.0	**Palos Verdes Estates** (city) Los Angeles County
14	101	36.4	**Moraga** (town) Contra Costa County
15	110	35.8	**Emeryville** (city) Alameda County
16	118	35.5	**La Cañada Flintridge** (city) Los Angeles County
16	118	35.5	**San Marino** (city) Los Angeles County
18	122	35.0	**Orinda** (city) Contra Costa County
19	133	34.4	**Lafayette** (city) Contra Costa County
20	135	34.2	**Mountain View** (city) Santa Clara County
21	161	33.0	**Tamalpais-Homestead Valley** (CDP) Marin County
22	191	31.8	**Manhattan Beach** (city) Los Angeles County
23	203	31.4	**Isla Vista** (CDP) Santa Barbara County
24	206	31.3	**Malibu** (city) Los Angeles County
25	230	30.3	**Los Gatos** (town) Santa Clara County
26	245	29.8	**Rancho Palos Verdes** (city) Los Angeles County
27	248	29.7	**South Pasadena** (city) Los Angeles County
28	255	29.4	**Larkspur** (city) Marin County
29	260	29.2	**Calabasas** (city) Los Angeles County
30	273	28.9	**El Cerrito** (city) Contra Costa County
30	273	28.9	**Laguna Beach** (city) Orange County
32	275	28.8	**Santa Monica** (city) Los Angeles County
33	280	28.7	**Claremont** (city) Los Angeles County
34	283	28.6	**Foster City** (city) San Mateo County
34	283	28.6	**Sierra Madre** (city) Los Angeles County
36	297	28.2	**Sunnyvale** (city) Santa Clara County
37	300	28.1	**Solana Beach** (city) San Diego County
38	308	27.9	**Coronado** (city) San Diego County
38	308	27.9	**Irvine** (city) Orange County
40	340	27.3	**San Carlos** (city) San Mateo County
41	347	27.2	**Alamo** (CDP) Contra Costa County
41	347	27.2	**Beverly Hills** (city) Los Angeles County
43	361	26.7	**View Park-Windsor Hills** (CDP) Los Angeles County
44	385	25.9	**Oak Park** (CDP) Ventura County
45	390	25.8	**Newport Beach** (city) Orange County
46	398	25.6	**Burlingame** (city) San Mateo County
47	408	25.3	**San Ramon** (city) Contra Costa County
48	418	25.0	**Belmont** (city) San Mateo County
49	430	24.7	**Walnut Creek** (city) Contra Costa County
50	444	24.4	**Ladera Ranch** (CDP) Orange County
51	462	24.0	**San Anselmo** (town) Marin County
52	477	23.6	**Hermosa Beach** (city) Los Angeles County
53	481	23.5	**Encinitas** (city) San Diego County
54	497	23.1	**Agoura Hills** (city) Los Angeles County
54	497	23.1	**Monterey** (city) Monterey County
56	503	23.0	**Fremont** (city) Alameda County
56	503	23.0	**Pleasanton** (city) Alameda County
56	503	23.0	**Santa Clara** (city) Santa Clara County
59	512	22.8	**Danville** (town) Contra Costa County
60	519	22.7	**Granite Bay** (CDP) Placer County
61	528	22.5	**Redondo Beach** (city) Los Angeles County
62	555	21.9	**Pasadena** (city) Los Angeles County
63	566	21.8	**North Tustin** (CDP) Orange County
63	566	21.8	**Rossmoor** (CDP) Orange County
65	594	21.4	**Goleta** (city) Santa Barbara County
65	594	21.4	**Pacific Grove** (city) Monterey County
65	594	21.4	**Santa Cruz** (city) Santa Cruz County
68	608	21.3	**Loma Linda** (city) San Bernardino County
68	608	21.3	**Stevenson Ranch** (CDP) Los Angeles County
70	624	21.0	**Carlsbad** (city) San Diego County
71	643	20.8	**Culver City** (city) Los Angeles County
72	653	20.7	**San Francisco** (city) San Francisco County
73	679	20.4	**Arcadia** (city) Los Angeles County
73	679	20.4	**Laguna Niguel** (city) Orange County
75	692	20.3	**Coto de Caza** (CDP) Orange County
76	711	20.0	**Thousand Oaks** (city) Ventura County
77	734	19.8	**Casa de Oro-Mount Helix** (CDP) San Diego County
77	734	19.8	**Half Moon Bay** (city) San Mateo County
79	753	19.6	**San Rafael** (city) Marin County
80	825	18.8	**Altadena** (CDP) Los Angeles County
80	825	18.8	**Seal Beach** (city) Orange County
80	825	18.8	**Yorba Linda** (city) Orange County
83	835	18.7	**San Luis Obispo** (city) San Luis Obispo County
84	859	18.4	**Alameda** (city) Alameda County
85	868	18.3	**La Crescenta-Montrose** (CDP) Los Angeles County
86	900	18.0	**Santa Barbara** (city) Santa Barbara County
87	928	17.7	**Bonita** (CDP) San Diego County
87	928	17.7	**Dublin** (city) Alameda County
87	928	17.7	**Rancho Mirage** (city) Riverside County
90	953	17.5	**Arcata** (city) Humboldt County
90	953	17.5	**San Mateo** (city) San Mateo County
92	966	17.4	**El Dorado Hills** (CDP) El Dorado County
92	966	17.4	**El Sobrante** (CDP) Riverside County
94	986	17.3	**Diamond Bar** (city) Los Angeles County
95	998	17.2	**Cerritos** (city) Los Angeles County
95	998	17.2	**West Hollywood** (city) Los Angeles County
97	1012	17.1	**Redlands** (city) San Bernardino County
98	1020	17.0	**Aliso Viejo** (city) Orange County
98	1020	17.0	**Dana Point** (city) Orange County
98	1020	17.0	**East San Gabriel** (CDP) Los Angeles County
101	1031	16.9	**Folsom** (city) Sacramento County
101	1031	16.9	**Laguna Woods** (city) Orange County
101	1031	16.9	**Novato** (city) Marin County
104	1045	16.8	**Laguna Hills** (city) Orange County
105	1055	16.7	**San Diego** (city) San Diego County
106	1060	16.6	**Oakland** (city) Alameda County
106	1060	16.6	**Poway** (city) San Diego County
108	1071	16.5	**El Segundo** (city) Los Angeles County
108	1071	16.5	**Scotts Valley** (city) Santa Cruz County
110	1088	16.4	**Campbell** (city) Santa Clara County
110	1088	16.4	**Rancho Santa Margarita** (city) Orange County
112	1101	16.3	**Clayton** (city) Contra Costa County
113	1114	16.2	**Mission Viejo** (city) Orange County
113	1114	16.2	**Redwood City** (city) San Mateo County
115	1134	16.0	**San Clemente** (city) Orange County
115	1134	16.0	**Walnut** (city) Los Angeles County
117	1199	15.5	**Fair Oaks** (CDP) Sacramento County
118	1232	15.2	**Pleasant Hill** (city) Contra Costa County
119	1256	15.0	**Torrance** (city) Los Angeles County
120	1280	14.8	**Benicia** (city) Solano County
121	1302	14.6	**Brea** (city) Orange County
121	1302	14.6	**Millbrae** (city) San Mateo County
123	1314	14.5	**Morro Bay** (city) San Luis Obispo County
124	1326	14.4	**Camarillo** (city) Ventura County
124	1326	14.4	**Chino Hills** (city) San Bernardino County
124	1326	14.4	**Healdsburg** (city) Sonoma County
127	1342	14.3	**Milpitas** (city) Santa Clara County
127	1342	14.3	**Tustin** (city) Orange County
129	1360	14.2	**Huntington Beach** (city) Orange County
130	1377	14.1	**Morgan Hill** (city) Santa Clara County
130	1377	14.1	**San Jose** (city) Santa Clara County
132	1389	14.0	**Sonoma** (city) Sonoma County
133	1428	13.8	**Los Alamitos** (city) Orange County
133	1428	13.8	**Los Osos** (CDP) San Luis Obispo County
135	1460	13.6	**Lake Arrowhead** (CDP) San Bernardino County
135	1460	13.6	**Palm Springs** (city) Riverside County
137	1476	13.5	**Lake Forest** (city) Orange County
137	1476	13.5	**Rancho San Diego** (CDP) San Diego County
139	1497	13.4	**Pacifica** (city) San Mateo County
140	1510	13.3	**Carmichael** (CDP) Sacramento County
140	1510	13.3	**Castro Valley** (CDP) Alameda County
142	1527	13.2	**Livermore** (city) Alameda County
143	1543	13.1	**Monrovia** (city) Los Angeles County
144	1561	13.0	**La Verne** (city) Los Angeles County
144	1561	13.0	**Live Oak** (CDP) Santa Cruz County
146	1579	12.9	**San Buenaventura (Ventura)** (city) Ventura County
146	1579	12.9	**Temple City** (city) Los Angeles County
148	1598	12.8	**Arden-Arcade** (CDP) Sacramento County
148	1598	12.8	**La Palma** (city) Orange County
148	1598	12.8	**San Dimas** (city) Los Angeles County

Note: *The state column ranks the top/bottom 150 places from all places in the state with population of 10,000 or more. The national column ranks the top/bottom 150 places from all places in the country with population of 10,000 or more. Places that are unincorporated were not considered in the rankings. Please refer to the User Guide for additional information.*

Educational Attainment: Graduate/Professional Degree or Higher

Top 150 Places Ranked in *Ascending* Order

State Rank	Nat'l Rank	Percent	Place
1	2	0.3	**Lemon Hill** (CDP) Sacramento County
2	3	0.5	**Arvin** (city) Kern County
3	5	0.6	**Avenal** (city) Kings County
4	6	0.7	**Maywood** (city) Los Angeles County
4	6	0.7	**Mendota** (city) Fresno County
4	6	0.7	**Muscoy** (CDP) San Bernardino County
7	10	0.8	**Florence-Graham** (CDP) Los Angeles County
7	10	0.8	**Soledad** (city) Monterey County
9	12	0.9	**Coachella** (city) Riverside County
9	12	0.9	**Corcoran** (city) Kings County
9	12	0.9	**Cudahy** (city) Los Angeles County
12	15	1.0	**Lamont** (CDP) Kern County
12	15	1.0	**Lennox** (CDP) Los Angeles County
12	15	1.0	**Mead Valley** (CDP) Riverside County
15	22	1.1	**Bell Gardens** (city) Los Angeles County
15	22	1.1	**Parlier** (city) Fresno County
17	25	1.2	**Bell** (city) Los Angeles County
17	25	1.2	**Bloomington** (CDP) San Bernardino County
17	25	1.2	**Garden Acres** (CDP) San Joaquin County
17	25	1.2	**Greenfield** (city) Monterey County
17	25	1.2	**Huntington Park** (city) Los Angeles County
17	25	1.2	**South San Jose Hills** (CDP) Los Angeles County
23	32	1.3	**East Los Angeles** (CDP) Los Angeles County
23	32	1.3	**East Rancho Dominguez** (CDP) Los Angeles County
23	32	1.3	**Linda** (CDP) Yuba County
23	32	1.3	**McFarland** (city) Kern County
23	32	1.3	**Walnut Park** (CDP) Los Angeles County
23	32	1.3	**Winton** (CDP) Merced County
29	40	1.4	**Delano** (city) Kern County
29	40	1.4	**South Gate** (city) Los Angeles County
29	40	1.4	**Willowbrook** (CDP) Los Angeles County
32	46	1.5	**Farmersville** (city) Tulare County
32	46	1.5	**Lynwood** (city) Los Angeles County
34	55	1.6	**Adelanto** (city) San Bernardino County
34	55	1.6	**Hawaiian Gardens** (city) Los Angeles County
34	55	1.6	**South El Monte** (city) Los Angeles County
37	63	1.7	**Dinuba** (city) Tulare County
37	63	1.7	**Paramount** (city) Los Angeles County
37	63	1.7	**Wasco** (city) Kern County
40	70	1.8	**Compton** (city) Los Angeles County
40	70	1.8	**Home Gardens** (CDP) Riverside County
40	70	1.8	**Shafter** (city) Kern County
43	75	1.9	**Lathrop** (city) San Joaquin County
43	75	1.9	**Lindsay** (city) Tulare County
45	81	2.0	**Delhi** (CDP) Merced County
45	81	2.0	**Tehachapi** (city) Kern County
45	81	2.0	**West Puente Valley** (CDP) Los Angeles County
48	86	2.1	**Bostonia** (CDP) San Diego County
48	86	2.1	**Clearlake** (city) Lake County
48	86	2.1	**Commerce** (city) Los Angeles County
48	86	2.1	**El Monte** (city) Los Angeles County
52	99	2.2	**Newman** (city) Stanislaus County
52	99	2.2	**Olivehurst** (CDP) Yuba County
54	106	2.3	**Ceres** (city) Stanislaus County
54	106	2.3	**King City** (city) Monterey County
54	106	2.3	**Lakeland Village** (CDP) Riverside County
54	106	2.3	**Montclair** (city) San Bernardino County
54	106	2.3	**Oildale** (CDP) Kern County
59	120	2.4	**Florin** (CDP) Sacramento County
59	120	2.4	**Madera** (city) Madera County
59	120	2.4	**Perris** (city) Riverside County
59	120	2.4	**Pico Rivera** (city) Los Angeles County
59	120	2.4	**Rio Linda** (CDP) Sacramento County
64	133	2.5	**Baldwin Park** (city) Los Angeles County
64	133	2.5	**Westmont** (CDP) Los Angeles County
66	144	2.6	**Chowchilla** (city) Madera County
66	144	2.6	**La Puente** (city) Los Angeles County
66	144	2.6	**Los Banos** (city) Merced County
66	144	2.6	**National City** (city) San Diego County
66	144	2.6	**North Highlands** (CDP) Sacramento County
66	144	2.6	**Oakley** (city) Contra Costa County
66	144	2.6	**Shasta Lake** (city) Shasta County
66	144	2.6	**West Whittier-Los Nietos** (CDP) Los Angeles County
74	163	2.7	**Blythe** (city) Riverside County
74	163	2.7	**Hollister** (city) San Benito County
74	163	2.7	**Sanger** (city) Fresno County
74	163	2.7	**Watsonville** (city) Santa Cruz County
78	180	2.8	**Kerman** (city) Fresno County
78	180	2.8	**Sun Village** (CDP) Los Angeles County
80	194	2.9	**Patterson** (city) Stanislaus County
81	205	3.0	**Bay Point** (CDP) Contra Costa County
81	205	3.0	**Livingston** (city) Merced County
81	205	3.0	**Phelan** (CDP) San Bernardino County
81	205	3.0	**Porterville** (city) Tulare County
81	205	3.0	**Salida** (CDP) Stanislaus County
86	229	3.1	**Alum Rock** (CDP) Santa Clara County
86	229	3.1	**Cherryland** (CDP) Alameda County
86	229	3.1	**Hesperia** (city) San Bernardino County
86	229	3.1	**Lake Los Angeles** (CDP) Los Angeles County
86	229	3.1	**Marysville** (city) Yuba County
86	229	3.1	**Parkway** (CDP) Sacramento County
92	248	3.2	**Susanville** (city) Lassen County
92	248	3.2	**Valinda** (CDP) Los Angeles County
94	266	3.3	**Brawley** (city) Imperial County
94	266	3.3	**Foothill Farms** (CDP) Sacramento County
94	266	3.3	**Ontario** (city) San Bernardino County
94	266	3.3	**Rosemead** (city) Los Angeles County
94	266	3.3	**San Fernando** (city) Los Angeles County
94	266	3.3	**San Pablo** (city) Contra Costa County
94	266	3.3	**Santa Ana** (city) Orange County
94	266	3.3	**Selma** (city) Fresno County
102	284	3.4	**Rialto** (city) San Bernardino County
103	304	3.5	**Galt** (city) Sacramento County
103	304	3.5	**Riverbank** (city) Stanislaus County
103	304	3.5	**Santa Fe Springs** (city) Los Angeles County
103	304	3.5	**Tulare** (city) Tulare County
107	326	3.6	**Bellflower** (city) Los Angeles County
107	326	3.6	**Red Bluff** (city) Tehama County
107	326	3.6	**San Bernardino** (city) San Bernardino County
110	351	3.7	**Calexico** (city) Imperial County
110	351	3.7	**Magalia** (CDP) Butte County
110	351	3.7	**San Lorenzo** (CDP) Alameda County
110	351	3.7	**Santa Maria** (city) Santa Barbara County
114	378	3.8	**Salinas** (city) Monterey County
115	398	3.9	**Citrus** (CDP) Los Angeles County
115	398	3.9	**Victorville** (city) San Bernardino County
117	415	4.0	**Exeter** (city) Tulare County
117	415	4.0	**Oroville** (city) Butte County
117	415	4.0	**Rosamond** (CDP) Kern County
120	456	4.1	**Ramona** (CDP) San Diego County
120	456	4.1	**South Whittier** (CDP) Los Angeles County
120	456	4.1	**Suisun City** (city) Solano County
123	481	4.2	**Barstow** (city) San Bernardino County
123	481	4.2	**Lemon Grove** (city) San Diego County
123	481	4.2	**Reedley** (city) Fresno County
126	497	4.3	**Ashland** (CDP) Alameda County
126	497	4.3	**Fontana** (city) San Bernardino County
126	497	4.3	**Moreno Valley** (city) Riverside County
129	525	4.4	**Big Bear City** (CDP) San Bernardino County
129	525	4.4	**Garden Grove** (city) Orange County
129	525	4.4	**Hawthorne** (city) Los Angeles County
129	525	4.4	**Hemet** (city) Riverside County
129	525	4.4	**Lawndale** (city) Los Angeles County
129	525	4.4	**Yucca Valley** (town) San Bernardino County
135	551	4.5	**Colton** (city) San Bernardino County
135	551	4.5	**Lake Elsinore** (city) Riverside County
135	551	4.5	**Manteca** (city) San Joaquin County
135	551	4.5	**Norwalk** (city) Los Angeles County
135	551	4.5	**Oxnard** (city) Ventura County
135	551	4.5	**San Jacinto** (city) Riverside County
135	551	4.5	**Tracy** (city) San Joaquin County
142	590	4.6	**Antioch** (city) Contra Costa County
142	590	4.6	**Stanton** (city) Orange County
144	620	4.7	**Atwater** (city) Merced County
144	620	4.7	**La Presa** (CDP) San Diego County
144	620	4.7	**Lompoc** (city) Santa Barbara County
144	620	4.7	**Santa Paula** (city) Ventura County
148	646	4.8	**Fortuna** (city) Humboldt County
149	679	4.9	**Citrus Heights** (city) Sacramento County
149	679	4.9	**Palmdale** (city) Los Angeles County

Note: *The state column ranks the top/bottom 150 places from all places in the state with population of 10,000 or more. The national column ranks the top/bottom 150 places from all places in the country with population of 10,000 or more. Places that are unincorporated were not considered in the rankings. Please refer to the User Guide for additional information.*

Homeownership Rate

Top 150 Places Ranked in *Descending* Order

State Rank	Nat'l Rank	Percent	Place
1	25	94.5	**Hillsborough** (town) San Mateo County
2	117	91.7	**Coto de Caza** (CDP) Orange County
3	125	91.5	**San Marino** (city) Los Angeles County
4	133	91.4	**Alamo** (CDP) Contra Costa County
4	133	91.4	**El Sobrante** (CDP) Riverside County
6	184	90.4	**Clayton** (city) Contra Costa County
7	204	90.0	**Rosedale** (CDP) Kern County
8	217	89.7	**Orinda** (city) Contra Costa County
9	240	89.4	**La Cañada Flintridge** (city) Los Angeles County
9	240	89.4	**North Tustin** (CDP) Orange County
11	259	89.0	**Granite Bay** (CDP) Placer County
12	269	88.9	**Woodcrest** (CDP) Riverside County
13	272	88.8	**Palos Verdes Estates** (city) Los Angeles County
13	272	88.8	**San Diego Country Estates** (CDP) San Diego County
15	298	88.3	**Piedmont** (city) Alameda County
15	298	88.3	**Walnut** (city) Los Angeles County
17	351	87.6	**Rossmoor** (CDP) Orange County
18	451	86.2	**Saratoga** (city) Santa Clara County
19	550	84.7	**El Dorado Hills** (CDP) El Dorado County
20	579	84.4	**Danville** (town) Contra Costa County
21	594	84.2	**Castaic** (CDP) Los Angeles County
22	614	83.9	**Moraga** (town) Contra Costa County
22	614	83.9	**Yorba Linda** (city) Orange County
24	628	83.8	**Los Altos** (city) Santa Clara County
25	709	82.8	**French Valley** (CDP) Riverside County
26	718	82.7	**Eastvale** (city) Riverside County
27	733	82.5	**Canyon Lake** (city) Riverside County
28	753	82.3	**Discovery Bay** (CDP) Contra Costa County
29	794	81.9	**Cerritos** (city) Los Angeles County
30	858	81.2	**Diamond Bar** (city) Los Angeles County
30	858	81.2	**Norco** (city) Riverside County
30	858	81.2	**West Puente Valley** (CDP) Los Angeles County
33	931	80.3	**Chino Hills** (city) San Bernardino County
33	931	80.3	**Rancho Mirage** (city) Riverside County
35	950	80.2	**Rancho Palos Verdes** (city) Los Angeles County
36	1015	79.5	**Hercules** (city) Contra Costa County
36	1015	79.5	**Lincoln** (city) Placer County
38	1046	79.1	**La Mirada** (city) Los Angeles County
39	1101	78.6	**American Canyon** (city) Napa County
39	1101	78.6	**Hacienda Heights** (CDP) Los Angeles County
41	1124	78.3	**Phelan** (CDP) San Bernardino County
42	1137	78.2	**Salida** (CDP) Stanislaus County
43	1143	78.1	**Orcutt** (CDP) Santa Barbara County
44	1156	78.0	**Agoura Hills** (city) Los Angeles County
44	1156	78.0	**Fairview** (CDP) Alameda County
44	1156	78.0	**Moorpark** (city) Ventura County
47	1169	77.9	**Mission Viejo** (city) Orange County
48	1178	77.8	**Vineyard** (CDP) Sacramento County
49	1226	77.2	**Laguna Woods** (city) Orange County
50	1248	77.0	**Avocado Heights** (CDP) Los Angeles County
50	1248	77.0	**Magalia** (CDP) Butte County
52	1261	76.9	**Menifee** (city) Riverside County
53	1275	76.8	**Carson** (city) Los Angeles County
54	1323	76.3	**Prunedale** (CDP) Monterey County
55	1337	76.2	**Brentwood** (city) Contra Costa County
55	1337	76.2	**Valinda** (CDP) Los Angeles County
55	1337	76.2	**West Carson** (CDP) Los Angeles County
58	1352	76.1	**Oakley** (city) Contra Costa County
58	1352	76.1	**South San Jose Hills** (CDP) Los Angeles County
60	1361	76.0	**Tamalpais-Homestead Valley** (CDP) Marin County
61	1377	75.8	**Windsor** (town) Sonoma County
62	1390	75.6	**Valle Vista** (CDP) Riverside County
63	1423	75.3	**La Quinta** (city) Riverside County
63	1423	75.3	**Lathrop** (city) San Joaquin County
65	1428	75.2	**Lafayette** (city) Contra Costa County
66	1442	75.0	**Beaumont** (city) Riverside County
66	1442	75.0	**San Lorenzo** (CDP) Alameda County
68	1469	74.7	**Laguna Hills** (city) Orange County
69	1480	74.6	**Elk Grove** (city) Sacramento County
69	1480	74.6	**Seal Beach** (city) Orange County
71	1492	74.5	**La Verne** (city) Los Angeles County
71	1492	74.5	**Oak Park** (CDP) Ventura County
71	1492	74.5	**Sun Village** (CDP) Los Angeles County
74	1505	74.4	**Poway** (city) San Diego County
75	1523	74.2	**San Juan Capistrano** (city) Orange County
76	1533	74.1	**Simi Valley** (city) Ventura County
76	1533	74.1	**Yucaipa** (city) San Bernardino County
78	1576	73.6	**Calabasas** (city) Los Angeles County
78	1576	73.6	**Galt** (city) Sacramento County
78	1576	73.6	**Stevenson Ranch** (CDP) Los Angeles County
81	1586	73.5	**Orangevale** (CDP) Sacramento County
82	1594	73.4	**Lake Arrowhead** (CDP) San Bernardino County
82	1594	73.4	**Scotts Valley** (city) Santa Cruz County
82	1594	73.4	**Wildomar** (city) Riverside County
85	1628	73.1	**Bonita** (CDP) San Diego County
85	1628	73.1	**Ladera Ranch** (CDP) Orange County
85	1628	73.1	**Thousand Oaks** (city) Ventura County
85	1628	73.1	**West Whittier-Los Nietos** (CDP) Los Angeles County
89	1655	72.8	**San Dimas** (city) Los Angeles County
90	1668	72.7	**Lake Los Angeles** (CDP) Los Angeles County
90	1668	72.7	**Ripon** (city) San Joaquin County
92	1678	72.6	**Rio Linda** (CDP) Sacramento County
93	1715	72.3	**Casa de Oro-Mount Helix** (CDP) San Diego County
93	1715	72.3	**Glendora** (city) Los Angeles County
93	1715	72.3	**Riverbank** (city) Stanislaus County
93	1715	72.3	**View Park-Windsor Hills** (CDP) Los Angeles County
97	1748	72.1	**Diamond Springs** (CDP) El Dorado County
97	1748	72.1	**Fountain Valley** (city) Orange County
97	1748	72.1	**Lakewood** (city) Los Angeles County
100	1768	72.0	**Laguna Niguel** (city) Orange County
101	1776	71.9	**La Palma** (city) Orange County
102	1792	71.8	**Pinole** (city) Contra Costa County
102	1792	71.8	**San Carlos** (city) San Mateo County
104	1809	71.6	**Altadena** (CDP) Los Angeles County
104	1809	71.6	**Crestline** (CDP) San Bernardino County
106	1823	71.5	**Rancho Santa Margarita** (city) Orange County
107	1835	71.4	**Morgan Hill** (city) Santa Clara County
107	1835	71.4	**San Ramon** (city) Contra Costa County
109	1852	71.2	**Nipomo** (CDP) San Luis Obispo County
109	1852	71.2	**Rancho San Diego** (CDP) San Diego County
109	1852	71.2	**Santa Clarita** (city) Los Angeles County
112	1865	71.1	**Imperial** (city) Imperial County
113	1887	70.9	**Citrus** (CDP) Los Angeles County
113	1887	70.9	**Half Moon Bay** (city) San Mateo County
113	1887	70.9	**Pleasanton** (city) Alameda County
116	1897	70.8	**Lake Forest** (city) Orange County
117	1906	70.7	**Home Gardens** (CDP) Riverside County
118	1923	70.5	**Benicia** (city) Solano County
118	1923	70.5	**Malibu** (city) Los Angeles County
118	1923	70.5	**Murrieta** (city) Riverside County
121	1937	70.4	**Santee** (city) San Diego County
122	1958	70.1	**Cypress** (city) Orange County
122	1958	70.1	**Livermore** (city) Alameda County
124	1978	69.9	**Folsom** (city) Sacramento County
125	2007	69.6	**Camarillo** (city) Ventura County
125	2007	69.6	**Quartz Hill** (CDP) Los Angeles County
127	2042	69.3	**Suisun City** (city) Solano County
128	2051	69.2	**Temecula** (city) Riverside County
129	2059	69.1	**Apple Valley** (town) San Bernardino County
129	2059	69.1	**Pico Rivera** (city) Los Angeles County
131	2075	69.0	**Castro Valley** (CDP) Alameda County
131	2075	69.0	**Lakeside** (CDP) San Diego County
131	2075	69.0	**Newark** (city) Alameda County
134	2088	68.9	**Bloomington** (CDP) San Bernardino County
134	2088	68.9	**Chino** (city) San Bernardino County
134	2088	68.9	**Del Aire** (CDP) Los Angeles County
134	2088	68.9	**Fontana** (city) San Bernardino County
138	2132	68.5	**Alpine** (CDP) San Diego County
139	2143	68.4	**Banning** (city) Riverside County
140	2145	68.3	**Antelope** (CDP) Sacramento County
140	2145	68.3	**Delhi** (CDP) Merced County
140	2145	68.3	**Pacifica** (city) San Mateo County
143	2159	68.2	**Cameron Park** (CDP) El Dorado County
143	2159	68.2	**Mead Valley** (CDP) Riverside County
143	2159	68.2	**Truckee** (town) Nevada County
146	2170	68.1	**Big Bear City** (CDP) San Bernardino County
147	2182	68.0	**San Jacinto** (city) Riverside County
148	2190	67.9	**Palmdale** (city) Los Angeles County
149	2206	67.8	**Rosamond** (CDP) Kern County
150	2215	67.7	**Los Osos** (CDP) San Luis Obispo County

Note: *The state column ranks the top/bottom 150 places from all places in the state with population of 10,000 or more. The national column ranks the top/bottom 150 places from all places in the country with population of 10,000 or more. Places that are unincorporated were not considered in the rankings. Please refer to the User Guide for additional information.*

Homeownership Rate

Top 150 Places Ranked in *Ascending* Order

State Rank	Nat'l Rank	Percent	Place
1	3	0.4	**Camp Pendleton South** (CDP) San Diego County
2	11	2.6	**Isla Vista** (CDP) Santa Barbara County
3	14	18.0	**Cudahy** (city) Los Angeles County
4	17	20.2	**Stanford** (CDP) Santa Clara County
5	21	22.1	**West Hollywood** (city) Los Angeles County
6	29	24.0	**Bell Gardens** (city) Los Angeles County
7	41	26.7	**Hawthorne** (city) Los Angeles County
8	43	27.0	**Huntington Park** (city) Los Angeles County
9	46	28.4	**Santa Monica** (city) Los Angeles County
10	54	29.0	**Bell** (city) Los Angeles County
11	59	29.9	**Lennox** (CDP) Los Angeles County
12	60	30.2	**Imperial Beach** (city) San Diego County
12	60	30.2	**Maywood** (city) Los Angeles County
14	67	31.1	**Westmont** (CDP) Los Angeles County
15	70	31.4	**Cherryland** (CDP) Alameda County
16	86	33.5	**National City** (city) San Diego County
17	92	33.8	**Twentynine Palms** (city) San Bernardino County
18	97	34.2	**Arcata** (city) Humboldt County
19	99	34.3	**Lawndale** (city) Los Angeles County
20	101	34.5	**Ashland** (CDP) Alameda County
21	114	35.4	**Emeryville** (city) Alameda County
22	118	35.7	**East Los Angeles** (CDP) Los Angeles County
22	118	35.7	**San Francisco** (city) San Francisco County
24	121	35.8	**Monterey** (city) Monterey County
25	129	36.7	**Florence-Graham** (CDP) Los Angeles County
26	131	36.9	**Inglewood** (city) Los Angeles County
27	153	38.1	**Glendale** (city) Los Angeles County
28	157	38.2	**Los Angeles** (city) Los Angeles County
29	175	38.8	**Lemon Hill** (CDP) Sacramento County
30	178	38.9	**Santa Barbara** (city) Santa Barbara County
30	178	38.9	**South Lake Tahoe** (city) El Dorado County
32	183	39.1	**Marysville** (city) Yuba County
33	185	39.2	**Loma Linda** (city) San Bernardino County
34	189	39.3	**San Luis Obispo** (city) San Luis Obispo County
35	195	39.4	**Grass Valley** (city) Nevada County
36	198	39.6	**Costa Mesa** (city) Orange County
37	202	40.0	**Bellflower** (city) Los Angeles County
38	215	40.8	**Alhambra** (city) Los Angeles County
39	217	41.0	**Berkeley** (city) Alameda County
39	217	41.0	**Oakland** (city) Alameda County
41	221	41.2	**El Cajon** (city) San Diego County
42	226	41.4	**Seaside** (city) Monterey County
43	236	41.6	**Long Beach** (city) Los Angeles County
44	242	41.7	**Mountain View** (city) Santa Clara County
45	254	42.0	**Bostonia** (CDP) San Diego County
46	260	42.2	**El Monte** (city) Los Angeles County
47	263	42.3	**Red Bluff** (city) Tehama County
48	280	42.7	**Chico** (city) Butte County
48	280	42.7	**Merced** (city) Merced County
50	285	42.8	**East Palo Alto** (city) San Mateo County
51	287	42.9	**El Segundo** (city) Los Angeles County
51	287	42.9	**Oroville** (city) Butte County
53	292	43.0	**Davis** (city) Yolo County
54	301	43.3	**Eureka** (city) Humboldt County
54	301	43.3	**Marina** (city) Monterey County
54	301	43.3	**Santa Cruz** (city) Santa Cruz County
57	310	43.4	**Oildale** (CDP) Kern County
57	310	43.4	**Paramount** (city) Los Angeles County
57	310	43.4	**Ukiah** (city) Mendocino County
60	322	43.6	**Mendota** (city) Fresno County
61	335	44.0	**Burbank** (city) Los Angeles County
61	335	44.0	**Watsonville** (city) Santa Cruz County
63	338	44.1	**Beverly Hills** (city) Los Angeles County
64	341	44.2	**Hawaiian Gardens** (city) Los Angeles County
65	350	44.6	**Hermosa Beach** (city) Los Angeles County
66	357	45.0	**Pasadena** (city) Los Angeles County
67	358	45.1	**Lamont** (CDP) Kern County
67	358	45.1	**Salinas** (city) Monterey County
69	376	45.5	**Avenal** (city) Kings County
70	380	45.6	**Pacific Grove** (city) Monterey County
71	384	45.7	**South Pasadena** (city) Los Angeles County
72	393	45.8	**La Mesa** (city) San Diego County
72	393	45.8	**South Gate** (city) Los Angeles County
74	404	46.0	**Santa Clara** (city) Santa Clara County
75	407	46.1	**Arden-Arcade** (CDP) Sacramento County
75	407	46.1	**Montebello** (city) Los Angeles County
75	407	46.1	**Parkway** (CDP) Sacramento County
78	411	46.2	**Parlier** (city) Fresno County
79	414	46.3	**Lomita** (city) Los Angeles County
80	422	46.4	**King City** (city) Monterey County
81	426	46.5	**Lynwood** (city) Los Angeles County
82	432	46.7	**Grover Beach** (city) San Luis Obispo County
82	432	46.7	**Los Alamitos** (city) Orange County
84	436	46.9	**North Fair Oaks** (CDP) San Mateo County
84	436	46.9	**San Pablo** (city) Contra Costa County
86	448	47.1	**Burlingame** (city) San Mateo County
87	462	47.5	**Santa Ana** (city) Orange County
88	483	47.9	**Commerce** (city) Los Angeles County
88	483	47.9	**Gardena** (city) Los Angeles County
90	492	48.0	**Sunnyvale** (city) Santa Clara County
91	498	48.1	**Alameda** (city) Alameda County
92	503	48.2	**Desert Hot Springs** (city) Riverside County
93	510	48.3	**Albany** (city) Alameda County
93	510	48.3	**Port Hueneme** (city) Ventura County
93	510	48.3	**San Diego** (city) San Diego County
96	516	48.4	**South El Monte** (city) Los Angeles County
97	522	48.5	**Anaheim** (city) Orange County
98	529	48.6	**Lompoc** (city) Santa Barbara County
99	536	48.8	**Coronado** (city) San Diego County
100	545	48.9	**North Highlands** (CDP) Sacramento County
101	548	49.0	**Barstow** (city) San Bernardino County
101	548	49.0	**Larkspur** (city) Marin County
101	548	49.0	**Rosemead** (city) Los Angeles County
104	558	49.1	**Fresno** (city) Fresno County
104	558	49.1	**Linda** (CDP) Yuba County
106	564	49.2	**San Gabriel** (city) Los Angeles County
107	574	49.3	**Carpinteria** (city) Santa Barbara County
108	582	49.4	**Sacramento** (city) Sacramento County
109	586	49.5	**El Centro** (city) Imperial County
109	586	49.5	**Monrovia** (city) Los Angeles County
111	613	50.0	**Stanton** (city) Orange County
112	617	50.1	**Campbell** (city) Santa Clara County
113	626	50.2	**Irvine** (city) Orange County
114	629	50.3	**San Bernardino** (city) San Bernardino County
115	637	50.5	**Downey** (city) Los Angeles County
116	645	50.6	**Lindsay** (city) Tulare County
116	645	50.6	**Redwood City** (city) San Mateo County
118	661	50.8	**Madera** (city) Madera County
118	661	50.8	**Tustin** (city) Orange County
120	683	51.2	**Coalinga** (city) Fresno County
121	696	51.4	**Redondo Beach** (city) Los Angeles County
122	700	51.5	**Corcoran** (city) Kings County
122	700	51.5	**Signal Hill** (city) Los Angeles County
122	700	51.5	**Susanville** (city) Lassen County
125	711	51.6	**Santa Maria** (city) Santa Barbara County
125	711	51.6	**Stockton** (city) San Joaquin County
127	717	51.7	**Richmond** (city) Contra Costa County
128	725	51.8	**Colton** (city) San Bernardino County
128	725	51.8	**Vista** (city) San Diego County
130	736	51.9	**Willowbrook** (CDP) Los Angeles County
131	750	52.1	**Brawley** (city) Imperial County
132	759	52.2	**Escondido** (city) San Diego County
132	759	52.2	**Wasco** (city) Kern County
134	767	52.3	**Blythe** (city) Riverside County
134	767	52.3	**San Mateo** (city) San Mateo County
134	767	52.3	**San Rafael** (city) Marin County
137	781	52.4	**Placerville** (city) El Dorado County
138	813	52.7	**Hayward** (city) Alameda County
138	813	52.7	**Lemoore** (city) Kings County
140	828	52.9	**Greenfield** (city) Monterey County
141	853	53.3	**Morro Bay** (city) San Luis Obispo County
141	853	53.3	**Walnut Park** (CDP) Los Angeles County
143	864	53.4	**Clearlake** (city) Lake County
143	864	53.4	**Winton** (CDP) Merced County
145	875	53.5	**Arvin** (city) Kern County
145	875	53.5	**Azusa** (city) Los Angeles County
145	875	53.5	**Chowchilla** (city) Madera County
148	885	53.6	**Goleta** (city) Santa Barbara County
149	896	53.7	**Calexico** (city) Imperial County
149	896	53.7	**Foothill Farms** (CDP) Sacramento County

Note: *The state column ranks the top/bottom 150 places from all places in the state with population of 10,000 or more. The national column ranks the top/bottom 150 places from all places in the country with population of 10,000 or more. Places that are unincorporated were not considered in the rankings. Please refer to the User Guide for additional information.*

Median Home Value

Top 150 Places Ranked in *Descending* Order

State Rank	Nat'l Rank	Dollars	Place
1	1	1 million+	**Alamo** (CDP) Contra Costa County
1	1	1 million+	**Beverly Hills** (city) Los Angeles County
1	1	1 million+	**Burlingame** (city) San Mateo County
1	1	1 million+	**Coronado** (city) San Diego County
1	1	1 million+	**Cupertino** (city) Santa Clara County
1	1	1 million+	**Hermosa Beach** (city) Los Angeles County
1	1	1 million+	**Hillsborough** (town) San Mateo County
1	1	1 million+	**La Cañada Flintridge** (city) Los Angeles County
1	1	1 million+	**Laguna Beach** (city) Orange County
1	1	1 million+	**Larkspur** (city) Marin County
1	1	1 million+	**Los Altos** (city) Santa Clara County
1	1	1 million+	**Los Gatos** (town) Santa Clara County
1	1	1 million+	**Malibu** (city) Los Angeles County
1	1	1 million+	**Manhattan Beach** (city) Los Angeles County
1	1	1 million+	**Menlo Park** (city) San Mateo County
1	1	1 million+	**Mill Valley** (city) Marin County
1	1	1 million+	**Newport Beach** (city) Orange County
1	1	1 million+	**Palo Alto** (city) Santa Clara County
1	1	1 million+	**Palos Verdes Estates** (city) Los Angeles County
1	1	1 million+	**Piedmont** (city) Alameda County
1	1	1 million+	**San Marino** (city) Los Angeles County
1	1	1 million+	**Saratoga** (city) Santa Clara County
1	1	1 million+	**Stanford** (CDP) Santa Clara County
24	35	999,900	**Santa Monica** (city) Los Angeles County
25	36	993,400	**Lafayette** (city) Contra Costa County
26	37	974,900	**Tamalpais-Homestead Valley** (CDP) Marin County
27	38	973,600	**Orinda** (city) Contra Costa County
28	40	954,900	**Solana Beach** (city) San Diego County
29	43	945,400	**Rancho Palos Verdes** (city) Los Angeles County
30	48	918,800	**San Carlos** (city) San Mateo County
31	50	901,700	**Millbrae** (city) San Mateo County
32	53	884,200	**Moraga** (town) Contra Costa County
33	54	882,400	**Belmont** (city) San Mateo County
34	56	874,500	**Coto de Caza** (CDP) Orange County
35	57	868,700	**Calabasas** (city) Los Angeles County
36	60	847,400	**Foster City** (city) San Mateo County
37	63	832,100	**Santa Barbara** (city) Santa Barbara County
38	65	827,600	**Danville** (town) Contra Costa County
39	66	827,200	**San Anselmo** (town) Marin County
40	68	820,200	**South Pasadena** (city) Los Angeles County
41	69	820,100	**Rossmoor** (CDP) Orange County
42	75	802,400	**Arcadia** (city) Los Angeles County
43	78	788,700	**Mountain View** (city) Santa Clara County
44	82	780,300	**Sierra Madre** (city) Los Angeles County
45	83	776,600	**North Tustin** (CDP) Orange County
46	85	765,400	**Redwood City** (city) San Mateo County
47	87	744,600	**San Francisco** (city) San Francisco County
48	90	736,500	**El Segundo** (city) Los Angeles County
49	95	715,000	**Redondo Beach** (city) Los Angeles County
50	96	713,600	**San Clemente** (city) Orange County
51	98	710,700	**San Mateo** (city) San Mateo County
51	98	710,700	**Sunnyvale** (city) Santa Clara County
53	101	709,400	**Pleasanton** (city) Alameda County
54	102	707,600	**Dana Point** (city) Orange County
55	105	699,600	**Half Moon Bay** (city) San Mateo County
56	107	698,600	**Berkeley** (city) Alameda County
57	110	695,800	**San Rafael** (city) Marin County
58	111	695,200	**Encinitas** (city) San Diego County
59	114	692,000	**San Ramon** (city) Contra Costa County
60	117	678,000	**Agoura Hills** (city) Los Angeles County
61	118	677,100	**Yorba Linda** (city) Orange County
62	122	667,000	**Pacific Grove** (city) Monterey County
63	123	666,900	**Campbell** (city) Santa Clara County
64	127	662,200	**Laguna Niguel** (city) Orange County
65	135	643,800	**Santa Cruz** (city) Santa Cruz County
66	137	643,200	**Irvine** (city) Orange County
67	140	635,100	**Oak Park** (CDP) Ventura County
68	145	625,100	**Walnut** (city) Los Angeles County
69	147	624,400	**Huntington Beach** (city) Orange County
70	148	624,100	**La Crescenta-Montrose** (CDP) Los Angeles County
71	152	621,900	**Albany** (city) Alameda County
72	154	618,800	**Alameda** (city) Alameda County
73	155	617,300	**Monterey** (city) Monterey County
74	159	614,000	**Carlsbad** (city) San Diego County
75	160	613,600	**Los Alamitos** (city) Orange County
75	160	613,600	**Torrance** (city) Los Angeles County
77	162	613,200	**Goleta** (city) Santa Barbara County
77	162	613,200	**Santa Clara** (city) Santa Clara County
79	164	612,600	**Ladera Ranch** (CDP) Orange County
80	165	610,700	**Granite Bay** (CDP) Placer County
81	167	610,000	**Pacifica** (city) San Mateo County
82	170	609,600	**Culver City** (city) Los Angeles County
83	174	604,100	**Fountain Valley** (city) Orange County
84	178	601,900	**West Hollywood** (city) Los Angeles County
85	180	601,500	**Pasadena** (city) Los Angeles County
86	181	600,900	**East San Gabriel** (CDP) Los Angeles County
87	182	600,300	**Fremont** (city) Alameda County
88	184	597,900	**San Bruno** (city) San Mateo County
89	187	593,900	**Thousand Oaks** (city) Ventura County
90	188	592,600	**Cerritos** (city) Los Angeles County
91	192	587,800	**Glendale** (city) Los Angeles County
92	194	586,100	**Scotts Valley** (city) Santa Cruz County
93	196	585,000	**South San Francisco** (city) San Mateo County
93	196	585,000	**Walnut Creek** (city) Contra Costa County
95	198	584,700	**Clayton** (city) Contra Costa County
96	201	583,900	**Stevenson Ranch** (CDP) Los Angeles County
97	205	580,700	**Costa Mesa** (city) Orange County
98	209	576,700	**Morgan Hill** (city) Santa Clara County
99	211	575,500	**Temple City** (city) Los Angeles County
100	213	573,700	**El Cerrito** (city) Contra Costa County
101	221	568,300	**La Palma** (city) Orange County
102	223	564,900	**Dublin** (city) Alameda County
103	226	562,900	**Laguna Hills** (city) Orange County
104	227	560,400	**San Jose** (city) Santa Clara County
105	228	560,300	**Novato** (city) Marin County
106	229	560,000	**Altadena** (CDP) Los Angeles County
107	235	555,900	**Casa de Oro-Mount Helix** (CDP) San Diego County
108	237	554,700	**Burbank** (city) Los Angeles County
109	241	552,900	**San Gabriel** (city) Los Angeles County
110	242	552,700	**Daly City** (city) San Mateo County
111	256	542,800	**Mission Viejo** (city) Orange County
112	259	540,200	**Live Oak** (CDP) Santa Cruz County
113	261	538,600	**North Fair Oaks** (CDP) San Mateo County
114	263	537,900	**Carpinteria** (city) Santa Barbara County
115	264	533,600	**Castro Valley** (CDP) Alameda County
115	264	533,600	**Claremont** (city) Los Angeles County
117	268	532,200	**Sonoma** (city) Sonoma County
118	271	529,300	**Davis** (city) Yolo County
119	278	522,000	**Brea** (city) Orange County
119	278	522,000	**San Juan Capistrano** (city) Orange County
121	280	521,900	**Diamond Bar** (city) Los Angeles County
122	281	520,300	**Moorpark** (city) Ventura County
123	283	519,500	**San Luis Obispo** (city) San Luis Obispo County
124	286	518,000	**Rancho Mirage** (city) Riverside County
125	288	516,800	**Rancho Santa Margarita** (city) Orange County
126	293	513,300	**Milpitas** (city) Santa Clara County
127	301	507,900	**Pleasant Hill** (city) Contra Costa County
128	303	505,700	**Monrovia** (city) Los Angeles County
129	305	504,400	**View Park-Windsor Hills** (CDP) Los Angeles County
130	310	499,000	**Bonita** (CDP) San Diego County
131	312	498,700	**Orange** (city) Orange County
132	316	496,600	**Cypress** (city) Orange County
133	321	495,100	**Poway** (city) San Diego County
134	324	493,200	**Placentia** (city) Orange County
135	328	491,600	**Tustin** (city) Orange County
136	330	490,800	**Lake Forest** (city) Orange County
137	337	484,800	**Morro Bay** (city) San Luis Obispo County
138	339	483,500	**Alpine** (CDP) San Diego County
139	346	478,900	**Fullerton** (city) Orange County
140	348	478,500	**Alhambra** (city) Los Angeles County
141	357	476,400	**Livermore** (city) Alameda County
142	358	476,200	**Chino Hills** (city) San Bernardino County
143	361	475,600	**Monterey Park** (city) Los Angeles County
144	363	474,300	**Union City** (city) Alameda County
145	367	473,300	**Healdsburg** (city) Sonoma County
146	370	472,900	**Rowland Heights** (CDP) Los Angeles County
147	372	470,200	**Rancho San Diego** (CDP) San Diego County
148	374	469,700	**El Dorado Hills** (CDP) El Dorado County
149	389	462,800	**Aliso Viejo** (city) Orange County
150	392	458,800	**Hacienda Heights** (CDP) Los Angeles County

Note: *The state column ranks the top/bottom 150 places from all places in the state with population of 10,000 or more. The national column ranks the top/bottom 150 places from all places in the country with population of 10,000 or more. Places that are unincorporated were not considered in the rankings. Please refer to the User Guide for additional information.*

Median Home Value

Top 150 Places Ranked in *Ascending* Order

State Rank	Nat'l Rank	Dollars	Place
1	254	83,200	**Lake Los Angeles** (CDP) Los Angeles County
2	383	89,800	**Lamont** (CDP) Kern County
3	462	93,600	**California City** (city) Kern County
4	487	95,100	**Clearlake** (city) Lake County
5	499	95,900	**Adelanto** (city) San Bernardino County
5	499	95,900	**Lemon Hill** (CDP) Sacramento County
7	523	97,400	**Barstow** (city) San Bernardino County
8	549	98,700	**Arvin** (city) Kern County
9	564	99,700	**Winton** (CDP) Merced County
10	633	103,300	**Garden Acres** (CDP) San Joaquin County
11	656	105,100	**Farmersville** (city) Tulare County
12	743	110,000	**Parlier** (city) Fresno County
13	754	110,600	**Mendota** (city) Fresno County
14	828	114,200	**Hemet** (city) Riverside County
15	864	115,600	**McFarland** (city) Kern County
16	995	121,100	**Lindsay** (city) Tulare County
17	999	121,300	**Avenal** (city) Kings County
18	1008	121,600	**Desert Hot Springs** (city) Riverside County
19	1044	123,400	**Corcoran** (city) Kings County
20	1058	124,200	**Rosamond** (CDP) Kern County
21	1070	124,800	**Oildale** (CDP) Kern County
22	1074	125,300	**Marysville** (city) Yuba County
23	1101	127,000	**Valle Vista** (CDP) Riverside County
24	1111	127,600	**Wasco** (city) Kern County
25	1144	129,300	**Phelan** (CDP) San Bernardino County
26	1155	129,500	**Shafter** (city) Kern County
27	1157	129,600	**Atwater** (city) Merced County
28	1192	131,200	**Blythe** (city) Riverside County
29	1213	132,100	**Linda** (CDP) Yuba County
30	1249	133,600	**Newman** (city) Stanislaus County
31	1266	134,300	**Delhi** (CDP) Merced County
32	1321	137,600	**Coachella** (city) Riverside County
33	1325	137,700	**Victorville** (city) San Bernardino County
34	1330	137,900	**Merced** (city) Merced County
35	1333	138,000	**Twentynine Palms** (city) San Bernardino County
36	1341	138,300	**San Jacinto** (city) Riverside County
37	1349	138,600	**Chowchilla** (city) Madera County
38	1371	140,100	**Delano** (city) Kern County
39	1398	141,700	**Muscoy** (CDP) San Bernardino County
40	1409	142,300	**Florin** (CDP) Sacramento County
41	1432	143,300	**North Highlands** (CDP) Sacramento County
42	1436	143,500	**Los Banos** (city) Merced County
43	1447	144,000	**Olivehurst** (CDP) Yuba County
44	1485	146,200	**Hesperia** (city) San Bernardino County
45	1506	147,500	**Brawley** (city) Imperial County
46	1512	147,900	**Yucca Valley** (town) San Bernardino County
47	1520	148,200	**Parkway** (CDP) Sacramento County
48	1530	148,600	**Dinuba** (city) Tulare County
49	1543	149,100	**Porterville** (city) Tulare County
50	1547	149,200	**El Centro** (city) Imperial County
51	1557	149,600	**Coalinga** (city) Fresno County
52	1579	150,500	**Sun Village** (CDP) Los Angeles County
53	1609	151,600	**Madera** (city) Madera County
54	1638	152,800	**San Bernardino** (city) San Bernardino County
55	1652	153,500	**Calexico** (city) Imperial County
55	1652	153,500	**East Hemet** (CDP) Riverside County
57	1673	154,600	**Magalia** (CDP) Butte County
58	1691	155,600	**Perris** (city) Riverside County
59	1702	156,300	**Oroville** (city) Butte County
59	1702	156,300	**Tehachapi** (city) Kern County
61	1720	157,100	**Ceres** (city) Stanislaus County
62	1737	157,600	**Tulare** (city) Tulare County
63	1747	158,100	**Red Bluff** (city) Tehama County
64	1758	158,500	**Sanger** (city) Fresno County
65	1763	158,700	**Colton** (city) San Bernardino County
66	1773	159,200	**Lancaster** (city) Los Angeles County
67	1779	159,300	**Banning** (city) Riverside County
68	1782	159,400	**King City** (city) Monterey County
69	1785	159,600	**Selma** (city) Fresno County
70	1790	159,700	**Exeter** (city) Tulare County
71	1825	161,400	**Foothill Farms** (CDP) Sacramento County
72	1835	161,900	**Livingston** (city) Merced County
73	1840	162,100	**Patterson** (city) Stanislaus County
74	1881	164,500	**Bay Point** (CDP) Contra Costa County
75	1901	165,400	**Kerman** (city) Fresno County
76	1923	166,300	**Greenfield** (city) Monterey County
77	1926	166,500	**Stockton** (city) San Joaquin County
78	1932	167,100	**Modesto** (city) Stanislaus County
79	1938	167,300	**Shasta Lake** (city) Shasta County
80	1941	167,400	**Mead Valley** (CDP) Riverside County
81	1954	167,800	**Lakeland Village** (CDP) Riverside County
82	1965	168,400	**Reedley** (city) Fresno County
83	1989	169,300	**Bloomington** (CDP) San Bernardino County
84	2018	171,400	**Susanville** (city) Lassen County
85	2020	171,600	**Apple Valley** (town) San Bernardino County
86	2038	172,000	**Palmdale** (city) Los Angeles County
87	2054	172,800	**Riverbank** (city) Stanislaus County
88	2098	175,100	**Imperial** (city) Imperial County
89	2133	177,100	**Visalia** (city) Tulare County
90	2141	178,100	**Salida** (CDP) Stanislaus County
91	2149	178,400	**Moreno Valley** (city) Riverside County
92	2154	178,800	**Hanford** (city) Kings County
93	2157	179,300	**Rio Linda** (CDP) Sacramento County
94	2162	179,500	**Cathedral City** (city) Riverside County
95	2170	179,700	**Bakersfield** (city) Kern County
96	2177	180,100	**Fresno** (city) Fresno County
97	2184	180,500	**Rialto** (city) San Bernardino County
98	2207	181,900	**Ridgecrest** (city) Kern County
99	2238	185,100	**Yuba City** (city) Sutter County
100	2241	185,300	**Rosemont** (CDP) Sacramento County
101	2271	187,000	**San Pablo** (city) Contra Costa County
102	2326	190,200	**Citrus Heights** (city) Sacramento County
103	2339	191,200	**Lathrop** (city) San Joaquin County
104	2341	191,300	**Rancho Cordova** (city) Sacramento County
105	2343	191,600	**Galt** (city) Sacramento County
106	2345	191,800	**Big Bear City** (CDP) San Bernardino County
107	2353	192,400	**Quartz Hill** (CDP) Los Angeles County
108	2355	192,600	**Indio** (city) Riverside County
109	2363	193,100	**Menifee** (city) Riverside County
110	2370	193,700	**Lemoore** (city) Kings County
111	2386	194,600	**Crestline** (CDP) San Bernardino County
112	2414	196,400	**Turlock** (city) Stanislaus County
113	2434	198,300	**Laguna Woods** (city) Orange County
114	2455	199,500	**Oakdale** (city) Stanislaus County
115	2503	203,700	**Soledad** (city) Monterey County
116	2530	206,400	**Cudahy** (city) Los Angeles County
117	2539	207,000	**Home Gardens** (CDP) Riverside County
118	2547	207,400	**Paradise** (town) Butte County
119	2568	209,000	**Lake Elsinore** (city) Riverside County
120	2593	210,400	**Antelope** (CDP) Sacramento County
121	2596	210,500	**La Riviera** (CDP) Sacramento County
122	2602	211,200	**Beaumont** (city) Riverside County
123	2626	212,600	**Kingsburg** (city) Fresno County
124	2629	212,900	**Manteca** (city) San Joaquin County
125	2662	215,300	**Suisun City** (city) Solano County
126	2695	218,300	**Vallejo** (city) Solano County
127	2704	218,900	**Yucaipa** (city) San Bernardino County
128	2714	219,800	**Willowbrook** (CDP) Los Angeles County
129	2723	220,500	**Wildomar** (city) Riverside County
130	2746	222,700	**Pittsburg** (city) Contra Costa County
131	2778	225,900	**Sacramento** (city) Sacramento County
132	2795	228,000	**Redding** (city) Shasta County
133	2800	228,600	**Lodi** (city) San Joaquin County
134	2837	232,300	**Grand Terrace** (city) San Bernardino County
135	2856	233,600	**Antioch** (city) Contra Costa County
136	2865	234,500	**Diamond Springs** (CDP) El Dorado County
137	2877	235,400	**Oakley** (city) Contra Costa County
138	2879	235,500	**Lompoc** (city) Santa Barbara County
139	2881	235,900	**Riverside** (city) Riverside County
140	2903	237,800	**Compton** (city) Los Angeles County
141	2910	238,500	**Placerville** (city) El Dorado County
142	2920	238,800	**East Rancho Dominguez** (CDP) Los Angeles County
143	2930	239,400	**North Auburn** (CDP) Placer County
144	2943	241,000	**West Sacramento** (city) Yolo County
145	2948	241,400	**Eureka** (city) Humboldt County
146	2968	243,000	**Florence-Graham** (CDP) Los Angeles County
147	2986	243,800	**Hawaiian Gardens** (city) Los Angeles County
148	2988	243,900	**Fontana** (city) San Bernardino County
149	3023	247,000	**Clovis** (city) Fresno County
150	3049	249,300	**Bostonia** (CDP) San Diego County

Note: *The state column ranks the top/bottom 150 places from all places in the state with population of 10,000 or more. The national column ranks the top/bottom 150 places from all places in the country with population of 10,000 or more. Places that are unincorporated were not considered in the rankings. Please refer to the User Guide for additional information.*

Median Year Structure Built

Top 150 Places Ranked in *Descending* Order

State Rank	Nat'l Rank	Year	Place
1	1	2005	**Eastvale** (city) Riverside County
1	1	2005	**French Valley** (CDP) Riverside County
1	1	2005	**Ladera Ranch** (CDP) Orange County
4	31	2003	**Camp Pendleton South** (CDP) San Diego County
4	31	2003	**Lincoln** (city) Placer County
6	56	2002	**Beaumont** (city) Riverside County
6	56	2002	**El Sobrante** (CDP) Riverside County
8	84	2001	**Brentwood** (city) Contra Costa County
8	84	2001	**Vineyard** (CDP) Sacramento County
10	121	2000	**Imperial** (city) Imperial County
10	121	2000	**Murrieta** (city) Riverside County
10	121	2000	**Patterson** (city) Stanislaus County
13	153	1999	**Coachella** (city) Riverside County
14	181	1998	**El Dorado Hills** (CDP) El Dorado County
14	181	1998	**Elk Grove** (city) Sacramento County
14	181	1998	**La Quinta** (city) Riverside County
14	181	1998	**Stevenson Ranch** (CDP) Los Angeles County
18	220	1997	**Adelanto** (city) San Bernardino County
18	220	1997	**American Canyon** (city) Napa County
18	220	1997	**Lathrop** (city) San Joaquin County
21	266	1996	**Lake Elsinore** (city) Riverside County
21	266	1996	**Perris** (city) Riverside County
21	266	1996	**Temecula** (city) Riverside County
24	312	1995	**Dublin** (city) Alameda County
24	312	1995	**Indio** (city) Riverside County
24	312	1995	**Menifee** (city) Riverside County
24	312	1995	**Rocklin** (city) Placer County
28	369	1994	**Aliso Viejo** (city) Orange County
28	369	1994	**Castaic** (CDP) Los Angeles County
28	369	1994	**Coto de Caza** (CDP) Orange County
28	369	1994	**Delhi** (CDP) Merced County
28	369	1994	**Folsom** (city) Sacramento County
28	369	1994	**Kerman** (city) Fresno County
28	369	1994	**Newman** (city) Stanislaus County
28	369	1994	**Riverbank** (city) Stanislaus County
28	369	1994	**Roseville** (city) Placer County
37	435	1993	**Antelope** (CDP) Sacramento County
37	435	1993	**Galt** (city) Sacramento County
37	435	1993	**Greenfield** (city) Monterey County
37	435	1993	**Rosedale** (CDP) Kern County
37	435	1993	**Salida** (CDP) Stanislaus County
37	435	1993	**Tracy** (city) San Joaquin County
37	435	1993	**Victorville** (city) San Bernardino County
44	501	1992	**Calexico** (city) Imperial County
44	501	1992	**California City** (city) Kern County
44	501	1992	**Los Banos** (city) Merced County
44	501	1992	**Rancho Santa Margarita** (city) Orange County
44	501	1992	**Soledad** (city) Monterey County
49	566	1991	**Irvine** (city) Orange County
49	566	1991	**Livingston** (city) Merced County
49	566	1991	**Oakley** (city) Contra Costa County
49	566	1991	**Parlier** (city) Fresno County
49	566	1991	**Rosamond** (CDP) Kern County
49	566	1991	**San Jacinto** (city) Riverside County
49	566	1991	**Wildomar** (city) Riverside County
56	651	1990	**Discovery Bay** (CDP) Contra Costa County
56	651	1990	**Ripon** (city) San Joaquin County
56	651	1990	**San Ramon** (city) Contra Costa County
56	651	1990	**Windsor** (town) Sonoma County
60	715	1989	**Chino Hills** (city) San Bernardino County
60	715	1989	**Clovis** (city) Fresno County
60	715	1989	**Corona** (city) Riverside County
60	715	1989	**McFarland** (city) Kern County
60	715	1989	**Palmdale** (city) Los Angeles County
65	778	1988	**Desert Hot Springs** (city) Riverside County
65	778	1988	**El Paso de Robles (Paso Robles)** (city) San Luis Obispo County
65	778	1988	**Nipomo** (CDP) San Luis Obispo County
65	778	1988	**Phelan** (CDP) San Bernardino County
65	778	1988	**San Marcos** (city) San Diego County
65	778	1988	**Truckee** (town) Nevada County
71	851	1987	**Cathedral City** (city) Riverside County
71	851	1987	**Fontana** (city) San Bernardino County
71	851	1987	**Hercules** (city) Contra Costa County
71	851	1987	**Hollister** (city) San Benito County
71	851	1987	**Moreno Valley** (city) Riverside County
71	851	1987	**Rancho Cucamonga** (city) San Bernardino County
71	851	1987	**San Diego Country Estates** (CDP) San Diego County
78	933	1986	**Apple Valley** (town) San Bernardino County
78	933	1986	**Arvin** (city) Kern County
78	933	1986	**Bakersfield** (city) Kern County
78	933	1986	**Cameron Park** (CDP) El Dorado County
78	933	1986	**Carlsbad** (city) San Diego County
78	933	1986	**Granite Bay** (CDP) Placer County
78	933	1986	**Lemoore** (city) Kings County
78	933	1986	**Madera** (city) Madera County
78	933	1986	**Moorpark** (city) Ventura County
78	933	1986	**Oak Park** (CDP) Ventura County
78	933	1986	**Oakdale** (city) Stanislaus County
89	1031	1985	**Alpine** (CDP) San Diego County
89	1031	1985	**Ceres** (city) Stanislaus County
89	1031	1985	**Chowchilla** (city) Madera County
89	1031	1985	**Delano** (city) Kern County
89	1031	1985	**Dixon** (city) Solano County
89	1031	1985	**Gilroy** (city) Santa Clara County
89	1031	1985	**Hesperia** (city) San Bernardino County
89	1031	1985	**Laguna Niguel** (city) Orange County
89	1031	1985	**Lancaster** (city) Los Angeles County
89	1031	1985	**Manteca** (city) San Joaquin County
89	1031	1985	**McKinleyville** (CDP) Humboldt County
89	1031	1985	**Rancho San Diego** (CDP) San Diego County
101	1133	1984	**Canyon Lake** (city) Riverside County
101	1133	1984	**Emeryville** (city) Alameda County
101	1133	1984	**Kingsburg** (city) Fresno County
101	1133	1984	**Lake Los Angeles** (CDP) Los Angeles County
101	1133	1984	**Morgan Hill** (city) Santa Clara County
101	1133	1984	**Palm Desert** (city) Riverside County
101	1133	1984	**Rancho Mirage** (city) Riverside County
101	1133	1984	**Suisun City** (city) Solano County
101	1133	1984	**Sun Village** (CDP) Los Angeles County
101	1133	1984	**Tulare** (city) Tulare County
101	1133	1984	**Turlock** (city) Stanislaus County
112	1238	1983	**Antioch** (city) Contra Costa County
112	1238	1983	**Banning** (city) Riverside County
112	1238	1983	**Calabasas** (city) Los Angeles County
112	1238	1983	**Fairfield** (city) Solano County
112	1238	1983	**Santa Clarita** (city) Los Angeles County
112	1238	1983	**Visalia** (city) Tulare County
112	1238	1983	**Winton** (CDP) Merced County
112	1238	1983	**Woodcrest** (CDP) Riverside County
112	1238	1983	**Yorba Linda** (city) Orange County
121	1344	1982	**Chula Vista** (city) San Diego County
121	1344	1982	**Diamond Springs** (CDP) El Dorado County
121	1344	1982	**Florin** (CDP) Sacramento County
121	1344	1982	**Hanford** (city) Kings County
121	1344	1982	**Hemet** (city) Riverside County
121	1344	1982	**Highland** (city) San Bernardino County
121	1344	1982	**King City** (city) Monterey County
121	1344	1982	**Loma Linda** (city) San Bernardino County
121	1344	1982	**Mead Valley** (CDP) Riverside County
121	1344	1982	**Oceanside** (city) San Diego County
121	1344	1982	**Pleasanton** (city) Alameda County
121	1344	1982	**Porterville** (city) Tulare County
121	1344	1982	**Sanger** (city) Fresno County
121	1344	1982	**Scotts Valley** (city) Santa Cruz County
121	1344	1982	**Vacaville** (city) Solano County
121	1344	1982	**Valle Vista** (CDP) Riverside County
121	1344	1982	**Walnut** (city) Los Angeles County
121	1344	1982	**West Sacramento** (city) Yolo County
121	1344	1982	**Yuba City** (city) Sutter County
140	1463	1981	**Chino** (city) San Bernardino County
140	1463	1981	**Clayton** (city) Contra Costa County
140	1463	1981	**Colton** (city) San Bernardino County
140	1463	1981	**Home Gardens** (CDP) Riverside County
140	1463	1981	**Lake Forest** (city) Orange County
140	1463	1981	**Lakeland Village** (CDP) Riverside County
140	1463	1981	**Magalia** (CDP) Butte County
140	1463	1981	**Mendota** (city) Fresno County
140	1463	1981	**Merced** (city) Merced County
140	1463	1981	**Redding** (city) Shasta County
140	1463	1981	**Rialto** (city) San Bernardino County

Note: *The state column ranks the top/bottom 150 places from all places in the state with population of 10,000 or more. The national column ranks the top/bottom 150 places from all places in the country with population of 10,000 or more. Places that are unincorporated were not considered in the rankings. Please refer to the User Guide for additional information.*

Median Year Structure Built

Top 150 Places Ranked in *Ascending* Order

State Rank	Nat'l Rank	Year	Place
1	1	<1940	**Berkeley** (city) Alameda County
1	1	<1940	**Piedmont** (city) Alameda County
1	1	<1940	**San Marino** (city) Los Angeles County
4	120	1941	**San Francisco** (city) San Francisco County
5	144	1943	**Walnut Park** (CDP) Los Angeles County
6	202	1947	**Altadena** (CDP) Los Angeles County
7	245	1949	**Oakland** (city) Alameda County
7	245	1949	**View Park-Windsor Hills** (CDP) Los Angeles County
9	270	1950	**East Los Angeles** (CDP) Los Angeles County
9	270	1950	**Huntington Park** (city) Los Angeles County
9	270	1950	**Maywood** (city) Los Angeles County
9	270	1950	**South Gate** (city) Los Angeles County
13	306	1951	**Del Aire** (CDP) Los Angeles County
13	306	1951	**Florence-Graham** (CDP) Los Angeles County
13	306	1951	**San Anselmo** (town) Marin County
13	306	1951	**South Pasadena** (city) Los Angeles County
17	344	1952	**Beverly Hills** (city) Los Angeles County
17	344	1952	**East Rancho Dominguez** (CDP) Los Angeles County
19	383	1953	**Albany** (city) Alameda County
19	383	1953	**Westmont** (CDP) Los Angeles County
21	425	1954	**Compton** (city) Los Angeles County
21	425	1954	**El Cerrito** (city) Contra Costa County
21	425	1954	**Eureka** (city) Humboldt County
21	425	1954	**Lynwood** (city) Los Angeles County
21	425	1954	**San Lorenzo** (CDP) Alameda County
26	482	1955	**Bell** (city) Los Angeles County
26	482	1955	**La Cañada Flintridge** (city) Los Angeles County
26	482	1955	**Pacific Grove** (city) Monterey County
26	482	1955	**West Whittier-Los Nietos** (CDP) Los Angeles County
30	544	1956	**Alhambra** (city) Los Angeles County
30	544	1956	**Alum Rock** (CDP) Santa Clara County
30	544	1956	**Burlingame** (city) San Mateo County
30	544	1956	**La Crescenta-Montrose** (CDP) Los Angeles County
30	544	1956	**Long Beach** (city) Los Angeles County
30	544	1956	**Pico Rivera** (city) Los Angeles County
30	544	1956	**San Fernando** (city) Los Angeles County
30	544	1956	**San Gabriel** (city) Los Angeles County
30	544	1956	**Sierra Madre** (city) Los Angeles County
30	544	1956	**West Puente Valley** (CDP) Los Angeles County
30	544	1956	**Whittier** (city) Los Angeles County
41	630	1957	**Burbank** (city) Los Angeles County
41	630	1957	**Citrus** (CDP) Los Angeles County
41	630	1957	**Commerce** (city) Los Angeles County
41	630	1957	**Lakewood** (city) Los Angeles County
41	630	1957	**Lennox** (CDP) Los Angeles County
41	630	1957	**Norwalk** (city) Los Angeles County
41	630	1957	**Pasadena** (city) Los Angeles County
41	630	1957	**South El Monte** (city) Los Angeles County
41	630	1957	**Temple City** (city) Los Angeles County
41	630	1957	**Valinda** (CDP) Los Angeles County
41	630	1957	**Willowbrook** (CDP) Los Angeles County
52	725	1958	**Downey** (city) Los Angeles County
52	725	1958	**North Fair Oaks** (CDP) San Mateo County
52	725	1958	**Rosemead** (city) Los Angeles County
52	725	1958	**San Carlos** (city) San Mateo County
52	725	1958	**San Leandro** (city) Alameda County
52	725	1958	**South Whittier** (CDP) Los Angeles County
58	808	1959	**Cherryland** (CDP) Alameda County
58	808	1959	**East San Gabriel** (CDP) Los Angeles County
58	808	1959	**Inglewood** (city) Los Angeles County
58	808	1959	**La Mirada** (city) Los Angeles County
58	808	1959	**La Puente** (city) Los Angeles County
58	808	1959	**Menlo Park** (city) San Mateo County
58	808	1959	**Mill Valley** (city) Marin County
58	808	1959	**Orinda** (city) Contra Costa County
58	808	1959	**Rossmoor** (CDP) Orange County
58	808	1959	**Santa Fe Springs** (city) Los Angeles County
68	886	1960	**Covina** (city) Los Angeles County
68	886	1960	**Gardena** (city) Los Angeles County
68	886	1960	**Lafayette** (city) Contra Costa County
68	886	1960	**Los Altos** (city) Santa Clara County
68	886	1960	**Los Angeles** (city) Los Angeles County
68	886	1960	**Manhattan Beach** (city) Los Angeles County
68	886	1960	**Monrovia** (city) Los Angeles County
68	886	1960	**Montebello** (city) Los Angeles County
68	886	1960	**Muscoy** (CDP) San Bernardino County
68	886	1960	**Palo Alto** (city) Santa Clara County
68	886	1960	**San Mateo** (city) San Mateo County
68	886	1960	**South San Jose Hills** (CDP) Los Angeles County
68	886	1960	**West Hollywood** (city) Los Angeles County
81	961	1961	**Alameda** (city) Alameda County
81	961	1961	**Bell Gardens** (city) Los Angeles County
81	961	1961	**Culver City** (city) Los Angeles County
81	961	1961	**Hillsborough** (town) San Mateo County
81	961	1961	**Millbrae** (city) San Mateo County
81	961	1961	**San Bruno** (city) San Mateo County
87	1018	1962	**Belmont** (city) San Mateo County
87	1018	1962	**Buena Park** (city) Orange County
87	1018	1962	**El Monte** (city) Los Angeles County
87	1018	1962	**El Segundo** (city) Los Angeles County
87	1018	1962	**Garden Acres** (CDP) San Joaquin County
87	1018	1962	**Glendale** (city) Los Angeles County
87	1018	1962	**Laguna Beach** (city) Orange County
87	1018	1962	**Lemon Hill** (CDP) Sacramento County
87	1018	1962	**Marysville** (city) Yuba County
87	1018	1962	**Monterey Park** (city) Los Angeles County
87	1018	1962	**Oroville** (city) Butte County
87	1018	1962	**Palos Verdes Estates** (city) Los Angeles County
87	1018	1962	**Richmond** (city) Contra Costa County
100	1097	1963	**Artesia** (city) Los Angeles County
100	1097	1963	**Crestline** (CDP) San Bernardino County
100	1097	1963	**Glendora** (city) Los Angeles County
100	1097	1963	**Lomita** (city) Los Angeles County
100	1097	1963	**Redwood City** (city) San Mateo County
100	1097	1963	**Santa Barbara** (city) Santa Barbara County
100	1097	1963	**Tamalpais-Homestead Valley** (CDP) Marin County
100	1097	1963	**Torrance** (city) Los Angeles County
108	1172	1964	**Ashland** (CDP) Alameda County
108	1172	1964	**Baldwin Park** (city) Los Angeles County
108	1172	1964	**Bellflower** (city) Los Angeles County
108	1172	1964	**East Palo Alto** (city) San Mateo County
108	1172	1964	**El Sobrante** (CDP) Contra Costa County
108	1172	1964	**Garden Grove** (city) Orange County
108	1172	1964	**Lemon Grove** (city) San Diego County
108	1172	1964	**North Tustin** (CDP) Orange County
108	1172	1964	**San Pablo** (city) Contra Costa County
108	1172	1964	**Santa Cruz** (city) Santa Cruz County
108	1172	1964	**Santa Monica** (city) Los Angeles County
108	1172	1964	**South San Francisco** (city) San Mateo County
120	1258	1965	**Arden-Arcade** (CDP) Sacramento County
120	1258	1965	**Carson** (city) Los Angeles County
120	1258	1965	**Castro Valley** (CDP) Alameda County
120	1258	1965	**Oildale** (CDP) Kern County
120	1258	1965	**Pacifica** (city) San Mateo County
120	1258	1965	**Parkway** (CDP) Sacramento County
120	1258	1965	**Pomona** (city) Los Angeles County
120	1258	1965	**San Rafael** (city) Marin County
120	1258	1965	**Seal Beach** (city) Orange County
120	1258	1965	**Seaside** (city) Monterey County
120	1258	1965	**West Covina** (city) Los Angeles County
131	1334	1966	**Arcadia** (city) Los Angeles County
131	1334	1966	**Avocado Heights** (CDP) Los Angeles County
131	1334	1966	**Daly City** (city) San Mateo County
131	1334	1966	**Duarte** (city) Los Angeles County
131	1334	1966	**Hermosa Beach** (city) Los Angeles County
136	1444	1967	**Claremont** (city) Los Angeles County
136	1444	1967	**Cudahy** (city) Los Angeles County
136	1444	1967	**Hawthorne** (city) Los Angeles County
136	1444	1967	**La Habra** (city) Orange County
136	1444	1967	**La Mesa** (city) San Diego County
136	1444	1967	**Larkspur** (city) Marin County
136	1444	1967	**Lawndale** (city) Los Angeles County
136	1444	1967	**North Highlands** (CDP) Sacramento County
136	1444	1967	**Rancho Palos Verdes** (city) Los Angeles County
136	1444	1967	**Santa Ana** (city) Orange County
136	1444	1967	**Saratoga** (city) Santa Clara County
147	1540	1968	**Barstow** (city) San Bernardino County
147	1540	1968	**Hawaiian Gardens** (city) Los Angeles County
147	1540	1968	**Laguna Woods** (city) Orange County
147	1540	1968	**Los Gatos** (town) Santa Clara County

Note: *The state column ranks the top/bottom 150 places from all places in the state with population of 10,000 or more. The national column ranks the top/bottom 150 places from all places in the country with population of 10,000 or more. Places that are unincorporated were not considered in the rankings. Please refer to the User Guide for additional information.*

Homeowner Vacancy Rate

Top 150 Places Ranked in *Descending* Order

State Rank	Nat'l Rank	Percent	Place
1	11	9.3	**Emeryville** (city) Alameda County
2	12	9.0	**Big Bear City** (CDP) San Bernardino County
3	16	8.6	**Desert Hot Springs** (city) Riverside County
4	21	8.3	**California City** (city) Kern County
5	28	7.9	**Lake Arrowhead** (CDP) San Bernardino County
6	51	6.7	**Crestline** (CDP) San Bernardino County
6	51	6.7	**Palm Springs** (city) Riverside County
8	58	6.6	**Adelanto** (city) San Bernardino County
9	61	6.5	**La Quinta** (city) Riverside County
10	67	6.4	**Coachella** (city) Riverside County
11	83	6.2	**Chowchilla** (city) Madera County
12	97	5.9	**Clearlake** (city) Lake County
12	97	5.9	**Newman** (city) Stanislaus County
14	109	5.7	**San Jacinto** (city) Riverside County
15	128	5.5	**Perris** (city) Riverside County
16	169	5.1	**Lemon Hill** (CDP) Sacramento County
16	169	5.1	**Wasco** (city) Kern County
18	185	5.0	**Barstow** (city) San Bernardino County
18	185	5.0	**Hemet** (city) Riverside County
18	185	5.0	**Indio** (city) Riverside County
18	185	5.0	**Palm Desert** (city) Riverside County
18	185	5.0	**Rancho Mirage** (city) Riverside County
23	206	4.9	**Victorville** (city) San Bernardino County
24	263	4.6	**Lake Elsinore** (city) Riverside County
24	263	4.6	**Yucca Valley** (town) San Bernardino County
26	287	4.5	**Imperial** (city) Imperial County
26	287	4.5	**Lake Los Angeles** (CDP) Los Angeles County
26	287	4.5	**Patterson** (city) Stanislaus County
26	287	4.5	**Rosamond** (CDP) Kern County
26	287	4.5	**South Lake Tahoe** (city) El Dorado County
31	318	4.4	**Valle Vista** (CDP) Riverside County
32	340	4.3	**Beaumont** (city) Riverside County
32	340	4.3	**Linda** (CDP) Yuba County
32	340	4.3	**Winton** (CDP) Merced County
35	367	4.2	**Cathedral City** (city) Riverside County
36	403	4.1	**Banning** (city) Riverside County
36	403	4.1	**Laguna Woods** (city) Orange County
36	403	4.1	**Los Banos** (city) Merced County
36	403	4.1	**Menifee** (city) Riverside County
40	444	4.0	**Apple Valley** (town) San Bernardino County
40	444	4.0	**Blythe** (city) Riverside County
40	444	4.0	**French Valley** (CDP) Riverside County
40	444	4.0	**Grass Valley** (city) Nevada County
40	444	4.0	**Oildale** (CDP) Kern County
45	485	3.9	**Parkway** (CDP) Sacramento County
46	539	3.8	**Coalinga** (city) Fresno County
46	539	3.8	**Lakeland Village** (CDP) Riverside County
46	539	3.8	**Lancaster** (city) Los Angeles County
46	539	3.8	**Olivehurst** (CDP) Yuba County
46	539	3.8	**Pacific Grove** (city) Monterey County
46	539	3.8	**Pittsburg** (city) Contra Costa County
52	589	3.7	**Lathrop** (city) San Joaquin County
52	589	3.7	**Muscoy** (CDP) San Bernardino County
54	641	3.6	**Hesperia** (city) San Bernardino County
54	641	3.6	**Oroville** (city) Butte County
54	641	3.6	**Twentynine Palms** (city) San Bernardino County
54	641	3.6	**West Hollywood** (city) Los Angeles County
58	702	3.5	**East Hemet** (CDP) Riverside County
58	702	3.5	**Madera** (city) Madera County
58	702	3.5	**Merced** (city) Merced County
58	702	3.5	**North Highlands** (CDP) Sacramento County
58	702	3.5	**Placerville** (city) El Dorado County
58	702	3.5	**Red Bluff** (city) Tehama County
64	765	3.4	**Diamond Springs** (CDP) El Dorado County
64	765	3.4	**Discovery Bay** (CDP) Contra Costa County
64	765	3.4	**Exeter** (city) Tulare County
64	765	3.4	**Greenfield** (city) Monterey County
64	765	3.4	**Moreno Valley** (city) Riverside County
64	765	3.4	**Oakley** (city) Contra Costa County
64	765	3.4	**Susanville** (city) Lassen County
71	841	3.3	**Atwater** (city) Merced County
71	841	3.3	**East Rancho Dominguez** (CDP) Los Angeles County
71	841	3.3	**Kerman** (city) Fresno County
71	841	3.3	**Morro Bay** (city) San Luis Obispo County
71	841	3.3	**Rancho Cordova** (city) Sacramento County
71	841	3.3	**Truckee** (town) Nevada County
77	932	3.2	**Bakersfield** (city) Kern County
77	932	3.2	**King City** (city) Monterey County
77	932	3.2	**Palmdale** (city) Los Angeles County
77	932	3.2	**San Bernardino** (city) San Bernardino County
77	932	3.2	**Stockton** (city) San Joaquin County
77	932	3.2	**Tehachapi** (city) Kern County
83	1014	3.1	**Eastvale** (city) Riverside County
83	1014	3.1	**Murrieta** (city) Riverside County
83	1014	3.1	**Rialto** (city) San Bernardino County
83	1014	3.1	**San Pablo** (city) Contra Costa County
83	1014	3.1	**Sanger** (city) Fresno County
88	1083	3.0	**Bay Point** (CDP) Contra Costa County
88	1083	3.0	**Fillmore** (city) Ventura County
88	1083	3.0	**Oakland** (city) Alameda County
88	1083	3.0	**Suisun City** (city) Solano County
88	1083	3.0	**Vallejo** (city) Solano County
88	1083	3.0	**West Sacramento** (city) Yolo County
88	1083	3.0	**Winter Gardens** (CDP) San Diego County
88	1083	3.0	**Yucaipa** (city) San Bernardino County
96	1191	2.9	**Avenal** (city) Kings County
96	1191	2.9	**Bostonia** (CDP) San Diego County
96	1191	2.9	**Canyon Lake** (city) Riverside County
96	1191	2.9	**Compton** (city) Los Angeles County
96	1191	2.9	**Delhi** (CDP) Merced County
96	1191	2.9	**Florence-Graham** (CDP) Los Angeles County
96	1191	2.9	**Lakeside** (CDP) San Diego County
96	1191	2.9	**North Auburn** (CDP) Placer County
96	1191	2.9	**Phelan** (CDP) San Bernardino County
96	1191	2.9	**Porterville** (city) Tulare County
96	1191	2.9	**Ridgecrest** (city) Kern County
96	1191	2.9	**Sun Village** (CDP) Los Angeles County
108	1296	2.8	**El Centro** (city) Imperial County
108	1296	2.8	**Kingsburg** (city) Fresno County
108	1296	2.8	**Malibu** (city) Los Angeles County
108	1296	2.8	**Modesto** (city) Stanislaus County
108	1296	2.8	**Paradise** (town) Butte County
108	1296	2.8	**Rio Linda** (CDP) Sacramento County
108	1296	2.8	**Riverbank** (city) Stanislaus County
108	1296	2.8	**Sacramento** (city) Sacramento County
108	1296	2.8	**Salida** (CDP) Stanislaus County
108	1296	2.8	**Tulare** (city) Tulare County
118	1413	2.7	**Antelope** (CDP) Sacramento County
118	1413	2.7	**Antioch** (city) Contra Costa County
118	1413	2.7	**Brentwood** (city) Contra Costa County
118	1413	2.7	**Citrus Heights** (city) Sacramento County
118	1413	2.7	**Healdsburg** (city) Sonoma County
118	1413	2.7	**Magalia** (CDP) Butte County
118	1413	2.7	**Manteca** (city) San Joaquin County
118	1413	2.7	**Marysville** (city) Yuba County
118	1413	2.7	**Mead Valley** (CDP) Riverside County
118	1413	2.7	**Oakdale** (city) Stanislaus County
118	1413	2.7	**Port Hueneme** (city) Ventura County
118	1413	2.7	**Temecula** (city) Riverside County
118	1413	2.7	**Wildomar** (city) Riverside County
131	1548	2.6	**American Canyon** (city) Napa County
131	1548	2.6	**Bloomington** (CDP) San Bernardino County
131	1548	2.6	**Calexico** (city) Imperial County
131	1548	2.6	**Colton** (city) San Bernardino County
131	1548	2.6	**Fontana** (city) San Bernardino County
131	1548	2.6	**Foothill Farms** (CDP) Sacramento County
131	1548	2.6	**Fresno** (city) Fresno County
131	1548	2.6	**Sonoma** (city) Sonoma County
131	1548	2.6	**Turlock** (city) Stanislaus County
131	1548	2.6	**Ukiah** (city) Mendocino County
131	1548	2.6	**Visalia** (city) Tulare County
142	1665	2.5	**Arvin** (city) Kern County
142	1665	2.5	**Ashland** (CDP) Alameda County
142	1665	2.5	**Ceres** (city) Stanislaus County
142	1665	2.5	**Dublin** (city) Alameda County
142	1665	2.5	**Fairfield** (city) Solano County
142	1665	2.5	**Farmersville** (city) Tulare County
142	1665	2.5	**Lincoln** (city) Placer County
142	1665	2.5	**Loma Linda** (city) San Bernardino County
142	1665	2.5	**Richmond** (city) Contra Costa County

***Note:** The state column ranks the top/bottom 150 places from all places in the state with population of 10,000 or more. The national column ranks the top/bottom 150 places from all places in the country with population of 10,000 or more. Places that are unincorporated were not considered in the rankings. Please refer to the User Guide for additional information.*

Homeowner Vacancy Rate

Top 150 Places Ranked in *Ascending* Order

State Rank	Nat'l Rank	Percent	Place
1	1	0.0	**Camp Pendleton South** (CDP) San Diego County
2	8	0.3	**La Palma** (city) Orange County
3	9	0.4	**El Segundo** (city) Los Angeles County
3	9	0.4	**Rossmoor** (CDP) Orange County
5	18	0.5	**Agoura Hills** (city) Los Angeles County
5	18	0.5	**Del Aire** (CDP) Los Angeles County
5	18	0.5	**Monterey Park** (city) Los Angeles County
5	18	0.5	**Piedmont** (city) Alameda County
5	18	0.5	**San Marino** (city) Los Angeles County
10	44	0.6	**La Crescenta-Montrose** (CDP) Los Angeles County
10	44	0.6	**Rancho Palos Verdes** (city) Los Angeles County
12	85	0.7	**Artesia** (city) Los Angeles County
12	85	0.7	**Avocado Heights** (CDP) Los Angeles County
12	85	0.7	**Belmont** (city) San Mateo County
12	85	0.7	**Cerritos** (city) Los Angeles County
12	85	0.7	**Clayton** (city) Contra Costa County
12	85	0.7	**Culver City** (city) Los Angeles County
12	85	0.7	**Lomita** (city) Los Angeles County
12	85	0.7	**Los Altos** (city) Santa Clara County
12	85	0.7	**Millbrae** (city) San Mateo County
12	85	0.7	**Moraga** (town) Contra Costa County
12	85	0.7	**Palos Verdes Estates** (city) Los Angeles County
12	85	0.7	**Saratoga** (city) Santa Clara County
12	85	0.7	**South El Monte** (city) Los Angeles County
12	85	0.7	**Temple City** (city) Los Angeles County
26	151	0.8	**Cupertino** (city) Santa Clara County
26	151	0.8	**Danville** (town) Contra Costa County
26	151	0.8	**Foster City** (city) San Mateo County
26	151	0.8	**Fountain Valley** (city) Orange County
26	151	0.8	**La Cañada Flintridge** (city) Los Angeles County
26	151	0.8	**La Mirada** (city) Los Angeles County
26	151	0.8	**Lafayette** (city) Contra Costa County
26	151	0.8	**Los Alamitos** (city) Orange County
26	151	0.8	**Manhattan Beach** (city) Los Angeles County
26	151	0.8	**Placentia** (city) Orange County
26	151	0.8	**Rancho San Diego** (CDP) San Diego County
26	151	0.8	**Rowland Heights** (CDP) Los Angeles County
26	151	0.8	**Thousand Oaks** (city) Ventura County
26	151	0.8	**Torrance** (city) Los Angeles County
26	151	0.8	**Walnut** (city) Los Angeles County
41	248	0.9	**Altadena** (CDP) Los Angeles County
41	248	0.9	**Claremont** (city) Los Angeles County
41	248	0.9	**Cypress** (city) Orange County
41	248	0.9	**Davis** (city) Yolo County
41	248	0.9	**Diamond Bar** (city) Los Angeles County
41	248	0.9	**Laguna Niguel** (city) Orange County
41	248	0.9	**Lennox** (CDP) Los Angeles County
41	248	0.9	**McFarland** (city) Kern County
41	248	0.9	**Mission Viejo** (city) Orange County
41	248	0.9	**Montebello** (city) Los Angeles County
41	248	0.9	**North Tustin** (CDP) Orange County
41	248	0.9	**Pacifica** (city) San Mateo County
41	248	0.9	**Pleasanton** (city) Alameda County
41	248	0.9	**Redondo Beach** (city) Los Angeles County
41	248	0.9	**Rosemead** (city) Los Angeles County
41	248	0.9	**Stanford** (CDP) Santa Clara County
41	248	0.9	**Valinda** (CDP) Los Angeles County
58	385	1.0	**Albany** (city) Alameda County
58	385	1.0	**Berkeley** (city) Alameda County
58	385	1.0	**Chino Hills** (city) San Bernardino County
58	385	1.0	**Commerce** (city) Los Angeles County
58	385	1.0	**Coto de Caza** (CDP) Orange County
58	385	1.0	**East San Gabriel** (CDP) Los Angeles County
58	385	1.0	**Encinitas** (city) San Diego County
58	385	1.0	**Glendora** (city) Los Angeles County
58	385	1.0	**Hacienda Heights** (CDP) Los Angeles County
58	385	1.0	**Half Moon Bay** (city) San Mateo County
58	385	1.0	**Hermosa Beach** (city) Los Angeles County
58	385	1.0	**La Puente** (city) Los Angeles County
58	385	1.0	**Los Gatos** (town) Santa Clara County
58	385	1.0	**Moorpark** (city) Ventura County
58	385	1.0	**Newark** (city) Alameda County
58	385	1.0	**North Fair Oaks** (CDP) San Mateo County
58	385	1.0	**Novato** (city) Marin County
58	385	1.0	**Pico Rivera** (city) Los Angeles County
58	385	1.0	**San Gabriel** (city) Los Angeles County
58	385	1.0	**Sierra Madre** (city) Los Angeles County
58	385	1.0	**South San Jose Hills** (CDP) Los Angeles County
58	385	1.0	**West Whittier-Los Nietos** (CDP) Los Angeles County
80	519	1.1	**Alameda** (city) Alameda County
80	519	1.1	**Arcadia** (city) Los Angeles County
80	519	1.1	**Bonita** (CDP) San Diego County
80	519	1.1	**Buena Park** (city) Orange County
80	519	1.1	**Covina** (city) Los Angeles County
80	519	1.1	**Duarte** (city) Los Angeles County
80	519	1.1	**El Cerrito** (city) Contra Costa County
80	519	1.1	**Fullerton** (city) Orange County
80	519	1.1	**Huntington Beach** (city) Orange County
80	519	1.1	**Lakewood** (city) Los Angeles County
80	519	1.1	**McKinleyville** (CDP) Humboldt County
80	519	1.1	**Menlo Park** (city) San Mateo County
80	519	1.1	**Orange** (city) Orange County
80	519	1.1	**Poway** (city) San Diego County
80	519	1.1	**San Bruno** (city) San Mateo County
80	519	1.1	**San Dimas** (city) Los Angeles County
80	519	1.1	**San Fernando** (city) Los Angeles County
80	519	1.1	**San Lorenzo** (CDP) Alameda County
80	519	1.1	**Santa Monica** (city) Los Angeles County
80	519	1.1	**South Pasadena** (city) Los Angeles County
80	519	1.1	**South Whittier** (CDP) Los Angeles County
80	519	1.1	**Sunnyvale** (city) Santa Clara County
80	519	1.1	**Walnut Park** (CDP) Los Angeles County
80	519	1.1	**West Covina** (city) Los Angeles County
104	672	1.2	**Alamo** (CDP) Contra Costa County
104	672	1.2	**Aliso Viejo** (city) Orange County
104	672	1.2	**Arcata** (city) Humboldt County
104	672	1.2	**Calabasas** (city) Los Angeles County
104	672	1.2	**Castaic** (CDP) Los Angeles County
104	672	1.2	**Costa Mesa** (city) Orange County
104	672	1.2	**East Los Angeles** (CDP) Los Angeles County
104	672	1.2	**Garden Grove** (city) Orange County
104	672	1.2	**Goleta** (city) Santa Barbara County
104	672	1.2	**Maywood** (city) Los Angeles County
104	672	1.2	**Mill Valley** (city) Marin County
104	672	1.2	**Milpitas** (city) Santa Clara County
104	672	1.2	**Oak Park** (CDP) Ventura County
104	672	1.2	**Orinda** (city) Contra Costa County
104	672	1.2	**Rancho Santa Margarita** (city) Orange County
104	672	1.2	**San Anselmo** (town) Marin County
104	672	1.2	**Santa Cruz** (city) Santa Cruz County
104	672	1.2	**Simi Valley** (city) Ventura County
104	672	1.2	**West Puente Valley** (CDP) Los Angeles County
104	672	1.2	**Yorba Linda** (city) Orange County
124	842	1.3	**Alhambra** (city) Los Angeles County
124	842	1.3	**Baldwin Park** (city) Los Angeles County
124	842	1.3	**Brea** (city) Orange County
124	842	1.3	**Burlingame** (city) San Mateo County
124	842	1.3	**Carson** (city) Los Angeles County
124	842	1.3	**Castro Valley** (CDP) Alameda County
124	842	1.3	**Cudahy** (city) Los Angeles County
124	842	1.3	**Fremont** (city) Alameda County
124	842	1.3	**Gardena** (city) Los Angeles County
124	842	1.3	**Glendale** (city) Los Angeles County
124	842	1.3	**Granite Bay** (CDP) Placer County
124	842	1.3	**Hillsborough** (town) San Mateo County
124	842	1.3	**Lake Forest** (city) Orange County
124	842	1.3	**Los Osos** (CDP) San Luis Obispo County
124	842	1.3	**Monrovia** (city) Los Angeles County
124	842	1.3	**Mountain View** (city) Santa Clara County
124	842	1.3	**Parlier** (city) Fresno County
124	842	1.3	**Petaluma** (city) Sonoma County
124	842	1.3	**Pleasant Hill** (city) Contra Costa County
124	842	1.3	**Redwood City** (city) San Mateo County
124	842	1.3	**San Buenaventura (Ventura)** (city) Ventura County
124	842	1.3	**San Clemente** (city) Orange County
124	842	1.3	**San Juan Capistrano** (city) Orange County
124	842	1.3	**San Ramon** (city) Contra Costa County
124	842	1.3	**Santa Barbara** (city) Santa Barbara County
124	842	1.3	**Santa Clara** (city) Santa Clara County
124	842	1.3	**South San Francisco** (city) San Mateo County

Note: *The state column ranks the top/bottom 150 places from all places in the state with population of 10,000 or more. The national column ranks the top/bottom 150 places from all places in the country with population of 10,000 or more. Places that are unincorporated were not considered in the rankings. Please refer to the User Guide for additional information.*

Median Gross Rent

Top 150 Places Ranked in *Descending* Order

State Rank	Nat'l Rank	Dollars	Place
1	1	2,000+	**Alamo** (CDP) Contra Costa County
1	1	2,000+	**Calabasas** (city) Los Angeles County
1	1	2,000+	**Clayton** (city) Contra Costa County
1	1	2,000+	**Coronado** (city) San Diego County
1	1	2,000+	**Coto de Caza** (CDP) Orange County
1	1	2,000+	**Cupertino** (city) Santa Clara County
1	1	2,000+	**Danville** (town) Contra Costa County
1	1	2,000+	**Discovery Bay** (CDP) Contra Costa County
1	1	2,000+	**Eastvale** (city) Riverside County
1	1	2,000+	**El Sobrante** (CDP) Riverside County
1	1	2,000+	**Foster City** (city) San Mateo County
1	1	2,000+	**Hillsborough** (town) San Mateo County
1	1	2,000+	**Los Altos** (city) Santa Clara County
1	1	2,000+	**Malibu** (city) Los Angeles County
1	1	2,000+	**Orinda** (city) Contra Costa County
1	1	2,000+	**Palos Verdes Estates** (city) Los Angeles County
1	1	2,000+	**Rancho Palos Verdes** (city) Los Angeles County
1	1	2,000+	**San Diego Country Estates** (CDP) San Diego County
1	1	2,000+	**San Marino** (city) Los Angeles County
1	1	2,000+	**Saratoga** (city) Santa Clara County
1	1	2,000+	**Tamalpais-Homestead Valley** (CDP) Marin County
22	76	1,996	**Oak Park** (CDP) Ventura County
23	77	1,995	**Manhattan Beach** (city) Los Angeles County
24	81	1,970	**Cerritos** (city) Los Angeles County
25	82	1,955	**Walnut** (city) Los Angeles County
26	84	1,953	**Piedmont** (city) Alameda County
27	86	1,948	**Scotts Valley** (city) Santa Cruz County
28	89	1,947	**Palo Alto** (city) Santa Clara County
29	94	1,924	**Agoura Hills** (city) Los Angeles County
29	94	1,924	**Newport Beach** (city) Orange County
31	102	1,906	**La Cañada Flintridge** (city) Los Angeles County
32	104	1,899	**Solana Beach** (city) San Diego County
33	109	1,896	**Ladera Ranch** (CDP) Orange County
34	112	1,893	**Beverly Hills** (city) Los Angeles County
35	114	1,887	**Camp Pendleton South** (CDP) San Diego County
35	114	1,887	**Laguna Beach** (city) Orange County
37	117	1,880	**Canyon Lake** (city) Riverside County
38	118	1,879	**French Valley** (CDP) Riverside County
39	121	1,872	**Brentwood** (city) Contra Costa County
40	129	1,846	**Aliso Viejo** (city) Orange County
40	129	1,846	**Irvine** (city) Orange County
42	131	1,845	**Hermosa Beach** (city) Los Angeles County
43	139	1,825	**Mission Viejo** (city) Orange County
43	139	1,825	**Thousand Oaks** (city) Ventura County
45	141	1,824	**Larkspur** (city) Marin County
46	146	1,817	**North Tustin** (CDP) Orange County
47	150	1,808	**Laguna Niguel** (city) Orange County
48	154	1,800	**Menlo Park** (city) San Mateo County
48	154	1,800	**Moraga** (town) Contra Costa County
50	159	1,794	**Mill Valley** (city) Marin County
51	168	1,787	**Dana Point** (city) Orange County
52	170	1,786	**Dublin** (city) Alameda County
52	170	1,786	**Stevenson Ranch** (CDP) Los Angeles County
54	174	1,783	**Chino Hills** (city) San Bernardino County
55	178	1,782	**Laguna Hills** (city) Orange County
56	187	1,768	**El Dorado Hills** (CDP) El Dorado County
57	195	1,761	**Diamond Bar** (city) Los Angeles County
58	206	1,744	**Yorba Linda** (city) Orange County
59	210	1,742	**Milpitas** (city) Santa Clara County
60	212	1,739	**Pacifica** (city) San Mateo County
61	214	1,736	**San Ramon** (city) Contra Costa County
62	219	1,734	**San Juan Capistrano** (city) Orange County
63	223	1,732	**Norco** (city) Riverside County
64	226	1,728	**Los Gatos** (town) Santa Clara County
65	230	1,724	**Millbrae** (city) San Mateo County
66	231	1,720	**Encinitas** (city) San Diego County
67	246	1,705	**Moorpark** (city) Ventura County
68	254	1,688	**Rancho Santa Margarita** (city) Orange County
69	260	1,682	**Half Moon Bay** (city) San Mateo County
69	260	1,682	**San Clemente** (city) Orange County
71	262	1,681	**Windsor** (town) Sonoma County
72	263	1,680	**Granite Bay** (CDP) Placer County
72	263	1,680	**Lake Forest** (city) Orange County
72	263	1,680	**Pleasanton** (city) Alameda County
75	268	1,679	**Redondo Beach** (city) Los Angeles County
76	274	1,675	**Simi Valley** (city) Ventura County
77	289	1,660	**San Mateo** (city) San Mateo County
78	297	1,646	**Camarillo** (city) Ventura County
79	300	1,643	**Rancho San Diego** (CDP) San Diego County
79	300	1,643	**San Bruno** (city) San Mateo County
81	312	1,636	**Rossmoor** (CDP) Orange County
82	314	1,631	**Carlsbad** (city) San Diego County
83	322	1,622	**American Canyon** (city) Napa County
83	322	1,622	**Bonita** (CDP) San Diego County
85	332	1,616	**Albany** (city) Alameda County
85	332	1,616	**Mountain View** (city) Santa Clara County
87	342	1,609	**Santa Clara** (city) Santa Clara County
88	345	1,607	**Goleta** (city) Santa Barbara County
88	345	1,607	**Morgan Hill** (city) Santa Clara County
90	348	1,606	**Culver City** (city) Los Angeles County
90	348	1,606	**Sunnyvale** (city) Santa Clara County
92	373	1,587	**Emeryville** (city) Alameda County
93	374	1,585	**Hacienda Heights** (CDP) Los Angeles County
94	382	1,578	**Fountain Valley** (city) Orange County
95	383	1,575	**Seal Beach** (city) Orange County
96	389	1,571	**San Dimas** (city) Los Angeles County
97	391	1,570	**Vineyard** (CDP) Sacramento County
98	394	1,569	**Novato** (city) Marin County
99	398	1,566	**Fremont** (city) Alameda County
100	401	1,564	**Belmont** (city) San Mateo County
101	405	1,561	**Lafayette** (city) Contra Costa County
102	406	1,560	**San Anselmo** (town) Marin County
103	407	1,559	**Huntington Beach** (city) Orange County
104	412	1,555	**Orcutt** (CDP) Santa Barbara County
105	416	1,549	**Lincoln** (city) Placer County
106	424	1,543	**Newark** (city) Alameda County
107	426	1,542	**Daly City** (city) San Mateo County
108	428	1,541	**Cypress** (city) Orange County
109	431	1,538	**San Carlos** (city) San Mateo County
110	432	1,537	**Lakewood** (city) Los Angeles County
111	435	1,533	**Santa Monica** (city) Los Angeles County
112	444	1,528	**Hercules** (city) Contra Costa County
113	448	1,524	**Costa Mesa** (city) Orange County
113	448	1,524	**San Lorenzo** (CDP) Alameda County
115	451	1,521	**Burlingame** (city) San Mateo County
116	457	1,519	**Oakley** (city) Contra Costa County
117	462	1,514	**Lathrop** (city) San Joaquin County
118	467	1,509	**Santa Clarita** (city) Los Angeles County
118	467	1,509	**Temecula** (city) Riverside County
120	472	1,503	**Seaside** (city) Monterey County
121	473	1,502	**Murrieta** (city) Riverside County
122	478	1,496	**Tustin** (city) Orange County
123	479	1,495	**Fairview** (CDP) Alameda County
124	480	1,494	**Campbell** (city) Santa Clara County
125	486	1,490	**El Segundo** (city) Los Angeles County
125	486	1,490	**Santa Cruz** (city) Santa Cruz County
127	491	1,488	**San Francisco** (city) San Francisco County
128	492	1,487	**Orange** (city) Orange County
129	493	1,486	**Redwood City** (city) San Mateo County
130	497	1,484	**Santa Barbara** (city) Santa Barbara County
131	499	1,483	**Sierra Madre** (city) Los Angeles County
131	499	1,483	**Sun Village** (CDP) Los Angeles County
133	503	1,481	**La Palma** (city) Orange County
134	505	1,479	**Poway** (city) San Diego County
135	506	1,478	**Los Alamitos** (city) Orange County
136	509	1,477	**Placentia** (city) Orange County
136	509	1,477	**South San Francisco** (city) San Mateo County
138	513	1,474	**San Jose** (city) Santa Clara County
139	529	1,464	**Brea** (city) Orange County
139	529	1,464	**West Puente Valley** (CDP) Los Angeles County
141	531	1,463	**Pleasant Hill** (city) Contra Costa County
142	536	1,461	**La Mirada** (city) Los Angeles County
143	552	1,451	**Union City** (city) Alameda County
144	560	1,448	**Livermore** (city) Alameda County
145	564	1,447	**Elk Grove** (city) Sacramento County
146	567	1,446	**Del Aire** (CDP) Los Angeles County
147	569	1,445	**Pacific Grove** (city) Monterey County
148	572	1,442	**Petaluma** (city) Sonoma County
148	572	1,442	**Rancho Cucamonga** (city) San Bernardino County
148	572	1,442	**Salida** (CDP) Stanislaus County

Note: *The state column ranks the top/bottom 150 places from all places in the state with population of 10,000 or more. The national column ranks the top/bottom 150 places from all places in the country with population of 10,000 or more. Places that are unincorporated were not considered in the rankings. Please refer to the User Guide for additional information.*

Median Gross Rent

Top 150 Places Ranked in *Ascending* Order

State Rank	Nat'l Rank	Dollars	Place
1	393	635	**Mendota** (city) Fresno County
2	513	655	**Wasco** (city) Kern County
3	769	701	**Avenal** (city) Kings County
4	894	724	**Lamont** (CDP) Kern County
5	921	728	**Farmersville** (city) Tulare County
6	929	729	**Lindsay** (city) Tulare County
7	945	732	**Brawley** (city) Imperial County
7	945	732	**Shafter** (city) Kern County
9	982	737	**Parlier** (city) Fresno County
9	982	737	**Red Bluff** (city) Tehama County
11	998	741	**El Centro** (city) Imperial County
12	1080	753	**Blythe** (city) Riverside County
13	1086	754	**Corcoran** (city) Kings County
14	1126	760	**Delano** (city) Kern County
14	1126	760	**Oroville** (city) Butte County
16	1197	772	**Porterville** (city) Tulare County
17	1214	776	**Barstow** (city) San Bernardino County
18	1224	777	**Selma** (city) Fresno County
19	1292	788	**Coalinga** (city) Fresno County
20	1300	789	**Calexico** (city) Imperial County
21	1365	800	**McFarland** (city) Kern County
22	1372	802	**Eureka** (city) Humboldt County
23	1383	804	**Tehachapi** (city) Kern County
24	1423	811	**Clearlake** (city) Lake County
25	1428	812	**Arvin** (city) Kern County
26	1435	813	**Susanville** (city) Lassen County
27	1452	818	**Kerman** (city) Fresno County
28	1460	819	**Fortuna** (city) Humboldt County
28	1460	819	**Merced** (city) Merced County
30	1480	822	**Olivehurst** (CDP) Yuba County
31	1494	824	**Oildale** (CDP) Kern County
32	1556	835	**Dinuba** (city) Tulare County
32	1556	835	**Marysville** (city) Yuba County
34	1622	846	**Lemon Hill** (CDP) Sacramento County
35	1641	848	**Exeter** (city) Tulare County
36	1680	854	**Reedley** (city) Fresno County
37	1689	855	**Linda** (CDP) Yuba County
38	1727	860	**Ridgecrest** (city) Kern County
38	1727	860	**Winton** (CDP) Merced County
40	1799	872	**Lemoore** (city) Kings County
41	1822	876	**Arden-Arcade** (CDP) Sacramento County
42	1835	878	**Coachella** (city) Riverside County
43	1843	879	**Commerce** (city) Los Angeles County
44	1880	884	**Fresno** (city) Fresno County
45	1897	887	**Sanger** (city) Fresno County
46	1917	890	**South Lake Tahoe** (city) El Dorado County
47	1924	891	**West Sacramento** (city) Yolo County
48	1927	892	**Yuba City** (city) Sutter County
49	1932	893	**Madera** (city) Madera County
50	1951	896	**Desert Hot Springs** (city) Riverside County
51	1965	898	**California City** (city) Kern County
52	1979	900	**Banning** (city) Riverside County
53	1989	901	**Kingsburg** (city) Fresno County
54	1996	902	**Arcata** (city) Humboldt County
55	2016	905	**Chowchilla** (city) Madera County
56	2022	906	**Atwater** (city) Merced County
57	2026	907	**Chico** (city) Butte County
58	2035	908	**Hanford** (city) Kings County
59	2054	911	**Paradise** (town) Butte County
60	2094	919	**Tulare** (city) Tulare County
60	2094	919	**Yucca Valley** (town) San Bernardino County
62	2110	922	**Woodland** (city) Yolo County
63	2116	923	**McKinleyville** (CDP) Humboldt County
64	2124	924	**Placerville** (city) El Dorado County
65	2136	925	**Grass Valley** (city) Nevada County
66	2142	926	**Ukiah** (city) Mendocino County
67	2160	929	**Twentynine Palms** (city) San Bernardino County
68	2167	930	**San Bernardino** (city) San Bernardino County
69	2181	932	**Garden Acres** (CDP) San Joaquin County
70	2191	934	**Parkway** (CDP) Sacramento County
71	2202	936	**Huntington Park** (city) Los Angeles County
72	2217	939	**Phelan** (CDP) San Bernardino County
73	2241	944	**Redding** (city) Shasta County
74	2245	945	**Carmichael** (CDP) Sacramento County
75	2254	946	**Valle Vista** (CDP) Riverside County
76	2263	948	**Hemet** (city) Riverside County
77	2279	950	**Palm Springs** (city) Riverside County
78	2296	954	**Ceres** (city) Stanislaus County
79	2302	955	**Delhi** (CDP) Merced County
80	2311	956	**North Highlands** (CDP) Sacramento County
80	2311	956	**Visalia** (city) Tulare County
82	2333	959	**Stockton** (city) San Joaquin County
83	2341	960	**Turlock** (city) Stanislaus County
84	2349	961	**Newman** (city) Stanislaus County
84	2349	961	**Rancho Cordova** (city) Sacramento County
86	2373	965	**Walnut Park** (CDP) Los Angeles County
87	2393	968	**East Los Angeles** (CDP) Los Angeles County
87	2393	968	**National City** (city) San Diego County
89	2407	969	**Florence-Graham** (CDP) Los Angeles County
89	2407	969	**Lompoc** (city) Santa Barbara County
91	2414	970	**Apple Valley** (town) San Bernardino County
92	2437	973	**King City** (city) Monterey County
93	2455	976	**Quartz Hill** (CDP) Los Angeles County
94	2460	977	**Colton** (city) San Bernardino County
94	2460	977	**Highland** (city) San Bernardino County
96	2463	978	**Auburn** (city) Placer County
96	2463	978	**Indio** (city) Riverside County
96	2463	978	**Westmont** (CDP) Los Angeles County
99	2478	979	**Bakersfield** (city) Kern County
99	2478	979	**Big Bear City** (CDP) San Bernardino County
101	2512	984	**Shasta Lake** (city) Shasta County
101	2512	984	**South Gate** (city) Los Angeles County
103	2524	986	**Adelanto** (city) San Bernardino County
104	2543	989	**Livingston** (city) Merced County
105	2552	990	**Lennox** (CDP) Los Angeles County
106	2557	991	**Florin** (CDP) Sacramento County
107	2563	992	**Magalia** (CDP) Butte County
107	2563	992	**North Auburn** (CDP) Placer County
109	2592	996	**Bell** (city) Los Angeles County
110	2613	998	**Lodi** (city) San Joaquin County
111	2619	999	**Sacramento** (city) Sacramento County
112	2623	1,000	**Rosamond** (CDP) Kern County
112	2623	1,000	**Willowbrook** (CDP) Los Angeles County
114	2648	1,006	**Citrus Heights** (city) Sacramento County
114	2648	1,006	**Maywood** (city) Los Angeles County
116	2664	1,011	**Lynwood** (city) Los Angeles County
117	2669	1,012	**Modesto** (city) Stanislaus County
118	2686	1,018	**Foothill Farms** (CDP) Sacramento County
119	2699	1,021	**Hawthorne** (city) Los Angeles County
120	2736	1,033	**Woodcrest** (CDP) Riverside County
121	2750	1,035	**La Riviera** (CDP) Sacramento County
122	2764	1,039	**Clovis** (city) Fresno County
123	2771	1,041	**Muscoy** (CDP) San Bernardino County
124	2776	1,043	**Compton** (city) Los Angeles County
125	2779	1,044	**Rosedale** (CDP) Kern County
126	2794	1,049	**Soledad** (city) Monterey County
127	2800	1,052	**Hesperia** (city) San Bernardino County
128	2807	1,053	**Fair Oaks** (CDP) Sacramento County
129	2813	1,054	**San Pablo** (city) Contra Costa County
130	2817	1,055	**Imperial** (city) Imperial County
130	2817	1,055	**Riverbank** (city) Stanislaus County
132	2830	1,057	**Fallbrook** (CDP) San Diego County
132	2830	1,057	**Mead Valley** (CDP) Riverside County
134	2837	1,058	**East Hemet** (CDP) Riverside County
135	2848	1,061	**Yucaipa** (city) San Bernardino County
136	2850	1,062	**Los Banos** (city) Merced County
137	2857	1,064	**San Jacinto** (city) Riverside County
138	2873	1,067	**Galt** (city) Sacramento County
139	2884	1,069	**Crestline** (CDP) San Bernardino County
139	2884	1,069	**Lancaster** (city) Los Angeles County
141	2894	1,071	**El Monte** (city) Los Angeles County
141	2894	1,071	**Lakeside** (CDP) San Diego County
143	2914	1,075	**Rosemont** (CDP) Sacramento County
144	2920	1,076	**Beaumont** (city) Riverside County
144	2920	1,076	**Inglewood** (city) Los Angeles County
146	2943	1,081	**Loma Linda** (city) San Bernardino County
146	2943	1,081	**Rialto** (city) San Bernardino County
148	2958	1,083	**Oakdale** (city) Stanislaus County
149	2981	1,087	**El Cajon** (city) San Diego County
149	2981	1,087	**Oakland** (city) Alameda County

***Note:** The state column ranks the top/bottom 150 places from all places in the state with population of 10,000 or more. The national column ranks the top/bottom 150 places from all places in the country with population of 10,000 or more. Places that are unincorporated were not considered in the rankings. Please refer to the User Guide for additional information.*

Rental Vacancy Rate

Top 150 Places Ranked in *Descending* Order

State Rank	Nat'l Rank	Percent	Place
1	27	22.5	**California City** (city) Kern County
2	102	17.5	**Hemet** (city) Riverside County
3	114	17.2	**Rancho Mirage** (city) Riverside County
4	125	16.8	**Palm Desert** (city) Riverside County
5	131	16.6	**Desert Hot Springs** (city) Riverside County
6	135	16.5	**La Quinta** (city) Riverside County
7	159	16.0	**Barstow** (city) San Bernardino County
8	193	15.5	**Palm Springs** (city) Riverside County
9	246	14.6	**Cameron Park** (CDP) El Dorado County
9	246	14.6	**South Lake Tahoe** (city) El Dorado County
11	303	14.0	**Big Bear City** (CDP) San Bernardino County
12	321	13.8	**Crestline** (CDP) San Bernardino County
13	385	13.3	**East Palo Alto** (city) San Mateo County
14	480	12.7	**Rosamond** (CDP) Kern County
15	512	12.5	**Indio** (city) Riverside County
16	530	12.4	**Lake Arrowhead** (CDP) San Bernardino County
17	543	12.3	**Adelanto** (city) San Bernardino County
18	561	12.2	**Tehachapi** (city) Kern County
19	582	12.1	**Clearlake** (city) Lake County
20	635	11.9	**Malibu** (city) Los Angeles County
21	656	11.8	**Corcoran** (city) Kings County
22	682	11.7	**Arden-Arcade** (CDP) Sacramento County
23	805	11.2	**Laguna Hills** (city) Orange County
24	831	11.1	**Victorville** (city) San Bernardino County
25	860	11.0	**Cathedral City** (city) Riverside County
26	896	10.9	**Atwater** (city) Merced County
26	896	10.9	**Banning** (city) Riverside County
28	991	10.6	**North Highlands** (CDP) Sacramento County
29	1024	10.5	**Oildale** (CDP) Kern County
30	1061	10.4	**Winton** (CDP) Merced County
31	1107	10.3	**Blythe** (city) Riverside County
31	1107	10.3	**Camp Pendleton South** (CDP) San Diego County
31	1107	10.3	**San Jacinto** (city) Riverside County
34	1151	10.2	**Emeryville** (city) Alameda County
34	1151	10.2	**Laguna Woods** (city) Orange County
34	1151	10.2	**Marysville** (city) Yuba County
37	1185	10.1	**East Hemet** (CDP) Riverside County
37	1185	10.1	**North Auburn** (CDP) Placer County
39	1220	10.0	**Apple Valley** (town) San Bernardino County
39	1220	10.0	**Lemon Hill** (CDP) Sacramento County
41	1258	9.9	**Loma Linda** (city) San Bernardino County
42	1291	9.8	**Carmichael** (CDP) Sacramento County
42	1291	9.8	**Valle Vista** (CDP) Riverside County
44	1340	9.7	**Parkway** (CDP) Sacramento County
44	1340	9.7	**Rialto** (city) San Bernardino County
46	1384	9.6	**Yucca Valley** (town) San Bernardino County
47	1415	9.5	**Linda** (CDP) Yuba County
47	1415	9.5	**San Bernardino** (city) San Bernardino County
49	1455	9.4	**Lancaster** (city) Los Angeles County
49	1455	9.4	**Palmdale** (city) Los Angeles County
49	1455	9.4	**Rosedale** (CDP) Kern County
49	1455	9.4	**Stockton** (city) San Joaquin County
49	1455	9.4	**Vallejo** (city) Solano County
54	1496	9.3	**Lakeland Village** (CDP) Riverside County
55	1541	9.2	**Colton** (city) San Bernardino County
55	1541	9.2	**Ridgecrest** (city) Kern County
55	1541	9.2	**Twentynine Palms** (city) San Bernardino County
58	1583	9.1	**Modesto** (city) Stanislaus County
59	1625	9.0	**Bakersfield** (city) Kern County
59	1625	9.0	**Turlock** (city) Stanislaus County
59	1625	9.0	**Yucaipa** (city) San Bernardino County
62	1674	8.9	**Florin** (CDP) Sacramento County
62	1674	8.9	**Rancho Cordova** (city) Sacramento County
64	1710	8.8	**Granite Bay** (CDP) Placer County
64	1710	8.8	**Westmont** (CDP) Los Angeles County
66	1755	8.7	**Highland** (city) San Bernardino County
67	1833	8.5	**Fallbrook** (CDP) San Diego County
67	1833	8.5	**Merced** (city) Merced County
67	1833	8.5	**Oakland** (city) Alameda County
67	1833	8.5	**Quartz Hill** (CDP) Los Angeles County
71	1892	8.4	**Coalinga** (city) Fresno County
71	1892	8.4	**Hesperia** (city) San Bernardino County
71	1892	8.4	**Los Banos** (city) Merced County
71	1892	8.4	**Oroville** (city) Butte County
75	1940	8.3	**Sacramento** (city) Sacramento County
75	1940	8.3	**San Pablo** (city) Contra Costa County
75	1940	8.3	**Upland** (city) San Bernardino County
78	1993	8.2	**Antioch** (city) Contra Costa County
78	1993	8.2	**Ceres** (city) Stanislaus County
78	1993	8.2	**Lodi** (city) San Joaquin County
78	1993	8.2	**Muscoy** (CDP) San Bernardino County
78	1993	8.2	**Rosemont** (CDP) Sacramento County
83	2058	8.1	**Richmond** (city) Contra Costa County
84	2115	8.0	**Beverly Hills** (city) Los Angeles County
84	2115	8.0	**Brawley** (city) Imperial County
84	2115	8.0	**Pinole** (city) Contra Costa County
87	2176	7.9	**Chowchilla** (city) Madera County
87	2176	7.9	**Orangevale** (CDP) Sacramento County
87	2176	7.9	**Redlands** (city) San Bernardino County
90	2225	7.8	**Citrus Heights** (city) Sacramento County
90	2225	7.8	**Murrieta** (city) Riverside County
90	2225	7.8	**Newport Beach** (city) Orange County
90	2225	7.8	**Placerville** (city) El Dorado County
90	2225	7.8	**Truckee** (town) Nevada County
95	2285	7.7	**Laguna Beach** (city) Orange County
95	2285	7.7	**Oakdale** (city) Stanislaus County
95	2285	7.7	**Susanville** (city) Lassen County
98	2325	7.6	**Bay Point** (CDP) Contra Costa County
98	2325	7.6	**Fresno** (city) Fresno County
98	2325	7.6	**La Riviera** (CDP) Sacramento County
101	2389	7.5	**Moreno Valley** (city) Riverside County
102	2440	7.4	**Lake Los Angeles** (CDP) Los Angeles County
102	2440	7.4	**Ripon** (city) San Joaquin County
102	2440	7.4	**Riverside** (city) Riverside County
105	2504	7.3	**Red Bluff** (city) Tehama County
105	2504	7.3	**Rocklin** (city) Placer County
105	2504	7.3	**Westminster** (city) Orange County
108	2558	7.2	**Anaheim** (city) Orange County
108	2558	7.2	**El Centro** (city) Imperial County
108	2558	7.2	**El Sobrante** (CDP) Contra Costa County
108	2558	7.2	**Foothill Farms** (CDP) Sacramento County
108	2558	7.2	**French Valley** (CDP) Riverside County
108	2558	7.2	**La Mesa** (city) San Diego County
108	2558	7.2	**Long Beach** (city) Los Angeles County
108	2558	7.2	**Rowland Heights** (CDP) Los Angeles County
116	2631	7.1	**Fairfield** (city) Solano County
116	2631	7.1	**Larkspur** (city) Marin County
116	2631	7.1	**Lompoc** (city) Santa Barbara County
116	2631	7.1	**Magalia** (CDP) Butte County
116	2631	7.1	**Temecula** (city) Riverside County
116	2631	7.1	**Yuba City** (city) Sutter County
122	2697	7.0	**Concord** (city) Contra Costa County
122	2697	7.0	**Dana Point** (city) Orange County
122	2697	7.0	**Fullerton** (city) Orange County
122	2697	7.0	**Garden Acres** (CDP) San Joaquin County
122	2697	7.0	**Grand Terrace** (city) San Bernardino County
122	2697	7.0	**Riverbank** (city) Stanislaus County
122	2697	7.0	**Sonoma** (city) Sonoma County
122	2697	7.0	**West Sacramento** (city) Yolo County
130	2763	6.9	**Newman** (city) Stanislaus County
130	2763	6.9	**Redding** (city) Shasta County
130	2763	6.9	**Shafter** (city) Kern County
133	2810	6.8	**Agoura Hills** (city) Los Angeles County
133	2810	6.8	**Lake Elsinore** (city) Riverside County
133	2810	6.8	**Menifee** (city) Riverside County
133	2810	6.8	**Perris** (city) Riverside County
133	2810	6.8	**Pittsburg** (city) Contra Costa County
133	2810	6.8	**Roseville** (city) Placer County
133	2810	6.8	**Vacaville** (city) Solano County
140	2865	6.7	**Arcadia** (city) Los Angeles County
140	2865	6.7	**Castaic** (CDP) Los Angeles County
140	2865	6.7	**Fair Oaks** (CDP) Sacramento County
140	2865	6.7	**Grass Valley** (city) Nevada County
140	2865	6.7	**Visalia** (city) Tulare County
140	2865	6.7	**Walnut Creek** (city) Contra Costa County
146	2931	6.6	**Azusa** (city) Los Angeles County
146	2931	6.6	**Hayward** (city) Alameda County
146	2931	6.6	**Lakeside** (CDP) San Diego County
146	2931	6.6	**Pasadena** (city) Los Angeles County
150	2977	6.5	**Alamo** (CDP) Contra Costa County

Note: *The state column ranks the top/bottom 150 places from all places in the state with population of 10,000 or more. The national column ranks the top/bottom 150 places from all places in the country with population of 10,000 or more. Places that are unincorporated were not considered in the rankings. Please refer to the User Guide for additional information.*

Rental Vacancy Rate

Top 150 Places Ranked in *Ascending* Order

State Rank	Nat'l Rank	Percent	Place
1	2	0.9	**Stanford** (CDP) Santa Clara County
2	9	1.5	**Coto de Caza** (CDP) Orange County
3	12	1.8	**Commerce** (city) Los Angeles County
4	13	1.9	**Half Moon Bay** (city) San Mateo County
4	13	1.9	**Isla Vista** (CDP) Santa Barbara County
4	13	1.9	**Live Oak** (CDP) Santa Cruz County
7	22	2.1	**West Puente Valley** (CDP) Los Angeles County
8	26	2.2	**Arcata** (city) Humboldt County
9	28	2.3	**Cudahy** (city) Los Angeles County
10	36	2.5	**Home Gardens** (CDP) Riverside County
10	36	2.5	**Watsonville** (city) Santa Cruz County
12	43	2.6	**Bell Gardens** (city) Los Angeles County
12	43	2.6	**Maywood** (city) Los Angeles County
12	43	2.6	**McFarland** (city) Kern County
12	43	2.6	**Morgan Hill** (city) Santa Clara County
16	53	2.7	**McKinleyville** (CDP) Humboldt County
16	53	2.7	**Windsor** (town) Sonoma County
18	66	2.9	**Moorpark** (city) Ventura County
19	85	3.1	**Avocado Heights** (CDP) Los Angeles County
19	85	3.1	**Calexico** (city) Imperial County
19	85	3.1	**Cerritos** (city) Los Angeles County
19	85	3.1	**Eastvale** (city) Riverside County
19	85	3.1	**Los Alamitos** (city) Orange County
19	85	3.1	**Milpitas** (city) Santa Clara County
19	85	3.1	**Nipomo** (CDP) San Luis Obispo County
26	104	3.2	**Alum Rock** (CDP) Santa Clara County
26	104	3.2	**Delhi** (CDP) Merced County
26	104	3.2	**East Los Angeles** (CDP) Los Angeles County
26	104	3.2	**Huntington Park** (city) Los Angeles County
26	104	3.2	**Rosemead** (city) Los Angeles County
26	104	3.2	**Scotts Valley** (city) Santa Cruz County
26	104	3.2	**South San Jose Hills** (CDP) Los Angeles County
33	130	3.3	**Baldwin Park** (city) Los Angeles County
33	130	3.3	**Bell** (city) Los Angeles County
33	130	3.3	**Lamont** (CDP) Kern County
33	130	3.3	**Valinda** (CDP) Los Angeles County
37	149	3.4	**King City** (city) Monterey County
37	149	3.4	**Lomita** (city) Los Angeles County
37	149	3.4	**North Tustin** (CDP) Orange County
37	149	3.4	**Santa Cruz** (city) Santa Cruz County
41	166	3.5	**Citrus** (CDP) Los Angeles County
41	166	3.5	**Cypress** (city) Orange County
41	166	3.5	**Davis** (city) Yolo County
41	166	3.5	**Delano** (city) Kern County
41	166	3.5	**Foster City** (city) San Mateo County
41	166	3.5	**Oak Park** (CDP) Ventura County
41	166	3.5	**South El Monte** (city) Los Angeles County
48	188	3.6	**Aliso Viejo** (city) Orange County
48	188	3.6	**Hacienda Heights** (CDP) Los Angeles County
48	188	3.6	**Marina** (city) Monterey County
48	188	3.6	**Rossmoor** (CDP) Orange County
48	188	3.6	**South Gate** (city) Los Angeles County
48	188	3.6	**Walnut Park** (CDP) Los Angeles County
54	211	3.7	**Artesia** (city) Los Angeles County
54	211	3.7	**Carson** (city) Los Angeles County
54	211	3.7	**El Sobrante** (CDP) Riverside County
54	211	3.7	**Eureka** (city) Humboldt County
54	211	3.7	**Grover Beach** (city) San Luis Obispo County
54	211	3.7	**Livingston** (city) Merced County
54	211	3.7	**Lynwood** (city) Los Angeles County
54	211	3.7	**Oxnard** (city) Ventura County
54	211	3.7	**Parlier** (city) Fresno County
54	211	3.7	**Piedmont** (city) Alameda County
54	211	3.7	**Reedley** (city) Fresno County
54	211	3.7	**San Mateo** (city) San Mateo County
54	211	3.7	**South Whittier** (CDP) Los Angeles County
54	211	3.7	**Ukiah** (city) Mendocino County
54	211	3.7	**Woodcrest** (CDP) Riverside County
69	240	3.8	**American Canyon** (city) Napa County
69	240	3.8	**Clayton** (city) Contra Costa County
69	240	3.8	**El Paso de Robles (Paso Robles)** (city) San Luis Obispo County
69	240	3.8	**Fountain Valley** (city) Orange County
69	240	3.8	**Lawndale** (city) Los Angeles County
69	240	3.8	**Norco** (city) Riverside County
69	240	3.8	**Norwalk** (city) Los Angeles County
69	240	3.8	**Prunedale** (CDP) Monterey County
69	240	3.8	**Santa Maria** (city) Santa Barbara County
78	274	3.9	**Antelope** (CDP) Sacramento County
78	274	3.9	**La Puente** (city) Los Angeles County
78	274	3.9	**Redwood City** (city) San Mateo County
78	274	3.9	**San Bruno** (city) San Mateo County
78	274	3.9	**San Fernando** (city) Los Angeles County
78	274	3.9	**Vineyard** (CDP) Sacramento County
84	304	4.0	**Arroyo Grande** (city) San Luis Obispo County
84	304	4.0	**La Mirada** (city) Los Angeles County
84	304	4.0	**Newark** (city) Alameda County
84	304	4.0	**San Diego Country Estates** (CDP) San Diego County
84	304	4.0	**San Ramon** (city) Contra Costa County
84	304	4.0	**Santee** (city) San Diego County
84	304	4.0	**South San Francisco** (city) San Mateo County
84	304	4.0	**Wasco** (city) Kern County
84	304	4.0	**Yorba Linda** (city) Orange County
93	332	4.1	**Culver City** (city) Los Angeles County
93	332	4.1	**El Dorado Hills** (CDP) El Dorado County
93	332	4.1	**El Segundo** (city) Los Angeles County
93	332	4.1	**La Crescenta-Montrose** (CDP) Los Angeles County
93	332	4.1	**Mendota** (city) Fresno County
93	332	4.1	**Montebello** (city) Los Angeles County
93	332	4.1	**Monterey Park** (city) Los Angeles County
93	332	4.1	**Moraga** (town) Contra Costa County
93	332	4.1	**Pico Rivera** (city) Los Angeles County
93	332	4.1	**Pleasanton** (city) Alameda County
93	332	4.1	**San Lorenzo** (CDP) Alameda County
93	332	4.1	**Santa Barbara** (city) Santa Barbara County
93	332	4.1	**Santa Paula** (city) Ventura County
93	332	4.1	**Soledad** (city) Monterey County
107	378	4.2	**Daly City** (city) San Mateo County
107	378	4.2	**Dinuba** (city) Tulare County
107	378	4.2	**Farmersville** (city) Tulare County
107	378	4.2	**Healdsburg** (city) Sonoma County
107	378	4.2	**Hillsborough** (town) San Mateo County
107	378	4.2	**Orinda** (city) Contra Costa County
113	419	4.3	**Hawaiian Gardens** (city) Los Angeles County
113	419	4.3	**Lake Forest** (city) Orange County
113	419	4.3	**Rio Linda** (CDP) Sacramento County
113	419	4.3	**San Jose** (city) Santa Clara County
113	419	4.3	**Saratoga** (city) Santa Clara County
113	419	4.3	**Stanton** (city) Orange County
113	419	4.3	**West Carson** (CDP) Los Angeles County
120	452	4.4	**Duarte** (city) Los Angeles County
120	452	4.4	**Hermosa Beach** (city) Los Angeles County
120	452	4.4	**Mountain View** (city) Santa Clara County
120	452	4.4	**Pacific Grove** (city) Monterey County
120	452	4.4	**Seal Beach** (city) Orange County
120	452	4.4	**Sunnyvale** (city) Santa Clara County
120	452	4.4	**Walnut** (city) Los Angeles County
127	484	4.5	**Ashland** (CDP) Alameda County
127	484	4.5	**Berkeley** (city) Alameda County
127	484	4.5	**Burlingame** (city) San Mateo County
127	484	4.5	**Chula Vista** (city) San Diego County
127	484	4.5	**Fillmore** (city) Ventura County
127	484	4.5	**Florence-Graham** (CDP) Los Angeles County
127	484	4.5	**Fremont** (city) Alameda County
127	484	4.5	**Goleta** (city) Santa Barbara County
127	484	4.5	**Imperial** (city) Imperial County
127	484	4.5	**Lennox** (CDP) Los Angeles County
127	484	4.5	**Los Gatos** (town) Santa Clara County
127	484	4.5	**Mead Valley** (CDP) Riverside County
127	484	4.5	**Mill Valley** (city) Marin County
127	484	4.5	**Orcutt** (CDP) Santa Barbara County
127	484	4.5	**San Anselmo** (town) Marin County
142	537	4.6	**Campbell** (city) Santa Clara County
142	537	4.6	**Carlsbad** (city) San Diego County
142	537	4.6	**El Monte** (city) Los Angeles County
142	537	4.6	**Garden Grove** (city) Orange County
142	537	4.6	**Gardena** (city) Los Angeles County
142	537	4.6	**Gilroy** (city) Santa Clara County
142	537	4.6	**Hanford** (city) Kings County
142	537	4.6	**Hawthorne** (city) Los Angeles County
142	537	4.6	**Montclair** (city) San Bernardino County

Note: *The state column ranks the top/bottom 150 places from all places in the state with population of 10,000 or more. The national column ranks the top/bottom 150 places from all places in the country with population of 10,000 or more. Places that are unincorporated were not considered in the rankings. Please refer to the User Guide for additional information.*

Population with Health Insurance

Top 150 Places Ranked in *Descending* Order

State Rank	Nat'l Rank	Percent	Place
1	10	99.0	**Camp Pendleton South** (CDP) San Diego County
1	10	99.0	**Piedmont** (city) Alameda County
3	14	98.9	**Hillsborough** (town) San Mateo County
4	37	98.4	**Alamo** (CDP) Contra Costa County
5	94	97.6	**Orinda** (city) Contra Costa County
5	94	97.6	**Saratoga** (city) Santa Clara County
7	108	97.5	**Los Altos** (city) Santa Clara County
7	108	97.5	**Mill Valley** (city) Marin County
9	121	97.4	**Clayton** (city) Contra Costa County
9	121	97.4	**Stanford** (CDP) Santa Clara County
11	145	97.2	**Coto de Caza** (CDP) Orange County
12	245	96.6	**Danville** (town) Contra Costa County
13	291	96.3	**Palos Verdes Estates** (city) Los Angeles County
14	335	96.1	**Lafayette** (city) Contra Costa County
14	335	96.1	**Laguna Woods** (city) Orange County
14	335	96.1	**Los Gatos** (town) Santa Clara County
14	335	96.1	**Malibu** (city) Los Angeles County
18	361	96.0	**Ladera Ranch** (CDP) Orange County
18	361	96.0	**Manhattan Beach** (city) Los Angeles County
20	387	95.9	**Foster City** (city) San Mateo County
20	387	95.9	**San Marino** (city) Los Angeles County
20	387	95.9	**Tamalpais-Homestead Valley** (CDP) Marin County
23	412	95.8	**Cupertino** (city) Santa Clara County
24	489	95.5	**Rancho Palos Verdes** (city) Los Angeles County
25	581	95.1	**El Dorado Hills** (CDP) El Dorado County
25	581	95.1	**Sierra Madre** (city) Los Angeles County
27	622	94.9	**San Diego Country Estates** (CDP) San Diego County
28	680	94.7	**San Ramon** (city) Contra Costa County
29	702	94.6	**Oak Park** (CDP) Ventura County
29	702	94.6	**Palo Alto** (city) Santa Clara County
31	779	94.3	**Larkspur** (city) Marin County
32	801	94.2	**Cameron Park** (CDP) El Dorado County
32	801	94.2	**Dublin** (city) Alameda County
32	801	94.2	**Moraga** (town) Contra Costa County
35	828	94.1	**La Cañada Flintridge** (city) Los Angeles County
36	864	94.0	**San Anselmo** (town) Marin County
37	886	93.9	**Discovery Bay** (CDP) Contra Costa County
38	926	93.7	**San Carlos** (city) San Mateo County
39	959	93.6	**Belmont** (city) San Mateo County
39	959	93.6	**Yorba Linda** (city) Orange County
41	989	93.5	**Coronado** (city) San Diego County
41	989	93.5	**Folsom** (city) Sacramento County
41	989	93.5	**North Tustin** (CDP) Orange County
41	989	93.5	**Rossmoor** (CDP) Orange County
45	1023	93.4	**Claremont** (city) Los Angeles County
45	1023	93.4	**Menlo Park** (city) San Mateo County
45	1023	93.4	**Scotts Valley** (city) Santa Cruz County
45	1023	93.4	**Seal Beach** (city) Orange County
49	1046	93.3	**Calabasas** (city) Los Angeles County
49	1046	93.3	**Granite Bay** (CDP) Placer County
51	1087	93.1	**Agoura Hills** (city) Los Angeles County
51	1087	93.1	**Brentwood** (city) Contra Costa County
51	1087	93.1	**Burlingame** (city) San Mateo County
54	1109	93.0	**Pleasanton** (city) Alameda County
54	1109	93.0	**Ripon** (city) San Joaquin County
56	1134	92.9	**Hermosa Beach** (city) Los Angeles County
56	1134	92.9	**Isla Vista** (CDP) Santa Barbara County
56	1134	92.9	**Rosedale** (CDP) Kern County
59	1199	92.7	**Albany** (city) Alameda County
59	1199	92.7	**Walnut Creek** (city) Contra Costa County
61	1236	92.6	**Stevenson Ranch** (CDP) Los Angeles County
62	1286	92.4	**Pacifica** (city) San Mateo County
63	1315	92.3	**Laguna Beach** (city) Orange County
64	1366	92.1	**Auburn** (city) Placer County
64	1366	92.1	**Martinez** (city) Contra Costa County
66	1391	92.0	**Davis** (city) Yolo County
66	1391	92.0	**Rancho Santa Margarita** (city) Orange County
66	1391	92.0	**Rocklin** (city) Placer County
69	1428	91.9	**Mission Viejo** (city) Orange County
70	1454	91.8	**Poway** (city) San Diego County
70	1454	91.8	**Windsor** (town) Sonoma County
72	1478	91.7	**El Segundo** (city) Los Angeles County
72	1478	91.7	**Sonoma** (city) Sonoma County
74	1525	91.5	**Fremont** (city) Alameda County
74	1525	91.5	**La Verne** (city) Los Angeles County
74	1525	91.5	**Newport Beach** (city) Orange County
74	1525	91.5	**Pleasant Hill** (city) Contra Costa County
78	1552	91.4	**Berkeley** (city) Alameda County
79	1579	91.3	**Benicia** (city) Solano County
79	1579	91.3	**Redondo Beach** (city) Los Angeles County
81	1606	91.2	**Livermore** (city) Alameda County
82	1634	91.1	**Castro Valley** (CDP) Alameda County
82	1634	91.1	**Hercules** (city) Contra Costa County
84	1675	90.9	**Goleta** (city) Santa Barbara County
84	1675	90.9	**Susanville** (city) Lassen County
84	1675	90.9	**Twentynine Palms** (city) San Bernardino County
87	1703	90.8	**Beverly Hills** (city) Los Angeles County
87	1703	90.8	**Roseville** (city) Placer County
89	1728	90.7	**Irvine** (city) Orange County
89	1728	90.7	**Millbrae** (city) San Mateo County
89	1728	90.7	**Santa Clara** (city) Santa Clara County
92	1759	90.6	**Elk Grove** (city) Sacramento County
92	1759	90.6	**Lincoln** (city) Placer County
94	1781	90.5	**Laguna Niguel** (city) Orange County
95	1807	90.4	**Fair Oaks** (CDP) Sacramento County
95	1807	90.4	**Vacaville** (city) Solano County
97	1830	90.3	**Novato** (city) Marin County
98	1847	90.2	**Carlsbad** (city) San Diego County
99	1876	90.1	**Aliso Viejo** (city) Orange County
99	1876	90.1	**Rancho Mirage** (city) Riverside County
101	1898	90.0	**Milpitas** (city) Santa Clara County
101	1898	90.0	**San Lorenzo** (CDP) Alameda County
103	1919	89.9	**Casa de Oro-Mount Helix** (CDP) San Diego County
103	1919	89.9	**Sunnyvale** (city) Santa Clara County
105	1948	89.8	**Alpine** (CDP) San Diego County
105	1948	89.8	**Arroyo Grande** (city) San Luis Obispo County
105	1948	89.8	**South San Francisco** (city) San Mateo County
108	1978	89.7	**La Crescenta-Montrose** (CDP) Los Angeles County
108	1978	89.7	**Newark** (city) Alameda County
110	2004	89.6	**Fairview** (CDP) Alameda County
110	2004	89.6	**View Park-Windsor Hills** (CDP) Los Angeles County
112	2021	89.5	**Campbell** (city) Santa Clara County
112	2021	89.5	**Fountain Valley** (city) Orange County
112	2021	89.5	**La Riviera** (CDP) Sacramento County
115	2044	89.4	**Camarillo** (city) Ventura County
115	2044	89.4	**Half Moon Bay** (city) San Mateo County
115	2044	89.4	**Mountain View** (city) Santa Clara County
115	2044	89.4	**Rancho San Diego** (CDP) San Diego County
119	2068	89.3	**San Bruno** (city) San Mateo County
119	2068	89.3	**Thousand Oaks** (city) Ventura County
121	2091	89.2	**Union City** (city) Alameda County
122	2144	89.0	**Santee** (city) San Diego County
123	2171	88.9	**Diamond Springs** (CDP) El Dorado County
123	2171	88.9	**San Clemente** (city) Orange County
123	2171	88.9	**San Francisco** (city) San Francisco County
123	2171	88.9	**Santa Monica** (city) Los Angeles County
127	2194	88.8	**Canyon Lake** (city) Riverside County
127	2194	88.8	**Castaic** (CDP) Los Angeles County
127	2194	88.8	**El Cerrito** (city) Contra Costa County
127	2194	88.8	**Petaluma** (city) Sonoma County
131	2223	88.7	**Ridgecrest** (city) Kern County
132	2245	88.6	**Glendora** (city) Los Angeles County
133	2264	88.5	**Alameda** (city) Alameda County
133	2264	88.5	**French Valley** (CDP) Riverside County
133	2264	88.5	**Pinole** (city) Contra Costa County
133	2264	88.5	**San Luis Obispo** (city) San Luis Obispo County
133	2264	88.5	**Simi Valley** (city) Ventura County
133	2264	88.5	**Walnut** (city) Los Angeles County
139	2285	88.4	**Los Alamitos** (city) Orange County
139	2285	88.4	**Suisun City** (city) Solano County
141	2303	88.3	**Morgan Hill** (city) Santa Clara County
141	2303	88.3	**San Mateo** (city) San Mateo County
143	2326	88.2	**Fairfield** (city) Solano County
143	2326	88.2	**Norco** (city) Riverside County
145	2351	88.1	**American Canyon** (city) Napa County
145	2351	88.1	**Atascadero** (city) San Luis Obispo County
145	2351	88.1	**Moorpark** (city) Ventura County
148	2375	88.0	**Huntington Beach** (city) Orange County
148	2375	88.0	**South Pasadena** (city) Los Angeles County
148	2375	88.0	**Torrance** (city) Los Angeles County

Note: *The state column ranks the top/bottom 150 places from all places in the state with population of 10,000 or more. The national column ranks the top/bottom 150 places from all places in the country with population of 10,000 or more. Places that are unincorporated were not considered in the rankings. Please refer to the User Guide for additional information.*

Population with Health Insurance

Top 150 Places Ranked in *Ascending* Order

State Rank	Nat'l Rank	Percent	Place
1	14	60.4	**Mead Valley** (CDP) Riverside County
2	15	60.6	**Mendota** (city) Fresno County
3	20	61.2	**Cudahy** (city) Los Angeles County
4	22	61.7	**Lennox** (CDP) Los Angeles County
5	23	61.8	**Bell Gardens** (city) Los Angeles County
6	27	62.0	**Maywood** (city) Los Angeles County
7	43	63.8	**East Los Angeles** (CDP) Los Angeles County
8	47	64.4	**Arvin** (city) Kern County
9	50	64.5	**Bell** (city) Los Angeles County
9	50	64.5	**Florence-Graham** (CDP) Los Angeles County
11	53	64.7	**East Rancho Dominguez** (CDP) Los Angeles County
12	54	64.9	**Coachella** (city) Riverside County
13	58	65.2	**McFarland** (city) Kern County
14	60	65.3	**Hawaiian Gardens** (city) Los Angeles County
15	65	65.7	**Muscoy** (CDP) San Bernardino County
16	68	65.8	**Lamont** (CDP) Kern County
17	70	66.0	**Huntington Park** (city) Los Angeles County
18	78	66.6	**King City** (city) Monterey County
18	78	66.6	**Lynwood** (city) Los Angeles County
20	80	66.7	**Santa Ana** (city) Orange County
21	94	68.2	**Walnut Park** (CDP) Los Angeles County
22	101	68.6	**Willowbrook** (CDP) Los Angeles County
23	103	68.7	**South San Jose Hills** (CDP) Los Angeles County
24	108	69.1	**Lawndale** (city) Los Angeles County
24	108	69.1	**South Gate** (city) Los Angeles County
26	112	69.2	**Bloomington** (CDP) San Bernardino County
27	114	69.3	**South El Monte** (city) Los Angeles County
28	121	69.5	**National City** (city) San Diego County
28	121	69.5	**Parlier** (city) Fresno County
30	124	69.6	**Avenal** (city) Kings County
30	124	69.6	**El Monte** (city) Los Angeles County
32	132	69.9	**Desert Hot Springs** (city) Riverside County
33	135	70.0	**Paramount** (city) Los Angeles County
34	157	70.9	**Greenfield** (city) Monterey County
35	160	71.0	**Cathedral City** (city) Riverside County
36	167	71.1	**Lakeland Village** (CDP) Riverside County
37	174	71.3	**Big Bear City** (CDP) San Bernardino County
38	178	71.5	**Home Gardens** (CDP) Riverside County
39	184	71.7	**Garden Acres** (CDP) San Joaquin County
40	197	72.0	**Citrus** (CDP) Los Angeles County
40	197	72.0	**Lindsay** (city) Tulare County
42	204	72.2	**Santa Maria** (city) Santa Barbara County
43	210	72.4	**Baldwin Park** (city) Los Angeles County
44	214	72.6	**Delano** (city) Kern County
45	216	72.7	**Perris** (city) Riverside County
46	224	73.0	**Calexico** (city) Imperial County
47	226	73.1	**Stanton** (city) Orange County
48	227	73.2	**Compton** (city) Los Angeles County
48	227	73.2	**Dinuba** (city) Tulare County
50	230	73.3	**Wasco** (city) Kern County
51	232	73.5	**Colton** (city) San Bernardino County
51	232	73.5	**Seaside** (city) Monterey County
53	237	73.6	**Westmont** (CDP) Los Angeles County
54	243	73.7	**Commerce** (city) Los Angeles County
54	243	73.7	**Montclair** (city) San Bernardino County
56	248	73.8	**La Puente** (city) Los Angeles County
57	256	73.9	**Inglewood** (city) Los Angeles County
58	263	74.0	**Newman** (city) Stanislaus County
58	263	74.0	**Pomona** (city) Los Angeles County
60	271	74.3	**Rosemead** (city) Los Angeles County
61	277	74.4	**Escondido** (city) San Diego County
61	277	74.4	**Hawthorne** (city) Los Angeles County
61	277	74.4	**Los Angeles** (city) Los Angeles County
64	284	74.5	**Avocado Heights** (CDP) Los Angeles County
64	284	74.5	**Lemon Hill** (CDP) Sacramento County
66	290	74.6	**Oxnard** (city) Ventura County
67	297	74.7	**Kerman** (city) Fresno County
68	298	74.8	**Rialto** (city) San Bernardino County
68	298	74.8	**San Pablo** (city) Contra Costa County
70	306	75.0	**Ontario** (city) San Bernardino County
70	306	75.0	**Salinas** (city) Monterey County
70	306	75.0	**San Fernando** (city) Los Angeles County
70	306	75.0	**Selma** (city) Fresno County
70	306	75.0	**Soledad** (city) Monterey County
75	317	75.1	**Fontana** (city) San Bernardino County
75	317	75.1	**Valinda** (CDP) Los Angeles County
77	327	75.3	**San Bernardino** (city) San Bernardino County
78	335	75.4	**Vista** (city) San Diego County
79	342	75.5	**Pico Rivera** (city) Los Angeles County
80	356	75.8	**Norwalk** (city) Los Angeles County
81	360	75.9	**Moreno Valley** (city) Riverside County
82	363	76.0	**East Palo Alto** (city) San Mateo County
83	373	76.1	**North Fair Oaks** (CDP) San Mateo County
84	380	76.2	**Artesia** (city) Los Angeles County
84	380	76.2	**Indio** (city) Riverside County
86	386	76.3	**Sun Village** (CDP) Los Angeles County
87	395	76.4	**Farmersville** (city) Tulare County
88	423	76.7	**Montebello** (city) Los Angeles County
88	423	76.7	**West Puente Valley** (CDP) Los Angeles County
88	423	76.7	**Winton** (CDP) Merced County
91	430	76.8	**Watsonville** (city) Santa Cruz County
92	436	76.9	**Madera** (city) Madera County
92	436	76.9	**Reedley** (city) Fresno County
94	440	77.0	**Azusa** (city) Los Angeles County
95	445	77.1	**Rowland Heights** (CDP) Los Angeles County
96	454	77.3	**Livingston** (city) Merced County
97	458	77.4	**Anaheim** (city) Orange County
97	458	77.4	**Signal Hill** (city) Los Angeles County
99	477	77.6	**San Gabriel** (city) Los Angeles County
100	487	77.7	**Shafter** (city) Kern County
101	500	77.9	**La Habra** (city) Orange County
101	500	77.9	**Santa Paula** (city) Ventura County
103	508	78.0	**Clearlake** (city) Lake County
103	508	78.0	**South Lake Tahoe** (city) El Dorado County
105	518	78.1	**Costa Mesa** (city) Orange County
105	518	78.1	**San Juan Capistrano** (city) Orange County
107	525	78.2	**Santa Fe Springs** (city) Los Angeles County
108	538	78.3	**Downey** (city) Los Angeles County
108	538	78.3	**Lake Los Angeles** (CDP) Los Angeles County
108	538	78.3	**Sanger** (city) Fresno County
111	549	78.4	**Linda** (CDP) Yuba County
111	549	78.4	**South Whittier** (CDP) Los Angeles County
113	559	78.5	**Ashland** (CDP) Alameda County
113	559	78.5	**Bellflower** (city) Los Angeles County
115	569	78.6	**Carpinteria** (city) Santa Barbara County
115	569	78.6	**Port Hueneme** (city) Ventura County
117	590	78.8	**Garden Grove** (city) Orange County
118	599	78.9	**Hesperia** (city) San Bernardino County
118	599	78.9	**Lake Elsinore** (city) Riverside County
118	599	78.9	**Lathrop** (city) San Joaquin County
118	599	78.9	**Santa Barbara** (city) Santa Barbara County
122	615	79.0	**Bay Point** (CDP) Contra Costa County
122	615	79.0	**Eureka** (city) Humboldt County
124	624	79.1	**Arcata** (city) Humboldt County
124	624	79.1	**Riverside** (city) Riverside County
126	641	79.3	**Gardena** (city) Los Angeles County
126	641	79.3	**Richmond** (city) Contra Costa County
128	655	79.4	**West Whittier-Los Nietos** (CDP) Los Angeles County
129	667	79.5	**Atwater** (city) Merced County
130	673	79.6	**El Cajon** (city) San Diego County
131	679	79.7	**Fullerton** (city) Orange County
131	679	79.7	**Los Banos** (city) Merced County
133	697	79.8	**East Hemet** (CDP) Riverside County
133	697	79.8	**North Highlands** (CDP) Sacramento County
133	697	79.8	**Palm Springs** (city) Riverside County
133	697	79.8	**Ramona** (CDP) San Diego County
137	707	79.9	**Tulare** (city) Tulare County
138	719	80.0	**Florin** (CDP) Sacramento County
138	719	80.0	**Monterey Park** (city) Los Angeles County
140	728	80.1	**Rosamond** (CDP) Kern County
141	739	80.2	**Porterville** (city) Tulare County
142	753	80.3	**Cherryland** (CDP) Alameda County
142	753	80.3	**Corcoran** (city) Kings County
142	753	80.3	**El Centro** (city) Imperial County
142	753	80.3	**La Presa** (CDP) San Diego County
142	753	80.3	**Lemon Grove** (city) San Diego County
147	774	80.4	**Buena Park** (city) Orange County
147	774	80.4	**Chowchilla** (city) Madera County
147	774	80.4	**Fresno** (city) Fresno County
147	774	80.4	**Glendale** (city) Los Angeles County

Note: *The state column ranks the top/bottom 150 places from all places in the state with population of 10,000 or more. The national column ranks the top/bottom 150 places from all places in the country with population of 10,000 or more. Places that are unincorporated were not considered in the rankings. Please refer to the User Guide for additional information.*

Population with Private Health Insurance

Top 150 Places Ranked in *Descending* Order

State Rank	Nat'l Rank	Percent	Place
1	1	98.0	**Camp Pendleton South** (CDP) San Diego County
2	9	95.3	**Stanford** (CDP) Santa Clara County
3	13	95.1	**Piedmont** (city) Alameda County
4	29	94.1	**Alamo** (CDP) Contra Costa County
5	44	93.4	**Coto de Caza** (CDP) Orange County
6	90	92.3	**Danville** (town) Contra Costa County
7	93	92.2	**Hillsborough** (town) San Mateo County
8	103	92.0	**Orinda** (city) Contra Costa County
9	111	91.9	**Manhattan Beach** (city) Los Angeles County
10	138	91.4	**Los Altos** (city) Santa Clara County
10	138	91.4	**Saratoga** (city) Santa Clara County
12	163	90.9	**Clayton** (city) Contra Costa County
12	163	90.9	**Ladera Ranch** (CDP) Orange County
14	174	90.7	**San Ramon** (city) Contra Costa County
15	207	90.4	**Tamalpais-Homestead Valley** (CDP) Marin County
16	217	90.3	**Lafayette** (city) Contra Costa County
17	224	90.2	**Oak Park** (CDP) Ventura County
18	286	89.5	**Palos Verdes Estates** (city) Los Angeles County
19	311	89.2	**Moraga** (town) Contra Costa County
20	315	89.1	**El Dorado Hills** (CDP) El Dorado County
20	315	89.1	**La Cañada Flintridge** (city) Los Angeles County
20	315	89.1	**Malibu** (city) Los Angeles County
23	353	88.7	**Los Gatos** (town) Santa Clara County
24	389	88.4	**Cupertino** (city) Santa Clara County
25	403	88.3	**Isla Vista** (CDP) Santa Barbara County
26	413	88.2	**Scotts Valley** (city) Santa Cruz County
27	437	88.0	**Hermosa Beach** (city) Los Angeles County
27	437	88.0	**Palo Alto** (city) Santa Clara County
29	461	87.8	**Mill Valley** (city) Marin County
30	475	87.7	**San Diego Country Estates** (CDP) San Diego County
31	510	87.5	**Dublin** (city) Alameda County
31	510	87.5	**Foster City** (city) San Mateo County
33	529	87.3	**Stevenson Ranch** (CDP) Los Angeles County
34	551	87.1	**Coronado** (city) San Diego County
34	551	87.1	**Granite Bay** (CDP) Placer County
36	559	87.0	**Folsom** (city) Sacramento County
36	559	87.0	**Pleasanton** (city) Alameda County
36	559	87.0	**Rancho Palos Verdes** (city) Los Angeles County
36	559	87.0	**San Marino** (city) Los Angeles County
40	600	86.7	**San Anselmo** (town) Marin County
41	608	86.6	**Larkspur** (city) Marin County
42	655	86.2	**Rossmoor** (CDP) Orange County
43	686	86.0	**San Carlos** (city) San Mateo County
44	733	85.7	**Sierra Madre** (city) Los Angeles County
45	743	85.6	**Burlingame** (city) San Mateo County
45	743	85.6	**Pacifica** (city) San Mateo County
47	754	85.5	**Calabasas** (city) Los Angeles County
48	779	85.3	**Davis** (city) Yolo County
48	779	85.3	**Discovery Bay** (CDP) Contra Costa County
50	826	84.9	**Yorba Linda** (city) Orange County
51	872	84.6	**Rancho Santa Margarita** (city) Orange County
52	890	84.4	**Agoura Hills** (city) Los Angeles County
52	890	84.4	**Albany** (city) Alameda County
52	890	84.4	**Belmont** (city) San Mateo County
55	902	84.3	**El Segundo** (city) Los Angeles County
56	957	83.9	**Walnut Creek** (city) Contra Costa County
57	1002	83.5	**Menlo Park** (city) San Mateo County
58	1018	83.4	**Rosedale** (CDP) Kern County
59	1047	83.2	**Aliso Viejo** (city) Orange County
60	1080	82.9	**Newport Beach** (city) Orange County
60	1080	82.9	**North Tustin** (CDP) Orange County
60	1080	82.9	**Rocklin** (city) Placer County
63	1110	82.7	**Laguna Beach** (city) Orange County
63	1110	82.7	**Livermore** (city) Alameda County
63	1110	82.7	**Pleasant Hill** (city) Contra Costa County
66	1131	82.5	**Cameron Park** (CDP) El Dorado County
66	1131	82.5	**Martinez** (city) Contra Costa County
68	1143	82.4	**Brentwood** (city) Contra Costa County
69	1170	82.2	**Poway** (city) San Diego County
70	1180	82.1	**Redondo Beach** (city) Los Angeles County
71	1206	81.9	**Irvine** (city) Orange County
72	1214	81.8	**Goleta** (city) Santa Barbara County
73	1235	81.6	**Berkeley** (city) Alameda County
74	1290	81.1	**Benicia** (city) Solano County
74	1290	81.1	**Laguna Niguel** (city) Orange County
74	1290	81.1	**Millbrae** (city) San Mateo County
77	1306	81.0	**Carlsbad** (city) San Diego County
78	1321	80.9	**Mission Viejo** (city) Orange County
79	1347	80.7	**Encinitas** (city) San Diego County
80	1368	80.6	**French Valley** (CDP) Riverside County
80	1368	80.6	**South Pasadena** (city) Los Angeles County
82	1384	80.5	**Castaic** (CDP) Los Angeles County
83	1405	80.3	**Sonoma** (city) Sonoma County
83	1405	80.3	**Windsor** (town) Sonoma County
85	1419	80.2	**Thousand Oaks** (city) Ventura County
86	1451	80.0	**Hercules** (city) Contra Costa County
87	1474	79.8	**Moorpark** (city) Ventura County
88	1493	79.7	**Beverly Hills** (city) Los Angeles County
89	1505	79.6	**San Luis Obispo** (city) San Luis Obispo County
89	1505	79.6	**View Park-Windsor Hills** (CDP) Los Angeles County
91	1514	79.5	**Claremont** (city) Los Angeles County
92	1577	79.0	**Campbell** (city) Santa Clara County
92	1577	79.0	**Mountain View** (city) Santa Clara County
92	1577	79.0	**Roseville** (city) Placer County
95	1603	78.8	**Castro Valley** (CDP) Alameda County
95	1603	78.8	**El Cerrito** (city) Contra Costa County
95	1603	78.8	**Sunnyvale** (city) Santa Clara County
98	1615	78.7	**Fremont** (city) Alameda County
98	1615	78.7	**La Crescenta-Montrose** (CDP) Los Angeles County
100	1629	78.6	**Santa Clara** (city) Santa Clara County
101	1638	78.5	**Pacific Grove** (city) Monterey County
102	1662	78.3	**Lincoln** (city) Placer County
103	1671	78.2	**San Clemente** (city) Orange County
104	1689	78.0	**Auburn** (city) Placer County
104	1689	78.0	**Camarillo** (city) Ventura County
106	1708	77.8	**San Bruno** (city) San Mateo County
107	1745	77.4	**Ripon** (city) San Joaquin County
108	1756	77.3	**Simi Valley** (city) Ventura County
109	1761	77.2	**Canyon Lake** (city) Riverside County
109	1761	77.2	**Los Alamitos** (city) Orange County
111	1777	77.1	**Chino Hills** (city) San Bernardino County
111	1777	77.1	**Elk Grove** (city) Sacramento County
111	1777	77.1	**Lake Forest** (city) Orange County
111	1777	77.1	**Novato** (city) Marin County
111	1777	77.1	**Walnut** (city) Los Angeles County
116	1796	77.0	**Arroyo Grande** (city) San Luis Obispo County
117	1805	76.9	**Fair Oaks** (CDP) Sacramento County
117	1805	76.9	**Rancho San Diego** (CDP) San Diego County
119	1825	76.7	**Half Moon Bay** (city) San Mateo County
120	1836	76.6	**El Sobrante** (CDP) Riverside County
120	1836	76.6	**Solana Beach** (city) San Diego County
122	1857	76.4	**Petaluma** (city) Sonoma County
123	1871	76.3	**Culver City** (city) Los Angeles County
123	1871	76.3	**Santa Monica** (city) Los Angeles County
123	1871	76.3	**Vacaville** (city) Solano County
126	1901	76.1	**Santee** (city) San Diego County
127	1943	75.7	**Atascadero** (city) San Luis Obispo County
128	1955	75.6	**Dana Point** (city) Orange County
129	1970	75.5	**Seal Beach** (city) Orange County
130	1978	75.4	**Diamond Bar** (city) Los Angeles County
130	1978	75.4	**La Verne** (city) Los Angeles County
132	1989	75.3	**South San Francisco** (city) San Mateo County
133	1998	75.2	**Alpine** (CDP) San Diego County
133	1998	75.2	**Huntington Beach** (city) Orange County
133	1998	75.2	**Salida** (CDP) Stanislaus County
133	1998	75.2	**San Mateo** (city) San Mateo County
137	2012	75.1	**Laguna Hills** (city) Orange County
138	2020	75.0	**Brea** (city) Orange County
138	2020	75.0	**Torrance** (city) Los Angeles County
140	2029	74.9	**Milpitas** (city) Santa Clara County
140	2029	74.9	**Rancho Cucamonga** (city) San Bernardino County
142	2044	74.8	**Murrieta** (city) Riverside County
143	2068	74.6	**Santa Cruz** (city) Santa Cruz County
144	2089	74.5	**Fairview** (CDP) Alameda County
145	2094	74.4	**Cerritos** (city) Los Angeles County
145	2094	74.4	**Santa Clarita** (city) Los Angeles County
147	2109	74.3	**Los Osos** (CDP) San Luis Obispo County
147	2109	74.3	**Morgan Hill** (city) Santa Clara County
149	2143	74.0	**Orangevale** (CDP) Sacramento County
150	2152	73.9	**Newark** (city) Alameda County

Note: *The state column ranks the top/bottom 150 places from all places in the state with population of 10,000 or more. The national column ranks the top/bottom 150 places from all places in the country with population of 10,000 or more. Places that are unincorporated were not considered in the rankings. Please refer to the User Guide for additional information.*

Population with Private Health Insurance

Top 150 Places Ranked in *Ascending* Order

State Rank	Nat'l Rank	Percent	Place
1	4	17.1	**Mendota** (city) Fresno County
2	10	21.8	**Muscoy** (CDP) San Bernardino County
3	12	23.4	**Parlier** (city) Fresno County
4	15	24.5	**McFarland** (city) Kern County
5	19	25.2	**Cudahy** (city) Los Angeles County
6	20	25.8	**Florence-Graham** (CDP) Los Angeles County
7	21	26.2	**Farmersville** (city) Tulare County
7	21	26.2	**Mead Valley** (CDP) Riverside County
9	26	26.4	**Willowbrook** (CDP) Los Angeles County
10	28	26.6	**East Rancho Dominguez** (CDP) Los Angeles County
11	33	27.7	**Bell Gardens** (city) Los Angeles County
12	35	27.8	**Lindsay** (city) Tulare County
13	37	28.3	**Huntington Park** (city) Los Angeles County
13	37	28.3	**Maywood** (city) Los Angeles County
15	39	28.5	**Avenal** (city) Kings County
15	39	28.5	**Lamont** (CDP) Kern County
17	41	28.8	**Arvin** (city) Kern County
18	43	28.9	**Lemon Hill** (CDP) Sacramento County
19	48	30.3	**Coachella** (city) Riverside County
20	51	30.7	**Bell** (city) Los Angeles County
21	54	31.3	**East Los Angeles** (CDP) Los Angeles County
22	61	32.3	**Clearlake** (city) Lake County
23	62	32.4	**Hawaiian Gardens** (city) Los Angeles County
24	63	32.6	**El Monte** (city) Los Angeles County
25	65	32.8	**South El Monte** (city) Los Angeles County
26	69	33.4	**Westmont** (CDP) Los Angeles County
27	74	33.6	**Dinuba** (city) Tulare County
28	76	33.8	**Lennox** (CDP) Los Angeles County
28	76	33.8	**South San Jose Hills** (CDP) Los Angeles County
30	81	34.0	**Walnut Park** (CDP) Los Angeles County
31	82	34.1	**Lynwood** (city) Los Angeles County
32	89	34.7	**Corcoran** (city) Kings County
32	89	34.7	**Desert Hot Springs** (city) Riverside County
34	92	34.8	**Compton** (city) Los Angeles County
35	94	35.0	**Wasco** (city) Kern County
36	96	35.2	**Garden Acres** (CDP) San Joaquin County
37	98	35.4	**Linda** (CDP) Yuba County
38	105	36.0	**Madera** (city) Madera County
39	111	36.5	**Delano** (city) Kern County
40	121	37.4	**Winton** (CDP) Merced County
41	127	37.8	**Calexico** (city) Imperial County
42	133	38.5	**Santa Ana** (city) Orange County
43	134	38.6	**Parkway** (CDP) Sacramento County
43	134	38.6	**Reedley** (city) Fresno County
45	138	38.7	**Selma** (city) Fresno County
46	141	38.8	**Greenfield** (city) Monterey County
46	141	38.8	**Paramount** (city) Los Angeles County
48	146	39.0	**Adelanto** (city) San Bernardino County
49	148	39.1	**South Gate** (city) Los Angeles County
50	154	39.4	**San Bernardino** (city) San Bernardino County
51	157	39.7	**Baldwin Park** (city) Los Angeles County
52	161	39.8	**National City** (city) San Diego County
53	163	39.9	**Perris** (city) Riverside County
54	165	40.0	**King City** (city) Monterey County
55	173	40.8	**Bloomington** (CDP) San Bernardino County
56	174	40.9	**Santa Maria** (city) Santa Barbara County
56	174	40.9	**Sun Village** (CDP) Los Angeles County
58	189	41.7	**Lake Los Angeles** (CDP) Los Angeles County
59	200	42.1	**Colton** (city) San Bernardino County
60	206	42.3	**North Highlands** (CDP) Sacramento County
61	214	42.6	**Kerman** (city) Fresno County
62	219	42.8	**Home Gardens** (CDP) Riverside County
63	223	42.9	**Commerce** (city) Los Angeles County
63	223	42.9	**Oildale** (CDP) Kern County
65	229	43.2	**Olivehurst** (CDP) Yuba County
66	232	43.3	**Rosemead** (city) Los Angeles County
67	235	43.4	**Marysville** (city) Yuba County
68	237	43.5	**Rialto** (city) San Bernardino County
69	241	43.8	**La Puente** (city) Los Angeles County
69	241	43.8	**Lawndale** (city) Los Angeles County
71	246	44.0	**Watsonville** (city) Santa Cruz County
72	252	44.2	**Cathedral City** (city) Riverside County
73	255	44.3	**Chowchilla** (city) Madera County
74	260	44.4	**El Centro** (city) Imperial County
74	260	44.4	**Pomona** (city) Los Angeles County
76	266	44.5	**Oroville** (city) Butte County
77	276	44.8	**Soledad** (city) Monterey County
78	281	44.9	**Cherryland** (CDP) Alameda County
79	291	45.1	**Hemet** (city) Riverside County
79	291	45.1	**North Fair Oaks** (CDP) San Mateo County
81	296	45.3	**Shafter** (city) Kern County
82	299	45.4	**Red Bluff** (city) Tehama County
83	310	45.8	**East Palo Alto** (city) San Mateo County
83	310	45.8	**San Fernando** (city) Los Angeles County
85	316	45.9	**Stanton** (city) Orange County
86	320	46.1	**Bay Point** (CDP) Contra Costa County
86	320	46.1	**Florin** (CDP) Sacramento County
88	337	46.5	**Sanger** (city) Fresno County
89	342	46.6	**Livingston** (city) Merced County
90	356	46.9	**Merced** (city) Merced County
91	362	47.0	**Fresno** (city) Fresno County
92	370	47.2	**Indio** (city) Riverside County
92	370	47.2	**Porterville** (city) Tulare County
94	382	47.6	**Hesperia** (city) San Bernardino County
94	382	47.6	**Montclair** (city) San Bernardino County
94	382	47.6	**Newman** (city) Stanislaus County
97	389	47.7	**Eureka** (city) Humboldt County
98	393	47.8	**Los Banos** (city) Merced County
99	398	47.9	**Brawley** (city) Imperial County
99	398	47.9	**Lompoc** (city) Santa Barbara County
101	403	48.1	**Banning** (city) Riverside County
101	403	48.1	**Citrus** (CDP) Los Angeles County
101	403	48.1	**El Cajon** (city) San Diego County
101	403	48.1	**Valinda** (CDP) Los Angeles County
105	415	48.3	**Salinas** (city) Monterey County
106	419	48.4	**Oxnard** (city) Ventura County
106	419	48.4	**West Puente Valley** (CDP) Los Angeles County
108	431	48.7	**Lakeland Village** (CDP) Riverside County
109	434	48.8	**Moreno Valley** (city) Riverside County
110	445	49.0	**San Pablo** (city) Contra Costa County
111	450	49.1	**Hawthorne** (city) Los Angeles County
112	454	49.2	**Inglewood** (city) Los Angeles County
112	454	49.2	**Tulare** (city) Tulare County
114	461	49.3	**Los Angeles** (city) Los Angeles County
115	467	49.4	**Montebello** (city) Los Angeles County
116	469	49.5	**Exeter** (city) Tulare County
117	475	49.6	**Ashland** (CDP) Alameda County
118	490	49.9	**Grass Valley** (city) Nevada County
119	492	50.0	**Atwater** (city) Merced County
119	492	50.0	**Foothill Farms** (CDP) Sacramento County
121	500	50.1	**Palmdale** (city) Los Angeles County
122	512	50.3	**Big Bear City** (CDP) San Bernardino County
123	516	50.4	**San Jacinto** (city) Riverside County
124	520	50.5	**Shasta Lake** (city) Shasta County
125	527	50.6	**Victorville** (city) San Bernardino County
126	529	50.7	**Westminster** (city) Orange County
126	529	50.7	**Yucca Valley** (town) San Bernardino County
128	535	50.8	**Stockton** (city) San Joaquin County
129	538	50.9	**Ontario** (city) San Bernardino County
129	538	50.9	**Ukiah** (city) Mendocino County
131	547	51.1	**Garden Grove** (city) Orange County
132	554	51.2	**East Hemet** (CDP) Riverside County
133	570	51.5	**Norwalk** (city) Los Angeles County
134	574	51.6	**Ceres** (city) Stanislaus County
134	574	51.6	**Pico Rivera** (city) Los Angeles County
136	579	51.7	**Fontana** (city) San Bernardino County
137	586	51.8	**California City** (city) Kern County
138	590	51.9	**Highland** (city) San Bernardino County
139	597	52.0	**Santa Paula** (city) Ventura County
140	618	52.6	**Yuba City** (city) Sutter County
141	644	53.1	**Bellflower** (city) Los Angeles County
142	653	53.2	**Anaheim** (city) Orange County
143	668	53.4	**Escondido** (city) San Diego County
144	675	53.6	**Glendale** (city) Los Angeles County
145	683	53.8	**Azusa** (city) Los Angeles County
146	694	53.9	**Barstow** (city) San Bernardino County
147	701	54.0	**Palm Springs** (city) Riverside County
148	708	54.1	**Valle Vista** (CDP) Riverside County
149	717	54.3	**Alum Rock** (CDP) Santa Clara County
150	739	54.6	**West Whittier-Los Nietos** (CDP) Los Angeles County

Note: *The state column ranks the top/bottom 150 places from all places in the state with population of 10,000 or more. The national column ranks the top/bottom 150 places from all places in the country with population of 10,000 or more. Places that are unincorporated were not considered in the rankings. Please refer to the User Guide for additional information.*

Population with Public Health Insurance

Top 150 Places Ranked in *Descending* Order

State Rank	Nat'l Rank	Percent	Place
1	2	79.8	**Laguna Woods** (city) Orange County
2	27	56.8	**Clearlake** (city) Lake County
3	52	53.3	**Red Bluff** (city) Tehama County
4	56	53.1	**Farmersville** (city) Tulare County
5	60	52.9	**Lemon Hill** (CDP) Sacramento County
6	63	52.5	**Marysville** (city) Yuba County
7	75	51.5	**Banning** (city) Riverside County
7	75	51.5	**Grass Valley** (city) Nevada County
9	83	51.3	**Linda** (CDP) Yuba County
10	86	51.2	**Parkway** (CDP) Sacramento County
11	96	50.6	**Magalia** (CDP) Butte County
11	96	50.6	**Oroville** (city) Butte County
13	102	50.4	**Parlier** (city) Fresno County
13	102	50.4	**Rancho Mirage** (city) Riverside County
15	123	49.3	**Corcoran** (city) Kings County
16	125	49.2	**Hemet** (city) Riverside County
17	146	48.2	**Placerville** (city) El Dorado County
17	146	48.2	**Shasta Lake** (city) Shasta County
19	172	47.5	**Olivehurst** (CDP) Yuba County
20	178	47.3	**Lindsay** (city) Tulare County
20	178	47.3	**Westmont** (CDP) Los Angeles County
22	184	47.2	**Muscoy** (CDP) San Bernardino County
23	186	47.1	**Madera** (city) Madera County
24	193	46.9	**Mendota** (city) Fresno County
25	204	46.7	**Adelanto** (city) San Bernardino County
26	232	46.0	**Winton** (CDP) Merced County
27	245	45.7	**North Highlands** (CDP) Sacramento County
28	248	45.6	**Reedley** (city) Fresno County
29	251	45.5	**Oildale** (CDP) Kern County
29	251	45.5	**Paradise** (town) Butte County
31	274	45.0	**Willowbrook** (CDP) Los Angeles County
32	287	44.7	**Merced** (city) Merced County
33	291	44.6	**California City** (city) Kern County
34	307	44.3	**Brawley** (city) Imperial County
34	307	44.3	**Dinuba** (city) Tulare County
36	320	44.2	**Ukiah** (city) Mendocino County
37	343	43.9	**Chowchilla** (city) Madera County
38	348	43.8	**Selma** (city) Fresno County
39	362	43.6	**Avenal** (city) Kings County
40	401	43.0	**Compton** (city) Los Angeles County
40	401	43.0	**Florin** (CDP) Sacramento County
40	401	43.0	**Garden Acres** (CDP) San Joaquin County
43	414	42.8	**Lake Los Angeles** (CDP) Los Angeles County
43	414	42.8	**Wasco** (city) Kern County
45	433	42.4	**Exeter** (city) Tulare County
46	443	42.3	**Fortuna** (city) Humboldt County
46	443	42.3	**Lompoc** (city) Santa Barbara County
48	452	42.2	**El Centro** (city) Imperial County
48	452	42.2	**Palm Desert** (city) Riverside County
50	457	42.1	**Barstow** (city) San Bernardino County
50	457	42.1	**Eureka** (city) Humboldt County
50	457	42.1	**Foothill Farms** (CDP) Sacramento County
50	457	42.1	**McFarland** (city) Kern County
54	468	42.0	**Yucca Valley** (town) San Bernardino County
55	486	41.7	**Cherryland** (CDP) Alameda County
55	486	41.7	**Desert Hot Springs** (city) Riverside County
57	499	41.5	**Fresno** (city) Fresno County
57	499	41.5	**Palm Springs** (city) Riverside County
59	512	41.4	**San Bernardino** (city) San Bernardino County
60	521	41.3	**Porterville** (city) Tulare County
61	526	41.2	**Florence-Graham** (CDP) Los Angeles County
62	538	41.1	**Sun Village** (CDP) Los Angeles County
63	543	41.0	**Delano** (city) Kern County
64	560	40.7	**East Rancho Dominguez** (CDP) Los Angeles County
65	575	40.5	**Lamont** (CDP) Kern County
65	575	40.5	**Seal Beach** (city) Orange County
67	590	40.3	**South El Monte** (city) Los Angeles County
68	595	40.2	**Valle Vista** (CDP) Riverside County
69	608	40.1	**Redding** (city) Shasta County
70	615	40.0	**El Monte** (city) Los Angeles County
71	629	39.8	**Huntington Park** (city) Los Angeles County
72	640	39.7	**Apple Valley** (town) San Bernardino County
73	655	39.5	**Watsonville** (city) Santa Cruz County
74	666	39.4	**Crestline** (CDP) San Bernardino County
75	677	39.3	**Calexico** (city) Imperial County
76	686	39.2	**Arvin** (city) Kern County
77	695	39.1	**Stockton** (city) San Joaquin County
78	705	39.0	**San Jacinto** (city) Riverside County
79	718	38.8	**El Cajon** (city) San Diego County
80	729	38.7	**Los Banos** (city) Merced County
81	736	38.6	**Bay Point** (CDP) Contra Costa County
82	746	38.5	**South San Jose Hills** (CDP) Los Angeles County
83	768	38.2	**Atwater** (city) Merced County
83	768	38.2	**Ceres** (city) Stanislaus County
83	768	38.2	**Hawaiian Gardens** (city) Los Angeles County
83	768	38.2	**Santa Maria** (city) Santa Barbara County
87	791	38.0	**Hesperia** (city) San Bernardino County
88	803	37.9	**Cudahy** (city) Los Angeles County
88	803	37.9	**Yuba City** (city) Sutter County
90	813	37.8	**East Hemet** (CDP) Riverside County
90	813	37.8	**North Fair Oaks** (CDP) San Mateo County
92	825	37.7	**Shafter** (city) Kern County
92	825	37.7	**Tulare** (city) Tulare County
94	857	37.4	**Indio** (city) Riverside County
94	857	37.4	**Sanger** (city) Fresno County
96	872	37.3	**Modesto** (city) Stanislaus County
96	872	37.3	**Morro Bay** (city) San Luis Obispo County
96	872	37.3	**Susanville** (city) Lassen County
96	872	37.3	**Victorville** (city) San Bernardino County
100	891	37.1	**Walnut Park** (CDP) Los Angeles County
100	891	37.1	**Westminster** (city) Orange County
102	924	36.8	**Mead Valley** (CDP) Riverside County
103	939	36.6	**Palmdale** (city) Los Angeles County
104	959	36.4	**Coachella** (city) Riverside County
104	959	36.4	**Highland** (city) San Bernardino County
106	966	36.3	**Bell Gardens** (city) Los Angeles County
106	966	36.3	**Commerce** (city) Los Angeles County
106	966	36.3	**Livingston** (city) Merced County
106	966	36.3	**Lodi** (city) San Joaquin County
110	980	36.2	**Colton** (city) San Bernardino County
110	980	36.2	**Greenfield** (city) Monterey County
110	980	36.2	**Kingsburg** (city) Fresno County
110	980	36.2	**National City** (city) San Diego County
114	1010	36.0	**Arden-Arcade** (CDP) Sacramento County
114	1010	36.0	**Kerman** (city) Fresno County
114	1010	36.0	**Lincoln** (city) Placer County
114	1010	36.0	**Rialto** (city) San Bernardino County
118	1025	35.9	**Bostonia** (CDP) San Diego County
118	1025	35.9	**Maywood** (city) Los Angeles County
118	1025	35.9	**Perris** (city) Riverside County
121	1077	35.5	**Baldwin Park** (city) Los Angeles County
121	1077	35.5	**Bell** (city) Los Angeles County
121	1077	35.5	**Cathedral City** (city) Riverside County
124	1085	35.4	**Diamond Springs** (CDP) El Dorado County
124	1085	35.4	**East Los Angeles** (CDP) Los Angeles County
124	1085	35.4	**Rancho Cordova** (city) Sacramento County
127	1112	35.2	**Lynwood** (city) Los Angeles County
127	1112	35.2	**Sacramento** (city) Sacramento County
127	1112	35.2	**Tehachapi** (city) Kern County
130	1129	35.1	**La Quinta** (city) Riverside County
131	1137	35.0	**North Auburn** (CDP) Placer County
132	1151	34.9	**Visalia** (city) Tulare County
133	1170	34.8	**Coalinga** (city) Fresno County
134	1178	34.7	**Rosemead** (city) Los Angeles County
135	1204	34.5	**La Riviera** (CDP) Sacramento County
135	1204	34.5	**Montebello** (city) Los Angeles County
137	1218	34.4	**Hanford** (city) Kings County
138	1235	34.3	**Blythe** (city) Riverside County
138	1235	34.3	**Paramount** (city) Los Angeles County
138	1235	34.3	**Phelan** (CDP) San Bernardino County
141	1253	34.2	**East Palo Alto** (city) San Mateo County
142	1263	34.1	**Soledad** (city) Monterey County
143	1279	34.0	**Menifee** (city) Riverside County
144	1292	33.9	**Galt** (city) Sacramento County
144	1292	33.9	**La Puente** (city) Los Angeles County
146	1310	33.8	**Carmichael** (CDP) Sacramento County
146	1310	33.8	**McKinleyville** (CDP) Humboldt County
148	1348	33.6	**Alum Rock** (CDP) Santa Clara County
148	1348	33.6	**Oakland** (city) Alameda County
150	1360	33.5	**Big Bear City** (CDP) San Bernardino County

Note: *The state column ranks the top/bottom 150 places from all places in the state with population of 10,000 or more. The national column ranks the top/bottom 150 places from all places in the country with population of 10,000 or more. Places that are unincorporated were not considered in the rankings. Please refer to the User Guide for additional information.*

Population with Public Health Insurance

Top 150 Places Ranked in *Ascending* Order

State Rank	Nat'l Rank	Percent	Place
1	1	2.1	**Camp Pendleton South** (CDP) San Diego County
2	15	7.3	**Stanford** (CDP) Santa Clara County
3	19	7.9	**Isla Vista** (CDP) Santa Barbara County
4	27	8.4	**Ladera Ranch** (CDP) Orange County
5	52	10.1	**Stevenson Ranch** (CDP) Los Angeles County
6	56	10.2	**San Ramon** (city) Contra Costa County
7	61	10.3	**El Sobrante** (CDP) Riverside County
8	88	11.3	**Aliso Viejo** (city) Orange County
9	93	11.5	**Oak Park** (CDP) Ventura County
10	109	11.9	**Coto de Caza** (CDP) Orange County
11	141	12.7	**Rancho Santa Margarita** (city) Orange County
12	150	12.9	**Castaic** (CDP) Los Angeles County
13	181	13.6	**Dublin** (city) Alameda County
14	206	14.0	**Davis** (city) Yolo County
14	206	14.0	**El Segundo** (city) Los Angeles County
16	220	14.2	**Chino Hills** (city) San Bernardino County
16	220	14.2	**Hermosa Beach** (city) Los Angeles County
18	230	14.3	**Irvine** (city) Orange County
19	237	14.4	**Piedmont** (city) Alameda County
20	245	14.5	**Manhattan Beach** (city) Los Angeles County
21	282	15.0	**South Pasadena** (city) Los Angeles County
22	320	15.5	**Pleasanton** (city) Alameda County
23	329	15.6	**Folsom** (city) Sacramento County
24	336	15.7	**Eastvale** (city) Riverside County
24	336	15.7	**Scotts Valley** (city) Santa Cruz County
26	347	15.8	**French Valley** (CDP) Riverside County
26	347	15.8	**Moorpark** (city) Ventura County
28	365	16.0	**Cupertino** (city) Santa Clara County
28	365	16.0	**Walnut** (city) Los Angeles County
30	417	16.6	**Redondo Beach** (city) Los Angeles County
31	430	16.7	**Lake Forest** (city) Orange County
32	441	16.8	**Granite Bay** (CDP) Placer County
32	441	16.8	**Salida** (CDP) Stanislaus County
34	450	16.9	**Yorba Linda** (city) Orange County
35	460	17.0	**Del Aire** (CDP) Los Angeles County
35	460	17.0	**La Cañada Flintridge** (city) Los Angeles County
35	460	17.0	**Tamalpais-Homestead Valley** (CDP) Marin County
38	478	17.1	**Albany** (city) Alameda County
38	478	17.1	**El Dorado Hills** (CDP) El Dorado County
40	491	17.2	**Danville** (town) Contra Costa County
40	491	17.2	**Encinitas** (city) San Diego County
42	512	17.4	**Alamo** (CDP) Contra Costa County
42	512	17.4	**Burlingame** (city) San Mateo County
44	553	17.8	**Mountain View** (city) Santa Clara County
45	566	17.9	**Agoura Hills** (city) Los Angeles County
46	578	18.0	**Pacifica** (city) San Mateo County
47	603	18.2	**Calabasas** (city) Los Angeles County
47	603	18.2	**San Diego Country Estates** (CDP) San Diego County
49	624	18.3	**Livermore** (city) Alameda County
49	624	18.3	**Rancho Cucamonga** (city) San Bernardino County
51	655	18.5	**Laguna Niguel** (city) Orange County
52	668	18.6	**Diamond Bar** (city) Los Angeles County
52	668	18.6	**Foster City** (city) San Mateo County
54	700	18.8	**Laguna Hills** (city) Orange County
55	737	19.0	**Sunnyvale** (city) Santa Clara County
56	747	19.1	**Palo Alto** (city) Santa Clara County
56	747	19.1	**Sierra Madre** (city) Los Angeles County
58	763	19.2	**Hercules** (city) Contra Costa County
58	763	19.2	**Menlo Park** (city) San Mateo County
58	763	19.2	**San Carlos** (city) San Mateo County
61	779	19.3	**Rocklin** (city) Placer County
62	797	19.4	**Fremont** (city) Alameda County
62	797	19.4	**San Luis Obispo** (city) San Luis Obispo County
62	797	19.4	**Temecula** (city) Riverside County
65	817	19.5	**Moraga** (town) Contra Costa County
66	834	19.6	**Berkeley** (city) Alameda County
67	850	19.7	**Campbell** (city) Santa Clara County
67	850	19.7	**Santa Cruz** (city) Santa Cruz County
69	865	19.8	**Hillsborough** (town) San Mateo County
69	865	19.8	**Truckee** (town) Nevada County
71	881	19.9	**Carlsbad** (city) San Diego County
71	881	19.9	**Poway** (city) San Diego County
71	881	19.9	**Santa Clara** (city) Santa Clara County
71	881	19.9	**Simi Valley** (city) Ventura County
75	897	20.0	**La Crescenta-Montrose** (CDP) Los Angeles County
75	897	20.0	**Los Altos** (city) Santa Clara County
75	897	20.0	**San Anselmo** (town) Marin County
78	913	20.1	**Lafayette** (city) Contra Costa County
79	936	20.2	**Santa Clarita** (city) Los Angeles County
80	954	20.3	**Clayton** (city) Contra Costa County
80	954	20.3	**Orinda** (city) Contra Costa County
80	954	20.3	**San Marino** (city) Los Angeles County
83	973	20.4	**Saratoga** (city) Santa Clara County
84	989	20.5	**Grand Terrace** (city) San Bernardino County
85	1007	20.6	**Brentwood** (city) Contra Costa County
85	1007	20.6	**Goleta** (city) Santa Barbara County
85	1007	20.6	**Rosedale** (CDP) Kern County
85	1007	20.6	**Thousand Oaks** (city) Ventura County
85	1007	20.6	**Tustin** (city) Orange County
90	1025	20.7	**Los Alamitos** (city) Orange County
90	1025	20.7	**Murrieta** (city) Riverside County
92	1057	20.9	**Malibu** (city) Los Angeles County
92	1057	20.9	**Windsor** (town) Sonoma County
94	1072	21.0	**Milpitas** (city) Santa Clara County
95	1104	21.2	**Chino** (city) San Bernardino County
96	1133	21.3	**Martinez** (city) Contra Costa County
96	1133	21.3	**San Clemente** (city) Orange County
96	1133	21.3	**Santa Monica** (city) Los Angeles County
99	1151	21.4	**Costa Mesa** (city) Orange County
99	1151	21.4	**Mission Viejo** (city) Orange County
99	1151	21.4	**San Bruno** (city) San Mateo County
102	1170	21.5	**Corona** (city) Riverside County
103	1206	21.7	**Belmont** (city) San Mateo County
103	1206	21.7	**Brea** (city) Orange County
103	1206	21.7	**West Hollywood** (city) Los Angeles County
106	1219	21.8	**Elk Grove** (city) Sacramento County
106	1219	21.8	**Morgan Hill** (city) Santa Clara County
106	1219	21.8	**Rossmoor** (CDP) Orange County
109	1242	21.9	**Benicia** (city) Solano County
110	1254	22.0	**Arcadia** (city) Los Angeles County
111	1272	22.1	**Burbank** (city) Los Angeles County
111	1272	22.1	**Pleasant Hill** (city) Contra Costa County
111	1272	22.1	**San Marcos** (city) San Diego County
114	1297	22.2	**Culver City** (city) Los Angeles County
114	1297	22.2	**Santee** (city) San Diego County
116	1321	22.3	**Cypress** (city) Orange County
116	1321	22.3	**Emeryville** (city) Alameda County
116	1321	22.3	**Lakewood** (city) Los Angeles County
116	1321	22.3	**Newport Beach** (city) Orange County
120	1364	22.6	**Monrovia** (city) Los Angeles County
120	1364	22.6	**San Dimas** (city) Los Angeles County
122	1380	22.7	**Canyon Lake** (city) Riverside County
122	1380	22.7	**Tracy** (city) San Joaquin County
124	1404	22.8	**Huntington Beach** (city) Orange County
124	1404	22.8	**Los Gatos** (town) Santa Clara County
124	1404	22.8	**Roseville** (city) Placer County
127	1435	23.0	**Torrance** (city) Los Angeles County
128	1451	23.1	**Beverly Hills** (city) Los Angeles County
128	1451	23.1	**Orange** (city) Orange County
128	1451	23.1	**Rohnert Park** (city) Sonoma County
131	1466	23.2	**Castro Valley** (CDP) Alameda County
131	1466	23.2	**Cerritos** (city) Los Angeles County
131	1466	23.2	**Woodcrest** (CDP) Riverside County
134	1491	23.3	**Palos Verdes Estates** (city) Los Angeles County
135	1515	23.4	**East San Gabriel** (CDP) Los Angeles County
135	1515	23.4	**La Mirada** (city) Los Angeles County
135	1515	23.4	**Petaluma** (city) Sonoma County
138	1540	23.5	**Laguna Beach** (city) Orange County
139	1567	23.6	**Dana Point** (city) Orange County
139	1567	23.6	**Discovery Bay** (CDP) Contra Costa County
139	1567	23.6	**Rancho San Diego** (CDP) San Diego County
142	1600	23.8	**North Tustin** (CDP) Orange County
143	1623	23.9	**Glendora** (city) Los Angeles County
144	1638	24.0	**American Canyon** (city) Napa County
145	1653	24.1	**Solana Beach** (city) San Diego County
146	1683	24.2	**Fullerton** (city) Orange County
146	1683	24.2	**Imperial** (city) Imperial County
148	1703	24.3	**Claremont** (city) Los Angeles County
148	1703	24.3	**El Cerrito** (city) Contra Costa County
150	1723	24.4	**Newark** (city) Alameda County

Note: *The state column ranks the top/bottom 150 places from all places in the state with population of 10,000 or more. The national column ranks the top/bottom 150 places from all places in the country with population of 10,000 or more. Places that are unincorporated were not considered in the rankings. Please refer to the User Guide for additional information.*

Population with No Health Insurance

Top 150 Places Ranked in *Descending* Order

State Rank	Nat'l Rank	Percent	Place
1	14	39.6	**Mead Valley** (CDP) Riverside County
2	15	39.4	**Mendota** (city) Fresno County
3	20	38.8	**Cudahy** (city) Los Angeles County
4	22	38.3	**Lennox** (CDP) Los Angeles County
5	23	38.2	**Bell Gardens** (city) Los Angeles County
6	27	38.0	**Maywood** (city) Los Angeles County
7	43	36.2	**East Los Angeles** (CDP) Los Angeles County
8	47	35.6	**Arvin** (city) Kern County
9	50	35.5	**Bell** (city) Los Angeles County
9	50	35.5	**Florence-Graham** (CDP) Los Angeles County
11	53	35.3	**East Rancho Dominguez** (CDP) Los Angeles County
12	54	35.1	**Coachella** (city) Riverside County
13	58	34.8	**McFarland** (city) Kern County
14	60	34.7	**Hawaiian Gardens** (city) Los Angeles County
15	65	34.3	**Muscoy** (CDP) San Bernardino County
16	68	34.2	**Lamont** (CDP) Kern County
17	70	34.0	**Huntington Park** (city) Los Angeles County
18	78	33.4	**King City** (city) Monterey County
18	78	33.4	**Lynwood** (city) Los Angeles County
20	80	33.3	**Santa Ana** (city) Orange County
21	94	31.8	**Walnut Park** (CDP) Los Angeles County
22	101	31.4	**Willowbrook** (CDP) Los Angeles County
23	103	31.3	**South San Jose Hills** (CDP) Los Angeles County
24	108	30.9	**Lawndale** (city) Los Angeles County
24	108	30.9	**South Gate** (city) Los Angeles County
26	112	30.8	**Bloomington** (CDP) San Bernardino County
27	114	30.7	**South El Monte** (city) Los Angeles County
28	121	30.5	**National City** (city) San Diego County
28	121	30.5	**Parlier** (city) Fresno County
30	124	30.4	**Avenal** (city) Kings County
30	124	30.4	**El Monte** (city) Los Angeles County
32	132	30.1	**Desert Hot Springs** (city) Riverside County
33	135	30.0	**Paramount** (city) Los Angeles County
34	157	29.1	**Greenfield** (city) Monterey County
35	160	29.0	**Cathedral City** (city) Riverside County
36	167	28.9	**Lakeland Village** (CDP) Riverside County
37	174	28.7	**Big Bear City** (CDP) San Bernardino County
38	178	28.5	**Home Gardens** (CDP) Riverside County
39	184	28.3	**Garden Acres** (CDP) San Joaquin County
40	197	28.0	**Citrus** (CDP) Los Angeles County
40	197	28.0	**Lindsay** (city) Tulare County
42	204	27.8	**Santa Maria** (city) Santa Barbara County
43	210	27.6	**Baldwin Park** (city) Los Angeles County
44	214	27.4	**Delano** (city) Kern County
45	216	27.3	**Perris** (city) Riverside County
46	224	27.0	**Calexico** (city) Imperial County
47	226	26.9	**Stanton** (city) Orange County
48	227	26.8	**Compton** (city) Los Angeles County
48	227	26.8	**Dinuba** (city) Tulare County
50	230	26.7	**Wasco** (city) Kern County
51	232	26.5	**Colton** (city) San Bernardino County
51	232	26.5	**Seaside** (city) Monterey County
53	237	26.4	**Westmont** (CDP) Los Angeles County
54	243	26.3	**Commerce** (city) Los Angeles County
54	243	26.3	**Montclair** (city) San Bernardino County
56	248	26.2	**La Puente** (city) Los Angeles County
57	256	26.1	**Inglewood** (city) Los Angeles County
58	263	26.0	**Newman** (city) Stanislaus County
58	263	26.0	**Pomona** (city) Los Angeles County
60	271	25.7	**Rosemead** (city) Los Angeles County
61	277	25.6	**Escondido** (city) San Diego County
61	277	25.6	**Hawthorne** (city) Los Angeles County
61	277	25.6	**Los Angeles** (city) Los Angeles County
64	284	25.5	**Avocado Heights** (CDP) Los Angeles County
64	284	25.5	**Lemon Hill** (CDP) Sacramento County
66	290	25.4	**Oxnard** (city) Ventura County
67	297	25.3	**Kerman** (city) Fresno County
68	298	25.2	**Rialto** (city) San Bernardino County
68	298	25.2	**San Pablo** (city) Contra Costa County
70	306	25.0	**Ontario** (city) San Bernardino County
70	306	25.0	**Salinas** (city) Monterey County
70	306	25.0	**San Fernando** (city) Los Angeles County
70	306	25.0	**Selma** (city) Fresno County
70	306	25.0	**Soledad** (city) Monterey County
75	317	24.9	**Fontana** (city) San Bernardino County
75	317	24.9	**Valinda** (CDP) Los Angeles County
77	327	24.7	**San Bernardino** (city) San Bernardino County
78	335	24.6	**Vista** (city) San Diego County
79	342	24.5	**Pico Rivera** (city) Los Angeles County
80	356	24.2	**Norwalk** (city) Los Angeles County
81	360	24.1	**Moreno Valley** (city) Riverside County
82	363	24.0	**East Palo Alto** (city) San Mateo County
83	373	23.9	**North Fair Oaks** (CDP) San Mateo County
84	380	23.8	**Artesia** (city) Los Angeles County
84	380	23.8	**Indio** (city) Riverside County
86	386	23.7	**Sun Village** (CDP) Los Angeles County
87	395	23.6	**Farmersville** (city) Tulare County
88	423	23.3	**Montebello** (city) Los Angeles County
88	423	23.3	**West Puente Valley** (CDP) Los Angeles County
88	423	23.3	**Winton** (CDP) Merced County
91	430	23.2	**Watsonville** (city) Santa Cruz County
92	436	23.1	**Madera** (city) Madera County
92	436	23.1	**Reedley** (city) Fresno County
94	440	23.0	**Azusa** (city) Los Angeles County
95	445	22.9	**Rowland Heights** (CDP) Los Angeles County
96	454	22.7	**Livingston** (city) Merced County
97	458	22.6	**Anaheim** (city) Orange County
97	458	22.6	**Signal Hill** (city) Los Angeles County
99	477	22.4	**San Gabriel** (city) Los Angeles County
100	487	22.3	**Shafter** (city) Kern County
101	500	22.1	**La Habra** (city) Orange County
101	500	22.1	**Santa Paula** (city) Ventura County
103	508	22.0	**Clearlake** (city) Lake County
103	508	22.0	**South Lake Tahoe** (city) El Dorado County
105	518	21.9	**Costa Mesa** (city) Orange County
105	518	21.9	**San Juan Capistrano** (city) Orange County
107	525	21.8	**Santa Fe Springs** (city) Los Angeles County
108	538	21.7	**Downey** (city) Los Angeles County
108	538	21.7	**Lake Los Angeles** (CDP) Los Angeles County
108	538	21.7	**Sanger** (city) Fresno County
111	549	21.6	**Linda** (CDP) Yuba County
111	549	21.6	**South Whittier** (CDP) Los Angeles County
113	559	21.5	**Ashland** (CDP) Alameda County
113	559	21.5	**Bellflower** (city) Los Angeles County
115	569	21.4	**Carpinteria** (city) Santa Barbara County
115	569	21.4	**Port Hueneme** (city) Ventura County
117	590	21.2	**Garden Grove** (city) Orange County
118	599	21.1	**Hesperia** (city) San Bernardino County
118	599	21.1	**Lake Elsinore** (city) Riverside County
118	599	21.1	**Lathrop** (city) San Joaquin County
118	599	21.1	**Santa Barbara** (city) Santa Barbara County
122	615	21.0	**Bay Point** (CDP) Contra Costa County
122	615	21.0	**Eureka** (city) Humboldt County
124	624	20.9	**Arcata** (city) Humboldt County
124	624	20.9	**Riverside** (city) Riverside County
126	641	20.7	**Gardena** (city) Los Angeles County
126	641	20.7	**Richmond** (city) Contra Costa County
128	655	20.6	**West Whittier-Los Nietos** (CDP) Los Angeles County
129	667	20.5	**Atwater** (city) Merced County
130	673	20.4	**El Cajon** (city) San Diego County
131	679	20.3	**Fullerton** (city) Orange County
131	679	20.3	**Los Banos** (city) Merced County
133	697	20.2	**East Hemet** (CDP) Riverside County
133	697	20.2	**North Highlands** (CDP) Sacramento County
133	697	20.2	**Palm Springs** (city) Riverside County
133	697	20.2	**Ramona** (CDP) San Diego County
137	707	20.1	**Tulare** (city) Tulare County
138	719	20.0	**Florin** (CDP) Sacramento County
138	719	20.0	**Monterey Park** (city) Los Angeles County
140	728	19.9	**Rosamond** (CDP) Kern County
141	739	19.8	**Porterville** (city) Tulare County
142	753	19.7	**Cherryland** (CDP) Alameda County
142	753	19.7	**Corcoran** (city) Kings County
142	753	19.7	**El Centro** (city) Imperial County
142	753	19.7	**La Presa** (CDP) San Diego County
142	753	19.7	**Lemon Grove** (city) San Diego County
147	774	19.6	**Buena Park** (city) Orange County
147	774	19.6	**Chowchilla** (city) Madera County
147	774	19.6	**Fresno** (city) Fresno County
147	774	19.6	**Glendale** (city) Los Angeles County

Note: *The state column ranks the top/bottom 150 places from all places in the state with population of 10,000 or more. The national column ranks the top/bottom 150 places from all places in the country with population of 10,000 or more. Places that are unincorporated were not considered in the rankings. Please refer to the User Guide for additional information.*

Population with No Health Insurance

Top 150 Places Ranked in *Ascending* Order

State Rank	Nat'l Rank	Percent	Place
1	10	1.0	**Camp Pendleton South** (CDP) San Diego County
1	10	1.0	**Piedmont** (city) Alameda County
3	14	1.1	**Hillsborough** (town) San Mateo County
4	37	1.6	**Alamo** (CDP) Contra Costa County
5	94	2.4	**Orinda** (city) Contra Costa County
5	94	2.4	**Saratoga** (city) Santa Clara County
7	108	2.5	**Los Altos** (city) Santa Clara County
7	108	2.5	**Mill Valley** (city) Marin County
9	121	2.6	**Clayton** (city) Contra Costa County
9	121	2.6	**Stanford** (CDP) Santa Clara County
11	145	2.8	**Coto de Caza** (CDP) Orange County
12	245	3.4	**Danville** (town) Contra Costa County
13	291	3.7	**Palos Verdes Estates** (city) Los Angeles County
14	335	3.9	**Lafayette** (city) Contra Costa County
14	335	3.9	**Laguna Woods** (city) Orange County
14	335	3.9	**Los Gatos** (town) Santa Clara County
14	335	3.9	**Malibu** (city) Los Angeles County
18	361	4.0	**Ladera Ranch** (CDP) Orange County
18	361	4.0	**Manhattan Beach** (city) Los Angeles County
20	387	4.1	**Foster City** (city) San Mateo County
20	387	4.1	**San Marino** (city) Los Angeles County
20	387	4.1	**Tamalpais-Homestead Valley** (CDP) Marin County
23	412	4.2	**Cupertino** (city) Santa Clara County
24	489	4.5	**Rancho Palos Verdes** (city) Los Angeles County
25	581	4.9	**El Dorado Hills** (CDP) El Dorado County
25	581	4.9	**Sierra Madre** (city) Los Angeles County
27	622	5.1	**San Diego Country Estates** (CDP) San Diego County
28	680	5.3	**San Ramon** (city) Contra Costa County
29	702	5.4	**Oak Park** (CDP) Ventura County
29	702	5.4	**Palo Alto** (city) Santa Clara County
31	779	5.7	**Larkspur** (city) Marin County
32	801	5.8	**Cameron Park** (CDP) El Dorado County
32	801	5.8	**Dublin** (city) Alameda County
32	801	5.8	**Moraga** (town) Contra Costa County
35	828	5.9	**La Cañada Flintridge** (city) Los Angeles County
36	864	6.0	**San Anselmo** (town) Marin County
37	886	6.1	**Discovery Bay** (CDP) Contra Costa County
38	926	6.3	**San Carlos** (city) San Mateo County
39	959	6.4	**Belmont** (city) San Mateo County
39	959	6.4	**Yorba Linda** (city) Orange County
41	989	6.5	**Coronado** (city) San Diego County
41	989	6.5	**Folsom** (city) Sacramento County
41	989	6.5	**North Tustin** (CDP) Orange County
41	989	6.5	**Rossmoor** (CDP) Orange County
45	1023	6.6	**Claremont** (city) Los Angeles County
45	1023	6.6	**Menlo Park** (city) San Mateo County
45	1023	6.6	**Scotts Valley** (city) Santa Cruz County
45	1023	6.6	**Seal Beach** (city) Orange County
49	1046	6.7	**Calabasas** (city) Los Angeles County
49	1046	6.7	**Granite Bay** (CDP) Placer County
51	1087	6.9	**Agoura Hills** (city) Los Angeles County
51	1087	6.9	**Brentwood** (city) Contra Costa County
51	1087	6.9	**Burlingame** (city) San Mateo County
54	1109	7.0	**Pleasanton** (city) Alameda County
54	1109	7.0	**Ripon** (city) San Joaquin County
56	1134	7.1	**Hermosa Beach** (city) Los Angeles County
56	1134	7.1	**Isla Vista** (CDP) Santa Barbara County
56	1134	7.1	**Rosedale** (CDP) Kern County
59	1199	7.3	**Albany** (city) Alameda County
59	1199	7.3	**Walnut Creek** (city) Contra Costa County
61	1236	7.4	**Stevenson Ranch** (CDP) Los Angeles County
62	1286	7.6	**Pacifica** (city) San Mateo County
63	1315	7.7	**Laguna Beach** (city) Orange County
64	1366	7.9	**Auburn** (city) Placer County
64	1366	7.9	**Martinez** (city) Contra Costa County
66	1391	8.0	**Davis** (city) Yolo County
66	1391	8.0	**Rancho Santa Margarita** (city) Orange County
66	1391	8.0	**Rocklin** (city) Placer County
69	1428	8.1	**Mission Viejo** (city) Orange County
70	1454	8.2	**Poway** (city) San Diego County
70	1454	8.2	**Windsor** (town) Sonoma County
72	1478	8.3	**El Segundo** (city) Los Angeles County
72	1478	8.3	**Sonoma** (city) Sonoma County
74	1525	8.5	**Fremont** (city) Alameda County
74	1525	8.5	**La Verne** (city) Los Angeles County
74	1525	8.5	**Newport Beach** (city) Orange County
74	1525	8.5	**Pleasant Hill** (city) Contra Costa County
78	1552	8.6	**Berkeley** (city) Alameda County
79	1579	8.7	**Benicia** (city) Solano County
79	1579	8.7	**Redondo Beach** (city) Los Angeles County
81	1606	8.8	**Livermore** (city) Alameda County
82	1634	8.9	**Castro Valley** (CDP) Alameda County
82	1634	8.9	**Hercules** (city) Contra Costa County
84	1675	9.1	**Goleta** (city) Santa Barbara County
84	1675	9.1	**Susanville** (city) Lassen County
84	1675	9.1	**Twentynine Palms** (city) San Bernardino County
87	1703	9.2	**Beverly Hills** (city) Los Angeles County
87	1703	9.2	**Roseville** (city) Placer County
89	1728	9.3	**Irvine** (city) Orange County
89	1728	9.3	**Millbrae** (city) San Mateo County
89	1728	9.3	**Santa Clara** (city) Santa Clara County
92	1759	9.4	**Elk Grove** (city) Sacramento County
92	1759	9.4	**Lincoln** (city) Placer County
94	1781	9.5	**Laguna Niguel** (city) Orange County
95	1807	9.6	**Fair Oaks** (CDP) Sacramento County
95	1807	9.6	**Vacaville** (city) Solano County
97	1830	9.7	**Novato** (city) Marin County
98	1847	9.8	**Carlsbad** (city) San Diego County
99	1876	9.9	**Aliso Viejo** (city) Orange County
99	1876	9.9	**Rancho Mirage** (city) Riverside County
101	1898	10.0	**Milpitas** (city) Santa Clara County
101	1898	10.0	**San Lorenzo** (CDP) Alameda County
103	1919	10.1	**Casa de Oro-Mount Helix** (CDP) San Diego County
103	1919	10.1	**Sunnyvale** (city) Santa Clara County
105	1948	10.2	**Alpine** (CDP) San Diego County
105	1948	10.2	**Arroyo Grande** (city) San Luis Obispo County
105	1948	10.2	**South San Francisco** (city) San Mateo County
108	1978	10.3	**La Crescenta-Montrose** (CDP) Los Angeles County
108	1978	10.3	**Newark** (city) Alameda County
110	2004	10.4	**Fairview** (CDP) Alameda County
110	2004	10.4	**View Park-Windsor Hills** (CDP) Los Angeles County
112	2021	10.5	**Campbell** (city) Santa Clara County
112	2021	10.5	**Fountain Valley** (city) Orange County
112	2021	10.5	**La Riviera** (CDP) Sacramento County
115	2044	10.6	**Camarillo** (city) Ventura County
115	2044	10.6	**Half Moon Bay** (city) San Mateo County
115	2044	10.6	**Mountain View** (city) Santa Clara County
115	2044	10.6	**Rancho San Diego** (CDP) San Diego County
119	2068	10.7	**San Bruno** (city) San Mateo County
119	2068	10.7	**Thousand Oaks** (city) Ventura County
121	2091	10.8	**Union City** (city) Alameda County
122	2144	11.0	**Santee** (city) San Diego County
123	2171	11.1	**Diamond Springs** (CDP) El Dorado County
123	2171	11.1	**San Clemente** (city) Orange County
123	2171	11.1	**San Francisco** (city) San Francisco County
123	2171	11.1	**Santa Monica** (city) Los Angeles County
127	2194	11.2	**Canyon Lake** (city) Riverside County
127	2194	11.2	**Castaic** (CDP) Los Angeles County
127	2194	11.2	**El Cerrito** (city) Contra Costa County
127	2194	11.2	**Petaluma** (city) Sonoma County
131	2223	11.3	**Ridgecrest** (city) Kern County
132	2245	11.4	**Glendora** (city) Los Angeles County
133	2264	11.5	**Alameda** (city) Alameda County
133	2264	11.5	**French Valley** (CDP) Riverside County
133	2264	11.5	**Pinole** (city) Contra Costa County
133	2264	11.5	**San Luis Obispo** (city) San Luis Obispo County
133	2264	11.5	**Simi Valley** (city) Ventura County
133	2264	11.5	**Walnut** (city) Los Angeles County
139	2285	11.6	**Los Alamitos** (city) Orange County
139	2285	11.6	**Suisun City** (city) Solano County
141	2303	11.7	**Morgan Hill** (city) Santa Clara County
141	2303	11.7	**San Mateo** (city) San Mateo County
143	2326	11.8	**Fairfield** (city) Solano County
143	2326	11.8	**Norco** (city) Riverside County
145	2351	11.9	**American Canyon** (city) Napa County
145	2351	11.9	**Atascadero** (city) San Luis Obispo County
145	2351	11.9	**Moorpark** (city) Ventura County
148	2375	12.0	**Huntington Beach** (city) Orange County
148	2375	12.0	**South Pasadena** (city) Los Angeles County
148	2375	12.0	**Torrance** (city) Los Angeles County

Note: *The state column ranks the top/bottom 150 places from all places in the state with population of 10,000 or more. The national column ranks the top/bottom 150 places from all places in the country with population of 10,000 or more. Places that are unincorporated were not considered in the rankings. Please refer to the User Guide for additional information.*

Population Under 18 Years Old with No Health Insurance

Top 150 Places Ranked in *Descending* Order

State Rank	Nat'l Rank	Percent	Place
1	22	24.6	**Mead Valley** (CDP) Riverside County
2	43	22.2	**Big Bear City** (CDP) San Bernardino County
3	56	21.1	**Lennox** (CDP) Los Angeles County
4	88	19.9	**Carpinteria** (city) Santa Barbara County
5	100	19.5	**Calexico** (city) Imperial County
6	114	18.9	**Banning** (city) Riverside County
7	133	17.9	**East Los Angeles** (CDP) Los Angeles County
8	142	17.6	**Lakeland Village** (CDP) Riverside County
8	142	17.6	**National City** (city) San Diego County
10	150	17.4	**Lamont** (CDP) Kern County
10	150	17.4	**Lynwood** (city) Los Angeles County
12	162	17.2	**Hawaiian Gardens** (city) Los Angeles County
13	182	16.7	**Coachella** (city) Riverside County
14	189	16.6	**Emeryville** (city) Alameda County
15	204	16.3	**Cudahy** (city) Los Angeles County
16	226	15.9	**Bell Gardens** (city) Los Angeles County
17	238	15.7	**Palm Springs** (city) Riverside County
18	245	15.6	**Arvin** (city) Kern County
19	258	15.4	**Desert Hot Springs** (city) Riverside County
20	280	15.1	**McFarland** (city) Kern County
21	288	15.0	**Bell** (city) Los Angeles County
22	294	14.8	**Santa Ana** (city) Orange County
22	294	14.8	**Willowbrook** (CDP) Los Angeles County
24	303	14.7	**Colton** (city) San Bernardino County
24	303	14.7	**Loma Linda** (city) San Bernardino County
26	311	14.6	**Montclair** (city) San Bernardino County
27	316	14.5	**Bloomington** (CDP) San Bernardino County
27	316	14.5	**Lake Los Angeles** (CDP) Los Angeles County
27	316	14.5	**Rosamond** (CDP) Kern County
30	327	14.4	**Avocado Heights** (CDP) Los Angeles County
30	327	14.4	**San Juan Capistrano** (city) Orange County
32	351	14.2	**Paramount** (city) Los Angeles County
32	351	14.2	**Santa Barbara** (city) Santa Barbara County
34	360	14.1	**Cathedral City** (city) Riverside County
34	360	14.1	**Santa Fe Springs** (city) Los Angeles County
34	360	14.1	**Seaside** (city) Monterey County
37	370	14.0	**Delano** (city) Kern County
38	372	13.9	**Maywood** (city) Los Angeles County
38	372	13.9	**Solana Beach** (city) San Diego County
40	380	13.8	**Escondido** (city) San Diego County
41	384	13.7	**East Rancho Dominguez** (CDP) Los Angeles County
41	384	13.7	**Signal Hill** (city) Los Angeles County
43	399	13.6	**Avenal** (city) Kings County
44	407	13.5	**Moreno Valley** (city) Riverside County
45	420	13.3	**Inglewood** (city) Los Angeles County
45	420	13.3	**Stanton** (city) Orange County
47	429	13.2	**Florence-Graham** (CDP) Los Angeles County
47	429	13.2	**Imperial Beach** (city) San Diego County
47	429	13.2	**Truckee** (town) Nevada County
50	438	13.1	**Del Aire** (CDP) Los Angeles County
51	447	13.0	**Fullerton** (city) Orange County
52	457	12.9	**Citrus** (CDP) Los Angeles County
53	466	12.8	**Clearlake** (city) Lake County
53	466	12.8	**La Presa** (CDP) San Diego County
55	478	12.6	**La Habra** (city) Orange County
55	478	12.6	**Ukiah** (city) Mendocino County
57	492	12.5	**El Sobrante** (CDP) Riverside County
58	497	12.4	**Fontana** (city) San Bernardino County
58	497	12.4	**Lemon Grove** (city) San Diego County
60	512	12.3	**Chowchilla** (city) Madera County
60	512	12.3	**King City** (city) Monterey County
62	532	12.1	**Home Gardens** (CDP) Riverside County
62	532	12.1	**Lindsay** (city) Tulare County
62	532	12.1	**Wildomar** (city) Riverside County
65	549	12.0	**Oxnard** (city) Ventura County
65	549	12.0	**Perris** (city) Riverside County
67	563	11.9	**Fillmore** (city) Ventura County
67	563	11.9	**Lathrop** (city) San Joaquin County
67	563	11.9	**Porterville** (city) Tulare County
67	563	11.9	**Prunedale** (CDP) Monterey County
67	563	11.9	**San Pablo** (city) Contra Costa County
67	563	11.9	**Walnut Park** (CDP) Los Angeles County
73	574	11.8	**North Auburn** (CDP) Placer County
73	574	11.8	**Rialto** (city) San Bernardino County
73	574	11.8	**South Gate** (city) Los Angeles County
76	588	11.7	**Ashland** (CDP) Alameda County
76	588	11.7	**Ontario** (city) San Bernardino County
78	598	11.6	**Hawthorne** (city) Los Angeles County
78	598	11.6	**Richmond** (city) Contra Costa County
78	598	11.6	**Yucca Valley** (town) San Bernardino County
81	618	11.5	**Napa** (city) Napa County
81	618	11.5	**Santa Maria** (city) Santa Barbara County
83	631	11.4	**Lemoore** (city) Kings County
83	631	11.4	**Yucaipa** (city) San Bernardino County
85	651	11.2	**Commerce** (city) Los Angeles County
85	651	11.2	**Indio** (city) Riverside County
85	651	11.2	**Rosemead** (city) Los Angeles County
85	651	11.2	**Sun Village** (CDP) Los Angeles County
89	666	11.1	**East Palo Alto** (city) San Mateo County
89	666	11.1	**Lawndale** (city) Los Angeles County
89	666	11.1	**Orcutt** (CDP) Santa Barbara County
89	666	11.1	**Sonoma** (city) Sonoma County
93	682	11.0	**El Cajon** (city) San Diego County
93	682	11.0	**Hesperia** (city) San Bernardino County
93	682	11.0	**Los Alamitos** (city) Orange County
93	682	11.0	**Quartz Hill** (CDP) Los Angeles County
97	698	10.9	**Paradise** (town) Butte County
97	698	10.9	**Tustin** (city) Orange County
97	698	10.9	**West Carson** (CDP) Los Angeles County
100	709	10.8	**Bonita** (CDP) San Diego County
100	709	10.8	**Riverside** (city) Riverside County
100	709	10.8	**Selma** (city) Fresno County
100	709	10.8	**Upland** (city) San Bernardino County
104	729	10.7	**Winter Gardens** (CDP) San Diego County
105	742	10.6	**Castaic** (CDP) Los Angeles County
105	742	10.6	**Hemet** (city) Riverside County
105	742	10.6	**Los Angeles** (city) Los Angeles County
105	742	10.6	**South El Monte** (city) Los Angeles County
109	761	10.5	**West Hollywood** (city) Los Angeles County
109	761	10.5	**Westmont** (CDP) Los Angeles County
111	773	10.4	**Greenfield** (city) Monterey County
111	773	10.4	**Vista** (city) San Diego County
113	790	10.3	**Bellflower** (city) Los Angeles County
113	790	10.3	**Corcoran** (city) Kings County
113	790	10.3	**Costa Mesa** (city) Orange County
113	790	10.3	**La Mirada** (city) Los Angeles County
113	790	10.3	**Redding** (city) Shasta County
113	790	10.3	**Wasco** (city) Kern County
119	806	10.2	**Artesia** (city) Los Angeles County
119	806	10.2	**Lancaster** (city) Los Angeles County
121	823	10.1	**La Quinta** (city) Riverside County
121	823	10.1	**Pico Rivera** (city) Los Angeles County
121	823	10.1	**San Bernardino** (city) San Bernardino County
124	845	10.0	**Bostonia** (CDP) San Diego County
124	845	10.0	**Imperial** (city) Imperial County
124	845	10.0	**Newman** (city) Stanislaus County
124	845	10.0	**Pomona** (city) Los Angeles County
128	868	9.9	**Azusa** (city) Los Angeles County
128	868	9.9	**Chula Vista** (city) San Diego County
128	868	9.9	**Huntington Park** (city) Los Angeles County
131	881	9.8	**Crestline** (CDP) San Bernardino County
131	881	9.8	**El Centro** (city) Imperial County
131	881	9.8	**Healdsburg** (city) Sonoma County
131	881	9.8	**Lake Elsinore** (city) Riverside County
131	881	9.8	**South Pasadena** (city) Los Angeles County
136	907	9.7	**Anaheim** (city) Orange County
136	907	9.7	**Compton** (city) Los Angeles County
136	907	9.7	**Murrieta** (city) Riverside County
136	907	9.7	**Norwalk** (city) Los Angeles County
136	907	9.7	**Sanger** (city) Fresno County
141	933	9.6	**Soledad** (city) Monterey County
141	933	9.6	**Valinda** (CDP) Los Angeles County
143	954	9.5	**Eureka** (city) Humboldt County
143	954	9.5	**Muscoy** (CDP) San Bernardino County
143	954	9.5	**Shafter** (city) Kern County
143	954	9.5	**Tulare** (city) Tulare County
147	976	9.4	**Altadena** (CDP) Los Angeles County
147	976	9.4	**Apple Valley** (town) San Bernardino County
147	976	9.4	**East Hemet** (CDP) Riverside County
147	976	9.4	**Vallejo** (city) Solano County

Note: *The state column ranks the top/bottom 150 places from all places in the state with population of 10,000 or more. The national column ranks the top/bottom 150 places from all places in the country with population of 10,000 or more. Places that are unincorporated were not considered in the rankings. Please refer to the User Guide for additional information.*

Population Under 18 Years Old with No Health Insurance

Top 150 Places Ranked in *Ascending* Order

State Rank	Nat'l Rank	Percent	Place
1	1	0.0	**Hillsborough** (town) San Mateo County
1	1	0.0	**Laguna Woods** (city) Orange County
1	1	0.0	**Scotts Valley** (city) Santa Cruz County
1	1	0.0	**Stanford** (CDP) Santa Clara County
5	89	0.2	**Malibu** (city) Los Angeles County
6	107	0.3	**Alamo** (CDP) Contra Costa County
6	107	0.3	**Piedmont** (city) Alameda County
8	210	0.7	**Mill Valley** (city) Marin County
8	210	0.7	**Orinda** (city) Contra Costa County
8	210	0.7	**San Diego Country Estates** (CDP) San Diego County
11	242	0.8	**Larkspur** (city) Marin County
11	242	0.8	**Los Gatos** (town) Santa Clara County
13	264	0.9	**Saratoga** (city) Santa Clara County
14	300	1.0	**Auburn** (city) Placer County
14	300	1.0	**Coto de Caza** (CDP) Orange County
16	344	1.1	**San Anselmo** (town) Marin County
17	382	1.2	**Belmont** (city) San Mateo County
18	424	1.3	**Cupertino** (city) Santa Clara County
18	424	1.3	**Lafayette** (city) Contra Costa County
18	424	1.3	**Los Altos** (city) Santa Clara County
21	469	1.4	**Agoura Hills** (city) Los Angeles County
21	469	1.4	**Oak Park** (CDP) Ventura County
21	469	1.4	**Placerville** (city) El Dorado County
24	528	1.5	**Diamond Springs** (CDP) El Dorado County
24	528	1.5	**Rancho Palos Verdes** (city) Los Angeles County
24	528	1.5	**View Park-Windsor Hills** (CDP) Los Angeles County
27	577	1.6	**Camp Pendleton South** (CDP) San Diego County
27	577	1.6	**Clayton** (city) Contra Costa County
27	577	1.6	**Dublin** (city) Alameda County
27	577	1.6	**Fair Oaks** (CDP) Sacramento County
27	577	1.6	**Foster City** (city) San Mateo County
32	627	1.7	**Manhattan Beach** (city) Los Angeles County
32	627	1.7	**Tamalpais-Homestead Valley** (CDP) Marin County
34	681	1.8	**Danville** (town) Contra Costa County
34	681	1.8	**Folsom** (city) Sacramento County
34	681	1.8	**Hermosa Beach** (city) Los Angeles County
34	681	1.8	**Ripon** (city) San Joaquin County
34	681	1.8	**Twentynine Palms** (city) San Bernardino County
39	729	1.9	**Fountain Valley** (city) Orange County
39	729	1.9	**La Riviera** (CDP) Sacramento County
41	835	2.1	**Mountain View** (city) Santa Clara County
42	876	2.2	**Palo Alto** (city) Santa Clara County
43	980	2.4	**Rocklin** (city) Placer County
44	1034	2.5	**Phelan** (CDP) San Bernardino County
45	1086	2.6	**San Lorenzo** (CDP) Alameda County
45	1086	2.6	**San Marino** (city) Los Angeles County
47	1133	2.7	**Campbell** (city) Santa Clara County
47	1133	2.7	**Castro Valley** (CDP) Alameda County
47	1133	2.7	**Patterson** (city) Stanislaus County
47	1133	2.7	**Santa Cruz** (city) Santa Cruz County
51	1185	2.8	**Menlo Park** (city) San Mateo County
51	1185	2.8	**Redondo Beach** (city) Los Angeles County
51	1185	2.8	**Sierra Madre** (city) Los Angeles County
54	1228	2.9	**El Dorado Hills** (CDP) El Dorado County
54	1228	2.9	**El Segundo** (city) Los Angeles County
54	1228	2.9	**Fremont** (city) Alameda County
54	1228	2.9	**San Ramon** (city) Contra Costa County
54	1228	2.9	**Santa Clara** (city) Santa Clara County
54	1228	2.9	**Walnut Creek** (city) Contra Costa County
60	1286	3.0	**Berkeley** (city) Alameda County
60	1286	3.0	**Burlingame** (city) San Mateo County
60	1286	3.0	**Laguna Beach** (city) Orange County
60	1286	3.0	**Rancho Santa Margarita** (city) Orange County
60	1286	3.0	**Susanville** (city) Lassen County
60	1286	3.0	**Windsor** (town) Sonoma County
60	1286	3.0	**Yorba Linda** (city) Orange County
67	1351	3.1	**American Canyon** (city) Napa County
67	1351	3.1	**La Verne** (city) Los Angeles County
67	1351	3.1	**Pleasanton** (city) Alameda County
70	1411	3.2	**Fairfield** (city) Solano County
70	1411	3.2	**Mission Viejo** (city) Orange County
72	1461	3.3	**Albany** (city) Alameda County
73	1506	3.4	**Cameron Park** (CDP) El Dorado County
73	1506	3.4	**San Rafael** (city) Marin County
75	1573	3.5	**Ladera Ranch** (CDP) Orange County
75	1573	3.5	**Pleasant Hill** (city) Contra Costa County
77	1621	3.6	**Milpitas** (city) Santa Clara County
77	1621	3.6	**Ridgecrest** (city) Kern County
77	1621	3.6	**San Mateo** (city) San Mateo County
80	1682	3.7	**Brawley** (city) Imperial County
80	1682	3.7	**Moraga** (town) Contra Costa County
82	1731	3.8	**Coronado** (city) San Diego County
82	1731	3.8	**Davis** (city) Yolo County
82	1731	3.8	**Oakdale** (city) Stanislaus County
82	1731	3.8	**Palos Verdes Estates** (city) Los Angeles County
82	1731	3.8	**Vacaville** (city) Solano County
87	1786	3.9	**Brentwood** (city) Contra Costa County
87	1786	3.9	**Oakley** (city) Contra Costa County
89	1832	4.0	**Casa de Oro-Mount Helix** (CDP) San Diego County
89	1832	4.0	**Hercules** (city) Contra Costa County
89	1832	4.0	**Newark** (city) Alameda County
89	1832	4.0	**Norco** (city) Riverside County
89	1832	4.0	**Roseville** (city) Placer County
94	1892	4.1	**San Carlos** (city) San Mateo County
94	1892	4.1	**San Francisco** (city) San Francisco County
96	1938	4.2	**Granite Bay** (CDP) Placer County
96	1938	4.2	**La Cañada Flintridge** (city) Los Angeles County
96	1938	4.2	**Newport Beach** (city) Orange County
99	1982	4.3	**Aliso Viejo** (city) Orange County
99	1982	4.3	**Brea** (city) Orange County
99	1982	4.3	**Cherryland** (CDP) Alameda County
99	1982	4.3	**Elk Grove** (city) Sacramento County
99	1982	4.3	**Glendora** (city) Los Angeles County
99	1982	4.3	**Martinez** (city) Contra Costa County
99	1982	4.3	**Monterey** (city) Monterey County
99	1982	4.3	**North Fair Oaks** (CDP) San Mateo County
99	1982	4.3	**Salida** (CDP) Stanislaus County
108	2041	4.4	**Kingsburg** (city) Fresno County
108	2041	4.4	**North Tustin** (CDP) Orange County
108	2041	4.4	**Petaluma** (city) Sonoma County
111	2079	4.5	**Calabasas** (city) Los Angeles County
111	2079	4.5	**Claremont** (city) Los Angeles County
113	2117	4.6	**Ceres** (city) Stanislaus County
113	2117	4.6	**Dana Point** (city) Orange County
113	2117	4.6	**Huntington Beach** (city) Orange County
113	2117	4.6	**La Crescenta-Montrose** (CDP) Los Angeles County
113	2117	4.6	**Sunnyvale** (city) Santa Clara County
118	2154	4.7	**Alum Rock** (CDP) Santa Clara County
118	2154	4.7	**Culver City** (city) Los Angeles County
118	2154	4.7	**Rohnert Park** (city) Sonoma County
118	2154	4.7	**Rossmoor** (CDP) Orange County
118	2154	4.7	**Union City** (city) Alameda County
123	2192	4.8	**French Valley** (CDP) Riverside County
124	2238	4.9	**Millbrae** (city) San Mateo County
124	2238	4.9	**Poway** (city) San Diego County
124	2238	4.9	**San Jose** (city) Santa Clara County
124	2238	4.9	**Tracy** (city) San Joaquin County
128	2279	5.0	**Adelanto** (city) San Bernardino County
128	2279	5.0	**Carlsbad** (city) San Diego County
128	2279	5.0	**Foothill Farms** (CDP) Sacramento County
128	2279	5.0	**Livermore** (city) Alameda County
128	2279	5.0	**Merced** (city) Merced County
128	2279	5.0	**San Dimas** (city) Los Angeles County
128	2279	5.0	**Stevenson Ranch** (CDP) Los Angeles County
135	2327	5.1	**Beaumont** (city) Riverside County
135	2327	5.1	**Riverbank** (city) Stanislaus County
135	2327	5.1	**South San Francisco** (city) San Mateo County
138	2368	5.2	**Magalia** (CDP) Butte County
138	2368	5.2	**Pacific Grove** (city) Monterey County
138	2368	5.2	**San Leandro** (city) Alameda County
141	2418	5.3	**Irvine** (city) Orange County
141	2418	5.3	**Rancho Cordova** (city) Sacramento County
141	2418	5.3	**Redwood City** (city) San Mateo County
144	2464	5.4	**Gilroy** (city) Santa Clara County
144	2464	5.4	**Goleta** (city) Santa Barbara County
144	2464	5.4	**Half Moon Bay** (city) San Mateo County
144	2464	5.4	**Orangevale** (CDP) Sacramento County
144	2464	5.4	**Pacifica** (city) San Mateo County
144	2464	5.4	**Rio Linda** (CDP) Sacramento County
144	2464	5.4	**San Buenaventura (Ventura)** (city) Ventura County

Note: *The state column ranks the top/bottom 150 places from all places in the state with population of 10,000 or more. The national column ranks the top/bottom 150 places from all places in the country with population of 10,000 or more. Places that are unincorporated were not considered in the rankings. Please refer to the User Guide for additional information.*

Commute to Work: Car

Top 150 Places Ranked in *Descending* Order

State Rank	Nat'l Rank	Percent	Place
1	29	97.3	**Salida** (CDP) Stanislaus County
2	102	96.5	**Imperial** (city) Imperial County
3	123	96.3	**Los Banos** (city) Merced County
4	168	96.0	**Riverbank** (city) Stanislaus County
5	177	95.9	**Lake Los Angeles** (CDP) Los Angeles County
6	228	95.7	**Kerman** (city) Fresno County
7	306	95.4	**Grand Terrace** (city) San Bernardino County
8	333	95.3	**Rosamond** (CDP) Kern County
9	390	95.1	**Rosedale** (CDP) Kern County
10	437	94.9	**Ripon** (city) San Joaquin County
11	469	94.8	**Exeter** (city) Tulare County
12	574	94.5	**Lemoore** (city) Kings County
12	574	94.5	**Patterson** (city) Stanislaus County
12	574	94.5	**Tulare** (city) Tulare County
15	609	94.4	**Galt** (city) Sacramento County
16	649	94.3	**Hanford** (city) Kings County
16	649	94.3	**Quartz Hill** (CDP) Los Angeles County
18	722	94.1	**Dixon** (city) Solano County
18	722	94.1	**Lancaster** (city) Los Angeles County
18	722	94.1	**Lathrop** (city) San Joaquin County
21	767	94.0	**Delano** (city) Kern County
21	767	94.0	**Delhi** (CDP) Merced County
23	816	93.9	**American Canyon** (city) Napa County
23	816	93.9	**Porterville** (city) Tulare County
25	865	93.8	**Coachella** (city) Riverside County
25	865	93.8	**Orcutt** (CDP) Santa Barbara County
25	865	93.8	**Perris** (city) Riverside County
28	917	93.7	**Vacaville** (city) Solano County
29	964	93.6	**Clovis** (city) Fresno County
29	964	93.6	**Manteca** (city) San Joaquin County
29	964	93.6	**Prunedale** (CDP) Monterey County
32	1000	93.5	**San Jacinto** (city) Riverside County
33	1043	93.4	**Castaic** (CDP) Los Angeles County
33	1043	93.4	**Colton** (city) San Bernardino County
33	1043	93.4	**Valle Vista** (CDP) Riverside County
36	1086	93.3	**Mead Valley** (CDP) Riverside County
36	1086	93.3	**Phelan** (CDP) San Bernardino County
38	1147	93.2	**Beaumont** (city) Riverside County
38	1147	93.2	**Fontana** (city) San Bernardino County
38	1147	93.2	**McFarland** (city) Kern County
38	1147	93.2	**Santa Paula** (city) Ventura County
42	1237	93.0	**Ontario** (city) San Bernardino County
43	1277	92.9	**Bakersfield** (city) Kern County
43	1277	92.9	**Cerritos** (city) Los Angeles County
43	1277	92.9	**Del Aire** (CDP) Los Angeles County
43	1277	92.9	**Santa Maria** (city) Santa Barbara County
47	1322	92.8	**Chino** (city) San Bernardino County
47	1322	92.8	**El Sobrante** (CDP) Riverside County
47	1322	92.8	**Hollister** (city) San Benito County
50	1371	92.7	**Lindsay** (city) Tulare County
50	1371	92.7	**Oxnard** (city) Ventura County
52	1416	92.6	**Dinuba** (city) Tulare County
52	1416	92.6	**Santa Fe Springs** (city) Los Angeles County
52	1416	92.6	**Sun Village** (CDP) Los Angeles County
55	1466	92.5	**Atwater** (city) Merced County
55	1466	92.5	**Diamond Springs** (CDP) El Dorado County
55	1466	92.5	**La Palma** (city) Orange County
55	1466	92.5	**Rossmoor** (CDP) Orange County
55	1466	92.5	**Shafter** (city) Kern County
55	1466	92.5	**Spring Valley** (CDP) San Diego County
61	1514	92.4	**Escondido** (city) San Diego County
61	1514	92.4	**Rialto** (city) San Bernardino County
61	1514	92.4	**Shasta Lake** (city) Shasta County
61	1514	92.4	**Turlock** (city) Stanislaus County
61	1514	92.4	**Yuba City** (city) Sutter County
66	1563	92.3	**Banning** (city) Riverside County
66	1563	92.3	**Nipomo** (CDP) San Luis Obispo County
66	1563	92.3	**Valinda** (CDP) Los Angeles County
66	1563	92.3	**Wildomar** (city) Riverside County
70	1608	92.2	**Chino Hills** (city) San Bernardino County
70	1608	92.2	**East Rancho Dominguez** (CDP) Los Angeles County
70	1608	92.2	**Garden Acres** (CDP) San Joaquin County
70	1608	92.2	**Indio** (city) Riverside County
74	1644	92.1	**Downey** (city) Los Angeles County
74	1644	92.1	**Eastvale** (city) Riverside County
74	1644	92.1	**Ridgecrest** (city) Kern County
74	1644	92.1	**Santee** (city) San Diego County
78	1695	92.0	**French Valley** (CDP) Riverside County
78	1695	92.0	**Lakewood** (city) Los Angeles County
78	1695	92.0	**Moreno Valley** (city) Riverside County
78	1695	92.0	**Rancho Cucamonga** (city) San Bernardino County
78	1695	92.0	**San Marcos** (city) San Diego County
83	1744	91.9	**Ceres** (city) Stanislaus County
83	1744	91.9	**Highland** (city) San Bernardino County
83	1744	91.9	**Lodi** (city) San Joaquin County
86	1782	91.8	**Arvin** (city) Kern County
86	1782	91.8	**Olivehurst** (CDP) Yuba County
86	1782	91.8	**Rancho San Diego** (CDP) San Diego County
86	1782	91.8	**Victorville** (city) San Bernardino County
90	1819	91.7	**Camarillo** (city) Ventura County
90	1819	91.7	**Garden Grove** (city) Orange County
90	1819	91.7	**Parkway** (CDP) Sacramento County
90	1819	91.7	**Stockton** (city) San Joaquin County
94	1857	91.6	**Commerce** (city) Los Angeles County
94	1857	91.6	**Cypress** (city) Orange County
94	1857	91.6	**Fountain Valley** (city) Orange County
94	1857	91.6	**Upland** (city) San Bernardino County
98	1892	91.5	**Glendora** (city) Los Angeles County
98	1892	91.5	**Lamont** (CDP) Kern County
98	1892	91.5	**Linda** (CDP) Yuba County
98	1892	91.5	**McKinleyville** (CDP) Humboldt County
98	1892	91.5	**Milpitas** (city) Santa Clara County
98	1892	91.5	**South Whittier** (CDP) Los Angeles County
104	1937	91.4	**Corcoran** (city) Kings County
104	1937	91.4	**Lakeland Village** (CDP) Riverside County
104	1937	91.4	**Winter Gardens** (CDP) San Diego County
107	1981	91.3	**Citrus Heights** (city) Sacramento County
107	1981	91.3	**Greenfield** (city) Monterey County
107	1981	91.3	**Montclair** (city) San Bernardino County
107	1981	91.3	**Vista** (city) San Diego County
107	1981	91.3	**Yucaipa** (city) San Bernardino County
112	2023	91.2	**Modesto** (city) Stanislaus County
112	2023	91.2	**Yorba Linda** (city) Orange County
114	2067	91.1	**Antelope** (CDP) Sacramento County
114	2067	91.1	**Norwalk** (city) Los Angeles County
114	2067	91.1	**West Carson** (CDP) Los Angeles County
117	2112	91.0	**Adelanto** (city) San Bernardino County
117	2112	91.0	**Canyon Lake** (city) Riverside County
117	2112	91.0	**King City** (city) Monterey County
117	2112	91.0	**Oildale** (CDP) Kern County
117	2112	91.0	**Palmdale** (city) Los Angeles County
117	2112	91.0	**Wasco** (city) Kern County
117	2112	91.0	**West Covina** (city) Los Angeles County
124	2149	90.9	**Brea** (city) Orange County
124	2149	90.9	**Carson** (city) Los Angeles County
124	2149	90.9	**Coalinga** (city) Fresno County
124	2149	90.9	**Murrieta** (city) Riverside County
124	2149	90.9	**San Diego Country Estates** (CDP) San Diego County
124	2149	90.9	**Visalia** (city) Tulare County
124	2149	90.9	**Westminster** (city) Orange County
131	2200	90.8	**Bloomington** (CDP) San Bernardino County
131	2200	90.8	**Blythe** (city) Riverside County
131	2200	90.8	**Corona** (city) Riverside County
131	2200	90.8	**Gardena** (city) Los Angeles County
131	2200	90.8	**Menifee** (city) Riverside County
131	2200	90.8	**Muscoy** (CDP) San Bernardino County
137	2240	90.7	**Alpine** (CDP) San Diego County
137	2240	90.7	**Hacienda Heights** (CDP) Los Angeles County
137	2240	90.7	**Hemet** (city) Riverside County
137	2240	90.7	**Lakeside** (CDP) San Diego County
137	2240	90.7	**Walnut** (city) Los Angeles County
142	2276	90.6	**Citrus** (CDP) Los Angeles County
142	2276	90.6	**Elk Grove** (city) Sacramento County
142	2276	90.6	**Tracy** (city) San Joaquin County
145	2308	90.5	**Scotts Valley** (city) Santa Cruz County
145	2308	90.5	**Suisun City** (city) Solano County
145	2308	90.5	**Vineyard** (CDP) Sacramento County
148	2347	90.4	**Fillmore** (city) Ventura County
148	2347	90.4	**Hesperia** (city) San Bernardino County
148	2347	90.4	**Lake Forest** (city) Orange County

Note: *The state column ranks the top/bottom 150 places from all places in the state with population of 10,000 or more. The national column ranks the top/bottom 150 places from all places in the country with population of 10,000 or more. Places that are unincorporated were not considered in the rankings. Please refer to the User Guide for additional information.*

Commute to Work: Car

Top 150 Places Ranked in *Ascending* Order

State Rank	Nat'l Rank	Percent	Place
1	3	24.1	**Stanford** (CDP) Santa Clara County
2	15	39.0	**Isla Vista** (CDP) Santa Barbara County
3	21	43.5	**Berkeley** (city) Alameda County
4	22	44.5	**San Francisco** (city) San Francisco County
5	55	57.4	**Albany** (city) Alameda County
6	82	61.9	**Emeryville** (city) Alameda County
7	103	63.7	**Davis** (city) Yolo County
7	103	63.7	**El Cerrito** (city) Contra Costa County
9	129	66.4	**Oakland** (city) Alameda County
10	135	67.0	**Arcata** (city) Humboldt County
11	150	67.8	**Santa Cruz** (city) Santa Cruz County
12	160	68.2	**Orinda** (city) Contra Costa County
13	167	68.7	**Malibu** (city) Los Angeles County
14	187	69.8	**Coronado** (city) San Diego County
15	189	70.1	**Mill Valley** (city) Marin County
16	202	70.8	**Alameda** (city) Alameda County
17	204	70.9	**Palo Alto** (city) Santa Clara County
18	211	71.4	**Moraga** (town) Contra Costa County
19	217	71.9	**Lafayette** (city) Contra Costa County
19	217	71.9	**Walnut Creek** (city) Contra Costa County
21	231	72.4	**San Anselmo** (town) Marin County
21	231	72.4	**San Rafael** (city) Marin County
23	259	73.4	**Piedmont** (city) Alameda County
24	278	74.3	**Solana Beach** (city) San Diego County
25	281	74.5	**Daly City** (city) San Mateo County
25	281	74.5	**Santa Barbara** (city) Santa Barbara County
27	286	74.7	**Camp Pendleton South** (CDP) San Diego County
28	305	75.3	**Tamalpais-Homestead Valley** (CDP) Marin County
29	320	75.7	**West Hollywood** (city) Los Angeles County
30	331	76.0	**Claremont** (city) Los Angeles County
30	331	76.0	**Santa Monica** (city) Los Angeles County
32	336	76.2	**Larkspur** (city) Marin County
33	346	76.6	**San Luis Obispo** (city) San Luis Obispo County
34	351	76.7	**Huntington Park** (city) Los Angeles County
35	361	77.0	**Menlo Park** (city) San Mateo County
35	361	77.0	**Pleasant Hill** (city) Contra Costa County
35	361	77.0	**Twentynine Palms** (city) San Bernardino County
38	372	77.2	**Los Angeles** (city) Los Angeles County
39	390	77.8	**Burlingame** (city) San Mateo County
40	401	78.0	**Carpinteria** (city) Santa Barbara County
41	405	78.1	**Beverly Hills** (city) Los Angeles County
42	432	78.8	**East Los Angeles** (CDP) Los Angeles County
42	432	78.8	**South Lake Tahoe** (city) El Dorado County
44	450	79.2	**North Fair Oaks** (CDP) San Mateo County
45	454	79.3	**Clearlake** (city) Lake County
45	454	79.3	**Westmont** (CDP) Los Angeles County
47	458	79.4	**Florence-Graham** (CDP) Los Angeles County
48	464	79.6	**Goleta** (city) Santa Barbara County
49	470	79.8	**Alamo** (CDP) Contra Costa County
49	470	79.8	**Healdsburg** (city) Sonoma County
49	470	79.8	**Tehachapi** (city) Kern County
52	482	79.9	**Richmond** (city) Contra Costa County
53	504	80.3	**Monterey** (city) Monterey County
53	504	80.3	**Rancho Mirage** (city) Riverside County
53	504	80.3	**Seaside** (city) Monterey County
56	510	80.4	**Pasadena** (city) Los Angeles County
56	510	80.4	**Sonoma** (city) Sonoma County
58	530	80.7	**Palm Springs** (city) Riverside County
59	535	80.8	**Maywood** (city) Los Angeles County
59	535	80.8	**Mountain View** (city) Santa Clara County
61	553	81.0	**Live Oak** (CDP) Santa Cruz County
62	576	81.4	**Dublin** (city) Alameda County
63	601	81.6	**National City** (city) San Diego County
64	606	81.7	**Chico** (city) Butte County
65	611	81.8	**Millbrae** (city) San Mateo County
66	617	81.9	**Fortuna** (city) Humboldt County
66	617	81.9	**Pleasanton** (city) Alameda County
66	617	81.9	**San Leandro** (city) Alameda County
69	624	82.0	**South San Francisco** (city) San Mateo County
70	634	82.1	**San Mateo** (city) San Mateo County
71	647	82.3	**South El Monte** (city) Los Angeles County
72	657	82.4	**Ashland** (CDP) Alameda County
72	657	82.4	**Belmont** (city) San Mateo County
72	657	82.4	**Concord** (city) Contra Costa County
72	657	82.4	**Pinole** (city) Contra Costa County
76	667	82.5	**Lennox** (CDP) Los Angeles County
76	667	82.5	**Walnut Park** (CDP) Los Angeles County
78	683	82.6	**Encinitas** (city) San Diego County
78	683	82.6	**Parlier** (city) Fresno County
80	692	82.7	**Azusa** (city) Los Angeles County
80	692	82.7	**Castro Valley** (CDP) Alameda County
80	692	82.7	**Long Beach** (city) Los Angeles County
83	702	82.8	**Laguna Woods** (city) Orange County
84	720	83.0	**San Bruno** (city) San Mateo County
84	720	83.0	**Susanville** (city) Lassen County
86	739	83.2	**San Ramon** (city) Contra Costa County
87	776	83.5	**Laguna Beach** (city) Orange County
87	776	83.5	**Morro Bay** (city) San Luis Obispo County
87	776	83.5	**Salinas** (city) Monterey County
87	776	83.5	**San Clemente** (city) Orange County
91	809	83.8	**Bell Gardens** (city) Los Angeles County
92	822	83.9	**Novato** (city) Marin County
92	822	83.9	**Pacifica** (city) San Mateo County
94	833	84.0	**Los Altos** (city) Santa Clara County
95	843	84.1	**Auburn** (city) Placer County
95	843	84.1	**Bell** (city) Los Angeles County
95	843	84.1	**Danville** (town) Contra Costa County
95	843	84.1	**Eureka** (city) Humboldt County
95	843	84.1	**Inglewood** (city) Los Angeles County
95	843	84.1	**San Diego** (city) San Diego County
101	855	84.2	**Martinez** (city) Contra Costa County
101	855	84.2	**Redwood City** (city) San Mateo County
103	873	84.3	**Cherryland** (CDP) Alameda County
103	873	84.3	**El Dorado Hills** (CDP) El Dorado County
105	884	84.4	**Bay Point** (CDP) Contra Costa County
105	884	84.4	**Glendale** (city) Los Angeles County
107	894	84.5	**Culver City** (city) Los Angeles County
107	894	84.5	**Port Hueneme** (city) Ventura County
109	908	84.6	**Clayton** (city) Contra Costa County
109	908	84.6	**Dana Point** (city) Orange County
109	908	84.6	**San Pablo** (city) Contra Costa County
112	922	84.7	**Hawaiian Gardens** (city) Los Angeles County
112	922	84.7	**Signal Hill** (city) Los Angeles County
114	936	84.8	**Manhattan Beach** (city) Los Angeles County
114	936	84.8	**Sacramento** (city) Sacramento County
116	962	85.0	**Newport Beach** (city) Orange County
116	962	85.0	**Pittsburg** (city) Contra Costa County
118	972	85.1	**Hermosa Beach** (city) Los Angeles County
119	998	85.3	**Arden-Arcade** (CDP) Sacramento County
119	998	85.3	**Crestline** (CDP) San Bernardino County
119	998	85.3	**Palos Verdes Estates** (city) Los Angeles County
122	1018	85.4	**Costa Mesa** (city) Orange County
122	1018	85.4	**Pacific Grove** (city) Monterey County
122	1018	85.4	**Sanger** (city) Fresno County
125	1025	85.5	**Cudahy** (city) Los Angeles County
125	1025	85.5	**Imperial Beach** (city) San Diego County
127	1041	85.6	**Irvine** (city) Orange County
127	1041	85.6	**Morgan Hill** (city) Santa Clara County
127	1041	85.6	**San Marino** (city) Los Angeles County
127	1041	85.6	**Yucca Valley** (town) San Bernardino County
131	1060	85.7	**Avenal** (city) Kings County
131	1060	85.7	**Carlsbad** (city) San Diego County
131	1060	85.7	**Casa de Oro-Mount Helix** (CDP) San Diego County
131	1060	85.7	**San Carlos** (city) San Mateo County
131	1060	85.7	**Watsonville** (city) Santa Cruz County
136	1080	85.8	**East Palo Alto** (city) San Mateo County
136	1080	85.8	**Hawthorne** (city) Los Angeles County
136	1080	85.8	**North Tustin** (CDP) Orange County
139	1095	85.9	**Fremont** (city) Alameda County
139	1095	85.9	**Grass Valley** (city) Nevada County
139	1095	85.9	**Hayward** (city) Alameda County
139	1095	85.9	**North Auburn** (CDP) Placer County
143	1111	86.0	**Stanton** (city) Orange County
144	1135	86.1	**Benicia** (city) Solano County
144	1135	86.1	**El Monte** (city) Los Angeles County
144	1135	86.1	**Laguna Hills** (city) Orange County
144	1135	86.1	**Lomita** (city) Los Angeles County
148	1153	86.2	**Coto de Caza** (CDP) Orange County
148	1153	86.2	**Marysville** (city) Yuba County
148	1153	86.2	**Rowland Heights** (CDP) Los Angeles County

Note: *The state column ranks the top/bottom 150 places from all places in the state with population of 10,000 or more. The national column ranks the top/bottom 150 places from all places in the country with population of 10,000 or more. Places that are unincorporated were not considered in the rankings. Please refer to the User Guide for additional information.*

Commute to Work: Public Transportation

Top 150 Places Ranked in *Descending* Order

State Rank	Nat'l Rank	Percent	Place
1	21	32.6	**San Francisco** (city) San Francisco County
2	63	24.1	**Albany** (city) Alameda County
3	81	22.3	**El Cerrito** (city) Contra Costa County
4	97	20.2	**Berkeley** (city) Alameda County
5	101	20.1	**Daly City** (city) San Mateo County
6	118	19.3	**Emeryville** (city) Alameda County
7	133	18.3	**Oakland** (city) Alameda County
8	187	15.6	**Orinda** (city) Contra Costa County
9	189	15.5	**Moraga** (town) Contra Costa County
10	194	15.4	**Walnut Creek** (city) Contra Costa County
11	203	15.2	**Alameda** (city) Alameda County
11	203	15.2	**Lafayette** (city) Contra Costa County
13	213	14.7	**Florence-Graham** (CDP) Los Angeles County
14	226	14.3	**Westmont** (CDP) Los Angeles County
15	250	13.2	**Huntington Park** (city) Los Angeles County
15	250	13.2	**Richmond** (city) Contra Costa County
17	258	13.0	**Pleasant Hill** (city) Contra Costa County
18	266	12.7	**East Los Angeles** (CDP) Los Angeles County
19	267	12.6	**Larkspur** (city) Marin County
20	277	12.3	**Burlingame** (city) San Mateo County
21	301	11.7	**Ashland** (CDP) Alameda County
22	311	11.4	**Piedmont** (city) Alameda County
22	311	11.4	**San Rafael** (city) Marin County
24	322	11.3	**San Anselmo** (town) Marin County
24	322	11.3	**San Bruno** (city) San Mateo County
26	332	11.2	**San Leandro** (city) Alameda County
27	345	11.0	**Los Angeles** (city) Los Angeles County
28	385	10.2	**South San Francisco** (city) San Mateo County
29	403	10.0	**San Pablo** (city) Contra Costa County
30	415	9.8	**Concord** (city) Contra Costa County
31	440	9.5	**Bay Point** (CDP) Contra Costa County
31	440	9.5	**Lennox** (CDP) Los Angeles County
33	450	9.3	**Millbrae** (city) San Mateo County
34	462	9.2	**Castro Valley** (CDP) Alameda County
34	462	9.2	**Dublin** (city) Alameda County
36	472	9.1	**Hercules** (city) Contra Costa County
37	479	9.0	**Pinole** (city) Contra Costa County
38	491	8.9	**Pittsburg** (city) Contra Costa County
39	499	8.8	**Walnut Park** (CDP) Los Angeles County
40	517	8.6	**Union City** (city) Alameda County
41	521	8.5	**Mill Valley** (city) Marin County
42	540	8.3	**North Fair Oaks** (CDP) San Mateo County
43	549	8.1	**Bell Gardens** (city) Los Angeles County
43	549	8.1	**Hayward** (city) Alameda County
45	575	7.8	**San Lorenzo** (CDP) Alameda County
46	586	7.7	**Long Beach** (city) Los Angeles County
47	600	7.6	**Fairview** (CDP) Alameda County
47	600	7.6	**Inglewood** (city) Los Angeles County
47	600	7.6	**San Mateo** (city) San Mateo County
50	611	7.5	**Maywood** (city) Los Angeles County
51	622	7.4	**Fremont** (city) Alameda County
52	632	7.3	**Avenal** (city) Kings County
52	632	7.3	**Hawthorne** (city) Los Angeles County
52	632	7.3	**National City** (city) San Diego County
55	648	7.1	**Cudahy** (city) Los Angeles County
55	648	7.1	**Pleasanton** (city) Alameda County
55	648	7.1	**Santa Ana** (city) Orange County
55	648	7.1	**Tamalpais-Homestead Valley** (CDP) Marin County
59	665	7.0	**El Sobrante** (CDP) Contra Costa County
59	665	7.0	**Pacifica** (city) San Mateo County
61	678	6.9	**South Gate** (city) Los Angeles County
62	696	6.8	**Bell** (city) Los Angeles County
63	718	6.6	**Clayton** (city) Contra Costa County
64	729	6.5	**Davis** (city) Yolo County
64	729	6.5	**Martinez** (city) Contra Costa County
66	740	6.4	**Alamo** (CDP) Contra Costa County
66	740	6.4	**Cherryland** (CDP) Alameda County
66	740	6.4	**Pasadena** (city) Los Angeles County
66	740	6.4	**Seaside** (city) Monterey County
66	740	6.4	**Willowbrook** (CDP) Los Angeles County
71	765	6.2	**Compton** (city) Los Angeles County
71	765	6.2	**El Monte** (city) Los Angeles County
71	765	6.2	**Isla Vista** (CDP) Santa Barbara County
71	765	6.2	**San Ramon** (city) Contra Costa County
75	780	6.1	**Santa Barbara** (city) Santa Barbara County
76	791	6.0	**Azusa** (city) Los Angeles County
77	803	5.9	**Montebello** (city) Los Angeles County
78	812	5.8	**Antioch** (city) Contra Costa County
79	831	5.7	**Hawaiian Gardens** (city) Los Angeles County
79	831	5.7	**Imperial Beach** (city) San Diego County
79	831	5.7	**Lynwood** (city) Los Angeles County
82	844	5.6	**Novato** (city) Marin County
83	872	5.4	**Rosemont** (CDP) Sacramento County
83	872	5.4	**Santa Cruz** (city) Santa Cruz County
83	872	5.4	**South Pasadena** (city) Los Angeles County
86	884	5.3	**Palo Alto** (city) Santa Clara County
87	905	5.2	**Mountain View** (city) Santa Clara County
87	905	5.2	**Paramount** (city) Los Angeles County
87	905	5.2	**Stanton** (city) Orange County
90	940	5.0	**Belmont** (city) San Mateo County
90	940	5.0	**Danville** (town) Contra Costa County
90	940	5.0	**East San Gabriel** (CDP) Los Angeles County
93	963	4.9	**La Riviera** (CDP) Sacramento County
93	963	4.9	**Santa Fe Springs** (city) Los Angeles County
93	963	4.9	**West Hollywood** (city) Los Angeles County
96	983	4.8	**Covina** (city) Los Angeles County
96	983	4.8	**Lompoc** (city) Santa Barbara County
96	983	4.8	**Newark** (city) Alameda County
99	1007	4.7	**East Palo Alto** (city) San Mateo County
99	1007	4.7	**San Carlos** (city) San Mateo County
99	1007	4.7	**Vallejo** (city) Solano County
102	1029	4.6	**Baldwin Park** (city) Los Angeles County
102	1029	4.6	**Bellflower** (city) Los Angeles County
102	1029	4.6	**Bostonia** (CDP) San Diego County
102	1029	4.6	**South El Monte** (city) Los Angeles County
106	1043	4.5	**Benicia** (city) Solano County
106	1043	4.5	**Glendale** (city) Los Angeles County
106	1043	4.5	**Lawndale** (city) Los Angeles County
106	1043	4.5	**Redwood City** (city) San Mateo County
106	1043	4.5	**Sunnyvale** (city) Santa Clara County
111	1060	4.4	**Anaheim** (city) Orange County
111	1060	4.4	**Carpinteria** (city) Santa Barbara County
113	1083	4.3	**Duarte** (city) Los Angeles County
113	1083	4.3	**Menlo Park** (city) San Mateo County
115	1107	4.2	**Rancho Cordova** (city) Sacramento County
115	1107	4.2	**Rowland Heights** (CDP) Los Angeles County
117	1126	4.1	**Alhambra** (city) Los Angeles County
117	1126	4.1	**East Rancho Dominguez** (CDP) Los Angeles County
119	1149	4.0	**Buena Park** (city) Orange County
119	1149	4.0	**Citrus** (CDP) Los Angeles County
119	1149	4.0	**Claremont** (city) Los Angeles County
119	1149	4.0	**La Habra** (city) Orange County
119	1149	4.0	**Lemon Grove** (city) San Diego County
119	1149	4.0	**Magalia** (CDP) Butte County
119	1149	4.0	**Sacramento** (city) Sacramento County
119	1149	4.0	**San Diego** (city) San Diego County
119	1149	4.0	**San Fernando** (city) Los Angeles County
128	1186	3.9	**Altadena** (CDP) Los Angeles County
128	1186	3.9	**Gardena** (city) Los Angeles County
128	1186	3.9	**Norwalk** (city) Los Angeles County
128	1186	3.9	**Oakley** (city) Contra Costa County
132	1208	3.8	**Alum Rock** (CDP) Santa Clara County
132	1208	3.8	**Arden-Arcade** (CDP) Sacramento County
132	1208	3.8	**Marina** (city) Monterey County
132	1208	3.8	**Santa Monica** (city) Los Angeles County
136	1242	3.7	**Foster City** (city) San Mateo County
136	1242	3.7	**Hillsborough** (town) San Mateo County
136	1242	3.7	**South San Jose Hills** (CDP) Los Angeles County
139	1272	3.6	**Fullerton** (city) Orange County
139	1272	3.6	**Lomita** (city) Los Angeles County
139	1272	3.6	**Monterey Park** (city) Los Angeles County
139	1272	3.6	**Santa Clara** (city) Santa Clara County
139	1272	3.6	**Sierra Madre** (city) Los Angeles County
139	1272	3.6	**Temple City** (city) Los Angeles County
145	1311	3.5	**El Cajon** (city) San Diego County
145	1311	3.5	**Montclair** (city) San Bernardino County
145	1311	3.5	**San Jose** (city) Santa Clara County
148	1345	3.4	**Commerce** (city) Los Angeles County
148	1345	3.4	**Live Oak** (CDP) Santa Cruz County
148	1345	3.4	**Pomona** (city) Los Angeles County

Note: *The state column ranks the top/bottom 150 places from all places in the state with population of 10,000 or more. The national column ranks the top/bottom 150 places from all places in the country with population of 10,000 or more. Places that are unincorporated were not considered in the rankings. Please refer to the User Guide for additional information.*

Commute to Work: Walk

Top 150 Places Ranked in *Descending* Order

State Rank	Nat'l Rank	Percent	Place
1	32	19.6	**Stanford** (CDP) Santa Clara County
2	56	16.0	**Arcata** (city) Humboldt County
3	62	15.4	**Berkeley** (city) Alameda County
4	72	14.7	**Isla Vista** (CDP) Santa Barbara County
5	74	14.6	**Tehachapi** (city) Kern County
6	81	13.7	**Camp Pendleton South** (CDP) San Diego County
7	96	12.7	**Twentynine Palms** (city) San Bernardino County
8	152	10.1	**San Francisco** (city) San Francisco County
8	152	10.1	**South Lake Tahoe** (city) El Dorado County
10	157	9.9	**Santa Cruz** (city) Santa Cruz County
11	168	9.6	**Claremont** (city) Los Angeles County
12	195	8.9	**Susanville** (city) Lassen County
13	235	8.0	**Emeryville** (city) Alameda County
14	239	7.9	**Port Hueneme** (city) Ventura County
15	261	7.5	**Sonoma** (city) Sonoma County
16	271	7.4	**San Luis Obispo** (city) San Luis Obispo County
17	292	7.1	**Azusa** (city) Los Angeles County
18	299	7.0	**Coronado** (city) San Diego County
18	299	7.0	**South El Monte** (city) Los Angeles County
20	314	6.8	**Santa Barbara** (city) Santa Barbara County
21	323	6.7	**Monterey** (city) Monterey County
22	367	6.2	**Barstow** (city) San Bernardino County
23	381	6.0	**Eureka** (city) Humboldt County
24	387	5.9	**Healdsburg** (city) Sonoma County
25	395	5.8	**Beverly Hills** (city) Los Angeles County
25	395	5.8	**Palo Alto** (city) Santa Clara County
27	403	5.7	**Clearlake** (city) Lake County
27	403	5.7	**West Hollywood** (city) Los Angeles County
29	413	5.6	**Loma Linda** (city) San Bernardino County
29	413	5.6	**Santa Monica** (city) Los Angeles County
31	427	5.5	**Huntington Park** (city) Los Angeles County
31	427	5.5	**Morro Bay** (city) San Luis Obispo County
33	438	5.4	**Chico** (city) Butte County
33	438	5.4	**Fortuna** (city) Humboldt County
35	471	5.2	**Carpinteria** (city) Santa Barbara County
35	471	5.2	**Maywood** (city) Los Angeles County
37	483	5.1	**Live Oak** (CDP) Santa Cruz County
37	483	5.1	**North Fair Oaks** (CDP) San Mateo County
39	493	5.0	**Malibu** (city) Los Angeles County
39	493	5.0	**Marysville** (city) Yuba County
41	520	4.8	**Hawaiian Gardens** (city) Los Angeles County
41	520	4.8	**San Rafael** (city) Marin County
43	538	4.7	**Auburn** (city) Placer County
43	538	4.7	**Newman** (city) Stanislaus County
45	560	4.6	**Albany** (city) Alameda County
45	560	4.6	**Pasadena** (city) Los Angeles County
47	589	4.4	**Fallbrook** (CDP) San Diego County
47	589	4.4	**Goleta** (city) Santa Barbara County
47	589	4.4	**Mill Valley** (city) Marin County
50	609	4.3	**Solana Beach** (city) San Diego County
51	637	4.2	**Alameda** (city) Alameda County
51	637	4.2	**Oakland** (city) Alameda County
51	637	4.2	**Ukiah** (city) Mendocino County
54	660	4.1	**Lake Arrowhead** (CDP) San Bernardino County
55	678	4.0	**East Los Angeles** (CDP) Los Angeles County
55	678	4.0	**Greenfield** (city) Monterey County
57	707	3.9	**Grass Valley** (city) Nevada County
58	731	3.8	**Cherryland** (CDP) Alameda County
58	731	3.8	**Crestline** (CDP) San Bernardino County
58	731	3.8	**Glendale** (city) Los Angeles County
58	731	3.8	**Kingsburg** (city) Fresno County
58	731	3.8	**Oroville** (city) Butte County
58	731	3.8	**South San Francisco** (city) San Mateo County
64	766	3.7	**Bell** (city) Los Angeles County
64	766	3.7	**Irvine** (city) Orange County
64	766	3.7	**Lennox** (CDP) Los Angeles County
64	766	3.7	**Los Angeles** (city) Los Angeles County
64	766	3.7	**Yucca Valley** (town) San Bernardino County
69	799	3.6	**Coalinga** (city) Fresno County
69	799	3.6	**El Segundo** (city) Los Angeles County
69	799	3.6	**Lompoc** (city) Santa Barbara County
69	799	3.6	**Moraga** (town) Contra Costa County
69	799	3.6	**San Anselmo** (town) Marin County
69	799	3.6	**San Gabriel** (city) Los Angeles County
75	839	3.5	**Fillmore** (city) Ventura County
75	839	3.5	**La Mirada** (city) Los Angeles County
75	839	3.5	**Redlands** (city) San Bernardino County
75	839	3.5	**San Mateo** (city) San Mateo County
75	839	3.5	**Seal Beach** (city) Orange County
75	839	3.5	**Willowbrook** (CDP) Los Angeles County
81	879	3.4	**Cudahy** (city) Los Angeles County
81	879	3.4	**Davis** (city) Yolo County
81	879	3.4	**Fullerton** (city) Orange County
81	879	3.4	**Walnut Park** (CDP) Los Angeles County
81	879	3.4	**Watsonville** (city) Santa Cruz County
86	925	3.3	**East Palo Alto** (city) San Mateo County
86	925	3.3	**National City** (city) San Diego County
86	925	3.3	**Paramount** (city) Los Angeles County
86	925	3.3	**Santa Clara** (city) Santa Clara County
86	925	3.3	**Stanton** (city) Orange County
86	925	3.3	**Walnut Creek** (city) Contra Costa County
92	965	3.2	**Fairfield** (city) Solano County
92	965	3.2	**La Crescenta-Montrose** (CDP) Los Angeles County
92	965	3.2	**Napa** (city) Napa County
92	965	3.2	**Parlier** (city) Fresno County
92	965	3.2	**Seaside** (city) Monterey County
97	1009	3.1	**Arroyo Grande** (city) San Luis Obispo County
97	1009	3.1	**Bell Gardens** (city) Los Angeles County
97	1009	3.1	**Lindsay** (city) Tulare County
97	1009	3.1	**Lynwood** (city) Los Angeles County
97	1009	3.1	**Sacramento** (city) Sacramento County
97	1009	3.1	**San Diego** (city) San Diego County
103	1053	3.0	**Agoura Hills** (city) Los Angeles County
103	1053	3.0	**Arden-Arcade** (CDP) Sacramento County
103	1053	3.0	**Buena Park** (city) Orange County
103	1053	3.0	**Burlingame** (city) San Mateo County
103	1053	3.0	**Madera** (city) Madera County
103	1053	3.0	**Pleasanton** (city) Alameda County
103	1053	3.0	**Redwood City** (city) San Mateo County
103	1053	3.0	**Santa Rosa** (city) Sonoma County
111	1105	2.9	**Burbank** (city) Los Angeles County
111	1105	2.9	**Dana Point** (city) Orange County
111	1105	2.9	**Duarte** (city) Los Angeles County
111	1105	2.9	**Grover Beach** (city) San Luis Obispo County
111	1105	2.9	**Pacific Grove** (city) Monterey County
111	1105	2.9	**Palm Springs** (city) Riverside County
111	1105	2.9	**Red Bluff** (city) Tehama County
111	1105	2.9	**San Fernando** (city) Los Angeles County
119	1164	2.8	**Corcoran** (city) Kings County
119	1164	2.8	**Gardena** (city) Los Angeles County
119	1164	2.8	**Mendota** (city) Fresno County
119	1164	2.8	**Riverside** (city) Riverside County
123	1218	2.7	**Menlo Park** (city) San Mateo County
123	1218	2.7	**Monrovia** (city) Los Angeles County
123	1218	2.7	**Mountain View** (city) Santa Clara County
123	1218	2.7	**Petaluma** (city) Sonoma County
127	1289	2.6	**El Monte** (city) Los Angeles County
127	1289	2.6	**Long Beach** (city) Los Angeles County
127	1289	2.6	**Rowland Heights** (CDP) Los Angeles County
127	1289	2.6	**Signal Hill** (city) Los Angeles County
131	1347	2.5	**Blythe** (city) Riverside County
131	1347	2.5	**Costa Mesa** (city) Orange County
131	1347	2.5	**Daly City** (city) San Mateo County
131	1347	2.5	**East Hemet** (CDP) Riverside County
131	1347	2.5	**Florence-Graham** (CDP) Los Angeles County
131	1347	2.5	**Imperial Beach** (city) San Diego County
131	1347	2.5	**Los Osos** (CDP) San Luis Obispo County
131	1347	2.5	**Pomona** (city) Los Angeles County
139	1439	2.4	**Brawley** (city) Imperial County
139	1439	2.4	**Chowchilla** (city) Madera County
139	1439	2.4	**Desert Hot Springs** (city) Riverside County
139	1439	2.4	**Lemon Hill** (CDP) Sacramento County
139	1439	2.4	**Manhattan Beach** (city) Los Angeles County
139	1439	2.4	**McFarland** (city) Kern County
139	1439	2.4	**Millbrae** (city) San Mateo County
139	1439	2.4	**Muscoy** (CDP) San Bernardino County
139	1439	2.4	**Oakdale** (city) Stanislaus County
139	1439	2.4	**Placerville** (city) El Dorado County
139	1439	2.4	**San Dimas** (city) Los Angeles County
139	1439	2.4	**San Jacinto** (city) Riverside County

Note: *The state column ranks the top/bottom 150 places from all places in the state with population of 10,000 or more. The national column ranks the top/bottom 150 places from all places in the country with population of 10,000 or more. Places that are unincorporated were not considered in the rankings. Please refer to the User Guide for additional information.*

Commute to Work: Walk

Top 150 Places Ranked in *Ascending* Order

State Rank	Nat'l Rank	Percent	Place
1	1	0.0	**Canyon Lake** (city) Riverside County
1	1	0.0	**Coto de Caza** (CDP) Orange County
1	1	0.0	**Garden Acres** (CDP) San Joaquin County
1	1	0.0	**Grand Terrace** (city) San Bernardino County
1	1	0.0	**Lake Los Angeles** (CDP) Los Angeles County
1	1	0.0	**Phelan** (CDP) San Bernardino County
1	1	0.0	**Quartz Hill** (CDP) Los Angeles County
1	1	0.0	**Sierra Madre** (city) Los Angeles County
9	93	0.1	**Lathrop** (city) San Joaquin County
9	93	0.1	**Rosedale** (CDP) Kern County
11	151	0.2	**French Valley** (CDP) Riverside County
11	151	0.2	**Kerman** (city) Fresno County
11	151	0.2	**Prunedale** (CDP) Monterey County
11	151	0.2	**Wildomar** (city) Riverside County
15	246	0.3	**Cerritos** (city) Los Angeles County
15	246	0.3	**Clayton** (city) Contra Costa County
15	246	0.3	**East San Gabriel** (CDP) Los Angeles County
15	246	0.3	**Eastvale** (city) Riverside County
15	246	0.3	**Granite Bay** (CDP) Placer County
15	246	0.3	**Oak Park** (CDP) Ventura County
15	246	0.3	**Orcutt** (CDP) Santa Barbara County
15	246	0.3	**Rancho Palos Verdes** (city) Los Angeles County
15	246	0.3	**Santa Fe Springs** (city) Los Angeles County
15	246	0.3	**Saratoga** (city) Santa Clara County
15	246	0.3	**Valle Vista** (CDP) Riverside County
26	358	0.4	**Antelope** (CDP) Sacramento County
26	358	0.4	**Brentwood** (city) Contra Costa County
26	358	0.4	**California City** (city) Kern County
26	358	0.4	**Hercules** (city) Contra Costa County
26	358	0.4	**Salida** (CDP) Stanislaus County
31	497	0.5	**Big Bear City** (CDP) San Bernardino County
31	497	0.5	**El Sobrante** (CDP) Contra Costa County
31	497	0.5	**El Sobrante** (CDP) Riverside County
31	497	0.5	**Mission Viejo** (city) Orange County
31	497	0.5	**Norco** (city) Riverside County
31	497	0.5	**Pinole** (city) Contra Costa County
31	497	0.5	**South Whittier** (CDP) Los Angeles County
31	497	0.5	**Winton** (CDP) Merced County
39	651	0.6	**Atascadero** (city) San Luis Obispo County
39	651	0.6	**Colton** (city) San Bernardino County
39	651	0.6	**Mead Valley** (CDP) Riverside County
39	651	0.6	**San Diego Country Estates** (CDP) San Diego County
39	651	0.6	**Vineyard** (CDP) Sacramento County
39	651	0.6	**Walnut** (city) Los Angeles County
39	651	0.6	**West Covina** (city) Los Angeles County
39	651	0.6	**Winter Gardens** (CDP) San Diego County
47	802	0.7	**Chino Hills** (city) San Bernardino County
47	802	0.7	**Imperial** (city) Imperial County
47	802	0.7	**Lakeland Village** (CDP) Riverside County
47	802	0.7	**Rialto** (city) San Bernardino County
47	802	0.7	**Rossmoor** (CDP) Orange County
47	802	0.7	**Shasta Lake** (city) Shasta County
47	802	0.7	**Spring Valley** (CDP) San Diego County
47	802	0.7	**Westmont** (CDP) Los Angeles County
47	802	0.7	**Yorba Linda** (city) Orange County
56	970	0.8	**Adelanto** (city) San Bernardino County
56	970	0.8	**Calabasas** (city) Los Angeles County
56	970	0.8	**Covina** (city) Los Angeles County
56	970	0.8	**El Dorado Hills** (CDP) El Dorado County
56	970	0.8	**Elk Grove** (city) Sacramento County
56	970	0.8	**Fontana** (city) San Bernardino County
56	970	0.8	**Hacienda Heights** (CDP) Los Angeles County
56	970	0.8	**La Cañada Flintridge** (city) Los Angeles County
56	970	0.8	**La Quinta** (city) Riverside County
56	970	0.8	**Lincoln** (city) Placer County
56	970	0.8	**Linda** (CDP) Yuba County
56	970	0.8	**Menifee** (city) Riverside County
56	970	0.8	**Milpitas** (city) Santa Clara County
56	970	0.8	**Nipomo** (CDP) San Luis Obispo County
56	970	0.8	**Palmdale** (city) Los Angeles County
56	970	0.8	**Rocklin** (city) Placer County
56	970	0.8	**Rosemont** (CDP) Sacramento County
56	970	0.8	**Santee** (city) San Diego County
56	970	0.8	**West Puente Valley** (CDP) Los Angeles County
75	1154	0.9	**Alum Rock** (CDP) Santa Clara County
75	1154	0.9	**Apple Valley** (town) San Bernardino County
75	1154	0.9	**Castaic** (CDP) Los Angeles County
75	1154	0.9	**Danville** (town) Contra Costa County
75	1154	0.9	**Delhi** (CDP) Merced County
75	1154	0.9	**Fair Oaks** (CDP) Sacramento County
75	1154	0.9	**Foothill Farms** (CDP) Sacramento County
75	1154	0.9	**Fountain Valley** (city) Orange County
75	1154	0.9	**Highland** (city) San Bernardino County
75	1154	0.9	**Ladera Ranch** (CDP) Orange County
75	1154	0.9	**Laguna Niguel** (city) Orange County
75	1154	0.9	**Los Banos** (city) Merced County
75	1154	0.9	**Murrieta** (city) Riverside County
75	1154	0.9	**Pacifica** (city) San Mateo County
75	1154	0.9	**Rohnert Park** (city) Sonoma County
75	1154	0.9	**Scotts Valley** (city) Santa Cruz County
75	1154	0.9	**Truckee** (town) Nevada County
75	1154	0.9	**Victorville** (city) San Bernardino County
75	1154	0.9	**View Park-Windsor Hills** (CDP) Los Angeles County
94	1324	1.0	**Banning** (city) Riverside County
94	1324	1.0	**Dixon** (city) Solano County
94	1324	1.0	**Fairview** (CDP) Alameda County
94	1324	1.0	**Farmersville** (city) Tulare County
94	1324	1.0	**Florin** (CDP) Sacramento County
94	1324	1.0	**Foster City** (city) San Mateo County
94	1324	1.0	**Laguna Hills** (city) Orange County
94	1324	1.0	**Lake Elsinore** (city) Riverside County
94	1324	1.0	**Moreno Valley** (city) Riverside County
94	1324	1.0	**Orinda** (city) Contra Costa County
94	1324	1.0	**Ripon** (city) San Joaquin County
94	1324	1.0	**Selma** (city) Fresno County
94	1324	1.0	**Simi Valley** (city) Ventura County
94	1324	1.0	**South Pasadena** (city) Los Angeles County
94	1324	1.0	**Temple City** (city) Los Angeles County
94	1324	1.0	**Union City** (city) Alameda County
110	1503	1.1	**Alpine** (CDP) San Diego County
110	1503	1.1	**Arcadia** (city) Los Angeles County
110	1503	1.1	**Carlsbad** (city) San Diego County
110	1503	1.1	**Casa de Oro-Mount Helix** (CDP) San Diego County
110	1503	1.1	**Cathedral City** (city) Riverside County
110	1503	1.1	**Coachella** (city) Riverside County
110	1503	1.1	**Del Aire** (CDP) Los Angeles County
110	1503	1.1	**Lancaster** (city) Los Angeles County
110	1503	1.1	**Magalia** (CDP) Butte County
110	1503	1.1	**Oakley** (city) Contra Costa County
110	1503	1.1	**Parkway** (CDP) Sacramento County
110	1503	1.1	**Pittsburg** (city) Contra Costa County
110	1503	1.1	**Pleasant Hill** (city) Contra Costa County
110	1503	1.1	**Porterville** (city) Tulare County
110	1503	1.1	**Salinas** (city) Monterey County
110	1503	1.1	**San Bruno** (city) San Mateo County
110	1503	1.1	**San Lorenzo** (CDP) Alameda County
110	1503	1.1	**Sun Village** (CDP) Los Angeles County
110	1503	1.1	**Valinda** (CDP) Los Angeles County
129	1681	1.2	**Atwater** (city) Merced County
129	1681	1.2	**Avocado Heights** (CDP) Los Angeles County
129	1681	1.2	**Bay Point** (CDP) Contra Costa County
129	1681	1.2	**Bloomington** (CDP) San Bernardino County
129	1681	1.2	**Corona** (city) Riverside County
129	1681	1.2	**Cupertino** (city) Santa Clara County
129	1681	1.2	**Folsom** (city) Sacramento County
129	1681	1.2	**Glendora** (city) Los Angeles County
129	1681	1.2	**Livermore** (city) Alameda County
129	1681	1.2	**Perris** (city) Riverside County
129	1681	1.2	**Rancho Santa Margarita** (city) Orange County
129	1681	1.2	**Soledad** (city) Monterey County
129	1681	1.2	**Upland** (city) San Bernardino County
129	1681	1.2	**West Sacramento** (city) Yolo County
129	1681	1.2	**Yucaipa** (city) San Bernardino County
144	1840	1.3	**American Canyon** (city) Napa County
144	1840	1.3	**Antioch** (city) Contra Costa County
144	1840	1.3	**Ashland** (CDP) Alameda County
144	1840	1.3	**Beaumont** (city) Riverside County
144	1840	1.3	**Ceres** (city) Stanislaus County
144	1840	1.3	**Chula Vista** (city) San Diego County
144	1840	1.3	**Clovis** (city) Fresno County

Note: *The state column ranks the top/bottom 150 places from all places in the state with population of 10,000 or more. The national column ranks the top/bottom 150 places from all places in the country with population of 10,000 or more. Places that are unincorporated were not considered in the rankings. Please refer to the User Guide for additional information.*

Commute to Work: Work from Home

Top 150 Places Ranked in *Descending* Order

State Rank	Nat'l Rank	Percent	Place
1	4	24.2	**Malibu** (city) Los Angeles County
2	17	16.0	**Solana Beach** (city) San Diego County
3	19	15.9	**Rancho Mirage** (city) Riverside County
4	26	14.7	**Coronado** (city) San Diego County
5	32	13.9	**Mill Valley** (city) Marin County
6	36	13.4	**Orinda** (city) Contra Costa County
7	37	13.2	**Tamalpais-Homestead Valley** (CDP) Marin County
8	38	13.1	**Coto de Caza** (CDP) Orange County
9	42	12.6	**Laguna Beach** (city) Orange County
10	45	12.4	**Clearlake** (city) Lake County
11	51	12.0	**Beverly Hills** (city) Los Angeles County
11	51	12.0	**El Dorado Hills** (CDP) El Dorado County
11	51	12.0	**West Hollywood** (city) Los Angeles County
14	57	11.9	**Palm Springs** (city) Riverside County
15	61	11.7	**San Marino** (city) Los Angeles County
16	67	11.4	**Alamo** (CDP) Contra Costa County
17	81	11.1	**Encinitas** (city) San Diego County
17	81	11.1	**Palos Verdes Estates** (city) Los Angeles County
19	92	10.9	**Berkeley** (city) Alameda County
19	92	10.9	**Granite Bay** (CDP) Placer County
19	92	10.9	**San Clemente** (city) Orange County
22	115	10.4	**Lafayette** (city) Contra Costa County
23	119	10.3	**North Tustin** (CDP) Orange County
24	130	10.1	**Truckee** (town) Nevada County
25	137	10.0	**Laguna Woods** (city) Orange County
26	139	9.9	**Casa de Oro-Mount Helix** (CDP) San Diego County
26	139	9.9	**North Auburn** (CDP) Placer County
26	139	9.9	**Oak Park** (CDP) Ventura County
29	148	9.7	**Newport Beach** (city) Orange County
29	148	9.7	**Piedmont** (city) Alameda County
31	152	9.6	**Big Bear City** (CDP) San Bernardino County
32	160	9.5	**Calabasas** (city) Los Angeles County
32	160	9.5	**Ladera Ranch** (CDP) Orange County
32	160	9.5	**San Anselmo** (town) Marin County
32	160	9.5	**Santa Monica** (city) Los Angeles County
36	167	9.4	**Carlsbad** (city) San Diego County
36	167	9.4	**Dana Point** (city) Orange County
36	167	9.4	**Manhattan Beach** (city) Los Angeles County
39	177	9.3	**Auburn** (city) Placer County
39	177	9.3	**California City** (city) Kern County
39	177	9.3	**Hermosa Beach** (city) Los Angeles County
42	187	9.2	**Saratoga** (city) Santa Clara County
43	190	9.1	**Laguna Niguel** (city) Orange County
44	200	9.0	**Belmont** (city) San Mateo County
44	200	9.0	**Los Altos** (city) Santa Clara County
46	209	8.9	**Danville** (town) Contra Costa County
47	221	8.7	**Menlo Park** (city) San Mateo County
47	221	8.7	**Mission Viejo** (city) Orange County
47	221	8.7	**Moraga** (town) Contra Costa County
50	234	8.6	**Laguna Hills** (city) Orange County
50	234	8.6	**Los Gatos** (town) Santa Clara County
50	234	8.6	**Los Osos** (CDP) San Luis Obispo County
50	234	8.6	**Palo Alto** (city) Santa Clara County
50	234	8.6	**Signal Hill** (city) Los Angeles County
55	244	8.5	**El Cerrito** (city) Contra Costa County
56	259	8.3	**Grass Valley** (city) Nevada County
56	259	8.3	**Sonoma** (city) Sonoma County
58	272	8.2	**Aliso Viejo** (city) Orange County
58	272	8.2	**Rancho Palos Verdes** (city) Los Angeles County
58	272	8.2	**Stevenson Ranch** (CDP) Los Angeles County
61	288	8.1	**Atascadero** (city) San Luis Obispo County
61	288	8.1	**San Rafael** (city) Marin County
63	304	8.0	**Yucca Valley** (town) San Bernardino County
64	313	7.9	**Lincoln** (city) Placer County
65	328	7.8	**Chowchilla** (city) Madera County
65	328	7.8	**Claremont** (city) Los Angeles County
65	328	7.8	**Clayton** (city) Contra Costa County
65	328	7.8	**Larkspur** (city) Marin County
65	328	7.8	**San Ramon** (city) Contra Costa County
65	328	7.8	**Thousand Oaks** (city) Ventura County
65	328	7.8	**View Park-Windsor Hills** (CDP) Los Angeles County
72	351	7.7	**Camp Pendleton South** (CDP) San Diego County
72	351	7.7	**Palm Desert** (city) Riverside County
74	366	7.6	**Brentwood** (city) Contra Costa County
74	366	7.6	**Canyon Lake** (city) Riverside County
74	366	7.6	**Hillsborough** (town) San Mateo County
74	366	7.6	**Novato** (city) Marin County
74	366	7.6	**Sierra Madre** (city) Los Angeles County
79	387	7.5	**Fair Oaks** (CDP) Sacramento County
79	387	7.5	**Walnut Creek** (city) Contra Costa County
81	404	7.4	**Stanford** (CDP) Santa Clara County
82	426	7.3	**Culver City** (city) Los Angeles County
82	426	7.3	**Healdsburg** (city) Sonoma County
82	426	7.3	**Pleasant Hill** (city) Contra Costa County
82	426	7.3	**Redondo Beach** (city) Los Angeles County
86	451	7.2	**Discovery Bay** (CDP) Contra Costa County
86	451	7.2	**La Cañada Flintridge** (city) Los Angeles County
86	451	7.2	**Magalia** (CDP) Butte County
86	451	7.2	**Norco** (city) Riverside County
86	451	7.2	**Paradise** (town) Butte County
91	475	7.1	**La Quinta** (city) Riverside County
92	497	7.0	**Half Moon Bay** (city) San Mateo County
92	497	7.0	**Morro Bay** (city) San Luis Obispo County
92	497	7.0	**North Highlands** (CDP) Sacramento County
92	497	7.0	**Placerville** (city) El Dorado County
92	497	7.0	**San Diego Country Estates** (CDP) San Diego County
92	497	7.0	**San Francisco** (city) San Francisco County
98	515	6.9	**Alpine** (CDP) San Diego County
98	515	6.9	**Irvine** (city) Orange County
98	515	6.9	**Morgan Hill** (city) Santa Clara County
98	515	6.9	**Ramona** (CDP) San Diego County
98	515	6.9	**Temecula** (city) Riverside County
98	515	6.9	**Woodcrest** (CDP) Riverside County
104	548	6.8	**Agoura Hills** (city) Los Angeles County
104	548	6.8	**Fortuna** (city) Humboldt County
104	548	6.8	**French Valley** (CDP) Riverside County
104	548	6.8	**Rancho Santa Margarita** (city) Orange County
108	572	6.7	**Diamond Bar** (city) Los Angeles County
108	572	6.7	**Monterey** (city) Monterey County
108	572	6.7	**Oakland** (city) Alameda County
108	572	6.7	**Pacifica** (city) San Mateo County
108	572	6.7	**Pleasanton** (city) Alameda County
108	572	6.7	**San Diego** (city) San Diego County
108	572	6.7	**San Juan Capistrano** (city) Orange County
108	572	6.7	**Scotts Valley** (city) Santa Cruz County
116	600	6.6	**Alameda** (city) Alameda County
116	600	6.6	**Cameron Park** (CDP) El Dorado County
116	600	6.6	**Twentynine Palms** (city) San Bernardino County
119	623	6.5	**Folsom** (city) Sacramento County
119	623	6.5	**Foster City** (city) San Mateo County
119	623	6.5	**Pacific Grove** (city) Monterey County
119	623	6.5	**Rocklin** (city) Placer County
119	623	6.5	**San Carlos** (city) San Mateo County
119	623	6.5	**Seaside** (city) Monterey County
125	649	6.4	**Albany** (city) Alameda County
125	649	6.4	**Crestline** (CDP) San Bernardino County
127	676	6.3	**Emeryville** (city) Alameda County
127	676	6.3	**Rio Linda** (CDP) Sacramento County
129	701	6.2	**Desert Hot Springs** (city) Riverside County
129	701	6.2	**Grover Beach** (city) San Luis Obispo County
129	701	6.2	**La Mesa** (city) San Diego County
129	701	6.2	**Menifee** (city) Riverside County
129	701	6.2	**Murrieta** (city) Riverside County
129	701	6.2	**National City** (city) San Diego County
129	701	6.2	**Roseville** (city) Placer County
136	739	6.1	**Antelope** (CDP) Sacramento County
136	739	6.1	**Benicia** (city) Solano County
136	739	6.1	**Cathedral City** (city) Riverside County
136	739	6.1	**El Segundo** (city) Los Angeles County
136	739	6.1	**Moorpark** (city) Ventura County
136	739	6.1	**Santa Cruz** (city) Santa Cruz County
142	769	6.0	**Lomita** (city) Los Angeles County
142	769	6.0	**Martinez** (city) Contra Costa County
142	769	6.0	**Petaluma** (city) Sonoma County
142	769	6.0	**San Dimas** (city) Los Angeles County
142	769	6.0	**Wildomar** (city) Riverside County
147	809	5.9	**Arcata** (city) Humboldt County
147	809	5.9	**Cupertino** (city) Santa Clara County
147	809	5.9	**Dublin** (city) Alameda County
147	809	5.9	**Fallbrook** (CDP) San Diego County

Note: *The state column ranks the top/bottom 150 places from all places in the state with population of 10,000 or more. The national column ranks the top/bottom 150 places from all places in the country with population of 10,000 or more. Places that are unincorporated were not considered in the rankings. Please refer to the User Guide for additional information.*

Commute to Work: Work from Home

Top 150 Places Ranked in *Ascending* Order

State Rank	Nat'l Rank	Percent	Place
1	5	0.2	**Mendota** (city) Fresno County
2	29	0.6	**McFarland** (city) Kern County
3	40	0.7	**Wasco** (city) Kern County
4	139	1.1	**Santa Fe Springs** (city) Los Angeles County
5	180	1.2	**East Rancho Dominguez** (CDP) Los Angeles County
5	180	1.2	**Gardena** (city) Los Angeles County
7	225	1.3	**King City** (city) Monterey County
7	225	1.3	**Lamont** (CDP) Kern County
7	225	1.3	**Lemoore** (city) Kings County
7	225	1.3	**Los Banos** (city) Merced County
11	272	1.4	**Artesia** (city) Los Angeles County
11	272	1.4	**Hawaiian Gardens** (city) Los Angeles County
11	272	1.4	**Santa Ana** (city) Orange County
14	327	1.5	**Avenal** (city) Kings County
14	327	1.5	**Delano** (city) Kern County
14	327	1.5	**Lynwood** (city) Los Angeles County
14	327	1.5	**Tehachapi** (city) Kern County
18	398	1.6	**Greenfield** (city) Monterey County
18	398	1.6	**Salida** (CDP) Stanislaus County
18	398	1.6	**San Fernando** (city) Los Angeles County
21	539	1.8	**Barstow** (city) San Bernardino County
21	539	1.8	**Dinuba** (city) Tulare County
21	539	1.8	**Hercules** (city) Contra Costa County
21	539	1.8	**Montclair** (city) San Bernardino County
21	539	1.8	**Santa Paula** (city) Ventura County
21	539	1.8	**Stanton** (city) Orange County
27	634	1.9	**Arvin** (city) Kern County
27	634	1.9	**Daly City** (city) San Mateo County
27	634	1.9	**Garden Grove** (city) Orange County
27	634	1.9	**Lindsay** (city) Tulare County
27	634	1.9	**Norwalk** (city) Los Angeles County
27	634	1.9	**Perris** (city) Riverside County
27	634	1.9	**Riverbank** (city) Stanislaus County
27	634	1.9	**Rosamond** (CDP) Kern County
35	710	2.0	**Colton** (city) San Bernardino County
35	710	2.0	**Commerce** (city) Los Angeles County
35	710	2.0	**Lennox** (CDP) Los Angeles County
38	818	2.1	**Alum Rock** (CDP) Santa Clara County
38	818	2.1	**Azusa** (city) Los Angeles County
38	818	2.1	**Lake Los Angeles** (CDP) Los Angeles County
38	818	2.1	**San Pablo** (city) Contra Costa County
38	818	2.1	**Santa Maria** (city) Santa Barbara County
38	818	2.1	**Tulare** (city) Tulare County
44	905	2.2	**Florence-Graham** (CDP) Los Angeles County
44	905	2.2	**Hanford** (city) Kings County
44	905	2.2	**Ontario** (city) San Bernardino County
44	905	2.2	**Porterville** (city) Tulare County
44	905	2.2	**Ridgecrest** (city) Kern County
49	1012	2.3	**East Los Angeles** (CDP) Los Angeles County
49	1012	2.3	**La Habra** (city) Orange County
49	1012	2.3	**Lompoc** (city) Santa Barbara County
49	1012	2.3	**South Gate** (city) Los Angeles County
49	1012	2.3	**West Whittier-Los Nietos** (CDP) Los Angeles County
54	1104	2.4	**Corcoran** (city) Kings County
54	1104	2.4	**Downey** (city) Los Angeles County
54	1104	2.4	**Hayward** (city) Alameda County
54	1104	2.4	**Home Gardens** (CDP) Riverside County
54	1104	2.4	**Imperial** (city) Imperial County
54	1104	2.4	**Lancaster** (city) Los Angeles County
54	1104	2.4	**Lathrop** (city) San Joaquin County
54	1104	2.4	**San Lorenzo** (CDP) Alameda County
54	1104	2.4	**Union City** (city) Alameda County
63	1206	2.5	**Covina** (city) Los Angeles County
63	1206	2.5	**Cudahy** (city) Los Angeles County
63	1206	2.5	**Exeter** (city) Tulare County
63	1206	2.5	**Huntington Park** (city) Los Angeles County
63	1206	2.5	**Kerman** (city) Fresno County
63	1206	2.5	**Lawndale** (city) Los Angeles County
63	1206	2.5	**Moreno Valley** (city) Riverside County
63	1206	2.5	**Oildale** (CDP) Kern County
63	1206	2.5	**Reedley** (city) Fresno County
63	1206	2.5	**South San Francisco** (city) San Mateo County
73	1321	2.6	**Bellflower** (city) Los Angeles County
73	1321	2.6	**Citrus** (CDP) Los Angeles County
73	1321	2.6	**Grand Terrace** (city) San Bernardino County
73	1321	2.6	**Oxnard** (city) Ventura County
73	1321	2.6	**Rosemont** (CDP) Sacramento County
73	1321	2.6	**Soledad** (city) Monterey County
73	1321	2.6	**Vacaville** (city) Solano County
80	1426	2.7	**Galt** (city) Sacramento County
80	1426	2.7	**Hawthorne** (city) Los Angeles County
80	1426	2.7	**Kingsburg** (city) Fresno County
80	1426	2.7	**La Palma** (city) Orange County
80	1426	2.7	**Manteca** (city) San Joaquin County
80	1426	2.7	**Newark** (city) Alameda County
80	1426	2.7	**Paramount** (city) Los Angeles County
80	1426	2.7	**Prunedale** (CDP) Monterey County
88	1547	2.8	**Bakersfield** (city) Kern County
88	1547	2.8	**Bell Gardens** (city) Los Angeles County
88	1547	2.8	**Brawley** (city) Imperial County
88	1547	2.8	**East Palo Alto** (city) San Mateo County
88	1547	2.8	**Fillmore** (city) Ventura County
88	1547	2.8	**Parlier** (city) Fresno County
88	1547	2.8	**Watsonville** (city) Santa Cruz County
88	1547	2.8	**Westminster** (city) Orange County
88	1547	2.8	**Whittier** (city) Los Angeles County
88	1547	2.8	**Willowbrook** (CDP) Los Angeles County
88	1547	2.8	**Winton** (CDP) Merced County
88	1547	2.8	**Woodland** (city) Yolo County
100	1631	2.9	**Ashland** (CDP) Alameda County
100	1631	2.9	**Chino** (city) San Bernardino County
100	1631	2.9	**Cypress** (city) Orange County
100	1631	2.9	**Del Aire** (CDP) Los Angeles County
100	1631	2.9	**Duarte** (city) Los Angeles County
100	1631	2.9	**Parkway** (CDP) Sacramento County
100	1631	2.9	**San Jacinto** (city) Riverside County
100	1631	2.9	**Shafter** (city) Kern County
100	1631	2.9	**South Whittier** (CDP) Los Angeles County
100	1631	2.9	**Yuba City** (city) Sutter County
110	1744	3.0	**Buena Park** (city) Orange County
110	1744	3.0	**Coachella** (city) Riverside County
110	1744	3.0	**Coalinga** (city) Fresno County
110	1744	3.0	**Compton** (city) Los Angeles County
110	1744	3.0	**Escondido** (city) San Diego County
110	1744	3.0	**Hollister** (city) San Benito County
110	1744	3.0	**Ripon** (city) San Joaquin County
110	1744	3.0	**San Leandro** (city) Alameda County
110	1744	3.0	**Upland** (city) San Bernardino County
119	1836	3.1	**Anaheim** (city) Orange County
119	1836	3.1	**Castaic** (CDP) Los Angeles County
119	1836	3.1	**Clovis** (city) Fresno County
119	1836	3.1	**Delhi** (CDP) Merced County
119	1836	3.1	**La Mirada** (city) Los Angeles County
119	1836	3.1	**La Puente** (city) Los Angeles County
119	1836	3.1	**Lakewood** (city) Los Angeles County
119	1836	3.1	**Pittsburg** (city) Contra Costa County
119	1836	3.1	**Rialto** (city) San Bernardino County
119	1836	3.1	**Richmond** (city) Contra Costa County
119	1836	3.1	**Suisun City** (city) Solano County
119	1836	3.1	**Valinda** (CDP) Los Angeles County
131	1928	3.2	**Bay Point** (CDP) Contra Costa County
131	1928	3.2	**Dixon** (city) Solano County
131	1928	3.2	**Fairview** (CDP) Alameda County
131	1928	3.2	**Fontana** (city) San Bernardino County
131	1928	3.2	**La Riviera** (CDP) Sacramento County
131	1928	3.2	**Maywood** (city) Los Angeles County
131	1928	3.2	**San Bruno** (city) San Mateo County
138	2036	3.3	**Bell** (city) Los Angeles County
138	2036	3.3	**Diamond Springs** (CDP) El Dorado County
138	2036	3.3	**Gilroy** (city) Santa Clara County
138	2036	3.3	**Imperial Beach** (city) San Diego County
138	2036	3.3	**South San Jose Hills** (CDP) Los Angeles County
143	2135	3.4	**American Canyon** (city) Napa County
143	2135	3.4	**Marina** (city) Monterey County
143	2135	3.4	**Patterson** (city) Stanislaus County
143	2135	3.4	**Quartz Hill** (CDP) Los Angeles County
143	2135	3.4	**West Carson** (CDP) Los Angeles County
148	2224	3.5	**Ceres** (city) Stanislaus County
148	2224	3.5	**Cherryland** (CDP) Alameda County
148	2224	3.5	**Citrus Heights** (city) Sacramento County

Note: *The state column ranks the top/bottom 150 places from all places in the state with population of 10,000 or more. The national column ranks the top/bottom 150 places from all places in the country with population of 10,000 or more. Places that are unincorporated were not considered in the rankings. Please refer to the User Guide for additional information.*

Median Travel Time to Work

Top 150 Places Ranked in *Descending* Order

State Rank	Nat'l Rank	Minutes	Place
1	5	47.0	**Sun Village** (CDP) Los Angeles County
2	8	46.0	**Discovery Bay** (CDP) Contra Costa County
3	10	45.8	**Lake Los Angeles** (CDP) Los Angeles County
4	13	43.4	**Canyon Lake** (city) Riverside County
4	13	43.4	**Phelan** (CDP) San Bernardino County
6	16	43.2	**Lake Elsinore** (city) Riverside County
7	24	42.4	**French Valley** (CDP) Riverside County
8	26	42.1	**Los Banos** (city) Merced County
9	35	41.4	**Eastvale** (city) Riverside County
10	40	41.0	**Patterson** (city) Stanislaus County
11	45	40.9	**Brentwood** (city) Contra Costa County
12	50	40.8	**Tracy** (city) San Joaquin County
13	59	40.5	**Lakeland Village** (CDP) Riverside County
13	59	40.5	**Palmdale** (city) Los Angeles County
15	65	40.2	**Oakley** (city) Contra Costa County
16	70	40.0	**Antioch** (city) Contra Costa County
17	76	39.4	**San Diego Country Estates** (CDP) San Diego County
18	96	38.6	**Hercules** (city) Contra Costa County
19	106	38.2	**Lathrop** (city) San Joaquin County
20	109	38.0	**Menifee** (city) Riverside County
21	139	37.1	**Chino Hills** (city) San Bernardino County
21	139	37.1	**Hesperia** (city) San Bernardino County
23	142	37.0	**Mead Valley** (CDP) Riverside County
23	142	37.0	**Perris** (city) Riverside County
25	150	36.9	**Adelanto** (city) San Bernardino County
26	156	36.7	**Stevenson Ranch** (CDP) Los Angeles County
27	175	36.4	**Woodcrest** (CDP) Riverside County
28	190	36.1	**Bay Point** (CDP) Contra Costa County
29	203	35.9	**San Jacinto** (city) Riverside County
30	209	35.8	**El Sobrante** (CDP) Riverside County
31	227	35.6	**Home Gardens** (CDP) Riverside County
31	227	35.6	**Victorville** (city) San Bernardino County
33	236	35.5	**Norco** (city) Riverside County
33	236	35.5	**Pittsburg** (city) Contra Costa County
35	254	35.2	**Corona** (city) Riverside County
35	254	35.2	**Hacienda Heights** (CDP) Los Angeles County
37	262	35.1	**Walnut** (city) Los Angeles County
37	262	35.1	**Wildomar** (city) Riverside County
39	271	35.0	**Palos Verdes Estates** (city) Los Angeles County
40	278	34.9	**Clayton** (city) Contra Costa County
41	290	34.7	**Murrieta** (city) Riverside County
41	290	34.7	**Pinole** (city) Contra Costa County
43	299	34.6	**Westmont** (CDP) Los Angeles County
44	315	34.4	**Crestline** (CDP) San Bernardino County
45	333	34.2	**Moreno Valley** (city) Riverside County
46	358	33.9	**Diamond Bar** (city) Los Angeles County
47	376	33.7	**Chino** (city) San Bernardino County
47	376	33.7	**Temecula** (city) Riverside County
49	387	33.6	**Montebello** (city) Los Angeles County
50	415	33.3	**Moraga** (town) Contra Costa County
50	415	33.3	**Rowland Heights** (CDP) Los Angeles County
50	415	33.3	**Valle Vista** (CDP) Riverside County
53	427	33.2	**Fairview** (CDP) Alameda County
53	427	33.2	**Newman** (city) Stanislaus County
53	427	33.2	**West Covina** (city) Los Angeles County
56	439	33.1	**Muscoy** (CDP) San Bernardino County
56	439	33.1	**South San Jose Hills** (CDP) Los Angeles County
58	449	33.0	**Vallejo** (city) Solano County
59	459	32.9	**Desert Hot Springs** (city) Riverside County
60	475	32.8	**California City** (city) Kern County
61	489	32.7	**East Hemet** (CDP) Riverside County
61	489	32.7	**San Ramon** (city) Contra Costa County
63	500	32.6	**Malibu** (city) Los Angeles County
63	500	32.6	**San Dimas** (city) Los Angeles County
65	521	32.4	**Cudahy** (city) Los Angeles County
65	521	32.4	**San Anselmo** (town) Marin County
65	521	32.4	**Valinda** (CDP) Los Angeles County
68	542	32.3	**Rialto** (city) San Bernardino County
68	542	32.3	**West Puente Valley** (CDP) Los Angeles County
70	565	32.2	**El Cerrito** (city) Contra Costa County
70	565	32.2	**Rancho Palos Verdes** (city) Los Angeles County
70	565	32.2	**Santa Clarita** (city) Los Angeles County
73	580	32.1	**Avenal** (city) Kings County
73	580	32.1	**Fontana** (city) San Bernardino County
75	602	32.0	**Beaumont** (city) Riverside County
75	602	32.0	**South El Monte** (city) Los Angeles County
77	623	31.8	**Coto de Caza** (CDP) Orange County
77	623	31.8	**East San Gabriel** (CDP) Los Angeles County
79	635	31.7	**American Canyon** (city) Napa County
79	635	31.7	**Manteca** (city) San Joaquin County
81	650	31.6	**Suisun City** (city) Solano County
82	670	31.5	**Glendora** (city) Los Angeles County
83	686	31.4	**Baldwin Park** (city) Los Angeles County
83	686	31.4	**Calabasas** (city) Los Angeles County
83	686	31.4	**Covina** (city) Los Angeles County
83	686	31.4	**Richmond** (city) Contra Costa County
87	704	31.3	**Dublin** (city) Alameda County
87	704	31.3	**La Puente** (city) Los Angeles County
89	721	31.2	**Alpine** (CDP) San Diego County
89	721	31.2	**El Sobrante** (CDP) Contra Costa County
91	755	31.0	**Florence-Graham** (CDP) Los Angeles County
91	755	31.0	**Morgan Hill** (city) Santa Clara County
93	777	30.9	**Avocado Heights** (CDP) Los Angeles County
93	777	30.9	**Fillmore** (city) Ventura County
93	777	30.9	**Hemet** (city) Riverside County
93	777	30.9	**Montclair** (city) San Bernardino County
97	795	30.8	**Castaic** (CDP) Los Angeles County
97	795	30.8	**Cerritos** (city) Los Angeles County
99	812	30.7	**Bloomington** (CDP) San Bernardino County
99	812	30.7	**Pleasant Hill** (city) Contra Costa County
99	812	30.7	**Walnut Creek** (city) Contra Costa County
99	812	30.7	**Yorba Linda** (city) Orange County
103	834	30.6	**Lancaster** (city) Los Angeles County
104	847	30.5	**Salida** (CDP) Stanislaus County
104	847	30.5	**San Francisco** (city) San Francisco County
106	875	30.4	**El Dorado Hills** (CDP) El Dorado County
106	875	30.4	**Rancho Cucamonga** (city) San Bernardino County
106	875	30.4	**San Pablo** (city) Contra Costa County
109	892	30.3	**Alamo** (CDP) Contra Costa County
109	892	30.3	**Danville** (town) Contra Costa County
109	892	30.3	**El Monte** (city) Los Angeles County
109	892	30.3	**Hollister** (city) San Benito County
109	892	30.3	**Ramona** (CDP) San Diego County
114	921	30.2	**Elk Grove** (city) Sacramento County
114	921	30.2	**Sierra Madre** (city) Los Angeles County
116	934	30.1	**Castro Valley** (CDP) Alameda County
116	934	30.1	**Quartz Hill** (CDP) Los Angeles County
116	934	30.1	**Union City** (city) Alameda County
116	934	30.1	**Walnut Park** (CDP) Los Angeles County
120	960	30.0	**Concord** (city) Contra Costa County
120	960	30.0	**Rosamond** (CDP) Kern County
120	960	30.0	**West Whittier-Los Nietos** (CDP) Los Angeles County
123	974	29.9	**Albany** (city) Alameda County
123	974	29.9	**Hermosa Beach** (city) Los Angeles County
123	974	29.9	**Huntington Park** (city) Los Angeles County
123	974	29.9	**Rossmoor** (CDP) Orange County
127	1000	29.8	**Benicia** (city) Solano County
127	1000	29.8	**La Palma** (city) Orange County
127	1000	29.8	**Upland** (city) San Bernardino County
127	1000	29.8	**Whittier** (city) Los Angeles County
131	1018	29.7	**Antelope** (CDP) Sacramento County
131	1018	29.7	**Brea** (city) Orange County
131	1018	29.7	**Fremont** (city) Alameda County
131	1018	29.7	**Ladera Ranch** (CDP) Orange County
135	1044	29.6	**Gilroy** (city) Santa Clara County
135	1044	29.6	**Pleasanton** (city) Alameda County
135	1044	29.6	**Temple City** (city) Los Angeles County
138	1068	29.5	**Citrus** (CDP) Los Angeles County
138	1068	29.5	**San Clemente** (city) Orange County
140	1101	29.3	**Alhambra** (city) Los Angeles County
140	1101	29.3	**Arcadia** (city) Los Angeles County
140	1101	29.3	**Cameron Park** (CDP) El Dorado County
140	1101	29.3	**La Mirada** (city) Los Angeles County
140	1101	29.3	**La Verne** (city) Los Angeles County
140	1101	29.3	**Mendota** (city) Fresno County
140	1101	29.3	**Petaluma** (city) Sonoma County
147	1131	29.2	**Agoura Hills** (city) Los Angeles County
147	1131	29.2	**Apple Valley** (town) San Bernardino County
147	1131	29.2	**Ashland** (CDP) Alameda County
147	1131	29.2	**Buena Park** (city) Orange County

Note: *The state column ranks the top/bottom 150 places from all places in the state with population of 10,000 or more. The national column ranks the top/bottom 150 places from all places in the country with population of 10,000 or more. Places that are unincorporated were not considered in the rankings. Please refer to the User Guide for additional information.*

Median Travel Time to Work

Top 150 Places Ranked in *Ascending* Order

State Rank	Nat'l Rank	Minutes	Place
1	36	12.5	**Stanford** (CDP) Santa Clara County
2	63	13.3	**Eureka** (city) Humboldt County
2	63	13.3	**Grass Valley** (city) Nevada County
4	86	13.8	**Isla Vista** (CDP) Santa Barbara County
5	93	13.9	**Ukiah** (city) Mendocino County
6	131	14.5	**South Lake Tahoe** (city) El Dorado County
7	162	14.8	**Blythe** (city) Riverside County
7	162	14.8	**San Luis Obispo** (city) San Luis Obispo County
9	174	14.9	**Arcata** (city) Humboldt County
9	174	14.9	**Ridgecrest** (city) Kern County
9	174	14.9	**Twentynine Palms** (city) San Bernardino County
12	254	15.6	**Susanville** (city) Lassen County
13	291	15.9	**Monterey** (city) Monterey County
14	336	16.2	**Goleta** (city) Santa Barbara County
15	397	16.7	**Santa Barbara** (city) Santa Barbara County
16	419	16.8	**Corcoran** (city) Kings County
17	441	16.9	**Redding** (city) Shasta County
18	484	17.2	**Oroville** (city) Butte County
19	507	17.3	**Chico** (city) Butte County
20	716	18.5	**Pacific Grove** (city) Monterey County
21	735	18.6	**McKinleyville** (CDP) Humboldt County
22	781	18.8	**Camp Pendleton South** (CDP) San Diego County
23	798	18.9	**Seaside** (city) Monterey County
24	811	19.0	**El Centro** (city) Imperial County
25	833	19.1	**Arroyo Grande** (city) San Luis Obispo County
25	833	19.1	**Brawley** (city) Imperial County
25	833	19.1	**Coalinga** (city) Fresno County
28	862	19.2	**Imperial** (city) Imperial County
28	862	19.2	**Loma Linda** (city) San Bernardino County
30	937	19.5	**Grover Beach** (city) San Luis Obispo County
30	937	19.5	**Shasta Lake** (city) Shasta County
32	973	19.6	**Tulare** (city) Tulare County
33	996	19.7	**Morro Bay** (city) San Luis Obispo County
34	1019	19.8	**Coronado** (city) San Diego County
34	1019	19.8	**Palm Desert** (city) Riverside County
36	1045	19.9	**Visalia** (city) Tulare County
37	1116	20.2	**Los Osos** (CDP) San Luis Obispo County
38	1151	20.3	**Hanford** (city) Kings County
39	1179	20.4	**Cathedral City** (city) Riverside County
39	1179	20.4	**Davis** (city) Yolo County
41	1204	20.5	**Clovis** (city) Fresno County
41	1204	20.5	**Tehachapi** (city) Kern County
43	1223	20.6	**Fortuna** (city) Humboldt County
43	1223	20.6	**Healdsburg** (city) Sonoma County
45	1247	20.7	**Lindsay** (city) Tulare County
45	1247	20.7	**Paradise** (town) Butte County
47	1298	20.9	**Woodland** (city) Yolo County
48	1348	21.1	**Clearlake** (city) Lake County
48	1348	21.1	**Livingston** (city) Merced County
48	1348	21.1	**Mountain View** (city) Santa Clara County
48	1348	21.1	**Porterville** (city) Tulare County
48	1348	21.1	**Santa Maria** (city) Santa Barbara County
53	1385	21.2	**Exeter** (city) Tulare County
54	1435	21.4	**Delano** (city) Kern County
54	1435	21.4	**Red Bluff** (city) Tehama County
56	1457	21.5	**Coachella** (city) Riverside County
56	1457	21.5	**Napa** (city) Napa County
56	1457	21.5	**Truckee** (town) Nevada County
59	1491	21.6	**Palm Springs** (city) Riverside County
59	1491	21.6	**Solana Beach** (city) San Diego County
61	1515	21.7	**Fresno** (city) Fresno County
62	1543	21.8	**Santa Clara** (city) Santa Clara County
63	1562	21.9	**Costa Mesa** (city) Orange County
63	1562	21.9	**Orcutt** (CDP) Santa Barbara County
63	1562	21.9	**Watsonville** (city) Santa Cruz County
66	1593	22.0	**El Segundo** (city) Los Angeles County
66	1593	22.0	**Santa Cruz** (city) Santa Cruz County
68	1619	22.1	**Dixon** (city) Solano County
68	1619	22.1	**Los Altos** (city) Santa Clara County
68	1619	22.1	**Menlo Park** (city) San Mateo County
68	1619	22.1	**Palo Alto** (city) Santa Clara County
72	1652	22.2	**Auburn** (city) Placer County
72	1652	22.2	**Carpinteria** (city) Santa Barbara County
74	1680	22.3	**Atwater** (city) Merced County
74	1680	22.3	**Camarillo** (city) Ventura County
74	1680	22.3	**King City** (city) Monterey County
74	1680	22.3	**Rancho Mirage** (city) Riverside County
74	1680	22.3	**Reedley** (city) Fresno County
79	1714	22.4	**Atascadero** (city) San Luis Obispo County
79	1714	22.4	**El Paso de Robles (Paso Robles)** (city) San Luis Obispo County
79	1714	22.4	**Kingsburg** (city) Fresno County
79	1714	22.4	**Lodi** (city) San Joaquin County
79	1714	22.4	**Merced** (city) Merced County
79	1714	22.4	**Shafter** (city) Kern County
85	1746	22.5	**Del Aire** (CDP) Los Angeles County
85	1746	22.5	**Oildale** (CDP) Kern County
85	1746	22.5	**San Buenaventura (Ventura)** (city) Ventura County
85	1746	22.5	**San Diego** (city) San Diego County
85	1746	22.5	**Turlock** (city) Stanislaus County
90	1786	22.6	**Live Oak** (CDP) Santa Cruz County
91	1812	22.7	**Arden-Arcade** (CDP) Sacramento County
91	1812	22.7	**Redlands** (city) San Bernardino County
93	1839	22.8	**Madera** (city) Madera County
93	1839	22.8	**Santa Rosa** (city) Sonoma County
93	1839	22.8	**West Sacramento** (city) Yolo County
96	1861	22.9	**Bakersfield** (city) Kern County
96	1861	22.9	**Indio** (city) Riverside County
96	1861	22.9	**Sanger** (city) Fresno County
99	1897	23.0	**Rosedale** (CDP) Kern County
99	1897	23.0	**Sunnyvale** (city) Santa Clara County
101	1916	23.1	**Oxnard** (city) Ventura County
102	1932	23.2	**Redwood City** (city) San Mateo County
102	1932	23.2	**Salinas** (city) Monterey County
104	1960	23.3	**Chowchilla** (city) Madera County
104	1960	23.3	**La Mesa** (city) San Diego County
104	1960	23.3	**Marina** (city) Monterey County
104	1960	23.3	**Milpitas** (city) Santa Clara County
104	1960	23.3	**Newport Beach** (city) Orange County
104	1960	23.3	**North Tustin** (CDP) Orange County
110	1993	23.4	**Farmersville** (city) Tulare County
110	1993	23.4	**North Fair Oaks** (CDP) San Mateo County
112	2016	23.5	**Windsor** (town) Sonoma County
113	2043	23.6	**Irvine** (city) Orange County
113	2043	23.6	**McFarland** (city) Kern County
115	2080	23.7	**North Auburn** (CDP) Placer County
115	2080	23.7	**Parlier** (city) Fresno County
117	2114	23.8	**Campbell** (city) Santa Clara County
117	2114	23.8	**Kerman** (city) Fresno County
117	2114	23.8	**La Quinta** (city) Riverside County
117	2114	23.8	**Lamont** (CDP) Kern County
117	2114	23.8	**South San Francisco** (city) San Mateo County
122	2147	23.9	**Banning** (city) Riverside County
122	2147	23.9	**Bonita** (CDP) San Diego County
122	2147	23.9	**East Palo Alto** (city) San Mateo County
122	2147	23.9	**Lemoore** (city) Kings County
122	2147	23.9	**Santee** (city) San Diego County
122	2147	23.9	**Vista** (city) San Diego County
128	2174	24.0	**Dinuba** (city) Tulare County
128	2174	24.0	**El Cajon** (city) San Diego County
128	2174	24.0	**Nipomo** (CDP) San Luis Obispo County
128	2174	24.0	**Port Hueneme** (city) Ventura County
128	2174	24.0	**Poway** (city) San Diego County
128	2174	24.0	**Sacramento** (city) Sacramento County
128	2174	24.0	**Tustin** (city) Orange County
135	2212	24.1	**Delhi** (CDP) Merced County
135	2212	24.1	**Lawndale** (city) Los Angeles County
135	2212	24.1	**San Juan Capistrano** (city) Orange County
138	2236	24.2	**Beverly Hills** (city) Los Angeles County
139	2271	24.3	**Barstow** (city) San Bernardino County
139	2271	24.3	**Casa de Oro-Mount Helix** (CDP) San Diego County
139	2271	24.3	**Grand Terrace** (city) San Bernardino County
139	2271	24.3	**Thousand Oaks** (city) Ventura County
143	2307	24.4	**Folsom** (city) Sacramento County
143	2307	24.4	**Rancho Cordova** (city) Sacramento County
145	2344	24.5	**Artesia** (city) Los Angeles County
145	2344	24.5	**Calexico** (city) Imperial County
145	2344	24.5	**Encinitas** (city) San Diego County
145	2344	24.5	**Garden Acres** (CDP) San Joaquin County
145	2344	24.5	**Highland** (city) San Bernardino County
145	2344	24.5	**Lennox** (CDP) Los Angeles County

Note: *The state column ranks the top/bottom 150 places from all places in the state with population of 10,000 or more. The national column ranks the top/bottom 150 places from all places in the country with population of 10,000 or more. Places that are unincorporated were not considered in the rankings. Please refer to the User Guide for additional information.*

Violent Crime Rate per 10,000 Population

Top 150 Places Ranked in *Descending* Order

State Rank	Nat'l Rank	Rate	Place
1	12	197.7	**Oakland** (city) Alameda County
2	66	126.9	**Compton** (city) Los Angeles County
3	68	126.7	**Emeryville** (city) Alameda County
4	85	120.8	**Stockton** (city) San Joaquin County
5	86	119.3	**East Palo Alto** (city) San Mateo County
6	119	103.6	**Richmond** (city) Contra Costa County
7	122	103.0	**Red Bluff** (city) Tehama County
8	138	99.2	**Desert Hot Springs** (city) Riverside County
9	139	98.9	**Barstow** (city) San Bernardino County
10	173	91.3	**Dinuba** (city) Tulare County
11	175	90.9	**San Bernardino** (city) San Bernardino County
12	176	90.2	**Madera** (city) Madera County
13	177	89.9	**Grass Valley** (city) Nevada County
14	180	88.9	**Antioch** (city) Contra Costa County
15	195	86.1	**Vallejo** (city) Solano County
16	200	84.7	**San Francisco** (city) San Francisco County
17	209	83.6	**Clearlake** (city) Lake County
18	210	83.4	**Modesto** (city) Stanislaus County
19	234	79.9	**Coalinga** (city) Fresno County
20	235	79.8	**Selma** (city) Fresno County
21	274	75.0	**Arvin** (city) Kern County
22	291	73.1	**Ukiah** (city) Mendocino County
23	304	71.5	**Marysville** (city) Yuba County
24	305	71.4	**Eureka** (city) Humboldt County
25	320	70.0	**Tulare** (city) Tulare County
26	339	68.4	**Merced** (city) Merced County
27	353	67.3	**Hawthorne** (city) Los Angeles County
28	356	66.9	**San Pablo** (city) Contra Costa County
29	364	66.2	**Inglewood** (city) Los Angeles County
30	367	65.6	**Sacramento** (city) Sacramento County
31	371	65.2	**California City** (city) Kern County
32	373	65.1	**Santa Cruz** (city) Santa Cruz County
33	377	64.3	**Redding** (city) Shasta County
33	377	64.3	**Salinas** (city) Monterey County
35	384	63.9	**Commerce** (city) Los Angeles County
36	389	63.5	**Adelanto** (city) San Bernardino County
37	399	63.0	**Atwater** (city) Merced County
38	402	62.8	**Reedley** (city) Fresno County
39	414	61.9	**West Hollywood** (city) Los Angeles County
40	424	61.3	**Lynwood** (city) Los Angeles County
40	424	61.3	**Parlier** (city) Fresno County
42	430	61.0	**Huntington Park** (city) Los Angeles County
43	433	60.9	**Placerville** (city) El Dorado County
44	455	59.2	**Delano** (city) Kern County
44	455	59.2	**Sanger** (city) Fresno County
46	470	58.3	**Indio** (city) Riverside County
47	474	57.9	**Bell** (city) Los Angeles County
48	508	55.4	**Lemon Grove** (city) San Diego County
49	512	55.1	**Palm Springs** (city) Riverside County
50	515	54.9	**Hanford** (city) Kings County
51	517	54.7	**Hemet** (city) Riverside County
52	519	54.6	**South Lake Tahoe** (city) El Dorado County
53	524	54.0	**Ridgecrest** (city) Kern County
54	532	53.6	**Hollister** (city) San Benito County
55	535	53.5	**Victorville** (city) San Bernardino County
56	537	53.4	**Pomona** (city) Los Angeles County
57	542	52.9	**McFarland** (city) Kern County
58	544	52.7	**National City** (city) San Diego County
59	548	52.6	**Greenfield** (city) Monterey County
60	558	52.1	**Lancaster** (city) Los Angeles County
61	562	52.0	**Rancho Cordova** (city) Sacramento County
62	564	51.9	**South Gate** (city) Los Angeles County
63	571	51.5	**Azusa** (city) Los Angeles County
64	579	51.3	**Bakersfield** (city) Kern County
64	579	51.3	**King City** (city) Monterey County
66	585	51.0	**Susanville** (city) Lassen County
67	596	50.2	**Fresno** (city) Fresno County
68	598	50.1	**Oroville** (city) Butte County
69	600	50.0	**Long Beach** (city) Los Angeles County
70	605	49.5	**Montclair** (city) San Bernardino County
71	610	49.3	**Imperial Beach** (city) San Diego County
72	621	48.7	**Lawndale** (city) Los Angeles County
73	628	48.5	**Palmdale** (city) Los Angeles County
74	630	48.4	**Berkeley** (city) Alameda County
75	635	48.1	**Woodland** (city) Yolo County
76	639	48.0	**Santa Maria** (city) Santa Barbara County
77	686	46.1	**Cudahy** (city) Los Angeles County
78	691	46.0	**Vista** (city) San Diego County
79	693	45.9	**Fairfield** (city) Solano County
80	695	45.8	**Chowchilla** (city) Madera County
81	709	45.5	**Watsonville** (city) Santa Cruz County
82	719	45.1	**Lodi** (city) San Joaquin County
83	724	45.0	**San Leandro** (city) Alameda County
84	727	44.8	**Lemoore** (city) Kings County
85	734	44.3	**Santa Fe Springs** (city) Los Angeles County
86	735	44.2	**Turlock** (city) Stanislaus County
87	744	43.6	**Farmersville** (city) Tulare County
87	744	43.6	**Rohnert Park** (city) Sonoma County
89	754	43.2	**South El Monte** (city) Los Angeles County
90	759	43.1	**Lompoc** (city) Santa Barbara County
91	765	42.8	**Carson** (city) Los Angeles County
92	769	42.6	**Los Angeles** (city) Los Angeles County
93	778	42.3	**Banning** (city) Riverside County
93	778	42.3	**Rialto** (city) San Bernardino County
95	783	42.1	**Avenal** (city) Kings County
96	785	42.0	**Riverside** (city) Riverside County
97	798	41.2	**West Sacramento** (city) Yolo County
98	803	41.0	**Gardena** (city) Los Angeles County
99	806	40.9	**Monterey** (city) Monterey County
100	809	40.8	**Culver City** (city) Los Angeles County
101	820	40.5	**Paramount** (city) Los Angeles County
101	820	40.5	**Yucca Valley** (town) San Bernardino County
103	825	40.4	**Maywood** (city) Los Angeles County
104	829	40.2	**Santa Barbara** (city) Santa Barbara County
105	830	40.1	**Escondido** (city) San Diego County
105	830	40.1	**Hesperia** (city) San Bernardino County
107	852	39.3	**San Diego** (city) San Diego County
108	864	39.1	**Visalia** (city) Tulare County
109	866	39.0	**Hayward** (city) Alameda County
110	872	38.8	**Hawaiian Gardens** (city) Los Angeles County
111	879	38.5	**Windsor** (town) Sonoma County
112	887	38.2	**Norwalk** (city) Los Angeles County
113	892	38.0	**El Cerrito** (city) Contra Costa County
114	898	37.8	**El Cajon** (city) San Diego County
115	901	37.6	**Arcata** (city) Humboldt County
115	901	37.6	**Artesia** (city) Los Angeles County
117	906	37.5	**Citrus Heights** (city) Sacramento County
118	934	36.7	**Oceanside** (city) San Diego County
119	937	36.6	**Pinole** (city) Contra Costa County
120	957	36.0	**Bellflower** (city) Los Angeles County
121	964	35.8	**Santa Paula** (city) Ventura County
122	969	35.6	**Auburn** (city) Placer County
122	969	35.6	**Fontana** (city) San Bernardino County
124	976	35.5	**San Fernando** (city) Los Angeles County
125	980	35.4	**La Puente** (city) Los Angeles County
126	989	35.1	**Gilroy** (city) Santa Clara County
126	989	35.1	**Highland** (city) San Bernardino County
126	989	35.1	**Porterville** (city) Tulare County
126	989	35.1	**San Rafael** (city) Marin County
126	989	35.1	**Seaside** (city) Monterey County
131	997	35.0	**Santa Monica** (city) Los Angeles County
132	1002	34.9	**San Luis Obispo** (city) San Luis Obispo County
133	1003	34.8	**Sonoma** (city) Sonoma County
134	1006	34.7	**Fortuna** (city) Humboldt County
135	1028	33.9	**Chico** (city) Butte County
136	1032	33.8	**Shafter** (city) Kern County
137	1034	33.7	**Newman** (city) Stanislaus County
137	1034	33.7	**Santa Ana** (city) Orange County
139	1044	33.5	**Atascadero** (city) San Luis Obispo County
140	1048	33.4	**El Paso de Robles (Paso Robles)** (city) San Luis Obispo County
140	1048	33.4	**Perris** (city) Riverside County
142	1054	33.3	**El Centro** (city) Imperial County
143	1059	33.1	**Mendota** (city) Fresno County
144	1076	32.7	**Anaheim** (city) Orange County
145	1080	32.5	**Pico Rivera** (city) Los Angeles County
146	1085	32.4	**Concord** (city) Contra Costa County
146	1085	32.4	**Napa** (city) Napa County
146	1085	32.4	**San Jose** (city) Santa Clara County
149	1097	32.1	**Oxnard** (city) Ventura County
150	1099	32.0	**Chino** (city) San Bernardino County

Note: *The state column ranks the top/bottom 150 places from all places in the state with population of 10,000 or more. The national column ranks the top/bottom 150 places from all places in the country with population of 10,000 or more. Places that are unincorporated were not considered in the rankings. Please refer to the User Guide for additional information.*

Violent Crime Rate per 10,000 Population

Top 150 Places Ranked in *Ascending* Order

State Rank	Nat'l Rank	Rate	Place
1	1	0.0	**Hillsborough** (town) San Mateo County
2	64	1.7	**Clayton** (city) Contra Costa County
3	143	2.7	**Canyon Lake** (city) Riverside County
4	162	3.0	**Laguna Woods** (city) Orange County
5	189	3.5	**Rancho Santa Margarita** (city) Orange County
6	200	3.6	**San Ramon** (city) Contra Costa County
7	220	3.9	**Danville** (town) Contra Costa County
8	266	4.4	**Imperial** (city) Imperial County
8	266	4.4	**Palos Verdes Estates** (city) Los Angeles County
8	266	4.4	**Yorba Linda** (city) Orange County
11	280	4.5	**Saratoga** (city) Santa Clara County
12	289	4.6	**Foster City** (city) San Mateo County
13	299	4.7	**Coronado** (city) San Diego County
14	307	4.8	**Irvine** (city) Orange County
15	326	5.0	**Aliso Viejo** (city) Orange County
16	362	5.4	**Orinda** (city) Contra Costa County
17	384	5.6	**Lincoln** (city) Placer County
18	407	5.8	**La Cañada Flintridge** (city) Los Angeles County
19	462	6.3	**La Palma** (city) Orange County
20	483	6.5	**Mission Viejo** (city) Orange County
20	483	6.5	**Murrieta** (city) Riverside County
20	483	6.5	**Seal Beach** (city) Orange County
23	492	6.6	**Moraga** (town) Contra Costa County
24	516	6.8	**Cupertino** (city) Santa Clara County
25	553	7.1	**Rancho Palos Verdes** (city) Los Angeles County
26	616	7.6	**Los Altos** (city) Santa Clara County
27	626	7.7	**Mill Valley** (city) Marin County
28	671	8.1	**Palo Alto** (city) Santa Clara County
29	682	8.2	**Chino Hills** (city) San Bernardino County
29	682	8.2	**Los Gatos** (town) Santa Clara County
29	682	8.2	**Pleasanton** (city) Alameda County
32	689	8.3	**Calabasas** (city) Los Angeles County
32	689	8.3	**Newport Beach** (city) Orange County
34	715	8.5	**Lafayette** (city) Contra Costa County
34	715	8.5	**Temecula** (city) Riverside County
36	725	8.6	**San Clemente** (city) Orange County
37	743	8.8	**Laguna Niguel** (city) Orange County
38	752	8.9	**Hercules** (city) Contra Costa County
39	777	9.2	**Agoura Hills** (city) Los Angeles County
40	786	9.3	**Glendale** (city) Los Angeles County
41	793	9.4	**Scotts Valley** (city) Santa Cruz County
42	826	9.7	**Sunnyvale** (city) Santa Clara County
43	858	10.1	**Belmont** (city) San Mateo County
43	858	10.1	**Corona** (city) Riverside County
43	858	10.1	**Ripon** (city) San Joaquin County
46	868	10.2	**Cypress** (city) Orange County
47	875	10.4	**Claremont** (city) Los Angeles County
47	875	10.4	**Rocklin** (city) Placer County
49	887	10.5	**Moorpark** (city) Ventura County
49	887	10.5	**Orange** (city) Orange County
49	887	10.5	**Simi Valley** (city) Ventura County
52	914	10.8	**Thousand Oaks** (city) Ventura County
53	920	10.9	**Benicia** (city) Solano County
54	927	11.0	**Camarillo** (city) Ventura County
54	927	11.0	**Diamond Bar** (city) Los Angeles County
56	933	11.1	**Truckee** (town) Nevada County
57	940	11.2	**South Pasadena** (city) Los Angeles County
58	962	11.5	**Eastvale** (city) Riverside County
59	988	11.8	**La Verne** (city) Los Angeles County
59	988	11.8	**Sierra Madre** (city) Los Angeles County
59	988	11.8	**Walnut Creek** (city) Contra Costa County
62	996	12.0	**Menifee** (city) Riverside County
62	996	12.0	**Wildomar** (city) Riverside County
64	1013	12.2	**Fremont** (city) Alameda County
64	1013	12.2	**Walnut** (city) Los Angeles County
66	1032	12.4	**Burlingame** (city) San Mateo County
67	1052	12.7	**Placentia** (city) Orange County
67	1052	12.7	**Torrance** (city) Los Angeles County
67	1052	12.7	**Tustin** (city) Orange County
70	1064	12.8	**Glendora** (city) Los Angeles County
71	1091	13.2	**Lake Forest** (city) Orange County
71	1091	13.2	**Temple City** (city) Los Angeles County
73	1103	13.3	**Arcadia** (city) Los Angeles County
73	1103	13.3	**Folsom** (city) Sacramento County
75	1113	13.4	**Milpitas** (city) Santa Clara County
76	1119	13.5	**Santa Clarita** (city) Los Angeles County
77	1128	13.6	**Hermosa Beach** (city) Los Angeles County
78	1162	14.1	**Dublin** (city) Alameda County
78	1162	14.1	**Goleta** (city) Santa Barbara County
80	1176	14.2	**Pacific Grove** (city) Monterey County
81	1185	14.3	**La Habra** (city) Orange County
81	1185	14.3	**Santa Clara** (city) Santa Clara County
83	1195	14.4	**Martinez** (city) Contra Costa County
84	1209	14.6	**La Mirada** (city) Los Angeles County
84	1209	14.6	**Rancho Mirage** (city) Riverside County
86	1243	15.0	**San Marino** (city) Los Angeles County
87	1256	15.2	**Albany** (city) Alameda County
88	1262	15.3	**Norco** (city) Riverside County
89	1270	15.4	**Monrovia** (city) Los Angeles County
90	1287	15.6	**Davis** (city) Yolo County
91	1306	15.8	**Brea** (city) Orange County
91	1306	15.8	**Carpinteria** (city) Santa Barbara County
91	1306	15.8	**Morgan Hill** (city) Santa Clara County
91	1306	15.8	**Riverbank** (city) Stanislaus County
95	1321	16.0	**Menlo Park** (city) San Mateo County
95	1321	16.0	**San Juan Capistrano** (city) Orange County
97	1337	16.2	**Fountain Valley** (city) Orange County
97	1337	16.2	**Pleasant Hill** (city) Contra Costa County
99	1348	16.3	**Burbank** (city) Los Angeles County
100	1354	16.4	**Brentwood** (city) Contra Costa County
101	1360	16.5	**Cerritos** (city) Los Angeles County
102	1392	17.0	**Laguna Hills** (city) Orange County
102	1392	17.0	**Monterey Park** (city) Los Angeles County
104	1404	17.1	**Fillmore** (city) Ventura County
104	1404	17.1	**Pacifica** (city) San Mateo County
106	1429	17.4	**La Quinta** (city) Riverside County
107	1441	17.6	**Arroyo Grande** (city) San Luis Obispo County
107	1441	17.6	**Laguna Beach** (city) Orange County
109	1450	17.8	**Manhattan Beach** (city) Los Angeles County
109	1450	17.8	**South San Francisco** (city) San Mateo County
109	1450	17.8	**Tracy** (city) San Joaquin County
112	1469	18.2	**Clovis** (city) Fresno County
112	1469	18.2	**Piedmont** (city) Alameda County
112	1469	18.2	**Poway** (city) San Diego County
115	1476	18.3	**Lake Elsinore** (city) Riverside County
116	1492	18.5	**Huntington Beach** (city) Orange County
116	1492	18.5	**Oakley** (city) Contra Costa County
118	1508	18.7	**Dixon** (city) Solano County
119	1519	18.8	**Duarte** (city) Los Angeles County
120	1531	19.0	**Exeter** (city) Tulare County
121	1548	19.2	**Alhambra** (city) Los Angeles County
121	1548	19.2	**Rancho Cucamonga** (city) San Bernardino County
121	1548	19.2	**San Dimas** (city) Los Angeles County
124	1573	19.7	**Kingsburg** (city) Fresno County
125	1581	19.8	**Patterson** (city) Stanislaus County
126	1587	19.9	**Novato** (city) Marin County
127	1593	20.0	**Carlsbad** (city) San Diego County
128	1609	20.3	**Mountain View** (city) Santa Clara County
129	1615	20.4	**Dana Point** (city) Orange County
129	1615	20.4	**Solana Beach** (city) San Diego County
129	1615	20.4	**Yucaipa** (city) San Bernardino County
132	1621	20.5	**Los Alamitos** (city) Orange County
133	1629	20.7	**Alameda** (city) Alameda County
133	1629	20.7	**Encinitas** (city) San Diego County
133	1629	20.7	**Roseville** (city) Placer County
136	1657	21.1	**Beaumont** (city) Riverside County
137	1677	21.3	**Daly City** (city) San Mateo County
137	1677	21.3	**Vacaville** (city) Solano County
139	1686	21.4	**West Covina** (city) Los Angeles County
140	1693	21.5	**Upland** (city) San Bernardino County
141	1707	21.7	**Malibu** (city) Los Angeles County
142	1713	21.8	**Healdsburg** (city) Sonoma County
142	1713	21.8	**Palm Desert** (city) Riverside County
144	1721	21.9	**El Segundo** (city) Los Angeles County
145	1730	22.1	**Beverly Hills** (city) Los Angeles County
146	1737	22.2	**Suisun City** (city) Solano County
147	1746	22.4	**Costa Mesa** (city) Orange County
148	1778	23.3	**Calexico** (city) Imperial County
148	1778	23.3	**Chula Vista** (city) San Diego County
150	1782	23.4	**Oakdale** (city) Stanislaus County

Note: *The state column ranks the top/bottom 150 places from all places in the state with population of 10,000 or more. The national column ranks the top/bottom 150 places from all places in the country with population of 10,000 or more. Places that are unincorporated were not considered in the rankings. Please refer to the User Guide for additional information.*

Property Crime Rate per 10,000 Population

Top 150 Places Ranked in *Descending* Order

State Rank	Nat'l Rank	Rate	Place
1	3	1,585.2	**Emeryville** (city) Alameda County
2	54	776.4	**Eureka** (city) Humboldt County
3	75	712.1	**Santa Fe Springs** (city) Los Angeles County
4	91	687.2	**Commerce** (city) Los Angeles County
5	110	662.0	**Red Bluff** (city) Tehama County
6	123	648.9	**Oroville** (city) Butte County
7	155	623.3	**Oakland** (city) Alameda County
8	194	587.1	**Grass Valley** (city) Nevada County
9	208	579.5	**San Francisco** (city) San Francisco County
10	333	512.0	**California City** (city) Kern County
11	344	507.8	**Palm Springs** (city) Riverside County
12	350	505.9	**Santa Cruz** (city) Santa Cruz County
13	360	503.0	**Stockton** (city) San Joaquin County
14	395	492.9	**Signal Hill** (city) Los Angeles County
15	407	489.1	**Modesto** (city) Stanislaus County
16	425	485.1	**Hemet** (city) Riverside County
17	428	484.6	**Vallejo** (city) Solano County
18	460	472.3	**Arcata** (city) Humboldt County
19	465	471.5	**El Centro** (city) Imperial County
20	468	470.2	**Brawley** (city) Imperial County
21	487	464.7	**Bakersfield** (city) Kern County
22	490	463.1	**El Cerrito** (city) Contra Costa County
23	495	462.7	**Berkeley** (city) Alameda County
24	497	461.5	**Clearlake** (city) Lake County
25	509	457.7	**Atwater** (city) Merced County
26	523	452.6	**San Leandro** (city) Alameda County
27	538	449.6	**Richmond** (city) Contra Costa County
28	556	443.8	**Fresno** (city) Fresno County
29	558	443.0	**Marysville** (city) Yuba County
30	566	441.2	**Selma** (city) Fresno County
31	570	439.0	**Palm Desert** (city) Riverside County
32	575	438.1	**San Bernardino** (city) San Bernardino County
33	600	431.5	**Pleasant Hill** (city) Contra Costa County
34	608	429.7	**Redlands** (city) San Bernardino County
35	610	429.5	**Montclair** (city) San Bernardino County
36	624	425.4	**Tulare** (city) Tulare County
37	656	417.1	**Antioch** (city) Contra Costa County
38	671	414.6	**Redding** (city) Shasta County
39	681	411.2	**West Hollywood** (city) Los Angeles County
40	689	409.6	**Culver City** (city) Los Angeles County
41	738	394.8	**Desert Hot Springs** (city) Riverside County
41	738	394.8	**San Jacinto** (city) Riverside County
43	758	391.4	**San Pablo** (city) Contra Costa County
44	775	387.1	**Oakdale** (city) Stanislaus County
45	782	385.5	**Campbell** (city) Santa Clara County
46	786	385.1	**San Luis Obispo** (city) San Luis Obispo County
47	796	383.2	**Santa Monica** (city) Los Angeles County
48	800	381.6	**La Quinta** (city) Riverside County
49	810	379.7	**Visalia** (city) Tulare County
50	815	377.7	**Monterey** (city) Monterey County
51	822	376.0	**Sacramento** (city) Sacramento County
52	823	375.3	**Turlock** (city) Stanislaus County
53	827	374.9	**Ceres** (city) Stanislaus County
54	832	373.5	**Manteca** (city) San Joaquin County
55	835	373.3	**Delano** (city) Kern County
56	836	372.9	**Calexico** (city) Imperial County
57	840	372.2	**San Buenaventura (Ventura)** (city) Ventura County
58	846	371.6	**Dinuba** (city) Tulare County
59	873	364.9	**Arvin** (city) Kern County
60	884	363.5	**Fortuna** (city) Humboldt County
61	885	363.4	**Pinole** (city) Contra Costa County
62	890	362.5	**Colton** (city) San Bernardino County
63	895	361.7	**Cerritos** (city) Los Angeles County
64	896	361.6	**Lodi** (city) San Joaquin County
65	918	357.0	**Rancho Mirage** (city) Riverside County
66	921	356.3	**Hanford** (city) Kings County
67	927	355.3	**Ukiah** (city) Mendocino County
68	963	347.3	**Concord** (city) Contra Costa County
69	978	343.9	**Salinas** (city) Monterey County
70	980	343.6	**Woodland** (city) Yolo County
71	984	342.2	**Clovis** (city) Fresno County
71	984	342.2	**Victorville** (city) San Bernardino County
73	1001	339.6	**Gilroy** (city) Santa Clara County
74	1003	339.2	**Barstow** (city) San Bernardino County
75	1005	339.0	**Beverly Hills** (city) Los Angeles County
76	1016	336.5	**La Mesa** (city) San Diego County
77	1018	336.4	**Indio** (city) Riverside County
78	1022	335.9	**Blythe** (city) Riverside County
79	1024	335.2	**Riverside** (city) Riverside County
80	1078	326.7	**Walnut Creek** (city) Contra Costa County
81	1083	325.9	**Fairfield** (city) Solano County
82	1084	325.6	**Rancho Cordova** (city) Sacramento County
83	1086	325.5	**Merced** (city) Merced County
84	1104	322.8	**Beaumont** (city) Riverside County
85	1118	320.9	**Hayward** (city) Alameda County
86	1132	318.1	**El Segundo** (city) Los Angeles County
87	1133	318.0	**Shafter** (city) Kern County
88	1138	316.9	**National City** (city) San Diego County
89	1141	316.6	**Coachella** (city) Riverside County
90	1146	316.0	**Costa Mesa** (city) Orange County
91	1164	312.4	**West Covina** (city) Los Angeles County
92	1171	310.9	**Citrus Heights** (city) Sacramento County
93	1187	308.6	**San Rafael** (city) Marin County
94	1195	307.9	**Huntington Park** (city) Los Angeles County
95	1202	306.8	**Los Alamitos** (city) Orange County
96	1216	304.6	**Pittsburg** (city) Contra Costa County
97	1218	304.3	**Patterson** (city) Stanislaus County
98	1219	304.2	**Loma Linda** (city) San Bernardino County
99	1220	304.0	**Yuba City** (city) Sutter County
100	1245	299.8	**Kerman** (city) Fresno County
101	1257	298.1	**West Sacramento** (city) Yolo County
102	1258	298.0	**Brea** (city) Orange County
103	1259	297.6	**Paramount** (city) Los Angeles County
104	1263	297.3	**Milpitas** (city) Santa Clara County
105	1270	296.6	**Santa Barbara** (city) Santa Barbara County
106	1274	295.8	**Coalinga** (city) Fresno County
107	1275	295.3	**Upland** (city) San Bernardino County
108	1278	294.6	**Madera** (city) Madera County
109	1279	294.5	**Sanger** (city) Fresno County
110	1297	291.8	**Riverbank** (city) Stanislaus County
111	1299	291.7	**Moreno Valley** (city) Riverside County
112	1300	291.6	**Albany** (city) Alameda County
113	1301	291.5	**Chico** (city) Butte County
114	1308	290.8	**Downey** (city) Los Angeles County
115	1314	290.3	**Pomona** (city) Los Angeles County
116	1327	287.5	**Santa Maria** (city) Santa Barbara County
117	1335	286.8	**Los Banos** (city) Merced County
118	1352	284.4	**Placerville** (city) El Dorado County
119	1355	284.3	**Adelanto** (city) San Bernardino County
120	1359	282.9	**Tehachapi** (city) Kern County
121	1363	282.4	**Perris** (city) Riverside County
122	1365	282.2	**South Gate** (city) Los Angeles County
123	1376	280.7	**Kingsburg** (city) Fresno County
124	1397	278.3	**Anaheim** (city) Orange County
125	1409	277.0	**Covina** (city) Los Angeles County
126	1410	276.8	**Long Beach** (city) Los Angeles County
127	1415	276.5	**Hermosa Beach** (city) Los Angeles County
128	1416	276.3	**Fullerton** (city) Orange County
129	1417	276.2	**Montebello** (city) Los Angeles County
130	1420	275.7	**Whittier** (city) Los Angeles County
131	1424	275.4	**El Paso de Robles (Paso Robles)** (city) San Luis Obispo County
131	1424	275.4	**South Lake Tahoe** (city) El Dorado County
133	1432	274.2	**Marina** (city) Monterey County
134	1449	272.5	**Porterville** (city) Tulare County
135	1452	271.9	**Pasadena** (city) Los Angeles County
136	1456	271.5	**Malibu** (city) Los Angeles County
137	1473	269.5	**Westminster** (city) Orange County
138	1480	268.7	**Davis** (city) Yolo County
139	1487	268.0	**Ontario** (city) San Bernardino County
140	1491	267.6	**El Cajon** (city) San Diego County
141	1494	267.0	**Temecula** (city) Riverside County
142	1496	266.7	**Escondido** (city) San Diego County
143	1497	266.4	**Piedmont** (city) Alameda County
144	1503	265.7	**Lake Elsinore** (city) Riverside County
145	1510	265.0	**Rialto** (city) San Bernardino County
146	1513	264.9	**Banning** (city) Riverside County
147	1514	264.8	**Roseville** (city) Placer County
148	1524	263.3	**Glendora** (city) Los Angeles County
149	1532	262.5	**Tracy** (city) San Joaquin County
150	1533	262.4	**Arcadia** (city) Los Angeles County

Note: *The state column ranks the top/bottom 150 places from all places in the state with population of 10,000 or more. The national column ranks the top/bottom 150 places from all places in the country with population of 10,000 or more. Places that are unincorporated were not considered in the rankings. Please refer to the User Guide for additional information.*

Property Crime Rate per 10,000 Population

Top 150 Places Ranked in *Ascending* Order

State Rank	Nat'l Rank	Rate	Place
1	56	50.7	**Hillsborough** (town) San Mateo County
2	67	53.9	**Imperial** (city) Imperial County
3	84	59.0	**Rancho Santa Margarita** (city) Orange County
4	99	63.0	**Aliso Viejo** (city) Orange County
5	137	71.9	**Saratoga** (city) Santa Clara County
6	181	79.6	**Laguna Woods** (city) Orange County
7	241	88.3	**Clayton** (city) Contra Costa County
8	256	90.0	**Moraga** (town) Contra Costa County
9	278	93.4	**Foster City** (city) San Mateo County
10	287	94.6	**Soledad** (city) Monterey County
11	292	95.1	**Danville** (town) Contra Costa County
12	300	96.2	**Laguna Niguel** (city) Orange County
13	320	98.7	**Windsor** (town) Sonoma County
14	329	99.9	**Avenal** (city) Kings County
15	331	100.0	**Fillmore** (city) Ventura County
16	346	102.1	**San Ramon** (city) Contra Costa County
17	350	102.5	**Lake Forest** (city) Orange County
18	359	103.7	**Yorba Linda** (city) Orange County
19	367	104.1	**Mission Viejo** (city) Orange County
20	393	107.1	**Truckee** (town) Nevada County
21	402	107.6	**Palos Verdes Estates** (city) Los Angeles County
22	422	110.3	**Hercules** (city) Contra Costa County
23	458	115.3	**Maywood** (city) Los Angeles County
24	462	115.6	**Orinda** (city) Contra Costa County
25	465	116.0	**Moorpark** (city) Ventura County
26	467	116.3	**Poway** (city) San Diego County
27	476	116.8	**Sierra Madre** (city) Los Angeles County
28	489	118.4	**Los Altos** (city) Santa Clara County
29	513	122.0	**La Puente** (city) Los Angeles County
30	527	123.4	**Lincoln** (city) Placer County
30	527	123.4	**San Juan Capistrano** (city) Orange County
32	537	124.5	**Thousand Oaks** (city) Ventura County
33	550	126.1	**Lawndale** (city) Los Angeles County
34	575	129.3	**San Clemente** (city) Orange County
35	584	129.8	**Calabasas** (city) Los Angeles County
36	593	131.2	**Temple City** (city) Los Angeles County
37	595	131.4	**Oakley** (city) Contra Costa County
38	605	132.2	**Chino Hills** (city) San Bernardino County
39	607	132.4	**Santa Clarita** (city) Los Angeles County
40	610	132.8	**Cudahy** (city) Los Angeles County
41	624	134.3	**Cupertino** (city) Santa Clara County
42	632	135.4	**Simi Valley** (city) Ventura County
43	633	136.2	**Twentynine Palms** (city) San Bernardino County
44	634	136.3	**Rancho Palos Verdes** (city) Los Angeles County
45	649	139.0	**Benicia** (city) Solano County
46	651	139.3	**Irvine** (city) Orange County
47	677	141.8	**Pacifica** (city) San Mateo County
48	682	142.0	**Hawaiian Gardens** (city) Los Angeles County
49	690	143.2	**Livingston** (city) Merced County
50	698	143.5	**Canyon Lake** (city) Riverside County
51	724	147.3	**La Cañada Flintridge** (city) Los Angeles County
52	727	147.4	**Agoura Hills** (city) Los Angeles County
53	736	148.4	**Dublin** (city) Alameda County
53	736	148.4	**Goleta** (city) Santa Barbara County
55	741	148.9	**Bell** (city) Los Angeles County
56	757	150.8	**Placentia** (city) Orange County
57	765	151.6	**King City** (city) Monterey County
58	768	152.2	**Murrieta** (city) Riverside County
59	774	152.9	**Walnut** (city) Los Angeles County
60	775	153.1	**Greenfield** (city) Monterey County
61	798	155.6	**Novato** (city) Marin County
62	801	156.3	**Corcoran** (city) Kings County
63	804	156.5	**Diamond Bar** (city) Los Angeles County
63	804	156.5	**Hollister** (city) San Benito County
65	834	159.6	**San Marcos** (city) San Diego County
66	839	160.2	**Wildomar** (city) Riverside County
67	841	160.8	**Mill Valley** (city) Marin County
68	855	163.2	**Laguna Hills** (city) Orange County
69	858	163.7	**Belmont** (city) San Mateo County
69	858	163.7	**Glendale** (city) Los Angeles County
71	860	164.2	**Morro Bay** (city) San Luis Obispo County
72	862	164.3	**Sunnyvale** (city) Santa Clara County
73	882	166.2	**Rohnert Park** (city) Sonoma County
74	883	166.3	**Lafayette** (city) Contra Costa County
75	887	166.6	**San Fernando** (city) Los Angeles County
76	904	168.2	**Duarte** (city) Los Angeles County
76	904	168.2	**Imperial Beach** (city) San Diego County
78	906	168.3	**San Marino** (city) Los Angeles County
79	918	169.4	**Morgan Hill** (city) Santa Clara County
80	919	169.6	**Rocklin** (city) Placer County
81	925	170.8	**Camarillo** (city) Ventura County
82	926	171.0	**Dana Point** (city) Orange County
82	926	171.0	**Petaluma** (city) Sonoma County
84	930	171.1	**La Mirada** (city) Los Angeles County
85	942	172.3	**Orange** (city) Orange County
86	946	173.1	**Seaside** (city) Monterey County
87	962	175.3	**Daly City** (city) San Mateo County
88	966	175.5	**Pleasanton** (city) Alameda County
89	969	176.0	**Encinitas** (city) San Diego County
90	972	176.3	**Yucaipa** (city) San Bernardino County
91	978	177.5	**Bell Gardens** (city) Los Angeles County
92	980	177.7	**Santa Paula** (city) Ventura County
93	983	178.5	**Baldwin Park** (city) Los Angeles County
94	987	178.9	**Napa** (city) Napa County
95	991	179.4	**Stanton** (city) Orange County
96	993	179.6	**South San Francisco** (city) San Mateo County
97	994	179.7	**San Gabriel** (city) Los Angeles County
98	1001	181.1	**Folsom** (city) Sacramento County
99	1003	181.5	**Los Gatos** (town) Santa Clara County
100	1012	182.5	**Fremont** (city) Alameda County
101	1017	183.1	**Eastvale** (city) Riverside County
102	1021	184.1	**Elk Grove** (city) Sacramento County
103	1027	184.8	**Port Hueneme** (city) Ventura County
104	1030	185.2	**Newman** (city) Stanislaus County
105	1042	186.3	**Seal Beach** (city) Orange County
106	1048	186.8	**Tustin** (city) Orange County
107	1052	187.1	**La Habra** (city) Orange County
108	1068	188.0	**Atascadero** (city) San Luis Obispo County
109	1075	188.7	**Carlsbad** (city) San Diego County
110	1078	188.8	**El Monte** (city) Los Angeles County
110	1078	188.8	**Torrance** (city) Los Angeles County
112	1097	190.0	**Monterey Park** (city) Los Angeles County
113	1101	190.4	**Cypress** (city) Orange County
114	1118	193.0	**Artesia** (city) Los Angeles County
114	1118	193.0	**Santa Ana** (city) Orange County
116	1126	193.6	**Garden Grove** (city) Orange County
117	1132	194.3	**Menlo Park** (city) San Mateo County
117	1132	194.3	**Sonoma** (city) Sonoma County
119	1135	194.6	**Lemon Grove** (city) San Diego County
120	1143	195.5	**Rosemead** (city) Los Angeles County
121	1149	196.4	**Carpinteria** (city) Santa Barbara County
122	1161	198.5	**Pacific Grove** (city) Monterey County
123	1170	199.7	**Ridgecrest** (city) Kern County
124	1183	200.8	**Lomita** (city) Los Angeles County
125	1184	201.0	**Fontana** (city) San Bernardino County
126	1188	201.2	**Laguna Beach** (city) Orange County
127	1196	202.1	**Paradise** (town) Butte County
128	1200	202.2	**Yucca Valley** (town) San Bernardino County
129	1214	203.3	**Menifee** (city) Riverside County
130	1227	204.4	**La Palma** (city) Orange County
130	1227	204.4	**Santa Rosa** (city) Sonoma County
132	1233	205.3	**East Palo Alto** (city) San Mateo County
133	1236	205.5	**Healdsburg** (city) Sonoma County
134	1240	205.6	**San Mateo** (city) San Mateo County
135	1247	206.0	**Fountain Valley** (city) Orange County
136	1254	207.2	**Chula Vista** (city) San Diego County
137	1263	208.3	**Santee** (city) San Diego County
138	1264	208.5	**San Dimas** (city) Los Angeles County
139	1275	209.4	**Alhambra** (city) Los Angeles County
140	1282	210.6	**Galt** (city) Sacramento County
141	1283	210.7	**Cathedral City** (city) Riverside County
142	1285	210.9	**Norwalk** (city) Los Angeles County
143	1296	211.4	**Reedley** (city) Fresno County
144	1297	211.5	**Vista** (city) San Diego County
145	1314	213.6	**Palmdale** (city) Los Angeles County
146	1328	214.7	**Corona** (city) Riverside County
147	1331	215.0	**Lynwood** (city) Los Angeles County
148	1343	216.0	**Norco** (city) Riverside County
149	1358	217.0	**Livermore** (city) Alameda County
150	1362	217.4	**Monrovia** (city) Los Angeles County

Note: *The state column ranks the top/bottom 150 places from all places in the state with population of 10,000 or more. The national column ranks the top/bottom 150 places from all places in the country with population of 10,000 or more. Places that are unincorporated were not considered in the rankings. Please refer to the User Guide for additional information.*

Education

California Public School Educational Profile

Category	Value	Category	Value
Schools *(2011-2012)*	10,214	**Diploma Recipients** *(2009-2010)*	404,987
Instructional Level		White, Non-Hispanic	132,893
Primary	5,874	Black, Non-Hispanic	27,580
Middle	1,435	Asian, Non-Hispanic	53,563
High	2,229	American Indian/Alaskan Native, Non-Hispanic	3,168
Other/Not Reported	676	Hawaiian Native/Pacific Islander, Non-Hispanic	2,661
Curriculum		Two or More Races, Non-Hispanic	11,034
Regular	8,671	Hispanic of Any Race	174,088
Special Education	147	**Staff** *(2011-2012)*	
Vocational	88	Teachers (FTE)	263,113.5
Alternative	1,308	Salary[1] ($)	70,126
Type		Librarians/Media Specialists (FTE)	797.5
Magnet	281	Guidance Counselors (FTE)	7,684.7
Charter	1,017	**Ratios** *(2011-2012)*	
Title I Eligible	8,565	Number of Students per Teacher	23.6 to 1
School-wide Title I	4,867	Number of Students per Librarian	7,792.1 to 1
Students *(2011-2012)*	6,214,203	Number of Students per Guidance Counselor	808.6 to 1
Gender (%)		**Finances** *(2010-2011)*	
Male	51.4	Current Expenditures ($ per student)	
Female	48.6	Total	9,146
Race/Ethnicity (%)		Instruction	5,514
White, Non-Hispanic	26.0	Support Services	3,246
Black, Non-Hispanic	6.5	Other	386
Asian, Non-Hispanic	11.2	General Revenue ($ per student)	
American Indian/Alaskan Native, Non-Hisp.	0.7	Total	10,790
Hawaiian Native/Pacific Islander, Non-Hisp.	0.6	From Federal Sources	1,470
Two or More Races, Non-Hispanic	2.9	From State Sources	6,107
Hispanic of Any Race	52.1	From Local Sources	3,212
Special Programs (%)		Long-Term Debt Outstanding ($ per student)	
Individual Education Program (IEP)	10.8	At Beginning of Fiscal Year	8,466
English Language Learner (ELL)	23.1	Issued During Fiscal Year	727
Eligible for Free Lunch Program	5.0	Retired During Fiscal Year	423
Eligible for Reduced-Price Lunch Program	0.0	At End of Fiscal Year	8,770
Average Freshman Grad. Rate (%) *(2009-2010)*	78.2	**College Entrance Exam Scores**	
White, Non-Hispanic	83.9	SAT Reasoning Test™ *(2013)*	
Black, Non-Hispanic	65.4	Participation Rate (%)	57
Asian/Pacific Islander, Non-Hispanic	90.1	Mean Critical Reading Score	498
American Indian/Alaskan Native, Non-Hispanic	75.1	Mean Math Score	512
Hispanic of Any Race	71.7	Mean Writing Score	495
High School Drop-out Rate (%) *(2009-2010)*	4.6	ACT *(2013)*	
White, Non-Hispanic	2.8	Participation Rate (%)	26
Black, Non-Hispanic	8.4	Mean Composite Score	22.2
Asian, Non-Hispanic	1.8	Mean English Score	21.6
American Indian/Alaskan Native, Non-Hispanic	6.5	Mean Math Score	22.8
Hawaiian Native/Pacific Islander, Non-Hispanic	5.0	Mean Reading Score	22.3
Two or More Races, Non-Hispanic	5.0	Mean Science Score	21.5
Hispanic of Any Race	5.8		

Note: *For an explanation of data, please refer to the User Guide in the front of the book; (1) Average salary for classroom teachers in 2013-14*

Number of Schools

Rank	Number	District Name	City
1	949	Los Angeles Unified	Los Angeles
2	225	San Diego Unified	San Diego
3	134	Oakland Unified	Oakland
4	116	San Francisco Unified	San Francisco
5	106	Fresno Unified	Fresno
6	92	Long Beach Unified	Long Beach
7	88	Sacramento City Unified	Sacramento
8	80	San Bernardino City Unified	San Bernardino
9	73	San Juan Unified	Carmichael
10	68	Garden Grove Unified	Garden Grove
11	66	Elk Grove Unified	Elk Grove
12	64	Capistrano Unified	SJ Capistrano
13	63	Stockton Unified	Stockton
14	60	Santa Ana Unified	Santa Ana
15	59	West Contra Costa Unified	Richmond
16	54	Lodi Unified	Lodi
16	54	Mt. Diablo Unified	Concord
16	54	Twin Rivers Unified	Mcclellan
19	53	San Jose Unified	San Jose
20	52	Corona-Norco Unified	Norco
21	49	Riverside Unified	Riverside
22	47	Clovis Unified	Clovis
23	46	Chula Vista Elementary	Chula Vista
24	44	Pomona Unified	Pomona
25	43	Fontana Unified	Fontana
26	41	Bakersfield City	Bakersfield
26	41	Fremont Unified	Fremont
26	41	Orange Unified	Orange
29	39	Moreno Valley Unified	Moreno Valley
29	39	Visalia Unified	Visalia
31	38	Compton Unified	Compton
31	38	Los Angeles County Office of Educ.	Downey
33	37	Poway Unified	San Diego
34	36	Chino Valley Unified	Chino
34	36	Hacienda La Puente Unified	City of Industry
36	35	Irvine Unified	Irvine
36	35	San Ramon Valley Unified	Danville
38	34	Desert Sands Unified	La Quinta
38	34	Placentia-Yorba Linda Unified	Placentia
38	34	Saddleback Valley Unified	Mission Viejo
38	34	Vista Unified	Vista
42	33	Folsom-Cordova Unified	Folsom
42	33	Glendale Unified	Glendale
42	33	Hayward Unified	Hayward
42	33	Napa Valley Unified	Napa
42	33	Pajaro Valley Unified	Watsonville
42	33	Temecula Valley Unified	Temecula
48	32	Ontario-Montclair Elementary	Ontario
49	31	ABC Unified	Cerritos
49	31	Hesperia Unified	Hesperia
49	31	Newport-Mesa Unified	Costa Mesa
49	31	Pasadena Unified	Pasadena
49	31	Torrance Unified	Torrance
54	30	Cajon Valley Union	El Cajon
54	30	Montebello Unified	Montebello
54	30	Rialto Unified	Rialto
54	30	Sweetwater Union High	Chula Vista
54	30	Ventura Unified	Ventura
59	29	Chico Unified	Chico
59	29	Fairfield-Suisun Unified	Fairfield
59	29	Manteca Unified	Manteca
59	29	Palm Springs Unified	Palm Springs
59	29	Simi Valley Unified	Simi Valley
59	29	Tustin Unified	Tustin
65	28	Alum Rock Union Elementary	San Jose
65	28	Antioch Unified	Antioch
65	28	Norwalk-La Mirada Unified	Norwalk
68	27	Colton Joint Unified	Colton
68	27	Conejo Valley Unified	Thousand Oaks
68	27	Hemet Unified	Hemet
68	27	Inglewood Unified	Inglewood
68	27	Madera Unified	Madera
68	27	Palmdale Elementary	Palmdale
68	27	Santa Barbara Unified	Santa Barbara
75	26	Modesto City Elementary	Modesto
75	26	Santa Clara Unified	Santa Clara
75	26	Vallejo City Unified	Vallejo
78	25	Cupertino Union	Cupertino
78	25	Escondido Union	Escondido
78	25	Jurupa Unified	Jurupa Valley
78	25	Kern Union High	Bakersfield
78	25	Lake Elsinore Unified	Lake Elsinore
78	25	Marysville Joint Unified	Marysville
78	25	Oceanside Unified	Oceanside
78	25	Redlands Unified	Redlands
86	24	Anaheim City	Anaheim
86	24	Ceres Unified	Ceres
86	24	Tracy Joint Unified	Tracy
89	23	Coachella Valley Unified	Thermal
89	23	East Side Union High	San Jose
89	23	Lancaster Elementary	Lancaster
89	23	Panama-Buena Vista Union	Bakersfield
93	22	Baldwin Park Unified	Baldwin Park
93	22	Burbank Unified	Burbank
93	22	La Mesa-Spring Valley	La Mesa
93	22	Monterey Peninsula Unified	Monterey
93	22	Porterville Unified	Porterville
93	22	Rowland Unified	Rowland Heights
99	21	Alvord Unified	Riverside
99	21	Anaheim Union High	Anaheim
99	21	Oxnard	Oxnard
99	21	Val Verde Unified	Perris
103	20	Alameda City Unified	Alameda
103	20	Central Unified	Fresno
103	20	Downey Unified	Downey
103	20	Fullerton Elementary	Fullerton
103	20	Grossmont Union High	La Mesa
103	20	Kings Canyon Joint Unified	Reedley
103	20	Murrieta Valley Unified	Murrieta
103	20	Oak Grove Elementary	San Jose
103	20	Rocklin Unified	Rocklin
103	20	San Mateo-Foster City	Foster City
103	20	Sanger Unified	Sanger
103	20	William S. Hart Union High	Santa Clarita
115	19	Berkeley Unified	Berkeley
115	19	Franklin-Mckinley Elementary	San Jose
115	19	Lynwood Unified	Lynwood
115	19	Palo Alto Unified	Palo Alto
115	19	Paramount Unified	Paramount
115	19	San Diego County Office of Educ.	San Diego
115	19	San Marcos Unified	San Marcos
115	19	Santa Maria-Bonita	Santa Maria
115	19	Yuba City Unified	Yuba City
124	18	Alhambra Unified	Alhambra
124	18	Evergreen Elementary	San Jose
124	18	Livermore Valley Joint Unified	Livermore
124	18	Lucia Mar Unified	Arroyo Grande
124	18	Merced City Elementary	Merced
124	18	Morongo Unified	Twentynine Plms
124	18	Natomas Unified	Sacramento
124	18	Palos Verdes Peninsula Unified	Palos Vrds Est
124	18	San Lorenzo Unified	San Lorenzo
124	18	Santa Clara County Office of Educ.	San Jose
124	18	Santa Rosa High	Santa Rosa
124	18	Victor Elementary	Victorville
124	18	Woodland Joint Unified	Woodland
137	17	Azusa Unified	Azusa
137	17	Covina-Valley Unified	Covina
137	17	Davis Joint Unified	Davis
137	17	Etiwanda Elementary	Etiwanda
137	17	Mountain Empire Unified	Pine Valley
137	17	Novato Unified	Novato
137	17	Roseville City Elementary	Roseville
137	17	San Luis Coastal Unified	San Luis Obispo
137	17	West Covina Unified	West Covina
137	17	Westminster Elementary	Westminster
147	16	Gilroy Unified	Gilroy
147	16	Las Virgenes Unified	Calabasas
147	16	Lompoc Unified	Lompoc
147	16	Redwood City Elementary	Redwood City
147	16	Santa Monica-Malibu Unified	Santa Monica
147	16	Tulare City	Tulare
147	16	Vacaville Unified	Vacaville
154	15	Apple Valley Unified	Apple Valley
154	15	Bellflower Unified	Bellflower
154	15	Carlsbad Unified	Carlsbad
154	15	Castro Valley Unified	Castro Valley
154	15	El Monte City Elementary	El Monte
154	15	El Rancho Unified	Pico Rivera
154	15	Jefferson Elementary	Daly City
154	15	Ocean View	Huntington Bch
154	15	Paradise Unified	Paradise
154	15	Pleasanton Unified	Pleasanton
154	15	Saugus Union	Santa Clarita
154	15	S San Francisco Unified	S San Francisco
154	15	Turlock Unified	Turlock
154	15	Walnut Valley Unified	Walnut
154	15	Washington Unified	West Sacramento
154	15	Yucaipa-Calimesa Joint Unified	Yucaipa
170	14	Adelanto Elementary	Adelanto
170	14	Antelope Valley Union High	Lancaster
170	14	Berryessa Union Elementary	San Jose
170	14	Bonita Unified	San Dimas
170	14	El Centro Elementary	El Centro
170	14	Los Banos Unified	Los Banos
170	14	Morgan Hill Unified	Morgan Hill
170	14	Nevada County Office of Education	Nevada City
170	14	New Haven Unified	Union City
170	14	San Jacinto Unified	San Jacinto
170	14	Sylvan Union Elementary	Modesto
170	14	Ukiah Unified	Ukiah
170	14	Upland Unified	Upland
183	13	Barstow Unified	Barstow
183	13	Calaveras Unified	San Andreas
183	13	Calexico Unified	Calexico
183	13	Campbell Union	Campbell
183	13	Delano Union Elementary	Delano
183	13	East Whittier City Elementary	Whittier
183	13	Lakeside Union Elementary	Lakeside
183	13	Milpitas Unified	Milpitas
183	13	Paso Robles Joint Unified	Paso Robles
183	13	Pittsburg Unified	Pittsburg
183	13	Pleasant Valley	Camarillo
183	13	Redondo Beach Unified	Redondo Beach
183	13	Salinas City Elementary	Salinas
183	13	Santa Rosa Elementary	Santa Rosa
183	13	Western Placer Unified	Lincoln
183	13	Willits Unified	Willits
183	13	Yosemite Unified	Oakhurst
200	12	Alisal Union	Salinas
200	12	Amador County Unified	Jackson
200	12	Atascadero Unified	Atascadero
200	12	Claremont Unified	Claremont
200	12	Cotati-Rohnert Park Unified	Rohnert Park
200	12	Del Norte County Unified	Crescent City
200	12	Gateway Unified	Redding
200	12	Greenfield Union	Bakersfield
200	12	Hanford Elementary	Hanford
200	12	Mariposa County Unified	Mariposa
200	12	Menifee Union Elementary	Menifee
200	12	Moorpark Unified	Moorpark
200	12	Mountain View Elementary	El Monte
200	12	Newark Unified	Newark
200	12	River Delta Joint Unified	Rio Vista
200	12	San Leandro Unified	San Leandro
200	12	Selma Unified	Selma
200	12	Snowline Joint Unified	Phelan
200	12	Sonoma Valley Unified	Sonoma
200	12	South Bay Union Elementary	Imperial Beach
200	12	Tahoe-Truckee Joint Unified	Truckee
200	12	Westside Union Elementary	Quartz Hill
200	12	Whittier City Elementary	Whittier
223	11	Alameda County Office of Education	Hayward
223	11	Arcadia Unified	Arcadia
223	11	Bishop Unified	Bishop
223	11	Coalinga-Huron Joint Unified	Coalinga
223	11	Cutler-Orosi Joint Unified	Orosi
223	11	Fountain Valley Elementary	Fountain Valley
223	11	Hawthorne	Hawthorne
223	11	Hueneme Elementary	Port Hueneme
223	11	Lincoln Unified	Stockton
223	11	Monrovia Unified	Monrovia
223	11	Mountain View Whisman	Mountain View
223	11	National Elementary	National City
223	11	Redding Elementary	Redding
223	11	Salinas Union High	Salinas
223	11	Santee Elementary	Santee
223	11	Shasta Union High	Redding
223	11	Sierra Sands Unified	Ridgecrest
223	11	Victor Valley Union High	Victorville
241	10	Alta Loma Elementary	Alta Loma
241	10	Atwater Elementary	Atwater
241	10	Banning Unified	Banning
241	10	Beaumont Unified	Beaumont
241	10	Brentwood Union Elementary	Brentwood
241	10	Chaffey Joint Union High	Ontario
241	10	Charter Oak Unified	Covina
241	10	Corcoran Joint Unified	Corcoran
241	10	Dinuba Unified	Dinuba
241	10	Dry Creek Joint Elementary	Roseville
241	10	Dublin Unified	Dublin
241	10	El Dorado Union High	Placerville

Note: This section only includes districts with 1,500 or more students; All categories are ranked from high to low

241	10	Fresno County Office of Education	Fresno
241	10	Garvey Elementary	Rosemead
241	10	Hollister	Hollister
241	10	Konocti Unified	Lower Lake
241	10	Lawndale Elementary	Lawndale
241	10	Lennox	Lennox
241	10	Lindsay Unified	Lindsay
241	10	Los Alamitos Unified	Los Alamitos
241	10	Nevada Joint Union High	Grass Valley
241	10	Newhall	Valencia
241	10	Ojai Unified	Ojai
241	10	Oxnard Union High	Oxnard
241	10	Petaluma Joint Union High	Petaluma
241	10	Ramona City Unified	Ramona
241	10	San Dieguito Union High	Encinitas
241	10	Santa Cruz City High	Soquel
241	10	Soledad Unified	Soledad
241	10	Sunnyvale	Sunnyvale
241	10	Travis Unified	Fairfield
241	10	Windsor Unified	Windsor
273	9	Brea-Olinda Unified	Brea
273	9	Buckeye Union Elementary	Shingle Springs
273	9	Center Joint Unified	Antelope
273	9	Encinitas Union Elementary	Encinitas
273	9	Fallbrook Union Elementary	Fallbrook
273	9	Fort Bragg Unified	Fort Bragg
273	9	Glendora Unified	Glendora
273	9	Golden Valley Unified	Madera
273	9	Goleta Union Elementary	Goleta
273	9	Huntington Bch City Elementary	Huntington Bch
273	9	Huntington Bch Union High	Huntington Bch
273	9	Kelseyville Unified	Kelseyville
273	9	La Habra City Elementary	La Habra
273	9	Little Lake City Elementary	Santa Fe Spgs
273	9	Los Altos Elementary	Los Altos
273	9	Magnolia Elementary	Anaheim
273	9	Martinez Unified	Martinez
273	9	Middletown Unified	Middletown
273	9	Newman-Crows Landing Unified	Newman
273	9	Oakdale Joint Unified	Oakdale
273	9	Orcutt Union Elementary	Orcutt
273	9	Petaluma City Elementary	Petaluma
273	9	Ravenswood City Elementary	East Palo Alto
273	9	Reef-Sunset Unified	Avenal
273	9	Rincon Valley Union Elementary	Santa Rosa
273	9	Rosedale Union Elementary	Bakersfield
273	9	San Bernardino Co. Office of Educ.	San Bernardino
273	9	San Gabriel Unified	San Gabriel
273	9	San Rafael City Elementary	San Rafael
273	9	Silver Valley Unified	Yermo
273	9	Sulphur Springs Union	Canyon Country
273	9	Valley Center-Pauma Unified	Valley Center
273	9	Washington Unified	Fresno
306	8	Benicia Unified	Benicia
306	8	Burton Elementary	Porterville
306	8	Carpinteria Unified	Carpinteria
306	8	Centralia Elementary	Buena Park
306	8	Culver City Unified	Culver City
306	8	Del Mar Union Elementary	San Diego
306	8	Denair Unified	Denair
306	8	Duarte Unified	Duarte
306	8	El Monte Union High	El Monte
306	8	Enterprise Elementary	Redding
306	8	Fillmore Unified	Fillmore
306	8	Fowler Unified	Fowler
306	8	Fullerton Joint Union High	Fullerton
306	8	Lake Tahoe Unified	S Lake Tahoe
306	8	Linden Unified	Linden
306	8	Loomis Union Elementary	Loomis
306	8	Merced Union High	Atwater
306	8	Modesto City High	Modesto
306	8	Mojave Unified	Mojave
306	8	North Monterey County Unified	Moss Landing
306	8	Nuview Union	Nuevo
306	8	Patterson Joint Unified	Patterson
306	8	Perris Elementary	Perris
306	8	Perris Union High	Perris
306	8	Rio Elementary	Oxnard
306	8	San Bruno Park Elementary	San Bruno
306	8	San Ysidro Elementary	San Ysidro
306	8	Sequoia Union High	Redwood City
306	8	Temple City Unified	Temple City
306	8	Templeton Unified	Templeton
306	8	Union Elementary	San Jose
306	8	Ventura County Office of Educ.	Camarillo
338	7	Alpine Union Elementary	Alpine
338	7	Anderson Union High	Anderson
338	7	Bassett Unified	La Puente
338	7	Bear Valley Unified	Big Bear Lake
338	7	Belmont-Redwood Shores Elem.	Belmont
338	7	Buena Park Elementary	Buena Park
338	7	Burlingame Elementary	Burlingame
338	7	Cabrillo Unified	Half Moon Bay
338	7	Campbell Union High	San Jose
338	7	Central Elementary	R Cucamonga
338	7	Dixon Unified	Dixon
338	7	Dos Palos Oro Loma Joint Unified	Dos Palos
338	7	Escalon Unified	Escalon
338	7	Escondido Union High	Escondido
338	7	Eureka City Schools	Eureka
338	7	Eureka Union	Granite Bay
338	7	Gridley Unified	Gridley
338	7	Hughson Unified	Hughson
338	7	Keppel Union Elementary	Pearblossom
338	7	Kerman Unified	Kerman
338	7	Kingsburg Elementary Charter	Kingsburg
338	7	Lemon Grove	Lemon Grove
338	7	Manhattan Beach Unified	Manhattan Beach
338	7	Merced County Office of Education	Merced
338	7	Monterey County Office of Educ.	Salinas
338	7	Northern Humboldt Union High	Mckinleyville
338	7	Oak Park Unified	Oak Park
338	7	Oakley Union Elementary	Oakley
338	7	Oroville City Elementary	Oroville
338	7	Pacifica	Pacifica
338	7	Palo Verde Unified	Blythe
338	7	Parlier Unified	Parlier
338	7	Rescue Union Elementary	Rescue
338	7	Rim of the World Unified	Blue Jay
338	7	Riverside County Office of Educ.	Riverside
338	7	Roseville Joint Union High	Roseville
338	7	San Carlos Elementary	San Carlos
338	7	San Joaquin County Office of Educ.	Stockton
338	7	San Lorenzo Valley Unified	Ben Lomond
338	7	San Mateo Union High	San Mateo
338	7	Santa Paula Elementary	Santa Paula
338	7	South Whittier Elementary	Whittier
338	7	Taft City	Taft
338	7	Tehachapi Unified	Tehachapi
338	7	Tulare County Office of Education	Visalia
338	7	Tulare Joint Union High	Tulare
338	7	Waterford Unified	Waterford
338	7	Whittier Union High	Whittier
386	6	Albany City Unified	Albany
386	6	Armona Union Elementary	Armona
386	6	Beverly Hills Unified	Beverly Hills
386	6	Black Oak Mine Unified	Georgetown
386	6	Carmel Unified	Carmel
386	6	Corning Union Elementary	Corning
386	6	Cypress Elementary	Cypress
386	6	Delhi Unified	Delhi
386	6	Empire Union Elementary	Modesto
386	6	Farmersville Unified	Farmersville
386	6	Firebaugh-Las Deltas Joint Unified	Firebaugh
386	6	Fremont Union High	Sunnyvale
386	6	Galt Joint Union Elementary	Galt
386	6	Golden Plains Unified	San Joaquin
386	6	Hanford Joint Union High	Hanford
386	6	Hilmar Unified	Hilmar
386	6	Imperial Unified	Imperial
386	6	Kern County Office of Education	Bakersfield
386	6	Lakeport Unified	Lakeport
386	6	Lemoore Union Elementary	Lemoore
386	6	Live Oak Elementary	Santa Cruz
386	6	Live Oak Unified	Live Oak
386	6	Lowell Joint	Whittier
386	6	Lucerne Valley Unified	Lucerne Valley
386	6	Mcfarland Unified	Mcfarland
386	6	Mendota Unified	Mendota
386	6	Mill Valley Elementary	Mill Valley
386	6	Moreland Elementary	San Jose
386	6	Orland Joint Unified	Orland
386	6	Piedmont City Unified	Piedmont
386	6	Placer Union High	Auburn
386	6	Red Bluff Union Elementary	Red Bluff
386	6	Ripon Unified	Ripon
386	6	Riverbank Unified	Riverbank
386	6	Santa Rita Union Elementary	Salinas
386	6	Sbc - Aspire Public Schools	Oakland
386	6	Solana Beach Elementary	Solana Beach
386	6	Southern Kern Unified	Rosamond
386	6	Stanislaus County Office of Educ.	Modesto
386	6	Stanislaus Union Elementary	Modesto
386	6	Tamalpais Union High	Larkspur
386	6	Walnut Creek Elementary	Walnut Creek
386	6	Wiseburn Elementary	Hawthorne
429	5	Acalanes Union High	Lafayette
429	5	Brawley Elementary	Brawley
429	5	Cambrian	San Jose
429	5	Centinela Valley Union High	Lawndale
429	5	Chowchilla Elementary	Chowchilla
429	5	Coronado Unified	Coronado
429	5	Delano Joint Union High	Delano
429	5	Eastside Union Elementary	Lancaster
429	5	El Segundo Unified	El Segundo
429	5	Fruitvale Elementary	Bakersfield
429	5	Greenfield Union Elementary	Greenfield
429	5	Gustine Unified	Gustine
429	5	Healdsburg Unified	Healdsburg
429	5	Holtville Unified	Holtville
429	5	Jefferson Union High	Daly City
429	5	Lafayette Elementary	Lafayette
429	5	Liberty Union High	Brentwood
429	5	Los Gatos Union Elementary	Los Gatos
429	5	Millbrae Elementary	Millbrae
429	5	Mt. Pleasant Elementary	San Jose
429	5	Norris Elementary	Bakersfield
429	5	Orinda Union Elementary	Orinda
429	5	Pacific Grove Unified	Pacific Grove
429	5	Piner-Olivet Union Elementary	Santa Rosa
429	5	Red Bluff Joint Union High	Red Bluff
429	5	Riverdale Joint Unified	Riverdale
429	5	Robla Elementary	Sacramento
429	5	Rosemead Elementary	Rosemead
429	5	Ross Valley Elementary	San Anselmo
429	5	Salida Union Elementary	Salida
429	5	Santa Cruz City Elementary	Soquel
429	5	Sbc - High Tech High	San Diego
429	5	South Pasadena Unified	South Pasadena
429	5	Wasco Union Elementary	Wasco
429	5	West Sonoma County Union High	Sebastopol
429	5	Winters Joint Unified	Winters
465	4	Acton-Agua Dulce Unified	Acton
465	4	Arvin Union Elementary	Arvin
465	4	Auburn Union Elementary	Auburn
465	4	Beardsley Elementary	Bakersfield
465	4	Bellevue Union Elementary	Santa Rosa
465	4	Bonsall Union Elementary	Bonsall
465	4	Castaic Union Elementary	Valencia
465	4	Central Union Elementary	Lemoore
465	4	Central Union High	El Centro
465	4	Cucamonga Elementary	R Cucamonga
465	4	Dixie Elementary	San Rafael
465	4	Earlimart Elementary	Earlimart
465	4	Exeter Union Elementary	Exeter
465	4	Gonzales Unified	Gonzales
465	4	Grass Valley Elementary	Grass Valley
465	4	Hermosa Beach City Elementary	Hermosa Beach
465	4	Hillsborough City Elementary	Hillsborough
465	4	Jefferson Elementary	Tracy
465	4	John Swett Unified	Rodeo
465	4	Julian Union Elementary	Julian
465	4	King City Union	King City
465	4	La Canada Unified	La Canada
465	4	Laguna Beach Unified	Laguna Beach
465	4	Lammersville Joint Unified	Mountain House
465	4	Lamont Elementary	Lamont
465	4	Livingston Union Elementary	Livingston
465	4	Los Nietos	Whittier
465	4	Menlo Park City Elementary	Atherton
465	4	Moraga Elementary	Moraga
465	4	Mountain View Elementary	Ontario
465	4	Muroc Joint Unified	North Edwards
465	4	Ocean View	Oxnard
465	4	Old Adobe Union	Petaluma
465	4	Orange County Dept of Education	Costa Mesa
465	4	Oroville Union High	Oroville
465	4	Richland Union Elementary	Shafter
465	4	Romoland Elementary	Homeland
465	4	Roseland Elementary	Santa Rosa
465	4	San Marino Unified	San Marino
465	4	Santa Maria Joint Union High	Santa Maria
465	4	Saratoga Union Elementary	Saratoga
465	4	Savanna Elementary	Anaheim
465	4	Scotts Valley Unified	Scotts Valley

Note: This section only includes districts with 1,500 or more students; All categories are ranked from high to low

465	4	Soquel Union Elementary	Capitola
465	4	South Monterey Co. Jt Union High	King City
465	4	Standard Elementary	Bakersfield
465	4	Willows Unified	Willows
465	4	Winton Elementary	Winton
513	3	Brawley Union High	Brawley
513	3	Byron Union Elementary	Byron
513	3	Dehesa Elementary	El Cajon
513	3	Fairfax Elementary	Bakersfield
513	3	Fallbrook Union High	Fallbrook
513	3	Galt Joint Union High	Galt
513	3	Lemoore Union High	Lemoore
513	3	Los Gatos-Saratoga Jt Union High	Los Gatos
513	3	Mountain View-Los Altos Union High	Mountain View
513	3	Oro Grande Elementary	Oro Grande
513	3	Pioneer Union Elementary	Hanford
513	3	San Rafael City High	San Rafael
513	3	Spencer Valley Elementary	Santa Ysabel
513	3	Weaver Union	Merced
513	3	Woodlake Union Elementary	Woodlake
513	3	Wright Elementary	Santa Rosa
529	2	Gorman Elementary	Gorman
529	2	Marcum-Illinois Union Elementary	East Nicolaus
529	2	San Benito High	Hollister
529	2	Santa Paula Union High	Santa Paula
529	2	Wasco Union High	Wasco

Number of Teachers

Rank	Number	District Name	City
1	28,769.0	Los Angeles Unified	Los Angeles
2	6,706.0	San Diego Unified	San Diego
3	3,134.8	Long Beach Unified	Long Beach
4	3,053.1	Fresno Unified	Fresno
5	2,921.0	San Francisco Unified	San Francisco
6	2,610.4	Elk Grove Unified	Elk Grove
7	2,341.1	San Bernardino City Unified	San Bernardino
8	2,275.6	Santa Ana Unified	Santa Ana
9	2,140.0	Corona-Norco Unified	Norco
10	2,096.6	Oakland Unified	Oakland
11	2,003.2	Capistrano Unified	SJ Capistrano
12	1,960.7	San Juan Unified	Carmichael
13	1,822.8	Garden Grove Unified	Garden Grove
14	1,672.6	Sacramento City Unified	Sacramento
15	1,639.7	Fontana Unified	Fontana
16	1,623.5	Stockton Unified	Stockton
17	1,619.7	Riverside Unified	Riverside
18	1,618.2	Sweetwater Union High	Chula Vista
19	1,500.0	Mt. Diablo Unified	Concord
20	1,489.5	Kern Union High	Bakersfield
21	1,482.7	Clovis Unified	Clovis
22	1,474.2	San Jose Unified	San Jose
23	1,456.0	Moreno Valley Unified	Moreno Valley
24	1,396.9	Fremont Unified	Fremont
25	1,351.9	Chula Vista Elementary	Chula Vista
25	1,351.9	West Contra Costa Unified	Richmond
27	1,322.2	Lodi Unified	Lodi
28	1,321.3	Twin Rivers Unified	Mcclellan
29	1,298.3	Bakersfield City	Bakersfield
30	1,264.1	Anaheim Union High	Anaheim
31	1,260.8	San Ramon Valley Unified	Danville
32	1,235.4	Temecula Valley Unified	Temecula
33	1,216.0	Poway Unified	San Diego
34	1,188.5	Montebello Unified	Montebello
35	1,180.5	Pomona Unified	Pomona
36	1,161.3	Chino Valley Unified	Chino
37	1,154.8	Orange Unified	Orange
38	1,125.1	Saddleback Valley Unified	Mission Viejo
39	1,115.6	Desert Sands Unified	La Quinta
40	1,113.4	Rialto Unified	Rialto
41	1,099.1	Glendale Unified	Glendale
42	1,088.9	East Side Union High	San Jose
43	1,071.2	Vista Unified	Vista
44	1,065.5	Compton Unified	Compton
45	1,052.5	Antelope Valley Union High	Lancaster
46	1,051.4	Visalia Unified	Visalia
47	1,028.6	William S. Hart Union High	Santa Clarita
48	1,019.9	Ontario-Montclair Elementary	Ontario
49	987.0	Colton Joint Unified	Colton
50	981.4	Irvine Unified	Irvine
51	977.5	Placentia-Yorba Linda Unified	Placentia
52	974.0	Grossmont Union High	La Mesa
53	923.7	Chaffey Joint Union High	Ontario
54	920.9	Newport-Mesa Unified	Costa Mesa
55	919.6	Manteca Unified	Manteca
56	904.3	Hacienda La Puente Unified	City of Industry
57	904.1	Palm Springs Unified	Palm Springs
58	901.6	Torrance Unified	Torrance
59	896.7	Lake Elsinore Unified	Lake Elsinore
60	893.8	Hayward Unified	Hayward
61	888.8	Pasadena Unified	Pasadena
62	888.2	Conejo Valley Unified	Thousand Oaks
63	887.8	Hemet Unified	Hemet
64	882.9	Murrieta Valley Unified	Murrieta
65	882.7	Baldwin Park Unified	Baldwin Park
66	882.1	Redlands Unified	Redlands
67	873.4	Hesperia Unified	Hesperia
68	862.3	Downey Unified	Downey
69	844.8	Oceanside Unified	Oceanside
70	833.7	Coachella Valley Unified	Thermal
71	833.6	Fairfield-Suisun Unified	Fairfield
72	822.8	ABC Unified	Cerritos
73	820.6	Jurupa Unified	Jurupa Valley
74	817.0	Norwalk-La Mirada Unified	Norwalk
75	811.2	Tustin Unified	Tustin
76	808.4	Escondido Union	Escondido
77	805.7	Antioch Unified	Antioch
78	804.7	Pajaro Valley Unified	Watsonville
79	793.9	Madera Unified	Madera
80	789.5	Simi Valley Unified	Simi Valley
81	788.9	Palmdale Elementary	Palmdale
82	769.2	Napa Valley Unified	Napa
83	768.3	Cupertino Union	Cupertino
84	767.2	Folsom-Cordova Unified	Folsom
85	755.6	Val Verde Unified	Perris
86	747.0	Anaheim City	Anaheim
87	733.0	Alvord Unified	Riverside
88	709.8	Tracy Joint Unified	Tracy
89	709.6	Modesto City Elementary	Modesto
90	708.9	Alhambra Unified	Alhambra
91	699.7	Ventura Unified	Ventura
92	672.7	Burbank Unified	Burbank
93	669.1	Vallejo City Unified	Vallejo
94	668.4	Oxnard Union High	Oxnard
95	668.3	San Marcos Unified	San Marcos
96	667.6	Cajon Valley Union	El Cajon
97	666.5	Palo Alto Unified	Palo Alto
98	658.8	Rowland Unified	Rowland Heights
99	653.8	Santa Barbara Unified	Santa Barbara
100	649.7	Alum Rock Union Elementary	San Jose
101	642.7	Santa Clara Unified	Santa Clara
102	637.7	Oxnard	Oxnard
103	633.9	Pleasanton Unified	Pleasanton
104	631.5	Huntington Bch Union High	Huntington Bch
105	625.2	Yuba City Unified	Yuba City
106	615.5	Paramount Unified	Paramount
107	613.1	Chico Unified	Chico
108	609.9	Turlock Unified	Turlock
109	608.7	West Covina Unified	West Covina
110	602.9	Victor Valley Union High	Victorville
111	601.2	Central Unified	Fresno
112	597.7	Salinas Union High	Salinas
113	592.3	Modesto City High	Modesto
114	591.8	Lynwood Unified	Lynwood
115	587.0	Panama-Buena Vista Union	Bakersfield
116	575.8	Walnut Valley Unified	Walnut
117	570.3	Livermore Valley Joint Unified	Livermore
118	569.6	Western Placer Unified	Lincoln
119	568.4	Santa Maria-Bonita	Santa Maria
120	557.4	Apple Valley Unified	Apple Valley
121	553.3	New Haven Unified	Union City
122	548.7	Porterville Unified	Porterville
123	542.4	Evergreen Elementary	San Jose
124	541.3	Covina-Valley Unified	Covina
125	537.9	Vacaville Unified	Vacaville
126	536.9	Fullerton Joint Union High	Fullerton
127	533.9	Lancaster Elementary	Lancaster
128	533.5	Fullerton Elementary	Fullerton
129	529.3	Bellflower Unified	Bellflower
130	526.0	Inglewood Unified	Inglewood
131	521.9	San Lorenzo Unified	San Lorenzo
132	517.6	Monterey Peninsula Unified	Monterey
133	517.1	Ceres Unified	Ceres
134	516.1	Santa Rosa High	Santa Rosa
135	515.4	Natomas Unified	Sacramento
136	511.6	Santa Monica-Malibu Unified	Santa Monica
137	497.3	Etiwanda Elementary	Etiwanda
138	490.6	Rocklin Unified	Rocklin
139	486.6	Alameda City Unified	Alameda
140	485.0	Sanger Unified	Sanger
141	482.2	Azusa Unified	Azusa
142	478.1	Lompoc Unified	Lompoc
143	477.3	Las Virgenes Unified	Calabasas
144	476.5	Berkeley Unified	Berkeley
145	475.8	Whittier Union High	Whittier
146	472.2	Oak Grove Elementary	San Jose
147	470.3	San Mateo-Foster City	Foster City
148	470.0	Upland Unified	Upland
149	465.4	Palos Verdes Peninsula Unified	Palos Vrds Est
150	465.3	San Dieguito Union High	Encinitas
151	457.1	Pittsburg Unified	Pittsburg
152	455.7	Gilroy Unified	Gilroy
153	453.4	Woodland Joint Unified	Woodland
154	447.3	Lucia Mar Unified	Arroyo Grande
155	438.9	Saugus Union	Santa Clarita
156	436.8	Marysville Joint Unified	Marysville
157	435.1	La Mesa-Spring Valley	La Mesa
158	435.0	Merced City Elementary	Merced
159	434.4	Merced Union High	Atwater
159	434.4	Riverside County Office of Educ.	Riverside
161	432.6	El Monte Union High	El Monte
162	430.4	Sequoia Union High	Redwood City
163	429.8	Fremont Union High	Sunnyvale
164	428.5	Roseville Joint Union High	Roseville
165	427.0	Carlsbad Unified	Carlsbad
166	426.9	Santa Clara County Office of Educ.	San Jose
167	418.5	Kings Canyon Joint Unified	Reedley
168	416.4	East Whittier City Elementary	Whittier
169	415.6	Roseville City Elementary	Roseville
170	413.0	Tulare City	Tulare
171	412.6	Franklin-Mckinley Elementary	San Jose
172	408.8	El Rancho Unified	Pico Rivera
173	405.5	Westminster Elementary	Westminster
174	404.5	Morongo Unified	Twentynine Plms
175	402.3	Yucaipa-Calimesa Joint Unified	Yucaipa
176	401.8	San Mateo Union High	San Mateo
177	400.7	San Leandro Unified	San Leandro
178	400.3	Redwood City Elementary	Redwood City
179	398.9	Milpitas Unified	Milpitas
180	397.6	Bonita Unified	San Dimas
181	397.2	S San Francisco Unified	S San Francisco
182	395.4	Menifee Union Elementary	Menifee
183	395.1	Perris Union High	Perris
184	393.0	Ocean View	Huntington Bch
185	390.8	Castro Valley Unified	Castro Valley
186	388.6	Davis Joint Unified	Davis
187	387.8	Arcadia Unified	Arcadia
188	387.6	Hawthorne	Hawthorne
189	385.3	Escondido Union High	Escondido
190	383.6	El Monte City Elementary	El Monte
191	380.4	Novato Unified	Novato
192	380.1	Victor Elementary	Victorville
193	379.6	Lincoln Unified	Stockton
194	379.1	San Luis Coastal Unified	San Luis Obispo
195	370.8	Calexico Unified	Calexico
196	357.2	Los Alamitos Unified	Los Alamitos
197	355.9	Morgan Hill Unified	Morgan Hill
198	355.8	Los Banos Unified	Los Banos
199	355.0	Washington Unified	West Sacramento
200	348.9	San Jacinto Unified	San Jacinto
201	347.0	Delano Union Elementary	Delano
202	342.5	Brentwood Union Elementary	Brentwood
203	342.1	Redondo Beach Unified	Redondo Beach
204	339.4	Campbell Union	Campbell
205	339.0	Berryessa Union Elementary	San Jose
206	337.5	Greenfield Union	Bakersfield
207	337.1	Salinas City Elementary	Salinas
208	325.8	Beaumont Unified	Beaumont
209	324.9	Orange County Dept of Education	Costa Mesa
210	322.9	Pleasant Valley	Camarillo
211	321.2	Westside Union Elementary	Quartz Hill
212	318.9	Sylvan Union Elementary	Modesto
213	318.8	Santa Maria Joint Union High	Santa Maria
214	314.1	Lennox	Lennox
215	314.0	Campbell Union High	San Jose
216	313.5	South Bay Union Elementary	Imperial Beach
217	312.8	Jefferson Elementary	Daly City
218	312.1	Hueneme Elementary	Port Hueneme
219	307.7	Liberty Union High	Brentwood
220	303.2	Adelanto Elementary	Adelanto
221	302.1	Dry Creek Joint Elementary	Roseville
222	302.0	Snowline Joint Unified	Phelan
223	295.1	Dublin Unified	Dublin
224	294.4	Dinuba Unified	Dinuba

Note: This section only includes districts with 1,500 or more students; All categories are ranked from high to low

Rank	Value	District	City
225	290.6	Sunnyvale	Sunnyvale
226	289.5	Alisal Union	Salinas
226	289.5	Paso Robles Joint Unified	Paso Robles
228	289.0	Newhall	Valencia
229	288.8	Claremont Unified	Claremont
230	288.4	Moorpark Unified	Moorpark
231	288.2	Glendora Unified	Glendora
232	286.7	Kern County Office of Education	Bakersfield
233	285.0	Mountain View Elementary	El Monte
234	284.5	Santee Elementary	Santee
235	282.5	Selma Unified	Selma
236	280.5	El Dorado Union High	Placerville
237	279.3	National Elementary	National City
238	277.5	Culver City Unified	Culver City
239	275.1	San Gabriel Unified	San Gabriel
240	271.7	Ukiah Unified	Ukiah
241	267.2	Newark Unified	Newark
242	266.1	Santa Rosa Elementary	Santa Rosa
243	265.0	Acalanes Union High	Lafayette
244	264.8	Hanford Elementary	Hanford
245	264.0	Manhattan Beach Unified	Manhattan Beach
246	259.3	Centinela Valley Union High	Lawndale
247	258.3	Barstow Unified	Barstow
248	257.8	Lawndale Elementary	Lawndale
249	256.7	Magnolia Elementary	Anaheim
250	255.9	San Bernardino Co. Office of Educ.	San Bernardino
251	254.5	Shasta Union High	Redding
252	252.5	Del Mar Union Elementary	San Diego
253	250.9	Petaluma Joint Union High	Petaluma
254	250.7	Encinitas Union Elementary	Encinitas
255	249.0	Monrovia Unified	Monrovia
256	247.0	Huntington Bch City Elementary	Huntington Bch
257	245.5	San Diego County Office of Educ.	San Diego
258	245.0	Perris Elementary	Perris
259	243.5	Whittier City Elementary	Whittier
260	243.2	Ramona City Unified	Ramona
261	240.5	Tulare Joint Union High	Tulare
262	239.7	Fountain Valley Elementary	Fountain Valley
263	239.2	Beverly Hills Unified	Beverly Hills
264	238.0	Windsor Unified	Windsor
265	235.9	Cotati-Rohnert Park Unified	Rohnert Park
266	235.3	Alta Loma Elementary	Alta Loma
267	233.0	Oakdale Joint Unified	Oakdale
268	231.3	Sonoma Valley Unified	Sonoma
269	228.9	Patterson Joint Unified	Patterson
270	227.8	Temple City Unified	Temple City
271	226.3	Garvey Elementary	Rosemead
271	226.3	Lakeside Union Elementary	Lakeside
273	225.2	Sulphur Springs Union	Canyon Country
274	223.5	El Centro Elementary	El Centro
275	220.6	Ravenswood City Elementary	East Palo Alto
276	220.3	Tamalpais Union High	Larkspur
277	220.1	Mountain View Whisman	Mountain View
278	219.0	Rosedale Union Elementary	Bakersfield
279	218.6	Sierra Sands Unified	Ridgecrest
280	218.0	Travis Unified	Fairfield
281	216.0	Fallbrook Union Elementary	Fallbrook
282	215.8	Charter Oak Unified	Covina
283	215.6	Buckeye Union Elementary	Shingle Springs
284	215.5	Atascadero Unified	Atascadero
285	212.8	Union Elementary	San Jose
286	211.5	Jefferson Union High	Daly City
287	209.4	Brea-Olinda Unified	Brea
288	207.8	Benicia Unified	Benicia
289	206.7	Paradise Unified	Paradise
290	203.3	Hollister	Hollister
291	203.2	Buena Park Elementary	Buena Park
291	203.2	Gateway Unified	Redding
293	201.8	Cutler-Orosi Joint Unified	Orosi
294	201.7	Banning Unified	Banning
295	200.7	Soledad Unified	Soledad
296	199.0	Orcutt Union Elementary	Orcutt
297	197.6	San Rafael City Elementary	San Rafael
298	195.8	Moreland Elementary	San Jose
299	195.1	Los Altos Elementary	Los Altos
300	194.8	Santa Cruz City High	Soquel
301	191.9	Center Joint Unified	Antelope
302	191.4	Little Lake City Elementary	Santa Fe Spgs
303	190.8	San Ysidro Elementary	San Ysidro
304	190.3	La Habra City Elementary	La Habra
305	190.0	Bassett Unified	La Puente
306	189.6	San Lorenzo Valley Unified	Ben Lomond
307	188.5	Galt Joint Union Elementary	Galt
308	187.8	Tehachapi Unified	Tehachapi
309	187.4	Kerman Unified	Kerman
309	187.4	Oakley Union Elementary	Oakley
311	186.3	Valley Center-Pauma Unified	Valley Center
312	185.9	Albany City Unified	Albany
312	185.9	Tahoe-Truckee Joint Unified	Truckee
314	184.3	Lake Tahoe Unified	S Lake Tahoe
315	183.9	Coalinga-Huron Joint Unified	Coalinga
316	183.0	Placer Union High	Auburn
317	182.7	Atwater Elementary	Atwater
317	182.7	Eureka City Schools	Eureka
319	181.7	South Pasadena Unified	South Pasadena
320	181.5	San Joaquin County Office of Educ.	Stockton
321	181.1	Central Elementary	R Cucamonga
322	181.0	Goleta Union Elementary	Goleta
323	180.2	Del Norte County Unified	Crescent City
324	179.3	Nevada County Office of Education	Nevada City
325	178.3	Mountain View-Los Altos Union High	Mountain View
326	176.5	Lindsay Unified	Lindsay
327	174.3	Rio Elementary	Oxnard
328	174.1	Rim of the World Unified	Blue Jay
329	173.5	Oak Park Unified	Oak Park
330	171.2	Central Union High	El Centro
331	171.0	Centralia Elementary	Buena Park
332	169.6	La Canada Unified	La Canada
333	169.0	North Monterey County Unified	Moss Landing
334	168.7	Delano Joint Union High	Delano
335	168.3	Burton Elementary	Porterville
336	167.3	Alameda County Office of Education	Hayward
337	167.0	Rescue Union Elementary	Rescue
338	166.6	Ventura County Office of Educ.	Camarillo
339	165.7	Martinez Unified	Martinez
340	163.1	Solana Beach Elementary	Solana Beach
341	162.9	Rincon Valley Union Elementary	Santa Rosa
342	162.1	Fillmore Unified	Fillmore
343	160.8	Waterford Unified	Waterford
344	159.9	Fresno County Office of Education	Fresno
345	158.7	Santa Paula Elementary	Santa Paula
346	158.6	Enterprise Elementary	Redding
347	156.5	Belmont-Redwood Shores Elem.	Belmont
348	156.4	Imperial Unified	Imperial
349	156.0	Norris Elementary	Bakersfield
350	155.7	Palo Verde Unified	Blythe
351	155.2	Duarte Unified	Duarte
352	155.1	Walnut Creek Elementary	Walnut Creek
353	155.0	Amador County Unified	Jackson
354	154.5	Menlo Park City Elementary	Atherton
355	154.3	Eureka Union	Granite Bay
355	154.3	Mcfarland Unified	Mcfarland
357	154.0	Parlier Unified	Parlier
358	153.2	Hanford Joint Union High	Hanford
359	153.0	Eastside Union Elementary	Lancaster
360	152.7	Cypress Elementary	Cypress
361	152.6	Piedmont City Unified	Piedmont
362	151.9	Calaveras Unified	San Andreas
362	151.9	Richland Union Elementary	Shafter
364	151.7	Lafayette Elementary	Lafayette
365	151.4	Nevada Joint Union High	Grass Valley
366	151.0	Mill Valley Elementary	Mill Valley
367	150.9	Wiseburn Elementary	Hawthorne
368	150.4	San Carlos Elementary	San Carlos
369	150.0	Los Gatos-Saratoga Jt Union High	Los Gatos
370	148.5	Oro Grande Elementary	Oro Grande
371	147.3	Dixon Unified	Dixon
372	146.7	Washington Unified	Fresno
373	144.9	Brawley Elementary	Brawley
374	144.5	Konocti Unified	Lower Lake
375	143.9	Corcoran Joint Unified	Corcoran
376	142.8	Cambrian	San Jose
377	142.7	Burlingame Elementary	Burlingame
378	141.4	Lemon Grove	Lemon Grove
379	141.3	Fruitvale Elementary	Bakersfield
380	140.9	Mountain Empire Unified	Pine Valley
381	139.6	San Marino Unified	San Marino
382	139.5	Loomis Union Elementary	Loomis
383	136.9	Los Gatos Union Elementary	Los Gatos
384	136.8	Cabrillo Unified	Half Moon Bay
385	135.7	Greenfield Union Elementary	Greenfield
386	135.5	Wasco Union Elementary	Wasco
387	135.0	Coronado Unified	Coronado
388	134.9	Redding Elementary	Redding
389	134.8	Laguna Beach Unified	Laguna Beach
390	134.7	Arvin Union Elementary	Arvin
391	134.2	Lemoore Union Elementary	Lemoore
392	133.2	Silver Valley Unified	Yermo
393	132.6	Castaic Union Elementary	Valencia
393	132.6	Pacifica	Pacifica
395	131.8	Tulare County Office of Education	Visalia
396	129.0	Carmel Unified	Carmel
397	128.3	Julian Union Elementary	Julian
398	128.1	King City Union	King City
399	126.8	Petaluma City Elementary	Petaluma
400	126.4	Empire Union Elementary	Modesto
401	125.5	El Segundo Unified	El Segundo
402	124.4	Stanislaus County Office of Educ.	Modesto
403	124.1	Fallbrook Union High	Fallbrook
404	124.0	Standard Elementary	Bakersfield
405	123.6	Riverbank Unified	Riverbank
406	123.2	Escalon Unified	Escalon
407	123.1	Southern Kern Unified	Rosamond
408	122.5	Monterey County Office of Educ.	Salinas
409	121.8	River Delta Joint Unified	Rio Vista
410	120.2	Ripon Unified	Ripon
411	119.9	Farmersville Unified	Farmersville
412	119.7	Newman-Crows Landing Unified	Newman
412	119.7	San Benito High	Hollister
414	119.1	Delhi Unified	Delhi
415	118.4	Jefferson Elementary	Tracy
416	118.2	Weaver Union	Merced
417	118.0	Romoland Elementary	Homeland
418	117.8	Lamont Elementary	Lamont
419	117.3	Reef-Sunset Unified	Avenal
420	116.7	Mendota Unified	Mendota
421	116.1	Oroville City Elementary	Oroville
422	116.0	Livingston Union Elementary	Livingston
422	116.0	South Whittier Elementary	Whittier
424	115.4	Lowell Joint	Whittier
425	115.0	Ocean View	Oxnard
425	115.0	Orinda Union Elementary	Orinda
427	114.5	Fort Bragg Unified	Fort Bragg
428	114.4	Stanislaus Union Elementary	Modesto
429	114.2	Ojai Unified	Ojai
430	113.9	Bear Valley Unified	Big Bear Lake
431	113.4	Lucerne Valley Unified	Lucerne Valley
432	113.0	Oroville Union High	Oroville
433	112.7	Hermosa Beach City Elementary	Hermosa Beach
434	112.5	Hilmar Unified	Hilmar
435	111.8	Mojave Unified	Mojave
436	110.7	Rosemead Elementary	Rosemead
437	109.1	Fowler Unified	Fowler
438	109.0	Nuview Union	Nuevo
439	108.6	Scotts Valley Unified	Scotts Valley
440	107.8	Ross Valley Elementary	San Anselmo
441	107.1	Willits Unified	Willits
442	106.8	Carpinteria Unified	Carpinteria
443	106.7	Salida Union Elementary	Salida
444	106.2	Mt. Pleasant Elementary	San Jose
445	106.1	Saratoga Union Elementary	Saratoga
446	105.2	Linden Unified	Linden
446	105.2	Merced County Office of Education	Merced
448	104.4	Lemoore Union High	Lemoore
449	104.0	Santa Rita Union Elementary	Salinas
450	103.9	Live Oak Elementary	Santa Cruz
451	103.2	Santa Cruz City Elementary	Soquel
452	102.7	Hillsborough City Elementary	Hillsborough
453	102.5	Cucamonga Elementary	R Cucamonga
454	102.1	Keppel Union Elementary	Pearblossom
455	101.8	Pacific Grove Unified	Pacific Grove
455	101.8	San Bruno Park Elementary	San Bruno
457	101.7	San Rafael City High	San Rafael
458	101.5	Mountain View Elementary	Ontario
458	101.5	Sbc - High Tech High	San Diego
460	101.3	Gonzales Unified	Gonzales
461	101.2	Kingsburg Elementary Charter	Kingsburg
462	100.9	Roseland Elementary	Santa Rosa
463	100.0	Fairfax Elementary	Bakersfield
464	99.8	Templeton Unified	Templeton
465	98.8	Taft City	Taft
466	98.5	Hughson Unified	Hughson
467	98.2	Auburn Union Elementary	Auburn
468	98.1	West Sonoma County Union High	Sebastopol
469	97.4	Yosemite Unified	Oakhurst
470	97.2	Lammersville Joint Unified	Mountain House
471	97.0	Red Bluff Union Elementary	Red Bluff
472	96.8	Gridley Unified	Gridley
473	96.4	Mariposa County Unified	Mariposa
474	96.0	Central Union Elementary	Lemoore
475	95.8	Galt Joint Union High	Galt
475	95.8	Orland Joint Unified	Orland
477	95.5	Armona Union Elementary	Armona
478	94.8	Muroc Joint Unified	North Edwards
479	94.7	Marcum-Illinois Union Elementary	East Nicolaus

Note: This section only includes districts with 1,500 or more students; All categories are ranked from high to low

480	94.5	Chowchilla Elementary	Chowchilla
481	94.3	Bishop Unified	Bishop
482	93.6	Firebaugh-Las Deltas Joint Unified	Firebaugh
483	91.3	Soquel Union Elementary	Capitola
484	91.0	Bonsall Union Elementary	Bonsall
485	90.9	Millbrae Elementary	Millbrae
486	90.0	Savanna Elementary	Anaheim
487	89.8	Spencer Valley Elementary	Santa Ysabel
488	89.0	Golden Plains Unified	San Joaquin
489	87.6	Bellevue Union Elementary	Santa Rosa
489	87.6	Dixie Elementary	San Rafael
491	87.1	Robla Elementary	Sacramento
492	86.4	Denair Unified	Denair
493	86.2	Anderson Union High	Anderson
494	85.9	Red Bluff Joint Union High	Red Bluff
495	85.3	Northern Humboldt Union High	Mckinleyville
496	85.0	Golden Valley Unified	Madera
496	85.0	Winton Elementary	Winton
498	84.9	Earlimart Elementary	Earlimart
499	84.8	Healdsburg Unified	Healdsburg
500	84.3	Grass Valley Elementary	Grass Valley
501	83.4	Moraga Elementary	Moraga
502	82.8	Alpine Union Elementary	Alpine
503	82.6	Kelseyville Unified	Kelseyville
504	82.1	Corning Union Elementary	Corning
505	81.4	Middletown Unified	Middletown
506	80.7	Dehesa Elementary	El Cajon
507	80.5	Dos Palos Oro Loma Joint Unified	Dos Palos
508	79.8	Los Nietos	Whittier
509	79.6	Gorman Elementary	Gorman
510	78.2	Wright Elementary	Santa Rosa
511	78.1	South Monterey Co. Jt Union High	King City
512	78.0	Sbc - Aspire Public Schools	Oakland
513	77.0	Riverdale Joint Unified	Riverdale
514	76.5	Black Oak Mine Unified	Georgetown
515	76.3	Woodlake Union Elementary	Woodlake
516	76.0	Brawley Union High	Brawley
517	75.6	Live Oak Unified	Live Oak
518	75.4	Gustine Unified	Gustine
519	74.9	John Swett Unified	Rodeo
520	74.6	Holtville Unified	Holtville
521	74.4	Winters Joint Unified	Winters
522	73.0	Wasco Union High	Wasco
523	72.6	Beardsley Elementary	Bakersfield
524	72.3	Lakeport Unified	Lakeport
525	65.8	Piner-Olivet Union Elementary	Santa Rosa
526	62.4	Byron Union Elementary	Byron
527	61.7	Old Adobe Union	Petaluma
528	61.5	Santa Paula Union High	Santa Paula
529	61.4	Acton-Agua Dulce Unified	Acton
530	60.5	Pioneer Union Elementary	Hanford
531	56.8	Willows Unified	Willows
n/a	n/a	Exeter Union Elementary	Exeter
n/a	n/a	Los Angeles County Office of Educ.	Downey

Number of Students

Rank	Number	District Name	City
1	659,639	Los Angeles Unified	Los Angeles
2	131,044	San Diego Unified	San Diego
3	83,691	Long Beach Unified	Long Beach
4	74,235	Fresno Unified	Fresno
5	62,126	Elk Grove Unified	Elk Grove
6	57,250	Santa Ana Unified	Santa Ana
7	56,310	San Francisco Unified	San Francisco
8	54,379	San Bernardino City Unified	San Bernardino
9	53,467	Corona-Norco Unified	Norco
10	53,170	Capistrano Unified	SJ Capistrano
11	47,999	Garden Grove Unified	Garden Grove
12	47,940	Sacramento City Unified	Sacramento
13	47,245	San Juan Unified	Carmichael
14	46,377	Oakland Unified	Oakland
15	42,406	Riverside Unified	Riverside
16	40,619	Sweetwater Union High	Chula Vista
17	40,592	Fontana Unified	Fontana
18	39,040	Clovis Unified	Clovis
19	38,803	Stockton Unified	Stockton
20	37,505	Kern Union High	Bakersfield
21	35,692	Moreno Valley Unified	Moreno Valley
22	34,569	Poway Unified	San Diego
23	33,977	Mt. Diablo Unified	Concord
24	33,308	San Jose Unified	San Jose
25	32,829	Fremont Unified	Fremont
26	32,704	Anaheim Union High	Anaheim
27	31,637	Twin Rivers Unified	Mcclellan
28	31,319	Montebello Unified	Montebello
29	31,313	Chino Valley Unified	Chino
30	30,885	Saddleback Valley Unified	Mission Viejo
31	30,319	Lodi Unified	Lodi
32	30,267	Temecula Valley Unified	Temecula
33	30,136	Orange Unified	Orange
34	29,884	San Ramon Valley Unified	Danville
35	29,883	West Contra Costa Unified	Richmond
36	29,199	Desert Sands Unified	La Quinta
37	28,321	Bakersfield City	Bakersfield
38	28,179	Irvine Unified	Irvine
39	28,101	Chula Vista Elementary	Chula Vista
40	27,737	Pomona Unified	Pomona
41	27,268	Visalia Unified	Visalia
42	26,764	Rialto Unified	Rialto
43	26,449	William S. Hart Union High	Santa Clarita
44	26,228	Glendale Unified	Glendale
45	25,747	Placentia-Yorba Linda Unified	Placentia
46	25,738	Vista Unified	Vista
47	25,638	East Side Union High	San Jose
48	25,543	Antelope Valley Union High	Lancaster
49	25,065	Chaffey Joint Union High	Ontario
50	24,781	Compton Unified	Compton
51	24,229	Torrance Unified	Torrance
52	23,677	Grossmont Union High	La Mesa
53	23,676	Palm Springs Unified	Palm Springs
54	23,507	Tustin Unified	Tustin
55	23,444	Hesperia Unified	Hesperia
56	23,309	Manteca Unified	Manteca
57	23,192	Colton Joint Unified	Colton
58	22,782	Downey Unified	Downey
59	22,693	Murrieta Valley Unified	Murrieta
60	22,569	Ontario-Montclair Elementary	Ontario
61	22,171	Lake Elsinore Unified	Lake Elsinore
62	21,977	Hemet Unified	Hemet
63	21,857	Newport-Mesa Unified	Costa Mesa
64	21,637	Hayward Unified	Hayward
65	21,577	Fairfield-Suisun Unified	Fairfield
66	21,408	Redlands Unified	Redlands
67	20,987	Oceanside Unified	Oceanside
68	20,849	Hacienda La Puente Unified	City of Industry
69	20,722	Conejo Valley Unified	Thousand Oaks
70	20,688	ABC Unified	Cerritos
71	20,585	Palmdale Elementary	Palmdale
72	20,208	Norwalk-La Mirada Unified	Norwalk
73	19,936	Madera Unified	Madera
74	19,914	Pajaro Valley Unified	Watsonville
75	19,884	Jurupa Unified	Jurupa Valley
76	19,802	Pasadena Unified	Pasadena
77	19,741	Alvord Unified	Riverside
78	19,615	Val Verde Unified	Perris
79	19,432	Simi Valley Unified	Simi Valley
80	19,312	Anaheim City	Anaheim
81	19,238	Baldwin Park Unified	Baldwin Park
82	19,154	Folsom-Cordova Unified	Folsom
83	19,117	San Marcos Unified	San Marcos
84	19,093	Escondido Union	Escondido
85	18,877	Antioch Unified	Antioch
86	18,650	Cupertino Union	Cupertino
87	18,406	Coachella Valley Unified	Thermal
88	18,290	Alhambra Unified	Alhambra
89	18,078	Napa Valley Unified	Napa
90	17,429	Ventura Unified	Ventura
91	17,422	Tracy Joint Unified	Tracy
92	16,810	Panama-Buena Vista Union	Bakersfield
93	16,790	Oxnard Union High	Oxnard
94	16,670	Burbank Unified	Burbank
95	16,442	Huntington Bch Union High	Huntington Bch
96	16,118	Oxnard	Oxnard
97	16,057	Cajon Valley Union	El Cajon
98	15,929	Paramount Unified	Paramount
99	15,738	Rowland Unified	Rowland Heights
100	15,515	Lynwood Unified	Lynwood
101	15,326	Santa Barbara Unified	Santa Barbara
102	15,313	Vallejo City Unified	Vallejo
103	15,302	West Covina Unified	West Covina
104	15,289	Santa Clara Unified	Santa Clara
105	15,254	Modesto City Elementary	Modesto
106	15,186	Victor Valley Union High	Victorville
107	14,899	Pleasanton Unified	Pleasanton
108	14,896	Central Unified	Fresno
109	14,783	Fullerton Joint Union High	Fullerton
110	14,735	Modesto City High	Modesto
111	14,676	Apple Valley Unified	Apple Valley
112	14,658	Walnut Valley Unified	Walnut
113	14,624	Santa Maria-Bonita	Santa Maria
114	14,430	Lancaster Elementary	Lancaster
115	14,279	Inglewood Unified	Inglewood
116	13,761	Salinas Union High	Salinas
117	13,736	Porterville Unified	Porterville
118	13,735	Turlock Unified	Turlock
119	13,734	Bellflower Unified	Bellflower
120	13,656	Fullerton Elementary	Fullerton
121	13,646	Chico Unified	Chico
122	13,538	Whittier Union High	Whittier
123	13,351	Evergreen Elementary	San Jose
124	13,256	Covina-Valley Unified	Covina
125	13,228	Yuba City Unified	Yuba City
126	13,031	Etiwanda Elementary	Etiwanda
127	12,951	New Haven Unified	Union City
128	12,941	Alum Rock Union Elementary	San Jose
129	12,781	Livermore Valley Joint Unified	Livermore
130	12,561	Vacaville Unified	Vacaville
131	12,532	Ceres Unified	Ceres
132	12,485	San Dieguito Union High	Encinitas
133	12,344	Natomas Unified	Sacramento
134	12,303	La Mesa-Spring Valley	La Mesa
135	12,205	Palo Alto Unified	Palo Alto
136	12,123	San Lorenzo Unified	San Lorenzo
137	11,927	Upland Unified	Upland
138	11,904	Rocklin Unified	Rocklin
139	11,840	Palos Verdes Peninsula Unified	Palos Vrds Est
140	11,531	Victor Elementary	Victorville
141	11,518	Oak Grove Elementary	San Jose
142	11,468	Santa Monica-Malibu Unified	Santa Monica
143	11,354	Santa Rosa High	Santa Rosa
144	11,319	Las Virgenes Unified	Calabasas
145	11,290	Gilroy Unified	Gilroy
146	11,204	San Mateo-Foster City	Foster City
147	11,063	Carlsbad Unified	Carlsbad
148	10,956	Monterey Peninsula Unified	Monterey
149	10,872	Sanger Unified	Sanger
150	10,805	Merced City Elementary	Merced
151	10,669	Alameda City Unified	Alameda
152	10,645	Perris Union High	Perris
153	10,620	Franklin-Mckinley Elementary	San Jose
154	10,588	Lucia Mar Unified	Arroyo Grande
155	10,535	Fremont Union High	Sunnyvale
156	10,381	Pittsburg Unified	Pittsburg
157	10,295	Saugus Union	Santa Clarita
158	10,293	Merced Union High	Atwater
159	10,252	Woodland Joint Unified	Woodland
160	10,163	Azusa Unified	Azusa
161	10,058	Roseville Joint Union High	Roseville
162	10,056	El Monte Union High	El Monte
163	9,953	El Rancho Unified	Pico Rivera
164	9,949	Milpitas Unified	Milpitas
165	9,879	Roseville City Elementary	Roseville
166	9,870	Bonita Unified	San Dimas
167	9,851	San Jacinto Unified	San Jacinto
168	9,841	Kings Canyon Joint Unified	Reedley
169	9,802	Lompoc Unified	Lompoc
170	9,784	Menifee Union Elementary	Menifee
171	9,782	Marysville Joint Unified	Marysville
172	9,719	Arcadia Unified	Arcadia
173	9,714	Los Alamitos Unified	Los Alamitos
174	9,655	Yucaipa-Calimesa Joint Unified	Yucaipa
175	9,637	Westminster Elementary	Westminster
176	9,545	Berkeley Unified	Berkeley
177	9,515	Los Banos Unified	Los Banos
178	9,461	Ocean View	Huntington Bch
179	9,369	El Monte City Elementary	El Monte
180	9,348	S San Francisco Unified	S San Francisco
181	9,312	Escondido Union High	Escondido
182	9,306	Morgan Hill Unified	Morgan Hill
183	9,297	Tulare City	Tulare
184	9,273	Redwood City Elementary	Redwood City
185	9,216	Calexico Unified	Calexico
186	9,170	Western Placer Unified	Lincoln
187	9,117	Adelanto Elementary	Adelanto
188	9,090	Morongo Unified	Twentynine Plms
189	9,052	Castro Valley Unified	Castro Valley
190	9,032	East Whittier City Elementary	Whittier
191	8,981	Lincoln Unified	Stockton
192	8,947	Sequoia Union High	Redwood City
193	8,870	San Leandro Unified	San Leandro
194	8,866	Hawthorne	Hawthorne
195	8,691	Los Angeles County Office of Educ.	Downey
196	8,660	Beaumont Unified	Beaumont

Note: This section only includes districts with 1,500 or more students; All categories are ranked from high to low

Rank	Number	District Name	City
197	8,658	Redondo Beach Unified	Redondo Beach
198	8,596	Davis Joint Unified	Davis
199	8,554	Alisal Union	Salinas
200	8,525	Westside Union Elementary	Quartz Hill
201	8,512	Greenfield Union	Bakersfield
202	8,511	Salinas City Elementary	Salinas
203	8,410	Sylvan Union Elementary	Modesto
204	8,336	Brentwood Union Elementary	Brentwood
205	8,289	Snowline Joint Unified	Phelan
206	8,250	Hueneme Elementary	Port Hueneme
207	8,247	San Mateo Union High	San Mateo
208	8,066	Berryessa Union Elementary	San Jose
209	7,999	Novato Unified	Novato
210	7,828	Mountain View Elementary	El Monte
211	7,796	Riverside County Office of Educ.	Riverside
212	7,712	Delano Union Elementary	Delano
213	7,683	Campbell Union	Campbell
214	7,682	South Bay Union Elementary	Imperial Beach
215	7,633	Santa Maria Joint Union High	Santa Maria
216	7,604	Liberty Union High	Brentwood
217	7,602	Orange County Dept of Education	Costa Mesa
218	7,574	Washington Unified	West Sacramento
219	7,488	Glendora Unified	Glendora
220	7,436	Jefferson Elementary	Daly City
221	7,408	Campbell Union High	San Jose
222	7,350	San Luis Coastal Unified	San Luis Obispo
223	7,348	Pleasant Valley	Camarillo
224	7,173	Huntington Bch City Elementary	Huntington Bch
225	7,107	Lennox	Lennox
226	7,091	Moorpark Unified	Moorpark
227	6,999	Dry Creek Joint Elementary	Roseville
228	6,941	Newhall	Valencia
229	6,936	Claremont Unified	Claremont
230	6,908	El Dorado Union High	Placerville
231	6,816	Culver City Unified	Culver City
232	6,748	Dublin Unified	Dublin
233	6,747	Paso Robles Joint Unified	Paso Robles
234	6,723	San Gabriel Unified	San Gabriel
235	6,716	Manhattan Beach Unified	Manhattan Beach
236	6,635	Sunnyvale	Sunnyvale
237	6,560	Newark Unified	Newark
238	6,547	Centinela Valley Union High	Lawndale
239	6,534	Santa Clara County Office of Educ.	San Jose
240	6,416	Santee Elementary	Santee
240	6,416	Whittier City Elementary	Whittier
242	6,415	Selma Unified	Selma
243	6,372	Magnolia Elementary	Anaheim
244	6,317	Fountain Valley Elementary	Fountain Valley
245	6,264	Alta Loma Elementary	Alta Loma
246	6,262	Lawndale Elementary	Lawndale
247	6,244	Ukiah Unified	Ukiah
248	6,151	Dinuba Unified	Dinuba
249	6,092	Ramona City Unified	Ramona
250	6,005	National Elementary	National City
251	5,991	Barstow Unified	Barstow
252	5,985	El Centro Elementary	El Centro
253	5,970	Monrovia Unified	Monrovia
254	5,960	Brea-Olinda Unified	Brea
255	5,946	Cotati-Rohnert Park Unified	Rohnert Park
256	5,834	Patterson Joint Unified	Patterson
257	5,816	Fallbrook Union Elementary	Fallbrook
257	5,816	Perris Elementary	Perris
259	5,795	Shasta Union High	Redding
260	5,739	Charter Oak Unified	Covina
261	5,705	Temple City Unified	Temple City
262	5,667	Hanford Elementary	Hanford
263	5,640	Hollister	Hollister
264	5,590	Sulphur Springs Union	Canyon Country
265	5,525	Windsor Unified	Windsor
266	5,475	Encinitas Union Elementary	Encinitas
267	5,402	Acalanes Union High	Lafayette
268	5,391	Travis Unified	Fairfield
269	5,360	Rosedale Union Elementary	Bakersfield
270	5,345	Buena Park Elementary	Buena Park
271	5,330	Oakdale Joint Unified	Oakdale
272	5,321	Garvey Elementary	Rosemead
273	5,286	Petaluma Joint Union High	Petaluma
274	5,252	San Ysidro Elementary	San Ysidro
275	5,240	Tulare Joint Union High	Tulare
276	5,234	La Habra City Elementary	La Habra
277	5,154	Lakeside Union Elementary	Lakeside
278	5,055	Sierra Sands Unified	Ridgecrest
279	5,045	Santa Rosa Elementary	Santa Rosa
280	5,029	Union Elementary	San Jose
281	5,004	Orcutt Union Elementary	Orcutt
282	4,997	Buckeye Union Elementary	Shingle Springs
283	4,969	Jefferson Union High	Daly City
283	4,969	Mountain View Whisman	Mountain View
285	4,923	Benicia Unified	Benicia
286	4,904	Atascadero Unified	Atascadero
287	4,849	Center Joint Unified	Antelope
288	4,781	Central Elementary	R Cucamonga
289	4,749	Kerman Unified	Kerman
290	4,726	Little Lake City Elementary	Santa Fe Spgs
291	4,691	Santa Cruz City High	Soquel
292	4,674	Sonoma Valley Unified	Sonoma
293	4,656	Oakley Union Elementary	Oakley
294	4,635	Soledad Unified	Soledad
295	4,608	Rio Elementary	Oxnard
296	4,588	South Pasadena Unified	South Pasadena
297	4,585	Beverly Hills Unified	Beverly Hills
298	4,584	Atwater Elementary	Atwater
299	4,503	Banning Unified	Banning
300	4,494	Tehachapi Unified	Tehachapi
301	4,486	Los Altos Elementary	Los Altos
302	4,440	Centralia Elementary	Buena Park
303	4,402	Moreland Elementary	San Jose
304	4,387	Del Mar Union Elementary	San Diego
305	4,384	Placer Union High	Auburn
306	4,367	North Monterey County Unified	Moss Landing
307	4,345	Paradise Unified	Paradise
308	4,340	Delano Joint Union High	Delano
309	4,305	Bassett Unified	La Puente
310	4,296	Ravenswood City Elementary	East Palo Alto
311	4,270	Coalinga-Huron Joint Unified	Coalinga
312	4,264	San Lorenzo Valley Unified	Ben Lomond
313	4,250	Kern County Office of Education	Bakersfield
314	4,202	Oak Park Unified	Oak Park
315	4,201	San Diego County Office of Educ.	San Diego
316	4,170	San Rafael City Elementary	San Rafael
317	4,168	Lindsay Unified	Lindsay
317	4,168	Valley Center-Pauma Unified	Valley Center
319	4,144	Martinez Unified	Martinez
320	4,133	Cutler-Orosi Joint Unified	Orosi
321	4,128	Rim of the World Unified	Blue Jay
322	4,083	Burton Elementary	Porterville
323	4,062	La Canada Unified	La Canada
324	4,056	Central Union High	El Centro
325	3,996	Gateway Unified	Redding
326	3,993	Rescue Union Elementary	Rescue
327	3,960	Amador County Unified	Jackson
328	3,916	Cypress Elementary	Cypress
329	3,883	Waterford Unified	Waterford
330	3,868	Duarte Unified	Duarte
331	3,858	Lake Tahoe Unified	S Lake Tahoe
332	3,855	Galt Joint Union Elementary	Galt
333	3,846	Fillmore Unified	Fillmore
334	3,841	Eureka City Schools	Eureka
335	3,839	Tahoe-Truckee Joint Unified	Truckee
335	3,839	Tamalpais Union High	Larkspur
337	3,813	Lemon Grove	Lemon Grove
338	3,803	Albany City Unified	Albany
338	3,803	Hanford Joint Union High	Hanford
340	3,744	Norris Elementary	Bakersfield
341	3,725	Brawley Elementary	Brawley
342	3,707	Del Norte County Unified	Crescent City
343	3,695	Imperial Unified	Imperial
344	3,694	Santa Paula Elementary	Santa Paula
345	3,681	Goleta Union Elementary	Goleta
346	3,652	Mountain View-Los Altos Union High	Mountain View
347	3,626	Wiseburn Elementary	Hawthorne
348	3,592	Dixon Unified	Dixon
349	3,554	Alameda County Office of Education	Hayward
350	3,532	Enterprise Elementary	Redding
351	3,530	Walnut Creek Elementary	Walnut Creek
352	3,486	Palo Verde Unified	Blythe
353	3,475	Nevada County Office of Education	Nevada City
354	3,462	South Whittier Elementary	Whittier
355	3,450	Eastside Union Elementary	Lancaster
356	3,412	Nevada Joint Union High	Grass Valley
357	3,396	Oro Grande Elementary	Oro Grande
358	3,380	Belmont-Redwood Shores Elem.	Belmont
358	3,380	Redding Elementary	Redding
360	3,375	Eureka Union	Granite Bay
361	3,365	Corcoran Joint Unified	Corcoran
362	3,353	Rincon Valley Union Elementary	Santa Rosa
363	3,329	Lafayette Elementary	Lafayette
364	3,324	Cambrian	San Jose
365	3,318	Parlier Unified	Parlier
366	3,317	Cabrillo Unified	Half Moon Bay
367	3,316	Fruitvale Elementary	Bakersfield
367	3,316	Wasco Union Elementary	Wasco
369	3,302	Calaveras Unified	San Andreas
369	3,302	Mcfarland Unified	Mcfarland
371	3,297	San Carlos Elementary	San Carlos
372	3,294	El Segundo Unified	El Segundo
373	3,290	Richland Union Elementary	Shafter
374	3,282	Lemoore Union Elementary	Lemoore
375	3,246	Los Gatos-Saratoga Jt Union High	Los Gatos
376	3,221	San Joaquin County Office of Educ.	Stockton
377	3,218	Pacifica	Pacifica
378	3,201	San Bernardino Co. Office of Educ.	San Bernardino
379	3,187	Arvin Union Elementary	Arvin
380	3,159	Lowell Joint	Whittier
381	3,122	Loomis Union Elementary	Loomis
382	3,116	Stanislaus Union Elementary	Modesto
383	3,113	San Marino Unified	San Marino
384	3,107	Coronado Unified	Coronado
384	3,107	Santa Rita Union Elementary	Salinas
386	3,106	Los Gatos Union Elementary	Los Gatos
387	3,099	Konocti Unified	Lower Lake
388	3,085	Ripon Unified	Ripon
389	3,060	Washington Unified	Fresno
390	3,050	San Benito High	Hollister
391	3,043	Southern Kern Unified	Rosamond
392	3,034	Laguna Beach Unified	Laguna Beach
393	3,032	Romoland Elementary	Homeland
394	2,997	Empire Union Elementary	Modesto
395	2,969	Greenfield Union Elementary	Greenfield
396	2,968	Mill Valley Elementary	Mill Valley
397	2,939	Castaic Union Elementary	Valencia
398	2,935	Ojai Unified	Ojai
399	2,906	Standard Elementary	Bakersfield
400	2,901	Burlingame Elementary	Burlingame
401	2,886	Escalon Unified	Escalon
402	2,879	Solana Beach Elementary	Solana Beach
403	2,873	Mendota Unified	Mendota
404	2,867	Fallbrook Union High	Fallbrook
405	2,850	Spencer Valley Elementary	Santa Ysabel
406	2,842	Lamont Elementary	Lamont
407	2,819	Newman-Crows Landing Unified	Newman
408	2,815	Rosemead Elementary	Rosemead
409	2,807	Mountain View Elementary	Ontario
410	2,777	Riverbank Unified	Riverbank
411	2,755	Mountain Empire Unified	Pine Valley
412	2,734	Mojave Unified	Mojave
413	2,719	Menlo Park City Elementary	Atherton
414	2,689	Bear Valley Unified	Big Bear Lake
415	2,687	Salida Union Elementary	Salida
416	2,677	Keppel Union Elementary	Pearblossom
417	2,665	Delhi Unified	Delhi
418	2,658	Oroville City Elementary	Oroville
419	2,629	Cucamonga Elementary	R Cucamonga
420	2,626	San Bruno Park Elementary	San Bruno
421	2,613	Mt. Pleasant Elementary	San Jose
422	2,612	Oroville Union High	Oroville
423	2,610	Reef-Sunset Unified	Avenal
424	2,602	Farmersville Unified	Farmersville
425	2,592	Julian Union Elementary	Julian
426	2,585	Lucerne Valley Unified	Lucerne Valley
427	2,582	Ocean View	Oxnard
428	2,564	Weaver Union	Merced
429	2,552	Piedmont City Unified	Piedmont
430	2,544	King City Union	King City
431	2,540	Ventura County Office of Educ.	Camarillo
432	2,537	Livingston Union Elementary	Livingston
433	2,535	Nuview Union	Nuevo
434	2,516	Jefferson Elementary	Tracy
435	2,506	Scotts Valley Unified	Scotts Valley
436	2,483	Petaluma City Elementary	Petaluma
437	2,442	Hermosa Beach City Elementary	Hermosa Beach
438	2,436	Silver Valley Unified	Yermo
439	2,397	Orinda Union Elementary	Orinda
440	2,377	Carmel Unified	Carmel
441	2,368	Gonzales Unified	Gonzales
442	2,366	Dos Palos Oro Loma Joint Unified	Dos Palos
443	2,363	Savanna Elementary	Anaheim
444	2,352	Fowler Unified	Fowler
445	2,347	Armona Union Elementary	Armona
446	2,340	Kingsburg Elementary Charter	Kingsburg
447	2,337	Carpinteria Unified	Carpinteria
448	2,336	Santa Cruz City Elementary	Soquel
449	2,322	Millbrae Elementary	Millbrae
450	2,307	Linden Unified	Linden
451	2,304	Roseland Elementary	Santa Rosa

Note: This section only includes districts with 1,500 or more students; All categories are ranked from high to low

452	2,302	River Delta Joint Unified	Rio Vista
453	2,294	Templeton Unified	Templeton
454	2,290	Fairfax Elementary	Bakersfield
455	2,287	Galt Joint Union High	Galt
456	2,277	Hilmar Unified	Hilmar
457	2,258	Marcum-Illinois Union Elementary	East Nicolaus
458	2,254	Lemoore Union High	Lemoore
459	2,232	Firebaugh-Las Deltas Joint Unified	Firebaugh
460	2,217	Sbc - High Tech High	San Diego
461	2,210	Ross Valley Elementary	San Anselmo
462	2,207	Yosemite Unified	Oakhurst
463	2,204	West Sonoma County Union High	Sebastopol
464	2,194	Orland Joint Unified	Orland
465	2,192	Stanislaus County Office of Educ.	Modesto
466	2,162	Lammersville Joint Unified	Mountain House
467	2,153	Hughson Unified	Hughson
468	2,138	Red Bluff Union Elementary	Red Bluff
469	2,128	Fresno County Office of Education	Fresno
470	2,115	Muroc Joint Unified	North Edwards
471	2,109	Saratoga Union Elementary	Saratoga
472	2,107	Taft City	Taft
473	2,100	Auburn Union Elementary	Auburn
474	2,072	Gridley Unified	Gridley
475	2,061	Live Oak Elementary	Santa Cruz
476	2,055	Robla Elementary	Sacramento
477	2,052	Chowchilla Elementary	Chowchilla
478	2,036	Anderson Union High	Anderson
479	2,003	Bishop Unified	Bishop
480	2,000	San Rafael City High	San Rafael
481	1,990	Alpine Union Elementary	Alpine
482	1,986	Tulare County Office of Education	Visalia
483	1,977	South Monterey Co. Jt Union High	King City
484	1,967	Bonsall Union Elementary	Bonsall
485	1,961	Exeter Union Elementary	Exeter
486	1,956	Pacific Grove Unified	Pacific Grove
487	1,945	Golden Valley Unified	Madera
488	1,944	Corning Union Elementary	Corning
489	1,934	Los Nietos	Whittier
490	1,919	Healdsburg Unified	Healdsburg
491	1,916	Mariposa County Unified	Mariposa
492	1,907	Dehesa Elementary	El Cajon
492	1,907	Willits Unified	Willits
494	1,904	Fort Bragg Unified	Fort Bragg
495	1,896	Central Union Elementary	Lemoore
496	1,895	Soquel Union Elementary	Capitola
497	1,872	Golden Plains Unified	San Joaquin
498	1,871	Sbc - Aspire Public Schools	Oakland
499	1,865	Earlimart Elementary	Earlimart
500	1,837	Winton Elementary	Winton
501	1,808	Brawley Union High	Brawley
502	1,792	Dixie Elementary	San Rafael
503	1,789	Live Oak Unified	Live Oak
504	1,775	Red Bluff Joint Union High	Red Bluff
505	1,773	Moraga Elementary	Moraga
505	1,773	Wasco Union High	Wasco
507	1,737	Bellevue Union Elementary	Santa Rosa
508	1,726	Kelseyville Unified	Kelseyville
509	1,718	Old Adobe Union	Petaluma
510	1,712	Gustine Unified	Gustine
511	1,711	Northern Humboldt Union High	Mckinleyville
512	1,705	Beardsley Elementary	Bakersfield
513	1,679	Grass Valley Elementary	Grass Valley
514	1,677	Byron Union Elementary	Byron
514	1,677	Middletown Unified	Middletown
516	1,655	John Swett Unified	Rodeo
517	1,637	Gorman Elementary	Gorman
518	1,609	Winters Joint Unified	Winters
519	1,600	Wright Elementary	Santa Rosa
520	1,596	Holtville Unified	Holtville
521	1,593	Santa Paula Union High	Santa Paula
522	1,577	Pioneer Union Elementary	Hanford
523	1,571	Riverdale Joint Unified	Riverdale
524	1,570	Lakeport Unified	Lakeport
525	1,569	Black Oak Mine Unified	Georgetown
526	1,559	Denair Unified	Denair
527	1,548	Monterey County Office of Educ.	Salinas
528	1,541	Merced County Office of Education	Merced
529	1,530	Piner-Olivet Union Elementary	Santa Rosa
530	1,525	Hillsborough City Elementary	Hillsborough
531	1,512	Woodlake Union Elementary	Woodlake
532	1,506	Acton-Agua Dulce Unified	Acton
532	1,506	Willows Unified	Willows

Male Students

Rank	Percent	District Name	City
1	69.9	San Bernardino Co. Office of Educ.	San Bernardino
2	63.3	Merced County Office of Education	Merced
3	62.9	Orange County Dept of Education	Costa Mesa
4	62.6	Fresno County Office of Education	Fresno
5	62.1	Stanislaus County Office of Educ.	Modesto
6	61.1	Kern County Office of Education	Bakersfield
7	60.7	San Diego County Office of Educ.	San Diego
8	60.4	San Joaquin County Office of Educ.	Stockton
9	60.3	Los Angeles County Office of Educ.	Downey
10	60.2	Nevada County Office of Education	Nevada City
11	60.1	Tulare County Office of Education	Visalia
12	58.0	Monterey County Office of Educ.	Salinas
13	55.3	Santa Clara County Office of Educ.	San Jose
14	54.9	Riverside County Office of Educ.	Riverside
14	54.9	Ventura County Office of Educ.	Camarillo
16	54.1	Centinela Valley Union High	Lawndale
17	54.0	Live Oak Elementary	Santa Cruz
18	53.6	Golden Valley Unified	Madera
19	53.5	Wasco Union High	Wasco
20	53.4	Lakeport Unified	Lakeport
20	53.4	Ripon Unified	Ripon
22	53.3	Holtville Unified	Holtville
22	53.3	Pacific Grove Unified	Pacific Grove
24	53.2	Healdsburg Unified	Healdsburg
24	53.2	Rincon Valley Union Elementary	Santa Rosa
26	53.0	Alpine Union Elementary	Alpine
26	53.0	Centralia Elementary	Buena Park
26	53.0	Delano Union Elementary	Delano
26	53.0	Golden Plains Unified	San Joaquin
26	53.0	Tehachapi Unified	Tehachapi
31	52.9	Denair Unified	Denair
31	52.9	Dixon Unified	Dixon
31	52.9	Firebaugh-Las Deltas Joint Unified	Firebaugh
31	52.9	Red Bluff Union Elementary	Red Bluff
31	52.9	Willows Unified	Willows
36	52.8	Oroville Union High	Oroville
36	52.8	Riverbank Unified	Riverbank
38	52.7	Dixie Elementary	San Rafael
39	52.6	Atwater Elementary	Atwater
39	52.6	Carmel Unified	Carmel
39	52.6	Fallbrook Union High	Fallbrook
39	52.6	La Canada Unified	La Canada
39	52.6	Salida Union Elementary	Salida
39	52.6	San Bruno Park Elementary	San Bruno
45	52.5	Gridley Unified	Gridley
45	52.5	Los Gatos-Saratoga Jt Union High	Los Gatos
45	52.5	Petaluma City Elementary	Petaluma
45	52.5	Piedmont City Unified	Piedmont
45	52.5	Valley Center-Pauma Unified	Valley Center
50	52.4	Alum Rock Union Elementary	San Jose
50	52.4	Beardsley Elementary	Bakersfield
50	52.4	Campbell Union	Campbell
50	52.4	Campbell Union High	San Jose
50	52.4	La Habra City Elementary	La Habra
50	52.4	Las Virgenes Unified	Calabasas
50	52.4	Sbc - High Tech High	San Diego
50	52.4	Willits Unified	Willits
58	52.3	Gateway Unified	Redding
58	52.3	Jefferson Union High	Daly City
58	52.3	Los Nietos	Whittier
58	52.3	Millbrae Elementary	Millbrae
58	52.3	Mountain View Whisman	Mountain View
58	52.3	Newport-Mesa Unified	Costa Mesa
58	52.3	Palo Verde Unified	Blythe
58	52.3	Rescue Union Elementary	Rescue
58	52.3	Rio Elementary	Oxnard
67	52.2	Acalanes Union High	Lafayette
67	52.2	Del Norte County Unified	Crescent City
67	52.2	Delhi Unified	Delhi
67	52.2	Garvey Elementary	Rosemead
67	52.2	Greenfield Union Elementary	Greenfield
67	52.2	Gustine Unified	Gustine
67	52.2	Huntington Bch City Elementary	Huntington Bch
67	52.2	Laguna Beach Unified	Laguna Beach
67	52.2	Monrovia Unified	Monrovia
67	52.2	New Haven Unified	Union City
67	52.2	Oroville City Elementary	Oroville
67	52.2	Ramona City Unified	Ramona
67	52.2	Rim of the World Unified	Blue Jay
67	52.2	River Delta Joint Unified	Rio Vista
67	52.2	San Ysidro Elementary	San Ysidro
67	52.2	Santa Maria Joint Union High	Santa Maria
67	52.2	Sunnyvale	Sunnyvale
67	52.2	Sweetwater Union High	Chula Vista
67	52.2	Wright Elementary	Santa Rosa
67	52.2	Yucaipa-Calimesa Joint Unified	Yucaipa
87	52.1	Alta Loma Elementary	Alta Loma
87	52.1	Berryessa Union Elementary	San Jose
87	52.1	Buena Park Elementary	Buena Park
87	52.1	Cajon Valley Union	El Cajon
87	52.1	Conejo Valley Unified	Thousand Oaks
87	52.1	El Monte City Elementary	El Monte
87	52.1	Grass Valley Elementary	Grass Valley
87	52.1	Menifee Union Elementary	Menifee
87	52.1	Mountain Empire Unified	Pine Valley
87	52.1	Perris Union High	Perris
87	52.1	Poway Unified	San Diego
87	52.1	Soledad Unified	Soledad
87	52.1	Stanislaus Union Elementary	Modesto
100	52.0	Adelanto Elementary	Adelanto
100	52.0	Apple Valley Unified	Apple Valley
100	52.0	Bear Valley Unified	Big Bear Lake
100	52.0	Benicia Unified	Benicia
100	52.0	Calaveras Unified	San Andreas
100	52.0	Castaic Union Elementary	Valencia
100	52.0	Eastside Union Elementary	Lancaster
100	52.0	Enterprise Elementary	Redding
100	52.0	Galt Joint Union Elementary	Galt
100	52.0	Mill Valley Elementary	Mill Valley
100	52.0	Monterey Peninsula Unified	Monterey
100	52.0	Oak Park Unified	Oak Park
100	52.0	Oakley Union Elementary	Oakley
100	52.0	Palos Verdes Peninsula Unified	Palos Vrds Est
100	52.0	Pasadena Unified	Pasadena
100	52.0	Redding Elementary	Redding
100	52.0	Riverdale Joint Unified	Riverdale
100	52.0	San Leandro Unified	San Leandro
100	52.0	San Marino Unified	San Marino
100	52.0	San Mateo-Foster City	Foster City
100	52.0	Scotts Valley Unified	Scotts Valley
100	52.0	S San Francisco Unified	S San Francisco
100	52.0	Westside Union Elementary	Quartz Hill
123	51.9	Bellflower Unified	Bellflower
123	51.9	Bishop Unified	Bishop
123	51.9	Buckeye Union Elementary	Shingle Springs
123	51.9	Carlsbad Unified	Carlsbad
123	51.9	Central Unified	Fresno
123	51.9	Coachella Valley Unified	Thermal
123	51.9	El Rancho Unified	Pico Rivera
123	51.9	Elk Grove Unified	Elk Grove
123	51.9	Fillmore Unified	Fillmore
123	51.9	Franklin-Mckinley Elementary	San Jose
123	51.9	Fruitvale Elementary	Bakersfield
123	51.9	Jefferson Elementary	Daly City
123	51.9	La Mesa-Spring Valley	La Mesa
123	51.9	Lake Tahoe Unified	S Lake Tahoe
123	51.9	Linden Unified	Linden
123	51.9	Loomis Union Elementary	Loomis
123	51.9	Modesto City Elementary	Modesto
123	51.9	Mountain View-Los Altos Union High	Mountain View
123	51.9	Ocean View	Huntington Bch
123	51.9	Oceanside Unified	Oceanside
123	51.9	Redondo Beach Unified	Redondo Beach
123	51.9	Rosedale Union Elementary	Bakersfield
123	51.9	Sierra Sands Unified	Ridgecrest
123	51.9	Vallejo City Unified	Vallejo
123	51.9	Walnut Creek Elementary	Walnut Creek
148	51.8	Barstow Unified	Barstow
148	51.8	Dinuba Unified	Dinuba
148	51.8	Dos Palos Oro Loma Joint Unified	Dos Palos
148	51.8	Dry Creek Joint Elementary	Roseville
148	51.8	Encinitas Union Elementary	Encinitas
148	51.8	Fremont Unified	Fremont
148	51.8	Huntington Bch Union High	Huntington Bch
148	51.8	Lafayette Elementary	Lafayette
148	51.8	Lancaster Elementary	Lancaster
148	51.8	Lindsay Unified	Lindsay
148	51.8	Lompoc Unified	Lompoc
148	51.8	Los Gatos Union Elementary	Los Gatos
148	51.8	Mt. Diablo Unified	Concord
148	51.8	Nevada Joint Union High	Grass Valley
148	51.8	Newark Unified	Newark
148	51.8	Newhall	Valencia
148	51.8	Newman-Crows Landing Unified	Newman
148	51.8	Paradise Unified	Paradise
148	51.8	Santa Monica-Malibu Unified	Santa Monica
148	51.8	Silver Valley Unified	Yermo

Note: This section only includes districts with 1,500 or more students; All categories are ranked from high to low

Rank	Value	District	City
148	51.8	Twin Rivers Unified	Mcclellan
148	51.8	Whittier City Elementary	Whittier
170	51.7	Brea-Olinda Unified	Brea
170	51.7	Cypress Elementary	Cypress
170	51.7	Glendale Unified	Glendale
170	51.7	Glendora Unified	Glendora
170	51.7	Keppel Union Elementary	Pearblossom
170	51.7	Mendota Unified	Mendota
170	51.7	Moreland Elementary	San Jose
170	51.7	North Monterey County Unified	Moss Landing
170	51.7	Reef-Sunset Unified	Avenal
170	51.7	Saddleback Valley Unified	Mission Viejo
170	51.7	San Francisco Unified	San Francisco
170	51.7	Santa Paula Elementary	Santa Paula
170	51.7	Saugus Union	Santa Clarita
170	51.7	Taft City	Taft
184	51.6	Albany City Unified	Albany
184	51.6	Central Union Elementary	Lemoore
184	51.6	Dublin Unified	Dublin
184	51.6	El Monte Union High	El Monte
184	51.6	Hesperia Unified	Hesperia
184	51.6	Irvine Unified	Irvine
184	51.6	Lake Elsinore Unified	Lake Elsinore
184	51.6	Palo Alto Unified	Palo Alto
184	51.6	Patterson Joint Unified	Patterson
184	51.6	Placentia-Yorba Linda Unified	Placentia
184	51.6	Rowland Unified	Rowland Heights
184	51.6	San Gabriel Unified	San Gabriel
184	51.6	San Jose Unified	San Jose
184	51.6	San Luis Coastal Unified	San Luis Obispo
184	51.6	San Rafael City High	San Rafael
184	51.6	South Whittier Elementary	Whittier
184	51.6	Sulphur Springs Union	Canyon Country
184	51.6	Turlock Unified	Turlock
184	51.6	Wasco Union Elementary	Wasco
203	51.5	Alisal Union	Salinas
203	51.5	Beaumont Unified	Beaumont
203	51.5	Colton Joint Unified	Colton
203	51.5	Del Mar Union Elementary	San Diego
203	51.5	East Side Union High	San Jose
203	51.5	Escondido Union	Escondido
203	51.5	Goleta Union Elementary	Goleta
203	51.5	Grossmont Union High	La Mesa
203	51.5	Hemet Unified	Hemet
203	51.5	Hollister	Hollister
203	51.5	Kerman Unified	Kerman
203	51.5	Konocti Unified	Lower Lake
203	51.5	Lammersville Joint Unified	Mountain House
203	51.5	Lennox	Lennox
203	51.5	Los Altos Elementary	Los Altos
203	51.5	Manteca Unified	Manteca
203	51.5	Merced City Elementary	Merced
203	51.5	Milpitas Unified	Milpitas
203	51.5	Moraga Elementary	Moraga
203	51.5	Norwalk-La Mirada Unified	Norwalk
203	51.5	Oakdale Joint Unified	Oakdale
203	51.5	Ocean View	Oxnard
203	51.5	Orange Unified	Orange
203	51.5	Pomona Unified	Pomona
203	51.5	Romoland Elementary	Homeland
203	51.5	San Dieguito Union High	Encinitas
203	51.5	San Lorenzo Valley Unified	Ben Lomond
203	51.5	San Ramon Valley Unified	Danville
203	51.5	South Pasadena Unified	South Pasadena
203	51.5	William S. Hart Union High	Santa Clarita
203	51.5	Yuba City Unified	Yuba City
234	51.4	Alameda City Unified	Alameda
234	51.4	Anaheim City	Anaheim
234	51.4	Anaheim Union High	Anaheim
234	51.4	Azusa Unified	Azusa
234	51.4	Central Union High	El Centro
234	51.4	Ceres Unified	Ceres
234	51.4	Charter Oak Unified	Covina
234	51.4	Compton Unified	Compton
234	51.4	El Centro Elementary	El Centro
234	51.4	Eureka Union	Granite Bay
234	51.4	Hilmar Unified	Hilmar
234	51.4	Imperial Unified	Imperial
234	51.4	Lemoore Union High	Lemoore
234	51.4	Lodi Unified	Lodi
234	51.4	Lynwood Unified	Lynwood
234	51.4	Napa Valley Unified	Napa
234	51.4	Oakland Unified	Oakland
234	51.4	Ojai Unified	Ojai
234	51.4	Orcutt Union Elementary	Orcutt
234	51.4	Pacifica	Pacifica
234	51.4	Perris Elementary	Perris
234	51.4	Piner-Olivet Union Elementary	Santa Rosa
234	51.4	Placer Union High	Auburn
234	51.4	San Bernardino City Unified	San Bernardino
234	51.4	San Diego Unified	San Diego
234	51.4	San Jacinto Unified	San Jacinto
234	51.4	Simi Valley Unified	Simi Valley
234	51.4	Snowline Joint Unified	Phelan
234	51.4	Walnut Valley Unified	Walnut
234	51.4	West Contra Costa Unified	Richmond
264	51.3	Alhambra Unified	Alhambra
264	51.3	Alvord Unified	Riverside
264	51.3	Beverly Hills Unified	Beverly Hills
264	51.3	Burton Elementary	Porterville
264	51.3	Chico Unified	Chico
264	51.3	Cupertino Union	Cupertino
264	51.3	East Whittier City Elementary	Whittier
264	51.3	El Dorado Union High	Placerville
264	51.3	Fallbrook Union Elementary	Fallbrook
264	51.3	Fontana Unified	Fontana
264	51.3	Fresno Unified	Fresno
264	51.3	Fullerton Elementary	Fullerton
264	51.3	Hayward Unified	Hayward
264	51.3	Kelseyville Unified	Kelseyville
264	51.3	Little Lake City Elementary	Santa Fe Spgs
264	51.3	Lucia Mar Unified	Arroyo Grande
264	51.3	Marysville Joint Unified	Marysville
264	51.3	Mojave Unified	Mojave
264	51.3	Ontario-Montclair Elementary	Ontario
264	51.3	Parlier Unified	Parlier
264	51.3	Pioneer Union Elementary	Hanford
264	51.3	Riverside Unified	Riverside
264	51.3	Rosemead Elementary	Rosemead
264	51.3	Torrance Unified	Torrance
264	51.3	Travis Unified	Fairfield
264	51.3	Ventura Unified	Ventura
290	51.2	Acton-Agua Dulce Unified	Acton
290	51.2	Antioch Unified	Antioch
290	51.2	Arcadia Unified	Arcadia
290	51.2	Carpinteria Unified	Carpinteria
290	51.2	Chino Valley Unified	Chino
290	51.2	Covina-Valley Unified	Covina
290	51.2	Downey Unified	Downey
290	51.2	El Segundo Unified	El Segundo
290	51.2	Etiwanda Elementary	Etiwanda
290	51.2	Farmersville Unified	Farmersville
290	51.2	Fowler Unified	Fowler
290	51.2	Fremont Union High	Sunnyvale
290	51.2	Galt Joint Union High	Galt
290	51.2	Hueneme Elementary	Port Hueneme
290	51.2	Hughson Unified	Hughson
290	51.2	Lemoore Union Elementary	Lemoore
290	51.2	Los Angeles Unified	Los Angeles
290	51.2	Morongo Unified	Twentynine Plms
290	51.2	Northern Humboldt Union High	Mckinleyville
290	51.2	Palmdale Elementary	Palmdale
290	51.2	Pittsburg Unified	Pittsburg
290	51.2	San Rafael City Elementary	San Rafael
290	51.2	Santa Clara Unified	Santa Clara
290	51.2	Santee Elementary	Santee
290	51.2	Temple City Unified	Temple City
290	51.2	Tracy Joint Unified	Tracy
290	51.2	Woodland Joint Unified	Woodland
317	51.1	ABC Unified	Cerritos
317	51.1	Bonita Unified	San Dimas
317	51.1	Chaffey Joint Union High	Ontario
317	51.1	Clovis Unified	Clovis
317	51.1	Coalinga-Huron Joint Unified	Coalinga
317	51.1	Eureka City Schools	Eureka
317	51.1	Fairfield-Suisun Unified	Fairfield
317	51.1	Garden Grove Unified	Garden Grove
317	51.1	Gilroy Unified	Gilroy
317	51.1	Inglewood Unified	Inglewood
317	51.1	Los Banos Unified	Los Banos
317	51.1	Madera Unified	Madera
317	51.1	Montebello Unified	Montebello
317	51.1	Moreno Valley Unified	Moreno Valley
317	51.1	Oxnard Union High	Oxnard
317	51.1	Palm Springs Unified	Palm Springs
317	51.1	Panama-Buena Vista Union	Bakersfield
317	51.1	San Carlos Elementary	San Carlos
317	51.1	Santa Barbara Unified	Santa Barbara
317	51.1	South Monterey Co. Jt Union High	King City
317	51.1	Vista Unified	Vista
317	51.1	Washington Unified	West Sacramento
317	51.1	Woodlake Union Elementary	Woodlake
340	51.0	Brawley Elementary	Brawley
340	51.0	Cabrillo Unified	Half Moon Bay
340	51.0	Corona-Norco Unified	Norco
340	51.0	Desert Sands Unified	La Quinta
340	51.0	Folsom-Cordova Unified	Folsom
340	51.0	Fountain Valley Elementary	Fountain Valley
340	51.0	Hacienda La Puente Unified	City of Industry
340	51.0	Kings Canyon Joint Unified	Reedley
340	51.0	Livermore Valley Joint Unified	Livermore
340	51.0	Long Beach Unified	Long Beach
340	51.0	Menlo Park City Elementary	Atherton
340	51.0	Muroc Joint Unified	North Edwards
340	51.0	National Elementary	National City
340	51.0	Novato Unified	Novato
340	51.0	Old Adobe Union	Petaluma
340	51.0	Pleasanton Unified	Pleasanton
340	51.0	Redwood City Elementary	Redwood City
340	51.0	San Juan Unified	Carmichael
340	51.0	San Lorenzo Unified	San Lorenzo
340	51.0	Santa Cruz City High	Soquel
340	51.0	Saratoga Union Elementary	Saratoga
340	51.0	Solana Beach Elementary	Solana Beach
340	51.0	Stockton Unified	Stockton
340	51.0	Union Elementary	San Jose
340	51.0	Vacaville Unified	Vacaville
340	51.0	Windsor Unified	Windsor
340	51.0	Winters Joint Unified	Winters
367	50.9	Armona Union Elementary	Armona
367	50.9	Arvin Union Elementary	Arvin
367	50.9	Calexico Unified	Calexico
367	50.9	Cambrian	San Jose
367	50.9	Cucamonga Elementary	R Cucamonga
367	50.9	Escalon Unified	Escalon
367	50.9	Fairfax Elementary	Bakersfield
367	50.9	Gonzales Unified	Gonzales
367	50.9	John Swett Unified	Rodeo
367	50.9	Lincoln Unified	Stockton
367	50.9	Murrieta Valley Unified	Murrieta
367	50.9	Oak Grove Elementary	San Jose
367	50.9	Porterville Unified	Porterville
367	50.9	Rocklin Unified	Rocklin
367	50.9	Roseville City Elementary	Roseville
367	50.9	Sacramento City Unified	Sacramento
367	50.9	Santa Maria-Bonita	Santa Maria
367	50.9	Sequoia Union High	Redwood City
367	50.9	Shasta Union High	Redding
367	50.9	Tustin Unified	Tustin
367	50.9	Upland Unified	Upland
367	50.9	Val Verde Unified	Perris
367	50.9	Victor Elementary	Victorville
367	50.9	Whittier Union High	Whittier
367	50.9	Winton Elementary	Winton
392	50.8	Alameda County Office of Education	Hayward
392	50.8	Antelope Valley Union High	Lancaster
392	50.8	Bakersfield City	Bakersfield
392	50.8	Belmont-Redwood Shores Elem.	Belmont
392	50.8	Brentwood Union Elementary	Brentwood
392	50.8	Capistrano Unified	SJ Capistrano
392	50.8	Chula Vista Elementary	Chula Vista
392	50.8	Cotati-Rohnert Park Unified	Rohnert Park
392	50.8	Davis Joint Unified	Davis
392	50.8	Fullerton Joint Union High	Fullerton
392	50.8	Moorpark Unified	Moorpark
392	50.8	Pajaro Valley Unified	Watsonville
392	50.8	Savanna Elementary	Anaheim
392	50.8	Temecula Valley Unified	Temecula
392	50.8	Ukiah Unified	Ukiah
407	50.7	Berkeley Unified	Berkeley
407	50.7	Burlingame Elementary	Burlingame
407	50.7	Chowchilla Elementary	Chowchilla
407	50.7	Duarte Unified	Duarte
407	50.7	Jurupa Unified	Jurupa Valley
407	50.7	Merced Union High	Atwater
407	50.7	Mountain View Elementary	Ontario
407	50.7	Oxnard	Oxnard
407	50.7	Robla Elementary	Sacramento
407	50.7	Roseville Joint Union High	Roseville
407	50.7	Salinas Union High	Salinas
407	50.7	Santa Rita Union Elementary	Salinas
407	50.7	Tamalpais Union High	Larkspur
407	50.7	Tulare City	Tulare
407	50.7	Western Placer Unified	Lincoln
422	50.6	Atascadero Unified	Atascadero

Note: This section only includes districts with 1,500 or more students; All categories are ranked from high to low

422	50.6	Banning Unified	Banning
422	50.6	Claremont Unified	Claremont
422	50.6	Corning Union Elementary	Corning
422	50.6	Fort Bragg Unified	Fort Bragg
422	50.6	King City Union	King City
422	50.6	Magnolia Elementary	Anaheim
422	50.6	Middletown Unified	Middletown
422	50.6	Ravenswood City Elementary	East Palo Alto
422	50.6	Redlands Unified	Redlands
422	50.6	Rialto Unified	Rialto
422	50.6	Salinas City Elementary	Salinas
422	50.6	San Marcos Unified	San Marcos
422	50.6	Selma Unified	Selma
422	50.6	Southern Kern Unified	Rosamond
422	50.6	Standard Elementary	Bakersfield
438	50.5	Castro Valley Unified	Castro Valley
438	50.5	Corcoran Joint Unified	Corcoran
438	50.5	Escondido Union High	Escondido
438	50.5	Evergreen Elementary	San Jose
438	50.5	Lamont Elementary	Lamont
438	50.5	Modesto City High	Modesto
438	50.5	Morgan Hill Unified	Morgan Hill
438	50.5	Natomas Unified	Sacramento
438	50.5	Orland Joint Unified	Orland
438	50.5	Paramount Unified	Paramount
438	50.5	Richland Union Elementary	Shafter
438	50.5	San Benito High	Hollister
438	50.5	Sonoma Valley Unified	Sonoma
438	50.5	South Bay Union Elementary	Imperial Beach
438	50.5	Yosemite Unified	Oakhurst
453	50.4	Black Oak Mine Unified	Georgetown
453	50.4	Burbank Unified	Burbank
453	50.4	Empire Union Elementary	Modesto
453	50.4	Hawthorne	Hawthorne
453	50.4	Jefferson Elementary	Tracy
453	50.4	Manhattan Beach Unified	Manhattan Beach
453	50.4	Orinda Union Elementary	Orinda
453	50.4	Pleasant Valley	Camarillo
453	50.4	Santa Cruz City Elementary	Soquel
453	50.4	Soquel Union Elementary	Capitola
453	50.4	Tahoe-Truckee Joint Unified	Truckee
453	50.4	Visalia Unified	Visalia
453	50.4	Westminster Elementary	Westminster
466	50.3	Kingsburg Elementary Charter	Kingsburg
466	50.3	Lowell Joint	Whittier
466	50.3	Norris Elementary	Bakersfield
466	50.3	West Covina Unified	West Covina
470	50.2	Culver City Unified	Culver City
470	50.2	Cutler-Orosi Joint Unified	Orosi
470	50.2	Earlimart Elementary	Earlimart
470	50.2	Kern Union High	Bakersfield
470	50.2	Liberty Union High	Brentwood
470	50.2	Livingston Union Elementary	Livingston
470	50.2	Petaluma Joint Union High	Petaluma
470	50.2	Roseland Elementary	Santa Rosa
470	50.2	San Mateo Union High	San Mateo
470	50.2	Santa Paula Union High	Santa Paula
470	50.2	Santa Rosa High	Santa Rosa
470	50.2	Tulare Joint Union High	Tulare
482	50.1	Bellevue Union Elementary	Santa Rosa
482	50.1	Center Joint Unified	Antelope
482	50.1	Lemon Grove	Lemon Grove
482	50.1	Martinez Unified	Martinez
486	50.0	Auburn Union Elementary	Auburn
486	50.0	Hanford Elementary	Hanford
486	50.0	Hillsborough City Elementary	Hillsborough
486	50.0	Lawndale Elementary	Lawndale
486	50.0	Live Oak Unified	Live Oak
486	50.0	Los Alamitos Unified	Los Alamitos
486	50.0	Paso Robles Joint Unified	Paso Robles
486	50.0	Sanger Unified	Sanger
486	50.0	Santa Ana Unified	Santa Ana
495	49.9	Baldwin Park Unified	Baldwin Park
495	49.9	Lakeside Union Elementary	Lakeside
497	49.8	Anderson Union High	Anderson
497	49.8	Delano Joint Union High	Delano
497	49.8	Mt. Pleasant Elementary	San Jose
497	49.8	Sylvan Union Elementary	Modesto
497	49.8	Washington Unified	Fresno
502	49.7	Exeter Union Elementary	Exeter
503	49.6	Bassett Unified	La Puente
503	49.6	Greenfield Union	Bakersfield
503	49.6	Mariposa County Unified	Mariposa
503	49.6	Mountain View Elementary	El Monte
503	49.6	Sbc - Aspire Public Schools	Oakland
503	49.6	West Sonoma County Union High	Sebastopol
509	49.5	Coronado Unified	Coronado
509	49.5	Mcfarland Unified	Mcfarland
509	49.5	Spencer Valley Elementary	Santa Ysabel
512	49.4	Brawley Union High	Brawley
512	49.4	Byron Union Elementary	Byron
512	49.4	Nuview Union	Nuevo
512	49.4	Ross Valley Elementary	San Anselmo
516	49.3	Central Elementary	R Cucamonga
516	49.3	Templeton Unified	Templeton
518	49.1	Julian Union Elementary	Julian
518	49.1	Red Bluff Joint Union High	Red Bluff
518	49.1	Santa Rosa Elementary	Santa Rosa
518	49.1	Waterford Unified	Waterford
522	49.0	Hanford Joint Union High	Hanford
522	49.0	Oro Grande Elementary	Oro Grande
524	48.9	Bonsall Union Elementary	Bonsall
524	48.9	Victor Valley Union High	Victorville
526	48.7	Lucerne Valley Unified	Lucerne Valley
527	48.6	Amador County Unified	Jackson
528	48.2	Marcum-Illinois Union Elementary	East Nicolaus
528	48.2	Wiseburn Elementary	Hawthorne
530	48.0	Hermosa Beach City Elementary	Hermosa Beach
531	47.7	Weaver Union	Merced
532	47.5	Dehesa Elementary	El Cajon
533	46.1	Gorman Elementary	Gorman

Female Students

Rank	Percent	District Name	City
1	53.9	Gorman Elementary	Gorman
2	52.5	Dehesa Elementary	El Cajon
3	52.3	Weaver Union	Merced
4	52.0	Hermosa Beach City Elementary	Hermosa Beach
5	51.8	Marcum-Illinois Union Elementary	East Nicolaus
5	51.8	Wiseburn Elementary	Hawthorne
7	51.4	Amador County Unified	Jackson
8	51.3	Lucerne Valley Unified	Lucerne Valley
9	51.1	Bonsall Union Elementary	Bonsall
9	51.1	Victor Valley Union High	Victorville
11	51.0	Hanford Joint Union High	Hanford
11	51.0	Oro Grande Elementary	Oro Grande
13	50.9	Julian Union Elementary	Julian
13	50.9	Red Bluff Joint Union High	Red Bluff
13	50.9	Santa Rosa Elementary	Santa Rosa
13	50.9	Waterford Unified	Waterford
17	50.7	Central Elementary	R Cucamonga
17	50.7	Templeton Unified	Templeton
19	50.6	Brawley Union High	Brawley
19	50.6	Byron Union Elementary	Byron
19	50.6	Nuview Union	Nuevo
19	50.6	Ross Valley Elementary	San Anselmo
23	50.5	Coronado Unified	Coronado
23	50.5	Mcfarland Unified	Mcfarland
23	50.5	Spencer Valley Elementary	Santa Ysabel
26	50.4	Bassett Unified	La Puente
26	50.4	Greenfield Union	Bakersfield
26	50.4	Mariposa County Unified	Mariposa
26	50.4	Mountain View Elementary	El Monte
26	50.4	Sbc - Aspire Public Schools	Oakland
26	50.4	West Sonoma County Union High	Sebastopol
32	50.3	Exeter Union Elementary	Exeter
33	50.2	Anderson Union High	Anderson
33	50.2	Delano Joint Union High	Delano
33	50.2	Mt. Pleasant Elementary	San Jose
33	50.2	Sylvan Union Elementary	Modesto
33	50.2	Washington Unified	Fresno
38	50.1	Baldwin Park Unified	Baldwin Park
38	50.1	Lakeside Union Elementary	Lakeside
40	50.0	Auburn Union Elementary	Auburn
40	50.0	Hanford Elementary	Hanford
40	50.0	Hillsborough City Elementary	Hillsborough
40	50.0	Lawndale Elementary	Lawndale
40	50.0	Live Oak Unified	Live Oak
40	50.0	Los Alamitos Unified	Los Alamitos
40	50.0	Paso Robles Joint Unified	Paso Robles
40	50.0	Sanger Unified	Sanger
40	50.0	Santa Ana Unified	Santa Ana
49	49.9	Bellevue Union Elementary	Santa Rosa
49	49.9	Center Joint Unified	Antelope
49	49.9	Lemon Grove	Lemon Grove
49	49.9	Martinez Unified	Martinez
53	49.8	Culver City Unified	Culver City
53	49.8	Cutler-Orosi Joint Unified	Orosi
53	49.8	Earlimart Elementary	Earlimart
53	49.8	Kern Union High	Bakersfield
53	49.8	Liberty Union High	Brentwood
53	49.8	Livingston Union Elementary	Livingston
53	49.8	Petaluma Joint Union High	Petaluma
53	49.8	Roseland Elementary	Santa Rosa
53	49.8	San Mateo Union High	San Mateo
53	49.8	Santa Paula Union High	Santa Paula
53	49.8	Santa Rosa High	Santa Rosa
53	49.8	Tulare Joint Union High	Tulare
65	49.7	Kingsburg Elementary Charter	Kingsburg
65	49.7	Lowell Joint	Whittier
65	49.7	Norris Elementary	Bakersfield
65	49.7	West Covina Unified	West Covina
69	49.6	Black Oak Mine Unified	Georgetown
69	49.6	Burbank Unified	Burbank
69	49.6	Empire Union Elementary	Modesto
69	49.6	Hawthorne	Hawthorne
69	49.6	Jefferson Elementary	Tracy
69	49.6	Manhattan Beach Unified	Manhattan Beach
69	49.6	Orinda Union Elementary	Orinda
69	49.6	Pleasant Valley	Camarillo
69	49.6	Santa Cruz City Elementary	Soquel
69	49.6	Soquel Union Elementary	Capitola
69	49.6	Tahoe-Truckee Joint Unified	Truckee
69	49.6	Visalia Unified	Visalia
69	49.6	Westminster Elementary	Westminster
82	49.5	Castro Valley Unified	Castro Valley
82	49.5	Corcoran Joint Unified	Corcoran
82	49.5	Escondido Union High	Escondido
82	49.5	Evergreen Elementary	San Jose
82	49.5	Lamont Elementary	Lamont
82	49.5	Modesto City High	Modesto
82	49.5	Morgan Hill Unified	Morgan Hill
82	49.5	Natomas Unified	Sacramento
82	49.5	Orland Joint Unified	Orland
82	49.5	Paramount Unified	Paramount
82	49.5	Richland Union Elementary	Shafter
82	49.5	San Benito High	Hollister
82	49.5	Sonoma Valley Unified	Sonoma
82	49.5	South Bay Union Elementary	Imperial Beach
82	49.5	Yosemite Unified	Oakhurst
97	49.4	Atascadero Unified	Atascadero
97	49.4	Banning Unified	Banning
97	49.4	Claremont Unified	Claremont
97	49.4	Corning Union Elementary	Corning
97	49.4	Fort Bragg Unified	Fort Bragg
97	49.4	King City Union	King City
97	49.4	Magnolia Elementary	Anaheim
97	49.4	Middletown Unified	Middletown
97	49.4	Ravenswood City Elementary	East Palo Alto
97	49.4	Redlands Unified	Redlands
97	49.4	Rialto Unified	Rialto
97	49.4	Salinas City Elementary	Salinas
97	49.4	San Marcos Unified	San Marcos
97	49.4	Selma Unified	Selma
97	49.4	Southern Kern Unified	Rosamond
97	49.4	Standard Elementary	Bakersfield
113	49.3	Berkeley Unified	Berkeley
113	49.3	Burlingame Elementary	Burlingame
113	49.3	Chowchilla Elementary	Chowchilla
113	49.3	Duarte Unified	Duarte
113	49.3	Jurupa Unified	Jurupa Valley
113	49.3	Merced Union High	Atwater
113	49.3	Mountain View Elementary	Ontario
113	49.3	Oxnard	Oxnard
113	49.3	Robla Elementary	Sacramento
113	49.3	Roseville Joint Union High	Roseville
113	49.3	Salinas Union High	Salinas
113	49.3	Santa Rita Union Elementary	Salinas
113	49.3	Tamalpais Union High	Larkspur
113	49.3	Tulare City	Tulare
113	49.3	Western Placer Unified	Lincoln
128	49.2	Alameda County Office of Education	Hayward
128	49.2	Antelope Valley Union High	Lancaster
128	49.2	Bakersfield City	Bakersfield
128	49.2	Belmont-Redwood Shores Elem.	Belmont
128	49.2	Brentwood Union Elementary	Brentwood
128	49.2	Capistrano Unified	SJ Capistrano
128	49.2	Chula Vista Elementary	Chula Vista
128	49.2	Cotati-Rohnert Park Unified	Rohnert Park
128	49.2	Davis Joint Unified	Davis
128	49.2	Fullerton Joint Union High	Fullerton
128	49.2	Moorpark Unified	Moorpark
128	49.2	Pajaro Valley Unified	Watsonville

Note: This section only includes districts with 1,500 or more students; All categories are ranked from high to low

Rank	Value	District	City
128	49.2	Savanna Elementary	Anaheim
128	49.2	Temecula Valley Unified	Temecula
128	49.2	Ukiah Unified	Ukiah
143	49.1	Armona Union Elementary	Armona
143	49.1	Arvin Union Elementary	Arvin
143	49.1	Calexico Unified	Calexico
143	49.1	Cambrian	San Jose
143	49.1	Cucamonga Elementary	R Cucamonga
143	49.1	Escalon Unified	Escalon
143	49.1	Fairfax Elementary	Bakersfield
143	49.1	Gonzales Unified	Gonzales
143	49.1	John Swett Unified	Rodeo
143	49.1	Lincoln Unified	Stockton
143	49.1	Murrieta Valley Unified	Murrieta
143	49.1	Oak Grove Elementary	San Jose
143	49.1	Porterville Unified	Porterville
143	49.1	Rocklin Unified	Rocklin
143	49.1	Roseville City Elementary	Roseville
143	49.1	Sacramento City Unified	Sacramento
143	49.1	Santa Maria-Bonita	Santa Maria
143	49.1	Sequoia Union High	Redwood City
143	49.1	Shasta Union High	Redding
143	49.1	Tustin Unified	Tustin
143	49.1	Upland Unified	Upland
143	49.1	Val Verde Unified	Perris
143	49.1	Victor Elementary	Victorville
143	49.1	Whittier Union High	Whittier
143	49.1	Winton Elementary	Winton
168	49.0	Brawley Elementary	Brawley
168	49.0	Cabrillo Unified	Half Moon Bay
168	49.0	Corona-Norco Unified	Norco
168	49.0	Desert Sands Unified	La Quinta
168	49.0	Folsom-Cordova Unified	Folsom
168	49.0	Fountain Valley Elementary	Fountain Valley
168	49.0	Hacienda La Puente Unified	City of Industry
168	49.0	Kings Canyon Joint Unified	Reedley
168	49.0	Livermore Valley Joint Unified	Livermore
168	49.0	Long Beach Unified	Long Beach
168	49.0	Menlo Park City Elementary	Atherton
168	49.0	Muroc Joint Unified	North Edwards
168	49.0	National Elementary	National City
168	49.0	Novato Unified	Novato
168	49.0	Old Adobe Union	Petaluma
168	49.0	Pleasanton Unified	Pleasanton
168	49.0	Redwood City Elementary	Redwood City
168	49.0	San Juan Unified	Carmichael
168	49.0	San Lorenzo Unified	San Lorenzo
168	49.0	Santa Cruz City High	Soquel
168	49.0	Saratoga Union Elementary	Saratoga
168	49.0	Solana Beach Elementary	Solana Beach
168	49.0	Stockton Unified	Stockton
168	49.0	Union Elementary	San Jose
168	49.0	Vacaville Unified	Vacaville
168	49.0	Windsor Unified	Windsor
168	49.0	Winters Joint Unified	Winters
195	48.9	ABC Unified	Cerritos
195	48.9	Bonita Unified	San Dimas
195	48.9	Chaffey Joint Union High	Ontario
195	48.9	Clovis Unified	Clovis
195	48.9	Coalinga-Huron Joint Unified	Coalinga
195	48.9	Eureka City Schools	Eureka
195	48.9	Fairfield-Suisun Unified	Fairfield
195	48.9	Garden Grove Unified	Garden Grove
195	48.9	Gilroy Unified	Gilroy
195	48.9	Inglewood Unified	Inglewood
195	48.9	Los Banos Unified	Los Banos
195	48.9	Madera Unified	Madera
195	48.9	Montebello Unified	Montebello
195	48.9	Moreno Valley Unified	Moreno Valley
195	48.9	Oxnard Union High	Oxnard
195	48.9	Palm Springs Unified	Palm Springs
195	48.9	Panama-Buena Vista Union	Bakersfield
195	48.9	San Carlos Elementary	San Carlos
195	48.9	Santa Barbara Unified	Santa Barbara
195	48.9	South Monterey Co. Jt Union High	King City
195	48.9	Vista Unified	Vista
195	48.9	Washington Unified	West Sacramento
195	48.9	Woodlake Union Elementary	Woodlake
218	48.8	Acton-Agua Dulce Unified	Acton
218	48.8	Antioch Unified	Antioch
218	48.8	Arcadia Unified	Arcadia
218	48.8	Carpinteria Unified	Carpinteria
218	48.8	Chino Valley Unified	Chino
218	48.8	Covina-Valley Unified	Covina
218	48.8	Downey Unified	Downey
218	48.8	El Segundo Unified	El Segundo
218	48.8	Etiwanda Elementary	Etiwanda
218	48.8	Farmersville Unified	Farmersville
218	48.8	Fowler Unified	Fowler
218	48.8	Fremont Union High	Sunnyvale
218	48.8	Galt Joint Union High	Galt
218	48.8	Hueneme Elementary	Port Hueneme
218	48.8	Hughson Unified	Hughson
218	48.8	Lemoore Union Elementary	Lemoore
218	48.8	Los Angeles Unified	Los Angeles
218	48.8	Morongo Unified	Twentynine Plms
218	48.8	Northern Humboldt Union High	Mckinleyville
218	48.8	Palmdale Elementary	Palmdale
218	48.8	Pittsburg Unified	Pittsburg
218	48.8	San Rafael City Elementary	San Rafael
218	48.8	Santa Clara Unified	Santa Clara
218	48.8	Santee Elementary	Santee
218	48.8	Temple City Unified	Temple City
218	48.8	Tracy Joint Unified	Tracy
218	48.8	Woodland Joint Unified	Woodland
245	48.7	Alhambra Unified	Alhambra
245	48.7	Alvord Unified	Riverside
245	48.7	Beverly Hills Unified	Beverly Hills
245	48.7	Burton Elementary	Porterville
245	48.7	Chico Unified	Chico
245	48.7	Cupertino Union	Cupertino
245	48.7	East Whittier City Elementary	Whittier
245	48.7	El Dorado Union High	Placerville
245	48.7	Fallbrook Union Elementary	Fallbrook
245	48.7	Fontana Unified	Fontana
245	48.7	Fresno Unified	Fresno
245	48.7	Fullerton Elementary	Fullerton
245	48.7	Hayward Unified	Hayward
245	48.7	Kelseyville Unified	Kelseyville
245	48.7	Little Lake City Elementary	Santa Fe Spgs
245	48.7	Lucia Mar Unified	Arroyo Grande
245	48.7	Marysville Joint Unified	Marysville
245	48.7	Mojave Unified	Mojave
245	48.7	Ontario-Montclair Elementary	Ontario
245	48.7	Parlier Unified	Parlier
245	48.7	Pioneer Union Elementary	Hanford
245	48.7	Riverside Unified	Riverside
245	48.7	Rosemead Elementary	Rosemead
245	48.7	Torrance Unified	Torrance
245	48.7	Travis Unified	Fairfield
245	48.7	Ventura Unified	Ventura
271	48.6	Alameda City Unified	Alameda
271	48.6	Anaheim City	Anaheim
271	48.6	Anaheim Union High	Anaheim
271	48.6	Azusa Unified	Azusa
271	48.6	Central Union High	El Centro
271	48.6	Ceres Unified	Ceres
271	48.6	Charter Oak Unified	Covina
271	48.6	Compton Unified	Compton
271	48.6	El Centro Elementary	El Centro
271	48.6	Eureka Union	Granite Bay
271	48.6	Hilmar Unified	Hilmar
271	48.6	Imperial Unified	Imperial
271	48.6	Lemoore Union High	Lemoore
271	48.6	Lodi Unified	Lodi
271	48.6	Lynwood Unified	Lynwood
271	48.6	Napa Valley Unified	Napa
271	48.6	Oakland Unified	Oakland
271	48.6	Ojai Unified	Ojai
271	48.6	Orcutt Union Elementary	Orcutt
271	48.6	Pacifica	Pacifica
271	48.6	Perris Elementary	Perris
271	48.6	Piner-Olivet Union Elementary	Santa Rosa
271	48.6	Placer Union High	Auburn
271	48.6	San Bernardino City Unified	San Bernardino
271	48.6	San Diego Unified	San Diego
271	48.6	San Jacinto Unified	San Jacinto
271	48.6	Simi Valley Unified	Simi Valley
271	48.6	Snowline Joint Unified	Phelan
271	48.6	Walnut Valley Unified	Walnut
271	48.6	West Contra Costa Unified	Richmond
301	48.5	Alisal Union	Salinas
301	48.5	Beaumont Unified	Beaumont
301	48.5	Colton Joint Unified	Colton
301	48.5	Del Mar Union Elementary	San Diego
301	48.5	East Side Union High	San Jose
301	48.5	Escondido Union	Escondido
301	48.5	Goleta Union Elementary	Goleta
301	48.5	Grossmont Union High	La Mesa
301	48.5	Hemet Unified	Hemet
301	48.5	Hollister	Hollister
301	48.5	Kerman Unified	Kerman
301	48.5	Konocti Unified	Lower Lake
301	48.5	Lammersville Joint Unified	Mountain House
301	48.5	Lennox	Lennox
301	48.5	Los Altos Elementary	Los Altos
301	48.5	Manteca Unified	Manteca
301	48.5	Merced City Elementary	Merced
301	48.5	Milpitas Unified	Milpitas
301	48.5	Moraga Elementary	Moraga
301	48.5	Norwalk-La Mirada Unified	Norwalk
301	48.5	Oakdale Joint Unified	Oakdale
301	48.5	Ocean View	Oxnard
301	48.5	Orange Unified	Orange
301	48.5	Pomona Unified	Pomona
301	48.5	Romoland Elementary	Homeland
301	48.5	San Dieguito Union High	Encinitas
301	48.5	San Lorenzo Valley Unified	Ben Lomond
301	48.5	San Ramon Valley Unified	Danville
301	48.5	South Pasadena Unified	South Pasadena
301	48.5	William S. Hart Union High	Santa Clarita
301	48.5	Yuba City Unified	Yuba City
332	48.4	Albany City Unified	Albany
332	48.4	Central Union Elementary	Lemoore
332	48.4	Dublin Unified	Dublin
332	48.4	El Monte Union High	El Monte
332	48.4	Hesperia Unified	Hesperia
332	48.4	Irvine Unified	Irvine
332	48.4	Lake Elsinore Unified	Lake Elsinore
332	48.4	Palo Alto Unified	Palo Alto
332	48.4	Patterson Joint Unified	Patterson
332	48.4	Placentia-Yorba Linda Unified	Placentia
332	48.4	Rowland Unified	Rowland Heights
332	48.4	San Gabriel Unified	San Gabriel
332	48.4	San Jose Unified	San Jose
332	48.4	San Luis Coastal Unified	San Luis Obispo
332	48.4	San Rafael City High	San Rafael
332	48.4	South Whittier Elementary	Whittier
332	48.4	Sulphur Springs Union	Canyon Country
332	48.4	Turlock Unified	Turlock
332	48.4	Wasco Union Elementary	Wasco
351	48.3	Brea-Olinda Unified	Brea
351	48.3	Cypress Elementary	Cypress
351	48.3	Glendale Unified	Glendale
351	48.3	Glendora Unified	Glendora
351	48.3	Keppel Union Elementary	Pearblossom
351	48.3	Mendota Unified	Mendota
351	48.3	Moreland Elementary	San Jose
351	48.3	North Monterey County Unified	Moss Landing
351	48.3	Reef-Sunset Unified	Avenal
351	48.3	Saddleback Valley Unified	Mission Viejo
351	48.3	San Francisco Unified	San Francisco
351	48.3	Santa Paula Elementary	Santa Paula
351	48.3	Saugus Union	Santa Clarita
351	48.3	Taft City	Taft
365	48.2	Barstow Unified	Barstow
365	48.2	Dinuba Unified	Dinuba
365	48.2	Dos Palos Oro Loma Joint Unified	Dos Palos
365	48.2	Dry Creek Joint Elementary	Roseville
365	48.2	Encinitas Union Elementary	Encinitas
365	48.2	Fremont Unified	Fremont
365	48.2	Huntington Bch Union High	Huntington Bch
365	48.2	Lafayette Elementary	Lafayette
365	48.2	Lancaster Elementary	Lancaster
365	48.2	Lindsay Unified	Lindsay
365	48.2	Lompoc Unified	Lompoc
365	48.2	Los Gatos Union Elementary	Los Gatos
365	48.2	Mt. Diablo Unified	Concord
365	48.2	Nevada Joint Union High	Grass Valley
365	48.2	Newark Unified	Newark
365	48.2	Newhall	Valencia
365	48.2	Newman-Crows Landing Unified	Newman
365	48.2	Paradise Unified	Paradise
365	48.2	Santa Monica-Malibu Unified	Santa Monica
365	48.2	Silver Valley Unified	Yermo
365	48.2	Twin Rivers Unified	Mcclellan
365	48.2	Whittier City Elementary	Whittier
387	48.1	Bellflower Unified	Bellflower
387	48.1	Bishop Unified	Bishop
387	48.1	Buckeye Union Elementary	Shingle Springs
387	48.1	Carlsbad Unified	Carlsbad
387	48.1	Central Unified	Fresno
387	48.1	Coachella Valley Unified	Thermal
387	48.1	El Rancho Unified	Pico Rivera
387	48.1	Elk Grove Unified	Elk Grove

Note: This section only includes districts with 1,500 or more students; All categories are ranked from high to low

387	48.1	Fillmore Unified	Fillmore
387	48.1	Franklin-Mckinley Elementary	San Jose
387	48.1	Fruitvale Elementary	Bakersfield
387	48.1	Jefferson Elementary	Daly City
387	48.1	La Mesa-Spring Valley	La Mesa
387	48.1	Lake Tahoe Unified	S Lake Tahoe
387	48.1	Linden Unified	Linden
387	48.1	Loomis Union Elementary	Loomis
387	48.1	Modesto City Elementary	Modesto
387	48.1	Mountain View-Los Altos Union High	Mountain View
387	48.1	Ocean View	Huntington Bch
387	48.1	Oceanside Unified	Oceanside
387	48.1	Redondo Beach Unified	Redondo Beach
387	48.1	Rosedale Union Elementary	Bakersfield
387	48.1	Sierra Sands Unified	Ridgecrest
387	48.1	Vallejo City Unified	Vallejo
387	48.1	Walnut Creek Elementary	Walnut Creek
412	48.0	Adelanto Elementary	Adelanto
412	48.0	Apple Valley Unified	Apple Valley
412	48.0	Bear Valley Unified	Big Bear Lake
412	48.0	Benicia Unified	Benicia
412	48.0	Calaveras Unified	San Andreas
412	48.0	Castaic Union Elementary	Valencia
412	48.0	Eastside Union Elementary	Lancaster
412	48.0	Enterprise Elementary	Redding
412	48.0	Galt Joint Union Elementary	Galt
412	48.0	Mill Valley Elementary	Mill Valley
412	48.0	Monterey Peninsula Unified	Monterey
412	48.0	Oak Park Unified	Oak Park
412	48.0	Oakley Union Elementary	Oakley
412	48.0	Palos Verdes Peninsula Unified	Palos Vrds Est
412	48.0	Pasadena Unified	Pasadena
412	48.0	Redding Elementary	Redding
412	48.0	Riverdale Joint Unified	Riverdale
412	48.0	San Leandro Unified	San Leandro
412	48.0	San Marino Unified	San Marino
412	48.0	San Mateo-Foster City	Foster City
412	48.0	Scotts Valley Unified	Scotts Valley
412	48.0	S San Francisco Unified	S San Francisco
412	48.0	Westside Union Elementary	Quartz Hill
435	47.9	Alta Loma Elementary	Alta Loma
435	47.9	Berryessa Union Elementary	San Jose
435	47.9	Buena Park Elementary	Buena Park
435	47.9	Cajon Valley Union	El Cajon
435	47.9	Conejo Valley Unified	Thousand Oaks
435	47.9	El Monte City Elementary	El Monte
435	47.9	Grass Valley Elementary	Grass Valley
435	47.9	Menifee Union Elementary	Menifee
435	47.9	Mountain Empire Unified	Pine Valley
435	47.9	Perris Union High	Perris
435	47.9	Poway Unified	San Diego
435	47.9	Soledad Unified	Soledad
435	47.9	Stanislaus Union Elementary	Modesto
448	47.8	Acalanes Union High	Lafayette
448	47.8	Del Norte County Unified	Crescent City
448	47.8	Delhi Unified	Delhi
448	47.8	Garvey Elementary	Rosemead
448	47.8	Greenfield Union Elementary	Greenfield
448	47.8	Gustine Unified	Gustine
448	47.8	Huntington Bch City Elementary	Huntington Bch
448	47.8	Laguna Beach Unified	Laguna Beach
448	47.8	Monrovia Unified	Monrovia
448	47.8	New Haven Unified	Union City
448	47.8	Oroville City Elementary	Oroville
448	47.8	Ramona City Unified	Ramona
448	47.8	Rim of the World Unified	Blue Jay
448	47.8	River Delta Joint Unified	Rio Vista
448	47.8	San Ysidro Elementary	San Ysidro
448	47.8	Santa Maria Joint Union High	Santa Maria
448	47.8	Sunnyvale	Sunnyvale
448	47.8	Sweetwater Union High	Chula Vista
448	47.8	Wright Elementary	Santa Rosa
448	47.8	Yucaipa-Calimesa Joint Unified	Yucaipa
468	47.7	Gateway Unified	Redding
468	47.7	Jefferson Union High	Daly City
468	47.7	La Habra City Elementary	La Habra
468	47.7	Los Nietos	Whittier
468	47.7	Millbrae Elementary	Millbrae
468	47.7	Mountain View Whisman	Mountain View
468	47.7	Newport-Mesa Unified	Costa Mesa
468	47.7	Palo Verde Unified	Blythe
468	47.7	Rescue Union Elementary	Rescue
468	47.7	Rio Elementary	Oxnard
478	47.6	Alum Rock Union Elementary	San Jose
478	47.6	Beardsley Elementary	Bakersfield
478	47.6	Campbell Union	Campbell
478	47.6	Campbell Union High	San Jose
478	47.6	Las Virgenes Unified	Calabasas
478	47.6	Sbc - High Tech High	San Diego
478	47.6	Willits Unified	Willits
485	47.5	Gridley Unified	Gridley
485	47.5	Los Gatos-Saratoga Jt Union High	Los Gatos
485	47.5	Petaluma City Elementary	Petaluma
485	47.5	Piedmont City Unified	Piedmont
485	47.5	Valley Center-Pauma Unified	Valley Center
490	47.4	Atwater Elementary	Atwater
490	47.4	Carmel Unified	Carmel
490	47.4	Fallbrook Union High	Fallbrook
490	47.4	La Canada Unified	La Canada
490	47.4	Salida Union Elementary	Salida
490	47.4	San Bruno Park Elementary	San Bruno
496	47.3	Dixie Elementary	San Rafael
497	47.2	Oroville Union High	Oroville
497	47.2	Riverbank Unified	Riverbank
499	47.1	Denair Unified	Denair
499	47.1	Dixon Unified	Dixon
499	47.1	Firebaugh-Las Deltas Joint Unified	Firebaugh
499	47.1	Red Bluff Union Elementary	Red Bluff
499	47.1	Willows Unified	Willows
504	47.0	Alpine Union Elementary	Alpine
504	47.0	Centralia Elementary	Buena Park
504	47.0	Delano Union Elementary	Delano
504	47.0	Golden Plains Unified	San Joaquin
504	47.0	Tehachapi Unified	Tehachapi
509	46.8	Healdsburg Unified	Healdsburg
509	46.8	Rincon Valley Union Elementary	Santa Rosa
511	46.7	Holtville Unified	Holtville
511	46.7	Pacific Grove Unified	Pacific Grove
513	46.6	Lakeport Unified	Lakeport
513	46.6	Ripon Unified	Ripon
515	46.5	Wasco Union High	Wasco
516	46.4	Golden Valley Unified	Madera
517	46.0	Live Oak Elementary	Santa Cruz
518	45.9	Centinela Valley Union High	Lawndale
519	45.1	Riverside County Office of Educ.	Riverside
519	45.1	Ventura County Office of Educ.	Camarillo
521	44.7	Santa Clara County Office of Educ.	San Jose
522	42.0	Monterey County Office of Educ.	Salinas
523	39.9	Tulare County Office of Education	Visalia
524	39.8	Nevada County Office of Education	Nevada City
525	39.7	Los Angeles County Office of Educ.	Downey
526	39.6	San Joaquin County Office of Educ.	Stockton
527	39.3	San Diego County Office of Educ.	San Diego
528	38.9	Kern County Office of Education	Bakersfield
529	37.9	Stanislaus County Office of Educ.	Modesto
530	37.4	Fresno County Office of Education	Fresno
531	37.1	Orange County Dept of Education	Costa Mesa
532	36.7	Merced County Office of Education	Merced
533	30.1	San Bernardino Co. Office of Educ.	San Bernardino

Individual Education Program Students

Rank	Percent	District Name	City
1	86.5	San Bernardino Co. Office of Educ.	San Bernardino
2	60.1	Fresno County Office of Education	Fresno
3	59.7	Tulare County Office of Education	Visalia
4	59.2	Merced County Office of Education	Merced
5	50.8	Stanislaus County Office of Educ.	Modesto
6	50.4	Los Angeles County Office of Educ.	Downey
7	42.3	Monterey County Office of Educ.	Salinas
8	29.4	Santa Clara County Office of Educ.	San Jose
9	28.4	Ventura County Office of Educ.	Camarillo
10	27.8	Kern County Office of Education	Bakersfield
11	24.2	San Joaquin County Office of Educ.	Stockton
12	18.3	Oroville City Elementary	Oroville
12	18.3	Riverside County Office of Educ.	Riverside
14	17.7	Acton-Agua Dulce Unified	Acton
15	17.3	Rincon Valley Union Elementary	Santa Rosa
15	17.3	West Sonoma County Union High	Sebastopol
17	16.7	Del Norte County Unified	Crescent City
18	16.6	San Diego County Office of Educ.	San Diego
19	16.5	Mariposa County Unified	Mariposa
20	16.0	Petaluma City Elementary	Petaluma
21	15.8	Windsor Unified	Windsor
22	15.5	Galt Joint Union Elementary	Galt
23	15.4	Northern Humboldt Union High	Mckinleyville
23	15.4	Oakley Union Elementary	Oakley
25	15.3	Santa Cruz City Elementary	Soquel
26	15.0	Mt. Pleasant Elementary	San Jose
27	14.5	Goleta Union Elementary	Goleta
27	14.5	Ojai Unified	Ojai
29	14.2	Silver Valley Unified	Yermo
30	14.0	King City Union	King City
30	14.0	Petaluma Joint Union High	Petaluma
32	13.9	Antelope Valley Union High	Lancaster
33	13.8	Santa Clara Unified	Santa Clara
34	13.6	Hemet Unified	Hemet
34	13.6	Livermore Valley Joint Unified	Livermore
34	13.6	San Marcos Unified	San Marcos
34	13.6	Southern Kern Unified	Rosamond
38	13.5	Lakeside Union Elementary	Lakeside
38	13.5	West Contra Costa Unified	Richmond
40	13.4	Center Joint Unified	Antelope
40	13.4	Mojave Unified	Mojave
40	13.4	Piedmont City Unified	Piedmont
43	13.3	Lake Tahoe Unified	S Lake Tahoe
43	13.3	Modesto City Elementary	Modesto
45	13.2	Morongo Unified	Twentynine Plms
45	13.2	Santa Paula Elementary	Santa Paula
47	13.1	Beverly Hills Unified	Beverly Hills
47	13.1	Konocti Unified	Lower Lake
47	13.1	Santa Rosa High	Santa Rosa
50	13.0	Brentwood Union Elementary	Brentwood
50	13.0	Solana Beach Elementary	Solana Beach
50	13.0	Vista Unified	Vista
53	12.9	Cotati-Rohnert Park Unified	Rohnert Park
53	12.9	Las Virgenes Unified	Calabasas
53	12.9	Los Nietos	Whittier
53	12.9	Paradise Unified	Paradise
53	12.9	San Rafael City Elementary	San Rafael
58	12.8	Paso Robles Joint Unified	Paso Robles
59	12.7	Eureka City Schools	Eureka
59	12.7	Pajaro Valley Unified	Watsonville
59	12.7	Redwood City Elementary	Redwood City
59	12.7	Rim of the World Unified	Blue Jay
59	12.7	River Delta Joint Unified	Rio Vista
59	12.7	San Leandro Unified	San Leandro
59	12.7	Sulphur Springs Union	Canyon Country
66	12.6	Cucamonga Elementary	R Cucamonga
66	12.6	Fillmore Unified	Fillmore
66	12.6	Live Oak Elementary	Santa Cruz
69	12.5	Bassett Unified	La Puente
69	12.5	Moorpark Unified	Moorpark
69	12.5	Pasadena Unified	Pasadena
69	12.5	Saugus Union	Santa Clarita
69	12.5	Sierra Sands Unified	Ridgecrest
74	12.4	Centinela Valley Union High	Lawndale
74	12.4	Covina-Valley Unified	Covina
74	12.4	Los Angeles Unified	Los Angeles
74	12.4	Orange County Dept of Education	Costa Mesa
74	12.4	Savanna Elementary	Anaheim
74	12.4	Soquel Union Elementary	Capitola
74	12.4	Sylvan Union Elementary	Modesto
74	12.4	Tehachapi Unified	Tehachapi
82	12.3	Belmont-Redwood Shores Elem.	Belmont
82	12.3	Empire Union Elementary	Modesto
82	12.3	Glendora Unified	Glendora
82	12.3	Grossmont Union High	La Mesa
82	12.3	Palmdale Elementary	Palmdale
82	12.3	Ramona City Unified	Ramona
88	12.2	Del Mar Union Elementary	San Diego
88	12.2	Etiwanda Elementary	Etiwanda
88	12.2	Modesto City High	Modesto
88	12.2	Old Adobe Union	Petaluma
88	12.2	Santa Barbara Unified	Santa Barbara
93	12.1	Cajon Valley Union	El Cajon
93	12.1	Hillsborough City Elementary	Hillsborough
93	12.1	La Mesa-Spring Valley	La Mesa
93	12.1	Lucia Mar Unified	Arroyo Grande
93	12.1	Santa Cruz City High	Soquel
98	12.0	East Whittier City Elementary	Whittier
98	12.0	Sonoma Valley Unified	Sonoma
100	11.9	Chino Valley Unified	Chino
100	11.9	Dixie Elementary	San Rafael
100	11.9	Folsom-Cordova Unified	Folsom
100	11.9	Grass Valley Elementary	Grass Valley
100	11.9	Mountain View Whisman	Mountain View
100	11.9	Newhall	Valencia
100	11.9	Ocean View	Huntington Bch
100	11.9	Redlands Unified	Redlands
100	11.9	Redondo Beach Unified	Redondo Beach
100	11.9	S San Francisco Unified	S San Francisco
100	11.9	Winters Joint Unified	Winters
111	11.8	Berkeley Unified	Berkeley

Note: This section only includes districts with 1,500 or more students; All categories are ranked from high to low

Rank	Value	District	City
111	11.8	Calaveras Unified	San Andreas
111	11.8	Duarte Unified	Duarte
111	11.8	Kelseyville Unified	Kelseyville
111	11.8	Sacramento City Unified	Sacramento
111	11.8	San Francisco Unified	San Francisco
111	11.8	Whittier City Elementary	Whittier
118	11.7	Antioch Unified	Antioch
118	11.7	Azusa Unified	Azusa
118	11.7	Bonsall Union Elementary	Bonsall
118	11.7	Fontana Unified	Fontana
118	11.7	Moreno Valley Unified	Moreno Valley
118	11.7	Robla Elementary	Sacramento
118	11.7	Sweetwater Union High	Chula Vista
118	11.7	Temecula Valley Unified	Temecula
118	11.7	Upland Unified	Upland
118	11.7	Walnut Creek Elementary	Walnut Creek
128	11.6	Encinitas Union Elementary	Encinitas
128	11.6	Gateway Unified	Redding
128	11.6	John Swett Unified	Rodeo
128	11.6	Lake Elsinore Unified	Lake Elsinore
128	11.6	Liberty Union High	Brentwood
128	11.6	Lowell Joint	Whittier
128	11.6	Mountain View-Los Altos Union High	Mountain View
128	11.6	Mt. Diablo Unified	Concord
128	11.6	Patterson Joint Unified	Patterson
128	11.6	Roseville City Elementary	Roseville
128	11.6	Santa Monica-Malibu Unified	Santa Monica
128	11.6	Sequoia Union High	Redwood City
128	11.6	Torrance Unified	Torrance
141	11.5	Murrieta Valley Unified	Murrieta
141	11.5	Novato Unified	Novato
141	11.5	Oceanside Unified	Oceanside
141	11.5	Placentia-Yorba Linda Unified	Placentia
141	11.5	San Dieguito Union High	Encinitas
141	11.5	Santa Rosa Elementary	Santa Rosa
147	11.4	Baldwin Park Unified	Baldwin Park
147	11.4	Pleasant Valley	Camarillo
147	11.4	San Luis Coastal Unified	San Luis Obispo
147	11.4	San Mateo Union High	San Mateo
147	11.4	Santee Elementary	Santee
147	11.4	Ukiah Unified	Ukiah
153	11.3	Alpine Union Elementary	Alpine
153	11.3	Anaheim City	Anaheim
153	11.3	Chaffey Joint Union High	Ontario
153	11.3	Chico Unified	Chico
153	11.3	Downey Unified	Downey
153	11.3	Lakeport Unified	Lakeport
153	11.3	Lawndale Elementary	Lawndale
153	11.3	Linden Unified	Linden
153	11.3	Lodi Unified	Lodi
153	11.3	Norwalk-La Mirada Unified	Norwalk
153	11.3	Paramount Unified	Paramount
153	11.3	San Diego Unified	San Diego
165	11.2	Adelanto Elementary	Adelanto
165	11.2	Auburn Union Elementary	Auburn
165	11.2	Centralia Elementary	Buena Park
165	11.2	Corona-Norco Unified	Norco
165	11.2	Lafayette Elementary	Lafayette
165	11.2	Middletown Unified	Middletown
165	11.2	Oakdale Joint Unified	Oakdale
165	11.2	San Carlos Elementary	San Carlos
165	11.2	San Jacinto Unified	San Jacinto
165	11.2	San Juan Unified	Carmichael
165	11.2	Travis Unified	Fairfield
165	11.2	Valley Center-Pauma Unified	Valley Center
165	11.2	Westminster Elementary	Westminster
165	11.2	William S. Hart Union High	Santa Clarita
165	11.2	Yucaipa-Calimesa Joint Unified	Yucaipa
180	11.1	Cambrian	San Jose
180	11.1	Coronado Unified	Coronado
180	11.1	Escondido Union	Escondido
180	11.1	Huntington Bch City Elementary	Huntington Bch
180	11.1	Morgan Hill Unified	Morgan Hill
180	11.1	San Rafael City High	San Rafael
180	11.1	Selma Unified	Selma
180	11.1	Simi Valley Unified	Simi Valley
180	11.1	Willits Unified	Willits
189	11.0	Carpinteria Unified	Carpinteria
189	11.0	La Habra City Elementary	La Habra
189	11.0	Orange Unified	Orange
189	11.0	Saratoga Union Elementary	Saratoga
189	11.0	South Bay Union Elementary	Imperial Beach
189	11.0	Stanislaus Union Elementary	Modesto
189	11.0	Tahoe-Truckee Joint Unified	Truckee
196	10.9	Claremont Unified	Claremont
196	10.9	Enterprise Elementary	Redding
196	10.9	Fallbrook Union Elementary	Fallbrook
196	10.9	Oakland Unified	Oakland
196	10.9	Oroville Union High	Oroville
196	10.9	Pleasanton Unified	Pleasanton
196	10.9	Winton Elementary	Winton
203	10.8	Barstow Unified	Barstow
203	10.8	Bellflower Unified	Bellflower
203	10.8	Fallbrook Union High	Fallbrook
203	10.8	Hilmar Unified	Hilmar
203	10.8	Manteca Unified	Manteca
203	10.8	Newport-Mesa Unified	Costa Mesa
203	10.8	Saddleback Valley Unified	Mission Viejo
203	10.8	South Monterey Co. Jt Union High	King City
203	10.8	Vallejo City Unified	Vallejo
212	10.7	Fullerton Elementary	Fullerton
212	10.7	Lincoln Unified	Stockton
212	10.7	Riverside Unified	Riverside
212	10.7	South Whittier Elementary	Whittier
212	10.7	Taft City	Taft
212	10.7	Twin Rivers Unified	Mcclellan
212	10.7	Woodland Joint Unified	Woodland
219	10.6	Burbank Unified	Burbank
219	10.6	Ceres Unified	Ceres
219	10.6	Dry Creek Joint Elementary	Roseville
219	10.6	Monrovia Unified	Monrovia
219	10.6	San Ysidro Elementary	San Ysidro
224	10.5	Alta Loma Elementary	Alta Loma
224	10.5	Campbell Union High	San Jose
224	10.5	Conejo Valley Unified	Thousand Oaks
224	10.5	Fountain Valley Elementary	Fountain Valley
224	10.5	Napa Valley Unified	Napa
224	10.5	Poway Unified	San Diego
224	10.5	San Bruno Park Elementary	San Bruno
231	10.4	Cabrillo Unified	Half Moon Bay
231	10.4	Dos Palos Oro Loma Joint Unified	Dos Palos
231	10.4	Fairfield-Suisun Unified	Fairfield
231	10.4	Garden Grove Unified	Garden Grove
231	10.4	Huntington Bch Union High	Huntington Bch
231	10.4	Jefferson Elementary	Tracy
231	10.4	Laguna Beach Unified	Laguna Beach
231	10.4	Lennox	Lennox
231	10.4	Monterey Peninsula Unified	Monterey
231	10.4	National Elementary	National City
241	10.3	Black Oak Mine Unified	Georgetown
241	10.3	Bonita Unified	San Dimas
241	10.3	Chula Vista Elementary	Chula Vista
241	10.3	Denair Unified	Denair
241	10.3	Dixon Unified	Dixon
241	10.3	Kerman Unified	Kerman
241	10.3	Los Altos Elementary	Los Altos
241	10.3	Natomas Unified	Sacramento
241	10.3	Palos Verdes Peninsula Unified	Palos Vrds Est
241	10.3	Santa Ana Unified	Santa Ana
241	10.3	Standard Elementary	Bakersfield
241	10.3	Wright Elementary	Santa Rosa
253	10.2	Alameda City Unified	Alameda
253	10.2	Anaheim Union High	Anaheim
253	10.2	Bear Valley Unified	Big Bear Lake
253	10.2	Beaumont Unified	Beaumont
253	10.2	Carlsbad Unified	Carlsbad
253	10.2	Elk Grove Unified	Elk Grove
253	10.2	Hollister	Hollister
253	10.2	Keppel Union Elementary	Pearblossom
253	10.2	Little Lake City Elementary	Santa Fe Spgs
253	10.2	Long Beach Unified	Long Beach
253	10.2	Mountain Empire Unified	Pine Valley
253	10.2	Orland Joint Unified	Orland
253	10.2	San Jose Unified	San Jose
253	10.2	Snowline Joint Unified	Phelan
253	10.2	Westside Union Elementary	Quartz Hill
253	10.2	Yuba City Unified	Yuba City
269	10.1	Alum Rock Union Elementary	San Jose
269	10.1	El Rancho Unified	Pico Rivera
269	10.1	Vacaville Unified	Vacaville
272	10.0	Buena Park Elementary	Buena Park
272	10.0	Jurupa Unified	Jurupa Valley
272	10.0	Lemon Grove	Lemon Grove
272	10.0	Newark Unified	Newark
272	10.0	Palo Alto Unified	Palo Alto
272	10.0	Panama-Buena Vista Union	Bakersfield
272	10.0	Red Bluff Union Elementary	Red Bluff
272	10.0	Rowland Unified	Rowland Heights
280	9.9	Benicia Unified	Benicia
280	9.9	Colton Joint Unified	Colton
280	9.9	Cypress Elementary	Cypress
280	9.9	Lancaster Elementary	Lancaster
280	9.9	Martinez Unified	Martinez
280	9.9	Merced Union High	Atwater
280	9.9	Mountain View Elementary	Ontario
280	9.9	Mountain View Elementary	El Monte
280	9.9	New Haven Unified	Union City
280	9.9	Oxnard Union High	Oxnard
280	9.9	Pittsburg Unified	Pittsburg
280	9.9	Santa Paula Union High	Santa Paula
292	9.8	Alvord Unified	Riverside
292	9.8	Berryessa Union Elementary	San Jose
292	9.8	Davis Joint Unified	Davis
292	9.8	Desert Sands Unified	La Quinta
292	9.8	Fruitvale Elementary	Bakersfield
292	9.8	Gridley Unified	Gridley
292	9.8	Moreland Elementary	San Jose
292	9.8	Soledad Unified	Soledad
300	9.7	Apple Valley Unified	Apple Valley
300	9.7	El Monte City Elementary	El Monte
300	9.7	Eureka Union	Granite Bay
300	9.7	Fresno Unified	Fresno
300	9.7	Menifee Union Elementary	Menifee
300	9.7	Newman-Crows Landing Unified	Newman
300	9.7	Pomona Unified	Pomona
307	9.6	Burlingame Elementary	Burlingame
307	9.6	Castaic Union Elementary	Valencia
307	9.6	Garvey Elementary	Rosemead
307	9.6	Gilroy Unified	Gilroy
307	9.6	Oak Grove Elementary	San Jose
307	9.6	Oak Park Unified	Oak Park
307	9.6	Pacifica	Pacifica
307	9.6	Palo Verde Unified	Blythe
307	9.6	Red Bluff Joint Union High	Red Bluff
307	9.6	San Lorenzo Unified	San Lorenzo
307	9.6	Turlock Unified	Turlock
307	9.6	Union Elementary	San Jose
319	9.5	Albany City Unified	Albany
319	9.5	Healdsburg Unified	Healdsburg
319	9.5	La Canada Unified	La Canada
319	9.5	Marysville Joint Unified	Marysville
319	9.5	Montebello Unified	Montebello
319	9.5	Ontario-Montclair Elementary	Ontario
319	9.5	Oxnard	Oxnard
319	9.5	Roseland Elementary	Santa Rosa
319	9.5	Temple City Unified	Temple City
319	9.5	Whittier Union High	Whittier
329	9.4	Acalanes Union High	Lafayette
329	9.4	Arvin Union Elementary	Arvin
329	9.4	Central Elementary	R Cucamonga
329	9.4	Culver City Unified	Culver City
329	9.4	East Side Union High	San Jose
329	9.4	Fremont Unified	Fremont
329	9.4	Galt Joint Union High	Galt
329	9.4	Hacienda La Puente Unified	City of Industry
329	9.4	Hueneme Elementary	Port Hueneme
329	9.4	Magnolia Elementary	Anaheim
329	9.4	Moraga Elementary	Moraga
329	9.4	Ocean View	Oxnard
329	9.4	Orcutt Union Elementary	Orcutt
329	9.4	Ravenswood City Elementary	East Palo Alto
329	9.4	Ross Valley Elementary	San Anselmo
329	9.4	Tracy Joint Unified	Tracy
329	9.4	Visalia Unified	Visalia
346	9.3	Charter Oak Unified	Covina
346	9.3	Dehesa Elementary	El Cajon
346	9.3	El Centro Elementary	El Centro
346	9.3	Glendale Unified	Glendale
346	9.3	Inglewood Unified	Inglewood
346	9.3	Nevada Joint Union High	Grass Valley
346	9.3	San Benito High	Hollister
346	9.3	Sunnyvale	Sunnyvale
354	9.2	Brea-Olinda Unified	Brea
354	9.2	Gonzales Unified	Gonzales
354	9.2	Hawthorne	Hawthorne
354	9.2	Jefferson Union High	Daly City
354	9.2	Lamont Elementary	Lamont
354	9.2	Mill Valley Elementary	Mill Valley
354	9.2	Pacific Grove Unified	Pacific Grove
354	9.2	Rocklin Unified	Rocklin
354	9.2	Rosemead Elementary	Rosemead
354	9.2	Salida Union Elementary	Salida
354	9.2	San Bernardino City Unified	San Bernardino
354	9.2	Val Verde Unified	Perris
366	9.1	ABC Unified	Cerritos

Note: This section only includes districts with 1,500 or more students; All categories are ranked from high to low

366	9.1	Muroc Joint Unified	North Edwards
366	9.1	San Lorenzo Valley Unified	Ben Lomond
366	9.1	Shasta Union High	Redding
366	9.1	Washington Unified	West Sacramento
371	9.0	Capistrano Unified	SJ Capistrano
371	9.0	Eastside Union Elementary	Lancaster
371	9.0	El Segundo Unified	El Segundo
371	9.0	Hayward Unified	Hayward
371	9.0	Holtville Unified	Holtville
371	9.0	Irvine Unified	Irvine
371	9.0	Palm Springs Unified	Palm Springs
371	9.0	Richland Union Elementary	Shafter
371	9.0	Victor Valley Union High	Victorville
380	8.9	Bellevue Union Elementary	Santa Rosa
380	8.9	Delhi Unified	Delhi
380	8.9	Julian Union Elementary	Julian
380	8.9	Lompoc Unified	Lompoc
380	8.9	Millbrae Elementary	Millbrae
385	8.8	Manhattan Beach Unified	Manhattan Beach
385	8.8	Placer Union High	Auburn
385	8.8	Redding Elementary	Redding
385	8.8	Romoland Elementary	Homeland
385	8.8	San Mateo-Foster City	Foster City
385	8.8	Stockton Unified	Stockton
391	8.7	Atwater Elementary	Atwater
391	8.7	Kingsburg Elementary Charter	Kingsburg
391	8.7	Lemoore Union High	Lemoore
391	8.7	Milpitas Unified	Milpitas
391	8.7	Tustin Unified	Tustin
391	8.7	Yosemite Unified	Oakhurst
397	8.6	Bakersfield City	Bakersfield
397	8.6	Coachella Valley Unified	Thermal
397	8.6	Escalon Unified	Escalon
397	8.6	Firebaugh-Las Deltas Joint Unified	Firebaugh
397	8.6	Franklin-Mckinley Elementary	San Jose
397	8.6	Fremont Union High	Sunnyvale
397	8.6	Fullerton Joint Union High	Fullerton
397	8.6	Lucerne Valley Unified	Lucerne Valley
397	8.6	Santa Maria Joint Union High	Santa Maria
406	8.5	Atascadero Unified	Atascadero
406	8.5	Bishop Unified	Bishop
406	8.5	Gustine Unified	Gustine
406	8.5	Hughson Unified	Hughson
406	8.5	Kern Union High	Bakersfield
406	8.5	Rialto Unified	Rialto
406	8.5	Rio Elementary	Oxnard
406	8.5	Salinas Union High	Salinas
406	8.5	Spencer Valley Elementary	Santa Ysabel
406	8.5	Ventura Unified	Ventura
406	8.5	West Covina Unified	West Covina
417	8.4	Beardsley Elementary	Bakersfield
417	8.4	El Dorado Union High	Placerville
417	8.4	El Monte Union High	El Monte
417	8.4	Escondido Union High	Escondido
417	8.4	San Marino Unified	San Marino
417	8.4	Scotts Valley Unified	Scotts Valley
423	8.3	Alhambra Unified	Alhambra
423	8.3	Banning Unified	Banning
423	8.3	Brawley Elementary	Brawley
423	8.3	Los Alamitos Unified	Los Alamitos
423	8.3	Nevada County Office of Education	Nevada City
423	8.3	Orinda Union Elementary	Orinda
423	8.3	Ripon Unified	Ripon
423	8.3	Western Placer Unified	Lincoln
431	8.2	Amador County Unified	Jackson
431	8.2	Campbell Union	Campbell
431	8.2	Castro Valley Unified	Castro Valley
431	8.2	Delano Union Elementary	Delano
431	8.2	Fairfax Elementary	Bakersfield
431	8.2	Golden Valley Unified	Madera
431	8.2	Los Banos Unified	Los Banos
431	8.2	Los Gatos-Saratoga Jt Union High	Los Gatos
439	8.1	Byron Union Elementary	Byron
439	8.1	Dublin Unified	Dublin
439	8.1	Greenfield Union	Bakersfield
439	8.1	South Pasadena Unified	South Pasadena
443	8.0	Anderson Union High	Anderson
443	8.0	Coalinga-Huron Joint Unified	Coalinga
443	8.0	Fort Bragg Unified	Fort Bragg
443	8.0	Hesperia Unified	Hesperia
443	8.0	Santa Rita Union Elementary	Salinas
443	8.0	Waterford Unified	Waterford
449	7.9	Arcadia Unified	Arcadia
449	7.9	Central Unified	Fresno
449	7.9	Fowler Unified	Fowler
449	7.9	Hanford Joint Union High	Hanford
449	7.9	Menlo Park City Elementary	Atherton
449	7.9	Rosedale Union Elementary	Bakersfield
449	7.9	Tamalpais Union High	Larkspur
456	7.8	Compton Unified	Compton
456	7.8	Walnut Valley Unified	Walnut
456	7.8	Weaver Union	Merced
459	7.7	Kings Canyon Joint Unified	Reedley
459	7.7	Mcfarland Unified	Mcfarland
459	7.7	Riverbank Unified	Riverbank
462	7.6	Carmel Unified	Carmel
462	7.6	Central Union High	El Centro
462	7.6	Clovis Unified	Clovis
462	7.6	Livingston Union Elementary	Livingston
462	7.6	San Ramon Valley Unified	Danville
467	7.5	Alisal Union	Salinas
467	7.5	Perris Union High	Perris
467	7.5	San Gabriel Unified	San Gabriel
470	7.4	Corning Union Elementary	Corning
470	7.4	Evergreen Elementary	San Jose
470	7.4	Lynwood Unified	Lynwood
473	7.3	Santa Maria-Bonita	Santa Maria
473	7.3	Victor Elementary	Victorville
475	7.2	Calexico Unified	Calexico
475	7.2	Delano Joint Union High	Delano
477	7.1	Wiseburn Elementary	Hawthorne
478	7.0	Imperial Unified	Imperial
478	7.0	Live Oak Unified	Live Oak
480	6.9	Cupertino Union	Cupertino
480	6.9	Merced City Elementary	Merced
480	6.9	Piner-Olivet Union Elementary	Santa Rosa
483	6.8	Corcoran Joint Unified	Corcoran
483	6.8	Greenfield Union Elementary	Greenfield
483	6.8	Hanford Elementary	Hanford
483	6.8	Salinas City Elementary	Salinas
487	6.7	Brawley Union High	Brawley
487	6.7	Sanger Unified	Sanger
487	6.7	Templeton Unified	Templeton
490	6.6	Tulare City	Tulare
491	6.5	Perris Elementary	Perris
492	6.4	Buckeye Union Elementary	Shingle Springs
492	6.4	North Monterey County Unified	Moss Landing
494	6.2	Roseville Joint Union High	Roseville
494	6.2	Washington Unified	Fresno
496	6.1	Burton Elementary	Porterville
496	6.1	Jefferson Elementary	Daly City
496	6.1	Tulare Joint Union High	Tulare
499	6.0	Loomis Union Elementary	Loomis
499	6.0	Madera Unified	Madera
499	6.0	Reef-Sunset Unified	Avenal
502	5.9	Central Union Elementary	Lemoore
502	5.9	Golden Plains Unified	San Joaquin
502	5.9	Parlier Unified	Parlier
502	5.9	Wasco Union Elementary	Wasco
506	5.8	Los Gatos Union Elementary	Los Gatos
506	5.8	Riverdale Joint Unified	Riverdale
508	5.7	Exeter Union Elementary	Exeter
508	5.7	Lemoore Union Elementary	Lemoore
508	5.7	Rescue Union Elementary	Rescue
508	5.7	Wasco Union High	Wasco
512	5.5	Marcum-Illinois Union Elementary	East Nicolaus
513	5.2	Oro Grande Elementary	Oro Grande
514	5.0	Hermosa Beach City Elementary	Hermosa Beach
514	5.0	Norris Elementary	Bakersfield
516	4.5	Nuview Union	Nuevo
517	4.3	Woodlake Union Elementary	Woodlake
518	4.2	Chowchilla Elementary	Chowchilla
519	4.1	Cutler-Orosi Joint Unified	Orosi
519	4.1	Porterville Unified	Porterville
521	4.0	Dinuba Unified	Dinuba
522	3.9	Pioneer Union Elementary	Hanford
523	3.8	Gorman Elementary	Gorman
524	3.6	Lindsay Unified	Lindsay
525	3.5	Mendota Unified	Mendota
526	3.3	Armona Union Elementary	Armona
526	3.3	Farmersville Unified	Farmersville
528	2.7	Alameda County Office of Education	Hayward
529	2.5	Earlimart Elementary	Earlimart
530	0.0	Lammersville Joint Unified	Mountain House
530	0.0	Sbc - Aspire Public Schools	Oakland
530	0.0	Sbc - High Tech High	San Diego
530	0.0	Willows Unified	Willows

English Language Learner Students

Rank	Percent	District Name	City
1	79.4	Mendota Unified	Mendota
2	74.0	Earlimart Elementary	Earlimart
3	72.1	Bellevue Union Elementary	Santa Rosa
4	70.4	Arvin Union Elementary	Arvin
5	69.2	Calexico Unified	Calexico
6	69.1	Greenfield Union Elementary	Greenfield
7	66.6	Lamont Elementary	Lamont
8	65.0	Alisal Union	Salinas
9	64.9	National Elementary	National City
10	64.8	Ocean View	Oxnard
11	64.4	Ravenswood City Elementary	East Palo Alto
12	63.8	Anaheim City	Anaheim
12	63.8	San Ysidro Elementary	San Ysidro
14	62.9	Parlier Unified	Parlier
15	62.1	Mountain View Elementary	El Monte
16	61.5	Roseland Elementary	Santa Rosa
17	61.4	King City Union	King City
18	61.3	Santa Maria-Bonita	Santa Maria
19	61.0	Golden Plains Unified	San Joaquin
20	59.1	Reef-Sunset Unified	Avenal
21	57.4	Coachella Valley Unified	Thermal
22	56.2	Santa Ana Unified	Santa Ana
23	55.8	Cutler-Orosi Joint Unified	Orosi
24	55.6	Westminster Elementary	Westminster
25	54.8	Salinas City Elementary	Salinas
26	54.2	Alum Rock Union Elementary	San Jose
27	53.4	Winton Elementary	Winton
28	53.3	Livingston Union Elementary	Livingston
28	53.3	Oxnard	Oxnard
30	53.0	Redwood City Elementary	Redwood City
31	52.6	Mt. Pleasant Elementary	San Jose
32	51.9	Coalinga-Huron Joint Unified	Coalinga
33	51.6	Lindsay Unified	Lindsay
34	51.3	Lennox	Lennox
34	51.3	Santa Paula Elementary	Santa Paula
34	51.3	Woodlake Union Elementary	Woodlake
37	51.0	Richland Union Elementary	Shafter
38	50.3	Pajaro Valley Unified	Watsonville
39	49.9	Franklin-Mckinley Elementary	San Jose
39	49.9	Soledad Unified	Soledad
41	49.0	Santa Rosa Elementary	Santa Rosa
42	48.8	Ontario-Montclair Elementary	Ontario
43	48.5	Mcfarland Unified	Mcfarland
44	48.3	Magnolia Elementary	Anaheim
45	48.0	El Monte City Elementary	El Monte
46	47.9	Savanna Elementary	Anaheim
47	47.7	Hueneme Elementary	Port Hueneme
48	46.4	Fairfax Elementary	Bakersfield
49	46.3	Wright Elementary	Santa Rosa
50	46.2	Rio Elementary	Oxnard
50	46.2	San Rafael City Elementary	San Rafael
52	45.9	El Centro Elementary	El Centro
52	45.9	Escondido Union	Escondido
54	45.8	Perris Elementary	Perris
55	45.7	Robla Elementary	Sacramento
56	45.5	Compton Unified	Compton
57	45.4	Riverbank Unified	Riverbank
58	45.3	South Whittier Elementary	Whittier
59	45.1	Gonzales Unified	Gonzales
60	44.9	Buena Park Elementary	Buena Park
61	44.7	South Bay Union Elementary	Imperial Beach
62	44.0	Santa Rita Union Elementary	Salinas
63	43.9	Delano Union Elementary	Delano
64	43.7	Garvey Elementary	Rosemead
65	43.5	Alvord Unified	Riverside
65	43.5	La Habra City Elementary	La Habra
67	43.2	Garden Grove Unified	Garden Grove
68	42.9	North Monterey County Unified	Moss Landing
69	42.8	Lynwood Unified	Lynwood
70	42.6	Delhi Unified	Delhi
71	41.6	Los Nietos	Whittier
72	41.4	Lawndale Elementary	Lawndale
73	41.3	Holtville Unified	Holtville
74	40.8	Wasco Union Elementary	Wasco
75	40.4	Brawley Elementary	Brawley
76	40.3	Firebaugh-Las Deltas Joint Unified	Firebaugh
76	40.3	Mountain View Whisman	Mountain View
78	40.0	Weaver Union	Merced
79	39.9	Modesto City Elementary	Modesto
80	39.6	Pomona Unified	Pomona
81	39.2	Sunnyvale	Sunnyvale
82	39.1	Farmersville Unified	Farmersville

Note: This section only includes districts with 1,500 or more students; All categories are ranked from high to low

Rank	Percent	District Name	City
83	39.0	Rosemead Elementary	Rosemead
84	38.5	San Bruno Park Elementary	San Bruno
84	38.5	Washington Unified	Fresno
86	38.4	Bassett Unified	La Puente
86	38.4	Gustine Unified	Gustine
88	38.2	Newman-Crows Landing Unified	Newman
89	38.0	Healdsburg Unified	Healdsburg
90	37.9	Fontana Unified	Fontana
90	37.9	Hawthorne	Hawthorne
92	37.3	Jurupa Unified	Jurupa Valley
93	37.2	Paramount Unified	Paramount
94	37.0	Berryessa Union Elementary	San Jose
95	36.9	Carpinteria Unified	Carpinteria
96	36.6	Chula Vista Elementary	Chula Vista
96	36.6	Corning Union Elementary	Corning
98	36.5	Santa Clara County Office of Educ.	San Jose
99	35.9	Atwater Elementary	Atwater
100	35.8	Madera Unified	Madera
101	35.7	Centralia Elementary	Buena Park
102	35.3	Hollister	Hollister
102	35.3	Pittsburg Unified	Pittsburg
104	35.1	Ceres Unified	Ceres
105	35.0	Campbell Union	Campbell
106	34.7	Patterson Joint Unified	Patterson
107	34.6	Azusa Unified	Azusa
107	34.6	Selma Unified	Selma
109	34.3	Old Adobe Union	Petaluma
110	34.2	Sonoma Valley Unified	Sonoma
110	34.2	West Contra Costa Unified	Richmond
112	34.0	Keppel Union Elementary	Pearblossom
112	34.0	Winters Joint Unified	Winters
114	33.4	Santa Barbara Unified	Santa Barbara
115	33.3	Cajon Valley Union	El Cajon
116	33.2	Goleta Union Elementary	Goleta
116	33.2	Hayward Unified	Hayward
118	33.0	Cabrillo Unified	Half Moon Bay
119	32.9	Orange County Dept of Education	Costa Mesa
119	32.9	Santa Paula Union High	Santa Paula
121	32.5	Montebello Unified	Montebello
121	32.5	Rowland Unified	Rowland Heights
123	32.2	Greenfield Union	Bakersfield
123	32.2	San Bernardino City Unified	San Bernardino
125	32.1	San Gabriel Unified	San Gabriel
126	32.0	Romoland Elementary	Homeland
127	31.9	Bakersfield City	Bakersfield
128	31.8	Fillmore Unified	Fillmore
128	31.8	Woodland Joint Unified	Woodland
130	31.7	Los Banos Unified	Los Banos
131	31.6	Live Oak Elementary	Santa Cruz
132	31.4	Lemon Grove	Lemon Grove
132	31.4	Oak Grove Elementary	San Jose
132	31.4	Riverdale Joint Unified	Riverdale
135	31.1	Palm Springs Unified	Palm Springs
136	31.0	Alhambra Unified	Alhambra
136	31.0	Santa Clara Unified	Santa Clara
138	30.8	Dinuba Unified	Dinuba
138	30.8	Oakland Unified	Oakland
140	30.7	Jefferson Elementary	Daly City
140	30.7	Kings Canyon Joint Unified	Reedley
142	30.6	Kerman Unified	Kerman
142	30.6	Monterey Peninsula Unified	Monterey
142	30.6	San Diego County Office of Educ.	San Diego
145	30.5	Dos Palos Oro Loma Joint Unified	Dos Palos
145	30.5	Fallbrook Union Elementary	Fallbrook
147	30.3	Delano Joint Union High	Delano
147	30.3	Palmdale Elementary	Palmdale
147	30.3	San Francisco Unified	San Francisco
150	29.8	Moreland Elementary	San Jose
150	29.8	Newhall	Valencia
150	29.8	South Monterey Co. Jt Union High	King City
153	29.6	Tulare City	Tulare
154	29.3	Piner-Olivet Union Elementary	Santa Rosa
154	29.3	Salinas Union High	Salinas
156	29.1	Chowchilla Elementary	Chowchilla
157	29.0	Milpitas Unified	Milpitas
158	28.9	Empire Union Elementary	Modesto
158	28.9	San Lorenzo Unified	San Lorenzo
160	28.8	Gilroy Unified	Gilroy
160	28.8	Merced City Elementary	Merced
160	28.8	San Leandro Unified	San Leandro
160	28.8	Sbc - Aspire Public Schools	Oakland
164	28.7	Baldwin Park Unified	Baldwin Park
165	28.5	Fowler Unified	Fowler
166	28.4	Alameda County Office of Education	Hayward
167	28.3	Colton Joint Unified	Colton
167	28.3	Lake Tahoe Unified	S Lake Tahoe
169	28.2	Corcoran Joint Unified	Corcoran
170	28.0	Millbrae Elementary	Millbrae
171	27.9	Inglewood Unified	Inglewood
171	27.9	Porterville Unified	Porterville
173	27.8	Orland Joint Unified	Orland
173	27.8	San Diego Unified	San Diego
175	27.6	Lodi Unified	Lodi
176	27.5	Central Union High	El Centro
176	27.5	Rialto Unified	Rialto
178	27.2	Glendale Unified	Glendale
178	27.2	Linden Unified	Linden
180	27.1	Mountain View Elementary	Ontario
180	27.1	Santa Cruz City Elementary	Soquel
180	27.1	S San Francisco Unified	S San Francisco
180	27.1	Vista Unified	Vista
184	27.0	Stockton Unified	Stockton
185	26.8	Twin Rivers Unified	Mcclellan
186	26.7	Eastside Union Elementary	Lancaster
187	26.6	River Delta Joint Unified	Rio Vista
187	26.6	San Jose Unified	San Jose
189	26.5	New Haven Unified	Union City
190	26.4	Turlock Unified	Turlock
191	26.3	Newport-Mesa Unified	Costa Mesa
191	26.3	San Mateo-Foster City	Foster City
193	26.2	Cucamonga Elementary	R Cucamonga
193	26.2	Hughson Unified	Hughson
193	26.2	Salida Union Elementary	Salida
196	26.0	Burton Elementary	Porterville
196	26.0	Newark Unified	Newark
198	25.9	Fullerton Elementary	Fullerton
199	25.7	Val Verde Unified	Perris
200	25.6	Orange Unified	Orange
200	25.6	Ukiah Unified	Ukiah
202	25.4	Hanford Elementary	Hanford
202	25.4	Lemoore Union Elementary	Lemoore
204	25.3	Duarte Unified	Duarte
204	25.3	Evergreen Elementary	San Jose
204	25.3	Sacramento City Unified	Sacramento
204	25.3	Stanislaus Union Elementary	Modesto
208	25.2	Centinela Valley Union High	Lawndale
208	25.2	Moreno Valley Unified	Moreno Valley
210	25.1	El Rancho Unified	Pico Rivera
210	25.1	Tustin Unified	Tustin
212	24.9	Valley Center-Pauma Unified	Valley Center
213	24.8	Gridley Unified	Gridley
213	24.8	Long Beach Unified	Long Beach
215	24.7	Desert Sands Unified	La Quinta
215	24.7	Dixon Unified	Dixon
215	24.7	Ocean View	Huntington Bch
218	24.5	El Monte Union High	El Monte
219	24.4	Imperial Unified	Imperial
219	24.4	Marysville Joint Unified	Marysville
219	24.4	Nuview Union	Nuevo
222	24.2	San Jacinto Unified	San Jacinto
223	24.1	Burlingame Elementary	Burlingame
224	24.0	Sweetwater Union High	Chula Vista
225	23.8	Tahoe-Truckee Joint Unified	Truckee
226	23.7	Tracy Joint Unified	Tracy
227	23.6	Cypress Elementary	Cypress
227	23.6	Fresno Unified	Fresno
229	23.5	Anaheim Union High	Anaheim
230	23.2	Los Angeles County Office of Educ.	Downey
230	23.2	Sanger Unified	Sanger
232	23.1	Los Angeles Unified	Los Angeles
233	22.8	Morgan Hill Unified	Morgan Hill
233	22.8	Petaluma City Elementary	Petaluma
233	22.8	Whittier City Elementary	Whittier
236	22.7	Santa Maria Joint Union High	Santa Maria
237	22.6	Monterey County Office of Educ.	Salinas
238	22.5	Galt Joint Union Elementary	Galt
238	22.5	San Marcos Unified	San Marcos
238	22.5	Willows Unified	Willows
241	22.4	Paso Robles Joint Unified	Paso Robles
241	22.4	Washington Unified	West Sacramento
243	22.3	Norwalk-La Mirada Unified	Norwalk
244	22.2	Alameda City Unified	Alameda
245	22.1	Hilmar Unified	Hilmar
246	21.9	Lompoc Unified	Lompoc
247	21.8	Bellflower Unified	Bellflower
248	21.7	Brawley Union High	Brawley
248	21.7	Wasco Union High	Wasco
250	21.6	Exeter Union Elementary	Exeter
251	21.5	Banning Unified	Banning
251	21.5	Yuba City Unified	Yuba City
253	21.4	Pasadena Unified	Pasadena
254	21.3	ABC Unified	Cerritos
255	21.1	Hacienda La Puente Unified	City of Industry
256	21.0	Fort Bragg Unified	Fort Bragg
257	20.9	La Mesa-Spring Valley	La Mesa
258	20.8	Escalon Unified	Escalon
259	20.6	Manteca Unified	Manteca
259	20.6	Sulphur Springs Union	Canyon Country
259	20.6	Temple City Unified	Temple City
262	20.5	Live Oak Unified	Live Oak
263	20.4	Albany City Unified	Albany
263	20.4	Fallbrook Union High	Fallbrook
265	20.3	Sequoia Union High	Redwood City
266	20.2	Merced County Office of Education	Merced
267	19.9	Oceanside Unified	Oceanside
268	19.7	Mt. Diablo Unified	Concord
268	19.7	Windsor Unified	Windsor
270	19.6	Lancaster Elementary	Lancaster
271	19.3	Hesperia Unified	Hesperia
271	19.3	Jefferson Elementary	Tracy
271	19.3	Oxnard Union High	Oxnard
274	19.1	Cotati-Rohnert Park Unified	Rohnert Park
275	19.0	Adelanto Elementary	Adelanto
276	18.9	Napa Valley Unified	Napa
276	18.9	San Bernardino Co. Office of Educ.	San Bernardino
278	18.8	East Side Union High	San Jose
279	18.7	Fresno County Office of Education	Fresno
280	18.6	Downey Unified	Downey
281	18.5	Mountain Empire Unified	Pine Valley
282	18.4	Moorpark Unified	Moorpark
283	18.2	Riverside Unified	Riverside
284	18.1	Escondido Union High	Escondido
284	18.1	Vallejo City Unified	Vallejo
286	17.6	Fremont Unified	Fremont
286	17.6	Kern County Office of Education	Bakersfield
288	17.5	Bonsall Union Elementary	Bonsall
288	17.5	Elk Grove Unified	Elk Grove
290	17.2	Natomas Unified	Sacramento
290	17.2	Visalia Unified	Visalia
292	17.0	Novato Unified	Novato
293	16.7	Victor Elementary	Victorville
294	16.6	Lincoln Unified	Stockton
294	16.6	Lucia Mar Unified	Arroyo Grande
294	16.6	Perris Union High	Perris
297	16.5	Dry Creek Joint Elementary	Roseville
298	16.4	Kingsburg Elementary Charter	Kingsburg
298	16.4	Oakley Union Elementary	Oakley
300	16.0	Konocti Unified	Lower Lake
301	15.9	Armona Union Elementary	Armona
301	15.9	Fairfield-Suisun Unified	Fairfield
303	15.8	East Whittier City Elementary	Whittier
303	15.8	Taft City	Taft
303	15.8	Ventura Unified	Ventura
306	15.6	John Swett Unified	Rodeo
307	15.5	Auburn Union Elementary	Auburn
308	15.4	Panama-Buena Vista Union	Bakersfield
308	15.4	San Rafael City High	San Rafael
310	15.3	Ramona City Unified	Ramona
311	15.2	Barstow Unified	Barstow
311	15.2	Irvine Unified	Irvine
311	15.2	Santa Rosa High	Santa Rosa
311	15.2	Solana Beach Elementary	Solana Beach
315	15.0	Torrance Unified	Torrance
316	14.9	Little Lake City Elementary	Santa Fe Spgs
317	14.8	Antioch Unified	Antioch
318	14.7	Hemet Unified	Hemet
318	14.7	Livermore Valley Joint Unified	Livermore
318	14.7	San Luis Coastal Unified	San Luis Obispo
321	14.6	Kelseyville Unified	Kelseyville
321	14.6	Saddleback Valley Unified	Mission Viejo
323	14.4	Beaumont Unified	Beaumont
323	14.4	Chino Valley Unified	Chino
325	14.3	Placentia-Yorba Linda Unified	Placentia
326	14.2	Lake Elsinore Unified	Lake Elsinore
327	14.1	Central Elementary	R Cucamonga
327	14.1	Corona-Norco Unified	Norco
327	14.1	Ripon Unified	Ripon
327	14.1	Tulare Joint Union High	Tulare
331	14.0	Mojave Unified	Mojave
331	14.0	San Joaquin County Office of Educ.	Stockton
331	14.0	Southern Kern Unified	Rosamond
334	13.9	Denair Unified	Denair
334	13.9	Fullerton Joint Union High	Fullerton
336	13.8	Red Bluff Union Elementary	Red Bluff
336	13.8	Sylvan Union Elementary	Modesto

Note: This section only includes districts with 1,500 or more students; All categories are ranked from high to low

Rank	Percent	District Name	City
338	13.7	Saugus Union	Santa Clarita
338	13.7	Upland Unified	Upland
340	13.6	Rincon Valley Union Elementary	Santa Rosa
341	13.5	Brentwood Union Elementary	Brentwood
342	13.4	Central Unified	Fresno
342	13.4	Central Union Elementary	Lemoore
344	13.3	Berkeley Unified	Berkeley
345	13.2	Antelope Valley Union High	Lancaster
345	13.2	Culver City Unified	Culver City
347	13.1	Waterford Unified	Waterford
348	12.8	Bear Valley Unified	Big Bear Lake
349	12.7	Roseville City Elementary	Roseville
350	12.6	Covina-Valley Unified	Covina
350	12.6	Encinitas Union Elementary	Encinitas
350	12.6	Grossmont Union High	La Mesa
353	12.5	Ojai Unified	Ojai
354	12.4	Palo Alto Unified	Palo Alto
355	12.3	Arcadia Unified	Arcadia
356	12.2	Chaffey Joint Union High	Ontario
356	12.2	San Benito High	Hollister
356	12.2	Soquel Union Elementary	Capitola
359	12.0	San Mateo Union High	San Mateo
360	11.9	Modesto City High	Modesto
360	11.9	Monrovia Unified	Monrovia
360	11.9	Poway Unified	San Diego
360	11.9	Riverside County Office of Educ.	Riverside
364	11.8	Center Joint Unified	Antelope
364	11.8	Lammersville Joint Unified	Mountain House
364	11.8	Menifee Union Elementary	Menifee
367	11.6	Fountain Valley Elementary	Fountain Valley
367	11.6	Merced Union High	Atwater
369	11.5	Lowell Joint	Whittier
369	11.5	Palo Verde Unified	Blythe
371	11.4	Snowline Joint Unified	Phelan
372	11.3	Wiseburn Elementary	Hawthorne
373	11.2	Brea-Olinda Unified	Brea
373	11.2	Eureka City Schools	Eureka
373	11.2	Union Elementary	San Jose
376	11.1	Bishop Unified	Bishop
376	11.1	Del Norte County Unified	Crescent City
376	11.1	Oakdale Joint Unified	Oakdale
379	11.0	Jefferson Union High	Daly City
380	10.9	Folsom-Cordova Unified	Folsom
380	10.9	Stanislaus County Office of Educ.	Modesto
380	10.9	Vacaville Unified	Vacaville
383	10.8	Cambrian	San Jose
383	10.8	Conejo Valley Unified	Thousand Oaks
383	10.8	Orcutt Union Elementary	Orcutt
383	10.8	Whittier Union High	Whittier
387	10.7	Burbank Unified	Burbank
387	10.7	Campbell Union High	San Jose
389	10.5	Lemoore Union High	Lemoore
389	10.5	Pleasant Valley	Camarillo
391	10.4	Davis Joint Unified	Davis
391	10.4	Petaluma Joint Union High	Petaluma
391	10.4	Walnut Creek Elementary	Walnut Creek
394	10.3	Capistrano Unified	SJ Capistrano
394	10.3	Castaic Union Elementary	Valencia
394	10.3	Dixie Elementary	San Rafael
397	10.2	Chico Unified	Chico
397	10.2	Rim of the World Unified	Blue Jay
397	10.2	Simi Valley Unified	Simi Valley
397	10.2	Ventura County Office of Educ.	Camarillo
401	10.1	Redlands Unified	Redlands
401	10.1	Willits Unified	Willits
403	10.0	Mountain View-Los Altos Union High	Mountain View
404	9.9	Fremont Union High	Sunnyvale
404	9.9	Hanford Joint Union High	Hanford
404	9.9	Oroville Union High	Oroville
404	9.9	Sbc - High Tech High	San Diego
408	9.8	Castro Valley Unified	Castro Valley
408	9.8	Pacifica	Pacifica
410	9.7	San Juan Unified	Carmichael
411	9.5	Huntington Bch Union High	Huntington Bch
411	9.5	Western Placer Unified	Lincoln
413	9.4	Oroville City Elementary	Oroville
414	9.3	Menlo Park City Elementary	Atherton
415	9.2	Galt Joint Union High	Galt
416	9.1	Beverly Hills Unified	Beverly Hills
416	9.1	Carlsbad Unified	Carlsbad
416	9.1	Yucaipa-Calimesa Joint Unified	Yucaipa
419	9.0	Apple Valley Unified	Apple Valley
419	9.0	Santa Monica-Malibu Unified	Santa Monica
419	9.0	Walnut Valley Unified	Walnut
422	8.9	Cupertino Union	Cupertino
423	8.8	Los Altos Elementary	Los Altos
423	8.8	Oro Grande Elementary	Oro Grande
425	8.7	Santa Cruz City High	Soquel
425	8.7	Victor Valley Union High	Victorville
425	8.7	William S. Hart Union High	Santa Clarita
428	8.5	Beardsley Elementary	Bakersfield
428	8.5	Belmont-Redwood Shores Elem.	Belmont
428	8.5	Kern Union High	Bakersfield
428	8.5	Sierra Sands Unified	Ridgecrest
428	8.5	Tulare County Office of Education	Visalia
433	8.4	Pacific Grove Unified	Pacific Grove
433	8.4	South Pasadena Unified	South Pasadena
435	8.3	San Carlos Elementary	San Carlos
436	8.1	Martinez Unified	Martinez
437	8.0	Del Mar Union Elementary	San Diego
438	7.9	Dehesa Elementary	El Cajon
439	7.8	Dublin Unified	Dublin
439	7.8	Pioneer Union Elementary	Hanford
439	7.8	Saratoga Union Elementary	Saratoga
439	7.8	Tehachapi Unified	Tehachapi
443	7.7	Santee Elementary	Santee
443	7.7	Westside Union Elementary	Quartz Hill
445	7.6	Acton-Agua Dulce Unified	Acton
445	7.6	Atascadero Unified	Atascadero
445	7.6	Lakeside Union Elementary	Lakeside
448	7.5	Etiwanda Elementary	Etiwanda
449	7.4	Middletown Unified	Middletown
449	7.4	West Covina Unified	West Covina
451	7.3	Charter Oak Unified	Covina
451	7.3	Liberty Union High	Brentwood
453	7.1	Redondo Beach Unified	Redondo Beach
454	6.9	Enterprise Elementary	Redding
454	6.9	Palos Verdes Peninsula Unified	Palos Vrds Est
456	6.6	Byron Union Elementary	Byron
457	6.5	Clovis Unified	Clovis
457	6.5	Pleasanton Unified	Pleasanton
459	6.4	Golden Valley Unified	Madera
460	6.1	Carmel Unified	Carmel
461	6.0	Lakeport Unified	Lakeport
462	5.9	El Segundo Unified	El Segundo
462	5.9	Las Virgenes Unified	Calabasas
464	5.8	Bonita Unified	San Dimas
464	5.8	Glendora Unified	Glendora
464	5.8	La Canada Unified	La Canada
467	5.6	Alta Loma Elementary	Alta Loma
467	5.6	Temecula Valley Unified	Temecula
469	5.5	Claremont Unified	Claremont
470	5.4	Rosedale Union Elementary	Bakersfield
471	5.3	Huntington Bch City Elementary	Huntington Bch
472	5.1	Grass Valley Elementary	Grass Valley
472	5.1	San Ramon Valley Unified	Danville
474	5.0	Fruitvale Elementary	Bakersfield
475	4.9	Nevada County Office of Education	Nevada City
476	4.7	Norris Elementary	Bakersfield
476	4.7	San Dieguito Union High	Encinitas
478	4.5	San Marino Unified	San Marino
479	4.4	Rocklin Unified	Rocklin
480	4.1	Murrieta Valley Unified	Murrieta
481	4.0	Ross Valley Elementary	San Anselmo
482	3.9	Laguna Beach Unified	Laguna Beach
483	3.8	Buckeye Union Elementary	Shingle Springs
483	3.8	Hermosa Beach City Elementary	Hermosa Beach
483	3.8	Templeton Unified	Templeton
486	3.6	Eureka Union	Granite Bay
486	3.6	Morongo Unified	Twentynine Plms
486	3.6	West Sonoma County Union High	Sebastopol
489	3.4	Alpine Union Elementary	Alpine
489	3.4	Hillsborough City Elementary	Hillsborough
489	3.4	Marcum-Illinois Union Elementary	East Nicolaus
492	3.3	Julian Union Elementary	Julian
492	3.3	Muroc Joint Unified	North Edwards
492	3.3	Standard Elementary	Bakersfield
495	3.2	Piedmont City Unified	Piedmont
495	3.2	Roseville Joint Union High	Roseville
495	3.2	Silver Valley Unified	Yermo
498	3.1	Lafayette Elementary	Lafayette
499	3.0	Mill Valley Elementary	Mill Valley
500	2.7	Travis Unified	Fairfield
501	2.6	Benicia Unified	Benicia
502	2.5	Red Bluff Joint Union High	Red Bluff
503	2.3	Rescue Union Elementary	Rescue
504	2.2	Amador County Unified	Jackson
504	2.2	Oak Park Unified	Oak Park
506	2.1	Coronado Unified	Coronado
506	2.1	Lucerne Valley Unified	Lucerne Valley
506	2.1	Redding Elementary	Redding
509	2.0	Mariposa County Unified	Mariposa
509	2.0	Scotts Valley Unified	Scotts Valley
511	1.9	Acalanes Union High	Lafayette
511	1.9	Los Alamitos Unified	Los Alamitos
513	1.8	Los Gatos Union Elementary	Los Gatos
514	1.7	Placer Union High	Auburn
515	1.6	Gateway Unified	Redding
515	1.6	Orinda Union Elementary	Orinda
517	1.5	Loomis Union Elementary	Loomis
517	1.5	Moraga Elementary	Moraga
519	1.3	Gorman Elementary	Gorman
520	1.2	Calaveras Unified	San Andreas
521	1.1	San Lorenzo Valley Unified	Ben Lomond
521	1.1	Tamalpais Union High	Larkspur
523	1.0	Anderson Union High	Anderson
523	1.0	Los Gatos-Saratoga Jt Union High	Los Gatos
523	1.0	Spencer Valley Elementary	Santa Ysabel
526	0.9	El Dorado Union High	Placerville
526	0.9	Paradise Unified	Paradise
528	0.8	Manhattan Beach Unified	Manhattan Beach
529	0.6	Northern Humboldt Union High	Mckinleyville
530	0.4	Black Oak Mine Unified	Georgetown
530	0.4	Nevada Joint Union High	Grass Valley
532	0.3	Shasta Union High	Redding
533	0.2	Yosemite Unified	Oakhurst

Students Eligible for Free Lunch

Rank	Percent	District Name	City
1	96.6	Mcfarland Unified	Mcfarland
2	88.3	Weaver Union	Merced
3	86.4	Arvin Union Elementary	Arvin
4	85.8	Gonzales Unified	Gonzales
5	82.4	Ontario-Montclair Elementary	Ontario
6	78.3	Hanford Elementary	Hanford
7	76.7	Bassett Unified	La Puente
7	76.7	Palm Springs Unified	Palm Springs
9	75.6	Coachella Valley Unified	Thermal
10	74.6	Jurupa Unified	Jurupa Valley
11	73.6	Oroville City Elementary	Oroville
12	73.4	Delhi Unified	Delhi
13	72.8	Riverbank Unified	Riverbank
14	72.4	Tulare City	Tulare
15	71.6	Banning Unified	Banning
16	71.3	Westminster Elementary	Westminster
17	67.7	Salida Union Elementary	Salida
18	67.3	Little Lake City Elementary	Santa Fe Spgs
19	67.0	Bellflower Unified	Bellflower
20	66.9	Enterprise Elementary	Redding
21	65.3	Brawley Union High	Brawley
22	64.8	Newman-Crows Landing Unified	Newman
23	61.2	Carpinteria Unified	Carpinteria
24	60.9	Lemoore Union Elementary	Lemoore
25	60.6	Apple Valley Unified	Apple Valley
26	60.3	Lake Tahoe Unified	S Lake Tahoe
27	57.7	Panama-Buena Vista Union	Bakersfield
28	57.1	Anderson Union High	Anderson
29	56.9	Monrovia Unified	Monrovia
30	56.3	Beaumont Unified	Beaumont
31	56.2	Hilmar Unified	Hilmar
32	56.1	Gateway Unified	Redding
33	55.4	Linden Unified	Linden
34	55.2	Grass Valley Elementary	Grass Valley
35	54.8	San Francisco Unified	San Francisco
36	53.5	Lincoln Unified	Stockton
37	53.4	Escondido Union High	Escondido
38	52.0	Oakland Unified	Oakland
39	51.1	San Lorenzo Unified	San Lorenzo
40	48.1	Sylvan Union Elementary	Modesto
41	47.4	Galt Joint Union High	Galt
42	47.2	Stanislaus County Office of Educ.	Modesto
43	45.6	Oro Grande Elementary	Oro Grande
44	45.1	Glendale Unified	Glendale
45	44.6	Sulphur Springs Union	Canyon Country
46	40.5	Ripon Unified	Ripon
47	40.1	Culver City Unified	Culver City
48	39.2	Gorman Elementary	Gorman
49	37.8	Menifee Union Elementary	Menifee
50	37.2	Westside Union Elementary	Quartz Hill
51	34.5	San Luis Coastal Unified	San Luis Obispo
52	34.3	Evergreen Elementary	San Jose
53	31.8	Moorpark Unified	Moorpark
54	31.0	Ramona City Unified	Ramona

Note: This section only includes districts with 1,500 or more students; All categories are ranked from high to low

55	28.7	Hanford Joint Union High	Hanford
56	27.8	Jefferson Elementary	Tracy
57	25.8	Old Adobe Union	Petaluma
58	24.2	Roseville Joint Union High	Roseville
59	17.3	Soquel Union Elementary	Capitola
60	15.6	Benicia Unified	Benicia
61	14.8	Nevada Joint Union High	Grass Valley
62	11.6	El Segundo Unified	El Segundo
63	9.6	Eureka Union	Granite Bay
64	8.9	Mountain View-Los Altos Union High	Mountain View
65	3.9	Los Altos Elementary	Los Altos
66	2.8	Lafayette Elementary	Lafayette
67	2.6	Palos Verdes Peninsula Unified	Palos Vrds Est
68	2.3	Manhattan Beach Unified	Manhattan Beach
69	1.6	Los Gatos-Saratoga Jt Union High	Los Gatos
69	1.6	Saratoga Union Elementary	Saratoga
71	1.0	Moraga Elementary	Moraga
n/a	n/a	ABC Unified	Cerritos
n/a	n/a	Acalanes Union High	Lafayette
n/a	n/a	Acton-Agua Dulce Unified	Acton
n/a	n/a	Adelanto Elementary	Adelanto
n/a	n/a	Alameda City Unified	Alameda
n/a	n/a	Alameda County Office of Education	Hayward
n/a	n/a	Albany City Unified	Albany
n/a	n/a	Alhambra Unified	Alhambra
n/a	n/a	Alisal Union	Salinas
n/a	n/a	Alpine Union Elementary	Alpine
n/a	n/a	Alta Loma Elementary	Alta Loma
n/a	n/a	Alum Rock Union Elementary	San Jose
n/a	n/a	Alvord Unified	Riverside
n/a	n/a	Amador County Unified	Jackson
n/a	n/a	Anaheim City	Anaheim
n/a	n/a	Anaheim Union High	Anaheim
n/a	n/a	Antelope Valley Union High	Lancaster
n/a	n/a	Antioch Unified	Antioch
n/a	n/a	Arcadia Unified	Arcadia
n/a	n/a	Armona Union Elementary	Armona
n/a	n/a	Atascadero Unified	Atascadero
n/a	n/a	Atwater Elementary	Atwater
n/a	n/a	Auburn Union Elementary	Auburn
n/a	n/a	Azusa Unified	Azusa
n/a	n/a	Bakersfield City	Bakersfield
n/a	n/a	Baldwin Park Unified	Baldwin Park
n/a	n/a	Barstow Unified	Barstow
n/a	n/a	Bear Valley Unified	Big Bear Lake
n/a	n/a	Beardsley Elementary	Bakersfield
n/a	n/a	Bellevue Union Elementary	Santa Rosa
n/a	n/a	Belmont-Redwood Shores Elem.	Belmont
n/a	n/a	Berkeley Unified	Berkeley
n/a	n/a	Berryessa Union Elementary	San Jose
n/a	n/a	Beverly Hills Unified	Beverly Hills
n/a	n/a	Bishop Unified	Bishop
n/a	n/a	Black Oak Mine Unified	Georgetown
n/a	n/a	Bonita Unified	San Dimas
n/a	n/a	Bonsall Union Elementary	Bonsall
n/a	n/a	Brawley Elementary	Brawley
n/a	n/a	Brea-Olinda Unified	Brea
n/a	n/a	Brentwood Union Elementary	Brentwood
n/a	n/a	Buckeye Union Elementary	Shingle Springs
n/a	n/a	Buena Park Elementary	Buena Park
n/a	n/a	Burbank Unified	Burbank
n/a	n/a	Burlingame Elementary	Burlingame
n/a	n/a	Burton Elementary	Porterville
n/a	n/a	Byron Union Elementary	Byron
n/a	n/a	Cabrillo Unified	Half Moon Bay
n/a	n/a	Cajon Valley Union	El Cajon
n/a	n/a	Calaveras Unified	San Andreas
n/a	n/a	Calexico Unified	Calexico
n/a	n/a	Cambrian	San Jose
n/a	n/a	Campbell Union	Campbell
n/a	n/a	Campbell Union High	San Jose
n/a	n/a	Capistrano Unified	SJ Capistrano
n/a	n/a	Carlsbad Unified	Carlsbad
n/a	n/a	Carmel Unified	Carmel
n/a	n/a	Castaic Union Elementary	Valencia
n/a	n/a	Castro Valley Unified	Castro Valley
n/a	n/a	Center Joint Unified	Antelope
n/a	n/a	Centinela Valley Union High	Lawndale
n/a	n/a	Central Elementary	R Cucamonga
n/a	n/a	Central Unified	Fresno
n/a	n/a	Central Union Elementary	Lemoore
n/a	n/a	Central Union High	El Centro
n/a	n/a	Centralia Elementary	Buena Park
n/a	n/a	Ceres Unified	Ceres
n/a	n/a	Chaffey Joint Union High	Ontario
n/a	n/a	Charter Oak Unified	Covina
n/a	n/a	Chico Unified	Chico
n/a	n/a	Chino Valley Unified	Chino
n/a	n/a	Chowchilla Elementary	Chowchilla
n/a	n/a	Chula Vista Elementary	Chula Vista
n/a	n/a	Claremont Unified	Claremont
n/a	n/a	Clovis Unified	Clovis
n/a	n/a	Coalinga-Huron Joint Unified	Coalinga
n/a	n/a	Colton Joint Unified	Colton
n/a	n/a	Compton Unified	Compton
n/a	n/a	Conejo Valley Unified	Thousand Oaks
n/a	n/a	Corcoran Joint Unified	Corcoran
n/a	n/a	Corning Union Elementary	Corning
n/a	n/a	Corona-Norco Unified	Norco
n/a	n/a	Coronado Unified	Coronado
n/a	n/a	Cotati-Rohnert Park Unified	Rohnert Park
n/a	n/a	Covina-Valley Unified	Covina
n/a	n/a	Cucamonga Elementary	R Cucamonga
n/a	n/a	Cupertino Union	Cupertino
n/a	n/a	Cutler-Orosi Joint Unified	Orosi
n/a	n/a	Cypress Elementary	Cypress
n/a	n/a	Davis Joint Unified	Davis
n/a	n/a	Dehesa Elementary	El Cajon
n/a	n/a	Del Mar Union Elementary	San Diego
n/a	n/a	Del Norte County Unified	Crescent City
n/a	n/a	Delano Joint Union High	Delano
n/a	n/a	Delano Union Elementary	Delano
n/a	n/a	Denair Unified	Denair
n/a	n/a	Desert Sands Unified	La Quinta
n/a	n/a	Dinuba Unified	Dinuba
n/a	n/a	Dixie Elementary	San Rafael
n/a	n/a	Dixon Unified	Dixon
n/a	n/a	Dos Palos Oro Loma Joint Unified	Dos Palos
n/a	n/a	Downey Unified	Downey
n/a	n/a	Dry Creek Joint Elementary	Roseville
n/a	n/a	Duarte Unified	Duarte
n/a	n/a	Dublin Unified	Dublin
n/a	n/a	Earlimart Elementary	Earlimart
n/a	n/a	East Side Union High	San Jose
n/a	n/a	East Whittier City Elementary	Whittier
n/a	n/a	Eastside Union Elementary	Lancaster
n/a	n/a	El Centro Elementary	El Centro
n/a	n/a	El Dorado Union High	Placerville
n/a	n/a	El Monte City Elementary	El Monte
n/a	n/a	El Monte Union High	El Monte
n/a	n/a	El Rancho Unified	Pico Rivera
n/a	n/a	Elk Grove Unified	Elk Grove
n/a	n/a	Empire Union Elementary	Modesto
n/a	n/a	Encinitas Union Elementary	Encinitas
n/a	n/a	Escalon Unified	Escalon
n/a	n/a	Escondido Union	Escondido
n/a	n/a	Etiwanda Elementary	Etiwanda
n/a	n/a	Eureka City Schools	Eureka
n/a	n/a	Exeter Union Elementary	Exeter
n/a	n/a	Fairfax Elementary	Bakersfield
n/a	n/a	Fairfield-Suisun Unified	Fairfield
n/a	n/a	Fallbrook Union Elementary	Fallbrook
n/a	n/a	Fallbrook Union High	Fallbrook
n/a	n/a	Farmersville Unified	Farmersville
n/a	n/a	Fillmore Unified	Fillmore
n/a	n/a	Firebaugh-Las Deltas Joint Unified	Firebaugh
n/a	n/a	Folsom-Cordova Unified	Folsom
n/a	n/a	Fontana Unified	Fontana
n/a	n/a	Fort Bragg Unified	Fort Bragg
n/a	n/a	Fountain Valley Elementary	Fountain Valley
n/a	n/a	Fowler Unified	Fowler
n/a	n/a	Franklin-Mckinley Elementary	San Jose
n/a	n/a	Fremont Unified	Fremont
n/a	n/a	Fremont Union High	Sunnyvale
n/a	n/a	Fresno County Office of Education	Fresno
n/a	n/a	Fresno Unified	Fresno
n/a	n/a	Fruitvale Elementary	Bakersfield
n/a	n/a	Fullerton Elementary	Fullerton
n/a	n/a	Fullerton Joint Union High	Fullerton
n/a	n/a	Galt Joint Union Elementary	Galt
n/a	n/a	Garden Grove Unified	Garden Grove
n/a	n/a	Garvey Elementary	Rosemead
n/a	n/a	Gilroy Unified	Gilroy
n/a	n/a	Glendora Unified	Glendora
n/a	n/a	Golden Plains Unified	San Joaquin
n/a	n/a	Golden Valley Unified	Madera
n/a	n/a	Goleta Union Elementary	Goleta
n/a	n/a	Greenfield Union	Bakersfield
n/a	n/a	Greenfield Union Elementary	Greenfield
n/a	n/a	Gridley Unified	Gridley
n/a	n/a	Grossmont Union High	La Mesa
n/a	n/a	Gustine Unified	Gustine
n/a	n/a	Hacienda La Puente Unified	City of Industry
n/a	n/a	Hawthorne	Hawthorne
n/a	n/a	Hayward Unified	Hayward
n/a	n/a	Healdsburg Unified	Healdsburg
n/a	n/a	Hemet Unified	Hemet
n/a	n/a	Hermosa Beach City Elementary	Hermosa Beach
n/a	n/a	Hesperia Unified	Hesperia
n/a	n/a	Hillsborough City Elementary	Hillsborough
n/a	n/a	Hollister	Hollister
n/a	n/a	Holtville Unified	Holtville
n/a	n/a	Hueneme Elementary	Port Hueneme
n/a	n/a	Hughson Unified	Hughson
n/a	n/a	Huntington Bch City Elementary	Huntington Bch
n/a	n/a	Huntington Bch Union High	Huntington Bch
n/a	n/a	Imperial Unified	Imperial
n/a	n/a	Inglewood Unified	Inglewood
n/a	n/a	Irvine Unified	Irvine
n/a	n/a	Jefferson Elementary	Daly City
n/a	n/a	Jefferson Union High	Daly City
n/a	n/a	John Swett Unified	Rodeo
n/a	n/a	Julian Union Elementary	Julian
n/a	n/a	Kelseyville Unified	Kelseyville
n/a	n/a	Keppel Union Elementary	Pearblossom
n/a	n/a	Kerman Unified	Kerman
n/a	n/a	Kern County Office of Education	Bakersfield
n/a	n/a	Kern Union High	Bakersfield
n/a	n/a	King City Union	King City
n/a	n/a	Kings Canyon Joint Unified	Reedley
n/a	n/a	Kingsburg Elementary Charter	Kingsburg
n/a	n/a	Konocti Unified	Lower Lake
n/a	n/a	La Canada Unified	La Canada
n/a	n/a	La Habra City Elementary	La Habra
n/a	n/a	La Mesa-Spring Valley	La Mesa
n/a	n/a	Laguna Beach Unified	Laguna Beach
n/a	n/a	Lake Elsinore Unified	Lake Elsinore
n/a	n/a	Lakeport Unified	Lakeport
n/a	n/a	Lakeside Union Elementary	Lakeside
n/a	n/a	Lammersville Joint Unified	Mountain House
n/a	n/a	Lamont Elementary	Lamont
n/a	n/a	Lancaster Elementary	Lancaster
n/a	n/a	Las Virgenes Unified	Calabasas
n/a	n/a	Lawndale Elementary	Lawndale
n/a	n/a	Lemon Grove	Lemon Grove
n/a	n/a	Lemoore Union High	Lemoore
n/a	n/a	Lennox	Lennox
n/a	n/a	Liberty Union High	Brentwood
n/a	n/a	Lindsay Unified	Lindsay
n/a	n/a	Live Oak Elementary	Santa Cruz
n/a	n/a	Live Oak Unified	Live Oak
n/a	n/a	Livermore Valley Joint Unified	Livermore
n/a	n/a	Livingston Union Elementary	Livingston
n/a	n/a	Lodi Unified	Lodi
n/a	n/a	Lompoc Unified	Lompoc
n/a	n/a	Long Beach Unified	Long Beach
n/a	n/a	Loomis Union Elementary	Loomis
n/a	n/a	Los Alamitos Unified	Los Alamitos
n/a	n/a	Los Angeles County Office of Educ.	Downey
n/a	n/a	Los Angeles Unified	Los Angeles
n/a	n/a	Los Banos Unified	Los Banos
n/a	n/a	Los Gatos Union Elementary	Los Gatos
n/a	n/a	Los Nietos	Whittier
n/a	n/a	Lowell Joint	Whittier
n/a	n/a	Lucerne Valley Unified	Lucerne Valley
n/a	n/a	Lucia Mar Unified	Arroyo Grande
n/a	n/a	Lynwood Unified	Lynwood
n/a	n/a	Madera Unified	Madera
n/a	n/a	Magnolia Elementary	Anaheim
n/a	n/a	Manteca Unified	Manteca
n/a	n/a	Marcum-Illinois Union Elementary	East Nicolaus
n/a	n/a	Mariposa County Unified	Mariposa
n/a	n/a	Martinez Unified	Martinez
n/a	n/a	Marysville Joint Unified	Marysville
n/a	n/a	Mendota Unified	Mendota
n/a	n/a	Menlo Park City Elementary	Atherton
n/a	n/a	Merced City Elementary	Merced
n/a	n/a	Merced County Office of Education	Merced
n/a	n/a	Merced Union High	Atwater
n/a	n/a	Middletown Unified	Middletown
n/a	n/a	Mill Valley Elementary	Mill Valley
n/a	n/a	Millbrae Elementary	Millbrae
n/a	n/a	Milpitas Unified	Milpitas
n/a	n/a	Modesto City Elementary	Modesto
n/a	n/a	Modesto City High	Modesto

Note: This section only includes districts with 1,500 or more students; All categories are ranked from high to low

n/a	n/a	Mojave Unified	Mojave
n/a	n/a	Montebello Unified	Montebello
n/a	n/a	Monterey County Office of Educ.	Salinas
n/a	n/a	Monterey Peninsula Unified	Monterey
n/a	n/a	Moreland Elementary	San Jose
n/a	n/a	Moreno Valley Unified	Moreno Valley
n/a	n/a	Morgan Hill Unified	Morgan Hill
n/a	n/a	Morongo Unified	Twentynine Plms
n/a	n/a	Mountain Empire Unified	Pine Valley
n/a	n/a	Mountain View Elementary	Ontario
n/a	n/a	Mountain View Elementary	El Monte
n/a	n/a	Mountain View Whisman	Mountain View
n/a	n/a	Mt. Diablo Unified	Concord
n/a	n/a	Mt. Pleasant Elementary	San Jose
n/a	n/a	Muroc Joint Unified	North Edwards
n/a	n/a	Murrieta Valley Unified	Murrieta
n/a	n/a	Napa Valley Unified	Napa
n/a	n/a	National Elementary	National City
n/a	n/a	Natomas Unified	Sacramento
n/a	n/a	Nevada County Office of Education	Nevada City
n/a	n/a	New Haven Unified	Union City
n/a	n/a	Newark Unified	Newark
n/a	n/a	Newhall	Valencia
n/a	n/a	Newport-Mesa Unified	Costa Mesa
n/a	n/a	Norris Elementary	Bakersfield
n/a	n/a	North Monterey County Unified	Moss Landing
n/a	n/a	Northern Humboldt Union High	Mckinleyville
n/a	n/a	Norwalk-La Mirada Unified	Norwalk
n/a	n/a	Novato Unified	Novato
n/a	n/a	Nuview Union	Nuevo
n/a	n/a	Oak Grove Elementary	San Jose
n/a	n/a	Oak Park Unified	Oak Park
n/a	n/a	Oakdale Joint Unified	Oakdale
n/a	n/a	Oakley Union Elementary	Oakley
n/a	n/a	Ocean View	Huntington Bch
n/a	n/a	Ocean View	Oxnard
n/a	n/a	Oceanside Unified	Oceanside
n/a	n/a	Ojai Unified	Ojai
n/a	n/a	Orange County Dept of Education	Costa Mesa
n/a	n/a	Orange Unified	Orange
n/a	n/a	Orcutt Union Elementary	Orcutt
n/a	n/a	Orinda Union Elementary	Orinda
n/a	n/a	Orland Joint Unified	Orland
n/a	n/a	Oroville Union High	Oroville
n/a	n/a	Oxnard	Oxnard
n/a	n/a	Oxnard Union High	Oxnard
n/a	n/a	Pacific Grove Unified	Pacific Grove
n/a	n/a	Pacifica	Pacifica
n/a	n/a	Pajaro Valley Unified	Watsonville
n/a	n/a	Palmdale Elementary	Palmdale
n/a	n/a	Palo Alto Unified	Palo Alto
n/a	n/a	Palo Verde Unified	Blythe
n/a	n/a	Paradise Unified	Paradise
n/a	n/a	Paramount Unified	Paramount
n/a	n/a	Parlier Unified	Parlier
n/a	n/a	Pasadena Unified	Pasadena
n/a	n/a	Paso Robles Joint Unified	Paso Robles
n/a	n/a	Patterson Joint Unified	Patterson
n/a	n/a	Perris Elementary	Perris
n/a	n/a	Perris Union High	Perris
n/a	n/a	Petaluma City Elementary	Petaluma
n/a	n/a	Petaluma Joint Union High	Petaluma
n/a	n/a	Piedmont City Unified	Piedmont
n/a	n/a	Piner-Olivet Union Elementary	Santa Rosa
n/a	n/a	Pioneer Union Elementary	Hanford
n/a	n/a	Pittsburg Unified	Pittsburg
n/a	n/a	Placentia-Yorba Linda Unified	Placentia
n/a	n/a	Placer Union High	Auburn
n/a	n/a	Pleasant Valley	Camarillo
n/a	n/a	Pleasanton Unified	Pleasanton
n/a	n/a	Pomona Unified	Pomona
n/a	n/a	Porterville Unified	Porterville
n/a	n/a	Poway Unified	San Diego
n/a	n/a	Ravenswood City Elementary	East Palo Alto
n/a	n/a	Red Bluff Joint Union High	Red Bluff
n/a	n/a	Red Bluff Union Elementary	Red Bluff
n/a	n/a	Redding Elementary	Redding
n/a	n/a	Redlands Unified	Redlands
n/a	n/a	Redondo Beach Unified	Redondo Beach
n/a	n/a	Redwood City Elementary	Redwood City
n/a	n/a	Reef-Sunset Unified	Avenal
n/a	n/a	Rescue Union Elementary	Rescue
n/a	n/a	Rialto Unified	Rialto
n/a	n/a	Richland Union Elementary	Shafter
n/a	n/a	Rim of the World Unified	Blue Jay
n/a	n/a	Rincon Valley Union Elementary	Santa Rosa
n/a	n/a	Rio Elementary	Oxnard
n/a	n/a	River Delta Joint Unified	Rio Vista
n/a	n/a	Riverdale Joint Unified	Riverdale
n/a	n/a	Riverside County Office of Educ.	Riverside
n/a	n/a	Riverside Unified	Riverside
n/a	n/a	Robla Elementary	Sacramento
n/a	n/a	Rocklin Unified	Rocklin
n/a	n/a	Romoland Elementary	Homeland
n/a	n/a	Rosedale Union Elementary	Bakersfield
n/a	n/a	Roseland Elementary	Santa Rosa
n/a	n/a	Rosemead Elementary	Rosemead
n/a	n/a	Roseville City Elementary	Roseville
n/a	n/a	Ross Valley Elementary	San Anselmo
n/a	n/a	Rowland Unified	Rowland Heights
n/a	n/a	Sacramento City Unified	Sacramento
n/a	n/a	Saddleback Valley Unified	Mission Viejo
n/a	n/a	Salinas City Elementary	Salinas
n/a	n/a	Salinas Union High	Salinas
n/a	n/a	San Benito High	Hollister
n/a	n/a	San Bernardino City Unified	San Bernardino
n/a	n/a	San Bernardino Co. Office of Educ.	San Bernardino
n/a	n/a	San Bruno Park Elementary	San Bruno
n/a	n/a	San Carlos Elementary	San Carlos
n/a	n/a	San Diego County Office of Educ.	San Diego
n/a	n/a	San Diego Unified	San Diego
n/a	n/a	San Dieguito Union High	Encinitas
n/a	n/a	San Gabriel Unified	San Gabriel
n/a	n/a	San Jacinto Unified	San Jacinto
n/a	n/a	San Joaquin County Office of Educ.	Stockton
n/a	n/a	San Jose Unified	San Jose
n/a	n/a	San Juan Unified	Carmichael
n/a	n/a	San Leandro Unified	San Leandro
n/a	n/a	San Lorenzo Valley Unified	Ben Lomond
n/a	n/a	San Marcos Unified	San Marcos
n/a	n/a	San Marino Unified	San Marino
n/a	n/a	San Mateo Union High	San Mateo
n/a	n/a	San Mateo-Foster City	Foster City
n/a	n/a	San Rafael City Elementary	San Rafael
n/a	n/a	San Rafael City High	San Rafael
n/a	n/a	San Ramon Valley Unified	Danville
n/a	n/a	San Ysidro Elementary	San Ysidro
n/a	n/a	Sanger Unified	Sanger
n/a	n/a	Santa Ana Unified	Santa Ana
n/a	n/a	Santa Barbara Unified	Santa Barbara
n/a	n/a	Santa Clara County Office of Educ.	San Jose
n/a	n/a	Santa Clara Unified	Santa Clara
n/a	n/a	Santa Cruz City Elementary	Soquel
n/a	n/a	Santa Cruz City High	Soquel
n/a	n/a	Santa Maria Joint Union High	Santa Maria
n/a	n/a	Santa Maria-Bonita	Santa Maria
n/a	n/a	Santa Monica-Malibu Unified	Santa Monica
n/a	n/a	Santa Paula Elementary	Santa Paula
n/a	n/a	Santa Paula Union High	Santa Paula
n/a	n/a	Santa Rita Union Elementary	Salinas
n/a	n/a	Santa Rosa Elementary	Santa Rosa
n/a	n/a	Santa Rosa High	Santa Rosa
n/a	n/a	Santee Elementary	Santee
n/a	n/a	Saugus Union	Santa Clarita
n/a	n/a	Savanna Elementary	Anaheim
n/a	n/a	Sbc - Aspire Public Schools	Oakland
n/a	n/a	Sbc - High Tech High	San Diego
n/a	n/a	Scotts Valley Unified	Scotts Valley
n/a	n/a	Selma Unified	Selma
n/a	n/a	Sequoia Union High	Redwood City
n/a	n/a	Shasta Union High	Redding
n/a	n/a	Sierra Sands Unified	Ridgecrest
n/a	n/a	Silver Valley Unified	Yermo
n/a	n/a	Simi Valley Unified	Simi Valley
n/a	n/a	Snowline Joint Unified	Phelan
n/a	n/a	Solana Beach Elementary	Solana Beach
n/a	n/a	Soledad Unified	Soledad
n/a	n/a	Sonoma Valley Unified	Sonoma
n/a	n/a	South Bay Union Elementary	Imperial Beach
n/a	n/a	South Monterey Co. Jt Union High	King City
n/a	n/a	South Pasadena Unified	South Pasadena
n/a	n/a	S San Francisco Unified	S San Francisco
n/a	n/a	South Whittier Elementary	Whittier
n/a	n/a	Southern Kern Unified	Rosamond
n/a	n/a	Spencer Valley Elementary	Santa Ysabel
n/a	n/a	Standard Elementary	Bakersfield
n/a	n/a	Stanislaus Union Elementary	Modesto
n/a	n/a	Stockton Unified	Stockton
n/a	n/a	Sunnyvale	Sunnyvale
n/a	n/a	Sweetwater Union High	Chula Vista
n/a	n/a	Taft City	Taft
n/a	n/a	Tahoe-Truckee Joint Unified	Truckee
n/a	n/a	Tamalpais Union High	Larkspur
n/a	n/a	Tehachapi Unified	Tehachapi
n/a	n/a	Temecula Valley Unified	Temecula
n/a	n/a	Temple City Unified	Temple City
n/a	n/a	Templeton Unified	Templeton
n/a	n/a	Torrance Unified	Torrance
n/a	n/a	Tracy Joint Unified	Tracy
n/a	n/a	Travis Unified	Fairfield
n/a	n/a	Tulare County Office of Education	Visalia
n/a	n/a	Tulare Joint Union High	Tulare
n/a	n/a	Turlock Unified	Turlock
n/a	n/a	Tustin Unified	Tustin
n/a	n/a	Twin Rivers Unified	Mcclellan
n/a	n/a	Ukiah Unified	Ukiah
n/a	n/a	Union Elementary	San Jose
n/a	n/a	Upland Unified	Upland
n/a	n/a	Vacaville Unified	Vacaville
n/a	n/a	Val Verde Unified	Perris
n/a	n/a	Vallejo City Unified	Vallejo
n/a	n/a	Valley Center-Pauma Unified	Valley Center
n/a	n/a	Ventura County Office of Educ.	Camarillo
n/a	n/a	Ventura Unified	Ventura
n/a	n/a	Victor Elementary	Victorville
n/a	n/a	Victor Valley Union High	Victorville
n/a	n/a	Visalia Unified	Visalia
n/a	n/a	Vista Unified	Vista
n/a	n/a	Walnut Creek Elementary	Walnut Creek
n/a	n/a	Walnut Valley Unified	Walnut
n/a	n/a	Wasco Union Elementary	Wasco
n/a	n/a	Wasco Union High	Wasco
n/a	n/a	Washington Unified	West Sacramento
n/a	n/a	Washington Unified	Fresno
n/a	n/a	Waterford Unified	Waterford
n/a	n/a	West Contra Costa Unified	Richmond
n/a	n/a	West Covina Unified	West Covina
n/a	n/a	West Sonoma County Union High	Sebastopol
n/a	n/a	Western Placer Unified	Lincoln
n/a	n/a	Whittier City Elementary	Whittier
n/a	n/a	Whittier Union High	Whittier
n/a	n/a	William S. Hart Union High	Santa Clarita
n/a	n/a	Willits Unified	Willits
n/a	n/a	Willows Unified	Willows
n/a	n/a	Windsor Unified	Windsor
n/a	n/a	Winters Joint Unified	Winters
n/a	n/a	Winton Elementary	Winton
n/a	n/a	Wiseburn Elementary	Hawthorne
n/a	n/a	Woodlake Union Elementary	Woodlake
n/a	n/a	Woodland Joint Unified	Woodland
n/a	n/a	Wright Elementary	Santa Rosa
n/a	n/a	Yosemite Unified	Oakhurst
n/a	n/a	Yuba City Unified	Yuba City
n/a	n/a	Yucaipa-Calimesa Joint Unified	Yucaipa

Students Eligible for Reduced-Price Lunch

Rank	Percent	District Name	City
1	7.7	Coachella Valley Unified	Thermal
2	6.4	Arvin Union Elementary	Arvin
3	2.6	Oroville City Elementary	Oroville
4	1.8	Oakland Unified	Oakland
5	0.9	Enterprise Elementary	Redding
6	0.8	Ontario-Montclair Elementary	Ontario
7	0.1	Lafayette Elementary	Lafayette
7	0.1	Mcfarland Unified	Mcfarland
7	0.1	Moraga Elementary	Moraga
7	0.1	Newman-Crows Landing Unified	Newman
7	0.1	Salida Union Elementary	Salida
7	0.1	Saratoga Union Elementary	Saratoga
13	0.0	Anderson Union High	Anderson
13	0.0	Apple Valley Unified	Apple Valley
13	0.0	Banning Unified	Banning
13	0.0	Bassett Unified	La Puente
13	0.0	Beaumont Unified	Beaumont
13	0.0	Bellflower Unified	Bellflower
13	0.0	Benicia Unified	Benicia
13	0.0	Brawley Union High	Brawley
13	0.0	Carpinteria Unified	Carpinteria
13	0.0	Culver City Unified	Culver City
13	0.0	Delhi Unified	Delhi
13	0.0	El Segundo Unified	El Segundo
13	0.0	Escondido Union High	Escondido

Note: This section only includes districts with 1,500 or more students; All categories are ranked from high to low

13	0.0	Eureka Union	Granite Bay
13	0.0	Evergreen Elementary	San Jose
13	0.0	Galt Joint Union High	Galt
13	0.0	Glendale Unified	Glendale
13	0.0	Gonzales Unified	Gonzales
13	0.0	Gorman Elementary	Gorman
13	0.0	Grass Valley Elementary	Grass Valley
13	0.0	Hanford Elementary	Hanford
13	0.0	Hanford Joint Union High	Hanford
13	0.0	Hilmar Unified	Hilmar
13	0.0	Jefferson Elementary	Tracy
13	0.0	Jurupa Unified	Jurupa Valley
13	0.0	Lake Tahoe Unified	S Lake Tahoe
13	0.0	Lemoore Union Elementary	Lemoore
13	0.0	Lincoln Unified	Stockton
13	0.0	Linden Unified	Linden
13	0.0	Little Lake City Elementary	Santa Fe Spgs
13	0.0	Los Altos Elementary	Los Altos
13	0.0	Los Gatos-Saratoga Jt Union High	Los Gatos
13	0.0	Manhattan Beach Unified	Manhattan Beach
13	0.0	Menifee Union Elementary	Menifee
13	0.0	Monrovia Unified	Monrovia
13	0.0	Moorpark Unified	Moorpark
13	0.0	Mountain View-Los Altos Union High	Mountain View
13	0.0	Nevada Joint Union High	Grass Valley
13	0.0	Old Adobe Union	Petaluma
13	0.0	Oro Grande Elementary	Oro Grande
13	0.0	Palm Springs Unified	Palm Springs
13	0.0	Palos Verdes Peninsula Unified	Palos Vrds Est
13	0.0	Panama-Buena Vista Union	Bakersfield
13	0.0	Ramona City Unified	Ramona
13	0.0	Ripon Unified	Ripon
13	0.0	Riverbank Unified	Riverbank
13	0.0	Roseville Joint Union High	Roseville
13	0.0	San Francisco Unified	San Francisco
13	0.0	San Lorenzo Unified	San Lorenzo
13	0.0	San Luis Coastal Unified	San Luis Obispo
13	0.0	Soquel Union Elementary	Capitola
13	0.0	Stanislaus County Office of Educ.	Modesto
13	0.0	Sulphur Springs Union	Canyon Country
13	0.0	Sylvan Union Elementary	Modesto
13	0.0	Tulare City	Tulare
13	0.0	Weaver Union	Merced
13	0.0	Westminster Elementary	Westminster
13	0.0	Westside Union Elementary	Quartz Hill
n/a	n/a	ABC Unified	Cerritos
n/a	n/a	Acalanes Union High	Lafayette
n/a	n/a	Acton-Agua Dulce Unified	Acton
n/a	n/a	Adelanto Elementary	Adelanto
n/a	n/a	Alameda City Unified	Alameda
n/a	n/a	Alameda County Office of Education	Hayward
n/a	n/a	Albany City Unified	Albany
n/a	n/a	Alhambra Unified	Alhambra
n/a	n/a	Alisal Union	Salinas
n/a	n/a	Alpine Union Elementary	Alpine
n/a	n/a	Alta Loma Elementary	Alta Loma
n/a	n/a	Alum Rock Union Elementary	San Jose
n/a	n/a	Alvord Unified	Riverside
n/a	n/a	Amador County Unified	Jackson
n/a	n/a	Anaheim City	Anaheim
n/a	n/a	Anaheim Union High	Anaheim
n/a	n/a	Antelope Valley Union High	Lancaster
n/a	n/a	Antioch Unified	Antioch
n/a	n/a	Arcadia Unified	Arcadia
n/a	n/a	Armona Union Elementary	Armona
n/a	n/a	Atascadero Unified	Atascadero
n/a	n/a	Atwater Elementary	Atwater
n/a	n/a	Auburn Union Elementary	Auburn
n/a	n/a	Azusa Unified	Azusa
n/a	n/a	Bakersfield City	Bakersfield
n/a	n/a	Baldwin Park Unified	Baldwin Park
n/a	n/a	Barstow Unified	Barstow
n/a	n/a	Bear Valley Unified	Big Bear Lake
n/a	n/a	Beardsley Elementary	Bakersfield
n/a	n/a	Bellevue Union Elementary	Santa Rosa
n/a	n/a	Belmont-Redwood Shores Elem.	Belmont
n/a	n/a	Berkeley Unified	Berkeley
n/a	n/a	Berryessa Union Elementary	San Jose
n/a	n/a	Beverly Hills Unified	Beverly Hills
n/a	n/a	Bishop Unified	Bishop
n/a	n/a	Black Oak Mine Unified	Georgetown
n/a	n/a	Bonita Unified	San Dimas
n/a	n/a	Bonsall Union Elementary	Bonsall
n/a	n/a	Brawley Elementary	Brawley
n/a	n/a	Brea-Olinda Unified	Brea

n/a	n/a	Brentwood Union Elementary	Brentwood
n/a	n/a	Buckeye Union Elementary	Shingle Springs
n/a	n/a	Buena Park Elementary	Buena Park
n/a	n/a	Burbank Unified	Burbank
n/a	n/a	Burlingame Elementary	Burlingame
n/a	n/a	Burton Elementary	Porterville
n/a	n/a	Byron Union Elementary	Byron
n/a	n/a	Cabrillo Unified	Half Moon Bay
n/a	n/a	Cajon Valley Union	El Cajon
n/a	n/a	Calaveras Unified	San Andreas
n/a	n/a	Calexico Unified	Calexico
n/a	n/a	Cambrian	San Jose
n/a	n/a	Campbell Union	Campbell
n/a	n/a	Campbell Union High	San Jose
n/a	n/a	Capistrano Unified	SJ Capistrano
n/a	n/a	Carlsbad Unified	Carlsbad
n/a	n/a	Carmel Unified	Carmel
n/a	n/a	Castaic Union Elementary	Valencia
n/a	n/a	Castro Valley Unified	Castro Valley
n/a	n/a	Center Joint Unified	Antelope
n/a	n/a	Centinela Valley Union High	Lawndale
n/a	n/a	Central Elementary	R Cucamonga
n/a	n/a	Central Unified	Fresno
n/a	n/a	Central Union Elementary	Lemoore
n/a	n/a	Central Union High	El Centro
n/a	n/a	Centralia Elementary	Buena Park
n/a	n/a	Ceres Unified	Ceres
n/a	n/a	Chaffey Joint Union High	Ontario
n/a	n/a	Charter Oak Unified	Covina
n/a	n/a	Chico Unified	Chico
n/a	n/a	Chino Valley Unified	Chino
n/a	n/a	Chowchilla Elementary	Chowchilla
n/a	n/a	Chula Vista Elementary	Chula Vista
n/a	n/a	Claremont Unified	Claremont
n/a	n/a	Clovis Unified	Clovis
n/a	n/a	Coalinga-Huron Joint Unified	Coalinga
n/a	n/a	Colton Joint Unified	Colton
n/a	n/a	Compton Unified	Compton
n/a	n/a	Conejo Valley Unified	Thousand Oaks
n/a	n/a	Corcoran Joint Unified	Corcoran
n/a	n/a	Corning Union Elementary	Corning
n/a	n/a	Corona-Norco Unified	Norco
n/a	n/a	Coronado Unified	Coronado
n/a	n/a	Cotati-Rohnert Park Unified	Rohnert Park
n/a	n/a	Covina-Valley Unified	Covina
n/a	n/a	Cucamonga Elementary	R Cucamonga
n/a	n/a	Cupertino Union	Cupertino
n/a	n/a	Cutler-Orosi Joint Unified	Orosi
n/a	n/a	Cypress Elementary	Cypress
n/a	n/a	Davis Joint Unified	Davis
n/a	n/a	Dehesa Elementary	El Cajon
n/a	n/a	Del Mar Union Elementary	San Diego
n/a	n/a	Del Norte County Unified	Crescent City
n/a	n/a	Delano Joint Union High	Delano
n/a	n/a	Delano Union Elementary	Delano
n/a	n/a	Denair Unified	Denair
n/a	n/a	Desert Sands Unified	La Quinta
n/a	n/a	Dinuba Unified	Dinuba
n/a	n/a	Dixie Elementary	San Rafael
n/a	n/a	Dixon Unified	Dixon
n/a	n/a	Dos Palos Oro Loma Joint Unified	Dos Palos
n/a	n/a	Downey Unified	Downey
n/a	n/a	Dry Creek Joint Elementary	Roseville
n/a	n/a	Duarte Unified	Duarte
n/a	n/a	Dublin Unified	Dublin
n/a	n/a	Earlimart Elementary	Earlimart
n/a	n/a	East Side Union High	San Jose
n/a	n/a	East Whittier City Elementary	Whittier
n/a	n/a	Eastside Union Elementary	Lancaster
n/a	n/a	El Centro Elementary	El Centro
n/a	n/a	El Dorado Union High	Placerville
n/a	n/a	El Monte City Elementary	El Monte
n/a	n/a	El Monte Union High	El Monte
n/a	n/a	El Rancho Unified	Pico Rivera
n/a	n/a	Elk Grove Unified	Elk Grove
n/a	n/a	Empire Union Elementary	Modesto
n/a	n/a	Encinitas Union Elementary	Encinitas
n/a	n/a	Escalon Unified	Escalon
n/a	n/a	Escondido Union	Escondido
n/a	n/a	Etiwanda Elementary	Etiwanda
n/a	n/a	Eureka City Schools	Eureka
n/a	n/a	Exeter Union Elementary	Exeter
n/a	n/a	Fairfax Elementary	Bakersfield
n/a	n/a	Fairfield-Suisun Unified	Fairfield
n/a	n/a	Fallbrook Union Elementary	Fallbrook

n/a	n/a	Fallbrook Union High	Fallbrook
n/a	n/a	Farmersville Unified	Farmersville
n/a	n/a	Fillmore Unified	Fillmore
n/a	n/a	Firebaugh-Las Deltas Joint Unified	Firebaugh
n/a	n/a	Folsom-Cordova Unified	Folsom
n/a	n/a	Fontana Unified	Fontana
n/a	n/a	Fort Bragg Unified	Fort Bragg
n/a	n/a	Fountain Valley Elementary	Fountain Valley
n/a	n/a	Fowler Unified	Fowler
n/a	n/a	Franklin-Mckinley Elementary	San Jose
n/a	n/a	Fremont Unified	Fremont
n/a	n/a	Fremont Union High	Sunnyvale
n/a	n/a	Fresno County Office of Education	Fresno
n/a	n/a	Fresno Unified	Fresno
n/a	n/a	Fruitvale Elementary	Bakersfield
n/a	n/a	Fullerton Elementary	Fullerton
n/a	n/a	Fullerton Joint Union High	Fullerton
n/a	n/a	Galt Joint Union Elementary	Galt
n/a	n/a	Garden Grove Unified	Garden Grove
n/a	n/a	Garvey Elementary	Rosemead
n/a	n/a	Gateway Unified	Redding
n/a	n/a	Gilroy Unified	Gilroy
n/a	n/a	Glendora Unified	Glendora
n/a	n/a	Golden Plains Unified	San Joaquin
n/a	n/a	Golden Valley Unified	Madera
n/a	n/a	Goleta Union Elementary	Goleta
n/a	n/a	Greenfield Union	Bakersfield
n/a	n/a	Greenfield Union Elementary	Greenfield
n/a	n/a	Gridley Unified	Gridley
n/a	n/a	Grossmont Union High	La Mesa
n/a	n/a	Gustine Unified	Gustine
n/a	n/a	Hacienda La Puente Unified	City of Industry
n/a	n/a	Hawthorne	Hawthorne
n/a	n/a	Hayward Unified	Hayward
n/a	n/a	Healdsburg Unified	Healdsburg
n/a	n/a	Hemet Unified	Hemet
n/a	n/a	Hermosa Beach City Elementary	Hermosa Beach
n/a	n/a	Hesperia Unified	Hesperia
n/a	n/a	Hillsborough City Elementary	Hillsborough
n/a	n/a	Hollister	Hollister
n/a	n/a	Holtville Unified	Holtville
n/a	n/a	Hueneme Elementary	Port Hueneme
n/a	n/a	Hughson Unified	Hughson
n/a	n/a	Huntington Bch City Elementary	Huntington Bch
n/a	n/a	Huntington Bch Union High	Huntington Bch
n/a	n/a	Imperial Unified	Imperial
n/a	n/a	Inglewood Unified	Inglewood
n/a	n/a	Irvine Unified	Irvine
n/a	n/a	Jefferson Elementary	Daly City
n/a	n/a	Jefferson Union High	Daly City
n/a	n/a	John Swett Unified	Rodeo
n/a	n/a	Julian Union Elementary	Julian
n/a	n/a	Kelseyville Unified	Kelseyville
n/a	n/a	Keppel Union Elementary	Pearblossom
n/a	n/a	Kerman Unified	Kerman
n/a	n/a	Kern County Office of Education	Bakersfield
n/a	n/a	Kern Union High	Bakersfield
n/a	n/a	King City Union	King City
n/a	n/a	Kings Canyon Joint Unified	Reedley
n/a	n/a	Kingsburg Elementary Charter	Kingsburg
n/a	n/a	Konocti Unified	Lower Lake
n/a	n/a	La Canada Unified	La Canada
n/a	n/a	La Habra City Elementary	La Habra
n/a	n/a	La Mesa-Spring Valley	La Mesa
n/a	n/a	Laguna Beach Unified	Laguna Beach
n/a	n/a	Lake Elsinore Unified	Lake Elsinore
n/a	n/a	Lakeport Unified	Lakeport
n/a	n/a	Lakeside Union Elementary	Lakeside
n/a	n/a	Lammersville Joint Unified	Mountain House
n/a	n/a	Lamont Elementary	Lamont
n/a	n/a	Lancaster Elementary	Lancaster
n/a	n/a	Las Virgenes Unified	Calabasas
n/a	n/a	Lawndale Elementary	Lawndale
n/a	n/a	Lemon Grove	Lemon Grove
n/a	n/a	Lemoore Union High	Lemoore
n/a	n/a	Lennox	Lennox
n/a	n/a	Liberty Union High	Brentwood
n/a	n/a	Lindsay Unified	Lindsay
n/a	n/a	Live Oak Elementary	Santa Cruz
n/a	n/a	Live Oak Unified	Live Oak
n/a	n/a	Livermore Valley Joint Unified	Livermore
n/a	n/a	Livingston Union Elementary	Livingston
n/a	n/a	Lodi Unified	Lodi
n/a	n/a	Lompoc Unified	Lompoc
n/a	n/a	Long Beach Unified	Long Beach

Note: This section only includes districts with 1,500 or more students; All categories are ranked from high to low

n/a	n/a	Loomis Union Elementary	Loomis
n/a	n/a	Los Alamitos Unified	Los Alamitos
n/a	n/a	Los Angeles County Office of Educ.	Downey
n/a	n/a	Los Angeles Unified	Los Angeles
n/a	n/a	Los Banos Unified	Los Banos
n/a	n/a	Los Gatos Union Elementary	Los Gatos
n/a	n/a	Los Nietos	Whittier
n/a	n/a	Lowell Joint	Whittier
n/a	n/a	Lucerne Valley Unified	Lucerne Valley
n/a	n/a	Lucia Mar Unified	Arroyo Grande
n/a	n/a	Lynwood Unified	Lynwood
n/a	n/a	Madera Unified	Madera
n/a	n/a	Magnolia Elementary	Anaheim
n/a	n/a	Manteca Unified	Manteca
n/a	n/a	Marcum-Illinois Union Elementary	East Nicolaus
n/a	n/a	Mariposa County Unified	Mariposa
n/a	n/a	Martinez Unified	Martinez
n/a	n/a	Marysville Joint Unified	Marysville
n/a	n/a	Mendota Unified	Mendota
n/a	n/a	Menlo Park City Elementary	Atherton
n/a	n/a	Merced City Elementary	Merced
n/a	n/a	Merced County Office of Education	Merced
n/a	n/a	Merced Union High	Atwater
n/a	n/a	Middletown Unified	Middletown
n/a	n/a	Mill Valley Elementary	Mill Valley
n/a	n/a	Millbrae Elementary	Millbrae
n/a	n/a	Milpitas Unified	Milpitas
n/a	n/a	Modesto City Elementary	Modesto
n/a	n/a	Modesto City High	Modesto
n/a	n/a	Mojave Unified	Mojave
n/a	n/a	Montebello Unified	Montebello
n/a	n/a	Monterey County Office of Educ.	Salinas
n/a	n/a	Monterey Peninsula Unified	Monterey
n/a	n/a	Moreland Elementary	San Jose
n/a	n/a	Moreno Valley Unified	Moreno Valley
n/a	n/a	Morgan Hill Unified	Morgan Hill
n/a	n/a	Morongo Unified	Twentynine Plms
n/a	n/a	Mountain Empire Unified	Pine Valley
n/a	n/a	Mountain View Elementary	Ontario
n/a	n/a	Mountain View Elementary	El Monte
n/a	n/a	Mountain View Whisman	Mountain View
n/a	n/a	Mt. Diablo Unified	Concord
n/a	n/a	Mt. Pleasant Elementary	San Jose
n/a	n/a	Muroc Joint Unified	North Edwards
n/a	n/a	Murrieta Valley Unified	Murrieta
n/a	n/a	Napa Valley Unified	Napa
n/a	n/a	National Elementary	National City
n/a	n/a	Natomas Unified	Sacramento
n/a	n/a	Nevada County Office of Education	Nevada City
n/a	n/a	New Haven Unified	Union City
n/a	n/a	Newark Unified	Newark
n/a	n/a	Newhall	Valencia
n/a	n/a	Newport-Mesa Unified	Costa Mesa
n/a	n/a	Norris Elementary	Bakersfield
n/a	n/a	North Monterey County Unified	Moss Landing
n/a	n/a	Northern Humboldt Union High	Mckinleyville
n/a	n/a	Norwalk-La Mirada Unified	Norwalk
n/a	n/a	Novato Unified	Novato
n/a	n/a	Nuview Union	Nuevo
n/a	n/a	Oak Grove Elementary	San Jose
n/a	n/a	Oak Park Unified	Oak Park
n/a	n/a	Oakdale Joint Unified	Oakdale
n/a	n/a	Oakley Union Elementary	Oakley
n/a	n/a	Ocean View	Huntington Bch
n/a	n/a	Ocean View	Oxnard
n/a	n/a	Oceanside Unified	Oceanside
n/a	n/a	Ojai Unified	Ojai
n/a	n/a	Orange County Dept of Education	Costa Mesa
n/a	n/a	Orange Unified	Orange
n/a	n/a	Orcutt Union Elementary	Orcutt
n/a	n/a	Orinda Union Elementary	Orinda
n/a	n/a	Orland Joint Unified	Orland
n/a	n/a	Oroville Union High	Oroville
n/a	n/a	Oxnard	Oxnard
n/a	n/a	Oxnard Union High	Oxnard
n/a	n/a	Pacific Grove Unified	Pacific Grove
n/a	n/a	Pacifica	Pacifica
n/a	n/a	Pajaro Valley Unified	Watsonville
n/a	n/a	Palmdale Elementary	Palmdale
n/a	n/a	Palo Alto Unified	Palo Alto
n/a	n/a	Palo Verde Unified	Blythe
n/a	n/a	Paradise Unified	Paradise
n/a	n/a	Paramount Unified	Paramount
n/a	n/a	Parlier Unified	Parlier
n/a	n/a	Pasadena Unified	Pasadena
n/a	n/a	Paso Robles Joint Unified	Paso Robles
n/a	n/a	Patterson Joint Unified	Patterson
n/a	n/a	Perris Elementary	Perris
n/a	n/a	Perris Union High	Perris
n/a	n/a	Petaluma City Elementary	Petaluma
n/a	n/a	Petaluma Joint Union High	Petaluma
n/a	n/a	Piedmont City Unified	Piedmont
n/a	n/a	Piner-Olivet Union Elementary	Santa Rosa
n/a	n/a	Pioneer Union Elementary	Hanford
n/a	n/a	Pittsburg Unified	Pittsburg
n/a	n/a	Placentia-Yorba Linda Unified	Placentia
n/a	n/a	Placer Union High	Auburn
n/a	n/a	Pleasant Valley	Camarillo
n/a	n/a	Pleasanton Unified	Pleasanton
n/a	n/a	Pomona Unified	Pomona
n/a	n/a	Porterville Unified	Porterville
n/a	n/a	Poway Unified	San Diego
n/a	n/a	Ravenswood City Elementary	East Palo Alto
n/a	n/a	Red Bluff Joint Union High	Red Bluff
n/a	n/a	Red Bluff Union Elementary	Red Bluff
n/a	n/a	Redding Elementary	Redding
n/a	n/a	Redlands Unified	Redlands
n/a	n/a	Redondo Beach Unified	Redondo Beach
n/a	n/a	Redwood City Elementary	Redwood City
n/a	n/a	Reef-Sunset Unified	Avenal
n/a	n/a	Rescue Union Elementary	Rescue
n/a	n/a	Rialto Unified	Rialto
n/a	n/a	Richland Union Elementary	Shafter
n/a	n/a	Rim of the World Unified	Blue Jay
n/a	n/a	Rincon Valley Union Elementary	Santa Rosa
n/a	n/a	Rio Elementary	Oxnard
n/a	n/a	River Delta Joint Unified	Rio Vista
n/a	n/a	Riverdale Joint Unified	Riverdale
n/a	n/a	Riverside County Office of Educ.	Riverside
n/a	n/a	Riverside Unified	Riverside
n/a	n/a	Robla Elementary	Sacramento
n/a	n/a	Rocklin Unified	Rocklin
n/a	n/a	Romoland Elementary	Homeland
n/a	n/a	Rosedale Union Elementary	Bakersfield
n/a	n/a	Roseland Elementary	Santa Rosa
n/a	n/a	Rosemead Elementary	Rosemead
n/a	n/a	Roseville City Elementary	Roseville
n/a	n/a	Ross Valley Elementary	San Anselmo
n/a	n/a	Rowland Unified	Rowland Heights
n/a	n/a	Sacramento City Unified	Sacramento
n/a	n/a	Saddleback Valley Unified	Mission Viejo
n/a	n/a	Salinas City Elementary	Salinas
n/a	n/a	Salinas Union High	Salinas
n/a	n/a	San Benito High	Hollister
n/a	n/a	San Bernardino City Unified	San Bernardino
n/a	n/a	San Bernardino Co. Office of Educ.	San Bernardino
n/a	n/a	San Bruno Park Elementary	San Bruno
n/a	n/a	San Carlos Elementary	San Carlos
n/a	n/a	San Diego County Office of Educ.	San Diego
n/a	n/a	San Diego Unified	San Diego
n/a	n/a	San Dieguito Union High	Encinitas
n/a	n/a	San Gabriel Unified	San Gabriel
n/a	n/a	San Jacinto Unified	San Jacinto
n/a	n/a	San Joaquin County Office of Educ.	Stockton
n/a	n/a	San Jose Unified	San Jose
n/a	n/a	San Juan Unified	Carmichael
n/a	n/a	San Leandro Unified	San Leandro
n/a	n/a	San Lorenzo Valley Unified	Ben Lomond
n/a	n/a	San Marcos Unified	San Marcos
n/a	n/a	San Marino Unified	San Marino
n/a	n/a	San Mateo Union High	San Mateo
n/a	n/a	San Mateo-Foster City	Foster City
n/a	n/a	San Rafael City Elementary	San Rafael
n/a	n/a	San Rafael City High	San Rafael
n/a	n/a	San Ramon Valley Unified	Danville
n/a	n/a	San Ysidro Elementary	San Ysidro
n/a	n/a	Sanger Unified	Sanger
n/a	n/a	Santa Ana Unified	Santa Ana
n/a	n/a	Santa Barbara Unified	Santa Barbara
n/a	n/a	Santa Clara County Office of Educ.	San Jose
n/a	n/a	Santa Clara Unified	Santa Clara
n/a	n/a	Santa Cruz City Elementary	Soquel
n/a	n/a	Santa Cruz City High	Soquel
n/a	n/a	Santa Maria Joint Union High	Santa Maria
n/a	n/a	Santa Maria-Bonita	Santa Maria
n/a	n/a	Santa Monica-Malibu Unified	Santa Monica
n/a	n/a	Santa Paula Elementary	Santa Paula
n/a	n/a	Santa Paula Union High	Santa Paula
n/a	n/a	Santa Rita Union Elementary	Salinas
n/a	n/a	Santa Rosa Elementary	Santa Rosa
n/a	n/a	Santa Rosa High	Santa Rosa
n/a	n/a	Santee Elementary	Santee
n/a	n/a	Saugus Union	Santa Clarita
n/a	n/a	Savanna Elementary	Anaheim
n/a	n/a	Sbc - Aspire Public Schools	Oakland
n/a	n/a	Sbc - High Tech High	San Diego
n/a	n/a	Scotts Valley Unified	Scotts Valley
n/a	n/a	Selma Unified	Selma
n/a	n/a	Sequoia Union High	Redwood City
n/a	n/a	Shasta Union High	Redding
n/a	n/a	Sierra Sands Unified	Ridgecrest
n/a	n/a	Silver Valley Unified	Yermo
n/a	n/a	Simi Valley Unified	Simi Valley
n/a	n/a	Snowline Joint Unified	Phelan
n/a	n/a	Solana Beach Elementary	Solana Beach
n/a	n/a	Soledad Unified	Soledad
n/a	n/a	Sonoma Valley Unified	Sonoma
n/a	n/a	South Bay Union Elementary	Imperial Beach
n/a	n/a	South Monterey Co. Jt Union High	King City
n/a	n/a	South Pasadena Unified	South Pasadena
n/a	n/a	S San Francisco Unified	S San Francisco
n/a	n/a	South Whittier Elementary	Whittier
n/a	n/a	Southern Kern Unified	Rosamond
n/a	n/a	Spencer Valley Elementary	Santa Ysabel
n/a	n/a	Standard Elementary	Bakersfield
n/a	n/a	Stanislaus Union Elementary	Modesto
n/a	n/a	Stockton Unified	Stockton
n/a	n/a	Sunnyvale	Sunnyvale
n/a	n/a	Sweetwater Union High	Chula Vista
n/a	n/a	Taft City	Taft
n/a	n/a	Tahoe-Truckee Joint Unified	Truckee
n/a	n/a	Tamalpais Union High	Larkspur
n/a	n/a	Tehachapi Unified	Tehachapi
n/a	n/a	Temecula Valley Unified	Temecula
n/a	n/a	Temple City Unified	Temple City
n/a	n/a	Templeton Unified	Templeton
n/a	n/a	Torrance Unified	Torrance
n/a	n/a	Tracy Joint Unified	Tracy
n/a	n/a	Travis Unified	Fairfield
n/a	n/a	Tulare County Office of Education	Visalia
n/a	n/a	Tulare Joint Union High	Tulare
n/a	n/a	Turlock Unified	Turlock
n/a	n/a	Tustin Unified	Tustin
n/a	n/a	Twin Rivers Unified	Mcclellan
n/a	n/a	Ukiah Unified	Ukiah
n/a	n/a	Union Elementary	San Jose
n/a	n/a	Upland Unified	Upland
n/a	n/a	Vacaville Unified	Vacaville
n/a	n/a	Val Verde Unified	Perris
n/a	n/a	Vallejo City Unified	Vallejo
n/a	n/a	Valley Center-Pauma Unified	Valley Center
n/a	n/a	Ventura County Office of Educ.	Camarillo
n/a	n/a	Ventura Unified	Ventura
n/a	n/a	Victor Elementary	Victorville
n/a	n/a	Victor Valley Union High	Victorville
n/a	n/a	Visalia Unified	Visalia
n/a	n/a	Vista Unified	Vista
n/a	n/a	Walnut Creek Elementary	Walnut Creek
n/a	n/a	Walnut Valley Unified	Walnut
n/a	n/a	Wasco Union Elementary	Wasco
n/a	n/a	Wasco Union High	Wasco
n/a	n/a	Washington Unified	West Sacramento
n/a	n/a	Washington Unified	Fresno
n/a	n/a	Waterford Unified	Waterford
n/a	n/a	West Contra Costa Unified	Richmond
n/a	n/a	West Covina Unified	West Covina
n/a	n/a	West Sonoma County Union High	Sebastopol
n/a	n/a	Western Placer Unified	Lincoln
n/a	n/a	Whittier City Elementary	Whittier
n/a	n/a	Whittier Union High	Whittier
n/a	n/a	William S. Hart Union High	Santa Clarita
n/a	n/a	Willits Unified	Willits
n/a	n/a	Willows Unified	Willows
n/a	n/a	Windsor Unified	Windsor
n/a	n/a	Winters Joint Unified	Winters
n/a	n/a	Winton Elementary	Winton
n/a	n/a	Wiseburn Elementary	Hawthorne
n/a	n/a	Woodlake Union Elementary	Woodlake
n/a	n/a	Woodland Joint Unified	Woodland
n/a	n/a	Wright Elementary	Santa Rosa
n/a	n/a	Yosemite Unified	Oakhurst
n/a	n/a	Yuba City Unified	Yuba City
n/a	n/a	Yucaipa-Calimesa Joint Unified	Yucaipa

Note: This section only includes districts with 1,500 or more students; All categories are ranked from high to low

Student/Teacher Ratio

(number of students per teacher)

Rank	Number	District Name	City
1	12.5	San Bernardino Co. Office of Educ.	San Bernardino
2	12.6	Monterey County Office of Educ.	Salinas
3	13.3	Fresno County Office of Education	Fresno
4	14.6	Merced County Office of Education	Merced
5	14.8	Hillsborough City Elementary	Hillsborough
5	14.8	Kern County Office of Education	Bakersfield
7	15.1	Tulare County Office of Education	Visalia
8	15.2	Ventura County Office of Educ.	Camarillo
9	15.3	Santa Clara County Office of Educ.	San Jose
10	16.1	Western Placer Unified	Lincoln
11	16.6	Fort Bragg Unified	Fort Bragg
12	16.7	Piedmont City Unified	Piedmont
13	17.1	San Diego County Office of Educ.	San Diego
14	17.4	Del Mar Union Elementary	San Diego
14	17.4	Tamalpais Union High	Larkspur
16	17.6	Menlo Park City Elementary	Atherton
16	17.6	Solana Beach Elementary	Solana Beach
16	17.6	Stanislaus County Office of Educ.	Modesto
19	17.8	San Joaquin County Office of Educ.	Stockton
19	17.8	Willits Unified	Willits
21	17.9	Riverside County Office of Educ.	Riverside
22	18.0	Denair Unified	Denair
23	18.3	Palo Alto Unified	Palo Alto
23	18.3	Silver Valley Unified	Yermo
25	18.4	Carmel Unified	Carmel
26	18.9	River Delta Joint Unified	Rio Vista
27	19.0	Santa Rosa Elementary	Santa Rosa
28	19.2	Beverly Hills Unified	Beverly Hills
28	19.2	Pacific Grove Unified	Pacific Grove
30	19.3	San Francisco Unified	San Francisco
31	19.4	Nevada County Office of Education	Nevada City
31	19.4	San Luis Coastal Unified	San Luis Obispo
33	19.5	Mountain Empire Unified	Pine Valley
33	19.5	Ravenswood City Elementary	East Palo Alto
33	19.5	San Diego Unified	San Diego
36	19.6	Petaluma City Elementary	Petaluma
37	19.7	Central Union Elementary	Lemoore
37	19.7	Gateway Unified	Redding
37	19.7	Mill Valley Elementary	Mill Valley
37	19.7	San Rafael City High	San Rafael
41	19.8	Bellevue Union Elementary	Santa Rosa
41	19.8	Live Oak Elementary	Santa Cruz
41	19.8	Woodlake Union Elementary	Woodlake
44	19.9	Alum Rock Union Elementary	San Jose
44	19.9	Grass Valley Elementary	Grass Valley
44	19.9	King City Union	King City
44	19.9	Mariposa County Unified	Mariposa
44	19.9	Saratoga Union Elementary	Saratoga
49	20.0	Berkeley Unified	Berkeley
50	20.1	Northern Humboldt Union High	Mckinleyville
51	20.2	Hilmar Unified	Hilmar
51	20.2	Julian Union Elementary	Julian
51	20.2	Sonoma Valley Unified	Sonoma
54	20.3	Burlingame Elementary	Burlingame
54	20.3	Goleta Union Elementary	Goleta
56	20.4	Acalanes Union High	Lafayette
56	20.4	Riverdale Joint Unified	Riverdale
56	20.4	Wright Elementary	Santa Rosa
59	20.5	Albany City Unified	Albany
59	20.5	Black Oak Mine Unified	Georgetown
59	20.5	Cutler-Orosi Joint Unified	Orosi
59	20.5	Dixie Elementary	San Rafael
59	20.5	Galt Joint Union Elementary	Galt
59	20.5	Lompoc Unified	Lompoc
59	20.5	Mountain View-Los Altos Union High	Mountain View
59	20.5	Ross Valley Elementary	San Anselmo
59	20.5	San Mateo Union High	San Mateo
68	20.6	Del Norte County Unified	Crescent City
68	20.6	Gorman Elementary	Gorman
68	20.6	Middletown Unified	Middletown
68	20.6	Rincon Valley Union Elementary	Santa Rosa
72	20.7	Red Bluff Joint Union High	Red Bluff
72	20.7	Tahoe-Truckee Joint Unified	Truckee
74	20.8	Chula Vista Elementary	Chula Vista
74	20.8	Orinda Union Elementary	Orinda
74	20.8	Sequoia Union High	Redwood City
74	20.8	Soquel Union Elementary	Capitola
78	20.9	Dinuba Unified	Dinuba
78	20.9	Kelseyville Unified	Kelseyville
78	20.9	Lake Tahoe Unified	S Lake Tahoe
78	20.9	Washington Unified	Fresno
82	21.0	Eureka City Schools	Eureka
82	21.0	Golden Plains Unified	San Joaquin
82	21.0	Novato Unified	Novato
82	21.0	Paradise Unified	Paradise
86	21.1	Azusa Unified	Azusa
86	21.1	Petaluma Joint Union High	Petaluma
86	21.1	San Rafael City Elementary	San Rafael
89	21.2	Alameda County Office of Education	Hayward
89	21.2	Monterey Peninsula Unified	Monterey
89	21.2	Yuba City Unified	Yuba City
92	21.3	Bishop Unified	Bishop
92	21.3	Jefferson Elementary	Tracy
92	21.3	Moraga Elementary	Moraga
92	21.3	Taft City	Taft
92	21.3	Washington Unified	West Sacramento
97	21.4	Auburn Union Elementary	Auburn
97	21.4	Gridley Unified	Gridley
97	21.4	Hanford Elementary	Hanford
97	21.4	Holtville Unified	Holtville
97	21.4	Mcfarland Unified	Mcfarland
102	21.5	Konocti Unified	Lower Lake
102	21.5	Modesto City Elementary	Modesto
102	21.5	National Elementary	National City
102	21.5	Parlier Unified	Parlier
106	21.6	Belmont-Redwood Shores Elem.	Belmont
106	21.6	Bonsall Union Elementary	Bonsall
106	21.6	Fowler Unified	Fowler
106	21.6	Lemoore Union High	Lemoore
106	21.6	Los Gatos-Saratoga Jt Union High	Los Gatos
106	21.6	Winters Joint Unified	Winters
106	21.6	Winton Elementary	Winton
113	21.7	Calaveras Unified	San Andreas
113	21.7	Chowchilla Elementary	Chowchilla
113	21.7	East Whittier City Elementary	Whittier
113	21.7	Farmersville Unified	Farmersville
113	21.7	Hermosa Beach City Elementary	Hermosa Beach
113	21.7	Lakeport Unified	Lakeport
113	21.7	Richland Union Elementary	Shafter
113	21.7	Weaver Union	Merced
121	21.8	Bakersfield City	Bakersfield
121	21.8	Baldwin Park Unified	Baldwin Park
121	21.8	Encinitas Union Elementary	Encinitas
121	21.8	Sbc - High Tech High	San Diego
121	21.8	Tulare Joint Union High	Tulare
126	21.9	Alameda City Unified	Alameda
126	21.9	Carpinteria Unified	Carpinteria
126	21.9	Eureka Union	Granite Bay
126	21.9	Greenfield Union Elementary	Greenfield
126	21.9	Hughson Unified	Hughson
126	21.9	Lafayette Elementary	Lafayette
126	21.9	Linden Unified	Linden
126	21.9	Livingston Union Elementary	Livingston
126	21.9	San Carlos Elementary	San Carlos
135	22.0	Earlimart Elementary	Earlimart
135	22.0	Red Bluff Union Elementary	Red Bluff
135	22.0	Santa Rosa High	Santa Rosa
138	22.1	Coachella Valley Unified	Thermal
138	22.1	Davis Joint Unified	Davis
138	22.1	John Swett Unified	Rodeo
138	22.1	Oakland Unified	Oakland
138	22.1	Ontario-Montclair Elementary	Ontario
138	22.1	San Leandro Unified	San Leandro
138	22.1	West Contra Costa Unified	Richmond
145	22.2	Castaic Union Elementary	Valencia
145	22.2	Delano Union Elementary	Delano
145	22.2	Lammersville Joint Unified	Mountain House
148	22.3	Banning Unified	Banning
148	22.3	Chico Unified	Chico
148	22.3	Enterprise Elementary	Redding
148	22.3	Muroc Joint Unified	North Edwards
148	22.3	Pasadena Unified	Pasadena
148	22.3	Reef-Sunset Unified	Avenal
148	22.3	San Marino Unified	San Marino
155	22.4	Delhi Unified	Delhi
155	22.4	Livermore Valley Joint Unified	Livermore
155	22.4	Loomis Union Elementary	Loomis
155	22.4	Marysville Joint Unified	Marysville
155	22.4	Palo Verde Unified	Blythe
155	22.4	Sanger Unified	Sanger
155	22.4	Santa Monica-Malibu Unified	Santa Monica
155	22.4	Valley Center-Pauma Unified	Valley Center
163	22.5	Eastside Union Elementary	Lancaster
163	22.5	Laguna Beach Unified	Laguna Beach
163	22.5	Moreland Elementary	San Jose
163	22.5	Morongo Unified	Twentynine Plms
163	22.5	Nevada Joint Union High	Grass Valley
163	22.5	Ocean View	Oxnard
163	22.5	Riverbank Unified	Riverbank
163	22.5	San Lorenzo Valley Unified	Ben Lomond
163	22.5	Santee Elementary	Santee
163	22.5	Tulare City	Tulare
163	22.5	Turlock Unified	Turlock
163	22.5	West Sonoma County Union High	Sebastopol
175	22.6	Campbell Union	Campbell
175	22.6	Healdsburg Unified	Healdsburg
175	22.6	Lennox	Lennox
175	22.6	Mountain View Whisman	Mountain View
175	22.6	San Jose Unified	San Jose
175	22.6	Santa Cruz City Elementary	Soquel
175	22.6	Woodland Joint Unified	Woodland
182	22.7	Bassett Unified	La Puente
182	22.7	Gustine Unified	Gustine
182	22.7	Los Gatos Union Elementary	Los Gatos
182	22.7	Mt. Diablo Unified	Concord
182	22.7	Pittsburg Unified	Pittsburg
182	22.7	Selma Unified	Selma
182	22.7	Yosemite Unified	Oakhurst
189	22.8	Atascadero Unified	Atascadero
189	22.8	Lakeside Union Elementary	Lakeside
189	22.8	Lucerne Valley Unified	Lucerne Valley
189	22.8	Pleasant Valley	Camarillo
189	22.8	Roseland Elementary	Santa Rosa
189	22.8	Shasta Union High	Redding
189	22.8	Sunnyvale	Sunnyvale
189	22.8	Walnut Creek Elementary	Walnut Creek
197	22.9	Dublin Unified	Dublin
197	22.9	Fairfax Elementary	Bakersfield
197	22.9	Golden Valley Unified	Madera
197	22.9	Hawthorne	Hawthorne
197	22.9	Lodi Unified	Lodi
197	22.9	Los Angeles Unified	Los Angeles
197	22.9	Oakdale Joint Unified	Oakdale
197	22.9	Orland Joint Unified	Orland
197	22.9	Oro Grande Elementary	Oro Grande
197	22.9	Oroville City Elementary	Oroville
197	22.9	Vallejo City Unified	Vallejo
208	23.0	Coronado Unified	Coronado
208	23.0	Los Altos Elementary	Los Altos
208	23.0	Salinas Union High	Salinas
208	23.0	Templeton Unified	Templeton
208	23.0	Ukiah Unified	Ukiah
213	23.1	Fallbrook Union High	Fallbrook
213	23.1	Hacienda La Puente Unified	City of Industry
213	23.1	Kingsburg Elementary Charter	Kingsburg
213	23.1	Oroville Union High	Oroville
213	23.1	Scotts Valley Unified	Scotts Valley
213	23.1	Sierra Sands Unified	Ridgecrest
213	23.1	Soledad Unified	Soledad
220	23.2	Barstow Unified	Barstow
220	23.2	Buckeye Union Elementary	Shingle Springs
220	23.2	Castro Valley Unified	Castro Valley
220	23.2	Coalinga-Huron Joint Unified	Coalinga
220	23.2	Dry Creek Joint Elementary	Roseville
220	23.2	El Monte Union High	El Monte
220	23.2	Redwood City Elementary	Redwood City
220	23.2	San Bernardino City Unified	San Bernardino
220	23.2	San Lorenzo Unified	San Lorenzo
220	23.2	Windsor Unified	Windsor
230	23.3	Cambrian	San Jose
230	23.3	Compton Unified	Compton
230	23.3	Conejo Valley Unified	Thousand Oaks
230	23.3	Nuview Union	Nuevo
230	23.3	Paso Robles Joint Unified	Paso Robles
230	23.3	Piner-Olivet Union Elementary	Santa Rosa
230	23.3	Santa Paula Elementary	Santa Paula
237	23.4	Antioch Unified	Antioch
237	23.4	Corcoran Joint Unified	Corcoran
237	23.4	Escalon Unified	Escalon
237	23.4	Gonzales Unified	Gonzales
237	23.4	New Haven Unified	Union City
237	23.4	Orange County Dept of Education	Costa Mesa
237	23.4	Santa Barbara Unified	Santa Barbara
237	23.4	Standard Elementary	Bakersfield
237	23.4	Vacaville Unified	Vacaville
246	23.5	Beardsley Elementary	Bakersfield
246	23.5	Colton Joint Unified	Colton
246	23.5	East Side Union High	San Jose
246	23.5	Fremont Unified	Fremont
246	23.5	Fruitvale Elementary	Bakersfield
246	23.5	Garvey Elementary	Rosemead

Note: This section only includes districts with 1,500 or more students; All categories are ranked from high to low

Rank	Value	District	City
246	23.5	Jefferson Union High	Daly City
246	23.5	Kings Canyon Joint Unified	Reedley
246	23.5	Napa Valley Unified	Napa
246	23.5	Pleasanton Unified	Pleasanton
246	23.5	Pomona Unified	Pomona
246	23.5	Roseville Joint Union High	Roseville
246	23.5	Saugus Union	Santa Clarita
246	23.5	S San Francisco Unified	S San Francisco
260	23.6	Anderson Union High	Anderson
260	23.6	Bear Valley Unified	Big Bear Lake
260	23.6	Campbell Union High	San Jose
260	23.6	Dehesa Elementary	El Cajon
260	23.6	Escondido Union	Escondido
260	23.6	Imperial Unified	Imperial
260	23.6	Lindsay Unified	Lindsay
260	23.6	Newman-Crows Landing Unified	Newman
260	23.6	Robla Elementary	Sacramento
260	23.6	Union Elementary	San Jose
270	23.7	Arvin Union Elementary	Arvin
270	23.7	Benicia Unified	Benicia
270	23.7	Central Union High	El Centro
270	23.7	Corning Union Elementary	Corning
270	23.7	Empire Union Elementary	Modesto
270	23.7	Fillmore Unified	Fillmore
270	23.7	Las Virgenes Unified	Calabasas
270	23.7	Lincoln Unified	Stockton
270	23.7	Live Oak Unified	Live Oak
270	23.7	Lucia Mar Unified	Arroyo Grande
270	23.7	Merced Union High	Atwater
270	23.7	Newport-Mesa Unified	Costa Mesa
270	23.7	Perris Elementary	Perris
270	23.7	Rim of the World Unified	Blue Jay
270	23.7	San Ramon Valley Unified	Danville
285	23.8	Berryessa Union Elementary	San Jose
285	23.8	Brawley Union High	Brawley
285	23.8	Elk Grove Unified	Elk Grove
285	23.8	Firebaugh-Las Deltas Joint Unified	Firebaugh
285	23.8	Jefferson Elementary	Daly City
285	23.8	Marcum-Illinois Union Elementary	East Nicolaus
285	23.8	Roseville City Elementary	Roseville
285	23.8	San Mateo-Foster City	Foster City
285	23.8	Santa Clara Unified	Santa Clara
285	23.8	Westminster Elementary	Westminster
295	23.9	Galt Joint Union High	Galt
295	23.9	Glendale Unified	Glendale
295	23.9	Natomas Unified	Sacramento
295	23.9	Rescue Union Elementary	Rescue
295	23.9	Rowland Unified	Rowland Heights
295	23.9	Santa Maria Joint Union High	Santa Maria
295	23.9	Stockton Unified	Stockton
295	23.9	Tehachapi Unified	Tehachapi
295	23.9	Twin Rivers Unified	Mcclellan
304	24.0	Alpine Union Elementary	Alpine
304	24.0	Claremont Unified	Claremont
304	24.0	La Canada Unified	La Canada
304	24.0	Monrovia Unified	Monrovia
304	24.0	Newhall	Valencia
304	24.0	Norris Elementary	Bakersfield
304	24.0	Placer Union High	Auburn
304	24.0	Rialto Unified	Rialto
304	24.0	Sbc - Aspire Public Schools	Oakland
304	24.0	Vista Unified	Vista
304	24.0	Wiseburn Elementary	Hawthorne
304	24.0	Yucaipa-Calimesa Joint Unified	Yucaipa
316	24.1	Cajon Valley Union	El Cajon
316	24.1	Lamont Elementary	Lamont
316	24.1	Ocean View	Huntington Bch
316	24.1	San Juan Unified	Carmichael
316	24.1	Santa Cruz City High	Soquel
321	24.2	Cabrillo Unified	Half Moon Bay
321	24.2	Ceres Unified	Ceres
321	24.2	Escondido Union High	Escondido
321	24.2	Hayward Unified	Hayward
321	24.2	Jurupa Unified	Jurupa Valley
321	24.2	Oak Park Unified	Oak Park
321	24.2	Waterford Unified	Waterford
328	24.3	Antelope Valley Union High	Lancaster
328	24.3	Brentwood Union Elementary	Brentwood
328	24.3	Burton Elementary	Porterville
328	24.3	Cupertino Union	Cupertino
328	24.3	El Rancho Unified	Pico Rivera
328	24.3	Fresno Unified	Fresno
328	24.3	Grossmont Union High	La Mesa
328	24.3	Lawndale Elementary	Lawndale
328	24.3	Los Nietos	Whittier
328	24.3	Pacifica	Pacifica
328	24.3	Redlands Unified	Redlands
328	24.3	Rocklin Unified	Rocklin
328	24.3	Wasco Union High	Wasco
341	24.4	Dixon Unified	Dixon
341	24.4	El Monte City Elementary	El Monte
341	24.4	Oak Grove Elementary	San Jose
341	24.4	San Gabriel Unified	San Gabriel
345	24.5	Acton-Agua Dulce Unified	Acton
345	24.5	Covina-Valley Unified	Covina
345	24.5	Fremont Union High	Sunnyvale
345	24.5	Lemoore Union Elementary	Lemoore
345	24.5	Mojave Unified	Mojave
345	24.5	Moreno Valley Unified	Moreno Valley
345	24.5	Rosedale Union Elementary	Bakersfield
345	24.5	South Bay Union Elementary	Imperial Beach
345	24.5	Temecula Valley Unified	Temecula
345	24.5	Tracy Joint Unified	Tracy
345	24.5	Wasco Union Elementary	Wasco
356	24.6	Armona Union Elementary	Armona
356	24.6	Culver City Unified	Culver City
356	24.6	El Dorado Union High	Placerville
356	24.6	Evergreen Elementary	San Jose
356	24.6	Mendota Unified	Mendota
356	24.6	Moorpark Unified	Moorpark
356	24.6	Mt. Pleasant Elementary	San Jose
356	24.6	Newark Unified	Newark
356	24.6	Simi Valley Unified	Simi Valley
365	24.7	Lake Elsinore Unified	Lake Elsinore
365	24.7	Liberty Union High	Brentwood
365	24.7	Little Lake City Elementary	Santa Fe Spgs
365	24.7	Menifee Union Elementary	Menifee
365	24.7	Norwalk-La Mirada Unified	Norwalk
365	24.7	Pajaro Valley Unified	Watsonville
365	24.7	Southern Kern Unified	Rosamond
365	24.7	Travis Unified	Fairfield
373	24.8	Bonita Unified	San Dimas
373	24.8	Burbank Unified	Burbank
373	24.8	Central Unified	Fresno
373	24.8	Fontana Unified	Fontana
373	24.8	Gilroy Unified	Gilroy
373	24.8	Hanford Joint Union High	Hanford
373	24.8	Hemet Unified	Hemet
373	24.8	Magnolia Elementary	Anaheim
373	24.8	Merced City Elementary	Merced
373	24.8	Oakley Union Elementary	Oakley
373	24.8	Oceanside Unified	Oceanside
373	24.8	Sulphur Springs Union	Canyon Country
385	24.9	Calexico Unified	Calexico
385	24.9	Duarte Unified	Duarte
385	24.9	Milpitas Unified	Milpitas
385	24.9	Modesto City High	Modesto
385	24.9	Ventura Unified	Ventura
390	25.0	Corona-Norco Unified	Norco
390	25.0	Folsom-Cordova Unified	Folsom
390	25.0	Martinez Unified	Martinez
390	25.0	Porterville Unified	Porterville
390	25.0	Temple City Unified	Temple City
395	25.1	ABC Unified	Cerritos
395	25.1	Arcadia Unified	Arcadia
395	25.1	Atwater Elementary	Atwater
395	25.1	Madera Unified	Madera
395	25.1	Orcutt Union Elementary	Orcutt
395	25.1	Oxnard Union High	Oxnard
395	25.1	Ramona City Unified	Ramona
395	25.1	Redding Elementary	Redding
395	25.1	Sweetwater Union High	Chula Vista
395	25.1	West Covina Unified	West Covina
405	25.2	Centinela Valley Union High	Lawndale
405	25.2	Cotati-Rohnert Park Unified	Rohnert Park
405	25.2	Greenfield Union	Bakersfield
405	25.2	Kern Union High	Bakersfield
405	25.2	Salida Union Elementary	Salida
405	25.2	Salinas City Elementary	Salinas
405	25.2	Santa Ana Unified	Santa Ana
405	25.2	Victor Valley Union High	Victorville
413	25.3	Center Joint Unified	Antelope
413	25.3	Kerman Unified	Kerman
413	25.3	Manteca Unified	Manteca
413	25.3	Oxnard	Oxnard
413	25.3	Redondo Beach Unified	Redondo Beach
413	25.3	South Monterey Co. Jt Union High	King City
413	25.3	South Pasadena Unified	South Pasadena
420	25.4	Manhattan Beach Unified	Manhattan Beach
420	25.4	Palos Verdes Peninsula Unified	Palos Vrds Est
420	25.4	Rosemead Elementary	Rosemead
420	25.4	Upland Unified	Upland
424	25.5	Amador County Unified	Jackson
424	25.5	Millbrae Elementary	Millbrae
424	25.5	Patterson Joint Unified	Patterson
424	25.5	San Benito High	Hollister
424	25.5	Walnut Valley Unified	Walnut
429	25.6	Cucamonga Elementary	R Cucamonga
429	25.6	Cypress Elementary	Cypress
429	25.6	Fullerton Elementary	Fullerton
432	25.7	Brawley Elementary	Brawley
432	25.7	Delano Joint Union High	Delano
432	25.7	Franklin-Mckinley Elementary	San Jose
432	25.7	Murrieta Valley Unified	Murrieta
432	25.7	Ojai Unified	Ojai
432	25.7	Ripon Unified	Ripon
432	25.7	Romoland Elementary	Homeland
432	25.7	Santa Maria-Bonita	Santa Maria
432	25.7	William S. Hart Union High	Santa Clarita
441	25.8	Alhambra Unified	Alhambra
441	25.8	North Monterey County Unified	Moss Landing
441	25.8	San Bruno Park Elementary	San Bruno
444	25.9	Anaheim City	Anaheim
444	25.9	Anaheim Union High	Anaheim
444	25.9	Bellflower Unified	Bellflower
444	25.9	Carlsbad Unified	Carlsbad
444	25.9	Fairfield-Suisun Unified	Fairfield
444	25.9	Paramount Unified	Paramount
444	25.9	Santa Paula Union High	Santa Paula
444	25.9	Visalia Unified	Visalia
452	26.0	Centralia Elementary	Buena Park
452	26.0	Glendora Unified	Glendora
452	26.0	Huntington Bch Union High	Huntington Bch
452	26.0	Val Verde Unified	Perris
456	26.1	Morgan Hill Unified	Morgan Hill
456	26.1	Orange Unified	Orange
456	26.1	Palmdale Elementary	Palmdale
456	26.1	Pioneer Union Elementary	Hanford
460	26.2	Desert Sands Unified	La Quinta
460	26.2	El Segundo Unified	El Segundo
460	26.2	Etiwanda Elementary	Etiwanda
460	26.2	Keppel Union Elementary	Pearblossom
460	26.2	Lynwood Unified	Lynwood
460	26.2	Palm Springs Unified	Palm Springs
460	26.2	Riverside Unified	Riverside
467	26.3	Apple Valley Unified	Apple Valley
467	26.3	Buena Park Elementary	Buena Park
467	26.3	Clovis Unified	Clovis
467	26.3	Garden Grove Unified	Garden Grove
467	26.3	Placentia-Yorba Linda Unified	Placentia
467	26.3	Savanna Elementary	Anaheim
467	26.3	Whittier City Elementary	Whittier
474	26.4	Central Elementary	R Cucamonga
474	26.4	Downey Unified	Downey
474	26.4	Fountain Valley Elementary	Fountain Valley
474	26.4	Hueneme Elementary	Port Hueneme
474	26.4	Montebello Unified	Montebello
474	26.4	Rio Elementary	Oxnard
474	26.4	Sylvan Union Elementary	Modesto
481	26.5	Capistrano Unified	SJ Capistrano
481	26.5	Westside Union Elementary	Quartz Hill
481	26.5	Willows Unified	Willows
484	26.6	Alta Loma Elementary	Alta Loma
484	26.6	Beaumont Unified	Beaumont
484	26.6	Charter Oak Unified	Covina
487	26.7	Long Beach Unified	Long Beach
487	26.7	Los Banos Unified	Los Banos
489	26.8	El Centro Elementary	El Centro
489	26.8	Hesperia Unified	Hesperia
489	26.8	San Dieguito Union High	Encinitas
492	26.9	Alvord Unified	Riverside
492	26.9	Byron Union Elementary	Byron
492	26.9	Fallbrook Union Elementary	Fallbrook
492	26.9	Perris Union High	Perris
492	26.9	Torrance Unified	Torrance
497	27.0	Chino Valley Unified	Chino
497	27.0	Lancaster Elementary	Lancaster
497	27.0	Lemon Grove	Lemon Grove
500	27.1	Chaffey Joint Union High	Ontario
500	27.1	Inglewood Unified	Inglewood
502	27.2	Los Alamitos Unified	Los Alamitos
502	27.2	Stanislaus Union Elementary	Modesto
504	27.4	Lowell Joint	Whittier
504	27.4	Snowline Joint Unified	Phelan
506	27.5	Fullerton Joint Union High	Fullerton

Note: This section only includes districts with 1,500 or more students; All categories are ranked from high to low

506	27.5	La Habra City Elementary	La Habra
506	27.5	Mountain View Elementary	El Monte
506	27.5	Saddleback Valley Unified	Mission Viejo
506	27.5	San Ysidro Elementary	San Ysidro
511	27.7	Hollister	Hollister
511	27.7	Mountain View Elementary	Ontario
513	27.8	Old Adobe Union	Petaluma
514	28.2	San Jacinto Unified	San Jacinto
515	28.3	La Mesa-Spring Valley	La Mesa
516	28.4	Poway Unified	San Diego
517	28.5	Brea-Olinda Unified	Brea
517	28.5	Whittier Union High	Whittier
519	28.6	Panama-Buena Vista Union	Bakersfield
519	28.6	San Marcos Unified	San Marcos
521	28.7	Irvine Unified	Irvine
521	28.7	Sacramento City Unified	Sacramento
523	29.0	Huntington Bch City Elementary	Huntington Bch
523	29.0	Tustin Unified	Tustin
525	29.4	Dos Palos Oro Loma Joint Unified	Dos Palos
526	29.5	Alisal Union	Salinas
527	29.8	South Whittier Elementary	Whittier
528	29.9	Santa Rita Union Elementary	Salinas
529	30.1	Adelanto Elementary	Adelanto
530	30.3	Victor Elementary	Victorville
531	31.7	Spencer Valley Elementary	Santa Ysabel
n/a	n/a	Exeter Union Elementary	Exeter
n/a	n/a	Los Angeles County Office of Educ.	Downey

Student/Librarian Ratio

(number of students per librarian)

Rank	Number	District Name	City
1	396.1	Hillsborough City Elementary	Hillsborough
2	671.6	Piedmont City Unified	Piedmont
3	679.8	Menlo Park City Elementary	Atherton
4	760.6	Albany City Unified	Albany
5	778.7	Santa Cruz City Elementary	Soquel
6	795.1	Santa Cruz City High	Soquel
7	854.7	Weaver Union	Merced
8	939.9	San Francisco Unified	San Francisco
9	961.2	Northern Humboldt Union High	Mckinleyville
10	1,000.0	San Rafael City High	San Rafael
11	1,086.7	Pacific Grove Unified	Pacific Grove
12	1,150.3	Fresno County Office of Education	Fresno
13	1,177.4	New Haven Unified	Union City
14	1,188.5	Carmel Unified	Carmel
15	1,279.7	Tamalpais Union High	Larkspur
16	1,287.2	Winters Joint Unified	Winters
17	1,312.4	Davis Joint Unified	Davis
18	1,321.5	Petaluma Joint Union High	Petaluma
19	1,350.5	Acalanes Union High	Lafayette
20	1,371.1	Tahoe-Truckee Joint Unified	Truckee
21	1,468.5	Berkeley Unified	Berkeley
22	1,470.0	San Luis Coastal Unified	San Luis Obispo
23	1,706.0	Nevada Joint Union High	Grass Valley
24	1,727.0	El Dorado Union High	Placerville
25	1,749.0	Alameda City Unified	Alameda
26	1,773.0	Wasco Union High	Wasco
27	1,792.0	Dixie Elementary	San Rafael
28	1,826.0	Mountain View-Los Altos Union High	Mountain View
29	1,945.0	Golden Valley Unified	Madera
30	1,955.6	Modesto City Elementary	Modesto
31	1,986.0	Tulare County Office of Education	Visalia
32	2,011.2	El Monte Union High	El Monte
33	2,031.0	Sweetwater Union High	Chula Vista
34	2,058.6	Merced Union High	Atwater
35	2,100.5	San Diego County Office of Educ.	San Diego
36	2,105.0	Modesto City High	Modesto
37	2,107.0	Fremont Union High	Sunnyvale
38	2,117.5	Roseville Joint Union High	Roseville
39	2,136.9	Mt. Diablo Unified	Concord
40	2,152.5	Grossmont Union High	La Mesa
41	2,189.4	Santa Barbara Unified	Santa Barbara
42	2,194.0	Orland Joint Unified	Orland
43	2,204.1	William S. Hart Union High	Santa Clarita
44	2,232.0	Firebaugh-Las Deltas Joint Unified	Firebaugh
45	2,236.8	Sequoia Union High	Redwood City
46	2,340.0	Kingsburg Elementary Charter	Kingsburg
47	2,432.9	Long Beach Unified	Long Beach
48	2,484.5	Jefferson Union High	Daly City
49	2,490.3	San Ramon Valley Unified	Danville
50	2,537.0	Livingston Union Elementary	Livingston
51	2,548.2	Santa Clara Unified	Santa Clara
52	2,612.0	Oroville Union High	Oroville
53	2,701.3	Merced City Elementary	Merced
54	2,711.9	Kern Union High	Bakersfield
55	2,798.3	Oxnard Union High	Oxnard
56	2,829.4	Ventura Unified	Ventura
57	3,106.0	Los Gatos Union Elementary	Los Gatos
58	3,167.9	San Leandro Unified	San Leandro
59	3,246.0	Los Gatos-Saratoga Jt Union High	Los Gatos
60	3,290.0	Richland Union Elementary	Shafter
61	3,290.2	Alvord Unified	Riverside
62	3,317.0	Cabrillo Unified	Half Moon Bay
63	3,329.0	Lafayette Elementary	Lafayette
64	3,382.3	Palm Springs Unified	Palm Springs
65	3,384.4	Ramona City Unified	Ramona
66	3,395.1	Irvine Unified	Irvine
67	3,398.7	San Bernardino City Unified	San Bernardino
68	3,411.5	Chico Unified	Chico
69	3,450.0	Eastside Union Elementary	Lancaster
70	3,596.2	Fairfield-Suisun Unified	Fairfield
71	3,600.4	Pasadena Unified	Pasadena
72	3,735.4	West Contra Costa Unified	Richmond
73	3,744.0	Norris Elementary	Bakersfield
74	3,797.0	Downey Unified	Downey
75	3,803.0	Hanford Joint Union High	Hanford
76	3,858.0	Lake Tahoe Unified	S Lake Tahoe
77	3,996.0	Gateway Unified	Redding
78	4,062.0	La Canada Unified	La Canada
79	4,127.5	Mcfarland Unified	Mcfarland
80	4,144.0	Martinez Unified	Martinez
81	4,168.0	Lindsay Unified	Lindsay
82	4,296.0	Ravenswood City Elementary	East Palo Alto
83	4,345.0	Paradise Unified	Paradise
84	4,494.0	Tehachapi Unified	Tehachapi
85	4,498.0	Paso Robles Joint Unified	Paso Robles
86	4,503.0	Banning Unified	Banning
87	4,519.6	Twin Rivers Unified	Mcclellan
88	4,527.6	Las Virgenes Unified	Calabasas
89	4,578.7	Porterville Unified	Porterville
90	4,585.0	Beverly Hills Unified	Beverly Hills
91	4,588.0	South Pasadena Unified	South Pasadena
92	4,635.0	Soledad Unified	Soledad
93	4,674.0	S San Francisco Unified	S San Francisco
94	4,711.8	Riverside Unified	Riverside
95	4,774.9	Sacramento City Unified	Sacramento
96	4,819.9	Vista Unified	Vista
97	4,849.0	Center Joint Unified	Antelope
98	4,901.0	Lompoc Unified	Lompoc
99	4,904.0	Atascadero Unified	Atascadero
100	4,920.5	Kings Canyon Joint Unified	Reedley
101	4,965.3	Central Unified	Fresno
102	5,055.0	Sierra Sands Unified	Ridgecrest
103	5,126.0	Woodland Joint Unified	Woodland
104	5,240.0	Tulare Joint Union High	Tulare
105	5,322.5	Perris Union High	Perris
106	5,352.0	Redlands Unified	Redlands
107	5,391.0	Travis Unified	Fairfield
108	5,479.3	Orange Unified	Orange
109	5,498.0	San Mateo Union High	San Mateo
110	5,525.0	Windsor Unified	Windsor
111	5,761.5	Poway Unified	San Diego
112	6,057.3	Torrance Unified	Torrance
113	6,096.7	Alhambra Unified	Alhambra
114	6,148.1	Los Alamitos Unified	Los Alamitos
115	6,186.3	Fresno Unified	Fresno
116	6,244.0	Ukiah Unified	Ukiah
117	6,415.0	Selma Unified	Selma
118	6,436.8	Placentia-Yorba Linda Unified	Placentia
119	6,534.0	Santa Clara County Office of Educ.	San Jose
120	6,560.0	Newark Unified	Newark
121	6,645.3	Madera Unified	Madera
122	6,716.0	Manhattan Beach Unified	Manhattan Beach
123	6,795.0	Sanger Unified	Sanger
124	6,867.0	Bellflower Unified	Bellflower
125	6,907.3	Conejo Valley Unified	Thousand Oaks
126	6,936.0	Claremont Unified	Claremont
127	6,936.1	San Dieguito Union High	Encinitas
128	7,070.1	Los Angeles Unified	Los Angeles
129	7,096.3	Santa Rosa High	Santa Rosa
130	7,242.6	Salinas Union High	Salinas
131	7,469.3	San Mateo-Foster City	Foster City
132	7,509.7	San Diego Unified	San Diego
133	7,579.8	Lodi Unified	Lodi
134	7,604.0	Liberty Union High	Brentwood
135	7,625.0	San Benito High	Hollister
136	7,869.0	Rowland Unified	Rowland Heights
137	8,066.0	Berryessa Union Elementary	San Jose
138	8,355.0	Chaffey Joint Union High	Ontario
139	8,410.0	Sylvan Union Elementary	Modesto
140	8,711.0	Tracy Joint Unified	Tracy
141	8,742.7	Glendale Unified	Glendale
142	8,981.0	Lincoln Unified	Stockton
143	9,039.0	Napa Valley Unified	Napa
144	9,052.0	Castro Valley Unified	Castro Valley
145	9,203.0	Coachella Valley Unified	Thermal
146	9,400.0	Morgan Hill Unified	Morgan Hill
147	9,449.0	San Juan Unified	Carmichael
148	9,655.0	Yucaipa-Calimesa Joint Unified	Yucaipa
149	9,719.0	Arcadia Unified	Arcadia
150	9,842.4	La Mesa-Spring Valley	La Mesa
151	10,381.0	Pittsburg Unified	Pittsburg
152	10,493.5	Oceanside Unified	Oceanside
153	10,551.4	Clovis Unified	Clovis
154	11,063.0	Carlsbad Unified	Carlsbad
155	11,290.0	Gilroy Unified	Gilroy
156	11,346.5	Murrieta Valley Unified	Murrieta
157	11,596.0	Colton Joint Unified	Colton
158	11,840.0	Palos Verdes Peninsula Unified	Palos Vrds Est
159	11,927.0	Upland Unified	Upland
160	11,940.0	Monrovia Unified	Monrovia
161	12,106.8	Temecula Valley Unified	Temecula
162	12,123.0	San Lorenzo Unified	San Lorenzo
163	12,227.5	Marysville Joint Unified	Marysville
164	12,532.0	Ceres Unified	Ceres
165	13,530.7	Fontana Unified	Fontana
166	13,634.0	Visalia Unified	Visalia
167	13,714.0	Garden Grove Unified	Garden Grove
168	14,243.3	East Side Union High	San Jose
169	14,279.0	Inglewood Unified	Inglewood
170	14,599.5	Desert Sands Unified	La Quinta
171	14,783.0	Fullerton Joint Union High	Fullerton
172	14,880.0	Rocklin Unified	Rocklin
173	15,186.0	Victor Valley Union High	Victorville
174	15,730.8	Antioch Unified	Antioch
175	15,929.0	Paramount Unified	Paramount
176	16,414.5	Fremont Unified	Fremont
177	16,442.0	Huntington Bch Union High	Huntington Bch
178	16,810.0	Panama-Buena Vista Union	Bakersfield
179	17,320.0	Beaumont Unified	Beaumont
180	17,374.7	Etiwanda Elementary	Etiwanda
181	19,323.8	Oakland Unified	Oakland
182	19,615.0	Val Verde Unified	Perris
183	21,010.2	Saddleback Valley Unified	Mission Viejo
184	21,591.1	Simi Valley Unified	Simi Valley
185	21,977.0	Hemet Unified	Hemet
186	22,171.0	Lake Elsinore Unified	Lake Elsinore
187	24,850.4	Elk Grove Unified	Elk Grove
188	25,225.0	Santa Rosa Elementary	Santa Rosa
189	26,702.0	Evergreen Elementary	San Jose
190	26,764.0	Rialto Unified	Rialto
191	31,313.0	Chino Valley Unified	Chino
192	38,186.0	Escondido Union	Escondido
193	57,250.0	Santa Ana Unified	Santa Ana
194	84,375.0	Eureka Union	Granite Bay
n/a	n/a	ABC Unified	Cerritos
n/a	n/a	Acton-Agua Dulce Unified	Acton
n/a	n/a	Adelanto Elementary	Adelanto
n/a	n/a	Alameda County Office of Education	Hayward
n/a	n/a	Alisal Union	Salinas
n/a	n/a	Alpine Union Elementary	Alpine
n/a	n/a	Alta Loma Elementary	Alta Loma
n/a	n/a	Alum Rock Union Elementary	San Jose
n/a	n/a	Amador County Unified	Jackson
n/a	n/a	Anaheim City	Anaheim
n/a	n/a	Anaheim Union High	Anaheim
n/a	n/a	Anderson Union High	Anderson
n/a	n/a	Antelope Valley Union High	Lancaster
n/a	n/a	Apple Valley Unified	Apple Valley
n/a	n/a	Armona Union Elementary	Armona
n/a	n/a	Arvin Union Elementary	Arvin
n/a	n/a	Atwater Elementary	Atwater
n/a	n/a	Auburn Union Elementary	Auburn
n/a	n/a	Azusa Unified	Azusa
n/a	n/a	Bakersfield City	Bakersfield
n/a	n/a	Baldwin Park Unified	Baldwin Park
n/a	n/a	Barstow Unified	Barstow
n/a	n/a	Bassett Unified	La Puente
n/a	n/a	Bear Valley Unified	Big Bear Lake
n/a	n/a	Beardsley Elementary	Bakersfield
n/a	n/a	Bellevue Union Elementary	Santa Rosa
n/a	n/a	Belmont-Redwood Shores Elem.	Belmont
n/a	n/a	Benicia Unified	Benicia

Note: This section only includes districts with 1,500 or more students; All categories are ranked from high to low

n/a	n/a	Bishop Unified	Bishop
n/a	n/a	Black Oak Mine Unified	Georgetown
n/a	n/a	Bonita Unified	San Dimas
n/a	n/a	Bonsall Union Elementary	Bonsall
n/a	n/a	Brawley Elementary	Brawley
n/a	n/a	Brawley Union High	Brawley
n/a	n/a	Brea-Olinda Unified	Brea
n/a	n/a	Brentwood Union Elementary	Brentwood
n/a	n/a	Buckeye Union Elementary	Shingle Springs
n/a	n/a	Buena Park Elementary	Buena Park
n/a	n/a	Burbank Unified	Burbank
n/a	n/a	Burlingame Elementary	Burlingame
n/a	n/a	Burton Elementary	Porterville
n/a	n/a	Byron Union Elementary	Byron
n/a	n/a	Cajon Valley Union	El Cajon
n/a	n/a	Calaveras Unified	San Andreas
n/a	n/a	Calexico Unified	Calexico
n/a	n/a	Cambrian	San Jose
n/a	n/a	Campbell Union	Campbell
n/a	n/a	Campbell Union High	San Jose
n/a	n/a	Capistrano Unified	SJ Capistrano
n/a	n/a	Carpinteria Unified	Carpinteria
n/a	n/a	Castaic Union Elementary	Valencia
n/a	n/a	Centinela Valley Union High	Lawndale
n/a	n/a	Central Elementary	R Cucamonga
n/a	n/a	Central Union Elementary	Lemoore
n/a	n/a	Central Union High	El Centro
n/a	n/a	Centralia Elementary	Buena Park
n/a	n/a	Charter Oak Unified	Covina
n/a	n/a	Chowchilla Elementary	Chowchilla
n/a	n/a	Chula Vista Elementary	Chula Vista
n/a	n/a	Coalinga-Huron Joint Unified	Coalinga
n/a	n/a	Compton Unified	Compton
n/a	n/a	Corcoran Joint Unified	Corcoran
n/a	n/a	Corning Union Elementary	Corning
n/a	n/a	Corona-Norco Unified	Norco
n/a	n/a	Coronado Unified	Coronado
n/a	n/a	Cotati-Rohnert Park Unified	Rohnert Park
n/a	n/a	Covina-Valley Unified	Covina
n/a	n/a	Cucamonga Elementary	R Cucamonga
n/a	n/a	Culver City Unified	Culver City
n/a	n/a	Cupertino Union	Cupertino
n/a	n/a	Cutler-Orosi Joint Unified	Orosi
n/a	n/a	Cypress Elementary	Cypress
n/a	n/a	Dehesa Elementary	El Cajon
n/a	n/a	Del Mar Union Elementary	San Diego
n/a	n/a	Del Norte County Unified	Crescent City
n/a	n/a	Delano Joint Union High	Delano
n/a	n/a	Delano Union Elementary	Delano
n/a	n/a	Delhi Unified	Delhi
n/a	n/a	Denair Unified	Denair
n/a	n/a	Dinuba Unified	Dinuba
n/a	n/a	Dixon Unified	Dixon
n/a	n/a	Dos Palos Oro Loma Joint Unified	Dos Palos
n/a	n/a	Dry Creek Joint Elementary	Roseville
n/a	n/a	Duarte Unified	Duarte
n/a	n/a	Dublin Unified	Dublin
n/a	n/a	Earlimart Elementary	Earlimart
n/a	n/a	East Whittier City Elementary	Whittier
n/a	n/a	El Centro Elementary	El Centro
n/a	n/a	El Monte City Elementary	El Monte
n/a	n/a	El Rancho Unified	Pico Rivera
n/a	n/a	El Segundo Unified	El Segundo
n/a	n/a	Empire Union Elementary	Modesto
n/a	n/a	Encinitas Union Elementary	Encinitas
n/a	n/a	Enterprise Elementary	Redding
n/a	n/a	Escalon Unified	Escalon
n/a	n/a	Escondido Union High	Escondido
n/a	n/a	Eureka City Schools	Eureka
n/a	n/a	Exeter Union Elementary	Exeter
n/a	n/a	Fairfax Elementary	Bakersfield
n/a	n/a	Fallbrook Union Elementary	Fallbrook
n/a	n/a	Fallbrook Union High	Fallbrook
n/a	n/a	Farmersville Unified	Farmersville
n/a	n/a	Fillmore Unified	Fillmore
n/a	n/a	Folsom-Cordova Unified	Folsom
n/a	n/a	Fort Bragg Unified	Fort Bragg
n/a	n/a	Fountain Valley Elementary	Fountain Valley
n/a	n/a	Fowler Unified	Fowler
n/a	n/a	Franklin-Mckinley Elementary	San Jose
n/a	n/a	Fruitvale Elementary	Bakersfield
n/a	n/a	Fullerton Elementary	Fullerton
n/a	n/a	Galt Joint Union Elementary	Galt
n/a	n/a	Galt Joint Union High	Galt
n/a	n/a	Garvey Elementary	Rosemead
n/a	n/a	Glendora Unified	Glendora
n/a	n/a	Golden Plains Unified	San Joaquin
n/a	n/a	Goleta Union Elementary	Goleta
n/a	n/a	Gonzales Unified	Gonzales
n/a	n/a	Gorman Elementary	Gorman
n/a	n/a	Grass Valley Elementary	Grass Valley
n/a	n/a	Greenfield Union	Bakersfield
n/a	n/a	Greenfield Union Elementary	Greenfield
n/a	n/a	Gridley Unified	Gridley
n/a	n/a	Gustine Unified	Gustine
n/a	n/a	Hacienda La Puente Unified	City of Industry
n/a	n/a	Hanford Elementary	Hanford
n/a	n/a	Hawthorne	Hawthorne
n/a	n/a	Hayward Unified	Hayward
n/a	n/a	Healdsburg Unified	Healdsburg
n/a	n/a	Hermosa Beach City Elementary	Hermosa Beach
n/a	n/a	Hesperia Unified	Hesperia
n/a	n/a	Hilmar Unified	Hilmar
n/a	n/a	Hollister	Hollister
n/a	n/a	Holtville Unified	Holtville
n/a	n/a	Hueneme Elementary	Port Hueneme
n/a	n/a	Hughson Unified	Hughson
n/a	n/a	Huntington Bch City Elementary	Huntington Bch
n/a	n/a	Imperial Unified	Imperial
n/a	n/a	Jefferson Elementary	Tracy
n/a	n/a	Jefferson Elementary	Daly City
n/a	n/a	John Swett Unified	Rodeo
n/a	n/a	Julian Union Elementary	Julian
n/a	n/a	Jurupa Unified	Jurupa Valley
n/a	n/a	Kelseyville Unified	Kelseyville
n/a	n/a	Keppel Union Elementary	Pearblossom
n/a	n/a	Kerman Unified	Kerman
n/a	n/a	Kern County Office of Education	Bakersfield
n/a	n/a	King City Union	King City
n/a	n/a	Konocti Unified	Lower Lake
n/a	n/a	La Habra City Elementary	La Habra
n/a	n/a	Laguna Beach Unified	Laguna Beach
n/a	n/a	Lakeport Unified	Lakeport
n/a	n/a	Lakeside Union Elementary	Lakeside
n/a	n/a	Lammersville Joint Unified	Mountain House
n/a	n/a	Lamont Elementary	Lamont
n/a	n/a	Lancaster Elementary	Lancaster
n/a	n/a	Lawndale Elementary	Lawndale
n/a	n/a	Lemon Grove	Lemon Grove
n/a	n/a	Lemoore Union Elementary	Lemoore
n/a	n/a	Lemoore Union High	Lemoore
n/a	n/a	Lennox	Lennox
n/a	n/a	Linden Unified	Linden
n/a	n/a	Little Lake City Elementary	Santa Fe Spgs
n/a	n/a	Live Oak Elementary	Santa Cruz
n/a	n/a	Live Oak Unified	Live Oak
n/a	n/a	Livermore Valley Joint Unified	Livermore
n/a	n/a	Loomis Union Elementary	Loomis
n/a	n/a	Los Altos Elementary	Los Altos
n/a	n/a	Los Angeles County Office of Educ.	Downey
n/a	n/a	Los Banos Unified	Los Banos
n/a	n/a	Los Nietos	Whittier
n/a	n/a	Lowell Joint	Whittier
n/a	n/a	Lucerne Valley Unified	Lucerne Valley
n/a	n/a	Lucia Mar Unified	Arroyo Grande
n/a	n/a	Lynwood Unified	Lynwood
n/a	n/a	Magnolia Elementary	Anaheim
n/a	n/a	Manteca Unified	Manteca
n/a	n/a	Marcum-Illinois Union Elementary	East Nicolaus
n/a	n/a	Mariposa County Unified	Mariposa
n/a	n/a	Mendota Unified	Mendota
n/a	n/a	Menifee Union Elementary	Menifee
n/a	n/a	Merced County Office of Education	Merced
n/a	n/a	Middletown Unified	Middletown
n/a	n/a	Mill Valley Elementary	Mill Valley
n/a	n/a	Millbrae Elementary	Millbrae
n/a	n/a	Milpitas Unified	Milpitas
n/a	n/a	Mojave Unified	Mojave
n/a	n/a	Montebello Unified	Montebello
n/a	n/a	Monterey County Office of Educ.	Salinas
n/a	n/a	Monterey Peninsula Unified	Monterey
n/a	n/a	Moorpark Unified	Moorpark
n/a	n/a	Moraga Elementary	Moraga
n/a	n/a	Moreland Elementary	San Jose
n/a	n/a	Moreno Valley Unified	Moreno Valley
n/a	n/a	Morongo Unified	Twentynine Plms
n/a	n/a	Mountain Empire Unified	Pine Valley
n/a	n/a	Mountain View Elementary	Ontario
n/a	n/a	Mountain View Elementary	El Monte
n/a	n/a	Mountain View Whisman	Mountain View
n/a	n/a	Mt. Pleasant Elementary	San Jose
n/a	n/a	Muroc Joint Unified	North Edwards
n/a	n/a	National Elementary	National City
n/a	n/a	Natomas Unified	Sacramento
n/a	n/a	Nevada County Office of Education	Nevada City
n/a	n/a	Newhall	Valencia
n/a	n/a	Newman-Crows Landing Unified	Newman
n/a	n/a	Newport-Mesa Unified	Costa Mesa
n/a	n/a	North Monterey County Unified	Moss Landing
n/a	n/a	Norwalk-La Mirada Unified	Norwalk
n/a	n/a	Novato Unified	Novato
n/a	n/a	Nuview Union	Nuevo
n/a	n/a	Oak Grove Elementary	San Jose
n/a	n/a	Oak Park Unified	Oak Park
n/a	n/a	Oakdale Joint Unified	Oakdale
n/a	n/a	Oakley Union Elementary	Oakley
n/a	n/a	Ocean View	Huntington Bch
n/a	n/a	Ocean View	Oxnard
n/a	n/a	Ojai Unified	Ojai
n/a	n/a	Old Adobe Union	Petaluma
n/a	n/a	Ontario-Montclair Elementary	Ontario
n/a	n/a	Orange County Dept of Education	Costa Mesa
n/a	n/a	Orcutt Union Elementary	Orcutt
n/a	n/a	Orinda Union Elementary	Orinda
n/a	n/a	Oro Grande Elementary	Oro Grande
n/a	n/a	Oroville City Elementary	Oroville
n/a	n/a	Oxnard	Oxnard
n/a	n/a	Pacifica	Pacifica
n/a	n/a	Pajaro Valley Unified	Watsonville
n/a	n/a	Palmdale Elementary	Palmdale
n/a	n/a	Palo Alto Unified	Palo Alto
n/a	n/a	Palo Verde Unified	Blythe
n/a	n/a	Parlier Unified	Parlier
n/a	n/a	Patterson Joint Unified	Patterson
n/a	n/a	Perris Elementary	Perris
n/a	n/a	Petaluma City Elementary	Petaluma
n/a	n/a	Piner-Olivet Union Elementary	Santa Rosa
n/a	n/a	Pioneer Union Elementary	Hanford
n/a	n/a	Placer Union High	Auburn
n/a	n/a	Pleasant Valley	Camarillo
n/a	n/a	Pleasanton Unified	Pleasanton
n/a	n/a	Pomona Unified	Pomona
n/a	n/a	Red Bluff Joint Union High	Red Bluff
n/a	n/a	Red Bluff Union Elementary	Red Bluff
n/a	n/a	Redding Elementary	Redding
n/a	n/a	Redondo Beach Unified	Redondo Beach
n/a	n/a	Redwood City Elementary	Redwood City
n/a	n/a	Reef-Sunset Unified	Avenal
n/a	n/a	Rescue Union Elementary	Rescue
n/a	n/a	Rim of the World Unified	Blue Jay
n/a	n/a	Rincon Valley Union Elementary	Santa Rosa
n/a	n/a	Rio Elementary	Oxnard
n/a	n/a	Ripon Unified	Ripon
n/a	n/a	River Delta Joint Unified	Rio Vista
n/a	n/a	Riverbank Unified	Riverbank
n/a	n/a	Riverdale Joint Unified	Riverdale
n/a	n/a	Riverside County Office of Educ.	Riverside
n/a	n/a	Robla Elementary	Sacramento
n/a	n/a	Romoland Elementary	Homeland
n/a	n/a	Rosedale Union Elementary	Bakersfield
n/a	n/a	Roseland Elementary	Santa Rosa
n/a	n/a	Rosemead Elementary	Rosemead
n/a	n/a	Roseville City Elementary	Roseville
n/a	n/a	Ross Valley Elementary	San Anselmo
n/a	n/a	Salida Union Elementary	Salida
n/a	n/a	Salinas City Elementary	Salinas
n/a	n/a	San Bernardino Co. Office of Educ.	San Bernardino
n/a	n/a	San Bruno Park Elementary	San Bruno
n/a	n/a	San Carlos Elementary	San Carlos
n/a	n/a	San Gabriel Unified	San Gabriel
n/a	n/a	San Jacinto Unified	San Jacinto
n/a	n/a	San Joaquin County Office of Educ.	Stockton
n/a	n/a	San Jose Unified	San Jose
n/a	n/a	San Lorenzo Valley Unified	Ben Lomond
n/a	n/a	San Marcos Unified	San Marcos
n/a	n/a	San Marino Unified	San Marino
n/a	n/a	San Rafael City Elementary	San Rafael
n/a	n/a	San Ysidro Elementary	San Ysidro
n/a	n/a	Santa Maria Joint Union High	Santa Maria
n/a	n/a	Santa Maria-Bonita	Santa Maria
n/a	n/a	Santa Monica-Malibu Unified	Santa Monica
n/a	n/a	Santa Paula Elementary	Santa Paula
n/a	n/a	Santa Paula Union High	Santa Paula
n/a	n/a	Santa Rita Union Elementary	Salinas
n/a	n/a	Santee Elementary	Santee

Note: This section only includes districts with 1,500 or more students; All categories are ranked from high to low

n/a	n/a	Saratoga Union Elementary	Saratoga
n/a	n/a	Saugus Union	Santa Clarita
n/a	n/a	Savanna Elementary	Anaheim
n/a	n/a	Sbc - Aspire Public Schools	Oakland
n/a	n/a	Sbc - High Tech High	San Diego
n/a	n/a	Scotts Valley Unified	Scotts Valley
n/a	n/a	Shasta Union High	Redding
n/a	n/a	Silver Valley Unified	Yermo
n/a	n/a	Snowline Joint Unified	Phelan
n/a	n/a	Solana Beach Elementary	Solana Beach
n/a	n/a	Sonoma Valley Unified	Sonoma
n/a	n/a	Soquel Union Elementary	Capitola
n/a	n/a	South Bay Union Elementary	Imperial Beach
n/a	n/a	South Monterey Co. Jt Union High	King City
n/a	n/a	South Whittier Elementary	Whittier
n/a	n/a	Southern Kern Unified	Rosamond
n/a	n/a	Spencer Valley Elementary	Santa Ysabel
n/a	n/a	Standard Elementary	Bakersfield
n/a	n/a	Stanislaus County Office of Educ.	Modesto
n/a	n/a	Stanislaus Union Elementary	Modesto
n/a	n/a	Stockton Unified	Stockton
n/a	n/a	Sulphur Springs Union	Canyon Country
n/a	n/a	Sunnyvale	Sunnyvale
n/a	n/a	Taft City	Taft
n/a	n/a	Temple City Unified	Temple City
n/a	n/a	Templeton Unified	Templeton
n/a	n/a	Tulare City	Tulare
n/a	n/a	Turlock Unified	Turlock
n/a	n/a	Tustin Unified	Tustin
n/a	n/a	Union Elementary	San Jose
n/a	n/a	Vacaville Unified	Vacaville
n/a	n/a	Vallejo City Unified	Vallejo
n/a	n/a	Valley Center-Pauma Unified	Valley Center
n/a	n/a	Ventura County Office of Educ.	Camarillo
n/a	n/a	Victor Elementary	Victorville
n/a	n/a	Walnut Creek Elementary	Walnut Creek
n/a	n/a	Walnut Valley Unified	Walnut
n/a	n/a	Wasco Union Elementary	Wasco
n/a	n/a	Washington Unified	West Sacramento
n/a	n/a	Washington Unified	Fresno
n/a	n/a	Waterford Unified	Waterford
n/a	n/a	West Covina Unified	West Covina
n/a	n/a	West Sonoma County Union High	Sebastopol
n/a	n/a	Western Placer Unified	Lincoln
n/a	n/a	Westminster Elementary	Westminster
n/a	n/a	Westside Union Elementary	Quartz Hill
n/a	n/a	Whittier City Elementary	Whittier
n/a	n/a	Whittier Union High	Whittier
n/a	n/a	Willits Unified	Willits
n/a	n/a	Willows Unified	Willows
n/a	n/a	Winton Elementary	Winton
n/a	n/a	Wiseburn Elementary	Hawthorne
n/a	n/a	Woodlake Union Elementary	Woodlake
n/a	n/a	Wright Elementary	Santa Rosa
n/a	n/a	Yosemite Unified	Oakhurst
n/a	n/a	Yuba City Unified	Yuba City

Student/Counselor Ratio

(number of students per counselor)

Rank	Number	District Name	City
1	139.0	Los Angeles County Office of Educ.	Downey
2	258.3	Brawley Union High	Brawley
3	261.0	San Mateo Union High	San Mateo
4	265.5	Santa Paula Union High	Santa Paula
5	280.1	Pleasanton Unified	Pleasanton
6	280.5	Northern Humboldt Union High	Mckinleyville
7	282.6	West Sonoma County Union High	Sebastopol
8	282.8	Anderson Union High	Anderson
9	290.0	Shasta Union High	Redding
10	294.1	San Rafael City High	San Rafael
11	295.3	Tamalpais Union High	Larkspur
12	295.8	El Monte Union High	El Monte
13	303.3	San Luis Coastal Unified	San Luis Obispo
14	314.0	Kern Union High	Bakersfield
15	323.2	San Diego County Office of Educ.	San Diego
16	323.5	Santa Rosa High	Santa Rosa
17	325.4	Acalanes Union High	Lafayette
18	327.9	Carmel Unified	Carmel
19	331.2	Los Gatos-Saratoga Jt Union High	Los Gatos
20	340.3	Jefferson Union High	Daly City
21	341.2	Santa Cruz City High	Soquel
22	341.9	Nevada Joint Union High	Grass Valley
23	343.9	Roseville Joint Union High	Roseville
24	344.6	Centinela Valley Union High	Lawndale
25	345.9	Sweetwater Union High	Chula Vista
26	346.3	Paramount Unified	Paramount
27	349.7	Central Union High	El Centro
28	354.6	Wasco Union High	Wasco
29	355.4	Monrovia Unified	Monrovia
30	361.9	Salinas Union High	Salinas
31	362.2	Tahoe-Truckee Joint Unified	Truckee
32	365.2	Mountain View-Los Altos Union High	Mountain View
33	366.6	Delano Joint Union High	Delano
34	373.1	Oroville Union High	Oroville
34	373.1	Oxnard Union High	Oxnard
36	374.3	Tulare Joint Union High	Tulare
37	375.9	Sequoia Union High	Redwood City
38	377.6	Petaluma Joint Union High	Petaluma
39	379.2	San Francisco Unified	San Francisco
40	380.3	Hanford Joint Union High	Hanford
41	382.3	Santa Monica-Malibu Unified	Santa Monica
42	385.9	Winters Joint Unified	Winters
43	392.6	Piedmont City Unified	Piedmont
44	392.7	Lemoore Union High	Lemoore
45	394.4	Red Bluff Joint Union High	Red Bluff
46	399.0	Holtville Unified	Holtville
47	400.5	El Dorado Union High	Placerville
48	406.2	La Canada Unified	La Canada
49	406.7	Hillsborough City Elementary	Hillsborough
50	418.3	Willows Unified	Willows
51	424.5	Beverly Hills Unified	Beverly Hills
52	424.9	Carpinteria Unified	Carpinteria
53	426.6	William S. Hart Union High	Santa Clarita
54	428.9	Merced Union High	Atwater
55	429.5	San Joaquin County Office of Educ.	Stockton
56	429.6	San Bernardino City Unified	San Bernardino
57	440.1	Grossmont Union High	La Mesa
58	449.0	Chaffey Joint Union High	Ontario
59	451.2	Ventura Unified	Ventura
60	452.1	Antelope Valley Union High	Lancaster
61	454.9	Pacific Grove Unified	Pacific Grove
62	458.8	Templeton Unified	Templeton
63	461.5	Placer Union High	Auburn
64	466.9	Oak Park Unified	Oak Park
65	475.2	Perris Union High	Perris
66	481.9	Riverdale Joint Unified	Riverdale
67	483.2	Fort Bragg Unified	Fort Bragg
68	486.8	Lennox	Lennox
69	489.1	Cutler-Orosi Joint Unified	Orosi
70	500.7	Fresno County Office of Education	Fresno
71	505.7	Laguna Beach Unified	Laguna Beach
72	506.1	Escondido Union High	Escondido
73	506.3	Redondo Beach Unified	Redondo Beach
74	507.8	Desert Sands Unified	La Quinta
75	508.2	Galt Joint Union High	Galt
76	512.5	Walnut Valley Unified	Walnut
77	515.2	Modesto City High	Modesto
78	518.6	Washington Unified	Fresno
79	521.0	Lindsay Unified	Lindsay
80	521.4	San Benito High	Hollister
81	523.3	Lakeport Unified	Lakeport
82	524.4	River Delta Joint Unified	Rio Vista
83	528.8	Los Angeles Unified	Los Angeles
84	534.1	San Diego Unified	San Diego
85	535.7	Coronado Unified	Coronado
86	535.8	San Dieguito Union High	Encinitas
87	539.8	South Pasadena Unified	South Pasadena
88	543.3	Temple City Unified	Temple City
89	544.7	Campbell Union High	San Jose
90	549.1	Santa Barbara Unified	Santa Barbara
91	549.5	Sierra Sands Unified	Ridgecrest
92	558.9	San Jose Unified	San Jose
93	566.4	Fremont Union High	Sunnyvale
94	568.3	Santa Paula Elementary	Santa Paula
95	569.2	Manhattan Beach Unified	Manhattan Beach
96	569.7	Compton Unified	Compton
97	571.7	Paradise Unified	Paradise
98	577.5	Fullerton Joint Union High	Fullerton
99	579.0	Palos Verdes Peninsula Unified	Palos Vrds Est
100	584.9	Liberty Union High	Brentwood
101	586.4	Spencer Valley Elementary	Santa Ysabel
102	594.2	Albany City Unified	Albany
103	598.7	San Marino Unified	San Marino
104	600.4	Mcfarland Unified	Mcfarland
105	601.1	Davis Joint Unified	Davis
106	603.5	Castro Valley Unified	Castro Valley
107	603.7	Arcadia Unified	Arcadia
108	605.0	Santa Clara County Office of Educ.	San Jose
109	607.1	Kern County Office of Education	Bakersfield
110	609.0	Silver Valley Unified	Yermo
111	610.0	Coalinga-Huron Joint Unified	Coalinga
112	611.6	Long Beach Unified	Long Beach
113	612.6	Lompoc Unified	Lompoc
114	614.1	Montebello Unified	Montebello
115	618.6	East Whittier City Elementary	Whittier
116	619.5	Gateway Unified	Redding
117	621.3	Sanger Unified	Sanger
118	622.3	Cabrillo Unified	Half Moon Bay
119	629.1	Palo Alto Unified	Palo Alto
120	631.2	Roseland Elementary	Santa Rosa
121	632.8	Victor Valley Union High	Victorville
122	634.3	Escalon Unified	Escalon
123	635.7	Willits Unified	Willits
124	638.8	Moorpark Unified	Moorpark
125	641.5	Lincoln Unified	Stockton
126	641.6	Denair Unified	Denair
127	644.9	Berkeley Unified	Berkeley
128	647.5	Dinuba Unified	Dinuba
129	650.5	Farmersville Unified	Farmersville
130	651.7	West Covina Unified	West Covina
131	654.1	Anaheim Union High	Anaheim
132	657.4	Coachella Valley Unified	Thermal
133	665.2	Snowline Joint Unified	Phelan
134	668.0	El Rancho Unified	Pico Rivera
135	674.0	Del Norte County Unified	Crescent City
136	674.7	Paso Robles Joint Unified	Paso Robles
137	681.6	Culver City Unified	Culver City
138	682.6	Hayward Unified	Hayward
139	688.0	Rim of the World Unified	Blue Jay
140	688.1	Hacienda La Puente Unified	City of Industry
141	689.9	North Monterey County Unified	Moss Landing
142	691.7	Moreno Valley Unified	Moreno Valley
143	696.5	Inglewood Unified	Inglewood
144	710.5	Torrance Unified	Torrance
145	710.9	Rialto Unified	Rialto
146	716.4	Las Virgenes Unified	Calabasas
147	716.8	Fallbrook Union High	Fallbrook
148	720.7	Twin Rivers Unified	Mcclellan
149	721.2	Mountain Empire Unified	Pine Valley
150	725.2	Wiseburn Elementary	Hawthorne
151	725.7	Redlands Unified	Redlands
152	728.5	Nevada County Office of Education	Nevada City
153	730.5	Clovis Unified	Clovis
154	730.7	Stanislaus County Office of Educ.	Modesto
155	730.8	Alameda City Unified	Alameda
156	733.6	Center Joint Unified	Antelope
157	735.7	Yosemite Unified	Oakhurst
158	739.6	Sonoma Valley Unified	Sonoma
159	739.7	Downey Unified	Downey
160	740.4	Stockton Unified	Stockton
161	742.0	Mill Valley Elementary	Mill Valley
162	744.0	Firebaugh-Las Deltas Joint Unified	Firebaugh
163	750.2	Murrieta Valley Unified	Murrieta
164	750.5	Banning Unified	Banning
165	758.2	San Rafael City Elementary	San Rafael
166	761.4	Delhi Unified	Delhi
167	761.8	Oceanside Unified	Oceanside
168	763.3	Santa Maria Joint Union High	Santa Maria
169	766.4	Mariposa County Unified	Mariposa
170	766.9	Oakdale Joint Unified	Oakdale
171	768.2	Eureka City Schools	Eureka
172	770.4	Bishop Unified	Bishop
173	770.5	Merced County Office of Education	Merced
174	774.5	Yuba City Unified	Yuba City
175	777.6	Vista Unified	Vista
176	778.3	Colton Joint Unified	Colton
177	781.8	Azusa Unified	Azusa
178	782.6	Monterey Peninsula Unified	Monterey
179	787.2	San Lorenzo Unified	San Lorenzo
180	789.3	Gonzales Unified	Gonzales
181	794.0	Bonita Unified	San Dimas
182	795.1	Upland Unified	Upland
183	797.0	Conejo Valley Unified	Thousand Oaks
184	801.7	Pasadena Unified	Pasadena
185	806.4	San Leandro Unified	San Leandro
186	807.9	Turlock Unified	Turlock
187	824.8	Beaumont Unified	Beaumont
188	828.2	Riverside Unified	Riverside
189	829.2	Temecula Valley Unified	Temecula
190	830.7	Madera Unified	Madera
191	841.6	Washington Unified	West Sacramento
192	842.3	Chico Unified	Chico
193	842.7	Soledad Unified	Soledad

Note: This section only includes districts with 1,500 or more students; All categories are ranked from high to low

Rank	Value	District	City
194	845.6	Palm Springs Unified	Palm Springs
195	847.5	Baldwin Park Unified	Baldwin Park
196	849.9	Tracy Joint Unified	Tracy
197	851.6	Amador County Unified	Jackson
198	852.1	Gilroy Unified	Gilroy
199	854.7	Weaver Union	Merced
200	855.9	Barstow Unified	Barstow
201	858.3	Alvord Unified	Riverside
202	863.6	Simi Valley Unified	Simi Valley
203	871.5	Palo Verde Unified	Blythe
204	874.1	Nuview Union	Nuevo
205	875.5	Fresno Unified	Fresno
206	878.2	San Juan Unified	Carmichael
207	878.6	Norwalk-La Mirada Unified	Norwalk
208	887.1	New Haven Unified	Union City
209	898.0	Dixon Unified	Dixon
210	898.5	Travis Unified	Fairfield
211	900.9	Martinez Unified	Martinez
212	902.7	East Side Union High	San Jose
213	903.7	Vacaville Unified	Vacaville
214	906.3	Menlo Park City Elementary	Atherton
215	910.9	Burbank Unified	Burbank
216	921.7	Parlier Unified	Parlier
217	922.1	Ocean View	Oxnard
218	923.0	Ramona City Unified	Ramona
219	923.8	Imperial Unified	Imperial
219	923.8	Lake Elsinore Unified	Lake Elsinore
221	932.5	Earlimart Elementary	Earlimart
222	934.0	Val Verde Unified	Perris
223	934.3	Alpine Union Elementary	Alpine
224	937.1	San Marcos Unified	San Marcos
225	937.9	Jurupa Unified	Jurupa Valley
226	942.0	San Carlos Elementary	San Carlos
227	954.8	Corona-Norco Unified	Norco
228	956.7	Bassett Unified	La Puente
229	959.5	Healdsburg Unified	Healdsburg
230	960.9	Windsor Unified	Windsor
231	963.9	Fillmore Unified	Fillmore
232	964.0	Dublin Unified	Dublin
233	966.2	Poway Unified	San Diego
234	972.5	Norris Elementary	Bakersfield
235	973.6	Santa Ana Unified	Santa Ana
236	974.0	Irvine Unified	Irvine
237	974.9	Newport-Mesa Unified	Costa Mesa
238	985.1	San Jacinto Unified	San Jacinto
239	990.9	Claremont Unified	Claremont
240	992.2	Ceres Unified	Ceres
241	995.9	Bear Valley Unified	Big Bear Lake
242	996.2	Hawthorne	Hawthorne
243	998.8	Napa Valley Unified	Napa
244	999.5	Alhambra Unified	Alhambra
245	1,002.1	Lake Tahoe Unified	S Lake Tahoe
246	1,003.5	Hemet Unified	Hemet
247	1,005.2	San Ramon Valley Unified	Danville
248	1,005.7	Carlsbad Unified	Carlsbad
249	1,018.8	Folsom-Cordova Unified	Folsom
250	1,020.6	Santa Clara Unified	Santa Clara
251	1,024.0	Rio Elementary	Oxnard
252	1,024.3	Lodi Unified	Lodi
253	1,025.2	Cotati-Rohnert Park Unified	Rohnert Park
254	1,034.3	Lynwood Unified	Lynwood
255	1,043.7	Lawndale Elementary	Lawndale
256	1,045.4	Charter Oak Unified	Covina
257	1,048.3	Apple Valley Unified	Apple Valley
258	1,049.1	Glendale Unified	Glendale
259	1,052.5	Campbell Union	Campbell
259	1,052.5	Novato Unified	Novato
261	1,056.6	Porterville Unified	Porterville
262	1,058.8	Lucia Mar Unified	Arroyo Grande
263	1,065.6	Hesperia Unified	Hesperia
264	1,066.8	Pomona Unified	Pomona
265	1,066.9	West Contra Costa Unified	Richmond
266	1,072.8	Yucaipa-Calimesa Joint Unified	Yucaipa
267	1,081.4	Pittsburg Unified	Pittsburg
268	1,090.5	Gridley Unified	Gridley
269	1,095.2	Chino Valley Unified	Chino
270	1,095.5	Covina-Valley Unified	Covina
271	1,096.7	Richland Union Elementary	Shafter
272	1,097.0	Orland Joint Unified	Orland
273	1,098.0	El Segundo Unified	El Segundo
274	1,103.3	John Swett Unified	Rodeo
275	1,104.5	Atascadero Unified	Atascadero
276	1,105.1	Duarte Unified	Duarte
277	1,113.7	Riverside County Office of Educ.	Riverside
278	1,114.9	Sacramento City Unified	Sacramento
279	1,120.0	Dixie Elementary	San Rafael
280	1,123.5	Tehachapi Unified	Tehachapi
281	1,126.6	Woodland Joint Unified	Woodland
282	1,126.7	Redding Elementary	Redding
283	1,133.2	Hughson Unified	Hughson
284	1,134.5	Glendora Unified	Glendora
285	1,145.8	Central Unified	Fresno
286	1,150.7	Kelseyville Unified	Kelseyville
287	1,152.0	Calexico Unified	Calexico
288	1,152.4	San Lorenzo Valley Unified	Ben Lomond
289	1,152.7	Empire Union Elementary	Modesto
290	1,153.5	Linden Unified	Linden
291	1,156.4	Los Alamitos Unified	Los Alamitos
292	1,176.0	Fowler Unified	Fowler
293	1,176.6	Elk Grove Unified	Elk Grove
294	1,180.5	Morongo Unified	Twentynine Plms
295	1,183.0	Dos Palos Oro Loma Joint Unified	Dos Palos
296	1,198.5	Orinda Union Elementary	Orinda
297	1,239.2	Rowland Unified	Rowland Heights
298	1,248.5	Bellflower Unified	Bellflower
299	1,248.9	Ojai Unified	Ojai
300	1,250.4	Tustin Unified	Tustin
301	1,251.4	Milpitas Unified	Milpitas
302	1,253.0	Scotts Valley Unified	Scotts Valley
303	1,263.1	Garden Grove Unified	Garden Grove
304	1,268.5	Livingston Union Elementary	Livingston
305	1,270.0	Ventura County Office of Educ.	Camarillo
306	1,272.5	Dry Creek Joint Elementary	Roseville
307	1,272.6	Natomas Unified	Sacramento
308	1,272.9	Escondido Union	Escondido
309	1,281.6	La Mesa-Spring Valley	La Mesa
310	1,287.4	Placentia-Yorba Linda Unified	Placentia
311	1,294.1	Alum Rock Union Elementary	San Jose
312	1,294.3	Waterford Unified	Waterford
313	1,298.1	Eureka Union	Granite Bay
314	1,299.3	Sbc - Aspire Public Schools	Oakland
315	1,312.0	Newark Unified	Newark
316	1,324.4	Brea-Olinda Unified	Brea
317	1,327.6	Pajaro Valley Unified	Watsonville
318	1,329.5	Santa Maria-Bonita	Santa Maria
319	1,340.0	Rosedale Union Elementary	Bakersfield
320	1,352.5	Hueneme Elementary	Port Hueneme
321	1,367.0	Mojave Unified	Mojave
322	1,379.9	Orange Unified	Orange
323	1,388.1	Buckeye Union Elementary	Shingle Springs
324	1,389.3	Valley Center-Pauma Unified	Valley Center
325	1,397.0	Armona Union Elementary	Armona
326	1,409.5	Newman-Crows Landing Unified	Newman
327	1,410.6	Ontario-Montclair Elementary	Ontario
328	1,422.9	Patterson Joint Unified	Patterson
329	1,425.8	Whittier City Elementary	Whittier
330	1,453.0	Standard Elementary	Bakersfield
331	1,479.1	Union Elementary	San Jose
332	1,484.5	Greenfield Union Elementary	Greenfield
333	1,490.0	Brawley Elementary	Brawley
334	1,493.8	Ukiah Unified	Ukiah
335	1,495.6	Corcoran Joint Unified	Corcoran
336	1,504.9	Marysville Joint Unified	Marysville
337	1,510.1	Mt. Diablo Unified	Concord
338	1,516.0	Romoland Elementary	Homeland
339	1,518.0	Hilmar Unified	Hilmar
340	1,531.3	Vallejo City Unified	Vallejo
341	1,533.5	Antioch Unified	Antioch
342	1,542.5	Ripon Unified	Ripon
343	1,556.1	San Mateo-Foster City	Foster City
344	1,563.3	Fremont Unified	Fremont
345	1,568.1	Burlingame Elementary	Burlingame
346	1,569.0	Black Oak Mine Unified	Georgetown
347	1,578.6	Ross Valley Elementary	San Anselmo
348	1,580.5	Cupertino Union	Cupertino
349	1,581.0	Western Placer Unified	Lincoln
350	1,593.7	Central Elementary	R Cucamonga
351	1,603.7	ABC Unified	Cerritos
352	1,609.0	Pacifica	Pacifica
353	1,637.0	Gorman Elementary	Gorman
354	1,640.2	Kings Canyon Joint Unified	Reedley
355	1,641.0	Benicia Unified	Benicia
355	1,641.0	Lemoore Union Elementary	Lemoore
357	1,645.4	Oak Grove Elementary	San Jose
358	1,659.8	Fairfield-Suisun Unified	Fairfield
359	1,662.0	Cambrian	San Jose
360	1,664.5	Lafayette Elementary	Lafayette
361	1,664.9	Manteca Unified	Manteca
362	1,677.0	Byron Union Elementary	Byron
363	1,679.0	Grass Valley Elementary	Grass Valley
364	1,707.0	Fullerton Elementary	Fullerton
365	1,725.0	Eastside Union Elementary	Lancaster
366	1,726.4	Saddleback Valley Unified	Mission Viejo
367	1,744.3	Hermosa Beach City Elementary	Hermosa Beach
368	1,750.7	San Ysidro Elementary	San Ysidro
369	1,765.0	Walnut Creek Elementary	Walnut Creek
370	1,773.0	Moraga Elementary	Moraga
371	1,773.7	Garvey Elementary	Rosemead
372	1,789.0	Live Oak Unified	Live Oak
373	1,792.4	Berryessa Union Elementary	San Jose
374	1,800.0	Morgan Hill Unified	Morgan Hill
375	1,837.0	Winton Elementary	Winton
376	1,851.3	Riverbank Unified	Riverbank
377	1,860.6	Adelanto Elementary	Adelanto
378	1,862.9	Merced City Elementary	Merced
379	1,870.5	Alameda County Office of Education	Hayward
380	1,872.0	Golden Plains Unified	San Joaquin
381	1,875.7	San Bruno Park Elementary	San Bruno
382	1,890.4	Little Lake City Elementary	Santa Fe Spgs
383	1,907.0	Dehesa Elementary	El Cajon
384	1,919.3	Solana Beach Elementary	Solana Beach
385	1,927.4	Westminster Elementary	Westminster
386	1,934.0	Los Nietos	Whittier
387	1,944.0	Corning Union Elementary	Corning
388	1,945.0	Golden Valley Unified	Madera
389	1,977.0	South Monterey Co. Jt Union High	King City
390	1,988.9	S San Francisco Unified	S San Francisco
391	1,996.5	Rescue Union Elementary	Rescue
392	1,997.0	Livermore Valley Joint Unified	Livermore
393	2,041.5	Burton Elementary	Porterville
394	2,055.3	Huntington Bch Union High	Huntington Bch
395	2,061.0	Live Oak Elementary	Santa Cruz
396	2,070.7	Los Gatos Union Elementary	Los Gatos
397	2,077.1	Fallbrook Union Elementary	Fallbrook
398	2,081.5	Visalia Unified	Visalia
399	2,090.0	Oakland Unified	Oakland
400	2,098.0	Redwood City Elementary	Redwood City
401	2,100.0	Auburn Union Elementary	Auburn
402	2,102.5	Sylvan Union Elementary	Modesto
403	2,109.0	Saratoga Union Elementary	Saratoga
404	2,138.0	Red Bluff Union Elementary	Red Bluff
405	2,140.0	Gustine Unified	Gustine
406	2,148.0	Ravenswood City Elementary	East Palo Alto
407	2,161.2	Pleasant Valley	Camarillo
408	2,201.0	Moreland Elementary	San Jose
409	2,293.9	Cajon Valley Union	El Cajon
410	2,302.6	Oxnard	Oxnard
411	2,324.3	Tulare City	Tulare
412	2,328.0	Oakley Union Elementary	Oakley
413	2,378.8	Los Banos Unified	Los Banos
414	2,514.1	Lakeside Union Elementary	Lakeside
415	2,544.0	King City Union	King City
416	2,560.7	South Bay Union Elementary	Imperial Beach
417	2,609.3	Mountain View Elementary	El Monte
418	2,610.0	Reef-Sunset Unified	Avenal
419	2,655.0	Franklin-Mckinley Elementary	San Jose
420	2,658.0	Oroville City Elementary	Oroville
421	2,677.0	Keppel Union Elementary	Pearblossom
422	2,795.4	Menifee Union Elementary	Menifee
423	2,815.0	Rosemead Elementary	Rosemead
424	2,837.3	Greenfield Union	Bakersfield
425	2,841.7	Westside Union Elementary	Quartz Hill
426	2,881.6	Encinitas Union Elementary	Encinitas
427	2,895.0	Bellevue Union Elementary	Santa Rosa
428	2,939.0	Castaic Union Elementary	Valencia
429	2,939.1	Jefferson Elementary	Daly City
430	2,992.5	El Centro Elementary	El Centro
431	3,002.5	National Elementary	National City
432	3,099.0	Konocti Unified	Lower Lake
433	3,132.6	Rocklin Unified	Rocklin
434	3,208.0	Santee Elementary	Santee
435	3,302.0	Calaveras Unified	San Andreas
436	3,316.0	Wasco Union Elementary	Wasco
437	3,361.5	San Gabriel Unified	San Gabriel
438	3,362.0	Panama-Buena Vista Union	Bakersfield
439	3,375.7	Savanna Elementary	Anaheim
440	3,380.0	Belmont-Redwood Shores Elem.	Belmont
441	3,431.7	Saugus Union	Santa Clarita
442	3,456.0	Julian Union Elementary	Julian
443	3,462.0	South Whittier Elementary	Whittier
444	3,532.0	Enterprise Elementary	Redding
445	3,540.1	Bakersfield City	Bakersfield
446	3,544.7	Capistrano Unified	SJ Capistrano
447	3,681.0	Goleta Union Elementary	Goleta
448	3,801.0	Orange County Dept of Education	Costa Mesa

Note: This section only includes districts with 1,500 or more students; All categories are ranked from high to low

449	3,855.0	Galt Joint Union Elementary	Galt
450	3,934.0	Bonsall Union Elementary	Bonsall
451	3,948.1	Fountain Valley Elementary	Fountain Valley
452	4,486.5	Modesto City Elementary	Modesto
453	4,516.0	Marcum-Illinois Union Elementary	East Nicolaus
454	4,684.5	El Monte City Elementary	El Monte
455	4,749.0	Kerman Unified	Kerman
456	4,957.9	Newhall	Valencia
457	5,004.0	Orcutt Union Elementary	Orcutt
458	5,045.0	Santa Rosa Elementary	Santa Rosa
459	5,193.3	Stanislaus Union Elementary	Modesto
460	5,203.3	Loomis Union Elementary	Loomis
461	5,345.0	Buena Park Elementary	Buena Park
462	5,590.0	Sulphur Springs Union	Canyon Country
463	5,640.0	Hollister	Hollister
464	6,372.0	Magnolia Elementary	Anaheim
465	6,415.0	Selma Unified	Selma
466	6,757.9	Ocean View	Huntington Bch
467	7,025.3	Chula Vista Elementary	Chula Vista
468	8,336.0	Brentwood Union Elementary	Brentwood
469	8,511.0	Salinas City Elementary	Salinas
470	8,972.0	Los Altos Elementary	Los Altos
471	10,292.5	Palmdale Elementary	Palmdale
472	10,340.0	Lucerne Valley Unified	Lucerne Valley
473	11,531.0	Victor Elementary	Victorville
474	13,351.0	Evergreen Elementary	San Jose
475	15,480.0	Monterey County Office of Educ.	Salinas
476	19,312.0	Anaheim City	Anaheim
n/a	n/a	Acton-Agua Dulce Unified	Acton
n/a	n/a	Alisal Union	Salinas
n/a	n/a	Alta Loma Elementary	Alta Loma
n/a	n/a	Arvin Union Elementary	Arvin
n/a	n/a	Atwater Elementary	Atwater
n/a	n/a	Beardsley Elementary	Bakersfield
n/a	n/a	Central Union Elementary	Lemoore
n/a	n/a	Centralia Elementary	Buena Park
n/a	n/a	Chowchilla Elementary	Chowchilla
n/a	n/a	Cucamonga Elementary	R Cucamonga
n/a	n/a	Cypress Elementary	Cypress
n/a	n/a	Del Mar Union Elementary	San Diego
n/a	n/a	Delano Union Elementary	Delano
n/a	n/a	Etiwanda Elementary	Etiwanda
n/a	n/a	Exeter Union Elementary	Exeter
n/a	n/a	Fairfax Elementary	Bakersfield
n/a	n/a	Fontana Unified	Fontana
n/a	n/a	Fruitvale Elementary	Bakersfield
n/a	n/a	Hanford Elementary	Hanford
n/a	n/a	Huntington Bch City Elementary	Huntington Bch
n/a	n/a	Jefferson Elementary	Tracy
n/a	n/a	Kingsburg Elementary Charter	Kingsburg
n/a	n/a	La Habra City Elementary	La Habra
n/a	n/a	Lammersville Joint Unified	Mountain House
n/a	n/a	Lamont Elementary	Lamont
n/a	n/a	Lancaster Elementary	Lancaster
n/a	n/a	Lemon Grove	Lemon Grove
n/a	n/a	Lowell Joint	Whittier
n/a	n/a	Mendota Unified	Mendota
n/a	n/a	Middletown Unified	Middletown
n/a	n/a	Millbrae Elementary	Millbrae
n/a	n/a	Mountain View Elementary	Ontario
n/a	n/a	Mountain View Whisman	Mountain View
n/a	n/a	Mt. Pleasant Elementary	San Jose
n/a	n/a	Muroc Joint Unified	North Edwards
n/a	n/a	Old Adobe Union	Petaluma
n/a	n/a	Oro Grande Elementary	Oro Grande
n/a	n/a	Perris Elementary	Perris
n/a	n/a	Petaluma City Elementary	Petaluma
n/a	n/a	Piner-Olivet Union Elementary	Santa Rosa
n/a	n/a	Pioneer Union Elementary	Hanford
n/a	n/a	Rincon Valley Union Elementary	Santa Rosa
n/a	n/a	Robla Elementary	Sacramento
n/a	n/a	Roseville City Elementary	Roseville
n/a	n/a	Salida Union Elementary	Salida
n/a	n/a	San Bernardino Co. Office of Educ.	San Bernardino
n/a	n/a	Santa Cruz City Elementary	Soquel
n/a	n/a	Santa Rita Union Elementary	Salinas
n/a	n/a	Sbc - High Tech High	San Diego
n/a	n/a	Soquel Union Elementary	Capitola
n/a	n/a	Southern Kern Unified	Rosamond
n/a	n/a	Sunnyvale	Sunnyvale
n/a	n/a	Taft City	Taft
n/a	n/a	Tulare County Office of Education	Visalia
n/a	n/a	Whittier Union High	Whittier
n/a	n/a	Woodlake Union Elementary	Woodlake
n/a	n/a	Wright Elementary	Santa Rosa

Current Expenditures per Student

Rank	Dollars	District Name	City
1	75,053	Los Angeles County Office of Educ.	Downey
2	64,656	Stanislaus County Office of Educ.	Modesto
3	61,030	Tulare County Office of Education	Visalia
4	60,543	Fresno County Office of Education	Fresno
5	60,394	San Diego County Office of Educ.	San Diego
6	60,071	Monterey County Office of Educ.	Salinas
7	57,888	San Bernardino Co. Office of Educ.	San Bernardino
8	48,020	Merced County Office of Education	Merced
9	39,112	Santa Clara County Office of Educ.	San Jose
10	34,737	Kern County Office of Education	Bakersfield
11	33,060	San Joaquin County Office of Educ.	Stockton
12	32,985	Ventura County Office of Educ.	Camarillo
13	29,726	Riverside County Office of Educ.	Riverside
14	23,865	Orange County Dept of Education	Costa Mesa
15	17,393	Carmel Unified	Carmel
16	14,590	Tamalpais Union High	Larkspur
17	13,741	Alameda County Office of Education	Hayward
18	13,649	Mountain View-Los Altos Union High	Mountain View
19	13,597	Laguna Beach Unified	Laguna Beach
20	13,534	Hillsborough City Elementary	Hillsborough
21	13,470	Palo Alto Unified	Palo Alto
22	13,035	Pacific Grove Unified	Pacific Grove
23	12,922	River Delta Joint Unified	Rio Vista
24	12,429	Berkeley Unified	Berkeley
25	12,141	Sequoia Union High	Redwood City
26	12,125	Tahoe-Truckee Joint Unified	Truckee
27	12,118	Piedmont City Unified	Piedmont
28	11,845	San Mateo Union High	San Mateo
29	11,844	San Rafael City High	San Rafael
30	11,828	Silver Valley Unified	Yermo
31	11,820	Solana Beach Elementary	Solana Beach
32	11,802	Beverly Hills Unified	Beverly Hills
33	11,742	Los Gatos-Saratoga Jt Union High	Los Gatos
34	11,554	Menlo Park City Elementary	Atherton
35	11,433	Saratoga Union Elementary	Saratoga
36	11,004	Newport-Mesa Unified	Costa Mesa
37	10,816	Los Angeles Unified	Los Angeles
38	10,669	Central Union Elementary	Lemoore
39	10,646	Golden Plains Unified	San Joaquin
40	10,643	Del Mar Union Elementary	San Diego
41	10,538	Ravenswood City Elementary	East Palo Alto
42	10,516	Goleta Union Elementary	Goleta
43	10,492	Riverbank Unified	Riverbank
44	10,454	Mill Valley Elementary	Mill Valley
45	10,443	Compton Unified	Compton
46	10,378	Santa Monica-Malibu Unified	Santa Monica
47	10,366	Bassett Unified	La Puente
48	10,275	Carpinteria Unified	Carpinteria
49	10,260	Northern Humboldt Union High	Mckinleyville
50	10,200	Roseland Elementary	Santa Rosa
51	10,168	El Monte City Elementary	El Monte
52	10,115	Delano Joint Union High	Delano
53	10,104	Dixie Elementary	San Rafael
54	10,024	Garvey Elementary	Rosemead
55	10,010	Centinela Valley Union High	Lawndale
56	9,993	Pomona Unified	Pomona
57	9,983	Los Altos Elementary	Los Altos
58	9,966	Mcfarland Unified	Mcfarland
59	9,932	Woodlake Union Elementary	Woodlake
60	9,930	Acalanes Union High	Lafayette
60	9,930	Fremont Union High	Sunnyvale
62	9,919	San Luis Coastal Unified	San Luis Obispo
63	9,915	Sunnyvale	Sunnyvale
64	9,881	Parlier Unified	Parlier
65	9,866	Cutler-Orosi Joint Unified	Orosi
66	9,839	San Francisco Unified	San Francisco
67	9,836	Fort Bragg Unified	Fort Bragg
68	9,806	El Monte Union High	El Monte
69	9,776	Pajaro Valley Unified	Watsonville
70	9,748	Mt. Pleasant Elementary	San Jose
70	9,748	Pasadena Unified	Pasadena
72	9,686	East Whittier City Elementary	Whittier
73	9,682	Sacramento City Unified	Sacramento
74	9,658	Mountain View Elementary	El Monte
75	9,604	Kern Union High	Bakersfield
76	9,593	Orinda Union Elementary	Orinda
77	9,515	Lindsay Unified	Lindsay
78	9,508	Santa Clara Unified	Santa Clara
79	9,505	San Diego Unified	San Diego
80	9,446	Delano Union Elementary	Delano
81	9,420	Live Oak Elementary	Santa Cruz
82	9,415	Fallbrook Union High	Fallbrook
83	9,406	Coachella Valley Unified	Thermal
84	9,390	Livingston Union Elementary	Livingston
85	9,357	Lennox	Lennox
86	9,344	Del Norte County Unified	Crescent City
87	9,341	Earlimart Elementary	Earlimart
88	9,323	West Contra Costa Unified	Richmond
89	9,322	Redwood City Elementary	Redwood City
90	9,320	Moreland Elementary	San Jose
90	9,320	Nevada County Office of Education	Nevada City
92	9,290	San Bernardino City Unified	San Bernardino
93	9,285	Farmersville Unified	Farmersville
94	9,277	National Elementary	National City
95	9,275	Konocti Unified	Lower Lake
96	9,274	Robla Elementary	Sacramento
97	9,272	Rincon Valley Union Elementary	Santa Rosa
98	9,269	San Ysidro Elementary	San Ysidro
99	9,263	Fresno Unified	Fresno
100	9,245	Bishop Unified	Bishop
101	9,244	Sonoma Valley Unified	Sonoma
102	9,200	Gateway Unified	Redding
102	9,200	Lawndale Elementary	Lawndale
102	9,200	Valley Center-Pauma Unified	Valley Center
105	9,199	Lamont Elementary	Lamont
106	9,168	Albany City Unified	Albany
107	9,156	Hacienda La Puente Unified	City of Industry
108	9,141	Oakland Unified	Oakland
109	9,131	South Monterey Co. Jt Union High	King City
110	9,122	South Bay Union Elementary	Imperial Beach
111	9,121	Mojave Unified	Mojave
111	9,121	Mountain View Whisman	Mountain View
113	9,104	Greenfield Union Elementary	Greenfield
114	9,094	Bakersfield City	Bakersfield
114	9,094	San Rafael City Elementary	San Rafael
116	9,090	Banning Unified	Banning
117	9,071	Healdsburg Unified	Healdsburg
118	9,065	Santa Ana Unified	Santa Ana
119	9,053	Rosemead Elementary	Rosemead
120	9,049	Ocean View	Oxnard
121	9,029	Santa Paula Elementary	Santa Paula
122	9,023	Anaheim Union High	Anaheim
123	9,020	Bellevue Union Elementary	Santa Rosa
124	9,017	Mariposa County Unified	Mariposa
125	9,016	San Jose Unified	San Jose
126	9,014	Monterey Peninsula Unified	Monterey
127	9,009	Alum Rock Union Elementary	San Jose
128	9,001	Sweetwater Union High	Chula Vista
129	8,996	San Marino Unified	San Marino
130	8,991	San Juan Unified	Carmichael
131	8,986	Red Bluff Joint Union High	Red Bluff
132	8,984	West Sonoma County Union High	Sebastopol
133	8,977	Yosemite Unified	Oakhurst
134	8,969	Dos Palos Oro Loma Joint Unified	Dos Palos
135	8,968	El Rancho Unified	Pico Rivera
136	8,950	Delhi Unified	Delhi
137	8,943	Riverdale Joint Unified	Riverdale
138	8,937	Hughson Unified	Hughson
139	8,932	Alhambra Unified	Alhambra
139	8,932	Duarte Unified	Duarte
141	8,927	Grass Valley Elementary	Grass Valley
142	8,923	Campbell Union High	San Jose
143	8,908	Moraga Elementary	Moraga
144	8,897	Holtville Unified	Holtville
145	8,889	Oxnard	Oxnard
146	8,885	Lake Tahoe Unified	S Lake Tahoe
147	8,880	Denair Unified	Denair
148	8,869	Marysville Joint Unified	Marysville
149	8,868	Eureka City Schools	Eureka
150	8,851	Rialto Unified	Rialto
151	8,819	Los Gatos Union Elementary	Los Gatos
152	8,814	Tulare Joint Union High	Tulare
153	8,793	Encinitas Union Elementary	Encinitas
154	8,791	Vallejo City Unified	Vallejo
155	8,786	Monrovia Unified	Monrovia
156	8,778	Taft City	Taft
157	8,764	Nuview Union	Nuevo
158	8,762	Firebaugh-Las Deltas Joint Unified	Firebaugh
159	8,760	Azusa Unified	Azusa
160	8,758	Norwalk-La Mirada Unified	Norwalk
161	8,757	Oroville City Elementary	Oroville
162	8,753	Jefferson Union High	Daly City
162	8,753	Porterville Unified	Porterville
164	8,743	Ontario-Montclair Elementary	Ontario
165	8,729	Empire Union Elementary	Modesto
166	8,726	Cabrillo Unified	Half Moon Bay
167	8,725	North Monterey County Unified	Moss Landing

Note: This section only includes districts with 1,500 or more students; All categories are ranked from high to low

Rank	Value	District	City
168	8,723	Kings Canyon Joint Unified	Reedley
169	8,717	Reef-Sunset Unified	Avenal
170	8,701	Wasco Union High	Wasco
171	8,699	Long Beach Unified	Long Beach
172	8,689	Stockton Unified	Stockton
173	8,688	Black Oak Mine Unified	Georgetown
174	8,680	Shasta Union High	Redding
175	8,667	Montebello Unified	Montebello
176	8,666	Willits Unified	Willits
177	8,663	Fullerton Joint Union High	Fullerton
178	8,657	Arvin Union Elementary	Arvin
179	8,646	Hayward Unified	Hayward
180	8,623	Paramount Unified	Paramount
181	8,622	Sanger Unified	Sanger
182	8,621	Redding Elementary	Redding
183	8,599	Huntington Bch Union High	Huntington Bch
183	8,599	Los Nietos	Whittier
185	8,581	Rowland Unified	Rowland Heights
186	8,573	Campbell Union	Campbell
187	8,568	Anderson Union High	Anderson
188	8,563	Paso Robles Joint Unified	Paso Robles
189	8,558	Pittsburg Unified	Pittsburg
190	8,553	Nevada Joint Union High	Grass Valley
191	8,550	Coalinga-Huron Joint Unified	Coalinga
192	8,544	John Swett Unified	Rodeo
193	8,543	Lemon Grove	Lemon Grove
194	8,542	Selma Unified	Selma
195	8,540	Brawley Union High	Brawley
196	8,534	New Haven Unified	Union City
197	8,528	Palm Springs Unified	Palm Springs
198	8,524	Coronado Unified	Coronado
198	8,524	Dublin Unified	Dublin
200	8,518	Galt Joint Union High	Galt
201	8,512	Glendale Unified	Glendale
202	8,508	Colton Joint Unified	Colton
203	8,495	Palos Verdes Peninsula Unified	Palos Vrds Est
204	8,493	Mendota Unified	Mendota
205	8,490	Mt. Diablo Unified	Concord
206	8,484	Palmdale Elementary	Palmdale
207	8,483	Ramona City Unified	Ramona
208	8,480	Muroc Joint Unified	North Edwards
209	8,474	Davis Joint Unified	Davis
210	8,467	Garden Grove Unified	Garden Grove
211	8,466	Perris Elementary	Perris
211	8,466	Whittier Union High	Whittier
213	8,459	Redondo Beach Unified	Redondo Beach
214	8,451	Lemoore Union High	Lemoore
215	8,449	Soledad Unified	Soledad
216	8,443	Kelseyville Unified	Kelseyville
217	8,423	San Bruno Park Elementary	San Bruno
218	8,422	Beardsley Elementary	Bakersfield
219	8,421	Alisal Union	Salinas
220	8,405	Santa Maria Joint Union High	Santa Maria
221	8,403	Sulphur Springs Union	Canyon Country
222	8,398	Merced City Elementary	Merced
223	8,394	Las Virgenes Unified	Calabasas
223	8,394	Merced Union High	Atwater
223	8,394	Wasco Union Elementary	Wasco
226	8,393	La Canada Unified	La Canada
227	8,391	ABC Unified	Cerritos
228	8,390	Sierra Sands Unified	Ridgecrest
229	8,388	Eastside Union Elementary	Lancaster
230	8,383	Enterprise Elementary	Redding
231	8,377	Inglewood Unified	Inglewood
232	8,375	Cajon Valley Union	El Cajon
233	8,370	Calexico Unified	Calexico
234	8,368	Belmont-Redwood Shores Elem.	Belmont
235	8,367	Washington Unified	West Sacramento
236	8,362	Ventura Unified	Ventura
237	8,359	Salinas Union High	Salinas
238	8,358	Corcoran Joint Unified	Corcoran
239	8,351	Hawthorne	Hawthorne
240	8,348	San Dieguito Union High	Encinitas
241	8,337	Lafayette Elementary	Lafayette
242	8,335	Wright Elementary	Santa Rosa
243	8,333	Oxnard Union High	Oxnard
244	8,326	Fillmore Unified	Fillmore
245	8,325	Oroville Union High	Oroville
246	8,316	Dinuba Unified	Dinuba
247	8,307	Manhattan Beach Unified	Manhattan Beach
248	8,300	Lakeside Union Elementary	Lakeside
249	8,297	Ross Valley Elementary	San Anselmo
250	8,295	Perris Union High	Perris
251	8,288	Placentia-Yorba Linda Unified	Placentia
252	8,282	Santa Paula Union High	Santa Paula
253	8,277	La Habra City Elementary	La Habra
254	8,273	La Mesa-Spring Valley	La Mesa
255	8,268	Ocean View	Huntington Bch
256	8,254	Antelope Valley Union High	Lancaster
257	8,251	Turlock Unified	Turlock
258	8,242	Cotati-Rohnert Park Unified	Rohnert Park
259	8,225	Alpine Union Elementary	Alpine
259	8,225	Livermore Valley Joint Unified	Livermore
261	8,223	Central Union High	El Centro
262	8,215	Winton Elementary	Winton
263	8,211	Auburn Union Elementary	Auburn
264	8,200	Calaveras Unified	San Andreas
265	8,198	Winters Joint Unified	Winters
266	8,196	San Carlos Elementary	San Carlos
267	8,193	Twin Rivers Unified	Mcclellan
268	8,181	South Whittier Elementary	Whittier
269	8,180	Palo Verde Unified	Blythe
270	8,174	Novato Unified	Novato
271	8,164	Gilroy Unified	Gilroy
272	8,163	Desert Sands Unified	La Quinta
273	8,162	Arcadia Unified	Arcadia
274	8,160	Grossmont Union High	La Mesa
275	8,158	Paradise Unified	Paradise
276	8,156	Fontana Unified	Fontana
277	8,153	Richland Union Elementary	Shafter
278	8,148	Bear Valley Unified	Big Bear Lake
278	8,148	Greenfield Union	Bakersfield
280	8,146	Salinas City Elementary	Salinas
281	8,142	Galt Joint Union Elementary	Galt
282	8,139	Savanna Elementary	Anaheim
283	8,135	Keppel Union Elementary	Pearblossom
283	8,135	Windsor Unified	Windsor
285	8,125	Morongo Unified	Twentynine Plms
286	8,117	Woodland Joint Unified	Woodland
287	8,116	Ceres Unified	Ceres
287	8,116	Rim of the World Unified	Blue Jay
289	8,113	Claremont Unified	Claremont
290	8,112	Castaic Union Elementary	Valencia
291	8,105	Westminster Elementary	Westminster
292	8,101	Newark Unified	Newark
293	8,096	Hemet Unified	Hemet
294	8,094	San Benito High	Hollister
295	8,078	Carlsbad Unified	Carlsbad
296	8,073	Fairfax Elementary	Bakersfield
297	8,058	Barstow Unified	Barstow
298	8,052	Lakeport Unified	Lakeport
299	8,050	Gridley Unified	Gridley
300	8,049	Eureka Union	Granite Bay
301	8,048	Hanford Elementary	Hanford
302	8,047	Lynwood Unified	Lynwood
303	8,037	Jurupa Unified	Jurupa Valley
304	8,028	Chico Unified	Chico
305	8,026	Newman-Crows Landing Unified	Newman
306	8,021	Magnolia Elementary	Anaheim
307	8,018	Clovis Unified	Clovis
308	8,015	Poway Unified	San Diego
309	8,013	Gonzales Unified	Gonzales
310	8,004	Downey Unified	Downey
311	8,001	Old Adobe Union	Petaluma
312	7,999	Fallbrook Union Elementary	Fallbrook
313	7,997	Corning Union Elementary	Corning
314	7,989	Pleasanton Unified	Pleasanton
315	7,986	Irvine Unified	Irvine
316	7,982	Ukiah Unified	Ukiah
317	7,971	Alvord Unified	Riverside
318	7,970	King City Union	King City
319	7,957	Buena Park Elementary	Buena Park
320	7,952	Linden Unified	Linden
321	7,941	San Leandro Unified	San Leandro
321	7,941	Soquel Union Elementary	Capitola
323	7,939	Burbank Unified	Burbank
324	7,928	Temple City Unified	Temple City
325	7,927	Chula Vista Elementary	Chula Vista
325	7,927	Orland Joint Unified	Orland
327	7,926	Golden Valley Unified	Madera
328	7,920	East Side Union High	San Jose
328	7,920	Ojai Unified	Ojai
330	7,913	Hueneme Elementary	Port Hueneme
331	7,912	Franklin-Mckinley Elementary	San Jose
332	7,911	Center Joint Unified	Antelope
333	7,910	Lake Elsinore Unified	Lake Elsinore
334	7,908	Little Lake City Elementary	Santa Fe Spgs
335	7,882	Saugus Union	Santa Clarita
336	7,881	Oak Park Unified	Oak Park
337	7,878	Santa Maria-Bonita	Santa Maria
338	7,876	Napa Valley Unified	Napa
339	7,875	Moreno Valley Unified	Moreno Valley
340	7,869	Riverside Unified	Riverside
341	7,863	Burlingame Elementary	Burlingame
342	7,858	Union Elementary	San Jose
343	7,844	Val Verde Unified	Perris
344	7,840	Oak Grove Elementary	San Jose
345	7,834	Red Bluff Union Elementary	Red Bluff
346	7,831	Elk Grove Unified	Elk Grove
347	7,824	Milpitas Unified	Milpitas
347	7,824	Mountain Empire Unified	Pine Valley
349	7,813	Escondido Union High	Escondido
350	7,798	Covina-Valley Unified	Covina
351	7,790	Hilmar Unified	Hilmar
352	7,786	El Dorado Union High	Placerville
353	7,782	Kingsburg Elementary Charter	Kingsburg
354	7,776	Kerman Unified	Kerman
355	7,775	San Ramon Valley Unified	Danville
356	7,774	Culver City Unified	Culver City
357	7,762	Conejo Valley Unified	Thousand Oaks
358	7,759	Fowler Unified	Fowler
359	7,757	Middletown Unified	Middletown
360	7,756	Standard Elementary	Bakersfield
361	7,755	Centralia Elementary	Buena Park
361	7,755	El Centro Elementary	El Centro
363	7,750	Placer Union High	Auburn
364	7,748	Live Oak Unified	Live Oak
365	7,743	Bellflower Unified	Bellflower
365	7,743	Burton Elementary	Porterville
365	7,743	El Segundo Unified	El Segundo
365	7,743	Oceanside Unified	Oceanside
369	7,741	San Mateo-Foster City	Foster City
369	7,741	South Pasadena Unified	South Pasadena
371	7,740	Pacifica	Pacifica
372	7,734	San Marcos Unified	San Marcos
373	7,729	Simi Valley Unified	Simi Valley
374	7,728	Alameda City Unified	Alameda
375	7,723	Madera Unified	Madera
375	7,723	Southern Kern Unified	Rosamond
377	7,722	Los Banos Unified	Los Banos
378	7,720	Acton-Agua Dulce Unified	Acton
379	7,713	Whittier City Elementary	Whittier
380	7,712	Escondido Union	Escondido
381	7,708	Salida Union Elementary	Salida
382	7,697	Castro Valley Unified	Castro Valley
383	7,696	Stanislaus Union Elementary	Modesto
384	7,695	Lucia Mar Unified	Arroyo Grande
385	7,686	Escalon Unified	Escalon
386	7,679	Oakdale Joint Unified	Oakdale
387	7,677	Lodi Unified	Lodi
388	7,675	Rio Elementary	Oxnard
389	7,673	Lancaster Elementary	Lancaster
390	7,672	Julian Union Elementary	Julian
391	7,663	Atascadero Unified	Atascadero
392	7,646	Bonita Unified	San Dimas
393	7,643	Panama-Buena Vista Union	Bakersfield
394	7,640	Fullerton Elementary	Fullerton
395	7,639	Roseville Joint Union High	Roseville
396	7,631	Willows Unified	Willows
397	7,628	Hanford Joint Union High	Hanford
398	7,625	Folsom-Cordova Unified	Folsom
399	7,622	Walnut Creek Elementary	Walnut Creek
400	7,620	Antioch Unified	Antioch
400	7,620	Moorpark Unified	Moorpark
402	7,619	Tulare City	Tulare
403	7,616	Hollister	Hollister
404	7,605	Cupertino Union	Cupertino
405	7,592	Brawley Elementary	Brawley
406	7,586	San Lorenzo Unified	San Lorenzo
407	7,576	Anaheim City	Anaheim
408	7,570	Vacaville Unified	Vacaville
409	7,569	Liberty Union High	Brentwood
410	7,566	Chaffey Joint Union High	Ontario
410	7,566	Romoland Elementary	Homeland
412	7,553	Visalia Unified	Visalia
413	7,541	Fremont Unified	Fremont
414	7,538	Murrieta Valley Unified	Murrieta
415	7,537	Atwater Elementary	Atwater
416	7,526	Yuba City Unified	Yuba City
417	7,522	Lompoc Unified	Lompoc
418	7,521	Piner-Olivet Union Elementary	Santa Rosa
419	7,480	Charter Oak Unified	Covina
420	7,478	Walnut Valley Unified	Walnut
421	7,468	Martinez Unified	Martinez
422	7,449	Brea-Olinda Unified	Brea

Note: This section only includes districts with 1,500 or more students; All categories are ranked from high to low

Rank	Dollars	District Name	City
423	7,445	Bonsall Union Elementary	Bonsall
424	7,441	Templeton Unified	Templeton
425	7,416	S San Francisco Unified	S San Francisco
426	7,408	Gustine Unified	Gustine
427	7,400	Berryessa Union Elementary	San Jose
428	7,398	Redlands Unified	Redlands
429	7,384	Chowchilla Elementary	Chowchilla
430	7,378	Baldwin Park Unified	Baldwin Park
431	7,377	San Jacinto Unified	San Jacinto
432	7,367	Fairfield-Suisun Unified	Fairfield
433	7,351	Evergreen Elementary	San Jose
434	7,335	Tehachapi Unified	Tehachapi
435	7,322	Cambrian	San Jose
436	7,312	Fountain Valley Elementary	Fountain Valley
437	7,303	Travis Unified	Fairfield
438	7,298	Orange Unified	Orange
439	7,285	Lemoore Union Elementary	Lemoore
440	7,276	Mountain View Elementary	Ontario
441	7,258	Patterson Joint Unified	Patterson
442	7,256	Cypress Elementary	Cypress
443	7,244	Snowline Joint Unified	Phelan
444	7,242	Chino Valley Unified	Chino
445	7,241	Capistrano Unified	SJ Capistrano
445	7,241	Central Unified	Fresno
447	7,239	Imperial Unified	Imperial
448	7,218	Oakley Union Elementary	Oakley
449	7,216	Santa Rita Union Elementary	Salinas
449	7,216	Santee Elementary	Santee
451	7,213	Corona-Norco Unified	Norco
452	7,204	Los Alamitos Unified	Los Alamitos
453	7,193	Exeter Union Elementary	Exeter
453	7,193	Newhall	Valencia
455	7,187	Millbrae Elementary	Millbrae
455	7,187	Westside Union Elementary	Quartz Hill
457	7,183	Roseville City Elementary	Roseville
458	7,173	Dixon Unified	Dixon
459	7,164	Yucaipa-Calimesa Joint Unified	Yucaipa
460	7,160	Vista Unified	Vista
461	7,159	Tracy Joint Unified	Tracy
462	7,157	Alta Loma Elementary	Alta Loma
463	7,144	Cucamonga Elementary	R Cucamonga
464	7,131	Lincoln Unified	Stockton
465	7,119	Weaver Union	Merced
466	7,116	Saddleback Valley Unified	Mission Viejo
467	7,112	Torrance Unified	Torrance
468	7,093	Victor Valley Union High	Victorville
469	7,083	Glendora Unified	Glendora
470	7,053	Scotts Valley Unified	Scotts Valley
471	7,043	Pioneer Union Elementary	Hanford
472	7,024	Orcutt Union Elementary	Orcutt
473	7,016	Morgan Hill Unified	Morgan Hill
474	7,012	Fruitvale Elementary	Bakersfield
475	7,002	Lowell Joint	Whittier
476	7,000	Jefferson Elementary	Tracy
477	6,982	Benicia Unified	Benicia
478	6,979	Central Elementary	R Cucamonga
479	6,966	Temecula Valley Unified	Temecula
480	6,950	William S. Hart Union High	Santa Clarita
481	6,947	Tustin Unified	Tustin
482	6,943	Brentwood Union Elementary	Brentwood
482	6,943	Manteca Unified	Manteca
484	6,941	Beaumont Unified	Beaumont
485	6,927	Pleasant Valley	Camarillo
486	6,867	Rosedale Union Elementary	Bakersfield
487	6,831	Rocklin Unified	Rocklin
488	6,823	Menifee Union Elementary	Menifee
489	6,809	Adelanto Elementary	Adelanto
490	6,802	Natomas Unified	Sacramento
491	6,771	Huntington Bch City Elementary	Huntington Bch
492	6,746	Buckeye Union Elementary	Shingle Springs
493	6,738	Ripon Unified	Ripon
494	6,700	Sylvan Union Elementary	Modesto
495	6,697	Byron Union Elementary	Byron
496	6,693	Apple Valley Unified	Apple Valley
497	6,674	Rescue Union Elementary	Rescue
498	6,612	Amador County Unified	Jackson
499	6,608	Dry Creek Joint Elementary	Roseville
500	6,603	Hesperia Unified	Hesperia
501	6,598	Victor Elementary	Victorville
502	6,577	San Gabriel Unified	San Gabriel
503	6,549	Loomis Union Elementary	Loomis
504	6,537	Jefferson Elementary	Daly City
505	6,378	Upland Unified	Upland
506	6,375	Etiwanda Elementary	Etiwanda
507	6,360	Norris Elementary	Bakersfield
508	5,958	West Covina Unified	West Covina
509	5,826	Western Placer Unified	Lincoln
510	5,694	Wiseburn Elementary	Hawthorne
511	5,306	San Lorenzo Valley Unified	Ben Lomond
512	5,014	Hermosa Beach City Elementary	Hermosa Beach
513	4,620	Waterford Unified	Waterford
514	4,198	Armona Union Elementary	Armona
515	3,314	Dehesa Elementary	El Cajon
516	3,313	Lucerne Valley Unified	Lucerne Valley
517	1,187	Oro Grande Elementary	Oro Grande
518	819	Marcum-Illinois Union Elementary	East Nicolaus
519	676	Gorman Elementary	Gorman
520	647	Spencer Valley Elementary	Santa Ysabel
n/a	n/a	Sbc - Aspire Public Schools	Oakland
n/a	n/a	Sbc - High Tech High	San Diego
n/a	n/a	Lammersville Joint Unified	Mountain House
n/a	n/a	Modesto City Elementary	Modesto
n/a	n/a	Modesto City High	Modesto
n/a	n/a	Petaluma City Elementary	Petaluma
n/a	n/a	Petaluma Joint Union High	Petaluma
n/a	n/a	Santa Barbara Unified	Santa Barbara
n/a	n/a	Santa Cruz City Elementary	Soquel
n/a	n/a	Santa Cruz City High	Soquel
n/a	n/a	Santa Rosa Elementary	Santa Rosa
n/a	n/a	Santa Rosa High	Santa Rosa
n/a	n/a	Washington Unified	Fresno

Total General Revenue per Student

Rank	Dollars	District Name	City
1	140,686	San Bernardino Co. Office of Educ.	San Bernardino
2	124,191	San Diego County Office of Educ.	San Diego
3	123,636	Tulare County Office of Education	Visalia
4	122,636	Los Angeles County Office of Educ.	Downey
5	121,564	Stanislaus County Office of Educ.	Modesto
6	89,222	Ventura County Office of Educ.	Camarillo
7	86,186	Monterey County Office of Educ.	Salinas
8	77,460	Fresno County Office of Education	Fresno
9	69,799	Merced County Office of Education	Merced
10	62,826	Santa Clara County Office of Educ.	San Jose
11	56,989	Kern County Office of Education	Bakersfield
12	49,460	San Joaquin County Office of Educ.	Stockton
13	38,824	Riverside County Office of Educ.	Riverside
14	38,047	Orange County Dept of Education	Costa Mesa
15	33,997	Mt. Pleasant Elementary	San Jose
16	21,065	Carmel Unified	Carmel
17	20,276	Tamalpais Union High	Larkspur
18	19,391	Roseland Elementary	Santa Rosa
19	19,249	Alameda County Office of Education	Hayward
20	17,662	Menlo Park City Elementary	Atherton
21	17,580	Lennox	Lennox
22	17,432	Val Verde Unified	Perris
23	16,941	Dublin Unified	Dublin
24	16,682	Mountain View-Los Altos Union High	Mountain View
25	16,443	San Mateo Union High	San Mateo
26	16,276	River Delta Joint Unified	Rio Vista
27	16,171	Pacific Grove Unified	Pacific Grove
28	16,078	Burton Elementary	Porterville
29	16,050	Piedmont City Unified	Piedmont
30	15,754	Laguna Beach Unified	Laguna Beach
31	15,464	Berkeley Unified	Berkeley
32	15,331	Sequoia Union High	Redwood City
33	15,298	Tahoe-Truckee Joint Unified	Truckee
34	15,283	Albany City Unified	Albany
35	15,255	Palo Alto Unified	Palo Alto
36	15,240	Beverly Hills Unified	Beverly Hills
37	15,087	Hillsborough City Elementary	Hillsborough
38	14,576	San Rafael City High	San Rafael
39	14,563	Lake Tahoe Unified	S Lake Tahoe
40	14,446	Centinela Valley Union High	Lawndale
41	14,400	Santee Elementary	Santee
42	14,391	Savanna Elementary	Anaheim
43	14,339	Solana Beach Elementary	Solana Beach
44	14,226	Los Gatos-Saratoga Jt Union High	Los Gatos
45	14,155	Los Angeles Unified	Los Angeles
46	13,993	Merced Union High	Atwater
47	13,875	San Rafael City Elementary	San Rafael
48	13,492	Grossmont Union High	La Mesa
49	13,488	Silver Valley Unified	Yermo
50	13,424	Santa Monica-Malibu Unified	Santa Monica
51	13,418	San Marino Unified	San Marino
52	13,264	Bishop Unified	Bishop
53	13,060	Central Union Elementary	Lemoore
54	12,804	Whittier Union High	Whittier
55	12,756	Jefferson Union High	Daly City
56	12,743	Belmont-Redwood Shores Elem.	Belmont
57	12,702	Dos Palos Oro Loma Joint Unified	Dos Palos
58	12,693	Castro Valley Unified	Castro Valley
59	12,587	Culver City Unified	Culver City
60	12,563	Desert Sands Unified	La Quinta
61	12,474	Los Altos Elementary	Los Altos
62	12,468	Mill Valley Elementary	Mill Valley
63	12,352	Acalanes Union High	Lafayette
64	12,331	Saratoga Union Elementary	Saratoga
65	12,317	San Francisco Unified	San Francisco
66	12,290	El Monte Union High	El Monte
67	12,265	Ross Valley Elementary	San Anselmo
68	12,254	Ceres Unified	Ceres
69	12,243	West Contra Costa Unified	Richmond
70	12,225	Bassett Unified	La Puente
71	12,164	Rowland Unified	Rowland Heights
72	12,145	Newport-Mesa Unified	Costa Mesa
73	12,102	Lindsay Unified	Lindsay
74	12,100	Marysville Joint Unified	Marysville
75	12,099	Arcadia Unified	Arcadia
76	12,082	Fremont Union High	Sunnyvale
77	12,066	Carpinteria Unified	Carpinteria
78	12,003	Novato Unified	Novato
79	11,961	Delano Joint Union High	Delano
80	11,944	Los Gatos Union Elementary	Los Gatos
81	11,903	Huntington Bch Union High	Huntington Bch
82	11,889	Pomona Unified	Pomona
83	11,882	Sweetwater Union High	Chula Vista
84	11,830	Adelanto Elementary	Adelanto
85	11,801	Kern Union High	Bakersfield
86	11,780	Pasadena Unified	Pasadena
86	11,780	San Mateo-Foster City	Foster City
88	11,754	Saugus Union	Santa Clarita
89	11,673	Oakland Unified	Oakland
90	11,581	Northern Humboldt Union High	Mckinleyville
91	11,562	Cutler-Orosi Joint Unified	Orosi
92	11,517	Golden Plains Unified	San Joaquin
93	11,502	Alhambra Unified	Alhambra
93	11,502	Redwood City Elementary	Redwood City
95	11,474	Healdsburg Unified	Healdsburg
96	11,434	Kerman Unified	Kerman
97	11,432	Nevada County Office of Education	Nevada City
98	11,413	Napa Valley Unified	Napa
99	11,396	Orland Joint Unified	Orland
100	11,367	Wasco Union High	Wasco
101	11,347	Oroville Union High	Oroville
102	11,327	Monrovia Unified	Monrovia
103	11,322	Santa Ana Unified	Santa Ana
104	11,311	Pittsburg Unified	Pittsburg
105	11,310	Del Mar Union Elementary	San Diego
106	11,297	Ravenswood City Elementary	East Palo Alto
107	11,278	Woodlake Union Elementary	Woodlake
108	11,271	San Carlos Elementary	San Carlos
109	11,270	El Monte City Elementary	El Monte
110	11,269	Goleta Union Elementary	Goleta
111	11,217	Moreland Elementary	San Jose
112	11,194	Cucamonga Elementary	R Cucamonga
113	11,186	San Diego Unified	San Diego
114	11,175	Central Union High	El Centro
115	11,150	Orinda Union Elementary	Orinda
116	11,144	Fort Bragg Unified	Fort Bragg
117	11,135	Byron Union Elementary	Byron
118	11,096	Mcfarland Unified	Mcfarland
119	11,084	Palmdale Elementary	Palmdale
120	11,079	Pleasanton Unified	Pleasanton
121	11,064	San Ysidro Elementary	San Ysidro
122	11,055	Rincon Valley Union Elementary	Santa Rosa
123	11,018	San Bernardino City Unified	San Bernardino
124	11,014	Garvey Elementary	Rosemead
125	11,011	Santa Clara Unified	Santa Clara
126	11,003	Coachella Valley Unified	Thermal
127	10,933	Santa Rita Union Elementary	Salinas
128	10,909	Riverbank Unified	Riverbank
129	10,886	East Side Union High	San Jose
130	10,884	Victor Valley Union High	Victorville
131	10,877	Sunnyvale	Sunnyvale
132	10,865	North Monterey County Unified	Moss Landing
133	10,864	San Luis Coastal Unified	San Luis Obispo
134	10,862	Banning Unified	Banning
135	10,848	Paramount Unified	Paramount
136	10,842	Fallbrook Union High	Fallbrook
137	10,837	Nevada Joint Union High	Grass Valley
138	10,822	Lamont Elementary	Lamont
139	10,815	Mountain View Whisman	Mountain View

Note: This section only includes districts with 1,500 or more students; All categories are ranked from high to low

Rank	Value	District	City
140	10,811	Compton Unified	Compton
141	10,774	Hacienda La Puente Unified	City of Industry
142	10,737	San Jose Unified	San Jose
143	10,708	Eureka City Schools	Eureka
144	10,700	Colton Joint Unified	Colton
145	10,696	Bellevue Union Elementary	Santa Rosa
145	10,696	Sacramento City Unified	Sacramento
147	10,669	Burlingame Elementary	Burlingame
148	10,653	Wright Elementary	Santa Rosa
149	10,650	Pajaro Valley Unified	Watsonville
150	10,641	Dixie Elementary	San Rafael
151	10,636	Fillmore Unified	Fillmore
152	10,609	Glendale Unified	Glendale
153	10,606	Rosedale Union Elementary	Bakersfield
154	10,604	Taft City	Taft
155	10,599	Tulare Joint Union High	Tulare
156	10,575	Earlimart Elementary	Earlimart
157	10,559	Campbell Union	Campbell
158	10,553	Duarte Unified	Duarte
158	10,553	Parlier Unified	Parlier
160	10,536	Oxnard	Oxnard
161	10,495	Redondo Beach Unified	Redondo Beach
162	10,475	Chico Unified	Chico
163	10,457	Castaic Union Elementary	Valencia
164	10,446	Gateway Unified	Redding
165	10,427	Palm Springs Unified	Palm Springs
166	10,413	Sierra Sands Unified	Ridgecrest
167	10,402	Norwalk-La Mirada Unified	Norwalk
168	10,391	Paso Robles Joint Unified	Paso Robles
169	10,390	Empire Union Elementary	Modesto
170	10,386	Campbell Union High	San Jose
171	10,382	Poway Unified	San Diego
172	10,356	Inglewood Unified	Inglewood
173	10,344	Bear Valley Unified	Big Bear Lake
174	10,328	Delano Union Elementary	Delano
175	10,325	South Bay Union Elementary	Imperial Beach
176	10,324	Live Oak Elementary	Santa Cruz
177	10,300	Reef-Sunset Unified	Avenal
178	10,296	Konocti Unified	Lower Lake
179	10,270	Fresno Unified	Fresno
180	10,256	Hughson Unified	Hughson
181	10,224	Clovis Unified	Clovis
182	10,208	Rosemead Elementary	Rosemead
183	10,182	Shasta Union High	Redding
184	10,166	Vallejo City Unified	Vallejo
185	10,165	Mendota Unified	Mendota
186	10,150	Manhattan Beach Unified	Manhattan Beach
187	10,133	Grass Valley Elementary	Grass Valley
188	10,130	Lemoore Union High	Lemoore
189	10,120	Dinuba Unified	Dinuba
189	10,120	Mojave Unified	Mojave
191	10,116	Auburn Union Elementary	Auburn
192	10,110	Las Virgenes Unified	Calabasas
193	10,109	Anaheim Union High	Anaheim
194	10,103	Hanford Joint Union High	Hanford
194	10,103	Red Bluff Joint Union High	Red Bluff
196	10,092	Irvine Unified	Irvine
197	10,080	Firebaugh-Las Deltas Joint Unified	Firebaugh
198	10,071	Moraga Elementary	Moraga
199	10,054	Mt. Diablo Unified	Concord
200	10,049	Turlock Unified	Turlock
201	10,046	Sonoma Valley Unified	Sonoma
202	10,045	Salinas Union High	Salinas
203	10,043	Long Beach Unified	Long Beach
204	10,035	El Segundo Unified	El Segundo
205	10,033	Claremont Unified	Claremont
206	10,029	Davis Joint Unified	Davis
207	10,022	Porterville Unified	Porterville
208	10,021	Farmersville Unified	Farmersville
209	10,017	Brawley Union High	Brawley
210	10,013	South Monterey Co. Jt Union High	King City
211	10,009	Azusa Unified	Azusa
212	10,004	Denair Unified	Denair
213	9,992	Livermore Valley Joint Unified	Livermore
214	9,988	Ocean View	Oxnard
215	9,976	Bakersfield City	Bakersfield
216	9,955	Holtville Unified	Holtville
217	9,954	San Marcos Unified	San Marcos
218	9,944	Ontario-Montclair Elementary	Ontario
219	9,941	Washington Unified	West Sacramento
220	9,930	John Swett Unified	Rodeo
221	9,912	San Ramon Valley Unified	Danville
222	9,898	Alisal Union	Salinas
222	9,898	Robla Elementary	Sacramento
224	9,894	Galt Joint Union High	Galt
225	9,887	Charter Oak Unified	Covina
226	9,883	Montebello Unified	Montebello
227	9,881	Hayward Unified	Hayward
227	9,881	Monterey Peninsula Unified	Monterey
229	9,879	Twin Rivers Unified	Mcclellan
230	9,874	Valley Center-Pauma Unified	Valley Center
231	9,873	Soledad Unified	Soledad
232	9,859	Coronado Unified	Coronado
233	9,842	Fontana Unified	Fontana
234	9,840	Morongo Unified	Twentynine Plms
235	9,827	Lawndale Elementary	Lawndale
236	9,824	Sulphur Springs Union	Canyon Country
237	9,818	East Whittier City Elementary	Whittier
237	9,818	South Pasadena Unified	South Pasadena
239	9,807	Chula Vista Elementary	Chula Vista
240	9,799	National Elementary	National City
241	9,793	Kings Canyon Joint Unified	Reedley
242	9,790	Standard Elementary	Bakersfield
243	9,770	Baldwin Park Unified	Baldwin Park
244	9,754	Palos Verdes Peninsula Unified	Palos Vrds Est
245	9,745	Anderson Union High	Anderson
246	9,740	Fullerton Joint Union High	Fullerton
247	9,738	Del Norte County Unified	Crescent City
248	9,736	Perris Elementary	Perris
249	9,734	Windsor Unified	Windsor
250	9,721	Pacifica	Pacifica
251	9,719	Jefferson Elementary	Daly City
252	9,717	Yosemite Unified	Oakhurst
253	9,708	Enterprise Elementary	Redding
254	9,701	San Leandro Unified	San Leandro
255	9,690	West Sonoma County Union High	Sebastopol
256	9,689	Mountain View Elementary	El Monte
257	9,687	Riverdale Joint Unified	Riverdale
258	9,675	Gilroy Unified	Gilroy
259	9,672	Millbrae Elementary	Millbrae
260	9,667	Los Nietos	Whittier
261	9,654	Chaffey Joint Union High	Ontario
262	9,652	Ukiah Unified	Ukiah
263	9,649	Redding Elementary	Redding
264	9,644	Beardsley Elementary	Bakersfield
265	9,633	Oceanside Unified	Oceanside
266	9,620	Santa Paula Union High	Santa Paula
267	9,619	ABC Unified	Cerritos
268	9,617	Mariposa County Unified	Mariposa
269	9,616	Encinitas Union Elementary	Encinitas
270	9,611	Buckeye Union Elementary	Shingle Springs
271	9,606	Bonita Unified	San Dimas
272	9,605	Eastside Union Elementary	Lancaster
273	9,599	Rim of the World Unified	Blue Jay
274	9,592	Oroville City Elementary	Oroville
275	9,581	Oxnard Union High	Oxnard
276	9,575	Lemon Grove	Lemon Grove
277	9,573	Alum Rock Union Elementary	San Jose
278	9,570	Salida Union Elementary	Salida
279	9,563	Martinez Unified	Martinez
279	9,563	Placer Union High	Auburn
279	9,563	Westminster Elementary	Westminster
282	9,561	Santa Paula Elementary	Santa Paula
283	9,558	Carlsbad Unified	Carlsbad
284	9,554	Cajon Valley Union	El Cajon
285	9,549	Wasco Union Elementary	Wasco
286	9,541	Greenfield Union Elementary	Greenfield
287	9,533	Coalinga-Huron Joint Unified	Coalinga
288	9,523	San Lorenzo Unified	San Lorenzo
289	9,514	Stockton Unified	Stockton
290	9,497	Liberty Union High	Brentwood
291	9,489	El Rancho Unified	Pico Rivera
292	9,487	Alameda City Unified	Alameda
293	9,486	Arvin Union Elementary	Arvin
294	9,472	Hawthorne	Hawthorne
295	9,460	New Haven Unified	Union City
296	9,457	Paradise Unified	Paradise
297	9,456	La Canada Unified	La Canada
298	9,442	Willits Unified	Willits
299	9,426	Covina-Valley Unified	Covina
299	9,426	San Benito High	Hollister
301	9,424	Riverside Unified	Riverside
302	9,416	Newark Unified	Newark
303	9,413	Union Elementary	San Jose
304	9,404	Hemet Unified	Hemet
305	9,395	Corcoran Joint Unified	Corcoran
306	9,383	Santa Maria Joint Union High	Santa Maria
307	9,380	Escondido Union High	Escondido
307	9,380	Nuview Union	Nuevo
307	9,380	Roseville Joint Union High	Roseville
310	9,377	Black Oak Mine Unified	Georgetown
311	9,376	Lynwood Unified	Lynwood
312	9,371	Cabrillo Unified	Half Moon Bay
313	9,363	Milpitas Unified	Milpitas
314	9,362	Gonzales Unified	Gonzales
315	9,341	El Dorado Union High	Placerville
316	9,332	Lafayette Elementary	Lafayette
317	9,326	Burbank Unified	Burbank
318	9,325	Richland Union Elementary	Shafter
319	9,324	Centralia Elementary	Buena Park
320	9,322	San Juan Unified	Carmichael
321	9,317	Muroc Joint Unified	North Edwards
322	9,307	Sanger Unified	Sanger
323	9,300	Palo Verde Unified	Blythe
324	9,291	Elk Grove Unified	Elk Grove
325	9,288	Livingston Union Elementary	Livingston
326	9,286	Calaveras Unified	San Andreas
327	9,282	Rio Elementary	Oxnard
328	9,274	Corona-Norco Unified	Norco
328	9,274	Winton Elementary	Winton
330	9,271	Tustin Unified	Tustin
331	9,270	Garden Grove Unified	Garden Grove
332	9,246	Gridley Unified	Gridley
333	9,242	Central Unified	Fresno
334	9,230	Downey Unified	Downey
335	9,226	Ventura Unified	Ventura
336	9,209	Vacaville Unified	Vacaville
337	9,205	Greenfield Union	Bakersfield
338	9,180	Antelope Valley Union High	Lancaster
339	9,178	Lodi Unified	Lodi
340	9,173	Oak Park Unified	Oak Park
341	9,170	Salinas City Elementary	Salinas
342	9,167	La Mesa-Spring Valley	La Mesa
343	9,166	Perris Union High	Perris
344	9,162	Old Adobe Union	Petaluma
345	9,155	Bellflower Unified	Bellflower
346	9,146	Fowler Unified	Fowler
347	9,139	Fallbrook Union Elementary	Fallbrook
348	9,137	Placentia-Yorba Linda Unified	Placentia
349	9,135	Merced City Elementary	Merced
350	9,130	Romoland Elementary	Homeland
351	9,129	Conejo Valley Unified	Thousand Oaks
352	9,122	Kelseyville Unified	Kelseyville
353	9,121	King City Union	King City
354	9,111	South Whittier Elementary	Whittier
355	9,107	San Dieguito Union High	Encinitas
356	9,100	Fremont Unified	Fremont
357	9,098	Calexico Unified	Calexico
358	9,096	Imperial Unified	Imperial
359	9,092	Middletown Unified	Middletown
360	9,088	Redlands Unified	Redlands
361	9,083	Rialto Unified	Rialto
361	9,083	Stanislaus Union Elementary	Modesto
363	9,078	Panama-Buena Vista Union	Bakersfield
364	9,059	Lucia Mar Unified	Arroyo Grande
365	9,054	Franklin-Mckinley Elementary	San Jose
365	9,054	Woodland Joint Unified	Woodland
367	9,027	Magnolia Elementary	Anaheim
368	9,013	Linden Unified	Linden
369	8,991	Hanford Elementary	Hanford
369	8,991	Simi Valley Unified	Simi Valley
371	8,990	Lakeside Union Elementary	Lakeside
372	8,977	Torrance Unified	Torrance
373	8,976	Fairfax Elementary	Bakersfield
374	8,974	Newman-Crows Landing Unified	Newman
375	8,963	Folsom-Cordova Unified	Folsom
376	8,962	Winters Joint Unified	Winters
377	8,948	Oakdale Joint Unified	Oakdale
378	8,945	Ramona City Unified	Ramona
379	8,944	Morgan Hill Unified	Morgan Hill
380	8,942	Selma Unified	Selma
381	8,936	Lake Elsinore Unified	Lake Elsinore
382	8,933	Soquel Union Elementary	Capitola
383	8,919	Moorpark Unified	Moorpark
384	8,915	Lakeport Unified	Lakeport
385	8,902	Orange Unified	Orange
386	8,888	Yuba City Unified	Yuba City
387	8,882	Live Oak Unified	Live Oak
388	8,874	Mountain Empire Unified	Pine Valley
389	8,857	Delhi Unified	Delhi
389	8,857	Saddleback Valley Unified	Mission Viejo
391	8,848	Cotati-Rohnert Park Unified	Rohnert Park
392	8,834	Walnut Creek Elementary	Walnut Creek
393	8,829	Los Banos Unified	Los Banos
394	8,791	Keppel Union Elementary	Pearblossom

Note: This section only includes districts with 1,500 or more students; All categories are ranked from high to low

395	8,779	Alpine Union Elementary	Alpine
395	8,779	Evergreen Elementary	San Jose
397	8,776	Visalia Unified	Visalia
398	8,775	Temple City Unified	Temple City
399	8,772	Murrieta Valley Unified	Murrieta
400	8,766	Willows Unified	Willows
401	8,759	Anaheim City	Anaheim
402	8,743	Southern Kern Unified	Rosamond
403	8,727	Jurupa Unified	Jurupa Valley
404	8,725	Little Lake City Elementary	Santa Fe Spgs
405	8,724	Walnut Valley Unified	Walnut
406	8,715	Travis Unified	Fairfield
407	8,706	Barstow Unified	Barstow
408	8,704	Corning Union Elementary	Corning
409	8,681	Kingsburg Elementary Charter	Kingsburg
410	8,674	Acton-Agua Dulce Unified	Acton
411	8,670	Buena Park Elementary	Buena Park
412	8,664	Alvord Unified	Riverside
412	8,664	Tehachapi Unified	Tehachapi
414	8,662	Pioneer Union Elementary	Hanford
414	8,662	Tracy Joint Unified	Tracy
416	8,641	Chino Valley Unified	Chino
417	8,639	Madera Unified	Madera
418	8,636	Bonsall Union Elementary	Bonsall
419	8,627	Rocklin Unified	Rocklin
420	8,626	Vista Unified	Vista
421	8,617	Atascadero Unified	Atascadero
422	8,615	Ojai Unified	Ojai
423	8,607	Brea-Olinda Unified	Brea
424	8,604	Hueneme Elementary	Port Hueneme
425	8,596	Moreno Valley Unified	Moreno Valley
426	8,594	Whittier City Elementary	Whittier
427	8,590	Cypress Elementary	Cypress
428	8,585	Atwater Elementary	Atwater
429	8,583	Red Bluff Union Elementary	Red Bluff
430	8,581	Ocean View	Huntington Bch
431	8,580	Escondido Union	Escondido
432	8,578	San Bruno Park Elementary	San Bruno
433	8,573	Golden Valley Unified	Madera
434	8,565	Manteca Unified	Manteca
435	8,560	Gustine Unified	Gustine
436	8,559	Oak Grove Elementary	San Jose
437	8,556	Fairfield-Suisun Unified	Fairfield
438	8,555	Center Joint Unified	Antelope
439	8,547	La Habra City Elementary	La Habra
440	8,538	Piner-Olivet Union Elementary	Santa Rosa
441	8,536	Cupertino Union	Cupertino
442	8,524	Brawley Elementary	Brawley
443	8,494	Fullerton Elementary	Fullerton
443	8,494	Lompoc Unified	Lompoc
445	8,467	Snowline Joint Unified	Phelan
446	8,453	Galt Joint Union Elementary	Galt
447	8,447	Benicia Unified	Benicia
447	8,447	Los Alamitos Unified	Los Alamitos
449	8,435	Etiwanda Elementary	Etiwanda
450	8,423	Lincoln Unified	Stockton
450	8,423	William S. Hart Union High	Santa Clarita
452	8,422	El Centro Elementary	El Centro
452	8,422	Hilmar Unified	Hilmar
454	8,419	Lancaster Elementary	Lancaster
455	8,416	Santa Maria-Bonita	Santa Maria
456	8,411	Patterson Joint Unified	Patterson
457	8,375	Glendora Unified	Glendora
458	8,357	Fruitvale Elementary	Bakersfield
459	8,335	Julian Union Elementary	Julian
460	8,329	Norris Elementary	Bakersfield
461	8,327	Hollister	Hollister
462	8,323	Mountain View Elementary	Ontario
463	8,318	Pleasant Valley	Camarillo
464	8,311	Natomas Unified	Sacramento
465	8,310	Yucaipa-Calimesa Joint Unified	Yucaipa
466	8,292	Wiseburn Elementary	Hawthorne
467	8,288	Tulare City	Tulare
468	8,276	Weaver Union	Merced
469	8,259	Cambrian	San Jose
470	8,255	Berryessa Union Elementary	San Jose
471	8,248	Exeter Union Elementary	Exeter
472	8,199	Dixon Unified	Dixon
473	8,142	Roseville City Elementary	Roseville
474	8,138	Escalon Unified	Escalon
475	8,136	Dry Creek Joint Elementary	Roseville
476	8,096	Alta Loma Elementary	Alta Loma
477	8,077	Orcutt Union Elementary	Orcutt
478	8,056	Antioch Unified	Antioch
479	8,055	Sylvan Union Elementary	Modesto
480	8,047	Eureka Union	Granite Bay
481	8,036	Newhall	Valencia
482	8,034	Brentwood Union Elementary	Brentwood
483	8,028	S San Francisco Unified	S San Francisco
484	8,027	Central Elementary	R Cucamonga
485	8,024	Oakley Union Elementary	Oakley
486	7,995	Chowchilla Elementary	Chowchilla
487	7,994	Ripon Unified	Ripon
488	7,993	Beaumont Unified	Beaumont
489	7,985	Temecula Valley Unified	Temecula
490	7,983	Huntington Bch City Elementary	Huntington Bch
491	7,943	Amador County Unified	Jackson
492	7,939	San Jacinto Unified	San Jacinto
493	7,899	Scotts Valley Unified	Scotts Valley
494	7,898	Templeton Unified	Templeton
495	7,864	Western Placer Unified	Lincoln
496	7,855	Victor Elementary	Victorville
497	7,854	Lemoore Union Elementary	Lemoore
498	7,839	Apple Valley Unified	Apple Valley
499	7,831	Westside Union Elementary	Quartz Hill
500	7,830	Capistrano Unified	SJ Capistrano
501	7,797	Menifee Union Elementary	Menifee
502	7,730	Fountain Valley Elementary	Fountain Valley
503	7,637	San Gabriel Unified	San Gabriel
504	7,587	Rescue Union Elementary	Rescue
505	7,561	Lowell Joint	Whittier
506	7,560	San Lorenzo Valley Unified	Ben Lomond
507	7,497	Hesperia Unified	Hesperia
508	7,454	Upland Unified	Upland
509	7,439	Loomis Union Elementary	Loomis
510	7,371	Jefferson Elementary	Tracy
511	6,673	West Covina Unified	West Covina
512	5,801	Hermosa Beach City Elementary	Hermosa Beach
513	5,594	Waterford Unified	Waterford
514	5,273	Armona Union Elementary	Armona
515	4,947	Lucerne Valley Unified	Lucerne Valley
516	4,177	Dehesa Elementary	El Cajon
517	3,244	Oro Grande Elementary	Oro Grande
518	1,391	Marcum-Illinois Union Elementary	East Nicolaus
519	909	Spencer Valley Elementary	Santa Ysabel
520	884	Gorman Elementary	Gorman
n/a	n/a	Sbc - Aspire Public Schools	Oakland
n/a	n/a	Sbc - High Tech High	San Diego
n/a	n/a	Lammersville Joint Unified	Mountain House
n/a	n/a	Modesto City Elementary	Modesto
n/a	n/a	Modesto City High	Modesto
n/a	n/a	Petaluma City Elementary	Petaluma
n/a	n/a	Petaluma Joint Union High	Petaluma
n/a	n/a	Santa Barbara Unified	Santa Barbara
n/a	n/a	Santa Cruz City Elementary	Soquel
n/a	n/a	Santa Cruz City High	Soquel
n/a	n/a	Santa Rosa Elementary	Santa Rosa
n/a	n/a	Santa Rosa High	Santa Rosa
n/a	n/a	Washington Unified	Fresno

Long-Term Debt per Student (end of FY)

Rank	Dollars	District Name	City
1	47,200	San Mateo Union High	San Mateo
2	45,147	Tamalpais Union High	Larkspur
3	44,569	Beverly Hills Unified	Beverly Hills
4	41,235	Hillsborough City Elementary	Hillsborough
5	39,598	Sequoia Union High	Redwood City
6	39,002	Menlo Park City Elementary	Atherton
7	33,765	Piedmont City Unified	Piedmont
8	32,445	Los Gatos Union Elementary	Los Gatos
9	32,356	Dublin Unified	Dublin
10	30,653	Santa Clara Unified	Santa Clara
11	29,751	Saratoga Union Elementary	Saratoga
12	29,282	San Rafael City High	San Rafael
13	27,530	San Ysidro Elementary	San Ysidro
14	27,423	West Contra Costa Unified	Richmond
15	26,371	Berkeley Unified	Berkeley
16	25,199	Tahoe-Truckee Joint Unified	Truckee
17	25,139	Wiseburn Elementary	Hawthorne
18	23,679	Pacific Grove Unified	Pacific Grove
19	23,623	Golden Valley Unified	Madera
20	23,020	Acalanes Union High	Lafayette
21	23,013	Carlsbad Unified	Carlsbad
22	22,469	Redondo Beach Unified	Redondo Beach
23	22,343	East Side Union High	San Jose
24	22,067	Campbell Union High	San Jose
25	22,027	Burlingame Elementary	Burlingame
26	21,206	Santa Monica-Malibu Unified	Santa Monica
27	20,790	Los Gatos-Saratoga Jt Union High	Los Gatos
28	20,651	Arcadia Unified	Arcadia
29	20,075	Palo Alto Unified	Palo Alto
30	19,728	Los Altos Elementary	Los Altos
31	19,708	Moreland Elementary	San Jose
32	19,538	Las Virgenes Unified	Calabasas
33	19,264	San Rafael City Elementary	San Rafael
34	19,234	Washington Unified	West Sacramento
35	19,178	Lake Tahoe Unified	S Lake Tahoe
36	19,136	San Jose Unified	San Jose
37	19,098	San Leandro Unified	San Leandro
38	19,070	Campbell Union	Campbell
39	19,043	Escondido Union High	Escondido
40	18,908	New Haven Unified	Union City
41	18,884	Healdsburg Unified	Healdsburg
42	18,854	Mill Valley Elementary	Mill Valley
43	18,839	Fremont Union High	Sunnyvale
44	18,802	Huntington Bch Union High	Huntington Bch
44	18,802	Mountain View Whisman	Mountain View
46	18,497	Grossmont Union High	La Mesa
47	18,413	Martinez Unified	Martinez
48	18,343	Auburn Union Elementary	Auburn
49	18,326	Pittsburg Unified	Pittsburg
50	18,311	Jefferson Union High	Daly City
51	18,145	Los Angeles Unified	Los Angeles
52	18,044	Sunnyvale	Sunnyvale
53	17,822	Carmel Unified	Carmel
54	16,954	San Carlos Elementary	San Carlos
55	16,913	El Segundo Unified	El Segundo
56	16,257	Mojave Unified	Mojave
57	16,220	Oakland Unified	Oakland
58	15,850	Natomas Unified	Sacramento
59	15,743	Western Placer Unified	Lincoln
60	15,608	Hanford Joint Union High	Hanford
61	15,541	Mountain View-Los Altos Union High	Mountain View
62	15,509	Rocklin Unified	Rocklin
63	15,462	Napa Valley Unified	Napa
64	15,233	Union Elementary	San Jose
65	14,916	Pasadena Unified	Pasadena
66	14,865	Monrovia Unified	Monrovia
67	14,787	Placentia-Yorba Linda Unified	Placentia
68	14,533	Centinela Valley Union High	Lawndale
69	14,364	Fort Bragg Unified	Fort Bragg
70	14,346	Live Oak Elementary	Santa Cruz
71	14,273	Palm Springs Unified	Palm Springs
72	14,202	Gilroy Unified	Gilroy
73	14,106	Denair Unified	Denair
74	13,459	Ross Valley Elementary	San Anselmo
75	13,428	El Monte Union High	El Monte
76	13,333	Piner-Olivet Union Elementary	Santa Rosa
77	13,207	Roseville Joint Union High	Roseville
78	13,164	Millbrae Elementary	Millbrae
79	13,119	Rosemead Elementary	Rosemead
80	13,060	River Delta Joint Unified	Rio Vista
81	13,043	San Marino Unified	San Marino
82	12,989	Delano Joint Union High	Delano
83	12,929	San Diego Unified	San Diego
84	12,710	Bellevue Union Elementary	Santa Rosa
85	12,703	South Monterey Co. Jt Union High	King City
86	12,689	Center Joint Unified	Antelope
87	12,666	Whittier Union High	Whittier
88	12,496	Cotati-Rohnert Park Unified	Rohnert Park
89	12,478	Galt Joint Union High	Galt
90	12,457	Folsom-Cordova Unified	Folsom
91	12,432	Calaveras Unified	San Andreas
92	12,308	Oro Grande Elementary	Oro Grande
93	12,128	Desert Sands Unified	La Quinta
94	12,039	El Monte City Elementary	El Monte
95	12,034	South Pasadena Unified	South Pasadena
96	11,986	Novato Unified	Novato
97	11,904	Belmont-Redwood Shores Elem.	Belmont
98	11,894	Duarte Unified	Duarte
99	11,806	Murrieta Valley Unified	Murrieta
100	11,686	Twin Rivers Unified	Mcclellan
101	11,634	Robla Elementary	Sacramento
102	11,632	Newport-Mesa Unified	Costa Mesa
103	11,610	Bonita Unified	San Dimas
104	11,595	Pacifica	Pacifica
105	11,517	Benicia Unified	Benicia
106	11,331	Willits Unified	Willits
107	11,328	Mt. Diablo Unified	Concord
108	11,313	San Francisco Unified	San Francisco
109	11,183	Santee Elementary	Santee
110	11,140	Alvord Unified	Riverside
111	11,102	San Bruno Park Elementary	San Bruno

Note: This section only includes districts with 1,500 or more students; All categories are ranked from high to low

Rank	Number	District Name	City
112	11,096	Morgan Hill Unified	Morgan Hill
113	11,065	Cypress Elementary	Cypress
114	11,055	Alameda City Unified	Alameda
115	11,005	Dixon Unified	Dixon
116	10,944	Banning Unified	Banning
117	10,943	Windsor Unified	Windsor
118	10,724	Davis Joint Unified	Davis
119	10,662	Oceanside Unified	Oceanside
120	10,520	Kern County Office of Education	Bakersfield
121	10,472	San Ramon Valley Unified	Danville
122	10,433	Newark Unified	Newark
123	10,424	Hemet Unified	Hemet
124	10,328	Laguna Beach Unified	Laguna Beach
125	10,250	Stockton Unified	Stockton
126	10,201	Eureka City Schools	Eureka
127	10,026	San Gabriel Unified	San Gabriel
128	9,869	Ukiah Unified	Ukiah
129	9,853	Kern Union High	Bakersfield
130	9,742	Oak Grove Elementary	San Jose
131	9,680	Placer Union High	Auburn
132	9,610	Rowland Unified	Rowland Heights
133	9,587	Acton-Agua Dulce Unified	Acton
134	9,533	Hayward Unified	Hayward
135	9,486	Oak Park Unified	Oak Park
136	9,478	Fowler Unified	Fowler
137	9,442	Bassett Unified	La Puente
138	9,410	Torrance Unified	Torrance
139	9,316	Westside Union Elementary	Quartz Hill
140	9,306	Walnut Creek Elementary	Walnut Creek
141	9,294	Castro Valley Unified	Castro Valley
142	9,218	Brea-Olinda Unified	Brea
143	9,212	Evergreen Elementary	San Jose
144	9,193	Poway Unified	San Diego
145	9,190	Bonsall Union Elementary	Bonsall
146	9,163	Gateway Unified	Redding
147	9,148	Coachella Valley Unified	Thermal
148	9,114	Beardsley Elementary	Bakersfield
149	9,068	San Jacinto Unified	San Jacinto
150	8,991	Rescue Union Elementary	Rescue
151	8,954	San Lorenzo Unified	San Lorenzo
152	8,931	San Lorenzo Valley Unified	Ben Lomond
153	8,927	Enterprise Elementary	Redding
154	8,833	Sweetwater Union High	Chula Vista
155	8,821	Central Unified	Fresno
156	8,810	Simi Valley Unified	Simi Valley
156	8,810	Wasco Union High	Wasco
158	8,785	El Dorado Union High	Placerville
159	8,773	Marysville Joint Unified	Marysville
160	8,754	Linden Unified	Linden
161	8,748	Rincon Valley Union Elementary	Santa Rosa
162	8,746	Azusa Unified	Azusa
163	8,689	Sonoma Valley Unified	Sonoma
164	8,678	Pomona Unified	Pomona
165	8,644	Sacramento City Unified	Sacramento
166	8,630	Sierra Sands Unified	Ridgecrest
167	8,614	Taft City	Taft
168	8,476	Manhattan Beach Unified	Manhattan Beach
169	8,360	Byron Union Elementary	Byron
170	8,357	San Mateo-Foster City	Foster City
171	8,351	Tulare Joint Union High	Tulare
172	8,333	Norwalk-La Mirada Unified	Norwalk
173	8,329	Scotts Valley Unified	Scotts Valley
174	8,300	Colton Joint Unified	Colton
175	8,287	Encinitas Union Elementary	Encinitas
176	8,278	Perris Union High	Perris
177	8,249	Garvey Elementary	Rosemead
178	8,222	John Swett Unified	Rodeo
179	8,204	Victor Valley Union High	Victorville
180	8,160	Inglewood Unified	Inglewood
181	8,142	Riverbank Unified	Riverbank
182	8,125	Alum Rock Union Elementary	San Jose
183	8,117	Merced Union High	Atwater
184	8,109	Liberty Union High	Brentwood
185	8,095	Middletown Unified	Middletown
186	8,093	Livermore Valley Joint Unified	Livermore
187	8,089	Buckeye Union Elementary	Shingle Springs
188	8,024	Vacaville Unified	Vacaville
189	8,011	William S. Hart Union High	Santa Clarita
190	7,996	Santa Maria Joint Union High	Santa Maria
191	7,984	Beaumont Unified	Beaumont
192	7,969	Chula Vista Elementary	Chula Vista
193	7,957	Franklin-Mckinley Elementary	San Jose
194	7,932	Alhambra Unified	Alhambra
195	7,930	Savanna Elementary	Anaheim
196	7,928	West Sonoma County Union High	Sebastopol
197	7,909	La Canada Unified	La Canada
198	7,897	Covina-Valley Unified	Covina
199	7,885	Soquel Union Elementary	Capitola
200	7,845	Anaheim City	Anaheim
201	7,843	Walnut Valley Unified	Walnut
202	7,833	Oxnard	Oxnard
203	7,824	Cajon Valley Union	El Cajon
204	7,810	Santa Rita Union Elementary	Salinas
205	7,716	Weaver Union	Merced
206	7,690	Glendora Unified	Glendora
207	7,646	Coronado Unified	Coronado
208	7,603	Cupertino Union	Cupertino
209	7,545	Saugus Union	Santa Clarita
210	7,512	Hawthorne	Hawthorne
211	7,431	Fruitvale Elementary	Bakersfield
212	7,396	Pleasanton Unified	Pleasanton
213	7,391	Southern Kern Unified	Rosamond
214	7,372	Oroville Union High	Oroville
215	7,357	Snowline Joint Unified	Phelan
216	7,284	Los Alamitos Unified	Los Alamitos
217	7,272	Newman-Crows Landing Unified	Newman
218	7,235	Albany City Unified	Albany
219	7,199	Victor Elementary	Victorville
220	7,195	North Monterey County Unified	Moss Landing
221	7,111	Richland Union Elementary	Shafter
222	7,086	Lakeside Union Elementary	Lakeside
223	6,970	Jefferson Elementary	Daly City
224	6,924	Long Beach Unified	Long Beach
225	6,843	Dry Creek Joint Elementary	Roseville
226	6,823	Vallejo City Unified	Vallejo
227	6,818	Moorpark Unified	Moorpark
228	6,796	Alisal Union	Salinas
229	6,791	Redwood City Elementary	Redwood City
230	6,780	Palos Verdes Peninsula Unified	Palos Vrds Est
231	6,764	Alpine Union Elementary	Alpine
232	6,691	Travis Unified	Fairfield
233	6,679	San Juan Unified	Carmichael
234	6,645	Santa Paula Union High	Santa Paula
235	6,619	Fallbrook Union High	Fallbrook
236	6,609	Baldwin Park Unified	Baldwin Park
236	6,609	Hughson Unified	Hughson
238	6,589	Santa Ana Unified	Santa Ana
239	6,586	Sulphur Springs Union	Canyon Country
240	6,562	Lindsay Unified	Lindsay
241	6,546	Del Mar Union Elementary	San Diego
242	6,543	Roseville City Elementary	Roseville
243	6,528	Huntington Bch City Elementary	Huntington Bch
244	6,526	Dinuba Unified	Dinuba
245	6,510	Claremont Unified	Claremont
246	6,505	Clovis Unified	Clovis
247	6,487	Brentwood Union Elementary	Brentwood
248	6,449	Fontana Unified	Fontana
249	6,396	Oxnard Union High	Oxnard
250	6,303	Little Lake City Elementary	Santa Fe Spgs
251	6,267	Fremont Unified	Fremont
252	6,254	Corona-Norco Unified	Norco
253	6,243	Lafayette Elementary	Lafayette
254	6,217	Val Verde Unified	Perris
255	6,176	Westminster Elementary	Westminster
256	6,163	Hermosa Beach City Elementary	Hermosa Beach
257	6,144	Konocti Unified	Lower Lake
258	6,095	El Rancho Unified	Pico Rivera
259	6,089	Yuba City Unified	Yuba City
260	6,088	Burbank Unified	Burbank
261	6,056	Lodi Unified	Lodi
262	6,019	Atascadero Unified	Atascadero
263	6,016	Orland Joint Unified	Orland
264	6,009	Fillmore Unified	Fillmore
265	5,973	Montebello Unified	Montebello
266	5,915	Delano Union Elementary	Delano
267	5,867	Shasta Union High	Redding
268	5,862	Carpinteria Unified	Carpinteria
269	5,815	Lincoln Unified	Stockton
270	5,695	Paramount Unified	Paramount
271	5,631	Upland Unified	Upland
272	5,627	Cambrian	San Jose
273	5,605	Menifee Union Elementary	Menifee
274	5,577	Orinda Union Elementary	Orinda
275	5,567	King City Union	King City
276	5,514	Ocean View	Oxnard
277	5,508	Tustin Unified	Tustin
278	5,497	Redlands Unified	Redlands
279	5,446	Fullerton Joint Union High	Fullerton
280	5,439	Chino Valley Unified	Chino
281	5,428	Goleta Union Elementary	Goleta
282	5,388	Pleasant Valley	Camarillo
283	5,377	Charter Oak Unified	Covina
284	5,373	Eastside Union Elementary	Lancaster
285	5,356	Vista Unified	Vista
286	5,328	Whittier City Elementary	Whittier
287	5,321	Mountain View Elementary	Ontario
288	5,257	Los Banos Unified	Los Banos
289	5,256	Rio Elementary	Oxnard
290	5,243	Old Adobe Union	Petaluma
291	5,205	Culver City Unified	Culver City
292	5,166	Moraga Elementary	Moraga
293	5,161	South Whittier Elementary	Whittier
294	5,157	Ceres Unified	Ceres
295	5,154	Fallbrook Union Elementary	Fallbrook
296	5,137	Pioneer Union Elementary	Hanford
297	5,112	Ventura County Office of Educ.	Camarillo
298	5,035	Coalinga-Huron Joint Unified	Coalinga
299	5,024	Kingsburg Elementary Charter	Kingsburg
300	5,017	Imperial Unified	Imperial
301	5,016	Glendale Unified	Glendale
302	5,007	Live Oak Unified	Live Oak
303	4,996	Lucia Mar Unified	Arroyo Grande
304	4,978	Northern Humboldt Union High	Mckinleyville
305	4,968	Oakley Union Elementary	Oakley
306	4,956	San Diego County Office of Educ.	San Diego
307	4,935	Hesperia Unified	Hesperia
308	4,888	Cucamonga Elementary	R Cucamonga
309	4,860	Dixie Elementary	San Rafael
310	4,787	Lakeport Unified	Lakeport
311	4,756	Berryessa Union Elementary	San Jose
312	4,691	Anaheim Union High	Anaheim
313	4,671	Sanger Unified	Sanger
314	4,655	Tracy Joint Unified	Tracy
315	4,647	Kings Canyon Joint Unified	Reedley
316	4,644	Milpitas Unified	Milpitas
317	4,603	Madera Unified	Madera
318	4,596	Castaic Union Elementary	Valencia
319	4,591	Hacienda La Puente Unified	City of Industry
320	4,576	Sylvan Union Elementary	Modesto
321	4,539	Holtville Unified	Holtville
322	4,537	Gustine Unified	Gustine
323	4,513	Lancaster Elementary	Lancaster
324	4,472	Palo Verde Unified	Blythe
325	4,467	Newhall	Valencia
326	4,439	San Bernardino City Unified	San Bernardino
327	4,400	Loomis Union Elementary	Loomis
328	4,355	Brawley Union High	Brawley
329	4,345	Cabrillo Unified	Half Moon Bay
330	4,280	Turlock Unified	Turlock
331	4,261	Adelanto Elementary	Adelanto
332	4,253	Saddleback Valley Unified	Mission Viejo
333	4,218	Calexico Unified	Calexico
334	4,217	Moreno Valley Unified	Moreno Valley
335	4,181	Chico Unified	Chico
336	4,178	Salinas Union High	Salinas
337	4,166	Black Oak Mine Unified	Georgetown
338	4,160	Ripon Unified	Ripon
339	4,154	Ramona City Unified	Ramona
340	4,150	Bishop Unified	Bishop
341	4,096	Redding Elementary	Redding
342	4,077	Wright Elementary	Santa Rosa
343	4,075	Woodland Joint Unified	Woodland
344	4,054	Salinas City Elementary	Salinas
345	4,051	Fairfield-Suisun Unified	Fairfield
346	4,020	Firebaugh-Las Deltas Joint Unified	Firebaugh
347	4,019	Ventura Unified	Ventura
348	3,997	Ojai Unified	Ojai
349	3,989	Tehachapi Unified	Tehachapi
350	3,988	Nevada Joint Union High	Grass Valley
351	3,984	Riverside Unified	Riverside
352	3,966	San Marcos Unified	San Marcos
353	3,964	Selma Unified	Selma
354	3,946	S San Francisco Unified	S San Francisco
355	3,944	Compton Unified	Compton
356	3,932	Standard Elementary	Bakersfield
357	3,814	Escondido Union	Escondido
358	3,770	Yosemite Unified	Oakhurst
359	3,743	Stanislaus Union Elementary	Modesto
360	3,680	Chaffey Joint Union High	Ontario
361	3,674	Fresno Unified	Fresno
362	3,589	Antelope Valley Union High	Lancaster
363	3,577	Red Bluff Joint Union High	Red Bluff
364	3,568	Central Union High	El Centro
365	3,545	Fullerton Elementary	Fullerton
366	3,514	Kerman Unified	Kerman

Note: This section only includes districts with 1,500 or more students; All categories are ranked from high to low

367	3,481	Palmdale Elementary	Palmdale
368	3,468	Rialto Unified	Rialto
369	3,451	Greenfield Union Elementary	Greenfield
370	3,445	Lawndale Elementary	Lawndale
371	3,435	Arvin Union Elementary	Arvin
372	3,434	Downey Unified	Downey
373	3,420	La Mesa-Spring Valley	La Mesa
374	3,366	Lemon Grove	Lemon Grove
375	3,338	Hueneme Elementary	Port Hueneme
376	3,337	Reef-Sunset Unified	Avenal
377	3,332	Jurupa Unified	Jurupa Valley
378	3,331	Temple City Unified	Temple City
379	3,305	Central Elementary	R Cucamonga
380	3,286	Lompoc Unified	Lompoc
381	3,261	Exeter Union Elementary	Exeter
382	3,248	Oakdale Joint Unified	Oakdale
383	3,215	Antioch Unified	Antioch
384	3,183	Gonzales Unified	Gonzales
385	3,144	ABC Unified	Cerritos
386	3,137	Winters Joint Unified	Winters
387	3,134	Monterey Peninsula Unified	Monterey
388	3,123	Paso Robles Joint Unified	Paso Robles
389	3,089	Morongo Unified	Twentynine Plms
390	3,074	Pajaro Valley Unified	Watsonville
391	3,068	Mt. Pleasant Elementary	San Jose
392	3,066	Escalon Unified	Escalon
393	3,060	Mcfarland Unified	Mcfarland
394	3,042	Manteca Unified	Manteca
395	2,992	East Whittier City Elementary	Whittier
396	2,982	Centralia Elementary	Buena Park
397	2,939	Conejo Valley Unified	Thousand Oaks
398	2,907	Lemoore Union High	Lemoore
399	2,887	Perris Elementary	Perris
400	2,793	Patterson Joint Unified	Patterson
401	2,767	Rim of the World Unified	Blue Jay
402	2,765	Alta Loma Elementary	Alta Loma
402	2,765	Los Angeles County Office of Educ.	Downey
404	2,761	Roseland Elementary	Santa Rosa
405	2,725	Ravenswood City Elementary	East Palo Alto
406	2,684	Orcutt Union Elementary	Orcutt
407	2,646	South Bay Union Elementary	Imperial Beach
408	2,643	Soledad Unified	Soledad
409	2,633	Greenfield Union	Bakersfield
410	2,593	Lucerne Valley Unified	Lucerne Valley
411	2,583	Lynwood Unified	Lynwood
412	2,572	Apple Valley Unified	Apple Valley
413	2,518	Amador County Unified	Jackson
414	2,506	Jefferson Elementary	Tracy
415	2,468	Santa Clara County Office of Educ.	San Jose
416	2,461	Buena Park Elementary	Buena Park
416	2,461	Santa Paula Elementary	Santa Paula
418	2,460	La Habra City Elementary	La Habra
419	2,439	Ontario-Montclair Elementary	Ontario
420	2,436	Salida Union Elementary	Salida
421	2,422	El Centro Elementary	El Centro
422	2,210	Oroville City Elementary	Oroville
423	2,173	Stanislaus County Office of Educ.	Modesto
424	2,171	West Covina Unified	West Covina
425	2,169	Galt Joint Union Elementary	Galt
426	2,093	Orange County Dept of Education	Costa Mesa
427	2,063	Panama-Buena Vista Union	Bakersfield
428	2,026	Atwater Elementary	Atwater
429	2,005	Nuview Union	Nuevo
430	2,002	Barstow Unified	Barstow
431	1,886	Dos Palos Oro Loma Joint Unified	Dos Palos
432	1,872	Porterville Unified	Porterville
433	1,861	Woodlake Union Elementary	Woodlake
434	1,791	Farmersville Unified	Farmersville
435	1,784	Parlier Unified	Parlier
436	1,769	Cutler-Orosi Joint Unified	Orosi
437	1,740	Fountain Valley Elementary	Fountain Valley
438	1,724	Wasco Union Elementary	Wasco
439	1,714	Eureka Union	Granite Bay
440	1,705	Norris Elementary	Bakersfield
441	1,677	Lake Elsinore Unified	Lake Elsinore
442	1,643	Riverdale Joint Unified	Riverdale
443	1,625	Orange Unified	Orange
444	1,610	Bakersfield City	Bakersfield
445	1,577	Livingston Union Elementary	Livingston
446	1,572	Earlimart Elementary	Earlimart
447	1,568	Lennox	Lennox
448	1,557	Hanford Elementary	Hanford
449	1,526	Santa Maria-Bonita	Santa Maria
450	1,523	Corning Union Elementary	Corning
450	1,523	Yucaipa-Calimesa Joint Unified	Yucaipa
452	1,519	Capistrano Unified	SJ Capistrano
453	1,505	Burton Elementary	Porterville
454	1,478	Fairfax Elementary	Bakersfield
455	1,416	Del Norte County Unified	Crescent City
456	1,399	Waterford Unified	Waterford
457	1,326	Mendota Unified	Mendota
458	1,319	Magnolia Elementary	Anaheim
459	1,312	Kelseyville Unified	Kelseyville
460	1,233	Lamont Elementary	Lamont
461	1,211	Delhi Unified	Delhi
462	1,185	San Dieguito Union High	Encinitas
463	1,182	Empire Union Elementary	Modesto
464	1,156	Muroc Joint Unified	North Edwards
465	1,131	Armona Union Elementary	Armona
466	1,130	Temecula Valley Unified	Temecula
467	950	Brawley Elementary	Brawley
468	926	Visalia Unified	Visalia
469	910	Mountain Empire Unified	Pine Valley
470	856	Riverside County Office of Educ.	Riverside
471	768	Bear Valley Unified	Big Bear Lake
472	696	Ocean View	Huntington Bch
473	690	Hollister	Hollister
474	685	Hilmar Unified	Hilmar
475	661	Bellflower Unified	Bellflower
476	504	Merced County Office of Education	Merced
477	451	Valley Center-Pauma Unified	Valley Center
478	395	Tulare City	Tulare
479	276	Paradise Unified	Paradise
480	133	Merced City Elementary	Merced
481	124	Rosedale Union Elementary	Bakersfield
482	65	Corcoran Joint Unified	Corcoran
483	0	Alameda County Office of Education	Hayward
483	0	Anderson Union High	Anderson
483	0	Central Union Elementary	Lemoore
483	0	Chowchilla Elementary	Chowchilla
483	0	Dehesa Elementary	El Cajon
483	0	Elk Grove Unified	Elk Grove
483	0	Etiwanda Elementary	Etiwanda
483	0	Fresno County Office of Education	Fresno
483	0	Garden Grove Unified	Garden Grove
483	0	Golden Plains Unified	San Joaquin
483	0	Gorman Elementary	Gorman
483	0	Grass Valley Elementary	Grass Valley
483	0	Gridley Unified	Gridley
483	0	Irvine Unified	Irvine
483	0	Julian Union Elementary	Julian
483	0	Keppel Union Elementary	Pearblossom
483	0	Lemoore Union Elementary	Lemoore
483	0	Los Nietos	Whittier
483	0	Lowell Joint	Whittier
483	0	Marcum-Illinois Union Elementary	East Nicolaus
483	0	Mariposa County Unified	Mariposa
483	0	Monterey County Office of Educ.	Salinas
483	0	Mountain View Elementary	El Monte
483	0	National Elementary	National City
483	0	Nevada County Office of Education	Nevada City
483	0	Red Bluff Union Elementary	Red Bluff
483	0	Romoland Elementary	Homeland
483	0	San Benito High	Hollister
483	0	San Bernardino Co. Office of Educ.	San Bernardino
483	0	San Joaquin County Office of Educ.	Stockton
483	0	San Luis Coastal Unified	San Luis Obispo
483	0	Sbc - Aspire Public Schools	Oakland
483	0	Sbc - High Tech High	San Diego
483	0	Silver Valley Unified	Yermo
483	0	Solana Beach Elementary	Solana Beach
483	0	Spencer Valley Elementary	Santa Ysabel
483	0	Templeton Unified	Templeton
483	0	Tulare County Office of Education	Visalia
483	0	Willows Unified	Willows
483	0	Winton Elementary	Winton
n/a	n/a	Lammersville Joint Unified	Mountain House
n/a	n/a	Modesto City Elementary	Modesto
n/a	n/a	Modesto City High	Modesto
n/a	n/a	Petaluma City Elementary	Petaluma
n/a	n/a	Petaluma Joint Union High	Petaluma
n/a	n/a	Santa Barbara Unified	Santa Barbara
n/a	n/a	Santa Cruz City Elementary	Soquel
n/a	n/a	Santa Cruz City High	Soquel
n/a	n/a	Santa Rosa Elementary	Santa Rosa
n/a	n/a	Santa Rosa High	Santa Rosa
n/a	n/a	Washington Unified	Fresno

Number of Diploma Recipients

Rank	Number	District Name	City
n/a	n/a	ABC Unified	Cerritos
n/a	n/a	Acalanes Union High	Lafayette
n/a	n/a	Acton-Agua Dulce Unified	Acton
n/a	n/a	Adelanto Elementary	Adelanto
n/a	n/a	Alameda City Unified	Alameda
n/a	n/a	Alameda County Office of Education	Hayward
n/a	n/a	Albany City Unified	Albany
n/a	n/a	Alhambra Unified	Alhambra
n/a	n/a	Alisal Union	Salinas
n/a	n/a	Alpine Union Elementary	Alpine
n/a	n/a	Alta Loma Elementary	Alta Loma
n/a	n/a	Alum Rock Union Elementary	San Jose
n/a	n/a	Alvord Unified	Riverside
n/a	n/a	Amador County Unified	Jackson
n/a	n/a	Anaheim City	Anaheim
n/a	n/a	Anaheim Union High	Anaheim
n/a	n/a	Anderson Union High	Anderson
n/a	n/a	Antelope Valley Union High	Lancaster
n/a	n/a	Antioch Unified	Antioch
n/a	n/a	Apple Valley Unified	Apple Valley
n/a	n/a	Arcadia Unified	Arcadia
n/a	n/a	Armona Union Elementary	Armona
n/a	n/a	Arvin Union Elementary	Arvin
n/a	n/a	Atascadero Unified	Atascadero
n/a	n/a	Atwater Elementary	Atwater
n/a	n/a	Auburn Union Elementary	Auburn
n/a	n/a	Azusa Unified	Azusa
n/a	n/a	Bakersfield City	Bakersfield
n/a	n/a	Baldwin Park Unified	Baldwin Park
n/a	n/a	Banning Unified	Banning
n/a	n/a	Barstow Unified	Barstow
n/a	n/a	Bassett Unified	La Puente
n/a	n/a	Bear Valley Unified	Big Bear Lake
n/a	n/a	Beardsley Elementary	Bakersfield
n/a	n/a	Beaumont Unified	Beaumont
n/a	n/a	Bellevue Union Elementary	Santa Rosa
n/a	n/a	Bellflower Unified	Bellflower
n/a	n/a	Belmont-Redwood Shores Elem.	Belmont
n/a	n/a	Benicia Unified	Benicia
n/a	n/a	Berkeley Unified	Berkeley
n/a	n/a	Berryessa Union Elementary	San Jose
n/a	n/a	Beverly Hills Unified	Beverly Hills
n/a	n/a	Bishop Unified	Bishop
n/a	n/a	Black Oak Mine Unified	Georgetown
n/a	n/a	Bonita Unified	San Dimas
n/a	n/a	Bonsall Union Elementary	Bonsall
n/a	n/a	Brawley Elementary	Brawley
n/a	n/a	Brawley Union High	Brawley
n/a	n/a	Brea-Olinda Unified	Brea
n/a	n/a	Brentwood Union Elementary	Brentwood
n/a	n/a	Buckeye Union Elementary	Shingle Springs
n/a	n/a	Buena Park Elementary	Buena Park
n/a	n/a	Burbank Unified	Burbank
n/a	n/a	Burlingame Elementary	Burlingame
n/a	n/a	Burton Elementary	Porterville
n/a	n/a	Byron Union Elementary	Byron
n/a	n/a	Cabrillo Unified	Half Moon Bay
n/a	n/a	Cajon Valley Union	El Cajon
n/a	n/a	Calaveras Unified	San Andreas
n/a	n/a	Calexico Unified	Calexico
n/a	n/a	Cambrian	San Jose
n/a	n/a	Campbell Union	Campbell
n/a	n/a	Campbell Union High	San Jose
n/a	n/a	Capistrano Unified	SJ Capistrano
n/a	n/a	Carlsbad Unified	Carlsbad
n/a	n/a	Carmel Unified	Carmel
n/a	n/a	Carpinteria Unified	Carpinteria
n/a	n/a	Castaic Union Elementary	Valencia
n/a	n/a	Castro Valley Unified	Castro Valley
n/a	n/a	Center Joint Unified	Antelope
n/a	n/a	Centinela Valley Union High	Lawndale
n/a	n/a	Central Elementary	R Cucamonga
n/a	n/a	Central Unified	Fresno
n/a	n/a	Central Union Elementary	Lemoore
n/a	n/a	Central Union High	El Centro
n/a	n/a	Centralia Elementary	Buena Park
n/a	n/a	Ceres Unified	Ceres
n/a	n/a	Chaffey Joint Union High	Ontario
n/a	n/a	Charter Oak Unified	Covina
n/a	n/a	Chico Unified	Chico
n/a	n/a	Chino Valley Unified	Chino
n/a	n/a	Chowchilla Elementary	Chowchilla

Note: This section only includes districts with 1,500 or more students; All categories are ranked from high to low

n/a	n/a	Chula Vista Elementary	Chula Vista
n/a	n/a	Claremont Unified	Claremont
n/a	n/a	Clovis Unified	Clovis
n/a	n/a	Coachella Valley Unified	Thermal
n/a	n/a	Coalinga-Huron Joint Unified	Coalinga
n/a	n/a	Colton Joint Unified	Colton
n/a	n/a	Compton Unified	Compton
n/a	n/a	Conejo Valley Unified	Thousand Oaks
n/a	n/a	Corcoran Joint Unified	Corcoran
n/a	n/a	Corning Union Elementary	Corning
n/a	n/a	Corona-Norco Unified	Norco
n/a	n/a	Coronado Unified	Coronado
n/a	n/a	Cotati-Rohnert Park Unified	Rohnert Park
n/a	n/a	Covina-Valley Unified	Covina
n/a	n/a	Cucamonga Elementary	R Cucamonga
n/a	n/a	Culver City Unified	Culver City
n/a	n/a	Cupertino Union	Cupertino
n/a	n/a	Cutler-Orosi Joint Unified	Orosi
n/a	n/a	Cypress Elementary	Cypress
n/a	n/a	Davis Joint Unified	Davis
n/a	n/a	Dehesa Elementary	El Cajon
n/a	n/a	Del Mar Union Elementary	San Diego
n/a	n/a	Del Norte County Unified	Crescent City
n/a	n/a	Delano Joint Union High	Delano
n/a	n/a	Delano Union Elementary	Delano
n/a	n/a	Delhi Unified	Delhi
n/a	n/a	Denair Unified	Denair
n/a	n/a	Desert Sands Unified	La Quinta
n/a	n/a	Dinuba Unified	Dinuba
n/a	n/a	Dixie Elementary	San Rafael
n/a	n/a	Dixon Unified	Dixon
n/a	n/a	Dos Palos Oro Loma Joint Unified	Dos Palos
n/a	n/a	Downey Unified	Downey
n/a	n/a	Dry Creek Joint Elementary	Roseville
n/a	n/a	Duarte Unified	Duarte
n/a	n/a	Dublin Unified	Dublin
n/a	n/a	Earlimart Elementary	Earlimart
n/a	n/a	East Side Union High	San Jose
n/a	n/a	East Whittier City Elementary	Whittier
n/a	n/a	Eastside Union Elementary	Lancaster
n/a	n/a	El Centro Elementary	El Centro
n/a	n/a	El Dorado Union High	Placerville
n/a	n/a	El Monte City Elementary	El Monte
n/a	n/a	El Monte Union High	El Monte
n/a	n/a	El Rancho Unified	Pico Rivera
n/a	n/a	El Segundo Unified	El Segundo
n/a	n/a	Elk Grove Unified	Elk Grove
n/a	n/a	Empire Union Elementary	Modesto
n/a	n/a	Encinitas Union Elementary	Encinitas
n/a	n/a	Enterprise Elementary	Redding
n/a	n/a	Escalon Unified	Escalon
n/a	n/a	Escondido Union	Escondido
n/a	n/a	Escondido Union High	Escondido
n/a	n/a	Etiwanda Elementary	Etiwanda
n/a	n/a	Eureka City Schools	Eureka
n/a	n/a	Eureka Union	Granite Bay
n/a	n/a	Evergreen Elementary	San Jose
n/a	n/a	Exeter Union Elementary	Exeter
n/a	n/a	Fairfax Elementary	Bakersfield
n/a	n/a	Fairfield-Suisun Unified	Fairfield
n/a	n/a	Fallbrook Union Elementary	Fallbrook
n/a	n/a	Fallbrook Union High	Fallbrook
n/a	n/a	Farmersville Unified	Farmersville
n/a	n/a	Fillmore Unified	Fillmore
n/a	n/a	Firebaugh-Las Deltas Joint Unified	Firebaugh
n/a	n/a	Folsom-Cordova Unified	Folsom
n/a	n/a	Fontana Unified	Fontana
n/a	n/a	Fort Bragg Unified	Fort Bragg
n/a	n/a	Fountain Valley Elementary	Fountain Valley
n/a	n/a	Fowler Unified	Fowler
n/a	n/a	Franklin-Mckinley Elementary	San Jose
n/a	n/a	Fremont Unified	Fremont
n/a	n/a	Fremont Union High	Sunnyvale
n/a	n/a	Fresno County Office of Education	Fresno
n/a	n/a	Fresno Unified	Fresno
n/a	n/a	Fruitvale Elementary	Bakersfield
n/a	n/a	Fullerton Elementary	Fullerton
n/a	n/a	Fullerton Joint Union High	Fullerton
n/a	n/a	Galt Joint Union Elementary	Galt
n/a	n/a	Galt Joint Union High	Galt
n/a	n/a	Garden Grove Unified	Garden Grove
n/a	n/a	Garvey Elementary	Rosemead
n/a	n/a	Gateway Unified	Redding
n/a	n/a	Gilroy Unified	Gilroy
n/a	n/a	Glendale Unified	Glendale
n/a	n/a	Glendora Unified	Glendora
n/a	n/a	Golden Plains Unified	San Joaquin
n/a	n/a	Golden Valley Unified	Madera
n/a	n/a	Goleta Union Elementary	Goleta
n/a	n/a	Gonzales Unified	Gonzales
n/a	n/a	Gorman Elementary	Gorman
n/a	n/a	Grass Valley Elementary	Grass Valley
n/a	n/a	Greenfield Union	Bakersfield
n/a	n/a	Greenfield Union Elementary	Greenfield
n/a	n/a	Gridley Unified	Gridley
n/a	n/a	Grossmont Union High	La Mesa
n/a	n/a	Gustine Unified	Gustine
n/a	n/a	Hacienda La Puente Unified	City of Industry
n/a	n/a	Hanford Elementary	Hanford
n/a	n/a	Hanford Joint Union High	Hanford
n/a	n/a	Hawthorne	Hawthorne
n/a	n/a	Hayward Unified	Hayward
n/a	n/a	Healdsburg Unified	Healdsburg
n/a	n/a	Hemet Unified	Hemet
n/a	n/a	Hermosa Beach City Elementary	Hermosa Beach
n/a	n/a	Hesperia Unified	Hesperia
n/a	n/a	Hillsborough City Elementary	Hillsborough
n/a	n/a	Hilmar Unified	Hilmar
n/a	n/a	Hollister	Hollister
n/a	n/a	Holtville Unified	Holtville
n/a	n/a	Hueneme Elementary	Port Hueneme
n/a	n/a	Hughson Unified	Hughson
n/a	n/a	Huntington Bch City Elementary	Huntington Bch
n/a	n/a	Huntington Bch Union High	Huntington Bch
n/a	n/a	Imperial Unified	Imperial
n/a	n/a	Inglewood Unified	Inglewood
n/a	n/a	Irvine Unified	Irvine
n/a	n/a	Jefferson Elementary	Tracy
n/a	n/a	Jefferson Elementary	Daly City
n/a	n/a	Jefferson Union High	Daly City
n/a	n/a	John Swett Unified	Rodeo
n/a	n/a	Julian Union Elementary	Julian
n/a	n/a	Jurupa Unified	Jurupa Valley
n/a	n/a	Kelseyville Unified	Kelseyville
n/a	n/a	Keppel Union Elementary	Pearblossom
n/a	n/a	Kerman Unified	Kerman
n/a	n/a	Kern County Office of Education	Bakersfield
n/a	n/a	Kern Union High	Bakersfield
n/a	n/a	King City Union	King City
n/a	n/a	Kings Canyon Joint Unified	Reedley
n/a	n/a	Kingsburg Elementary Charter	Kingsburg
n/a	n/a	Konocti Unified	Lower Lake
n/a	n/a	La Canada Unified	La Canada
n/a	n/a	La Habra City Elementary	La Habra
n/a	n/a	La Mesa-Spring Valley	La Mesa
n/a	n/a	Lafayette Elementary	Lafayette
n/a	n/a	Laguna Beach Unified	Laguna Beach
n/a	n/a	Lake Elsinore Unified	Lake Elsinore
n/a	n/a	Lake Tahoe Unified	S Lake Tahoe
n/a	n/a	Lakeport Unified	Lakeport
n/a	n/a	Lakeside Union Elementary	Lakeside
n/a	n/a	Lammersville Joint Unified	Mountain House
n/a	n/a	Lamont Elementary	Lamont
n/a	n/a	Lancaster Elementary	Lancaster
n/a	n/a	Las Virgenes Unified	Calabasas
n/a	n/a	Lawndale Elementary	Lawndale
n/a	n/a	Lemon Grove	Lemon Grove
n/a	n/a	Lemoore Union Elementary	Lemoore
n/a	n/a	Lemoore Union High	Lemoore
n/a	n/a	Lennox	Lennox
n/a	n/a	Liberty Union High	Brentwood
n/a	n/a	Lincoln Unified	Stockton
n/a	n/a	Linden Unified	Linden
n/a	n/a	Lindsay Unified	Lindsay
n/a	n/a	Little Lake City Elementary	Santa Fe Spgs
n/a	n/a	Live Oak Elementary	Santa Cruz
n/a	n/a	Live Oak Unified	Live Oak
n/a	n/a	Livermore Valley Joint Unified	Livermore
n/a	n/a	Livingston Union Elementary	Livingston
n/a	n/a	Lodi Unified	Lodi
n/a	n/a	Lompoc Unified	Lompoc
n/a	n/a	Long Beach Unified	Long Beach
n/a	n/a	Loomis Union Elementary	Loomis
n/a	n/a	Los Alamitos Unified	Los Alamitos
n/a	n/a	Los Altos Elementary	Los Altos
n/a	n/a	Los Angeles County Office of Educ.	Downey
n/a	n/a	Los Angeles Unified	Los Angeles
n/a	n/a	Los Banos Unified	Los Banos
n/a	n/a	Los Gatos Union Elementary	Los Gatos
n/a	n/a	Los Gatos-Saratoga Jt Union High	Los Gatos
n/a	n/a	Los Nietos	Whittier
n/a	n/a	Lowell Joint	Whittier
n/a	n/a	Lucerne Valley Unified	Lucerne Valley
n/a	n/a	Lucia Mar Unified	Arroyo Grande
n/a	n/a	Lynwood Unified	Lynwood
n/a	n/a	Madera Unified	Madera
n/a	n/a	Magnolia Elementary	Anaheim
n/a	n/a	Manhattan Beach Unified	Manhattan Beach
n/a	n/a	Manteca Unified	Manteca
n/a	n/a	Marcum-Illinois Union Elementary	East Nicolaus
n/a	n/a	Mariposa County Unified	Mariposa
n/a	n/a	Martinez Unified	Martinez
n/a	n/a	Marysville Joint Unified	Marysville
n/a	n/a	Mcfarland Unified	Mcfarland
n/a	n/a	Mendota Unified	Mendota
n/a	n/a	Menifee Union Elementary	Menifee
n/a	n/a	Menlo Park City Elementary	Atherton
n/a	n/a	Merced City Elementary	Merced
n/a	n/a	Merced County Office of Education	Merced
n/a	n/a	Merced Union High	Atwater
n/a	n/a	Middletown Unified	Middletown
n/a	n/a	Mill Valley Elementary	Mill Valley
n/a	n/a	Millbrae Elementary	Millbrae
n/a	n/a	Milpitas Unified	Milpitas
n/a	n/a	Modesto City Elementary	Modesto
n/a	n/a	Modesto City High	Modesto
n/a	n/a	Mojave Unified	Mojave
n/a	n/a	Monrovia Unified	Monrovia
n/a	n/a	Montebello Unified	Montebello
n/a	n/a	Monterey County Office of Educ.	Salinas
n/a	n/a	Monterey Peninsula Unified	Monterey
n/a	n/a	Moorpark Unified	Moorpark
n/a	n/a	Moraga Elementary	Moraga
n/a	n/a	Moreland Elementary	San Jose
n/a	n/a	Moreno Valley Unified	Moreno Valley
n/a	n/a	Morgan Hill Unified	Morgan Hill
n/a	n/a	Morongo Unified	Twentynine Plms
n/a	n/a	Mountain Empire Unified	Pine Valley
n/a	n/a	Mountain View Elementary	Ontario
n/a	n/a	Mountain View Elementary	El Monte
n/a	n/a	Mountain View Whisman	Mountain View
n/a	n/a	Mountain View-Los Altos Union High	Mountain View
n/a	n/a	Mt. Diablo Unified	Concord
n/a	n/a	Mt. Pleasant Elementary	San Jose
n/a	n/a	Muroc Joint Unified	North Edwards
n/a	n/a	Murrieta Valley Unified	Murrieta
n/a	n/a	Napa Valley Unified	Napa
n/a	n/a	National Elementary	National City
n/a	n/a	Natomas Unified	Sacramento
n/a	n/a	Nevada County Office of Education	Nevada City
n/a	n/a	Nevada Joint Union High	Grass Valley
n/a	n/a	New Haven Unified	Union City
n/a	n/a	Newark Unified	Newark
n/a	n/a	Newhall	Valencia
n/a	n/a	Newman-Crows Landing Unified	Newman
n/a	n/a	Newport-Mesa Unified	Costa Mesa
n/a	n/a	Norris Elementary	Bakersfield
n/a	n/a	North Monterey County Unified	Moss Landing
n/a	n/a	Northern Humboldt Union High	Mckinleyville
n/a	n/a	Norwalk-La Mirada Unified	Norwalk
n/a	n/a	Novato Unified	Novato
n/a	n/a	Nuview Union	Nuevo
n/a	n/a	Oak Grove Elementary	San Jose
n/a	n/a	Oak Park Unified	Oak Park
n/a	n/a	Oakdale Joint Unified	Oakdale
n/a	n/a	Oakland Unified	Oakland
n/a	n/a	Oakley Union Elementary	Oakley
n/a	n/a	Ocean View	Huntington Bch
n/a	n/a	Ocean View	Oxnard
n/a	n/a	Oceanside Unified	Oceanside
n/a	n/a	Ojai Unified	Ojai
n/a	n/a	Old Adobe Union	Petaluma
n/a	n/a	Ontario-Montclair Elementary	Ontario
n/a	n/a	Orange County Dept of Education	Costa Mesa
n/a	n/a	Orange Unified	Orange
n/a	n/a	Orcutt Union Elementary	Orcutt
n/a	n/a	Orinda Union Elementary	Orinda
n/a	n/a	Orland Joint Unified	Orland
n/a	n/a	Oro Grande Elementary	Oro Grande
n/a	n/a	Oroville City Elementary	Oroville
n/a	n/a	Oroville Union High	Oroville
n/a	n/a	Oxnard	Oxnard
n/a	n/a	Oxnard Union High	Oxnard
n/a	n/a	Pacific Grove Unified	Pacific Grove
n/a	n/a	Pacifica	Pacifica

Note: This section only includes districts with 1,500 or more students; All categories are ranked from high to low

n/a	n/a	Pajaro Valley Unified	Watsonville
n/a	n/a	Palm Springs Unified	Palm Springs
n/a	n/a	Palmdale Elementary	Palmdale
n/a	n/a	Palo Alto Unified	Palo Alto
n/a	n/a	Palo Verde Unified	Blythe
n/a	n/a	Palos Verdes Peninsula Unified	Palos Vrds Est
n/a	n/a	Panama-Buena Vista Union	Bakersfield
n/a	n/a	Paradise Unified	Paradise
n/a	n/a	Paramount Unified	Paramount
n/a	n/a	Parlier Unified	Parlier
n/a	n/a	Pasadena Unified	Pasadena
n/a	n/a	Paso Robles Joint Unified	Paso Robles
n/a	n/a	Patterson Joint Unified	Patterson
n/a	n/a	Perris Elementary	Perris
n/a	n/a	Perris Union High	Perris
n/a	n/a	Petaluma City Elementary	Petaluma
n/a	n/a	Petaluma Joint Union High	Petaluma
n/a	n/a	Piedmont City Unified	Piedmont
n/a	n/a	Piner-Olivet Union Elementary	Santa Rosa
n/a	n/a	Pioneer Union Elementary	Hanford
n/a	n/a	Pittsburg Unified	Pittsburg
n/a	n/a	Placentia-Yorba Linda Unified	Placentia
n/a	n/a	Placer Union High	Auburn
n/a	n/a	Pleasant Valley	Camarillo
n/a	n/a	Pleasanton Unified	Pleasanton
n/a	n/a	Pomona Unified	Pomona
n/a	n/a	Porterville Unified	Porterville
n/a	n/a	Poway Unified	San Diego
n/a	n/a	Ramona City Unified	Ramona
n/a	n/a	Ravenswood City Elementary	East Palo Alto
n/a	n/a	Red Bluff Joint Union High	Red Bluff
n/a	n/a	Red Bluff Union Elementary	Red Bluff
n/a	n/a	Redding Elementary	Redding
n/a	n/a	Redlands Unified	Redlands
n/a	n/a	Redondo Beach Unified	Redondo Beach
n/a	n/a	Redwood City Elementary	Redwood City
n/a	n/a	Reef-Sunset Unified	Avenal
n/a	n/a	Rescue Union Elementary	Rescue
n/a	n/a	Rialto Unified	Rialto
n/a	n/a	Richland Union Elementary	Shafter
n/a	n/a	Rim of the World Unified	Blue Jay
n/a	n/a	Rincon Valley Union Elementary	Santa Rosa
n/a	n/a	Rio Elementary	Oxnard
n/a	n/a	Ripon Unified	Ripon
n/a	n/a	River Delta Joint Unified	Rio Vista
n/a	n/a	Riverbank Unified	Riverbank
n/a	n/a	Riverdale Joint Unified	Riverdale
n/a	n/a	Riverside County Office of Educ.	Riverside
n/a	n/a	Riverside Unified	Riverside
n/a	n/a	Robla Elementary	Sacramento
n/a	n/a	Rocklin Unified	Rocklin
n/a	n/a	Romoland Elementary	Homeland
n/a	n/a	Rosedale Union Elementary	Bakersfield
n/a	n/a	Roseland Elementary	Santa Rosa
n/a	n/a	Rosemead Elementary	Rosemead
n/a	n/a	Roseville City Elementary	Roseville
n/a	n/a	Roseville Joint Union High	Roseville
n/a	n/a	Ross Valley Elementary	San Anselmo
n/a	n/a	Rowland Unified	Rowland Heights
n/a	n/a	Sacramento City Unified	Sacramento
n/a	n/a	Saddleback Valley Unified	Mission Viejo
n/a	n/a	Salida Union Elementary	Salida
n/a	n/a	Salinas City Elementary	Salinas
n/a	n/a	Salinas Union High	Salinas
n/a	n/a	San Benito High	Hollister
n/a	n/a	San Bernardino City Unified	San Bernardino
n/a	n/a	San Bernardino Co. Office of Educ.	San Bernardino
n/a	n/a	San Bruno Park Elementary	San Bruno
n/a	n/a	San Carlos Elementary	San Carlos
n/a	n/a	San Diego County Office of Educ.	San Diego
n/a	n/a	San Diego Unified	San Diego
n/a	n/a	San Dieguito Union High	Encinitas
n/a	n/a	San Francisco Unified	San Francisco
n/a	n/a	San Gabriel Unified	San Gabriel
n/a	n/a	San Jacinto Unified	San Jacinto
n/a	n/a	San Joaquin County Office of Educ.	Stockton
n/a	n/a	San Jose Unified	San Jose
n/a	n/a	San Juan Unified	Carmichael
n/a	n/a	San Leandro Unified	San Leandro
n/a	n/a	San Lorenzo Unified	San Lorenzo
n/a	n/a	San Lorenzo Valley Unified	Ben Lomond
n/a	n/a	San Luis Coastal Unified	San Luis Obispo
n/a	n/a	San Marcos Unified	San Marcos
n/a	n/a	San Marino Unified	San Marino
n/a	n/a	San Mateo Union High	San Mateo
n/a	n/a	San Mateo-Foster City	Foster City
n/a	n/a	San Rafael City Elementary	San Rafael
n/a	n/a	San Rafael City High	San Rafael
n/a	n/a	San Ramon Valley Unified	Danville
n/a	n/a	San Ysidro Elementary	San Ysidro
n/a	n/a	Sanger Unified	Sanger
n/a	n/a	Santa Ana Unified	Santa Ana
n/a	n/a	Santa Barbara Unified	Santa Barbara
n/a	n/a	Santa Clara County Office of Educ.	San Jose
n/a	n/a	Santa Clara Unified	Santa Clara
n/a	n/a	Santa Cruz City Elementary	Soquel
n/a	n/a	Santa Cruz City High	Soquel
n/a	n/a	Santa Maria Joint Union High	Santa Maria
n/a	n/a	Santa Maria-Bonita	Santa Maria
n/a	n/a	Santa Monica-Malibu Unified	Santa Monica
n/a	n/a	Santa Paula Elementary	Santa Paula
n/a	n/a	Santa Paula Union High	Santa Paula
n/a	n/a	Santa Rita Union Elementary	Salinas
n/a	n/a	Santa Rosa Elementary	Santa Rosa
n/a	n/a	Santa Rosa High	Santa Rosa
n/a	n/a	Santee Elementary	Santee
n/a	n/a	Saratoga Union Elementary	Saratoga
n/a	n/a	Saugus Union	Santa Clarita
n/a	n/a	Savanna Elementary	Anaheim
n/a	n/a	Sbc - Aspire Public Schools	Oakland
n/a	n/a	Sbc - High Tech High	San Diego
n/a	n/a	Scotts Valley Unified	Scotts Valley
n/a	n/a	Selma Unified	Selma
n/a	n/a	Sequoia Union High	Redwood City
n/a	n/a	Shasta Union High	Redding
n/a	n/a	Sierra Sands Unified	Ridgecrest
n/a	n/a	Silver Valley Unified	Yermo
n/a	n/a	Simi Valley Unified	Simi Valley
n/a	n/a	Snowline Joint Unified	Phelan
n/a	n/a	Solana Beach Elementary	Solana Beach
n/a	n/a	Soledad Unified	Soledad
n/a	n/a	Sonoma Valley Unified	Sonoma
n/a	n/a	Soquel Union Elementary	Capitola
n/a	n/a	South Bay Union Elementary	Imperial Beach
n/a	n/a	South Monterey Co. Jt Union High	King City
n/a	n/a	South Pasadena Unified	South Pasadena
n/a	n/a	S San Francisco Unified	S San Francisco
n/a	n/a	South Whittier Elementary	Whittier
n/a	n/a	Southern Kern Unified	Rosamond
n/a	n/a	Spencer Valley Elementary	Santa Ysabel
n/a	n/a	Standard Elementary	Bakersfield
n/a	n/a	Stanislaus County Office of Educ.	Modesto
n/a	n/a	Stanislaus Union Elementary	Modesto
n/a	n/a	Stockton Unified	Stockton
n/a	n/a	Sulphur Springs Union	Canyon Country
n/a	n/a	Sunnyvale	Sunnyvale
n/a	n/a	Sweetwater Union High	Chula Vista
n/a	n/a	Sylvan Union Elementary	Modesto
n/a	n/a	Taft City	Taft
n/a	n/a	Tahoe-Truckee Joint Unified	Truckee
n/a	n/a	Tamalpais Union High	Larkspur
n/a	n/a	Tehachapi Unified	Tehachapi
n/a	n/a	Temecula Valley Unified	Temecula
n/a	n/a	Temple City Unified	Temple City
n/a	n/a	Templeton Unified	Templeton
n/a	n/a	Torrance Unified	Torrance
n/a	n/a	Tracy Joint Unified	Tracy
n/a	n/a	Travis Unified	Fairfield
n/a	n/a	Tulare City	Tulare
n/a	n/a	Tulare County Office of Education	Visalia
n/a	n/a	Tulare Joint Union High	Tulare
n/a	n/a	Turlock Unified	Turlock
n/a	n/a	Tustin Unified	Tustin
n/a	n/a	Twin Rivers Unified	Mcclellan
n/a	n/a	Ukiah Unified	Ukiah
n/a	n/a	Union Elementary	San Jose
n/a	n/a	Upland Unified	Upland
n/a	n/a	Vacaville Unified	Vacaville
n/a	n/a	Val Verde Unified	Perris
n/a	n/a	Vallejo City Unified	Vallejo
n/a	n/a	Valley Center-Pauma Unified	Valley Center
n/a	n/a	Ventura County Office of Educ.	Camarillo
n/a	n/a	Ventura Unified	Ventura
n/a	n/a	Victor Elementary	Victorville
n/a	n/a	Victor Valley Union High	Victorville
n/a	n/a	Visalia Unified	Visalia
n/a	n/a	Vista Unified	Vista
n/a	n/a	Walnut Creek Elementary	Walnut Creek
n/a	n/a	Walnut Valley Unified	Walnut
n/a	n/a	Wasco Union Elementary	Wasco
n/a	n/a	Wasco Union High	Wasco
n/a	n/a	Washington Unified	West Sacramento
n/a	n/a	Washington Unified	Fresno
n/a	n/a	Waterford Unified	Waterford
n/a	n/a	Weaver Union	Merced
n/a	n/a	West Contra Costa Unified	Richmond
n/a	n/a	West Covina Unified	West Covina
n/a	n/a	West Sonoma County Union High	Sebastopol
n/a	n/a	Western Placer Unified	Lincoln
n/a	n/a	Westminster Elementary	Westminster
n/a	n/a	Westside Union Elementary	Quartz Hill
n/a	n/a	Whittier City Elementary	Whittier
n/a	n/a	Whittier Union High	Whittier
n/a	n/a	William S. Hart Union High	Santa Clarita
n/a	n/a	Willits Unified	Willits
n/a	n/a	Willows Unified	Willows
n/a	n/a	Windsor Unified	Windsor
n/a	n/a	Winters Joint Unified	Winters
n/a	n/a	Winton Elementary	Winton
n/a	n/a	Wiseburn Elementary	Hawthorne
n/a	n/a	Woodlake Union Elementary	Woodlake
n/a	n/a	Woodland Joint Unified	Woodland
n/a	n/a	Wright Elementary	Santa Rosa
n/a	n/a	Yosemite Unified	Oakhurst
n/a	n/a	Yuba City Unified	Yuba City
n/a	n/a	Yucaipa-Calimesa Joint Unified	Yucaipa

High School Drop-out Rate

Rank	Percent	District Name	City
n/a	n/a	ABC Unified	Cerritos
n/a	n/a	Acalanes Union High	Lafayette
n/a	n/a	Acton-Agua Dulce Unified	Acton
n/a	n/a	Alameda City Unified	Alameda
n/a	n/a	Alameda County Office of Education	Hayward
n/a	n/a	Albany City Unified	Albany
n/a	n/a	Alhambra Unified	Alhambra
n/a	n/a	Alvord Unified	Riverside
n/a	n/a	Amador County Unified	Jackson
n/a	n/a	Anaheim Union High	Anaheim
n/a	n/a	Anderson Union High	Anderson
n/a	n/a	Antelope Valley Union High	Lancaster
n/a	n/a	Antioch Unified	Antioch
n/a	n/a	Apple Valley Unified	Apple Valley
n/a	n/a	Arcadia Unified	Arcadia
n/a	n/a	Armona Union Elementary	Armona
n/a	n/a	Atascadero Unified	Atascadero
n/a	n/a	Azusa Unified	Azusa
n/a	n/a	Baldwin Park Unified	Baldwin Park
n/a	n/a	Banning Unified	Banning
n/a	n/a	Barstow Unified	Barstow
n/a	n/a	Bassett Unified	La Puente
n/a	n/a	Bear Valley Unified	Big Bear Lake
n/a	n/a	Beaumont Unified	Beaumont
n/a	n/a	Bellflower Unified	Bellflower
n/a	n/a	Benicia Unified	Benicia
n/a	n/a	Berkeley Unified	Berkeley
n/a	n/a	Beverly Hills Unified	Beverly Hills
n/a	n/a	Bishop Unified	Bishop
n/a	n/a	Black Oak Mine Unified	Georgetown
n/a	n/a	Bonita Unified	San Dimas
n/a	n/a	Brawley Union High	Brawley
n/a	n/a	Brea-Olinda Unified	Brea
n/a	n/a	Burbank Unified	Burbank
n/a	n/a	Cabrillo Unified	Half Moon Bay
n/a	n/a	Calaveras Unified	San Andreas
n/a	n/a	Calexico Unified	Calexico
n/a	n/a	Campbell Union High	San Jose
n/a	n/a	Capistrano Unified	SJ Capistrano
n/a	n/a	Carlsbad Unified	Carlsbad
n/a	n/a	Carmel Unified	Carmel
n/a	n/a	Carpinteria Unified	Carpinteria
n/a	n/a	Castro Valley Unified	Castro Valley
n/a	n/a	Center Joint Unified	Antelope
n/a	n/a	Centinela Valley Union High	Lawndale
n/a	n/a	Central Unified	Fresno
n/a	n/a	Central Union High	El Centro
n/a	n/a	Ceres Unified	Ceres
n/a	n/a	Chaffey Joint Union High	Ontario
n/a	n/a	Charter Oak Unified	Covina
n/a	n/a	Chico Unified	Chico
n/a	n/a	Chino Valley Unified	Chino
n/a	n/a	Claremont Unified	Claremont
n/a	n/a	Clovis Unified	Clovis

n/a	n/a	Coachella Valley Unified	Thermal
n/a	n/a	Coalinga-Huron Joint Unified	Coalinga
n/a	n/a	Colton Joint Unified	Colton
n/a	n/a	Compton Unified	Compton
n/a	n/a	Conejo Valley Unified	Thousand Oaks
n/a	n/a	Corcoran Joint Unified	Corcoran
n/a	n/a	Corona-Norco Unified	Norco
n/a	n/a	Coronado Unified	Coronado
n/a	n/a	Cotati-Rohnert Park Unified	Rohnert Park
n/a	n/a	Covina-Valley Unified	Covina
n/a	n/a	Culver City Unified	Culver City
n/a	n/a	Cutler-Orosi Joint Unified	Orosi
n/a	n/a	Davis Joint Unified	Davis
n/a	n/a	Dehesa Elementary	El Cajon
n/a	n/a	Del Norte County Unified	Crescent City
n/a	n/a	Delano Joint Union High	Delano
n/a	n/a	Delhi Unified	Delhi
n/a	n/a	Denair Unified	Denair
n/a	n/a	Desert Sands Unified	La Quinta
n/a	n/a	Dinuba Unified	Dinuba
n/a	n/a	Dixon Unified	Dixon
n/a	n/a	Dos Palos Oro Loma Joint Unified	Dos Palos
n/a	n/a	Downey Unified	Downey
n/a	n/a	Duarte Unified	Duarte
n/a	n/a	Dublin Unified	Dublin
n/a	n/a	East Side Union High	San Jose
n/a	n/a	El Dorado Union High	Placerville
n/a	n/a	El Monte Union High	El Monte
n/a	n/a	El Rancho Unified	Pico Rivera
n/a	n/a	El Segundo Unified	El Segundo
n/a	n/a	Elk Grove Unified	Elk Grove
n/a	n/a	Escalon Unified	Escalon
n/a	n/a	Escondido Union High	Escondido
n/a	n/a	Eureka City Schools	Eureka
n/a	n/a	Fairfield-Suisun Unified	Fairfield
n/a	n/a	Fallbrook Union High	Fallbrook
n/a	n/a	Farmersville Unified	Farmersville
n/a	n/a	Fillmore Unified	Fillmore
n/a	n/a	Firebaugh-Las Deltas Joint Unified	Firebaugh
n/a	n/a	Folsom-Cordova Unified	Folsom
n/a	n/a	Fontana Unified	Fontana
n/a	n/a	Fort Bragg Unified	Fort Bragg
n/a	n/a	Fowler Unified	Fowler
n/a	n/a	Fremont Unified	Fremont
n/a	n/a	Fremont Union High	Sunnyvale
n/a	n/a	Fresno County Office of Education	Fresno
n/a	n/a	Fresno Unified	Fresno
n/a	n/a	Fullerton Joint Union High	Fullerton
n/a	n/a	Galt Joint Union High	Galt
n/a	n/a	Garden Grove Unified	Garden Grove
n/a	n/a	Gateway Unified	Redding
n/a	n/a	Gilroy Unified	Gilroy
n/a	n/a	Glendale Unified	Glendale
n/a	n/a	Glendora Unified	Glendora
n/a	n/a	Golden Plains Unified	San Joaquin
n/a	n/a	Golden Valley Unified	Madera
n/a	n/a	Gonzales Unified	Gonzales
n/a	n/a	Gorman Elementary	Gorman
n/a	n/a	Gridley Unified	Gridley
n/a	n/a	Grossmont Union High	La Mesa
n/a	n/a	Gustine Unified	Gustine
n/a	n/a	Hacienda La Puente Unified	City of Industry
n/a	n/a	Hanford Joint Union High	Hanford
n/a	n/a	Hawthorne	Hawthorne
n/a	n/a	Hayward Unified	Hayward
n/a	n/a	Healdsburg Unified	Healdsburg
n/a	n/a	Hemet Unified	Hemet
n/a	n/a	Hesperia Unified	Hesperia
n/a	n/a	Hilmar Unified	Hilmar
n/a	n/a	Holtville Unified	Holtville
n/a	n/a	Hughson Unified	Hughson
n/a	n/a	Huntington Bch Union High	Huntington Bch
n/a	n/a	Imperial Unified	Imperial
n/a	n/a	Inglewood Unified	Inglewood
n/a	n/a	Irvine Unified	Irvine
n/a	n/a	Jefferson Elementary	Daly City
n/a	n/a	Jefferson Union High	Daly City
n/a	n/a	John Swett Unified	Rodeo
n/a	n/a	Julian Union Elementary	Julian
n/a	n/a	Jurupa Unified	Jurupa Valley
n/a	n/a	Kelseyville Unified	Kelseyville
n/a	n/a	Kerman Unified	Kerman
n/a	n/a	Kern County Office of Education	Bakersfield
n/a	n/a	Kern Union High	Bakersfield
n/a	n/a	Kings Canyon Joint Unified	Reedley
n/a	n/a	Konocti Unified	Lower Lake
n/a	n/a	La Canada Unified	La Canada
n/a	n/a	Laguna Beach Unified	Laguna Beach
n/a	n/a	Lake Elsinore Unified	Lake Elsinore
n/a	n/a	Lake Tahoe Unified	S Lake Tahoe
n/a	n/a	Lakeport Unified	Lakeport
n/a	n/a	Lakeside Union Elementary	Lakeside
n/a	n/a	Lammersville Joint Unified	Mountain House
n/a	n/a	Las Virgenes Unified	Calabasas
n/a	n/a	Lawndale Elementary	Lawndale
n/a	n/a	Lemoore Union High	Lemoore
n/a	n/a	Lennox	Lennox
n/a	n/a	Liberty Union High	Brentwood
n/a	n/a	Lincoln Unified	Stockton
n/a	n/a	Linden Unified	Linden
n/a	n/a	Lindsay Unified	Lindsay
n/a	n/a	Live Oak Elementary	Santa Cruz
n/a	n/a	Live Oak Unified	Live Oak
n/a	n/a	Livermore Valley Joint Unified	Livermore
n/a	n/a	Lodi Unified	Lodi
n/a	n/a	Lompoc Unified	Lompoc
n/a	n/a	Long Beach Unified	Long Beach
n/a	n/a	Los Alamitos Unified	Los Alamitos
n/a	n/a	Los Angeles County Office of Educ.	Downey
n/a	n/a	Los Angeles Unified	Los Angeles
n/a	n/a	Los Banos Unified	Los Banos
n/a	n/a	Los Gatos-Saratoga Jt Union High	Los Gatos
n/a	n/a	Lucerne Valley Unified	Lucerne Valley
n/a	n/a	Lucia Mar Unified	Arroyo Grande
n/a	n/a	Lynwood Unified	Lynwood
n/a	n/a	Madera Unified	Madera
n/a	n/a	Manhattan Beach Unified	Manhattan Beach
n/a	n/a	Manteca Unified	Manteca
n/a	n/a	Marcum-Illinois Union Elementary	East Nicolaus
n/a	n/a	Mariposa County Unified	Mariposa
n/a	n/a	Martinez Unified	Martinez
n/a	n/a	Marysville Joint Unified	Marysville
n/a	n/a	Mcfarland Unified	Mcfarland
n/a	n/a	Mendota Unified	Mendota
n/a	n/a	Menifee Union Elementary	Menifee
n/a	n/a	Merced County Office of Education	Merced
n/a	n/a	Merced Union High	Atwater
n/a	n/a	Middletown Unified	Middletown
n/a	n/a	Milpitas Unified	Milpitas
n/a	n/a	Modesto City High	Modesto
n/a	n/a	Mojave Unified	Mojave
n/a	n/a	Monrovia Unified	Monrovia
n/a	n/a	Montebello Unified	Montebello
n/a	n/a	Monterey County Office of Educ.	Salinas
n/a	n/a	Monterey Peninsula Unified	Monterey
n/a	n/a	Moorpark Unified	Moorpark
n/a	n/a	Moreno Valley Unified	Moreno Valley
n/a	n/a	Morgan Hill Unified	Morgan Hill
n/a	n/a	Morongo Unified	Twentynine Plms
n/a	n/a	Mountain Empire Unified	Pine Valley
n/a	n/a	Mountain View-Los Altos Union High	Mountain View
n/a	n/a	Mt. Diablo Unified	Concord
n/a	n/a	Muroc Joint Unified	North Edwards
n/a	n/a	Murrieta Valley Unified	Murrieta
n/a	n/a	Napa Valley Unified	Napa
n/a	n/a	Natomas Unified	Sacramento
n/a	n/a	Nevada County Office of Education	Nevada City
n/a	n/a	Nevada Joint Union High	Grass Valley
n/a	n/a	New Haven Unified	Union City
n/a	n/a	Newark Unified	Newark
n/a	n/a	Newman-Crows Landing Unified	Newman
n/a	n/a	Newport-Mesa Unified	Costa Mesa
n/a	n/a	North Monterey County Unified	Moss Landing
n/a	n/a	Northern Humboldt Union High	Mckinleyville
n/a	n/a	Norwalk-La Mirada Unified	Norwalk
n/a	n/a	Novato Unified	Novato
n/a	n/a	Nuview Union	Nuevo
n/a	n/a	Oak Park Unified	Oak Park
n/a	n/a	Oakdale Joint Unified	Oakdale
n/a	n/a	Oakland Unified	Oakland
n/a	n/a	Oceanside Unified	Oceanside
n/a	n/a	Ojai Unified	Ojai
n/a	n/a	Orange County Dept of Education	Costa Mesa
n/a	n/a	Orange Unified	Orange
n/a	n/a	Orland Joint Unified	Orland
n/a	n/a	Oro Grande Elementary	Oro Grande
n/a	n/a	Oroville Union High	Oroville
n/a	n/a	Oxnard Union High	Oxnard
n/a	n/a	Pacific Grove Unified	Pacific Grove
n/a	n/a	Pajaro Valley Unified	Watsonville
n/a	n/a	Palm Springs Unified	Palm Springs
n/a	n/a	Palo Alto Unified	Palo Alto
n/a	n/a	Palo Verde Unified	Blythe
n/a	n/a	Palos Verdes Peninsula Unified	Palos Vrds Est
n/a	n/a	Paradise Unified	Paradise
n/a	n/a	Paramount Unified	Paramount
n/a	n/a	Parlier Unified	Parlier
n/a	n/a	Pasadena Unified	Pasadena
n/a	n/a	Paso Robles Joint Unified	Paso Robles
n/a	n/a	Patterson Joint Unified	Patterson
n/a	n/a	Perris Union High	Perris
n/a	n/a	Petaluma Joint Union High	Petaluma
n/a	n/a	Piedmont City Unified	Piedmont
n/a	n/a	Piner-Olivet Union Elementary	Santa Rosa
n/a	n/a	Pittsburg Unified	Pittsburg
n/a	n/a	Placentia-Yorba Linda Unified	Placentia
n/a	n/a	Placer Union High	Auburn
n/a	n/a	Pleasanton Unified	Pleasanton
n/a	n/a	Pomona Unified	Pomona
n/a	n/a	Porterville Unified	Porterville
n/a	n/a	Poway Unified	San Diego
n/a	n/a	Ramona City Unified	Ramona
n/a	n/a	Ravenswood City Elementary	East Palo Alto
n/a	n/a	Red Bluff Joint Union High	Red Bluff
n/a	n/a	Redding Elementary	Redding
n/a	n/a	Redlands Unified	Redlands
n/a	n/a	Redondo Beach Unified	Redondo Beach
n/a	n/a	Reef-Sunset Unified	Avenal
n/a	n/a	Rialto Unified	Rialto
n/a	n/a	Rim of the World Unified	Blue Jay
n/a	n/a	Ripon Unified	Ripon
n/a	n/a	River Delta Joint Unified	Rio Vista
n/a	n/a	Riverbank Unified	Riverbank
n/a	n/a	Riverdale Joint Unified	Riverdale
n/a	n/a	Riverside County Office of Educ.	Riverside
n/a	n/a	Riverside Unified	Riverside
n/a	n/a	Rocklin Unified	Rocklin
n/a	n/a	Roseland Elementary	Santa Rosa
n/a	n/a	Roseville Joint Union High	Roseville
n/a	n/a	Rowland Unified	Rowland Heights
n/a	n/a	Sacramento City Unified	Sacramento
n/a	n/a	Saddleback Valley Unified	Mission Viejo
n/a	n/a	Salinas Union High	Salinas
n/a	n/a	San Benito High	Hollister
n/a	n/a	San Bernardino City Unified	San Bernardino
n/a	n/a	San Bernardino Co. Office of Educ.	San Bernardino
n/a	n/a	San Diego County Office of Educ.	San Diego
n/a	n/a	San Diego Unified	San Diego
n/a	n/a	San Dieguito Union High	Encinitas
n/a	n/a	San Francisco Unified	San Francisco
n/a	n/a	San Gabriel Unified	San Gabriel
n/a	n/a	San Jacinto Unified	San Jacinto
n/a	n/a	San Joaquin County Office of Educ.	Stockton
n/a	n/a	San Jose Unified	San Jose
n/a	n/a	San Juan Unified	Carmichael
n/a	n/a	San Leandro Unified	San Leandro
n/a	n/a	San Lorenzo Unified	San Lorenzo
n/a	n/a	San Lorenzo Valley Unified	Ben Lomond
n/a	n/a	San Luis Coastal Unified	San Luis Obispo
n/a	n/a	San Marcos Unified	San Marcos
n/a	n/a	San Marino Unified	San Marino
n/a	n/a	San Mateo Union High	San Mateo
n/a	n/a	San Rafael City High	San Rafael
n/a	n/a	San Ramon Valley Unified	Danville
n/a	n/a	Sanger Unified	Sanger
n/a	n/a	Santa Ana Unified	Santa Ana
n/a	n/a	Santa Barbara Unified	Santa Barbara
n/a	n/a	Santa Clara County Office of Educ.	San Jose
n/a	n/a	Santa Clara Unified	Santa Clara
n/a	n/a	Santa Cruz City High	Soquel
n/a	n/a	Santa Maria Joint Union High	Santa Maria
n/a	n/a	Santa Monica-Malibu Unified	Santa Monica
n/a	n/a	Santa Paula Union High	Santa Paula
n/a	n/a	Santa Rosa High	Santa Rosa
n/a	n/a	Scotts Valley Unified	Scotts Valley
n/a	n/a	Selma Unified	Selma
n/a	n/a	Sequoia Union High	Redwood City
n/a	n/a	Shasta Union High	Redding
n/a	n/a	Sierra Sands Unified	Ridgecrest
n/a	n/a	Silver Valley Unified	Yermo
n/a	n/a	Simi Valley Unified	Simi Valley
n/a	n/a	Snowline Joint Unified	Phelan
n/a	n/a	Soledad Unified	Soledad
n/a	n/a	Sonoma Valley Unified	Sonoma
n/a	n/a	South Monterey Co. Jt Union High	King City

Note: This section only includes districts with 1,500 or more students; All categories are ranked from high to low

n/a	n/a	South Pasadena Unified	South Pasadena
n/a	n/a	S San Francisco Unified	S San Francisco
n/a	n/a	Southern Kern Unified	Rosamond
n/a	n/a	Spencer Valley Elementary	Santa Ysabel
n/a	n/a	Stanislaus County Office of Educ.	Modesto
n/a	n/a	Stockton Unified	Stockton
n/a	n/a	Sweetwater Union High	Chula Vista
n/a	n/a	Tahoe-Truckee Joint Unified	Truckee
n/a	n/a	Tamalpais Union High	Larkspur
n/a	n/a	Tehachapi Unified	Tehachapi
n/a	n/a	Temecula Valley Unified	Temecula
n/a	n/a	Temple City Unified	Temple City
n/a	n/a	Templeton Unified	Templeton
n/a	n/a	Torrance Unified	Torrance
n/a	n/a	Tracy Joint Unified	Tracy
n/a	n/a	Travis Unified	Fairfield
n/a	n/a	Tulare County Office of Education	Visalia
n/a	n/a	Tulare Joint Union High	Tulare
n/a	n/a	Turlock Unified	Turlock
n/a	n/a	Tustin Unified	Tustin
n/a	n/a	Twin Rivers Unified	Mcclellan
n/a	n/a	Ukiah Unified	Ukiah
n/a	n/a	Upland Unified	Upland
n/a	n/a	Vacaville Unified	Vacaville
n/a	n/a	Val Verde Unified	Perris
n/a	n/a	Vallejo City Unified	Vallejo
n/a	n/a	Valley Center-Pauma Unified	Valley Center
n/a	n/a	Ventura County Office of Educ.	Camarillo
n/a	n/a	Ventura Unified	Ventura
n/a	n/a	Victor Valley Union High	Victorville
n/a	n/a	Visalia Unified	Visalia
n/a	n/a	Vista Unified	Vista
n/a	n/a	Walnut Valley Unified	Walnut
n/a	n/a	Wasco Union High	Wasco
n/a	n/a	Washington Unified	West Sacramento
n/a	n/a	Washington Unified	Fresno
n/a	n/a	Waterford Unified	Waterford
n/a	n/a	West Contra Costa Unified	Richmond
n/a	n/a	West Covina Unified	West Covina
n/a	n/a	West Sonoma County Union High	Sebastopol
n/a	n/a	Western Placer Unified	Lincoln
n/a	n/a	Whittier Union High	Whittier
n/a	n/a	William S. Hart Union High	Santa Clarita
n/a	n/a	Willits Unified	Willits
n/a	n/a	Willows Unified	Willows
n/a	n/a	Windsor Unified	Windsor
n/a	n/a	Winters Joint Unified	Winters
n/a	n/a	Woodland Joint Unified	Woodland
n/a	n/a	Yosemite Unified	Oakhurst
n/a	n/a	Yuba City Unified	Yuba City
n/a	n/a	Yucaipa-Calimesa Joint Unified	Yucaipa
n/a	n/a	Adelanto Elementary	Adelanto
n/a	n/a	Alisal Union	Salinas
n/a	n/a	Alpine Union Elementary	Alpine
n/a	n/a	Alta Loma Elementary	Alta Loma
n/a	n/a	Alum Rock Union Elementary	San Jose
n/a	n/a	Anaheim City	Anaheim
n/a	n/a	Arvin Union Elementary	Arvin
n/a	n/a	Atwater Elementary	Atwater
n/a	n/a	Auburn Union Elementary	Auburn
n/a	n/a	Bakersfield City	Bakersfield
n/a	n/a	Beardsley Elementary	Bakersfield
n/a	n/a	Bellevue Union Elementary	Santa Rosa
n/a	n/a	Belmont-Redwood Shores Elem.	Belmont
n/a	n/a	Berryessa Union Elementary	San Jose
n/a	n/a	Bonsall Union Elementary	Bonsall
n/a	n/a	Brawley Elementary	Brawley
n/a	n/a	Brentwood Union Elementary	Brentwood
n/a	n/a	Buckeye Union Elementary	Shingle Springs
n/a	n/a	Buena Park Elementary	Buena Park
n/a	n/a	Burlingame Elementary	Burlingame
n/a	n/a	Burton Elementary	Porterville
n/a	n/a	Byron Union Elementary	Byron
n/a	n/a	Cajon Valley Union	El Cajon
n/a	n/a	Cambrian	San Jose
n/a	n/a	Campbell Union	Campbell
n/a	n/a	Castaic Union Elementary	Valencia
n/a	n/a	Central Elementary	R Cucamonga
n/a	n/a	Central Union Elementary	Lemoore
n/a	n/a	Centralia Elementary	Buena Park
n/a	n/a	Chowchilla Elementary	Chowchilla
n/a	n/a	Chula Vista Elementary	Chula Vista
n/a	n/a	Corning Union Elementary	Corning
n/a	n/a	Cucamonga Elementary	R Cucamonga
n/a	n/a	Cupertino Union	Cupertino
n/a	n/a	Cypress Elementary	Cypress
n/a	n/a	Del Mar Union Elementary	San Diego
n/a	n/a	Delano Union Elementary	Delano
n/a	n/a	Dixie Elementary	San Rafael
n/a	n/a	Dry Creek Joint Elementary	Roseville
n/a	n/a	Earlimart Elementary	Earlimart
n/a	n/a	East Whittier City Elementary	Whittier
n/a	n/a	Eastside Union Elementary	Lancaster
n/a	n/a	El Centro Elementary	El Centro
n/a	n/a	El Monte City Elementary	El Monte
n/a	n/a	Empire Union Elementary	Modesto
n/a	n/a	Encinitas Union Elementary	Encinitas
n/a	n/a	Enterprise Elementary	Redding
n/a	n/a	Escondido Union	Escondido
n/a	n/a	Etiwanda Elementary	Etiwanda
n/a	n/a	Eureka Union	Granite Bay
n/a	n/a	Evergreen Elementary	San Jose
n/a	n/a	Exeter Union Elementary	Exeter
n/a	n/a	Fairfax Elementary	Bakersfield
n/a	n/a	Fallbrook Union Elementary	Fallbrook
n/a	n/a	Fountain Valley Elementary	Fountain Valley
n/a	n/a	Franklin-Mckinley Elementary	San Jose
n/a	n/a	Fruitvale Elementary	Bakersfield
n/a	n/a	Fullerton Elementary	Fullerton
n/a	n/a	Galt Joint Union Elementary	Galt
n/a	n/a	Garvey Elementary	Rosemead
n/a	n/a	Goleta Union Elementary	Goleta
n/a	n/a	Grass Valley Elementary	Grass Valley
n/a	n/a	Greenfield Union	Bakersfield
n/a	n/a	Greenfield Union Elementary	Greenfield
n/a	n/a	Hanford Elementary	Hanford
n/a	n/a	Hermosa Beach City Elementary	Hermosa Beach
n/a	n/a	Hillsborough City Elementary	Hillsborough
n/a	n/a	Hollister	Hollister
n/a	n/a	Hueneme Elementary	Port Hueneme
n/a	n/a	Huntington Bch City Elementary	Huntington Bch
n/a	n/a	Jefferson Elementary	Tracy
n/a	n/a	Keppel Union Elementary	Pearblossom
n/a	n/a	King City Union	King City
n/a	n/a	Kingsburg Elementary Charter	Kingsburg
n/a	n/a	La Habra City Elementary	La Habra
n/a	n/a	La Mesa-Spring Valley	La Mesa
n/a	n/a	Lafayette Elementary	Lafayette
n/a	n/a	Lamont Elementary	Lamont
n/a	n/a	Lancaster Elementary	Lancaster
n/a	n/a	Lemon Grove	Lemon Grove
n/a	n/a	Lemoore Union Elementary	Lemoore
n/a	n/a	Little Lake City Elementary	Santa Fe Spgs
n/a	n/a	Livingston Union Elementary	Livingston
n/a	n/a	Loomis Union Elementary	Loomis
n/a	n/a	Los Altos Elementary	Los Altos
n/a	n/a	Los Gatos Union Elementary	Los Gatos
n/a	n/a	Los Nietos	Whittier
n/a	n/a	Lowell Joint	Whittier
n/a	n/a	Magnolia Elementary	Anaheim
n/a	n/a	Menlo Park City Elementary	Atherton
n/a	n/a	Merced City Elementary	Merced
n/a	n/a	Mill Valley Elementary	Mill Valley
n/a	n/a	Millbrae Elementary	Millbrae
n/a	n/a	Modesto City Elementary	Modesto
n/a	n/a	Moraga Elementary	Moraga
n/a	n/a	Moreland Elementary	San Jose
n/a	n/a	Mountain View Elementary	Ontario
n/a	n/a	Mountain View Elementary	El Monte
n/a	n/a	Mountain View Whisman	Mountain View
n/a	n/a	Mt. Pleasant Elementary	San Jose
n/a	n/a	National Elementary	National City
n/a	n/a	Newhall	Valencia
n/a	n/a	Norris Elementary	Bakersfield
n/a	n/a	Oak Grove Elementary	San Jose
n/a	n/a	Oakley Union Elementary	Oakley
n/a	n/a	Ocean View	Huntington Bch
n/a	n/a	Ocean View	Oxnard
n/a	n/a	Old Adobe Union	Petaluma
n/a	n/a	Ontario-Montclair Elementary	Ontario
n/a	n/a	Orcutt Union Elementary	Orcutt
n/a	n/a	Orinda Union Elementary	Orinda
n/a	n/a	Oroville City Elementary	Oroville
n/a	n/a	Oxnard	Oxnard
n/a	n/a	Pacifica	Pacifica
n/a	n/a	Palmdale Elementary	Palmdale
n/a	n/a	Panama-Buena Vista Union	Bakersfield
n/a	n/a	Perris Elementary	Perris
n/a	n/a	Petaluma City Elementary	Petaluma
n/a	n/a	Pioneer Union Elementary	Hanford
n/a	n/a	Pleasant Valley	Camarillo
n/a	n/a	Red Bluff Union Elementary	Red Bluff
n/a	n/a	Redwood City Elementary	Redwood City
n/a	n/a	Rescue Union Elementary	Rescue
n/a	n/a	Richland Union Elementary	Shafter
n/a	n/a	Rincon Valley Union Elementary	Santa Rosa
n/a	n/a	Rio Elementary	Oxnard
n/a	n/a	Robla Elementary	Sacramento
n/a	n/a	Romoland Elementary	Homeland
n/a	n/a	Rosedale Union Elementary	Bakersfield
n/a	n/a	Rosemead Elementary	Rosemead
n/a	n/a	Roseville City Elementary	Roseville
n/a	n/a	Ross Valley Elementary	San Anselmo
n/a	n/a	Salida Union Elementary	Salida
n/a	n/a	Salinas City Elementary	Salinas
n/a	n/a	San Bruno Park Elementary	San Bruno
n/a	n/a	San Carlos Elementary	San Carlos
n/a	n/a	San Mateo-Foster City	Foster City
n/a	n/a	San Rafael City Elementary	San Rafael
n/a	n/a	San Ysidro Elementary	San Ysidro
n/a	n/a	Santa Cruz City Elementary	Soquel
n/a	n/a	Santa Maria-Bonita	Santa Maria
n/a	n/a	Santa Paula Elementary	Santa Paula
n/a	n/a	Santa Rita Union Elementary	Salinas
n/a	n/a	Santa Rosa Elementary	Santa Rosa
n/a	n/a	Santee Elementary	Santee
n/a	n/a	Saratoga Union Elementary	Saratoga
n/a	n/a	Saugus Union	Santa Clarita
n/a	n/a	Savanna Elementary	Anaheim
n/a	n/a	Sbc - Aspire Public Schools	Oakland
n/a	n/a	Sbc - High Tech High	San Diego
n/a	n/a	Solana Beach Elementary	Solana Beach
n/a	n/a	Soquel Union Elementary	Capitola
n/a	n/a	South Bay Union Elementary	Imperial Beach
n/a	n/a	South Whittier Elementary	Whittier
n/a	n/a	Standard Elementary	Bakersfield
n/a	n/a	Stanislaus Union Elementary	Modesto
n/a	n/a	Sulphur Springs Union	Canyon Country
n/a	n/a	Sunnyvale	Sunnyvale
n/a	n/a	Sylvan Union Elementary	Modesto
n/a	n/a	Taft City	Taft
n/a	n/a	Tulare City	Tulare
n/a	n/a	Union Elementary	San Jose
n/a	n/a	Victor Elementary	Victorville
n/a	n/a	Walnut Creek Elementary	Walnut Creek
n/a	n/a	Wasco Union Elementary	Wasco
n/a	n/a	Weaver Union	Merced
n/a	n/a	Westminster Elementary	Westminster
n/a	n/a	Westside Union Elementary	Quartz Hill
n/a	n/a	Whittier City Elementary	Whittier
n/a	n/a	Winton Elementary	Winton
n/a	n/a	Wiseburn Elementary	Hawthorne
n/a	n/a	Woodlake Union Elementary	Woodlake
n/a	n/a	Wright Elementary	Santa Rosa

Average Freshman Graduation Rate

Rank	Percent	District Name	City
n/a	n/a	ABC Unified	Cerritos
n/a	n/a	Acalanes Union High	Lafayette
n/a	n/a	Acton-Agua Dulce Unified	Acton
n/a	n/a	Adelanto Elementary	Adelanto
n/a	n/a	Alameda City Unified	Alameda
n/a	n/a	Alameda County Office of Education	Hayward
n/a	n/a	Albany City Unified	Albany
n/a	n/a	Alhambra Unified	Alhambra
n/a	n/a	Alisal Union	Salinas
n/a	n/a	Alpine Union Elementary	Alpine
n/a	n/a	Alta Loma Elementary	Alta Loma
n/a	n/a	Alum Rock Union Elementary	San Jose
n/a	n/a	Alvord Unified	Riverside
n/a	n/a	Amador County Unified	Jackson
n/a	n/a	Anaheim City	Anaheim
n/a	n/a	Anaheim Union High	Anaheim
n/a	n/a	Anderson Union High	Anderson
n/a	n/a	Antelope Valley Union High	Lancaster
n/a	n/a	Antioch Unified	Antioch
n/a	n/a	Apple Valley Unified	Apple Valley
n/a	n/a	Arcadia Unified	Arcadia
n/a	n/a	Armona Union Elementary	Armona
n/a	n/a	Arvin Union Elementary	Arvin
n/a	n/a	Atascadero Unified	Atascadero
n/a	n/a	Atwater Elementary	Atwater
n/a	n/a	Auburn Union Elementary	Auburn

Note: This section only includes districts with 1,500 or more students; All categories are ranked from high to low

n/a	n/a	Azusa Unified	Azusa
n/a	n/a	Bakersfield City	Bakersfield
n/a	n/a	Baldwin Park Unified	Baldwin Park
n/a	n/a	Banning Unified	Banning
n/a	n/a	Barstow Unified	Barstow
n/a	n/a	Bassett Unified	La Puente
n/a	n/a	Bear Valley Unified	Big Bear Lake
n/a	n/a	Beardsley Elementary	Bakersfield
n/a	n/a	Beaumont Unified	Beaumont
n/a	n/a	Bellevue Union Elementary	Santa Rosa
n/a	n/a	Bellflower Unified	Bellflower
n/a	n/a	Belmont-Redwood Shores Elem.	Belmont
n/a	n/a	Benicia Unified	Benicia
n/a	n/a	Berkeley Unified	Berkeley
n/a	n/a	Berryessa Union Elementary	San Jose
n/a	n/a	Beverly Hills Unified	Beverly Hills
n/a	n/a	Bishop Unified	Bishop
n/a	n/a	Black Oak Mine Unified	Georgetown
n/a	n/a	Bonita Unified	San Dimas
n/a	n/a	Bonsall Union Elementary	Bonsall
n/a	n/a	Brawley Elementary	Brawley
n/a	n/a	Brawley Union High	Brawley
n/a	n/a	Brea-Olinda Unified	Brea
n/a	n/a	Brentwood Union Elementary	Brentwood
n/a	n/a	Buckeye Union Elementary	Shingle Springs
n/a	n/a	Buena Park Elementary	Buena Park
n/a	n/a	Burbank Unified	Burbank
n/a	n/a	Burlingame Elementary	Burlingame
n/a	n/a	Burton Elementary	Porterville
n/a	n/a	Byron Union Elementary	Byron
n/a	n/a	Cabrillo Unified	Half Moon Bay
n/a	n/a	Cajon Valley Union	El Cajon
n/a	n/a	Calaveras Unified	San Andreas
n/a	n/a	Calexico Unified	Calexico
n/a	n/a	Cambrian	San Jose
n/a	n/a	Campbell Union	Campbell
n/a	n/a	Campbell Union High	San Jose
n/a	n/a	Capistrano Unified	SJ Capistrano
n/a	n/a	Carlsbad Unified	Carlsbad
n/a	n/a	Carmel Unified	Carmel
n/a	n/a	Carpinteria Unified	Carpinteria
n/a	n/a	Castaic Union Elementary	Valencia
n/a	n/a	Castro Valley Unified	Castro Valley
n/a	n/a	Center Joint Unified	Antelope
n/a	n/a	Centinela Valley Union High	Lawndale
n/a	n/a	Central Elementary	R Cucamonga
n/a	n/a	Central Unified	Fresno
n/a	n/a	Central Union Elementary	Lemoore
n/a	n/a	Central Union High	El Centro
n/a	n/a	Centralia Elementary	Buena Park
n/a	n/a	Ceres Unified	Ceres
n/a	n/a	Chaffey Joint Union High	Ontario
n/a	n/a	Charter Oak Unified	Covina
n/a	n/a	Chico Unified	Chico
n/a	n/a	Chino Valley Unified	Chino
n/a	n/a	Chowchilla Elementary	Chowchilla
n/a	n/a	Chula Vista Elementary	Chula Vista
n/a	n/a	Claremont Unified	Claremont
n/a	n/a	Clovis Unified	Clovis
n/a	n/a	Coachella Valley Unified	Thermal
n/a	n/a	Coalinga-Huron Joint Unified	Coalinga
n/a	n/a	Colton Joint Unified	Colton
n/a	n/a	Compton Unified	Compton
n/a	n/a	Conejo Valley Unified	Thousand Oaks
n/a	n/a	Corcoran Joint Unified	Corcoran
n/a	n/a	Corning Union Elementary	Corning
n/a	n/a	Corona-Norco Unified	Norco
n/a	n/a	Coronado Unified	Coronado
n/a	n/a	Cotati-Rohnert Park Unified	Rohnert Park
n/a	n/a	Covina-Valley Unified	Covina
n/a	n/a	Cucamonga Elementary	R Cucamonga
n/a	n/a	Culver City Unified	Culver City
n/a	n/a	Cupertino Union	Cupertino
n/a	n/a	Cutler-Orosi Joint Unified	Orosi
n/a	n/a	Cypress Elementary	Cypress
n/a	n/a	Davis Joint Unified	Davis
n/a	n/a	Dehesa Elementary	El Cajon
n/a	n/a	Del Mar Union Elementary	San Diego
n/a	n/a	Del Norte County Unified	Crescent City
n/a	n/a	Delano Joint Union High	Delano
n/a	n/a	Delano Union Elementary	Delano
n/a	n/a	Delhi Unified	Delhi
n/a	n/a	Denair Unified	Denair
n/a	n/a	Desert Sands Unified	La Quinta
n/a	n/a	Dinuba Unified	Dinuba

n/a	n/a	Dixie Elementary	San Rafael
n/a	n/a	Dixon Unified	Dixon
n/a	n/a	Dos Palos Oro Loma Joint Unified	Dos Palos
n/a	n/a	Downey Unified	Downey
n/a	n/a	Dry Creek Joint Elementary	Roseville
n/a	n/a	Duarte Unified	Duarte
n/a	n/a	Dublin Unified	Dublin
n/a	n/a	Earlimart Elementary	Earlimart
n/a	n/a	East Side Union High	San Jose
n/a	n/a	East Whittier City Elementary	Whittier
n/a	n/a	Eastside Union Elementary	Lancaster
n/a	n/a	El Centro Elementary	El Centro
n/a	n/a	El Dorado Union High	Placerville
n/a	n/a	El Monte City Elementary	El Monte
n/a	n/a	El Monte Union High	El Monte
n/a	n/a	El Rancho Unified	Pico Rivera
n/a	n/a	El Segundo Unified	El Segundo
n/a	n/a	Elk Grove Unified	Elk Grove
n/a	n/a	Empire Union Elementary	Modesto
n/a	n/a	Encinitas Union Elementary	Encinitas
n/a	n/a	Enterprise Elementary	Redding
n/a	n/a	Escalon Unified	Escalon
n/a	n/a	Escondido Union	Escondido
n/a	n/a	Escondido Union High	Escondido
n/a	n/a	Etiwanda Elementary	Etiwanda
n/a	n/a	Eureka City Schools	Eureka
n/a	n/a	Eureka Union	Granite Bay
n/a	n/a	Evergreen Elementary	San Jose
n/a	n/a	Exeter Union Elementary	Exeter
n/a	n/a	Fairfax Elementary	Bakersfield
n/a	n/a	Fairfield-Suisun Unified	Fairfield
n/a	n/a	Fallbrook Union Elementary	Fallbrook
n/a	n/a	Fallbrook Union High	Fallbrook
n/a	n/a	Farmersville Unified	Farmersville
n/a	n/a	Fillmore Unified	Fillmore
n/a	n/a	Firebaugh-Las Deltas Joint Unified	Firebaugh
n/a	n/a	Folsom-Cordova Unified	Folsom
n/a	n/a	Fontana Unified	Fontana
n/a	n/a	Fort Bragg Unified	Fort Bragg
n/a	n/a	Fountain Valley Elementary	Fountain Valley
n/a	n/a	Fowler Unified	Fowler
n/a	n/a	Franklin-Mckinley Elementary	San Jose
n/a	n/a	Fremont Unified	Fremont
n/a	n/a	Fremont Union High	Sunnyvale
n/a	n/a	Fresno County Office of Education	Fresno
n/a	n/a	Fresno Unified	Fresno
n/a	n/a	Fruitvale Elementary	Bakersfield
n/a	n/a	Fullerton Elementary	Fullerton
n/a	n/a	Fullerton Joint Union High	Fullerton
n/a	n/a	Galt Joint Union Elementary	Galt
n/a	n/a	Galt Joint Union High	Galt
n/a	n/a	Garden Grove Unified	Garden Grove
n/a	n/a	Garvey Elementary	Rosemead
n/a	n/a	Gateway Unified	Redding
n/a	n/a	Gilroy Unified	Gilroy
n/a	n/a	Glendale Unified	Glendale
n/a	n/a	Glendora Unified	Glendora
n/a	n/a	Golden Plains Unified	San Joaquin
n/a	n/a	Golden Valley Unified	Madera
n/a	n/a	Goleta Union Elementary	Goleta
n/a	n/a	Gonzales Unified	Gonzales
n/a	n/a	Gorman Elementary	Gorman
n/a	n/a	Grass Valley Elementary	Grass Valley
n/a	n/a	Greenfield Union	Bakersfield
n/a	n/a	Greenfield Union Elementary	Greenfield
n/a	n/a	Gridley Unified	Gridley
n/a	n/a	Grossmont Union High	La Mesa
n/a	n/a	Gustine Unified	Gustine
n/a	n/a	Hacienda La Puente Unified	City of Industry
n/a	n/a	Hanford Elementary	Hanford
n/a	n/a	Hanford Joint Union High	Hanford
n/a	n/a	Hawthorne	Hawthorne
n/a	n/a	Hayward Unified	Hayward
n/a	n/a	Healdsburg Unified	Healdsburg
n/a	n/a	Hemet Unified	Hemet
n/a	n/a	Hermosa Beach City Elementary	Hermosa Beach
n/a	n/a	Hesperia Unified	Hesperia
n/a	n/a	Hillsborough City Elementary	Hillsborough
n/a	n/a	Hilmar Unified	Hilmar
n/a	n/a	Hollister	Hollister
n/a	n/a	Holtville Unified	Holtville
n/a	n/a	Hueneme Elementary	Port Hueneme
n/a	n/a	Hughson Unified	Hughson
n/a	n/a	Huntington Bch City Elementary	Huntington Bch
n/a	n/a	Huntington Bch Union High	Huntington Bch

n/a	n/a	Imperial Unified	Imperial
n/a	n/a	Inglewood Unified	Inglewood
n/a	n/a	Irvine Unified	Irvine
n/a	n/a	Jefferson Elementary	Tracy
n/a	n/a	Jefferson Elementary	Daly City
n/a	n/a	Jefferson Union High	Daly City
n/a	n/a	John Swett Unified	Rodeo
n/a	n/a	Julian Union Elementary	Julian
n/a	n/a	Jurupa Unified	Jurupa Valley
n/a	n/a	Kelseyville Unified	Kelseyville
n/a	n/a	Keppel Union Elementary	Pearblossom
n/a	n/a	Kerman Unified	Kerman
n/a	n/a	Kern County Office of Education	Bakersfield
n/a	n/a	Kern Union High	Bakersfield
n/a	n/a	King City Union	King City
n/a	n/a	Kings Canyon Joint Unified	Reedley
n/a	n/a	Kingsburg Elementary Charter	Kingsburg
n/a	n/a	Konocti Unified	Lower Lake
n/a	n/a	La Canada Unified	La Canada
n/a	n/a	La Habra City Elementary	La Habra
n/a	n/a	La Mesa-Spring Valley	La Mesa
n/a	n/a	Lafayette Elementary	Lafayette
n/a	n/a	Laguna Beach Unified	Laguna Beach
n/a	n/a	Lake Elsinore Unified	Lake Elsinore
n/a	n/a	Lake Tahoe Unified	S Lake Tahoe
n/a	n/a	Lakeport Unified	Lakeport
n/a	n/a	Lakeside Union Elementary	Lakeside
n/a	n/a	Lammersville Joint Unified	Mountain House
n/a	n/a	Lamont Elementary	Lamont
n/a	n/a	Lancaster Elementary	Lancaster
n/a	n/a	Las Virgenes Unified	Calabasas
n/a	n/a	Lawndale Elementary	Lawndale
n/a	n/a	Lemon Grove	Lemon Grove
n/a	n/a	Lemoore Union Elementary	Lemoore
n/a	n/a	Lemoore Union High	Lemoore
n/a	n/a	Lennox	Lennox
n/a	n/a	Liberty Union High	Brentwood
n/a	n/a	Lincoln Unified	Stockton
n/a	n/a	Linden Unified	Linden
n/a	n/a	Lindsay Unified	Lindsay
n/a	n/a	Little Lake City Elementary	Santa Fe Spgs
n/a	n/a	Live Oak Elementary	Santa Cruz
n/a	n/a	Live Oak Unified	Live Oak
n/a	n/a	Livermore Valley Joint Unified	Livermore
n/a	n/a	Livingston Union Elementary	Livingston
n/a	n/a	Lodi Unified	Lodi
n/a	n/a	Lompoc Unified	Lompoc
n/a	n/a	Long Beach Unified	Long Beach
n/a	n/a	Loomis Union Elementary	Loomis
n/a	n/a	Los Alamitos Unified	Los Alamitos
n/a	n/a	Los Altos Elementary	Los Altos
n/a	n/a	Los Angeles County Office of Educ.	Downey
n/a	n/a	Los Angeles Unified	Los Angeles
n/a	n/a	Los Banos Unified	Los Banos
n/a	n/a	Los Gatos Union Elementary	Los Gatos
n/a	n/a	Los Gatos-Saratoga Jt Union High	Los Gatos
n/a	n/a	Los Nietos	Whittier
n/a	n/a	Lowell Joint	Whittier
n/a	n/a	Lucerne Valley Unified	Lucerne Valley
n/a	n/a	Lucia Mar Unified	Arroyo Grande
n/a	n/a	Lynwood Unified	Lynwood
n/a	n/a	Madera Unified	Madera
n/a	n/a	Magnolia Elementary	Anaheim
n/a	n/a	Manhattan Beach Unified	Manhattan Beach
n/a	n/a	Manteca Unified	Manteca
n/a	n/a	Marcum-Illinois Union Elementary	East Nicolaus
n/a	n/a	Mariposa County Unified	Mariposa
n/a	n/a	Martinez Unified	Martinez
n/a	n/a	Marysville Joint Unified	Marysville
n/a	n/a	Mcfarland Unified	Mcfarland
n/a	n/a	Mendota Unified	Mendota
n/a	n/a	Menifee Union Elementary	Menifee
n/a	n/a	Menlo Park City Elementary	Atherton
n/a	n/a	Merced City Elementary	Merced
n/a	n/a	Merced County Office of Education	Merced
n/a	n/a	Merced Union High	Atwater
n/a	n/a	Middletown Unified	Middletown
n/a	n/a	Mill Valley Elementary	Mill Valley
n/a	n/a	Millbrae Elementary	Millbrae
n/a	n/a	Milpitas Unified	Milpitas
n/a	n/a	Modesto City Elementary	Modesto
n/a	n/a	Modesto City High	Modesto
n/a	n/a	Mojave Unified	Mojave
n/a	n/a	Monrovia Unified	Monrovia
n/a	n/a	Montebello Unified	Montebello

Note: This section only includes districts with 1,500 or more students; All categories are ranked from high to low

n/a	n/a	Monterey County Office of Educ.	Salinas
n/a	n/a	Monterey Peninsula Unified	Monterey
n/a	n/a	Moorpark Unified	Moorpark
n/a	n/a	Moraga Elementary	Moraga
n/a	n/a	Moreland Elementary	San Jose
n/a	n/a	Moreno Valley Unified	Moreno Valley
n/a	n/a	Morgan Hill Unified	Morgan Hill
n/a	n/a	Morongo Unified	Twentynine Plms
n/a	n/a	Mountain Empire Unified	Pine Valley
n/a	n/a	Mountain View Elementary	Ontario
n/a	n/a	Mountain View Elementary	El Monte
n/a	n/a	Mountain View Whisman	Mountain View
n/a	n/a	Mountain View-Los Altos Union High	Mountain View
n/a	n/a	Mt. Diablo Unified	Concord
n/a	n/a	Mt. Pleasant Elementary	San Jose
n/a	n/a	Muroc Joint Unified	North Edwards
n/a	n/a	Murrieta Valley Unified	Murrieta
n/a	n/a	Napa Valley Unified	Napa
n/a	n/a	National Elementary	National City
n/a	n/a	Natomas Unified	Sacramento
n/a	n/a	Nevada County Office of Education	Nevada City
n/a	n/a	Nevada Joint Union High	Grass Valley
n/a	n/a	New Haven Unified	Union City
n/a	n/a	Newark Unified	Newark
n/a	n/a	Newhall	Valencia
n/a	n/a	Newman-Crows Landing Unified	Newman
n/a	n/a	Newport-Mesa Unified	Costa Mesa
n/a	n/a	Norris Elementary	Bakersfield
n/a	n/a	North Monterey County Unified	Moss Landing
n/a	n/a	Northern Humboldt Union High	Mckinleyville
n/a	n/a	Norwalk-La Mirada Unified	Norwalk
n/a	n/a	Novato Unified	Novato
n/a	n/a	Nuview Union	Nuevo
n/a	n/a	Oak Grove Elementary	San Jose
n/a	n/a	Oak Park Unified	Oak Park
n/a	n/a	Oakdale Joint Unified	Oakdale
n/a	n/a	Oakland Unified	Oakland
n/a	n/a	Oakley Union Elementary	Oakley
n/a	n/a	Ocean View	Huntington Bch
n/a	n/a	Ocean View	Oxnard
n/a	n/a	Oceanside Unified	Oceanside
n/a	n/a	Ojai Unified	Ojai
n/a	n/a	Old Adobe Union	Petaluma
n/a	n/a	Ontario-Montclair Elementary	Ontario
n/a	n/a	Orange County Dept of Education	Costa Mesa
n/a	n/a	Orange Unified	Orange
n/a	n/a	Orcutt Union Elementary	Orcutt
n/a	n/a	Orinda Union Elementary	Orinda
n/a	n/a	Orland Joint Unified	Orland
n/a	n/a	Oro Grande Elementary	Oro Grande
n/a	n/a	Oroville City Elementary	Oroville
n/a	n/a	Oroville Union High	Oroville
n/a	n/a	Oxnard	Oxnard
n/a	n/a	Oxnard Union High	Oxnard
n/a	n/a	Pacific Grove Unified	Pacific Grove
n/a	n/a	Pacifica	Pacifica
n/a	n/a	Pajaro Valley Unified	Watsonville
n/a	n/a	Palm Springs Unified	Palm Springs
n/a	n/a	Palmdale Elementary	Palmdale
n/a	n/a	Palo Alto Unified	Palo Alto
n/a	n/a	Palo Verde Unified	Blythe
n/a	n/a	Palos Verdes Peninsula Unified	Palos Vrds Est
n/a	n/a	Panama-Buena Vista Union	Bakersfield
n/a	n/a	Paradise Unified	Paradise
n/a	n/a	Paramount Unified	Paramount
n/a	n/a	Parlier Unified	Parlier
n/a	n/a	Pasadena Unified	Pasadena
n/a	n/a	Paso Robles Joint Unified	Paso Robles
n/a	n/a	Patterson Joint Unified	Patterson
n/a	n/a	Perris Elementary	Perris
n/a	n/a	Perris Union High	Perris
n/a	n/a	Petaluma City Elementary	Petaluma
n/a	n/a	Petaluma Joint Union High	Petaluma
n/a	n/a	Piedmont City Unified	Piedmont
n/a	n/a	Piner-Olivet Union Elementary	Santa Rosa
n/a	n/a	Pioneer Union Elementary	Hanford
n/a	n/a	Pittsburg Unified	Pittsburg
n/a	n/a	Placentia-Yorba Linda Unified	Placentia
n/a	n/a	Placer Union High	Auburn
n/a	n/a	Pleasant Valley	Camarillo
n/a	n/a	Pleasanton Unified	Pleasanton
n/a	n/a	Pomona Unified	Pomona
n/a	n/a	Porterville Unified	Porterville
n/a	n/a	Poway Unified	San Diego

n/a	n/a	Ramona City Unified	Ramona
n/a	n/a	Ravenswood City Elementary	East Palo Alto
n/a	n/a	Red Bluff Joint Union High	Red Bluff
n/a	n/a	Red Bluff Union Elementary	Red Bluff
n/a	n/a	Redding Elementary	Redding
n/a	n/a	Redlands Unified	Redlands
n/a	n/a	Redondo Beach Unified	Redondo Beach
n/a	n/a	Redwood City Elementary	Redwood City
n/a	n/a	Reef-Sunset Unified	Avenal
n/a	n/a	Rescue Union Elementary	Rescue
n/a	n/a	Rialto Unified	Rialto
n/a	n/a	Richland Union Elementary	Shafter
n/a	n/a	Rim of the World Unified	Blue Jay
n/a	n/a	Rincon Valley Union Elementary	Santa Rosa
n/a	n/a	Rio Elementary	Oxnard
n/a	n/a	Ripon Unified	Ripon
n/a	n/a	River Delta Joint Unified	Rio Vista
n/a	n/a	Riverbank Unified	Riverbank
n/a	n/a	Riverdale Joint Unified	Riverdale
n/a	n/a	Riverside County Office of Educ.	Riverside
n/a	n/a	Riverside Unified	Riverside
n/a	n/a	Robla Elementary	Sacramento
n/a	n/a	Rocklin Unified	Rocklin
n/a	n/a	Romoland Elementary	Homeland
n/a	n/a	Rosedale Union Elementary	Bakersfield
n/a	n/a	Roseland Elementary	Santa Rosa
n/a	n/a	Rosemead Elementary	Rosemead
n/a	n/a	Roseville City Elementary	Roseville
n/a	n/a	Roseville Joint Union High	Roseville
n/a	n/a	Ross Valley Elementary	San Anselmo
n/a	n/a	Rowland Unified	Rowland Heights
n/a	n/a	Sacramento City Unified	Sacramento
n/a	n/a	Saddleback Valley Unified	Mission Viejo
n/a	n/a	Salida Union Elementary	Salida
n/a	n/a	Salinas City Elementary	Salinas
n/a	n/a	Salinas Union High	Salinas
n/a	n/a	San Benito High	Hollister
n/a	n/a	San Bernardino City Unified	San Bernardino
n/a	n/a	San Bernardino Co. Office of Educ.	San Bernardino
n/a	n/a	San Bruno Park Elementary	San Bruno
n/a	n/a	San Carlos Elementary	San Carlos
n/a	n/a	San Diego County Office of Educ.	San Diego
n/a	n/a	San Diego Unified	San Diego
n/a	n/a	San Dieguito Union High	Encinitas
n/a	n/a	San Francisco Unified	San Francisco
n/a	n/a	San Gabriel Unified	San Gabriel
n/a	n/a	San Jacinto Unified	San Jacinto
n/a	n/a	San Joaquin County Office of Educ.	Stockton
n/a	n/a	San Jose Unified	San Jose
n/a	n/a	San Juan Unified	Carmichael
n/a	n/a	San Leandro Unified	San Leandro
n/a	n/a	San Lorenzo Unified	San Lorenzo
n/a	n/a	San Lorenzo Valley Unified	Ben Lomond
n/a	n/a	San Luis Coastal Unified	San Luis Obispo
n/a	n/a	San Marcos Unified	San Marcos
n/a	n/a	San Marino Unified	San Marino
n/a	n/a	San Mateo Union High	San Mateo
n/a	n/a	San Mateo-Foster City	Foster City
n/a	n/a	San Rafael City Elementary	San Rafael
n/a	n/a	San Rafael City High	San Rafael
n/a	n/a	San Ramon Valley Unified	Danville
n/a	n/a	San Ysidro Elementary	San Ysidro
n/a	n/a	Sanger Unified	Sanger
n/a	n/a	Santa Ana Unified	Santa Ana
n/a	n/a	Santa Barbara Unified	Santa Barbara
n/a	n/a	Santa Clara County Office of Educ.	San Jose
n/a	n/a	Santa Clara Unified	Santa Clara
n/a	n/a	Santa Cruz City Elementary	Soquel
n/a	n/a	Santa Cruz City High	Soquel
n/a	n/a	Santa Maria Joint Union High	Santa Maria
n/a	n/a	Santa Maria-Bonita	Santa Maria
n/a	n/a	Santa Monica-Malibu Unified	Santa Monica
n/a	n/a	Santa Paula Elementary	Santa Paula
n/a	n/a	Santa Paula Union High	Santa Paula
n/a	n/a	Santa Rita Union Elementary	Salinas
n/a	n/a	Santa Rosa Elementary	Santa Rosa
n/a	n/a	Santa Rosa High	Santa Rosa
n/a	n/a	Santee Elementary	Santee
n/a	n/a	Saratoga Union Elementary	Saratoga
n/a	n/a	Saugus Union	Santa Clarita
n/a	n/a	Savanna Elementary	Anaheim
n/a	n/a	Sbc - Aspire Public Schools	Oakland
n/a	n/a	Sbc - High Tech High	San Diego
n/a	n/a	Scotts Valley Unified	Scotts Valley

n/a	n/a	Selma Unified	Selma
n/a	n/a	Sequoia Union High	Redwood City
n/a	n/a	Shasta Union High	Redding
n/a	n/a	Sierra Sands Unified	Ridgecrest
n/a	n/a	Silver Valley Unified	Yermo
n/a	n/a	Simi Valley Unified	Simi Valley
n/a	n/a	Snowline Joint Unified	Phelan
n/a	n/a	Solana Beach Elementary	Solana Beach
n/a	n/a	Soledad Unified	Soledad
n/a	n/a	Sonoma Valley Unified	Sonoma
n/a	n/a	Soquel Union Elementary	Capitola
n/a	n/a	South Bay Union Elementary	Imperial Beach
n/a	n/a	South Monterey Co. Jt Union High	King City
n/a	n/a	South Pasadena Unified	South Pasadena
n/a	n/a	S San Francisco Unified	S San Francisco
n/a	n/a	South Whittier Elementary	Whittier
n/a	n/a	Southern Kern Unified	Rosamond
n/a	n/a	Spencer Valley Elementary	Santa Ysabel
n/a	n/a	Standard Elementary	Bakersfield
n/a	n/a	Stanislaus County Office of Educ.	Modesto
n/a	n/a	Stanislaus Union Elementary	Modesto
n/a	n/a	Stockton Unified	Stockton
n/a	n/a	Sulphur Springs Union	Canyon Country
n/a	n/a	Sunnyvale	Sunnyvale
n/a	n/a	Sweetwater Union High	Chula Vista
n/a	n/a	Sylvan Union Elementary	Modesto
n/a	n/a	Taft City	Taft
n/a	n/a	Tahoe-Truckee Joint Unified	Truckee
n/a	n/a	Tamalpais Union High	Larkspur
n/a	n/a	Tehachapi Unified	Tehachapi
n/a	n/a	Temecula Valley Unified	Temecula
n/a	n/a	Temple City Unified	Temple City
n/a	n/a	Templeton Unified	Templeton
n/a	n/a	Torrance Unified	Torrance
n/a	n/a	Tracy Joint Unified	Tracy
n/a	n/a	Travis Unified	Fairfield
n/a	n/a	Tulare City	Tulare
n/a	n/a	Tulare County Office of Education	Visalia
n/a	n/a	Tulare Joint Union High	Tulare
n/a	n/a	Turlock Unified	Turlock
n/a	n/a	Tustin Unified	Tustin
n/a	n/a	Twin Rivers Unified	Mcclellan
n/a	n/a	Ukiah Unified	Ukiah
n/a	n/a	Union Elementary	San Jose
n/a	n/a	Upland Unified	Upland
n/a	n/a	Vacaville Unified	Vacaville
n/a	n/a	Val Verde Unified	Perris
n/a	n/a	Vallejo City Unified	Vallejo
n/a	n/a	Valley Center-Pauma Unified	Valley Center
n/a	n/a	Ventura County Office of Educ.	Camarillo
n/a	n/a	Ventura Unified	Ventura
n/a	n/a	Victor Elementary	Victorville
n/a	n/a	Victor Valley Union High	Victorville
n/a	n/a	Visalia Unified	Visalia
n/a	n/a	Vista Unified	Vista
n/a	n/a	Walnut Creek Elementary	Walnut Creek
n/a	n/a	Walnut Valley Unified	Walnut
n/a	n/a	Wasco Union Elementary	Wasco
n/a	n/a	Wasco Union High	Wasco
n/a	n/a	Washington Unified	West Sacramento
n/a	n/a	Washington Unified	Fresno
n/a	n/a	Waterford Unified	Waterford
n/a	n/a	Weaver Union	Merced
n/a	n/a	West Contra Costa Unified	Richmond
n/a	n/a	West Covina Unified	West Covina
n/a	n/a	West Sonoma County Union High	Sebastopol
n/a	n/a	Western Placer Unified	Lincoln
n/a	n/a	Westminster Elementary	Westminster
n/a	n/a	Westside Union Elementary	Quartz Hill
n/a	n/a	Whittier City Elementary	Whittier
n/a	n/a	Whittier Union High	Whittier
n/a	n/a	William S. Hart Union High	Santa Clarita
n/a	n/a	Willits Unified	Willits
n/a	n/a	Willows Unified	Willows
n/a	n/a	Windsor Unified	Windsor
n/a	n/a	Winters Joint Unified	Winters
n/a	n/a	Winton Elementary	Winton
n/a	n/a	Wiseburn Elementary	Hawthorne
n/a	n/a	Woodlake Union Elementary	Woodlake
n/a	n/a	Woodland Joint Unified	Woodland
n/a	n/a	Wright Elementary	Santa Rosa
n/a	n/a	Yosemite Unified	Oakhurst
n/a	n/a	Yuba City Unified	Yuba City
n/a	n/a	Yucaipa-Calimesa Joint Unified	Yucaipa

Note: This section only includes districts with 1,500 or more students; All categories are ranked from high to low

Overall Results

- In 2013, the average score of fourth-grade students in California was 234. This was lower than the average score of 241 for public school students in the nation.
- The average score for students in California in 2013 (234) was not significantly different from their average score in 2011 (234) and was higher than their average score in 1992 (208).
- The score gap between higher performing students in California (those at the 75th percentile) and lower performing students (those at the 25th percentile) was 43 points in 2013. This performance gap was not significantly different from that in 1992 (49 points).
- The percentage of students in California who performed at or above the NAEP *Proficient* level was 33 percent in 2013. This percentage was not significantly different from that in 2011 (34 percent) and was greater than that in 1992 (12 percent).
- The percentage of students in California who performed at or above the NAEP *Basic* level was 74 percent in 2013. This percentage was not significantly different from that in 2011 (74 percent) and was greater than that in 1992 (46 percent).

Achievement-Level Percentages and Average Score Results

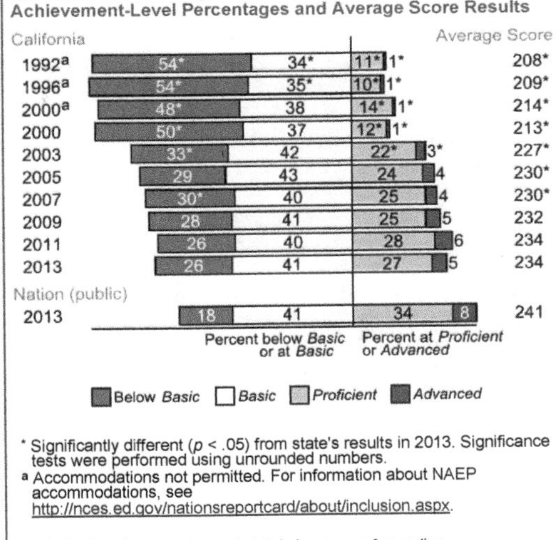

* Significantly different ($p < .05$) from state's results in 2013. Significance tests were performed using unrounded numbers.
[a] Accommodations not permitted. For information about NAEP accommodations, see http://nces.ed.gov/nationsreportcard/about/inclusion.aspx.

NOTE: Detail may not sum to totals because of rounding.

Compare the Average Score in 2013 to Other States/Jurisdictions

District of Columbia
DoDEA[1]

[1] Department of Defense Education Activity (overseas and domestic schools).

In 2013, the average score in California (234) was

- lower than those in 42 states/jurisdictions
- higher than that in 1 state/jurisdiction
- not significantly different from those in 8 states/jurisdictions

Average Scores for State/Jurisdiction and Nation (public)

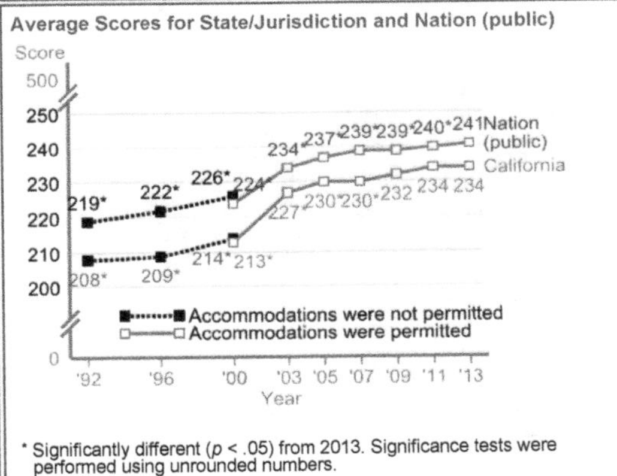

* Significantly different ($p < .05$) from 2013. Significance tests were performed using unrounded numbers.

NOTE: For information about NAEP accommodations, see http://nces.ed.gov/nationsreportcard/about/inclusion.aspx.

Results for Student Groups in 2013

Reporting Groups	Percent of students	Avg. score	Percentages at or above *Basic*	Percentages at or above *Proficient*	Percent at *Advanced*
Race/Ethnicity					
White	26	249	89	53	9
Black	6	221	60	18	1
Hispanic	54	224	65	19	1
Asian	11	255	91	60	20
American Indian/Alaska Native	1	‡	‡	‡	‡
Native Hawaiian/Pacific Islander	1	‡	‡	‡	‡
Two or more races	1	244	79	50	15
Gender					
Male	51	235	75	35	6
Female	49	232	72	30	4
National School Lunch Program					
Eligible	60	224	64	19	2
Not eligible	39	249	89	53	11

‡ Reporting standards not met.

NOTE: Detail may not sum to totals because of rounding, and because the "Information not available" category for the National School Lunch Program, which provides free/reduced-price lunches, is not displayed. Black includes African American and Hispanic includes Latino. Race categories exclude Hispanic origin.

Score Gaps for Student Groups

- In 2013, Black students had an average score that was 27 points lower than White students. This performance gap was narrower than that in 1992 (39 points).
- In 2013, Hispanic students had an average score that was 25 points lower than White students. This performance gap was not significantly different from that in 1992 (31 points).
- In 2013, male students in California had an average score that was not significantly different from female students.
- In 2013, students who were eligible for free/reduced-price school lunch, an indicator of low family income, had an average score that was 25 points lower than students who were not eligible for free/reduced-price school lunch. This performance gap was not significantly different from that in 1996 (28 points).

NOTE: Statistical comparisons are calculated on the basis of unrounded scale scores or percentages.
SOURCE: U.S. Department of Education, Institute of Education Sciences, National Center for Education Statistics, National Assessment of Educational Progress (NAEP), various years, 1992–2013 Mathematics Assessments.

Overall Results

- In 2013, the average score of eighth-grade students in California was 276. This was lower than the average score of 284 for public school students in the nation.
- The average score for students in California in 2013 (276) was not significantly different from their average score in 2011 (273) and was higher than their average score in 1990 (256).
- The score gap between higher performing students in California (those at the 75th percentile) and lower performing students (those at the 25th percentile) was 51 points in 2013. This performance gap was not significantly different from that in 1990 (51 points).
- The percentage of students in California who performed at or above the NAEP *Proficient* level was 28 percent in 2013. This percentage was not significantly different from that in 2011 (25 percent) and was greater than that in 1990 (12 percent).
- The percentage of students in California who performed at or above the NAEP *Basic* level was 65 percent in 2013. This percentage was not significantly different from that in 2011 (61 percent) and was greater than that in 1990 (45 percent).

Achievement-Level Percentages and Average Score Results

* Significantly different ($p < .05$) from state's results in 2013. Significance tests were performed using unrounded numbers.

[a] Accommodations not permitted. For information about NAEP accommodations, see http://nces.ed.gov/nationsreportcard/about/inclusion.aspx.

NOTE: Detail may not sum to totals because of rounding.

Compare the Average Score in 2013 to Other States/Jurisdictions

[1] Department of Defense Education Activity (overseas and domestic schools).

In 2013, the average score in California (276) was

- lower than those in 40 states/jurisdictions
- higher than those in 5 states/jurisdictions
- not significantly different from those in 6 states/jurisdictions

Average Scores for State/Jurisdiction and Nation (public)

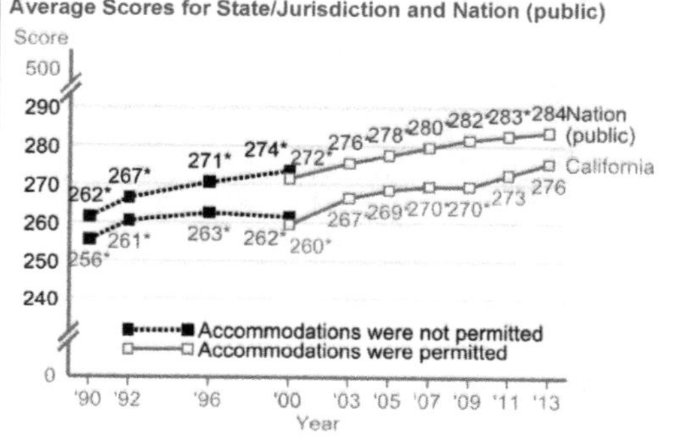

* Significantly different ($p < .05$) from 2013. Significance tests were performed using unrounded numbers.

NOTE: For information about NAEP accommodations, see http://nces.ed.gov/nationsreportcard/about/inclusion.aspx.

Results for Student Groups in 2013

Reporting Groups	Percent of students	Avg. score	Percentages at or above *Basic*	Percentages at or above *Proficient*	Percent at *Advanced*
Race/Ethnicity					
White	28	291	82	42	10
Black	6	258	45	11	2
Hispanic	53	263	53	15	2
Asian	12	307	88	61	24
American Indian/Alaska Native	1	‡	‡	‡	‡
Native Hawaiian/Pacific Islander	1	‡	‡	‡	‡
Two or more races	1	300	89	55	13
Gender					
Male	51	277	66	29	7
Female	49	275	63	26	5
National School Lunch Program					
Eligible	58	264	54	15	2
Not eligible	41	293	80	45	13

‡ Reporting standards not met.

NOTE: Detail may not sum to totals because of rounding, and because the "Information not available" category for the National School Lunch Program, which provides free/reduced-price lunches, is not displayed. Black includes African American and Hispanic includes Latino. Race categories exclude Hispanic origin.

Score Gaps for Student Groups

- In 2013, Black students had an average score that was 33 points lower than White students. This performance gap was not significantly different from that in 1990 (38 points).
- In 2013, Hispanic students had an average score that was 28 points lower than White students. This performance gap was not significantly different from that in 1990 (34 points).
- In 2013, male students in California had an average score that was not significantly different from female students.
- In 2013, students who were eligible for free/reduced-price school lunch, an indicator of low family income, had an average score that was 29 points lower than students who were not eligible for free/reduced-price school lunch. This performance gap was not significantly different from that in 1996 (30 points).

ies National Center for Education Statistics, Institute of Education Sciences

NOTE: Statistical comparisons are calculated on the basis of unrounded scale scores or percentages.
SOURCE: U.S. Department of Education, Institute of Education Sciences, National Center for Education Statistics, National Assessment of Educational Progress (NAEP), various years, 1990–2013 Mathematics Assessments.

Overall Results

- In 2013, the average score of fourth-grade students in California was 213. This was lower than the average score of 221 for public school students in the nation.
- The average score for students in California in 2013 (213) was not significantly different from their average score in 2011 (211) and was higher than their average score in 1992 (202).
- The score gap between higher performing students in California (those at the 75th percentile) and lower performing students (those at the 25th percentile) was 52 points in 2013. This performance gap was not significantly different from that in 1992 (55 points).
- The percentage of students in California who performed at or above the NAEP *Proficient* level was 27 percent in 2013. This percentage was not significantly different from that in 2011 (25 percent) and was greater than that in 1992 (19 percent).
- The percentage of students in California who performed at or above the NAEP *Basic* level was 58 percent in 2013. This percentage was not significantly different from that in 2011 (56 percent) and was greater than that in 1992 (48 percent).

Achievement-Level Percentages and Average Score Results

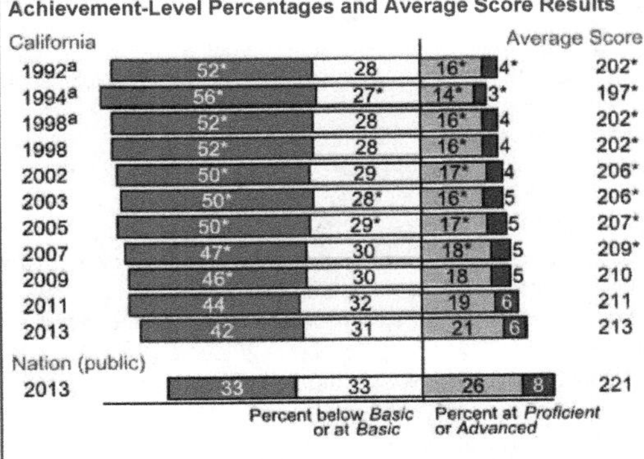

* Significantly different ($p < .05$) from state's results in 2013. Significance tests were performed using unrounded numbers.

a Accommodations not permitted. For information about NAEP accommodations, see http://nces.ed.gov/nationsreportcard/about/inclusion.aspx.

NOTE: Detail may not sum to totals because of rounding.

Compare the Average Score in 2013 to Other States/Jurisdictions

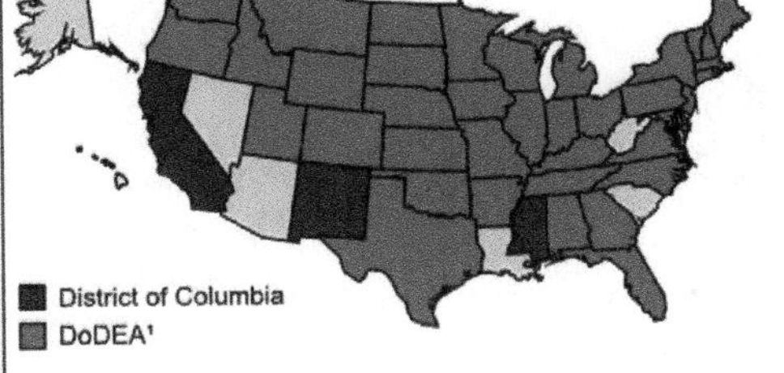

District of Columbia

DoDEA[1]

[1] Department of Defense Education Activity (overseas and domestic schools).

In 2013, the average score in California (213) was

- lower than those in 41 states/jurisdictions
- higher than those in 3 states/jurisdictions
- not significantly different from those in 7 states/jurisdictions

Average Scores for State/Jurisdiction and Nation (public)

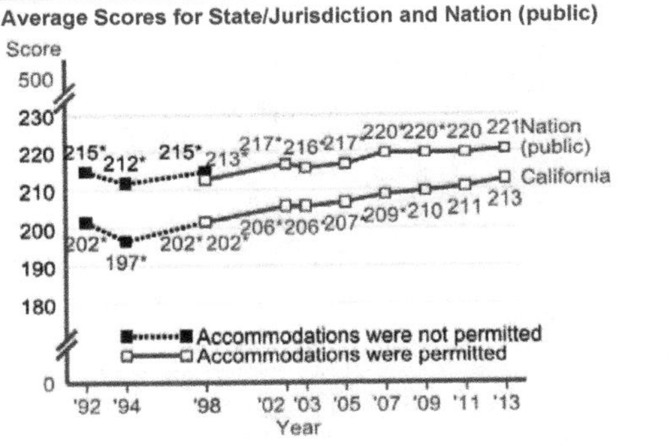

* Significantly different ($p < .05$) from 2013. Significance tests were performed using unrounded numbers.

NOTE: For information about NAEP accommodations, see http://nces.ed.gov/nationsreportcard/about/inclusion.aspx.

Results for Student Groups in 2013

Reporting Groups	Percent of students	Avg. score	Percentages at or above *Basic*	Percentages at or above *Proficient*	Percent at *Advanced*
Race/Ethnicity					
White	26	232	79	46	13
Black	6	202	44	13	1
Hispanic	54	201	46	16	2
Asian	11	229	77	43	11
American Indian/Alaska Native	1	‡	‡	‡	‡
Native Hawaiian/Pacific Islander	1	‡	‡	‡	‡
Two or more races	1	226	70	38	16
Gender					
Male	51	210	55	25	5
Female	49	216	61	29	7
National School Lunch Program					
Eligible	60	200	45	15	2
Not eligible	39	232	79	46	12

‡ Reporting standards not met.

NOTE: Detail may not sum to totals because of rounding, and because the "Information not available" category for the National School Lunch Program, which provides free/reduced-price lunches, is not displayed. Black includes African American and Hispanic includes Latino. Race categories exclude Hispanic origin.

Score Gaps for Student Groups

- In 2013, Black students had an average score that was 30 points lower than White students. This performance gap was not significantly different from that in 1992 (36 points).
- In 2013, Hispanic students had an average score that was 31 points lower than White students. This performance gap was not significantly different from that in 1992 (37 points).
- In 2013, female students in California had an average score that was higher than male students by 6 points.
- In 2013, students who were eligible for free/reduced-price school lunch, an indicator of low family income, had an average score that was 32 points lower than students who were not eligible for free/reduced-price school lunch. This performance gap was not significantly different from that in 1998 (36 points).

NOTE: Statistical comparisons are calculated on the basis of unrounded scale scores or percentages.
SOURCE: U.S. Department of Education, Institute of Education Sciences, National Center for Education Statistics, National Assessment of Educational Progress (NAEP), various years, 1992–2013 Reading Assessments.

The Nation's Report Card Reading 2013 State Snapshot Report

California
Grade 8
Public Schools

Overall Results

- In 2013, the average score of eighth-grade students in California was 262. This was lower than the average score of 266 for public school students in the nation.
- The average score for students in California in 2013 (262) was higher than their average score in 2011 (255) and in 1998 (252).
- The score gap between higher performing students in California (those at the 75th percentile) and lower performing students (those at the 25th percentile) was 45 points in 2013. This performance gap was not significantly different from that in 1998 (46 points).
- The percentage of students in California who performed at or above the NAEP *Proficient* level was 29 percent in 2013. This percentage was greater than that in 2011 (24 percent) and in 1998 (21 percent).
- The percentage of students in California who performed at or above the NAEP *Basic* level was 72 percent in 2013. This percentage was greater than that in 2011 (65 percent) and in 1998 (63 percent).

Achievement-Level Percentages and Average Score Results

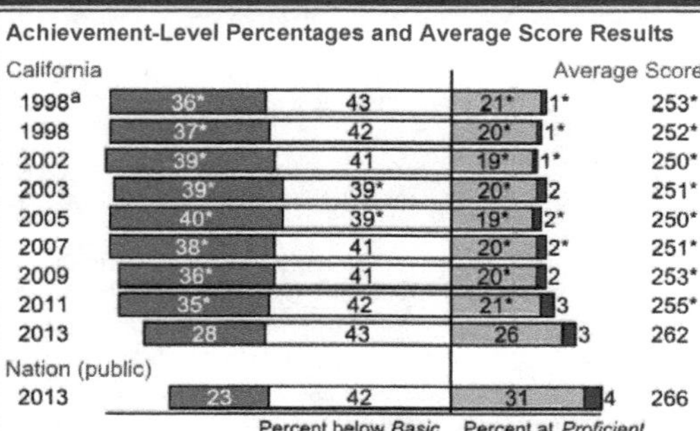

* Significantly different ($p < .05$) from state's results in 2013. Significance tests were performed using unrounded numbers.
[a] Accommodations not permitted. For information about NAEP accommodations, see http://nces.ed.gov/nationsreportcard/about/inclusion.aspx.

NOTE: Detail may not sum to totals because of rounding.

Compare the Average Score in 2013 to Other States/Jurisdictions

District of Columbia
DoDEA[1]

[1] Department of Defense Education Activity (overseas and domestic schools).

In 2013, the average score in California (262) was

- lower than those in 35 states/jurisdictions
- higher than those in 6 states/jurisdictions
- not significantly different from those in 10 states/jurisdictions

Average Scores for State/Jurisdiction and Nation (public)

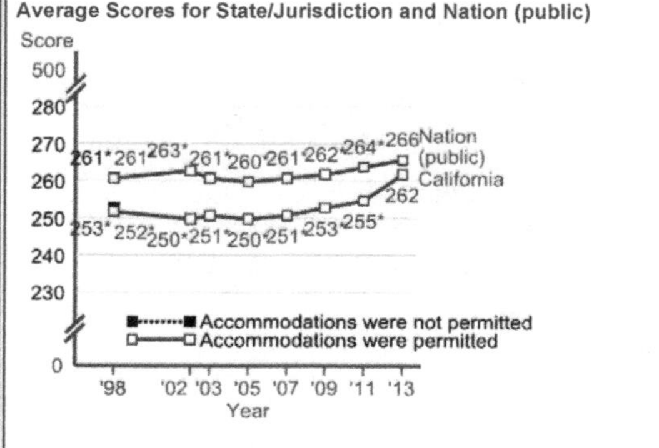

* Significantly different ($p < .05$) from 2013. Significance tests were performed using unrounded numbers.

NOTE: For information about NAEP accommodations, see http://nces.ed.gov/nationsreportcard/about/inclusion.aspx.

Results for Student Groups in 2013

Reporting Groups	Percent of students	Avg. score	Percentages at or above *Basic*	Percentages at or above *Proficient*	Percent at *Advanced*
Race/Ethnicity					
White	27	275	85	44	5
Black	6	247	56	15	#
Hispanic	52	252	64	18	1
Asian	12	280	86	51	9
American Indian/Alaska Native	1	‡	‡	‡	‡
Native Hawaiian/Pacific Islander	1	‡	‡	‡	‡
Two or more races	1	270	84	36	7
Gender					
Male	51	257	68	25	2
Female	49	267	77	34	4
National School Lunch Program					
Eligible	58	251	63	17	1
Not eligible	41	276	85	46	6

Rounds to zero. ‡ Reporting standards not met.

NOTE: Detail may not sum to totals because of rounding, and because the "Information not available" category for the National School Lunch Program, which provides free/reduced-price lunches, is not displayed. Black includes African American and Hispanic includes Latino. Race categories exclude Hispanic origin.

Score Gaps for Student Groups

- In 2013, Black students had an average score that was 28 points lower than White students. This performance gap was not significantly different from that in 1998 (30 points).
- In 2013, Hispanic students had an average score that was 23 points lower than White students. This performance gap was narrower than that in 1998 (30 points).
- In 2013, female students in California had an average score that was higher than male students by 10 points.
- In 2013, students who were eligible for free/reduced-price school lunch, an indicator of low family income, had an average score that was 25 points lower than students who were not eligible for free/reduced-price school lunch. This performance gap was narrower than that in 1998 (32 points).

NOTE: Statistical comparisons are calculated on the basis of unrounded scale scores or percentages.
SOURCE: U.S. Department of Education, Institute of Education Sciences, National Center for Education Statistics, National Assessment of Educational Progress (NAEP), various years, 1998–2013 Reading Assessments.

Science 2009

State Snapshot Report

California
Grade 4
Public Schools

2009 Science Assessment Content

Guided by a new framework, the NAEP science assessment was updated in 2009 to keep the content current with key developments in science, curriculum standards, assessments, and research. The 2009 framework organizes science content into three broad content areas.

Physical science includes concepts related to properties and changes of matter, forms of energy, energy transfer and conservation, position and motion of objects, and forces affecting motion.

Life science includes concepts related to organization and development, matter and energy transformations, interdependence, heredity and reproduction, and evolution and diversity.

Earth and space sciences includes concepts related to objects in the universe, the history of the Earth, properties of Earth materials, tectonics, energy in Earth systems, climate and weather, and biogeochemical cycles.

The 2009 science assessment was composed of 143 questions at grade 4, 162 at grade 8, and 179 at grade 12. Students responded to only a portion of the questions, which included both multiple-choice questions and questions that required a written response.

Compare the Average Score in 2009 to Other States/Jurisdictions

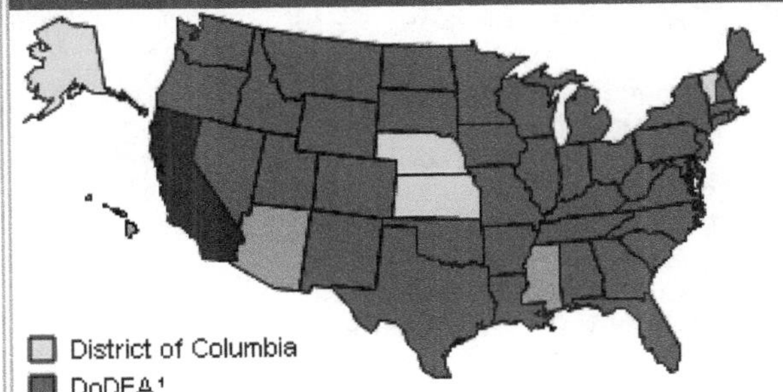

[1] Department of Defense Education Activity (overseas and domestic schools).

In 2009, the average score in **California** was

- lower than those in 43 states/jurisdictions
- higher than that in 0 states/jurisdictions
- not significantly different from those in 3 states/jurisdictions
- 5 states/jurisdictions did not participate

Overall Results

- In 2009, the average score of fourth-grade students in California was 136. This was lower than the average score of 149 for public school students in the nation.
- The percentage of students in California who performed at or above the NAEP *Proficient* level was 22 percent in 2009. This percentage was smaller than the nation (32 percent).
- The percentage of students in California who performed at or above the NAEP *Basic* level was 58 percent in 2009. This percentage was smaller than the nation (71 percent).

Achievement-Level Percentages and Average Score Results

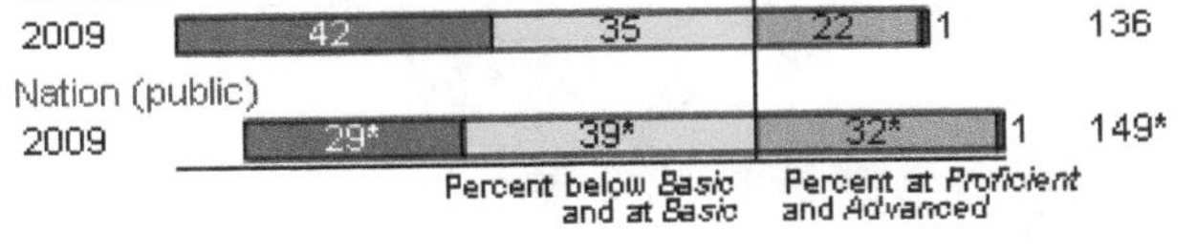

* Significantly different ($p < .05$) from California. Significance tests were performed using unrounded numbers.

NOTE: Detail may not sum to totals because of rounding.

Results for Student Groups in 2009

Reporting Groups	Percent of students	Avg. score	Percentages at or above Basic	Percentages at or above Proficient	Percent at Advanced
Gender					
Male	52	136	57	22	#
Female	48	137	58	22	1
Race/Ethnicity					
White	28	157	81	41	1
Black	7	122	41	9	#
Hispanic	51	121	42	8	#
Asian/Pacific Islander	11	160	81	45	3
American Indian/Alaska Native	1	‡	‡	‡	‡
National School Lunch Program					
Eligible	53	122	43	10	#
Not eligible	45	154	76	38	1

Rounds to zero. ‡ Reporting standards not met.

NOTE: Detail may not sum to totals because of rounding, and because the "Information not available" category for the National School Lunch Program, which provides free/reduced-price lunches, and the "Unclassified" category for race/ethnicity are not displayed.

Score Gaps for Student Groups

- In 2009, female students in California had an average score that was not significantly different from male students.
- In 2009, Black students had an average score that was 35 points lower than White students. This performance gap was not significantly different from the nation (35 points).
- In 2009, Hispanic students had an average score that was 36 points lower than White students. This performance gap was not significantly different from the nation (32 points).
- In 2009, students who were eligible for free/reduced-price school lunch, an indicator of low family income, had an average score that was 32 points lower than students who were not eligible for free/reduced-price school lunch. This performance gap was not significantly different from the nation (29 points).

NOTE: Statistical comparisons are calculated on the basis of unrounded scale scores or percentages.
SOURCE: U.S. Department of Education, Institute of Education Sciences, National Center for Education Statistics, National Assessment of Educational Progress (NAEP), 2009 Science Assessment.

The Nation's Report Card Science 2011 State Snapshot Report

California Grade 8 Public Schools

Overall Results

- In 2011, the average score of eighth-grade students in California was 140. This was lower than the average score of 151 for public school students in the nation.
- The average score for students in California in 2011 (140) was not significantly different from their average score in 2009 (137).
- In 2011, the score gap between students in California at the 75th percentile and students at the 25th percentile was 50 points. This performance gap was not significantly different from that of 2009 (51 points).
- The percentage of students in California who performed at or above the NAEP *Proficient* level was 22 percent in 2011. This percentage was not significantly different from that in 2009 (20 percent).
- The percentage of students in California who performed at or above the NAEP *Basic* level was 53 percent in 2011. This percentage was not significantly different from that in 2009 (48 percent).

Achievement-Level Percentages and Average Score Results

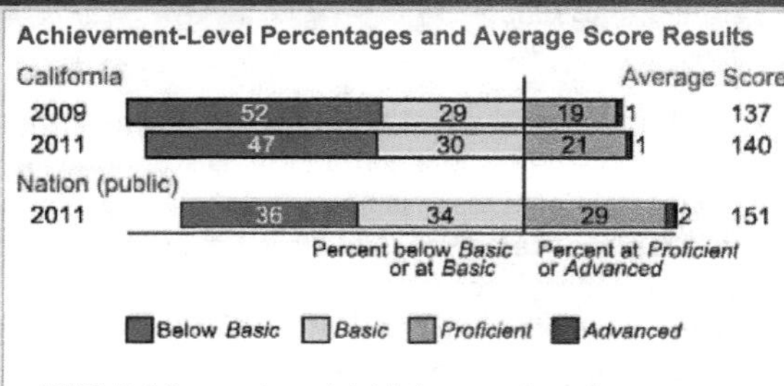

NOTE: Detail may not sum to totals because of rounding.

Compare the Average Score in 2011 to Other States/Jurisdictions

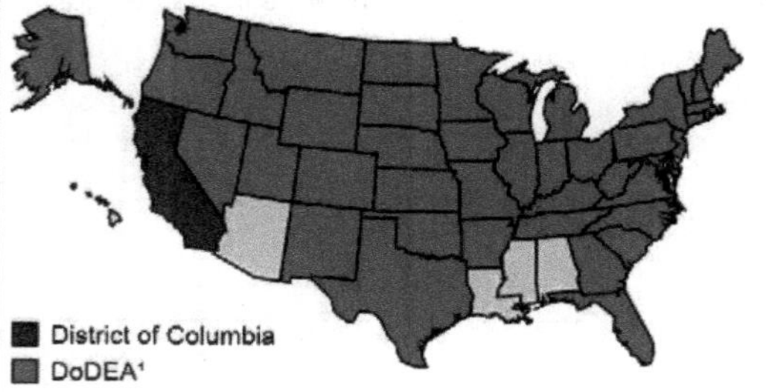

[1] Department of Defense Education Activity (overseas and domestic schools).

In 2011, the average score in California (140) was

- lower than those in 45 states/jurisdictions
- higher than that in 1 state/jurisdiction
- not significantly different from those in 5 states/jurisdictions

Average Scores for State/Jurisdiction and Nation (public)

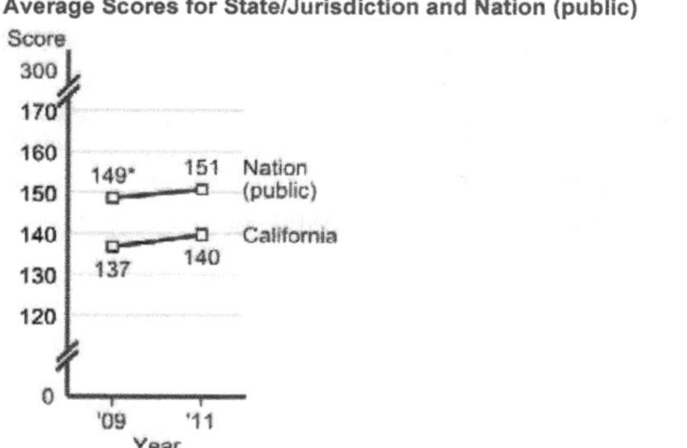

* Significantly different ($p < .05$) from 2011. Significance tests were performed using unrounded numbers.

Results for Student Groups in 2011

Reporting Groups	Percent of students	Avg. score	Percentages at or above *Basic*	Percentages at or above *Proficient*	Percent at *Advanced*
Race/Ethnicity					
White	26	159	74	39	2
Black	7	124	32	8	#
Hispanic	51	128	39	11	#
Asian	14	158	73	41	2
American Indian/Alaska Native	1	‡	‡	‡	‡
Native Hawaiian/Pacific Islander	1	‡	‡	‡	‡
Two or more races	#	‡	‡	‡	‡
Gender					
Male	51	143	55	25	1
Female	49	138	50	20	1
National School Lunch Program					
Eligible	55	127	37	10	#
Not eligible	44	157	71	38	2

Rounds to zero. ‡ Reporting standards not met.

NOTE: Detail may not sum to totals because of rounding, and because the "Information not available" category for the National School Lunch Program, which provides free/reduced-price lunches, is not displayed. Black includes African American and Hispanic includes Latino. Race categories exclude Hispanic origin.

Score Gaps for Student Groups

- In 2011, Black students had an average score that was 36 points lower than White students. This performance gap was not significantly different from that in 2009 (35 points).
- In 2011, Hispanic students had an average score that was 31 points lower than White students. This performance gap was not significantly different from that in 2009 (35 points).
- In 2011, male students in California had an average score that was not significantly different from female students.
- In 2011, students who were eligible for free/reduced-price school lunch, an indicator of low family income, had an average score that was 30 points lower than students who were not eligible for free/reduced-price school lunch. This performance gap was not significantly different from that in 2009 (31 points).

NOTE: Statistical comparisons are calculated on the basis of unrounded scale scores or percentages.
SOURCE: U.S. Department of Education, Institute of Education Sciences, National Center for Education Statistics, National Assessment of Educational Progress (NAEP), 2009 and 2011 Science Assessments.

NCES National Center for Education Statistics · The Nation's Report Card NAEP

The Nation's Report Card
State **Writing 2002**
Snapshot Report

California
Grade 4
Public School

NCES 2003-532CA4

The writing assessment of the National Assessment of Educational Progress (NAEP) measures narrative, informative, and persuasive writing–three purposes identified in the NAEP framework. The NAEP writing scale ranges from 0 to 300.

Overall Writing Results for California

- The average scale score for fourth-grade students in California was 146.
- California's average score (146) was lower[1] than that of the nation's public schools (153).
- Students' average scale scores in California were higher than those in 3 jurisdictions[2], not significantly different from those in 23 jurisdictions, and lower than those in 21 jurisdictions.
- The percentage of students who performed at or above the NAEP *Proficient* level was 23 percent. The percentage of students who performed at or above the *Basic* level was 80 percent.

Student Percentage at Each Achievement Level

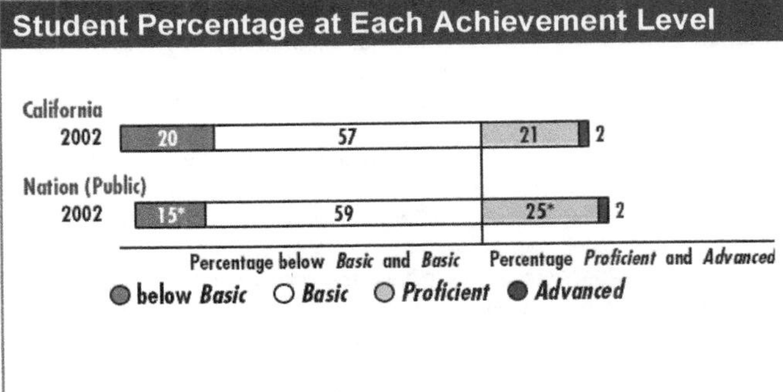

Performance of NAEP Reporting Groups in California

Reporting groups	Percentage of students	Average Score	Below *Basic*	*Basic*	*Proficient*	*Advanced*
Male	52	136 ↓	27 ↑	60	13 ↓	1
Female	48	157	13	55	30	3
White	35	158	11	57	29	2
Black	7	138	27	59	14	1
Hispanic	46	135	28	58	13 ↓	1
Asian/Pacific Islander	10	164	8	54	35	3
American Indian/Alaska Native	1	---	---	---	---	---
Free/reduced-priced school lunch						
Eligible	46	134	29	59	12 ↓	#
Not eligible	37	162	10	54	33	3
Information not available	17	147	18	60	20	2

Average Score Gaps Between Selected Groups

- Female students in California had an average score that was higher than that of male students (21 points). This performance gap was not significantly different from that of the Nation (18 points).
- White students had an average score that was higher than that of Black students (21 points). This performance gap was not significantly different from that of the Nation (20 points).
- White students had an average score that was higher than that of Hispanic students (23 points). This performance gap was not significantly different from that of the Nation (19 points).
- Students who were not eligible for free/reduced-price school lunch had an average score that was higher than that of students who were eligible (28 points). This performance gap was not significantly different from that of the Nation (22 points).

Writing Scale Scores at Selected Percentiles

Scale Score Distribution

	25th Percentile	50th Percentile	75th Percentile
California	*121* ↓	*147* ↓	*173* ↓
Nation (Public)	*128*	*153*	*178*

An examination of scores at different percentiles on the 0-300 NAEP writing scale at each grade indicates how well students at lower, middle, and higher levels of the distribution performed. For example, the data above shows that 75 percent of students in public schools nationally scored below *178,* while 75 percent of students in California scored below *173.*

\# Percentage rounds to zero.
--- Reporting standards not met; sample size insufficient to permit a reliable estimate.
* Significantly different from California.
↑ Significantly higher than, ↓ lower than appropriate subgroup in the nation (public).
[1] Comparisons (higher/lower/not different) are based on statistical tests. The .05 level was used for testing statistical significance.
[2] "Jurisdictions" includes participating states and other jurisdictions (such as Guam or the District of Columbia).
NOTE: Detail may not sum to totals because of rounding. Score gaps are calculated based on differences between unrounded average scale scores.
Visit http://nces.ed.gov/nationsreportcard/states/ for additional results and detailed information.
SOURCE: U.S. Department of Education, Institute of Education Sciences, National Center for Education Statistics, National Assessment of Educational Progress (NAEP), 2002 Writing Assessment.

ies NATIONAL CENTER FOR EDUCATION STATISTICS Institute of Education Sciences

NCES 2008-470CA8

The Nation's Report Card **Writing 2007** State Snapshot Report

California
Grade 8
Public Schools

The National Assessment of Educational Progress (NAEP) assesses writing for three purposes identified in the NAEP framework: narrative, informative, and persuasive. The NAEP writing scale ranges from 0 to 300.

Overall Writing Results for California

- In 2007, the average scale score for eighth-grade students in California was 148. This was not significantly different from their average score in 2002 (144) and was higher than their average score in 1998 (141).[1]
- California's average score (148) in 2007 was lower than that of the nation's public schools (154).
- Of the 45 states and one other jurisdiction that participated in the 2007 eighth-grade assessment, students' average scale score in California was higher than those in 4 jurisdictions, not significantly different from those in 6 jurisdictions, and lower than those in 35 jurisdictions.[2]
- The percentage of students in California who performed at or above the NAEP *Proficient* level was 25 percent in 2007. This percentage was not significantly different from that in 2002 (23 percent) and was greater than that in 1998 (20 percent).
- The percentage of students in California who performed at or above the NAEP *Basic* level was 83 percent in 2007. This percentage was greater than that in 2002 (78 percent) and was greater than that in 1998 (76 percent).

Percentages at NAEP Achievement Levels and Average Score

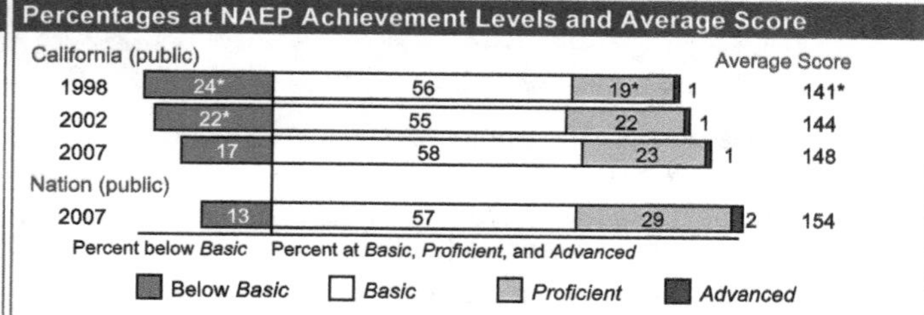

Below *Basic* | *Basic* | *Proficient* | *Advanced*

NOTE: The NAEP grade 8 writing achievement levels correspond to the following scale points: Below *Basic*, 113 or lower; *Basic*, 114–172; *Proficient*, 173–223; *Advanced*, 224 or above.

Performance of NAEP Reporting Groups in California: 2007

Reporting groups	Percent of students	Average score	Percent below *Basic*	Percent of students at or above *Basic*	Percent of students at or above *Proficient*	Percent *Advanced*
Male	52	139	23	77	17	1
Female	48	157↑	11↓	89↑	33	2
White	31	161	9	91	38	2
Black	7	138	23	77	13	#
Hispanic	48	137	23	77	13	#
Asian/Pacific Islander	12	164	10	90	44	4
American Indian/Alaska Native	1	136	29	71	17	1
Eligible for National School Lunch Program	47↑	136	24	76	13	#
Not eligible for National School Lunch Program	49	159	10	90	36	2

Average Score Gaps Between Selected Groups

- In 2007, male students in California had an average score that was lower than that of female students by 18 points. This performance gap was not significantly different from that of 1998 (15 points).
- In 2007, Black students had an average score that was lower than that of White students by 23 points. This performance gap was not significantly different from that of 1998 (20 points).
- In 2007, Hispanic students had an average score that was lower than that of White students by 24 points. This performance gap was narrower than that of 1998 (30 points).
- In 2007, students who were eligible for free/reduced-price school lunch, an indicator of poverty, had an average score that was lower than that of students who were not eligible for free/reduced-price school lunch by 23 points. This performance gap was narrower than that of 1998 (33 points).
- In 2007, the score gap between students at the 75th percentile and students at the 25th percentile was 48 points. This performance gap was not significantly different from that of 1998 (51 points).

Writing Scores at Selected Percentiles in California

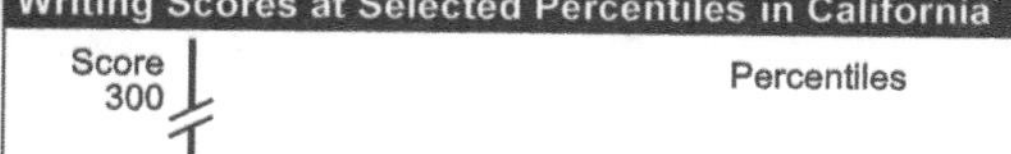

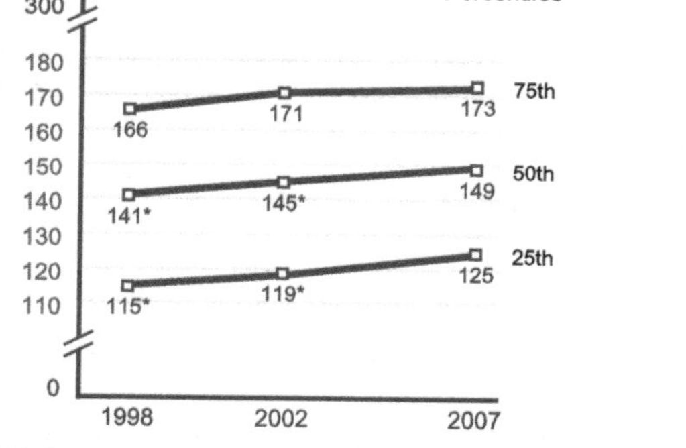

NOTE: Scores at selected percentiles on the NAEP writing scale indicate how well students at lower, middle, and higher levels performed.

\# Rounds to zero.
‡ Reporting standards not met.
* Significantly different from 2007.
↑ Significantly higher than 2002. ↓ Significantly lower than 2002.

[1] Comparisons (higher/lower/narrower/wider/not different) are based on statistical tests. The .05 level with appropriate adjustments for multiple comparisons was used for testing statistical significance. Statistical comparisons are calculated on the basis of unrounded scale scores or percentages. Comparisons across jurisdictions and comparisons with the nation or within a jurisdiction across years may be affected by differences in exclusion rates for students with disabilities (SD) and English language learners (ELL). The exclusion rates for SD and ELL in California were 1 percent and 1 percent in 2007, respectively. For more information on NAEP significance testing, see http://nces.ed.gov/nationsreportcard/writing/interpret-results.asp#statistical.

[2] "Jurisdiction" refers to states, the District of Columbia, and the Department of Defense Education Activity schools.

NOTE: Detail may not sum to totals because of rounding and because the "Information not available" category for the National School Lunch Program, which provides free and reduced-price lunches, and the "Unclassified" category for race/ethnicity are not displayed. Visit http://nces.ed.gov/nationsreportcard/states/ for additional results and detailed information.

SOURCE: U.S. Department of Education, Institute of Education Sciences, National Center for Education Statistics, National Assessment of Educational Progress (NAEP), 1998, 2002, and 2007 Writing Assessments.

CAASPP Reporting » 2014 CAASPP » About 2014 CAASPP

2014 CAASPP Paper-based Test Results

About 2014 CAASPP

The 2014 California Assessment of Student Performance and Progress (CAASPP) System includes four paper-based tests:

- California Standards Tests - Science
- California Modified Assessment - Science
- California Alternate Performance Assessment – English language arts (ELA), mathematics, and science
- Standards-based Tests in Spanish – Reading/language arts (RLA)

California Standards Tests (CSTs)

The CSTs for science in grades five, eight, and ten are administered only to students in California public schools. All questions are multiple–choice. These tests were developed specifically to assess students' knowledge of the California content standards in science. The 2014 CSTs were required for students who were enrolled in grades 5, 8, and 10 at the time of testing.

Science
The CSTs for science were administered by grade to students in grades five, eight, and ten.

- Grade five—Covers grades four and five science content standards
- Grade eight—Covers grade eight science content standards
- Grade ten (CST for Life Science)—Covers middle school life science and high school biology content standards

All CSTs for Science have 60 multiple-choice questions.

California Modified Assessment (CMA)

The CMA for science was administered to eligible students in grades five, eight, and ten. The CMA is a standards-based test for students with an individualized education program who meet the eligibility criteria adopted by the State Board of Education. The Elementary and Secondary Education Act called for a range of assessments appropriate to students' abilities. The CMA provides an appropriate assessment for a small percentage of students allowing them to demonstrate their knowledge of skills in the California academic content standards for science.

The CMA for Science tests were administered by grade to eligible students in grades five, eight, and ten.

- Grade five—Covers grades four and five science content standards
- Grade eight—Covers grade eight science content standards
- Grade ten (CST for Life Science)—Covers middle school life science and high school biology content standards

California Alternate Performance Assessment (CAPA)

Students with significant cognitive disabilities who are unable to take the Smarter Balanced Field Test even with designated supports and accommodations participated in the CAASPP system by taking the CAPA. The CAPA is an individually administered performance assessment with all tasks linked to the California ELA, mathematics, and science content standards.

The CAPA is organized into five levels, representing specific grade spans. Most students eligible for the CAPA take the level corresponding to their enrollment grade. The CAPA tests were administered to eligible students in grades two through eleven.

- Level I
  - Students in grades two through eleven (students with the most significant cognitive disabilities)

- Level II
  - Students in grades two and three
- Level III
  - Students in grades four and five
- Level IV
  - Students in grades six through eight
- Level V
  - Students in grades nine through eleven

Standards-based Tests in Spanish (STS)

The STS consists of multiple–choice tests in Spanish that assess RLA in grades two through eleven. Local education agencies had the option of administering the STS for RLA to the Spanish-speaking English learners (ELs) in grades two through eleven who either were receiving instruction in Spanish or had been enrolled in school in the United States for less than 12 months when testing began.

California Department of Education
1430 N Street
Sacramento, CA 95814

2014 CAASPP Test Results

State of California

All Students - California Standards Test Scores

County Name: ----

District Name: ----

School Name: ----

CDS Code: ----

Total Number Tested: 1,418,901

Total Number Tested in Selected Subgroup: 1,418,901

Note: The first row in each table contains numbers 2 through 11 which represent grades two through eleven respectively. EOC stands for end-of-course.

An asterisk (*) appears on the Internet reports to protect student privacy when 10 or fewer students had valid test scores.

CST Science - Grade 5, Grade 8, and Grade 10 Life Science

Result Type	2	3	4	5	6	7	8	9	10	11	EOC
Students Tested				433,443			436,946		437,677		
Students with Scores				432,471			435,237		435,884		
Mean Scale Score				367.8			392.2		359.9		
% Advanced				27 %			44 %		28 %		
% Proficient				33 %			22 %		28 %		
% Basic				24 %			18 %		26 %		
% Below Basic				11 %			9 %		11 %		
% Far Below Basic				6 %			7 %		7 %		

California Department of Education

Page generated 3/5/2015 7:48:09 AM

2014 CAASPP Test Results

State of California

All Students - California Modified Assessment

County Name: ----

District Name: ----

School Name: ----

CDS Code: ----

Total Number Tested: 1,418,901

Total Number Tested in Selected Subgroup: 1,418,901

Note: The first row in each table contains numbers 2 through 11 which represent grades two through eleven respectively. EOC stands for end-of-course.

An asterisk (*) appears on the Internet reports to protect student privacy when 10 or fewer students had valid test scores.

CMA Science - Grade 5, Grade 8, and Grade 10 Life Science

Result Type	2	3	4	5	6	7	8	9	10	11
Students Tested				27,032			22,494		12,951	
Students with Scores				26,744			22,046		12,752	
Mean Scale Score				345.0			334.5		309.8	
% Advanced				15 %			15 %		6 %	
% Proficient				31 %			24 %		20 %	
% Basic				31 %			31 %		29 %	
% Below Basic				20 %			18 %		29 %	
% Far Below Basic				3 %			12 %		16 %	

California Department of Education

Page generated 3/5/2015 7:48:45 AM

2014 CAASPP Test Results

State of California

All Students - California Alternate Performance Assessment Scores

Total Number Tested in CAPA: 48358

Percent Tested: (48358 / 1418901) 3 %

County Name: ----

District Name: ----

School Name: ----

CDS Code: ----

Total Number Tested: 1,418,901

Total Number Tested in Selected Subgroup: 1,418,901

Note: The first row in each table contains numbers 2 through 11 which represent grades two through eleven respectively.

An asterisk (*) appears on the Internet reports to protect student privacy when 10 or fewer students had valid test scores.

CAPA English-Language Arts

	Level I									
Result Type	2	3	4	5	6	7	8	9	10	11
Students Tested	2236	1743	1653	1537	1441	1321	1264	1269	1247	1211
Students with Scores	2236	1743	1653	1537	1441	1321	1264	1269	1247	1211
Mean Scale Score	41.8	41.1	41.4	41.8	41.1	41.6	41.6	41.0	41.8	41.1
% Advanced	59 %	59 %	57 %	59 %	57 %	58 %	57 %	57 %	57 %	56 %
% Proficient	25 %	24 %	27 %	25 %	24 %	24 %	25 %	25 %	24 %	24 %
% Basic	7 %	7 %	6 %	7 %	7 %	7 %	7 %	7 %	6 %	7 %
% Below Basic	5 %	5 %	6 %	6 %	6 %	7 %	7 %	6 %	6 %	6 %
% Far Below Basic	3 %	5 %	4 %	3 %	5 %	4 %	5 %	6 %	6 %	7 %

CAPA Mathematics

	Level I									
Result Type	2	3	4	5	6	7	8	9	10	11
Students Tested	2227	1737	1650	1530	1435	1315	1256	1266	1240	1210
Students with Scores	2227	1737	1650	1530	1435	1315	1256	1266	1240	1210
Mean Scale Score	36.9	36.3	36.6	36.9	36.4	36.7	36.7	36.1	36.7	36.6
% Advanced	38 %	36 %	37 %	39 %	36 %	39 %	39 %	37 %	41 %	39 %
% Proficient	33 %	33 %	31 %	30 %	32 %	29 %	28 %	30 %	28 %	28 %
% Basic	16 %	17 %	18 %	17 %	16 %	17 %	16 %	15 %	12 %	15 %
% Below Basic	8 %	8 %	8 %	8 %	9 %	8 %	10 %	9 %	10 %	9 %
% Far Below Basic	5 %	7 %	6 %	6 %	6 %	7 %	7 %	9 %	8 %	9 %

CAPA Science

	Level I									
Result Type	2	3	4	5	6	7	8	9	10	11
Students Tested				1442			1196		1162	
Students with Scores				1442			1196		1162	
Mean Scale Score				37.4			37.7		37.7	
% Advanced				41 %			42 %		42 %	
% Proficient				28 %			23 %		24 %	
% Basic				16 %			18 %		17 %	
% Below Basic				8 %			8 %		9 %	
% Far Below Basic				7 %			8 %		9 %	

CAPA English-Language Arts

	Level II		Level III		Level IV			Level V		
Result Type	2	3	4	5	6	7	8	9	10	11
Students Tested	2462	3410	3346	3622	3314	3449	3371	3388	3566	3414
Students with Scores	2462	3410	3346	3622	3314	3449	3371	3388	3566	3414
Mean Scale Score	37.4	38.9	38.8	40.0	37.9	39.1	39.8	38.0	38.9	39.1
% Advanced	36 %	47 %	46 %	55 %	34 %	42 %	47 %	38 %	47 %	48 %
% Proficient	40 %	35 %	36 %	32 %	36 %	34 %	30 %	39 %	33 %	32 %
% Basic	18 %	13 %	13 %	10 %	19 %	15 %	14 %	18 %	16 %	15 %
% Below Basic	5 %	4 %	3 %	2 %	8 %	7 %	6 %	4 %	3 %	3 %
% Far Below Basic	2 %	1 %	2 %	1 %	3 %	3 %	3 %	2 %	2 %	2 %

CAPA Mathematics

	Level II		Level III		Level IV			Level V		
Result Type	2	3	4	5	6	7	8	9	10	11
Students Tested	2457	3407	3337	3615	3304	3438	3361	3370	3555	3399
Students with Scores	2457	3407	3337	3615	3304	3438	3361	3370	3555	3399
Mean Scale Score	36.0	38.1	35.7	36.7	35.3	36.7	37.6	36.3	37.5	37.9
% Advanced	26 %	39 %	23 %	31 %	23 %	30 %	36 %	30 %	39 %	42 %
% Proficient	35 %	31 %	37 %	36 %	34 %	36 %	35 %	37 %	33 %	32 %
% Basic	20 %	16 %	31 %	26 %	27 %	21 %	19 %	19 %	17 %	15 %
% Below Basic	16 %	13 %	7 %	6 %	15 %	11 %	9 %	11 %	9 %	9 %
% Far Below Basic	3 %	2 %	1 %	1 %	2 %	2 %	2 %	2 %	2 %	3 %

CAPA Science

	Level II		Level III		Level IV			Level V		
Result Type	2	3	4	5	6	7	8	9	10	11
Students Tested				3551			3290		3450	
Students with Scores				3551			3290		3450	
Mean Scale Score				36.1			35.7		35.9	
% Advanced				16 %			18 %		24 %	
% Proficient				54 %			48 %		41 %	
% Basic				25 %			25 %		30 %	
% Below Basic				4 %			9 %		5 %	
% Far Below Basic				1 %			1 %		1 %	

California Department of Education

Page generated 3/5/2015 7:49:05 AM

2014 CAASPP Test Results

State of California

All Students - Standards-based Tests in Spanish

County Name: ----

District Name: ----

School Name: ----

CDS Code: ----

Total Number Tested: 1,418,901

Total Number Tested in Selected Subgroup: 1,418,901

Note: The first row in each table contains numbers 2 through 11 which represent grades two through eleven respectively. EOC stands for end-of-course.

An asterisk (*) appears on the Internet reports to protect student privacy when 10 or fewer students had valid test scores.

STS Reading-Language Arts

Result Type	2	3	4	5	6	7	8	9	10	11
Students Tested	2,742	1,835	1,082	800	462	458	434	941	391	187
Students with Scores	2,695	1,819	1,077	793	458	453	430	922	389	187
Mean Scale Score	318.3	311.1	315.0	307.9	320.0	323.1	324.7	320.0	314.7	316.2
% Advanced	10 %	4 %	9 %	7 %	11 %	9 %	10 %	9 %	9 %	10 %
% Proficient	20 %	14 %	19 %	18 %	23 %	21 %	23 %	23 %	20 %	25 %
% Basic	33 %	39 %	32 %	24 %	26 %	34 %	33 %	33 %	33 %	30 %
% Below Basic	31 %	34 %	24 %	20 %	21 %	25 %	26 %	26 %	27 %	22 %
% Far Below Basic	7 %	8 %	16 %	31 %	19 %	11 %	9 %	9 %	12 %	12 %

California Department of Education

Page generated 3/5/2015 7:50:19 AM

Ancestry and Ethnicity

State Profile

Population: 37,253,956

Ancestry	Population	%
Afghan (31,291)	33,216	0.09
African, Sub-Saharan (211,499)	265,745	0.73
African (138,676)	181,250	0.49
Cape Verdean (1,322)	2,514	0.01
Ethiopian (22,305)	24,586	0.07
Ghanaian (2,126)	2,383	0.01
Kenyan (3,027)	3,397	0.01
Liberian (1,031)	1,184	<0.01
Nigerian (19,694)	21,824	0.06
Senegalese (473)	644	<0.01
Sierra Leonean (458)	667	<0.01
Somalian (6,660)	7,150	0.02
South African (5,978)	8,602	0.02
Sudanese (2,776)	3,028	0.01
Ugandan (1,082)	1,202	<0.01
Zimbabwean (525)	726	<0.01
Other Sub-Saharan African (5,366)	6,588	0.02
Albanian (2,159)	3,854	0.01
Alsatian (256)	926	<0.01
American (889,435)	889,435	2.43
Arab (178,290)	247,243	0.67
Arab (31,197)	41,438	0.11
Egyptian (31,633)	37,531	0.10
Iraqi (11,109)	15,029	0.04
Jordanian (10,962)	13,108	0.04
Lebanese (33,893)	58,107	0.16
Moroccan (5,465)	8,147	0.02
Palestinian (14,035)	18,442	0.05
Syrian (11,044)	19,307	0.05
Other Arab (28,952)	36,134	0.10
Armenian (199,725)	241,323	0.66
Assyrian/Chaldean/Syriac (22,514)	27,563	0.08
Australian (9,511)	19,471	0.05
Austrian (21,461)	81,470	0.22
Basque (8,463)	20,606	0.06
Belgian (9,074)	27,884	0.08
Brazilian (19,862)	30,167	0.08
British (80,256)	150,588	0.41
Bulgarian (7,944)	11,242	0.03
Cajun (1,411)	2,987	0.01
Canadian (44,744)	90,905	0.25
Carpatho Rusyn (64)	374	<0.01
Celtic (3,816)	7,889	0.02
Croatian (19,225)	45,537	0.12
Cypriot (474)	604	<0.01
Czech (25,930)	94,047	0.26
Czechoslovakian (11,160)	25,946	0.07
Danish (52,530)	194,960	0.53
Dutch (105,296)	422,077	1.15
Eastern European (48,975)	56,408	0.15
English (696,517)	2,482,263	6.78
Estonian (1,725)	3,744	0.01
European (387,618)	469,275	1.28
Finnish (17,635)	54,331	0.15
French, ex. Basque (126,540)	775,213	2.12
French Canadian (47,219)	117,231	0.32
German (933,090)	3,506,466	9.57
German Russian (612)	1,616	<0.01
Greek (60,205)	138,194	0.38
Guyanese (1,916)	2,932	0.01
Hungarian (45,512)	131,741	0.36
Icelander (3,058)	7,372	0.02
Iranian (175,122)	203,656	0.56
Irish (678,425)	2,748,155	7.50
Israeli (21,339)	28,074	0.08
Italian (570,968)	1,543,300	4.21
Latvian (4,764)	11,443	0.03
Lithuanian (17,224)	51,747	0.14
Luxemburger (782)	2,948	0.01
Macedonian (1,545)	2,776	0.01
Maltese (3,742)	7,582	0.02
New Zealander (2,696)	4,604	0.01
Northern European (41,001)	45,938	0.13
Norwegian (125,259)	401,548	1.10
Pennsylvania German (3,427)	7,691	0.02
Polish (154,032)	515,633	1.41
Portuguese (170,785)	374,875	1.02
Romanian (38,673)	67,491	0.18
Russian (204,639)	446,376	1.22
Scandinavian (31,728)	67,697	0.18
Scotch-Irish (147,602)	435,810	1.19
Scottish (155,163)	565,334	1.54
Serbian (7,715)	15,315	0.04
Slavic (4,984)	13,137	0.04
Slovak (9,123)	24,859	0.07
Slovene (2,813)	8,956	0.02
Soviet Union (293)	334	<0.01
Swedish (113,350)	456,603	1.25
Swiss (27,062)	114,687	0.31
Turkish (13,579)	22,091	0.06
Ukrainian (56,056)	93,449	0.26
Welsh (30,899)	180,792	0.49
West Indian, ex. Hispanic (46,550)	73,694	0.20
Bahamian (424)	775	<0.01
Barbadian (734)	1,235	<0.01
Belizean (14,852)	19,627	0.05
Bermudan (177)	308	<0.01
British West Indian (1,147)	1,757	<0.01
Dutch West Indian (625)	2,806	0.01
Haitian (4,912)	7,538	0.02
Jamaican (16,117)	25,882	0.07
Trinidadian/Tobagonian (2,671)	4,439	0.01
U.S. Virgin Islander (305)	450	<0.01
West Indian (4,457)	8,589	0.02
Other West Indian (129)	288	<0.01
Yugoslavian (18,028)	37,235	0.10

Hispanic Origin	Population	%
Hispanic or Latino (of any race)	14,013,719	37.62
Central American, ex. Mexican	1,132,520	3.04
Costa Rican	22,469	0.06
Guatemalan	332,737	0.89
Honduran	72,795	0.20
Nicaraguan	100,790	0.27
Panamanian	17,768	0.05
Salvadoran	573,956	1.54
Other Central American	12,005	0.03
Cuban	88,607	0.24
Dominican Republic	11,455	0.03
Mexican	11,423,146	30.66
Puerto Rican	189,945	0.51
South American	293,880	0.79
Argentinean	44,410	0.12
Bolivian	13,351	0.04
Chilean	24,006	0.06
Colombian	64,416	0.17
Ecuadorian	35,750	0.10
Paraguayan	1,228	<0.01
Peruvian	91,511	0.25
Uruguayan	4,110	0.01
Venezuelan	11,100	0.03
Other South American	3,998	0.01
Other Hispanic or Latino	874,166	2.35

Race*	Population	%
African-American/Black (2,299,072)	2,683,914	7.20
Not Hispanic (2,163,804)	2,436,082	6.54
Hispanic (135,268)	247,832	0.67
American Indian/Alaska Native (362,801)	723,225	1.94
Not Hispanic (162,250)	383,957	1.03
Hispanic (200,551)	339,268	0.91
Alaska Athabascan *(Ala. Nat.)* (378)	697	<0.01
Aleut *(Alaska Native)* (488)	1,107	<0.01
Apache (10,803)	24,799	0.07
Arapaho (316)	727	<0.01
Blackfeet (2,498)	15,420	0.04
Canadian/French Am. Ind. (597)	1,645	<0.01
Central American Ind. (2,412)	4,329	0.01
Cherokee (20,969)	92,246	0.25
Cheyenne (543)	1,546	<0.01
Chickasaw (1,822)	4,827	0.01
Chippewa (3,095)	7,250	0.02
Choctaw (7,389)	23,403	0.06
Colville (211)	368	<0.01
Comanche (1,150)	2,920	0.01
Cree (221)	1,053	<0.01
Creek (2,213)	6,195	0.02
Crow (283)	866	<0.01
Delaware (487)	1,289	<0.01
Hopi (1,022)	2,238	0.01
Houma (72)	137	<0.01
Inupiat *(Alaska Native)* (469)	1,019	<0.01
Iroquois (1,636)	5,443	0.01
Kiowa (388)	784	<0.01
Lumbee (413)	855	<0.01
Menominee (148)	316	<0.01
Mexican American Ind. (45,933)	66,424	0.18
Navajo (8,796)	17,080	0.05
Osage (657)	2,168	0.01
Ottawa (286)	651	<0.01
Paiute (2,390)	4,153	0.01
Pima (1,192)	2,127	0.01
Potawatomi (1,393)	2,962	0.01
Pueblo (2,973)	5,569	0.01
Puget Sound Salish (401)	749	<0.01
Seminole (640)	2,992	0.01
Shoshone (1,011)	2,217	0.01
Sioux (5,075)	12,439	0.03
South American Ind. (1,592)	4,121	0.01
Spanish American Ind. (2,854)	4,271	0.01
Tlingit-Haida *(Alaska Native)* (739)	1,571	<0.01
Tohono O'Odham (1,408)	2,359	0.01
Tsimshian *(Alaska Native)* (73)	190	<0.01
Ute (440)	1,111	<0.01
Yakama (168)	385	<0.01
Yaqui (5,279)	10,375	0.03
Yuman (2,263)	2,988	0.01
Yup'ik *(Alaska Native)* (157)	323	<0.01
Asian (4,861,007)	5,556,592	14.92
Not Hispanic (4,775,070)	5,324,591	14.29
Hispanic (85,937)	232,001	0.62
Bangladeshi (9,268)	10,494	0.03
Bhutanese (694)	750	<0.01
Burmese (15,035)	17,978	0.05
Cambodian (86,244)	102,317	0.27
Chinese, ex. Taiwanese (1,150,206)	1,349,111	3.62
Filipino (1,195,580)	1,474,707	3.96
Hmong (86,989)	91,224	0.24
Indian (528,176)	590,445	1.58
Indonesian (25,398)	39,506	0.11
Japanese (272,528)	428,014	1.15
Korean (451,892)	505,225	1.36
Laotian (58,424)	69,303	0.19
Malaysian (2,979)	5,595	0.02
Nepalese (5,618)	6,231	0.02
Pakistani (46,780)	53,474	0.14
Sri Lankan (10,240)	11,929	0.03
Taiwanese (96,009)	109,928	0.30
Thai (51,509)	67,707	0.18
Vietnamese (581,946)	647,589	1.74
Hawaii Native/Pacific Islander (144,386)	286,145	0.77
Not Hispanic (128,577)	233,405	0.63
Hispanic (15,809)	52,740	0.14
Fijian (19,355)	24,059	0.06
Guamanian/Chamorro (24,299)	44,425	0.12
Marshallese (1,559)	1,761	<0.01
Native Hawaiian (21,423)	74,932	0.20
Samoan (40,900)	60,876	0.16
Tongan (18,329)	22,893	0.06
White (21,453,934)	22,953,374	61.61
Not Hispanic (14,956,253)	15,763,625	42.31
Hispanic (6,497,681)	7,189,749	19.30

*Notes: † The Census 2010 population figure is used to calculate the percentages in the Hispanic Origin and Race categories. Ancestry percentages are based on the 2006-2010 American Community Survey population (not shown); ‡ Numbers in parentheses indicate the number of people reporting a single ancestry; * Numbers in parentheses indicate the number of persons reporting this race alone, not in combination with any other race; Please refer to the Explanation of Data for more information.*

County Profiles

Alameda County

Population: 1,510,271

Ancestry	Population	%
Afghan (7,036)	7,342	0.50
African, Sub-Saharan (16,057)	18,815	1.27
African (8,284)	10,272	0.70
Cape Verdean (99)	128	0.01
Ethiopian (3,352)	3,580	0.24
Ghanaian (148)	158	0.01
Kenyan (436)	535	0.04
Liberian (226)	226	0.02
Nigerian (2,265)	2,437	0.16
Senegalese (43)	56	<0.01
Sierra Leonean (76)	127	0.01
Somalian (91)	179	0.01
South African (132)	160	0.01
Sudanese (113)	121	0.01
Ugandan (21)	21	<0.01
Zimbabwean (44)	44	<0.01
Other Sub-Saharan African (727)	771	0.05
Albanian (39)	160	0.01
Alsatian (10)	41	<0.01
American (20,054)	20,054	1.36
Arab (7,648)	10,129	0.69
Arab (1,311)	1,635	0.11
Egyptian (917)	1,131	0.08
Iraqi (145)	193	0.01
Jordanian (319)	496	0.03
Lebanese (808)	1,440	0.10
Moroccan (216)	379	0.03
Palestinian (1,195)	1,477	0.10
Syrian (69)	320	0.02
Other Arab (2,668)	3,058	0.21
Armenian (1,268)	2,235	0.15
Assyrian/Chaldean/Syriac (269)	319	0.02
Australian (233)	566	0.04
Austrian (682)	3,183	0.22
Basque (325)	515	0.03
Belgian (573)	1,465	0.10
Brazilian (788)	1,381	0.09
British (3,957)	7,875	0.53
Bulgarian (209)	311	0.02
Cajun (33)	95	0.01
Canadian (1,326)	2,902	0.20
Carpatho Rusyn (0)	48	<0.01
Celtic (209)	573	0.04
Croatian (766)	2,016	0.14
Cypriot (61)	61	<0.01
Czech (479)	2,970	0.20
Czechoslovakian (270)	679	0.05
Danish (1,481)	8,333	0.56
Dutch (2,884)	12,456	0.84
Eastern European (3,289)	3,919	0.27
English (19,543)	85,809	5.81
Estonian (102)	225	0.02
European (19,430)	22,988	1.56
Finnish (578)	2,137	0.14
French, ex. Basque (5,313)	27,499	1.86
French Canadian (1,390)	3,945	0.27
German (25,578)	114,070	7.72
German Russian (0)	23	<0.01
Greek (2,858)	6,105	0.41
Guyanese (108)	148	0.01
Hungarian (1,281)	4,173	0.28
Icelander (112)	303	0.02
Iranian (5,172)	6,055	0.41
Irish (23,101)	96,625	6.54
Israeli (533)	749	0.05
Italian (18,031)	55,154	3.73
Latvian (223)	459	0.03
Lithuanian (803)	2,319	0.16
Luxemburger (22)	138	0.01
Macedonian (21)	62	<0.01
Maltese (126)	228	0.02
New Zealander (103)	195	0.01
Northern European (2,419)	2,747	0.19
Norwegian (3,191)	13,927	0.94
Pennsylvania German (40)	136	0.01
Polish (5,192)	19,584	1.33
Portuguese (15,425)	33,204	2.25
Romanian (1,130)	2,328	0.16
Russian (7,504)	18,510	1.25
Scandinavian (1,121)	2,345	0.16
Scotch-Irish (4,624)	16,795	1.14
Scottish (4,591)	20,544	1.39
Serbian (82)	323	0.02
Slavic (233)	486	0.03
Slovak (323)	1,292	0.09
Slovene (144)	408	0.03
Soviet Union (0)	0	<0.01
Swedish (4,036)	17,517	1.19
Swiss (990)	4,296	0.29
Turkish (762)	1,188	0.08
Ukrainian (1,085)	2,877	0.19
Welsh (753)	6,309	0.43
West Indian, ex. Hispanic (1,837)	3,047	0.21
Bahamian (0)	16	<0.01
Barbadian (25)	25	<0.01
Belizean (94)	143	0.01
Bermudan (11)	51	<0.01
British West Indian (0)	29	<0.01
Dutch West Indian (0)	0	<0.01
Haitian (179)	295	0.02
Jamaican (703)	1,137	0.08
Trinidadian/Tobagonian (285)	508	0.03
U.S. Virgin Islander (16)	16	<0.01
West Indian (524)	827	0.06
Other West Indian (0)	0	<0.01
Yugoslavian (946)	1,701	0.12

Hispanic Origin	Population	%
Hispanic or Latino (of any race)	339,889	22.51
Central American, ex. Mexican	37,643	2.49
Costa Rican	658	0.04
Guatemalan	9,300	0.62
Honduran	2,203	0.15
Nicaraguan	6,384	0.42
Panamanian	878	0.06
Salvadoran	17,851	1.18
Other Central American	369	0.02
Cuban	2,448	0.16
Dominican Republic	499	0.03
Mexican	248,180	16.43
Puerto Rican	12,201	0.81
South American	11,609	0.77
Argentinean	1,271	0.08
Bolivian	591	0.04
Chilean	1,211	0.08
Colombian	2,168	0.14
Ecuadorian	703	0.05
Paraguayan	36	<0.01
Peruvian	4,700	0.31
Uruguayan	151	0.01
Venezuelan	606	0.04
Other South American	172	0.01
Other Hispanic or Latino	27,309	1.81

Race*	Population	%
African-American/Black (190,451)	214,841	14.23
Not Hispanic (184,126)	202,681	13.42
Hispanic (6,325)	12,160	0.81
American Indian/Alaska Native (9,799)	26,089	1.73
Not Hispanic (4,189)	14,785	0.98
Hispanic (5,610)	11,304	0.75
Alaska Athabascan *(Ala. Nat.)* (9)	19	<0.01
Aleut *(Alaska Native)* (20)	52	<0.01
Apache (322)	904	0.06
Arapaho (24)	47	<0.01
Blackfeet (120)	859	0.06
Canadian/French Am. Ind. (14)	73	<0.01
Central American Ind. (149)	285	0.02
Cherokee (457)	3,532	0.23
Cheyenne (24)	84	0.01
Chickasaw (45)	155	0.01
Chippewa (124)	314	0.02
Choctaw (163)	939	0.06
Colville (8)	13	<0.01
Comanche (55)	127	0.01
Cree (6)	48	<0.01
Creek (54)	233	0.02
Crow (17)	43	<0.01
Delaware (15)	49	<0.01
Hopi (34)	94	0.01
Houma (1)	6	<0.01
Inupiat *(Alaska Native)* (20)	55	<0.01
Iroquois (57)	276	0.02
Kiowa (33)	57	<0.01
Lumbee (6)	22	<0.01
Menominee (1)	4	<0.01
Mexican American Ind. (1,446)	2,334	0.15
Navajo (339)	655	0.04
Osage (14)	55	<0.01
Ottawa (5)	7	<0.01
Paiute (60)	123	0.01
Pima (39)	65	<0.01
Potawatomi (27)	86	0.01
Pueblo (124)	257	0.02
Puget Sound Salish (7)	21	<0.01
Seminole (21)	183	0.01
Shoshone (39)	73	<0.01
Sioux (262)	639	0.04
South American Ind. (110)	330	0.02
Spanish American Ind. (66)	111	0.01
Tlingit-Haida *(Alaska Native)* (36)	98	0.01
Tohono O'Odham (51)	86	0.01
Tsimshian *(Alaska Native)* (3)	13	<0.01
Ute (16)	61	<0.01
Yakama (9)	18	<0.01
Yaqui (94)	259	0.02
Yuman (11)	33	<0.01
Yup'ik *(Alaska Native)* (5)	15	<0.01
Asian (394,560)	440,869	29.19
Not Hispanic (390,524)	429,864	28.46
Hispanic (4,036)	11,005	0.73
Bangladeshi (466)	514	0.03
Bhutanese (316)	345	0.02
Burmese (2,369)	2,712	0.18
Cambodian (4,325)	5,246	0.35
Chinese, ex. Taiwanese (138,824)	154,987	10.26
Filipino (82,406)	99,665	6.60
Hmong (344)	369	0.02
Indian (72,278)	78,208	5.18
Indonesian (1,066)	1,794	0.12
Japanese (11,344)	20,090	1.33
Korean (17,464)	20,444	1.35
Laotian (3,674)	4,194	0.28
Malaysian (241)	481	0.03
Nepalese (894)	1,005	0.07
Pakistani (4,274)	4,819	0.32
Sri Lankan (495)	599	0.04
Taiwanese (7,531)	8,580	0.57
Thai (1,737)	2,439	0.16
Vietnamese (30,533)	34,823	2.31
Hawaii Native/Pacific Islander (12,802)	22,322	1.48
Not Hispanic (11,931)	19,499	1.29
Hispanic (871)	2,823	0.19
Fijian (3,630)	4,394	0.29
Guamanian/Chamorro (1,455)	2,703	0.18
Marshallese (27)	37	<0.01
Native Hawaiian (1,318)	4,905	0.32
Samoan (2,022)	3,076	0.20
Tongan (2,861)	3,381	0.22
White (649,122)	719,942	47.67
Not Hispanic (514,559)	561,927	37.21
Hispanic (134,563)	158,015	10.46

*Notes: † The Census 2010 population figure is used to calculate the percentages in the Hispanic Origin and Race categories. Ancestry percentages are based on the 2006-2010 American Community Survey population (not shown); ‡ Numbers in parentheses indicate the number of people reporting a single ancestry; * Numbers in parentheses indicate the number of persons reporting this race alone, not in combination with any other race; Please refer to the Explanation of Data for more information.*

Alpine County

Population: 1,175

Ancestry	Population	%
Afghan (0)	0	<0.01
African, Sub-Saharan (0)	0	<0.01
African (0)	0	<0.01
Cape Verdean (0)	0	<0.01
Ethiopian (0)	0	<0.01
Ghanaian (0)	0	<0.01
Kenyan (0)	0	<0.01
Liberian (0)	0	<0.01
Nigerian (0)	0	<0.01
Senegalese (0)	0	<0.01
Sierra Leonean (0)	0	<0.01
Somalian (0)	0	<0.01
South African (0)	0	<0.01
Sudanese (0)	0	<0.01
Ugandan (0)	0	<0.01
Zimbabwean (0)	0	<0.01
Other Sub-Saharan African (0)	0	<0.01
Albanian (0)	0	<0.01
Alsatian (0)	0	<0.01
American (15)	15	1.28
Arab (0)	0	<0.01
Arab (0)	0	<0.01
Egyptian (0)	0	<0.01
Iraqi (0)	0	<0.01
Jordanian (0)	0	<0.01
Lebanese (0)	0	<0.01
Moroccan (0)	0	<0.01
Palestinian (0)	0	<0.01
Syrian (0)	0	<0.01
Other Arab (0)	0	<0.01
Armenian (0)	0	<0.01
Assyrian/Chaldean/Syriac (0)	0	<0.01
Australian (0)	5	0.43
Austrian (0)	0	<0.01
Basque (0)	0	<0.01
Belgian (0)	0	<0.01
Brazilian (0)	0	<0.01
British (0)	0	<0.01
Bulgarian (0)	0	<0.01
Cajun (0)	0	<0.01
Canadian (13)	13	1.11
Carpatho Rusyn (0)	0	<0.01
Celtic (0)	0	<0.01
Croatian (0)	0	<0.01
Cypriot (0)	0	<0.01
Czech (0)	3	0.26
Czechoslovakian (0)	0	<0.01
Danish (0)	3	0.26
Dutch (12)	32	2.72
Eastern European (0)	0	<0.01
English (19)	132	11.22
Estonian (0)	0	<0.01
European (104)	104	8.84
Finnish (3)	7	0.60
French, ex. Basque (0)	44	3.74
French Canadian (0)	9	0.77
German (55)	180	15.31
German Russian (0)	0	<0.01
Greek (0)	0	<0.01
Guyanese (0)	0	<0.01
Hungarian (0)	0	<0.01
Icelander (0)	0	<0.01
Iranian (0)	0	<0.01
Irish (49)	171	14.54
Israeli (0)	4	0.34
Italian (34)	132	11.22
Latvian (0)	0	<0.01
Lithuanian (0)	0	<0.01
Luxemburger (0)	0	<0.01
Macedonian (0)	0	<0.01
Maltese (0)	0	<0.01
New Zealander (0)	0	<0.01
Northern European (0)	0	<0.01
Norwegian (0)	0	<0.01
Pennsylvania German (0)	0	<0.01
Polish (0)	22	1.87
Portuguese (4)	4	0.34
Romanian (0)	0	<0.01
Russian (0)	0	<0.01
Scandinavian (6)	6	0.51
Scotch-Irish (0)	20	1.70
Scottish (10)	32	2.72
Serbian (0)	0	<0.01
Slavic (0)	0	<0.01
Slovak (0)	0	<0.01
Slovene (0)	0	<0.01
Soviet Union (0)	0	<0.01
Swedish (26)	38	3.23
Swiss (2)	10	0.85
Turkish (0)	0	<0.01
Ukrainian (0)	0	<0.01
Welsh (0)	18	1.53
West Indian, ex. Hispanic (0)	0	<0.01
Bahamian (0)	0	<0.01
Barbadian (0)	0	<0.01
Belizean (0)	0	<0.01
Bermudan (0)	0	<0.01
British West Indian (0)	0	<0.01
Dutch West Indian (0)	0	<0.01
Haitian (0)	0	<0.01
Jamaican (0)	0	<0.01
Trinidadian/Tobagonian (0)	0	<0.01
U.S. Virgin Islander (0)	0	<0.01
West Indian (0)	0	<0.01
Other West Indian (0)	0	<0.01
Yugoslavian (0)	0	<0.01

Hispanic Origin	Population	%
Hispanic or Latino (of any race)	84	7.15
Central American, ex. Mexican	6	0.51
Costa Rican	0	<0.01
Guatemalan	2	0.17
Honduran	0	<0.01
Nicaraguan	0	<0.01
Panamanian	0	<0.01
Salvadoran	4	0.34
Other Central American	0	<0.01
Cuban	0	<0.01
Dominican Republic	0	<0.01
Mexican	63	5.36
Puerto Rican	1	0.09
South American	1	0.09
Argentinean	1	0.09
Bolivian	0	<0.01
Chilean	0	<0.01
Colombian	0	<0.01
Ecuadorian	0	<0.01
Paraguayan	0	<0.01
Peruvian	0	<0.01
Uruguayan	0	<0.01
Venezuelan	0	<0.01
Other South American	0	<0.01
Other Hispanic or Latino	13	1.11

Race*	Population	%
African-American/Black (0)	1	0.09
Not Hispanic (0)	1	0.09
Hispanic (0)	0	<0.01
American Indian/Alaska Native (240)	262	22.30
Not Hispanic (210)	228	19.40
Hispanic (30)	34	2.89
Alaska Athabascan *(Ala. Nat.)* (0)	0	<0.01
Aleut *(Alaska Native)* (0)	0	<0.01
Apache (2)	4	0.34
Arapaho (0)	0	<0.01
Blackfeet (0)	0	<0.01
Canadian/French Am. Ind. (0)	0	<0.01
Central American Ind. (0)	0	<0.01
Cherokee (8)	10	0.85
Cheyenne (0)	0	<0.01
Chickasaw (3)	3	0.26
Chippewa (0)	0	<0.01
Choctaw (0)	0	<0.01
Colville (0)	0	<0.01
Comanche (0)	0	<0.01
Cree (0)	0	<0.01
Creek (3)	3	0.26
Crow (0)	0	<0.01
Delaware (0)	0	<0.01
Hopi (0)	0	<0.01
Houma (0)	0	<0.01
Inupiat *(Alaska Native)* (0)	0	<0.01
Iroquois (0)	0	<0.01
Kiowa (0)	0	<0.01
Lumbee (0)	0	<0.01
Menominee (0)	0	<0.01
Mexican American Ind. (0)	0	<0.01
Navajo (1)	3	0.26
Osage (0)	0	<0.01
Ottawa (0)	0	<0.01
Paiute (7)	12	1.02
Pima (0)	3	0.26
Potawatomi (0)	0	<0.01
Pueblo (0)	1	0.09
Puget Sound Salish (0)	0	<0.01
Seminole (0)	0	<0.01
Shoshone (2)	3	0.26
Sioux (4)	5	0.43
South American Ind. (0)	0	<0.01
Spanish American Ind. (0)	0	<0.01
Tlingit-Haida *(Alaska Native)* (0)	0	<0.01
Tohono O'Odham (0)	0	<0.01
Tsimshian *(Alaska Native)* (0)	0	<0.01
Ute (0)	0	<0.01
Yakama (0)	0	<0.01
Yaqui (0)	0	<0.01
Yuman (2)	2	0.17
Yup'ik *(Alaska Native)* (0)	0	<0.01
Asian (7)	15	1.28
Not Hispanic (7)	12	1.02
Hispanic (0)	3	0.26
Bangladeshi (0)	0	<0.01
Bhutanese (0)	0	<0.01
Burmese (0)	0	<0.01
Cambodian (0)	0	<0.01
Chinese, ex. Taiwanese (3)	6	0.51
Filipino (1)	5	0.43
Hmong (0)	0	<0.01
Indian (0)	0	<0.01
Indonesian (0)	0	<0.01
Japanese (1)	4	0.34
Korean (0)	0	<0.01
Laotian (0)	0	<0.01
Malaysian (0)	0	<0.01
Nepalese (0)	0	<0.01
Pakistani (0)	0	<0.01
Sri Lankan (0)	0	<0.01
Taiwanese (0)	0	<0.01
Thai (0)	0	<0.01
Vietnamese (1)	4	0.34
Hawaii Native/Pacific Islander (0)	0	<0.01
Not Hispanic (0)	0	<0.01
Hispanic (0)	0	<0.01
Fijian (0)	0	<0.01
Guamanian/Chamorro (0)	0	<0.01
Marshallese (0)	0	<0.01
Native Hawaiian (0)	0	<0.01
Samoan (0)	0	<0.01
Tongan (0)	0	<0.01
White (881)	908	77.28
Not Hispanic (852)	872	74.21
Hispanic (29)	36	3.06

*Notes: † The Census 2010 population figure is used to calculate the percentages in the Hispanic Origin and Race categories. Ancestry percentages are based on the 2006-2010 American Community Survey population (not shown); ‡ Numbers in parentheses indicate the number of people reporting a single ancestry; * Numbers in parentheses indicate the number of persons reporting this race alone, not in combination with any other race; Please refer to the Explanation of Data for more information.*

Amador County

Population: 38,091

Ancestry	Population	%
Afghan (0)	0	<0.01
African, Sub-Saharan (17)	49	0.13
African (17)	49	0.13
Cape Verdean (0)	0	<0.01
Ethiopian (0)	0	<0.01
Ghanaian (0)	0	<0.01
Kenyan (0)	0	<0.01
Liberian (0)	0	<0.01
Nigerian (0)	0	<0.01
Senegalese (0)	0	<0.01
Sierra Leonean (0)	0	<0.01
Somalian (0)	0	<0.01
South African (0)	0	<0.01
Sudanese (0)	0	<0.01
Ugandan (0)	0	<0.01
Zimbabwean (0)	0	<0.01
Other Sub-Saharan African (0)	0	<0.01
Albanian (0)	0	<0.01
Alsatian (0)	0	<0.01
American (1,529)	1,529	3.99
Arab (67)	119	0.31
Arab (43)	43	0.11
Egyptian (8)	22	0.06
Iraqi (0)	0	<0.01
Jordanian (0)	0	<0.01
Lebanese (16)	48	0.13
Moroccan (0)	0	<0.01
Palestinian (0)	6	0.02
Syrian (0)	0	<0.01
Other Arab (0)	0	<0.01
Armenian (5)	20	0.05
Assyrian/Chaldean/Syriac (28)	38	0.10
Australian (43)	43	0.11
Austrian (16)	78	0.20
Basque (41)	87	0.23
Belgian (76)	80	0.21
Brazilian (0)	0	<0.01
British (82)	221	0.58
Bulgarian (0)	0	<0.01
Cajun (0)	0	<0.01
Canadian (64)	122	0.32
Carpatho Rusyn (0)	0	<0.01
Celtic (0)	11	0.03
Croatian (18)	26	0.07
Cypriot (0)	0	<0.01
Czech (32)	61	0.16
Czechoslovakian (0)	39	0.10
Danish (125)	889	2.32
Dutch (75)	1,165	3.04
Eastern European (50)	50	0.13
English (1,495)	5,841	15.24
Estonian (0)	0	<0.01
European (767)	853	2.23
Finnish (31)	52	0.14
French, ex. Basque (309)	1,987	5.18
French Canadian (300)	657	1.71
German (1,702)	7,596	19.82
German Russian (0)	0	<0.01
Greek (97)	292	0.76
Guyanese (0)	0	<0.01
Hungarian (142)	259	0.68
Icelander (0)	10	0.03
Iranian (76)	93	0.24
Irish (1,524)	7,114	18.56
Israeli (0)	0	<0.01
Italian (1,106)	3,595	9.38
Latvian (0)	35	0.09
Lithuanian (7)	43	0.11
Luxemburger (0)	16	0.04
Macedonian (0)	0	<0.01
Maltese (37)	37	0.10
New Zealander (0)	0	<0.01
Northern European (64)	64	0.17
Norwegian (301)	969	2.53
Pennsylvania German (0)	7	0.02
Polish (151)	383	1.00
Portuguese (318)	942	2.46
Romanian (0)	0	<0.01
Russian (203)	388	1.01
Scandinavian (77)	218	0.57
Scotch-Irish (273)	1,142	2.98
Scottish (367)	1,124	2.93
Serbian (21)	21	0.05
Slavic (14)	19	0.05
Slovak (0)	0	<0.01
Slovene (0)	0	<0.01
Soviet Union (0)	0	<0.01
Swedish (215)	1,620	4.23
Swiss (65)	259	0.68
Turkish (0)	0	<0.01
Ukrainian (54)	97	0.25
Welsh (47)	245	0.64
West Indian, ex. Hispanic (0)	8	0.02
Bahamian (0)	0	<0.01
Barbadian (0)	0	<0.01
Belizean (0)	0	<0.01
Bermudan (0)	0	<0.01
British West Indian (0)	0	<0.01
Dutch West Indian (0)	8	0.02
Haitian (0)	0	<0.01
Jamaican (0)	0	<0.01
Trinidadian/Tobagonian (0)	0	<0.01
U.S. Virgin Islander (0)	0	<0.01
West Indian (0)	0	<0.01
Other West Indian (0)	0	<0.01
Yugoslavian (35)	89	0.23

Hispanic Origin	Population	%
Hispanic or Latino (of any race)	4,756	12.49
Central American, ex. Mexican	104	0.27
Costa Rican	8	0.02
Guatemalan	11	0.03
Honduran	12	0.03
Nicaraguan	21	0.06
Panamanian	2	0.01
Salvadoran	45	0.12
Other Central American	5	0.01
Cuban	21	0.06
Dominican Republic	0	<0.01
Mexican	3,750	9.84
Puerto Rican	123	0.32
South American	50	0.13
Argentinean	13	0.03
Bolivian	0	<0.01
Chilean	9	0.02
Colombian	9	0.02
Ecuadorian	3	0.01
Paraguayan	1	<0.01
Peruvian	13	0.03
Uruguayan	0	<0.01
Venezuelan	2	0.01
Other South American	0	<0.01
Other Hispanic or Latino	708	1.86

Race*	Population	%
African-American/Black (962)	1,109	2.91
Not Hispanic (938)	1,065	2.80
Hispanic (24)	44	0.12
American Indian/Alaska Native (678)	1,402	3.68
Not Hispanic (547)	1,129	2.96
Hispanic (131)	273	0.72
Alaska Athabascan *(Ala. Nat.)* (0)	0	<0.01
Aleut *(Alaska Native)* (0)	1	<0.01
Apache (19)	33	0.09
Arapaho (0)	2	0.01
Blackfeet (6)	29	0.08
Canadian/French Am. Ind. (0)	0	<0.01
Central American Ind. (1)	1	<0.01
Cherokee (85)	319	0.84
Cheyenne (4)	6	0.02
Chickasaw (2)	13	0.03
Chippewa (14)	21	0.06
Choctaw (17)	69	0.18
Colville (0)	0	<0.01
Comanche (3)	11	0.03
Cree (0)	0	<0.01
Creek (11)	12	0.03
Crow (0)	2	0.01
Delaware (6)	9	0.02
Hopi (1)	3	0.01
Houma (0)	0	<0.01
Inupiat *(Alaska Native)* (1)	2	0.01
Iroquois (1)	17	0.04
Kiowa (0)	2	0.01
Lumbee (0)	0	<0.01
Menominee (0)	0	<0.01
Mexican American Ind. (12)	19	0.05
Navajo (8)	14	0.04
Osage (0)	2	0.01
Ottawa (6)	7	0.02
Paiute (2)	4	0.01
Pima (1)	5	0.01
Potawatomi (7)	7	0.02
Pueblo (2)	4	0.01
Puget Sound Salish (1)	1	<0.01
Seminole (5)	6	0.02
Shoshone (0)	4	0.01
Sioux (7)	23	0.06
South American Ind. (0)	0	<0.01
Spanish American Ind. (0)	0	<0.01
Tlingit-Haida *(Alaska Native)* (5)	7	0.02
Tohono O'Odham (0)	0	<0.01
Tsimshian *(Alaska Native)* (0)	0	<0.01
Ute (0)	3	0.01
Yakama (0)	0	<0.01
Yaqui (3)	10	0.03
Yuman (1)	2	0.01
Yup'ik *(Alaska Native)* (0)	0	<0.01
Asian (419)	739	1.94
Not Hispanic (396)	644	1.69
Hispanic (23)	95	0.25
Bangladeshi (0)	0	<0.01
Bhutanese (0)	0	<0.01
Burmese (1)	4	0.01
Cambodian (2)	2	0.01
Chinese, ex. Taiwanese (64)	104	0.27
Filipino (136)	300	0.79
Hmong (4)	5	0.01
Indian (35)	57	0.15
Indonesian (2)	7	0.02
Japanese (59)	120	0.32
Korean (31)	49	0.13
Laotian (1)	1	<0.01
Malaysian (0)	0	<0.01
Nepalese (0)	0	<0.01
Pakistani (5)	5	0.01
Sri Lankan (0)	0	<0.01
Taiwanese (1)	2	0.01
Thai (7)	22	0.06
Vietnamese (31)	40	0.11
Hawaii Native/Pacific Islander (77)	177	0.46
Not Hispanic (63)	136	0.36
Hispanic (14)	41	0.11
Fijian (11)	12	0.03
Guamanian/Chamorro (10)	20	0.05
Marshallese (0)	0	<0.01
Native Hawaiian (31)	81	0.21
Samoan (9)	20	0.05
Tongan (1)	9	0.02
White (33,149)	34,388	90.28
Not Hispanic (30,325)	31,206	81.92
Hispanic (2,824)	3,182	8.35

*Notes: † The Census 2010 population figure is used to calculate the percentages in the Hispanic Origin and Race categories. Ancestry percentages are based on the 2006-2010 American Community Survey population (not shown); ‡ Numbers in parentheses indicate the number of people reporting a single ancestry; * Numbers in parentheses indicate the number of persons reporting this race alone, not in combination with any other race; Please refer to the Explanation of Data for more information.*

Butte County

Population: 220,000

Ancestry	Population	%
Afghan (0)	0	<0.01
African, Sub-Saharan (247)	391	0.18
African (202)	316	0.14
Cape Verdean (0)	0	<0.01
Ethiopian (9)	22	0.01
Ghanaian (0)	0	<0.01
Kenyan (29)	29	0.01
Liberian (0)	0	<0.01
Nigerian (0)	0	<0.01
Senegalese (0)	0	<0.01
Sierra Leonean (0)	0	<0.01
Somalian (0)	0	<0.01
South African (7)	21	0.01
Sudanese (0)	0	<0.01
Ugandan (0)	0	<0.01
Zimbabwean (0)	0	<0.01
Other Sub-Saharan African (0)	3	<0.01
Albanian (0)	0	<0.01
Alsatian (0)	0	<0.01
American (16,200)	16,200	7.41
Arab (281)	457	0.21
Arab (41)	41	0.02
Egyptian (11)	11	0.01
Iraqi (3)	25	0.01
Jordanian (4)	4	<0.01
Lebanese (14)	137	0.06
Moroccan (31)	31	0.01
Palestinian (22)	38	0.02
Syrian (30)	45	0.02
Other Arab (125)	125	0.06
Armenian (353)	533	0.24
Assyrian/Chaldean/Syriac (35)	48	0.02
Australian (76)	121	0.06
Austrian (298)	704	0.32
Basque (66)	176	0.08
Belgian (63)	206	0.09
Brazilian (0)	89	0.04
British (588)	1,015	0.46
Bulgarian (187)	187	0.09
Cajun (0)	0	<0.01
Canadian (228)	924	0.42
Carpatho Rusyn (0)	0	<0.01
Celtic (0)	0	<0.01
Croatian (150)	255	0.12
Cypriot (0)	0	<0.01
Czech (238)	1,148	0.53
Czechoslovakian (202)	276	0.13
Danish (719)	3,053	1.40
Dutch (914)	5,400	2.47
Eastern European (95)	109	0.05
English (6,852)	29,512	13.50
Estonian (0)	0	<0.01
European (4,066)	4,544	2.08
Finnish (159)	463	0.21
French, ex. Basque (1,084)	8,900	4.07
French Canadian (539)	1,375	0.63
German (11,744)	43,688	19.98
German Russian (0)	0	<0.01
Greek (397)	1,237	0.57
Guyanese (0)	50	0.02
Hungarian (278)	998	0.46
Icelander (38)	64	0.03
Iranian (116)	224	0.10
Irish (6,977)	31,158	14.25
Israeli (0)	7	<0.01
Italian (4,635)	14,063	6.43
Latvian (20)	32	0.01
Lithuanian (48)	318	0.15
Luxemburger (12)	18	0.01
Macedonian (0)	0	<0.01
Maltese (17)	73	0.03
New Zealander (0)	4	<0.01
Northern European (488)	494	0.23
Norwegian (1,457)	5,034	2.30
Pennsylvania German (19)	91	0.04
Polish (680)	3,001	1.37
Portuguese (2,081)	5,059	2.31
Romanian (209)	339	0.16
Russian (444)	1,829	0.84
Scandinavian (379)	1,041	0.48
Scotch-Irish (1,979)	6,323	2.89
Scottish (1,388)	6,222	2.85
Serbian (0)	4	<0.01
Slavic (44)	44	0.02
Slovak (7)	163	0.07
Slovene (9)	74	0.03
Soviet Union (0)	0	<0.01
Swedish (1,251)	5,060	2.31
Swiss (356)	1,596	0.73
Turkish (20)	69	0.03
Ukrainian (106)	314	0.14
Welsh (242)	1,845	0.84
West Indian, ex. Hispanic (107)	163	0.07
Bahamian (0)	0	<0.01
Barbadian (0)	0	<0.01
Belizean (0)	0	<0.01
Bermudan (0)	0	<0.01
British West Indian (0)	0	<0.01
Dutch West Indian (42)	77	0.04
Haitian (5)	26	0.01
Jamaican (0)	0	<0.01
Trinidadian/Tobagonian (27)	27	0.01
U.S. Virgin Islander (0)	0	<0.01
West Indian (33)	33	0.02
Other West Indian (0)	0	<0.01
Yugoslavian (135)	327	0.15

Hispanic Origin	Population	%
Hispanic or Latino (of any race)	31,116	14.14
Central American, ex. Mexican	736	0.33
Costa Rican	54	0.02
Guatemalan	154	0.07
Honduran	58	0.03
Nicaraguan	150	0.07
Panamanian	35	0.02
Salvadoran	271	0.12
Other Central American	14	0.01
Cuban	191	0.09
Dominican Republic	15	0.01
Mexican	26,204	11.91
Puerto Rican	725	0.33
South American	447	0.20
Argentinean	47	0.02
Bolivian	33	0.02
Chilean	66	0.03
Colombian	92	0.04
Ecuadorian	31	0.01
Paraguayan	3	<0.01
Peruvian	130	0.06
Uruguayan	7	<0.01
Venezuelan	27	0.01
Other South American	11	0.01
Other Hispanic or Latino	2,798	1.27

Race*	Population	%
African-American/Black (3,415)	5,386	2.45
Not Hispanic (3,133)	4,757	2.16
Hispanic (282)	629	0.29
American Indian/Alaska Native (4,395)	9,067	4.12
Not Hispanic (3,395)	7,209	3.28
Hispanic (1,000)	1,858	0.84
Alaska Athabascan *(Ala. Nat.)* (9)	13	0.01
Aleut *(Alaska Native)* (8)	12	0.01
Apache (81)	186	0.08
Arapaho (10)	17	0.01
Blackfeet (46)	275	0.13
Canadian/French Am. Ind. (2)	10	<0.01
Central American Ind. (6)	10	<0.01
Cherokee (449)	1,592	0.72
Cheyenne (6)	21	0.01
Chickasaw (28)	59	0.03
Chippewa (46)	111	0.05
Choctaw (111)	361	0.16
Colville (4)	4	<0.01
Comanche (7)	26	0.01
Cree (11)	21	0.01
Creek (28)	59	0.03
Crow (8)	19	0.01
Delaware (6)	13	0.01
Hopi (9)	18	0.01
Houma (9)	9	<0.01
Inupiat *(Alaska Native)* (8)	15	0.01
Iroquois (9)	49	0.02
Kiowa (3)	5	<0.01
Lumbee (1)	5	<0.01
Menominee (0)	2	<0.01
Mexican American Ind. (122)	210	0.10
Navajo (37)	83	0.04
Osage (13)	34	0.02
Ottawa (4)	7	<0.01
Paiute (30)	59	0.03
Pima (3)	8	<0.01
Potawatomi (22)	56	0.03
Pueblo (16)	31	0.01
Puget Sound Salish (11)	18	0.01
Seminole (7)	27	0.01
Shoshone (27)	45	0.02
Sioux (85)	217	0.10
South American Ind. (1)	6	<0.01
Spanish American Ind. (4)	9	<0.01
Tlingit-Haida *(Alaska Native)* (10)	23	0.01
Tohono O'Odham (7)	9	<0.01
Tsimshian *(Alaska Native)* (8)	9	<0.01
Ute (2)	3	<0.01
Yakama (0)	6	<0.01
Yaqui (18)	61	0.03
Yuman (10)	14	0.01
Yup'ik *(Alaska Native)* (8)	10	<0.01
Asian (9,057)	11,480	5.22
Not Hispanic (8,921)	10,994	5.00
Hispanic (136)	486	0.22
Bangladeshi (4)	4	<0.01
Bhutanese (0)	0	<0.01
Burmese (16)	21	0.01
Cambodian (47)	78	0.04
Chinese, ex. Taiwanese (828)	1,210	0.55
Filipino (841)	1,598	0.73
Hmong (4,139)	4,354	1.98
Indian (703)	911	0.41
Indonesian (20)	47	0.02
Japanese (493)	1,092	0.50
Korean (293)	451	0.21
Laotian (595)	704	0.32
Malaysian (9)	16	0.01
Nepalese (6)	7	<0.01
Pakistani (186)	205	0.09
Sri Lankan (25)	26	0.01
Taiwanese (33)	49	0.02
Thai (58)	104	0.05
Vietnamese (258)	349	0.16
Hawaii Native/Pacific Islander (452)	1,156	0.53
Not Hispanic (401)	953	0.43
Hispanic (51)	203	0.09
Fijian (16)	29	0.01
Guamanian/Chamorro (73)	138	0.06
Marshallese (0)	5	<0.01
Native Hawaiian (155)	510	0.23
Samoan (94)	160	0.07
Tongan (21)	22	0.01
White (180,096)	189,669	86.21
Not Hispanic (165,416)	172,223	78.28
Hispanic (14,680)	17,446	7.93

*Notes: † The Census 2010 population figure is used to calculate the percentages in the Hispanic Origin and Race categories. Ancestry percentages are based on the 2006-2010 American Community Survey population (not shown); ‡ Numbers in parentheses indicate the number of people reporting a single ancestry; * Numbers in parentheses indicate the number of persons reporting this race alone, not in combination with any other race; Please refer to the Explanation of Data for more information.*

Calaveras County

Population: 45,578

Ancestry	Population	%
Afghan (0)	0	<0.01
African, Sub-Saharan (0)	19	0.04
African (0)	19	0.04
Cape Verdean (0)	0	<0.01
Ethiopian (0)	0	<0.01
Ghanaian (0)	0	<0.01
Kenyan (0)	0	<0.01
Liberian (0)	0	<0.01
Nigerian (0)	0	<0.01
Senegalese (0)	0	<0.01
Sierra Leonean (0)	0	<0.01
Somalian (0)	0	<0.01
South African (0)	0	<0.01
Sudanese (0)	0	<0.01
Ugandan (0)	0	<0.01
Zimbabwean (0)	0	<0.01
Other Sub-Saharan African (0)	0	<0.01
Albanian (0)	0	<0.01
Alsatian (0)	0	<0.01
American (2,323)	2,323	5.05
Arab (0)	49	0.11
Arab (0)	0	<0.01
Egyptian (0)	0	<0.01
Iraqi (0)	0	<0.01
Jordanian (0)	0	<0.01
Lebanese (0)	0	<0.01
Moroccan (0)	0	<0.01
Palestinian (0)	0	<0.01
Syrian (0)	49	0.11
Other Arab (0)	0	<0.01
Armenian (51)	93	0.20
Assyrian/Chaldean/Syriac (0)	0	<0.01
Australian (13)	134	0.29
Austrian (0)	92	0.20
Basque (0)	8	0.02
Belgian (0)	12	0.03
Brazilian (0)	0	<0.01
British (103)	216	0.47
Bulgarian (0)	0	<0.01
Cajun (0)	0	<0.01
Canadian (35)	184	0.40
Carpatho Rusyn (0)	0	<0.01
Celtic (0)	0	<0.01
Croatian (46)	93	0.20
Cypriot (0)	0	<0.01
Czech (92)	193	0.42
Czechoslovakian (0)	0	<0.01
Danish (107)	306	0.67
Dutch (241)	1,500	3.26
Eastern European (21)	21	0.05
English (1,772)	6,976	15.17
Estonian (0)	0	<0.01
European (1,057)	1,303	2.83
Finnish (10)	103	0.22
French, ex. Basque (487)	2,628	5.71
French Canadian (98)	227	0.49
German (3,182)	10,349	22.50
German Russian (0)	0	<0.01
Greek (77)	428	0.93
Guyanese (0)	0	<0.01
Hungarian (135)	318	0.69
Icelander (0)	0	<0.01
Iranian (0)	0	<0.01
Irish (1,516)	7,843	17.05
Israeli (0)	0	<0.01
Italian (1,277)	4,106	8.93
Latvian (0)	0	<0.01
Lithuanian (45)	97	0.21
Luxemburger (0)	0	<0.01
Macedonian (0)	0	<0.01
Maltese (0)	27	0.06
New Zealander (0)	0	<0.01
Northern European (123)	156	0.34
Norwegian (684)	1,379	3.00
Pennsylvania German (19)	19	0.04
Polish (110)	704	1.53
Portuguese (519)	1,216	2.64
Romanian (22)	22	0.05
Russian (126)	613	1.33
Scandinavian (128)	341	0.74
Scotch-Irish (521)	1,307	2.84
Scottish (606)	1,680	3.65
Serbian (37)	90	0.20
Slavic (0)	0	<0.01
Slovak (0)	0	<0.01
Slovene (11)	11	0.02
Soviet Union (0)	0	<0.01
Swedish (470)	1,408	3.06
Swiss (38)	261	0.57
Turkish (81)	81	0.18
Ukrainian (17)	65	0.14
Welsh (155)	574	1.25
West Indian, ex. Hispanic (0)	0	<0.01
Bahamian (0)	0	<0.01
Barbadian (0)	0	<0.01
Belizean (0)	0	<0.01
Bermudan (0)	0	<0.01
British West Indian (0)	0	<0.01
Dutch West Indian (0)	0	<0.01
Haitian (0)	0	<0.01
Jamaican (0)	0	<0.01
Trinidadian/Tobagonian (0)	0	<0.01
U.S. Virgin Islander (0)	0	<0.01
West Indian (0)	0	<0.01
Other West Indian (0)	0	<0.01
Yugoslavian (60)	76	0.17

Hispanic Origin	Population	%
Hispanic or Latino (of any race)	4,703	10.32
Central American, ex. Mexican	108	0.24
Costa Rican	3	0.01
Guatemalan	20	0.04
Honduran	7	0.02
Nicaraguan	19	0.04
Panamanian	13	0.03
Salvadoran	46	0.10
Other Central American	0	<0.01
Cuban	43	0.09
Dominican Republic	0	<0.01
Mexican	3,560	7.81
Puerto Rican	171	0.38
South American	76	0.17
Argentinean	24	0.05
Bolivian	1	<0.01
Chilean	13	0.03
Colombian	11	0.02
Ecuadorian	1	<0.01
Paraguayan	1	<0.01
Peruvian	24	0.05
Uruguayan	0	<0.01
Venezuelan	1	<0.01
Other South American	0	<0.01
Other Hispanic or Latino	745	1.63

Race*	Population	%
African-American/Black (383)	590	1.29
Not Hispanic (355)	532	1.17
Hispanic (28)	58	0.13
American Indian/Alaska Native (689)	1,618	3.55
Not Hispanic (526)	1,310	2.87
Hispanic (163)	308	0.68
Alaska Athabascan *(Ala. Nat.)* (4)	5	0.01
Aleut *(Alaska Native)* (0)	3	0.01
Apache (25)	46	0.10
Arapaho (0)	0	<0.01
Blackfeet (8)	27	0.06
Canadian/French Am. Ind. (4)	7	0.02
Central American Ind. (0)	0	<0.01
Cherokee (96)	422	0.93
Cheyenne (3)	4	0.01
Chickasaw (12)	28	0.06
Chippewa (9)	35	0.08
Choctaw (37)	132	0.29
Colville (0)	0	<0.01
Comanche (1)	4	0.01
Cree (0)	6	0.01
Creek (7)	13	0.03
Crow (1)	1	<0.01
Delaware (2)	2	<0.01
Hopi (1)	5	0.01
Houma (0)	0	<0.01
Inupiat *(Alaska Native)* (3)	4	0.01
Iroquois (6)	21	0.05
Kiowa (1)	1	<0.01
Lumbee (4)	5	0.01
Menominee (5)	5	0.01
Mexican American Ind. (27)	37	0.08
Navajo (18)	26	0.06
Osage (1)	3	0.01
Ottawa (4)	5	0.01
Paiute (0)	2	<0.01
Pima (0)	0	<0.01
Potawatomi (5)	6	0.01
Pueblo (3)	8	0.02
Puget Sound Salish (4)	5	0.01
Seminole (1)	4	0.01
Shoshone (1)	5	0.01
Sioux (13)	34	0.07
South American Ind. (1)	6	0.01
Spanish American Ind. (3)	3	0.01
Tlingit-Haida *(Alaska Native)* (3)	6	0.01
Tohono O'Odham (0)	0	<0.01
Tsimshian *(Alaska Native)* (0)	0	<0.01
Ute (0)	1	<0.01
Yakama (0)	2	<0.01
Yaqui (2)	23	0.05
Yuman (0)	2	<0.01
Yup'ik *(Alaska Native)* (0)	0	<0.01
Asian (571)	944	2.07
Not Hispanic (529)	823	1.81
Hispanic (42)	121	0.27
Bangladeshi (0)	0	<0.01
Bhutanese (0)	0	<0.01
Burmese (2)	2	<0.01
Cambodian (8)	11	0.02
Chinese, ex. Taiwanese (87)	151	0.33
Filipino (197)	368	0.81
Hmong (32)	33	0.07
Indian (54)	75	0.16
Indonesian (6)	9	0.02
Japanese (90)	177	0.39
Korean (24)	57	0.13
Laotian (8)	8	0.02
Malaysian (0)	0	<0.01
Nepalese (0)	0	<0.01
Pakistani (1)	1	<0.01
Sri Lankan (0)	2	<0.01
Taiwanese (2)	5	0.01
Thai (10)	21	0.05
Vietnamese (23)	32	0.07
Hawaii Native/Pacific Islander (79)	173	0.38
Not Hispanic (71)	149	0.33
Hispanic (8)	24	0.05
Fijian (1)	4	0.01
Guamanian/Chamorro (19)	29	0.06
Marshallese (1)	1	<0.01
Native Hawaiian (38)	103	0.23
Samoan (4)	8	0.02
Tongan (0)	1	<0.01
White (40,522)	42,216	92.62
Not Hispanic (38,074)	39,265	86.15
Hispanic (2,448)	2,951	6.47

*Notes: † The Census 2010 population figure is used to calculate the percentages in the Hispanic Origin and Race categories. Ancestry percentages are based on the 2006-2010 American Community Survey population (not shown); ‡ Numbers in parentheses indicate the number of people reporting a single ancestry; * Numbers in parentheses indicate the number of persons reporting this race alone, not in combination with any other race; Please refer to the Explanation of Data for more information.*

Colusa County

Population: 21,419

Ancestry	Population	%
Afghan (0)	0	<0.01
African, Sub-Saharan (0)	6	0.03
African (0)	6	0.03
Cape Verdean (0)	0	<0.01
Ethiopian (0)	0	<0.01
Ghanaian (0)	0	<0.01
Kenyan (0)	0	<0.01
Liberian (0)	0	<0.01
Nigerian (0)	0	<0.01
Senegalese (0)	0	<0.01
Sierra Leonean (0)	0	<0.01
Somalian (0)	0	<0.01
South African (0)	0	<0.01
Sudanese (0)	0	<0.01
Ugandan (0)	0	<0.01
Zimbabwean (0)	0	<0.01
Other Sub-Saharan African (0)	0	<0.01
Albanian (0)	0	<0.01
Alsatian (0)	0	<0.01
American (1,035)	1,035	4.89
Arab (0)	8	0.04
Arab (0)	8	0.04
Egyptian (0)	0	<0.01
Iraqi (0)	0	<0.01
Jordanian (0)	0	<0.01
Lebanese (0)	0	<0.01
Moroccan (0)	0	<0.01
Palestinian (0)	0	<0.01
Syrian (0)	0	<0.01
Other Arab (0)	0	<0.01
Armenian (0)	4	0.02
Assyrian/Chaldean/Syriac (0)	0	<0.01
Australian (0)	0	<0.01
Austrian (0)	21	0.10
Basque (0)	0	<0.01
Belgian (0)	9	0.04
Brazilian (0)	0	<0.01
British (4)	4	0.02
Bulgarian (0)	0	<0.01
Cajun (0)	0	<0.01
Canadian (20)	51	0.24
Carpatho Rusyn (0)	0	<0.01
Celtic (0)	0	<0.01
Croatian (0)	24	0.11
Cypriot (0)	0	<0.01
Czech (3)	20	0.09
Czechoslovakian (0)	12	0.06
Danish (0)	154	0.73
Dutch (33)	348	1.64
Eastern European (0)	0	<0.01
English (257)	1,352	6.39
Estonian (0)	0	<0.01
European (114)	114	0.54
Finnish (12)	12	0.06
French, ex. Basque (41)	494	2.33
French Canadian (12)	57	0.27
German (857)	2,795	13.21
German Russian (0)	0	<0.01
Greek (10)	52	0.25
Guyanese (0)	0	<0.01
Hungarian (7)	40	0.19
Icelander (0)	0	<0.01
Iranian (0)	0	<0.01
Irish (247)	1,600	7.56
Israeli (0)	0	<0.01
Italian (342)	666	3.15
Latvian (5)	5	0.02
Lithuanian (0)	0	<0.01
Luxemburger (0)	8	0.04
Macedonian (0)	0	<0.01
Maltese (0)	0	<0.01
New Zealander (0)	0	<0.01
Northern European (0)	0	<0.01
Norwegian (29)	177	0.84
Pennsylvania German (0)	0	<0.01
Polish (0)	31	0.15
Portuguese (238)	460	2.17
Romanian (0)	0	<0.01
Russian (0)	17	0.08
Scandinavian (8)	18	0.09
Scotch-Irish (89)	239	1.13
Scottish (124)	378	1.79
Serbian (8)	8	0.04
Slavic (0)	0	<0.01
Slovak (0)	0	<0.01
Slovene (0)	0	<0.01
Soviet Union (0)	0	<0.01
Swedish (23)	319	1.51
Swiss (39)	173	0.82
Turkish (0)	0	<0.01
Ukrainian (4)	4	0.02
Welsh (0)	47	0.22
West Indian, ex. Hispanic (11)	11	0.05
Bahamian (0)	0	<0.01
Barbadian (0)	0	<0.01
Belizean (0)	0	<0.01
Bermudan (0)	0	<0.01
British West Indian (0)	0	<0.01
Dutch West Indian (11)	11	0.05
Haitian (0)	0	<0.01
Jamaican (0)	0	<0.01
Trinidadian/Tobagonian (0)	0	<0.01
U.S. Virgin Islander (0)	0	<0.01
West Indian (0)	0	<0.01
Other West Indian (0)	0	<0.01
Yugoslavian (0)	0	<0.01

Hispanic Origin	Population	%
Hispanic or Latino (of any race)	11,804	55.11
Central American, ex. Mexican	103	0.48
Costa Rican	2	0.01
Guatemalan	18	0.08
Honduran	17	0.08
Nicaraguan	12	0.06
Panamanian	1	<0.01
Salvadoran	53	0.25
Other Central American	0	<0.01
Cuban	6	0.03
Dominican Republic	4	0.02
Mexican	10,834	50.58
Puerto Rican	60	0.28
South American	13	0.06
Argentinean	1	<0.01
Bolivian	0	<0.01
Chilean	0	<0.01
Colombian	3	0.01
Ecuadorian	0	<0.01
Paraguayan	0	<0.01
Peruvian	9	0.04
Uruguayan	0	<0.01
Venezuelan	0	<0.01
Other South American	0	<0.01
Other Hispanic or Latino	784	3.66

Race*	Population	%
African-American/Black (195)	286	1.34
Not Hispanic (168)	225	1.05
Hispanic (27)	61	0.28
American Indian/Alaska Native (419)	608	2.84
Not Hispanic (296)	426	1.99
Hispanic (123)	182	0.85
Alaska Athabascan *(Ala. Nat.)* (0)	0	<0.01
Aleut *(Alaska Native)* (0)	0	<0.01
Apache (8)	10	0.05
Arapaho (0)	0	<0.01
Blackfeet (2)	6	0.03
Canadian/French Am. Ind. (0)	0	<0.01
Central American Ind. (3)	3	0.01
Cherokee (41)	82	0.38
Cheyenne (0)	1	<0.01
Chickasaw (0)	0	<0.01
Chippewa (6)	6	0.03
Choctaw (3)	14	0.07
Colville (0)	0	<0.01
Comanche (1)	1	<0.01
Cree (0)	0	<0.01
Creek (0)	0	<0.01
Crow (2)	3	0.01
Delaware (0)	0	<0.01
Hopi (0)	0	<0.01
Houma (0)	0	<0.01
Inupiat *(Alaska Native)* (0)	1	<0.01
Iroquois (0)	2	0.01
Kiowa (0)	0	<0.01
Lumbee (0)	0	<0.01
Menominee (4)	6	0.03
Mexican American Ind. (34)	38	0.18
Navajo (0)	1	<0.01
Osage (0)	0	<0.01
Ottawa (0)	0	<0.01
Paiute (6)	9	0.04
Pima (0)	0	<0.01
Potawatomi (5)	7	0.03
Pueblo (0)	0	<0.01
Puget Sound Salish (0)	0	<0.01
Seminole (1)	3	0.01
Shoshone (5)	5	0.02
Sioux (3)	3	0.01
South American Ind. (0)	0	<0.01
Spanish American Ind. (0)	1	<0.01
Tlingit-Haida *(Alaska Native)* (0)	0	<0.01
Tohono O'Odham (0)	0	<0.01
Tsimshian *(Alaska Native)* (0)	0	<0.01
Ute (0)	0	<0.01
Yakama (0)	0	<0.01
Yaqui (0)	0	<0.01
Yuman (1)	1	<0.01
Yup'ik *(Alaska Native)* (0)	0	<0.01
Asian (281)	436	2.04
Not Hispanic (267)	364	1.70
Hispanic (14)	72	0.34
Bangladeshi (0)	0	<0.01
Bhutanese (0)	0	<0.01
Burmese (0)	0	<0.01
Cambodian (3)	3	0.01
Chinese, ex. Taiwanese (27)	49	0.23
Filipino (48)	97	0.45
Hmong (8)	8	0.04
Indian (119)	153	0.71
Indonesian (0)	1	<0.01
Japanese (29)	40	0.19
Korean (16)	20	0.09
Laotian (2)	2	0.01
Malaysian (0)	0	<0.01
Nepalese (0)	0	<0.01
Pakistani (3)	3	0.01
Sri Lankan (0)	0	<0.01
Taiwanese (0)	0	<0.01
Thai (4)	10	0.05
Vietnamese (7)	10	0.05
Hawaii Native/Pacific Islander (68)	138	0.64
Not Hispanic (59)	92	0.43
Hispanic (9)	46	0.21
Fijian (33)	42	0.20
Guamanian/Chamorro (10)	15	0.07
Marshallese (0)	0	<0.01
Native Hawaiian (14)	44	0.21
Samoan (0)	0	<0.01
Tongan (0)	0	<0.01
White (13,854)	14,505	67.72
Not Hispanic (8,524)	8,758	40.89
Hispanic (5,330)	5,747	26.83

*Notes: † The Census 2010 population figure is used to calculate the percentages in the Hispanic Origin and Race categories. Ancestry percentages are based on the 2006-2010 American Community Survey population (not shown); ‡ Numbers in parentheses indicate the number of people reporting a single ancestry; * Numbers in parentheses indicate the number of persons reporting this race alone, not in combination with any other race; Please refer to the Explanation of Data for more information.*

Contra Costa County

Population: 1,049,025

Ancestry	Population	%
Afghan (3,514)	3,689	0.36
African, Sub-Saharan (12,193)	15,309	1.49
African (7,826)	10,494	1.02
Cape Verdean (89)	148	0.01
Ethiopian (1,183)	1,360	0.13
Ghanaian (128)	150	0.01
Kenyan (353)	374	0.04
Liberian (94)	94	0.01
Nigerian (1,750)	1,821	0.18
Senegalese (11)	11	<0.01
Sierra Leonean (0)	0	<0.01
Somalian (7)	37	<0.01
South African (273)	285	0.03
Sudanese (7)	7	<0.01
Ugandan (121)	121	0.01
Zimbabwean (35)	68	0.01
Other Sub-Saharan African (316)	339	0.03
Albanian (29)	63	0.01
Alsatian (42)	61	0.01
American (24,136)	24,136	2.36
Arab (5,133)	6,855	0.67
Arab (632)	957	0.09
Egyptian (813)	1,064	0.10
Iraqi (219)	282	0.03
Jordanian (157)	157	0.02
Lebanese (619)	1,235	0.12
Moroccan (151)	291	0.03
Palestinian (1,169)	1,274	0.12
Syrian (157)	277	0.03
Other Arab (1,216)	1,318	0.13
Armenian (1,615)	2,362	0.23
Assyrian/Chaldean/Syriac (147)	159	0.02
Australian (380)	743	0.07
Austrian (721)	2,778	0.27
Basque (255)	912	0.09
Belgian (272)	993	0.10
Brazilian (2,030)	2,272	0.22
British (2,777)	5,885	0.57
Bulgarian (427)	623	0.06
Cajun (92)	92	0.01
Canadian (938)	2,155	0.21
Carpatho Rusyn (0)	0	<0.01
Celtic (133)	257	0.03
Croatian (560)	1,562	0.15
Cypriot (0)	0	<0.01
Czech (827)	3,368	0.33
Czechoslovakian (264)	670	0.07
Danish (1,987)	7,841	0.77
Dutch (2,999)	13,682	1.34
Eastern European (1,506)	1,667	0.16
English (22,567)	89,726	8.76
Estonian (35)	99	0.01
European (15,492)	18,159	1.77
Finnish (743)	2,582	0.25
French, ex. Basque (3,214)	26,695	2.60
French Canadian (1,273)	3,263	0.32
German (27,962)	119,356	11.65
German Russian (32)	32	<0.01
Greek (1,988)	5,414	0.53
Guyanese (161)	161	0.02
Hungarian (1,183)	4,201	0.41
Icelander (144)	338	0.03
Iranian (6,490)	7,236	0.71
Irish (22,195)	100,252	9.78
Israeli (486)	607	0.06
Italian (22,856)	62,820	6.13
Latvian (183)	609	0.06
Lithuanian (650)	1,904	0.19
Luxemburger (82)	197	0.02
Macedonian (25)	62	0.01
Maltese (329)	754	0.07
New Zealander (50)	101	0.01
Northern European (2,893)	3,133	0.31
Norwegian (4,388)	15,334	1.50
Pennsylvania German (39)	68	0.01
Polish (4,434)	15,430	1.51
Portuguese (8,419)	22,397	2.19
Romanian (642)	1,517	0.15
Russian (7,080)	13,869	1.35
Scandinavian (1,624)	3,257	0.32
Scotch-Irish (4,901)	15,795	1.54
Scottish (5,462)	21,135	2.06
Serbian (301)	511	0.05
Slavic (180)	547	0.05
Slovak (412)	881	0.09
Slovene (143)	242	0.02
Soviet Union (0)	0	<0.01
Swedish (3,968)	16,741	1.63
Swiss (910)	4,083	0.40
Turkish (374)	480	0.05
Ukrainian (1,611)	2,994	0.29
Welsh (821)	6,915	0.67
West Indian, ex. Hispanic (1,273)	2,399	0.23
Bahamian (18)	51	<0.01
Barbadian (10)	117	0.01
Belizean (311)	395	0.04
Bermudan (0)	0	<0.01
British West Indian (10)	24	<0.01
Dutch West Indian (0)	45	<0.01
Haitian (99)	183	0.02
Jamaican (536)	1,035	0.10
Trinidadian/Tobagonian (106)	166	0.02
U.S. Virgin Islander (0)	0	<0.01
West Indian (183)	362	0.04
Other West Indian (0)	21	<0.01
Yugoslavian (623)	1,471	0.14

Hispanic Origin	Population	%
Hispanic or Latino (of any race)	255,560	24.36
Central American, ex. Mexican	36,056	3.44
Costa Rican	623	0.06
Guatemalan	5,539	0.53
Honduran	1,154	0.11
Nicaraguan	7,512	0.72
Panamanian	681	0.06
Salvadoran	20,304	1.94
Other Central American	243	0.02
Cuban	1,671	0.16
Dominican Republic	296	0.03
Mexican	179,192	17.08
Puerto Rican	7,170	0.68
South American	10,520	1.00
Argentinean	944	0.09
Bolivian	420	0.04
Chilean	965	0.09
Colombian	1,604	0.15
Ecuadorian	537	0.05
Paraguayan	66	0.01
Peruvian	5,349	0.51
Uruguayan	117	0.01
Venezuelan	409	0.04
Other South American	109	0.01
Other Hispanic or Latino	20,655	1.97

Race*	Population	%
African-American/Black (97,161)	112,381	10.71
Not Hispanic (93,604)	105,105	10.02
Hispanic (3,557)	7,276	0.69
American Indian/Alaska Native (6,122)	17,327	1.65
Not Hispanic (2,984)	10,549	1.01
Hispanic (3,138)	6,778	0.65
Alaska Athabascan *(Ala. Nat.)* (7)	16	<0.01
Aleut *(Alaska Native)* (10)	29	<0.01
Apache (174)	533	0.05
Arapaho (12)	25	<0.01
Blackfeet (64)	566	0.05
Canadian/French Am. Ind. (7)	41	<0.01
Central American Ind. (54)	116	0.01
Cherokee (481)	2,997	0.29
Cheyenne (8)	37	<0.01
Chickasaw (33)	129	0.01
Chippewa (91)	253	0.02
Choctaw (225)	829	0.08
Colville (1)	9	<0.01
Comanche (25)	84	0.01
Cree (6)	26	<0.01
Creek (54)	200	0.02
Crow (3)	24	<0.01
Delaware (22)	48	<0.01
Hopi (18)	52	<0.01
Houma (14)	16	<0.01
Inupiat *(Alaska Native)* (12)	29	<0.01
Iroquois (47)	166	0.02
Kiowa (3)	33	<0.01
Lumbee (10)	25	<0.01
Menominee (2)	3	<0.01
Mexican American Ind. (748)	1,232	0.12
Navajo (140)	379	0.04
Osage (15)	60	0.01
Ottawa (8)	29	<0.01
Paiute (42)	94	0.01
Pima (19)	35	<0.01
Potawatomi (39)	73	0.01
Pueblo (83)	159	0.02
Puget Sound Salish (17)	29	<0.01
Seminole (13)	90	0.01
Shoshone (9)	47	<0.01
Sioux (120)	394	0.04
South American Ind. (69)	173	0.02
Spanish American Ind. (61)	104	0.01
Tlingit-Haida *(Alaska Native)* (16)	48	<0.01
Tohono O'Odham (27)	50	<0.01
Tsimshian *(Alaska Native)* (3)	9	<0.01
Ute (27)	70	0.01
Yakama (2)	6	<0.01
Yaqui (69)	170	0.02
Yuman (13)	17	<0.01
Yup'ik *(Alaska Native)* (1)	2	<0.01
Asian (151,469)	180,773	17.23
Not Hispanic (148,881)	173,195	16.51
Hispanic (2,588)	7,578	0.72
Bangladeshi (168)	189	0.02
Bhutanese (9)	11	<0.01
Burmese (384)	487	0.05
Cambodian (908)	1,177	0.11
Chinese, ex. Taiwanese (38,233)	47,038	4.48
Filipino (48,418)	61,161	5.83
Hmong (89)	99	0.01
Indian (22,328)	24,816	2.37
Indonesian (872)	1,384	0.13
Japanese (7,389)	13,321	1.27
Korean (8,216)	10,048	0.96
Laotian (4,084)	4,636	0.44
Malaysian (105)	227	0.02
Nepalese (464)	499	0.05
Pakistani (2,326)	2,653	0.25
Sri Lankan (304)	353	0.03
Taiwanese (1,975)	2,334	0.22
Thai (1,004)	1,526	0.15
Vietnamese (7,401)	8,941	0.85
Hawaii Native/Pacific Islander (4,845)	10,153	0.97
Not Hispanic (4,382)	8,414	0.80
Hispanic (463)	1,739	0.17
Fijian (745)	988	0.09
Guamanian/Chamorro (696)	1,466	0.14
Marshallese (0)	3	<0.01
Native Hawaiian (648)	2,904	0.28
Samoan (901)	1,534	0.15
Tongan (1,118)	1,363	0.13
White (614,512)	665,881	63.48
Not Hispanic (500,923)	533,891	50.89
Hispanic (113,589)	131,990	12.58

*Notes: † The Census 2010 population figure is used to calculate the percentages in the Hispanic Origin and Race categories. Ancestry percentages are based on the 2006-2010 American Community Survey population (not shown); ‡ Numbers in parentheses indicate the number of people reporting a single ancestry; * Numbers in parentheses indicate the number of persons reporting this race alone, not in combination with any other race; Please refer to the Explanation of Data for more information.*

Del Norte County

Population: 28,610

Ancestry	Population	%
Afghan (0)	0	<0.01
African, Sub-Saharan (133)	240	0.84
African (130)	237	0.83
Cape Verdean (0)	0	<0.01
Ethiopian (0)	0	<0.01
Ghanaian (0)	0	<0.01
Kenyan (0)	0	<0.01
Liberian (0)	0	<0.01
Nigerian (0)	0	<0.01
Senegalese (0)	0	<0.01
Sierra Leonean (0)	0	<0.01
Somalian (0)	0	<0.01
South African (0)	0	<0.01
Sudanese (0)	0	<0.01
Ugandan (0)	0	<0.01
Zimbabwean (0)	0	<0.01
Other Sub-Saharan African (3)	3	0.01
Albanian (0)	0	<0.01
Alsatian (0)	0	<0.01
American (1,588)	1,588	5.58
Arab (52)	80	0.28
Arab (0)	14	0.05
Egyptian (0)	0	<0.01
Iraqi (0)	0	<0.01
Jordanian (0)	0	<0.01
Lebanese (0)	0	<0.01
Moroccan (0)	0	<0.01
Palestinian (31)	45	0.16
Syrian (11)	11	0.04
Other Arab (10)	10	0.04
Armenian (0)	13	0.05
Assyrian/Chaldean/Syriac (0)	0	<0.01
Australian (0)	0	<0.01
Austrian (0)	51	0.18
Basque (0)	0	<0.01
Belgian (21)	21	0.07
Brazilian (0)	18	0.06
British (31)	110	0.39
Bulgarian (0)	0	<0.01
Cajun (0)	0	<0.01
Canadian (30)	204	0.72
Carpatho Rusyn (0)	0	<0.01
Celtic (0)	85	0.30
Croatian (0)	0	<0.01
Cypriot (0)	0	<0.01
Czech (21)	142	0.50
Czechoslovakian (0)	0	<0.01
Danish (188)	248	0.87
Dutch (92)	520	1.83
Eastern European (0)	0	<0.01
English (896)	3,337	11.72
Estonian (0)	0	<0.01
European (361)	395	1.39
Finnish (35)	97	0.34
French, ex. Basque (89)	905	3.18
French Canadian (71)	174	0.61
German (1,283)	4,996	17.55
German Russian (0)	0	<0.01
Greek (60)	139	0.49
Guyanese (0)	0	<0.01
Hungarian (11)	33	0.12
Icelander (0)	0	<0.01
Iranian (96)	96	0.34
Irish (940)	4,362	15.32
Israeli (0)	0	<0.01
Italian (583)	1,424	5.00
Latvian (9)	9	0.03
Lithuanian (0)	50	0.18
Luxemburger (0)	0	<0.01
Macedonian (0)	0	<0.01
Maltese (0)	0	<0.01
New Zealander (0)	0	<0.01
Northern European (41)	41	0.14
Norwegian (183)	648	2.28
Pennsylvania German (0)	0	<0.01
Polish (119)	430	1.51
Portuguese (50)	139	0.49
Romanian (0)	0	<0.01
Russian (35)	89	0.31
Scandinavian (71)	84	0.30
Scotch-Irish (276)	705	2.48
Scottish (191)	746	2.62
Serbian (0)	52	0.18
Slavic (0)	0	<0.01
Slovak (0)	20	0.07
Slovene (0)	0	<0.01
Soviet Union (0)	0	<0.01
Swedish (120)	741	2.60
Swiss (37)	125	0.44
Turkish (0)	0	<0.01
Ukrainian (0)	12	0.04
Welsh (14)	120	0.42
West Indian, ex. Hispanic (7)	7	0.02
Bahamian (0)	0	<0.01
Barbadian (0)	0	<0.01
Belizean (7)	7	0.02
Bermudan (0)	0	<0.01
British West Indian (0)	0	<0.01
Dutch West Indian (0)	0	<0.01
Haitian (0)	0	<0.01
Jamaican (0)	0	<0.01
Trinidadian/Tobagonian (0)	0	<0.01
U.S. Virgin Islander (0)	0	<0.01
West Indian (0)	0	<0.01
Other West Indian (0)	0	<0.01
Yugoslavian (0)	0	<0.01

Hispanic Origin	Population	%
Hispanic or Latino (of any race)	5,093	17.80
Central American, ex. Mexican	67	0.23
Costa Rican	2	0.01
Guatemalan	15	0.05
Honduran	6	0.02
Nicaraguan	13	0.05
Panamanian	5	0.02
Salvadoran	26	0.09
Other Central American	0	<0.01
Cuban	9	0.03
Dominican Republic	0	<0.01
Mexican	4,155	14.52
Puerto Rican	88	0.31
South American	34	0.12
Argentinean	10	0.03
Bolivian	7	0.02
Chilean	3	0.01
Colombian	10	0.03
Ecuadorian	0	<0.01
Paraguayan	0	<0.01
Peruvian	3	0.01
Uruguayan	1	<0.01
Venezuelan	0	<0.01
Other South American	0	<0.01
Other Hispanic or Latino	740	2.59

Race*	Population	%
African-American/Black (993)	1,106	3.87
Not Hispanic (967)	1,068	3.73
Hispanic (26)	38	0.13
American Indian/Alaska Native (2,244)	3,118	10.90
Not Hispanic (1,935)	2,639	9.22
Hispanic (309)	479	1.67
Alaska Athabascan *(Ala. Nat.)* (1)	1	<0.01
Aleut *(Alaska Native)* (14)	22	0.08
Apache (13)	34	0.12
Arapaho (0)	0	<0.01
Blackfeet (5)	21	0.07
Canadian/French Am. Ind. (2)	3	0.01
Central American Ind. (2)	5	0.02
Cherokee (126)	294	1.03
Cheyenne (2)	4	0.01
Chickasaw (3)	11	0.04
Chippewa (18)	24	0.08
Choctaw (22)	41	0.14
Colville (1)	1	<0.01
Comanche (6)	11	0.04
Cree (1)	4	0.01
Creek (7)	17	0.06
Crow (0)	1	<0.01
Delaware (0)	1	<0.01
Hopi (2)	4	0.01
Houma (0)	0	<0.01
Inupiat *(Alaska Native)* (2)	5	0.02
Iroquois (12)	20	0.07
Kiowa (0)	1	<0.01
Lumbee (1)	1	<0.01
Menominee (1)	1	<0.01
Mexican American Ind. (63)	86	0.30
Navajo (3)	18	0.06
Osage (1)	11	0.04
Ottawa (1)	2	0.01
Paiute (11)	13	0.05
Pima (0)	2	0.01
Potawatomi (2)	4	0.01
Pueblo (4)	6	0.02
Puget Sound Salish (3)	3	0.01
Seminole (2)	9	0.03
Shoshone (2)	3	0.01
Sioux (27)	49	0.17
South American Ind. (1)	5	0.02
Spanish American Ind. (0)	0	<0.01
Tlingit-Haida *(Alaska Native)* (9)	20	0.07
Tohono O'Odham (7)	7	0.02
Tsimshian *(Alaska Native)* (1)	1	<0.01
Ute (1)	1	<0.01
Yakama (2)	2	0.01
Yaqui (5)	10	0.03
Yuman (4)	4	0.01
Yup'ik *(Alaska Native)* (3)	6	0.02
Asian (965)	1,206	4.22
Not Hispanic (938)	1,127	3.94
Hispanic (27)	79	0.28
Bangladeshi (0)	0	<0.01
Bhutanese (0)	0	<0.01
Burmese (0)	1	<0.01
Cambodian (1)	2	0.01
Chinese, ex. Taiwanese (49)	93	0.33
Filipino (99)	198	0.69
Hmong (593)	616	2.15
Indian (28)	41	0.14
Indonesian (0)	1	<0.01
Japanese (35)	81	0.28
Korean (27)	54	0.19
Laotian (43)	54	0.19
Malaysian (0)	0	<0.01
Nepalese (0)	0	<0.01
Pakistani (0)	0	<0.01
Sri Lankan (0)	0	<0.01
Taiwanese (0)	0	<0.01
Thai (12)	13	0.05
Vietnamese (36)	44	0.15
Hawaii Native/Pacific Islander (32)	81	0.28
Not Hispanic (26)	65	0.23
Hispanic (6)	16	0.06
Fijian (0)	0	<0.01
Guamanian/Chamorro (2)	3	0.01
Marshallese (0)	0	<0.01
Native Hawaiian (18)	43	0.15
Samoan (7)	14	0.05
Tongan (2)	3	0.01
White (21,098)	22,285	77.89
Not Hispanic (18,513)	19,421	67.88
Hispanic (2,585)	2,864	10.01

*Notes: † The Census 2010 population figure is used to calculate the percentages in the Hispanic Origin and Race categories. Ancestry percentages are based on the 2006-2010 American Community Survey population (not shown); ‡ Numbers in parentheses indicate the number of people reporting a single ancestry; * Numbers in parentheses indicate the number of persons reporting this race alone, not in combination with any other race; Please refer to the Explanation of Data for more information.*

El Dorado County

Population: 181,058

Ancestry	Population	%
Afghan (0)	0	<0.01
African, Sub-Saharan (225)	378	0.21
African (211)	347	0.19
Cape Verdean (0)	0	<0.01
Ethiopian (0)	0	<0.01
Ghanaian (0)	0	<0.01
Kenyan (0)	0	<0.01
Liberian (0)	0	<0.01
Nigerian (0)	17	0.01
Senegalese (0)	0	<0.01
Sierra Leonean (0)	0	<0.01
Somalian (0)	0	<0.01
South African (14)	14	0.01
Sudanese (0)	0	<0.01
Ugandan (0)	0	<0.01
Zimbabwean (0)	0	<0.01
Other Sub-Saharan African (0)	0	<0.01
Albanian (0)	33	0.02
Alsatian (12)	12	0.01
American (7,520)	7,520	4.20
Arab (251)	537	0.30
Arab (0)	21	0.01
Egyptian (20)	48	0.03
Iraqi (0)	0	<0.01
Jordanian (0)	0	<0.01
Lebanese (140)	238	0.13
Moroccan (0)	0	<0.01
Palestinian (0)	0	<0.01
Syrian (4)	31	0.02
Other Arab (87)	199	0.11
Armenian (274)	388	0.22
Assyrian/Chaldean/Syriac (25)	29	0.02
Australian (25)	58	0.03
Austrian (242)	714	0.40
Basque (0)	159	0.09
Belgian (72)	204	0.11
Brazilian (43)	69	0.04
British (650)	1,396	0.78
Bulgarian (127)	201	0.11
Cajun (0)	0	<0.01
Canadian (295)	592	0.33
Carpatho Rusyn (0)	0	<0.01
Celtic (37)	47	0.03
Croatian (293)	531	0.30
Cypriot (0)	0	<0.01
Czech (114)	649	0.36
Czechoslovakian (223)	351	0.20
Danish (578)	2,522	1.41
Dutch (821)	3,707	2.07
Eastern European (168)	168	0.09
English (7,274)	26,583	14.85
Estonian (0)	0	<0.01
European (3,714)	4,342	2.42
Finnish (204)	652	0.36
French, ex. Basque (1,134)	7,625	4.26
French Canadian (775)	1,575	0.88
German (9,802)	38,333	21.41
German Russian (0)	0	<0.01
Greek (445)	1,069	0.60
Guyanese (0)	0	<0.01
Hungarian (541)	1,175	0.66
Icelander (12)	73	0.04
Iranian (620)	646	0.36
Irish (5,838)	26,470	14.78
Israeli (36)	51	0.03
Italian (4,755)	14,222	7.94
Latvian (0)	70	0.04
Lithuanian (67)	172	0.10
Luxemburger (0)	11	0.01
Macedonian (0)	4	<0.01
Maltese (16)	103	0.06
New Zealander (0)	51	0.03
Northern European (314)	340	0.19
Norwegian (1,830)	4,973	2.78
Pennsylvania German (70)	99	0.06
Polish (982)	3,418	1.91
Portuguese (1,603)	3,685	2.06
Romanian (123)	325	0.18
Russian (427)	1,852	1.03
Scandinavian (289)	722	0.40
Scotch-Irish (1,457)	4,490	2.51
Scottish (1,608)	6,485	3.62
Serbian (0)	80	0.04
Slavic (24)	55	0.03
Slovak (112)	199	0.11
Slovene (20)	36	0.02
Soviet Union (0)	0	<0.01
Swedish (1,359)	5,686	3.18
Swiss (296)	1,591	0.89
Turkish (99)	118	0.07
Ukrainian (184)	441	0.25
Welsh (338)	1,950	1.09
West Indian, ex. Hispanic (0)	0	<0.01
Bahamian (0)	0	<0.01
Barbadian (0)	0	<0.01
Belizean (0)	0	<0.01
Bermudan (0)	0	<0.01
British West Indian (0)	0	<0.01
Dutch West Indian (0)	0	<0.01
Haitian (0)	0	<0.01
Jamaican (0)	0	<0.01
Trinidadian/Tobagonian (0)	0	<0.01
U.S. Virgin Islander (0)	0	<0.01
West Indian (0)	0	<0.01
Other West Indian (0)	0	<0.01
Yugoslavian (131)	318	0.18

Hispanic Origin	Population	%
Hispanic or Latino (of any race)	21,875	12.08
Central American, ex. Mexican	983	0.54
Costa Rican	49	0.03
Guatemalan	145	0.08
Honduran	39	0.02
Nicaraguan	142	0.08
Panamanian	51	0.03
Salvadoran	550	0.30
Other Central American	7	<0.01
Cuban	148	0.08
Dominican Republic	21	0.01
Mexican	16,682	9.21
Puerto Rican	574	0.32
South American	535	0.30
Argentinean	119	0.07
Bolivian	29	0.02
Chilean	70	0.04
Colombian	152	0.08
Ecuadorian	33	0.02
Paraguayan	4	<0.01
Peruvian	89	0.05
Uruguayan	3	<0.01
Venezuelan	18	0.01
Other South American	18	0.01
Other Hispanic or Latino	2,932	1.62

Race*	Population	%
African-American/Black (1,409)	2,282	1.26
Not Hispanic (1,296)	1,999	1.10
Hispanic (113)	283	0.16
American Indian/Alaska Native (2,070)	4,704	2.60
Not Hispanic (1,553)	3,663	2.02
Hispanic (517)	1,041	0.57
Alaska Athabascan *(Ala. Nat.)* (2)	3	<0.01
Aleut *(Alaska Native)* (2)	5	<0.01
Apache (54)	117	0.06
Arapaho (0)	4	<0.01
Blackfeet (17)	116	0.06
Canadian/French Am. Ind. (8)	16	0.01
Central American Ind. (1)	1	<0.01
Cherokee (266)	983	0.54
Cheyenne (5)	14	0.01
Chickasaw (25)	61	0.03
Chippewa (46)	86	0.05
Choctaw (90)	285	0.16
Colville (1)	3	<0.01
Comanche (7)	17	0.01
Cree (2)	7	<0.01
Creek (11)	38	0.02
Crow (2)	15	0.01
Delaware (9)	20	0.01
Hopi (0)	11	0.01
Houma (0)	0	<0.01
Inupiat *(Alaska Native)* (3)	13	0.01
Iroquois (17)	64	0.04
Kiowa (3)	4	<0.01
Lumbee (0)	2	<0.01
Menominee (1)	1	<0.01
Mexican American Ind. (117)	174	0.10
Navajo (26)	82	0.05
Osage (6)	29	0.02
Ottawa (2)	4	<0.01
Paiute (8)	31	0.02
Pima (10)	17	0.01
Potawatomi (14)	24	0.01
Pueblo (22)	40	0.02
Puget Sound Salish (4)	10	0.01
Seminole (1)	16	0.01
Shoshone (11)	37	0.02
Sioux (43)	128	0.07
South American Ind. (6)	6	<0.01
Spanish American Ind. (10)	12	0.01
Tlingit-Haida *(Alaska Native)* (3)	15	0.01
Tohono O'Odham (1)	6	<0.01
Tsimshian *(Alaska Native)* (0)	0	<0.01
Ute (2)	8	<0.01
Yakama (0)	1	<0.01
Yaqui (11)	22	0.01
Yuman (1)	2	<0.01
Yup'ik *(Alaska Native)* (0)	1	<0.01
Asian (6,297)	8,788	4.85
Not Hispanic (6,143)	8,242	4.55
Hispanic (154)	546	0.30
Bangladeshi (15)	15	0.01
Bhutanese (0)	0	<0.01
Burmese (13)	14	0.01
Cambodian (47)	60	0.03
Chinese, ex. Taiwanese (1,119)	1,605	0.89
Filipino (2,077)	3,067	1.69
Hmong (47)	53	0.03
Indian (1,060)	1,200	0.66
Indonesian (29)	74	0.04
Japanese (533)	1,215	0.67
Korean (560)	787	0.43
Laotian (16)	27	0.01
Malaysian (1)	4	<0.01
Nepalese (2)	3	<0.01
Pakistani (61)	67	0.04
Sri Lankan (15)	18	0.01
Taiwanese (52)	61	0.03
Thai (44)	80	0.04
Vietnamese (367)	497	0.27
Hawaii Native/Pacific Islander (294)	830	0.46
Not Hispanic (261)	679	0.38
Hispanic (33)	151	0.08
Fijian (25)	32	0.02
Guamanian/Chamorro (62)	149	0.08
Marshallese (2)	2	<0.01
Native Hawaiian (117)	369	0.20
Samoan (20)	59	0.03
Tongan (10)	23	0.01
White (156,793)	163,235	90.16
Not Hispanic (144,689)	149,371	82.50
Hispanic (12,104)	13,864	7.66

*Notes: † The Census 2010 population figure is used to calculate the percentages in the Hispanic Origin and Race categories. Ancestry percentages are based on the 2006-2010 American Community Survey population (not shown); ‡ Numbers in parentheses indicate the number of people reporting a single ancestry; * Numbers in parentheses indicate the number of persons reporting this race alone, not in combination with any other race; Please refer to the Explanation of Data for more information.*

Fresno County

Population: 930,450

Ancestry	Population	%
Afghan (124)	136	0.01
African, Sub-Saharan (2,509)	3,174	0.35
African (1,540)	2,154	0.24
Cape Verdean (0)	0	<0.01
Ethiopian (320)	339	0.04
Ghanaian (5)	25	<0.01
Kenyan (0)	0	<0.01
Liberian (0)	0	<0.01
Nigerian (394)	394	0.04
Senegalese (0)	0	<0.01
Sierra Leonean (0)	0	<0.01
Somalian (70)	70	0.01
South African (7)	19	<0.01
Sudanese (109)	109	0.01
Ugandan (0)	0	<0.01
Zimbabwean (0)	0	<0.01
Other Sub-Saharan African (64)	64	0.01
Albanian (4)	27	<0.01
Alsatian (0)	13	<0.01
American (14,898)	14,898	1.64
Arab (5,214)	6,193	0.68
Arab (2,049)	2,320	0.26
Egyptian (401)	417	0.05
Iraqi (99)	99	0.01
Jordanian (794)	794	0.09
Lebanese (317)	628	0.07
Moroccan (11)	23	<0.01
Palestinian (143)	190	0.02
Syrian (264)	540	0.06
Other Arab (1,136)	1,182	0.13
Armenian (7,814)	10,602	1.17
Assyrian/Chaldean/Syriac (95)	195	0.02
Australian (23)	39	<0.01
Austrian (187)	837	0.09
Basque (489)	811	0.09
Belgian (99)	419	0.05
Brazilian (137)	503	0.06
British (526)	1,505	0.17
Bulgarian (0)	0	<0.01
Cajun (4)	36	<0.01
Canadian (756)	1,300	0.14
Carpatho Rusyn (0)	0	<0.01
Celtic (57)	195	0.02
Croatian (97)	269	0.03
Cypriot (0)	0	<0.01
Czech (487)	1,614	0.18
Czechoslovakian (264)	600	0.07
Danish (1,904)	5,435	0.60
Dutch (2,086)	9,488	1.04
Eastern European (150)	196	0.02
English (13,309)	47,700	5.25
Estonian (20)	28	<0.01
European (5,353)	6,443	0.71
Finnish (222)	1,062	0.12
French, ex. Basque (2,177)	14,157	1.56
French Canadian (870)	1,758	0.19
German (24,256)	79,534	8.75
German Russian (86)	148	0.02
Greek (820)	1,867	0.21
Guyanese (0)	0	<0.01
Hungarian (176)	901	0.10
Icelander (17)	61	0.01
Iranian (943)	1,392	0.15
Irish (13,371)	52,878	5.82
Israeli (208)	263	0.03
Italian (11,494)	31,467	3.46
Latvian (10)	62	0.01
Lithuanian (74)	260	0.03
Luxemburger (12)	68	0.01
Macedonian (0)	22	<0.01
Maltese (8)	8	<0.01
New Zealander (73)	144	0.02
Northern European (648)	751	0.08
Norwegian (1,937)	6,035	0.66
Pennsylvania German (219)	256	0.03
Polish (1,380)	4,529	0.50
Portuguese (6,038)	11,721	1.29
Romanian (282)	530	0.06
Russian (2,246)	5,245	0.58
Scandinavian (408)	915	0.10
Scotch-Irish (3,104)	9,106	1.00
Scottish (3,123)	9,885	1.09
Serbian (55)	171	0.02
Slavic (135)	304	0.03
Slovak (45)	140	0.02
Slovene (12)	71	0.01
Soviet Union (0)	0	<0.01
Swedish (2,467)	9,241	1.02
Swiss (381)	2,214	0.24
Turkish (98)	109	0.01
Ukrainian (1,344)	1,665	0.18
Welsh (552)	4,002	0.44
West Indian, ex. Hispanic (245)	717	0.08
Bahamian (66)	66	0.01
Barbadian (0)	14	<0.01
Belizean (0)	39	<0.01
Bermudan (0)	0	<0.01
British West Indian (11)	11	<0.01
Dutch West Indian (25)	177	0.02
Haitian (0)	0	<0.01
Jamaican (132)	268	0.03
Trinidadian/Tobagonian (0)	0	<0.01
U.S. Virgin Islander (0)	0	<0.01
West Indian (11)	129	0.01
Other West Indian (0)	13	<0.01
Yugoslavian (151)	401	0.04

Hispanic Origin	Population	%
Hispanic or Latino (of any race)	468,070	50.31
Central American, ex. Mexican	9,183	0.99
Costa Rican	185	0.02
Guatemalan	1,154	0.12
Honduran	991	0.11
Nicaraguan	520	0.06
Panamanian	172	0.02
Salvadoran	6,102	0.66
Other Central American	59	0.01
Cuban	615	0.07
Dominican Republic	111	0.01
Mexican	428,191	46.02
Puerto Rican	2,790	0.30
South American	1,687	0.18
Argentinean	221	0.02
Bolivian	65	0.01
Chilean	200	0.02
Colombian	508	0.05
Ecuadorian	145	0.02
Paraguayan	16	<0.01
Peruvian	403	0.04
Uruguayan	28	<0.01
Venezuelan	80	0.01
Other South American	21	<0.01
Other Hispanic or Latino	25,493	2.74

Race*	Population	%
African-American/Black (49,523)	57,795	6.21
Not Hispanic (45,005)	50,062	5.38
Hispanic (4,518)	7,733	0.83
American Indian/Alaska Native (15,649)	25,501	2.74
Not Hispanic (5,979)	11,630	1.25
Hispanic (9,670)	13,871	1.49
Alaska Athabascan *(Ala. Nat.)* (13)	23	<0.01
Aleut *(Alaska Native)* (12)	14	<0.01
Apache (576)	1,035	0.11
Arapaho (1)	7	<0.01
Blackfeet (78)	346	0.04
Canadian/French Am. Ind. (18)	38	<0.01
Central American Ind. (32)	53	0.01
Cherokee (834)	2,740	0.29
Cheyenne (19)	48	0.01
Chickasaw (51)	172	0.02
Chippewa (67)	131	0.01
Choctaw (344)	844	0.09
Colville (11)	13	<0.01
Comanche (61)	137	0.01
Cree (9)	20	<0.01
Creek (125)	316	0.03
Crow (14)	31	<0.01
Delaware (20)	26	<0.01
Hopi (21)	57	0.01
Houma (1)	3	<0.01
Inupiat *(Alaska Native)* (5)	13	<0.01
Iroquois (47)	115	0.01
Kiowa (20)	35	<0.01
Lumbee (9)	21	<0.01
Menominee (12)	15	<0.01
Mexican American Ind. (2,503)	3,145	0.34
Navajo (249)	450	0.05
Osage (8)	44	<0.01
Ottawa (4)	8	<0.01
Paiute (41)	116	0.01
Pima (42)	62	0.01
Potawatomi (65)	116	0.01
Pueblo (67)	110	0.01
Puget Sound Salish (17)	24	<0.01
Seminole (31)	78	0.01
Shoshone (43)	62	0.01
Sioux (119)	248	0.03
South American Ind. (14)	35	<0.01
Spanish American Ind. (72)	88	0.01
Tlingit-Haida *(Alaska Native)* (3)	11	<0.01
Tohono O'Odham (53)	80	0.01
Tsimshian *(Alaska Native)* (1)	1	<0.01
Ute (12)	28	<0.01
Yakama (1)	3	<0.01
Yaqui (487)	723	0.08
Yuman (45)	69	0.01
Yup'ik *(Alaska Native)* (3)	7	<0.01
Asian (89,357)	101,134	10.87
Not Hispanic (86,856)	94,804	10.19
Hispanic (2,501)	6,330	0.68
Bangladeshi (32)	35	<0.01
Bhutanese (1)	1	<0.01
Burmese (67)	86	0.01
Cambodian (5,015)	5,618	0.60
Chinese, ex. Taiwanese (5,638)	7,429	0.80
Filipino (9,720)	13,491	1.45
Hmong (30,648)	31,771	3.41
Indian (15,469)	17,111	1.84
Indonesian (216)	352	0.04
Japanese (4,980)	7,487	0.80
Korean (1,586)	2,139	0.23
Laotian (7,088)	7,967	0.86
Malaysian (31)	51	0.01
Nepalese (33)	41	<0.01
Pakistani (519)	611	0.07
Sri Lankan (73)	91	0.01
Taiwanese (193)	219	0.02
Thai (505)	769	0.08
Vietnamese (3,114)	3,609	0.39
Hawaii Native/Pacific Islander (1,405)	3,572	0.38
Not Hispanic (1,066)	2,339	0.25
Hispanic (339)	1,233	0.13
Fijian (143)	185	0.02
Guamanian/Chamorro (253)	475	0.05
Marshallese (6)	8	<0.01
Native Hawaiian (288)	1,064	0.11
Samoan (383)	608	0.07
Tongan (39)	78	0.01
White (515,145)	548,884	58.99
Not Hispanic (304,522)	318,333	34.21
Hispanic (210,623)	230,551	24.78

*Notes: † The Census 2010 population figure is used to calculate the percentages in the Hispanic Origin and Race categories. Ancestry percentages are based on the 2006-2010 American Community Survey population (not shown); ‡ Numbers in parentheses indicate the number of people reporting a single ancestry; * Numbers in parentheses indicate the number of persons reporting this race alone, not in combination with any other race; Please refer to the Explanation of Data for more information.*

Glenn County

Population: 28,122

Ancestry	Population	%
Afghan (0)	0	<0.01
African, Sub-Saharan (26)	38	0.14
African (26)	38	0.14
Cape Verdean (0)	0	<0.01
Ethiopian (0)	0	<0.01
Ghanaian (0)	0	<0.01
Kenyan (0)	0	<0.01
Liberian (0)	0	<0.01
Nigerian (0)	0	<0.01
Senegalese (0)	0	<0.01
Sierra Leonean (0)	0	<0.01
Somalian (0)	0	<0.01
South African (0)	0	<0.01
Sudanese (0)	0	<0.01
Ugandan (0)	0	<0.01
Zimbabwean (0)	0	<0.01
Other Sub-Saharan African (0)	0	<0.01
Albanian (0)	0	<0.01
Alsatian (0)	0	<0.01
American (1,345)	1,345	4.81
Arab (380)	468	1.68
Arab (79)	79	0.28
Egyptian (0)	0	<0.01
Iraqi (0)	0	<0.01
Jordanian (0)	0	<0.01
Lebanese (12)	12	0.04
Moroccan (0)	0	<0.01
Palestinian (240)	282	1.01
Syrian (0)	46	0.16
Other Arab (49)	49	0.18
Armenian (0)	0	<0.01
Assyrian/Chaldean/Syriac (0)	0	<0.01
Australian (17)	17	0.06
Austrian (0)	39	0.14
Basque (36)	129	0.46
Belgian (0)	11	0.04
Brazilian (0)	46	0.16
British (91)	126	0.45
Bulgarian (0)	0	<0.01
Cajun (0)	0	<0.01
Canadian (11)	119	0.43
Carpatho Rusyn (0)	0	<0.01
Celtic (0)	29	0.10
Croatian (0)	0	<0.01
Cypriot (0)	0	<0.01
Czech (27)	40	0.14
Czechoslovakian (0)	0	<0.01
Danish (30)	144	0.52
Dutch (251)	835	2.99
Eastern European (0)	0	<0.01
English (554)	1,777	6.36
Estonian (0)	0	<0.01
European (149)	258	0.92
Finnish (46)	56	0.20
French, ex. Basque (117)	564	2.02
French Canadian (64)	124	0.44
German (1,196)	3,567	12.77
German Russian (0)	0	<0.01
Greek (41)	48	0.17
Guyanese (0)	0	<0.01
Hungarian (86)	98	0.35
Icelander (0)	0	<0.01
Iranian (0)	0	<0.01
Irish (489)	2,586	9.26
Israeli (0)	0	<0.01
Italian (411)	944	3.38
Latvian (0)	0	<0.01
Lithuanian (66)	66	0.24
Luxemburger (0)	0	<0.01
Macedonian (0)	0	<0.01
Maltese (0)	0	<0.01
New Zealander (0)	0	<0.01
Northern European (7)	7	0.03
Norwegian (55)	224	0.80
Pennsylvania German (0)	0	<0.01
Polish (122)	194	0.69
Portuguese (499)	1,026	3.67
Romanian (0)	0	<0.01
Russian (3)	74	0.26
Scandinavian (16)	35	0.13
Scotch-Irish (166)	301	1.08
Scottish (302)	670	2.40
Serbian (0)	0	<0.01
Slavic (9)	29	0.10
Slovak (4)	5	0.02
Slovene (0)	0	<0.01
Soviet Union (0)	0	<0.01
Swedish (119)	391	1.40
Swiss (32)	165	0.59
Turkish (0)	0	<0.01
Ukrainian (35)	52	0.19
Welsh (12)	162	0.58
West Indian, ex. Hispanic (31)	57	0.20
Bahamian (0)	0	<0.01
Barbadian (0)	0	<0.01
Belizean (0)	0	<0.01
Bermudan (0)	0	<0.01
British West Indian (0)	0	<0.01
Dutch West Indian (0)	0	<0.01
Haitian (21)	47	0.17
Jamaican (10)	10	0.04
Trinidadian/Tobagonian (0)	0	<0.01
U.S. Virgin Islander (0)	0	<0.01
West Indian (0)	0	<0.01
Other West Indian (0)	0	<0.01
Yugoslavian (12)	12	0.04

Hispanic Origin	Population	%
Hispanic or Latino (of any race)	10,539	37.48
Central American, ex. Mexican	84	0.30
Costa Rican	3	0.01
Guatemalan	28	0.10
Honduran	11	0.04
Nicaraguan	5	0.02
Panamanian	1	<0.01
Salvadoran	33	0.12
Other Central American	3	0.01
Cuban	4	0.01
Dominican Republic	0	<0.01
Mexican	9,970	35.45
Puerto Rican	41	0.15
South American	28	0.10
Argentinean	2	0.01
Bolivian	0	<0.01
Chilean	4	0.01
Colombian	3	0.01
Ecuadorian	1	<0.01
Paraguayan	0	<0.01
Peruvian	13	0.05
Uruguayan	0	<0.01
Venezuelan	4	0.01
Other South American	1	<0.01
Other Hispanic or Latino	412	1.47

Race*	Population	%
African-American/Black (231)	359	1.28
Not Hispanic (192)	281	1.00
Hispanic (39)	78	0.28
American Indian/Alaska Native (619)	1,036	3.68
Not Hispanic (477)	751	2.67
Hispanic (142)	285	1.01
Alaska Athabascan *(Ala. Nat.)* (1)	1	<0.01
Aleut *(Alaska Native)* (0)	0	<0.01
Apache (4)	10	0.04
Arapaho (0)	0	<0.01
Blackfeet (2)	13	0.05
Canadian/French Am. Ind. (0)	2	0.01
Central American Ind. (0)	0	<0.01
Cherokee (31)	91	0.32
Cheyenne (0)	0	<0.01
Chickasaw (0)	0	<0.01
Chippewa (6)	16	0.06
Choctaw (18)	40	0.14
Colville (0)	0	<0.01
Comanche (1)	4	0.01
Cree (0)	0	<0.01
Creek (1)	2	0.01
Crow (0)	0	<0.01
Delaware (1)	2	0.01
Hopi (0)	0	<0.01
Houma (0)	0	<0.01
Inupiat *(Alaska Native)* (0)	0	<0.01
Iroquois (4)	4	0.01
Kiowa (2)	3	0.01
Lumbee (0)	3	0.01
Menominee (0)	0	<0.01
Mexican American Ind. (11)	31	0.11
Navajo (0)	5	0.02
Osage (1)	1	<0.01
Ottawa (0)	0	<0.01
Paiute (2)	4	0.01
Pima (0)	0	<0.01
Potawatomi (6)	6	0.02
Pueblo (0)	1	<0.01
Puget Sound Salish (0)	3	0.01
Seminole (0)	3	0.01
Shoshone (2)	2	0.01
Sioux (21)	27	0.10
South American Ind. (0)	0	<0.01
Spanish American Ind. (4)	4	0.01
Tlingit-Haida *(Alaska Native)* (2)	4	0.01
Tohono O'Odham (2)	2	0.01
Tsimshian *(Alaska Native)* (0)	0	<0.01
Ute (0)	0	<0.01
Yakama (1)	1	<0.01
Yaqui (1)	1	<0.01
Yuman (0)	0	<0.01
Yup'ik *(Alaska Native)* (0)	0	<0.01
Asian (722)	889	3.16
Not Hispanic (674)	797	2.83
Hispanic (48)	92	0.33
Bangladeshi (0)	0	<0.01
Bhutanese (0)	0	<0.01
Burmese (0)	0	<0.01
Cambodian (6)	8	0.03
Chinese, ex. Taiwanese (49)	69	0.25
Filipino (69)	127	0.45
Hmong (180)	183	0.65
Indian (102)	117	0.42
Indonesian (5)	5	0.02
Japanese (20)	44	0.16
Korean (7)	21	0.07
Laotian (206)	244	0.87
Malaysian (0)	0	<0.01
Nepalese (0)	0	<0.01
Pakistani (16)	16	0.06
Sri Lankan (0)	1	<0.01
Taiwanese (0)	0	<0.01
Thai (4)	8	0.03
Vietnamese (11)	17	0.06
Hawaii Native/Pacific Islander (24)	68	0.24
Not Hispanic (22)	42	0.15
Hispanic (2)	26	0.09
Fijian (5)	8	0.03
Guamanian/Chamorro (2)	3	0.01
Marshallese (0)	0	<0.01
Native Hawaiian (4)	15	0.05
Samoan (4)	6	0.02
Tongan (0)	0	<0.01
White (19,990)	20,893	74.29
Not Hispanic (15,717)	16,149	57.42
Hispanic (4,273)	4,744	16.87

*Notes: † The Census 2010 population figure is used to calculate the percentages in the Hispanic Origin and Race categories. Ancestry percentages are based on the 2006-2010 American Community Survey population (not shown); ‡ Numbers in parentheses indicate the number of people reporting a single ancestry; * Numbers in parentheses indicate the number of persons reporting this race alone, not in combination with any other race; Please refer to the Explanation of Data for more information.*

Humboldt County

Population: 134,623

Ancestry	Population	%
Afghan (141)	141	0.11
African, Sub-Saharan (267)	670	0.50
African (185)	573	0.43
Cape Verdean (5)	5	<0.01
Ethiopian (0)	0	<0.01
Ghanaian (5)	5	<0.01
Kenyan (0)	0	<0.01
Liberian (0)	0	<0.01
Nigerian (70)	76	0.06
Senegalese (0)	0	<0.01
Sierra Leonean (0)	0	<0.01
Somalian (0)	0	<0.01
South African (0)	9	0.01
Sudanese (0)	0	<0.01
Ugandan (2)	2	<0.01
Zimbabwean (0)	0	<0.01
Other Sub-Saharan African (0)	0	<0.01
Albanian (0)	0	<0.01
Alsatian (0)	37	0.03
American (4,598)	4,598	3.46
Arab (159)	318	0.24
Arab (102)	102	0.08
Egyptian (14)	14	0.01
Iraqi (0)	0	<0.01
Jordanian (0)	0	<0.01
Lebanese (16)	151	0.11
Moroccan (0)	0	<0.01
Palestinian (0)	0	<0.01
Syrian (27)	27	0.02
Other Arab (0)	24	0.02
Armenian (103)	200	0.15
Assyrian/Chaldean/Syriac (12)	12	0.01
Australian (36)	74	0.06
Austrian (180)	573	0.43
Basque (14)	36	0.03
Belgian (44)	214	0.16
Brazilian (60)	60	0.05
British (345)	700	0.53
Bulgarian (0)	12	0.01
Cajun (18)	18	0.01
Canadian (128)	494	0.37
Carpatho Rusyn (0)	0	<0.01
Celtic (69)	100	0.08
Croatian (157)	232	0.17
Cypriot (0)	0	<0.01
Czech (63)	445	0.33
Czechoslovakian (48)	226	0.17
Danish (620)	1,808	1.36
Dutch (508)	2,563	1.93
Eastern European (187)	218	0.16
English (4,314)	16,079	12.08
Estonian (0)	2	<0.01
European (9,405)	11,253	8.46
Finnish (232)	577	0.43
French, ex. Basque (633)	5,666	4.26
French Canadian (365)	918	0.69
German (5,265)	20,855	15.67
German Russian (0)	10	0.01
Greek (141)	449	0.34
Guyanese (0)	0	<0.01
Hungarian (134)	560	0.42
Icelander (23)	30	0.02
Iranian (86)	108	0.08
Irish (4,706)	17,875	13.43
Israeli (0)	0	<0.01
Italian (3,361)	8,971	6.74
Latvian (0)	30	0.02
Lithuanian (91)	208	0.16
Luxemburger (0)	8	0.01
Macedonian (0)	0	<0.01
Maltese (0)	0	<0.01
New Zealander (23)	51	0.04
Northern European (180)	180	0.14
Norwegian (998)	3,371	2.53
Pennsylvania German (8)	66	0.05
Polish (757)	2,508	1.88
Portuguese (1,545)	3,289	2.47
Romanian (54)	110	0.08
Russian (696)	1,770	1.33
Scandinavian (539)	856	0.64
Scotch-Irish (1,395)	3,744	2.81
Scottish (1,021)	4,584	3.45
Serbian (9)	19	0.01
Slavic (12)	69	0.05
Slovak (110)	197	0.15
Slovene (0)	25	0.02
Soviet Union (0)	0	<0.01
Swedish (857)	3,645	2.74
Swiss (225)	1,275	0.96
Turkish (4)	8	0.01
Ukrainian (126)	199	0.15
Welsh (205)	1,079	0.81
West Indian, ex. Hispanic (69)	460	0.35
Bahamian (0)	0	<0.01
Barbadian (0)	0	<0.01
Belizean (0)	0	<0.01
Bermudan (0)	0	<0.01
British West Indian (0)	0	<0.01
Dutch West Indian (60)	97	0.07
Haitian (0)	0	<0.01
Jamaican (9)	9	0.01
Trinidadian/Tobagonian (0)	311	0.23
U.S. Virgin Islander (0)	0	<0.01
West Indian (0)	43	0.03
Other West Indian (0)	0	<0.01
Yugoslavian (85)	158	0.12

Hispanic Origin	Population	%
Hispanic or Latino (of any race)	13,211	9.81
Central American, ex. Mexican	473	0.35
Costa Rican	30	0.02
Guatemalan	145	0.11
Honduran	49	0.04
Nicaraguan	69	0.05
Panamanian	17	0.01
Salvadoran	158	0.12
Other Central American	5	<0.01
Cuban	170	0.13
Dominican Republic	17	0.01
Mexican	10,332	7.67
Puerto Rican	370	0.27
South American	340	0.25
Argentinean	39	0.03
Bolivian	20	0.01
Chilean	72	0.05
Colombian	64	0.05
Ecuadorian	45	0.03
Paraguayan	2	<0.01
Peruvian	67	0.05
Uruguayan	5	<0.01
Venezuelan	17	0.01
Other South American	9	0.01
Other Hispanic or Latino	1,509	1.12

Race*	Population	%
African-American/Black (1,505)	2,642	1.96
Not Hispanic (1,393)	2,307	1.71
Hispanic (112)	335	0.25
American Indian/Alaska Native (7,726)	11,972	8.89
Not Hispanic (6,961)	10,534	7.82
Hispanic (765)	1,438	1.07
Alaska Athabascan *(Ala. Nat.)* (19)	24	0.02
Aleut *(Alaska Native)* (12)	19	0.01
Apache (73)	172	0.13
Arapaho (1)	5	<0.01
Blackfeet (27)	170	0.13
Canadian/French Am. Ind. (11)	24	0.02
Central American Ind. (9)	16	0.01
Cherokee (253)	1,094	0.81
Cheyenne (7)	25	0.02
Chickasaw (20)	67	0.05
Chippewa (33)	77	0.06
Choctaw (82)	256	0.19
Colville (1)	3	<0.01
Comanche (10)	28	0.02
Cree (1)	9	0.01
Creek (15)	52	0.04
Crow (6)	17	0.01
Delaware (1)	2	<0.01
Hopi (11)	13	0.01
Houma (0)	0	<0.01
Inupiat *(Alaska Native)* (11)	15	0.01
Iroquois (29)	80	0.06
Kiowa (2)	7	0.01
Lumbee (3)	4	<0.01
Menominee (0)	4	<0.01
Mexican American Ind. (103)	162	0.12
Navajo (51)	84	0.06
Osage (11)	27	0.02
Ottawa (11)	17	0.01
Paiute (26)	42	0.03
Pima (21)	22	0.02
Potawatomi (18)	33	0.02
Pueblo (7)	12	0.01
Puget Sound Salish (6)	8	0.01
Seminole (0)	8	0.01
Shoshone (17)	31	0.02
Sioux (54)	139	0.10
South American Ind. (10)	28	0.02
Spanish American Ind. (3)	5	<0.01
Tlingit-Haida *(Alaska Native)* (17)	29	0.02
Tohono O'Odham (6)	11	0.01
Tsimshian *(Alaska Native)* (1)	4	<0.01
Ute (6)	20	0.01
Yakama (3)	4	<0.01
Yaqui (25)	52	0.04
Yuman (31)	36	0.03
Yup'ik *(Alaska Native)* (1)	5	<0.01
Asian (2,944)	4,438	3.30
Not Hispanic (2,854)	4,106	3.05
Hispanic (90)	332	0.25
Bangladeshi (7)	7	0.01
Bhutanese (1)	1	<0.01
Burmese (6)	6	<0.01
Cambodian (28)	38	0.03
Chinese, ex. Taiwanese (503)	801	0.59
Filipino (401)	896	0.67
Hmong (698)	721	0.54
Indian (204)	288	0.21
Indonesian (17)	43	0.03
Japanese (294)	735	0.55
Korean (182)	301	0.22
Laotian (234)	292	0.22
Malaysian (1)	2	<0.01
Nepalese (4)	5	<0.01
Pakistani (21)	34	0.03
Sri Lankan (2)	3	<0.01
Taiwanese (9)	13	0.01
Thai (49)	81	0.06
Vietnamese (125)	183	0.14
Hawaii Native/Pacific Islander (352)	768	0.57
Not Hispanic (332)	680	0.51
Hispanic (20)	88	0.07
Fijian (3)	8	0.01
Guamanian/Chamorro (16)	50	0.04
Marshallese (0)	1	<0.01
Native Hawaiian (117)	345	0.26
Samoan (62)	144	0.11
Tongan (4)	12	0.01
White (109,920)	116,614	86.62
Not Hispanic (103,958)	109,242	81.15
Hispanic (5,962)	7,372	5.48

*Notes: † The Census 2010 population figure is used to calculate the percentages in the Hispanic Origin and Race categories. Ancestry percentages are based on the 2006-2010 American Community Survey population (not shown); ‡ Numbers in parentheses indicate the number of people reporting a single ancestry; * Numbers in parentheses indicate the number of persons reporting this race alone, not in combination with any other race; Please refer to the Explanation of Data for more information.*

Imperial County

Population: 174,528

Ancestry	Population	%
Afghan (0)	15	0.01
African, Sub-Saharan (368)	438	0.26
African (351)	421	0.25
Cape Verdean (0)	0	<0.01
Ethiopian (0)	0	<0.01
Ghanaian (0)	0	<0.01
Kenyan (0)	0	<0.01
Liberian (0)	0	<0.01
Nigerian (17)	17	0.01
Senegalese (0)	0	<0.01
Sierra Leonean (0)	0	<0.01
Somalian (0)	0	<0.01
South African (0)	0	<0.01
Sudanese (0)	0	<0.01
Ugandan (0)	0	<0.01
Zimbabwean (0)	0	<0.01
Other Sub-Saharan African (0)	0	<0.01
Albanian (0)	0	<0.01
Alsatian (0)	0	<0.01
American (2,074)	2,074	1.23
Arab (558)	599	0.36
Arab (25)	25	0.01
Egyptian (0)	12	0.01
Iraqi (0)	0	<0.01
Jordanian (0)	0	<0.01
Lebanese (25)	45	0.03
Moroccan (38)	38	0.02
Palestinian (0)	9	0.01
Syrian (85)	85	0.05
Other Arab (385)	385	0.23
Armenian (55)	55	0.03
Assyrian/Chaldean/Syriac (0)	0	<0.01
Australian (0)	0	<0.01
Austrian (0)	42	0.02
Basque (11)	110	0.07
Belgian (0)	3	<0.01
Brazilian (0)	0	<0.01
British (78)	223	0.13
Bulgarian (0)	0	<0.01
Cajun (0)	0	<0.01
Canadian (84)	153	0.09
Carpatho Rusyn (0)	0	<0.01
Celtic (0)	0	<0.01
Croatian (19)	24	0.01
Cypriot (0)	0	<0.01
Czech (32)	72	0.04
Czechoslovakian (32)	89	0.05
Danish (31)	77	0.05
Dutch (80)	822	0.49
Eastern European (18)	27	0.02
English (1,119)	3,434	2.04
Estonian (0)	0	<0.01
European (251)	353	0.21
Finnish (0)	52	0.03
French, ex. Basque (265)	1,717	1.02
French Canadian (32)	91	0.05
German (1,810)	6,486	3.86
German Russian (0)	9	0.01
Greek (29)	82	0.05
Guyanese (0)	0	<0.01
Hungarian (6)	181	0.11
Icelander (0)	7	<0.01
Iranian (0)	0	<0.01
Irish (1,140)	4,518	2.69
Israeli (0)	0	<0.01
Italian (579)	2,059	1.23
Latvian (0)	40	0.02
Lithuanian (0)	10	0.01
Luxemburger (0)	21	0.01
Macedonian (0)	0	<0.01
Maltese (0)	0	<0.01
New Zealander (0)	0	<0.01
Northern European (96)	96	0.06
Norwegian (141)	348	0.21
Pennsylvania German (0)	0	<0.01
Polish (234)	675	0.40
Portuguese (34)	178	0.11
Romanian (10)	10	0.01
Russian (20)	263	0.16
Scandinavian (58)	61	0.04
Scotch-Irish (255)	737	0.44
Scottish (292)	731	0.43
Serbian (30)	30	0.02
Slavic (8)	8	<0.01
Slovak (0)	11	0.01
Slovene (0)	4	<0.01
Soviet Union (0)	0	<0.01
Swedish (151)	550	0.33
Swiss (159)	380	0.23
Turkish (0)	0	<0.01
Ukrainian (14)	79	0.05
Welsh (8)	345	0.21
West Indian, ex. Hispanic (46)	95	0.06
Bahamian (0)	0	<0.01
Barbadian (0)	0	<0.01
Belizean (18)	52	0.03
Bermudan (0)	0	<0.01
British West Indian (19)	19	0.01
Dutch West Indian (0)	8	<0.01
Haitian (0)	0	<0.01
Jamaican (9)	16	0.01
Trinidadian/Tobagonian (0)	0	<0.01
U.S. Virgin Islander (0)	0	<0.01
West Indian (0)	0	<0.01
Other West Indian (0)	0	<0.01
Yugoslavian (52)	52	0.03

Hispanic Origin	Population	%
Hispanic or Latino (of any race)	140,271	80.37
Central American, ex. Mexican	632	0.36
Costa Rican	11	0.01
Guatemalan	93	0.05
Honduran	23	0.01
Nicaraguan	87	0.05
Panamanian	23	0.01
Salvadoran	384	0.22
Other Central American	11	0.01
Cuban	121	0.07
Dominican Republic	20	0.01
Mexican	134,797	77.24
Puerto Rican	467	0.27
South American	249	0.14
Argentinean	22	0.01
Bolivian	5	<0.01
Chilean	42	0.02
Colombian	63	0.04
Ecuadorian	27	0.02
Paraguayan	1	<0.01
Peruvian	73	0.04
Uruguayan	0	<0.01
Venezuelan	11	0.01
Other South American	5	<0.01
Other Hispanic or Latino	3,985	2.28

Race*	Population	%
African-American/Black (5,773)	6,617	3.79
Not Hispanic (5,114)	5,445	3.12
Hispanic (659)	1,172	0.67
American Indian/Alaska Native (3,059)	4,137	2.37
Not Hispanic (1,642)	2,084	1.19
Hispanic (1,417)	2,053	1.18
Alaska Athabascan *(Ala. Nat.)* (0)	0	<0.01
Aleut *(Alaska Native)* (0)	0	<0.01
Apache (21)	56	0.03
Arapaho (5)	6	<0.01
Blackfeet (15)	35	0.02
Canadian/French Am. Ind. (0)	2	<0.01
Central American Ind. (4)	5	<0.01
Cherokee (53)	184	0.11
Cheyenne (3)	3	<0.01
Chickasaw (12)	14	0.01
Chippewa (7)	11	0.01
Choctaw (39)	91	0.05
Colville (0)	0	<0.01
Comanche (5)	7	<0.01
Cree (0)	0	<0.01
Creek (4)	6	<0.01
Crow (0)	4	<0.01
Delaware (2)	2	<0.01
Hopi (3)	6	<0.01
Houma (0)	0	<0.01
Inupiat *(Alaska Native)* (1)	1	<0.01
Iroquois (6)	12	0.01
Kiowa (0)	1	<0.01
Lumbee (0)	5	<0.01
Menominee (0)	0	<0.01
Mexican American Ind. (239)	341	0.20
Navajo (31)	65	0.04
Osage (1)	4	<0.01
Ottawa (2)	2	<0.01
Paiute (15)	20	0.01
Pima (15)	17	0.01
Potawatomi (2)	2	<0.01
Pueblo (4)	7	<0.01
Puget Sound Salish (0)	0	<0.01
Seminole (2)	4	<0.01
Shoshone (3)	6	<0.01
Sioux (23)	45	0.03
South American Ind. (1)	7	<0.01
Spanish American Ind. (4)	20	0.01
Tlingit-Haida *(Alaska Native)* (0)	1	<0.01
Tohono O'Odham (19)	20	0.01
Tsimshian *(Alaska Native)* (0)	0	<0.01
Ute (0)	0	<0.01
Yakama (0)	0	<0.01
Yaqui (117)	185	0.11
Yuman (1,143)	1,263	0.72
Yup'ik *(Alaska Native)* (0)	0	<0.01
Asian (2,843)	4,194	2.40
Not Hispanic (2,201)	2,620	1.50
Hispanic (642)	1,574	0.90
Bangladeshi (5)	5	<0.01
Bhutanese (0)	0	<0.01
Burmese (2)	2	<0.01
Cambodian (43)	54	0.03
Chinese, ex. Taiwanese (644)	900	0.52
Filipino (995)	1,684	0.96
Hmong (14)	16	0.01
Indian (324)	453	0.26
Indonesian (3)	3	<0.01
Japanese (134)	253	0.14
Korean (345)	401	0.23
Laotian (9)	14	0.01
Malaysian (2)	2	<0.01
Nepalese (0)	0	<0.01
Pakistani (22)	33	0.02
Sri Lankan (2)	2	<0.01
Taiwanese (26)	32	0.02
Thai (3)	12	0.01
Vietnamese (155)	191	0.11
Hawaii Native/Pacific Islander (165)	369	0.21
Not Hispanic (87)	159	0.09
Hispanic (78)	210	0.12
Fijian (2)	4	<0.01
Guamanian/Chamorro (40)	61	0.03
Marshallese (0)	0	<0.01
Native Hawaiian (33)	102	0.06
Samoan (47)	74	0.04
Tongan (10)	16	0.01
White (102,553)	109,149	62.54
Not Hispanic (23,927)	24,837	14.23
Hispanic (78,626)	84,312	48.31

*Notes: † The Census 2010 population figure is used to calculate the percentages in the Hispanic Origin and Race categories. Ancestry percentages are based on the 2006-2010 American Community Survey population (not shown); ‡ Numbers in parentheses indicate the number of people reporting a single ancestry; * Numbers in parentheses indicate the number of persons reporting this race alone, not in combination with any other race; Please refer to the Explanation of Data for more information.*

Inyo County

Population: 18,546

Ancestry	Population	%
Afghan (0)	0	<0.01
African, Sub-Saharan (22)	89	0.48
African (22)	89	0.48
Cape Verdean (0)	0	<0.01
Ethiopian (0)	0	<0.01
Ghanaian (0)	0	<0.01
Kenyan (0)	0	<0.01
Liberian (0)	0	<0.01
Nigerian (0)	0	<0.01
Senegalese (0)	0	<0.01
Sierra Leonean (0)	0	<0.01
Somalian (0)	0	<0.01
South African (0)	0	<0.01
Sudanese (0)	0	<0.01
Ugandan (0)	0	<0.01
Zimbabwean (0)	0	<0.01
Other Sub-Saharan African (0)	0	<0.01
Albanian (0)	0	<0.01
Alsatian (0)	0	<0.01
American (731)	731	3.97
Arab (0)	8	0.04
Arab (0)	0	<0.01
Egyptian (0)	0	<0.01
Iraqi (0)	0	<0.01
Jordanian (0)	0	<0.01
Lebanese (0)	4	0.02
Moroccan (0)	0	<0.01
Palestinian (0)	0	<0.01
Syrian (0)	4	0.02
Other Arab (0)	0	<0.01
Armenian (16)	16	0.09
Assyrian/Chaldean/Syriac (11)	11	0.06
Australian (0)	0	<0.01
Austrian (27)	58	0.31
Basque (35)	35	0.19
Belgian (94)	99	0.54
Brazilian (0)	0	<0.01
British (94)	110	0.60
Bulgarian (0)	0	<0.01
Cajun (0)	0	<0.01
Canadian (0)	45	0.24
Carpatho Rusyn (0)	0	<0.01
Celtic (0)	51	0.28
Croatian (0)	18	0.10
Cypriot (0)	0	<0.01
Czech (41)	109	0.59
Czechoslovakian (10)	10	0.05
Danish (140)	330	1.79
Dutch (206)	642	3.48
Eastern European (14)	14	0.08
English (834)	2,272	12.33
Estonian (0)	7	0.04
European (161)	237	1.29
Finnish (9)	13	0.07
French, ex. Basque (300)	962	5.22
French Canadian (43)	70	0.38
German (939)	3,058	16.59
German Russian (0)	0	<0.01
Greek (31)	31	0.17
Guyanese (0)	0	<0.01
Hungarian (24)	58	0.31
Icelander (0)	0	<0.01
Iranian (0)	0	<0.01
Irish (741)	2,623	14.23
Israeli (0)	0	<0.01
Italian (137)	625	3.39
Latvian (5)	5	0.03
Lithuanian (13)	29	0.16
Luxemburger (0)	0	<0.01
Macedonian (0)	0	<0.01
Maltese (0)	0	<0.01
New Zealander (0)	0	<0.01
Northern European (28)	28	0.15
Norwegian (91)	334	1.81
Pennsylvania German (7)	10	0.05
Polish (64)	240	1.30
Portuguese (61)	131	0.71
Romanian (13)	17	0.09
Russian (22)	56	0.30
Scandinavian (64)	131	0.71
Scotch-Irish (199)	416	2.26
Scottish (176)	507	2.75
Serbian (0)	0	<0.01
Slavic (0)	0	<0.01
Slovak (0)	31	0.17
Slovene (0)	0	<0.01
Soviet Union (0)	0	<0.01
Swedish (75)	308	1.67
Swiss (29)	46	0.25
Turkish (0)	0	<0.01
Ukrainian (28)	74	0.40
Welsh (54)	204	1.11
West Indian, ex. Hispanic (16)	40	0.22
Bahamian (0)	0	<0.01
Barbadian (0)	0	<0.01
Belizean (0)	0	<0.01
Bermudan (0)	0	<0.01
British West Indian (0)	0	<0.01
Dutch West Indian (0)	0	<0.01
Haitian (16)	40	0.22
Jamaican (0)	0	<0.01
Trinidadian/Tobagonian (0)	0	<0.01
U.S. Virgin Islander (0)	0	<0.01
West Indian (0)	0	<0.01
Other West Indian (0)	0	<0.01
Yugoslavian (0)	13	0.07

Hispanic Origin	Population	%
Hispanic or Latino (of any race)	3,597	19.40
Central American, ex. Mexican	90	0.49
Costa Rican	2	0.01
Guatemalan	20	0.11
Honduran	5	0.03
Nicaraguan	9	0.05
Panamanian	2	0.01
Salvadoran	50	0.27
Other Central American	2	0.01
Cuban	13	0.07
Dominican Republic	0	<0.01
Mexican	3,030	16.34
Puerto Rican	32	0.17
South American	47	0.25
Argentinean	1	0.01
Bolivian	0	<0.01
Chilean	3	0.02
Colombian	10	0.05
Ecuadorian	3	0.02
Paraguayan	0	<0.01
Peruvian	24	0.13
Uruguayan	0	<0.01
Venezuelan	5	0.03
Other South American	1	0.01
Other Hispanic or Latino	385	2.08

Race*	Population	%
African-American/Black (109)	156	0.84
Not Hispanic (102)	130	0.70
Hispanic (7)	26	0.14
American Indian/Alaska Native (2,121)	2,492	13.44
Not Hispanic (1,895)	2,165	11.67
Hispanic (226)	327	1.76
Alaska Athabascan *(Ala. Nat.)* (1)	1	0.01
Aleut *(Alaska Native)* (0)	1	0.01
Apache (19)	26	0.14
Arapaho (8)	10	0.05
Blackfeet (2)	5	0.03
Canadian/French Am. Ind. (0)	1	0.01
Central American Ind. (0)	0	<0.01
Cherokee (18)	56	0.30
Cheyenne (0)	1	0.01
Chickasaw (1)	4	0.02
Chippewa (6)	15	0.08
Choctaw (6)	14	0.08
Colville (0)	2	0.01
Comanche (0)	3	0.02
Cree (2)	3	0.02
Creek (1)	1	0.01
Crow (1)	2	0.01
Delaware (0)	0	<0.01
Hopi (2)	2	0.01
Houma (0)	0	<0.01
Inupiat *(Alaska Native)* (0)	0	<0.01
Iroquois (1)	4	0.02
Kiowa (5)	9	0.05
Lumbee (0)	0	<0.01
Menominee (0)	0	<0.01
Mexican American Ind. (24)	30	0.16
Navajo (3)	9	0.05
Osage (0)	3	0.02
Ottawa (0)	0	<0.01
Paiute (172)	253	1.36
Pima (2)	2	0.01
Potawatomi (4)	11	0.06
Pueblo (2)	4	0.02
Puget Sound Salish (0)	0	<0.01
Seminole (1)	1	0.01
Shoshone (58)	80	0.43
Sioux (11)	14	0.08
South American Ind. (5)	6	0.03
Spanish American Ind. (0)	0	<0.01
Tlingit-Haida *(Alaska Native)* (4)	4	0.02
Tohono O'Odham (4)	6	0.03
Tsimshian *(Alaska Native)* (0)	0	<0.01
Ute (2)	2	0.01
Yakama (0)	1	0.01
Yaqui (6)	8	0.04
Yuman (17)	27	0.15
Yup'ik *(Alaska Native)* (0)	0	<0.01
Asian (243)	357	1.92
Not Hispanic (229)	319	1.72
Hispanic (14)	38	0.20
Bangladeshi (5)	5	0.03
Bhutanese (0)	0	<0.01
Burmese (0)	0	<0.01
Cambodian (9)	10	0.05
Chinese, ex. Taiwanese (34)	52	0.28
Filipino (30)	58	0.31
Hmong (0)	0	<0.01
Indian (59)	65	0.35
Indonesian (1)	7	0.04
Japanese (45)	99	0.53
Korean (11)	18	0.10
Laotian (2)	3	0.02
Malaysian (0)	0	<0.01
Nepalese (0)	0	<0.01
Pakistani (7)	7	0.04
Sri Lankan (6)	6	0.03
Taiwanese (1)	2	0.01
Thai (7)	7	0.04
Vietnamese (13)	18	0.10
Hawaii Native/Pacific Islander (16)	46	0.25
Not Hispanic (15)	40	0.22
Hispanic (1)	6	0.03
Fijian (0)	0	<0.01
Guamanian/Chamorro (2)	2	0.01
Marshallese (0)	0	<0.01
Native Hawaiian (9)	31	0.17
Samoan (1)	2	0.01
Tongan (0)	0	<0.01
White (13,741)	14,322	77.22
Not Hispanic (12,296)	12,666	68.30
Hispanic (1,445)	1,656	8.93

*Notes: † The Census 2010 population figure is used to calculate the percentages in the Hispanic Origin and Race categories. Ancestry percentages are based on the 2006-2010 American Community Survey population (not shown); ‡ Numbers in parentheses indicate the number of people reporting a single ancestry; * Numbers in parentheses indicate the number of persons reporting this race alone, not in combination with any other race; Please refer to the Explanation of Data for more information.*

Kern County

Population: 839,631

Ancestry	Population	%
Afghan (59)	59	0.01
African, Sub-Saharan (2,232)	2,671	0.33
African (1,358)	1,756	0.22
Cape Verdean (0)	0	<0.01
Ethiopian (170)	170	0.02
Ghanaian (0)	0	<0.01
Kenyan (56)	73	0.01
Liberian (0)	0	<0.01
Nigerian (431)	455	0.06
Senegalese (0)	0	<0.01
Sierra Leonean (0)	0	<0.01
Somalian (58)	58	0.01
South African (74)	74	0.01
Sudanese (20)	20	<0.01
Ugandan (0)	0	<0.01
Zimbabwean (0)	0	<0.01
Other Sub-Saharan African (65)	65	0.01
Albanian (9)	18	<0.01
Alsatian (0)	0	<0.01
American (22,284)	22,284	2.73
Arab (4,075)	5,511	0.68
Arab (1,899)	2,334	0.29
Egyptian (346)	422	0.05
Iraqi (0)	8	<0.01
Jordanian (203)	450	0.06
Lebanese (288)	620	0.08
Moroccan (25)	56	0.01
Palestinian (64)	237	0.03
Syrian (197)	271	0.03
Other Arab (1,053)	1,113	0.14
Armenian (514)	961	0.12
Assyrian/Chaldean/Syriac (63)	63	0.01
Australian (129)	228	0.03
Austrian (150)	642	0.08
Basque (894)	1,918	0.24
Belgian (103)	537	0.07
Brazilian (135)	205	0.03
British (913)	1,804	0.22
Bulgarian (37)	50	0.01
Cajun (82)	214	0.03
Canadian (836)	1,433	0.18
Carpatho Rusyn (0)	0	<0.01
Celtic (91)	149	0.02
Croatian (175)	514	0.06
Cypriot (0)	0	<0.01
Czech (253)	1,345	0.16
Czechoslovakian (172)	564	0.07
Danish (1,138)	3,289	0.40
Dutch (1,582)	10,151	1.24
Eastern European (144)	199	0.02
English (17,810)	51,971	6.37
Estonian (19)	38	<0.01
European (7,122)	8,791	1.08
Finnish (215)	881	0.11
French, ex. Basque (2,567)	14,456	1.77
French Canadian (859)	2,383	0.29
German (23,604)	77,395	9.49
German Russian (8)	8	<0.01
Greek (455)	1,708	0.21
Guyanese (55)	138	0.02
Hungarian (313)	1,008	0.12
Icelander (0)	120	0.01
Iranian (639)	724	0.09
Irish (15,688)	63,538	7.79
Israeli (10)	46	0.01
Italian (7,915)	21,914	2.69
Latvian (9)	35	<0.01
Lithuanian (183)	594	0.07
Luxemburger (17)	17	<0.01
Macedonian (0)	0	<0.01
Maltese (46)	90	0.01
New Zealander (34)	34	<0.01
Northern European (532)	559	0.07
Norwegian (2,411)	7,488	0.92
Pennsylvania German (80)	244	0.03
Polish (1,579)	6,012	0.74
Portuguese (1,454)	4,029	0.49
Romanian (132)	344	0.04
Russian (1,105)	2,682	0.33
Scandinavian (404)	1,178	0.14
Scotch-Irish (3,590)	9,938	1.22
Scottish (3,045)	12,326	1.51
Serbian (37)	76	0.01
Slavic (69)	203	0.02
Slovak (58)	172	0.02
Slovene (20)	134	0.02
Soviet Union (0)	0	<0.01
Swedish (2,031)	8,566	1.05
Swiss (411)	1,450	0.18
Turkish (41)	160	0.02
Ukrainian (333)	683	0.08
Welsh (545)	3,404	0.42
West Indian, ex. Hispanic (572)	1,556	0.19
Bahamian (0)	4	<0.01
Barbadian (0)	0	<0.01
Belizean (24)	49	0.01
Bermudan (0)	0	<0.01
British West Indian (5)	5	<0.01
Dutch West Indian (18)	563	0.07
Haitian (234)	357	0.04
Jamaican (161)	282	0.03
Trinidadian/Tobagonian (0)	45	0.01
U.S. Virgin Islander (0)	0	<0.01
West Indian (121)	242	0.03
Other West Indian (9)	9	<0.01
Yugoslavian (318)	634	0.08

Hispanic Origin	Population	%
Hispanic or Latino (of any race)	413,033	49.19
Central American, ex. Mexican	13,995	1.67
Costa Rican	267	0.03
Guatemalan	3,388	0.40
Honduran	1,080	0.13
Nicaraguan	522	0.06
Panamanian	148	0.02
Salvadoran	8,485	1.01
Other Central American	105	0.01
Cuban	808	0.10
Dominican Republic	148	0.02
Mexican	364,524	43.41
Puerto Rican	4,172	0.50
South American	2,717	0.32
Argentinean	318	0.04
Bolivian	69	0.01
Chilean	155	0.02
Colombian	632	0.08
Ecuadorian	246	0.03
Paraguayan	1	<0.01
Peruvian	917	0.11
Uruguayan	40	<0.01
Venezuelan	308	0.04
Other South American	31	<0.01
Other Hispanic or Latino	26,669	3.18

Race*	Population	%
African-American/Black (48,921)	56,494	6.73
Not Hispanic (45,377)	50,417	6.00
Hispanic (3,544)	6,077	0.72
American Indian/Alaska Native (12,676)	22,612	2.69
Not Hispanic (5,893)	12,381	1.47
Hispanic (6,783)	10,231	1.22
Alaska Athabascan *(Ala. Nat.)* (6)	14	<0.01
Aleut *(Alaska Native)* (24)	41	<0.01
Apache (403)	818	0.10
Arapaho (19)	38	<0.01
Blackfeet (111)	436	0.05
Canadian/French Am. Ind. (3)	20	<0.01
Central American Ind. (23)	46	0.01
Cherokee (1,191)	3,826	0.46
Cheyenne (23)	33	<0.01
Chickasaw (142)	273	0.03
Chippewa (52)	141	0.02
Choctaw (505)	1,190	0.14
Colville (11)	15	<0.01
Comanche (68)	139	0.02
Cree (3)	29	<0.01
Creek (134)	315	0.04
Crow (8)	16	<0.01
Delaware (10)	26	<0.01
Hopi (26)	40	<0.01
Houma (1)	4	<0.01
Inupiat *(Alaska Native)* (12)	19	<0.01
Iroquois (33)	102	0.01
Kiowa (10)	30	<0.01
Lumbee (17)	27	<0.01
Menominee (1)	5	<0.01
Mexican American Ind. (1,388)	1,831	0.22
Navajo (263)	462	0.06
Osage (13)	56	0.01
Ottawa (5)	10	<0.01
Paiute (357)	613	0.07
Pima (49)	92	0.01
Potawatomi (63)	118	0.01
Pueblo (84)	126	0.02
Puget Sound Salish (18)	31	<0.01
Seminole (26)	85	0.01
Shoshone (49)	91	0.01
Sioux (105)	252	0.03
South American Ind. (19)	41	<0.01
Spanish American Ind. (43)	64	0.01
Tlingit-Haida *(Alaska Native)* (18)	31	<0.01
Tohono O'Odham (44)	58	0.01
Tsimshian *(Alaska Native)* (1)	1	<0.01
Ute (13)	30	<0.01
Yakama (7)	11	<0.01
Yaqui (227)	358	0.04
Yuman (19)	30	<0.01
Yup'ik *(Alaska Native)* (5)	9	<0.01
Asian (34,846)	43,382	5.17
Not Hispanic (33,100)	38,641	4.60
Hispanic (1,746)	4,741	0.56
Bangladeshi (50)	53	0.01
Bhutanese (2)	2	<0.01
Burmese (281)	323	0.04
Cambodian (652)	832	0.10
Chinese, ex. Taiwanese (2,383)	3,466	0.41
Filipino (15,948)	20,296	2.42
Hmong (50)	60	0.01
Indian (8,604)	9,437	1.12
Indonesian (171)	249	0.03
Japanese (1,105)	2,285	0.27
Korean (1,770)	2,271	0.27
Laotian (285)	420	0.05
Malaysian (17)	34	<0.01
Nepalese (10)	11	<0.01
Pakistani (323)	391	0.05
Sri Lankan (37)	52	0.01
Taiwanese (119)	150	0.02
Thai (403)	564	0.07
Vietnamese (1,512)	1,869	0.22
Hawaii Native/Pacific Islander (1,252)	3,027	0.36
Not Hispanic (995)	2,030	0.24
Hispanic (257)	997	0.12
Fijian (15)	30	<0.01
Guamanian/Chamorro (337)	615	0.07
Marshallese (17)	18	<0.01
Native Hawaiian (324)	994	0.12
Samoan (305)	555	0.07
Tongan (55)	83	0.01
White (499,766)	531,609	63.31
Not Hispanic (323,794)	337,608	40.21
Hispanic (175,972)	194,001	23.11

*Notes: † The Census 2010 population figure is used to calculate the percentages in the Hispanic Origin and Race categories. Ancestry percentages are based on the 2006-2010 American Community Survey population (not shown); ‡ Numbers in parentheses indicate the number of people reporting a single ancestry; * Numbers in parentheses indicate the number of persons reporting this race alone, not in combination with any other race; Please refer to the Explanation of Data for more information.*

Kings County

Population: 152,982

Ancestry	Population	%
Afghan (7)	7	<0.01
African, Sub-Saharan (712)	1,082	0.72
African (567)	937	0.62
Cape Verdean (0)	0	<0.01
Ethiopian (46)	46	0.03
Ghanaian (0)	0	<0.01
Kenyan (0)	0	<0.01
Liberian (0)	0	<0.01
Nigerian (5)	5	<0.01
Senegalese (0)	0	<0.01
Sierra Leonean (0)	0	<0.01
Somalian (0)	0	<0.01
South African (0)	0	<0.01
Sudanese (0)	0	<0.01
Ugandan (0)	0	<0.01
Zimbabwean (0)	0	<0.01
Other Sub-Saharan African (94)	94	0.06
Albanian (0)	0	<0.01
Alsatian (0)	0	<0.01
American (4,339)	4,339	2.87
Arab (245)	310	0.21
Arab (41)	89	0.06
Egyptian (7)	7	<0.01
Iraqi (0)	0	<0.01
Jordanian (55)	55	0.04
Lebanese (4)	21	0.01
Moroccan (0)	0	<0.01
Palestinian (0)	0	<0.01
Syrian (0)	0	<0.01
Other Arab (138)	138	0.09
Armenian (73)	124	0.08
Assyrian/Chaldean/Syriac (14)	14	0.01
Australian (31)	50	0.03
Austrian (14)	47	0.03
Basque (59)	182	0.12
Belgian (7)	58	0.04
Brazilian (23)	34	0.02
British (166)	316	0.21
Bulgarian (0)	0	<0.01
Cajun (8)	13	0.01
Canadian (76)	234	0.15
Carpatho Rusyn (0)	0	<0.01
Celtic (45)	45	0.03
Croatian (30)	64	0.04
Cypriot (0)	0	<0.01
Czech (32)	159	0.11
Czechoslovakian (60)	116	0.08
Danish (133)	492	0.33
Dutch (830)	2,297	1.52
Eastern European (12)	12	0.01
English (2,991)	7,477	4.95
Estonian (0)	0	<0.01
European (1,269)	1,403	0.93
Finnish (26)	209	0.14
French, ex. Basque (322)	2,136	1.41
French Canadian (37)	129	0.09
German (3,402)	11,221	7.43
German Russian (0)	8	0.01
Greek (85)	284	0.19
Guyanese (30)	50	0.03
Hungarian (26)	141	0.09
Icelander (0)	0	<0.01
Iranian (44)	44	0.03
Irish (2,952)	10,001	6.62
Israeli (0)	0	<0.01
Italian (1,395)	4,075	2.70
Latvian (0)	0	<0.01
Lithuanian (0)	8	0.01
Luxemburger (0)	0	<0.01
Macedonian (0)	0	<0.01
Maltese (0)	0	<0.01
New Zealander (0)	57	0.04
Northern European (98)	98	0.06
Norwegian (198)	811	0.54
Pennsylvania German (9)	30	0.02
Polish (346)	1,168	0.77
Portuguese (4,642)	6,354	4.20
Romanian (16)	16	0.01
Russian (21)	226	0.15
Scandinavian (28)	40	0.03
Scotch-Irish (521)	1,745	1.15
Scottish (408)	1,212	0.80
Serbian (37)	53	0.04
Slavic (0)	0	<0.01
Slovak (29)	39	0.03
Slovene (0)	9	0.01
Soviet Union (0)	0	<0.01
Swedish (230)	1,069	0.71
Swiss (89)	234	0.15
Turkish (16)	16	0.01
Ukrainian (12)	20	0.01
Welsh (36)	462	0.31
West Indian, ex. Hispanic (140)	259	0.17
Bahamian (0)	0	<0.01
Barbadian (19)	19	0.01
Belizean (39)	39	0.03
Bermudan (0)	0	<0.01
British West Indian (0)	0	<0.01
Dutch West Indian (0)	49	0.03
Haitian (7)	30	0.02
Jamaican (13)	25	0.02
Trinidadian/Tobagonian (16)	16	0.01
U.S. Virgin Islander (0)	0	<0.01
West Indian (46)	81	0.05
Other West Indian (0)	0	<0.01
Yugoslavian (9)	31	0.02

Hispanic Origin	Population	%
Hispanic or Latino (of any race)	77,866	50.90
Central American, ex. Mexican	794	0.52
Costa Rican	11	0.01
Guatemalan	173	0.11
Honduran	154	0.10
Nicaraguan	77	0.05
Panamanian	44	0.03
Salvadoran	311	0.20
Other Central American	24	0.02
Cuban	128	0.08
Dominican Republic	50	0.03
Mexican	69,740	45.59
Puerto Rican	572	0.37
South American	274	0.18
Argentinean	15	0.01
Bolivian	20	0.01
Chilean	18	0.01
Colombian	63	0.04
Ecuadorian	38	0.02
Paraguayan	1	<0.01
Peruvian	93	0.06
Uruguayan	0	<0.01
Venezuelan	17	0.01
Other South American	9	0.01
Other Hispanic or Latino	6,308	4.12

Race*	Population	%
African-American/Black (11,014)	12,701	8.30
Not Hispanic (10,314)	11,433	7.47
Hispanic (700)	1,268	0.83
American Indian/Alaska Native (2,562)	3,976	2.60
Not Hispanic (1,297)	2,057	1.34
Hispanic (1,265)	1,919	1.25
Alaska Athabascan *(Ala. Nat.)* (0)	0	<0.01
Aleut *(Alaska Native)* (0)	0	<0.01
Apache (61)	128	0.08
Arapaho (3)	5	<0.01
Blackfeet (6)	40	0.03
Canadian/French Am. Ind. (1)	7	<0.01
Central American Ind. (4)	8	0.01
Cherokee (131)	437	0.29
Cheyenne (1)	2	<0.01
Chickasaw (6)	23	0.02
Chippewa (12)	17	0.01
Choctaw (71)	141	0.09
Colville (0)	0	<0.01
Comanche (7)	15	0.01
Cree (2)	5	<0.01
Creek (20)	29	0.02
Crow (1)	2	<0.01
Delaware (0)	2	<0.01
Hopi (2)	10	0.01
Houma (0)	0	<0.01
Inupiat *(Alaska Native)* (0)	3	<0.01
Iroquois (4)	12	0.01
Kiowa (0)	1	<0.01
Lumbee (2)	7	<0.01
Menominee (0)	0	<0.01
Mexican American Ind. (173)	233	0.15
Navajo (48)	93	0.06
Osage (1)	4	<0.01
Ottawa (0)	1	<0.01
Paiute (11)	14	0.01
Pima (37)	41	0.03
Potawatomi (9)	14	0.01
Pueblo (4)	10	0.01
Puget Sound Salish (3)	3	<0.01
Seminole (1)	4	<0.01
Shoshone (11)	15	0.01
Sioux (12)	35	0.02
South American Ind. (9)	11	0.01
Spanish American Ind. (8)	12	0.01
Tlingit-Haida *(Alaska Native)* (2)	4	<0.01
Tohono O'Odham (7)	8	0.01
Tsimshian *(Alaska Native)* (0)	0	<0.01
Ute (2)	5	<0.01
Yakama (1)	1	<0.01
Yaqui (33)	55	0.04
Yuman (0)	0	<0.01
Yup'ik *(Alaska Native)* (0)	0	<0.01
Asian (5,620)	7,735	5.06
Not Hispanic (5,339)	6,895	4.51
Hispanic (281)	840	0.55
Bangladeshi (2)	4	<0.01
Bhutanese (0)	0	<0.01
Burmese (2)	4	<0.01
Cambodian (90)	110	0.07
Chinese, ex. Taiwanese (364)	575	0.38
Filipino (3,664)	4,881	3.19
Hmong (204)	234	0.15
Indian (419)	539	0.35
Indonesian (12)	17	0.01
Japanese (282)	671	0.44
Korean (119)	237	0.15
Laotian (57)	77	0.05
Malaysian (0)	1	<0.01
Nepalese (0)	0	<0.01
Pakistani (22)	27	0.02
Sri Lankan (7)	8	0.01
Taiwanese (8)	12	0.01
Thai (35)	64	0.04
Vietnamese (123)	183	0.12
Hawaii Native/Pacific Islander (271)	724	0.47
Not Hispanic (228)	537	0.35
Hispanic (43)	187	0.12
Fijian (2)	2	<0.01
Guamanian/Chamorro (91)	147	0.10
Marshallese (5)	5	<0.01
Native Hawaiian (70)	246	0.16
Samoan (38)	74	0.05
Tongan (4)	7	<0.01
White (83,027)	89,444	58.47
Not Hispanic (53,879)	56,792	37.12
Hispanic (29,148)	32,652	21.34

*Notes: † The Census 2010 population figure is used to calculate the percentages in the Hispanic Origin and Race categories. Ancestry percentages are based on the 2006-2010 American Community Survey population (not shown); ‡ Numbers in parentheses indicate the number of people reporting a single ancestry; * Numbers in parentheses indicate the number of persons reporting this race alone, not in combination with any other race; Please refer to the Explanation of Data for more information.*

Lake County

Population: 64,665

Ancestry	Population	%
Afghan (0)	0	<0.01
African, Sub-Saharan (176)	378	0.59
African (137)	296	0.46
Cape Verdean (0)	0	<0.01
Ethiopian (34)	34	0.05
Ghanaian (0)	0	<0.01
Kenyan (5)	5	0.01
Liberian (0)	0	<0.01
Nigerian (0)	0	<0.01
Senegalese (0)	0	<0.01
Sierra Leonean (0)	0	<0.01
Somalian (0)	0	<0.01
South African (0)	43	0.07
Sudanese (0)	0	<0.01
Ugandan (0)	0	<0.01
Zimbabwean (0)	0	<0.01
Other Sub-Saharan African (0)	0	<0.01
Albanian (0)	0	<0.01
Alsatian (0)	0	<0.01
American (2,208)	2,208	3.43
Arab (82)	146	0.23
Arab (0)	0	<0.01
Egyptian (82)	82	0.13
Iraqi (0)	12	0.02
Jordanian (0)	0	<0.01
Lebanese (0)	0	<0.01
Moroccan (0)	0	<0.01
Palestinian (0)	11	0.02
Syrian (0)	31	0.05
Other Arab (0)	10	0.02
Armenian (10)	10	0.02
Assyrian/Chaldean/Syriac (0)	0	<0.01
Australian (30)	177	0.27
Austrian (15)	83	0.13
Basque (0)	56	0.09
Belgian (72)	110	0.17
Brazilian (0)	0	<0.01
British (124)	245	0.38
Bulgarian (36)	36	0.06
Cajun (48)	48	0.07
Canadian (28)	75	0.12
Carpatho Rusyn (0)	0	<0.01
Celtic (0)	19	0.03
Croatian (56)	94	0.15
Cypriot (0)	0	<0.01
Czech (19)	257	0.40
Czechoslovakian (1)	10	0.02
Danish (284)	1,035	1.61
Dutch (431)	1,427	2.22
Eastern European (15)	15	0.02
English (2,205)	9,470	14.71
Estonian (0)	0	<0.01
European (414)	477	0.74
Finnish (81)	207	0.32
French, ex. Basque (528)	3,190	4.96
French Canadian (53)	296	0.46
German (3,026)	12,694	19.72
German Russian (0)	0	<0.01
Greek (194)	419	0.65
Guyanese (0)	0	<0.01
Hungarian (53)	239	0.37
Icelander (49)	49	0.08
Iranian (14)	53	0.08
Irish (2,811)	11,631	18.07
Israeli (0)	0	<0.01
Italian (1,646)	4,687	7.28
Latvian (0)	0	<0.01
Lithuanian (81)	140	0.22
Luxemburger (0)	0	<0.01
Macedonian (56)	56	0.09
Maltese (54)	54	0.08
New Zealander (0)	0	<0.01
Northern European (43)	43	0.07
Norwegian (497)	1,309	2.03
Pennsylvania German (21)	41	0.06
Polish (181)	761	1.18
Portuguese (500)	1,834	2.85
Romanian (75)	94	0.15
Russian (149)	327	0.51
Scandinavian (26)	120	0.19
Scotch-Irish (855)	1,706	2.65
Scottish (438)	1,891	2.94
Serbian (0)	0	<0.01
Slavic (0)	7	0.01
Slovak (0)	0	<0.01
Slovene (0)	0	<0.01
Soviet Union (0)	0	<0.01
Swedish (400)	1,877	2.92
Swiss (94)	417	0.65
Turkish (0)	0	<0.01
Ukrainian (6)	83	0.13
Welsh (108)	687	1.07
West Indian, ex. Hispanic (24)	24	0.04
Bahamian (0)	0	<0.01
Barbadian (0)	0	<0.01
Belizean (24)	24	0.04
Bermudan (0)	0	<0.01
British West Indian (0)	0	<0.01
Dutch West Indian (0)	0	<0.01
Haitian (0)	0	<0.01
Jamaican (0)	0	<0.01
Trinidadian/Tobagonian (0)	0	<0.01
U.S. Virgin Islander (0)	0	<0.01
West Indian (0)	0	<0.01
Other West Indian (0)	0	<0.01
Yugoslavian (9)	61	0.09

Hispanic Origin	Population	%
Hispanic or Latino (of any race)	11,088	17.15
Central American, ex. Mexican	354	0.55
Costa Rican	3	<0.01
Guatemalan	71	0.11
Honduran	26	0.04
Nicaraguan	47	0.07
Panamanian	8	0.01
Salvadoran	194	0.30
Other Central American	5	0.01
Cuban	42	0.06
Dominican Republic	7	0.01
Mexican	9,258	14.32
Puerto Rican	269	0.42
South American	93	0.14
Argentinean	10	0.02
Bolivian	3	<0.01
Chilean	14	0.02
Colombian	14	0.02
Ecuadorian	7	0.01
Paraguayan	1	<0.01
Peruvian	38	0.06
Uruguayan	2	<0.01
Venezuelan	2	<0.01
Other South American	2	<0.01
Other Hispanic or Latino	1,065	1.65

Race*	Population	%
African-American/Black (1,232)	1,787	2.76
Not Hispanic (1,186)	1,652	2.55
Hispanic (46)	135	0.21
American Indian/Alaska Native (2,049)	3,654	5.65
Not Hispanic (1,530)	2,756	4.26
Hispanic (519)	898	1.39
Alaska Athabascan *(Ala. Nat.)* (4)	4	0.01
Aleut *(Alaska Native)* (11)	16	0.02
Apache (31)	84	0.13
Arapaho (1)	1	<0.01
Blackfeet (14)	74	0.11
Canadian/French Am. Ind. (1)	4	0.01
Central American Ind. (5)	5	0.01
Cherokee (108)	459	0.71
Cheyenne (7)	23	0.04
Chickasaw (3)	13	0.02
Chippewa (7)	29	0.04
Choctaw (43)	133	0.21
Colville (3)	6	0.01
Comanche (2)	20	0.03
Cree (0)	12	0.02
Creek (21)	46	0.07
Crow (1)	2	<0.01
Delaware (2)	10	0.02
Hopi (9)	12	0.02
Houma (0)	0	<0.01
Inupiat *(Alaska Native)* (9)	14	0.02
Iroquois (7)	16	0.02
Kiowa (0)	0	<0.01
Lumbee (4)	6	0.01
Menominee (1)	5	0.01
Mexican American Ind. (49)	78	0.12
Navajo (27)	68	0.11
Osage (2)	17	0.03
Ottawa (4)	7	0.01
Paiute (12)	24	0.04
Pima (5)	10	0.02
Potawatomi (2)	9	0.01
Pueblo (6)	7	0.01
Puget Sound Salish (2)	2	<0.01
Seminole (0)	9	0.01
Shoshone (7)	17	0.03
Sioux (15)	60	0.09
South American Ind. (3)	5	0.01
Spanish American Ind. (7)	11	0.02
Tlingit-Haida *(Alaska Native)* (3)	6	0.01
Tohono O'Odham (1)	3	<0.01
Tsimshian *(Alaska Native)* (0)	0	<0.01
Ute (0)	4	0.01
Yakama (0)	2	<0.01
Yaqui (5)	11	0.02
Yuman (1)	4	0.01
Yup'ik *(Alaska Native)* (0)	0	<0.01
Asian (724)	1,219	1.89
Not Hispanic (695)	1,085	1.68
Hispanic (29)	134	0.21
Bangladeshi (0)	0	<0.01
Bhutanese (0)	0	<0.01
Burmese (0)	1	<0.01
Cambodian (16)	18	0.03
Chinese, ex. Taiwanese (129)	170	0.26
Filipino (264)	498	0.77
Hmong (0)	0	<0.01
Indian (81)	104	0.16
Indonesian (1)	5	0.01
Japanese (78)	211	0.33
Korean (40)	75	0.12
Laotian (17)	20	0.03
Malaysian (0)	1	<0.01
Nepalese (2)	2	<0.01
Pakistani (6)	6	0.01
Sri Lankan (0)	0	<0.01
Taiwanese (7)	8	0.01
Thai (27)	34	0.05
Vietnamese (35)	43	0.07
Hawaii Native/Pacific Islander (108)	381	0.59
Not Hispanic (97)	301	0.47
Hispanic (11)	80	0.12
Fijian (3)	5	0.01
Guamanian/Chamorro (9)	35	0.05
Marshallese (0)	0	<0.01
Native Hawaiian (60)	238	0.37
Samoan (15)	40	0.06
Tongan (5)	7	0.01
White (52,033)	54,779	84.71
Not Hispanic (47,938)	49,825	77.05
Hispanic (4,095)	4,954	7.66

*Notes: † The Census 2010 population figure is used to calculate the percentages in the Hispanic Origin and Race categories. Ancestry percentages are based on the 2006-2010 American Community Survey population (not shown); ‡ Numbers in parentheses indicate the number of people reporting a single ancestry; * Numbers in parentheses indicate the number of persons reporting this race alone, not in combination with any other race; Please refer to the Explanation of Data for more information.*

Lassen County

Population: 34,895

Ancestry	Population	%
Afghan (0)	0	<0.01
African, Sub-Saharan (160)	234	0.67
African (156)	211	0.60
Cape Verdean (0)	0	<0.01
Ethiopian (0)	0	<0.01
Ghanaian (0)	0	<0.01
Kenyan (0)	0	<0.01
Liberian (0)	0	<0.01
Nigerian (0)	0	<0.01
Senegalese (0)	0	<0.01
Sierra Leonean (0)	0	<0.01
Somalian (0)	0	<0.01
South African (4)	23	0.07
Sudanese (0)	0	<0.01
Ugandan (0)	0	<0.01
Zimbabwean (0)	0	<0.01
Other Sub-Saharan African (0)	0	<0.01
Albanian (0)	0	<0.01
Alsatian (0)	0	<0.01
American (1,321)	1,321	3.77
Arab (8)	48	0.14
Arab (0)	0	<0.01
Egyptian (0)	0	<0.01
Iraqi (0)	0	<0.01
Jordanian (0)	0	<0.01
Lebanese (0)	9	0.03
Moroccan (0)	0	<0.01
Palestinian (8)	8	0.02
Syrian (0)	31	0.09
Other Arab (0)	0	<0.01
Armenian (50)	53	0.15
Assyrian/Chaldean/Syriac (0)	0	<0.01
Australian (0)	0	<0.01
Austrian (0)	10	0.03
Basque (60)	120	0.34
Belgian (0)	0	<0.01
Brazilian (0)	0	<0.01
British (34)	88	0.25
Bulgarian (0)	0	<0.01
Cajun (0)	0	<0.01
Canadian (45)	104	0.30
Carpatho Rusyn (0)	0	<0.01
Celtic (0)	16	0.05
Croatian (0)	0	<0.01
Cypriot (0)	0	<0.01
Czech (121)	225	0.64
Czechoslovakian (46)	46	0.13
Danish (71)	185	0.53
Dutch (89)	485	1.38
Eastern European (0)	0	<0.01
English (630)	3,099	8.83
Estonian (0)	0	<0.01
European (749)	892	2.54
Finnish (14)	51	0.15
French, ex. Basque (200)	1,039	2.96
French Canadian (36)	87	0.25
German (1,740)	5,583	15.91
German Russian (0)	0	<0.01
Greek (0)	81	0.23
Guyanese (0)	0	<0.01
Hungarian (28)	116	0.33
Icelander (0)	0	<0.01
Iranian (29)	70	0.20
Irish (1,670)	5,039	14.36
Israeli (0)	0	<0.01
Italian (927)	1,699	4.84
Latvian (44)	44	0.13
Lithuanian (2)	2	0.01
Luxemburger (0)	0	<0.01
Macedonian (0)	0	<0.01
Maltese (0)	0	<0.01
New Zealander (0)	0	<0.01
Northern European (49)	49	0.14
Norwegian (241)	617	1.76
Pennsylvania German (0)	0	<0.01
Polish (168)	466	1.33
Portuguese (156)	595	1.70
Romanian (0)	10	0.03
Russian (69)	168	0.48
Scandinavian (23)	51	0.15
Scotch-Irish (203)	532	1.52
Scottish (493)	1,098	3.13
Serbian (30)	30	0.09
Slavic (0)	50	0.14
Slovak (0)	5	0.01
Slovene (0)	0	<0.01
Soviet Union (0)	0	<0.01
Swedish (267)	692	1.97
Swiss (64)	165	0.47
Turkish (0)	0	<0.01
Ukrainian (43)	59	0.17
Welsh (23)	249	0.71
West Indian, ex. Hispanic (116)	200	0.57
Bahamian (0)	0	<0.01
Barbadian (0)	0	<0.01
Belizean (86)	93	0.27
Bermudan (0)	0	<0.01
British West Indian (0)	0	<0.01
Dutch West Indian (0)	55	0.16
Haitian (14)	22	0.06
Jamaican (0)	13	0.04
Trinidadian/Tobagonian (16)	16	0.05
U.S. Virgin Islander (0)	0	<0.01
West Indian (0)	1	<0.01
Other West Indian (0)	0	<0.01
Yugoslavian (69)	77	0.22

Hispanic Origin	Population	%
Hispanic or Latino (of any race)	6,117	17.53
Central American, ex. Mexican	64	0.18
Costa Rican	5	0.01
Guatemalan	9	0.03
Honduran	4	0.01
Nicaraguan	12	0.03
Panamanian	4	0.01
Salvadoran	30	0.09
Other Central American	0	<0.01
Cuban	21	0.06
Dominican Republic	4	0.01
Mexican	4,215	12.08
Puerto Rican	88	0.25
South American	21	0.06
Argentinean	1	<0.01
Bolivian	0	<0.01
Chilean	2	0.01
Colombian	3	0.01
Ecuadorian	5	0.01
Paraguayan	0	<0.01
Peruvian	4	0.01
Uruguayan	0	<0.01
Venezuelan	6	0.02
Other South American	0	<0.01
Other Hispanic or Latino	1,704	4.88

Race*	Population	%
African-American/Black (2,834)	3,036	8.70
Not Hispanic (2,790)	2,954	8.47
Hispanic (44)	82	0.23
American Indian/Alaska Native (1,234)	1,905	5.46
Not Hispanic (999)	1,553	4.45
Hispanic (235)	352	1.01
Alaska Athabascan *(Ala. Nat.)* (1)	3	0.01
Aleut *(Alaska Native)* (3)	7	0.02
Apache (15)	32	0.09
Arapaho (2)	4	0.01
Blackfeet (6)	33	0.09
Canadian/French Am. Ind. (2)	3	0.01
Central American Ind. (0)	0	<0.01
Cherokee (66)	227	0.65
Cheyenne (5)	7	0.02
Chickasaw (9)	14	0.04
Chippewa (13)	29	0.08
Choctaw (33)	60	0.17
Colville (1)	1	<0.01
Comanche (0)	1	<0.01
Cree (0)	1	<0.01
Creek (3)	5	0.01
Crow (2)	3	0.01
Delaware (1)	4	0.01
Hopi (5)	5	0.01
Houma (0)	0	<0.01
Inupiat *(Alaska Native)* (1)	3	0.01
Iroquois (9)	19	0.05
Kiowa (0)	0	<0.01
Lumbee (2)	3	0.01
Menominee (0)	1	<0.01
Mexican American Ind. (27)	33	0.09
Navajo (14)	19	0.05
Osage (2)	7	0.02
Ottawa (0)	2	0.01
Paiute (155)	227	0.65
Pima (2)	2	0.01
Potawatomi (1)	1	<0.01
Pueblo (4)	4	0.01
Puget Sound Salish (3)	6	0.02
Seminole (0)	3	0.01
Shoshone (7)	16	0.05
Sioux (14)	24	0.07
South American Ind. (1)	1	<0.01
Spanish American Ind. (1)	2	0.01
Tlingit-Haida *(Alaska Native)* (8)	8	0.02
Tohono O'Odham (3)	3	0.01
Tsimshian *(Alaska Native)* (0)	0	<0.01
Ute (1)	5	0.01
Yakama (1)	1	<0.01
Yaqui (5)	19	0.05
Yuman (0)	0	<0.01
Yup'ik *(Alaska Native)* (0)	0	<0.01
Asian (356)	543	1.56
Not Hispanic (337)	479	1.37
Hispanic (19)	64	0.18
Bangladeshi (0)	4	0.01
Bhutanese (0)	0	<0.01
Burmese (0)	0	<0.01
Cambodian (3)	3	0.01
Chinese, ex. Taiwanese (47)	86	0.25
Filipino (133)	198	0.57
Hmong (3)	3	0.01
Indian (31)	54	0.15
Indonesian (0)	0	<0.01
Japanese (28)	71	0.20
Korean (19)	45	0.13
Laotian (13)	14	0.04
Malaysian (1)	1	<0.01
Nepalese (0)	0	<0.01
Pakistani (1)	1	<0.01
Sri Lankan (0)	3	0.01
Taiwanese (0)	1	<0.01
Thai (8)	10	0.03
Vietnamese (34)	42	0.12
Hawaii Native/Pacific Islander (165)	246	0.70
Not Hispanic (163)	228	0.65
Hispanic (2)	18	0.05
Fijian (4)	5	0.01
Guamanian/Chamorro (6)	14	0.04
Marshallese (0)	0	<0.01
Native Hawaiian (21)	65	0.19
Samoan (14)	26	0.07
Tongan (3)	8	0.02
White (25,532)	26,651	76.37
Not Hispanic (23,270)	24,077	69.00
Hispanic (2,262)	2,574	7.38

*Notes: † The Census 2010 population figure is used to calculate the percentages in the Hispanic Origin and Race categories. Ancestry percentages are based on the 2006-2010 American Community Survey population (not shown); ‡ Numbers in parentheses indicate the number of people reporting a single ancestry; * Numbers in parentheses indicate the number of persons reporting this race alone, not in combination with any other race; Please refer to the Explanation of Data for more information.*

Los Angeles County

Population: 9,818,605

Ancestry	Population	%
Afghan (3,586)	3,885	0.04
African, Sub-Saharan (89,059)	107,677	1.10
African (68,574)	83,772	0.86
Cape Verdean (198)	505	0.01
Ethiopian (6,170)	6,825	0.07
Ghanaian (979)	1,064	0.01
Kenyan (576)	642	0.01
Liberian (143)	157	<0.01
Nigerian (7,223)	8,243	0.08
Senegalese (247)	247	<0.01
Sierra Leonean (207)	261	<0.01
Somalian (185)	203	<0.01
South African (1,522)	2,280	0.02
Sudanese (400)	475	<0.01
Ugandan (484)	540	0.01
Zimbabwean (225)	252	<0.01
Other Sub-Saharan African (1,926)	2,211	0.02
Albanian (404)	849	0.01
Alsatian (20)	199	<0.01
American (207,551)	207,551	2.13
Arab (52,410)	73,301	0.75
Arab (6,425)	9,005	0.09
Egyptian (12,749)	14,836	0.15
Iraqi (1,709)	2,948	0.03
Jordanian (2,775)	3,202	0.03
Lebanese (13,068)	20,855	0.21
Moroccan (2,528)	3,671	0.04
Palestinian (1,587)	2,306	0.02
Syrian (5,354)	7,941	0.08
Other Arab (6,215)	8,537	0.09
Armenian (159,300)	179,279	1.84
Assyrian/Chaldean/Syriac (1,906)	2,481	0.03
Australian (2,575)	4,526	0.05
Austrian (5,962)	21,738	0.22
Basque (1,007)	2,375	0.02
Belgian (1,783)	5,269	0.05
Brazilian (5,641)	8,009	0.08
British (15,980)	29,486	0.30
Bulgarian (2,784)	3,728	0.04
Cajun (212)	552	0.01
Canadian (10,274)	19,984	0.20
Carpatho Rusyn (7)	142	<0.01
Celtic (572)	1,527	0.02
Croatian (6,573)	12,846	0.13
Cypriot (146)	201	<0.01
Czech (4,794)	17,303	0.18
Czechoslovakian (1,866)	4,357	0.04
Danish (7,060)	27,500	0.28
Dutch (16,381)	64,362	0.66
Eastern European (19,207)	21,516	0.22
English (106,288)	389,248	3.99
Estonian (434)	856	0.01
European (64,536)	79,863	0.82
Finnish (2,673)	8,063	0.08
French, ex. Basque (22,328)	126,336	1.29
French Canadian (8,398)	20,430	0.21
German (138,013)	537,107	5.50
German Russian (166)	445	<0.01
Greek (14,677)	30,178	0.31
Guyanese (631)	987	0.01
Hungarian (13,787)	34,997	0.36
Icelander (683)	1,199	0.01
Iranian (78,796)	92,297	0.95
Irish (105,063)	424,072	4.35
Israeli (12,245)	15,672	0.16
Italian (105,330)	276,030	2.83
Latvian (1,620)	3,394	0.03
Lithuanian (5,184)	13,941	0.14
Luxemburger (134)	556	0.01
Macedonian (530)	799	0.01
Maltese (310)	511	0.01
New Zealander (678)	1,135	0.01
Northern European (5,669)	6,263	0.06
Norwegian (18,795)	60,602	0.62
Pennsylvania German (442)	1,226	0.01
Polish (38,999)	126,154	1.29
Portuguese (9,288)	23,003	0.24
Romanian (9,826)	18,616	0.19
Russian (75,729)	157,023	1.61
Scandinavian (5,140)	10,425	0.11
Scotch-Irish (21,963)	66,233	0.68
Scottish (23,509)	89,406	0.92
Serbian (1,888)	3,669	0.04
Slavic (694)	2,321	0.02
Slovak (1,621)	4,761	0.05
Slovene (514)	1,945	0.02
Soviet Union (129)	152	<0.01
Swedish (17,429)	69,428	0.71
Swiss (3,848)	15,922	0.16
Turkish (3,745)	6,292	0.06
Ukrainian (11,706)	20,562	0.21
Welsh (4,902)	28,387	0.29
West Indian, ex. Hispanic (23,898)	33,917	0.35
Bahamian (204)	371	<0.01
Barbadian (224)	368	<0.01
Belizean (11,345)	14,545	0.15
Bermudan (88)	127	<0.01
British West Indian (521)	677	0.01
Dutch West Indian (62)	313	<0.01
Haitian (1,857)	2,754	0.03
Jamaican (6,705)	10,077	0.10
Trinidadian/Tobagonian (950)	1,372	0.01
U.S. Virgin Islander (106)	174	<0.01
West Indian (1,800)	3,059	0.03
Other West Indian (36)	80	<0.01
Yugoslavian (2,977)	6,496	0.07

Hispanic Origin	Population	%
Hispanic or Latino (of any race)	4,687,889	47.74
Central American, ex. Mexican	675,832	6.88
Costa Rican	9,365	0.10
Guatemalan	214,939	2.19
Honduran	42,901	0.44
Nicaraguan	37,205	0.38
Panamanian	5,402	0.06
Salvadoran	358,825	3.65
Other Central American	7,195	0.07
Cuban	41,350	0.42
Dominican Republic	3,609	0.04
Mexican	3,510,677	35.76
Puerto Rican	44,609	0.45
South American	118,776	1.21
Argentinean	19,540	0.20
Bolivian	4,857	0.05
Chilean	8,573	0.09
Colombian	25,272	0.26
Ecuadorian	19,588	0.20
Paraguayan	413	<0.01
Peruvian	34,135	0.35
Uruguayan	1,628	0.02
Venezuelan	3,279	0.03
Other South American	1,491	0.02
Other Hispanic or Latino	293,036	2.98

Race*	Population	%
African-American/Black (856,874)	948,337	9.66
Not Hispanic (815,086)	876,512	8.93
Hispanic (41,788)	71,825	0.73
American Indian/Alaska Native (72,828)	140,764	1.43
Not Hispanic (18,886)	53,563	0.55
Hispanic (53,942)	87,201	0.89
Alaska Athabascan *(Ala. Nat.)* (59)	113	<0.01
Aleut *(Alaska Native)* (42)	110	<0.01
Apache (2,316)	4,932	0.05
Arapaho (69)	139	<0.01
Blackfeet (420)	2,759	0.03
Canadian/French Am. Ind. (140)	320	<0.01
Central American Ind. (1,349)	2,364	0.02
Cherokee (2,608)	13,054	0.13
Cheyenne (120)	294	<0.01
Chickasaw (181)	698	0.01
Chippewa (427)	1,043	0.01
Choctaw (866)	3,241	0.03
Colville (42)	72	<0.01
Comanche (211)	445	<0.01
Cree (44)	197	<0.01
Creek (378)	1,062	0.01
Crow (33)	120	<0.01
Delaware (76)	200	<0.01
Hopi (295)	582	0.01
Houma (3)	19	<0.01
Inupiat *(Alaska Native)* (58)	158	<0.01
Iroquois (288)	969	0.01
Kiowa (93)	147	<0.01
Lumbee (81)	156	<0.01
Menominee (20)	49	<0.01
Mexican American Ind. (13,885)	19,953	0.20
Navajo (2,338)	4,133	0.04
Osage (92)	323	<0.01
Ottawa (42)	113	<0.01
Paiute (174)	332	<0.01
Pima (327)	564	0.01
Potawatomi (141)	370	<0.01
Pueblo (746)	1,421	0.01
Puget Sound Salish (31)	81	<0.01
Seminole (114)	618	0.01
Shoshone (173)	354	<0.01
Sioux (851)	2,040	0.02
South American Ind. (476)	1,271	0.01
Spanish American Ind. (929)	1,442	0.01
Tlingit-Haida *(Alaska Native)* (79)	186	<0.01
Tohono O'Odham (413)	656	0.01
Tsimshian *(Alaska Native)* (14)	29	<0.01
Ute (90)	202	<0.01
Yakama (23)	60	<0.01
Yaqui (1,045)	2,142	0.02
Yuman (209)	333	<0.01
Yup'ik *(Alaska Native)* (19)	40	<0.01
Asian (1,346,865)	1,497,960	15.26
Not Hispanic (1,325,671)	1,443,258	14.70
Hispanic (21,194)	54,702	0.56
Bangladeshi (4,550)	5,162	0.05
Bhutanese (40)	42	<0.01
Burmese (4,375)	5,254	0.05
Cambodian (32,125)	37,450	0.38
Chinese, ex. Taiwanese (350,119)	403,730	4.11
Filipino (322,110)	374,285	3.81
Hmong (660)	760	0.01
Indian (79,169)	92,179	0.94
Indonesian (8,804)	13,001	0.13
Japanese (102,287)	138,983	1.42
Korean (216,501)	230,876	2.35
Laotian (2,847)	4,067	0.04
Malaysian (883)	1,496	0.02
Nepalese (1,104)	1,229	0.01
Pakistani (9,530)	10,930	0.11
Sri Lankan (4,680)	5,380	0.05
Taiwanese (40,336)	45,808	0.47
Thai (25,014)	29,792	0.30
Vietnamese (87,468)	104,024	1.06
Hawaii Native/Pacific Islander (26,094)	54,169	0.55
Not Hispanic (22,464)	42,249	0.43
Hispanic (3,630)	11,920	0.12
Fijian (983)	1,306	0.01
Guamanian/Chamorro (3,447)	6,084	0.06
Marshallese (12)	27	<0.01
Native Hawaiian (4,013)	13,257	0.14
Samoan (12,115)	16,535	0.17
Tongan (2,571)	3,253	0.03
White (4,936,599)	5,292,966	53.91
Not Hispanic (2,728,321)	2,884,958	29.38
Hispanic (2,208,278)	2,408,008	24.52

*Notes: † The Census 2010 population figure is used to calculate the percentages in the Hispanic Origin and Race categories. Ancestry percentages are based on the 2006-2010 American Community Survey population (not shown); ‡ Numbers in parentheses indicate the number of people reporting a single ancestry; * Numbers in parentheses indicate the number of persons reporting this race alone, not in combination with any other race; Please refer to the Explanation of Data for more information.*

Madera County

Population: 150,865

Ancestry	Population	%
Afghan (0)	0	<0.01
African, Sub-Saharan (100)	204	0.14
African (71)	175	0.12
Cape Verdean (0)	0	<0.01
Ethiopian (29)	29	0.02
Ghanaian (0)	0	<0.01
Kenyan (0)	0	<0.01
Liberian (0)	0	<0.01
Nigerian (0)	0	<0.01
Senegalese (0)	0	<0.01
Sierra Leonean (0)	0	<0.01
Somalian (0)	0	<0.01
South African (0)	0	<0.01
Sudanese (0)	0	<0.01
Ugandan (0)	0	<0.01
Zimbabwean (0)	0	<0.01
Other Sub-Saharan African (0)	0	<0.01
Albanian (0)	9	0.01
Alsatian (0)	0	<0.01
American (2,764)	2,764	1.87
Arab (483)	713	0.48
Arab (101)	147	0.10
Egyptian (0)	0	<0.01
Iraqi (0)	0	<0.01
Jordanian (87)	87	0.06
Lebanese (75)	148	0.10
Moroccan (0)	0	<0.01
Palestinian (111)	126	0.09
Syrian (0)	60	0.04
Other Arab (109)	145	0.10
Armenian (36)	188	0.13
Assyrian/Chaldean/Syriac (49)	100	0.07
Australian (24)	52	0.04
Austrian (0)	130	0.09
Basque (108)	211	0.14
Belgian (12)	36	0.02
Brazilian (0)	0	<0.01
British (143)	331	0.22
Bulgarian (0)	25	0.02
Cajun (0)	0	<0.01
Canadian (152)	193	0.13
Carpatho Rusyn (0)	0	<0.01
Celtic (10)	20	0.01
Croatian (32)	49	0.03
Cypriot (0)	0	<0.01
Czech (10)	207	0.14
Czechoslovakian (44)	44	0.03
Danish (175)	656	0.44
Dutch (635)	1,937	1.31
Eastern European (27)	27	0.02
English (2,895)	9,841	6.66
Estonian (13)	13	0.01
European (602)	809	0.55
Finnish (28)	45	0.03
French, ex. Basque (413)	2,425	1.64
French Canadian (189)	417	0.28
German (3,550)	12,609	8.53
German Russian (0)	11	0.01
Greek (89)	304	0.21
Guyanese (0)	0	<0.01
Hungarian (20)	181	0.12
Icelander (0)	0	<0.01
Iranian (15)	46	0.03
Irish (3,107)	10,333	6.99
Israeli (224)	260	0.18
Italian (1,949)	4,820	3.26
Latvian (0)	65	0.04
Lithuanian (11)	112	0.08
Luxemburger (0)	0	<0.01
Macedonian (0)	0	<0.01
Maltese (22)	32	0.02
New Zealander (0)	0	<0.01
Northern European (43)	52	0.04
Norwegian (558)	1,321	0.89
Pennsylvania German (0)	0	<0.01
Polish (321)	802	0.54
Portuguese (1,784)	2,710	1.83
Romanian (64)	104	0.07
Russian (252)	624	0.42
Scandinavian (68)	136	0.09
Scotch-Irish (545)	1,848	1.25
Scottish (715)	2,302	1.56
Serbian (0)	0	<0.01
Slavic (0)	2	<0.01
Slovak (19)	30	0.02
Slovene (0)	0	<0.01
Soviet Union (0)	0	<0.01
Swedish (467)	1,336	0.90
Swiss (100)	332	0.22
Turkish (0)	0	<0.01
Ukrainian (161)	259	0.18
Welsh (177)	771	0.52
West Indian, ex. Hispanic (21)	97	0.07
Bahamian (0)	0	<0.01
Barbadian (0)	0	<0.01
Belizean (0)	9	0.01
Bermudan (0)	0	<0.01
British West Indian (0)	0	<0.01
Dutch West Indian (12)	67	0.05
Haitian (0)	12	0.01
Jamaican (9)	9	0.01
Trinidadian/Tobagonian (0)	0	<0.01
U.S. Virgin Islander (0)	0	<0.01
West Indian (0)	0	<0.01
Other West Indian (0)	0	<0.01
Yugoslavian (9)	61	0.04

Hispanic Origin	Population	%
Hispanic or Latino (of any race)	80,992	53.69
Central American, ex. Mexican	940	0.62
Costa Rican	22	0.01
Guatemalan	191	0.13
Honduran	91	0.06
Nicaraguan	67	0.04
Panamanian	17	0.01
Salvadoran	542	0.36
Other Central American	10	0.01
Cuban	124	0.08
Dominican Republic	8	0.01
Mexican	74,580	49.43
Puerto Rican	576	0.38
South American	223	0.15
Argentinean	48	0.03
Bolivian	11	0.01
Chilean	25	0.02
Colombian	52	0.03
Ecuadorian	14	0.01
Paraguayan	1	<0.01
Peruvian	54	0.04
Uruguayan	4	<0.01
Venezuelan	13	0.01
Other South American	1	<0.01
Other Hispanic or Latino	4,541	3.01

Race*	Population	%
African-American/Black (5,629)	6,452	4.28
Not Hispanic (5,009)	5,453	3.61
Hispanic (620)	999	0.66
American Indian/Alaska Native (4,136)	6,154	4.08
Not Hispanic (1,790)	3,101	2.06
Hispanic (2,346)	3,053	2.02
Alaska Athabascan *(Ala. Nat.)* (0)	0	<0.01
Aleut *(Alaska Native)* (0)	1	<0.01
Apache (74)	148	0.10
Arapaho (1)	7	<0.01
Blackfeet (22)	57	0.04
Canadian/French Am. Ind. (3)	8	0.01
Central American Ind. (11)	15	0.01
Cherokee (183)	674	0.45
Cheyenne (2)	9	0.01
Chickasaw (16)	29	0.02
Chippewa (13)	37	0.02
Choctaw (80)	188	0.12
Colville (0)	5	<0.01
Comanche (11)	30	0.02
Cree (2)	6	<0.01
Creek (10)	25	0.02
Crow (0)	6	<0.01
Delaware (7)	17	0.01
Hopi (4)	7	<0.01
Houma (0)	0	<0.01
Inupiat *(Alaska Native)* (9)	12	0.01
Iroquois (3)	10	0.01
Kiowa (3)	6	<0.01
Lumbee (1)	1	<0.01
Menominee (0)	0	<0.01
Mexican American Ind. (933)	1,086	0.72
Navajo (33)	60	0.04
Osage (6)	9	0.01
Ottawa (0)	0	<0.01
Paiute (17)	24	0.02
Pima (1)	8	0.01
Potawatomi (6)	19	0.01
Pueblo (5)	13	0.01
Puget Sound Salish (1)	4	<0.01
Seminole (5)	13	0.01
Shoshone (7)	9	0.01
Sioux (25)	54	0.04
South American Ind. (19)	23	0.02
Spanish American Ind. (7)	8	0.01
Tlingit-Haida *(Alaska Native)* (7)	8	0.01
Tohono O'Odham (1)	2	<0.01
Tsimshian *(Alaska Native)* (1)	1	<0.01
Ute (2)	5	<0.01
Yakama (6)	6	<0.01
Yaqui (28)	65	0.04
Yuman (6)	9	0.01
Yup'ik *(Alaska Native)* (0)	4	<0.01
Asian (2,802)	3,832	2.54
Not Hispanic (2,533)	3,180	2.11
Hispanic (269)	652	0.43
Bangladeshi (0)	2	<0.01
Bhutanese (0)	0	<0.01
Burmese (4)	4	<0.01
Cambodian (73)	87	0.06
Chinese, ex. Taiwanese (252)	364	0.24
Filipino (664)	1,090	0.72
Hmong (143)	148	0.10
Indian (985)	1,144	0.76
Indonesian (12)	22	0.01
Japanese (183)	350	0.23
Korean (111)	159	0.11
Laotian (37)	42	0.03
Malaysian (0)	1	<0.01
Nepalese (0)	0	<0.01
Pakistani (108)	124	0.08
Sri Lankan (0)	0	<0.01
Taiwanese (5)	6	<0.01
Thai (17)	33	0.02
Vietnamese (75)	93	0.06
Hawaii Native/Pacific Islander (162)	476	0.32
Not Hispanic (107)	250	0.17
Hispanic (55)	226	0.15
Fijian (4)	7	<0.01
Guamanian/Chamorro (20)	45	0.03
Marshallese (2)	2	<0.01
Native Hawaiian (63)	197	0.13
Samoan (34)	65	0.04
Tongan (1)	5	<0.01
White (94,456)	99,840	66.18
Not Hispanic (57,380)	59,556	39.48
Hispanic (37,076)	40,284	26.70

*Notes: † The Census 2010 population figure is used to calculate the percentages in the Hispanic Origin and Race categories. Ancestry percentages are based on the 2006-2010 American Community Survey population (not shown); ‡ Numbers in parentheses indicate the number of people reporting a single ancestry; * Numbers in parentheses indicate the number of persons reporting this race alone, not in combination with any other race; Please refer to the Explanation of Data for more information.*

Marin County

Population: 252,409

Ancestry	Population	%
Afghan (0)	0	<0.01
African, Sub-Saharan (725)	1,040	0.42
African (363)	511	0.21
Cape Verdean (0)	0	<0.01
Ethiopian (82)	154	0.06
Ghanaian (0)	0	<0.01
Kenyan (101)	101	0.04
Liberian (63)	63	0.03
Nigerian (22)	36	0.01
Senegalese (0)	0	<0.01
Sierra Leonean (0)	0	<0.01
Somalian (7)	7	<0.01
South African (46)	110	0.04
Sudanese (0)	0	<0.01
Ugandan (0)	0	<0.01
Zimbabwean (0)	0	<0.01
Other Sub-Saharan African (41)	58	0.02
Albanian (11)	25	0.01
Alsatian (0)	13	0.01
American (5,316)	5,316	2.14
Arab (798)	1,421	0.57
Arab (16)	16	0.01
Egyptian (273)	340	0.14
Iraqi (11)	16	0.01
Jordanian (55)	64	0.03
Lebanese (115)	423	0.17
Moroccan (85)	161	0.06
Palestinian (116)	190	0.08
Syrian (33)	72	0.03
Other Arab (94)	139	0.06
Armenian (618)	786	0.32
Assyrian/Chaldean/Syriac (13)	50	0.02
Australian (158)	424	0.17
Austrian (502)	1,760	0.71
Basque (187)	425	0.17
Belgian (179)	440	0.18
Brazilian (553)	725	0.29
British (2,137)	3,141	1.26
Bulgarian (147)	239	0.10
Cajun (0)	0	<0.01
Canadian (866)	1,686	0.68
Carpatho Rusyn (0)	0	<0.01
Celtic (96)	156	0.06
Croatian (478)	1,170	0.47
Cypriot (0)	0	<0.01
Czech (397)	1,475	0.59
Czechoslovakian (137)	382	0.15
Danish (1,000)	3,028	1.22
Dutch (827)	3,912	1.57
Eastern European (1,679)	1,859	0.75
English (8,637)	33,241	13.37
Estonian (48)	106	0.04
European (6,115)	7,057	2.84
Finnish (295)	756	0.30
French, ex. Basque (2,091)	9,816	3.95
French Canadian (425)	1,103	0.44
German (9,458)	37,776	15.20
German Russian (0)	0	<0.01
Greek (774)	1,777	0.71
Guyanese (0)	0	<0.01
Hungarian (408)	1,814	0.73
Icelander (78)	121	0.05
Iranian (1,876)	2,253	0.91
Irish (11,130)	37,352	15.02
Israeli (201)	261	0.10
Italian (8,369)	23,065	9.28
Latvian (69)	172	0.07
Lithuanian (355)	1,153	0.46
Luxemburger (20)	53	0.02
Macedonian (42)	99	0.04
Maltese (18)	75	0.03
New Zealander (133)	175	0.07
Northern European (1,014)	1,106	0.44
Norwegian (1,329)	4,796	1.93
Pennsylvania German (32)	103	0.04
Polish (1,656)	6,257	2.52
Portuguese (1,145)	3,242	1.30
Romanian (387)	1,321	0.53
Russian (3,639)	9,201	3.70
Scandinavian (537)	1,049	0.42
Scotch-Irish (1,920)	5,711	2.30
Scottish (2,031)	8,817	3.55
Serbian (67)	132	0.05
Slavic (40)	160	0.06
Slovak (236)	331	0.13
Slovene (60)	139	0.06
Soviet Union (0)	0	<0.01
Swedish (1,543)	7,054	2.84
Swiss (746)	2,541	1.02
Turkish (55)	251	0.10
Ukrainian (497)	1,033	0.42
Welsh (342)	2,309	0.93
West Indian, ex. Hispanic (376)	545	0.22
Bahamian (0)	0	<0.01
Barbadian (0)	0	<0.01
Belizean (0)	0	<0.01
Bermudan (14)	14	0.01
British West Indian (0)	0	<0.01
Dutch West Indian (0)	0	<0.01
Haitian (85)	89	0.04
Jamaican (266)	424	0.17
Trinidadian/Tobagonian (0)	7	<0.01
U.S. Virgin Islander (8)	8	<0.01
West Indian (3)	3	<0.01
Other West Indian (0)	0	<0.01
Yugoslavian (134)	408	0.16

Hispanic Origin	Population	%
Hispanic or Latino (of any race)	39,069	15.48
Central American, ex. Mexican	12,273	4.86
Costa Rican	114	0.05
Guatemalan	7,938	3.14
Honduran	164	0.06
Nicaraguan	631	0.25
Panamanian	71	0.03
Salvadoran	3,255	1.29
Other Central American	100	0.04
Cuban	455	0.18
Dominican Republic	90	0.04
Mexican	18,029	7.14
Puerto Rican	856	0.34
South American	2,610	1.03
Argentinean	355	0.14
Bolivian	86	0.03
Chilean	222	0.09
Colombian	464	0.18
Ecuadorian	145	0.06
Paraguayan	11	<0.01
Peruvian	1,110	0.44
Uruguayan	67	0.03
Venezuelan	103	0.04
Other South American	47	0.02
Other Hispanic or Latino	4,756	1.88

Race*	Population	%
African-American/Black (6,987)	8,941	3.54
Not Hispanic (6,621)	8,243	3.27
Hispanic (366)	698	0.28
American Indian/Alaska Native (1,523)	3,787	1.50
Not Hispanic (531)	1,974	0.78
Hispanic (992)	1,813	0.72
Alaska Athabascan *(Ala. Nat.)* (2)	3	<0.01
Aleut *(Alaska Native)* (1)	8	<0.01
Apache (17)	56	0.02
Arapaho (0)	2	<0.01
Blackfeet (10)	68	0.03
Canadian/French Am. Ind. (1)	6	<0.01
Central American Ind. (43)	73	0.03
Cherokee (77)	475	0.19
Cheyenne (1)	13	0.01
Chickasaw (4)	20	0.01
Chippewa (7)	33	0.01
Choctaw (17)	95	0.04
Colville (0)	0	<0.01
Comanche (4)	19	0.01
Cree (0)	8	<0.01
Creek (13)	26	0.01
Crow (0)	2	<0.01
Delaware (2)	21	0.01
Hopi (0)	2	<0.01
Houma (0)	0	<0.01
Inupiat *(Alaska Native)* (5)	6	<0.01
Iroquois (10)	48	0.02
Kiowa (0)	2	<0.01
Lumbee (1)	4	<0.01
Menominee (0)	1	<0.01
Mexican American Ind. (296)	429	0.17
Navajo (22)	64	0.03
Osage (1)	13	0.01
Ottawa (1)	3	<0.01
Paiute (1)	3	<0.01
Pima (4)	8	<0.01
Potawatomi (2)	18	0.01
Pueblo (9)	18	0.01
Puget Sound Salish (2)	11	<0.01
Seminole (1)	21	0.01
Shoshone (0)	7	<0.01
Sioux (15)	44	0.02
South American Ind. (19)	41	0.02
Spanish American Ind. (20)	25	0.01
Tlingit-Haida *(Alaska Native)* (2)	9	<0.01
Tohono O'Odham (1)	8	<0.01
Tsimshian *(Alaska Native)* (0)	0	<0.01
Ute (3)	9	<0.01
Yakama (2)	4	<0.01
Yaqui (4)	22	0.01
Yuman (4)	5	<0.01
Yup'ik *(Alaska Native)* (0)	0	<0.01
Asian (13,761)	18,750	7.43
Not Hispanic (13,577)	18,024	7.14
Hispanic (184)	726	0.29
Bangladeshi (9)	10	<0.01
Bhutanese (5)	9	<0.01
Burmese (14)	28	0.01
Cambodian (117)	146	0.06
Chinese, ex. Taiwanese (3,986)	5,718	2.27
Filipino (1,870)	3,058	1.21
Hmong (8)	10	<0.01
Indian (2,015)	2,399	0.95
Indonesian (67)	111	0.04
Japanese (1,677)	2,967	1.18
Korean (1,312)	1,756	0.70
Laotian (48)	69	0.03
Malaysian (8)	18	0.01
Nepalese (38)	44	0.02
Pakistani (124)	154	0.06
Sri Lankan (24)	29	0.01
Taiwanese (131)	181	0.07
Thai (268)	392	0.16
Vietnamese (1,339)	1,601	0.63
Hawaii Native/Pacific Islander (509)	1,132	0.45
Not Hispanic (436)	930	0.37
Hispanic (73)	202	0.08
Fijian (188)	207	0.08
Guamanian/Chamorro (77)	141	0.06
Marshallese (0)	0	<0.01
Native Hawaiian (107)	430	0.17
Samoan (47)	100	0.04
Tongan (34)	43	0.02
White (201,963)	211,647	83.85
Not Hispanic (183,830)	190,585	75.51
Hispanic (18,133)	21,062	8.34

*Notes: † The Census 2010 population figure is used to calculate the percentages in the Hispanic Origin and Race categories. Ancestry percentages are based on the 2006-2010 American Community Survey population (not shown); ‡ Numbers in parentheses indicate the number of people reporting a single ancestry; * Numbers in parentheses indicate the number of persons reporting this race alone, not in combination with any other race; Please refer to the Explanation of Data for more information.*

Mariposa County

Population: 18,251

Ancestry	Population	%
Afghan (0)	0	<0.01
African, Sub-Saharan (22)	22	0.12
African (9)	9	0.05
Cape Verdean (0)	0	<0.01
Ethiopian (0)	0	<0.01
Ghanaian (0)	0	<0.01
Kenyan (0)	0	<0.01
Liberian (0)	0	<0.01
Nigerian (0)	0	<0.01
Senegalese (0)	0	<0.01
Sierra Leonean (0)	0	<0.01
Somalian (0)	0	<0.01
South African (13)	13	0.07
Sudanese (0)	0	<0.01
Ugandan (0)	0	<0.01
Zimbabwean (0)	0	<0.01
Other Sub-Saharan African (0)	0	<0.01
Albanian (0)	0	<0.01
Alsatian (0)	0	<0.01
American (598)	598	3.27
Arab (0)	0	<0.01
Arab (0)	0	<0.01
Egyptian (0)	0	<0.01
Iraqi (0)	0	<0.01
Jordanian (0)	0	<0.01
Lebanese (0)	0	<0.01
Moroccan (0)	0	<0.01
Palestinian (0)	0	<0.01
Syrian (0)	0	<0.01
Other Arab (0)	0	<0.01
Armenian (0)	0	<0.01
Assyrian/Chaldean/Syriac (0)	0	<0.01
Australian (0)	0	<0.01
Austrian (0)	46	0.25
Basque (0)	0	<0.01
Belgian (0)	31	0.17
Brazilian (0)	0	<0.01
British (29)	149	0.81
Bulgarian (0)	0	<0.01
Cajun (0)	1	0.01
Canadian (11)	46	0.25
Carpatho Rusyn (0)	0	<0.01
Celtic (0)	0	<0.01
Croatian (27)	142	0.78
Cypriot (0)	0	<0.01
Czech (0)	0	<0.01
Czechoslovakian (44)	44	0.24
Danish (97)	213	1.16
Dutch (86)	457	2.50
Eastern European (41)	41	0.22
English (906)	2,915	15.94
Estonian (0)	42	0.23
European (379)	442	2.42
Finnish (0)	20	0.11
French, ex. Basque (25)	948	5.18
French Canadian (21)	39	0.21
German (1,065)	4,024	22.00
German Russian (0)	0	<0.01
Greek (0)	0	<0.01
Guyanese (0)	0	<0.01
Hungarian (0)	0	<0.01
Icelander (0)	0	<0.01
Iranian (0)	12	0.07
Irish (1,096)	3,998	21.86
Israeli (10)	10	0.05
Italian (346)	1,142	6.24
Latvian (0)	0	<0.01
Lithuanian (0)	0	<0.01
Luxemburger (0)	0	<0.01
Macedonian (0)	0	<0.01
Maltese (0)	0	<0.01
New Zealander (0)	0	<0.01
Northern European (36)	36	0.20
Norwegian (23)	192	1.05
Pennsylvania German (0)	0	<0.01
Polish (97)	646	3.53
Portuguese (137)	302	1.65
Romanian (9)	13	0.07
Russian (55)	278	1.52
Scandinavian (43)	58	0.32
Scotch-Irish (223)	615	3.36
Scottish (208)	527	2.88
Serbian (0)	0	<0.01
Slavic (3)	3	0.02
Slovak (0)	0	<0.01
Slovene (0)	0	<0.01
Soviet Union (0)	0	<0.01
Swedish (52)	344	1.88
Swiss (0)	0	<0.01
Turkish (0)	0	<0.01
Ukrainian (12)	12	0.07
Welsh (23)	139	0.76
West Indian, ex. Hispanic (75)	75	0.41
Bahamian (0)	0	<0.01
Barbadian (0)	0	<0.01
Belizean (0)	0	<0.01
Bermudan (0)	0	<0.01
British West Indian (0)	0	<0.01
Dutch West Indian (62)	62	0.34
Haitian (0)	0	<0.01
Jamaican (13)	13	0.07
Trinidadian/Tobagonian (0)	0	<0.01
U.S. Virgin Islander (0)	0	<0.01
West Indian (0)	0	<0.01
Other West Indian (0)	0	<0.01
Yugoslavian (0)	51	0.28

Hispanic Origin	Population	%
Hispanic or Latino (of any race)	1,676	9.18
Central American, ex. Mexican	54	0.30
Costa Rican	1	0.01
Guatemalan	8	0.04
Honduran	7	0.04
Nicaraguan	15	0.08
Panamanian	6	0.03
Salvadoran	16	0.09
Other Central American	1	0.01
Cuban	9	0.05
Dominican Republic	0	<0.01
Mexican	1,248	6.84
Puerto Rican	66	0.36
South American	39	0.21
Argentinean	3	0.02
Bolivian	1	0.01
Chilean	4	0.02
Colombian	20	0.11
Ecuadorian	0	<0.01
Paraguayan	0	<0.01
Peruvian	11	0.06
Uruguayan	0	<0.01
Venezuelan	0	<0.01
Other South American	0	<0.01
Other Hispanic or Latino	260	1.42

Race*	Population	%
African-American/Black (138)	249	1.36
Not Hispanic (129)	214	1.17
Hispanic (9)	35	0.19
American Indian/Alaska Native (527)	983	5.39
Not Hispanic (459)	846	4.64
Hispanic (68)	137	0.75
Alaska Athabascan *(Ala. Nat.)* (0)	1	0.01
Aleut *(Alaska Native)* (0)	0	<0.01
Apache (9)	16	0.09
Arapaho (0)	0	<0.01
Blackfeet (1)	17	0.09
Canadian/French Am. Ind. (0)	0	<0.01
Central American Ind. (0)	0	<0.01
Cherokee (34)	145	0.79
Cheyenne (0)	2	0.01
Chickasaw (12)	16	0.09
Chippewa (4)	8	0.04
Choctaw (15)	47	0.26
Colville (0)	0	<0.01
Comanche (1)	2	0.01
Cree (0)	0	<0.01
Creek (0)	1	0.01
Crow (0)	4	0.02
Delaware (0)	1	0.01
Hopi (0)	0	<0.01
Houma (0)	0	<0.01
Inupiat *(Alaska Native)* (3)	3	0.02
Iroquois (2)	5	0.03
Kiowa (0)	0	<0.01
Lumbee (0)	0	<0.01
Menominee (0)	0	<0.01
Mexican American Ind. (13)	17	0.09
Navajo (7)	11	0.06
Osage (0)	2	0.01
Ottawa (0)	0	<0.01
Paiute (6)	17	0.09
Pima (0)	0	<0.01
Potawatomi (0)	3	0.02
Pueblo (0)	1	0.01
Puget Sound Salish (0)	0	<0.01
Seminole (1)	1	0.01
Shoshone (1)	2	0.01
Sioux (7)	16	0.09
South American Ind. (5)	9	0.05
Spanish American Ind. (1)	1	0.01
Tlingit-Haida *(Alaska Native)* (1)	1	0.01
Tohono O'Odham (5)	5	0.03
Tsimshian *(Alaska Native)* (0)	0	<0.01
Ute (0)	0	<0.01
Yakama (0)	0	<0.01
Yaqui (1)	4	0.02
Yuman (0)	0	<0.01
Yup'ik *(Alaska Native)* (0)	0	<0.01
Asian (204)	317	1.74
Not Hispanic (201)	288	1.58
Hispanic (3)	29	0.16
Bangladeshi (0)	0	<0.01
Bhutanese (0)	0	<0.01
Burmese (0)	0	<0.01
Cambodian (2)	2	0.01
Chinese, ex. Taiwanese (23)	35	0.19
Filipino (69)	113	0.62
Hmong (3)	3	0.02
Indian (19)	30	0.16
Indonesian (2)	9	0.05
Japanese (37)	74	0.41
Korean (14)	19	0.10
Laotian (0)	0	<0.01
Malaysian (0)	0	<0.01
Nepalese (1)	1	0.01
Pakistani (3)	3	0.02
Sri Lankan (2)	2	0.01
Taiwanese (6)	6	0.03
Thai (9)	15	0.08
Vietnamese (2)	3	0.02
Hawaii Native/Pacific Islander (26)	53	0.29
Not Hispanic (26)	47	0.26
Hispanic (0)	6	0.03
Fijian (0)	0	<0.01
Guamanian/Chamorro (3)	8	0.04
Marshallese (0)	0	<0.01
Native Hawaiian (13)	25	0.14
Samoan (0)	2	0.01
Tongan (0)	0	<0.01
White (16,103)	16,794	92.02
Not Hispanic (15,192)	15,708	86.07
Hispanic (911)	1,086	5.95

*Notes: † The Census 2010 population figure is used to calculate the percentages in the Hispanic Origin and Race categories. Ancestry percentages are based on the 2006-2010 American Community Survey population (not shown); ‡ Numbers in parentheses indicate the number of people reporting a single ancestry; * Numbers in parentheses indicate the number of persons reporting this race alone, not in combination with any other race; Please refer to the Explanation of Data for more information.*

Mendocino County

Population: 87,841

Ancestry	Population	%
Afghan (0)	0	<0.01
African, Sub-Saharan (34)	56	0.06
African (34)	39	0.04
Cape Verdean (0)	0	<0.01
Ethiopian (0)	2	<0.01
Ghanaian (0)	0	<0.01
Kenyan (0)	0	<0.01
Liberian (0)	0	<0.01
Nigerian (0)	0	<0.01
Senegalese (0)	0	<0.01
Sierra Leonean (0)	0	<0.01
Somalian (0)	0	<0.01
South African (0)	0	<0.01
Sudanese (0)	0	<0.01
Ugandan (0)	0	<0.01
Zimbabwean (0)	0	<0.01
Other Sub-Saharan African (0)	15	0.02
Albanian (0)	0	<0.01
Alsatian (0)	0	<0.01
American (3,046)	3,046	3.48
Arab (69)	123	0.14
Arab (27)	27	0.03
Egyptian (0)	18	0.02
Iraqi (0)	0	<0.01
Jordanian (0)	0	<0.01
Lebanese (0)	16	0.02
Moroccan (0)	0	<0.01
Palestinian (42)	42	0.05
Syrian (0)	20	0.02
Other Arab (0)	0	<0.01
Armenian (73)	116	0.13
Assyrian/Chaldean/Syriac (0)	0	<0.01
Australian (34)	117	0.13
Austrian (17)	337	0.39
Basque (9)	27	0.03
Belgian (27)	32	0.04
Brazilian (26)	66	0.08
British (250)	403	0.46
Bulgarian (0)	50	0.06
Cajun (0)	0	<0.01
Canadian (89)	276	0.32
Carpatho Rusyn (0)	0	<0.01
Celtic (43)	94	0.11
Croatian (46)	89	0.10
Cypriot (0)	0	<0.01
Czech (97)	612	0.70
Czechoslovakian (34)	101	0.12
Danish (341)	1,133	1.30
Dutch (284)	2,402	2.75
Eastern European (224)	224	0.26
English (2,661)	11,734	13.41
Estonian (0)	0	<0.01
European (1,568)	1,739	1.99
Finnish (253)	1,144	1.31
French, ex. Basque (550)	3,592	4.11
French Canadian (78)	465	0.53
German (3,537)	14,452	16.52
German Russian (0)	40	0.05
Greek (186)	425	0.49
Guyanese (0)	0	<0.01
Hungarian (193)	568	0.65
Icelander (0)	56	0.06
Iranian (0)	84	0.10
Irish (2,592)	11,641	13.31
Israeli (3)	5	0.01
Italian (2,225)	5,935	6.78
Latvian (12)	75	0.09
Lithuanian (19)	108	0.12
Luxemburger (0)	0	<0.01
Macedonian (9)	18	0.02
Maltese (0)	19	0.02
New Zealander (50)	50	0.06
Northern European (149)	158	0.18
Norwegian (441)	1,403	1.60
Pennsylvania German (0)	7	0.01
Polish (281)	1,185	1.35
Portuguese (744)	1,785	2.04
Romanian (7)	147	0.17
Russian (286)	1,130	1.29
Scandinavian (88)	304	0.35
Scotch-Irish (759)	1,956	2.24
Scottish (598)	2,593	2.96
Serbian (0)	10	0.01
Slavic (0)	7	0.01
Slovak (56)	56	0.06
Slovene (0)	0	<0.01
Soviet Union (0)	0	<0.01
Swedish (434)	1,985	2.27
Swiss (130)	554	0.63
Turkish (0)	19	0.02
Ukrainian (62)	130	0.15
Welsh (96)	1,060	1.21
West Indian, ex. Hispanic (0)	167	0.19
Bahamian (0)	0	<0.01
Barbadian (0)	0	<0.01
Belizean (0)	0	<0.01
Bermudan (0)	0	<0.01
British West Indian (0)	0	<0.01
Dutch West Indian (0)	10	0.01
Haitian (0)	0	<0.01
Jamaican (0)	157	0.18
Trinidadian/Tobagonian (0)	0	<0.01
U.S. Virgin Islander (0)	0	<0.01
West Indian (0)	0	<0.01
Other West Indian (0)	0	<0.01
Yugoslavian (0)	49	0.06

Hispanic Origin	Population	%
Hispanic or Latino (of any race)	19,505	22.20
Central American, ex. Mexican	239	0.27
Costa Rican	12	0.01
Guatemalan	43	0.05
Honduran	31	0.04
Nicaraguan	42	0.05
Panamanian	10	0.01
Salvadoran	92	0.10
Other Central American	9	0.01
Cuban	44	0.05
Dominican Republic	12	0.01
Mexican	17,593	20.03
Puerto Rican	221	0.25
South American	177	0.20
Argentinean	24	0.03
Bolivian	7	0.01
Chilean	20	0.02
Colombian	29	0.03
Ecuadorian	36	0.04
Paraguayan	1	<0.01
Peruvian	40	0.05
Uruguayan	3	<0.01
Venezuelan	13	0.01
Other South American	4	<0.01
Other Hispanic or Latino	1,219	1.39

Race*	Population	%
African-American/Black (622)	1,145	1.30
Not Hispanic (544)	965	1.10
Hispanic (78)	180	0.20
American Indian/Alaska Native (4,277)	6,365	7.25
Not Hispanic (3,486)	5,049	5.75
Hispanic (791)	1,316	1.50
Alaska Athabascan *(Ala. Nat.)* (6)	10	0.01
Aleut *(Alaska Native)* (0)	4	<0.01
Apache (39)	85	0.10
Arapaho (6)	9	0.01
Blackfeet (16)	84	0.10
Canadian/French Am. Ind. (9)	12	0.01
Central American Ind. (1)	3	<0.01
Cherokee (147)	540	0.61
Cheyenne (3)	8	0.01
Chickasaw (5)	15	0.02
Chippewa (16)	31	0.04
Choctaw (63)	136	0.15
Colville (3)	3	<0.01
Comanche (0)	3	<0.01
Cree (0)	5	0.01
Creek (4)	16	0.02
Crow (1)	4	<0.01
Delaware (6)	7	0.01
Hopi (1)	3	<0.01
Houma (1)	1	<0.01
Inupiat *(Alaska Native)* (4)	4	<0.01
Iroquois (10)	24	0.03
Kiowa (0)	0	<0.01
Lumbee (2)	2	<0.01
Menominee (0)	0	<0.01
Mexican American Ind. (207)	259	0.29
Navajo (23)	45	0.05
Osage (2)	12	0.01
Ottawa (0)	6	0.01
Paiute (23)	28	0.03
Pima (2)	5	0.01
Potawatomi (1)	15	0.02
Pueblo (2)	9	0.01
Puget Sound Salish (2)	7	0.01
Seminole (2)	16	0.02
Shoshone (5)	9	0.01
Sioux (27)	68	0.08
South American Ind. (0)	4	<0.01
Spanish American Ind. (19)	25	0.03
Tlingit-Haida *(Alaska Native)* (2)	7	0.01
Tohono O'Odham (3)	6	0.01
Tsimshian *(Alaska Native)* (2)	2	<0.01
Ute (0)	1	<0.01
Yakama (1)	5	0.01
Yaqui (12)	32	0.04
Yuman (3)	3	<0.01
Yup'ik *(Alaska Native)* (0)	1	<0.01
Asian (1,450)	2,084	2.37
Not Hispanic (1,402)	1,932	2.20
Hispanic (48)	152	0.17
Bangladeshi (1)	2	<0.01
Bhutanese (0)	0	<0.01
Burmese (15)	20	0.02
Cambodian (20)	30	0.03
Chinese, ex. Taiwanese (454)	604	0.69
Filipino (372)	640	0.73
Hmong (1)	1	<0.01
Indian (117)	174	0.20
Indonesian (2)	12	0.01
Japanese (115)	217	0.25
Korean (76)	119	0.14
Laotian (4)	5	0.01
Malaysian (3)	4	<0.01
Nepalese (5)	8	0.01
Pakistani (31)	31	0.04
Sri Lankan (1)	2	<0.01
Taiwanese (13)	14	0.02
Thai (42)	55	0.06
Vietnamese (110)	132	0.15
Hawaii Native/Pacific Islander (119)	332	0.38
Not Hispanic (92)	247	0.28
Hispanic (27)	85	0.10
Fijian (2)	2	<0.01
Guamanian/Chamorro (18)	37	0.04
Marshallese (0)	0	<0.01
Native Hawaiian (58)	188	0.21
Samoan (15)	31	0.04
Tongan (1)	4	<0.01
White (67,218)	70,790	80.59
Not Hispanic (60,249)	62,523	71.18
Hispanic (6,969)	8,267	9.41

*Notes: † The Census 2010 population figure is used to calculate the percentages in the Hispanic Origin and Race categories. Ancestry percentages are based on the 2006-2010 American Community Survey population (not shown); ‡ Numbers in parentheses indicate the number of people reporting a single ancestry; * Numbers in parentheses indicate the number of persons reporting this race alone, not in combination with any other race; Please refer to the Explanation of Data for more information.*

Merced County

Population: 255,793

Ancestry	Population	%
Afghan (37)	97	0.04
African, Sub-Saharan (291)	371	0.15
African (233)	313	0.12
Cape Verdean (0)	0	<0.01
Ethiopian (12)	12	<0.01
Ghanaian (0)	0	<0.01
Kenyan (0)	0	<0.01
Liberian (0)	0	<0.01
Nigerian (26)	26	0.01
Senegalese (0)	0	<0.01
Sierra Leonean (0)	0	<0.01
Somalian (0)	0	<0.01
South African (20)	20	0.01
Sudanese (0)	0	<0.01
Ugandan (0)	0	<0.01
Zimbabwean (0)	0	<0.01
Other Sub-Saharan African (0)	0	<0.01
Albanian (0)	6	<0.01
Alsatian (0)	12	<0.01
American (5,875)	5,875	2.34
Arab (315)	453	0.18
Arab (89)	89	0.04
Egyptian (0)	0	<0.01
Iraqi (0)	8	<0.01
Jordanian (0)	0	<0.01
Lebanese (16)	60	0.02
Moroccan (4)	14	0.01
Palestinian (38)	38	0.02
Syrian (7)	40	0.02
Other Arab (161)	204	0.08
Armenian (46)	107	0.04
Assyrian/Chaldean/Syriac (0)	28	0.01
Australian (33)	33	0.01
Austrian (21)	96	0.04
Basque (133)	229	0.09
Belgian (40)	81	0.03
Brazilian (15)	120	0.05
British (236)	353	0.14
Bulgarian (0)	0	<0.01
Cajun (0)	29	0.01
Canadian (83)	175	0.07
Carpatho Rusyn (0)	0	<0.01
Celtic (26)	26	0.01
Croatian (0)	17	0.01
Cypriot (0)	0	<0.01
Czech (79)	159	0.06
Czechoslovakian (0)	49	0.02
Danish (170)	702	0.28
Dutch (897)	2,641	1.05
Eastern European (56)	66	0.03
English (2,751)	10,201	4.07
Estonian (0)	0	<0.01
European (1,058)	1,322	0.53
Finnish (86)	201	0.08
French, ex. Basque (554)	3,257	1.30
French Canadian (120)	416	0.17
German (4,205)	15,795	6.30
German Russian (0)	0	<0.01
Greek (84)	295	0.12
Guyanese (0)	0	<0.01
Hungarian (176)	480	0.19
Icelander (0)	13	0.01
Iranian (307)	307	0.12
Irish (2,915)	12,914	5.15
Israeli (0)	0	<0.01
Italian (2,166)	6,365	2.54
Latvian (0)	0	<0.01
Lithuanian (41)	112	0.04
Luxemburger (0)	0	<0.01
Macedonian (0)	11	<0.01
Maltese (0)	0	<0.01
New Zealander (0)	0	<0.01
Northern European (128)	128	0.05
Norwegian (804)	2,009	0.80
Pennsylvania German (0)	3	<0.01
Polish (267)	1,197	0.48
Portuguese (9,769)	13,998	5.58
Romanian (3)	46	0.02
Russian (262)	685	0.27
Scandinavian (84)	117	0.05
Scotch-Irish (535)	1,731	0.69
Scottish (593)	1,884	0.75
Serbian (0)	0	<0.01
Slavic (13)	17	0.01
Slovak (0)	17	0.01
Slovene (0)	0	<0.01
Soviet Union (0)	0	<0.01
Swedish (515)	2,016	0.80
Swiss (220)	771	0.31
Turkish (12)	12	<0.01
Ukrainian (0)	84	0.03
Welsh (57)	522	0.21
West Indian, ex. Hispanic (75)	89	0.04
Bahamian (0)	0	<0.01
Barbadian (0)	0	<0.01
Belizean (0)	0	<0.01
Bermudan (0)	0	<0.01
British West Indian (0)	0	<0.01
Dutch West Indian (0)	6	<0.01
Haitian (9)	9	<0.01
Jamaican (46)	54	0.02
Trinidadian/Tobagonian (9)	9	<0.01
U.S. Virgin Islander (0)	0	<0.01
West Indian (11)	11	<0.01
Other West Indian (0)	0	<0.01
Yugoslavian (18)	33	0.01

Hispanic Origin	Population	%
Hispanic or Latino (of any race)	140,485	54.92
Central American, ex. Mexican	1,748	0.68
Costa Rican	55	0.02
Guatemalan	293	0.11
Honduran	133	0.05
Nicaraguan	304	0.12
Panamanian	62	0.02
Salvadoran	887	0.35
Other Central American	14	0.01
Cuban	173	0.07
Dominican Republic	24	0.01
Mexican	130,663	51.08
Puerto Rican	1,025	0.40
South American	465	0.18
Argentinean	59	0.02
Bolivian	19	0.01
Chilean	44	0.02
Colombian	90	0.04
Ecuadorian	29	0.01
Paraguayan	1	<0.01
Peruvian	184	0.07
Uruguayan	10	<0.01
Venezuelan	20	0.01
Other South American	9	<0.01
Other Hispanic or Latino	6,387	2.50

Race*	Population	%
African-American/Black (9,926)	12,189	4.77
Not Hispanic (8,785)	10,195	3.99
Hispanic (1,141)	1,994	0.78
American Indian/Alaska Native (3,473)	5,939	2.32
Not Hispanic (1,126)	2,574	1.01
Hispanic (2,347)	3,365	1.32
Alaska Athabascan *(Ala. Nat.)* (0)	1	<0.01
Aleut *(Alaska Native)* (4)	4	<0.01
Apache (128)	244	0.10
Arapaho (1)	1	<0.01
Blackfeet (20)	97	0.04
Canadian/French Am. Ind. (0)	4	<0.01
Central American Ind. (7)	8	<0.01
Cherokee (223)	828	0.32
Cheyenne (3)	9	<0.01
Chickasaw (13)	33	0.01
Chippewa (26)	38	0.01
Choctaw (76)	191	0.07
Colville (1)	2	<0.01
Comanche (7)	16	0.01
Cree (4)	8	<0.01
Creek (16)	34	0.01
Crow (5)	8	<0.01
Delaware (6)	11	<0.01
Hopi (5)	15	0.01
Houma (0)	0	<0.01
Inupiat *(Alaska Native)* (1)	2	<0.01
Iroquois (5)	14	0.01
Kiowa (0)	0	<0.01
Lumbee (1)	1	<0.01
Menominee (1)	1	<0.01
Mexican American Ind. (411)	572	0.22
Navajo (48)	86	0.03
Osage (6)	16	0.01
Ottawa (1)	1	<0.01
Paiute (32)	49	0.02
Pima (4)	18	0.01
Potawatomi (23)	45	0.02
Pueblo (11)	18	0.01
Puget Sound Salish (2)	4	<0.01
Seminole (2)	22	0.01
Shoshone (7)	15	0.01
Sioux (50)	86	0.03
South American Ind. (11)	13	0.01
Spanish American Ind. (270)	279	0.11
Tlingit-Haida *(Alaska Native)* (6)	14	0.01
Tohono O'Odham (12)	13	0.01
Tsimshian *(Alaska Native)* (0)	0	<0.01
Ute (3)	5	<0.01
Yakama (1)	4	<0.01
Yaqui (60)	90	0.04
Yuman (1)	2	<0.01
Yup'ik *(Alaska Native)* (0)	0	<0.01
Asian (18,836)	21,902	8.56
Not Hispanic (18,183)	20,284	7.93
Hispanic (653)	1,618	0.63
Bangladeshi (7)	7	<0.01
Bhutanese (0)	0	<0.01
Burmese (18)	20	0.01
Cambodian (115)	154	0.06
Chinese, ex. Taiwanese (1,026)	1,360	0.53
Filipino (2,487)	3,684	1.44
Hmong (6,920)	7,254	2.84
Indian (4,162)	4,596	1.80
Indonesian (20)	43	0.02
Japanese (555)	1,010	0.39
Korean (344)	519	0.20
Laotian (1,606)	1,810	0.71
Malaysian (1)	4	<0.01
Nepalese (8)	8	<0.01
Pakistani (109)	132	0.05
Sri Lankan (12)	13	0.01
Taiwanese (55)	70	0.03
Thai (155)	279	0.11
Vietnamese (420)	516	0.20
Hawaii Native/Pacific Islander (583)	1,406	0.55
Not Hispanic (476)	1,018	0.40
Hispanic (107)	388	0.15
Fijian (52)	74	0.03
Guamanian/Chamorro (146)	224	0.09
Marshallese (3)	3	<0.01
Native Hawaiian (144)	436	0.17
Samoan (131)	227	0.09
Tongan (23)	30	0.01
White (148,381)	158,310	61.89
Not Hispanic (81,599)	85,380	33.38
Hispanic (66,782)	72,930	28.51

*Notes: † The Census 2010 population figure is used to calculate the percentages in the Hispanic Origin and Race categories. Ancestry percentages are based on the 2006-2010 American Community Survey population (not shown); ‡ Numbers in parentheses indicate the number of people reporting a single ancestry; * Numbers in parentheses indicate the number of persons reporting this race alone, not in combination with any other race; Please refer to the Explanation of Data for more information.*

Modoc County

Population: 9,686

Ancestry	Population	%
Afghan (0)	0	<0.01
African, Sub-Saharan (5)	5	0.05
African (0)	0	<0.01
Cape Verdean (0)	0	<0.01
Ethiopian (0)	0	<0.01
Ghanaian (0)	0	<0.01
Kenyan (0)	0	<0.01
Liberian (0)	0	<0.01
Nigerian (0)	0	<0.01
Senegalese (0)	0	<0.01
Sierra Leonean (0)	0	<0.01
Somalian (0)	0	<0.01
South African (5)	5	0.05
Sudanese (0)	0	<0.01
Ugandan (0)	0	<0.01
Zimbabwean (0)	0	<0.01
Other Sub-Saharan African (0)	0	<0.01
Albanian (0)	0	<0.01
Alsatian (0)	0	<0.01
American (253)	253	2.63
Arab (0)	6	0.06
Arab (0)	0	<0.01
Egyptian (0)	0	<0.01
Iraqi (0)	0	<0.01
Jordanian (0)	0	<0.01
Lebanese (0)	0	<0.01
Moroccan (0)	0	<0.01
Palestinian (0)	0	<0.01
Syrian (0)	6	0.06
Other Arab (0)	0	<0.01
Armenian (8)	8	0.08
Assyrian/Chaldean/Syriac (0)	0	<0.01
Australian (0)	0	<0.01
Austrian (0)	26	0.27
Basque (89)	92	0.96
Belgian (0)	0	<0.01
Brazilian (0)	0	<0.01
British (12)	63	0.66
Bulgarian (0)	0	<0.01
Cajun (0)	0	<0.01
Canadian (0)	5	0.05
Carpatho Rusyn (0)	0	<0.01
Celtic (0)	0	<0.01
Croatian (0)	0	<0.01
Cypriot (0)	0	<0.01
Czech (36)	69	0.72
Czechoslovakian (15)	15	0.16
Danish (62)	107	1.11
Dutch (15)	191	1.99
Eastern European (16)	16	0.17
English (578)	1,883	19.60
Estonian (0)	0	<0.01
European (32)	55	0.57
Finnish (0)	28	0.29
French, ex. Basque (136)	365	3.80
French Canadian (16)	16	0.17
German (610)	2,453	25.54
German Russian (0)	0	<0.01
Greek (11)	30	0.31
Guyanese (0)	0	<0.01
Hungarian (0)	78	0.81
Icelander (0)	0	<0.01
Iranian (0)	0	<0.01
Irish (249)	1,725	17.96
Israeli (0)	0	<0.01
Italian (133)	290	3.02
Latvian (0)	0	<0.01
Lithuanian (0)	0	<0.01
Luxemburger (0)	0	<0.01
Macedonian (0)	0	<0.01
Maltese (0)	0	<0.01
New Zealander (0)	0	<0.01
Northern European (25)	25	0.26
Norwegian (8)	168	1.75
Pennsylvania German (0)	4	0.04
Polish (0)	0	<0.01
Portuguese (94)	153	1.59
Romanian (0)	0	<0.01
Russian (74)	123	1.28
Scandinavian (14)	27	0.28
Scotch-Irish (107)	221	2.30
Scottish (177)	490	5.10
Serbian (0)	0	<0.01
Slavic (0)	0	<0.01
Slovak (0)	0	<0.01
Slovene (6)	6	0.06
Soviet Union (0)	0	<0.01
Swedish (78)	216	2.25
Swiss (37)	44	0.46
Turkish (0)	0	<0.01
Ukrainian (0)	0	<0.01
Welsh (5)	133	1.38
West Indian, ex. Hispanic (7)	24	0.25
Bahamian (0)	0	<0.01
Barbadian (0)	0	<0.01
Belizean (0)	0	<0.01
Bermudan (0)	0	<0.01
British West Indian (0)	0	<0.01
Dutch West Indian (7)	24	0.25
Haitian (0)	0	<0.01
Jamaican (0)	0	<0.01
Trinidadian/Tobagonian (0)	0	<0.01
U.S. Virgin Islander (0)	0	<0.01
West Indian (0)	0	<0.01
Other West Indian (0)	0	<0.01
Yugoslavian (0)	0	<0.01

Hispanic Origin	Population	%
Hispanic or Latino (of any race)	1,342	13.86
Central American, ex. Mexican	29	0.30
Costa Rican	2	0.02
Guatemalan	3	0.03
Honduran	3	0.03
Nicaraguan	0	<0.01
Panamanian	0	<0.01
Salvadoran	20	0.21
Other Central American	1	0.01
Cuban	2	0.02
Dominican Republic	1	0.01
Mexican	1,143	11.80
Puerto Rican	3	0.03
South American	29	0.30
Argentinean	6	0.06
Bolivian	4	0.04
Chilean	1	0.01
Colombian	7	0.07
Ecuadorian	1	0.01
Paraguayan	0	<0.01
Peruvian	5	0.05
Uruguayan	0	<0.01
Venezuelan	0	<0.01
Other South American	5	0.05
Other Hispanic or Latino	135	1.39

Race*	Population	%
African-American/Black (82)	121	1.25
Not Hispanic (77)	110	1.14
Hispanic (5)	11	0.11
American Indian/Alaska Native (370)	590	6.09
Not Hispanic (293)	463	4.78
Hispanic (77)	127	1.31
Alaska Athabascan *(Ala. Nat.)* (0)	0	<0.01
Aleut *(Alaska Native)* (1)	1	0.01
Apache (1)	10	0.10
Arapaho (0)	0	<0.01
Blackfeet (4)	18	0.19
Canadian/French Am. Ind. (0)	1	0.01
Central American Ind. (0)	0	<0.01
Cherokee (24)	79	0.82
Cheyenne (0)	1	0.01
Chickasaw (2)	3	0.03
Chippewa (1)	3	0.03
Choctaw (11)	15	0.15
Colville (0)	0	<0.01
Comanche (3)	6	0.06
Cree (1)	2	0.02
Creek (0)	2	0.02
Crow (0)	0	<0.01
Delaware (0)	0	<0.01
Hopi (0)	0	<0.01
Houma (0)	0	<0.01
Inupiat *(Alaska Native)* (0)	0	<0.01
Iroquois (0)	2	0.02
Kiowa (0)	0	<0.01
Lumbee (1)	2	0.02
Menominee (0)	0	<0.01
Mexican American Ind. (18)	28	0.29
Navajo (3)	9	0.09
Osage (0)	0	<0.01
Ottawa (0)	0	<0.01
Paiute (65)	87	0.90
Pima (0)	0	<0.01
Potawatomi (2)	5	0.05
Pueblo (0)	0	<0.01
Puget Sound Salish (0)	4	0.04
Seminole (0)	0	<0.01
Shoshone (1)	2	0.02
Sioux (11)	16	0.17
South American Ind. (1)	1	0.01
Spanish American Ind. (0)	0	<0.01
Tlingit-Haida *(Alaska Native)* (1)	1	0.01
Tohono O'Odham (1)	1	0.01
Tsimshian *(Alaska Native)* (0)	0	<0.01
Ute (2)	2	0.02
Yakama (0)	0	<0.01
Yaqui (1)	1	0.01
Yuman (0)	0	<0.01
Yup'ik *(Alaska Native)* (0)	0	<0.01
Asian (78)	119	1.23
Not Hispanic (70)	92	0.95
Hispanic (8)	27	0.28
Bangladeshi (0)	0	<0.01
Bhutanese (0)	0	<0.01
Burmese (0)	0	<0.01
Cambodian (0)	0	<0.01
Chinese, ex. Taiwanese (25)	28	0.29
Filipino (17)	36	0.37
Hmong (0)	0	<0.01
Indian (14)	16	0.17
Indonesian (1)	4	0.04
Japanese (11)	24	0.25
Korean (1)	1	0.01
Laotian (0)	0	<0.01
Malaysian (0)	0	<0.01
Nepalese (0)	0	<0.01
Pakistani (0)	0	<0.01
Sri Lankan (0)	0	<0.01
Taiwanese (0)	0	<0.01
Thai (2)	2	0.02
Vietnamese (1)	1	0.01
Hawaii Native/Pacific Islander (21)	39	0.40
Not Hispanic (21)	30	0.31
Hispanic (0)	9	0.09
Fijian (0)	0	<0.01
Guamanian/Chamorro (4)	5	0.05
Marshallese (0)	0	<0.01
Native Hawaiian (12)	22	0.23
Samoan (3)	5	0.05
Tongan (0)	0	<0.01
White (8,084)	8,419	86.92
Not Hispanic (7,649)	7,860	81.15
Hispanic (435)	559	5.77

*Notes: † The Census 2010 population figure is used to calculate the percentages in the Hispanic Origin and Race categories. Ancestry percentages are based on the 2006-2010 American Community Survey population (not shown); ‡ Numbers in parentheses indicate the number of people reporting a single ancestry; * Numbers in parentheses indicate the number of persons reporting this race alone, not in combination with any other race; Please refer to the Explanation of Data for more information.*

Mono County

Population: 14,202

Ancestry	Population	%
Afghan (0)	0	<0.01
African, Sub-Saharan (0)	0	<0.01
African (0)	0	<0.01
Cape Verdean (0)	0	<0.01
Ethiopian (0)	0	<0.01
Ghanaian (0)	0	<0.01
Kenyan (0)	0	<0.01
Liberian (0)	0	<0.01
Nigerian (0)	0	<0.01
Senegalese (0)	0	<0.01
Sierra Leonean (0)	0	<0.01
Somalian (0)	0	<0.01
South African (0)	0	<0.01
Sudanese (0)	0	<0.01
Ugandan (0)	0	<0.01
Zimbabwean (0)	0	<0.01
Other Sub-Saharan African (0)	0	<0.01
Albanian (0)	0	<0.01
Alsatian (0)	0	<0.01
American (308)	308	2.22
Arab (42)	42	0.30
Arab (0)	0	<0.01
Egyptian (0)	0	<0.01
Iraqi (0)	0	<0.01
Jordanian (0)	0	<0.01
Lebanese (42)	42	0.30
Moroccan (0)	0	<0.01
Palestinian (0)	0	<0.01
Syrian (0)	0	<0.01
Other Arab (0)	0	<0.01
Armenian (122)	122	0.88
Assyrian/Chaldean/Syriac (0)	0	<0.01
Australian (0)	0	<0.01
Austrian (0)	50	0.36
Basque (0)	206	1.48
Belgian (0)	0	<0.01
Brazilian (0)	0	<0.01
British (30)	30	0.22
Bulgarian (0)	0	<0.01
Cajun (0)	0	<0.01
Canadian (0)	55	0.40
Carpatho Rusyn (0)	0	<0.01
Celtic (0)	0	<0.01
Croatian (16)	63	0.45
Cypriot (0)	0	<0.01
Czech (5)	12	0.09
Czechoslovakian (0)	0	<0.01
Danish (67)	130	0.93
Dutch (145)	222	1.60
Eastern European (0)	0	<0.01
English (505)	1,676	12.05
Estonian (0)	0	<0.01
European (404)	519	3.73
Finnish (0)	0	<0.01
French, ex. Basque (222)	548	3.94
French Canadian (0)	13	0.09
German (626)	1,898	13.65
German Russian (0)	0	<0.01
Greek (36)	36	0.26
Guyanese (0)	0	<0.01
Hungarian (0)	20	0.14
Icelander (35)	35	0.25
Iranian (20)	20	0.14
Irish (561)	1,792	12.89
Israeli (0)	0	<0.01
Italian (343)	1,027	7.39
Latvian (0)	0	<0.01
Lithuanian (134)	134	0.96
Luxemburger (0)	0	<0.01
Macedonian (0)	0	<0.01
Maltese (0)	0	<0.01
New Zealander (0)	0	<0.01
Northern European (0)	0	<0.01
Norwegian (36)	357	2.57
Pennsylvania German (53)	118	0.85
Polish (52)	282	2.03
Portuguese (56)	69	0.50
Romanian (0)	0	<0.01
Russian (234)	259	1.86
Scandinavian (0)	0	<0.01
Scotch-Irish (141)	486	3.50
Scottish (157)	379	2.73
Serbian (0)	0	<0.01
Slavic (0)	0	<0.01
Slovak (0)	0	<0.01
Slovene (0)	21	0.15
Soviet Union (0)	0	<0.01
Swedish (200)	434	3.12
Swiss (24)	134	0.96
Turkish (0)	0	<0.01
Ukrainian (0)	0	<0.01
Welsh (18)	86	0.62
West Indian, ex. Hispanic (0)	3	0.02
Bahamian (0)	0	<0.01
Barbadian (0)	0	<0.01
Belizean (0)	0	<0.01
Bermudan (0)	0	<0.01
British West Indian (0)	0	<0.01
Dutch West Indian (0)	0	<0.01
Haitian (0)	3	0.02
Jamaican (0)	0	<0.01
Trinidadian/Tobagonian (0)	0	<0.01
U.S. Virgin Islander (0)	0	<0.01
West Indian (0)	0	<0.01
Other West Indian (0)	0	<0.01
Yugoslavian (0)	20	0.14

Hispanic Origin	Population	%
Hispanic or Latino (of any race)	3,762	26.49
Central American, ex. Mexican	86	0.61
Costa Rican	7	0.05
Guatemalan	23	0.16
Honduran	14	0.10
Nicaraguan	3	0.02
Panamanian	2	0.01
Salvadoran	37	0.26
Other Central American	0	<0.01
Cuban	16	0.11
Dominican Republic	4	0.03
Mexican	3,261	22.96
Puerto Rican	34	0.24
South American	69	0.49
Argentinean	9	0.06
Bolivian	0	<0.01
Chilean	32	0.23
Colombian	14	0.10
Ecuadorian	2	0.01
Paraguayan	0	<0.01
Peruvian	8	0.06
Uruguayan	3	0.02
Venezuelan	1	0.01
Other South American	0	<0.01
Other Hispanic or Latino	292	2.06

Race*	Population	%
African-American/Black (47)	104	0.73
Not Hispanic (42)	91	0.64
Hispanic (5)	13	0.09
American Indian/Alaska Native (302)	433	3.05
Not Hispanic (239)	337	2.37
Hispanic (63)	96	0.68
Alaska Athabascan *(Ala. Nat.)* (0)	0	<0.01
Aleut *(Alaska Native)* (0)	0	<0.01
Apache (3)	9	0.06
Arapaho (0)	0	<0.01
Blackfeet (1)	1	0.01
Canadian/French Am. Ind. (0)	0	<0.01
Central American Ind. (0)	0	<0.01
Cherokee (7)	25	0.18
Cheyenne (0)	0	<0.01
Chickasaw (0)	0	<0.01
Chippewa (2)	2	0.01
Choctaw (2)	9	0.06
Colville (0)	0	<0.01
Comanche (0)	2	0.01
Cree (0)	1	0.01
Creek (4)	4	0.03
Crow (0)	0	<0.01
Delaware (0)	0	<0.01
Hopi (0)	4	0.03
Houma (0)	0	<0.01
Inupiat *(Alaska Native)* (1)	1	0.01
Iroquois (1)	2	0.01
Kiowa (0)	0	<0.01
Lumbee (0)	0	<0.01
Menominee (0)	1	0.01
Mexican American Ind. (12)	22	0.15
Navajo (1)	2	0.01
Osage (0)	0	<0.01
Ottawa (0)	0	<0.01
Paiute (117)	133	0.94
Pima (0)	0	<0.01
Potawatomi (0)	0	<0.01
Pueblo (0)	1	0.01
Puget Sound Salish (1)	1	0.01
Seminole (1)	1	0.01
Shoshone (6)	12	0.08
Sioux (9)	13	0.09
South American Ind. (1)	1	0.01
Spanish American Ind. (0)	0	<0.01
Tlingit-Haida *(Alaska Native)* (0)	2	0.01
Tohono O'Odham (0)	0	<0.01
Tsimshian *(Alaska Native)* (0)	0	<0.01
Ute (0)	0	<0.01
Yakama (0)	2	0.01
Yaqui (3)	3	0.02
Yuman (0)	0	<0.01
Yup'ik *(Alaska Native)* (0)	0	<0.01
Asian (192)	307	2.16
Not Hispanic (191)	284	2.00
Hispanic (1)	23	0.16
Bangladeshi (0)	0	<0.01
Bhutanese (0)	0	<0.01
Burmese (0)	0	<0.01
Cambodian (2)	4	0.03
Chinese, ex. Taiwanese (25)	52	0.37
Filipino (27)	74	0.52
Hmong (8)	8	0.06
Indian (12)	14	0.10
Indonesian (2)	4	0.03
Japanese (52)	95	0.67
Korean (27)	31	0.22
Laotian (0)	1	0.01
Malaysian (0)	1	0.01
Nepalese (0)	0	<0.01
Pakistani (0)	0	<0.01
Sri Lankan (2)	2	0.01
Taiwanese (0)	0	<0.01
Thai (9)	20	0.14
Vietnamese (4)	9	0.06
Hawaii Native/Pacific Islander (11)	36	0.25
Not Hispanic (11)	31	0.22
Hispanic (0)	5	0.04
Fijian (0)	0	<0.01
Guamanian/Chamorro (0)	0	<0.01
Marshallese (0)	0	<0.01
Native Hawaiian (4)	20	0.14
Samoan (2)	3	0.02
Tongan (0)	0	<0.01
White (11,697)	12,067	84.97
Not Hispanic (9,687)	9,905	69.74
Hispanic (2,010)	2,162	15.22

*Notes: † The Census 2010 population figure is used to calculate the percentages in the Hispanic Origin and Race categories. Ancestry percentages are based on the 2006-2010 American Community Survey population (not shown); ‡ Numbers in parentheses indicate the number of people reporting a single ancestry; * Numbers in parentheses indicate the number of persons reporting this race alone, not in combination with any other race; Please refer to the Explanation of Data for more information.*

Monterey County

Population: 415,057

Ancestry	Population	%
Afghan (134)	134	0.03
African, Sub-Saharan (1,168)	1,606	0.39
African (662)	999	0.25
Cape Verdean (14)	14	<0.01
Ethiopian (15)	51	0.01
Ghanaian (0)	0	<0.01
Kenyan (0)	3	<0.01
Liberian (0)	0	<0.01
Nigerian (60)	60	0.01
Senegalese (151)	151	0.04
Sierra Leonean (0)	0	<0.01
Somalian (0)	0	<0.01
South African (38)	38	0.01
Sudanese (213)	265	0.07
Ugandan (0)	0	<0.01
Zimbabwean (0)	10	<0.01
Other Sub-Saharan African (15)	15	<0.01
Albanian (0)	0	<0.01
Alsatian (0)	0	<0.01
American (6,346)	6,346	1.56
Arab (1,327)	2,088	0.51
Arab (140)	195	0.05
Egyptian (272)	272	0.07
Iraqi (128)	241	0.06
Jordanian (7)	99	0.02
Lebanese (113)	301	0.07
Moroccan (102)	149	0.04
Palestinian (54)	171	0.04
Syrian (136)	167	0.04
Other Arab (375)	493	0.12
Armenian (173)	370	0.09
Assyrian/Chaldean/Syriac (87)	99	0.02
Australian (63)	159	0.04
Austrian (266)	906	0.22
Basque (82)	255	0.06
Belgian (132)	363	0.09
Brazilian (79)	411	0.10
British (704)	1,300	0.32
Bulgarian (25)	40	0.01
Cajun (14)	30	0.01
Canadian (391)	771	0.19
Carpatho Rusyn (0)	0	<0.01
Celtic (19)	47	0.01
Croatian (78)	284	0.07
Cypriot (0)	0	<0.01
Czech (378)	1,296	0.32
Czechoslovakian (102)	221	0.05
Danish (795)	2,402	0.59
Dutch (817)	3,678	0.90
Eastern European (370)	479	0.12
English (7,244)	26,146	6.42
Estonian (63)	117	0.03
European (3,329)	4,070	1.00
Finnish (111)	463	0.11
French, ex. Basque (1,027)	7,840	1.92
French Canadian (552)	1,252	0.31
German (8,486)	31,768	7.80
German Russian (29)	65	0.02
Greek (395)	1,297	0.32
Guyanese (23)	27	0.01
Hungarian (393)	1,090	0.27
Icelander (33)	65	0.02
Iranian (248)	299	0.07
Irish (7,334)	27,887	6.84
Israeli (24)	63	0.02
Italian (7,299)	17,078	4.19
Latvian (11)	151	0.04
Lithuanian (126)	528	0.13
Luxemburger (14)	66	0.02
Macedonian (50)	50	0.01
Maltese (44)	120	0.03
New Zealander (25)	25	0.01
Northern European (787)	873	0.21
Norwegian (1,233)	3,599	0.88
Pennsylvania German (32)	101	0.02
Polish (1,278)	3,860	0.95
Portuguese (2,380)	5,168	1.27
Romanian (186)	292	0.07
Russian (980)	2,538	0.62
Scandinavian (361)	696	0.17
Scotch-Irish (2,277)	6,053	1.49
Scottish (1,397)	5,851	1.44
Serbian (44)	59	0.01
Slavic (115)	140	0.03
Slovak (123)	439	0.11
Slovene (25)	197	0.05
Soviet Union (0)	0	<0.01
Swedish (1,047)	4,154	1.02
Swiss (895)	3,051	0.75
Turkish (215)	268	0.07
Ukrainian (237)	450	0.11
Welsh (479)	2,120	0.52
West Indian, ex. Hispanic (306)	431	0.11
Bahamian (0)	0	<0.01
Barbadian (0)	26	0.01
Belizean (121)	127	0.03
Bermudan (0)	0	<0.01
British West Indian (0)	0	<0.01
Dutch West Indian (0)	0	<0.01
Haitian (0)	0	<0.01
Jamaican (165)	254	0.06
Trinidadian/Tobagonian (12)	12	<0.01
U.S. Virgin Islander (0)	0	<0.01
West Indian (8)	12	<0.01
Other West Indian (0)	0	<0.01
Yugoslavian (113)	259	0.06

Hispanic Origin	Population	%
Hispanic or Latino (of any race)	230,003	55.41
Central American, ex. Mexican	4,829	1.16
Costa Rican	81	0.02
Guatemalan	447	0.11
Honduran	337	0.08
Nicaraguan	168	0.04
Panamanian	314	0.08
Salvadoran	3,444	0.83
Other Central American	38	0.01
Cuban	364	0.09
Dominican Republic	72	0.02
Mexican	208,521	50.24
Puerto Rican	2,037	0.49
South American	1,374	0.33
Argentinean	180	0.04
Bolivian	55	0.01
Chilean	184	0.04
Colombian	297	0.07
Ecuadorian	110	0.03
Paraguayan	38	0.01
Peruvian	407	0.10
Uruguayan	9	<0.01
Venezuelan	71	0.02
Other South American	23	0.01
Other Hispanic or Latino	12,806	3.09

Race*	Population	%
African-American/Black (12,785)	16,554	3.99
Not Hispanic (11,300)	13,858	3.34
Hispanic (1,485)	2,696	0.65
American Indian/Alaska Native (5,464)	9,603	2.31
Not Hispanic (1,361)	3,496	0.84
Hispanic (4,103)	6,107	1.47
Alaska Athabascan *(Ala. Nat.)* (1)	7	<0.01
Aleut *(Alaska Native)* (3)	14	<0.01
Apache (114)	249	0.06
Arapaho (1)	11	<0.01
Blackfeet (16)	144	0.03
Canadian/French Am. Ind. (1)	11	<0.01
Central American Ind. (12)	32	0.01
Cherokee (208)	905	0.22
Cheyenne (2)	5	<0.01
Chickasaw (25)	52	0.01
Chippewa (17)	63	0.02
Choctaw (77)	191	0.05
Colville (3)	4	<0.01
Comanche (12)	36	0.01
Cree (2)	11	<0.01
Creek (36)	60	0.01
Crow (3)	9	<0.01
Delaware (4)	17	<0.01
Hopi (19)	33	0.01
Houma (1)	1	<0.01
Inupiat *(Alaska Native)* (6)	13	<0.01
Iroquois (11)	51	0.01
Kiowa (1)	6	<0.01
Lumbee (2)	6	<0.01
Menominee (2)	3	<0.01
Mexican American Ind. (1,549)	1,985	0.48
Navajo (71)	137	0.03
Osage (10)	20	<0.01
Ottawa (0)	1	<0.01
Paiute (20)	31	0.01
Pima (3)	10	<0.01
Potawatomi (15)	37	0.01
Pueblo (25)	63	0.02
Puget Sound Salish (3)	12	<0.01
Seminole (3)	27	0.01
Shoshone (17)	31	0.01
Sioux (31)	102	0.02
South American Ind. (9)	28	0.01
Spanish American Ind. (32)	57	0.01
Tlingit-Haida *(Alaska Native)* (6)	14	<0.01
Tohono O'Odham (6)	20	<0.01
Tsimshian *(Alaska Native)* (0)	1	<0.01
Ute (7)	12	<0.01
Yakama (0)	4	<0.01
Yaqui (35)	91	0.02
Yuman (7)	10	<0.01
Yup'ik *(Alaska Native)* (1)	9	<0.01
Asian (25,258)	33,552	8.08
Not Hispanic (23,777)	29,614	7.13
Hispanic (1,481)	3,938	0.95
Bangladeshi (9)	9	<0.01
Bhutanese (0)	0	<0.01
Burmese (43)	64	0.02
Cambodian (63)	81	0.02
Chinese, ex. Taiwanese (2,372)	3,445	0.83
Filipino (11,754)	15,916	3.83
Hmong (36)	38	0.01
Indian (1,590)	2,120	0.51
Indonesian (97)	159	0.04
Japanese (2,623)	4,711	1.14
Korean (2,816)	3,790	0.91
Laotian (17)	30	0.01
Malaysian (3)	23	0.01
Nepalese (64)	70	0.02
Pakistani (80)	132	0.03
Sri Lankan (22)	26	0.01
Taiwanese (131)	180	0.04
Thai (250)	367	0.09
Vietnamese (1,633)	1,953	0.47
Hawaii Native/Pacific Islander (2,071)	3,859	0.93
Not Hispanic (1,868)	3,202	0.77
Hispanic (203)	657	0.16
Fijian (283)	364	0.09
Guamanian/Chamorro (462)	866	0.21
Marshallese (3)	3	<0.01
Native Hawaiian (261)	993	0.24
Samoan (395)	664	0.16
Tongan (291)	334	0.08
White (230,717)	248,209	59.80
Not Hispanic (136,435)	144,345	34.78
Hispanic (94,282)	103,864	25.02

*Notes: † The Census 2010 population figure is used to calculate the percentages in the Hispanic Origin and Race categories. Ancestry percentages are based on the 2006-2010 American Community Survey population (not shown); ‡ Numbers in parentheses indicate the number of people reporting a single ancestry; * Numbers in parentheses indicate the number of persons reporting this race alone, not in combination with any other race; Please refer to the Explanation of Data for more information.*

Napa County

Population: 136,484

Ancestry	Population	%
Afghan (0)	0	<0.01
African, Sub-Saharan (220)	323	0.24
African (7)	58	0.04
Cape Verdean (36)	80	0.06
Ethiopian (0)	0	<0.01
Ghanaian (15)	15	0.01
Kenyan (12)	12	0.01
Liberian (0)	0	<0.01
Nigerian (70)	70	0.05
Senegalese (0)	0	<0.01
Sierra Leonean (0)	0	<0.01
Somalian (0)	0	<0.01
South African (8)	16	0.01
Sudanese (0)	0	<0.01
Ugandan (0)	0	<0.01
Zimbabwean (0)	0	<0.01
Other Sub-Saharan African (72)	72	0.05
Albanian (0)	0	<0.01
Alsatian (0)	0	<0.01
American (3,623)	3,623	2.70
Arab (186)	408	0.30
Arab (56)	144	0.11
Egyptian (41)	41	0.03
Iraqi (7)	7	0.01
Jordanian (20)	31	0.02
Lebanese (14)	76	0.06
Moroccan (0)	0	<0.01
Palestinian (0)	6	<0.01
Syrian (19)	74	0.06
Other Arab (29)	29	0.02
Armenian (88)	150	0.11
Assyrian/Chaldean/Syriac (26)	51	0.04
Australian (64)	80	0.06
Austrian (80)	416	0.31
Basque (32)	168	0.13
Belgian (111)	171	0.13
Brazilian (21)	40	0.03
British (441)	717	0.53
Bulgarian (0)	10	0.01
Cajun (0)	0	<0.01
Canadian (120)	379	0.28
Carpatho Rusyn (0)	0	<0.01
Celtic (10)	30	0.02
Croatian (45)	173	0.13
Cypriot (0)	0	<0.01
Czech (105)	297	0.22
Czechoslovakian (130)	219	0.16
Danish (320)	1,357	1.01
Dutch (556)	2,098	1.57
Eastern European (134)	134	0.10
English (3,328)	12,697	9.47
Estonian (0)	20	0.01
European (1,826)	2,087	1.56
Finnish (73)	303	0.23
French, ex. Basque (881)	5,115	3.82
French Canadian (125)	331	0.25
German (4,195)	18,264	13.62
German Russian (0)	0	<0.01
Greek (339)	800	0.60
Guyanese (0)	0	<0.01
Hungarian (177)	538	0.40
Icelander (0)	12	0.01
Iranian (44)	103	0.08
Irish (3,980)	14,289	10.66
Israeli (20)	20	0.01
Italian (3,084)	8,455	6.31
Latvian (0)	26	0.02
Lithuanian (0)	117	0.09
Luxemburger (14)	26	0.02
Macedonian (13)	13	0.01
Maltese (11)	11	0.01
New Zealander (87)	129	0.10
Northern European (255)	272	0.20
Norwegian (965)	2,463	1.84
Pennsylvania German (0)	38	0.03
Polish (311)	1,779	1.33
Portuguese (823)	2,283	1.70
Romanian (0)	69	0.05
Russian (652)	1,437	1.07
Scandinavian (365)	495	0.37
Scotch-Irish (760)	2,512	1.87
Scottish (797)	3,279	2.45
Serbian (37)	63	0.05
Slavic (9)	17	0.01
Slovak (19)	49	0.04
Slovene (74)	150	0.11
Soviet Union (0)	0	<0.01
Swedish (592)	2,636	1.97
Swiss (195)	906	0.68
Turkish (53)	125	0.09
Ukrainian (58)	248	0.19
Welsh (200)	1,132	0.84
West Indian, ex. Hispanic (26)	36	0.03
Bahamian (0)	0	<0.01
Barbadian (0)	0	<0.01
Belizean (0)	0	<0.01
Bermudan (0)	0	<0.01
British West Indian (0)	0	<0.01
Dutch West Indian (0)	0	<0.01
Haitian (0)	0	<0.01
Jamaican (19)	19	0.01
Trinidadian/Tobagonian (0)	10	0.01
U.S. Virgin Islander (0)	0	<0.01
West Indian (7)	7	0.01
Other West Indian (0)	0	<0.01
Yugoslavian (149)	294	0.22

Hispanic Origin	Population	%
Hispanic or Latino (of any race)	44,010	32.25
Central American, ex. Mexican	1,625	1.19
Costa Rican	67	0.05
Guatemalan	541	0.40
Honduran	84	0.06
Nicaraguan	197	0.14
Panamanian	33	0.02
Salvadoran	689	0.50
Other Central American	14	0.01
Cuban	152	0.11
Dominican Republic	23	0.02
Mexican	38,738	28.38
Puerto Rican	478	0.35
South American	508	0.37
Argentinean	64	0.05
Bolivian	12	0.01
Chilean	84	0.06
Colombian	110	0.08
Ecuadorian	27	0.02
Paraguayan	5	<0.01
Peruvian	158	0.12
Uruguayan	11	0.01
Venezuelan	27	0.02
Other South American	10	0.01
Other Hispanic or Latino	2,486	1.82

Race*	Population	%
African-American/Black (2,668)	3,488	2.56
Not Hispanic (2,440)	3,070	2.25
Hispanic (228)	418	0.31
American Indian/Alaska Native (1,058)	2,402	1.76
Not Hispanic (544)	1,476	1.08
Hispanic (514)	926	0.68
Alaska Athabascan *(Ala. Nat.)* (1)	2	<0.01
Aleut *(Alaska Native)* (0)	1	<0.01
Apache (15)	56	0.04
Arapaho (0)	0	<0.01
Blackfeet (13)	72	0.05
Canadian/French Am. Ind. (0)	4	<0.01
Central American Ind. (1)	2	<0.01
Cherokee (102)	417	0.31
Cheyenne (1)	1	<0.01
Chickasaw (6)	17	0.01
Chippewa (12)	32	0.02
Choctaw (39)	106	0.08
Colville (1)	3	<0.01
Comanche (0)	5	<0.01
Cree (3)	5	<0.01
Creek (7)	13	0.01
Crow (2)	15	0.01
Delaware (6)	9	0.01
Hopi (0)	2	<0.01
Houma (3)	3	<0.01
Inupiat *(Alaska Native)* (1)	5	<0.01
Iroquois (8)	22	0.02
Kiowa (1)	3	<0.01
Lumbee (1)	4	<0.01
Menominee (3)	6	<0.01
Mexican American Ind. (140)	198	0.15
Navajo (6)	27	0.02
Osage (11)	14	0.01
Ottawa (4)	10	0.01
Paiute (6)	9	0.01
Pima (3)	8	0.01
Potawatomi (14)	15	0.01
Pueblo (7)	9	0.01
Puget Sound Salish (0)	0	<0.01
Seminole (1)	7	0.01
Shoshone (0)	1	<0.01
Sioux (18)	46	0.03
South American Ind. (3)	6	<0.01
Spanish American Ind. (6)	12	0.01
Tlingit-Haida *(Alaska Native)* (5)	5	<0.01
Tohono O'Odham (0)	4	<0.01
Tsimshian *(Alaska Native)* (0)	0	<0.01
Ute (0)	1	<0.01
Yakama (0)	3	<0.01
Yaqui (3)	4	<0.01
Yuman (2)	4	<0.01
Yup'ik *(Alaska Native)* (9)	10	0.01
Asian (9,223)	11,116	8.14
Not Hispanic (8,986)	10,503	7.70
Hispanic (237)	613	0.45
Bangladeshi (11)	11	0.01
Bhutanese (0)	0	<0.01
Burmese (22)	36	0.03
Cambodian (28)	42	0.03
Chinese, ex. Taiwanese (837)	1,252	0.92
Filipino (5,824)	6,915	5.07
Hmong (10)	13	0.01
Indian (672)	801	0.59
Indonesian (34)	64	0.05
Japanese (498)	874	0.64
Korean (388)	516	0.38
Laotian (62)	71	0.05
Malaysian (2)	16	0.01
Nepalese (5)	6	<0.01
Pakistani (115)	121	0.09
Sri Lankan (7)	10	0.01
Taiwanese (28)	32	0.02
Thai (56)	79	0.06
Vietnamese (303)	382	0.28
Hawaii Native/Pacific Islander (372)	820	0.60
Not Hispanic (313)	657	0.48
Hispanic (59)	163	0.12
Fijian (17)	24	0.02
Guamanian/Chamorro (167)	263	0.19
Marshallese (0)	0	<0.01
Native Hawaiian (80)	267	0.20
Samoan (38)	81	0.06
Tongan (15)	25	0.02
White (97,525)	102,414	75.04
Not Hispanic (76,967)	79,611	58.33
Hispanic (20,558)	22,803	16.71

*Notes: † The Census 2010 population figure is used to calculate the percentages in the Hispanic Origin and Race categories. Ancestry percentages are based on the 2006-2010 American Community Survey population (not shown); ‡ Numbers in parentheses indicate the number of people reporting a single ancestry; * Numbers in parentheses indicate the number of persons reporting this race alone, not in combination with any other race; Please refer to the Explanation of Data for more information.*

Nevada County

Population: 98,764

Ancestry	Population	%
Afghan (0)	0	<0.01
African, Sub-Saharan (54)	76	0.08
African (0)	9	0.01
Cape Verdean (0)	0	<0.01
Ethiopian (0)	0	<0.01
Ghanaian (0)	0	<0.01
Kenyan (0)	0	<0.01
Liberian (0)	0	<0.01
Nigerian (0)	0	<0.01
Senegalese (0)	0	<0.01
Sierra Leonean (0)	0	<0.01
Somalian (0)	0	<0.01
South African (54)	67	0.07
Sudanese (0)	0	<0.01
Ugandan (0)	0	<0.01
Zimbabwean (0)	0	<0.01
Other Sub-Saharan African (0)	0	<0.01
Albanian (34)	34	0.03
Alsatian (0)	6	0.01
American (4,132)	4,132	4.21
Arab (6)	26	0.03
Arab (0)	0	<0.01
Egyptian (0)	0	<0.01
Iraqi (0)	0	<0.01
Jordanian (6)	6	0.01
Lebanese (0)	6	0.01
Moroccan (0)	0	<0.01
Palestinian (0)	0	<0.01
Syrian (0)	14	0.01
Other Arab (0)	0	<0.01
Armenian (284)	518	0.53
Assyrian/Chaldean/Syriac (0)	225	0.23
Australian (31)	83	0.08
Austrian (60)	298	0.30
Basque (37)	131	0.13
Belgian (12)	89	0.09
Brazilian (8)	17	0.02
British (397)	664	0.68
Bulgarian (0)	7	0.01
Cajun (0)	0	<0.01
Canadian (233)	631	0.64
Carpatho Rusyn (0)	0	<0.01
Celtic (47)	52	0.05
Croatian (61)	153	0.16
Cypriot (0)	0	<0.01
Czech (227)	474	0.48
Czechoslovakian (18)	154	0.16
Danish (302)	1,705	1.74
Dutch (555)	2,146	2.19
Eastern European (74)	74	0.08
English (5,057)	18,704	19.05
Estonian (8)	28	0.03
European (1,723)	2,047	2.08
Finnish (133)	633	0.64
French, ex. Basque (388)	4,264	4.34
French Canadian (281)	784	0.80
German (4,974)	19,910	20.28
German Russian (0)	0	<0.01
Greek (111)	505	0.51
Guyanese (15)	15	0.02
Hungarian (84)	385	0.39
Icelander (0)	20	0.02
Iranian (67)	72	0.07
Irish (4,208)	17,905	18.24
Israeli (0)	0	<0.01
Italian (2,849)	7,983	8.13
Latvian (27)	37	0.04
Lithuanian (70)	171	0.17
Luxemburger (13)	27	0.03
Macedonian (0)	0	<0.01
Maltese (0)	0	<0.01
New Zealander (47)	113	0.12
Northern European (369)	409	0.42
Norwegian (909)	2,624	2.67
Pennsylvania German (96)	102	0.10
Polish (444)	1,922	1.96
Portuguese (585)	2,037	2.07
Romanian (45)	167	0.17
Russian (318)	889	0.91
Scandinavian (242)	649	0.66
Scotch-Irish (1,272)	3,499	3.56
Scottish (1,231)	3,887	3.96
Serbian (10)	60	0.06
Slavic (0)	20	0.02
Slovak (34)	92	0.09
Slovene (4)	4	<0.01
Soviet Union (0)	0	<0.01
Swedish (758)	3,631	3.70
Swiss (354)	1,006	1.02
Turkish (0)	10	0.01
Ukrainian (55)	314	0.32
Welsh (282)	1,457	1.48
West Indian, ex. Hispanic (55)	74	0.08
Bahamian (0)	0	<0.01
Barbadian (0)	0	<0.01
Belizean (55)	55	0.06
Bermudan (0)	0	<0.01
British West Indian (0)	0	<0.01
Dutch West Indian (0)	19	0.02
Haitian (0)	0	<0.01
Jamaican (0)	0	<0.01
Trinidadian/Tobagonian (0)	0	<0.01
U.S. Virgin Islander (0)	0	<0.01
West Indian (0)	0	<0.01
Other West Indian (0)	0	<0.01
Yugoslavian (53)	413	0.42

Hispanic Origin	Population	%
Hispanic or Latino (of any race)	8,439	8.54
Central American, ex. Mexican	243	0.25
Costa Rican	17	0.02
Guatemalan	41	0.04
Honduran	19	0.02
Nicaraguan	41	0.04
Panamanian	21	0.02
Salvadoran	103	0.10
Other Central American	1	<0.01
Cuban	79	0.08
Dominican Republic	8	0.01
Mexican	6,652	6.74
Puerto Rican	276	0.28
South American	188	0.19
Argentinean	40	0.04
Bolivian	8	0.01
Chilean	38	0.04
Colombian	31	0.03
Ecuadorian	16	0.02
Paraguayan	2	<0.01
Peruvian	35	0.04
Uruguayan	4	<0.01
Venezuelan	8	0.01
Other South American	6	0.01
Other Hispanic or Latino	993	1.01

Race*	Population	%
African-American/Black (389)	767	0.78
Not Hispanic (341)	668	0.68
Hispanic (48)	99	0.10
American Indian/Alaska Native (1,044)	2,696	2.73
Not Hispanic (793)	2,136	2.16
Hispanic (251)	560	0.57
Alaska Athabascan *(Ala. Nat.)* (3)	4	<0.01
Aleut *(Alaska Native)* (2)	3	<0.01
Apache (24)	72	0.07
Arapaho (0)	2	<0.01
Blackfeet (23)	73	0.07
Canadian/French Am. Ind. (1)	8	0.01
Central American Ind. (3)	5	0.01
Cherokee (150)	609	0.62
Cheyenne (2)	9	0.01
Chickasaw (13)	28	0.03
Chippewa (23)	55	0.06
Choctaw (32)	124	0.13
Colville (0)	0	<0.01
Comanche (3)	16	0.02
Cree (0)	8	0.01
Creek (12)	24	0.02
Crow (2)	2	<0.01
Delaware (4)	11	0.01
Hopi (2)	4	<0.01
Houma (0)	0	<0.01
Inupiat *(Alaska Native)* (0)	1	<0.01
Iroquois (14)	42	0.04
Kiowa (2)	6	0.01
Lumbee (0)	0	<0.01
Menominee (0)	0	<0.01
Mexican American Ind. (45)	74	0.07
Navajo (15)	44	0.04
Osage (5)	16	0.02
Ottawa (0)	4	<0.01
Paiute (29)	43	0.04
Pima (1)	1	<0.01
Potawatomi (5)	18	0.02
Pueblo (6)	13	0.01
Puget Sound Salish (8)	15	0.02
Seminole (0)	4	<0.01
Shoshone (12)	15	0.02
Sioux (22)	60	0.06
South American Ind. (1)	7	0.01
Spanish American Ind. (3)	6	0.01
Tlingit-Haida *(Alaska Native)* (0)	9	0.01
Tohono O'Odham (0)	1	<0.01
Tsimshian *(Alaska Native)* (0)	2	<0.01
Ute (1)	13	0.01
Yakama (2)	4	<0.01
Yaqui (12)	22	0.02
Yuman (0)	0	<0.01
Yup'ik *(Alaska Native)* (0)	0	<0.01
Asian (1,187)	2,008	2.03
Not Hispanic (1,124)	1,855	1.88
Hispanic (63)	153	0.15
Bangladeshi (0)	0	<0.01
Bhutanese (0)	0	<0.01
Burmese (3)	3	<0.01
Cambodian (22)	24	0.02
Chinese, ex. Taiwanese (326)	476	0.48
Filipino (208)	467	0.47
Hmong (3)	4	<0.01
Indian (113)	197	0.20
Indonesian (14)	33	0.03
Japanese (248)	488	0.49
Korean (71)	118	0.12
Laotian (10)	15	0.02
Malaysian (3)	4	<0.01
Nepalese (12)	15	0.02
Pakistani (4)	13	0.01
Sri Lankan (0)	2	<0.01
Taiwanese (1)	3	<0.01
Thai (45)	74	0.07
Vietnamese (48)	77	0.08
Hawaii Native/Pacific Islander (110)	352	0.36
Not Hispanic (96)	295	0.30
Hispanic (14)	57	0.06
Fijian (6)	12	0.01
Guamanian/Chamorro (17)	39	0.04
Marshallese (1)	1	<0.01
Native Hawaiian (38)	184	0.19
Samoan (4)	20	0.02
Tongan (12)	15	0.02
White (90,233)	93,177	94.34
Not Hispanic (85,477)	87,733	88.83
Hispanic (4,756)	5,444	5.51

*Notes: † The Census 2010 population figure is used to calculate the percentages in the Hispanic Origin and Race categories. Ancestry percentages are based on the 2006-2010 American Community Survey population (not shown); ‡ Numbers in parentheses indicate the number of people reporting a single ancestry; * Numbers in parentheses indicate the number of persons reporting this race alone, not in combination with any other race; Please refer to the Explanation of Data for more information.*

Orange County

Population: 3,010,232

Ancestry	Population	%
Afghan (3,426)	3,614	0.12
African, Sub-Saharan (5,868)	7,587	0.26
African (2,441)	3,475	0.12
Cape Verdean (15)	15	<0.01
Ethiopian (997)	1,042	0.04
Ghanaian (116)	116	<0.01
Kenyan (165)	165	0.01
Liberian (0)	0	<0.01
Nigerian (628)	646	0.02
Senegalese (0)	17	<0.01
Sierra Leonean (0)	0	<0.01
Somalian (193)	193	0.01
South African (904)	1,407	0.05
Sudanese (74)	74	<0.01
Ugandan (0)	0	<0.01
Zimbabwean (19)	32	<0.01
Other Sub-Saharan African (316)	405	0.01
Albanian (367)	547	0.02
Alsatian (0)	68	<0.01
American (84,492)	84,492	2.85
Arab (20,915)	26,749	0.90
Arab (3,192)	4,126	0.14
Egyptian (5,635)	6,152	0.21
Iraqi (474)	675	0.02
Jordanian (1,919)	2,191	0.07
Lebanese (4,126)	6,364	0.21
Moroccan (358)	518	0.02
Palestinian (1,103)	1,391	0.05
Syrian (1,448)	2,132	0.07
Other Arab (2,660)	3,200	0.11
Armenian (6,675)	10,226	0.34
Assyrian/Chaldean/Syriac (487)	760	0.03
Australian (748)	1,702	0.06
Austrian (2,312)	7,636	0.26
Basque (440)	1,049	0.04
Belgian (1,164)	2,894	0.10
Brazilian (1,749)	2,502	0.08
British (8,255)	16,379	0.55
Bulgarian (537)	780	0.03
Cajun (83)	142	<0.01
Canadian (4,625)	9,565	0.32
Carpatho Rusyn (0)	13	<0.01
Celtic (308)	687	0.02
Croatian (1,352)	3,882	0.13
Cypriot (0)	0	<0.01
Czech (2,648)	9,262	0.31
Czechoslovakian (1,055)	2,537	0.09
Danish (4,360)	16,191	0.55
Dutch (11,725)	40,170	1.35
Eastern European (3,491)	4,021	0.14
English (68,867)	231,022	7.79
Estonian (98)	199	0.01
European (29,941)	35,307	1.19
Finnish (1,194)	4,108	0.14
French, ex. Basque (11,616)	67,853	2.29
French Canadian (4,761)	10,511	0.35
German (90,554)	330,533	11.15
German Russian (17)	25	<0.01
Greek (6,556)	13,213	0.45
Guyanese (87)	181	0.01
Hungarian (4,970)	15,034	0.51
Icelander (201)	536	0.02
Iranian (28,163)	30,670	1.03
Irish (63,692)	250,388	8.44
Israeli (1,198)	1,790	0.06
Italian (52,258)	133,374	4.50
Latvian (326)	782	0.03
Lithuanian (1,595)	4,878	0.16
Luxemburger (92)	274	0.01
Macedonian (154)	330	0.01
Maltese (200)	376	0.01
New Zealander (219)	415	0.01
Northern European (2,521)	3,065	0.10
Norwegian (11,809)	36,593	1.23
Pennsylvania German (261)	521	0.02
Polish (16,517)	53,033	1.79
Portuguese (4,318)	11,274	0.38
Romanian (6,273)	9,485	0.32
Russian (14,775)	34,615	1.17
Scandinavian (2,491)	5,815	0.20
Scotch-Irish (13,465)	36,929	1.25
Scottish (15,104)	50,476	1.70
Serbian (1,103)	1,981	0.07
Slavic (667)	1,563	0.05
Slovak (1,114)	3,112	0.10
Slovene (217)	904	0.03
Soviet Union (14)	14	<0.01
Swedish (11,294)	43,340	1.46
Swiss (1,705)	8,044	0.27
Turkish (1,897)	2,877	0.10
Ukrainian (2,385)	5,494	0.19
Welsh (3,158)	16,156	0.54
West Indian, ex. Hispanic (1,379)	2,249	0.08
Bahamian (0)	0	<0.01
Barbadian (55)	71	<0.01
Belizean (180)	313	0.01
Bermudan (0)	10	<0.01
British West Indian (81)	93	<0.01
Dutch West Indian (41)	60	<0.01
Haitian (52)	163	0.01
Jamaican (744)	1,025	0.03
Trinidadian/Tobagonian (106)	202	0.01
U.S. Virgin Islander (10)	10	<0.01
West Indian (94)	286	0.01
Other West Indian (16)	16	<0.01
Yugoslavian (1,498)	3,185	0.11

Hispanic Origin	Population	%
Hispanic or Latino (of any race)	1,012,973	33.65
Central American, ex. Mexican	49,115	1.63
Costa Rican	2,006	0.07
Guatemalan	16,365	0.54
Honduran	3,143	0.10
Nicaraguan	3,402	0.11
Panamanian	951	0.03
Salvadoran	22,694	0.75
Other Central American	554	0.02
Cuban	8,352	0.28
Dominican Republic	749	0.02
Mexican	858,068	28.51
Puerto Rican	11,090	0.37
South American	32,274	1.07
Argentinean	5,566	0.18
Bolivian	2,211	0.07
Chilean	1,898	0.06
Colombian	7,832	0.26
Ecuadorian	3,530	0.12
Paraguayan	96	<0.01
Peruvian	9,333	0.31
Uruguayan	475	0.02
Venezuelan	901	0.03
Other South American	432	0.01
Other Hispanic or Latino	53,325	1.77

Race*	Population	%
African-American/Black (50,744)	67,729	2.25
Not Hispanic (44,000)	55,919	1.86
Hispanic (6,744)	11,810	0.39
American Indian/Alaska Native (18,132)	37,580	1.25
Not Hispanic (6,216)	17,346	0.58
Hispanic (11,916)	20,234	0.67
Alaska Athabascan *(Ala. Nat.)* (9)	25	<0.01
Aleut *(Alaska Native)* (30)	62	<0.01
Apache (615)	1,542	0.05
Arapaho (12)	27	<0.01
Blackfeet (127)	726	0.02
Canadian/French Am. Ind. (39)	98	<0.01
Central American Ind. (51)	97	<0.01
Cherokee (1,026)	4,738	0.16
Cheyenne (31)	72	<0.01
Chickasaw (119)	273	0.01
Chippewa (153)	404	0.01
Choctaw (341)	1,057	0.04
Colville (14)	24	<0.01
Comanche (54)	160	0.01
Cree (11)	39	<0.01
Creek (116)	330	0.01
Crow (11)	43	<0.01
Delaware (24)	89	<0.01
Hopi (62)	146	<0.01
Houma (4)	5	<0.01
Inupiat *(Alaska Native)* (16)	33	<0.01
Iroquois (106)	364	0.01
Kiowa (29)	52	<0.01
Lumbee (40)	87	<0.01
Menominee (13)	21	<0.01
Mexican American Ind. (2,532)	3,646	0.12
Navajo (495)	994	0.03
Osage (70)	187	0.01
Ottawa (24)	42	<0.01
Paiute (37)	82	<0.01
Pima (60)	106	<0.01
Potawatomi (91)	182	0.01
Pueblo (166)	325	0.01
Puget Sound Salish (29)	39	<0.01
Seminole (32)	150	<0.01
Shoshone (81)	159	0.01
Sioux (210)	575	0.02
South American Ind. (93)	256	0.01
Spanish American Ind. (227)	350	0.01
Tlingit-Haida *(Alaska Native)* (23)	54	<0.01
Tohono O'Odham (54)	109	<0.01
Tsimshian *(Alaska Native)* (3)	17	<0.01
Ute (17)	50	<0.01
Yakama (6)	14	<0.01
Yaqui (247)	556	0.02
Yuman (53)	72	<0.01
Yup'ik *(Alaska Native)* (4)	14	<0.01
Asian (537,804)	597,748	19.86
Not Hispanic (532,477)	582,791	19.36
Hispanic (5,327)	14,957	0.50
Bangladeshi (863)	945	0.03
Bhutanese (1)	1	<0.01
Burmese (655)	855	0.03
Cambodian (5,718)	7,072	0.23
Chinese, ex. Taiwanese (65,923)	84,170	2.80
Filipino (71,060)	89,341	2.97
Hmong (1,102)	1,200	0.04
Indian (40,732)	45,044	1.50
Indonesian (2,631)	4,356	0.14
Japanese (32,276)	48,226	1.60
Korean (87,697)	93,710	3.11
Laotian (2,554)	3,053	0.10
Malaysian (270)	456	0.02
Nepalese (274)	300	0.01
Pakistani (5,318)	6,057	0.20
Sri Lankan (1,385)	1,523	0.05
Taiwanese (13,159)	14,670	0.49
Thai (4,015)	5,288	0.18
Vietnamese (183,766)	194,423	6.46
Hawaii Native/Pacific Islander (9,354)	19,484	0.65
Not Hispanic (8,357)	16,210	0.54
Hispanic (997)	3,274	0.11
Fijian (197)	296	0.01
Guamanian/Chamorro (1,382)	2,510	0.08
Marshallese (447)	495	0.02
Native Hawaiian (1,901)	6,256	0.21
Samoan (3,632)	5,205	0.17
Tongan (662)	883	0.03
White (1,830,758)	1,941,890	64.51
Not Hispanic (1,328,499)	1,392,127	46.25
Hispanic (502,259)	549,763	18.26

*Notes: † The Census 2010 population figure is used to calculate the percentages in the Hispanic Origin and Race categories. Ancestry percentages are based on the 2006-2010 American Community Survey population (not shown); ‡ Numbers in parentheses indicate the number of people reporting a single ancestry; * Numbers in parentheses indicate the number of persons reporting this race alone, not in combination with any other race; Please refer to the Explanation of Data for more information.*

Placer County

Population: 348,432

Ancestry	Population	%
Afghan (244)	244	0.07
African, Sub-Saharan (477)	619	0.18
African (159)	265	0.08
Cape Verdean (9)	9	<0.01
Ethiopian (0)	0	<0.01
Ghanaian (48)	48	0.01
Kenyan (0)	0	<0.01
Liberian (0)	0	<0.01
Nigerian (11)	11	<0.01
Senegalese (0)	0	<0.01
Sierra Leonean (0)	0	<0.01
Somalian (0)	0	<0.01
South African (202)	224	0.07
Sudanese (48)	48	0.01
Ugandan (0)	14	<0.01
Zimbabwean (0)	0	<0.01
Other Sub-Saharan African (0)	0	<0.01
Albanian (26)	26	0.01
Alsatian (15)	27	0.01
American (12,633)	12,633	3.75
Arab (800)	1,618	0.48
Arab (194)	274	0.08
Egyptian (294)	346	0.10
Iraqi (14)	155	0.05
Jordanian (87)	87	0.03
Lebanese (158)	586	0.17
Moroccan (0)	0	<0.01
Palestinian (36)	52	0.02
Syrian (0)	61	0.02
Other Arab (17)	57	0.02
Armenian (321)	661	0.20
Assyrian/Chaldean/Syriac (74)	167	0.05
Australian (193)	328	0.10
Austrian (230)	1,079	0.32
Basque (95)	249	0.07
Belgian (162)	388	0.12
Brazilian (114)	255	0.08
British (1,111)	2,006	0.60
Bulgarian (124)	134	0.04
Cajun (21)	64	0.02
Canadian (399)	1,167	0.35
Carpatho Rusyn (0)	0	<0.01
Celtic (0)	6	<0.01
Croatian (168)	378	0.11
Cypriot (0)	0	<0.01
Czech (489)	1,402	0.42
Czechoslovakian (132)	293	0.09
Danish (910)	4,276	1.27
Dutch (1,173)	6,073	1.80
Eastern European (272)	323	0.10
English (14,112)	52,266	15.53
Estonian (12)	46	0.01
European (7,387)	8,278	2.46
Finnish (559)	1,352	0.40
French, ex. Basque (1,781)	13,035	3.87
French Canadian (500)	1,359	0.40
German (17,973)	66,825	19.86
German Russian (0)	21	0.01
Greek (995)	2,911	0.87
Guyanese (0)	0	<0.01
Hungarian (282)	1,039	0.31
Icelander (24)	38	0.01
Iranian (1,490)	1,735	0.52
Irish (12,236)	52,745	15.68
Israeli (11)	11	<0.01
Italian (9,187)	26,493	7.87
Latvian (69)	89	0.03
Lithuanian (181)	708	0.21
Luxemburger (11)	20	0.01
Macedonian (81)	81	0.02
Maltese (99)	309	0.09
New Zealander (57)	79	0.02
Northern European (611)	611	0.18
Norwegian (3,442)	9,863	2.93
Pennsylvania German (58)	228	0.07
Polish (1,567)	6,939	2.06
Portuguese (2,308)	6,782	2.02
Romanian (642)	860	0.26
Russian (1,356)	3,414	1.01
Scandinavian (683)	1,240	0.37
Scotch-Irish (2,447)	6,747	2.01
Scottish (2,859)	10,580	3.14
Serbian (0)	75	0.02
Slavic (34)	200	0.06
Slovak (156)	345	0.10
Slovene (124)	225	0.07
Soviet Union (0)	0	<0.01
Swedish (2,440)	9,307	2.77
Swiss (554)	2,050	0.61
Turkish (96)	144	0.04
Ukrainian (1,920)	2,466	0.73
Welsh (471)	2,695	0.80
West Indian, ex. Hispanic (105)	193	0.06
Bahamian (0)	0	<0.01
Barbadian (0)	28	0.01
Belizean (0)	0	<0.01
Bermudan (0)	0	<0.01
British West Indian (0)	0	<0.01
Dutch West Indian (0)	18	0.01
Haitian (0)	14	<0.01
Jamaican (56)	84	0.02
Trinidadian/Tobagonian (15)	15	<0.01
U.S. Virgin Islander (0)	0	<0.01
West Indian (29)	29	0.01
Other West Indian (5)	5	<0.01
Yugoslavian (472)	929	0.28

Hispanic Origin	Population	%
Hispanic or Latino (of any race)	44,710	12.83
Central American, ex. Mexican	2,113	0.61
Costa Rican	122	0.04
Guatemalan	486	0.14
Honduran	105	0.03
Nicaraguan	338	0.10
Panamanian	112	0.03
Salvadoran	926	0.27
Other Central American	24	0.01
Cuban	376	0.11
Dominican Republic	63	0.02
Mexican	33,954	9.74
Puerto Rican	1,552	0.45
South American	1,273	0.37
Argentinean	207	0.06
Bolivian	50	0.01
Chilean	177	0.05
Colombian	299	0.09
Ecuadorian	69	0.02
Paraguayan	7	<0.01
Peruvian	357	0.10
Uruguayan	16	<0.01
Venezuelan	74	0.02
Other South American	17	<0.01
Other Hispanic or Latino	5,379	1.54

Race*	Population	%
African-American/Black (4,751)	7,237	2.08
Not Hispanic (4,427)	6,466	1.86
Hispanic (324)	771	0.22
American Indian/Alaska Native (3,011)	7,287	2.09
Not Hispanic (2,080)	5,346	1.53
Hispanic (931)	1,941	0.56
Alaska Athabascan *(Ala. Nat.)* (9)	14	<0.01
Aleut *(Alaska Native)* (10)	17	<0.01
Apache (91)	201	0.06
Arapaho (5)	13	<0.01
Blackfeet (26)	171	0.05
Canadian/French Am. Ind. (3)	17	<0.01
Central American Ind. (6)	7	<0.01
Cherokee (389)	1,533	0.44
Cheyenne (9)	21	0.01
Chickasaw (41)	99	0.03
Chippewa (51)	116	0.03
Choctaw (124)	358	0.10
Colville (5)	10	<0.01
Comanche (10)	25	0.01
Cree (2)	16	<0.01
Creek (31)	87	0.02
Crow (2)	13	<0.01
Delaware (3)	23	0.01
Hopi (8)	28	0.01
Houma (1)	2	<0.01
Inupiat *(Alaska Native)* (6)	8	<0.01
Iroquois (28)	81	0.02
Kiowa (2)	6	<0.01
Lumbee (10)	25	0.01
Menominee (0)	9	<0.01
Mexican American Ind. (132)	224	0.06
Navajo (39)	86	0.02
Osage (6)	21	0.01
Ottawa (1)	12	<0.01
Paiute (28)	53	0.02
Pima (5)	10	<0.01
Potawatomi (30)	53	0.02
Pueblo (26)	58	0.02
Puget Sound Salish (3)	15	<0.01
Seminole (1)	17	<0.01
Shoshone (16)	40	0.01
Sioux (82)	178	0.05
South American Ind. (7)	21	0.01
Spanish American Ind. (17)	23	0.01
Tlingit-Haida *(Alaska Native)* (13)	25	0.01
Tohono O'Odham (4)	11	<0.01
Tsimshian *(Alaska Native)* (0)	0	<0.01
Ute (10)	12	<0.01
Yakama (1)	4	<0.01
Yaqui (22)	46	0.01
Yuman (8)	16	<0.01
Yup'ik *(Alaska Native)* (4)	6	<0.01
Asian (20,435)	27,034	7.76
Not Hispanic (19,963)	25,540	7.33
Hispanic (472)	1,494	0.43
Bangladeshi (18)	26	0.01
Bhutanese (0)	0	<0.01
Burmese (52)	70	0.02
Cambodian (97)	147	0.04
Chinese, ex. Taiwanese (2,783)	4,207	1.21
Filipino (6,534)	9,138	2.62
Hmong (103)	131	0.04
Indian (4,370)	4,768	1.37
Indonesian (123)	199	0.06
Japanese (1,965)	3,735	1.07
Korean (1,301)	1,810	0.52
Laotian (102)	142	0.04
Malaysian (15)	35	0.01
Nepalese (19)	20	0.01
Pakistani (272)	312	0.09
Sri Lankan (62)	69	0.02
Taiwanese (162)	208	0.06
Thai (144)	294	0.08
Vietnamese (1,381)	1,686	0.48
Hawaii Native/Pacific Islander (778)	1,963	0.56
Not Hispanic (697)	1,611	0.46
Hispanic (81)	352	0.10
Fijian (86)	108	0.03
Guamanian/Chamorro (190)	402	0.12
Marshallese (1)	3	<0.01
Native Hawaiian (223)	840	0.24
Samoan (75)	167	0.05
Tongan (44)	64	0.02
White (290,977)	304,752	87.46
Not Hispanic (265,294)	275,177	78.98
Hispanic (25,683)	29,575	8.49

*Notes: † The Census 2010 population figure is used to calculate the percentages in the Hispanic Origin and Race categories. Ancestry percentages are based on the 2006-2010 American Community Survey population (not shown); ‡ Numbers in parentheses indicate the number of people reporting a single ancestry; * Numbers in parentheses indicate the number of persons reporting this race alone, not in combination with any other race; Please refer to the Explanation of Data for more information.*

Plumas County

Population: 20,007

Ancestry	Population	%
Afghan (0)	0	<0.01
African, Sub-Saharan (10)	10	0.05
African (10)	10	0.05
Cape Verdean (0)	0	<0.01
Ethiopian (0)	0	<0.01
Ghanaian (0)	0	<0.01
Kenyan (0)	0	<0.01
Liberian (0)	0	<0.01
Nigerian (0)	0	<0.01
Senegalese (0)	0	<0.01
Sierra Leonean (0)	0	<0.01
Somalian (0)	0	<0.01
South African (0)	0	<0.01
Sudanese (0)	0	<0.01
Ugandan (0)	0	<0.01
Zimbabwean (0)	0	<0.01
Other Sub-Saharan African (0)	0	<0.01
Albanian (0)	0	<0.01
Alsatian (0)	0	<0.01
American (694)	694	3.40
Arab (80)	80	0.39
Arab (0)	0	<0.01
Egyptian (0)	0	<0.01
Iraqi (0)	0	<0.01
Jordanian (0)	0	<0.01
Lebanese (66)	66	0.32
Moroccan (0)	0	<0.01
Palestinian (14)	14	0.07
Syrian (0)	0	<0.01
Other Arab (0)	0	<0.01
Armenian (0)	33	0.16
Assyrian/Chaldean/Syriac (0)	0	<0.01
Australian (0)	0	<0.01
Austrian (0)	36	0.18
Basque (6)	15	0.07
Belgian (0)	0	<0.01
Brazilian (0)	0	<0.01
British (61)	151	0.74
Bulgarian (9)	36	0.18
Cajun (0)	0	<0.01
Canadian (67)	67	0.33
Carpatho Rusyn (0)	0	<0.01
Celtic (10)	10	0.05
Croatian (0)	0	<0.01
Cypriot (0)	0	<0.01
Czech (124)	245	1.20
Czechoslovakian (8)	8	0.04
Danish (86)	148	0.73
Dutch (96)	653	3.20
Eastern European (0)	0	<0.01
English (933)	3,080	15.10
Estonian (15)	15	0.07
European (959)	1,143	5.61
Finnish (265)	299	1.47
French, ex. Basque (134)	996	4.88
French Canadian (78)	133	0.65
German (888)	3,760	18.44
German Russian (0)	34	0.17
Greek (0)	0	<0.01
Guyanese (0)	0	<0.01
Hungarian (78)	130	0.64
Icelander (0)	0	<0.01
Iranian (0)	0	<0.01
Irish (775)	3,133	15.36
Israeli (0)	0	<0.01
Italian (813)	1,436	7.04
Latvian (0)	0	<0.01
Lithuanian (0)	12	0.06
Luxemburger (0)	0	<0.01
Macedonian (0)	0	<0.01
Maltese (0)	0	<0.01
New Zealander (0)	0	<0.01
Northern European (51)	51	0.25
Norwegian (102)	314	1.54
Pennsylvania German (0)	11	0.05
Polish (57)	168	0.82
Portuguese (103)	277	1.36
Romanian (0)	0	<0.01
Russian (123)	288	1.41
Scandinavian (0)	49	0.24
Scotch-Irish (255)	587	2.88
Scottish (360)	1,038	5.09
Serbian (0)	16	0.08
Slavic (0)	10	0.05
Slovak (0)	0	<0.01
Slovene (0)	15	0.07
Soviet Union (0)	0	<0.01
Swedish (314)	357	1.75
Swiss (39)	152	0.75
Turkish (0)	0	<0.01
Ukrainian (23)	32	0.16
Welsh (11)	153	0.75
West Indian, ex. Hispanic (0)	0	<0.01
Bahamian (0)	0	<0.01
Barbadian (0)	0	<0.01
Belizean (0)	0	<0.01
Bermudan (0)	0	<0.01
British West Indian (0)	0	<0.01
Dutch West Indian (0)	0	<0.01
Haitian (0)	0	<0.01
Jamaican (0)	0	<0.01
Trinidadian/Tobagonian (0)	0	<0.01
U.S. Virgin Islander (0)	0	<0.01
West Indian (0)	0	<0.01
Other West Indian (0)	0	<0.01
Yugoslavian (64)	76	0.37

Hispanic Origin	Population	%
Hispanic or Latino (of any race)	1,605	8.02
Central American, ex. Mexican	25	0.12
Costa Rican	2	0.01
Guatemalan	2	0.01
Honduran	2	0.01
Nicaraguan	6	0.03
Panamanian	1	<0.01
Salvadoran	12	0.06
Other Central American	0	<0.01
Cuban	14	0.07
Dominican Republic	0	<0.01
Mexican	1,285	6.42
Puerto Rican	35	0.17
South American	20	0.10
Argentinean	4	0.02
Bolivian	0	<0.01
Chilean	0	<0.01
Colombian	7	0.03
Ecuadorian	5	0.02
Paraguayan	0	<0.01
Peruvian	2	0.01
Uruguayan	0	<0.01
Venezuelan	1	<0.01
Other South American	1	<0.01
Other Hispanic or Latino	226	1.13

Race*	Population	%
African-American/Black (192)	289	1.44
Not Hispanic (181)	268	1.34
Hispanic (11)	21	0.10
American Indian/Alaska Native (539)	988	4.94
Not Hispanic (460)	850	4.25
Hispanic (79)	138	0.69
Alaska Athabascan *(Ala. Nat.)* (0)	0	<0.01
Aleut *(Alaska Native)* (0)	0	<0.01
Apache (9)	18	0.09
Arapaho (3)	4	0.02
Blackfeet (4)	21	0.10
Canadian/French Am. Ind. (1)	3	0.01
Central American Ind. (0)	0	<0.01
Cherokee (39)	151	0.75
Cheyenne (0)	0	<0.01
Chickasaw (0)	3	0.01
Chippewa (13)	29	0.14
Choctaw (16)	33	0.16
Colville (0)	0	<0.01
Comanche (0)	3	0.01
Cree (4)	5	0.02
Creek (5)	8	0.04
Crow (1)	6	0.03
Delaware (0)	1	<0.01
Hopi (0)	0	<0.01
Houma (0)	0	<0.01
Inupiat *(Alaska Native)* (1)	1	<0.01
Iroquois (1)	6	0.03
Kiowa (0)	0	<0.01
Lumbee (1)	1	<0.01
Menominee (0)	0	<0.01
Mexican American Ind. (9)	16	0.08
Navajo (8)	13	0.06
Osage (0)	1	<0.01
Ottawa (0)	0	<0.01
Paiute (12)	13	0.06
Pima (2)	4	0.02
Potawatomi (3)	8	0.04
Pueblo (1)	9	0.04
Puget Sound Salish (0)	0	<0.01
Seminole (0)	0	<0.01
Shoshone (9)	15	0.07
Sioux (7)	15	0.07
South American Ind. (1)	1	<0.01
Spanish American Ind. (0)	0	<0.01
Tlingit-Haida *(Alaska Native)* (2)	2	0.01
Tohono O'Odham (8)	8	0.04
Tsimshian *(Alaska Native)* (0)	0	<0.01
Ute (3)	3	0.01
Yakama (0)	0	<0.01
Yaqui (7)	12	0.06
Yuman (1)	3	0.01
Yup'ik *(Alaska Native)* (0)	0	<0.01
Asian (134)	258	1.29
Not Hispanic (127)	233	1.16
Hispanic (7)	25	0.12
Bangladeshi (0)	0	<0.01
Bhutanese (0)	0	<0.01
Burmese (0)	5	0.02
Cambodian (1)	1	<0.01
Chinese, ex. Taiwanese (26)	46	0.23
Filipino (39)	93	0.46
Hmong (1)	4	0.02
Indian (16)	21	0.10
Indonesian (0)	0	<0.01
Japanese (15)	57	0.28
Korean (12)	20	0.10
Laotian (1)	1	<0.01
Malaysian (0)	0	<0.01
Nepalese (0)	0	<0.01
Pakistani (0)	0	<0.01
Sri Lankan (0)	0	<0.01
Taiwanese (1)	2	0.01
Thai (3)	3	0.01
Vietnamese (7)	11	0.05
Hawaii Native/Pacific Islander (18)	43	0.21
Not Hispanic (18)	42	0.21
Hispanic (0)	1	<0.01
Fijian (1)	4	0.02
Guamanian/Chamorro (2)	2	0.01
Marshallese (1)	1	<0.01
Native Hawaiian (9)	21	0.10
Samoan (3)	13	0.06
Tongan (0)	0	<0.01
White (17,797)	18,493	92.43
Not Hispanic (17,015)	17,583	87.88
Hispanic (782)	910	4.55

*Notes: † The Census 2010 population figure is used to calculate the percentages in the Hispanic Origin and Race categories. Ancestry percentages are based on the 2006-2010 American Community Survey population (not shown); ‡ Numbers in parentheses indicate the number of people reporting a single ancestry; * Numbers in parentheses indicate the number of persons reporting this race alone, not in combination with any other race; Please refer to the Explanation of Data for more information.*

Riverside County

Population: 2,189,641

Ancestry	Population	%
Afghan (867)	1,046	0.05
African, Sub-Saharan (8,427)	10,578	0.50
African (5,836)	7,567	0.36
Cape Verdean (32)	66	<0.01
Ethiopian (320)	341	0.02
Ghanaian (0)	0	<0.01
Kenyan (234)	275	0.01
Liberian (29)	29	<0.01
Nigerian (1,386)	1,413	0.07
Senegalese (7)	7	<0.01
Sierra Leonean (12)	12	<0.01
Somalian (10)	56	<0.01
South African (221)	298	0.01
Sudanese (113)	113	0.01
Ugandan (113)	131	0.01
Zimbabwean (30)	98	<0.01
Other Sub-Saharan African (84)	172	0.01
Albanian (107)	202	0.01
Alsatian (0)	12	<0.01
American (53,424)	53,424	2.53
Arab (9,104)	11,743	0.56
Arab (1,199)	1,531	0.07
Egyptian (2,491)	2,896	0.14
Iraqi (507)	643	0.03
Jordanian (855)	929	0.04
Lebanese (2,424)	3,364	0.16
Moroccan (231)	290	0.01
Palestinian (546)	670	0.03
Syrian (238)	572	0.03
Other Arab (613)	848	0.04
Armenian (1,263)	2,665	0.13
Assyrian/Chaldean/Syriac (194)	411	0.02
Australian (261)	873	0.04
Austrian (1,325)	4,326	0.21
Basque (428)	816	0.04
Belgian (390)	1,495	0.07
Brazilian (722)	1,193	0.06
British (4,026)	6,389	0.30
Bulgarian (259)	395	0.02
Cajun (94)	160	0.01
Canadian (3,857)	7,046	0.33
Carpatho Rusyn (0)	0	<0.01
Celtic (77)	180	0.01
Croatian (767)	1,702	0.08
Cypriot (0)	0	<0.01
Czech (1,615)	5,028	0.24
Czechoslovakian (720)	1,485	0.07
Danish (3,136)	9,948	0.47
Dutch (8,056)	30,919	1.47
Eastern European (890)	1,013	0.05
English (47,746)	152,574	7.23
Estonian (89)	154	0.01
European (19,103)	24,340	1.15
Finnish (1,063)	2,922	0.14
French, ex. Basque (8,325)	49,353	2.34
French Canadian (4,555)	10,131	0.48
German (62,552)	220,860	10.47
German Russian (21)	31	<0.01
Greek (2,749)	6,163	0.29
Guyanese (144)	215	0.01
Hungarian (3,245)	8,533	0.40
Icelander (173)	312	0.01
Iranian (2,960)	3,575	0.17
Irish (41,515)	161,809	7.67
Israeli (315)	478	0.02
Italian (31,637)	82,762	3.92
Latvian (235)	375	0.02
Lithuanian (968)	2,430	0.12
Luxemburger (97)	169	0.01
Macedonian (102)	169	0.01
Maltese (335)	538	0.03
New Zealander (108)	268	0.01
Northern European (1,127)	1,231	0.06
Norwegian (9,005)	25,328	1.20
Pennsylvania German (281)	619	0.03
Polish (10,302)	29,431	1.40
Portuguese (3,329)	8,421	0.40
Romanian (2,940)	4,720	0.22
Russian (5,996)	14,684	0.70
Scandinavian (1,948)	3,935	0.19
Scotch-Irish (8,925)	25,005	1.19
Scottish (8,407)	30,351	1.44
Serbian (218)	660	0.03
Slavic (290)	731	0.03
Slovak (702)	1,461	0.07
Slovene (128)	408	0.02
Soviet Union (34)	34	<0.01
Swedish (7,464)	26,905	1.28
Swiss (1,083)	4,031	0.19
Turkish (201)	485	0.02
Ukrainian (1,275)	2,825	0.13
Welsh (2,234)	10,024	0.48
West Indian, ex. Hispanic (2,605)	4,206	0.20
Bahamian (0)	19	<0.01
Barbadian (22)	38	<0.01
Belizean (456)	708	0.03
Bermudan (13)	13	<0.01
British West Indian (93)	232	0.01
Dutch West Indian (25)	126	0.01
Haitian (313)	549	0.03
Jamaican (1,280)	1,922	0.09
Trinidadian/Tobagonian (173)	198	0.01
U.S. Virgin Islander (0)	0	<0.01
West Indian (230)	401	0.02
Other West Indian (0)	0	<0.01
Yugoslavian (679)	1,652	0.08

Hispanic Origin	Population	%
Hispanic or Latino (of any race)	995,257	45.45
Central American, ex. Mexican	41,151	1.88
Costa Rican	1,383	0.06
Guatemalan	14,388	0.66
Honduran	2,452	0.11
Nicaraguan	3,631	0.17
Panamanian	1,221	0.06
Salvadoran	17,616	0.80
Other Central American	460	0.02
Cuban	5,825	0.27
Dominican Republic	720	0.03
Mexican	865,117	39.51
Puerto Rican	13,622	0.62
South American	15,322	0.70
Argentinean	2,367	0.11
Bolivian	630	0.03
Chilean	1,080	0.05
Colombian	3,898	0.18
Ecuadorian	2,103	0.10
Paraguayan	55	<0.01
Peruvian	4,161	0.19
Uruguayan	270	0.01
Venezuelan	542	0.02
Other South American	216	0.01
Other Hispanic or Latino	53,500	2.44

Race*	Population	%
African-American/Black (140,543)	166,032	7.58
Not Hispanic (130,823)	148,460	6.78
Hispanic (9,720)	17,572	0.80
American Indian/Alaska Native (23,710)	43,724	2.00
Not Hispanic (10,931)	22,543	1.03
Hispanic (12,779)	21,181	0.97
Alaska Athabascan *(Ala. Nat.)* (40)	54	<0.01
Aleut *(Alaska Native)* (33)	60	<0.01
Apache (720)	1,571	0.07
Arapaho (17)	38	<0.01
Blackfeet (138)	828	0.04
Canadian/French Am. Ind. (35)	109	<0.01
Central American Ind. (107)	174	0.01
Cherokee (1,141)	4,646	0.21
Cheyenne (24)	75	<0.01
Chickasaw (138)	283	0.01
Chippewa (213)	471	0.02
Choctaw (468)	1,300	0.06
Colville (10)	13	<0.01
Comanche (72)	160	0.01
Cree (8)	46	<0.01
Creek (169)	392	0.02
Crow (15)	47	<0.01
Delaware (39)	85	<0.01
Hopi (96)	170	0.01
Houma (4)	5	<0.01
Inupiat *(Alaska Native)* (26)	47	<0.01
Iroquois (103)	315	0.01
Kiowa (24)	38	<0.01
Lumbee (39)	75	<0.01
Menominee (15)	22	<0.01
Mexican American Ind. (2,218)	3,332	0.15
Navajo (610)	1,186	0.05
Osage (45)	129	0.01
Ottawa (29)	59	<0.01
Paiute (74)	144	0.01
Pima (95)	202	0.01
Potawatomi (67)	185	0.01
Pueblo (183)	337	0.02
Puget Sound Salish (41)	50	<0.01
Seminole (56)	210	0.01
Shoshone (42)	92	<0.01
Sioux (274)	657	0.03
South American Ind. (93)	179	0.01
Spanish American Ind. (170)	273	0.01
Tlingit-Haida *(Alaska Native)* (35)	65	<0.01
Tohono O'Odham (129)	190	0.01
Tsimshian *(Alaska Native)* (1)	6	<0.01
Ute (22)	78	<0.01
Yakama (4)	16	<0.01
Yaqui (370)	694	0.03
Yuman (123)	165	0.01
Yup'ik *(Alaska Native)* (2)	17	<0.01
Asian (130,468)	161,542	7.38
Not Hispanic (125,921)	148,597	6.79
Hispanic (4,547)	12,945	0.59
Bangladeshi (343)	413	0.02
Bhutanese (1)	1	<0.01
Burmese (155)	215	0.01
Cambodian (2,820)	3,491	0.16
Chinese, ex. Taiwanese (15,341)	20,873	0.95
Filipino (51,003)	65,440	2.99
Hmong (1,223)	1,369	0.06
Indian (11,509)	13,588	0.62
Indonesian (1,153)	2,004	0.09
Japanese (5,196)	11,328	0.52
Korean (12,189)	14,384	0.66
Laotian (2,628)	3,173	0.14
Malaysian (72)	151	0.01
Nepalese (90)	98	<0.01
Pakistani (2,350)	2,693	0.12
Sri Lankan (488)	555	0.03
Taiwanese (1,759)	2,068	0.09
Thai (1,965)	2,880	0.13
Vietnamese (14,623)	16,986	0.78
Hawaii Native/Pacific Islander (6,874)	14,108	0.64
Not Hispanic (5,849)	10,911	0.50
Hispanic (1,025)	3,197	0.15
Fijian (189)	251	0.01
Guamanian/Chamorro (1,615)	2,819	0.13
Marshallese (9)	11	<0.01
Native Hawaiian (1,246)	4,187	0.19
Samoan (2,135)	3,431	0.16
Tongan (804)	977	0.04
White (1,335,147)	1,422,477	64.96
Not Hispanic (869,068)	909,581	41.54
Hispanic (466,079)	512,896	23.42

*Notes: † The Census 2010 population figure is used to calculate the percentages in the Hispanic Origin and Race categories. Ancestry percentages are based on the 2006-2010 American Community Survey population (not shown); ‡ Numbers in parentheses indicate the number of people reporting a single ancestry; * Numbers in parentheses indicate the number of persons reporting this race alone, not in combination with any other race; Please refer to the Explanation of Data for more information.*

Sacramento County

Population: 1,418,788

Ancestry	Population	%
Afghan (2,071)	2,149	0.15
African, Sub-Saharan (8,446)	12,074	0.87
African (4,855)	7,737	0.55
Cape Verdean (259)	587	0.04
Ethiopian (1,345)	1,525	0.11
Ghanaian (51)	51	<0.01
Kenyan (292)	292	0.02
Liberian (13)	13	<0.01
Nigerian (934)	976	0.07
Senegalese (0)	0	<0.01
Sierra Leonean (0)	15	<0.01
Somalian (148)	156	0.01
South African (282)	325	0.02
Sudanese (48)	60	<0.01
Ugandan (116)	148	0.01
Zimbabwean (0)	0	<0.01
Other Sub-Saharan African (103)	189	0.01
Albanian (121)	205	0.01
Alsatian (15)	37	<0.01
American (32,678)	32,678	2.34
Arab (4,536)	7,185	0.52
Arab (1,200)	1,641	0.12
Egyptian (400)	659	0.05
Iraqi (97)	138	0.01
Jordanian (345)	392	0.03
Lebanese (707)	1,594	0.11
Moroccan (194)	281	0.02
Palestinian (631)	827	0.06
Syrian (98)	398	0.03
Other Arab (864)	1,255	0.09
Armenian (2,224)	3,318	0.24
Assyrian/Chaldean/Syriac (143)	281	0.02
Australian (192)	767	0.05
Austrian (612)	2,164	0.16
Basque (293)	675	0.05
Belgian (261)	886	0.06
Brazilian (175)	456	0.03
British (2,392)	5,245	0.38
Bulgarian (400)	523	0.04
Cajun (0)	17	<0.01
Canadian (1,262)	3,125	0.22
Carpatho Rusyn (0)	19	<0.01
Celtic (132)	509	0.04
Croatian (661)	2,170	0.16
Cypriot (10)	22	<0.01
Czech (943)	3,992	0.29
Czechoslovakian (490)	1,216	0.09
Danish (1,955)	8,713	0.62
Dutch (3,713)	19,590	1.40
Eastern European (837)	953	0.07
English (30,054)	116,473	8.35
Estonian (20)	85	0.01
European (13,496)	17,206	1.23
Finnish (725)	2,288	0.16
French, ex. Basque (4,368)	35,655	2.56
French Canadian (1,729)	4,921	0.35
German (45,008)	174,008	12.47
German Russian (34)	108	0.01
Greek (2,748)	6,573	0.47
Guyanese (23)	23	<0.01
Hungarian (1,334)	4,410	0.32
Icelander (193)	476	0.03
Iranian (3,192)	4,143	0.30
Irish (29,298)	134,151	9.62
Israeli (200)	314	0.02
Italian (23,438)	70,684	5.07
Latvian (108)	293	0.02
Lithuanian (367)	1,566	0.11
Luxemburger (0)	125	0.01
Macedonian (0)	23	<0.01
Maltese (43)	205	0.01
New Zealander (20)	20	<0.01
Northern European (1,817)	2,104	0.15
Norwegian (6,143)	20,434	1.46
Pennsylvania German (117)	372	0.03
Polish (4,812)	18,395	1.32
Portuguese (8,958)	25,666	1.84
Romanian (4,944)	6,256	0.45
Russian (12,366)	20,532	1.47
Scandinavian (1,722)	3,808	0.27
Scotch-Irish (7,692)	21,377	1.53
Scottish (7,493)	28,489	2.04
Serbian (381)	714	0.05
Slavic (360)	754	0.05
Slovak (273)	740	0.05
Slovene (106)	358	0.03
Soviet Union (0)	0	<0.01
Swedish (4,785)	21,078	1.51
Swiss (1,020)	4,949	0.35
Turkish (546)	742	0.05
Ukrainian (16,695)	19,547	1.40
Welsh (1,562)	9,424	0.68
West Indian, ex. Hispanic (1,235)	2,205	0.16
Bahamian (44)	44	<0.01
Barbadian (18)	28	<0.01
Belizean (175)	229	0.02
Bermudan (5)	30	<0.01
British West Indian (2)	51	<0.01
Dutch West Indian (16)	65	<0.01
Haitian (14)	110	0.01
Jamaican (591)	923	0.07
Trinidadian/Tobagonian (106)	208	0.01
U.S. Virgin Islander (0)	9	<0.01
West Indian (264)	508	0.04
Other West Indian (0)	0	<0.01
Yugoslavian (1,842)	3,085	0.22

Hispanic Origin	Population	%
Hispanic or Latino (of any race)	306,196	21.58
Central American, ex. Mexican	14,594	1.03
Costa Rican	513	0.04
Guatemalan	2,950	0.21
Honduran	981	0.07
Nicaraguan	2,565	0.18
Panamanian	918	0.06
Salvadoran	6,509	0.46
Other Central American	158	0.01
Cuban	1,873	0.13
Dominican Republic	433	0.03
Mexican	249,431	17.58
Puerto Rican	9,267	0.65
South American	5,380	0.38
Argentinean	619	0.04
Bolivian	220	0.02
Chilean	609	0.04
Colombian	1,170	0.08
Ecuadorian	401	0.03
Paraguayan	37	<0.01
Peruvian	1,818	0.13
Uruguayan	76	0.01
Venezuelan	351	0.02
Other South American	79	0.01
Other Hispanic or Latino	25,218	1.78

Race*	Population	%
African-American/Black (147,058)	178,580	12.59
Not Hispanic (139,949)	164,091	11.57
Hispanic (7,109)	14,489	1.02
American Indian/Alaska Native (14,308)	36,825	2.60
Not Hispanic (7,875)	23,676	1.67
Hispanic (6,433)	13,149	0.93
Alaska Athabascan *(Ala. Nat.)* (24)	34	<0.01
Aleut *(Alaska Native)* (15)	62	<0.01
Apache (489)	1,251	0.09
Arapaho (11)	43	<0.01
Blackfeet (184)	1,316	0.09
Canadian/French Am. Ind. (27)	69	<0.01
Central American Ind. (29)	64	<0.01
Cherokee (1,237)	6,324	0.45
Cheyenne (24)	103	0.01
Chickasaw (88)	300	0.02
Chippewa (217)	480	0.03
Choctaw (350)	1,488	0.10
Colville (10)	24	<0.01
Comanche (48)	138	0.01
Cree (18)	90	0.01
Creek (95)	374	0.03
Crow (22)	76	0.01
Delaware (24)	77	0.01
Hopi (28)	83	0.01
Houma (5)	10	<0.01
Inupiat *(Alaska Native)* (37)	73	0.01
Iroquois (102)	312	0.02
Kiowa (33)	53	<0.01
Lumbee (30)	45	<0.01
Menominee (10)	27	<0.01
Mexican American Ind. (1,014)	1,657	0.12
Navajo (391)	893	0.06
Osage (14)	90	0.01
Ottawa (22)	38	<0.01
Paiute (159)	277	0.02
Pima (42)	67	<0.01
Potawatomi (74)	192	0.01
Pueblo (122)	222	0.02
Puget Sound Salish (27)	43	<0.01
Seminole (36)	191	0.01
Shoshone (61)	178	0.01
Sioux (359)	882	0.06
South American Ind. (35)	130	0.01
Spanish American Ind. (80)	135	0.01
Tlingit-Haida *(Alaska Native)* (61)	151	0.01
Tohono O'Odham (43)	77	0.01
Tsimshian *(Alaska Native)* (5)	28	<0.01
Ute (18)	42	<0.01
Yakama (19)	34	<0.01
Yaqui (194)	376	0.03
Yuman (25)	39	<0.01
Yup'ik *(Alaska Native)* (8)	24	<0.01
Asian (203,211)	241,160	17.00
Not Hispanic (198,944)	229,376	16.17
Hispanic (4,267)	11,784	0.83
Bangladeshi (249)	267	0.02
Bhutanese (167)	178	0.01
Burmese (145)	196	0.01
Cambodian (2,024)	2,610	0.18
Chinese, ex. Taiwanese (39,016)	47,588	3.35
Filipino (41,455)	56,966	4.02
Hmong (25,184)	26,324	1.86
Indian (26,560)	31,750	2.24
Indonesian (496)	900	0.06
Japanese (10,708)	18,981	1.34
Korean (6,049)	8,421	0.59
Laotian (10,396)	11,872	0.84
Malaysian (115)	179	0.01
Nepalese (230)	282	0.02
Pakistani (3,638)	4,016	0.28
Sri Lankan (275)	314	0.02
Taiwanese (799)	1,014	0.07
Thai (1,190)	2,184	0.15
Vietnamese (25,030)	28,261	1.99
Hawaii Native/Pacific Islander (13,858)	24,138	1.70
Not Hispanic (13,099)	21,536	1.52
Hispanic (759)	2,602	0.18
Fijian (5,618)	6,771	0.48
Guamanian/Chamorro (1,291)	2,446	0.17
Marshallese (707)	736	0.05
Native Hawaiian (988)	3,903	0.28
Samoan (1,684)	2,655	0.19
Tongan (1,747)	2,169	0.15
White (815,151)	887,564	62.56
Not Hispanic (687,166)	735,226	51.82
Hispanic (127,985)	152,338	10.74

*Notes: † The Census 2010 population figure is used to calculate the percentages in the Hispanic Origin and Race categories. Ancestry percentages are based on the 2006-2010 American Community Survey population (not shown); ‡ Numbers in parentheses indicate the number of people reporting a single ancestry; * Numbers in parentheses indicate the number of persons reporting this race alone, not in combination with any other race; Please refer to the Explanation of Data for more information.*

San Benito County

Population: 55,269

Ancestry	Population	%
Afghan (0)	0	<0.01
African, Sub-Saharan (44)	89	0.16
African (31)	76	0.14
Cape Verdean (0)	0	<0.01
Ethiopian (0)	0	<0.01
Ghanaian (0)	0	<0.01
Kenyan (0)	0	<0.01
Liberian (0)	0	<0.01
Nigerian (0)	0	<0.01
Senegalese (0)	0	<0.01
Sierra Leonean (0)	0	<0.01
Somalian (0)	0	<0.01
South African (11)	11	0.02
Sudanese (0)	0	<0.01
Ugandan (0)	0	<0.01
Zimbabwean (0)	0	<0.01
Other Sub-Saharan African (2)	2	<0.01
Albanian (0)	0	<0.01
Alsatian (0)	0	<0.01
American (1,236)	1,236	2.27
Arab (165)	191	0.35
Arab (48)	74	0.14
Egyptian (0)	0	<0.01
Iraqi (0)	0	<0.01
Jordanian (0)	0	<0.01
Lebanese (113)	113	0.21
Moroccan (0)	0	<0.01
Palestinian (0)	0	<0.01
Syrian (4)	4	0.01
Other Arab (0)	0	<0.01
Armenian (10)	10	0.02
Assyrian/Chaldean/Syriac (3)	3	0.01
Australian (84)	84	0.15
Austrian (23)	24	0.04
Basque (37)	131	0.24
Belgian (0)	11	0.02
Brazilian (0)	0	<0.01
British (125)	210	0.39
Bulgarian (4)	14	0.03
Cajun (0)	31	0.06
Canadian (31)	118	0.22
Carpatho Rusyn (0)	0	<0.01
Celtic (20)	22	0.04
Croatian (23)	41	0.08
Cypriot (0)	0	<0.01
Czech (83)	264	0.48
Czechoslovakian (3)	31	0.06
Danish (69)	304	0.56
Dutch (111)	520	0.95
Eastern European (0)	17	0.03
English (743)	3,765	6.91
Estonian (0)	0	<0.01
European (431)	824	1.51
Finnish (0)	15	0.03
French, ex. Basque (18)	1,215	2.23
French Canadian (0)	111	0.20
German (1,007)	4,956	9.09
German Russian (0)	0	<0.01
Greek (52)	105	0.19
Guyanese (0)	0	<0.01
Hungarian (0)	171	0.31
Icelander (0)	0	<0.01
Iranian (6)	97	0.18
Irish (1,091)	4,634	8.50
Israeli (0)	0	<0.01
Italian (1,360)	3,973	7.29
Latvian (0)	0	<0.01
Lithuanian (0)	87	0.16
Luxemburger (0)	0	<0.01
Macedonian (0)	5	0.01
Maltese (17)	17	0.03
New Zealander (0)	0	<0.01
Northern European (29)	29	0.05
Norwegian (173)	448	0.82
Pennsylvania German (21)	21	0.04
Polish (91)	525	0.96
Portuguese (543)	1,734	3.18
Romanian (0)	0	<0.01
Russian (19)	159	0.29
Scandinavian (119)	174	0.32
Scotch-Irish (282)	650	1.19
Scottish (263)	998	1.83
Serbian (0)	4	0.01
Slavic (0)	2	<0.01
Slovak (12)	12	0.02
Slovene (0)	23	0.04
Soviet Union (0)	0	<0.01
Swedish (132)	501	0.92
Swiss (56)	341	0.63
Turkish (0)	0	<0.01
Ukrainian (12)	90	0.17
Welsh (10)	214	0.39
West Indian, ex. Hispanic (0)	0	<0.01
Bahamian (0)	0	<0.01
Barbadian (0)	0	<0.01
Belizean (0)	0	<0.01
Bermudan (0)	0	<0.01
British West Indian (0)	0	<0.01
Dutch West Indian (0)	0	<0.01
Haitian (0)	0	<0.01
Jamaican (0)	0	<0.01
Trinidadian/Tobagonian (0)	0	<0.01
U.S. Virgin Islander (0)	0	<0.01
West Indian (0)	0	<0.01
Other West Indian (0)	0	<0.01
Yugoslavian (0)	26	0.05

Hispanic Origin	Population	%
Hispanic or Latino (of any race)	31,186	56.43
Central American, ex. Mexican	405	0.73
Costa Rican	17	0.03
Guatemalan	84	0.15
Honduran	58	0.10
Nicaraguan	61	0.11
Panamanian	13	0.02
Salvadoran	171	0.31
Other Central American	1	<0.01
Cuban	41	0.07
Dominican Republic	12	0.02
Mexican	28,694	51.92
Puerto Rican	237	0.43
South American	141	0.26
Argentinean	13	0.02
Bolivian	1	<0.01
Chilean	27	0.05
Colombian	31	0.06
Ecuadorian	7	0.01
Paraguayan	4	0.01
Peruvian	36	0.07
Uruguayan	6	0.01
Venezuelan	16	0.03
Other South American	0	<0.01
Other Hispanic or Latino	1,656	3.00

Race*	Population	%
African-American/Black (483)	825	1.49
Not Hispanic (355)	522	0.94
Hispanic (128)	303	0.55
American Indian/Alaska Native (895)	1,603	2.90
Not Hispanic (231)	544	0.98
Hispanic (664)	1,059	1.92
Alaska Athabascan *(Ala. Nat.)* (0)	0	<0.01
Aleut *(Alaska Native)* (0)	0	<0.01
Apache (22)	57	0.10
Arapaho (1)	1	<0.01
Blackfeet (9)	38	0.07
Canadian/French Am. Ind. (2)	8	0.01
Central American Ind. (0)	0	<0.01
Cherokee (47)	179	0.32
Cheyenne (0)	0	<0.01
Chickasaw (3)	5	0.01
Chippewa (11)	27	0.05
Choctaw (4)	31	0.06
Colville (0)	0	<0.01
Comanche (3)	7	0.01
Cree (0)	1	<0.01
Creek (1)	3	0.01
Crow (0)	0	<0.01
Delaware (0)	0	<0.01
Hopi (6)	10	0.02
Houma (0)	0	<0.01
Inupiat *(Alaska Native)* (1)	3	0.01
Iroquois (1)	3	0.01
Kiowa (0)	0	<0.01
Lumbee (0)	0	<0.01
Menominee (0)	0	<0.01
Mexican American Ind. (237)	304	0.55
Navajo (14)	26	0.05
Osage (0)	4	0.01
Ottawa (0)	1	<0.01
Paiute (4)	5	0.01
Pima (2)	12	0.02
Potawatomi (5)	14	0.03
Pueblo (4)	19	0.03
Puget Sound Salish (1)	7	0.01
Seminole (3)	6	0.01
Shoshone (1)	2	<0.01
Sioux (7)	12	0.02
South American Ind. (1)	1	<0.01
Spanish American Ind. (11)	27	0.05
Tlingit-Haida *(Alaska Native)* (3)	4	0.01
Tohono O'Odham (1)	3	0.01
Tsimshian *(Alaska Native)* (0)	0	<0.01
Ute (0)	0	<0.01
Yakama (0)	0	<0.01
Yaqui (5)	19	0.03
Yuman (0)	0	<0.01
Yup'ik *(Alaska Native)* (0)	0	<0.01
Asian (1,443)	2,265	4.10
Not Hispanic (1,298)	1,771	3.20
Hispanic (145)	494	0.89
Bangladeshi (1)	1	<0.01
Bhutanese (0)	0	<0.01
Burmese (0)	3	0.01
Cambodian (15)	23	0.04
Chinese, ex. Taiwanese (155)	254	0.46
Filipino (690)	1,169	2.12
Hmong (0)	0	<0.01
Indian (115)	144	0.26
Indonesian (3)	24	0.04
Japanese (193)	371	0.67
Korean (82)	124	0.22
Laotian (8)	13	0.02
Malaysian (0)	0	<0.01
Nepalese (0)	0	<0.01
Pakistani (23)	28	0.05
Sri Lankan (0)	0	<0.01
Taiwanese (3)	8	0.01
Thai (7)	8	0.01
Vietnamese (79)	113	0.20
Hawaii Native/Pacific Islander (94)	255	0.46
Not Hispanic (65)	151	0.27
Hispanic (29)	104	0.19
Fijian (2)	4	0.01
Guamanian/Chamorro (26)	49	0.09
Marshallese (0)	0	<0.01
Native Hawaiian (31)	106	0.19
Samoan (8)	12	0.02
Tongan (2)	4	0.01
White (35,181)	37,450	67.76
Not Hispanic (21,154)	21,962	39.74
Hispanic (14,027)	15,488	28.02

*Notes: † The Census 2010 population figure is used to calculate the percentages in the Hispanic Origin and Race categories. Ancestry percentages are based on the 2006-2010 American Community Survey population (not shown); ‡ Numbers in parentheses indicate the number of people reporting a single ancestry; * Numbers in parentheses indicate the number of persons reporting this race alone, not in combination with any other race; Please refer to the Explanation of Data for more information.*

San Bernardino County

Population: 2,035,210

Ancestry	Population	%
Afghan (834)	834	0.04
African, Sub-Saharan (11,199)	14,621	0.73
African (7,799)	10,295	0.51
Cape Verdean (98)	126	0.01
Ethiopian (281)	411	0.02
Ghanaian (276)	308	0.02
Kenyan (105)	113	0.01
Liberian (27)	27	<0.01
Nigerian (2,063)	2,436	0.12
Senegalese (0)	0	<0.01
Sierra Leonean (0)	0	<0.01
Somalian (16)	101	0.01
South African (196)	300	0.01
Sudanese (7)	23	<0.01
Ugandan (24)	24	<0.01
Zimbabwean (22)	22	<0.01
Other Sub-Saharan African (285)	435	0.02
Albanian (195)	249	0.01
Alsatian (16)	55	<0.01
American (53,059)	53,059	2.65
Arab (10,426)	14,870	0.74
Arab (2,165)	3,104	0.15
Egyptian (2,125)	2,273	0.11
Iraqi (264)	413	0.02
Jordanian (711)	945	0.05
Lebanese (1,557)	3,006	0.15
Moroccan (193)	246	0.01
Palestinian (1,119)	1,827	0.09
Syrian (826)	1,239	0.06
Other Arab (1,466)	1,817	0.09
Armenian (1,816)	2,703	0.13
Assyrian/Chaldean/Syriac (259)	315	0.02
Australian (358)	857	0.04
Austrian (493)	2,137	0.11
Basque (461)	1,137	0.06
Belgian (238)	1,037	0.05
Brazilian (463)	809	0.04
British (2,149)	4,607	0.23
Bulgarian (37)	186	0.01
Cajun (27)	148	0.01
Canadian (2,266)	4,601	0.23
Carpatho Rusyn (0)	0	<0.01
Celtic (149)	211	0.01
Croatian (225)	742	0.04
Cypriot (0)	0	<0.01
Czech (900)	3,408	0.17
Czechoslovakian (403)	1,190	0.06
Danish (1,764)	6,608	0.33
Dutch (6,917)	23,919	1.19
Eastern European (487)	609	0.03
English (37,247)	119,126	5.94
Estonian (51)	51	<0.01
European (15,172)	20,161	1.01
Finnish (755)	2,060	0.10
French, ex. Basque (6,371)	40,945	2.04
French Canadian (2,584)	6,518	0.33
German (49,149)	182,043	9.08
German Russian (29)	40	<0.01
Greek (1,551)	4,832	0.24
Guyanese (110)	124	0.01
Hungarian (1,906)	5,944	0.30
Icelander (250)	820	0.04
Iranian (3,177)	3,630	0.18
Irish (33,990)	138,700	6.92
Israeli (241)	279	0.01
Italian (24,383)	72,680	3.62
Latvian (87)	170	0.01
Lithuanian (608)	1,653	0.08
Luxemburger (21)	53	<0.01
Macedonian (13)	25	<0.01
Maltese (59)	95	<0.01
New Zealander (8)	81	<0.01
Northern European (1,116)	1,333	0.07
Norwegian (5,227)	17,630	0.88
Pennsylvania German (270)	530	0.03
Polish (6,699)	22,930	1.14
Portuguese (3,619)	8,296	0.41
Romanian (1,767)	2,441	0.12
Russian (2,776)	8,437	0.42
Scandinavian (1,575)	3,269	0.16
Scotch-Irish (7,376)	20,035	1.00
Scottish (7,301)	23,581	1.18
Serbian (184)	436	0.02
Slavic (152)	469	0.02
Slovak (325)	835	0.04
Slovene (177)	399	0.02
Soviet Union (0)	0	<0.01
Swedish (5,189)	19,297	0.96
Swiss (662)	3,193	0.16
Turkish (123)	394	0.02
Ukrainian (767)	2,226	0.11
Welsh (1,461)	8,205	0.41
West Indian, ex. Hispanic (3,600)	5,635	0.28
Bahamian (14)	71	<0.01
Barbadian (225)	241	0.01
Belizean (1,229)	1,650	0.08
Bermudan (0)	0	<0.01
British West Indian (139)	158	0.01
Dutch West Indian (46)	57	<0.01
Haitian (269)	490	0.02
Jamaican (1,152)	1,993	0.10
Trinidadian/Tobagonian (149)	186	0.01
U.S. Virgin Islander (165)	180	0.01
West Indian (189)	586	0.03
Other West Indian (23)	23	<0.01
Yugoslavian (668)	1,497	0.07

Hispanic Origin	Population	%
Hispanic or Latino (of any race)	1,001,145	49.19
Central American, ex. Mexican	53,571	2.63
Costa Rican	1,742	0.09
Guatemalan	14,338	0.70
Honduran	4,221	0.21
Nicaraguan	6,162	0.30
Panamanian	1,335	0.07
Salvadoran	25,056	1.23
Other Central American	717	0.04
Cuban	6,291	0.31
Dominican Republic	739	0.04
Mexican	848,541	41.69
Puerto Rican	14,179	0.70
South American	16,165	0.79
Argentinean	2,910	0.14
Bolivian	484	0.02
Chilean	986	0.05
Colombian	3,961	0.19
Ecuadorian	2,559	0.13
Paraguayan	53	<0.01
Peruvian	4,257	0.21
Uruguayan	229	0.01
Venezuelan	492	0.02
Other South American	234	0.01
Other Hispanic or Latino	61,659	3.03

Race*	Population	%
African-American/Black (181,862)	208,806	10.26
Not Hispanic (170,700)	188,484	9.26
Hispanic (11,162)	20,322	1.00
American Indian/Alaska Native (22,689)	43,859	2.16
Not Hispanic (8,523)	20,463	1.01
Hispanic (14,166)	23,396	1.15
Alaska Athabascan *(Ala. Nat.)* (20)	42	<0.01
Aleut *(Alaska Native)* (20)	48	<0.01
Apache (934)	2,028	0.10
Arapaho (19)	47	<0.01
Blackfeet (191)	1,158	0.06
Canadian/French Am. Ind. (35)	97	<0.01
Central American Ind. (89)	185	0.01
Cherokee (1,258)	5,491	0.27
Cheyenne (44)	122	0.01
Chickasaw (72)	272	0.01
Chippewa (199)	414	0.02
Choctaw (415)	1,267	0.06
Colville (15)	28	<0.01
Comanche (94)	197	0.01
Cree (5)	35	<0.01
Creek (134)	376	0.02
Crow (25)	56	<0.01
Delaware (28)	69	<0.01
Hopi (95)	197	0.01
Houma (7)	11	<0.01
Inupiat *(Alaska Native)* (32)	61	<0.01
Iroquois (104)	295	0.01
Kiowa (28)	47	<0.01
Lumbee (28)	56	<0.01
Menominee (8)	22	<0.01
Mexican American Ind. (2,369)	3,719	0.18
Navajo (871)	1,511	0.07
Osage (56)	159	0.01
Ottawa (17)	52	<0.01
Paiute (86)	166	0.01
Pima (136)	229	0.01
Potawatomi (115)	208	0.01
Pueblo (453)	701	0.03
Puget Sound Salish (17)	23	<0.01
Seminole (51)	184	0.01
Shoshone (62)	128	0.01
Sioux (374)	778	0.04
South American Ind. (77)	173	0.01
Spanish American Ind. (169)	246	0.01
Tlingit-Haida *(Alaska Native)* (46)	70	<0.01
Tohono O'Odham (139)	208	0.01
Tsimshian *(Alaska Native)* (0)	2	<0.01
Ute (30)	64	<0.01
Yakama (6)	13	<0.01
Yaqui (544)	971	0.05
Yuman (275)	407	0.02
Yup'ik *(Alaska Native)* (20)	29	<0.01
Asian (128,603)	154,710	7.60
Not Hispanic (123,978)	142,112	6.98
Hispanic (4,625)	12,598	0.62
Bangladeshi (682)	807	0.04
Bhutanese (6)	6	<0.01
Burmese (361)	440	0.02
Cambodian (3,202)	3,904	0.19
Chinese, ex. Taiwanese (19,540)	25,054	1.23
Filipino (41,702)	52,488	2.58
Hmong (209)	229	0.01
Indian (12,078)	14,183	0.70
Indonesian (4,814)	6,256	0.31
Japanese (4,652)	9,973	0.49
Korean (13,720)	16,027	0.79
Laotian (788)	1,039	0.05
Malaysian (141)	254	0.01
Nepalese (80)	84	<0.01
Pakistani (2,146)	2,537	0.12
Sri Lankan (286)	340	0.02
Taiwanese (3,359)	3,845	0.19
Thai (2,332)	3,230	0.16
Vietnamese (12,819)	14,550	0.71
Hawaii Native/Pacific Islander (6,870)	13,517	0.66
Not Hispanic (5,845)	10,259	0.50
Hispanic (1,025)	3,258	0.16
Fijian (145)	220	0.01
Guamanian/Chamorro (1,186)	2,003	0.10
Marshallese (34)	41	<0.01
Native Hawaiian (1,210)	3,506	0.17
Samoan (2,476)	3,787	0.19
Tongan (1,022)	1,376	0.07
White (1,153,161)	1,236,552	60.76
Not Hispanic (677,598)	712,879	35.03
Hispanic (475,563)	523,673	25.73

*Notes: † The Census 2010 population figure is used to calculate the percentages in the Hispanic Origin and Race categories. Ancestry percentages are based on the 2006-2010 American Community Survey population (not shown); ‡ Numbers in parentheses indicate the number of people reporting a single ancestry; * Numbers in parentheses indicate the number of persons reporting this race alone, not in combination with any other race; Please refer to the Explanation of Data for more information.*

San Diego County

Population: 3,095,313

Ancestry	Population	%
Afghan (3,046)	3,230	0.11
African, Sub-Saharan (21,920)	27,025	0.89
African (9,957)	13,814	0.46
Cape Verdean (247)	313	0.01
Ethiopian (2,550)	2,871	0.09
Ghanaian (98)	98	<0.01
Kenyan (150)	166	0.01
Liberian (40)	40	<0.01
Nigerian (903)	948	0.03
Senegalese (0)	141	<0.01
Sierra Leonean (0)	0	<0.01
Somalian (5,111)	5,264	0.17
South African (992)	1,307	0.04
Sudanese (1,123)	1,129	0.04
Ugandan (31)	31	<0.01
Zimbabwean (71)	71	<0.01
Other Sub-Saharan African (647)	832	0.03
Albanian (306)	520	0.02
Alsatian (9)	27	<0.01
American (76,031)	76,031	2.52
Arab (18,286)	25,920	0.86
Arab (2,485)	3,445	0.11
Egyptian (798)	1,011	0.03
Iraqi (5,546)	7,019	0.23
Jordanian (314)	501	0.02
Lebanese (3,464)	5,894	0.20
Moroccan (663)	863	0.03
Palestinian (875)	1,385	0.05
Syrian (677)	1,649	0.05
Other Arab (3,464)	4,153	0.14
Armenian (3,369)	5,503	0.18
Assyrian/Chaldean/Syriac (6,616)	8,320	0.28
Australian (1,305)	2,070	0.07
Austrian (1,937)	8,059	0.27
Basque (360)	1,171	0.04
Belgian (858)	3,374	0.11
Brazilian (2,331)	3,445	0.11
British (8,090)	15,558	0.51
Bulgarian (672)	1,093	0.04
Cajun (168)	384	0.01
Canadian (4,310)	8,478	0.28
Carpatho Rusyn (0)	61	<0.01
Celtic (545)	861	0.03
Croatian (884)	2,851	0.09
Cypriot (69)	69	<0.01
Czech (3,323)	11,946	0.40
Czechoslovakian (1,128)	2,592	0.09
Danish (4,709)	17,527	0.58
Dutch (9,463)	38,405	1.27
Eastern European (3,546)	4,059	0.13
English (80,967)	262,378	8.68
Estonian (114)	295	0.01
European (37,362)	44,927	1.49
Finnish (1,528)	5,311	0.18
French, ex. Basque (13,934)	82,112	2.72
French Canadian (5,448)	13,359	0.44
German (102,184)	377,344	12.48
German Russian (39)	108	<0.01
Greek (4,668)	12,143	0.40
Guyanese (224)	359	0.01
Hungarian (4,469)	14,031	0.46
Icelander (478)	1,069	0.04
Iranian (10,967)	13,154	0.44
Irish (70,470)	282,766	9.36
Israeli (973)	1,362	0.05
Italian (53,344)	144,389	4.78
Latvian (544)	1,307	0.04
Lithuanian (1,797)	5,771	0.19
Luxemburger (56)	245	0.01
Macedonian (214)	300	0.01
Maltese (159)	430	0.01
New Zealander (261)	375	0.01
Northern European (3,228)	3,522	0.12
Norwegian (14,038)	43,505	1.44
Pennsylvania German (423)	803	0.03
Polish (19,488)	62,094	2.05
Portuguese (8,723)	21,246	0.70
Romanian (1,904)	4,090	0.14
Russian (14,970)	34,609	1.15
Scandinavian (3,273)	7,191	0.24
Scotch-Irish (15,936)	46,116	1.53
Scottish (16,563)	59,926	1.98
Serbian (1,310)	2,258	0.07
Slavic (562)	1,316	0.04
Slovak (1,104)	3,129	0.10
Slovene (331)	988	0.03
Soviet Union (25)	25	<0.01
Swedish (11,286)	46,391	1.53
Swiss (2,328)	9,616	0.32
Turkish (1,342)	2,273	0.08
Ukrainian (3,341)	6,956	0.23
Welsh (3,758)	20,179	0.67
West Indian, ex. Hispanic (3,579)	5,586	0.18
Bahamian (60)	86	<0.01
Barbadian (86)	137	<0.01
Belizean (275)	437	0.01
Bermudan (46)	63	<0.01
British West Indian (154)	201	0.01
Dutch West Indian (51)	87	<0.01
Haitian (766)	1,068	0.04
Jamaican (1,440)	2,171	0.07
Trinidadian/Tobagonian (200)	297	0.01
U.S. Virgin Islander (0)	43	<0.01
West Indian (467)	940	0.03
Other West Indian (34)	56	<0.01
Yugoslavian (1,657)	3,139	0.10

Hispanic Origin	Population	%
Hispanic or Latino (of any race)	991,348	32.03
Central American, ex. Mexican	22,187	0.72
Costa Rican	1,749	0.06
Guatemalan	7,305	0.24
Honduran	2,504	0.08
Nicaraguan	2,025	0.07
Panamanian	2,144	0.07
Salvadoran	6,137	0.20
Other Central American	323	0.01
Cuban	5,674	0.18
Dominican Republic	1,862	0.06
Mexican	869,868	28.10
Puerto Rican	20,468	0.66
South American	17,491	0.57
Argentinean	2,432	0.08
Bolivian	808	0.03
Chilean	1,730	0.06
Colombian	5,046	0.16
Ecuadorian	1,716	0.06
Paraguayan	100	<0.01
Peruvian	4,105	0.13
Uruguayan	250	0.01
Venezuelan	1,080	0.03
Other South American	224	0.01
Other Hispanic or Latino	53,798	1.74

Race*	Population	%
African-American/Black (158,213)	194,788	6.29
Not Hispanic (146,600)	173,327	5.60
Hispanic (11,613)	21,461	0.69
American Indian/Alaska Native (26,340)	52,749	1.70
Not Hispanic (14,098)	30,681	0.99
Hispanic (12,242)	22,068	0.71
Alaska Athabascan *(Ala. Nat.)* (40)	75	<0.01
Aleut *(Alaska Native)* (59)	103	<0.01
Apache (653)	1,619	0.05
Arapaho (18)	53	<0.01
Blackfeet (173)	1,024	0.03
Canadian/French Am. Ind. (73)	168	0.01
Central American Ind. (96)	177	0.01
Cherokee (1,292)	5,948	0.19
Cheyenne (45)	109	<0.01
Chickasaw (177)	407	0.01
Chippewa (294)	637	0.02
Choctaw (443)	1,341	0.04
Colville (9)	20	<0.01
Comanche (89)	217	0.01
Cree (19)	78	<0.01
Creek (150)	424	0.01
Crow (32)	66	<0.01
Delaware (40)	96	<0.01
Hopi (66)	146	<0.01
Houma (7)	17	<0.01
Inupiat *(Alaska Native)* (47)	94	<0.01
Iroquois (182)	541	0.02
Kiowa (15)	40	<0.01
Lumbee (55)	108	<0.01
Menominee (18)	44	<0.01
Mexican American Ind. (2,931)	4,357	0.14
Navajo (890)	1,510	0.05
Osage (71)	204	0.01
Ottawa (39)	66	<0.01
Paiute (57)	112	<0.01
Pima (65)	121	<0.01
Potawatomi (109)	200	0.01
Pueblo (254)	418	0.01
Puget Sound Salish (41)	85	<0.01
Seminole (62)	254	0.01
Shoshone (47)	142	<0.01
Sioux (407)	938	0.03
South American Ind. (93)	253	0.01
Spanish American Ind. (125)	194	0.01
Tlingit-Haida *(Alaska Native)* (72)	125	<0.01
Tohono O'Odham (105)	206	0.01
Tsimshian *(Alaska Native)* (10)	15	<0.01
Ute (41)	78	<0.01
Yakama (12)	28	<0.01
Yaqui (383)	835	0.03
Yuman (109)	156	0.01
Yup'ik *(Alaska Native)* (20)	34	<0.01
Asian (336,091)	407,984	13.18
Not Hispanic (328,058)	385,992	12.47
Hispanic (8,033)	21,992	0.71
Bangladeshi (348)	404	0.01
Bhutanese (82)	83	<0.01
Burmese (986)	1,077	0.03
Cambodian (4,924)	5,963	0.19
Chinese, ex. Taiwanese (45,138)	58,962	1.90
Filipino (146,618)	182,248	5.89
Hmong (1,269)	1,388	0.04
Indian (24,306)	27,854	0.90
Indonesian (837)	1,699	0.05
Japanese (18,687)	34,574	1.12
Korean (20,738)	25,387	0.82
Laotian (6,859)	8,079	0.26
Malaysian (161)	485	0.02
Nepalese (193)	222	0.01
Pakistani (1,435)	1,803	0.06
Sri Lankan (350)	451	0.01
Taiwanese (4,008)	4,722	0.15
Thai (2,459)	3,806	0.12
Vietnamese (44,202)	49,764	1.61
Hawaii Native/Pacific Islander (15,337)	30,626	0.99
Not Hispanic (13,504)	24,878	0.80
Hispanic (1,833)	5,748	0.19
Fijian (98)	193	0.01
Guamanian/Chamorro (5,567)	9,792	0.32
Marshallese (168)	199	0.01
Native Hawaiian (2,482)	8,273	0.27
Samoan (4,875)	7,451	0.24
Tongan (298)	514	0.02
White (1,981,442)	2,113,354	68.28
Not Hispanic (1,500,047)	1,580,816	51.07
Hispanic (481,395)	532,538	17.20

*Notes: † The Census 2010 population figure is used to calculate the percentages in the Hispanic Origin and Race categories. Ancestry percentages are based on the 2006-2010 American Community Survey population (not shown); ‡ Numbers in parentheses indicate the number of people reporting a single ancestry; * Numbers in parentheses indicate the number of persons reporting this race alone, not in combination with any other race; Please refer to the Explanation of Data for more information.*

San Francisco County

Population: 805,235

Ancestry	Population	%
Afghan (118)	158	0.02
African, Sub-Saharan (3,082)	4,541	0.58
African (1,941)	3,031	0.38
Cape Verdean (0)	0	<0.01
Ethiopian (561)	585	0.07
Ghanaian (91)	123	0.02
Kenyan (0)	0	<0.01
Liberian (7)	18	<0.01
Nigerian (170)	211	0.03
Senegalese (0)	0	<0.01
Sierra Leonean (0)	0	<0.01
Somalian (47)	72	0.01
South African (78)	247	0.03
Sudanese (0)	30	<0.01
Ugandan (6)	6	<0.01
Zimbabwean (0)	0	<0.01
Other Sub-Saharan African (181)	218	0.03
Albanian (53)	143	0.02
Alsatian (24)	49	0.01
American (8,041)	8,041	1.02
Arab (3,899)	5,672	0.72
Arab (727)	1,106	0.14
Egyptian (360)	483	0.06
Iraqi (32)	60	0.01
Jordanian (296)	353	0.04
Lebanese (541)	1,112	0.14
Moroccan (65)	135	0.02
Palestinian (520)	705	0.09
Syrian (77)	159	0.02
Other Arab (1,281)	1,559	0.20
Armenian (1,496)	2,149	0.27
Assyrian/Chaldean/Syriac (154)	196	0.02
Australian (626)	954	0.12
Austrian (916)	3,588	0.45
Basque (206)	508	0.06
Belgian (294)	783	0.10
Brazilian (1,266)	1,569	0.20
British (3,363)	6,050	0.77
Bulgarian (402)	468	0.06
Cajun (155)	219	0.03
Canadian (801)	1,697	0.22
Carpatho Rusyn (0)	16	<0.01
Celtic (91)	194	0.02
Croatian (578)	1,466	0.19
Cypriot (6)	50	0.01
Czech (960)	2,987	0.38
Czechoslovakian (268)	422	0.05
Danish (973)	3,739	0.47
Dutch (1,691)	7,416	0.94
Eastern European (3,092)	3,844	0.49
English (10,682)	45,268	5.74
Estonian (98)	227	0.03
European (13,269)	15,818	2.00
Finnish (390)	1,264	0.16
French, ex. Basque (4,299)	17,757	2.25
French Canadian (1,190)	2,726	0.35
German (16,144)	65,133	8.25
German Russian (0)	16	<0.01
Greek (2,266)	4,216	0.53
Guyanese (0)	0	<0.01
Hungarian (1,208)	3,416	0.43
Icelander (67)	223	0.03
Iranian (1,848)	2,263	0.29
Irish (20,894)	64,487	8.17
Israeli (279)	437	0.06
Italian (15,657)	38,913	4.93
Latvian (243)	632	0.08
Lithuanian (500)	1,821	0.23
Luxemburger (0)	126	0.02
Macedonian (68)	156	0.02
Maltese (385)	608	0.08
New Zealander (74)	123	0.02
Northern European (1,907)	2,060	0.26
Norwegian (1,935)	7,582	0.96
Pennsylvania German (19)	111	0.01
Polish (4,793)	16,127	2.04
Portuguese (1,615)	4,497	0.57
Romanian (810)	1,943	0.25
Russian (11,670)	21,435	2.72
Scandinavian (523)	1,088	0.14
Scotch-Irish (2,897)	8,480	1.07
Scottish (3,767)	13,167	1.67
Serbian (204)	435	0.06
Slavic (197)	627	0.08
Slovak (268)	861	0.11
Slovene (187)	400	0.05
Soviet Union (75)	75	0.01
Swedish (2,218)	8,924	1.13
Swiss (906)	3,264	0.41
Turkish (525)	721	0.09
Ukrainian (3,286)	4,917	0.62
Welsh (850)	3,806	0.48
West Indian, ex. Hispanic (689)	1,316	0.17
Bahamian (9)	9	<0.01
Barbadian (0)	20	<0.01
Belizean (90)	140	0.02
Bermudan (0)	0	<0.01
British West Indian (27)	36	<0.01
Dutch West Indian (0)	0	<0.01
Haitian (49)	49	0.01
Jamaican (399)	714	0.09
Trinidadian/Tobagonian (25)	140	0.02
U.S. Virgin Islander (0)	0	<0.01
West Indian (90)	208	0.03
Other West Indian (0)	0	<0.01
Yugoslavian (279)	538	0.07

Hispanic Origin	Population	%
Hispanic or Latino (of any race)	121,774	15.12
Central American, ex. Mexican	33,834	4.20
Costa Rican	487	0.06
Guatemalan	6,154	0.76
Honduran	2,611	0.32
Nicaraguan	7,604	0.94
Panamanian	399	0.05
Salvadoran	16,165	2.01
Other Central American	414	0.05
Cuban	1,992	0.25
Dominican Republic	289	0.04
Mexican	59,675	7.41
Puerto Rican	4,204	0.52
South American	8,618	1.07
Argentinean	1,100	0.14
Bolivian	416	0.05
Chilean	754	0.09
Colombian	1,717	0.21
Ecuadorian	577	0.07
Paraguayan	43	0.01
Peruvian	3,260	0.40
Uruguayan	118	0.01
Venezuelan	496	0.06
Other South American	137	0.02
Other Hispanic or Latino	13,162	1.63

Race*	Population	%
African-American/Black (48,870)	57,810	7.18
Not Hispanic (46,781)	53,760	6.68
Hispanic (2,089)	4,050	0.50
American Indian/Alaska Native (4,024)	10,873	1.35
Not Hispanic (1,828)	6,241	0.78
Hispanic (2,196)	4,632	0.58
Alaska Athabascan *(Ala. Nat.)* (5)	9	<0.01
Aleut *(Alaska Native)* (10)	30	<0.01
Apache (105)	271	0.03
Arapaho (8)	17	<0.01
Blackfeet (27)	284	0.04
Canadian/French Am. Ind. (9)	42	0.01
Central American Ind. (83)	144	0.02
Cherokee (223)	1,441	0.18
Cheyenne (5)	14	<0.01
Chickasaw (17)	80	0.01
Chippewa (72)	167	0.02
Choctaw (64)	318	0.04
Colville (5)	8	<0.01
Comanche (6)	47	0.01
Cree (5)	35	<0.01
Creek (27)	108	0.01
Crow (9)	23	<0.01
Delaware (5)	38	<0.01
Hopi (8)	23	<0.01
Houma (4)	5	<0.01
Inupiat *(Alaska Native)* (12)	22	<0.01
Iroquois (43)	133	0.02
Kiowa (1)	10	<0.01
Lumbee (5)	11	<0.01
Menominee (1)	3	<0.01
Mexican American Ind. (752)	1,209	0.15
Navajo (151)	242	0.03
Osage (5)	26	<0.01
Ottawa (1)	7	<0.01
Paiute (28)	44	0.01
Pima (19)	36	<0.01
Potawatomi (11)	34	<0.01
Pueblo (19)	83	0.01
Puget Sound Salish (6)	11	<0.01
Seminole (10)	68	0.01
Shoshone (5)	25	<0.01
Sioux (94)	251	0.03
South American Ind. (73)	198	0.02
Spanish American Ind. (27)	41	0.01
Tlingit-Haida *(Alaska Native)* (19)	29	<0.01
Tohono O'Odham (19)	27	<0.01
Tsimshian *(Alaska Native)* (3)	8	<0.01
Ute (5)	18	<0.01
Yakama (2)	7	<0.01
Yaqui (45)	90	0.01
Yuman (6)	10	<0.01
Yup'ik *(Alaska Native)* (3)	5	<0.01
Asian (267,915)	288,529	35.83
Not Hispanic (265,700)	283,435	35.20
Hispanic (2,215)	5,094	0.63
Bangladeshi (98)	113	0.01
Bhutanese (7)	8	<0.01
Burmese (1,296)	1,579	0.20
Cambodian (1,213)	1,518	0.19
Chinese, ex. Taiwanese (169,642)	181,707	22.57
Filipino (36,347)	43,646	5.42
Hmong (95)	109	0.01
Indian (9,747)	11,583	1.44
Indonesian (946)	1,349	0.17
Japanese (10,121)	15,278	1.90
Korean (9,670)	11,558	1.44
Laotian (529)	651	0.08
Malaysian (202)	358	0.04
Nepalese (352)	388	0.05
Pakistani (831)	1,012	0.13
Sri Lankan (141)	191	0.02
Taiwanese (2,332)	2,806	0.35
Thai (2,336)	2,879	0.36
Vietnamese (12,871)	16,075	2.00
Hawaii Native/Pacific Islander (3,359)	6,173	0.77
Not Hispanic (3,128)	5,432	0.67
Hispanic (231)	741	0.09
Fijian (176)	250	0.03
Guamanian/Chamorro (313)	566	0.07
Marshallese (3)	5	<0.01
Native Hawaiian (410)	1,489	0.18
Samoan (1,988)	2,542	0.32
Tongan (163)	220	0.03
White (390,387)	420,823	52.26
Not Hispanic (337,451)	358,844	44.56
Hispanic (52,936)	61,979	7.70

*Notes: † The Census 2010 population figure is used to calculate the percentages in the Hispanic Origin and Race categories. Ancestry percentages are based on the 2006-2010 American Community Survey population (not shown); ‡ Numbers in parentheses indicate the number of people reporting a single ancestry; * Numbers in parentheses indicate the number of persons reporting this race alone, not in combination with any other race; Please refer to the Explanation of Data for more information.*

San Joaquin County

Population: 685,306

Ancestry	Population	%
Afghan (2,077)	2,219	0.33
African, Sub-Saharan (1,965)	2,605	0.39
African (1,147)	1,652	0.25
Cape Verdean (28)	39	0.01
Ethiopian (320)	320	0.05
Ghanaian (0)	0	<0.01
Kenyan (0)	0	<0.01
Liberian (81)	91	0.01
Nigerian (225)	257	0.04
Senegalese (0)	0	<0.01
Sierra Leonean (28)	28	<0.01
Somalian (6)	6	<0.01
South African (0)	7	<0.01
Sudanese (62)	62	0.01
Ugandan (0)	0	<0.01
Zimbabwean (68)	118	0.02
Other Sub-Saharan African (0)	25	<0.01
Albanian (0)	0	<0.01
Alsatian (0)	17	<0.01
American (14,961)	14,961	2.22
Arab (2,698)	3,375	0.50
Arab (897)	999	0.15
Egyptian (373)	397	0.06
Iraqi (0)	0	<0.01
Jordanian (43)	43	0.01
Lebanese (268)	581	0.09
Moroccan (18)	55	0.01
Palestinian (578)	614	0.09
Syrian (105)	234	0.03
Other Arab (416)	452	0.07
Armenian (261)	521	0.08
Assyrian/Chaldean/Syriac (20)	51	0.01
Australian (28)	197	0.03
Austrian (92)	655	0.10
Basque (319)	661	0.10
Belgian (71)	325	0.05
Brazilian (153)	383	0.06
British (659)	1,682	0.25
Bulgarian (56)	100	0.01
Cajun (0)	20	<0.01
Canadian (594)	1,141	0.17
Carpatho Rusyn (0)	0	<0.01
Celtic (26)	52	0.01
Croatian (152)	422	0.06
Cypriot (0)	0	<0.01
Czech (249)	974	0.14
Czechoslovakian (136)	195	0.03
Danish (580)	2,844	0.42
Dutch (3,316)	9,420	1.40
Eastern European (157)	190	0.03
English (9,400)	36,413	5.41
Estonian (8)	8	<0.01
European (4,433)	5,522	0.82
Finnish (294)	727	0.11
French, ex. Basque (1,847)	13,636	2.02
French Canadian (619)	1,566	0.23
German (20,588)	69,509	10.32
German Russian (0)	117	0.02
Greek (779)	2,102	0.31
Guyanese (0)	0	<0.01
Hungarian (440)	1,181	0.18
Icelander (18)	63	0.01
Iranian (721)	970	0.14
Irish (9,873)	46,260	6.87
Israeli (28)	102	0.02
Italian (13,061)	33,937	5.04
Latvian (43)	56	0.01
Lithuanian (94)	388	0.06
Luxemburger (0)	54	0.01
Macedonian (0)	0	<0.01
Maltese (93)	184	0.03
New Zealander (26)	83	0.01
Northern European (378)	580	0.09
Norwegian (1,960)	6,634	0.98
Pennsylvania German (52)	97	0.01
Polish (1,266)	4,774	0.71
Portuguese (9,263)	18,838	2.80
Romanian (319)	427	0.06
Russian (824)	3,390	0.50
Scandinavian (177)	556	0.08
Scotch-Irish (1,900)	6,866	1.02
Scottish (2,265)	7,194	1.07
Serbian (82)	138	0.02
Slavic (63)	251	0.04
Slovak (142)	402	0.06
Slovene (16)	121	0.02
Soviet Union (0)	0	<0.01
Swedish (1,447)	7,238	1.07
Swiss (652)	2,701	0.40
Turkish (104)	159	0.02
Ukrainian (122)	437	0.06
Welsh (306)	2,274	0.34
West Indian, ex. Hispanic (300)	734	0.11
Bahamian (0)	0	<0.01
Barbadian (0)	42	0.01
Belizean (82)	107	0.02
Bermudan (0)	0	<0.01
British West Indian (0)	0	<0.01
Dutch West Indian (19)	69	0.01
Haitian (15)	29	<0.01
Jamaican (56)	199	0.03
Trinidadian/Tobagonian (83)	83	0.01
U.S. Virgin Islander (0)	0	<0.01
West Indian (45)	184	0.03
Other West Indian (0)	21	<0.01
Yugoslavian (170)	570	0.08

Hispanic Origin	Population	%
Hispanic or Latino (of any race)	266,341	38.86
Central American, ex. Mexican	7,408	1.08
Costa Rican	193	0.03
Guatemalan	1,529	0.22
Honduran	419	0.06
Nicaraguan	1,710	0.25
Panamanian	267	0.04
Salvadoran	3,234	0.47
Other Central American	56	0.01
Cuban	614	0.09
Dominican Republic	140	0.02
Mexican	233,442	34.06
Puerto Rican	4,727	0.69
South American	2,579	0.38
Argentinean	248	0.04
Bolivian	112	0.02
Chilean	386	0.06
Colombian	461	0.07
Ecuadorian	202	0.03
Paraguayan	10	<0.01
Peruvian	979	0.14
Uruguayan	32	<0.01
Venezuelan	115	0.02
Other South American	34	<0.01
Other Hispanic or Latino	17,431	2.54

Race*	Population	%
African-American/Black (51,744)	61,726	9.01
Not Hispanic (48,540)	55,241	8.06
Hispanic (3,204)	6,485	0.95
American Indian/Alaska Native (7,196)	16,436	2.40
Not Hispanic (3,179)	8,905	1.30
Hispanic (4,017)	7,531	1.10
Alaska Athabascan *(Ala. Nat.)* (8)	12	<0.01
Aleut *(Alaska Native)* (15)	41	0.01
Apache (305)	767	0.11
Arapaho (3)	11	<0.01
Blackfeet (71)	423	0.06
Canadian/French Am. Ind. (12)	40	0.01
Central American Ind. (15)	26	<0.01
Cherokee (568)	2,798	0.41
Cheyenne (10)	29	<0.01
Chickasaw (45)	121	0.02
Chippewa (54)	123	0.02
Choctaw (215)	731	0.11
Colville (4)	5	<0.01
Comanche (18)	47	0.01
Cree (8)	21	<0.01
Creek (43)	114	0.02
Crow (3)	15	<0.01
Delaware (25)	47	0.01
Hopi (11)	44	0.01
Houma (1)	5	<0.01
Inupiat *(Alaska Native)* (9)	19	<0.01
Iroquois (23)	78	0.01
Kiowa (7)	12	<0.01
Lumbee (9)	17	<0.01
Menominee (1)	2	<0.01
Mexican American Ind. (747)	1,137	0.17
Navajo (196)	442	0.06
Osage (26)	55	0.01
Ottawa (7)	9	<0.01
Paiute (71)	129	0.02
Pima (27)	51	0.01
Potawatomi (26)	77	0.01
Pueblo (53)	145	0.02
Puget Sound Salish (31)	42	0.01
Seminole (24)	83	0.01
Shoshone (11)	44	0.01
Sioux (196)	408	0.06
South American Ind. (38)	73	0.01
Spanish American Ind. (33)	51	0.01
Tlingit-Haida *(Alaska Native)* (19)	47	0.01
Tohono O'Odham (15)	40	0.01
Tsimshian *(Alaska Native)* (0)	1	<0.01
Ute (19)	49	0.01
Yakama (10)	23	<0.01
Yaqui (118)	274	0.04
Yuman (13)	29	<0.01
Yup'ik *(Alaska Native)* (2)	6	<0.01
Asian (98,472)	116,818	17.05
Not Hispanic (94,547)	106,877	15.60
Hispanic (3,925)	9,941	1.45
Bangladeshi (21)	24	<0.01
Bhutanese (0)	0	<0.01
Burmese (116)	149	0.02
Cambodian (11,119)	12,557	1.83
Chinese, ex. Taiwanese (7,633)	10,204	1.49
Filipino (35,476)	46,447	6.78
Hmong (6,651)	6,968	1.02
Indian (12,951)	14,676	2.14
Indonesian (116)	280	0.04
Japanese (2,894)	5,143	0.75
Korean (1,289)	1,904	0.28
Laotian (3,500)	4,266	0.62
Malaysian (19)	40	0.01
Nepalese (50)	50	0.01
Pakistani (4,147)	4,533	0.66
Sri Lankan (48)	59	0.01
Taiwanese (175)	226	0.03
Thai (284)	591	0.09
Vietnamese (7,812)	8,674	1.27
Hawaii Native/Pacific Islander (3,758)	7,689	1.12
Not Hispanic (3,248)	5,999	0.88
Hispanic (510)	1,690	0.25
Fijian (1,056)	1,224	0.18
Guamanian/Chamorro (627)	1,157	0.17
Marshallese (2)	10	<0.01
Native Hawaiian (578)	2,127	0.31
Samoan (756)	1,214	0.18
Tongan (276)	391	0.06
White (349,287)	382,934	55.88
Not Hispanic (245,919)	263,100	38.39
Hispanic (103,368)	119,834	17.49

*Notes: † The Census 2010 population figure is used to calculate the percentages in the Hispanic Origin and Race categories. Ancestry percentages are based on the 2006-2010 American Community Survey population (not shown); ‡ Numbers in parentheses indicate the number of people reporting a single ancestry; * Numbers in parentheses indicate the number of persons reporting this race alone, not in combination with any other race; Please refer to the Explanation of Data for more information.*

San Luis Obispo County

Population: 269,637

Ancestry	Population	%
Afghan (0)	0	<0.01
African, Sub-Saharan (484)	562	0.21
African (337)	415	0.16
Cape Verdean (0)	0	<0.01
Ethiopian (48)	48	0.02
Ghanaian (16)	16	0.01
Kenyan (0)	0	<0.01
Liberian (0)	0	<0.01
Nigerian (33)	33	0.01
Senegalese (0)	0	<0.01
Sierra Leonean (0)	0	<0.01
Somalian (0)	0	<0.01
South African (50)	50	0.02
Sudanese (0)	0	<0.01
Ugandan (0)	0	<0.01
Zimbabwean (0)	0	<0.01
Other Sub-Saharan African (0)	0	<0.01
Albanian (15)	53	0.02
Alsatian (0)	11	<0.01
American (9,767)	9,767	3.68
Arab (592)	1,418	0.53
Arab (130)	209	0.08
Egyptian (65)	411	0.15
Iraqi (0)	0	<0.01
Jordanian (116)	116	0.04
Lebanese (79)	318	0.12
Moroccan (0)	0	<0.01
Palestinian (36)	65	0.02
Syrian (43)	123	0.05
Other Arab (123)	176	0.07
Armenian (246)	617	0.23
Assyrian/Chaldean/Syriac (24)	48	0.02
Australian (104)	222	0.08
Austrian (120)	918	0.35
Basque (208)	336	0.13
Belgian (25)	266	0.10
Brazilian (57)	144	0.05
British (1,094)	2,252	0.85
Bulgarian (0)	14	0.01
Cajun (106)	119	0.04
Canadian (691)	1,040	0.39
Carpatho Rusyn (0)	0	<0.01
Celtic (25)	63	0.02
Croatian (200)	490	0.18
Cypriot (0)	0	<0.01
Czech (561)	1,516	0.57
Czechoslovakian (133)	358	0.13
Danish (958)	3,697	1.39
Dutch (1,655)	6,302	2.37
Eastern European (220)	261	0.10
English (10,394)	34,612	13.03
Estonian (31)	44	0.02
European (5,912)	6,764	2.55
Finnish (211)	485	0.18
French, ex. Basque (1,679)	9,400	3.54
French Canadian (430)	1,548	0.58
German (13,192)	45,786	17.24
German Russian (0)	17	0.01
Greek (564)	1,306	0.49
Guyanese (0)	0	<0.01
Hungarian (497)	1,374	0.52
Icelander (18)	45	0.02
Iranian (191)	291	0.11
Irish (7,926)	32,940	12.40
Israeli (140)	140	0.05
Italian (5,812)	16,261	6.12
Latvian (56)	123	0.05
Lithuanian (249)	717	0.27
Luxemburger (10)	50	0.02
Macedonian (0)	0	<0.01
Maltese (15)	25	0.01
New Zealander (0)	14	0.01
Northern European (572)	590	0.22
Norwegian (1,815)	5,984	2.25
Pennsylvania German (123)	260	0.10
Polish (1,462)	5,268	1.98
Portuguese (2,980)	6,139	2.31
Romanian (113)	326	0.12
Russian (972)	3,074	1.16
Scandinavian (736)	1,220	0.46
Scotch-Irish (2,264)	6,839	2.58
Scottish (2,819)	8,607	3.24
Serbian (30)	158	0.06
Slavic (71)	209	0.08
Slovak (99)	227	0.09
Slovene (10)	136	0.05
Soviet Union (0)	0	<0.01
Swedish (1,830)	6,459	2.43
Swiss (519)	2,740	1.03
Turkish (23)	94	0.04
Ukrainian (115)	443	0.17
Welsh (488)	2,712	1.02
West Indian, ex. Hispanic (121)	405	0.15
Bahamian (0)	0	<0.01
Barbadian (0)	0	<0.01
Belizean (38)	64	0.02
Bermudan (0)	0	<0.01
British West Indian (0)	15	0.01
Dutch West Indian (0)	20	0.01
Haitian (28)	66	0.02
Jamaican (42)	185	0.07
Trinidadian/Tobagonian (13)	13	<0.01
U.S. Virgin Islander (0)	0	<0.01
West Indian (0)	42	0.02
Other West Indian (0)	0	<0.01
Yugoslavian (137)	369	0.14

Hispanic Origin	Population	%
Hispanic or Latino (of any race)	55,973	20.76
Central American, ex. Mexican	1,184	0.44
Costa Rican	102	0.04
Guatemalan	332	0.12
Honduran	75	0.03
Nicaraguan	147	0.05
Panamanian	61	0.02
Salvadoran	455	0.17
Other Central American	12	<0.01
Cuban	290	0.11
Dominican Republic	33	0.01
Mexican	47,680	17.68
Puerto Rican	882	0.33
South American	915	0.34
Argentinean	157	0.06
Bolivian	28	0.01
Chilean	115	0.04
Colombian	175	0.06
Ecuadorian	78	0.03
Paraguayan	2	<0.01
Peruvian	294	0.11
Uruguayan	6	<0.01
Venezuelan	45	0.02
Other South American	15	0.01
Other Hispanic or Latino	4,989	1.85

Race*	Population	%
African-American/Black (5,550)	7,089	2.63
Not Hispanic (5,128)	6,254	2.32
Hispanic (422)	835	0.31
American Indian/Alaska Native (2,536)	5,878	2.18
Not Hispanic (1,367)	3,591	1.33
Hispanic (1,169)	2,287	0.85
Alaska Athabascan *(Ala. Nat.)* (0)	1	<0.01
Aleut *(Alaska Native)* (0)	8	<0.01
Apache (67)	169	0.06
Arapaho (1)	1	<0.01
Blackfeet (35)	180	0.07
Canadian/French Am. Ind. (4)	11	<0.01
Central American Ind. (4)	12	<0.01
Cherokee (249)	1,062	0.39
Cheyenne (8)	17	0.01
Chickasaw (25)	59	0.02
Chippewa (38)	69	0.03
Choctaw (83)	262	0.10
Colville (0)	1	<0.01
Comanche (7)	35	0.01
Cree (1)	14	0.01
Creek (12)	48	0.02
Crow (1)	5	<0.01
Delaware (4)	11	<0.01
Hopi (3)	12	<0.01
Houma (0)	0	<0.01
Inupiat *(Alaska Native)* (2)	10	<0.01
Iroquois (20)	65	0.02
Kiowa (4)	8	<0.01
Lumbee (0)	1	<0.01
Menominee (1)	2	<0.01
Mexican American Ind. (242)	371	0.14
Navajo (48)	138	0.05
Osage (12)	38	0.01
Ottawa (4)	10	<0.01
Paiute (20)	32	0.01
Pima (2)	6	<0.01
Potawatomi (23)	46	0.02
Pueblo (19)	54	0.02
Puget Sound Salish (5)	9	<0.01
Seminole (10)	26	0.01
Shoshone (1)	6	<0.01
Sioux (46)	102	0.04
South American Ind. (19)	36	0.01
Spanish American Ind. (12)	17	0.01
Tlingit-Haida *(Alaska Native)* (15)	22	0.01
Tohono O'Odham (7)	10	<0.01
Tsimshian *(Alaska Native)* (0)	2	<0.01
Ute (4)	12	<0.01
Yakama (3)	7	<0.01
Yaqui (53)	101	0.04
Yuman (7)	8	<0.01
Yup'ik *(Alaska Native)* (0)	1	<0.01
Asian (8,507)	12,159	4.51
Not Hispanic (8,106)	11,029	4.09
Hispanic (401)	1,130	0.42
Bangladeshi (6)	7	<0.01
Bhutanese (3)	3	<0.01
Burmese (17)	30	0.01
Cambodian (93)	123	0.05
Chinese, ex. Taiwanese (1,638)	2,449	0.91
Filipino (2,906)	4,483	1.66
Hmong (14)	19	0.01
Indian (767)	978	0.36
Indonesian (69)	158	0.06
Japanese (1,046)	2,019	0.75
Korean (675)	925	0.34
Laotian (58)	74	0.03
Malaysian (5)	16	0.01
Nepalese (2)	8	<0.01
Pakistani (54)	76	0.03
Sri Lankan (24)	30	0.01
Taiwanese (72)	104	0.04
Thai (146)	211	0.08
Vietnamese (431)	558	0.21
Hawaii Native/Pacific Islander (389)	1,069	0.40
Not Hispanic (346)	877	0.33
Hispanic (43)	192	0.07
Fijian (20)	26	0.01
Guamanian/Chamorro (55)	117	0.04
Marshallese (2)	5	<0.01
Native Hawaiian (130)	493	0.18
Samoan (82)	160	0.06
Tongan (14)	22	0.01
White (222,756)	231,936	86.02
Not Hispanic (191,696)	197,515	73.25
Hispanic (31,060)	34,421	12.77

*Notes: † The Census 2010 population figure is used to calculate the percentages in the Hispanic Origin and Race categories. Ancestry percentages are based on the 2006-2010 American Community Survey population (not shown); ‡ Numbers in parentheses indicate the number of people reporting a single ancestry; * Numbers in parentheses indicate the number of persons reporting this race alone, not in combination with any other race; Please refer to the Explanation of Data for more information.*

San Mateo County

Population: 718,451

Ancestry	Population	%
Afghan (133)	169	0.02
African, Sub-Saharan (1,329)	2,124	0.30
African (646)	1,153	0.16
Cape Verdean (0)	0	<0.01
Ethiopian (129)	149	0.02
Ghanaian (22)	22	<0.01
Kenyan (25)	57	0.01
Liberian (90)	136	0.02
Nigerian (182)	302	0.04
Senegalese (0)	0	<0.01
Sierra Leonean (0)	0	<0.01
Somalian (0)	0	<0.01
South African (159)	229	0.03
Sudanese (0)	0	<0.01
Ugandan (0)	0	<0.01
Zimbabwean (0)	0	<0.01
Other Sub-Saharan African (76)	76	0.01
Albanian (30)	91	0.01
Alsatian (7)	45	0.01
American (11,173)	11,173	1.59
Arab (8,714)	10,873	1.54
Arab (2,101)	2,455	0.35
Egyptian (688)	763	0.11
Iraqi (567)	567	0.08
Jordanian (691)	945	0.13
Lebanese (1,189)	2,000	0.28
Moroccan (175)	214	0.03
Palestinian (1,835)	2,063	0.29
Syrian (214)	370	0.05
Other Arab (1,254)	1,496	0.21
Armenian (1,997)	2,791	0.40
Assyrian/Chaldean/Syriac (159)	260	0.04
Australian (295)	479	0.07
Austrian (553)	2,140	0.30
Basque (275)	832	0.12
Belgian (208)	602	0.09
Brazilian (1,454)	1,880	0.27
British (2,434)	3,978	0.56
Bulgarian (135)	194	0.03
Cajun (0)	0	<0.01
Canadian (1,144)	2,105	0.30
Carpatho Rusyn (0)	18	<0.01
Celtic (202)	224	0.03
Croatian (756)	1,730	0.25
Cypriot (34)	53	0.01
Czech (637)	2,129	0.30
Czechoslovakian (273)	649	0.09
Danish (1,209)	4,510	0.64
Dutch (1,612)	6,875	0.98
Eastern European (1,457)	1,644	0.23
English (12,238)	48,076	6.83
Estonian (125)	228	0.03
European (11,291)	13,240	1.88
Finnish (435)	1,282	0.18
French, ex. Basque (3,011)	16,961	2.41
French Canadian (747)	1,751	0.25
German (16,906)	64,292	9.13
German Russian (18)	18	<0.01
Greek (3,299)	6,042	0.86
Guyanese (38)	48	0.01
Hungarian (1,125)	2,813	0.40
Icelander (36)	151	0.02
Iranian (4,221)	4,741	0.67
Irish (15,540)	60,636	8.61
Israeli (214)	383	0.05
Italian (19,266)	48,563	6.89
Latvian (133)	329	0.05
Lithuanian (275)	1,131	0.16
Luxemburger (0)	14	<0.01
Macedonian (8)	33	<0.01
Maltese (870)	1,532	0.22
New Zealander (180)	216	0.03
Northern European (1,067)	1,211	0.17
Norwegian (2,241)	7,172	1.02
Pennsylvania German (41)	86	0.01
Polish (3,498)	10,638	1.51
Portuguese (2,129)	5,851	0.83
Romanian (521)	985	0.14
Russian (7,001)	12,572	1.78
Scandinavian (618)	1,108	0.16
Scotch-Irish (2,405)	7,378	1.05
Scottish (3,369)	12,051	1.71
Serbian (71)	237	0.03
Slavic (42)	75	0.01
Slovak (203)	477	0.07
Slovene (50)	187	0.03
Soviet Union (0)	0	<0.01
Swedish (2,273)	9,730	1.38
Swiss (859)	2,962	0.42
Turkish (966)	1,349	0.19
Ukrainian (1,361)	2,376	0.34
Welsh (455)	3,202	0.45
West Indian, ex. Hispanic (424)	680	0.10
Bahamian (0)	0	<0.01
Barbadian (10)	10	<0.01
Belizean (18)	30	<0.01
Bermudan (0)	0	<0.01
British West Indian (0)	37	0.01
Dutch West Indian (0)	0	<0.01
Haitian (120)	120	0.02
Jamaican (191)	325	0.05
Trinidadian/Tobagonian (61)	88	0.01
U.S. Virgin Islander (0)	0	<0.01
West Indian (18)	64	0.01
Other West Indian (6)	6	<0.01
Yugoslavian (383)	796	0.11

Hispanic Origin	Population	%
Hispanic or Latino (of any race)	182,502	25.40
Central American, ex. Mexican	39,500	5.50
Costa Rican	439	0.06
Guatemalan	8,769	1.22
Honduran	1,281	0.18
Nicaraguan	8,676	1.21
Panamanian	355	0.05
Salvadoran	19,574	2.72
Other Central American	406	0.06
Cuban	1,193	0.17
Dominican Republic	156	0.02
Mexican	112,444	15.65
Puerto Rican	3,962	0.55
South American	9,713	1.35
Argentinean	1,056	0.15
Bolivian	565	0.08
Chilean	848	0.12
Colombian	1,304	0.18
Ecuadorian	502	0.07
Paraguayan	35	<0.01
Peruvian	4,761	0.66
Uruguayan	109	0.02
Venezuelan	318	0.04
Other South American	215	0.03
Other Hispanic or Latino	15,534	2.16

Race*	Population	%
African-American/Black (20,436)	26,338	3.67
Not Hispanic (18,763)	23,054	3.21
Hispanic (1,673)	3,284	0.46
American Indian/Alaska Native (3,306)	8,367	1.16
Not Hispanic (1,125)	4,070	0.57
Hispanic (2,181)	4,297	0.60
Alaska Athabascan *(Ala. Nat.)* (5)	14	<0.01
Aleut *(Alaska Native)* (6)	22	<0.01
Apache (88)	266	0.04
Arapaho (21)	38	0.01
Blackfeet (12)	216	0.03
Canadian/French Am. Ind. (10)	34	<0.01
Central American Ind. (54)	103	0.01
Cherokee (134)	966	0.13
Cheyenne (2)	20	<0.01
Chickasaw (14)	45	0.01
Chippewa (40)	118	0.02
Choctaw (83)	269	0.04
Colville (4)	6	<0.01
Comanche (7)	36	0.01
Cree (1)	9	<0.01
Creek (16)	60	0.01
Crow (0)	0	<0.01
Delaware (2)	17	<0.01
Hopi (8)	19	<0.01
Houma (0)	1	<0.01
Inupiat *(Alaska Native)* (4)	11	<0.01
Iroquois (14)	101	0.01
Kiowa (3)	16	<0.01
Lumbee (3)	13	<0.01
Menominee (0)	2	<0.01
Mexican American Ind. (541)	832	0.12
Navajo (106)	254	0.04
Osage (2)	23	<0.01
Ottawa (2)	5	<0.01
Paiute (13)	34	<0.01
Pima (3)	16	<0.01
Potawatomi (4)	13	<0.01
Pueblo (23)	61	0.01
Puget Sound Salish (2)	3	<0.01
Seminole (5)	47	0.01
Shoshone (6)	16	<0.01
Sioux (60)	184	0.03
South American Ind. (38)	125	0.02
Spanish American Ind. (56)	82	0.01
Tlingit-Haida *(Alaska Native)* (20)	45	0.01
Tohono O'Odham (7)	21	<0.01
Tsimshian *(Alaska Native)* (2)	3	<0.01
Ute (1)	19	<0.01
Yakama (4)	4	<0.01
Yaqui (29)	65	0.01
Yuman (4)	18	<0.01
Yup'ik *(Alaska Native)* (0)	0	<0.01
Asian (178,118)	199,294	27.74
Not Hispanic (175,934)	193,418	26.92
Hispanic (2,184)	5,876	0.82
Bangladeshi (59)	69	0.01
Bhutanese (3)	3	<0.01
Burmese (2,263)	2,577	0.36
Cambodian (345)	493	0.07
Chinese, ex. Taiwanese (62,372)	71,857	10.00
Filipino (70,191)	80,349	11.18
Hmong (74)	93	0.01
Indian (13,486)	15,933	2.22
Indonesian (717)	1,079	0.15
Japanese (8,779)	13,294	1.85
Korean (5,496)	7,061	0.98
Laotian (211)	300	0.04
Malaysian (85)	162	0.02
Nepalese (245)	260	0.04
Pakistani (779)	927	0.13
Sri Lankan (129)	169	0.02
Taiwanese (2,229)	2,648	0.37
Thai (952)	1,295	0.18
Vietnamese (3,492)	4,680	0.65
Hawaii Native/Pacific Islander (10,317)	15,069	2.10
Not Hispanic (9,884)	13,667	1.90
Hispanic (433)	1,402	0.20
Fijian (1,732)	2,168	0.30
Guamanian/Chamorro (339)	685	0.10
Marshallese (10)	14	<0.01
Native Hawaiian (525)	2,032	0.28
Samoan (1,972)	2,792	0.39
Tongan (4,594)	5,312	0.74
White (383,535)	414,430	57.68
Not Hispanic (303,609)	323,113	44.97
Hispanic (79,926)	91,317	12.71

*Notes: † The Census 2010 population figure is used to calculate the percentages in the Hispanic Origin and Race categories. Ancestry percentages are based on the 2006-2010 American Community Survey population (not shown); ‡ Numbers in parentheses indicate the number of people reporting a single ancestry; * Numbers in parentheses indicate the number of persons reporting this race alone, not in combination with any other race; Please refer to the Explanation of Data for more information.*

Santa Barbara County

Population: 423,895

Ancestry	Population	%
Afghan (165)	165	0.04
African, Sub-Saharan (641)	937	0.23
African (389)	597	0.14
Cape Verdean (12)	12	<0.01
Ethiopian (80)	93	0.02
Ghanaian (0)	0	<0.01
Kenyan (8)	8	<0.01
Liberian (0)	0	<0.01
Nigerian (20)	53	0.01
Senegalese (0)	0	<0.01
Sierra Leonean (0)	0	<0.01
Somalian (0)	0	<0.01
South African (73)	115	0.03
Sudanese (36)	36	0.01
Ugandan (0)	0	<0.01
Zimbabwean (0)	0	<0.01
Other Sub-Saharan African (23)	23	0.01
Albanian (8)	8	<0.01
Alsatian (0)	13	<0.01
American (10,185)	10,185	2.45
Arab (1,120)	1,720	0.41
Arab (490)	638	0.15
Egyptian (57)	146	0.04
Iraqi (0)	0	<0.01
Jordanian (0)	0	<0.01
Lebanese (325)	550	0.13
Moroccan (37)	61	0.01
Palestinian (43)	56	0.01
Syrian (18)	111	0.03
Other Arab (150)	158	0.04
Armenian (315)	552	0.13
Assyrian/Chaldean/Syriac (25)	25	0.01
Australian (94)	438	0.11
Austrian (401)	1,360	0.33
Basque (248)	648	0.16
Belgian (251)	637	0.15
Brazilian (81)	234	0.06
British (1,461)	2,640	0.63
Bulgarian (57)	82	0.02
Cajun (31)	74	0.02
Canadian (608)	1,629	0.39
Carpatho Rusyn (0)	0	<0.01
Celtic (57)	76	0.02
Croatian (193)	674	0.16
Cypriot (12)	12	<0.01
Czech (332)	1,358	0.33
Czechoslovakian (332)	738	0.18
Danish (1,783)	4,635	1.11
Dutch (1,703)	5,763	1.39
Eastern European (632)	751	0.18
English (9,788)	37,935	9.12
Estonian (0)	49	0.01
European (5,580)	6,458	1.55
Finnish (147)	755	0.18
French, ex. Basque (2,016)	12,087	2.91
French Canadian (604)	1,565	0.38
German (12,868)	50,213	12.07
German Russian (0)	12	<0.01
Greek (832)	1,872	0.45
Guyanese (111)	111	0.03
Hungarian (712)	1,762	0.42
Icelander (10)	114	0.03
Iranian (810)	1,002	0.24
Irish (9,215)	38,755	9.31
Israeli (161)	237	0.06
Italian (6,557)	19,606	4.71
Latvian (92)	180	0.04
Lithuanian (224)	639	0.15
Luxemburger (0)	18	<0.01
Macedonian (0)	51	0.01
Maltese (19)	58	0.01
New Zealander (9)	48	0.01
Northern European (452)	614	0.15
Norwegian (2,400)	6,575	1.58
Pennsylvania German (39)	118	0.03
Polish (1,764)	7,078	1.70
Portuguese (1,861)	4,510	1.08
Romanian (69)	500	0.12
Russian (2,174)	5,855	1.41
Scandinavian (444)	857	0.21
Scotch-Irish (2,620)	7,268	1.75
Scottish (2,267)	8,026	1.93
Serbian (166)	244	0.06
Slavic (70)	163	0.04
Slovak (210)	419	0.10
Slovene (15)	36	0.01
Soviet Union (0)	0	<0.01
Swedish (2,351)	7,329	1.76
Swiss (478)	2,451	0.59
Turkish (324)	473	0.11
Ukrainian (705)	1,223	0.29
Welsh (410)	3,424	0.82
West Indian, ex. Hispanic (246)	544	0.13
Bahamian (0)	0	<0.01
Barbadian (0)	0	<0.01
Belizean (0)	16	<0.01
Bermudan (0)	0	<0.01
British West Indian (42)	104	0.02
Dutch West Indian (0)	32	0.01
Haitian (9)	55	0.01
Jamaican (161)	303	0.07
Trinidadian/Tobagonian (11)	11	<0.01
U.S. Virgin Islander (0)	0	<0.01
West Indian (23)	23	0.01
Other West Indian (0)	0	<0.01
Yugoslavian (117)	196	0.05

Hispanic Origin	Population	%
Hispanic or Latino (of any race)	181,687	42.86
Central American, ex. Mexican	4,203	0.99
Costa Rican	198	0.05
Guatemalan	1,547	0.36
Honduran	414	0.10
Nicaraguan	257	0.06
Panamanian	125	0.03
Salvadoran	1,611	0.38
Other Central American	51	0.01
Cuban	446	0.11
Dominican Republic	75	0.02
Mexican	163,356	38.54
Puerto Rican	1,398	0.33
South American	2,061	0.49
Argentinean	428	0.10
Bolivian	60	0.01
Chilean	303	0.07
Colombian	492	0.12
Ecuadorian	134	0.03
Paraguayan	20	<0.01
Peruvian	475	0.11
Uruguayan	24	0.01
Venezuelan	107	0.03
Other South American	18	<0.01
Other Hispanic or Latino	10,148	2.39

Race*	Population	%
African-American/Black (8,513)	11,731	2.77
Not Hispanic (7,242)	9,405	2.22
Hispanic (1,271)	2,326	0.55
American Indian/Alaska Native (5,485)	10,110	2.39
Not Hispanic (1,843)	4,045	0.95
Hispanic (3,642)	6,065	1.43
Alaska Athabascan *(Ala. Nat.)* (7)	8	<0.01
Aleut *(Alaska Native)* (7)	20	<0.01
Apache (152)	309	0.07
Arapaho (1)	4	<0.01
Blackfeet (24)	122	0.03
Canadian/French Am. Ind. (11)	33	0.01
Central American Ind. (18)	29	0.01
Cherokee (184)	877	0.21
Cheyenne (9)	24	0.01
Chickasaw (22)	60	0.01
Chippewa (29)	85	0.02
Choctaw (105)	293	0.07
Colville (0)	1	<0.01
Comanche (15)	44	0.01
Cree (2)	10	<0.01
Creek (28)	75	0.02
Crow (2)	9	<0.01
Delaware (13)	20	<0.01
Hopi (5)	25	0.01
Houma (0)	1	<0.01
Inupiat *(Alaska Native)* (10)	15	<0.01
Iroquois (17)	65	0.02
Kiowa (4)	10	<0.01
Lumbee (5)	7	<0.01
Menominee (1)	1	<0.01
Mexican American Ind. (1,011)	1,450	0.34
Navajo (63)	146	0.03
Osage (11)	32	0.01
Ottawa (0)	0	<0.01
Paiute (13)	22	0.01
Pima (15)	29	0.01
Potawatomi (4)	23	0.01
Pueblo (43)	65	0.02
Puget Sound Salish (4)	8	<0.01
Seminole (3)	19	<0.01
Shoshone (7)	25	0.01
Sioux (51)	165	0.04
South American Ind. (16)	35	0.01
Spanish American Ind. (42)	52	0.01
Tlingit-Haida *(Alaska Native)* (16)	29	0.01
Tohono O'Odham (6)	22	0.01
Tsimshian *(Alaska Native)* (1)	1	<0.01
Ute (4)	5	<0.01
Yakama (6)	11	<0.01
Yaqui (86)	165	0.04
Yuman (12)	17	<0.01
Yup'ik *(Alaska Native)* (5)	6	<0.01
Asian (20,665)	27,475	6.48
Not Hispanic (19,591)	24,549	5.79
Hispanic (1,074)	2,926	0.69
Bangladeshi (36)	39	0.01
Bhutanese (13)	14	<0.01
Burmese (7)	17	<0.01
Cambodian (144)	198	0.05
Chinese, ex. Taiwanese (3,814)	5,317	1.25
Filipino (6,802)	9,693	2.29
Hmong (491)	517	0.12
Indian (1,777)	2,212	0.52
Indonesian (152)	250	0.06
Japanese (2,121)	3,797	0.90
Korean (1,928)	2,399	0.57
Laotian (189)	221	0.05
Malaysian (12)	37	0.01
Nepalese (23)	31	0.01
Pakistani (123)	151	0.04
Sri Lankan (98)	125	0.03
Taiwanese (314)	394	0.09
Thai (304)	440	0.10
Vietnamese (1,428)	1,794	0.42
Hawaii Native/Pacific Islander (806)	1,991	0.47
Not Hispanic (680)	1,511	0.36
Hispanic (126)	480	0.11
Fijian (13)	24	0.01
Guamanian/Chamorro (251)	387	0.09
Marshallese (6)	7	<0.01
Native Hawaiian (263)	907	0.21
Samoan (129)	239	0.06
Tongan (29)	55	0.01
White (295,124)	311,913	73.58
Not Hispanic (203,122)	211,098	49.80
Hispanic (92,002)	100,815	23.78

*Notes: † The Census 2010 population figure is used to calculate the percentages in the Hispanic Origin and Race categories. Ancestry percentages are based on the 2006-2010 American Community Survey population (not shown); ‡ Numbers in parentheses indicate the number of people reporting a single ancestry; * Numbers in parentheses indicate the number of persons reporting this race alone, not in combination with any other race; Please refer to the Explanation of Data for more information.*

Santa Clara County

Population: 1,781,642

Ancestry	Population	%
Afghan (1,728)	1,855	0.11
African, Sub-Saharan (7,126)	9,162	0.53
African (2,224)	3,339	0.19
Cape Verdean (21)	115	0.01
Ethiopian (3,125)	3,336	0.19
Ghanaian (0)	31	<0.01
Kenyan (174)	217	0.01
Liberian (145)	198	0.01
Nigerian (359)	400	0.02
Senegalese (14)	14	<0.01
Sierra Leonean (44)	117	0.01
Somalian (371)	408	0.02
South African (245)	407	0.02
Sudanese (139)	181	0.01
Ugandan (18)	18	<0.01
Zimbabwean (0)	0	<0.01
Other Sub-Saharan African (247)	381	0.02
Albanian (149)	181	0.01
Alsatian (45)	68	<0.01
American (25,124)	25,124	1.44
Arab (7,136)	10,279	0.59
Arab (897)	1,416	0.08
Egyptian (1,455)	1,780	0.10
Iraqi (340)	428	0.02
Jordanian (400)	415	0.02
Lebanese (1,498)	2,397	0.14
Moroccan (200)	508	0.03
Palestinian (671)	983	0.06
Syrian (383)	575	0.03
Other Arab (1,292)	1,777	0.10
Armenian (2,471)	3,349	0.19
Assyrian/Chaldean/Syriac (2,481)	2,880	0.17
Australian (258)	547	0.03
Austrian (789)	3,009	0.17
Basque (136)	510	0.03
Belgian (707)	1,636	0.09
Brazilian (843)	1,320	0.08
British (5,359)	9,433	0.54
Bulgarian (846)	1,039	0.06
Cajun (47)	130	0.01
Canadian (2,768)	4,802	0.28
Carpatho Rusyn (57)	57	<0.01
Celtic (185)	436	0.03
Croatian (1,963)	4,206	0.24
Cypriot (125)	125	0.01
Czech (1,668)	4,729	0.27
Czechoslovakian (633)	1,266	0.07
Danish (2,340)	8,907	0.51
Dutch (4,564)	16,619	0.96
Eastern European (2,478)	2,982	0.17
English (27,603)	104,760	6.02
Estonian (134)	270	0.02
European (20,926)	25,240	1.45
Finnish (786)	2,617	0.15
French, ex. Basque (7,152)	34,726	2.00
French Canadian (1,705)	4,653	0.27
German (35,838)	141,974	8.16
German Russian (35)	43	<0.01
Greek (3,101)	6,895	0.40
Guyanese (144)	236	0.01
Hungarian (1,951)	5,194	0.30
Icelander (74)	215	0.01
Iranian (14,349)	15,726	0.90
Irish (25,686)	104,278	6.00
Israeli (2,488)	2,935	0.17
Italian (32,189)	80,529	4.63
Latvian (309)	695	0.04
Lithuanian (613)	1,962	0.11
Luxemburger (74)	271	0.02
Macedonian (121)	201	0.01
Maltese (177)	341	0.02
New Zealander (173)	240	0.01
Northern European (2,991)	3,297	0.19
Norwegian (5,265)	18,759	1.08
Pennsylvania German (139)	273	0.02
Polish (6,973)	21,479	1.23
Portuguese (14,656)	28,163	1.62
Romanian (1,887)	3,300	0.19
Russian (11,325)	19,909	1.14
Scandinavian (1,099)	2,684	0.15
Scotch-Irish (4,816)	16,315	0.94
Scottish (6,187)	24,367	1.40
Serbian (809)	1,321	0.08
Slavic (311)	779	0.04
Slovak (505)	1,427	0.08
Slovene (173)	398	0.02
Soviet Union (0)	9	<0.01
Swedish (4,284)	20,141	1.16
Swiss (1,850)	6,916	0.40
Turkish (983)	1,438	0.08
Ukrainian (3,106)	5,116	0.29
Welsh (1,466)	8,208	0.47
West Indian, ex. Hispanic (859)	1,455	0.08
Bahamian (0)	0	<0.01
Barbadian (13)	13	<0.01
Belizean (0)	41	<0.01
Bermudan (0)	0	<0.01
British West Indian (0)	0	<0.01
Dutch West Indian (0)	14	<0.01
Haitian (219)	278	0.02
Jamaican (404)	706	0.04
Trinidadian/Tobagonian (120)	174	0.01
U.S. Virgin Islander (0)	10	<0.01
West Indian (103)	181	0.01
Other West Indian (0)	38	<0.01
Yugoslavian (2,033)	3,282	0.19

Hispanic Origin	Population	%
Hispanic or Latino (of any race)	479,210	26.90
Central American, ex. Mexican	24,783	1.39
Costa Rican	545	0.03
Guatemalan	4,479	0.25
Honduran	2,498	0.14
Nicaraguan	4,479	0.25
Panamanian	629	0.04
Salvadoran	11,914	0.67
Other Central American	239	0.01
Cuban	2,292	0.13
Dominican Republic	459	0.03
Mexican	400,402	22.47
Puerto Rican	7,798	0.44
South American	12,719	0.71
Argentinean	1,538	0.09
Bolivian	897	0.05
Chilean	1,370	0.08
Colombian	2,436	0.14
Ecuadorian	723	0.04
Paraguayan	53	<0.01
Peruvian	4,618	0.26
Uruguayan	135	0.01
Venezuelan	780	0.04
Other South American	169	0.01
Other Hispanic or Latino	30,757	1.73

Race*	Population	%
African-American/Black (46,428)	59,787	3.36
Not Hispanic (42,331)	51,686	2.90
Hispanic (4,097)	8,101	0.45
American Indian/Alaska Native (12,960)	26,569	1.49
Not Hispanic (4,042)	11,390	0.64
Hispanic (8,918)	15,179	0.85
Alaska Athabascan *(Ala. Nat.)* (10)	32	<0.01
Aleut *(Alaska Native)* (23)	48	<0.01
Apache (634)	1,446	0.08
Arapaho (6)	15	<0.01
Blackfeet (71)	474	0.03
Canadian/French Am. Ind. (28)	81	<0.01
Central American Ind. (61)	99	0.01
Cherokee (582)	2,961	0.17
Cheyenne (12)	38	<0.01
Chickasaw (46)	111	0.01
Chippewa (155)	354	0.02
Choctaw (175)	659	0.04
Colville (12)	18	<0.01
Comanche (61)	134	0.01
Cree (6)	37	<0.01
Creek (62)	206	0.01
Crow (5)	27	<0.01
Delaware (11)	48	<0.01
Hopi (32)	81	<0.01
Houma (2)	4	<0.01
Inupiat *(Alaska Native)* (18)	48	<0.01
Iroquois (55)	214	0.01
Kiowa (25)	40	<0.01
Lumbee (8)	19	<0.01
Menominee (10)	16	<0.01
Mexican American Ind. (1,763)	2,582	0.14
Navajo (369)	782	0.04
Osage (22)	78	<0.01
Ottawa (5)	14	<0.01
Paiute (54)	100	0.01
Pima (41)	56	<0.01
Potawatomi (49)	123	0.01
Pueblo (117)	220	0.01
Puget Sound Salish (6)	26	<0.01
Seminole (17)	96	0.01
Shoshone (37)	92	0.01
Sioux (250)	515	0.03
South American Ind. (85)	225	0.01
Spanish American Ind. (74)	110	0.01
Tlingit-Haida *(Alaska Native)* (42)	87	<0.01
Tohono O'Odham (59)	101	0.01
Tsimshian *(Alaska Native)* (3)	8	<0.01
Ute (14)	41	<0.01
Yakama (7)	14	<0.01
Yaqui (301)	585	0.03
Yuman (30)	47	<0.01
Yup'ik *(Alaska Native)* (7)	11	<0.01
Asian (570,524)	618,242	34.70
Not Hispanic (565,466)	605,123	33.96
Hispanic (5,058)	13,119	0.74
Bangladeshi (935)	1,033	0.06
Bhutanese (31)	34	<0.01
Burmese (1,011)	1,205	0.07
Cambodian (4,798)	5,842	0.33
Chinese, ex. Taiwanese (136,593)	156,637	8.79
Filipino (87,412)	104,234	5.85
Hmong (323)	362	0.02
Indian (117,596)	123,182	6.91
Indonesian (1,121)	1,897	0.11
Japanese (25,075)	36,389	2.04
Korean (27,946)	31,591	1.77
Laotian (1,562)	1,999	0.11
Malaysian (441)	740	0.04
Nepalese (707)	747	0.04
Pakistani (4,488)	5,063	0.28
Sri Lankan (745)	869	0.05
Taiwanese (15,067)	17,117	0.96
Thai (1,827)	2,466	0.14
Vietnamese (125,695)	134,525	7.55
Hawaii Native/Pacific Islander (7,060)	14,468	0.81
Not Hispanic (6,252)	11,834	0.66
Hispanic (808)	2,634	0.15
Fijian (756)	947	0.05
Guamanian/Chamorro (1,209)	2,363	0.13
Marshallese (22)	30	<0.01
Native Hawaiian (964)	3,937	0.22
Samoan (2,057)	2,927	0.16
Tongan (1,078)	1,355	0.08
White (836,616)	908,082	50.97
Not Hispanic (626,909)	671,521	37.69
Hispanic (209,707)	236,561	13.28

*Notes: † The Census 2010 population figure is used to calculate the percentages in the Hispanic Origin and Race categories. Ancestry percentages are based on the 2006-2010 American Community Survey population (not shown); ‡ Numbers in parentheses indicate the number of people reporting a single ancestry; * Numbers in parentheses indicate the number of persons reporting this race alone, not in combination with any other race; Please refer to the Explanation of Data for more information.*

Santa Cruz County

Population: 262,382

Ancestry	Population	%
Afghan (105)	118	0.05
African, Sub-Saharan (245)	424	0.17
African (163)	311	0.12
Cape Verdean (0)	0	<0.01
Ethiopian (26)	26	0.01
Ghanaian (0)	0	<0.01
Kenyan (0)	0	<0.01
Liberian (0)	0	<0.01
Nigerian (17)	17	0.01
Senegalese (0)	0	<0.01
Sierra Leonean (0)	0	<0.01
Somalian (0)	0	<0.01
South African (39)	59	0.02
Sudanese (0)	11	<0.01
Ugandan (0)	0	<0.01
Zimbabwean (0)	0	<0.01
Other Sub-Saharan African (0)	0	<0.01
Albanian (0)	10	<0.01
Alsatian (0)	15	0.01
American (6,274)	6,274	2.44
Arab (426)	982	0.38
Arab (32)	147	0.06
Egyptian (0)	74	0.03
Iraqi (16)	19	0.01
Jordanian (0)	0	<0.01
Lebanese (163)	412	0.16
Moroccan (37)	37	0.01
Palestinian (68)	77	0.03
Syrian (8)	64	0.02
Other Arab (102)	152	0.06
Armenian (249)	468	0.18
Assyrian/Chaldean/Syriac (0)	0	<0.01
Australian (105)	193	0.08
Austrian (275)	1,067	0.42
Basque (66)	178	0.07
Belgian (63)	317	0.12
Brazilian (79)	380	0.15
British (1,154)	2,205	0.86
Bulgarian (42)	104	0.04
Cajun (35)	58	0.02
Canadian (387)	817	0.32
Carpatho Rusyn (0)	0	<0.01
Celtic (131)	200	0.08
Croatian (369)	895	0.35
Cypriot (0)	0	<0.01
Czech (213)	1,255	0.49
Czechoslovakian (149)	403	0.16
Danish (655)	2,577	1.00
Dutch (862)	4,612	1.80
Eastern European (516)	746	0.29
English (7,163)	30,202	11.76
Estonian (54)	98	0.04
European (5,326)	6,915	2.69
Finnish (259)	755	0.29
French, ex. Basque (1,094)	9,645	3.75
French Canadian (486)	1,517	0.59
German (8,574)	37,764	14.70
German Russian (7)	7	<0.01
Greek (442)	1,500	0.58
Guyanese (0)	0	<0.01
Hungarian (269)	1,235	0.48
Icelander (27)	97	0.04
Iranian (333)	493	0.19
Irish (6,323)	29,996	11.68
Israeli (103)	198	0.08
Italian (6,176)	18,437	7.18
Latvian (33)	114	0.04
Lithuanian (68)	421	0.16
Luxemburger (8)	16	0.01
Macedonian (0)	39	0.02
Maltese (20)	29	0.01
New Zealander (45)	100	0.04
Northern European (2,312)	2,667	1.04
Norwegian (1,673)	4,652	1.81
Pennsylvania German (45)	50	0.02
Polish (1,158)	5,485	2.14
Portuguese (2,185)	5,936	2.31
Romanian (228)	577	0.22
Russian (1,419)	5,046	1.96
Scandinavian (527)	1,082	0.42
Scotch-Irish (1,779)	4,963	1.93
Scottish (2,242)	8,767	3.41
Serbian (57)	78	0.03
Slavic (101)	233	0.09
Slovak (153)	327	0.13
Slovene (18)	218	0.08
Soviet Union (0)	9	<0.01
Swedish (1,128)	6,501	2.53
Swiss (235)	1,663	0.65
Turkish (128)	245	0.10
Ukrainian (215)	555	0.22
Welsh (315)	2,453	0.95
West Indian, ex. Hispanic (10)	71	0.03
Bahamian (0)	0	<0.01
Barbadian (1)	2	<0.01
Belizean (0)	0	<0.01
Bermudan (0)	0	<0.01
British West Indian (0)	0	<0.01
Dutch West Indian (0)	0	<0.01
Haitian (0)	0	<0.01
Jamaican (0)	0	<0.01
Trinidadian/Tobagonian (0)	18	0.01
U.S. Virgin Islander (0)	0	<0.01
West Indian (9)	51	0.02
Other West Indian (0)	0	<0.01
Yugoslavian (131)	413	0.16

Hispanic Origin	Population	%
Hispanic or Latino (of any race)	84,092	32.05
Central American, ex. Mexican	2,429	0.93
Costa Rican	76	0.03
Guatemalan	302	0.12
Honduran	80	0.03
Nicaraguan	189	0.07
Panamanian	72	0.03
Salvadoran	1,689	0.64
Other Central American	21	0.01
Cuban	311	0.12
Dominican Republic	47	0.02
Mexican	73,848	28.15
Puerto Rican	756	0.29
South American	1,249	0.48
Argentinean	231	0.09
Bolivian	61	0.02
Chilean	159	0.06
Colombian	262	0.10
Ecuadorian	83	0.03
Paraguayan	7	<0.01
Peruvian	346	0.13
Uruguayan	23	0.01
Venezuelan	62	0.02
Other South American	15	0.01
Other Hispanic or Latino	5,452	2.08

Race*	Population	%
African-American/Black (2,766)	4,757	1.81
Not Hispanic (2,304)	3,800	1.45
Hispanic (462)	957	0.36
American Indian/Alaska Native (2,253)	5,511	2.10
Not Hispanic (978)	3,134	1.19
Hispanic (1,275)	2,377	0.91
Alaska Athabascan *(Ala. Nat.)* (1)	1	<0.01
Aleut *(Alaska Native)* (1)	12	<0.01
Apache (95)	223	0.08
Arapaho (1)	8	<0.01
Blackfeet (18)	111	0.04
Canadian/French Am. Ind. (3)	21	0.01
Central American Ind. (16)	23	0.01
Cherokee (150)	872	0.33
Cheyenne (7)	18	0.01
Chickasaw (7)	22	0.01
Chippewa (36)	91	0.03
Choctaw (43)	180	0.07
Colville (0)	0	<0.01
Comanche (19)	54	0.02
Cree (5)	28	0.01
Creek (10)	64	0.02
Crow (0)	3	<0.01
Delaware (1)	9	<0.01
Hopi (10)	23	0.01
Houma (0)	0	<0.01
Inupiat *(Alaska Native)* (7)	13	<0.01
Iroquois (12)	66	0.03
Kiowa (0)	5	<0.01
Lumbee (1)	2	<0.01
Menominee (2)	3	<0.01
Mexican American Ind. (349)	522	0.20
Navajo (31)	94	0.04
Osage (4)	16	0.01
Ottawa (3)	7	<0.01
Paiute (8)	21	0.01
Pima (6)	13	<0.01
Potawatomi (12)	27	0.01
Pueblo (19)	42	0.02
Puget Sound Salish (0)	1	<0.01
Seminole (3)	19	0.01
Shoshone (3)	18	0.01
Sioux (26)	115	0.04
South American Ind. (12)	43	0.02
Spanish American Ind. (14)	23	0.01
Tlingit-Haida *(Alaska Native)* (9)	19	0.01
Tohono O'Odham (10)	22	0.01
Tsimshian *(Alaska Native)* (0)	1	<0.01
Ute (0)	5	<0.01
Yakama (1)	4	<0.01
Yaqui (58)	109	0.04
Yuman (1)	1	<0.01
Yup'ik *(Alaska Native)* (5)	7	<0.01
Asian (11,112)	15,683	5.98
Not Hispanic (10,658)	14,235	5.43
Hispanic (454)	1,448	0.55
Bangladeshi (5)	5	<0.01
Bhutanese (0)	0	<0.01
Burmese (16)	21	0.01
Cambodian (119)	149	0.06
Chinese, ex. Taiwanese (2,957)	4,080	1.55
Filipino (2,733)	4,432	1.69
Hmong (30)	31	0.01
Indian (1,077)	1,400	0.53
Indonesian (44)	134	0.05
Japanese (1,685)	3,048	1.16
Korean (785)	1,083	0.41
Laotian (22)	34	0.01
Malaysian (8)	33	0.01
Nepalese (24)	30	0.01
Pakistani (50)	78	0.03
Sri Lankan (32)	41	0.02
Taiwanese (152)	190	0.07
Thai (196)	285	0.11
Vietnamese (629)	821	0.31
Hawaii Native/Pacific Islander (349)	1,213	0.46
Not Hispanic (292)	943	0.36
Hispanic (57)	270	0.10
Fijian (11)	23	0.01
Guamanian/Chamorro (47)	148	0.06
Marshallese (0)	0	<0.01
Native Hawaiian (155)	581	0.22
Samoan (48)	146	0.06
Tongan (11)	23	0.01
White (190,208)	201,193	76.68
Not Hispanic (156,397)	162,962	62.11
Hispanic (33,811)	38,231	14.57

*Notes: † The Census 2010 population figure is used to calculate the percentages in the Hispanic Origin and Race categories. Ancestry percentages are based on the 2006-2010 American Community Survey population (not shown); ‡ Numbers in parentheses indicate the number of people reporting a single ancestry; * Numbers in parentheses indicate the number of persons reporting this race alone, not in combination with any other race; Please refer to the Explanation of Data for more information.*

Shasta County

Population: 177,223

Ancestry	Population	%
Afghan (10)	10	0.01
African, Sub-Saharan (90)	234	0.13
African (0)	82	0.05
Cape Verdean (0)	0	<0.01
Ethiopian (0)	43	0.02
Ghanaian (0)	0	<0.01
Kenyan (0)	0	<0.01
Liberian (34)	34	0.02
Nigerian (39)	56	0.03
Senegalese (0)	0	<0.01
Sierra Leonean (0)	0	<0.01
Somalian (0)	0	<0.01
South African (17)	17	0.01
Sudanese (0)	0	<0.01
Ugandan (0)	0	<0.01
Zimbabwean (0)	0	<0.01
Other Sub-Saharan African (0)	2	<0.01
Albanian (0)	0	<0.01
Alsatian (10)	10	0.01
American (13,920)	13,920	7.87
Arab (499)	616	0.35
Arab (41)	41	0.02
Egyptian (0)	0	<0.01
Iraqi (178)	197	0.11
Jordanian (157)	157	0.09
Lebanese (106)	204	0.12
Moroccan (0)	0	<0.01
Palestinian (0)	0	<0.01
Syrian (17)	17	0.01
Other Arab (0)	0	<0.01
Armenian (162)	182	0.10
Assyrian/Chaldean/Syriac (0)	10	0.01
Australian (88)	203	0.11
Austrian (131)	572	0.32
Basque (90)	139	0.08
Belgian (18)	86	0.05
Brazilian (34)	44	0.02
British (399)	832	0.47
Bulgarian (0)	13	0.01
Cajun (24)	35	0.02
Canadian (176)	430	0.24
Carpatho Rusyn (0)	0	<0.01
Celtic (37)	37	0.02
Croatian (96)	211	0.12
Cypriot (0)	0	<0.01
Czech (152)	756	0.43
Czechoslovakian (150)	418	0.24
Danish (552)	1,853	1.05
Dutch (835)	4,314	2.44
Eastern European (87)	117	0.07
English (7,164)	23,731	13.41
Estonian (0)	0	<0.01
European (2,185)	2,425	1.37
Finnish (595)	1,140	0.64
French, ex. Basque (919)	6,997	3.96
French Canadian (404)	1,261	0.71
German (11,327)	35,911	20.30
German Russian (9)	70	0.04
Greek (381)	680	0.38
Guyanese (0)	0	<0.01
Hungarian (129)	587	0.33
Icelander (30)	119	0.07
Iranian (124)	188	0.11
Irish (7,255)	27,365	15.47
Israeli (0)	0	<0.01
Italian (3,696)	9,636	5.45
Latvian (11)	21	0.01
Lithuanian (79)	236	0.13
Luxemburger (0)	41	0.02
Macedonian (0)	8	<0.01
Maltese (0)	55	0.03
New Zealander (0)	0	<0.01
Northern European (336)	342	0.19
Norwegian (1,041)	4,284	2.42
Pennsylvania German (100)	184	0.10
Polish (839)	2,633	1.49
Portuguese (819)	2,459	1.39
Romanian (46)	109	0.06
Russian (744)	1,858	1.05
Scandinavian (520)	751	0.42
Scotch-Irish (1,325)	4,460	2.52
Scottish (1,289)	4,272	2.41
Serbian (0)	111	0.06
Slavic (13)	68	0.04
Slovak (31)	142	0.08
Slovene (17)	33	0.02
Soviet Union (0)	0	<0.01
Swedish (1,252)	5,418	3.06
Swiss (194)	929	0.53
Turkish (56)	103	0.06
Ukrainian (144)	373	0.21
Welsh (252)	1,707	0.96
West Indian, ex. Hispanic (6)	97	0.05
Bahamian (0)	0	<0.01
Barbadian (0)	0	<0.01
Belizean (0)	0	<0.01
Bermudan (0)	0	<0.01
British West Indian (0)	0	<0.01
Dutch West Indian (6)	80	0.05
Haitian (0)	0	<0.01
Jamaican (0)	8	<0.01
Trinidadian/Tobagonian (0)	0	<0.01
U.S. Virgin Islander (0)	0	<0.01
West Indian (0)	9	0.01
Other West Indian (0)	0	<0.01
Yugoslavian (153)	250	0.14

Hispanic Origin	Population	%
Hispanic or Latino (of any race)	14,878	8.40
Central American, ex. Mexican	453	0.26
Costa Rican	38	0.02
Guatemalan	94	0.05
Honduran	27	0.02
Nicaraguan	69	0.04
Panamanian	24	0.01
Salvadoran	198	0.11
Other Central American	3	<0.01
Cuban	99	0.06
Dominican Republic	25	0.01
Mexican	11,384	6.42
Puerto Rican	478	0.27
South American	230	0.13
Argentinean	21	0.01
Bolivian	17	0.01
Chilean	19	0.01
Colombian	58	0.03
Ecuadorian	26	0.01
Paraguayan	2	<0.01
Peruvian	62	0.03
Uruguayan	3	<0.01
Venezuelan	19	0.01
Other South American	3	<0.01
Other Hispanic or Latino	2,209	1.25

Race*	Population	%
African-American/Black (1,548)	2,784	1.57
Not Hispanic (1,438)	2,473	1.40
Hispanic (110)	311	0.18
American Indian/Alaska Native (4,950)	9,381	5.29
Not Hispanic (4,162)	7,901	4.46
Hispanic (788)	1,480	0.84
Alaska Athabascan *(Ala. Nat.)* (16)	27	0.02
Aleut *(Alaska Native)* (18)	34	0.02
Apache (54)	143	0.08
Arapaho (2)	9	0.01
Blackfeet (35)	185	0.10
Canadian/French Am. Ind. (7)	11	0.01
Central American Ind. (4)	10	0.01
Cherokee (430)	1,414	0.80
Cheyenne (14)	29	0.02
Chickasaw (24)	65	0.04
Chippewa (62)	130	0.07
Choctaw (134)	378	0.21
Colville (1)	3	<0.01
Comanche (10)	30	0.02
Cree (2)	20	0.01
Creek (21)	67	0.04
Crow (2)	15	0.01
Delaware (6)	13	0.01
Hopi (7)	11	0.01
Houma (0)	0	<0.01
Inupiat *(Alaska Native)* (9)	29	0.02
Iroquois (25)	62	0.03
Kiowa (1)	7	<0.01
Lumbee (3)	13	0.01
Menominee (0)	1	<0.01
Mexican American Ind. (94)	152	0.09
Navajo (58)	129	0.07
Osage (12)	28	0.02
Ottawa (2)	5	<0.01
Paiute (41)	59	0.03
Pima (4)	12	0.01
Potawatomi (30)	57	0.03
Pueblo (17)	21	0.01
Puget Sound Salish (4)	7	<0.01
Seminole (3)	19	0.01
Shoshone (9)	19	0.01
Sioux (75)	155	0.09
South American Ind. (1)	4	<0.01
Spanish American Ind. (1)	3	<0.01
Tlingit-Haida *(Alaska Native)* (23)	42	0.02
Tohono O'Odham (3)	4	<0.01
Tsimshian *(Alaska Native)* (1)	5	<0.01
Ute (1)	7	<0.01
Yakama (3)	8	<0.01
Yaqui (14)	29	0.02
Yuman (12)	17	0.01
Yup'ik *(Alaska Native)* (1)	2	<0.01
Asian (4,391)	5,928	3.34
Not Hispanic (4,297)	5,623	3.17
Hispanic (94)	305	0.17
Bangladeshi (8)	9	0.01
Bhutanese (0)	0	<0.01
Burmese (5)	7	<0.01
Cambodian (41)	68	0.04
Chinese, ex. Taiwanese (488)	790	0.45
Filipino (642)	1,249	0.70
Hmong (81)	99	0.06
Indian (475)	568	0.32
Indonesian (11)	34	0.02
Japanese (276)	676	0.38
Korean (205)	311	0.18
Laotian (1,589)	1,743	0.98
Malaysian (0)	0	<0.01
Nepalese (4)	4	<0.01
Pakistani (26)	29	0.02
Sri Lankan (3)	3	<0.01
Taiwanese (14)	19	0.01
Thai (77)	120	0.07
Vietnamese (148)	198	0.11
Hawaii Native/Pacific Islander (271)	718	0.41
Not Hispanic (232)	595	0.34
Hispanic (39)	123	0.07
Fijian (8)	9	0.01
Guamanian/Chamorro (48)	98	0.06
Marshallese (1)	5	<0.01
Native Hawaiian (122)	399	0.23
Samoan (35)	67	0.04
Tongan (4)	8	<0.01
White (153,726)	161,106	90.91
Not Hispanic (146,044)	151,737	85.62
Hispanic (7,682)	9,369	5.29

*Notes: † The Census 2010 population figure is used to calculate the percentages in the Hispanic Origin and Race categories. Ancestry percentages are based on the 2006-2010 American Community Survey population (not shown); ‡ Numbers in parentheses indicate the number of people reporting a single ancestry; * Numbers in parentheses indicate the number of persons reporting this race alone, not in combination with any other race; Please refer to the Explanation of Data for more information.*

Sierra County

Population: 3,240

Ancestry	Population	%
Afghan (0)	0	<0.01
African, Sub-Saharan (0)	0	<0.01
African (0)	0	<0.01
Cape Verdean (0)	0	<0.01
Ethiopian (0)	0	<0.01
Ghanaian (0)	0	<0.01
Kenyan (0)	0	<0.01
Liberian (0)	0	<0.01
Nigerian (0)	0	<0.01
Senegalese (0)	0	<0.01
Sierra Leonean (0)	0	<0.01
Somalian (0)	0	<0.01
South African (0)	0	<0.01
Sudanese (0)	0	<0.01
Ugandan (0)	0	<0.01
Zimbabwean (0)	0	<0.01
Other Sub-Saharan African (0)	0	<0.01
Albanian (0)	0	<0.01
Alsatian (0)	0	<0.01
American (123)	123	3.65
Arab (0)	7	0.21
Arab (0)	0	<0.01
Egyptian (0)	0	<0.01
Iraqi (0)	0	<0.01
Jordanian (0)	0	<0.01
Lebanese (0)	7	0.21
Moroccan (0)	0	<0.01
Palestinian (0)	0	<0.01
Syrian (0)	0	<0.01
Other Arab (0)	0	<0.01
Armenian (0)	0	<0.01
Assyrian/Chaldean/Syriac (0)	0	<0.01
Australian (0)	0	<0.01
Austrian (0)	0	<0.01
Basque (0)	8	0.24
Belgian (0)	0	<0.01
Brazilian (0)	0	<0.01
British (0)	14	0.42
Bulgarian (0)	0	<0.01
Cajun (0)	0	<0.01
Canadian (0)	0	<0.01
Carpatho Rusyn (0)	0	<0.01
Celtic (0)	0	<0.01
Croatian (0)	0	<0.01
Cypriot (0)	0	<0.01
Czech (0)	28	0.83
Czechoslovakian (7)	33	0.98
Danish (0)	6	0.18
Dutch (0)	82	2.44
Eastern European (6)	6	0.18
English (166)	459	13.64
Estonian (0)	0	<0.01
European (136)	136	4.04
Finnish (0)	0	<0.01
French, ex. Basque (30)	188	5.59
French Canadian (34)	34	1.01
German (203)	781	23.20
German Russian (0)	0	<0.01
Greek (0)	10	0.30
Guyanese (0)	0	<0.01
Hungarian (0)	0	<0.01
Icelander (0)	0	<0.01
Iranian (0)	0	<0.01
Irish (109)	427	12.69
Israeli (0)	0	<0.01
Italian (98)	276	8.20
Latvian (0)	0	<0.01
Lithuanian (0)	20	0.59
Luxemburger (0)	0	<0.01
Macedonian (0)	0	<0.01
Maltese (0)	0	<0.01
New Zealander (0)	0	<0.01
Northern European (0)	0	<0.01
Norwegian (22)	107	3.18
Pennsylvania German (0)	0	<0.01
Polish (23)	58	1.72
Portuguese (45)	90	2.67
Romanian (0)	0	<0.01
Russian (0)	7	0.21
Scandinavian (0)	0	<0.01
Scotch-Irish (73)	171	5.08
Scottish (64)	263	7.81
Serbian (0)	0	<0.01
Slavic (0)	0	<0.01
Slovak (0)	0	<0.01
Slovene (0)	0	<0.01
Soviet Union (0)	0	<0.01
Swedish (143)	331	9.83
Swiss (118)	143	4.25
Turkish (0)	0	<0.01
Ukrainian (0)	0	<0.01
Welsh (0)	0	<0.01
West Indian, ex. Hispanic (0)	0	<0.01
Bahamian (0)	0	<0.01
Barbadian (0)	0	<0.01
Belizean (0)	0	<0.01
Bermudan (0)	0	<0.01
British West Indian (0)	0	<0.01
Dutch West Indian (0)	0	<0.01
Haitian (0)	0	<0.01
Jamaican (0)	0	<0.01
Trinidadian/Tobagonian (0)	0	<0.01
U.S. Virgin Islander (0)	0	<0.01
West Indian (0)	0	<0.01
Other West Indian (0)	0	<0.01
Yugoslavian (15)	41	1.22

Hispanic Origin	Population	%
Hispanic or Latino (of any race)	269	8.30
Central American, ex. Mexican	4	0.12
Costa Rican	0	<0.01
Guatemalan	0	<0.01
Honduran	0	<0.01
Nicaraguan	0	<0.01
Panamanian	4	0.12
Salvadoran	0	<0.01
Other Central American	0	<0.01
Cuban	5	0.15
Dominican Republic	0	<0.01
Mexican	216	6.67
Puerto Rican	3	0.09
South American	2	0.06
Argentinean	1	0.03
Bolivian	0	<0.01
Chilean	0	<0.01
Colombian	1	0.03
Ecuadorian	0	<0.01
Paraguayan	0	<0.01
Peruvian	0	<0.01
Uruguayan	0	<0.01
Venezuelan	0	<0.01
Other South American	0	<0.01
Other Hispanic or Latino	39	1.20

Race*	Population	%
African-American/Black (6)	17	0.52
Not Hispanic (5)	12	0.37
Hispanic (1)	5	0.15
American Indian/Alaska Native (44)	86	2.65
Not Hispanic (41)	78	2.41
Hispanic (3)	8	0.25
Alaska Athabascan *(Ala. Nat.)* (0)	0	<0.01
Aleut *(Alaska Native)* (0)	0	<0.01
Apache (2)	2	0.06
Arapaho (0)	0	<0.01
Blackfeet (1)	3	0.09
Canadian/French Am. Ind. (0)	0	<0.01
Central American Ind. (0)	0	<0.01
Cherokee (4)	15	0.46
Cheyenne (0)	0	<0.01
Chickasaw (0)	0	<0.01
Chippewa (0)	0	<0.01
Choctaw (2)	4	0.12
Colville (0)	0	<0.01
Comanche (0)	0	<0.01
Cree (0)	1	0.03
Creek (0)	0	<0.01
Crow (0)	0	<0.01
Delaware (0)	0	<0.01
Hopi (0)	0	<0.01
Houma (0)	0	<0.01
Inupiat *(Alaska Native)* (0)	0	<0.01
Iroquois (2)	2	0.06
Kiowa (0)	0	<0.01
Lumbee (1)	1	0.03
Menominee (0)	0	<0.01
Mexican American Ind. (0)	1	0.03
Navajo (0)	0	<0.01
Osage (0)	1	0.03
Ottawa (0)	0	<0.01
Paiute (1)	1	0.03
Pima (0)	0	<0.01
Potawatomi (0)	0	<0.01
Pueblo (0)	0	<0.01
Puget Sound Salish (0)	0	<0.01
Seminole (2)	3	0.09
Shoshone (0)	0	<0.01
Sioux (1)	5	0.15
South American Ind. (0)	0	<0.01
Spanish American Ind. (0)	0	<0.01
Tlingit-Haida *(Alaska Native)* (0)	0	<0.01
Tohono O'Odham (0)	0	<0.01
Tsimshian *(Alaska Native)* (0)	0	<0.01
Ute (0)	0	<0.01
Yakama (0)	0	<0.01
Yaqui (0)	0	<0.01
Yuman (0)	0	<0.01
Yup'ik *(Alaska Native)* (0)	0	<0.01
Asian (12)	25	0.77
Not Hispanic (12)	21	0.65
Hispanic (0)	4	0.12
Bangladeshi (0)	0	<0.01
Bhutanese (0)	0	<0.01
Burmese (0)	0	<0.01
Cambodian (0)	0	<0.01
Chinese, ex. Taiwanese (2)	2	0.06
Filipino (3)	10	0.31
Hmong (1)	2	0.06
Indian (0)	3	0.09
Indonesian (0)	0	<0.01
Japanese (1)	3	0.09
Korean (1)	1	0.03
Laotian (0)	0	<0.01
Malaysian (0)	0	<0.01
Nepalese (0)	0	<0.01
Pakistani (0)	0	<0.01
Sri Lankan (0)	0	<0.01
Taiwanese (0)	0	<0.01
Thai (2)	2	0.06
Vietnamese (2)	2	0.06
Hawaii Native/Pacific Islander (2)	9	0.28
Not Hispanic (2)	7	0.22
Hispanic (0)	2	0.06
Fijian (0)	0	<0.01
Guamanian/Chamorro (0)	1	0.03
Marshallese (0)	0	<0.01
Native Hawaiian (2)	5	0.15
Samoan (0)	2	0.06
Tongan (0)	0	<0.01
White (3,022)	3,097	95.59
Not Hispanic (2,855)	2,907	89.72
Hispanic (167)	190	5.86

*Notes: † The Census 2010 population figure is used to calculate the percentages in the Hispanic Origin and Race categories. Ancestry percentages are based on the 2006-2010 American Community Survey population (not shown); ‡ Numbers in parentheses indicate the number of people reporting a single ancestry; * Numbers in parentheses indicate the number of persons reporting this race alone, not in combination with any other race; Please refer to the Explanation of Data for more information.*

Siskiyou County

Population: 44,900

Ancestry	Population	%
Afghan (0)	0	<0.01
African, Sub-Saharan (35)	67	0.15
African (31)	63	0.14
Cape Verdean (0)	0	<0.01
Ethiopian (0)	0	<0.01
Ghanaian (0)	0	<0.01
Kenyan (0)	0	<0.01
Liberian (0)	0	<0.01
Nigerian (0)	0	<0.01
Senegalese (0)	0	<0.01
Sierra Leonean (0)	0	<0.01
Somalian (0)	0	<0.01
South African (4)	4	0.01
Sudanese (0)	0	<0.01
Ugandan (0)	0	<0.01
Zimbabwean (0)	0	<0.01
Other Sub-Saharan African (0)	0	<0.01
Albanian (0)	0	<0.01
Alsatian (0)	5	0.01
American (1,751)	1,751	3.92
Arab (30)	141	0.32
Arab (6)	6	0.01
Egyptian (0)	0	<0.01
Iraqi (20)	36	0.08
Jordanian (0)	0	<0.01
Lebanese (0)	30	0.07
Moroccan (0)	0	<0.01
Palestinian (0)	0	<0.01
Syrian (4)	69	0.15
Other Arab (0)	0	<0.01
Armenian (0)	0	<0.01
Assyrian/Chaldean/Syriac (3)	3	0.01
Australian (3)	15	0.03
Austrian (45)	81	0.18
Basque (3)	37	0.08
Belgian (13)	58	0.13
Brazilian (20)	22	0.05
British (114)	160	0.36
Bulgarian (57)	66	0.15
Cajun (0)	0	<0.01
Canadian (37)	90	0.20
Carpatho Rusyn (0)	0	<0.01
Celtic (13)	73	0.16
Croatian (20)	85	0.19
Cypriot (0)	0	<0.01
Czech (115)	221	0.49
Czechoslovakian (19)	26	0.06
Danish (147)	500	1.12
Dutch (284)	1,252	2.80
Eastern European (61)	61	0.14
English (2,178)	6,897	15.43
Estonian (0)	0	<0.01
European (419)	487	1.09
Finnish (55)	93	0.21
French, ex. Basque (385)	1,969	4.41
French Canadian (273)	567	1.27
German (2,869)	8,725	19.52
German Russian (0)	0	<0.01
Greek (76)	125	0.28
Guyanese (0)	0	<0.01
Hungarian (95)	210	0.47
Icelander (3)	3	0.01
Iranian (110)	110	0.25
Irish (1,639)	6,696	14.98
Israeli (14)	14	0.03
Italian (1,463)	3,346	7.49
Latvian (0)	40	0.09
Lithuanian (5)	56	0.13
Luxemburger (0)	0	<0.01
Macedonian (0)	0	<0.01
Maltese (4)	15	0.03
New Zealander (3)	3	0.01
Northern European (137)	145	0.32
Norwegian (340)	1,067	2.39
Pennsylvania German (6)	89	0.20
Polish (186)	590	1.32
Portuguese (470)	1,229	2.75
Romanian (76)	89	0.20
Russian (200)	551	1.23
Scandinavian (69)	150	0.34
Scotch-Irish (466)	1,254	2.81
Scottish (523)	1,624	3.63
Serbian (0)	7	0.02
Slavic (0)	9	0.02
Slovak (4)	24	0.05
Slovene (28)	50	0.11
Soviet Union (0)	0	<0.01
Swedish (349)	1,244	2.78
Swiss (71)	238	0.53
Turkish (0)	0	<0.01
Ukrainian (14)	62	0.14
Welsh (97)	470	1.05
West Indian, ex. Hispanic (0)	19	0.04
Bahamian (0)	0	<0.01
Barbadian (0)	0	<0.01
Belizean (0)	0	<0.01
Bermudan (0)	0	<0.01
British West Indian (0)	0	<0.01
Dutch West Indian (0)	8	0.02
Haitian (0)	2	<0.01
Jamaican (0)	9	0.02
Trinidadian/Tobagonian (0)	0	<0.01
U.S. Virgin Islander (0)	0	<0.01
West Indian (0)	0	<0.01
Other West Indian (0)	0	<0.01
Yugoslavian (12)	43	0.10

Hispanic Origin	Population	%
Hispanic or Latino (of any race)	4,615	10.28
Central American, ex. Mexican	108	0.24
Costa Rican	8	0.02
Guatemalan	19	0.04
Honduran	2	<0.01
Nicaraguan	27	0.06
Panamanian	11	0.02
Salvadoran	41	0.09
Other Central American	0	<0.01
Cuban	32	0.07
Dominican Republic	15	0.03
Mexican	3,777	8.41
Puerto Rican	124	0.28
South American	57	0.13
Argentinean	19	0.04
Bolivian	0	<0.01
Chilean	12	0.03
Colombian	9	0.02
Ecuadorian	3	0.01
Paraguayan	0	<0.01
Peruvian	9	0.02
Uruguayan	1	<0.01
Venezuelan	4	0.01
Other South American	0	<0.01
Other Hispanic or Latino	502	1.12

Race*	Population	%
African-American/Black (571)	904	2.01
Not Hispanic (552)	821	1.83
Hispanic (19)	83	0.18
American Indian/Alaska Native (1,814)	3,407	7.59
Not Hispanic (1,549)	2,922	6.51
Hispanic (265)	485	1.08
Alaska Athabascan *(Ala. Nat.)* (0)	0	<0.01
Aleut *(Alaska Native)* (4)	4	0.01
Apache (26)	79	0.18
Arapaho (0)	0	<0.01
Blackfeet (6)	59	0.13
Canadian/French Am. Ind. (1)	4	0.01
Central American Ind. (1)	1	<0.01
Cherokee (95)	426	0.95
Cheyenne (2)	13	0.03
Chickasaw (4)	9	0.02
Chippewa (8)	21	0.05
Choctaw (29)	91	0.20
Colville (1)	1	<0.01
Comanche (2)	12	0.03
Cree (0)	1	<0.01
Creek (7)	24	0.05
Crow (0)	2	<0.01
Delaware (0)	3	0.01
Hopi (0)	0	<0.01
Houma (0)	0	<0.01
Inupiat *(Alaska Native)* (8)	9	0.02
Iroquois (5)	14	0.03
Kiowa (0)	5	0.01
Lumbee (1)	7	0.02
Menominee (0)	0	<0.01
Mexican American Ind. (37)	57	0.13
Navajo (15)	42	0.09
Osage (6)	11	0.02
Ottawa (1)	2	<0.01
Paiute (7)	17	0.04
Pima (0)	1	<0.01
Potawatomi (4)	7	0.02
Pueblo (4)	6	0.01
Puget Sound Salish (1)	1	<0.01
Seminole (4)	9	0.02
Shoshone (8)	13	0.03
Sioux (17)	72	0.16
South American Ind. (0)	0	<0.01
Spanish American Ind. (0)	0	<0.01
Tlingit-Haida *(Alaska Native)* (7)	8	0.02
Tohono O'Odham (3)	4	0.01
Tsimshian *(Alaska Native)* (1)	1	<0.01
Ute (7)	7	0.02
Yakama (1)	3	0.01
Yaqui (2)	9	0.02
Yuman (5)	6	0.01
Yup'ik *(Alaska Native)* (1)	4	0.01
Asian (540)	878	1.96
Not Hispanic (528)	815	1.82
Hispanic (12)	63	0.14
Bangladeshi (0)	0	<0.01
Bhutanese (0)	0	<0.01
Burmese (2)	4	0.01
Cambodian (25)	33	0.07
Chinese, ex. Taiwanese (75)	123	0.27
Filipino (81)	195	0.43
Hmong (0)	0	<0.01
Indian (68)	105	0.23
Indonesian (4)	8	0.02
Japanese (69)	134	0.30
Korean (29)	54	0.12
Laotian (126)	159	0.35
Malaysian (2)	3	0.01
Nepalese (0)	0	<0.01
Pakistani (5)	5	0.01
Sri Lankan (1)	1	<0.01
Taiwanese (0)	1	<0.01
Thai (12)	19	0.04
Vietnamese (11)	19	0.04
Hawaii Native/Pacific Islander (80)	214	0.48
Not Hispanic (69)	184	0.41
Hispanic (11)	30	0.07
Fijian (3)	3	0.01
Guamanian/Chamorro (6)	16	0.04
Marshallese (0)	3	0.01
Native Hawaiian (23)	104	0.23
Samoan (27)	47	0.10
Tongan (0)	3	0.01
White (38,030)	40,225	89.59
Not Hispanic (35,683)	37,407	83.31
Hispanic (2,347)	2,818	6.28

*Notes: † The Census 2010 population figure is used to calculate the percentages in the Hispanic Origin and Race categories. Ancestry percentages are based on the 2006-2010 American Community Survey population (not shown); ‡ Numbers in parentheses indicate the number of people reporting a single ancestry; * Numbers in parentheses indicate the number of persons reporting this race alone, not in combination with any other race; Please refer to the Explanation of Data for more information.*

Solano County

Population: 413,344

Ancestry	Population	%
Afghan (366)	424	0.10
African, Sub-Saharan (7,692)	9,818	2.39
African (6,779)	8,683	2.12
Cape Verdean (91)	228	0.06
Ethiopian (134)	143	0.03
Ghanaian (0)	8	<0.01
Kenyan (167)	167	0.04
Liberian (39)	58	0.01
Nigerian (64)	73	0.02
Senegalese (0)	0	<0.01
Sierra Leonean (91)	91	0.02
Somalian (203)	203	0.05
South African (33)	65	0.02
Sudanese (28)	28	0.01
Ugandan (0)	0	<0.01
Zimbabwean (0)	0	<0.01
Other Sub-Saharan African (63)	71	0.02
Albanian (0)	0	<0.01
Alsatian (0)	17	<0.01
American (9,146)	9,146	2.23
Arab (1,150)	2,083	0.51
Arab (256)	380	0.09
Egyptian (76)	267	0.07
Iraqi (46)	46	0.01
Jordanian (118)	124	0.03
Lebanese (137)	372	0.09
Moroccan (0)	9	<0.01
Palestinian (334)	409	0.10
Syrian (80)	275	0.07
Other Arab (103)	201	0.05
Armenian (245)	462	0.11
Assyrian/Chaldean/Syriac (57)	67	0.02
Australian (73)	137	0.03
Austrian (213)	517	0.13
Basque (139)	361	0.09
Belgian (36)	266	0.06
Brazilian (167)	247	0.06
British (751)	1,421	0.35
Bulgarian (64)	92	0.02
Cajun (9)	9	<0.01
Canadian (448)	828	0.20
Carpatho Rusyn (0)	0	<0.01
Celtic (76)	96	0.02
Croatian (162)	304	0.07
Cypriot (0)	0	<0.01
Czech (98)	571	0.14
Czechoslovakian (121)	235	0.06
Danish (911)	2,707	0.66
Dutch (996)	4,028	0.98
Eastern European (191)	248	0.06
English (9,182)	29,486	7.19
Estonian (0)	0	<0.01
European (7,525)	9,518	2.32
Finnish (406)	1,108	0.27
French, ex. Basque (1,032)	8,042	1.96
French Canadian (530)	1,491	0.36
German (13,423)	42,466	10.36
German Russian (25)	25	0.01
Greek (940)	2,051	0.50
Guyanese (0)	16	<0.01
Hungarian (381)	1,264	0.31
Icelander (15)	49	0.01
Iranian (754)	834	0.20
Irish (8,880)	34,048	8.30
Israeli (8)	8	<0.01
Italian (5,997)	16,844	4.11
Latvian (66)	265	0.06
Lithuanian (216)	655	0.16
Luxemburger (14)	54	0.01
Macedonian (0)	0	<0.01
Maltese (25)	149	0.04
New Zealander (8)	8	<0.01
Northern European (293)	323	0.08
Norwegian (1,832)	5,326	1.30
Pennsylvania German (78)	181	0.04
Polish (1,348)	4,695	1.15
Portuguese (2,477)	5,745	1.40
Romanian (169)	241	0.06
Russian (695)	2,390	0.58
Scandinavian (321)	768	0.19
Scotch-Irish (1,607)	5,248	1.28
Scottish (2,476)	7,785	1.90
Serbian (56)	67	0.02
Slavic (71)	152	0.04
Slovak (70)	513	0.13
Slovene (8)	75	0.02
Soviet Union (7)	7	<0.01
Swedish (1,257)	4,433	1.08
Swiss (294)	1,393	0.34
Turkish (141)	206	0.05
Ukrainian (186)	461	0.11
Welsh (207)	1,851	0.45
West Indian, ex. Hispanic (565)	1,099	0.27
Bahamian (0)	0	<0.01
Barbadian (0)	0	<0.01
Belizean (8)	63	0.02
Bermudan (0)	0	<0.01
British West Indian (43)	65	0.02
Dutch West Indian (0)	0	<0.01
Haitian (14)	58	0.01
Jamaican (327)	647	0.16
Trinidadian/Tobagonian (93)	130	0.03
U.S. Virgin Islander (0)	0	<0.01
West Indian (80)	136	0.03
Other West Indian (0)	0	<0.01
Yugoslavian (127)	525	0.13

Hispanic Origin	Population	%
Hispanic or Latino (of any race)	99,356	24.04
Central American, ex. Mexican	8,398	2.03
Costa Rican	154	0.04
Guatemalan	1,470	0.36
Honduran	366	0.09
Nicaraguan	1,750	0.42
Panamanian	345	0.08
Salvadoran	4,229	1.02
Other Central American	84	0.02
Cuban	677	0.16
Dominican Republic	149	0.04
Mexican	75,276	18.21
Puerto Rican	3,716	0.90
South American	1,985	0.48
Argentinean	167	0.04
Bolivian	68	0.02
Chilean	171	0.04
Colombian	389	0.09
Ecuadorian	133	0.03
Paraguayan	34	0.01
Peruvian	847	0.20
Uruguayan	19	<0.01
Venezuelan	127	0.03
Other South American	30	0.01
Other Hispanic or Latino	9,155	2.21

Race*	Population	%
African-American/Black (60,750)	71,375	17.27
Not Hispanic (58,743)	67,000	16.21
Hispanic (2,007)	4,375	1.06
American Indian/Alaska Native (3,212)	9,401	2.27
Not Hispanic (1,864)	6,347	1.54
Hispanic (1,348)	3,054	0.74
Alaska Athabascan *(Ala. Nat.)* (7)	12	<0.01
Aleut *(Alaska Native)* (16)	47	0.01
Apache (105)	307	0.07
Arapaho (3)	6	<0.01
Blackfeet (31)	276	0.07
Canadian/French Am. Ind. (8)	25	0.01
Central American Ind. (6)	21	0.01
Cherokee (279)	1,589	0.38
Cheyenne (1)	14	<0.01
Chickasaw (32)	69	0.02
Chippewa (46)	113	0.03
Choctaw (91)	416	0.10
Colville (3)	6	<0.01
Comanche (7)	43	0.01
Cree (3)	29	0.01
Creek (39)	146	0.04
Crow (7)	16	<0.01
Delaware (7)	17	<0.01
Hopi (10)	35	0.01
Houma (0)	0	<0.01
Inupiat *(Alaska Native)* (9)	23	0.01
Iroquois (22)	80	0.02
Kiowa (7)	10	<0.01
Lumbee (2)	3	<0.01
Menominee (1)	2	<0.01
Mexican American Ind. (251)	485	0.12
Navajo (104)	245	0.06
Osage (5)	38	0.01
Ottawa (4)	9	<0.01
Paiute (20)	49	0.01
Pima (3)	11	<0.01
Potawatomi (28)	41	0.01
Pueblo (27)	49	0.01
Puget Sound Salish (4)	9	<0.01
Seminole (11)	73	0.02
Shoshone (6)	18	<0.01
Sioux (69)	232	0.06
South American Ind. (11)	44	0.01
Spanish American Ind. (17)	26	0.01
Tlingit-Haida *(Alaska Native)* (11)	46	0.01
Tohono O'Odham (9)	25	0.01
Tsimshian *(Alaska Native)* (4)	5	<0.01
Ute (7)	20	<0.01
Yakama (1)	3	<0.01
Yaqui (18)	56	0.01
Yuman (5)	20	<0.01
Yup'ik *(Alaska Native)* (2)	4	<0.01
Asian (60,473)	74,750	18.08
Not Hispanic (59,027)	70,483	17.05
Hispanic (1,446)	4,267	1.03
Bangladeshi (8)	18	<0.01
Bhutanese (0)	0	<0.01
Burmese (55)	86	0.02
Cambodian (177)	244	0.06
Chinese, ex. Taiwanese (3,719)	6,084	1.47
Filipino (43,366)	52,641	12.74
Hmong (302)	342	0.08
Indian (4,214)	4,951	1.20
Indonesian (115)	239	0.06
Japanese (1,795)	4,418	1.07
Korean (1,179)	2,047	0.50
Laotian (839)	1,046	0.25
Malaysian (20)	61	0.01
Nepalese (43)	48	0.01
Pakistani (320)	386	0.09
Sri Lankan (18)	27	0.01
Taiwanese (142)	200	0.05
Thai (434)	824	0.20
Vietnamese (1,984)	2,490	0.60
Hawaii Native/Pacific Islander (3,564)	7,727	1.87
Not Hispanic (3,243)	6,569	1.59
Hispanic (321)	1,158	0.28
Fijian (367)	499	0.12
Guamanian/Chamorro (1,443)	2,799	0.68
Marshallese (5)	6	<0.01
Native Hawaiian (506)	2,231	0.54
Samoan (669)	1,178	0.28
Tongan (189)	266	0.06
White (210,751)	235,002	56.85
Not Hispanic (168,628)	185,034	44.77
Hispanic (42,123)	49,968	12.09

*Notes: † The Census 2010 population figure is used to calculate the percentages in the Hispanic Origin and Race categories. Ancestry percentages are based on the 2006-2010 American Community Survey population (not shown); ‡ Numbers in parentheses indicate the number of people reporting a single ancestry; * Numbers in parentheses indicate the number of persons reporting this race alone, not in combination with any other race; Please refer to the Explanation of Data for more information.*

Sonoma County

Population: 483,878

Ancestry	Population	%
Afghan (16)	16	<0.01
African, Sub-Saharan (1,414)	1,841	0.39
African (466)	824	0.17
Cape Verdean (0)	0	<0.01
Ethiopian (512)	549	0.12
Ghanaian (0)	0	<0.01
Kenyan (0)	10	<0.01
Liberian (0)	0	<0.01
Nigerian (0)	0	<0.01
Senegalese (0)	0	<0.01
Sierra Leonean (0)	16	<0.01
Somalian (0)	0	<0.01
South African (54)	60	0.01
Sudanese (236)	236	0.05
Ugandan (146)	146	0.03
Zimbabwean (0)	0	<0.01
Other Sub-Saharan African (0)	0	<0.01
Albanian (0)	18	<0.01
Alsatian (11)	11	<0.01
American (13,241)	13,241	2.79
Arab (907)	1,552	0.33
Arab (195)	267	0.06
Egyptian (242)	295	0.06
Iraqi (0)	0	<0.01
Jordanian (59)	96	0.02
Lebanese (118)	453	0.10
Moroccan (16)	16	<0.01
Palestinian (206)	217	0.05
Syrian (10)	121	0.03
Other Arab (61)	87	0.02
Armenian (176)	589	0.12
Assyrian/Chaldean/Syriac (136)	158	0.03
Australian (218)	439	0.09
Austrian (254)	1,432	0.30
Basque (122)	241	0.05
Belgian (171)	513	0.11
Brazilian (125)	187	0.04
British (1,920)	3,174	0.67
Bulgarian (125)	145	0.03
Cajun (38)	86	0.02
Canadian (718)	1,550	0.33
Carpatho Rusyn (0)	0	<0.01
Celtic (114)	170	0.04
Croatian (321)	685	0.14
Cypriot (0)	0	<0.01
Czech (252)	2,011	0.42
Czechoslovakian (277)	590	0.12
Danish (1,868)	6,057	1.28
Dutch (1,537)	7,984	1.68
Eastern European (945)	1,046	0.22
English (13,428)	55,635	11.74
Estonian (57)	94	0.02
European (12,339)	14,139	2.98
Finnish (436)	1,726	0.36
French, ex. Basque (2,125)	17,922	3.78
French Canadian (824)	1,998	0.42
German (19,085)	75,044	15.83
German Russian (0)	0	<0.01
Greek (820)	2,798	0.59
Guyanese (0)	14	<0.01
Hungarian (577)	2,083	0.44
Icelander (11)	70	0.01
Iranian (831)	1,130	0.24
Irish (16,077)	64,914	13.69
Israeli (174)	257	0.05
Italian (16,680)	44,163	9.32
Latvian (78)	341	0.07
Lithuanian (472)	1,269	0.27
Luxemburger (28)	41	0.01
Macedonian (38)	47	0.01
Maltese (135)	361	0.08
New Zealander (121)	121	0.03
Northern European (1,350)	1,563	0.33
Norwegian (2,473)	8,932	1.88
Pennsylvania German (11)	57	0.01
Polish (2,062)	8,261	1.74
Portuguese (3,285)	9,049	1.91
Romanian (176)	577	0.12
Russian (2,436)	7,541	1.59
Scandinavian (769)	1,421	0.30
Scotch-Irish (3,957)	11,108	2.34
Scottish (3,634)	14,331	3.02
Serbian (90)	306	0.06
Slavic (99)	187	0.04
Slovak (105)	373	0.08
Slovene (64)	160	0.03
Soviet Union (0)	0	<0.01
Swedish (2,505)	10,479	2.21
Swiss (676)	4,332	0.91
Turkish (160)	312	0.07
Ukrainian (384)	888	0.19
Welsh (635)	4,244	0.90
West Indian, ex. Hispanic (563)	705	0.15
Bahamian (9)	9	<0.01
Barbadian (0)	0	<0.01
Belizean (109)	109	0.02
Bermudan (0)	0	<0.01
British West Indian (0)	0	<0.01
Dutch West Indian (0)	25	0.01
Haitian (420)	431	0.09
Jamaican (17)	92	0.02
Trinidadian/Tobagonian (5)	19	<0.01
U.S. Virgin Islander (0)	0	<0.01
West Indian (3)	20	<0.01
Other West Indian (0)	0	<0.01
Yugoslavian (300)	749	0.16

Hispanic Origin	Population	%
Hispanic or Latino (of any race)	120,430	24.89
Central American, ex. Mexican	5,856	1.21
Costa Rican	187	0.04
Guatemalan	1,197	0.25
Honduran	290	0.06
Nicaraguan	883	0.18
Panamanian	112	0.02
Salvadoran	3,138	0.65
Other Central American	49	0.01
Cuban	510	0.11
Dominican Republic	73	0.02
Mexican	101,905	21.06
Puerto Rican	1,786	0.37
South American	2,427	0.50
Argentinean	282	0.06
Bolivian	71	0.01
Chilean	218	0.05
Colombian	627	0.13
Ecuadorian	210	0.04
Paraguayan	23	<0.01
Peruvian	797	0.16
Uruguayan	32	0.01
Venezuelan	119	0.02
Other South American	48	0.01
Other Hispanic or Latino	7,873	1.63

Race*	Population	%
African-American/Black (7,610)	11,661	2.41
Not Hispanic (6,769)	9,979	2.06
Hispanic (841)	1,682	0.35
American Indian/Alaska Native (6,489)	13,307	2.75
Not Hispanic (3,584)	8,066	1.67
Hispanic (2,905)	5,241	1.08
Alaska Athabascan *(Ala. Nat.)* (10)	19	<0.01
Aleut *(Alaska Native)* (18)	55	0.01
Apache (113)	399	0.08
Arapaho (2)	6	<0.01
Blackfeet (38)	241	0.05
Canadian/French Am. Ind. (15)	41	0.01
Central American Ind. (14)	24	<0.01
Cherokee (304)	1,588	0.33
Cheyenne (10)	33	0.01
Chickasaw (32)	78	0.02
Chippewa (61)	177	0.04
Choctaw (142)	450	0.09
Colville (6)	7	<0.01
Comanche (23)	66	0.01
Cree (3)	19	<0.01
Creek (27)	77	0.02
Crow (2)	17	<0.01
Delaware (4)	28	0.01
Hopi (8)	25	0.01
Houma (1)	4	<0.01
Inupiat *(Alaska Native)* (13)	38	0.01
Iroquois (16)	87	0.02
Kiowa (2)	7	<0.01
Lumbee (10)	12	<0.01
Menominee (2)	7	<0.01
Mexican American Ind. (665)	970	0.20
Navajo (85)	213	0.04
Osage (11)	66	0.01
Ottawa (2)	13	<0.01
Paiute (23)	46	0.01
Pima (7)	12	<0.01
Potawatomi (21)	48	0.01
Pueblo (24)	53	0.01
Puget Sound Salish (5)	19	<0.01
Seminole (5)	33	0.01
Shoshone (13)	30	0.01
Sioux (80)	243	0.05
South American Ind. (21)	54	0.01
Spanish American Ind. (43)	64	0.01
Tlingit-Haida *(Alaska Native)* (18)	42	0.01
Tohono O'Odham (4)	12	<0.01
Tsimshian *(Alaska Native)* (3)	13	<0.01
Ute (5)	27	0.01
Yakama (6)	14	<0.01
Yaqui (39)	109	0.02
Yuman (4)	9	<0.01
Yup'ik *(Alaska Native)* (12)	13	<0.01
Asian (18,341)	25,180	5.20
Not Hispanic (17,777)	23,434	4.84
Hispanic (564)	1,746	0.36
Bangladeshi (21)	23	<0.01
Bhutanese (0)	0	<0.01
Burmese (48)	68	0.01
Cambodian (1,130)	1,316	0.27
Chinese, ex. Taiwanese (3,578)	5,187	1.07
Filipino (3,693)	6,188	1.28
Hmong (108)	126	0.03
Indian (2,157)	2,660	0.55
Indonesian (107)	202	0.04
Japanese (1,595)	3,248	0.67
Korean (1,050)	1,476	0.31
Laotian (1,076)	1,322	0.27
Malaysian (21)	32	0.01
Nepalese (254)	280	0.06
Pakistani (200)	233	0.05
Sri Lankan (25)	33	0.01
Taiwanese (151)	197	0.04
Thai (325)	488	0.10
Vietnamese (1,899)	2,249	0.46
Hawaii Native/Pacific Islander (1,558)	3,244	0.67
Not Hispanic (1,434)	2,755	0.57
Hispanic (124)	489	0.10
Fijian (592)	676	0.14
Guamanian/Chamorro (115)	263	0.05
Marshallese (3)	4	<0.01
Native Hawaiian (320)	1,190	0.25
Samoan (279)	540	0.11
Tongan (65)	118	0.02
White (371,412)	390,658	80.73
Not Hispanic (320,027)	331,918	68.60
Hispanic (51,385)	58,740	12.14

*Notes: † The Census 2010 population figure is used to calculate the percentages in the Hispanic Origin and Race categories. Ancestry percentages are based on the 2006-2010 American Community Survey population (not shown); ‡ Numbers in parentheses indicate the number of people reporting a single ancestry; * Numbers in parentheses indicate the number of persons reporting this race alone, not in combination with any other race; Please refer to the Explanation of Data for more information.*

Stanislaus County

Population: 514,453

Ancestry	Population	%
Afghan (256)	256	0.05
African, Sub-Saharan (858)	1,160	0.23
African (504)	723	0.14
Cape Verdean (0)	33	0.01
Ethiopian (136)	136	0.03
Ghanaian (0)	0	<0.01
Kenyan (107)	107	0.02
Liberian (0)	0	<0.01
Nigerian (89)	89	0.02
Senegalese (0)	0	<0.01
Sierra Leonean (0)	0	<0.01
Somalian (22)	22	<0.01
South African (0)	19	<0.01
Sudanese (0)	0	<0.01
Ugandan (0)	0	<0.01
Zimbabwean (0)	0	<0.01
Other Sub-Saharan African (0)	31	0.01
Albanian (0)	0	<0.01
Alsatian (0)	0	<0.01
American (16,650)	16,650	3.27
Arab (2,283)	2,745	0.54
Arab (602)	736	0.14
Egyptian (69)	95	0.02
Iraqi (560)	641	0.13
Jordanian (0)	0	<0.01
Lebanese (140)	207	0.04
Moroccan (0)	12	<0.01
Palestinian (270)	270	0.05
Syrian (117)	169	0.03
Other Arab (525)	615	0.12
Armenian (726)	1,201	0.24
Assyrian/Chaldean/Syriac (8,697)	9,352	1.83
Australian (61)	166	0.03
Austrian (125)	695	0.14
Basque (195)	380	0.07
Belgian (101)	295	0.06
Brazilian (129)	204	0.04
British (459)	941	0.18
Bulgarian (0)	13	<0.01
Cajun (7)	41	0.01
Canadian (478)	762	0.15
Carpatho Rusyn (0)	0	<0.01
Celtic (15)	50	0.01
Croatian (99)	209	0.04
Cypriot (0)	0	<0.01
Czech (134)	530	0.10
Czechoslovakian (59)	225	0.04
Danish (733)	2,811	0.55
Dutch (2,903)	10,263	2.01
Eastern European (130)	139	0.03
English (9,638)	33,569	6.59
Estonian (23)	197	0.04
European (3,629)	4,502	0.88
Finnish (83)	528	0.10
French, ex. Basque (1,123)	10,373	2.04
French Canadian (426)	1,197	0.23
German (14,109)	53,078	10.41
German Russian (0)	62	0.01
Greek (639)	1,354	0.27
Guyanese (0)	0	<0.01
Hungarian (298)	810	0.16
Icelander (101)	162	0.03
Iranian (981)	1,333	0.26
Irish (10,366)	45,309	8.89
Israeli (0)	17	<0.01
Italian (7,178)	20,481	4.02
Latvian (0)	13	<0.01
Lithuanian (105)	341	0.07
Luxemburger (22)	56	0.01
Macedonian (0)	0	<0.01
Maltese (31)	74	0.01
New Zealander (9)	17	<0.01
Northern European (310)	332	0.07
Norwegian (1,779)	5,849	1.15
Pennsylvania German (36)	72	0.01
Polish (1,169)	3,753	0.74
Portuguese (14,023)	25,212	4.95
Romanian (827)	962	0.19
Russian (562)	1,599	0.31
Scandinavian (473)	956	0.19
Scotch-Irish (2,229)	6,770	1.33
Scottish (2,069)	7,595	1.49
Serbian (5)	66	0.01
Slavic (35)	102	0.02
Slovak (20)	58	0.01
Slovene (10)	52	0.01
Soviet Union (0)	0	<0.01
Swedish (2,242)	7,929	1.56
Swiss (731)	2,805	0.55
Turkish (0)	41	0.01
Ukrainian (178)	458	0.09
Welsh (418)	2,848	0.56
West Indian, ex. Hispanic (129)	329	0.06
Bahamian (0)	0	<0.01
Barbadian (0)	0	<0.01
Belizean (0)	63	0.01
Bermudan (0)	0	<0.01
British West Indian (0)	0	<0.01
Dutch West Indian (42)	143	0.03
Haitian (0)	20	<0.01
Jamaican (74)	90	0.02
Trinidadian/Tobagonian (0)	0	<0.01
U.S. Virgin Islander (0)	0	<0.01
West Indian (13)	13	<0.01
Other West Indian (0)	0	<0.01
Yugoslavian (290)	504	0.10

Hispanic Origin	Population	%
Hispanic or Latino (of any race)	215,658	41.92
Central American, ex. Mexican	5,378	1.05
Costa Rican	153	0.03
Guatemalan	1,134	0.22
Honduran	347	0.07
Nicaraguan	1,012	0.20
Panamanian	128	0.02
Salvadoran	2,555	0.50
Other Central American	49	0.01
Cuban	386	0.08
Dominican Republic	58	0.01
Mexican	193,368	37.59
Puerto Rican	3,124	0.61
South American	1,530	0.30
Argentinean	150	0.03
Bolivian	65	0.01
Chilean	181	0.04
Colombian	504	0.10
Ecuadorian	94	0.02
Paraguayan	6	<0.01
Peruvian	458	0.09
Uruguayan	18	<0.01
Venezuelan	45	0.01
Other South American	9	<0.01
Other Hispanic or Latino	11,814	2.30

Race*	Population	%
African-American/Black (14,721)	19,606	3.81
Not Hispanic (13,065)	16,376	3.18
Hispanic (1,656)	3,230	0.63
American Indian/Alaska Native (5,902)	12,658	2.46
Not Hispanic (2,870)	7,335	1.43
Hispanic (3,032)	5,323	1.03
Alaska Athabascan *(Ala. Nat.)* (4)	20	<0.01
Aleut *(Alaska Native)* (16)	34	0.01
Apache (232)	559	0.11
Arapaho (5)	11	<0.01
Blackfeet (39)	296	0.06
Canadian/French Am. Ind. (6)	12	<0.01
Central American Ind. (3)	11	<0.01
Cherokee (749)	2,621	0.51
Cheyenne (4)	20	<0.01
Chickasaw (84)	161	0.03
Chippewa (32)	124	0.02
Choctaw (290)	842	0.16
Colville (6)	8	<0.01
Comanche (10)	41	0.01
Cree (10)	23	<0.01
Creek (86)	213	0.04
Crow (5)	8	<0.01
Delaware (9)	18	<0.01
Hopi (19)	34	0.01
Houma (0)	1	<0.01
Inupiat *(Alaska Native)* (13)	19	<0.01
Iroquois (27)	91	0.02
Kiowa (6)	12	<0.01
Lumbee (2)	4	<0.01
Menominee (1)	2	<0.01
Mexican American Ind. (480)	712	0.14
Navajo (124)	299	0.06
Osage (10)	38	0.01
Ottawa (13)	19	<0.01
Paiute (76)	125	0.02
Pima (16)	31	0.01
Potawatomi (29)	46	0.01
Pueblo (34)	84	0.02
Puget Sound Salish (5)	9	<0.01
Seminole (11)	52	0.01
Shoshone (9)	25	<0.01
Sioux (90)	248	0.05
South American Ind. (24)	58	0.01
Spanish American Ind. (43)	55	0.01
Tlingit-Haida *(Alaska Native)* (7)	11	<0.01
Tohono O'Odham (35)	59	0.01
Tsimshian *(Alaska Native)* (1)	1	<0.01
Ute (12)	20	<0.01
Yakama (0)	2	<0.01
Yaqui (95)	184	0.04
Yuman (9)	15	<0.01
Yup'ik *(Alaska Native)* (0)	3	<0.01
Asian (26,090)	34,573	6.72
Not Hispanic (24,712)	31,006	6.03
Hispanic (1,378)	3,567	0.69
Bangladeshi (6)	12	<0.01
Bhutanese (0)	0	<0.01
Burmese (38)	42	0.01
Cambodian (3,413)	3,934	0.76
Chinese, ex. Taiwanese (2,368)	3,333	0.65
Filipino (5,747)	9,011	1.75
Hmong (567)	611	0.12
Indian (7,571)	9,022	1.75
Indonesian (38)	105	0.02
Japanese (723)	1,885	0.37
Korean (598)	898	0.17
Laotian (1,639)	1,983	0.39
Malaysian (7)	18	<0.01
Nepalese (10)	10	<0.01
Pakistani (282)	330	0.06
Sri Lankan (12)	15	<0.01
Taiwanese (85)	118	0.02
Thai (158)	297	0.06
Vietnamese (1,651)	1,991	0.39
Hawaii Native/Pacific Islander (3,401)	6,353	1.23
Not Hispanic (3,016)	5,209	1.01
Hispanic (385)	1,144	0.22
Fijian (1,550)	1,902	0.37
Guamanian/Chamorro (305)	633	0.12
Marshallese (0)	1	<0.01
Native Hawaiian (454)	1,366	0.27
Samoan (536)	802	0.16
Tongan (94)	132	0.03
White (337,342)	360,337	70.04
Not Hispanic (240,423)	251,811	48.95
Hispanic (96,919)	108,526	21.10

*Notes: † The Census 2010 population figure is used to calculate the percentages in the Hispanic Origin and Race categories. Ancestry percentages are based on the 2006-2010 American Community Survey population (not shown); ‡ Numbers in parentheses indicate the number of people reporting a single ancestry; * Numbers in parentheses indicate the number of persons reporting this race alone, not in combination with any other race; Please refer to the Explanation of Data for more information.*

Sutter County

Population: 94,737

Ancestry	Population	%
Afghan (0)	0	<0.01
African, Sub-Saharan (103)	148	0.16
African (71)	102	0.11
Cape Verdean (0)	0	<0.01
Ethiopian (0)	0	<0.01
Ghanaian (0)	0	<0.01
Kenyan (7)	21	0.02
Liberian (0)	0	<0.01
Nigerian (0)	0	<0.01
Senegalese (0)	0	<0.01
Sierra Leonean (0)	0	<0.01
Somalian (0)	0	<0.01
South African (14)	14	0.01
Sudanese (0)	0	<0.01
Ugandan (0)	0	<0.01
Zimbabwean (11)	11	0.01
Other Sub-Saharan African (0)	0	<0.01
Albanian (0)	0	<0.01
Alsatian (0)	0	<0.01
American (5,520)	5,520	5.91
Arab (68)	188	0.20
Arab (66)	66	0.07
Egyptian (0)	0	<0.01
Iraqi (0)	0	<0.01
Jordanian (0)	0	<0.01
Lebanese (0)	110	0.12
Moroccan (0)	0	<0.01
Palestinian (0)	0	<0.01
Syrian (2)	12	0.01
Other Arab (0)	0	<0.01
Armenian (165)	193	0.21
Assyrian/Chaldean/Syriac (0)	0	<0.01
Australian (0)	0	<0.01
Austrian (9)	65	0.07
Basque (80)	128	0.14
Belgian (7)	37	0.04
Brazilian (37)	99	0.11
British (86)	185	0.20
Bulgarian (3)	3	<0.01
Cajun (9)	23	0.02
Canadian (34)	175	0.19
Carpatho Rusyn (0)	0	<0.01
Celtic (10)	22	0.02
Croatian (3)	20	0.02
Cypriot (0)	0	<0.01
Czech (149)	315	0.34
Czechoslovakian (25)	282	0.30
Danish (382)	903	0.97
Dutch (317)	1,723	1.84
Eastern European (6)	18	0.02
English (2,131)	7,361	7.88
Estonian (0)	0	<0.01
European (663)	818	0.88
Finnish (83)	175	0.19
French, ex. Basque (372)	2,275	2.44
French Canadian (31)	192	0.21
German (3,215)	12,455	13.33
German Russian (57)	57	0.06
Greek (142)	352	0.38
Guyanese (0)	0	<0.01
Hungarian (21)	55	0.06
Icelander (0)	0	<0.01
Iranian (12)	61	0.07
Irish (1,789)	9,065	9.70
Israeli (0)	0	<0.01
Italian (1,490)	3,692	3.95
Latvian (0)	0	<0.01
Lithuanian (46)	117	0.13
Luxemburger (0)	43	0.05
Macedonian (0)	0	<0.01
Maltese (14)	14	0.01
New Zealander (0)	12	0.01
Northern European (50)	50	0.05
Norwegian (403)	1,345	1.44
Pennsylvania German (13)	13	0.01
Polish (229)	816	0.87
Portuguese (743)	1,717	1.84
Romanian (20)	31	0.03
Russian (77)	422	0.45
Scandinavian (111)	289	0.31
Scotch-Irish (544)	1,167	1.25
Scottish (492)	1,643	1.76
Serbian (0)	15	0.02
Slavic (0)	7	0.01
Slovak (0)	104	0.11
Slovene (0)	0	<0.01
Soviet Union (0)	0	<0.01
Swedish (140)	849	0.91
Swiss (109)	473	0.51
Turkish (33)	42	0.04
Ukrainian (23)	84	0.09
Welsh (92)	457	0.49
West Indian, ex. Hispanic (18)	91	0.10
Bahamian (0)	0	<0.01
Barbadian (0)	0	<0.01
Belizean (0)	0	<0.01
Bermudan (0)	0	<0.01
British West Indian (0)	0	<0.01
Dutch West Indian (0)	9	0.01
Haitian (0)	0	<0.01
Jamaican (18)	68	0.07
Trinidadian/Tobagonian (0)	0	<0.01
U.S. Virgin Islander (0)	0	<0.01
West Indian (0)	14	0.01
Other West Indian (0)	0	<0.01
Yugoslavian (31)	178	0.19

Hispanic Origin	Population	%
Hispanic or Latino (of any race)	27,251	28.76
Central American, ex. Mexican	371	0.39
Costa Rican	23	0.02
Guatemalan	55	0.06
Honduran	40	0.04
Nicaraguan	85	0.09
Panamanian	20	0.02
Salvadoran	147	0.16
Other Central American	1	<0.01
Cuban	69	0.07
Dominican Republic	4	<0.01
Mexican	24,468	25.83
Puerto Rican	356	0.38
South American	141	0.15
Argentinean	21	0.02
Bolivian	1	<0.01
Chilean	6	0.01
Colombian	34	0.04
Ecuadorian	13	0.01
Paraguayan	3	<0.01
Peruvian	54	0.06
Uruguayan	5	0.01
Venezuelan	0	<0.01
Other South American	4	<0.01
Other Hispanic or Latino	1,842	1.94

Race*	Population	%
African-American/Black (1,919)	2,756	2.91
Not Hispanic (1,713)	2,348	2.48
Hispanic (206)	408	0.43
American Indian/Alaska Native (1,365)	2,919	3.08
Not Hispanic (925)	2,074	2.19
Hispanic (440)	845	0.89
Alaska Athabascan *(Ala. Nat.)* (0)	1	<0.01
Aleut *(Alaska Native)* (0)	1	<0.01
Apache (36)	78	0.08
Arapaho (0)	0	<0.01
Blackfeet (11)	76	0.08
Canadian/French Am. Ind. (4)	8	0.01
Central American Ind. (2)	2	<0.01
Cherokee (280)	717	0.76
Cheyenne (0)	4	<0.01
Chickasaw (10)	17	0.02
Chippewa (26)	47	0.05
Choctaw (54)	130	0.14
Colville (0)	0	<0.01
Comanche (1)	8	0.01
Cree (0)	0	<0.01
Creek (18)	32	0.03
Crow (0)	1	<0.01
Delaware (2)	9	0.01
Hopi (6)	15	0.02
Houma (0)	0	<0.01
Inupiat *(Alaska Native)* (1)	1	<0.01
Iroquois (4)	11	0.01
Kiowa (0)	1	<0.01
Lumbee (1)	2	<0.01
Menominee (2)	2	<0.01
Mexican American Ind. (86)	126	0.13
Navajo (14)	60	0.06
Osage (1)	7	0.01
Ottawa (1)	2	<0.01
Paiute (3)	7	0.01
Pima (0)	4	<0.01
Potawatomi (9)	14	0.01
Pueblo (9)	23	0.02
Puget Sound Salish (1)	1	<0.01
Seminole (0)	3	<0.01
Shoshone (5)	8	0.01
Sioux (22)	46	0.05
South American Ind. (7)	10	0.01
Spanish American Ind. (5)	6	0.01
Tlingit-Haida *(Alaska Native)* (2)	12	0.01
Tohono O'Odham (2)	4	<0.01
Tsimshian *(Alaska Native)* (0)	0	<0.01
Ute (1)	1	<0.01
Yakama (0)	0	<0.01
Yaqui (10)	23	0.02
Yuman (3)	6	0.01
Yup'ik *(Alaska Native)* (0)	0	<0.01
Asian (13,663)	15,572	16.44
Not Hispanic (13,442)	14,996	15.83
Hispanic (221)	576	0.61
Bangladeshi (2)	5	0.01
Bhutanese (0)	0	<0.01
Burmese (8)	9	0.01
Cambodian (60)	73	0.08
Chinese, ex. Taiwanese (325)	487	0.51
Filipino (714)	1,226	1.29
Hmong (360)	370	0.39
Indian (10,513)	11,118	11.74
Indonesian (20)	37	0.04
Japanese (382)	686	0.72
Korean (156)	254	0.27
Laotian (52)	76	0.08
Malaysian (2)	2	<0.01
Nepalese (9)	9	0.01
Pakistani (565)	615	0.65
Sri Lankan (8)	15	0.02
Taiwanese (1)	6	0.01
Thai (49)	103	0.11
Vietnamese (184)	228	0.24
Hawaii Native/Pacific Islander (281)	655	0.69
Not Hispanic (256)	549	0.58
Hispanic (25)	106	0.11
Fijian (34)	48	0.05
Guamanian/Chamorro (147)	219	0.23
Marshallese (1)	1	<0.01
Native Hawaiian (48)	164	0.17
Samoan (15)	59	0.06
Tongan (1)	5	0.01
White (57,749)	62,080	65.53
Not Hispanic (47,782)	50,319	53.11
Hispanic (9,967)	11,761	12.41

*Notes: † The Census 2010 population figure is used to calculate the percentages in the Hispanic Origin and Race categories. Ancestry percentages are based on the 2006-2010 American Community Survey population (not shown); ‡ Numbers in parentheses indicate the number of people reporting a single ancestry; * Numbers in parentheses indicate the number of persons reporting this race alone, not in combination with any other race; Please refer to the Explanation of Data for more information.*

Tehama County

Population: 63,463

Ancestry	Population	%
Afghan (0)	0	<0.01
African, Sub-Saharan (128)	164	0.26
African (109)	145	0.23
Cape Verdean (19)	19	0.03
Ethiopian (0)	0	<0.01
Ghanaian (0)	0	<0.01
Kenyan (0)	0	<0.01
Liberian (0)	0	<0.01
Nigerian (0)	0	<0.01
Senegalese (0)	0	<0.01
Sierra Leonean (0)	0	<0.01
Somalian (0)	0	<0.01
South African (0)	0	<0.01
Sudanese (0)	0	<0.01
Ugandan (0)	0	<0.01
Zimbabwean (0)	0	<0.01
Other Sub-Saharan African (0)	0	<0.01
Albanian (14)	14	0.02
Alsatian (0)	0	<0.01
American (3,996)	3,996	6.39
Arab (21)	74	0.12
Arab (9)	51	0.08
Egyptian (0)	0	<0.01
Iraqi (0)	0	<0.01
Jordanian (12)	12	0.02
Lebanese (0)	11	0.02
Moroccan (0)	0	<0.01
Palestinian (0)	0	<0.01
Syrian (0)	0	<0.01
Other Arab (0)	0	<0.01
Armenian (40)	40	0.06
Assyrian/Chaldean/Syriac (22)	93	0.15
Australian (15)	71	0.11
Austrian (0)	119	0.19
Basque (1)	2	<0.01
Belgian (3)	35	0.06
Brazilian (0)	0	<0.01
British (105)	191	0.31
Bulgarian (20)	20	0.03
Cajun (0)	0	<0.01
Canadian (40)	76	0.12
Carpatho Rusyn (0)	0	<0.01
Celtic (0)	0	<0.01
Croatian (6)	62	0.10
Cypriot (0)	0	<0.01
Czech (20)	134	0.21
Czechoslovakian (0)	47	0.08
Danish (117)	345	0.55
Dutch (283)	1,537	2.46
Eastern European (0)	10	0.02
English (2,193)	7,375	11.79
Estonian (13)	13	0.02
European (612)	723	1.16
Finnish (71)	146	0.23
French, ex. Basque (273)	2,060	3.29
French Canadian (155)	236	0.38
German (2,542)	9,632	15.39
German Russian (0)	0	<0.01
Greek (105)	338	0.54
Guyanese (0)	0	<0.01
Hungarian (17)	45	0.07
Icelander (8)	18	0.03
Iranian (199)	231	0.37
Irish (2,811)	9,322	14.90
Israeli (62)	62	0.10
Italian (976)	2,360	3.77
Latvian (0)	11	0.02
Lithuanian (14)	46	0.07
Luxemburger (0)	0	<0.01
Macedonian (0)	9	0.01
Maltese (0)	0	<0.01
New Zealander (0)	0	<0.01
Northern European (49)	54	0.09
Norwegian (328)	1,178	1.88
Pennsylvania German (22)	32	0.05
Polish (278)	716	1.14
Portuguese (750)	1,362	2.18
Romanian (0)	91	0.15
Russian (226)	671	1.07
Scandinavian (34)	320	0.51
Scotch-Irish (391)	1,182	1.89
Scottish (338)	1,427	2.28
Serbian (15)	28	0.04
Slavic (0)	7	0.01
Slovak (2)	2	<0.01
Slovene (0)	0	<0.01
Soviet Union (0)	0	<0.01
Swedish (301)	1,299	2.08
Swiss (98)	239	0.38
Turkish (0)	35	0.06
Ukrainian (25)	155	0.25
Welsh (50)	383	0.61
West Indian, ex. Hispanic (0)	10	0.02
Bahamian (0)	0	<0.01
Barbadian (0)	0	<0.01
Belizean (0)	0	<0.01
Bermudan (0)	0	<0.01
British West Indian (0)	0	<0.01
Dutch West Indian (0)	10	0.02
Haitian (0)	0	<0.01
Jamaican (0)	0	<0.01
Trinidadian/Tobagonian (0)	0	<0.01
U.S. Virgin Islander (0)	0	<0.01
West Indian (0)	0	<0.01
Other West Indian (0)	0	<0.01
Yugoslavian (16)	40	0.06

Hispanic Origin	Population	%
Hispanic or Latino (of any race)	13,906	21.91
Central American, ex. Mexican	236	0.37
Costa Rican	23	0.04
Guatemalan	29	0.05
Honduran	23	0.04
Nicaraguan	17	0.03
Panamanian	12	0.02
Salvadoran	129	0.20
Other Central American	3	<0.01
Cuban	12	0.02
Dominican Republic	1	<0.01
Mexican	12,398	19.54
Puerto Rican	177	0.28
South American	65	0.10
Argentinean	11	0.02
Bolivian	2	<0.01
Chilean	9	0.01
Colombian	10	0.02
Ecuadorian	3	<0.01
Paraguayan	1	<0.01
Peruvian	13	0.02
Uruguayan	3	<0.01
Venezuelan	10	0.02
Other South American	3	<0.01
Other Hispanic or Latino	1,017	1.60

Race*	Population	%
African-American/Black (406)	716	1.13
Not Hispanic (349)	606	0.95
Hispanic (57)	110	0.17
American Indian/Alaska Native (1,644)	3,034	4.78
Not Hispanic (1,205)	2,326	3.67
Hispanic (439)	708	1.12
Alaska Athabascan *(Ala. Nat.)* (3)	3	<0.01
Aleut *(Alaska Native)* (0)	0	<0.01
Apache (27)	60	0.09
Arapaho (0)	1	<0.01
Blackfeet (12)	58	0.09
Canadian/French Am. Ind. (3)	7	0.01
Central American Ind. (0)	1	<0.01
Cherokee (163)	520	0.82
Cheyenne (1)	14	0.02
Chickasaw (10)	18	0.03
Chippewa (25)	63	0.10
Choctaw (50)	132	0.21
Colville (0)	0	<0.01
Comanche (0)	10	0.02
Cree (1)	6	0.01
Creek (9)	22	0.03
Crow (0)	0	<0.01
Delaware (5)	6	0.01
Hopi (1)	5	0.01
Houma (0)	0	<0.01
Inupiat *(Alaska Native)* (2)	3	<0.01
Iroquois (3)	8	0.01
Kiowa (1)	2	<0.01
Lumbee (0)	5	0.01
Menominee (0)	0	<0.01
Mexican American Ind. (84)	110	0.17
Navajo (19)	39	0.06
Osage (5)	8	0.01
Ottawa (0)	1	<0.01
Paiute (11)	21	0.03
Pima (0)	0	<0.01
Potawatomi (12)	19	0.03
Pueblo (5)	8	0.01
Puget Sound Salish (1)	6	0.01
Seminole (5)	15	0.02
Shoshone (6)	7	0.01
Sioux (22)	59	0.09
South American Ind. (1)	1	<0.01
Spanish American Ind. (7)	8	0.01
Tlingit-Haida *(Alaska Native)* (3)	5	0.01
Tohono O'Odham (0)	1	<0.01
Tsimshian *(Alaska Native)* (0)	0	<0.01
Ute (6)	9	0.01
Yakama (0)	5	0.01
Yaqui (12)	33	0.05
Yuman (0)	0	<0.01
Yup'ik *(Alaska Native)* (1)	2	<0.01
Asian (656)	1,040	1.64
Not Hispanic (625)	910	1.43
Hispanic (31)	130	0.20
Bangladeshi (0)	0	<0.01
Bhutanese (0)	0	<0.01
Burmese (4)	8	0.01
Cambodian (1)	1	<0.01
Chinese, ex. Taiwanese (87)	121	0.19
Filipino (185)	358	0.56
Hmong (27)	30	0.05
Indian (114)	143	0.23
Indonesian (4)	5	0.01
Japanese (52)	121	0.19
Korean (40)	67	0.11
Laotian (63)	89	0.14
Malaysian (0)	0	<0.01
Nepalese (0)	0	<0.01
Pakistani (5)	8	0.01
Sri Lankan (0)	0	<0.01
Taiwanese (4)	5	0.01
Thai (4)	8	0.01
Vietnamese (35)	42	0.07
Hawaii Native/Pacific Islander (76)	195	0.31
Not Hispanic (64)	145	0.23
Hispanic (12)	50	0.08
Fijian (0)	2	<0.01
Guamanian/Chamorro (12)	24	0.04
Marshallese (0)	0	<0.01
Native Hawaiian (26)	85	0.13
Samoan (19)	38	0.06
Tongan (1)	5	0.01
White (51,721)	54,255	85.49
Not Hispanic (45,603)	47,181	74.34
Hispanic (6,118)	7,074	11.15

*Notes: † The Census 2010 population figure is used to calculate the percentages in the Hispanic Origin and Race categories. Ancestry percentages are based on the 2006-2010 American Community Survey population (not shown); ‡ Numbers in parentheses indicate the number of people reporting a single ancestry; * Numbers in parentheses indicate the number of persons reporting this race alone, not in combination with any other race; Please refer to the Explanation of Data for more information.*

Trinity County

Population: 13,786

Ancestry	Population	%
Afghan (0)	0	<0.01
African, Sub-Saharan (23)	23	0.17
African (23)	23	0.17
Cape Verdean (0)	0	<0.01
Ethiopian (0)	0	<0.01
Ghanaian (0)	0	<0.01
Kenyan (0)	0	<0.01
Liberian (0)	0	<0.01
Nigerian (0)	0	<0.01
Senegalese (0)	0	<0.01
Sierra Leonean (0)	0	<0.01
Somalian (0)	0	<0.01
South African (0)	0	<0.01
Sudanese (0)	0	<0.01
Ugandan (0)	0	<0.01
Zimbabwean (0)	0	<0.01
Other Sub-Saharan African (0)	0	<0.01
Albanian (0)	0	<0.01
Alsatian (0)	0	<0.01
American (352)	352	2.57
Arab (10)	32	0.23
Arab (6)	22	0.16
Egyptian (0)	0	<0.01
Iraqi (0)	0	<0.01
Jordanian (0)	0	<0.01
Lebanese (4)	4	0.03
Moroccan (0)	0	<0.01
Palestinian (0)	0	<0.01
Syrian (0)	6	0.04
Other Arab (0)	0	<0.01
Armenian (0)	0	<0.01
Assyrian/Chaldean/Syriac (0)	0	<0.01
Australian (0)	0	<0.01
Austrian (5)	19	0.14
Basque (0)	67	0.49
Belgian (0)	37	0.27
Brazilian (0)	0	<0.01
British (13)	36	0.26
Bulgarian (0)	0	<0.01
Cajun (21)	21	0.15
Canadian (25)	25	0.18
Carpatho Rusyn (0)	0	<0.01
Celtic (0)	0	<0.01
Croatian (0)	0	<0.01
Cypriot (0)	0	<0.01
Czech (66)	110	0.80
Czechoslovakian (0)	9	0.07
Danish (65)	402	2.93
Dutch (26)	315	2.30
Eastern European (0)	0	<0.01
English (374)	2,638	19.25
Estonian (0)	0	<0.01
European (255)	316	2.31
Finnish (22)	129	0.94
French, ex. Basque (69)	762	5.56
French Canadian (21)	37	0.27
German (789)	3,470	25.33
German Russian (0)	0	<0.01
Greek (0)	18	0.13
Guyanese (0)	0	<0.01
Hungarian (88)	147	1.07
Icelander (0)	0	<0.01
Iranian (95)	95	0.69
Irish (538)	3,143	22.94
Israeli (0)	0	<0.01
Italian (326)	813	5.93
Latvian (0)	0	<0.01
Lithuanian (0)	58	0.42
Luxemburger (0)	0	<0.01
Macedonian (0)	0	<0.01
Maltese (4)	4	0.03
New Zealander (0)	0	<0.01
Northern European (61)	72	0.53
Norwegian (73)	447	3.26
Pennsylvania German (0)	0	<0.01
Polish (47)	261	1.90
Portuguese (76)	177	1.29
Romanian (0)	0	<0.01
Russian (61)	234	1.71
Scandinavian (20)	20	0.15
Scotch-Irish (187)	630	4.60
Scottish (234)	778	5.68
Serbian (0)	0	<0.01
Slavic (0)	5	0.04
Slovak (0)	0	<0.01
Slovene (0)	0	<0.01
Soviet Union (0)	0	<0.01
Swedish (117)	461	3.36
Swiss (24)	213	1.55
Turkish (0)	0	<0.01
Ukrainian (7)	7	0.05
Welsh (67)	381	2.78
West Indian, ex. Hispanic (0)	1	0.01
Bahamian (0)	0	<0.01
Barbadian (0)	0	<0.01
Belizean (0)	0	<0.01
Bermudan (0)	0	<0.01
British West Indian (0)	0	<0.01
Dutch West Indian (0)	0	<0.01
Haitian (0)	0	<0.01
Jamaican (0)	1	0.01
Trinidadian/Tobagonian (0)	0	<0.01
U.S. Virgin Islander (0)	0	<0.01
West Indian (0)	0	<0.01
Other West Indian (0)	0	<0.01
Yugoslavian (0)	0	<0.01

Hispanic Origin	Population	%
Hispanic or Latino (of any race)	959	6.96
Central American, ex. Mexican	18	0.13
Costa Rican	1	0.01
Guatemalan	0	<0.01
Honduran	0	<0.01
Nicaraguan	5	0.04
Panamanian	4	0.03
Salvadoran	8	0.06
Other Central American	0	<0.01
Cuban	12	0.09
Dominican Republic	0	<0.01
Mexican	704	5.11
Puerto Rican	29	0.21
South American	22	0.16
Argentinean	3	0.02
Bolivian	0	<0.01
Chilean	11	0.08
Colombian	6	0.04
Ecuadorian	0	<0.01
Paraguayan	0	<0.01
Peruvian	2	0.01
Uruguayan	0	<0.01
Venezuelan	0	<0.01
Other South American	0	<0.01
Other Hispanic or Latino	174	1.26

Race*	Population	%
African-American/Black (59)	109	0.79
Not Hispanic (45)	91	0.66
Hispanic (14)	18	0.13
American Indian/Alaska Native (655)	1,180	8.56
Not Hispanic (558)	1,008	7.31
Hispanic (97)	172	1.25
Alaska Athabascan *(Ala. Nat.)* (0)	2	0.01
Aleut *(Alaska Native)* (0)	1	0.01
Apache (6)	18	0.13
Arapaho (0)	0	<0.01
Blackfeet (5)	23	0.17
Canadian/French Am. Ind. (0)	0	<0.01
Central American Ind. (0)	0	<0.01
Cherokee (63)	216	1.57
Cheyenne (1)	3	0.02
Chickasaw (0)	7	0.05
Chippewa (4)	6	0.04
Choctaw (10)	31	0.22
Colville (0)	0	<0.01
Comanche (3)	4	0.03
Cree (0)	1	0.01
Creek (3)	8	0.06
Crow (0)	0	<0.01
Delaware (5)	7	0.05
Hopi (0)	0	<0.01
Houma (0)	0	<0.01
Inupiat *(Alaska Native)* (0)	0	<0.01
Iroquois (0)	3	0.02
Kiowa (1)	1	0.01
Lumbee (0)	0	<0.01
Menominee (0)	0	<0.01
Mexican American Ind. (15)	23	0.17
Navajo (3)	7	0.05
Osage (1)	8	0.06
Ottawa (0)	0	<0.01
Paiute (5)	5	0.04
Pima (0)	0	<0.01
Potawatomi (1)	2	0.01
Pueblo (0)	2	0.01
Puget Sound Salish (2)	3	0.02
Seminole (2)	11	0.08
Shoshone (1)	1	0.01
Sioux (6)	23	0.17
South American Ind. (0)	1	0.01
Spanish American Ind. (1)	2	0.01
Tlingit-Haida *(Alaska Native)* (1)	3	0.02
Tohono O'Odham (0)	0	<0.01
Tsimshian *(Alaska Native)* (0)	0	<0.01
Ute (1)	1	0.01
Yakama (2)	3	0.02
Yaqui (2)	3	0.02
Yuman (0)	1	0.01
Yup'ik *(Alaska Native)* (0)	0	<0.01
Asian (94)	190	1.38
Not Hispanic (93)	173	1.25
Hispanic (1)	17	0.12
Bangladeshi (0)	0	<0.01
Bhutanese (0)	0	<0.01
Burmese (1)	1	0.01
Cambodian (0)	2	0.01
Chinese, ex. Taiwanese (9)	36	0.26
Filipino (23)	51	0.37
Hmong (0)	0	<0.01
Indian (10)	20	0.15
Indonesian (4)	7	0.05
Japanese (16)	33	0.24
Korean (4)	13	0.09
Laotian (15)	15	0.11
Malaysian (0)	0	<0.01
Nepalese (0)	0	<0.01
Pakistani (0)	0	<0.01
Sri Lankan (0)	0	<0.01
Taiwanese (1)	1	0.01
Thai (4)	12	0.09
Vietnamese (0)	3	0.02
Hawaii Native/Pacific Islander (16)	66	0.48
Not Hispanic (16)	60	0.44
Hispanic (0)	6	0.04
Fijian (1)	1	0.01
Guamanian/Chamorro (2)	7	0.05
Marshallese (0)	0	<0.01
Native Hawaiian (10)	47	0.34
Samoan (2)	4	0.03
Tongan (0)	1	0.01
White (12,033)	12,708	92.18
Not Hispanic (11,518)	12,078	87.61
Hispanic (515)	630	4.57

*Notes: † The Census 2010 population figure is used to calculate the percentages in the Hispanic Origin and Race categories. Ancestry percentages are based on the 2006-2010 American Community Survey population (not shown); ‡ Numbers in parentheses indicate the number of people reporting a single ancestry; * Numbers in parentheses indicate the number of persons reporting this race alone, not in combination with any other race; Please refer to the Explanation of Data for more information.*

Tulare County

Population: 442,179

Ancestry	Population	%
Afghan (0)	0	<0.01
African, Sub-Saharan (457)	606	0.14
African (211)	360	0.08
Cape Verdean (0)	0	<0.01
Ethiopian (143)	143	0.03
Ghanaian (0)	0	<0.01
Kenyan (0)	0	<0.01
Liberian (0)	0	<0.01
Nigerian (93)	93	0.02
Senegalese (0)	0	<0.01
Sierra Leonean (0)	0	<0.01
Somalian (0)	0	<0.01
South African (10)	10	<0.01
Sudanese (0)	0	<0.01
Ugandan (0)	0	<0.01
Zimbabwean (0)	0	<0.01
Other Sub-Saharan African (0)	0	<0.01
Albanian (0)	0	<0.01
Alsatian (0)	0	<0.01
American (11,215)	11,215	2.61
Arab (982)	1,134	0.26
Arab (415)	475	0.11
Egyptian (73)	78	0.02
Iraqi (0)	0	<0.01
Jordanian (34)	34	0.01
Lebanese (192)	231	0.05
Moroccan (0)	0	<0.01
Palestinian (178)	187	0.04
Syrian (35)	58	0.01
Other Arab (55)	71	0.02
Armenian (593)	909	0.21
Assyrian/Chaldean/Syriac (71)	81	0.02
Australian (52)	73	0.02
Austrian (74)	230	0.05
Basque (53)	143	0.03
Belgian (48)	225	0.05
Brazilian (85)	95	0.02
British (264)	392	0.09
Bulgarian (18)	18	<0.01
Cajun (0)	0	<0.01
Canadian (215)	476	0.11
Carpatho Rusyn (0)	0	<0.01
Celtic (57)	63	0.01
Croatian (66)	151	0.04
Cypriot (0)	0	<0.01
Czech (287)	528	0.12
Czechoslovakian (138)	203	0.05
Danish (199)	1,114	0.26
Dutch (2,645)	6,007	1.40
Eastern European (48)	66	0.02
English (7,794)	19,581	4.56
Estonian (0)	0	<0.01
European (2,306)	2,601	0.61
Finnish (176)	296	0.07
French, ex. Basque (866)	4,597	1.07
French Canadian (254)	543	0.13
German (8,783)	26,403	6.15
German Russian (0)	0	<0.01
Greek (203)	512	0.12
Guyanese (0)	0	<0.01
Hungarian (131)	315	0.07
Icelander (39)	76	0.02
Iranian (134)	189	0.04
Irish (6,046)	20,686	4.82
Israeli (140)	150	0.03
Italian (2,357)	6,726	1.57
Latvian (0)	14	<0.01
Lithuanian (32)	47	0.01
Luxemburger (0)	0	<0.01
Macedonian (0)	0	<0.01
Maltese (0)	0	<0.01
New Zealander (10)	10	<0.01
Northern European (385)	457	0.11
Norwegian (981)	2,031	0.47
Pennsylvania German (2)	10	<0.01
Polish (634)	1,765	0.41
Portuguese (7,231)	9,681	2.25
Romanian (10)	66	0.02
Russian (540)	1,084	0.25
Scandinavian (147)	281	0.07
Scotch-Irish (971)	2,842	0.66
Scottish (1,152)	3,354	0.78
Serbian (4)	25	0.01
Slavic (38)	72	0.02
Slovak (20)	74	0.02
Slovene (11)	19	<0.01
Soviet Union (0)	0	<0.01
Swedish (1,106)	2,880	0.67
Swiss (118)	691	0.16
Turkish (0)	0	<0.01
Ukrainian (49)	105	0.02
Welsh (161)	1,199	0.28
West Indian, ex. Hispanic (135)	301	0.07
Bahamian (0)	0	<0.01
Barbadian (0)	10	<0.01
Belizean (0)	0	<0.01
Bermudan (0)	0	<0.01
British West Indian (0)	0	<0.01
Dutch West Indian (74)	206	0.05
Haitian (36)	60	0.01
Jamaican (25)	25	0.01
Trinidadian/Tobagonian (0)	0	<0.01
U.S. Virgin Islander (0)	0	<0.01
West Indian (0)	0	<0.01
Other West Indian (0)	0	<0.01
Yugoslavian (42)	142	0.03

Hispanic Origin	Population	%
Hispanic or Latino (of any race)	268,065	60.62
Central American, ex. Mexican	2,368	0.54
Costa Rican	78	0.02
Guatemalan	480	0.11
Honduran	218	0.05
Nicaraguan	216	0.05
Panamanian	64	0.01
Salvadoran	1,297	0.29
Other Central American	15	<0.01
Cuban	242	0.05
Dominican Republic	54	0.01
Mexican	250,262	56.60
Puerto Rican	1,418	0.32
South American	570	0.13
Argentinean	100	0.02
Bolivian	30	0.01
Chilean	51	0.01
Colombian	123	0.03
Ecuadorian	29	0.01
Paraguayan	2	<0.01
Peruvian	171	0.04
Uruguayan	7	<0.01
Venezuelan	56	0.01
Other South American	1	<0.01
Other Hispanic or Latino	13,151	2.97

Race*	Population	%
African-American/Black (7,196)	9,720	2.20
Not Hispanic (5,497)	6,840	1.55
Hispanic (1,699)	2,880	0.65
American Indian/Alaska Native (6,993)	11,521	2.61
Not Hispanic (3,323)	5,948	1.35
Hispanic (3,670)	5,573	1.26
Alaska Athabascan *(Ala. Nat.)* (1)	3	<0.01
Aleut *(Alaska Native)* (2)	6	<0.01
Apache (195)	341	0.08
Arapaho (8)	14	<0.01
Blackfeet (35)	125	0.03
Canadian/French Am. Ind. (14)	22	<0.01
Central American Ind. (4)	7	<0.01
Cherokee (461)	1,417	0.32
Cheyenne (14)	23	0.01
Chickasaw (55)	116	0.03
Chippewa (24)	34	0.01
Choctaw (223)	490	0.11
Colville (5)	10	<0.01
Comanche (24)	57	0.01
Cree (1)	9	<0.01
Creek (51)	96	0.02
Crow (5)	5	<0.01
Delaware (4)	11	<0.01
Hopi (26)	31	0.01
Houma (0)	0	<0.01
Inupiat *(Alaska Native)* (2)	12	<0.01
Iroquois (19)	52	0.01
Kiowa (4)	23	0.01
Lumbee (6)	9	<0.01
Menominee (1)	1	<0.01
Mexican American Ind. (644)	895	0.20
Navajo (68)	149	0.03
Osage (2)	17	<0.01
Ottawa (1)	15	<0.01
Paiute (54)	77	0.02
Pima (35)	55	0.01
Potawatomi (53)	93	0.02
Pueblo (20)	43	0.01
Puget Sound Salish (13)	20	<0.01
Seminole (24)	62	0.01
Shoshone (10)	21	<0.01
Sioux (58)	159	0.04
South American Ind. (4)	10	<0.01
Spanish American Ind. (34)	60	0.01
Tlingit-Haida *(Alaska Native)* (5)	14	<0.01
Tohono O'Odham (24)	35	0.01
Tsimshian *(Alaska Native)* (0)	0	<0.01
Ute (7)	10	<0.01
Yakama (1)	3	<0.01
Yaqui (120)	195	0.04
Yuman (18)	35	0.01
Yup'ik *(Alaska Native)* (1)	7	<0.01
Asian (15,176)	18,948	4.29
Not Hispanic (14,204)	16,425	3.71
Hispanic (972)	2,523	0.57
Bangladeshi (15)	15	<0.01
Bhutanese (0)	0	<0.01
Burmese (40)	51	0.01
Cambodian (135)	180	0.04
Chinese, ex. Taiwanese (1,073)	1,541	0.35
Filipino (5,605)	7,363	1.67
Hmong (1,005)	1,086	0.25
Indian (1,659)	1,917	0.43
Indonesian (19)	46	0.01
Japanese (696)	1,217	0.28
Korean (318)	505	0.11
Laotian (1,669)	1,978	0.45
Malaysian (7)	7	<0.01
Nepalese (8)	11	<0.01
Pakistani (195)	222	0.05
Sri Lankan (8)	17	<0.01
Taiwanese (25)	45	0.01
Thai (1,562)	1,714	0.39
Vietnamese (405)	506	0.11
Hawaii Native/Pacific Islander (509)	1,395	0.32
Not Hispanic (370)	866	0.20
Hispanic (139)	529	0.12
Fijian (16)	38	0.01
Guamanian/Chamorro (82)	154	0.03
Marshallese (49)	54	0.01
Native Hawaiian (114)	449	0.10
Samoan (72)	139	0.03
Tongan (27)	45	0.01
White (265,618)	281,270	63.61
Not Hispanic (143,935)	149,459	33.80
Hispanic (121,683)	131,811	29.81

*Notes: † The Census 2010 population figure is used to calculate the percentages in the Hispanic Origin and Race categories. Ancestry percentages are based on the 2006-2010 American Community Survey population (not shown); ‡ Numbers in parentheses indicate the number of people reporting a single ancestry; * Numbers in parentheses indicate the number of persons reporting this race alone, not in combination with any other race; Please refer to the Explanation of Data for more information.*

Tuolumne County

Population: 55,365

Ancestry	Population	%
Afghan (0)	0	<0.01
African, Sub-Saharan (109)	119	0.21
African (109)	119	0.21
Cape Verdean (0)	0	<0.01
Ethiopian (0)	0	<0.01
Ghanaian (0)	0	<0.01
Kenyan (0)	0	<0.01
Liberian (0)	0	<0.01
Nigerian (0)	0	<0.01
Senegalese (0)	0	<0.01
Sierra Leonean (0)	0	<0.01
Somalian (0)	0	<0.01
South African (0)	0	<0.01
Sudanese (0)	0	<0.01
Ugandan (0)	0	<0.01
Zimbabwean (0)	0	<0.01
Other Sub-Saharan African (0)	0	<0.01
Albanian (0)	0	<0.01
Alsatian (0)	0	<0.01
American (2,360)	2,360	4.21
Arab (25)	63	0.11
Arab (0)	0	<0.01
Egyptian (0)	20	0.04
Iraqi (0)	0	<0.01
Jordanian (0)	0	<0.01
Lebanese (25)	41	0.07
Moroccan (0)	2	<0.01
Palestinian (0)	0	<0.01
Syrian (0)	0	<0.01
Other Arab (0)	0	<0.01
Armenian (14)	23	0.04
Assyrian/Chaldean/Syriac (0)	0	<0.01
Australian (0)	7	0.01
Austrian (100)	313	0.56
Basque (0)	41	0.07
Belgian (0)	54	0.10
Brazilian (0)	8	0.01
British (88)	160	0.29
Bulgarian (0)	0	<0.01
Cajun (0)	0	<0.01
Canadian (106)	236	0.42
Carpatho Rusyn (0)	0	<0.01
Celtic (0)	0	<0.01
Croatian (16)	53	0.09
Cypriot (0)	0	<0.01
Czech (55)	211	0.38
Czechoslovakian (20)	161	0.29
Danish (264)	957	1.71
Dutch (309)	1,469	2.62
Eastern European (22)	22	0.04
English (2,242)	8,855	15.79
Estonian (8)	8	0.01
European (716)	834	1.49
Finnish (29)	190	0.34
French, ex. Basque (398)	1,850	3.30
French Canadian (115)	241	0.43
German (3,410)	11,539	20.58
German Russian (0)	0	<0.01
Greek (98)	194	0.35
Guyanese (0)	0	<0.01
Hungarian (4)	159	0.28
Icelander (0)	0	<0.01
Iranian (5)	33	0.06
Irish (2,241)	8,997	16.04
Israeli (0)	0	<0.01
Italian (1,859)	4,875	8.69
Latvian (7)	26	0.05
Lithuanian (2)	2	<0.01
Luxemburger (0)	0	<0.01
Macedonian (0)	0	<0.01
Maltese (0)	0	<0.01
New Zealander (0)	8	0.01
Northern European (85)	94	0.17
Norwegian (553)	1,618	2.89
Pennsylvania German (0)	39	0.07
Polish (346)	911	1.62
Portuguese (618)	1,657	2.96
Romanian (12)	56	0.10
Russian (139)	538	0.96
Scandinavian (101)	530	0.95
Scotch-Irish (414)	1,544	2.75
Scottish (442)	1,983	3.54
Serbian (0)	0	<0.01
Slavic (36)	67	0.12
Slovak (78)	133	0.24
Slovene (0)	20	0.04
Soviet Union (0)	0	<0.01
Swedish (432)	1,969	3.51
Swiss (176)	393	0.70
Turkish (0)	0	<0.01
Ukrainian (7)	32	0.06
Welsh (60)	429	0.77
West Indian, ex. Hispanic (14)	14	0.02
Bahamian (0)	0	<0.01
Barbadian (0)	0	<0.01
Belizean (8)	8	0.01
Bermudan (0)	0	<0.01
British West Indian (0)	0	<0.01
Dutch West Indian (0)	0	<0.01
Haitian (6)	6	0.01
Jamaican (0)	0	<0.01
Trinidadian/Tobagonian (0)	0	<0.01
U.S. Virgin Islander (0)	0	<0.01
West Indian (0)	0	<0.01
Other West Indian (0)	0	<0.01
Yugoslavian (93)	169	0.30

Hispanic Origin	Population	%
Hispanic or Latino (of any race)	5,918	10.69
Central American, ex. Mexican	134	0.24
Costa Rican	7	0.01
Guatemalan	27	0.05
Honduran	10	0.02
Nicaraguan	22	0.04
Panamanian	16	0.03
Salvadoran	48	0.09
Other Central American	4	0.01
Cuban	46	0.08
Dominican Republic	2	<0.01
Mexican	4,134	7.47
Puerto Rican	161	0.29
South American	59	0.11
Argentinean	11	0.02
Bolivian	1	<0.01
Chilean	13	0.02
Colombian	10	0.02
Ecuadorian	6	0.01
Paraguayan	0	<0.01
Peruvian	13	0.02
Uruguayan	4	0.01
Venezuelan	0	<0.01
Other South American	1	<0.01
Other Hispanic or Latino	1,382	2.50

Race*	Population	%
African-American/Black (1,143)	1,342	2.42
Not Hispanic (1,114)	1,265	2.28
Hispanic (29)	77	0.14
American Indian/Alaska Native (1,039)	2,190	3.96
Not Hispanic (830)	1,718	3.10
Hispanic (209)	472	0.85
Alaska Athabascan *(Ala. Nat.)* (2)	3	0.01
Aleut *(Alaska Native)* (4)	5	0.01
Apache (25)	55	0.10
Arapaho (0)	1	<0.01
Blackfeet (14)	53	0.10
Canadian/French Am. Ind. (0)	3	0.01
Central American Ind. (1)	1	<0.01
Cherokee (136)	492	0.89
Cheyenne (3)	16	0.03
Chickasaw (12)	32	0.06
Chippewa (4)	12	0.02
Choctaw (50)	128	0.23
Colville (0)	0	<0.01
Comanche (3)	12	0.02
Cree (0)	3	0.01
Creek (6)	28	0.05
Crow (3)	6	0.01
Delaware (2)	5	0.01
Hopi (3)	4	0.01
Houma (0)	0	<0.01
Inupiat *(Alaska Native)* (0)	1	<0.01
Iroquois (2)	8	0.01
Kiowa (2)	2	<0.01
Lumbee (0)	5	0.01
Menominee (1)	1	<0.01
Mexican American Ind. (43)	55	0.10
Navajo (15)	31	0.06
Osage (7)	14	0.03
Ottawa (0)	2	<0.01
Paiute (2)	13	0.02
Pima (1)	2	<0.01
Potawatomi (11)	14	0.03
Pueblo (1)	8	0.01
Puget Sound Salish (1)	1	<0.01
Seminole (1)	9	0.02
Shoshone (1)	7	0.01
Sioux (13)	46	0.08
South American Ind. (3)	5	0.01
Spanish American Ind. (1)	10	0.02
Tlingit-Haida *(Alaska Native)* (8)	9	0.02
Tohono O'Odham (7)	12	0.02
Tsimshian *(Alaska Native)* (0)	0	<0.01
Ute (5)	10	0.02
Yakama (1)	2	<0.01
Yaqui (17)	36	0.07
Yuman (0)	0	<0.01
Yup'ik *(Alaska Native)* (0)	2	<0.01
Asian (572)	996	1.80
Not Hispanic (530)	827	1.49
Hispanic (42)	169	0.31
Bangladeshi (0)	0	<0.01
Bhutanese (0)	0	<0.01
Burmese (0)	0	<0.01
Cambodian (9)	10	0.02
Chinese, ex. Taiwanese (129)	213	0.38
Filipino (214)	381	0.69
Hmong (0)	3	0.01
Indian (51)	69	0.12
Indonesian (3)	11	0.02
Japanese (79)	185	0.33
Korean (30)	59	0.11
Laotian (3)	7	0.01
Malaysian (1)	1	<0.01
Nepalese (0)	0	<0.01
Pakistani (0)	2	<0.01
Sri Lankan (0)	0	<0.01
Taiwanese (3)	6	0.01
Thai (6)	18	0.03
Vietnamese (11)	20	0.04
Hawaii Native/Pacific Islander (76)	217	0.39
Not Hispanic (62)	163	0.29
Hispanic (14)	54	0.10
Fijian (4)	6	0.01
Guamanian/Chamorro (6)	14	0.03
Marshallese (0)	0	<0.01
Native Hawaiian (44)	156	0.28
Samoan (5)	9	0.02
Tongan (2)	5	0.01
White (48,274)	50,133	90.55
Not Hispanic (45,325)	46,616	84.20
Hispanic (2,949)	3,517	6.35

*Notes: † The Census 2010 population figure is used to calculate the percentages in the Hispanic Origin and Race categories. Ancestry percentages are based on the 2006-2010 American Community Survey population (not shown); ‡ Numbers in parentheses indicate the number of people reporting a single ancestry; * Numbers in parentheses indicate the number of persons reporting this race alone, not in combination with any other race; Please refer to the Explanation of Data for more information.*

Ventura County

Population: 823,318

Ancestry	Population	%
Afghan (785)	798	0.10
African, Sub-Saharan (1,190)	1,673	0.21
African (705)	1,105	0.14
Cape Verdean (24)	46	0.01
Ethiopian (31)	31	<0.01
Ghanaian (128)	128	0.02
Kenyan (25)	25	<0.01
Liberian (0)	0	<0.01
Nigerian (121)	129	0.02
Senegalese (0)	0	<0.01
Sierra Leonean (0)	0	<0.01
Somalian (24)	24	<0.01
South African (116)	169	0.02
Sudanese (0)	0	<0.01
Ugandan (0)	0	<0.01
Zimbabwean (0)	0	<0.01
Other Sub-Saharan African (16)	16	<0.01
Albanian (238)	293	0.04
Alsatian (8)	33	<0.01
American (33,594)	33,594	4.15
Arab (3,232)	4,895	0.61
Arab (721)	859	0.11
Egyptian (478)	605	0.07
Iraqi (96)	122	0.02
Jordanian (285)	285	0.04
Lebanese (725)	1,394	0.17
Moroccan (87)	87	0.01
Palestinian (97)	119	0.01
Syrian (225)	682	0.08
Other Arab (518)	742	0.09
Armenian (1,680)	2,465	0.30
Assyrian/Chaldean/Syriac (91)	132	0.02
Australian (150)	384	0.05
Austrian (864)	2,877	0.36
Basque (101)	433	0.05
Belgian (133)	513	0.06
Brazilian (121)	487	0.06
British (2,962)	4,785	0.59
Bulgarian (83)	167	0.02
Cajun (0)	23	<0.01
Canadian (1,334)	3,084	0.38
Carpatho Rusyn (0)	0	<0.01
Celtic (25)	50	0.01
Croatian (288)	977	0.12
Cypriot (0)	0	<0.01
Czech (629)	2,761	0.34
Czechoslovakian (415)	856	0.11
Danish (1,479)	5,706	0.71
Dutch (2,386)	10,376	1.28
Eastern European (1,523)	1,749	0.22
English (19,805)	72,215	8.93
Estonian (21)	70	0.01
European (9,855)	11,664	1.44
Finnish (615)	1,215	0.15
French, ex. Basque (2,623)	20,840	2.58
French Canadian (1,274)	3,681	0.45
German (24,439)	99,365	12.28
German Russian (0)	6	<0.01
Greek (1,404)	3,540	0.44
Guyanese (12)	29	<0.01
Hungarian (1,485)	4,454	0.55
Icelander (31)	113	0.01
Iranian (3,059)	3,944	0.49
Irish (17,925)	75,690	9.36
Israeli (463)	740	0.09
Italian (14,328)	41,056	5.07
Latvian (25)	141	0.02
Lithuanian (557)	1,738	0.21
Luxemburger (0)	7	<0.01
Macedonian (0)	92	0.01
Maltese (0)	21	<0.01
New Zealander (35)	52	0.01
Northern European (846)	937	0.12
Norwegian (3,574)	11,852	1.46
Pennsylvania German (54)	115	0.01
Polish (5,231)	18,700	2.31
Portuguese (1,379)	3,811	0.47
Romanian (738)	1,722	0.21
Russian (5,848)	14,702	1.82
Scandinavian (741)	1,862	0.23
Scotch-Irish (3,790)	12,033	1.49
Scottish (4,655)	15,987	1.98
Serbian (144)	355	0.04
Slavic (137)	493	0.06
Slovak (270)	571	0.07
Slovene (81)	216	0.03
Soviet Union (9)	9	<0.01
Swedish (2,980)	13,012	1.61
Swiss (463)	2,430	0.30
Turkish (210)	546	0.07
Ukrainian (855)	1,961	0.24
Welsh (1,047)	5,098	0.63
West Indian, ex. Hispanic (568)	1,085	0.13
Bahamian (0)	29	<0.01
Barbadian (26)	26	<0.01
Belizean (60)	72	0.01
Bermudan (0)	0	<0.01
British West Indian (0)	0	<0.01
Dutch West Indian (6)	148	0.02
Haitian (48)	87	0.01
Jamaican (285)	485	0.06
Trinidadian/Tobagonian (90)	154	0.02
U.S. Virgin Islander (0)	0	<0.01
West Indian (53)	84	0.01
Other West Indian (0)	0	<0.01
Yugoslavian (598)	1,113	0.14

Hispanic Origin	Population	%
Hispanic or Latino (of any race)	331,567	40.27
Central American, ex. Mexican	11,312	1.37
Costa Rican	480	0.06
Guatemalan	4,014	0.49
Honduran	807	0.10
Nicaraguan	893	0.11
Panamanian	288	0.03
Salvadoran	4,713	0.57
Other Central American	117	0.01
Cuban	1,474	0.18
Dominican Republic	192	0.02
Mexican	292,777	35.56
Puerto Rican	3,195	0.39
South American	6,310	0.77
Argentinean	1,141	0.14
Bolivian	191	0.02
Chilean	615	0.07
Colombian	1,454	0.18
Ecuadorian	638	0.08
Paraguayan	23	<0.01
Peruvian	1,841	0.22
Uruguayan	127	0.02
Venezuelan	189	0.02
Other South American	91	0.01
Other Hispanic or Latino	16,307	1.98

Race*	Population	%
African-American/Black (15,163)	20,931	2.54
Not Hispanic (13,082)	16,949	2.06
Hispanic (2,081)	3,982	0.48
American Indian/Alaska Native (8,068)	15,942	1.94
Not Hispanic (2,389)	6,915	0.84
Hispanic (5,679)	9,027	1.10
Alaska Athabascan *(Ala. Nat.)* (5)	9	<0.01
Aleut *(Alaska Native)* (8)	10	<0.01
Apache (265)	644	0.08
Arapaho (2)	10	<0.01
Blackfeet (50)	293	0.04
Canadian/French Am. Ind. (9)	33	<0.01
Central American Ind. (22)	42	0.01
Cherokee (506)	2,362	0.29
Cheyenne (9)	32	<0.01
Chickasaw (39)	98	0.01
Chippewa (69)	149	0.02
Choctaw (167)	570	0.07
Colville (6)	11	<0.01
Comanche (48)	92	0.01
Cree (4)	16	<0.01
Creek (29)	96	0.01
Crow (8)	22	<0.01
Delaware (8)	20	<0.01
Hopi (25)	71	0.01
Houma (2)	2	<0.01
Inupiat *(Alaska Native)* (2)	13	<0.01
Iroquois (38)	148	0.02
Kiowa (5)	16	<0.01
Lumbee (2)	13	<0.01
Menominee (3)	10	<0.01
Mexican American Ind. (1,808)	2,387	0.29
Navajo (114)	255	0.03
Osage (25)	67	0.01
Ottawa (4)	7	<0.01
Paiute (14)	37	<0.01
Pima (13)	27	<0.01
Potawatomi (38)	67	0.01
Pueblo (73)	122	0.01
Puget Sound Salish (4)	6	<0.01
Seminole (12)	56	0.01
Shoshone (10)	41	<0.01
Sioux (99)	299	0.04
South American Ind. (39)	90	0.01
Spanish American Ind. (36)	73	0.01
Tlingit-Haida *(Alaska Native)* (6)	23	<0.01
Tohono O'Odham (37)	76	0.01
Tsimshian *(Alaska Native)* (0)	0	<0.01
Ute (7)	26	<0.01
Yakama (3)	3	<0.01
Yaqui (128)	260	0.03
Yuman (8)	18	<0.01
Yup'ik *(Alaska Native)* (2)	3	<0.01
Asian (55,446)	69,252	8.41
Not Hispanic (54,099)	64,962	7.89
Hispanic (1,347)	4,290	0.52
Bangladeshi (134)	152	0.02
Bhutanese (5)	7	<0.01
Burmese (78)	110	0.01
Cambodian (412)	536	0.07
Chinese, ex. Taiwanese (8,395)	11,185	1.36
Filipino (19,703)	25,103	3.05
Hmong (38)	46	0.01
Indian (9,107)	10,146	1.23
Indonesian (301)	640	0.08
Japanese (4,518)	8,190	0.99
Korean (4,222)	5,213	0.63
Laotian (215)	272	0.03
Malaysian (42)	105	0.01
Nepalese (61)	77	0.01
Pakistani (525)	612	0.07
Sri Lankan (285)	332	0.04
Taiwanese (760)	887	0.11
Thai (672)	930	0.11
Vietnamese (4,189)	4,814	0.58
Hawaii Native/Pacific Islander (1,643)	4,070	0.49
Not Hispanic (1,353)	3,050	0.37
Hispanic (290)	1,020	0.12
Fijian (31)	50	0.01
Guamanian/Chamorro (379)	691	0.08
Marshallese (2)	5	<0.01
Native Hawaiian (434)	1,409	0.17
Samoan (487)	890	0.11
Tongan (66)	127	0.02
White (565,804)	597,984	72.63
Not Hispanic (400,868)	417,477	50.71
Hispanic (164,936)	180,507	21.92

*Notes: † The Census 2010 population figure is used to calculate the percentages in the Hispanic Origin and Race categories. Ancestry percentages are based on the 2006-2010 American Community Survey population (not shown); ‡ Numbers in parentheses indicate the number of people reporting a single ancestry; * Numbers in parentheses indicate the number of persons reporting this race alone, not in combination with any other race; Please refer to the Explanation of Data for more information.*

Yolo County

Population: 200,849

Ancestry	Population	%
Afghan (346)	346	0.18
African, Sub-Saharan (1,038)	1,358	0.69
African (691)	969	0.49
Cape Verdean (26)	26	0.01
Ethiopian (145)	170	0.09
Ghanaian (0)	17	0.01
Kenyan (0)	0	<0.01
Liberian (0)	0	<0.01
Nigerian (24)	24	0.01
Senegalese (0)	0	<0.01
Sierra Leonean (0)	0	<0.01
Somalian (91)	91	0.05
South African (61)	61	0.03
Sudanese (0)	0	<0.01
Ugandan (0)	0	<0.01
Zimbabwean (0)	0	<0.01
Other Sub-Saharan African (0)	0	<0.01
Albanian (0)	70	0.04
Alsatian (12)	12	0.01
American (4,087)	4,087	2.08
Arab (397)	596	0.30
Arab (47)	79	0.04
Egyptian (0)	37	0.02
Iraqi (31)	31	0.02
Jordanian (38)	38	0.02
Lebanese (66)	151	0.08
Moroccan (0)	0	<0.01
Palestinian (55)	55	0.03
Syrian (22)	45	0.02
Other Arab (138)	160	0.08
Armenian (251)	369	0.19
Assyrian/Chaldean/Syriac (18)	28	0.01
Australian (96)	450	0.23
Austrian (99)	463	0.24
Basque (126)	221	0.11
Belgian (60)	161	0.08
Brazilian (80)	105	0.05
British (373)	869	0.44
Bulgarian (15)	24	0.01
Cajun (0)	20	0.01
Canadian (177)	392	0.20
Carpatho Rusyn (0)	0	<0.01
Celtic (9)	30	0.02
Croatian (108)	375	0.19
Cypriot (11)	11	0.01
Czech (180)	556	0.28
Czechoslovakian (62)	172	0.09
Danish (236)	1,188	0.60
Dutch (622)	2,682	1.37
Eastern European (359)	419	0.21
English (5,302)	19,812	10.09
Estonian (12)	12	0.01
European (4,484)	5,626	2.86
Finnish (128)	378	0.19
French, ex. Basque (923)	4,391	2.24
French Canadian (303)	713	0.36
German (6,773)	24,905	12.68
German Russian (0)	0	<0.01
Greek (319)	718	0.37
Guyanese (0)	0	<0.01
Hungarian (68)	551	0.28
Icelander (27)	27	0.01
Iranian (692)	784	0.40
Irish (4,332)	18,488	9.41
Israeli (113)	113	0.06
Italian (2,668)	9,547	4.86
Latvian (41)	60	0.03
Lithuanian (69)	307	0.16
Luxemburger (0)	23	0.01
Macedonian (0)	11	0.01
Maltese (0)	0	<0.01
New Zealander (27)	34	0.02
Northern European (382)	437	0.22
Norwegian (680)	2,733	1.39
Pennsylvania German (30)	30	0.02
Polish (657)	3,447	1.75
Portuguese (1,175)	2,715	1.38
Romanian (187)	391	0.20
Russian (2,608)	4,209	2.14
Scandinavian (211)	486	0.25
Scotch-Irish (972)	4,094	2.08
Scottish (1,062)	4,692	2.39
Serbian (51)	59	0.03
Slavic (33)	78	0.04
Slovak (40)	144	0.07
Slovene (0)	39	0.02
Soviet Union (0)	0	<0.01
Swedish (718)	3,265	1.66
Swiss (235)	1,128	0.57
Turkish (146)	206	0.10
Ukrainian (951)	1,155	0.59
Welsh (233)	1,401	0.71
West Indian, ex. Hispanic (67)	107	0.05
Bahamian (0)	0	<0.01
Barbadian (0)	0	<0.01
Belizean (0)	0	<0.01
Bermudan (0)	0	<0.01
British West Indian (0)	0	<0.01
Dutch West Indian (0)	0	<0.01
Haitian (8)	16	0.01
Jamaican (59)	87	0.04
Trinidadian/Tobagonian (0)	4	<0.01
U.S. Virgin Islander (0)	0	<0.01
West Indian (0)	0	<0.01
Other West Indian (0)	0	<0.01
Yugoslavian (107)	137	0.07

Hispanic Origin	Population	%
Hispanic or Latino (of any race)	60,953	30.35
Central American, ex. Mexican	1,657	0.82
Costa Rican	76	0.04
Guatemalan	399	0.20
Honduran	164	0.08
Nicaraguan	224	0.11
Panamanian	70	0.03
Salvadoran	716	0.36
Other Central American	8	<0.01
Cuban	194	0.10
Dominican Republic	47	0.02
Mexican	53,114	26.44
Puerto Rican	755	0.38
South American	1,220	0.61
Argentinean	200	0.10
Bolivian	34	0.02
Chilean	178	0.09
Colombian	258	0.13
Ecuadorian	103	0.05
Paraguayan	5	<0.01
Peruvian	301	0.15
Uruguayan	29	0.01
Venezuelan	96	0.05
Other South American	16	0.01
Other Hispanic or Latino	3,966	1.97

Race*	Population	%
African-American/Black (5,208)	7,037	3.50
Not Hispanic (4,752)	6,083	3.03
Hispanic (456)	954	0.47
American Indian/Alaska Native (2,214)	4,774	2.38
Not Hispanic (1,098)	2,685	1.34
Hispanic (1,116)	2,089	1.04
Alaska Athabascan *(Ala. Nat.)* (2)	5	<0.01
Aleut *(Alaska Native)* (2)	3	<0.01
Apache (66)	166	0.08
Arapaho (0)	1	<0.01
Blackfeet (18)	78	0.04
Canadian/French Am. Ind. (10)	15	0.01
Central American Ind. (6)	13	0.01
Cherokee (174)	701	0.35
Cheyenne (2)	11	0.01
Chickasaw (16)	30	0.01
Chippewa (26)	52	0.03
Choctaw (57)	186	0.09
Colville (0)	1	<0.01
Comanche (2)	13	0.01
Cree (0)	11	0.01
Creek (11)	33	0.02
Crow (10)	24	0.01
Delaware (2)	4	<0.01
Hopi (8)	14	0.01
Houma (0)	2	<0.01
Inupiat *(Alaska Native)* (4)	8	<0.01
Iroquois (14)	47	0.02
Kiowa (2)	2	<0.01
Lumbee (0)	0	<0.01
Menominee (0)	0	<0.01
Mexican American Ind. (215)	337	0.17
Navajo (55)	112	0.06
Osage (3)	15	0.01
Ottawa (0)	8	<0.01
Paiute (17)	29	0.01
Pima (3)	6	<0.01
Potawatomi (13)	20	0.01
Pueblo (9)	24	0.01
Puget Sound Salish (1)	2	<0.01
Seminole (1)	7	<0.01
Shoshone (16)	25	0.01
Sioux (49)	129	0.06
South American Ind. (4)	25	0.01
Spanish American Ind. (29)	32	0.02
Tlingit-Haida *(Alaska Native)* (5)	10	<0.01
Tohono O'Odham (4)	7	<0.01
Tsimshian *(Alaska Native)* (0)	0	<0.01
Ute (1)	4	<0.01
Yakama (7)	7	<0.01
Yaqui (29)	64	0.03
Yuman (0)	0	<0.01
Yup'ik *(Alaska Native)* (1)	3	<0.01
Asian (26,052)	31,145	15.51
Not Hispanic (25,640)	29,827	14.85
Hispanic (412)	1,318	0.66
Bangladeshi (58)	58	0.03
Bhutanese (1)	1	<0.01
Burmese (38)	59	0.03
Cambodian (305)	371	0.18
Chinese, ex. Taiwanese (8,652)	10,311	5.13
Filipino (3,093)	4,695	2.34
Hmong (460)	488	0.24
Indian (3,923)	4,513	2.25
Indonesian (70)	120	0.06
Japanese (1,501)	2,767	1.38
Korean (2,004)	2,354	1.17
Laotian (613)	717	0.36
Malaysian (20)	33	0.02
Nepalese (288)	318	0.16
Pakistani (1,037)	1,137	0.57
Sri Lankan (98)	117	0.06
Taiwanese (567)	644	0.32
Thai (206)	309	0.15
Vietnamese (1,894)	2,291	1.14
Hawaii Native/Pacific Islander (910)	1,984	0.99
Not Hispanic (817)	1,603	0.80
Hispanic (93)	381	0.19
Fijian (455)	546	0.27
Guamanian/Chamorro (98)	239	0.12
Marshallese (7)	8	<0.01
Native Hawaiian (97)	397	0.20
Samoan (71)	136	0.07
Tongan (45)	58	0.03
White (126,883)	136,861	68.14
Not Hispanic (100,240)	106,214	52.88
Hispanic (26,643)	30,647	15.26

*Notes: † The Census 2010 population figure is used to calculate the percentages in the Hispanic Origin and Race categories. Ancestry percentages are based on the 2006-2010 American Community Survey population (not shown); ‡ Numbers in parentheses indicate the number of people reporting a single ancestry; * Numbers in parentheses indicate the number of persons reporting this race alone, not in combination with any other race; Please refer to the Explanation of Data for more information.*

Yuba County

Population: 72,155

Ancestry	Population	%
Afghan (60)	60	0.08
African, Sub-Saharan (77)	215	0.30
African (77)	215	0.30
Cape Verdean (0)	0	<0.01
Ethiopian (0)	0	<0.01
Ghanaian (0)	0	<0.01
Kenyan (0)	0	<0.01
Liberian (0)	0	<0.01
Nigerian (0)	0	<0.01
Senegalese (0)	0	<0.01
Sierra Leonean (0)	0	<0.01
Somalian (0)	0	<0.01
South African (0)	0	<0.01
Sudanese (0)	0	<0.01
Ugandan (0)	0	<0.01
Zimbabwean (0)	0	<0.01
Other Sub-Saharan African (0)	0	<0.01
Albanian (0)	0	<0.01
Alsatian (0)	0	<0.01
American (5,698)	5,698	8.01
Arab (0)	26	0.04
Arab (0)	0	<0.01
Egyptian (0)	6	0.01
Iraqi (0)	0	<0.01
Jordanian (0)	0	<0.01
Lebanese (0)	20	0.03
Moroccan (0)	0	<0.01
Palestinian (0)	0	<0.01
Syrian (0)	0	<0.01
Other Arab (0)	0	<0.01
Armenian (11)	11	0.02
Assyrian/Chaldean/Syriac (0)	0	<0.01
Australian (86)	86	0.12
Austrian (24)	134	0.19
Basque (6)	116	0.16
Belgian (0)	0	<0.01
Brazilian (18)	34	0.05
British (67)	167	0.23
Bulgarian (0)	0	<0.01
Cajun (25)	35	0.05
Canadian (14)	78	0.11
Carpatho Rusyn (0)	0	<0.01
Celtic (38)	38	0.05
Croatian (26)	48	0.07
Cypriot (0)	0	<0.01
Czech (39)	96	0.13
Czechoslovakian (22)	32	0.04
Danish (165)	710	1.00
Dutch (164)	1,223	1.72
Eastern European (25)	43	0.06
English (1,692)	5,866	8.24
Estonian (0)	0	<0.01
European (356)	424	0.60
Finnish (53)	98	0.14
French, ex. Basque (362)	2,401	3.37
French Canadian (117)	267	0.38
German (2,576)	9,880	13.88
German Russian (0)	0	<0.01
Greek (46)	279	0.39
Guyanese (0)	0	<0.01
Hungarian (70)	144	0.20
Icelander (0)	0	<0.01
Iranian (0)	0	<0.01
Irish (1,703)	8,135	11.43
Israeli (14)	29	0.04
Italian (1,137)	2,635	3.70
Latvian (11)	11	0.02
Lithuanian (18)	75	0.11
Luxemburger (9)	18	0.03
Macedonian (0)	0	<0.01
Maltese (0)	0	<0.01
New Zealander (0)	13	0.02
Northern European (40)	59	0.08
Norwegian (219)	794	1.12
Pennsylvania German (0)	0	<0.01
Polish (331)	1,023	1.44
Portuguese (713)	1,328	1.87
Romanian (760)	809	1.14
Russian (106)	386	0.54
Scandinavian (65)	412	0.58
Scotch-Irish (707)	1,846	2.59
Scottish (409)	1,317	1.85
Serbian (42)	60	0.08
Slavic (0)	0	<0.01
Slovak (9)	17	0.02
Slovene (0)	0	<0.01
Soviet Union (0)	0	<0.01
Swedish (193)	833	1.17
Swiss (43)	206	0.29
Turkish (0)	0	<0.01
Ukrainian (115)	195	0.27
Welsh (131)	462	0.65
West Indian, ex. Hispanic (0)	56	0.08
Bahamian (0)	0	<0.01
Barbadian (0)	0	<0.01
Belizean (0)	0	<0.01
Bermudan (0)	0	<0.01
British West Indian (0)	0	<0.01
Dutch West Indian (0)	38	0.05
Haitian (0)	0	<0.01
Jamaican (0)	18	0.03
Trinidadian/Tobagonian (0)	0	<0.01
U.S. Virgin Islander (0)	0	<0.01
West Indian (0)	0	<0.01
Other West Indian (0)	0	<0.01
Yugoslavian (26)	86	0.12

Hispanic Origin	Population	%
Hispanic or Latino (of any race)	18,051	25.02
Central American, ex. Mexican	352	0.49
Costa Rican	8	0.01
Guatemalan	37	0.05
Honduran	34	0.05
Nicaraguan	61	0.08
Panamanian	44	0.06
Salvadoran	167	0.23
Other Central American	1	<0.01
Cuban	38	0.05
Dominican Republic	15	0.02
Mexican	15,776	21.86
Puerto Rican	351	0.49
South American	143	0.20
Argentinean	20	0.03
Bolivian	5	0.01
Chilean	6	0.01
Colombian	47	0.07
Ecuadorian	10	0.01
Paraguayan	2	<0.01
Peruvian	45	0.06
Uruguayan	0	<0.01
Venezuelan	7	0.01
Other South American	1	<0.01
Other Hispanic or Latino	1,376	1.91

Race*	Population	%
African-American/Black (2,361)	3,516	4.87
Not Hispanic (2,122)	3,009	4.17
Hispanic (239)	507	0.70
American Indian/Alaska Native (1,675)	3,870	5.36
Not Hispanic (1,260)	2,945	4.08
Hispanic (415)	925	1.28
Alaska Athabascan *(Ala. Nat.)* (1)	4	0.01
Aleut *(Alaska Native)* (2)	6	0.01
Apache (31)	105	0.15
Arapaho (3)	6	0.01
Blackfeet (18)	121	0.17
Canadian/French Am. Ind. (0)	8	0.01
Central American Ind. (0)	0	<0.01
Cherokee (349)	1,085	1.50
Cheyenne (1)	8	0.01
Chickasaw (18)	37	0.05
Chippewa (28)	76	0.11
Choctaw (74)	186	0.26
Colville (3)	4	0.01
Comanche (3)	13	0.02
Cree (3)	8	0.01
Creek (28)	70	0.10
Crow (1)	6	0.01
Delaware (6)	8	0.01
Hopi (1)	2	<0.01
Houma (0)	0	<0.01
Inupiat *(Alaska Native)* (2)	8	0.01
Iroquois (7)	23	0.03
Kiowa (0)	0	<0.01
Lumbee (2)	2	<0.01
Menominee (3)	3	<0.01
Mexican American Ind. (69)	119	0.16
Navajo (15)	48	0.07
Osage (3)	5	0.01
Ottawa (0)	0	<0.01
Paiute (5)	17	0.02
Pima (0)	3	<0.01
Potawatomi (21)	31	0.04
Pueblo (5)	14	0.02
Puget Sound Salish (0)	0	<0.01
Seminole (4)	7	0.01
Shoshone (6)	21	0.03
Sioux (27)	67	0.09
South American Ind. (1)	6	0.01
Spanish American Ind. (7)	7	0.01
Tlingit-Haida *(Alaska Native)* (0)	1	<0.01
Tohono O'Odham (0)	0	<0.01
Tsimshian *(Alaska Native)* (0)	0	<0.01
Ute (0)	2	<0.01
Yakama (0)	2	<0.01
Yaqui (19)	33	0.05
Yuman (1)	1	<0.01
Yup'ik *(Alaska Native)* (1)	1	<0.01
Asian (4,862)	6,126	8.49
Not Hispanic (4,710)	5,686	7.88
Hispanic (152)	440	0.61
Bangladeshi (11)	11	0.02
Bhutanese (0)	0	<0.01
Burmese (1)	2	<0.01
Cambodian (134)	168	0.23
Chinese, ex. Taiwanese (265)	438	0.61
Filipino (694)	1,203	1.67
Hmong (2,426)	2,513	3.48
Indian (461)	595	0.82
Indonesian (4)	7	0.01
Japanese (187)	449	0.62
Korean (108)	247	0.34
Laotian (153)	192	0.27
Malaysian (0)	0	<0.01
Nepalese (0)	0	<0.01
Pakistani (69)	90	0.12
Sri Lankan (3)	3	<0.01
Taiwanese (2)	9	0.01
Thai (54)	131	0.18
Vietnamese (86)	129	0.18
Hawaii Native/Pacific Islander (293)	587	0.81
Not Hispanic (270)	490	0.68
Hispanic (23)	97	0.13
Fijian (21)	26	0.04
Guamanian/Chamorro (112)	184	0.26
Marshallese (0)	1	<0.01
Native Hawaiian (50)	194	0.27
Samoan (53)	91	0.13
Tongan (10)	33	0.05
White (49,332)	53,808	74.57
Not Hispanic (42,416)	45,336	62.83
Hispanic (6,916)	8,472	11.74

*Notes: † The Census 2010 population figure is used to calculate the percentages in the Hispanic Origin and Race categories. Ancestry percentages are based on the 2006-2010 American Community Survey population (not shown); ‡ Numbers in parentheses indicate the number of people reporting a single ancestry; * Numbers in parentheses indicate the number of persons reporting this race alone, not in combination with any other race; Please refer to the Explanation of Data for more information.*

Place Profiles

Alameda

Place Type: City
County: Alameda
Population: 73,812

Ancestry	Population	%
Afghan (290)	337	0.46
African, Sub-Saharan (573)	586	0.81
African (69)	82	0.11
Cape Verdean (0)	0	<0.01
Ethiopian (326)	326	0.45
Ghanaian (0)	0	<0.01
Kenyan (0)	0	<0.01
Liberian (8)	8	0.01
Nigerian (71)	71	0.10
Senegalese (0)	0	<0.01
Sierra Leonean (0)	0	<0.01
Somalian (0)	0	<0.01
South African (0)	0	<0.01
Sudanese (0)	0	<0.01
Ugandan (0)	0	<0.01
Zimbabwean (0)	0	<0.01
Other Sub-Saharan African (99)	99	0.14
Albanian (0)	25	0.03
Alsatian (0)	12	0.02
American (837)	837	1.15
Arab (268)	478	0.66
Arab (0)	0	<0.01
Egyptian (0)	0	<0.01
Iraqi (0)	0	<0.01
Jordanian (0)	0	<0.01
Lebanese (0)	100	0.14
Moroccan (69)	119	0.16
Palestinian (136)	136	0.19
Syrian (0)	32	0.04
Other Arab (63)	91	0.13
Armenian (93)	127	0.18
Assyrian/Chaldean/Syriac (0)	9	0.01
Australian (0)	45	0.06
Austrian (44)	221	0.30
Basque (89)	119	0.16
Belgian (8)	27	0.04
Brazilian (33)	52	0.07
British (371)	578	0.80
Bulgarian (25)	43	0.06
Cajun (0)	0	<0.01
Canadian (39)	126	0.17
Carpatho Rusyn (0)	0	<0.01
Celtic (11)	50	0.07
Croatian (62)	104	0.14
Cypriot (51)	51	0.07
Czech (20)	139	0.19
Czechoslovakian (0)	7	0.01
Danish (117)	599	0.83
Dutch (306)	1,050	1.45
Eastern European (240)	341	0.47
English (1,325)	6,400	8.83
Estonian (27)	27	0.04
European (1,216)	1,553	2.14
Finnish (9)	222	0.31
French, ex. Basque (220)	1,806	2.49
French Canadian (83)	347	0.48
German (1,719)	7,596	10.48
German Russian (0)	0	<0.01
Greek (40)	262	0.36
Guyanese (0)	0	<0.01
Hungarian (105)	298	0.41
Icelander (0)	0	<0.01
Iranian (0)	13	0.02
Irish (1,927)	7,529	10.38
Israeli (0)	0	<0.01
Italian (1,237)	3,647	5.03
Latvian (0)	0	<0.01
Lithuanian (14)	128	0.18
Luxemburger (0)	0	<0.01
Macedonian (0)	0	<0.01
Maltese (0)	0	<0.01
New Zealander (25)	62	0.09
Northern European (249)	269	0.37
Norwegian (378)	1,270	1.75
Pennsylvania German (0)	17	0.02
Polish (348)	1,627	2.24
Portuguese (396)	1,093	1.51
Romanian (54)	93	0.13
Russian (444)	1,295	1.79
Scandinavian (45)	210	0.29
Scotch-Irish (442)	1,426	1.97
Scottish (296)	1,309	1.81
Serbian (6)	35	0.05
Slavic (11)	25	0.03
Slovak (0)	23	0.03
Slovene (47)	47	0.06
Soviet Union (0)	0	<0.01
Swedish (214)	1,104	1.52
Swiss (38)	317	0.44
Turkish (15)	57	0.08
Ukrainian (106)	215	0.30
Welsh (146)	596	0.82
West Indian, ex. Hispanic (160)	190	0.26
Bahamian (0)	0	<0.01
Barbadian (0)	0	<0.01
Belizean (0)	0	<0.01
Bermudan (0)	0	<0.01
British West Indian (0)	0	<0.01
Dutch West Indian (0)	0	<0.01
Haitian (65)	65	0.09
Jamaican (48)	78	0.11
Trinidadian/Tobagonian (0)	0	<0.01
U.S. Virgin Islander (0)	0	<0.01
West Indian (47)	47	0.06
Other West Indian (0)	0	<0.01
Yugoslavian (144)	226	0.31

Hispanic Origin	Population	%
Hispanic or Latino (of any race)	8,092	10.96
Central American, ex. Mexican	841	1.14
Costa Rican	18	0.02
Guatemalan	178	0.24
Honduran	41	0.06
Nicaraguan	213	0.29
Panamanian	33	0.04
Salvadoran	352	0.48
Other Central American	6	0.01
Cuban	158	0.21
Dominican Republic	36	0.05
Mexican	4,765	6.46
Puerto Rican	487	0.66
South American	701	0.95
Argentinean	50	0.07
Bolivian	16	0.02
Chilean	74	0.10
Colombian	172	0.23
Ecuadorian	41	0.06
Paraguayan	2	<0.01
Peruvian	285	0.39
Uruguayan	8	0.01
Venezuelan	40	0.05
Other South American	13	0.02
Other Hispanic or Latino	1,104	1.50

Race*	Population	%
African-American/Black (4,759)	6,149	8.33
Not Hispanic (4,516)	5,645	7.65
Hispanic (243)	504	0.68
American Indian/Alaska Native (426)	1,397	1.89
Not Hispanic (247)	916	1.24
Hispanic (179)	481	0.65
Alaska Athabascan *(Ala. Nat.)* (1)	1	<0.01
Aleut *(Alaska Native)* (4)	4	0.01
Apache (15)	56	0.08
Arapaho (1)	1	<0.01
Blackfeet (5)	61	0.08
Canadian/French Am. Ind. (3)	5	0.01
Central American Ind. (4)	9	0.01
Cherokee (15)	206	0.28
Cheyenne (1)	8	0.01
Chickasaw (3)	9	0.01
Chippewa (7)	20	0.03
Choctaw (8)	60	0.08
Colville (0)	1	<0.01
Comanche (4)	8	0.01
Cree (0)	2	<0.01
Creek (4)	20	0.03
Crow (0)	1	<0.01
Delaware (2)	10	0.01
Hopi (1)	6	0.01
Houma (0)	0	<0.01
Inupiat *(Alaska Native)* (1)	2	<0.01
Iroquois (3)	22	0.03
Kiowa (1)	1	<0.01
Lumbee (0)	0	<0.01
Menominee (0)	0	<0.01
Mexican American Ind. (29)	65	0.09
Navajo (27)	60	0.08
Osage (0)	5	0.01
Ottawa (0)	0	<0.01
Paiute (7)	10	0.01
Pima (2)	4	0.01
Potawatomi (0)	0	<0.01
Pueblo (4)	9	0.01
Puget Sound Salish (0)	0	<0.01
Seminole (1)	10	0.01
Shoshone (0)	1	<0.01
Sioux (27)	53	0.07
South American Ind. (3)	12	0.02
Spanish American Ind. (3)	8	0.01
Tlingit-Haida *(Alaska Native)* (3)	11	0.01
Tohono O'Odham (1)	1	<0.01
Tsimshian *(Alaska Native)* (0)	0	<0.01
Ute (0)	2	<0.01
Yakama (0)	0	<0.01
Yaqui (4)	10	0.01
Yuman (1)	2	<0.01
Yup'ik *(Alaska Native)* (1)	2	<0.01
Asian (23,058)	26,240	35.55
Not Hispanic (22,822)	25,552	34.62
Hispanic (236)	688	0.93
Bangladeshi (9)	9	0.01
Bhutanese (59)	71	0.10
Burmese (21)	28	0.04
Cambodian (127)	175	0.24
Chinese, ex. Taiwanese (10,485)	11,760	15.93
Filipino (5,419)	6,809	9.22
Hmong (7)	7	0.01
Indian (793)	954	1.29
Indonesian (40)	84	0.11
Japanese (836)	1,496	2.03
Korean (1,496)	1,751	2.37
Laotian (71)	96	0.13
Malaysian (11)	28	0.04
Nepalese (79)	99	0.13
Pakistani (59)	73	0.10
Sri Lankan (16)	24	0.03
Taiwanese (136)	179	0.24
Thai (92)	141	0.19
Vietnamese (2,041)	2,379	3.22
Hawaii Native/Pacific Islander (381)	834	1.13
Not Hispanic (342)	708	0.96
Hispanic (39)	126	0.17
Fijian (20)	27	0.04
Guamanian/Chamorro (129)	223	0.30
Marshallese (0)	0	<0.01
Native Hawaiian (77)	307	0.42
Samoan (86)	150	0.20
Tongan (24)	36	0.05
White (37,460)	41,810	56.64
Not Hispanic (33,468)	36,910	50.01
Hispanic (3,992)	4,900	6.64

*Notes: † The Census 2010 population figure is used to calculate the percentages in the Hispanic Origin and Race categories. Ancestry percentages are based on the 2006-2010 American Community Survey population (not shown); ‡ Numbers in parentheses indicate the number of people reporting a single ancestry; * Numbers in parentheses indicate the number of persons reporting this race alone, not in combination with any other race; Please refer to the Explanation of Data for more information.*

Alhambra

Place Type: City
County: Los Angeles
Population: 83,089

Ancestry	Population	%
Afghan (8)	8	0.01
African, Sub-Saharan (62)	72	0.09
African (24)	34	0.04
Cape Verdean (0)	0	<0.01
Ethiopian (0)	0	<0.01
Ghanaian (0)	0	<0.01
Kenyan (0)	0	<0.01
Liberian (0)	0	<0.01
Nigerian (0)	0	<0.01
Senegalese (0)	0	<0.01
Sierra Leonean (0)	0	<0.01
Somalian (0)	0	<0.01
South African (15)	15	0.02
Sudanese (0)	0	<0.01
Ugandan (0)	0	<0.01
Zimbabwean (0)	0	<0.01
Other Sub-Saharan African (23)	23	0.03
Albanian (73)	73	0.09
Alsatian (0)	0	<0.01
American (366)	366	0.44
Arab (111)	158	0.19
Arab (0)	0	<0.01
Egyptian (46)	93	0.11
Iraqi (0)	0	<0.01
Jordanian (0)	0	<0.01
Lebanese (65)	65	0.08
Moroccan (0)	0	<0.01
Palestinian (0)	0	<0.01
Syrian (0)	0	<0.01
Other Arab (0)	0	<0.01
Armenian (23)	142	0.17
Assyrian/Chaldean/Syriac (12)	12	0.01
Australian (0)	8	0.01
Austrian (20)	46	0.06
Basque (14)	35	0.04
Belgian (21)	59	0.07
Brazilian (53)	53	0.06
British (34)	62	0.07
Bulgarian (0)	0	<0.01
Cajun (0)	0	<0.01
Canadian (64)	102	0.12
Carpatho Rusyn (0)	0	<0.01
Celtic (9)	9	0.01
Croatian (42)	64	0.08
Cypriot (0)	0	<0.01
Czech (0)	7	0.01
Czechoslovakian (0)	0	<0.01
Danish (59)	112	0.13
Dutch (22)	178	0.21
Eastern European (8)	8	0.01
English (315)	1,360	1.63
Estonian (10)	10	0.01
European (244)	308	0.37
Finnish (0)	7	0.01
French, ex. Basque (37)	534	0.64
French Canadian (0)	71	0.09
German (384)	1,376	1.65
German Russian (0)	0	<0.01
Greek (63)	203	0.24
Guyanese (0)	0	<0.01
Hungarian (50)	134	0.16
Icelander (6)	6	0.01
Iranian (213)	384	0.46
Irish (293)	1,140	1.37
Israeli (0)	0	<0.01
Italian (936)	1,521	1.82
Latvian (18)	72	0.09
Lithuanian (50)	57	0.07
Luxemburger (0)	0	<0.01
Macedonian (0)	0	<0.01
Maltese (0)	0	<0.01
New Zealander (0)	0	<0.01
Northern European (0)	0	<0.01
Norwegian (108)	200	0.24
Pennsylvania German (0)	0	<0.01
Polish (148)	364	0.44
Portuguese (61)	212	0.25
Romanian (81)	108	0.13
Russian (93)	206	0.25
Scandinavian (16)	16	0.02
Scotch-Irish (77)	329	0.39
Scottish (94)	233	0.28
Serbian (0)	0	<0.01
Slavic (36)	36	0.04
Slovak (26)	26	0.03
Slovene (0)	0	<0.01
Soviet Union (0)	0	<0.01
Swedish (17)	218	0.26
Swiss (0)	47	0.06
Turkish (0)	0	<0.01
Ukrainian (59)	142	0.17
Welsh (14)	14	0.02
West Indian, ex. Hispanic (16)	16	0.02
Bahamian (0)	0	<0.01
Barbadian (0)	0	<0.01
Belizean (16)	16	0.02
Bermudan (0)	0	<0.01
British West Indian (0)	0	<0.01
Dutch West Indian (0)	0	<0.01
Haitian (0)	0	<0.01
Jamaican (0)	0	<0.01
Trinidadian/Tobagonian (0)	0	<0.01
U.S. Virgin Islander (0)	0	<0.01
West Indian (0)	0	<0.01
Other West Indian (0)	0	<0.01
Yugoslavian (46)	63	0.08

Hispanic Origin	Population	%
Hispanic or Latino (of any race)	28,582	34.40
Central American, ex. Mexican	2,842	3.42
Costa Rican	110	0.13
Guatemalan	713	0.86
Honduran	128	0.15
Nicaraguan	509	0.61
Panamanian	45	0.05
Salvadoran	1,286	1.55
Other Central American	51	0.06
Cuban	417	0.50
Dominican Republic	21	0.03
Mexican	22,159	26.67
Puerto Rican	346	0.42
South American	961	1.16
Argentinean	112	0.13
Bolivian	19	0.02
Chilean	47	0.06
Colombian	225	0.27
Ecuadorian	249	0.30
Paraguayan	7	0.01
Peruvian	248	0.30
Uruguayan	2	<0.01
Venezuelan	40	0.05
Other South American	12	0.01
Other Hispanic or Latino	1,836	2.21

Race*	Population	%
African-American/Black (1,281)	1,703	2.05
Not Hispanic (1,078)	1,308	1.57
Hispanic (203)	395	0.48
American Indian/Alaska Native (538)	1,037	1.25
Not Hispanic (116)	301	0.36
Hispanic (422)	736	0.89
Alaska Athabascan (*Ala. Nat.*) (2)	2	<0.01
Aleut (*Alaska Native*) (0)	1	<0.01
Apache (34)	66	0.08
Arapaho (1)	1	<0.01
Blackfeet (2)	22	0.03
Canadian/French Am. Ind. (0)	0	<0.01
Central American Ind. (5)	11	0.01
Cherokee (12)	55	0.07
Cheyenne (1)	2	<0.01
Chickasaw (0)	3	<0.01
Chippewa (1)	1	<0.01
Choctaw (9)	20	0.02
Colville (0)	1	<0.01
Comanche (3)	5	0.01
Cree (0)	0	<0.01
Creek (1)	2	<0.01
Crow (0)	3	<0.01
Delaware (2)	2	<0.01
Hopi (4)	17	0.02
Houma (0)	0	<0.01
Inupiat (*Alaska Native*) (0)	1	<0.01
Iroquois (0)	4	<0.01
Kiowa (0)	0	<0.01
Lumbee (9)	9	0.01
Menominee (0)	1	<0.01
Mexican American Ind. (82)	133	0.16
Navajo (9)	26	0.03
Osage (0)	0	<0.01
Ottawa (0)	0	<0.01
Paiute (0)	0	<0.01
Pima (1)	1	<0.01
Potawatomi (2)	2	<0.01
Pueblo (7)	24	0.03
Puget Sound Salish (0)	0	<0.01
Seminole (2)	12	0.01
Shoshone (1)	1	<0.01
Sioux (8)	13	0.02
South American Ind. (4)	7	0.01
Spanish American Ind. (22)	28	0.03
Tlingit-Haida (*Alaska Native*) (0)	0	<0.01
Tohono O'Odham (4)	4	<0.01
Tsimshian (*Alaska Native*) (0)	1	<0.01
Ute (0)	0	<0.01
Yakama (0)	0	<0.01
Yaqui (19)	36	0.04
Yuman (0)	1	<0.01
Yup'ik (*Alaska Native*) (0)	0	<0.01
Asian (43,957)	45,395	54.63
Not Hispanic (43,614)	44,579	53.65
Hispanic (343)	816	0.98
Bangladeshi (13)	17	0.02
Bhutanese (0)	0	<0.01
Burmese (433)	528	0.64
Cambodian (342)	497	0.60
Chinese, ex. Taiwanese (29,201)	31,493	37.90
Filipino (2,109)	2,592	3.12
Hmong (9)	9	0.01
Indian (451)	557	0.67
Indonesian (508)	647	0.78
Japanese (1,224)	1,642	1.98
Korean (844)	969	1.17
Laotian (51)	85	0.10
Malaysian (35)	57	0.07
Nepalese (49)	51	0.06
Pakistani (50)	56	0.07
Sri Lankan (35)	43	0.05
Taiwanese (1,659)	1,866	2.25
Thai (494)	561	0.68
Vietnamese (4,212)	5,348	6.44
Hawaii Native/Pacific Islander (81)	308	0.37
Not Hispanic (54)	213	0.26
Hispanic (27)	95	0.11
Fijian (0)	0	<0.01
Guamanian/Chamorro (17)	40	0.05
Marshallese (1)	2	<0.01
Native Hawaiian (31)	94	0.11
Samoan (23)	39	0.05
Tongan (1)	2	<0.01
White (23,521)	25,700	30.93
Not Hispanic (8,346)	9,217	11.09
Hispanic (15,175)	16,483	19.84

*Notes: † The Census 2010 population figure is used to calculate the percentages in the Hispanic Origin and Race categories. Ancestry percentages are based on the 2006-2010 American Community Survey population (not shown); ‡ Numbers in parentheses indicate the number of people reporting a single ancestry; * Numbers in parentheses indicate the number of persons reporting this race alone, not in combination with any other race; Please refer to the Explanation of Data for more information.*

Anaheim

Place Type: City
County: Orange
Population: 336,265

Ancestry	Population	%
Afghan (200)	308	0.09
African, Sub-Saharan (1,449)	1,577	0.47
African (387)	474	0.14
Cape Verdean (0)	0	<0.01
Ethiopian (642)	642	0.19
Ghanaian (0)	0	<0.01
Kenyan (60)	60	0.02
Liberian (0)	0	<0.01
Nigerian (104)	104	0.03
Senegalese (0)	0	<0.01
Sierra Leonean (0)	0	<0.01
Somalian (72)	72	0.02
South African (0)	27	0.01
Sudanese (0)	0	<0.01
Ugandan (0)	0	<0.01
Zimbabwean (9)	9	<0.01
Other Sub-Saharan African (175)	189	0.06
Albanian (182)	207	0.06
Alsatian (0)	0	<0.01
American (5,167)	5,167	1.55
Arab (3,389)	4,077	1.22
Arab (404)	607	0.18
Egyptian (1,042)	1,072	0.32
Iraqi (89)	89	0.03
Jordanian (548)	575	0.17
Lebanese (590)	816	0.25
Moroccan (31)	31	0.01
Palestinian (199)	226	0.07
Syrian (344)	399	0.12
Other Arab (142)	262	0.08
Armenian (568)	802	0.24
Assyrian/Chaldean/Syriac (34)	85	0.03
Australian (9)	49	0.01
Austrian (133)	609	0.18
Basque (34)	71	0.02
Belgian (139)	254	0.08
Brazilian (271)	387	0.12
British (398)	629	0.19
Bulgarian (111)	147	0.04
Cajun (0)	0	<0.01
Canadian (412)	756	0.23
Carpatho Rusyn (0)	0	<0.01
Celtic (18)	81	0.02
Croatian (134)	232	0.07
Cypriot (0)	0	<0.01
Czech (215)	680	0.20
Czechoslovakian (112)	234	0.07
Danish (188)	945	0.28
Dutch (858)	2,724	0.82
Eastern European (106)	146	0.04
English (4,688)	15,386	4.62
Estonian (0)	9	<0.01
European (1,666)	2,073	0.62
Finnish (88)	256	0.08
French, ex. Basque (1,036)	5,575	1.67
French Canadian (331)	662	0.20
German (7,063)	23,531	7.07
German Russian (0)	0	<0.01
Greek (607)	908	0.27
Guyanese (44)	44	0.01
Hungarian (348)	834	0.25
Icelander (0)	9	<0.01
Iranian (1,814)	2,070	0.62
Irish (4,205)	17,503	5.26
Israeli (43)	104	0.03
Italian (4,368)	9,767	2.93
Latvian (35)	68	0.02
Lithuanian (108)	278	0.08
Luxemburger (44)	44	0.01
Macedonian (67)	87	0.03
Maltese (0)	0	<0.01
New Zealander (0)	13	<0.01
Northern European (75)	126	0.04
Norwegian (1,047)	2,965	0.89
Pennsylvania German (36)	64	0.02
Polish (941)	3,304	0.99
Portuguese (516)	1,035	0.31
Romanian (1,567)	1,744	0.52
Russian (642)	1,973	0.59
Scandinavian (124)	281	0.08
Scotch-Irish (844)	2,321	0.70
Scottish (744)	2,711	0.81
Serbian (42)	158	0.05
Slavic (36)	68	0.02
Slovak (87)	176	0.05
Slovene (25)	43	0.01
Soviet Union (0)	0	<0.01
Swedish (711)	2,803	0.84
Swiss (71)	491	0.15
Turkish (31)	59	0.02
Ukrainian (88)	218	0.07
Welsh (223)	930	0.28
West Indian, ex. Hispanic (284)	345	0.10
Bahamian (0)	0	<0.01
Barbadian (0)	0	<0.01
Belizean (24)	24	0.01
Bermudan (0)	0	<0.01
British West Indian (6)	6	<0.01
Dutch West Indian (0)	0	<0.01
Haitian (15)	15	<0.01
Jamaican (215)	225	0.07
Trinidadian/Tobagonian (13)	13	<0.01
U.S. Virgin Islander (0)	0	<0.01
West Indian (11)	62	0.02
Other West Indian (0)	0	<0.01
Yugoslavian (216)	258	0.08

Hispanic Origin	Population	%
Hispanic or Latino (of any race)	177,467	52.78
Central American, ex. Mexican	9,074	2.70
Costa Rican	296	0.09
Guatemalan	3,474	1.03
Honduran	636	0.19
Nicaraguan	543	0.16
Panamanian	100	0.03
Salvadoran	3,957	1.18
Other Central American	68	0.02
Cuban	945	0.28
Dominican Republic	114	0.03
Mexican	154,554	45.96
Puerto Rican	1,439	0.43
South American	3,763	1.12
Argentinean	519	0.15
Bolivian	211	0.06
Chilean	181	0.05
Colombian	884	0.26
Ecuadorian	417	0.12
Paraguayan	9	<0.01
Peruvian	1,365	0.41
Uruguayan	66	0.02
Venezuelan	80	0.02
Other South American	31	0.01
Other Hispanic or Latino	7,578	2.25

Race*	Population	%
African-American/Black (9,347)	11,478	3.41
Not Hispanic (8,209)	9,560	2.84
Hispanic (1,138)	1,918	0.57
American Indian/Alaska Native (2,648)	4,684	1.39
Not Hispanic (743)	1,773	0.53
Hispanic (1,905)	2,911	0.87
Alaska Athabascan *(Ala. Nat.)* (0)	3	<0.01
Aleut *(Alaska Native)* (6)	9	<0.01
Apache (113)	228	0.07
Arapaho (0)	3	<0.01
Blackfeet (9)	68	0.02
Canadian/French Am. Ind. (7)	14	<0.01
Central American Ind. (7)	14	<0.01
Cherokee (92)	408	0.12
Cheyenne (5)	9	<0.01
Chickasaw (8)	25	0.01
Chippewa (16)	25	0.01
Choctaw (24)	72	0.02
Colville (4)	5	<0.01
Comanche (4)	16	<0.01
Cree (0)	5	<0.01
Creek (12)	37	0.01
Crow (2)	6	<0.01
Delaware (2)	6	<0.01
Hopi (13)	25	0.01
Houma (0)	0	<0.01
Inupiat *(Alaska Native)* (0)	1	<0.01
Iroquois (4)	32	0.01
Kiowa (5)	8	<0.01
Lumbee (4)	7	<0.01
Menominee (10)	10	<0.01
Mexican American Ind. (450)	592	0.18
Navajo (71)	149	0.04
Osage (3)	10	<0.01
Ottawa (2)	8	<0.01
Paiute (5)	17	0.01
Pima (12)	18	0.01
Potawatomi (6)	23	0.01
Pueblo (21)	34	0.01
Puget Sound Salish (3)	3	<0.01
Seminole (3)	21	0.01
Shoshone (20)	30	0.01
Sioux (17)	51	0.02
South American Ind. (11)	27	0.01
Spanish American Ind. (34)	46	0.01
Tlingit-Haida *(Alaska Native)* (6)	9	<0.01
Tohono O'Odham (10)	23	0.01
Tsimshian *(Alaska Native)* (2)	3	<0.01
Ute (1)	2	<0.01
Yakama (3)	6	<0.01
Yaqui (50)	84	0.02
Yuman (22)	26	0.01
Yup'ik *(Alaska Native)* (0)	0	<0.01
Asian (49,857)	55,024	16.36
Not Hispanic (49,210)	53,269	15.84
Hispanic (647)	1,755	0.52
Bangladeshi (227)	240	0.07
Bhutanese (0)	0	<0.01
Burmese (85)	97	0.03
Cambodian (680)	831	0.25
Chinese, ex. Taiwanese (4,042)	5,374	1.60
Filipino (11,956)	13,813	4.11
Hmong (118)	132	0.04
Indian (4,456)	4,915	1.46
Indonesian (306)	462	0.14
Japanese (2,082)	3,145	0.94
Korean (6,575)	6,999	2.08
Laotian (648)	749	0.22
Malaysian (22)	53	0.02
Nepalese (79)	80	0.02
Pakistani (705)	782	0.23
Sri Lankan (214)	237	0.07
Taiwanese (657)	740	0.22
Thai (480)	632	0.19
Vietnamese (14,706)	15,674	4.66
Hawaii Native/Pacific Islander (1,607)	2,778	0.83
Not Hispanic (1,437)	2,238	0.67
Hispanic (170)	540	0.16
Fijian (35)	65	0.02
Guamanian/Chamorro (184)	328	0.10
Marshallese (0)	0	<0.01
Native Hawaiian (227)	653	0.19
Samoan (766)	1,023	0.30
Tongan (209)	259	0.08
White (177,237)	189,689	56.41
Not Hispanic (92,362)	97,490	28.99
Hispanic (84,875)	92,199	27.42

*Notes: † The Census 2010 population figure is used to calculate the percentages in the Hispanic Origin and Race categories. Ancestry percentages are based on the 2006-2010 American Community Survey population (not shown); ‡ Numbers in parentheses indicate the number of people reporting a single ancestry; * Numbers in parentheses indicate the number of persons reporting this race alone, not in combination with any other race; Please refer to the Explanation of Data for more information.*

Antioch

Place Type: City
County: Contra Costa
Population: 102,372

Ancestry	Population	%
Afghan (706)	725	0.73
African, Sub-Saharan (1,577)	2,459	2.47
African (836)	1,700	1.70
Cape Verdean (0)	0	<0.01
Ethiopian (217)	217	0.22
Ghanaian (20)	20	0.02
Kenyan (0)	0	<0.01
Liberian (0)	0	<0.01
Nigerian (504)	522	0.52
Senegalese (0)	0	<0.01
Sierra Leonean (0)	0	<0.01
Somalian (0)	0	<0.01
South African (0)	0	<0.01
Sudanese (0)	0	<0.01
Ugandan (0)	0	<0.01
Zimbabwean (0)	0	<0.01
Other Sub-Saharan African (0)	0	<0.01
Albanian (0)	0	<0.01
Alsatian (0)	0	<0.01
American (1,716)	1,716	1.72
Arab (514)	695	0.70
Arab (61)	87	0.09
Egyptian (206)	206	0.21
Iraqi (0)	0	<0.01
Jordanian (0)	0	<0.01
Lebanese (18)	143	0.14
Moroccan (0)	0	<0.01
Palestinian (212)	229	0.23
Syrian (17)	30	0.03
Other Arab (0)	0	<0.01
Armenian (110)	110	0.11
Assyrian/Chaldean/Syriac (0)	0	<0.01
Australian (14)	14	0.01
Austrian (0)	70	0.07
Basque (0)	122	0.12
Belgian (23)	52	0.05
Brazilian (196)	239	0.24
British (95)	446	0.45
Bulgarian (0)	0	<0.01
Cajun (40)	40	0.04
Canadian (39)	79	0.08
Carpatho Rusyn (0)	0	<0.01
Celtic (0)	0	<0.01
Croatian (12)	90	0.09
Cypriot (0)	0	<0.01
Czech (44)	199	0.20
Czechoslovakian (0)	110	0.11
Danish (143)	664	0.67
Dutch (246)	2,152	2.16
Eastern European (10)	18	0.02
English (1,520)	5,508	5.52
Estonian (0)	0	<0.01
European (706)	938	0.94
Finnish (19)	236	0.24
French, ex. Basque (335)	1,789	1.79
French Canadian (30)	318	0.32
German (2,025)	10,160	10.19
German Russian (0)	0	<0.01
Greek (76)	282	0.28
Guyanese (40)	40	0.04
Hungarian (49)	145	0.15
Icelander (14)	14	0.01
Iranian (90)	90	0.09
Irish (1,479)	8,778	8.80
Israeli (13)	13	0.01
Italian (1,870)	4,791	4.80
Latvian (0)	0	<0.01
Lithuanian (4)	43	0.04
Luxemburger (0)	0	<0.01
Macedonian (0)	0	<0.01
Maltese (30)	40	0.04
New Zealander (38)	38	0.04
Northern European (17)	36	0.04
Norwegian (216)	730	0.73
Pennsylvania German (9)	9	0.01
Polish (212)	954	0.96
Portuguese (709)	1,994	2.00
Romanian (23)	64	0.06
Russian (137)	426	0.43
Scandinavian (31)	174	0.17
Scotch-Irish (363)	1,142	1.15
Scottish (301)	1,711	1.72
Serbian (0)	23	0.02
Slavic (0)	13	0.01
Slovak (0)	21	0.02
Slovene (0)	8	0.01
Soviet Union (0)	0	<0.01
Swedish (103)	1,179	1.18
Swiss (21)	102	0.10
Turkish (0)	0	<0.01
Ukrainian (52)	78	0.08
Welsh (20)	587	0.59
West Indian, ex. Hispanic (97)	358	0.36
Bahamian (0)	33	0.03
Barbadian (10)	93	0.09
Belizean (9)	9	0.01
Bermudan (0)	0	<0.01
British West Indian (0)	0	<0.01
Dutch West Indian (0)	10	0.01
Haitian (0)	0	<0.01
Jamaican (20)	79	0.08
Trinidadian/Tobagonian (37)	37	0.04
U.S. Virgin Islander (0)	0	<0.01
West Indian (21)	97	0.10
Other West Indian (0)	0	<0.01
Yugoslavian (0)	96	0.10

Hispanic Origin	Population	%
Hispanic or Latino (of any race)	32,436	31.68
Central American, ex. Mexican	4,289	4.19
Costa Rican	94	0.09
Guatemalan	452	0.44
Honduran	150	0.15
Nicaraguan	1,269	1.24
Panamanian	85	0.08
Salvadoran	2,212	2.16
Other Central American	27	0.03
Cuban	185	0.18
Dominican Republic	61	0.06
Mexican	23,110	22.57
Puerto Rican	1,204	1.18
South American	1,083	1.06
Argentinean	47	0.05
Bolivian	54	0.05
Chilean	46	0.04
Colombian	86	0.08
Ecuadorian	46	0.04
Paraguayan	3	<0.01
Peruvian	748	0.73
Uruguayan	11	0.01
Venezuelan	32	0.03
Other South American	10	0.01
Other Hispanic or Latino	2,504	2.45

Race*	Population	%
African-American/Black (17,667)	20,329	19.86
Not Hispanic (17,045)	19,064	18.62
Hispanic (622)	1,265	1.24
American Indian/Alaska Native (887)	2,514	2.46
Not Hispanic (455)	1,532	1.50
Hispanic (432)	982	0.96
Alaska Athabascan *(Ala. Nat.)* (0)	0	<0.01
Aleut *(Alaska Native)* (1)	2	<0.01
Apache (23)	64	0.06
Arapaho (5)	5	<0.01
Blackfeet (13)	89	0.09
Canadian/French Am. Ind. (0)	6	0.01
Central American Ind. (5)	9	0.01
Cherokee (65)	489	0.48
Cheyenne (4)	9	0.01
Chickasaw (3)	8	0.01
Chippewa (11)	26	0.03
Choctaw (24)	136	0.13
Colville (0)	0	<0.01
Comanche (2)	3	<0.01
Cree (0)	0	<0.01
Creek (8)	31	0.03
Crow (0)	0	<0.01
Delaware (5)	10	0.01
Hopi (11)	19	0.02
Houma (0)	0	<0.01
Inupiat *(Alaska Native)* (0)	8	0.01
Iroquois (6)	11	0.01
Kiowa (0)	3	<0.01
Lumbee (1)	7	0.01
Menominee (0)	0	<0.01
Mexican American Ind. (130)	224	0.22
Navajo (13)	49	0.05
Osage (2)	3	<0.01
Ottawa (0)	7	0.01
Paiute (16)	27	0.03
Pima (5)	7	0.01
Potawatomi (2)	14	0.01
Pueblo (10)	12	0.01
Puget Sound Salish (0)	1	<0.01
Seminole (6)	13	0.01
Shoshone (0)	1	<0.01
Sioux (15)	46	0.04
South American Ind. (8)	12	0.01
Spanish American Ind. (9)	13	0.01
Tlingit-Haida *(Alaska Native)* (1)	5	<0.01
Tohono O'Odham (2)	10	0.01
Tsimshian *(Alaska Native)* (0)	0	<0.01
Ute (4)	9	0.01
Yakama (0)	3	<0.01
Yaqui (20)	37	0.04
Yuman (2)	2	<0.01
Yup'ik *(Alaska Native)* (0)	0	<0.01
Asian (10,709)	13,704	13.39
Not Hispanic (10,322)	12,608	12.32
Hispanic (387)	1,096	1.07
Bangladeshi (43)	43	0.04
Bhutanese (0)	0	<0.01
Burmese (48)	53	0.05
Cambodian (148)	198	0.19
Chinese, ex. Taiwanese (1,356)	1,953	1.91
Filipino (5,850)	7,541	7.37
Hmong (16)	16	0.02
Indian (964)	1,197	1.17
Indonesian (76)	116	0.11
Japanese (212)	604	0.59
Korean (214)	306	0.30
Laotian (153)	204	0.20
Malaysian (9)	13	0.01
Nepalese (10)	10	0.01
Pakistani (223)	272	0.27
Sri Lankan (30)	32	0.03
Taiwanese (35)	42	0.04
Thai (95)	147	0.14
Vietnamese (733)	886	0.87
Hawaii Native/Pacific Islander (817)	1,529	1.49
Not Hispanic (743)	1,271	1.24
Hispanic (74)	258	0.25
Fijian (109)	139	0.14
Guamanian/Chamorro (137)	272	0.27
Marshallese (0)	0	<0.01
Native Hawaiian (81)	352	0.34
Samoan (210)	325	0.32
Tongan (178)	226	0.22
White (50,083)	56,308	55.00
Not Hispanic (36,490)	40,125	39.20
Hispanic (13,593)	16,183	15.81

*Notes: † The Census 2010 population figure is used to calculate the percentages in the Hispanic Origin and Race categories. Ancestry percentages are based on the 2006-2010 American Community Survey population (not shown); ‡ Numbers in parentheses indicate the number of people reporting a single ancestry; * Numbers in parentheses indicate the number of persons reporting this race alone, not in combination with any other race; Please refer to the Explanation of Data for more information.*

Apple Valley

Place Type: Town
County: San Bernardino
Population: 69,135

Ancestry	Population	%
Afghan (0)	0	<0.01
African, Sub-Saharan (627)	656	0.97
African (570)	588	0.87
Cape Verdean (0)	0	<0.01
Ethiopian (33)	33	0.05
Ghanaian (0)	0	<0.01
Kenyan (0)	0	<0.01
Liberian (0)	0	<0.01
Nigerian (24)	24	0.04
Senegalese (0)	0	<0.01
Sierra Leonean (0)	0	<0.01
Somalian (0)	0	<0.01
South African (0)	11	0.02
Sudanese (0)	0	<0.01
Ugandan (0)	0	<0.01
Zimbabwean (0)	0	<0.01
Other Sub-Saharan African (0)	0	<0.01
Albanian (10)	10	0.01
Alsatian (0)	0	<0.01
American (2,597)	2,597	3.85
Arab (305)	332	0.49
Arab (7)	7	0.01
Egyptian (178)	178	0.26
Iraqi (0)	0	<0.01
Jordanian (11)	22	0.03
Lebanese (0)	16	0.02
Moroccan (0)	0	<0.01
Palestinian (0)	0	<0.01
Syrian (0)	0	<0.01
Other Arab (109)	109	0.16
Armenian (72)	148	0.22
Assyrian/Chaldean/Syriac (0)	0	<0.01
Australian (26)	26	0.04
Austrian (57)	88	0.13
Basque (0)	70	0.10
Belgian (0)	70	0.10
Brazilian (14)	24	0.04
British (68)	149	0.22
Bulgarian (0)	0	<0.01
Cajun (0)	0	<0.01
Canadian (62)	212	0.31
Carpatho Rusyn (0)	0	<0.01
Celtic (0)	20	0.03
Croatian (0)	51	0.08
Cypriot (0)	0	<0.01
Czech (24)	156	0.23
Czechoslovakian (18)	25	0.04
Danish (111)	418	0.62
Dutch (286)	1,143	1.70
Eastern European (18)	18	0.03
English (3,110)	8,389	12.45
Estonian (0)	0	<0.01
European (524)	706	1.05
Finnish (82)	116	0.17
French, ex. Basque (387)	2,805	4.16
French Canadian (167)	497	0.74
German (2,383)	9,749	14.47
German Russian (0)	0	<0.01
Greek (0)	64	0.09
Guyanese (16)	16	0.02
Hungarian (17)	168	0.25
Icelander (0)	27	0.04
Iranian (65)	65	0.10
Irish (2,094)	7,835	11.63
Israeli (0)	0	<0.01
Italian (1,470)	4,017	5.96
Latvian (0)	0	<0.01
Lithuanian (8)	38	0.06
Luxemburger (0)	9	0.01
Macedonian (0)	0	<0.01
Maltese (0)	0	<0.01
New Zealander (0)	6	0.01
Northern European (13)	38	0.06
Norwegian (390)	1,319	1.96
Pennsylvania German (54)	68	0.10
Polish (251)	1,530	2.27
Portuguese (63)	239	0.35
Romanian (81)	91	0.14
Russian (161)	399	0.59
Scandinavian (64)	143	0.21
Scotch-Irish (339)	912	1.35
Scottish (178)	1,144	1.70
Serbian (0)	0	<0.01
Slavic (0)	45	0.07
Slovak (8)	29	0.04
Slovene (0)	0	<0.01
Soviet Union (0)	0	<0.01
Swedish (232)	1,023	1.52
Swiss (28)	239	0.35
Turkish (0)	0	<0.01
Ukrainian (0)	58	0.09
Welsh (85)	459	0.68
West Indian, ex. Hispanic (39)	39	0.06
Bahamian (0)	0	<0.01
Barbadian (0)	0	<0.01
Belizean (10)	10	0.01
Bermudan (0)	0	<0.01
British West Indian (12)	12	0.02
Dutch West Indian (0)	0	<0.01
Haitian (0)	0	<0.01
Jamaican (0)	0	<0.01
Trinidadian/Tobagonian (17)	17	0.03
U.S. Virgin Islander (0)	0	<0.01
West Indian (0)	0	<0.01
Other West Indian (0)	0	<0.01
Yugoslavian (74)	74	0.11

Hispanic Origin	Population	%
Hispanic or Latino (of any race)	20,156	29.15
Central American, ex. Mexican	986	1.43
Costa Rican	47	0.07
Guatemalan	329	0.48
Honduran	58	0.08
Nicaraguan	76	0.11
Panamanian	37	0.05
Salvadoran	421	0.61
Other Central American	18	0.03
Cuban	214	0.31
Dominican Republic	19	0.03
Mexican	16,217	23.46
Puerto Rican	518	0.75
South American	288	0.42
Argentinean	54	0.08
Bolivian	3	<0.01
Chilean	16	0.02
Colombian	89	0.13
Ecuadorian	61	0.09
Paraguayan	2	<0.01
Peruvian	52	0.08
Uruguayan	0	<0.01
Venezuelan	7	0.01
Other South American	4	0.01
Other Hispanic or Latino	1,914	2.77

Race*	Population	%
African-American/Black (6,321)	7,434	10.75
Not Hispanic (5,967)	6,802	9.84
Hispanic (354)	632	0.91
American Indian/Alaska Native (779)	1,871	2.71
Not Hispanic (363)	1,060	1.53
Hispanic (416)	811	1.17
Alaska Athabascan *(Ala. Nat.)* (0)	0	<0.01
Aleut *(Alaska Native)* (1)	1	<0.01
Apache (37)	84	0.12
Arapaho (1)	9	0.01
Blackfeet (5)	54	0.08
Canadian/French Am. Ind. (2)	7	0.01
Central American Ind. (1)	3	<0.01
Cherokee (52)	287	0.42
Cheyenne (5)	15	0.02
Chickasaw (1)	19	0.03
Chippewa (10)	23	0.03
Choctaw (32)	67	0.10
Colville (0)	1	<0.01
Comanche (3)	7	0.01
Cree (0)	2	<0.01
Creek (2)	7	0.01
Crow (1)	2	<0.01
Delaware (1)	2	<0.01
Hopi (2)	14	0.02
Houma (0)	0	<0.01
Inupiat *(Alaska Native)* (1)	1	<0.01
Iroquois (10)	22	0.03
Kiowa (0)	0	<0.01
Lumbee (0)	1	<0.01
Menominee (0)	1	<0.01
Mexican American Ind. (59)	119	0.17
Navajo (36)	60	0.09
Osage (3)	8	0.01
Ottawa (0)	0	<0.01
Paiute (5)	16	0.02
Pima (5)	7	0.01
Potawatomi (12)	15	0.02
Pueblo (30)	58	0.08
Puget Sound Salish (0)	2	<0.01
Seminole (5)	10	0.01
Shoshone (5)	15	0.02
Sioux (11)	40	0.06
South American Ind. (1)	2	<0.01
Spanish American Ind. (2)	10	0.01
Tlingit-Haida *(Alaska Native)* (1)	1	<0.01
Tohono O'Odham (5)	8	0.01
Tsimshian *(Alaska Native)* (0)	0	<0.01
Ute (1)	1	<0.01
Yakama (0)	0	<0.01
Yaqui (11)	30	0.04
Yuman (6)	11	0.02
Yup'ik *(Alaska Native)* (0)	0	<0.01
Asian (2,020)	2,782	4.02
Not Hispanic (1,934)	2,497	3.61
Hispanic (86)	285	0.41
Bangladeshi (6)	8	0.01
Bhutanese (0)	0	<0.01
Burmese (0)	0	<0.01
Cambodian (50)	57	0.08
Chinese, ex. Taiwanese (179)	290	0.42
Filipino (741)	1,088	1.57
Hmong (0)	0	<0.01
Indian (272)	323	0.47
Indonesian (11)	32	0.05
Japanese (154)	324	0.47
Korean (327)	385	0.56
Laotian (3)	7	0.01
Malaysian (1)	6	0.01
Nepalese (0)	0	<0.01
Pakistani (25)	29	0.04
Sri Lankan (12)	13	0.02
Taiwanese (16)	21	0.03
Thai (37)	47	0.07
Vietnamese (122)	147	0.21
Hawaii Native/Pacific Islander (294)	508	0.73
Not Hispanic (265)	431	0.62
Hispanic (29)	77	0.11
Fijian (0)	0	<0.01
Guamanian/Chamorro (45)	79	0.11
Marshallese (0)	0	<0.01
Native Hawaiian (78)	157	0.23
Samoan (141)	188	0.27
Tongan (17)	20	0.03
White (47,762)	50,821	73.51
Not Hispanic (38,374)	40,088	57.99
Hispanic (9,388)	10,733	15.52

*Notes: † The Census 2010 population figure is used to calculate the percentages in the Hispanic Origin and Race categories. Ancestry percentages are based on the 2006-2010 American Community Survey population (not shown); ‡ Numbers in parentheses indicate the number of people reporting a single ancestry; * Numbers in parentheses indicate the number of persons reporting this race alone, not in combination with any other race; Please refer to the Explanation of Data for more information.*

Arcadia

Place Type: City
County: Los Angeles
Population: 56,364

Ancestry	Population	%
Afghan (0)	0	<0.01
African, Sub-Saharan (35)	45	0.08
African (13)	23	0.04
Cape Verdean (0)	0	<0.01
Ethiopian (11)	11	0.02
Ghanaian (0)	0	<0.01
Kenyan (0)	0	<0.01
Liberian (0)	0	<0.01
Nigerian (11)	11	0.02
Senegalese (0)	0	<0.01
Sierra Leonean (0)	0	<0.01
Somalian (0)	0	<0.01
South African (0)	0	<0.01
Sudanese (0)	0	<0.01
Ugandan (0)	0	<0.01
Zimbabwean (0)	0	<0.01
Other Sub-Saharan African (0)	0	<0.01
Albanian (0)	0	<0.01
Alsatian (0)	0	<0.01
American (874)	874	1.57
Arab (347)	506	0.91
Arab (7)	24	0.04
Egyptian (196)	275	0.49
Iraqi (0)	0	<0.01
Jordanian (13)	66	0.12
Lebanese (45)	55	0.10
Moroccan (0)	0	<0.01
Palestinian (0)	0	<0.01
Syrian (30)	30	0.05
Other Arab (56)	56	0.10
Armenian (260)	287	0.52
Assyrian/Chaldean/Syriac (0)	0	<0.01
Australian (3)	34	0.06
Austrian (26)	52	0.09
Basque (11)	11	0.02
Belgian (0)	12	0.02
Brazilian (0)	31	0.06
British (91)	136	0.24
Bulgarian (11)	11	0.02
Cajun (0)	0	<0.01
Canadian (109)	210	0.38
Carpatho Rusyn (0)	0	<0.01
Celtic (0)	0	<0.01
Croatian (44)	44	0.08
Cypriot (0)	0	<0.01
Czech (16)	27	0.05
Czechoslovakian (0)	9	0.02
Danish (33)	139	0.25
Dutch (127)	470	0.84
Eastern European (62)	62	0.11
English (862)	2,810	5.04
Estonian (0)	0	<0.01
European (256)	316	0.57
Finnish (10)	10	0.02
French, ex. Basque (42)	792	1.42
French Canadian (53)	63	0.11
German (974)	3,062	5.50
German Russian (0)	0	<0.01
Greek (190)	275	0.49
Guyanese (0)	0	<0.01
Hungarian (62)	81	0.15
Icelander (0)	0	<0.01
Iranian (202)	211	0.38
Irish (488)	2,040	3.66
Israeli (36)	36	0.06
Italian (785)	1,823	3.27
Latvian (10)	24	0.04
Lithuanian (30)	93	0.17
Luxemburger (0)	0	<0.01
Macedonian (0)	0	<0.01
Maltese (0)	0	<0.01
New Zealander (0)	0	<0.01
Northern European (38)	38	0.07
Norwegian (132)	536	0.96
Pennsylvania German (0)	5	0.01
Polish (161)	421	0.76
Portuguese (27)	35	0.06
Romanian (61)	71	0.13
Russian (101)	232	0.42
Scandinavian (0)	31	0.06
Scotch-Irish (110)	413	0.74
Scottish (168)	599	1.08
Serbian (0)	0	<0.01
Slavic (0)	0	<0.01
Slovak (0)	32	0.06
Slovene (0)	0	<0.01
Soviet Union (0)	0	<0.01
Swedish (78)	249	0.45
Swiss (11)	75	0.13
Turkish (0)	0	<0.01
Ukrainian (23)	36	0.06
Welsh (31)	86	0.15
West Indian, ex. Hispanic (21)	21	0.04
Bahamian (0)	0	<0.01
Barbadian (0)	0	<0.01
Belizean (0)	0	<0.01
Bermudan (0)	0	<0.01
British West Indian (0)	0	<0.01
Dutch West Indian (0)	0	<0.01
Haitian (0)	0	<0.01
Jamaican (0)	0	<0.01
Trinidadian/Tobagonian (21)	21	0.04
U.S. Virgin Islander (0)	0	<0.01
West Indian (0)	0	<0.01
Other West Indian (0)	0	<0.01
Yugoslavian (0)	65	0.12

Hispanic Origin	Population	%
Hispanic or Latino (of any race)	6,799	12.06
Central American, ex. Mexican	490	0.87
Costa Rican	16	0.03
Guatemalan	140	0.25
Honduran	26	0.05
Nicaraguan	71	0.13
Panamanian	20	0.04
Salvadoran	211	0.37
Other Central American	6	0.01
Cuban	131	0.23
Dominican Republic	3	0.01
Mexican	4,438	7.87
Puerto Rican	141	0.25
South American	516	0.92
Argentinean	124	0.22
Bolivian	28	0.05
Chilean	31	0.05
Colombian	126	0.22
Ecuadorian	48	0.09
Paraguayan	6	0.01
Peruvian	134	0.24
Uruguayan	2	<0.01
Venezuelan	11	0.02
Other South American	6	0.01
Other Hispanic or Latino	1,080	1.92

Race*	Population	%
African-American/Black (681)	896	1.59
Not Hispanic (628)	778	1.38
Hispanic (53)	118	0.21
American Indian/Alaska Native (186)	426	0.76
Not Hispanic (73)	200	0.35
Hispanic (113)	226	0.40
Alaska Athabascan *(Ala. Nat.)* (0)	0	<0.01
Aleut *(Alaska Native)* (0)	1	<0.01
Apache (5)	9	0.02
Arapaho (0)	1	<0.01
Blackfeet (0)	5	0.01
Canadian/French Am. Ind. (1)	4	0.01
Central American Ind. (0)	0	<0.01
Cherokee (9)	31	0.05
Cheyenne (0)	2	<0.01
Chickasaw (0)	1	<0.01
Chippewa (1)	8	0.01
Choctaw (0)	3	0.01
Colville (0)	0	<0.01
Comanche (0)	0	<0.01
Cree (0)	0	<0.01
Creek (0)	2	<0.01
Crow (0)	0	<0.01
Delaware (0)	0	<0.01
Hopi (1)	1	<0.01
Houma (0)	0	<0.01
Inupiat *(Alaska Native)* (0)	0	<0.01
Iroquois (0)	1	<0.01
Kiowa (0)	0	<0.01
Lumbee (0)	1	<0.01
Menominee (0)	0	<0.01
Mexican American Ind. (47)	49	0.09
Navajo (3)	11	0.02
Osage (0)	2	<0.01
Ottawa (0)	1	<0.01
Paiute (0)	2	<0.01
Pima (0)	0	<0.01
Potawatomi (1)	1	<0.01
Pueblo (1)	5	0.01
Puget Sound Salish (0)	0	<0.01
Seminole (0)	1	<0.01
Shoshone (0)	0	<0.01
Sioux (5)	10	0.02
South American Ind. (3)	11	0.02
Spanish American Ind. (0)	0	<0.01
Tlingit-Haida *(Alaska Native)* (1)	1	<0.01
Tohono O'Odham (0)	0	<0.01
Tsimshian *(Alaska Native)* (0)	0	<0.01
Ute (1)	6	0.01
Yakama (0)	0	<0.01
Yaqui (1)	4	0.01
Yuman (0)	0	<0.01
Yup'ik *(Alaska Native)* (0)	0	<0.01
Asian (33,353)	34,416	61.06
Not Hispanic (33,224)	34,096	60.49
Hispanic (129)	320	0.57
Bangladeshi (41)	41	0.07
Bhutanese (0)	0	<0.01
Burmese (325)	376	0.67
Cambodian (64)	98	0.17
Chinese, ex. Taiwanese (20,345)	21,744	38.58
Filipino (1,087)	1,342	2.38
Hmong (1)	1	<0.01
Indian (1,377)	1,473	2.61
Indonesian (328)	422	0.75
Japanese (883)	1,235	2.19
Korean (1,937)	2,094	3.72
Laotian (17)	25	0.04
Malaysian (59)	80	0.14
Nepalese (2)	3	0.01
Pakistani (97)	111	0.20
Sri Lankan (59)	67	0.12
Taiwanese (4,400)	4,846	8.60
Thai (248)	301	0.53
Vietnamese (776)	1,042	1.85
Hawaii Native/Pacific Islander (16)	191	0.34
Not Hispanic (15)	168	0.30
Hispanic (1)	23	0.04
Fijian (3)	8	0.01
Guamanian/Chamorro (2)	11	0.02
Marshallese (0)	0	<0.01
Native Hawaiian (4)	28	0.05
Samoan (3)	5	0.01
Tongan (0)	0	<0.01
White (18,191)	19,390	34.40
Not Hispanic (14,467)	15,275	27.10
Hispanic (3,724)	4,115	7.30

*Notes: † The Census 2010 population figure is used to calculate the percentages in the Hispanic Origin and Race categories. Ancestry percentages are based on the 2006-2010 American Community Survey population (not shown); ‡ Numbers in parentheses indicate the number of people reporting a single ancestry; * Numbers in parentheses indicate the number of persons reporting this race alone, not in combination with any other race; Please refer to the Explanation of Data for more information.*

Arden-Arcade

Place Type: CDP
County: Sacramento
Population: 92,186

Ancestry	Population	%
Afghan (26)	26	0.03
African, Sub-Saharan (446)	575	0.63
African (316)	350	0.38
Cape Verdean (15)	31	0.03
Ethiopian (55)	71	0.08
Ghanaian (0)	0	<0.01
Kenyan (19)	19	0.02
Liberian (0)	0	<0.01
Nigerian (24)	39	0.04
Senegalese (0)	0	<0.01
Sierra Leonean (0)	0	<0.01
Somalian (0)	0	<0.01
South African (0)	0	<0.01
Sudanese (0)	0	<0.01
Ugandan (8)	40	0.04
Zimbabwean (0)	0	<0.01
Other Sub-Saharan African (9)	25	0.03
Albanian (0)	0	<0.01
Alsatian (15)	23	0.03
American (3,234)	3,234	3.56
Arab (185)	335	0.37
Arab (111)	111	0.12
Egyptian (31)	31	0.03
Iraqi (0)	0	<0.01
Jordanian (0)	0	<0.01
Lebanese (27)	106	0.12
Moroccan (0)	0	<0.01
Palestinian (16)	29	0.03
Syrian (0)	13	0.01
Other Arab (0)	45	0.05
Armenian (303)	337	0.37
Assyrian/Chaldean/Syriac (19)	30	0.03
Australian (53)	53	0.06
Austrian (105)	230	0.25
Basque (50)	159	0.17
Belgian (34)	67	0.07
Brazilian (31)	31	0.03
British (157)	327	0.36
Bulgarian (17)	17	0.02
Cajun (0)	0	<0.01
Canadian (196)	265	0.29
Carpatho Rusyn (0)	0	<0.01
Celtic (17)	205	0.23
Croatian (191)	471	0.52
Cypriot (0)	0	<0.01
Czech (93)	450	0.49
Czechoslovakian (46)	180	0.20
Danish (245)	826	0.91
Dutch (279)	1,654	1.82
Eastern European (243)	273	0.30
English (2,973)	10,809	11.89
Estonian (0)	7	0.01
European (1,031)	1,324	1.46
Finnish (51)	208	0.23
French, ex. Basque (266)	3,429	3.77
French Canadian (190)	454	0.50
German (3,662)	13,842	15.22
German Russian (0)	0	<0.01
Greek (176)	390	0.43
Guyanese (0)	0	<0.01
Hungarian (114)	373	0.41
Icelander (0)	30	0.03
Iranian (368)	461	0.51
Irish (2,278)	10,656	11.72
Israeli (94)	94	0.10
Italian (1,992)	5,574	6.13
Latvian (0)	0	<0.01
Lithuanian (19)	121	0.13
Luxemburger (0)	9	0.01
Macedonian (0)	0	<0.01
Maltese (10)	22	0.02
New Zealander (0)	0	<0.01
Northern European (268)	285	0.31
Norwegian (586)	1,936	2.13
Pennsylvania German (0)	0	<0.01
Polish (657)	1,804	1.98
Portuguese (328)	1,403	1.54
Romanian (239)	297	0.33
Russian (974)	1,489	1.64
Scandinavian (229)	481	0.53
Scotch-Irish (1,032)	2,677	2.94
Scottish (709)	2,817	3.10
Serbian (15)	60	0.07
Slavic (9)	60	0.07
Slovak (19)	70	0.08
Slovene (0)	0	<0.01
Soviet Union (0)	0	<0.01
Swedish (525)	1,652	1.82
Swiss (167)	523	0.58
Turkish (29)	45	0.05
Ukrainian (597)	761	0.84
Welsh (86)	693	0.76
West Indian, ex. Hispanic (39)	62	0.07
Bahamian (0)	0	<0.01
Barbadian (0)	0	<0.01
Belizean (0)	0	<0.01
Bermudan (0)	10	0.01
British West Indian (0)	0	<0.01
Dutch West Indian (16)	23	0.03
Haitian (14)	20	0.02
Jamaican (9)	9	0.01
Trinidadian/Tobagonian (0)	0	<0.01
U.S. Virgin Islander (0)	0	<0.01
West Indian (0)	0	<0.01
Other West Indian (0)	0	<0.01
Yugoslavian (92)	201	0.22

Hispanic Origin	Population	%
Hispanic or Latino (of any race)	17,147	18.60
Central American, ex. Mexican	952	1.03
Costa Rican	35	0.04
Guatemalan	178	0.19
Honduran	171	0.19
Nicaraguan	118	0.13
Panamanian	53	0.06
Salvadoran	382	0.41
Other Central American	15	0.02
Cuban	135	0.15
Dominican Republic	20	0.02
Mexican	13,469	14.61
Puerto Rican	548	0.59
South American	455	0.49
Argentinean	36	0.04
Bolivian	14	0.02
Chilean	58	0.06
Colombian	90	0.10
Ecuadorian	24	0.03
Paraguayan	3	<0.01
Peruvian	178	0.19
Uruguayan	9	0.01
Venezuelan	32	0.03
Other South American	11	0.01
Other Hispanic or Latino	1,568	1.70

Race*	Population	%
African-American/Black (7,977)	9,974	10.82
Not Hispanic (7,527)	9,091	9.86
Hispanic (450)	883	0.96
American Indian/Alaska Native (948)	2,418	2.62
Not Hispanic (584)	1,628	1.77
Hispanic (364)	790	0.86
Alaska Athabascan *(Ala. Nat.)* (1)	2	<0.01
Aleut *(Alaska Native)* (5)	6	0.01
Apache (27)	52	0.06
Arapaho (0)	2	<0.01
Blackfeet (4)	77	0.08
Canadian/French Am. Ind. (2)	5	0.01
Central American Ind. (0)	1	<0.01
Cherokee (91)	441	0.48
Cheyenne (1)	13	0.01
Chickasaw (4)	16	0.02
Chippewa (22)	34	0.04
Choctaw (16)	90	0.10
Colville (0)	1	<0.01
Comanche (5)	5	0.01
Cree (0)	4	<0.01
Creek (4)	20	0.02
Crow (1)	9	0.01
Delaware (4)	5	0.01
Hopi (0)	6	0.01
Houma (0)	3	<0.01
Inupiat *(Alaska Native)* (2)	4	<0.01
Iroquois (12)	36	0.04
Kiowa (1)	2	<0.01
Lumbee (2)	2	<0.01
Menominee (2)	3	<0.01
Mexican American Ind. (64)	108	0.12
Navajo (15)	39	0.04
Osage (1)	11	0.01
Ottawa (1)	1	<0.01
Paiute (8)	11	0.01
Pima (9)	11	0.01
Potawatomi (6)	9	0.01
Pueblo (11)	20	0.02
Puget Sound Salish (2)	3	<0.01
Seminole (3)	11	0.01
Shoshone (4)	14	0.02
Sioux (34)	76	0.08
South American Ind. (1)	10	0.01
Spanish American Ind. (1)	5	0.01
Tlingit-Haida *(Alaska Native)* (4)	8	0.01
Tohono O'Odham (3)	6	0.01
Tsimshian *(Alaska Native)* (0)	4	<0.01
Ute (0)	0	<0.01
Yakama (0)	1	<0.01
Yaqui (8)	28	0.03
Yuman (0)	0	<0.01
Yup'ik *(Alaska Native)* (0)	3	<0.01
Asian (5,152)	6,976	7.57
Not Hispanic (4,990)	6,493	7.04
Hispanic (162)	483	0.52
Bangladeshi (5)	5	0.01
Bhutanese (135)	142	0.15
Burmese (9)	12	0.01
Cambodian (57)	75	0.08
Chinese, ex. Taiwanese (893)	1,213	1.32
Filipino (1,233)	1,926	2.09
Hmong (261)	292	0.32
Indian (569)	713	0.77
Indonesian (35)	62	0.07
Japanese (468)	868	0.94
Korean (351)	488	0.53
Laotian (183)	209	0.23
Malaysian (5)	7	0.01
Nepalese (20)	41	0.04
Pakistani (63)	76	0.08
Sri Lankan (10)	11	0.01
Taiwanese (65)	81	0.09
Thai (90)	129	0.14
Vietnamese (366)	434	0.47
Hawaii Native/Pacific Islander (531)	988	1.07
Not Hispanic (491)	857	0.93
Hispanic (40)	131	0.14
Fijian (224)	262	0.28
Guamanian/Chamorro (60)	103	0.11
Marshallese (0)	1	<0.01
Native Hawaiian (62)	253	0.27
Samoan (76)	146	0.16
Tongan (54)	74	0.08
White (64,688)	69,251	75.12
Not Hispanic (57,529)	60,628	65.77
Hispanic (7,159)	8,623	9.35

*Notes: † The Census 2010 population figure is used to calculate the percentages in the Hispanic Origin and Race categories. Ancestry percentages are based on the 2006-2010 American Community Survey population (not shown); ‡ Numbers in parentheses indicate the number of people reporting a single ancestry; * Numbers in parentheses indicate the number of persons reporting this race alone, not in combination with any other race; Please refer to the Explanation of Data for more information.*

Bakersfield

Place Type: City
County: Kern
Population: 347,483

Ancestry	Population	%
Afghan (41)	41	0.01
African, Sub-Saharan (1,554)	1,907	0.57
African (834)	1,163	0.35
Cape Verdean (0)	0	<0.01
Ethiopian (162)	162	0.05
Ghanaian (0)	0	<0.01
Kenyan (0)	0	<0.01
Liberian (0)	0	<0.01
Nigerian (416)	440	0.13
Senegalese (0)	0	<0.01
Sierra Leonean (0)	0	<0.01
Somalian (58)	58	0.02
South African (66)	66	0.02
Sudanese (0)	0	<0.01
Ugandan (0)	0	<0.01
Zimbabwean (0)	0	<0.01
Other Sub-Saharan African (18)	18	0.01
Albanian (0)	9	<0.01
Alsatian (0)	0	<0.01
American (8,205)	8,205	2.47
Arab (1,749)	2,702	0.81
Arab (788)	1,040	0.31
Egyptian (291)	364	0.11
Iraqi (0)	8	<0.01
Jordanian (105)	352	0.11
Lebanese (199)	359	0.11
Moroccan (17)	40	0.01
Palestinian (56)	165	0.05
Syrian (38)	103	0.03
Other Arab (255)	271	0.08
Armenian (310)	557	0.17
Assyrian/Chaldean/Syriac (63)	63	0.02
Australian (9)	58	0.02
Austrian (40)	218	0.07
Basque (602)	1,084	0.33
Belgian (29)	110	0.03
Brazilian (96)	166	0.05
British (401)	632	0.19
Bulgarian (29)	42	0.01
Cajun (40)	139	0.04
Canadian (388)	598	0.18
Carpatho Rusyn (0)	0	<0.01
Celtic (55)	86	0.03
Croatian (95)	284	0.09
Cypriot (0)	0	<0.01
Czech (124)	578	0.17
Czechoslovakian (47)	177	0.05
Danish (416)	1,382	0.42
Dutch (599)	4,032	1.21
Eastern European (33)	71	0.02
English (6,915)	21,066	6.35
Estonian (19)	38	0.01
European (3,013)	3,718	1.12
Finnish (59)	298	0.09
French, ex. Basque (902)	5,286	1.59
French Canadian (321)	934	0.28
German (9,945)	31,918	9.62
German Russian (8)	8	<0.01
Greek (272)	1,029	0.31
Guyanese (38)	121	0.04
Hungarian (152)	408	0.12
Icelander (0)	0	<0.01
Iranian (562)	641	0.19
Irish (6,524)	25,483	7.68
Israeli (0)	36	0.01
Italian (3,512)	9,902	2.98
Latvian (9)	35	0.01
Lithuanian (100)	286	0.09
Luxemburger (9)	9	<0.01
Macedonian (0)	0	<0.01
Maltese (9)	9	<0.01
New Zealander (8)	8	<0.01
Northern European (125)	152	0.05
Norwegian (744)	2,750	0.83
Pennsylvania German (9)	72	0.02
Polish (569)	2,502	0.75
Portuguese (545)	1,586	0.48
Romanian (66)	184	0.06
Russian (336)	948	0.29
Scandinavian (171)	543	0.16
Scotch-Irish (1,166)	3,607	1.09
Scottish (1,140)	4,779	1.44
Serbian (0)	9	<0.01
Slavic (43)	65	0.02
Slovak (14)	37	0.01
Slovene (0)	0	<0.01
Soviet Union (0)	0	<0.01
Swedish (904)	4,065	1.22
Swiss (154)	750	0.23
Turkish (25)	73	0.02
Ukrainian (142)	285	0.09
Welsh (259)	1,244	0.37
West Indian, ex. Hispanic (160)	425	0.13
Bahamian (0)	0	<0.01
Barbadian (0)	0	<0.01
Belizean (0)	0	<0.01
Bermudan (0)	0	<0.01
British West Indian (0)	0	<0.01
Dutch West Indian (18)	201	0.06
Haitian (71)	71	0.02
Jamaican (43)	80	0.02
Trinidadian/Tobagonian (0)	45	0.01
U.S. Virgin Islander (0)	0	<0.01
West Indian (19)	19	0.01
Other West Indian (9)	9	<0.01
Yugoslavian (260)	365	0.11

Hispanic Origin	Population	%
Hispanic or Latino (of any race)	158,205	45.53
Central American, ex. Mexican	7,497	2.16
Costa Rican	139	0.04
Guatemalan	1,804	0.52
Honduran	545	0.16
Nicaraguan	239	0.07
Panamanian	66	0.02
Salvadoran	4,654	1.34
Other Central American	50	0.01
Cuban	405	0.12
Dominican Republic	77	0.02
Mexican	137,102	39.46
Puerto Rican	1,860	0.54
South American	1,747	0.50
Argentinean	212	0.06
Bolivian	50	0.01
Chilean	89	0.03
Colombian	425	0.12
Ecuadorian	136	0.04
Paraguayan	0	<0.01
Peruvian	534	0.15
Uruguayan	21	0.01
Venezuelan	259	0.07
Other South American	21	0.01
Other Hispanic or Latino	9,517	2.74

Race*	Population	%
African-American/Black (28,368)	32,437	9.33
Not Hispanic (26,677)	29,390	8.46
Hispanic (1,691)	3,047	0.88
American Indian/Alaska Native (5,102)	9,097	2.62
Not Hispanic (2,265)	4,742	1.36
Hispanic (2,837)	4,355	1.25
Alaska Athabascan *(Ala. Nat.)* (3)	11	<0.01
Aleut *(Alaska Native)* (1)	1	<0.01
Apache (173)	336	0.10
Arapaho (6)	13	<0.01
Blackfeet (54)	186	0.05
Canadian/French Am. Ind. (2)	6	<0.01
Central American Ind. (12)	29	0.01
Cherokee (497)	1,444	0.42
Cheyenne (12)	15	<0.01
Chickasaw (53)	112	0.03
Chippewa (13)	47	0.01
Choctaw (202)	467	0.13
Colville (4)	6	<0.01
Comanche (36)	57	0.02
Cree (1)	6	<0.01
Creek (53)	143	0.04
Crow (3)	7	<0.01
Delaware (2)	4	<0.01
Hopi (18)	27	0.01
Houma (0)	1	<0.01
Inupiat *(Alaska Native)* (9)	11	<0.01
Iroquois (4)	20	0.01
Kiowa (6)	19	0.01
Lumbee (3)	6	<0.01
Menominee (0)	0	<0.01
Mexican American Ind. (338)	474	0.14
Navajo (104)	176	0.05
Osage (5)	19	0.01
Ottawa (3)	5	<0.01
Paiute (125)	214	0.06
Pima (23)	41	0.01
Potawatomi (35)	52	0.01
Pueblo (35)	58	0.02
Puget Sound Salish (11)	14	<0.01
Seminole (11)	42	0.01
Shoshone (22)	45	0.01
Sioux (42)	99	0.03
South American Ind. (15)	24	0.01
Spanish American Ind. (19)	24	0.01
Tlingit-Haida *(Alaska Native)* (3)	4	<0.01
Tohono O'Odham (26)	32	0.01
Tsimshian *(Alaska Native)* (0)	0	<0.01
Ute (3)	5	<0.01
Yakama (0)	4	<0.01
Yaqui (88)	154	0.04
Yuman (1)	3	<0.01
Yup'ik *(Alaska Native)* (0)	2	<0.01
Asian (21,432)	25,815	7.43
Not Hispanic (20,496)	23,435	6.74
Hispanic (936)	2,380	0.68
Bangladeshi (44)	44	0.01
Bhutanese (2)	2	<0.01
Burmese (255)	294	0.08
Cambodian (396)	520	0.15
Chinese, ex. Taiwanese (1,721)	2,341	0.67
Filipino (7,046)	9,074	2.61
Hmong (15)	21	0.01
Indian (7,328)	7,896	2.27
Indonesian (123)	167	0.05
Japanese (551)	1,128	0.32
Korean (1,352)	1,619	0.47
Laotian (204)	297	0.09
Malaysian (14)	24	0.01
Nepalese (7)	8	<0.01
Pakistani (245)	289	0.08
Sri Lankan (31)	45	0.01
Taiwanese (92)	110	0.03
Thai (188)	264	0.08
Vietnamese (1,140)	1,368	0.39
Hawaii Native/Pacific Islander (478)	1,202	0.35
Not Hispanic (357)	792	0.23
Hispanic (121)	410	0.12
Fijian (12)	21	0.01
Guamanian/Chamorro (111)	221	0.06
Marshallese (15)	16	<0.01
Native Hawaiian (132)	408	0.12
Samoan (104)	224	0.06
Tongan (21)	29	0.01
White (197,349)	211,351	60.82
Not Hispanic (131,311)	137,595	39.60
Hispanic (66,038)	73,756	21.23

*Notes: † The Census 2010 population figure is used to calculate the percentages in the Hispanic Origin and Race categories. Ancestry percentages are based on the 2006-2010 American Community Survey population (not shown); ‡ Numbers in parentheses indicate the number of people reporting a single ancestry; * Numbers in parentheses indicate the number of persons reporting this race alone, not in combination with any other race; Please refer to the Explanation of Data for more information.*

Baldwin Park

Place Type: City
County: Los Angeles
Population: 75,390

Ancestry	Population	%
Afghan (0)	0	<0.01
African, Sub-Saharan (106)	116	0.15
African (14)	24	0.03
Cape Verdean (0)	0	<0.01
Ethiopian (0)	0	<0.01
Ghanaian (0)	0	<0.01
Kenyan (0)	0	<0.01
Liberian (0)	0	<0.01
Nigerian (92)	92	0.12
Senegalese (0)	0	<0.01
Sierra Leonean (0)	0	<0.01
Somalian (0)	0	<0.01
South African (0)	0	<0.01
Sudanese (0)	0	<0.01
Ugandan (0)	0	<0.01
Zimbabwean (0)	0	<0.01
Other Sub-Saharan African (0)	0	<0.01
Albanian (0)	0	<0.01
Alsatian (0)	0	<0.01
American (501)	501	0.66
Arab (37)	37	0.05
Arab (0)	0	<0.01
Egyptian (0)	0	<0.01
Iraqi (0)	0	<0.01
Jordanian (0)	0	<0.01
Lebanese (0)	0	<0.01
Moroccan (0)	0	<0.01
Palestinian (0)	0	<0.01
Syrian (37)	37	0.05
Other Arab (0)	0	<0.01
Armenian (50)	50	0.07
Assyrian/Chaldean/Syriac (0)	0	<0.01
Australian (0)	0	<0.01
Austrian (0)	27	0.04
Basque (0)	0	<0.01
Belgian (0)	9	0.01
Brazilian (0)	0	<0.01
British (32)	53	0.07
Bulgarian (60)	93	0.12
Cajun (0)	0	<0.01
Canadian (0)	0	<0.01
Carpatho Rusyn (0)	0	<0.01
Celtic (0)	0	<0.01
Croatian (0)	0	<0.01
Cypriot (0)	0	<0.01
Czech (0)	0	<0.01
Czechoslovakian (0)	0	<0.01
Danish (0)	73	0.10
Dutch (17)	278	0.37
Eastern European (12)	12	0.02
English (89)	366	0.49
Estonian (0)	0	<0.01
European (9)	30	0.04
Finnish (0)	0	<0.01
French, ex. Basque (41)	250	0.33
French Canadian (4)	18	0.02
German (147)	722	0.96
German Russian (0)	0	<0.01
Greek (11)	47	0.06
Guyanese (0)	0	<0.01
Hungarian (0)	36	0.05
Icelander (0)	0	<0.01
Iranian (17)	60	0.08
Irish (237)	731	0.97
Israeli (0)	0	<0.01
Italian (108)	407	0.54
Latvian (0)	0	<0.01
Lithuanian (0)	0	<0.01
Luxemburger (0)	0	<0.01
Macedonian (0)	0	<0.01
Maltese (0)	0	<0.01
New Zealander (0)	0	<0.01
Northern European (0)	0	<0.01
Norwegian (39)	81	0.11
Pennsylvania German (0)	0	<0.01
Polish (60)	159	0.21
Portuguese (5)	39	0.05
Romanian (0)	0	<0.01
Russian (41)	96	0.13
Scandinavian (0)	0	<0.01
Scotch-Irish (25)	242	0.32
Scottish (44)	161	0.21
Serbian (0)	0	<0.01
Slavic (0)	0	<0.01
Slovak (0)	0	<0.01
Slovene (0)	0	<0.01
Soviet Union (0)	0	<0.01
Swedish (16)	44	0.06
Swiss (0)	63	0.08
Turkish (7)	7	0.01
Ukrainian (18)	18	0.02
Welsh (33)	160	0.21
West Indian, ex. Hispanic (0)	0	<0.01
Bahamian (0)	0	<0.01
Barbadian (0)	0	<0.01
Belizean (0)	0	<0.01
Bermudan (0)	0	<0.01
British West Indian (0)	0	<0.01
Dutch West Indian (0)	0	<0.01
Haitian (0)	0	<0.01
Jamaican (0)	0	<0.01
Trinidadian/Tobagonian (0)	0	<0.01
U.S. Virgin Islander (0)	0	<0.01
West Indian (0)	0	<0.01
Other West Indian (0)	0	<0.01
Yugoslavian (0)	14	0.02

Hispanic Origin	Population	%
Hispanic or Latino (of any race)	60,403	80.12
Central American, ex. Mexican	4,065	5.39
Costa Rican	70	0.09
Guatemalan	924	1.23
Honduran	262	0.35
Nicaraguan	440	0.58
Panamanian	30	0.04
Salvadoran	2,272	3.01
Other Central American	67	0.09
Cuban	173	0.23
Dominican Republic	21	0.03
Mexican	52,803	70.04
Puerto Rican	267	0.35
South American	526	0.70
Argentinean	42	0.06
Bolivian	44	0.06
Chilean	20	0.03
Colombian	147	0.19
Ecuadorian	113	0.15
Paraguayan	4	0.01
Peruvian	144	0.19
Uruguayan	8	0.01
Venezuelan	4	0.01
Other South American	0	<0.01
Other Hispanic or Latino	2,548	3.38

Race*	Population	%
African-American/Black (913)	1,142	1.51
Not Hispanic (662)	737	0.98
Hispanic (251)	405	0.54
American Indian/Alaska Native (674)	1,134	1.50
Not Hispanic (91)	169	0.22
Hispanic (583)	965	1.28
Alaska Athabascan *(Ala. Nat.)* (0)	0	<0.01
Aleut *(Alaska Native)* (0)	0	<0.01
Apache (28)	66	0.09
Arapaho (0)	0	<0.01
Blackfeet (2)	14	0.02
Canadian/French Am. Ind. (0)	0	<0.01
Central American Ind. (4)	14	0.02
Cherokee (11)	36	0.05
Cheyenne (0)	0	<0.01
Chickasaw (3)	5	0.01
Chippewa (3)	3	<0.01
Choctaw (6)	10	0.01
Colville (0)	0	<0.01
Comanche (7)	8	0.01
Cree (0)	0	<0.01
Creek (0)	3	<0.01
Crow (0)	1	<0.01
Delaware (0)	0	<0.01
Hopi (0)	0	<0.01
Houma (0)	0	<0.01
Inupiat *(Alaska Native)* (0)	0	<0.01
Iroquois (0)	0	<0.01
Kiowa (0)	0	<0.01
Lumbee (1)	1	<0.01
Menominee (0)	0	<0.01
Mexican American Ind. (106)	175	0.23
Navajo (8)	23	0.03
Osage (0)	1	<0.01
Ottawa (0)	0	<0.01
Paiute (4)	4	0.01
Pima (2)	2	<0.01
Potawatomi (0)	5	0.01
Pueblo (13)	21	0.03
Puget Sound Salish (0)	0	<0.01
Seminole (0)	0	<0.01
Shoshone (7)	7	0.01
Sioux (7)	10	0.01
South American Ind. (1)	5	0.01
Spanish American Ind. (12)	16	0.02
Tlingit-Haida *(Alaska Native)* (0)	0	<0.01
Tohono O'Odham (1)	3	<0.01
Tsimshian *(Alaska Native)* (0)	0	<0.01
Ute (0)	0	<0.01
Yakama (0)	0	<0.01
Yaqui (8)	21	0.03
Yuman (10)	10	0.01
Yup'ik *(Alaska Native)* (0)	0	<0.01
Asian (10,696)	11,190	14.84
Not Hispanic (10,495)	10,715	14.21
Hispanic (201)	475	0.63
Bangladeshi (0)	0	<0.01
Bhutanese (0)	0	<0.01
Burmese (90)	97	0.13
Cambodian (312)	350	0.46
Chinese, ex. Taiwanese (3,654)	4,086	5.42
Filipino (3,439)	3,733	4.95
Hmong (3)	3	<0.01
Indian (62)	109	0.14
Indonesian (47)	79	0.10
Japanese (122)	188	0.25
Korean (119)	132	0.18
Laotian (104)	114	0.15
Malaysian (0)	10	0.01
Nepalese (0)	0	<0.01
Pakistani (6)	6	0.01
Sri Lankan (6)	6	0.01
Taiwanese (217)	259	0.34
Thai (155)	169	0.22
Vietnamese (1,895)	2,178	2.89
Hawaii Native/Pacific Islander (85)	178	0.24
Not Hispanic (66)	125	0.17
Hispanic (19)	53	0.07
Fijian (0)	0	<0.01
Guamanian/Chamorro (15)	20	0.03
Marshallese (0)	0	<0.01
Native Hawaiian (12)	30	0.04
Samoan (24)	35	0.05
Tongan (6)	7	0.01
White (33,119)	35,388	46.94
Not Hispanic (3,232)	3,464	4.59
Hispanic (29,887)	31,924	42.35

*Notes: † The Census 2010 population figure is used to calculate the percentages in the Hispanic Origin and Race categories. Ancestry percentages are based on the 2006-2010 American Community Survey population (not shown); ‡ Numbers in parentheses indicate the number of people reporting a single ancestry; * Numbers in parentheses indicate the number of persons reporting this race alone, not in combination with any other race; Please refer to the Explanation of Data for more information.*

Bellflower

Place Type: City
County: Los Angeles
Population: 76,616

Ancestry	Population	%
Afghan (0)	0	<0.01
African, Sub-Saharan (640)	704	0.93
African (215)	270	0.36
Cape Verdean (0)	0	<0.01
Ethiopian (0)	0	<0.01
Ghanaian (0)	9	0.01
Kenyan (0)	0	<0.01
Liberian (0)	0	<0.01
Nigerian (402)	402	0.53
Senegalese (0)	0	<0.01
Sierra Leonean (0)	0	<0.01
Somalian (0)	0	<0.01
South African (12)	12	0.02
Sudanese (0)	0	<0.01
Ugandan (0)	0	<0.01
Zimbabwean (0)	0	<0.01
Other Sub-Saharan African (11)	11	0.01
Albanian (0)	0	<0.01
Alsatian (0)	0	<0.01
American (1,467)	1,467	1.93
Arab (476)	594	0.78
Arab (17)	17	0.02
Egyptian (415)	494	0.65
Iraqi (0)	0	<0.01
Jordanian (0)	0	<0.01
Lebanese (27)	51	0.07
Moroccan (0)	0	<0.01
Palestinian (0)	0	<0.01
Syrian (0)	5	0.01
Other Arab (17)	27	0.04
Armenian (13)	24	0.03
Assyrian/Chaldean/Syriac (0)	69	0.09
Australian (0)	0	<0.01
Austrian (10)	48	0.06
Basque (0)	0	<0.01
Belgian (21)	21	0.03
Brazilian (0)	0	<0.01
British (64)	91	0.12
Bulgarian (0)	0	<0.01
Cajun (11)	11	0.01
Canadian (28)	57	0.08
Carpatho Rusyn (0)	0	<0.01
Celtic (0)	0	<0.01
Croatian (0)	0	<0.01
Cypriot (0)	0	<0.01
Czech (52)	128	0.17
Czechoslovakian (0)	5	0.01
Danish (21)	120	0.16
Dutch (1,081)	1,961	2.58
Eastern European (21)	21	0.03
English (766)	2,373	3.12
Estonian (0)	0	<0.01
European (168)	214	0.28
Finnish (5)	30	0.04
French, ex. Basque (116)	753	0.99
French Canadian (180)	340	0.45
German (828)	3,485	4.59
German Russian (13)	13	0.02
Greek (0)	28	0.04
Guyanese (0)	0	<0.01
Hungarian (0)	129	0.17
Icelander (0)	0	<0.01
Iranian (0)	0	<0.01
Irish (732)	2,761	3.64
Israeli (0)	0	<0.01
Italian (498)	1,449	1.91
Latvian (0)	25	0.03
Lithuanian (114)	114	0.15
Luxemburger (0)	0	<0.01
Macedonian (0)	0	<0.01
Maltese (0)	0	<0.01
New Zealander (0)	0	<0.01
Northern European (0)	0	<0.01
Norwegian (48)	189	0.25
Pennsylvania German (0)	9	0.01
Polish (107)	338	0.45
Portuguese (45)	143	0.19
Romanian (71)	145	0.19
Russian (17)	68	0.09
Scandinavian (59)	127	0.17
Scotch-Irish (94)	267	0.35
Scottish (21)	270	0.36
Serbian (0)	0	<0.01
Slavic (0)	0	<0.01
Slovak (0)	4	0.01
Slovene (0)	0	<0.01
Soviet Union (0)	0	<0.01
Swedish (121)	368	0.48
Swiss (0)	45	0.06
Turkish (18)	28	0.04
Ukrainian (4)	4	0.01
Welsh (49)	135	0.18
West Indian, ex. Hispanic (108)	108	0.14
Bahamian (0)	0	<0.01
Barbadian (0)	0	<0.01
Belizean (0)	0	<0.01
Bermudan (0)	0	<0.01
British West Indian (56)	56	0.07
Dutch West Indian (0)	0	<0.01
Haitian (0)	0	<0.01
Jamaican (26)	26	0.03
Trinidadian/Tobagonian (12)	12	0.02
U.S. Virgin Islander (14)	14	0.02
West Indian (0)	0	<0.01
Other West Indian (0)	0	<0.01
Yugoslavian (28)	49	0.06

Hispanic Origin	Population	%
Hispanic or Latino (of any race)	40,085	52.32
Central American, ex. Mexican	3,104	4.05
Costa Rican	74	0.10
Guatemalan	898	1.17
Honduran	184	0.24
Nicaraguan	297	0.39
Panamanian	62	0.08
Salvadoran	1,563	2.04
Other Central American	26	0.03
Cuban	295	0.39
Dominican Republic	44	0.06
Mexican	32,587	42.53
Puerto Rican	445	0.58
South American	867	1.13
Argentinean	116	0.15
Bolivian	22	0.03
Chilean	58	0.08
Colombian	203	0.26
Ecuadorian	174	0.23
Paraguayan	3	<0.01
Peruvian	250	0.33
Uruguayan	6	0.01
Venezuelan	23	0.03
Other South American	12	0.02
Other Hispanic or Latino	2,743	3.58

Race*	Population	%
African-American/Black (10,760)	11,788	15.39
Not Hispanic (10,374)	11,032	14.40
Hispanic (386)	756	0.99
American Indian/Alaska Native (731)	1,286	1.68
Not Hispanic (229)	543	0.71
Hispanic (502)	743	0.97
Alaska Athabascan *(Ala. Nat.)* (2)	2	<0.01
Aleut *(Alaska Native)* (0)	0	<0.01
Apache (21)	34	0.04
Arapaho (1)	1	<0.01
Blackfeet (9)	21	0.03
Canadian/French Am. Ind. (4)	8	0.01
Central American Ind. (5)	7	0.01
Cherokee (51)	137	0.18
Cheyenne (5)	8	0.01
Chickasaw (1)	3	<0.01
Chippewa (3)	13	0.02
Choctaw (27)	50	0.07
Colville (0)	0	<0.01
Comanche (7)	9	0.01
Cree (0)	1	<0.01
Creek (4)	11	0.01
Crow (0)	7	0.01
Delaware (1)	6	0.01
Hopi (4)	4	0.01
Houma (0)	0	<0.01
Inupiat *(Alaska Native)* (0)	0	<0.01
Iroquois (2)	11	0.01
Kiowa (0)	3	<0.01
Lumbee (0)	1	<0.01
Menominee (0)	0	<0.01
Mexican American Ind. (113)	152	0.20
Navajo (28)	50	0.07
Osage (0)	5	0.01
Ottawa (0)	1	<0.01
Paiute (2)	3	<0.01
Pima (3)	4	0.01
Potawatomi (1)	1	<0.01
Pueblo (12)	16	0.02
Puget Sound Salish (0)	0	<0.01
Seminole (0)	9	0.01
Shoshone (0)	2	<0.01
Sioux (4)	13	0.02
South American Ind. (1)	2	<0.01
Spanish American Ind. (11)	14	0.02
Tlingit-Haida *(Alaska Native)* (0)	0	<0.01
Tohono O'Odham (0)	0	<0.01
Tsimshian *(Alaska Native)* (0)	0	<0.01
Ute (1)	1	<0.01
Yakama (2)	2	<0.01
Yaqui (3)	10	0.01
Yuman (0)	0	<0.01
Yup'ik *(Alaska Native)* (0)	0	<0.01
Asian (8,865)	9,846	12.85
Not Hispanic (8,720)	9,404	12.27
Hispanic (145)	442	0.58
Bangladeshi (51)	55	0.07
Bhutanese (0)	0	<0.01
Burmese (4)	4	0.01
Cambodian (810)	978	1.28
Chinese, ex. Taiwanese (453)	710	0.93
Filipino (4,563)	5,088	6.64
Hmong (3)	4	0.01
Indian (416)	515	0.67
Indonesian (75)	109	0.14
Japanese (195)	337	0.44
Korean (826)	866	1.13
Laotian (13)	25	0.03
Malaysian (4)	4	0.01
Nepalese (6)	7	0.01
Pakistani (52)	57	0.07
Sri Lankan (36)	37	0.05
Taiwanese (30)	33	0.04
Thai (485)	552	0.72
Vietnamese (453)	538	0.70
Hawaii Native/Pacific Islander (615)	954	1.25
Not Hispanic (567)	805	1.05
Hispanic (48)	149	0.19
Fijian (34)	52	0.07
Guamanian/Chamorro (45)	90	0.12
Marshallese (0)	1	<0.01
Native Hawaiian (38)	135	0.18
Samoan (400)	507	0.66
Tongan (57)	81	0.11
White (32,337)	35,015	45.70
Not Hispanic (14,971)	16,072	20.98
Hispanic (17,366)	18,943	24.72

*Notes: † The Census 2010 population figure is used to calculate the percentages in the Hispanic Origin and Race categories. Ancestry percentages are based on the 2006-2010 American Community Survey population (not shown); ‡ Numbers in parentheses indicate the number of people reporting a single ancestry; * Numbers in parentheses indicate the number of persons reporting this race alone, not in combination with any other race; Please refer to the Explanation of Data for more information.*

Berkeley

Place Type: City
County: Alameda
Population: 112,580

Ancestry	Population	%
Afghan (8)	29	0.03
African, Sub-Saharan (1,047)	1,312	1.20
African (437)	668	0.61
Cape Verdean (0)	0	<0.01
Ethiopian (217)	222	0.20
Ghanaian (0)	0	<0.01
Kenyan (70)	70	0.06
Liberian (0)	0	<0.01
Nigerian (36)	65	0.06
Senegalese (0)	0	<0.01
Sierra Leonean (23)	23	0.02
Somalian (0)	0	<0.01
South African (92)	92	0.08
Sudanese (0)	0	<0.01
Ugandan (0)	0	<0.01
Zimbabwean (0)	0	<0.01
Other Sub-Saharan African (172)	172	0.16
Albanian (0)	0	<0.01
Alsatian (0)	19	0.02
American (1,220)	1,220	1.12
Arab (672)	882	0.81
Arab (153)	157	0.14
Egyptian (41)	41	0.04
Iraqi (17)	26	0.02
Jordanian (50)	50	0.05
Lebanese (49)	93	0.09
Moroccan (101)	136	0.12
Palestinian (34)	47	0.04
Syrian (10)	29	0.03
Other Arab (217)	303	0.28
Armenian (256)	381	0.35
Assyrian/Chaldean/Syriac (51)	51	0.05
Australian (47)	58	0.05
Austrian (108)	539	0.49
Basque (0)	22	0.02
Belgian (86)	209	0.19
Brazilian (118)	229	0.21
British (349)	975	0.89
Bulgarian (40)	72	0.07
Cajun (6)	6	0.01
Canadian (171)	307	0.28
Carpatho Rusyn (0)	11	0.01
Celtic (38)	86	0.08
Croatian (28)	158	0.14
Cypriot (0)	0	<0.01
Czech (53)	502	0.46
Czechoslovakian (10)	36	0.03
Danish (153)	851	0.78
Dutch (193)	1,041	0.95
Eastern European (869)	1,046	0.96
English (1,717)	8,474	7.75
Estonian (9)	57	0.05
European (2,467)	2,914	2.66
Finnish (63)	327	0.30
French, ex. Basque (707)	3,051	2.79
French Canadian (66)	282	0.26
German (1,772)	9,475	8.66
German Russian (0)	0	<0.01
Greek (294)	648	0.59
Guyanese (8)	8	0.01
Hungarian (187)	640	0.58
Icelander (0)	68	0.06
Iranian (741)	925	0.85
Irish (1,927)	7,959	7.27
Israeli (153)	214	0.20
Italian (999)	4,172	3.81
Latvian (78)	100	0.09
Lithuanian (105)	302	0.28
Luxemburger (0)	0	<0.01
Macedonian (0)	41	0.04
Maltese (10)	30	0.03
New Zealander (10)	36	0.03
Northern European (263)	305	0.28
Norwegian (286)	1,315	1.20
Pennsylvania German (8)	8	0.01
Polish (759)	3,058	2.80
Portuguese (258)	793	0.72
Romanian (195)	449	0.41
Russian (1,605)	4,125	3.77
Scandinavian (225)	399	0.36
Scotch-Irish (356)	1,478	1.35
Scottish (435)	2,473	2.26
Serbian (19)	25	0.02
Slavic (23)	128	0.12
Slovak (39)	220	0.20
Slovene (23)	57	0.05
Soviet Union (0)	0	<0.01
Swedish (321)	1,340	1.22
Swiss (132)	784	0.72
Turkish (64)	86	0.08
Ukrainian (139)	561	0.51
Welsh (63)	795	0.73
West Indian, ex. Hispanic (142)	248	0.23
Bahamian (0)	0	<0.01
Barbadian (0)	0	<0.01
Belizean (0)	0	<0.01
Bermudan (0)	0	<0.01
British West Indian (0)	0	<0.01
Dutch West Indian (0)	0	<0.01
Haitian (54)	64	0.06
Jamaican (19)	32	0.03
Trinidadian/Tobagonian (10)	23	0.02
U.S. Virgin Islander (0)	0	<0.01
West Indian (59)	129	0.12
Other West Indian (0)	0	<0.01
Yugoslavian (9)	68	0.06

Hispanic Origin	Population	%
Hispanic or Latino (of any race)	12,209	10.84
Central American, ex. Mexican	1,220	1.08
Costa Rican	76	0.07
Guatemalan	346	0.31
Honduran	81	0.07
Nicaraguan	186	0.17
Panamanian	63	0.06
Salvadoran	451	0.40
Other Central American	17	0.02
Cuban	248	0.22
Dominican Republic	59	0.05
Mexican	7,680	6.82
Puerto Rican	521	0.46
South American	1,319	1.17
Argentinean	232	0.21
Bolivian	41	0.04
Chilean	201	0.18
Colombian	236	0.21
Ecuadorian	84	0.07
Paraguayan	7	0.01
Peruvian	382	0.34
Uruguayan	21	0.02
Venezuelan	91	0.08
Other South American	24	0.02
Other Hispanic or Latino	1,162	1.03

Race*	Population	%
African-American/Black (11,241)	13,317	11.83
Not Hispanic (10,896)	12,524	11.12
Hispanic (345)	793	0.70
American Indian/Alaska Native (479)	1,836	1.63
Not Hispanic (228)	1,119	0.99
Hispanic (251)	717	0.64
Alaska Athabascan *(Ala. Nat.)* (0)	1	<0.01
Aleut *(Alaska Native)* (2)	4	<0.01
Apache (20)	57	0.05
Arapaho (0)	1	<0.01
Blackfeet (10)	45	0.04
Canadian/French Am. Ind. (2)	6	0.01
Central American Ind. (11)	22	0.02
Cherokee (21)	257	0.23
Cheyenne (0)	5	<0.01
Chickasaw (1)	6	0.01
Chippewa (4)	19	0.02
Choctaw (8)	107	0.10
Colville (0)	1	<0.01
Comanche (2)	3	<0.01
Cree (1)	8	0.01
Creek (3)	23	0.02
Crow (0)	1	<0.01
Delaware (1)	1	<0.01
Hopi (4)	4	<0.01
Houma (0)	0	<0.01
Inupiat *(Alaska Native)* (1)	7	0.01
Iroquois (8)	43	0.04
Kiowa (4)	6	0.01
Lumbee (0)	7	0.01
Menominee (0)	1	<0.01
Mexican American Ind. (81)	164	0.15
Navajo (19)	44	0.04
Osage (0)	7	0.01
Ottawa (0)	0	<0.01
Paiute (0)	0	<0.01
Pima (1)	6	0.01
Potawatomi (5)	13	0.01
Pueblo (2)	14	0.01
Puget Sound Salish (0)	1	<0.01
Seminole (0)	15	0.01
Shoshone (1)	3	<0.01
Sioux (19)	44	0.04
South American Ind. (6)	47	0.04
Spanish American Ind. (5)	9	0.01
Tlingit-Haida *(Alaska Native)* (1)	2	<0.01
Tohono O'Odham (4)	5	<0.01
Tsimshian *(Alaska Native)* (0)	1	<0.01
Ute (1)	2	<0.01
Yakama (0)	0	<0.01
Yaqui (14)	29	0.03
Yuman (2)	5	<0.01
Yup'ik *(Alaska Native)* (0)	1	<0.01
Asian (21,690)	25,707	22.83
Not Hispanic (21,499)	25,158	22.35
Hispanic (191)	549	0.49
Bangladeshi (64)	72	0.06
Bhutanese (2)	2	<0.01
Burmese (43)	66	0.06
Cambodian (100)	132	0.12
Chinese, ex. Taiwanese (8,655)	10,374	9.21
Filipino (1,640)	2,446	2.17
Hmong (56)	59	0.05
Indian (2,712)	3,197	2.84
Indonesian (94)	179	0.16
Japanese (1,752)	2,948	2.62
Korean (2,392)	2,754	2.45
Laotian (84)	101	0.09
Malaysian (20)	47	0.04
Nepalese (190)	211	0.19
Pakistani (349)	428	0.38
Sri Lankan (57)	71	0.06
Taiwanese (918)	1,066	0.95
Thai (323)	410	0.36
Vietnamese (1,110)	1,394	1.24
Hawaii Native/Pacific Islander (186)	577	0.51
Not Hispanic (170)	496	0.44
Hispanic (16)	81	0.07
Fijian (21)	36	0.03
Guamanian/Chamorro (30)	53	0.05
Marshallese (0)	0	<0.01
Native Hawaiian (30)	195	0.17
Samoan (43)	77	0.07
Tongan (31)	48	0.04
White (66,996)	72,950	64.80
Not Hispanic (61,539)	66,337	58.92
Hispanic (5,457)	6,613	5.87

*Notes: † The Census 2010 population figure is used to calculate the percentages in the Hispanic Origin and Race categories. Ancestry percentages are based on the 2006-2010 American Community Survey population (not shown); ‡ Numbers in parentheses indicate the number of people reporting a single ancestry; * Numbers in parentheses indicate the number of persons reporting this race alone, not in combination with any other race; Please refer to the Explanation of Data for more information.*

Brentwood

Place Type: City
County: Contra Costa
Population: 51,481

Ancestry	Population	%
Afghan (200)	200	0.43
African, Sub-Saharan (137)	174	0.38
African (28)	35	0.08
Cape Verdean (0)	0	<0.01
Ethiopian (0)	0	<0.01
Ghanaian (0)	0	<0.01
Kenyan (0)	0	<0.01
Liberian (0)	0	<0.01
Nigerian (109)	109	0.24
Senegalese (0)	0	<0.01
Sierra Leonean (0)	0	<0.01
Somalian (0)	30	0.06
South African (0)	0	<0.01
Sudanese (0)	0	<0.01
Ugandan (0)	0	<0.01
Zimbabwean (0)	0	<0.01
Other Sub-Saharan African (0)	0	<0.01
Albanian (0)	0	<0.01
Alsatian (0)	0	<0.01
American (984)	984	2.13
Arab (223)	336	0.73
Arab (53)	164	0.35
Egyptian (76)	78	0.17
Iraqi (0)	0	<0.01
Jordanian (0)	0	<0.01
Lebanese (14)	14	0.03
Moroccan (0)	0	<0.01
Palestinian (80)	80	0.17
Syrian (0)	0	<0.01
Other Arab (0)	0	<0.01
Armenian (11)	93	0.20
Assyrian/Chaldean/Syriac (0)	0	<0.01
Australian (13)	13	0.03
Austrian (15)	175	0.38
Basque (0)	0	<0.01
Belgian (0)	0	<0.01
Brazilian (17)	17	0.04
British (68)	213	0.46
Bulgarian (0)	0	<0.01
Cajun (0)	0	<0.01
Canadian (29)	87	0.19
Carpatho Rusyn (0)	0	<0.01
Celtic (0)	12	0.03
Croatian (24)	133	0.29
Cypriot (0)	0	<0.01
Czech (0)	76	0.16
Czechoslovakian (2)	19	0.04
Danish (62)	365	0.79
Dutch (204)	747	1.61
Eastern European (11)	11	0.02
English (975)	4,704	10.16
Estonian (0)	0	<0.01
European (719)	913	1.97
Finnish (22)	87	0.19
French, ex. Basque (54)	1,423	3.07
French Canadian (181)	283	0.61
German (1,388)	6,490	14.02
German Russian (0)	0	<0.01
Greek (15)	133	0.29
Guyanese (0)	0	<0.01
Hungarian (53)	89	0.19
Icelander (0)	0	<0.01
Iranian (116)	116	0.25
Irish (1,189)	5,755	12.43
Israeli (0)	0	<0.01
Italian (1,248)	3,962	8.56
Latvian (0)	25	0.05
Lithuanian (0)	39	0.08
Luxemburger (0)	11	0.02
Macedonian (0)	0	<0.01
Maltese (0)	0	<0.01
New Zealander (0)	0	<0.01
Northern European (38)	38	0.08
Norwegian (184)	863	1.86
Pennsylvania German (0)	0	<0.01
Polish (145)	965	2.08
Portuguese (897)	2,149	4.64
Romanian (0)	61	0.13
Russian (72)	427	0.92
Scandinavian (124)	287	0.62
Scotch-Irish (170)	439	0.95
Scottish (223)	803	1.73
Serbian (22)	66	0.14
Slavic (14)	41	0.09
Slovak (13)	22	0.05
Slovene (0)	30	0.06
Soviet Union (0)	0	<0.01
Swedish (271)	1,111	2.40
Swiss (37)	240	0.52
Turkish (0)	0	<0.01
Ukrainian (72)	85	0.18
Welsh (38)	268	0.58
West Indian, ex. Hispanic (141)	193	0.42
Bahamian (0)	0	<0.01
Barbadian (0)	0	<0.01
Belizean (0)	34	0.07
Bermudan (0)	0	<0.01
British West Indian (0)	0	<0.01
Dutch West Indian (0)	0	<0.01
Haitian (0)	0	<0.01
Jamaican (141)	159	0.34
Trinidadian/Tobagonian (0)	0	<0.01
U.S. Virgin Islander (0)	0	<0.01
West Indian (0)	0	<0.01
Other West Indian (0)	0	<0.01
Yugoslavian (14)	14	0.03

Hispanic Origin	Population	%
Hispanic or Latino (of any race)	13,779	26.77
Central American, ex. Mexican	934	1.81
Costa Rican	17	0.03
Guatemalan	183	0.36
Honduran	34	0.07
Nicaraguan	233	0.45
Panamanian	29	0.06
Salvadoran	438	0.85
Other Central American	0	<0.01
Cuban	82	0.16
Dominican Republic	10	0.02
Mexican	10,521	20.44
Puerto Rican	618	1.20
South American	348	0.68
Argentinean	50	0.10
Bolivian	32	0.06
Chilean	48	0.09
Colombian	46	0.09
Ecuadorian	30	0.06
Paraguayan	0	<0.01
Peruvian	112	0.22
Uruguayan	6	0.01
Venezuelan	15	0.03
Other South American	9	0.02
Other Hispanic or Latino	1,266	2.46

Race*	Population	%
African-American/Black (3,389)	4,184	8.13
Not Hispanic (3,197)	3,825	7.43
Hispanic (192)	359	0.70
American Indian/Alaska Native (333)	992	1.93
Not Hispanic (178)	633	1.23
Hispanic (155)	359	0.70
Alaska Athabascan *(Ala. Nat.)* (0)	0	<0.01
Aleut *(Alaska Native)* (0)	0	<0.01
Apache (5)	28	0.05
Arapaho (0)	0	<0.01
Blackfeet (2)	34	0.07
Canadian/French Am. Ind. (0)	1	<0.01
Central American Ind. (3)	5	0.01
Cherokee (35)	192	0.37
Cheyenne (0)	0	<0.01
Chickasaw (1)	13	0.03
Chippewa (13)	22	0.04
Choctaw (16)	67	0.13
Colville (0)	2	<0.01
Comanche (3)	9	0.02
Cree (0)	1	<0.01
Creek (1)	18	0.03
Crow (0)	7	0.01
Delaware (0)	2	<0.01
Hopi (0)	5	0.01
Houma (0)	0	<0.01
Inupiat *(Alaska Native)* (0)	0	<0.01
Iroquois (0)	10	0.02
Kiowa (0)	8	0.02
Lumbee (1)	1	<0.01
Menominee (0)	0	<0.01
Mexican American Ind. (14)	37	0.07
Navajo (12)	34	0.07
Osage (0)	2	<0.01
Ottawa (0)	0	<0.01
Paiute (1)	2	<0.01
Pima (1)	1	<0.01
Potawatomi (2)	2	<0.01
Pueblo (2)	11	0.02
Puget Sound Salish (5)	8	0.02
Seminole (1)	7	0.01
Shoshone (2)	6	0.01
Sioux (6)	19	0.04
South American Ind. (1)	1	<0.01
Spanish American Ind. (4)	6	0.01
Tlingit-Haida *(Alaska Native)* (0)	0	<0.01
Tohono O'Odham (1)	1	<0.01
Tsimshian *(Alaska Native)* (0)	0	<0.01
Ute (1)	4	0.01
Yakama (0)	0	<0.01
Yaqui (5)	9	0.02
Yuman (0)	0	<0.01
Yup'ik *(Alaska Native)* (0)	0	<0.01
Asian (4,051)	5,630	10.94
Not Hispanic (3,903)	5,151	10.01
Hispanic (148)	479	0.93
Bangladeshi (12)	15	0.03
Bhutanese (0)	0	<0.01
Burmese (13)	15	0.03
Cambodian (29)	38	0.07
Chinese, ex. Taiwanese (459)	740	1.44
Filipino (2,159)	2,958	5.75
Hmong (11)	11	0.02
Indian (441)	530	1.03
Indonesian (24)	46	0.09
Japanese (141)	434	0.84
Korean (166)	231	0.45
Laotian (18)	38	0.07
Malaysian (2)	2	<0.01
Nepalese (2)	2	<0.01
Pakistani (82)	87	0.17
Sri Lankan (3)	3	0.01
Taiwanese (33)	36	0.07
Thai (17)	45	0.09
Vietnamese (224)	303	0.59
Hawaii Native/Pacific Islander (202)	560	1.09
Not Hispanic (170)	461	0.90
Hispanic (32)	99	0.19
Fijian (20)	40	0.08
Guamanian/Chamorro (54)	119	0.23
Marshallese (0)	0	<0.01
Native Hawaiian (45)	238	0.46
Samoan (28)	70	0.14
Tongan (16)	26	0.05
White (34,969)	38,011	73.84
Not Hispanic (27,944)	29,819	57.92
Hispanic (7,025)	8,192	15.91

*Notes: † The Census 2010 population figure is used to calculate the percentages in the Hispanic Origin and Race categories. Ancestry percentages are based on the 2006-2010 American Community Survey population (not shown); ‡ Numbers in parentheses indicate the number of people reporting a single ancestry; * Numbers in parentheses indicate the number of persons reporting this race alone, not in combination with any other race; Please refer to the Explanation of Data for more information.*

Buena Park

Place Type: City
County: Orange
Population: 80,530

Ancestry	Population	%
Afghan (89)	89	0.11
African, Sub-Saharan (39)	39	0.05
African (39)	39	0.05
Cape Verdean (0)	0	<0.01
Ethiopian (0)	0	<0.01
Ghanaian (0)	0	<0.01
Kenyan (0)	0	<0.01
Liberian (0)	0	<0.01
Nigerian (0)	0	<0.01
Senegalese (0)	0	<0.01
Sierra Leonean (0)	0	<0.01
Somalian (0)	0	<0.01
South African (0)	0	<0.01
Sudanese (0)	0	<0.01
Ugandan (0)	0	<0.01
Zimbabwean (0)	0	<0.01
Other Sub-Saharan African (0)	0	<0.01
Albanian (0)	0	<0.01
Alsatian (0)	0	<0.01
American (1,428)	1,428	1.79
Arab (344)	464	0.58
Arab (113)	113	0.14
Egyptian (40)	40	0.05
Iraqi (0)	0	<0.01
Jordanian (121)	142	0.18
Lebanese (17)	52	0.07
Moroccan (27)	27	0.03
Palestinian (0)	0	<0.01
Syrian (0)	43	0.05
Other Arab (26)	47	0.06
Armenian (0)	27	0.03
Assyrian/Chaldean/Syriac (0)	0	<0.01
Australian (0)	0	<0.01
Austrian (45)	78	0.10
Basque (0)	0	<0.01
Belgian (7)	44	0.06
Brazilian (70)	70	0.09
British (116)	176	0.22
Bulgarian (0)	0	<0.01
Cajun (0)	0	<0.01
Canadian (82)	102	0.13
Carpatho Rusyn (0)	0	<0.01
Celtic (0)	26	0.03
Croatian (0)	0	<0.01
Cypriot (0)	0	<0.01
Czech (10)	32	0.04
Czechoslovakian (36)	45	0.06
Danish (59)	186	0.23
Dutch (259)	900	1.13
Eastern European (17)	17	0.02
English (960)	3,677	4.61
Estonian (0)	0	<0.01
European (318)	318	0.40
Finnish (17)	71	0.09
French, ex. Basque (177)	1,236	1.55
French Canadian (78)	225	0.28
German (1,743)	6,207	7.78
German Russian (0)	0	<0.01
Greek (152)	270	0.34
Guyanese (0)	0	<0.01
Hungarian (111)	336	0.42
Icelander (9)	19	0.02
Iranian (160)	178	0.22
Irish (1,232)	5,376	6.74
Israeli (0)	0	<0.01
Italian (973)	2,728	3.42
Latvian (0)	0	<0.01
Lithuanian (0)	9	0.01
Luxemburger (0)	0	<0.01
Macedonian (0)	0	<0.01
Maltese (0)	0	<0.01
New Zealander (0)	0	<0.01
Northern European (0)	0	<0.01
Norwegian (223)	642	0.81
Pennsylvania German (0)	0	<0.01
Polish (317)	1,005	1.26
Portuguese (154)	439	0.55
Romanian (274)	274	0.34
Russian (121)	260	0.33
Scandinavian (125)	219	0.27
Scotch-Irish (182)	702	0.88
Scottish (198)	737	0.92
Serbian (33)	146	0.18
Slavic (0)	0	<0.01
Slovak (0)	120	0.15
Slovene (0)	0	<0.01
Soviet Union (0)	0	<0.01
Swedish (167)	715	0.90
Swiss (16)	25	0.03
Turkish (0)	0	<0.01
Ukrainian (56)	91	0.11
Welsh (0)	312	0.39
West Indian, ex. Hispanic (38)	46	0.06
Bahamian (0)	0	<0.01
Barbadian (0)	0	<0.01
Belizean (0)	0	<0.01
Bermudan (0)	0	<0.01
British West Indian (4)	4	0.01
Dutch West Indian (0)	0	<0.01
Haitian (0)	0	<0.01
Jamaican (34)	42	0.05
Trinidadian/Tobagonian (0)	0	<0.01
U.S. Virgin Islander (0)	0	<0.01
West Indian (0)	0	<0.01
Other West Indian (0)	0	<0.01
Yugoslavian (0)	108	0.14

Hispanic Origin	Population	%
Hispanic or Latino (of any race)	31,638	39.29
Central American, ex. Mexican	1,700	2.11
Costa Rican	47	0.06
Guatemalan	592	0.74
Honduran	119	0.15
Nicaraguan	206	0.26
Panamanian	22	0.03
Salvadoran	679	0.84
Other Central American	35	0.04
Cuban	261	0.32
Dominican Republic	20	0.02
Mexican	26,549	32.97
Puerto Rican	422	0.52
South American	930	1.15
Argentinean	112	0.14
Bolivian	22	0.03
Chilean	40	0.05
Colombian	209	0.26
Ecuadorian	146	0.18
Paraguayan	6	0.01
Peruvian	374	0.46
Uruguayan	1	<0.01
Venezuelan	15	0.02
Other South American	5	0.01
Other Hispanic or Latino	1,756	2.18

Race*	Population	%
African-American/Black (3,073)	3,761	4.67
Not Hispanic (2,809)	3,239	4.02
Hispanic (264)	522	0.65
American Indian/Alaska Native (862)	1,602	1.99
Not Hispanic (188)	473	0.59
Hispanic (674)	1,129	1.40
Alaska Athabascan *(Ala. Nat.)* (0)	0	<0.01
Aleut *(Alaska Native)* (0)	1	<0.01
Apache (28)	67	0.08
Arapaho (0)	0	<0.01
Blackfeet (5)	29	0.04
Canadian/French Am. Ind. (1)	2	<0.01
Central American Ind. (2)	3	<0.01
Cherokee (33)	143	0.18
Cheyenne (0)	0	<0.01
Chickasaw (0)	8	0.01
Chippewa (4)	10	0.01
Choctaw (11)	25	0.03
Colville (0)	0	<0.01
Comanche (1)	6	0.01
Cree (0)	0	<0.01
Creek (6)	8	0.01
Crow (0)	0	<0.01
Delaware (0)	0	<0.01
Hopi (5)	12	0.01
Houma (0)	0	<0.01
Inupiat *(Alaska Native)* (0)	0	<0.01
Iroquois (4)	6	0.01
Kiowa (0)	0	<0.01
Lumbee (0)	0	<0.01
Menominee (1)	1	<0.01
Mexican American Ind. (93)	142	0.18
Navajo (15)	44	0.05
Osage (0)	1	<0.01
Ottawa (0)	0	<0.01
Paiute (0)	0	<0.01
Pima (2)	2	<0.01
Potawatomi (4)	6	0.01
Pueblo (3)	11	0.01
Puget Sound Salish (0)	0	<0.01
Seminole (0)	0	<0.01
Shoshone (7)	10	0.01
Sioux (8)	20	0.02
South American Ind. (0)	2	<0.01
Spanish American Ind. (2)	2	<0.01
Tlingit-Haida *(Alaska Native)* (7)	7	0.01
Tohono O'Odham (3)	6	0.01
Tsimshian *(Alaska Native)* (0)	0	<0.01
Ute (1)	8	0.01
Yakama (0)	0	<0.01
Yaqui (10)	28	0.03
Yuman (4)	6	0.01
Yup'ik *(Alaska Native)* (0)	0	<0.01
Asian (21,488)	23,063	28.64
Not Hispanic (21,232)	22,417	27.84
Hispanic (256)	646	0.80
Bangladeshi (32)	32	0.04
Bhutanese (0)	0	<0.01
Burmese (47)	52	0.06
Cambodian (227)	282	0.35
Chinese, ex. Taiwanese (1,179)	1,538	1.91
Filipino (6,767)	7,506	9.32
Hmong (26)	27	0.03
Indian (2,054)	2,247	2.79
Indonesian (60)	123	0.15
Japanese (636)	996	1.24
Korean (7,806)	8,001	9.94
Laotian (92)	97	0.12
Malaysian (3)	3	<0.01
Nepalese (16)	16	0.02
Pakistani (169)	197	0.24
Sri Lankan (43)	45	0.06
Taiwanese (296)	332	0.41
Thai (255)	288	0.36
Vietnamese (1,317)	1,479	1.84
Hawaii Native/Pacific Islander (455)	814	1.01
Not Hispanic (389)	653	0.81
Hispanic (66)	161	0.20
Fijian (44)	50	0.06
Guamanian/Chamorro (80)	118	0.15
Marshallese (0)	0	<0.01
Native Hawaiian (62)	182	0.23
Samoan (173)	241	0.30
Tongan (43)	59	0.07
White (36,454)	39,761	49.37
Not Hispanic (22,302)	23,728	29.46
Hispanic (14,152)	16,033	19.91

*Notes: † The Census 2010 population figure is used to calculate the percentages in the Hispanic Origin and Race categories. Ancestry percentages are based on the 2006-2010 American Community Survey population (not shown); ‡ Numbers in parentheses indicate the number of people reporting a single ancestry; * Numbers in parentheses indicate the number of persons reporting this race alone, not in combination with any other race; Please refer to the Explanation of Data for more information.*

Burbank

Place Type: City
County: Los Angeles
Population: 103,340

Ancestry	Population	%
Afghan (0)	0	<0.01
African, Sub-Saharan (60)	102	0.10
African (60)	82	0.08
Cape Verdean (0)	0	<0.01
Ethiopian (0)	0	<0.01
Ghanaian (0)	0	<0.01
Kenyan (0)	0	<0.01
Liberian (0)	0	<0.01
Nigerian (0)	0	<0.01
Senegalese (0)	0	<0.01
Sierra Leonean (0)	0	<0.01
Somalian (0)	0	<0.01
South African (0)	20	0.02
Sudanese (0)	0	<0.01
Ugandan (0)	0	<0.01
Zimbabwean (0)	0	<0.01
Other Sub-Saharan African (0)	0	<0.01
Albanian (12)	30	0.03
Alsatian (0)	0	<0.01
American (2,962)	2,962	2.88
Arab (1,402)	1,768	1.72
Arab (334)	383	0.37
Egyptian (157)	244	0.24
Iraqi (0)	0	<0.01
Jordanian (47)	47	0.05
Lebanese (333)	470	0.46
Moroccan (0)	0	<0.01
Palestinian (28)	70	0.07
Syrian (373)	409	0.40
Other Arab (130)	145	0.14
Armenian (11,652)	12,490	12.16
Assyrian/Chaldean/Syriac (49)	74	0.07
Australian (9)	20	0.02
Austrian (115)	450	0.44
Basque (0)	12	0.01
Belgian (93)	176	0.17
Brazilian (34)	49	0.05
British (199)	465	0.45
Bulgarian (84)	84	0.08
Cajun (0)	0	<0.01
Canadian (173)	292	0.28
Carpatho Rusyn (0)	0	<0.01
Celtic (0)	0	<0.01
Croatian (49)	110	0.11
Cypriot (0)	0	<0.01
Czech (95)	271	0.26
Czechoslovakian (93)	156	0.15
Danish (162)	591	0.58
Dutch (72)	1,006	0.98
Eastern European (58)	80	0.08
English (1,652)	6,949	6.76
Estonian (0)	0	<0.01
European (1,096)	1,652	1.61
Finnish (61)	223	0.22
French, ex. Basque (331)	2,066	2.01
French Canadian (116)	424	0.41
German (2,257)	9,613	9.36
German Russian (0)	0	<0.01
Greek (412)	766	0.75
Guyanese (8)	8	0.01
Hungarian (225)	523	0.51
Icelander (0)	12	0.01
Iranian (915)	1,583	1.54
Irish (1,958)	8,539	8.31
Israeli (18)	39	0.04
Italian (3,124)	6,982	6.80
Latvian (15)	15	0.01
Lithuanian (89)	231	0.22
Luxemburger (0)	30	0.03
Macedonian (34)	47	0.05
Maltese (0)	0	<0.01
New Zealander (24)	24	0.02
Northern European (220)	220	0.21
Norwegian (332)	891	0.87
Pennsylvania German (7)	25	0.02
Polish (401)	1,721	1.68
Portuguese (133)	376	0.37
Romanian (83)	222	0.22
Russian (461)	1,617	1.57
Scandinavian (70)	148	0.14
Scotch-Irish (607)	1,680	1.64
Scottish (710)	2,020	1.97
Serbian (198)	198	0.19
Slavic (0)	0	<0.01
Slovak (82)	136	0.13
Slovene (13)	55	0.05
Soviet Union (0)	0	<0.01
Swedish (356)	1,536	1.50
Swiss (69)	339	0.33
Turkish (114)	161	0.16
Ukrainian (151)	288	0.28
Welsh (147)	631	0.61
West Indian, ex. Hispanic (145)	280	0.27
Bahamian (0)	0	<0.01
Barbadian (13)	13	0.01
Belizean (0)	0	<0.01
Bermudan (0)	0	<0.01
British West Indian (0)	0	<0.01
Dutch West Indian (0)	0	<0.01
Haitian (10)	80	0.08
Jamaican (122)	179	0.17
Trinidadian/Tobagonian (0)	0	<0.01
U.S. Virgin Islander (0)	0	<0.01
West Indian (0)	8	0.01
Other West Indian (0)	0	<0.01
Yugoslavian (15)	73	0.07

Hispanic Origin	Population	%
Hispanic or Latino (of any race)	25,310	24.49
Central American, ex. Mexican	4,331	4.19
Costa Rican	199	0.19
Guatemalan	1,238	1.20
Honduran	165	0.16
Nicaraguan	406	0.39
Panamanian	66	0.06
Salvadoran	2,231	2.16
Other Central American	26	0.03
Cuban	1,087	1.05
Dominican Republic	62	0.06
Mexican	14,706	14.23
Puerto Rican	601	0.58
South American	2,548	2.47
Argentinean	406	0.39
Bolivian	208	0.20
Chilean	165	0.16
Colombian	677	0.66
Ecuadorian	376	0.36
Paraguayan	7	0.01
Peruvian	589	0.57
Uruguayan	24	0.02
Venezuelan	65	0.06
Other South American	31	0.03
Other Hispanic or Latino	1,975	1.91

Race*	Population	%
African-American/Black (2,600)	3,478	3.37
Not Hispanic (2,443)	3,098	3.00
Hispanic (157)	380	0.37
American Indian/Alaska Native (486)	1,210	1.17
Not Hispanic (196)	609	0.59
Hispanic (290)	601	0.58
Alaska Athabascan *(Ala. Nat.)* (0)	0	<0.01
Aleut *(Alaska Native)* (1)	1	<0.01
Apache (25)	47	0.05
Arapaho (2)	2	<0.01
Blackfeet (1)	13	0.01
Canadian/French Am. Ind. (0)	1	<0.01
Central American Ind. (1)	5	<0.01
Cherokee (21)	171	0.17
Cheyenne (0)	0	<0.01
Chickasaw (1)	11	0.01
Chippewa (9)	15	0.01
Choctaw (11)	46	0.04
Colville (0)	0	<0.01
Comanche (1)	5	<0.01
Cree (0)	3	<0.01
Creek (7)	19	0.02
Crow (6)	11	0.01
Delaware (2)	2	<0.01
Hopi (4)	6	0.01
Houma (0)	0	<0.01
Inupiat *(Alaska Native)* (1)	1	<0.01
Iroquois (7)	20	0.02
Kiowa (0)	1	<0.01
Lumbee (1)	1	<0.01
Menominee (0)	0	<0.01
Mexican American Ind. (81)	130	0.13
Navajo (25)	35	0.03
Osage (3)	7	0.01
Ottawa (0)	0	<0.01
Paiute (2)	8	0.01
Pima (1)	1	<0.01
Potawatomi (2)	15	0.01
Pueblo (9)	15	0.01
Puget Sound Salish (2)	3	<0.01
Seminole (1)	9	0.01
Shoshone (1)	1	<0.01
Sioux (6)	40	0.04
South American Ind. (12)	23	0.02
Spanish American Ind. (2)	3	<0.01
Tlingit-Haida *(Alaska Native)* (0)	1	<0.01
Tohono O'Odham (5)	7	0.01
Tsimshian *(Alaska Native)* (0)	0	<0.01
Ute (2)	4	<0.01
Yakama (0)	0	<0.01
Yaqui (5)	13	0.01
Yuman (0)	2	<0.01
Yup'ik *(Alaska Native)* (0)	1	<0.01
Asian (12,007)	14,398	13.93
Not Hispanic (11,753)	13,797	13.35
Hispanic (254)	601	0.58
Bangladeshi (15)	17	0.02
Bhutanese (0)	0	<0.01
Burmese (0)	4	<0.01
Cambodian (30)	55	0.05
Chinese, ex. Taiwanese (1,029)	1,520	1.47
Filipino (4,835)	5,612	5.43
Hmong (0)	1	<0.01
Indian (1,502)	1,643	1.59
Indonesian (37)	72	0.07
Japanese (716)	1,102	1.07
Korean (2,140)	2,324	2.25
Laotian (5)	11	0.01
Malaysian (5)	14	0.01
Nepalese (10)	10	0.01
Pakistani (35)	41	0.04
Sri Lankan (62)	82	0.08
Taiwanese (55)	74	0.07
Thai (470)	538	0.52
Vietnamese (673)	763	0.74
Hawaii Native/Pacific Islander (89)	405	0.39
Not Hispanic (76)	332	0.32
Hispanic (13)	73	0.07
Fijian (4)	6	0.01
Guamanian/Chamorro (13)	46	0.04
Marshallese (0)	0	<0.01
Native Hawaiian (28)	150	0.15
Samoan (14)	29	0.03
Tongan (0)	1	<0.01
White (75,167)	79,609	77.04
Not Hispanic (60,265)	63,038	61.00
Hispanic (14,902)	16,571	16.04

*Notes: † The Census 2010 population figure is used to calculate the percentages in the Hispanic Origin and Race categories. Ancestry percentages are based on the 2006-2010 American Community Survey population (not shown); ‡ Numbers in parentheses indicate the number of people reporting a single ancestry; * Numbers in parentheses indicate the number of persons reporting this race alone, not in combination with any other race; Please refer to the Explanation of Data for more information.*

Camarillo

Place Type: City
County: Ventura
Population: 65,201

Ancestry	Population	%
Afghan (0)	0	<0.01
African, Sub-Saharan (89)	147	0.23
African (37)	80	0.13
Cape Verdean (0)	0	<0.01
Ethiopian (0)	0	<0.01
Ghanaian (0)	0	<0.01
Kenyan (0)	0	<0.01
Liberian (0)	0	<0.01
Nigerian (0)	0	<0.01
Senegalese (0)	0	<0.01
Sierra Leonean (0)	0	<0.01
Somalian (24)	24	0.04
South African (28)	43	0.07
Sudanese (0)	0	<0.01
Ugandan (0)	0	<0.01
Zimbabwean (0)	0	<0.01
Other Sub-Saharan African (0)	0	<0.01
Albanian (0)	0	<0.01
Alsatian (0)	0	<0.01
American (2,022)	2,022	3.18
Arab (415)	568	0.89
Arab (196)	233	0.37
Egyptian (61)	61	0.10
Iraqi (0)	15	0.02
Jordanian (0)	0	<0.01
Lebanese (80)	147	0.23
Moroccan (0)	0	<0.01
Palestinian (10)	10	0.02
Syrian (25)	46	0.07
Other Arab (43)	56	0.09
Armenian (269)	390	0.61
Assyrian/Chaldean/Syriac (0)	0	<0.01
Australian (0)	0	<0.01
Austrian (139)	271	0.43
Basque (7)	34	0.05
Belgian (0)	16	0.03
Brazilian (0)	0	<0.01
British (296)	386	0.61
Bulgarian (0)	0	<0.01
Cajun (0)	0	<0.01
Canadian (103)	418	0.66
Carpatho Rusyn (0)	0	<0.01
Celtic (0)	0	<0.01
Croatian (21)	78	0.12
Cypriot (0)	0	<0.01
Czech (83)	214	0.34
Czechoslovakian (6)	42	0.07
Danish (80)	375	0.59
Dutch (345)	1,169	1.84
Eastern European (164)	190	0.30
English (1,755)	7,679	12.07
Estonian (0)	0	<0.01
European (921)	1,152	1.81
Finnish (53)	243	0.38
French, ex. Basque (225)	2,257	3.55
French Canadian (120)	467	0.73
German (2,680)	11,389	17.91
German Russian (0)	0	<0.01
Greek (47)	235	0.37
Guyanese (0)	0	<0.01
Hungarian (85)	338	0.53
Icelander (10)	28	0.04
Iranian (241)	267	0.42
Irish (1,729)	7,412	11.65
Israeli (7)	17	0.03
Italian (1,324)	3,773	5.93
Latvian (0)	0	<0.01
Lithuanian (44)	151	0.24
Luxemburger (0)	7	0.01
Macedonian (0)	49	0.08
Maltese (0)	0	<0.01
New Zealander (11)	11	0.02
Northern European (101)	101	0.16
Norwegian (354)	1,167	1.83
Pennsylvania German (0)	24	0.04
Polish (597)	2,076	3.26
Portuguese (164)	382	0.60
Romanian (146)	185	0.29
Russian (557)	1,682	2.64
Scandinavian (90)	124	0.19
Scotch-Irish (380)	1,198	1.88
Scottish (367)	1,525	2.40
Serbian (0)	0	<0.01
Slavic (28)	42	0.07
Slovak (8)	27	0.04
Slovene (22)	57	0.09
Soviet Union (0)	0	<0.01
Swedish (249)	1,247	1.96
Swiss (63)	219	0.34
Turkish (23)	23	0.04
Ukrainian (55)	186	0.29
Welsh (153)	510	0.80
West Indian, ex. Hispanic (0)	12	0.02
Bahamian (0)	0	<0.01
Barbadian (0)	0	<0.01
Belizean (0)	12	0.02
Bermudan (0)	0	<0.01
British West Indian (0)	0	<0.01
Dutch West Indian (0)	0	<0.01
Haitian (0)	0	<0.01
Jamaican (0)	0	<0.01
Trinidadian/Tobagonian (0)	0	<0.01
U.S. Virgin Islander (0)	0	<0.01
West Indian (0)	0	<0.01
Other West Indian (0)	0	<0.01
Yugoslavian (226)	301	0.47

Hispanic Origin	Population	%
Hispanic or Latino (of any race)	14,958	22.94
Central American, ex. Mexican	502	0.77
Costa Rican	20	0.03
Guatemalan	156	0.24
Honduran	30	0.05
Nicaraguan	84	0.13
Panamanian	27	0.04
Salvadoran	183	0.28
Other Central American	2	<0.01
Cuban	100	0.15
Dominican Republic	12	0.02
Mexican	12,613	19.34
Puerto Rican	271	0.42
South American	487	0.75
Argentinean	88	0.13
Bolivian	24	0.04
Chilean	57	0.09
Colombian	91	0.14
Ecuadorian	52	0.08
Paraguayan	1	<0.01
Peruvian	116	0.18
Uruguayan	9	0.01
Venezuelan	36	0.06
Other South American	13	0.02
Other Hispanic or Latino	973	1.49

Race*	Population	%
African-American/Black (1,216)	1,760	2.70
Not Hispanic (1,106)	1,519	2.33
Hispanic (110)	241	0.37
American Indian/Alaska Native (397)	1,018	1.56
Not Hispanic (139)	521	0.80
Hispanic (258)	497	0.76
Alaska Athabascan *(Ala. Nat.)* (0)	1	<0.01
Aleut *(Alaska Native)* (0)	0	<0.01
Apache (26)	52	0.08
Arapaho (1)	3	<0.01
Blackfeet (4)	19	0.03
Canadian/French Am. Ind. (1)	1	<0.01
Central American Ind. (0)	1	<0.01
Cherokee (26)	162	0.25
Cheyenne (1)	4	0.01
Chickasaw (2)	6	0.01
Chippewa (8)	17	0.03
Choctaw (16)	45	0.07
Colville (2)	6	0.01
Comanche (1)	2	<0.01
Cree (0)	0	<0.01
Creek (2)	7	0.01
Crow (0)	1	<0.01
Delaware (1)	2	<0.01
Hopi (1)	6	0.01
Houma (0)	0	<0.01
Inupiat *(Alaska Native)* (0)	3	<0.01
Iroquois (7)	13	0.02
Kiowa (0)	0	<0.01
Lumbee (0)	1	<0.01
Menominee (0)	0	<0.01
Mexican American Ind. (37)	79	0.12
Navajo (4)	12	0.02
Osage (3)	9	0.01
Ottawa (1)	1	<0.01
Paiute (1)	2	<0.01
Pima (0)	0	<0.01
Potawatomi (10)	13	0.02
Pueblo (4)	12	0.02
Puget Sound Salish (1)	1	<0.01
Seminole (1)	3	<0.01
Shoshone (0)	0	<0.01
Sioux (6)	24	0.04
South American Ind. (0)	1	<0.01
Spanish American Ind. (3)	7	0.01
Tlingit-Haida *(Alaska Native)* (0)	5	0.01
Tohono O'Odham (0)	0	<0.01
Tsimshian *(Alaska Native)* (0)	0	<0.01
Ute (0)	1	<0.01
Yakama (0)	0	<0.01
Yaqui (2)	8	0.01
Yuman (0)	0	<0.01
Yup'ik *(Alaska Native)* (0)	0	<0.01
Asian (6,633)	8,150	12.50
Not Hispanic (6,491)	7,751	11.89
Hispanic (142)	399	0.61
Bangladeshi (17)	20	0.03
Bhutanese (1)	3	<0.01
Burmese (10)	13	0.02
Cambodian (32)	54	0.08
Chinese, ex. Taiwanese (945)	1,306	2.00
Filipino (2,437)	3,087	4.73
Hmong (14)	14	0.02
Indian (795)	876	1.34
Indonesian (22)	61	0.09
Japanese (777)	1,266	1.94
Korean (614)	768	1.18
Laotian (27)	39	0.06
Malaysian (3)	12	0.02
Nepalese (5)	5	0.01
Pakistani (37)	48	0.07
Sri Lankan (9)	12	0.02
Taiwanese (113)	133	0.20
Thai (72)	110	0.17
Vietnamese (451)	516	0.79
Hawaii Native/Pacific Islander (116)	365	0.56
Not Hispanic (107)	307	0.47
Hispanic (9)	58	0.09
Fijian (3)	3	<0.01
Guamanian/Chamorro (48)	91	0.14
Marshallese (0)	0	<0.01
Native Hawaiian (23)	127	0.19
Samoan (24)	55	0.08
Tongan (6)	9	0.01
White (48,947)	51,689	79.28
Not Hispanic (40,324)	42,083	64.54
Hispanic (8,623)	9,606	14.73

*Notes: † The Census 2010 population figure is used to calculate the percentages in the Hispanic Origin and Race categories. Ancestry percentages are based on the 2006-2010 American Community Survey population (not shown); ‡ Numbers in parentheses indicate the number of people reporting a single ancestry; * Numbers in parentheses indicate the number of persons reporting this race alone, not in combination with any other race; Please refer to the Explanation of Data for more information.*

Carlsbad

Place Type: City
County: San Diego
Population: 105,328

Ancestry	Population	%
Afghan (278)	302	0.30
African, Sub-Saharan (21)	90	0.09
African (13)	22	0.02
Cape Verdean (0)	0	<0.01
Ethiopian (0)	0	<0.01
Ghanaian (0)	0	<0.01
Kenyan (0)	0	<0.01
Liberian (0)	0	<0.01
Nigerian (0)	0	<0.01
Senegalese (0)	0	<0.01
Sierra Leonean (0)	0	<0.01
Somalian (0)	0	<0.01
South African (8)	68	0.07
Sudanese (0)	0	<0.01
Ugandan (0)	0	<0.01
Zimbabwean (0)	0	<0.01
Other Sub-Saharan African (0)	0	<0.01
Albanian (28)	40	0.04
Alsatian (0)	0	<0.01
American (2,866)	2,866	2.87
Arab (429)	811	0.81
Arab (35)	61	0.06
Egyptian (85)	96	0.10
Iraqi (0)	0	<0.01
Jordanian (0)	0	<0.01
Lebanese (124)	443	0.44
Moroccan (0)	9	0.01
Palestinian (23)	23	0.02
Syrian (65)	82	0.08
Other Arab (97)	97	0.10
Armenian (129)	265	0.27
Assyrian/Chaldean/Syriac (0)	0	<0.01
Australian (92)	101	0.10
Austrian (179)	596	0.60
Basque (0)	152	0.15
Belgian (17)	82	0.08
Brazilian (76)	166	0.17
British (286)	710	0.71
Bulgarian (30)	30	0.03
Cajun (0)	0	<0.01
Canadian (216)	525	0.53
Carpatho Rusyn (0)	0	<0.01
Celtic (20)	44	0.04
Croatian (68)	257	0.26
Cypriot (18)	18	0.02
Czech (114)	593	0.59
Czechoslovakian (56)	189	0.19
Danish (429)	1,413	1.42
Dutch (569)	1,883	1.89
Eastern European (216)	267	0.27
English (6,452)	16,407	16.45
Estonian (9)	22	0.02
European (2,439)	2,706	2.71
Finnish (109)	298	0.30
French, ex. Basque (401)	3,531	3.54
French Canadian (202)	850	0.85
German (4,403)	17,307	17.35
German Russian (0)	0	<0.01
Greek (160)	619	0.62
Guyanese (0)	10	0.01
Hungarian (289)	885	0.89
Icelander (8)	83	0.08
Iranian (469)	598	0.60
Irish (3,209)	13,677	13.71
Israeli (15)	54	0.05
Italian (2,890)	7,825	7.84
Latvian (38)	70	0.07
Lithuanian (74)	212	0.21
Luxemburger (0)	24	0.02
Macedonian (116)	127	0.13
Maltese (0)	45	0.05
New Zealander (0)	8	0.01
Northern European (91)	91	0.09
Norwegian (804)	2,375	2.38
Pennsylvania German (19)	19	0.02
Polish (1,202)	3,666	3.68
Portuguese (181)	696	0.70
Romanian (56)	146	0.15
Russian (879)	2,346	2.35
Scandinavian (242)	325	0.33
Scotch-Irish (511)	1,837	1.84
Scottish (643)	2,720	2.73
Serbian (235)	288	0.29
Slavic (29)	93	0.09
Slovak (63)	151	0.15
Slovene (9)	18	0.02
Soviet Union (0)	0	<0.01
Swedish (701)	2,833	2.84
Swiss (135)	577	0.58
Turkish (58)	94	0.09
Ukrainian (554)	832	0.83
Welsh (184)	963	0.97
West Indian, ex. Hispanic (0)	9	0.01
Bahamian (0)	0	<0.01
Barbadian (0)	0	<0.01
Belizean (0)	9	0.01
Bermudan (0)	0	<0.01
British West Indian (0)	0	<0.01
Dutch West Indian (0)	0	<0.01
Haitian (0)	0	<0.01
Jamaican (0)	0	<0.01
Trinidadian/Tobagonian (0)	0	<0.01
U.S. Virgin Islander (0)	0	<0.01
West Indian (0)	0	<0.01
Other West Indian (0)	0	<0.01
Yugoslavian (28)	191	0.19

Hispanic Origin	Population	%
Hispanic or Latino (of any race)	13,988	13.28
Central American, ex. Mexican	471	0.45
Costa Rican	41	0.04
Guatemalan	129	0.12
Honduran	56	0.05
Nicaraguan	69	0.07
Panamanian	52	0.05
Salvadoran	117	0.11
Other Central American	7	0.01
Cuban	213	0.20
Dominican Republic	34	0.03
Mexican	10,695	10.15
Puerto Rican	449	0.43
South American	898	0.85
Argentinean	124	0.12
Bolivian	35	0.03
Chilean	113	0.11
Colombian	208	0.20
Ecuadorian	90	0.09
Paraguayan	14	0.01
Peruvian	221	0.21
Uruguayan	4	<0.01
Venezuelan	67	0.06
Other South American	22	0.02
Other Hispanic or Latino	1,228	1.17

Race*	Population	%
African-American/Black (1,379)	2,048	1.94
Not Hispanic (1,232)	1,796	1.71
Hispanic (147)	252	0.24
American Indian/Alaska Native (514)	1,111	1.05
Not Hispanic (271)	665	0.63
Hispanic (243)	446	0.42
Alaska Athabascan *(Ala. Nat.)* (0)	0	<0.01
Aleut *(Alaska Native)* (1)	2	<0.01
Apache (8)	30	0.03
Arapaho (0)	0	<0.01
Blackfeet (1)	16	0.02
Canadian/French Am. Ind. (2)	3	<0.01
Central American Ind. (0)	0	<0.01
Cherokee (40)	163	0.15
Cheyenne (0)	0	<0.01
Chickasaw (5)	7	0.01
Chippewa (9)	17	0.02
Choctaw (17)	41	0.04
Colville (0)	0	<0.01
Comanche (1)	3	<0.01
Cree (0)	1	<0.01
Creek (3)	5	<0.01
Crow (1)	2	<0.01
Delaware (2)	2	<0.01
Hopi (0)	1	<0.01
Houma (0)	0	<0.01
Inupiat *(Alaska Native)* (0)	1	<0.01
Iroquois (7)	17	0.02
Kiowa (1)	1	<0.01
Lumbee (0)	3	<0.01
Menominee (0)	0	<0.01
Mexican American Ind. (64)	81	0.08
Navajo (8)	20	0.02
Osage (2)	6	0.01
Ottawa (3)	3	<0.01
Paiute (1)	7	0.01
Pima (0)	2	<0.01
Potawatomi (5)	13	0.01
Pueblo (5)	8	0.01
Puget Sound Salish (0)	0	<0.01
Seminole (0)	6	0.01
Shoshone (2)	3	<0.01
Sioux (7)	20	0.02
South American Ind. (7)	17	0.02
Spanish American Ind. (1)	8	0.01
Tlingit-Haida *(Alaska Native)* (0)	0	<0.01
Tohono O'Odham (1)	2	<0.01
Tsimshian *(Alaska Native)* (0)	0	<0.01
Ute (1)	3	<0.01
Yakama (0)	1	<0.01
Yaqui (5)	7	0.01
Yuman (1)	1	<0.01
Yup'ik *(Alaska Native)* (0)	0	<0.01
Asian (7,460)	10,058	9.55
Not Hispanic (7,336)	9,624	9.14
Hispanic (124)	434	0.41
Bangladeshi (27)	27	0.03
Bhutanese (0)	0	<0.01
Burmese (6)	6	0.01
Cambodian (33)	41	0.04
Chinese, ex. Taiwanese (1,815)	2,420	2.30
Filipino (1,225)	2,049	1.95
Hmong (2)	3	<0.01
Indian (1,195)	1,401	1.33
Indonesian (27)	84	0.08
Japanese (852)	1,528	1.45
Korean (926)	1,173	1.11
Laotian (16)	27	0.03
Malaysian (5)	11	0.01
Nepalese (2)	3	<0.01
Pakistani (49)	63	0.06
Sri Lankan (8)	12	0.01
Taiwanese (182)	215	0.20
Thai (89)	132	0.13
Vietnamese (675)	817	0.78
Hawaii Native/Pacific Islander (198)	607	0.58
Not Hispanic (182)	500	0.47
Hispanic (16)	107	0.10
Fijian (5)	11	0.01
Guamanian/Chamorro (45)	103	0.10
Marshallese (0)	0	<0.01
Native Hawaiian (56)	271	0.26
Samoan (51)	122	0.12
Tongan (1)	16	0.02
White (87,205)	91,202	86.59
Not Hispanic (78,879)	81,860	77.72
Hispanic (8,326)	9,342	8.87

*Notes: † The Census 2010 population figure is used to calculate the percentages in the Hispanic Origin and Race categories. Ancestry percentages are based on the 2006-2010 American Community Survey population (not shown); ‡ Numbers in parentheses indicate the number of people reporting a single ancestry; * Numbers in parentheses indicate the number of persons reporting this race alone, not in combination with any other race; Please refer to the Explanation of Data for more information.*

Carmichael

Place Type: CDP
County: Sacramento
Population: 61,762

Ancestry	Population	%
Afghan (0)	0	<0.01
African, Sub-Saharan (467)	794	1.28
African (276)	500	0.81
Cape Verdean (0)	22	0.04
Ethiopian (0)	0	<0.01
Ghanaian (0)	0	<0.01
Kenyan (0)	0	<0.01
Liberian (0)	0	<0.01
Nigerian (0)	0	<0.01
Senegalese (0)	0	<0.01
Sierra Leonean (0)	0	<0.01
Somalian (0)	0	<0.01
South African (128)	152	0.25
Sudanese (0)	0	<0.01
Ugandan (0)	0	<0.01
Zimbabwean (0)	0	<0.01
Other Sub-Saharan African (63)	120	0.19
Albanian (102)	102	0.17
Alsatian (0)	0	<0.01
American (1,894)	1,894	3.06
Arab (293)	407	0.66
Arab (45)	73	0.12
Egyptian (0)	0	<0.01
Iraqi (12)	12	0.02
Jordanian (24)	24	0.04
Lebanese (42)	73	0.12
Moroccan (59)	87	0.14
Palestinian (0)	0	<0.01
Syrian (8)	35	0.06
Other Arab (103)	103	0.17
Armenian (240)	266	0.43
Assyrian/Chaldean/Syriac (0)	0	<0.01
Australian (0)	12	0.02
Austrian (33)	94	0.15
Basque (24)	123	0.20
Belgian (36)	145	0.23
Brazilian (0)	0	<0.01
British (73)	280	0.45
Bulgarian (30)	30	0.05
Cajun (0)	0	<0.01
Canadian (22)	68	0.11
Carpatho Rusyn (0)	0	<0.01
Celtic (8)	20	0.03
Croatian (46)	150	0.24
Cypriot (0)	0	<0.01
Czech (63)	271	0.44
Czechoslovakian (50)	133	0.22
Danish (154)	503	0.81
Dutch (151)	1,299	2.10
Eastern European (56)	56	0.09
English (2,303)	9,670	15.65
Estonian (0)	0	<0.01
European (941)	1,322	2.14
Finnish (62)	134	0.22
French, ex. Basque (234)	2,078	3.36
French Canadian (97)	207	0.33
German (2,567)	11,501	18.61
German Russian (11)	11	0.02
Greek (158)	337	0.55
Guyanese (0)	0	<0.01
Hungarian (87)	302	0.49
Icelander (38)	88	0.14
Iranian (256)	420	0.68
Irish (2,308)	9,857	15.95
Israeli (0)	24	0.04
Italian (1,860)	4,932	7.98
Latvian (0)	11	0.02
Lithuanian (13)	64	0.10
Luxemburger (0)	0	<0.01
Macedonian (0)	0	<0.01
Maltese (7)	7	0.01
New Zealander (0)	0	<0.01
Northern European (94)	105	0.17
Norwegian (278)	1,301	2.10
Pennsylvania German (0)	43	0.07
Polish (310)	1,041	1.68
Portuguese (483)	1,497	2.42
Romanian (455)	629	1.02
Russian (515)	1,052	1.70
Scandinavian (53)	149	0.24
Scotch-Irish (413)	1,728	2.80
Scottish (448)	1,827	2.96
Serbian (47)	47	0.08
Slavic (29)	55	0.09
Slovak (20)	43	0.07
Slovene (16)	50	0.08
Soviet Union (0)	0	<0.01
Swedish (366)	1,233	1.99
Swiss (103)	509	0.82
Turkish (58)	80	0.13
Ukrainian (581)	819	1.33
Welsh (204)	664	1.07
West Indian, ex. Hispanic (14)	110	0.18
Bahamian (0)	0	<0.01
Barbadian (0)	0	<0.01
Belizean (0)	33	0.05
Bermudan (0)	0	<0.01
British West Indian (2)	12	0.02
Dutch West Indian (0)	0	<0.01
Haitian (0)	17	0.03
Jamaican (0)	36	0.06
Trinidadian/Tobagonian (0)	0	<0.01
U.S. Virgin Islander (0)	0	<0.01
West Indian (12)	12	0.02
Other West Indian (0)	0	<0.01
Yugoslavian (250)	272	0.44

Hispanic Origin	Population	%
Hispanic or Latino (of any race)	7,218	11.69
Central American, ex. Mexican	372	0.60
Costa Rican	26	0.04
Guatemalan	87	0.14
Honduran	18	0.03
Nicaraguan	60	0.10
Panamanian	28	0.05
Salvadoran	138	0.22
Other Central American	15	0.02
Cuban	90	0.15
Dominican Republic	19	0.03
Mexican	5,130	8.31
Puerto Rican	335	0.54
South American	257	0.42
Argentinean	49	0.08
Bolivian	11	0.02
Chilean	28	0.05
Colombian	73	0.12
Ecuadorian	19	0.03
Paraguayan	2	<0.01
Peruvian	54	0.09
Uruguayan	8	0.01
Venezuelan	9	0.01
Other South American	4	0.01
Other Hispanic or Latino	1,015	1.64

Race*	Population	%
African-American/Black (2,972)	4,101	6.64
Not Hispanic (2,795)	3,694	5.98
Hispanic (177)	407	0.66
American Indian/Alaska Native (546)	1,530	2.48
Not Hispanic (382)	1,114	1.80
Hispanic (164)	416	0.67
Alaska Athabascan *(Ala. Nat.)* (2)	2	<0.01
Aleut *(Alaska Native)* (0)	2	<0.01
Apache (23)	51	0.08
Arapaho (0)	1	<0.01
Blackfeet (11)	65	0.11
Canadian/French Am. Ind. (0)	7	0.01
Central American Ind. (0)	2	<0.01
Cherokee (61)	303	0.49
Cheyenne (2)	9	0.01
Chickasaw (9)	22	0.04
Chippewa (16)	38	0.06
Choctaw (19)	54	0.09
Colville (3)	4	0.01
Comanche (1)	5	0.01
Cree (0)	4	0.01
Creek (5)	26	0.04
Crow (1)	3	<0.01
Delaware (0)	5	0.01
Hopi (1)	1	<0.01
Houma (0)	0	<0.01
Inupiat *(Alaska Native)* (2)	8	0.01
Iroquois (10)	24	0.04
Kiowa (3)	3	<0.01
Lumbee (3)	3	<0.01
Menominee (0)	1	<0.01
Mexican American Ind. (21)	45	0.07
Navajo (18)	38	0.06
Osage (0)	2	<0.01
Ottawa (4)	5	0.01
Paiute (3)	6	0.01
Pima (0)	0	<0.01
Potawatomi (9)	17	0.03
Pueblo (8)	14	0.02
Puget Sound Salish (5)	5	0.01
Seminole (5)	10	0.02
Shoshone (7)	14	0.02
Sioux (13)	42	0.07
South American Ind. (0)	2	<0.01
Spanish American Ind. (1)	2	<0.01
Tlingit-Haida *(Alaska Native)* (2)	7	0.01
Tohono O'Odham (2)	4	0.01
Tsimshian *(Alaska Native)* (1)	1	<0.01
Ute (2)	2	<0.01
Yakama (2)	4	0.01
Yaqui (8)	11	0.02
Yuman (4)	4	0.01
Yup'ik *(Alaska Native)* (0)	0	<0.01
Asian (2,653)	3,865	6.26
Not Hispanic (2,546)	3,563	5.77
Hispanic (107)	302	0.49
Bangladeshi (2)	2	<0.01
Bhutanese (20)	24	0.04
Burmese (5)	6	0.01
Cambodian (16)	31	0.05
Chinese, ex. Taiwanese (505)	725	1.17
Filipino (566)	1,055	1.71
Hmong (43)	49	0.08
Indian (330)	408	0.66
Indonesian (31)	45	0.07
Japanese (319)	643	1.04
Korean (363)	430	0.70
Laotian (15)	26	0.04
Malaysian (2)	8	0.01
Nepalese (7)	12	0.02
Pakistani (22)	31	0.05
Sri Lankan (9)	9	0.01
Taiwanese (29)	29	0.05
Thai (26)	49	0.08
Vietnamese (198)	240	0.39
Hawaii Native/Pacific Islander (287)	532	0.86
Not Hispanic (250)	429	0.69
Hispanic (37)	103	0.17
Fijian (50)	61	0.10
Guamanian/Chamorro (67)	115	0.19
Marshallese (2)	2	<0.01
Native Hawaiian (62)	168	0.27
Samoan (60)	103	0.17
Tongan (16)	28	0.05
White (49,776)	52,877	85.61
Not Hispanic (45,979)	48,212	78.06
Hispanic (3,797)	4,665	7.55

*Notes: † The Census 2010 population figure is used to calculate the percentages in the Hispanic Origin and Race categories. Ancestry percentages are based on the 2006-2010 American Community Survey population (not shown); ‡ Numbers in parentheses indicate the number of people reporting a single ancestry; * Numbers in parentheses indicate the number of persons reporting this race alone, not in combination with any other race; Please refer to the Explanation of Data for more information.*

Carson

Place Type: City
County: Los Angeles
Population: 91,714

Ancestry	Population	%
Afghan (61)	61	0.07
African, Sub-Saharan (3,966)	4,806	5.26
African (3,517)	4,332	4.74
Cape Verdean (0)	0	<0.01
Ethiopian (64)	79	0.09
Ghanaian (0)	0	<0.01
Kenyan (0)	0	<0.01
Liberian (0)	0	<0.01
Nigerian (359)	369	0.40
Senegalese (0)	0	<0.01
Sierra Leonean (0)	0	<0.01
Somalian (26)	26	0.03
South African (0)	0	<0.01
Sudanese (0)	0	<0.01
Ugandan (0)	0	<0.01
Zimbabwean (0)	0	<0.01
Other Sub-Saharan African (0)	0	<0.01
Albanian (0)	0	<0.01
Alsatian (0)	0	<0.01
American (4,135)	4,135	4.53
Arab (133)	210	0.23
Arab (18)	50	0.05
Egyptian (10)	10	0.01
Iraqi (0)	0	<0.01
Jordanian (44)	69	0.08
Lebanese (0)	12	0.01
Moroccan (0)	0	<0.01
Palestinian (38)	46	0.05
Syrian (23)	23	0.03
Other Arab (0)	0	<0.01
Armenian (0)	16	0.02
Assyrian/Chaldean/Syriac (0)	0	<0.01
Australian (10)	10	0.01
Austrian (15)	15	0.02
Basque (0)	0	<0.01
Belgian (0)	31	0.03
Brazilian (13)	13	0.01
British (54)	90	0.10
Bulgarian (0)	0	<0.01
Cajun (0)	0	<0.01
Canadian (31)	70	0.08
Carpatho Rusyn (0)	0	<0.01
Celtic (0)	0	<0.01
Croatian (0)	27	0.03
Cypriot (0)	0	<0.01
Czech (20)	65	0.07
Czechoslovakian (0)	0	<0.01
Danish (6)	32	0.04
Dutch (40)	147	0.16
Eastern European (0)	0	<0.01
English (261)	1,196	1.31
Estonian (0)	0	<0.01
European (77)	176	0.19
Finnish (11)	59	0.06
French, ex. Basque (272)	805	0.88
French Canadian (39)	78	0.09
German (401)	2,300	2.52
German Russian (31)	88	0.10
Greek (20)	29	0.03
Guyanese (0)	0	<0.01
Hungarian (12)	32	0.04
Icelander (0)	0	<0.01
Iranian (19)	19	0.02
Irish (179)	1,115	1.22
Israeli (0)	0	<0.01
Italian (235)	1,033	1.13
Latvian (0)	0	<0.01
Lithuanian (0)	0	<0.01
Luxemburger (0)	0	<0.01
Macedonian (0)	0	<0.01
Maltese (0)	0	<0.01
New Zealander (0)	0	<0.01
Northern European (0)	0	<0.01
Norwegian (61)	227	0.25
Pennsylvania German (0)	0	<0.01
Polish (139)	248	0.27
Portuguese (42)	117	0.13
Romanian (0)	14	0.02
Russian (40)	52	0.06
Scandinavian (0)	0	<0.01
Scotch-Irish (94)	313	0.34
Scottish (35)	246	0.27
Serbian (0)	0	<0.01
Slavic (4)	4	<0.01
Slovak (23)	31	0.03
Slovene (0)	0	<0.01
Soviet Union (0)	0	<0.01
Swedish (40)	222	0.24
Swiss (0)	10	0.01
Turkish (19)	19	0.02
Ukrainian (16)	74	0.08
Welsh (13)	23	0.03
West Indian, ex. Hispanic (203)	316	0.35
Bahamian (0)	0	<0.01
Barbadian (0)	25	0.03
Belizean (44)	47	0.05
Bermudan (0)	0	<0.01
British West Indian (0)	0	<0.01
Dutch West Indian (0)	0	<0.01
Haitian (0)	0	<0.01
Jamaican (159)	198	0.22
Trinidadian/Tobagonian (0)	0	<0.01
U.S. Virgin Islander (0)	0	<0.01
West Indian (0)	46	0.05
Other West Indian (0)	0	<0.01
Yugoslavian (0)	0	<0.01

Hispanic Origin	Population	%
Hispanic or Latino (of any race)	35,417	38.62
Central American, ex. Mexican	2,402	2.62
Costa Rican	88	0.10
Guatemalan	896	0.98
Honduran	170	0.19
Nicaraguan	113	0.12
Panamanian	81	0.09
Salvadoran	1,033	1.13
Other Central American	21	0.02
Cuban	274	0.30
Dominican Republic	24	0.03
Mexican	29,896	32.60
Puerto Rican	576	0.63
South American	627	0.68
Argentinean	69	0.08
Bolivian	14	0.02
Chilean	48	0.05
Colombian	110	0.12
Ecuadorian	139	0.15
Paraguayan	8	0.01
Peruvian	204	0.22
Uruguayan	2	<0.01
Venezuelan	18	0.02
Other South American	15	0.02
Other Hispanic or Latino	1,618	1.76

Race*	Population	%
African-American/Black (21,856)	23,090	25.18
Not Hispanic (21,385)	22,263	24.27
Hispanic (471)	827	0.90
American Indian/Alaska Native (518)	1,207	1.32
Not Hispanic (152)	581	0.63
Hispanic (366)	626	0.68
Alaska Athabascan *(Ala. Nat.)* (0)	0	<0.01
Aleut *(Alaska Native)* (0)	1	<0.01
Apache (15)	36	0.04
Arapaho (8)	8	0.01
Blackfeet (1)	43	0.05
Canadian/French Am. Ind. (1)	1	<0.01
Central American Ind. (14)	16	0.02
Cherokee (21)	134	0.15
Cheyenne (0)	0	<0.01
Chickasaw (0)	2	<0.01
Chippewa (6)	7	0.01
Choctaw (6)	50	0.05
Colville (0)	0	<0.01
Comanche (0)	0	<0.01
Cree (0)	1	<0.01
Creek (2)	20	0.02
Crow (0)	0	<0.01
Delaware (2)	2	<0.01
Hopi (0)	0	<0.01
Houma (0)	2	<0.01
Inupiat *(Alaska Native)* (0)	1	<0.01
Iroquois (0)	1	<0.01
Kiowa (0)	0	<0.01
Lumbee (0)	1	<0.01
Menominee (0)	0	<0.01
Mexican American Ind. (66)	105	0.11
Navajo (30)	49	0.05
Osage (1)	3	<0.01
Ottawa (1)	7	0.01
Paiute (1)	4	<0.01
Pima (0)	2	<0.01
Potawatomi (1)	6	0.01
Pueblo (3)	9	0.01
Puget Sound Salish (0)	0	<0.01
Seminole (0)	4	<0.01
Shoshone (3)	3	<0.01
Sioux (16)	30	0.03
South American Ind. (1)	8	0.01
Spanish American Ind. (13)	17	0.02
Tlingit-Haida *(Alaska Native)* (0)	2	<0.01
Tohono O'Odham (0)	2	<0.01
Tsimshian *(Alaska Native)* (0)	0	<0.01
Ute (4)	6	0.01
Yakama (0)	0	<0.01
Yaqui (11)	27	0.03
Yuman (0)	1	<0.01
Yup'ik *(Alaska Native)* (0)	0	<0.01
Asian (23,522)	25,296	27.58
Not Hispanic (23,105)	24,363	26.56
Hispanic (417)	933	1.02
Bangladeshi (9)	10	0.01
Bhutanese (0)	0	<0.01
Burmese (4)	7	0.01
Cambodian (209)	236	0.26
Chinese, ex. Taiwanese (397)	719	0.78
Filipino (20,092)	21,539	23.48
Hmong (1)	2	<0.01
Indian (275)	381	0.42
Indonesian (34)	69	0.08
Japanese (730)	1,079	1.18
Korean (754)	822	0.90
Laotian (15)	37	0.04
Malaysian (2)	8	0.01
Nepalese (19)	23	0.03
Pakistani (86)	92	0.10
Sri Lankan (47)	47	0.05
Taiwanese (28)	41	0.04
Thai (61)	94	0.10
Vietnamese (325)	417	0.45
Hawaii Native/Pacific Islander (2,386)	3,088	3.37
Not Hispanic (2,291)	2,773	3.02
Hispanic (95)	315	0.34
Fijian (33)	43	0.05
Guamanian/Chamorro (148)	261	0.28
Marshallese (0)	0	<0.01
Native Hawaiian (109)	355	0.39
Samoan (1,982)	2,352	2.56
Tongan (24)	40	0.04
White (21,864)	24,707	26.94
Not Hispanic (7,022)	8,238	8.98
Hispanic (14,842)	16,469	17.96

*Notes: † The Census 2010 population figure is used to calculate the percentages in the Hispanic Origin and Race categories. Ancestry percentages are based on the 2006-2010 American Community Survey population (not shown); ‡ Numbers in parentheses indicate the number of people reporting a single ancestry; * Numbers in parentheses indicate the number of persons reporting this race alone, not in combination with any other race; Please refer to the Explanation of Data for more information.*

Castro Valley

Place Type: CDP
County: Alameda
Population: 61,388

Ancestry	Population	%
Afghan (316)	316	0.52
African, Sub-Saharan (586)	638	1.05
African (422)	461	0.76
Cape Verdean (0)	0	<0.01
Ethiopian (13)	13	0.02
Ghanaian (0)	0	<0.01
Kenyan (29)	42	0.07
Liberian (0)	0	<0.01
Nigerian (122)	122	0.20
Senegalese (0)	0	<0.01
Sierra Leonean (0)	0	<0.01
Somalian (0)	0	<0.01
South African (0)	0	<0.01
Sudanese (0)	0	<0.01
Ugandan (0)	0	<0.01
Zimbabwean (0)	0	<0.01
Other Sub-Saharan African (0)	0	<0.01
Albanian (0)	0	<0.01
Alsatian (0)	0	<0.01
American (1,191)	1,191	1.96
Arab (364)	530	0.87
Arab (35)	76	0.13
Egyptian (134)	151	0.25
Iraqi (0)	0	<0.01
Jordanian (66)	66	0.11
Lebanese (24)	35	0.06
Moroccan (0)	0	<0.01
Palestinian (11)	55	0.09
Syrian (9)	51	0.08
Other Arab (85)	96	0.16
Armenian (79)	142	0.23
Assyrian/Chaldean/Syriac (21)	21	0.03
Australian (0)	0	<0.01
Austrian (105)	230	0.38
Basque (0)	0	<0.01
Belgian (41)	216	0.36
Brazilian (0)	20	0.03
British (226)	363	0.60
Bulgarian (0)	0	<0.01
Cajun (0)	0	<0.01
Canadian (24)	60	0.10
Carpatho Rusyn (0)	0	<0.01
Celtic (0)	21	0.03
Croatian (29)	101	0.17
Cypriot (0)	0	<0.01
Czech (92)	276	0.46
Czechoslovakian (12)	28	0.05
Danish (141)	720	1.19
Dutch (162)	946	1.56
Eastern European (24)	24	0.04
English (1,294)	5,839	9.63
Estonian (21)	21	0.03
European (1,135)	1,372	2.26
Finnish (26)	56	0.09
French, ex. Basque (238)	1,685	2.78
French Canadian (67)	288	0.48
German (1,613)	7,285	12.02
German Russian (0)	0	<0.01
Greek (233)	409	0.67
Guyanese (0)	0	<0.01
Hungarian (199)	334	0.55
Icelander (0)	21	0.03
Iranian (330)	410	0.68
Irish (1,306)	6,837	11.28
Israeli (0)	40	0.07
Italian (1,484)	4,134	6.82
Latvian (0)	30	0.05
Lithuanian (101)	180	0.30
Luxemburger (0)	0	<0.01
Macedonian (0)	0	<0.01
Maltese (13)	41	0.07
New Zealander (0)	0	<0.01
Northern European (19)	46	0.08
Norwegian (200)	1,178	1.94
Pennsylvania German (0)	3	<0.01
Polish (227)	719	1.19
Portuguese (1,246)	2,665	4.40
Romanian (61)	112	0.18
Russian (429)	777	1.28
Scandinavian (32)	77	0.13
Scotch-Irish (195)	1,119	1.85
Scottish (413)	1,147	1.89
Serbian (12)	23	0.04
Slavic (0)	0	<0.01
Slovak (0)	54	0.09
Slovene (0)	0	<0.01
Soviet Union (0)	0	<0.01
Swedish (151)	738	1.22
Swiss (46)	280	0.46
Turkish (0)	21	0.03
Ukrainian (135)	177	0.29
Welsh (37)	351	0.58
West Indian, ex. Hispanic (111)	158	0.26
Bahamian (0)	0	<0.01
Barbadian (0)	0	<0.01
Belizean (51)	51	0.08
Bermudan (0)	0	<0.01
British West Indian (0)	0	<0.01
Dutch West Indian (0)	0	<0.01
Haitian (0)	0	<0.01
Jamaican (60)	60	0.10
Trinidadian/Tobagonian (0)	0	<0.01
U.S. Virgin Islander (0)	0	<0.01
West Indian (0)	47	0.08
Other West Indian (0)	0	<0.01
Yugoslavian (132)	161	0.27

Hispanic Origin	Population	%
Hispanic or Latino (of any race)	10,689	17.41
Central American, ex. Mexican	984	1.60
Costa Rican	27	0.04
Guatemalan	137	0.22
Honduran	36	0.06
Nicaraguan	335	0.55
Panamanian	23	0.04
Salvadoran	403	0.66
Other Central American	23	0.04
Cuban	90	0.15
Dominican Republic	12	0.02
Mexican	6,929	11.29
Puerto Rican	665	1.08
South American	522	0.85
Argentinean	53	0.09
Bolivian	22	0.04
Chilean	39	0.06
Colombian	81	0.13
Ecuadorian	26	0.04
Paraguayan	0	<0.01
Peruvian	284	0.46
Uruguayan	2	<0.01
Venezuelan	12	0.02
Other South American	3	<0.01
Other Hispanic or Latino	1,487	2.42

Race*	Population	%
African-American/Black (4,260)	5,171	8.42
Not Hispanic (4,064)	4,740	7.72
Hispanic (196)	431	0.70
American Indian/Alaska Native (329)	1,106	1.80
Not Hispanic (160)	659	1.07
Hispanic (169)	447	0.73
Alaska Athabascan *(Ala. Nat.)* (0)	0	<0.01
Aleut *(Alaska Native)* (3)	6	0.01
Apache (24)	70	0.11
Arapaho (0)	0	<0.01
Blackfeet (13)	46	0.07
Canadian/French Am. Ind. (0)	7	0.01
Central American Ind. (1)	1	<0.01
Cherokee (30)	190	0.31
Cheyenne (2)	8	0.01
Chickasaw (1)	14	0.02
Chippewa (8)	21	0.03
Choctaw (27)	68	0.11
Colville (0)	0	<0.01
Comanche (3)	3	<0.01
Cree (0)	3	<0.01
Creek (1)	3	<0.01
Crow (0)	0	<0.01
Delaware (0)	0	<0.01
Hopi (1)	2	<0.01
Houma (0)	0	<0.01
Inupiat *(Alaska Native)* (1)	3	<0.01
Iroquois (1)	9	0.01
Kiowa (3)	6	0.01
Lumbee (0)	0	<0.01
Menominee (0)	0	<0.01
Mexican American Ind. (35)	63	0.10
Navajo (8)	21	0.03
Osage (0)	2	<0.01
Ottawa (0)	0	<0.01
Paiute (3)	7	0.01
Pima (3)	4	0.01
Potawatomi (1)	2	<0.01
Pueblo (1)	7	0.01
Puget Sound Salish (0)	2	<0.01
Seminole (0)	4	0.01
Shoshone (1)	2	<0.01
Sioux (9)	38	0.06
South American Ind. (6)	13	0.02
Spanish American Ind. (1)	3	<0.01
Tlingit-Haida *(Alaska Native)* (0)	4	0.01
Tohono O'Odham (0)	4	0.01
Tsimshian *(Alaska Native)* (0)	0	<0.01
Ute (0)	1	<0.01
Yakama (0)	0	<0.01
Yaqui (0)	8	0.01
Yuman (0)	0	<0.01
Yup'ik *(Alaska Native)* (0)	0	<0.01
Asian (13,140)	15,080	24.57
Not Hispanic (12,975)	14,567	23.73
Hispanic (165)	513	0.84
Bangladeshi (13)	13	0.02
Bhutanese (0)	0	<0.01
Burmese (12)	13	0.02
Cambodian (103)	126	0.21
Chinese, ex. Taiwanese (6,919)	7,718	12.57
Filipino (1,938)	2,794	4.55
Hmong (6)	6	0.01
Indian (1,008)	1,177	1.92
Indonesian (57)	90	0.15
Japanese (536)	1,009	1.64
Korean (969)	1,088	1.77
Laotian (61)	86	0.14
Malaysian (8)	29	0.05
Nepalese (52)	53	0.09
Pakistani (42)	55	0.09
Sri Lankan (12)	13	0.02
Taiwanese (139)	161	0.26
Thai (57)	77	0.13
Vietnamese (673)	826	1.35
Hawaii Native/Pacific Islander (417)	818	1.33
Not Hispanic (374)	688	1.12
Hispanic (43)	130	0.21
Fijian (85)	110	0.18
Guamanian/Chamorro (57)	112	0.18
Marshallese (0)	0	<0.01
Native Hawaiian (57)	258	0.42
Samoan (48)	81	0.13
Tongan (99)	129	0.21
White (35,602)	38,920	63.40
Not Hispanic (30,398)	32,622	53.14
Hispanic (5,204)	6,298	10.26

*Notes: † The Census 2010 population figure is used to calculate the percentages in the Hispanic Origin and Race categories. Ancestry percentages are based on the 2006-2010 American Community Survey population (not shown); ‡ Numbers in parentheses indicate the number of people reporting a single ancestry; * Numbers in parentheses indicate the number of persons reporting this race alone, not in combination with any other race; Please refer to the Explanation of Data for more information.*

Cathedral City

Place Type: City
County: Riverside
Population: 51,200

Ancestry	Population	%
Afghan (0)	0	<0.01
African, Sub-Saharan (69)	103	0.20
African (24)	24	0.05
Cape Verdean (2)	16	0.03
Ethiopian (0)	0	<0.01
Ghanaian (0)	0	<0.01
Kenyan (0)	0	<0.01
Liberian (0)	0	<0.01
Nigerian (17)	19	0.04
Senegalese (0)	0	<0.01
Sierra Leonean (0)	0	<0.01
Somalian (0)	0	<0.01
South African (26)	26	0.05
Sudanese (0)	0	<0.01
Ugandan (0)	0	<0.01
Zimbabwean (0)	0	<0.01
Other Sub-Saharan African (0)	18	0.04
Albanian (0)	0	<0.01
Alsatian (0)	0	<0.01
American (1,580)	1,580	3.12
Arab (54)	74	0.15
Arab (0)	11	0.02
Egyptian (0)	0	<0.01
Iraqi (0)	0	<0.01
Jordanian (0)	0	<0.01
Lebanese (39)	46	0.09
Moroccan (0)	0	<0.01
Palestinian (0)	0	<0.01
Syrian (12)	14	0.03
Other Arab (3)	3	0.01
Armenian (46)	84	0.17
Assyrian/Chaldean/Syriac (21)	24	0.05
Australian (10)	10	0.02
Austrian (120)	174	0.34
Basque (9)	9	0.02
Belgian (5)	5	0.01
Brazilian (38)	60	0.12
British (70)	235	0.46
Bulgarian (0)	11	0.02
Cajun (4)	17	0.03
Canadian (300)	404	0.80
Carpatho Rusyn (0)	0	<0.01
Celtic (0)	0	<0.01
Croatian (13)	79	0.16
Cypriot (0)	0	<0.01
Czech (53)	122	0.24
Czechoslovakian (21)	21	0.04
Danish (31)	202	0.40
Dutch (93)	481	0.95
Eastern European (30)	30	0.06
English (931)	3,120	6.17
Estonian (0)	0	<0.01
European (311)	395	0.78
Finnish (6)	21	0.04
French, ex. Basque (202)	840	1.66
French Canadian (185)	299	0.59
German (1,303)	4,032	7.97
German Russian (0)	0	<0.01
Greek (46)	152	0.30
Guyanese (0)	0	<0.01
Hungarian (88)	255	0.50
Icelander (11)	11	0.02
Iranian (20)	23	0.05
Irish (1,210)	3,584	7.08
Israeli (0)	0	<0.01
Italian (963)	1,724	3.41
Latvian (2)	4	0.01
Lithuanian (57)	98	0.19
Luxemburger (0)	0	<0.01
Macedonian (0)	0	<0.01
Maltese (0)	70	0.14
New Zealander (0)	0	<0.01
Northern European (28)	28	0.06
Norwegian (241)	494	0.98
Pennsylvania German (0)	19	0.04
Polish (217)	540	1.07
Portuguese (65)	127	0.25
Romanian (125)	156	0.31
Russian (236)	536	1.06
Scandinavian (99)	99	0.20
Scotch-Irish (110)	421	0.83
Scottish (189)	528	1.04
Serbian (0)	61	0.12
Slavic (5)	5	0.01
Slovak (2)	34	0.07
Slovene (20)	24	0.05
Soviet Union (0)	0	<0.01
Swedish (107)	484	0.96
Swiss (10)	103	0.20
Turkish (0)	11	0.02
Ukrainian (21)	80	0.16
Welsh (20)	230	0.45
West Indian, ex. Hispanic (75)	83	0.16
Bahamian (0)	0	<0.01
Barbadian (0)	0	<0.01
Belizean (37)	45	0.09
Bermudan (0)	0	<0.01
British West Indian (0)	0	<0.01
Dutch West Indian (0)	0	<0.01
Haitian (0)	0	<0.01
Jamaican (0)	0	<0.01
Trinidadian/Tobagonian (0)	0	<0.01
U.S. Virgin Islander (0)	0	<0.01
West Indian (38)	38	0.08
Other West Indian (0)	0	<0.01
Yugoslavian (2)	21	0.04

Hispanic Origin	Population	%
Hispanic or Latino (of any race)	30,085	58.76
Central American, ex. Mexican	1,927	3.76
Costa Rican	6	0.01
Guatemalan	994	1.94
Honduran	70	0.14
Nicaraguan	122	0.24
Panamanian	22	0.04
Salvadoran	704	1.38
Other Central American	9	0.02
Cuban	91	0.18
Dominican Republic	5	0.01
Mexican	26,165	51.10
Puerto Rican	222	0.43
South American	390	0.76
Argentinean	51	0.10
Bolivian	2	<0.01
Chilean	54	0.11
Colombian	62	0.12
Ecuadorian	17	0.03
Paraguayan	7	0.01
Peruvian	159	0.31
Uruguayan	22	0.04
Venezuelan	15	0.03
Other South American	1	<0.01
Other Hispanic or Latino	1,285	2.51

Race*	Population	%
African-American/Black (1,344)	1,737	3.39
Not Hispanic (1,108)	1,329	2.60
Hispanic (236)	408	0.80
American Indian/Alaska Native (540)	902	1.76
Not Hispanic (228)	406	0.79
Hispanic (312)	496	0.97
Alaska Athabascan *(Ala. Nat.)* (1)	1	<0.01
Aleut *(Alaska Native)* (0)	0	<0.01
Apache (9)	18	0.04
Arapaho (0)	0	<0.01
Blackfeet (1)	14	0.03
Canadian/French Am. Ind. (1)	2	<0.01
Central American Ind. (2)	2	<0.01
Cherokee (32)	95	0.19
Cheyenne (0)	0	<0.01
Chickasaw (6)	7	0.01
Chippewa (1)	8	0.02
Choctaw (7)	21	0.04
Colville (0)	0	<0.01
Comanche (4)	5	0.01
Cree (0)	0	<0.01
Creek (6)	11	0.02
Crow (0)	0	<0.01
Delaware (0)	0	<0.01
Hopi (0)	1	<0.01
Houma (0)	1	<0.01
Inupiat *(Alaska Native)* (2)	2	<0.01
Iroquois (3)	4	0.01
Kiowa (7)	7	0.01
Lumbee (0)	0	<0.01
Menominee (0)	0	<0.01
Mexican American Ind. (73)	104	0.20
Navajo (11)	18	0.04
Osage (5)	5	0.01
Ottawa (0)	0	<0.01
Paiute (1)	5	0.01
Pima (0)	2	<0.01
Potawatomi (1)	9	0.02
Pueblo (3)	7	0.01
Puget Sound Salish (2)	2	<0.01
Seminole (0)	2	<0.01
Shoshone (0)	1	<0.01
Sioux (1)	7	0.01
South American Ind. (9)	16	0.03
Spanish American Ind. (8)	16	0.03
Tlingit-Haida *(Alaska Native)* (0)	0	<0.01
Tohono O'Odham (0)	0	<0.01
Tsimshian *(Alaska Native)* (0)	0	<0.01
Ute (0)	0	<0.01
Yakama (0)	0	<0.01
Yaqui (15)	17	0.03
Yuman (1)	1	<0.01
Yup'ik *(Alaska Native)* (0)	1	<0.01
Asian (2,562)	3,035	5.93
Not Hispanic (2,449)	2,734	5.34
Hispanic (113)	301	0.59
Bangladeshi (1)	1	<0.01
Bhutanese (0)	0	<0.01
Burmese (1)	1	<0.01
Cambodian (17)	25	0.05
Chinese, ex. Taiwanese (168)	233	0.46
Filipino (1,771)	2,083	4.07
Hmong (0)	0	<0.01
Indian (131)	174	0.34
Indonesian (11)	15	0.03
Japanese (70)	147	0.29
Korean (61)	71	0.14
Laotian (12)	16	0.03
Malaysian (0)	3	0.01
Nepalese (1)	2	<0.01
Pakistani (11)	17	0.03
Sri Lankan (26)	38	0.07
Taiwanese (1)	4	0.01
Thai (16)	21	0.04
Vietnamese (189)	197	0.38
Hawaii Native/Pacific Islander (55)	154	0.30
Not Hispanic (47)	116	0.23
Hispanic (8)	38	0.07
Fijian (0)	0	<0.01
Guamanian/Chamorro (16)	31	0.06
Marshallese (0)	0	<0.01
Native Hawaiian (12)	51	0.10
Samoan (12)	17	0.03
Tongan (0)	1	<0.01
White (32,537)	34,379	67.15
Not Hispanic (16,531)	17,129	33.46
Hispanic (16,006)	17,250	33.69

*Notes: † The Census 2010 population figure is used to calculate the percentages in the Hispanic Origin and Race categories. Ancestry percentages are based on the 2006-2010 American Community Survey population (not shown); ‡ Numbers in parentheses indicate the number of people reporting a single ancestry; * Numbers in parentheses indicate the number of persons reporting this race alone, not in combination with any other race; Please refer to the Explanation of Data for more information.*

Chico

Place Type: City
County: Butte
Population: 86,187

Ancestry	Population	%
Afghan (0)	0	<0.01
African, Sub-Saharan (201)	280	0.33
African (163)	226	0.27
Cape Verdean (0)	0	<0.01
Ethiopian (9)	22	0.03
Ghanaian (0)	0	<0.01
Kenyan (29)	29	0.03
Liberian (0)	0	<0.01
Nigerian (0)	0	<0.01
Senegalese (0)	0	<0.01
Sierra Leonean (0)	0	<0.01
Somalian (0)	0	<0.01
South African (0)	0	<0.01
Sudanese (0)	0	<0.01
Ugandan (0)	0	<0.01
Zimbabwean (0)	0	<0.01
Other Sub-Saharan African (0)	3	<0.01
Albanian (0)	0	<0.01
Alsatian (0)	0	<0.01
American (5,798)	5,798	6.81
Arab (236)	356	0.42
Arab (13)	13	0.02
Egyptian (11)	11	0.01
Iraqi (0)	22	0.03
Jordanian (4)	4	<0.01
Lebanese (0)	83	0.10
Moroccan (31)	31	0.04
Palestinian (22)	22	0.03
Syrian (30)	45	0.05
Other Arab (125)	125	0.15
Armenian (150)	266	0.31
Assyrian/Chaldean/Syriac (15)	28	0.03
Australian (65)	83	0.10
Austrian (106)	305	0.36
Basque (46)	55	0.06
Belgian (0)	44	0.05
Brazilian (0)	51	0.06
British (172)	449	0.53
Bulgarian (187)	187	0.22
Cajun (0)	0	<0.01
Canadian (137)	455	0.53
Carpatho Rusyn (0)	0	<0.01
Celtic (0)	0	<0.01
Croatian (96)	201	0.24
Cypriot (0)	0	<0.01
Czech (135)	442	0.52
Czechoslovakian (43)	106	0.12
Danish (248)	1,185	1.39
Dutch (282)	1,808	2.12
Eastern European (61)	61	0.07
English (2,206)	10,783	12.67
Estonian (0)	0	<0.01
European (1,466)	1,705	2.00
Finnish (46)	168	0.20
French, ex. Basque (322)	3,374	3.96
French Canadian (204)	488	0.57
German (4,083)	16,596	19.49
German Russian (0)	0	<0.01
Greek (250)	808	0.95
Guyanese (0)	50	0.06
Hungarian (116)	308	0.36
Icelander (38)	64	0.08
Iranian (15)	66	0.08
Irish (2,818)	12,531	14.72
Israeli (0)	0	<0.01
Italian (2,050)	6,333	7.44
Latvian (6)	6	0.01
Lithuanian (33)	233	0.27
Luxemburger (0)	0	<0.01
Macedonian (0)	0	<0.01
Maltese (17)	73	0.09
New Zealander (0)	0	<0.01
Northern European (135)	136	0.16
Norwegian (525)	2,139	2.51
Pennsylvania German (0)	0	<0.01
Polish (385)	1,428	1.68
Portuguese (800)	2,352	2.76
Romanian (52)	116	0.14
Russian (110)	812	0.95
Scandinavian (128)	336	0.39
Scotch-Irish (641)	2,302	2.70
Scottish (478)	2,710	3.18
Serbian (0)	4	<0.01
Slavic (44)	44	0.05
Slovak (0)	65	0.08
Slovene (9)	59	0.07
Soviet Union (0)	0	<0.01
Swedish (458)	1,980	2.33
Swiss (82)	467	0.55
Turkish (20)	53	0.06
Ukrainian (44)	171	0.20
Welsh (109)	736	0.86
West Indian, ex. Hispanic (65)	79	0.09
Bahamian (0)	0	<0.01
Barbadian (0)	0	<0.01
Belizean (0)	0	<0.01
Bermudan (0)	0	<0.01
British West Indian (0)	0	<0.01
Dutch West Indian (0)	0	<0.01
Haitian (5)	19	0.02
Jamaican (0)	0	<0.01
Trinidadian/Tobagonian (27)	27	0.03
U.S. Virgin Islander (0)	0	<0.01
West Indian (33)	33	0.04
Other West Indian (0)	0	<0.01
Yugoslavian (25)	148	0.17

Hispanic Origin	Population	%
Hispanic or Latino (of any race)	13,315	15.45
Central American, ex. Mexican	391	0.45
Costa Rican	37	0.04
Guatemalan	89	0.10
Honduran	29	0.03
Nicaraguan	80	0.09
Panamanian	20	0.02
Salvadoran	127	0.15
Other Central American	9	0.01
Cuban	91	0.11
Dominican Republic	11	0.01
Mexican	11,051	12.82
Puerto Rican	322	0.37
South American	286	0.33
Argentinean	28	0.03
Bolivian	18	0.02
Chilean	49	0.06
Colombian	60	0.07
Ecuadorian	16	0.02
Paraguayan	3	<0.01
Peruvian	77	0.09
Uruguayan	4	<0.01
Venezuelan	24	0.03
Other South American	7	0.01
Other Hispanic or Latino	1,163	1.35

Race*	Population	%
African-American/Black (1,771)	2,798	3.25
Not Hispanic (1,636)	2,468	2.86
Hispanic (135)	330	0.38
American Indian/Alaska Native (1,167)	2,666	3.09
Not Hispanic (791)	1,922	2.23
Hispanic (376)	744	0.86
Alaska Athabascan *(Ala. Nat.)* (6)	6	0.01
Aleut *(Alaska Native)* (3)	4	<0.01
Apache (21)	56	0.06
Arapaho (4)	7	0.01
Blackfeet (6)	81	0.09
Canadian/French Am. Ind. (0)	4	<0.01
Central American Ind. (1)	5	0.01
Cherokee (107)	431	0.50
Cheyenne (3)	7	0.01
Chickasaw (7)	26	0.03
Chippewa (19)	46	0.05
Choctaw (22)	96	0.11
Colville (2)	2	<0.01
Comanche (1)	3	<0.01
Cree (3)	6	0.01
Creek (5)	24	0.03
Crow (0)	2	<0.01
Delaware (2)	7	0.01
Hopi (0)	0	<0.01
Houma (0)	0	<0.01
Inupiat *(Alaska Native)* (1)	3	<0.01
Iroquois (4)	15	0.02
Kiowa (0)	2	<0.01
Lumbee (0)	1	<0.01
Menominee (0)	1	<0.01
Mexican American Ind. (54)	84	0.10
Navajo (20)	41	0.05
Osage (5)	18	0.02
Ottawa (1)	1	<0.01
Paiute (5)	17	0.02
Pima (1)	1	<0.01
Potawatomi (9)	22	0.03
Pueblo (8)	16	0.02
Puget Sound Salish (2)	3	<0.01
Seminole (3)	10	0.01
Shoshone (9)	23	0.03
Sioux (38)	89	0.10
South American Ind. (1)	4	<0.01
Spanish American Ind. (1)	3	<0.01
Tlingit-Haida *(Alaska Native)* (6)	11	0.01
Tohono O'Odham (1)	2	<0.01
Tsimshian *(Alaska Native)* (7)	7	0.01
Ute (1)	2	<0.01
Yakama (0)	5	0.01
Yaqui (7)	31	0.04
Yuman (2)	2	<0.01
Yup'ik *(Alaska Native)* (2)	3	<0.01
Asian (3,656)	4,948	5.74
Not Hispanic (3,589)	4,700	5.45
Hispanic (67)	248	0.29
Bangladeshi (4)	4	<0.01
Bhutanese (0)	0	<0.01
Burmese (4)	6	0.01
Cambodian (27)	42	0.05
Chinese, ex. Taiwanese (584)	806	0.94
Filipino (419)	800	0.93
Hmong (1,157)	1,225	1.42
Indian (325)	413	0.48
Indonesian (10)	21	0.02
Japanese (293)	642	0.74
Korean (174)	264	0.31
Laotian (141)	177	0.21
Malaysian (5)	7	0.01
Nepalese (6)	7	0.01
Pakistani (89)	97	0.11
Sri Lankan (25)	25	0.03
Taiwanese (28)	41	0.05
Thai (30)	57	0.07
Vietnamese (164)	195	0.23
Hawaii Native/Pacific Islander (210)	516	0.60
Not Hispanic (189)	434	0.50
Hispanic (21)	82	0.10
Fijian (6)	16	0.02
Guamanian/Chamorro (48)	78	0.09
Marshallese (0)	5	0.01
Native Hawaiian (44)	192	0.22
Samoan (40)	58	0.07
Tongan (5)	5	0.01
White (69,606)	73,535	85.32
Not Hispanic (63,561)	66,261	76.88
Hispanic (6,045)	7,274	8.44

*Notes: † The Census 2010 population figure is used to calculate the percentages in the Hispanic Origin and Race categories. Ancestry percentages are based on the 2006-2010 American Community Survey population (not shown); ‡ Numbers in parentheses indicate the number of people reporting a single ancestry; * Numbers in parentheses indicate the number of persons reporting this race alone, not in combination with any other race; Please refer to the Explanation of Data for more information.*

Chino

Place Type: City
County: San Bernardino
Population: 77,983

Ancestry	Population	%
Afghan (0)	0	<0.01
African, Sub-Saharan (296)	433	0.56
African (165)	242	0.31
Cape Verdean (0)	0	<0.01
Ethiopian (81)	133	0.17
Ghanaian (0)	0	<0.01
Kenyan (0)	0	<0.01
Liberian (0)	0	<0.01
Nigerian (50)	50	0.06
Senegalese (0)	0	<0.01
Sierra Leonean (0)	0	<0.01
Somalian (0)	0	<0.01
South African (0)	8	0.01
Sudanese (0)	0	<0.01
Ugandan (0)	0	<0.01
Zimbabwean (0)	0	<0.01
Other Sub-Saharan African (0)	0	<0.01
Albanian (0)	0	<0.01
Alsatian (0)	0	<0.01
American (2,824)	2,824	3.63
Arab (187)	313	0.40
Arab (7)	16	0.02
Egyptian (7)	7	0.01
Iraqi (0)	0	<0.01
Jordanian (0)	0	<0.01
Lebanese (42)	99	0.13
Moroccan (0)	8	0.01
Palestinian (0)	9	0.01
Syrian (131)	174	0.22
Other Arab (0)	0	<0.01
Armenian (117)	143	0.18
Assyrian/Chaldean/Syriac (13)	22	0.03
Australian (33)	59	0.08
Austrian (21)	95	0.12
Basque (66)	103	0.13
Belgian (0)	20	0.03
Brazilian (4)	4	0.01
British (0)	0	<0.01
Bulgarian (0)	0	<0.01
Cajun (0)	0	<0.01
Canadian (68)	210	0.27
Carpatho Rusyn (0)	0	<0.01
Celtic (0)	0	<0.01
Croatian (0)	13	0.02
Cypriot (0)	0	<0.01
Czech (0)	49	0.06
Czechoslovakian (8)	8	0.01
Danish (76)	200	0.26
Dutch (631)	1,087	1.40
Eastern European (15)	15	0.02
English (1,260)	3,717	4.78
Estonian (0)	0	<0.01
European (469)	730	0.94
Finnish (0)	135	0.17
French, ex. Basque (169)	1,185	1.52
French Canadian (237)	282	0.36
German (1,466)	5,550	7.14
German Russian (0)	0	<0.01
Greek (29)	98	0.13
Guyanese (19)	19	0.02
Hungarian (58)	115	0.15
Icelander (5)	5	0.01
Iranian (44)	53	0.07
Irish (980)	4,246	5.46
Israeli (0)	0	<0.01
Italian (758)	2,698	3.47
Latvian (0)	0	<0.01
Lithuanian (18)	49	0.06
Luxemburger (0)	0	<0.01
Macedonian (0)	0	<0.01
Maltese (0)	0	<0.01
New Zealander (0)	0	<0.01
Northern European (26)	26	0.03
Norwegian (173)	461	0.59
Pennsylvania German (0)	0	<0.01
Polish (193)	721	0.93
Portuguese (729)	1,174	1.51
Romanian (153)	153	0.20
Russian (97)	254	0.33
Scandinavian (17)	26	0.03
Scotch-Irish (255)	678	0.87
Scottish (375)	827	1.06
Serbian (0)	7	0.01
Slavic (16)	69	0.09
Slovak (0)	0	<0.01
Slovene (0)	0	<0.01
Soviet Union (0)	0	<0.01
Swedish (60)	414	0.53
Swiss (8)	66	0.08
Turkish (0)	0	<0.01
Ukrainian (0)	26	0.03
Welsh (20)	235	0.30
West Indian, ex. Hispanic (77)	167	0.21
Bahamian (0)	0	<0.01
Barbadian (0)	0	<0.01
Belizean (24)	93	0.12
Bermudan (0)	0	<0.01
British West Indian (0)	0	<0.01
Dutch West Indian (0)	0	<0.01
Haitian (0)	0	<0.01
Jamaican (13)	21	0.03
Trinidadian/Tobagonian (0)	8	0.01
U.S. Virgin Islander (0)	0	<0.01
West Indian (40)	45	0.06
Other West Indian (0)	0	<0.01
Yugoslavian (0)	34	0.04

Hispanic Origin	Population	%
Hispanic or Latino (of any race)	41,993	53.85
Central American, ex. Mexican	1,792	2.30
Costa Rican	106	0.14
Guatemalan	432	0.55
Honduran	145	0.19
Nicaraguan	221	0.28
Panamanian	28	0.04
Salvadoran	849	1.09
Other Central American	11	0.01
Cuban	355	0.46
Dominican Republic	17	0.02
Mexican	36,069	46.25
Puerto Rican	490	0.63
South American	874	1.12
Argentinean	229	0.29
Bolivian	20	0.03
Chilean	41	0.05
Colombian	182	0.23
Ecuadorian	151	0.19
Paraguayan	2	<0.01
Peruvian	213	0.27
Uruguayan	6	0.01
Venezuelan	17	0.02
Other South American	13	0.02
Other Hispanic or Latino	2,396	3.07

Race*	Population	%
African-American/Black (4,829)	5,459	7.00
Not Hispanic (4,529)	4,913	6.30
Hispanic (300)	546	0.70
American Indian/Alaska Native (786)	1,381	1.77
Not Hispanic (256)	536	0.69
Hispanic (530)	845	1.08
Alaska Athabascan *(Ala. Nat.)* (1)	1	<0.01
Aleut *(Alaska Native)* (0)	0	<0.01
Apache (25)	68	0.09
Arapaho (1)	1	<0.01
Blackfeet (6)	27	0.03
Canadian/French Am. Ind. (0)	2	<0.01
Central American Ind. (4)	4	0.01
Cherokee (38)	144	0.18
Cheyenne (4)	6	0.01
Chickasaw (1)	3	<0.01
Chippewa (2)	4	0.01
Choctaw (13)	40	0.05
Colville (0)	0	<0.01
Comanche (3)	3	<0.01
Cree (0)	1	<0.01
Creek (18)	20	0.03
Crow (2)	4	0.01
Delaware (1)	1	<0.01
Hopi (0)	2	<0.01
Houma (0)	0	<0.01
Inupiat *(Alaska Native)* (3)	5	0.01
Iroquois (0)	4	0.01
Kiowa (2)	2	<0.01
Lumbee (1)	2	<0.01
Menominee (0)	0	<0.01
Mexican American Ind. (76)	108	0.14
Navajo (22)	44	0.06
Osage (3)	3	<0.01
Ottawa (0)	0	<0.01
Paiute (2)	3	<0.01
Pima (5)	9	0.01
Potawatomi (4)	4	0.01
Pueblo (6)	16	0.02
Puget Sound Salish (0)	0	<0.01
Seminole (1)	4	0.01
Shoshone (3)	9	0.01
Sioux (15)	34	0.04
South American Ind. (11)	11	0.01
Spanish American Ind. (1)	5	0.01
Tlingit-Haida *(Alaska Native)* (6)	10	0.01
Tohono O'Odham (3)	8	0.01
Tsimshian *(Alaska Native)* (0)	0	<0.01
Ute (0)	6	0.01
Yakama (0)	0	<0.01
Yaqui (20)	37	0.05
Yuman (8)	11	0.01
Yup'ik *(Alaska Native)* (0)	0	<0.01
Asian (8,159)	9,279	11.90
Not Hispanic (7,932)	8,632	11.07
Hispanic (227)	647	0.83
Bangladeshi (39)	45	0.06
Bhutanese (5)	5	0.01
Burmese (25)	28	0.04
Cambodian (102)	116	0.15
Chinese, ex. Taiwanese (1,909)	2,258	2.90
Filipino (2,821)	3,361	4.31
Hmong (4)	4	0.01
Indian (626)	710	0.91
Indonesian (99)	177	0.23
Japanese (244)	516	0.66
Korean (606)	683	0.88
Laotian (46)	58	0.07
Malaysian (21)	30	0.04
Nepalese (0)	1	<0.01
Pakistani (96)	118	0.15
Sri Lankan (13)	18	0.02
Taiwanese (448)	503	0.65
Thai (99)	136	0.17
Vietnamese (537)	652	0.84
Hawaii Native/Pacific Islander (168)	419	0.54
Not Hispanic (112)	261	0.33
Hispanic (56)	158	0.20
Fijian (4)	6	0.01
Guamanian/Chamorro (33)	56	0.07
Marshallese (0)	0	<0.01
Native Hawaiian (35)	138	0.18
Samoan (62)	104	0.13
Tongan (20)	21	0.03
White (43,981)	46,869	60.10
Not Hispanic (21,659)	22,700	29.11
Hispanic (22,322)	24,169	30.99

*Notes: † The Census 2010 population figure is used to calculate the percentages in the Hispanic Origin and Race categories. Ancestry percentages are based on the 2006-2010 American Community Survey population (not shown); ‡ Numbers in parentheses indicate the number of people reporting a single ancestry; * Numbers in parentheses indicate the number of persons reporting this race alone, not in combination with any other race; Please refer to the Explanation of Data for more information.*

Chino Hills

Place Type: City
County: San Bernardino
Population: 74,799

Ancestry	Population	%
Afghan (41)	41	0.06
African, Sub-Saharan (323)	534	0.72
African (125)	271	0.36
Cape Verdean (0)	0	<0.01
Ethiopian (0)	65	0.09
Ghanaian (35)	35	0.05
Kenyan (0)	0	<0.01
Liberian (0)	0	<0.01
Nigerian (148)	148	0.20
Senegalese (0)	0	<0.01
Sierra Leonean (0)	0	<0.01
Somalian (0)	0	<0.01
South African (0)	0	<0.01
Sudanese (0)	0	<0.01
Ugandan (0)	0	<0.01
Zimbabwean (0)	0	<0.01
Other Sub-Saharan African (15)	15	0.02
Albanian (0)	0	<0.01
Alsatian (0)	0	<0.01
American (2,017)	2,017	2.71
Arab (1,231)	1,497	2.01
Arab (184)	405	0.54
Egyptian (340)	371	0.50
Iraqi (0)	0	<0.01
Jordanian (15)	15	0.02
Lebanese (369)	383	0.51
Moroccan (0)	0	<0.01
Palestinian (175)	175	0.24
Syrian (11)	11	0.01
Other Arab (137)	137	0.18
Armenian (154)	248	0.33
Assyrian/Chaldean/Syriac (8)	26	0.03
Australian (0)	0	<0.01
Austrian (0)	55	0.07
Basque (18)	65	0.09
Belgian (0)	26	0.03
Brazilian (21)	32	0.04
British (80)	142	0.19
Bulgarian (30)	30	0.04
Cajun (0)	0	<0.01
Canadian (160)	385	0.52
Carpatho Rusyn (0)	0	<0.01
Celtic (0)	0	<0.01
Croatian (11)	70	0.09
Cypriot (0)	0	<0.01
Czech (34)	117	0.16
Czechoslovakian (12)	21	0.03
Danish (80)	422	0.57
Dutch (244)	1,384	1.86
Eastern European (39)	39	0.05
English (1,282)	4,488	6.03
Estonian (0)	0	<0.01
European (832)	1,235	1.66
Finnish (13)	57	0.08
French, ex. Basque (170)	1,267	1.70
French Canadian (42)	364	0.49
German (1,361)	6,506	8.74
German Russian (0)	0	<0.01
Greek (127)	277	0.37
Guyanese (0)	0	<0.01
Hungarian (152)	239	0.32
Icelander (0)	9	0.01
Iranian (131)	187	0.25
Irish (879)	4,584	6.16
Israeli (91)	91	0.12
Italian (1,322)	3,811	5.12
Latvian (0)	0	<0.01
Lithuanian (22)	35	0.05
Luxemburger (0)	0	<0.01
Macedonian (0)	0	<0.01
Maltese (0)	0	<0.01
New Zealander (8)	8	0.01
Northern European (51)	51	0.07
Norwegian (249)	740	0.99
Pennsylvania German (15)	47	0.06
Polish (186)	881	1.18
Portuguese (49)	181	0.24
Romanian (39)	60	0.08
Russian (121)	560	0.75
Scandinavian (159)	270	0.36
Scotch-Irish (430)	1,089	1.46
Scottish (341)	1,236	1.66
Serbian (14)	53	0.07
Slavic (0)	13	0.02
Slovak (27)	52	0.07
Slovene (0)	0	<0.01
Soviet Union (0)	0	<0.01
Swedish (141)	674	0.91
Swiss (65)	214	0.29
Turkish (0)	0	<0.01
Ukrainian (68)	226	0.30
Welsh (65)	347	0.47
West Indian, ex. Hispanic (170)	193	0.26
Bahamian (0)	0	<0.01
Barbadian (0)	0	<0.01
Belizean (116)	116	0.16
Bermudan (0)	0	<0.01
British West Indian (0)	0	<0.01
Dutch West Indian (0)	0	<0.01
Haitian (27)	41	0.06
Jamaican (27)	36	0.05
Trinidadian/Tobagonian (0)	0	<0.01
U.S. Virgin Islander (0)	0	<0.01
West Indian (0)	0	<0.01
Other West Indian (0)	0	<0.01
Yugoslavian (10)	10	0.01

Hispanic Origin	Population	%
Hispanic or Latino (of any race)	21,802	29.15
Central American, ex. Mexican	1,180	1.58
Costa Rican	92	0.12
Guatemalan	278	0.37
Honduran	51	0.07
Nicaraguan	169	0.23
Panamanian	20	0.03
Salvadoran	547	0.73
Other Central American	23	0.03
Cuban	383	0.51
Dominican Republic	23	0.03
Mexican	17,678	23.63
Puerto Rican	389	0.52
South American	965	1.29
Argentinean	167	0.22
Bolivian	23	0.03
Chilean	73	0.10
Colombian	273	0.36
Ecuadorian	191	0.26
Paraguayan	7	0.01
Peruvian	171	0.23
Uruguayan	8	0.01
Venezuelan	33	0.04
Other South American	19	0.03
Other Hispanic or Latino	1,184	1.58

Race*	Population	%
African-American/Black (3,415)	3,986	5.33
Not Hispanic (3,225)	3,644	4.87
Hispanic (190)	342	0.46
American Indian/Alaska Native (379)	816	1.09
Not Hispanic (143)	350	0.47
Hispanic (236)	466	0.62
Alaska Athabascan *(Ala. Nat.)* (0)	0	<0.01
Aleut *(Alaska Native)* (0)	0	<0.01
Apache (13)	42	0.06
Arapaho (0)	0	<0.01
Blackfeet (7)	18	0.02
Canadian/French Am. Ind. (1)	2	<0.01
Central American Ind. (0)	0	<0.01
Cherokee (25)	105	0.14
Cheyenne (0)	1	<0.01
Chickasaw (4)	17	0.02
Chippewa (1)	6	0.01
Choctaw (11)	28	0.04
Colville (0)	0	<0.01
Comanche (3)	8	0.01
Cree (0)	0	<0.01
Creek (0)	4	0.01
Crow (5)	5	0.01
Delaware (1)	4	0.01
Hopi (3)	5	0.01
Houma (0)	0	<0.01
Inupiat *(Alaska Native)* (0)	0	<0.01
Iroquois (0)	3	<0.01
Kiowa (0)	0	<0.01
Lumbee (0)	0	<0.01
Menominee (0)	0	<0.01
Mexican American Ind. (30)	50	0.07
Navajo (15)	40	0.05
Osage (0)	0	<0.01
Ottawa (0)	0	<0.01
Paiute (1)	1	<0.01
Pima (4)	10	0.01
Potawatomi (3)	4	0.01
Pueblo (7)	21	0.03
Puget Sound Salish (0)	0	<0.01
Seminole (0)	1	<0.01
Shoshone (0)	0	<0.01
Sioux (7)	15	0.02
South American Ind. (0)	3	<0.01
Spanish American Ind. (6)	9	0.01
Tlingit-Haida *(Alaska Native)* (0)	0	<0.01
Tohono O'Odham (0)	0	<0.01
Tsimshian *(Alaska Native)* (0)	0	<0.01
Ute (0)	0	<0.01
Yakama (0)	0	<0.01
Yaqui (6)	12	0.02
Yuman (0)	0	<0.01
Yup'ik *(Alaska Native)* (0)	0	<0.01
Asian (22,676)	24,637	32.94
Not Hispanic (22,351)	23,813	31.84
Hispanic (325)	824	1.10
Bangladeshi (26)	32	0.04
Bhutanese (0)	0	<0.01
Burmese (41)	51	0.07
Cambodian (106)	145	0.19
Chinese, ex. Taiwanese (6,012)	6,895	9.22
Filipino (6,277)	7,257	9.70
Hmong (8)	9	0.01
Indian (2,003)	2,139	2.86
Indonesian (288)	389	0.52
Japanese (660)	1,162	1.55
Korean (3,401)	3,662	4.90
Laotian (70)	79	0.11
Malaysian (27)	34	0.05
Nepalese (5)	5	0.01
Pakistani (334)	375	0.50
Sri Lankan (42)	47	0.06
Taiwanese (1,242)	1,422	1.90
Thai (244)	323	0.43
Vietnamese (996)	1,168	1.56
Hawaii Native/Pacific Islander (115)	360	0.48
Not Hispanic (99)	291	0.39
Hispanic (16)	69	0.09
Fijian (5)	8	0.01
Guamanian/Chamorro (25)	43	0.06
Marshallese (0)	0	<0.01
Native Hawaiian (36)	118	0.16
Samoan (28)	44	0.06
Tongan (0)	0	<0.01
White (38,035)	41,076	54.92
Not Hispanic (25,017)	26,656	35.64
Hispanic (13,018)	14,420	19.28

*Notes: † The Census 2010 population figure is used to calculate the percentages in the Hispanic Origin and Race categories. Ancestry percentages are based on the 2006-2010 American Community Survey population (not shown); ‡ Numbers in parentheses indicate the number of people reporting a single ancestry; * Numbers in parentheses indicate the number of persons reporting this race alone, not in combination with any other race; Please refer to the Explanation of Data for more information.*

Chula Vista

Place Type: City
County: San Diego
Population: 243,916

Ancestry	Population	%
Afghan (39)	39	0.02
African, Sub-Saharan (633)	806	0.35
African (344)	517	0.23
Cape Verdean (8)	8	<0.01
Ethiopian (209)	209	0.09
Ghanaian (0)	0	<0.01
Kenyan (0)	0	<0.01
Liberian (0)	0	<0.01
Nigerian (25)	25	0.01
Senegalese (0)	0	<0.01
Sierra Leonean (0)	0	<0.01
Somalian (0)	0	<0.01
South African (27)	27	0.01
Sudanese (0)	0	<0.01
Ugandan (20)	20	0.01
Zimbabwean (0)	0	<0.01
Other Sub-Saharan African (0)	0	<0.01
Albanian (0)	0	<0.01
Alsatian (0)	0	<0.01
American (3,413)	3,413	1.49
Arab (479)	892	0.39
Arab (23)	134	0.06
Egyptian (0)	34	0.01
Iraqi (56)	77	0.03
Jordanian (22)	22	0.01
Lebanese (86)	219	0.10
Moroccan (95)	113	0.05
Palestinian (34)	52	0.02
Syrian (0)	10	<0.01
Other Arab (163)	231	0.10
Armenian (113)	218	0.09
Assyrian/Chaldean/Syriac (15)	37	0.02
Australian (26)	78	0.03
Austrian (51)	287	0.12
Basque (42)	80	0.03
Belgian (0)	40	0.02
Brazilian (35)	35	0.02
British (682)	895	0.39
Bulgarian (49)	61	0.03
Cajun (0)	0	<0.01
Canadian (232)	288	0.13
Carpatho Rusyn (0)	0	<0.01
Celtic (28)	34	0.01
Croatian (10)	36	0.02
Cypriot (0)	0	<0.01
Czech (89)	422	0.18
Czechoslovakian (21)	101	0.04
Danish (170)	625	0.27
Dutch (168)	996	0.43
Eastern European (39)	39	0.02
English (2,584)	8,433	3.67
Estonian (0)	0	<0.01
European (1,437)	1,658	0.72
Finnish (38)	166	0.07
French, ex. Basque (483)	3,717	1.62
French Canadian (206)	463	0.20
German (4,095)	14,147	6.16
German Russian (0)	0	<0.01
Greek (152)	657	0.29
Guyanese (16)	46	0.02
Hungarian (29)	385	0.17
Icelander (16)	16	0.01
Iranian (153)	350	0.15
Irish (3,144)	11,613	5.06
Israeli (44)	44	0.02
Italian (2,180)	5,093	2.22
Latvian (24)	32	0.01
Lithuanian (0)	106	0.05
Luxemburger (0)	8	<0.01
Macedonian (0)	28	0.01
Maltese (0)	0	<0.01
New Zealander (0)	0	<0.01
Northern European (45)	55	0.02
Norwegian (557)	1,588	0.69
Pennsylvania German (35)	35	0.02
Polish (517)	1,875	0.82
Portuguese (533)	1,363	0.59
Romanian (39)	101	0.04
Russian (125)	580	0.25
Scandinavian (58)	198	0.09
Scotch-Irish (630)	1,819	0.79
Scottish (603)	1,755	0.76
Serbian (11)	32	0.01
Slavic (35)	35	0.02
Slovak (32)	128	0.06
Slovene (8)	25	0.01
Soviet Union (0)	0	<0.01
Swedish (392)	1,254	0.55
Swiss (129)	277	0.12
Turkish (58)	169	0.07
Ukrainian (90)	192	0.08
Welsh (255)	703	0.31
West Indian, ex. Hispanic (341)	600	0.26
Bahamian (0)	0	<0.01
Barbadian (12)	12	0.01
Belizean (0)	15	0.01
Bermudan (0)	0	<0.01
British West Indian (13)	34	0.01
Dutch West Indian (0)	13	0.01
Haitian (18)	104	0.05
Jamaican (298)	345	0.15
Trinidadian/Tobagonian (0)	14	0.01
U.S. Virgin Islander (0)	16	0.01
West Indian (0)	47	0.02
Other West Indian (0)	0	<0.01
Yugoslavian (16)	46	0.02

Hispanic Origin	Population	%
Hispanic or Latino (of any race)	142,066	58.24
Central American, ex. Mexican	1,619	0.66
Costa Rican	181	0.07
Guatemalan	320	0.13
Honduran	176	0.07
Nicaraguan	236	0.10
Panamanian	203	0.08
Salvadoran	489	0.20
Other Central American	14	0.01
Cuban	532	0.22
Dominican Republic	193	0.08
Mexican	130,413	53.47
Puerto Rican	2,282	0.94
South American	1,763	0.72
Argentinean	202	0.08
Bolivian	113	0.05
Chilean	168	0.07
Colombian	572	0.23
Ecuadorian	176	0.07
Paraguayan	4	<0.01
Peruvian	408	0.17
Uruguayan	25	0.01
Venezuelan	81	0.03
Other South American	14	0.01
Other Hispanic or Latino	5,264	2.16

Race*	Population	%
African-American/Black (11,219)	14,196	5.82
Not Hispanic (9,972)	11,893	4.88
Hispanic (1,247)	2,303	0.94
American Indian/Alaska Native (1,880)	3,421	1.40
Not Hispanic (600)	1,420	0.58
Hispanic (1,280)	2,001	0.82
Alaska Athabascan *(Ala. Nat.)* (5)	5	<0.01
Aleut *(Alaska Native)* (3)	5	<0.01
Apache (45)	128	0.05
Arapaho (0)	0	<0.01
Blackfeet (12)	63	0.03
Canadian/French Am. Ind. (2)	6	<0.01
Central American Ind. (8)	13	0.01
Cherokee (68)	296	0.12
Cheyenne (2)	9	<0.01
Chickasaw (19)	25	0.01
Chippewa (10)	24	0.01
Choctaw (39)	89	0.04
Colville (0)	0	<0.01
Comanche (12)	25	0.01
Cree (2)	3	<0.01
Creek (9)	26	0.01
Crow (4)	13	0.01
Delaware (0)	2	<0.01
Hopi (3)	3	<0.01
Houma (1)	2	<0.01
Inupiat *(Alaska Native)* (3)	8	<0.01
Iroquois (16)	36	0.01
Kiowa (2)	6	<0.01
Lumbee (3)	7	<0.01
Menominee (0)	0	<0.01
Mexican American Ind. (296)	451	0.18
Navajo (100)	158	0.06
Osage (5)	8	<0.01
Ottawa (1)	2	<0.01
Paiute (0)	2	<0.01
Pima (9)	14	0.01
Potawatomi (4)	6	<0.01
Pueblo (23)	35	0.01
Puget Sound Salish (2)	5	<0.01
Seminole (1)	5	<0.01
Shoshone (0)	4	<0.01
Sioux (15)	34	0.01
South American Ind. (3)	11	<0.01
Spanish American Ind. (8)	10	<0.01
Tlingit-Haida *(Alaska Native)* (1)	2	<0.01
Tohono O'Odham (20)	28	0.01
Tsimshian *(Alaska Native)* (2)	3	<0.01
Ute (1)	1	<0.01
Yakama (0)	3	<0.01
Yaqui (34)	77	0.03
Yuman (6)	10	<0.01
Yup'ik *(Alaska Native)* (1)	3	<0.01
Asian (35,042)	41,840	17.15
Not Hispanic (33,581)	38,101	15.62
Hispanic (1,461)	3,739	1.53
Bangladeshi (19)	20	0.01
Bhutanese (0)	0	<0.01
Burmese (13)	15	0.01
Cambodian (95)	135	0.06
Chinese, ex. Taiwanese (1,558)	2,441	1.00
Filipino (26,597)	31,344	12.85
Hmong (3)	6	<0.01
Indian (582)	784	0.32
Indonesian (33)	74	0.03
Japanese (1,951)	3,369	1.38
Korean (2,028)	2,397	0.98
Laotian (113)	162	0.07
Malaysian (8)	32	0.01
Nepalese (11)	13	0.01
Pakistani (105)	145	0.06
Sri Lankan (41)	46	0.02
Taiwanese (116)	164	0.07
Thai (102)	191	0.08
Vietnamese (888)	1,108	0.45
Hawaii Native/Pacific Islander (1,351)	2,746	1.13
Not Hispanic (1,105)	1,993	0.82
Hispanic (246)	753	0.31
Fijian (10)	11	<0.01
Guamanian/Chamorro (780)	1,389	0.57
Marshallese (1)	6	<0.01
Native Hawaiian (155)	577	0.24
Samoan (237)	396	0.16
Tongan (61)	72	0.03
White (130,991)	142,343	58.36
Not Hispanic (49,641)	54,966	22.53
Hispanic (81,350)	87,377	35.82

*Notes: † The Census 2010 population figure is used to calculate the percentages in the Hispanic Origin and Race categories. Ancestry percentages are based on the 2006-2010 American Community Survey population (not shown); ‡ Numbers in parentheses indicate the number of people reporting a single ancestry; * Numbers in parentheses indicate the number of persons reporting this race alone, not in combination with any other race; Please refer to the Explanation of Data for more information.*

Citrus Heights

Place Type: City
County: Sacramento
Population: 83,301

Ancestry	Population	%
Afghan (0)	0	<0.01
African, Sub-Saharan (131)	197	0.23
African (90)	148	0.18
Cape Verdean (7)	7	0.01
Ethiopian (21)	29	0.03
Ghanaian (0)	0	<0.01
Kenyan (0)	0	<0.01
Liberian (13)	13	0.02
Nigerian (0)	0	<0.01
Senegalese (0)	0	<0.01
Sierra Leonean (0)	0	<0.01
Somalian (0)	0	<0.01
South African (0)	0	<0.01
Sudanese (0)	0	<0.01
Ugandan (0)	0	<0.01
Zimbabwean (0)	0	<0.01
Other Sub-Saharan African (0)	0	<0.01
Albanian (0)	0	<0.01
Alsatian (0)	14	0.02
American (2,380)	2,380	2.82
Arab (208)	280	0.33
Arab (6)	40	0.05
Egyptian (11)	11	0.01
Iraqi (39)	39	0.05
Jordanian (0)	0	<0.01
Lebanese (9)	9	0.01
Moroccan (29)	29	0.03
Palestinian (0)	0	<0.01
Syrian (0)	0	<0.01
Other Arab (114)	152	0.18
Armenian (123)	234	0.28
Assyrian/Chaldean/Syriac (0)	37	0.04
Australian (0)	80	0.09
Austrian (88)	122	0.14
Basque (35)	44	0.05
Belgian (0)	49	0.06
Brazilian (68)	105	0.12
British (226)	349	0.41
Bulgarian (0)	14	0.02
Cajun (0)	0	<0.01
Canadian (124)	294	0.35
Carpatho Rusyn (0)	19	0.02
Celtic (8)	8	0.01
Croatian (55)	211	0.25
Cypriot (0)	0	<0.01
Czech (78)	290	0.34
Czechoslovakian (52)	75	0.09
Danish (209)	1,123	1.33
Dutch (451)	2,006	2.38
Eastern European (0)	0	<0.01
English (3,422)	11,463	13.59
Estonian (0)	0	<0.01
European (940)	1,044	1.24
Finnish (116)	226	0.27
French, ex. Basque (252)	2,853	3.38
French Canadian (130)	286	0.34
German (4,168)	15,987	18.95
German Russian (0)	0	<0.01
Greek (191)	547	0.65
Guyanese (0)	0	<0.01
Hungarian (152)	522	0.62
Icelander (12)	63	0.07
Iranian (240)	339	0.40
Irish (2,736)	12,491	14.81
Israeli (0)	0	<0.01
Italian (1,647)	5,358	6.35
Latvian (0)	0	<0.01
Lithuanian (21)	75	0.09
Luxemburger (0)	0	<0.01
Macedonian (0)	0	<0.01
Maltese (0)	27	0.03
New Zealander (0)	0	<0.01
Northern European (139)	139	0.16
Norwegian (561)	2,043	2.42
Pennsylvania German (34)	75	0.09
Polish (310)	1,260	1.49
Portuguese (427)	1,645	1.95
Romanian (462)	533	0.63
Russian (1,283)	1,916	2.27
Scandinavian (125)	318	0.38
Scotch-Irish (778)	1,532	1.82
Scottish (692)	1,893	2.24
Serbian (45)	54	0.06
Slavic (19)	82	0.10
Slovak (29)	87	0.10
Slovene (0)	0	<0.01
Soviet Union (0)	0	<0.01
Swedish (350)	1,968	2.33
Swiss (18)	289	0.34
Turkish (38)	72	0.09
Ukrainian (1,796)	1,833	2.17
Welsh (114)	766	0.91
West Indian, ex. Hispanic (0)	0	<0.01
Bahamian (0)	0	<0.01
Barbadian (0)	0	<0.01
Belizean (0)	0	<0.01
Bermudan (0)	0	<0.01
British West Indian (0)	0	<0.01
Dutch West Indian (0)	0	<0.01
Haitian (0)	0	<0.01
Jamaican (0)	0	<0.01
Trinidadian/Tobagonian (0)	0	<0.01
U.S. Virgin Islander (0)	0	<0.01
West Indian (0)	0	<0.01
Other West Indian (0)	0	<0.01
Yugoslavian (321)	447	0.53

Hispanic Origin	Population	%
Hispanic or Latino (of any race)	13,734	16.49
Central American, ex. Mexican	775	0.93
Costa Rican	18	0.02
Guatemalan	290	0.35
Honduran	25	0.03
Nicaraguan	102	0.12
Panamanian	45	0.05
Salvadoran	290	0.35
Other Central American	5	0.01
Cuban	102	0.12
Dominican Republic	18	0.02
Mexican	10,321	12.39
Puerto Rican	458	0.55
South American	332	0.40
Argentinean	51	0.06
Bolivian	4	<0.01
Chilean	66	0.08
Colombian	54	0.06
Ecuadorian	32	0.04
Paraguayan	3	<0.01
Peruvian	92	0.11
Uruguayan	8	0.01
Venezuelan	17	0.02
Other South American	5	0.01
Other Hispanic or Latino	1,728	2.07

Race*	Population	%
African-American/Black (2,751)	3,849	4.62
Not Hispanic (2,542)	3,416	4.10
Hispanic (209)	433	0.52
American Indian/Alaska Native (753)	2,187	2.63
Not Hispanic (507)	1,579	1.90
Hispanic (246)	608	0.73
Alaska Athabascan *(Ala. Nat.)* (1)	3	<0.01
Aleut *(Alaska Native)* (1)	5	0.01
Apache (18)	69	0.08
Arapaho (0)	0	<0.01
Blackfeet (11)	62	0.07
Canadian/French Am. Ind. (2)	4	<0.01
Central American Ind. (6)	6	0.01
Cherokee (83)	439	0.53
Cheyenne (1)	6	0.01
Chickasaw (6)	27	0.03
Chippewa (10)	32	0.04
Choctaw (16)	102	0.12
Colville (3)	3	<0.01
Comanche (1)	25	0.03
Cree (2)	3	<0.01
Creek (8)	28	0.03
Crow (0)	1	<0.01
Delaware (1)	2	<0.01
Hopi (2)	4	<0.01
Houma (2)	2	<0.01
Inupiat *(Alaska Native)* (2)	4	<0.01
Iroquois (7)	18	0.02
Kiowa (0)	0	<0.01
Lumbee (0)	1	<0.01
Menominee (1)	2	<0.01
Mexican American Ind. (35)	60	0.07
Navajo (15)	36	0.04
Osage (1)	8	0.01
Ottawa (2)	2	<0.01
Paiute (11)	18	0.02
Pima (1)	1	<0.01
Potawatomi (13)	25	0.03
Pueblo (7)	14	0.02
Puget Sound Salish (2)	2	<0.01
Seminole (3)	14	0.02
Shoshone (5)	15	0.02
Sioux (28)	62	0.07
South American Ind. (3)	8	0.01
Spanish American Ind. (5)	11	0.01
Tlingit-Haida *(Alaska Native)* (4)	7	0.01
Tohono O'Odham (9)	15	0.02
Tsimshian *(Alaska Native)* (0)	1	<0.01
Ute (0)	0	<0.01
Yakama (1)	1	<0.01
Yaqui (8)	15	0.02
Yuman (1)	2	<0.01
Yup'ik *(Alaska Native)* (1)	1	<0.01
Asian (2,714)	4,218	5.06
Not Hispanic (2,577)	3,805	4.57
Hispanic (137)	413	0.50
Bangladeshi (4)	4	<0.01
Bhutanese (0)	0	<0.01
Burmese (1)	1	<0.01
Cambodian (34)	48	0.06
Chinese, ex. Taiwanese (309)	532	0.64
Filipino (1,027)	1,627	1.95
Hmong (51)	57	0.07
Indian (338)	431	0.52
Indonesian (10)	27	0.03
Japanese (280)	664	0.80
Korean (180)	286	0.34
Laotian (37)	60	0.07
Malaysian (4)	4	<0.01
Nepalese (5)	7	0.01
Pakistani (40)	54	0.06
Sri Lankan (9)	9	0.01
Taiwanese (9)	19	0.02
Thai (44)	83	0.10
Vietnamese (200)	261	0.31
Hawaii Native/Pacific Islander (363)	766	0.92
Not Hispanic (325)	623	0.75
Hispanic (38)	143	0.17
Fijian (50)	58	0.07
Guamanian/Chamorro (103)	164	0.20
Marshallese (7)	7	0.01
Native Hawaiian (58)	273	0.33
Samoan (52)	86	0.10
Tongan (52)	62	0.07
White (66,856)	70,911	85.13
Not Hispanic (60,438)	63,235	75.91
Hispanic (6,418)	7,676	9.21

*Notes: † The Census 2010 population figure is used to calculate the percentages in the Hispanic Origin and Race categories. Ancestry percentages are based on the 2006-2010 American Community Survey population (not shown); ‡ Numbers in parentheses indicate the number of people reporting a single ancestry; * Numbers in parentheses indicate the number of persons reporting this race alone, not in combination with any other race; Please refer to the Explanation of Data for more information.*

Clovis

Place Type: City
County: Fresno
Population: 95,631

Ancestry	Population	%
Afghan (0)	0	<0.01
African, Sub-Saharan (438)	482	0.53
African (140)	164	0.18
Cape Verdean (0)	0	<0.01
Ethiopian (66)	66	0.07
Ghanaian (0)	20	0.02
Kenyan (0)	0	<0.01
Liberian (0)	0	<0.01
Nigerian (232)	232	0.25
Senegalese (0)	0	<0.01
Sierra Leonean (0)	0	<0.01
Somalian (0)	0	<0.01
South African (0)	0	<0.01
Sudanese (0)	0	<0.01
Ugandan (0)	0	<0.01
Zimbabwean (0)	0	<0.01
Other Sub-Saharan African (0)	0	<0.01
Albanian (0)	0	<0.01
Alsatian (0)	0	<0.01
American (2,525)	2,525	2.77
Arab (559)	676	0.74
Arab (235)	253	0.28
Egyptian (78)	78	0.09
Iraqi (0)	0	<0.01
Jordanian (75)	75	0.08
Lebanese (37)	95	0.10
Moroccan (11)	23	0.03
Palestinian (0)	0	<0.01
Syrian (13)	42	0.05
Other Arab (110)	110	0.12
Armenian (602)	984	1.08
Assyrian/Chaldean/Syriac (43)	108	0.12
Australian (0)	0	<0.01
Austrian (36)	141	0.15
Basque (86)	100	0.11
Belgian (24)	82	0.09
Brazilian (55)	350	0.38
British (186)	351	0.39
Bulgarian (0)	0	<0.01
Cajun (0)	0	<0.01
Canadian (73)	155	0.17
Carpatho Rusyn (0)	0	<0.01
Celtic (0)	0	<0.01
Croatian (21)	51	0.06
Cypriot (0)	0	<0.01
Czech (181)	329	0.36
Czechoslovakian (87)	275	0.30
Danish (355)	812	0.89
Dutch (142)	1,248	1.37
Eastern European (0)	0	<0.01
English (2,126)	8,109	8.89
Estonian (0)	0	<0.01
European (1,368)	1,560	1.71
Finnish (84)	148	0.16
French, ex. Basque (302)	2,289	2.51
French Canadian (188)	388	0.43
German (3,493)	13,881	15.23
German Russian (12)	12	0.01
Greek (65)	235	0.26
Guyanese (0)	0	<0.01
Hungarian (95)	142	0.16
Icelander (9)	53	0.06
Iranian (132)	234	0.26
Irish (2,460)	9,216	10.11
Israeli (0)	17	0.02
Italian (2,246)	6,461	7.09
Latvian (0)	41	0.04
Lithuanian (7)	26	0.03
Luxemburger (0)	0	<0.01
Macedonian (0)	9	0.01
Maltese (0)	0	<0.01
New Zealander (23)	23	0.03
Northern European (128)	185	0.20
Norwegian (304)	1,114	1.22
Pennsylvania German (122)	122	0.13
Polish (110)	907	0.99
Portuguese (540)	1,490	1.63
Romanian (85)	162	0.18
Russian (196)	759	0.83
Scandinavian (35)	48	0.05
Scotch-Irish (555)	1,955	2.14
Scottish (442)	1,829	2.01
Serbian (0)	26	0.03
Slavic (89)	96	0.11
Slovak (9)	57	0.06
Slovene (0)	14	0.02
Soviet Union (0)	0	<0.01
Swedish (343)	1,423	1.56
Swiss (76)	596	0.65
Turkish (11)	11	0.01
Ukrainian (291)	369	0.40
Welsh (80)	788	0.86
West Indian, ex. Hispanic (66)	117	0.13
Bahamian (66)	66	0.07
Barbadian (0)	0	<0.01
Belizean (0)	27	0.03
Bermudan (0)	0	<0.01
British West Indian (0)	0	<0.01
Dutch West Indian (0)	10	0.01
Haitian (0)	0	<0.01
Jamaican (0)	0	<0.01
Trinidadian/Tobagonian (0)	0	<0.01
U.S. Virgin Islander (0)	0	<0.01
West Indian (0)	14	0.02
Other West Indian (0)	0	<0.01
Yugoslavian (20)	76	0.08

Hispanic Origin	Population	%
Hispanic or Latino (of any race)	24,514	25.63
Central American, ex. Mexican	556	0.58
Costa Rican	59	0.06
Guatemalan	96	0.10
Honduran	38	0.04
Nicaraguan	85	0.09
Panamanian	34	0.04
Salvadoran	230	0.24
Other Central American	14	0.01
Cuban	66	0.07
Dominican Republic	8	0.01
Mexican	21,360	22.34
Puerto Rican	307	0.32
South American	275	0.29
Argentinean	41	0.04
Bolivian	11	0.01
Chilean	38	0.04
Colombian	86	0.09
Ecuadorian	21	0.02
Paraguayan	1	<0.01
Peruvian	50	0.05
Uruguayan	11	0.01
Venezuelan	16	0.02
Other South American	0	<0.01
Other Hispanic or Latino	1,942	2.03

Race*	Population	%
African-American/Black (2,618)	3,481	3.64
Not Hispanic (2,360)	3,002	3.14
Hispanic (258)	479	0.50
American Indian/Alaska Native (1,320)	2,580	2.70
Not Hispanic (754)	1,616	1.69
Hispanic (566)	964	1.01
Alaska Athabascan *(Ala. Nat.)* (0)	1	<0.01
Aleut *(Alaska Native)* (4)	4	<0.01
Apache (61)	95	0.10
Arapaho (0)	0	<0.01
Blackfeet (10)	53	0.06
Canadian/French Am. Ind. (2)	6	0.01
Central American Ind. (1)	4	<0.01
Cherokee (129)	405	0.42
Cheyenne (1)	12	0.01
Chickasaw (9)	28	0.03
Chippewa (5)	16	0.02
Choctaw (75)	150	0.16
Colville (4)	5	0.01
Comanche (5)	18	0.02
Cree (2)	2	<0.01
Creek (10)	31	0.03
Crow (3)	7	0.01
Delaware (4)	4	<0.01
Hopi (6)	8	0.01
Houma (0)	0	<0.01
Inupiat *(Alaska Native)* (0)	3	<0.01
Iroquois (10)	29	0.03
Kiowa (2)	3	<0.01
Lumbee (0)	7	0.01
Menominee (0)	0	<0.01
Mexican American Ind. (67)	110	0.12
Navajo (10)	26	0.03
Osage (1)	7	0.01
Ottawa (0)	0	<0.01
Paiute (9)	18	0.02
Pima (8)	8	0.01
Potawatomi (7)	14	0.01
Pueblo (16)	20	0.02
Puget Sound Salish (2)	2	<0.01
Seminole (2)	7	0.01
Shoshone (2)	6	0.01
Sioux (15)	42	0.04
South American Ind. (0)	2	<0.01
Spanish American Ind. (3)	4	<0.01
Tlingit-Haida *(Alaska Native)* (0)	1	<0.01
Tohono O'Odham (2)	4	<0.01
Tsimshian *(Alaska Native)* (0)	0	<0.01
Ute (1)	1	<0.01
Yakama (0)	0	<0.01
Yaqui (15)	31	0.03
Yuman (0)	0	<0.01
Yup'ik *(Alaska Native)* (2)	2	<0.01
Asian (10,233)	11,971	12.52
Not Hispanic (9,965)	11,264	11.78
Hispanic (268)	707	0.74
Bangladeshi (2)	2	<0.01
Bhutanese (0)	0	<0.01
Burmese (9)	12	0.01
Cambodian (208)	254	0.27
Chinese, ex. Taiwanese (920)	1,216	1.27
Filipino (1,826)	2,407	2.52
Hmong (2,887)	3,001	3.14
Indian (1,553)	1,750	1.83
Indonesian (42)	69	0.07
Japanese (660)	1,111	1.16
Korean (318)	428	0.45
Laotian (359)	417	0.44
Malaysian (1)	3	<0.01
Nepalese (0)	0	<0.01
Pakistani (87)	106	0.11
Sri Lankan (27)	33	0.03
Taiwanese (17)	18	0.02
Thai (103)	148	0.15
Vietnamese (721)	836	0.87
Hawaii Native/Pacific Islander (218)	493	0.52
Not Hispanic (187)	390	0.41
Hispanic (31)	103	0.11
Fijian (31)	36	0.04
Guamanian/Chamorro (57)	87	0.09
Marshallese (0)	0	<0.01
Native Hawaiian (49)	184	0.19
Samoan (55)	93	0.10
Tongan (0)	0	<0.01
White (67,758)	71,689	74.96
Not Hispanic (55,021)	57,330	59.95
Hispanic (12,737)	14,359	15.02

*Notes: † The Census 2010 population figure is used to calculate the percentages in the Hispanic Origin and Race categories. Ancestry percentages are based on the 2006-2010 American Community Survey population (not shown); ‡ Numbers in parentheses indicate the number of people reporting a single ancestry; * Numbers in parentheses indicate the number of persons reporting this race alone, not in combination with any other race; Please refer to the Explanation of Data for more information.*

Colton

Place Type: City
County: San Bernardino
Population: 52,154

Ancestry	Population	%
Afghan (0)	0	<0.01
African, Sub-Saharan (530)	585	1.12
African (195)	226	0.43
Cape Verdean (0)	0	<0.01
Ethiopian (0)	0	<0.01
Ghanaian (0)	0	<0.01
Kenyan (0)	0	<0.01
Liberian (0)	0	<0.01
Nigerian (335)	335	0.64
Senegalese (0)	0	<0.01
Sierra Leonean (0)	0	<0.01
Somalian (0)	0	<0.01
South African (0)	24	0.05
Sudanese (0)	0	<0.01
Ugandan (0)	0	<0.01
Zimbabwean (0)	0	<0.01
Other Sub-Saharan African (0)	0	<0.01
Albanian (0)	0	<0.01
Alsatian (0)	0	<0.01
American (610)	610	1.17
Arab (301)	331	0.63
Arab (34)	34	0.07
Egyptian (177)	189	0.36
Iraqi (0)	0	<0.01
Jordanian (44)	44	0.08
Lebanese (13)	31	0.06
Moroccan (0)	0	<0.01
Palestinian (0)	0	<0.01
Syrian (33)	33	0.06
Other Arab (0)	0	<0.01
Armenian (122)	122	0.23
Assyrian/Chaldean/Syriac (0)	0	<0.01
Australian (0)	0	<0.01
Austrian (0)	0	<0.01
Basque (0)	53	0.10
Belgian (0)	0	<0.01
Brazilian (22)	34	0.07
British (70)	111	0.21
Bulgarian (0)	0	<0.01
Cajun (0)	22	0.04
Canadian (0)	0	<0.01
Carpatho Rusyn (0)	0	<0.01
Celtic (0)	0	<0.01
Croatian (0)	0	<0.01
Cypriot (0)	0	<0.01
Czech (13)	46	0.09
Czechoslovakian (0)	0	<0.01
Danish (13)	79	0.15
Dutch (53)	178	0.34
Eastern European (0)	0	<0.01
English (143)	684	1.31
Estonian (0)	0	<0.01
European (110)	110	0.21
Finnish (0)	50	0.10
French, ex. Basque (156)	384	0.74
French Canadian (0)	0	<0.01
German (477)	1,525	2.92
German Russian (0)	0	<0.01
Greek (0)	0	<0.01
Guyanese (0)	0	<0.01
Hungarian (35)	54	0.10
Icelander (0)	0	<0.01
Iranian (54)	54	0.10
Irish (352)	1,431	2.74
Israeli (0)	0	<0.01
Italian (458)	998	1.91
Latvian (0)	0	<0.01
Lithuanian (0)	0	<0.01
Luxemburger (0)	0	<0.01
Macedonian (0)	0	<0.01
Maltese (0)	0	<0.01
New Zealander (0)	0	<0.01
Northern European (0)	0	<0.01
Norwegian (14)	175	0.34
Pennsylvania German (0)	0	<0.01
Polish (50)	172	0.33
Portuguese (64)	224	0.43
Romanian (184)	184	0.35
Russian (0)	20	0.04
Scandinavian (7)	27	0.05
Scotch-Irish (55)	259	0.50
Scottish (196)	347	0.66
Serbian (0)	0	<0.01
Slavic (11)	11	0.02
Slovak (0)	9	0.02
Slovene (0)	0	<0.01
Soviet Union (0)	0	<0.01
Swedish (82)	182	0.35
Swiss (0)	0	<0.01
Turkish (0)	0	<0.01
Ukrainian (11)	20	0.04
Welsh (0)	42	0.08
West Indian, ex. Hispanic (178)	218	0.42
Bahamian (0)	0	<0.01
Barbadian (0)	0	<0.01
Belizean (56)	96	0.18
Bermudan (0)	0	<0.01
British West Indian (0)	0	<0.01
Dutch West Indian (13)	13	0.02
Haitian (46)	46	0.09
Jamaican (63)	63	0.12
Trinidadian/Tobagonian (0)	0	<0.01
U.S. Virgin Islander (0)	0	<0.01
West Indian (0)	0	<0.01
Other West Indian (0)	0	<0.01
Yugoslavian (9)	37	0.07

Hispanic Origin	Population	%
Hispanic or Latino (of any race)	37,039	71.02
Central American, ex. Mexican	1,397	2.68
Costa Rican	21	0.04
Guatemalan	406	0.78
Honduran	93	0.18
Nicaraguan	157	0.30
Panamanian	40	0.08
Salvadoran	656	1.26
Other Central American	24	0.05
Cuban	119	0.23
Dominican Republic	26	0.05
Mexican	32,985	63.25
Puerto Rican	397	0.76
South American	289	0.55
Argentinean	32	0.06
Bolivian	13	0.02
Chilean	13	0.02
Colombian	83	0.16
Ecuadorian	44	0.08
Paraguayan	0	<0.01
Peruvian	80	0.15
Uruguayan	7	0.01
Venezuelan	16	0.03
Other South American	1	<0.01
Other Hispanic or Latino	1,826	3.50

Race*	Population	%
African-American/Black (5,055)	5,750	11.03
Not Hispanic (4,648)	5,060	9.70
Hispanic (407)	690	1.32
American Indian/Alaska Native (661)	1,122	2.15
Not Hispanic (126)	334	0.64
Hispanic (535)	788	1.51
Alaska Athabascan *(Ala. Nat.)* (3)	3	0.01
Aleut *(Alaska Native)* (0)	3	0.01
Apache (29)	53	0.10
Arapaho (0)	0	<0.01
Blackfeet (4)	18	0.03
Canadian/French Am. Ind. (2)	2	<0.01
Central American Ind. (5)	14	0.03
Cherokee (20)	108	0.21
Cheyenne (2)	3	0.01
Chickasaw (1)	6	0.01
Chippewa (2)	11	0.02
Choctaw (10)	28	0.05
Colville (0)	0	<0.01
Comanche (3)	5	0.01
Cree (0)	0	<0.01
Creek (8)	16	0.03
Crow (0)	0	<0.01
Delaware (0)	0	<0.01
Hopi (0)	1	<0.01
Houma (0)	0	<0.01
Inupiat *(Alaska Native)* (0)	0	<0.01
Iroquois (2)	6	0.01
Kiowa (0)	0	<0.01
Lumbee (0)	0	<0.01
Menominee (0)	0	<0.01
Mexican American Ind. (88)	134	0.26
Navajo (12)	29	0.06
Osage (0)	1	<0.01
Ottawa (1)	1	<0.01
Paiute (0)	2	<0.01
Pima (4)	4	0.01
Potawatomi (2)	7	0.01
Pueblo (5)	6	0.01
Puget Sound Salish (0)	0	<0.01
Seminole (0)	0	<0.01
Shoshone (0)	1	<0.01
Sioux (10)	13	0.02
South American Ind. (0)	1	<0.01
Spanish American Ind. (7)	7	0.01
Tlingit-Haida *(Alaska Native)* (0)	0	<0.01
Tohono O'Odham (0)	1	<0.01
Tsimshian *(Alaska Native)* (0)	0	<0.01
Ute (0)	0	<0.01
Yakama (0)	0	<0.01
Yaqui (20)	29	0.06
Yuman (6)	14	0.03
Yup'ik *(Alaska Native)* (0)	0	<0.01
Asian (2,590)	3,151	6.04
Not Hispanic (2,430)	2,780	5.33
Hispanic (160)	371	0.71
Bangladeshi (10)	14	0.03
Bhutanese (0)	0	<0.01
Burmese (6)	6	0.01
Cambodian (57)	76	0.15
Chinese, ex. Taiwanese (191)	283	0.54
Filipino (943)	1,160	2.22
Hmong (16)	16	0.03
Indian (257)	338	0.65
Indonesian (319)	429	0.82
Japanese (73)	140	0.27
Korean (149)	186	0.36
Laotian (15)	21	0.04
Malaysian (0)	2	<0.01
Nepalese (6)	6	0.01
Pakistani (30)	40	0.08
Sri Lankan (3)	6	0.01
Taiwanese (6)	6	0.01
Thai (38)	54	0.10
Vietnamese (308)	343	0.66
Hawaii Native/Pacific Islander (176)	337	0.65
Not Hispanic (136)	232	0.44
Hispanic (40)	105	0.20
Fijian (1)	1	<0.01
Guamanian/Chamorro (24)	39	0.07
Marshallese (0)	0	<0.01
Native Hawaiian (29)	73	0.14
Samoan (67)	101	0.19
Tongan (41)	49	0.09
White (22,613)	24,634	47.23
Not Hispanic (6,803)	7,413	14.21
Hispanic (15,810)	17,221	33.02

*Notes: † The Census 2010 population figure is used to calculate the percentages in the Hispanic Origin and Race categories. Ancestry percentages are based on the 2006-2010 American Community Survey population (not shown); ‡ Numbers in parentheses indicate the number of people reporting a single ancestry; * Numbers in parentheses indicate the number of persons reporting this race alone, not in combination with any other race; Please refer to the Explanation of Data for more information.*

Compton

Place Type: City
County: Los Angeles
Population: 96,455

Ancestry	Population	%
Afghan (0)	0	<0.01
African, Sub-Saharan (3,208)	4,191	4.38
African (3,199)	4,112	4.29
Cape Verdean (0)	0	<0.01
Ethiopian (9)	9	0.01
Ghanaian (0)	0	<0.01
Kenyan (0)	0	<0.01
Liberian (0)	0	<0.01
Nigerian (0)	70	0.07
Senegalese (0)	0	<0.01
Sierra Leonean (0)	0	<0.01
Somalian (0)	0	<0.01
South African (0)	0	<0.01
Sudanese (0)	0	<0.01
Ugandan (0)	0	<0.01
Zimbabwean (0)	0	<0.01
Other Sub-Saharan African (0)	0	<0.01
Albanian (0)	0	<0.01
Alsatian (0)	0	<0.01
American (1,113)	1,113	1.16
Arab (0)	0	<0.01
Arab (0)	0	<0.01
Egyptian (0)	0	<0.01
Iraqi (0)	0	<0.01
Jordanian (0)	0	<0.01
Lebanese (0)	0	<0.01
Moroccan (0)	0	<0.01
Palestinian (0)	0	<0.01
Syrian (0)	0	<0.01
Other Arab (0)	0	<0.01
Armenian (0)	0	<0.01
Assyrian/Chaldean/Syriac (0)	0	<0.01
Australian (0)	0	<0.01
Austrian (0)	0	<0.01
Basque (0)	0	<0.01
Belgian (0)	0	<0.01
Brazilian (0)	0	<0.01
British (48)	58	0.06
Bulgarian (0)	0	<0.01
Cajun (0)	0	<0.01
Canadian (0)	0	<0.01
Carpatho Rusyn (0)	0	<0.01
Celtic (0)	0	<0.01
Croatian (0)	0	<0.01
Cypriot (0)	0	<0.01
Czech (0)	14	0.01
Czechoslovakian (0)	0	<0.01
Danish (0)	20	0.02
Dutch (0)	31	0.03
Eastern European (0)	0	<0.01
English (51)	127	0.13
Estonian (0)	0	<0.01
European (23)	149	0.16
Finnish (0)	11	0.01
French, ex. Basque (5)	80	0.08
French Canadian (0)	0	<0.01
German (8)	71	0.07
German Russian (0)	0	<0.01
Greek (7)	7	0.01
Guyanese (64)	64	0.07
Hungarian (9)	9	0.01
Icelander (0)	0	<0.01
Iranian (0)	0	<0.01
Irish (28)	162	0.17
Israeli (0)	0	<0.01
Italian (48)	182	0.19
Latvian (0)	0	<0.01
Lithuanian (0)	0	<0.01
Luxemburger (0)	0	<0.01
Macedonian (0)	0	<0.01
Maltese (0)	0	<0.01
New Zealander (0)	0	<0.01
Northern European (12)	51	0.05
Norwegian (35)	35	0.04
Pennsylvania German (0)	0	<0.01
Polish (0)	0	<0.01
Portuguese (24)	110	0.11
Romanian (0)	0	<0.01
Russian (0)	0	<0.01
Scandinavian (0)	0	<0.01
Scotch-Irish (0)	0	<0.01
Scottish (0)	8	0.01
Serbian (0)	0	<0.01
Slavic (0)	0	<0.01
Slovak (0)	0	<0.01
Slovene (0)	0	<0.01
Soviet Union (0)	0	<0.01
Swedish (0)	0	<0.01
Swiss (0)	0	<0.01
Turkish (0)	0	<0.01
Ukrainian (0)	0	<0.01
Welsh (0)	0	<0.01
West Indian, ex. Hispanic (192)	458	0.48
Bahamian (11)	11	0.01
Barbadian (0)	0	<0.01
Belizean (158)	308	0.32
Bermudan (0)	0	<0.01
British West Indian (0)	0	<0.01
Dutch West Indian (0)	0	<0.01
Haitian (0)	0	<0.01
Jamaican (23)	122	0.13
Trinidadian/Tobagonian (0)	0	<0.01
U.S. Virgin Islander (0)	0	<0.01
West Indian (0)	17	0.02
Other West Indian (0)	0	<0.01
Yugoslavian (0)	0	<0.01

Hispanic Origin	Population	%
Hispanic or Latino (of any race)	62,669	64.97
Central American, ex. Mexican	4,910	5.09
Costa Rican	39	0.04
Guatemalan	1,471	1.53
Honduran	571	0.59
Nicaraguan	215	0.22
Panamanian	30	0.03
Salvadoran	2,470	2.56
Other Central American	114	0.12
Cuban	77	0.08
Dominican Republic	27	0.03
Mexican	54,084	56.07
Puerto Rican	218	0.23
South American	209	0.22
Argentinean	12	0.01
Bolivian	7	0.01
Chilean	15	0.02
Colombian	46	0.05
Ecuadorian	54	0.06
Paraguayan	1	<0.01
Peruvian	66	0.07
Uruguayan	0	<0.01
Venezuelan	3	<0.01
Other South American	5	0.01
Other Hispanic or Latino	3,144	3.26

Race*	Population	%
African-American/Black (31,688)	32,800	34.01
Not Hispanic (30,992)	31,687	32.85
Hispanic (696)	1,113	1.15
American Indian/Alaska Native (655)	1,182	1.23
Not Hispanic (175)	468	0.49
Hispanic (480)	714	0.74
Alaska Athabascan *(Ala. Nat.)* (0)	0	<0.01
Aleut *(Alaska Native)* (0)	0	<0.01
Apache (7)	14	0.01
Arapaho (0)	0	<0.01
Blackfeet (3)	42	0.04
Canadian/French Am. Ind. (13)	13	0.01
Central American Ind. (4)	8	0.01
Cherokee (23)	88	0.09
Cheyenne (0)	4	<0.01
Chickasaw (0)	0	<0.01
Chippewa (1)	4	<0.01
Choctaw (19)	47	0.05
Colville (0)	0	<0.01
Comanche (0)	0	<0.01
Cree (0)	1	<0.01
Creek (1)	8	0.01
Crow (0)	0	<0.01
Delaware (0)	0	<0.01
Hopi (0)	0	<0.01
Houma (0)	0	<0.01
Inupiat *(Alaska Native)* (0)	0	<0.01
Iroquois (0)	1	<0.01
Kiowa (0)	0	<0.01
Lumbee (0)	0	<0.01
Menominee (0)	0	<0.01
Mexican American Ind. (127)	185	0.19
Navajo (29)	31	0.03
Osage (0)	0	<0.01
Ottawa (0)	0	<0.01
Paiute (3)	3	<0.01
Pima (2)	4	<0.01
Potawatomi (0)	0	<0.01
Pueblo (3)	4	<0.01
Puget Sound Salish (0)	0	<0.01
Seminole (0)	2	<0.01
Shoshone (0)	0	<0.01
Sioux (7)	11	0.01
South American Ind. (4)	4	<0.01
Spanish American Ind. (28)	31	0.03
Tlingit-Haida *(Alaska Native)* (0)	0	<0.01
Tohono O'Odham (0)	0	<0.01
Tsimshian *(Alaska Native)* (0)	0	<0.01
Ute (0)	0	<0.01
Yakama (0)	0	<0.01
Yaqui (3)	8	0.01
Yuman (3)	3	<0.01
Yup'ik *(Alaska Native)* (0)	0	<0.01
Asian (292)	617	0.64
Not Hispanic (222)	391	0.41
Hispanic (70)	226	0.23
Bangladeshi (0)	0	<0.01
Bhutanese (0)	0	<0.01
Burmese (0)	1	<0.01
Cambodian (11)	25	0.03
Chinese, ex. Taiwanese (18)	59	0.06
Filipino (137)	257	0.27
Hmong (1)	1	<0.01
Indian (31)	67	0.07
Indonesian (3)	9	0.01
Japanese (23)	46	0.05
Korean (13)	26	0.03
Laotian (1)	3	<0.01
Malaysian (0)	0	<0.01
Nepalese (0)	0	<0.01
Pakistani (11)	11	0.01
Sri Lankan (2)	2	<0.01
Taiwanese (0)	1	<0.01
Thai (8)	9	0.01
Vietnamese (23)	30	0.03
Hawaii Native/Pacific Islander (718)	899	0.93
Not Hispanic (684)	805	0.83
Hispanic (34)	94	0.10
Fijian (1)	1	<0.01
Guamanian/Chamorro (6)	18	0.02
Marshallese (0)	0	<0.01
Native Hawaiian (9)	52	0.05
Samoan (624)	735	0.76
Tongan (33)	42	0.04
White (24,942)	27,200	28.20
Not Hispanic (782)	1,117	1.16
Hispanic (24,160)	26,083	27.04

*Notes: † The Census 2010 population figure is used to calculate the percentages in the Hispanic Origin and Race categories. Ancestry percentages are based on the 2006-2010 American Community Survey population (not shown); ‡ Numbers in parentheses indicate the number of people reporting a single ancestry; * Numbers in parentheses indicate the number of persons reporting this race alone, not in combination with any other race; Please refer to the Explanation of Data for more information.*

Concord

Place Type: City
County: Contra Costa
Population: 122,067

Ancestry	Population	%
Afghan (1,608)	1,655	1.36
African, Sub-Saharan (736)	931	0.77
African (229)	347	0.29
Cape Verdean (89)	114	0.09
Ethiopian (55)	55	0.05
Ghanaian (0)	0	<0.01
Kenyan (17)	38	0.03
Liberian (64)	64	0.05
Nigerian (104)	135	0.11
Senegalese (0)	0	<0.01
Sierra Leonean (0)	0	<0.01
Somalian (0)	0	<0.01
South African (100)	100	0.08
Sudanese (0)	0	<0.01
Ugandan (66)	66	0.05
Zimbabwean (0)	0	<0.01
Other Sub-Saharan African (12)	12	0.01
Albanian (0)	0	<0.01
Alsatian (29)	29	0.02
American (4,147)	4,147	3.42
Arab (145)	182	0.15
Arab (0)	0	<0.01
Egyptian (10)	10	0.01
Iraqi (0)	0	<0.01
Jordanian (0)	0	<0.01
Lebanese (28)	56	0.05
Moroccan (0)	0	<0.01
Palestinian (60)	60	0.05
Syrian (0)	9	0.01
Other Arab (47)	47	0.04
Armenian (66)	205	0.17
Assyrian/Chaldean/Syriac (0)	0	<0.01
Australian (62)	95	0.08
Austrian (92)	211	0.17
Basque (0)	30	0.02
Belgian (30)	154	0.13
Brazilian (271)	327	0.27
British (217)	585	0.48
Bulgarian (149)	294	0.24
Cajun (16)	16	0.01
Canadian (121)	216	0.18
Carpatho Rusyn (0)	0	<0.01
Celtic (7)	21	0.02
Croatian (87)	175	0.14
Cypriot (0)	0	<0.01
Czech (106)	379	0.31
Czechoslovakian (0)	10	0.01
Danish (215)	892	0.74
Dutch (273)	1,529	1.26
Eastern European (108)	119	0.10
English (2,562)	10,528	8.68
Estonian (0)	0	<0.01
European (1,816)	2,204	1.82
Finnish (13)	80	0.07
French, ex. Basque (403)	3,477	2.87
French Canadian (189)	517	0.43
German (3,705)	14,696	12.11
German Russian (0)	0	<0.01
Greek (180)	813	0.67
Guyanese (71)	71	0.06
Hungarian (134)	633	0.52
Icelander (16)	16	0.01
Iranian (589)	714	0.59
Irish (2,774)	12,170	10.03
Israeli (109)	109	0.09
Italian (2,759)	7,426	6.12
Latvian (0)	28	0.02
Lithuanian (98)	231	0.19
Luxemburger (0)	16	0.01
Macedonian (0)	37	0.03
Maltese (24)	166	0.14
New Zealander (0)	13	0.01
Northern European (164)	180	0.15
Norwegian (860)	2,059	1.70
Pennsylvania German (0)	13	0.01
Polish (577)	1,834	1.51
Portuguese (832)	2,291	1.89
Romanian (124)	164	0.14
Russian (1,443)	2,149	1.77
Scandinavian (323)	517	0.43
Scotch-Irish (753)	2,110	1.74
Scottish (639)	2,161	1.78
Serbian (15)	29	0.02
Slavic (22)	51	0.04
Slovak (122)	194	0.16
Slovene (0)	17	0.01
Soviet Union (0)	0	<0.01
Swedish (562)	1,845	1.52
Swiss (46)	288	0.24
Turkish (41)	49	0.04
Ukrainian (287)	529	0.44
Welsh (131)	975	0.80
West Indian, ex. Hispanic (51)	131	0.11
Bahamian (0)	0	<0.01
Barbadian (0)	0	<0.01
Belizean (0)	0	<0.01
Bermudan (0)	0	<0.01
British West Indian (10)	10	0.01
Dutch West Indian (0)	0	<0.01
Haitian (0)	0	<0.01
Jamaican (11)	74	0.06
Trinidadian/Tobagonian (12)	12	0.01
U.S. Virgin Islander (0)	0	<0.01
West Indian (18)	35	0.03
Other West Indian (0)	0	<0.01
Yugoslavian (16)	48	0.04

Hispanic Origin	Population	%
Hispanic or Latino (of any race)	37,311	30.57
Central American, ex. Mexican	4,761	3.90
Costa Rican	118	0.10
Guatemalan	592	0.48
Honduran	116	0.10
Nicaraguan	886	0.73
Panamanian	119	0.10
Salvadoran	2,904	2.38
Other Central American	26	0.02
Cuban	214	0.18
Dominican Republic	30	0.02
Mexican	26,779	21.94
Puerto Rican	892	0.73
South American	1,845	1.51
Argentinean	146	0.12
Bolivian	53	0.04
Chilean	101	0.08
Colombian	279	0.23
Ecuadorian	111	0.09
Paraguayan	9	0.01
Peruvian	1,056	0.87
Uruguayan	15	0.01
Venezuelan	55	0.05
Other South American	20	0.02
Other Hispanic or Latino	2,790	2.29

Race*	Population	%
African-American/Black (4,371)	5,791	4.74
Not Hispanic (3,991)	5,064	4.15
Hispanic (380)	727	0.60
American Indian/Alaska Native (852)	2,298	1.88
Not Hispanic (366)	1,287	1.05
Hispanic (486)	1,011	0.83
Alaska Athabascan *(Ala. Nat.)* (1)	2	<0.01
Aleut *(Alaska Native)* (2)	4	<0.01
Apache (38)	95	0.08
Arapaho (1)	8	0.01
Blackfeet (8)	79	0.06
Canadian/French Am. Ind. (2)	6	<0.01
Central American Ind. (3)	21	0.02
Cherokee (64)	438	0.36
Cheyenne (1)	5	<0.01
Chickasaw (9)	25	0.02
Chippewa (8)	35	0.03
Choctaw (28)	111	0.09
Colville (0)	2	<0.01
Comanche (6)	14	0.01
Cree (0)	3	<0.01
Creek (3)	12	0.01
Crow (0)	1	<0.01
Delaware (6)	7	0.01
Hopi (2)	4	<0.01
Houma (0)	0	<0.01
Inupiat *(Alaska Native)* (0)	0	<0.01
Iroquois (17)	27	0.02
Kiowa (2)	4	<0.01
Lumbee (0)	0	<0.01
Menominee (0)	1	<0.01
Mexican American Ind. (105)	160	0.13
Navajo (35)	77	0.06
Osage (2)	6	<0.01
Ottawa (0)	0	<0.01
Paiute (8)	15	0.01
Pima (0)	0	<0.01
Potawatomi (12)	15	0.01
Pueblo (15)	27	0.02
Puget Sound Salish (1)	4	<0.01
Seminole (2)	9	0.01
Shoshone (0)	4	<0.01
Sioux (20)	70	0.06
South American Ind. (9)	24	0.02
Spanish American Ind. (2)	5	<0.01
Tlingit-Haida *(Alaska Native)* (3)	8	0.01
Tohono O'Odham (4)	5	<0.01
Tsimshian *(Alaska Native)* (0)	2	<0.01
Ute (7)	16	0.01
Yakama (2)	3	<0.01
Yaqui (5)	18	0.01
Yuman (0)	2	<0.01
Yup'ik *(Alaska Native)* (0)	0	<0.01
Asian (13,538)	17,105	14.01
Not Hispanic (13,219)	16,144	13.23
Hispanic (319)	961	0.79
Bangladeshi (8)	9	0.01
Bhutanese (0)	0	<0.01
Burmese (75)	96	0.08
Cambodian (48)	68	0.06
Chinese, ex. Taiwanese (2,795)	3,601	2.95
Filipino (5,333)	6,837	5.60
Hmong (8)	9	0.01
Indian (1,628)	1,872	1.53
Indonesian (132)	201	0.16
Japanese (749)	1,382	1.13
Korean (686)	873	0.72
Laotian (101)	121	0.10
Malaysian (4)	17	0.01
Nepalese (16)	17	0.01
Pakistani (188)	218	0.18
Sri Lankan (34)	39	0.03
Taiwanese (99)	126	0.10
Thai (112)	162	0.13
Vietnamese (799)	944	0.77
Hawaii Native/Pacific Islander (816)	1,445	1.18
Not Hispanic (744)	1,172	0.96
Hispanic (72)	273	0.22
Fijian (28)	36	0.03
Guamanian/Chamorro (90)	161	0.13
Marshallese (0)	0	<0.01
Native Hawaiian (88)	369	0.30
Samoan (121)	232	0.19
Tongan (341)	380	0.31
White (78,767)	85,528	70.07
Not Hispanic (61,416)	65,567	53.71
Hispanic (17,351)	19,961	16.35

*Notes: † The Census 2010 population figure is used to calculate the percentages in the Hispanic Origin and Race categories. Ancestry percentages are based on the 2006-2010 American Community Survey population (not shown); ‡ Numbers in parentheses indicate the number of people reporting a single ancestry; * Numbers in parentheses indicate the number of persons reporting this race alone, not in combination with any other race; Please refer to the Explanation of Data for more information.*

Corona

Place Type: City
County: Riverside
Population: 152,374

Ancestry	Population	%
Afghan (22)	94	0.06
African, Sub-Saharan (398)	600	0.40
African (237)	407	0.27
Cape Verdean (0)	0	<0.01
Ethiopian (26)	26	0.02
Ghanaian (0)	0	<0.01
Kenyan (0)	0	<0.01
Liberian (0)	0	<0.01
Nigerian (65)	82	0.05
Senegalese (0)	0	<0.01
Sierra Leonean (0)	0	<0.01
Somalian (0)	0	<0.01
South African (0)	0	<0.01
Sudanese (40)	40	0.03
Ugandan (0)	0	<0.01
Zimbabwean (30)	30	0.02
Other Sub-Saharan African (0)	15	0.01
Albanian (0)	0	<0.01
Alsatian (0)	0	<0.01
American (3,027)	3,027	2.01
Arab (2,818)	3,365	2.24
Arab (379)	463	0.31
Egyptian (1,053)	1,103	0.73
Iraqi (151)	239	0.16
Jordanian (58)	88	0.06
Lebanese (715)	845	0.56
Moroccan (148)	148	0.10
Palestinian (149)	195	0.13
Syrian (0)	46	0.03
Other Arab (165)	238	0.16
Armenian (187)	313	0.21
Assyrian/Chaldean/Syriac (34)	34	0.02
Australian (0)	47	0.03
Austrian (46)	137	0.09
Basque (37)	57	0.04
Belgian (28)	71	0.05
Brazilian (83)	183	0.12
British (182)	309	0.21
Bulgarian (6)	20	0.01
Cajun (0)	27	0.02
Canadian (103)	296	0.20
Carpatho Rusyn (0)	0	<0.01
Celtic (0)	6	<0.01
Croatian (12)	80	0.05
Cypriot (0)	0	<0.01
Czech (178)	286	0.19
Czechoslovakian (27)	49	0.03
Danish (256)	758	0.50
Dutch (365)	1,911	1.27
Eastern European (0)	10	0.01
English (2,697)	8,970	5.96
Estonian (0)	0	<0.01
European (1,754)	2,049	1.36
Finnish (43)	153	0.10
French, ex. Basque (649)	3,872	2.57
French Canadian (456)	892	0.59
German (4,083)	16,019	10.64
German Russian (0)	0	<0.01
Greek (140)	725	0.48
Guyanese (0)	11	0.01
Hungarian (220)	458	0.30
Icelander (9)	23	0.02
Iranian (961)	1,065	0.71
Irish (2,074)	11,652	7.74
Israeli (32)	62	0.04
Italian (1,921)	6,284	4.18
Latvian (69)	78	0.05
Lithuanian (100)	223	0.15
Luxemburger (11)	11	0.01
Macedonian (34)	49	0.03
Maltese (0)	0	<0.01
New Zealander (8)	24	0.02
Northern European (30)	43	0.03
Norwegian (429)	1,808	1.20
Pennsylvania German (0)	0	<0.01
Polish (912)	2,224	1.48
Portuguese (209)	639	0.42
Romanian (145)	221	0.15
Russian (269)	776	0.52
Scandinavian (257)	681	0.45
Scotch-Irish (486)	1,758	1.17
Scottish (518)	1,904	1.27
Serbian (0)	95	0.06
Slavic (0)	36	0.02
Slovak (24)	107	0.07
Slovene (12)	29	0.02
Soviet Union (0)	0	<0.01
Swedish (380)	1,857	1.23
Swiss (59)	168	0.11
Turkish (0)	19	0.01
Ukrainian (78)	136	0.09
Welsh (49)	466	0.31
West Indian, ex. Hispanic (67)	101	0.07
Bahamian (0)	0	<0.01
Barbadian (8)	8	0.01
Belizean (20)	20	0.01
Bermudan (0)	0	<0.01
British West Indian (0)	0	<0.01
Dutch West Indian (0)	0	<0.01
Haitian (0)	0	<0.01
Jamaican (13)	47	0.03
Trinidadian/Tobagonian (0)	0	<0.01
U.S. Virgin Islander (0)	0	<0.01
West Indian (26)	26	0.02
Other West Indian (0)	0	<0.01
Yugoslavian (20)	115	0.08

Hispanic Origin	Population	%
Hispanic or Latino (of any race)	66,447	43.61
Central American, ex. Mexican	3,118	2.05
Costa Rican	173	0.11
Guatemalan	934	0.61
Honduran	215	0.14
Nicaraguan	296	0.19
Panamanian	111	0.07
Salvadoran	1,350	0.89
Other Central American	39	0.03
Cuban	651	0.43
Dominican Republic	54	0.04
Mexican	56,979	37.39
Puerto Rican	899	0.59
South American	1,740	1.14
Argentinean	244	0.16
Bolivian	82	0.05
Chilean	140	0.09
Colombian	396	0.26
Ecuadorian	239	0.16
Paraguayan	0	<0.01
Peruvian	513	0.34
Uruguayan	27	0.02
Venezuelan	70	0.05
Other South American	29	0.02
Other Hispanic or Latino	3,006	1.97

Race*	Population	%
African-American/Black (8,934)	10,450	6.86
Not Hispanic (8,333)	9,399	6.17
Hispanic (601)	1,051	0.69
American Indian/Alaska Native (1,153)	2,256	1.48
Not Hispanic (422)	992	0.65
Hispanic (731)	1,264	0.83
Alaska Athabascan *(Ala. Nat.)* (0)	0	<0.01
Aleut *(Alaska Native)* (0)	2	<0.01
Apache (46)	86	0.06
Arapaho (0)	0	<0.01
Blackfeet (13)	41	0.03
Canadian/French Am. Ind. (0)	1	<0.01
Central American Ind. (3)	3	<0.01
Cherokee (75)	265	0.17
Cheyenne (1)	1	<0.01
Chickasaw (24)	32	0.02
Chippewa (15)	23	0.02
Choctaw (29)	81	0.05
Colville (1)	1	<0.01
Comanche (3)	17	0.01
Cree (1)	1	<0.01
Creek (9)	16	0.01
Crow (5)	9	0.01
Delaware (0)	0	<0.01
Hopi (8)	14	0.01
Houma (0)	0	<0.01
Inupiat *(Alaska Native)* (0)	0	<0.01
Iroquois (6)	23	0.02
Kiowa (6)	7	<0.01
Lumbee (1)	2	<0.01
Menominee (1)	1	<0.01
Mexican American Ind. (117)	171	0.11
Navajo (33)	66	0.04
Osage (4)	9	0.01
Ottawa (0)	0	<0.01
Paiute (2)	9	0.01
Pima (6)	7	<0.01
Potawatomi (3)	4	<0.01
Pueblo (6)	13	0.01
Puget Sound Salish (0)	0	<0.01
Seminole (1)	19	0.01
Shoshone (1)	3	<0.01
Sioux (16)	40	0.03
South American Ind. (6)	15	0.01
Spanish American Ind. (5)	35	0.02
Tlingit-Haida *(Alaska Native)* (0)	1	<0.01
Tohono O'Odham (5)	8	0.01
Tsimshian *(Alaska Native)* (0)	0	<0.01
Ute (4)	12	0.01
Yakama (0)	1	<0.01
Yaqui (27)	56	0.04
Yuman (6)	11	0.01
Yup'ik *(Alaska Native)* (0)	0	<0.01
Asian (15,048)	17,899	11.75
Not Hispanic (14,650)	16,857	11.06
Hispanic (398)	1,042	0.68
Bangladeshi (55)	77	0.05
Bhutanese (0)	0	<0.01
Burmese (11)	17	0.01
Cambodian (284)	332	0.22
Chinese, ex. Taiwanese (1,287)	1,843	1.21
Filipino (4,570)	5,660	3.71
Hmong (21)	34	0.02
Indian (2,436)	2,693	1.77
Indonesian (153)	227	0.15
Japanese (465)	1,012	0.66
Korean (1,756)	1,993	1.31
Laotian (139)	182	0.12
Malaysian (2)	8	0.01
Nepalese (2)	2	<0.01
Pakistani (666)	731	0.48
Sri Lankan (86)	88	0.06
Taiwanese (156)	172	0.11
Thai (130)	198	0.13
Vietnamese (2,215)	2,520	1.65
Hawaii Native/Pacific Islander (552)	1,098	0.72
Not Hispanic (496)	887	0.58
Hispanic (56)	211	0.14
Fijian (38)	47	0.03
Guamanian/Chamorro (127)	222	0.15
Marshallese (5)	5	<0.01
Native Hawaiian (101)	301	0.20
Samoan (161)	260	0.17
Tongan (50)	58	0.04
White (90,925)	97,516	64.00
Not Hispanic (58,087)	61,175	40.15
Hispanic (32,838)	36,341	23.85

*Notes: † The Census 2010 population figure is used to calculate the percentages in the Hispanic Origin and Race categories. Ancestry percentages are based on the 2006-2010 American Community Survey population (not shown); ‡ Numbers in parentheses indicate the number of people reporting a single ancestry; * Numbers in parentheses indicate the number of persons reporting this race alone, not in combination with any other race; Please refer to the Explanation of Data for more information.*

Costa Mesa

Place Type: City
County: Orange
Population: 109,960

Ancestry	Population	%
Afghan (9)	9	0.01
African, Sub-Saharan (119)	155	0.14
African (77)	95	0.09
Cape Verdean (0)	0	<0.01
Ethiopian (0)	0	<0.01
Ghanaian (0)	0	<0.01
Kenyan (0)	0	<0.01
Liberian (0)	0	<0.01
Nigerian (0)	0	<0.01
Senegalese (0)	0	<0.01
Sierra Leonean (0)	0	<0.01
Somalian (0)	0	<0.01
South African (8)	26	0.02
Sudanese (0)	0	<0.01
Ugandan (0)	0	<0.01
Zimbabwean (0)	0	<0.01
Other Sub-Saharan African (34)	34	0.03
Albanian (0)	0	<0.01
Alsatian (0)	33	0.03
American (2,803)	2,803	2.56
Arab (615)	746	0.68
Arab (138)	181	0.17
Egyptian (206)	206	0.19
Iraqi (0)	0	<0.01
Jordanian (53)	53	0.05
Lebanese (96)	136	0.12
Moroccan (7)	7	0.01
Palestinian (53)	53	0.05
Syrian (9)	25	0.02
Other Arab (53)	85	0.08
Armenian (221)	674	0.62
Assyrian/Chaldean/Syriac (0)	0	<0.01
Australian (13)	95	0.09
Austrian (43)	256	0.23
Basque (9)	23	0.02
Belgian (17)	44	0.04
Brazilian (134)	193	0.18
British (394)	826	0.76
Bulgarian (25)	38	0.03
Cajun (0)	0	<0.01
Canadian (147)	482	0.44
Carpatho Rusyn (0)	0	<0.01
Celtic (19)	19	0.02
Croatian (124)	201	0.18
Cypriot (0)	0	<0.01
Czech (92)	533	0.49
Czechoslovakian (9)	42	0.04
Danish (86)	513	0.47
Dutch (395)	1,668	1.53
Eastern European (205)	237	0.22
English (2,957)	9,779	8.95
Estonian (12)	12	0.01
European (1,178)	1,511	1.38
Finnish (59)	170	0.16
French, ex. Basque (284)	3,000	2.74
French Canadian (232)	661	0.60
German (3,505)	14,780	13.52
German Russian (0)	0	<0.01
Greek (247)	727	0.67
Guyanese (0)	0	<0.01
Hungarian (131)	640	0.59
Icelander (27)	35	0.03
Iranian (244)	361	0.33
Irish (2,670)	10,915	9.98
Israeli (54)	84	0.08
Italian (2,113)	5,902	5.40
Latvian (25)	60	0.05
Lithuanian (98)	245	0.22
Luxemburger (0)	0	<0.01
Macedonian (8)	8	0.01
Maltese (11)	11	0.01
New Zealander (55)	55	0.05
Northern European (158)	171	0.16
Norwegian (500)	1,924	1.76
Pennsylvania German (0)	15	0.01
Polish (912)	2,415	2.21
Portuguese (183)	704	0.64
Romanian (39)	93	0.09
Russian (437)	1,496	1.37
Scandinavian (161)	473	0.43
Scotch-Irish (567)	1,748	1.60
Scottish (568)	2,293	2.10
Serbian (32)	32	0.03
Slavic (10)	21	0.02
Slovak (128)	207	0.19
Slovene (7)	48	0.04
Soviet Union (0)	0	<0.01
Swedish (615)	2,201	2.01
Swiss (141)	467	0.43
Turkish (54)	78	0.07
Ukrainian (100)	211	0.19
Welsh (138)	710	0.65
West Indian, ex. Hispanic (151)	218	0.20
Bahamian (0)	0	<0.01
Barbadian (8)	8	0.01
Belizean (0)	0	<0.01
Bermudan (0)	0	<0.01
British West Indian (61)	61	0.06
Dutch West Indian (0)	0	<0.01
Haitian (0)	0	<0.01
Jamaican (48)	115	0.11
Trinidadian/Tobagonian (34)	34	0.03
U.S. Virgin Islander (0)	0	<0.01
West Indian (0)	0	<0.01
Other West Indian (0)	0	<0.01
Yugoslavian (50)	112	0.10

Hispanic Origin	Population	%
Hispanic or Latino (of any race)	39,403	35.83
Central American, ex. Mexican	3,497	3.18
Costa Rican	47	0.04
Guatemalan	1,134	1.03
Honduran	174	0.16
Nicaraguan	108	0.10
Panamanian	22	0.02
Salvadoran	1,983	1.80
Other Central American	29	0.03
Cuban	233	0.21
Dominican Republic	23	0.02
Mexican	31,646	28.78
Puerto Rican	433	0.39
South American	1,146	1.04
Argentinean	239	0.22
Bolivian	70	0.06
Chilean	54	0.05
Colombian	299	0.27
Ecuadorian	153	0.14
Paraguayan	8	0.01
Peruvian	251	0.23
Uruguayan	35	0.03
Venezuelan	22	0.02
Other South American	15	0.01
Other Hispanic or Latino	2,425	2.21

Race*	Population	%
African-American/Black (1,640)	2,337	2.13
Not Hispanic (1,352)	1,895	1.72
Hispanic (288)	442	0.40
American Indian/Alaska Native (686)	1,651	1.50
Not Hispanic (266)	772	0.70
Hispanic (420)	879	0.80
Alaska Athabascan *(Ala. Nat.)* (0)	0	<0.01
Aleut *(Alaska Native)* (5)	6	0.01
Apache (21)	49	0.04
Arapaho (2)	2	<0.01
Blackfeet (4)	35	0.03
Canadian/French Am. Ind. (1)	1	<0.01
Central American Ind. (1)	1	<0.01
Cherokee (63)	252	0.23
Cheyenne (0)	0	<0.01
Chickasaw (4)	16	0.01
Chippewa (2)	15	0.01
Choctaw (16)	52	0.05
Colville (2)	2	<0.01
Comanche (1)	5	<0.01
Cree (1)	4	<0.01
Creek (0)	6	0.01
Crow (0)	1	<0.01
Delaware (2)	3	<0.01
Hopi (3)	5	<0.01
Houma (0)	0	<0.01
Inupiat *(Alaska Native)* (0)	1	<0.01
Iroquois (1)	6	0.01
Kiowa (0)	0	<0.01
Lumbee (2)	3	<0.01
Menominee (0)	0	<0.01
Mexican American Ind. (100)	197	0.18
Navajo (20)	41	0.04
Osage (3)	7	0.01
Ottawa (0)	0	<0.01
Paiute (5)	7	0.01
Pima (3)	6	0.01
Potawatomi (5)	8	0.01
Pueblo (6)	9	0.01
Puget Sound Salish (5)	6	0.01
Seminole (4)	8	0.01
Shoshone (1)	6	0.01
Sioux (4)	10	0.01
South American Ind. (11)	18	0.02
Spanish American Ind. (7)	10	0.01
Tlingit-Haida *(Alaska Native)* (1)	2	<0.01
Tohono O'Odham (0)	2	<0.01
Tsimshian *(Alaska Native)* (0)	0	<0.01
Ute (2)	2	<0.01
Yakama (0)	4	<0.01
Yaqui (12)	21	0.02
Yuman (4)	5	<0.01
Yup'ik *(Alaska Native)* (1)	1	<0.01
Asian (8,654)	10,662	9.70
Not Hispanic (8,483)	10,160	9.24
Hispanic (171)	502	0.46
Bangladeshi (10)	10	0.01
Bhutanese (0)	0	<0.01
Burmese (8)	9	0.01
Cambodian (93)	137	0.12
Chinese, ex. Taiwanese (981)	1,427	1.30
Filipino (1,814)	2,500	2.27
Hmong (14)	18	0.02
Indian (617)	740	0.67
Indonesian (57)	131	0.12
Japanese (1,312)	1,905	1.73
Korean (730)	907	0.82
Laotian (24)	25	0.02
Malaysian (9)	9	0.01
Nepalese (7)	8	0.01
Pakistani (61)	84	0.08
Sri Lankan (48)	51	0.05
Taiwanese (112)	137	0.12
Thai (121)	167	0.15
Vietnamese (2,255)	2,475	2.25
Hawaii Native/Pacific Islander (527)	995	0.90
Not Hispanic (486)	879	0.80
Hispanic (41)	116	0.11
Fijian (9)	15	0.01
Guamanian/Chamorro (42)	87	0.08
Marshallese (164)	177	0.16
Native Hawaiian (140)	380	0.35
Samoan (86)	155	0.14
Tongan (4)	6	0.01
White (75,335)	79,899	72.66
Not Hispanic (56,993)	59,439	54.06
Hispanic (18,342)	20,460	18.61

*Notes: † The Census 2010 population figure is used to calculate the percentages in the Hispanic Origin and Race categories. Ancestry percentages are based on the 2006-2010 American Community Survey population (not shown); ‡ Numbers in parentheses indicate the number of people reporting a single ancestry; * Numbers in parentheses indicate the number of persons reporting this race alone, not in combination with any other race; Please refer to the Explanation of Data for more information.*

Cupertino

Place Type: City
County: Santa Clara
Population: 58,302

Ancestry	Population	%
Afghan (60)	60	0.11
African, Sub-Saharan (17)	95	0.17
African (0)	34	0.06
Cape Verdean (0)	0	<0.01
Ethiopian (17)	61	0.11
Ghanaian (0)	0	<0.01
Kenyan (0)	0	<0.01
Liberian (0)	0	<0.01
Nigerian (0)	0	<0.01
Senegalese (0)	0	<0.01
Sierra Leonean (0)	0	<0.01
Somalian (0)	0	<0.01
South African (0)	0	<0.01
Sudanese (0)	0	<0.01
Ugandan (0)	0	<0.01
Zimbabwean (0)	0	<0.01
Other Sub-Saharan African (0)	0	<0.01
Albanian (13)	25	0.04
Alsatian (0)	0	<0.01
American (594)	594	1.05
Arab (307)	399	0.71
Arab (0)	13	0.02
Egyptian (205)	227	0.40
Iraqi (0)	0	<0.01
Jordanian (25)	25	0.04
Lebanese (14)	40	0.07
Moroccan (0)	0	<0.01
Palestinian (0)	0	<0.01
Syrian (63)	94	0.17
Other Arab (0)	0	<0.01
Armenian (162)	201	0.36
Assyrian/Chaldean/Syriac (168)	168	0.30
Australian (0)	0	<0.01
Austrian (59)	102	0.18
Basque (0)	0	<0.01
Belgian (21)	51	0.09
Brazilian (14)	14	0.02
British (145)	272	0.48
Bulgarian (55)	55	0.10
Cajun (0)	0	<0.01
Canadian (75)	133	0.24
Carpatho Rusyn (0)	0	<0.01
Celtic (11)	11	0.02
Croatian (102)	228	0.40
Cypriot (0)	0	<0.01
Czech (128)	319	0.56
Czechoslovakian (8)	31	0.05
Danish (29)	226	0.40
Dutch (37)	463	0.82
Eastern European (79)	79	0.14
English (716)	2,908	5.15
Estonian (0)	0	<0.01
European (619)	678	1.20
Finnish (0)	124	0.22
French, ex. Basque (151)	1,037	1.84
French Canadian (73)	162	0.29
German (1,074)	3,754	6.64
German Russian (0)	0	<0.01
Greek (109)	303	0.54
Guyanese (0)	0	<0.01
Hungarian (63)	122	0.22
Icelander (0)	0	<0.01
Iranian (1,005)	1,005	1.78
Irish (595)	2,479	4.39
Israeli (354)	363	0.64
Italian (802)	1,477	2.61
Latvian (29)	60	0.11
Lithuanian (16)	63	0.11
Luxemburger (0)	0	<0.01
Macedonian (44)	44	0.08
Maltese (0)	0	<0.01
New Zealander (0)	0	<0.01
Northern European (111)	124	0.22
Norwegian (207)	492	0.87
Pennsylvania German (0)	0	<0.01
Polish (146)	595	1.05
Portuguese (105)	320	0.57
Romanian (22)	76	0.13
Russian (792)	1,192	2.11
Scandinavian (34)	58	0.10
Scotch-Irish (162)	553	0.98
Scottish (216)	629	1.11
Serbian (15)	30	0.05
Slavic (0)	45	0.08
Slovak (39)	39	0.07
Slovene (14)	14	0.02
Soviet Union (0)	0	<0.01
Swedish (90)	373	0.66
Swiss (119)	274	0.48
Turkish (11)	11	0.02
Ukrainian (190)	240	0.42
Welsh (51)	96	0.17
West Indian, ex. Hispanic (54)	77	0.14
Bahamian (0)	0	<0.01
Barbadian (0)	0	<0.01
Belizean (0)	0	<0.01
Bermudan (0)	0	<0.01
British West Indian (0)	0	<0.01
Dutch West Indian (0)	0	<0.01
Haitian (54)	54	0.10
Jamaican (0)	23	0.04
Trinidadian/Tobagonian (0)	0	<0.01
U.S. Virgin Islander (0)	0	<0.01
West Indian (0)	0	<0.01
Other West Indian (0)	0	<0.01
Yugoslavian (149)	194	0.34

Hispanic Origin	Population	%
Hispanic or Latino (of any race)	2,113	3.62
Central American, ex. Mexican	111	0.19
Costa Rican	7	0.01
Guatemalan	28	0.05
Honduran	4	0.01
Nicaraguan	24	0.04
Panamanian	4	0.01
Salvadoran	41	0.07
Other Central American	3	0.01
Cuban	26	0.04
Dominican Republic	3	0.01
Mexican	1,373	2.35
Puerto Rican	70	0.12
South American	241	0.41
Argentinean	28	0.05
Bolivian	23	0.04
Chilean	23	0.04
Colombian	56	0.10
Ecuadorian	12	0.02
Paraguayan	0	<0.01
Peruvian	62	0.11
Uruguayan	7	0.01
Venezuelan	27	0.05
Other South American	3	0.01
Other Hispanic or Latino	289	0.50

Race*	Population	%
African-American/Black (344)	515	0.88
Not Hispanic (322)	473	0.81
Hispanic (22)	42	0.07
American Indian/Alaska Native (117)	310	0.53
Not Hispanic (80)	228	0.39
Hispanic (37)	82	0.14
Alaska Athabascan *(Ala. Nat.)* (1)	1	<0.01
Aleut *(Alaska Native)* (0)	0	<0.01
Apache (1)	2	<0.01
Arapaho (0)	0	<0.01
Blackfeet (1)	11	0.02
Canadian/French Am. Ind. (0)	1	<0.01
Central American Ind. (2)	2	<0.01
Cherokee (7)	41	0.07
Cheyenne (0)	0	<0.01
Chickasaw (0)	0	<0.01
Chippewa (1)	7	0.01
Choctaw (7)	15	0.03
Colville (1)	1	<0.01
Comanche (1)	2	<0.01
Cree (0)	0	<0.01
Creek (2)	2	<0.01
Crow (0)	0	<0.01
Delaware (0)	3	0.01
Hopi (0)	0	<0.01
Houma (0)	0	<0.01
Inupiat *(Alaska Native)* (0)	1	<0.01
Iroquois (2)	5	0.01
Kiowa (0)	0	<0.01
Lumbee (0)	0	<0.01
Menominee (0)	0	<0.01
Mexican American Ind. (3)	8	0.01
Navajo (2)	7	0.01
Osage (0)	1	<0.01
Ottawa (0)	0	<0.01
Paiute (0)	0	<0.01
Pima (0)	0	<0.01
Potawatomi (0)	0	<0.01
Pueblo (2)	2	<0.01
Puget Sound Salish (0)	2	<0.01
Seminole (0)	0	<0.01
Shoshone (0)	0	<0.01
Sioux (1)	4	0.01
South American Ind. (1)	5	0.01
Spanish American Ind. (0)	0	<0.01
Tlingit-Haida *(Alaska Native)* (0)	0	<0.01
Tohono O'Odham (0)	0	<0.01
Tsimshian *(Alaska Native)* (0)	0	<0.01
Ute (0)	1	<0.01
Yakama (0)	1	<0.01
Yaqui (2)	10	0.02
Yuman (0)	0	<0.01
Yup'ik *(Alaska Native)* (0)	0	<0.01
Asian (36,895)	38,503	66.04
Not Hispanic (36,815)	38,342	65.76
Hispanic (80)	161	0.28
Bangladeshi (66)	67	0.11
Bhutanese (0)	0	<0.01
Burmese (52)	59	0.10
Cambodian (18)	27	0.05
Chinese, ex. Taiwanese (13,953)	14,930	25.61
Filipino (535)	777	1.33
Hmong (3)	4	0.01
Indian (13,179)	13,415	23.01
Indonesian (74)	110	0.19
Japanese (1,951)	2,489	4.27
Korean (2,709)	2,876	4.93
Laotian (2)	2	<0.01
Malaysian (27)	38	0.07
Nepalese (25)	25	0.04
Pakistani (233)	248	0.43
Sri Lankan (32)	37	0.06
Taiwanese (2,467)	2,753	4.72
Thai (70)	102	0.17
Vietnamese (745)	850	1.46
Hawaii Native/Pacific Islander (54)	191	0.33
Not Hispanic (39)	162	0.28
Hispanic (15)	29	0.05
Fijian (2)	2	<0.01
Guamanian/Chamorro (21)	39	0.07
Marshallese (0)	0	<0.01
Native Hawaiian (13)	43	0.07
Samoan (8)	10	0.02
Tongan (2)	3	0.01
White (18,270)	19,846	34.04
Not Hispanic (17,085)	18,483	31.70
Hispanic (1,185)	1,363	2.34

*Notes: † The Census 2010 population figure is used to calculate the percentages in the Hispanic Origin and Race categories. Ancestry percentages are based on the 2006-2010 American Community Survey population (not shown); ‡ Numbers in parentheses indicate the number of people reporting a single ancestry; * Numbers in parentheses indicate the number of persons reporting this race alone, not in combination with any other race; Please refer to the Explanation of Data for more information.*

Daly City

Place Type: City
County: San Mateo
Population: 101,123

Ancestry	Population	%
Afghan (0)	0	<0.01
African, Sub-Saharan (215)	358	0.36
African (179)	322	0.32
Cape Verdean (0)	0	<0.01
Ethiopian (0)	0	<0.01
Ghanaian (0)	0	<0.01
Kenyan (0)	0	<0.01
Liberian (0)	0	<0.01
Nigerian (16)	16	0.02
Senegalese (0)	0	<0.01
Sierra Leonean (0)	0	<0.01
Somalian (0)	0	<0.01
South African (0)	0	<0.01
Sudanese (0)	0	<0.01
Ugandan (0)	0	<0.01
Zimbabwean (0)	0	<0.01
Other Sub-Saharan African (20)	20	0.02
Albanian (0)	0	<0.01
Alsatian (0)	0	<0.01
American (434)	434	0.43
Arab (2,071)	2,327	2.33
Arab (929)	991	0.99
Egyptian (70)	70	0.07
Iraqi (230)	230	0.23
Jordanian (62)	97	0.10
Lebanese (102)	191	0.19
Moroccan (0)	0	<0.01
Palestinian (511)	555	0.56
Syrian (0)	26	0.03
Other Arab (167)	167	0.17
Armenian (183)	183	0.18
Assyrian/Chaldean/Syriac (0)	0	<0.01
Australian (0)	16	0.02
Austrian (12)	55	0.06
Basque (25)	99	0.10
Belgian (0)	0	<0.01
Brazilian (274)	311	0.31
British (150)	164	0.16
Bulgarian (40)	40	0.04
Cajun (0)	0	<0.01
Canadian (56)	141	0.14
Carpatho Rusyn (0)	0	<0.01
Celtic (15)	15	0.02
Croatian (32)	102	0.10
Cypriot (0)	0	<0.01
Czech (43)	105	0.11
Czechoslovakian (16)	47	0.05
Danish (59)	136	0.14
Dutch (103)	289	0.29
Eastern European (0)	0	<0.01
English (159)	1,064	1.07
Estonian (20)	20	0.02
European (699)	962	0.96
Finnish (0)	47	0.05
French, ex. Basque (171)	654	0.66
French Canadian (13)	44	0.04
German (604)	2,613	2.62
German Russian (0)	0	<0.01
Greek (104)	197	0.20
Guyanese (0)	0	<0.01
Hungarian (41)	172	0.17
Icelander (11)	19	0.02
Iranian (150)	179	0.18
Irish (683)	2,435	2.44
Israeli (0)	0	<0.01
Italian (1,150)	2,546	2.55
Latvian (0)	5	0.01
Lithuanian (0)	12	0.01
Luxemburger (0)	0	<0.01
Macedonian (0)	0	<0.01
Maltese (0)	0	<0.01
New Zealander (14)	14	0.01
Northern European (0)	0	<0.01
Norwegian (101)	216	0.22
Pennsylvania German (0)	0	<0.01
Polish (129)	516	0.52
Portuguese (184)	404	0.40
Romanian (0)	25	0.03
Russian (429)	527	0.53
Scandinavian (0)	27	0.03
Scotch-Irish (69)	396	0.40
Scottish (134)	280	0.28
Serbian (0)	14	0.01
Slavic (0)	7	0.01
Slovak (0)	22	0.02
Slovene (0)	27	0.03
Soviet Union (0)	0	<0.01
Swedish (103)	425	0.43
Swiss (34)	97	0.10
Turkish (0)	14	0.01
Ukrainian (85)	100	0.10
Welsh (0)	96	0.10
West Indian, ex. Hispanic (11)	23	0.02
Bahamian (0)	0	<0.01
Barbadian (0)	0	<0.01
Belizean (0)	12	0.01
Bermudan (0)	0	<0.01
British West Indian (0)	0	<0.01
Dutch West Indian (0)	0	<0.01
Haitian (0)	0	<0.01
Jamaican (11)	11	0.01
Trinidadian/Tobagonian (0)	0	<0.01
U.S. Virgin Islander (0)	0	<0.01
West Indian (0)	0	<0.01
Other West Indian (0)	0	<0.01
Yugoslavian (83)	142	0.14

Hispanic Origin	Population	%
Hispanic or Latino (of any race)	23,929	23.66
Central American, ex. Mexican	9,813	9.70
Costa Rican	79	0.08
Guatemalan	1,363	1.35
Honduran	479	0.47
Nicaraguan	2,764	2.73
Panamanian	48	0.05
Salvadoran	5,000	4.94
Other Central American	80	0.08
Cuban	131	0.13
Dominican Republic	20	0.02
Mexican	9,535	9.43
Puerto Rican	684	0.68
South American	1,233	1.22
Argentinean	61	0.06
Bolivian	87	0.09
Chilean	64	0.06
Colombian	143	0.14
Ecuadorian	67	0.07
Paraguayan	2	<0.01
Peruvian	738	0.73
Uruguayan	6	0.01
Venezuelan	32	0.03
Other South American	33	0.03
Other Hispanic or Latino	2,513	2.49

Race*	Population	%
African-American/Black (3,600)	4,612	4.56
Not Hispanic (3,284)	4,005	3.96
Hispanic (316)	607	0.60
American Indian/Alaska Native (404)	992	0.98
Not Hispanic (115)	453	0.45
Hispanic (289)	539	0.53
Alaska Athabascan *(Ala. Nat.)* (0)	4	<0.01
Aleut *(Alaska Native)* (2)	3	<0.01
Apache (12)	35	0.03
Arapaho (3)	5	<0.01
Blackfeet (1)	34	0.03
Canadian/French Am. Ind. (1)	1	<0.01
Central American Ind. (4)	11	0.01
Cherokee (6)	113	0.11
Cheyenne (0)	2	<0.01
Chickasaw (0)	1	<0.01
Chippewa (4)	11	0.01
Choctaw (4)	17	0.02
Colville (0)	0	<0.01
Comanche (0)	2	<0.01
Cree (0)	0	<0.01
Creek (0)	5	<0.01
Crow (0)	0	<0.01
Delaware (0)	1	<0.01
Hopi (0)	0	<0.01
Houma (0)	0	<0.01
Inupiat *(Alaska Native)* (1)	1	<0.01
Iroquois (0)	12	0.01
Kiowa (0)	0	<0.01
Lumbee (0)	1	<0.01
Menominee (0)	0	<0.01
Mexican American Ind. (71)	108	0.11
Navajo (16)	33	0.03
Osage (0)	8	0.01
Ottawa (0)	0	<0.01
Paiute (2)	7	0.01
Pima (0)	0	<0.01
Potawatomi (1)	1	<0.01
Pueblo (6)	9	0.01
Puget Sound Salish (0)	0	<0.01
Seminole (2)	8	0.01
Shoshone (1)	1	<0.01
Sioux (15)	23	0.02
South American Ind. (9)	16	0.02
Spanish American Ind. (14)	23	0.02
Tlingit-Haida *(Alaska Native)* (0)	4	<0.01
Tohono O'Odham (6)	6	0.01
Tsimshian *(Alaska Native)* (0)	0	<0.01
Ute (0)	3	<0.01
Yakama (0)	0	<0.01
Yaqui (4)	6	0.01
Yuman (1)	1	<0.01
Yup'ik *(Alaska Native)* (0)	0	<0.01
Asian (56,267)	59,093	58.44
Not Hispanic (55,711)	57,841	57.20
Hispanic (556)	1,252	1.24
Bangladeshi (11)	12	0.01
Bhutanese (2)	2	<0.01
Burmese (1,829)	2,023	2.00
Cambodian (98)	135	0.13
Chinese, ex. Taiwanese (15,438)	16,992	16.80
Filipino (33,649)	36,028	35.63
Hmong (23)	30	0.03
Indian (637)	851	0.84
Indonesian (217)	281	0.28
Japanese (611)	1,022	1.01
Korean (629)	764	0.76
Laotian (44)	62	0.06
Malaysian (22)	47	0.05
Nepalese (29)	30	0.03
Pakistani (169)	189	0.19
Sri Lankan (17)	20	0.02
Taiwanese (167)	185	0.18
Thai (200)	257	0.25
Vietnamese (1,037)	1,331	1.32
Hawaii Native/Pacific Islander (805)	1,396	1.38
Not Hispanic (752)	1,203	1.19
Hispanic (53)	193	0.19
Fijian (126)	178	0.18
Guamanian/Chamorro (43)	123	0.12
Marshallese (2)	6	0.01
Native Hawaiian (58)	230	0.23
Samoan (467)	603	0.60
Tongan (16)	37	0.04
White (23,842)	27,266	26.96
Not Hispanic (14,031)	15,942	15.76
Hispanic (9,811)	11,324	11.20

*Notes: † The Census 2010 population figure is used to calculate the percentages in the Hispanic Origin and Race categories. Ancestry percentages are based on the 2006-2010 American Community Survey population (not shown); ‡ Numbers in parentheses indicate the number of people reporting a single ancestry; * Numbers in parentheses indicate the number of persons reporting this race alone, not in combination with any other race; Please refer to the Explanation of Data for more information.*

Davis

Place Type: City
County: Yolo
Population: 65,622

Ancestry	Population	%
Afghan (154)	154	0.24
African, Sub-Saharan (434)	531	0.82
African (285)	340	0.52
Cape Verdean (0)	0	<0.01
Ethiopian (49)	74	0.11
Ghanaian (0)	17	0.03
Kenyan (0)	0	<0.01
Liberian (0)	0	<0.01
Nigerian (9)	9	0.01
Senegalese (0)	0	<0.01
Sierra Leonean (0)	0	<0.01
Somalian (91)	91	0.14
South African (0)	0	<0.01
Sudanese (0)	0	<0.01
Ugandan (0)	0	<0.01
Zimbabwean (0)	0	<0.01
Other Sub-Saharan African (0)	0	<0.01
Albanian (0)	40	0.06
Alsatian (12)	12	0.02
American (992)	992	1.53
Arab (272)	370	0.57
Arab (45)	50	0.08
Egyptian (0)	14	0.02
Iraqi (0)	0	<0.01
Jordanian (23)	23	0.04
Lebanese (57)	111	0.17
Moroccan (0)	0	<0.01
Palestinian (32)	32	0.05
Syrian (0)	13	0.02
Other Arab (115)	127	0.20
Armenian (122)	192	0.30
Assyrian/Chaldean/Syriac (0)	0	<0.01
Australian (50)	269	0.41
Austrian (50)	273	0.42
Basque (65)	77	0.12
Belgian (60)	136	0.21
Brazilian (67)	86	0.13
British (227)	551	0.85
Bulgarian (0)	9	0.01
Cajun (0)	9	0.01
Canadian (49)	190	0.29
Carpatho Rusyn (0)	0	<0.01
Celtic (0)	21	0.03
Croatian (27)	104	0.16
Cypriot (11)	11	0.02
Czech (113)	307	0.47
Czechoslovakian (0)	27	0.04
Danish (87)	410	0.63
Dutch (276)	988	1.52
Eastern European (199)	235	0.36
English (2,047)	8,175	12.61
Estonian (12)	12	0.02
European (2,445)	3,038	4.69
Finnish (34)	121	0.19
French, ex. Basque (381)	1,809	2.79
French Canadian (101)	249	0.38
German (1,961)	9,304	14.35
German Russian (0)	0	<0.01
Greek (105)	363	0.56
Guyanese (0)	0	<0.01
Hungarian (26)	275	0.42
Icelander (12)	12	0.02
Iranian (447)	530	0.82
Irish (1,860)	7,023	10.83
Israeli (104)	104	0.16
Italian (869)	3,874	5.97
Latvian (41)	60	0.09
Lithuanian (60)	202	0.31
Luxemburger (0)	0	<0.01
Macedonian (0)	11	0.02
Maltese (0)	0	<0.01
New Zealander (27)	27	0.04
Northern European (295)	337	0.52
Norwegian (234)	959	1.48
Pennsylvania German (13)	13	0.02
Polish (342)	1,591	2.45
Portuguese (302)	659	1.02
Romanian (54)	247	0.38
Russian (533)	1,289	1.99
Scandinavian (85)	209	0.32
Scotch-Irish (387)	1,809	2.79
Scottish (268)	1,993	3.07
Serbian (13)	21	0.03
Slavic (33)	67	0.10
Slovak (25)	61	0.09
Slovene (0)	32	0.05
Soviet Union (0)	0	<0.01
Swedish (284)	1,200	1.85
Swiss (128)	722	1.11
Turkish (126)	163	0.25
Ukrainian (155)	259	0.40
Welsh (140)	742	1.14
West Indian, ex. Hispanic (41)	45	0.07
Bahamian (0)	0	<0.01
Barbadian (0)	0	<0.01
Belizean (0)	0	<0.01
Bermudan (0)	0	<0.01
British West Indian (0)	0	<0.01
Dutch West Indian (0)	0	<0.01
Haitian (0)	0	<0.01
Jamaican (41)	41	0.06
Trinidadian/Tobagonian (0)	4	0.01
U.S. Virgin Islander (0)	0	<0.01
West Indian (0)	0	<0.01
Other West Indian (0)	0	<0.01
Yugoslavian (31)	61	0.09

Hispanic Origin	Population	%
Hispanic or Latino (of any race)	8,172	12.45
Central American, ex. Mexican	708	1.08
Costa Rican	40	0.06
Guatemalan	182	0.28
Honduran	24	0.04
Nicaraguan	97	0.15
Panamanian	24	0.04
Salvadoran	336	0.51
Other Central American	5	0.01
Cuban	80	0.12
Dominican Republic	14	0.02
Mexican	5,618	8.56
Puerto Rican	221	0.34
South American	711	1.08
Argentinean	128	0.20
Bolivian	19	0.03
Chilean	123	0.19
Colombian	141	0.21
Ecuadorian	57	0.09
Paraguayan	4	0.01
Peruvian	159	0.24
Uruguayan	17	0.03
Venezuelan	58	0.09
Other South American	5	0.01
Other Hispanic or Latino	820	1.25

Race*	Population	%
African-American/Black (1,528)	2,086	3.18
Not Hispanic (1,415)	1,859	2.83
Hispanic (113)	227	0.35
American Indian/Alaska Native (339)	983	1.50
Not Hispanic (166)	602	0.92
Hispanic (173)	381	0.58
Alaska Athabascan *(Ala. Nat.)* (1)	1	<0.01
Aleut *(Alaska Native)* (0)	0	<0.01
Apache (24)	44	0.07
Arapaho (0)	0	<0.01
Blackfeet (2)	22	0.03
Canadian/French Am. Ind. (3)	4	0.01
Central American Ind. (4)	8	0.01
Cherokee (24)	163	0.25
Cheyenne (0)	4	0.01
Chickasaw (6)	10	0.02
Chippewa (2)	7	0.01
Choctaw (11)	52	0.08
Colville (0)	1	<0.01
Comanche (0)	4	0.01
Cree (0)	6	0.01
Creek (4)	10	0.02
Crow (0)	0	<0.01
Delaware (1)	1	<0.01
Hopi (0)	0	<0.01
Houma (0)	1	<0.01
Inupiat *(Alaska Native)* (0)	0	<0.01
Iroquois (4)	14	0.02
Kiowa (0)	0	<0.01
Lumbee (0)	0	<0.01
Menominee (0)	0	<0.01
Mexican American Ind. (40)	65	0.10
Navajo (15)	27	0.04
Osage (1)	7	0.01
Ottawa (0)	5	0.01
Paiute (0)	4	0.01
Pima (0)	1	<0.01
Potawatomi (2)	3	<0.01
Pueblo (0)	5	0.01
Puget Sound Salish (0)	1	<0.01
Seminole (1)	2	<0.01
Shoshone (1)	3	<0.01
Sioux (11)	26	0.04
South American Ind. (2)	14	0.02
Spanish American Ind. (6)	7	0.01
Tlingit-Haida *(Alaska Native)* (2)	3	<0.01
Tohono O'Odham (0)	0	<0.01
Tsimshian *(Alaska Native)* (0)	0	<0.01
Ute (0)	0	<0.01
Yakama (1)	1	<0.01
Yaqui (4)	9	0.01
Yuman (0)	0	<0.01
Yup'ik *(Alaska Native)* (1)	3	<0.01
Asian (14,355)	16,574	25.26
Not Hispanic (14,213)	16,170	24.64
Hispanic (142)	404	0.62
Bangladeshi (41)	41	0.06
Bhutanese (1)	1	<0.01
Burmese (30)	50	0.08
Cambodian (63)	87	0.13
Chinese, ex. Taiwanese (5,969)	7,009	10.68
Filipino (1,033)	1,615	2.46
Hmong (201)	204	0.31
Indian (1,631)	1,793	2.73
Indonesian (55)	76	0.12
Japanese (953)	1,674	2.55
Korean (1,560)	1,766	2.69
Laotian (90)	97	0.15
Malaysian (14)	19	0.03
Nepalese (134)	150	0.23
Pakistani (172)	194	0.30
Sri Lankan (59)	64	0.10
Taiwanese (394)	446	0.68
Thai (104)	148	0.23
Vietnamese (1,185)	1,403	2.14
Hawaii Native/Pacific Islander (136)	344	0.52
Not Hispanic (120)	279	0.43
Hispanic (16)	65	0.10
Fijian (35)	42	0.06
Guamanian/Chamorro (23)	60	0.09
Marshallese (6)	6	0.01
Native Hawaiian (22)	113	0.17
Samoan (19)	41	0.06
Tongan (2)	5	0.01
White (42,571)	45,794	69.78
Not Hispanic (38,641)	41,141	62.69
Hispanic (3,930)	4,653	7.09

*Notes: † The Census 2010 population figure is used to calculate the percentages in the Hispanic Origin and Race categories. Ancestry percentages are based on the 2006-2010 American Community Survey population (not shown); ‡ Numbers in parentheses indicate the number of people reporting a single ancestry; * Numbers in parentheses indicate the number of persons reporting this race alone, not in combination with any other race; Please refer to the Explanation of Data for more information.*

Delano

Place Type: City
County: Kern
Population: 53,041

Ancestry	Population	%
Afghan (0)	0	<0.01
African, Sub-Saharan (51)	58	0.11
African (40)	47	0.09
Cape Verdean (0)	0	<0.01
Ethiopian (0)	0	<0.01
Ghanaian (0)	0	<0.01
Kenyan (0)	0	<0.01
Liberian (0)	0	<0.01
Nigerian (0)	0	<0.01
Senegalese (0)	0	<0.01
Sierra Leonean (0)	0	<0.01
Somalian (0)	0	<0.01
South African (0)	0	<0.01
Sudanese (0)	0	<0.01
Ugandan (0)	0	<0.01
Zimbabwean (0)	0	<0.01
Other Sub-Saharan African (11)	11	0.02
Albanian (0)	0	<0.01
Alsatian (0)	0	<0.01
American (355)	355	0.69
Arab (84)	110	0.21
Arab (7)	24	0.05
Egyptian (0)	0	<0.01
Iraqi (0)	0	<0.01
Jordanian (32)	32	0.06
Lebanese (0)	0	<0.01
Moroccan (0)	0	<0.01
Palestinian (8)	8	0.02
Syrian (0)	0	<0.01
Other Arab (37)	46	0.09
Armenian (41)	57	0.11
Assyrian/Chaldean/Syriac (0)	0	<0.01
Australian (0)	0	<0.01
Austrian (0)	16	0.03
Basque (0)	0	<0.01
Belgian (0)	0	<0.01
Brazilian (9)	9	0.02
British (0)	18	0.04
Bulgarian (0)	0	<0.01
Cajun (0)	0	<0.01
Canadian (14)	22	0.04
Carpatho Rusyn (0)	0	<0.01
Celtic (0)	0	<0.01
Croatian (23)	23	0.04
Cypriot (0)	0	<0.01
Czech (0)	8	0.02
Czechoslovakian (0)	0	<0.01
Danish (10)	47	0.09
Dutch (47)	121	0.24
Eastern European (0)	0	<0.01
English (176)	502	0.98
Estonian (0)	0	<0.01
European (129)	137	0.27
Finnish (10)	20	0.04
French, ex. Basque (26)	185	0.36
French Canadian (11)	27	0.05
German (151)	916	1.79
German Russian (0)	0	<0.01
Greek (0)	37	0.07
Guyanese (0)	0	<0.01
Hungarian (0)	5	0.01
Icelander (0)	0	<0.01
Iranian (15)	15	0.03
Irish (174)	936	1.82
Israeli (0)	0	<0.01
Italian (182)	538	1.05
Latvian (0)	0	<0.01
Lithuanian (0)	0	<0.01
Luxemburger (0)	0	<0.01
Macedonian (0)	0	<0.01
Maltese (8)	8	0.02
New Zealander (0)	0	<0.01
Northern European (9)	9	0.02
Norwegian (9)	68	0.13
Pennsylvania German (0)	0	<0.01
Polish (17)	83	0.16
Portuguese (63)	104	0.20
Romanian (23)	38	0.07
Russian (23)	70	0.14
Scandinavian (0)	15	0.03
Scotch-Irish (52)	128	0.25
Scottish (16)	135	0.26
Serbian (0)	0	<0.01
Slavic (0)	0	<0.01
Slovak (0)	0	<0.01
Slovene (0)	0	<0.01
Soviet Union (0)	0	<0.01
Swedish (0)	23	0.04
Swiss (0)	0	<0.01
Turkish (0)	0	<0.01
Ukrainian (0)	0	<0.01
Welsh (0)	59	0.11
West Indian, ex. Hispanic (20)	71	0.14
Bahamian (0)	0	<0.01
Barbadian (0)	0	<0.01
Belizean (8)	33	0.06
Bermudan (0)	0	<0.01
British West Indian (0)	0	<0.01
Dutch West Indian (0)	0	<0.01
Haitian (12)	12	0.02
Jamaican (0)	26	0.05
Trinidadian/Tobagonian (0)	0	<0.01
U.S. Virgin Islander (0)	0	<0.01
West Indian (0)	0	<0.01
Other West Indian (0)	0	<0.01
Yugoslavian (0)	0	<0.01

Hispanic Origin	Population	%
Hispanic or Latino (of any race)	37,913	71.48
Central American, ex. Mexican	427	0.81
Costa Rican	13	0.02
Guatemalan	121	0.23
Honduran	37	0.07
Nicaraguan	12	0.02
Panamanian	5	0.01
Salvadoran	238	0.45
Other Central American	1	<0.01
Cuban	14	0.03
Dominican Republic	0	<0.01
Mexican	34,658	65.34
Puerto Rican	197	0.37
South American	34	0.06
Argentinean	1	<0.01
Bolivian	1	<0.01
Chilean	10	0.02
Colombian	0	<0.01
Ecuadorian	10	0.02
Paraguayan	0	<0.01
Peruvian	7	0.01
Uruguayan	0	<0.01
Venezuelan	5	0.01
Other South American	0	<0.01
Other Hispanic or Latino	2,583	4.87

Race*	Population	%
African-American/Black (4,191)	4,360	8.22
Not Hispanic (4,007)	4,088	7.71
Hispanic (184)	272	0.51
American Indian/Alaska Native (501)	666	1.26
Not Hispanic (154)	220	0.41
Hispanic (347)	446	0.84
Alaska Athabascan *(Ala. Nat.)* (0)	0	<0.01
Aleut *(Alaska Native)* (1)	2	<0.01
Apache (14)	19	0.04
Arapaho (0)	0	<0.01
Blackfeet (0)	1	<0.01
Canadian/French Am. Ind. (0)	0	<0.01
Central American Ind. (0)	0	<0.01
Cherokee (7)	21	0.04
Cheyenne (0)	1	<0.01
Chickasaw (3)	3	0.01
Chippewa (0)	0	<0.01
Choctaw (8)	13	0.02
Colville (0)	0	<0.01
Comanche (0)	0	<0.01
Cree (0)	0	<0.01
Creek (4)	5	0.01
Crow (0)	0	<0.01
Delaware (0)	0	<0.01
Hopi (0)	0	<0.01
Houma (0)	0	<0.01
Inupiat *(Alaska Native)* (0)	0	<0.01
Iroquois (0)	0	<0.01
Kiowa (0)	0	<0.01
Lumbee (0)	0	<0.01
Menominee (0)	0	<0.01
Mexican American Ind. (95)	111	0.21
Navajo (6)	18	0.03
Osage (0)	0	<0.01
Ottawa (0)	0	<0.01
Paiute (3)	10	0.02
Pima (0)	0	<0.01
Potawatomi (1)	1	<0.01
Pueblo (7)	8	0.02
Puget Sound Salish (0)	0	<0.01
Seminole (4)	4	0.01
Shoshone (0)	0	<0.01
Sioux (1)	1	<0.01
South American Ind. (0)	0	<0.01
Spanish American Ind. (0)	0	<0.01
Tlingit-Haida *(Alaska Native)* (1)	1	<0.01
Tohono O'Odham (2)	4	0.01
Tsimshian *(Alaska Native)* (0)	0	<0.01
Ute (0)	0	<0.01
Yakama (0)	0	<0.01
Yaqui (28)	33	0.06
Yuman (4)	8	0.02
Yup'ik *(Alaska Native)* (1)	2	<0.01
Asian (6,757)	7,493	14.13
Not Hispanic (6,436)	6,795	12.81
Hispanic (321)	698	1.32
Bangladeshi (3)	3	0.01
Bhutanese (0)	0	<0.01
Burmese (0)	0	<0.01
Cambodian (19)	25	0.05
Chinese, ex. Taiwanese (34)	62	0.12
Filipino (6,280)	6,927	13.06
Hmong (1)	3	0.01
Indian (324)	375	0.71
Indonesian (0)	0	<0.01
Japanese (21)	36	0.07
Korean (28)	28	0.05
Laotian (5)	6	0.01
Malaysian (0)	0	<0.01
Nepalese (0)	0	<0.01
Pakistani (0)	0	<0.01
Sri Lankan (0)	0	<0.01
Taiwanese (0)	0	<0.01
Thai (0)	0	<0.01
Vietnamese (7)	9	0.02
Hawaii Native/Pacific Islander (30)	156	0.29
Not Hispanic (22)	89	0.17
Hispanic (8)	67	0.13
Fijian (0)	0	<0.01
Guamanian/Chamorro (9)	25	0.05
Marshallese (0)	0	<0.01
Native Hawaiian (8)	45	0.08
Samoan (1)	9	0.02
Tongan (0)	1	<0.01
White (19,304)	20,721	39.07
Not Hispanic (3,980)	4,243	8.00
Hispanic (15,324)	16,478	31.07

*Notes: † The Census 2010 population figure is used to calculate the percentages in the Hispanic Origin and Race categories. Ancestry percentages are based on the 2006-2010 American Community Survey population (not shown); ‡ Numbers in parentheses indicate the number of people reporting a single ancestry; * Numbers in parentheses indicate the number of persons reporting this race alone, not in combination with any other race; Please refer to the Explanation of Data for more information.*

Diamond Bar

Place Type: City
County: Los Angeles
Population: 55,544

Ancestry	Population	%
Afghan (0)	0	<0.01
African, Sub-Saharan (286)	355	0.64
African (268)	326	0.59
Cape Verdean (0)	0	<0.01
Ethiopian (0)	0	<0.01
Ghanaian (0)	0	<0.01
Kenyan (0)	0	<0.01
Liberian (0)	0	<0.01
Nigerian (18)	18	0.03
Senegalese (0)	0	<0.01
Sierra Leonean (0)	0	<0.01
Somalian (0)	0	<0.01
South African (0)	0	<0.01
Sudanese (0)	0	<0.01
Ugandan (0)	0	<0.01
Zimbabwean (0)	0	<0.01
Other Sub-Saharan African (0)	11	0.02
Albanian (0)	0	<0.01
Alsatian (0)	0	<0.01
American (1,298)	1,298	2.33
Arab (357)	461	0.83
Arab (150)	156	0.28
Egyptian (100)	100	0.18
Iraqi (0)	0	<0.01
Jordanian (0)	0	<0.01
Lebanese (54)	110	0.20
Moroccan (0)	0	<0.01
Palestinian (0)	0	<0.01
Syrian (0)	0	<0.01
Other Arab (53)	95	0.17
Armenian (312)	447	0.80
Assyrian/Chaldean/Syriac (0)	0	<0.01
Australian (0)	0	<0.01
Austrian (31)	63	0.11
Basque (0)	72	0.13
Belgian (0)	31	0.06
Brazilian (0)	0	<0.01
British (73)	83	0.15
Bulgarian (23)	23	0.04
Cajun (0)	0	<0.01
Canadian (8)	58	0.10
Carpatho Rusyn (0)	0	<0.01
Celtic (10)	22	0.04
Croatian (14)	42	0.08
Cypriot (0)	0	<0.01
Czech (0)	102	0.18
Czechoslovakian (0)	55	0.10
Danish (24)	145	0.26
Dutch (100)	521	0.94
Eastern European (120)	120	0.22
English (632)	2,450	4.40
Estonian (0)	0	<0.01
European (224)	420	0.75
Finnish (8)	25	0.04
French, ex. Basque (79)	537	0.96
French Canadian (110)	129	0.23
German (724)	3,311	5.94
German Russian (0)	0	<0.01
Greek (143)	325	0.58
Guyanese (13)	13	0.02
Hungarian (27)	104	0.19
Icelander (0)	0	<0.01
Iranian (128)	128	0.23
Irish (660)	2,305	4.14
Israeli (0)	0	<0.01
Italian (649)	1,832	3.29
Latvian (0)	0	<0.01
Lithuanian (0)	24	0.04
Luxemburger (0)	0	<0.01
Macedonian (0)	19	0.03
Maltese (0)	0	<0.01
New Zealander (0)	0	<0.01
Northern European (11)	17	0.03
Norwegian (64)	194	0.35
Pennsylvania German (8)	16	0.03
Polish (152)	499	0.90
Portuguese (60)	123	0.22
Romanian (9)	21	0.04
Russian (94)	241	0.43
Scandinavian (8)	71	0.13
Scotch-Irish (70)	396	0.71
Scottish (253)	641	1.15
Serbian (10)	10	0.02
Slavic (0)	0	<0.01
Slovak (0)	0	<0.01
Slovene (13)	13	0.02
Soviet Union (0)	0	<0.01
Swedish (63)	197	0.35
Swiss (30)	76	0.14
Turkish (0)	26	0.05
Ukrainian (11)	48	0.09
Welsh (15)	85	0.15
West Indian, ex. Hispanic (36)	36	0.06
Bahamian (0)	0	<0.01
Barbadian (0)	0	<0.01
Belizean (9)	9	0.02
Bermudan (0)	0	<0.01
British West Indian (0)	0	<0.01
Dutch West Indian (0)	0	<0.01
Haitian (12)	12	0.02
Jamaican (0)	0	<0.01
Trinidadian/Tobagonian (15)	15	0.03
U.S. Virgin Islander (0)	0	<0.01
West Indian (0)	0	<0.01
Other West Indian (0)	0	<0.01
Yugoslavian (0)	9	0.02

Hispanic Origin	Population	%
Hispanic or Latino (of any race)	11,138	20.05
Central American, ex. Mexican	675	1.22
Costa Rican	54	0.10
Guatemalan	174	0.31
Honduran	41	0.07
Nicaraguan	118	0.21
Panamanian	20	0.04
Salvadoran	255	0.46
Other Central American	13	0.02
Cuban	193	0.35
Dominican Republic	6	0.01
Mexican	8,766	15.78
Puerto Rican	185	0.33
South American	640	1.15
Argentinean	86	0.15
Bolivian	16	0.03
Chilean	50	0.09
Colombian	163	0.29
Ecuadorian	120	0.22
Paraguayan	1	<0.01
Peruvian	174	0.31
Uruguayan	7	0.01
Venezuelan	21	0.04
Other South American	2	<0.01
Other Hispanic or Latino	673	1.21

Race*	Population	%
African-American/Black (2,288)	2,620	4.72
Not Hispanic (2,194)	2,437	4.39
Hispanic (94)	183	0.33
American Indian/Alaska Native (178)	455	0.82
Not Hispanic (67)	203	0.37
Hispanic (111)	252	0.45
Alaska Athabascan *(Ala. Nat.)* (0)	1	<0.01
Aleut *(Alaska Native)* (0)	1	<0.01
Apache (10)	22	0.04
Arapaho (0)	0	<0.01
Blackfeet (1)	4	0.01
Canadian/French Am. Ind. (0)	0	<0.01
Central American Ind. (0)	1	<0.01
Cherokee (8)	34	0.06
Cheyenne (0)	0	<0.01
Chickasaw (2)	3	0.01
Chippewa (1)	1	<0.01
Choctaw (5)	17	0.03
Colville (0)	0	<0.01
Comanche (0)	0	<0.01
Cree (0)	1	<0.01
Creek (0)	5	0.01
Crow (0)	1	<0.01
Delaware (0)	0	<0.01
Hopi (0)	2	<0.01
Houma (0)	0	<0.01
Inupiat *(Alaska Native)* (0)	0	<0.01
Iroquois (0)	0	<0.01
Kiowa (0)	0	<0.01
Lumbee (0)	0	<0.01
Menominee (0)	0	<0.01
Mexican American Ind. (5)	13	0.02
Navajo (8)	32	0.06
Osage (1)	2	<0.01
Ottawa (0)	0	<0.01
Paiute (0)	0	<0.01
Pima (5)	5	0.01
Potawatomi (2)	2	<0.01
Pueblo (0)	2	<0.01
Puget Sound Salish (0)	0	<0.01
Seminole (1)	6	0.01
Shoshone (1)	3	0.01
Sioux (1)	6	0.01
South American Ind. (1)	7	0.01
Spanish American Ind. (8)	8	0.01
Tlingit-Haida *(Alaska Native)* (0)	0	<0.01
Tohono O'Odham (1)	2	<0.01
Tsimshian *(Alaska Native)* (0)	0	<0.01
Ute (0)	0	<0.01
Yakama (0)	0	<0.01
Yaqui (1)	4	0.01
Yuman (2)	2	<0.01
Yup'ik *(Alaska Native)* (0)	0	<0.01
Asian (29,144)	30,478	54.87
Not Hispanic (28,883)	29,892	53.82
Hispanic (261)	586	1.06
Bangladeshi (27)	27	0.05
Bhutanese (0)	0	<0.01
Burmese (131)	166	0.30
Cambodian (63)	100	0.18
Chinese, ex. Taiwanese (11,587)	12,547	22.59
Filipino (3,277)	3,767	6.78
Hmong (3)	3	0.01
Indian (2,086)	2,205	3.97
Indonesian (277)	350	0.63
Japanese (870)	1,194	2.15
Korean (5,782)	5,961	10.73
Laotian (19)	31	0.06
Malaysian (17)	31	0.06
Nepalese (4)	4	0.01
Pakistani (301)	337	0.61
Sri Lankan (42)	43	0.08
Taiwanese (2,808)	3,162	5.69
Thai (170)	203	0.37
Vietnamese (717)	906	1.63
Hawaii Native/Pacific Islander (106)	335	0.60
Not Hispanic (92)	287	0.52
Hispanic (14)	48	0.09
Fijian (2)	9	0.02
Guamanian/Chamorro (18)	20	0.04
Marshallese (0)	0	<0.01
Native Hawaiian (28)	84	0.15
Samoan (44)	52	0.09
Tongan (3)	8	0.01
White (18,434)	20,044	36.09
Not Hispanic (11,812)	12,743	22.94
Hispanic (6,622)	7,301	13.14

*Notes: † The Census 2010 population figure is used to calculate the percentages in the Hispanic Origin and Race categories. Ancestry percentages are based on the 2006-2010 American Community Survey population (not shown); ‡ Numbers in parentheses indicate the number of people reporting a single ancestry; * Numbers in parentheses indicate the number of persons reporting this race alone, not in combination with any other race; Please refer to the Explanation of Data for more information.*

Downey

Place Type: City
County: Los Angeles
Population: 111,772

Ancestry	Population	%
Afghan (0)	0	<0.01
African, Sub-Saharan (343)	402	0.36
African (197)	226	0.20
Cape Verdean (0)	0	<0.01
Ethiopian (7)	7	0.01
Ghanaian (93)	93	0.08
Kenyan (0)	23	0.02
Liberian (0)	0	<0.01
Nigerian (46)	46	0.04
Senegalese (0)	0	<0.01
Sierra Leonean (0)	0	<0.01
Somalian (0)	0	<0.01
South African (0)	0	<0.01
Sudanese (0)	0	<0.01
Ugandan (0)	0	<0.01
Zimbabwean (0)	0	<0.01
Other Sub-Saharan African (0)	7	0.01
Albanian (43)	52	0.05
Alsatian (0)	0	<0.01
American (1,718)	1,718	1.55
Arab (792)	1,007	0.91
Arab (40)	92	0.08
Egyptian (549)	603	0.54
Iraqi (0)	0	<0.01
Jordanian (0)	0	<0.01
Lebanese (62)	137	0.12
Moroccan (23)	48	0.04
Palestinian (0)	0	<0.01
Syrian (55)	64	0.06
Other Arab (63)	63	0.06
Armenian (133)	178	0.16
Assyrian/Chaldean/Syriac (0)	0	<0.01
Australian (0)	0	<0.01
Austrian (37)	37	0.03
Basque (15)	15	0.01
Belgian (9)	39	0.04
Brazilian (11)	45	0.04
British (59)	118	0.11
Bulgarian (0)	0	<0.01
Cajun (7)	7	0.01
Canadian (66)	111	0.10
Carpatho Rusyn (0)	0	<0.01
Celtic (0)	0	<0.01
Croatian (0)	41	0.04
Cypriot (0)	0	<0.01
Czech (72)	157	0.14
Czechoslovakian (55)	84	0.08
Danish (53)	151	0.14
Dutch (167)	477	0.43
Eastern European (0)	0	<0.01
English (1,021)	3,050	2.75
Estonian (0)	0	<0.01
European (340)	409	0.37
Finnish (0)	0	<0.01
French, ex. Basque (171)	1,126	1.02
French Canadian (190)	273	0.25
German (1,220)	4,386	3.95
German Russian (0)	0	<0.01
Greek (461)	579	0.52
Guyanese (22)	22	0.02
Hungarian (78)	111	0.10
Icelander (0)	0	<0.01
Iranian (365)	379	0.34
Irish (585)	2,704	2.44
Israeli (0)	0	<0.01
Italian (1,234)	2,250	2.03
Latvian (17)	17	0.02
Lithuanian (28)	28	0.03
Luxemburger (0)	15	0.01
Macedonian (0)	0	<0.01
Maltese (0)	0	<0.01
New Zealander (0)	0	<0.01
Northern European (33)	33	0.03
Norwegian (87)	523	0.47
Pennsylvania German (14)	43	0.04
Polish (328)	620	0.56
Portuguese (32)	253	0.23
Romanian (62)	75	0.07
Russian (393)	600	0.54
Scandinavian (36)	54	0.05
Scotch-Irish (165)	631	0.57
Scottish (211)	637	0.57
Serbian (0)	0	<0.01
Slavic (0)	78	0.07
Slovak (0)	21	0.02
Slovene (0)	6	0.01
Soviet Union (0)	0	<0.01
Swedish (120)	473	0.43
Swiss (43)	104	0.09
Turkish (0)	0	<0.01
Ukrainian (0)	0	<0.01
Welsh (58)	154	0.14
West Indian, ex. Hispanic (72)	109	0.10
Bahamian (0)	0	<0.01
Barbadian (0)	0	<0.01
Belizean (0)	4	<0.01
Bermudan (0)	0	<0.01
British West Indian (0)	0	<0.01
Dutch West Indian (0)	0	<0.01
Haitian (0)	0	<0.01
Jamaican (61)	71	0.06
Trinidadian/Tobagonian (11)	11	0.01
U.S. Virgin Islander (0)	0	<0.01
West Indian (0)	23	0.02
Other West Indian (0)	0	<0.01
Yugoslavian (184)	201	0.18

Hispanic Origin	Population	%
Hispanic or Latino (of any race)	78,996	70.68
Central American, ex. Mexican	8,546	7.65
Costa Rican	263	0.24
Guatemalan	2,180	1.95
Honduran	505	0.45
Nicaraguan	1,092	0.98
Panamanian	71	0.06
Salvadoran	4,356	3.90
Other Central American	79	0.07
Cuban	2,283	2.04
Dominican Republic	70	0.06
Mexican	60,331	53.98
Puerto Rican	745	0.67
South American	3,506	3.14
Argentinean	429	0.38
Bolivian	134	0.12
Chilean	120	0.11
Colombian	733	0.66
Ecuadorian	678	0.61
Paraguayan	4	<0.01
Peruvian	1,277	1.14
Uruguayan	29	0.03
Venezuelan	67	0.06
Other South American	35	0.03
Other Hispanic or Latino	3,515	3.14

Race*	Population	%
African-American/Black (4,329)	4,933	4.41
Not Hispanic (3,834)	4,105	3.67
Hispanic (495)	828	0.74
American Indian/Alaska Native (820)	1,439	1.29
Not Hispanic (212)	408	0.37
Hispanic (608)	1,031	0.92
Alaska Athabascan *(Ala. Nat.)* (0)	0	<0.01
Aleut *(Alaska Native)* (1)	2	<0.01
Apache (30)	52	0.05
Arapaho (0)	0	<0.01
Blackfeet (10)	21	0.02
Canadian/French Am. Ind. (2)	5	<0.01
Central American Ind. (5)	15	0.01
Cherokee (26)	93	0.08
Cheyenne (2)	3	<0.01
Chickasaw (2)	7	0.01
Chippewa (7)	10	0.01
Choctaw (29)	51	0.05
Colville (0)	0	<0.01
Comanche (10)	11	0.01
Cree (0)	0	<0.01
Creek (7)	16	0.01
Crow (0)	1	<0.01
Delaware (4)	4	<0.01
Hopi (12)	17	0.02
Houma (0)	0	<0.01
Inupiat *(Alaska Native)* (0)	1	<0.01
Iroquois (2)	4	<0.01
Kiowa (3)	3	<0.01
Lumbee (1)	1	<0.01
Menominee (1)	1	<0.01
Mexican American Ind. (119)	158	0.14
Navajo (51)	80	0.07
Osage (0)	3	<0.01
Ottawa (0)	0	<0.01
Paiute (1)	1	<0.01
Pima (7)	11	0.01
Potawatomi (0)	2	<0.01
Pueblo (9)	15	0.01
Puget Sound Salish (0)	0	<0.01
Seminole (0)	3	<0.01
Shoshone (1)	14	0.01
Sioux (8)	16	0.01
South American Ind. (13)	19	0.02
Spanish American Ind. (11)	18	0.02
Tlingit-Haida *(Alaska Native)* (0)	1	<0.01
Tohono O'Odham (6)	9	0.01
Tsimshian *(Alaska Native)* (0)	0	<0.01
Ute (0)	0	<0.01
Yakama (1)	3	<0.01
Yaqui (11)	28	0.03
Yuman (5)	6	0.01
Yup'ik *(Alaska Native)* (0)	0	<0.01
Asian (7,804)	8,898	7.96
Not Hispanic (7,484)	8,088	7.24
Hispanic (320)	810	0.72
Bangladeshi (37)	52	0.05
Bhutanese (0)	0	<0.01
Burmese (13)	25	0.02
Cambodian (145)	217	0.19
Chinese, ex. Taiwanese (477)	671	0.60
Filipino (2,470)	2,869	2.57
Hmong (5)	9	0.01
Indian (657)	771	0.69
Indonesian (30)	51	0.05
Japanese (322)	557	0.50
Korean (2,508)	2,619	2.34
Laotian (10)	11	0.01
Malaysian (1)	3	<0.01
Nepalese (5)	5	<0.01
Pakistani (129)	155	0.14
Sri Lankan (23)	24	0.02
Taiwanese (106)	115	0.10
Thai (254)	289	0.26
Vietnamese (367)	423	0.38
Hawaii Native/Pacific Islander (221)	494	0.44
Not Hispanic (170)	327	0.29
Hispanic (51)	167	0.15
Fijian (20)	28	0.03
Guamanian/Chamorro (33)	61	0.05
Marshallese (0)	0	<0.01
Native Hawaiian (46)	149	0.13
Samoan (83)	133	0.12
Tongan (10)	14	0.01
White (63,255)	66,983	59.93
Not Hispanic (19,786)	20,652	18.48
Hispanic (43,469)	46,331	41.45

*Notes: † The Census 2010 population figure is used to calculate the percentages in the Hispanic Origin and Race categories. Ancestry percentages are based on the 2006-2010 American Community Survey population (not shown); ‡ Numbers in parentheses indicate the number of people reporting a single ancestry; * Numbers in parentheses indicate the number of persons reporting this race alone, not in combination with any other race; Please refer to the Explanation of Data for more information.*

East Los Angeles

Place Type: CDP
County: Los Angeles
Population: 126,496

Ancestry	Population	%
Afghan (0)	0	<0.01
African, Sub-Saharan (0)	13	0.01
African (0)	13	0.01
Cape Verdean (0)	0	<0.01
Ethiopian (0)	0	<0.01
Ghanaian (0)	0	<0.01
Kenyan (0)	0	<0.01
Liberian (0)	0	<0.01
Nigerian (0)	0	<0.01
Senegalese (0)	0	<0.01
Sierra Leonean (0)	0	<0.01
Somalian (0)	0	<0.01
South African (0)	0	<0.01
Sudanese (0)	0	<0.01
Ugandan (0)	0	<0.01
Zimbabwean (0)	0	<0.01
Other Sub-Saharan African (0)	0	<0.01
Albanian (0)	0	<0.01
Alsatian (0)	0	<0.01
American (2,082)	2,082	1.69
Arab (13)	60	0.05
Arab (13)	60	0.05
Egyptian (0)	0	<0.01
Iraqi (0)	0	<0.01
Jordanian (0)	0	<0.01
Lebanese (0)	0	<0.01
Moroccan (0)	0	<0.01
Palestinian (0)	0	<0.01
Syrian (0)	0	<0.01
Other Arab (0)	0	<0.01
Armenian (59)	70	0.06
Assyrian/Chaldean/Syriac (0)	0	<0.01
Australian (0)	0	<0.01
Austrian (0)	0	<0.01
Basque (22)	22	0.02
Belgian (0)	0	<0.01
Brazilian (0)	0	<0.01
British (0)	0	<0.01
Bulgarian (0)	0	<0.01
Cajun (0)	0	<0.01
Canadian (0)	0	<0.01
Carpatho Rusyn (0)	0	<0.01
Celtic (0)	0	<0.01
Croatian (0)	0	<0.01
Cypriot (0)	0	<0.01
Czech (0)	3	<0.01
Czechoslovakian (0)	0	<0.01
Danish (6)	6	<0.01
Dutch (0)	0	<0.01
Eastern European (0)	0	<0.01
English (71)	191	0.16
Estonian (0)	0	<0.01
European (0)	89	0.07
Finnish (0)	0	<0.01
French, ex. Basque (8)	134	0.11
French Canadian (0)	23	0.02
German (117)	335	0.27
German Russian (0)	0	<0.01
Greek (8)	8	0.01
Guyanese (0)	0	<0.01
Hungarian (7)	27	0.02
Icelander (0)	0	<0.01
Iranian (0)	0	<0.01
Irish (23)	117	0.10
Israeli (0)	0	<0.01
Italian (33)	190	0.15
Latvian (0)	0	<0.01
Lithuanian (0)	0	<0.01
Luxemburger (0)	0	<0.01
Macedonian (0)	0	<0.01
Maltese (0)	0	<0.01
New Zealander (23)	23	0.02
Northern European (0)	0	<0.01
Norwegian (0)	17	0.01
Pennsylvania German (0)	0	<0.01
Polish (141)	176	0.14
Portuguese (0)	12	0.01
Romanian (0)	0	<0.01
Russian (89)	97	0.08
Scandinavian (13)	13	0.01
Scotch-Irish (0)	0	<0.01
Scottish (36)	121	0.10
Serbian (15)	15	0.01
Slavic (0)	0	<0.01
Slovak (0)	0	<0.01
Slovene (0)	0	<0.01
Soviet Union (0)	0	<0.01
Swedish (0)	10	0.01
Swiss (0)	0	<0.01
Turkish (0)	0	<0.01
Ukrainian (32)	32	0.03
Welsh (0)	37	0.03
West Indian, ex. Hispanic (56)	111	0.09
Bahamian (0)	0	<0.01
Barbadian (0)	0	<0.01
Belizean (0)	0	<0.01
Bermudan (0)	0	<0.01
British West Indian (0)	0	<0.01
Dutch West Indian (0)	0	<0.01
Haitian (49)	104	0.08
Jamaican (0)	0	<0.01
Trinidadian/Tobagonian (0)	0	<0.01
U.S. Virgin Islander (0)	0	<0.01
West Indian (7)	7	0.01
Other West Indian (0)	0	<0.01
Yugoslavian (0)	26	0.02

Hispanic Origin	Population	%
Hispanic or Latino (of any race)	122,784	97.07
Central American, ex. Mexican	5,994	4.74
Costa Rican	29	0.02
Guatemalan	1,825	1.44
Honduran	494	0.39
Nicaraguan	283	0.22
Panamanian	21	0.02
Salvadoran	3,274	2.59
Other Central American	68	0.05
Cuban	132	0.10
Dominican Republic	9	0.01
Mexican	111,441	88.10
Puerto Rican	264	0.21
South American	458	0.36
Argentinean	43	0.03
Bolivian	11	0.01
Chilean	29	0.02
Colombian	90	0.07
Ecuadorian	163	0.13
Paraguayan	0	<0.01
Peruvian	100	0.08
Uruguayan	11	0.01
Venezuelan	3	<0.01
Other South American	8	0.01
Other Hispanic or Latino	4,486	3.55

Race*	Population	%
African-American/Black (817)	1,073	0.85
Not Hispanic (322)	354	0.28
Hispanic (495)	719	0.57
American Indian/Alaska Native (1,549)	2,088	1.65
Not Hispanic (167)	219	0.17
Hispanic (1,382)	1,869	1.48
Alaska Athabascan *(Ala. Nat.)* (0)	0	<0.01
Aleut *(Alaska Native)* (0)	0	<0.01
Apache (58)	74	0.06
Arapaho (0)	0	<0.01
Blackfeet (1)	5	<0.01
Canadian/French Am. Ind. (0)	0	<0.01
Central American Ind. (10)	21	0.02
Cherokee (27)	71	0.06
Cheyenne (0)	1	<0.01
Chickasaw (0)	0	<0.01
Chippewa (8)	9	0.01
Choctaw (4)	7	0.01
Colville (0)	0	<0.01
Comanche (3)	3	<0.01
Cree (0)	0	<0.01
Creek (3)	4	<0.01
Crow (1)	1	<0.01
Delaware (0)	0	<0.01
Hopi (4)	8	0.01
Houma (0)	0	<0.01
Inupiat *(Alaska Native)* (1)	2	<0.01
Iroquois (1)	1	<0.01
Kiowa (0)	0	<0.01
Lumbee (0)	0	<0.01
Menominee (0)	0	<0.01
Mexican American Ind. (384)	487	0.38
Navajo (40)	69	0.05
Osage (0)	0	<0.01
Ottawa (0)	0	<0.01
Paiute (6)	6	<0.01
Pima (11)	12	0.01
Potawatomi (0)	0	<0.01
Pueblo (22)	26	0.02
Puget Sound Salish (0)	0	<0.01
Seminole (0)	0	<0.01
Shoshone (1)	1	<0.01
Sioux (9)	10	0.01
South American Ind. (1)	3	<0.01
Spanish American Ind. (26)	33	0.03
Tlingit-Haida *(Alaska Native)* (0)	0	<0.01
Tohono O'Odham (7)	16	0.01
Tsimshian *(Alaska Native)* (0)	0	<0.01
Ute (4)	4	<0.01
Yakama (0)	0	<0.01
Yaqui (45)	66	0.05
Yuman (4)	4	<0.01
Yup'ik *(Alaska Native)* (0)	0	<0.01
Asian (1,144)	1,531	1.21
Not Hispanic (962)	1,045	0.83
Hispanic (182)	486	0.38
Bangladeshi (0)	0	<0.01
Bhutanese (0)	0	<0.01
Burmese (2)	2	<0.01
Cambodian (14)	16	0.01
Chinese, ex. Taiwanese (377)	453	0.36
Filipino (209)	311	0.25
Hmong (0)	0	<0.01
Indian (38)	66	0.05
Indonesian (4)	7	0.01
Japanese (258)	335	0.26
Korean (60)	75	0.06
Laotian (14)	21	0.02
Malaysian (2)	2	<0.01
Nepalese (0)	0	<0.01
Pakistani (4)	5	<0.01
Sri Lankan (0)	1	<0.01
Taiwanese (7)	10	0.01
Thai (20)	29	0.02
Vietnamese (73)	90	0.07
Hawaii Native/Pacific Islander (63)	149	0.12
Not Hispanic (13)	21	0.02
Hispanic (50)	128	0.10
Fijian (0)	0	<0.01
Guamanian/Chamorro (25)	31	0.02
Marshallese (0)	0	<0.01
Native Hawaiian (21)	49	0.04
Samoan (8)	20	0.02
Tongan (0)	0	<0.01
White (63,934)	67,508	53.37
Not Hispanic (1,917)	2,062	1.63
Hispanic (62,017)	65,446	51.74

*Notes: † The Census 2010 population figure is used to calculate the percentages in the Hispanic Origin and Race categories. Ancestry percentages are based on the 2006-2010 American Community Survey population (not shown); ‡ Numbers in parentheses indicate the number of people reporting a single ancestry; * Numbers in parentheses indicate the number of persons reporting this race alone, not in combination with any other race; Please refer to the Explanation of Data for more information.*

Eastvale

Place Type: CDP
County: Riverside
Population: 53,668

Ancestry	Population	%
Afghan (0)	0	<0.01
African, Sub-Saharan (791)	811	1.65
African (197)	217	0.44
Cape Verdean (0)	0	<0.01
Ethiopian (29)	29	0.06
Ghanaian (0)	0	<0.01
Kenyan (0)	0	<0.01
Liberian (0)	0	<0.01
Nigerian (565)	565	1.15
Senegalese (0)	0	<0.01
Sierra Leonean (0)	0	<0.01
Somalian (0)	0	<0.01
South African (0)	0	<0.01
Sudanese (0)	0	<0.01
Ugandan (0)	0	<0.01
Zimbabwean (0)	0	<0.01
Other Sub-Saharan African (0)	0	<0.01
Albanian (0)	0	<0.01
Alsatian (0)	0	<0.01
American (1,166)	1,166	2.37
Arab (327)	403	0.82
Arab (0)	0	<0.01
Egyptian (261)	308	0.63
Iraqi (0)	0	<0.01
Jordanian (0)	0	<0.01
Lebanese (18)	47	0.10
Moroccan (0)	0	<0.01
Palestinian (0)	0	<0.01
Syrian (0)	0	<0.01
Other Arab (48)	48	0.10
Armenian (48)	85	0.17
Assyrian/Chaldean/Syriac (0)	0	<0.01
Australian (0)	0	<0.01
Austrian (0)	97	0.20
Basque (0)	0	<0.01
Belgian (0)	12	0.02
Brazilian (0)	27	0.05
British (38)	68	0.14
Bulgarian (0)	0	<0.01
Cajun (0)	0	<0.01
Canadian (90)	162	0.33
Carpatho Rusyn (0)	0	<0.01
Celtic (0)	0	<0.01
Croatian (0)	10	0.02
Cypriot (0)	0	<0.01
Czech (0)	17	0.03
Czechoslovakian (10)	33	0.07
Danish (11)	148	0.30
Dutch (156)	460	0.94
Eastern European (21)	21	0.04
English (250)	1,608	3.27
Estonian (0)	0	<0.01
European (367)	560	1.14
Finnish (0)	9	0.02
French, ex. Basque (73)	837	1.70
French Canadian (28)	173	0.35
German (841)	3,555	7.24
German Russian (0)	0	<0.01
Greek (20)	30	0.06
Guyanese (0)	0	<0.01
Hungarian (69)	152	0.31
Icelander (0)	0	<0.01
Iranian (105)	116	0.24
Irish (564)	2,485	5.06
Israeli (0)	0	<0.01
Italian (383)	1,433	2.92
Latvian (0)	6	0.01
Lithuanian (0)	0	<0.01
Luxemburger (0)	0	<0.01
Macedonian (0)	0	<0.01
Maltese (0)	0	<0.01
New Zealander (0)	0	<0.01
Northern European (63)	63	0.13
Norwegian (113)	292	0.59
Pennsylvania German (0)	0	<0.01
Polish (53)	280	0.57
Portuguese (182)	344	0.70
Romanian (88)	88	0.18
Russian (62)	161	0.33
Scandinavian (45)	87	0.18
Scotch-Irish (51)	212	0.43
Scottish (8)	359	0.73
Serbian (0)	0	<0.01
Slavic (0)	0	<0.01
Slovak (0)	0	<0.01
Slovene (0)	0	<0.01
Soviet Union (0)	0	<0.01
Swedish (52)	154	0.31
Swiss (12)	56	0.11
Turkish (0)	0	<0.01
Ukrainian (36)	57	0.12
Welsh (0)	115	0.23
West Indian, ex. Hispanic (62)	62	0.13
Bahamian (0)	0	<0.01
Barbadian (0)	0	<0.01
Belizean (0)	0	<0.01
Bermudan (0)	0	<0.01
British West Indian (24)	24	0.05
Dutch West Indian (0)	0	<0.01
Haitian (0)	0	<0.01
Jamaican (19)	19	0.04
Trinidadian/Tobagonian (0)	0	<0.01
U.S. Virgin Islander (0)	0	<0.01
West Indian (19)	19	0.04
Other West Indian (0)	0	<0.01
Yugoslavian (13)	163	0.33

Hispanic Origin	Population	%
Hispanic or Latino (of any race)	21,445	39.96
Central American, ex. Mexican	1,198	2.23
Costa Rican	53	0.10
Guatemalan	311	0.58
Honduran	69	0.13
Nicaraguan	149	0.28
Panamanian	43	0.08
Salvadoran	561	1.05
Other Central American	12	0.02
Cuban	277	0.52
Dominican Republic	10	0.02
Mexican	17,575	32.75
Puerto Rican	356	0.66
South American	739	1.38
Argentinean	76	0.14
Bolivian	44	0.08
Chilean	43	0.08
Colombian	200	0.37
Ecuadorian	145	0.27
Paraguayan	0	<0.01
Peruvian	199	0.37
Uruguayan	12	0.02
Venezuelan	16	0.03
Other South American	4	0.01
Other Hispanic or Latino	1,290	2.40

Race*	Population	%
African-American/Black (5,190)	5,892	10.98
Not Hispanic (4,914)	5,411	10.08
Hispanic (276)	481	0.90
American Indian/Alaska Native (290)	650	1.21
Not Hispanic (102)	321	0.60
Hispanic (188)	329	0.61
Alaska Athabascan *(Ala. Nat.)* (0)	0	<0.01
Aleut *(Alaska Native)* (3)	3	0.01
Apache (10)	32	0.06
Arapaho (2)	2	<0.01
Blackfeet (1)	16	0.03
Canadian/French Am. Ind. (0)	2	<0.01
Central American Ind. (0)	1	<0.01
Cherokee (15)	85	0.16
Cheyenne (0)	0	<0.01
Chickasaw (7)	21	0.04
Chippewa (5)	9	0.02
Choctaw (7)	19	0.04
Colville (0)	0	<0.01
Comanche (1)	1	<0.01
Cree (0)	0	<0.01
Creek (0)	0	<0.01
Crow (0)	0	<0.01
Delaware (0)	4	0.01
Hopi (0)	2	<0.01
Houma (0)	0	<0.01
Inupiat *(Alaska Native)* (0)	0	<0.01
Iroquois (2)	7	0.01
Kiowa (0)	0	<0.01
Lumbee (0)	0	<0.01
Menominee (0)	0	<0.01
Mexican American Ind. (25)	37	0.07
Navajo (6)	16	0.03
Osage (0)	0	<0.01
Ottawa (0)	0	<0.01
Paiute (0)	0	<0.01
Pima (0)	1	<0.01
Potawatomi (4)	4	0.01
Pueblo (5)	17	0.03
Puget Sound Salish (0)	0	<0.01
Seminole (1)	2	<0.01
Shoshone (0)	0	<0.01
Sioux (0)	3	0.01
South American Ind. (1)	1	<0.01
Spanish American Ind. (6)	6	0.01
Tlingit-Haida *(Alaska Native)* (0)	1	<0.01
Tohono O'Odham (3)	3	0.01
Tsimshian *(Alaska Native)* (0)	0	<0.01
Ute (0)	0	<0.01
Yakama (0)	0	<0.01
Yaqui (0)	0	<0.01
Yuman (0)	0	<0.01
Yup'ik *(Alaska Native)* (0)	0	<0.01
Asian (13,003)	14,244	26.54
Not Hispanic (12,770)	13,719	25.56
Hispanic (233)	525	0.98
Bangladeshi (19)	23	0.04
Bhutanese (0)	0	<0.01
Burmese (9)	10	0.02
Cambodian (291)	367	0.68
Chinese, ex. Taiwanese (3,158)	3,625	6.75
Filipino (3,417)	3,973	7.40
Hmong (71)	75	0.14
Indian (1,456)	1,593	2.97
Indonesian (109)	172	0.32
Japanese (128)	334	0.62
Korean (1,108)	1,194	2.22
Laotian (148)	167	0.31
Malaysian (11)	15	0.03
Nepalese (22)	22	0.04
Pakistani (319)	342	0.64
Sri Lankan (39)	42	0.08
Taiwanese (518)	622	1.16
Thai (112)	153	0.29
Vietnamese (1,517)	1,756	3.27
Hawaii Native/Pacific Islander (198)	443	0.83
Not Hispanic (156)	322	0.60
Hispanic (42)	121	0.23
Fijian (4)	5	0.01
Guamanian/Chamorro (31)	52	0.10
Marshallese (0)	0	<0.01
Native Hawaiian (13)	75	0.14
Samoan (62)	99	0.18
Tongan (62)	69	0.13
White (22,998)	25,136	46.84
Not Hispanic (12,712)	13,792	25.70
Hispanic (10,286)	11,344	21.14

*Notes: † The Census 2010 population figure is used to calculate the percentages in the Hispanic Origin and Race categories. Ancestry percentages are based on the 2006-2010 American Community Survey population (not shown); ‡ Numbers in parentheses indicate the number of people reporting a single ancestry; * Numbers in parentheses indicate the number of persons reporting this race alone, not in combination with any other race; Please refer to the Explanation of Data for more information.*

El Cajon

Place Type: City
County: San Diego
Population: 99,478

Ancestry	Population	%
Afghan (403)	484	0.49
African, Sub-Saharan (330)	459	0.47
African (306)	377	0.38
Cape Verdean (14)	14	0.01
Ethiopian (0)	0	<0.01
Ghanaian (0)	0	<0.01
Kenyan (0)	0	<0.01
Liberian (0)	0	<0.01
Nigerian (10)	10	0.01
Senegalese (0)	0	<0.01
Sierra Leonean (0)	0	<0.01
Somalian (0)	48	0.05
South African (0)	0	<0.01
Sudanese (0)	0	<0.01
Ugandan (0)	0	<0.01
Zimbabwean (0)	0	<0.01
Other Sub-Saharan African (0)	10	0.01
Albanian (0)	0	<0.01
Alsatian (0)	0	<0.01
American (2,287)	2,287	2.34
Arab (3,598)	4,795	4.90
Arab (386)	560	0.57
Egyptian (37)	37	0.04
Iraqi (2,221)	3,081	3.15
Jordanian (49)	49	0.05
Lebanese (49)	62	0.06
Moroccan (0)	0	<0.01
Palestinian (38)	38	0.04
Syrian (10)	10	0.01
Other Arab (808)	958	0.98
Armenian (161)	169	0.17
Assyrian/Chaldean/Syriac (3,849)	4,776	4.88
Australian (13)	24	0.02
Austrian (21)	167	0.17
Basque (21)	21	0.02
Belgian (0)	45	0.05
Brazilian (0)	9	0.01
British (93)	287	0.29
Bulgarian (0)	31	0.03
Cajun (0)	0	<0.01
Canadian (26)	330	0.34
Carpatho Rusyn (0)	0	<0.01
Celtic (0)	0	<0.01
Croatian (20)	57	0.06
Cypriot (0)	0	<0.01
Czech (118)	368	0.38
Czechoslovakian (35)	46	0.05
Danish (110)	373	0.38
Dutch (237)	1,371	1.40
Eastern European (22)	22	0.02
English (1,724)	7,754	7.92
Estonian (0)	0	<0.01
European (724)	791	0.81
Finnish (14)	134	0.14
French, ex. Basque (381)	2,749	2.81
French Canadian (284)	433	0.44
German (3,319)	13,339	13.62
German Russian (0)	0	<0.01
Greek (208)	376	0.38
Guyanese (0)	0	<0.01
Hungarian (64)	302	0.31
Icelander (0)	56	0.06
Iranian (138)	158	0.16
Irish (2,105)	10,107	10.32
Israeli (9)	22	0.02
Italian (2,033)	5,053	5.16
Latvian (0)	41	0.04
Lithuanian (74)	222	0.23
Luxemburger (12)	12	0.01
Macedonian (0)	0	<0.01
Maltese (0)	39	0.04
New Zealander (0)	17	0.02
Northern European (27)	27	0.03
Norwegian (285)	1,066	1.09
Pennsylvania German (15)	47	0.05
Polish (426)	1,672	1.71
Portuguese (151)	427	0.44
Romanian (9)	22	0.02
Russian (297)	812	0.83
Scandinavian (93)	310	0.32
Scotch-Irish (377)	1,493	1.52
Scottish (452)	1,771	1.81
Serbian (13)	13	0.01
Slavic (18)	86	0.09
Slovak (8)	52	0.05
Slovene (26)	26	0.03
Soviet Union (0)	0	<0.01
Swedish (368)	1,478	1.51
Swiss (7)	150	0.15
Turkish (0)	0	<0.01
Ukrainian (107)	257	0.26
Welsh (150)	634	0.65
West Indian, ex. Hispanic (127)	224	0.23
Bahamian (0)	0	<0.01
Barbadian (0)	0	<0.01
Belizean (21)	36	0.04
Bermudan (0)	0	<0.01
British West Indian (0)	0	<0.01
Dutch West Indian (0)	0	<0.01
Haitian (17)	94	0.10
Jamaican (7)	7	0.01
Trinidadian/Tobagonian (0)	0	<0.01
U.S. Virgin Islander (0)	0	<0.01
West Indian (82)	87	0.09
Other West Indian (0)	0	<0.01
Yugoslavian (105)	116	0.12

Hispanic Origin	Population	%
Hispanic or Latino (of any race)	28,036	28.18
Central American, ex. Mexican	694	0.70
Costa Rican	54	0.05
Guatemalan	225	0.23
Honduran	51	0.05
Nicaraguan	62	0.06
Panamanian	67	0.07
Salvadoran	219	0.22
Other Central American	16	0.02
Cuban	99	0.10
Dominican Republic	37	0.04
Mexican	24,534	24.66
Puerto Rican	646	0.65
South American	339	0.34
Argentinean	30	0.03
Bolivian	15	0.02
Chilean	44	0.04
Colombian	99	0.10
Ecuadorian	34	0.03
Paraguayan	0	<0.01
Peruvian	97	0.10
Uruguayan	2	<0.01
Venezuelan	18	0.02
Other South American	0	<0.01
Other Hispanic or Latino	1,687	1.70

Race*	Population	%
African-American/Black (6,306)	8,058	8.10
Not Hispanic (5,939)	7,213	7.25
Hispanic (367)	845	0.85
American Indian/Alaska Native (835)	2,017	2.03
Not Hispanic (455)	1,236	1.24
Hispanic (380)	781	0.79
Alaska Athabascan *(Ala. Nat.)* (1)	2	<0.01
Aleut *(Alaska Native)* (0)	3	<0.01
Apache (27)	61	0.06
Arapaho (2)	8	0.01
Blackfeet (10)	66	0.07
Canadian/French Am. Ind. (2)	13	0.01
Central American Ind. (5)	7	0.01
Cherokee (61)	306	0.31
Cheyenne (7)	12	0.01
Chickasaw (3)	10	0.01
Chippewa (21)	30	0.03
Choctaw (20)	63	0.06
Colville (0)	0	<0.01
Comanche (3)	7	0.01
Cree (1)	8	0.01
Creek (1)	24	0.02
Crow (1)	3	<0.01
Delaware (0)	1	<0.01
Hopi (1)	3	<0.01
Houma (0)	0	<0.01
Inupiat *(Alaska Native)* (0)	1	<0.01
Iroquois (5)	17	0.02
Kiowa (2)	2	<0.01
Lumbee (1)	3	<0.01
Menominee (2)	2	<0.01
Mexican American Ind. (55)	105	0.11
Navajo (14)	34	0.03
Osage (1)	8	0.01
Ottawa (6)	6	0.01
Paiute (2)	2	<0.01
Pima (2)	5	0.01
Potawatomi (0)	2	<0.01
Pueblo (17)	37	0.04
Puget Sound Salish (0)	3	<0.01
Seminole (1)	6	0.01
Shoshone (2)	7	0.01
Sioux (18)	47	0.05
South American Ind. (3)	6	0.01
Spanish American Ind. (4)	5	0.01
Tlingit-Haida *(Alaska Native)* (0)	0	<0.01
Tohono O'Odham (3)	8	0.01
Tsimshian *(Alaska Native)* (0)	0	<0.01
Ute (0)	0	<0.01
Yakama (1)	3	<0.01
Yaqui (23)	45	0.05
Yuman (7)	8	0.01
Yup'ik *(Alaska Native)* (0)	0	<0.01
Asian (3,561)	6,496	6.53
Not Hispanic (3,375)	5,904	5.93
Hispanic (186)	592	0.60
Bangladeshi (0)	0	<0.01
Bhutanese (2)	2	<0.01
Burmese (122)	124	0.12
Cambodian (102)	132	0.13
Chinese, ex. Taiwanese (443)	638	0.64
Filipino (1,740)	2,678	2.69
Hmong (7)	10	0.01
Indian (119)	229	0.23
Indonesian (27)	39	0.04
Japanese (193)	536	0.54
Korean (88)	180	0.18
Laotian (28)	41	0.04
Malaysian (2)	2	<0.01
Nepalese (0)	0	<0.01
Pakistani (32)	36	0.04
Sri Lankan (6)	15	0.02
Taiwanese (10)	12	0.01
Thai (43)	73	0.07
Vietnamese (412)	520	0.52
Hawaii Native/Pacific Islander (495)	1,210	1.22
Not Hispanic (440)	978	0.98
Hispanic (55)	232	0.23
Fijian (1)	3	<0.01
Guamanian/Chamorro (230)	404	0.41
Marshallese (0)	0	<0.01
Native Hawaiian (72)	258	0.26
Samoan (120)	227	0.23
Tongan (4)	13	0.01
White (68,897)	74,773	75.17
Not Hispanic (56,462)	60,466	60.78
Hispanic (12,435)	14,307	14.38

*Notes: † The Census 2010 population figure is used to calculate the percentages in the Hispanic Origin and Race categories. Ancestry percentages are based on the 2006-2010 American Community Survey population (not shown); ‡ Numbers in parentheses indicate the number of people reporting a single ancestry; * Numbers in parentheses indicate the number of persons reporting this race alone, not in combination with any other race; Please refer to the Explanation of Data for more information.*

El Monte

Place Type: City
County: Los Angeles
Population: 113,475

Ancestry	Population	%
Afghan (0)	0	<0.01
African, Sub-Saharan (120)	132	0.12
African (29)	41	0.04
Cape Verdean (0)	0	<0.01
Ethiopian (36)	36	0.03
Ghanaian (0)	0	<0.01
Kenyan (0)	0	<0.01
Liberian (0)	0	<0.01
Nigerian (55)	55	0.05
Senegalese (0)	0	<0.01
Sierra Leonean (0)	0	<0.01
Somalian (0)	0	<0.01
South African (0)	0	<0.01
Sudanese (0)	0	<0.01
Ugandan (0)	0	<0.01
Zimbabwean (0)	0	<0.01
Other Sub-Saharan African (0)	0	<0.01
Albanian (0)	0	<0.01
Alsatian (0)	0	<0.01
American (547)	547	0.48
Arab (22)	22	0.02
Arab (0)	0	<0.01
Egyptian (10)	10	0.01
Iraqi (0)	0	<0.01
Jordanian (0)	0	<0.01
Lebanese (12)	12	0.01
Moroccan (0)	0	<0.01
Palestinian (0)	0	<0.01
Syrian (0)	0	<0.01
Other Arab (0)	0	<0.01
Armenian (8)	34	0.03
Assyrian/Chaldean/Syriac (0)	0	<0.01
Australian (0)	0	<0.01
Austrian (0)	5	<0.01
Basque (0)	19	0.02
Belgian (0)	0	<0.01
Brazilian (21)	21	0.02
British (0)	6	0.01
Bulgarian (11)	26	0.02
Cajun (0)	0	<0.01
Canadian (5)	5	<0.01
Carpatho Rusyn (0)	0	<0.01
Celtic (0)	0	<0.01
Croatian (0)	0	<0.01
Cypriot (0)	0	<0.01
Czech (7)	27	0.02
Czechoslovakian (13)	13	0.01
Danish (0)	39	0.03
Dutch (20)	251	0.22
Eastern European (0)	0	<0.01
English (240)	708	0.62
Estonian (0)	0	<0.01
European (110)	115	0.10
Finnish (0)	51	0.04
French, ex. Basque (94)	336	0.30
French Canadian (18)	18	0.02
German (297)	1,228	1.08
German Russian (0)	0	<0.01
Greek (0)	23	0.02
Guyanese (0)	0	<0.01
Hungarian (13)	22	0.02
Icelander (0)	0	<0.01
Iranian (11)	11	0.01
Irish (236)	826	0.73
Israeli (0)	0	<0.01
Italian (160)	539	0.47
Latvian (0)	0	<0.01
Lithuanian (17)	60	0.05
Luxemburger (0)	0	<0.01
Macedonian (0)	0	<0.01
Maltese (0)	0	<0.01
New Zealander (0)	0	<0.01
Northern European (0)	0	<0.01
Norwegian (45)	92	0.08
Pennsylvania German (0)	0	<0.01
Polish (13)	43	0.04
Portuguese (34)	34	0.03
Romanian (0)	0	<0.01
Russian (48)	76	0.07
Scandinavian (7)	17	0.01
Scotch-Irish (51)	137	0.12
Scottish (0)	37	0.03
Serbian (0)	0	<0.01
Slavic (0)	0	<0.01
Slovak (0)	0	<0.01
Slovene (0)	0	<0.01
Soviet Union (0)	0	<0.01
Swedish (24)	194	0.17
Swiss (0)	23	0.02
Turkish (0)	0	<0.01
Ukrainian (0)	0	<0.01
Welsh (0)	0	<0.01
West Indian, ex. Hispanic (37)	59	0.05
Bahamian (0)	0	<0.01
Barbadian (0)	0	<0.01
Belizean (25)	25	0.02
Bermudan (0)	0	<0.01
British West Indian (0)	0	<0.01
Dutch West Indian (0)	0	<0.01
Haitian (0)	0	<0.01
Jamaican (12)	34	0.03
Trinidadian/Tobagonian (0)	0	<0.01
U.S. Virgin Islander (0)	0	<0.01
West Indian (0)	0	<0.01
Other West Indian (0)	0	<0.01
Yugoslavian (0)	0	<0.01

Hispanic Origin	Population	%
Hispanic or Latino (of any race)	78,317	69.02
Central American, ex. Mexican	4,961	4.37
Costa Rican	67	0.06
Guatemalan	1,393	1.23
Honduran	388	0.34
Nicaraguan	450	0.40
Panamanian	31	0.03
Salvadoran	2,570	2.26
Other Central American	62	0.05
Cuban	350	0.31
Dominican Republic	8	0.01
Mexican	69,053	60.85
Puerto Rican	232	0.20
South American	565	0.50
Argentinean	103	0.09
Bolivian	9	0.01
Chilean	17	0.01
Colombian	93	0.08
Ecuadorian	102	0.09
Paraguayan	1	<0.01
Peruvian	209	0.18
Uruguayan	12	0.01
Venezuelan	7	0.01
Other South American	12	0.01
Other Hispanic or Latino	3,148	2.77

Race*	Population	%
African-American/Black (870)	1,178	1.04
Not Hispanic (502)	582	0.51
Hispanic (368)	596	0.53
American Indian/Alaska Native (1,083)	1,569	1.38
Not Hispanic (133)	272	0.24
Hispanic (950)	1,297	1.14
Alaska Athabascan *(Ala. Nat.)* (0)	0	<0.01
Aleut *(Alaska Native)* (1)	1	<0.01
Apache (29)	61	0.05
Arapaho (1)	1	<0.01
Blackfeet (2)	2	<0.01
Canadian/French Am. Ind. (0)	0	<0.01
Central American Ind. (16)	29	0.03
Cherokee (10)	52	0.05
Cheyenne (10)	10	0.01
Chickasaw (0)	4	<0.01
Chippewa (4)	7	0.01
Choctaw (2)	6	0.01
Colville (0)	0	<0.01
Comanche (0)	0	<0.01
Cree (0)	0	<0.01
Creek (3)	6	0.01
Crow (0)	0	<0.01
Delaware (0)	0	<0.01
Hopi (4)	6	0.01
Houma (0)	0	<0.01
Inupiat *(Alaska Native)* (0)	0	<0.01
Iroquois (1)	5	<0.01
Kiowa (0)	0	<0.01
Lumbee (0)	0	<0.01
Menominee (0)	0	<0.01
Mexican American Ind. (200)	277	0.24
Navajo (9)	19	0.02
Osage (1)	1	<0.01
Ottawa (0)	0	<0.01
Paiute (2)	3	<0.01
Pima (7)	7	0.01
Potawatomi (1)	1	<0.01
Pueblo (2)	11	0.01
Puget Sound Salish (0)	0	<0.01
Seminole (0)	3	<0.01
Shoshone (0)	0	<0.01
Sioux (5)	10	0.01
South American Ind. (3)	5	<0.01
Spanish American Ind. (19)	27	0.02
Tlingit-Haida *(Alaska Native)* (0)	0	<0.01
Tohono O'Odham (5)	7	0.01
Tsimshian *(Alaska Native)* (0)	0	<0.01
Ute (0)	0	<0.01
Yakama (0)	0	<0.01
Yaqui (31)	55	0.05
Yuman (5)	10	0.01
Yup'ik *(Alaska Native)* (0)	0	<0.01
Asian (28,503)	29,188	25.72
Not Hispanic (28,264)	28,605	25.21
Hispanic (239)	583	0.51
Bangladeshi (1)	11	0.01
Bhutanese (0)	0	<0.01
Burmese (225)	241	0.21
Cambodian (481)	632	0.56
Chinese, ex. Taiwanese (14,665)	16,151	14.23
Filipino (1,384)	1,565	1.38
Hmong (0)	1	<0.01
Indian (184)	282	0.25
Indonesian (113)	135	0.12
Japanese (210)	320	0.28
Korean (199)	236	0.21
Laotian (40)	65	0.06
Malaysian (24)	42	0.04
Nepalese (24)	24	0.02
Pakistani (14)	18	0.02
Sri Lankan (12)	16	0.01
Taiwanese (730)	816	0.72
Thai (201)	230	0.20
Vietnamese (8,433)	9,667	8.52
Hawaii Native/Pacific Islander (131)	282	0.25
Not Hispanic (84)	153	0.13
Hispanic (47)	129	0.11
Fijian (0)	1	<0.01
Guamanian/Chamorro (21)	30	0.03
Marshallese (0)	0	<0.01
Native Hawaiian (39)	78	0.07
Samoan (37)	59	0.05
Tongan (5)	7	0.01
White (44,058)	47,011	41.43
Not Hispanic (5,556)	5,890	5.19
Hispanic (38,502)	41,121	36.24

*Notes: † The Census 2010 population figure is used to calculate the percentages in the Hispanic Origin and Race categories. Ancestry percentages are based on the 2006-2010 American Community Survey population (not shown); ‡ Numbers in parentheses indicate the number of people reporting a single ancestry; * Numbers in parentheses indicate the number of persons reporting this race alone, not in combination with any other race; Please refer to the Explanation of Data for more information.*

Elk Grove

Place Type: City
County: Sacramento
Population: 153,015

Ancestry	Population	%
Afghan (1,204)	1,211	0.86
African, Sub-Saharan (1,669)	2,477	1.75
African (619)	1,331	0.94
Cape Verdean (38)	106	0.08
Ethiopian (486)	492	0.35
Ghanaian (10)	10	0.01
Kenyan (0)	0	<0.01
Liberian (0)	0	<0.01
Nigerian (354)	363	0.26
Senegalese (0)	0	<0.01
Sierra Leonean (0)	0	<0.01
Somalian (148)	148	0.10
South African (14)	14	0.01
Sudanese (0)	0	<0.01
Ugandan (0)	0	<0.01
Zimbabwean (0)	0	<0.01
Other Sub-Saharan African (0)	13	0.01
Albanian (0)	8	0.01
Alsatian (0)	0	<0.01
American (2,130)	2,130	1.51
Arab (1,044)	1,444	1.02
Arab (132)	206	0.15
Egyptian (101)	110	0.08
Iraqi (46)	46	0.03
Jordanian (115)	115	0.08
Lebanese (233)	397	0.28
Moroccan (0)	0	<0.01
Palestinian (267)	396	0.28
Syrian (80)	80	0.06
Other Arab (70)	94	0.07
Armenian (53)	202	0.14
Assyrian/Chaldean/Syriac (13)	13	0.01
Australian (26)	48	0.03
Austrian (109)	317	0.22
Basque (52)	52	0.04
Belgian (13)	45	0.03
Brazilian (34)	73	0.05
British (70)	463	0.33
Bulgarian (0)	0	<0.01
Cajun (0)	0	<0.01
Canadian (127)	446	0.32
Carpatho Rusyn (0)	0	<0.01
Celtic (0)	15	0.01
Croatian (64)	231	0.16
Cypriot (0)	0	<0.01
Czech (76)	261	0.18
Czechoslovakian (22)	62	0.04
Danish (127)	739	0.52
Dutch (349)	1,801	1.28
Eastern European (22)	48	0.03
English (2,030)	9,477	6.71
Estonian (0)	0	<0.01
European (1,024)	1,413	1.00
Finnish (25)	120	0.08
French, ex. Basque (309)	3,063	2.17
French Canadian (209)	740	0.52
German (3,692)	15,493	10.97
German Russian (0)	0	<0.01
Greek (247)	837	0.59
Guyanese (23)	23	0.02
Hungarian (81)	286	0.20
Icelander (8)	8	0.01
Iranian (221)	271	0.19
Irish (1,957)	11,046	7.82
Israeli (0)	0	<0.01
Italian (2,182)	6,741	4.77
Latvian (0)	15	0.01
Lithuanian (25)	75	0.05
Luxemburger (0)	0	<0.01
Macedonian (0)	0	<0.01
Maltese (10)	47	0.03
New Zealander (8)	8	0.01
Northern European (177)	200	0.14
Norwegian (477)	1,360	0.96
Pennsylvania German (0)	0	<0.01
Polish (249)	1,258	0.89
Portuguese (865)	2,750	1.95
Romanian (132)	400	0.28
Russian (344)	945	0.67
Scandinavian (142)	321	0.23
Scotch-Irish (536)	1,675	1.19
Scottish (412)	2,583	1.83
Serbian (8)	17	0.01
Slavic (0)	40	0.03
Slovak (0)	63	0.04
Slovene (0)	39	0.03
Soviet Union (0)	0	<0.01
Swedish (386)	2,091	1.48
Swiss (38)	322	0.23
Turkish (0)	8	0.01
Ukrainian (271)	385	0.27
Welsh (222)	1,020	0.72
West Indian, ex. Hispanic (154)	387	0.27
Bahamian (44)	44	0.03
Barbadian (0)	0	<0.01
Belizean (0)	0	<0.01
Bermudan (0)	15	0.01
British West Indian (0)	0	<0.01
Dutch West Indian (0)	42	0.03
Haitian (0)	53	0.04
Jamaican (37)	51	0.04
Trinidadian/Tobagonian (23)	79	0.06
U.S. Virgin Islander (0)	0	<0.01
West Indian (50)	103	0.07
Other West Indian (0)	0	<0.01
Yugoslavian (119)	358	0.25

Hispanic Origin	Population	%
Hispanic or Latino (of any race)	27,581	18.03
Central American, ex. Mexican	1,882	1.23
Costa Rican	73	0.05
Guatemalan	255	0.17
Honduran	73	0.05
Nicaraguan	453	0.30
Panamanian	175	0.11
Salvadoran	831	0.54
Other Central American	22	0.01
Cuban	222	0.15
Dominican Republic	56	0.04
Mexican	21,186	13.85
Puerto Rican	1,064	0.70
South American	699	0.46
Argentinean	63	0.04
Bolivian	39	0.03
Chilean	63	0.04
Colombian	140	0.09
Ecuadorian	55	0.04
Paraguayan	2	<0.01
Peruvian	275	0.18
Uruguayan	8	0.01
Venezuelan	50	0.03
Other South American	4	<0.01
Other Hispanic or Latino	2,472	1.62

Race*	Population	%
African-American/Black (17,172)	20,952	13.69
Not Hispanic (16,462)	19,426	12.70
Hispanic (710)	1,526	1.00
American Indian/Alaska Native (965)	2,996	1.96
Not Hispanic (507)	1,962	1.28
Hispanic (458)	1,034	0.68
Alaska Athabascan *(Ala. Nat.)* (1)	2	<0.01
Aleut *(Alaska Native)* (0)	8	0.01
Apache (36)	96	0.06
Arapaho (0)	0	<0.01
Blackfeet (10)	95	0.06
Canadian/French Am. Ind. (1)	2	<0.01
Central American Ind. (3)	5	<0.01
Cherokee (93)	555	0.36
Cheyenne (0)	6	<0.01
Chickasaw (7)	18	0.01
Chippewa (14)	36	0.02
Choctaw (18)	137	0.09
Colville (1)	1	<0.01
Comanche (1)	12	0.01
Cree (1)	8	0.01
Creek (10)	44	0.03
Crow (0)	0	<0.01
Delaware (5)	8	0.01
Hopi (0)	8	0.01
Houma (0)	0	<0.01
Inupiat *(Alaska Native)* (1)	2	<0.01
Iroquois (7)	21	0.01
Kiowa (2)	5	<0.01
Lumbee (2)	3	<0.01
Menominee (0)	0	<0.01
Mexican American Ind. (65)	108	0.07
Navajo (18)	63	0.04
Osage (1)	4	<0.01
Ottawa (3)	3	<0.01
Paiute (6)	17	0.01
Pima (0)	1	<0.01
Potawatomi (8)	19	0.01
Pueblo (3)	13	0.01
Puget Sound Salish (0)	1	<0.01
Seminole (5)	20	0.01
Shoshone (3)	7	<0.01
Sioux (22)	58	0.04
South American Ind. (4)	16	0.01
Spanish American Ind. (3)	8	0.01
Tlingit-Haida *(Alaska Native)* (5)	17	0.01
Tohono O'Odham (2)	2	<0.01
Tsimshian *(Alaska Native)* (1)	4	<0.01
Ute (0)	0	<0.01
Yakama (1)	1	<0.01
Yaqui (18)	32	0.02
Yuman (5)	7	<0.01
Yup'ik *(Alaska Native)* (0)	6	<0.01
Asian (40,261)	46,861	30.63
Not Hispanic (39,479)	44,901	29.34
Hispanic (782)	1,960	1.28
Bangladeshi (13)	20	0.01
Bhutanese (0)	0	<0.01
Burmese (24)	30	0.02
Cambodian (311)	384	0.25
Chinese, ex. Taiwanese (8,806)	10,629	6.95
Filipino (11,769)	14,891	9.73
Hmong (1,696)	1,789	1.17
Indian (4,968)	5,856	3.83
Indonesian (65)	125	0.08
Japanese (1,346)	2,725	1.78
Korean (658)	1,028	0.67
Laotian (777)	937	0.61
Malaysian (16)	26	0.02
Nepalese (28)	31	0.02
Pakistani (581)	645	0.42
Sri Lankan (35)	41	0.03
Taiwanese (150)	198	0.13
Thai (118)	257	0.17
Vietnamese (7,024)	7,796	5.09
Hawaii Native/Pacific Islander (1,807)	3,319	2.17
Not Hispanic (1,731)	3,048	1.99
Hispanic (76)	271	0.18
Fijian (1,103)	1,279	0.84
Guamanian/Chamorro (171)	350	0.23
Marshallese (18)	26	0.02
Native Hawaiian (77)	402	0.26
Samoan (99)	191	0.12
Tongan (101)	133	0.09
White (70,478)	79,401	51.89
Not Hispanic (58,305)	64,620	42.23
Hispanic (12,173)	14,781	9.66

*Notes: † The Census 2010 population figure is used to calculate the percentages in the Hispanic Origin and Race categories. Ancestry percentages are based on the 2006-2010 American Community Survey population (not shown); ‡ Numbers in parentheses indicate the number of people reporting a single ancestry; * Numbers in parentheses indicate the number of persons reporting this race alone, not in combination with any other race; Please refer to the Explanation of Data for more information.*

Encinitas

Place Type: City
County: San Diego
Population: 59,518

Ancestry	Population	%
Afghan (0)	0	<0.01
African, Sub-Saharan (0)	0	<0.01
African (0)	0	<0.01
Cape Verdean (0)	0	<0.01
Ethiopian (0)	0	<0.01
Ghanaian (0)	0	<0.01
Kenyan (0)	0	<0.01
Liberian (0)	0	<0.01
Nigerian (0)	0	<0.01
Senegalese (0)	0	<0.01
Sierra Leonean (0)	0	<0.01
Somalian (0)	0	<0.01
South African (0)	0	<0.01
Sudanese (0)	0	<0.01
Ugandan (0)	0	<0.01
Zimbabwean (0)	0	<0.01
Other Sub-Saharan African (0)	0	<0.01
Albanian (0)	28	0.05
Alsatian (0)	0	<0.01
American (1,648)	1,648	2.80
Arab (100)	249	0.42
Arab (17)	17	0.03
Egyptian (0)	0	<0.01
Iraqi (0)	27	0.05
Jordanian (0)	0	<0.01
Lebanese (53)	146	0.25
Moroccan (7)	30	0.05
Palestinian (0)	0	<0.01
Syrian (23)	29	0.05
Other Arab (0)	0	<0.01
Armenian (24)	59	0.10
Assyrian/Chaldean/Syriac (0)	0	<0.01
Australian (118)	133	0.23
Austrian (66)	184	0.31
Basque (8)	31	0.05
Belgian (0)	24	0.04
Brazilian (74)	111	0.19
British (283)	666	1.13
Bulgarian (0)	0	<0.01
Cajun (0)	0	<0.01
Canadian (123)	214	0.36
Carpatho Rusyn (0)	0	<0.01
Celtic (30)	30	0.05
Croatian (28)	85	0.14
Cypriot (0)	0	<0.01
Czech (95)	252	0.43
Czechoslovakian (74)	114	0.19
Danish (94)	407	0.69
Dutch (209)	665	1.13
Eastern European (181)	220	0.37
English (3,152)	9,494	16.16
Estonian (0)	0	<0.01
European (1,158)	1,308	2.23
Finnish (12)	21	0.04
French, ex. Basque (434)	2,779	4.73
French Canadian (218)	482	0.82
German (2,452)	10,401	17.70
German Russian (0)	0	<0.01
Greek (193)	395	0.67
Guyanese (0)	0	<0.01
Hungarian (152)	478	0.81
Icelander (10)	22	0.04
Iranian (306)	393	0.67
Irish (2,059)	7,825	13.32
Israeli (25)	25	0.04
Italian (1,591)	4,259	7.25
Latvian (21)	66	0.11
Lithuanian (58)	190	0.32
Luxemburger (0)	0	<0.01
Macedonian (0)	0	<0.01
Maltese (0)	0	<0.01
New Zealander (8)	8	0.01
Northern European (183)	183	0.31
Norwegian (706)	1,880	3.20
Pennsylvania German (69)	69	0.12
Polish (461)	1,809	3.08
Portuguese (268)	450	0.77
Romanian (14)	106	0.18
Russian (935)	1,863	3.17
Scandinavian (144)	377	0.64
Scotch-Irish (490)	1,740	2.96
Scottish (734)	2,179	3.71
Serbian (21)	81	0.14
Slavic (0)	64	0.11
Slovak (51)	160	0.27
Slovene (0)	14	0.02
Soviet Union (0)	0	<0.01
Swedish (336)	1,466	2.49
Swiss (54)	251	0.43
Turkish (52)	52	0.09
Ukrainian (47)	205	0.35
Welsh (45)	575	0.98
West Indian, ex. Hispanic (15)	30	0.05
Bahamian (0)	0	<0.01
Barbadian (0)	15	0.03
Belizean (0)	0	<0.01
Bermudan (0)	0	<0.01
British West Indian (0)	0	<0.01
Dutch West Indian (0)	0	<0.01
Haitian (0)	0	<0.01
Jamaican (15)	15	0.03
Trinidadian/Tobagonian (0)	0	<0.01
U.S. Virgin Islander (0)	0	<0.01
West Indian (0)	0	<0.01
Other West Indian (0)	0	<0.01
Yugoslavian (34)	87	0.15

Hispanic Origin	Population	%
Hispanic or Latino (of any race)	8,138	13.67
Central American, ex. Mexican	403	0.68
Costa Rican	24	0.04
Guatemalan	205	0.34
Honduran	34	0.06
Nicaraguan	22	0.04
Panamanian	27	0.05
Salvadoran	85	0.14
Other Central American	6	0.01
Cuban	91	0.15
Dominican Republic	12	0.02
Mexican	6,412	10.77
Puerto Rican	186	0.31
South American	366	0.61
Argentinean	64	0.11
Bolivian	13	0.02
Chilean	50	0.08
Colombian	105	0.18
Ecuadorian	20	0.03
Paraguayan	0	<0.01
Peruvian	69	0.12
Uruguayan	0	<0.01
Venezuelan	39	0.07
Other South American	6	0.01
Other Hispanic or Latino	668	1.12

Race*	Population	%
African-American/Black (361)	618	1.04
Not Hispanic (316)	515	0.87
Hispanic (45)	103	0.17
American Indian/Alaska Native (301)	729	1.22
Not Hispanic (159)	437	0.73
Hispanic (142)	292	0.49
Alaska Athabascan *(Ala. Nat.)* (1)	4	0.01
Aleut *(Alaska Native)* (0)	0	<0.01
Apache (7)	22	0.04
Arapaho (0)	0	<0.01
Blackfeet (2)	14	0.02
Canadian/French Am. Ind. (0)	2	<0.01
Central American Ind. (0)	1	<0.01
Cherokee (19)	96	0.16
Cheyenne (0)	0	<0.01
Chickasaw (2)	6	0.01
Chippewa (4)	16	0.03
Choctaw (6)	23	0.04
Colville (0)	0	<0.01
Comanche (1)	1	<0.01
Cree (0)	0	<0.01
Creek (2)	3	0.01
Crow (2)	2	<0.01
Delaware (0)	0	<0.01
Hopi (1)	3	0.01
Houma (0)	0	<0.01
Inupiat *(Alaska Native)* (0)	0	<0.01
Iroquois (6)	14	0.02
Kiowa (0)	0	<0.01
Lumbee (3)	3	0.01
Menominee (0)	0	<0.01
Mexican American Ind. (60)	85	0.14
Navajo (3)	14	0.02
Osage (0)	4	0.01
Ottawa (0)	0	<0.01
Paiute (2)	2	<0.01
Pima (0)	0	<0.01
Potawatomi (0)	1	<0.01
Pueblo (3)	8	0.01
Puget Sound Salish (6)	7	0.01
Seminole (1)	6	0.01
Shoshone (0)	0	<0.01
Sioux (10)	19	0.03
South American Ind. (1)	8	0.01
Spanish American Ind. (0)	1	<0.01
Tlingit-Haida *(Alaska Native)* (3)	4	0.01
Tohono O'Odham (0)	2	<0.01
Tsimshian *(Alaska Native)* (1)	1	<0.01
Ute (0)	0	<0.01
Yakama (0)	0	<0.01
Yaqui (3)	6	0.01
Yuman (0)	0	<0.01
Yup'ik *(Alaska Native)* (1)	1	<0.01
Asian (2,323)	3,390	5.70
Not Hispanic (2,291)	3,258	5.47
Hispanic (32)	132	0.22
Bangladeshi (4)	6	0.01
Bhutanese (0)	0	<0.01
Burmese (4)	4	0.01
Cambodian (8)	10	0.02
Chinese, ex. Taiwanese (546)	804	1.35
Filipino (353)	634	1.07
Hmong (0)	0	<0.01
Indian (351)	422	0.71
Indonesian (9)	39	0.07
Japanese (447)	816	1.37
Korean (218)	326	0.55
Laotian (13)	17	0.03
Malaysian (2)	3	0.01
Nepalese (1)	1	<0.01
Pakistani (10)	23	0.04
Sri Lankan (8)	9	0.02
Taiwanese (52)	62	0.10
Thai (44)	58	0.10
Vietnamese (136)	191	0.32
Hawaii Native/Pacific Islander (91)	253	0.43
Not Hispanic (81)	225	0.38
Hispanic (10)	28	0.05
Fijian (1)	3	0.01
Guamanian/Chamorro (21)	48	0.08
Marshallese (0)	0	<0.01
Native Hawaiian (39)	120	0.20
Samoan (2)	6	0.01
Tongan (1)	4	0.01
White (51,067)	52,974	89.01
Not Hispanic (46,881)	48,279	81.12
Hispanic (4,186)	4,695	7.89

*Notes: † The Census 2010 population figure is used to calculate the percentages in the Hispanic Origin and Race categories. Ancestry percentages are based on the 2006-2010 American Community Survey population (not shown); ‡ Numbers in parentheses indicate the number of people reporting a single ancestry; * Numbers in parentheses indicate the number of persons reporting this race alone, not in combination with any other race; Please refer to the Explanation of Data for more information.*

Escondido

Place Type: City
County: San Diego
Population: 143,911

Ancestry	Population	%
Afghan (47)	63	0.04
African, Sub-Saharan (365)	511	0.36
African (47)	193	0.14
Cape Verdean (0)	0	<0.01
Ethiopian (16)	16	0.01
Ghanaian (8)	8	0.01
Kenyan (0)	0	<0.01
Liberian (0)	0	<0.01
Nigerian (90)	90	0.06
Senegalese (0)	0	<0.01
Sierra Leonean (0)	0	<0.01
Somalian (0)	0	<0.01
South African (60)	60	0.04
Sudanese (0)	0	<0.01
Ugandan (11)	11	0.01
Zimbabwean (0)	0	<0.01
Other Sub-Saharan African (133)	133	0.09
Albanian (11)	11	0.01
Alsatian (0)	0	<0.01
American (2,997)	2,997	2.13
Arab (432)	612	0.43
Arab (68)	128	0.09
Egyptian (125)	125	0.09
Iraqi (49)	71	0.05
Jordanian (0)	0	<0.01
Lebanese (33)	46	0.03
Moroccan (0)	0	<0.01
Palestinian (26)	51	0.04
Syrian (75)	127	0.09
Other Arab (56)	64	0.05
Armenian (44)	78	0.06
Assyrian/Chaldean/Syriac (0)	7	<0.01
Australian (0)	10	0.01
Austrian (71)	254	0.18
Basque (0)	60	0.04
Belgian (21)	114	0.08
Brazilian (60)	118	0.08
British (322)	564	0.40
Bulgarian (54)	54	0.04
Cajun (0)	0	<0.01
Canadian (145)	270	0.19
Carpatho Rusyn (0)	49	0.03
Celtic (8)	8	0.01
Croatian (4)	60	0.04
Cypriot (0)	0	<0.01
Czech (91)	357	0.25
Czechoslovakian (21)	57	0.04
Danish (185)	785	0.56
Dutch (553)	1,634	1.16
Eastern European (41)	53	0.04
English (4,576)	12,343	8.75
Estonian (0)	10	0.01
European (1,014)	1,168	0.83
Finnish (59)	232	0.16
French, ex. Basque (632)	3,026	2.15
French Canadian (240)	465	0.33
German (4,627)	14,458	10.25
German Russian (0)	12	0.01
Greek (203)	513	0.36
Guyanese (0)	0	<0.01
Hungarian (248)	456	0.32
Icelander (0)	0	<0.01
Iranian (408)	500	0.35
Irish (2,276)	9,651	6.84
Israeli (18)	46	0.03
Italian (1,959)	5,156	3.66
Latvian (10)	10	0.01
Lithuanian (29)	215	0.15
Luxemburger (0)	26	0.02
Macedonian (0)	0	<0.01
Maltese (10)	10	0.01
New Zealander (0)	0	<0.01
Northern European (176)	176	0.12
Norwegian (634)	1,880	1.33
Pennsylvania German (18)	37	0.03
Polish (877)	2,368	1.68
Portuguese (253)	889	0.63
Romanian (252)	303	0.21
Russian (316)	858	0.61
Scandinavian (72)	132	0.09
Scotch-Irish (783)	1,965	1.39
Scottish (618)	2,609	1.85
Serbian (83)	105	0.07
Slavic (10)	36	0.03
Slovak (93)	117	0.08
Slovene (17)	98	0.07
Soviet Union (0)	0	<0.01
Swedish (494)	1,894	1.34
Swiss (123)	442	0.31
Turkish (0)	28	0.02
Ukrainian (11)	130	0.09
Welsh (168)	918	0.65
West Indian, ex. Hispanic (30)	55	0.04
Bahamian (0)	0	<0.01
Barbadian (0)	0	<0.01
Belizean (9)	9	0.01
Bermudan (0)	0	<0.01
British West Indian (0)	0	<0.01
Dutch West Indian (0)	0	<0.01
Haitian (0)	8	0.01
Jamaican (7)	24	0.02
Trinidadian/Tobagonian (14)	14	0.01
U.S. Virgin Islander (0)	0	<0.01
West Indian (0)	0	<0.01
Other West Indian (0)	0	<0.01
Yugoslavian (137)	210	0.15

Hispanic Origin	Population	%
Hispanic or Latino (of any race)	70,326	48.87
Central American, ex. Mexican	1,816	1.26
Costa Rican	66	0.05
Guatemalan	872	0.61
Honduran	101	0.07
Nicaraguan	79	0.05
Panamanian	46	0.03
Salvadoran	616	0.43
Other Central American	36	0.03
Cuban	173	0.12
Dominican Republic	57	0.04
Mexican	63,552	44.16
Puerto Rican	863	0.60
South American	535	0.37
Argentinean	68	0.05
Bolivian	21	0.01
Chilean	33	0.02
Colombian	155	0.11
Ecuadorian	67	0.05
Paraguayan	4	<0.01
Peruvian	126	0.09
Uruguayan	15	0.01
Venezuelan	43	0.03
Other South American	3	<0.01
Other Hispanic or Latino	3,330	2.31

Race*	Population	%
African-American/Black (3,585)	4,844	3.37
Not Hispanic (3,046)	3,894	2.71
Hispanic (539)	950	0.66
American Indian/Alaska Native (1,472)	2,829	1.97
Not Hispanic (577)	1,242	0.86
Hispanic (895)	1,587	1.10
Alaska Athabascan *(Ala. Nat.)* (0)	0	<0.01
Aleut *(Alaska Native)* (2)	3	<0.01
Apache (28)	69	0.05
Arapaho (1)	1	<0.01
Blackfeet (7)	28	0.02
Canadian/French Am. Ind. (1)	3	<0.01
Central American Ind. (12)	26	0.02
Cherokee (67)	237	0.16
Cheyenne (0)	2	<0.01
Chickasaw (2)	11	0.01
Chippewa (14)	29	0.02
Choctaw (10)	49	0.03
Colville (3)	6	<0.01
Comanche (4)	6	<0.01
Cree (0)	0	<0.01
Creek (7)	16	0.01
Crow (5)	6	<0.01
Delaware (4)	5	<0.01
Hopi (5)	6	<0.01
Houma (0)	0	<0.01
Inupiat *(Alaska Native)* (5)	7	<0.01
Iroquois (16)	41	0.03
Kiowa (0)	1	<0.01
Lumbee (3)	3	<0.01
Menominee (0)	1	<0.01
Mexican American Ind. (278)	374	0.26
Navajo (47)	66	0.05
Osage (0)	8	0.01
Ottawa (1)	1	<0.01
Paiute (0)	0	<0.01
Pima (2)	3	<0.01
Potawatomi (4)	4	<0.01
Pueblo (9)	14	0.01
Puget Sound Salish (1)	1	<0.01
Seminole (1)	6	<0.01
Shoshone (4)	14	0.01
Sioux (12)	34	0.02
South American Ind. (6)	11	0.01
Spanish American Ind. (13)	16	0.01
Tlingit-Haida *(Alaska Native)* (2)	2	<0.01
Tohono O'Odham (8)	13	0.01
Tsimshian *(Alaska Native)* (0)	0	<0.01
Ute (1)	6	<0.01
Yakama (0)	0	<0.01
Yaqui (21)	44	0.03
Yuman (5)	5	<0.01
Yup'ik *(Alaska Native)* (0)	0	<0.01
Asian (8,740)	10,679	7.42
Not Hispanic (8,491)	9,970	6.93
Hispanic (249)	709	0.49
Bangladeshi (2)	12	0.01
Bhutanese (0)	0	<0.01
Burmese (12)	13	0.01
Cambodian (72)	98	0.07
Chinese, ex. Taiwanese (691)	993	0.69
Filipino (3,807)	4,768	3.31
Hmong (25)	25	0.02
Indian (479)	626	0.43
Indonesian (17)	42	0.03
Japanese (381)	739	0.51
Korean (382)	527	0.37
Laotian (489)	557	0.39
Malaysian (4)	6	<0.01
Nepalese (0)	0	<0.01
Pakistani (71)	79	0.05
Sri Lankan (7)	9	0.01
Taiwanese (51)	72	0.05
Thai (128)	158	0.11
Vietnamese (1,755)	1,947	1.35
Hawaii Native/Pacific Islander (350)	761	0.53
Not Hispanic (306)	576	0.40
Hispanic (44)	185	0.13
Fijian (1)	1	<0.01
Guamanian/Chamorro (112)	209	0.15
Marshallese (2)	2	<0.01
Native Hawaiian (91)	246	0.17
Samoan (95)	157	0.11
Tongan (7)	11	0.01
White (86,876)	92,390	64.20
Not Hispanic (58,142)	60,637	42.14
Hispanic (28,734)	31,753	22.06

*Notes: † The Census 2010 population figure is used to calculate the percentages in the Hispanic Origin and Race categories. Ancestry percentages are based on the 2006-2010 American Community Survey population (not shown); ‡ Numbers in parentheses indicate the number of people reporting a single ancestry; * Numbers in parentheses indicate the number of persons reporting this race alone, not in combination with any other race; Please refer to the Explanation of Data for more information.*

Fairfield

Place Type: City
County: Solano
Population: 105,321

Ancestry	Population	%
Afghan (213)	271	0.26
African, Sub-Saharan (1,989)	2,343	2.26
African (1,706)	2,042	1.97
Cape Verdean (57)	57	0.05
Ethiopian (32)	41	0.04
Ghanaian (0)	0	<0.01
Kenyan (135)	135	0.13
Liberian (0)	0	<0.01
Nigerian (31)	40	0.04
Senegalese (0)	0	<0.01
Sierra Leonean (0)	0	<0.01
Somalian (0)	0	<0.01
South African (0)	0	<0.01
Sudanese (28)	28	0.03
Ugandan (0)	0	<0.01
Zimbabwean (0)	0	<0.01
Other Sub-Saharan African (0)	0	<0.01
Albanian (0)	0	<0.01
Alsatian (0)	0	<0.01
American (1,938)	1,938	1.87
Arab (489)	898	0.87
Arab (0)	0	<0.01
Egyptian (37)	135	0.13
Iraqi (12)	12	0.01
Jordanian (107)	113	0.11
Lebanese (69)	163	0.16
Moroccan (0)	9	0.01
Palestinian (191)	226	0.22
Syrian (19)	88	0.08
Other Arab (54)	152	0.15
Armenian (28)	83	0.08
Assyrian/Chaldean/Syriac (0)	0	<0.01
Australian (0)	0	<0.01
Austrian (48)	122	0.12
Basque (28)	62	0.06
Belgian (12)	42	0.04
Brazilian (127)	127	0.12
British (141)	248	0.24
Bulgarian (0)	0	<0.01
Cajun (0)	0	<0.01
Canadian (116)	200	0.19
Carpatho Rusyn (0)	0	<0.01
Celtic (0)	0	<0.01
Croatian (32)	43	0.04
Cypriot (0)	0	<0.01
Czech (22)	152	0.15
Czechoslovakian (0)	36	0.03
Danish (83)	435	0.42
Dutch (176)	915	0.88
Eastern European (51)	68	0.07
English (1,747)	5,395	5.20
Estonian (0)	0	<0.01
European (1,472)	1,595	1.54
Finnish (0)	58	0.06
French, ex. Basque (223)	1,914	1.85
French Canadian (109)	396	0.38
German (2,662)	8,597	8.29
German Russian (19)	19	0.02
Greek (237)	516	0.50
Guyanese (0)	16	0.02
Hungarian (82)	236	0.23
Icelander (15)	49	0.05
Iranian (62)	120	0.12
Irish (1,847)	7,191	6.93
Israeli (0)	0	<0.01
Italian (1,375)	3,714	3.58
Latvian (29)	29	0.03
Lithuanian (17)	49	0.05
Luxemburger (14)	14	0.01
Macedonian (0)	0	<0.01
Maltese (25)	32	0.03
New Zealander (0)	0	<0.01
Northern European (53)	53	0.05
Norwegian (405)	1,515	1.46
Pennsylvania German (25)	43	0.04
Polish (255)	1,196	1.15
Portuguese (470)	1,208	1.16
Romanian (0)	0	<0.01
Russian (49)	233	0.22
Scandinavian (66)	206	0.20
Scotch-Irish (273)	1,080	1.04
Scottish (513)	1,715	1.65
Serbian (0)	11	0.01
Slavic (65)	128	0.12
Slovak (0)	160	0.15
Slovene (0)	0	<0.01
Soviet Union (7)	7	0.01
Swedish (250)	1,213	1.17
Swiss (31)	173	0.17
Turkish (80)	103	0.10
Ukrainian (50)	89	0.09
Welsh (17)	321	0.31
West Indian, ex. Hispanic (88)	245	0.24
Bahamian (0)	0	<0.01
Barbadian (0)	0	<0.01
Belizean (0)	0	<0.01
Bermudan (0)	0	<0.01
British West Indian (0)	0	<0.01
Dutch West Indian (0)	0	<0.01
Haitian (0)	0	<0.01
Jamaican (88)	229	0.22
Trinidadian/Tobagonian (0)	16	0.02
U.S. Virgin Islander (0)	0	<0.01
West Indian (0)	0	<0.01
Other West Indian (0)	0	<0.01
Yugoslavian (0)	94	0.09

Hispanic Origin	Population	%
Hispanic or Latino (of any race)	28,789	27.33
Central American, ex. Mexican	2,099	1.99
Costa Rican	63	0.06
Guatemalan	275	0.26
Honduran	106	0.10
Nicaraguan	478	0.45
Panamanian	89	0.08
Salvadoran	1,068	1.01
Other Central American	20	0.02
Cuban	179	0.17
Dominican Republic	60	0.06
Mexican	22,360	21.23
Puerto Rican	1,184	1.12
South American	566	0.54
Argentinean	31	0.03
Bolivian	12	0.01
Chilean	45	0.04
Colombian	136	0.13
Ecuadorian	38	0.04
Paraguayan	4	<0.01
Peruvian	254	0.24
Uruguayan	4	<0.01
Venezuelan	30	0.03
Other South American	12	0.01
Other Hispanic or Latino	2,341	2.22

Race*	Population	%
African-American/Black (16,586)	20,028	19.02
Not Hispanic (15,979)	18,660	17.72
Hispanic (607)	1,368	1.30
American Indian/Alaska Native (869)	2,529	2.40
Not Hispanic (462)	1,683	1.60
Hispanic (407)	846	0.80
Alaska Athabascan *(Ala. Nat.)* (1)	3	<0.01
Aleut *(Alaska Native)* (2)	3	<0.01
Apache (40)	84	0.08
Arapaho (0)	0	<0.01
Blackfeet (2)	70	0.07
Canadian/French Am. Ind. (0)	3	<0.01
Central American Ind. (0)	6	0.01
Cherokee (76)	414	0.39
Cheyenne (0)	2	<0.01
Chickasaw (7)	16	0.02
Chippewa (16)	34	0.03
Choctaw (21)	111	0.11
Colville (1)	1	<0.01
Comanche (0)	9	0.01
Cree (0)	6	0.01
Creek (7)	35	0.03
Crow (1)	4	<0.01
Delaware (0)	1	<0.01
Hopi (1)	3	<0.01
Houma (0)	0	<0.01
Inupiat *(Alaska Native)* (2)	7	0.01
Iroquois (8)	23	0.02
Kiowa (2)	2	<0.01
Lumbee (0)	0	<0.01
Menominee (1)	1	<0.01
Mexican American Ind. (58)	109	0.10
Navajo (37)	54	0.05
Osage (0)	7	0.01
Ottawa (0)	0	<0.01
Paiute (6)	18	0.02
Pima (0)	0	<0.01
Potawatomi (12)	13	0.01
Pueblo (9)	10	0.01
Puget Sound Salish (1)	2	<0.01
Seminole (3)	16	0.02
Shoshone (2)	5	<0.01
Sioux (17)	55	0.05
South American Ind. (3)	10	0.01
Spanish American Ind. (6)	7	0.01
Tlingit-Haida *(Alaska Native)* (2)	9	0.01
Tohono O'Odham (5)	9	0.01
Tsimshian *(Alaska Native)* (0)	1	<0.01
Ute (1)	2	<0.01
Yakama (0)	0	<0.01
Yaqui (4)	18	0.02
Yuman (4)	4	<0.01
Yup'ik *(Alaska Native)* (0)	1	<0.01
Asian (15,700)	20,062	19.05
Not Hispanic (15,265)	18,804	17.85
Hispanic (435)	1,258	1.19
Bangladeshi (2)	5	<0.01
Bhutanese (0)	0	<0.01
Burmese (9)	16	0.02
Cambodian (37)	63	0.06
Chinese, ex. Taiwanese (1,049)	1,783	1.69
Filipino (9,590)	12,265	11.65
Hmong (141)	170	0.16
Indian (1,846)	2,051	1.95
Indonesian (24)	47	0.04
Japanese (616)	1,452	1.38
Korean (446)	775	0.74
Laotian (357)	437	0.41
Malaysian (5)	8	0.01
Nepalese (22)	23	0.02
Pakistani (121)	137	0.13
Sri Lankan (8)	10	0.01
Taiwanese (63)	92	0.09
Thai (161)	323	0.31
Vietnamese (632)	808	0.77
Hawaii Native/Pacific Islander (1,149)	2,503	2.38
Not Hispanic (1,049)	2,140	2.03
Hispanic (100)	363	0.34
Fijian (143)	183	0.17
Guamanian/Chamorro (539)	1,013	0.96
Marshallese (4)	5	<0.01
Native Hawaiian (119)	668	0.63
Samoan (194)	348	0.33
Tongan (44)	57	0.05
White (48,407)	55,602	52.79
Not Hispanic (37,091)	42,174	40.04
Hispanic (11,316)	13,428	12.75

*Notes: † The Census 2010 population figure is used to calculate the percentages in the Hispanic Origin and Race categories. Ancestry percentages are based on the 2006-2010 American Community Survey population (not shown); ‡ Numbers in parentheses indicate the number of people reporting a single ancestry; * Numbers in parentheses indicate the number of persons reporting this race alone, not in combination with any other race; Please refer to the Explanation of Data for more information.*

Florence-Graham

Place Type: CDP
County: Los Angeles
Population: 63,387

Ancestry	Population	%
Afghan (0)	0	<0.01
African, Sub-Saharan (167)	167	0.27
African (161)	161	0.26
Cape Verdean (0)	0	<0.01
Ethiopian (0)	0	<0.01
Ghanaian (0)	0	<0.01
Kenyan (0)	0	<0.01
Liberian (0)	0	<0.01
Nigerian (6)	6	0.01
Senegalese (0)	0	<0.01
Sierra Leonean (0)	0	<0.01
Somalian (0)	0	<0.01
South African (0)	0	<0.01
Sudanese (0)	0	<0.01
Ugandan (0)	0	<0.01
Zimbabwean (0)	0	<0.01
Other Sub-Saharan African (0)	0	<0.01
Albanian (0)	0	<0.01
Alsatian (0)	0	<0.01
American (497)	497	0.82
Arab (7)	22	0.04
Arab (0)	0	<0.01
Egyptian (0)	0	<0.01
Iraqi (0)	0	<0.01
Jordanian (0)	0	<0.01
Lebanese (0)	0	<0.01
Moroccan (0)	6	0.01
Palestinian (0)	0	<0.01
Syrian (0)	0	<0.01
Other Arab (7)	16	0.03
Armenian (0)	0	<0.01
Assyrian/Chaldean/Syriac (0)	0	<0.01
Australian (0)	0	<0.01
Austrian (0)	0	<0.01
Basque (0)	0	<0.01
Belgian (0)	0	<0.01
Brazilian (0)	0	<0.01
British (20)	20	0.03
Bulgarian (0)	0	<0.01
Cajun (0)	0	<0.01
Canadian (0)	0	<0.01
Carpatho Rusyn (0)	0	<0.01
Celtic (0)	0	<0.01
Croatian (0)	0	<0.01
Cypriot (0)	0	<0.01
Czech (0)	0	<0.01
Czechoslovakian (0)	0	<0.01
Danish (0)	0	<0.01
Dutch (0)	57	0.09
Eastern European (27)	27	0.04
English (0)	0	<0.01
Estonian (0)	0	<0.01
European (0)	0	<0.01
Finnish (0)	0	<0.01
French, ex. Basque (10)	136	0.22
French Canadian (0)	0	<0.01
German (0)	99	0.16
German Russian (0)	0	<0.01
Greek (0)	0	<0.01
Guyanese (0)	0	<0.01
Hungarian (0)	0	<0.01
Icelander (0)	0	<0.01
Iranian (0)	0	<0.01
Irish (11)	94	0.15
Israeli (0)	0	<0.01
Italian (8)	16	0.03
Latvian (0)	0	<0.01
Lithuanian (8)	18	0.03
Luxemburger (0)	0	<0.01
Macedonian (0)	0	<0.01
Maltese (0)	0	<0.01
New Zealander (0)	0	<0.01
Northern European (0)	0	<0.01
Norwegian (0)	0	<0.01
Pennsylvania German (0)	0	<0.01
Polish (0)	0	<0.01
Portuguese (0)	0	<0.01
Romanian (0)	0	<0.01
Russian (0)	0	<0.01
Scandinavian (0)	0	<0.01
Scotch-Irish (0)	0	<0.01
Scottish (18)	18	0.03
Serbian (0)	0	<0.01
Slavic (0)	0	<0.01
Slovak (0)	0	<0.01
Slovene (0)	0	<0.01
Soviet Union (0)	0	<0.01
Swedish (0)	0	<0.01
Swiss (0)	0	<0.01
Turkish (0)	0	<0.01
Ukrainian (0)	0	<0.01
Welsh (0)	0	<0.01
West Indian, ex. Hispanic (33)	72	0.12
Bahamian (0)	0	<0.01
Barbadian (0)	0	<0.01
Belizean (11)	50	0.08
Bermudan (0)	0	<0.01
British West Indian (0)	0	<0.01
Dutch West Indian (0)	0	<0.01
Haitian (22)	22	0.04
Jamaican (0)	0	<0.01
Trinidadian/Tobagonian (0)	0	<0.01
U.S. Virgin Islander (0)	0	<0.01
West Indian (0)	0	<0.01
Other West Indian (0)	0	<0.01
Yugoslavian (0)	0	<0.01

Hispanic Origin	Population	%
Hispanic or Latino (of any race)	57,066	90.03
Central American, ex. Mexican	5,736	9.05
Costa Rican	11	0.02
Guatemalan	1,685	2.66
Honduran	505	0.80
Nicaraguan	196	0.31
Panamanian	4	0.01
Salvadoran	3,239	5.11
Other Central American	96	0.15
Cuban	47	0.07
Dominican Republic	4	0.01
Mexican	47,862	75.51
Puerto Rican	143	0.23
South American	120	0.19
Argentinean	10	0.02
Bolivian	1	<0.01
Chilean	12	0.02
Colombian	9	0.01
Ecuadorian	43	0.07
Paraguayan	0	<0.01
Peruvian	41	0.06
Uruguayan	0	<0.01
Venezuelan	0	<0.01
Other South American	4	0.01
Other Hispanic or Latino	3,154	4.98

Race*	Population	%
African-American/Black (5,861)	6,163	9.72
Not Hispanic (5,517)	5,620	8.87
Hispanic (344)	543	0.86
American Indian/Alaska Native (498)	788	1.24
Not Hispanic (50)	100	0.16
Hispanic (448)	688	1.09
Alaska Athabascan *(Ala. Nat.)* (0)	0	<0.01
Aleut *(Alaska Native)* (0)	0	<0.01
Apache (2)	4	0.01
Arapaho (0)	2	<0.01
Blackfeet (1)	5	0.01
Canadian/French Am. Ind. (0)	1	<0.01
Central American Ind. (9)	26	0.04
Cherokee (9)	26	0.04
Cheyenne (0)	0	<0.01
Chickasaw (0)	0	<0.01
Chippewa (0)	0	<0.01
Choctaw (4)	11	0.02
Colville (0)	0	<0.01
Comanche (0)	0	<0.01
Cree (1)	1	<0.01
Creek (1)	3	<0.01
Crow (0)	0	<0.01
Delaware (0)	0	<0.01
Hopi (0)	0	<0.01
Houma (0)	0	<0.01
Inupiat *(Alaska Native)* (0)	0	<0.01
Iroquois (0)	0	<0.01
Kiowa (6)	6	0.01
Lumbee (5)	5	0.01
Menominee (0)	0	<0.01
Mexican American Ind. (154)	213	0.34
Navajo (8)	11	0.02
Osage (0)	1	<0.01
Ottawa (0)	0	<0.01
Paiute (0)	0	<0.01
Pima (3)	3	<0.01
Potawatomi (0)	0	<0.01
Pueblo (0)	0	<0.01
Puget Sound Salish (0)	0	<0.01
Seminole (0)	1	<0.01
Shoshone (0)	0	<0.01
Sioux (0)	0	<0.01
South American Ind. (4)	5	0.01
Spanish American Ind. (13)	34	0.05
Tlingit-Haida *(Alaska Native)* (0)	3	<0.01
Tohono O'Odham (2)	2	<0.01
Tsimshian *(Alaska Native)* (0)	0	<0.01
Ute (0)	0	<0.01
Yakama (0)	0	<0.01
Yaqui (2)	3	<0.01
Yuman (1)	1	<0.01
Yup'ik *(Alaska Native)* (0)	0	<0.01
Asian (150)	290	0.46
Not Hispanic (91)	110	0.17
Hispanic (59)	180	0.28
Bangladeshi (0)	12	0.02
Bhutanese (0)	0	<0.01
Burmese (0)	0	<0.01
Cambodian (5)	9	0.01
Chinese, ex. Taiwanese (15)	22	0.03
Filipino (40)	67	0.11
Hmong (0)	0	<0.01
Indian (23)	41	0.06
Indonesian (0)	0	<0.01
Japanese (22)	43	0.07
Korean (11)	19	0.03
Laotian (4)	4	0.01
Malaysian (0)	0	<0.01
Nepalese (0)	0	<0.01
Pakistani (0)	0	<0.01
Sri Lankan (0)	0	<0.01
Taiwanese (0)	0	<0.01
Thai (2)	2	<0.01
Vietnamese (1)	1	<0.01
Hawaii Native/Pacific Islander (25)	89	0.14
Not Hispanic (9)	22	0.03
Hispanic (16)	67	0.11
Fijian (0)	0	<0.01
Guamanian/Chamorro (6)	10	0.02
Marshallese (0)	0	<0.01
Native Hawaiian (10)	16	0.03
Samoan (7)	17	0.03
Tongan (0)	0	<0.01
White (23,895)	25,713	40.57
Not Hispanic (422)	496	0.78
Hispanic (23,473)	25,217	39.78

*Notes: † The Census 2010 population figure is used to calculate the percentages in the Hispanic Origin and Race categories. Ancestry percentages are based on the 2006-2010 American Community Survey population (not shown); ‡ Numbers in parentheses indicate the number of people reporting a single ancestry; * Numbers in parentheses indicate the number of persons reporting this race alone, not in combination with any other race; Please refer to the Explanation of Data for more information.*

Folsom

Place Type: City
County: Sacramento
Population: 72,203

Ancestry	Population	%
Afghan (17)	17	0.02
African, Sub-Saharan (222)	266	0.39
African (189)	233	0.34
Cape Verdean (0)	0	<0.01
Ethiopian (10)	10	0.01
Ghanaian (0)	0	<0.01
Kenyan (0)	0	<0.01
Liberian (0)	0	<0.01
Nigerian (13)	13	0.02
Senegalese (0)	0	<0.01
Sierra Leonean (0)	0	<0.01
Somalian (0)	0	<0.01
South African (10)	10	0.01
Sudanese (0)	0	<0.01
Ugandan (0)	0	<0.01
Zimbabwean (0)	0	<0.01
Other Sub-Saharan African (0)	0	<0.01
Albanian (11)	33	0.05
Alsatian (0)	0	<0.01
American (1,838)	1,838	2.66
Arab (166)	359	0.52
Arab (29)	29	0.04
Egyptian (44)	93	0.13
Iraqi (0)	0	<0.01
Jordanian (0)	0	<0.01
Lebanese (24)	168	0.24
Moroccan (11)	11	0.02
Palestinian (29)	29	0.04
Syrian (0)	0	<0.01
Other Arab (29)	29	0.04
Armenian (70)	179	0.26
Assyrian/Chaldean/Syriac (0)	0	<0.01
Australian (13)	27	0.04
Austrian (11)	114	0.17
Basque (12)	12	0.02
Belgian (16)	79	0.11
Brazilian (0)	0	<0.01
British (179)	353	0.51
Bulgarian (0)	58	0.08
Cajun (0)	0	<0.01
Canadian (131)	239	0.35
Carpatho Rusyn (0)	0	<0.01
Celtic (28)	28	0.04
Croatian (43)	134	0.19
Cypriot (0)	0	<0.01
Czech (48)	329	0.48
Czechoslovakian (0)	45	0.07
Danish (219)	823	1.19
Dutch (358)	1,411	2.04
Eastern European (24)	40	0.06
English (1,923)	7,950	11.51
Estonian (0)	0	<0.01
European (998)	1,269	1.84
Finnish (0)	148	0.21
French, ex. Basque (207)	1,979	2.87
French Canadian (150)	391	0.57
German (3,744)	12,307	17.82
German Russian (0)	0	<0.01
Greek (132)	308	0.45
Guyanese (0)	0	<0.01
Hungarian (52)	258	0.37
Icelander (0)	33	0.05
Iranian (444)	531	0.77
Irish (1,793)	9,088	13.16
Israeli (0)	0	<0.01
Italian (1,857)	6,013	8.71
Latvian (21)	65	0.09
Lithuanian (24)	89	0.13
Luxemburger (0)	0	<0.01
Macedonian (0)	0	<0.01
Maltese (0)	0	<0.01
New Zealander (0)	0	<0.01
Northern European (158)	168	0.24
Norwegian (540)	1,785	2.58
Pennsylvania German (0)	39	0.06
Polish (399)	1,910	2.77
Portuguese (411)	1,023	1.48
Romanian (41)	77	0.11
Russian (226)	740	1.07
Scandinavian (76)	190	0.28
Scotch-Irish (448)	984	1.42
Scottish (549)	1,948	2.82
Serbian (0)	0	<0.01
Slavic (8)	54	0.08
Slovak (33)	42	0.06
Slovene (27)	44	0.06
Soviet Union (0)	0	<0.01
Swedish (328)	1,282	1.86
Swiss (32)	355	0.51
Turkish (18)	29	0.04
Ukrainian (284)	343	0.50
Welsh (128)	634	0.92
West Indian, ex. Hispanic (37)	151	0.22
Bahamian (0)	0	<0.01
Barbadian (0)	0	<0.01
Belizean (14)	23	0.03
Bermudan (0)	0	<0.01
British West Indian (0)	0	<0.01
Dutch West Indian (0)	0	<0.01
Haitian (0)	0	<0.01
Jamaican (23)	38	0.06
Trinidadian/Tobagonian (0)	0	<0.01
U.S. Virgin Islander (0)	0	<0.01
West Indian (0)	90	0.13
Other West Indian (0)	0	<0.01
Yugoslavian (88)	144	0.21

Hispanic Origin	Population	%
Hispanic or Latino (of any race)	8,064	11.17
Central American, ex. Mexican	392	0.54
Costa Rican	57	0.08
Guatemalan	43	0.06
Honduran	27	0.04
Nicaraguan	78	0.11
Panamanian	25	0.03
Salvadoran	158	0.22
Other Central American	4	0.01
Cuban	63	0.09
Dominican Republic	16	0.02
Mexican	5,422	7.51
Puerto Rican	283	0.39
South American	381	0.53
Argentinean	58	0.08
Bolivian	20	0.03
Chilean	30	0.04
Colombian	117	0.16
Ecuadorian	23	0.03
Paraguayan	3	<0.01
Peruvian	90	0.12
Uruguayan	7	0.01
Venezuelan	26	0.04
Other South American	7	0.01
Other Hispanic or Latino	1,507	2.09

Race*	Population	%
African-American/Black (4,140)	4,587	6.35
Not Hispanic (4,080)	4,436	6.14
Hispanic (60)	151	0.21
American Indian/Alaska Native (427)	1,011	1.40
Not Hispanic (289)	728	1.01
Hispanic (138)	283	0.39
Alaska Athabascan *(Ala. Nat.)* (0)	0	<0.01
Aleut *(Alaska Native)* (0)	1	<0.01
Apache (15)	39	0.05
Arapaho (1)	3	<0.01
Blackfeet (4)	16	0.02
Canadian/French Am. Ind. (0)	0	<0.01
Central American Ind. (0)	0	<0.01
Cherokee (46)	168	0.23
Cheyenne (0)	1	<0.01
Chickasaw (2)	7	0.01
Chippewa (11)	18	0.02
Choctaw (19)	38	0.05
Colville (0)	0	<0.01
Comanche (0)	1	<0.01
Cree (0)	0	<0.01
Creek (2)	12	0.02
Crow (0)	0	<0.01
Delaware (1)	5	0.01
Hopi (0)	4	0.01
Houma (0)	0	<0.01
Inupiat *(Alaska Native)* (2)	3	<0.01
Iroquois (2)	12	0.02
Kiowa (1)	1	<0.01
Lumbee (0)	0	<0.01
Menominee (2)	2	<0.01
Mexican American Ind. (26)	40	0.06
Navajo (4)	12	0.02
Osage (0)	5	0.01
Ottawa (0)	0	<0.01
Paiute (6)	6	0.01
Pima (1)	1	<0.01
Potawatomi (2)	4	0.01
Pueblo (4)	5	0.01
Puget Sound Salish (0)	0	<0.01
Seminole (0)	3	<0.01
Shoshone (0)	1	<0.01
Sioux (7)	26	0.04
South American Ind. (2)	7	0.01
Spanish American Ind. (3)	5	0.01
Tlingit-Haida *(Alaska Native)* (4)	12	0.02
Tohono O'Odham (0)	0	<0.01
Tsimshian *(Alaska Native)* (0)	0	<0.01
Ute (0)	0	<0.01
Yakama (3)	4	0.01
Yaqui (3)	8	0.01
Yuman (1)	1	<0.01
Yup'ik *(Alaska Native)* (1)	1	<0.01
Asian (9,000)	10,710	14.83
Not Hispanic (8,917)	10,393	14.39
Hispanic (83)	317	0.44
Bangladeshi (95)	99	0.14
Bhutanese (4)	4	0.01
Burmese (8)	11	0.02
Cambodian (29)	43	0.06
Chinese, ex. Taiwanese (1,530)	1,974	2.73
Filipino (1,128)	1,738	2.41
Hmong (19)	24	0.03
Indian (3,801)	3,981	5.51
Indonesian (26)	43	0.06
Japanese (347)	762	1.06
Korean (734)	868	1.20
Laotian (22)	32	0.04
Malaysian (30)	38	0.05
Nepalese (38)	38	0.05
Pakistani (146)	168	0.23
Sri Lankan (62)	66	0.09
Taiwanese (86)	108	0.15
Thai (50)	72	0.10
Vietnamese (463)	587	0.81
Hawaii Native/Pacific Islander (173)	447	0.62
Not Hispanic (156)	382	0.53
Hispanic (17)	65	0.09
Fijian (71)	79	0.11
Guamanian/Chamorro (32)	70	0.10
Marshallese (0)	0	<0.01
Native Hawaiian (37)	160	0.22
Samoan (3)	9	0.01
Tongan (9)	13	0.02
White (53,627)	56,318	78.00
Not Hispanic (48,009)	50,013	69.27
Hispanic (5,618)	6,305	8.73

*Notes: † The Census 2010 population figure is used to calculate the percentages in the Hispanic Origin and Race categories. Ancestry percentages are based on the 2006-2010 American Community Survey population (not shown); ‡ Numbers in parentheses indicate the number of people reporting a single ancestry; * Numbers in parentheses indicate the number of persons reporting this race alone, not in combination with any other race; Please refer to the Explanation of Data for more information.*

Fontana

Place Type: City
County: San Bernardino
Population: 196,069

Ancestry	Population	%
Afghan (238)	238	0.13
African, Sub-Saharan (1,756)	2,139	1.13
African (1,360)	1,703	0.90
Cape Verdean (68)	96	0.05
Ethiopian (48)	48	0.03
Ghanaian (35)	47	0.02
Kenyan (0)	0	<0.01
Liberian (0)	0	<0.01
Nigerian (180)	180	0.10
Senegalese (0)	0	<0.01
Sierra Leonean (0)	0	<0.01
Somalian (0)	0	<0.01
South African (0)	0	<0.01
Sudanese (0)	0	<0.01
Ugandan (0)	0	<0.01
Zimbabwean (0)	0	<0.01
Other Sub-Saharan African (65)	65	0.03
Albanian (0)	0	<0.01
Alsatian (0)	0	<0.01
American (3,822)	3,822	2.02
Arab (676)	1,107	0.58
Arab (110)	368	0.19
Egyptian (95)	164	0.09
Iraqi (17)	49	0.03
Jordanian (5)	5	<0.01
Lebanese (34)	59	0.03
Moroccan (132)	132	0.07
Palestinian (131)	131	0.07
Syrian (0)	13	0.01
Other Arab (152)	186	0.10
Armenian (49)	49	0.03
Assyrian/Chaldean/Syriac (60)	60	0.03
Australian (0)	0	<0.01
Austrian (31)	130	0.07
Basque (12)	12	0.01
Belgian (57)	112	0.06
Brazilian (0)	31	0.02
British (77)	208	0.11
Bulgarian (0)	54	0.03
Cajun (0)	0	<0.01
Canadian (29)	233	0.12
Carpatho Rusyn (0)	0	<0.01
Celtic (0)	0	<0.01
Croatian (14)	14	0.01
Cypriot (0)	0	<0.01
Czech (46)	144	0.08
Czechoslovakian (0)	22	0.01
Danish (33)	228	0.12
Dutch (144)	846	0.45
Eastern European (56)	56	0.03
English (1,144)	4,852	2.56
Estonian (0)	0	<0.01
European (697)	1,048	0.55
Finnish (16)	34	0.02
French, ex. Basque (491)	1,887	1.00
French Canadian (103)	292	0.15
German (1,723)	8,399	4.43
German Russian (0)	0	<0.01
Greek (47)	198	0.10
Guyanese (0)	0	<0.01
Hungarian (167)	381	0.20
Icelander (47)	47	0.02
Iranian (127)	171	0.09
Irish (997)	6,960	3.67
Israeli (0)	10	0.01
Italian (1,451)	4,478	2.36
Latvian (0)	0	<0.01
Lithuanian (0)	75	0.04
Luxemburger (0)	13	0.01
Macedonian (0)	0	<0.01
Maltese (0)	0	<0.01
New Zealander (0)	0	<0.01
Northern European (16)	16	0.01
Norwegian (222)	618	0.33
Pennsylvania German (0)	0	<0.01
Polish (193)	1,072	0.57
Portuguese (199)	620	0.33
Romanian (87)	118	0.06
Russian (132)	351	0.19
Scandinavian (17)	198	0.10
Scotch-Irish (153)	564	0.30
Scottish (283)	1,204	0.64
Serbian (50)	82	0.04
Slavic (0)	8	<0.01
Slovak (0)	55	0.03
Slovene (36)	76	0.04
Soviet Union (0)	0	<0.01
Swedish (83)	401	0.21
Swiss (0)	247	0.13
Turkish (0)	0	<0.01
Ukrainian (14)	24	0.01
Welsh (46)	371	0.20
West Indian, ex. Hispanic (531)	618	0.33
Bahamian (0)	0	<0.01
Barbadian (56)	72	0.04
Belizean (198)	198	0.10
Bermudan (0)	0	<0.01
British West Indian (8)	27	0.01
Dutch West Indian (0)	0	<0.01
Haitian (13)	13	0.01
Jamaican (199)	251	0.13
Trinidadian/Tobagonian (0)	0	<0.01
U.S. Virgin Islander (24)	24	0.01
West Indian (33)	33	0.02
Other West Indian (0)	0	<0.01
Yugoslavian (51)	151	0.08

Hispanic Origin	Population	%
Hispanic or Latino (of any race)	130,957	66.79
Central American, ex. Mexican	8,860	4.52
Costa Rican	187	0.10
Guatemalan	2,230	1.14
Honduran	636	0.32
Nicaraguan	1,152	0.59
Panamanian	179	0.09
Salvadoran	4,382	2.23
Other Central American	94	0.05
Cuban	617	0.31
Dominican Republic	42	0.02
Mexican	111,818	57.03
Puerto Rican	1,344	0.69
South American	2,245	1.15
Argentinean	323	0.16
Bolivian	58	0.03
Chilean	134	0.07
Colombian	545	0.28
Ecuadorian	415	0.21
Paraguayan	10	0.01
Peruvian	646	0.33
Uruguayan	54	0.03
Venezuelan	34	0.02
Other South American	26	0.01
Other Hispanic or Latino	6,031	3.08

Race*	Population	%
African-American/Black (19,574)	21,881	11.16
Not Hispanic (18,157)	19,507	9.95
Hispanic (1,417)	2,374	1.21
American Indian/Alaska Native (1,957)	3,482	1.78
Not Hispanic (454)	1,084	0.55
Hispanic (1,503)	2,398	1.22
Alaska Athabascan *(Ala. Nat.)* (0)	1	<0.01
Aleut *(Alaska Native)* (0)	1	<0.01
Apache (67)	162	0.08
Arapaho (0)	0	<0.01
Blackfeet (19)	84	0.04
Canadian/French Am. Ind. (2)	2	<0.01
Central American Ind. (12)	23	0.01
Cherokee (60)	309	0.16
Cheyenne (2)	9	<0.01
Chickasaw (4)	9	<0.01
Chippewa (15)	22	0.01
Choctaw (25)	78	0.04
Colville (0)	0	<0.01
Comanche (5)	10	0.01
Cree (0)	0	<0.01
Creek (3)	19	0.01
Crow (0)	2	<0.01
Delaware (1)	3	<0.01
Hopi (1)	8	<0.01
Houma (0)	4	<0.01
Inupiat *(Alaska Native)* (0)	0	<0.01
Iroquois (3)	21	0.01
Kiowa (4)	6	<0.01
Lumbee (0)	3	<0.01
Menominee (0)	0	<0.01
Mexican American Ind. (254)	374	0.19
Navajo (57)	100	0.05
Osage (8)	13	0.01
Ottawa (2)	2	<0.01
Paiute (0)	0	<0.01
Pima (4)	8	<0.01
Potawatomi (4)	9	<0.01
Pueblo (45)	56	0.03
Puget Sound Salish (0)	0	<0.01
Seminole (8)	18	0.01
Shoshone (11)	13	0.01
Sioux (30)	46	0.02
South American Ind. (6)	15	0.01
Spanish American Ind. (23)	37	0.02
Tlingit-Haida *(Alaska Native)* (0)	1	<0.01
Tohono O'Odham (15)	21	0.01
Tsimshian *(Alaska Native)* (0)	0	<0.01
Ute (5)	5	<0.01
Yakama (0)	0	<0.01
Yaqui (50)	86	0.04
Yuman (10)	17	0.01
Yup'ik *(Alaska Native)* (0)	0	<0.01
Asian (12,948)	15,084	7.69
Not Hispanic (12,456)	13,826	7.05
Hispanic (492)	1,258	0.64
Bangladeshi (64)	73	0.04
Bhutanese (0)	0	<0.01
Burmese (43)	48	0.02
Cambodian (290)	358	0.18
Chinese, ex. Taiwanese (1,347)	1,783	0.91
Filipino (6,047)	7,014	3.58
Hmong (3)	5	<0.01
Indian (1,294)	1,455	0.74
Indonesian (398)	503	0.26
Japanese (270)	659	0.34
Korean (1,022)	1,174	0.60
Laotian (89)	122	0.06
Malaysian (3)	6	<0.01
Nepalese (3)	3	<0.01
Pakistani (195)	221	0.11
Sri Lankan (40)	48	0.02
Taiwanese (123)	152	0.08
Thai (133)	200	0.10
Vietnamese (1,095)	1,252	0.64
Hawaii Native/Pacific Islander (547)	1,032	0.53
Not Hispanic (474)	764	0.39
Hispanic (73)	268	0.14
Fijian (16)	22	0.01
Guamanian/Chamorro (50)	95	0.05
Marshallese (0)	0	<0.01
Native Hawaiian (77)	241	0.12
Samoan (195)	290	0.15
Tongan (157)	176	0.09
White (92,978)	100,668	51.34
Not Hispanic (30,279)	32,526	16.59
Hispanic (62,699)	68,142	34.75

*Notes: † The Census 2010 population figure is used to calculate the percentages in the Hispanic Origin and Race categories. Ancestry percentages are based on the 2006-2010 American Community Survey population (not shown); ‡ Numbers in parentheses indicate the number of people reporting a single ancestry; * Numbers in parentheses indicate the number of persons reporting this race alone, not in combination with any other race; Please refer to the Explanation of Data for more information.*

Fountain Valley

Place Type: City
County: Orange
Population: 55,313

Ancestry	Population	%
Afghan (54)	54	0.10
African, Sub-Saharan (103)	214	0.39
African (103)	214	0.39
Cape Verdean (0)	0	<0.01
Ethiopian (0)	0	<0.01
Ghanaian (0)	0	<0.01
Kenyan (0)	0	<0.01
Liberian (0)	0	<0.01
Nigerian (0)	0	<0.01
Senegalese (0)	0	<0.01
Sierra Leonean (0)	0	<0.01
Somalian (0)	0	<0.01
South African (0)	0	<0.01
Sudanese (0)	0	<0.01
Ugandan (0)	0	<0.01
Zimbabwean (0)	0	<0.01
Other Sub-Saharan African (0)	0	<0.01
Albanian (0)	0	<0.01
Alsatian (0)	0	<0.01
American (1,134)	1,134	2.06
Arab (564)	636	1.16
Arab (252)	252	0.46
Egyptian (72)	80	0.15
Iraqi (0)	0	<0.01
Jordanian (92)	92	0.17
Lebanese (36)	85	0.15
Moroccan (0)	0	<0.01
Palestinian (13)	28	0.05
Syrian (0)	0	<0.01
Other Arab (99)	99	0.18
Armenian (335)	378	0.69
Assyrian/Chaldean/Syriac (0)	0	<0.01
Australian (32)	70	0.13
Austrian (66)	203	0.37
Basque (0)	0	<0.01
Belgian (82)	82	0.15
Brazilian (34)	34	0.06
British (120)	274	0.50
Bulgarian (0)	0	<0.01
Cajun (14)	29	0.05
Canadian (39)	146	0.27
Carpatho Rusyn (0)	0	<0.01
Celtic (0)	0	<0.01
Croatian (118)	198	0.36
Cypriot (0)	0	<0.01
Czech (71)	235	0.43
Czechoslovakian (24)	50	0.09
Danish (63)	440	0.80
Dutch (290)	923	1.68
Eastern European (66)	66	0.12
English (1,440)	5,281	9.61
Estonian (0)	0	<0.01
European (785)	880	1.60
Finnish (14)	129	0.23
French, ex. Basque (258)	1,420	2.58
French Canadian (123)	264	0.48
German (1,742)	6,635	12.07
German Russian (0)	0	<0.01
Greek (89)	272	0.49
Guyanese (19)	59	0.11
Hungarian (50)	195	0.35
Icelander (0)	21	0.04
Iranian (63)	63	0.11
Irish (1,253)	5,738	10.44
Israeli (9)	9	0.02
Italian (1,099)	2,448	4.45
Latvian (0)	10	0.02
Lithuanian (11)	82	0.15
Luxemburger (0)	0	<0.01
Macedonian (0)	0	<0.01
Maltese (0)	0	<0.01
New Zealander (10)	24	0.04
Northern European (73)	73	0.13
Norwegian (235)	989	1.80
Pennsylvania German (0)	0	<0.01
Polish (360)	1,160	2.11
Portuguese (83)	199	0.36
Romanian (147)	196	0.36
Russian (232)	804	1.46
Scandinavian (9)	33	0.06
Scotch-Irish (161)	864	1.57
Scottish (381)	1,341	2.44
Serbian (0)	14	0.03
Slavic (0)	12	0.02
Slovak (0)	0	<0.01
Slovene (6)	21	0.04
Soviet Union (0)	0	<0.01
Swedish (306)	1,089	1.98
Swiss (82)	157	0.29
Turkish (136)	136	0.25
Ukrainian (28)	82	0.15
Welsh (89)	440	0.80
West Indian, ex. Hispanic (49)	49	0.09
Bahamian (0)	0	<0.01
Barbadian (0)	0	<0.01
Belizean (8)	8	0.01
Bermudan (0)	0	<0.01
British West Indian (0)	0	<0.01
Dutch West Indian (0)	0	<0.01
Haitian (0)	0	<0.01
Jamaican (41)	41	0.07
Trinidadian/Tobagonian (0)	0	<0.01
U.S. Virgin Islander (0)	0	<0.01
West Indian (0)	0	<0.01
Other West Indian (0)	0	<0.01
Yugoslavian (51)	51	0.09

Hispanic Origin	Population	%
Hispanic or Latino (of any race)	7,250	13.11
Central American, ex. Mexican	337	0.61
Costa Rican	25	0.05
Guatemalan	73	0.13
Honduran	30	0.05
Nicaraguan	42	0.08
Panamanian	23	0.04
Salvadoran	135	0.24
Other Central American	9	0.02
Cuban	154	0.28
Dominican Republic	6	0.01
Mexican	5,463	9.88
Puerto Rican	175	0.32
South American	503	0.91
Argentinean	97	0.18
Bolivian	40	0.07
Chilean	41	0.07
Colombian	107	0.19
Ecuadorian	64	0.12
Paraguayan	0	<0.01
Peruvian	137	0.25
Uruguayan	5	0.01
Venezuelan	4	0.01
Other South American	8	0.01
Other Hispanic or Latino	612	1.11

Race*	Population	%
African-American/Black (510)	767	1.39
Not Hispanic (473)	681	1.23
Hispanic (37)	86	0.16
American Indian/Alaska Native (229)	635	1.15
Not Hispanic (127)	403	0.73
Hispanic (102)	232	0.42
Alaska Athabascan *(Ala. Nat.)* (0)	0	<0.01
Aleut *(Alaska Native)* (0)	1	<0.01
Apache (11)	26	0.05
Arapaho (0)	0	<0.01
Blackfeet (5)	16	0.03
Canadian/French Am. Ind. (5)	6	0.01
Central American Ind. (0)	0	<0.01
Cherokee (30)	152	0.27
Cheyenne (4)	4	0.01
Chickasaw (3)	11	0.02
Chippewa (1)	2	<0.01
Choctaw (8)	29	0.05
Colville (0)	0	<0.01
Comanche (0)	4	0.01
Cree (0)	1	<0.01
Creek (0)	11	0.02
Crow (0)	0	<0.01
Delaware (0)	2	<0.01
Hopi (0)	0	<0.01
Houma (0)	0	<0.01
Inupiat *(Alaska Native)* (0)	0	<0.01
Iroquois (0)	7	0.01
Kiowa (0)	0	<0.01
Lumbee (3)	3	0.01
Menominee (0)	0	<0.01
Mexican American Ind. (32)	39	0.07
Navajo (3)	10	0.02
Osage (0)	0	<0.01
Ottawa (1)	1	<0.01
Paiute (0)	1	<0.01
Pima (0)	1	<0.01
Potawatomi (2)	3	0.01
Pueblo (5)	13	0.02
Puget Sound Salish (0)	0	<0.01
Seminole (0)	1	<0.01
Shoshone (0)	0	<0.01
Sioux (7)	18	0.03
South American Ind. (0)	3	0.01
Spanish American Ind. (2)	2	<0.01
Tlingit-Haida *(Alaska Native)* (0)	0	<0.01
Tohono O'Odham (0)	0	<0.01
Tsimshian *(Alaska Native)* (0)	0	<0.01
Ute (0)	0	<0.01
Yakama (0)	0	<0.01
Yaqui (6)	16	0.03
Yuman (0)	0	<0.01
Yup'ik *(Alaska Native)* (0)	5	0.01
Asian (18,418)	19,755	35.71
Not Hispanic (18,324)	19,481	35.22
Hispanic (94)	274	0.50
Bangladeshi (10)	10	0.02
Bhutanese (0)	0	<0.01
Burmese (23)	32	0.06
Cambodian (120)	170	0.31
Chinese, ex. Taiwanese (1,851)	2,421	4.38
Filipino (838)	1,190	2.15
Hmong (56)	59	0.11
Indian (544)	608	1.10
Indonesian (45)	86	0.16
Japanese (1,312)	1,817	3.28
Korean (894)	1,019	1.84
Laotian (62)	79	0.14
Malaysian (2)	6	0.01
Nepalese (0)	0	<0.01
Pakistani (111)	134	0.24
Sri Lankan (4)	4	0.01
Taiwanese (483)	529	0.96
Thai (63)	92	0.17
Vietnamese (11,431)	11,861	21.44
Hawaii Native/Pacific Islander (171)	435	0.79
Not Hispanic (159)	384	0.69
Hispanic (12)	51	0.09
Fijian (2)	2	<0.01
Guamanian/Chamorro (27)	56	0.10
Marshallese (2)	2	<0.01
Native Hawaiian (38)	169	0.31
Samoan (73)	108	0.20
Tongan (13)	26	0.05
White (31,225)	33,287	60.18
Not Hispanic (27,234)	28,713	51.91
Hispanic (3,991)	4,574	8.27

*Notes: † The Census 2010 population figure is used to calculate the percentages in the Hispanic Origin and Race categories. Ancestry percentages are based on the 2006-2010 American Community Survey population (not shown); ‡ Numbers in parentheses indicate the number of people reporting a single ancestry; * Numbers in parentheses indicate the number of persons reporting this race alone, not in combination with any other race; Please refer to the Explanation of Data for more information.*

Fremont

Place Type: City
County: Alameda
Population: 214,089

Ancestry	Population	%
Afghan (2,638)	2,760	1.32
African, Sub-Saharan (890)	1,187	0.57
African (629)	795	0.38
Cape Verdean (0)	13	0.01
Ethiopian (97)	125	0.06
Ghanaian (20)	20	0.01
Kenyan (0)	42	0.02
Liberian (0)	0	<0.01
Nigerian (0)	0	<0.01
Senegalese (0)	0	<0.01
Sierra Leonean (0)	0	<0.01
Somalian (0)	20	0.01
South African (4)	32	0.02
Sudanese (27)	27	0.01
Ugandan (0)	0	<0.01
Zimbabwean (0)	0	<0.01
Other Sub-Saharan African (113)	113	0.05
Albanian (0)	0	<0.01
Alsatian (0)	0	<0.01
American (2,512)	2,512	1.20
Arab (1,877)	2,346	1.12
Arab (322)	396	0.19
Egyptian (268)	391	0.19
Iraqi (71)	110	0.05
Jordanian (14)	14	0.01
Lebanese (348)	454	0.22
Moroccan (0)	0	<0.01
Palestinian (300)	391	0.19
Syrian (0)	0	<0.01
Other Arab (554)	590	0.28
Armenian (161)	247	0.12
Assyrian/Chaldean/Syriac (81)	81	0.04
Australian (5)	5	<0.01
Austrian (109)	281	0.13
Basque (27)	38	0.02
Belgian (31)	133	0.06
Brazilian (82)	105	0.05
British (771)	1,345	0.64
Bulgarian (49)	56	0.03
Cajun (0)	11	0.01
Canadian (163)	493	0.24
Carpatho Rusyn (0)	0	<0.01
Celtic (80)	80	0.04
Croatian (81)	187	0.09
Cypriot (0)	0	<0.01
Czech (56)	233	0.11
Czechoslovakian (26)	84	0.04
Danish (118)	1,000	0.48
Dutch (517)	1,554	0.74
Eastern European (32)	61	0.03
English (2,243)	9,623	4.60
Estonian (12)	36	0.02
European (1,577)	1,837	0.88
Finnish (68)	289	0.14
French, ex. Basque (483)	2,524	1.21
French Canadian (206)	449	0.21
German (3,496)	14,843	7.09
German Russian (0)	0	<0.01
Greek (211)	590	0.28
Guyanese (0)	0	<0.01
Hungarian (117)	419	0.20
Icelander (0)	0	<0.01
Iranian (652)	800	0.38
Irish (2,636)	9,938	4.75
Israeli (0)	34	0.02
Italian (2,010)	5,357	2.56
Latvian (0)	44	0.02
Lithuanian (79)	306	0.15
Luxemburger (0)	30	0.01
Macedonian (0)	0	<0.01
Maltese (0)	0	<0.01
New Zealander (0)	0	<0.01
Northern European (254)	297	0.14
Norwegian (251)	1,499	0.72
Pennsylvania German (0)	10	<0.01
Polish (618)	2,165	1.03
Portuguese (2,427)	4,754	2.27
Romanian (134)	164	0.08
Russian (828)	1,958	0.94
Scandinavian (125)	238	0.11
Scotch-Irish (634)	2,074	0.99
Scottish (686)	2,689	1.29
Serbian (0)	29	0.01
Slavic (45)	45	0.02
Slovak (40)	98	0.05
Slovene (21)	21	0.01
Soviet Union (0)	0	<0.01
Swedish (743)	2,362	1.13
Swiss (24)	307	0.15
Turkish (56)	74	0.04
Ukrainian (184)	465	0.22
Welsh (81)	537	0.26
West Indian, ex. Hispanic (87)	126	0.06
Bahamian (0)	0	<0.01
Barbadian (0)	0	<0.01
Belizean (0)	0	<0.01
Bermudan (0)	0	<0.01
British West Indian (0)	0	<0.01
Dutch West Indian (0)	0	<0.01
Haitian (0)	0	<0.01
Jamaican (41)	46	0.02
Trinidadian/Tobagonian (34)	68	0.03
U.S. Virgin Islander (0)	0	<0.01
West Indian (12)	12	0.01
Other West Indian (0)	0	<0.01
Yugoslavian (70)	140	0.07

Hispanic Origin	Population	%
Hispanic or Latino (of any race)	31,698	14.81
Central American, ex. Mexican	2,429	1.13
Costa Rican	63	0.03
Guatemalan	430	0.20
Honduran	73	0.03
Nicaraguan	645	0.30
Panamanian	94	0.04
Salvadoran	1,102	0.51
Other Central American	22	0.01
Cuban	165	0.08
Dominican Republic	26	0.01
Mexican	23,600	11.02
Puerto Rican	1,241	0.58
South American	1,344	0.63
Argentinean	103	0.05
Bolivian	80	0.04
Chilean	124	0.06
Colombian	228	0.11
Ecuadorian	80	0.04
Paraguayan	2	<0.01
Peruvian	616	0.29
Uruguayan	22	0.01
Venezuelan	78	0.04
Other South American	11	0.01
Other Hispanic or Latino	2,893	1.35

Race*	Population	%
African-American/Black (7,103)	8,842	4.13
Not Hispanic (6,743)	8,086	3.78
Hispanic (360)	756	0.35
American Indian/Alaska Native (976)	2,463	1.15
Not Hispanic (458)	1,436	0.67
Hispanic (518)	1,027	0.48
Alaska Athabascan *(Ala. Nat.)* (2)	3	<0.01
Aleut *(Alaska Native)* (3)	9	<0.01
Apache (29)	98	0.05
Arapaho (0)	2	<0.01
Blackfeet (10)	70	0.03
Canadian/French Am. Ind. (1)	6	<0.01
Central American Ind. (0)	3	<0.01
Cherokee (56)	374	0.17
Cheyenne (0)	6	<0.01
Chickasaw (11)	22	0.01
Chippewa (10)	34	0.02
Choctaw (20)	77	0.04
Colville (0)	0	<0.01
Comanche (6)	16	0.01
Cree (0)	6	<0.01
Creek (8)	24	0.01
Crow (0)	0	<0.01
Delaware (3)	5	<0.01
Hopi (2)	7	<0.01
Houma (0)	0	<0.01
Inupiat *(Alaska Native)* (2)	5	<0.01
Iroquois (4)	15	0.01
Kiowa (8)	9	<0.01
Lumbee (0)	0	<0.01
Menominee (0)	0	<0.01
Mexican American Ind. (113)	179	0.08
Navajo (30)	63	0.03
Osage (4)	7	<0.01
Ottawa (0)	0	<0.01
Paiute (3)	8	<0.01
Pima (0)	2	<0.01
Potawatomi (5)	13	0.01
Pueblo (11)	25	0.01
Puget Sound Salish (0)	0	<0.01
Seminole (2)	12	0.01
Shoshone (2)	2	<0.01
Sioux (17)	53	0.02
South American Ind. (4)	12	0.01
Spanish American Ind. (15)	20	0.01
Tlingit-Haida *(Alaska Native)* (9)	20	0.01
Tohono O'Odham (7)	10	<0.01
Tsimshian *(Alaska Native)* (0)	1	<0.01
Ute (0)	4	<0.01
Yakama (0)	0	<0.01
Yaqui (9)	37	0.02
Yuman (1)	1	<0.01
Yup'ik *(Alaska Native)* (0)	1	<0.01
Asian (108,332)	116,755	54.54
Not Hispanic (107,679)	115,097	53.76
Hispanic (653)	1,658	0.77
Bangladeshi (216)	231	0.11
Bhutanese (0)	0	<0.01
Burmese (1,314)	1,450	0.68
Cambodian (153)	215	0.10
Chinese, ex. Taiwanese (33,706)	36,484	17.04
Filipino (14,285)	17,070	7.97
Hmong (112)	117	0.05
Indian (38,711)	40,010	18.69
Indonesian (237)	360	0.17
Japanese (1,716)	2,852	1.33
Korean (3,059)	3,459	1.62
Laotian (152)	208	0.10
Malaysian (96)	158	0.07
Nepalese (142)	152	0.07
Pakistani (2,081)	2,242	1.05
Sri Lankan (151)	172	0.08
Taiwanese (4,131)	4,572	2.14
Thai (264)	400	0.19
Vietnamese (5,249)	5,952	2.78
Hawaii Native/Pacific Islander (1,169)	2,514	1.17
Not Hispanic (1,064)	2,174	1.02
Hispanic (105)	340	0.16
Fijian (291)	348	0.16
Guamanian/Chamorro (238)	458	0.21
Marshallese (11)	17	0.01
Native Hawaiian (195)	735	0.34
Samoan (166)	255	0.12
Tongan (149)	192	0.09
White (70,320)	80,195	37.46
Not Hispanic (56,766)	64,017	29.90
Hispanic (13,554)	16,178	7.56

*Notes: † The Census 2010 population figure is used to calculate the percentages in the Hispanic Origin and Race categories. Ancestry percentages are based on the 2006-2010 American Community Survey population (not shown); ‡ Numbers in parentheses indicate the number of people reporting a single ancestry; * Numbers in parentheses indicate the number of persons reporting this race alone, not in combination with any other race; Please refer to the Explanation of Data for more information.*

Fresno

Place Type: City
County: Fresno
Population: 494,665

Ancestry	Population	%
Afghan (46)	58	0.01
African, Sub-Saharan (1,907)	2,412	0.50
African (1,344)	1,818	0.38
Cape Verdean (0)	0	<0.01
Ethiopian (221)	240	0.05
Ghanaian (5)	5	<0.01
Kenyan (0)	0	<0.01
Liberian (0)	0	<0.01
Nigerian (157)	157	0.03
Senegalese (0)	0	<0.01
Sierra Leonean (0)	0	<0.01
Somalian (0)	0	<0.01
South African (7)	19	<0.01
Sudanese (109)	109	0.02
Ugandan (0)	0	<0.01
Zimbabwean (0)	0	<0.01
Other Sub-Saharan African (64)	64	0.01
Albanian (0)	23	<0.01
Alsatian (0)	0	<0.01
American (6,280)	6,280	1.30
Arab (3,658)	4,301	0.89
Arab (1,557)	1,720	0.36
Egyptian (305)	313	0.06
Iraqi (91)	91	0.02
Jordanian (708)	708	0.15
Lebanese (153)	372	0.08
Moroccan (0)	0	<0.01
Palestinian (123)	170	0.04
Syrian (203)	363	0.07
Other Arab (518)	564	0.12
Armenian (5,389)	7,000	1.45
Assyrian/Chaldean/Syriac (52)	79	0.02
Australian (23)	39	0.01
Austrian (129)	451	0.09
Basque (203)	359	0.07
Belgian (42)	195	0.04
Brazilian (71)	142	0.03
British (211)	841	0.17
Bulgarian (0)	0	<0.01
Cajun (4)	36	0.01
Canadian (535)	874	0.18
Carpatho Rusyn (0)	0	<0.01
Celtic (55)	183	0.04
Croatian (76)	154	0.03
Cypriot (0)	0	<0.01
Czech (207)	825	0.17
Czechoslovakian (104)	213	0.04
Danish (678)	2,292	0.47
Dutch (878)	4,720	0.98
Eastern European (119)	165	0.03
English (6,805)	24,262	5.01
Estonian (20)	28	0.01
European (2,498)	3,030	0.63
Finnish (81)	640	0.13
French, ex. Basque (1,231)	7,784	1.61
French Canadian (441)	914	0.19
German (11,561)	39,420	8.14
German Russian (9)	23	<0.01
Greek (505)	1,082	0.22
Guyanese (0)	0	<0.01
Hungarian (58)	465	0.10
Icelander (0)	0	<0.01
Iranian (695)	995	0.21
Irish (6,748)	26,731	5.52
Israeli (193)	231	0.05
Italian (5,935)	16,181	3.34
Latvian (10)	21	<0.01
Lithuanian (29)	168	0.03
Luxemburger (0)	25	0.01
Macedonian (0)	13	<0.01
Maltese (0)	0	<0.01
New Zealander (0)	42	0.01
Northern European (362)	387	0.08
Norwegian (991)	2,869	0.59
Pennsylvania German (55)	82	0.02
Polish (924)	2,612	0.54
Portuguese (2,751)	5,315	1.10
Romanian (98)	235	0.05
Russian (1,323)	3,100	0.64
Scandinavian (177)	487	0.10
Scotch-Irish (1,672)	4,450	0.92
Scottish (1,729)	4,988	1.03
Serbian (31)	91	0.02
Slavic (39)	144	0.03
Slovak (33)	80	0.02
Slovene (12)	42	0.01
Soviet Union (0)	0	<0.01
Swedish (1,055)	4,491	0.93
Swiss (186)	1,010	0.21
Turkish (87)	87	0.02
Ukrainian (891)	1,067	0.22
Welsh (437)	1,973	0.41
West Indian, ex. Hispanic (122)	510	0.11
Bahamian (0)	0	<0.01
Barbadian (0)	6	<0.01
Belizean (0)	12	<0.01
Bermudan (0)	0	<0.01
British West Indian (0)	0	<0.01
Dutch West Indian (16)	133	0.03
Haitian (0)	0	<0.01
Jamaican (95)	231	0.05
Trinidadian/Tobagonian (0)	0	<0.01
U.S. Virgin Islander (0)	0	<0.01
West Indian (11)	115	0.02
Other West Indian (0)	13	<0.01
Yugoslavian (57)	119	0.02

Hispanic Origin	Population	%
Hispanic or Latino (of any race)	232,055	46.91
Central American, ex. Mexican	3,381	0.68
Costa Rican	98	0.02
Guatemalan	678	0.14
Honduran	318	0.06
Nicaraguan	320	0.06
Panamanian	107	0.02
Salvadoran	1,833	0.37
Other Central American	27	0.01
Cuban	406	0.08
Dominican Republic	79	0.02
Mexican	211,431	42.74
Puerto Rican	1,825	0.37
South American	1,084	0.22
Argentinean	148	0.03
Bolivian	47	0.01
Chilean	113	0.02
Colombian	318	0.06
Ecuadorian	88	0.02
Paraguayan	7	<0.01
Peruvian	283	0.06
Uruguayan	15	<0.01
Venezuelan	49	0.01
Other South American	16	<0.01
Other Hispanic or Latino	13,849	2.80

Race*	Population	%
African-American/Black (40,960)	46,895	9.48
Not Hispanic (37,885)	41,526	8.39
Hispanic (3,075)	5,369	1.09
American Indian/Alaska Native (8,525)	14,161	2.86
Not Hispanic (3,127)	6,241	1.26
Hispanic (5,398)	7,920	1.60
Alaska Athabascan *(Ala. Nat.)* (7)	7	<0.01
Aleut *(Alaska Native)* (7)	8	<0.01
Apache (355)	648	0.13
Arapaho (0)	4	<0.01
Blackfeet (44)	216	0.04
Canadian/French Am. Ind. (14)	21	<0.01
Central American Ind. (19)	34	0.01
Cherokee (422)	1,408	0.28
Cheyenne (9)	22	<0.01
Chickasaw (13)	71	0.01
Chippewa (33)	68	0.01
Choctaw (136)	411	0.08
Colville (5)	6	<0.01
Comanche (41)	77	0.02
Cree (5)	15	<0.01
Creek (52)	162	0.03
Crow (11)	18	<0.01
Delaware (10)	16	<0.01
Hopi (12)	45	0.01
Houma (1)	3	<0.01
Inupiat *(Alaska Native)* (3)	5	<0.01
Iroquois (23)	44	0.01
Kiowa (13)	21	<0.01
Lumbee (4)	7	<0.01
Menominee (6)	6	<0.01
Mexican American Ind. (1,282)	1,666	0.34
Navajo (165)	294	0.06
Osage (6)	24	<0.01
Ottawa (4)	7	<0.01
Paiute (19)	67	0.01
Pima (24)	41	0.01
Potawatomi (29)	47	0.01
Pueblo (37)	68	0.01
Puget Sound Salish (3)	7	<0.01
Seminole (19)	49	0.01
Shoshone (25)	36	0.01
Sioux (68)	149	0.03
South American Ind. (9)	22	<0.01
Spanish American Ind. (46)	58	0.01
Tlingit-Haida *(Alaska Native)* (1)	5	<0.01
Tohono O'Odham (43)	62	0.01
Tsimshian *(Alaska Native)* (1)	1	<0.01
Ute (9)	20	<0.01
Yakama (1)	3	<0.01
Yaqui (353)	522	0.11
Yuman (15)	26	0.01
Yup'ik *(Alaska Native)* (1)	4	<0.01
Asian (62,528)	69,765	14.10
Not Hispanic (60,939)	65,854	13.31
Hispanic (1,589)	3,911	0.79
Bangladeshi (28)	30	0.01
Bhutanese (1)	1	<0.01
Burmese (50)	66	0.01
Cambodian (4,310)	4,798	0.97
Chinese, ex. Taiwanese (3,605)	4,726	0.96
Filipino (6,359)	8,726	1.76
Hmong (23,449)	24,328	4.92
Indian (8,814)	9,825	1.99
Indonesian (158)	253	0.05
Japanese (2,401)	3,787	0.77
Korean (1,106)	1,434	0.29
Laotian (6,007)	6,733	1.36
Malaysian (30)	43	0.01
Nepalese (29)	34	0.01
Pakistani (326)	378	0.08
Sri Lankan (35)	45	0.01
Taiwanese (140)	154	0.03
Thai (337)	515	0.10
Vietnamese (2,093)	2,412	0.49
Hawaii Native/Pacific Islander (849)	2,133	0.43
Not Hispanic (663)	1,431	0.29
Hispanic (186)	702	0.14
Fijian (93)	114	0.02
Guamanian/Chamorro (152)	264	0.05
Marshallese (5)	6	<0.01
Native Hawaiian (164)	608	0.12
Samoan (234)	388	0.08
Tongan (23)	48	0.01
White (245,306)	263,929	53.36
Not Hispanic (148,598)	156,548	31.65
Hispanic (96,708)	107,381	21.71

*Notes: † The Census 2010 population figure is used to calculate the percentages in the Hispanic Origin and Race categories. Ancestry percentages are based on the 2006-2010 American Community Survey population (not shown); ‡ Numbers in parentheses indicate the number of people reporting a single ancestry; * Numbers in parentheses indicate the number of persons reporting this race alone, not in combination with any other race; Please refer to the Explanation of Data for more information.*

Fullerton

Place Type: City
County: Orange
Population: 135,161

Ancestry	Population	%
Afghan (176)	188	0.14
African, Sub-Saharan (304)	607	0.46
African (77)	126	0.09
Cape Verdean (0)	0	<0.01
Ethiopian (94)	139	0.10
Ghanaian (0)	0	<0.01
Kenyan (0)	0	<0.01
Liberian (0)	0	<0.01
Nigerian (119)	119	0.09
Senegalese (0)	0	<0.01
Sierra Leonean (0)	0	<0.01
Somalian (0)	0	<0.01
South African (14)	198	0.15
Sudanese (0)	0	<0.01
Ugandan (0)	0	<0.01
Zimbabwean (0)	0	<0.01
Other Sub-Saharan African (0)	25	0.02
Albanian (0)	0	<0.01
Alsatian (0)	9	0.01
American (2,569)	2,569	1.93
Arab (447)	770	0.58
Arab (0)	238	0.18
Egyptian (60)	74	0.06
Iraqi (27)	33	0.02
Jordanian (15)	20	0.02
Lebanese (232)	280	0.21
Moroccan (0)	0	<0.01
Palestinian (41)	41	0.03
Syrian (0)	12	0.01
Other Arab (72)	72	0.05
Armenian (215)	338	0.25
Assyrian/Chaldean/Syriac (0)	8	0.01
Australian (24)	46	0.03
Austrian (31)	370	0.28
Basque (50)	50	0.04
Belgian (50)	161	0.12
Brazilian (16)	37	0.03
British (200)	634	0.48
Bulgarian (0)	0	<0.01
Cajun (0)	0	<0.01
Canadian (270)	474	0.36
Carpatho Rusyn (0)	0	<0.01
Celtic (37)	111	0.08
Croatian (85)	190	0.14
Cypriot (0)	0	<0.01
Czech (34)	193	0.15
Czechoslovakian (0)	107	0.08
Danish (125)	638	0.48
Dutch (724)	1,891	1.42
Eastern European (29)	67	0.05
English (2,822)	9,591	7.22
Estonian (0)	0	<0.01
European (758)	950	0.71
Finnish (82)	211	0.16
French, ex. Basque (310)	2,297	1.73
French Canadian (254)	442	0.33
German (3,722)	13,529	10.18
German Russian (7)	7	0.01
Greek (496)	828	0.62
Guyanese (0)	0	<0.01
Hungarian (208)	770	0.58
Icelander (0)	53	0.04
Iranian (528)	537	0.40
Irish (2,271)	9,523	7.17
Israeli (53)	53	0.04
Italian (1,793)	4,838	3.64
Latvian (0)	15	0.01
Lithuanian (27)	83	0.06
Luxemburger (0)	12	0.01
Macedonian (0)	0	<0.01
Maltese (0)	0	<0.01
New Zealander (16)	51	0.04
Northern European (127)	127	0.10
Norwegian (410)	1,353	1.02
Pennsylvania German (0)	10	0.01
Polish (496)	1,688	1.27
Portuguese (252)	539	0.41
Romanian (574)	663	0.50
Russian (508)	989	0.74
Scandinavian (98)	257	0.19
Scotch-Irish (725)	2,049	1.54
Scottish (402)	1,926	1.45
Serbian (62)	80	0.06
Slavic (47)	75	0.06
Slovak (70)	86	0.06
Slovene (24)	49	0.04
Soviet Union (0)	0	<0.01
Swedish (481)	1,929	1.45
Swiss (43)	302	0.23
Turkish (60)	74	0.06
Ukrainian (105)	314	0.24
Welsh (171)	986	0.74
West Indian, ex. Hispanic (16)	80	0.06
Bahamian (0)	0	<0.01
Barbadian (0)	0	<0.01
Belizean (0)	31	0.02
Bermudan (0)	0	<0.01
British West Indian (0)	0	<0.01
Dutch West Indian (0)	0	<0.01
Haitian (0)	21	0.02
Jamaican (0)	0	<0.01
Trinidadian/Tobagonian (0)	2	<0.01
U.S. Virgin Islander (0)	0	<0.01
West Indian (0)	10	0.01
Other West Indian (16)	16	0.01
Yugoslavian (30)	59	0.04

Hispanic Origin	Population	%
Hispanic or Latino (of any race)	46,501	34.40
Central American, ex. Mexican	2,039	1.51
Costa Rican	117	0.09
Guatemalan	594	0.44
Honduran	163	0.12
Nicaraguan	274	0.20
Panamanian	31	0.02
Salvadoran	800	0.59
Other Central American	60	0.04
Cuban	413	0.31
Dominican Republic	24	0.02
Mexican	39,718	29.39
Puerto Rican	594	0.44
South American	1,291	0.96
Argentinean	244	0.18
Bolivian	49	0.04
Chilean	70	0.05
Colombian	269	0.20
Ecuadorian	161	0.12
Paraguayan	7	0.01
Peruvian	423	0.31
Uruguayan	10	0.01
Venezuelan	15	0.01
Other South American	43	0.03
Other Hispanic or Latino	2,422	1.79

Race*	Population	%
African-American/Black (3,138)	3,968	2.94
Not Hispanic (2,791)	3,321	2.46
Hispanic (347)	647	0.48
American Indian/Alaska Native (842)	1,859	1.38
Not Hispanic (251)	796	0.59
Hispanic (591)	1,063	0.79
Alaska Athabascan *(Ala. Nat.)* (0)	1	<0.01
Aleut *(Alaska Native)* (0)	1	<0.01
Apache (34)	77	0.06
Arapaho (0)	3	<0.01
Blackfeet (7)	43	0.03
Canadian/French Am. Ind. (0)	2	<0.01
Central American Ind. (2)	4	<0.01
Cherokee (50)	238	0.18
Cheyenne (2)	4	<0.01
Chickasaw (1)	5	<0.01
Chippewa (4)	9	0.01
Choctaw (10)	48	0.04
Colville (0)	2	<0.01
Comanche (6)	13	0.01
Cree (0)	1	<0.01
Creek (3)	27	0.02
Crow (0)	0	<0.01
Delaware (1)	5	<0.01
Hopi (1)	2	<0.01
Houma (0)	0	<0.01
Inupiat *(Alaska Native)* (1)	2	<0.01
Iroquois (3)	15	0.01
Kiowa (4)	5	<0.01
Lumbee (1)	1	<0.01
Menominee (0)	1	<0.01
Mexican American Ind. (114)	172	0.13
Navajo (25)	52	0.04
Osage (2)	4	<0.01
Ottawa (0)	0	<0.01
Paiute (3)	5	<0.01
Pima (5)	8	0.01
Potawatomi (3)	17	0.01
Pueblo (11)	19	0.01
Puget Sound Salish (1)	1	<0.01
Seminole (0)	8	0.01
Shoshone (1)	6	<0.01
Sioux (12)	46	0.03
South American Ind. (3)	7	0.01
Spanish American Ind. (9)	15	0.01
Tlingit-Haida *(Alaska Native)* (0)	0	<0.01
Tohono O'Odham (4)	6	<0.01
Tsimshian *(Alaska Native)* (0)	0	<0.01
Ute (0)	2	<0.01
Yakama (0)	0	<0.01
Yaqui (21)	53	0.04
Yuman (1)	1	<0.01
Yup'ik *(Alaska Native)* (0)	0	<0.01
Asian (30,788)	33,256	24.60
Not Hispanic (30,486)	32,479	24.03
Hispanic (302)	777	0.57
Bangladeshi (49)	54	0.04
Bhutanese (0)	0	<0.01
Burmese (51)	67	0.05
Cambodian (153)	215	0.16
Chinese, ex. Taiwanese (3,339)	4,235	3.13
Filipino (3,380)	4,263	3.15
Hmong (20)	25	0.02
Indian (2,494)	2,714	2.01
Indonesian (194)	278	0.21
Japanese (1,260)	1,966	1.45
Korean (15,544)	16,004	11.84
Laotian (157)	196	0.15
Malaysian (24)	37	0.03
Nepalese (20)	20	0.01
Pakistani (254)	306	0.23
Sri Lankan (51)	55	0.04
Taiwanese (697)	782	0.58
Thai (218)	284	0.21
Vietnamese (1,945)	2,277	1.68
Hawaii Native/Pacific Islander (321)	790	0.58
Not Hispanic (270)	653	0.48
Hispanic (51)	137	0.10
Fijian (3)	7	0.01
Guamanian/Chamorro (40)	112	0.08
Marshallese (0)	0	<0.01
Native Hawaiian (77)	271	0.20
Samoan (132)	196	0.15
Tongan (15)	24	0.02
White (72,845)	77,699	57.49
Not Hispanic (51,656)	54,164	40.07
Hispanic (21,189)	23,535	17.41

*Notes: † The Census 2010 population figure is used to calculate the percentages in the Hispanic Origin and Race categories. Ancestry percentages are based on the 2006-2010 American Community Survey population (not shown); ‡ Numbers in parentheses indicate the number of people reporting a single ancestry; * Numbers in parentheses indicate the number of persons reporting this race alone, not in combination with any other race; Please refer to the Explanation of Data for more information.*

Garden Grove

Place Type: City
County: Orange
Population: 170,883

Ancestry	Population	%
Afghan (434)	434	0.26
African, Sub-Saharan (87)	131	0.08
African (68)	86	0.05
Cape Verdean (0)	0	<0.01
Ethiopian (0)	0	<0.01
Ghanaian (0)	0	<0.01
Kenyan (0)	0	<0.01
Liberian (0)	0	<0.01
Nigerian (0)	0	<0.01
Senegalese (0)	0	<0.01
Sierra Leonean (0)	0	<0.01
Somalian (0)	0	<0.01
South African (0)	26	0.02
Sudanese (8)	8	<0.01
Ugandan (0)	0	<0.01
Zimbabwean (0)	0	<0.01
Other Sub-Saharan African (11)	11	0.01
Albanian (0)	8	<0.01
Alsatian (0)	0	<0.01
American (3,323)	3,323	1.97
Arab (509)	585	0.35
Arab (20)	20	0.01
Egyptian (118)	118	0.07
Iraqi (9)	9	0.01
Jordanian (69)	69	0.04
Lebanese (3)	40	0.02
Moroccan (108)	108	0.06
Palestinian (60)	60	0.04
Syrian (113)	113	0.07
Other Arab (9)	48	0.03
Armenian (88)	165	0.10
Assyrian/Chaldean/Syriac (29)	29	0.02
Australian (42)	62	0.04
Austrian (11)	79	0.05
Basque (12)	31	0.02
Belgian (9)	56	0.03
Brazilian (47)	47	0.03
British (225)	369	0.22
Bulgarian (0)	22	0.01
Cajun (0)	0	<0.01
Canadian (119)	217	0.13
Carpatho Rusyn (0)	0	<0.01
Celtic (7)	19	0.01
Croatian (40)	81	0.05
Cypriot (0)	0	<0.01
Czech (23)	195	0.12
Czechoslovakian (8)	82	0.05
Danish (78)	434	0.26
Dutch (295)	1,260	0.75
Eastern European (27)	27	0.02
English (2,038)	7,102	4.20
Estonian (0)	0	<0.01
European (592)	786	0.47
Finnish (26)	103	0.06
French, ex. Basque (480)	2,112	1.25
French Canadian (176)	394	0.23
German (2,843)	10,090	5.97
German Russian (10)	10	0.01
Greek (228)	376	0.22
Guyanese (0)	0	<0.01
Hungarian (80)	342	0.20
Icelander (0)	0	<0.01
Iranian (81)	86	0.05
Irish (1,980)	7,908	4.68
Israeli (10)	10	0.01
Italian (1,194)	2,886	1.71
Latvian (0)	34	0.02
Lithuanian (87)	174	0.10
Luxemburger (0)	0	<0.01
Macedonian (0)	0	<0.01
Maltese (0)	21	0.01
New Zealander (0)	0	<0.01
Northern European (17)	17	0.01
Norwegian (321)	848	0.50
Pennsylvania German (15)	26	0.02
Polish (658)	1,608	0.95
Portuguese (146)	461	0.27
Romanian (325)	355	0.21
Russian (254)	679	0.40
Scandinavian (103)	141	0.08
Scotch-Irish (375)	1,179	0.70
Scottish (359)	1,354	0.80
Serbian (29)	29	0.02
Slavic (14)	27	0.02
Slovak (40)	53	0.03
Slovene (0)	0	<0.01
Soviet Union (0)	0	<0.01
Swedish (359)	1,052	0.62
Swiss (60)	225	0.13
Turkish (121)	165	0.10
Ukrainian (97)	138	0.08
Welsh (174)	486	0.29
West Indian, ex. Hispanic (67)	96	0.06
Bahamian (0)	0	<0.01
Barbadian (0)	0	<0.01
Belizean (0)	6	<0.01
Bermudan (0)	0	<0.01
British West Indian (0)	0	<0.01
Dutch West Indian (0)	0	<0.01
Haitian (0)	0	<0.01
Jamaican (67)	90	0.05
Trinidadian/Tobagonian (0)	0	<0.01
U.S. Virgin Islander (0)	0	<0.01
West Indian (0)	0	<0.01
Other West Indian (0)	0	<0.01
Yugoslavian (13)	65	0.04

Hispanic Origin	Population	%
Hispanic or Latino (of any race)	63,079	36.91
Central American, ex. Mexican	2,968	1.74
Costa Rican	89	0.05
Guatemalan	841	0.49
Honduran	210	0.12
Nicaraguan	156	0.09
Panamanian	55	0.03
Salvadoran	1,609	0.94
Other Central American	8	<0.01
Cuban	341	0.20
Dominican Republic	44	0.03
Mexican	54,565	31.93
Puerto Rican	524	0.31
South American	1,465	0.86
Argentinean	169	0.10
Bolivian	110	0.06
Chilean	88	0.05
Colombian	327	0.19
Ecuadorian	149	0.09
Paraguayan	2	<0.01
Peruvian	569	0.33
Uruguayan	19	0.01
Venezuelan	23	0.01
Other South American	9	0.01
Other Hispanic or Latino	3,172	1.86

Race*	Population	%
African-American/Black (2,155)	2,919	1.71
Not Hispanic (1,752)	2,267	1.33
Hispanic (403)	652	0.38
American Indian/Alaska Native (983)	1,826	1.07
Not Hispanic (286)	724	0.42
Hispanic (697)	1,102	0.64
Alaska Athabascan *(Ala. Nat.)* (0)	0	<0.01
Aleut *(Alaska Native)* (0)	0	<0.01
Apache (33)	88	0.05
Arapaho (0)	2	<0.01
Blackfeet (3)	15	0.01
Canadian/French Am. Ind. (0)	3	<0.01
Central American Ind. (3)	3	<0.01
Cherokee (54)	153	0.09
Cheyenne (3)	10	0.01
Chickasaw (9)	10	0.01
Chippewa (8)	16	0.01
Choctaw (9)	29	0.02
Colville (0)	0	<0.01
Comanche (2)	4	<0.01
Cree (0)	2	<0.01
Creek (1)	3	<0.01
Crow (0)	3	<0.01
Delaware (4)	7	<0.01
Hopi (4)	10	0.01
Houma (0)	0	<0.01
Inupiat *(Alaska Native)* (0)	0	<0.01
Iroquois (7)	23	0.01
Kiowa (1)	1	<0.01
Lumbee (0)	4	<0.01
Menominee (0)	1	<0.01
Mexican American Ind. (126)	175	0.10
Navajo (22)	51	0.03
Osage (0)	5	<0.01
Ottawa (0)	1	<0.01
Paiute (1)	2	<0.01
Pima (7)	10	0.01
Potawatomi (0)	0	<0.01
Pueblo (5)	14	0.01
Puget Sound Salish (4)	4	<0.01
Seminole (7)	10	0.01
Shoshone (2)	4	<0.01
Sioux (12)	24	0.01
South American Ind. (2)	5	<0.01
Spanish American Ind. (20)	23	0.01
Tlingit-Haida *(Alaska Native)* (0)	2	<0.01
Tohono O'Odham (5)	6	<0.01
Tsimshian *(Alaska Native)* (0)	0	<0.01
Ute (0)	0	<0.01
Yakama (0)	0	<0.01
Yaqui (3)	20	0.01
Yuman (2)	2	<0.01
Yup'ik *(Alaska Native)* (0)	2	<0.01
Asian (63,451)	65,923	38.58
Not Hispanic (63,118)	65,071	38.08
Hispanic (333)	852	0.50
Bangladeshi (42)	47	0.03
Bhutanese (0)	0	<0.01
Burmese (99)	104	0.06
Cambodian (627)	753	0.44
Chinese, ex. Taiwanese (2,084)	3,035	1.78
Filipino (3,177)	3,944	2.31
Hmong (200)	212	0.12
Indian (676)	895	0.52
Indonesian (152)	223	0.13
Japanese (895)	1,297	0.76
Korean (5,717)	5,951	3.48
Laotian (355)	412	0.24
Malaysian (8)	20	0.01
Nepalese (3)	3	<0.01
Pakistani (384)	416	0.24
Sri Lankan (50)	60	0.04
Taiwanese (106)	134	0.08
Thai (202)	256	0.15
Vietnamese (47,331)	48,774	28.54
Hawaii Native/Pacific Islander (1,110)	1,673	0.98
Not Hispanic (1,030)	1,460	0.85
Hispanic (80)	213	0.12
Fijian (8)	10	0.01
Guamanian/Chamorro (140)	218	0.13
Marshallese (103)	109	0.06
Native Hawaiian (134)	366	0.21
Samoan (617)	760	0.44
Tongan (48)	56	0.03
White (68,149)	73,273	42.88
Not Hispanic (38,558)	40,865	23.91
Hispanic (29,591)	32,408	18.97

*Notes: † The Census 2010 population figure is used to calculate the percentages in the Hispanic Origin and Race categories. Ancestry percentages are based on the 2006-2010 American Community Survey population (not shown); ‡ Numbers in parentheses indicate the number of people reporting a single ancestry; * Numbers in parentheses indicate the number of persons reporting this race alone, not in combination with any other race; Please refer to the Explanation of Data for more information.*

Gardena

Place Type: City
County: Los Angeles
Population: 58,829

Ancestry	Population	%
Afghan (0)	0	<0.01
African, Sub-Saharan (531)	580	0.99
African (428)	477	0.81
Cape Verdean (0)	0	<0.01
Ethiopian (23)	23	0.04
Ghanaian (0)	0	<0.01
Kenyan (0)	0	<0.01
Liberian (0)	0	<0.01
Nigerian (80)	80	0.14
Senegalese (0)	0	<0.01
Sierra Leonean (0)	0	<0.01
Somalian (0)	0	<0.01
South African (0)	0	<0.01
Sudanese (0)	0	<0.01
Ugandan (0)	0	<0.01
Zimbabwean (0)	0	<0.01
Other Sub-Saharan African (0)	0	<0.01
Albanian (0)	0	<0.01
Alsatian (0)	0	<0.01
American (1,792)	1,792	3.05
Arab (37)	37	0.06
Arab (0)	0	<0.01
Egyptian (18)	18	0.03
Iraqi (0)	0	<0.01
Jordanian (0)	0	<0.01
Lebanese (11)	11	0.02
Moroccan (0)	0	<0.01
Palestinian (0)	0	<0.01
Syrian (0)	0	<0.01
Other Arab (8)	8	0.01
Armenian (10)	10	0.02
Assyrian/Chaldean/Syriac (0)	0	<0.01
Australian (0)	0	<0.01
Austrian (6)	28	0.05
Basque (0)	0	<0.01
Belgian (0)	0	<0.01
Brazilian (9)	9	0.02
British (66)	129	0.22
Bulgarian (0)	0	<0.01
Cajun (8)	8	0.01
Canadian (26)	42	0.07
Carpatho Rusyn (0)	0	<0.01
Celtic (0)	0	<0.01
Croatian (22)	33	0.06
Cypriot (0)	0	<0.01
Czech (0)	0	<0.01
Czechoslovakian (10)	10	0.02
Danish (17)	25	0.04
Dutch (18)	192	0.33
Eastern European (0)	0	<0.01
English (217)	1,001	1.71
Estonian (0)	0	<0.01
European (99)	119	0.20
Finnish (0)	0	<0.01
French, ex. Basque (25)	257	0.44
French Canadian (36)	36	0.06
German (526)	1,768	3.01
German Russian (0)	0	<0.01
Greek (0)	0	<0.01
Guyanese (0)	0	<0.01
Hungarian (19)	47	0.08
Icelander (0)	0	<0.01
Iranian (42)	53	0.09
Irish (235)	1,390	2.37
Israeli (0)	0	<0.01
Italian (371)	608	1.04
Latvian (0)	0	<0.01
Lithuanian (0)	0	<0.01
Luxemburger (0)	0	<0.01
Macedonian (0)	0	<0.01
Maltese (0)	0	<0.01
New Zealander (0)	0	<0.01
Northern European (0)	0	<0.01
Norwegian (49)	209	0.36
Pennsylvania German (0)	0	<0.01
Polish (69)	92	0.16
Portuguese (34)	131	0.22
Romanian (0)	0	<0.01
Russian (59)	93	0.16
Scandinavian (0)	7	0.01
Scotch-Irish (10)	111	0.19
Scottish (26)	151	0.26
Serbian (0)	24	0.04
Slavic (0)	0	<0.01
Slovak (10)	21	0.04
Slovene (0)	0	<0.01
Soviet Union (0)	0	<0.01
Swedish (23)	170	0.29
Swiss (5)	65	0.11
Turkish (0)	0	<0.01
Ukrainian (11)	18	0.03
Welsh (7)	83	0.14
West Indian, ex. Hispanic (226)	332	0.57
Bahamian (0)	0	<0.01
Barbadian (0)	0	<0.01
Belizean (203)	203	0.35
Bermudan (0)	0	<0.01
British West Indian (0)	16	0.03
Dutch West Indian (0)	0	<0.01
Haitian (0)	0	<0.01
Jamaican (9)	9	0.02
Trinidadian/Tobagonian (14)	75	0.13
U.S. Virgin Islander (0)	0	<0.01
West Indian (0)	29	0.05
Other West Indian (0)	0	<0.01
Yugoslavian (0)	0	<0.01

Hispanic Origin	Population	%
Hispanic or Latino (of any race)	22,151	37.65
Central American, ex. Mexican	2,934	4.99
Costa Rican	69	0.12
Guatemalan	1,080	1.84
Honduran	170	0.29
Nicaraguan	190	0.32
Panamanian	48	0.08
Salvadoran	1,341	2.28
Other Central American	36	0.06
Cuban	225	0.38
Dominican Republic	36	0.06
Mexican	16,462	27.98
Puerto Rican	356	0.61
South American	867	1.47
Argentinean	51	0.09
Bolivian	13	0.02
Chilean	36	0.06
Colombian	122	0.21
Ecuadorian	176	0.30
Paraguayan	2	<0.01
Peruvian	439	0.75
Uruguayan	3	0.01
Venezuelan	16	0.03
Other South American	9	0.02
Other Hispanic or Latino	1,271	2.16

Race*	Population	%
African-American/Black (14,352)	15,136	25.73
Not Hispanic (14,034)	14,571	24.77
Hispanic (318)	565	0.96
American Indian/Alaska Native (348)	735	1.25
Not Hispanic (100)	333	0.57
Hispanic (248)	402	0.68
Alaska Athabascan *(Ala. Nat.)* (0)	0	<0.01
Aleut *(Alaska Native)* (0)	0	<0.01
Apache (11)	16	0.03
Arapaho (0)	0	<0.01
Blackfeet (1)	18	0.03
Canadian/French Am. Ind. (0)	1	<0.01
Central American Ind. (5)	11	0.02
Cherokee (12)	56	0.10
Cheyenne (1)	1	<0.01
Chickasaw (1)	3	0.01
Chippewa (9)	10	0.02
Choctaw (7)	28	0.05
Colville (0)	0	<0.01
Comanche (3)	4	0.01
Cree (0)	0	<0.01
Creek (0)	4	0.01
Crow (0)	0	<0.01
Delaware (0)	0	<0.01
Hopi (0)	0	<0.01
Houma (0)	3	0.01
Inupiat *(Alaska Native)* (0)	1	<0.01
Iroquois (0)	0	<0.01
Kiowa (0)	0	<0.01
Lumbee (0)	0	<0.01
Menominee (0)	0	<0.01
Mexican American Ind. (45)	78	0.13
Navajo (11)	27	0.05
Osage (1)	4	0.01
Ottawa (0)	1	<0.01
Paiute (1)	1	<0.01
Pima (1)	1	<0.01
Potawatomi (0)	1	<0.01
Pueblo (7)	16	0.03
Puget Sound Salish (0)	0	<0.01
Seminole (0)	2	<0.01
Shoshone (0)	1	<0.01
Sioux (8)	9	0.02
South American Ind. (5)	12	0.02
Spanish American Ind. (5)	7	0.01
Tlingit-Haida *(Alaska Native)* (0)	0	<0.01
Tohono O'Odham (6)	10	0.02
Tsimshian *(Alaska Native)* (0)	0	<0.01
Ute (0)	0	<0.01
Yakama (0)	1	<0.01
Yaqui (1)	2	<0.01
Yuman (0)	0	<0.01
Yup'ik *(Alaska Native)* (0)	4	0.01
Asian (15,400)	16,602	28.22
Not Hispanic (15,149)	16,023	27.24
Hispanic (251)	579	0.98
Bangladeshi (0)	0	<0.01
Bhutanese (0)	0	<0.01
Burmese (18)	23	0.04
Cambodian (86)	96	0.16
Chinese, ex. Taiwanese (957)	1,316	2.24
Filipino (2,346)	2,853	4.85
Hmong (1)	1	<0.01
Indian (193)	277	0.47
Indonesian (50)	74	0.13
Japanese (5,726)	6,584	11.19
Korean (3,457)	3,636	6.18
Laotian (8)	14	0.02
Malaysian (2)	6	0.01
Nepalese (20)	23	0.04
Pakistani (30)	32	0.05
Sri Lankan (61)	66	0.11
Taiwanese (95)	113	0.19
Thai (175)	210	0.36
Vietnamese (1,624)	1,737	2.95
Hawaii Native/Pacific Islander (426)	767	1.30
Not Hispanic (382)	643	1.09
Hispanic (44)	124	0.21
Fijian (14)	19	0.03
Guamanian/Chamorro (28)	46	0.08
Marshallese (1)	1	<0.01
Native Hawaiian (122)	324	0.55
Samoan (191)	269	0.46
Tongan (40)	51	0.09
White (14,498)	16,293	27.70
Not Hispanic (5,484)	6,344	10.78
Hispanic (9,014)	9,949	16.91

*Notes: † The Census 2010 population figure is used to calculate the percentages in the Hispanic Origin and Race categories. Ancestry percentages are based on the 2006-2010 American Community Survey population (not shown); ‡ Numbers in parentheses indicate the number of people reporting a single ancestry; * Numbers in parentheses indicate the number of persons reporting this race alone, not in combination with any other race; Please refer to the Explanation of Data for more information.*

Glendale

Place Type: City
County: Los Angeles
Population: 191,719

Ancestry	Population	%
Afghan (92)	92	0.05
African, Sub-Saharan (273)	342	0.18
African (67)	109	0.06
Cape Verdean (0)	0	<0.01
Ethiopian (0)	0	<0.01
Ghanaian (0)	0	<0.01
Kenyan (0)	0	<0.01
Liberian (0)	0	<0.01
Nigerian (109)	109	0.06
Senegalese (0)	0	<0.01
Sierra Leonean (34)	34	0.02
Somalian (0)	0	<0.01
South African (0)	27	0.01
Sudanese (10)	10	0.01
Ugandan (0)	0	<0.01
Zimbabwean (0)	0	<0.01
Other Sub-Saharan African (53)	53	0.03
Albanian (0)	95	0.05
Alsatian (0)	0	<0.01
American (3,450)	3,450	1.80
Arab (2,910)	4,218	2.19
Arab (291)	420	0.22
Egyptian (282)	329	0.17
Iraqi (429)	715	0.37
Jordanian (0)	0	<0.01
Lebanese (1,470)	2,062	1.07
Moroccan (32)	32	0.02
Palestinian (27)	96	0.05
Syrian (238)	340	0.18
Other Arab (141)	224	0.12
Armenian (58,115)	65,434	34.05
Assyrian/Chaldean/Syriac (121)	235	0.12
Australian (74)	89	0.05
Austrian (125)	402	0.21
Basque (39)	39	0.02
Belgian (21)	69	0.04
Brazilian (109)	120	0.06
British (541)	895	0.47
Bulgarian (35)	115	0.06
Cajun (0)	0	<0.01
Canadian (164)	383	0.20
Carpatho Rusyn (0)	0	<0.01
Celtic (0)	14	0.01
Croatian (95)	190	0.10
Cypriot (0)	0	<0.01
Czech (55)	298	0.16
Czechoslovakian (0)	67	0.03
Danish (171)	767	0.40
Dutch (277)	958	0.50
Eastern European (89)	103	0.05
English (1,981)	7,611	3.96
Estonian (18)	18	0.01
European (802)	933	0.49
Finnish (113)	236	0.12
French, ex. Basque (324)	2,100	1.09
French Canadian (66)	362	0.19
German (2,361)	9,882	5.14
German Russian (0)	0	<0.01
Greek (467)	1,214	0.63
Guyanese (0)	0	<0.01
Hungarian (257)	512	0.27
Icelander (0)	15	0.01
Iranian (5,079)	10,199	5.31
Irish (2,203)	7,669	3.99
Israeli (20)	92	0.05
Italian (2,119)	5,077	2.64
Latvian (0)	10	0.01
Lithuanian (163)	265	0.14
Luxemburger (0)	86	0.04
Macedonian (11)	22	0.01
Maltese (0)	0	<0.01
New Zealander (11)	11	0.01
Northern European (47)	60	0.03
Norwegian (202)	942	0.49
Pennsylvania German (0)	27	0.01
Polish (561)	1,916	1.00
Portuguese (28)	155	0.08
Romanian (471)	576	0.30
Russian (826)	1,837	0.96
Scandinavian (153)	286	0.15
Scotch-Irish (426)	1,306	0.68
Scottish (674)	1,836	0.96
Serbian (55)	67	0.03
Slavic (15)	96	0.05
Slovak (55)	124	0.06
Slovene (0)	0	<0.01
Soviet Union (0)	0	<0.01
Swedish (323)	1,349	0.70
Swiss (34)	231	0.12
Turkish (40)	72	0.04
Ukrainian (319)	541	0.28
Welsh (109)	737	0.38
West Indian, ex. Hispanic (194)	236	0.12
Bahamian (0)	0	<0.01
Barbadian (0)	0	<0.01
Belizean (38)	38	0.02
Bermudan (0)	0	<0.01
British West Indian (15)	31	0.02
Dutch West Indian (0)	0	<0.01
Haitian (61)	70	0.04
Jamaican (80)	97	0.05
Trinidadian/Tobagonian (0)	0	<0.01
U.S. Virgin Islander (0)	0	<0.01
West Indian (0)	0	<0.01
Other West Indian (0)	0	<0.01
Yugoslavian (54)	78	0.04

Hispanic Origin	Population	%
Hispanic or Latino (of any race)	33,414	17.43
Central American, ex. Mexican	6,392	3.33
Costa Rican	145	0.08
Guatemalan	1,723	0.90
Honduran	367	0.19
Nicaraguan	526	0.27
Panamanian	72	0.04
Salvadoran	3,481	1.82
Other Central American	78	0.04
Cuban	1,513	0.79
Dominican Republic	69	0.04
Mexican	19,126	9.98
Puerto Rican	575	0.30
South American	3,287	1.71
Argentinean	539	0.28
Bolivian	150	0.08
Chilean	230	0.12
Colombian	841	0.44
Ecuadorian	542	0.28
Paraguayan	20	0.01
Peruvian	803	0.42
Uruguayan	53	0.03
Venezuelan	82	0.04
Other South American	27	0.01
Other Hispanic or Latino	2,452	1.28

Race*	Population	%
African-American/Black (2,573)	3,445	1.80
Not Hispanic (2,325)	2,932	1.53
Hispanic (248)	513	0.27
American Indian/Alaska Native (531)	1,185	0.62
Not Hispanic (192)	567	0.30
Hispanic (339)	618	0.32
Alaska Athabascan *(Ala. Nat.)* (0)	0	<0.01
Aleut *(Alaska Native)* (0)	4	<0.01
Apache (18)	43	0.02
Arapaho (1)	1	<0.01
Blackfeet (3)	21	0.01
Canadian/French Am. Ind. (1)	1	<0.01
Central American Ind. (14)	16	0.01
Cherokee (21)	122	0.06
Cheyenne (0)	2	<0.01
Chickasaw (0)	7	<0.01
Chippewa (0)	1	<0.01
Choctaw (7)	23	0.01
Colville (1)	1	<0.01
Comanche (5)	8	<0.01
Cree (2)	3	<0.01
Creek (3)	5	<0.01
Crow (0)	0	<0.01
Delaware (1)	1	<0.01
Hopi (7)	20	0.01
Houma (0)	0	<0.01
Inupiat *(Alaska Native)* (0)	0	<0.01
Iroquois (1)	15	0.01
Kiowa (0)	0	<0.01
Lumbee (1)	1	<0.01
Menominee (0)	0	<0.01
Mexican American Ind. (75)	131	0.07
Navajo (31)	46	0.02
Osage (4)	11	0.01
Ottawa (1)	1	<0.01
Paiute (0)	0	<0.01
Pima (1)	3	<0.01
Potawatomi (0)	3	<0.01
Pueblo (5)	14	0.01
Puget Sound Salish (0)	3	<0.01
Seminole (0)	4	<0.01
Shoshone (1)	5	<0.01
Sioux (11)	19	0.01
South American Ind. (9)	27	0.01
Spanish American Ind. (5)	18	0.01
Tlingit-Haida *(Alaska Native)* (2)	4	<0.01
Tohono O'Odham (3)	11	0.01
Tsimshian *(Alaska Native)* (0)	0	<0.01
Ute (0)	1	<0.01
Yakama (0)	3	<0.01
Yaqui (7)	19	0.01
Yuman (1)	1	<0.01
Yup'ik *(Alaska Native)* (0)	0	<0.01
Asian (31,434)	36,832	19.21
Not Hispanic (31,073)	35,949	18.75
Hispanic (361)	883	0.46
Bangladeshi (154)	182	0.09
Bhutanese (0)	0	<0.01
Burmese (34)	41	0.02
Cambodian (32)	51	0.03
Chinese, ex. Taiwanese (2,313)	3,008	1.57
Filipino (13,238)	14,442	7.53
Hmong (0)	1	<0.01
Indian (1,747)	1,996	1.04
Indonesian (77)	137	0.07
Japanese (1,222)	1,785	0.93
Korean (10,315)	10,650	5.56
Laotian (23)	33	0.02
Malaysian (8)	10	0.01
Nepalese (6)	6	<0.01
Pakistani (111)	141	0.07
Sri Lankan (44)	49	0.03
Taiwanese (122)	136	0.07
Thai (525)	592	0.31
Vietnamese (686)	807	0.42
Hawaii Native/Pacific Islander (122)	915	0.48
Not Hispanic (105)	835	0.44
Hispanic (17)	80	0.04
Fijian (5)	9	<0.01
Guamanian/Chamorro (31)	64	0.03
Marshallese (1)	2	<0.01
Native Hawaiian (52)	170	0.09
Samoan (4)	17	0.01
Tongan (2)	5	<0.01
White (136,226)	144,049	75.14
Not Hispanic (117,929)	123,773	64.56
Hispanic (18,297)	20,276	10.58

*Notes: † The Census 2010 population figure is used to calculate the percentages in the Hispanic Origin and Race categories. Ancestry percentages are based on the 2006-2010 American Community Survey population (not shown); ‡ Numbers in parentheses indicate the number of people reporting a single ancestry; * Numbers in parentheses indicate the number of persons reporting this race alone, not in combination with any other race; Please refer to the Explanation of Data for more information.*

Glendora

Place Type: City
County: Los Angeles
Population: 50,073

Ancestry	Population	%
Afghan (0)	0	<0.01
African, Sub-Saharan (39)	39	0.08
African (14)	14	0.03
Cape Verdean (0)	0	<0.01
Ethiopian (12)	12	0.02
Ghanaian (0)	0	<0.01
Kenyan (0)	0	<0.01
Liberian (0)	0	<0.01
Nigerian (13)	13	0.03
Senegalese (0)	0	<0.01
Sierra Leonean (0)	0	<0.01
Somalian (0)	0	<0.01
South African (0)	0	<0.01
Sudanese (0)	0	<0.01
Ugandan (0)	0	<0.01
Zimbabwean (0)	0	<0.01
Other Sub-Saharan African (0)	0	<0.01
Albanian (0)	0	<0.01
Alsatian (0)	0	<0.01
American (1,867)	1,867	3.74
Arab (1,048)	1,087	2.18
Arab (112)	112	0.22
Egyptian (136)	161	0.32
Iraqi (0)	0	<0.01
Jordanian (0)	0	<0.01
Lebanese (455)	455	0.91
Moroccan (0)	0	<0.01
Palestinian (4)	4	0.01
Syrian (269)	283	0.57
Other Arab (72)	72	0.14
Armenian (192)	315	0.63
Assyrian/Chaldean/Syriac (33)	33	0.07
Australian (13)	13	0.03
Austrian (38)	79	0.16
Basque (52)	106	0.21
Belgian (0)	15	0.03
Brazilian (0)	0	<0.01
British (59)	160	0.32
Bulgarian (0)	0	<0.01
Cajun (0)	18	0.04
Canadian (139)	245	0.49
Carpatho Rusyn (0)	0	<0.01
Celtic (15)	66	0.13
Croatian (31)	40	0.08
Cypriot (0)	0	<0.01
Czech (132)	325	0.65
Czechoslovakian (15)	26	0.05
Danish (115)	481	0.96
Dutch (216)	1,481	2.97
Eastern European (16)	16	0.03
English (1,362)	4,870	9.76
Estonian (0)	0	<0.01
European (495)	736	1.48
Finnish (0)	39	0.08
French, ex. Basque (144)	1,500	3.01
French Canadian (87)	159	0.32
German (2,077)	7,755	15.55
German Russian (0)	0	<0.01
Greek (107)	325	0.65
Guyanese (0)	0	<0.01
Hungarian (120)	247	0.50
Icelander (0)	10	0.02
Iranian (130)	135	0.27
Irish (1,113)	4,549	9.12
Israeli (0)	0	<0.01
Italian (1,476)	4,208	8.44
Latvian (0)	0	<0.01
Lithuanian (0)	49	0.10
Luxemburger (0)	0	<0.01
Macedonian (0)	0	<0.01
Maltese (10)	10	0.02
New Zealander (0)	0	<0.01
Northern European (28)	65	0.13
Norwegian (175)	735	1.47
Pennsylvania German (6)	54	0.11
Polish (371)	1,096	2.20
Portuguese (56)	170	0.34
Romanian (55)	75	0.15
Russian (231)	475	0.95
Scandinavian (38)	223	0.45
Scotch-Irish (340)	927	1.86
Scottish (328)	1,354	2.71
Serbian (23)	23	0.05
Slavic (10)	62	0.12
Slovak (22)	80	0.16
Slovene (9)	9	0.02
Soviet Union (0)	0	<0.01
Swedish (236)	758	1.52
Swiss (46)	74	0.15
Turkish (75)	75	0.15
Ukrainian (41)	137	0.27
Welsh (105)	297	0.60
West Indian, ex. Hispanic (77)	90	0.18
Bahamian (0)	0	<0.01
Barbadian (0)	0	<0.01
Belizean (0)	0	<0.01
Bermudan (0)	0	<0.01
British West Indian (0)	0	<0.01
Dutch West Indian (0)	0	<0.01
Haitian (0)	0	<0.01
Jamaican (65)	65	0.13
Trinidadian/Tobagonian (0)	0	<0.01
U.S. Virgin Islander (0)	0	<0.01
West Indian (12)	25	0.05
Other West Indian (0)	0	<0.01
Yugoslavian (23)	128	0.26

Hispanic Origin	Population	%
Hispanic or Latino (of any race)	15,348	30.65
Central American, ex. Mexican	898	1.79
Costa Rican	49	0.10
Guatemalan	205	0.41
Honduran	39	0.08
Nicaraguan	175	0.35
Panamanian	18	0.04
Salvadoran	401	0.80
Other Central American	11	0.02
Cuban	259	0.52
Dominican Republic	16	0.03
Mexican	12,151	24.27
Puerto Rican	274	0.55
South American	622	1.24
Argentinean	142	0.28
Bolivian	25	0.05
Chilean	50	0.10
Colombian	148	0.30
Ecuadorian	83	0.17
Paraguayan	2	<0.01
Peruvian	148	0.30
Uruguayan	3	0.01
Venezuelan	11	0.02
Other South American	10	0.02
Other Hispanic or Latino	1,128	2.25

Race*	Population	%
African-American/Black (930)	1,278	2.55
Not Hispanic (834)	1,068	2.13
Hispanic (96)	210	0.42
American Indian/Alaska Native (345)	759	1.52
Not Hispanic (102)	315	0.63
Hispanic (243)	444	0.89
Alaska Athabascan *(Ala. Nat.)* (0)	0	<0.01
Aleut *(Alaska Native)* (1)	2	<0.01
Apache (23)	49	0.10
Arapaho (0)	2	<0.01
Blackfeet (0)	10	0.02
Canadian/French Am. Ind. (0)	1	<0.01
Central American Ind. (3)	4	0.01
Cherokee (15)	95	0.19
Cheyenne (0)	5	0.01
Chickasaw (0)	2	<0.01
Chippewa (3)	6	0.01
Choctaw (1)	15	0.03
Colville (0)	0	<0.01
Comanche (2)	9	0.02
Cree (0)	2	<0.01
Creek (2)	4	0.01
Crow (0)	0	<0.01
Delaware (0)	1	<0.01
Hopi (1)	3	0.01
Houma (0)	0	<0.01
Inupiat *(Alaska Native)* (0)	0	<0.01
Iroquois (4)	13	0.03
Kiowa (0)	0	<0.01
Lumbee (0)	0	<0.01
Menominee (0)	0	<0.01
Mexican American Ind. (35)	48	0.10
Navajo (11)	28	0.06
Osage (0)	1	<0.01
Ottawa (1)	2	<0.01
Paiute (3)	5	0.01
Pima (1)	4	0.01
Potawatomi (0)	2	<0.01
Pueblo (2)	3	0.01
Puget Sound Salish (0)	0	<0.01
Seminole (0)	1	<0.01
Shoshone (1)	1	<0.01
Sioux (10)	14	0.03
South American Ind. (0)	3	0.01
Spanish American Ind. (6)	6	0.01
Tlingit-Haida *(Alaska Native)* (0)	0	<0.01
Tohono O'Odham (7)	12	0.02
Tsimshian *(Alaska Native)* (0)	0	<0.01
Ute (0)	3	0.01
Yakama (0)	0	<0.01
Yaqui (12)	21	0.04
Yuman (2)	5	0.01
Yup'ik *(Alaska Native)* (0)	0	<0.01
Asian (3,999)	4,980	9.95
Not Hispanic (3,898)	4,634	9.25
Hispanic (101)	346	0.69
Bangladeshi (10)	12	0.02
Bhutanese (0)	0	<0.01
Burmese (3)	6	0.01
Cambodian (18)	26	0.05
Chinese, ex. Taiwanese (944)	1,207	2.41
Filipino (1,352)	1,694	3.38
Hmong (15)	15	0.03
Indian (499)	548	1.09
Indonesian (76)	149	0.30
Japanese (303)	564	1.13
Korean (185)	237	0.47
Laotian (3)	8	0.02
Malaysian (1)	2	<0.01
Nepalese (0)	4	0.01
Pakistani (29)	36	0.07
Sri Lankan (21)	28	0.06
Taiwanese (116)	137	0.27
Thai (80)	95	0.19
Vietnamese (159)	221	0.44
Hawaii Native/Pacific Islander (52)	222	0.44
Not Hispanic (42)	183	0.37
Hispanic (10)	39	0.08
Fijian (1)	1	<0.01
Guamanian/Chamorro (6)	11	0.02
Marshallese (0)	0	<0.01
Native Hawaiian (22)	102	0.20
Samoan (7)	35	0.07
Tongan (1)	5	0.01
White (37,582)	39,711	79.31
Not Hispanic (28,565)	29,628	59.17
Hispanic (9,017)	10,083	20.14

*Notes: † The Census 2010 population figure is used to calculate the percentages in the Hispanic Origin and Race categories. Ancestry percentages are based on the 2006-2010 American Community Survey population (not shown); ‡ Numbers in parentheses indicate the number of people reporting a single ancestry; * Numbers in parentheses indicate the number of persons reporting this race alone, not in combination with any other race; Please refer to the Explanation of Data for more information.*

Hacienda Heights

Place Type: CDP
County: Los Angeles
Population: 54,038

Ancestry	Population	%
Afghan (0)	0	<0.01
African, Sub-Saharan (30)	30	0.06
African (30)	30	0.06
Cape Verdean (0)	0	<0.01
Ethiopian (0)	0	<0.01
Ghanaian (0)	0	<0.01
Kenyan (0)	0	<0.01
Liberian (0)	0	<0.01
Nigerian (0)	0	<0.01
Senegalese (0)	0	<0.01
Sierra Leonean (0)	0	<0.01
Somalian (0)	0	<0.01
South African (0)	0	<0.01
Sudanese (0)	0	<0.01
Ugandan (0)	0	<0.01
Zimbabwean (0)	0	<0.01
Other Sub-Saharan African (0)	0	<0.01
Albanian (0)	0	<0.01
Alsatian (0)	0	<0.01
American (1,338)	1,338	2.49
Arab (235)	260	0.48
Arab (82)	82	0.15
Egyptian (143)	143	0.27
Iraqi (0)	0	<0.01
Jordanian (0)	0	<0.01
Lebanese (0)	25	0.05
Moroccan (0)	0	<0.01
Palestinian (0)	0	<0.01
Syrian (0)	0	<0.01
Other Arab (10)	10	0.02
Armenian (146)	173	0.32
Assyrian/Chaldean/Syriac (0)	0	<0.01
Australian (0)	7	0.01
Austrian (18)	74	0.14
Basque (0)	0	<0.01
Belgian (0)	6	0.01
Brazilian (11)	11	0.02
British (10)	10	0.02
Bulgarian (0)	0	<0.01
Cajun (47)	47	0.09
Canadian (83)	147	0.27
Carpatho Rusyn (0)	0	<0.01
Celtic (0)	11	0.02
Croatian (10)	50	0.09
Cypriot (0)	0	<0.01
Czech (0)	50	0.09
Czechoslovakian (15)	26	0.05
Danish (17)	75	0.14
Dutch (37)	429	0.80
Eastern European (7)	7	0.01
English (316)	1,152	2.15
Estonian (21)	21	0.04
European (150)	196	0.37
Finnish (19)	113	0.21
French, ex. Basque (33)	367	0.68
French Canadian (17)	54	0.10
German (638)	2,335	4.35
German Russian (0)	0	<0.01
Greek (188)	229	0.43
Guyanese (0)	0	<0.01
Hungarian (25)	51	0.10
Icelander (0)	0	<0.01
Iranian (113)	126	0.23
Irish (258)	1,584	2.95
Israeli (0)	0	<0.01
Italian (406)	1,068	1.99
Latvian (11)	11	0.02
Lithuanian (0)	0	<0.01
Luxemburger (0)	0	<0.01
Macedonian (0)	0	<0.01
Maltese (0)	0	<0.01
New Zealander (0)	0	<0.01
Northern European (7)	7	0.01
Norwegian (53)	134	0.25
Pennsylvania German (0)	0	<0.01
Polish (151)	373	0.70
Portuguese (59)	114	0.21
Romanian (28)	38	0.07
Russian (194)	250	0.47
Scandinavian (27)	39	0.07
Scotch-Irish (57)	275	0.51
Scottish (156)	418	0.78
Serbian (0)	0	<0.01
Slavic (0)	15	0.03
Slovak (8)	19	0.04
Slovene (0)	8	0.01
Soviet Union (0)	0	<0.01
Swedish (70)	401	0.75
Swiss (0)	31	0.06
Turkish (0)	0	<0.01
Ukrainian (35)	63	0.12
Welsh (13)	62	0.12
West Indian, ex. Hispanic (90)	113	0.21
Bahamian (0)	0	<0.01
Barbadian (0)	0	<0.01
Belizean (15)	38	0.07
Bermudan (0)	0	<0.01
British West Indian (0)	0	<0.01
Dutch West Indian (0)	0	<0.01
Haitian (46)	46	0.09
Jamaican (0)	0	<0.01
Trinidadian/Tobagonian (0)	0	<0.01
U.S. Virgin Islander (0)	0	<0.01
West Indian (29)	29	0.05
Other West Indian (0)	0	<0.01
Yugoslavian (12)	12	0.02

Hispanic Origin	Population	%
Hispanic or Latino (of any race)	24,608	45.54
Central American, ex. Mexican	1,511	2.80
Costa Rican	64	0.12
Guatemalan	378	0.70
Honduran	69	0.13
Nicaraguan	157	0.29
Panamanian	12	0.02
Salvadoran	807	1.49
Other Central American	24	0.04
Cuban	157	0.29
Dominican Republic	6	0.01
Mexican	20,994	38.85
Puerto Rican	215	0.40
South American	660	1.22
Argentinean	117	0.22
Bolivian	30	0.06
Chilean	31	0.06
Colombian	142	0.26
Ecuadorian	135	0.25
Paraguayan	1	<0.01
Peruvian	182	0.34
Uruguayan	7	0.01
Venezuelan	11	0.02
Other South American	4	0.01
Other Hispanic or Latino	1,065	1.97

Race*	Population	%
African-American/Black (743)	916	1.70
Not Hispanic (644)	726	1.34
Hispanic (99)	190	0.35
American Indian/Alaska Native (315)	567	1.05
Not Hispanic (69)	175	0.32
Hispanic (246)	392	0.73
Alaska Athabascan *(Ala. Nat.)* (0)	0	<0.01
Aleut *(Alaska Native)* (0)	0	<0.01
Apache (13)	37	0.07
Arapaho (0)	0	<0.01
Blackfeet (4)	10	0.02
Canadian/French Am. Ind. (0)	2	<0.01
Central American Ind. (0)	0	<0.01
Cherokee (4)	33	0.06
Cheyenne (1)	1	<0.01
Chickasaw (0)	4	0.01
Chippewa (9)	9	0.02
Choctaw (2)	7	0.01
Colville (0)	1	<0.01
Comanche (0)	0	<0.01
Cree (0)	1	<0.01
Creek (0)	4	0.01
Crow (0)	0	<0.01
Delaware (1)	1	<0.01
Hopi (5)	5	0.01
Houma (0)	0	<0.01
Inupiat *(Alaska Native)* (1)	1	<0.01
Iroquois (2)	4	0.01
Kiowa (1)	1	<0.01
Lumbee (0)	0	<0.01
Menominee (0)	0	<0.01
Mexican American Ind. (52)	67	0.12
Navajo (11)	17	0.03
Osage (1)	1	<0.01
Ottawa (0)	0	<0.01
Paiute (2)	3	0.01
Pima (1)	4	0.01
Potawatomi (0)	0	<0.01
Pueblo (6)	12	0.02
Puget Sound Salish (1)	1	<0.01
Seminole (0)	2	<0.01
Shoshone (3)	3	0.01
Sioux (0)	0	<0.01
South American Ind. (2)	5	0.01
Spanish American Ind. (8)	15	0.03
Tlingit-Haida *(Alaska Native)* (1)	1	<0.01
Tohono O'Odham (5)	10	0.02
Tsimshian *(Alaska Native)* (0)	0	<0.01
Ute (5)	5	0.01
Yakama (0)	0	<0.01
Yaqui (3)	7	0.01
Yuman (0)	0	<0.01
Yup'ik *(Alaska Native)* (5)	5	0.01
Asian (20,065)	20,891	38.66
Not Hispanic (19,878)	20,414	37.78
Hispanic (187)	477	0.88
Bangladeshi (7)	9	0.02
Bhutanese (0)	0	<0.01
Burmese (49)	57	0.11
Cambodian (96)	115	0.21
Chinese, ex. Taiwanese (10,497)	11,348	21.00
Filipino (1,212)	1,504	2.78
Hmong (8)	8	0.01
Indian (265)	319	0.59
Indonesian (147)	205	0.38
Japanese (1,158)	1,449	2.68
Korean (2,483)	2,609	4.83
Laotian (43)	47	0.09
Malaysian (19)	39	0.07
Nepalese (0)	0	<0.01
Pakistani (41)	42	0.08
Sri Lankan (5)	9	0.02
Taiwanese (2,547)	2,944	5.45
Thai (231)	287	0.53
Vietnamese (417)	563	1.04
Hawaii Native/Pacific Islander (99)	290	0.54
Not Hispanic (63)	212	0.39
Hispanic (36)	78	0.14
Fijian (4)	7	0.01
Guamanian/Chamorro (7)	11	0.02
Marshallese (0)	0	<0.01
Native Hawaiian (30)	69	0.13
Samoan (29)	47	0.09
Tongan (19)	20	0.04
White (21,873)	23,196	42.93
Not Hispanic (8,035)	8,495	15.72
Hispanic (13,838)	14,701	27.20

*Notes: † The Census 2010 population figure is used to calculate the percentages in the Hispanic Origin and Race categories. Ancestry percentages are based on the 2006-2010 American Community Survey population (not shown); ‡ Numbers in parentheses indicate the number of people reporting a single ancestry; * Numbers in parentheses indicate the number of persons reporting this race alone, not in combination with any other race; Please refer to the Explanation of Data for more information.*

Hanford

Place Type: City
County: Kings
Population: 53,967

Ancestry	Population	%
Afghan (0)	0	<0.01
African, Sub-Saharan (252)	287	0.55
African (130)	165	0.32
Cape Verdean (0)	0	<0.01
Ethiopian (28)	28	0.05
Ghanaian (0)	0	<0.01
Kenyan (0)	0	<0.01
Liberian (0)	0	<0.01
Nigerian (0)	0	<0.01
Senegalese (0)	0	<0.01
Sierra Leonean (0)	0	<0.01
Somalian (0)	0	<0.01
South African (0)	0	<0.01
Sudanese (0)	0	<0.01
Ugandan (0)	0	<0.01
Zimbabwean (0)	0	<0.01
Other Sub-Saharan African (94)	94	0.18
Albanian (0)	0	<0.01
Alsatian (0)	0	<0.01
American (1,723)	1,723	3.29
Arab (160)	177	0.34
Arab (41)	41	0.08
Egyptian (7)	7	0.01
Iraqi (0)	0	<0.01
Jordanian (0)	0	<0.01
Lebanese (4)	21	0.04
Moroccan (0)	0	<0.01
Palestinian (0)	0	<0.01
Syrian (0)	0	<0.01
Other Arab (108)	108	0.21
Armenian (10)	19	0.04
Assyrian/Chaldean/Syriac (0)	0	<0.01
Australian (19)	29	0.06
Austrian (14)	27	0.05
Basque (27)	65	0.12
Belgian (0)	33	0.06
Brazilian (0)	0	<0.01
British (38)	98	0.19
Bulgarian (0)	0	<0.01
Cajun (8)	13	0.02
Canadian (54)	54	0.10
Carpatho Rusyn (0)	0	<0.01
Celtic (45)	45	0.09
Croatian (26)	32	0.06
Cypriot (0)	0	<0.01
Czech (0)	123	0.24
Czechoslovakian (14)	53	0.10
Danish (68)	245	0.47
Dutch (415)	1,162	2.22
Eastern European (0)	0	<0.01
English (1,228)	3,523	6.73
Estonian (0)	0	<0.01
European (487)	551	1.05
Finnish (17)	176	0.34
French, ex. Basque (187)	944	1.80
French Canadian (10)	39	0.07
German (1,412)	4,900	9.37
German Russian (0)	0	<0.01
Greek (39)	150	0.29
Guyanese (0)	20	0.04
Hungarian (18)	74	0.14
Icelander (0)	0	<0.01
Iranian (0)	0	<0.01
Irish (1,196)	3,870	7.40
Israeli (0)	0	<0.01
Italian (618)	1,825	3.49
Latvian (0)	0	<0.01
Lithuanian (0)	0	<0.01
Luxemburger (0)	0	<0.01
Macedonian (0)	0	<0.01
Maltese (0)	0	<0.01
New Zealander (0)	57	0.11
Northern European (48)	48	0.09
Norwegian (36)	244	0.47
Pennsylvania German (0)	0	<0.01
Polish (91)	299	0.57
Portuguese (2,268)	3,147	6.02
Romanian (8)	8	0.02
Russian (21)	80	0.15
Scandinavian (0)	0	<0.01
Scotch-Irish (225)	852	1.63
Scottish (186)	550	1.05
Serbian (0)	0	<0.01
Slavic (0)	0	<0.01
Slovak (18)	18	0.03
Slovene (0)	0	<0.01
Soviet Union (0)	0	<0.01
Swedish (68)	402	0.77
Swiss (31)	102	0.19
Turkish (16)	16	0.03
Ukrainian (12)	12	0.02
Welsh (10)	270	0.52
West Indian, ex. Hispanic (35)	63	0.12
Bahamian (0)	0	<0.01
Barbadian (19)	19	0.04
Belizean (0)	0	<0.01
Bermudan (0)	0	<0.01
British West Indian (0)	0	<0.01
Dutch West Indian (0)	28	0.05
Haitian (0)	0	<0.01
Jamaican (0)	0	<0.01
Trinidadian/Tobagonian (16)	16	0.03
U.S. Virgin Islander (0)	0	<0.01
West Indian (0)	0	<0.01
Other West Indian (0)	0	<0.01
Yugoslavian (0)	14	0.03

Hispanic Origin	Population	%
Hispanic or Latino (of any race)	25,419	47.10
Central American, ex. Mexican	282	0.52
Costa Rican	7	0.01
Guatemalan	60	0.11
Honduran	47	0.09
Nicaraguan	36	0.07
Panamanian	15	0.03
Salvadoran	117	0.22
Other Central American	0	<0.01
Cuban	40	0.07
Dominican Republic	16	0.03
Mexican	23,269	43.12
Puerto Rican	180	0.33
South American	93	0.17
Argentinean	8	0.01
Bolivian	11	0.02
Chilean	7	0.01
Colombian	18	0.03
Ecuadorian	10	0.02
Paraguayan	1	<0.01
Peruvian	36	0.07
Uruguayan	0	<0.01
Venezuelan	2	<0.01
Other South American	0	<0.01
Other Hispanic or Latino	1,539	2.85

Race*	Population	%
African-American/Black (2,632)	3,320	6.15
Not Hispanic (2,367)	2,837	5.26
Hispanic (265)	483	0.89
American Indian/Alaska Native (712)	1,247	2.31
Not Hispanic (331)	612	1.13
Hispanic (381)	635	1.18
Alaska Athabascan *(Ala. Nat.)* (0)	0	<0.01
Aleut *(Alaska Native)* (0)	0	<0.01
Apache (24)	58	0.11
Arapaho (2)	4	0.01
Blackfeet (4)	15	0.03
Canadian/French Am. Ind. (0)	6	0.01
Central American Ind. (0)	0	<0.01
Cherokee (57)	185	0.34
Cheyenne (0)	0	<0.01
Chickasaw (3)	6	0.01
Chippewa (6)	6	0.01
Choctaw (33)	45	0.08
Colville (0)	0	<0.01
Comanche (2)	2	<0.01
Cree (2)	5	0.01
Creek (8)	13	0.02
Crow (1)	1	<0.01
Delaware (0)	1	<0.01
Hopi (1)	3	0.01
Houma (0)	0	<0.01
Inupiat *(Alaska Native)* (0)	0	<0.01
Iroquois (4)	5	0.01
Kiowa (0)	0	<0.01
Lumbee (0)	1	<0.01
Menominee (0)	0	<0.01
Mexican American Ind. (63)	75	0.14
Navajo (14)	26	0.05
Osage (0)	3	0.01
Ottawa (0)	1	<0.01
Paiute (3)	5	0.01
Pima (23)	25	0.05
Potawatomi (0)	0	<0.01
Pueblo (0)	2	<0.01
Puget Sound Salish (2)	2	<0.01
Seminole (0)	0	<0.01
Shoshone (5)	7	0.01
Sioux (4)	12	0.02
South American Ind. (1)	1	<0.01
Spanish American Ind. (1)	1	<0.01
Tlingit-Haida *(Alaska Native)* (1)	2	<0.01
Tohono O'Odham (2)	3	0.01
Tsimshian *(Alaska Native)* (0)	0	<0.01
Ute (1)	2	<0.01
Yakama (0)	0	<0.01
Yaqui (12)	22	0.04
Yuman (0)	0	<0.01
Yup'ik *(Alaska Native)* (0)	0	<0.01
Asian (2,322)	3,071	5.69
Not Hispanic (2,205)	2,738	5.07
Hispanic (117)	333	0.62
Bangladeshi (2)	4	0.01
Bhutanese (0)	0	<0.01
Burmese (0)	0	<0.01
Cambodian (33)	40	0.07
Chinese, ex. Taiwanese (214)	317	0.59
Filipino (1,354)	1,751	3.24
Hmong (104)	126	0.23
Indian (217)	274	0.51
Indonesian (7)	8	0.01
Japanese (117)	238	0.44
Korean (41)	72	0.13
Laotian (26)	38	0.07
Malaysian (0)	1	<0.01
Nepalese (0)	0	<0.01
Pakistani (18)	23	0.04
Sri Lankan (4)	5	0.01
Taiwanese (3)	4	0.01
Thai (15)	27	0.05
Vietnamese (66)	104	0.19
Hawaii Native/Pacific Islander (53)	205	0.38
Not Hispanic (43)	150	0.28
Hispanic (10)	55	0.10
Fijian (0)	0	<0.01
Guamanian/Chamorro (8)	18	0.03
Marshallese (3)	3	0.01
Native Hawaiian (19)	79	0.15
Samoan (8)	17	0.03
Tongan (0)	0	<0.01
White (33,713)	36,283	67.23
Not Hispanic (22,205)	23,331	43.23
Hispanic (11,508)	12,952	24.00

*Notes: † The Census 2010 population figure is used to calculate the percentages in the Hispanic Origin and Race categories. Ancestry percentages are based on the 2006-2010 American Community Survey population (not shown); ‡ Numbers in parentheses indicate the number of people reporting a single ancestry; * Numbers in parentheses indicate the number of persons reporting this race alone, not in combination with any other race; Please refer to the Explanation of Data for more information.*

Hawthorne

Place Type: City
County: Los Angeles
Population: 84,293

Ancestry	Population	%
Afghan (113)	113	0.13
African, Sub-Saharan (2,260)	2,790	3.31
African (1,323)	1,719	2.04
Cape Verdean (0)	0	<0.01
Ethiopian (409)	409	0.49
Ghanaian (69)	69	0.08
Kenyan (5)	5	0.01
Liberian (0)	0	<0.01
Nigerian (325)	447	0.53
Senegalese (0)	0	<0.01
Sierra Leonean (27)	27	0.03
Somalian (0)	0	<0.01
South African (0)	12	0.01
Sudanese (102)	102	0.12
Ugandan (0)	0	<0.01
Zimbabwean (0)	0	<0.01
Other Sub-Saharan African (0)	0	<0.01
Albanian (0)	9	0.01
Alsatian (0)	0	<0.01
American (12,456)	12,456	14.79
Arab (595)	717	0.85
Arab (54)	78	0.09
Egyptian (305)	329	0.39
Iraqi (0)	0	<0.01
Jordanian (7)	7	0.01
Lebanese (0)	49	0.06
Moroccan (33)	33	0.04
Palestinian (89)	89	0.11
Syrian (0)	25	0.03
Other Arab (107)	107	0.13
Armenian (78)	87	0.10
Assyrian/Chaldean/Syriac (22)	22	0.03
Australian (0)	0	<0.01
Austrian (0)	21	0.02
Basque (0)	0	<0.01
Belgian (0)	0	<0.01
Brazilian (97)	108	0.13
British (72)	78	0.09
Bulgarian (0)	0	<0.01
Cajun (0)	0	<0.01
Canadian (12)	32	0.04
Carpatho Rusyn (0)	0	<0.01
Celtic (0)	0	<0.01
Croatian (0)	12	0.01
Cypriot (0)	0	<0.01
Czech (22)	99	0.12
Czechoslovakian (0)	6	0.01
Danish (0)	80	0.10
Dutch (41)	230	0.27
Eastern European (0)	0	<0.01
English (212)	984	1.17
Estonian (0)	0	<0.01
European (145)	238	0.28
Finnish (0)	0	<0.01
French, ex. Basque (66)	301	0.36
French Canadian (44)	101	0.12
German (532)	1,993	2.37
German Russian (0)	0	<0.01
Greek (32)	58	0.07
Guyanese (0)	0	<0.01
Hungarian (44)	126	0.15
Icelander (0)	26	0.03
Iranian (64)	64	0.08
Irish (136)	1,248	1.48
Israeli (0)	0	<0.01
Italian (386)	878	1.04
Latvian (0)	0	<0.01
Lithuanian (0)	9	0.01
Luxemburger (9)	17	0.02
Macedonian (0)	0	<0.01
Maltese (0)	0	<0.01
New Zealander (17)	17	0.02
Northern European (22)	22	0.03
Norwegian (0)	28	0.03
Pennsylvania German (0)	0	<0.01
Polish (52)	298	0.35
Portuguese (18)	129	0.15
Romanian (21)	21	0.02
Russian (21)	132	0.16
Scandinavian (11)	53	0.06
Scotch-Irish (53)	152	0.18
Scottish (17)	117	0.14
Serbian (29)	29	0.03
Slavic (0)	0	<0.01
Slovak (0)	11	0.01
Slovene (0)	0	<0.01
Soviet Union (0)	0	<0.01
Swedish (33)	270	0.32
Swiss (0)	43	0.05
Turkish (10)	10	0.01
Ukrainian (34)	48	0.06
Welsh (0)	24	0.03
West Indian, ex. Hispanic (556)	645	0.77
Bahamian (0)	0	<0.01
Barbadian (0)	0	<0.01
Belizean (292)	341	0.41
Bermudan (0)	0	<0.01
British West Indian (0)	0	<0.01
Dutch West Indian (0)	0	<0.01
Haitian (42)	42	0.05
Jamaican (183)	201	0.24
Trinidadian/Tobagonian (0)	22	0.03
U.S. Virgin Islander (0)	0	<0.01
West Indian (39)	39	0.05
Other West Indian (0)	0	<0.01
Yugoslavian (0)	0	<0.01

Hispanic Origin	Population	%
Hispanic or Latino (of any race)	44,572	52.88
Central American, ex. Mexican	8,547	10.14
Costa Rican	169	0.20
Guatemalan	3,669	4.35
Honduran	584	0.69
Nicaraguan	556	0.66
Panamanian	130	0.15
Salvadoran	3,335	3.96
Other Central American	104	0.12
Cuban	752	0.89
Dominican Republic	55	0.07
Mexican	29,371	34.84
Puerto Rican	689	0.82
South American	1,826	2.17
Argentinean	123	0.15
Bolivian	31	0.04
Chilean	61	0.07
Colombian	487	0.58
Ecuadorian	280	0.33
Paraguayan	3	<0.01
Peruvian	768	0.91
Uruguayan	29	0.03
Venezuelan	29	0.03
Other South American	15	0.02
Other Hispanic or Latino	3,332	3.95

Race*	Population	%
African-American/Black (23,385)	24,674	29.27
Not Hispanic (22,579)	23,386	27.74
Hispanic (806)	1,288	1.53
American Indian/Alaska Native (565)	1,214	1.44
Not Hispanic (172)	449	0.53
Hispanic (393)	765	0.91
Alaska Athabascan *(Ala. Nat.)* (0)	0	<0.01
Aleut *(Alaska Native)* (0)	0	<0.01
Apache (15)	34	0.04
Arapaho (0)	1	<0.01
Blackfeet (4)	36	0.04
Canadian/French Am. Ind. (1)	2	<0.01
Central American Ind. (6)	20	0.02
Cherokee (26)	95	0.11
Cheyenne (0)	0	<0.01
Chickasaw (0)	5	0.01
Chippewa (2)	8	0.01
Choctaw (1)	28	0.03
Colville (1)	3	<0.01
Comanche (5)	8	0.01
Cree (0)	0	<0.01
Creek (0)	5	0.01
Crow (0)	0	<0.01
Delaware (0)	1	<0.01
Hopi (2)	2	<0.01
Houma (0)	0	<0.01
Inupiat *(Alaska Native)* (0)	4	<0.01
Iroquois (1)	9	0.01
Kiowa (0)	0	<0.01
Lumbee (0)	0	<0.01
Menominee (0)	0	<0.01
Mexican American Ind. (130)	203	0.24
Navajo (13)	23	0.03
Osage (0)	3	<0.01
Ottawa (0)	0	<0.01
Paiute (0)	0	<0.01
Pima (1)	7	0.01
Potawatomi (0)	0	<0.01
Pueblo (7)	15	0.02
Puget Sound Salish (0)	0	<0.01
Seminole (0)	18	0.02
Shoshone (0)	1	<0.01
Sioux (11)	17	0.02
South American Ind. (6)	22	0.03
Spanish American Ind. (7)	13	0.02
Tlingit-Haida *(Alaska Native)* (0)	0	<0.01
Tohono O'Odham (3)	4	<0.01
Tsimshian *(Alaska Native)* (0)	0	<0.01
Ute (2)	2	<0.01
Yakama (0)	0	<0.01
Yaqui (9)	16	0.02
Yuman (0)	4	<0.01
Yup'ik *(Alaska Native)* (0)	0	<0.01
Asian (5,642)	6,624	7.86
Not Hispanic (5,492)	6,203	7.36
Hispanic (150)	421	0.50
Bangladeshi (31)	31	0.04
Bhutanese (0)	0	<0.01
Burmese (31)	34	0.04
Cambodian (21)	28	0.03
Chinese, ex. Taiwanese (392)	583	0.69
Filipino (2,317)	2,697	3.20
Hmong (1)	1	<0.01
Indian (519)	663	0.79
Indonesian (36)	67	0.08
Japanese (339)	533	0.63
Korean (308)	363	0.43
Laotian (2)	2	<0.01
Malaysian (2)	5	0.01
Nepalese (13)	13	0.02
Pakistani (246)	288	0.34
Sri Lankan (29)	36	0.04
Taiwanese (18)	26	0.03
Thai (63)	77	0.09
Vietnamese (1,058)	1,136	1.35
Hawaii Native/Pacific Islander (974)	1,337	1.59
Not Hispanic (919)	1,176	1.40
Hispanic (55)	161	0.19
Fijian (108)	126	0.15
Guamanian/Chamorro (33)	42	0.05
Marshallese (0)	0	<0.01
Native Hawaiian (51)	164	0.19
Samoan (123)	214	0.25
Tongan (575)	656	0.78
White (27,678)	30,467	36.14
Not Hispanic (8,642)	9,609	11.40
Hispanic (19,036)	20,858	24.74

*Notes: † The Census 2010 population figure is used to calculate the percentages in the Hispanic Origin and Race categories. Ancestry percentages are based on the 2006-2010 American Community Survey population (not shown); ‡ Numbers in parentheses indicate the number of people reporting a single ancestry; * Numbers in parentheses indicate the number of persons reporting this race alone, not in combination with any other race; Please refer to the Explanation of Data for more information.*

Hayward

Place Type: City
County: Alameda
Population: 144,186

Ancestry	Population	%
Afghan (798)	826	0.58
African, Sub-Saharan (1,732)	1,985	1.40
African (682)	840	0.59
Cape Verdean (0)	0	<0.01
Ethiopian (260)	331	0.23
Ghanaian (43)	43	0.03
Kenyan (54)	66	0.05
Liberian (129)	129	0.09
Nigerian (543)	543	0.38
Senegalese (0)	0	<0.01
Sierra Leonean (0)	0	<0.01
Somalian (0)	0	<0.01
South African (0)	0	<0.01
Sudanese (0)	0	<0.01
Ugandan (21)	21	0.01
Zimbabwean (0)	0	<0.01
Other Sub-Saharan African (0)	12	0.01
Albanian (0)	0	<0.01
Alsatian (0)	0	<0.01
American (1,373)	1,373	0.97
Arab (500)	580	0.41
Arab (157)	157	0.11
Egyptian (140)	140	0.10
Iraqi (15)	15	0.01
Jordanian (0)	0	<0.01
Lebanese (0)	9	0.01
Moroccan (0)	0	<0.01
Palestinian (150)	165	0.12
Syrian (21)	77	0.05
Other Arab (17)	17	0.01
Armenian (63)	119	0.08
Assyrian/Chaldean/Syriac (0)	0	<0.01
Australian (9)	31	0.02
Austrian (13)	79	0.06
Basque (10)	17	0.01
Belgian (17)	61	0.04
Brazilian (28)	75	0.05
British (159)	357	0.25
Bulgarian (0)	12	0.01
Cajun (0)	0	<0.01
Canadian (41)	135	0.10
Carpatho Rusyn (0)	0	<0.01
Celtic (28)	28	0.02
Croatian (103)	119	0.08
Cypriot (0)	0	<0.01
Czech (34)	113	0.08
Czechoslovakian (22)	44	0.03
Danish (78)	580	0.41
Dutch (363)	1,029	0.73
Eastern European (49)	49	0.03
English (940)	4,609	3.26
Estonian (8)	8	0.01
European (743)	916	0.65
Finnish (43)	133	0.09
French, ex. Basque (319)	1,623	1.15
French Canadian (75)	118	0.08
German (1,716)	6,298	4.45
German Russian (0)	0	<0.01
Greek (134)	420	0.30
Guyanese (0)	0	<0.01
Hungarian (42)	223	0.16
Icelander (0)	0	<0.01
Iranian (300)	353	0.25
Irish (1,107)	5,694	4.02
Israeli (0)	22	0.02
Italian (993)	2,611	1.85
Latvian (0)	0	<0.01
Lithuanian (0)	19	0.01
Luxemburger (0)	0	<0.01
Macedonian (0)	0	<0.01
Maltese (11)	11	0.01
New Zealander (0)	0	<0.01
Northern European (8)	8	0.01
Norwegian (125)	500	0.35
Pennsylvania German (0)	9	0.01
Polish (279)	736	0.52
Portuguese (2,043)	4,390	3.10
Romanian (113)	244	0.17
Russian (242)	601	0.42
Scandinavian (44)	54	0.04
Scotch-Irish (249)	880	0.62
Scottish (193)	805	0.57
Serbian (0)	8	0.01
Slavic (18)	18	0.01
Slovak (10)	54	0.04
Slovene (0)	13	0.01
Soviet Union (0)	0	<0.01
Swedish (209)	904	0.64
Swiss (11)	108	0.08
Turkish (100)	108	0.08
Ukrainian (49)	114	0.08
Welsh (47)	202	0.14
West Indian, ex. Hispanic (47)	154	0.11
Bahamian (0)	16	0.01
Barbadian (0)	0	<0.01
Belizean (0)	0	<0.01
Bermudan (0)	0	<0.01
British West Indian (0)	0	<0.01
Dutch West Indian (0)	0	<0.01
Haitian (15)	64	0.05
Jamaican (32)	58	0.04
Trinidadian/Tobagonian (0)	0	<0.01
U.S. Virgin Islander (0)	0	<0.01
West Indian (0)	16	0.01
Other West Indian (0)	0	<0.01
Yugoslavian (72)	83	0.06

Hispanic Origin	Population	%
Hispanic or Latino (of any race)	58,730	40.73
Central American, ex. Mexican	7,505	5.21
Costa Rican	96	0.07
Guatemalan	1,504	1.04
Honduran	329	0.23
Nicaraguan	1,745	1.21
Panamanian	100	0.07
Salvadoran	3,676	2.55
Other Central American	55	0.04
Cuban	217	0.15
Dominican Republic	40	0.03
Mexican	43,597	30.24
Puerto Rican	2,232	1.55
South American	1,300	0.90
Argentinean	65	0.05
Bolivian	86	0.06
Chilean	82	0.06
Colombian	196	0.14
Ecuadorian	61	0.04
Paraguayan	3	<0.01
Peruvian	761	0.53
Uruguayan	4	<0.01
Venezuelan	28	0.02
Other South American	14	0.01
Other Hispanic or Latino	3,839	2.66

Race*	Population	%
African-American/Black (17,099)	19,451	13.49
Not Hispanic (16,297)	17,898	12.41
Hispanic (802)	1,553	1.08
American Indian/Alaska Native (1,396)	2,973	2.06
Not Hispanic (492)	1,414	0.98
Hispanic (904)	1,559	1.08
Alaska Athabascan *(Ala. Nat.)* (0)	0	<0.01
Aleut *(Alaska Native)* (1)	3	<0.01
Apache (45)	118	0.08
Arapaho (6)	10	0.01
Blackfeet (9)	79	0.05
Canadian/French Am. Ind. (1)	3	<0.01
Central American Ind. (8)	16	0.01
Cherokee (39)	303	0.21
Cheyenne (6)	9	0.01
Chickasaw (1)	9	0.01
Chippewa (15)	22	0.02
Choctaw (10)	68	0.05
Colville (3)	3	<0.01
Comanche (9)	14	0.01
Cree (0)	0	<0.01
Creek (3)	13	0.01
Crow (1)	6	<0.01
Delaware (0)	1	<0.01
Hopi (7)	20	0.01
Houma (0)	0	<0.01
Inupiat *(Alaska Native)* (1)	4	<0.01
Iroquois (2)	20	0.01
Kiowa (1)	4	<0.01
Lumbee (0)	2	<0.01
Menominee (0)	0	<0.01
Mexican American Ind. (202)	309	0.21
Navajo (50)	104	0.07
Osage (0)	3	<0.01
Ottawa (0)	0	<0.01
Paiute (14)	21	0.01
Pima (5)	6	<0.01
Potawatomi (1)	6	<0.01
Pueblo (22)	34	0.02
Puget Sound Salish (0)	0	<0.01
Seminole (3)	17	0.01
Shoshone (2)	4	<0.01
Sioux (43)	84	0.06
South American Ind. (6)	14	0.01
Spanish American Ind. (8)	15	0.01
Tlingit-Haida *(Alaska Native)* (3)	10	0.01
Tohono O'Odham (3)	9	0.01
Tsimshian *(Alaska Native)* (3)	4	<0.01
Ute (3)	5	<0.01
Yakama (1)	5	<0.01
Yaqui (7)	26	0.02
Yuman (1)	2	<0.01
Yup'ik *(Alaska Native)* (1)	1	<0.01
Asian (31,666)	36,334	25.20
Not Hispanic (31,090)	34,827	24.15
Hispanic (576)	1,507	1.05
Bangladeshi (19)	20	0.01
Bhutanese (0)	0	<0.01
Burmese (105)	120	0.08
Cambodian (229)	312	0.22
Chinese, ex. Taiwanese (5,421)	6,398	4.44
Filipino (15,058)	17,134	11.88
Hmong (37)	38	0.03
Indian (4,260)	5,409	3.75
Indonesian (121)	195	0.14
Japanese (715)	1,276	0.88
Korean (662)	846	0.59
Laotian (73)	106	0.07
Malaysian (23)	43	0.03
Nepalese (59)	63	0.04
Pakistani (183)	224	0.16
Sri Lankan (18)	19	0.01
Taiwanese (169)	206	0.14
Thai (120)	170	0.12
Vietnamese (3,416)	3,712	2.57
Hawaii Native/Pacific Islander (4,535)	6,708	4.65
Not Hispanic (4,290)	6,093	4.23
Hispanic (245)	615	0.43
Fijian (2,188)	2,535	1.76
Guamanian/Chamorro (271)	470	0.33
Marshallese (0)	2	<0.01
Native Hawaiian (261)	784	0.54
Samoan (673)	859	0.60
Tongan (627)	719	0.50
White (49,309)	56,207	38.98
Not Hispanic (27,178)	30,682	21.28
Hispanic (22,131)	25,525	17.70

*Notes: † The Census 2010 population figure is used to calculate the percentages in the Hispanic Origin and Race categories. Ancestry percentages are based on the 2006-2010 American Community Survey population (not shown); ‡ Numbers in parentheses indicate the number of people reporting a single ancestry; * Numbers in parentheses indicate the number of persons reporting this race alone, not in combination with any other race; Please refer to the Explanation of Data for more information.*

Hemet

Place Type: City
County: Riverside
Population: 78,657

Ancestry	Population	%
Afghan (0)	0	<0.01
African, Sub-Saharan (73)	212	0.28
African (36)	130	0.17
Cape Verdean (0)	0	<0.01
Ethiopian (0)	0	<0.01
Ghanaian (0)	0	<0.01
Kenyan (0)	0	<0.01
Liberian (0)	0	<0.01
Nigerian (0)	0	<0.01
Senegalese (0)	0	<0.01
Sierra Leonean (0)	0	<0.01
Somalian (0)	0	<0.01
South African (0)	0	<0.01
Sudanese (0)	0	<0.01
Ugandan (37)	37	0.05
Zimbabwean (0)	0	<0.01
Other Sub-Saharan African (0)	45	0.06
Albanian (12)	32	0.04
Alsatian (0)	0	<0.01
American (2,937)	2,937	3.84
Arab (131)	155	0.20
Arab (9)	33	0.04
Egyptian (9)	9	0.01
Iraqi (0)	0	<0.01
Jordanian (100)	100	0.13
Lebanese (13)	13	0.02
Moroccan (0)	0	<0.01
Palestinian (0)	0	<0.01
Syrian (0)	0	<0.01
Other Arab (0)	0	<0.01
Armenian (11)	61	0.08
Assyrian/Chaldean/Syriac (0)	13	0.02
Australian (49)	57	0.07
Austrian (94)	231	0.30
Basque (0)	146	0.19
Belgian (25)	99	0.13
Brazilian (26)	26	0.03
British (224)	255	0.33
Bulgarian (0)	0	<0.01
Cajun (0)	0	<0.01
Canadian (235)	358	0.47
Carpatho Rusyn (0)	0	<0.01
Celtic (0)	12	0.02
Croatian (19)	28	0.04
Cypriot (0)	0	<0.01
Czech (92)	237	0.31
Czechoslovakian (64)	112	0.15
Danish (178)	479	0.63
Dutch (345)	1,094	1.43
Eastern European (0)	0	<0.01
English (2,926)	8,359	10.94
Estonian (0)	0	<0.01
European (345)	572	0.75
Finnish (18)	113	0.15
French, ex. Basque (394)	2,368	3.10
French Canadian (312)	470	0.62
German (2,855)	9,886	12.94
German Russian (0)	0	<0.01
Greek (91)	201	0.26
Guyanese (0)	0	<0.01
Hungarian (126)	395	0.52
Icelander (15)	15	0.02
Iranian (0)	0	<0.01
Irish (2,050)	7,059	9.24
Israeli (0)	0	<0.01
Italian (1,430)	2,635	3.45
Latvian (44)	78	0.10
Lithuanian (84)	231	0.30
Luxemburger (7)	7	0.01
Macedonian (0)	0	<0.01
Maltese (0)	0	<0.01
New Zealander (0)	0	<0.01
Northern European (22)	30	0.04
Norwegian (531)	1,283	1.68
Pennsylvania German (32)	71	0.09
Polish (377)	1,184	1.55
Portuguese (122)	326	0.43
Romanian (171)	229	0.30
Russian (166)	358	0.47
Scandinavian (195)	265	0.35
Scotch-Irish (348)	1,333	1.74
Scottish (296)	1,238	1.62
Serbian (15)	25	0.03
Slavic (0)	0	<0.01
Slovak (77)	113	0.15
Slovene (0)	0	<0.01
Soviet Union (34)	34	0.04
Swedish (351)	1,443	1.89
Swiss (9)	117	0.15
Turkish (12)	34	0.04
Ukrainian (137)	153	0.20
Welsh (160)	548	0.72
West Indian, ex. Hispanic (66)	119	0.16
Bahamian (0)	0	<0.01
Barbadian (0)	0	<0.01
Belizean (0)	12	0.02
Bermudan (0)	0	<0.01
British West Indian (0)	0	<0.01
Dutch West Indian (0)	0	<0.01
Haitian (0)	27	0.04
Jamaican (66)	66	0.09
Trinidadian/Tobagonian (0)	14	0.02
U.S. Virgin Islander (0)	0	<0.01
West Indian (0)	0	<0.01
Other West Indian (0)	0	<0.01
Yugoslavian (6)	71	0.09

Hispanic Origin	Population	%
Hispanic or Latino (of any race)	28,150	35.79
Central American, ex. Mexican	788	1.00
Costa Rican	34	0.04
Guatemalan	235	0.30
Honduran	42	0.05
Nicaraguan	102	0.13
Panamanian	38	0.05
Salvadoran	330	0.42
Other Central American	7	0.01
Cuban	203	0.26
Dominican Republic	22	0.03
Mexican	24,271	30.86
Puerto Rican	627	0.80
South American	357	0.45
Argentinean	53	0.07
Bolivian	17	0.02
Chilean	11	0.01
Colombian	101	0.13
Ecuadorian	48	0.06
Paraguayan	3	<0.01
Peruvian	98	0.12
Uruguayan	8	0.01
Venezuelan	9	0.01
Other South American	9	0.01
Other Hispanic or Latino	1,882	2.39

Race*	Population	%
African-American/Black (5,049)	6,236	7.93
Not Hispanic (4,711)	5,503	7.00
Hispanic (338)	733	0.93
American Indian/Alaska Native (1,223)	2,237	2.84
Not Hispanic (549)	1,176	1.50
Hispanic (674)	1,061	1.35
Alaska Athabascan *(Ala. Nat.)* (6)	6	0.01
Aleut *(Alaska Native)* (1)	2	<0.01
Apache (58)	109	0.14
Arapaho (0)	8	0.01
Blackfeet (8)	54	0.07
Canadian/French Am. Ind. (5)	6	0.01
Central American Ind. (1)	3	<0.01
Cherokee (54)	267	0.34
Cheyenne (1)	10	0.01
Chickasaw (7)	15	0.02
Chippewa (9)	17	0.02
Choctaw (21)	81	0.10
Colville (1)	1	<0.01
Comanche (5)	7	0.01
Cree (0)	0	<0.01
Creek (15)	22	0.03
Crow (0)	2	<0.01
Delaware (0)	1	<0.01
Hopi (0)	7	0.01
Houma (0)	0	<0.01
Inupiat *(Alaska Native)* (0)	0	<0.01
Iroquois (3)	14	0.02
Kiowa (0)	0	<0.01
Lumbee (4)	11	0.01
Menominee (6)	6	0.01
Mexican American Ind. (81)	115	0.15
Navajo (39)	64	0.08
Osage (4)	9	0.01
Ottawa (8)	15	0.02
Paiute (10)	14	0.02
Pima (3)	5	0.01
Potawatomi (4)	5	0.01
Pueblo (1)	9	0.01
Puget Sound Salish (0)	0	<0.01
Seminole (2)	7	0.01
Shoshone (2)	5	0.01
Sioux (12)	25	0.03
South American Ind. (1)	1	<0.01
Spanish American Ind. (11)	13	0.02
Tlingit-Haida *(Alaska Native)* (1)	1	<0.01
Tohono O'Odham (4)	4	0.01
Tsimshian *(Alaska Native)* (0)	0	<0.01
Ute (1)	7	0.01
Yakama (0)	0	<0.01
Yaqui (7)	37	0.05
Yuman (14)	14	0.02
Yup'ik *(Alaska Native)* (0)	0	<0.01
Asian (2,352)	3,324	4.23
Not Hispanic (2,197)	2,876	3.66
Hispanic (155)	448	0.57
Bangladeshi (1)	1	<0.01
Bhutanese (0)	0	<0.01
Burmese (5)	9	0.01
Cambodian (82)	108	0.14
Chinese, ex. Taiwanese (202)	284	0.36
Filipino (1,233)	1,733	2.20
Hmong (14)	15	0.02
Indian (176)	218	0.28
Indonesian (21)	57	0.07
Japanese (137)	313	0.40
Korean (78)	130	0.17
Laotian (41)	50	0.06
Malaysian (3)	6	0.01
Nepalese (3)	3	<0.01
Pakistani (29)	32	0.04
Sri Lankan (3)	5	0.01
Taiwanese (25)	25	0.03
Thai (44)	82	0.10
Vietnamese (166)	207	0.26
Hawaii Native/Pacific Islander (284)	606	0.77
Not Hispanic (239)	474	0.60
Hispanic (45)	132	0.17
Fijian (0)	1	<0.01
Guamanian/Chamorro (61)	129	0.16
Marshallese (0)	0	<0.01
Native Hawaiian (72)	187	0.24
Samoan (82)	133	0.17
Tongan (28)	50	0.06
White (53,259)	56,784	72.19
Not Hispanic (40,723)	42,479	54.01
Hispanic (12,536)	14,305	18.19

*Notes: † The Census 2010 population figure is used to calculate the percentages in the Hispanic Origin and Race categories. Ancestry percentages are based on the 2006-2010 American Community Survey population (not shown); ‡ Numbers in parentheses indicate the number of people reporting a single ancestry; * Numbers in parentheses indicate the number of persons reporting this race alone, not in combination with any other race; Please refer to the Explanation of Data for more information.*

Hesperia

Place Type: City
County: San Bernardino
Population: 90,173

Ancestry	Population	%
Afghan (40)	40	0.05
African, Sub-Saharan (129)	176	0.20
African (97)	144	0.17
Cape Verdean (0)	0	<0.01
Ethiopian (32)	32	0.04
Ghanaian (0)	0	<0.01
Kenyan (0)	0	<0.01
Liberian (0)	0	<0.01
Nigerian (0)	0	<0.01
Senegalese (0)	0	<0.01
Sierra Leonean (0)	0	<0.01
Somalian (0)	0	<0.01
South African (0)	0	<0.01
Sudanese (0)	0	<0.01
Ugandan (0)	0	<0.01
Zimbabwean (0)	0	<0.01
Other Sub-Saharan African (0)	0	<0.01
Albanian (0)	0	<0.01
Alsatian (0)	0	<0.01
American (2,195)	2,195	2.54
Arab (150)	150	0.17
Arab (43)	43	0.05
Egyptian (39)	39	0.05
Iraqi (0)	0	<0.01
Jordanian (46)	46	0.05
Lebanese (22)	22	0.03
Moroccan (0)	0	<0.01
Palestinian (0)	0	<0.01
Syrian (0)	0	<0.01
Other Arab (0)	0	<0.01
Armenian (11)	36	0.04
Assyrian/Chaldean/Syriac (0)	0	<0.01
Australian (0)	38	0.04
Austrian (64)	110	0.13
Basque (26)	44	0.05
Belgian (17)	17	0.02
Brazilian (22)	31	0.04
British (115)	213	0.25
Bulgarian (0)	0	<0.01
Cajun (0)	0	<0.01
Canadian (54)	131	0.15
Carpatho Rusyn (0)	0	<0.01
Celtic (31)	31	0.04
Croatian (43)	78	0.09
Cypriot (0)	0	<0.01
Czech (26)	170	0.20
Czechoslovakian (0)	12	0.01
Danish (81)	265	0.31
Dutch (218)	1,308	1.51
Eastern European (0)	0	<0.01
English (2,453)	6,901	7.99
Estonian (0)	0	<0.01
European (858)	910	1.05
Finnish (0)	31	0.04
French, ex. Basque (380)	2,174	2.52
French Canadian (88)	289	0.33
German (2,408)	9,140	10.58
German Russian (0)	0	<0.01
Greek (44)	393	0.45
Guyanese (0)	0	<0.01
Hungarian (78)	132	0.15
Icelander (0)	0	<0.01
Iranian (0)	0	<0.01
Irish (1,701)	7,883	9.12
Israeli (0)	0	<0.01
Italian (1,108)	3,697	4.28
Latvian (0)	0	<0.01
Lithuanian (10)	77	0.09
Luxemburger (0)	0	<0.01
Macedonian (0)	0	<0.01
Maltese (0)	21	0.02
New Zealander (0)	0	<0.01
Northern European (13)	13	0.02
Norwegian (218)	930	1.08
Pennsylvania German (31)	63	0.07
Polish (235)	1,045	1.21
Portuguese (302)	504	0.58
Romanian (0)	37	0.04
Russian (255)	547	0.63
Scandinavian (7)	76	0.09
Scotch-Irish (233)	743	0.86
Scottish (359)	998	1.16
Serbian (0)	0	<0.01
Slavic (0)	27	0.03
Slovak (24)	56	0.06
Slovene (0)	0	<0.01
Soviet Union (0)	0	<0.01
Swedish (179)	882	1.02
Swiss (28)	127	0.15
Turkish (0)	0	<0.01
Ukrainian (0)	19	0.02
Welsh (0)	287	0.33
West Indian, ex. Hispanic (93)	162	0.19
Bahamian (0)	0	<0.01
Barbadian (0)	0	<0.01
Belizean (0)	17	0.02
Bermudan (0)	0	<0.01
British West Indian (0)	0	<0.01
Dutch West Indian (0)	0	<0.01
Haitian (0)	0	<0.01
Jamaican (93)	145	0.17
Trinidadian/Tobagonian (0)	0	<0.01
U.S. Virgin Islander (0)	0	<0.01
West Indian (0)	0	<0.01
Other West Indian (0)	0	<0.01
Yugoslavian (0)	0	<0.01

Hispanic Origin	Population	%
Hispanic or Latino (of any race)	44,091	48.90
Central American, ex. Mexican	2,847	3.16
Costa Rican	55	0.06
Guatemalan	863	0.96
Honduran	183	0.20
Nicaraguan	202	0.22
Panamanian	39	0.04
Salvadoran	1,450	1.61
Other Central American	55	0.06
Cuban	237	0.26
Dominican Republic	18	0.02
Mexican	36,486	40.46
Puerto Rican	626	0.69
South American	454	0.50
Argentinean	86	0.10
Bolivian	13	0.01
Chilean	37	0.04
Colombian	107	0.12
Ecuadorian	65	0.07
Paraguayan	0	<0.01
Peruvian	128	0.14
Uruguayan	3	<0.01
Venezuelan	8	0.01
Other South American	7	0.01
Other Hispanic or Latino	3,423	3.80

Race*	Population	%
African-American/Black (5,226)	6,214	6.89
Not Hispanic (4,853)	5,484	6.08
Hispanic (373)	730	0.81
American Indian/Alaska Native (1,118)	2,050	2.27
Not Hispanic (412)	923	1.02
Hispanic (706)	1,127	1.25
Alaska Athabascan *(Ala. Nat.)* (0)	0	<0.01
Aleut *(Alaska Native)* (1)	1	<0.01
Apache (66)	126	0.14
Arapaho (0)	1	<0.01
Blackfeet (2)	30	0.03
Canadian/French Am. Ind. (0)	1	<0.01
Central American Ind. (2)	6	0.01
Cherokee (75)	281	0.31
Cheyenne (3)	8	0.01
Chickasaw (2)	18	0.02
Chippewa (12)	20	0.02
Choctaw (22)	50	0.06
Colville (0)	0	<0.01
Comanche (2)	6	0.01
Cree (0)	1	<0.01
Creek (6)	16	0.02
Crow (0)	0	<0.01
Delaware (3)	4	<0.01
Hopi (15)	17	0.02
Houma (0)	0	<0.01
Inupiat *(Alaska Native)* (0)	3	<0.01
Iroquois (1)	12	0.01
Kiowa (0)	4	<0.01
Lumbee (2)	2	<0.01
Menominee (0)	0	<0.01
Mexican American Ind. (118)	164	0.18
Navajo (25)	49	0.05
Osage (2)	2	<0.01
Ottawa (0)	1	<0.01
Paiute (3)	9	0.01
Pima (14)	20	0.02
Potawatomi (8)	14	0.02
Pueblo (10)	21	0.02
Puget Sound Salish (0)	0	<0.01
Seminole (2)	5	0.01
Shoshone (3)	8	0.01
Sioux (19)	40	0.04
South American Ind. (3)	5	0.01
Spanish American Ind. (11)	15	0.02
Tlingit-Haida *(Alaska Native)* (9)	9	0.01
Tohono O'Odham (9)	19	0.02
Tsimshian *(Alaska Native)* (0)	0	<0.01
Ute (5)	6	0.01
Yakama (0)	0	<0.01
Yaqui (32)	59	0.07
Yuman (2)	3	<0.01
Yup'ik *(Alaska Native)* (0)	1	<0.01
Asian (1,884)	2,851	3.16
Not Hispanic (1,704)	2,337	2.59
Hispanic (180)	514	0.57
Bangladeshi (7)	7	0.01
Bhutanese (0)	0	<0.01
Burmese (0)	2	<0.01
Cambodian (89)	105	0.12
Chinese, ex. Taiwanese (129)	244	0.27
Filipino (604)	954	1.06
Hmong (0)	0	<0.01
Indian (194)	268	0.30
Indonesian (41)	71	0.08
Japanese (143)	371	0.41
Korean (249)	348	0.39
Laotian (6)	9	0.01
Malaysian (6)	14	0.02
Nepalese (0)	0	<0.01
Pakistani (8)	11	0.01
Sri Lankan (6)	6	0.01
Taiwanese (0)	5	0.01
Thai (20)	57	0.06
Vietnamese (309)	349	0.39
Hawaii Native/Pacific Islander (270)	563	0.62
Not Hispanic (205)	395	0.44
Hispanic (65)	168	0.19
Fijian (1)	3	<0.01
Guamanian/Chamorro (35)	71	0.08
Marshallese (0)	0	<0.01
Native Hawaiian (78)	175	0.19
Samoan (95)	163	0.18
Tongan (24)	32	0.04
White (55,129)	58,853	65.27
Not Hispanic (37,027)	38,508	42.70
Hispanic (18,102)	20,345	22.56

*Notes: † The Census 2010 population figure is used to calculate the percentages in the Hispanic Origin and Race categories. Ancestry percentages are based on the 2006-2010 American Community Survey population (not shown); ‡ Numbers in parentheses indicate the number of people reporting a single ancestry; * Numbers in parentheses indicate the number of persons reporting this race alone, not in combination with any other race; Please refer to the Explanation of Data for more information.*

Highland

Place Type: City
County: San Bernardino
Population: 53,104

Ancestry	Population	%
Afghan (0)	0	<0.01
African, Sub-Saharan (291)	385	0.74
African (25)	75	0.14
Cape Verdean (0)	0	<0.01
Ethiopian (0)	0	<0.01
Ghanaian (41)	41	0.08
Kenyan (0)	0	<0.01
Liberian (0)	0	<0.01
Nigerian (180)	180	0.34
Senegalese (0)	0	<0.01
Sierra Leonean (0)	0	<0.01
Somalian (0)	44	0.08
South African (0)	0	<0.01
Sudanese (0)	0	<0.01
Ugandan (0)	0	<0.01
Zimbabwean (0)	0	<0.01
Other Sub-Saharan African (45)	45	0.09
Albanian (0)	0	<0.01
Alsatian (0)	0	<0.01
American (1,040)	1,040	1.99
Arab (410)	466	0.89
Arab (184)	184	0.35
Egyptian (0)	0	<0.01
Iraqi (0)	0	<0.01
Jordanian (33)	33	0.06
Lebanese (66)	109	0.21
Moroccan (0)	0	<0.01
Palestinian (16)	16	0.03
Syrian (106)	117	0.22
Other Arab (5)	7	0.01
Armenian (10)	68	0.13
Assyrian/Chaldean/Syriac (0)	0	<0.01
Australian (11)	11	0.02
Austrian (0)	27	0.05
Basque (46)	79	0.15
Belgian (0)	9	0.02
Brazilian (0)	0	<0.01
British (4)	91	0.17
Bulgarian (0)	0	<0.01
Cajun (0)	0	<0.01
Canadian (32)	39	0.07
Carpatho Rusyn (0)	0	<0.01
Celtic (0)	0	<0.01
Croatian (0)	15	0.03
Cypriot (0)	0	<0.01
Czech (32)	69	0.13
Czechoslovakian (0)	48	0.09
Danish (0)	85	0.16
Dutch (56)	495	0.95
Eastern European (0)	0	<0.01
English (735)	2,809	5.37
Estonian (0)	0	<0.01
European (136)	163	0.31
Finnish (0)	5	0.01
French, ex. Basque (122)	1,103	2.11
French Canadian (132)	188	0.36
German (1,212)	4,860	9.29
German Russian (0)	0	<0.01
Greek (0)	21	0.04
Guyanese (0)	0	<0.01
Hungarian (29)	241	0.46
Icelander (28)	28	0.05
Iranian (0)	23	0.04
Irish (1,025)	3,993	7.63
Israeli (0)	0	<0.01
Italian (611)	1,689	3.23
Latvian (0)	13	0.02
Lithuanian (96)	96	0.18
Luxemburger (0)	0	<0.01
Macedonian (0)	0	<0.01
Maltese (0)	0	<0.01
New Zealander (0)	0	<0.01
Northern European (36)	36	0.07
Norwegian (172)	681	1.30
Pennsylvania German (0)	0	<0.01
Polish (166)	663	1.27
Portuguese (16)	197	0.38
Romanian (49)	49	0.09
Russian (276)	455	0.87
Scandinavian (0)	48	0.09
Scotch-Irish (73)	375	0.72
Scottish (145)	555	1.06
Serbian (0)	0	<0.01
Slavic (3)	14	0.03
Slovak (22)	22	0.04
Slovene (0)	15	0.03
Soviet Union (0)	0	<0.01
Swedish (86)	302	0.58
Swiss (11)	22	0.04
Turkish (0)	0	<0.01
Ukrainian (10)	34	0.06
Welsh (0)	193	0.37
West Indian, ex. Hispanic (41)	55	0.11
Bahamian (0)	0	<0.01
Barbadian (0)	0	<0.01
Belizean (0)	0	<0.01
Bermudan (0)	0	<0.01
British West Indian (12)	12	0.02
Dutch West Indian (0)	0	<0.01
Haitian (21)	21	0.04
Jamaican (0)	0	<0.01
Trinidadian/Tobagonian (0)	0	<0.01
U.S. Virgin Islander (0)	0	<0.01
West Indian (8)	22	0.04
Other West Indian (0)	0	<0.01
Yugoslavian (74)	74	0.14

Hispanic Origin	Population	%
Hispanic or Latino (of any race)	25,556	48.12
Central American, ex. Mexican	911	1.72
Costa Rican	35	0.07
Guatemalan	278	0.52
Honduran	94	0.18
Nicaraguan	113	0.21
Panamanian	25	0.05
Salvadoran	352	0.66
Other Central American	14	0.03
Cuban	156	0.29
Dominican Republic	15	0.03
Mexican	22,430	42.24
Puerto Rican	294	0.55
South American	252	0.47
Argentinean	45	0.08
Bolivian	5	0.01
Chilean	23	0.04
Colombian	45	0.08
Ecuadorian	39	0.07
Paraguayan	0	<0.01
Peruvian	72	0.14
Uruguayan	10	0.02
Venezuelan	11	0.02
Other South American	2	<0.01
Other Hispanic or Latino	1,498	2.82

Race*	Population	%
African-American/Black (5,887)	6,795	12.80
Not Hispanic (5,584)	6,220	11.71
Hispanic (303)	575	1.08
American Indian/Alaska Native (542)	1,092	2.06
Not Hispanic (233)	543	1.02
Hispanic (309)	549	1.03
Alaska Athabascan *(Ala. Nat.)* (1)	3	0.01
Aleut *(Alaska Native)* (0)	2	<0.01
Apache (26)	38	0.07
Arapaho (1)	2	<0.01
Blackfeet (10)	62	0.12
Canadian/French Am. Ind. (0)	2	<0.01
Central American Ind. (1)	1	<0.01
Cherokee (33)	116	0.22
Cheyenne (2)	2	<0.01
Chickasaw (0)	7	0.01
Chippewa (6)	16	0.03
Choctaw (6)	39	0.07
Colville (1)	1	<0.01
Comanche (0)	1	<0.01
Cree (0)	0	<0.01
Creek (7)	14	0.03
Crow (0)	0	<0.01
Delaware (0)	0	<0.01
Hopi (2)	7	0.01
Houma (0)	0	<0.01
Inupiat *(Alaska Native)* (0)	0	<0.01
Iroquois (5)	7	0.01
Kiowa (0)	0	<0.01
Lumbee (0)	0	<0.01
Menominee (0)	0	<0.01
Mexican American Ind. (55)	77	0.14
Navajo (18)	24	0.05
Osage (1)	3	0.01
Ottawa (0)	1	<0.01
Paiute (3)	3	0.01
Pima (1)	1	<0.01
Potawatomi (2)	5	0.01
Pueblo (11)	16	0.03
Puget Sound Salish (0)	0	<0.01
Seminole (2)	7	0.01
Shoshone (0)	2	<0.01
Sioux (10)	22	0.04
South American Ind. (1)	3	0.01
Spanish American Ind. (0)	1	<0.01
Tlingit-Haida *(Alaska Native)* (1)	1	<0.01
Tohono O'Odham (4)	8	0.02
Tsimshian *(Alaska Native)* (0)	0	<0.01
Ute (0)	0	<0.01
Yakama (0)	0	<0.01
Yaqui (21)	30	0.06
Yuman (0)	0	<0.01
Yup'ik *(Alaska Native)* (0)	0	<0.01
Asian (3,954)	4,775	8.99
Not Hispanic (3,812)	4,431	8.34
Hispanic (142)	344	0.65
Bangladeshi (35)	35	0.07
Bhutanese (0)	0	<0.01
Burmese (1)	1	<0.01
Cambodian (186)	230	0.43
Chinese, ex. Taiwanese (278)	425	0.80
Filipino (1,044)	1,405	2.65
Hmong (0)	0	<0.01
Indian (328)	379	0.71
Indonesian (163)	206	0.39
Japanese (120)	264	0.50
Korean (198)	250	0.47
Laotian (21)	33	0.06
Malaysian (3)	7	0.01
Nepalese (0)	0	<0.01
Pakistani (70)	92	0.17
Sri Lankan (0)	0	<0.01
Taiwanese (18)	24	0.05
Thai (126)	158	0.30
Vietnamese (1,222)	1,312	2.47
Hawaii Native/Pacific Islander (168)	370	0.70
Not Hispanic (159)	287	0.54
Hispanic (9)	83	0.16
Fijian (14)	14	0.03
Guamanian/Chamorro (20)	51	0.10
Marshallese (0)	0	<0.01
Native Hawaiian (28)	108	0.20
Samoan (80)	121	0.23
Tongan (11)	14	0.03
White (27,836)	30,159	56.79
Not Hispanic (16,347)	17,384	32.74
Hispanic (11,489)	12,775	24.06

*Notes: † The Census 2010 population figure is used to calculate the percentages in the Hispanic Origin and Race categories. Ancestry percentages are based on the 2006-2010 American Community Survey population (not shown); ‡ Numbers in parentheses indicate the number of people reporting a single ancestry; * Numbers in parentheses indicate the number of persons reporting this race alone, not in combination with any other race; Please refer to the Explanation of Data for more information.*

Huntington Beach

Place Type: City
County: Orange
Population: 189,992

Ancestry	Population	%
Afghan (24)	24	0.01
African, Sub-Saharan (156)	268	0.14
African (82)	183	0.10
Cape Verdean (0)	0	<0.01
Ethiopian (10)	10	0.01
Ghanaian (0)	0	<0.01
Kenyan (0)	0	<0.01
Liberian (0)	0	<0.01
Nigerian (0)	11	0.01
Senegalese (0)	0	<0.01
Sierra Leonean (0)	0	<0.01
Somalian (0)	0	<0.01
South African (48)	48	0.03
Sudanese (0)	0	<0.01
Ugandan (0)	0	<0.01
Zimbabwean (0)	0	<0.01
Other Sub-Saharan African (16)	16	0.01
Albanian (0)	15	0.01
Alsatian (0)	10	0.01
American (6,150)	6,150	3.26
Arab (1,895)	2,455	1.30
Arab (197)	255	0.13
Egyptian (1,048)	1,048	0.55
Iraqi (9)	46	0.02
Jordanian (171)	171	0.09
Lebanese (158)	453	0.24
Moroccan (0)	80	0.04
Palestinian (53)	98	0.05
Syrian (88)	114	0.06
Other Arab (171)	190	0.10
Armenian (472)	695	0.37
Assyrian/Chaldean/Syriac (16)	16	0.01
Australian (110)	391	0.21
Austrian (198)	728	0.39
Basque (11)	23	0.01
Belgian (29)	168	0.09
Brazilian (307)	450	0.24
British (597)	1,185	0.63
Bulgarian (9)	60	0.03
Cajun (17)	28	0.01
Canadian (256)	799	0.42
Carpatho Rusyn (0)	0	<0.01
Celtic (14)	21	0.01
Croatian (169)	618	0.33
Cypriot (0)	0	<0.01
Czech (333)	1,079	0.57
Czechoslovakian (46)	214	0.11
Danish (483)	1,987	1.05
Dutch (1,103)	4,608	2.44
Eastern European (251)	274	0.15
English (6,172)	21,837	11.56
Estonian (0)	11	0.01
European (2,703)	3,207	1.70
Finnish (41)	445	0.24
French, ex. Basque (950)	6,793	3.60
French Canadian (401)	1,008	0.53
German (9,715)	32,622	17.27
German Russian (0)	0	<0.01
Greek (561)	1,199	0.63
Guyanese (0)	0	<0.01
Hungarian (605)	1,920	1.02
Icelander (54)	61	0.03
Iranian (435)	478	0.25
Irish (6,383)	24,675	13.06
Israeli (48)	197	0.10
Italian (6,522)	15,311	8.10
Latvian (0)	77	0.04
Lithuanian (154)	629	0.33
Luxemburger (15)	73	0.04
Macedonian (0)	48	0.03
Maltese (9)	49	0.03
New Zealander (7)	80	0.04
Northern European (199)	273	0.14
Norwegian (1,463)	3,981	2.11
Pennsylvania German (35)	94	0.05
Polish (1,553)	4,968	2.63
Portuguese (473)	1,256	0.66
Romanian (408)	1,012	0.54
Russian (1,461)	3,421	1.81
Scandinavian (230)	539	0.29
Scotch-Irish (1,179)	3,816	2.02
Scottish (1,735)	5,014	2.65
Serbian (46)	75	0.04
Slavic (35)	95	0.05
Slovak (188)	427	0.23
Slovene (23)	159	0.08
Soviet Union (0)	0	<0.01
Swedish (882)	4,208	2.23
Swiss (177)	688	0.36
Turkish (161)	185	0.10
Ukrainian (296)	732	0.39
Welsh (258)	1,786	0.95
West Indian, ex. Hispanic (32)	71	0.04
Bahamian (0)	0	<0.01
Barbadian (0)	0	<0.01
Belizean (0)	0	<0.01
Bermudan (0)	0	<0.01
British West Indian (0)	0	<0.01
Dutch West Indian (0)	0	<0.01
Haitian (0)	23	0.01
Jamaican (15)	15	0.01
Trinidadian/Tobagonian (0)	0	<0.01
U.S. Virgin Islander (0)	0	<0.01
West Indian (17)	33	0.02
Other West Indian (0)	0	<0.01
Yugoslavian (208)	514	0.27

Hispanic Origin	Population	%
Hispanic or Latino (of any race)	32,411	17.06
Central American, ex. Mexican	1,216	0.64
Costa Rican	118	0.06
Guatemalan	373	0.20
Honduran	107	0.06
Nicaraguan	137	0.07
Panamanian	62	0.03
Salvadoran	397	0.21
Other Central American	22	0.01
Cuban	633	0.33
Dominican Republic	38	0.02
Mexican	25,139	13.23
Puerto Rican	844	0.44
South American	1,805	0.95
Argentinean	394	0.21
Bolivian	75	0.04
Chilean	159	0.08
Colombian	418	0.22
Ecuadorian	216	0.11
Paraguayan	4	<0.01
Peruvian	411	0.22
Uruguayan	34	0.02
Venezuelan	67	0.04
Other South American	27	0.01
Other Hispanic or Latino	2,736	1.44

Race*	Population	%
African-American/Black (1,813)	2,774	1.46
Not Hispanic (1,635)	2,400	1.26
Hispanic (178)	374	0.20
American Indian/Alaska Native (992)	2,759	1.45
Not Hispanic (532)	1,778	0.94
Hispanic (460)	981	0.52
Alaska Athabascan *(Ala. Nat.)* (0)	2	<0.01
Aleut *(Alaska Native)* (2)	6	<0.01
Apache (50)	138	0.07
Arapaho (0)	0	<0.01
Blackfeet (8)	79	0.04
Canadian/French Am. Ind. (6)	13	0.01
Central American Ind. (0)	2	<0.01
Cherokee (93)	470	0.25
Cheyenne (4)	7	<0.01
Chickasaw (8)	20	0.01
Chippewa (29)	68	0.04
Choctaw (30)	139	0.07
Colville (0)	1	<0.01
Comanche (4)	21	0.01
Cree (2)	6	<0.01
Creek (19)	40	0.02
Crow (0)	8	<0.01
Delaware (4)	12	0.01
Hopi (7)	14	0.01
Houma (0)	0	<0.01
Inupiat *(Alaska Native)* (7)	12	0.01
Iroquois (5)	37	0.02
Kiowa (1)	3	<0.01
Lumbee (8)	10	0.01
Menominee (0)	3	<0.01
Mexican American Ind. (104)	147	0.08
Navajo (26)	64	0.03
Osage (4)	21	0.01
Ottawa (2)	3	<0.01
Paiute (2)	8	<0.01
Pima (5)	7	<0.01
Potawatomi (12)	19	0.01
Pueblo (12)	26	0.01
Puget Sound Salish (2)	3	<0.01
Seminole (6)	19	0.01
Shoshone (8)	25	0.01
Sioux (25)	61	0.03
South American Ind. (3)	14	0.01
Spanish American Ind. (2)	8	<0.01
Tlingit-Haida *(Alaska Native)* (2)	5	<0.01
Tohono O'Odham (2)	7	<0.01
Tsimshian *(Alaska Native)* (0)	0	<0.01
Ute (2)	2	<0.01
Yakama (1)	1	<0.01
Yaqui (16)	46	0.02
Yuman (7)	11	0.01
Yup'ik *(Alaska Native)* (2)	5	<0.01
Asian (21,070)	25,619	13.48
Not Hispanic (20,792)	24,694	13.00
Hispanic (278)	925	0.49
Bangladeshi (17)	18	0.01
Bhutanese (0)	0	<0.01
Burmese (29)	32	0.02
Cambodian (171)	227	0.12
Chinese, ex. Taiwanese (3,203)	4,507	2.37
Filipino (2,474)	3,863	2.03
Hmong (25)	32	0.02
Indian (967)	1,173	0.62
Indonesian (98)	263	0.14
Japanese (2,953)	4,451	2.34
Korean (1,610)	1,990	1.05
Laotian (45)	64	0.03
Malaysian (22)	33	0.02
Nepalese (2)	2	<0.01
Pakistani (145)	161	0.08
Sri Lankan (55)	66	0.03
Taiwanese (503)	548	0.29
Thai (293)	403	0.21
Vietnamese (7,585)	8,215	4.32
Hawaii Native/Pacific Islander (635)	1,578	0.83
Not Hispanic (595)	1,374	0.72
Hispanic (40)	204	0.11
Fijian (2)	7	<0.01
Guamanian/Chamorro (105)	209	0.11
Marshallese (19)	24	0.01
Native Hawaiian (183)	668	0.35
Samoan (195)	327	0.17
Tongan (46)	61	0.03
White (145,661)	153,515	80.80
Not Hispanic (127,640)	133,155	70.08
Hispanic (18,021)	20,360	10.72

*Notes: † The Census 2010 population figure is used to calculate the percentages in the Hispanic Origin and Race categories. Ancestry percentages are based on the 2006-2010 American Community Survey population (not shown); ‡ Numbers in parentheses indicate the number of people reporting a single ancestry; * Numbers in parentheses indicate the number of persons reporting this race alone, not in combination with any other race; Please refer to the Explanation of Data for more information.*

Huntington Park

Place Type: City
County: Los Angeles
Population: 58,114

Ancestry	Population	%
Afghan (0)	0	<0.01
African, Sub-Saharan (23)	23	0.04
African (23)	23	0.04
Cape Verdean (0)	0	<0.01
Ethiopian (0)	0	<0.01
Ghanaian (0)	0	<0.01
Kenyan (0)	0	<0.01
Liberian (0)	0	<0.01
Nigerian (0)	0	<0.01
Senegalese (0)	0	<0.01
Sierra Leonean (0)	0	<0.01
Somalian (0)	0	<0.01
South African (0)	0	<0.01
Sudanese (0)	0	<0.01
Ugandan (0)	0	<0.01
Zimbabwean (0)	0	<0.01
Other Sub-Saharan African (0)	0	<0.01
Albanian (0)	0	<0.01
Alsatian (0)	0	<0.01
American (707)	707	1.21
Arab (0)	0	<0.01
Arab (0)	0	<0.01
Egyptian (0)	0	<0.01
Iraqi (0)	0	<0.01
Jordanian (0)	0	<0.01
Lebanese (0)	0	<0.01
Moroccan (0)	0	<0.01
Palestinian (0)	0	<0.01
Syrian (0)	0	<0.01
Other Arab (0)	0	<0.01
Armenian (0)	36	0.06
Assyrian/Chaldean/Syriac (0)	0	<0.01
Australian (0)	0	<0.01
Austrian (0)	0	<0.01
Basque (0)	0	<0.01
Belgian (0)	0	<0.01
Brazilian (0)	0	<0.01
British (11)	11	0.02
Bulgarian (11)	11	0.02
Cajun (0)	0	<0.01
Canadian (8)	8	0.01
Carpatho Rusyn (0)	0	<0.01
Celtic (0)	0	<0.01
Croatian (0)	0	<0.01
Cypriot (0)	0	<0.01
Czech (0)	0	<0.01
Czechoslovakian (0)	0	<0.01
Danish (0)	0	<0.01
Dutch (0)	72	0.12
Eastern European (0)	0	<0.01
English (0)	39	0.07
Estonian (14)	14	0.02
European (0)	0	<0.01
Finnish (0)	0	<0.01
French, ex. Basque (0)	42	0.07
French Canadian (0)	0	<0.01
German (28)	170	0.29
German Russian (0)	0	<0.01
Greek (0)	0	<0.01
Guyanese (0)	0	<0.01
Hungarian (0)	0	<0.01
Icelander (0)	0	<0.01
Iranian (0)	23	0.04
Irish (61)	75	0.13
Israeli (0)	0	<0.01
Italian (34)	148	0.25
Latvian (0)	0	<0.01
Lithuanian (0)	0	<0.01
Luxemburger (0)	0	<0.01
Macedonian (0)	0	<0.01
Maltese (0)	0	<0.01
New Zealander (0)	0	<0.01
Northern European (0)	0	<0.01
Norwegian (0)	0	<0.01
Pennsylvania German (0)	0	<0.01
Polish (22)	22	0.04
Portuguese (34)	34	0.06
Romanian (0)	0	<0.01
Russian (0)	0	<0.01
Scandinavian (0)	0	<0.01
Scotch-Irish (0)	7	0.01
Scottish (0)	16	0.03
Serbian (0)	0	<0.01
Slavic (0)	0	<0.01
Slovak (0)	0	<0.01
Slovene (0)	0	<0.01
Soviet Union (0)	0	<0.01
Swedish (4)	4	0.01
Swiss (0)	0	<0.01
Turkish (19)	40	0.07
Ukrainian (0)	0	<0.01
Welsh (0)	9	0.02
West Indian, ex. Hispanic (0)	0	<0.01
Bahamian (0)	0	<0.01
Barbadian (0)	0	<0.01
Belizean (0)	0	<0.01
Bermudan (0)	0	<0.01
British West Indian (0)	0	<0.01
Dutch West Indian (0)	0	<0.01
Haitian (0)	0	<0.01
Jamaican (0)	0	<0.01
Trinidadian/Tobagonian (0)	0	<0.01
U.S. Virgin Islander (0)	0	<0.01
West Indian (0)	0	<0.01
Other West Indian (0)	0	<0.01
Yugoslavian (0)	0	<0.01

Hispanic Origin	Population	%
Hispanic or Latino (of any race)	56,445	97.13
Central American, ex. Mexican	6,404	11.02
Costa Rican	79	0.14
Guatemalan	1,822	3.14
Honduran	487	0.84
Nicaraguan	546	0.94
Panamanian	18	0.03
Salvadoran	3,381	5.82
Other Central American	71	0.12
Cuban	442	0.76
Dominican Republic	13	0.02
Mexican	46,467	79.96
Puerto Rican	188	0.32
South American	447	0.77
Argentinean	39	0.07
Bolivian	17	0.03
Chilean	16	0.03
Colombian	115	0.20
Ecuadorian	142	0.24
Paraguayan	2	<0.01
Peruvian	112	0.19
Uruguayan	1	<0.01
Venezuelan	3	0.01
Other South American	0	<0.01
Other Hispanic or Latino	2,484	4.27

Race*	Population	%
African-American/Black (440)	572	0.98
Not Hispanic (211)	228	0.39
Hispanic (229)	344	0.59
American Indian/Alaska Native (752)	1,000	1.72
Not Hispanic (29)	46	0.08
Hispanic (723)	954	1.64
Alaska Athabascan *(Ala. Nat.)* (0)	0	<0.01
Aleut *(Alaska Native)* (0)	0	<0.01
Apache (8)	16	0.03
Arapaho (0)	0	<0.01
Blackfeet (3)	11	0.02
Canadian/French Am. Ind. (0)	0	<0.01
Central American Ind. (11)	21	0.04
Cherokee (5)	18	0.03
Cheyenne (0)	0	<0.01
Chickasaw (0)	0	<0.01
Chippewa (1)	1	<0.01
Choctaw (1)	2	<0.01
Colville (0)	0	<0.01
Comanche (4)	4	0.01
Cree (0)	0	<0.01
Creek (0)	0	<0.01
Crow (0)	0	<0.01
Delaware (0)	0	<0.01
Hopi (0)	0	<0.01
Houma (0)	0	<0.01
Inupiat *(Alaska Native)* (0)	0	<0.01
Iroquois (0)	0	<0.01
Kiowa (0)	0	<0.01
Lumbee (0)	0	<0.01
Menominee (0)	0	<0.01
Mexican American Ind. (243)	286	0.49
Navajo (6)	11	0.02
Osage (0)	0	<0.01
Ottawa (0)	0	<0.01
Paiute (0)	0	<0.01
Pima (4)	7	0.01
Potawatomi (0)	0	<0.01
Pueblo (5)	12	0.02
Puget Sound Salish (0)	0	<0.01
Seminole (0)	0	<0.01
Shoshone (3)	3	0.01
Sioux (7)	8	0.01
South American Ind. (1)	4	0.01
Spanish American Ind. (5)	12	0.02
Tlingit-Haida *(Alaska Native)* (0)	0	<0.01
Tohono O'Odham (6)	12	0.02
Tsimshian *(Alaska Native)* (0)	0	<0.01
Ute (0)	0	<0.01
Yakama (0)	0	<0.01
Yaqui (3)	5	0.01
Yuman (0)	3	0.01
Yup'ik *(Alaska Native)* (0)	0	<0.01
Asian (393)	529	0.91
Not Hispanic (320)	343	0.59
Hispanic (73)	186	0.32
Bangladeshi (4)	4	0.01
Bhutanese (0)	0	<0.01
Burmese (0)	0	<0.01
Cambodian (3)	5	0.01
Chinese, ex. Taiwanese (34)	51	0.09
Filipino (187)	222	0.38
Hmong (1)	1	<0.01
Indian (45)	72	0.12
Indonesian (0)	0	<0.01
Japanese (13)	17	0.03
Korean (19)	23	0.04
Laotian (7)	7	0.01
Malaysian (0)	0	<0.01
Nepalese (0)	0	<0.01
Pakistani (0)	0	<0.01
Sri Lankan (0)	0	<0.01
Taiwanese (4)	4	0.01
Thai (12)	16	0.03
Vietnamese (48)	54	0.09
Hawaii Native/Pacific Islander (28)	78	0.13
Not Hispanic (15)	29	0.05
Hispanic (13)	49	0.08
Fijian (2)	3	0.01
Guamanian/Chamorro (5)	15	0.03
Marshallese (0)	0	<0.01
Native Hawaiian (11)	21	0.04
Samoan (7)	12	0.02
Tongan (0)	1	<0.01
White (29,776)	31,657	54.47
Not Hispanic (935)	979	1.68
Hispanic (28,841)	30,678	52.79

*Notes: † The Census 2010 population figure is used to calculate the percentages in the Hispanic Origin and Race categories. Ancestry percentages are based on the 2006-2010 American Community Survey population (not shown); ‡ Numbers in parentheses indicate the number of people reporting a single ancestry; * Numbers in parentheses indicate the number of persons reporting this race alone, not in combination with any other race; Please refer to the Explanation of Data for more information.*

Indio

Place Type: City
County: Riverside
Population: 76,036

Ancestry	Population	%
Afghan (0)	0	<0.01
African, Sub-Saharan (430)	508	0.70
African (367)	445	0.61
Cape Verdean (0)	0	<0.01
Ethiopian (0)	0	<0.01
Ghanaian (0)	0	<0.01
Kenyan (0)	0	<0.01
Liberian (26)	26	0.04
Nigerian (0)	0	<0.01
Senegalese (0)	0	<0.01
Sierra Leonean (0)	0	<0.01
Somalian (0)	0	<0.01
South African (37)	37	0.05
Sudanese (0)	0	<0.01
Ugandan (0)	0	<0.01
Zimbabwean (0)	0	<0.01
Other Sub-Saharan African (0)	0	<0.01
Albanian (0)	0	<0.01
Alsatian (0)	0	<0.01
American (1,476)	1,476	2.04
Arab (9)	18	0.02
Arab (0)	0	<0.01
Egyptian (0)	0	<0.01
Iraqi (0)	0	<0.01
Jordanian (0)	0	<0.01
Lebanese (0)	9	0.01
Moroccan (0)	0	<0.01
Palestinian (9)	9	0.01
Syrian (0)	0	<0.01
Other Arab (0)	0	<0.01
Armenian (21)	31	0.04
Assyrian/Chaldean/Syriac (0)	0	<0.01
Australian (0)	10	0.01
Austrian (6)	60	0.08
Basque (5)	5	0.01
Belgian (23)	23	0.03
Brazilian (0)	0	<0.01
British (80)	229	0.32
Bulgarian (0)	0	<0.01
Cajun (0)	0	<0.01
Canadian (99)	153	0.21
Carpatho Rusyn (0)	0	<0.01
Celtic (0)	0	<0.01
Croatian (21)	29	0.04
Cypriot (0)	0	<0.01
Czech (36)	49	0.07
Czechoslovakian (0)	11	0.02
Danish (117)	375	0.52
Dutch (192)	724	1.00
Eastern European (46)	46	0.06
English (1,272)	3,682	5.08
Estonian (10)	10	0.01
European (211)	225	0.31
Finnish (55)	66	0.09
French, ex. Basque (206)	1,054	1.45
French Canadian (39)	94	0.13
German (1,498)	4,555	6.28
German Russian (0)	0	<0.01
Greek (30)	137	0.19
Guyanese (0)	0	<0.01
Hungarian (69)	186	0.26
Icelander (0)	0	<0.01
Iranian (0)	0	<0.01
Irish (1,312)	3,517	4.85
Israeli (0)	0	<0.01
Italian (962)	1,829	2.52
Latvian (0)	14	0.02
Lithuanian (52)	114	0.16
Luxemburger (0)	0	<0.01
Macedonian (0)	0	<0.01
Maltese (0)	0	<0.01
New Zealander (0)	0	<0.01
Northern European (20)	20	0.03
Norwegian (139)	563	0.78
Pennsylvania German (0)	0	<0.01
Polish (263)	706	0.97
Portuguese (127)	253	0.35
Romanian (0)	61	0.08
Russian (236)	508	0.70
Scandinavian (48)	66	0.09
Scotch-Irish (279)	646	0.89
Scottish (228)	555	0.77
Serbian (0)	0	<0.01
Slavic (0)	42	0.06
Slovak (26)	71	0.10
Slovene (0)	9	0.01
Soviet Union (0)	0	<0.01
Swedish (236)	504	0.70
Swiss (65)	119	0.16
Turkish (0)	26	0.04
Ukrainian (55)	74	0.10
Welsh (35)	169	0.23
West Indian, ex. Hispanic (0)	11	0.02
Bahamian (0)	0	<0.01
Barbadian (0)	0	<0.01
Belizean (0)	0	<0.01
Bermudan (0)	0	<0.01
British West Indian (0)	0	<0.01
Dutch West Indian (0)	0	<0.01
Haitian (0)	0	<0.01
Jamaican (0)	0	<0.01
Trinidadian/Tobagonian (0)	0	<0.01
U.S. Virgin Islander (0)	0	<0.01
West Indian (0)	11	0.02
Other West Indian (0)	0	<0.01
Yugoslavian (0)	11	0.02

Hispanic Origin	Population	%
Hispanic or Latino (of any race)	51,540	67.78
Central American, ex. Mexican	876	1.15
Costa Rican	20	0.03
Guatemalan	180	0.24
Honduran	43	0.06
Nicaraguan	88	0.12
Panamanian	39	0.05
Salvadoran	492	0.65
Other Central American	14	0.02
Cuban	91	0.12
Dominican Republic	12	0.02
Mexican	48,095	63.25
Puerto Rican	232	0.31
South American	289	0.38
Argentinean	74	0.10
Bolivian	8	0.01
Chilean	35	0.05
Colombian	80	0.11
Ecuadorian	27	0.04
Paraguayan	2	<0.01
Peruvian	46	0.06
Uruguayan	7	0.01
Venezuelan	8	0.01
Other South American	2	<0.01
Other Hispanic or Latino	1,945	2.56

Race*	Population	%
African-American/Black (1,805)	2,264	2.98
Not Hispanic (1,521)	1,752	2.30
Hispanic (284)	512	0.67
American Indian/Alaska Native (741)	1,121	1.47
Not Hispanic (209)	349	0.46
Hispanic (532)	772	1.02
Alaska Athabascan *(Ala. Nat.)* (0)	0	<0.01
Aleut *(Alaska Native)* (2)	2	<0.01
Apache (20)	44	0.06
Arapaho (0)	0	<0.01
Blackfeet (3)	20	0.03
Canadian/French Am. Ind. (0)	1	<0.01
Central American Ind. (9)	17	0.02
Cherokee (26)	82	0.11
Cheyenne (0)	0	<0.01
Chickasaw (3)	10	0.01
Chippewa (2)	5	0.01
Choctaw (12)	27	0.04
Colville (0)	0	<0.01
Comanche (0)	2	<0.01
Cree (0)	0	<0.01
Creek (5)	11	0.01
Crow (0)	0	<0.01
Delaware (0)	1	<0.01
Hopi (0)	0	<0.01
Houma (0)	0	<0.01
Inupiat *(Alaska Native)* (1)	1	<0.01
Iroquois (2)	2	<0.01
Kiowa (0)	0	<0.01
Lumbee (0)	0	<0.01
Menominee (0)	0	<0.01
Mexican American Ind. (124)	179	0.24
Navajo (26)	40	0.05
Osage (0)	0	<0.01
Ottawa (1)	6	0.01
Paiute (0)	3	<0.01
Pima (14)	15	0.02
Potawatomi (1)	2	<0.01
Pueblo (0)	0	<0.01
Puget Sound Salish (3)	3	<0.01
Seminole (2)	3	<0.01
Shoshone (0)	2	<0.01
Sioux (4)	10	0.01
South American Ind. (1)	2	<0.01
Spanish American Ind. (9)	12	0.02
Tlingit-Haida *(Alaska Native)* (0)	0	<0.01
Tohono O'Odham (5)	7	0.01
Tsimshian *(Alaska Native)* (0)	0	<0.01
Ute (0)	1	<0.01
Yakama (0)	0	<0.01
Yaqui (14)	25	0.03
Yuman (4)	5	0.01
Yup'ik *(Alaska Native)* (0)	1	<0.01
Asian (1,693)	2,314	3.04
Not Hispanic (1,467)	1,784	2.35
Hispanic (226)	530	0.70
Bangladeshi (0)	0	<0.01
Bhutanese (0)	0	<0.01
Burmese (1)	1	<0.01
Cambodian (28)	36	0.05
Chinese, ex. Taiwanese (212)	291	0.38
Filipino (765)	1,093	1.44
Hmong (0)	0	<0.01
Indian (166)	198	0.26
Indonesian (20)	31	0.04
Japanese (112)	200	0.26
Korean (101)	130	0.17
Laotian (1)	5	0.01
Malaysian (1)	1	<0.01
Nepalese (0)	0	<0.01
Pakistani (13)	22	0.03
Sri Lankan (9)	10	0.01
Taiwanese (10)	17	0.02
Thai (20)	38	0.05
Vietnamese (151)	179	0.24
Hawaii Native/Pacific Islander (55)	174	0.23
Not Hispanic (40)	93	0.12
Hispanic (15)	81	0.11
Fijian (2)	2	<0.01
Guamanian/Chamorro (12)	36	0.05
Marshallese (0)	0	<0.01
Native Hawaiian (21)	72	0.09
Samoan (3)	10	0.01
Tongan (0)	0	<0.01
White (46,735)	48,900	64.31
Not Hispanic (20,512)	21,090	27.74
Hispanic (26,223)	27,810	36.57

*Notes: † The Census 2010 population figure is used to calculate the percentages in the Hispanic Origin and Race categories. Ancestry percentages are based on the 2006-2010 American Community Survey population (not shown); ‡ Numbers in parentheses indicate the number of people reporting a single ancestry; * Numbers in parentheses indicate the number of persons reporting this race alone, not in combination with any other race; Please refer to the Explanation of Data for more information.*

Inglewood

Place Type: City
County: Los Angeles
Population: 109,673

Ancestry	Population	%
Afghan (0)	0	<0.01
African, Sub-Saharan (2,554)	3,108	2.82
African (1,767)	2,163	1.97
Cape Verdean (0)	16	0.01
Ethiopian (316)	399	0.36
Ghanaian (15)	15	0.01
Kenyan (0)	0	<0.01
Liberian (9)	9	0.01
Nigerian (356)	415	0.38
Senegalese (0)	0	<0.01
Sierra Leonean (0)	0	<0.01
Somalian (0)	0	<0.01
South African (0)	0	<0.01
Sudanese (0)	0	<0.01
Ugandan (0)	0	<0.01
Zimbabwean (0)	0	<0.01
Other Sub-Saharan African (91)	91	0.08
Albanian (0)	0	<0.01
Alsatian (0)	0	<0.01
American (2,663)	2,663	2.42
Arab (235)	328	0.30
Arab (115)	148	0.13
Egyptian (97)	129	0.12
Iraqi (0)	0	<0.01
Jordanian (0)	0	<0.01
Lebanese (23)	51	0.05
Moroccan (0)	0	<0.01
Palestinian (0)	0	<0.01
Syrian (0)	0	<0.01
Other Arab (0)	0	<0.01
Armenian (41)	130	0.12
Assyrian/Chaldean/Syriac (0)	0	<0.01
Australian (0)	0	<0.01
Austrian (0)	33	0.03
Basque (0)	15	0.01
Belgian (0)	8	0.01
Brazilian (84)	264	0.24
British (0)	82	0.07
Bulgarian (0)	0	<0.01
Cajun (0)	0	<0.01
Canadian (0)	27	0.02
Carpatho Rusyn (0)	0	<0.01
Celtic (15)	15	0.01
Croatian (0)	57	0.05
Cypriot (0)	0	<0.01
Czech (0)	8	0.01
Czechoslovakian (0)	14	0.01
Danish (18)	18	0.02
Dutch (37)	100	0.09
Eastern European (13)	13	0.01
English (190)	663	0.60
Estonian (55)	55	0.05
European (106)	208	0.19
Finnish (0)	0	<0.01
French, ex. Basque (14)	644	0.59
French Canadian (0)	35	0.03
German (229)	1,216	1.10
German Russian (0)	0	<0.01
Greek (8)	17	0.02
Guyanese (40)	53	0.05
Hungarian (14)	119	0.11
Icelander (0)	0	<0.01
Iranian (8)	8	0.01
Irish (253)	958	0.87
Israeli (0)	0	<0.01
Italian (168)	543	0.49
Latvian (0)	0	<0.01
Lithuanian (0)	0	<0.01
Luxemburger (0)	0	<0.01
Macedonian (0)	0	<0.01
Maltese (0)	0	<0.01
New Zealander (0)	0	<0.01
Northern European (7)	7	0.01
Norwegian (25)	55	0.05
Pennsylvania German (0)	0	<0.01
Polish (34)	129	0.12
Portuguese (0)	26	0.02
Romanian (11)	11	0.01
Russian (7)	7	0.01
Scandinavian (30)	30	0.03
Scotch-Irish (105)	277	0.25
Scottish (38)	126	0.11
Serbian (0)	0	<0.01
Slavic (0)	0	<0.01
Slovak (0)	0	<0.01
Slovene (0)	0	<0.01
Soviet Union (0)	0	<0.01
Swedish (18)	71	0.06
Swiss (7)	7	0.01
Turkish (0)	39	0.04
Ukrainian (17)	17	0.02
Welsh (0)	91	0.08
West Indian, ex. Hispanic (1,362)	1,770	1.61
Bahamian (88)	88	0.08
Barbadian (16)	16	0.01
Belizean (505)	711	0.65
Bermudan (0)	0	<0.01
British West Indian (0)	0	<0.01
Dutch West Indian (0)	0	<0.01
Haitian (48)	48	0.04
Jamaican (612)	766	0.70
Trinidadian/Tobagonian (14)	14	0.01
U.S. Virgin Islander (22)	46	0.04
West Indian (57)	81	0.07
Other West Indian (0)	0	<0.01
Yugoslavian (90)	102	0.09

Hispanic Origin	Population	%
Hispanic or Latino (of any race)	55,449	50.56
Central American, ex. Mexican	8,697	7.93
Costa Rican	70	0.06
Guatemalan	3,593	3.28
Honduran	649	0.59
Nicaraguan	337	0.31
Panamanian	119	0.11
Salvadoran	3,869	3.53
Other Central American	60	0.05
Cuban	362	0.33
Dominican Republic	74	0.07
Mexican	41,983	38.28
Puerto Rican	578	0.53
South American	505	0.46
Argentinean	45	0.04
Bolivian	18	0.02
Chilean	14	0.01
Colombian	140	0.13
Ecuadorian	105	0.10
Paraguayan	3	<0.01
Peruvian	161	0.15
Uruguayan	3	<0.01
Venezuelan	13	0.01
Other South American	3	<0.01
Other Hispanic or Latino	3,250	2.96

Race*	Population	%
African-American/Black (48,164)	50,219	45.79
Not Hispanic (47,029)	48,512	44.23
Hispanic (1,135)	1,707	1.56
American Indian/Alaska Native (751)	1,699	1.55
Not Hispanic (220)	846	0.77
Hispanic (531)	853	0.78
Alaska Athabascan *(Ala. Nat.)* (0)	0	<0.01
Aleut *(Alaska Native)* (0)	0	<0.01
Apache (3)	17	0.02
Arapaho (0)	0	<0.01
Blackfeet (7)	70	0.06
Canadian/French Am. Ind. (0)	4	<0.01
Central American Ind. (4)	33	0.03
Cherokee (23)	208	0.19
Cheyenne (0)	0	<0.01
Chickasaw (0)	9	0.01
Chippewa (1)	2	<0.01
Choctaw (11)	57	0.05
Colville (0)	0	<0.01
Comanche (1)	3	<0.01
Cree (2)	2	<0.01
Creek (2)	18	0.02
Crow (0)	0	<0.01
Delaware (1)	1	<0.01
Hopi (0)	5	<0.01
Houma (0)	0	<0.01
Inupiat *(Alaska Native)* (0)	0	<0.01
Iroquois (0)	4	<0.01
Kiowa (0)	0	<0.01
Lumbee (0)	0	<0.01
Menominee (0)	0	<0.01
Mexican American Ind. (178)	268	0.24
Navajo (19)	30	0.03
Osage (0)	0	<0.01
Ottawa (0)	0	<0.01
Paiute (1)	1	<0.01
Pima (1)	1	<0.01
Potawatomi (0)	1	<0.01
Pueblo (8)	10	0.01
Puget Sound Salish (0)	0	<0.01
Seminole (4)	12	0.01
Shoshone (0)	1	<0.01
Sioux (2)	13	0.01
South American Ind. (2)	11	0.01
Spanish American Ind. (6)	9	0.01
Tlingit-Haida *(Alaska Native)* (4)	6	0.01
Tohono O'Odham (11)	14	0.01
Tsimshian *(Alaska Native)* (0)	0	<0.01
Ute (0)	0	<0.01
Yakama (1)	1	<0.01
Yaqui (12)	23	0.02
Yuman (0)	3	<0.01
Yup'ik *(Alaska Native)* (0)	0	<0.01
Asian (1,484)	2,104	1.92
Not Hispanic (1,374)	1,815	1.65
Hispanic (110)	289	0.26
Bangladeshi (14)	15	0.01
Bhutanese (0)	0	<0.01
Burmese (14)	15	0.01
Cambodian (15)	21	0.02
Chinese, ex. Taiwanese (92)	168	0.15
Filipino (593)	771	0.70
Hmong (2)	4	<0.01
Indian (257)	364	0.33
Indonesian (19)	35	0.03
Japanese (150)	271	0.25
Korean (51)	84	0.08
Laotian (3)	21	0.02
Malaysian (0)	0	<0.01
Nepalese (0)	2	<0.01
Pakistani (106)	135	0.12
Sri Lankan (42)	44	0.04
Taiwanese (10)	10	0.01
Thai (23)	37	0.03
Vietnamese (28)	47	0.04
Hawaii Native/Pacific Islander (350)	597	0.54
Not Hispanic (323)	497	0.45
Hispanic (27)	100	0.09
Fijian (62)	75	0.07
Guamanian/Chamorro (14)	16	0.01
Marshallese (0)	0	<0.01
Native Hawaiian (11)	54	0.05
Samoan (33)	67	0.06
Tongan (196)	221	0.20
White (25,562)	28,634	26.11
Not Hispanic (3,165)	4,080	3.72
Hispanic (22,397)	24,554	22.39

*Notes: † The Census 2010 population figure is used to calculate the percentages in the Hispanic Origin and Race categories. Ancestry percentages are based on the 2006-2010 American Community Survey population (not shown); ‡ Numbers in parentheses indicate the number of people reporting a single ancestry; * Numbers in parentheses indicate the number of persons reporting this race alone, not in combination with any other race; Please refer to the Explanation of Data for more information.*

Irvine

Place Type: City
County: Orange
Population: 212,375

Ancestry	Population	%
Afghan (1,177)	1,177	0.59
African, Sub-Saharan (763)	879	0.44
African (284)	350	0.18
Cape Verdean (15)	15	0.01
Ethiopian (33)	33	0.02
Ghanaian (0)	0	<0.01
Kenyan (0)	0	<0.01
Liberian (0)	0	<0.01
Nigerian (54)	54	0.03
Senegalese (0)	0	<0.01
Sierra Leonean (0)	0	<0.01
Somalian (75)	75	0.04
South African (302)	339	0.17
Sudanese (0)	0	<0.01
Ugandan (0)	0	<0.01
Zimbabwean (0)	13	0.01
Other Sub-Saharan African (0)	0	<0.01
Albanian (12)	27	0.01
Alsatian (0)	0	<0.01
American (7,327)	7,327	3.68
Arab (2,568)	3,229	1.62
Arab (557)	667	0.33
Egyptian (448)	463	0.23
Iraqi (41)	59	0.03
Jordanian (154)	239	0.12
Lebanese (558)	661	0.33
Moroccan (98)	133	0.07
Palestinian (35)	61	0.03
Syrian (161)	346	0.17
Other Arab (516)	600	0.30
Armenian (556)	838	0.42
Assyrian/Chaldean/Syriac (69)	87	0.04
Australian (164)	256	0.13
Austrian (160)	463	0.23
Basque (37)	111	0.06
Belgian (150)	271	0.14
Brazilian (58)	73	0.04
British (435)	1,176	0.59
Bulgarian (141)	141	0.07
Cajun (4)	4	<0.01
Canadian (460)	1,087	0.55
Carpatho Rusyn (0)	0	<0.01
Celtic (36)	48	0.02
Croatian (90)	243	0.12
Cypriot (0)	0	<0.01
Czech (322)	775	0.39
Czechoslovakian (116)	169	0.08
Danish (197)	858	0.43
Dutch (511)	1,650	0.83
Eastern European (724)	851	0.43
English (3,487)	12,960	6.51
Estonian (0)	0	<0.01
European (2,728)	3,236	1.63
Finnish (124)	303	0.15
French, ex. Basque (946)	4,184	2.10
French Canadian (307)	655	0.33
German (4,413)	17,426	8.75
German Russian (0)	0	<0.01
Greek (320)	835	0.42
Guyanese (24)	24	0.01
Hungarian (391)	1,365	0.69
Icelander (16)	57	0.03
Iranian (7,475)	7,908	3.97
Irish (3,783)	12,827	6.44
Israeli (442)	525	0.26
Italian (2,730)	7,135	3.58
Latvian (51)	131	0.07
Lithuanian (124)	335	0.17
Luxemburger (0)	7	<0.01
Macedonian (17)	31	0.02
Maltese (10)	10	0.01
New Zealander (7)	7	<0.01
Northern European (134)	164	0.08
Norwegian (546)	1,936	0.97
Pennsylvania German (8)	8	<0.01
Polish (1,202)	3,697	1.86
Portuguese (273)	743	0.37
Romanian (340)	617	0.31
Russian (2,106)	4,120	2.07
Scandinavian (168)	294	0.15
Scotch-Irish (735)	1,932	0.97
Scottish (614)	2,827	1.42
Serbian (96)	223	0.11
Slavic (10)	37	0.02
Slovak (26)	128	0.06
Slovene (32)	66	0.03
Soviet Union (0)	0	<0.01
Swedish (916)	2,808	1.41
Swiss (241)	835	0.42
Turkish (496)	612	0.31
Ukrainian (272)	465	0.23
Welsh (165)	736	0.37
West Indian, ex. Hispanic (46)	104	0.05
Bahamian (0)	0	<0.01
Barbadian (0)	0	<0.01
Belizean (0)	0	<0.01
Bermudan (0)	0	<0.01
British West Indian (0)	0	<0.01
Dutch West Indian (0)	0	<0.01
Haitian (0)	9	<0.01
Jamaican (46)	58	0.03
Trinidadian/Tobagonian (0)	28	0.01
U.S. Virgin Islander (0)	0	<0.01
West Indian (0)	9	<0.01
Other West Indian (0)	0	<0.01
Yugoslavian (121)	176	0.09

Hispanic Origin	Population	%
Hispanic or Latino (of any race)	19,621	9.24
Central American, ex. Mexican	1,461	0.69
Costa Rican	172	0.08
Guatemalan	334	0.16
Honduran	84	0.04
Nicaraguan	176	0.08
Panamanian	99	0.05
Salvadoran	585	0.28
Other Central American	11	0.01
Cuban	467	0.22
Dominican Republic	69	0.03
Mexican	12,807	6.03
Puerto Rican	641	0.30
South American	2,418	1.14
Argentinean	440	0.21
Bolivian	123	0.06
Chilean	198	0.09
Colombian	662	0.31
Ecuadorian	249	0.12
Paraguayan	8	<0.01
Peruvian	557	0.26
Uruguayan	26	0.01
Venezuelan	115	0.05
Other South American	40	0.02
Other Hispanic or Latino	1,758	0.83

Race*	Population	%
African-American/Black (3,718)	5,104	2.40
Not Hispanic (3,494)	4,618	2.17
Hispanic (224)	486	0.23
American Indian/Alaska Native (355)	1,362	0.64
Not Hispanic (199)	889	0.42
Hispanic (156)	473	0.22
Alaska Athabascan *(Ala. Nat.)* (0)	0	<0.01
Aleut *(Alaska Native)* (3)	8	<0.01
Apache (16)	57	0.03
Arapaho (0)	1	<0.01
Blackfeet (1)	29	0.01
Canadian/French Am. Ind. (0)	3	<0.01
Central American Ind. (0)	1	<0.01
Cherokee (38)	260	0.12
Cheyenne (2)	5	<0.01
Chickasaw (6)	14	0.01
Chippewa (4)	20	0.01
Choctaw (10)	41	0.02
Colville (0)	0	<0.01
Comanche (3)	10	<0.01
Cree (0)	3	<0.01
Creek (4)	20	0.01
Crow (0)	6	<0.01
Delaware (1)	1	<0.01
Hopi (3)	6	<0.01
Houma (1)	1	<0.01
Inupiat *(Alaska Native)* (0)	0	<0.01
Iroquois (1)	16	0.01
Kiowa (1)	6	<0.01
Lumbee (2)	3	<0.01
Menominee (0)	2	<0.01
Mexican American Ind. (43)	75	0.04
Navajo (13)	40	0.02
Osage (5)	17	0.01
Ottawa (2)	2	<0.01
Paiute (2)	2	<0.01
Pima (0)	3	<0.01
Potawatomi (0)	3	<0.01
Pueblo (4)	9	<0.01
Puget Sound Salish (0)	0	<0.01
Seminole (2)	5	<0.01
Shoshone (3)	6	<0.01
Sioux (10)	30	0.01
South American Ind. (5)	31	0.01
Spanish American Ind. (2)	2	<0.01
Tlingit-Haida *(Alaska Native)* (1)	1	<0.01
Tohono O'Odham (0)	0	<0.01
Tsimshian *(Alaska Native)* (0)	1	<0.01
Ute (0)	0	<0.01
Yakama (0)	0	<0.01
Yaqui (8)	16	0.01
Yuman (0)	0	<0.01
Yup'ik *(Alaska Native)* (0)	0	<0.01
Asian (83,176)	91,896	43.27
Not Hispanic (82,722)	90,762	42.74
Hispanic (454)	1,134	0.53
Bangladeshi (122)	136	0.06
Bhutanese (0)	0	<0.01
Burmese (93)	127	0.06
Cambodian (234)	336	0.16
Chinese, ex. Taiwanese (21,783)	25,177	11.85
Filipino (6,192)	8,085	3.81
Hmong (50)	56	0.03
Indian (10,687)	11,325	5.33
Indonesian (320)	498	0.23
Japanese (6,474)	8,797	4.14
Korean (18,445)	19,473	9.17
Laotian (74)	117	0.06
Malaysian (52)	84	0.04
Nepalese (50)	62	0.03
Pakistani (1,490)	1,631	0.77
Sri Lankan (195)	217	0.10
Taiwanese (5,284)	5,790	2.73
Thai (464)	598	0.28
Vietnamese (7,882)	9,000	4.24
Hawaii Native/Pacific Islander (334)	1,067	0.50
Not Hispanic (295)	953	0.45
Hispanic (39)	114	0.05
Fijian (18)	23	0.01
Guamanian/Chamorro (94)	163	0.08
Marshallese (8)	9	<0.01
Native Hawaiian (75)	347	0.16
Samoan (85)	146	0.07
Tongan (11)	18	0.01
White (107,215)	117,576	55.36
Not Hispanic (95,822)	104,511	49.21
Hispanic (11,393)	13,065	6.15

*Notes: † The Census 2010 population figure is used to calculate the percentages in the Hispanic Origin and Race categories. Ancestry percentages are based on the 2006-2010 American Community Survey population (not shown); ‡ Numbers in parentheses indicate the number of people reporting a single ancestry; * Numbers in parentheses indicate the number of persons reporting this race alone, not in combination with any other race; Please refer to the Explanation of Data for more information.*

La Habra

Place Type: City
County: Orange
Population: 60,239

Ancestry	Population	%
Afghan (77)	77	0.13
African, Sub-Saharan (12)	12	0.02
African (12)	12	0.02
Cape Verdean (0)	0	<0.01
Ethiopian (0)	0	<0.01
Ghanaian (0)	0	<0.01
Kenyan (0)	0	<0.01
Liberian (0)	0	<0.01
Nigerian (0)	0	<0.01
Senegalese (0)	0	<0.01
Sierra Leonean (0)	0	<0.01
Somalian (0)	0	<0.01
South African (0)	0	<0.01
Sudanese (0)	0	<0.01
Ugandan (0)	0	<0.01
Zimbabwean (0)	0	<0.01
Other Sub-Saharan African (0)	0	<0.01
Albanian (0)	12	0.02
Alsatian (0)	0	<0.01
American (1,343)	1,343	2.25
Arab (84)	179	0.30
Arab (10)	46	0.08
Egyptian (10)	18	0.03
Iraqi (0)	0	<0.01
Jordanian (0)	0	<0.01
Lebanese (30)	51	0.09
Moroccan (0)	0	<0.01
Palestinian (0)	20	0.03
Syrian (34)	44	0.07
Other Arab (0)	0	<0.01
Armenian (194)	244	0.41
Assyrian/Chaldean/Syriac (33)	85	0.14
Australian (0)	0	<0.01
Austrian (26)	144	0.24
Basque (35)	67	0.11
Belgian (0)	0	<0.01
Brazilian (17)	28	0.05
British (90)	185	0.31
Bulgarian (0)	0	<0.01
Cajun (0)	0	<0.01
Canadian (75)	104	0.17
Carpatho Rusyn (0)	0	<0.01
Celtic (21)	21	0.04
Croatian (0)	12	0.02
Cypriot (0)	0	<0.01
Czech (58)	206	0.34
Czechoslovakian (9)	17	0.03
Danish (47)	444	0.74
Dutch (301)	764	1.28
Eastern European (0)	0	<0.01
English (857)	3,431	5.74
Estonian (0)	16	0.03
European (582)	604	1.01
Finnish (31)	69	0.12
French, ex. Basque (143)	854	1.43
French Canadian (157)	203	0.34
German (1,324)	5,078	8.50
German Russian (0)	0	<0.01
Greek (46)	64	0.11
Guyanese (0)	0	<0.01
Hungarian (95)	177	0.30
Icelander (0)	0	<0.01
Iranian (202)	202	0.34
Irish (966)	4,339	7.26
Israeli (0)	25	0.04
Italian (634)	1,696	2.84
Latvian (0)	0	<0.01
Lithuanian (0)	13	0.02
Luxemburger (0)	0	<0.01
Macedonian (0)	0	<0.01
Maltese (13)	13	0.02
New Zealander (0)	0	<0.01
Northern European (28)	45	0.08
Norwegian (118)	545	0.91
Pennsylvania German (35)	35	0.06
Polish (124)	577	0.97
Portuguese (63)	136	0.23
Romanian (48)	98	0.16
Russian (274)	426	0.71
Scandinavian (24)	34	0.06
Scotch-Irish (222)	553	0.93
Scottish (105)	598	1.00
Serbian (43)	43	0.07
Slavic (41)	41	0.07
Slovak (14)	62	0.10
Slovene (0)	0	<0.01
Soviet Union (0)	0	<0.01
Swedish (115)	644	1.08
Swiss (0)	43	0.07
Turkish (0)	26	0.04
Ukrainian (5)	35	0.06
Welsh (43)	170	0.28
West Indian, ex. Hispanic (64)	64	0.11
Bahamian (0)	0	<0.01
Barbadian (0)	0	<0.01
Belizean (49)	49	0.08
Bermudan (0)	0	<0.01
British West Indian (0)	0	<0.01
Dutch West Indian (10)	10	0.02
Haitian (0)	0	<0.01
Jamaican (5)	5	0.01
Trinidadian/Tobagonian (0)	0	<0.01
U.S. Virgin Islander (0)	0	<0.01
West Indian (0)	0	<0.01
Other West Indian (0)	0	<0.01
Yugoslavian (41)	74	0.12

Hispanic Origin	Population	%
Hispanic or Latino (of any race)	34,449	57.19
Central American, ex. Mexican	1,283	2.13
Costa Rican	83	0.14
Guatemalan	418	0.69
Honduran	52	0.09
Nicaraguan	119	0.20
Panamanian	15	0.02
Salvadoran	577	0.96
Other Central American	19	0.03
Cuban	279	0.46
Dominican Republic	15	0.02
Mexican	30,316	50.33
Puerto Rican	313	0.52
South American	634	1.05
Argentinean	123	0.20
Bolivian	32	0.05
Chilean	30	0.05
Colombian	162	0.27
Ecuadorian	101	0.17
Paraguayan	7	0.01
Peruvian	151	0.25
Uruguayan	10	0.02
Venezuelan	8	0.01
Other South American	10	0.02
Other Hispanic or Latino	1,609	2.67

Race*	Population	%
African-American/Black (1,025)	1,349	2.24
Not Hispanic (836)	1,018	1.69
Hispanic (189)	331	0.55
American Indian/Alaska Native (531)	960	1.59
Not Hispanic (148)	368	0.61
Hispanic (383)	592	0.98
Alaska Athabascan *(Ala. Nat.)* (1)	1	<0.01
Aleut *(Alaska Native)* (0)	0	<0.01
Apache (15)	55	0.09
Arapaho (0)	1	<0.01
Blackfeet (0)	13	0.02
Canadian/French Am. Ind. (0)	0	<0.01
Central American Ind. (7)	8	0.01
Cherokee (28)	129	0.21
Cheyenne (0)	0	<0.01
Chickasaw (10)	13	0.02
Chippewa (7)	8	0.01
Choctaw (13)	38	0.06
Colville (0)	0	<0.01
Comanche (1)	3	<0.01
Cree (0)	0	<0.01
Creek (3)	11	0.02
Crow (1)	1	<0.01
Delaware (0)	7	0.01
Hopi (2)	6	0.01
Houma (0)	0	<0.01
Inupiat *(Alaska Native)* (0)	1	<0.01
Iroquois (0)	4	0.01
Kiowa (3)	3	<0.01
Lumbee (3)	7	0.01
Menominee (0)	0	<0.01
Mexican American Ind. (56)	79	0.13
Navajo (28)	47	0.08
Osage (5)	7	0.01
Ottawa (0)	0	<0.01
Paiute (5)	5	0.01
Pima (7)	10	0.02
Potawatomi (5)	5	0.01
Pueblo (14)	15	0.02
Puget Sound Salish (5)	5	0.01
Seminole (1)	1	<0.01
Shoshone (0)	0	<0.01
Sioux (8)	17	0.03
South American Ind. (1)	4	0.01
Spanish American Ind. (4)	4	0.01
Tlingit-Haida *(Alaska Native)* (0)	4	0.01
Tohono O'Odham (2)	6	0.01
Tsimshian *(Alaska Native)* (0)	0	<0.01
Ute (1)	1	<0.01
Yakama (0)	0	<0.01
Yaqui (7)	17	0.03
Yuman (1)	1	<0.01
Yup'ik *(Alaska Native)* (0)	0	<0.01
Asian (5,653)	6,415	10.65
Not Hispanic (5,501)	6,021	10.00
Hispanic (152)	394	0.65
Bangladeshi (15)	21	0.03
Bhutanese (0)	0	<0.01
Burmese (15)	17	0.03
Cambodian (43)	64	0.11
Chinese, ex. Taiwanese (695)	856	1.42
Filipino (1,137)	1,421	2.36
Hmong (2)	6	0.01
Indian (384)	430	0.71
Indonesian (61)	86	0.14
Japanese (352)	561	0.93
Korean (2,306)	2,375	3.94
Laotian (17)	18	0.03
Malaysian (5)	6	0.01
Nepalese (5)	5	0.01
Pakistani (37)	52	0.09
Sri Lankan (12)	12	0.02
Taiwanese (119)	148	0.25
Thai (83)	110	0.18
Vietnamese (197)	235	0.39
Hawaii Native/Pacific Islander (103)	288	0.48
Not Hispanic (80)	210	0.35
Hispanic (23)	78	0.13
Fijian (2)	3	<0.01
Guamanian/Chamorro (24)	39	0.06
Marshallese (0)	0	<0.01
Native Hawaiian (44)	129	0.21
Samoan (26)	47	0.08
Tongan (3)	6	0.01
White (35,147)	37,363	62.02
Not Hispanic (18,178)	19,022	31.58
Hispanic (16,969)	18,341	30.45

*Notes: † The Census 2010 population figure is used to calculate the percentages in the Hispanic Origin and Race categories. Ancestry percentages are based on the 2006-2010 American Community Survey population (not shown); ‡ Numbers in parentheses indicate the number of people reporting a single ancestry; * Numbers in parentheses indicate the number of persons reporting this race alone, not in combination with any other race; Please refer to the Explanation of Data for more information.*

La Mesa

Place Type: City
County: San Diego
Population: 57,065

Ancestry	Population	%
Afghan (73)	73	0.13
African, Sub-Saharan (608)	729	1.30
African (178)	281	0.50
Cape Verdean (0)	0	<0.01
Ethiopian (133)	133	0.24
Ghanaian (0)	0	<0.01
Kenyan (0)	0	<0.01
Liberian (0)	0	<0.01
Nigerian (64)	64	0.11
Senegalese (0)	0	<0.01
Sierra Leonean (0)	0	<0.01
Somalian (233)	233	0.41
South African (0)	18	0.03
Sudanese (0)	0	<0.01
Ugandan (0)	0	<0.01
Zimbabwean (0)	0	<0.01
Other Sub-Saharan African (0)	0	<0.01
Albanian (0)	0	<0.01
Alsatian (0)	0	<0.01
American (1,485)	1,485	2.64
Arab (233)	307	0.55
Arab (25)	25	0.04
Egyptian (49)	62	0.11
Iraqi (12)	12	0.02
Jordanian (79)	79	0.14
Lebanese (30)	56	0.10
Moroccan (0)	0	<0.01
Palestinian (0)	0	<0.01
Syrian (0)	11	0.02
Other Arab (38)	62	0.11
Armenian (74)	144	0.26
Assyrian/Chaldean/Syriac (94)	94	0.17
Australian (19)	62	0.11
Austrian (43)	103	0.18
Basque (0)	0	<0.01
Belgian (40)	141	0.25
Brazilian (0)	28	0.05
British (129)	318	0.57
Bulgarian (10)	10	0.02
Cajun (0)	0	<0.01
Canadian (55)	261	0.46
Carpatho Rusyn (0)	0	<0.01
Celtic (39)	39	0.07
Croatian (27)	27	0.05
Cypriot (0)	0	<0.01
Czech (34)	291	0.52
Czechoslovakian (88)	104	0.18
Danish (60)	404	0.72
Dutch (175)	854	1.52
Eastern European (12)	12	0.02
English (1,480)	6,214	11.05
Estonian (0)	0	<0.01
European (491)	617	1.10
Finnish (0)	168	0.30
French, ex. Basque (246)	1,923	3.42
French Canadian (116)	283	0.50
German (2,222)	10,278	18.27
German Russian (0)	43	0.08
Greek (73)	271	0.48
Guyanese (0)	0	<0.01
Hungarian (109)	421	0.75
Icelander (0)	14	0.02
Iranian (190)	277	0.49
Irish (2,145)	7,663	13.62
Israeli (12)	30	0.05
Italian (1,237)	3,706	6.59
Latvian (17)	17	0.03
Lithuanian (70)	166	0.30
Luxemburger (0)	0	<0.01
Macedonian (0)	18	0.03
Maltese (0)	0	<0.01
New Zealander (15)	15	0.03
Northern European (16)	16	0.03
Norwegian (441)	1,179	2.10
Pennsylvania German (32)	62	0.11
Polish (526)	1,674	2.98
Portuguese (267)	604	1.07
Romanian (51)	84	0.15
Russian (532)	917	1.63
Scandinavian (0)	320	0.57
Scotch-Irish (299)	1,262	2.24
Scottish (596)	1,903	3.38
Serbian (18)	18	0.03
Slavic (0)	16	0.03
Slovak (59)	116	0.21
Slovene (0)	14	0.02
Soviet Union (0)	0	<0.01
Swedish (407)	1,513	2.69
Swiss (29)	221	0.39
Turkish (19)	28	0.05
Ukrainian (146)	194	0.34
Welsh (103)	470	0.84
West Indian, ex. Hispanic (239)	419	0.74
Bahamian (0)	0	<0.01
Barbadian (12)	23	0.04
Belizean (65)	65	0.12
Bermudan (0)	0	<0.01
British West Indian (0)	0	<0.01
Dutch West Indian (0)	0	<0.01
Haitian (89)	89	0.16
Jamaican (73)	147	0.26
Trinidadian/Tobagonian (0)	0	<0.01
U.S. Virgin Islander (0)	0	<0.01
West Indian (0)	95	0.17
Other West Indian (0)	0	<0.01
Yugoslavian (45)	83	0.15

Hispanic Origin	Population	%
Hispanic or Latino (of any race)	11,696	20.50
Central American, ex. Mexican	339	0.59
Costa Rican	48	0.08
Guatemalan	66	0.12
Honduran	40	0.07
Nicaraguan	38	0.07
Panamanian	75	0.13
Salvadoran	69	0.12
Other Central American	3	0.01
Cuban	124	0.22
Dominican Republic	59	0.10
Mexican	9,496	16.64
Puerto Rican	402	0.70
South American	349	0.61
Argentinean	39	0.07
Bolivian	9	0.02
Chilean	28	0.05
Colombian	114	0.20
Ecuadorian	38	0.07
Paraguayan	1	<0.01
Peruvian	108	0.19
Uruguayan	0	<0.01
Venezuelan	10	0.02
Other South American	2	<0.01
Other Hispanic or Latino	927	1.62

Race*	Population	%
African-American/Black (4,399)	5,458	9.56
Not Hispanic (4,102)	4,914	8.61
Hispanic (297)	544	0.95
American Indian/Alaska Native (431)	1,104	1.93
Not Hispanic (249)	676	1.18
Hispanic (182)	428	0.75
Alaska Athabascan *(Ala. Nat.)* (1)	1	<0.01
Aleut *(Alaska Native)* (4)	4	0.01
Apache (18)	33	0.06
Arapaho (0)	0	<0.01
Blackfeet (7)	34	0.06
Canadian/French Am. Ind. (1)	2	<0.01
Central American Ind. (1)	3	0.01
Cherokee (22)	158	0.28
Cheyenne (0)	6	0.01
Chickasaw (4)	9	0.02
Chippewa (9)	19	0.03
Choctaw (11)	36	0.06
Colville (0)	0	<0.01
Comanche (4)	6	0.01
Cree (0)	1	<0.01
Creek (5)	17	0.03
Crow (1)	1	<0.01
Delaware (3)	5	0.01
Hopi (0)	4	0.01
Houma (0)	0	<0.01
Inupiat *(Alaska Native)* (1)	1	<0.01
Iroquois (9)	23	0.04
Kiowa (1)	3	0.01
Lumbee (2)	2	<0.01
Menominee (0)	0	<0.01
Mexican American Ind. (26)	46	0.08
Navajo (9)	30	0.05
Osage (6)	6	0.01
Ottawa (0)	0	<0.01
Paiute (2)	2	<0.01
Pima (4)	5	0.01
Potawatomi (3)	3	0.01
Pueblo (6)	12	0.02
Puget Sound Salish (1)	1	<0.01
Seminole (1)	7	0.01
Shoshone (0)	0	<0.01
Sioux (21)	33	0.06
South American Ind. (0)	4	0.01
Spanish American Ind. (5)	11	0.02
Tlingit-Haida *(Alaska Native)* (4)	5	0.01
Tohono O'Odham (1)	2	<0.01
Tsimshian *(Alaska Native)* (0)	0	<0.01
Ute (0)	7	0.01
Yakama (0)	0	<0.01
Yaqui (9)	29	0.05
Yuman (3)	4	0.01
Yup'ik *(Alaska Native)* (0)	0	<0.01
Asian (3,289)	4,584	8.03
Not Hispanic (3,152)	4,192	7.35
Hispanic (137)	392	0.69
Bangladeshi (0)	0	<0.01
Bhutanese (0)	0	<0.01
Burmese (1)	7	0.01
Cambodian (71)	97	0.17
Chinese, ex. Taiwanese (560)	756	1.32
Filipino (994)	1,591	2.79
Hmong (4)	4	0.01
Indian (206)	283	0.50
Indonesian (28)	46	0.08
Japanese (328)	641	1.12
Korean (186)	256	0.45
Laotian (58)	68	0.12
Malaysian (0)	1	<0.01
Nepalese (11)	11	0.02
Pakistani (16)	25	0.04
Sri Lankan (2)	3	0.01
Taiwanese (28)	33	0.06
Thai (61)	106	0.19
Vietnamese (567)	660	1.16
Hawaii Native/Pacific Islander (318)	622	1.09
Not Hispanic (272)	519	0.91
Hispanic (46)	103	0.18
Fijian (4)	4	0.01
Guamanian/Chamorro (149)	241	0.42
Marshallese (0)	0	<0.01
Native Hawaiian (36)	121	0.21
Samoan (92)	162	0.28
Tongan (2)	8	0.01
White (40,964)	43,761	76.69
Not Hispanic (35,295)	37,130	65.07
Hispanic (5,669)	6,631	11.62

*Notes: † The Census 2010 population figure is used to calculate the percentages in the Hispanic Origin and Race categories. Ancestry percentages are based on the 2006-2010 American Community Survey population (not shown); ‡ Numbers in parentheses indicate the number of people reporting a single ancestry; * Numbers in parentheses indicate the number of persons reporting this race alone, not in combination with any other race; Please refer to the Explanation of Data for more information.*

Laguna Niguel

Place Type: City
County: Orange
Population: 62,979

Ancestry	Population	%
Afghan (178)	178	0.28
African, Sub-Saharan (110)	116	0.19
African (23)	29	0.05
Cape Verdean (0)	0	<0.01
Ethiopian (0)	0	<0.01
Ghanaian (0)	0	<0.01
Kenyan (0)	0	<0.01
Liberian (0)	0	<0.01
Nigerian (0)	0	<0.01
Senegalese (0)	0	<0.01
Sierra Leonean (0)	0	<0.01
Somalian (0)	0	<0.01
South African (78)	78	0.12
Sudanese (9)	9	0.01
Ugandan (0)	0	<0.01
Zimbabwean (0)	0	<0.01
Other Sub-Saharan African (0)	0	<0.01
Albanian (0)	16	0.03
Alsatian (0)	0	<0.01
American (1,805)	1,805	2.88
Arab (527)	730	1.17
Arab (53)	53	0.08
Egyptian (156)	211	0.34
Iraqi (36)	51	0.08
Jordanian (14)	14	0.02
Lebanese (157)	258	0.41
Moroccan (0)	0	<0.01
Palestinian (9)	9	0.01
Syrian (65)	97	0.15
Other Arab (37)	37	0.06
Armenian (233)	387	0.62
Assyrian/Chaldean/Syriac (10)	10	0.02
Australian (0)	20	0.03
Austrian (119)	298	0.48
Basque (51)	67	0.11
Belgian (63)	91	0.15
Brazilian (50)	90	0.14
British (273)	778	1.24
Bulgarian (72)	72	0.11
Cajun (0)	0	<0.01
Canadian (98)	206	0.33
Carpatho Rusyn (0)	0	<0.01
Celtic (0)	0	<0.01
Croatian (60)	123	0.20
Cypriot (0)	0	<0.01
Czech (173)	337	0.54
Czechoslovakian (26)	60	0.10
Danish (175)	342	0.55
Dutch (258)	1,061	1.69
Eastern European (188)	188	0.30
English (2,540)	7,457	11.91
Estonian (11)	19	0.03
European (1,145)	1,430	2.28
Finnish (82)	228	0.36
French, ex. Basque (452)	2,235	3.57
French Canadian (93)	255	0.41
German (3,686)	10,822	17.28
German Russian (0)	0	<0.01
Greek (326)	557	0.89
Guyanese (0)	0	<0.01
Hungarian (224)	419	0.67
Icelander (0)	0	<0.01
Iranian (3,045)	3,258	5.20
Irish (2,506)	8,818	14.08
Israeli (0)	20	0.03
Italian (1,851)	4,797	7.66
Latvian (11)	11	0.02
Lithuanian (86)	227	0.36
Luxemburger (6)	6	0.01
Macedonian (0)	0	<0.01
Maltese (14)	41	0.07
New Zealander (50)	60	0.10
Northern European (59)	59	0.09
Norwegian (248)	845	1.35
Pennsylvania German (0)	18	0.03
Polish (751)	2,004	3.20
Portuguese (358)	526	0.84
Romanian (170)	421	0.67
Russian (809)	1,915	3.06
Scandinavian (43)	64	0.10
Scotch-Irish (428)	1,122	1.79
Scottish (378)	1,251	2.00
Serbian (0)	9	0.01
Slavic (58)	117	0.19
Slovak (33)	140	0.22
Slovene (0)	37	0.06
Soviet Union (0)	0	<0.01
Swedish (286)	1,257	2.01
Swiss (41)	289	0.46
Turkish (10)	48	0.08
Ukrainian (102)	272	0.43
Welsh (57)	423	0.68
West Indian, ex. Hispanic (42)	61	0.10
Bahamian (0)	0	<0.01
Barbadian (17)	17	0.03
Belizean (0)	0	<0.01
Bermudan (0)	0	<0.01
British West Indian (0)	0	<0.01
Dutch West Indian (25)	44	0.07
Haitian (0)	0	<0.01
Jamaican (0)	0	<0.01
Trinidadian/Tobagonian (0)	0	<0.01
U.S. Virgin Islander (0)	0	<0.01
West Indian (0)	0	<0.01
Other West Indian (0)	0	<0.01
Yugoslavian (48)	64	0.10

Hispanic Origin	Population	%
Hispanic or Latino (of any race)	8,761	13.91
Central American, ex. Mexican	479	0.76
Costa Rican	34	0.05
Guatemalan	191	0.30
Honduran	18	0.03
Nicaraguan	62	0.10
Panamanian	39	0.06
Salvadoran	115	0.18
Other Central American	20	0.03
Cuban	212	0.34
Dominican Republic	18	0.03
Mexican	6,264	9.95
Puerto Rican	214	0.34
South American	813	1.29
Argentinean	159	0.25
Bolivian	39	0.06
Chilean	42	0.07
Colombian	196	0.31
Ecuadorian	78	0.12
Paraguayan	1	<0.01
Peruvian	240	0.38
Uruguayan	3	<0.01
Venezuelan	38	0.06
Other South American	17	0.03
Other Hispanic or Latino	761	1.21

Race*	Population	%
African-American/Black (777)	1,113	1.77
Not Hispanic (693)	952	1.51
Hispanic (84)	161	0.26
American Indian/Alaska Native (219)	571	0.91
Not Hispanic (115)	355	0.56
Hispanic (104)	216	0.34
Alaska Athabascan *(Ala. Nat.)* (1)	1	<0.01
Aleut *(Alaska Native)* (0)	0	<0.01
Apache (7)	33	0.05
Arapaho (0)	0	<0.01
Blackfeet (0)	12	0.02
Canadian/French Am. Ind. (1)	1	<0.01
Central American Ind. (0)	0	<0.01
Cherokee (13)	96	0.15
Cheyenne (1)	2	<0.01
Chickasaw (2)	7	0.01
Chippewa (3)	14	0.02
Choctaw (7)	23	0.04
Colville (0)	3	<0.01
Comanche (4)	12	0.02
Cree (1)	1	<0.01
Creek (1)	1	<0.01
Crow (0)	0	<0.01
Delaware (0)	7	0.01
Hopi (2)	5	0.01
Houma (0)	0	<0.01
Inupiat *(Alaska Native)* (1)	1	<0.01
Iroquois (0)	1	<0.01
Kiowa (0)	0	<0.01
Lumbee (0)	0	<0.01
Menominee (0)	0	<0.01
Mexican American Ind. (18)	41	0.07
Navajo (10)	13	0.02
Osage (2)	2	<0.01
Ottawa (2)	2	<0.01
Paiute (0)	1	<0.01
Pima (1)	1	<0.01
Potawatomi (0)	3	<0.01
Pueblo (5)	6	0.01
Puget Sound Salish (0)	1	<0.01
Seminole (0)	1	<0.01
Shoshone (1)	3	<0.01
Sioux (0)	6	0.01
South American Ind. (1)	5	0.01
Spanish American Ind. (0)	0	<0.01
Tlingit-Haida *(Alaska Native)* (0)	2	<0.01
Tohono O'Odham (0)	0	<0.01
Tsimshian *(Alaska Native)* (0)	0	<0.01
Ute (1)	4	0.01
Yakama (0)	0	<0.01
Yaqui (2)	4	0.01
Yuman (0)	0	<0.01
Yup'ik *(Alaska Native)* (0)	0	<0.01
Asian (5,459)	7,236	11.49
Not Hispanic (5,390)	7,000	11.11
Hispanic (69)	236	0.37
Bangladeshi (6)	11	0.02
Bhutanese (0)	0	<0.01
Burmese (2)	3	<0.01
Cambodian (32)	56	0.09
Chinese, ex. Taiwanese (1,225)	1,558	2.47
Filipino (1,125)	1,529	2.43
Hmong (2)	2	<0.01
Indian (488)	547	0.87
Indonesian (83)	116	0.18
Japanese (779)	1,151	1.83
Korean (573)	699	1.11
Laotian (13)	16	0.03
Malaysian (6)	13	0.02
Nepalese (6)	9	0.01
Pakistani (60)	74	0.12
Sri Lankan (16)	16	0.03
Taiwanese (201)	235	0.37
Thai (78)	106	0.17
Vietnamese (520)	642	1.02
Hawaii Native/Pacific Islander (87)	290	0.46
Not Hispanic (79)	262	0.42
Hispanic (8)	28	0.04
Fijian (3)	9	0.01
Guamanian/Chamorro (9)	24	0.04
Marshallese (0)	0	<0.01
Native Hawaiian (31)	102	0.16
Samoan (17)	49	0.08
Tongan (6)	10	0.02
White (50,625)	53,168	84.42
Not Hispanic (45,682)	47,688	75.72
Hispanic (4,943)	5,480	8.70

*Notes: † The Census 2010 population figure is used to calculate the percentages in the Hispanic Origin and Race categories. Ancestry percentages are based on the 2006-2010 American Community Survey population (not shown); ‡ Numbers in parentheses indicate the number of people reporting a single ancestry; * Numbers in parentheses indicate the number of persons reporting this race alone, not in combination with any other race; Please refer to the Explanation of Data for more information.*

Lake Elsinore

Place Type: City
County: Riverside
Population: 51,821

Ancestry	Population	%
Afghan (0)	12	0.02
African, Sub-Saharan (129)	366	0.75
African (53)	244	0.50
Cape Verdean (0)	0	<0.01
Ethiopian (0)	0	<0.01
Ghanaian (0)	0	<0.01
Kenyan (0)	0	<0.01
Liberian (0)	0	<0.01
Nigerian (76)	76	0.16
Senegalese (0)	0	<0.01
Sierra Leonean (0)	0	<0.01
Somalian (0)	46	0.09
South African (0)	0	<0.01
Sudanese (0)	0	<0.01
Ugandan (0)	0	<0.01
Zimbabwean (0)	0	<0.01
Other Sub-Saharan African (0)	0	<0.01
Albanian (0)	0	<0.01
Alsatian (0)	0	<0.01
American (1,132)	1,132	2.33
Arab (121)	281	0.58
Arab (11)	11	0.02
Egyptian (0)	27	0.06
Iraqi (0)	0	<0.01
Jordanian (29)	29	0.06
Lebanese (15)	130	0.27
Moroccan (0)	0	<0.01
Palestinian (25)	25	0.05
Syrian (41)	59	0.12
Other Arab (0)	0	<0.01
Armenian (12)	120	0.25
Assyrian/Chaldean/Syriac (0)	0	<0.01
Australian (0)	0	<0.01
Austrian (22)	46	0.09
Basque (0)	0	<0.01
Belgian (0)	0	<0.01
Brazilian (0)	26	0.05
British (33)	51	0.10
Bulgarian (0)	9	0.02
Cajun (0)	0	<0.01
Canadian (147)	176	0.36
Carpatho Rusyn (0)	0	<0.01
Celtic (0)	0	<0.01
Croatian (34)	45	0.09
Cypriot (0)	0	<0.01
Czech (60)	205	0.42
Czechoslovakian (0)	6	0.01
Danish (14)	365	0.75
Dutch (411)	1,108	2.28
Eastern European (22)	22	0.05
English (911)	2,988	6.14
Estonian (0)	0	<0.01
European (317)	456	0.94
Finnish (51)	111	0.23
French, ex. Basque (394)	1,370	2.82
French Canadian (62)	202	0.42
German (1,297)	4,777	9.82
German Russian (0)	0	<0.01
Greek (18)	132	0.27
Guyanese (0)	0	<0.01
Hungarian (70)	175	0.36
Icelander (0)	7	0.01
Iranian (12)	53	0.11
Irish (623)	3,621	7.44
Israeli (0)	0	<0.01
Italian (909)	2,321	4.77
Latvian (0)	0	<0.01
Lithuanian (0)	14	0.03
Luxemburger (0)	0	<0.01
Macedonian (0)	0	<0.01
Maltese (0)	0	<0.01
New Zealander (0)	40	0.08
Northern European (0)	0	<0.01
Norwegian (198)	552	1.13
Pennsylvania German (0)	0	<0.01
Polish (251)	668	1.37
Portuguese (41)	134	0.28
Romanian (26)	45	0.09
Russian (42)	197	0.40
Scandinavian (60)	126	0.26
Scotch-Irish (154)	490	1.01
Scottish (152)	510	1.05
Serbian (0)	0	<0.01
Slavic (0)	0	<0.01
Slovak (0)	21	0.04
Slovene (0)	6	0.01
Soviet Union (0)	0	<0.01
Swedish (36)	496	1.02
Swiss (9)	105	0.22
Turkish (0)	0	<0.01
Ukrainian (26)	54	0.11
Welsh (28)	189	0.39
West Indian, ex. Hispanic (166)	297	0.61
Bahamian (0)	0	<0.01
Barbadian (0)	0	<0.01
Belizean (17)	111	0.23
Bermudan (0)	0	<0.01
British West Indian (0)	0	<0.01
Dutch West Indian (0)	0	<0.01
Haitian (0)	0	<0.01
Jamaican (149)	186	0.38
Trinidadian/Tobagonian (0)	0	<0.01
U.S. Virgin Islander (0)	0	<0.01
West Indian (0)	0	<0.01
Other West Indian (0)	0	<0.01
Yugoslavian (25)	40	0.08

Hispanic Origin	Population	%
Hispanic or Latino (of any race)	25,073	48.38
Central American, ex. Mexican	1,935	3.73
Costa Rican	46	0.09
Guatemalan	1,268	2.45
Honduran	49	0.09
Nicaraguan	73	0.14
Panamanian	51	0.10
Salvadoran	433	0.84
Other Central American	15	0.03
Cuban	150	0.29
Dominican Republic	23	0.04
Mexican	20,497	39.55
Puerto Rican	319	0.62
South American	558	1.08
Argentinean	142	0.27
Bolivian	16	0.03
Chilean	29	0.06
Colombian	136	0.26
Ecuadorian	71	0.14
Paraguayan	9	0.02
Peruvian	130	0.25
Uruguayan	6	0.01
Venezuelan	18	0.03
Other South American	1	<0.01
Other Hispanic or Latino	1,591	3.07

Race*	Population	%
African-American/Black (2,738)	3,544	6.84
Not Hispanic (2,488)	3,011	5.81
Hispanic (250)	533	1.03
American Indian/Alaska Native (483)	1,054	2.03
Not Hispanic (190)	515	0.99
Hispanic (293)	539	1.04
Alaska Athabascan *(Ala. Nat.)* (0)	0	<0.01
Aleut *(Alaska Native)* (6)	6	0.01
Apache (20)	48	0.09
Arapaho (0)	0	<0.01
Blackfeet (5)	33	0.06
Canadian/French Am. Ind. (3)	3	0.01
Central American Ind. (5)	5	0.01
Cherokee (17)	130	0.25
Cheyenne (3)	7	0.01
Chickasaw (1)	4	0.01
Chippewa (4)	11	0.02
Choctaw (4)	27	0.05
Colville (0)	0	<0.01
Comanche (3)	11	0.02
Cree (0)	0	<0.01
Creek (5)	14	0.03
Crow (0)	2	<0.01
Delaware (5)	8	0.02
Hopi (1)	5	0.01
Houma (0)	0	<0.01
Inupiat *(Alaska Native)* (0)	1	<0.01
Iroquois (2)	10	0.02
Kiowa (0)	0	<0.01
Lumbee (0)	1	<0.01
Menominee (0)	0	<0.01
Mexican American Ind. (71)	103	0.20
Navajo (11)	14	0.03
Osage (1)	4	0.01
Ottawa (0)	2	<0.01
Paiute (0)	1	<0.01
Pima (0)	1	<0.01
Potawatomi (0)	0	<0.01
Pueblo (4)	6	0.01
Puget Sound Salish (5)	5	0.01
Seminole (3)	4	0.01
Shoshone (3)	9	0.02
Sioux (9)	29	0.06
South American Ind. (0)	2	<0.01
Spanish American Ind. (1)	1	<0.01
Tlingit-Haida *(Alaska Native)* (0)	1	<0.01
Tohono O'Odham (1)	4	0.01
Tsimshian *(Alaska Native)* (0)	1	<0.01
Ute (0)	0	<0.01
Yakama (0)	0	<0.01
Yaqui (12)	20	0.04
Yuman (3)	3	0.01
Yup'ik *(Alaska Native)* (0)	0	<0.01
Asian (2,996)	3,768	7.27
Not Hispanic (2,895)	3,431	6.62
Hispanic (101)	337	0.65
Bangladeshi (0)	0	<0.01
Bhutanese (0)	0	<0.01
Burmese (6)	7	0.01
Cambodian (213)	230	0.44
Chinese, ex. Taiwanese (258)	383	0.74
Filipino (1,272)	1,681	3.24
Hmong (8)	9	0.02
Indian (153)	173	0.33
Indonesian (8)	24	0.05
Japanese (118)	271	0.52
Korean (270)	333	0.64
Laotian (51)	62	0.12
Malaysian (2)	7	0.01
Nepalese (1)	1	<0.01
Pakistani (47)	54	0.10
Sri Lankan (2)	4	0.01
Taiwanese (9)	12	0.02
Thai (38)	60	0.12
Vietnamese (427)	504	0.97
Hawaii Native/Pacific Islander (174)	409	0.79
Not Hispanic (144)	309	0.60
Hispanic (30)	100	0.19
Fijian (4)	8	0.02
Guamanian/Chamorro (22)	50	0.10
Marshallese (0)	0	<0.01
Native Hawaiian (47)	155	0.30
Samoan (71)	141	0.27
Tongan (4)	4	0.01
White (31,067)	33,819	65.26
Not Hispanic (19,604)	20,757	40.06
Hispanic (11,463)	13,062	25.21

*Notes: † The Census 2010 population figure is used to calculate the percentages in the Hispanic Origin and Race categories. Ancestry percentages are based on the 2006-2010 American Community Survey population (not shown); ‡ Numbers in parentheses indicate the number of people reporting a single ancestry; * Numbers in parentheses indicate the number of persons reporting this race alone, not in combination with any other race; Please refer to the Explanation of Data for more information.*

Lake Forest

Place Type: City
County: Orange
Population: 77,264

Ancestry	Population	%
Afghan (106)	150	0.20
African, Sub-Saharan (250)	250	0.33
African (148)	148	0.19
Cape Verdean (0)	0	<0.01
Ethiopian (0)	0	<0.01
Ghanaian (0)	0	<0.01
Kenyan (0)	0	<0.01
Liberian (0)	0	<0.01
Nigerian (0)	0	<0.01
Senegalese (0)	0	<0.01
Sierra Leonean (0)	0	<0.01
Somalian (46)	46	0.06
South African (56)	56	0.07
Sudanese (0)	0	<0.01
Ugandan (0)	0	<0.01
Zimbabwean (0)	0	<0.01
Other Sub-Saharan African (0)	0	<0.01
Albanian (11)	11	0.01
Alsatian (0)	16	0.02
American (2,803)	2,803	3.65
Arab (365)	481	0.63
Arab (46)	46	0.06
Egyptian (132)	186	0.24
Iraqi (0)	0	<0.01
Jordanian (0)	0	<0.01
Lebanese (151)	213	0.28
Moroccan (0)	0	<0.01
Palestinian (0)	0	<0.01
Syrian (17)	17	0.02
Other Arab (19)	19	0.02
Armenian (164)	269	0.35
Assyrian/Chaldean/Syriac (0)	0	<0.01
Australian (42)	112	0.15
Austrian (26)	209	0.27
Basque (0)	19	0.02
Belgian (37)	109	0.14
Brazilian (66)	92	0.12
British (381)	891	1.16
Bulgarian (0)	0	<0.01
Cajun (0)	0	<0.01
Canadian (138)	263	0.34
Carpatho Rusyn (0)	0	<0.01
Celtic (0)	0	<0.01
Croatian (61)	153	0.20
Cypriot (0)	0	<0.01
Czech (96)	255	0.33
Czechoslovakian (21)	47	0.06
Danish (88)	400	0.52
Dutch (468)	1,646	2.15
Eastern European (128)	141	0.18
English (2,574)	7,581	9.88
Estonian (0)	0	<0.01
European (989)	1,247	1.63
Finnish (49)	243	0.32
French, ex. Basque (524)	2,611	3.40
French Canadian (214)	423	0.55
German (3,106)	11,350	14.79
German Russian (0)	0	<0.01
Greek (131)	366	0.48
Guyanese (0)	0	<0.01
Hungarian (126)	325	0.42
Icelander (16)	16	0.02
Iranian (984)	1,167	1.52
Irish (2,297)	8,071	10.52
Israeli (57)	57	0.07
Italian (1,754)	4,292	5.59
Latvian (0)	13	0.02
Lithuanian (0)	79	0.10
Luxemburger (0)	0	<0.01
Macedonian (0)	0	<0.01
Maltese (0)	31	0.04
New Zealander (0)	0	<0.01
Northern European (57)	92	0.12
Norwegian (493)	1,272	1.66
Pennsylvania German (0)	0	<0.01
Polish (444)	1,967	2.56
Portuguese (80)	255	0.33
Romanian (199)	250	0.33
Russian (570)	1,310	1.71
Scandinavian (150)	230	0.30
Scotch-Irish (454)	1,120	1.46
Scottish (369)	1,503	1.96
Serbian (7)	33	0.04
Slavic (8)	18	0.02
Slovak (0)	44	0.06
Slovene (0)	7	0.01
Soviet Union (0)	0	<0.01
Swedish (386)	1,761	2.30
Swiss (4)	340	0.44
Turkish (52)	100	0.13
Ukrainian (48)	148	0.19
Welsh (67)	508	0.66
West Indian, ex. Hispanic (14)	14	0.02
Bahamian (0)	0	<0.01
Barbadian (0)	0	<0.01
Belizean (0)	0	<0.01
Bermudan (0)	0	<0.01
British West Indian (0)	0	<0.01
Dutch West Indian (0)	0	<0.01
Haitian (0)	0	<0.01
Jamaican (14)	14	0.02
Trinidadian/Tobagonian (0)	0	<0.01
U.S. Virgin Islander (0)	0	<0.01
West Indian (0)	0	<0.01
Other West Indian (0)	0	<0.01
Yugoslavian (0)	82	0.11

Hispanic Origin	Population	%
Hispanic or Latino (of any race)	19,024	24.62
Central American, ex. Mexican	1,595	2.06
Costa Rican	70	0.09
Guatemalan	855	1.11
Honduran	60	0.08
Nicaraguan	83	0.11
Panamanian	38	0.05
Salvadoran	474	0.61
Other Central American	15	0.02
Cuban	200	0.26
Dominican Republic	13	0.02
Mexican	14,299	18.51
Puerto Rican	354	0.46
South American	1,430	1.85
Argentinean	261	0.34
Bolivian	85	0.11
Chilean	60	0.08
Colombian	454	0.59
Ecuadorian	120	0.16
Paraguayan	2	<0.01
Peruvian	371	0.48
Uruguayan	19	0.02
Venezuelan	39	0.05
Other South American	19	0.02
Other Hispanic or Latino	1,133	1.47

Race*	Population	%
African-American/Black (1,295)	1,794	2.32
Not Hispanic (1,158)	1,544	2.00
Hispanic (137)	250	0.32
American Indian/Alaska Native (384)	951	1.23
Not Hispanic (195)	548	0.71
Hispanic (189)	403	0.52
Alaska Athabascan *(Ala. Nat.)* (1)	1	<0.01
Aleut *(Alaska Native)* (0)	2	<0.01
Apache (7)	29	0.04
Arapaho (1)	1	<0.01
Blackfeet (6)	26	0.03
Canadian/French Am. Ind. (5)	8	0.01
Central American Ind. (0)	4	0.01
Cherokee (23)	164	0.21
Cheyenne (0)	2	<0.01
Chickasaw (0)	7	0.01
Chippewa (7)	11	0.01
Choctaw (10)	36	0.05
Colville (0)	0	<0.01
Comanche (0)	3	<0.01
Cree (0)	0	<0.01
Creek (6)	11	0.01
Crow (0)	0	<0.01
Delaware (1)	6	0.01
Hopi (0)	2	<0.01
Houma (0)	0	<0.01
Inupiat *(Alaska Native)* (0)	0	<0.01
Iroquois (9)	12	0.02
Kiowa (0)	6	0.01
Lumbee (1)	1	<0.01
Menominee (1)	1	<0.01
Mexican American Ind. (44)	70	0.09
Navajo (9)	18	0.02
Osage (9)	20	0.03
Ottawa (0)	0	<0.01
Paiute (1)	2	<0.01
Pima (0)	1	<0.01
Potawatomi (3)	8	0.01
Pueblo (10)	20	0.03
Puget Sound Salish (0)	0	<0.01
Seminole (0)	5	0.01
Shoshone (0)	2	<0.01
Sioux (4)	15	0.02
South American Ind. (4)	13	0.02
Spanish American Ind. (3)	9	0.01
Tlingit-Haida *(Alaska Native)* (0)	0	<0.01
Tohono O'Odham (1)	1	<0.01
Tsimshian *(Alaska Native)* (0)	0	<0.01
Ute (1)	1	<0.01
Yakama (0)	0	<0.01
Yaqui (5)	11	0.01
Yuman (0)	0	<0.01
Yup'ik *(Alaska Native)* (0)	0	<0.01
Asian (10,115)	12,091	15.65
Not Hispanic (9,985)	11,699	15.14
Hispanic (130)	392	0.51
Bangladeshi (8)	13	0.02
Bhutanese (0)	0	<0.01
Burmese (5)	13	0.02
Cambodian (35)	51	0.07
Chinese, ex. Taiwanese (1,432)	1,946	2.52
Filipino (2,625)	3,232	4.18
Hmong (15)	17	0.02
Indian (1,610)	1,739	2.25
Indonesian (189)	266	0.34
Japanese (764)	1,267	1.64
Korean (827)	983	1.27
Laotian (61)	72	0.09
Malaysian (16)	24	0.03
Nepalese (0)	0	<0.01
Pakistani (116)	127	0.16
Sri Lankan (93)	100	0.13
Taiwanese (228)	293	0.38
Thai (108)	145	0.19
Vietnamese (1,617)	1,819	2.35
Hawaii Native/Pacific Islander (191)	509	0.66
Not Hispanic (172)	425	0.55
Hispanic (19)	84	0.11
Fijian (2)	2	<0.01
Guamanian/Chamorro (43)	92	0.12
Marshallese (0)	0	<0.01
Native Hawaiian (59)	182	0.24
Samoan (46)	73	0.09
Tongan (2)	4	0.01
White (54,341)	57,595	74.54
Not Hispanic (44,177)	46,333	59.97
Hispanic (10,164)	11,262	14.58

*Notes: † The Census 2010 population figure is used to calculate the percentages in the Hispanic Origin and Race categories. Ancestry percentages are based on the 2006-2010 American Community Survey population (not shown); ‡ Numbers in parentheses indicate the number of people reporting a single ancestry; * Numbers in parentheses indicate the number of persons reporting this race alone, not in combination with any other race; Please refer to the Explanation of Data for more information.*

Lakewood

Place Type: City
County: Los Angeles
Population: 80,048

Ancestry	Population	%
Afghan (0)	0	<0.01
African, Sub-Saharan (457)	542	0.68
African (242)	302	0.38
Cape Verdean (25)	50	0.06
Ethiopian (0)	0	<0.01
Ghanaian (0)	0	<0.01
Kenyan (0)	0	<0.01
Liberian (0)	0	<0.01
Nigerian (45)	45	0.06
Senegalese (0)	0	<0.01
Sierra Leonean (0)	0	<0.01
Somalian (0)	0	<0.01
South African (12)	12	0.02
Sudanese (0)	0	<0.01
Ugandan (0)	0	<0.01
Zimbabwean (0)	0	<0.01
Other Sub-Saharan African (133)	133	0.17
Albanian (0)	0	<0.01
Alsatian (0)	0	<0.01
American (1,588)	1,588	1.99
Arab (461)	668	0.84
Arab (110)	147	0.18
Egyptian (93)	129	0.16
Iraqi (0)	0	<0.01
Jordanian (52)	68	0.09
Lebanese (34)	45	0.06
Moroccan (121)	149	0.19
Palestinian (0)	16	0.02
Syrian (38)	63	0.08
Other Arab (13)	51	0.06
Armenian (80)	216	0.27
Assyrian/Chaldean/Syriac (0)	0	<0.01
Australian (45)	45	0.06
Austrian (12)	171	0.21
Basque (0)	0	<0.01
Belgian (0)	23	0.03
Brazilian (41)	41	0.05
British (77)	158	0.20
Bulgarian (0)	0	<0.01
Cajun (0)	0	<0.01
Canadian (135)	253	0.32
Carpatho Rusyn (0)	0	<0.01
Celtic (11)	23	0.03
Croatian (0)	39	0.05
Cypriot (11)	11	0.01
Czech (11)	124	0.16
Czechoslovakian (24)	42	0.05
Danish (136)	436	0.55
Dutch (557)	1,430	1.79
Eastern European (84)	84	0.11
English (1,789)	5,414	6.78
Estonian (0)	0	<0.01
European (900)	1,113	1.39
Finnish (77)	160	0.20
French, ex. Basque (190)	1,245	1.56
French Canadian (101)	241	0.30
German (2,537)	8,127	10.18
German Russian (0)	0	<0.01
Greek (11)	115	0.14
Guyanese (23)	45	0.06
Hungarian (56)	392	0.49
Icelander (64)	64	0.08
Iranian (17)	39	0.05
Irish (1,401)	6,044	7.57
Israeli (29)	29	0.04
Italian (851)	2,493	3.12
Latvian (11)	11	0.01
Lithuanian (0)	39	0.05
Luxemburger (0)	0	<0.01
Macedonian (0)	0	<0.01
Maltese (0)	0	<0.01
New Zealander (0)	0	<0.01
Northern European (33)	43	0.05
Norwegian (270)	992	1.24
Pennsylvania German (36)	48	0.06
Polish (342)	922	1.15
Portuguese (161)	443	0.55
Romanian (123)	185	0.23
Russian (308)	624	0.78
Scandinavian (85)	130	0.16
Scotch-Irish (115)	823	1.03
Scottish (385)	1,067	1.34
Serbian (0)	12	0.02
Slavic (0)	0	<0.01
Slovak (0)	0	<0.01
Slovene (0)	35	0.04
Soviet Union (0)	0	<0.01
Swedish (273)	821	1.03
Swiss (54)	170	0.21
Turkish (13)	26	0.03
Ukrainian (10)	38	0.05
Welsh (56)	249	0.31
West Indian, ex. Hispanic (257)	321	0.40
Bahamian (0)	0	<0.01
Barbadian (0)	0	<0.01
Belizean (153)	153	0.19
Bermudan (0)	0	<0.01
British West Indian (0)	0	<0.01
Dutch West Indian (0)	0	<0.01
Haitian (0)	0	<0.01
Jamaican (75)	75	0.09
Trinidadian/Tobagonian (9)	9	0.01
U.S. Virgin Islander (0)	0	<0.01
West Indian (20)	84	0.11
Other West Indian (0)	0	<0.01
Yugoslavian (19)	54	0.07

Hispanic Origin	Population	%
Hispanic or Latino (of any race)	24,101	30.11
Central American, ex. Mexican	1,566	1.96
Costa Rican	106	0.13
Guatemalan	394	0.49
Honduran	153	0.19
Nicaraguan	170	0.21
Panamanian	65	0.08
Salvadoran	662	0.83
Other Central American	16	0.02
Cuban	315	0.39
Dominican Republic	63	0.08
Mexican	19,252	24.05
Puerto Rican	537	0.67
South American	824	1.03
Argentinean	151	0.19
Bolivian	18	0.02
Chilean	57	0.07
Colombian	193	0.24
Ecuadorian	136	0.17
Paraguayan	0	<0.01
Peruvian	227	0.28
Uruguayan	24	0.03
Venezuelan	9	0.01
Other South American	9	0.01
Other Hispanic or Latino	1,544	1.93

Race*	Population	%
African-American/Black (6,973)	8,044	10.05
Not Hispanic (6,663)	7,424	9.27
Hispanic (310)	620	0.77
American Indian/Alaska Native (564)	1,320	1.65
Not Hispanic (234)	704	0.88
Hispanic (330)	616	0.77
Alaska Athabascan *(Ala. Nat.)* (0)	0	<0.01
Aleut *(Alaska Native)* (0)	0	<0.01
Apache (20)	62	0.08
Arapaho (1)	3	<0.01
Blackfeet (5)	31	0.04
Canadian/French Am. Ind. (1)	2	<0.01
Central American Ind. (0)	3	<0.01
Cherokee (46)	209	0.26
Cheyenne (2)	7	0.01
Chickasaw (7)	25	0.03
Chippewa (15)	33	0.04
Choctaw (11)	53	0.07
Colville (0)	0	<0.01
Comanche (1)	6	0.01
Cree (4)	7	0.01
Creek (11)	20	0.02
Crow (0)	4	<0.01
Delaware (4)	4	<0.01
Hopi (0)	7	0.01
Houma (0)	0	<0.01
Inupiat *(Alaska Native)* (0)	10	0.01
Iroquois (4)	16	0.02
Kiowa (3)	5	0.01
Lumbee (5)	8	0.01
Menominee (0)	1	<0.01
Mexican American Ind. (63)	81	0.10
Navajo (32)	57	0.07
Osage (2)	3	<0.01
Ottawa (0)	1	<0.01
Paiute (0)	1	<0.01
Pima (0)	1	<0.01
Potawatomi (1)	8	0.01
Pueblo (5)	10	0.01
Puget Sound Salish (0)	2	<0.01
Seminole (0)	5	0.01
Shoshone (2)	3	<0.01
Sioux (17)	30	0.04
South American Ind. (8)	13	0.02
Spanish American Ind. (6)	10	0.01
Tlingit-Haida *(Alaska Native)* (2)	7	0.01
Tohono O'Odham (0)	4	<0.01
Tsimshian *(Alaska Native)* (2)	2	<0.01
Ute (1)	1	<0.01
Yakama (0)	0	<0.01
Yaqui (3)	12	0.01
Yuman (6)	6	0.01
Yup'ik *(Alaska Native)* (3)	3	<0.01
Asian (13,115)	15,136	18.91
Not Hispanic (12,811)	14,352	17.93
Hispanic (304)	784	0.98
Bangladeshi (17)	19	0.02
Bhutanese (0)	0	<0.01
Burmese (5)	14	0.02
Cambodian (1,144)	1,317	1.65
Chinese, ex. Taiwanese (1,042)	1,561	1.95
Filipino (6,504)	7,715	9.64
Hmong (9)	9	0.01
Indian (509)	590	0.74
Indonesian (69)	130	0.16
Japanese (571)	1,039	1.30
Korean (1,177)	1,327	1.66
Laotian (41)	67	0.08
Malaysian (8)	10	0.01
Nepalese (4)	6	0.01
Pakistani (59)	65	0.08
Sri Lankan (42)	53	0.07
Taiwanese (116)	131	0.16
Thai (299)	386	0.48
Vietnamese (947)	1,101	1.38
Hawaii Native/Pacific Islander (744)	1,265	1.58
Not Hispanic (686)	1,100	1.37
Hispanic (58)	165	0.21
Fijian (7)	7	0.01
Guamanian/Chamorro (148)	275	0.34
Marshallese (1)	1	<0.01
Native Hawaiian (93)	288	0.36
Samoan (403)	534	0.67
Tongan (48)	57	0.07
White (44,820)	48,522	60.62
Not Hispanic (32,774)	34,872	43.56
Hispanic (12,046)	13,650	17.05

*Notes: † The Census 2010 population figure is used to calculate the percentages in the Hispanic Origin and Race categories. Ancestry percentages are based on the 2006-2010 American Community Survey population (not shown); ‡ Numbers in parentheses indicate the number of people reporting a single ancestry; * Numbers in parentheses indicate the number of persons reporting this race alone, not in combination with any other race; Please refer to the Explanation of Data for more information.*

Lancaster

Place Type: City
County: Los Angeles
Population: 156,633

Ancestry	Population	%
Afghan (0)	0	<0.01
African, Sub-Saharan (1,621)	2,125	1.42
African (1,357)	1,803	1.20
Cape Verdean (17)	17	0.01
Ethiopian (26)	36	0.02
Ghanaian (0)	0	<0.01
Kenyan (17)	34	0.02
Liberian (0)	0	<0.01
Nigerian (138)	151	0.10
Senegalese (0)	0	<0.01
Sierra Leonean (0)	0	<0.01
Somalian (22)	32	0.02
South African (44)	44	0.03
Sudanese (0)	0	<0.01
Ugandan (0)	0	<0.01
Zimbabwean (0)	0	<0.01
Other Sub-Saharan African (0)	8	0.01
Albanian (0)	0	<0.01
Alsatian (0)	0	<0.01
American (2,966)	2,966	1.98
Arab (1,011)	1,111	0.74
Arab (133)	153	0.10
Egyptian (152)	152	0.10
Iraqi (0)	0	<0.01
Jordanian (7)	7	<0.01
Lebanese (154)	213	0.14
Moroccan (0)	0	<0.01
Palestinian (0)	0	<0.01
Syrian (515)	536	0.36
Other Arab (50)	50	0.03
Armenian (315)	576	0.38
Assyrian/Chaldean/Syriac (0)	0	<0.01
Australian (0)	0	<0.01
Austrian (154)	318	0.21
Basque (29)	29	0.02
Belgian (20)	50	0.03
Brazilian (0)	0	<0.01
British (275)	455	0.30
Bulgarian (20)	26	0.02
Cajun (20)	20	0.01
Canadian (292)	631	0.42
Carpatho Rusyn (0)	0	<0.01
Celtic (0)	0	<0.01
Croatian (23)	110	0.07
Cypriot (0)	0	<0.01
Czech (143)	288	0.19
Czechoslovakian (0)	46	0.03
Danish (99)	694	0.46
Dutch (346)	1,398	0.93
Eastern European (134)	160	0.11
English (2,398)	8,112	5.42
Estonian (27)	110	0.07
European (1,118)	1,245	0.83
Finnish (33)	155	0.10
French, ex. Basque (711)	3,197	2.14
French Canadian (152)	361	0.24
German (3,738)	12,246	8.18
German Russian (0)	27	0.02
Greek (169)	357	0.24
Guyanese (17)	52	0.03
Hungarian (177)	377	0.25
Icelander (0)	10	0.01
Iranian (65)	268	0.18
Irish (2,004)	8,889	5.94
Israeli (0)	0	<0.01
Italian (2,827)	5,661	3.78
Latvian (0)	0	<0.01
Lithuanian (0)	58	0.04
Luxemburger (0)	0	<0.01
Macedonian (0)	0	<0.01
Maltese (0)	0	<0.01
New Zealander (0)	0	<0.01
Northern European (42)	42	0.03
Norwegian (529)	1,007	0.67
Pennsylvania German (6)	31	0.02
Polish (379)	1,418	0.95
Portuguese (222)	512	0.34
Romanian (106)	179	0.12
Russian (152)	718	0.48
Scandinavian (70)	194	0.13
Scotch-Irish (619)	1,311	0.88
Scottish (527)	2,064	1.38
Serbian (0)	87	0.06
Slavic (24)	67	0.04
Slovak (0)	23	0.02
Slovene (9)	9	0.01
Soviet Union (0)	0	<0.01
Swedish (268)	1,047	0.70
Swiss (83)	351	0.23
Turkish (0)	0	<0.01
Ukrainian (89)	211	0.14
Welsh (125)	426	0.28
West Indian, ex. Hispanic (618)	1,053	0.70
Bahamian (0)	0	<0.01
Barbadian (0)	10	0.01
Belizean (567)	876	0.59
Bermudan (0)	0	<0.01
British West Indian (22)	22	0.01
Dutch West Indian (0)	7	<0.01
Haitian (18)	18	0.01
Jamaican (0)	46	0.03
Trinidadian/Tobagonian (0)	34	0.02
U.S. Virgin Islander (0)	0	<0.01
West Indian (11)	40	0.03
Other West Indian (0)	0	<0.01
Yugoslavian (70)	104	0.07

Hispanic Origin	Population	%
Hispanic or Latino (of any race)	59,596	38.05
Central American, ex. Mexican	8,114	5.18
Costa Rican	156	0.10
Guatemalan	2,075	1.32
Honduran	474	0.30
Nicaraguan	442	0.28
Panamanian	170	0.11
Salvadoran	4,713	3.01
Other Central American	84	0.05
Cuban	514	0.33
Dominican Republic	63	0.04
Mexican	42,115	26.89
Puerto Rican	1,105	0.71
South American	1,345	0.86
Argentinean	204	0.13
Bolivian	25	0.02
Chilean	162	0.10
Colombian	227	0.14
Ecuadorian	181	0.12
Paraguayan	3	<0.01
Peruvian	457	0.29
Uruguayan	29	0.02
Venezuelan	29	0.02
Other South American	28	0.02
Other Hispanic or Latino	6,340	4.05

Race*	Population	%
African-American/Black (32,083)	35,558	22.70
Not Hispanic (30,859)	33,469	21.37
Hispanic (1,224)	2,089	1.33
American Indian/Alaska Native (1,519)	3,310	2.11
Not Hispanic (663)	1,843	1.18
Hispanic (856)	1,467	0.94
Alaska Athabascan *(Ala. Nat.)* (1)	1	<0.01
Aleut *(Alaska Native)* (1)	4	<0.01
Apache (46)	151	0.10
Arapaho (7)	12	0.01
Blackfeet (20)	168	0.11
Canadian/French Am. Ind. (8)	12	0.01
Central American Ind. (13)	22	0.01
Cherokee (105)	487	0.31
Cheyenne (2)	12	0.01
Chickasaw (11)	28	0.02
Chippewa (9)	16	0.01
Choctaw (28)	99	0.06
Colville (0)	0	<0.01
Comanche (2)	9	0.01
Cree (1)	2	<0.01
Creek (8)	41	0.03
Crow (0)	3	<0.01
Delaware (0)	3	<0.01
Hopi (8)	13	0.01
Houma (0)	0	<0.01
Inupiat *(Alaska Native)* (8)	12	0.01
Iroquois (4)	36	0.02
Kiowa (0)	1	<0.01
Lumbee (0)	0	<0.01
Menominee (0)	2	<0.01
Mexican American Ind. (159)	245	0.16
Navajo (58)	85	0.05
Osage (6)	13	0.01
Ottawa (8)	11	0.01
Paiute (7)	18	0.01
Pima (4)	5	<0.01
Potawatomi (5)	9	0.01
Pueblo (7)	16	0.01
Puget Sound Salish (0)	0	<0.01
Seminole (9)	25	0.02
Shoshone (2)	25	0.02
Sioux (21)	56	0.04
South American Ind. (3)	9	0.01
Spanish American Ind. (12)	14	0.01
Tlingit-Haida *(Alaska Native)* (0)	4	<0.01
Tohono O'Odham (5)	7	<0.01
Tsimshian *(Alaska Native)* (0)	0	<0.01
Ute (1)	6	<0.01
Yakama (0)	0	<0.01
Yaqui (34)	62	0.04
Yuman (1)	4	<0.01
Yup'ik *(Alaska Native)* (0)	0	<0.01
Asian (6,810)	8,839	5.64
Not Hispanic (6,474)	7,925	5.06
Hispanic (336)	914	0.58
Bangladeshi (26)	26	0.02
Bhutanese (0)	0	<0.01
Burmese (6)	10	0.01
Cambodian (147)	165	0.11
Chinese, ex. Taiwanese (581)	874	0.56
Filipino (3,444)	4,399	2.81
Hmong (21)	21	0.01
Indian (593)	716	0.46
Indonesian (47)	89	0.06
Japanese (297)	718	0.46
Korean (503)	691	0.44
Laotian (22)	33	0.02
Malaysian (1)	1	<0.01
Nepalese (5)	5	<0.01
Pakistani (59)	65	0.04
Sri Lankan (96)	107	0.07
Taiwanese (25)	28	0.02
Thai (106)	160	0.10
Vietnamese (529)	616	0.39
Hawaii Native/Pacific Islander (362)	877	0.56
Not Hispanic (295)	632	0.40
Hispanic (67)	245	0.16
Fijian (7)	18	0.01
Guamanian/Chamorro (112)	160	0.10
Marshallese (0)	0	<0.01
Native Hawaiian (93)	290	0.19
Samoan (81)	176	0.11
Tongan (34)	48	0.03
White (77,734)	84,210	53.76
Not Hispanic (53,576)	57,150	36.49
Hispanic (24,158)	27,060	17.28

*Notes: † The Census 2010 population figure is used to calculate the percentages in the Hispanic Origin and Race categories. Ancestry percentages are based on the 2006-2010 American Community Survey population (not shown); ‡ Numbers in parentheses indicate the number of people reporting a single ancestry; * Numbers in parentheses indicate the number of persons reporting this race alone, not in combination with any other race; Please refer to the Explanation of Data for more information.*

Livermore

Place Type: City
County: Alameda
Population: 80,968

Ancestry	Population	%
Afghan (179)	179	0.23
African, Sub-Saharan (291)	419	0.53
African (197)	231	0.29
Cape Verdean (0)	0	<0.01
Ethiopian (0)	0	<0.01
Ghanaian (0)	0	<0.01
Kenyan (0)	0	<0.01
Liberian (0)	0	<0.01
Nigerian (79)	136	0.17
Senegalese (0)	0	<0.01
Sierra Leonean (15)	52	0.07
Somalian (0)	0	<0.01
South African (0)	0	<0.01
Sudanese (0)	0	<0.01
Ugandan (0)	0	<0.01
Zimbabwean (0)	0	<0.01
Other Sub-Saharan African (0)	0	<0.01
Albanian (0)	0	<0.01
Alsatian (0)	0	<0.01
American (2,742)	2,742	3.49
Arab (273)	682	0.87
Arab (33)	33	0.04
Egyptian (0)	0	<0.01
Iraqi (0)	0	<0.01
Jordanian (73)	250	0.32
Lebanese (115)	169	0.22
Moroccan (0)	0	<0.01
Palestinian (32)	100	0.13
Syrian (20)	24	0.03
Other Arab (0)	106	0.13
Armenian (152)	304	0.39
Assyrian/Chaldean/Syriac (62)	62	0.08
Australian (8)	8	0.01
Austrian (32)	171	0.22
Basque (139)	156	0.20
Belgian (0)	58	0.07
Brazilian (122)	122	0.16
British (168)	322	0.41
Bulgarian (0)	0	<0.01
Cajun (17)	17	0.02
Canadian (154)	361	0.46
Carpatho Rusyn (0)	0	<0.01
Celtic (9)	9	0.01
Croatian (69)	261	0.33
Cypriot (0)	0	<0.01
Czech (10)	227	0.29
Czechoslovakian (13)	83	0.11
Danish (154)	1,107	1.41
Dutch (338)	1,350	1.72
Eastern European (8)	16	0.02
English (2,607)	9,374	11.94
Estonian (0)	0	<0.01
European (1,365)	1,485	1.89
Finnish (46)	167	0.21
French, ex. Basque (633)	2,682	3.42
French Canadian (355)	541	0.69
German (2,823)	12,945	16.49
German Russian (0)	0	<0.01
Greek (110)	471	0.60
Guyanese (0)	0	<0.01
Hungarian (171)	492	0.63
Icelander (23)	35	0.04
Iranian (288)	288	0.37
Irish (2,140)	9,994	12.73
Israeli (0)	0	<0.01
Italian (1,865)	6,299	8.02
Latvian (0)	0	<0.01
Lithuanian (80)	255	0.32
Luxemburger (0)	0	<0.01
Macedonian (0)	0	<0.01
Maltese (18)	18	0.02
New Zealander (0)	0	<0.01
Northern European (156)	156	0.20
Norwegian (433)	1,586	2.02
Pennsylvania German (12)	12	0.02
Polish (404)	1,492	1.90
Portuguese (1,100)	2,934	3.74
Romanian (35)	189	0.24
Russian (319)	637	0.81
Scandinavian (169)	322	0.41
Scotch-Irish (569)	2,051	2.61
Scottish (526)	2,365	3.01
Serbian (0)	36	0.05
Slavic (9)	18	0.02
Slovak (21)	107	0.14
Slovene (14)	79	0.10
Soviet Union (0)	0	<0.01
Swedish (365)	2,279	2.90
Swiss (60)	247	0.31
Turkish (8)	15	0.02
Ukrainian (10)	100	0.13
Welsh (117)	796	1.01
West Indian, ex. Hispanic (11)	11	0.01
Bahamian (0)	0	<0.01
Barbadian (11)	11	0.01
Belizean (0)	0	<0.01
Bermudan (0)	0	<0.01
British West Indian (0)	0	<0.01
Dutch West Indian (0)	0	<0.01
Haitian (0)	0	<0.01
Jamaican (0)	0	<0.01
Trinidadian/Tobagonian (0)	0	<0.01
U.S. Virgin Islander (0)	0	<0.01
West Indian (0)	0	<0.01
Other West Indian (0)	0	<0.01
Yugoslavian (13)	103	0.13

Hispanic Origin	Population	%
Hispanic or Latino (of any race)	16,920	20.90
Central American, ex. Mexican	730	0.90
Costa Rican	18	0.02
Guatemalan	73	0.09
Honduran	27	0.03
Nicaraguan	174	0.21
Panamanian	42	0.05
Salvadoran	385	0.48
Other Central American	11	0.01
Cuban	105	0.13
Dominican Republic	12	0.01
Mexican	13,296	16.42
Puerto Rican	586	0.72
South American	499	0.62
Argentinean	57	0.07
Bolivian	38	0.05
Chilean	40	0.05
Colombian	109	0.13
Ecuadorian	26	0.03
Paraguayan	1	<0.01
Peruvian	195	0.24
Uruguayan	5	0.01
Venezuelan	14	0.02
Other South American	14	0.02
Other Hispanic or Latino	1,692	2.09

Race*	Population	%
African-American/Black (1,702)	2,365	2.92
Not Hispanic (1,562)	2,058	2.54
Hispanic (140)	307	0.38
American Indian/Alaska Native (476)	1,312	1.62
Not Hispanic (251)	789	0.97
Hispanic (225)	523	0.65
Alaska Athabascan *(Ala. Nat.)* (0)	1	<0.01
Aleut *(Alaska Native)* (2)	7	0.01
Apache (21)	74	0.09
Arapaho (0)	3	<0.01
Blackfeet (4)	37	0.05
Canadian/French Am. Ind. (0)	5	0.01
Central American Ind. (4)	4	<0.01
Cherokee (45)	250	0.31
Cheyenne (0)	0	<0.01
Chickasaw (2)	6	0.01
Chippewa (13)	24	0.03
Choctaw (12)	62	0.08
Colville (0)	0	<0.01
Comanche (6)	10	0.01
Cree (1)	1	<0.01
Creek (2)	6	0.01
Crow (0)	2	<0.01
Delaware (0)	0	<0.01
Hopi (0)	2	<0.01
Houma (0)	0	<0.01
Inupiat *(Alaska Native)* (0)	0	<0.01
Iroquois (3)	14	0.02
Kiowa (0)	7	0.01
Lumbee (0)	0	<0.01
Menominee (0)	1	<0.01
Mexican American Ind. (30)	53	0.07
Navajo (9)	24	0.03
Osage (2)	6	0.01
Ottawa (0)	0	<0.01
Paiute (6)	9	0.01
Pima (2)	2	<0.01
Potawatomi (4)	5	0.01
Pueblo (5)	15	0.02
Puget Sound Salish (2)	2	<0.01
Seminole (1)	9	0.01
Shoshone (3)	9	0.01
Sioux (11)	28	0.03
South American Ind. (4)	7	0.01
Spanish American Ind. (3)	4	<0.01
Tlingit-Haida *(Alaska Native)* (8)	14	0.02
Tohono O'Odham (0)	0	<0.01
Tsimshian *(Alaska Native)* (0)	0	<0.01
Ute (1)	11	0.01
Yakama (0)	0	<0.01
Yaqui (4)	14	0.02
Yuman (0)	0	<0.01
Yup'ik *(Alaska Native)* (1)	1	<0.01
Asian (6,802)	8,916	11.01
Not Hispanic (6,643)	8,390	10.36
Hispanic (159)	526	0.65
Bangladeshi (8)	8	0.01
Bhutanese (0)	0	<0.01
Burmese (4)	6	0.01
Cambodian (37)	60	0.07
Chinese, ex. Taiwanese (1,223)	1,712	2.11
Filipino (2,245)	3,153	3.89
Hmong (4)	4	<0.01
Indian (1,578)	1,729	2.14
Indonesian (20)	36	0.04
Japanese (379)	825	1.02
Korean (346)	519	0.64
Laotian (6)	8	0.01
Malaysian (12)	20	0.02
Nepalese (6)	6	0.01
Pakistani (103)	115	0.14
Sri Lankan (25)	25	0.03
Taiwanese (73)	91	0.11
Thai (60)	81	0.10
Vietnamese (393)	504	0.62
Hawaii Native/Pacific Islander (277)	684	0.84
Not Hispanic (231)	524	0.65
Hispanic (46)	160	0.20
Fijian (32)	56	0.07
Guamanian/Chamorro (66)	106	0.13
Marshallese (0)	0	<0.01
Native Hawaiian (90)	326	0.40
Samoan (50)	87	0.11
Tongan (14)	20	0.02
White (60,418)	64,320	79.44
Not Hispanic (52,397)	54,902	67.81
Hispanic (8,021)	9,418	11.63

*Notes: † The Census 2010 population figure is used to calculate the percentages in the Hispanic Origin and Race categories. Ancestry percentages are based on the 2006-2010 American Community Survey population (not shown); ‡ Numbers in parentheses indicate the number of people reporting a single ancestry; * Numbers in parentheses indicate the number of persons reporting this race alone, not in combination with any other race; Please refer to the Explanation of Data for more information.*

Lodi

Place Type: City
County: San Joaquin
Population: 62,134

Ancestry	Population	%
Afghan (0)	0	<0.01
African, Sub-Saharan (131)	227	0.36
African (131)	227	0.36
Cape Verdean (0)	0	<0.01
Ethiopian (0)	0	<0.01
Ghanaian (0)	0	<0.01
Kenyan (0)	0	<0.01
Liberian (0)	0	<0.01
Nigerian (0)	0	<0.01
Senegalese (0)	0	<0.01
Sierra Leonean (0)	0	<0.01
Somalian (0)	0	<0.01
South African (0)	0	<0.01
Sudanese (0)	0	<0.01
Ugandan (0)	0	<0.01
Zimbabwean (0)	0	<0.01
Other Sub-Saharan African (0)	0	<0.01
Albanian (0)	0	<0.01
Alsatian (0)	0	<0.01
American (1,479)	1,479	2.38
Arab (502)	640	1.03
Arab (0)	0	<0.01
Egyptian (0)	0	<0.01
Iraqi (0)	0	<0.01
Jordanian (21)	21	0.03
Lebanese (12)	52	0.08
Moroccan (0)	0	<0.01
Palestinian (464)	464	0.75
Syrian (5)	103	0.17
Other Arab (0)	0	<0.01
Armenian (16)	93	0.15
Assyrian/Chaldean/Syriac (0)	0	<0.01
Australian (0)	29	0.05
Austrian (14)	96	0.15
Basque (0)	56	0.09
Belgian (31)	89	0.14
Brazilian (0)	0	<0.01
British (51)	153	0.25
Bulgarian (0)	0	<0.01
Cajun (0)	0	<0.01
Canadian (72)	214	0.34
Carpatho Rusyn (0)	0	<0.01
Celtic (0)	0	<0.01
Croatian (9)	52	0.08
Cypriot (0)	0	<0.01
Czech (35)	225	0.36
Czechoslovakian (37)	37	0.06
Danish (69)	489	0.79
Dutch (171)	1,050	1.69
Eastern European (24)	29	0.05
English (1,257)	4,928	7.92
Estonian (0)	0	<0.01
European (418)	532	0.85
Finnish (55)	72	0.12
French, ex. Basque (266)	1,373	2.21
French Canadian (178)	228	0.37
German (5,630)	12,805	20.58
German Russian (0)	0	<0.01
Greek (105)	327	0.53
Guyanese (0)	0	<0.01
Hungarian (21)	45	0.07
Icelander (0)	0	<0.01
Iranian (167)	205	0.33
Irish (1,434)	6,226	10.01
Israeli (0)	0	<0.01
Italian (1,589)	4,435	7.13
Latvian (0)	0	<0.01
Lithuanian (0)	0	<0.01
Luxemburger (0)	0	<0.01
Macedonian (0)	0	<0.01
Maltese (17)	17	0.03
New Zealander (0)	0	<0.01
Northern European (86)	86	0.14
Norwegian (253)	1,021	1.64
Pennsylvania German (0)	0	<0.01
Polish (139)	584	0.94
Portuguese (552)	1,106	1.78
Romanian (7)	20	0.03
Russian (65)	500	0.80
Scandinavian (21)	85	0.14
Scotch-Irish (321)	1,106	1.78
Scottish (325)	978	1.57
Serbian (0)	0	<0.01
Slavic (63)	90	0.14
Slovak (11)	11	0.02
Slovene (0)	11	0.02
Soviet Union (0)	0	<0.01
Swedish (231)	1,055	1.70
Swiss (27)	294	0.47
Turkish (0)	0	<0.01
Ukrainian (6)	49	0.08
Welsh (30)	351	0.56
West Indian, ex. Hispanic (0)	0	<0.01
Bahamian (0)	0	<0.01
Barbadian (0)	0	<0.01
Belizean (0)	0	<0.01
Bermudan (0)	0	<0.01
British West Indian (0)	0	<0.01
Dutch West Indian (0)	0	<0.01
Haitian (0)	0	<0.01
Jamaican (0)	0	<0.01
Trinidadian/Tobagonian (0)	0	<0.01
U.S. Virgin Islander (0)	0	<0.01
West Indian (0)	0	<0.01
Other West Indian (0)	0	<0.01
Yugoslavian (43)	72	0.12

Hispanic Origin	Population	%
Hispanic or Latino (of any race)	22,613	36.39
Central American, ex. Mexican	285	0.46
Costa Rican	15	0.02
Guatemalan	77	0.12
Honduran	24	0.04
Nicaraguan	48	0.08
Panamanian	5	0.01
Salvadoran	115	0.19
Other Central American	1	<0.01
Cuban	39	0.06
Dominican Republic	3	<0.01
Mexican	20,579	33.12
Puerto Rican	246	0.40
South American	91	0.15
Argentinean	14	0.02
Bolivian	3	<0.01
Chilean	8	0.01
Colombian	26	0.04
Ecuadorian	6	0.01
Paraguayan	0	<0.01
Peruvian	26	0.04
Uruguayan	4	0.01
Venezuelan	3	<0.01
Other South American	1	<0.01
Other Hispanic or Latino	1,370	2.20

Race*	Population	%
African-American/Black (517)	834	1.34
Not Hispanic (388)	587	0.94
Hispanic (129)	247	0.40
American Indian/Alaska Native (560)	1,255	2.02
Not Hispanic (248)	724	1.17
Hispanic (312)	531	0.85
Alaska Athabascan *(Ala. Nat.)* (0)	0	<0.01
Aleut *(Alaska Native)* (3)	4	0.01
Apache (13)	36	0.06
Arapaho (0)	0	<0.01
Blackfeet (4)	17	0.03
Canadian/French Am. Ind. (0)	0	<0.01
Central American Ind. (0)	0	<0.01
Cherokee (40)	201	0.32
Cheyenne (0)	2	<0.01
Chickasaw (4)	16	0.03
Chippewa (7)	9	0.01
Choctaw (13)	52	0.08
Colville (0)	1	<0.01
Comanche (3)	5	0.01
Cree (2)	7	0.01
Creek (3)	7	0.01
Crow (0)	1	<0.01
Delaware (0)	3	<0.01
Hopi (0)	0	<0.01
Houma (0)	0	<0.01
Inupiat *(Alaska Native)* (1)	1	<0.01
Iroquois (0)	2	<0.01
Kiowa (2)	3	<0.01
Lumbee (0)	4	0.01
Menominee (0)	0	<0.01
Mexican American Ind. (109)	142	0.23
Navajo (4)	12	0.02
Osage (5)	6	0.01
Ottawa (0)	0	<0.01
Paiute (1)	4	0.01
Pima (0)	1	<0.01
Potawatomi (1)	3	<0.01
Pueblo (2)	4	0.01
Puget Sound Salish (3)	4	0.01
Seminole (1)	1	<0.01
Shoshone (1)	5	0.01
Sioux (10)	26	0.04
South American Ind. (0)	1	<0.01
Spanish American Ind. (1)	2	<0.01
Tlingit-Haida *(Alaska Native)* (3)	8	0.01
Tohono O'Odham (2)	2	<0.01
Tsimshian *(Alaska Native)* (0)	0	<0.01
Ute (1)	5	0.01
Yakama (7)	11	0.02
Yaqui (8)	16	0.03
Yuman (0)	6	0.01
Yup'ik *(Alaska Native)* (0)	0	<0.01
Asian (4,293)	5,250	8.45
Not Hispanic (4,167)	4,834	7.78
Hispanic (126)	416	0.67
Bangladeshi (0)	0	<0.01
Bhutanese (0)	0	<0.01
Burmese (12)	16	0.03
Cambodian (34)	39	0.06
Chinese, ex. Taiwanese (206)	299	0.48
Filipino (706)	1,162	1.87
Hmong (27)	28	0.05
Indian (812)	914	1.47
Indonesian (4)	16	0.03
Japanese (482)	663	1.07
Korean (67)	106	0.17
Laotian (39)	43	0.07
Malaysian (2)	2	<0.01
Nepalese (9)	9	0.01
Pakistani (1,603)	1,709	2.75
Sri Lankan (4)	9	0.01
Taiwanese (5)	5	0.01
Thai (9)	14	0.02
Vietnamese (72)	96	0.15
Hawaii Native/Pacific Islander (105)	302	0.49
Not Hispanic (88)	233	0.37
Hispanic (17)	69	0.11
Fijian (29)	37	0.06
Guamanian/Chamorro (17)	39	0.06
Marshallese (0)	0	<0.01
Native Hawaiian (45)	122	0.20
Samoan (1)	21	0.03
Tongan (0)	6	0.01
White (42,662)	45,122	72.62
Not Hispanic (33,194)	34,352	55.29
Hispanic (9,468)	10,770	17.33

*Notes: † The Census 2010 population figure is used to calculate the percentages in the Hispanic Origin and Race categories. Ancestry percentages are based on the 2006-2010 American Community Survey population (not shown); ‡ Numbers in parentheses indicate the number of people reporting a single ancestry; * Numbers in parentheses indicate the number of persons reporting this race alone, not in combination with any other race; Please refer to the Explanation of Data for more information.*

Long Beach

Place Type: City
County: Los Angeles
Population: 462,257

Ancestry	Population	%
Afghan (18)	18	<0.01
African, Sub-Saharan (7,542)	10,870	2.35
African (6,339)	9,464	2.05
Cape Verdean (6)	47	0.01
Ethiopian (142)	229	0.05
Ghanaian (9)	9	<0.01
Kenyan (100)	117	0.03
Liberian (0)	0	<0.01
Nigerian (485)	528	0.11
Senegalese (0)	0	<0.01
Sierra Leonean (12)	27	0.01
Somalian (0)	0	<0.01
South African (59)	59	0.01
Sudanese (126)	126	0.03
Ugandan (29)	29	0.01
Zimbabwean (0)	0	<0.01
Other Sub-Saharan African (235)	235	0.05
Albanian (16)	63	0.01
Alsatian (0)	0	<0.01
American (7,230)	7,230	1.57
Arab (1,478)	2,244	0.49
Arab (321)	537	0.12
Egyptian (250)	263	0.06
Iraqi (0)	18	<0.01
Jordanian (10)	22	<0.01
Lebanese (340)	588	0.13
Moroccan (37)	51	0.01
Palestinian (42)	111	0.02
Syrian (50)	68	0.01
Other Arab (428)	586	0.13
Armenian (467)	889	0.19
Assyrian/Chaldean/Syriac (43)	65	0.01
Australian (32)	165	0.04
Austrian (222)	617	0.13
Basque (39)	153	0.03
Belgian (53)	267	0.06
Brazilian (232)	281	0.06
British (800)	1,611	0.35
Bulgarian (60)	95	0.02
Cajun (31)	157	0.03
Canadian (435)	887	0.19
Carpatho Rusyn (0)	34	0.01
Celtic (117)	170	0.04
Croatian (220)	485	0.11
Cypriot (70)	94	0.02
Czech (243)	854	0.18
Czechoslovakian (127)	369	0.08
Danish (340)	1,179	0.26
Dutch (1,498)	4,630	1.00
Eastern European (262)	285	0.06
English (7,163)	23,359	5.06
Estonian (0)	0	<0.01
European (4,306)	5,522	1.20
Finnish (158)	479	0.10
French, ex. Basque (1,221)	8,425	1.82
French Canadian (470)	1,161	0.25
German (8,982)	33,099	7.17
German Russian (11)	50	0.01
Greek (832)	1,580	0.34
Guyanese (15)	15	<0.01
Hungarian (830)	1,825	0.40
Icelander (58)	76	0.02
Iranian (507)	613	0.13
Irish (8,000)	27,445	5.94
Israeli (98)	208	0.05
Italian (5,745)	14,721	3.19
Latvian (50)	99	0.02
Lithuanian (113)	463	0.10
Luxemburger (15)	15	<0.01
Macedonian (0)	0	<0.01
Maltese (0)	0	<0.01
New Zealander (11)	11	<0.01
Northern European (460)	485	0.11
Norwegian (1,542)	4,263	0.92
Pennsylvania German (23)	65	0.01
Polish (1,909)	6,373	1.38
Portuguese (441)	1,460	0.32
Romanian (302)	621	0.13
Russian (1,491)	4,610	1.00
Scandinavian (304)	561	0.12
Scotch-Irish (1,750)	4,933	1.07
Scottish (1,699)	6,072	1.31
Serbian (110)	263	0.06
Slavic (11)	157	0.03
Slovak (23)	183	0.04
Slovene (37)	105	0.02
Soviet Union (0)	0	<0.01
Swedish (864)	4,170	0.90
Swiss (142)	763	0.17
Turkish (254)	288	0.06
Ukrainian (193)	552	0.12
Welsh (520)	1,823	0.39
West Indian, ex. Hispanic (1,055)	1,815	0.39
Bahamian (17)	92	0.02
Barbadian (0)	0	<0.01
Belizean (240)	336	0.07
Bermudan (0)	0	<0.01
British West Indian (43)	69	0.01
Dutch West Indian (0)	47	0.01
Haitian (49)	102	0.02
Jamaican (320)	557	0.12
Trinidadian/Tobagonian (163)	168	0.04
U.S. Virgin Islander (37)	37	0.01
West Indian (186)	407	0.09
Other West Indian (0)	0	<0.01
Yugoslavian (73)	238	0.05

Hispanic Origin	Population	%
Hispanic or Latino (of any race)	188,412	40.76
Central American, ex. Mexican	16,486	3.57
Costa Rican	467	0.10
Guatemalan	5,134	1.11
Honduran	2,696	0.58
Nicaraguan	1,007	0.22
Panamanian	313	0.07
Salvadoran	6,657	1.44
Other Central American	212	0.05
Cuban	1,264	0.27
Dominican Republic	194	0.04
Mexican	151,983	32.88
Puerto Rican	3,025	0.65
South American	4,123	0.89
Argentinean	650	0.14
Bolivian	125	0.03
Chilean	288	0.06
Colombian	1,037	0.22
Ecuadorian	679	0.15
Paraguayan	12	<0.01
Peruvian	1,109	0.24
Uruguayan	51	0.01
Venezuelan	123	0.03
Other South American	49	0.01
Other Hispanic or Latino	11,337	2.45

Race*	Population	%
African-American/Black (62,603)	69,744	15.09
Not Hispanic (59,925)	65,067	14.08
Hispanic (2,678)	4,677	1.01
American Indian/Alaska Native (3,458)	7,958	1.72
Not Hispanic (1,349)	4,002	0.87
Hispanic (2,109)	3,956	0.86
Alaska Athabascan *(Ala. Nat.)* (9)	11	<0.01
Aleut *(Alaska Native)* (2)	13	<0.01
Apache (89)	244	0.05
Arapaho (5)	6	<0.01
Blackfeet (27)	214	0.05
Canadian/French Am. Ind. (4)	30	0.01
Central American Ind. (46)	78	0.02
Cherokee (185)	947	0.20
Cheyenne (13)	22	<0.01
Chickasaw (14)	43	0.01
Chippewa (40)	108	0.02
Choctaw (59)	240	0.05
Colville (0)	0	<0.01
Comanche (8)	15	<0.01
Cree (2)	13	<0.01
Creek (32)	98	0.02
Crow (4)	6	<0.01
Delaware (5)	13	<0.01
Hopi (7)	22	<0.01
Houma (0)	0	<0.01
Inupiat *(Alaska Native)* (2)	8	<0.01
Iroquois (23)	79	0.02
Kiowa (3)	5	<0.01
Lumbee (7)	10	<0.01
Menominee (1)	1	<0.01
Mexican American Ind. (578)	840	0.18
Navajo (175)	320	0.07
Osage (13)	29	0.01
Ottawa (4)	7	<0.01
Paiute (7)	7	<0.01
Pima (17)	25	0.01
Potawatomi (11)	27	0.01
Pueblo (34)	83	0.02
Puget Sound Salish (1)	1	<0.01
Seminole (6)	48	0.01
Shoshone (5)	29	0.01
Sioux (56)	166	0.04
South American Ind. (18)	77	0.02
Spanish American Ind. (32)	62	0.01
Tlingit-Haida *(Alaska Native)* (9)	13	<0.01
Tohono O'Odham (5)	18	<0.01
Tsimshian *(Alaska Native)* (0)	0	<0.01
Ute (15)	19	<0.01
Yakama (1)	7	<0.01
Yaqui (61)	130	0.03
Yuman (19)	37	0.01
Yup'ik *(Alaska Native)* (1)	2	<0.01
Asian (59,496)	67,961	14.70
Not Hispanic (58,268)	64,834	14.03
Hispanic (1,228)	3,127	0.68
Bangladeshi (153)	180	0.04
Bhutanese (0)	0	<0.01
Burmese (69)	89	0.02
Cambodian (18,051)	19,998	4.33
Chinese, ex. Taiwanese (3,478)	5,734	1.24
Filipino (20,964)	24,963	5.40
Hmong (299)	327	0.07
Indian (1,916)	2,591	0.56
Indonesian (143)	304	0.07
Japanese (2,883)	4,683	1.01
Korean (1,888)	2,385	0.52
Laotian (536)	893	0.19
Malaysian (39)	60	0.01
Nepalese (26)	31	0.01
Pakistani (131)	181	0.04
Sri Lankan (176)	212	0.05
Taiwanese (289)	356	0.08
Thai (780)	1,266	0.27
Vietnamese (4,204)	4,952	1.07
Hawaii Native/Pacific Islander (5,253)	7,498	1.62
Not Hispanic (4,915)	6,549	1.42
Hispanic (338)	949	0.21
Fijian (32)	50	0.01
Guamanian/Chamorro (534)	937	0.20
Marshallese (0)	0	<0.01
Native Hawaiian (336)	1,018	0.22
Samoan (3,736)	4,513	0.98
Tongan (295)	371	0.08
White (213,066)	231,897	50.17
Not Hispanic (135,698)	145,170	31.40
Hispanic (77,368)	86,727	18.76

*Notes: † The Census 2010 population figure is used to calculate the percentages in the Hispanic Origin and Race categories. Ancestry percentages are based on the 2006-2010 American Community Survey population (not shown); ‡ Numbers in parentheses indicate the number of people reporting a single ancestry; * Numbers in parentheses indicate the number of persons reporting this race alone, not in combination with any other race; Please refer to the Explanation of Data for more information.*

Los Angeles

Place Type: City
County: Los Angeles
Population: 3,792,621

Ancestry	Population	%
Afghan (2,245)	2,434	0.06
African, Sub-Saharan (44,842)	51,431	1.36
African (34,439)	39,515	1.05
Cape Verdean (118)	198	0.01
Ethiopian (3,611)	3,896	0.10
Ghanaian (548)	587	0.02
Kenyan (327)	336	0.01
Liberian (76)	76	<0.01
Nigerian (2,870)	3,268	0.09
Senegalese (164)	164	<0.01
Sierra Leonean (82)	121	<0.01
Somalian (0)	0	<0.01
South African (1,120)	1,463	0.04
Sudanese (109)	184	<0.01
Ugandan (455)	491	0.01
Zimbabwean (74)	101	<0.01
Other Sub-Saharan African (849)	1,031	0.03
Albanian (164)	335	0.01
Alsatian (20)	78	<0.01
American (68,094)	68,094	1.81
Arab (20,422)	30,066	0.80
Arab (2,382)	3,096	0.08
Egyptian (4,964)	6,033	0.16
Iraqi (659)	1,444	0.04
Jordanian (1,094)	1,238	0.03
Lebanese (4,390)	8,079	0.21
Moroccan (1,441)	2,098	0.06
Palestinian (625)	947	0.03
Syrian (1,761)	2,954	0.08
Other Arab (3,106)	4,177	0.11
Armenian (67,869)	73,256	1.94
Assyrian/Chaldean/Syriac (1,238)	1,479	0.04
Australian (1,627)	2,486	0.07
Austrian (3,249)	11,090	0.29
Basque (195)	741	0.02
Belgian (819)	2,001	0.05
Brazilian (2,864)	3,962	0.11
British (6,774)	12,180	0.32
Bulgarian (1,850)	2,293	0.06
Cajun (50)	153	<0.01
Canadian (4,548)	7,817	0.21
Carpatho Rusyn (7)	80	<0.01
Celtic (192)	654	0.02
Croatian (3,875)	6,277	0.17
Cypriot (52)	69	<0.01
Czech (1,893)	6,899	0.18
Czechoslovakian (816)	1,806	0.05
Danish (2,465)	9,510	0.25
Dutch (4,418)	17,897	0.47
Eastern European (12,383)	14,001	0.37
English (32,884)	129,873	3.44
Estonian (186)	347	0.01
European (27,406)	33,149	0.88
Finnish (1,054)	2,919	0.08
French, ex. Basque (9,775)	46,698	1.24
French Canadian (3,034)	6,978	0.18
German (45,269)	177,061	4.69
German Russian (111)	145	<0.01
Greek (6,423)	12,497	0.33
Guyanese (250)	437	0.01
Hungarian (6,434)	16,285	0.43
Icelander (269)	380	0.01
Iranian (47,100)	51,547	1.37
Irish (36,683)	147,342	3.91
Israeli (9,984)	12,294	0.33
Italian (39,779)	101,064	2.68
Latvian (1,116)	2,043	0.05
Lithuanian (2,509)	6,875	0.18
Luxemburger (73)	253	0.01
Macedonian (352)	473	0.01
Maltese (164)	279	0.01
New Zealander (351)	502	0.01
Northern European (1,712)	1,975	0.05
Norwegian (6,731)	20,565	0.55
Pennsylvania German (196)	440	0.01
Polish (17,994)	60,010	1.59
Portuguese (2,915)	7,722	0.20
Romanian (5,610)	10,676	0.28
Russian (49,568)	96,251	2.55
Scandinavian (2,082)	4,130	0.11
Scotch-Irish (7,498)	21,996	0.58
Scottish (7,629)	29,120	0.77
Serbian (774)	1,315	0.03
Slavic (271)	742	0.02
Slovak (654)	1,904	0.05
Slovene (175)	730	0.02
Soviet Union (82)	105	<0.01
Swedish (6,007)	23,723	0.63
Swiss (1,678)	5,328	0.14
Turkish (1,961)	3,354	0.09
Ukrainian (7,070)	11,493	0.30
Welsh (1,655)	10,583	0.28
West Indian, ex. Hispanic (13,757)	17,886	0.47
Bahamian (88)	166	<0.01
Barbadian (128)	202	0.01
Belizean (7,369)	8,719	0.23
Bermudan (80)	118	<0.01
British West Indian (235)	308	0.01
Dutch West Indian (0)	71	<0.01
Haitian (1,109)	1,526	0.04
Jamaican (3,172)	4,559	0.12
Trinidadian/Tobagonian (469)	631	0.02
U.S. Virgin Islander (33)	77	<0.01
West Indian (1,056)	1,476	0.04
Other West Indian (18)	33	<0.01
Yugoslavian (1,137)	2,313	0.06

Hispanic Origin	Population	%
Hispanic or Latino (of any race)	1,838,822	48.48
Central American, ex. Mexican	415,913	10.97
Costa Rican	3,182	0.08
Guatemalan	138,139	3.64
Honduran	23,919	0.63
Nicaraguan	15,572	0.41
Panamanian	2,131	0.06
Salvadoran	228,990	6.04
Other Central American	3,980	0.10
Cuban	13,494	0.36
Dominican Republic	1,602	0.04
Mexican	1,209,573	31.89
Puerto Rican	15,565	0.41
South American	49,352	1.30
Argentinean	8,570	0.23
Bolivian	2,561	0.07
Chilean	4,112	0.11
Colombian	9,766	0.26
Ecuadorian	7,314	0.19
Paraguayan	180	<0.01
Peruvian	14,033	0.37
Uruguayan	697	0.02
Venezuelan	1,490	0.04
Other South American	629	0.02
Other Hispanic or Latino	133,323	3.52

Race*	Population	%
African-American/Black (365,118)	402,448	10.61
Not Hispanic (347,380)	372,821	9.83
Hispanic (17,738)	29,627	0.78
American Indian/Alaska Native (28,215)	54,236	1.43
Not Hispanic (6,589)	19,510	0.51
Hispanic (21,626)	34,726	0.92
Alaska Athabascan *(Ala. Nat.)* (23)	49	<0.01
Aleut *(Alaska Native)* (14)	35	<0.01
Apache (691)	1,531	0.04
Arapaho (10)	24	<0.01
Blackfeet (108)	966	0.03
Canadian/French Am. Ind. (57)	119	<0.01
Central American Ind. (959)	1,602	0.04
Cherokee (881)	4,661	0.12
Cheyenne (22)	77	<0.01
Chickasaw (65)	207	0.01
Chippewa (134)	331	0.01
Choctaw (243)	1,133	0.03
Colville (12)	27	<0.01
Comanche (58)	145	<0.01
Cree (15)	66	<0.01
Creek (108)	334	0.01
Crow (11)	44	<0.01
Delaware (28)	80	<0.01
Hopi (85)	163	<0.01
Houma (0)	10	<0.01
Inupiat *(Alaska Native)* (23)	56	<0.01
Iroquois (112)	321	0.01
Kiowa (35)	49	<0.01
Lumbee (20)	59	<0.01
Menominee (11)	18	<0.01
Mexican American Ind. (6,740)	9,589	0.25
Navajo (740)	1,260	0.03
Osage (27)	107	<0.01
Ottawa (9)	24	<0.01
Paiute (45)	86	<0.01
Pima (69)	152	<0.01
Potawatomi (40)	115	<0.01
Pueblo (261)	493	0.01
Puget Sound Salish (7)	22	<0.01
Seminole (41)	234	0.01
Shoshone (74)	116	<0.01
Sioux (267)	661	0.02
South American Ind. (243)	595	0.02
Spanish American Ind. (351)	564	0.01
Tlingit-Haida *(Alaska Native)* (30)	69	<0.01
Tohono O'Odham (150)	220	0.01
Tsimshian *(Alaska Native)* (6)	14	<0.01
Ute (27)	48	<0.01
Yakama (7)	15	<0.01
Yaqui (314)	647	0.02
Yuman (75)	105	<0.01
Yup'ik *(Alaska Native)* (5)	17	<0.01
Asian (426,959)	483,585	12.75
Not Hispanic (420,212)	465,942	12.29
Hispanic (6,747)	17,643	0.47
Bangladeshi (3,098)	3,483	0.09
Bhutanese (35)	36	<0.01
Burmese (673)	842	0.02
Cambodian (3,446)	4,280	0.11
Chinese, ex. Taiwanese (61,950)	75,827	2.00
Filipino (122,787)	139,859	3.69
Hmong (131)	149	<0.01
Indian (32,996)	38,574	1.02
Indonesian (2,544)	3,670	0.10
Japanese (32,619)	43,978	1.16
Korean (108,282)	114,140	3.01
Laotian (635)	871	0.02
Malaysian (190)	342	0.01
Nepalese (347)	387	0.01
Pakistani (3,411)	3,973	0.10
Sri Lankan (2,058)	2,358	0.06
Taiwanese (4,559)	5,282	0.14
Thai (12,349)	14,122	0.37
Vietnamese (19,969)	23,325	0.62
Hawaii Native/Pacific Islander (5,577)	15,031	0.40
Not Hispanic (4,300)	10,779	0.28
Hispanic (1,277)	4,252	0.11
Fijian (329)	420	0.01
Guamanian/Chamorro (1,103)	1,840	0.05
Marshallese (2)	3	<0.01
Native Hawaiian (1,209)	4,062	0.11
Samoan (1,504)	2,480	0.07
Tongan (502)	649	0.02
White (1,888,158)	2,031,586	53.57
Not Hispanic (1,086,908)	1,148,305	30.28
Hispanic (801,250)	883,281	23.29

*Notes: † The Census 2010 population figure is used to calculate the percentages in the Hispanic Origin and Race categories. Ancestry percentages are based on the 2006-2010 American Community Survey population (not shown); ‡ Numbers in parentheses indicate the number of people reporting a single ancestry; * Numbers in parentheses indicate the number of persons reporting this race alone, not in combination with any other race; Please refer to the Explanation of Data for more information.*

Lynwood

Place Type: City
County: Los Angeles
Population: 69,772

Ancestry	Population	%
Afghan (0)	0	<0.01
African, Sub-Saharan (525)	662	0.95
African (525)	662	0.95
Cape Verdean (0)	0	<0.01
Ethiopian (0)	0	<0.01
Ghanaian (0)	0	<0.01
Kenyan (0)	0	<0.01
Liberian (0)	0	<0.01
Nigerian (0)	0	<0.01
Senegalese (0)	0	<0.01
Sierra Leonean (0)	0	<0.01
Somalian (0)	0	<0.01
South African (0)	0	<0.01
Sudanese (0)	0	<0.01
Ugandan (0)	0	<0.01
Zimbabwean (0)	0	<0.01
Other Sub-Saharan African (0)	0	<0.01
Albanian (0)	0	<0.01
Alsatian (0)	0	<0.01
American (1,380)	1,380	1.98
Arab (34)	62	0.09
Arab (0)	0	<0.01
Egyptian (0)	0	<0.01
Iraqi (28)	28	0.04
Jordanian (0)	0	<0.01
Lebanese (6)	6	0.01
Moroccan (0)	0	<0.01
Palestinian (0)	0	<0.01
Syrian (0)	0	<0.01
Other Arab (0)	28	0.04
Armenian (6)	6	0.01
Assyrian/Chaldean/Syriac (0)	0	<0.01
Australian (0)	0	<0.01
Austrian (0)	0	<0.01
Basque (0)	0	<0.01
Belgian (0)	0	<0.01
Brazilian (0)	0	<0.01
British (0)	0	<0.01
Bulgarian (0)	0	<0.01
Cajun (0)	0	<0.01
Canadian (0)	0	<0.01
Carpatho Rusyn (0)	0	<0.01
Celtic (0)	0	<0.01
Croatian (0)	0	<0.01
Cypriot (0)	0	<0.01
Czech (10)	10	0.01
Czechoslovakian (0)	0	<0.01
Danish (0)	9	0.01
Dutch (0)	9	0.01
Eastern European (0)	0	<0.01
English (113)	263	0.38
Estonian (0)	0	<0.01
European (0)	9	0.01
Finnish (0)	0	<0.01
French, ex. Basque (8)	75	0.11
French Canadian (8)	14	0.02
German (189)	390	0.56
German Russian (0)	0	<0.01
Greek (22)	30	0.04
Guyanese (0)	0	<0.01
Hungarian (0)	16	0.02
Icelander (0)	0	<0.01
Iranian (6)	6	0.01
Irish (29)	307	0.44
Israeli (0)	8	0.01
Italian (36)	186	0.27
Latvian (0)	0	<0.01
Lithuanian (0)	0	<0.01
Luxemburger (0)	0	<0.01
Macedonian (0)	0	<0.01
Maltese (0)	0	<0.01
New Zealander (0)	0	<0.01
Northern European (0)	0	<0.01
Norwegian (0)	42	0.06
Pennsylvania German (0)	11	0.02
Polish (55)	84	0.12
Portuguese (0)	28	0.04
Romanian (0)	0	<0.01
Russian (93)	101	0.14
Scandinavian (0)	0	<0.01
Scotch-Irish (28)	28	0.04
Scottish (0)	75	0.11
Serbian (0)	0	<0.01
Slavic (0)	0	<0.01
Slovak (0)	0	<0.01
Slovene (0)	0	<0.01
Soviet Union (0)	0	<0.01
Swedish (0)	14	0.02
Swiss (0)	0	<0.01
Turkish (0)	0	<0.01
Ukrainian (0)	8	0.01
Welsh (0)	7	0.01
West Indian, ex. Hispanic (68)	120	0.17
Bahamian (0)	0	<0.01
Barbadian (0)	0	<0.01
Belizean (40)	48	0.07
Bermudan (0)	0	<0.01
British West Indian (0)	0	<0.01
Dutch West Indian (0)	0	<0.01
Haitian (0)	0	<0.01
Jamaican (16)	16	0.02
Trinidadian/Tobagonian (0)	44	0.06
U.S. Virgin Islander (0)	0	<0.01
West Indian (12)	12	0.02
Other West Indian (0)	0	<0.01
Yugoslavian (0)	0	<0.01

Hispanic Origin	Population	%
Hispanic or Latino (of any race)	60,452	86.64
Central American, ex. Mexican	5,761	8.26
Costa Rican	15	0.02
Guatemalan	1,754	2.51
Honduran	420	0.60
Nicaraguan	315	0.45
Panamanian	25	0.04
Salvadoran	3,154	4.52
Other Central American	78	0.11
Cuban	110	0.16
Dominican Republic	13	0.02
Mexican	51,021	73.13
Puerto Rican	192	0.28
South American	349	0.50
Argentinean	26	0.04
Bolivian	13	0.02
Chilean	9	0.01
Colombian	29	0.04
Ecuadorian	128	0.18
Paraguayan	0	<0.01
Peruvian	137	0.20
Uruguayan	3	<0.01
Venezuelan	3	<0.01
Other South American	1	<0.01
Other Hispanic or Latino	3,006	4.31

Race*	Population	%
African-American/Black (7,168)	7,602	10.90
Not Hispanic (6,752)	6,922	9.92
Hispanic (416)	680	0.97
American Indian/Alaska Native (464)	753	1.08
Not Hispanic (76)	152	0.22
Hispanic (388)	601	0.86
Alaska Athabascan *(Ala. Nat.)* (0)	0	<0.01
Aleut *(Alaska Native)* (0)	0	<0.01
Apache (3)	7	0.01
Arapaho (0)	0	<0.01
Blackfeet (0)	3	<0.01
Canadian/French Am. Ind. (0)	1	<0.01
Central American Ind. (6)	10	0.01
Cherokee (9)	37	0.05
Cheyenne (0)	0	<0.01
Chickasaw (0)	0	<0.01
Chippewa (0)	4	0.01
Choctaw (8)	15	0.02
Colville (0)	0	<0.01
Comanche (0)	0	<0.01
Cree (0)	3	<0.01
Creek (0)	1	<0.01
Crow (0)	0	<0.01
Delaware (1)	2	<0.01
Hopi (0)	0	<0.01
Houma (0)	0	<0.01
Inupiat *(Alaska Native)* (0)	0	<0.01
Iroquois (0)	0	<0.01
Kiowa (0)	0	<0.01
Lumbee (0)	0	<0.01
Menominee (0)	0	<0.01
Mexican American Ind. (128)	190	0.27
Navajo (9)	18	0.03
Osage (0)	0	<0.01
Ottawa (0)	0	<0.01
Paiute (0)	0	<0.01
Pima (1)	3	<0.01
Potawatomi (0)	0	<0.01
Pueblo (3)	7	0.01
Puget Sound Salish (0)	0	<0.01
Seminole (0)	0	<0.01
Shoshone (0)	0	<0.01
Sioux (3)	3	<0.01
South American Ind. (1)	1	<0.01
Spanish American Ind. (4)	13	0.02
Tlingit-Haida *(Alaska Native)* (0)	0	<0.01
Tohono O'Odham (6)	6	0.01
Tsimshian *(Alaska Native)* (0)	0	<0.01
Ute (0)	0	<0.01
Yakama (0)	0	<0.01
Yaqui (0)	0	<0.01
Yuman (0)	3	<0.01
Yup'ik *(Alaska Native)* (0)	0	<0.01
Asian (457)	603	0.86
Not Hispanic (390)	442	0.63
Hispanic (67)	161	0.23
Bangladeshi (0)	0	<0.01
Bhutanese (0)	0	<0.01
Burmese (0)	0	<0.01
Cambodian (6)	8	0.01
Chinese, ex. Taiwanese (31)	50	0.07
Filipino (120)	174	0.25
Hmong (0)	0	<0.01
Indian (91)	106	0.15
Indonesian (5)	6	0.01
Japanese (12)	18	0.03
Korean (44)	51	0.07
Laotian (67)	73	0.10
Malaysian (0)	0	<0.01
Nepalese (0)	0	<0.01
Pakistani (1)	1	<0.01
Sri Lankan (0)	0	<0.01
Taiwanese (0)	1	<0.01
Thai (40)	57	0.08
Vietnamese (18)	19	0.03
Hawaii Native/Pacific Islander (206)	294	0.42
Not Hispanic (170)	204	0.29
Hispanic (36)	90	0.13
Fijian (0)	1	<0.01
Guamanian/Chamorro (10)	21	0.03
Marshallese (0)	0	<0.01
Native Hawaiian (6)	23	0.03
Samoan (171)	198	0.28
Tongan (12)	14	0.02
White (27,444)	29,384	42.11
Not Hispanic (1,539)	1,673	2.40
Hispanic (25,905)	27,711	39.72

*Notes: † The Census 2010 population figure is used to calculate the percentages in the Hispanic Origin and Race categories. Ancestry percentages are based on the 2006-2010 American Community Survey population (not shown); ‡ Numbers in parentheses indicate the number of people reporting a single ancestry; * Numbers in parentheses indicate the number of persons reporting this race alone, not in combination with any other race; Please refer to the Explanation of Data for more information.*

Madera

Place Type: City
County: Madera
Population: 61,416

Ancestry	Population	%
Afghan (0)	0	<0.01
African, Sub-Saharan (15)	111	0.19
African (15)	111	0.19
Cape Verdean (0)	0	<0.01
Ethiopian (0)	0	<0.01
Ghanaian (0)	0	<0.01
Kenyan (0)	0	<0.01
Liberian (0)	0	<0.01
Nigerian (0)	0	<0.01
Senegalese (0)	0	<0.01
Sierra Leonean (0)	0	<0.01
Somalian (0)	0	<0.01
South African (0)	0	<0.01
Sudanese (0)	0	<0.01
Ugandan (0)	0	<0.01
Zimbabwean (0)	0	<0.01
Other Sub-Saharan African (0)	0	<0.01
Albanian (0)	0	<0.01
Alsatian (0)	0	<0.01
American (565)	565	0.96
Arab (103)	148	0.25
Arab (91)	111	0.19
Egyptian (0)	0	<0.01
Iraqi (0)	0	<0.01
Jordanian (0)	0	<0.01
Lebanese (12)	37	0.06
Moroccan (0)	0	<0.01
Palestinian (0)	0	<0.01
Syrian (0)	0	<0.01
Other Arab (0)	0	<0.01
Armenian (0)	40	0.07
Assyrian/Chaldean/Syriac (0)	0	<0.01
Australian (0)	0	<0.01
Austrian (0)	0	<0.01
Basque (28)	28	0.05
Belgian (0)	0	<0.01
Brazilian (0)	0	<0.01
British (10)	121	0.21
Bulgarian (0)	0	<0.01
Cajun (0)	0	<0.01
Canadian (0)	11	0.02
Carpatho Rusyn (0)	0	<0.01
Celtic (0)	0	<0.01
Croatian (0)	0	<0.01
Cypriot (0)	0	<0.01
Czech (0)	19	0.03
Czechoslovakian (0)	0	<0.01
Danish (36)	140	0.24
Dutch (152)	447	0.76
Eastern European (0)	0	<0.01
English (402)	1,229	2.08
Estonian (0)	0	<0.01
European (177)	240	0.41
Finnish (0)	0	<0.01
French, ex. Basque (107)	350	0.59
French Canadian (97)	141	0.24
German (517)	1,921	3.26
German Russian (0)	0	<0.01
Greek (0)	25	0.04
Guyanese (0)	0	<0.01
Hungarian (0)	0	<0.01
Icelander (0)	0	<0.01
Iranian (0)	0	<0.01
Irish (960)	2,219	3.76
Israeli (0)	0	<0.01
Italian (515)	881	1.49
Latvian (0)	0	<0.01
Lithuanian (0)	0	<0.01
Luxemburger (0)	0	<0.01
Macedonian (0)	0	<0.01
Maltese (16)	16	0.03
New Zealander (0)	0	<0.01
Northern European (0)	9	0.02
Norwegian (83)	225	0.38
Pennsylvania German (0)	0	<0.01
Polish (88)	117	0.20
Portuguese (573)	827	1.40
Romanian (0)	0	<0.01
Russian (44)	135	0.23
Scandinavian (26)	39	0.07
Scotch-Irish (62)	256	0.43
Scottish (11)	262	0.44
Serbian (0)	0	<0.01
Slavic (0)	0	<0.01
Slovak (0)	11	0.02
Slovene (0)	0	<0.01
Soviet Union (0)	0	<0.01
Swedish (53)	211	0.36
Swiss (39)	98	0.17
Turkish (0)	0	<0.01
Ukrainian (18)	40	0.07
Welsh (9)	141	0.24
West Indian, ex. Hispanic (0)	0	<0.01
Bahamian (0)	0	<0.01
Barbadian (0)	0	<0.01
Belizean (0)	0	<0.01
Bermudan (0)	0	<0.01
British West Indian (0)	0	<0.01
Dutch West Indian (0)	0	<0.01
Haitian (0)	0	<0.01
Jamaican (0)	0	<0.01
Trinidadian/Tobagonian (0)	0	<0.01
U.S. Virgin Islander (0)	0	<0.01
West Indian (0)	0	<0.01
Other West Indian (0)	0	<0.01
Yugoslavian (0)	0	<0.01

Hispanic Origin	Population	%
Hispanic or Latino (of any race)	47,103	76.69
Central American, ex. Mexican	491	0.80
Costa Rican	4	0.01
Guatemalan	104	0.17
Honduran	53	0.09
Nicaraguan	33	0.05
Panamanian	6	0.01
Salvadoran	287	0.47
Other Central American	4	0.01
Cuban	48	0.08
Dominican Republic	4	0.01
Mexican	44,444	72.37
Puerto Rican	227	0.37
South American	96	0.16
Argentinean	25	0.04
Bolivian	6	0.01
Chilean	5	0.01
Colombian	13	0.02
Ecuadorian	7	0.01
Paraguayan	0	<0.01
Peruvian	31	0.05
Uruguayan	2	<0.01
Venezuelan	7	0.01
Other South American	0	<0.01
Other Hispanic or Latino	1,793	2.92

Race*	Population	%
African-American/Black (2,069)	2,477	4.03
Not Hispanic (1,661)	1,861	3.03
Hispanic (408)	616	1.00
American Indian/Alaska Native (1,933)	2,471	4.02
Not Hispanic (335)	567	0.92
Hispanic (1,598)	1,904	3.10
Alaska Athabascan *(Ala. Nat.)* (0)	0	<0.01
Aleut *(Alaska Native)* (0)	0	<0.01
Apache (32)	59	0.10
Arapaho (0)	0	<0.01
Blackfeet (3)	9	0.01
Canadian/French Am. Ind. (2)	2	<0.01
Central American Ind. (8)	10	0.02
Cherokee (28)	110	0.18
Cheyenne (0)	3	<0.01
Chickasaw (1)	1	<0.01
Chippewa (9)	13	0.02
Choctaw (23)	43	0.07
Colville (0)	0	<0.01
Comanche (5)	11	0.02
Cree (1)	1	<0.01
Creek (4)	5	0.01
Crow (0)	0	<0.01
Delaware (0)	1	<0.01
Hopi (1)	1	<0.01
Houma (0)	0	<0.01
Inupiat *(Alaska Native)* (0)	0	<0.01
Iroquois (2)	3	<0.01
Kiowa (2)	2	<0.01
Lumbee (0)	0	<0.01
Menominee (0)	0	<0.01
Mexican American Ind. (780)	891	1.45
Navajo (18)	28	0.05
Osage (0)	0	<0.01
Ottawa (0)	0	<0.01
Paiute (11)	13	0.02
Pima (0)	4	0.01
Potawatomi (1)	2	<0.01
Pueblo (4)	9	0.01
Puget Sound Salish (0)	0	<0.01
Seminole (0)	1	<0.01
Shoshone (1)	1	<0.01
Sioux (6)	14	0.02
South American Ind. (9)	9	0.01
Spanish American Ind. (7)	7	0.01
Tlingit-Haida *(Alaska Native)* (0)	0	<0.01
Tohono O'Odham (1)	1	<0.01
Tsimshian *(Alaska Native)* (0)	0	<0.01
Ute (0)	0	<0.01
Yakama (6)	6	0.01
Yaqui (14)	27	0.04
Yuman (4)	7	0.01
Yup'ik *(Alaska Native)* (0)	3	<0.01
Asian (1,369)	1,825	2.97
Not Hispanic (1,199)	1,452	2.36
Hispanic (170)	373	0.61
Bangladeshi (0)	0	<0.01
Bhutanese (0)	0	<0.01
Burmese (0)	0	<0.01
Cambodian (32)	40	0.07
Chinese, ex. Taiwanese (109)	147	0.24
Filipino (328)	510	0.83
Hmong (48)	51	0.08
Indian (563)	638	1.04
Indonesian (8)	17	0.03
Japanese (46)	105	0.17
Korean (39)	62	0.10
Laotian (16)	16	0.03
Malaysian (0)	0	<0.01
Nepalese (0)	0	<0.01
Pakistani (80)	86	0.14
Sri Lankan (0)	0	<0.01
Taiwanese (0)	0	<0.01
Thai (11)	20	0.03
Vietnamese (30)	37	0.06
Hawaii Native/Pacific Islander (72)	207	0.34
Not Hispanic (35)	75	0.12
Hispanic (37)	132	0.21
Fijian (3)	6	0.01
Guamanian/Chamorro (4)	11	0.02
Marshallese (0)	0	<0.01
Native Hawaiian (33)	69	0.11
Samoan (16)	25	0.04
Tongan (0)	1	<0.01
White (30,640)	32,872	53.52
Not Hispanic (10,402)	10,927	17.79
Hispanic (20,238)	21,945	35.73

*Notes: † The Census 2010 population figure is used to calculate the percentages in the Hispanic Origin and Race categories. Ancestry percentages are based on the 2006-2010 American Community Survey population (not shown); ‡ Numbers in parentheses indicate the number of people reporting a single ancestry; * Numbers in parentheses indicate the number of persons reporting this race alone, not in combination with any other race; Please refer to the Explanation of Data for more information.*

Manteca

Place Type: City
County: San Joaquin
Population: 67,096

Ancestry	Population	%
Afghan (313)	416	0.64
African, Sub-Saharan (45)	70	0.11
African (17)	42	0.06
Cape Verdean (0)	0	<0.01
Ethiopian (0)	0	<0.01
Ghanaian (0)	0	<0.01
Kenyan (0)	0	<0.01
Liberian (0)	0	<0.01
Nigerian (0)	0	<0.01
Senegalese (0)	0	<0.01
Sierra Leonean (28)	28	0.04
Somalian (0)	0	<0.01
South African (0)	0	<0.01
Sudanese (0)	0	<0.01
Ugandan (0)	0	<0.01
Zimbabwean (0)	0	<0.01
Other Sub-Saharan African (0)	0	<0.01
Albanian (0)	0	<0.01
Alsatian (0)	0	<0.01
American (1,786)	1,786	2.75
Arab (122)	140	0.22
Arab (0)	0	<0.01
Egyptian (30)	30	0.05
Iraqi (0)	0	<0.01
Jordanian (0)	0	<0.01
Lebanese (0)	0	<0.01
Moroccan (9)	18	0.03
Palestinian (0)	0	<0.01
Syrian (0)	0	<0.01
Other Arab (83)	92	0.14
Armenian (44)	90	0.14
Assyrian/Chaldean/Syriac (0)	31	0.05
Australian (0)	30	0.05
Austrian (8)	61	0.09
Basque (0)	11	0.02
Belgian (27)	83	0.13
Brazilian (0)	47	0.07
British (95)	213	0.33
Bulgarian (0)	0	<0.01
Cajun (0)	0	<0.01
Canadian (59)	167	0.26
Carpatho Rusyn (0)	0	<0.01
Celtic (0)	7	0.01
Croatian (27)	197	0.30
Cypriot (0)	0	<0.01
Czech (0)	126	0.19
Czechoslovakian (18)	24	0.04
Danish (37)	245	0.38
Dutch (361)	1,269	1.95
Eastern European (0)	0	<0.01
English (1,343)	4,615	7.10
Estonian (0)	0	<0.01
European (595)	671	1.03
Finnish (0)	14	0.02
French, ex. Basque (196)	1,558	2.40
French Canadian (42)	185	0.28
German (2,084)	9,462	14.57
German Russian (0)	0	<0.01
Greek (92)	250	0.38
Guyanese (0)	0	<0.01
Hungarian (41)	183	0.28
Icelander (10)	34	0.05
Iranian (0)	0	<0.01
Irish (1,540)	6,490	9.99
Israeli (0)	0	<0.01
Italian (1,313)	4,017	6.18
Latvian (0)	0	<0.01
Lithuanian (0)	38	0.06
Luxemburger (0)	0	<0.01
Macedonian (0)	0	<0.01
Maltese (0)	14	0.02
New Zealander (0)	0	<0.01
Northern European (27)	27	0.04
Norwegian (262)	924	1.42
Pennsylvania German (0)	11	0.02
Polish (109)	546	0.84
Portuguese (1,563)	3,310	5.10
Romanian (36)	36	0.06
Russian (37)	265	0.41
Scandinavian (0)	23	0.04
Scotch-Irish (185)	671	1.03
Scottish (204)	818	1.26
Serbian (0)	0	<0.01
Slavic (0)	117	0.18
Slovak (51)	151	0.23
Slovene (0)	17	0.03
Soviet Union (0)	0	<0.01
Swedish (204)	844	1.30
Swiss (91)	323	0.50
Turkish (20)	75	0.12
Ukrainian (0)	44	0.07
Welsh (47)	141	0.22
West Indian, ex. Hispanic (83)	122	0.19
Bahamian (0)	0	<0.01
Barbadian (0)	0	<0.01
Belizean (0)	16	0.02
Bermudan (0)	0	<0.01
British West Indian (0)	0	<0.01
Dutch West Indian (0)	0	<0.01
Haitian (0)	0	<0.01
Jamaican (0)	23	0.04
Trinidadian/Tobagonian (83)	83	0.13
U.S. Virgin Islander (0)	0	<0.01
West Indian (0)	0	<0.01
Other West Indian (0)	0	<0.01
Yugoslavian (8)	25	0.04

Hispanic Origin	Population	%
Hispanic or Latino (of any race)	25,317	37.73
Central American, ex. Mexican	882	1.31
Costa Rican	18	0.03
Guatemalan	175	0.26
Honduran	52	0.08
Nicaraguan	210	0.31
Panamanian	22	0.03
Salvadoran	396	0.59
Other Central American	9	0.01
Cuban	88	0.13
Dominican Republic	24	0.04
Mexican	20,962	31.24
Puerto Rican	844	1.26
South American	315	0.47
Argentinean	19	0.03
Bolivian	7	0.01
Chilean	27	0.04
Colombian	42	0.06
Ecuadorian	35	0.05
Paraguayan	1	<0.01
Peruvian	173	0.26
Uruguayan	3	<0.01
Venezuelan	7	0.01
Other South American	1	<0.01
Other Hispanic or Latino	2,202	3.28

Race*	Population	%
African-American/Black (2,869)	3,724	5.55
Not Hispanic (2,669)	3,204	4.78
Hispanic (200)	520	0.78
American Indian/Alaska Native (735)	1,801	2.68
Not Hispanic (359)	941	1.40
Hispanic (376)	860	1.28
Alaska Athabascan *(Ala. Nat.)* (1)	1	<0.01
Aleut *(Alaska Native)* (1)	4	0.01
Apache (27)	87	0.13
Arapaho (0)	0	<0.01
Blackfeet (4)	39	0.06
Canadian/French Am. Ind. (0)	9	0.01
Central American Ind. (1)	2	<0.01
Cherokee (68)	343	0.51
Cheyenne (0)	1	<0.01
Chickasaw (6)	8	0.01
Chippewa (9)	29	0.04
Choctaw (34)	102	0.15
Colville (2)	2	<0.01
Comanche (1)	2	<0.01
Cree (0)	0	<0.01
Creek (3)	8	0.01
Crow (0)	0	<0.01
Delaware (0)	2	<0.01
Hopi (0)	5	0.01
Houma (1)	5	0.01
Inupiat *(Alaska Native)* (0)	3	<0.01
Iroquois (1)	19	0.03
Kiowa (3)	5	0.01
Lumbee (0)	0	<0.01
Menominee (0)	0	<0.01
Mexican American Ind. (47)	95	0.14
Navajo (14)	40	0.06
Osage (6)	12	0.02
Ottawa (0)	0	<0.01
Paiute (19)	33	0.05
Pima (0)	0	<0.01
Potawatomi (3)	12	0.02
Pueblo (6)	13	0.02
Puget Sound Salish (5)	7	0.01
Seminole (6)	17	0.03
Shoshone (1)	7	0.01
Sioux (29)	52	0.08
South American Ind. (5)	13	0.02
Spanish American Ind. (7)	8	0.01
Tlingit-Haida *(Alaska Native)* (1)	1	<0.01
Tohono O'Odham (0)	0	<0.01
Tsimshian *(Alaska Native)* (0)	0	<0.01
Ute (3)	18	0.03
Yakama (1)	4	0.01
Yaqui (20)	37	0.06
Yuman (2)	2	<0.01
Yup'ik *(Alaska Native)* (0)	0	<0.01
Asian (4,780)	6,532	9.74
Not Hispanic (4,549)	5,757	8.58
Hispanic (231)	775	1.16
Bangladeshi (0)	0	<0.01
Bhutanese (0)	0	<0.01
Burmese (17)	19	0.03
Cambodian (134)	164	0.24
Chinese, ex. Taiwanese (349)	571	0.85
Filipino (1,899)	2,953	4.40
Hmong (49)	52	0.08
Indian (1,622)	1,746	2.60
Indonesian (15)	36	0.05
Japanese (133)	351	0.52
Korean (86)	146	0.22
Laotian (72)	95	0.14
Malaysian (1)	3	<0.01
Nepalese (0)	0	<0.01
Pakistani (40)	54	0.08
Sri Lankan (0)	1	<0.01
Taiwanese (4)	6	0.01
Thai (18)	42	0.06
Vietnamese (167)	226	0.34
Hawaii Native/Pacific Islander (384)	890	1.33
Not Hispanic (302)	624	0.93
Hispanic (82)	266	0.40
Fijian (99)	106	0.16
Guamanian/Chamorro (81)	182	0.27
Marshallese (0)	0	<0.01
Native Hawaiian (93)	340	0.51
Samoan (51)	106	0.16
Tongan (9)	16	0.02
White (41,840)	45,863	68.35
Not Hispanic (31,476)	33,402	49.78
Hispanic (10,364)	12,461	18.57

*Notes: † The Census 2010 population figure is used to calculate the percentages in the Hispanic Origin and Race categories. Ancestry percentages are based on the 2006-2010 American Community Survey population (not shown); ‡ Numbers in parentheses indicate the number of people reporting a single ancestry; * Numbers in parentheses indicate the number of persons reporting this race alone, not in combination with any other race; Please refer to the Explanation of Data for more information.*

Menifee

Place Type: City
County: Riverside
Population: 77,519

Ancestry	Population	%
Afghan (11)	11	0.02
African, Sub-Saharan (266)	289	0.40
African (266)	289	0.40
Cape Verdean (0)	0	<0.01
Ethiopian (0)	0	<0.01
Ghanaian (0)	0	<0.01
Kenyan (0)	0	<0.01
Liberian (0)	0	<0.01
Nigerian (0)	0	<0.01
Senegalese (0)	0	<0.01
Sierra Leonean (0)	0	<0.01
Somalian (0)	0	<0.01
South African (0)	0	<0.01
Sudanese (0)	0	<0.01
Ugandan (0)	0	<0.01
Zimbabwean (0)	0	<0.01
Other Sub-Saharan African (0)	0	<0.01
Albanian (0)	0	<0.01
Alsatian (0)	0	<0.01
American (2,194)	2,194	3.03
Arab (233)	266	0.37
Arab (10)	10	0.01
Egyptian (0)	0	<0.01
Iraqi (8)	8	0.01
Jordanian (163)	163	0.22
Lebanese (0)	19	0.03
Moroccan (0)	0	<0.01
Palestinian (0)	0	<0.01
Syrian (0)	14	0.02
Other Arab (52)	52	0.07
Armenian (57)	76	0.10
Assyrian/Chaldean/Syriac (0)	0	<0.01
Australian (13)	75	0.10
Austrian (49)	144	0.20
Basque (85)	85	0.12
Belgian (13)	45	0.06
Brazilian (8)	37	0.05
British (157)	226	0.31
Bulgarian (26)	26	0.04
Cajun (0)	0	<0.01
Canadian (113)	325	0.45
Carpatho Rusyn (0)	0	<0.01
Celtic (0)	32	0.04
Croatian (68)	100	0.14
Cypriot (0)	0	<0.01
Czech (70)	256	0.35
Czechoslovakian (23)	33	0.05
Danish (121)	433	0.60
Dutch (381)	2,084	2.87
Eastern European (21)	21	0.03
English (2,163)	7,360	10.15
Estonian (0)	0	<0.01
European (762)	997	1.38
Finnish (82)	251	0.35
French, ex. Basque (351)	2,493	3.44
French Canadian (190)	556	0.77
German (3,084)	10,602	14.62
German Russian (0)	0	<0.01
Greek (121)	241	0.33
Guyanese (41)	53	0.07
Hungarian (117)	278	0.38
Icelander (0)	9	0.01
Iranian (0)	20	0.03
Irish (1,896)	6,860	9.46
Israeli (0)	0	<0.01
Italian (1,717)	3,985	5.50
Latvian (0)	0	<0.01
Lithuanian (13)	62	0.09
Luxemburger (13)	26	0.04
Macedonian (23)	23	0.03
Maltese (34)	34	0.05
New Zealander (0)	0	<0.01
Northern European (11)	24	0.03
Norwegian (652)	1,218	1.68
Pennsylvania German (13)	28	0.04
Polish (649)	1,414	1.95
Portuguese (77)	232	0.32
Romanian (235)	386	0.53
Russian (268)	550	0.76
Scandinavian (62)	106	0.15
Scotch-Irish (402)	1,449	2.00
Scottish (351)	1,348	1.86
Serbian (15)	27	0.04
Slavic (39)	39	0.05
Slovak (25)	78	0.11
Slovene (0)	10	0.01
Soviet Union (0)	0	<0.01
Swedish (398)	1,169	1.61
Swiss (34)	149	0.21
Turkish (0)	0	<0.01
Ukrainian (64)	176	0.24
Welsh (77)	412	0.57
West Indian, ex. Hispanic (133)	218	0.30
Bahamian (0)	0	<0.01
Barbadian (0)	0	<0.01
Belizean (121)	121	0.17
Bermudan (0)	0	<0.01
British West Indian (0)	0	<0.01
Dutch West Indian (0)	0	<0.01
Haitian (0)	14	0.02
Jamaican (12)	83	0.11
Trinidadian/Tobagonian (0)	0	<0.01
U.S. Virgin Islander (0)	0	<0.01
West Indian (0)	0	<0.01
Other West Indian (0)	0	<0.01
Yugoslavian (51)	69	0.10

Hispanic Origin	Population	%
Hispanic or Latino (of any race)	25,551	32.96
Central American, ex. Mexican	730	0.94
Costa Rican	33	0.04
Guatemalan	194	0.25
Honduran	51	0.07
Nicaraguan	117	0.15
Panamanian	46	0.06
Salvadoran	284	0.37
Other Central American	5	0.01
Cuban	212	0.27
Dominican Republic	15	0.02
Mexican	21,690	27.98
Puerto Rican	591	0.76
South American	488	0.63
Argentinean	75	0.10
Bolivian	21	0.03
Chilean	27	0.03
Colombian	163	0.21
Ecuadorian	73	0.09
Paraguayan	0	<0.01
Peruvian	92	0.12
Uruguayan	13	0.02
Venezuelan	13	0.02
Other South American	11	0.01
Other Hispanic or Latino	1,825	2.35

Race*	Population	%
African-American/Black (3,858)	4,717	6.08
Not Hispanic (3,630)	4,288	5.53
Hispanic (228)	429	0.55
American Indian/Alaska Native (655)	1,483	1.91
Not Hispanic (314)	852	1.10
Hispanic (341)	631	0.81
Alaska Athabascan *(Ala. Nat.)* (1)	2	<0.01
Aleut *(Alaska Native)* (2)	2	<0.01
Apache (21)	48	0.06
Arapaho (0)	0	<0.01
Blackfeet (5)	30	0.04
Canadian/French Am. Ind. (1)	7	0.01
Central American Ind. (4)	4	0.01
Cherokee (46)	169	0.22
Cheyenne (0)	2	<0.01
Chickasaw (4)	13	0.02
Chippewa (15)	27	0.03
Choctaw (17)	43	0.06
Colville (0)	1	<0.01
Comanche (2)	6	0.01
Cree (0)	0	<0.01
Creek (6)	15	0.02
Crow (0)	2	<0.01
Delaware (4)	12	0.02
Hopi (7)	8	0.01
Houma (0)	0	<0.01
Inupiat *(Alaska Native)* (0)	1	<0.01
Iroquois (2)	12	0.02
Kiowa (0)	0	<0.01
Lumbee (2)	5	0.01
Menominee (0)	0	<0.01
Mexican American Ind. (42)	77	0.10
Navajo (14)	44	0.06
Osage (0)	2	<0.01
Ottawa (0)	0	<0.01
Paiute (5)	5	0.01
Pima (3)	5	0.01
Potawatomi (3)	9	0.01
Pueblo (3)	5	0.01
Puget Sound Salish (0)	0	<0.01
Seminole (0)	0	<0.01
Shoshone (0)	0	<0.01
Sioux (15)	30	0.04
South American Ind. (2)	6	0.01
Spanish American Ind. (0)	0	<0.01
Tlingit-Haida *(Alaska Native)* (1)	1	<0.01
Tohono O'Odham (5)	5	0.01
Tsimshian *(Alaska Native)* (0)	0	<0.01
Ute (1)	2	<0.01
Yakama (1)	1	<0.01
Yaqui (6)	21	0.03
Yuman (1)	1	<0.01
Yup'ik *(Alaska Native)* (0)	0	<0.01
Asian (3,788)	5,094	6.57
Not Hispanic (3,597)	4,559	5.88
Hispanic (191)	535	0.69
Bangladeshi (3)	11	0.01
Bhutanese (0)	0	<0.01
Burmese (1)	2	<0.01
Cambodian (137)	157	0.20
Chinese, ex. Taiwanese (232)	394	0.51
Filipino (2,042)	2,690	3.47
Hmong (3)	3	<0.01
Indian (162)	243	0.31
Indonesian (33)	85	0.11
Japanese (231)	498	0.64
Korean (138)	214	0.28
Laotian (150)	181	0.23
Malaysian (0)	7	0.01
Nepalese (0)	1	<0.01
Pakistani (23)	35	0.05
Sri Lankan (9)	10	0.01
Taiwanese (8)	11	0.01
Thai (58)	101	0.13
Vietnamese (424)	484	0.62
Hawaii Native/Pacific Islander (295)	609	0.79
Not Hispanic (262)	513	0.66
Hispanic (33)	96	0.12
Fijian (6)	7	0.01
Guamanian/Chamorro (93)	142	0.18
Marshallese (0)	0	<0.01
Native Hawaiian (42)	188	0.24
Samoan (72)	130	0.17
Tongan (43)	52	0.07
White (55,444)	58,760	75.80
Not Hispanic (41,988)	43,744	56.43
Hispanic (13,456)	15,016	19.37

*Notes: † The Census 2010 population figure is used to calculate the percentages in the Hispanic Origin and Race categories. Ancestry percentages are based on the 2006-2010 American Community Survey population (not shown); ‡ Numbers in parentheses indicate the number of people reporting a single ancestry; * Numbers in parentheses indicate the number of persons reporting this race alone, not in combination with any other race; Please refer to the Explanation of Data for more information.*

Merced

Place Type: City
County: Merced
Population: 78,958

Ancestry	Population	%
Afghan (0)	0	<0.01
African, Sub-Saharan (108)	119	0.15
African (76)	87	0.11
Cape Verdean (0)	0	<0.01
Ethiopian (0)	0	<0.01
Ghanaian (0)	0	<0.01
Kenyan (0)	0	<0.01
Liberian (0)	0	<0.01
Nigerian (12)	12	0.02
Senegalese (0)	0	<0.01
Sierra Leonean (0)	0	<0.01
Somalian (0)	0	<0.01
South African (20)	20	0.03
Sudanese (0)	0	<0.01
Ugandan (0)	0	<0.01
Zimbabwean (0)	0	<0.01
Other Sub-Saharan African (0)	0	<0.01
Albanian (0)	6	0.01
Alsatian (0)	12	0.02
American (1,590)	1,590	2.06
Arab (103)	164	0.21
Arab (0)	0	<0.01
Egyptian (0)	0	<0.01
Iraqi (0)	8	0.01
Jordanian (0)	0	<0.01
Lebanese (0)	10	0.01
Moroccan (0)	10	0.01
Palestinian (38)	38	0.05
Syrian (7)	40	0.05
Other Arab (58)	58	0.08
Armenian (10)	35	0.05
Assyrian/Chaldean/Syriac (0)	0	<0.01
Australian (33)	33	0.04
Austrian (8)	40	0.05
Basque (46)	53	0.07
Belgian (0)	41	0.05
Brazilian (0)	57	0.07
British (107)	128	0.17
Bulgarian (0)	0	<0.01
Cajun (0)	0	<0.01
Canadian (19)	36	0.05
Carpatho Rusyn (0)	0	<0.01
Celtic (26)	26	0.03
Croatian (0)	8	0.01
Cypriot (0)	0	<0.01
Czech (19)	38	0.05
Czechoslovakian (0)	8	0.01
Danish (54)	259	0.34
Dutch (61)	455	0.59
Eastern European (47)	57	0.07
English (810)	3,102	4.02
Estonian (0)	0	<0.01
European (263)	321	0.42
Finnish (60)	94	0.12
French, ex. Basque (266)	1,482	1.92
French Canadian (38)	174	0.23
German (1,214)	4,733	6.14
German Russian (0)	0	<0.01
Greek (0)	102	0.13
Guyanese (0)	0	<0.01
Hungarian (32)	150	0.19
Icelander (0)	13	0.02
Iranian (75)	75	0.10
Irish (926)	4,161	5.40
Israeli (0)	0	<0.01
Italian (439)	1,718	2.23
Latvian (0)	0	<0.01
Lithuanian (12)	56	0.07
Luxemburger (0)	0	<0.01
Macedonian (0)	0	<0.01
Maltese (0)	0	<0.01
New Zealander (0)	0	<0.01
Northern European (0)	0	<0.01
Norwegian (322)	658	0.85
Pennsylvania German (0)	0	<0.01
Polish (52)	272	0.35
Portuguese (733)	1,645	2.13
Romanian (0)	0	<0.01
Russian (156)	251	0.33
Scandinavian (41)	50	0.06
Scotch-Irish (126)	492	0.64
Scottish (257)	674	0.87
Serbian (0)	0	<0.01
Slavic (0)	0	<0.01
Slovak (0)	0	<0.01
Slovene (0)	0	<0.01
Soviet Union (0)	0	<0.01
Swedish (108)	378	0.49
Swiss (68)	224	0.29
Turkish (0)	0	<0.01
Ukrainian (0)	0	<0.01
Welsh (16)	224	0.29
West Indian, ex. Hispanic (11)	11	0.01
Bahamian (0)	0	<0.01
Barbadian (0)	0	<0.01
Belizean (0)	0	<0.01
Bermudan (0)	0	<0.01
British West Indian (0)	0	<0.01
Dutch West Indian (0)	0	<0.01
Haitian (0)	0	<0.01
Jamaican (0)	0	<0.01
Trinidadian/Tobagonian (0)	0	<0.01
U.S. Virgin Islander (0)	0	<0.01
West Indian (11)	11	0.01
Other West Indian (0)	0	<0.01
Yugoslavian (0)	0	<0.01

Hispanic Origin	Population	%
Hispanic or Latino (of any race)	39,140	49.57
Central American, ex. Mexican	502	0.64
Costa Rican	18	0.02
Guatemalan	57	0.07
Honduran	37	0.05
Nicaraguan	120	0.15
Panamanian	17	0.02
Salvadoran	248	0.31
Other Central American	5	0.01
Cuban	75	0.09
Dominican Republic	7	0.01
Mexican	35,593	45.08
Puerto Rican	384	0.49
South American	152	0.19
Argentinean	31	0.04
Bolivian	4	0.01
Chilean	19	0.02
Colombian	32	0.04
Ecuadorian	3	<0.01
Paraguayan	1	<0.01
Peruvian	41	0.05
Uruguayan	5	0.01
Venezuelan	15	0.02
Other South American	1	<0.01
Other Hispanic or Latino	2,427	3.07

Race*	Population	%
African-American/Black (4,958)	6,059	7.67
Not Hispanic (4,483)	5,200	6.59
Hispanic (475)	859	1.09
American Indian/Alaska Native (1,153)	2,091	2.65
Not Hispanic (399)	966	1.22
Hispanic (754)	1,125	1.42
Alaska Athabascan *(Ala. Nat.)* (0)	0	<0.01
Aleut *(Alaska Native)* (0)	0	<0.01
Apache (42)	75	0.09
Arapaho (0)	0	<0.01
Blackfeet (11)	36	0.05
Canadian/French Am. Ind. (0)	0	<0.01
Central American Ind. (5)	5	0.01
Cherokee (91)	332	0.42
Cheyenne (1)	6	0.01
Chickasaw (2)	12	0.02
Chippewa (11)	17	0.02
Choctaw (28)	77	0.10
Colville (0)	0	<0.01
Comanche (0)	1	<0.01
Cree (1)	4	0.01
Creek (5)	12	0.02
Crow (3)	6	0.01
Delaware (0)	3	<0.01
Hopi (1)	3	<0.01
Houma (0)	0	<0.01
Inupiat *(Alaska Native)* (0)	0	<0.01
Iroquois (2)	5	0.01
Kiowa (0)	0	<0.01
Lumbee (0)	0	<0.01
Menominee (0)	0	<0.01
Mexican American Ind. (121)	176	0.22
Navajo (24)	32	0.04
Osage (3)	6	0.01
Ottawa (0)	0	<0.01
Paiute (17)	32	0.04
Pima (3)	5	0.01
Potawatomi (2)	4	0.01
Pueblo (2)	4	0.01
Puget Sound Salish (1)	1	<0.01
Seminole (1)	9	0.01
Shoshone (4)	10	0.01
Sioux (17)	40	0.05
South American Ind. (1)	1	<0.01
Spanish American Ind. (18)	26	0.03
Tlingit-Haida *(Alaska Native)* (5)	9	0.01
Tohono O'Odham (3)	4	0.01
Tsimshian *(Alaska Native)* (0)	0	<0.01
Ute (2)	3	<0.01
Yakama (0)	0	<0.01
Yaqui (23)	35	0.04
Yuman (1)	1	<0.01
Yup'ik *(Alaska Native)* (0)	0	<0.01
Asian (9,342)	10,509	13.31
Not Hispanic (9,116)	9,934	12.58
Hispanic (226)	575	0.73
Bangladeshi (0)	0	<0.01
Bhutanese (0)	0	<0.01
Burmese (9)	10	0.01
Cambodian (31)	43	0.05
Chinese, ex. Taiwanese (535)	684	0.87
Filipino (1,046)	1,451	1.84
Hmong (4,552)	4,741	6.00
Indian (597)	725	0.92
Indonesian (6)	16	0.02
Japanese (223)	391	0.50
Korean (137)	201	0.25
Laotian (1,323)	1,482	1.88
Malaysian (0)	0	<0.01
Nepalese (8)	8	0.01
Pakistani (54)	69	0.09
Sri Lankan (5)	6	0.01
Taiwanese (41)	50	0.06
Thai (63)	137	0.17
Vietnamese (188)	225	0.28
Hawaii Native/Pacific Islander (174)	392	0.50
Not Hispanic (131)	259	0.33
Hispanic (43)	133	0.17
Fijian (18)	27	0.03
Guamanian/Chamorro (38)	66	0.08
Marshallese (3)	3	<0.01
Native Hawaiian (43)	132	0.17
Samoan (33)	55	0.07
Tongan (0)	0	<0.01
White (41,177)	44,776	56.71
Not Hispanic (23,702)	25,220	31.94
Hispanic (17,475)	19,556	24.77

*Notes: † The Census 2010 population figure is used to calculate the percentages in the Hispanic Origin and Race categories. Ancestry percentages are based on the 2006-2010 American Community Survey population (not shown); ‡ Numbers in parentheses indicate the number of people reporting a single ancestry; * Numbers in parentheses indicate the number of persons reporting this race alone, not in combination with any other race; Please refer to the Explanation of Data for more information.*

Milpitas

Place Type: City
County: Santa Clara
Population: 66,790

Ancestry	Population	%
Afghan (444)	454	0.70
African, Sub-Saharan (325)	336	0.52
African (94)	103	0.16
Cape Verdean (0)	0	<0.01
Ethiopian (91)	91	0.14
Ghanaian (0)	0	<0.01
Kenyan (0)	0	<0.01
Liberian (104)	104	0.16
Nigerian (0)	2	<0.01
Senegalese (0)	0	<0.01
Sierra Leonean (0)	0	<0.01
Somalian (36)	36	0.06
South African (0)	0	<0.01
Sudanese (0)	0	<0.01
Ugandan (0)	0	<0.01
Zimbabwean (0)	0	<0.01
Other Sub-Saharan African (0)	0	<0.01
Albanian (0)	0	<0.01
Alsatian (0)	0	<0.01
American (413)	413	0.63
Arab (180)	256	0.39
Arab (73)	83	0.13
Egyptian (0)	0	<0.01
Iraqi (11)	11	0.02
Jordanian (0)	0	<0.01
Lebanese (39)	52	0.08
Moroccan (0)	10	0.02
Palestinian (9)	52	0.08
Syrian (43)	43	0.07
Other Arab (5)	5	0.01
Armenian (23)	36	0.06
Assyrian/Chaldean/Syriac (31)	62	0.10
Australian (11)	11	0.02
Austrian (12)	40	0.06
Basque (0)	0	<0.01
Belgian (0)	23	0.04
Brazilian (0)	0	<0.01
British (113)	302	0.46
Bulgarian (30)	38	0.06
Cajun (0)	0	<0.01
Canadian (0)	0	<0.01
Carpatho Rusyn (0)	0	<0.01
Celtic (0)	0	<0.01
Croatian (7)	7	0.01
Cypriot (0)	0	<0.01
Czech (10)	45	0.07
Czechoslovakian (12)	12	0.02
Danish (5)	86	0.13
Dutch (59)	456	0.70
Eastern European (0)	0	<0.01
English (361)	1,722	2.64
Estonian (3)	3	<0.01
European (224)	321	0.49
Finnish (0)	22	0.03
French, ex. Basque (97)	1,203	1.85
French Canadian (11)	33	0.05
German (715)	3,221	4.94
German Russian (0)	0	<0.01
Greek (37)	54	0.08
Guyanese (0)	0	<0.01
Hungarian (56)	103	0.16
Icelander (0)	0	<0.01
Iranian (217)	217	0.33
Irish (536)	2,065	3.17
Israeli (15)	60	0.09
Italian (437)	1,411	2.17
Latvian (0)	0	<0.01
Lithuanian (13)	13	0.02
Luxemburger (0)	0	<0.01
Macedonian (0)	0	<0.01
Maltese (0)	0	<0.01
New Zealander (0)	0	<0.01
Northern European (10)	10	0.02
Norwegian (99)	447	0.69
Pennsylvania German (0)	0	<0.01
Polish (144)	360	0.55
Portuguese (236)	530	0.81
Romanian (84)	106	0.16
Russian (50)	96	0.15
Scandinavian (19)	68	0.10
Scotch-Irish (60)	382	0.59
Scottish (97)	284	0.44
Serbian (0)	0	<0.01
Slavic (15)	15	0.02
Slovak (21)	105	0.16
Slovene (15)	15	0.02
Soviet Union (0)	0	<0.01
Swedish (39)	325	0.50
Swiss (17)	48	0.07
Turkish (63)	63	0.10
Ukrainian (9)	45	0.07
Welsh (5)	127	0.19
West Indian, ex. Hispanic (54)	75	0.12
Bahamian (0)	0	<0.01
Barbadian (0)	0	<0.01
Belizean (0)	0	<0.01
Bermudan (0)	0	<0.01
British West Indian (0)	0	<0.01
Dutch West Indian (0)	0	<0.01
Haitian (0)	0	<0.01
Jamaican (54)	60	0.09
Trinidadian/Tobagonian (0)	0	<0.01
U.S. Virgin Islander (0)	0	<0.01
West Indian (0)	15	0.02
Other West Indian (0)	0	<0.01
Yugoslavian (15)	15	0.02

Hispanic Origin	Population	%
Hispanic or Latino (of any race)	11,240	16.83
Central American, ex. Mexican	608	0.91
Costa Rican	20	0.03
Guatemalan	70	0.10
Honduran	23	0.03
Nicaraguan	237	0.35
Panamanian	31	0.05
Salvadoran	217	0.32
Other Central American	10	0.01
Cuban	44	0.07
Dominican Republic	21	0.03
Mexican	9,257	13.86
Puerto Rican	209	0.31
South American	315	0.47
Argentinean	66	0.10
Bolivian	5	0.01
Chilean	25	0.04
Colombian	26	0.04
Ecuadorian	16	0.02
Paraguayan	0	<0.01
Peruvian	139	0.21
Uruguayan	3	<0.01
Venezuelan	28	0.04
Other South American	7	0.01
Other Hispanic or Latino	786	1.18

Race*	Population	%
African-American/Black (1,969)	2,588	3.87
Not Hispanic (1,836)	2,290	3.43
Hispanic (133)	298	0.45
American Indian/Alaska Native (309)	792	1.19
Not Hispanic (137)	434	0.65
Hispanic (172)	358	0.54
Alaska Athabascan *(Ala. Nat.)* (0)	0	<0.01
Aleut *(Alaska Native)* (2)	6	0.01
Apache (19)	36	0.05
Arapaho (0)	0	<0.01
Blackfeet (4)	30	0.04
Canadian/French Am. Ind. (1)	3	<0.01
Central American Ind. (1)	1	<0.01
Cherokee (14)	82	0.12
Cheyenne (1)	1	<0.01
Chickasaw (1)	3	<0.01
Chippewa (5)	29	0.04
Choctaw (1)	25	0.04
Colville (0)	0	<0.01
Comanche (0)	0	<0.01
Cree (0)	0	<0.01
Creek (0)	7	0.01
Crow (0)	1	<0.01
Delaware (1)	6	0.01
Hopi (1)	1	<0.01
Houma (0)	0	<0.01
Inupiat *(Alaska Native)* (1)	1	<0.01
Iroquois (7)	12	0.02
Kiowa (3)	3	<0.01
Lumbee (0)	0	<0.01
Menominee (5)	5	0.01
Mexican American Ind. (13)	36	0.05
Navajo (13)	23	0.03
Osage (2)	2	<0.01
Ottawa (0)	0	<0.01
Paiute (1)	3	<0.01
Pima (0)	0	<0.01
Potawatomi (3)	3	<0.01
Pueblo (0)	1	<0.01
Puget Sound Salish (1)	1	<0.01
Seminole (1)	3	<0.01
Shoshone (0)	2	<0.01
Sioux (2)	17	0.03
South American Ind. (1)	4	0.01
Spanish American Ind. (1)	3	<0.01
Tlingit-Haida *(Alaska Native)* (1)	6	0.01
Tohono O'Odham (2)	2	<0.01
Tsimshian *(Alaska Native)* (0)	0	<0.01
Ute (1)	4	0.01
Yakama (1)	2	<0.01
Yaqui (8)	19	0.03
Yuman (0)	0	<0.01
Yup'ik *(Alaska Native)* (3)	3	<0.01
Asian (41,536)	43,466	65.08
Not Hispanic (41,308)	42,929	64.27
Hispanic (228)	537	0.80
Bangladeshi (56)	58	0.09
Bhutanese (0)	0	<0.01
Burmese (123)	135	0.20
Cambodian (177)	220	0.33
Chinese, ex. Taiwanese (9,182)	10,156	15.21
Filipino (11,546)	12,649	18.94
Hmong (31)	35	0.05
Indian (6,351)	6,602	9.88
Indonesian (52)	79	0.12
Japanese (404)	681	1.02
Korean (711)	816	1.22
Laotian (101)	146	0.22
Malaysian (43)	81	0.12
Nepalese (21)	23	0.03
Pakistani (380)	408	0.61
Sri Lankan (13)	16	0.02
Taiwanese (758)	860	1.29
Thai (92)	124	0.19
Vietnamese (10,356)	11,042	16.53
Hawaii Native/Pacific Islander (346)	739	1.11
Not Hispanic (316)	619	0.93
Hispanic (30)	120	0.18
Fijian (42)	57	0.09
Guamanian/Chamorro (107)	177	0.27
Marshallese (0)	0	<0.01
Native Hawaiian (30)	145	0.22
Samoan (78)	126	0.19
Tongan (39)	50	0.07
White (13,725)	15,892	23.79
Not Hispanic (9,751)	11,226	16.81
Hispanic (3,974)	4,666	6.99

*Notes: † The Census 2010 population figure is used to calculate the percentages in the Hispanic Origin and Race categories. Ancestry percentages are based on the 2006-2010 American Community Survey population (not shown); ‡ Numbers in parentheses indicate the number of people reporting a single ancestry; * Numbers in parentheses indicate the number of persons reporting this race alone, not in combination with any other race; Please refer to the Explanation of Data for more information.*

Mission Viejo

Place Type: City
County: Orange
Population: 93,305

Ancestry	Population	%
Afghan (55)	55	0.06
African, Sub-Saharan (292)	325	0.35
African (189)	193	0.21
Cape Verdean (0)	0	<0.01
Ethiopian (0)	0	<0.01
Ghanaian (0)	0	<0.01
Kenyan (0)	0	<0.01
Liberian (0)	0	<0.01
Nigerian (17)	17	0.02
Senegalese (0)	17	0.02
Sierra Leonean (0)	0	<0.01
Somalian (0)	0	<0.01
South African (65)	77	0.08
Sudanese (0)	0	<0.01
Ugandan (0)	0	<0.01
Zimbabwean (0)	0	<0.01
Other Sub-Saharan African (21)	21	0.02
Albanian (0)	0	<0.01
Alsatian (0)	0	<0.01
American (4,003)	4,003	4.32
Arab (962)	1,264	1.36
Arab (314)	324	0.35
Egyptian (161)	177	0.19
Iraqi (0)	0	<0.01
Jordanian (37)	57	0.06
Lebanese (360)	507	0.55
Moroccan (0)	0	<0.01
Palestinian (30)	66	0.07
Syrian (0)	35	0.04
Other Arab (60)	98	0.11
Armenian (386)	462	0.50
Assyrian/Chaldean/Syriac (0)	0	<0.01
Australian (0)	17	0.02
Austrian (90)	401	0.43
Basque (31)	122	0.13
Belgian (16)	92	0.10
Brazilian (11)	17	0.02
British (543)	1,204	1.30
Bulgarian (17)	17	0.02
Cajun (33)	33	0.04
Canadian (351)	559	0.60
Carpatho Rusyn (0)	0	<0.01
Celtic (16)	16	0.02
Croatian (47)	214	0.23
Cypriot (0)	0	<0.01
Czech (115)	480	0.52
Czechoslovakian (0)	69	0.07
Danish (228)	942	1.02
Dutch (563)	1,707	1.84
Eastern European (161)	173	0.19
English (3,141)	11,373	12.28
Estonian (11)	25	0.03
European (1,439)	1,673	1.81
Finnish (45)	211	0.23
French, ex. Basque (629)	3,375	3.64
French Canadian (254)	553	0.60
German (4,059)	15,874	17.14
German Russian (0)	0	<0.01
Greek (185)	547	0.59
Guyanese (0)	28	0.03
Hungarian (128)	754	0.81
Icelander (0)	32	0.03
Iranian (2,404)	2,460	2.66
Irish (3,696)	13,315	14.38
Israeli (9)	9	0.01
Italian (2,530)	6,660	7.19
Latvian (27)	60	0.06
Lithuanian (99)	388	0.42
Luxemburger (8)	20	0.02
Macedonian (0)	14	0.02
Maltese (11)	20	0.02
New Zealander (22)	22	0.02
Northern European (74)	74	0.08
Norwegian (526)	1,730	1.87
Pennsylvania German (0)	0	<0.01
Polish (781)	3,283	3.54
Portuguese (102)	243	0.26
Romanian (247)	592	0.64
Russian (834)	2,070	2.24
Scandinavian (100)	315	0.34
Scotch-Irish (736)	1,675	1.81
Scottish (1,029)	2,724	2.94
Serbian (64)	88	0.10
Slavic (20)	20	0.02
Slovak (13)	181	0.20
Slovene (27)	65	0.07
Soviet Union (0)	0	<0.01
Swedish (280)	2,055	2.22
Swiss (110)	346	0.37
Turkish (98)	122	0.13
Ukrainian (71)	201	0.22
Welsh (251)	763	0.82
West Indian, ex. Hispanic (23)	78	0.08
Bahamian (0)	0	<0.01
Barbadian (6)	22	0.02
Belizean (7)	7	0.01
Bermudan (0)	0	<0.01
British West Indian (0)	12	0.01
Dutch West Indian (0)	0	<0.01
Haitian (0)	0	<0.01
Jamaican (10)	10	0.01
Trinidadian/Tobagonian (0)	0	<0.01
U.S. Virgin Islander (0)	0	<0.01
West Indian (0)	27	0.03
Other West Indian (0)	0	<0.01
Yugoslavian (50)	172	0.19

Hispanic Origin	Population	%
Hispanic or Latino (of any race)	15,877	17.02
Central American, ex. Mexican	823	0.88
Costa Rican	71	0.08
Guatemalan	300	0.32
Honduran	50	0.05
Nicaraguan	78	0.08
Panamanian	40	0.04
Salvadoran	276	0.30
Other Central American	8	0.01
Cuban	325	0.35
Dominican Republic	32	0.03
Mexican	11,559	12.39
Puerto Rican	396	0.42
South American	1,569	1.68
Argentinean	313	0.34
Bolivian	72	0.08
Chilean	92	0.10
Colombian	446	0.48
Ecuadorian	173	0.19
Paraguayan	3	<0.01
Peruvian	379	0.41
Uruguayan	18	0.02
Venezuelan	50	0.05
Other South American	23	0.02
Other Hispanic or Latino	1,173	1.26

Race*	Population	%
African-American/Black (1,210)	1,847	1.98
Not Hispanic (1,129)	1,654	1.77
Hispanic (81)	193	0.21
American Indian/Alaska Native (379)	925	0.99
Not Hispanic (176)	568	0.61
Hispanic (203)	357	0.38
Alaska Athabascan *(Ala. Nat.)* (0)	0	<0.01
Aleut *(Alaska Native)* (0)	3	<0.01
Apache (8)	19	0.02
Arapaho (1)	1	<0.01
Blackfeet (4)	29	0.03
Canadian/French Am. Ind. (0)	0	<0.01
Central American Ind. (1)	2	<0.01
Cherokee (35)	171	0.18
Cheyenne (1)	2	<0.01
Chickasaw (4)	9	0.01
Chippewa (3)	4	<0.01
Choctaw (7)	26	0.03
Colville (1)	1	<0.01
Comanche (1)	2	<0.01
Cree (1)	1	<0.01
Creek (6)	8	0.01
Crow (0)	0	<0.01
Delaware (0)	0	<0.01
Hopi (0)	1	<0.01
Houma (2)	2	<0.01
Inupiat *(Alaska Native)* (1)	1	<0.01
Iroquois (7)	13	0.01
Kiowa (2)	2	<0.01
Lumbee (2)	2	<0.01
Menominee (1)	1	<0.01
Mexican American Ind. (35)	58	0.06
Navajo (19)	34	0.04
Osage (4)	8	0.01
Ottawa (1)	6	0.01
Paiute (1)	5	0.01
Pima (1)	2	<0.01
Potawatomi (1)	8	0.01
Pueblo (7)	9	0.01
Puget Sound Salish (3)	3	<0.01
Seminole (0)	4	<0.01
Shoshone (0)	1	<0.01
Sioux (5)	13	0.01
South American Ind. (1)	8	0.01
Spanish American Ind. (2)	3	<0.01
Tlingit-Haida *(Alaska Native)* (0)	0	<0.01
Tohono O'Odham (2)	4	<0.01
Tsimshian *(Alaska Native)* (0)	0	<0.01
Ute (0)	5	0.01
Yakama (0)	0	<0.01
Yaqui (3)	7	0.01
Yuman (0)	0	<0.01
Yup'ik *(Alaska Native)* (1)	1	<0.01
Asian (8,462)	11,030	11.82
Not Hispanic (8,312)	10,616	11.38
Hispanic (150)	414	0.44
Bangladeshi (24)	24	0.03
Bhutanese (0)	0	<0.01
Burmese (24)	33	0.04
Cambodian (71)	91	0.10
Chinese, ex. Taiwanese (1,403)	1,889	2.02
Filipino (2,240)	2,946	3.16
Hmong (5)	5	0.01
Indian (852)	990	1.06
Indonesian (97)	172	0.18
Japanese (959)	1,639	1.76
Korean (743)	931	1.00
Laotian (12)	13	0.01
Malaysian (1)	2	<0.01
Nepalese (13)	13	0.01
Pakistani (143)	175	0.19
Sri Lankan (40)	45	0.05
Taiwanese (171)	201	0.22
Thai (120)	159	0.17
Vietnamese (1,146)	1,315	1.41
Hawaii Native/Pacific Islander (153)	437	0.47
Not Hispanic (146)	403	0.43
Hispanic (7)	34	0.04
Fijian (7)	9	0.01
Guamanian/Chamorro (38)	73	0.08
Marshallese (0)	0	<0.01
Native Hawaiian (47)	191	0.20
Samoan (26)	55	0.06
Tongan (7)	9	0.01
White (74,493)	78,381	84.01
Not Hispanic (64,276)	67,222	72.05
Hispanic (10,217)	11,159	11.96

*Notes: † The Census 2010 population figure is used to calculate the percentages in the Hispanic Origin and Race categories. Ancestry percentages are based on the 2006-2010 American Community Survey population (not shown); ‡ Numbers in parentheses indicate the number of people reporting a single ancestry; * Numbers in parentheses indicate the number of persons reporting this race alone, not in combination with any other race; Please refer to the Explanation of Data for more information.*

Modesto

Place Type: City
County: Stanislaus
Population: 201,165

Ancestry	Population	%
Afghan (256)	256	0.13
African, Sub-Saharan (211)	387	0.19
African (98)	274	0.14
Cape Verdean (0)	0	<0.01
Ethiopian (76)	76	0.04
Ghanaian (0)	0	<0.01
Kenyan (0)	0	<0.01
Liberian (0)	0	<0.01
Nigerian (37)	37	0.02
Senegalese (0)	0	<0.01
Sierra Leonean (0)	0	<0.01
Somalian (0)	0	<0.01
South African (0)	0	<0.01
Sudanese (0)	0	<0.01
Ugandan (0)	0	<0.01
Zimbabwean (0)	0	<0.01
Other Sub-Saharan African (0)	0	<0.01
Albanian (0)	0	<0.01
Alsatian (0)	0	<0.01
American (6,546)	6,546	3.24
Arab (1,267)	1,485	0.74
Arab (108)	223	0.11
Egyptian (25)	41	0.02
Iraqi (491)	547	0.27
Jordanian (0)	0	<0.01
Lebanese (49)	59	0.03
Moroccan (0)	12	0.01
Palestinian (270)	270	0.13
Syrian (75)	75	0.04
Other Arab (249)	258	0.13
Armenian (341)	565	0.28
Assyrian/Chaldean/Syriac (2,367)	2,553	1.26
Australian (40)	94	0.05
Austrian (10)	243	0.12
Basque (63)	116	0.06
Belgian (13)	66	0.03
Brazilian (50)	98	0.05
British (205)	393	0.19
Bulgarian (0)	13	0.01
Cajun (0)	16	0.01
Canadian (184)	271	0.13
Carpatho Rusyn (0)	0	<0.01
Celtic (15)	50	0.02
Croatian (26)	81	0.04
Cypriot (0)	0	<0.01
Czech (72)	254	0.13
Czechoslovakian (28)	113	0.06
Danish (270)	1,066	0.53
Dutch (1,198)	4,037	2.00
Eastern European (107)	116	0.06
English (4,395)	14,727	7.29
Estonian (23)	54	0.03
European (1,640)	2,029	1.00
Finnish (62)	368	0.18
French, ex. Basque (604)	5,489	2.72
French Canadian (155)	501	0.25
German (6,429)	22,747	11.27
German Russian (0)	21	0.01
Greek (330)	820	0.41
Guyanese (0)	0	<0.01
Hungarian (154)	380	0.19
Icelander (47)	96	0.05
Iranian (393)	554	0.27
Irish (4,509)	19,237	9.53
Israeli (0)	17	0.01
Italian (3,470)	8,823	4.37
Latvian (0)	0	<0.01
Lithuanian (35)	147	0.07
Luxemburger (0)	21	0.01
Macedonian (0)	0	<0.01
Maltese (0)	28	0.01
New Zealander (9)	9	<0.01
Northern European (93)	93	0.05
Norwegian (812)	2,570	1.27
Pennsylvania German (15)	42	0.02
Polish (633)	1,744	0.86
Portuguese (3,878)	7,250	3.59
Romanian (747)	791	0.39
Russian (259)	756	0.37
Scandinavian (213)	375	0.19
Scotch-Irish (1,083)	3,409	1.69
Scottish (890)	2,625	1.30
Serbian (0)	53	0.03
Slavic (24)	37	0.02
Slovak (0)	17	0.01
Slovene (0)	32	0.02
Soviet Union (0)	0	<0.01
Swedish (888)	3,260	1.61
Swiss (371)	1,072	0.53
Turkish (0)	5	<0.01
Ukrainian (160)	320	0.16
Welsh (175)	1,523	0.75
West Indian, ex. Hispanic (67)	179	0.09
Bahamian (0)	0	<0.01
Barbadian (0)	0	<0.01
Belizean (0)	58	0.03
Bermudan (0)	0	<0.01
British West Indian (0)	0	<0.01
Dutch West Indian (0)	24	0.01
Haitian (0)	20	0.01
Jamaican (54)	64	0.03
Trinidadian/Tobagonian (0)	0	<0.01
U.S. Virgin Islander (0)	0	<0.01
West Indian (13)	13	0.01
Other West Indian (0)	0	<0.01
Yugoslavian (43)	78	0.04

Hispanic Origin	Population	%
Hispanic or Latino (of any race)	71,381	35.48
Central American, ex. Mexican	2,341	1.16
Costa Rican	55	0.03
Guatemalan	421	0.21
Honduran	126	0.06
Nicaraguan	510	0.25
Panamanian	82	0.04
Salvadoran	1,134	0.56
Other Central American	13	0.01
Cuban	196	0.10
Dominican Republic	18	0.01
Mexican	62,010	30.83
Puerto Rican	1,447	0.72
South American	749	0.37
Argentinean	73	0.04
Bolivian	29	0.01
Chilean	97	0.05
Colombian	239	0.12
Ecuadorian	38	0.02
Paraguayan	0	<0.01
Peruvian	230	0.11
Uruguayan	15	0.01
Venezuelan	24	0.01
Other South American	4	<0.01
Other Hispanic or Latino	4,620	2.30

Race*	Population	%
African-American/Black (8,396)	11,151	5.54
Not Hispanic (7,539)	9,455	4.70
Hispanic (857)	1,696	0.84
American Indian/Alaska Native (2,494)	5,569	2.77
Not Hispanic (1,141)	3,080	1.53
Hispanic (1,353)	2,489	1.24
Alaska Athabascan *(Ala. Nat.)* (0)	16	0.01
Aleut *(Alaska Native)* (11)	16	0.01
Apache (97)	266	0.13
Arapaho (0)	1	<0.01
Blackfeet (10)	129	0.06
Canadian/French Am. Ind. (2)	4	<0.01
Central American Ind. (0)	4	<0.01
Cherokee (277)	1,004	0.50
Cheyenne (3)	12	0.01
Chickasaw (31)	76	0.04
Chippewa (9)	50	0.02
Choctaw (130)	385	0.19
Colville (3)	5	<0.01
Comanche (4)	24	0.01
Cree (4)	8	<0.01
Creek (28)	85	0.04
Crow (0)	1	<0.01
Delaware (5)	7	<0.01
Hopi (7)	11	0.01
Houma (0)	1	<0.01
Inupiat *(Alaska Native)* (3)	5	<0.01
Iroquois (14)	41	0.02
Kiowa (1)	5	<0.01
Lumbee (0)	1	<0.01
Menominee (0)	0	<0.01
Mexican American Ind. (212)	323	0.16
Navajo (70)	158	0.08
Osage (2)	15	0.01
Ottawa (0)	2	<0.01
Paiute (39)	70	0.03
Pima (7)	20	0.01
Potawatomi (12)	22	0.01
Pueblo (12)	37	0.02
Puget Sound Salish (2)	6	<0.01
Seminole (7)	27	0.01
Shoshone (3)	13	0.01
Sioux (39)	105	0.05
South American Ind. (9)	21	0.01
Spanish American Ind. (19)	27	0.01
Tlingit-Haida *(Alaska Native)* (3)	4	<0.01
Tohono O'Odham (10)	21	0.01
Tsimshian *(Alaska Native)* (0)	0	<0.01
Ute (1)	6	<0.01
Yakama (0)	0	<0.01
Yaqui (51)	100	0.05
Yuman (1)	4	<0.01
Yup'ik *(Alaska Native)* (0)	1	<0.01
Asian (13,557)	17,695	8.80
Not Hispanic (12,899)	15,978	7.94
Hispanic (658)	1,717	0.85
Bangladeshi (1)	7	<0.01
Bhutanese (0)	0	<0.01
Burmese (29)	30	0.01
Cambodian (2,402)	2,752	1.37
Chinese, ex. Taiwanese (1,358)	1,901	0.94
Filipino (3,021)	4,614	2.29
Hmong (261)	287	0.14
Indian (2,599)	3,403	1.69
Indonesian (12)	37	0.02
Japanese (356)	924	0.46
Korean (314)	450	0.22
Laotian (1,035)	1,257	0.62
Malaysian (2)	7	<0.01
Nepalese (4)	4	<0.01
Pakistani (132)	157	0.08
Sri Lankan (3)	5	<0.01
Taiwanese (48)	63	0.03
Thai (88)	162	0.08
Vietnamese (1,183)	1,394	0.69
Hawaii Native/Pacific Islander (1,924)	3,467	1.72
Not Hispanic (1,747)	2,976	1.48
Hispanic (177)	491	0.24
Fijian (1,109)	1,355	0.67
Guamanian/Chamorro (144)	324	0.16
Marshallese (0)	1	<0.01
Native Hawaiian (173)	567	0.28
Samoan (202)	334	0.17
Tongan (22)	34	0.02
White (130,833)	140,979	70.08
Not Hispanic (99,347)	104,608	52.00
Hispanic (31,486)	36,371	18.08

*Notes: † The Census 2010 population figure is used to calculate the percentages in the Hispanic Origin and Race categories. Ancestry percentages are based on the 2006-2010 American Community Survey population (not shown); ‡ Numbers in parentheses indicate the number of people reporting a single ancestry; * Numbers in parentheses indicate the number of persons reporting this race alone, not in combination with any other race; Please refer to the Explanation of Data for more information.*

Montebello

Place Type: City
County: Los Angeles
Population: 62,500

Ancestry	Population	%
Afghan (0)	0	<0.01
African, Sub-Saharan (13)	39	0.06
African (13)	39	0.06
Cape Verdean (0)	0	<0.01
Ethiopian (0)	0	<0.01
Ghanaian (0)	0	<0.01
Kenyan (0)	0	<0.01
Liberian (0)	0	<0.01
Nigerian (0)	0	<0.01
Senegalese (0)	0	<0.01
Sierra Leonean (0)	0	<0.01
Somalian (0)	0	<0.01
South African (0)	0	<0.01
Sudanese (0)	0	<0.01
Ugandan (0)	0	<0.01
Zimbabwean (0)	0	<0.01
Other Sub-Saharan African (0)	0	<0.01
Albanian (0)	0	<0.01
Alsatian (0)	0	<0.01
American (922)	922	1.48
Arab (77)	151	0.24
Arab (0)	0	<0.01
Egyptian (18)	18	0.03
Iraqi (0)	0	<0.01
Jordanian (0)	0	<0.01
Lebanese (6)	46	0.07
Moroccan (0)	0	<0.01
Palestinian (45)	45	0.07
Syrian (8)	28	0.04
Other Arab (0)	14	0.02
Armenian (1,686)	1,885	3.02
Assyrian/Chaldean/Syriac (0)	0	<0.01
Australian (0)	0	<0.01
Austrian (9)	9	0.01
Basque (0)	17	0.03
Belgian (22)	22	0.04
Brazilian (0)	0	<0.01
British (0)	27	0.04
Bulgarian (16)	16	0.03
Cajun (0)	0	<0.01
Canadian (0)	0	<0.01
Carpatho Rusyn (0)	0	<0.01
Celtic (0)	0	<0.01
Croatian (0)	0	<0.01
Cypriot (0)	0	<0.01
Czech (0)	0	<0.01
Czechoslovakian (0)	0	<0.01
Danish (0)	0	<0.01
Dutch (36)	122	0.20
Eastern European (2)	2	<0.01
English (117)	411	0.66
Estonian (0)	0	<0.01
European (78)	201	0.32
Finnish (0)	5	0.01
French, ex. Basque (12)	117	0.19
French Canadian (22)	30	0.05
German (133)	559	0.90
German Russian (0)	0	<0.01
Greek (75)	96	0.15
Guyanese (0)	0	<0.01
Hungarian (13)	19	0.03
Icelander (0)	0	<0.01
Iranian (98)	172	0.28
Irish (123)	495	0.79
Israeli (0)	0	<0.01
Italian (400)	935	1.50
Latvian (0)	0	<0.01
Lithuanian (0)	0	<0.01
Luxemburger (0)	0	<0.01
Macedonian (0)	0	<0.01
Maltese (0)	0	<0.01
New Zealander (0)	0	<0.01
Northern European (2)	2	<0.01
Norwegian (7)	24	0.04
Pennsylvania German (0)	9	0.01
Polish (46)	80	0.13
Portuguese (0)	36	0.06
Romanian (14)	42	0.07
Russian (206)	316	0.51
Scandinavian (0)	0	<0.01
Scotch-Irish (40)	86	0.14
Scottish (15)	60	0.10
Serbian (7)	7	0.01
Slavic (0)	0	<0.01
Slovak (0)	0	<0.01
Slovene (16)	16	0.03
Soviet Union (0)	0	<0.01
Swedish (0)	8	0.01
Swiss (10)	17	0.03
Turkish (18)	30	0.05
Ukrainian (38)	38	0.06
Welsh (0)	9	0.01
West Indian, ex. Hispanic (31)	40	0.06
Bahamian (0)	0	<0.01
Barbadian (0)	0	<0.01
Belizean (0)	0	<0.01
Bermudan (0)	0	<0.01
British West Indian (31)	31	0.05
Dutch West Indian (0)	0	<0.01
Haitian (0)	9	0.01
Jamaican (0)	0	<0.01
Trinidadian/Tobagonian (0)	0	<0.01
U.S. Virgin Islander (0)	0	<0.01
West Indian (0)	0	<0.01
Other West Indian (0)	0	<0.01
Yugoslavian (0)	11	0.02

Hispanic Origin	Population	%
Hispanic or Latino (of any race)	49,578	79.32
Central American, ex. Mexican	3,219	5.15
Costa Rican	53	0.08
Guatemalan	789	1.26
Honduran	210	0.34
Nicaraguan	341	0.55
Panamanian	3	<0.01
Salvadoran	1,780	2.85
Other Central American	43	0.07
Cuban	127	0.20
Dominican Republic	14	0.02
Mexican	43,662	69.86
Puerto Rican	212	0.34
South American	654	1.05
Argentinean	106	0.17
Bolivian	28	0.04
Chilean	39	0.06
Colombian	128	0.20
Ecuadorian	124	0.20
Paraguayan	10	0.02
Peruvian	194	0.31
Uruguayan	7	0.01
Venezuelan	13	0.02
Other South American	5	0.01
Other Hispanic or Latino	1,690	2.70

Race*	Population	%
African-American/Black (567)	781	1.25
Not Hispanic (380)	431	0.69
Hispanic (187)	350	0.56
American Indian/Alaska Native (634)	948	1.52
Not Hispanic (99)	167	0.27
Hispanic (535)	781	1.25
Alaska Athabascan *(Ala. Nat.)* (0)	0	<0.01
Aleut *(Alaska Native)* (0)	0	<0.01
Apache (40)	61	0.10
Arapaho (0)	0	<0.01
Blackfeet (11)	12	0.02
Canadian/French Am. Ind. (0)	1	<0.01
Central American Ind. (0)	0	<0.01
Cherokee (26)	57	0.09
Cheyenne (2)	2	<0.01
Chickasaw (0)	0	<0.01
Chippewa (0)	4	0.01
Choctaw (2)	6	0.01
Colville (0)	0	<0.01
Comanche (1)	1	<0.01
Cree (1)	1	<0.01
Creek (0)	1	<0.01
Crow (0)	1	<0.01
Delaware (1)	2	<0.01
Hopi (6)	10	0.02
Houma (0)	0	<0.01
Inupiat *(Alaska Native)* (0)	0	<0.01
Iroquois (0)	1	<0.01
Kiowa (0)	0	<0.01
Lumbee (0)	0	<0.01
Menominee (0)	0	<0.01
Mexican American Ind. (109)	162	0.26
Navajo (37)	51	0.08
Osage (0)	0	<0.01
Ottawa (0)	0	<0.01
Paiute (4)	4	0.01
Pima (5)	7	0.01
Potawatomi (0)	1	<0.01
Pueblo (2)	4	0.01
Puget Sound Salish (0)	0	<0.01
Seminole (0)	0	<0.01
Shoshone (0)	0	<0.01
Sioux (7)	10	0.02
South American Ind. (0)	1	<0.01
Spanish American Ind. (9)	10	0.02
Tlingit-Haida *(Alaska Native)* (0)	0	<0.01
Tohono O'Odham (16)	16	0.03
Tsimshian *(Alaska Native)* (3)	4	0.01
Ute (0)	0	<0.01
Yakama (0)	0	<0.01
Yaqui (18)	34	0.05
Yuman (0)	0	<0.01
Yup'ik *(Alaska Native)* (0)	0	<0.01
Asian (6,850)	7,359	11.77
Not Hispanic (6,646)	6,886	11.02
Hispanic (204)	473	0.76
Bangladeshi (50)	54	0.09
Bhutanese (0)	0	<0.01
Burmese (16)	21	0.03
Cambodian (54)	98	0.16
Chinese, ex. Taiwanese (2,469)	2,749	4.40
Filipino (932)	1,132	1.81
Hmong (0)	0	<0.01
Indian (481)	517	0.83
Indonesian (24)	25	0.04
Japanese (1,462)	1,669	2.67
Korean (586)	624	1.00
Laotian (5)	6	0.01
Malaysian (9)	11	0.02
Nepalese (2)	2	<0.01
Pakistani (5)	7	0.01
Sri Lankan (3)	3	<0.01
Taiwanese (74)	82	0.13
Thai (143)	175	0.28
Vietnamese (231)	287	0.46
Hawaii Native/Pacific Islander (58)	190	0.30
Not Hispanic (37)	101	0.16
Hispanic (21)	89	0.14
Fijian (0)	1	<0.01
Guamanian/Chamorro (17)	26	0.04
Marshallese (0)	0	<0.01
Native Hawaiian (12)	39	0.06
Samoan (22)	36	0.06
Tongan (0)	0	<0.01
White (33,633)	35,555	56.89
Not Hispanic (5,325)	5,613	8.98
Hispanic (28,308)	29,942	47.91

*Notes: † The Census 2010 population figure is used to calculate the percentages in the Hispanic Origin and Race categories. Ancestry percentages are based on the 2006-2010 American Community Survey population (not shown); ‡ Numbers in parentheses indicate the number of people reporting a single ancestry; * Numbers in parentheses indicate the number of persons reporting this race alone, not in combination with any other race; Please refer to the Explanation of Data for more information.*

Monterey Park

Place Type: City
County: Los Angeles
Population: 60,269

Ancestry	Population	%
Afghan (0)	0	<0.01
African, Sub-Saharan (0)	0	<0.01
African (0)	0	<0.01
Cape Verdean (0)	0	<0.01
Ethiopian (0)	0	<0.01
Ghanaian (0)	0	<0.01
Kenyan (0)	0	<0.01
Liberian (0)	0	<0.01
Nigerian (0)	0	<0.01
Senegalese (0)	0	<0.01
Sierra Leonean (0)	0	<0.01
Somalian (0)	0	<0.01
South African (0)	0	<0.01
Sudanese (0)	0	<0.01
Ugandan (0)	0	<0.01
Zimbabwean (0)	0	<0.01
Other Sub-Saharan African (0)	0	<0.01
Albanian (0)	0	<0.01
Alsatian (0)	0	<0.01
American (225)	225	0.37
Arab (171)	268	0.45
Arab (0)	0	<0.01
Egyptian (0)	0	<0.01
Iraqi (20)	40	0.07
Jordanian (0)	0	<0.01
Lebanese (151)	212	0.35
Moroccan (0)	0	<0.01
Palestinian (0)	0	<0.01
Syrian (0)	0	<0.01
Other Arab (0)	16	0.03
Armenian (273)	273	0.45
Assyrian/Chaldean/Syriac (0)	0	<0.01
Australian (0)	0	<0.01
Austrian (0)	0	<0.01
Basque (0)	0	<0.01
Belgian (0)	0	<0.01
Brazilian (18)	18	0.03
British (12)	12	0.02
Bulgarian (0)	0	<0.01
Cajun (0)	0	<0.01
Canadian (0)	37	0.06
Carpatho Rusyn (0)	0	<0.01
Celtic (0)	0	<0.01
Croatian (7)	7	0.01
Cypriot (0)	0	<0.01
Czech (9)	9	0.01
Czechoslovakian (0)	0	<0.01
Danish (47)	74	0.12
Dutch (6)	35	0.06
Eastern European (18)	37	0.06
English (76)	263	0.44
Estonian (0)	0	<0.01
European (72)	154	0.26
Finnish (0)	0	<0.01
French, ex. Basque (0)	270	0.45
French Canadian (0)	0	<0.01
German (150)	887	1.47
German Russian (0)	0	<0.01
Greek (15)	18	0.03
Guyanese (22)	22	0.04
Hungarian (6)	18	0.03
Icelander (0)	0	<0.01
Iranian (11)	11	0.02
Irish (185)	508	0.84
Israeli (0)	8	0.01
Italian (165)	479	0.80
Latvian (0)	0	<0.01
Lithuanian (0)	23	0.04
Luxemburger (0)	0	<0.01
Macedonian (0)	0	<0.01
Maltese (0)	0	<0.01
New Zealander (0)	0	<0.01
Northern European (0)	0	<0.01
Norwegian (11)	11	0.02
Pennsylvania German (0)	0	<0.01
Polish (26)	54	0.09
Portuguese (28)	41	0.07
Romanian (31)	54	0.09
Russian (64)	72	0.12
Scandinavian (0)	0	<0.01
Scotch-Irish (96)	150	0.25
Scottish (31)	65	0.11
Serbian (0)	51	0.08
Slavic (0)	0	<0.01
Slovak (0)	0	<0.01
Slovene (0)	0	<0.01
Soviet Union (0)	0	<0.01
Swedish (31)	47	0.08
Swiss (11)	11	0.02
Turkish (0)	0	<0.01
Ukrainian (0)	14	0.02
Welsh (11)	72	0.12
West Indian, ex. Hispanic (15)	15	0.02
Bahamian (0)	0	<0.01
Barbadian (0)	0	<0.01
Belizean (15)	15	0.02
Bermudan (0)	0	<0.01
British West Indian (0)	0	<0.01
Dutch West Indian (0)	0	<0.01
Haitian (0)	0	<0.01
Jamaican (0)	0	<0.01
Trinidadian/Tobagonian (0)	0	<0.01
U.S. Virgin Islander (0)	0	<0.01
West Indian (0)	0	<0.01
Other West Indian (0)	0	<0.01
Yugoslavian (12)	12	0.02

Hispanic Origin	Population	%
Hispanic or Latino (of any race)	16,218	26.91
Central American, ex. Mexican	1,183	1.96
Costa Rican	19	0.03
Guatemalan	275	0.46
Honduran	52	0.09
Nicaraguan	164	0.27
Panamanian	16	0.03
Salvadoran	641	1.06
Other Central American	16	0.03
Cuban	108	0.18
Dominican Republic	2	<0.01
Mexican	13,659	22.66
Puerto Rican	124	0.21
South American	326	0.54
Argentinean	33	0.05
Bolivian	10	0.02
Chilean	10	0.02
Colombian	60	0.10
Ecuadorian	103	0.17
Paraguayan	0	<0.01
Peruvian	96	0.16
Uruguayan	0	<0.01
Venezuelan	9	0.01
Other South American	5	0.01
Other Hispanic or Latino	816	1.35

Race*	Population	%
African-American/Black (252)	458	0.76
Not Hispanic (194)	301	0.50
Hispanic (58)	157	0.26
American Indian/Alaska Native (242)	516	0.86
Not Hispanic (51)	181	0.30
Hispanic (191)	335	0.56
Alaska Athabascan *(Ala. Nat.)* (0)	0	<0.01
Aleut *(Alaska Native)* (0)	0	<0.01
Apache (16)	22	0.04
Arapaho (0)	0	<0.01
Blackfeet (4)	14	0.02
Canadian/French Am. Ind. (0)	2	<0.01
Central American Ind. (0)	1	<0.01
Cherokee (2)	33	0.05
Cheyenne (0)	4	0.01
Chickasaw (0)	0	<0.01
Chippewa (0)	0	<0.01
Choctaw (0)	2	<0.01
Colville (0)	3	<0.01
Comanche (0)	1	<0.01
Cree (0)	0	<0.01
Creek (0)	0	<0.01
Crow (0)	0	<0.01
Delaware (0)	0	<0.01
Hopi (1)	5	0.01
Houma (0)	0	<0.01
Inupiat *(Alaska Native)* (0)	0	<0.01
Iroquois (3)	6	0.01
Kiowa (0)	0	<0.01
Lumbee (0)	0	<0.01
Menominee (0)	0	<0.01
Mexican American Ind. (29)	80	0.13
Navajo (34)	43	0.07
Osage (0)	0	<0.01
Ottawa (0)	0	<0.01
Paiute (0)	1	<0.01
Pima (1)	3	<0.01
Potawatomi (0)	0	<0.01
Pueblo (2)	4	0.01
Puget Sound Salish (0)	0	<0.01
Seminole (0)	1	<0.01
Shoshone (0)	0	<0.01
Sioux (7)	10	0.02
South American Ind. (0)	3	<0.01
Spanish American Ind. (1)	5	0.01
Tlingit-Haida *(Alaska Native)* (0)	1	<0.01
Tohono O'Odham (3)	6	0.01
Tsimshian *(Alaska Native)* (0)	2	<0.01
Ute (0)	0	<0.01
Yakama (1)	1	<0.01
Yaqui (4)	10	0.02
Yuman (3)	7	0.01
Yup'ik *(Alaska Native)* (0)	0	<0.01
Asian (40,301)	41,284	68.50
Not Hispanic (39,974)	40,660	67.46
Hispanic (327)	624	1.04
Bangladeshi (8)	8	0.01
Bhutanese (0)	0	<0.01
Burmese (236)	279	0.46
Cambodian (495)	676	1.12
Chinese, ex. Taiwanese (27,734)	29,537	49.01
Filipino (1,165)	1,437	2.38
Hmong (0)	0	<0.01
Indian (152)	217	0.36
Indonesian (223)	284	0.47
Japanese (3,515)	4,034	6.69
Korean (768)	890	1.48
Laotian (51)	68	0.11
Malaysian (29)	49	0.08
Nepalese (1)	2	<0.01
Pakistani (6)	8	0.01
Sri Lankan (9)	10	0.02
Taiwanese (1,025)	1,233	2.05
Thai (529)	569	0.94
Vietnamese (2,629)	3,323	5.51
Hawaii Native/Pacific Islander (28)	176	0.29
Not Hispanic (19)	149	0.25
Hispanic (9)	27	0.04
Fijian (4)	4	0.01
Guamanian/Chamorro (7)	12	0.02
Marshallese (0)	2	<0.01
Native Hawaiian (8)	58	0.10
Samoan (2)	5	0.01
Tongan (0)	0	<0.01
White (11,680)	12,942	21.47
Not Hispanic (2,998)	3,504	5.81
Hispanic (8,682)	9,438	15.66

*Notes: † The Census 2010 population figure is used to calculate the percentages in the Hispanic Origin and Race categories. Ancestry percentages are based on the 2006-2010 American Community Survey population (not shown); ‡ Numbers in parentheses indicate the number of people reporting a single ancestry; * Numbers in parentheses indicate the number of persons reporting this race alone, not in combination with any other race; Please refer to the Explanation of Data for more information.*

Moreno Valley

Place Type: City
County: Riverside
Population: 193,365

Ancestry	Population	%
Afghan (245)	337	0.18
African, Sub-Saharan (1,207)	1,405	0.75
African (941)	1,113	0.59
Cape Verdean (0)	0	<0.01
Ethiopian (106)	106	0.06
Ghanaian (0)	0	<0.01
Kenyan (25)	51	0.03
Liberian (0)	0	<0.01
Nigerian (135)	135	0.07
Senegalese (0)	0	<0.01
Sierra Leonean (0)	0	<0.01
Somalian (0)	0	<0.01
South African (0)	0	<0.01
Sudanese (0)	0	<0.01
Ugandan (0)	0	<0.01
Zimbabwean (0)	0	<0.01
Other Sub-Saharan African (0)	0	<0.01
Albanian (0)	0	<0.01
Alsatian (0)	0	<0.01
American (2,619)	2,619	1.40
Arab (957)	1,107	0.59
Arab (241)	241	0.13
Egyptian (189)	271	0.14
Iraqi (12)	12	0.01
Jordanian (35)	35	0.02
Lebanese (195)	195	0.10
Moroccan (0)	0	<0.01
Palestinian (230)	259	0.14
Syrian (12)	19	0.01
Other Arab (43)	75	0.04
Armenian (28)	64	0.03
Assyrian/Chaldean/Syriac (0)	0	<0.01
Australian (0)	0	<0.01
Austrian (0)	57	0.03
Basque (0)	0	<0.01
Belgian (3)	63	0.03
Brazilian (6)	6	<0.01
British (113)	320	0.17
Bulgarian (8)	8	<0.01
Cajun (0)	0	<0.01
Canadian (100)	336	0.18
Carpatho Rusyn (0)	0	<0.01
Celtic (0)	24	0.01
Croatian (20)	97	0.05
Cypriot (0)	0	<0.01
Czech (25)	93	0.05
Czechoslovakian (17)	47	0.03
Danish (159)	437	0.23
Dutch (341)	1,238	0.66
Eastern European (9)	9	<0.01
English (1,547)	5,560	2.97
Estonian (0)	0	<0.01
European (687)	935	0.50
Finnish (13)	82	0.04
French, ex. Basque (514)	2,513	1.34
French Canadian (300)	863	0.46
German (2,632)	9,981	5.33
German Russian (0)	0	<0.01
Greek (42)	133	0.07
Guyanese (10)	10	0.01
Hungarian (36)	247	0.13
Icelander (50)	50	0.03
Iranian (263)	263	0.14
Irish (1,546)	6,755	3.60
Israeli (0)	0	<0.01
Italian (1,157)	3,337	1.78
Latvian (0)	0	<0.01
Lithuanian (10)	92	0.05
Luxemburger (0)	0	<0.01
Macedonian (10)	10	0.01
Maltese (0)	0	<0.01
New Zealander (0)	0	<0.01
Northern European (62)	62	0.03
Norwegian (235)	943	0.50
Pennsylvania German (13)	62	0.03
Polish (441)	1,186	0.63
Portuguese (214)	570	0.30
Romanian (50)	50	0.03
Russian (221)	531	0.28
Scandinavian (49)	155	0.08
Scotch-Irish (147)	688	0.37
Scottish (372)	1,029	0.55
Serbian (0)	53	0.03
Slavic (0)	102	0.05
Slovak (13)	16	0.01
Slovene (0)	0	<0.01
Soviet Union (0)	0	<0.01
Swedish (205)	1,010	0.54
Swiss (32)	141	0.08
Turkish (0)	0	<0.01
Ukrainian (63)	168	0.09
Welsh (26)	367	0.20
West Indian, ex. Hispanic (439)	717	0.38
Bahamian (0)	8	<0.01
Barbadian (0)	0	<0.01
Belizean (144)	236	0.13
Bermudan (0)	0	<0.01
British West Indian (10)	10	0.01
Dutch West Indian (8)	23	0.01
Haitian (0)	0	<0.01
Jamaican (226)	353	0.19
Trinidadian/Tobagonian (0)	11	0.01
U.S. Virgin Islander (0)	0	<0.01
West Indian (51)	76	0.04
Other West Indian (0)	0	<0.01
Yugoslavian (16)	55	0.03

Hispanic Origin	Population	%
Hispanic or Latino (of any race)	105,169	54.39
Central American, ex. Mexican	5,710	2.95
Costa Rican	185	0.10
Guatemalan	1,562	0.81
Honduran	386	0.20
Nicaraguan	528	0.27
Panamanian	186	0.10
Salvadoran	2,794	1.44
Other Central American	69	0.04
Cuban	606	0.31
Dominican Republic	65	0.03
Mexican	90,054	46.57
Puerto Rican	1,636	0.85
South American	1,587	0.82
Argentinean	233	0.12
Bolivian	85	0.04
Chilean	59	0.03
Colombian	355	0.18
Ecuadorian	296	0.15
Paraguayan	4	<0.01
Peruvian	463	0.24
Uruguayan	39	0.02
Venezuelan	39	0.02
Other South American	14	0.01
Other Hispanic or Latino	5,511	2.85

Race*	Population	%
African-American/Black (34,889)	39,019	20.18
Not Hispanic (33,195)	36,134	18.69
Hispanic (1,694)	2,885	1.49
American Indian/Alaska Native (1,721)	3,611	1.87
Not Hispanic (573)	1,681	0.87
Hispanic (1,148)	1,930	1.00
Alaska Athabascan *(Ala. Nat.)* (2)	2	<0.01
Aleut *(Alaska Native)* (2)	8	<0.01
Apache (55)	125	0.06
Arapaho (1)	2	<0.01
Blackfeet (16)	77	0.04
Canadian/French Am. Ind. (6)	12	0.01
Central American Ind. (10)	11	0.01
Cherokee (96)	367	0.19
Cheyenne (3)	6	<0.01
Chickasaw (2)	8	<0.01
Chippewa (14)	38	0.02
Choctaw (36)	136	0.07
Colville (0)	0	<0.01
Comanche (2)	2	<0.01
Cree (0)	7	<0.01
Creek (9)	38	0.02
Crow (2)	5	<0.01
Delaware (1)	5	<0.01
Hopi (4)	7	<0.01
Houma (0)	0	<0.01
Inupiat *(Alaska Native)* (0)	0	<0.01
Iroquois (2)	14	0.01
Kiowa (1)	1	<0.01
Lumbee (5)	7	<0.01
Menominee (1)	4	<0.01
Mexican American Ind. (237)	338	0.17
Navajo (84)	146	0.08
Osage (5)	9	<0.01
Ottawa (2)	4	<0.01
Paiute (6)	20	0.01
Pima (0)	6	<0.01
Potawatomi (5)	10	0.01
Pueblo (7)	12	0.01
Puget Sound Salish (1)	1	<0.01
Seminole (3)	36	0.02
Shoshone (4)	7	<0.01
Sioux (17)	53	0.03
South American Ind. (9)	21	0.01
Spanish American Ind. (27)	30	0.02
Tlingit-Haida *(Alaska Native)* (2)	4	<0.01
Tohono O'Odham (12)	27	0.01
Tsimshian *(Alaska Native)* (1)	3	<0.01
Ute (0)	4	<0.01
Yakama (0)	0	<0.01
Yaqui (27)	59	0.03
Yuman (3)	11	0.01
Yup'ik *(Alaska Native)* (0)	3	<0.01
Asian (11,867)	14,814	7.66
Not Hispanic (11,423)	13,509	6.99
Hispanic (444)	1,305	0.67
Bangladeshi (105)	115	0.06
Bhutanese (0)	0	<0.01
Burmese (14)	15	0.01
Cambodian (398)	496	0.26
Chinese, ex. Taiwanese (831)	1,301	0.67
Filipino (5,437)	6,788	3.51
Hmong (138)	143	0.07
Indian (794)	999	0.52
Indonesian (98)	149	0.08
Japanese (362)	874	0.45
Korean (678)	920	0.48
Laotian (396)	454	0.23
Malaysian (8)	18	0.01
Nepalese (3)	3	<0.01
Pakistani (264)	298	0.15
Sri Lankan (26)	28	0.01
Taiwanese (88)	102	0.05
Thai (277)	427	0.22
Vietnamese (1,394)	1,604	0.83
Hawaii Native/Pacific Islander (1,117)	1,760	0.91
Not Hispanic (990)	1,409	0.73
Hispanic (127)	351	0.18
Fijian (20)	30	0.02
Guamanian/Chamorro (220)	344	0.18
Marshallese (0)	1	<0.01
Native Hawaiian (138)	372	0.19
Samoan (455)	628	0.32
Tongan (158)	187	0.10
White (80,969)	89,407	46.24
Not Hispanic (36,573)	40,399	20.89
Hispanic (44,396)	49,008	25.34

*Notes: † The Census 2010 population figure is used to calculate the percentages in the Hispanic Origin and Race categories. Ancestry percentages are based on the 2006-2010 American Community Survey population (not shown); ‡ Numbers in parentheses indicate the number of people reporting a single ancestry; * Numbers in parentheses indicate the number of persons reporting this race alone, not in combination with any other race; Please refer to the Explanation of Data for more information.*

Mountain View

Place Type: City
County: Santa Clara
Population: 74,066

Ancestry	Population	%
Afghan (0)	0	<0.01
African, Sub-Saharan (268)	479	0.66
African (90)	231	0.32
Cape Verdean (0)	0	<0.01
Ethiopian (7)	7	0.01
Ghanaian (0)	16	0.02
Kenyan (55)	74	0.10
Liberian (0)	0	<0.01
Nigerian (9)	9	0.01
Senegalese (0)	0	<0.01
Sierra Leonean (0)	0	<0.01
Somalian (0)	0	<0.01
South African (48)	83	0.11
Sudanese (40)	40	0.06
Ugandan (0)	0	<0.01
Zimbabwean (0)	0	<0.01
Other Sub-Saharan African (19)	19	0.03
Albanian (0)	0	<0.01
Alsatian (0)	0	<0.01
American (924)	924	1.27
Arab (530)	756	1.04
Arab (96)	129	0.18
Egyptian (51)	79	0.11
Iraqi (0)	0	<0.01
Jordanian (0)	0	<0.01
Lebanese (46)	83	0.11
Moroccan (15)	101	0.14
Palestinian (186)	193	0.27
Syrian (0)	0	<0.01
Other Arab (136)	171	0.24
Armenian (90)	99	0.14
Assyrian/Chaldean/Syriac (0)	0	<0.01
Australian (39)	78	0.11
Austrian (34)	114	0.16
Basque (5)	14	0.02
Belgian (10)	49	0.07
Brazilian (97)	139	0.19
British (508)	927	1.28
Bulgarian (108)	108	0.15
Cajun (0)	0	<0.01
Canadian (71)	186	0.26
Carpatho Rusyn (0)	0	<0.01
Celtic (50)	50	0.07
Croatian (75)	194	0.27
Cypriot (0)	0	<0.01
Czech (50)	125	0.17
Czechoslovakian (19)	43	0.06
Danish (98)	783	1.08
Dutch (301)	1,158	1.60
Eastern European (165)	189	0.26
English (1,373)	5,882	8.11
Estonian (11)	26	0.04
European (1,527)	1,647	2.27
Finnish (47)	139	0.19
French, ex. Basque (601)	2,008	2.77
French Canadian (140)	320	0.44
German (1,944)	7,661	10.57
German Russian (0)	8	0.01
Greek (108)	249	0.34
Guyanese (0)	24	0.03
Hungarian (341)	690	0.95
Icelander (0)	0	<0.01
Iranian (506)	606	0.84
Irish (1,217)	5,012	6.91
Israeli (96)	134	0.18
Italian (1,046)	3,361	4.64
Latvian (23)	31	0.04
Lithuanian (55)	113	0.16
Luxemburger (0)	0	<0.01
Macedonian (0)	0	<0.01
Maltese (6)	6	0.01
New Zealander (8)	8	0.01
Northern European (86)	86	0.12
Norwegian (264)	1,278	1.76
Pennsylvania German (0)	13	0.02
Polish (402)	1,195	1.65
Portuguese (314)	765	1.06
Romanian (100)	231	0.32
Russian (1,191)	1,976	2.73
Scandinavian (119)	343	0.47
Scotch-Irish (248)	970	1.34
Scottish (415)	1,478	2.04
Serbian (91)	135	0.19
Slavic (0)	49	0.07
Slovak (67)	109	0.15
Slovene (22)	53	0.07
Soviet Union (0)	0	<0.01
Swedish (221)	971	1.34
Swiss (107)	591	0.82
Turkish (131)	163	0.22
Ukrainian (610)	680	0.94
Welsh (108)	498	0.69
West Indian, ex. Hispanic (45)	69	0.10
Bahamian (0)	0	<0.01
Barbadian (0)	0	<0.01
Belizean (0)	0	<0.01
Bermudan (0)	0	<0.01
British West Indian (0)	0	<0.01
Dutch West Indian (0)	0	<0.01
Haitian (0)	0	<0.01
Jamaican (29)	53	0.07
Trinidadian/Tobagonian (8)	8	0.01
U.S. Virgin Islander (0)	0	<0.01
West Indian (8)	8	0.01
Other West Indian (0)	0	<0.01
Yugoslavian (180)	180	0.25

Hispanic Origin	Population	%
Hispanic or Latino (of any race)	16,071	21.70
Central American, ex. Mexican	1,910	2.58
Costa Rican	28	0.04
Guatemalan	474	0.64
Honduran	81	0.11
Nicaraguan	109	0.15
Panamanian	46	0.06
Salvadoran	1,155	1.56
Other Central American	17	0.02
Cuban	90	0.12
Dominican Republic	24	0.03
Mexican	11,523	15.56
Puerto Rican	338	0.46
South American	874	1.18
Argentinean	96	0.13
Bolivian	53	0.07
Chilean	91	0.12
Colombian	137	0.18
Ecuadorian	41	0.06
Paraguayan	3	<0.01
Peruvian	395	0.53
Uruguayan	11	0.01
Venezuelan	32	0.04
Other South American	15	0.02
Other Hispanic or Latino	1,312	1.77

Race*	Population	%
African-American/Black (1,629)	2,201	2.97
Not Hispanic (1,468)	1,906	2.57
Hispanic (161)	295	0.40
American Indian/Alaska Native (344)	823	1.11
Not Hispanic (116)	396	0.53
Hispanic (228)	427	0.58
Alaska Athabascan *(Ala. Nat.)* (0)	0	<0.01
Aleut *(Alaska Native)* (0)	2	<0.01
Apache (8)	20	0.03
Arapaho (0)	0	<0.01
Blackfeet (1)	17	0.02
Canadian/French Am. Ind. (2)	2	<0.01
Central American Ind. (1)	1	<0.01
Cherokee (22)	105	0.14
Cheyenne (0)	2	<0.01
Chickasaw (2)	5	0.01
Chippewa (4)	11	0.01
Choctaw (4)	19	0.03
Colville (1)	1	<0.01
Comanche (0)	0	<0.01
Cree (1)	2	<0.01
Creek (1)	7	0.01
Crow (0)	0	<0.01
Delaware (1)	2	<0.01
Hopi (0)	0	<0.01
Houma (0)	0	<0.01
Inupiat *(Alaska Native)* (1)	3	<0.01
Iroquois (5)	16	0.02
Kiowa (2)	4	0.01
Lumbee (0)	0	<0.01
Menominee (0)	1	<0.01
Mexican American Ind. (60)	92	0.12
Navajo (7)	29	0.04
Osage (0)	2	<0.01
Ottawa (0)	1	<0.01
Paiute (0)	2	<0.01
Pima (0)	0	<0.01
Potawatomi (2)	3	<0.01
Pueblo (8)	10	0.01
Puget Sound Salish (0)	0	<0.01
Seminole (1)	8	0.01
Shoshone (0)	6	0.01
Sioux (6)	11	0.01
South American Ind. (5)	12	0.02
Spanish American Ind. (1)	1	<0.01
Tlingit-Haida *(Alaska Native)* (1)	2	<0.01
Tohono O'Odham (0)	1	<0.01
Tsimshian *(Alaska Native)* (1)	1	<0.01
Ute (0)	1	<0.01
Yakama (0)	0	<0.01
Yaqui (5)	16	0.02
Yuman (0)	0	<0.01
Yup'ik *(Alaska Native)* (0)	1	<0.01
Asian (19,232)	21,527	29.06
Not Hispanic (19,064)	21,116	28.51
Hispanic (168)	411	0.55
Bangladeshi (11)	11	0.01
Bhutanese (1)	1	<0.01
Burmese (47)	73	0.10
Cambodian (23)	27	0.04
Chinese, ex. Taiwanese (7,303)	8,277	11.18
Filipino (2,499)	3,086	4.17
Hmong (7)	7	0.01
Indian (4,344)	4,612	6.23
Indonesian (89)	136	0.18
Japanese (1,548)	2,091	2.82
Korean (1,031)	1,236	1.67
Laotian (12)	15	0.02
Malaysian (17)	23	0.03
Nepalese (101)	108	0.15
Pakistani (136)	163	0.22
Sri Lankan (53)	65	0.09
Taiwanese (648)	757	1.02
Thai (126)	162	0.22
Vietnamese (694)	798	1.08
Hawaii Native/Pacific Islander (391)	694	0.94
Not Hispanic (372)	612	0.83
Hispanic (19)	82	0.11
Fijian (56)	64	0.09
Guamanian/Chamorro (44)	77	0.10
Marshallese (0)	0	<0.01
Native Hawaiian (29)	161	0.22
Samoan (43)	69	0.09
Tongan (171)	202	0.27
White (41,468)	44,694	60.34
Not Hispanic (34,052)	36,381	49.12
Hispanic (7,416)	8,313	11.22

*Notes: † The Census 2010 population figure is used to calculate the percentages in the Hispanic Origin and Race categories. Ancestry percentages are based on the 2006-2010 American Community Survey population (not shown); ‡ Numbers in parentheses indicate the number of people reporting a single ancestry; * Numbers in parentheses indicate the number of persons reporting this race alone, not in combination with any other race; Please refer to the Explanation of Data for more information.*

Murrieta

Place Type: City
County: Riverside
Population: 103,466

Ancestry	Population	%
Afghan (165)	165	0.17
African, Sub-Saharan (1,218)	1,396	1.46
African (995)	1,154	1.21
Cape Verdean (0)	0	<0.01
Ethiopian (0)	0	<0.01
Ghanaian (0)	0	<0.01
Kenyan (48)	48	0.05
Liberian (0)	0	<0.01
Nigerian (0)	0	<0.01
Senegalese (0)	0	<0.01
Sierra Leonean (0)	0	<0.01
Somalian (0)	0	<0.01
South African (99)	118	0.12
Sudanese (0)	0	<0.01
Ugandan (0)	0	<0.01
Zimbabwean (0)	0	<0.01
Other Sub-Saharan African (76)	76	0.08
Albanian (0)	0	<0.01
Alsatian (0)	12	0.01
American (2,317)	2,317	2.42
Arab (176)	424	0.44
Arab (0)	10	0.01
Egyptian (0)	0	<0.01
Iraqi (15)	42	0.04
Jordanian (0)	0	<0.01
Lebanese (65)	215	0.22
Moroccan (0)	37	0.04
Palestinian (35)	47	0.05
Syrian (42)	42	0.04
Other Arab (19)	31	0.03
Armenian (37)	137	0.14
Assyrian/Chaldean/Syriac (20)	76	0.08
Australian (28)	295	0.31
Austrian (0)	189	0.20
Basque (0)	0	<0.01
Belgian (0)	91	0.10
Brazilian (9)	55	0.06
British (323)	528	0.55
Bulgarian (48)	69	0.07
Cajun (0)	0	<0.01
Canadian (251)	324	0.34
Carpatho Rusyn (0)	0	<0.01
Celtic (0)	0	<0.01
Croatian (25)	57	0.06
Cypriot (0)	0	<0.01
Czech (25)	174	0.18
Czechoslovakian (16)	86	0.09
Danish (149)	777	0.81
Dutch (274)	1,801	1.88
Eastern European (83)	167	0.17
English (2,434)	9,682	10.12
Estonian (0)	0	<0.01
European (2,043)	2,477	2.59
Finnish (39)	171	0.18
French, ex. Basque (457)	3,255	3.40
French Canadian (331)	745	0.78
German (3,542)	15,477	16.18
German Russian (0)	0	<0.01
Greek (64)	293	0.31
Guyanese (23)	23	0.02
Hungarian (152)	521	0.54
Icelander (0)	21	0.02
Iranian (228)	361	0.38
Irish (2,002)	10,350	10.82
Israeli (19)	60	0.06
Italian (2,076)	6,261	6.54
Latvian (31)	51	0.05
Lithuanian (55)	196	0.20
Luxemburger (0)	0	<0.01
Macedonian (0)	0	<0.01
Maltese (17)	37	0.04
New Zealander (0)	0	<0.01
Northern European (27)	27	0.03
Norwegian (639)	2,314	2.42
Pennsylvania German (12)	38	0.04
Polish (340)	1,615	1.69
Portuguese (137)	324	0.34
Romanian (73)	179	0.19
Russian (206)	791	0.83
Scandinavian (92)	173	0.18
Scotch-Irish (558)	1,431	1.50
Scottish (516)	2,207	2.31
Serbian (13)	16	0.02
Slavic (0)	49	0.05
Slovak (38)	70	0.07
Slovene (0)	32	0.03
Soviet Union (0)	0	<0.01
Swedish (472)	1,401	1.46
Swiss (118)	325	0.34
Turkish (0)	0	<0.01
Ukrainian (75)	216	0.23
Welsh (24)	563	0.59
West Indian, ex. Hispanic (81)	183	0.19
Bahamian (0)	0	<0.01
Barbadian (0)	16	0.02
Belizean (0)	0	<0.01
Bermudan (0)	0	<0.01
British West Indian (0)	0	<0.01
Dutch West Indian (17)	17	0.02
Haitian (10)	60	0.06
Jamaican (28)	56	0.06
Trinidadian/Tobagonian (26)	26	0.03
U.S. Virgin Islander (0)	0	<0.01
West Indian (0)	8	0.01
Other West Indian (0)	0	<0.01
Yugoslavian (11)	91	0.10

Hispanic Origin	Population	%
Hispanic or Latino (of any race)	26,792	25.89
Central American, ex. Mexican	1,151	1.11
Costa Rican	96	0.09
Guatemalan	273	0.26
Honduran	82	0.08
Nicaraguan	123	0.12
Panamanian	121	0.12
Salvadoran	445	0.43
Other Central American	11	0.01
Cuban	375	0.36
Dominican Republic	61	0.06
Mexican	21,400	20.68
Puerto Rican	1,025	0.99
South American	905	0.87
Argentinean	144	0.14
Bolivian	28	0.03
Chilean	63	0.06
Colombian	228	0.22
Ecuadorian	137	0.13
Paraguayan	3	<0.01
Peruvian	240	0.23
Uruguayan	18	0.02
Venezuelan	35	0.03
Other South American	9	0.01
Other Hispanic or Latino	1,875	1.81

Race*	Population	%
African-American/Black (5,601)	7,178	6.94
Not Hispanic (5,162)	6,335	6.12
Hispanic (439)	843	0.81
American Indian/Alaska Native (741)	1,753	1.69
Not Hispanic (389)	1,001	0.97
Hispanic (352)	752	0.73
Alaska Athabascan *(Ala. Nat.)* (4)	5	<0.01
Aleut *(Alaska Native)* (1)	2	<0.01
Apache (13)	62	0.06
Arapaho (0)	3	<0.01
Blackfeet (10)	42	0.04
Canadian/French Am. Ind. (0)	7	0.01
Central American Ind. (10)	17	0.02
Cherokee (52)	248	0.24
Cheyenne (2)	5	<0.01
Chickasaw (2)	7	0.01
Chippewa (5)	27	0.03
Choctaw (10)	40	0.04
Colville (3)	3	<0.01
Comanche (2)	2	<0.01
Cree (1)	2	<0.01
Creek (11)	20	0.02
Crow (0)	0	<0.01
Delaware (0)	0	<0.01
Hopi (6)	8	0.01
Houma (1)	1	<0.01
Inupiat *(Alaska Native)* (0)	0	<0.01
Iroquois (7)	32	0.03
Kiowa (0)	1	<0.01
Lumbee (2)	2	<0.01
Menominee (2)	2	<0.01
Mexican American Ind. (58)	102	0.10
Navajo (32)	67	0.06
Osage (1)	2	<0.01
Ottawa (0)	1	<0.01
Paiute (0)	1	<0.01
Pima (3)	12	0.01
Potawatomi (1)	6	0.01
Pueblo (23)	36	0.03
Puget Sound Salish (5)	7	0.01
Seminole (0)	3	<0.01
Shoshone (2)	5	<0.01
Sioux (14)	35	0.03
South American Ind. (6)	11	0.01
Spanish American Ind. (3)	5	<0.01
Tlingit-Haida *(Alaska Native)* (6)	7	0.01
Tohono O'Odham (0)	2	<0.01
Tsimshian *(Alaska Native)* (0)	0	<0.01
Ute (0)	5	<0.01
Yakama (0)	3	<0.01
Yaqui (17)	22	0.02
Yuman (0)	0	<0.01
Yup'ik *(Alaska Native)* (1)	1	<0.01
Asian (9,556)	12,457	12.04
Not Hispanic (9,304)	11,498	11.11
Hispanic (252)	959	0.93
Bangladeshi (15)	15	0.01
Bhutanese (0)	0	<0.01
Burmese (14)	26	0.03
Cambodian (234)	268	0.26
Chinese, ex. Taiwanese (639)	1,092	1.06
Filipino (4,966)	6,449	6.23
Hmong (35)	43	0.04
Indian (464)	577	0.56
Indonesian (45)	112	0.11
Japanese (390)	1,048	1.01
Korean (748)	931	0.90
Laotian (323)	402	0.39
Malaysian (4)	11	0.01
Nepalese (2)	2	<0.01
Pakistani (63)	84	0.08
Sri Lankan (15)	20	0.02
Taiwanese (50)	71	0.07
Thai (119)	185	0.18
Vietnamese (1,045)	1,248	1.21
Hawaii Native/Pacific Islander (391)	923	0.89
Not Hispanic (332)	750	0.72
Hispanic (59)	173	0.17
Fijian (5)	5	<0.01
Guamanian/Chamorro (176)	296	0.29
Marshallese (0)	0	<0.01
Native Hawaiian (73)	298	0.29
Samoan (80)	161	0.16
Tongan (16)	28	0.03
White (72,137)	77,562	74.96
Not Hispanic (57,590)	60,850	58.81
Hispanic (14,547)	16,712	16.15

*Notes: † The Census 2010 population figure is used to calculate the percentages in the Hispanic Origin and Race categories. Ancestry percentages are based on the 2006-2010 American Community Survey population (not shown); ‡ Numbers in parentheses indicate the number of people reporting a single ancestry; * Numbers in parentheses indicate the number of persons reporting this race alone, not in combination with any other race; Please refer to the Explanation of Data for more information.*

Napa

Place Type: City
County: Napa
Population: 76,915

Ancestry	Population	%
Afghan (0)	0	<0.01
African, Sub-Saharan (139)	147	0.19
African (7)	7	0.01
Cape Verdean (36)	36	0.05
Ethiopian (0)	0	<0.01
Ghanaian (15)	15	0.02
Kenyan (0)	0	<0.01
Liberian (0)	0	<0.01
Nigerian (52)	52	0.07
Senegalese (0)	0	<0.01
Sierra Leonean (0)	0	<0.01
Somalian (0)	0	<0.01
South African (8)	16	0.02
Sudanese (0)	0	<0.01
Ugandan (0)	0	<0.01
Zimbabwean (0)	0	<0.01
Other Sub-Saharan African (21)	21	0.03
Albanian (0)	0	<0.01
Alsatian (0)	0	<0.01
American (2,121)	2,121	2.79
Arab (91)	238	0.31
Arab (18)	64	0.08
Egyptian (13)	13	0.02
Iraqi (0)	0	<0.01
Jordanian (0)	0	<0.01
Lebanese (14)	65	0.09
Moroccan (0)	0	<0.01
Palestinian (0)	6	0.01
Syrian (17)	61	0.08
Other Arab (29)	29	0.04
Armenian (35)	97	0.13
Assyrian/Chaldean/Syriac (0)	0	<0.01
Australian (12)	28	0.04
Austrian (56)	292	0.38
Basque (32)	130	0.17
Belgian (32)	69	0.09
Brazilian (9)	24	0.03
British (220)	341	0.45
Bulgarian (0)	10	0.01
Cajun (0)	0	<0.01
Canadian (48)	194	0.26
Carpatho Rusyn (0)	0	<0.01
Celtic (0)	10	0.01
Croatian (33)	121	0.16
Cypriot (0)	0	<0.01
Czech (83)	153	0.20
Czechoslovakian (28)	94	0.12
Danish (225)	821	1.08
Dutch (302)	1,285	1.69
Eastern European (104)	104	0.14
English (1,491)	6,981	9.18
Estonian (0)	20	0.03
European (1,169)	1,297	1.71
Finnish (54)	110	0.14
French, ex. Basque (474)	2,562	3.37
French Canadian (79)	237	0.31
German (2,248)	10,127	13.32
German Russian (0)	0	<0.01
Greek (125)	340	0.45
Guyanese (0)	0	<0.01
Hungarian (6)	236	0.31
Icelander (0)	12	0.02
Iranian (26)	26	0.03
Irish (1,819)	7,872	10.36
Israeli (0)	0	<0.01
Italian (1,721)	4,849	6.38
Latvian (0)	26	0.03
Lithuanian (0)	68	0.09
Luxemburger (14)	26	0.03
Macedonian (0)	0	<0.01
Maltese (11)	11	0.01
New Zealander (0)	0	<0.01
Northern European (135)	135	0.18
Norwegian (649)	1,587	2.09
Pennsylvania German (0)	0	<0.01
Polish (198)	835	1.10
Portuguese (330)	1,298	1.71
Romanian (0)	60	0.08
Russian (336)	659	0.87
Scandinavian (229)	303	0.40
Scotch-Irish (442)	1,489	1.96
Scottish (355)	1,823	2.40
Serbian (12)	38	0.05
Slavic (0)	8	0.01
Slovak (0)	0	<0.01
Slovene (58)	73	0.10
Soviet Union (0)	0	<0.01
Swedish (326)	1,424	1.87
Swiss (106)	425	0.56
Turkish (48)	91	0.12
Ukrainian (30)	178	0.23
Welsh (132)	853	1.12
West Indian, ex. Hispanic (0)	10	0.01
Bahamian (0)	0	<0.01
Barbadian (0)	0	<0.01
Belizean (0)	0	<0.01
Bermudan (0)	0	<0.01
British West Indian (0)	0	<0.01
Dutch West Indian (0)	0	<0.01
Haitian (0)	0	<0.01
Jamaican (0)	0	<0.01
Trinidadian/Tobagonian (0)	10	0.01
U.S. Virgin Islander (0)	0	<0.01
West Indian (0)	0	<0.01
Other West Indian (0)	0	<0.01
Yugoslavian (143)	257	0.34

Hispanic Origin	Population	%
Hispanic or Latino (of any race)	28,923	37.60
Central American, ex. Mexican	693	0.90
Costa Rican	51	0.07
Guatemalan	258	0.34
Honduran	47	0.06
Nicaraguan	75	0.10
Panamanian	10	0.01
Salvadoran	248	0.32
Other Central American	4	0.01
Cuban	70	0.09
Dominican Republic	12	0.02
Mexican	26,246	34.12
Puerto Rican	220	0.29
South American	268	0.35
Argentinean	23	0.03
Bolivian	5	0.01
Chilean	48	0.06
Colombian	69	0.09
Ecuadorian	19	0.02
Paraguayan	0	<0.01
Peruvian	81	0.11
Uruguayan	5	0.01
Venezuelan	15	0.02
Other South American	3	<0.01
Other Hispanic or Latino	1,414	1.84

Race*	Population	%
African-American/Black (486)	808	1.05
Not Hispanic (370)	617	0.80
Hispanic (116)	191	0.25
American Indian/Alaska Native (637)	1,419	1.84
Not Hispanic (312)	856	1.11
Hispanic (325)	563	0.73
Alaska Athabascan *(Ala. Nat.)* (0)	1	<0.01
Aleut *(Alaska Native)* (0)	1	<0.01
Apache (6)	32	0.04
Arapaho (0)	0	<0.01
Blackfeet (2)	30	0.04
Canadian/French Am. Ind. (0)	3	<0.01
Central American Ind. (1)	1	<0.01
Cherokee (58)	244	0.32
Cheyenne (1)	1	<0.01
Chickasaw (4)	10	0.01
Chippewa (9)	13	0.02
Choctaw (30)	70	0.09
Colville (0)	1	<0.01
Comanche (0)	5	0.01
Cree (3)	5	0.01
Creek (5)	7	0.01
Crow (0)	9	0.01
Delaware (2)	5	0.01
Hopi (0)	0	<0.01
Houma (3)	3	<0.01
Inupiat *(Alaska Native)* (0)	0	<0.01
Iroquois (5)	15	0.02
Kiowa (1)	3	<0.01
Lumbee (0)	3	<0.01
Menominee (3)	3	<0.01
Mexican American Ind. (97)	124	0.16
Navajo (5)	16	0.02
Osage (4)	4	0.01
Ottawa (4)	9	0.01
Paiute (2)	4	0.01
Pima (1)	2	<0.01
Potawatomi (11)	11	0.01
Pueblo (4)	5	0.01
Puget Sound Salish (0)	0	<0.01
Seminole (1)	6	0.01
Shoshone (0)	1	<0.01
Sioux (9)	24	0.03
South American Ind. (3)	6	0.01
Spanish American Ind. (6)	12	0.02
Tlingit-Haida *(Alaska Native)* (1)	1	<0.01
Tohono O'Odham (0)	3	<0.01
Tsimshian *(Alaska Native)* (0)	0	<0.01
Ute (0)	0	<0.01
Yakama (0)	0	<0.01
Yaqui (2)	2	<0.01
Yuman (0)	0	<0.01
Yup'ik *(Alaska Native)* (2)	3	<0.01
Asian (1,755)	2,535	3.30
Not Hispanic (1,685)	2,302	2.99
Hispanic (70)	233	0.30
Bangladeshi (5)	5	0.01
Bhutanese (0)	0	<0.01
Burmese (7)	12	0.02
Cambodian (6)	6	0.01
Chinese, ex. Taiwanese (282)	455	0.59
Filipino (551)	866	1.13
Hmong (1)	2	<0.01
Indian (186)	253	0.33
Indonesian (16)	30	0.04
Japanese (302)	486	0.63
Korean (153)	217	0.28
Laotian (4)	7	0.01
Malaysian (0)	7	0.01
Nepalese (0)	0	<0.01
Pakistani (44)	46	0.06
Sri Lankan (5)	7	0.01
Taiwanese (17)	18	0.02
Thai (19)	27	0.04
Vietnamese (75)	96	0.12
Hawaii Native/Pacific Islander (144)	345	0.45
Not Hispanic (116)	261	0.34
Hispanic (28)	84	0.11
Fijian (6)	6	0.01
Guamanian/Chamorro (51)	94	0.12
Marshallese (0)	0	<0.01
Native Hawaiian (46)	147	0.19
Samoan (3)	24	0.03
Tongan (12)	21	0.03
White (57,754)	60,375	78.50
Not Hispanic (43,963)	45,310	58.91
Hispanic (13,791)	15,065	19.59

*Notes: † The Census 2010 population figure is used to calculate the percentages in the Hispanic Origin and Race categories. Ancestry percentages are based on the 2006-2010 American Community Survey population (not shown); ‡ Numbers in parentheses indicate the number of people reporting a single ancestry; * Numbers in parentheses indicate the number of persons reporting this race alone, not in combination with any other race; Please refer to the Explanation of Data for more information.*

National City

Place Type: City
County: San Diego
Population: 58,582

Ancestry	Population	%
Afghan (0)	0	<0.01
African, Sub-Saharan (106)	130	0.23
African (96)	109	0.19
Cape Verdean (0)	0	<0.01
Ethiopian (0)	0	<0.01
Ghanaian (0)	0	<0.01
Kenyan (0)	0	<0.01
Liberian (0)	0	<0.01
Nigerian (10)	21	0.04
Senegalese (0)	0	<0.01
Sierra Leonean (0)	0	<0.01
Somalian (0)	0	<0.01
South African (0)	0	<0.01
Sudanese (0)	0	<0.01
Ugandan (0)	0	<0.01
Zimbabwean (0)	0	<0.01
Other Sub-Saharan African (0)	0	<0.01
Albanian (0)	0	<0.01
Alsatian (0)	0	<0.01
American (456)	456	0.80
Arab (143)	203	0.35
Arab (143)	143	0.25
Egyptian (0)	0	<0.01
Iraqi (0)	0	<0.01
Jordanian (0)	0	<0.01
Lebanese (0)	48	0.08
Moroccan (0)	0	<0.01
Palestinian (0)	0	<0.01
Syrian (0)	12	0.02
Other Arab (0)	0	<0.01
Armenian (0)	12	0.02
Assyrian/Chaldean/Syriac (0)	0	<0.01
Australian (0)	0	<0.01
Austrian (25)	50	0.09
Basque (0)	0	<0.01
Belgian (21)	21	0.04
Brazilian (0)	0	<0.01
British (0)	55	0.10
Bulgarian (0)	0	<0.01
Cajun (0)	0	<0.01
Canadian (0)	19	0.03
Carpatho Rusyn (0)	0	<0.01
Celtic (0)	0	<0.01
Croatian (0)	0	<0.01
Cypriot (0)	0	<0.01
Czech (0)	1	<0.01
Czechoslovakian (0)	0	<0.01
Danish (0)	66	0.12
Dutch (28)	148	0.26
Eastern European (0)	0	<0.01
English (371)	1,349	2.35
Estonian (0)	0	<0.01
European (12)	34	0.06
Finnish (0)	0	<0.01
French, ex. Basque (57)	349	0.61
French Canadian (0)	10	0.02
German (370)	1,402	2.44
German Russian (0)	0	<0.01
Greek (0)	37	0.06
Guyanese (0)	0	<0.01
Hungarian (10)	67	0.12
Icelander (0)	0	<0.01
Iranian (0)	9	0.02
Irish (169)	1,270	2.21
Israeli (15)	15	0.03
Italian (169)	639	1.11
Latvian (0)	0	<0.01
Lithuanian (10)	10	0.02
Luxemburger (0)	0	<0.01
Macedonian (0)	0	<0.01
Maltese (0)	0	<0.01
New Zealander (0)	0	<0.01
Northern European (0)	0	<0.01
Norwegian (59)	256	0.45
Pennsylvania German (0)	0	<0.01
Polish (48)	162	0.28
Portuguese (32)	239	0.42
Romanian (0)	10	0.02
Russian (34)	44	0.08
Scandinavian (0)	9	0.02
Scotch-Irish (148)	273	0.48
Scottish (54)	272	0.47
Serbian (0)	0	<0.01
Slavic (0)	0	<0.01
Slovak (0)	0	<0.01
Slovene (0)	30	0.05
Soviet Union (0)	0	<0.01
Swedish (115)	220	0.38
Swiss (0)	0	<0.01
Turkish (0)	0	<0.01
Ukrainian (25)	25	0.04
Welsh (0)	24	0.04
West Indian, ex. Hispanic (15)	71	0.12
Bahamian (0)	0	<0.01
Barbadian (0)	0	<0.01
Belizean (0)	0	<0.01
Bermudan (0)	0	<0.01
British West Indian (0)	0	<0.01
Dutch West Indian (0)	0	<0.01
Haitian (0)	0	<0.01
Jamaican (0)	39	0.07
Trinidadian/Tobagonian (0)	17	0.03
U.S. Virgin Islander (0)	0	<0.01
West Indian (15)	15	0.03
Other West Indian (0)	0	<0.01
Yugoslavian (41)	41	0.07

Hispanic Origin	Population	%
Hispanic or Latino (of any race)	36,911	63.01
Central American, ex. Mexican	504	0.86
Costa Rican	47	0.08
Guatemalan	101	0.17
Honduran	97	0.17
Nicaraguan	55	0.09
Panamanian	60	0.10
Salvadoran	141	0.24
Other Central American	3	0.01
Cuban	109	0.19
Dominican Republic	54	0.09
Mexican	34,473	58.85
Puerto Rican	489	0.83
South American	206	0.35
Argentinean	25	0.04
Bolivian	33	0.06
Chilean	12	0.02
Colombian	54	0.09
Ecuadorian	26	0.04
Paraguayan	0	<0.01
Peruvian	37	0.06
Uruguayan	4	0.01
Venezuelan	14	0.02
Other South American	1	<0.01
Other Hispanic or Latino	1,076	1.84

Race*	Population	%
African-American/Black (3,054)	3,638	6.21
Not Hispanic (2,660)	3,023	5.16
Hispanic (394)	615	1.05
American Indian/Alaska Native (618)	1,006	1.72
Not Hispanic (168)	367	0.63
Hispanic (450)	639	1.09
Alaska Athabascan *(Ala. Nat.)* (0)	1	<0.01
Aleut *(Alaska Native)* (0)	0	<0.01
Apache (32)	52	0.09
Arapaho (1)	4	0.01
Blackfeet (2)	15	0.03
Canadian/French Am. Ind. (0)	1	<0.01
Central American Ind. (0)	1	<0.01
Cherokee (19)	67	0.11
Cheyenne (0)	0	<0.01
Chickasaw (1)	7	0.01
Chippewa (8)	14	0.02
Choctaw (9)	12	0.02
Colville (0)	0	<0.01
Comanche (0)	2	<0.01
Cree (1)	1	<0.01
Creek (3)	4	0.01
Crow (1)	3	0.01
Delaware (0)	1	<0.01
Hopi (1)	1	<0.01
Houma (0)	0	<0.01
Inupiat *(Alaska Native)* (2)	3	0.01
Iroquois (1)	4	0.01
Kiowa (0)	0	<0.01
Lumbee (1)	1	<0.01
Menominee (0)	0	<0.01
Mexican American Ind. (71)	106	0.18
Navajo (29)	38	0.06
Osage (0)	0	<0.01
Ottawa (1)	2	<0.01
Paiute (0)	0	<0.01
Pima (0)	1	<0.01
Potawatomi (0)	1	<0.01
Pueblo (5)	6	0.01
Puget Sound Salish (0)	0	<0.01
Seminole (0)	4	0.01
Shoshone (1)	4	0.01
Sioux (2)	10	0.02
South American Ind. (6)	7	0.01
Spanish American Ind. (3)	4	0.01
Tlingit-Haida *(Alaska Native)* (2)	2	<0.01
Tohono O'Odham (2)	3	0.01
Tsimshian *(Alaska Native)* (0)	0	<0.01
Ute (0)	0	<0.01
Yakama (0)	0	<0.01
Yaqui (6)	8	0.01
Yuman (2)	2	<0.01
Yup'ik *(Alaska Native)* (0)	1	<0.01
Asian (10,699)	11,771	20.09
Not Hispanic (10,401)	11,148	19.03
Hispanic (298)	623	1.06
Bangladeshi (1)	1	<0.01
Bhutanese (0)	0	<0.01
Burmese (1)	1	<0.01
Cambodian (33)	46	0.08
Chinese, ex. Taiwanese (165)	255	0.44
Filipino (9,772)	10,695	18.26
Hmong (19)	20	0.03
Indian (68)	123	0.21
Indonesian (6)	11	0.02
Japanese (120)	286	0.49
Korean (72)	100	0.17
Laotian (111)	139	0.24
Malaysian (1)	21	0.04
Nepalese (1)	1	<0.01
Pakistani (5)	8	0.01
Sri Lankan (0)	4	0.01
Taiwanese (2)	4	0.01
Thai (11)	20	0.03
Vietnamese (127)	145	0.25
Hawaii Native/Pacific Islander (482)	777	1.33
Not Hispanic (413)	604	1.03
Hispanic (69)	173	0.30
Fijian (1)	2	<0.01
Guamanian/Chamorro (212)	303	0.52
Marshallese (12)	12	0.02
Native Hawaiian (27)	90	0.15
Samoan (176)	238	0.41
Tongan (14)	24	0.04
White (24,725)	26,830	45.80
Not Hispanic (6,872)	7,597	12.97
Hispanic (17,853)	19,233	32.83

*Notes: † The Census 2010 population figure is used to calculate the percentages in the Hispanic Origin and Race categories. Ancestry percentages are based on the 2006-2010 American Community Survey population (not shown); ‡ Numbers in parentheses indicate the number of people reporting a single ancestry; * Numbers in parentheses indicate the number of persons reporting this race alone, not in combination with any other race; Please refer to the Explanation of Data for more information.*

Newport Beach

Place Type: City
County: Orange
Population: 85,186

Ancestry	Population	%
Afghan (0)	0	<0.01
African, Sub-Saharan (160)	314	0.38
African (50)	151	0.18
Cape Verdean (0)	0	<0.01
Ethiopian (0)	0	<0.01
Ghanaian (0)	0	<0.01
Kenyan (0)	0	<0.01
Liberian (0)	0	<0.01
Nigerian (0)	0	<0.01
Senegalese (0)	0	<0.01
Sierra Leonean (0)	0	<0.01
Somalian (0)	0	<0.01
South African (83)	125	0.15
Sudanese (0)	0	<0.01
Ugandan (0)	0	<0.01
Zimbabwean (0)	0	<0.01
Other Sub-Saharan African (27)	38	0.05
Albanian (0)	7	0.01
Alsatian (0)	0	<0.01
American (3,741)	3,741	4.48
Arab (603)	997	1.19
Arab (12)	12	0.01
Egyptian (77)	160	0.19
Iraqi (35)	83	0.10
Jordanian (17)	49	0.06
Lebanese (175)	301	0.36
Moroccan (0)	0	<0.01
Palestinian (36)	36	0.04
Syrian (28)	59	0.07
Other Arab (223)	297	0.36
Armenian (332)	581	0.70
Assyrian/Chaldean/Syriac (0)	0	<0.01
Australian (17)	17	0.02
Austrian (293)	601	0.72
Basque (0)	20	0.02
Belgian (54)	192	0.23
Brazilian (20)	20	0.02
British (333)	734	0.88
Bulgarian (28)	54	0.06
Cajun (0)	5	0.01
Canadian (258)	516	0.62
Carpatho Rusyn (0)	13	0.02
Celtic (0)	0	<0.01
Croatian (58)	197	0.24
Cypriot (0)	0	<0.01
Czech (122)	356	0.43
Czechoslovakian (30)	167	0.20
Danish (205)	702	0.84
Dutch (359)	1,588	1.90
Eastern European (148)	148	0.18
English (4,258)	14,515	17.37
Estonian (11)	11	0.01
European (2,170)	2,427	2.90
Finnish (26)	96	0.11
French, ex. Basque (490)	3,333	3.99
French Canadian (175)	459	0.55
German (3,890)	15,533	18.59
German Russian (0)	0	<0.01
Greek (272)	560	0.67
Guyanese (0)	0	<0.01
Hungarian (434)	870	1.04
Icelander (0)	0	<0.01
Iranian (2,099)	2,378	2.85
Irish (2,968)	12,812	15.33
Israeli (96)	123	0.15
Italian (2,721)	7,119	8.52
Latvian (11)	24	0.03
Lithuanian (24)	304	0.36
Luxemburger (0)	11	0.01
Macedonian (0)	0	<0.01
Maltese (0)	0	<0.01
New Zealander (21)	33	0.04
Northern European (107)	132	0.16
Norwegian (595)	1,963	2.35
Pennsylvania German (0)	0	<0.01
Polish (666)	2,431	2.91
Portuguese (144)	484	0.58
Romanian (126)	312	0.37
Russian (964)	1,996	2.39
Scandinavian (80)	205	0.25
Scotch-Irish (1,112)	2,750	3.29
Scottish (877)	2,846	3.41
Serbian (9)	20	0.02
Slavic (0)	63	0.08
Slovak (28)	91	0.11
Slovene (13)	38	0.05
Soviet Union (0)	0	<0.01
Swedish (543)	2,439	2.92
Swiss (184)	730	0.87
Turkish (142)	204	0.24
Ukrainian (238)	362	0.43
Welsh (162)	1,134	1.36
West Indian, ex. Hispanic (24)	24	0.03
Bahamian (0)	0	<0.01
Barbadian (24)	24	0.03
Belizean (0)	0	<0.01
Bermudan (0)	0	<0.01
British West Indian (0)	0	<0.01
Dutch West Indian (0)	0	<0.01
Haitian (0)	0	<0.01
Jamaican (0)	0	<0.01
Trinidadian/Tobagonian (0)	0	<0.01
U.S. Virgin Islander (0)	0	<0.01
West Indian (0)	0	<0.01
Other West Indian (0)	0	<0.01
Yugoslavian (100)	143	0.17

Hispanic Origin	Population	%
Hispanic or Latino (of any race)	6,174	7.25
Central American, ex. Mexican	350	0.41
Costa Rican	36	0.04
Guatemalan	108	0.13
Honduran	14	0.02
Nicaraguan	58	0.07
Panamanian	21	0.02
Salvadoran	98	0.12
Other Central American	15	0.02
Cuban	216	0.25
Dominican Republic	19	0.02
Mexican	3,861	4.53
Puerto Rican	220	0.26
South American	628	0.74
Argentinean	141	0.17
Bolivian	30	0.04
Chilean	66	0.08
Colombian	155	0.18
Ecuadorian	80	0.09
Paraguayan	3	<0.01
Peruvian	87	0.10
Uruguayan	18	0.02
Venezuelan	33	0.04
Other South American	15	0.02
Other Hispanic or Latino	880	1.03

Race*	Population	%
African-American/Black (616)	880	1.03
Not Hispanic (571)	795	0.93
Hispanic (45)	85	0.10
American Indian/Alaska Native (223)	603	0.71
Not Hispanic (152)	414	0.49
Hispanic (71)	189	0.22
Alaska Athabascan *(Ala. Nat.)* (0)	1	<0.01
Aleut *(Alaska Native)* (0)	0	<0.01
Apache (11)	24	0.03
Arapaho (1)	1	<0.01
Blackfeet (2)	16	0.02
Canadian/French Am. Ind. (4)	5	0.01
Central American Ind. (0)	0	<0.01
Cherokee (29)	110	0.13
Cheyenne (0)	1	<0.01
Chickasaw (4)	6	0.01
Chippewa (6)	11	0.01
Choctaw (9)	19	0.02
Colville (0)	1	<0.01
Comanche (0)	0	<0.01
Cree (0)	0	<0.01
Creek (3)	6	0.01
Crow (2)	2	<0.01
Delaware (1)	2	<0.01
Hopi (0)	0	<0.01
Houma (0)	0	<0.01
Inupiat *(Alaska Native)* (0)	0	<0.01
Iroquois (3)	15	0.02
Kiowa (0)	0	<0.01
Lumbee (1)	2	<0.01
Menominee (0)	0	<0.01
Mexican American Ind. (4)	22	0.03
Navajo (13)	21	0.02
Osage (0)	4	<0.01
Ottawa (2)	3	<0.01
Paiute (3)	4	<0.01
Pima (0)	0	<0.01
Potawatomi (2)	3	<0.01
Pueblo (2)	9	0.01
Puget Sound Salish (1)	4	<0.01
Seminole (0)	0	<0.01
Shoshone (1)	1	<0.01
Sioux (1)	13	0.02
South American Ind. (0)	1	<0.01
Spanish American Ind. (0)	0	<0.01
Tlingit-Haida *(Alaska Native)* (0)	0	<0.01
Tohono O'Odham (1)	1	<0.01
Tsimshian *(Alaska Native)* (0)	1	<0.01
Ute (0)	0	<0.01
Yakama (0)	0	<0.01
Yaqui (2)	7	0.01
Yuman (0)	0	<0.01
Yup'ik *(Alaska Native)* (0)	0	<0.01
Asian (5,982)	7,587	8.91
Not Hispanic (5,925)	7,382	8.67
Hispanic (57)	205	0.24
Bangladeshi (11)	11	0.01
Bhutanese (0)	0	<0.01
Burmese (13)	20	0.02
Cambodian (15)	29	0.03
Chinese, ex. Taiwanese (1,480)	1,945	2.28
Filipino (619)	918	1.08
Hmong (3)	3	<0.01
Indian (691)	826	0.97
Indonesian (17)	48	0.06
Japanese (821)	1,230	1.44
Korean (843)	1,030	1.21
Laotian (7)	13	0.02
Malaysian (4)	13	0.02
Nepalese (0)	0	<0.01
Pakistani (54)	66	0.08
Sri Lankan (11)	13	0.02
Taiwanese (320)	369	0.43
Thai (69)	89	0.10
Vietnamese (668)	815	0.96
Hawaii Native/Pacific Islander (114)	327	0.38
Not Hispanic (95)	274	0.32
Hispanic (19)	53	0.06
Fijian (1)	3	<0.01
Guamanian/Chamorro (20)	42	0.05
Marshallese (0)	0	<0.01
Native Hawaiian (49)	150	0.18
Samoan (22)	40	0.05
Tongan (2)	2	<0.01
White (74,357)	76,656	89.99
Not Hispanic (70,142)	71,976	84.49
Hispanic (4,215)	4,680	5.49

*Notes: † The Census 2010 population figure is used to calculate the percentages in the Hispanic Origin and Race categories. Ancestry percentages are based on the 2006-2010 American Community Survey population (not shown); ‡ Numbers in parentheses indicate the number of people reporting a single ancestry; * Numbers in parentheses indicate the number of persons reporting this race alone, not in combination with any other race; Please refer to the Explanation of Data for more information.*

Norwalk

Place Type: City
County: Los Angeles
Population: 105,549

Ancestry	Population	%
Afghan (0)	0	<0.01
African, Sub-Saharan (244)	319	0.30
African (244)	319	0.30
Cape Verdean (0)	0	<0.01
Ethiopian (0)	0	<0.01
Ghanaian (0)	0	<0.01
Kenyan (0)	0	<0.01
Liberian (0)	0	<0.01
Nigerian (0)	0	<0.01
Senegalese (0)	0	<0.01
Sierra Leonean (0)	0	<0.01
Somalian (0)	0	<0.01
South African (0)	0	<0.01
Sudanese (0)	0	<0.01
Ugandan (0)	0	<0.01
Zimbabwean (0)	0	<0.01
Other Sub-Saharan African (0)	0	<0.01
Albanian (0)	0	<0.01
Alsatian (0)	0	<0.01
American (1,903)	1,903	1.81
Arab (184)	209	0.20
Arab (0)	0	<0.01
Egyptian (114)	114	0.11
Iraqi (0)	0	<0.01
Jordanian (0)	0	<0.01
Lebanese (46)	60	0.06
Moroccan (0)	0	<0.01
Palestinian (0)	0	<0.01
Syrian (0)	11	0.01
Other Arab (24)	24	0.02
Armenian (44)	65	0.06
Assyrian/Chaldean/Syriac (0)	0	<0.01
Australian (0)	0	<0.01
Austrian (0)	0	<0.01
Basque (0)	0	<0.01
Belgian (17)	42	0.04
Brazilian (0)	15	0.01
British (0)	43	0.04
Bulgarian (8)	8	0.01
Cajun (15)	15	0.01
Canadian (25)	71	0.07
Carpatho Rusyn (0)	0	<0.01
Celtic (0)	0	<0.01
Croatian (7)	14	0.01
Cypriot (0)	0	<0.01
Czech (5)	38	0.04
Czechoslovakian (0)	0	<0.01
Danish (57)	118	0.11
Dutch (180)	675	0.64
Eastern European (0)	0	<0.01
English (851)	2,538	2.41
Estonian (22)	22	0.02
European (152)	152	0.14
Finnish (11)	35	0.03
French, ex. Basque (254)	938	0.89
French Canadian (31)	42	0.04
German (644)	2,455	2.34
German Russian (0)	0	<0.01
Greek (0)	49	0.05
Guyanese (0)	0	<0.01
Hungarian (94)	143	0.14
Icelander (0)	0	<0.01
Iranian (152)	198	0.19
Irish (474)	2,447	2.33
Israeli (0)	0	<0.01
Italian (519)	1,477	1.41
Latvian (104)	104	0.10
Lithuanian (0)	21	0.02
Luxemburger (0)	0	<0.01
Macedonian (0)	0	<0.01
Maltese (0)	0	<0.01
New Zealander (9)	9	0.01
Northern European (0)	0	<0.01
Norwegian (200)	462	0.44
Pennsylvania German (0)	0	<0.01
Polish (198)	539	0.51
Portuguese (169)	366	0.35
Romanian (66)	66	0.06
Russian (87)	187	0.18
Scandinavian (14)	14	0.01
Scotch-Irish (76)	322	0.31
Scottish (122)	420	0.40
Serbian (0)	0	<0.01
Slavic (0)	0	<0.01
Slovak (17)	17	0.02
Slovene (0)	0	<0.01
Soviet Union (0)	0	<0.01
Swedish (62)	235	0.22
Swiss (0)	7	0.01
Turkish (0)	0	<0.01
Ukrainian (17)	17	0.02
Welsh (12)	111	0.11
West Indian, ex. Hispanic (58)	90	0.09
Bahamian (0)	0	<0.01
Barbadian (0)	0	<0.01
Belizean (16)	16	0.02
Bermudan (0)	0	<0.01
British West Indian (0)	21	0.02
Dutch West Indian (0)	0	<0.01
Haitian (0)	0	<0.01
Jamaican (0)	0	<0.01
Trinidadian/Tobagonian (0)	0	<0.01
U.S. Virgin Islander (0)	0	<0.01
West Indian (42)	53	0.05
Other West Indian (0)	0	<0.01
Yugoslavian (0)	0	<0.01

Hispanic Origin	Population	%
Hispanic or Latino (of any race)	74,041	70.15
Central American, ex. Mexican	5,460	5.17
Costa Rican	158	0.15
Guatemalan	1,411	1.34
Honduran	330	0.31
Nicaraguan	603	0.57
Panamanian	52	0.05
Salvadoran	2,871	2.72
Other Central American	35	0.03
Cuban	386	0.37
Dominican Republic	49	0.05
Mexican	63,299	59.97
Puerto Rican	488	0.46
South American	1,333	1.26
Argentinean	120	0.11
Bolivian	26	0.02
Chilean	42	0.04
Colombian	303	0.29
Ecuadorian	325	0.31
Paraguayan	0	<0.01
Peruvian	453	0.43
Uruguayan	22	0.02
Venezuelan	24	0.02
Other South American	18	0.02
Other Hispanic or Latino	3,026	2.87

Race*	Population	%
African-American/Black (4,593)	5,240	4.96
Not Hispanic (4,135)	4,451	4.22
Hispanic (458)	789	0.75
American Indian/Alaska Native (1,213)	1,916	1.82
Not Hispanic (281)	570	0.54
Hispanic (932)	1,346	1.28
Alaska Athabascan *(Ala. Nat.)* (1)	3	<0.01
Aleut *(Alaska Native)* (2)	2	<0.01
Apache (46)	100	0.09
Arapaho (1)	4	<0.01
Blackfeet (3)	31	0.03
Canadian/French Am. Ind. (0)	0	<0.01
Central American Ind. (10)	17	0.02
Cherokee (27)	110	0.10
Cheyenne (0)	1	<0.01
Chickasaw (3)	6	0.01
Chippewa (10)	15	0.01
Choctaw (19)	40	0.04
Colville (9)	9	0.01
Comanche (9)	12	0.01
Cree (0)	1	<0.01
Creek (20)	23	0.02
Crow (0)	1	<0.01
Delaware (0)	2	<0.01
Hopi (16)	18	0.02
Houma (0)	0	<0.01
Inupiat *(Alaska Native)* (0)	2	<0.01
Iroquois (1)	1	<0.01
Kiowa (1)	1	<0.01
Lumbee (1)	1	<0.01
Menominee (0)	4	<0.01
Mexican American Ind. (155)	232	0.22
Navajo (40)	96	0.09
Osage (0)	0	<0.01
Ottawa (1)	1	<0.01
Paiute (10)	10	0.01
Pima (14)	18	0.02
Potawatomi (0)	1	<0.01
Pueblo (11)	19	0.02
Puget Sound Salish (0)	0	<0.01
Seminole (5)	10	0.01
Shoshone (0)	4	<0.01
Sioux (16)	37	0.04
South American Ind. (4)	8	0.01
Spanish American Ind. (13)	18	0.02
Tlingit-Haida *(Alaska Native)* (0)	0	<0.01
Tohono O'Odham (8)	12	0.01
Tsimshian *(Alaska Native)* (0)	0	<0.01
Ute (1)	4	<0.01
Yakama (0)	0	<0.01
Yaqui (7)	25	0.02
Yuman (0)	0	<0.01
Yup'ik *(Alaska Native)* (0)	1	<0.01
Asian (12,700)	13,787	13.06
Not Hispanic (12,387)	13,032	12.35
Hispanic (313)	755	0.72
Bangladeshi (31)	41	0.04
Bhutanese (2)	2	<0.01
Burmese (19)	22	0.02
Cambodian (677)	743	0.70
Chinese, ex. Taiwanese (813)	1,047	0.99
Filipino (5,581)	6,135	5.81
Hmong (6)	17	0.02
Indian (870)	997	0.94
Indonesian (67)	105	0.10
Japanese (260)	427	0.40
Korean (2,610)	2,678	2.54
Laotian (31)	42	0.04
Malaysian (2)	8	0.01
Nepalese (49)	49	0.05
Pakistani (78)	89	0.08
Sri Lankan (34)	45	0.04
Taiwanese (88)	112	0.11
Thai (282)	344	0.33
Vietnamese (822)	900	0.85
Hawaii Native/Pacific Islander (431)	752	0.71
Not Hispanic (366)	559	0.53
Hispanic (65)	193	0.18
Fijian (22)	30	0.03
Guamanian/Chamorro (55)	98	0.09
Marshallese (0)	0	<0.01
Native Hawaiian (62)	148	0.14
Samoan (173)	252	0.24
Tongan (65)	74	0.07
White (52,089)	55,720	52.79
Not Hispanic (13,007)	13,808	13.08
Hispanic (39,082)	41,912	39.71

*Notes: † The Census 2010 population figure is used to calculate the percentages in the Hispanic Origin and Race categories. Ancestry percentages are based on the 2006-2010 American Community Survey population (not shown); ‡ Numbers in parentheses indicate the number of people reporting a single ancestry; * Numbers in parentheses indicate the number of persons reporting this race alone, not in combination with any other race; Please refer to the Explanation of Data for more information.*

Novato

Place Type: City
County: Marin
Population: 51,904

Ancestry	Population	%
Afghan (0)	0	<0.01
African, Sub-Saharan (271)	320	0.63
African (108)	145	0.29
Cape Verdean (0)	0	<0.01
Ethiopian (0)	0	<0.01
Ghanaian (0)	0	<0.01
Kenyan (101)	101	0.20
Liberian (0)	0	<0.01
Nigerian (0)	0	<0.01
Senegalese (0)	0	<0.01
Sierra Leonean (0)	0	<0.01
Somalian (0)	0	<0.01
South African (21)	33	0.07
Sudanese (0)	0	<0.01
Ugandan (0)	0	<0.01
Zimbabwean (0)	0	<0.01
Other Sub-Saharan African (41)	41	0.08
Albanian (0)	0	<0.01
Alsatian (0)	0	<0.01
American (918)	918	1.82
Arab (103)	337	0.67
Arab (0)	0	<0.01
Egyptian (0)	29	0.06
Iraqi (0)	0	<0.01
Jordanian (0)	0	<0.01
Lebanese (0)	115	0.23
Moroccan (50)	108	0.21
Palestinian (0)	19	0.04
Syrian (33)	33	0.07
Other Arab (20)	33	0.07
Armenian (97)	97	0.19
Assyrian/Chaldean/Syriac (0)	0	<0.01
Australian (16)	28	0.06
Austrian (78)	272	0.54
Basque (11)	78	0.15
Belgian (123)	164	0.32
Brazilian (316)	316	0.63
British (389)	521	1.03
Bulgarian (84)	84	0.17
Cajun (0)	0	<0.01
Canadian (208)	539	1.07
Carpatho Rusyn (0)	0	<0.01
Celtic (14)	27	0.05
Croatian (116)	269	0.53
Cypriot (0)	0	<0.01
Czech (42)	245	0.49
Czechoslovakian (50)	91	0.18
Danish (160)	675	1.34
Dutch (139)	576	1.14
Eastern European (116)	155	0.31
English (1,224)	5,507	10.91
Estonian (0)	37	0.07
European (1,274)	1,496	2.96
Finnish (60)	84	0.17
French, ex. Basque (365)	1,751	3.47
French Canadian (113)	261	0.52
German (1,873)	7,318	14.49
German Russian (0)	0	<0.01
Greek (166)	396	0.78
Guyanese (0)	0	<0.01
Hungarian (49)	262	0.52
Icelander (0)	0	<0.01
Iranian (476)	500	0.99
Irish (2,372)	7,264	14.39
Israeli (19)	19	0.04
Italian (1,977)	5,410	10.72
Latvian (57)	89	0.18
Lithuanian (38)	98	0.19
Luxemburger (0)	0	<0.01
Macedonian (0)	0	<0.01
Maltese (18)	18	0.04
New Zealander (0)	16	0.03
Northern European (47)	68	0.13
Norwegian (197)	1,014	2.01
Pennsylvania German (0)	0	<0.01
Polish (244)	1,011	2.00
Portuguese (469)	1,163	2.30
Romanian (56)	180	0.36
Russian (413)	1,297	2.57
Scandinavian (46)	122	0.24
Scotch-Irish (336)	1,315	2.60
Scottish (231)	1,496	2.96
Serbian (0)	11	0.02
Slavic (0)	22	0.04
Slovak (42)	66	0.13
Slovene (0)	58	0.11
Soviet Union (0)	0	<0.01
Swedish (332)	1,525	3.02
Swiss (90)	319	0.63
Turkish (0)	12	0.02
Ukrainian (161)	263	0.52
Welsh (59)	396	0.78
West Indian, ex. Hispanic (138)	145	0.29
Bahamian (0)	0	<0.01
Barbadian (0)	0	<0.01
Belizean (0)	0	<0.01
Bermudan (0)	0	<0.01
British West Indian (0)	0	<0.01
Dutch West Indian (0)	0	<0.01
Haitian (50)	50	0.10
Jamaican (88)	88	0.17
Trinidadian/Tobagonian (0)	7	0.01
U.S. Virgin Islander (0)	0	<0.01
West Indian (0)	0	<0.01
Other West Indian (0)	0	<0.01
Yugoslavian (23)	37	0.07

Hispanic Origin	Population	%
Hispanic or Latino (of any race)	11,046	21.28
Central American, ex. Mexican	2,892	5.57
Costa Rican	30	0.06
Guatemalan	1,412	2.72
Honduran	36	0.07
Nicaraguan	206	0.40
Panamanian	9	0.02
Salvadoran	1,156	2.23
Other Central American	43	0.08
Cuban	70	0.13
Dominican Republic	13	0.03
Mexican	5,941	11.45
Puerto Rican	239	0.46
South American	829	1.60
Argentinean	64	0.12
Bolivian	28	0.05
Chilean	38	0.07
Colombian	103	0.20
Ecuadorian	31	0.06
Paraguayan	4	0.01
Peruvian	496	0.96
Uruguayan	32	0.06
Venezuelan	20	0.04
Other South American	13	0.03
Other Hispanic or Latino	1,062	2.05

Race*	Population	%
African-American/Black (1,419)	1,971	3.80
Not Hispanic (1,321)	1,785	3.44
Hispanic (98)	186	0.36
American Indian/Alaska Native (286)	759	1.46
Not Hispanic (108)	425	0.82
Hispanic (178)	334	0.64
Alaska Athabascan *(Ala. Nat.)* (1)	1	<0.01
Aleut *(Alaska Native)* (0)	4	0.01
Apache (2)	7	0.01
Arapaho (0)	0	<0.01
Blackfeet (3)	19	0.04
Canadian/French Am. Ind. (0)	1	<0.01
Central American Ind. (0)	0	<0.01
Cherokee (28)	103	0.20
Cheyenne (1)	3	0.01
Chickasaw (1)	2	<0.01
Chippewa (6)	11	0.02
Choctaw (7)	19	0.04
Colville (0)	0	<0.01
Comanche (0)	3	0.01
Cree (0)	3	0.01
Creek (2)	5	0.01
Crow (0)	1	<0.01
Delaware (1)	2	<0.01
Hopi (0)	1	<0.01
Houma (0)	0	<0.01
Inupiat *(Alaska Native)* (1)	1	<0.01
Iroquois (0)	9	0.02
Kiowa (0)	0	<0.01
Lumbee (0)	0	<0.01
Menominee (0)	0	<0.01
Mexican American Ind. (59)	89	0.17
Navajo (5)	17	0.03
Osage (0)	2	<0.01
Ottawa (0)	0	<0.01
Paiute (0)	1	<0.01
Pima (2)	2	<0.01
Potawatomi (1)	4	0.01
Pueblo (2)	2	<0.01
Puget Sound Salish (1)	1	<0.01
Seminole (1)	9	0.02
Shoshone (0)	2	<0.01
Sioux (0)	6	0.01
South American Ind. (1)	5	0.01
Spanish American Ind. (14)	15	0.03
Tlingit-Haida *(Alaska Native)* (1)	1	<0.01
Tohono O'Odham (1)	8	0.02
Tsimshian *(Alaska Native)* (0)	0	<0.01
Ute (0)	1	<0.01
Yakama (0)	0	<0.01
Yaqui (0)	8	0.02
Yuman (0)	0	<0.01
Yup'ik *(Alaska Native)* (0)	0	<0.01
Asian (3,428)	4,541	8.75
Not Hispanic (3,367)	4,310	8.30
Hispanic (61)	231	0.45
Bangladeshi (3)	3	0.01
Bhutanese (0)	0	<0.01
Burmese (6)	13	0.03
Cambodian (66)	75	0.14
Chinese, ex. Taiwanese (1,009)	1,390	2.68
Filipino (608)	956	1.84
Hmong (0)	0	<0.01
Indian (578)	644	1.24
Indonesian (11)	26	0.05
Japanese (301)	595	1.15
Korean (237)	319	0.61
Laotian (20)	24	0.05
Malaysian (0)	2	<0.01
Nepalese (3)	3	0.01
Pakistani (37)	41	0.08
Sri Lankan (3)	4	0.01
Taiwanese (30)	61	0.12
Thai (69)	106	0.20
Vietnamese (283)	354	0.68
Hawaii Native/Pacific Islander (117)	286	0.55
Not Hispanic (103)	230	0.44
Hispanic (14)	56	0.11
Fijian (33)	38	0.07
Guamanian/Chamorro (14)	28	0.05
Marshallese (0)	0	<0.01
Native Hawaiian (35)	123	0.24
Samoan (15)	38	0.07
Tongan (5)	8	0.02
White (39,443)	41,688	80.32
Not Hispanic (34,141)	35,651	68.69
Hispanic (5,302)	6,037	11.63

*Notes: † The Census 2010 population figure is used to calculate the percentages in the Hispanic Origin and Race categories. Ancestry percentages are based on the 2006-2010 American Community Survey population (not shown); ‡ Numbers in parentheses indicate the number of people reporting a single ancestry; * Numbers in parentheses indicate the number of persons reporting this race alone, not in combination with any other race; Please refer to the Explanation of Data for more information.*

Oakland

Place Type: City
County: Alameda
Population: 390,724

Ancestry	Population	%
Afghan (536)	551	0.14
African, Sub-Saharan (7,268)	8,436	2.18
African (4,055)	4,978	1.29
Cape Verdean (99)	115	0.03
Ethiopian (1,867)	1,983	0.51
Ghanaian (69)	79	0.02
Kenyan (115)	115	0.03
Liberian (89)	89	0.02
Nigerian (509)	542	0.14
Senegalese (10)	10	<0.01
Sierra Leonean (0)	0	<0.01
Somalian (54)	105	0.03
South African (32)	32	0.01
Sudanese (78)	78	0.02
Ugandan (0)	0	<0.01
Zimbabwean (0)	0	<0.01
Other Sub-Saharan African (291)	310	0.08
Albanian (8)	22	0.01
Alsatian (10)	10	<0.01
American (3,822)	3,822	0.99
Arab (2,249)	2,646	0.68
Arab (446)	515	0.13
Egyptian (20)	65	0.02
Iraqi (42)	42	0.01
Jordanian (21)	21	0.01
Lebanese (118)	237	0.06
Moroccan (27)	78	0.02
Palestinian (125)	137	0.04
Syrian (0)	31	0.01
Other Arab (1,450)	1,520	0.39
Armenian (186)	359	0.09
Assyrian/Chaldean/Syriac (0)	11	<0.01
Australian (105)	216	0.06
Austrian (132)	843	0.22
Basque (14)	24	0.01
Belgian (259)	370	0.10
Brazilian (149)	347	0.09
British (780)	1,790	0.46
Bulgarian (61)	61	0.02
Cajun (10)	47	0.01
Canadian (287)	558	0.14
Carpatho Rusyn (0)	37	0.01
Celtic (43)	235	0.06
Croatian (106)	455	0.12
Cypriot (0)	0	<0.01
Czech (61)	719	0.19
Czechoslovakian (60)	123	0.03
Danish (260)	1,221	0.32
Dutch (417)	2,131	0.55
Eastern European (1,444)	1,717	0.44
English (3,496)	15,955	4.12
Estonian (14)	65	0.02
European (5,453)	6,403	1.65
Finnish (190)	514	0.13
French, ex. Basque (1,070)	5,368	1.39
French Canadian (173)	1,004	0.26
German (4,317)	21,071	5.45
German Russian (0)	23	0.01
Greek (710)	1,246	0.32
Guyanese (78)	106	0.03
Hungarian (206)	939	0.24
Icelander (12)	57	0.01
Iranian (798)	1,056	0.27
Irish (4,548)	18,855	4.87
Israeli (183)	235	0.06
Italian (3,259)	10,620	2.74
Latvian (67)	201	0.05
Lithuanian (179)	701	0.18
Luxemburger (0)	46	0.01
Macedonian (21)	21	0.01
Maltese (8)	44	0.01
New Zealander (34)	63	0.02
Northern European (699)	853	0.22
Norwegian (466)	2,538	0.66
Pennsylvania German (11)	26	0.01
Polish (929)	4,296	1.11
Portuguese (1,028)	2,276	0.59
Romanian (117)	466	0.12
Russian (1,984)	5,358	1.38
Scandinavian (192)	419	0.11
Scotch-Irish (977)	3,269	0.84
Scottish (950)	4,325	1.12
Serbian (11)	99	0.03
Slavic (16)	54	0.01
Slovak (175)	359	0.09
Slovene (23)	66	0.02
Soviet Union (0)	0	<0.01
Swedish (1,029)	3,653	0.94
Swiss (149)	856	0.22
Turkish (299)	575	0.15
Ukrainian (204)	579	0.15
Welsh (65)	1,353	0.35
West Indian, ex. Hispanic (1,073)	1,774	0.46
Bahamian (0)	0	<0.01
Barbadian (9)	9	<0.01
Belizean (12)	61	0.02
Bermudan (11)	39	0.01
British West Indian (0)	29	0.01
Dutch West Indian (0)	0	<0.01
Haitian (45)	102	0.03
Jamaican (393)	705	0.18
Trinidadian/Tobagonian (229)	387	0.10
U.S. Virgin Islander (16)	16	<0.01
West Indian (358)	426	0.11
Other West Indian (0)	0	<0.01
Yugoslavian (125)	277	0.07

Hispanic Origin	Population	%
Hispanic or Latino (of any race)	99,068	25.35
Central American, ex. Mexican	15,387	3.94
Costa Rican	145	0.04
Guatemalan	5,223	1.34
Honduran	1,160	0.30
Nicaraguan	1,156	0.30
Panamanian	301	0.08
Salvadoran	7,246	1.85
Other Central American	156	0.04
Cuban	862	0.22
Dominican Republic	183	0.05
Mexican	70,799	18.12
Puerto Rican	2,737	0.70
South American	2,371	0.61
Argentinean	334	0.09
Bolivian	93	0.02
Chilean	297	0.08
Colombian	493	0.13
Ecuadorian	193	0.05
Paraguayan	9	<0.01
Peruvian	690	0.18
Uruguayan	42	0.01
Venezuelan	176	0.05
Other South American	44	0.01
Other Hispanic or Latino	6,729	1.72

Race*	Population	%
African-American/Black (109,471)	119,122	30.49
Not Hispanic (106,637)	114,212	29.23
Hispanic (2,834)	4,910	1.26
American Indian/Alaska Native (3,040)	8,322	2.13
Not Hispanic (1,214)	4,795	1.23
Hispanic (1,826)	3,527	0.90
Alaska Athabascan *(Ala. Nat.)* (6)	11	<0.01
Aleut *(Alaska Native)* (2)	9	<0.01
Apache (69)	174	0.04
Arapaho (6)	16	<0.01
Blackfeet (30)	328	0.08
Canadian/French Am. Ind. (4)	27	0.01
Central American Ind. (111)	199	0.05
Cherokee (94)	971	0.25
Cheyenne (11)	28	0.01
Chickasaw (5)	45	0.01
Chippewa (33)	80	0.02
Choctaw (36)	282	0.07
Colville (0)	1	<0.01
Comanche (4)	24	0.01
Cree (3)	14	<0.01
Creek (13)	97	0.02
Crow (13)	22	0.01
Delaware (5)	18	<0.01
Hopi (10)	26	0.01
Houma (1)	2	<0.01
Inupiat *(Alaska Native)* (10)	26	0.01
Iroquois (21)	95	0.02
Kiowa (9)	11	<0.01
Lumbee (3)	7	<0.01
Menominee (1)	2	<0.01
Mexican American Ind. (621)	945	0.24
Navajo (111)	184	0.05
Osage (6)	13	<0.01
Ottawa (4)	6	<0.01
Paiute (14)	31	0.01
Pima (14)	25	0.01
Potawatomi (5)	21	0.01
Pueblo (45)	83	0.02
Puget Sound Salish (3)	9	<0.01
Seminole (7)	86	0.02
Shoshone (13)	29	0.01
Sioux (94)	213	0.05
South American Ind. (49)	134	0.03
Spanish American Ind. (21)	32	0.01
Tlingit-Haida *(Alaska Native)* (5)	16	<0.01
Tohono O'Odham (13)	29	0.01
Tsimshian *(Alaska Native)* (0)	2	<0.01
Ute (5)	8	<0.01
Yakama (6)	7	<0.01
Yaqui (33)	67	0.02
Yuman (4)	15	<0.01
Yup'ik *(Alaska Native)* (0)	1	<0.01
Asian (65,811)	73,775	18.88
Not Hispanic (65,127)	71,892	18.40
Hispanic (684)	1,883	0.48
Bangladeshi (23)	33	0.01
Bhutanese (255)	272	0.07
Burmese (335)	377	0.10
Cambodian (2,746)	3,175	0.81
Chinese, ex. Taiwanese (33,734)	37,235	9.53
Filipino (6,070)	8,661	2.22
Hmong (40)	49	0.01
Indian (2,114)	2,879	0.74
Indonesian (102)	196	0.05
Japanese (2,031)	3,667	0.94
Korean (2,446)	3,096	0.79
Laotian (2,815)	3,071	0.79
Malaysian (19)	55	0.01
Nepalese (171)	204	0.05
Pakistani (187)	243	0.06
Sri Lankan (71)	97	0.02
Taiwanese (308)	401	0.10
Thai (308)	472	0.12
Vietnamese (8,766)	10,038	2.57
Hawaii Native/Pacific Islander (2,222)	3,574	0.91
Not Hispanic (2,081)	3,073	0.79
Hispanic (141)	501	0.13
Fijian (107)	174	0.04
Guamanian/Chamorro (142)	305	0.08
Marshallese (2)	4	<0.01
Native Hawaiian (168)	664	0.17
Samoan (238)	460	0.12
Tongan (1,299)	1,463	0.37
White (134,925)	151,162	38.69
Not Hispanic (101,308)	111,751	28.60
Hispanic (33,617)	39,411	10.09

*Notes: † The Census 2010 population figure is used to calculate the percentages in the Hispanic Origin and Race categories. Ancestry percentages are based on the 2006-2010 American Community Survey population (not shown); ‡ Numbers in parentheses indicate the number of people reporting a single ancestry; * Numbers in parentheses indicate the number of persons reporting this race alone, not in combination with any other race; Please refer to the Explanation of Data for more information.*

Oceanside

Place Type: City
County: San Diego
Population: 167,086

Ancestry	Population	%
Afghan (12)	12	0.01
African, Sub-Saharan (1,447)	2,090	1.27
African (1,070)	1,713	1.04
Cape Verdean (0)	0	<0.01
Ethiopian (208)	208	0.13
Ghanaian (0)	0	<0.01
Kenyan (0)	0	<0.01
Liberian (0)	0	<0.01
Nigerian (13)	13	0.01
Senegalese (0)	0	<0.01
Sierra Leonean (0)	0	<0.01
Somalian (139)	139	0.08
South African (0)	0	<0.01
Sudanese (0)	0	<0.01
Ugandan (0)	0	<0.01
Zimbabwean (0)	0	<0.01
Other Sub-Saharan African (17)	17	0.01
Albanian (11)	11	0.01
Alsatian (0)	0	<0.01
American (3,408)	3,408	2.07
Arab (266)	543	0.33
Arab (67)	112	0.07
Egyptian (11)	11	0.01
Iraqi (94)	141	0.09
Jordanian (0)	0	<0.01
Lebanese (52)	172	0.10
Moroccan (0)	18	0.01
Palestinian (29)	58	0.04
Syrian (0)	18	0.01
Other Arab (13)	13	0.01
Armenian (93)	275	0.17
Assyrian/Chaldean/Syriac (0)	0	<0.01
Australian (21)	21	0.01
Austrian (110)	373	0.23
Basque (30)	54	0.03
Belgian (36)	420	0.25
Brazilian (86)	133	0.08
British (408)	781	0.47
Bulgarian (0)	12	0.01
Cajun (0)	74	0.04
Canadian (291)	517	0.31
Carpatho Rusyn (0)	0	<0.01
Celtic (13)	103	0.06
Croatian (54)	146	0.09
Cypriot (0)	0	<0.01
Czech (159)	679	0.41
Czechoslovakian (35)	35	0.02
Danish (358)	1,549	0.94
Dutch (538)	2,641	1.60
Eastern European (37)	37	0.02
English (4,137)	14,231	8.64
Estonian (0)	0	<0.01
European (2,290)	2,689	1.63
Finnish (47)	295	0.18
French, ex. Basque (870)	4,599	2.79
French Canadian (300)	656	0.40
German (6,091)	21,019	12.76
German Russian (0)	0	<0.01
Greek (227)	693	0.42
Guyanese (0)	0	<0.01
Hungarian (162)	939	0.57
Icelander (0)	24	0.01
Iranian (263)	326	0.20
Irish (3,927)	16,680	10.13
Israeli (0)	0	<0.01
Italian (2,681)	7,600	4.61
Latvian (8)	105	0.06
Lithuanian (127)	277	0.17
Luxemburger (19)	31	0.02
Macedonian (34)	34	0.02
Maltese (0)	0	<0.01
New Zealander (0)	0	<0.01
Northern European (213)	213	0.13
Norwegian (646)	2,418	1.47
Pennsylvania German (7)	20	0.01
Polish (1,195)	3,389	2.06
Portuguese (345)	923	0.56
Romanian (87)	199	0.12
Russian (701)	1,689	1.03
Scandinavian (192)	376	0.23
Scotch-Irish (1,099)	2,838	1.72
Scottish (851)	3,104	1.88
Serbian (31)	91	0.06
Slavic (26)	71	0.04
Slovak (33)	78	0.05
Slovene (0)	11	0.01
Soviet Union (0)	0	<0.01
Swedish (655)	2,512	1.53
Swiss (60)	354	0.21
Turkish (99)	139	0.08
Ukrainian (262)	406	0.25
Welsh (130)	1,055	0.64
West Indian, ex. Hispanic (122)	219	0.13
Bahamian (0)	0	<0.01
Barbadian (0)	9	0.01
Belizean (0)	40	0.02
Bermudan (0)	0	<0.01
British West Indian (0)	0	<0.01
Dutch West Indian (0)	0	<0.01
Haitian (40)	40	0.02
Jamaican (82)	106	0.06
Trinidadian/Tobagonian (0)	12	0.01
U.S. Virgin Islander (0)	0	<0.01
West Indian (0)	12	0.01
Other West Indian (0)	0	<0.01
Yugoslavian (69)	95	0.06

Hispanic Origin	Population	%
Hispanic or Latino (of any race)	59,947	35.88
Central American, ex. Mexican	1,547	0.93
Costa Rican	131	0.08
Guatemalan	371	0.22
Honduran	138	0.08
Nicaraguan	127	0.08
Panamanian	175	0.10
Salvadoran	589	0.35
Other Central American	16	0.01
Cuban	288	0.17
Dominican Republic	154	0.09
Mexican	52,217	31.25
Puerto Rican	1,602	0.96
South American	1,084	0.65
Argentinean	116	0.07
Bolivian	46	0.03
Chilean	64	0.04
Colombian	316	0.19
Ecuadorian	130	0.08
Paraguayan	3	<0.01
Peruvian	301	0.18
Uruguayan	12	0.01
Venezuelan	77	0.05
Other South American	19	0.01
Other Hispanic or Latino	3,055	1.83

Race*	Population	%
African-American/Black (7,873)	10,278	6.15
Not Hispanic (7,101)	8,838	5.29
Hispanic (772)	1,440	0.86
American Indian/Alaska Native (1,385)	2,998	1.79
Not Hispanic (613)	1,563	0.94
Hispanic (772)	1,435	0.86
Alaska Athabascan *(Ala. Nat.)* (0)	0	<0.01
Aleut *(Alaska Native)* (2)	4	<0.01
Apache (56)	124	0.07
Arapaho (1)	1	<0.01
Blackfeet (8)	45	0.03
Canadian/French Am. Ind. (7)	11	0.01
Central American Ind. (11)	19	0.01
Cherokee (62)	335	0.20
Cheyenne (0)	3	<0.01
Chickasaw (12)	32	0.02
Chippewa (16)	30	0.02
Choctaw (30)	84	0.05
Colville (2)	3	<0.01
Comanche (4)	14	0.01
Cree (0)	7	<0.01
Creek (8)	23	0.01
Crow (1)	2	<0.01
Delaware (1)	4	<0.01
Hopi (8)	14	0.01
Houma (0)	0	<0.01
Inupiat *(Alaska Native)* (5)	6	<0.01
Iroquois (5)	24	0.01
Kiowa (0)	0	<0.01
Lumbee (3)	8	<0.01
Menominee (0)	1	<0.01
Mexican American Ind. (229)	338	0.20
Navajo (64)	101	0.06
Osage (2)	6	<0.01
Ottawa (2)	5	<0.01
Paiute (8)	10	0.01
Pima (1)	4	<0.01
Potawatomi (2)	3	<0.01
Pueblo (19)	33	0.02
Puget Sound Salish (4)	5	<0.01
Seminole (6)	21	0.01
Shoshone (4)	14	0.01
Sioux (20)	59	0.04
South American Ind. (7)	19	0.01
Spanish American Ind. (18)	23	0.01
Tlingit-Haida *(Alaska Native)* (4)	7	<0.01
Tohono O'Odham (1)	1	<0.01
Tsimshian *(Alaska Native)* (0)	0	<0.01
Ute (1)	7	<0.01
Yakama (1)	1	<0.01
Yaqui (9)	29	0.02
Yuman (5)	9	0.01
Yup'ik *(Alaska Native)* (1)	1	<0.01
Asian (11,081)	15,112	9.04
Not Hispanic (10,638)	13,827	8.28
Hispanic (443)	1,285	0.77
Bangladeshi (8)	8	<0.01
Bhutanese (0)	0	<0.01
Burmese (33)	42	0.03
Cambodian (98)	126	0.08
Chinese, ex. Taiwanese (929)	1,548	0.93
Filipino (5,705)	7,853	4.70
Hmong (28)	30	0.02
Indian (407)	531	0.32
Indonesian (52)	104	0.06
Japanese (1,243)	2,376	1.42
Korean (609)	874	0.52
Laotian (61)	87	0.05
Malaysian (13)	17	0.01
Nepalese (16)	21	0.01
Pakistani (24)	27	0.02
Sri Lankan (15)	15	0.01
Taiwanese (79)	106	0.06
Thai (132)	198	0.12
Vietnamese (1,178)	1,388	0.83
Hawaii Native/Pacific Islander (2,144)	3,428	2.05
Not Hispanic (1,999)	2,962	1.77
Hispanic (145)	466	0.28
Fijian (3)	11	0.01
Guamanian/Chamorro (325)	525	0.31
Marshallese (3)	3	<0.01
Native Hawaiian (261)	877	0.52
Samoan (1,330)	1,781	1.07
Tongan (33)	60	0.04
White (109,020)	117,020	70.04
Not Hispanic (80,849)	85,536	51.19
Hispanic (28,171)	31,484	18.84

*Notes: † The Census 2010 population figure is used to calculate the percentages in the Hispanic Origin and Race categories. Ancestry percentages are based on the 2006-2010 American Community Survey population (not shown); ‡ Numbers in parentheses indicate the number of people reporting a single ancestry; * Numbers in parentheses indicate the number of persons reporting this race alone, not in combination with any other race; Please refer to the Explanation of Data for more information.*

Ontario

Place Type: City
County: San Bernardino
Population: 163,924

Ancestry	Population	%
Afghan (63)	63	0.04
African, Sub-Saharan (777)	916	0.55
African (480)	609	0.37
Cape Verdean (0)	0	<0.01
Ethiopian (0)	0	<0.01
Ghanaian (0)	0	<0.01
Kenyan (0)	0	<0.01
Liberian (0)	0	<0.01
Nigerian (297)	307	0.19
Senegalese (0)	0	<0.01
Sierra Leonean (0)	0	<0.01
Somalian (0)	0	<0.01
South African (0)	0	<0.01
Sudanese (0)	0	<0.01
Ugandan (0)	0	<0.01
Zimbabwean (0)	0	<0.01
Other Sub-Saharan African (0)	0	<0.01
Albanian (0)	0	<0.01
Alsatian (0)	25	0.02
American (4,023)	4,023	2.44
Arab (376)	451	0.27
Arab (57)	57	0.03
Egyptian (79)	79	0.05
Iraqi (0)	0	<0.01
Jordanian (0)	0	<0.01
Lebanese (81)	100	0.06
Moroccan (0)	0	<0.01
Palestinian (78)	90	0.05
Syrian (81)	125	0.08
Other Arab (0)	0	<0.01
Armenian (102)	134	0.08
Assyrian/Chaldean/Syriac (77)	77	0.05
Australian (0)	0	<0.01
Austrian (0)	130	0.08
Basque (33)	116	0.07
Belgian (0)	0	<0.01
Brazilian (98)	107	0.06
British (83)	237	0.14
Bulgarian (0)	0	<0.01
Cajun (0)	48	0.03
Canadian (57)	267	0.16
Carpatho Rusyn (0)	0	<0.01
Celtic (0)	0	<0.01
Croatian (71)	82	0.05
Cypriot (0)	0	<0.01
Czech (29)	135	0.08
Czechoslovakian (0)	21	0.01
Danish (34)	472	0.29
Dutch (1,120)	1,980	1.20
Eastern European (27)	27	0.02
English (1,471)	5,887	3.56
Estonian (0)	0	<0.01
European (784)	1,108	0.67
Finnish (38)	120	0.07
French, ex. Basque (243)	2,359	1.43
French Canadian (188)	270	0.16
German (2,077)	8,373	5.07
German Russian (0)	0	<0.01
Greek (19)	137	0.08
Guyanese (0)	0	<0.01
Hungarian (101)	554	0.34
Icelander (75)	75	0.05
Iranian (138)	157	0.10
Irish (1,320)	6,161	3.73
Israeli (0)	0	<0.01
Italian (1,213)	4,032	2.44
Latvian (0)	0	<0.01
Lithuanian (11)	106	0.06
Luxemburger (0)	0	<0.01
Macedonian (0)	0	<0.01
Maltese (0)	0	<0.01
New Zealander (0)	0	<0.01
Northern European (26)	37	0.02
Norwegian (434)	1,328	0.80
Pennsylvania German (41)	80	0.05
Polish (344)	1,301	0.79
Portuguese (459)	597	0.36
Romanian (0)	13	0.01
Russian (49)	328	0.20
Scandinavian (0)	37	0.02
Scotch-Irish (377)	851	0.52
Scottish (261)	1,583	0.96
Serbian (0)	15	0.01
Slavic (24)	24	0.01
Slovak (0)	41	0.02
Slovene (0)	17	0.01
Soviet Union (0)	0	<0.01
Swedish (240)	1,152	0.70
Swiss (22)	170	0.10
Turkish (15)	86	0.05
Ukrainian (28)	141	0.09
Welsh (106)	349	0.21
West Indian, ex. Hispanic (249)	591	0.36
Bahamian (0)	0	<0.01
Barbadian (0)	0	<0.01
Belizean (52)	155	0.09
Bermudan (0)	0	<0.01
British West Indian (107)	107	0.06
Dutch West Indian (0)	0	<0.01
Haitian (0)	0	<0.01
Jamaican (69)	162	0.10
Trinidadian/Tobagonian (0)	0	<0.01
U.S. Virgin Islander (12)	12	0.01
West Indian (9)	155	0.09
Other West Indian (0)	0	<0.01
Yugoslavian (39)	127	0.08

Hispanic Origin	Population	%
Hispanic or Latino (of any race)	113,085	68.99
Central American, ex. Mexican	6,264	3.82
Costa Rican	175	0.11
Guatemalan	1,676	1.02
Honduran	793	0.48
Nicaraguan	658	0.40
Panamanian	102	0.06
Salvadoran	2,791	1.70
Other Central American	69	0.04
Cuban	592	0.36
Dominican Republic	56	0.03
Mexican	98,596	60.15
Puerto Rican	1,001	0.61
South American	1,519	0.93
Argentinean	243	0.15
Bolivian	62	0.04
Chilean	65	0.04
Colombian	376	0.23
Ecuadorian	270	0.16
Paraguayan	6	<0.01
Peruvian	404	0.25
Uruguayan	30	0.02
Venezuelan	36	0.02
Other South American	27	0.02
Other Hispanic or Latino	5,057	3.08

Race*	Population	%
African-American/Black (10,561)	12,096	7.38
Not Hispanic (9,598)	10,529	6.42
Hispanic (963)	1,567	0.96
American Indian/Alaska Native (1,686)	2,949	1.80
Not Hispanic (361)	848	0.52
Hispanic (1,325)	2,101	1.28
Alaska Athabascan *(Ala. Nat.)* (1)	1	<0.01
Aleut *(Alaska Native)* (0)	0	<0.01
Apache (59)	98	0.06
Arapaho (7)	7	<0.01
Blackfeet (12)	60	0.04
Canadian/French Am. Ind. (1)	7	<0.01
Central American Ind. (14)	20	0.01
Cherokee (82)	264	0.16
Cheyenne (1)	3	<0.01
Chickasaw (9)	16	0.01
Chippewa (6)	20	0.01
Choctaw (15)	57	0.03
Colville (0)	0	<0.01
Comanche (10)	15	0.01
Cree (0)	0	<0.01
Creek (2)	3	<0.01
Crow (0)	0	<0.01
Delaware (4)	7	<0.01
Hopi (6)	12	0.01
Houma (0)	0	<0.01
Inupiat *(Alaska Native)* (0)	0	<0.01
Iroquois (2)	5	<0.01
Kiowa (3)	4	<0.01
Lumbee (3)	3	<0.01
Menominee (0)	0	<0.01
Mexican American Ind. (211)	417	0.25
Navajo (61)	98	0.06
Osage (0)	8	<0.01
Ottawa (3)	4	<0.01
Paiute (6)	6	<0.01
Pima (9)	12	0.01
Potawatomi (5)	7	<0.01
Pueblo (15)	25	0.02
Puget Sound Salish (0)	0	<0.01
Seminole (2)	10	0.01
Shoshone (6)	8	<0.01
Sioux (18)	37	0.02
South American Ind. (7)	7	<0.01
Spanish American Ind. (21)	29	0.02
Tlingit-Haida *(Alaska Native)* (1)	2	<0.01
Tohono O'Odham (10)	10	0.01
Tsimshian *(Alaska Native)* (0)	0	<0.01
Ute (0)	2	<0.01
Yakama (0)	0	<0.01
Yaqui (53)	84	0.05
Yuman (3)	16	0.01
Yup'ik *(Alaska Native)* (0)	0	<0.01
Asian (8,453)	10,009	6.11
Not Hispanic (8,078)	8,965	5.47
Hispanic (375)	1,044	0.64
Bangladeshi (59)	64	0.04
Bhutanese (0)	0	<0.01
Burmese (20)	27	0.02
Cambodian (276)	309	0.19
Chinese, ex. Taiwanese (1,074)	1,422	0.87
Filipino (2,909)	3,566	2.18
Hmong (37)	38	0.02
Indian (640)	757	0.46
Indonesian (267)	344	0.21
Japanese (263)	543	0.33
Korean (488)	610	0.37
Laotian (33)	48	0.03
Malaysian (3)	9	0.01
Nepalese (0)	0	<0.01
Pakistani (129)	163	0.10
Sri Lankan (15)	16	0.01
Taiwanese (174)	197	0.12
Thai (107)	157	0.10
Vietnamese (1,612)	1,752	1.07
Hawaii Native/Pacific Islander (514)	962	0.59
Not Hispanic (448)	686	0.42
Hispanic (66)	276	0.17
Fijian (10)	13	0.01
Guamanian/Chamorro (45)	79	0.05
Marshallese (1)	2	<0.01
Native Hawaiian (69)	228	0.14
Samoan (128)	206	0.13
Tongan (200)	237	0.14
White (83,683)	89,915	54.85
Not Hispanic (29,898)	31,518	19.23
Hispanic (53,785)	58,397	35.62

*Notes: † The Census 2010 population figure is used to calculate the percentages in the Hispanic Origin and Race categories. Ancestry percentages are based on the 2006-2010 American Community Survey population (not shown); ‡ Numbers in parentheses indicate the number of people reporting a single ancestry; * Numbers in parentheses indicate the number of persons reporting this race alone, not in combination with any other race; Please refer to the Explanation of Data for more information.*

Orange

Place Type: City
County: Orange
Population: 136,416

Ancestry	Population	%
Afghan (42)	42	0.03
African, Sub-Saharan (156)	194	0.14
African (97)	128	0.10
Cape Verdean (0)	0	<0.01
Ethiopian (2)	2	<0.01
Ghanaian (0)	0	<0.01
Kenyan (0)	0	<0.01
Liberian (0)	0	<0.01
Nigerian (12)	19	0.01
Senegalese (0)	0	<0.01
Sierra Leonean (0)	0	<0.01
Somalian (0)	0	<0.01
South African (0)	0	<0.01
Sudanese (21)	21	0.02
Ugandan (0)	0	<0.01
Zimbabwean (0)	0	<0.01
Other Sub-Saharan African (24)	24	0.02
Albanian (20)	41	0.03
Alsatian (0)	0	<0.01
American (10,395)	10,395	7.72
Arab (870)	1,076	0.80
Arab (37)	37	0.03
Egyptian (76)	89	0.07
Iraqi (39)	39	0.03
Jordanian (187)	219	0.16
Lebanese (196)	309	0.23
Moroccan (0)	0	<0.01
Palestinian (0)	0	<0.01
Syrian (244)	268	0.20
Other Arab (91)	115	0.09
Armenian (650)	781	0.58
Assyrian/Chaldean/Syriac (0)	38	0.03
Australian (3)	20	0.01
Austrian (34)	271	0.20
Basque (8)	22	0.02
Belgian (19)	124	0.09
Brazilian (14)	14	0.01
British (359)	640	0.48
Bulgarian (18)	27	0.02
Cajun (0)	0	<0.01
Canadian (127)	254	0.19
Carpatho Rusyn (0)	0	<0.01
Celtic (10)	49	0.04
Croatian (38)	132	0.10
Cypriot (0)	0	<0.01
Czech (48)	407	0.30
Czechoslovakian (64)	106	0.08
Danish (189)	572	0.43
Dutch (488)	1,907	1.42
Eastern European (146)	146	0.11
English (2,686)	9,623	7.15
Estonian (17)	17	0.01
European (1,034)	1,228	0.91
Finnish (122)	239	0.18
French, ex. Basque (371)	2,532	1.88
French Canadian (209)	409	0.30
German (4,069)	14,807	11.00
German Russian (0)	0	<0.01
Greek (366)	670	0.50
Guyanese (0)	13	0.01
Hungarian (108)	400	0.30
Icelander (0)	22	0.02
Iranian (503)	626	0.47
Irish (2,322)	10,224	7.60
Israeli (10)	10	0.01
Italian (2,072)	5,575	4.14
Latvian (64)	113	0.08
Lithuanian (22)	125	0.09
Luxemburger (0)	0	<0.01
Macedonian (0)	0	<0.01
Maltese (10)	35	0.03
New Zealander (0)	7	0.01
Northern European (105)	135	0.10
Norwegian (488)	1,652	1.23
Pennsylvania German (0)	0	<0.01
Polish (525)	1,808	1.34
Portuguese (81)	437	0.32
Romanian (377)	549	0.41
Russian (379)	978	0.73
Scandinavian (107)	289	0.21
Scotch-Irish (569)	1,558	1.16
Scottish (530)	2,126	1.58
Serbian (24)	83	0.06
Slavic (17)	61	0.05
Slovak (54)	95	0.07
Slovene (12)	51	0.04
Soviet Union (0)	0	<0.01
Swedish (390)	1,764	1.31
Swiss (46)	289	0.21
Turkish (102)	123	0.09
Ukrainian (67)	150	0.11
Welsh (184)	589	0.44
West Indian, ex. Hispanic (102)	187	0.14
Bahamian (0)	0	<0.01
Barbadian (0)	0	<0.01
Belizean (14)	14	0.01
Bermudan (0)	0	<0.01
British West Indian (0)	0	<0.01
Dutch West Indian (0)	0	<0.01
Haitian (2)	2	<0.01
Jamaican (66)	127	0.09
Trinidadian/Tobagonian (0)	0	<0.01
U.S. Virgin Islander (0)	0	<0.01
West Indian (20)	44	0.03
Other West Indian (0)	0	<0.01
Yugoslavian (64)	116	0.09

Hispanic Origin	Population	%
Hispanic or Latino (of any race)	52,014	38.13
Central American, ex. Mexican	2,152	1.58
Costa Rican	94	0.07
Guatemalan	790	0.58
Honduran	163	0.12
Nicaraguan	163	0.12
Panamanian	55	0.04
Salvadoran	851	0.62
Other Central American	36	0.03
Cuban	414	0.30
Dominican Republic	49	0.04
Mexican	45,074	33.04
Puerto Rican	488	0.36
South American	1,349	0.99
Argentinean	257	0.19
Bolivian	157	0.12
Chilean	72	0.05
Colombian	257	0.19
Ecuadorian	158	0.12
Paraguayan	3	<0.01
Peruvian	371	0.27
Uruguayan	25	0.02
Venezuelan	32	0.02
Other South American	17	0.01
Other Hispanic or Latino	2,488	1.82

Race*	Population	%
African-American/Black (2,227)	3,007	2.20
Not Hispanic (1,895)	2,425	1.78
Hispanic (332)	582	0.43
American Indian/Alaska Native (993)	1,939	1.42
Not Hispanic (357)	869	0.64
Hispanic (636)	1,070	0.78
Alaska Athabascan *(Ala. Nat.)* (0)	1	<0.01
Aleut *(Alaska Native)* (3)	8	0.01
Apache (60)	106	0.08
Arapaho (2)	5	<0.01
Blackfeet (10)	42	0.03
Canadian/French Am. Ind. (0)	6	<0.01
Central American Ind. (3)	13	0.01
Cherokee (51)	249	0.18
Cheyenne (4)	5	<0.01
Chickasaw (9)	17	0.01
Chippewa (6)	29	0.02
Choctaw (20)	63	0.05
Colville (0)	0	<0.01
Comanche (5)	10	0.01
Cree (0)	1	<0.01
Creek (4)	16	0.01
Crow (2)	4	<0.01
Delaware (0)	0	<0.01
Hopi (0)	2	<0.01
Houma (0)	0	<0.01
Inupiat *(Alaska Native)* (2)	4	<0.01
Iroquois (13)	20	0.01
Kiowa (0)	0	<0.01
Lumbee (3)	3	<0.01
Menominee (0)	0	<0.01
Mexican American Ind. (129)	179	0.13
Navajo (31)	47	0.03
Osage (3)	7	0.01
Ottawa (0)	0	<0.01
Paiute (0)	5	<0.01
Pima (4)	11	0.01
Potawatomi (10)	12	0.01
Pueblo (4)	8	0.01
Puget Sound Salish (2)	3	<0.01
Seminole (2)	6	<0.01
Shoshone (8)	13	0.01
Sioux (10)	32	0.02
South American Ind. (1)	14	0.01
Spanish American Ind. (10)	19	0.01
Tlingit-Haida *(Alaska Native)* (1)	3	<0.01
Tohono O'Odham (5)	11	0.01
Tsimshian *(Alaska Native)* (0)	0	<0.01
Ute (0)	2	<0.01
Yakama (0)	0	<0.01
Yaqui (15)	30	0.02
Yuman (0)	0	<0.01
Yup'ik *(Alaska Native)* (0)	0	<0.01
Asian (15,350)	17,473	12.81
Not Hispanic (15,116)	16,795	12.31
Hispanic (234)	678	0.50
Bangladeshi (22)	22	0.02
Bhutanese (0)	0	<0.01
Burmese (9)	21	0.02
Cambodian (313)	351	0.26
Chinese, ex. Taiwanese (1,791)	2,444	1.79
Filipino (2,892)	3,607	2.64
Hmong (12)	18	0.01
Indian (1,460)	1,597	1.17
Indonesian (114)	162	0.12
Japanese (1,106)	1,772	1.30
Korean (1,830)	2,039	1.49
Laotian (41)	51	0.04
Malaysian (4)	15	0.01
Nepalese (1)	2	<0.01
Pakistani (170)	194	0.14
Sri Lankan (67)	70	0.05
Taiwanese (420)	477	0.35
Thai (144)	185	0.14
Vietnamese (4,310)	4,664	3.42
Hawaii Native/Pacific Islander (352)	720	0.53
Not Hispanic (321)	604	0.44
Hispanic (31)	116	0.09
Fijian (4)	7	0.01
Guamanian/Chamorro (59)	99	0.07
Marshallese (5)	8	0.01
Native Hawaiian (98)	270	0.20
Samoan (99)	155	0.11
Tongan (41)	58	0.04
White (91,522)	96,270	70.57
Not Hispanic (63,805)	66,180	48.51
Hispanic (27,717)	30,090	22.06

*Notes: † The Census 2010 population figure is used to calculate the percentages in the Hispanic Origin and Race categories. Ancestry percentages are based on the 2006-2010 American Community Survey population (not shown); ‡ Numbers in parentheses indicate the number of people reporting a single ancestry; * Numbers in parentheses indicate the number of persons reporting this race alone, not in combination with any other race; Please refer to the Explanation of Data for more information.*

Oxnard

Place Type: City
County: Ventura
Population: 197,899

Ancestry	Population	%
Afghan (32)	32	0.02
African, Sub-Saharan (434)	496	0.26
African (385)	439	0.23
Cape Verdean (0)	0	<0.01
Ethiopian (0)	0	<0.01
Ghanaian (0)	0	<0.01
Kenyan (0)	0	<0.01
Liberian (0)	0	<0.01
Nigerian (15)	23	0.01
Senegalese (0)	0	<0.01
Sierra Leonean (0)	0	<0.01
Somalian (0)	0	<0.01
South African (34)	34	0.02
Sudanese (0)	0	<0.01
Ugandan (0)	0	<0.01
Zimbabwean (0)	0	<0.01
Other Sub-Saharan African (0)	0	<0.01
Albanian (31)	31	0.02
Alsatian (0)	0	<0.01
American (1,962)	1,962	1.02
Arab (137)	170	0.09
Arab (45)	45	0.02
Egyptian (13)	35	0.02
Iraqi (0)	0	<0.01
Jordanian (0)	0	<0.01
Lebanese (0)	11	0.01
Moroccan (0)	0	<0.01
Palestinian (0)	0	<0.01
Syrian (16)	16	0.01
Other Arab (63)	63	0.03
Armenian (34)	67	0.03
Assyrian/Chaldean/Syriac (0)	0	<0.01
Australian (7)	24	0.01
Austrian (64)	226	0.12
Basque (8)	48	0.02
Belgian (8)	87	0.05
Brazilian (0)	27	0.01
British (196)	353	0.18
Bulgarian (83)	106	0.06
Cajun (0)	0	<0.01
Canadian (69)	245	0.13
Carpatho Rusyn (0)	0	<0.01
Celtic (0)	0	<0.01
Croatian (93)	110	0.06
Cypriot (0)	0	<0.01
Czech (37)	127	0.07
Czechoslovakian (0)	19	0.01
Danish (68)	405	0.21
Dutch (108)	753	0.39
Eastern European (88)	107	0.06
English (1,691)	5,380	2.79
Estonian (0)	0	<0.01
European (573)	807	0.42
Finnish (56)	56	0.03
French, ex. Basque (172)	1,779	0.92
French Canadian (77)	251	0.13
German (2,491)	8,448	4.39
German Russian (0)	6	<0.01
Greek (85)	138	0.07
Guyanese (12)	29	0.02
Hungarian (115)	336	0.17
Icelander (12)	12	0.01
Iranian (150)	181	0.09
Irish (1,706)	7,202	3.74
Israeli (0)	0	<0.01
Italian (905)	2,897	1.50
Latvian (0)	0	<0.01
Lithuanian (84)	119	0.06
Luxemburger (0)	0	<0.01
Macedonian (0)	19	0.01
Maltese (0)	21	0.01
New Zealander (11)	28	0.01
Northern European (80)	113	0.06
Norwegian (306)	774	0.40
Pennsylvania German (13)	13	0.01
Polish (318)	1,543	0.80
Portuguese (117)	550	0.29
Romanian (0)	41	0.02
Russian (396)	1,056	0.55
Scandinavian (33)	111	0.06
Scotch-Irish (392)	1,253	0.65
Scottish (374)	1,368	0.71
Serbian (7)	85	0.04
Slavic (9)	51	0.03
Slovak (26)	62	0.03
Slovene (0)	0	<0.01
Soviet Union (0)	0	<0.01
Swedish (391)	1,002	0.52
Swiss (35)	171	0.09
Turkish (9)	9	<0.01
Ukrainian (54)	117	0.06
Welsh (38)	345	0.18
West Indian, ex. Hispanic (177)	232	0.12
Bahamian (0)	0	<0.01
Barbadian (0)	0	<0.01
Belizean (0)	0	<0.01
Bermudan (0)	0	<0.01
British West Indian (0)	0	<0.01
Dutch West Indian (6)	6	<0.01
Haitian (0)	6	<0.01
Jamaican (89)	116	0.06
Trinidadian/Tobagonian (82)	104	0.05
U.S. Virgin Islander (0)	0	<0.01
West Indian (0)	0	<0.01
Other West Indian (0)	0	<0.01
Yugoslavian (0)	82	0.04

Hispanic Origin	Population	%
Hispanic or Latino (of any race)	145,551	73.55
Central American, ex. Mexican	2,288	1.16
Costa Rican	52	0.03
Guatemalan	630	0.32
Honduran	204	0.10
Nicaraguan	138	0.07
Panamanian	72	0.04
Salvadoran	1,172	0.59
Other Central American	20	0.01
Cuban	166	0.08
Dominican Republic	39	0.02
Mexican	136,991	69.22
Puerto Rican	678	0.34
South American	686	0.35
Argentinean	105	0.05
Bolivian	36	0.02
Chilean	80	0.04
Colombian	183	0.09
Ecuadorian	55	0.03
Paraguayan	0	<0.01
Peruvian	185	0.09
Uruguayan	25	0.01
Venezuelan	13	0.01
Other South American	4	<0.01
Other Hispanic or Latino	4,703	2.38

Race*	Population	%
African-American/Black (5,771)	7,324	3.70
Not Hispanic (4,754)	5,591	2.83
Hispanic (1,017)	1,733	0.88
American Indian/Alaska Native (2,953)	4,494	2.27
Not Hispanic (424)	1,023	0.52
Hispanic (2,529)	3,471	1.75
Alaska Athabascan *(Ala. Nat.)* (0)	2	<0.01
Aleut *(Alaska Native)* (4)	5	<0.01
Apache (55)	146	0.07
Arapaho (0)	0	<0.01
Blackfeet (9)	52	0.03
Canadian/French Am. Ind. (1)	3	<0.01
Central American Ind. (8)	11	0.01
Cherokee (80)	295	0.15
Cheyenne (4)	4	<0.01
Chickasaw (7)	9	<0.01
Chippewa (11)	18	0.01
Choctaw (22)	48	0.02
Colville (0)	0	<0.01
Comanche (17)	20	0.01
Cree (1)	1	<0.01
Creek (2)	11	0.01
Crow (0)	2	<0.01
Delaware (3)	8	<0.01
Hopi (5)	15	0.01
Houma (0)	0	<0.01
Inupiat *(Alaska Native)* (0)	0	<0.01
Iroquois (4)	12	0.01
Kiowa (3)	10	0.01
Lumbee (0)	1	<0.01
Menominee (0)	0	<0.01
Mexican American Ind. (1,129)	1,377	0.70
Navajo (35)	59	0.03
Osage (2)	15	0.01
Ottawa (1)	2	<0.01
Paiute (7)	14	0.01
Pima (0)	4	<0.01
Potawatomi (0)	1	<0.01
Pueblo (21)	36	0.02
Puget Sound Salish (0)	0	<0.01
Seminole (3)	17	0.01
Shoshone (0)	1	<0.01
Sioux (23)	54	0.03
South American Ind. (8)	24	0.01
Spanish American Ind. (16)	32	0.02
Tlingit-Haida *(Alaska Native)* (0)	4	<0.01
Tohono O'Odham (9)	20	0.01
Tsimshian *(Alaska Native)* (0)	0	<0.01
Ute (2)	5	<0.01
Yakama (1)	1	<0.01
Yaqui (49)	91	0.05
Yuman (4)	4	<0.01
Yup'ik *(Alaska Native)* (2)	2	<0.01
Asian (14,550)	17,273	8.73
Not Hispanic (14,084)	15,805	7.99
Hispanic (466)	1,468	0.74
Bangladeshi (31)	33	0.02
Bhutanese (0)	0	<0.01
Burmese (6)	6	<0.01
Cambodian (81)	107	0.05
Chinese, ex. Taiwanese (605)	948	0.48
Filipino (10,166)	11,788	5.96
Hmong (8)	9	<0.01
Indian (586)	741	0.37
Indonesian (25)	47	0.02
Japanese (801)	1,411	0.71
Korean (465)	570	0.29
Laotian (92)	113	0.06
Malaysian (1)	21	0.01
Nepalese (13)	19	0.01
Pakistani (9)	12	0.01
Sri Lankan (20)	26	0.01
Taiwanese (47)	65	0.03
Thai (78)	129	0.07
Vietnamese (1,203)	1,343	0.68
Hawaii Native/Pacific Islander (658)	1,241	0.63
Not Hispanic (537)	867	0.44
Hispanic (121)	374	0.19
Fijian (4)	8	<0.01
Guamanian/Chamorro (172)	275	0.14
Marshallese (0)	0	<0.01
Native Hawaiian (87)	262	0.13
Samoan (327)	474	0.24
Tongan (7)	11	0.01
White (95,346)	102,814	51.95
Not Hispanic (29,410)	31,821	16.08
Hispanic (65,936)	70,993	35.87

*Notes: † The Census 2010 population figure is used to calculate the percentages in the Hispanic Origin and Race categories. Ancestry percentages are based on the 2006-2010 American Community Survey population (not shown); ‡ Numbers in parentheses indicate the number of people reporting a single ancestry; * Numbers in parentheses indicate the number of persons reporting this race alone, not in combination with any other race; Please refer to the Explanation of Data for more information.*

Palmdale

Place Type: City
County: Los Angeles
Population: 152,750

Ancestry	Population	%
Afghan (0)	0	<0.01
African, Sub-Saharan (2,709)	3,168	2.17
African (2,530)	2,924	2.00
Cape Verdean (0)	0	<0.01
Ethiopian (99)	99	0.07
Ghanaian (0)	0	<0.01
Kenyan (0)	0	<0.01
Liberian (0)	0	<0.01
Nigerian (50)	50	0.03
Senegalese (0)	0	<0.01
Sierra Leonean (0)	0	<0.01
Somalian (0)	0	<0.01
South African (30)	83	0.06
Sudanese (0)	0	<0.01
Ugandan (0)	0	<0.01
Zimbabwean (0)	0	<0.01
Other Sub-Saharan African (0)	12	0.01
Albanian (0)	0	<0.01
Alsatian (0)	0	<0.01
American (2,904)	2,904	1.99
Arab (615)	840	0.57
Arab (80)	137	0.09
Egyptian (277)	277	0.19
Iraqi (0)	0	<0.01
Jordanian (66)	66	0.05
Lebanese (64)	204	0.14
Moroccan (10)	28	0.02
Palestinian (0)	0	<0.01
Syrian (59)	69	0.05
Other Arab (59)	59	0.04
Armenian (456)	776	0.53
Assyrian/Chaldean/Syriac (26)	26	0.02
Australian (10)	57	0.04
Austrian (0)	29	0.02
Basque (0)	0	<0.01
Belgian (23)	129	0.09
Brazilian (0)	0	<0.01
British (289)	366	0.25
Bulgarian (0)	9	0.01
Cajun (0)	0	<0.01
Canadian (265)	441	0.30
Carpatho Rusyn (0)	0	<0.01
Celtic (0)	0	<0.01
Croatian (16)	90	0.06
Cypriot (0)	0	<0.01
Czech (55)	228	0.16
Czechoslovakian (26)	96	0.07
Danish (122)	436	0.30
Dutch (260)	1,408	0.96
Eastern European (61)	101	0.07
English (1,994)	6,570	4.49
Estonian (0)	0	<0.01
European (896)	1,113	0.76
Finnish (47)	140	0.10
French, ex. Basque (295)	1,925	1.32
French Canadian (278)	585	0.40
German (1,873)	8,673	5.93
German Russian (0)	21	0.01
Greek (119)	303	0.21
Guyanese (0)	0	<0.01
Hungarian (258)	526	0.36
Icelander (204)	204	0.14
Iranian (294)	321	0.22
Irish (1,648)	7,527	5.15
Israeli (12)	12	0.01
Italian (1,232)	4,553	3.11
Latvian (15)	15	0.01
Lithuanian (0)	0	<0.01
Luxemburger (0)	0	<0.01
Macedonian (63)	63	0.04
Maltese (0)	14	0.01
New Zealander (0)	0	<0.01
Northern European (0)	0	<0.01
Norwegian (433)	1,327	0.91
Pennsylvania German (12)	12	0.01
Polish (407)	1,434	0.98
Portuguese (83)	188	0.13
Romanian (11)	34	0.02
Russian (355)	882	0.60
Scandinavian (22)	22	0.02
Scotch-Irish (240)	1,169	0.80
Scottish (321)	1,567	1.07
Serbian (0)	9	0.01
Slavic (0)	0	<0.01
Slovak (0)	11	0.01
Slovene (0)	13	0.01
Soviet Union (0)	0	<0.01
Swedish (297)	1,308	0.89
Swiss (42)	107	0.07
Turkish (35)	35	0.02
Ukrainian (67)	141	0.10
Welsh (30)	558	0.38
West Indian, ex. Hispanic (176)	535	0.37
Bahamian (0)	0	<0.01
Barbadian (0)	0	<0.01
Belizean (89)	128	0.09
Bermudan (0)	0	<0.01
British West Indian (0)	0	<0.01
Dutch West Indian (0)	27	0.02
Haitian (0)	0	<0.01
Jamaican (67)	344	0.24
Trinidadian/Tobagonian (20)	20	0.01
U.S. Virgin Islander (0)	0	<0.01
West Indian (0)	16	0.01
Other West Indian (0)	0	<0.01
Yugoslavian (72)	224	0.15

Hispanic Origin	Population	%
Hispanic or Latino (of any race)	83,097	54.40
Central American, ex. Mexican	14,815	9.70
Costa Rican	176	0.12
Guatemalan	3,618	2.37
Honduran	656	0.43
Nicaraguan	650	0.43
Panamanian	124	0.08
Salvadoran	9,488	6.21
Other Central American	103	0.07
Cuban	705	0.46
Dominican Republic	48	0.03
Mexican	58,207	38.11
Puerto Rican	1,138	0.75
South American	1,951	1.28
Argentinean	307	0.20
Bolivian	58	0.04
Chilean	172	0.11
Colombian	385	0.25
Ecuadorian	385	0.25
Paraguayan	0	<0.01
Peruvian	573	0.38
Uruguayan	22	0.01
Venezuelan	31	0.02
Other South American	18	0.01
Other Hispanic or Latino	6,233	4.08

Race*	Population	%
African-American/Black (22,677)	25,272	16.54
Not Hispanic (21,595)	23,302	15.25
Hispanic (1,082)	1,970	1.29
American Indian/Alaska Native (1,316)	2,842	1.86
Not Hispanic (477)	1,403	0.92
Hispanic (839)	1,439	0.94
Alaska Athabascan *(Ala. Nat.)* (3)	5	<0.01
Aleut *(Alaska Native)* (0)	0	<0.01
Apache (52)	121	0.08
Arapaho (0)	1	<0.01
Blackfeet (13)	107	0.07
Canadian/French Am. Ind. (4)	7	<0.01
Central American Ind. (9)	18	0.01
Cherokee (90)	406	0.27
Cheyenne (10)	16	0.01
Chickasaw (13)	21	0.01
Chippewa (8)	23	0.02
Choctaw (26)	97	0.06
Colville (0)	0	<0.01
Comanche (2)	4	<0.01
Cree (1)	2	<0.01
Creek (9)	34	0.02
Crow (0)	4	<0.01
Delaware (4)	8	0.01
Hopi (11)	23	0.02
Houma (0)	0	<0.01
Inupiat *(Alaska Native)* (2)	5	<0.01
Iroquois (0)	17	0.01
Kiowa (0)	2	<0.01
Lumbee (2)	7	<0.01
Menominee (0)	0	<0.01
Mexican American Ind. (150)	212	0.14
Navajo (41)	78	0.05
Osage (2)	10	0.01
Ottawa (3)	5	<0.01
Paiute (10)	14	0.01
Pima (2)	4	<0.01
Potawatomi (0)	10	0.01
Pueblo (23)	33	0.02
Puget Sound Salish (0)	2	<0.01
Seminole (1)	11	0.01
Shoshone (1)	6	<0.01
Sioux (22)	49	0.03
South American Ind. (4)	11	0.01
Spanish American Ind. (10)	20	0.01
Tlingit-Haida *(Alaska Native)* (1)	1	<0.01
Tohono O'Odham (15)	19	0.01
Tsimshian *(Alaska Native)* (0)	0	<0.01
Ute (0)	0	<0.01
Yakama (0)	0	<0.01
Yaqui (38)	51	0.03
Yuman (2)	8	0.01
Yup'ik *(Alaska Native)* (0)	0	<0.01
Asian (6,548)	8,430	5.52
Not Hispanic (6,223)	7,479	4.90
Hispanic (325)	951	0.62
Bangladeshi (32)	38	0.02
Bhutanese (0)	0	<0.01
Burmese (22)	27	0.02
Cambodian (63)	72	0.05
Chinese, ex. Taiwanese (422)	689	0.45
Filipino (3,394)	4,273	2.80
Hmong (4)	6	<0.01
Indian (621)	779	0.51
Indonesian (48)	106	0.07
Japanese (265)	620	0.41
Korean (609)	776	0.51
Laotian (20)	31	0.02
Malaysian (7)	8	0.01
Nepalese (14)	14	0.01
Pakistani (126)	145	0.09
Sri Lankan (87)	88	0.06
Taiwanese (27)	31	0.02
Thai (130)	172	0.11
Vietnamese (414)	495	0.32
Hawaii Native/Pacific Islander (335)	763	0.50
Not Hispanic (211)	472	0.31
Hispanic (124)	291	0.19
Fijian (13)	14	0.01
Guamanian/Chamorro (97)	155	0.10
Marshallese (0)	0	<0.01
Native Hawaiian (85)	240	0.16
Samoan (38)	112	0.07
Tongan (29)	36	0.02
White (74,901)	81,397	53.29
Not Hispanic (37,390)	40,028	26.20
Hispanic (37,511)	41,369	27.08

*Notes: † The Census 2010 population figure is used to calculate the percentages in the Hispanic Origin and Race categories. Ancestry percentages are based on the 2006-2010 American Community Survey population (not shown); ‡ Numbers in parentheses indicate the number of people reporting a single ancestry; * Numbers in parentheses indicate the number of persons reporting this race alone, not in combination with any other race; Please refer to the Explanation of Data for more information.*

Palo Alto

Place Type: City
County: Santa Clara
Population: 64,403

Ancestry	Population	%
Afghan (65)	65	0.10
African, Sub-Saharan (408)	642	1.03
African (175)	175	0.28
Cape Verdean (0)	10	0.02
Ethiopian (220)	360	0.58
Ghanaian (0)	0	<0.01
Kenyan (0)	0	<0.01
Liberian (0)	0	<0.01
Nigerian (0)	0	<0.01
Senegalese (0)	0	<0.01
Sierra Leonean (0)	0	<0.01
Somalian (0)	0	<0.01
South African (13)	97	0.16
Sudanese (0)	0	<0.01
Ugandan (0)	0	<0.01
Zimbabwean (0)	0	<0.01
Other Sub-Saharan African (0)	0	<0.01
Albanian (0)	0	<0.01
Alsatian (0)	0	<0.01
American (1,058)	1,058	1.69
Arab (265)	680	1.09
Arab (9)	9	0.01
Egyptian (17)	108	0.17
Iraqi (15)	58	0.09
Jordanian (21)	21	0.03
Lebanese (5)	42	0.07
Moroccan (88)	181	0.29
Palestinian (10)	28	0.04
Syrian (22)	50	0.08
Other Arab (78)	183	0.29
Armenian (131)	200	0.32
Assyrian/Chaldean/Syriac (87)	126	0.20
Australian (21)	71	0.11
Austrian (153)	343	0.55
Basque (0)	0	<0.01
Belgian (97)	141	0.23
Brazilian (63)	73	0.12
British (538)	1,004	1.61
Bulgarian (24)	76	0.12
Cajun (0)	11	0.02
Canadian (262)	324	0.52
Carpatho Rusyn (0)	0	<0.01
Celtic (6)	13	0.02
Croatian (41)	144	0.23
Cypriot (0)	0	<0.01
Czech (359)	554	0.89
Czechoslovakian (20)	46	0.07
Danish (187)	546	0.87
Dutch (402)	934	1.49
Eastern European (431)	452	0.72
English (2,149)	7,653	12.25
Estonian (0)	0	<0.01
European (2,509)	2,712	4.34
Finnish (78)	130	0.21
French, ex. Basque (811)	2,308	3.69
French Canadian (95)	239	0.38
German (1,994)	7,260	11.62
German Russian (0)	0	<0.01
Greek (125)	375	0.60
Guyanese (16)	68	0.11
Hungarian (106)	452	0.72
Icelander (0)	11	0.02
Iranian (599)	720	1.15
Irish (988)	4,757	7.61
Israeli (356)	421	0.67
Italian (845)	2,273	3.64
Latvian (36)	49	0.08
Lithuanian (62)	185	0.30
Luxemburger (0)	30	0.05
Macedonian (27)	39	0.06
Maltese (0)	0	<0.01
New Zealander (78)	103	0.16
Northern European (369)	369	0.59
Norwegian (327)	1,072	1.72
Pennsylvania German (0)	19	0.03
Polish (492)	1,629	2.61
Portuguese (126)	364	0.58
Romanian (48)	159	0.25
Russian (1,390)	2,425	3.88
Scandinavian (88)	206	0.33
Scotch-Irish (256)	953	1.53
Scottish (391)	1,822	2.92
Serbian (29)	51	0.08
Slavic (0)	13	0.02
Slovak (16)	38	0.06
Slovene (0)	42	0.07
Soviet Union (0)	9	0.01
Swedish (411)	1,522	2.44
Swiss (187)	490	0.78
Turkish (92)	144	0.23
Ukrainian (341)	563	0.90
Welsh (47)	510	0.82
West Indian, ex. Hispanic (94)	146	0.23
Bahamian (0)	0	<0.01
Barbadian (0)	0	<0.01
Belizean (0)	0	<0.01
Bermudan (0)	0	<0.01
British West Indian (0)	0	<0.01
Dutch West Indian (0)	0	<0.01
Haitian (0)	0	<0.01
Jamaican (74)	126	0.20
Trinidadian/Tobagonian (0)	0	<0.01
U.S. Virgin Islander (0)	0	<0.01
West Indian (20)	20	0.03
Other West Indian (0)	0	<0.01
Yugoslavian (23)	54	0.09

Hispanic Origin	Population	%
Hispanic or Latino (of any race)	3,974	6.17
Central American, ex. Mexican	414	0.64
Costa Rican	25	0.04
Guatemalan	87	0.14
Honduran	30	0.05
Nicaraguan	51	0.08
Panamanian	17	0.03
Salvadoran	194	0.30
Other Central American	10	0.02
Cuban	82	0.13
Dominican Republic	18	0.03
Mexican	2,265	3.52
Puerto Rican	113	0.18
South American	588	0.91
Argentinean	111	0.17
Bolivian	37	0.06
Chilean	82	0.13
Colombian	94	0.15
Ecuadorian	37	0.06
Paraguayan	4	0.01
Peruvian	157	0.24
Uruguayan	19	0.03
Venezuelan	44	0.07
Other South American	3	<0.01
Other Hispanic or Latino	494	0.77

Race*	Population	%
African-American/Black (1,197)	1,559	2.42
Not Hispanic (1,131)	1,441	2.24
Hispanic (66)	118	0.18
American Indian/Alaska Native (121)	371	0.58
Not Hispanic (65)	269	0.42
Hispanic (56)	102	0.16
Alaska Athabascan *(Ala. Nat.)* (0)	5	0.01
Aleut *(Alaska Native)* (0)	6	0.01
Apache (5)	6	0.01
Arapaho (0)	0	<0.01
Blackfeet (2)	11	0.02
Canadian/French Am. Ind. (0)	1	<0.01
Central American Ind. (2)	7	0.01
Cherokee (7)	68	0.11
Cheyenne (0)	0	<0.01
Chickasaw (0)	5	0.01
Chippewa (0)	2	<0.01
Choctaw (4)	14	0.02
Colville (0)	0	<0.01
Comanche (1)	1	<0.01
Cree (1)	2	<0.01
Creek (4)	4	0.01
Crow (0)	0	<0.01
Delaware (0)	2	<0.01
Hopi (0)	0	<0.01
Houma (0)	0	<0.01
Inupiat *(Alaska Native)* (1)	2	<0.01
Iroquois (1)	4	0.01
Kiowa (0)	0	<0.01
Lumbee (0)	0	<0.01
Menominee (0)	0	<0.01
Mexican American Ind. (15)	26	0.04
Navajo (4)	11	0.02
Osage (0)	1	<0.01
Ottawa (0)	1	<0.01
Paiute (0)	4	0.01
Pima (0)	0	<0.01
Potawatomi (0)	6	0.01
Pueblo (0)	0	<0.01
Puget Sound Salish (0)	0	<0.01
Seminole (1)	1	<0.01
Shoshone (0)	0	<0.01
Sioux (2)	7	0.01
South American Ind. (2)	3	<0.01
Spanish American Ind. (1)	1	<0.01
Tlingit-Haida *(Alaska Native)* (5)	6	0.01
Tohono O'Odham (0)	1	<0.01
Tsimshian *(Alaska Native)* (0)	0	<0.01
Ute (1)	1	<0.01
Yakama (0)	0	<0.01
Yaqui (1)	2	<0.01
Yuman (1)	1	<0.01
Yup'ik *(Alaska Native)* (0)	1	<0.01
Asian (17,461)	19,492	30.27
Not Hispanic (17,404)	19,336	30.02
Hispanic (57)	156	0.24
Bangladeshi (10)	17	0.03
Bhutanese (0)	0	<0.01
Burmese (20)	26	0.04
Cambodian (18)	26	0.04
Chinese, ex. Taiwanese (8,695)	9,739	15.12
Filipino (581)	852	1.32
Hmong (0)	0	<0.01
Indian (2,776)	3,099	4.81
Indonesian (44)	58	0.09
Japanese (1,319)	1,831	2.84
Korean (1,791)	1,978	3.07
Laotian (8)	14	0.02
Malaysian (5)	29	0.05
Nepalese (18)	21	0.03
Pakistani (159)	200	0.31
Sri Lankan (32)	43	0.07
Taiwanese (946)	1,061	1.65
Thai (109)	135	0.21
Vietnamese (401)	514	0.80
Hawaii Native/Pacific Islander (142)	295	0.46
Not Hispanic (135)	272	0.42
Hispanic (7)	23	0.04
Fijian (13)	16	0.02
Guamanian/Chamorro (12)	25	0.04
Marshallese (0)	0	<0.01
Native Hawaiian (16)	80	0.12
Samoan (20)	27	0.04
Tongan (68)	85	0.13
White (41,359)	43,815	68.03
Not Hispanic (39,052)	41,247	64.05
Hispanic (2,307)	2,568	3.99

*Notes: † The Census 2010 population figure is used to calculate the percentages in the Hispanic Origin and Race categories. Ancestry percentages are based on the 2006-2010 American Community Survey population (not shown); ‡ Numbers in parentheses indicate the number of people reporting a single ancestry; * Numbers in parentheses indicate the number of persons reporting this race alone, not in combination with any other race; Please refer to the Explanation of Data for more information.*

Paramount

Place Type: City
County: Los Angeles
Population: 54,098

Ancestry	Population	%
Afghan (0)	0	<0.01
African, Sub-Saharan (363)	407	0.75
African (222)	266	0.49
Cape Verdean (0)	0	<0.01
Ethiopian (141)	141	0.26
Ghanaian (0)	0	<0.01
Kenyan (0)	0	<0.01
Liberian (0)	0	<0.01
Nigerian (0)	0	<0.01
Senegalese (0)	0	<0.01
Sierra Leonean (0)	0	<0.01
Somalian (0)	0	<0.01
South African (0)	0	<0.01
Sudanese (0)	0	<0.01
Ugandan (0)	0	<0.01
Zimbabwean (0)	0	<0.01
Other Sub-Saharan African (0)	0	<0.01
Albanian (0)	0	<0.01
Alsatian (0)	0	<0.01
American (672)	672	1.24
Arab (397)	431	0.80
Arab (0)	0	<0.01
Egyptian (364)	364	0.67
Iraqi (0)	0	<0.01
Jordanian (0)	0	<0.01
Lebanese (33)	46	0.08
Moroccan (0)	0	<0.01
Palestinian (0)	21	0.04
Syrian (0)	0	<0.01
Other Arab (0)	0	<0.01
Armenian (30)	30	0.06
Assyrian/Chaldean/Syriac (0)	0	<0.01
Australian (0)	26	0.05
Austrian (0)	0	<0.01
Basque (0)	0	<0.01
Belgian (0)	0	<0.01
Brazilian (0)	0	<0.01
British (10)	21	0.04
Bulgarian (0)	0	<0.01
Cajun (0)	0	<0.01
Canadian (0)	0	<0.01
Carpatho Rusyn (0)	0	<0.01
Celtic (0)	0	<0.01
Croatian (0)	0	<0.01
Cypriot (0)	0	<0.01
Czech (0)	47	0.09
Czechoslovakian (0)	0	<0.01
Danish (45)	84	0.16
Dutch (21)	129	0.24
Eastern European (0)	0	<0.01
English (87)	337	0.62
Estonian (0)	0	<0.01
European (29)	174	0.32
Finnish (0)	0	<0.01
French, ex. Basque (26)	281	0.52
French Canadian (10)	30	0.06
German (337)	1,101	2.03
German Russian (0)	13	0.02
Greek (0)	0	<0.01
Guyanese (0)	0	<0.01
Hungarian (44)	66	0.12
Icelander (0)	0	<0.01
Iranian (8)	8	0.01
Irish (208)	643	1.19
Israeli (53)	53	0.10
Italian (202)	596	1.10
Latvian (0)	0	<0.01
Lithuanian (0)	0	<0.01
Luxemburger (0)	0	<0.01
Macedonian (0)	0	<0.01
Maltese (0)	0	<0.01
New Zealander (0)	0	<0.01
Northern European (0)	0	<0.01
Norwegian (30)	67	0.12
Pennsylvania German (0)	0	<0.01
Polish (80)	190	0.35
Portuguese (20)	20	0.04
Romanian (0)	0	<0.01
Russian (0)	0	<0.01
Scandinavian (0)	0	<0.01
Scotch-Irish (10)	69	0.13
Scottish (11)	128	0.24
Serbian (0)	14	0.03
Slavic (0)	0	<0.01
Slovak (0)	0	<0.01
Slovene (0)	0	<0.01
Soviet Union (0)	0	<0.01
Swedish (10)	32	0.06
Swiss (0)	0	<0.01
Turkish (0)	0	<0.01
Ukrainian (0)	0	<0.01
Welsh (0)	86	0.16
West Indian, ex. Hispanic (167)	197	0.36
Bahamian (0)	0	<0.01
Barbadian (0)	0	<0.01
Belizean (58)	77	0.14
Bermudan (0)	0	<0.01
British West Indian (0)	0	<0.01
Dutch West Indian (0)	0	<0.01
Haitian (0)	0	<0.01
Jamaican (109)	109	0.20
Trinidadian/Tobagonian (0)	11	0.02
U.S. Virgin Islander (0)	0	<0.01
West Indian (0)	0	<0.01
Other West Indian (0)	0	<0.01
Yugoslavian (0)	9	0.02

Hispanic Origin	Population	%
Hispanic or Latino (of any race)	42,547	78.65
Central American, ex. Mexican	2,962	5.48
Costa Rican	32	0.06
Guatemalan	943	1.74
Honduran	206	0.38
Nicaraguan	249	0.46
Panamanian	38	0.07
Salvadoran	1,463	2.70
Other Central American	31	0.06
Cuban	133	0.25
Dominican Republic	29	0.05
Mexican	37,077	68.54
Puerto Rican	234	0.43
South American	426	0.79
Argentinean	24	0.04
Bolivian	10	0.02
Chilean	22	0.04
Colombian	90	0.17
Ecuadorian	95	0.18
Paraguayan	3	0.01
Peruvian	169	0.31
Uruguayan	6	0.01
Venezuelan	7	0.01
Other South American	0	<0.01
Other Hispanic or Latino	1,686	3.12

Race*	Population	%
African-American/Black (6,334)	6,748	12.47
Not Hispanic (5,980)	6,230	11.52
Hispanic (354)	518	0.96
American Indian/Alaska Native (440)	716	1.32
Not Hispanic (86)	211	0.39
Hispanic (354)	505	0.93
Alaska Athabascan *(Ala. Nat.)* (0)	0	<0.01
Aleut *(Alaska Native)* (0)	0	<0.01
Apache (10)	19	0.04
Arapaho (0)	0	<0.01
Blackfeet (0)	10	0.02
Canadian/French Am. Ind. (0)	0	<0.01
Central American Ind. (5)	13	0.02
Cherokee (7)	25	0.05
Cheyenne (0)	2	<0.01
Chickasaw (0)	2	<0.01
Chippewa (1)	8	0.01
Choctaw (0)	8	0.01
Colville (0)	0	<0.01
Comanche (3)	3	0.01
Cree (0)	0	<0.01
Creek (2)	3	0.01
Crow (0)	1	<0.01
Delaware (0)	0	<0.01
Hopi (0)	0	<0.01
Houma (0)	0	<0.01
Inupiat *(Alaska Native)* (0)	0	<0.01
Iroquois (2)	4	0.01
Kiowa (0)	0	<0.01
Lumbee (1)	1	<0.01
Menominee (0)	0	<0.01
Mexican American Ind. (90)	159	0.29
Navajo (13)	16	0.03
Osage (0)	0	<0.01
Ottawa (0)	0	<0.01
Paiute (2)	2	<0.01
Pima (0)	0	<0.01
Potawatomi (0)	0	<0.01
Pueblo (4)	6	0.01
Puget Sound Salish (0)	0	<0.01
Seminole (0)	3	0.01
Shoshone (0)	0	<0.01
Sioux (4)	7	0.01
South American Ind. (1)	7	0.01
Spanish American Ind. (5)	6	0.01
Tlingit-Haida *(Alaska Native)* (0)	0	<0.01
Tohono O'Odham (0)	1	<0.01
Tsimshian *(Alaska Native)* (0)	0	<0.01
Ute (0)	0	<0.01
Yakama (0)	0	<0.01
Yaqui (1)	7	0.01
Yuman (0)	3	0.01
Yup'ik *(Alaska Native)* (0)	0	<0.01
Asian (1,629)	1,999	3.70
Not Hispanic (1,531)	1,727	3.19
Hispanic (98)	272	0.50
Bangladeshi (9)	15	0.03
Bhutanese (0)	0	<0.01
Burmese (0)	0	<0.01
Cambodian (249)	275	0.51
Chinese, ex. Taiwanese (69)	123	0.23
Filipino (731)	859	1.59
Hmong (8)	8	0.01
Indian (113)	146	0.27
Indonesian (5)	10	0.02
Japanese (63)	114	0.21
Korean (100)	114	0.21
Laotian (20)	26	0.05
Malaysian (0)	0	<0.01
Nepalese (2)	3	0.01
Pakistani (28)	33	0.06
Sri Lankan (4)	4	0.01
Taiwanese (0)	3	0.01
Thai (88)	115	0.21
Vietnamese (54)	63	0.12
Hawaii Native/Pacific Islander (419)	574	1.06
Not Hispanic (396)	508	0.94
Hispanic (23)	66	0.12
Fijian (6)	7	0.01
Guamanian/Chamorro (38)	53	0.10
Marshallese (0)	0	<0.01
Native Hawaiian (14)	47	0.09
Samoan (318)	360	0.67
Tongan (15)	23	0.04
White (22,988)	24,788	45.82
Not Hispanic (3,015)	3,295	6.09
Hispanic (19,973)	21,493	39.73

*Notes: † The Census 2010 population figure is used to calculate the percentages in the Hispanic Origin and Race categories. Ancestry percentages are based on the 2006-2010 American Community Survey population (not shown); ‡ Numbers in parentheses indicate the number of people reporting a single ancestry; * Numbers in parentheses indicate the number of persons reporting this race alone, not in combination with any other race; Please refer to the Explanation of Data for more information.*

Pasadena

Place Type: City
County: Los Angeles
Population: 137,122

Ancestry	Population	%
Afghan (0)	0	<0.01
African, Sub-Saharan (757)	900	0.66
African (506)	616	0.45
Cape Verdean (0)	0	<0.01
Ethiopian (116)	116	0.09
Ghanaian (0)	0	<0.01
Kenyan (11)	11	0.01
Liberian (0)	0	<0.01
Nigerian (19)	37	0.03
Senegalese (0)	0	<0.01
Sierra Leonean (0)	0	<0.01
Somalian (0)	0	<0.01
South African (0)	15	0.01
Sudanese (0)	0	<0.01
Ugandan (0)	0	<0.01
Zimbabwean (105)	105	0.08
Other Sub-Saharan African (0)	0	<0.01
Albanian (0)	0	<0.01
Alsatian (0)	0	<0.01
American (1,965)	1,965	1.44
Arab (1,410)	2,003	1.47
Arab (170)	383	0.28
Egyptian (98)	98	0.07
Iraqi (0)	0	<0.01
Jordanian (325)	356	0.26
Lebanese (254)	467	0.34
Moroccan (0)	0	<0.01
Palestinian (73)	79	0.06
Syrian (333)	428	0.31
Other Arab (157)	192	0.14
Armenian (4,606)	5,017	3.68
Assyrian/Chaldean/Syriac (0)	0	<0.01
Australian (0)	43	0.03
Austrian (104)	383	0.28
Basque (0)	72	0.05
Belgian (36)	134	0.10
Brazilian (108)	176	0.13
British (365)	812	0.60
Bulgarian (116)	116	0.09
Cajun (6)	6	<0.01
Canadian (15)	134	0.10
Carpatho Rusyn (0)	0	<0.01
Celtic (21)	37	0.03
Croatian (40)	77	0.06
Cypriot (0)	0	<0.01
Czech (30)	217	0.16
Czechoslovakian (11)	45	0.03
Danish (187)	569	0.42
Dutch (454)	1,370	1.00
Eastern European (144)	168	0.12
English (2,727)	9,624	7.05
Estonian (0)	27	0.02
European (1,322)	1,616	1.18
Finnish (87)	280	0.21
French, ex. Basque (508)	3,027	2.22
French Canadian (84)	389	0.29
German (2,679)	9,864	7.23
German Russian (0)	0	<0.01
Greek (279)	709	0.52
Guyanese (36)	36	0.03
Hungarian (179)	558	0.41
Icelander (23)	31	0.02
Iranian (519)	573	0.42
Irish (2,776)	8,963	6.57
Israeli (25)	31	0.02
Italian (1,654)	5,139	3.77
Latvian (24)	24	0.02
Lithuanian (58)	192	0.14
Luxemburger (37)	37	0.03
Macedonian (0)	0	<0.01
Maltese (9)	29	0.02
New Zealander (15)	15	0.01
Northern European (229)	242	0.18
Norwegian (310)	1,113	0.82
Pennsylvania German (0)	0	<0.01
Polish (761)	2,127	1.56
Portuguese (13)	129	0.09
Romanian (434)	517	0.38
Russian (597)	1,461	1.07
Scandinavian (149)	307	0.22
Scotch-Irish (600)	1,644	1.20
Scottish (640)	2,177	1.60
Serbian (29)	62	0.05
Slavic (26)	49	0.04
Slovak (45)	90	0.07
Slovene (20)	101	0.07
Soviet Union (0)	0	<0.01
Swedish (339)	1,383	1.01
Swiss (70)	494	0.36
Turkish (10)	21	0.02
Ukrainian (103)	298	0.22
Welsh (104)	726	0.53
West Indian, ex. Hispanic (136)	159	0.12
Bahamian (0)	0	<0.01
Barbadian (14)	14	0.01
Belizean (23)	23	0.02
Bermudan (8)	8	0.01
British West Indian (0)	0	<0.01
Dutch West Indian (0)	6	<0.01
Haitian (16)	16	0.01
Jamaican (73)	90	0.07
Trinidadian/Tobagonian (0)	0	<0.01
U.S. Virgin Islander (0)	0	<0.01
West Indian (2)	2	<0.01
Other West Indian (0)	0	<0.01
Yugoslavian (85)	108	0.08

Hispanic Origin	Population	%
Hispanic or Latino (of any race)	46,174	33.67
Central American, ex. Mexican	5,724	4.17
Costa Rican	178	0.13
Guatemalan	1,367	1.00
Honduran	897	0.65
Nicaraguan	357	0.26
Panamanian	170	0.12
Salvadoran	2,689	1.96
Other Central American	66	0.05
Cuban	627	0.46
Dominican Republic	48	0.04
Mexican	34,168	24.92
Puerto Rican	624	0.46
South American	2,283	1.66
Argentinean	404	0.29
Bolivian	101	0.07
Chilean	171	0.12
Colombian	540	0.39
Ecuadorian	334	0.24
Paraguayan	4	<0.01
Peruvian	584	0.43
Uruguayan	15	0.01
Venezuelan	100	0.07
Other South American	30	0.02
Other Hispanic or Latino	2,700	1.97

Race*	Population	%
African-American/Black (14,650)	16,498	12.03
Not Hispanic (13,912)	15,192	11.08
Hispanic (738)	1,306	0.95
American Indian/Alaska Native (827)	2,033	1.48
Not Hispanic (211)	874	0.64
Hispanic (616)	1,159	0.85
Alaska Athabascan *(Ala. Nat.)* (0)	0	<0.01
Aleut *(Alaska Native)* (2)	2	<0.01
Apache (24)	62	0.05
Arapaho (4)	9	0.01
Blackfeet (6)	45	0.03
Canadian/French Am. Ind. (4)	6	<0.01
Central American Ind. (8)	20	0.01
Cherokee (18)	219	0.16
Cheyenne (1)	1	<0.01
Chickasaw (1)	15	0.01
Chippewa (3)	16	0.01
Choctaw (5)	32	0.02
Colville (2)	2	<0.01
Comanche (2)	8	0.01
Cree (1)	8	0.01
Creek (2)	13	0.01
Crow (0)	1	<0.01
Delaware (0)	1	<0.01
Hopi (5)	11	0.01
Houma (0)	1	<0.01
Inupiat *(Alaska Native)* (0)	1	<0.01
Iroquois (3)	13	0.01
Kiowa (0)	0	<0.01
Lumbee (0)	1	<0.01
Menominee (0)	3	<0.01
Mexican American Ind. (135)	249	0.18
Navajo (18)	36	0.03
Osage (0)	7	0.01
Ottawa (4)	4	<0.01
Paiute (3)	8	0.01
Pima (8)	17	0.01
Potawatomi (2)	5	<0.01
Pueblo (3)	11	0.01
Puget Sound Salish (0)	3	<0.01
Seminole (0)	12	0.01
Shoshone (3)	5	<0.01
Sioux (15)	30	0.02
South American Ind. (6)	23	0.02
Spanish American Ind. (11)	26	0.02
Tlingit-Haida *(Alaska Native)* (0)	4	<0.01
Tohono O'Odham (2)	2	<0.01
Tsimshian *(Alaska Native)* (0)	0	<0.01
Ute (1)	3	<0.01
Yakama (0)	0	<0.01
Yaqui (9)	26	0.02
Yuman (5)	8	0.01
Yup'ik *(Alaska Native)* (0)	0	<0.01
Asian (19,595)	22,513	16.42
Not Hispanic (19,293)	21,709	15.83
Hispanic (302)	804	0.59
Bangladeshi (28)	30	0.02
Bhutanese (0)	0	<0.01
Burmese (42)	58	0.04
Cambodian (36)	63	0.05
Chinese, ex. Taiwanese (6,168)	7,316	5.34
Filipino (3,692)	4,632	3.38
Hmong (1)	2	<0.01
Indian (1,742)	2,008	1.46
Indonesian (230)	325	0.24
Japanese (2,013)	2,808	2.05
Korean (2,709)	3,017	2.20
Laotian (10)	18	0.01
Malaysian (15)	34	0.02
Nepalese (17)	20	0.01
Pakistani (143)	165	0.12
Sri Lankan (169)	182	0.13
Taiwanese (777)	887	0.65
Thai (261)	347	0.25
Vietnamese (632)	812	0.59
Hawaii Native/Pacific Islander (134)	476	0.35
Not Hispanic (106)	387	0.28
Hispanic (28)	89	0.06
Fijian (2)	4	<0.01
Guamanian/Chamorro (21)	47	0.03
Marshallese (0)	0	<0.01
Native Hawaiian (50)	180	0.13
Samoan (13)	21	0.02
Tongan (1)	3	<0.01
White (76,550)	81,968	59.78
Not Hispanic (53,135)	56,332	41.08
Hispanic (23,415)	25,636	18.70

*Notes: † The Census 2010 population figure is used to calculate the percentages in the Hispanic Origin and Race categories. Ancestry percentages are based on the 2006-2010 American Community Survey population (not shown); ‡ Numbers in parentheses indicate the number of people reporting a single ancestry; * Numbers in parentheses indicate the number of persons reporting this race alone, not in combination with any other race; Please refer to the Explanation of Data for more information.*

Perris

Place Type: City
County: Riverside
Population: 68,386

Ancestry	Population	%
Afghan (0)	0	<0.01
African, Sub-Saharan (386)	386	0.61
African (343)	343	0.54
Cape Verdean (0)	0	<0.01
Ethiopian (0)	0	<0.01
Ghanaian (0)	0	<0.01
Kenyan (0)	0	<0.01
Liberian (0)	0	<0.01
Nigerian (43)	43	0.07
Senegalese (0)	0	<0.01
Sierra Leonean (0)	0	<0.01
Somalian (0)	0	<0.01
South African (0)	0	<0.01
Sudanese (0)	0	<0.01
Ugandan (0)	0	<0.01
Zimbabwean (0)	0	<0.01
Other Sub-Saharan African (0)	0	<0.01
Albanian (0)	0	<0.01
Alsatian (0)	0	<0.01
American (653)	653	1.03
Arab (209)	284	0.45
Arab (12)	12	0.02
Egyptian (115)	115	0.18
Iraqi (41)	41	0.06
Jordanian (0)	0	<0.01
Lebanese (0)	0	<0.01
Moroccan (0)	0	<0.01
Palestinian (0)	0	<0.01
Syrian (18)	93	0.15
Other Arab (23)	23	0.04
Armenian (0)	0	<0.01
Assyrian/Chaldean/Syriac (0)	0	<0.01
Australian (0)	0	<0.01
Austrian (0)	12	0.02
Basque (0)	29	0.05
Belgian (0)	63	0.10
Brazilian (59)	59	0.09
British (18)	42	0.07
Bulgarian (0)	0	<0.01
Cajun (0)	0	<0.01
Canadian (28)	132	0.21
Carpatho Rusyn (0)	0	<0.01
Celtic (0)	0	<0.01
Croatian (13)	33	0.05
Cypriot (0)	0	<0.01
Czech (11)	45	0.07
Czechoslovakian (0)	0	<0.01
Danish (16)	36	0.06
Dutch (32)	210	0.33
Eastern European (47)	47	0.07
English (329)	1,015	1.59
Estonian (0)	0	<0.01
European (302)	445	0.70
Finnish (0)	16	0.03
French, ex. Basque (12)	311	0.49
French Canadian (21)	134	0.21
German (786)	2,855	4.49
German Russian (0)	0	<0.01
Greek (0)	13	0.02
Guyanese (0)	0	<0.01
Hungarian (28)	44	0.07
Icelander (0)	0	<0.01
Iranian (21)	101	0.16
Irish (393)	1,637	2.57
Israeli (0)	0	<0.01
Italian (161)	711	1.12
Latvian (0)	0	<0.01
Lithuanian (11)	22	0.03
Luxemburger (0)	0	<0.01
Macedonian (0)	0	<0.01
Maltese (0)	0	<0.01
New Zealander (0)	0	<0.01
Northern European (0)	0	<0.01
Norwegian (64)	377	0.59
Pennsylvania German (0)	16	0.03
Polish (187)	394	0.62
Portuguese (14)	103	0.16
Romanian (13)	27	0.04
Russian (80)	215	0.34
Scandinavian (0)	14	0.02
Scotch-Irish (38)	433	0.68
Scottish (19)	241	0.38
Serbian (0)	10	0.02
Slavic (0)	8	0.01
Slovak (0)	0	<0.01
Slovene (0)	0	<0.01
Soviet Union (0)	0	<0.01
Swedish (7)	28	0.04
Swiss (0)	0	<0.01
Turkish (0)	36	0.06
Ukrainian (0)	14	0.02
Welsh (11)	64	0.10
West Indian, ex. Hispanic (241)	255	0.40
Bahamian (0)	0	<0.01
Barbadian (0)	0	<0.01
Belizean (80)	80	0.13
Bermudan (0)	0	<0.01
British West Indian (0)	0	<0.01
Dutch West Indian (0)	14	0.02
Haitian (0)	0	<0.01
Jamaican (67)	67	0.11
Trinidadian/Tobagonian (74)	74	0.12
U.S. Virgin Islander (0)	0	<0.01
West Indian (20)	20	0.03
Other West Indian (0)	0	<0.01
Yugoslavian (0)	9	0.01

Hispanic Origin	Population	%
Hispanic or Latino (of any race)	49,079	71.77
Central American, ex. Mexican	2,089	3.05
Costa Rican	36	0.05
Guatemalan	704	1.03
Honduran	102	0.15
Nicaraguan	195	0.29
Panamanian	40	0.06
Salvadoran	997	1.46
Other Central American	15	0.02
Cuban	211	0.31
Dominican Republic	18	0.03
Mexican	43,641	63.82
Puerto Rican	410	0.60
South American	403	0.59
Argentinean	43	0.06
Bolivian	28	0.04
Chilean	13	0.02
Colombian	98	0.14
Ecuadorian	76	0.11
Paraguayan	0	<0.01
Peruvian	119	0.17
Uruguayan	0	<0.01
Venezuelan	21	0.03
Other South American	5	0.01
Other Hispanic or Latino	2,307	3.37

Race*	Population	%
African-American/Black (8,307)	9,393	13.74
Not Hispanic (7,763)	8,471	12.39
Hispanic (544)	922	1.35
American Indian/Alaska Native (589)	1,070	1.56
Not Hispanic (154)	387	0.57
Hispanic (435)	683	1.00
Alaska Athabascan *(Ala. Nat.)* (0)	0	<0.01
Aleut *(Alaska Native)* (0)	0	<0.01
Apache (9)	36	0.05
Arapaho (0)	0	<0.01
Blackfeet (0)	26	0.04
Canadian/French Am. Ind. (0)	9	0.01
Central American Ind. (6)	6	0.01
Cherokee (19)	103	0.15
Cheyenne (0)	0	<0.01
Chickasaw (1)	5	0.01
Chippewa (2)	3	<0.01
Choctaw (9)	28	0.04
Colville (0)	0	<0.01
Comanche (0)	0	<0.01
Cree (0)	0	<0.01
Creek (0)	2	<0.01
Crow (0)	1	<0.01
Delaware (0)	1	<0.01
Hopi (3)	3	<0.01
Houma (0)	0	<0.01
Inupiat *(Alaska Native)* (1)	1	<0.01
Iroquois (0)	6	0.01
Kiowa (0)	0	<0.01
Lumbee (0)	0	<0.01
Menominee (0)	0	<0.01
Mexican American Ind. (102)	141	0.21
Navajo (21)	35	0.05
Osage (0)	1	<0.01
Ottawa (0)	4	0.01
Paiute (4)	8	0.01
Pima (1)	4	0.01
Potawatomi (0)	1	<0.01
Pueblo (11)	11	0.02
Puget Sound Salish (2)	2	<0.01
Seminole (0)	0	<0.01
Shoshone (6)	6	0.01
Sioux (8)	10	0.01
South American Ind. (1)	3	<0.01
Spanish American Ind. (3)	14	0.02
Tlingit-Haida *(Alaska Native)* (0)	1	<0.01
Tohono O'Odham (0)	1	<0.01
Tsimshian *(Alaska Native)* (0)	0	<0.01
Ute (0)	4	0.01
Yakama (0)	0	<0.01
Yaqui (6)	6	0.01
Yuman (0)	3	<0.01
Yup'ik *(Alaska Native)* (0)	0	<0.01
Asian (2,461)	3,166	4.63
Not Hispanic (2,285)	2,747	4.02
Hispanic (176)	419	0.61
Bangladeshi (27)	38	0.06
Bhutanese (0)	0	<0.01
Burmese (0)	0	<0.01
Cambodian (80)	100	0.15
Chinese, ex. Taiwanese (159)	280	0.41
Filipino (1,172)	1,512	2.21
Hmong (7)	8	0.01
Indian (193)	272	0.40
Indonesian (13)	28	0.04
Japanese (54)	145	0.21
Korean (49)	99	0.14
Laotian (60)	98	0.14
Malaysian (0)	0	<0.01
Nepalese (3)	3	<0.01
Pakistani (64)	77	0.11
Sri Lankan (5)	5	0.01
Taiwanese (19)	20	0.03
Thai (46)	73	0.11
Vietnamese (354)	397	0.58
Hawaii Native/Pacific Islander (286)	504	0.74
Not Hispanic (259)	409	0.60
Hispanic (27)	95	0.14
Fijian (32)	33	0.05
Guamanian/Chamorro (28)	61	0.09
Marshallese (0)	0	<0.01
Native Hawaiian (23)	77	0.11
Samoan (140)	192	0.28
Tongan (33)	40	0.06
White (28,937)	31,662	46.30
Not Hispanic (7,499)	8,387	12.26
Hispanic (21,438)	23,275	34.03

*Notes: † The Census 2010 population figure is used to calculate the percentages in the Hispanic Origin and Race categories. Ancestry percentages are based on the 2006-2010 American Community Survey population (not shown); ‡ Numbers in parentheses indicate the number of people reporting a single ancestry; * Numbers in parentheses indicate the number of persons reporting this race alone, not in combination with any other race; Please refer to the Explanation of Data for more information.*

Petaluma

Place Type: City
County: Sonoma
Population: 57,941

Ancestry	Population	%
Afghan (16)	16	0.03
African, Sub-Saharan (27)	27	0.05
African (27)	27	0.05
Cape Verdean (0)	0	<0.01
Ethiopian (0)	0	<0.01
Ghanaian (0)	0	<0.01
Kenyan (0)	0	<0.01
Liberian (0)	0	<0.01
Nigerian (0)	0	<0.01
Senegalese (0)	0	<0.01
Sierra Leonean (0)	0	<0.01
Somalian (0)	0	<0.01
South African (0)	0	<0.01
Sudanese (0)	0	<0.01
Ugandan (0)	0	<0.01
Zimbabwean (0)	0	<0.01
Other Sub-Saharan African (0)	0	<0.01
Albanian (0)	10	0.02
Alsatian (11)	11	0.02
American (1,354)	1,354	2.39
Arab (162)	245	0.43
Arab (17)	17	0.03
Egyptian (0)	0	<0.01
Iraqi (0)	0	<0.01
Jordanian (0)	11	0.02
Lebanese (9)	58	0.10
Moroccan (0)	0	<0.01
Palestinian (98)	109	0.19
Syrian (0)	0	<0.01
Other Arab (38)	50	0.09
Armenian (58)	113	0.20
Assyrian/Chaldean/Syriac (31)	31	0.05
Australian (0)	54	0.10
Austrian (20)	137	0.24
Basque (0)	6	0.01
Belgian (23)	99	0.17
Brazilian (0)	0	<0.01
British (358)	492	0.87
Bulgarian (0)	0	<0.01
Cajun (0)	0	<0.01
Canadian (95)	165	0.29
Carpatho Rusyn (0)	0	<0.01
Celtic (16)	25	0.04
Croatian (46)	112	0.20
Cypriot (0)	0	<0.01
Czech (34)	195	0.34
Czechoslovakian (10)	79	0.14
Danish (199)	845	1.49
Dutch (115)	913	1.61
Eastern European (188)	198	0.35
English (1,377)	6,894	12.16
Estonian (8)	20	0.04
European (1,247)	1,396	2.46
Finnish (0)	107	0.19
French, ex. Basque (271)	2,369	4.18
French Canadian (69)	283	0.50
German (2,634)	9,221	16.27
German Russian (0)	0	<0.01
Greek (138)	383	0.68
Guyanese (0)	0	<0.01
Hungarian (93)	375	0.66
Icelander (0)	0	<0.01
Iranian (174)	213	0.38
Irish (1,995)	9,046	15.96
Israeli (84)	93	0.16
Italian (1,718)	5,480	9.67
Latvian (14)	28	0.05
Lithuanian (45)	131	0.23
Luxemburger (0)	0	<0.01
Macedonian (0)	0	<0.01
Maltese (65)	99	0.17
New Zealander (0)	0	<0.01
Northern European (102)	155	0.27
Norwegian (234)	1,109	1.96
Pennsylvania German (0)	13	0.02
Polish (278)	872	1.54
Portuguese (538)	1,755	3.10
Romanian (18)	138	0.24
Russian (540)	1,179	2.08
Scandinavian (82)	190	0.34
Scotch-Irish (715)	1,773	3.13
Scottish (363)	1,355	2.39
Serbian (0)	41	0.07
Slavic (0)	0	<0.01
Slovak (0)	17	0.03
Slovene (15)	22	0.04
Soviet Union (0)	0	<0.01
Swedish (265)	1,230	2.17
Swiss (103)	697	1.23
Turkish (79)	114	0.20
Ukrainian (0)	9	0.02
Welsh (105)	636	1.12
West Indian, ex. Hispanic (229)	229	0.40
Bahamian (0)	0	<0.01
Barbadian (0)	0	<0.01
Belizean (0)	0	<0.01
Bermudan (0)	0	<0.01
British West Indian (0)	0	<0.01
Dutch West Indian (0)	0	<0.01
Haitian (229)	229	0.40
Jamaican (0)	0	<0.01
Trinidadian/Tobagonian (0)	0	<0.01
U.S. Virgin Islander (0)	0	<0.01
West Indian (0)	0	<0.01
Other West Indian (0)	0	<0.01
Yugoslavian (21)	81	0.14

Hispanic Origin	Population	%
Hispanic or Latino (of any race)	12,453	21.49
Central American, ex. Mexican	1,342	2.32
Costa Rican	25	0.04
Guatemalan	375	0.65
Honduran	46	0.08
Nicaraguan	178	0.31
Panamanian	16	0.03
Salvadoran	688	1.19
Other Central American	14	0.02
Cuban	40	0.07
Dominican Republic	8	0.01
Mexican	9,378	16.19
Puerto Rican	164	0.28
South American	472	0.81
Argentinean	31	0.05
Bolivian	4	0.01
Chilean	43	0.07
Colombian	135	0.23
Ecuadorian	30	0.05
Paraguayan	4	0.01
Peruvian	200	0.35
Uruguayan	6	0.01
Venezuelan	11	0.02
Other South American	8	0.01
Other Hispanic or Latino	1,049	1.81

Race*	Population	%
African-American/Black (801)	1,167	2.01
Not Hispanic (719)	1,028	1.77
Hispanic (82)	139	0.24
American Indian/Alaska Native (353)	924	1.59
Not Hispanic (198)	602	1.04
Hispanic (155)	322	0.56
Alaska Athabascan *(Ala. Nat.)* (1)	2	<0.01
Aleut *(Alaska Native)* (0)	4	0.01
Apache (10)	40	0.07
Arapaho (0)	0	<0.01
Blackfeet (3)	21	0.04
Canadian/French Am. Ind. (0)	0	<0.01
Central American Ind. (5)	6	0.01
Cherokee (34)	144	0.25
Cheyenne (2)	3	0.01
Chickasaw (1)	8	0.01
Chippewa (7)	23	0.04
Choctaw (17)	55	0.09
Colville (0)	0	<0.01
Comanche (2)	2	<0.01
Cree (0)	1	<0.01
Creek (2)	4	0.01
Crow (0)	1	<0.01
Delaware (0)	4	0.01
Hopi (0)	1	<0.01
Houma (0)	2	<0.01
Inupiat *(Alaska Native)* (0)	2	<0.01
Iroquois (1)	8	0.01
Kiowa (0)	0	<0.01
Lumbee (6)	6	0.01
Menominee (0)	0	<0.01
Mexican American Ind. (49)	64	0.11
Navajo (4)	17	0.03
Osage (2)	7	0.01
Ottawa (0)	0	<0.01
Paiute (1)	6	0.01
Pima (1)	1	<0.01
Potawatomi (3)	6	0.01
Pueblo (2)	2	<0.01
Puget Sound Salish (0)	5	0.01
Seminole (1)	3	0.01
Shoshone (0)	2	<0.01
Sioux (3)	18	0.03
South American Ind. (3)	4	0.01
Spanish American Ind. (2)	3	0.01
Tlingit-Haida *(Alaska Native)* (1)	1	<0.01
Tohono O'Odham (0)	0	<0.01
Tsimshian *(Alaska Native)* (0)	0	<0.01
Ute (0)	2	<0.01
Yakama (0)	1	<0.01
Yaqui (4)	9	0.02
Yuman (0)	0	<0.01
Yup'ik *(Alaska Native)* (0)	0	<0.01
Asian (2,607)	3,571	6.16
Not Hispanic (2,550)	3,382	5.84
Hispanic (57)	189	0.33
Bangladeshi (7)	7	0.01
Bhutanese (0)	0	<0.01
Burmese (9)	13	0.02
Cambodian (23)	27	0.05
Chinese, ex. Taiwanese (727)	979	1.69
Filipino (546)	881	1.52
Hmong (18)	21	0.04
Indian (444)	492	0.85
Indonesian (22)	32	0.06
Japanese (211)	473	0.82
Korean (127)	193	0.33
Laotian (62)	68	0.12
Malaysian (0)	3	0.01
Nepalese (6)	6	0.01
Pakistani (66)	73	0.13
Sri Lankan (7)	13	0.02
Taiwanese (35)	42	0.07
Thai (42)	67	0.12
Vietnamese (152)	188	0.32
Hawaii Native/Pacific Islander (129)	362	0.62
Not Hispanic (119)	299	0.52
Hispanic (10)	63	0.11
Fijian (34)	46	0.08
Guamanian/Chamorro (21)	49	0.08
Marshallese (1)	1	<0.01
Native Hawaiian (29)	181	0.31
Samoan (15)	31	0.05
Tongan (3)	17	0.03
White (46,566)	48,767	84.17
Not Hispanic (40,226)	41,698	71.97
Hispanic (6,340)	7,069	12.20

*Notes: † The Census 2010 population figure is used to calculate the percentages in the Hispanic Origin and Race categories. Ancestry percentages are based on the 2006-2010 American Community Survey population (not shown); ‡ Numbers in parentheses indicate the number of people reporting a single ancestry; * Numbers in parentheses indicate the number of persons reporting this race alone, not in combination with any other race; Please refer to the Explanation of Data for more information.*

Pico Rivera

Place Type: City
County: Los Angeles
Population: 62,942

Ancestry	Population	%
Afghan (0)	0	<0.01
African, Sub-Saharan (79)	122	0.19
African (79)	122	0.19
Cape Verdean (0)	0	<0.01
Ethiopian (0)	0	<0.01
Ghanaian (0)	0	<0.01
Kenyan (0)	0	<0.01
Liberian (0)	0	<0.01
Nigerian (0)	0	<0.01
Senegalese (0)	0	<0.01
Sierra Leonean (0)	0	<0.01
Somalian (0)	0	<0.01
South African (0)	0	<0.01
Sudanese (0)	0	<0.01
Ugandan (0)	0	<0.01
Zimbabwean (0)	0	<0.01
Other Sub-Saharan African (0)	0	<0.01
Albanian (0)	0	<0.01
Alsatian (0)	0	<0.01
American (459)	459	0.73
Arab (82)	82	0.13
Arab (0)	0	<0.01
Egyptian (82)	82	0.13
Iraqi (0)	0	<0.01
Jordanian (0)	0	<0.01
Lebanese (0)	0	<0.01
Moroccan (0)	0	<0.01
Palestinian (0)	0	<0.01
Syrian (0)	0	<0.01
Other Arab (0)	0	<0.01
Armenian (227)	272	0.43
Assyrian/Chaldean/Syriac (0)	0	<0.01
Australian (0)	0	<0.01
Austrian (9)	60	0.10
Basque (0)	25	0.04
Belgian (0)	0	<0.01
Brazilian (0)	0	<0.01
British (36)	58	0.09
Bulgarian (0)	0	<0.01
Cajun (0)	0	<0.01
Canadian (40)	45	0.07
Carpatho Rusyn (0)	0	<0.01
Celtic (9)	9	0.01
Croatian (11)	11	0.02
Cypriot (0)	0	<0.01
Czech (0)	0	<0.01
Czechoslovakian (0)	12	0.02
Danish (0)	12	0.02
Dutch (40)	87	0.14
Eastern European (0)	0	<0.01
English (222)	638	1.01
Estonian (0)	0	<0.01
European (0)	0	<0.01
Finnish (0)	0	<0.01
French, ex. Basque (64)	270	0.43
French Canadian (11)	24	0.04
German (124)	698	1.11
German Russian (0)	0	<0.01
Greek (14)	22	0.03
Guyanese (0)	0	<0.01
Hungarian (12)	25	0.04
Icelander (0)	0	<0.01
Iranian (9)	9	0.01
Irish (140)	579	0.92
Israeli (0)	0	<0.01
Italian (156)	521	0.83
Latvian (0)	0	<0.01
Lithuanian (0)	0	<0.01
Luxemburger (0)	0	<0.01
Macedonian (0)	0	<0.01
Maltese (0)	0	<0.01
New Zealander (0)	0	<0.01
Northern European (0)	0	<0.01
Norwegian (0)	64	0.10
Pennsylvania German (0)	9	0.01
Polish (0)	24	0.04
Portuguese (26)	152	0.24
Romanian (0)	0	<0.01
Russian (40)	50	0.08
Scandinavian (0)	21	0.03
Scotch-Irish (0)	102	0.16
Scottish (29)	100	0.16
Serbian (0)	19	0.03
Slavic (0)	0	<0.01
Slovak (0)	27	0.04
Slovene (0)	0	<0.01
Soviet Union (0)	0	<0.01
Swedish (26)	136	0.22
Swiss (0)	12	0.02
Turkish (0)	0	<0.01
Ukrainian (28)	47	0.07
Welsh (14)	33	0.05
West Indian, ex. Hispanic (0)	11	0.02
Bahamian (0)	0	<0.01
Barbadian (0)	0	<0.01
Belizean (0)	11	0.02
Bermudan (0)	0	<0.01
British West Indian (0)	0	<0.01
Dutch West Indian (0)	0	<0.01
Haitian (0)	0	<0.01
Jamaican (0)	0	<0.01
Trinidadian/Tobagonian (0)	0	<0.01
U.S. Virgin Islander (0)	0	<0.01
West Indian (0)	0	<0.01
Other West Indian (0)	0	<0.01
Yugoslavian (0)	0	<0.01

Hispanic Origin	Population	%
Hispanic or Latino (of any race)	57,400	91.20
Central American, ex. Mexican	3,059	4.86
Costa Rican	66	0.10
Guatemalan	761	1.21
Honduran	154	0.24
Nicaraguan	281	0.45
Panamanian	14	0.02
Salvadoran	1,733	2.75
Other Central American	50	0.08
Cuban	166	0.26
Dominican Republic	13	0.02
Mexican	51,337	81.56
Puerto Rican	268	0.43
South American	530	0.84
Argentinean	65	0.10
Bolivian	12	0.02
Chilean	12	0.02
Colombian	154	0.24
Ecuadorian	114	0.18
Paraguayan	0	<0.01
Peruvian	155	0.25
Uruguayan	7	0.01
Venezuelan	7	0.01
Other South American	4	0.01
Other Hispanic or Latino	2,027	3.22

Race*	Population	%
African-American/Black (602)	834	1.33
Not Hispanic (366)	424	0.67
Hispanic (236)	410	0.65
American Indian/Alaska Native (871)	1,207	1.92
Not Hispanic (114)	170	0.27
Hispanic (757)	1,037	1.65
Alaska Athabascan *(Ala. Nat.)* (2)	2	<0.01
Aleut *(Alaska Native)* (0)	0	<0.01
Apache (55)	90	0.14
Arapaho (2)	2	<0.01
Blackfeet (0)	1	<0.01
Canadian/French Am. Ind. (2)	2	<0.01
Central American Ind. (0)	0	<0.01
Cherokee (13)	43	0.07
Cheyenne (1)	2	<0.01
Chickasaw (0)	7	0.01
Chippewa (2)	6	0.01
Choctaw (7)	12	0.02
Colville (0)	0	<0.01
Comanche (7)	7	0.01
Cree (0)	0	<0.01
Creek (0)	1	<0.01
Crow (1)	5	0.01
Delaware (0)	0	<0.01
Hopi (1)	3	<0.01
Houma (0)	0	<0.01
Inupiat *(Alaska Native)* (0)	0	<0.01
Iroquois (0)	0	<0.01
Kiowa (4)	9	0.01
Lumbee (0)	0	<0.01
Menominee (0)	0	<0.01
Mexican American Ind. (152)	189	0.30
Navajo (20)	35	0.06
Osage (0)	0	<0.01
Ottawa (0)	0	<0.01
Paiute (2)	9	0.01
Pima (7)	9	0.01
Potawatomi (0)	0	<0.01
Pueblo (1)	1	<0.01
Puget Sound Salish (0)	0	<0.01
Seminole (0)	5	0.01
Shoshone (2)	2	<0.01
Sioux (13)	16	0.03
South American Ind. (0)	4	0.01
Spanish American Ind. (5)	15	0.02
Tlingit-Haida *(Alaska Native)* (0)	3	<0.01
Tohono O'Odham (2)	3	<0.01
Tsimshian *(Alaska Native)* (0)	0	<0.01
Ute (1)	4	0.01
Yakama (0)	0	<0.01
Yaqui (33)	56	0.09
Yuman (1)	2	<0.01
Yup'ik *(Alaska Native)* (0)	0	<0.01
Asian (1,614)	1,921	3.05
Not Hispanic (1,463)	1,579	2.51
Hispanic (151)	342	0.54
Bangladeshi (3)	3	<0.01
Bhutanese (0)	0	<0.01
Burmese (11)	11	0.02
Cambodian (67)	80	0.13
Chinese, ex. Taiwanese (218)	255	0.41
Filipino (772)	900	1.43
Hmong (0)	1	<0.01
Indian (69)	99	0.16
Indonesian (1)	6	0.01
Japanese (134)	223	0.35
Korean (64)	84	0.13
Laotian (0)	3	<0.01
Malaysian (2)	2	<0.01
Nepalese (3)	3	<0.01
Pakistani (3)	6	0.01
Sri Lankan (1)	2	<0.01
Taiwanese (25)	27	0.04
Thai (48)	50	0.08
Vietnamese (144)	166	0.26
Hawaii Native/Pacific Islander (42)	160	0.25
Not Hispanic (15)	65	0.10
Hispanic (27)	95	0.15
Fijian (1)	1	<0.01
Guamanian/Chamorro (13)	18	0.03
Marshallese (0)	0	<0.01
Native Hawaiian (15)	61	0.10
Samoan (5)	21	0.03
Tongan (1)	4	0.01
White (37,411)	39,388	62.58
Not Hispanic (3,281)	3,467	5.51
Hispanic (34,130)	35,921	57.07

*Notes: † The Census 2010 population figure is used to calculate the percentages in the Hispanic Origin and Race categories. Ancestry percentages are based on the 2006-2010 American Community Survey population (not shown); ‡ Numbers in parentheses indicate the number of people reporting a single ancestry; * Numbers in parentheses indicate the number of persons reporting this race alone, not in combination with any other race; Please refer to the Explanation of Data for more information.*

Pittsburg

Place Type: City
County: Contra Costa
Population: 63,264

Ancestry	Population	%
Afghan (147)	147	0.24
African, Sub-Saharan (864)	1,533	2.48
African (478)	1,147	1.86
Cape Verdean (0)	0	<0.01
Ethiopian (0)	0	<0.01
Ghanaian (0)	0	<0.01
Kenyan (0)	0	<0.01
Liberian (0)	0	<0.01
Nigerian (84)	84	0.14
Senegalese (0)	0	<0.01
Sierra Leonean (0)	0	<0.01
Somalian (0)	0	<0.01
South African (41)	41	0.07
Sudanese (0)	0	<0.01
Ugandan (55)	55	0.09
Zimbabwean (0)	0	<0.01
Other Sub-Saharan African (206)	206	0.33
Albanian (0)	0	<0.01
Alsatian (0)	0	<0.01
American (582)	582	0.94
Arab (218)	218	0.35
Arab (123)	123	0.20
Egyptian (47)	47	0.08
Iraqi (0)	0	<0.01
Jordanian (0)	0	<0.01
Lebanese (15)	15	0.02
Moroccan (12)	12	0.02
Palestinian (0)	0	<0.01
Syrian (0)	0	<0.01
Other Arab (21)	21	0.03
Armenian (11)	11	0.02
Assyrian/Chaldean/Syriac (0)	0	<0.01
Australian (0)	0	<0.01
Austrian (15)	65	0.11
Basque (53)	87	0.14
Belgian (0)	0	<0.01
Brazilian (0)	0	<0.01
British (42)	161	0.26
Bulgarian (0)	0	<0.01
Cajun (0)	0	<0.01
Canadian (0)	0	<0.01
Carpatho Rusyn (0)	0	<0.01
Celtic (0)	0	<0.01
Croatian (0)	11	0.02
Cypriot (0)	0	<0.01
Czech (23)	94	0.15
Czechoslovakian (0)	0	<0.01
Danish (22)	265	0.43
Dutch (202)	460	0.75
Eastern European (10)	10	0.02
English (288)	1,695	2.75
Estonian (0)	0	<0.01
European (126)	200	0.32
Finnish (0)	15	0.02
French, ex. Basque (69)	683	1.11
French Canadian (30)	49	0.08
German (555)	2,679	4.34
German Russian (23)	23	0.04
Greek (10)	64	0.10
Guyanese (18)	18	0.03
Hungarian (63)	135	0.22
Icelander (0)	0	<0.01
Iranian (31)	31	0.05
Irish (503)	2,638	4.27
Israeli (0)	0	<0.01
Italian (1,209)	2,501	4.05
Latvian (0)	0	<0.01
Lithuanian (0)	44	0.07
Luxemburger (0)	0	<0.01
Macedonian (0)	0	<0.01
Maltese (0)	0	<0.01
New Zealander (0)	0	<0.01
Northern European (0)	0	<0.01
Norwegian (99)	293	0.47
Pennsylvania German (0)	9	0.01
Polish (168)	385	0.62
Portuguese (223)	1,176	1.91
Romanian (0)	14	0.02
Russian (38)	158	0.26
Scandinavian (73)	126	0.20
Scotch-Irish (278)	576	0.93
Scottish (141)	425	0.69
Serbian (0)	0	<0.01
Slavic (0)	0	<0.01
Slovak (27)	27	0.04
Slovene (0)	0	<0.01
Soviet Union (0)	0	<0.01
Swedish (26)	376	0.61
Swiss (0)	34	0.06
Turkish (0)	0	<0.01
Ukrainian (26)	40	0.06
Welsh (16)	105	0.17
West Indian, ex. Hispanic (66)	66	0.11
Bahamian (0)	0	<0.01
Barbadian (0)	0	<0.01
Belizean (0)	0	<0.01
Bermudan (0)	0	<0.01
British West Indian (0)	0	<0.01
Dutch West Indian (0)	0	<0.01
Haitian (0)	0	<0.01
Jamaican (57)	57	0.09
Trinidadian/Tobagonian (0)	0	<0.01
U.S. Virgin Islander (0)	0	<0.01
West Indian (9)	9	0.01
Other West Indian (0)	0	<0.01
Yugoslavian (117)	174	0.28

Hispanic Origin	Population	%
Hispanic or Latino (of any race)	26,841	42.43
Central American, ex. Mexican	3,513	5.55
Costa Rican	37	0.06
Guatemalan	354	0.56
Honduran	91	0.14
Nicaraguan	879	1.39
Panamanian	54	0.09
Salvadoran	2,076	3.28
Other Central American	22	0.03
Cuban	98	0.15
Dominican Republic	30	0.05
Mexican	20,109	31.79
Puerto Rican	890	1.41
South American	610	0.96
Argentinean	21	0.03
Bolivian	28	0.04
Chilean	33	0.05
Colombian	112	0.18
Ecuadorian	24	0.04
Paraguayan	4	0.01
Peruvian	348	0.55
Uruguayan	5	0.01
Venezuelan	31	0.05
Other South American	4	0.01
Other Hispanic or Latino	1,591	2.51

Race*	Population	%
African-American/Black (11,187)	12,770	20.19
Not Hispanic (10,756)	11,831	18.70
Hispanic (431)	939	1.48
American Indian/Alaska Native (517)	1,263	2.00
Not Hispanic (202)	638	1.01
Hispanic (315)	625	0.99
Alaska Athabascan *(Ala. Nat.)* (0)	0	<0.01
Aleut *(Alaska Native)* (1)	1	<0.01
Apache (19)	62	0.10
Arapaho (0)	0	<0.01
Blackfeet (2)	43	0.07
Canadian/French Am. Ind. (0)	1	<0.01
Central American Ind. (1)	2	<0.01
Cherokee (26)	148	0.23
Cheyenne (0)	8	0.01
Chickasaw (0)	3	<0.01
Chippewa (1)	3	<0.01
Choctaw (8)	33	0.05
Colville (0)	0	<0.01
Comanche (0)	5	0.01
Cree (0)	4	0.01
Creek (8)	12	0.02
Crow (0)	2	<0.01
Delaware (0)	0	<0.01
Hopi (2)	6	0.01
Houma (1)	1	<0.01
Inupiat *(Alaska Native)* (3)	4	0.01
Iroquois (0)	5	0.01
Kiowa (0)	4	0.01
Lumbee (0)	0	<0.01
Menominee (0)	0	<0.01
Mexican American Ind. (99)	146	0.23
Navajo (8)	23	0.04
Osage (3)	7	0.01
Ottawa (2)	5	0.01
Paiute (0)	9	0.01
Pima (1)	1	<0.01
Potawatomi (1)	1	<0.01
Pueblo (0)	3	<0.01
Puget Sound Salish (0)	0	<0.01
Seminole (1)	4	0.01
Shoshone (1)	3	<0.01
Sioux (13)	35	0.06
South American Ind. (4)	9	0.01
Spanish American Ind. (1)	2	<0.01
Tlingit-Haida *(Alaska Native)* (0)	0	<0.01
Tohono O'Odham (0)	5	0.01
Tsimshian *(Alaska Native)* (0)	0	<0.01
Ute (2)	6	0.01
Yakama (0)	0	<0.01
Yaqui (2)	13	0.02
Yuman (3)	4	0.01
Yup'ik *(Alaska Native)* (0)	0	<0.01
Asian (9,891)	11,659	18.43
Not Hispanic (9,654)	10,933	17.28
Hispanic (237)	726	1.15
Bangladeshi (17)	18	0.03
Bhutanese (0)	0	<0.01
Burmese (9)	11	0.02
Cambodian (128)	146	0.23
Chinese, ex. Taiwanese (721)	995	1.57
Filipino (6,253)	7,301	11.54
Hmong (1)	3	<0.01
Indian (1,251)	1,465	2.32
Indonesian (33)	66	0.10
Japanese (114)	310	0.49
Korean (120)	198	0.31
Laotian (92)	117	0.18
Malaysian (1)	7	0.01
Nepalese (8)	8	0.01
Pakistani (99)	116	0.18
Sri Lankan (7)	7	0.01
Taiwanese (12)	16	0.03
Thai (54)	87	0.14
Vietnamese (717)	787	1.24
Hawaii Native/Pacific Islander (645)	1,126	1.78
Not Hispanic (614)	976	1.54
Hispanic (31)	150	0.24
Fijian (175)	234	0.37
Guamanian/Chamorro (42)	116	0.18
Marshallese (0)	0	<0.01
Native Hawaiian (42)	184	0.29
Samoan (108)	164	0.26
Tongan (202)	235	0.37
White (23,106)	26,446	41.80
Not Hispanic (12,684)	14,289	22.59
Hispanic (10,422)	12,157	19.22

*Notes: † The Census 2010 population figure is used to calculate the percentages in the Hispanic Origin and Race categories. Ancestry percentages are based on the 2006-2010 American Community Survey population (not shown); ‡ Numbers in parentheses indicate the number of people reporting a single ancestry; * Numbers in parentheses indicate the number of persons reporting this race alone, not in combination with any other race; Please refer to the Explanation of Data for more information.*

Placentia

Place Type: City
County: Orange
Population: 50,533

Ancestry	Population	%
Afghan (8)	8	0.02
African, Sub-Saharan (233)	260	0.52
African (30)	42	0.08
Cape Verdean (0)	0	<0.01
Ethiopian (15)	15	0.03
Ghanaian (0)	0	<0.01
Kenyan (0)	0	<0.01
Liberian (0)	0	<0.01
Nigerian (175)	175	0.35
Senegalese (0)	0	<0.01
Sierra Leonean (0)	0	<0.01
Somalian (0)	0	<0.01
South African (13)	28	0.06
Sudanese (0)	0	<0.01
Ugandan (0)	0	<0.01
Zimbabwean (0)	0	<0.01
Other Sub-Saharan African (0)	0	<0.01
Albanian (0)	0	<0.01
Alsatian (0)	0	<0.01
American (1,409)	1,409	2.84
Arab (274)	407	0.82
Arab (40)	40	0.08
Egyptian (0)	33	0.07
Iraqi (0)	23	0.05
Jordanian (110)	118	0.24
Lebanese (80)	149	0.30
Moroccan (0)	0	<0.01
Palestinian (0)	0	<0.01
Syrian (31)	31	0.06
Other Arab (13)	13	0.03
Armenian (101)	196	0.40
Assyrian/Chaldean/Syriac (0)	0	<0.01
Australian (0)	0	<0.01
Austrian (26)	90	0.18
Basque (0)	0	<0.01
Belgian (0)	14	0.03
Brazilian (16)	16	0.03
British (88)	218	0.44
Bulgarian (0)	9	0.02
Cajun (0)	0	<0.01
Canadian (160)	213	0.43
Carpatho Rusyn (0)	0	<0.01
Celtic (0)	0	<0.01
Croatian (33)	117	0.24
Cypriot (0)	0	<0.01
Czech (30)	167	0.34
Czechoslovakian (32)	80	0.16
Danish (115)	435	0.88
Dutch (161)	533	1.08
Eastern European (38)	84	0.17
English (1,022)	3,982	8.03
Estonian (0)	0	<0.01
European (517)	613	1.24
Finnish (23)	33	0.07
French, ex. Basque (113)	983	1.98
French Canadian (54)	148	0.30
German (1,664)	6,630	13.38
German Russian (0)	0	<0.01
Greek (49)	196	0.40
Guyanese (0)	0	<0.01
Hungarian (145)	429	0.87
Icelander (0)	17	0.03
Iranian (280)	287	0.58
Irish (1,085)	4,986	10.06
Israeli (0)	0	<0.01
Italian (937)	2,352	4.75
Latvian (0)	0	<0.01
Lithuanian (56)	77	0.16
Luxemburger (0)	0	<0.01
Macedonian (0)	0	<0.01
Maltese (0)	0	<0.01
New Zealander (0)	0	<0.01
Northern European (64)	64	0.13
Norwegian (276)	533	1.08
Pennsylvania German (9)	31	0.06
Polish (329)	1,097	2.21
Portuguese (35)	49	0.10
Romanian (94)	148	0.30
Russian (206)	388	0.78
Scandinavian (43)	55	0.11
Scotch-Irish (189)	611	1.23
Scottish (216)	909	1.83
Serbian (9)	9	0.02
Slavic (10)	70	0.14
Slovak (28)	93	0.19
Slovene (0)	21	0.04
Soviet Union (0)	0	<0.01
Swedish (78)	814	1.64
Swiss (0)	55	0.11
Turkish (0)	0	<0.01
Ukrainian (52)	136	0.27
Welsh (0)	152	0.31
West Indian, ex. Hispanic (32)	32	0.06
Bahamian (0)	0	<0.01
Barbadian (0)	0	<0.01
Belizean (22)	22	0.04
Bermudan (0)	0	<0.01
British West Indian (0)	0	<0.01
Dutch West Indian (0)	0	<0.01
Haitian (10)	10	0.02
Jamaican (0)	0	<0.01
Trinidadian/Tobagonian (0)	0	<0.01
U.S. Virgin Islander (0)	0	<0.01
West Indian (0)	0	<0.01
Other West Indian (0)	0	<0.01
Yugoslavian (0)	16	0.03

Hispanic Origin	Population	%
Hispanic or Latino (of any race)	18,416	36.44
Central American, ex. Mexican	934	1.85
Costa Rican	32	0.06
Guatemalan	492	0.97
Honduran	34	0.07
Nicaraguan	73	0.14
Panamanian	21	0.04
Salvadoran	272	0.54
Other Central American	10	0.02
Cuban	172	0.34
Dominican Republic	13	0.03
Mexican	15,464	30.60
Puerto Rican	163	0.32
South American	554	1.10
Argentinean	93	0.18
Bolivian	30	0.06
Chilean	37	0.07
Colombian	129	0.26
Ecuadorian	63	0.12
Paraguayan	4	0.01
Peruvian	179	0.35
Uruguayan	5	0.01
Venezuelan	7	0.01
Other South American	7	0.01
Other Hispanic or Latino	1,116	2.21

Race*	Population	%
African-American/Black (914)	1,185	2.35
Not Hispanic (818)	997	1.97
Hispanic (96)	188	0.37
American Indian/Alaska Native (386)	722	1.43
Not Hispanic (123)	289	0.57
Hispanic (263)	433	0.86
Alaska Athabascan *(Ala. Nat.)* (0)	0	<0.01
Aleut *(Alaska Native)* (1)	4	0.01
Apache (6)	25	0.05
Arapaho (0)	0	<0.01
Blackfeet (1)	6	0.01
Canadian/French Am. Ind. (2)	3	0.01
Central American Ind. (0)	0	<0.01
Cherokee (24)	80	0.16
Cheyenne (1)	4	0.01
Chickasaw (1)	4	0.01
Chippewa (3)	9	0.02
Choctaw (4)	30	0.06
Colville (0)	0	<0.01
Comanche (2)	2	<0.01
Cree (0)	0	<0.01
Creek (1)	6	0.01
Crow (0)	0	<0.01
Delaware (0)	0	<0.01
Hopi (2)	3	0.01
Houma (0)	0	<0.01
Inupiat *(Alaska Native)* (0)	0	<0.01
Iroquois (1)	3	0.01
Kiowa (4)	4	0.01
Lumbee (0)	3	0.01
Menominee (0)	0	<0.01
Mexican American Ind. (39)	63	0.12
Navajo (13)	19	0.04
Osage (1)	1	<0.01
Ottawa (1)	1	<0.01
Paiute (0)	1	<0.01
Pima (0)	0	<0.01
Potawatomi (3)	5	0.01
Pueblo (2)	7	0.01
Puget Sound Salish (0)	0	<0.01
Seminole (0)	0	<0.01
Shoshone (2)	3	0.01
Sioux (1)	1	<0.01
South American Ind. (0)	1	<0.01
Spanish American Ind. (5)	9	0.02
Tlingit-Haida *(Alaska Native)* (0)	2	<0.01
Tohono O'Odham (4)	5	0.01
Tsimshian *(Alaska Native)* (0)	1	<0.01
Ute (1)	3	0.01
Yakama (1)	1	<0.01
Yaqui (6)	13	0.03
Yuman (0)	0	<0.01
Yup'ik *(Alaska Native)* (0)	0	<0.01
Asian (7,531)	8,389	16.60
Not Hispanic (7,457)	8,122	16.07
Hispanic (74)	267	0.53
Bangladeshi (14)	17	0.03
Bhutanese (0)	0	<0.01
Burmese (10)	13	0.03
Cambodian (76)	95	0.19
Chinese, ex. Taiwanese (1,135)	1,438	2.85
Filipino (1,569)	1,894	3.75
Hmong (9)	11	0.02
Indian (922)	1,007	1.99
Indonesian (90)	146	0.29
Japanese (506)	762	1.51
Korean (978)	1,055	2.09
Laotian (32)	47	0.09
Malaysian (16)	18	0.04
Nepalese (3)	3	0.01
Pakistani (60)	75	0.15
Sri Lankan (29)	29	0.06
Taiwanese (331)	358	0.71
Thai (73)	93	0.18
Vietnamese (1,349)	1,467	2.90
Hawaii Native/Pacific Islander (74)	179	0.35
Not Hispanic (58)	135	0.27
Hispanic (16)	44	0.09
Fijian (7)	7	0.01
Guamanian/Chamorro (12)	21	0.04
Marshallese (0)	0	<0.01
Native Hawaiian (23)	68	0.13
Samoan (17)	25	0.05
Tongan (5)	5	0.01
White (31,373)	33,091	65.48
Not Hispanic (22,590)	23,449	46.40
Hispanic (8,783)	9,642	19.08

*Notes: † The Census 2010 population figure is used to calculate the percentages in the Hispanic Origin and Race categories. Ancestry percentages are based on the 2006-2010 American Community Survey population (not shown); ‡ Numbers in parentheses indicate the number of people reporting a single ancestry; * Numbers in parentheses indicate the number of persons reporting this race alone, not in combination with any other race; Please refer to the Explanation of Data for more information.*

Pleasanton

Place Type: City
County: Alameda
Population: 70,285

Ancestry	Population	%
Afghan (121)	153	0.22
African, Sub-Saharan (59)	167	0.24
African (59)	167	0.24
Cape Verdean (0)	0	<0.01
Ethiopian (0)	0	<0.01
Ghanaian (0)	0	<0.01
Kenyan (0)	0	<0.01
Liberian (0)	0	<0.01
Nigerian (0)	0	<0.01
Senegalese (0)	0	<0.01
Sierra Leonean (0)	0	<0.01
Somalian (0)	0	<0.01
South African (0)	0	<0.01
Sudanese (0)	0	<0.01
Ugandan (0)	0	<0.01
Zimbabwean (0)	0	<0.01
Other Sub-Saharan African (0)	0	<0.01
Albanian (0)	0	<0.01
Alsatian (0)	0	<0.01
American (1,331)	1,331	1.95
Arab (225)	345	0.51
Arab (0)	0	<0.01
Egyptian (86)	86	0.13
Iraqi (0)	0	<0.01
Jordanian (0)	0	<0.01
Lebanese (33)	86	0.13
Moroccan (0)	0	<0.01
Palestinian (78)	117	0.17
Syrian (9)	21	0.03
Other Arab (19)	35	0.05
Armenian (88)	177	0.26
Assyrian/Chaldean/Syriac (10)	40	0.06
Australian (0)	67	0.10
Austrian (19)	155	0.23
Basque (20)	28	0.04
Belgian (46)	148	0.22
Brazilian (65)	87	0.13
British (393)	655	0.96
Bulgarian (0)	0	<0.01
Cajun (0)	0	<0.01
Canadian (135)	227	0.33
Carpatho Rusyn (0)	0	<0.01
Celtic (0)	0	<0.01
Croatian (70)	224	0.33
Cypriot (10)	10	0.01
Czech (26)	273	0.40
Czechoslovakian (31)	80	0.12
Danish (98)	768	1.13
Dutch (82)	746	1.09
Eastern European (104)	104	0.15
English (1,740)	8,006	11.74
Estonian (0)	0	<0.01
European (1,011)	1,320	1.94
Finnish (47)	107	0.16
French, ex. Basque (230)	2,067	3.03
French Canadian (108)	263	0.39
German (2,021)	9,821	14.40
German Russian (0)	0	<0.01
Greek (172)	489	0.72
Guyanese (0)	0	<0.01
Hungarian (76)	258	0.38
Icelander (0)	8	0.01
Iranian (862)	870	1.28
Irish (1,774)	8,737	12.81
Israeli (62)	62	0.09
Italian (1,866)	5,716	8.38
Latvian (0)	0	<0.01
Lithuanian (109)	135	0.20
Luxemburger (0)	10	0.01
Macedonian (0)	0	<0.01
Maltese (0)	0	<0.01
New Zealander (34)	34	0.05
Northern European (234)	234	0.34
Norwegian (331)	1,137	1.67
Pennsylvania German (9)	23	0.03
Polish (206)	1,037	1.52
Portuguese (396)	1,733	2.54
Romanian (141)	184	0.27
Russian (313)	713	1.05
Scandinavian (84)	151	0.22
Scotch-Irish (332)	1,218	1.79
Scottish (376)	1,738	2.55
Serbian (0)	22	0.03
Slavic (0)	6	0.01
Slovak (33)	106	0.16
Slovene (16)	16	0.02
Soviet Union (0)	0	<0.01
Swedish (207)	1,893	2.78
Swiss (123)	308	0.45
Turkish (32)	32	0.05
Ukrainian (74)	224	0.33
Welsh (58)	543	0.80
West Indian, ex. Hispanic (39)	96	0.14
Bahamian (0)	0	<0.01
Barbadian (0)	0	<0.01
Belizean (0)	0	<0.01
Bermudan (0)	0	<0.01
British West Indian (0)	0	<0.01
Dutch West Indian (0)	0	<0.01
Haitian (0)	0	<0.01
Jamaican (0)	0	<0.01
Trinidadian/Tobagonian (0)	0	<0.01
U.S. Virgin Islander (0)	0	<0.01
West Indian (39)	96	0.14
Other West Indian (0)	0	<0.01
Yugoslavian (111)	252	0.37

Hispanic Origin	Population	%
Hispanic or Latino (of any race)	7,264	10.34
Central American, ex. Mexican	418	0.59
Costa Rican	24	0.03
Guatemalan	60	0.09
Honduran	24	0.03
Nicaraguan	101	0.14
Panamanian	39	0.06
Salvadoran	166	0.24
Other Central American	4	0.01
Cuban	98	0.14
Dominican Republic	17	0.02
Mexican	4,903	6.98
Puerto Rican	331	0.47
South American	470	0.67
Argentinean	68	0.10
Bolivian	22	0.03
Chilean	55	0.08
Colombian	128	0.18
Ecuadorian	22	0.03
Paraguayan	3	<0.01
Peruvian	148	0.21
Uruguayan	0	<0.01
Venezuelan	20	0.03
Other South American	4	0.01
Other Hispanic or Latino	1,027	1.46

Race*	Population	%
African-American/Black (1,190)	1,616	2.30
Not Hispanic (1,116)	1,456	2.07
Hispanic (74)	160	0.23
American Indian/Alaska Native (226)	713	1.01
Not Hispanic (143)	488	0.69
Hispanic (83)	225	0.32
Alaska Athabascan *(Ala. Nat.)* (0)	1	<0.01
Aleut *(Alaska Native)* (0)	0	<0.01
Apache (2)	14	0.02
Arapaho (2)	2	<0.01
Blackfeet (4)	10	0.01
Canadian/French Am. Ind. (1)	3	<0.01
Central American Ind. (0)	2	<0.01
Cherokee (22)	134	0.19
Cheyenne (0)	2	<0.01
Chickasaw (1)	3	<0.01
Chippewa (4)	12	0.02
Choctaw (7)	41	0.06
Colville (1)	1	<0.01
Comanche (1)	5	0.01
Cree (0)	1	<0.01
Creek (5)	8	0.01
Crow (0)	5	0.01
Delaware (3)	5	0.01
Hopi (0)	3	<0.01
Houma (0)	0	<0.01
Inupiat *(Alaska Native)* (0)	0	<0.01
Iroquois (1)	6	0.01
Kiowa (0)	2	<0.01
Lumbee (0)	0	<0.01
Menominee (0)	0	<0.01
Mexican American Ind. (17)	29	0.04
Navajo (8)	14	0.02
Osage (0)	2	<0.01
Ottawa (0)	0	<0.01
Paiute (2)	3	<0.01
Pima (1)	3	<0.01
Potawatomi (3)	10	0.01
Pueblo (0)	1	<0.01
Puget Sound Salish (1)	1	<0.01
Seminole (1)	4	0.01
Shoshone (0)	1	<0.01
Sioux (3)	10	0.01
South American Ind. (3)	7	0.01
Spanish American Ind. (0)	0	<0.01
Tlingit-Haida *(Alaska Native)* (0)	0	<0.01
Tohono O'Odham (1)	1	<0.01
Tsimshian *(Alaska Native)* (0)	0	<0.01
Ute (0)	3	<0.01
Yakama (0)	2	<0.01
Yaqui (1)	5	0.01
Yuman (0)	0	<0.01
Yup'ik *(Alaska Native)* (0)	3	<0.01
Asian (16,322)	18,484	26.30
Not Hispanic (16,209)	18,108	25.76
Hispanic (113)	376	0.53
Bangladeshi (34)	36	0.05
Bhutanese (0)	0	<0.01
Burmese (35)	42	0.06
Cambodian (27)	37	0.05
Chinese, ex. Taiwanese (5,198)	5,928	8.43
Filipino (1,521)	2,234	3.18
Hmong (6)	6	0.01
Indian (5,214)	5,476	7.79
Indonesian (62)	107	0.15
Japanese (624)	1,155	1.64
Korean (1,882)	2,046	2.91
Laotian (19)	27	0.04
Malaysian (7)	21	0.03
Nepalese (10)	14	0.02
Pakistani (262)	299	0.43
Sri Lankan (33)	34	0.05
Taiwanese (438)	478	0.68
Thai (56)	80	0.11
Vietnamese (429)	528	0.75
Hawaii Native/Pacific Islander (134)	393	0.56
Not Hispanic (125)	345	0.49
Hispanic (9)	48	0.07
Fijian (21)	25	0.04
Guamanian/Chamorro (29)	70	0.10
Marshallese (0)	0	<0.01
Native Hawaiian (32)	191	0.27
Samoan (11)	23	0.03
Tongan (20)	25	0.04
White (47,058)	50,027	71.18
Not Hispanic (42,738)	44,995	64.02
Hispanic (4,320)	5,032	7.16

*Notes: † The Census 2010 population figure is used to calculate the percentages in the Hispanic Origin and Race categories. Ancestry percentages are based on the 2006-2010 American Community Survey population (not shown); ‡ Numbers in parentheses indicate the number of people reporting a single ancestry; * Numbers in parentheses indicate the number of persons reporting this race alone, not in combination with any other race; Please refer to the Explanation of Data for more information.*

Pomona

Place Type: City
County: Los Angeles
Population: 149,058

Ancestry	Population	%
Afghan (72)	72	0.05
African, Sub-Saharan (516)	574	0.39
African (233)	272	0.18
Cape Verdean (0)	12	0.01
Ethiopian (61)	61	0.04
Ghanaian (10)	10	0.01
Kenyan (36)	36	0.02
Liberian (0)	0	<0.01
Nigerian (28)	28	0.02
Senegalese (0)	0	<0.01
Sierra Leonean (0)	0	<0.01
Somalian (99)	99	0.07
South African (0)	0	<0.01
Sudanese (0)	0	<0.01
Ugandan (0)	0	<0.01
Zimbabwean (0)	0	<0.01
Other Sub-Saharan African (49)	56	0.04
Albanian (0)	0	<0.01
Alsatian (0)	0	<0.01
American (2,429)	2,429	1.63
Arab (962)	1,005	0.68
Arab (14)	14	0.01
Egyptian (18)	18	0.01
Iraqi (0)	0	<0.01
Jordanian (15)	28	0.02
Lebanese (905)	935	0.63
Moroccan (0)	0	<0.01
Palestinian (0)	0	<0.01
Syrian (0)	0	<0.01
Other Arab (10)	10	0.01
Armenian (78)	78	0.05
Assyrian/Chaldean/Syriac (0)	0	<0.01
Australian (0)	0	<0.01
Austrian (13)	113	0.08
Basque (16)	28	0.02
Belgian (0)	111	0.07
Brazilian (9)	21	0.01
British (71)	129	0.09
Bulgarian (0)	18	0.01
Cajun (0)	0	<0.01
Canadian (73)	120	0.08
Carpatho Rusyn (0)	0	<0.01
Celtic (0)	0	<0.01
Croatian (0)	17	0.01
Cypriot (0)	0	<0.01
Czech (0)	35	0.02
Czechoslovakian (0)	0	<0.01
Danish (74)	173	0.12
Dutch (165)	672	0.45
Eastern European (8)	16	0.01
English (883)	3,009	2.02
Estonian (0)	0	<0.01
European (250)	297	0.20
Finnish (62)	132	0.09
French, ex. Basque (194)	1,165	0.78
French Canadian (80)	146	0.10
German (1,009)	4,622	3.11
German Russian (0)	0	<0.01
Greek (75)	119	0.08
Guyanese (0)	0	<0.01
Hungarian (77)	180	0.12
Icelander (0)	0	<0.01
Iranian (485)	508	0.34
Irish (629)	3,841	2.58
Israeli (0)	0	<0.01
Italian (687)	2,572	1.73
Latvian (0)	0	<0.01
Lithuanian (0)	0	<0.01
Luxemburger (0)	0	<0.01
Macedonian (0)	0	<0.01
Maltese (10)	10	0.01
New Zealander (0)	0	<0.01
Northern European (0)	0	<0.01
Norwegian (146)	450	0.30
Pennsylvania German (0)	0	<0.01
Polish (247)	492	0.33
Portuguese (90)	204	0.14
Romanian (0)	30	0.02
Russian (229)	472	0.32
Scandinavian (42)	42	0.03
Scotch-Irish (112)	343	0.23
Scottish (110)	597	0.40
Serbian (0)	0	<0.01
Slavic (0)	9	0.01
Slovak (0)	31	0.02
Slovene (0)	0	<0.01
Soviet Union (0)	0	<0.01
Swedish (132)	337	0.23
Swiss (0)	53	0.04
Turkish (26)	64	0.04
Ukrainian (86)	118	0.08
Welsh (44)	152	0.10
West Indian, ex. Hispanic (166)	286	0.19
Bahamian (0)	0	<0.01
Barbadian (0)	0	<0.01
Belizean (36)	67	0.05
Bermudan (0)	0	<0.01
British West Indian (0)	0	<0.01
Dutch West Indian (0)	0	<0.01
Haitian (0)	0	<0.01
Jamaican (117)	206	0.14
Trinidadian/Tobagonian (13)	13	0.01
U.S. Virgin Islander (0)	0	<0.01
West Indian (0)	0	<0.01
Other West Indian (0)	0	<0.01
Yugoslavian (8)	21	0.01

Hispanic Origin	Population	%
Hispanic or Latino (of any race)	105,135	70.53
Central American, ex. Mexican	6,907	4.63
Costa Rican	85	0.06
Guatemalan	1,885	1.26
Honduran	632	0.42
Nicaraguan	625	0.42
Panamanian	75	0.05
Salvadoran	3,518	2.36
Other Central American	87	0.06
Cuban	404	0.27
Dominican Republic	23	0.02
Mexican	90,988	61.04
Puerto Rican	725	0.49
South American	1,007	0.68
Argentinean	154	0.10
Bolivian	33	0.02
Chilean	47	0.03
Colombian	200	0.13
Ecuadorian	219	0.15
Paraguayan	2	<0.01
Peruvian	288	0.19
Uruguayan	11	0.01
Venezuelan	28	0.02
Other South American	25	0.02
Other Hispanic or Latino	5,081	3.41

Race*	Population	%
African-American/Black (10,924)	12,276	8.24
Not Hispanic (10,107)	10,915	7.32
Hispanic (817)	1,361	0.91
American Indian/Alaska Native (1,763)	2,949	1.98
Not Hispanic (320)	769	0.52
Hispanic (1,443)	2,180	1.46
Alaska Athabascan *(Ala. Nat.)* (0)	0	<0.01
Aleut *(Alaska Native)* (0)	7	<0.01
Apache (66)	129	0.09
Arapaho (5)	5	<0.01
Blackfeet (8)	46	0.03
Canadian/French Am. Ind. (1)	3	<0.01
Central American Ind. (11)	28	0.02
Cherokee (47)	183	0.12
Cheyenne (1)	3	<0.01
Chickasaw (4)	19	0.01
Chippewa (5)	14	0.01
Choctaw (10)	35	0.02
Colville (0)	0	<0.01
Comanche (10)	13	0.01
Cree (1)	3	<0.01
Creek (3)	9	0.01
Crow (0)	0	<0.01
Delaware (1)	4	<0.01
Hopi (5)	15	0.01
Houma (0)	0	<0.01
Inupiat *(Alaska Native)* (2)	7	<0.01
Iroquois (2)	4	<0.01
Kiowa (0)	1	<0.01
Lumbee (1)	2	<0.01
Menominee (0)	2	<0.01
Mexican American Ind. (265)	355	0.24
Navajo (61)	114	0.08
Osage (2)	3	<0.01
Ottawa (0)	0	<0.01
Paiute (1)	4	<0.01
Pima (8)	12	0.01
Potawatomi (3)	3	<0.01
Pueblo (8)	30	0.02
Puget Sound Salish (0)	1	<0.01
Seminole (4)	9	0.01
Shoshone (10)	11	0.01
Sioux (20)	38	0.03
South American Ind. (6)	15	0.01
Spanish American Ind. (27)	33	0.02
Tlingit-Haida *(Alaska Native)* (0)	0	<0.01
Tohono O'Odham (7)	8	0.01
Tsimshian *(Alaska Native)* (0)	0	<0.01
Ute (0)	4	<0.01
Yakama (0)	1	<0.01
Yaqui (13)	21	0.01
Yuman (14)	19	0.01
Yup'ik *(Alaska Native)* (0)	0	<0.01
Asian (12,688)	14,312	9.60
Not Hispanic (12,303)	13,374	8.97
Hispanic (385)	938	0.63
Bangladeshi (35)	39	0.03
Bhutanese (0)	0	<0.01
Burmese (41)	44	0.03
Cambodian (768)	836	0.56
Chinese, ex. Taiwanese (2,945)	3,460	2.32
Filipino (3,250)	3,879	2.60
Hmong (37)	41	0.03
Indian (684)	807	0.54
Indonesian (150)	219	0.15
Japanese (400)	740	0.50
Korean (1,038)	1,130	0.76
Laotian (217)	244	0.16
Malaysian (30)	41	0.03
Nepalese (3)	3	<0.01
Pakistani (148)	163	0.11
Sri Lankan (16)	22	0.01
Taiwanese (378)	445	0.30
Thai (245)	312	0.21
Vietnamese (1,777)	1,966	1.32
Hawaii Native/Pacific Islander (282)	681	0.46
Not Hispanic (240)	474	0.32
Hispanic (42)	207	0.14
Fijian (13)	15	0.01
Guamanian/Chamorro (30)	59	0.04
Marshallese (0)	0	<0.01
Native Hawaiian (58)	147	0.10
Samoan (135)	224	0.15
Tongan (23)	33	0.02
White (71,564)	76,897	51.59
Not Hispanic (18,672)	20,142	13.51
Hispanic (52,892)	56,755	38.08

*Notes: † The Census 2010 population figure is used to calculate the percentages in the Hispanic Origin and Race categories. Ancestry percentages are based on the 2006-2010 American Community Survey population (not shown); ‡ Numbers in parentheses indicate the number of people reporting a single ancestry; * Numbers in parentheses indicate the number of persons reporting this race alone, not in combination with any other race; Please refer to the Explanation of Data for more information.*

Porterville

Place Type: City
County: Tulare
Population: 54,165

Ancestry	Population	%
Afghan (0)	0	<0.01
African, Sub-Saharan (24)	24	0.05
African (12)	12	0.02
Cape Verdean (0)	0	<0.01
Ethiopian (0)	0	<0.01
Ghanaian (0)	0	<0.01
Kenyan (0)	0	<0.01
Liberian (0)	0	<0.01
Nigerian (12)	12	0.02
Senegalese (0)	0	<0.01
Sierra Leonean (0)	0	<0.01
Somalian (0)	0	<0.01
South African (0)	0	<0.01
Sudanese (0)	0	<0.01
Ugandan (0)	0	<0.01
Zimbabwean (0)	0	<0.01
Other Sub-Saharan African (0)	0	<0.01
Albanian (0)	0	<0.01
Alsatian (0)	0	<0.01
American (1,683)	1,683	3.19
Arab (77)	77	0.15
Arab (44)	44	0.08
Egyptian (0)	0	<0.01
Iraqi (0)	0	<0.01
Jordanian (0)	0	<0.01
Lebanese (33)	33	0.06
Moroccan (0)	0	<0.01
Palestinian (0)	0	<0.01
Syrian (0)	0	<0.01
Other Arab (0)	0	<0.01
Armenian (0)	25	0.05
Assyrian/Chaldean/Syriac (0)	0	<0.01
Australian (12)	12	0.02
Austrian (13)	55	0.10
Basque (0)	0	<0.01
Belgian (0)	32	0.06
Brazilian (31)	36	0.07
British (0)	28	0.05
Bulgarian (0)	0	<0.01
Cajun (0)	0	<0.01
Canadian (0)	10	0.02
Carpatho Rusyn (0)	0	<0.01
Celtic (0)	0	<0.01
Croatian (9)	9	0.02
Cypriot (0)	0	<0.01
Czech (0)	14	0.03
Czechoslovakian (12)	53	0.10
Danish (18)	112	0.21
Dutch (89)	369	0.70
Eastern European (0)	0	<0.01
English (788)	2,382	4.51
Estonian (0)	0	<0.01
European (230)	280	0.53
Finnish (115)	167	0.32
French, ex. Basque (159)	694	1.32
French Canadian (24)	112	0.21
German (1,219)	3,829	7.26
German Russian (0)	0	<0.01
Greek (27)	74	0.14
Guyanese (0)	0	<0.01
Hungarian (0)	36	0.07
Icelander (0)	33	0.06
Iranian (0)	0	<0.01
Irish (816)	2,918	5.53
Israeli (0)	0	<0.01
Italian (248)	1,314	2.49
Latvian (0)	0	<0.01
Lithuanian (0)	0	<0.01
Luxemburger (0)	0	<0.01
Macedonian (0)	0	<0.01
Maltese (0)	0	<0.01
New Zealander (0)	0	<0.01
Northern European (0)	0	<0.01
Norwegian (185)	250	0.47
Pennsylvania German (0)	8	0.02
Polish (40)	145	0.27
Portuguese (93)	108	0.20
Romanian (0)	0	<0.01
Russian (52)	130	0.25
Scandinavian (26)	97	0.18
Scotch-Irish (73)	388	0.74
Scottish (10)	393	0.74
Serbian (0)	11	0.02
Slavic (15)	49	0.09
Slovak (10)	10	0.02
Slovene (0)	0	<0.01
Soviet Union (0)	0	<0.01
Swedish (131)	393	0.74
Swiss (9)	26	0.05
Turkish (0)	0	<0.01
Ukrainian (7)	7	0.01
Welsh (0)	265	0.50
West Indian, ex. Hispanic (60)	109	0.21
Bahamian (0)	0	<0.01
Barbadian (0)	0	<0.01
Belizean (0)	0	<0.01
Bermudan (0)	0	<0.01
British West Indian (0)	0	<0.01
Dutch West Indian (60)	109	0.21
Haitian (0)	0	<0.01
Jamaican (0)	0	<0.01
Trinidadian/Tobagonian (0)	0	<0.01
U.S. Virgin Islander (0)	0	<0.01
West Indian (0)	0	<0.01
Other West Indian (0)	0	<0.01
Yugoslavian (24)	24	0.05

Hispanic Origin	Population	%
Hispanic or Latino (of any race)	33,549	61.94
Central American, ex. Mexican	236	0.44
Costa Rican	12	0.02
Guatemalan	57	0.11
Honduran	26	0.05
Nicaraguan	20	0.04
Panamanian	15	0.03
Salvadoran	104	0.19
Other Central American	2	<0.01
Cuban	30	0.06
Dominican Republic	5	0.01
Mexican	31,421	58.01
Puerto Rican	173	0.32
South American	40	0.07
Argentinean	2	<0.01
Bolivian	2	<0.01
Chilean	5	0.01
Colombian	10	0.02
Ecuadorian	0	<0.01
Paraguayan	0	<0.01
Peruvian	21	0.04
Uruguayan	0	<0.01
Venezuelan	0	<0.01
Other South American	0	<0.01
Other Hispanic or Latino	1,644	3.04

Race*	Population	%
African-American/Black (673)	960	1.77
Not Hispanic (454)	586	1.08
Hispanic (219)	374	0.69
American Indian/Alaska Native (1,007)	1,675	3.09
Not Hispanic (461)	824	1.52
Hispanic (546)	851	1.57
Alaska Athabascan *(Ala. Nat.)* (0)	0	<0.01
Aleut *(Alaska Native)* (1)	4	0.01
Apache (11)	20	0.04
Arapaho (3)	4	0.01
Blackfeet (4)	14	0.03
Canadian/French Am. Ind. (1)	3	0.01
Central American Ind. (1)	1	<0.01
Cherokee (57)	190	0.35
Cheyenne (2)	2	<0.01
Chickasaw (2)	5	0.01
Chippewa (5)	5	0.01
Choctaw (17)	42	0.08
Colville (0)	1	<0.01
Comanche (1)	5	0.01
Cree (0)	0	<0.01
Creek (1)	10	0.02
Crow (0)	0	<0.01
Delaware (3)	4	0.01
Hopi (6)	9	0.02
Houma (0)	0	<0.01
Inupiat *(Alaska Native)* (1)	4	0.01
Iroquois (0)	2	<0.01
Kiowa (2)	19	0.04
Lumbee (0)	0	<0.01
Menominee (0)	0	<0.01
Mexican American Ind. (66)	105	0.19
Navajo (4)	8	0.01
Osage (0)	0	<0.01
Ottawa (0)	1	<0.01
Paiute (7)	10	0.02
Pima (15)	23	0.04
Potawatomi (1)	5	0.01
Pueblo (1)	5	0.01
Puget Sound Salish (0)	0	<0.01
Seminole (0)	0	<0.01
Shoshone (3)	9	0.02
Sioux (10)	21	0.04
South American Ind. (0)	0	<0.01
Spanish American Ind. (8)	9	0.02
Tlingit-Haida *(Alaska Native)* (2)	6	0.01
Tohono O'Odham (5)	5	0.01
Tsimshian *(Alaska Native)* (0)	0	<0.01
Ute (1)	4	0.01
Yakama (0)	0	<0.01
Yaqui (18)	25	0.05
Yuman (12)	17	0.03
Yup'ik *(Alaska Native)* (0)	0	<0.01
Asian (2,521)	3,153	5.82
Not Hispanic (2,349)	2,707	5.00
Hispanic (172)	446	0.82
Bangladeshi (2)	2	<0.01
Bhutanese (0)	0	<0.01
Burmese (2)	2	<0.01
Cambodian (23)	34	0.06
Chinese, ex. Taiwanese (124)	170	0.31
Filipino (1,256)	1,643	3.03
Hmong (192)	203	0.37
Indian (218)	266	0.49
Indonesian (1)	5	0.01
Japanese (38)	98	0.18
Korean (35)	57	0.11
Laotian (352)	429	0.79
Malaysian (3)	3	0.01
Nepalese (0)	0	<0.01
Pakistani (63)	73	0.13
Sri Lankan (1)	1	<0.01
Taiwanese (1)	7	0.01
Thai (22)	63	0.12
Vietnamese (38)	43	0.08
Hawaii Native/Pacific Islander (64)	157	0.29
Not Hispanic (49)	98	0.18
Hispanic (15)	59	0.11
Fijian (1)	1	<0.01
Guamanian/Chamorro (5)	13	0.02
Marshallese (5)	5	0.01
Native Hawaiian (19)	59	0.11
Samoan (21)	27	0.05
Tongan (0)	0	<0.01
White (31,847)	34,025	62.82
Not Hispanic (16,423)	17,160	31.68
Hispanic (15,424)	16,865	31.14

*Notes: † The Census 2010 population figure is used to calculate the percentages in the Hispanic Origin and Race categories. Ancestry percentages are based on the 2006-2010 American Community Survey population (not shown); ‡ Numbers in parentheses indicate the number of people reporting a single ancestry; * Numbers in parentheses indicate the number of persons reporting this race alone, not in combination with any other race; Please refer to the Explanation of Data for more information.*

Rancho Cordova

Place Type: City
County: Sacramento
Population: 64,776

Ancestry	Population	%
Afghan (13)	13	0.02
African, Sub-Saharan (505)	562	0.89
African (224)	281	0.44
Cape Verdean (0)	0	<0.01
Ethiopian (22)	22	0.03
Ghanaian (0)	0	<0.01
Kenyan (129)	129	0.20
Liberian (0)	0	<0.01
Nigerian (22)	22	0.03
Senegalese (0)	0	<0.01
Sierra Leonean (0)	0	<0.01
Somalian (0)	0	<0.01
South African (0)	0	<0.01
Sudanese (0)	0	<0.01
Ugandan (108)	108	0.17
Zimbabwean (0)	0	<0.01
Other Sub-Saharan African (0)	0	<0.01
Albanian (0)	0	<0.01
Alsatian (0)	0	<0.01
American (1,885)	1,885	2.98
Arab (313)	399	0.63
Arab (8)	8	0.01
Egyptian (52)	52	0.08
Iraqi (0)	0	<0.01
Jordanian (33)	33	0.05
Lebanese (10)	10	0.02
Moroccan (44)	59	0.09
Palestinian (0)	0	<0.01
Syrian (0)	32	0.05
Other Arab (166)	205	0.32
Armenian (768)	900	1.42
Assyrian/Chaldean/Syriac (0)	0	<0.01
Australian (0)	9	0.01
Austrian (36)	82	0.13
Basque (22)	22	0.03
Belgian (15)	38	0.06
Brazilian (9)	9	0.01
British (158)	291	0.46
Bulgarian (30)	30	0.05
Cajun (0)	0	<0.01
Canadian (89)	166	0.26
Carpatho Rusyn (0)	0	<0.01
Celtic (0)	0	<0.01
Croatian (0)	30	0.05
Cypriot (10)	22	0.03
Czech (20)	215	0.34
Czechoslovakian (24)	62	0.10
Danish (46)	343	0.54
Dutch (91)	832	1.31
Eastern European (0)	0	<0.01
English (1,022)	4,461	7.05
Estonian (0)	0	<0.01
European (654)	722	1.14
Finnish (39)	73	0.12
French, ex. Basque (330)	1,573	2.49
French Canadian (85)	251	0.40
German (1,818)	7,424	11.73
German Russian (0)	0	<0.01
Greek (152)	294	0.46
Guyanese (0)	0	<0.01
Hungarian (29)	108	0.17
Icelander (14)	14	0.02
Iranian (130)	130	0.21
Irish (1,356)	5,396	8.52
Israeli (0)	38	0.06
Italian (988)	3,128	4.94
Latvian (0)	9	0.01
Lithuanian (0)	57	0.09
Luxemburger (0)	0	<0.01
Macedonian (0)	0	<0.01
Maltese (0)	37	0.06
New Zealander (0)	0	<0.01
Northern European (89)	133	0.21
Norwegian (213)	819	1.29
Pennsylvania German (46)	46	0.07
Polish (151)	930	1.47
Portuguese (429)	895	1.41
Romanian (640)	682	1.08
Russian (929)	1,137	1.80
Scandinavian (78)	196	0.31
Scotch-Irish (386)	1,003	1.58
Scottish (366)	1,063	1.68
Serbian (0)	0	<0.01
Slavic (0)	7	0.01
Slovak (17)	46	0.07
Slovene (0)	16	0.03
Soviet Union (0)	0	<0.01
Swedish (107)	618	0.98
Swiss (7)	87	0.14
Turkish (20)	20	0.03
Ukrainian (2,675)	2,814	4.45
Welsh (19)	491	0.78
West Indian, ex. Hispanic (123)	123	0.19
Bahamian (0)	0	<0.01
Barbadian (0)	0	<0.01
Belizean (0)	0	<0.01
Bermudan (5)	5	0.01
British West Indian (0)	0	<0.01
Dutch West Indian (0)	0	<0.01
Haitian (0)	0	<0.01
Jamaican (20)	20	0.03
Trinidadian/Tobagonian (0)	0	<0.01
U.S. Virgin Islander (0)	0	<0.01
West Indian (98)	98	0.15
Other West Indian (0)	0	<0.01
Yugoslavian (0)	85	0.13

Hispanic Origin	Population	%
Hispanic or Latino (of any race)	12,740	19.67
Central American, ex. Mexican	970	1.50
Costa Rican	31	0.05
Guatemalan	225	0.35
Honduran	53	0.08
Nicaraguan	166	0.26
Panamanian	26	0.04
Salvadoran	454	0.70
Other Central American	15	0.02
Cuban	66	0.10
Dominican Republic	23	0.04
Mexican	9,862	15.22
Puerto Rican	468	0.72
South American	260	0.40
Argentinean	23	0.04
Bolivian	26	0.04
Chilean	25	0.04
Colombian	55	0.08
Ecuadorian	17	0.03
Paraguayan	2	<0.01
Peruvian	99	0.15
Uruguayan	0	<0.01
Venezuelan	13	0.02
Other South American	0	<0.01
Other Hispanic or Latino	1,091	1.68

Race*	Population	%
African-American/Black (6,561)	8,361	12.91
Not Hispanic (6,286)	7,710	11.90
Hispanic (275)	651	1.01
American Indian/Alaska Native (668)	1,651	2.55
Not Hispanic (398)	1,126	1.74
Hispanic (270)	525	0.81
Alaska Athabascan *(Ala. Nat.)* (0)	1	<0.01
Aleut *(Alaska Native)* (2)	5	0.01
Apache (31)	75	0.12
Arapaho (6)	7	0.01
Blackfeet (11)	77	0.12
Canadian/French Am. Ind. (0)	3	<0.01
Central American Ind. (1)	7	0.01
Cherokee (67)	341	0.53
Cheyenne (0)	1	<0.01
Chickasaw (8)	21	0.03
Chippewa (14)	22	0.03
Choctaw (23)	70	0.11
Colville (0)	1	<0.01
Comanche (5)	5	0.01
Cree (0)	6	0.01
Creek (10)	35	0.05
Crow (0)	3	<0.01
Delaware (1)	7	0.01
Hopi (3)	3	<0.01
Houma (0)	0	<0.01
Inupiat *(Alaska Native)* (1)	3	<0.01
Iroquois (5)	10	0.02
Kiowa (6)	8	0.01
Lumbee (0)	0	<0.01
Menominee (1)	3	<0.01
Mexican American Ind. (39)	57	0.09
Navajo (22)	48	0.07
Osage (2)	2	<0.01
Ottawa (0)	0	<0.01
Paiute (9)	19	0.03
Pima (2)	2	<0.01
Potawatomi (4)	10	0.02
Pueblo (4)	9	0.01
Puget Sound Salish (0)	0	<0.01
Seminole (0)	5	0.01
Shoshone (2)	8	0.01
Sioux (26)	56	0.09
South American Ind. (4)	6	0.01
Spanish American Ind. (2)	6	0.01
Tlingit-Haida *(Alaska Native)* (5)	5	0.01
Tohono O'Odham (1)	1	<0.01
Tsimshian *(Alaska Native)* (0)	0	<0.01
Ute (1)	1	<0.01
Yakama (2)	2	<0.01
Yaqui (2)	6	0.01
Yuman (1)	2	<0.01
Yup'ik *(Alaska Native)* (0)	0	<0.01
Asian (7,831)	9,610	14.84
Not Hispanic (7,645)	9,124	14.09
Hispanic (186)	486	0.75
Bangladeshi (49)	50	0.08
Bhutanese (0)	0	<0.01
Burmese (1)	1	<0.01
Cambodian (78)	103	0.16
Chinese, ex. Taiwanese (852)	1,197	1.85
Filipino (2,330)	3,110	4.80
Hmong (420)	440	0.68
Indian (1,325)	1,530	2.36
Indonesian (67)	102	0.16
Japanese (269)	639	0.99
Korean (678)	810	1.25
Laotian (131)	154	0.24
Malaysian (19)	27	0.04
Nepalese (8)	9	0.01
Pakistani (100)	122	0.19
Sri Lankan (21)	22	0.03
Taiwanese (22)	28	0.04
Thai (77)	118	0.18
Vietnamese (1,031)	1,188	1.83
Hawaii Native/Pacific Islander (556)	1,044	1.61
Not Hispanic (506)	910	1.40
Hispanic (50)	134	0.21
Fijian (172)	233	0.36
Guamanian/Chamorro (66)	138	0.21
Marshallese (1)	4	0.01
Native Hawaiian (40)	211	0.33
Samoan (89)	168	0.26
Tongan (16)	31	0.05
White (39,123)	42,728	65.96
Not Hispanic (33,863)	36,418	56.22
Hispanic (5,260)	6,310	9.74

*Notes: † The Census 2010 population figure is used to calculate the percentages in the Hispanic Origin and Race categories. Ancestry percentages are based on the 2006-2010 American Community Survey population (not shown); ‡ Numbers in parentheses indicate the number of people reporting a single ancestry; * Numbers in parentheses indicate the number of persons reporting this race alone, not in combination with any other race; Please refer to the Explanation of Data for more information.*

Rancho Cucamonga

Place Type: City
County: San Bernardino
Population: 165,269

Ancestry	Population	%
Afghan (219)	219	0.14
African, Sub-Saharan (1,505)	2,103	1.31
African (1,220)	1,716	1.07
Cape Verdean (0)	0	<0.01
Ethiopian (0)	13	0.01
Ghanaian (0)	0	<0.01
Kenyan (59)	59	0.04
Liberian (15)	15	0.01
Nigerian (200)	277	0.17
Senegalese (0)	0	<0.01
Sierra Leonean (0)	0	<0.01
Somalian (0)	0	<0.01
South African (0)	0	<0.01
Sudanese (0)	0	<0.01
Ugandan (0)	0	<0.01
Zimbabwean (0)	0	<0.01
Other Sub-Saharan African (11)	23	0.01
Albanian (99)	114	0.07
Alsatian (0)	0	<0.01
American (5,809)	5,809	3.61
Arab (1,368)	2,065	1.28
Arab (330)	454	0.28
Egyptian (434)	434	0.27
Iraqi (0)	17	0.01
Jordanian (86)	161	0.10
Lebanese (176)	495	0.31
Moroccan (45)	81	0.05
Palestinian (153)	168	0.10
Syrian (114)	225	0.14
Other Arab (30)	30	0.02
Armenian (279)	444	0.28
Assyrian/Chaldean/Syriac (0)	16	0.01
Australian (53)	150	0.09
Austrian (51)	237	0.15
Basque (87)	221	0.14
Belgian (0)	42	0.03
Brazilian (73)	206	0.13
British (324)	595	0.37
Bulgarian (7)	40	0.02
Cajun (0)	0	<0.01
Canadian (270)	526	0.33
Carpatho Rusyn (0)	0	<0.01
Celtic (13)	26	0.02
Croatian (24)	132	0.08
Cypriot (0)	0	<0.01
Czech (158)	627	0.39
Czechoslovakian (116)	165	0.10
Danish (246)	647	0.40
Dutch (594)	2,719	1.69
Eastern European (85)	157	0.10
English (3,195)	11,740	7.30
Estonian (0)	0	<0.01
European (1,576)	2,309	1.44
Finnish (142)	330	0.21
French, ex. Basque (397)	4,318	2.69
French Canadian (166)	846	0.53
German (3,885)	18,604	11.57
German Russian (0)	0	<0.01
Greek (215)	666	0.41
Guyanese (0)	0	<0.01
Hungarian (183)	864	0.54
Icelander (47)	87	0.05
Iranian (810)	903	0.56
Irish (2,771)	12,938	8.05
Israeli (80)	80	0.05
Italian (3,668)	10,720	6.67
Latvian (0)	0	<0.01
Lithuanian (103)	239	0.15
Luxemburger (0)	0	<0.01
Macedonian (0)	2	<0.01
Maltese (0)	0	<0.01
New Zealander (0)	0	<0.01
Northern European (87)	97	0.06
Norwegian (622)	1,790	1.11
Pennsylvania German (17)	17	0.01
Polish (790)	2,686	1.67
Portuguese (239)	695	0.43
Romanian (101)	284	0.18
Russian (157)	850	0.53
Scandinavian (148)	395	0.25
Scotch-Irish (253)	1,566	0.97
Scottish (565)	2,037	1.27
Serbian (44)	73	0.05
Slavic (0)	71	0.04
Slovak (0)	35	0.02
Slovene (30)	55	0.03
Soviet Union (0)	0	<0.01
Swedish (387)	2,344	1.46
Swiss (13)	293	0.18
Turkish (61)	160	0.10
Ukrainian (39)	361	0.22
Welsh (173)	1,323	0.82
West Indian, ex. Hispanic (336)	698	0.43
Bahamian (0)	34	0.02
Barbadian (10)	10	0.01
Belizean (71)	179	0.11
Bermudan (0)	0	<0.01
British West Indian (0)	0	<0.01
Dutch West Indian (24)	24	0.01
Haitian (26)	95	0.06
Jamaican (70)	145	0.09
Trinidadian/Tobagonian (61)	61	0.04
U.S. Virgin Islander (0)	0	<0.01
West Indian (51)	127	0.08
Other West Indian (23)	23	0.01
Yugoslavian (44)	222	0.14

Hispanic Origin	Population	%
Hispanic or Latino (of any race)	57,688	34.91
Central American, ex. Mexican	3,487	2.11
Costa Rican	245	0.15
Guatemalan	907	0.55
Honduran	211	0.13
Nicaraguan	598	0.36
Panamanian	100	0.06
Salvadoran	1,396	0.84
Other Central American	30	0.02
Cuban	820	0.50
Dominican Republic	64	0.04
Mexican	45,369	27.45
Puerto Rican	1,214	0.73
South American	2,823	1.71
Argentinean	561	0.34
Bolivian	75	0.05
Chilean	146	0.09
Colombian	694	0.42
Ecuadorian	399	0.24
Paraguayan	9	0.01
Peruvian	800	0.48
Uruguayan	19	0.01
Venezuelan	73	0.04
Other South American	47	0.03
Other Hispanic or Latino	3,911	2.37

Race*	Population	%
African-American/Black (15,246)	17,582	10.64
Not Hispanic (14,486)	16,162	9.78
Hispanic (760)	1,420	0.86
American Indian/Alaska Native (1,134)	2,611	1.58
Not Hispanic (409)	1,235	0.75
Hispanic (725)	1,376	0.83
Alaska Athabascan *(Ala. Nat.)* (0)	5	<0.01
Aleut *(Alaska Native)* (1)	3	<0.01
Apache (49)	113	0.07
Arapaho (0)	1	<0.01
Blackfeet (8)	80	0.05
Canadian/French Am. Ind. (2)	6	<0.01
Central American Ind. (7)	16	0.01
Cherokee (67)	362	0.22
Cheyenne (1)	4	<0.01
Chickasaw (3)	25	0.02
Chippewa (12)	30	0.02
Choctaw (26)	80	0.05
Colville (2)	8	<0.01
Comanche (4)	16	0.01
Cree (0)	1	<0.01
Creek (8)	37	0.02
Crow (0)	2	<0.01
Delaware (0)	5	<0.01
Hopi (5)	11	0.01
Houma (1)	1	<0.01
Inupiat *(Alaska Native)* (1)	2	<0.01
Iroquois (9)	21	0.01
Kiowa (7)	9	0.01
Lumbee (4)	4	<0.01
Menominee (0)	0	<0.01
Mexican American Ind. (100)	176	0.11
Navajo (46)	92	0.06
Osage (4)	11	0.01
Ottawa (0)	5	<0.01
Paiute (11)	14	0.01
Pima (1)	8	<0.01
Potawatomi (3)	24	0.01
Pueblo (9)	24	0.01
Puget Sound Salish (6)	8	<0.01
Seminole (1)	9	0.01
Shoshone (2)	8	<0.01
Sioux (18)	43	0.03
South American Ind. (12)	16	0.01
Spanish American Ind. (7)	14	0.01
Tlingit-Haida *(Alaska Native)* (1)	1	<0.01
Tohono O'Odham (10)	10	0.01
Tsimshian *(Alaska Native)* (0)	0	<0.01
Ute (6)	9	0.01
Yakama (3)	6	<0.01
Yaqui (30)	73	0.04
Yuman (6)	11	0.01
Yup'ik *(Alaska Native)* (5)	9	0.01
Asian (17,208)	20,512	12.41
Not Hispanic (16,741)	19,216	11.63
Hispanic (467)	1,296	0.78
Bangladeshi (131)	144	0.09
Bhutanese (1)	1	<0.01
Burmese (58)	72	0.04
Cambodian (142)	180	0.11
Chinese, ex. Taiwanese (2,916)	3,715	2.25
Filipino (5,513)	6,762	4.09
Hmong (22)	27	0.02
Indian (1,869)	2,133	1.29
Indonesian (494)	723	0.44
Japanese (559)	1,224	0.74
Korean (2,189)	2,443	1.48
Laotian (36)	42	0.03
Malaysian (22)	31	0.02
Nepalese (8)	8	<0.01
Pakistani (466)	521	0.32
Sri Lankan (42)	49	0.03
Taiwanese (533)	609	0.37
Thai (297)	403	0.24
Vietnamese (1,159)	1,350	0.82
Hawaii Native/Pacific Islander (443)	1,132	0.68
Not Hispanic (383)	909	0.55
Hispanic (60)	223	0.13
Fijian (6)	22	0.01
Guamanian/Chamorro (53)	94	0.06
Marshallese (0)	0	<0.01
Native Hawaiian (75)	286	0.17
Samoan (109)	207	0.13
Tongan (145)	195	0.12
White (102,401)	109,730	66.39
Not Hispanic (70,572)	74,326	44.97
Hispanic (31,829)	35,404	21.42

*Notes: † The Census 2010 population figure is used to calculate the percentages in the Hispanic Origin and Race categories. Ancestry percentages are based on the 2006-2010 American Community Survey population (not shown); ‡ Numbers in parentheses indicate the number of people reporting a single ancestry; * Numbers in parentheses indicate the number of persons reporting this race alone, not in combination with any other race; Please refer to the Explanation of Data for more information.*

Redding

Place Type: City
County: Shasta
Population: 89,861

Ancestry	Population	%
Afghan (10)	10	0.01
African, Sub-Saharan (51)	166	0.19
African (0)	72	0.08
Cape Verdean (0)	0	<0.01
Ethiopian (0)	43	0.05
Ghanaian (0)	0	<0.01
Kenyan (0)	0	<0.01
Liberian (34)	34	0.04
Nigerian (0)	0	<0.01
Senegalese (0)	0	<0.01
Sierra Leonean (0)	0	<0.01
Somalian (0)	0	<0.01
South African (17)	17	0.02
Sudanese (0)	0	<0.01
Ugandan (0)	0	<0.01
Zimbabwean (0)	0	<0.01
Other Sub-Saharan African (0)	0	<0.01
Albanian (0)	0	<0.01
Alsatian (0)	0	<0.01
American (5,979)	5,979	6.69
Arab (96)	150	0.17
Arab (0)	0	<0.01
Egyptian (0)	0	<0.01
Iraqi (0)	0	<0.01
Jordanian (3)	3	<0.01
Lebanese (76)	130	0.15
Moroccan (0)	0	<0.01
Palestinian (0)	0	<0.01
Syrian (17)	17	0.02
Other Arab (0)	0	<0.01
Armenian (159)	171	0.19
Assyrian/Chaldean/Syriac (0)	0	<0.01
Australian (34)	87	0.10
Austrian (66)	239	0.27
Basque (90)	106	0.12
Belgian (0)	9	0.01
Brazilian (25)	35	0.04
British (198)	506	0.57
Bulgarian (0)	13	0.01
Cajun (24)	35	0.04
Canadian (77)	184	0.21
Carpatho Rusyn (0)	0	<0.01
Celtic (0)	0	<0.01
Croatian (37)	119	0.13
Cypriot (0)	0	<0.01
Czech (80)	417	0.47
Czechoslovakian (35)	235	0.26
Danish (207)	1,008	1.13
Dutch (489)	2,024	2.26
Eastern European (81)	111	0.12
English (3,773)	12,433	13.91
Estonian (0)	0	<0.01
European (958)	1,111	1.24
Finnish (533)	836	0.94
French, ex. Basque (499)	3,512	3.93
French Canadian (164)	635	0.71
German (5,347)	17,567	19.65
German Russian (0)	61	0.07
Greek (127)	321	0.36
Guyanese (0)	0	<0.01
Hungarian (60)	381	0.43
Icelander (0)	6	0.01
Iranian (16)	80	0.09
Irish (3,778)	13,432	15.03
Israeli (0)	0	<0.01
Italian (2,032)	5,117	5.72
Latvian (11)	11	0.01
Lithuanian (48)	72	0.08
Luxemburger (0)	31	0.03
Macedonian (0)	0	<0.01
Maltese (0)	18	0.02
New Zealander (0)	0	<0.01
Northern European (269)	275	0.31
Norwegian (350)	2,132	2.39
Pennsylvania German (38)	53	0.06
Polish (591)	1,610	1.80
Portuguese (393)	1,436	1.61
Romanian (35)	77	0.09
Russian (551)	1,237	1.38
Scandinavian (297)	428	0.48
Scotch-Irish (676)	2,305	2.58
Scottish (516)	2,023	2.26
Serbian (0)	8	0.01
Slavic (0)	33	0.04
Slovak (0)	29	0.03
Slovene (0)	0	<0.01
Soviet Union (0)	0	<0.01
Swedish (662)	3,053	3.42
Swiss (54)	280	0.31
Turkish (0)	0	<0.01
Ukrainian (0)	201	0.22
Welsh (131)	853	0.95
West Indian, ex. Hispanic (0)	38	0.04
Bahamian (0)	0	<0.01
Barbadian (0)	0	<0.01
Belizean (0)	0	<0.01
Bermudan (0)	0	<0.01
British West Indian (0)	0	<0.01
Dutch West Indian (0)	38	0.04
Haitian (0)	0	<0.01
Jamaican (0)	0	<0.01
Trinidadian/Tobagonian (0)	0	<0.01
U.S. Virgin Islander (0)	0	<0.01
West Indian (0)	0	<0.01
Other West Indian (0)	0	<0.01
Yugoslavian (54)	131	0.15

Hispanic Origin	Population	%
Hispanic or Latino (of any race)	7,787	8.67
Central American, ex. Mexican	244	0.27
Costa Rican	20	0.02
Guatemalan	43	0.05
Honduran	15	0.02
Nicaraguan	39	0.04
Panamanian	11	0.01
Salvadoran	113	0.13
Other Central American	3	<0.01
Cuban	56	0.06
Dominican Republic	18	0.02
Mexican	5,767	6.42
Puerto Rican	307	0.34
South American	143	0.16
Argentinean	13	0.01
Bolivian	6	0.01
Chilean	12	0.01
Colombian	41	0.05
Ecuadorian	9	0.01
Paraguayan	1	<0.01
Peruvian	44	0.05
Uruguayan	1	<0.01
Venezuelan	13	0.01
Other South American	3	<0.01
Other Hispanic or Latino	1,252	1.39

Race*	Population	%
African-American/Black (1,092)	1,971	2.19
Not Hispanic (1,025)	1,757	1.96
Hispanic (67)	214	0.24
American Indian/Alaska Native (2,034)	4,059	4.52
Not Hispanic (1,665)	3,383	3.76
Hispanic (369)	676	0.75
Alaska Athabascan *(Ala. Nat.)* (10)	15	0.02
Aleut *(Alaska Native)* (2)	7	0.01
Apache (33)	79	0.09
Arapaho (2)	6	0.01
Blackfeet (21)	94	0.10
Canadian/French Am. Ind. (2)	5	0.01
Central American Ind. (1)	2	<0.01
Cherokee (170)	599	0.67
Cheyenne (6)	9	0.01
Chickasaw (8)	25	0.03
Chippewa (24)	63	0.07
Choctaw (61)	175	0.19
Colville (1)	1	<0.01
Comanche (3)	15	0.02
Cree (1)	5	0.01
Creek (12)	38	0.04
Crow (1)	6	0.01
Delaware (1)	5	0.01
Hopi (3)	7	0.01
Houma (0)	0	<0.01
Inupiat *(Alaska Native)* (6)	20	0.02
Iroquois (9)	17	0.02
Kiowa (1)	5	0.01
Lumbee (3)	7	0.01
Menominee (0)	1	<0.01
Mexican American Ind. (37)	65	0.07
Navajo (22)	48	0.05
Osage (4)	10	0.01
Ottawa (2)	3	<0.01
Paiute (22)	33	0.04
Pima (2)	5	0.01
Potawatomi (14)	29	0.03
Pueblo (6)	9	0.01
Puget Sound Salish (1)	3	<0.01
Seminole (1)	5	0.01
Shoshone (1)	5	0.01
Sioux (34)	71	0.08
South American Ind. (0)	3	<0.01
Spanish American Ind. (0)	2	<0.01
Tlingit-Haida *(Alaska Native)* (6)	19	0.02
Tohono O'Odham (2)	2	<0.01
Tsimshian *(Alaska Native)* (1)	5	0.01
Ute (0)	1	<0.01
Yakama (3)	4	<0.01
Yaqui (7)	12	0.01
Yuman (4)	6	0.01
Yup'ik *(Alaska Native)* (0)	1	<0.01
Asian (3,034)	3,925	4.37
Not Hispanic (2,974)	3,752	4.18
Hispanic (60)	173	0.19
Bangladeshi (8)	9	0.01
Bhutanese (0)	0	<0.01
Burmese (5)	6	0.01
Cambodian (29)	49	0.05
Chinese, ex. Taiwanese (390)	566	0.63
Filipino (425)	762	0.85
Hmong (52)	68	0.08
Indian (370)	428	0.48
Indonesian (7)	25	0.03
Japanese (158)	405	0.45
Korean (143)	208	0.23
Laotian (1,023)	1,124	1.25
Malaysian (0)	0	<0.01
Nepalese (2)	2	<0.01
Pakistani (25)	27	0.03
Sri Lankan (3)	3	<0.01
Taiwanese (9)	13	0.01
Thai (44)	66	0.07
Vietnamese (120)	156	0.17
Hawaii Native/Pacific Islander (156)	413	0.46
Not Hispanic (128)	334	0.37
Hispanic (28)	79	0.09
Fijian (7)	7	0.01
Guamanian/Chamorro (28)	57	0.06
Marshallese (1)	5	0.01
Native Hawaiian (63)	217	0.24
Samoan (25)	49	0.05
Tongan (3)	6	0.01
White (77,117)	80,967	90.10
Not Hispanic (73,038)	75,994	84.57
Hispanic (4,079)	4,973	5.53

*Notes: † The Census 2010 population figure is used to calculate the percentages in the Hispanic Origin and Race categories. Ancestry percentages are based on the 2006-2010 American Community Survey population (not shown); ‡ Numbers in parentheses indicate the number of people reporting a single ancestry; * Numbers in parentheses indicate the number of persons reporting this race alone, not in combination with any other race; Please refer to the Explanation of Data for more information.*

Redlands

Place Type: City
County: San Bernardino
Population: 68,747

Ancestry	Population	%
Afghan (0)	0	<0.01
African, Sub-Saharan (807)	844	1.23
African (706)	727	1.06
Cape Verdean (0)	0	<0.01
Ethiopian (20)	20	0.03
Ghanaian (0)	0	<0.01
Kenyan (21)	21	0.03
Liberian (0)	0	<0.01
Nigerian (0)	0	<0.01
Senegalese (0)	0	<0.01
Sierra Leonean (0)	0	<0.01
Somalian (0)	0	<0.01
South African (53)	53	0.08
Sudanese (7)	23	0.03
Ugandan (0)	0	<0.01
Zimbabwean (0)	0	<0.01
Other Sub-Saharan African (0)	0	<0.01
Albanian (0)	0	<0.01
Alsatian (16)	16	0.02
American (1,811)	1,811	2.63
Arab (468)	603	0.88
Arab (0)	0	<0.01
Egyptian (113)	149	0.22
Iraqi (11)	11	0.02
Jordanian (111)	111	0.16
Lebanese (51)	77	0.11
Moroccan (0)	0	<0.01
Palestinian (29)	29	0.04
Syrian (135)	208	0.30
Other Arab (18)	18	0.03
Armenian (71)	153	0.22
Assyrian/Chaldean/Syriac (0)	0	<0.01
Australian (42)	100	0.15
Austrian (29)	207	0.30
Basque (12)	18	0.03
Belgian (0)	35	0.05
Brazilian (1)	14	0.02
British (341)	701	1.02
Bulgarian (0)	17	0.02
Cajun (16)	16	0.02
Canadian (88)	220	0.32
Carpatho Rusyn (0)	0	<0.01
Celtic (0)	0	<0.01
Croatian (0)	29	0.04
Cypriot (0)	0	<0.01
Czech (29)	139	0.20
Czechoslovakian (14)	68	0.10
Danish (185)	487	0.71
Dutch (631)	1,575	2.29
Eastern European (30)	41	0.06
English (1,727)	6,746	9.80
Estonian (0)	0	<0.01
European (994)	1,249	1.81
Finnish (51)	142	0.21
French, ex. Basque (457)	1,821	2.64
French Canadian (193)	445	0.65
German (3,381)	10,844	15.75
German Russian (0)	0	<0.01
Greek (173)	326	0.47
Guyanese (0)	0	<0.01
Hungarian (139)	467	0.68
Icelander (0)	0	<0.01
Iranian (186)	186	0.27
Irish (1,672)	7,443	10.81
Israeli (27)	27	0.04
Italian (1,262)	3,665	5.32
Latvian (14)	24	0.03
Lithuanian (25)	118	0.17
Luxemburger (0)	0	<0.01
Macedonian (0)	0	<0.01
Maltese (0)	0	<0.01
New Zealander (0)	18	0.03
Northern European (78)	78	0.11
Norwegian (297)	1,224	1.78
Pennsylvania German (0)	12	0.02
Polish (340)	1,394	2.02
Portuguese (179)	460	0.67
Romanian (162)	168	0.24
Russian (208)	725	1.05
Scandinavian (94)	135	0.20
Scotch-Irish (481)	1,059	1.54
Scottish (316)	1,357	1.97
Serbian (24)	53	0.08
Slavic (19)	38	0.06
Slovak (12)	28	0.04
Slovene (0)	14	0.02
Soviet Union (0)	0	<0.01
Swedish (545)	1,411	2.05
Swiss (81)	292	0.42
Turkish (0)	0	<0.01
Ukrainian (0)	69	0.10
Welsh (102)	566	0.82
West Indian, ex. Hispanic (52)	140	0.20
Bahamian (0)	23	0.03
Barbadian (0)	0	<0.01
Belizean (0)	0	<0.01
Bermudan (0)	0	<0.01
British West Indian (0)	0	<0.01
Dutch West Indian (0)	0	<0.01
Haitian (0)	0	<0.01
Jamaican (38)	103	0.15
Trinidadian/Tobagonian (0)	0	<0.01
U.S. Virgin Islander (0)	0	<0.01
West Indian (14)	14	0.02
Other West Indian (0)	0	<0.01
Yugoslavian (38)	63	0.09

Hispanic Origin	Population	%
Hispanic or Latino (of any race)	20,810	30.27
Central American, ex. Mexican	611	0.89
Costa Rican	56	0.08
Guatemalan	127	0.18
Honduran	51	0.07
Nicaraguan	61	0.09
Panamanian	44	0.06
Salvadoran	255	0.37
Other Central American	17	0.02
Cuban	137	0.20
Dominican Republic	35	0.05
Mexican	17,460	25.40
Puerto Rican	477	0.69
South American	462	0.67
Argentinean	97	0.14
Bolivian	18	0.03
Chilean	45	0.07
Colombian	141	0.21
Ecuadorian	36	0.05
Paraguayan	2	<0.01
Peruvian	106	0.15
Uruguayan	4	0.01
Venezuelan	9	0.01
Other South American	4	0.01
Other Hispanic or Latino	1,628	2.37

Race*	Population	%
African-American/Black (3,564)	4,411	6.42
Not Hispanic (3,326)	3,900	5.67
Hispanic (238)	511	0.74
American Indian/Alaska Native (625)	1,313	1.91
Not Hispanic (236)	636	0.93
Hispanic (389)	677	0.98
Alaska Athabascan *(Ala. Nat.)* (0)	2	<0.01
Aleut *(Alaska Native)* (1)	2	<0.01
Apache (12)	39	0.06
Arapaho (0)	2	<0.01
Blackfeet (6)	27	0.04
Canadian/French Am. Ind. (0)	4	0.01
Central American Ind. (1)	7	0.01
Cherokee (28)	174	0.25
Cheyenne (1)	6	0.01
Chickasaw (2)	5	0.01
Chippewa (6)	17	0.02
Choctaw (19)	54	0.08
Colville (0)	0	<0.01
Comanche (0)	0	<0.01
Cree (0)	0	<0.01
Creek (4)	9	0.01
Crow (0)	4	0.01
Delaware (1)	1	<0.01
Hopi (9)	9	0.01
Houma (0)	0	<0.01
Inupiat *(Alaska Native)* (0)	1	<0.01
Iroquois (4)	8	0.01
Kiowa (0)	0	<0.01
Lumbee (1)	4	0.01
Menominee (0)	0	<0.01
Mexican American Ind. (59)	87	0.13
Navajo (28)	44	0.06
Osage (6)	8	0.01
Ottawa (1)	5	0.01
Paiute (0)	0	<0.01
Pima (0)	2	<0.01
Potawatomi (1)	5	0.01
Pueblo (13)	18	0.03
Puget Sound Salish (2)	2	<0.01
Seminole (0)	3	<0.01
Shoshone (1)	2	<0.01
Sioux (10)	22	0.03
South American Ind. (1)	8	0.01
Spanish American Ind. (8)	8	0.01
Tlingit-Haida *(Alaska Native)* (1)	1	<0.01
Tohono O'Odham (5)	8	0.01
Tsimshian *(Alaska Native)* (0)	0	<0.01
Ute (0)	0	<0.01
Yakama (0)	0	<0.01
Yaqui (23)	47	0.07
Yuman (4)	5	0.01
Yup'ik *(Alaska Native)* (0)	0	<0.01
Asian (5,216)	6,487	9.44
Not Hispanic (5,100)	6,075	8.84
Hispanic (116)	412	0.60
Bangladeshi (53)	71	0.10
Bhutanese (0)	0	<0.01
Burmese (16)	23	0.03
Cambodian (101)	134	0.19
Chinese, ex. Taiwanese (718)	979	1.42
Filipino (1,209)	1,623	2.36
Hmong (0)	0	<0.01
Indian (856)	1,007	1.46
Indonesian (375)	434	0.63
Japanese (233)	528	0.77
Korean (532)	657	0.96
Laotian (12)	17	0.02
Malaysian (5)	12	0.02
Nepalese (13)	13	0.02
Pakistani (127)	161	0.23
Sri Lankan (17)	21	0.03
Taiwanese (96)	113	0.16
Thai (153)	195	0.28
Vietnamese (456)	528	0.77
Hawaii Native/Pacific Islander (235)	504	0.73
Not Hispanic (201)	403	0.59
Hispanic (34)	101	0.15
Fijian (0)	2	<0.01
Guamanian/Chamorro (18)	50	0.07
Marshallese (0)	2	<0.01
Native Hawaiian (60)	181	0.26
Samoan (102)	143	0.21
Tongan (3)	11	0.02
White (47,452)	50,342	73.23
Not Hispanic (37,103)	38,703	56.30
Hispanic (10,349)	11,639	16.93

*Notes: † The Census 2010 population figure is used to calculate the percentages in the Hispanic Origin and Race categories. Ancestry percentages are based on the 2006-2010 American Community Survey population (not shown); ‡ Numbers in parentheses indicate the number of people reporting a single ancestry; * Numbers in parentheses indicate the number of persons reporting this race alone, not in combination with any other race; Please refer to the Explanation of Data for more information.*

Redondo Beach

Place Type: City
County: Los Angeles
Population: 66,748

Ancestry	Population	%
Afghan (210)	210	0.32
African, Sub-Saharan (285)	308	0.47
African (171)	172	0.26
Cape Verdean (32)	32	0.05
Ethiopian (48)	48	0.07
Ghanaian (12)	12	0.02
Kenyan (22)	22	0.03
Liberian (0)	0	<0.01
Nigerian (0)	10	0.02
Senegalese (0)	0	<0.01
Sierra Leonean (0)	0	<0.01
Somalian (0)	0	<0.01
South African (0)	0	<0.01
Sudanese (0)	0	<0.01
Ugandan (0)	0	<0.01
Zimbabwean (0)	0	<0.01
Other Sub-Saharan African (0)	12	0.02
Albanian (0)	0	<0.01
Alsatian (0)	0	<0.01
American (2,768)	2,768	4.19
Arab (550)	795	1.20
Arab (12)	12	0.02
Egyptian (61)	61	0.09
Iraqi (13)	13	0.02
Jordanian (0)	0	<0.01
Lebanese (339)	545	0.83
Moroccan (15)	15	0.02
Palestinian (14)	14	0.02
Syrian (82)	105	0.16
Other Arab (14)	30	0.05
Armenian (594)	659	1.00
Assyrian/Chaldean/Syriac (17)	17	0.03
Australian (11)	41	0.06
Austrian (95)	291	0.44
Basque (11)	11	0.02
Belgian (22)	58	0.09
Brazilian (302)	302	0.46
British (392)	730	1.11
Bulgarian (15)	40	0.06
Cajun (0)	0	<0.01
Canadian (141)	265	0.40
Carpatho Rusyn (0)	15	0.02
Celtic (0)	42	0.06
Croatian (66)	95	0.14
Cypriot (0)	0	<0.01
Czech (140)	391	0.59
Czechoslovakian (0)	22	0.03
Danish (76)	310	0.47
Dutch (187)	1,197	1.81
Eastern European (365)	380	0.58
English (1,906)	6,401	9.69
Estonian (0)	39	0.06
European (1,530)	1,770	2.68
Finnish (90)	289	0.44
French, ex. Basque (292)	1,768	2.68
French Canadian (253)	574	0.87
German (3,122)	10,689	16.18
German Russian (0)	0	<0.01
Greek (193)	440	0.67
Guyanese (0)	0	<0.01
Hungarian (186)	576	0.87
Icelander (0)	14	0.02
Iranian (672)	672	1.02
Irish (2,544)	8,764	13.27
Israeli (18)	18	0.03
Italian (1,331)	4,623	7.00
Latvian (39)	95	0.14
Lithuanian (72)	164	0.25
Luxemburger (0)	1	<0.01
Macedonian (0)	0	<0.01
Maltese (8)	17	0.03
New Zealander (0)	0	<0.01
Northern European (41)	47	0.07
Norwegian (412)	1,399	2.12
Pennsylvania German (0)	0	<0.01
Polish (789)	2,078	3.15
Portuguese (266)	430	0.65
Romanian (33)	212	0.32
Russian (568)	1,509	2.28
Scandinavian (130)	250	0.38
Scotch-Irish (192)	662	1.00
Scottish (296)	1,368	2.07
Serbian (69)	106	0.16
Slavic (98)	110	0.17
Slovak (0)	142	0.21
Slovene (0)	52	0.08
Soviet Union (0)	0	<0.01
Swedish (258)	1,304	1.97
Swiss (22)	523	0.79
Turkish (132)	139	0.21
Ukrainian (83)	190	0.29
Welsh (84)	499	0.76
West Indian, ex. Hispanic (52)	67	0.10
Bahamian (0)	0	<0.01
Barbadian (0)	0	<0.01
Belizean (17)	17	0.03
Bermudan (0)	0	<0.01
British West Indian (0)	0	<0.01
Dutch West Indian (0)	0	<0.01
Haitian (10)	10	0.02
Jamaican (11)	11	0.02
Trinidadian/Tobagonian (0)	0	<0.01
U.S. Virgin Islander (0)	0	<0.01
West Indian (14)	29	0.04
Other West Indian (0)	0	<0.01
Yugoslavian (30)	88	0.13

Hispanic Origin	Population	%
Hispanic or Latino (of any race)	10,142	15.19
Central American, ex. Mexican	930	1.39
Costa Rican	73	0.11
Guatemalan	302	0.45
Honduran	69	0.10
Nicaraguan	117	0.18
Panamanian	33	0.05
Salvadoran	305	0.46
Other Central American	31	0.05
Cuban	338	0.51
Dominican Republic	28	0.04
Mexican	6,193	9.28
Puerto Rican	399	0.60
South American	1,230	1.84
Argentinean	232	0.35
Bolivian	41	0.06
Chilean	104	0.16
Colombian	243	0.36
Ecuadorian	124	0.19
Paraguayan	5	0.01
Peruvian	375	0.56
Uruguayan	29	0.04
Venezuelan	61	0.09
Other South American	16	0.02
Other Hispanic or Latino	1,024	1.53

Race*	Population	%
African-American/Black (1,852)	2,558	3.83
Not Hispanic (1,772)	2,323	3.48
Hispanic (80)	235	0.35
American Indian/Alaska Native (291)	767	1.15
Not Hispanic (163)	494	0.74
Hispanic (128)	273	0.41
Alaska Athabascan *(Ala. Nat.)* (0)	1	<0.01
Aleut *(Alaska Native)* (2)	2	<0.01
Apache (8)	19	0.03
Arapaho (0)	3	<0.01
Blackfeet (10)	23	0.03
Canadian/French Am. Ind. (0)	1	<0.01
Central American Ind. (5)	5	0.01
Cherokee (35)	128	0.19
Cheyenne (2)	6	0.01
Chickasaw (2)	6	0.01
Chippewa (5)	18	0.03
Choctaw (14)	39	0.06
Colville (1)	1	<0.01
Comanche (1)	5	0.01
Cree (1)	4	0.01
Creek (3)	12	0.02
Crow (0)	1	<0.01
Delaware (0)	4	0.01
Hopi (0)	2	<0.01
Houma (0)	0	<0.01
Inupiat *(Alaska Native)* (2)	2	<0.01
Iroquois (1)	9	0.01
Kiowa (0)	0	<0.01
Lumbee (0)	1	<0.01
Menominee (0)	1	<0.01
Mexican American Ind. (16)	30	0.04
Navajo (24)	47	0.07
Osage (0)	1	<0.01
Ottawa (0)	0	<0.01
Paiute (1)	3	<0.01
Pima (0)	4	0.01
Potawatomi (1)	4	0.01
Pueblo (6)	10	0.01
Puget Sound Salish (0)	2	<0.01
Seminole (1)	5	0.01
Shoshone (0)	1	<0.01
Sioux (8)	23	0.03
South American Ind. (1)	7	0.01
Spanish American Ind. (3)	3	<0.01
Tlingit-Haida *(Alaska Native)* (0)	2	<0.01
Tohono O'Odham (0)	1	<0.01
Tsimshian *(Alaska Native)* (0)	0	<0.01
Ute (0)	1	<0.01
Yakama (0)	6	0.01
Yaqui (4)	10	0.01
Yuman (2)	2	<0.01
Yup'ik *(Alaska Native)* (0)	0	<0.01
Asian (8,004)	10,324	15.47
Not Hispanic (7,858)	9,865	14.78
Hispanic (146)	459	0.69
Bangladeshi (6)	6	0.01
Bhutanese (0)	0	<0.01
Burmese (8)	14	0.02
Cambodian (23)	28	0.04
Chinese, ex. Taiwanese (1,567)	2,247	3.37
Filipino (1,159)	1,937	2.90
Hmong (3)	3	<0.01
Indian (736)	870	1.30
Indonesian (55)	114	0.17
Japanese (1,836)	2,658	3.98
Korean (1,020)	1,282	1.92
Laotian (7)	10	0.01
Malaysian (7)	13	0.02
Nepalese (4)	4	0.01
Pakistani (165)	185	0.28
Sri Lankan (15)	26	0.04
Taiwanese (187)	219	0.33
Thai (124)	180	0.27
Vietnamese (599)	746	1.12
Hawaii Native/Pacific Islander (199)	580	0.87
Not Hispanic (177)	469	0.70
Hispanic (22)	111	0.17
Fijian (8)	13	0.02
Guamanian/Chamorro (48)	79	0.12
Marshallese (0)	0	<0.01
Native Hawaiian (56)	248	0.37
Samoan (52)	100	0.15
Tongan (10)	19	0.03
White (49,805)	53,210	79.72
Not Hispanic (43,531)	46,077	69.03
Hispanic (6,274)	7,133	10.69

*Notes: † The Census 2010 population figure is used to calculate the percentages in the Hispanic Origin and Race categories. Ancestry percentages are based on the 2006-2010 American Community Survey population (not shown); ‡ Numbers in parentheses indicate the number of people reporting a single ancestry; * Numbers in parentheses indicate the number of persons reporting this race alone, not in combination with any other race; Please refer to the Explanation of Data for more information.*

Redwood City

Place Type: City
County: San Mateo
Population: 76,815

Ancestry	Population	%
Afghan (0)	0	<0.01
African, Sub-Saharan (29)	120	0.16
African (13)	95	0.13
Cape Verdean (0)	0	<0.01
Ethiopian (0)	0	<0.01
Ghanaian (0)	0	<0.01
Kenyan (0)	0	<0.01
Liberian (0)	0	<0.01
Nigerian (0)	0	<0.01
Senegalese (0)	0	<0.01
Sierra Leonean (0)	0	<0.01
Somalian (0)	0	<0.01
South African (9)	18	0.02
Sudanese (0)	0	<0.01
Ugandan (0)	0	<0.01
Zimbabwean (0)	0	<0.01
Other Sub-Saharan African (7)	7	0.01
Albanian (14)	14	0.02
Alsatian (0)	0	<0.01
American (1,474)	1,474	1.96
Arab (533)	695	0.92
Arab (141)	155	0.21
Egyptian (35)	55	0.07
Iraqi (100)	100	0.13
Jordanian (0)	0	<0.01
Lebanese (119)	218	0.29
Moroccan (23)	23	0.03
Palestinian (47)	66	0.09
Syrian (20)	30	0.04
Other Arab (48)	48	0.06
Armenian (55)	79	0.11
Assyrian/Chaldean/Syriac (16)	38	0.05
Australian (13)	61	0.08
Austrian (26)	216	0.29
Basque (33)	43	0.06
Belgian (0)	58	0.08
Brazilian (46)	87	0.12
British (269)	409	0.54
Bulgarian (42)	42	0.06
Cajun (0)	0	<0.01
Canadian (124)	299	0.40
Carpatho Rusyn (0)	0	<0.01
Celtic (115)	115	0.15
Croatian (112)	342	0.45
Cypriot (0)	0	<0.01
Czech (91)	239	0.32
Czechoslovakian (34)	109	0.14
Danish (99)	698	0.93
Dutch (244)	903	1.20
Eastern European (187)	226	0.30
English (1,454)	5,306	7.06
Estonian (44)	76	0.10
European (924)	1,231	1.64
Finnish (63)	134	0.18
French, ex. Basque (285)	1,924	2.56
French Canadian (56)	147	0.20
German (2,419)	7,186	9.56
German Russian (0)	0	<0.01
Greek (456)	799	1.06
Guyanese (0)	0	<0.01
Hungarian (56)	278	0.37
Icelander (0)	0	<0.01
Iranian (485)	491	0.65
Irish (1,866)	6,552	8.71
Israeli (90)	102	0.14
Italian (2,202)	5,505	7.32
Latvian (15)	54	0.07
Lithuanian (27)	70	0.09
Luxemburger (0)	0	<0.01
Macedonian (0)	0	<0.01
Maltese (32)	121	0.16
New Zealander (10)	10	0.01
Northern European (53)	62	0.08
Norwegian (289)	752	1.00
Pennsylvania German (0)	12	0.02
Polish (393)	984	1.31
Portuguese (375)	676	0.90
Romanian (91)	135	0.18
Russian (532)	1,013	1.35
Scandinavian (94)	114	0.15
Scotch-Irish (245)	857	1.14
Scottish (591)	1,603	2.13
Serbian (0)	0	<0.01
Slavic (0)	0	<0.01
Slovak (13)	45	0.06
Slovene (14)	14	0.02
Soviet Union (0)	0	<0.01
Swedish (266)	1,137	1.51
Swiss (250)	556	0.74
Turkish (223)	283	0.38
Ukrainian (44)	181	0.24
Welsh (45)	414	0.55
West Indian, ex. Hispanic (0)	37	0.05
Bahamian (0)	0	<0.01
Barbadian (0)	0	<0.01
Belizean (0)	0	<0.01
Bermudan (0)	0	<0.01
British West Indian (0)	0	<0.01
Dutch West Indian (0)	0	<0.01
Haitian (0)	0	<0.01
Jamaican (0)	0	<0.01
Trinidadian/Tobagonian (0)	0	<0.01
U.S. Virgin Islander (0)	0	<0.01
West Indian (0)	37	0.05
Other West Indian (0)	0	<0.01
Yugoslavian (117)	169	0.22

Hispanic Origin	Population	%
Hispanic or Latino (of any race)	29,810	38.81
Central American, ex. Mexican	5,032	6.55
Costa Rican	62	0.08
Guatemalan	1,756	2.29
Honduran	135	0.18
Nicaraguan	565	0.74
Panamanian	37	0.05
Salvadoran	2,432	3.17
Other Central American	45	0.06
Cuban	167	0.22
Dominican Republic	24	0.03
Mexican	21,132	27.51
Puerto Rican	384	0.50
South American	1,166	1.52
Argentinean	149	0.19
Bolivian	90	0.12
Chilean	89	0.12
Colombian	133	0.17
Ecuadorian	43	0.06
Paraguayan	0	<0.01
Peruvian	578	0.75
Uruguayan	21	0.03
Venezuelan	41	0.05
Other South American	22	0.03
Other Hispanic or Latino	1,905	2.48

Race*	Population	%
African-American/Black (1,881)	2,531	3.29
Not Hispanic (1,655)	2,131	2.77
Hispanic (226)	400	0.52
American Indian/Alaska Native (511)	1,101	1.43
Not Hispanic (152)	484	0.63
Hispanic (359)	617	0.80
Alaska Athabascan *(Ala. Nat.)* (0)	0	<0.01
Aleut *(Alaska Native)* (1)	2	<0.01
Apache (13)	42	0.05
Arapaho (1)	2	<0.01
Blackfeet (4)	20	0.03
Canadian/French Am. Ind. (1)	3	<0.01
Central American Ind. (17)	25	0.03
Cherokee (15)	101	0.13
Cheyenne (0)	0	<0.01
Chickasaw (2)	9	0.01
Chippewa (5)	13	0.02
Choctaw (5)	30	0.04
Colville (3)	3	<0.01
Comanche (0)	3	<0.01
Cree (0)	0	<0.01
Creek (3)	4	0.01
Crow (0)	0	<0.01
Delaware (1)	1	<0.01
Hopi (1)	1	<0.01
Houma (0)	0	<0.01
Inupiat *(Alaska Native)* (1)	3	<0.01
Iroquois (2)	5	0.01
Kiowa (0)	1	<0.01
Lumbee (0)	0	<0.01
Menominee (0)	0	<0.01
Mexican American Ind. (123)	169	0.22
Navajo (8)	33	0.04
Osage (0)	2	<0.01
Ottawa (1)	1	<0.01
Paiute (2)	7	0.01
Pima (0)	0	<0.01
Potawatomi (0)	1	<0.01
Pueblo (2)	6	0.01
Puget Sound Salish (1)	1	<0.01
Seminole (0)	2	<0.01
Shoshone (0)	3	<0.01
Sioux (8)	25	0.03
South American Ind. (6)	12	0.02
Spanish American Ind. (7)	7	0.01
Tlingit-Haida *(Alaska Native)* (8)	12	0.02
Tohono O'Odham (0)	0	<0.01
Tsimshian *(Alaska Native)* (0)	0	<0.01
Ute (0)	1	<0.01
Yakama (1)	1	<0.01
Yaqui (3)	8	0.01
Yuman (0)	7	0.01
Yup'ik *(Alaska Native)* (0)	0	<0.01
Asian (8,216)	10,083	13.13
Not Hispanic (8,063)	9,620	12.52
Hispanic (153)	463	0.60
Bangladeshi (4)	5	0.01
Bhutanese (0)	0	<0.01
Burmese (5)	15	0.02
Cambodian (37)	56	0.07
Chinese, ex. Taiwanese (2,870)	3,628	4.72
Filipino (1,665)	2,331	3.03
Hmong (2)	2	<0.01
Indian (1,440)	1,673	2.18
Indonesian (45)	78	0.10
Japanese (647)	1,038	1.35
Korean (405)	541	0.70
Laotian (22)	34	0.04
Malaysian (5)	13	0.02
Nepalese (6)	6	0.01
Pakistani (69)	84	0.11
Sri Lankan (15)	19	0.02
Taiwanese (179)	227	0.30
Thai (53)	82	0.11
Vietnamese (331)	423	0.55
Hawaii Native/Pacific Islander (795)	1,242	1.62
Not Hispanic (732)	1,092	1.42
Hispanic (63)	150	0.20
Fijian (121)	156	0.20
Guamanian/Chamorro (45)	77	0.10
Marshallese (0)	0	<0.01
Native Hawaiian (33)	156	0.20
Samoan (69)	107	0.14
Tongan (459)	539	0.70
White (46,255)	49,787	64.81
Not Hispanic (33,801)	35,757	46.55
Hispanic (12,454)	14,030	18.26

*Notes: † The Census 2010 population figure is used to calculate the percentages in the Hispanic Origin and Race categories. Ancestry percentages are based on the 2006-2010 American Community Survey population (not shown); ‡ Numbers in parentheses indicate the number of people reporting a single ancestry; * Numbers in parentheses indicate the number of persons reporting this race alone, not in combination with any other race; Please refer to the Explanation of Data for more information.*

Rialto

Place Type: City
County: San Bernardino
Population: 99,171

Ancestry	Population	%
Afghan (0)	0	<0.01
African, Sub-Saharan (641)	868	0.87
African (544)	771	0.78
Cape Verdean (0)	0	<0.01
Ethiopian (22)	22	0.02
Ghanaian (12)	12	0.01
Kenyan (17)	17	0.02
Liberian (0)	0	<0.01
Nigerian (46)	46	0.05
Senegalese (0)	0	<0.01
Sierra Leonean (0)	0	<0.01
Somalian (0)	0	<0.01
South African (0)	0	<0.01
Sudanese (0)	0	<0.01
Ugandan (0)	0	<0.01
Zimbabwean (0)	0	<0.01
Other Sub-Saharan African (0)	0	<0.01
Albanian (0)	0	<0.01
Alsatian (0)	0	<0.01
American (2,257)	2,257	2.27
Arab (397)	421	0.42
Arab (0)	24	0.02
Egyptian (208)	208	0.21
Iraqi (0)	0	<0.01
Jordanian (0)	0	<0.01
Lebanese (0)	0	<0.01
Moroccan (0)	0	<0.01
Palestinian (153)	153	0.15
Syrian (36)	36	0.04
Other Arab (0)	0	<0.01
Armenian (0)	0	<0.01
Assyrian/Chaldean/Syriac (0)	0	<0.01
Australian (0)	0	<0.01
Austrian (0)	0	<0.01
Basque (0)	0	<0.01
Belgian (0)	0	<0.01
Brazilian (36)	95	0.10
British (35)	170	0.17
Bulgarian (0)	0	<0.01
Cajun (0)	0	<0.01
Canadian (25)	25	0.03
Carpatho Rusyn (0)	0	<0.01
Celtic (0)	0	<0.01
Croatian (0)	0	<0.01
Cypriot (0)	0	<0.01
Czech (0)	65	0.07
Czechoslovakian (7)	7	0.01
Danish (22)	131	0.13
Dutch (0)	238	0.24
Eastern European (0)	0	<0.01
English (578)	2,205	2.22
Estonian (0)	0	<0.01
European (262)	353	0.36
Finnish (0)	22	0.02
French, ex. Basque (109)	975	0.98
French Canadian (16)	47	0.05
German (1,299)	4,375	4.41
German Russian (0)	0	<0.01
Greek (13)	44	0.04
Guyanese (0)	0	<0.01
Hungarian (11)	67	0.07
Icelander (0)	0	<0.01
Iranian (0)	0	<0.01
Irish (817)	2,925	2.95
Israeli (0)	0	<0.01
Italian (429)	1,402	1.41
Latvian (0)	0	<0.01
Lithuanian (46)	71	0.07
Luxemburger (0)	0	<0.01
Macedonian (0)	0	<0.01
Maltese (0)	0	<0.01
New Zealander (0)	0	<0.01
Northern European (0)	0	<0.01
Norwegian (32)	398	0.40
Pennsylvania German (16)	16	0.02
Polish (71)	187	0.19
Portuguese (42)	42	0.04
Romanian (0)	0	<0.01
Russian (32)	114	0.11
Scandinavian (40)	50	0.05
Scotch-Irish (81)	260	0.26
Scottish (75)	234	0.24
Serbian (0)	0	<0.01
Slavic (0)	0	<0.01
Slovak (24)	69	0.07
Slovene (25)	33	0.03
Soviet Union (0)	0	<0.01
Swedish (58)	169	0.17
Swiss (35)	136	0.14
Turkish (0)	0	<0.01
Ukrainian (0)	0	<0.01
Welsh (9)	40	0.04
West Indian, ex. Hispanic (527)	572	0.58
Bahamian (0)	0	<0.01
Barbadian (159)	159	0.16
Belizean (223)	231	0.23
Bermudan (0)	0	<0.01
British West Indian (0)	0	<0.01
Dutch West Indian (0)	0	<0.01
Haitian (0)	0	<0.01
Jamaican (145)	182	0.18
Trinidadian/Tobagonian (0)	0	<0.01
U.S. Virgin Islander (0)	0	<0.01
West Indian (0)	0	<0.01
Other West Indian (0)	0	<0.01
Yugoslavian (0)	0	<0.01

Hispanic Origin	Population	%
Hispanic or Latino (of any race)	67,038	67.60
Central American, ex. Mexican	4,402	4.44
Costa Rican	102	0.10
Guatemalan	1,111	1.12
Honduran	324	0.33
Nicaraguan	482	0.49
Panamanian	86	0.09
Salvadoran	2,246	2.26
Other Central American	51	0.05
Cuban	251	0.25
Dominican Republic	39	0.04
Mexican	57,699	58.18
Puerto Rican	687	0.69
South American	747	0.75
Argentinean	97	0.10
Bolivian	35	0.04
Chilean	35	0.04
Colombian	201	0.20
Ecuadorian	127	0.13
Paraguayan	0	<0.01
Peruvian	207	0.21
Uruguayan	4	<0.01
Venezuelan	30	0.03
Other South American	11	0.01
Other Hispanic or Latino	3,213	3.24

Race*	Population	%
African-American/Black (16,236)	17,754	17.90
Not Hispanic (15,457)	16,367	16.50
Hispanic (779)	1,387	1.40
American Indian/Alaska Native (1,062)	1,855	1.87
Not Hispanic (237)	640	0.65
Hispanic (825)	1,215	1.23
Alaska Athabascan *(Ala. Nat.)* (0)	0	<0.01
Aleut *(Alaska Native)* (0)	1	<0.01
Apache (36)	79	0.08
Arapaho (0)	1	<0.01
Blackfeet (3)	56	0.06
Canadian/French Am. Ind. (0)	0	<0.01
Central American Ind. (12)	27	0.03
Cherokee (20)	152	0.15
Cheyenne (0)	0	<0.01
Chickasaw (2)	16	0.02
Chippewa (11)	17	0.02
Choctaw (13)	32	0.03
Colville (0)	0	<0.01
Comanche (2)	3	<0.01
Cree (0)	0	<0.01
Creek (1)	6	0.01
Crow (0)	1	<0.01
Delaware (1)	4	<0.01
Hopi (3)	7	0.01
Houma (3)	3	<0.01
Inupiat *(Alaska Native)* (1)	1	<0.01
Iroquois (2)	8	0.01
Kiowa (1)	1	<0.01
Lumbee (0)	0	<0.01
Menominee (0)	0	<0.01
Mexican American Ind. (141)	198	0.20
Navajo (17)	44	0.04
Osage (4)	11	0.01
Ottawa (0)	5	0.01
Paiute (10)	19	0.02
Pima (5)	7	0.01
Potawatomi (4)	4	<0.01
Pueblo (28)	36	0.04
Puget Sound Salish (0)	0	<0.01
Seminole (2)	19	0.02
Shoshone (4)	9	0.01
Sioux (11)	25	0.03
South American Ind. (0)	3	<0.01
Spanish American Ind. (13)	13	0.01
Tlingit-Haida *(Alaska Native)* (0)	0	<0.01
Tohono O'Odham (1)	3	<0.01
Tsimshian *(Alaska Native)* (0)	0	<0.01
Ute (0)	0	<0.01
Yakama (0)	4	<0.01
Yaqui (48)	63	0.06
Yuman (1)	2	<0.01
Yup'ik *(Alaska Native)* (0)	0	<0.01
Asian (2,258)	2,950	2.97
Not Hispanic (2,037)	2,435	2.46
Hispanic (221)	515	0.52
Bangladeshi (4)	4	<0.01
Bhutanese (0)	0	<0.01
Burmese (25)	26	0.03
Cambodian (257)	310	0.31
Chinese, ex. Taiwanese (185)	324	0.33
Filipino (814)	1,102	1.11
Hmong (0)	0	<0.01
Indian (168)	222	0.22
Indonesian (76)	107	0.11
Japanese (94)	199	0.20
Korean (90)	117	0.12
Laotian (45)	57	0.06
Malaysian (2)	3	<0.01
Nepalese (0)	0	<0.01
Pakistani (50)	61	0.06
Sri Lankan (1)	2	<0.01
Taiwanese (18)	20	0.02
Thai (60)	79	0.08
Vietnamese (239)	279	0.28
Hawaii Native/Pacific Islander (361)	635	0.64
Not Hispanic (313)	476	0.48
Hispanic (48)	159	0.16
Fijian (20)	22	0.02
Guamanian/Chamorro (28)	39	0.04
Marshallese (8)	8	0.01
Native Hawaiian (66)	168	0.17
Samoan (139)	209	0.21
Tongan (50)	66	0.07
White (43,592)	47,165	47.56
Not Hispanic (12,475)	13,465	13.58
Hispanic (31,117)	33,700	33.98

*Notes: † The Census 2010 population figure is used to calculate the percentages in the Hispanic Origin and Race categories. Ancestry percentages are based on the 2006-2010 American Community Survey population (not shown); ‡ Numbers in parentheses indicate the number of people reporting a single ancestry; * Numbers in parentheses indicate the number of persons reporting this race alone, not in combination with any other race; Please refer to the Explanation of Data for more information.*

Richmond

Place Type: City
County: Contra Costa
Population: 103,701

Ancestry	Population	%
Afghan (12)	12	0.01
African, Sub-Saharan (5,295)	5,853	5.72
African (4,590)	4,973	4.86
Cape Verdean (0)	22	0.02
Ethiopian (321)	474	0.46
Ghanaian (0)	0	<0.01
Kenyan (0)	0	<0.01
Liberian (0)	0	<0.01
Nigerian (326)	326	0.32
Senegalese (11)	11	0.01
Sierra Leonean (0)	0	<0.01
Somalian (0)	0	<0.01
South African (0)	0	<0.01
Sudanese (0)	0	<0.01
Ugandan (0)	0	<0.01
Zimbabwean (0)	0	<0.01
Other Sub-Saharan African (47)	47	0.05
Albanian (0)	0	<0.01
Alsatian (0)	0	<0.01
American (886)	886	0.87
Arab (624)	670	0.66
Arab (43)	43	0.04
Egyptian (0)	0	<0.01
Iraqi (8)	8	0.01
Jordanian (0)	0	<0.01
Lebanese (18)	24	0.02
Moroccan (26)	37	0.04
Palestinian (529)	539	0.53
Syrian (0)	10	0.01
Other Arab (0)	9	0.01
Armenian (45)	60	0.06
Assyrian/Chaldean/Syriac (0)	0	<0.01
Australian (10)	32	0.03
Austrian (19)	229	0.22
Basque (11)	11	0.01
Belgian (13)	96	0.09
Brazilian (547)	547	0.53
British (126)	181	0.18
Bulgarian (0)	0	<0.01
Cajun (0)	0	<0.01
Canadian (26)	43	0.04
Carpatho Rusyn (0)	0	<0.01
Celtic (31)	73	0.07
Croatian (8)	42	0.04
Cypriot (0)	0	<0.01
Czech (21)	146	0.14
Czechoslovakian (30)	43	0.04
Danish (100)	237	0.23
Dutch (129)	434	0.42
Eastern European (150)	150	0.15
English (642)	2,649	2.59
Estonian (0)	0	<0.01
European (457)	623	0.61
Finnish (0)	38	0.04
French, ex. Basque (114)	1,261	1.23
French Canadian (32)	82	0.08
German (1,031)	4,058	3.97
German Russian (0)	0	<0.01
Greek (66)	180	0.18
Guyanese (0)	0	<0.01
Hungarian (146)	273	0.27
Icelander (0)	20	0.02
Iranian (419)	485	0.47
Irish (596)	2,693	2.63
Israeli (44)	44	0.04
Italian (919)	2,181	2.13
Latvian (9)	9	0.01
Lithuanian (35)	78	0.08
Luxemburger (0)	0	<0.01
Macedonian (0)	0	<0.01
Maltese (0)	0	<0.01
New Zealander (0)	0	<0.01
Northern European (187)	187	0.18
Norwegian (100)	494	0.48
Pennsylvania German (0)	0	<0.01
Polish (108)	548	0.54
Portuguese (475)	817	0.80
Romanian (42)	63	0.06
Russian (253)	609	0.60
Scandinavian (57)	122	0.12
Scotch-Irish (301)	882	0.86
Scottish (235)	789	0.77
Serbian (0)	0	<0.01
Slavic (63)	75	0.07
Slovak (48)	61	0.06
Slovene (13)	13	0.01
Soviet Union (0)	0	<0.01
Swedish (151)	703	0.69
Swiss (28)	84	0.08
Turkish (0)	0	<0.01
Ukrainian (61)	115	0.11
Welsh (19)	229	0.22
West Indian, ex. Hispanic (190)	334	0.33
Bahamian (0)	0	<0.01
Barbadian (0)	0	<0.01
Belizean (0)	0	<0.01
Bermudan (0)	0	<0.01
British West Indian (0)	0	<0.01
Dutch West Indian (0)	0	<0.01
Haitian (77)	101	0.10
Jamaican (98)	177	0.17
Trinidadian/Tobagonian (0)	0	<0.01
U.S. Virgin Islander (0)	0	<0.01
West Indian (15)	56	0.05
Other West Indian (0)	0	<0.01
Yugoslavian (24)	190	0.19

Hispanic Origin	Population	%
Hispanic or Latino (of any race)	40,921	39.46
Central American, ex. Mexican	8,329	8.03
Costa Rican	36	0.03
Guatemalan	1,717	1.66
Honduran	319	0.31
Nicaraguan	1,209	1.17
Panamanian	87	0.08
Salvadoran	4,888	4.71
Other Central American	73	0.07
Cuban	141	0.14
Dominican Republic	27	0.03
Mexican	28,275	27.27
Puerto Rican	534	0.51
South American	942	0.91
Argentinean	53	0.05
Bolivian	22	0.02
Chilean	136	0.13
Colombian	107	0.10
Ecuadorian	37	0.04
Paraguayan	0	<0.01
Peruvian	548	0.53
Uruguayan	6	0.01
Venezuelan	26	0.03
Other South American	7	0.01
Other Hispanic or Latino	2,673	2.58

Race*	Population	%
African-American/Black (27,542)	29,796	28.73
Not Hispanic (26,872)	28,533	27.51
Hispanic (670)	1,263	1.22
American Indian/Alaska Native (662)	1,735	1.67
Not Hispanic (250)	962	0.93
Hispanic (412)	773	0.75
Alaska Athabascan *(Ala. Nat.)* (1)	1	<0.01
Aleut *(Alaska Native)* (0)	1	<0.01
Apache (18)	50	0.05
Arapaho (0)	0	<0.01
Blackfeet (0)	51	0.05
Canadian/French Am. Ind. (1)	6	0.01
Central American Ind. (18)	31	0.03
Cherokee (33)	204	0.20
Cheyenne (0)	0	<0.01
Chickasaw (2)	13	0.01
Chippewa (5)	7	0.01
Choctaw (13)	64	0.06
Colville (1)	1	<0.01
Comanche (2)	10	0.01
Cree (4)	7	0.01
Creek (5)	15	0.01
Crow (0)	3	<0.01
Delaware (1)	2	<0.01
Hopi (0)	1	<0.01
Houma (2)	2	<0.01
Inupiat *(Alaska Native)* (3)	3	<0.01
Iroquois (7)	19	0.02
Kiowa (1)	1	<0.01
Lumbee (0)	0	<0.01
Menominee (0)	0	<0.01
Mexican American Ind. (115)	173	0.17
Navajo (16)	24	0.02
Osage (0)	1	<0.01
Ottawa (0)	0	<0.01
Paiute (5)	9	0.01
Pima (0)	0	<0.01
Potawatomi (0)	0	<0.01
Pueblo (14)	19	0.02
Puget Sound Salish (0)	1	<0.01
Seminole (0)	10	0.01
Shoshone (0)	1	<0.01
Sioux (11)	24	0.02
South American Ind. (9)	20	0.02
Spanish American Ind. (12)	14	0.01
Tlingit-Haida *(Alaska Native)* (1)	5	<0.01
Tohono O'Odham (1)	3	<0.01
Tsimshian *(Alaska Native)* (0)	0	<0.01
Ute (1)	2	<0.01
Yakama (0)	0	<0.01
Yaqui (13)	25	0.02
Yuman (0)	0	<0.01
Yup'ik *(Alaska Native)* (0)	1	<0.01
Asian (13,984)	15,852	15.29
Not Hispanic (13,783)	15,261	14.72
Hispanic (201)	591	0.57
Bangladeshi (2)	2	<0.01
Bhutanese (0)	0	<0.01
Burmese (46)	54	0.05
Cambodian (107)	150	0.14
Chinese, ex. Taiwanese (4,009)	4,581	4.42
Filipino (3,678)	4,500	4.34
Hmong (16)	18	0.02
Indian (1,295)	1,469	1.42
Indonesian (46)	84	0.08
Japanese (657)	1,073	1.03
Korean (405)	494	0.48
Laotian (1,703)	1,886	1.82
Malaysian (25)	45	0.04
Nepalese (68)	75	0.07
Pakistani (244)	261	0.25
Sri Lankan (39)	48	0.05
Taiwanese (169)	190	0.18
Thai (137)	217	0.21
Vietnamese (689)	816	0.79
Hawaii Native/Pacific Islander (537)	977	0.94
Not Hispanic (462)	768	0.74
Hispanic (75)	209	0.20
Fijian (110)	132	0.13
Guamanian/Chamorro (58)	111	0.11
Marshallese (0)	0	<0.01
Native Hawaiian (47)	189	0.18
Samoan (157)	230	0.22
Tongan (102)	130	0.13
White (32,590)	36,803	35.49
Not Hispanic (17,769)	19,814	19.11
Hispanic (14,821)	16,989	16.38

*Notes: † The Census 2010 population figure is used to calculate the percentages in the Hispanic Origin and Race categories. Ancestry percentages are based on the 2006-2010 American Community Survey population (not shown); ‡ Numbers in parentheses indicate the number of people reporting a single ancestry; * Numbers in parentheses indicate the number of persons reporting this race alone, not in combination with any other race; Please refer to the Explanation of Data for more information.*

Riverside

Place Type: City
County: Riverside
Population: 303,871

Ancestry	Population	%
Afghan (69)	69	0.02
African, Sub-Saharan (1,292)	1,585	0.53
African (846)	1,076	0.36
Cape Verdean (0)	0	<0.01
Ethiopian (0)	0	<0.01
Ghanaian (0)	0	<0.01
Kenyan (85)	100	0.03
Liberian (0)	0	<0.01
Nigerian (351)	351	0.12
Senegalese (0)	0	<0.01
Sierra Leonean (0)	0	<0.01
Somalian (10)	10	<0.01
South African (0)	20	0.01
Sudanese (0)	0	<0.01
Ugandan (0)	18	0.01
Zimbabwean (0)	0	<0.01
Other Sub-Saharan African (0)	10	<0.01
Albanian (0)	0	<0.01
Alsatian (0)	0	<0.01
American (7,297)	7,297	2.43
Arab (1,846)	2,242	0.75
Arab (127)	127	0.04
Egyptian (320)	349	0.12
Iraqi (237)	258	0.09
Jordanian (367)	367	0.12
Lebanese (567)	789	0.26
Moroccan (28)	28	0.01
Palestinian (12)	21	0.01
Syrian (8)	86	0.03
Other Arab (180)	217	0.07
Armenian (188)	357	0.12
Assyrian/Chaldean/Syriac (22)	99	0.03
Australian (31)	56	0.02
Austrian (251)	607	0.20
Basque (55)	120	0.04
Belgian (165)	285	0.09
Brazilian (97)	166	0.06
British (432)	697	0.23
Bulgarian (116)	130	0.04
Cajun (16)	16	0.01
Canadian (325)	620	0.21
Carpatho Rusyn (0)	0	<0.01
Celtic (9)	9	<0.01
Croatian (32)	164	0.05
Cypriot (0)	0	<0.01
Czech (58)	676	0.22
Czechoslovakian (76)	204	0.07
Danish (335)	1,079	0.36
Dutch (754)	3,659	1.22
Eastern European (74)	101	0.03
English (6,029)	18,993	6.32
Estonian (0)	10	<0.01
European (1,634)	2,080	0.69
Finnish (179)	494	0.16
French, ex. Basque (1,101)	7,394	2.46
French Canadian (405)	1,155	0.38
German (7,904)	29,153	9.70
German Russian (0)	0	<0.01
Greek (364)	723	0.24
Guyanese (21)	21	0.01
Hungarian (318)	799	0.27
Icelander (0)	0	<0.01
Iranian (372)	456	0.15
Irish (5,516)	20,754	6.91
Israeli (136)	146	0.05
Italian (4,273)	12,257	4.08
Latvian (0)	0	<0.01
Lithuanian (76)	176	0.06
Luxemburger (0)	0	<0.01
Macedonian (0)	0	<0.01
Maltese (0)	94	0.03
New Zealander (24)	73	0.02
Northern European (273)	295	0.10
Norwegian (818)	2,285	0.76
Pennsylvania German (59)	82	0.03
Polish (911)	3,752	1.25
Portuguese (514)	914	0.30
Romanian (909)	1,063	0.35
Russian (398)	1,525	0.51
Scandinavian (175)	548	0.18
Scotch-Irish (1,349)	3,461	1.15
Scottish (959)	3,263	1.09
Serbian (25)	90	0.03
Slavic (0)	112	0.04
Slovak (113)	178	0.06
Slovene (10)	98	0.03
Soviet Union (0)	0	<0.01
Swedish (1,140)	3,367	1.12
Swiss (135)	643	0.21
Turkish (59)	59	0.02
Ukrainian (105)	218	0.07
Welsh (304)	1,170	0.39
West Indian, ex. Hispanic (311)	670	0.22
Bahamian (0)	0	<0.01
Barbadian (0)	0	<0.01
Belizean (13)	13	<0.01
Bermudan (0)	0	<0.01
British West Indian (0)	0	<0.01
Dutch West Indian (0)	9	<0.01
Haitian (72)	89	0.03
Jamaican (218)	502	0.17
Trinidadian/Tobagonian (0)	0	<0.01
U.S. Virgin Islander (0)	0	<0.01
West Indian (8)	57	0.02
Other West Indian (0)	0	<0.01
Yugoslavian (34)	106	0.04

Hispanic Origin	Population	%
Hispanic or Latino (of any race)	148,953	49.02
Central American, ex. Mexican	7,792	2.56
Costa Rican	249	0.08
Guatemalan	3,338	1.10
Honduran	367	0.12
Nicaraguan	600	0.20
Panamanian	144	0.05
Salvadoran	2,995	0.99
Other Central American	99	0.03
Cuban	912	0.30
Dominican Republic	76	0.03
Mexican	127,165	41.85
Puerto Rican	2,115	0.70
South American	2,540	0.84
Argentinean	379	0.12
Bolivian	102	0.03
Chilean	236	0.08
Colombian	660	0.22
Ecuadorian	317	0.10
Paraguayan	2	<0.01
Peruvian	702	0.23
Uruguayan	19	0.01
Venezuelan	98	0.03
Other South American	25	0.01
Other Hispanic or Latino	8,353	2.75

Race*	Population	%
African-American/Black (21,421)	25,409	8.36
Not Hispanic (19,917)	22,636	7.45
Hispanic (1,504)	2,773	0.91
American Indian/Alaska Native (3,467)	6,447	2.12
Not Hispanic (1,297)	2,862	0.94
Hispanic (2,170)	3,585	1.18
Alaska Athabascan *(Ala. Nat.)* (8)	11	<0.01
Aleut *(Alaska Native)* (4)	5	<0.01
Apache (122)	256	0.08
Arapaho (5)	9	<0.01
Blackfeet (33)	139	0.05
Canadian/French Am. Ind. (4)	5	<0.01
Central American Ind. (19)	32	0.01
Cherokee (182)	693	0.23
Cheyenne (3)	13	<0.01
Chickasaw (13)	34	0.01
Chippewa (10)	42	0.01
Choctaw (68)	182	0.06
Colville (3)	5	<0.01
Comanche (10)	26	0.01
Cree (1)	5	<0.01
Creek (28)	48	0.02
Crow (6)	8	<0.01
Delaware (6)	13	<0.01
Hopi (38)	59	0.02
Houma (2)	2	<0.01
Inupiat *(Alaska Native)* (4)	7	<0.01
Iroquois (3)	35	0.01
Kiowa (3)	4	<0.01
Lumbee (9)	12	<0.01
Menominee (4)	4	<0.01
Mexican American Ind. (400)	633	0.21
Navajo (106)	201	0.07
Osage (8)	20	0.01
Ottawa (2)	2	<0.01
Paiute (10)	17	0.01
Pima (23)	51	0.02
Potawatomi (3)	31	0.01
Pueblo (37)	66	0.02
Puget Sound Salish (1)	1	<0.01
Seminole (12)	43	0.01
Shoshone (6)	15	<0.01
Sioux (43)	93	0.03
South American Ind. (29)	45	0.01
Spanish American Ind. (29)	52	0.02
Tlingit-Haida *(Alaska Native)* (2)	14	<0.01
Tohono O'Odham (21)	29	0.01
Tsimshian *(Alaska Native)* (0)	2	<0.01
Ute (7)	16	0.01
Yakama (0)	0	<0.01
Yaqui (60)	103	0.03
Yuman (38)	48	0.02
Yup'ik *(Alaska Native)* (1)	1	<0.01
Asian (22,566)	26,675	8.78
Not Hispanic (21,934)	24,912	8.20
Hispanic (632)	1,763	0.58
Bangladeshi (69)	76	0.03
Bhutanese (0)	0	<0.01
Burmese (45)	60	0.02
Cambodian (275)	373	0.12
Chinese, ex. Taiwanese (4,422)	5,471	1.80
Filipino (5,124)	6,761	2.22
Hmong (76)	83	0.03
Indian (2,396)	2,712	0.89
Indonesian (213)	370	0.12
Japanese (948)	1,907	0.63
Korean (3,220)	3,557	1.17
Laotian (303)	369	0.12
Malaysian (14)	25	0.01
Nepalese (17)	18	0.01
Pakistani (331)	377	0.12
Sri Lankan (114)	122	0.04
Taiwanese (484)	547	0.18
Thai (307)	427	0.14
Vietnamese (3,135)	3,544	1.17
Hawaii Native/Pacific Islander (1,219)	2,283	0.75
Not Hispanic (1,019)	1,762	0.58
Hispanic (200)	521	0.17
Fijian (34)	54	0.02
Guamanian/Chamorro (218)	384	0.13
Marshallese (4)	4	<0.01
Native Hawaiian (162)	586	0.19
Samoan (434)	618	0.20
Tongan (240)	281	0.09
White (171,669)	184,386	60.68
Not Hispanic (103,398)	109,018	35.88
Hispanic (68,271)	75,368	24.80

*Notes: † The Census 2010 population figure is used to calculate the percentages in the Hispanic Origin and Race categories. Ancestry percentages are based on the 2006-2010 American Community Survey population (not shown); ‡ Numbers in parentheses indicate the number of people reporting a single ancestry; * Numbers in parentheses indicate the number of persons reporting this race alone, not in combination with any other race; Please refer to the Explanation of Data for more information.*

Rocklin

Place Type: City
County: Placer
Population: 56,974

Ancestry	Population	%
Afghan (216)	216	0.40
African, Sub-Saharan (232)	260	0.48
African (96)	110	0.20
Cape Verdean (0)	0	<0.01
Ethiopian (0)	0	<0.01
Ghanaian (0)	0	<0.01
Kenyan (0)	0	<0.01
Liberian (0)	0	<0.01
Nigerian (11)	11	0.02
Senegalese (0)	0	<0.01
Sierra Leonean (0)	0	<0.01
Somalian (0)	0	<0.01
South African (77)	77	0.14
Sudanese (48)	48	0.09
Ugandan (0)	14	0.03
Zimbabwean (0)	0	<0.01
Other Sub-Saharan African (0)	0	<0.01
Albanian (0)	0	<0.01
Alsatian (0)	12	0.02
American (2,289)	2,289	4.22
Arab (177)	245	0.45
Arab (15)	15	0.03
Egyptian (127)	127	0.23
Iraqi (0)	0	<0.01
Jordanian (0)	0	<0.01
Lebanese (21)	21	0.04
Moroccan (0)	0	<0.01
Palestinian (14)	30	0.06
Syrian (0)	52	0.10
Other Arab (0)	0	<0.01
Armenian (80)	137	0.25
Assyrian/Chaldean/Syriac (0)	0	<0.01
Australian (7)	14	0.03
Austrian (12)	152	0.28
Basque (12)	115	0.21
Belgian (55)	133	0.25
Brazilian (43)	43	0.08
British (183)	326	0.60
Bulgarian (11)	21	0.04
Cajun (0)	29	0.05
Canadian (85)	244	0.45
Carpatho Rusyn (0)	0	<0.01
Celtic (0)	0	<0.01
Croatian (23)	39	0.07
Cypriot (0)	0	<0.01
Czech (88)	286	0.53
Czechoslovakian (38)	48	0.09
Danish (97)	663	1.22
Dutch (196)	1,019	1.88
Eastern European (42)	63	0.12
English (2,099)	8,010	14.76
Estonian (0)	14	0.03
European (1,281)	1,482	2.73
Finnish (89)	257	0.47
French, ex. Basque (385)	2,223	4.10
French Canadian (58)	237	0.44
German (2,380)	10,333	19.04
German Russian (0)	0	<0.01
Greek (28)	364	0.67
Guyanese (0)	0	<0.01
Hungarian (0)	90	0.17
Icelander (12)	26	0.05
Iranian (258)	322	0.59
Irish (1,865)	7,830	14.43
Israeli (0)	0	<0.01
Italian (1,855)	4,789	8.82
Latvian (0)	0	<0.01
Lithuanian (48)	85	0.16
Luxemburger (0)	0	<0.01
Macedonian (48)	48	0.09
Maltese (0)	0	<0.01
New Zealander (11)	33	0.06
Northern European (66)	66	0.12
Norwegian (546)	1,640	3.02
Pennsylvania German (0)	0	<0.01
Polish (289)	1,249	2.30
Portuguese (370)	1,045	1.93
Romanian (147)	224	0.41
Russian (153)	325	0.60
Scandinavian (48)	110	0.20
Scotch-Irish (295)	888	1.64
Scottish (439)	1,480	2.73
Serbian (0)	25	0.05
Slavic (9)	19	0.04
Slovak (0)	38	0.07
Slovene (22)	64	0.12
Soviet Union (0)	0	<0.01
Swedish (459)	1,645	3.03
Swiss (77)	266	0.49
Turkish (16)	16	0.03
Ukrainian (612)	685	1.26
Welsh (84)	424	0.78
West Indian, ex. Hispanic (26)	26	0.05
Bahamian (0)	0	<0.01
Barbadian (0)	0	<0.01
Belizean (0)	0	<0.01
Bermudan (0)	0	<0.01
British West Indian (0)	0	<0.01
Dutch West Indian (0)	0	<0.01
Haitian (0)	0	<0.01
Jamaican (12)	12	0.02
Trinidadian/Tobagonian (0)	0	<0.01
U.S. Virgin Islander (0)	0	<0.01
West Indian (14)	14	0.03
Other West Indian (0)	0	<0.01
Yugoslavian (164)	299	0.55

Hispanic Origin	Population	%
Hispanic or Latino (of any race)	6,555	11.51
Central American, ex. Mexican	355	0.62
Costa Rican	28	0.05
Guatemalan	70	0.12
Honduran	21	0.04
Nicaraguan	73	0.13
Panamanian	21	0.04
Salvadoran	134	0.24
Other Central American	8	0.01
Cuban	83	0.15
Dominican Republic	15	0.03
Mexican	4,685	8.22
Puerto Rican	317	0.56
South American	277	0.49
Argentinean	39	0.07
Bolivian	13	0.02
Chilean	35	0.06
Colombian	75	0.13
Ecuadorian	21	0.04
Paraguayan	0	<0.01
Peruvian	67	0.12
Uruguayan	8	0.01
Venezuelan	16	0.03
Other South American	3	0.01
Other Hispanic or Latino	823	1.44

Race*	Population	%
African-American/Black (858)	1,262	2.22
Not Hispanic (809)	1,133	1.99
Hispanic (49)	129	0.23
American Indian/Alaska Native (410)	1,042	1.83
Not Hispanic (270)	719	1.26
Hispanic (140)	323	0.57
Alaska Athabascan *(Ala. Nat.)* (1)	2	<0.01
Aleut *(Alaska Native)* (2)	3	0.01
Apache (22)	39	0.07
Arapaho (1)	2	<0.01
Blackfeet (2)	16	0.03
Canadian/French Am. Ind. (0)	1	<0.01
Central American Ind. (1)	2	<0.01
Cherokee (40)	192	0.34
Cheyenne (0)	6	0.01
Chickasaw (4)	13	0.02
Chippewa (4)	18	0.03
Choctaw (4)	29	0.05
Colville (2)	5	0.01
Comanche (1)	4	0.01
Cree (0)	4	0.01
Creek (9)	24	0.04
Crow (0)	3	0.01
Delaware (0)	4	0.01
Hopi (0)	4	0.01
Houma (0)	0	<0.01
Inupiat *(Alaska Native)* (1)	1	<0.01
Iroquois (3)	17	0.03
Kiowa (1)	2	<0.01
Lumbee (1)	9	0.02
Menominee (0)	0	<0.01
Mexican American Ind. (22)	35	0.06
Navajo (4)	14	0.02
Osage (0)	2	<0.01
Ottawa (0)	1	<0.01
Paiute (4)	9	0.02
Pima (0)	0	<0.01
Potawatomi (8)	10	0.02
Pueblo (10)	14	0.02
Puget Sound Salish (2)	3	0.01
Seminole (1)	1	<0.01
Shoshone (1)	5	0.01
Sioux (14)	29	0.05
South American Ind. (0)	3	0.01
Spanish American Ind. (1)	1	<0.01
Tlingit-Haida *(Alaska Native)* (1)	1	<0.01
Tohono O'Odham (3)	6	0.01
Tsimshian *(Alaska Native)* (0)	0	<0.01
Ute (6)	6	0.01
Yakama (0)	0	<0.01
Yaqui (4)	8	0.01
Yuman (4)	5	0.01
Yup'ik *(Alaska Native)* (0)	0	<0.01
Asian (4,105)	5,644	9.91
Not Hispanic (4,024)	5,336	9.37
Hispanic (81)	308	0.54
Bangladeshi (8)	12	0.02
Bhutanese (0)	0	<0.01
Burmese (14)	17	0.03
Cambodian (40)	54	0.09
Chinese, ex. Taiwanese (617)	970	1.70
Filipino (1,051)	1,671	2.93
Hmong (5)	7	0.01
Indian (837)	924	1.62
Indonesian (43)	68	0.12
Japanese (415)	827	1.45
Korean (332)	473	0.83
Laotian (33)	45	0.08
Malaysian (6)	16	0.03
Nepalese (8)	8	0.01
Pakistani (41)	49	0.09
Sri Lankan (25)	25	0.04
Taiwanese (44)	50	0.09
Thai (19)	41	0.07
Vietnamese (328)	407	0.71
Hawaii Native/Pacific Islander (150)	404	0.71
Not Hispanic (138)	323	0.57
Hispanic (12)	81	0.14
Fijian (20)	25	0.04
Guamanian/Chamorro (36)	73	0.13
Marshallese (0)	1	<0.01
Native Hawaiian (30)	174	0.31
Samoan (22)	42	0.07
Tongan (7)	7	0.01
White (47,047)	49,657	87.16
Not Hispanic (43,008)	44,930	78.86
Hispanic (4,039)	4,727	8.30

*Notes: † The Census 2010 population figure is used to calculate the percentages in the Hispanic Origin and Race categories. Ancestry percentages are based on the 2006-2010 American Community Survey population (not shown); ‡ Numbers in parentheses indicate the number of people reporting a single ancestry; * Numbers in parentheses indicate the number of persons reporting this race alone, not in combination with any other race; Please refer to the Explanation of Data for more information.*

Rosemead

Place Type: City
County: Los Angeles
Population: 53,764

Ancestry	Population	%
Afghan (0)	0	<0.01
African, Sub-Saharan (121)	128	0.24
African (42)	49	0.09
Cape Verdean (0)	0	<0.01
Ethiopian (0)	0	<0.01
Ghanaian (0)	0	<0.01
Kenyan (0)	0	<0.01
Liberian (0)	0	<0.01
Nigerian (0)	0	<0.01
Senegalese (0)	0	<0.01
Sierra Leonean (0)	0	<0.01
Somalian (0)	0	<0.01
South African (0)	0	<0.01
Sudanese (0)	0	<0.01
Ugandan (0)	0	<0.01
Zimbabwean (0)	0	<0.01
Other Sub-Saharan African (79)	79	0.15
Albanian (0)	0	<0.01
Alsatian (0)	0	<0.01
American (281)	281	0.52
Arab (49)	49	0.09
Arab (49)	49	0.09
Egyptian (0)	0	<0.01
Iraqi (0)	0	<0.01
Jordanian (0)	0	<0.01
Lebanese (0)	0	<0.01
Moroccan (0)	0	<0.01
Palestinian (0)	0	<0.01
Syrian (0)	0	<0.01
Other Arab (0)	0	<0.01
Armenian (37)	37	0.07
Assyrian/Chaldean/Syriac (0)	0	<0.01
Australian (0)	0	<0.01
Austrian (7)	7	0.01
Basque (0)	8	0.01
Belgian (0)	0	<0.01
Brazilian (17)	51	0.10
British (8)	19	0.04
Bulgarian (0)	0	<0.01
Cajun (0)	0	<0.01
Canadian (0)	22	0.04
Carpatho Rusyn (0)	0	<0.01
Celtic (0)	0	<0.01
Croatian (0)	0	<0.01
Cypriot (0)	0	<0.01
Czech (5)	16	0.03
Czechoslovakian (0)	0	<0.01
Danish (0)	14	0.03
Dutch (0)	23	0.04
Eastern European (21)	21	0.04
English (60)	324	0.60
Estonian (0)	0	<0.01
European (49)	78	0.15
Finnish (0)	35	0.07
French, ex. Basque (31)	240	0.45
French Canadian (0)	0	<0.01
German (95)	525	0.98
German Russian (0)	0	<0.01
Greek (0)	0	<0.01
Guyanese (0)	0	<0.01
Hungarian (0)	0	<0.01
Icelander (0)	0	<0.01
Iranian (0)	0	<0.01
Irish (107)	533	0.99
Israeli (0)	0	<0.01
Italian (284)	521	0.97
Latvian (0)	0	<0.01
Lithuanian (0)	0	<0.01
Luxemburger (0)	0	<0.01
Macedonian (0)	0	<0.01
Maltese (0)	0	<0.01
New Zealander (0)	0	<0.01
Northern European (0)	0	<0.01
Norwegian (18)	63	0.12
Pennsylvania German (0)	0	<0.01
Polish (10)	31	0.06
Portuguese (0)	11	0.02
Romanian (19)	19	0.04
Russian (16)	50	0.09
Scandinavian (0)	0	<0.01
Scotch-Irish (52)	140	0.26
Scottish (32)	86	0.16
Serbian (0)	0	<0.01
Slavic (0)	0	<0.01
Slovak (0)	0	<0.01
Slovene (0)	0	<0.01
Soviet Union (0)	0	<0.01
Swedish (9)	44	0.08
Swiss (10)	33	0.06
Turkish (0)	0	<0.01
Ukrainian (0)	0	<0.01
Welsh (0)	0	<0.01
West Indian, ex. Hispanic (10)	44	0.08
Bahamian (0)	0	<0.01
Barbadian (0)	0	<0.01
Belizean (10)	44	0.08
Bermudan (0)	0	<0.01
British West Indian (0)	0	<0.01
Dutch West Indian (0)	0	<0.01
Haitian (0)	0	<0.01
Jamaican (0)	0	<0.01
Trinidadian/Tobagonian (0)	0	<0.01
U.S. Virgin Islander (0)	0	<0.01
West Indian (0)	0	<0.01
Other West Indian (0)	0	<0.01
Yugoslavian (18)	18	0.03

Hispanic Origin	Population	%
Hispanic or Latino (of any race)	18,147	33.75
Central American, ex. Mexican	1,188	2.21
Costa Rican	24	0.04
Guatemalan	306	0.57
Honduran	81	0.15
Nicaraguan	143	0.27
Panamanian	9	0.02
Salvadoran	594	1.10
Other Central American	31	0.06
Cuban	153	0.28
Dominican Republic	3	0.01
Mexican	15,469	28.77
Puerto Rican	113	0.21
South American	251	0.47
Argentinean	51	0.09
Bolivian	8	0.01
Chilean	5	0.01
Colombian	49	0.09
Ecuadorian	42	0.08
Paraguayan	0	<0.01
Peruvian	74	0.14
Uruguayan	6	0.01
Venezuelan	11	0.02
Other South American	5	0.01
Other Hispanic or Latino	970	1.80

Race*	Population	%
African-American/Black (273)	363	0.68
Not Hispanic (176)	218	0.41
Hispanic (97)	145	0.27
American Indian/Alaska Native (396)	600	1.12
Not Hispanic (56)	122	0.23
Hispanic (340)	478	0.89
Alaska Athabascan *(Ala. Nat.)* (0)	0	<0.01
Aleut *(Alaska Native)* (0)	0	<0.01
Apache (10)	21	0.04
Arapaho (0)	0	<0.01
Blackfeet (1)	4	0.01
Canadian/French Am. Ind. (0)	0	<0.01
Central American Ind. (0)	0	<0.01
Cherokee (17)	25	0.05
Cheyenne (0)	0	<0.01
Chickasaw (0)	0	<0.01
Chippewa (1)	3	0.01
Choctaw (0)	4	0.01
Colville (0)	0	<0.01
Comanche (0)	0	<0.01
Cree (0)	0	<0.01
Creek (1)	1	<0.01
Crow (0)	0	<0.01
Delaware (0)	0	<0.01
Hopi (0)	0	<0.01
Houma (0)	0	<0.01
Inupiat *(Alaska Native)* (0)	0	<0.01
Iroquois (1)	1	<0.01
Kiowa (0)	0	<0.01
Lumbee (0)	0	<0.01
Menominee (0)	0	<0.01
Mexican American Ind. (73)	119	0.22
Navajo (8)	23	0.04
Osage (0)	0	<0.01
Ottawa (0)	0	<0.01
Paiute (1)	1	<0.01
Pima (0)	0	<0.01
Potawatomi (0)	0	<0.01
Pueblo (8)	9	0.02
Puget Sound Salish (0)	0	<0.01
Seminole (1)	1	<0.01
Shoshone (0)	0	<0.01
Sioux (7)	8	0.01
South American Ind. (0)	1	<0.01
Spanish American Ind. (2)	2	<0.01
Tlingit-Haida *(Alaska Native)* (0)	0	<0.01
Tohono O'Odham (8)	8	0.01
Tsimshian *(Alaska Native)* (0)	0	<0.01
Ute (0)	2	<0.01
Yakama (0)	0	<0.01
Yaqui (9)	20	0.04
Yuman (0)	0	<0.01
Yup'ik *(Alaska Native)* (0)	0	<0.01
Asian (32,617)	33,107	61.58
Not Hispanic (32,439)	32,749	60.91
Hispanic (178)	358	0.67
Bangladeshi (5)	7	0.01
Bhutanese (0)	0	<0.01
Burmese (336)	376	0.70
Cambodian (749)	994	1.85
Chinese, ex. Taiwanese (18,352)	20,548	38.22
Filipino (816)	974	1.81
Hmong (3)	3	0.01
Indian (202)	269	0.50
Indonesian (71)	100	0.19
Japanese (590)	684	1.27
Korean (270)	293	0.54
Laotian (26)	42	0.08
Malaysian (12)	18	0.03
Nepalese (4)	4	0.01
Pakistani (3)	3	0.01
Sri Lankan (8)	11	0.02
Taiwanese (407)	461	0.86
Thai (205)	235	0.44
Vietnamese (8,268)	10,046	18.69
Hawaii Native/Pacific Islander (32)	92	0.17
Not Hispanic (14)	53	0.10
Hispanic (18)	39	0.07
Fijian (0)	0	<0.01
Guamanian/Chamorro (11)	18	0.03
Marshallese (0)	0	<0.01
Native Hawaiian (6)	21	0.04
Samoan (9)	13	0.02
Tongan (1)	2	<0.01
White (11,348)	12,192	22.68
Not Hispanic (2,549)	2,788	5.19
Hispanic (8,799)	9,404	17.49

*Notes: † The Census 2010 population figure is used to calculate the percentages in the Hispanic Origin and Race categories. Ancestry percentages are based on the 2006-2010 American Community Survey population (not shown); ‡ Numbers in parentheses indicate the number of people reporting a single ancestry; * Numbers in parentheses indicate the number of persons reporting this race alone, not in combination with any other race; Please refer to the Explanation of Data for more information.*

Roseville

Place Type: City
County: Placer
Population: 118,788

Ancestry	Population	%
Afghan (28)	28	0.02
African, Sub-Saharan (110)	121	0.11
African (13)	24	0.02
Cape Verdean (9)	9	0.01
Ethiopian (0)	0	<0.01
Ghanaian (48)	48	0.04
Kenyan (0)	0	<0.01
Liberian (0)	0	<0.01
Nigerian (0)	0	<0.01
Senegalese (0)	0	<0.01
Sierra Leonean (0)	0	<0.01
Somalian (0)	0	<0.01
South African (40)	40	0.04
Sudanese (0)	0	<0.01
Ugandan (0)	0	<0.01
Zimbabwean (0)	0	<0.01
Other Sub-Saharan African (0)	0	<0.01
Albanian (0)	0	<0.01
Alsatian (0)	0	<0.01
American (3,835)	3,835	3.37
Arab (319)	604	0.53
Arab (117)	153	0.13
Egyptian (87)	115	0.10
Iraqi (0)	141	0.12
Jordanian (0)	0	<0.01
Lebanese (88)	145	0.13
Moroccan (0)	0	<0.01
Palestinian (10)	10	0.01
Syrian (0)	0	<0.01
Other Arab (17)	40	0.04
Armenian (150)	229	0.20
Assyrian/Chaldean/Syriac (5)	98	0.09
Australian (162)	256	0.22
Austrian (113)	366	0.32
Basque (39)	57	0.05
Belgian (33)	114	0.10
Brazilian (11)	11	0.01
British (254)	577	0.51
Bulgarian (84)	84	0.07
Cajun (9)	9	0.01
Canadian (143)	383	0.34
Carpatho Rusyn (0)	0	<0.01
Celtic (0)	0	<0.01
Croatian (29)	122	0.11
Cypriot (0)	0	<0.01
Czech (208)	597	0.52
Czechoslovakian (21)	101	0.09
Danish (337)	1,567	1.38
Dutch (296)	1,546	1.36
Eastern European (101)	101	0.09
English (4,230)	15,474	13.60
Estonian (12)	12	0.01
European (2,354)	2,574	2.26
Finnish (192)	530	0.47
French, ex. Basque (328)	3,671	3.23
French Canadian (110)	371	0.33
German (5,977)	20,919	18.38
German Russian (0)	0	<0.01
Greek (363)	1,029	0.90
Guyanese (0)	0	<0.01
Hungarian (43)	317	0.28
Icelander (12)	12	0.01
Iranian (589)	767	0.67
Irish (3,967)	18,023	15.83
Israeli (0)	0	<0.01
Italian (2,933)	8,689	7.63
Latvian (69)	84	0.07
Lithuanian (41)	217	0.19
Luxemburger (0)	0	<0.01
Macedonian (33)	33	0.03
Maltese (67)	181	0.16
New Zealander (0)	0	<0.01
Northern European (229)	229	0.20
Norwegian (1,062)	3,331	2.93
Pennsylvania German (14)	27	0.02
Polish (569)	2,528	2.22
Portuguese (544)	2,134	1.87
Romanian (309)	415	0.36
Russian (762)	1,431	1.26
Scandinavian (257)	423	0.37
Scotch-Irish (766)	2,143	1.88
Scottish (707)	3,159	2.78
Serbian (0)	31	0.03
Slavic (8)	78	0.07
Slovak (108)	196	0.17
Slovene (9)	25	0.02
Soviet Union (0)	0	<0.01
Swedish (620)	2,780	2.44
Swiss (171)	691	0.61
Turkish (21)	21	0.02
Ukrainian (748)	830	0.73
Welsh (94)	817	0.72
West Indian, ex. Hispanic (51)	107	0.09
Bahamian (0)	0	<0.01
Barbadian (0)	28	0.02
Belizean (0)	0	<0.01
Bermudan (0)	0	<0.01
British West Indian (0)	0	<0.01
Dutch West Indian (0)	0	<0.01
Haitian (0)	0	<0.01
Jamaican (44)	72	0.06
Trinidadian/Tobagonian (0)	0	<0.01
U.S. Virgin Islander (0)	0	<0.01
West Indian (7)	7	0.01
Other West Indian (0)	0	<0.01
Yugoslavian (253)	348	0.31

Hispanic Origin	Population	%
Hispanic or Latino (of any race)	17,359	14.61
Central American, ex. Mexican	837	0.70
Costa Rican	46	0.04
Guatemalan	236	0.20
Honduran	49	0.04
Nicaraguan	130	0.11
Panamanian	40	0.03
Salvadoran	331	0.28
Other Central American	5	<0.01
Cuban	137	0.12
Dominican Republic	23	0.02
Mexican	13,096	11.02
Puerto Rican	619	0.52
South American	504	0.42
Argentinean	58	0.05
Bolivian	19	0.02
Chilean	74	0.06
Colombian	115	0.10
Ecuadorian	32	0.03
Paraguayan	2	<0.01
Peruvian	157	0.13
Uruguayan	7	0.01
Venezuelan	31	0.03
Other South American	9	0.01
Other Hispanic or Latino	2,143	1.80

Race*	Population	%
African-American/Black (2,329)	3,470	2.92
Not Hispanic (2,157)	3,058	2.57
Hispanic (172)	412	0.35
American Indian/Alaska Native (885)	2,157	1.82
Not Hispanic (568)	1,509	1.27
Hispanic (317)	648	0.55
Alaska Athabascan *(Ala. Nat.)* (3)	3	<0.01
Aleut *(Alaska Native)* (0)	0	<0.01
Apache (38)	82	0.07
Arapaho (3)	9	0.01
Blackfeet (7)	49	0.04
Canadian/French Am. Ind. (1)	1	<0.01
Central American Ind. (0)	0	<0.01
Cherokee (87)	380	0.32
Cheyenne (7)	12	0.01
Chickasaw (13)	27	0.02
Chippewa (19)	28	0.02
Choctaw (36)	107	0.09
Colville (2)	2	<0.01
Comanche (2)	11	0.01
Cree (1)	2	<0.01
Creek (9)	29	0.02
Crow (1)	2	<0.01
Delaware (2)	6	0.01
Hopi (4)	10	0.01
Houma (1)	1	<0.01
Inupiat *(Alaska Native)* (1)	1	<0.01
Iroquois (8)	18	0.02
Kiowa (0)	0	<0.01
Lumbee (2)	7	0.01
Menominee (0)	1	<0.01
Mexican American Ind. (56)	88	0.07
Navajo (17)	30	0.03
Osage (1)	4	<0.01
Ottawa (1)	8	0.01
Paiute (9)	16	0.01
Pima (1)	2	<0.01
Potawatomi (6)	15	0.01
Pueblo (2)	10	0.01
Puget Sound Salish (1)	4	<0.01
Seminole (0)	7	0.01
Shoshone (8)	15	0.01
Sioux (30)	64	0.05
South American Ind. (1)	8	0.01
Spanish American Ind. (0)	2	<0.01
Tlingit-Haida *(Alaska Native)* (1)	4	<0.01
Tohono O'Odham (1)	3	<0.01
Tsimshian *(Alaska Native)* (0)	0	<0.01
Ute (0)	0	<0.01
Yakama (1)	2	<0.01
Yaqui (10)	15	0.01
Yuman (4)	10	0.01
Yup'ik *(Alaska Native)* (2)	3	<0.01
Asian (10,026)	12,853	10.82
Not Hispanic (9,785)	12,117	10.20
Hispanic (241)	736	0.62
Bangladeshi (8)	9	0.01
Bhutanese (0)	0	<0.01
Burmese (26)	37	0.03
Cambodian (45)	64	0.05
Chinese, ex. Taiwanese (1,144)	1,766	1.49
Filipino (3,637)	4,791	4.03
Hmong (52)	71	0.06
Indian (2,337)	2,501	2.11
Indonesian (40)	71	0.06
Japanese (674)	1,400	1.18
Korean (583)	842	0.71
Laotian (38)	50	0.04
Malaysian (9)	10	0.01
Nepalese (5)	5	<0.01
Pakistani (151)	176	0.15
Sri Lankan (26)	30	0.03
Taiwanese (80)	110	0.09
Thai (65)	131	0.11
Vietnamese (676)	834	0.70
Hawaii Native/Pacific Islander (346)	829	0.70
Not Hispanic (294)	653	0.55
Hispanic (52)	176	0.15
Fijian (46)	55	0.05
Guamanian/Chamorro (99)	205	0.17
Marshallese (0)	1	<0.01
Native Hawaiian (95)	337	0.28
Samoan (31)	68	0.06
Tongan (17)	32	0.03
White (94,199)	99,504	83.77
Not Hispanic (84,349)	88,043	74.12
Hispanic (9,850)	11,461	9.65

*Notes: † The Census 2010 population figure is used to calculate the percentages in the Hispanic Origin and Race categories. Ancestry percentages are based on the 2006-2010 American Community Survey population (not shown); ‡ Numbers in parentheses indicate the number of people reporting a single ancestry; * Numbers in parentheses indicate the number of persons reporting this race alone, not in combination with any other race; Please refer to the Explanation of Data for more information.*

Sacramento

Place Type: City
County: Sacramento
Population: 466,488

Ancestry	Population	%
Afghan (580)	580	0.13
African, Sub-Saharan (3,143)	4,175	0.91
African (1,896)	2,618	0.57
Cape Verdean (112)	299	0.07
Ethiopian (605)	692	0.15
Ghanaian (41)	41	0.01
Kenyan (9)	9	<0.01
Liberian (0)	0	<0.01
Nigerian (350)	359	0.08
Senegalese (0)	0	<0.01
Sierra Leonean (0)	0	<0.01
Somalian (0)	8	<0.01
South African (130)	149	0.03
Sudanese (0)	0	<0.01
Ugandan (0)	0	<0.01
Zimbabwean (0)	0	<0.01
Other Sub-Saharan African (0)	0	<0.01
Albanian (8)	27	0.01
Alsatian (0)	0	<0.01
American (7,542)	7,542	1.64
Arab (922)	1,877	0.41
Arab (348)	597	0.13
Egyptian (68)	201	0.04
Iraqi (0)	9	<0.01
Jordanian (152)	199	0.04
Lebanese (101)	323	0.07
Moroccan (23)	46	0.01
Palestinian (105)	159	0.03
Syrian (10)	37	0.01
Other Arab (115)	306	0.07
Armenian (317)	711	0.15
Assyrian/Chaldean/Syriac (85)	151	0.03
Australian (93)	357	0.08
Austrian (116)	709	0.15
Basque (32)	101	0.02
Belgian (19)	205	0.04
Brazilian (26)	175	0.04
British (654)	1,493	0.32
Bulgarian (278)	304	0.07
Cajun (0)	17	<0.01
Canadian (262)	634	0.14
Carpatho Rusyn (0)	0	<0.01
Celtic (56)	97	0.02
Croatian (167)	483	0.11
Cypriot (0)	0	<0.01
Czech (303)	1,164	0.25
Czechoslovakian (87)	294	0.06
Danish (409)	1,908	0.42
Dutch (950)	4,826	1.05
Eastern European (370)	414	0.09
English (6,966)	28,086	6.11
Estonian (0)	34	0.01
European (3,938)	5,277	1.15
Finnish (145)	567	0.12
French, ex. Basque (1,089)	9,645	2.10
French Canadian (412)	1,254	0.27
German (10,093)	41,408	9.01
German Russian (14)	38	0.01
Greek (1,009)	2,242	0.49
Guyanese (0)	0	<0.01
Hungarian (284)	1,189	0.26
Icelander (87)	189	0.04
Iranian (629)	1,001	0.22
Irish (8,354)	35,916	7.82
Israeli (76)	94	0.02
Italian (6,196)	18,754	4.08
Latvian (52)	101	0.02
Lithuanian (165)	593	0.13
Luxemburger (0)	35	0.01
Macedonian (0)	0	<0.01
Maltese (16)	44	0.01
New Zealander (0)	0	<0.01
Northern European (479)	493	0.11
Norwegian (1,904)	5,382	1.17
Pennsylvania German (21)	73	0.02
Polish (1,235)	4,573	1.00
Portuguese (2,792)	7,182	1.56
Romanian (888)	1,087	0.24
Russian (2,507)	4,916	1.07
Scandinavian (384)	989	0.22
Scotch-Irish (1,629)	5,314	1.16
Scottish (1,719)	7,694	1.67
Serbian (122)	312	0.07
Slavic (45)	161	0.04
Slovak (33)	179	0.04
Slovene (14)	120	0.03
Soviet Union (0)	0	<0.01
Swedish (1,103)	5,613	1.22
Swiss (437)	1,686	0.37
Turkish (258)	279	0.06
Ukrainian (1,425)	2,189	0.48
Welsh (289)	2,314	0.50
West Indian, ex. Hispanic (412)	812	0.18
Bahamian (0)	0	<0.01
Barbadian (10)	10	<0.01
Belizean (92)	104	0.02
Bermudan (0)	0	<0.01
British West Indian (0)	21	<0.01
Dutch West Indian (0)	0	<0.01
Haitian (0)	20	<0.01
Jamaican (133)	376	0.08
Trinidadian/Tobagonian (73)	90	0.02
U.S. Virgin Islander (0)	0	<0.01
West Indian (104)	191	0.04
Other West Indian (0)	0	<0.01
Yugoslavian (574)	900	0.20

Hispanic Origin	Population	%
Hispanic or Latino (of any race)	125,276	26.86
Central American, ex. Mexican	5,184	1.11
Costa Rican	162	0.03
Guatemalan	977	0.21
Honduran	357	0.08
Nicaraguan	895	0.19
Panamanian	325	0.07
Salvadoran	2,425	0.52
Other Central American	43	0.01
Cuban	640	0.14
Dominican Republic	190	0.04
Mexican	105,467	22.61
Puerto Rican	3,344	0.72
South American	1,777	0.38
Argentinean	179	0.04
Bolivian	66	0.01
Chilean	205	0.04
Colombian	400	0.09
Ecuadorian	116	0.02
Paraguayan	12	<0.01
Peruvian	614	0.13
Uruguayan	27	0.01
Venezuelan	118	0.03
Other South American	40	0.01
Other Hispanic or Latino	8,674	1.86

Race*	Population	%
African-American/Black (68,335)	80,469	17.25
Not Hispanic (64,967)	74,051	15.87
Hispanic (3,368)	6,418	1.38
American Indian/Alaska Native (5,291)	13,242	2.84
Not Hispanic (2,586)	7,885	1.69
Hispanic (2,705)	5,357	1.15
Alaska Athabascan *(Ala. Nat.)* (7)	11	<0.01
Aleut *(Alaska Native)* (2)	20	<0.01
Apache (197)	476	0.10
Arapaho (1)	10	<0.01
Blackfeet (82)	485	0.10
Canadian/French Am. Ind. (12)	21	<0.01
Central American Ind. (6)	23	<0.01
Cherokee (371)	2,019	0.43
Cheyenne (12)	46	0.01
Chickasaw (27)	96	0.02
Chippewa (65)	151	0.03
Choctaw (84)	426	0.09
Colville (3)	12	<0.01
Comanche (11)	44	0.01
Cree (10)	39	0.01
Creek (22)	114	0.02
Crow (12)	37	0.01
Delaware (8)	20	<0.01
Hopi (12)	28	0.01
Houma (3)	3	<0.01
Inupiat *(Alaska Native)* (14)	27	0.01
Iroquois (31)	92	0.02
Kiowa (7)	15	<0.01
Lumbee (10)	19	<0.01
Menominee (1)	7	<0.01
Mexican American Ind. (469)	746	0.16
Navajo (155)	355	0.08
Osage (3)	30	0.01
Ottawa (1)	6	<0.01
Paiute (62)	107	0.02
Pima (20)	33	0.01
Potawatomi (16)	54	0.01
Pueblo (47)	81	0.02
Puget Sound Salish (11)	21	<0.01
Seminole (10)	63	0.01
Shoshone (17)	49	0.01
Sioux (118)	302	0.06
South American Ind. (12)	43	0.01
Spanish American Ind. (45)	65	0.01
Tlingit-Haida *(Alaska Native)* (20)	55	0.01
Tohono O'Odham (12)	26	0.01
Tsimshian *(Alaska Native)* (1)	5	<0.01
Ute (12)	21	<0.01
Yakama (4)	6	<0.01
Yaqui (125)	207	0.04
Yuman (9)	15	<0.01
Yup'ik *(Alaska Native)* (1)	3	<0.01
Asian (85,503)	98,705	21.16
Not Hispanic (83,841)	94,141	20.18
Hispanic (1,662)	4,564	0.98
Bangladeshi (68)	70	0.02
Bhutanese (8)	8	<0.01
Burmese (49)	71	0.02
Cambodian (840)	1,082	0.23
Chinese, ex. Taiwanese (19,989)	23,350	5.01
Filipino (13,468)	18,503	3.97
Hmong (15,984)	16,676	3.57
Indian (8,514)	10,700	2.29
Indonesian (147)	278	0.06
Japanese (5,730)	8,759	1.88
Korean (1,265)	1,994	0.43
Laotian (5,904)	6,675	1.43
Malaysian (26)	45	0.01
Nepalese (84)	90	0.02
Pakistani (1,927)	2,061	0.44
Sri Lankan (76)	94	0.02
Taiwanese (310)	367	0.08
Thai (415)	784	0.17
Vietnamese (6,682)	7,730	1.66
Hawaii Native/Pacific Islander (6,655)	10,699	2.29
Not Hispanic (6,392)	9,762	2.09
Hispanic (263)	937	0.20
Fijian (2,703)	3,244	0.70
Guamanian/Chamorro (366)	707	0.15
Marshallese (387)	400	0.09
Native Hawaiian (346)	1,236	0.26
Samoan (819)	1,233	0.26
Tongan (1,141)	1,382	0.30
White (210,006)	233,865	50.13
Not Hispanic (161,062)	175,948	37.72
Hispanic (48,944)	57,917	12.42

*Notes: † The Census 2010 population figure is used to calculate the percentages in the Hispanic Origin and Race categories. Ancestry percentages are based on the 2006-2010 American Community Survey population (not shown); ‡ Numbers in parentheses indicate the number of people reporting a single ancestry; * Numbers in parentheses indicate the number of persons reporting this race alone, not in combination with any other race; Please refer to the Explanation of Data for more information.*

Salinas

Place Type: City
County: Monterey
Population: 150,441

Ancestry	Population	%
Afghan (15)	15	0.01
African, Sub-Saharan (315)	345	0.23
African (242)	272	0.18
Cape Verdean (0)	0	<0.01
Ethiopian (0)	0	<0.01
Ghanaian (0)	0	<0.01
Kenyan (0)	0	<0.01
Liberian (0)	0	<0.01
Nigerian (0)	0	<0.01
Senegalese (20)	20	0.01
Sierra Leonean (0)	0	<0.01
Somalian (0)	0	<0.01
South African (38)	38	0.03
Sudanese (0)	0	<0.01
Ugandan (0)	0	<0.01
Zimbabwean (0)	0	<0.01
Other Sub-Saharan African (15)	15	0.01
Albanian (0)	0	<0.01
Alsatian (0)	0	<0.01
American (1,553)	1,553	1.06
Arab (151)	190	0.13
Arab (8)	8	0.01
Egyptian (53)	53	0.04
Iraqi (0)	0	<0.01
Jordanian (0)	0	<0.01
Lebanese (0)	25	0.02
Moroccan (0)	0	<0.01
Palestinian (9)	9	0.01
Syrian (11)	25	0.02
Other Arab (70)	70	0.05
Armenian (24)	69	0.05
Assyrian/Chaldean/Syriac (0)	0	<0.01
Australian (10)	77	0.05
Austrian (30)	153	0.10
Basque (25)	55	0.04
Belgian (0)	27	0.02
Brazilian (0)	86	0.06
British (127)	217	0.15
Bulgarian (0)	15	0.01
Cajun (14)	30	0.02
Canadian (100)	146	0.10
Carpatho Rusyn (0)	-0	<0.01
Celtic (0)	28	0.02
Croatian (20)	20	0.01
Cypriot (0)	0	<0.01
Czech (39)	133	0.09
Czechoslovakian (9)	81	0.06
Danish (174)	511	0.35
Dutch (117)	760	0.52
Eastern European (12)	12	0.01
English (1,181)	3,789	2.58
Estonian (0)	0	<0.01
European (660)	753	0.51
Finnish (32)	77	0.05
French, ex. Basque (50)	1,160	0.79
French Canadian (61)	166	0.11
German (1,452)	6,020	4.09
German Russian (0)	11	0.01
Greek (20)	119	0.08
Guyanese (0)	0	<0.01
Hungarian (57)	169	0.11
Icelander (0)	0	<0.01
Iranian (17)	17	0.01
Irish (1,271)	5,253	3.57
Israeli (0)	39	0.03
Italian (1,257)	3,230	2.20
Latvian (0)	0	<0.01
Lithuanian (7)	7	<0.01
Luxemburger (0)	0	<0.01
Macedonian (0)	0	<0.01
Maltese (0)	0	<0.01
New Zealander (0)	0	<0.01
Northern European (58)	69	0.05
Norwegian (173)	491	0.33
Pennsylvania German (12)	12	0.01
Polish (104)	393	0.27
Portuguese (281)	746	0.51
Romanian (88)	111	0.08
Russian (86)	224	0.15
Scandinavian (138)	151	0.10
Scotch-Irish (501)	1,035	0.70
Scottish (236)	895	0.61
Serbian (0)	0	<0.01
Slavic (14)	14	0.01
Slovak (0)	41	0.03
Slovene (0)	10	0.01
Soviet Union (0)	0	<0.01
Swedish (235)	762	0.52
Swiss (155)	567	0.39
Turkish (85)	85	0.06
Ukrainian (28)	38	0.03
Welsh (19)	290	0.20
West Indian, ex. Hispanic (132)	132	0.09
Bahamian (0)	0	<0.01
Barbadian (0)	0	<0.01
Belizean (0)	0	<0.01
Bermudan (0)	0	<0.01
British West Indian (0)	0	<0.01
Dutch West Indian (0)	0	<0.01
Haitian (0)	0	<0.01
Jamaican (132)	132	0.09
Trinidadian/Tobagonian (0)	0	<0.01
U.S. Virgin Islander (0)	0	<0.01
West Indian (0)	0	<0.01
Other West Indian (0)	0	<0.01
Yugoslavian (0)	12	0.01

Hispanic Origin	Population	%
Hispanic or Latino (of any race)	112,799	74.98
Central American, ex. Mexican	1,800	1.20
Costa Rican	24	0.02
Guatemalan	177	0.12
Honduran	136	0.09
Nicaraguan	58	0.04
Panamanian	93	0.06
Salvadoran	1,302	0.87
Other Central American	10	0.01
Cuban	94	0.06
Dominican Republic	21	0.01
Mexican	104,237	69.29
Puerto Rican	715	0.48
South American	420	0.28
Argentinean	53	0.04
Bolivian	5	<0.01
Chilean	61	0.04
Colombian	74	0.05
Ecuadorian	36	0.02
Paraguayan	0	<0.01
Peruvian	179	0.12
Uruguayan	0	<0.01
Venezuelan	12	0.01
Other South American	0	<0.01
Other Hispanic or Latino	5,512	3.66

Race*	Population	%
African-American/Black (2,993)	4,054	2.69
Not Hispanic (2,343)	2,934	1.95
Hispanic (650)	1,120	0.74
American Indian/Alaska Native (1,888)	3,125	2.08
Not Hispanic (418)	892	0.59
Hispanic (1,470)	2,233	1.48
Alaska Athabascan *(Ala. Nat.)* (0)	2	<0.01
Aleut *(Alaska Native)* (2)	5	<0.01
Apache (50)	93	0.06
Arapaho (0)	4	<0.01
Blackfeet (3)	22	0.01
Canadian/French Am. Ind. (0)	2	<0.01
Central American Ind. (1)	4	<0.01
Cherokee (76)	230	0.15
Cheyenne (1)	1	<0.01
Chickasaw (10)	21	0.01
Chippewa (5)	21	0.01
Choctaw (35)	55	0.04
Colville (0)	0	<0.01
Comanche (9)	16	0.01
Cree (0)	4	<0.01
Creek (13)	24	0.02
Crow (1)	2	<0.01
Delaware (0)	0	<0.01
Hopi (6)	12	0.01
Houma (0)	0	<0.01
Inupiat *(Alaska Native)* (1)	2	<0.01
Iroquois (1)	18	0.01
Kiowa (1)	1	<0.01
Lumbee (0)	2	<0.01
Menominee (0)	0	<0.01
Mexican American Ind. (320)	508	0.34
Navajo (23)	32	0.02
Osage (1)	6	<0.01
Ottawa (0)	0	<0.01
Paiute (17)	25	0.02
Pima (0)	2	<0.01
Potawatomi (1)	5	<0.01
Pueblo (7)	15	0.01
Puget Sound Salish (2)	3	<0.01
Seminole (1)	5	<0.01
Shoshone (12)	16	0.01
Sioux (12)	18	0.01
South American Ind. (2)	6	<0.01
Spanish American Ind. (8)	12	0.01
Tlingit-Haida *(Alaska Native)* (2)	8	0.01
Tohono O'Odham (5)	8	0.01
Tsimshian *(Alaska Native)* (0)	0	<0.01
Ute (4)	4	<0.01
Yakama (0)	0	<0.01
Yaqui (19)	41	0.03
Yuman (1)	1	<0.01
Yup'ik *(Alaska Native)* (0)	4	<0.01
Asian (9,438)	12,058	8.02
Not Hispanic (8,677)	10,123	6.73
Hispanic (761)	1,935	1.29
Bangladeshi (4)	4	<0.01
Bhutanese (0)	0	<0.01
Burmese (30)	35	0.02
Cambodian (18)	26	0.02
Chinese, ex. Taiwanese (815)	1,147	0.76
Filipino (6,041)	7,740	5.14
Hmong (11)	11	0.01
Indian (582)	722	0.48
Indonesian (12)	21	0.01
Japanese (659)	1,193	0.79
Korean (500)	699	0.46
Laotian (5)	11	0.01
Malaysian (0)	6	<0.01
Nepalese (3)	3	<0.01
Pakistani (5)	23	0.02
Sri Lankan (3)	3	<0.01
Taiwanese (15)	22	0.01
Thai (29)	61	0.04
Vietnamese (383)	463	0.31
Hawaii Native/Pacific Islander (478)	1,047	0.70
Not Hispanic (383)	748	0.50
Hispanic (95)	299	0.20
Fijian (17)	17	0.01
Guamanian/Chamorro (158)	281	0.19
Marshallese (0)	0	<0.01
Native Hawaiian (92)	349	0.23
Samoan (72)	125	0.08
Tongan (50)	65	0.04
White (68,973)	75,011	49.86
Not Hispanic (23,333)	25,121	16.70
Hispanic (45,640)	49,890	33.16

*Notes: † The Census 2010 population figure is used to calculate the percentages in the Hispanic Origin and Race categories. Ancestry percentages are based on the 2006-2010 American Community Survey population (not shown); ‡ Numbers in parentheses indicate the number of people reporting a single ancestry; * Numbers in parentheses indicate the number of persons reporting this race alone, not in combination with any other race; Please refer to the Explanation of Data for more information.*

San Bernardino

Place Type: City
County: San Bernardino
Population: 209,924

Ancestry	Population	%
Afghan (0)	0	<0.01
African, Sub-Saharan (815)	955	0.46
African (517)	625	0.30
Cape Verdean (30)	30	0.01
Ethiopian (22)	22	0.01
Ghanaian (56)	56	0.03
Kenyan (0)	0	<0.01
Liberian (0)	0	<0.01
Nigerian (148)	148	0.07
Senegalese (0)	0	<0.01
Sierra Leonean (0)	0	<0.01
Somalian (0)	0	<0.01
South African (5)	5	<0.01
Sudanese (0)	0	<0.01
Ugandan (24)	24	0.01
Zimbabwean (0)	0	<0.01
Other Sub-Saharan African (13)	45	0.02
Albanian (0)	0	<0.01
Alsatian (0)	0	<0.01
American (2,621)	2,621	1.25
Arab (1,577)	3,403	1.63
Arab (472)	574	0.27
Egyptian (46)	46	0.02
Iraqi (45)	114	0.05
Jordanian (111)	250	0.12
Lebanese (389)	1,107	0.53
Moroccan (0)	0	<0.01
Palestinian (70)	670	0.32
Syrian (0)	71	0.03
Other Arab (444)	571	0.27
Armenian (22)	22	0.01
Assyrian/Chaldean/Syriac (38)	51	0.02
Australian (5)	5	<0.01
Austrian (59)	144	0.07
Basque (0)	48	0.02
Belgian (8)	113	0.05
Brazilian (38)	68	0.03
British (93)	237	0.11
Bulgarian (0)	13	0.01
Cajun (0)	0	<0.01
Canadian (109)	199	0.10
Carpatho Rusyn (0)	0	<0.01
Celtic (0)	0	<0.01
Croatian (20)	48	0.02
Cypriot (0)	0	<0.01
Czech (55)	166	0.08
Czechoslovakian (13)	47	0.02
Danish (34)	297	0.14
Dutch (305)	984	0.47
Eastern European (35)	35	0.02
English (1,914)	6,889	3.29
Estonian (17)	17	0.01
European (813)	1,029	0.49
Finnish (23)	54	0.03
French, ex. Basque (463)	2,526	1.21
French Canadian (197)	436	0.21
German (3,435)	10,589	5.06
German Russian (0)	0	<0.01
Greek (48)	376	0.18
Guyanese (15)	29	0.01
Hungarian (58)	189	0.09
Icelander (0)	9	<0.01
Iranian (49)	135	0.06
Irish (2,295)	8,158	3.90
Israeli (0)	0	<0.01
Italian (893)	3,379	1.62
Latvian (39)	39	0.02
Lithuanian (0)	49	0.02
Luxemburger (0)	10	<0.01
Macedonian (0)	0	<0.01
Maltese (0)	0	<0.01
New Zealander (0)	0	<0.01
Northern European (128)	128	0.06
Norwegian (286)	861	0.41
Pennsylvania German (11)	11	0.01
Polish (339)	1,174	0.56
Portuguese (137)	423	0.20
Romanian (63)	63	0.03
Russian (376)	834	0.40
Scandinavian (29)	82	0.04
Scotch-Irish (399)	1,361	0.65
Scottish (386)	1,478	0.71
Serbian (0)	0	<0.01
Slavic (0)	6	<0.01
Slovak (0)	32	0.02
Slovene (44)	94	0.04
Soviet Union (0)	0	<0.01
Swedish (299)	850	0.41
Swiss (8)	137	0.07
Turkish (37)	80	0.04
Ukrainian (34)	143	0.07
Welsh (126)	284	0.14
West Indian, ex. Hispanic (150)	213	0.10
Bahamian (0)	0	<0.01
Barbadian (0)	0	<0.01
Belizean (72)	72	0.03
Bermudan (0)	0	<0.01
British West Indian (0)	0	<0.01
Dutch West Indian (0)	0	<0.01
Haitian (0)	0	<0.01
Jamaican (78)	126	0.06
Trinidadian/Tobagonian (0)	0	<0.01
U.S. Virgin Islander (0)	15	0.01
West Indian (0)	0	<0.01
Other West Indian (0)	0	<0.01
Yugoslavian (19)	19	0.01

Hispanic Origin	Population	%
Hispanic or Latino (of any race)	125,994	60.02
Central American, ex. Mexican	5,616	2.68
Costa Rican	159	0.08
Guatemalan	1,509	0.72
Honduran	528	0.25
Nicaraguan	559	0.27
Panamanian	152	0.07
Salvadoran	2,641	1.26
Other Central American	68	0.03
Cuban	412	0.20
Dominican Republic	60	0.03
Mexican	109,448	52.14
Puerto Rican	1,495	0.71
South American	764	0.36
Argentinean	132	0.06
Bolivian	20	0.01
Chilean	41	0.02
Colombian	203	0.10
Ecuadorian	106	0.05
Paraguayan	0	<0.01
Peruvian	205	0.10
Uruguayan	8	<0.01
Venezuelan	36	0.02
Other South American	13	0.01
Other Hispanic or Latino	8,199	3.91

Race*	Population	%
African-American/Black (31,582)	35,348	16.84
Not Hispanic (29,897)	32,292	15.38
Hispanic (1,685)	3,056	1.46
American Indian/Alaska Native (2,822)	4,997	2.38
Not Hispanic (867)	1,993	0.95
Hispanic (1,955)	3,004	1.43
Alaska Athabascan *(Ala. Nat.)* (5)	7	<0.01
Aleut *(Alaska Native)* (5)	11	0.01
Apache (107)	254	0.12
Arapaho (0)	5	<0.01
Blackfeet (26)	112	0.05
Canadian/French Am. Ind. (3)	12	0.01
Central American Ind. (10)	14	0.01
Cherokee (151)	512	0.24
Cheyenne (12)	14	0.01
Chickasaw (0)	13	0.01
Chippewa (25)	34	0.02
Choctaw (28)	146	0.07
Colville (1)	2	<0.01
Comanche (18)	27	0.01
Cree (0)	7	<0.01
Creek (26)	76	0.04
Crow (0)	7	<0.01
Delaware (2)	3	<0.01
Hopi (19)	27	0.01
Houma (0)	0	<0.01
Inupiat *(Alaska Native)* (3)	7	<0.01
Iroquois (12)	28	0.01
Kiowa (0)	0	<0.01
Lumbee (1)	2	<0.01
Menominee (1)	1	<0.01
Mexican American Ind. (372)	540	0.26
Navajo (93)	165	0.08
Osage (4)	14	0.01
Ottawa (2)	3	<0.01
Paiute (8)	20	0.01
Pima (18)	27	0.01
Potawatomi (18)	22	0.01
Pueblo (46)	61	0.03
Puget Sound Salish (1)	1	<0.01
Seminole (2)	10	<0.01
Shoshone (9)	10	<0.01
Sioux (58)	92	0.04
South American Ind. (7)	23	0.01
Spanish American Ind. (19)	25	0.01
Tlingit-Haida *(Alaska Native)* (4)	5	<0.01
Tohono O'Odham (3)	14	0.01
Tsimshian *(Alaska Native)* (0)	0	<0.01
Ute (0)	10	<0.01
Yakama (0)	0	<0.01
Yaqui (63)	108	0.05
Yuman (15)	27	0.01
Yup'ik *(Alaska Native)* (0)	0	<0.01
Asian (8,454)	10,503	5.00
Not Hispanic (8,027)	9,389	4.47
Hispanic (427)	1,114	0.53
Bangladeshi (90)	114	0.05
Bhutanese (0)	0	<0.01
Burmese (10)	15	0.01
Cambodian (852)	1,014	0.48
Chinese, ex. Taiwanese (642)	968	0.46
Filipino (2,495)	3,260	1.55
Hmong (41)	41	0.02
Indian (584)	786	0.37
Indonesian (650)	769	0.37
Japanese (271)	667	0.32
Korean (429)	578	0.28
Laotian (208)	260	0.12
Malaysian (0)	0	<0.01
Nepalese (10)	10	<0.01
Pakistani (103)	134	0.06
Sri Lankan (26)	26	0.01
Taiwanese (47)	57	0.03
Thai (231)	286	0.14
Vietnamese (1,221)	1,397	0.67
Hawaii Native/Pacific Islander (839)	1,497	0.71
Not Hispanic (704)	1,120	0.53
Hispanic (135)	377	0.18
Fijian (35)	51	0.02
Guamanian/Chamorro (130)	186	0.09
Marshallese (15)	16	0.01
Native Hawaiian (107)	303	0.14
Samoan (388)	594	0.28
Tongan (82)	151	0.07
White (95,734)	103,895	49.49
Not Hispanic (39,977)	43,018	20.49
Hispanic (55,757)	60,877	29.00

*Notes: † The Census 2010 population figure is used to calculate the percentages in the Hispanic Origin and Race categories. Ancestry percentages are based on the 2006-2010 American Community Survey population (not shown); ‡ Numbers in parentheses indicate the number of people reporting a single ancestry; * Numbers in parentheses indicate the number of persons reporting this race alone, not in combination with any other race; Please refer to the Explanation of Data for more information.*

San Buenaventura (Ventura)

Place Type: City
County: Ventura
Population: 106,433

Ancestry	Population	%
Afghan (0)	0	<0.01
African, Sub-Saharan (66)	98	0.09
African (37)	56	0.05
Cape Verdean (0)	0	<0.01
Ethiopian (0)	0	<0.01
Ghanaian (0)	0	<0.01
Kenyan (13)	13	0.01
Liberian (0)	0	<0.01
Nigerian (0)	0	<0.01
Senegalese (0)	0	<0.01
Sierra Leonean (0)	0	<0.01
Somalian (0)	0	<0.01
South African (0)	13	0.01
Sudanese (0)	0	<0.01
Ugandan (0)	0	<0.01
Zimbabwean (0)	0	<0.01
Other Sub-Saharan African (16)	16	0.02
Albanian (10)	10	0.01
Alsatian (0)	0	<0.01
American (2,859)	2,859	2.72
Arab (428)	697	0.66
Arab (241)	271	0.26
Egyptian (104)	115	0.11
Iraqi (0)	0	<0.01
Jordanian (0)	0	<0.01
Lebanese (43)	227	0.22
Moroccan (0)	0	<0.01
Palestinian (0)	0	<0.01
Syrian (0)	28	0.03
Other Arab (40)	56	0.05
Armenian (122)	152	0.14
Assyrian/Chaldean/Syriac (0)	0	<0.01
Australian (11)	68	0.06
Austrian (65)	458	0.44
Basque (24)	67	0.06
Belgian (65)	100	0.10
Brazilian (27)	39	0.04
British (208)	369	0.35
Bulgarian (0)	0	<0.01
Cajun (0)	0	<0.01
Canadian (152)	410	0.39
Carpatho Rusyn (0)	0	<0.01
Celtic (0)	12	0.01
Croatian (0)	43	0.04
Cypriot (0)	0	<0.01
Czech (61)	389	0.37
Czechoslovakian (36)	36	0.03
Danish (379)	1,189	1.13
Dutch (314)	1,869	1.78
Eastern European (159)	159	0.15
English (3,493)	13,161	12.51
Estonian (0)	10	0.01
European (1,511)	1,777	1.69
Finnish (112)	187	0.18
French, ex. Basque (511)	3,912	3.72
French Canadian (283)	734	0.70
German (3,897)	17,580	16.71
German Russian (0)	0	<0.01
Greek (194)	609	0.58
Guyanese (0)	0	<0.01
Hungarian (227)	786	0.75
Icelander (9)	24	0.02
Iranian (157)	317	0.30
Irish (2,917)	12,972	12.33
Israeli (39)	49	0.05
Italian (1,633)	5,364	5.10
Latvian (0)	34	0.03
Lithuanian (41)	197	0.19
Luxemburger (0)	0	<0.01
Macedonian (0)	0	<0.01
Maltese (0)	0	<0.01
New Zealander (0)	0	<0.01
Northern European (91)	91	0.09
Norwegian (593)	1,826	1.74
Pennsylvania German (41)	60	0.06
Polish (694)	2,459	2.34
Portuguese (274)	728	0.69
Romanian (41)	278	0.26
Russian (539)	1,625	1.54
Scandinavian (38)	261	0.25
Scotch-Irish (827)	2,369	2.25
Scottish (773)	2,873	2.73
Serbian (0)	0	<0.01
Slavic (27)	153	0.15
Slovak (78)	98	0.09
Slovene (0)	0	<0.01
Soviet Union (0)	0	<0.01
Swedish (372)	2,104	2.00
Swiss (80)	637	0.61
Turkish (84)	150	0.14
Ukrainian (161)	303	0.29
Welsh (265)	968	0.92
West Indian, ex. Hispanic (47)	130	0.12
Bahamian (0)	0	<0.01
Barbadian (0)	0	<0.01
Belizean (0)	0	<0.01
Bermudan (0)	0	<0.01
British West Indian (0)	0	<0.01
Dutch West Indian (0)	75	0.07
Haitian (30)	30	0.03
Jamaican (17)	17	0.02
Trinidadian/Tobagonian (0)	0	<0.01
U.S. Virgin Islander (0)	0	<0.01
West Indian (0)	8	0.01
Other West Indian (0)	0	<0.01
Yugoslavian (120)	247	0.23

Hispanic Origin	Population	%
Hispanic or Latino (of any race)	33,874	31.83
Central American, ex. Mexican	758	0.71
Costa Rican	44	0.04
Guatemalan	277	0.26
Honduran	36	0.03
Nicaraguan	86	0.08
Panamanian	44	0.04
Salvadoran	262	0.25
Other Central American	9	0.01
Cuban	144	0.14
Dominican Republic	24	0.02
Mexican	29,837	28.03
Puerto Rican	396	0.37
South American	674	0.63
Argentinean	111	0.10
Bolivian	28	0.03
Chilean	94	0.09
Colombian	149	0.14
Ecuadorian	40	0.04
Paraguayan	1	<0.01
Peruvian	183	0.17
Uruguayan	19	0.02
Venezuelan	37	0.03
Other South American	12	0.01
Other Hispanic or Latino	2,041	1.92

Race*	Population	%
African-American/Black (1,724)	2,660	2.50
Not Hispanic (1,466)	2,132	2.00
Hispanic (258)	528	0.50
American Indian/Alaska Native (1,287)	2,858	2.69
Not Hispanic (545)	1,512	1.42
Hispanic (742)	1,346	1.26
Alaska Athabascan *(Ala. Nat.)* (1)	1	<0.01
Aleut *(Alaska Native)* (3)	3	<0.01
Apache (52)	131	0.12
Arapaho (0)	1	<0.01
Blackfeet (4)	61	0.06
Canadian/French Am. Ind. (1)	8	0.01
Central American Ind. (2)	6	0.01
Cherokee (128)	536	0.50
Cheyenne (1)	3	<0.01
Chickasaw (9)	27	0.03
Chippewa (13)	33	0.03
Choctaw (38)	155	0.15
Colville (0)	0	<0.01
Comanche (12)	21	0.02
Cree (0)	2	<0.01
Creek (8)	21	0.02
Crow (0)	7	0.01
Delaware (1)	5	<0.01
Hopi (2)	17	0.02
Houma (0)	0	<0.01
Inupiat *(Alaska Native)* (1)	1	<0.01
Iroquois (9)	32	0.03
Kiowa (1)	3	<0.01
Lumbee (0)	2	<0.01
Menominee (1)	5	<0.01
Mexican American Ind. (123)	178	0.17
Navajo (16)	53	0.05
Osage (5)	14	0.01
Ottawa (0)	1	<0.01
Paiute (6)	11	0.01
Pima (6)	10	0.01
Potawatomi (7)	19	0.02
Pueblo (17)	27	0.03
Puget Sound Salish (0)	0	<0.01
Seminole (1)	4	<0.01
Shoshone (4)	5	<0.01
Sioux (25)	51	0.05
South American Ind. (7)	14	0.01
Spanish American Ind. (2)	7	0.01
Tlingit-Haida *(Alaska Native)* (4)	7	0.01
Tohono O'Odham (10)	17	0.02
Tsimshian *(Alaska Native)* (0)	0	<0.01
Ute (1)	4	<0.01
Yakama (2)	2	<0.01
Yaqui (19)	52	0.05
Yuman (2)	2	<0.01
Yup'ik *(Alaska Native)* (0)	1	<0.01
Asian (3,663)	5,321	5.00
Not Hispanic (3,523)	4,769	4.48
Hispanic (140)	552	0.52
Bangladeshi (19)	25	0.02
Bhutanese (0)	0	<0.01
Burmese (0)	7	0.01
Cambodian (86)	99	0.09
Chinese, ex. Taiwanese (560)	908	0.85
Filipino (930)	1,551	1.46
Hmong (2)	3	<0.01
Indian (467)	576	0.54
Indonesian (21)	57	0.05
Japanese (395)	873	0.82
Korean (450)	550	0.52
Laotian (52)	58	0.05
Malaysian (9)	11	0.01
Nepalese (23)	27	0.03
Pakistani (45)	48	0.05
Sri Lankan (50)	55	0.05
Taiwanese (35)	41	0.04
Thai (70)	97	0.09
Vietnamese (281)	339	0.32
Hawaii Native/Pacific Islander (206)	548	0.51
Not Hispanic (167)	389	0.37
Hispanic (39)	159	0.15
Fijian (4)	4	<0.01
Guamanian/Chamorro (35)	80	0.08
Marshallese (0)	0	<0.01
Native Hawaiian (80)	254	0.24
Samoan (36)	96	0.09
Tongan (3)	11	0.01
White (81,553)	86,489	81.26
Not Hispanic (63,879)	66,463	62.45
Hispanic (17,674)	20,026	18.82

*Notes: † The Census 2010 population figure is used to calculate the percentages in the Hispanic Origin and Race categories. Ancestry percentages are based on the 2006-2010 American Community Survey population (not shown); ‡ Numbers in parentheses indicate the number of people reporting a single ancestry; * Numbers in parentheses indicate the number of persons reporting this race alone, not in combination with any other race; Please refer to the Explanation of Data for more information.*

San Clemente

Place Type: City
County: Orange
Population: 63,522

Ancestry	Population	%
Afghan (44)	44	0.07
African, Sub-Saharan (36)	96	0.16
African (36)	57	0.09
Cape Verdean (0)	0	<0.01
Ethiopian (0)	0	<0.01
Ghanaian (0)	0	<0.01
Kenyan (0)	0	<0.01
Liberian (0)	0	<0.01
Nigerian (0)	0	<0.01
Senegalese (0)	0	<0.01
Sierra Leonean (0)	0	<0.01
Somalian (0)	0	<0.01
South African (0)	0	<0.01
Sudanese (0)	0	<0.01
Ugandan (0)	0	<0.01
Zimbabwean (0)	0	<0.01
Other Sub-Saharan African (0)	39	0.06
Albanian (0)	0	<0.01
Alsatian (0)	0	<0.01
American (1,902)	1,902	3.13
Arab (250)	308	0.51
Arab (25)	25	0.04
Egyptian (92)	101	0.17
Iraqi (0)	9	0.01
Jordanian (27)	36	0.06
Lebanese (73)	97	0.16
Moroccan (0)	0	<0.01
Palestinian (0)	0	<0.01
Syrian (15)	15	0.02
Other Arab (18)	25	0.04
Armenian (161)	267	0.44
Assyrian/Chaldean/Syriac (13)	26	0.04
Australian (42)	147	0.24
Austrian (48)	177	0.29
Basque (0)	18	0.03
Belgian (118)	278	0.46
Brazilian (169)	182	0.30
British (313)	433	0.71
Bulgarian (0)	8	0.01
Cajun (0)	0	<0.01
Canadian (143)	267	0.44
Carpatho Rusyn (0)	0	<0.01
Celtic (22)	22	0.04
Croatian (59)	172	0.28
Cypriot (0)	0	<0.01
Czech (21)	140	0.23
Czechoslovakian (47)	61	0.10
Danish (106)	633	1.04
Dutch (492)	1,526	2.51
Eastern European (46)	46	0.08
English (3,284)	8,898	14.64
Estonian (0)	0	<0.01
European (948)	1,142	1.88
Finnish (40)	107	0.18
French, ex. Basque (413)	2,064	3.40
French Canadian (184)	343	0.56
German (3,203)	11,693	19.24
German Russian (0)	8	0.01
Greek (91)	275	0.45
Guyanese (0)	0	<0.01
Hungarian (185)	408	0.67
Icelander (0)	14	0.02
Iranian (367)	465	0.77
Irish (2,611)	9,417	15.50
Israeli (19)	19	0.03
Italian (1,774)	5,107	8.40
Latvian (0)	11	0.02
Lithuanian (15)	120	0.20
Luxemburger (0)	12	0.02
Macedonian (14)	50	0.08
Maltese (0)	6	0.01
New Zealander (0)	8	0.01
Northern European (73)	86	0.14
Norwegian (413)	1,175	1.93
Pennsylvania German (0)	0	<0.01
Polish (654)	1,824	3.00
Portuguese (118)	225	0.37
Romanian (134)	206	0.34
Russian (524)	1,447	2.38
Scandinavian (126)	256	0.42
Scotch-Irish (671)	1,276	2.10
Scottish (889)	2,113	3.48
Serbian (20)	80	0.13
Slavic (129)	160	0.26
Slovak (39)	85	0.14
Slovene (0)	0	<0.01
Soviet Union (0)	0	<0.01
Swedish (581)	1,632	2.69
Swiss (48)	156	0.26
Turkish (28)	114	0.19
Ukrainian (13)	79	0.13
Welsh (94)	562	0.92
West Indian, ex. Hispanic (0)	0	<0.01
Bahamian (0)	0	<0.01
Barbadian (0)	0	<0.01
Belizean (0)	0	<0.01
Bermudan (0)	0	<0.01
British West Indian (0)	0	<0.01
Dutch West Indian (0)	0	<0.01
Haitian (0)	0	<0.01
Jamaican (0)	0	<0.01
Trinidadian/Tobagonian (0)	0	<0.01
U.S. Virgin Islander (0)	0	<0.01
West Indian (0)	0	<0.01
Other West Indian (0)	0	<0.01
Yugoslavian (33)	75	0.12

Hispanic Origin	Population	%
Hispanic or Latino (of any race)	10,702	16.85
Central American, ex. Mexican	298	0.47
Costa Rican	34	0.05
Guatemalan	82	0.13
Honduran	16	0.03
Nicaraguan	31	0.05
Panamanian	23	0.04
Salvadoran	110	0.17
Other Central American	2	<0.01
Cuban	148	0.23
Dominican Republic	17	0.03
Mexican	8,471	13.34
Puerto Rican	260	0.41
South American	606	0.95
Argentinean	162	0.26
Bolivian	24	0.04
Chilean	53	0.08
Colombian	108	0.17
Ecuadorian	62	0.10
Paraguayan	4	0.01
Peruvian	140	0.22
Uruguayan	7	0.01
Venezuelan	40	0.06
Other South American	6	0.01
Other Hispanic or Latino	902	1.42

Race*	Population	%
African-American/Black (411)	689	1.08
Not Hispanic (349)	586	0.92
Hispanic (62)	103	0.16
American Indian/Alaska Native (363)	829	1.31
Not Hispanic (193)	545	0.86
Hispanic (170)	284	0.45
Alaska Athabascan *(Ala. Nat.)* (2)	2	<0.01
Aleut *(Alaska Native)* (0)	0	<0.01
Apache (9)	23	0.04
Arapaho (0)	0	<0.01
Blackfeet (3)	20	0.03
Canadian/French Am. Ind. (1)	2	<0.01
Central American Ind. (0)	1	<0.01
Cherokee (34)	135	0.21
Cheyenne (0)	0	<0.01
Chickasaw (2)	7	0.01
Chippewa (4)	13	0.02
Choctaw (13)	35	0.06
Colville (1)	1	<0.01
Comanche (0)	5	0.01
Cree (0)	0	<0.01
Creek (1)	7	0.01
Crow (0)	0	<0.01
Delaware (1)	5	0.01
Hopi (0)	0	<0.01
Houma (0)	0	<0.01
Inupiat *(Alaska Native)* (1)	1	<0.01
Iroquois (3)	18	0.03
Kiowa (3)	3	<0.01
Lumbee (0)	8	0.01
Menominee (0)	0	<0.01
Mexican American Ind. (18)	28	0.04
Navajo (9)	18	0.03
Osage (1)	7	0.01
Ottawa (1)	1	<0.01
Paiute (0)	0	<0.01
Pima (0)	0	<0.01
Potawatomi (0)	2	<0.01
Pueblo (1)	9	0.01
Puget Sound Salish (1)	1	<0.01
Seminole (0)	10	0.02
Shoshone (3)	3	<0.01
Sioux (12)	18	0.03
South American Ind. (2)	5	0.01
Spanish American Ind. (2)	7	0.01
Tlingit-Haida *(Alaska Native)* (0)	1	<0.01
Tohono O'Odham (1)	3	<0.01
Tsimshian *(Alaska Native)* (0)	0	<0.01
Ute (0)	2	<0.01
Yakama (0)	0	<0.01
Yaqui (3)	8	0.01
Yuman (2)	3	<0.01
Yup'ik *(Alaska Native)* (0)	0	<0.01
Asian (2,333)	3,461	5.45
Not Hispanic (2,269)	3,265	5.14
Hispanic (64)	196	0.31
Bangladeshi (14)	15	0.02
Bhutanese (0)	0	<0.01
Burmese (1)	2	<0.01
Cambodian (16)	22	0.03
Chinese, ex. Taiwanese (391)	644	1.01
Filipino (550)	887	1.40
Hmong (0)	0	<0.01
Indian (278)	338	0.53
Indonesian (10)	51	0.08
Japanese (318)	618	0.97
Korean (267)	383	0.60
Laotian (4)	7	0.01
Malaysian (3)	3	<0.01
Nepalese (4)	4	0.01
Pakistani (17)	23	0.04
Sri Lankan (3)	3	<0.01
Taiwanese (31)	41	0.06
Thai (62)	92	0.14
Vietnamese (212)	285	0.45
Hawaii Native/Pacific Islander (90)	263	0.41
Not Hispanic (78)	222	0.35
Hispanic (12)	41	0.06
Fijian (6)	8	0.01
Guamanian/Chamorro (9)	24	0.04
Marshallese (1)	2	<0.01
Native Hawaiian (45)	134	0.21
Samoan (12)	30	0.05
Tongan (0)	8	0.01
White (54,605)	56,749	89.34
Not Hispanic (48,254)	49,759	78.33
Hispanic (6,351)	6,990	11.00

*Notes: † The Census 2010 population figure is used to calculate the percentages in the Hispanic Origin and Race categories. Ancestry percentages are based on the 2006-2010 American Community Survey population (not shown); ‡ Numbers in parentheses indicate the number of people reporting a single ancestry; * Numbers in parentheses indicate the number of persons reporting this race alone, not in combination with any other race; Please refer to the Explanation of Data for more information.*

San Diego

Place Type: City
County: San Diego
Population: 1,307,402

Ancestry	Population	%
Afghan (1,808)	1,850	0.14
African, Sub-Saharan (12,871)	15,315	1.19
African (3,942)	5,572	0.43
Cape Verdean (217)	270	0.02
Ethiopian (1,688)	1,985	0.15
Ghanaian (79)	79	0.01
Kenyan (144)	160	0.01
Liberian (40)	40	<0.01
Nigerian (624)	658	0.05
Senegalese (0)	141	0.01
Sierra Leonean (0)	0	<0.01
Somalian (4,076)	4,090	0.32
South African (671)	869	0.07
Sudanese (1,036)	1,036	0.08
Ugandan (0)	0	<0.01
Zimbabwean (39)	39	<0.01
Other Sub-Saharan African (315)	376	0.03
Albanian (98)	193	0.02
Alsatian (0)	0	<0.01
American (32,627)	32,627	2.54
Arab (6,874)	10,030	0.78
Arab (678)	944	0.07
Egyptian (342)	430	0.03
Iraqi (1,155)	1,390	0.11
Jordanian (152)	185	0.01
Lebanese (2,299)	3,545	0.28
Moroccan (540)	611	0.05
Palestinian (448)	828	0.06
Syrian (254)	762	0.06
Other Arab (1,006)	1,335	0.10
Armenian (2,071)	3,045	0.24
Assyrian/Chaldean/Syriac (234)	463	0.04
Australian (713)	1,114	0.09
Austrian (851)	3,861	0.30
Basque (178)	498	0.04
Belgian (536)	1,571	0.12
Brazilian (1,760)	2,350	0.18
British (3,433)	6,683	0.52
Bulgarian (359)	474	0.04
Cajun (131)	217	0.02
Canadian (1,944)	3,425	0.27
Carpatho Rusyn (0)	12	<0.01
Celtic (109)	224	0.02
Croatian (424)	1,378	0.11
Cypriot (51)	51	<0.01
Czech (1,630)	5,144	0.40
Czechoslovakian (358)	1,044	0.08
Danish (1,455)	5,944	0.46
Dutch (3,510)	14,365	1.12
Eastern European (2,350)	2,599	0.20
English (24,452)	92,418	7.20
Estonian (60)	164	0.01
European (16,404)	19,955	1.56
Finnish (701)	2,374	0.19
French, ex. Basque (6,144)	32,028	2.50
French Canadian (2,164)	5,134	0.40
German (39,229)	140,941	10.99
German Russian (39)	53	<0.01
Greek (2,169)	5,154	0.40
Guyanese (173)	260	0.02
Hungarian (2,197)	6,397	0.50
Icelander (224)	408	0.03
Iranian (6,731)	7,595	0.59
Irish (28,310)	108,215	8.44
Israeli (782)	990	0.08
Italian (22,861)	61,669	4.81
Latvian (250)	596	0.05
Lithuanian (876)	2,852	0.22
Luxemburger (25)	130	0.01
Macedonian (25)	47	<0.01
Maltese (77)	146	0.01
New Zealander (142)	193	0.02
Northern European (1,318)	1,520	0.12
Norwegian (5,525)	16,955	1.32
Pennsylvania German (164)	308	0.02
Polish (8,465)	26,533	2.07
Portuguese (4,518)	9,505	0.74
Romanian (788)	2,000	0.16
Russian (8,529)	18,222	1.42
Scandinavian (1,432)	2,796	0.22
Scotch-Irish (6,291)	17,899	1.40
Scottish (6,292)	24,212	1.89
Serbian (564)	935	0.07
Slavic (248)	468	0.04
Slovak (466)	1,472	0.11
Slovene (203)	455	0.04
Soviet Union (25)	25	<0.01
Swedish (4,230)	17,467	1.36
Swiss (931)	4,165	0.32
Turkish (825)	1,280	0.10
Ukrainian (1,576)	3,425	0.27
Welsh (1,673)	8,167	0.64
West Indian, ex. Hispanic (1,820)	2,607	0.20
Bahamian (60)	74	0.01
Barbadian (31)	39	<0.01
Belizean (83)	122	0.01
Bermudan (46)	46	<0.01
British West Indian (101)	112	0.01
Dutch West Indian (51)	74	0.01
Haitian (355)	413	0.03
Jamaican (703)	1,036	0.08
Trinidadian/Tobagonian (144)	156	0.01
U.S. Virgin Islander (0)	27	<0.01
West Indian (212)	474	0.04
Other West Indian (34)	34	<0.01
Yugoslavian (585)	1,142	0.09

Hispanic Origin	Population	%
Hispanic or Latino (of any race)	376,020	28.76
Central American, ex. Mexican	9,188	0.70
Costa Rican	723	0.06
Guatemalan	2,696	0.21
Honduran	1,293	0.10
Nicaraguan	895	0.07
Panamanian	1,018	0.08
Salvadoran	2,415	0.18
Other Central American	148	0.01
Cuban	2,694	0.21
Dominican Republic	903	0.07
Mexican	325,812	24.92
Puerto Rican	8,220	0.63
South American	8,220	0.63
Argentinean	1,322	0.10
Bolivian	345	0.03
Chilean	876	0.07
Colombian	2,214	0.17
Ecuadorian	737	0.06
Paraguayan	52	<0.01
Peruvian	1,901	0.15
Uruguayan	141	0.01
Venezuelan	525	0.04
Other South American	107	0.01
Other Hispanic or Latino	20,983	1.60

Race*	Population	%
African-American/Black (87,949)	104,374	7.98
Not Hispanic (82,497)	94,818	7.25
Hispanic (5,452)	9,556	0.73
American Indian/Alaska Native (7,696)	17,865	1.37
Not Hispanic (3,545)	10,117	0.77
Hispanic (4,151)	7,748	0.59
Alaska Athabascan *(Ala. Nat.)* (19)	39	<0.01
Aleut *(Alaska Native)* (23)	51	<0.01
Apache (239)	616	0.05
Arapaho (5)	16	<0.01
Blackfeet (64)	426	0.03
Canadian/French Am. Ind. (22)	53	<0.01
Central American Ind. (27)	59	<0.01
Cherokee (456)	2,342	0.18
Cheyenne (13)	31	<0.01
Chickasaw (47)	141	0.01
Chippewa (124)	238	0.02
Choctaw (153)	487	0.04
Colville (1)	3	<0.01
Comanche (27)	79	0.01
Cree (11)	40	<0.01
Creek (49)	163	0.01
Crow (8)	20	<0.01
Delaware (10)	26	<0.01
Hopi (30)	57	<0.01
Houma (3)	12	<0.01
Inupiat *(Alaska Native)* (19)	41	<0.01
Iroquois (61)	183	0.01
Kiowa (7)	16	<0.01
Lumbee (20)	45	<0.01
Menominee (7)	19	<0.01
Mexican American Ind. (1,020)	1,561	0.12
Navajo (314)	532	0.04
Osage (21)	70	0.01
Ottawa (12)	22	<0.01
Paiute (29)	62	<0.01
Pima (24)	44	<0.01
Potawatomi (44)	80	0.01
Pueblo (93)	150	0.01
Puget Sound Salish (16)	32	<0.01
Seminole (28)	114	0.01
Shoshone (18)	51	<0.01
Sioux (138)	335	0.03
South American Ind. (31)	106	0.01
Spanish American Ind. (20)	51	<0.01
Tlingit-Haida *(Alaska Native)* (35)	70	0.01
Tohono O'Odham (27)	69	0.01
Tsimshian *(Alaska Native)* (3)	7	<0.01
Ute (13)	22	<0.01
Yakama (5)	12	<0.01
Yaqui (157)	310	0.02
Yuman (27)	48	<0.01
Yup'ik *(Alaska Native)* (15)	20	<0.01
Asian (207,944)	241,293	18.46
Not Hispanic (204,347)	232,029	17.75
Hispanic (3,597)	9,264	0.71
Bangladeshi (223)	254	0.02
Bhutanese (80)	81	0.01
Burmese (766)	824	0.06
Cambodian (3,922)	4,650	0.36
Chinese, ex. Taiwanese (32,525)	40,557	3.10
Filipino (76,738)	92,828	7.10
Hmong (1,081)	1,166	0.09
Indian (17,255)	19,096	1.46
Indonesian (470)	879	0.07
Japanese (9,625)	16,815	1.29
Korean (13,559)	15,883	1.21
Laotian (5,260)	6,058	0.46
Malaysian (103)	315	0.02
Nepalese (131)	146	0.01
Pakistani (919)	1,132	0.09
Sri Lankan (194)	248	0.02
Taiwanese (2,953)	3,400	0.26
Thai (1,367)	2,061	0.16
Vietnamese (33,149)	36,713	2.81
Hawaii Native/Pacific Islander (5,908)	11,945	0.91
Not Hispanic (5,178)	9,844	0.75
Hispanic (730)	2,101	0.16
Fijian (43)	79	0.01
Guamanian/Chamorro (2,301)	3,999	0.31
Marshallese (145)	164	0.01
Native Hawaiian (1,005)	3,194	0.24
Samoan (1,567)	2,490	0.19
Tongan (115)	180	0.01
White (769,971)	824,542	63.07
Not Hispanic (589,702)	625,399	47.84
Hispanic (180,269)	199,143	15.23

*Notes: † The Census 2010 population figure is used to calculate the percentages in the Hispanic Origin and Race categories. Ancestry percentages are based on the 2006-2010 American Community Survey population (not shown); ‡ Numbers in parentheses indicate the number of people reporting a single ancestry; * Numbers in parentheses indicate the number of persons reporting this race alone, not in combination with any other race; Please refer to the Explanation of Data for more information.*

San Francisco

Place Type: City
County: San Francisco
Population: 805,235

Ancestry	Population	%
Afghan (118)	158	0.02
African, Sub-Saharan (3,082)	4,541	0.58
African (1,941)	3,031	0.38
Cape Verdean (0)	0	<0.01
Ethiopian (561)	585	0.07
Ghanaian (91)	123	0.02
Kenyan (0)	0	<0.01
Liberian (7)	18	<0.01
Nigerian (170)	211	0.03
Senegalese (0)	0	<0.01
Sierra Leonean (0)	0	<0.01
Somalian (47)	72	0.01
South African (78)	247	0.03
Sudanese (0)	30	<0.01
Ugandan (6)	6	<0.01
Zimbabwean (0)	0	<0.01
Other Sub-Saharan African (181)	218	0.03
Albanian (53)	143	0.02
Alsatian (24)	49	0.01
American (8,041)	8,041	1.02
Arab (3,899)	5,672	0.72
Arab (727)	1,106	0.14
Egyptian (360)	483	0.06
Iraqi (32)	60	0.01
Jordanian (296)	353	0.04
Lebanese (541)	1,112	0.14
Moroccan (65)	135	0.02
Palestinian (520)	705	0.09
Syrian (77)	159	0.02
Other Arab (1,281)	1,559	0.20
Armenian (1,496)	2,149	0.27
Assyrian/Chaldean/Syriac (154)	196	0.02
Australian (626)	954	0.12
Austrian (916)	3,588	0.45
Basque (206)	508	0.06
Belgian (294)	783	0.10
Brazilian (1,266)	1,569	0.20
British (3,363)	6,050	0.77
Bulgarian (402)	468	0.06
Cajun (155)	219	0.03
Canadian (801)	1,697	0.22
Carpatho Rusyn (0)	16	<0.01
Celtic (91)	194	0.02
Croatian (578)	1,466	0.19
Cypriot (6)	50	0.01
Czech (960)	2,987	0.38
Czechoslovakian (268)	422	0.05
Danish (973)	3,739	0.47
Dutch (1,691)	7,416	0.94
Eastern European (3,092)	3,844	0.49
English (10,682)	45,268	5.74
Estonian (98)	227	0.03
European (13,269)	15,818	2.00
Finnish (390)	1,264	0.16
French, ex. Basque (4,299)	17,757	2.25
French Canadian (1,190)	2,726	0.35
German (16,144)	65,133	8.25
German Russian (0)	16	<0.01
Greek (2,266)	4,216	0.53
Guyanese (0)	0	<0.01
Hungarian (1,208)	3,416	0.43
Icelander (67)	223	0.03
Iranian (1,848)	2,263	0.29
Irish (20,894)	64,487	8.17
Israeli (279)	437	0.06
Italian (15,657)	38,913	4.93
Latvian (243)	632	0.08
Lithuanian (500)	1,821	0.23
Luxemburger (0)	126	0.02
Macedonian (68)	156	0.02
Maltese (385)	608	0.08
New Zealander (74)	123	0.02
Northern European (1,907)	2,060	0.26
Norwegian (1,935)	7,582	0.96
Pennsylvania German (19)	111	0.01
Polish (4,793)	16,127	2.04
Portuguese (1,615)	4,497	0.57
Romanian (810)	1,943	0.25
Russian (11,670)	21,435	2.72
Scandinavian (523)	1,088	0.14
Scotch-Irish (2,897)	8,480	1.07
Scottish (3,767)	13,167	1.67
Serbian (204)	435	0.06
Slavic (197)	627	0.08
Slovak (268)	861	0.11
Slovene (187)	400	0.05
Soviet Union (75)	75	0.01
Swedish (2,218)	8,924	1.13
Swiss (906)	3,264	0.41
Turkish (525)	721	0.09
Ukrainian (3,286)	4,917	0.62
Welsh (850)	3,806	0.48
West Indian, ex. Hispanic (689)	1,316	0.17
Bahamian (9)	9	<0.01
Barbadian (0)	20	<0.01
Belizean (90)	140	0.02
Bermudan (0)	0	<0.01
British West Indian (27)	36	<0.01
Dutch West Indian (0)	0	<0.01
Haitian (49)	49	0.01
Jamaican (399)	714	0.09
Trinidadian/Tobagonian (25)	140	0.02
U.S. Virgin Islander (0)	0	<0.01
West Indian (90)	208	0.03
Other West Indian (0)	0	<0.01
Yugoslavian (279)	538	0.07

Hispanic Origin	Population	%
Hispanic or Latino (of any race)	121,774	15.12
Central American, ex. Mexican	33,834	4.20
Costa Rican	487	0.06
Guatemalan	6,154	0.76
Honduran	2,611	0.32
Nicaraguan	7,604	0.94
Panamanian	399	0.05
Salvadoran	16,165	2.01
Other Central American	414	0.05
Cuban	1,992	0.25
Dominican Republic	289	0.04
Mexican	59,675	7.41
Puerto Rican	4,204	0.52
South American	8,618	1.07
Argentinean	1,100	0.14
Bolivian	416	0.05
Chilean	754	0.09
Colombian	1,717	0.21
Ecuadorian	577	0.07
Paraguayan	43	0.01
Peruvian	3,260	0.40
Uruguayan	118	0.01
Venezuelan	496	0.06
Other South American	137	0.02
Other Hispanic or Latino	13,162	1.63

Race*	Population	%
African-American/Black (48,870)	57,810	7.18
Not Hispanic (46,781)	53,760	6.68
Hispanic (2,089)	4,050	0.50
American Indian/Alaska Native (4,024)	10,873	1.35
Not Hispanic (1,828)	6,241	0.78
Hispanic (2,196)	4,632	0.58
Alaska Athabascan *(Ala. Nat.)* (5)	9	<0.01
Aleut *(Alaska Native)* (10)	30	<0.01
Apache (105)	271	0.03
Arapaho (8)	17	<0.01
Blackfeet (27)	284	0.04
Canadian/French Am. Ind. (9)	42	0.01
Central American Ind. (83)	144	0.02
Cherokee (223)	1,441	0.18
Cheyenne (5)	14	<0.01
Chickasaw (17)	80	0.01
Chippewa (72)	167	0.02
Choctaw (64)	318	0.04
Colville (5)	8	<0.01
Comanche (6)	47	0.01
Cree (5)	35	<0.01
Creek (27)	108	0.01
Crow (9)	23	<0.01
Delaware (5)	38	<0.01
Hopi (8)	23	<0.01
Houma (4)	5	<0.01
Inupiat *(Alaska Native)* (12)	22	<0.01
Iroquois (43)	133	0.02
Kiowa (1)	10	<0.01
Lumbee (5)	11	<0.01
Menominee (1)	3	<0.01
Mexican American Ind. (752)	1,209	0.15
Navajo (151)	242	0.03
Osage (5)	26	<0.01
Ottawa (1)	7	<0.01
Paiute (28)	44	0.01
Pima (19)	36	<0.01
Potawatomi (11)	34	<0.01
Pueblo (19)	83	0.01
Puget Sound Salish (6)	11	<0.01
Seminole (10)	68	0.01
Shoshone (5)	25	<0.01
Sioux (94)	251	0.03
South American Ind. (73)	198	0.02
Spanish American Ind. (27)	41	0.01
Tlingit-Haida *(Alaska Native)* (19)	29	<0.01
Tohono O'Odham (19)	27	<0.01
Tsimshian *(Alaska Native)* (3)	8	<0.01
Ute (5)	18	<0.01
Yakama (2)	7	<0.01
Yaqui (45)	90	0.01
Yuman (6)	10	<0.01
Yup'ik *(Alaska Native)* (3)	5	<0.01
Asian (267,915)	288,529	35.83
Not Hispanic (265,700)	283,435	35.20
Hispanic (2,215)	5,094	0.63
Bangladeshi (98)	113	0.01
Bhutanese (7)	8	<0.01
Burmese (1,296)	1,579	0.20
Cambodian (1,213)	1,518	0.19
Chinese, ex. Taiwanese (169,642)	181,707	22.57
Filipino (36,347)	43,646	5.42
Hmong (95)	109	0.01
Indian (9,747)	11,583	1.44
Indonesian (946)	1,349	0.17
Japanese (10,121)	15,278	1.90
Korean (9,670)	11,558	1.44
Laotian (529)	651	0.08
Malaysian (202)	358	0.04
Nepalese (352)	388	0.05
Pakistani (831)	1,012	0.13
Sri Lankan (141)	191	0.02
Taiwanese (2,332)	2,806	0.35
Thai (2,336)	2,879	0.36
Vietnamese (12,871)	16,075	2.00
Hawaii Native/Pacific Islander (3,359)	6,173	0.77
Not Hispanic (3,128)	5,432	0.67
Hispanic (231)	741	0.09
Fijian (176)	250	0.03
Guamanian/Chamorro (313)	566	0.07
Marshallese (3)	5	<0.01
Native Hawaiian (410)	1,489	0.18
Samoan (1,988)	2,542	0.32
Tongan (163)	220	0.03
White (390,387)	420,823	52.26
Not Hispanic (337,451)	358,844	44.56
Hispanic (52,936)	61,979	7.70

*Notes: † The Census 2010 population figure is used to calculate the percentages in the Hispanic Origin and Race categories. Ancestry percentages are based on the 2006-2010 American Community Survey population (not shown); ‡ Numbers in parentheses indicate the number of people reporting a single ancestry; * Numbers in parentheses indicate the number of persons reporting this race alone, not in combination with any other race; Please refer to the Explanation of Data for more information.*

San Jose

Place Type: City
County: Santa Clara
Population: 945,942

Ancestry	Population	%
Afghan (808)	925	0.10
African, Sub-Saharan (4,478)	5,552	0.60
African (1,313)	1,999	0.22
Cape Verdean (21)	105	0.01
Ethiopian (1,993)	2,008	0.22
Ghanaian (0)	0	<0.01
Kenyan (69)	69	0.01
Liberian (41)	94	0.01
Nigerian (221)	229	0.02
Senegalese (0)	0	<0.01
Sierra Leonean (44)	117	0.01
Somalian (324)	324	0.04
South African (184)	211	0.02
Sudanese (39)	81	0.01
Ugandan (18)	18	<0.01
Zimbabwean (0)	0	<0.01
Other Sub-Saharan African (211)	297	0.03
Albanian (56)	64	0.01
Alsatian (38)	61	0.01
American (11,998)	11,998	1.30
Arab (3,514)	4,802	0.52
Arab (441)	698	0.08
Egyptian (733)	847	0.09
Iraqi (140)	177	0.02
Jordanian (204)	219	0.02
Lebanese (1,025)	1,317	0.14
Moroccan (38)	91	0.01
Palestinian (361)	587	0.06
Syrian (111)	171	0.02
Other Arab (461)	695	0.08
Armenian (1,238)	1,585	0.17
Assyrian/Chaldean/Syriac (1,732)	2,016	0.22
Australian (17)	80	0.01
Austrian (197)	1,045	0.11
Basque (73)	259	0.03
Belgian (274)	693	0.07
Brazilian (470)	683	0.07
British (1,711)	3,157	0.34
Bulgarian (202)	264	0.03
Cajun (13)	68	0.01
Canadian (875)	1,796	0.19
Carpatho Rusyn (0)	0	<0.01
Celtic (60)	243	0.03
Croatian (742)	1,692	0.18
Cypriot (0)	0	<0.01
Czech (449)	1,653	0.18
Czechoslovakian (217)	484	0.05
Danish (858)	3,362	0.36
Dutch (2,072)	7,446	0.80
Eastern European (900)	1,162	0.13
English (11,113)	42,150	4.56
Estonian (37)	54	0.01
European (8,084)	9,840	1.06
Finnish (309)	892	0.10
French, ex. Basque (2,199)	14,068	1.52
French Canadian (614)	1,741	0.19
German (15,618)	61,487	6.65
German Russian (7)	7	<0.01
Greek (1,635)	3,018	0.33
Guyanese (59)	59	0.01
Hungarian (651)	1,873	0.20
Icelander (47)	121	0.01
Iranian (6,703)	7,389	0.80
Irish (11,484)	46,086	4.98
Israeli (529)	641	0.07
Italian (16,922)	40,876	4.42
Latvian (29)	155	0.02
Lithuanian (223)	644	0.07
Luxemburger (74)	168	0.02
Macedonian (43)	65	0.01
Maltese (106)	179	0.02
New Zealander (59)	59	0.01
Northern European (958)	1,065	0.12
Norwegian (2,111)	8,087	0.87
Pennsylvania German (49)	60	0.01
Polish (2,946)	8,895	0.96
Portuguese (8,414)	15,480	1.67
Romanian (836)	1,307	0.14
Russian (3,533)	6,163	0.67
Scandinavian (435)	980	0.11
Scotch-Irish (2,309)	7,094	0.77
Scottish (2,187)	9,176	0.99
Serbian (201)	398	0.04
Slavic (57)	235	0.03
Slovak (227)	702	0.08
Slovene (39)	107	0.01
Soviet Union (0)	0	<0.01
Swedish (1,742)	8,620	0.93
Swiss (541)	2,530	0.27
Turkish (361)	539	0.06
Ukrainian (1,060)	1,748	0.19
Welsh (725)	3,304	0.36
West Indian, ex. Hispanic (356)	684	0.07
Bahamian (0)	0	<0.01
Barbadian (0)	0	<0.01
Belizean (0)	41	<0.01
Bermudan (0)	0	<0.01
British West Indian (0)	0	<0.01
Dutch West Indian (0)	14	<0.01
Haitian (87)	87	0.01
Jamaican (123)	252	0.03
Trinidadian/Tobagonian (97)	140	0.02
U.S. Virgin Islander (0)	0	<0.01
West Indian (49)	112	0.01
Other West Indian (0)	38	<0.01
Yugoslavian (1,112)	1,585	0.17

Hispanic Origin	Population	%
Hispanic or Latino (of any race)	313,636	33.16
Central American, ex. Mexican	14,697	1.55
Costa Rican	258	0.03
Guatemalan	2,294	0.24
Honduran	1,890	0.20
Nicaraguan	2,917	0.31
Panamanian	371	0.04
Salvadoran	6,829	0.72
Other Central American	138	0.01
Cuban	1,194	0.13
Dominican Republic	235	0.02
Mexican	268,538	28.39
Puerto Rican	4,763	0.50
South American	6,035	0.64
Argentinean	666	0.07
Bolivian	459	0.05
Chilean	632	0.07
Colombian	1,266	0.13
Ecuadorian	368	0.04
Paraguayan	31	<0.01
Peruvian	2,128	0.22
Uruguayan	45	<0.01
Venezuelan	350	0.04
Other South American	90	0.01
Other Hispanic or Latino	18,174	1.92

Race*	Population	%
African-American/Black (30,242)	37,836	4.00
Not Hispanic (27,508)	32,533	3.44
Hispanic (2,734)	5,303	0.56
American Indian/Alaska Native (8,297)	16,064	1.70
Not Hispanic (2,255)	6,164	0.65
Hispanic (6,042)	9,900	1.05
Alaska Athabascan *(Ala. Nat.)* (3)	11	<0.01
Aleut *(Alaska Native)* (21)	33	<0.01
Apache (445)	959	0.10
Arapaho (4)	9	<0.01
Blackfeet (44)	267	0.03
Canadian/French Am. Ind. (16)	45	<0.01
Central American Ind. (32)	51	0.01
Cherokee (331)	1,622	0.17
Cheyenne (4)	16	<0.01
Chickasaw (26)	53	0.01
Chippewa (85)	181	0.02
Choctaw (100)	371	0.04
Colville (7)	7	<0.01
Comanche (52)	91	0.01
Cree (1)	18	<0.01
Creek (36)	115	0.01
Crow (1)	6	<0.01
Delaware (8)	25	<0.01
Hopi (19)	58	0.01
Houma (2)	4	<0.01
Inupiat *(Alaska Native)* (8)	26	<0.01
Iroquois (27)	117	0.01
Kiowa (17)	25	<0.01
Lumbee (4)	11	<0.01
Menominee (4)	9	<0.01
Mexican American Ind. (1,208)	1,697	0.18
Navajo (233)	476	0.05
Osage (8)	35	<0.01
Ottawa (5)	8	<0.01
Paiute (30)	58	0.01
Pima (24)	38	<0.01
Potawatomi (23)	52	0.01
Pueblo (54)	114	0.01
Puget Sound Salish (1)	11	<0.01
Seminole (12)	54	0.01
Shoshone (25)	46	<0.01
Sioux (168)	313	0.03
South American Ind. (50)	133	0.01
Spanish American Ind. (55)	82	0.01
Tlingit-Haida *(Alaska Native)* (18)	40	<0.01
Tohono O'Odham (41)	68	0.01
Tsimshian *(Alaska Native)* (0)	3	<0.01
Ute (6)	17	<0.01
Yakama (5)	7	<0.01
Yaqui (183)	354	0.04
Yuman (28)	41	<0.01
Yup'ik *(Alaska Native)* (2)	3	<0.01
Asian (303,138)	326,627	34.53
Not Hispanic (300,022)	318,607	33.68
Hispanic (3,116)	8,020	0.85
Bangladeshi (519)	576	0.06
Bhutanese (0)	0	<0.01
Burmese (510)	602	0.06
Cambodian (4,106)	4,934	0.52
Chinese, ex. Taiwanese (57,189)	67,093	7.09
Filipino (53,008)	62,549	6.61
Hmong (199)	219	0.02
Indian (43,827)	46,410	4.91
Indonesian (580)	948	0.10
Japanese (10,998)	16,322	1.73
Korean (11,342)	12,929	1.37
Laotian (1,275)	1,590	0.17
Malaysian (194)	304	0.03
Nepalese (134)	139	0.01
Pakistani (1,890)	2,131	0.23
Sri Lankan (316)	358	0.04
Taiwanese (5,834)	6,579	0.70
Thai (848)	1,178	0.12
Vietnamese (100,486)	106,647	11.27
Hawaii Native/Pacific Islander (4,017)	8,116	0.86
Not Hispanic (3,492)	6,460	0.68
Hispanic (525)	1,656	0.18
Fijian (396)	490	0.05
Guamanian/Chamorro (689)	1,396	0.15
Marshallese (13)	20	<0.01
Native Hawaiian (547)	2,161	0.23
Samoan (1,389)	1,954	0.21
Tongan (381)	526	0.06
White (404,437)	442,231	46.75
Not Hispanic (271,382)	292,431	30.91
Hispanic (133,055)	149,800	15.84

*Notes: † The Census 2010 population figure is used to calculate the percentages in the Hispanic Origin and Race categories. Ancestry percentages are based on the 2006-2010 American Community Survey population (not shown); ‡ Numbers in parentheses indicate the number of people reporting a single ancestry; * Numbers in parentheses indicate the number of persons reporting this race alone, not in combination with any other race; Please refer to the Explanation of Data for more information.*

San Leandro

Place Type: City
County: Alameda
Population: 84,950

Ancestry	Population	%
Afghan (35)	35	0.04
African, Sub-Saharan (1,952)	2,077	2.51
African (893)	951	1.15
Cape Verdean (0)	0	<0.01
Ethiopian (350)	350	0.42
Ghanaian (0)	0	<0.01
Kenyan (0)	0	<0.01
Liberian (0)	0	<0.01
Nigerian (676)	729	0.88
Senegalese (33)	33	0.04
Sierra Leonean (0)	14	0.02
Somalian (0)	0	<0.01
South African (0)	0	<0.01
Sudanese (0)	0	<0.01
Ugandan (0)	0	<0.01
Zimbabwean (0)	0	<0.01
Other Sub-Saharan African (0)	0	<0.01
Albanian (10)	10	0.01
Alsatian (0)	0	<0.01
American (1,334)	1,334	1.61
Arab (391)	479	0.58
Arab (67)	99	0.12
Egyptian (66)	66	0.08
Iraqi (0)	0	<0.01
Jordanian (26)	26	0.03
Lebanese (6)	40	0.05
Moroccan (19)	19	0.02
Palestinian (55)	55	0.07
Syrian (0)	22	0.03
Other Arab (152)	152	0.18
Armenian (48)	118	0.14
Assyrian/Chaldean/Syriac (0)	0	<0.01
Australian (15)	15	0.02
Austrian (24)	143	0.17
Basque (0)	23	0.03
Belgian (0)	15	0.02
Brazilian (0)	0	<0.01
British (30)	67	0.08
Bulgarian (0)	0	<0.01
Cajun (0)	0	<0.01
Canadian (13)	84	0.10
Carpatho Rusyn (0)	0	<0.01
Celtic (0)	0	<0.01
Croatian (106)	163	0.20
Cypriot (0)	0	<0.01
Czech (27)	129	0.16
Czechoslovakian (15)	56	0.07
Danish (62)	298	0.36
Dutch (79)	511	0.62
Eastern European (96)	96	0.12
English (920)	3,223	3.89
Estonian (11)	11	0.01
European (1,214)	1,367	1.65
Finnish (18)	102	0.12
French, ex. Basque (323)	1,355	1.64
French Canadian (53)	72	0.09
German (1,470)	4,418	5.33
German Russian (0)	0	<0.01
Greek (219)	292	0.35
Guyanese (0)	0	<0.01
Hungarian (5)	31	0.04
Icelander (0)	0	<0.01
Iranian (23)	47	0.06
Irish (1,451)	4,357	5.26
Israeli (0)	0	<0.01
Italian (1,019)	2,702	3.26
Latvian (61)	61	0.07
Lithuanian (0)	17	0.02
Luxemburger (0)	0	<0.01
Macedonian (0)	0	<0.01
Maltese (37)	37	0.04
New Zealander (0)	0	<0.01
Northern European (68)	76	0.09
Norwegian (186)	710	0.86
Pennsylvania German (0)	0	<0.01
Polish (514)	1,134	1.37
Portuguese (1,880)	3,314	4.00
Romanian (24)	33	0.04
Russian (208)	459	0.55
Scandinavian (14)	93	0.11
Scotch-Irish (240)	766	0.92
Scottish (91)	690	0.83
Serbian (0)	0	<0.01
Slavic (39)	68	0.08
Slovak (5)	14	0.02
Slovene (0)	16	0.02
Soviet Union (0)	0	<0.01
Swedish (226)	580	0.70
Swiss (135)	249	0.30
Turkish (0)	0	<0.01
Ukrainian (72)	122	0.15
Welsh (12)	164	0.20
West Indian, ex. Hispanic (14)	37	0.04
Bahamian (0)	0	<0.01
Barbadian (0)	0	<0.01
Belizean (0)	0	<0.01
Bermudan (0)	0	<0.01
British West Indian (0)	0	<0.01
Dutch West Indian (0)	0	<0.01
Haitian (0)	0	<0.01
Jamaican (14)	28	0.03
Trinidadian/Tobagonian (0)	0	<0.01
U.S. Virgin Islander (0)	0	<0.01
West Indian (0)	9	0.01
Other West Indian (0)	0	<0.01
Yugoslavian (135)	157	0.19

Hispanic Origin	Population	%
Hispanic or Latino (of any race)	23,237	27.35
Central American, ex. Mexican	2,371	2.79
Costa Rican	62	0.07
Guatemalan	455	0.54
Honduran	118	0.14
Nicaraguan	444	0.52
Panamanian	41	0.05
Salvadoran	1,229	1.45
Other Central American	22	0.03
Cuban	121	0.14
Dominican Republic	22	0.03
Mexican	17,102	20.13
Puerto Rican	831	0.98
South American	668	0.79
Argentinean	80	0.09
Bolivian	30	0.04
Chilean	50	0.06
Colombian	135	0.16
Ecuadorian	16	0.02
Paraguayan	1	<0.01
Peruvian	298	0.35
Uruguayan	6	0.01
Venezuelan	39	0.05
Other South American	13	0.02
Other Hispanic or Latino	2,122	2.50

Race*	Population	%
African-American/Black (10,437)	11,838	13.94
Not Hispanic (10,052)	11,051	13.01
Hispanic (385)	787	0.93
American Indian/Alaska Native (669)	1,578	1.86
Not Hispanic (246)	791	0.93
Hispanic (423)	787	0.93
Alaska Athabascan *(Ala. Nat.)* (0)	1	<0.01
Aleut *(Alaska Native)* (1)	4	<0.01
Apache (28)	60	0.07
Arapaho (1)	1	<0.01
Blackfeet (6)	45	0.05
Canadian/French Am. Ind. (0)	1	<0.01
Central American Ind. (5)	10	0.01
Cherokee (27)	203	0.24
Cheyenne (1)	2	<0.01
Chickasaw (0)	3	<0.01
Chippewa (5)	26	0.03
Choctaw (13)	42	0.05
Colville (0)	2	<0.01
Comanche (5)	10	0.01
Cree (0)	5	0.01
Creek (2)	8	0.01
Crow (0)	0	<0.01
Delaware (0)	1	<0.01
Hopi (2)	9	0.01
Houma (0)	4	<0.01
Inupiat *(Alaska Native)* (0)	0	<0.01
Iroquois (6)	17	0.02
Kiowa (2)	4	<0.01
Lumbee (0)	0	<0.01
Menominee (0)	0	<0.01
Mexican American Ind. (94)	170	0.20
Navajo (31)	55	0.06
Osage (0)	3	<0.01
Ottawa (1)	1	<0.01
Paiute (3)	14	0.02
Pima (4)	4	<0.01
Potawatomi (1)	1	<0.01
Pueblo (16)	29	0.03
Puget Sound Salish (1)	1	<0.01
Seminole (2)	4	<0.01
Shoshone (1)	3	<0.01
Sioux (15)	33	0.04
South American Ind. (8)	23	0.03
Spanish American Ind. (3)	4	<0.01
Tlingit-Haida *(Alaska Native)* (3)	8	0.01
Tohono O'Odham (4)	6	0.01
Tsimshian *(Alaska Native)* (0)	1	<0.01
Ute (0)	4	<0.01
Yakama (0)	0	<0.01
Yaqui (6)	13	0.02
Yuman (1)	2	<0.01
Yup'ik *(Alaska Native)* (1)	1	<0.01
Asian (25,206)	27,280	32.11
Not Hispanic (24,924)	26,490	31.18
Hispanic (282)	790	0.93
Bangladeshi (2)	2	<0.01
Bhutanese (0)	0	<0.01
Burmese (37)	57	0.07
Cambodian (277)	335	0.39
Chinese, ex. Taiwanese (11,551)	12,337	14.52
Filipino (7,935)	9,060	10.67
Hmong (2)	2	<0.01
Indian (638)	767	0.90
Indonesian (47)	81	0.10
Japanese (462)	817	0.96
Korean (491)	635	0.75
Laotian (95)	112	0.13
Malaysian (9)	16	0.02
Nepalese (32)	32	0.04
Pakistani (43)	49	0.06
Sri Lankan (11)	11	0.01
Taiwanese (97)	116	0.14
Thai (47)	75	0.09
Vietnamese (2,715)	3,000	3.53
Hawaii Native/Pacific Islander (642)	1,182	1.39
Not Hispanic (596)	996	1.17
Hispanic (46)	186	0.22
Fijian (72)	104	0.12
Guamanian/Chamorro (159)	252	0.30
Marshallese (0)	0	<0.01
Native Hawaiian (81)	314	0.37
Samoan (162)	222	0.26
Tongan (88)	109	0.13
White (31,946)	35,526	41.82
Not Hispanic (23,006)	25,040	29.48
Hispanic (8,940)	10,486	12.34

*Notes: † The Census 2010 population figure is used to calculate the percentages in the Hispanic Origin and Race categories. Ancestry percentages are based on the 2006-2010 American Community Survey population (not shown); ‡ Numbers in parentheses indicate the number of people reporting a single ancestry; * Numbers in parentheses indicate the number of persons reporting this race alone, not in combination with any other race; Please refer to the Explanation of Data for more information.*

San Marcos

Place Type: City
County: San Diego
Population: 83,781

Ancestry	Population	%
Afghan (47)	47	0.06
African, Sub-Saharan (341)	480	0.61
African (163)	211	0.27
Cape Verdean (0)	0	<0.01
Ethiopian (66)	66	0.08
Ghanaian (11)	11	0.01
Kenyan (0)	0	<0.01
Liberian (0)	0	<0.01
Nigerian (0)	0	<0.01
Senegalese (0)	0	<0.01
Sierra Leonean (0)	0	<0.01
Somalian (38)	129	0.17
South African (25)	25	0.03
Sudanese (0)	0	<0.01
Ugandan (0)	0	<0.01
Zimbabwean (0)	0	<0.01
Other Sub-Saharan African (38)	38	0.05
Albanian (0)	0	<0.01
Alsatian (0)	0	<0.01
American (1,241)	1,241	1.59
Arab (525)	535	0.68
Arab (156)	156	0.20
Egyptian (0)	0	<0.01
Iraqi (59)	59	0.08
Jordanian (0)	0	<0.01
Lebanese (10)	10	0.01
Moroccan (0)	10	0.01
Palestinian (89)	89	0.11
Syrian (98)	98	0.13
Other Arab (113)	113	0.14
Armenian (103)	188	0.24
Assyrian/Chaldean/Syriac (0)	25	0.03
Australian (0)	13	0.02
Austrian (33)	235	0.30
Basque (0)	11	0.01
Belgian (0)	22	0.03
Brazilian (22)	33	0.04
British (181)	277	0.35
Bulgarian (35)	35	0.04
Cajun (0)	0	<0.01
Canadian (71)	224	0.29
Carpatho Rusyn (0)	0	<0.01
Celtic (0)	0	<0.01
Croatian (4)	72	0.09
Cypriot (0)	0	<0.01
Czech (72)	259	0.33
Czechoslovakian (16)	57	0.07
Danish (62)	346	0.44
Dutch (545)	1,532	1.96
Eastern European (43)	50	0.06
English (4,414)	10,282	13.16
Estonian (15)	44	0.06
European (1,207)	1,412	1.81
Finnish (16)	127	0.16
French, ex. Basque (346)	1,858	2.38
French Canadian (147)	352	0.45
German (2,706)	9,355	11.97
German Russian (0)	0	<0.01
Greek (149)	360	0.46
Guyanese (0)	8	0.01
Hungarian (70)	467	0.60
Icelander (0)	11	0.01
Iranian (293)	444	0.57
Irish (1,697)	6,333	8.11
Israeli (25)	25	0.03
Italian (1,703)	4,747	6.08
Latvian (19)	34	0.04
Lithuanian (20)	129	0.17
Luxemburger (0)	0	<0.01
Macedonian (0)	0	<0.01
Maltese (10)	19	0.02
New Zealander (11)	11	0.01
Northern European (46)	63	0.08
Norwegian (320)	956	1.22
Pennsylvania German (0)	0	<0.01
Polish (648)	1,633	2.09
Portuguese (184)	428	0.55
Romanian (79)	116	0.15
Russian (329)	783	1.00
Scandinavian (127)	234	0.30
Scotch-Irish (300)	881	1.13
Scottish (263)	1,086	1.39
Serbian (42)	81	0.10
Slavic (12)	51	0.07
Slovak (33)	78	0.10
Slovene (0)	0	<0.01
Soviet Union (0)	0	<0.01
Swedish (370)	1,059	1.36
Swiss (20)	167	0.21
Turkish (26)	111	0.14
Ukrainian (30)	53	0.07
Welsh (55)	438	0.56
West Indian, ex. Hispanic (124)	222	0.28
Bahamian (0)	0	<0.01
Barbadian (0)	0	<0.01
Belizean (11)	11	0.01
Bermudan (0)	0	<0.01
British West Indian (7)	7	0.01
Dutch West Indian (0)	0	<0.01
Haitian (67)	83	0.11
Jamaican (0)	52	0.07
Trinidadian/Tobagonian (9)	17	0.02
U.S. Virgin Islander (0)	0	<0.01
West Indian (30)	30	0.04
Other West Indian (0)	22	0.03
Yugoslavian (0)	19	0.02

Hispanic Origin	Population	%
Hispanic or Latino (of any race)	30,697	36.64
Central American, ex. Mexican	634	0.76
Costa Rican	35	0.04
Guatemalan	203	0.24
Honduran	62	0.07
Nicaraguan	53	0.06
Panamanian	35	0.04
Salvadoran	231	0.28
Other Central American	15	0.02
Cuban	170	0.20
Dominican Republic	27	0.03
Mexican	27,350	32.64
Puerto Rican	455	0.54
South American	544	0.65
Argentinean	84	0.10
Bolivian	30	0.04
Chilean	37	0.04
Colombian	156	0.19
Ecuadorian	42	0.05
Paraguayan	2	<0.01
Peruvian	155	0.19
Uruguayan	2	<0.01
Venezuelan	36	0.04
Other South American	0	<0.01
Other Hispanic or Latino	1,517	1.81

Race*	Population	%
African-American/Black (1,967)	2,775	3.31
Not Hispanic (1,756)	2,305	2.75
Hispanic (211)	470	0.56
American Indian/Alaska Native (591)	1,176	1.40
Not Hispanic (255)	596	0.71
Hispanic (336)	580	0.69
Alaska Athabascan *(Ala. Nat.)* (2)	2	<0.01
Aleut *(Alaska Native)* (2)	2	<0.01
Apache (16)	30	0.04
Arapaho (1)	7	0.01
Blackfeet (2)	20	0.02
Canadian/French Am. Ind. (1)	3	<0.01
Central American Ind. (0)	0	<0.01
Cherokee (30)	129	0.15
Cheyenne (0)	0	<0.01
Chickasaw (1)	11	0.01
Chippewa (13)	17	0.02
Choctaw (12)	31	0.04
Colville (0)	2	<0.01
Comanche (2)	5	0.01
Cree (0)	0	<0.01
Creek (5)	6	0.01
Crow (1)	2	<0.01
Delaware (0)	0	<0.01
Hopi (1)	5	0.01
Houma (0)	0	<0.01
Inupiat *(Alaska Native)* (0)	0	<0.01
Iroquois (4)	9	0.01
Kiowa (0)	0	<0.01
Lumbee (2)	6	0.01
Menominee (0)	0	<0.01
Mexican American Ind. (100)	143	0.17
Navajo (6)	16	0.02
Osage (0)	1	<0.01
Ottawa (0)	0	<0.01
Paiute (1)	3	<0.01
Pima (1)	6	0.01
Potawatomi (1)	6	0.01
Pueblo (3)	4	<0.01
Puget Sound Salish (0)	1	<0.01
Seminole (1)	4	<0.01
Shoshone (0)	3	<0.01
Sioux (7)	15	0.02
South American Ind. (1)	5	0.01
Spanish American Ind. (0)	0	<0.01
Tlingit-Haida *(Alaska Native)* (1)	2	<0.01
Tohono O'Odham (0)	4	<0.01
Tsimshian *(Alaska Native)* (0)	0	<0.01
Ute (1)	2	<0.01
Yakama (0)	0	<0.01
Yaqui (6)	19	0.02
Yuman (1)	1	<0.01
Yup'ik *(Alaska Native)* (0)	0	<0.01
Asian (7,518)	9,503	11.34
Not Hispanic (7,363)	9,047	10.80
Hispanic (155)	456	0.54
Bangladeshi (2)	5	0.01
Bhutanese (0)	0	<0.01
Burmese (5)	8	0.01
Cambodian (40)	64	0.08
Chinese, ex. Taiwanese (1,093)	1,482	1.77
Filipino (2,817)	3,575	4.27
Hmong (10)	12	0.01
Indian (700)	834	1.00
Indonesian (18)	47	0.06
Japanese (451)	897	1.07
Korean (410)	555	0.66
Laotian (200)	248	0.30
Malaysian (5)	13	0.02
Nepalese (0)	1	<0.01
Pakistani (38)	49	0.06
Sri Lankan (11)	19	0.02
Taiwanese (69)	89	0.11
Thai (69)	124	0.15
Vietnamese (1,175)	1,372	1.64
Hawaii Native/Pacific Islander (322)	708	0.85
Not Hispanic (289)	574	0.69
Hispanic (33)	134	0.16
Fijian (11)	15	0.02
Guamanian/Chamorro (80)	142	0.17
Marshallese (0)	0	<0.01
Native Hawaiian (57)	225	0.27
Samoan (126)	181	0.22
Tongan (18)	33	0.04
White (53,235)	56,959	67.99
Not Hispanic (40,736)	42,954	51.27
Hispanic (12,499)	14,005	16.72

*Notes: † The Census 2010 population figure is used to calculate the percentages in the Hispanic Origin and Race categories. Ancestry percentages are based on the 2006-2010 American Community Survey population (not shown); ‡ Numbers in parentheses indicate the number of people reporting a single ancestry; * Numbers in parentheses indicate the number of persons reporting this race alone, not in combination with any other race; Please refer to the Explanation of Data for more information.*

San Mateo

Place Type: City
County: San Mateo
Population: 97,207

Ancestry	Population	%
Afghan (10)	32	0.03
African, Sub-Saharan (212)	316	0.33
African (135)	196	0.21
Cape Verdean (0)	0	<0.01
Ethiopian (0)	10	0.01
Ghanaian (0)	0	<0.01
Kenyan (0)	0	<0.01
Liberian (16)	16	0.02
Nigerian (0)	33	0.03
Senegalese (0)	0	<0.01
Sierra Leonean (0)	0	<0.01
Somalian (0)	0	<0.01
South African (48)	48	0.05
Sudanese (0)	0	<0.01
Ugandan (0)	0	<0.01
Zimbabwean (0)	0	<0.01
Other Sub-Saharan African (13)	13	0.01
Albanian (0)	28	0.03
Alsatian (7)	7	0.01
American (1,430)	1,430	1.51
Arab (1,101)	1,409	1.49
Arab (127)	162	0.17
Egyptian (90)	121	0.13
Iraqi (61)	61	0.06
Jordanian (134)	134	0.14
Lebanese (150)	273	0.29
Moroccan (78)	78	0.08
Palestinian (219)	265	0.28
Syrian (42)	58	0.06
Other Arab (200)	257	0.27
Armenian (585)	755	0.80
Assyrian/Chaldean/Syriac (37)	37	0.04
Australian (58)	87	0.09
Austrian (84)	281	0.30
Basque (57)	125	0.13
Belgian (56)	124	0.13
Brazilian (83)	164	0.17
British (366)	618	0.65
Bulgarian (29)	29	0.03
Cajun (0)	0	<0.01
Canadian (145)	265	0.28
Carpatho Rusyn (0)	0	<0.01
Celtic (38)	51	0.05
Croatian (133)	302	0.32
Cypriot (0)	0	<0.01
Czech (156)	497	0.52
Czechoslovakian (49)	68	0.07
Danish (136)	565	0.60
Dutch (249)	995	1.05
Eastern European (155)	183	0.19
English (1,618)	6,445	6.80
Estonian (19)	36	0.04
European (1,172)	1,261	1.33
Finnish (61)	202	0.21
French, ex. Basque (271)	2,461	2.60
French Canadian (168)	321	0.34
German (2,428)	9,474	10.00
German Russian (0)	0	<0.01
Greek (398)	776	0.82
Guyanese (38)	38	0.04
Hungarian (170)	428	0.45
Icelander (14)	43	0.05
Iranian (884)	1,015	1.07
Irish (2,306)	9,085	9.59
Israeli (0)	49	0.05
Italian (3,176)	7,619	8.04
Latvian (20)	59	0.06
Lithuanian (18)	107	0.11
Luxemburger (0)	0	<0.01
Macedonian (0)	0	<0.01
Maltese (101)	203	0.21
New Zealander (23)	23	0.02
Northern European (111)	111	0.12
Norwegian (202)	864	0.91
Pennsylvania German (8)	8	0.01
Polish (624)	1,746	1.84
Portuguese (486)	947	1.00
Romanian (123)	207	0.22
Russian (1,448)	2,375	2.51
Scandinavian (69)	87	0.09
Scotch-Irish (388)	1,420	1.50
Scottish (527)	1,966	2.07
Serbian (0)	18	0.02
Slavic (21)	37	0.04
Slovak (10)	73	0.08
Slovene (11)	21	0.02
Soviet Union (0)	0	<0.01
Swedish (331)	1,100	1.16
Swiss (57)	334	0.35
Turkish (401)	501	0.53
Ukrainian (159)	327	0.35
Welsh (64)	410	0.43
West Indian, ex. Hispanic (9)	47	0.05
Bahamian (0)	0	<0.01
Barbadian (0)	0	<0.01
Belizean (0)	0	<0.01
Bermudan (0)	0	<0.01
British West Indian (0)	14	0.01
Dutch West Indian (0)	0	<0.01
Haitian (0)	0	<0.01
Jamaican (0)	24	0.03
Trinidadian/Tobagonian (9)	9	0.01
U.S. Virgin Islander (0)	0	<0.01
West Indian (0)	0	<0.01
Other West Indian (0)	0	<0.01
Yugoslavian (10)	42	0.04

Hispanic Origin	Population	%
Hispanic or Latino (of any race)	25,815	26.56
Central American, ex. Mexican	6,575	6.76
Costa Rican	42	0.04
Guatemalan	2,755	2.83
Honduran	189	0.19
Nicaraguan	910	0.94
Panamanian	43	0.04
Salvadoran	2,571	2.64
Other Central American	65	0.07
Cuban	189	0.19
Dominican Republic	34	0.03
Mexican	13,959	14.36
Puerto Rican	519	0.53
South American	2,228	2.29
Argentinean	225	0.23
Bolivian	131	0.13
Chilean	258	0.27
Colombian	244	0.25
Ecuadorian	92	0.09
Paraguayan	10	0.01
Peruvian	1,163	1.20
Uruguayan	22	0.02
Venezuelan	44	0.05
Other South American	39	0.04
Other Hispanic or Latino	2,311	2.38

Race*	Population	%
African-American/Black (2,296)	3,102	3.19
Not Hispanic (2,099)	2,672	2.75
Hispanic (197)	430	0.44
American Indian/Alaska Native (505)	1,173	1.21
Not Hispanic (140)	502	0.52
Hispanic (365)	671	0.69
Alaska Athabascan *(Ala. Nat.)* (0)	1	<0.01
Aleut *(Alaska Native)* (2)	2	<0.01
Apache (9)	29	0.03
Arapaho (0)	0	<0.01
Blackfeet (1)	12	0.01
Canadian/French Am. Ind. (1)	5	0.01
Central American Ind. (13)	22	0.02
Cherokee (23)	146	0.15
Cheyenne (1)	2	<0.01
Chickasaw (0)	5	0.01
Chippewa (3)	11	0.01
Choctaw (8)	31	0.03
Colville (0)	2	<0.01
Comanche (0)	2	<0.01
Cree (0)	3	<0.01
Creek (2)	6	0.01
Crow (0)	0	<0.01
Delaware (0)	4	<0.01
Hopi (1)	1	<0.01
Houma (0)	0	<0.01
Inupiat *(Alaska Native)* (0)	1	<0.01
Iroquois (0)	10	0.01
Kiowa (2)	5	0.01
Lumbee (0)	0	<0.01
Menominee (0)	0	<0.01
Mexican American Ind. (103)	141	0.15
Navajo (18)	36	0.04
Osage (0)	1	<0.01
Ottawa (0)	0	<0.01
Paiute (0)	0	<0.01
Pima (0)	0	<0.01
Potawatomi (2)	4	<0.01
Pueblo (5)	13	0.01
Puget Sound Salish (0)	0	<0.01
Seminole (1)	4	<0.01
Shoshone (2)	2	<0.01
Sioux (6)	25	0.03
South American Ind. (4)	27	0.03
Spanish American Ind. (1)	2	<0.01
Tlingit-Haida *(Alaska Native)* (4)	8	0.01
Tohono O'Odham (0)	0	<0.01
Tsimshian *(Alaska Native)* (0)	0	<0.01
Ute (0)	5	0.01
Yakama (1)	1	<0.01
Yaqui (3)	3	<0.01
Yuman (1)	1	<0.01
Yup'ik *(Alaska Native)* (0)	0	<0.01
Asian (18,384)	21,349	21.96
Not Hispanic (18,153)	20,645	21.24
Hispanic (231)	704	0.72
Bangladeshi (3)	3	<0.01
Bhutanese (0)	0	<0.01
Burmese (38)	52	0.05
Cambodian (47)	63	0.06
Chinese, ex. Taiwanese (7,377)	8,674	8.92
Filipino (4,478)	5,611	5.77
Hmong (7)	7	0.01
Indian (1,713)	2,076	2.14
Indonesian (86)	129	0.13
Japanese (2,093)	2,835	2.92
Korean (776)	1,002	1.03
Laotian (15)	26	0.03
Malaysian (6)	17	0.02
Nepalese (70)	72	0.07
Pakistani (60)	73	0.08
Sri Lankan (20)	25	0.03
Taiwanese (350)	433	0.45
Thai (146)	186	0.19
Vietnamese (336)	475	0.49
Hawaii Native/Pacific Islander (1,998)	2,803	2.88
Not Hispanic (1,937)	2,588	2.66
Hispanic (61)	215	0.22
Fijian (322)	390	0.40
Guamanian/Chamorro (73)	119	0.12
Marshallese (0)	0	<0.01
Native Hawaiian (100)	345	0.35
Samoan (161)	261	0.27
Tongan (1,111)	1,324	1.36
White (56,214)	60,800	62.55
Not Hispanic (45,240)	48,139	49.52
Hispanic (10,974)	12,661	13.02

*Notes: † The Census 2010 population figure is used to calculate the percentages in the Hispanic Origin and Race categories. Ancestry percentages are based on the 2006-2010 American Community Survey population (not shown); ‡ Numbers in parentheses indicate the number of people reporting a single ancestry; * Numbers in parentheses indicate the number of persons reporting this race alone, not in combination with any other race; Please refer to the Explanation of Data for more information.*

San Rafael

Place Type: City
County: Marin
Population: 57,713

Ancestry	Population	%
Afghan (0)	0	<0.01
African, Sub-Saharan (97)	149	0.26
African (34)	55	0.10
Cape Verdean (0)	0	<0.01
Ethiopian (0)	0	<0.01
Ghanaian (0)	0	<0.01
Kenyan (0)	0	<0.01
Liberian (63)	63	0.11
Nigerian (0)	14	0.02
Senegalese (0)	0	<0.01
Sierra Leonean (0)	0	<0.01
Somalian (0)	0	<0.01
South African (0)	17	0.03
Sudanese (0)	0	<0.01
Ugandan (0)	0	<0.01
Zimbabwean (0)	0	<0.01
Other Sub-Saharan African (0)	0	<0.01
Albanian (0)	14	0.02
Alsatian (0)	0	<0.01
American (1,101)	1,101	1.93
Arab (249)	329	0.58
Arab (0)	0	<0.01
Egyptian (85)	85	0.15
Iraqi (0)	0	<0.01
Jordanian (41)	41	0.07
Lebanese (33)	78	0.14
Moroccan (0)	0	<0.01
Palestinian (81)	116	0.20
Syrian (0)	0	<0.01
Other Arab (9)	9	0.02
Armenian (43)	65	0.11
Assyrian/Chaldean/Syriac (0)	0	<0.01
Australian (15)	26	0.05
Austrian (188)	601	1.06
Basque (0)	35	0.06
Belgian (0)	44	0.08
Brazilian (62)	180	0.32
British (436)	672	1.18
Bulgarian (0)	0	<0.01
Cajun (0)	0	<0.01
Canadian (174)	233	0.41
Carpatho Rusyn (0)	0	<0.01
Celtic (10)	10	0.02
Croatian (27)	112	0.20
Cypriot (0)	0	<0.01
Czech (49)	118	0.21
Czechoslovakian (0)	95	0.17
Danish (226)	775	1.36
Dutch (106)	767	1.35
Eastern European (346)	360	0.63
English (1,335)	5,692	10.00
Estonian (0)	0	<0.01
European (958)	1,146	2.01
Finnish (67)	185	0.32
French, ex. Basque (455)	2,043	3.59
French Canadian (40)	115	0.20
German (2,120)	7,191	12.63
German Russian (0)	0	<0.01
Greek (138)	363	0.64
Guyanese (0)	0	<0.01
Hungarian (70)	281	0.49
Icelander (15)	29	0.05
Iranian (341)	384	0.67
Irish (2,295)	7,471	13.12
Israeli (35)	52	0.09
Italian (1,545)	4,405	7.74
Latvian (0)	0	<0.01
Lithuanian (184)	450	0.79
Luxemburger (0)	7	0.01
Macedonian (0)	0	<0.01
Maltese (0)	0	<0.01
New Zealander (0)	0	<0.01
Northern European (149)	175	0.31
Norwegian (215)	865	1.52
Pennsylvania German (0)	13	0.02
Polish (339)	1,346	2.36
Portuguese (166)	471	0.83
Romanian (166)	425	0.75
Russian (777)	2,027	3.56
Scandinavian (193)	293	0.51
Scotch-Irish (487)	1,330	2.34
Scottish (399)	1,490	2.62
Serbian (7)	22	0.04
Slavic (21)	47	0.08
Slovak (15)	15	0.03
Slovene (16)	37	0.06
Soviet Union (0)	0	<0.01
Swedish (268)	1,493	2.62
Swiss (198)	561	0.99
Turkish (13)	141	0.25
Ukrainian (48)	225	0.40
Welsh (102)	560	0.98
West Indian, ex. Hispanic (171)	240	0.42
Bahamian (0)	0	<0.01
Barbadian (0)	0	<0.01
Belizean (0)	0	<0.01
Bermudan (0)	0	<0.01
British West Indian (0)	0	<0.01
Dutch West Indian (0)	0	<0.01
Haitian (35)	35	0.06
Jamaican (128)	197	0.35
Trinidadian/Tobagonian (0)	0	<0.01
U.S. Virgin Islander (8)	8	0.01
West Indian (0)	0	<0.01
Other West Indian (0)	0	<0.01
Yugoslavian (44)	169	0.30

Hispanic Origin	Population	%
Hispanic or Latino (of any race)	17,302	29.98
Central American, ex. Mexican	7,740	13.41
Costa Rican	36	0.06
Guatemalan	5,895	10.21
Honduran	93	0.16
Nicaraguan	175	0.30
Panamanian	19	0.03
Salvadoran	1,478	2.56
Other Central American	44	0.08
Cuban	96	0.17
Dominican Republic	31	0.05
Mexican	7,011	12.15
Puerto Rican	173	0.30
South American	586	1.02
Argentinean	60	0.10
Bolivian	24	0.04
Chilean	55	0.10
Colombian	112	0.19
Ecuadorian	37	0.06
Paraguayan	4	0.01
Peruvian	251	0.43
Uruguayan	17	0.03
Venezuelan	19	0.03
Other South American	7	0.01
Other Hispanic or Latino	1,665	2.88

Race*	Population	%
African-American/Black (1,154)	1,614	2.80
Not Hispanic (1,024)	1,371	2.38
Hispanic (130)	243	0.42
American Indian/Alaska Native (709)	1,417	2.46
Not Hispanic (107)	421	0.73
Hispanic (602)	996	1.73
Alaska Athabascan *(Ala. Nat.)* (0)	0	<0.01
Aleut *(Alaska Native)* (0)	3	0.01
Apache (6)	17	0.03
Arapaho (0)	0	<0.01
Blackfeet (1)	19	0.03
Canadian/French Am. Ind. (0)	3	0.01
Central American Ind. (32)	56	0.10
Cherokee (11)	121	0.21
Cheyenne (0)	3	0.01
Chickasaw (1)	4	0.01
Chippewa (1)	3	0.01
Choctaw (1)	9	0.02
Colville (0)	0	<0.01
Comanche (1)	6	0.01
Cree (0)	1	<0.01
Creek (2)	4	0.01
Crow (0)	0	<0.01
Delaware (1)	12	0.02
Hopi (0)	1	<0.01
Houma (0)	0	<0.01
Inupiat *(Alaska Native)* (2)	2	<0.01
Iroquois (3)	13	0.02
Kiowa (0)	2	<0.01
Lumbee (0)	0	<0.01
Menominee (0)	1	<0.01
Mexican American Ind. (182)	248	0.43
Navajo (4)	13	0.02
Osage (0)	4	0.01
Ottawa (1)	1	<0.01
Paiute (1)	2	<0.01
Pima (1)	3	0.01
Potawatomi (0)	0	<0.01
Pueblo (5)	9	0.02
Puget Sound Salish (0)	2	<0.01
Seminole (0)	2	<0.01
Shoshone (0)	1	<0.01
Sioux (4)	8	0.01
South American Ind. (7)	12	0.02
Spanish American Ind. (1)	3	0.01
Tlingit-Haida *(Alaska Native)* (0)	1	<0.01
Tohono O'Odham (0)	0	<0.01
Tsimshian *(Alaska Native)* (0)	0	<0.01
Ute (3)	3	0.01
Yakama (1)	1	<0.01
Yaqui (4)	6	0.01
Yuman (4)	4	0.01
Yup'ik *(Alaska Native)* (0)	0	<0.01
Asian (3,513)	4,503	7.80
Not Hispanic (3,463)	4,331	7.50
Hispanic (50)	172	0.30
Bangladeshi (3)	3	0.01
Bhutanese (0)	0	<0.01
Burmese (0)	0	<0.01
Cambodian (32)	44	0.08
Chinese, ex. Taiwanese (858)	1,242	2.15
Filipino (533)	780	1.35
Hmong (6)	8	0.01
Indian (494)	567	0.98
Indonesian (27)	35	0.06
Japanese (323)	550	0.95
Korean (244)	335	0.58
Laotian (16)	23	0.04
Malaysian (2)	2	<0.01
Nepalese (15)	15	0.03
Pakistani (25)	28	0.05
Sri Lankan (10)	10	0.02
Taiwanese (35)	37	0.06
Thai (50)	74	0.13
Vietnamese (652)	734	1.27
Hawaii Native/Pacific Islander (126)	290	0.50
Not Hispanic (93)	213	0.37
Hispanic (33)	77	0.13
Fijian (45)	48	0.08
Guamanian/Chamorro (30)	49	0.08
Marshallese (0)	0	<0.01
Native Hawaiian (16)	90	0.16
Samoan (15)	30	0.05
Tongan (13)	16	0.03
White (40,734)	43,379	75.16
Not Hispanic (34,031)	35,399	61.34
Hispanic (6,703)	7,980	13.83

*Notes: † The Census 2010 population figure is used to calculate the percentages in the Hispanic Origin and Race categories. Ancestry percentages are based on the 2006-2010 American Community Survey population (not shown); ‡ Numbers in parentheses indicate the number of people reporting a single ancestry; * Numbers in parentheses indicate the number of persons reporting this race alone, not in combination with any other race; Please refer to the Explanation of Data for more information.*

San Ramon

Place Type: City
County: Contra Costa
Population: 72,148

Ancestry	Population	%
Afghan (118)	118	0.18
African, Sub-Saharan (417)	457	0.68
African (0)	7	0.01
Cape Verdean (0)	0	<0.01
Ethiopian (13)	13	0.02
Ghanaian (17)	17	0.03
Kenyan (336)	336	0.50
Liberian (0)	0	<0.01
Nigerian (44)	44	0.07
Senegalese (0)	0	<0.01
Sierra Leonean (0)	0	<0.01
Somalian (0)	0	<0.01
South African (0)	0	<0.01
Sudanese (7)	7	0.01
Ugandan (0)	0	<0.01
Zimbabwean (0)	33	0.05
Other Sub-Saharan African (0)	0	<0.01
Albanian (0)	0	<0.01
Alsatian (0)	0	<0.01
American (1,383)	1,383	2.07
Arab (690)	830	1.24
Arab (0)	0	<0.01
Egyptian (103)	232	0.35
Iraqi (0)	0	<0.01
Jordanian (141)	141	0.21
Lebanese (251)	262	0.39
Moroccan (0)	0	<0.01
Palestinian (58)	58	0.09
Syrian (0)	0	<0.01
Other Arab (137)	137	0.21
Armenian (219)	256	0.38
Assyrian/Chaldean/Syriac (21)	27	0.04
Australian (59)	59	0.09
Austrian (22)	311	0.47
Basque (9)	176	0.26
Belgian (0)	128	0.19
Brazilian (35)	35	0.05
British (267)	421	0.63
Bulgarian (0)	0	<0.01
Cajun (0)	0	<0.01
Canadian (204)	307	0.46
Carpatho Rusyn (0)	0	<0.01
Celtic (0)	0	<0.01
Croatian (40)	72	0.11
Cypriot (0)	0	<0.01
Czech (44)	245	0.37
Czechoslovakian (0)	9	0.01
Danish (179)	533	0.80
Dutch (189)	687	1.03
Eastern European (81)	97	0.15
English (1,043)	5,990	8.96
Estonian (0)	6	0.01
European (875)	1,042	1.56
Finnish (28)	111	0.17
French, ex. Basque (249)	1,706	2.55
French Canadian (86)	246	0.37
German (1,764)	8,449	12.64
German Russian (0)	0	<0.01
Greek (158)	522	0.78
Guyanese (0)	0	<0.01
Hungarian (149)	410	0.61
Icelander (46)	116	0.17
Iranian (934)	973	1.46
Irish (1,482)	6,828	10.22
Israeli (0)	16	0.02
Italian (1,665)	4,640	6.94
Latvian (0)	17	0.03
Lithuanian (41)	171	0.26
Luxemburger (0)	0	<0.01
Macedonian (25)	25	0.04
Maltese (0)	15	0.02
New Zealander (12)	12	0.02
Northern European (237)	237	0.35
Norwegian (202)	1,035	1.55
Pennsylvania German (0)	0	<0.01
Polish (322)	1,360	2.04
Portuguese (493)	1,836	2.75
Romanian (179)	279	0.42
Russian (668)	1,246	1.86
Scandinavian (66)	131	0.20
Scotch-Irish (225)	736	1.10
Scottish (395)	1,297	1.94
Serbian (0)	12	0.02
Slavic (0)	38	0.06
Slovak (0)	55	0.08
Slovene (15)	15	0.02
Soviet Union (0)	0	<0.01
Swedish (202)	768	1.15
Swiss (85)	289	0.43
Turkish (13)	57	0.09
Ukrainian (143)	379	0.57
Welsh (58)	451	0.67
West Indian, ex. Hispanic (56)	122	0.18
Bahamian (0)	0	<0.01
Barbadian (0)	0	<0.01
Belizean (0)	0	<0.01
Bermudan (0)	0	<0.01
British West Indian (0)	0	<0.01
Dutch West Indian (0)	0	<0.01
Haitian (0)	0	<0.01
Jamaican (36)	69	0.10
Trinidadian/Tobagonian (20)	53	0.08
U.S. Virgin Islander (0)	0	<0.01
West Indian (0)	0	<0.01
Other West Indian (0)	0	<0.01
Yugoslavian (83)	160	0.24

Hispanic Origin	Population	%
Hispanic or Latino (of any race)	6,250	8.66
Central American, ex. Mexican	586	0.81
Costa Rican	31	0.04
Guatemalan	71	0.10
Honduran	7	0.01
Nicaraguan	176	0.24
Panamanian	45	0.06
Salvadoran	250	0.35
Other Central American	6	0.01
Cuban	111	0.15
Dominican Republic	15	0.02
Mexican	3,729	5.17
Puerto Rican	309	0.43
South American	628	0.87
Argentinean	76	0.11
Bolivian	40	0.06
Chilean	65	0.09
Colombian	140	0.19
Ecuadorian	30	0.04
Paraguayan	0	<0.01
Peruvian	222	0.31
Uruguayan	6	0.01
Venezuelan	38	0.05
Other South American	11	0.02
Other Hispanic or Latino	872	1.21

Race*	Population	%
African-American/Black (2,043)	2,657	3.68
Not Hispanic (1,946)	2,419	3.35
Hispanic (97)	238	0.33
American Indian/Alaska Native (205)	645	0.89
Not Hispanic (128)	415	0.58
Hispanic (77)	230	0.32
Alaska Athabascan *(Ala. Nat.)* (2)	2	<0.01
Aleut *(Alaska Native)* (1)	4	0.01
Apache (1)	16	0.02
Arapaho (0)	0	<0.01
Blackfeet (4)	17	0.02
Canadian/French Am. Ind. (2)	3	<0.01
Central American Ind. (0)	0	<0.01
Cherokee (17)	121	0.17
Cheyenne (0)	0	<0.01
Chickasaw (2)	5	0.01
Chippewa (1)	7	0.01
Choctaw (10)	38	0.05
Colville (0)	0	<0.01
Comanche (0)	1	<0.01
Cree (0)	1	<0.01
Creek (1)	5	0.01
Crow (1)	3	<0.01
Delaware (1)	3	<0.01
Hopi (0)	6	0.01
Houma (0)	0	<0.01
Inupiat *(Alaska Native)* (0)	0	<0.01
Iroquois (4)	11	0.02
Kiowa (0)	2	<0.01
Lumbee (0)	1	<0.01
Menominee (0)	0	<0.01
Mexican American Ind. (10)	28	0.04
Navajo (1)	7	0.01
Osage (0)	3	<0.01
Ottawa (0)	0	<0.01
Paiute (0)	0	<0.01
Pima (3)	3	<0.01
Potawatomi (1)	5	0.01
Pueblo (4)	4	0.01
Puget Sound Salish (1)	1	<0.01
Seminole (0)	0	<0.01
Shoshone (0)	4	0.01
Sioux (7)	25	0.03
South American Ind. (3)	8	0.01
Spanish American Ind. (1)	3	<0.01
Tlingit-Haida *(Alaska Native)* (0)	2	<0.01
Tohono O'Odham (3)	3	<0.01
Tsimshian *(Alaska Native)* (0)	0	<0.01
Ute (1)	5	0.01
Yakama (0)	0	<0.01
Yaqui (2)	7	0.01
Yuman (3)	3	<0.01
Yup'ik *(Alaska Native)* (0)	0	<0.01
Asian (25,713)	28,406	39.37
Not Hispanic (25,531)	27,937	38.72
Hispanic (182)	469	0.65
Bangladeshi (40)	47	0.07
Bhutanese (0)	0	<0.01
Burmese (27)	35	0.05
Cambodian (44)	57	0.08
Chinese, ex. Taiwanese (8,040)	9,284	12.87
Filipino (3,412)	4,416	6.12
Hmong (6)	9	0.01
Indian (8,179)	8,468	11.74
Indonesian (146)	199	0.28
Japanese (648)	1,266	1.75
Korean (2,285)	2,548	3.53
Laotian (23)	30	0.04
Malaysian (12)	29	0.04
Nepalese (18)	19	0.03
Pakistani (469)	525	0.73
Sri Lankan (49)	58	0.08
Taiwanese (420)	480	0.67
Thai (71)	102	0.14
Vietnamese (827)	1,083	1.50
Hawaii Native/Pacific Islander (156)	502	0.70
Not Hispanic (141)	423	0.59
Hispanic (15)	79	0.11
Fijian (31)	41	0.06
Guamanian/Chamorro (54)	104	0.14
Marshallese (0)	0	<0.01
Native Hawaiian (30)	222	0.31
Samoan (8)	28	0.04
Tongan (16)	19	0.03
White (38,639)	41,924	58.11
Not Hispanic (34,956)	37,605	52.12
Hispanic (3,683)	4,319	5.99

*Notes: † The Census 2010 population figure is used to calculate the percentages in the Hispanic Origin and Race categories. Ancestry percentages are based on the 2006-2010 American Community Survey population (not shown); ‡ Numbers in parentheses indicate the number of people reporting a single ancestry; * Numbers in parentheses indicate the number of persons reporting this race alone, not in combination with any other race; Please refer to the Explanation of Data for more information.*

Santa Ana

Place Type: City
County: Orange
Population: 324,528

Ancestry	Population	%
Afghan (93)	93	0.03
African, Sub-Saharan (591)	696	0.21
African (259)	339	0.10
Cape Verdean (0)	0	<0.01
Ethiopian (79)	79	0.02
Ghanaian (72)	72	0.02
Kenyan (88)	88	0.03
Liberian (0)	0	<0.01
Nigerian (0)	0	<0.01
Senegalese (0)	0	<0.01
Sierra Leonean (0)	0	<0.01
Somalian (0)	0	<0.01
South African (93)	118	0.04
Sudanese (0)	0	<0.01
Ugandan (0)	0	<0.01
Zimbabwean (0)	0	<0.01
Other Sub-Saharan African (0)	0	<0.01
Albanian (0)	0	<0.01
Alsatian (0)	0	<0.01
American (4,922)	4,922	1.51
Arab (759)	951	0.29
Arab (84)	166	0.05
Egyptian (211)	222	0.07
Iraqi (0)	0	<0.01
Jordanian (8)	8	<0.01
Lebanese (106)	188	0.06
Moroccan (47)	47	0.01
Palestinian (205)	216	0.07
Syrian (50)	50	0.02
Other Arab (48)	54	0.02
Armenian (100)	186	0.06
Assyrian/Chaldean/Syriac (19)	19	0.01
Australian (7)	7	<0.01
Austrian (16)	95	0.03
Basque (52)	68	0.02
Belgian (15)	37	0.01
Brazilian (17)	41	0.01
British (98)	287	0.09
Bulgarian (18)	18	0.01
Cajun (0)	0	<0.01
Canadian (44)	166	0.05
Carpatho Rusyn (0)	0	<0.01
Celtic (0)	10	<0.01
Croatian (13)	67	0.02
Cypriot (0)	0	<0.01
Czech (59)	221	0.07
Czechoslovakian (12)	49	0.02
Danish (47)	372	0.11
Dutch (248)	882	0.27
Eastern European (19)	19	0.01
English (1,483)	4,960	1.53
Estonian (0)	0	<0.01
European (1,024)	1,123	0.35
Finnish (31)	40	0.01
French, ex. Basque (307)	1,971	0.61
French Canadian (102)	251	0.08
German (1,785)	6,659	2.05
German Russian (0)	0	<0.01
Greek (166)	287	0.09
Guyanese (0)	0	<0.01
Hungarian (131)	242	0.07
Icelander (0)	0	<0.01
Iranian (245)	251	0.08
Irish (1,396)	4,904	1.51
Israeli (14)	14	<0.01
Italian (1,323)	2,776	0.85
Latvian (2)	5	<0.01
Lithuanian (117)	174	0.05
Luxemburger (0)	0	<0.01
Macedonian (0)	0	<0.01
Maltese (0)	0	<0.01
New Zealander (0)	0	<0.01
Northern European (54)	96	0.03
Norwegian (133)	717	0.22
Pennsylvania German (25)	25	0.01
Polish (341)	1,105	0.34
Portuguese (87)	248	0.08
Romanian (93)	115	0.04
Russian (193)	486	0.15
Scandinavian (13)	64	0.02
Scotch-Irish (201)	809	0.25
Scottish (508)	1,520	0.47
Serbian (49)	57	0.02
Slavic (13)	33	0.01
Slovak (23)	67	0.02
Slovene (0)	0	<0.01
Soviet Union (0)	0	<0.01
Swedish (229)	796	0.24
Swiss (16)	113	0.03
Turkish (72)	131	0.04
Ukrainian (36)	121	0.04
Welsh (105)	470	0.14
West Indian, ex. Hispanic (44)	86	0.03
Bahamian (0)	0	<0.01
Barbadian (0)	0	<0.01
Belizean (0)	0	<0.01
Bermudan (0)	0	<0.01
British West Indian (0)	0	<0.01
Dutch West Indian (0)	0	<0.01
Haitian (8)	8	<0.01
Jamaican (9)	21	0.01
Trinidadian/Tobagonian (10)	21	0.01
U.S. Virgin Islander (10)	10	<0.01
West Indian (7)	26	0.01
Other West Indian (0)	0	<0.01
Yugoslavian (38)	61	0.02

Hispanic Origin	Population	%
Hispanic or Latino (of any race)	253,928	78.25
Central American, ex. Mexican	11,011	3.39
Costa Rican	117	0.04
Guatemalan	3,300	1.02
Honduran	663	0.20
Nicaraguan	375	0.12
Panamanian	54	0.02
Salvadoran	6,389	1.97
Other Central American	113	0.03
Cuban	506	0.16
Dominican Republic	36	0.01
Mexican	230,381	70.99
Puerto Rican	667	0.21
South American	2,303	0.71
Argentinean	276	0.09
Bolivian	398	0.12
Chilean	99	0.03
Colombian	532	0.16
Ecuadorian	224	0.07
Paraguayan	3	<0.01
Peruvian	651	0.20
Uruguayan	47	0.01
Venezuelan	38	0.01
Other South American	35	0.01
Other Hispanic or Latino	9,024	2.78

Race*	Population	%
African-American/Black (4,856)	6,162	1.90
Not Hispanic (3,177)	3,659	1.13
Hispanic (1,679)	2,503	0.77
American Indian/Alaska Native (3,260)	4,916	1.51
Not Hispanic (507)	960	0.30
Hispanic (2,753)	3,956	1.22
Alaska Athabascan *(Ala. Nat.)* (0)	3	<0.01
Aleut *(Alaska Native)* (1)	1	<0.01
Apache (62)	143	0.04
Arapaho (1)	1	<0.01
Blackfeet (17)	35	0.01
Canadian/French Am. Ind. (1)	5	<0.01
Central American Ind. (9)	17	0.01
Cherokee (65)	216	0.07
Cheyenne (1)	1	<0.01
Chickasaw (13)	13	<0.01
Chippewa (9)	18	0.01
Choctaw (17)	36	0.01
Colville (0)	0	<0.01
Comanche (5)	11	<0.01
Cree (0)	0	<0.01
Creek (4)	10	<0.01
Crow (0)	2	<0.01
Delaware (1)	1	<0.01
Hopi (7)	14	<0.01
Houma (1)	1	<0.01
Inupiat *(Alaska Native)* (0)	2	<0.01
Iroquois (6)	14	<0.01
Kiowa (3)	4	<0.01
Lumbee (2)	3	<0.01
Menominee (0)	0	<0.01
Mexican American Ind. (721)	974	0.30
Navajo (65)	105	0.03
Osage (4)	10	<0.01
Ottawa (0)	0	<0.01
Paiute (0)	2	<0.01
Pima (4)	14	<0.01
Potawatomi (0)	1	<0.01
Pueblo (15)	27	0.01
Puget Sound Salish (0)	0	<0.01
Seminole (2)	13	<0.01
Shoshone (11)	14	<0.01
Sioux (17)	34	0.01
South American Ind. (11)	22	0.01
Spanish American Ind. (107)	170	0.05
Tlingit-Haida *(Alaska Native)* (2)	2	<0.01
Tohono O'Odham (10)	16	<0.01
Tsimshian *(Alaska Native)* (0)	1	<0.01
Ute (1)	3	<0.01
Yakama (0)	0	<0.01
Yaqui (22)	38	0.01
Yuman (2)	7	<0.01
Yup'ik *(Alaska Native)* (0)	0	<0.01
Asian (34,138)	36,324	11.19
Not Hispanic (33,618)	34,961	10.77
Hispanic (520)	1,363	0.42
Bangladeshi (18)	21	0.01
Bhutanese (0)	0	<0.01
Burmese (27)	47	0.01
Cambodian (1,583)	1,818	0.56
Chinese, ex. Taiwanese (1,874)	2,634	0.81
Filipino (2,512)	3,101	0.96
Hmong (344)	361	0.11
Indian (1,016)	1,241	0.38
Indonesian (59)	116	0.04
Japanese (741)	1,151	0.35
Korean (690)	836	0.26
Laotian (478)	527	0.16
Malaysian (14)	16	<0.01
Nepalese (11)	12	<0.01
Pakistani (98)	106	0.03
Sri Lankan (34)	35	0.01
Taiwanese (105)	119	0.04
Thai (160)	232	0.07
Vietnamese (23,167)	24,260	7.48
Hawaii Native/Pacific Islander (976)	1,576	0.49
Not Hispanic (826)	1,109	0.34
Hispanic (150)	467	0.14
Fijian (10)	16	<0.01
Guamanian/Chamorro (52)	98	0.03
Marshallese (70)	82	0.03
Native Hawaiian (113)	307	0.09
Samoan (545)	695	0.21
Tongan (92)	104	0.03
White (148,838)	158,778	48.93
Not Hispanic (29,950)	31,646	9.75
Hispanic (118,888)	127,132	39.17

*Notes: † The Census 2010 population figure is used to calculate the percentages in the Hispanic Origin and Race categories. Ancestry percentages are based on the 2006-2010 American Community Survey population (not shown); ‡ Numbers in parentheses indicate the number of people reporting a single ancestry; * Numbers in parentheses indicate the number of persons reporting this race alone, not in combination with any other race; Please refer to the Explanation of Data for more information.*

Santa Barbara

Place Type: City
County: Santa Barbara
Population: 88,410

Ancestry	Population	%
Afghan (73)	73	0.08
African, Sub-Saharan (142)	307	0.35
African (68)	209	0.24
Cape Verdean (0)	0	<0.01
Ethiopian (44)	44	0.05
Ghanaian (0)	0	<0.01
Kenyan (0)	0	<0.01
Liberian (0)	0	<0.01
Nigerian (0)	16	0.02
Senegalese (0)	0	<0.01
Sierra Leonean (0)	0	<0.01
Somalian (0)	0	<0.01
South African (30)	38	0.04
Sudanese (0)	0	<0.01
Ugandan (0)	0	<0.01
Zimbabwean (0)	0	<0.01
Other Sub-Saharan African (0)	0	<0.01
Albanian (0)	0	<0.01
Alsatian (0)	13	0.01
American (2,069)	2,069	2.35
Arab (169)	329	0.37
Arab (10)	21	0.02
Egyptian (49)	68	0.08
Iraqi (0)	0	<0.01
Jordanian (0)	0	<0.01
Lebanese (48)	112	0.13
Moroccan (0)	0	<0.01
Palestinian (0)	0	<0.01
Syrian (0)	66	0.08
Other Arab (62)	62	0.07
Armenian (112)	188	0.21
Assyrian/Chaldean/Syriac (0)	0	<0.01
Australian (23)	212	0.24
Austrian (195)	443	0.50
Basque (101)	276	0.31
Belgian (81)	197	0.22
Brazilian (24)	51	0.06
British (371)	773	0.88
Bulgarian (27)	27	0.03
Cajun (0)	9	0.01
Canadian (87)	327	0.37
Carpatho Rusyn (0)	0	<0.01
Celtic (0)	0	<0.01
Croatian (23)	107	0.12
Cypriot (12)	12	0.01
Czech (71)	278	0.32
Czechoslovakian (106)	206	0.23
Danish (382)	743	0.85
Dutch (334)	1,097	1.25
Eastern European (239)	302	0.34
English (2,262)	8,688	9.89
Estonian (0)	38	0.04
European (1,266)	1,428	1.63
Finnish (6)	183	0.21
French, ex. Basque (532)	2,968	3.38
French Canadian (131)	313	0.36
German (2,496)	11,279	12.84
German Russian (0)	0	<0.01
Greek (152)	458	0.52
Guyanese (0)	0	<0.01
Hungarian (192)	451	0.51
Icelander (0)	0	<0.01
Iranian (295)	340	0.39
Irish (2,086)	9,140	10.40
Israeli (13)	40	0.05
Italian (1,881)	5,514	6.28
Latvian (40)	70	0.08
Lithuanian (85)	153	0.17
Luxemburger (0)	0	<0.01
Macedonian (0)	28	0.03
Maltese (0)	15	0.02
New Zealander (0)	0	<0.01
Northern European (138)	138	0.16
Norwegian (495)	1,855	2.11
Pennsylvania German (0)	9	0.01
Polish (490)	2,208	2.51
Portuguese (97)	430	0.49
Romanian (34)	214	0.24
Russian (902)	2,018	2.30
Scandinavian (240)	350	0.40
Scotch-Irish (860)	2,241	2.55
Scottish (796)	2,272	2.59
Serbian (22)	76	0.09
Slavic (13)	34	0.04
Slovak (46)	115	0.13
Slovene (0)	0	<0.01
Soviet Union (0)	0	<0.01
Swedish (690)	2,060	2.34
Swiss (137)	644	0.73
Turkish (183)	226	0.26
Ukrainian (119)	284	0.32
Welsh (127)	1,017	1.16
West Indian, ex. Hispanic (0)	20	0.02
Bahamian (0)	0	<0.01
Barbadian (0)	0	<0.01
Belizean (0)	0	<0.01
Bermudan (0)	0	<0.01
British West Indian (0)	0	<0.01
Dutch West Indian (0)	0	<0.01
Haitian (0)	20	0.02
Jamaican (0)	0	<0.01
Trinidadian/Tobagonian (0)	0	<0.01
U.S. Virgin Islander (0)	0	<0.01
West Indian (0)	0	<0.01
Other West Indian (0)	0	<0.01
Yugoslavian (0)	0	<0.01

Hispanic Origin	Population	%
Hispanic or Latino (of any race)	33,591	37.99
Central American, ex. Mexican	1,013	1.15
Costa Rican	40	0.05
Guatemalan	546	0.62
Honduran	85	0.10
Nicaraguan	54	0.06
Panamanian	27	0.03
Salvadoran	244	0.28
Other Central American	17	0.02
Cuban	106	0.12
Dominican Republic	28	0.03
Mexican	29,502	33.37
Puerto Rican	197	0.22
South American	651	0.74
Argentinean	121	0.14
Bolivian	19	0.02
Chilean	79	0.09
Colombian	151	0.17
Ecuadorian	44	0.05
Paraguayan	4	<0.01
Peruvian	176	0.20
Uruguayan	10	0.01
Venezuelan	36	0.04
Other South American	11	0.01
Other Hispanic or Latino	2,094	2.37

Race*	Population	%
African-American/Black (1,420)	1,977	2.24
Not Hispanic (1,177)	1,530	1.73
Hispanic (243)	447	0.51
American Indian/Alaska Native (892)	1,771	2.00
Not Hispanic (313)	752	0.85
Hispanic (579)	1,019	1.15
Alaska Athabascan *(Ala. Nat.)* (1)	2	<0.01
Aleut *(Alaska Native)* (1)	3	<0.01
Apache (27)	53	0.06
Arapaho (0)	1	<0.01
Blackfeet (4)	24	0.03
Canadian/French Am. Ind. (0)	3	<0.01
Central American Ind. (7)	9	0.01
Cherokee (27)	171	0.19
Cheyenne (1)	8	0.01
Chickasaw (6)	16	0.02
Chippewa (10)	18	0.02
Choctaw (13)	47	0.05
Colville (0)	0	<0.01
Comanche (7)	18	0.02
Cree (0)	3	<0.01
Creek (4)	9	0.01
Crow (1)	2	<0.01
Delaware (3)	4	<0.01
Hopi (0)	8	0.01
Houma (0)	0	<0.01
Inupiat *(Alaska Native)* (1)	3	<0.01
Iroquois (0)	13	0.01
Kiowa (1)	2	<0.01
Lumbee (0)	1	<0.01
Menominee (0)	0	<0.01
Mexican American Ind. (98)	155	0.18
Navajo (9)	18	0.02
Osage (1)	3	<0.01
Ottawa (0)	0	<0.01
Paiute (2)	5	0.01
Pima (1)	5	0.01
Potawatomi (0)	3	<0.01
Pueblo (4)	11	0.01
Puget Sound Salish (0)	0	<0.01
Seminole (0)	4	<0.01
Shoshone (1)	5	0.01
Sioux (16)	35	0.04
South American Ind. (6)	9	0.01
Spanish American Ind. (3)	3	<0.01
Tlingit-Haida *(Alaska Native)* (4)	4	<0.01
Tohono O'Odham (0)	4	<0.01
Tsimshian *(Alaska Native)* (0)	0	<0.01
Ute (1)	1	<0.01
Yakama (0)	0	<0.01
Yaqui (19)	33	0.04
Yuman (0)	0	<0.01
Yup'ik *(Alaska Native)* (0)	0	<0.01
Asian (3,062)	4,281	4.84
Not Hispanic (2,927)	3,907	4.42
Hispanic (135)	374	0.42
Bangladeshi (5)	7	0.01
Bhutanese (9)	10	0.01
Burmese (1)	4	<0.01
Cambodian (35)	44	0.05
Chinese, ex. Taiwanese (848)	1,129	1.28
Filipino (554)	894	1.01
Hmong (7)	9	0.01
Indian (326)	434	0.49
Indonesian (30)	46	0.05
Japanese (474)	780	0.88
Korean (335)	431	0.49
Laotian (14)	17	0.02
Malaysian (4)	7	0.01
Nepalese (4)	12	0.01
Pakistani (13)	16	0.02
Sri Lankan (21)	25	0.03
Taiwanese (48)	62	0.07
Thai (66)	87	0.10
Vietnamese (158)	215	0.24
Hawaii Native/Pacific Islander (116)	285	0.32
Not Hispanic (94)	219	0.25
Hispanic (22)	66	0.07
Fijian (3)	7	0.01
Guamanian/Chamorro (18)	33	0.04
Marshallese (0)	1	<0.01
Native Hawaiian (53)	145	0.16
Samoan (18)	36	0.04
Tongan (0)	6	0.01
White (66,411)	69,489	78.60
Not Hispanic (48,417)	49,972	56.52
Hispanic (17,994)	19,517	22.08

*Notes: † The Census 2010 population figure is used to calculate the percentages in the Hispanic Origin and Race categories. Ancestry percentages are based on the 2006-2010 American Community Survey population (not shown); ‡ Numbers in parentheses indicate the number of people reporting a single ancestry; * Numbers in parentheses indicate the number of persons reporting this race alone, not in combination with any other race; Please refer to the Explanation of Data for more information.*

Santa Clara

Place Type: City
County: Santa Clara
Population: 116,468

Ancestry	Population	%
Afghan (160)	160	0.14
African, Sub-Saharan (1,007)	1,089	0.97
African (170)	252	0.22
Cape Verdean (0)	0	<0.01
Ethiopian (692)	692	0.62
Ghanaian (0)	0	<0.01
Kenyan (38)	38	0.03
Liberian (0)	0	<0.01
Nigerian (47)	47	0.04
Senegalese (0)	0	<0.01
Sierra Leonean (0)	0	<0.01
Somalian (0)	0	<0.01
South African (0)	0	<0.01
Sudanese (60)	60	0.05
Ugandan (0)	0	<0.01
Zimbabwean (0)	0	<0.01
Other Sub-Saharan African (0)	0	<0.01
Albanian (41)	41	0.04
Alsatian (0)	0	<0.01
American (1,390)	1,390	1.24
Arab (973)	1,195	1.06
Arab (101)	101	0.09
Egyptian (64)	98	0.09
Iraqi (174)	174	0.15
Jordanian (86)	86	0.08
Lebanese (135)	261	0.23
Moroccan (55)	91	0.08
Palestinian (10)	21	0.02
Syrian (109)	109	0.10
Other Arab (239)	254	0.23
Armenian (174)	253	0.22
Assyrian/Chaldean/Syriac (219)	219	0.19
Australian (22)	22	0.02
Austrian (58)	260	0.23
Basque (17)	116	0.10
Belgian (52)	70	0.06
Brazilian (16)	132	0.12
British (365)	624	0.55
Bulgarian (45)	45	0.04
Cajun (0)	0	<0.01
Canadian (135)	351	0.31
Carpatho Rusyn (0)	0	<0.01
Celtic (0)	0	<0.01
Croatian (52)	142	0.13
Cypriot (115)	115	0.10
Czech (160)	336	0.30
Czechoslovakian (24)	81	0.07
Danish (46)	300	0.27
Dutch (252)	1,268	1.13
Eastern European (111)	111	0.10
English (1,864)	7,015	6.24
Estonian (32)	53	0.05
European (892)	1,074	0.95
Finnish (36)	120	0.11
French, ex. Basque (619)	2,503	2.23
French Canadian (142)	343	0.30
German (2,097)	9,325	8.29
German Russian (15)	15	0.01
Greek (163)	422	0.38
Guyanese (0)	0	<0.01
Hungarian (96)	325	0.29
Icelander (0)	10	0.01
Iranian (684)	713	0.63
Irish (2,225)	7,836	6.97
Israeli (27)	76	0.07
Italian (1,708)	4,479	3.98
Latvian (11)	11	0.01
Lithuanian (23)	134	0.12
Luxemburger (0)	14	0.01
Macedonian (0)	0	<0.01
Maltese (0)	0	<0.01
New Zealander (0)	32	0.03
Northern European (85)	98	0.09
Norwegian (203)	878	0.78
Pennsylvania German (79)	93	0.08
Polish (572)	1,615	1.44
Portuguese (2,266)	3,654	3.25
Romanian (285)	345	0.31
Russian (588)	1,028	0.91
Scandinavian (65)	122	0.11
Scotch-Irish (266)	1,090	0.97
Scottish (354)	1,603	1.43
Serbian (187)	187	0.17
Slavic (0)	0	<0.01
Slovak (11)	62	0.06
Slovene (8)	35	0.03
Soviet Union (0)	0	<0.01
Swedish (236)	1,390	1.24
Swiss (60)	301	0.27
Turkish (85)	85	0.08
Ukrainian (195)	289	0.26
Welsh (38)	490	0.44
West Indian, ex. Hispanic (13)	45	0.04
Bahamian (0)	0	<0.01
Barbadian (13)	13	0.01
Belizean (0)	0	<0.01
Bermudan (0)	0	<0.01
British West Indian (0)	0	<0.01
Dutch West Indian (0)	0	<0.01
Haitian (0)	0	<0.01
Jamaican (0)	32	0.03
Trinidadian/Tobagonian (0)	0	<0.01
U.S. Virgin Islander (0)	0	<0.01
West Indian (0)	0	<0.01
Other West Indian (0)	0	<0.01
Yugoslavian (161)	264	0.23

Hispanic Origin	Population	%
Hispanic or Latino (of any race)	22,589	19.40
Central American, ex. Mexican	1,668	1.43
Costa Rican	37	0.03
Guatemalan	341	0.29
Honduran	104	0.09
Nicaraguan	368	0.32
Panamanian	48	0.04
Salvadoran	760	0.65
Other Central American	10	0.01
Cuban	216	0.19
Dominican Republic	23	0.02
Mexican	17,037	14.63
Puerto Rican	421	0.36
South American	1,142	0.98
Argentinean	101	0.09
Bolivian	105	0.09
Chilean	112	0.10
Colombian	172	0.15
Ecuadorian	47	0.04
Paraguayan	2	<0.01
Peruvian	503	0.43
Uruguayan	10	0.01
Venezuelan	79	0.07
Other South American	11	0.01
Other Hispanic or Latino	2,082	1.79

Race*	Population	%
African-American/Black (3,154)	4,150	3.56
Not Hispanic (2,929)	3,690	3.17
Hispanic (225)	460	0.39
American Indian/Alaska Native (579)	1,397	1.20
Not Hispanic (240)	706	0.61
Hispanic (339)	691	0.59
Alaska Athabascan *(Ala. Nat.)* (0)	0	<0.01
Aleut *(Alaska Native)* (0)	0	<0.01
Apache (24)	60	0.05
Arapaho (1)	2	<0.01
Blackfeet (3)	29	0.02
Canadian/French Am. Ind. (1)	3	<0.01
Central American Ind. (2)	3	<0.01
Cherokee (29)	185	0.16
Cheyenne (0)	6	0.01
Chickasaw (2)	6	0.01
Chippewa (7)	14	0.01
Choctaw (5)	29	0.02
Colville (0)	0	<0.01
Comanche (2)	9	0.01
Cree (0)	6	0.01
Creek (2)	8	0.01
Crow (1)	5	<0.01
Delaware (0)	1	<0.01
Hopi (0)	0	<0.01
Houma (0)	0	<0.01
Inupiat *(Alaska Native)* (0)	1	<0.01
Iroquois (4)	16	0.01
Kiowa (1)	1	<0.01
Lumbee (2)	4	<0.01
Menominee (1)	1	<0.01
Mexican American Ind. (57)	124	0.11
Navajo (18)	30	0.03
Osage (5)	9	0.01
Ottawa (0)	1	<0.01
Paiute (0)	2	<0.01
Pima (1)	1	<0.01
Potawatomi (1)	8	0.01
Pueblo (4)	8	0.01
Puget Sound Salish (0)	5	<0.01
Seminole (2)	12	0.01
Shoshone (2)	2	<0.01
Sioux (8)	46	0.04
South American Ind. (7)	20	0.02
Spanish American Ind. (4)	4	<0.01
Tlingit-Haida *(Alaska Native)* (3)	9	0.01
Tohono O'Odham (10)	17	0.01
Tsimshian *(Alaska Native)* (0)	0	<0.01
Ute (0)	1	<0.01
Yakama (1)	1	<0.01
Yaqui (18)	32	0.03
Yuman (0)	0	<0.01
Yup'ik *(Alaska Native)* (1)	1	<0.01
Asian (43,889)	47,564	40.84
Not Hispanic (43,531)	46,702	40.10
Hispanic (358)	862	0.74
Bangladeshi (159)	177	0.15
Bhutanese (19)	22	0.02
Burmese (96)	115	0.10
Cambodian (92)	119	0.10
Chinese, ex. Taiwanese (7,396)	8,652	7.43
Filipino (7,222)	8,558	7.35
Hmong (31)	38	0.03
Indian (15,890)	16,412	14.09
Indonesian (114)	209	0.18
Japanese (1,731)	2,617	2.25
Korean (3,506)	3,789	3.25
Laotian (44)	73	0.06
Malaysian (47)	71	0.06
Nepalese (69)	80	0.07
Pakistani (904)	974	0.84
Sri Lankan (68)	81	0.07
Taiwanese (718)	862	0.74
Thai (154)	206	0.18
Vietnamese (4,498)	4,924	4.23
Hawaii Native/Pacific Islander (651)	1,248	1.07
Not Hispanic (604)	1,094	0.94
Hispanic (47)	154	0.13
Fijian (97)	123	0.11
Guamanian/Chamorro (116)	164	0.14
Marshallese (0)	0	<0.01
Native Hawaiian (88)	359	0.31
Samoan (148)	240	0.21
Tongan (128)	140	0.12
White (52,359)	57,309	49.21
Not Hispanic (42,026)	45,351	38.94
Hispanic (10,333)	11,958	10.27

*Notes: † The Census 2010 population figure is used to calculate the percentages in the Hispanic Origin and Race categories. Ancestry percentages are based on the 2006-2010 American Community Survey population (not shown); ‡ Numbers in parentheses indicate the number of people reporting a single ancestry; * Numbers in parentheses indicate the number of persons reporting this race alone, not in combination with any other race; Please refer to the Explanation of Data for more information.*

Santa Clarita

Place Type: City
County: Los Angeles
Population: 176,320

Ancestry	Population	%
Afghan (154)	180	0.10
African, Sub-Saharan (844)	1,039	0.60
African (347)	385	0.22
Cape Verdean (0)	0	<0.01
Ethiopian (0)	0	<0.01
Ghanaian (0)	0	<0.01
Kenyan (0)	0	<0.01
Liberian (0)	14	0.01
Nigerian (451)	517	0.30
Senegalese (0)	0	<0.01
Sierra Leonean (0)	0	<0.01
Somalian (0)	0	<0.01
South African (46)	123	0.07
Sudanese (0)	0	<0.01
Ugandan (0)	0	<0.01
Zimbabwean (0)	0	<0.01
Other Sub-Saharan African (0)	0	<0.01
Albanian (7)	7	<0.01
Alsatian (0)	17	0.01
American (5,155)	5,155	2.99
Arab (1,230)	1,891	1.10
Arab (6)	62	0.04
Egyptian (605)	636	0.37
Iraqi (0)	0	<0.01
Jordanian (167)	167	0.10
Lebanese (96)	503	0.29
Moroccan (0)	0	<0.01
Palestinian (91)	125	0.07
Syrian (130)	252	0.15
Other Arab (135)	146	0.08
Armenian (1,026)	1,403	0.81
Assyrian/Chaldean/Syriac (113)	162	0.09
Australian (38)	166	0.10
Austrian (44)	468	0.27
Basque (15)	50	0.03
Belgian (67)	231	0.13
Brazilian (83)	168	0.10
British (415)	831	0.48
Bulgarian (42)	56	0.03
Cajun (17)	56	0.03
Canadian (223)	540	0.31
Carpatho Rusyn (0)	0	<0.01
Celtic (0)	157	0.09
Croatian (103)	241	0.14
Cypriot (0)	0	<0.01
Czech (138)	603	0.35
Czechoslovakian (8)	106	0.06
Danish (245)	1,078	0.63
Dutch (419)	2,024	1.18
Eastern European (268)	365	0.21
English (4,835)	17,821	10.35
Estonian (0)	10	0.01
European (2,306)	2,946	1.71
Finnish (21)	381	0.22
French, ex. Basque (686)	5,259	3.05
French Canadian (448)	860	0.50
German (5,990)	26,730	15.52
German Russian (0)	0	<0.01
Greek (305)	1,243	0.72
Guyanese (12)	21	0.01
Hungarian (501)	1,257	0.73
Icelander (0)	27	0.02
Iranian (647)	799	0.46
Irish (3,607)	19,220	11.16
Israeli (126)	157	0.09
Italian (4,328)	13,153	7.64
Latvian (9)	24	0.01
Lithuanian (241)	411	0.24
Luxemburger (0)	0	<0.01
Macedonian (0)	13	0.01
Maltese (0)	0	<0.01
New Zealander (0)	0	<0.01
Northern European (204)	226	0.13
Norwegian (775)	3,508	2.04
Pennsylvania German (0)	0	<0.01
Polish (1,433)	5,110	2.97
Portuguese (262)	912	0.53
Romanian (133)	319	0.19
Russian (1,729)	4,252	2.47
Scandinavian (214)	459	0.27
Scotch-Irish (1,167)	3,817	2.22
Scottish (1,090)	4,327	2.51
Serbian (0)	10	0.01
Slavic (0)	21	0.01
Slovak (80)	192	0.11
Slovene (25)	137	0.08
Soviet Union (0)	0	<0.01
Swedish (745)	4,096	2.38
Swiss (133)	896	0.52
Turkish (42)	157	0.09
Ukrainian (125)	388	0.23
Welsh (109)	1,502	0.87
West Indian, ex. Hispanic (78)	483	0.28
Bahamian (0)	14	0.01
Barbadian (0)	0	<0.01
Belizean (0)	145	0.08
Bermudan (0)	1	<0.01
British West Indian (0)	0	<0.01
Dutch West Indian (20)	75	0.04
Haitian (0)	14	0.01
Jamaican (58)	111	0.06
Trinidadian/Tobagonian (0)	0	<0.01
U.S. Virgin Islander (0)	0	<0.01
West Indian (0)	123	0.07
Other West Indian (0)	0	<0.01
Yugoslavian (165)	311	0.18

Hispanic Origin	Population	%
Hispanic or Latino (of any race)	51,941	29.46
Central American, ex. Mexican	5,657	3.21
Costa Rican	185	0.10
Guatemalan	2,410	1.37
Honduran	276	0.16
Nicaraguan	324	0.18
Panamanian	82	0.05
Salvadoran	2,272	1.29
Other Central American	108	0.06
Cuban	1,053	0.60
Dominican Republic	60	0.03
Mexican	36,666	20.80
Puerto Rican	1,004	0.57
South American	3,311	1.88
Argentinean	621	0.35
Bolivian	124	0.07
Chilean	284	0.16
Colombian	773	0.44
Ecuadorian	509	0.29
Paraguayan	6	<0.01
Peruvian	831	0.47
Uruguayan	47	0.03
Venezuelan	57	0.03
Other South American	59	0.03
Other Hispanic or Latino	4,190	2.38

Race*	Population	%
African-American/Black (5,623)	7,209	4.09
Not Hispanic (5,157)	6,337	3.59
Hispanic (466)	872	0.49
American Indian/Alaska Native (1,013)	2,380	1.35
Not Hispanic (435)	1,313	0.74
Hispanic (578)	1,067	0.61
Alaska Athabascan *(Ala. Nat.)* (1)	6	<0.01
Aleut *(Alaska Native)* (0)	0	<0.01
Apache (42)	105	0.06
Arapaho (1)	1	<0.01
Blackfeet (10)	59	0.03
Canadian/French Am. Ind. (2)	6	<0.01
Central American Ind. (4)	9	0.01
Cherokee (64)	359	0.20
Cheyenne (0)	2	<0.01
Chickasaw (11)	37	0.02
Chippewa (13)	28	0.02
Choctaw (21)	102	0.06
Colville (0)	0	<0.01
Comanche (7)	15	0.01
Cree (0)	0	<0.01
Creek (16)	33	0.02
Crow (0)	2	<0.01
Delaware (2)	2	<0.01
Hopi (2)	8	<0.01
Houma (0)	0	<0.01
Inupiat *(Alaska Native)* (3)	3	<0.01
Iroquois (17)	37	0.02
Kiowa (0)	0	<0.01
Lumbee (1)	3	<0.01
Menominee (1)	1	<0.01
Mexican American Ind. (111)	179	0.10
Navajo (28)	65	0.04
Osage (0)	1	<0.01
Ottawa (0)	0	<0.01
Paiute (6)	11	0.01
Pima (4)	6	<0.01
Potawatomi (12)	17	0.01
Pueblo (16)	31	0.02
Puget Sound Salish (1)	3	<0.01
Seminole (1)	15	0.01
Shoshone (2)	4	<0.01
Sioux (24)	54	0.03
South American Ind. (4)	20	0.01
Spanish American Ind. (9)	19	0.01
Tlingit-Haida *(Alaska Native)* (1)	4	<0.01
Tohono O'Odham (5)	10	0.01
Tsimshian *(Alaska Native)* (0)	0	<0.01
Ute (2)	11	0.01
Yakama (2)	2	<0.01
Yaqui (20)	43	0.02
Yuman (0)	0	<0.01
Yup'ik *(Alaska Native)* (3)	3	<0.01
Asian (15,025)	18,381	10.42
Not Hispanic (14,689)	17,448	9.90
Hispanic (336)	933	0.53
Bangladeshi (61)	79	0.04
Bhutanese (2)	3	<0.01
Burmese (41)	47	0.03
Cambodian (39)	58	0.03
Chinese, ex. Taiwanese (1,328)	2,131	1.21
Filipino (6,063)	7,378	4.18
Hmong (4)	7	<0.01
Indian (1,401)	1,601	0.91
Indonesian (133)	236	0.13
Japanese (1,053)	1,892	1.07
Korean (2,937)	3,238	1.84
Laotian (14)	23	0.01
Malaysian (12)	27	0.02
Nepalese (12)	12	0.01
Pakistani (187)	223	0.13
Sri Lankan (129)	147	0.08
Taiwanese (83)	119	0.07
Thai (337)	456	0.26
Vietnamese (484)	643	0.36
Hawaii Native/Pacific Islander (272)	795	0.45
Not Hispanic (235)	642	0.36
Hispanic (37)	153	0.09
Fijian (12)	12	0.01
Guamanian/Chamorro (59)	125	0.07
Marshallese (2)	2	<0.01
Native Hawaiian (85)	308	0.17
Samoan (22)	88	0.05
Tongan (13)	15	0.01
White (125,005)	132,184	74.97
Not Hispanic (98,838)	102,899	58.36
Hispanic (26,167)	29,285	16.61

*Notes: † The Census 2010 population figure is used to calculate the percentages in the Hispanic Origin and Race categories. Ancestry percentages are based on the 2006-2010 American Community Survey population (not shown); ‡ Numbers in parentheses indicate the number of people reporting a single ancestry; * Numbers in parentheses indicate the number of persons reporting this race alone, not in combination with any other race; Please refer to the Explanation of Data for more information.*

Santa Cruz

Place Type: City
County: Santa Cruz
Population: 59,946

Ancestry	Population	%
Afghan (91)	91	0.16
African, Sub-Saharan (90)	194	0.33
African (30)	114	0.20
Cape Verdean (0)	0	<0.01
Ethiopian (26)	26	0.04
Ghanaian (0)	0	<0.01
Kenyan (0)	0	<0.01
Liberian (0)	0	<0.01
Nigerian (17)	17	0.03
Senegalese (0)	0	<0.01
Sierra Leonean (0)	0	<0.01
Somalian (0)	0	<0.01
South African (17)	37	0.06
Sudanese (0)	0	<0.01
Ugandan (0)	0	<0.01
Zimbabwean (0)	0	<0.01
Other Sub-Saharan African (0)	0	<0.01
Albanian (0)	0	<0.01
Alsatian (0)	0	<0.01
American (1,492)	1,492	2.56
Arab (146)	364	0.62
Arab (0)	57	0.10
Egyptian (0)	0	<0.01
Iraqi (16)	16	0.03
Jordanian (0)	0	<0.01
Lebanese (59)	156	0.27
Moroccan (37)	37	0.06
Palestinian (0)	0	<0.01
Syrian (0)	50	0.09
Other Arab (34)	48	0.08
Armenian (153)	279	0.48
Assyrian/Chaldean/Syriac (0)	0	<0.01
Australian (14)	60	0.10
Austrian (9)	226	0.39
Basque (36)	73	0.13
Belgian (12)	66	0.11
Brazilian (0)	32	0.05
British (285)	597	1.02
Bulgarian (14)	28	0.05
Cajun (0)	0	<0.01
Canadian (113)	289	0.50
Carpatho Rusyn (0)	0	<0.01
Celtic (35)	89	0.15
Croatian (28)	141	0.24
Cypriot (0)	0	<0.01
Czech (24)	337	0.58
Czechoslovakian (46)	60	0.10
Danish (189)	597	1.02
Dutch (357)	1,210	2.08
Eastern European (213)	297	0.51
English (1,509)	7,257	12.45
Estonian (16)	16	0.03
European (1,670)	2,354	4.04
Finnish (71)	148	0.25
French, ex. Basque (291)	2,565	4.40
French Canadian (117)	383	0.66
German (2,172)	9,157	15.72
German Russian (0)	0	<0.01
Greek (137)	389	0.67
Guyanese (0)	0	<0.01
Hungarian (117)	414	0.71
Icelander (0)	38	0.07
Iranian (124)	150	0.26
Irish (1,655)	8,382	14.39
Israeli (73)	135	0.23
Italian (1,485)	4,528	7.77
Latvian (0)	14	0.02
Lithuanian (39)	153	0.26
Luxemburger (8)	16	0.03
Macedonian (0)	0	<0.01
Maltese (20)	20	0.03
New Zealander (0)	0	<0.01
Northern European (970)	1,071	1.84
Norwegian (628)	1,311	2.25
Pennsylvania German (0)	0	<0.01
Polish (186)	1,760	3.02
Portuguese (429)	1,273	2.18
Romanian (70)	187	0.32
Russian (514)	1,732	2.97
Scandinavian (212)	451	0.77
Scotch-Irish (704)	1,514	2.60
Scottish (436)	2,581	4.43
Serbian (19)	19	0.03
Slavic (0)	14	0.02
Slovak (0)	41	0.07
Slovene (0)	158	0.27
Soviet Union (0)	0	<0.01
Swedish (399)	2,135	3.66
Swiss (33)	371	0.64
Turkish (10)	61	0.10
Ukrainian (85)	193	0.33
Welsh (147)	617	1.06
West Indian, ex. Hispanic (1)	28	0.05
Bahamian (0)	0	<0.01
Barbadian (1)	2	<0.01
Belizean (0)	0	<0.01
Bermudan (0)	0	<0.01
British West Indian (0)	0	<0.01
Dutch West Indian (0)	0	<0.01
Haitian (0)	0	<0.01
Jamaican (0)	0	<0.01
Trinidadian/Tobagonian (0)	0	<0.01
U.S. Virgin Islander (0)	0	<0.01
West Indian (0)	26	0.04
Other West Indian (0)	0	<0.01
Yugoslavian (33)	138	0.24

Hispanic Origin	Population	%
Hispanic or Latino (of any race)	11,624	19.39
Central American, ex. Mexican	943	1.57
Costa Rican	26	0.04
Guatemalan	127	0.21
Honduran	22	0.04
Nicaraguan	73	0.12
Panamanian	18	0.03
Salvadoran	669	1.12
Other Central American	8	0.01
Cuban	117	0.20
Dominican Republic	16	0.03
Mexican	8,953	14.94
Puerto Rican	242	0.40
South American	455	0.76
Argentinean	83	0.14
Bolivian	16	0.03
Chilean	66	0.11
Colombian	96	0.16
Ecuadorian	31	0.05
Paraguayan	0	<0.01
Peruvian	115	0.19
Uruguayan	10	0.02
Venezuelan	28	0.05
Other South American	10	0.02
Other Hispanic or Latino	898	1.50

Race*	Population	%
African-American/Black (1,071)	1,709	2.85
Not Hispanic (979)	1,501	2.50
Hispanic (92)	208	0.35
American Indian/Alaska Native (440)	1,292	2.16
Not Hispanic (238)	825	1.38
Hispanic (202)	467	0.78
Alaska Athabascan *(Ala. Nat.)* (1)	1	<0.01
Aleut *(Alaska Native)* (1)	4	0.01
Apache (17)	43	0.07
Arapaho (1)	1	<0.01
Blackfeet (3)	31	0.05
Canadian/French Am. Ind. (1)	3	0.01
Central American Ind. (3)	4	0.01
Cherokee (23)	205	0.34
Cheyenne (2)	6	0.01
Chickasaw (2)	7	0.01
Chippewa (3)	10	0.02
Choctaw (13)	44	0.07
Colville (0)	0	<0.01
Comanche (4)	13	0.02
Cree (0)	8	0.01
Creek (0)	17	0.03
Crow (0)	1	<0.01
Delaware (0)	2	<0.01
Hopi (2)	3	0.01
Houma (0)	0	<0.01
Inupiat *(Alaska Native)* (5)	6	0.01
Iroquois (1)	17	0.03
Kiowa (0)	4	0.01
Lumbee (0)	1	<0.01
Menominee (0)	1	<0.01
Mexican American Ind. (47)	78	0.13
Navajo (7)	19	0.03
Osage (1)	3	0.01
Ottawa (0)	0	<0.01
Paiute (0)	3	0.01
Pima (0)	0	<0.01
Potawatomi (3)	12	0.02
Pueblo (2)	4	0.01
Puget Sound Salish (0)	1	<0.01
Seminole (1)	8	0.01
Shoshone (1)	5	0.01
Sioux (7)	31	0.05
South American Ind. (3)	20	0.03
Spanish American Ind. (7)	9	0.02
Tlingit-Haida *(Alaska Native)* (4)	8	0.01
Tohono O'Odham (4)	10	0.02
Tsimshian *(Alaska Native)* (0)	1	<0.01
Ute (0)	3	0.01
Yakama (0)	0	<0.01
Yaqui (11)	23	0.04
Yuman (0)	0	<0.01
Yup'ik *(Alaska Native)* (0)	1	<0.01
Asian (4,591)	6,182	10.31
Not Hispanic (4,476)	5,825	9.72
Hispanic (115)	357	0.60
Bangladeshi (4)	4	0.01
Bhutanese (0)	0	<0.01
Burmese (5)	8	0.01
Cambodian (18)	27	0.05
Chinese, ex. Taiwanese (1,798)	2,345	3.91
Filipino (666)	1,108	1.85
Hmong (18)	18	0.03
Indian (453)	584	0.97
Indonesian (11)	42	0.07
Japanese (401)	932	1.55
Korean (352)	478	0.80
Laotian (17)	25	0.04
Malaysian (2)	13	0.02
Nepalese (9)	11	0.02
Pakistani (25)	39	0.07
Sri Lankan (13)	15	0.03
Taiwanese (98)	117	0.20
Thai (75)	110	0.18
Vietnamese (315)	431	0.72
Hawaii Native/Pacific Islander (108)	328	0.55
Not Hispanic (97)	282	0.47
Hispanic (11)	46	0.08
Fijian (5)	14	0.02
Guamanian/Chamorro (10)	41	0.07
Marshallese (0)	0	<0.01
Native Hawaiian (44)	146	0.24
Samoan (20)	46	0.08
Tongan (5)	8	0.01
White (44,661)	47,737	79.63
Not Hispanic (39,985)	42,171	70.35
Hispanic (4,676)	5,566	9.29

*Notes: † The Census 2010 population figure is used to calculate the percentages in the Hispanic Origin and Race categories. Ancestry percentages are based on the 2006-2010 American Community Survey population (not shown); ‡ Numbers in parentheses indicate the number of people reporting a single ancestry; * Numbers in parentheses indicate the number of persons reporting this race alone, not in combination with any other race; Please refer to the Explanation of Data for more information.*

Santa Maria

Place Type: City
County: Santa Barbara
Population: 99,553

Ancestry	Population	%
Afghan (8)	8	0.01
African, Sub-Saharan (86)	105	0.11
African (86)	105	0.11
Cape Verdean (0)	0	<0.01
Ethiopian (0)	0	<0.01
Ghanaian (0)	0	<0.01
Kenyan (0)	0	<0.01
Liberian (0)	0	<0.01
Nigerian (0)	0	<0.01
Senegalese (0)	0	<0.01
Sierra Leonean (0)	0	<0.01
Somalian (0)	0	<0.01
South African (0)	0	<0.01
Sudanese (0)	0	<0.01
Ugandan (0)	0	<0.01
Zimbabwean (0)	0	<0.01
Other Sub-Saharan African (0)	0	<0.01
Albanian (0)	0	<0.01
Alsatian (0)	0	<0.01
American (1,686)	1,686	1.78
Arab (248)	278	0.29
Arab (217)	217	0.23
Egyptian (0)	30	0.03
Iraqi (0)	0	<0.01
Jordanian (0)	0	<0.01
Lebanese (0)	0	<0.01
Moroccan (19)	19	0.02
Palestinian (12)	12	0.01
Syrian (0)	0	<0.01
Other Arab (0)	0	<0.01
Armenian (20)	20	0.02
Assyrian/Chaldean/Syriac (0)	0	<0.01
Australian (9)	9	0.01
Austrian (15)	154	0.16
Basque (30)	30	0.03
Belgian (47)	61	0.06
Brazilian (0)	21	0.02
British (56)	89	0.09
Bulgarian (0)	7	0.01
Cajun (0)	0	<0.01
Canadian (68)	88	0.09
Carpatho Rusyn (0)	0	<0.01
Celtic (0)	0	<0.01
Croatian (0)	29	0.03
Cypriot (0)	0	<0.01
Czech (33)	86	0.09
Czechoslovakian (42)	42	0.04
Danish (207)	452	0.48
Dutch (231)	508	0.54
Eastern European (0)	9	0.01
English (1,229)	3,622	3.83
Estonian (0)	0	<0.01
European (472)	538	0.57
Finnish (0)	20	0.02
French, ex. Basque (215)	1,041	1.10
French Canadian (105)	317	0.33
German (1,352)	5,411	5.72
German Russian (0)	0	<0.01
Greek (16)	161	0.17
Guyanese (0)	0	<0.01
Hungarian (129)	195	0.21
Icelander (0)	10	0.01
Iranian (9)	55	0.06
Irish (1,002)	4,211	4.45
Israeli (0)	0	<0.01
Italian (654)	1,639	1.73
Latvian (25)	54	0.06
Lithuanian (9)	28	0.03
Luxemburger (0)	13	0.01
Macedonian (0)	0	<0.01
Maltese (0)	0	<0.01
New Zealander (0)	0	<0.01
Northern European (77)	77	0.08
Norwegian (344)	692	0.73
Pennsylvania German (0)	0	<0.01
Polish (76)	393	0.42
Portuguese (660)	1,229	1.30
Romanian (0)	21	0.02
Russian (66)	295	0.31
Scandinavian (24)	93	0.10
Scotch-Irish (149)	569	0.60
Scottish (190)	657	0.69
Serbian (0)	0	<0.01
Slavic (0)	7	0.01
Slovak (9)	9	0.01
Slovene (0)	10	0.01
Soviet Union (0)	0	<0.01
Swedish (322)	707	0.75
Swiss (22)	332	0.35
Turkish (8)	8	0.01
Ukrainian (97)	144	0.15
Welsh (70)	280	0.30
West Indian, ex. Hispanic (92)	108	0.11
Bahamian (0)	0	<0.01
Barbadian (0)	0	<0.01
Belizean (0)	16	0.02
Bermudan (0)	0	<0.01
British West Indian (0)	0	<0.01
Dutch West Indian (0)	0	<0.01
Haitian (0)	0	<0.01
Jamaican (92)	92	0.10
Trinidadian/Tobagonian (0)	0	<0.01
U.S. Virgin Islander (0)	0	<0.01
West Indian (0)	0	<0.01
Other West Indian (0)	0	<0.01
Yugoslavian (23)	23	0.02

Hispanic Origin	Population	%
Hispanic or Latino (of any race)	70,114	70.43
Central American, ex. Mexican	962	0.97
Costa Rican	32	0.03
Guatemalan	225	0.23
Honduran	115	0.12
Nicaraguan	26	0.03
Panamanian	16	0.02
Salvadoran	536	0.54
Other Central American	12	0.01
Cuban	63	0.06
Dominican Republic	10	0.01
Mexican	65,188	65.48
Puerto Rican	362	0.36
South American	178	0.18
Argentinean	31	0.03
Bolivian	13	0.01
Chilean	26	0.03
Colombian	57	0.06
Ecuadorian	7	0.01
Paraguayan	0	<0.01
Peruvian	29	0.03
Uruguayan	1	<0.01
Venezuelan	14	0.01
Other South American	0	<0.01
Other Hispanic or Latino	3,351	3.37

Race*	Population	%
African-American/Black (1,656)	2,260	2.27
Not Hispanic (1,193)	1,516	1.52
Hispanic (463)	744	0.75
American Indian/Alaska Native (1,818)	2,866	2.88
Not Hispanic (345)	727	0.73
Hispanic (1,473)	2,139	2.15
Alaska Athabascan *(Ala. Nat.)* (0)	0	<0.01
Aleut *(Alaska Native)* (2)	2	<0.01
Apache (46)	69	0.07
Arapaho (0)	0	<0.01
Blackfeet (4)	28	0.03
Canadian/French Am. Ind. (5)	7	0.01
Central American Ind. (1)	8	0.01
Cherokee (38)	153	0.15
Cheyenne (3)	5	0.01
Chickasaw (2)	6	0.01
Chippewa (4)	10	0.01
Choctaw (27)	71	0.07
Colville (0)	0	<0.01
Comanche (2)	3	<0.01
Cree (0)	1	<0.01
Creek (7)	18	0.02
Crow (0)	1	<0.01
Delaware (1)	1	<0.01
Hopi (2)	5	0.01
Houma (0)	0	<0.01
Inupiat *(Alaska Native)* (2)	2	<0.01
Iroquois (1)	3	<0.01
Kiowa (2)	7	0.01
Lumbee (2)	3	<0.01
Menominee (0)	0	<0.01
Mexican American Ind. (626)	868	0.87
Navajo (13)	38	0.04
Osage (0)	1	<0.01
Ottawa (0)	0	<0.01
Paiute (2)	4	<0.01
Pima (2)	4	<0.01
Potawatomi (2)	8	0.01
Pueblo (6)	6	0.01
Puget Sound Salish (1)	2	<0.01
Seminole (1)	3	<0.01
Shoshone (1)	1	<0.01
Sioux (15)	32	0.03
South American Ind. (2)	4	<0.01
Spanish American Ind. (34)	40	0.04
Tlingit-Haida *(Alaska Native)* (5)	12	0.01
Tohono O'Odham (2)	2	<0.01
Tsimshian *(Alaska Native)* (0)	0	<0.01
Ute (1)	2	<0.01
Yakama (0)	0	<0.01
Yaqui (24)	40	0.04
Yuman (5)	5	0.01
Yup'ik *(Alaska Native)* (0)	0	<0.01
Asian (5,054)	6,418	6.45
Not Hispanic (4,652)	5,354	5.38
Hispanic (402)	1,064	1.07
Bangladeshi (0)	0	<0.01
Bhutanese (0)	0	<0.01
Burmese (1)	3	<0.01
Cambodian (30)	42	0.04
Chinese, ex. Taiwanese (215)	352	0.35
Filipino (3,595)	4,514	4.53
Hmong (4)	5	0.01
Indian (277)	361	0.36
Indonesian (26)	32	0.03
Japanese (289)	521	0.52
Korean (250)	316	0.32
Laotian (29)	34	0.03
Malaysian (1)	2	<0.01
Nepalese (1)	1	<0.01
Pakistani (12)	14	0.01
Sri Lankan (16)	19	0.02
Taiwanese (6)	7	0.01
Thai (28)	46	0.05
Vietnamese (141)	177	0.18
Hawaii Native/Pacific Islander (161)	402	0.40
Not Hispanic (132)	286	0.29
Hispanic (29)	116	0.12
Fijian (0)	0	<0.01
Guamanian/Chamorro (38)	71	0.07
Marshallese (0)	0	<0.01
Native Hawaiian (38)	182	0.18
Samoan (35)	71	0.07
Tongan (12)	19	0.02
White (55,983)	60,167	60.44
Not Hispanic (21,626)	22,747	22.85
Hispanic (34,357)	37,420	37.59

*Notes: † The Census 2010 population figure is used to calculate the percentages in the Hispanic Origin and Race categories. Ancestry percentages are based on the 2006-2010 American Community Survey population (not shown); ‡ Numbers in parentheses indicate the number of people reporting a single ancestry; * Numbers in parentheses indicate the number of persons reporting this race alone, not in combination with any other race; Please refer to the Explanation of Data for more information.*

Santa Monica

Place Type: City
County: Los Angeles
Population: 89,736

Ancestry	Population	%
Afghan (0)	0	<0.01
African, Sub-Saharan (518)	884	1.00
African (273)	447	0.50
Cape Verdean (0)	67	0.08
Ethiopian (134)	225	0.25
Ghanaian (0)	0	<0.01
Kenyan (0)	0	<0.01
Liberian (0)	0	<0.01
Nigerian (0)	0	<0.01
Senegalese (0)	0	<0.01
Sierra Leonean (0)	0	<0.01
Somalian (0)	0	<0.01
South African (65)	77	0.09
Sudanese (0)	0	<0.01
Ugandan (0)	0	<0.01
Zimbabwean (46)	46	0.05
Other Sub-Saharan African (0)	22	0.02
Albanian (17)	17	0.02
Alsatian (0)	14	0.02
American (3,633)	3,633	4.10
Arab (716)	1,138	1.28
Arab (24)	24	0.03
Egyptian (263)	278	0.31
Iraqi (36)	71	0.08
Jordanian (0)	0	<0.01
Lebanese (122)	323	0.36
Moroccan (54)	82	0.09
Palestinian (0)	19	0.02
Syrian (61)	123	0.14
Other Arab (156)	218	0.25
Armenian (102)	220	0.25
Assyrian/Chaldean/Syriac (0)	0	<0.01
Australian (51)	188	0.21
Austrian (198)	793	0.89
Basque (49)	49	0.06
Belgian (130)	300	0.34
Brazilian (43)	75	0.08
British (533)	914	1.03
Bulgarian (38)	38	0.04
Cajun (0)	14	0.02
Canadian (342)	592	0.67
Carpatho Rusyn (0)	0	<0.01
Celtic (31)	31	0.03
Croatian (149)	427	0.48
Cypriot (0)	0	<0.01
Czech (307)	602	0.68
Czechoslovakian (22)	54	0.06
Danish (142)	564	0.64
Dutch (343)	1,320	1.49
Eastern European (875)	988	1.11
English (2,882)	9,074	10.23
Estonian (13)	24	0.03
European (1,280)	1,445	1.63
Finnish (80)	167	0.19
French, ex. Basque (647)	2,837	3.20
French Canadian (245)	379	0.43
German (3,193)	10,958	12.36
German Russian (0)	0	<0.01
Greek (281)	488	0.55
Guyanese (18)	58	0.07
Hungarian (400)	1,147	1.29
Icelander (0)	0	<0.01
Iranian (2,544)	2,587	2.92
Irish (2,989)	10,235	11.54
Israeli (251)	277	0.31
Italian (2,293)	6,432	7.25
Latvian (24)	136	0.15
Lithuanian (494)	1,080	1.22
Luxemburger (0)	19	0.02
Macedonian (0)	0	<0.01
Maltese (0)	12	0.01
New Zealander (35)	76	0.09
Northern European (193)	193	0.22
Norwegian (206)	1,013	1.14
Pennsylvania German (0)	22	0.02
Polish (1,642)	4,188	4.72
Portuguese (32)	87	0.10
Romanian (229)	500	0.56
Russian (2,029)	5,142	5.80
Scandinavian (139)	266	0.30
Scotch-Irish (480)	1,249	1.41
Scottish (645)	2,269	2.56
Serbian (31)	163	0.18
Slavic (9)	167	0.19
Slovak (87)	177	0.20
Slovene (26)	51	0.06
Soviet Union (20)	20	0.02
Swedish (579)	1,921	2.17
Swiss (158)	400	0.45
Turkish (131)	165	0.19
Ukrainian (539)	957	1.08
Welsh (203)	1,075	1.21
West Indian, ex. Hispanic (117)	178	0.20
Bahamian (0)	0	<0.01
Barbadian (0)	0	<0.01
Belizean (0)	0	<0.01
Bermudan (0)	0	<0.01
British West Indian (18)	18	0.02
Dutch West Indian (0)	0	<0.01
Haitian (0)	0	<0.01
Jamaican (47)	68	0.08
Trinidadian/Tobagonian (0)	0	<0.01
U.S. Virgin Islander (0)	0	<0.01
West Indian (52)	92	0.10
Other West Indian (0)	0	<0.01
Yugoslavian (53)	207	0.23

Hispanic Origin	Population	%
Hispanic or Latino (of any race)	11,716	13.06
Central American, ex. Mexican	1,120	1.25
Costa Rican	49	0.05
Guatemalan	318	0.35
Honduran	75	0.08
Nicaraguan	80	0.09
Panamanian	40	0.04
Salvadoran	543	0.61
Other Central American	15	0.02
Cuban	267	0.30
Dominican Republic	32	0.04
Mexican	7,686	8.57
Puerto Rican	366	0.41
South American	1,152	1.28
Argentinean	271	0.30
Bolivian	28	0.03
Chilean	131	0.15
Colombian	263	0.29
Ecuadorian	105	0.12
Paraguayan	4	<0.01
Peruvian	184	0.21
Uruguayan	36	0.04
Venezuelan	107	0.12
Other South American	23	0.03
Other Hispanic or Latino	1,093	1.22

Race*	Population	%
African-American/Black (3,526)	4,475	4.99
Not Hispanic (3,364)	4,157	4.63
Hispanic (162)	318	0.35
American Indian/Alaska Native (338)	974	1.09
Not Hispanic (173)	646	0.72
Hispanic (165)	328	0.37
Alaska Athabascan *(Ala. Nat.)* (1)	3	<0.01
Aleut *(Alaska Native)* (1)	2	<0.01
Apache (9)	23	0.03
Arapaho (0)	0	<0.01
Blackfeet (2)	17	0.02
Canadian/French Am. Ind. (1)	2	<0.01
Central American Ind. (3)	4	<0.01
Cherokee (30)	164	0.18
Cheyenne (2)	2	<0.01
Chickasaw (0)	6	0.01
Chippewa (5)	15	0.02
Choctaw (6)	31	0.03
Colville (1)	1	<0.01
Comanche (1)	6	0.01
Cree (1)	2	<0.01
Creek (4)	12	0.01
Crow (0)	0	<0.01
Delaware (0)	2	<0.01
Hopi (1)	2	<0.01
Houma (0)	0	<0.01
Inupiat *(Alaska Native)* (1)	3	<0.01
Iroquois (1)	17	0.02
Kiowa (1)	4	<0.01
Lumbee (1)	2	<0.01
Menominee (0)	0	<0.01
Mexican American Ind. (42)	55	0.06
Navajo (19)	31	0.03
Osage (1)	5	0.01
Ottawa (0)	0	<0.01
Paiute (0)	0	<0.01
Pima (3)	4	<0.01
Potawatomi (4)	5	0.01
Pueblo (8)	12	0.01
Puget Sound Salish (0)	2	<0.01
Seminole (1)	9	0.01
Shoshone (0)	2	<0.01
Sioux (6)	22	0.02
South American Ind. (7)	24	0.03
Spanish American Ind. (2)	4	<0.01
Tlingit-Haida *(Alaska Native)* (1)	4	<0.01
Tohono O'Odham (1)	1	<0.01
Tsimshian *(Alaska Native)* (1)	1	<0.01
Ute (0)	3	<0.01
Yakama (0)	0	<0.01
Yaqui (1)	11	0.01
Yuman (3)	3	<0.01
Yup'ik *(Alaska Native)* (1)	1	<0.01
Asian (8,053)	10,262	11.44
Not Hispanic (7,960)	10,015	11.16
Hispanic (93)	247	0.28
Bangladeshi (19)	24	0.03
Bhutanese (1)	1	<0.01
Burmese (9)	13	0.01
Cambodian (27)	40	0.04
Chinese, ex. Taiwanese (2,159)	2,740	3.05
Filipino (829)	1,212	1.35
Hmong (2)	2	<0.01
Indian (1,034)	1,264	1.41
Indonesian (47)	84	0.09
Japanese (1,343)	1,924	2.14
Korean (1,296)	1,541	1.72
Laotian (7)	17	0.02
Malaysian (6)	11	0.01
Nepalese (16)	19	0.02
Pakistani (101)	137	0.15
Sri Lankan (25)	28	0.03
Taiwanese (303)	370	0.41
Thai (120)	148	0.16
Vietnamese (281)	381	0.42
Hawaii Native/Pacific Islander (124)	361	0.40
Not Hispanic (116)	313	0.35
Hispanic (8)	48	0.05
Fijian (34)	38	0.04
Guamanian/Chamorro (9)	24	0.03
Marshallese (0)	0	<0.01
Native Hawaiian (31)	115	0.13
Samoan (16)	23	0.03
Tongan (5)	10	0.01
White (69,663)	73,215	81.59
Not Hispanic (62,917)	65,793	73.32
Hispanic (6,746)	7,422	8.27

*Notes: † The Census 2010 population figure is used to calculate the percentages in the Hispanic Origin and Race categories. Ancestry percentages are based on the 2006-2010 American Community Survey population (not shown); ‡ Numbers in parentheses indicate the number of people reporting a single ancestry; * Numbers in parentheses indicate the number of persons reporting this race alone, not in combination with any other race; Please refer to the Explanation of Data for more information.*

Santa Rosa

Place Type: City
County: Sonoma
Population: 167,815

Ancestry	Population	%
Afghan (0)	0	<0.01
African, Sub-Saharan (844)	1,077	0.66
African (197)	395	0.24
Cape Verdean (0)	0	<0.01
Ethiopian (466)	491	0.30
Ghanaian (0)	0	<0.01
Kenyan (0)	10	0.01
Liberian (0)	0	<0.01
Nigerian (0)	0	<0.01
Senegalese (0)	0	<0.01
Sierra Leonean (0)	0	<0.01
Somalian (0)	0	<0.01
South African (35)	35	0.02
Sudanese (0)	0	<0.01
Ugandan (146)	146	0.09
Zimbabwean (0)	0	<0.01
Other Sub-Saharan African (0)	0	<0.01
Albanian (0)	0	<0.01
Alsatian (0)	0	<0.01
American (4,123)	4,123	2.53
Arab (156)	335	0.21
Arab (22)	36	0.02
Egyptian (7)	60	0.04
Iraqi (0)	0	<0.01
Jordanian (51)	51	0.03
Lebanese (10)	62	0.04
Moroccan (0)	0	<0.01
Palestinian (66)	66	0.04
Syrian (0)	46	0.03
Other Arab (0)	14	0.01
Armenian (16)	165	0.10
Assyrian/Chaldean/Syriac (24)	24	0.01
Australian (28)	54	0.03
Austrian (46)	458	0.28
Basque (0)	10	0.01
Belgian (87)	174	0.11
Brazilian (53)	103	0.06
British (542)	857	0.53
Bulgarian (27)	27	0.02
Cajun (38)	56	0.03
Canadian (213)	428	0.26
Carpatho Rusyn (0)	0	<0.01
Celtic (27)	37	0.02
Croatian (64)	194	0.12
Cypriot (0)	0	<0.01
Czech (70)	519	0.32
Czechoslovakian (117)	142	0.09
Danish (772)	2,234	1.37
Dutch (514)	2,452	1.51
Eastern European (376)	419	0.26
English (4,071)	15,897	9.77
Estonian (0)	0	<0.01
European (5,651)	6,559	4.03
Finnish (116)	527	0.32
French, ex. Basque (649)	5,081	3.12
French Canadian (430)	862	0.53
German (5,853)	21,836	13.43
German Russian (0)	0	<0.01
Greek (213)	939	0.58
Guyanese (0)	0	<0.01
Hungarian (279)	820	0.50
Icelander (0)	25	0.02
Iranian (487)	586	0.36
Irish (4,991)	18,711	11.50
Israeli (22)	22	0.01
Italian (4,798)	12,226	7.52
Latvian (16)	42	0.03
Lithuanian (143)	411	0.25
Luxemburger (19)	19	0.01
Macedonian (38)	47	0.03
Maltese (0)	56	0.03
New Zealander (96)	96	0.06
Northern European (303)	330	0.20
Norwegian (610)	2,551	1.57
Pennsylvania German (0)	13	0.01
Polish (537)	2,273	1.40
Portuguese (722)	2,415	1.48
Romanian (86)	201	0.12
Russian (484)	1,888	1.16
Scandinavian (315)	542	0.33
Scotch-Irish (1,249)	3,352	2.06
Scottish (1,098)	4,346	2.67
Serbian (0)	72	0.04
Slavic (47)	59	0.04
Slovak (46)	86	0.05
Slovene (25)	70	0.04
Soviet Union (0)	0	<0.01
Swedish (669)	3,092	1.90
Swiss (151)	924	0.57
Turkish (18)	38	0.02
Ukrainian (179)	318	0.20
Welsh (181)	1,242	0.76
West Indian, ex. Hispanic (34)	131	0.08
Bahamian (9)	9	0.01
Barbadian (0)	0	<0.01
Belizean (15)	15	0.01
Bermudan (0)	0	<0.01
British West Indian (0)	0	<0.01
Dutch West Indian (0)	5	<0.01
Haitian (0)	0	<0.01
Jamaican (10)	85	0.05
Trinidadian/Tobagonian (0)	0	<0.01
U.S. Virgin Islander (0)	0	<0.01
West Indian (0)	17	0.01
Other West Indian (0)	0	<0.01
Yugoslavian (60)	161	0.10

Hispanic Origin	Population	%
Hispanic or Latino (of any race)	47,970	28.59
Central American, ex. Mexican	2,239	1.33
Costa Rican	54	0.03
Guatemalan	348	0.21
Honduran	132	0.08
Nicaraguan	325	0.19
Panamanian	51	0.03
Salvadoran	1,311	0.78
Other Central American	18	0.01
Cuban	178	0.11
Dominican Republic	22	0.01
Mexican	40,889	24.37
Puerto Rican	661	0.39
South American	845	0.50
Argentinean	91	0.05
Bolivian	41	0.02
Chilean	81	0.05
Colombian	207	0.12
Ecuadorian	66	0.04
Paraguayan	11	0.01
Peruvian	290	0.17
Uruguayan	9	0.01
Venezuelan	32	0.02
Other South American	17	0.01
Other Hispanic or Latino	3,136	1.87

Race*	Population	%
African-American/Black (4,079)	5,938	3.54
Not Hispanic (3,660)	5,142	3.06
Hispanic (419)	796	0.47
American Indian/Alaska Native (2,808)	5,575	3.32
Not Hispanic (1,511)	3,221	1.92
Hispanic (1,297)	2,354	1.40
Alaska Athabascan *(Ala. Nat.)* (5)	8	<0.01
Aleut *(Alaska Native)* (6)	21	0.01
Apache (40)	184	0.11
Arapaho (0)	2	<0.01
Blackfeet (9)	97	0.06
Canadian/French Am. Ind. (5)	12	0.01
Central American Ind. (6)	10	0.01
Cherokee (95)	511	0.30
Cheyenne (3)	14	0.01
Chickasaw (12)	35	0.02
Chippewa (20)	62	0.04
Choctaw (50)	143	0.09
Colville (1)	1	<0.01
Comanche (16)	39	0.02
Cree (1)	13	0.01
Creek (10)	26	0.02
Crow (2)	10	0.01
Delaware (0)	11	0.01
Hopi (5)	6	<0.01
Houma (1)	1	<0.01
Inupiat *(Alaska Native)* (6)	20	0.01
Iroquois (9)	32	0.02
Kiowa (1)	1	<0.01
Lumbee (1)	1	<0.01
Menominee (2)	5	<0.01
Mexican American Ind. (267)	410	0.24
Navajo (40)	92	0.05
Osage (1)	14	0.01
Ottawa (0)	4	<0.01
Paiute (5)	12	0.01
Pima (3)	7	<0.01
Potawatomi (4)	13	0.01
Pueblo (11)	26	0.02
Puget Sound Salish (0)	6	<0.01
Seminole (4)	24	0.01
Shoshone (4)	9	0.01
Sioux (36)	97	0.06
South American Ind. (4)	13	0.01
Spanish American Ind. (14)	26	0.02
Tlingit-Haida *(Alaska Native)* (4)	16	0.01
Tohono O'Odham (0)	7	<0.01
Tsimshian *(Alaska Native)* (0)	2	<0.01
Ute (1)	10	0.01
Yakama (0)	2	<0.01
Yaqui (16)	55	0.03
Yuman (4)	7	<0.01
Yup'ik *(Alaska Native)* (4)	5	<0.01
Asian (8,746)	11,319	6.74
Not Hispanic (8,521)	10,606	6.32
Hispanic (225)	713	0.42
Bangladeshi (5)	5	<0.01
Bhutanese (0)	0	<0.01
Burmese (22)	32	0.02
Cambodian (808)	931	0.55
Chinese, ex. Taiwanese (1,542)	2,144	1.28
Filipino (1,549)	2,451	1.46
Hmong (63)	76	0.05
Indian (941)	1,154	0.69
Indonesian (32)	64	0.04
Japanese (471)	1,016	0.61
Korean (467)	653	0.39
Laotian (698)	849	0.51
Malaysian (9)	12	0.01
Nepalese (137)	153	0.09
Pakistani (82)	94	0.06
Sri Lankan (14)	16	0.01
Taiwanese (68)	96	0.06
Thai (141)	187	0.11
Vietnamese (1,239)	1,431	0.85
Hawaii Native/Pacific Islander (810)	1,420	0.85
Not Hispanic (750)	1,221	0.73
Hispanic (60)	199	0.12
Fijian (375)	419	0.25
Guamanian/Chamorro (47)	78	0.05
Marshallese (1)	2	<0.01
Native Hawaiian (130)	428	0.26
Samoan (157)	264	0.16
Tongan (15)	27	0.02
White (119,158)	126,600	75.44
Not Hispanic (100,126)	104,546	62.30
Hispanic (19,032)	22,054	13.14

*Notes: † The Census 2010 population figure is used to calculate the percentages in the Hispanic Origin and Race categories. Ancestry percentages are based on the 2006-2010 American Community Survey population (not shown); ‡ Numbers in parentheses indicate the number of people reporting a single ancestry; * Numbers in parentheses indicate the number of persons reporting this race alone, not in combination with any other race; Please refer to the Explanation of Data for more information.*

Santee

Place Type: City
County: San Diego
Population: 53,413

Ancestry	Population	%
Afghan (0)	0	<0.01
African, Sub-Saharan (109)	141	0.27
African (96)	118	0.22
Cape Verdean (0)	0	<0.01
Ethiopian (0)	0	<0.01
Ghanaian (0)	0	<0.01
Kenyan (0)	0	<0.01
Liberian (0)	0	<0.01
Nigerian (0)	0	<0.01
Senegalese (0)	0	<0.01
Sierra Leonean (0)	0	<0.01
Somalian (0)	0	<0.01
South African (9)	19	0.04
Sudanese (0)	0	<0.01
Ugandan (0)	0	<0.01
Zimbabwean (0)	0	<0.01
Other Sub-Saharan African (4)	4	0.01
Albanian (118)	118	0.22
Alsatian (0)	0	<0.01
American (1,791)	1,791	3.38
Arab (887)	1,287	2.43
Arab (148)	219	0.41
Egyptian (12)	39	0.07
Iraqi (117)	148	0.28
Jordanian (6)	160	0.30
Lebanese (118)	137	0.26
Moroccan (0)	19	0.04
Palestinian (0)	0	<0.01
Syrian (0)	67	0.13
Other Arab (486)	498	0.94
Armenian (103)	135	0.25
Assyrian/Chaldean/Syriac (110)	110	0.21
Australian (0)	15	0.03
Austrian (47)	197	0.37
Basque (0)	13	0.02
Belgian (0)	101	0.19
Brazilian (0)	100	0.19
British (145)	424	0.80
Bulgarian (20)	20	0.04
Cajun (0)	0	<0.01
Canadian (107)	191	0.36
Carpatho Rusyn (0)	0	<0.01
Celtic (15)	23	0.04
Croatian (26)	26	0.05
Cypriot (0)	0	<0.01
Czech (72)	392	0.74
Czechoslovakian (22)	22	0.04
Danish (143)	285	0.54
Dutch (121)	926	1.75
Eastern European (11)	22	0.04
English (1,867)	6,595	12.45
Estonian (0)	0	<0.01
European (532)	708	1.34
Finnish (46)	65	0.12
French, ex. Basque (509)	2,200	4.15
French Canadian (159)	452	0.85
German (3,367)	11,882	22.43
German Russian (0)	0	<0.01
Greek (132)	291	0.55
Guyanese (0)	0	<0.01
Hungarian (43)	352	0.66
Icelander (14)	14	0.03
Iranian (142)	154	0.29
Irish (1,543)	8,278	15.63
Israeli (0)	33	0.06
Italian (1,077)	3,637	6.87
Latvian (0)	0	<0.01
Lithuanian (17)	52	0.10
Luxemburger (0)	0	<0.01
Macedonian (0)	0	<0.01
Maltese (0)	0	<0.01
New Zealander (0)	0	<0.01
Northern European (27)	27	0.05
Norwegian (425)	1,295	2.44
Pennsylvania German (0)	12	0.02
Polish (357)	1,454	2.75
Portuguese (276)	713	1.35
Romanian (61)	73	0.14
Russian (52)	481	0.91
Scandinavian (34)	82	0.15
Scotch-Irish (475)	1,204	2.27
Scottish (378)	1,277	2.41
Serbian (0)	11	0.02
Slavic (0)	0	<0.01
Slovak (37)	114	0.22
Slovene (0)	0	<0.01
Soviet Union (0)	0	<0.01
Swedish (264)	1,090	2.06
Swiss (0)	88	0.17
Turkish (0)	31	0.06
Ukrainian (49)	100	0.19
Welsh (56)	411	0.78
West Indian, ex. Hispanic (8)	25	0.05
Bahamian (0)	0	<0.01
Barbadian (0)	0	<0.01
Belizean (0)	0	<0.01
Bermudan (0)	17	0.03
British West Indian (0)	0	<0.01
Dutch West Indian (0)	0	<0.01
Haitian (0)	0	<0.01
Jamaican (8)	8	0.02
Trinidadian/Tobagonian (0)	0	<0.01
U.S. Virgin Islander (0)	0	<0.01
West Indian (0)	0	<0.01
Other West Indian (0)	0	<0.01
Yugoslavian (16)	43	0.08

Hispanic Origin	Population	%
Hispanic or Latino (of any race)	8,699	16.29
Central American, ex. Mexican	210	0.39
Costa Rican	54	0.10
Guatemalan	43	0.08
Honduran	12	0.02
Nicaraguan	29	0.05
Panamanian	23	0.04
Salvadoran	45	0.08
Other Central American	4	0.01
Cuban	49	0.09
Dominican Republic	7	0.01
Mexican	7,086	13.27
Puerto Rican	318	0.60
South American	209	0.39
Argentinean	16	0.03
Bolivian	23	0.04
Chilean	33	0.06
Colombian	45	0.08
Ecuadorian	11	0.02
Paraguayan	5	0.01
Peruvian	58	0.11
Uruguayan	5	0.01
Venezuelan	12	0.02
Other South American	1	<0.01
Other Hispanic or Latino	820	1.54

Race*	Population	%
African-American/Black (1,057)	1,620	3.03
Not Hispanic (971)	1,426	2.67
Hispanic (86)	194	0.36
American Indian/Alaska Native (409)	999	1.87
Not Hispanic (290)	676	1.27
Hispanic (119)	323	0.60
Alaska Athabascan *(Ala. Nat.)* (2)	3	0.01
Aleut *(Alaska Native)* (1)	1	<0.01
Apache (17)	48	0.09
Arapaho (0)	1	<0.01
Blackfeet (14)	47	0.09
Canadian/French Am. Ind. (1)	3	0.01
Central American Ind. (0)	0	<0.01
Cherokee (37)	146	0.27
Cheyenne (1)	2	<0.01
Chickasaw (7)	11	0.02
Chippewa (13)	30	0.06
Choctaw (10)	36	0.07
Colville (0)	0	<0.01
Comanche (0)	9	0.02
Cree (1)	4	0.01
Creek (3)	8	0.01
Crow (0)	0	<0.01
Delaware (1)	2	<0.01
Hopi (0)	0	<0.01
Houma (0)	0	<0.01
Inupiat *(Alaska Native)* (2)	2	<0.01
Iroquois (1)	11	0.02
Kiowa (0)	0	<0.01
Lumbee (2)	4	0.01
Menominee (1)	1	<0.01
Mexican American Ind. (15)	30	0.06
Navajo (18)	44	0.08
Osage (0)	12	0.02
Ottawa (1)	3	0.01
Paiute (0)	1	<0.01
Pima (0)	0	<0.01
Potawatomi (2)	12	0.02
Pueblo (6)	10	0.02
Puget Sound Salish (0)	1	<0.01
Seminole (1)	4	0.01
Shoshone (1)	1	<0.01
Sioux (7)	21	0.04
South American Ind. (0)	0	<0.01
Spanish American Ind. (1)	1	<0.01
Tlingit-Haida *(Alaska Native)* (0)	0	<0.01
Tohono O'Odham (1)	5	0.01
Tsimshian *(Alaska Native)* (0)	0	<0.01
Ute (0)	0	<0.01
Yakama (0)	0	<0.01
Yaqui (12)	25	0.05
Yuman (3)	6	0.01
Yup'ik *(Alaska Native)* (1)	1	<0.01
Asian (2,044)	3,247	6.08
Not Hispanic (1,974)	2,949	5.52
Hispanic (70)	298	0.56
Bangladeshi (2)	2	<0.01
Bhutanese (0)	0	<0.01
Burmese (0)	0	<0.01
Cambodian (25)	31	0.06
Chinese, ex. Taiwanese (194)	355	0.66
Filipino (971)	1,605	3.00
Hmong (0)	0	<0.01
Indian (92)	130	0.24
Indonesian (22)	43	0.08
Japanese (168)	475	0.89
Korean (101)	160	0.30
Laotian (32)	46	0.09
Malaysian (3)	4	0.01
Nepalese (2)	3	0.01
Pakistani (4)	8	0.01
Sri Lankan (3)	4	0.01
Taiwanese (16)	22	0.04
Thai (47)	70	0.13
Vietnamese (255)	307	0.57
Hawaii Native/Pacific Islander (253)	632	1.18
Not Hispanic (232)	526	0.98
Hispanic (21)	106	0.20
Fijian (2)	12	0.02
Guamanian/Chamorro (132)	276	0.52
Marshallese (0)	0	<0.01
Native Hawaiian (52)	194	0.36
Samoan (34)	88	0.16
Tongan (2)	3	0.01
White (44,083)	46,684	87.40
Not Hispanic (39,312)	41,021	76.80
Hispanic (4,771)	5,663	10.60

*Notes: † The Census 2010 population figure is used to calculate the percentages in the Hispanic Origin and Race categories. Ancestry percentages are based on the 2006-2010 American Community Survey population (not shown); ‡ Numbers in parentheses indicate the number of people reporting a single ancestry; * Numbers in parentheses indicate the number of persons reporting this race alone, not in combination with any other race; Please refer to the Explanation of Data for more information.*

Simi Valley

Place Type: City
County: Ventura
Population: 124,237

Ancestry	Population	%
Afghan (625)	638	0.52
African, Sub-Saharan (153)	360	0.30
African (27)	212	0.17
Cape Verdean (24)	46	0.04
Ethiopian (5)	5	<0.01
Ghanaian (0)	0	<0.01
Kenyan (0)	0	<0.01
Liberian (0)	0	<0.01
Nigerian (97)	97	0.08
Senegalese (0)	0	<0.01
Sierra Leonean (0)	0	<0.01
Somalian (0)	0	<0.01
South African (0)	0	<0.01
Sudanese (0)	0	<0.01
Ugandan (0)	0	<0.01
Zimbabwean (0)	0	<0.01
Other Sub-Saharan African (0)	0	<0.01
Albanian (91)	102	0.08
Alsatian (0)	0	<0.01
American (11,845)	11,845	9.74
Arab (952)	1,258	1.03
Arab (66)	70	0.06
Egyptian (84)	107	0.09
Iraqi (96)	107	0.09
Jordanian (120)	120	0.10
Lebanese (238)	341	0.28
Moroccan (75)	75	0.06
Palestinian (61)	73	0.06
Syrian (97)	236	0.19
Other Arab (115)	129	0.11
Armenian (459)	599	0.49
Assyrian/Chaldean/Syriac (38)	53	0.04
Australian (39)	66	0.05
Austrian (199)	452	0.37
Basque (8)	19	0.02
Belgian (14)	72	0.06
Brazilian (51)	197	0.16
British (577)	962	0.79
Bulgarian (0)	8	0.01
Cajun (0)	0	<0.01
Canadian (271)	571	0.47
Carpatho Rusyn (0)	0	<0.01
Celtic (0)	0	<0.01
Croatian (55)	188	0.15
Cypriot (0)	0	<0.01
Czech (107)	512	0.42
Czechoslovakian (106)	196	0.16
Danish (268)	922	0.76
Dutch (549)	2,067	1.70
Eastern European (187)	246	0.20
English (3,293)	12,807	10.53
Estonian (13)	19	0.02
European (1,642)	1,895	1.56
Finnish (244)	325	0.27
French, ex. Basque (359)	3,650	3.00
French Canadian (271)	768	0.63
German (4,527)	17,975	14.77
German Russian (0)	0	<0.01
Greek (276)	720	0.59
Guyanese (0)	0	<0.01
Hungarian (240)	785	0.65
Icelander (0)	40	0.03
Iranian (658)	767	0.63
Irish (2,690)	13,019	10.70
Israeli (22)	123	0.10
Italian (3,376)	8,720	7.17
Latvian (12)	12	0.01
Lithuanian (124)	422	0.35
Luxemburger (0)	0	<0.01
Macedonian (0)	11	0.01
Maltese (0)	0	<0.01
New Zealander (0)	0	<0.01
Northern European (99)	99	0.08
Norwegian (460)	2,034	1.67
Pennsylvania German (0)	0	<0.01
Polish (922)	3,350	2.75
Portuguese (169)	483	0.40
Romanian (212)	375	0.31
Russian (1,105)	2,408	1.98
Scandinavian (157)	397	0.33
Scotch-Irish (522)	2,020	1.66
Scottish (536)	2,221	1.83
Serbian (55)	71	0.06
Slavic (30)	51	0.04
Slovak (17)	57	0.05
Slovene (20)	39	0.03
Soviet Union (0)	0	<0.01
Swedish (559)	2,433	2.00
Swiss (24)	287	0.24
Turkish (36)	57	0.05
Ukrainian (106)	264	0.22
Welsh (152)	899	0.74
West Indian, ex. Hispanic (161)	279	0.23
Bahamian (0)	0	<0.01
Barbadian (16)	16	0.01
Belizean (37)	37	0.03
Bermudan (0)	0	<0.01
British West Indian (0)	0	<0.01
Dutch West Indian (0)	0	<0.01
Haitian (0)	0	<0.01
Jamaican (90)	143	0.12
Trinidadian/Tobagonian (8)	50	0.04
U.S. Virgin Islander (0)	0	<0.01
West Indian (10)	33	0.03
Other West Indian (0)	0	<0.01
Yugoslavian (108)	208	0.17

Hispanic Origin	Population	%
Hispanic or Latino (of any race)	28,938	23.29
Central American, ex. Mexican	3,370	2.71
Costa Rican	164	0.13
Guatemalan	1,082	0.87
Honduran	265	0.21
Nicaraguan	234	0.19
Panamanian	55	0.04
Salvadoran	1,520	1.22
Other Central American	50	0.04
Cuban	431	0.35
Dominican Republic	30	0.02
Mexican	20,165	16.23
Puerto Rican	698	0.56
South American	2,077	1.67
Argentinean	351	0.28
Bolivian	52	0.04
Chilean	132	0.11
Colombian	502	0.40
Ecuadorian	226	0.18
Paraguayan	11	0.01
Peruvian	716	0.58
Uruguayan	31	0.02
Venezuelan	28	0.02
Other South American	28	0.02
Other Hispanic or Latino	2,167	1.74

Race*	Population	%
African-American/Black (1,739)	2,588	2.08
Not Hispanic (1,602)	2,224	1.79
Hispanic (137)	364	0.29
American Indian/Alaska Native (761)	2,042	1.64
Not Hispanic (356)	1,228	0.99
Hispanic (405)	814	0.66
Alaska Athabascan *(Ala. Nat.)* (0)	0	<0.01
Aleut *(Alaska Native)* (0)	0	<0.01
Apache (22)	66	0.05
Arapaho (0)	1	<0.01
Blackfeet (8)	50	0.04
Canadian/French Am. Ind. (0)	1	<0.01
Central American Ind. (1)	6	<0.01
Cherokee (80)	439	0.35
Cheyenne (0)	4	<0.01
Chickasaw (3)	12	0.01
Chippewa (16)	31	0.02
Choctaw (18)	99	0.08
Colville (3)	4	<0.01
Comanche (3)	9	0.01
Cree (1)	5	<0.01
Creek (2)	19	0.02
Crow (0)	0	<0.01
Delaware (0)	1	<0.01
Hopi (1)	2	<0.01
Houma (0)	0	<0.01
Inupiat *(Alaska Native)* (0)	4	<0.01
Iroquois (12)	40	0.03
Kiowa (1)	2	<0.01
Lumbee (1)	2	<0.01
Menominee (0)	0	<0.01
Mexican American Ind. (95)	150	0.12
Navajo (15)	42	0.03
Osage (9)	15	0.01
Ottawa (0)	0	<0.01
Paiute (0)	3	<0.01
Pima (0)	0	<0.01
Potawatomi (5)	9	0.01
Pueblo (10)	14	0.01
Puget Sound Salish (2)	2	<0.01
Seminole (3)	16	0.01
Shoshone (1)	4	<0.01
Sioux (13)	48	0.04
South American Ind. (7)	15	0.01
Spanish American Ind. (12)	16	0.01
Tlingit-Haida *(Alaska Native)* (0)	0	<0.01
Tohono O'Odham (7)	15	0.01
Tsimshian *(Alaska Native)* (0)	0	<0.01
Ute (2)	8	0.01
Yakama (0)	0	<0.01
Yaqui (7)	17	0.01
Yuman (2)	9	0.01
Yup'ik *(Alaska Native)* (0)	0	<0.01
Asian (11,555)	14,147	11.39
Not Hispanic (11,328)	13,519	10.88
Hispanic (227)	628	0.51
Bangladeshi (30)	30	0.02
Bhutanese (0)	0	<0.01
Burmese (35)	44	0.04
Cambodian (68)	85	0.07
Chinese, ex. Taiwanese (1,417)	1,957	1.58
Filipino (2,710)	3,612	2.91
Hmong (3)	5	<0.01
Indian (3,381)	3,617	2.91
Indonesian (123)	220	0.18
Japanese (662)	1,220	0.98
Korean (876)	1,101	0.89
Laotian (11)	20	0.02
Malaysian (10)	18	0.01
Nepalese (14)	17	0.01
Pakistani (165)	189	0.15
Sri Lankan (78)	82	0.07
Taiwanese (91)	128	0.10
Thai (243)	308	0.25
Vietnamese (1,240)	1,403	1.13
Hawaii Native/Pacific Islander (178)	546	0.44
Not Hispanic (148)	446	0.36
Hispanic (30)	100	0.08
Fijian (11)	13	0.01
Guamanian/Chamorro (43)	71	0.06
Marshallese (1)	4	<0.01
Native Hawaiian (67)	210	0.17
Samoan (15)	48	0.04
Tongan (20)	29	0.02
White (93,597)	98,635	79.39
Not Hispanic (78,009)	81,189	65.35
Hispanic (15,588)	17,446	14.04

*Notes: † The Census 2010 population figure is used to calculate the percentages in the Hispanic Origin and Race categories. Ancestry percentages are based on the 2006-2010 American Community Survey population (not shown); ‡ Numbers in parentheses indicate the number of people reporting a single ancestry; * Numbers in parentheses indicate the number of persons reporting this race alone, not in combination with any other race; Please refer to the Explanation of Data for more information.*

South Gate

Place Type: City
County: Los Angeles
Population: 94,396

Ancestry	Population	%
Afghan (0)	0	<0.01
African, Sub-Saharan (22)	39	0.04
African (22)	39	0.04
Cape Verdean (0)	0	<0.01
Ethiopian (0)	0	<0.01
Ghanaian (0)	0	<0.01
Kenyan (0)	0	<0.01
Liberian (0)	0	<0.01
Nigerian (0)	0	<0.01
Senegalese (0)	0	<0.01
Sierra Leonean (0)	0	<0.01
Somalian (0)	0	<0.01
South African (0)	0	<0.01
Sudanese (0)	0	<0.01
Ugandan (0)	0	<0.01
Zimbabwean (0)	0	<0.01
Other Sub-Saharan African (0)	0	<0.01
Albanian (0)	0	<0.01
Alsatian (0)	0	<0.01
American (1,715)	1,715	1.81
Arab (36)	90	0.10
Arab (27)	73	0.08
Egyptian (9)	9	0.01
Iraqi (0)	0	<0.01
Jordanian (0)	0	<0.01
Lebanese (0)	8	0.01
Moroccan (0)	0	<0.01
Palestinian (0)	0	<0.01
Syrian (0)	0	<0.01
Other Arab (0)	0	<0.01
Armenian (0)	0	<0.01
Assyrian/Chaldean/Syriac (0)	0	<0.01
Australian (0)	0	<0.01
Austrian (23)	23	0.02
Basque (0)	16	0.02
Belgian (0)	0	<0.01
Brazilian (29)	50	0.05
British (0)	9	0.01
Bulgarian (0)	0	<0.01
Cajun (0)	0	<0.01
Canadian (0)	13	0.01
Carpatho Rusyn (0)	0	<0.01
Celtic (0)	0	<0.01
Croatian (9)	22	0.02
Cypriot (0)	0	<0.01
Czech (6)	6	0.01
Czechoslovakian (15)	15	0.02
Danish (6)	13	0.01
Dutch (0)	64	0.07
Eastern European (0)	0	<0.01
English (206)	513	0.54
Estonian (0)	0	<0.01
European (0)	11	0.01
Finnish (0)	12	0.01
French, ex. Basque (134)	235	0.25
French Canadian (46)	77	0.08
German (187)	710	0.75
German Russian (0)	0	<0.01
Greek (119)	131	0.14
Guyanese (0)	0	<0.01
Hungarian (0)	0	<0.01
Icelander (0)	0	<0.01
Iranian (0)	19	0.02
Irish (138)	732	0.77
Israeli (0)	0	<0.01
Italian (114)	323	0.34
Latvian (0)	0	<0.01
Lithuanian (0)	8	0.01
Luxemburger (0)	0	<0.01
Macedonian (0)	0	<0.01
Maltese (0)	0	<0.01
New Zealander (0)	0	<0.01
Northern European (0)	0	<0.01
Norwegian (43)	66	0.07
Pennsylvania German (0)	0	<0.01
Polish (14)	86	0.09
Portuguese (34)	63	0.07
Romanian (0)	0	<0.01
Russian (82)	121	0.13
Scandinavian (13)	13	0.01
Scotch-Irish (12)	41	0.04
Scottish (19)	69	0.07
Serbian (0)	0	<0.01
Slavic (0)	0	<0.01
Slovak (0)	0	<0.01
Slovene (0)	0	<0.01
Soviet Union (0)	0	<0.01
Swedish (26)	33	0.03
Swiss (0)	0	<0.01
Turkish (0)	0	<0.01
Ukrainian (19)	19	0.02
Welsh (0)	26	0.03
West Indian, ex. Hispanic (0)	14	0.01
Bahamian (0)	0	<0.01
Barbadian (0)	0	<0.01
Belizean (0)	0	<0.01
Bermudan (0)	0	<0.01
British West Indian (0)	0	<0.01
Dutch West Indian (0)	0	<0.01
Haitian (0)	0	<0.01
Jamaican (0)	0	<0.01
Trinidadian/Tobagonian (0)	14	0.01
U.S. Virgin Islander (0)	0	<0.01
West Indian (0)	0	<0.01
Other West Indian (0)	0	<0.01
Yugoslavian (0)	31	0.03

Hispanic Origin	Population	%
Hispanic or Latino (of any race)	89,442	94.75
Central American, ex. Mexican	9,777	10.36
Costa Rican	97	0.10
Guatemalan	2,629	2.79
Honduran	507	0.54
Nicaraguan	983	1.04
Panamanian	18	0.02
Salvadoran	5,407	5.73
Other Central American	136	0.14
Cuban	754	0.80
Dominican Republic	25	0.03
Mexican	73,677	78.05
Puerto Rican	464	0.49
South American	1,216	1.29
Argentinean	112	0.12
Bolivian	13	0.01
Chilean	46	0.05
Colombian	237	0.25
Ecuadorian	348	0.37
Paraguayan	1	<0.01
Peruvian	431	0.46
Uruguayan	7	0.01
Venezuelan	12	0.01
Other South American	9	0.01
Other Hispanic or Latino	3,529	3.74

Race*	Population	%
African-American/Black (890)	1,201	1.27
Not Hispanic (585)	630	0.67
Hispanic (305)	571	0.60
American Indian/Alaska Native (878)	1,269	1.34
Not Hispanic (110)	161	0.17
Hispanic (768)	1,108	1.17
Alaska Athabascan *(Ala. Nat.)* (2)	2	<0.01
Aleut *(Alaska Native)* (0)	0	<0.01
Apache (16)	24	0.03
Arapaho (0)	0	<0.01
Blackfeet (8)	15	0.02
Canadian/French Am. Ind. (2)	2	<0.01
Central American Ind. (12)	20	0.02
Cherokee (9)	47	0.05
Cheyenne (0)	0	<0.01
Chickasaw (0)	1	<0.01
Chippewa (0)	1	<0.01
Choctaw (4)	15	0.02
Colville (0)	0	<0.01
Comanche (0)	0	<0.01
Cree (0)	5	0.01
Creek (7)	9	0.01
Crow (3)	3	<0.01
Delaware (0)	1	<0.01
Hopi (2)	5	0.01
Houma (0)	0	<0.01
Inupiat *(Alaska Native)* (0)	0	<0.01
Iroquois (0)	2	<0.01
Kiowa (0)	0	<0.01
Lumbee (1)	1	<0.01
Menominee (0)	1	<0.01
Mexican American Ind. (215)	290	0.31
Navajo (9)	28	0.03
Osage (0)	0	<0.01
Ottawa (0)	0	<0.01
Paiute (1)	3	<0.01
Pima (15)	15	0.02
Potawatomi (0)	1	<0.01
Pueblo (16)	21	0.02
Puget Sound Salish (6)	6	0.01
Seminole (1)	1	<0.01
Shoshone (1)	1	<0.01
Sioux (6)	16	0.02
South American Ind. (2)	6	0.01
Spanish American Ind. (14)	17	0.02
Tlingit-Haida *(Alaska Native)* (3)	3	<0.01
Tohono O'Odham (5)	6	0.01
Tsimshian *(Alaska Native)* (0)	0	<0.01
Ute (0)	0	<0.01
Yakama (0)	0	<0.01
Yaqui (12)	19	0.02
Yuman (0)	0	<0.01
Yup'ik *(Alaska Native)* (0)	0	<0.01
Asian (732)	991	1.05
Not Hispanic (647)	707	0.75
Hispanic (85)	284	0.30
Bangladeshi (2)	2	<0.01
Bhutanese (0)	0	<0.01
Burmese (5)	5	0.01
Cambodian (29)	31	0.03
Chinese, ex. Taiwanese (40)	70	0.07
Filipino (223)	299	0.32
Hmong (2)	4	<0.01
Indian (95)	118	0.13
Indonesian (2)	3	<0.01
Japanese (39)	74	0.08
Korean (176)	205	0.22
Laotian (16)	18	0.02
Malaysian (0)	0	<0.01
Nepalese (0)	0	<0.01
Pakistani (2)	2	<0.01
Sri Lankan (1)	1	<0.01
Taiwanese (10)	10	0.01
Thai (50)	58	0.06
Vietnamese (11)	33	0.03
Hawaii Native/Pacific Islander (99)	185	0.20
Not Hispanic (69)	87	0.09
Hispanic (30)	98	0.10
Fijian (0)	0	<0.01
Guamanian/Chamorro (15)	22	0.02
Marshallese (0)	0	<0.01
Native Hawaiian (21)	34	0.04
Samoan (44)	66	0.07
Tongan (7)	7	0.01
White (47,645)	50,671	53.68
Not Hispanic (3,233)	3,363	3.56
Hispanic (44,412)	47,308	50.12

*Notes: † The Census 2010 population figure is used to calculate the percentages in the Hispanic Origin and Race categories. Ancestry percentages are based on the 2006-2010 American Community Survey population (not shown); ‡ Numbers in parentheses indicate the number of people reporting a single ancestry; * Numbers in parentheses indicate the number of persons reporting this race alone, not in combination with any other race; Please refer to the Explanation of Data for more information.*

South San Francisco

Place Type: City
County: San Mateo
Population: 63,632

Ancestry	Population	%
Afghan (0)	0	<0.01
African, Sub-Saharan (211)	282	0.45
African (76)	76	0.12
Cape Verdean (0)	0	<0.01
Ethiopian (0)	0	<0.01
Ghanaian (0)	0	<0.01
Kenyan (0)	0	<0.01
Liberian (0)	0	<0.01
Nigerian (135)	206	0.33
Senegalese (0)	0	<0.01
Sierra Leonean (0)	0	<0.01
Somalian (0)	0	<0.01
South African (0)	0	<0.01
Sudanese (0)	0	<0.01
Ugandan (0)	0	<0.01
Zimbabwean (0)	0	<0.01
Other Sub-Saharan African (0)	0	<0.01
Albanian (0)	0	<0.01
Alsatian (0)	0	<0.01
American (491)	491	0.79
Arab (1,028)	1,248	2.01
Arab (353)	363	0.59
Egyptian (0)	0	<0.01
Iraqi (0)	0	<0.01
Jordanian (107)	278	0.45
Lebanese (132)	132	0.21
Moroccan (16)	33	0.05
Palestinian (298)	320	0.52
Syrian (0)	0	<0.01
Other Arab (122)	122	0.20
Armenian (84)	95	0.15
Assyrian/Chaldean/Syriac (0)	12	0.02
Australian (0)	11	0.02
Austrian (10)	40	0.06
Basque (0)	11	0.02
Belgian (0)	0	<0.01
Brazilian (27)	62	0.10
British (0)	62	0.10
Bulgarian (0)	0	<0.01
Cajun (0)	0	<0.01
Canadian (23)	23	0.04
Carpatho Rusyn (0)	0	<0.01
Celtic (0)	0	<0.01
Croatian (72)	90	0.15
Cypriot (34)	34	0.05
Czech (30)	45	0.07
Czechoslovakian (29)	76	0.12
Danish (78)	171	0.28
Dutch (35)	188	0.30
Eastern European (0)	22	0.04
English (452)	1,790	2.89
Estonian (0)	0	<0.01
European (280)	301	0.49
Finnish (38)	103	0.17
French, ex. Basque (233)	976	1.57
French Canadian (28)	86	0.14
German (475)	2,398	3.87
German Russian (18)	18	0.03
Greek (342)	486	0.78
Guyanese (0)	0	<0.01
Hungarian (45)	85	0.14
Icelander (0)	0	<0.01
Iranian (0)	9	0.01
Irish (671)	2,998	4.83
Israeli (0)	0	<0.01
Italian (1,991)	3,794	6.12
Latvian (22)	37	0.06
Lithuanian (22)	165	0.27
Luxemburger (0)	0	<0.01
Macedonian (0)	0	<0.01
Maltese (69)	100	0.16
New Zealander (0)	0	<0.01
Northern European (68)	68	0.11
Norwegian (107)	314	0.51
Pennsylvania German (12)	34	0.05
Polish (172)	453	0.73
Portuguese (154)	400	0.64
Romanian (34)	52	0.08
Russian (115)	316	0.51
Scandinavian (10)	10	0.02
Scotch-Irish (123)	234	0.38
Scottish (102)	312	0.50
Serbian (0)	0	<0.01
Slavic (10)	10	0.02
Slovak (0)	0	<0.01
Slovene (0)	0	<0.01
Soviet Union (0)	0	<0.01
Swedish (44)	263	0.42
Swiss (33)	42	0.07
Turkish (0)	0	<0.01
Ukrainian (137)	165	0.27
Welsh (13)	144	0.23
West Indian, ex. Hispanic (10)	10	0.02
Bahamian (0)	0	<0.01
Barbadian (0)	0	<0.01
Belizean (0)	0	<0.01
Bermudan (0)	0	<0.01
British West Indian (0)	0	<0.01
Dutch West Indian (0)	0	<0.01
Haitian (0)	0	<0.01
Jamaican (10)	10	0.02
Trinidadian/Tobagonian (0)	0	<0.01
U.S. Virgin Islander (0)	0	<0.01
West Indian (0)	0	<0.01
Other West Indian (0)	0	<0.01
Yugoslavian (28)	43	0.07

Hispanic Origin	Population	%
Hispanic or Latino (of any race)	21,645	34.02
Central American, ex. Mexican	5,381	8.46
Costa Rican	43	0.07
Guatemalan	576	0.91
Honduran	140	0.22
Nicaraguan	1,639	2.58
Panamanian	36	0.06
Salvadoran	2,897	4.55
Other Central American	50	0.08
Cuban	92	0.14
Dominican Republic	12	0.02
Mexican	13,194	20.73
Puerto Rican	571	0.90
South American	815	1.28
Argentinean	51	0.08
Bolivian	37	0.06
Chilean	34	0.05
Colombian	152	0.24
Ecuadorian	64	0.10
Paraguayan	3	<0.01
Peruvian	424	0.67
Uruguayan	4	0.01
Venezuelan	26	0.04
Other South American	20	0.03
Other Hispanic or Latino	1,580	2.48

Race*	Population	%
African-American/Black (1,625)	2,190	3.44
Not Hispanic (1,480)	1,851	2.91
Hispanic (145)	339	0.53
American Indian/Alaska Native (395)	927	1.46
Not Hispanic (138)	412	0.65
Hispanic (257)	515	0.81
Alaska Athabascan *(Ala. Nat.)* (1)	2	<0.01
Aleut *(Alaska Native)* (0)	1	<0.01
Apache (9)	29	0.05
Arapaho (0)	5	0.01
Blackfeet (3)	28	0.04
Canadian/French Am. Ind. (0)	4	0.01
Central American Ind. (10)	16	0.03
Cherokee (11)	68	0.11
Cheyenne (0)	8	0.01
Chickasaw (1)	6	0.01
Chippewa (13)	19	0.03
Choctaw (21)	41	0.06
Colville (1)	1	<0.01
Comanche (0)	1	<0.01
Cree (0)	0	<0.01
Creek (6)	11	0.02
Crow (0)	0	<0.01
Delaware (0)	2	<0.01
Hopi (0)	0	<0.01
Houma (0)	0	<0.01
Inupiat *(Alaska Native)* (1)	1	<0.01
Iroquois (0)	8	0.01
Kiowa (0)	0	<0.01
Lumbee (0)	0	<0.01
Menominee (0)	1	<0.01
Mexican American Ind. (38)	72	0.11
Navajo (21)	44	0.07
Osage (1)	1	<0.01
Ottawa (0)	0	<0.01
Paiute (2)	3	<0.01
Pima (1)	4	0.01
Potawatomi (0)	1	<0.01
Pueblo (2)	9	0.01
Puget Sound Salish (0)	0	<0.01
Seminole (1)	11	0.02
Shoshone (0)	2	<0.01
Sioux (9)	16	0.03
South American Ind. (1)	8	0.01
Spanish American Ind. (9)	11	0.02
Tlingit-Haida *(Alaska Native)* (1)	3	<0.01
Tohono O'Odham (0)	2	<0.01
Tsimshian *(Alaska Native)* (1)	2	<0.01
Ute (1)	2	<0.01
Yakama (2)	2	<0.01
Yaqui (5)	5	0.01
Yuman (0)	0	<0.01
Yup'ik *(Alaska Native)* (0)	0	<0.01
Asian (23,293)	25,409	39.93
Not Hispanic (22,923)	24,507	38.51
Hispanic (370)	902	1.42
Bangladeshi (0)	0	<0.01
Bhutanese (0)	0	<0.01
Burmese (139)	168	0.26
Cambodian (50)	65	0.10
Chinese, ex. Taiwanese (6,843)	7,687	12.08
Filipino (12,829)	14,358	22.56
Hmong (4)	4	0.01
Indian (989)	1,311	2.06
Indonesian (111)	160	0.25
Japanese (429)	743	1.17
Korean (374)	498	0.78
Laotian (24)	32	0.05
Malaysian (13)	17	0.03
Nepalese (60)	61	0.10
Pakistani (117)	138	0.22
Sri Lankan (7)	7	0.01
Taiwanese (106)	126	0.20
Thai (104)	129	0.20
Vietnamese (395)	515	0.81
Hawaii Native/Pacific Islander (1,111)	1,797	2.82
Not Hispanic (1,054)	1,595	2.51
Hispanic (57)	202	0.32
Fijian (332)	414	0.65
Guamanian/Chamorro (32)	75	0.12
Marshallese (0)	0	<0.01
Native Hawaiian (69)	237	0.37
Samoan (340)	473	0.74
Tongan (171)	250	0.39
White (23,760)	26,496	41.64
Not Hispanic (14,016)	15,403	24.21
Hispanic (9,744)	11,093	17.43

*Notes: † The Census 2010 population figure is used to calculate the percentages in the Hispanic Origin and Race categories. Ancestry percentages are based on the 2006-2010 American Community Survey population (not shown); ‡ Numbers in parentheses indicate the number of people reporting a single ancestry; * Numbers in parentheses indicate the number of persons reporting this race alone, not in combination with any other race; Please refer to the Explanation of Data for more information.*

South Whittier

Place Type: CDP
County: Los Angeles
Population: 57,156

Ancestry	Population	%
Afghan (0)	0	<0.01
African, Sub-Saharan (56)	151	0.27
African (56)	151	0.27
Cape Verdean (0)	0	<0.01
Ethiopian (0)	0	<0.01
Ghanaian (0)	0	<0.01
Kenyan (0)	0	<0.01
Liberian (0)	0	<0.01
Nigerian (0)	0	<0.01
Senegalese (0)	0	<0.01
Sierra Leonean (0)	0	<0.01
Somalian (0)	0	<0.01
South African (0)	0	<0.01
Sudanese (0)	0	<0.01
Ugandan (0)	0	<0.01
Zimbabwean (0)	0	<0.01
Other Sub-Saharan African (0)	0	<0.01
Albanian (0)	0	<0.01
Alsatian (0)	0	<0.01
American (986)	986	1.73
Arab (112)	177	0.31
Arab (0)	15	0.03
Egyptian (47)	54	0.09
Iraqi (0)	0	<0.01
Jordanian (0)	0	<0.01
Lebanese (37)	80	0.14
Moroccan (0)	0	<0.01
Palestinian (0)	0	<0.01
Syrian (15)	15	0.03
Other Arab (13)	13	0.02
Armenian (99)	158	0.28
Assyrian/Chaldean/Syriac (0)	0	<0.01
Australian (0)	0	<0.01
Austrian (6)	18	0.03
Basque (0)	0	<0.01
Belgian (0)	0	<0.01
Brazilian (137)	137	0.24
British (63)	177	0.31
Bulgarian (0)	0	<0.01
Cajun (0)	0	<0.01
Canadian (31)	63	0.11
Carpatho Rusyn (0)	0	<0.01
Celtic (0)	0	<0.01
Croatian (10)	36	0.06
Cypriot (0)	0	<0.01
Czech (32)	45	0.08
Czechoslovakian (9)	9	0.02
Danish (51)	166	0.29
Dutch (54)	300	0.53
Eastern European (97)	97	0.17
English (421)	1,591	2.80
Estonian (0)	0	<0.01
European (344)	445	0.78
Finnish (11)	19	0.03
French, ex. Basque (31)	450	0.79
French Canadian (33)	176	0.31
German (590)	2,377	4.18
German Russian (0)	0	<0.01
Greek (64)	187	0.33
Guyanese (0)	0	<0.01
Hungarian (49)	62	0.11
Icelander (0)	0	<0.01
Iranian (0)	0	<0.01
Irish (376)	1,867	3.28
Israeli (0)	0	<0.01
Italian (254)	872	1.53
Latvian (0)	0	<0.01
Lithuanian (0)	9	0.02
Luxemburger (0)	0	<0.01
Macedonian (0)	0	<0.01
Maltese (0)	0	<0.01
New Zealander (0)	0	<0.01
Northern European (0)	0	<0.01
Norwegian (23)	292	0.51
Pennsylvania German (9)	20	0.04
Polish (70)	414	0.73
Portuguese (52)	135	0.24
Romanian (0)	0	<0.01
Russian (170)	300	0.53
Scandinavian (21)	21	0.04
Scotch-Irish (97)	454	0.80
Scottish (156)	373	0.66
Serbian (0)	0	<0.01
Slavic (0)	0	<0.01
Slovak (0)	15	0.03
Slovene (0)	0	<0.01
Soviet Union (0)	0	<0.01
Swedish (62)	287	0.50
Swiss (44)	153	0.27
Turkish (0)	0	<0.01
Ukrainian (25)	54	0.09
Welsh (34)	133	0.23
West Indian, ex. Hispanic (43)	71	0.12
Bahamian (0)	0	<0.01
Barbadian (0)	0	<0.01
Belizean (0)	28	0.05
Bermudan (0)	0	<0.01
British West Indian (0)	0	<0.01
Dutch West Indian (0)	0	<0.01
Haitian (0)	0	<0.01
Jamaican (11)	11	0.02
Trinidadian/Tobagonian (8)	8	0.01
U.S. Virgin Islander (0)	0	<0.01
West Indian (24)	24	0.04
Other West Indian (0)	0	<0.01
Yugoslavian (0)	0	<0.01

Hispanic Origin	Population	%
Hispanic or Latino (of any race)	44,094	77.15
Central American, ex. Mexican	2,217	3.88
Costa Rican	59	0.10
Guatemalan	612	1.07
Honduran	103	0.18
Nicaraguan	299	0.52
Panamanian	24	0.04
Salvadoran	1,110	1.94
Other Central American	10	0.02
Cuban	206	0.36
Dominican Republic	10	0.02
Mexican	38,766	67.82
Puerto Rican	354	0.62
South American	548	0.96
Argentinean	70	0.12
Bolivian	11	0.02
Chilean	34	0.06
Colombian	136	0.24
Ecuadorian	108	0.19
Paraguayan	0	<0.01
Peruvian	170	0.30
Uruguayan	9	0.02
Venezuelan	5	0.01
Other South American	5	0.01
Other Hispanic or Latino	1,993	3.49

Race*	Population	%
African-American/Black (859)	1,176	2.06
Not Hispanic (601)	711	1.24
Hispanic (258)	465	0.81
American Indian/Alaska Native (743)	1,209	2.12
Not Hispanic (139)	276	0.48
Hispanic (604)	933	1.63
Alaska Athabascan *(Ala. Nat.)* (0)	0	<0.01
Aleut *(Alaska Native)* (2)	2	<0.01
Apache (54)	91	0.16
Arapaho (2)	5	0.01
Blackfeet (13)	26	0.05
Canadian/French Am. Ind. (1)	1	<0.01
Central American Ind. (12)	12	0.02
Cherokee (18)	72	0.13
Cheyenne (2)	2	<0.01
Chickasaw (0)	4	0.01
Chippewa (5)	17	0.03
Choctaw (3)	15	0.03
Colville (1)	1	<0.01
Comanche (3)	10	0.02
Cree (0)	0	<0.01
Creek (3)	6	0.01
Crow (0)	0	<0.01
Delaware (0)	0	<0.01
Hopi (5)	10	0.02
Houma (0)	0	<0.01
Inupiat *(Alaska Native)* (0)	0	<0.01
Iroquois (2)	3	0.01
Kiowa (0)	0	<0.01
Lumbee (0)	5	0.01
Menominee (0)	0	<0.01
Mexican American Ind. (71)	111	0.19
Navajo (27)	46	0.08
Osage (0)	0	<0.01
Ottawa (0)	0	<0.01
Paiute (1)	4	0.01
Pima (5)	7	0.01
Potawatomi (3)	5	0.01
Pueblo (9)	13	0.02
Puget Sound Salish (0)	0	<0.01
Seminole (1)	7	0.01
Shoshone (1)	1	<0.01
Sioux (7)	14	0.02
South American Ind. (8)	11	0.02
Spanish American Ind. (0)	1	<0.01
Tlingit-Haida *(Alaska Native)* (0)	5	0.01
Tohono O'Odham (15)	22	0.04
Tsimshian *(Alaska Native)* (0)	0	<0.01
Ute (0)	1	<0.01
Yakama (0)	0	<0.01
Yaqui (13)	42	0.07
Yuman (1)	1	<0.01
Yup'ik *(Alaska Native)* (0)	0	<0.01
Asian (2,305)	2,791	4.88
Not Hispanic (2,151)	2,418	4.23
Hispanic (154)	373	0.65
Bangladeshi (4)	4	0.01
Bhutanese (0)	0	<0.01
Burmese (7)	11	0.02
Cambodian (54)	58	0.10
Chinese, ex. Taiwanese (222)	321	0.56
Filipino (1,164)	1,406	2.46
Hmong (0)	0	<0.01
Indian (103)	135	0.24
Indonesian (13)	21	0.04
Japanese (159)	273	0.48
Korean (165)	185	0.32
Laotian (67)	83	0.15
Malaysian (0)	0	<0.01
Nepalese (16)	16	0.03
Pakistani (2)	5	0.01
Sri Lankan (12)	12	0.02
Taiwanese (21)	26	0.05
Thai (78)	113	0.20
Vietnamese (129)	155	0.27
Hawaii Native/Pacific Islander (147)	282	0.49
Not Hispanic (76)	145	0.25
Hispanic (71)	137	0.24
Fijian (0)	0	<0.01
Guamanian/Chamorro (26)	41	0.07
Marshallese (0)	0	<0.01
Native Hawaiian (21)	86	0.15
Samoan (43)	74	0.13
Tongan (32)	34	0.06
White (33,663)	35,650	62.37
Not Hispanic (9,526)	9,959	17.42
Hispanic (24,137)	25,691	44.95

*Notes: † The Census 2010 population figure is used to calculate the percentages in the Hispanic Origin and Race categories. Ancestry percentages are based on the 2006-2010 American Community Survey population (not shown); ‡ Numbers in parentheses indicate the number of people reporting a single ancestry; * Numbers in parentheses indicate the number of persons reporting this race alone, not in combination with any other race; Please refer to the Explanation of Data for more information.*

Stockton

Place Type: City
County: San Joaquin
Population: 291,707

Ancestry	Population	%
Afghan (150)	150	0.05
African, Sub-Saharan (1,061)	1,447	0.50
African (575)	876	0.30
Cape Verdean (0)	0	<0.01
Ethiopian (256)	256	0.09
Ghanaian (0)	0	<0.01
Kenyan (0)	0	<0.01
Liberian (81)	91	0.03
Nigerian (81)	81	0.03
Senegalese (0)	0	<0.01
Sierra Leonean (0)	0	<0.01
Somalian (0)	0	<0.01
South African (0)	0	<0.01
Sudanese (0)	0	<0.01
Ugandan (0)	0	<0.01
Zimbabwean (68)	118	0.04
Other Sub-Saharan African (0)	25	0.01
Albanian (0)	0	<0.01
Alsatian (0)	0	<0.01
American (4,367)	4,367	1.52
Arab (1,504)	1,750	0.61
Arab (802)	879	0.31
Egyptian (251)	251	0.09
Iraqi (0)	0	<0.01
Jordanian (22)	22	0.01
Lebanese (151)	274	0.10
Moroccan (0)	10	<0.01
Palestinian (78)	78	0.03
Syrian (100)	131	0.05
Other Arab (100)	105	0.04
Armenian (118)	136	0.05
Assyrian/Chaldean/Syriac (0)	0	<0.01
Australian (0)	0	<0.01
Austrian (37)	199	0.07
Basque (135)	280	0.10
Belgian (0)	32	0.01
Brazilian (79)	142	0.05
British (203)	475	0.17
Bulgarian (0)	16	0.01
Cajun (0)	20	0.01
Canadian (217)	285	0.10
Carpatho Rusyn (0)	0	<0.01
Celtic (13)	25	0.01
Croatian (73)	118	0.04
Cypriot (0)	0	<0.01
Czech (19)	197	0.07
Czechoslovakian (38)	91	0.03
Danish (251)	995	0.35
Dutch (341)	1,770	0.62
Eastern European (96)	115	0.04
English (2,649)	10,748	3.74
Estonian (8)	8	<0.01
European (1,559)	2,042	0.71
Finnish (150)	343	0.12
French, ex. Basque (606)	4,378	1.52
French Canadian (117)	443	0.15
German (4,830)	18,204	6.33
German Russian (0)	117	0.04
Greek (312)	600	0.21
Guyanese (0)	0	<0.01
Hungarian (112)	354	0.12
Icelander (0)	0	<0.01
Iranian (336)	359	0.12
Irish (3,122)	13,023	4.53
Israeli (28)	93	0.03
Italian (4,441)	10,289	3.58
Latvian (16)	29	0.01
Lithuanian (54)	198	0.07
Luxemburger (0)	39	0.01
Macedonian (0)	0	<0.01
Maltese (27)	77	0.03
New Zealander (0)	0	<0.01
Northern European (85)	231	0.08
Norwegian (602)	1,663	0.58
Pennsylvania German (7)	41	0.01
Polish (409)	1,488	0.52
Portuguese (1,432)	3,256	1.13
Romanian (113)	149	0.05
Russian (335)	1,618	0.56
Scandinavian (22)	55	0.02
Scotch-Irish (504)	1,824	0.63
Scottish (668)	2,160	0.75
Serbian (62)	70	0.02
Slavic (0)	0	<0.01
Slovak (16)	67	0.02
Slovene (16)	93	0.03
Soviet Union (0)	0	<0.01
Swedish (386)	1,893	0.66
Swiss (68)	414	0.14
Turkish (76)	76	0.03
Ukrainian (76)	128	0.04
Welsh (159)	807	0.28
West Indian, ex. Hispanic (204)	303	0.11
Bahamian (0)	0	<0.01
Barbadian (0)	15	0.01
Belizean (73)	73	0.03
Bermudan (0)	0	<0.01
British West Indian (0)	0	<0.01
Dutch West Indian (19)	19	0.01
Haitian (15)	29	0.01
Jamaican (52)	73	0.03
Trinidadian/Tobagonian (0)	0	<0.01
U.S. Virgin Islander (0)	0	<0.01
West Indian (45)	73	0.03
Other West Indian (0)	21	0.01
Yugoslavian (39)	176	0.06

Hispanic Origin	Population	%
Hispanic or Latino (of any race)	117,590	40.31
Central American, ex. Mexican	3,302	1.13
Costa Rican	78	0.03
Guatemalan	793	0.27
Honduran	205	0.07
Nicaraguan	786	0.27
Panamanian	131	0.04
Salvadoran	1,296	0.44
Other Central American	13	<0.01
Cuban	245	0.08
Dominican Republic	75	0.03
Mexican	104,172	35.71
Puerto Rican	1,831	0.63
South American	962	0.33
Argentinean	72	0.02
Bolivian	37	0.01
Chilean	207	0.07
Colombian	211	0.07
Ecuadorian	86	0.03
Paraguayan	1	<0.01
Peruvian	273	0.09
Uruguayan	11	<0.01
Venezuelan	53	0.02
Other South American	11	<0.01
Other Hispanic or Latino	7,003	2.40

Race*	Population	%
African-American/Black (35,548)	41,432	14.20
Not Hispanic (33,507)	37,389	12.82
Hispanic (2,041)	4,043	1.39
American Indian/Alaska Native (3,086)	7,284	2.50
Not Hispanic (1,237)	3,819	1.31
Hispanic (1,849)	3,465	1.19
Alaska Athabascan *(Ala. Nat.)* (6)	7	<0.01
Aleut *(Alaska Native)* (5)	17	0.01
Apache (140)	384	0.13
Arapaho (3)	9	<0.01
Blackfeet (38)	229	0.08
Canadian/French Am. Ind. (5)	17	0.01
Central American Ind. (7)	14	<0.01
Cherokee (203)	1,176	0.40
Cheyenne (5)	16	0.01
Chickasaw (11)	37	0.01
Chippewa (22)	54	0.02
Choctaw (53)	276	0.09
Colville (1)	1	<0.01
Comanche (2)	13	<0.01
Cree (2)	6	<0.01
Creek (9)	38	0.01
Crow (3)	12	<0.01
Delaware (15)	19	0.01
Hopi (8)	16	0.01
Houma (0)	0	<0.01
Inupiat *(Alaska Native)* (4)	4	<0.01
Iroquois (12)	25	0.01
Kiowa (1)	2	<0.01
Lumbee (2)	4	<0.01
Menominee (0)	1	<0.01
Mexican American Ind. (305)	485	0.17
Navajo (109)	233	0.08
Osage (10)	21	0.01
Ottawa (3)	4	<0.01
Paiute (8)	24	0.01
Pima (18)	31	0.01
Potawatomi (12)	35	0.01
Pueblo (26)	65	0.02
Puget Sound Salish (7)	9	<0.01
Seminole (10)	46	0.02
Shoshone (5)	17	0.01
Sioux (97)	185	0.06
South American Ind. (7)	29	0.01
Spanish American Ind. (14)	21	0.01
Tlingit-Haida *(Alaska Native)* (7)	18	0.01
Tohono O'Odham (5)	15	0.01
Tsimshian *(Alaska Native)* (0)	1	<0.01
Ute (8)	15	0.01
Yakama (1)	2	<0.01
Yaqui (60)	166	0.06
Yuman (7)	12	<0.01
Yup'ik *(Alaska Native)* (1)	4	<0.01
Asian (62,716)	71,852	24.63
Not Hispanic (60,323)	65,993	22.62
Hispanic (2,393)	5,859	2.01
Bangladeshi (5)	5	<0.01
Bhutanese (0)	0	<0.01
Burmese (27)	35	0.01
Cambodian (10,170)	11,429	3.92
Chinese, ex. Taiwanese (5,067)	6,382	2.19
Filipino (21,133)	27,113	9.29
Hmong (5,819)	6,073	2.08
Indian (4,735)	5,630	1.93
Indonesian (25)	77	0.03
Japanese (1,362)	2,344	0.80
Korean (638)	912	0.31
Laotian (2,961)	3,581	1.23
Malaysian (10)	25	0.01
Nepalese (0)	0	<0.01
Pakistani (1,706)	1,904	0.65
Sri Lankan (7)	9	<0.01
Taiwanese (112)	133	0.05
Thai (148)	357	0.12
Vietnamese (6,044)	6,552	2.25
Hawaii Native/Pacific Islander (1,822)	3,566	1.22
Not Hispanic (1,622)	2,869	0.98
Hispanic (200)	697	0.24
Fijian (579)	665	0.23
Guamanian/Chamorro (250)	414	0.14
Marshallese (1)	4	<0.01
Native Hawaiian (178)	800	0.27
Samoan (424)	637	0.22
Tongan (133)	188	0.06
White (108,044)	122,069	41.85
Not Hispanic (66,836)	73,943	25.35
Hispanic (41,208)	48,126	16.50

*Notes: † The Census 2010 population figure is used to calculate the percentages in the Hispanic Origin and Race categories. Ancestry percentages are based on the 2006-2010 American Community Survey population (not shown); ‡ Numbers in parentheses indicate the number of people reporting a single ancestry; * Numbers in parentheses indicate the number of persons reporting this race alone, not in combination with any other race; Please refer to the Explanation of Data for more information.*

Sunnyvale

Place Type: City
County: Santa Clara
Population: 140,081

Ancestry	Population	%
Afghan (82)	82	0.06
African, Sub-Saharan (138)	198	0.15
African (116)	116	0.08
Cape Verdean (0)	0	<0.01
Ethiopian (10)	10	0.01
Ghanaian (0)	0	<0.01
Kenyan (12)	24	0.02
Liberian (0)	0	<0.01
Nigerian (0)	0	<0.01
Senegalese (0)	0	<0.01
Sierra Leonean (0)	0	<0.01
Somalian (0)	0	<0.01
South African (0)	0	<0.01
Sudanese (0)	0	<0.01
Ugandan (0)	0	<0.01
Zimbabwean (0)	0	<0.01
Other Sub-Saharan African (0)	48	0.04
Albanian (0)	12	0.01
Alsatian (0)	0	<0.01
American (1,943)	1,943	1.42
Arab (559)	832	0.61
Arab (134)	227	0.17
Egyptian (142)	165	0.12
Iraqi (0)	0	<0.01
Jordanian (7)	7	0.01
Lebanese (11)	91	0.07
Moroccan (0)	0	<0.01
Palestinian (40)	47	0.03
Syrian (0)	28	0.02
Other Arab (225)	267	0.20
Armenian (291)	419	0.31
Assyrian/Chaldean/Syriac (103)	141	0.10
Australian (35)	70	0.05
Austrian (73)	257	0.19
Basque (0)	16	0.01
Belgian (80)	177	0.13
Brazilian (19)	71	0.05
British (406)	836	0.61
Bulgarian (301)	308	0.23
Cajun (0)	0	<0.01
Canadian (452)	738	0.54
Carpatho Rusyn (0)	0	<0.01
Celtic (16)	31	0.02
Croatian (262)	388	0.28
Cypriot (0)	0	<0.01
Czech (127)	461	0.34
Czechoslovakian (67)	155	0.11
Danish (198)	851	0.62
Dutch (196)	1,131	0.83
Eastern European (111)	149	0.11
English (2,131)	8,447	6.19
Estonian (16)	36	0.03
European (1,661)	2,236	1.64
Finnish (50)	245	0.18
French, ex. Basque (815)	3,053	2.24
French Canadian (189)	492	0.36
German (2,920)	11,118	8.15
German Russian (0)	0	<0.01
Greek (136)	383	0.28
Guyanese (69)	69	0.05
Hungarian (274)	643	0.47
Icelander (27)	40	0.03
Iranian (1,081)	1,120	0.82
Irish (1,706)	7,804	5.72
Israeli (727)	796	0.58
Italian (2,253)	4,899	3.59
Latvian (28)	46	0.03
Lithuanian (51)	95	0.07
Luxemburger (0)	34	0.02
Macedonian (0)	14	0.01
Maltese (0)	8	0.01
New Zealander (0)	0	<0.01
Northern European (260)	360	0.26
Norwegian (461)	1,476	1.08
Pennsylvania German (11)	33	0.02
Polish (600)	1,878	1.38
Portuguese (500)	1,117	0.82
Romanian (271)	594	0.44
Russian (947)	1,478	1.08
Scandinavian (131)	314	0.23
Scotch-Irish (302)	1,082	0.79
Scottish (583)	1,926	1.41
Serbian (151)	183	0.13
Slavic (145)	228	0.17
Slovak (37)	102	0.07
Slovene (19)	36	0.03
Soviet Union (0)	0	<0.01
Swedish (302)	1,794	1.31
Swiss (193)	568	0.42
Turkish (88)	183	0.13
Ukrainian (228)	386	0.28
Welsh (94)	687	0.50
West Indian, ex. Hispanic (13)	13	0.01
Bahamian (0)	0	<0.01
Barbadian (0)	0	<0.01
Belizean (0)	0	<0.01
Bermudan (0)	0	<0.01
British West Indian (0)	0	<0.01
Dutch West Indian (0)	0	<0.01
Haitian (13)	13	0.01
Jamaican (0)	0	<0.01
Trinidadian/Tobagonian (0)	0	<0.01
U.S. Virgin Islander (0)	0	<0.01
West Indian (0)	0	<0.01
Other West Indian (0)	0	<0.01
Yugoslavian (153)	322	0.24

Hispanic Origin	Population	%
Hispanic or Latino (of any race)	26,517	18.93
Central American, ex. Mexican	2,609	1.86
Costa Rican	38	0.03
Guatemalan	684	0.49
Honduran	82	0.06
Nicaraguan	289	0.21
Panamanian	34	0.02
Salvadoran	1,460	1.04
Other Central American	22	0.02
Cuban	116	0.08
Dominican Republic	33	0.02
Mexican	19,939	14.23
Puerto Rican	559	0.40
South American	1,241	0.89
Argentinean	125	0.09
Bolivian	82	0.06
Chilean	83	0.06
Colombian	207	0.15
Ecuadorian	33	0.02
Paraguayan	2	<0.01
Peruvian	607	0.43
Uruguayan	19	0.01
Venezuelan	74	0.05
Other South American	9	0.01
Other Hispanic or Latino	2,020	1.44

Race*	Population	%
African-American/Black (2,735)	3,630	2.59
Not Hispanic (2,533)	3,192	2.28
Hispanic (202)	438	0.31
American Indian/Alaska Native (662)	1,438	1.03
Not Hispanic (292)	789	0.56
Hispanic (370)	649	0.46
Alaska Athabascan *(Ala. Nat.)* (3)	5	<0.01
Aleut *(Alaska Native)* (0)	0	<0.01
Apache (21)	50	0.04
Arapaho (0)	0	<0.01
Blackfeet (2)	17	0.01
Canadian/French Am. Ind. (3)	8	0.01
Central American Ind. (1)	2	<0.01
Cherokee (43)	200	0.14
Cheyenne (0)	0	<0.01
Chickasaw (2)	10	0.01
Chippewa (11)	17	0.01
Choctaw (17)	43	0.03
Colville (2)	2	<0.01
Comanche (0)	10	0.01
Cree (1)	3	<0.01
Creek (5)	12	0.01
Crow (0)	2	<0.01
Delaware (0)	1	<0.01
Hopi (2)	4	<0.01
Houma (0)	0	<0.01
Inupiat *(Alaska Native)* (4)	7	<0.01
Iroquois (4)	8	0.01
Kiowa (1)	2	<0.01
Lumbee (0)	2	<0.01
Menominee (0)	0	<0.01
Mexican American Ind. (68)	102	0.07
Navajo (15)	33	0.02
Osage (4)	10	0.01
Ottawa (0)	0	<0.01
Paiute (0)	0	<0.01
Pima (5)	5	<0.01
Potawatomi (4)	6	<0.01
Pueblo (3)	6	<0.01
Puget Sound Salish (0)	0	<0.01
Seminole (0)	5	<0.01
Shoshone (3)	7	<0.01
Sioux (6)	16	0.01
South American Ind. (6)	14	0.01
Spanish American Ind. (4)	8	0.01
Tlingit-Haida *(Alaska Native)* (4)	7	<0.01
Tohono O'Odham (1)	1	<0.01
Tsimshian *(Alaska Native)* (0)	0	<0.01
Ute (0)	4	<0.01
Yakama (0)	1	<0.01
Yaqui (13)	22	0.02
Yuman (1)	4	<0.01
Yup'ik *(Alaska Native)* (0)	0	<0.01
Asian (57,320)	61,253	43.73
Not Hispanic (57,012)	60,435	43.14
Hispanic (308)	818	0.58
Bangladeshi (52)	61	0.04
Bhutanese (1)	1	<0.01
Burmese (110)	125	0.09
Cambodian (87)	137	0.10
Chinese, ex. Taiwanese (15,745)	17,556	12.53
Filipino (6,599)	7,847	5.60
Hmong (30)	34	0.02
Indian (21,737)	22,285	15.91
Indonesian (103)	178	0.13
Japanese (2,985)	3,950	2.82
Korean (2,996)	3,294	2.35
Laotian (34)	42	0.03
Malaysian (66)	96	0.07
Nepalese (298)	305	0.22
Pakistani (330)	398	0.28
Sri Lankan (103)	108	0.08
Taiwanese (1,527)	1,736	1.24
Thai (206)	252	0.18
Vietnamese (3,030)	3,433	2.45
Hawaii Native/Pacific Islander (638)	1,177	0.84
Not Hispanic (594)	1,022	0.73
Hispanic (44)	155	0.11
Fijian (66)	86	0.06
Guamanian/Chamorro (77)	144	0.10
Marshallese (0)	0	<0.01
Native Hawaiian (66)	288	0.21
Samoan (188)	241	0.17
Tongan (161)	186	0.13
White (60,193)	65,362	46.66
Not Hispanic (48,323)	51,946	37.08
Hispanic (11,870)	13,416	9.58

*Notes: † The Census 2010 population figure is used to calculate the percentages in the Hispanic Origin and Race categories. Ancestry percentages are based on the 2006-2010 American Community Survey population (not shown); ‡ Numbers in parentheses indicate the number of people reporting a single ancestry; * Numbers in parentheses indicate the number of persons reporting this race alone, not in combination with any other race; Please refer to the Explanation of Data for more information.*

Temecula

Place Type: City
County: Riverside
Population: 100,097

Ancestry	Population	%
Afghan (237)	240	0.25
African, Sub-Saharan (284)	401	0.42
African (95)	131	0.14
Cape Verdean (15)	15	0.02
Ethiopian (31)	31	0.03
Ghanaian (0)	0	<0.01
Kenyan (0)	0	<0.01
Liberian (0)	0	<0.01
Nigerian (0)	0	<0.01
Senegalese (0)	0	<0.01
Sierra Leonean (12)	12	0.01
Somalian (0)	0	<0.01
South African (0)	13	0.01
Sudanese (55)	55	0.06
Ugandan (76)	76	0.08
Zimbabwean (0)	68	0.07
Other Sub-Saharan African (0)	0	<0.01
Albanian (70)	70	0.07
Alsatian (0)	0	<0.01
American (2,275)	2,275	2.37
Arab (254)	424	0.44
Arab (61)	146	0.15
Egyptian (84)	131	0.14
Iraqi (0)	0	<0.01
Jordanian (57)	62	0.06
Lebanese (19)	52	0.05
Moroccan (0)	0	<0.01
Palestinian (33)	33	0.03
Syrian (0)	0	<0.01
Other Arab (0)	0	<0.01
Armenian (0)	108	0.11
Assyrian/Chaldean/Syriac (0)	0	<0.01
Australian (0)	69	0.07
Austrian (66)	237	0.25
Basque (54)	54	0.06
Belgian (23)	76	0.08
Brazilian (0)	11	0.01
British (261)	480	0.50
Bulgarian (23)	23	0.02
Cajun (17)	43	0.04
Canadian (264)	608	0.63
Carpatho Rusyn (0)	0	<0.01
Celtic (0)	0	<0.01
Croatian (27)	107	0.11
Cypriot (0)	0	<0.01
Czech (169)	430	0.45
Czechoslovakian (87)	132	0.14
Danish (77)	399	0.42
Dutch (318)	1,765	1.84
Eastern European (41)	41	0.04
English (3,223)	10,374	10.83
Estonian (14)	14	0.01
European (2,627)	3,436	3.59
Finnish (24)	115	0.12
French, ex. Basque (505)	3,211	3.35
French Canadian (289)	466	0.49
German (3,673)	13,609	14.20
German Russian (0)	0	<0.01
Greek (242)	740	0.77
Guyanese (0)	0	<0.01
Hungarian (133)	573	0.60
Icelander (0)	0	<0.01
Iranian (154)	167	0.17
Irish (2,260)	10,882	11.36
Israeli (10)	10	0.01
Italian (2,206)	7,284	7.60
Latvian (13)	13	0.01
Lithuanian (32)	59	0.06
Luxemburger (0)	0	<0.01
Macedonian (11)	20	0.02
Maltese (0)	0	<0.01
New Zealander (0)	27	0.03
Northern European (89)	117	0.12
Norwegian (449)	1,297	1.35
Pennsylvania German (12)	12	0.01
Polish (904)	3,023	3.15
Portuguese (289)	692	0.72
Romanian (28)	123	0.13
Russian (400)	953	0.99
Scandinavian (159)	245	0.26
Scotch-Irish (463)	1,154	1.20
Scottish (572)	2,456	2.56
Serbian (7)	30	0.03
Slavic (48)	48	0.05
Slovak (46)	112	0.12
Slovene (15)	15	0.02
Soviet Union (0)	0	<0.01
Swedish (480)	1,668	1.74
Swiss (19)	134	0.14
Turkish (0)	9	0.01
Ukrainian (121)	219	0.23
Welsh (204)	773	0.81
West Indian, ex. Hispanic (92)	231	0.24
Bahamian (0)	0	<0.01
Barbadian (0)	0	<0.01
Belizean (0)	0	<0.01
Bermudan (0)	0	<0.01
British West Indian (59)	198	0.21
Dutch West Indian (0)	0	<0.01
Haitian (0)	0	<0.01
Jamaican (0)	0	<0.01
Trinidadian/Tobagonian (9)	9	0.01
U.S. Virgin Islander (0)	0	<0.01
West Indian (24)	24	0.03
Other West Indian (0)	0	<0.01
Yugoslavian (75)	125	0.13

Hispanic Origin	Population	%
Hispanic or Latino (of any race)	24,727	24.70
Central American, ex. Mexican	1,027	1.03
Costa Rican	68	0.07
Guatemalan	334	0.33
Honduran	61	0.06
Nicaraguan	87	0.09
Panamanian	91	0.09
Salvadoran	368	0.37
Other Central American	18	0.02
Cuban	249	0.25
Dominican Republic	77	0.08
Mexican	19,928	19.91
Puerto Rican	970	0.97
South American	848	0.85
Argentinean	131	0.13
Bolivian	23	0.02
Chilean	70	0.07
Colombian	219	0.22
Ecuadorian	109	0.11
Paraguayan	6	0.01
Peruvian	205	0.20
Uruguayan	25	0.02
Venezuelan	38	0.04
Other South American	22	0.02
Other Hispanic or Latino	1,628	1.63

Race*	Population	%
African-American/Black (4,132)	5,496	5.49
Not Hispanic (3,794)	4,828	4.82
Hispanic (338)	668	0.67
American Indian/Alaska Native (1,079)	2,038	2.04
Not Hispanic (655)	1,244	1.24
Hispanic (424)	794	0.79
Alaska Athabascan *(Ala. Nat.)* (0)	0	<0.01
Aleut *(Alaska Native)* (5)	5	<0.01
Apache (24)	65	0.06
Arapaho (1)	1	<0.01
Blackfeet (4)	30	0.03
Canadian/French Am. Ind. (0)	7	0.01
Central American Ind. (2)	4	<0.01
Cherokee (59)	211	0.21
Cheyenne (2)	9	0.01
Chickasaw (1)	9	0.01
Chippewa (11)	29	0.03
Choctaw (11)	29	0.03
Colville (0)	0	<0.01
Comanche (0)	3	<0.01
Cree (0)	0	<0.01
Creek (5)	17	0.02
Crow (1)	2	<0.01
Delaware (5)	6	0.01
Hopi (1)	1	<0.01
Houma (0)	0	<0.01
Inupiat *(Alaska Native)* (0)	3	<0.01
Iroquois (8)	24	0.02
Kiowa (3)	3	<0.01
Lumbee (1)	2	<0.01
Menominee (0)	0	<0.01
Mexican American Ind. (52)	75	0.07
Navajo (31)	75	0.07
Osage (2)	3	<0.01
Ottawa (0)	2	<0.01
Paiute (2)	2	<0.01
Pima (6)	20	0.02
Potawatomi (12)	24	0.02
Pueblo (10)	18	0.02
Puget Sound Salish (0)	0	<0.01
Seminole (7)	8	0.01
Shoshone (1)	5	<0.01
Sioux (7)	25	0.02
South American Ind. (3)	8	0.01
Spanish American Ind. (1)	2	<0.01
Tlingit-Haida *(Alaska Native)* (0)	0	<0.01
Tohono O'Odham (2)	2	<0.01
Tsimshian *(Alaska Native)* (0)	0	<0.01
Ute (4)	4	<0.01
Yakama (2)	5	<0.01
Yaqui (3)	9	0.01
Yuman (6)	7	0.01
Yup'ik *(Alaska Native)* (0)	4	<0.01
Asian (9,765)	12,633	12.62
Not Hispanic (9,524)	11,786	11.77
Hispanic (241)	847	0.85
Bangladeshi (7)	7	0.01
Bhutanese (0)	0	<0.01
Burmese (6)	13	0.01
Cambodian (165)	208	0.21
Chinese, ex. Taiwanese (742)	1,184	1.18
Filipino (5,494)	6,969	6.96
Hmong (34)	46	0.05
Indian (478)	609	0.61
Indonesian (53)	116	0.12
Japanese (384)	1,005	1.00
Korean (859)	1,061	1.06
Laotian (281)	322	0.32
Malaysian (6)	10	0.01
Nepalese (22)	22	0.02
Pakistani (40)	46	0.05
Sri Lankan (5)	10	0.01
Taiwanese (50)	64	0.06
Thai (211)	303	0.30
Vietnamese (581)	777	0.78
Hawaii Native/Pacific Islander (368)	890	0.89
Not Hispanic (319)	716	0.72
Hispanic (49)	174	0.17
Fijian (5)	7	0.01
Guamanian/Chamorro (167)	303	0.30
Marshallese (0)	0	<0.01
Native Hawaiian (73)	305	0.30
Samoan (76)	155	0.15
Tongan (8)	11	0.01
White (70,880)	75,939	75.87
Not Hispanic (57,246)	60,422	60.36
Hispanic (13,634)	15,517	15.50

*Notes: † The Census 2010 population figure is used to calculate the percentages in the Hispanic Origin and Race categories. Ancestry percentages are based on the 2006-2010 American Community Survey population (not shown); ‡ Numbers in parentheses indicate the number of people reporting a single ancestry; * Numbers in parentheses indicate the number of persons reporting this race alone, not in combination with any other race; Please refer to the Explanation of Data for more information.*

Thousand Oaks

Place Type: City
County: Ventura
Population: 126,683

Ancestry	Population	%
Afghan (22)	22	0.02
African, Sub-Saharan (236)	301	0.24
African (72)	112	0.09
Cape Verdean (0)	0	<0.01
Ethiopian (0)	0	<0.01
Ghanaian (128)	128	0.10
Kenyan (0)	0	<0.01
Liberian (0)	0	<0.01
Nigerian (0)	0	<0.01
Senegalese (0)	0	<0.01
Sierra Leonean (0)	0	<0.01
Somalian (0)	0	<0.01
South African (36)	61	0.05
Sudanese (0)	0	<0.01
Ugandan (0)	0	<0.01
Zimbabwean (0)	0	<0.01
Other Sub-Saharan African (0)	0	<0.01
Albanian (92)	92	0.07
Alsatian (0)	25	0.02
American (5,973)	5,973	4.79
Arab (597)	1,219	0.98
Arab (104)	154	0.12
Egyptian (110)	166	0.13
Iraqi (0)	0	<0.01
Jordanian (0)	0	<0.01
Lebanese (216)	451	0.36
Moroccan (12)	12	0.01
Palestinian (0)	10	0.01
Syrian (19)	162	0.13
Other Arab (136)	264	0.21
Armenian (352)	578	0.46
Assyrian/Chaldean/Syriac (11)	22	0.02
Australian (63)	172	0.14
Austrian (212)	836	0.67
Basque (12)	28	0.02
Belgian (32)	109	0.09
Brazilian (26)	56	0.04
British (1,019)	1,514	1.21
Bulgarian (0)	11	0.01
Cajun (0)	23	0.02
Canadian (421)	725	0.58
Carpatho Rusyn (0)	0	<0.01
Celtic (13)	13	0.01
Croatian (58)	398	0.32
Cypriot (0)	0	<0.01
Czech (174)	661	0.53
Czechoslovakian (88)	189	0.15
Danish (406)	1,405	1.13
Dutch (540)	1,995	1.60
Eastern European (621)	674	0.54
English (3,710)	14,138	11.34
Estonian (8)	13	0.01
European (2,520)	2,952	2.37
Finnish (73)	238	0.19
French, ex. Basque (630)	3,983	3.19
French Canadian (186)	745	0.60
German (4,973)	18,494	14.83
German Russian (0)	0	<0.01
Greek (532)	929	0.75
Guyanese (0)	0	<0.01
Hungarian (420)	1,124	0.90
Icelander (0)	9	0.01
Iranian (1,111)	1,536	1.23
Irish (3,922)	15,400	12.35
Israeli (245)	384	0.31
Italian (3,917)	10,438	8.37
Latvian (0)	36	0.03
Lithuanian (153)	403	0.32
Luxemburger (0)	0	<0.01
Macedonian (0)	0	<0.01
Maltese (0)	0	<0.01
New Zealander (0)	0	<0.01
Northern European (234)	252	0.20
Norwegian (939)	2,592	2.08
Pennsylvania German (0)	10	0.01
Polish (1,457)	4,985	4.00
Portuguese (326)	647	0.52
Romanian (220)	494	0.40
Russian (1,888)	4,469	3.58
Scandinavian (158)	403	0.32
Scotch-Irish (766)	2,095	1.68
Scottish (1,076)	3,283	2.63
Serbian (38)	68	0.05
Slavic (31)	56	0.04
Slovak (81)	180	0.14
Slovene (21)	94	0.08
Soviet Union (0)	0	<0.01
Swedish (737)	3,155	2.53
Swiss (59)	279	0.22
Turkish (11)	145	0.12
Ukrainian (192)	544	0.44
Welsh (205)	1,003	0.80
West Indian, ex. Hispanic (70)	184	0.15
Bahamian (0)	29	0.02
Barbadian (0)	0	<0.01
Belizean (23)	23	0.02
Bermudan (0)	0	<0.01
British West Indian (0)	0	<0.01
Dutch West Indian (0)	10	0.01
Haitian (13)	46	0.04
Jamaican (13)	55	0.04
Trinidadian/Tobagonian (0)	0	<0.01
U.S. Virgin Islander (0)	0	<0.01
West Indian (21)	21	0.02
Other West Indian (0)	0	<0.01
Yugoslavian (75)	126	0.10

Hispanic Origin	Population	%
Hispanic or Latino (of any race)	21,341	16.85
Central American, ex. Mexican	2,441	1.93
Costa Rican	87	0.07
Guatemalan	1,173	0.93
Honduran	102	0.08
Nicaraguan	231	0.18
Panamanian	37	0.03
Salvadoran	793	0.63
Other Central American	18	0.01
Cuban	280	0.22
Dominican Republic	31	0.02
Mexican	14,671	11.58
Puerto Rican	466	0.37
South American	1,325	1.05
Argentinean	278	0.22
Bolivian	22	0.02
Chilean	112	0.09
Colombian	285	0.22
Ecuadorian	145	0.11
Paraguayan	4	<0.01
Peruvian	390	0.31
Uruguayan	23	0.02
Venezuelan	42	0.03
Other South American	24	0.02
Other Hispanic or Latino	2,127	1.68

Race*	Population	%
African-American/Black (1,674)	2,375	1.87
Not Hispanic (1,508)	2,047	1.62
Hispanic (166)	328	0.26
American Indian/Alaska Native (497)	1,385	1.09
Not Hispanic (231)	806	0.64
Hispanic (266)	579	0.46
Alaska Athabascan *(Ala. Nat.)* (0)	0	<0.01
Aleut *(Alaska Native)* (1)	1	<0.01
Apache (18)	60	0.05
Arapaho (1)	1	<0.01
Blackfeet (1)	20	0.02
Canadian/French Am. Ind. (0)	4	<0.01
Central American Ind. (5)	11	0.01
Cherokee (61)	265	0.21
Cheyenne (0)	8	0.01
Chickasaw (5)	14	0.01
Chippewa (10)	19	0.01
Choctaw (16)	76	0.06
Colville (1)	1	<0.01
Comanche (3)	9	0.01
Cree (1)	6	<0.01
Creek (0)	6	<0.01
Crow (3)	4	<0.01
Delaware (0)	1	<0.01
Hopi (1)	5	<0.01
Houma (0)	0	<0.01
Inupiat *(Alaska Native)* (0)	0	<0.01
Iroquois (2)	19	0.01
Kiowa (0)	1	<0.01
Lumbee (0)	4	<0.01
Menominee (0)	1	<0.01
Mexican American Ind. (94)	148	0.12
Navajo (8)	24	0.02
Osage (4)	6	<0.01
Ottawa (0)	0	<0.01
Paiute (0)	2	<0.01
Pima (1)	3	<0.01
Potawatomi (3)	3	<0.01
Pueblo (4)	6	<0.01
Puget Sound Salish (0)	0	<0.01
Seminole (0)	1	<0.01
Shoshone (1)	2	<0.01
Sioux (7)	38	0.03
South American Ind. (10)	21	0.02
Spanish American Ind. (1)	4	<0.01
Tlingit-Haida *(Alaska Native)* (0)	2	<0.01
Tohono O'Odham (8)	9	0.01
Tsimshian *(Alaska Native)* (0)	0	<0.01
Ute (2)	5	<0.01
Yakama (0)	0	<0.01
Yaqui (9)	15	0.01
Yuman (0)	1	<0.01
Yup'ik *(Alaska Native)* (0)	0	<0.01
Asian (11,043)	13,559	10.70
Not Hispanic (10,928)	13,169	10.40
Hispanic (115)	390	0.31
Bangladeshi (23)	28	0.02
Bhutanese (4)	4	<0.01
Burmese (12)	23	0.02
Cambodian (50)	69	0.05
Chinese, ex. Taiwanese (3,460)	4,113	3.25
Filipino (1,324)	1,967	1.55
Hmong (4)	7	0.01
Indian (2,518)	2,753	2.17
Indonesian (52)	129	0.10
Japanese (916)	1,640	1.29
Korean (1,097)	1,310	1.03
Laotian (7)	10	0.01
Malaysian (13)	26	0.02
Nepalese (5)	8	0.01
Pakistani (164)	187	0.15
Sri Lankan (95)	115	0.09
Taiwanese (321)	346	0.27
Thai (117)	147	0.12
Vietnamese (514)	613	0.48
Hawaii Native/Pacific Islander (146)	488	0.39
Not Hispanic (134)	419	0.33
Hispanic (12)	69	0.05
Fijian (2)	7	0.01
Guamanian/Chamorro (14)	50	0.04
Marshallese (1)	1	<0.01
Native Hawaiian (66)	210	0.17
Samoan (22)	54	0.04
Tongan (20)	37	0.03
White (101,702)	105,955	83.64
Not Hispanic (88,970)	91,960	72.59
Hispanic (12,732)	13,995	11.05

*Notes: † The Census 2010 population figure is used to calculate the percentages in the Hispanic Origin and Race categories. Ancestry percentages are based on the 2006-2010 American Community Survey population (not shown); ‡ Numbers in parentheses indicate the number of people reporting a single ancestry; * Numbers in parentheses indicate the number of persons reporting this race alone, not in combination with any other race; Please refer to the Explanation of Data for more information.*

Torrance

Place Type: City
County: Los Angeles
Population: 145,438

Ancestry	Population	%
Afghan (273)	298	0.21
African, Sub-Saharan (748)	923	0.64
African (413)	550	0.38
Cape Verdean (0)	0	<0.01
Ethiopian (63)	63	0.04
Ghanaian (0)	0	<0.01
Kenyan (15)	15	0.01
Liberian (23)	23	0.02
Nigerian (201)	219	0.15
Senegalese (0)	0	<0.01
Sierra Leonean (0)	0	<0.01
Somalian (0)	0	<0.01
South African (16)	16	0.01
Sudanese (0)	0	<0.01
Ugandan (0)	20	0.01
Zimbabwean (0)	0	<0.01
Other Sub-Saharan African (17)	17	0.01
Albanian (6)	6	<0.01
Alsatian (0)	15	0.01
American (5,526)	5,526	3.84
Arab (930)	1,417	0.98
Arab (86)	310	0.22
Egyptian (312)	341	0.24
Iraqi (0)	0	<0.01
Jordanian (43)	86	0.06
Lebanese (178)	246	0.17
Moroccan (174)	174	0.12
Palestinian (0)	43	0.03
Syrian (104)	153	0.11
Other Arab (33)	64	0.04
Armenian (353)	485	0.34
Assyrian/Chaldean/Syriac (0)	0	<0.01
Australian (54)	122	0.08
Austrian (135)	316	0.22
Basque (9)	16	0.01
Belgian (28)	132	0.09
Brazilian (182)	280	0.19
British (413)	692	0.48
Bulgarian (12)	70	0.05
Cajun (0)	0	<0.01
Canadian (393)	769	0.53
Carpatho Rusyn (0)	13	0.01
Celtic (34)	34	0.02
Croatian (117)	390	0.27
Cypriot (0)	0	<0.01
Czech (156)	657	0.46
Czechoslovakian (65)	100	0.07
Danish (278)	1,058	0.73
Dutch (516)	1,908	1.33
Eastern European (170)	175	0.12
English (2,960)	11,936	8.29
Estonian (12)	48	0.03
European (918)	1,147	0.80
Finnish (138)	367	0.25
French, ex. Basque (471)	3,284	2.28
French Canadian (240)	677	0.47
German (3,990)	15,947	11.08
German Russian (0)	0	<0.01
Greek (562)	900	0.63
Guyanese (14)	14	0.01
Hungarian (258)	780	0.54
Icelander (0)	42	0.03
Iranian (886)	1,102	0.77
Irish (3,625)	12,483	8.67
Israeli (65)	102	0.07
Italian (2,694)	7,293	5.07
Latvian (8)	112	0.08
Lithuanian (264)	536	0.37
Luxemburger (0)	22	0.02
Macedonian (0)	0	<0.01
Maltese (9)	9	0.01
New Zealander (14)	154	0.11
Northern European (159)	172	0.12
Norwegian (516)	1,798	1.25
Pennsylvania German (29)	70	0.05
Polish (665)	2,184	1.52
Portuguese (260)	666	0.46
Romanian (148)	387	0.27
Russian (678)	1,918	1.33
Scandinavian (202)	466	0.32
Scotch-Irish (401)	1,637	1.14
Scottish (710)	2,577	1.79
Serbian (138)	151	0.10
Slavic (0)	0	<0.01
Slovak (98)	181	0.13
Slovene (0)	108	0.08
Soviet Union (0)	0	<0.01
Swedish (556)	1,859	1.29
Swiss (66)	339	0.24
Turkish (140)	459	0.32
Ukrainian (126)	270	0.19
Welsh (73)	671	0.47
West Indian, ex. Hispanic (141)	198	0.14
Bahamian (0)	0	<0.01
Barbadian (0)	0	<0.01
Belizean (48)	88	0.06
Bermudan (0)	0	<0.01
British West Indian (0)	0	<0.01
Dutch West Indian (29)	38	0.03
Haitian (0)	0	<0.01
Jamaican (0)	8	0.01
Trinidadian/Tobagonian (29)	29	0.02
U.S. Virgin Islander (0)	0	<0.01
West Indian (35)	35	0.02
Other West Indian (0)	0	<0.01
Yugoslavian (136)	320	0.22

Hispanic Origin	Population	%
Hispanic or Latino (of any race)	23,440	16.12
Central American, ex. Mexican	2,147	1.48
Costa Rican	218	0.15
Guatemalan	630	0.43
Honduran	168	0.12
Nicaraguan	342	0.24
Panamanian	50	0.03
Salvadoran	723	0.50
Other Central American	16	0.01
Cuban	882	0.61
Dominican Republic	71	0.05
Mexican	14,880	10.23
Puerto Rican	731	0.50
South American	2,540	1.75
Argentinean	371	0.26
Bolivian	49	0.03
Chilean	221	0.15
Colombian	498	0.34
Ecuadorian	295	0.20
Paraguayan	2	<0.01
Peruvian	955	0.66
Uruguayan	23	0.02
Venezuelan	84	0.06
Other South American	42	0.03
Other Hispanic or Latino	2,189	1.51

Race*	Population	%
African-American/Black (3,955)	5,072	3.49
Not Hispanic (3,740)	4,587	3.15
Hispanic (215)	485	0.33
American Indian/Alaska Native (554)	1,532	1.05
Not Hispanic (304)	927	0.64
Hispanic (250)	605	0.42
Alaska Athabascan *(Ala. Nat.)* (0)	1	<0.01
Aleut *(Alaska Native)* (3)	6	<0.01
Apache (17)	62	0.04
Arapaho (0)	1	<0.01
Blackfeet (13)	40	0.03
Canadian/French Am. Ind. (1)	4	<0.01
Central American Ind. (3)	6	<0.01
Cherokee (53)	297	0.20
Cheyenne (0)	16	0.01
Chickasaw (7)	22	0.02
Chippewa (11)	26	0.02
Choctaw (24)	54	0.04
Colville (1)	1	<0.01
Comanche (1)	7	<0.01
Cree (2)	7	<0.01
Creek (5)	16	0.01
Crow (0)	0	<0.01
Delaware (2)	5	<0.01
Hopi (0)	3	<0.01
Houma (0)	0	<0.01
Inupiat *(Alaska Native)* (1)	1	<0.01
Iroquois (7)	19	0.01
Kiowa (1)	1	<0.01
Lumbee (4)	4	<0.01
Menominee (2)	2	<0.01
Mexican American Ind. (39)	77	0.05
Navajo (27)	42	0.03
Osage (4)	13	0.01
Ottawa (0)	0	<0.01
Paiute (3)	4	<0.01
Pima (1)	1	<0.01
Potawatomi (7)	11	0.01
Pueblo (7)	8	0.01
Puget Sound Salish (6)	13	0.01
Seminole (1)	10	0.01
Shoshone (0)	4	<0.01
Sioux (6)	32	0.02
South American Ind. (7)	26	0.02
Spanish American Ind. (11)	13	0.01
Tlingit-Haida *(Alaska Native)* (3)	3	<0.01
Tohono O'Odham (1)	8	0.01
Tsimshian *(Alaska Native)* (1)	1	<0.01
Ute (3)	3	<0.01
Yakama (0)	1	<0.01
Yaqui (10)	26	0.02
Yuman (0)	0	<0.01
Yup'ik *(Alaska Native)* (0)	0	<0.01
Asian (50,240)	55,499	38.16
Not Hispanic (49,707)	54,136	37.22
Hispanic (533)	1,363	0.94
Bangladeshi (53)	58	0.04
Bhutanese (0)	0	<0.01
Burmese (81)	103	0.07
Cambodian (77)	100	0.07
Chinese, ex. Taiwanese (6,373)	8,045	5.53
Filipino (4,965)	6,715	4.62
Hmong (16)	19	0.01
Indian (3,921)	4,290	2.95
Indonesian (112)	221	0.15
Japanese (15,465)	18,532	12.74
Korean (12,092)	12,779	8.79
Laotian (17)	28	0.02
Malaysian (27)	33	0.02
Nepalese (29)	33	0.02
Pakistani (943)	1,050	0.72
Sri Lankan (238)	266	0.18
Taiwanese (1,271)	1,436	0.99
Thai (389)	524	0.36
Vietnamese (2,137)	2,369	1.63
Hawaii Native/Pacific Islander (530)	1,363	0.94
Not Hispanic (473)	1,118	0.77
Hispanic (57)	245	0.17
Fijian (8)	14	0.01
Guamanian/Chamorro (59)	137	0.09
Marshallese (0)	0	<0.01
Native Hawaiian (163)	634	0.44
Samoan (219)	380	0.26
Tongan (8)	17	0.01
White (74,333)	81,103	55.76
Not Hispanic (61,591)	66,475	45.71
Hispanic (12,742)	14,628	10.06

*Notes: † The Census 2010 population figure is used to calculate the percentages in the Hispanic Origin and Race categories. Ancestry percentages are based on the 2006-2010 American Community Survey population (not shown); ‡ Numbers in parentheses indicate the number of people reporting a single ancestry; * Numbers in parentheses indicate the number of persons reporting this race alone, not in combination with any other race; Please refer to the Explanation of Data for more information.*

Tracy

Place Type: City
County: San Joaquin
Population: 82,922

Ancestry	Population	%
Afghan (945)	953	1.20
African, Sub-Saharan (314)	335	0.42
African (314)	324	0.41
Cape Verdean (0)	11	0.01
Ethiopian (0)	0	<0.01
Ghanaian (0)	0	<0.01
Kenyan (0)	0	<0.01
Liberian (0)	0	<0.01
Nigerian (0)	0	<0.01
Senegalese (0)	0	<0.01
Sierra Leonean (0)	0	<0.01
Somalian (0)	0	<0.01
South African (0)	0	<0.01
Sudanese (0)	0	<0.01
Ugandan (0)	0	<0.01
Zimbabwean (0)	0	<0.01
Other Sub-Saharan African (0)	0	<0.01
Albanian (0)	0	<0.01
Alsatian (0)	0	<0.01
American (1,188)	1,188	1.50
Arab (332)	402	0.51
Arab (55)	55	0.07
Egyptian (92)	116	0.15
Iraqi (0)	0	<0.01
Jordanian (0)	0	<0.01
Lebanese (0)	46	0.06
Moroccan (9)	9	0.01
Palestinian (29)	29	0.04
Syrian (0)	0	<0.01
Other Arab (147)	147	0.19
Armenian (0)	54	0.07
Assyrian/Chaldean/Syriac (0)	0	<0.01
Australian (0)	0	<0.01
Austrian (0)	9	0.01
Basque (77)	134	0.17
Belgian (13)	88	0.11
Brazilian (28)	28	0.04
British (28)	133	0.17
Bulgarian (9)	18	0.02
Cajun (0)	0	<0.01
Canadian (58)	194	0.24
Carpatho Rusyn (0)	0	<0.01
Celtic (0)	0	<0.01
Croatian (11)	23	0.03
Cypriot (0)	0	<0.01
Czech (55)	132	0.17
Czechoslovakian (43)	43	0.05
Danish (11)	300	0.38
Dutch (64)	536	0.67
Eastern European (10)	10	0.01
English (668)	3,870	4.87
Estonian (0)	0	<0.01
European (501)	612	0.77
Finnish (59)	168	0.21
French, ex. Basque (112)	1,994	2.51
French Canadian (37)	59	0.07
German (1,639)	7,749	9.76
German Russian (0)	0	<0.01
Greek (26)	417	0.53
Guyanese (0)	0	<0.01
Hungarian (142)	224	0.28
Icelander (0)	0	<0.01
Iranian (32)	116	0.15
Irish (1,034)	5,930	7.47
Israeli (0)	0	<0.01
Italian (1,195)	4,587	5.78
Latvian (0)	0	<0.01
Lithuanian (0)	0	<0.01
Luxemburger (0)	15	0.02
Macedonian (0)	0	<0.01
Maltese (5)	5	0.01
New Zealander (0)	0	<0.01
Northern European (17)	17	0.02
Norwegian (134)	701	0.88
Pennsylvania German (0)	0	<0.01
Polish (185)	836	1.05
Portuguese (1,632)	3,855	4.85
Romanian (20)	52	0.07
Russian (77)	272	0.34
Scandinavian (51)	116	0.15
Scotch-Irish (266)	764	0.96
Scottish (453)	1,036	1.30
Serbian (20)	68	0.09
Slavic (0)	0	<0.01
Slovak (41)	63	0.08
Slovene (0)	0	<0.01
Soviet Union (0)	0	<0.01
Swedish (151)	1,195	1.50
Swiss (12)	190	0.24
Turkish (0)	0	<0.01
Ukrainian (23)	31	0.04
Welsh (13)	412	0.52
West Indian, ex. Hispanic (9)	125	0.16
Bahamian (0)	0	<0.01
Barbadian (0)	27	0.03
Belizean (9)	18	0.02
Bermudan (0)	0	<0.01
British West Indian (0)	0	<0.01
Dutch West Indian (0)	0	<0.01
Haitian (0)	0	<0.01
Jamaican (0)	27	0.03
Trinidadian/Tobagonian (0)	0	<0.01
U.S. Virgin Islander (0)	0	<0.01
West Indian (0)	53	0.07
Other West Indian (0)	0	<0.01
Yugoslavian (20)	68	0.09

Hispanic Origin	Population	%
Hispanic or Latino (of any race)	30,557	36.85
Central American, ex. Mexican	1,690	2.04
Costa Rican	33	0.04
Guatemalan	260	0.31
Honduran	65	0.08
Nicaraguan	427	0.51
Panamanian	58	0.07
Salvadoran	835	1.01
Other Central American	12	0.01
Cuban	136	0.16
Dominican Republic	17	0.02
Mexican	25,099	30.27
Puerto Rican	906	1.09
South American	632	0.76
Argentinean	47	0.06
Bolivian	42	0.05
Chilean	66	0.08
Colombian	68	0.08
Ecuadorian	34	0.04
Paraguayan	3	<0.01
Peruvian	337	0.41
Uruguayan	5	0.01
Venezuelan	19	0.02
Other South American	11	0.01
Other Hispanic or Latino	2,077	2.50

Race*	Population	%
African-American/Black (5,953)	7,315	8.82
Not Hispanic (5,636)	6,639	8.01
Hispanic (317)	676	0.82
American Indian/Alaska Native (715)	1,749	2.11
Not Hispanic (297)	923	1.11
Hispanic (418)	826	1.00
Alaska Athabascan *(Ala. Nat.)* (0)	1	<0.01
Aleut *(Alaska Native)* (3)	7	0.01
Apache (23)	75	0.09
Arapaho (0)	0	<0.01
Blackfeet (4)	66	0.08
Canadian/French Am. Ind. (3)	5	0.01
Central American Ind. (3)	6	0.01
Cherokee (67)	269	0.32
Cheyenne (0)	1	<0.01
Chickasaw (1)	13	0.02
Chippewa (5)	16	0.02
Choctaw (31)	84	0.10
Colville (0)	0	<0.01
Comanche (9)	13	0.02
Cree (1)	3	<0.01
Creek (2)	13	0.02
Crow (0)	0	<0.01
Delaware (0)	2	<0.01
Hopi (1)	5	0.01
Houma (0)	0	<0.01
Inupiat *(Alaska Native)* (1)	6	0.01
Iroquois (2)	8	0.01
Kiowa (0)	0	<0.01
Lumbee (5)	5	0.01
Menominee (0)	0	<0.01
Mexican American Ind. (69)	112	0.14
Navajo (30)	71	0.09
Osage (1)	1	<0.01
Ottawa (0)	0	<0.01
Paiute (17)	32	0.04
Pima (1)	3	<0.01
Potawatomi (3)	11	0.01
Pueblo (6)	32	0.04
Puget Sound Salish (4)	5	0.01
Seminole (4)	7	0.01
Shoshone (0)	7	0.01
Sioux (19)	47	0.06
South American Ind. (11)	12	0.01
Spanish American Ind. (3)	6	0.01
Tlingit-Haida *(Alaska Native)* (2)	2	<0.01
Tohono O'Odham (5)	10	0.01
Tsimshian *(Alaska Native)* (0)	0	<0.01
Ute (0)	4	<0.01
Yakama (0)	3	<0.01
Yaqui (9)	13	0.02
Yuman (0)	0	<0.01
Yup'ik *(Alaska Native)* (0)	0	<0.01
Asian (12,229)	15,260	18.40
Not Hispanic (11,803)	14,196	17.12
Hispanic (426)	1,064	1.28
Bangladeshi (7)	7	0.01
Bhutanese (0)	0	<0.01
Burmese (49)	62	0.07
Cambodian (237)	299	0.36
Chinese, ex. Taiwanese (1,033)	1,528	1.84
Filipino (5,319)	6,666	8.04
Hmong (12)	17	0.02
Indian (3,088)	3,395	4.09
Indonesian (48)	101	0.12
Japanese (239)	629	0.76
Korean (245)	370	0.45
Laotian (133)	167	0.20
Malaysian (5)	6	0.01
Nepalese (19)	19	0.02
Pakistani (330)	360	0.43
Sri Lankan (33)	35	0.04
Taiwanese (33)	47	0.06
Thai (60)	98	0.12
Vietnamese (889)	1,046	1.26
Hawaii Native/Pacific Islander (747)	1,466	1.77
Not Hispanic (641)	1,155	1.39
Hispanic (106)	311	0.38
Fijian (182)	222	0.27
Guamanian/Chamorro (140)	254	0.31
Marshallese (0)	2	<0.01
Native Hawaiian (113)	393	0.47
Samoan (172)	280	0.34
Tongan (70)	97	0.12
White (43,724)	48,862	58.93
Not Hispanic (30,005)	33,032	39.84
Hispanic (13,719)	15,830	19.09

*Notes: † The Census 2010 population figure is used to calculate the percentages in the Hispanic Origin and Race categories. Ancestry percentages are based on the 2006-2010 American Community Survey population (not shown); ‡ Numbers in parentheses indicate the number of people reporting a single ancestry; * Numbers in parentheses indicate the number of persons reporting this race alone, not in combination with any other race; Please refer to the Explanation of Data for more information.*

Tulare

Place Type: City
County: Tulare
Population: 59,278

Ancestry	Population	%
Afghan (0)	0	<0.01
African, Sub-Saharan (50)	82	0.14
African (26)	58	0.10
Cape Verdean (0)	0	<0.01
Ethiopian (24)	24	0.04
Ghanaian (0)	0	<0.01
Kenyan (0)	0	<0.01
Liberian (0)	0	<0.01
Nigerian (0)	0	<0.01
Senegalese (0)	0	<0.01
Sierra Leonean (0)	0	<0.01
Somalian (0)	0	<0.01
South African (0)	0	<0.01
Sudanese (0)	0	<0.01
Ugandan (0)	0	<0.01
Zimbabwean (0)	0	<0.01
Other Sub-Saharan African (0)	0	<0.01
Albanian (0)	0	<0.01
Alsatian (0)	0	<0.01
American (1,939)	1,939	3.41
Arab (18)	60	0.11
Arab (0)	0	<0.01
Egyptian (0)	5	0.01
Iraqi (0)	0	<0.01
Jordanian (0)	0	<0.01
Lebanese (8)	20	0.04
Moroccan (0)	0	<0.01
Palestinian (10)	19	0.03
Syrian (0)	0	<0.01
Other Arab (0)	16	0.03
Armenian (44)	116	0.20
Assyrian/Chaldean/Syriac (0)	10	0.02
Australian (26)	34	0.06
Austrian (0)	24	0.04
Basque (0)	0	<0.01
Belgian (5)	107	0.19
Brazilian (44)	44	0.08
British (0)	19	0.03
Bulgarian (0)	0	<0.01
Cajun (0)	0	<0.01
Canadian (38)	63	0.11
Carpatho Rusyn (0)	0	<0.01
Celtic (0)	0	<0.01
Croatian (0)	46	0.08
Cypriot (0)	0	<0.01
Czech (99)	99	0.17
Czechoslovakian (0)	0	<0.01
Danish (34)	62	0.11
Dutch (286)	856	1.50
Eastern European (0)	0	<0.01
English (1,582)	3,009	5.28
Estonian (0)	0	<0.01
European (117)	117	0.21
Finnish (0)	0	<0.01
French, ex. Basque (107)	434	0.76
French Canadian (24)	53	0.09
German (895)	3,096	5.44
German Russian (0)	0	<0.01
Greek (0)	24	0.04
Guyanese (0)	0	<0.01
Hungarian (14)	39	0.07
Icelander (0)	0	<0.01
Iranian (26)	26	0.05
Irish (786)	2,856	5.02
Israeli (140)	140	0.25
Italian (187)	629	1.10
Latvian (0)	0	<0.01
Lithuanian (15)	25	0.04
Luxemburger (0)	0	<0.01
Macedonian (0)	0	<0.01
Maltese (0)	0	<0.01
New Zealander (0)	0	<0.01
Northern European (138)	138	0.24
Norwegian (31)	272	0.48
Pennsylvania German (0)	0	<0.01
Polish (141)	338	0.59
Portuguese (3,625)	4,347	7.63
Romanian (7)	19	0.03
Russian (39)	95	0.17
Scandinavian (0)	7	0.01
Scotch-Irish (179)	504	0.89
Scottish (81)	253	0.44
Serbian (0)	0	<0.01
Slavic (9)	9	0.02
Slovak (0)	0	<0.01
Slovene (0)	0	<0.01
Soviet Union (0)	0	<0.01
Swedish (31)	290	0.51
Swiss (0)	38	0.07
Turkish (0)	0	<0.01
Ukrainian (0)	0	<0.01
Welsh (28)	221	0.39
West Indian, ex. Hispanic (36)	46	0.08
Bahamian (0)	0	<0.01
Barbadian (0)	10	0.02
Belizean (0)	0	<0.01
Bermudan (0)	0	<0.01
British West Indian (0)	0	<0.01
Dutch West Indian (0)	0	<0.01
Haitian (36)	36	0.06
Jamaican (0)	0	<0.01
Trinidadian/Tobagonian (0)	0	<0.01
U.S. Virgin Islander (0)	0	<0.01
West Indian (0)	0	<0.01
Other West Indian (0)	0	<0.01
Yugoslavian (0)	0	<0.01

Hispanic Origin	Population	%
Hispanic or Latino (of any race)	34,062	57.46
Central American, ex. Mexican	364	0.61
Costa Rican	8	0.01
Guatemalan	88	0.15
Honduran	21	0.04
Nicaraguan	46	0.08
Panamanian	4	0.01
Salvadoran	194	0.33
Other Central American	3	0.01
Cuban	28	0.05
Dominican Republic	6	0.01
Mexican	31,539	53.21
Puerto Rican	210	0.35
South American	78	0.13
Argentinean	11	0.02
Bolivian	8	0.01
Chilean	4	0.01
Colombian	11	0.02
Ecuadorian	2	<0.01
Paraguayan	0	<0.01
Peruvian	35	0.06
Uruguayan	2	<0.01
Venezuelan	5	0.01
Other South American	0	<0.01
Other Hispanic or Latino	1,837	3.10

Race*	Population	%
African-American/Black (2,328)	2,898	4.89
Not Hispanic (1,987)	2,297	3.87
Hispanic (341)	601	1.01
American Indian/Alaska Native (694)	1,374	2.32
Not Hispanic (296)	688	1.16
Hispanic (398)	686	1.16
Alaska Athabascan *(Ala. Nat.)* (0)	0	<0.01
Aleut *(Alaska Native)* (0)	1	<0.01
Apache (20)	32	0.05
Arapaho (0)	0	<0.01
Blackfeet (5)	14	0.02
Canadian/French Am. Ind. (2)	3	0.01
Central American Ind. (1)	2	<0.01
Cherokee (45)	178	0.30
Cheyenne (1)	7	0.01
Chickasaw (13)	19	0.03
Chippewa (4)	7	0.01
Choctaw (59)	106	0.18
Colville (0)	2	<0.01
Comanche (3)	8	0.01
Cree (0)	0	<0.01
Creek (6)	12	0.02
Crow (1)	1	<0.01
Delaware (0)	0	<0.01
Hopi (9)	9	0.02
Houma (0)	0	<0.01
Inupiat *(Alaska Native)* (0)	4	0.01
Iroquois (0)	1	<0.01
Kiowa (0)	1	<0.01
Lumbee (0)	1	<0.01
Menominee (0)	0	<0.01
Mexican American Ind. (42)	63	0.11
Navajo (2)	12	0.02
Osage (1)	1	<0.01
Ottawa (0)	13	0.02
Paiute (2)	2	<0.01
Pima (1)	5	0.01
Potawatomi (4)	11	0.02
Pueblo (2)	8	0.01
Puget Sound Salish (0)	6	0.01
Seminole (4)	15	0.03
Shoshone (0)	0	<0.01
Sioux (14)	34	0.06
South American Ind. (1)	4	0.01
Spanish American Ind. (1)	1	<0.01
Tlingit-Haida *(Alaska Native)* (0)	1	<0.01
Tohono O'Odham (2)	5	0.01
Tsimshian *(Alaska Native)* (0)	0	<0.01
Ute (0)	0	<0.01
Yakama (0)	0	<0.01
Yaqui (16)	27	0.05
Yuman (2)	4	0.01
Yup'ik *(Alaska Native)* (0)	0	<0.01
Asian (1,276)	1,752	2.96
Not Hispanic (1,144)	1,457	2.46
Hispanic (132)	295	0.50
Bangladeshi (0)	0	<0.01
Bhutanese (0)	0	<0.01
Burmese (0)	0	<0.01
Cambodian (14)	21	0.04
Chinese, ex. Taiwanese (121)	203	0.34
Filipino (318)	523	0.88
Hmong (77)	79	0.13
Indian (313)	350	0.59
Indonesian (3)	5	0.01
Japanese (38)	101	0.17
Korean (26)	37	0.06
Laotian (53)	63	0.11
Malaysian (0)	0	<0.01
Nepalese (0)	0	<0.01
Pakistani (9)	9	0.02
Sri Lankan (0)	0	<0.01
Taiwanese (1)	1	<0.01
Thai (199)	210	0.35
Vietnamese (53)	65	0.11
Hawaii Native/Pacific Islander (80)	258	0.44
Not Hispanic (52)	168	0.28
Hispanic (28)	90	0.15
Fijian (0)	0	<0.01
Guamanian/Chamorro (12)	30	0.05
Marshallese (1)	1	<0.01
Native Hawaiian (10)	78	0.13
Samoan (6)	22	0.04
Tongan (19)	31	0.05
White (36,347)	38,776	65.41
Not Hispanic (20,597)	21,558	36.37
Hispanic (15,750)	17,218	29.05

*Notes: † The Census 2010 population figure is used to calculate the percentages in the Hispanic Origin and Race categories. Ancestry percentages are based on the 2006-2010 American Community Survey population (not shown); ‡ Numbers in parentheses indicate the number of people reporting a single ancestry; * Numbers in parentheses indicate the number of persons reporting this race alone, not in combination with any other race; Please refer to the Explanation of Data for more information.*

Turlock

Place Type: City
County: Stanislaus
Population: 68,549

Ancestry	Population	%
Afghan (0)	0	<0.01
African, Sub-Saharan (156)	194	0.29
African (127)	157	0.23
Cape Verdean (0)	0	<0.01
Ethiopian (0)	0	<0.01
Ghanaian (0)	0	<0.01
Kenyan (29)	29	0.04
Liberian (0)	0	<0.01
Nigerian (0)	0	<0.01
Senegalese (0)	0	<0.01
Sierra Leonean (0)	0	<0.01
Somalian (0)	0	<0.01
South African (0)	0	<0.01
Sudanese (0)	0	<0.01
Ugandan (0)	0	<0.01
Zimbabwean (0)	0	<0.01
Other Sub-Saharan African (0)	8	0.01
Albanian (0)	0	<0.01
Alsatian (0)	0	<0.01
American (1,476)	1,476	2.19
Arab (175)	190	0.28
Arab (0)	0	<0.01
Egyptian (0)	0	<0.01
Iraqi (46)	61	0.09
Jordanian (0)	0	<0.01
Lebanese (59)	59	0.09
Moroccan (0)	0	<0.01
Palestinian (0)	0	<0.01
Syrian (4)	4	0.01
Other Arab (66)	66	0.10
Armenian (75)	219	0.33
Assyrian/Chaldean/Syriac (5,495)	5,798	8.61
Australian (10)	23	0.03
Austrian (60)	92	0.14
Basque (22)	22	0.03
Belgian (25)	37	0.05
Brazilian (12)	12	0.02
British (84)	173	0.26
Bulgarian (0)	0	<0.01
Cajun (0)	0	<0.01
Canadian (50)	72	0.11
Carpatho Rusyn (0)	0	<0.01
Celtic (0)	0	<0.01
Croatian (14)	28	0.04
Cypriot (0)	0	<0.01
Czech (10)	31	0.05
Czechoslovakian (9)	31	0.05
Danish (177)	331	0.49
Dutch (307)	1,316	1.95
Eastern European (8)	8	0.01
English (1,090)	4,549	6.75
Estonian (0)	8	0.01
European (393)	474	0.70
Finnish (14)	41	0.06
French, ex. Basque (125)	1,172	1.74
French Canadian (17)	82	0.12
German (2,022)	8,224	12.21
German Russian (0)	0	<0.01
Greek (48)	82	0.12
Guyanese (0)	0	<0.01
Hungarian (0)	8	0.01
Icelander (0)	0	<0.01
Iranian (578)	721	1.07
Irish (831)	5,148	7.64
Israeli (0)	0	<0.01
Italian (677)	2,785	4.13
Latvian (0)	0	<0.01
Lithuanian (60)	136	0.20
Luxemburger (0)	0	<0.01
Macedonian (0)	0	<0.01
Maltese (0)	0	<0.01
New Zealander (0)	0	<0.01
Northern European (137)	150	0.22
Norwegian (250)	855	1.27
Pennsylvania German (21)	30	0.04
Polish (56)	332	0.49
Portuguese (2,885)	5,184	7.69
Romanian (0)	13	0.02
Russian (97)	128	0.19
Scandinavian (137)	238	0.35
Scotch-Irish (113)	611	0.91
Scottish (255)	1,504	2.23
Serbian (0)	0	<0.01
Slavic (11)	45	0.07
Slovak (0)	0	<0.01
Slovene (0)	0	<0.01
Soviet Union (0)	0	<0.01
Swedish (528)	1,746	2.59
Swiss (65)	249	0.37
Turkish (0)	0	<0.01
Ukrainian (10)	10	0.01
Welsh (38)	383	0.57
West Indian, ex. Hispanic (0)	10	0.01
Bahamian (0)	0	<0.01
Barbadian (0)	0	<0.01
Belizean (0)	0	<0.01
Bermudan (0)	0	<0.01
British West Indian (0)	0	<0.01
Dutch West Indian (0)	10	0.01
Haitian (0)	0	<0.01
Jamaican (0)	0	<0.01
Trinidadian/Tobagonian (0)	0	<0.01
U.S. Virgin Islander (0)	0	<0.01
West Indian (0)	0	<0.01
Other West Indian (0)	0	<0.01
Yugoslavian (48)	48	0.07

Hispanic Origin	Population	%
Hispanic or Latino (of any race)	24,957	36.41
Central American, ex. Mexican	482	0.70
Costa Rican	10	0.01
Guatemalan	162	0.24
Honduran	44	0.06
Nicaraguan	89	0.13
Panamanian	9	0.01
Salvadoran	164	0.24
Other Central American	4	0.01
Cuban	27	0.04
Dominican Republic	5	0.01
Mexican	22,605	32.98
Puerto Rican	324	0.47
South American	240	0.35
Argentinean	21	0.03
Bolivian	11	0.02
Chilean	30	0.04
Colombian	112	0.16
Ecuadorian	10	0.01
Paraguayan	0	<0.01
Peruvian	53	0.08
Uruguayan	0	<0.01
Venezuelan	2	<0.01
Other South American	1	<0.01
Other Hispanic or Latino	1,274	1.86

Race*	Population	%
African-American/Black (1,160)	1,595	2.33
Not Hispanic (1,018)	1,337	1.95
Hispanic (142)	258	0.38
American Indian/Alaska Native (601)	1,291	1.88
Not Hispanic (316)	767	1.12
Hispanic (285)	524	0.76
Alaska Athabascan *(Ala. Nat.)* (1)	1	<0.01
Aleut *(Alaska Native)* (2)	6	0.01
Apache (20)	48	0.07
Arapaho (1)	6	0.01
Blackfeet (8)	26	0.04
Canadian/French Am. Ind. (0)	3	<0.01
Central American Ind. (0)	2	<0.01
Cherokee (83)	304	0.44
Cheyenne (1)	3	<0.01
Chickasaw (5)	10	0.01
Chippewa (10)	21	0.03
Choctaw (23)	72	0.11
Colville (0)	0	<0.01
Comanche (0)	2	<0.01
Cree (0)	0	<0.01
Creek (15)	26	0.04
Crow (0)	0	<0.01
Delaware (3)	7	0.01
Hopi (7)	9	0.01
Houma (0)	0	<0.01
Inupiat *(Alaska Native)* (0)	0	<0.01
Iroquois (5)	8	0.01
Kiowa (0)	0	<0.01
Lumbee (0)	0	<0.01
Menominee (0)	0	<0.01
Mexican American Ind. (41)	64	0.09
Navajo (11)	44	0.06
Osage (2)	6	0.01
Ottawa (1)	1	<0.01
Paiute (0)	0	<0.01
Pima (0)	0	<0.01
Potawatomi (2)	3	<0.01
Pueblo (1)	3	<0.01
Puget Sound Salish (1)	1	<0.01
Seminole (3)	9	0.01
Shoshone (0)	2	<0.01
Sioux (4)	17	0.02
South American Ind. (4)	14	0.02
Spanish American Ind. (10)	11	0.02
Tlingit-Haida *(Alaska Native)* (2)	3	<0.01
Tohono O'Odham (1)	5	0.01
Tsimshian *(Alaska Native)* (0)	0	<0.01
Ute (1)	1	<0.01
Yakama (0)	0	<0.01
Yaqui (5)	14	0.02
Yuman (0)	0	<0.01
Yup'ik *(Alaska Native)* (0)	0	<0.01
Asian (3,865)	5,135	7.49
Not Hispanic (3,728)	4,810	7.02
Hispanic (137)	325	0.47
Bangladeshi (0)	0	<0.01
Bhutanese (0)	0	<0.01
Burmese (3)	3	<0.01
Cambodian (61)	85	0.12
Chinese, ex. Taiwanese (333)	415	0.61
Filipino (501)	855	1.25
Hmong (115)	120	0.18
Indian (2,292)	2,501	3.65
Indonesian (11)	19	0.03
Japanese (140)	297	0.43
Korean (116)	149	0.22
Laotian (27)	34	0.05
Malaysian (0)	0	<0.01
Nepalese (6)	6	0.01
Pakistani (30)	32	0.05
Sri Lankan (7)	7	0.01
Taiwanese (13)	14	0.02
Thai (9)	20	0.03
Vietnamese (109)	125	0.18
Hawaii Native/Pacific Islander (313)	674	0.98
Not Hispanic (271)	557	0.81
Hispanic (42)	117	0.17
Fijian (120)	156	0.23
Guamanian/Chamorro (41)	69	0.10
Marshallese (0)	0	<0.01
Native Hawaiian (73)	183	0.27
Samoan (23)	38	0.06
Tongan (1)	1	<0.01
White (47,864)	50,830	74.15
Not Hispanic (36,220)	37,886	55.27
Hispanic (11,644)	12,944	18.88

*Notes: † The Census 2010 population figure is used to calculate the percentages in the Hispanic Origin and Race categories. Ancestry percentages are based on the 2006-2010 American Community Survey population (not shown); ‡ Numbers in parentheses indicate the number of people reporting a single ancestry; * Numbers in parentheses indicate the number of persons reporting this race alone, not in combination with any other race; Please refer to the Explanation of Data for more information.*

Tustin

Place Type: City
County: Orange
Population: 75,540

Ancestry	Population	%
Afghan (111)	111	0.15
African, Sub-Saharan (261)	340	0.46
African (134)	155	0.21
Cape Verdean (0)	0	<0.01
Ethiopian (0)	0	<0.01
Ghanaian (44)	44	0.06
Kenyan (0)	0	<0.01
Liberian (0)	0	<0.01
Nigerian (66)	66	0.09
Senegalese (0)	0	<0.01
Sierra Leonean (0)	0	<0.01
Somalian (0)	0	<0.01
South African (17)	75	0.10
Sudanese (0)	0	<0.01
Ugandan (0)	0	<0.01
Zimbabwean (0)	0	<0.01
Other Sub-Saharan African (0)	0	<0.01
Albanian (0)	0	<0.01
Alsatian (0)	0	<0.01
American (2,328)	2,328	3.16
Arab (558)	669	0.91
Arab (39)	73	0.10
Egyptian (230)	230	0.31
Iraqi (0)	0	<0.01
Jordanian (0)	0	<0.01
Lebanese (67)	111	0.15
Moroccan (0)	9	0.01
Palestinian (76)	76	0.10
Syrian (43)	43	0.06
Other Arab (103)	127	0.17
Armenian (118)	170	0.23
Assyrian/Chaldean/Syriac (41)	41	0.06
Australian (14)	28	0.04
Austrian (0)	42	0.06
Basque (16)	16	0.02
Belgian (6)	45	0.06
Brazilian (78)	159	0.22
British (169)	291	0.39
Bulgarian (0)	16	0.02
Cajun (0)	0	<0.01
Canadian (77)	119	0.16
Carpatho Rusyn (0)	0	<0.01
Celtic (0)	0	<0.01
Croatian (14)	28	0.04
Cypriot (0)	0	<0.01
Czech (63)	200	0.27
Czechoslovakian (48)	80	0.11
Danish (66)	262	0.36
Dutch (338)	865	1.17
Eastern European (87)	87	0.12
English (1,252)	4,369	5.93
Estonian (0)	0	<0.01
European (680)	729	0.99
Finnish (0)	34	0.05
French, ex. Basque (361)	1,441	1.95
French Canadian (42)	84	0.11
German (1,586)	6,048	8.20
German Russian (0)	0	<0.01
Greek (220)	382	0.52
Guyanese (0)	0	<0.01
Hungarian (6)	209	0.28
Icelander (0)	0	<0.01
Iranian (619)	677	0.92
Irish (1,530)	4,813	6.53
Israeli (0)	0	<0.01
Italian (805)	2,188	2.97
Latvian (0)	0	<0.01
Lithuanian (0)	56	0.08
Luxemburger (11)	23	0.03
Macedonian (0)	0	<0.01
Maltese (0)	0	<0.01
New Zealander (0)	0	<0.01
Northern European (37)	37	0.05
Norwegian (260)	643	0.87
Pennsylvania German (19)	21	0.03
Polish (373)	1,037	1.41
Portuguese (37)	192	0.26
Romanian (66)	66	0.09
Russian (415)	702	0.95
Scandinavian (99)	151	0.20
Scotch-Irish (263)	800	1.09
Scottish (411)	1,044	1.42
Serbian (45)	83	0.11
Slavic (0)	86	0.12
Slovak (0)	16	0.02
Slovene (0)	0	<0.01
Soviet Union (0)	0	<0.01
Swedish (153)	735	1.00
Swiss (25)	126	0.17
Turkish (54)	84	0.11
Ukrainian (10)	101	0.14
Welsh (15)	238	0.32
West Indian, ex. Hispanic (49)	57	0.08
Bahamian (0)	0	<0.01
Barbadian (0)	0	<0.01
Belizean (0)	0	<0.01
Bermudan (0)	0	<0.01
British West Indian (0)	0	<0.01
Dutch West Indian (0)	0	<0.01
Haitian (0)	0	<0.01
Jamaican (35)	43	0.06
Trinidadian/Tobagonian (0)	0	<0.01
U.S. Virgin Islander (0)	0	<0.01
West Indian (14)	14	0.02
Other West Indian (0)	0	<0.01
Yugoslavian (46)	161	0.22

Hispanic Origin	Population	%
Hispanic or Latino (of any race)	30,024	39.75
Central American, ex. Mexican	1,738	2.30
Costa Rican	42	0.06
Guatemalan	577	0.76
Honduran	114	0.15
Nicaraguan	100	0.13
Panamanian	27	0.04
Salvadoran	871	1.15
Other Central American	7	0.01
Cuban	169	0.22
Dominican Republic	29	0.04
Mexican	24,715	32.72
Puerto Rican	233	0.31
South American	1,443	1.91
Argentinean	150	0.20
Bolivian	285	0.38
Chilean	69	0.09
Colombian	298	0.39
Ecuadorian	113	0.15
Paraguayan	4	0.01
Peruvian	463	0.61
Uruguayan	29	0.04
Venezuelan	20	0.03
Other South American	12	0.02
Other Hispanic or Latino	1,697	2.25

Race*	Population	%
African-American/Black (1,722)	2,247	2.97
Not Hispanic (1,535)	1,873	2.48
Hispanic (187)	374	0.50
American Indian/Alaska Native (442)	887	1.17
Not Hispanic (142)	373	0.49
Hispanic (300)	514	0.68
Alaska Athabascan *(Ala. Nat.)* (0)	1	<0.01
Aleut *(Alaska Native)* (1)	3	<0.01
Apache (18)	33	0.04
Arapaho (0)	2	<0.01
Blackfeet (0)	16	0.02
Canadian/French Am. Ind. (1)	6	0.01
Central American Ind. (10)	10	0.01
Cherokee (18)	84	0.11
Cheyenne (0)	0	<0.01
Chickasaw (0)	3	<0.01
Chippewa (3)	13	0.02
Choctaw (11)	29	0.04
Colville (0)	1	<0.01
Comanche (3)	3	<0.01
Cree (1)	1	<0.01
Creek (1)	4	0.01
Crow (0)	2	<0.01
Delaware (0)	2	<0.01
Hopi (0)	2	<0.01
Houma (0)	0	<0.01
Inupiat *(Alaska Native)* (0)	0	<0.01
Iroquois (4)	13	0.02
Kiowa (1)	1	<0.01
Lumbee (0)	0	<0.01
Menominee (0)	0	<0.01
Mexican American Ind. (54)	79	0.10
Navajo (21)	41	0.05
Osage (0)	2	<0.01
Ottawa (0)	1	<0.01
Paiute (0)	2	<0.01
Pima (0)	1	<0.01
Potawatomi (0)	1	<0.01
Pueblo (14)	21	0.03
Puget Sound Salish (0)	0	<0.01
Seminole (0)	0	<0.01
Shoshone (1)	3	<0.01
Sioux (7)	18	0.02
South American Ind. (10)	15	0.02
Spanish American Ind. (3)	5	0.01
Tlingit-Haida *(Alaska Native)* (1)	1	<0.01
Tohono O'Odham (1)	1	<0.01
Tsimshian *(Alaska Native)* (0)	0	<0.01
Ute (0)	0	<0.01
Yakama (0)	0	<0.01
Yaqui (10)	22	0.03
Yuman (0)	0	<0.01
Yup'ik *(Alaska Native)* (0)	0	<0.01
Asian (15,299)	16,973	22.47
Not Hispanic (15,147)	16,578	21.95
Hispanic (152)	395	0.52
Bangladeshi (70)	81	0.11
Bhutanese (0)	0	<0.01
Burmese (30)	36	0.05
Cambodian (284)	336	0.44
Chinese, ex. Taiwanese (2,564)	3,125	4.14
Filipino (2,364)	2,870	3.80
Hmong (18)	18	0.02
Indian (2,181)	2,332	3.09
Indonesian (65)	92	0.12
Japanese (895)	1,343	1.78
Korean (2,159)	2,422	3.21
Laotian (52)	63	0.08
Malaysian (8)	10	0.01
Nepalese (8)	10	0.01
Pakistani (198)	229	0.30
Sri Lankan (65)	73	0.10
Taiwanese (684)	741	0.98
Thai (85)	114	0.15
Vietnamese (2,907)	3,244	4.29
Hawaii Native/Pacific Islander (268)	530	0.70
Not Hispanic (244)	438	0.58
Hispanic (24)	92	0.12
Fijian (7)	8	0.01
Guamanian/Chamorro (32)	78	0.10
Marshallese (74)	77	0.10
Native Hawaiian (35)	129	0.17
Samoan (56)	85	0.11
Tongan (23)	33	0.04
White (39,729)	42,774	56.62
Not Hispanic (26,317)	27,983	37.04
Hispanic (13,412)	14,791	19.58

*Notes: † The Census 2010 population figure is used to calculate the percentages in the Hispanic Origin and Race categories. Ancestry percentages are based on the 2006-2010 American Community Survey population (not shown); ‡ Numbers in parentheses indicate the number of people reporting a single ancestry; * Numbers in parentheses indicate the number of persons reporting this race alone, not in combination with any other race; Please refer to the Explanation of Data for more information.*

Union City

Place Type: City
County: Alameda
Population: 69,516

Ancestry	Population	%
Afghan (1,085)	1,085	1.59
African, Sub-Saharan (305)	377	0.55
African (154)	181	0.27
Cape Verdean (0)	0	<0.01
Ethiopian (77)	77	0.11
Ghanaian (5)	5	0.01
Kenyan (13)	45	0.07
Liberian (0)	0	<0.01
Nigerian (19)	19	0.03
Senegalese (0)	0	<0.01
Sierra Leonean (0)	0	<0.01
Somalian (37)	37	0.05
South African (0)	0	<0.01
Sudanese (0)	0	<0.01
Ugandan (0)	0	<0.01
Zimbabwean (0)	0	<0.01
Other Sub-Saharan African (0)	13	0.02
Albanian (0)	0	<0.01
Alsatian (0)	0	<0.01
American (591)	591	0.87
Arab (215)	284	0.42
Arab (9)	52	0.08
Egyptian (0)	0	<0.01
Iraqi (0)	0	<0.01
Jordanian (69)	69	0.10
Lebanese (49)	49	0.07
Moroccan (0)	0	<0.01
Palestinian (40)	40	0.06
Syrian (0)	0	<0.01
Other Arab (48)	74	0.11
Armenian (0)	0	<0.01
Assyrian/Chaldean/Syriac (0)	0	<0.01
Australian (0)	0	<0.01
Austrian (6)	21	0.03
Basque (15)	15	0.02
Belgian (0)	0	<0.01
Brazilian (14)	40	0.06
British (214)	285	0.42
Bulgarian (0)	0	<0.01
Cajun (0)	0	<0.01
Canadian (68)	83	0.12
Carpatho Rusyn (0)	0	<0.01
Celtic (0)	0	<0.01
Croatian (8)	17	0.02
Cypriot (0)	0	<0.01
Czech (5)	5	0.01
Czechoslovakian (8)	17	0.02
Danish (10)	67	0.10
Dutch (107)	217	0.32
Eastern European (0)	6	0.01
English (696)	1,884	2.77
Estonian (0)	0	<0.01
European (213)	276	0.41
Finnish (0)	0	<0.01
French, ex. Basque (277)	704	1.03
French Canadian (71)	91	0.13
German (736)	2,937	4.31
German Russian (0)	0	<0.01
Greek (116)	245	0.36
Guyanese (9)	21	0.03
Hungarian (33)	64	0.09
Icelander (0)	0	<0.01
Iranian (71)	71	0.10
Irish (349)	1,814	2.66
Israeli (26)	33	0.05
Italian (490)	1,444	2.12
Latvian (0)	0	<0.01
Lithuanian (14)	51	0.07
Luxemburger (0)	0	<0.01
Macedonian (0)	0	<0.01
Maltese (0)	0	<0.01
New Zealander (0)	0	<0.01
Northern European (23)	23	0.03
Norwegian (22)	76	0.11
Pennsylvania German (0)	0	<0.01
Polish (84)	282	0.41
Portuguese (694)	1,114	1.64
Romanian (28)	28	0.04
Russian (32)	210	0.31
Scandinavian (0)	0	<0.01
Scotch-Irish (65)	374	0.55
Scottish (102)	294	0.43
Serbian (0)	0	<0.01
Slavic (0)	0	<0.01
Slovak (0)	0	<0.01
Slovene (0)	0	<0.01
Soviet Union (0)	0	<0.01
Swedish (48)	178	0.26
Swiss (27)	53	0.08
Turkish (0)	11	0.02
Ukrainian (0)	14	0.02
Welsh (8)	102	0.15
West Indian, ex. Hispanic (114)	138	0.20
Bahamian (0)	0	<0.01
Barbadian (0)	0	<0.01
Belizean (31)	31	0.05
Bermudan (0)	12	0.02
British West Indian (0)	0	<0.01
Dutch West Indian (0)	0	<0.01
Haitian (0)	0	<0.01
Jamaican (71)	83	0.12
Trinidadian/Tobagonian (12)	12	0.02
U.S. Virgin Islander (0)	0	<0.01
West Indian (0)	0	<0.01
Other West Indian (0)	0	<0.01
Yugoslavian (0)	0	<0.01

Hispanic Origin	Population	%
Hispanic or Latino (of any race)	15,895	22.87
Central American, ex. Mexican	1,208	1.74
Costa Rican	25	0.04
Guatemalan	137	0.20
Honduran	83	0.12
Nicaraguan	299	0.43
Panamanian	50	0.07
Salvadoran	605	0.87
Other Central American	9	0.01
Cuban	55	0.08
Dominican Republic	10	0.01
Mexican	12,652	18.20
Puerto Rican	611	0.88
South American	372	0.54
Argentinean	24	0.03
Bolivian	36	0.05
Chilean	31	0.04
Colombian	52	0.07
Ecuadorian	13	0.02
Paraguayan	3	<0.01
Peruvian	184	0.26
Uruguayan	15	0.02
Venezuelan	12	0.02
Other South American	2	<0.01
Other Hispanic or Latino	987	1.42

Race*	Population	%
African-American/Black (4,402)	5,185	7.46
Not Hispanic (4,194)	4,770	6.86
Hispanic (208)	415	0.60
American Indian/Alaska Native (329)	830	1.19
Not Hispanic (116)	418	0.60
Hispanic (213)	412	0.59
Alaska Athabascan *(Ala. Nat.)* (0)	0	<0.01
Aleut *(Alaska Native)* (1)	1	<0.01
Apache (15)	41	0.06
Arapaho (0)	3	<0.01
Blackfeet (0)	12	0.02
Canadian/French Am. Ind. (0)	0	<0.01
Central American Ind. (0)	0	<0.01
Cherokee (25)	145	0.21
Cheyenne (1)	6	0.01
Chickasaw (5)	11	0.02
Chippewa (3)	9	0.01
Choctaw (2)	27	0.04
Colville (0)	0	<0.01
Comanche (3)	10	0.01
Cree (1)	1	<0.01
Creek (3)	5	0.01
Crow (0)	0	<0.01
Delaware (0)	2	<0.01
Hopi (0)	0	<0.01
Houma (0)	0	<0.01
Inupiat *(Alaska Native)* (0)	0	<0.01
Iroquois (2)	3	<0.01
Kiowa (1)	1	<0.01
Lumbee (0)	3	<0.01
Menominee (0)	0	<0.01
Mexican American Ind. (48)	81	0.12
Navajo (4)	7	0.01
Osage (0)	1	<0.01
Ottawa (0)	0	<0.01
Paiute (0)	0	<0.01
Pima (1)	1	<0.01
Potawatomi (0)	0	<0.01
Pueblo (0)	12	0.02
Puget Sound Salish (0)	2	<0.01
Seminole (2)	5	0.01
Shoshone (1)	2	<0.01
Sioux (4)	22	0.03
South American Ind. (5)	9	0.01
Spanish American Ind. (1)	2	<0.01
Tlingit-Haida *(Alaska Native)* (0)	0	<0.01
Tohono O'Odham (0)	0	<0.01
Tsimshian *(Alaska Native)* (0)	0	<0.01
Ute (2)	9	0.01
Yakama (0)	0	<0.01
Yaqui (8)	13	0.02
Yuman (1)	4	0.01
Yup'ik *(Alaska Native)* (0)	0	<0.01
Asian (35,363)	38,427	55.28
Not Hispanic (35,052)	37,720	54.26
Hispanic (311)	707	1.02
Bangladeshi (18)	27	0.04
Bhutanese (0)	0	<0.01
Burmese (275)	314	0.45
Cambodian (183)	248	0.36
Chinese, ex. Taiwanese (7,186)	8,102	11.65
Filipino (13,953)	15,289	21.99
Hmong (38)	40	0.06
Indian (7,966)	8,570	12.33
Indonesian (128)	207	0.30
Japanese (385)	751	1.08
Korean (650)	758	1.09
Laotian (82)	105	0.15
Malaysian (10)	21	0.03
Nepalese (40)	42	0.06
Pakistani (403)	450	0.65
Sri Lankan (32)	45	0.06
Taiwanese (391)	441	0.63
Thai (135)	167	0.24
Vietnamese (2,559)	2,851	4.10
Hawaii Native/Pacific Islander (892)	1,563	2.25
Not Hispanic (839)	1,374	1.98
Hispanic (53)	189	0.27
Fijian (323)	403	0.58
Guamanian/Chamorro (94)	187	0.27
Marshallese (0)	0	<0.01
Native Hawaiian (104)	332	0.48
Samoan (146)	251	0.36
Tongan (137)	168	0.24
White (16,640)	19,918	28.65
Not Hispanic (10,009)	12,283	17.67
Hispanic (6,631)	7,635	10.98

*Notes: † The Census 2010 population figure is used to calculate the percentages in the Hispanic Origin and Race categories. Ancestry percentages are based on the 2006-2010 American Community Survey population (not shown); ‡ Numbers in parentheses indicate the number of people reporting a single ancestry; * Numbers in parentheses indicate the number of persons reporting this race alone, not in combination with any other race; Please refer to the Explanation of Data for more information.*

Upland

Place Type: City
County: San Bernardino
Population: 73,732

Ancestry	Population	%
Afghan (85)	85	0.12
African, Sub-Saharan (250)	277	0.37
African (177)	186	0.25
Cape Verdean (0)	0	<0.01
Ethiopian (7)	7	0.01
Ghanaian (7)	7	0.01
Kenyan (0)	0	<0.01
Liberian (0)	0	<0.01
Nigerian (0)	0	<0.01
Senegalese (0)	0	<0.01
Sierra Leonean (0)	0	<0.01
Somalian (0)	0	<0.01
South African (0)	0	<0.01
Sudanese (0)	0	<0.01
Ugandan (0)	0	<0.01
Zimbabwean (0)	0	<0.01
Other Sub-Saharan African (59)	77	0.10
Albanian (0)	22	0.03
Alsatian (0)	14	0.02
American (3,521)	3,521	4.77
Arab (574)	794	1.07
Arab (159)	217	0.29
Egyptian (86)	86	0.12
Iraqi (0)	31	0.04
Jordanian (19)	28	0.04
Lebanese (121)	121	0.16
Moroccan (0)	0	<0.01
Palestinian (20)	38	0.05
Syrian (10)	46	0.06
Other Arab (159)	227	0.31
Armenian (148)	172	0.23
Assyrian/Chaldean/Syriac (0)	0	<0.01
Australian (17)	17	0.02
Austrian (0)	92	0.12
Basque (101)	202	0.27
Belgian (0)	21	0.03
Brazilian (62)	62	0.08
British (80)	270	0.37
Bulgarian (0)	0	<0.01
Cajun (0)	16	0.02
Canadian (116)	208	0.28
Carpatho Rusyn (0)	0	<0.01
Celtic (12)	25	0.03
Croatian (28)	45	0.06
Cypriot (0)	0	<0.01
Czech (13)	115	0.16
Czechoslovakian (0)	191	0.26
Danish (73)	355	0.48
Dutch (210)	744	1.01
Eastern European (18)	18	0.02
English (1,353)	5,011	6.78
Estonian (0)	0	<0.01
European (991)	1,387	1.88
Finnish (67)	219	0.30
French, ex. Basque (191)	1,763	2.39
French Canadian (90)	279	0.38
German (2,236)	9,289	12.57
German Russian (0)	0	<0.01
Greek (177)	298	0.40
Guyanese (0)	0	<0.01
Hungarian (91)	437	0.59
Icelander (0)	0	<0.01
Iranian (798)	798	1.08
Irish (1,458)	6,384	8.64
Israeli (34)	34	0.05
Italian (1,596)	4,901	6.63
Latvian (0)	0	<0.01
Lithuanian (11)	51	0.07
Luxemburger (0)	0	<0.01
Macedonian (0)	10	0.01
Maltese (0)	0	<0.01
New Zealander (0)	19	0.03
Northern European (36)	36	0.05
Norwegian (347)	1,132	1.53
Pennsylvania German (15)	15	0.02
Polish (268)	1,377	1.86
Portuguese (27)	126	0.17
Romanian (59)	168	0.23
Russian (120)	266	0.36
Scandinavian (9)	38	0.05
Scotch-Irish (448)	1,085	1.47
Scottish (290)	1,242	1.68
Serbian (27)	118	0.16
Slavic (10)	32	0.04
Slovak (30)	107	0.14
Slovene (0)	0	<0.01
Soviet Union (0)	0	<0.01
Swedish (231)	1,246	1.69
Swiss (42)	140	0.19
Turkish (0)	0	<0.01
Ukrainian (44)	150	0.20
Welsh (64)	577	0.78
West Indian, ex. Hispanic (113)	189	0.26
Bahamian (0)	0	<0.01
Barbadian (0)	0	<0.01
Belizean (0)	0	<0.01
Bermudan (0)	0	<0.01
British West Indian (0)	0	<0.01
Dutch West Indian (0)	0	<0.01
Haitian (0)	0	<0.01
Jamaican (113)	113	0.15
Trinidadian/Tobagonian (0)	0	<0.01
U.S. Virgin Islander (0)	0	<0.01
West Indian (0)	76	0.10
Other West Indian (0)	0	<0.01
Yugoslavian (73)	122	0.17

Hispanic Origin	Population	%
Hispanic or Latino (of any race)	28,035	38.02
Central American, ex. Mexican	1,628	2.21
Costa Rican	75	0.10
Guatemalan	402	0.55
Honduran	115	0.16
Nicaraguan	250	0.34
Panamanian	45	0.06
Salvadoran	719	0.98
Other Central American	22	0.03
Cuban	363	0.49
Dominican Republic	47	0.06
Mexican	22,727	30.82
Puerto Rican	443	0.60
South American	1,040	1.41
Argentinean	222	0.30
Bolivian	32	0.04
Chilean	79	0.11
Colombian	193	0.26
Ecuadorian	161	0.22
Paraguayan	3	<0.01
Peruvian	299	0.41
Uruguayan	8	0.01
Venezuelan	33	0.04
Other South American	10	0.01
Other Hispanic or Latino	1,787	2.42

Race*	Population	%
African-American/Black (5,400)	6,234	8.45
Not Hispanic (5,031)	5,553	7.53
Hispanic (369)	681	0.92
American Indian/Alaska Native (522)	1,218	1.65
Not Hispanic (184)	535	0.73
Hispanic (338)	683	0.93
Alaska Athabascan *(Ala. Nat.)* (0)	0	<0.01
Aleut *(Alaska Native)* (3)	3	<0.01
Apache (25)	63	0.09
Arapaho (0)	0	<0.01
Blackfeet (2)	22	0.03
Canadian/French Am. Ind. (0)	0	<0.01
Central American Ind. (4)	17	0.02
Cherokee (18)	153	0.21
Cheyenne (0)	0	<0.01
Chickasaw (1)	8	0.01
Chippewa (2)	6	0.01
Choctaw (12)	41	0.06
Colville (0)	1	<0.01
Comanche (5)	12	0.02
Cree (1)	3	<0.01
Creek (11)	18	0.02
Crow (1)	1	<0.01
Delaware (1)	2	<0.01
Hopi (0)	1	<0.01
Houma (0)	0	<0.01
Inupiat *(Alaska Native)* (0)	0	<0.01
Iroquois (3)	7	0.01
Kiowa (0)	0	<0.01
Lumbee (1)	1	<0.01
Menominee (0)	0	<0.01
Mexican American Ind. (37)	91	0.12
Navajo (27)	46	0.06
Osage (1)	3	<0.01
Ottawa (0)	0	<0.01
Paiute (2)	2	<0.01
Pima (3)	7	0.01
Potawatomi (10)	15	0.02
Pueblo (16)	25	0.03
Puget Sound Salish (2)	4	0.01
Seminole (4)	4	0.01
Shoshone (0)	0	<0.01
Sioux (10)	19	0.03
South American Ind. (4)	14	0.02
Spanish American Ind. (4)	6	0.01
Tlingit-Haida *(Alaska Native)* (1)	1	<0.01
Tohono O'Odham (4)	9	0.01
Tsimshian *(Alaska Native)* (0)	2	<0.01
Ute (0)	0	<0.01
Yakama (0)	0	<0.01
Yaqui (20)	30	0.04
Yuman (1)	1	<0.01
Yup'ik *(Alaska Native)* (0)	0	<0.01
Asian (6,217)	7,410	10.05
Not Hispanic (6,057)	6,915	9.38
Hispanic (160)	495	0.67
Bangladeshi (19)	23	0.03
Bhutanese (0)	0	<0.01
Burmese (75)	81	0.11
Cambodian (27)	44	0.06
Chinese, ex. Taiwanese (1,149)	1,431	1.94
Filipino (1,435)	1,882	2.55
Hmong (2)	2	<0.01
Indian (674)	772	1.05
Indonesian (285)	371	0.50
Japanese (329)	566	0.77
Korean (773)	889	1.21
Laotian (17)	26	0.04
Malaysian (13)	24	0.03
Nepalese (13)	13	0.02
Pakistani (148)	163	0.22
Sri Lankan (24)	25	0.03
Taiwanese (358)	382	0.52
Thai (107)	127	0.17
Vietnamese (542)	607	0.82
Hawaii Native/Pacific Islander (159)	415	0.56
Not Hispanic (134)	281	0.38
Hispanic (25)	134	0.18
Fijian (7)	13	0.02
Guamanian/Chamorro (24)	55	0.07
Marshallese (0)	2	<0.01
Native Hawaiian (39)	140	0.19
Samoan (26)	52	0.07
Tongan (32)	51	0.07
White (48,364)	51,343	69.63
Not Hispanic (32,564)	33,874	45.94
Hispanic (15,800)	17,469	23.69

*Notes: † The Census 2010 population figure is used to calculate the percentages in the Hispanic Origin and Race categories. Ancestry percentages are based on the 2006-2010 American Community Survey population (not shown); ‡ Numbers in parentheses indicate the number of people reporting a single ancestry; * Numbers in parentheses indicate the number of persons reporting this race alone, not in combination with any other race; Please refer to the Explanation of Data for more information.*

Vacaville

Place Type: City
County: Solano
Population: 92,428

Ancestry	Population	%
Afghan (85)	85	0.09
African, Sub-Saharan (1,702)	2,233	2.43
African (1,541)	2,024	2.20
Cape Verdean (0)	0	<0.01
Ethiopian (28)	28	0.03
Ghanaian (0)	8	0.01
Kenyan (0)	0	<0.01
Liberian (0)	0	<0.01
Nigerian (0)	0	<0.01
Senegalese (0)	0	<0.01
Sierra Leonean (91)	91	0.10
Somalian (0)	0	<0.01
South African (33)	65	0.07
Sudanese (0)	0	<0.01
Ugandan (0)	0	<0.01
Zimbabwean (0)	0	<0.01
Other Sub-Saharan African (9)	17	0.02
Albanian (0)	0	<0.01
Alsatian (0)	17	0.02
American (2,594)	2,594	2.82
Arab (116)	197	0.21
Arab (84)	84	0.09
Egyptian (8)	8	0.01
Iraqi (0)	0	<0.01
Jordanian (11)	11	0.01
Lebanese (0)	0	<0.01
Moroccan (0)	0	<0.01
Palestinian (0)	0	<0.01
Syrian (0)	81	0.09
Other Arab (13)	13	0.01
Armenian (31)	99	0.11
Assyrian/Chaldean/Syriac (57)	57	0.06
Australian (30)	37	0.04
Austrian (92)	200	0.22
Basque (24)	108	0.12
Belgian (0)	82	0.09
Brazilian (0)	11	0.01
British (250)	477	0.52
Bulgarian (0)	0	<0.01
Cajun (9)	9	0.01
Canadian (152)	163	0.18
Carpatho Rusyn (0)	0	<0.01
Celtic (23)	23	0.03
Croatian (22)	59	0.06
Cypriot (0)	0	<0.01
Czech (14)	133	0.14
Czechoslovakian (50)	78	0.08
Danish (201)	809	0.88
Dutch (374)	1,283	1.40
Eastern European (41)	58	0.06
English (2,637)	9,319	10.14
Estonian (0)	0	<0.01
European (2,028)	2,390	2.60
Finnish (110)	277	0.30
French, ex. Basque (353)	2,425	2.64
French Canadian (169)	348	0.38
German (5,076)	14,207	15.45
German Russian (6)	6	0.01
Greek (262)	551	0.60
Guyanese (0)	0	<0.01
Hungarian (156)	414	0.45
Icelander (0)	0	<0.01
Iranian (541)	541	0.59
Irish (3,369)	10,180	11.07
Israeli (8)	8	0.01
Italian (1,927)	5,228	5.69
Latvian (0)	143	0.16
Lithuanian (98)	195	0.21
Luxemburger (0)	15	0.02
Macedonian (0)	0	<0.01
Maltese (0)	59	0.06
New Zealander (0)	0	<0.01
Northern European (25)	25	0.03
Norwegian (446)	1,150	1.25
Pennsylvania German (0)	71	0.08
Polish (316)	1,225	1.33
Portuguese (911)	1,625	1.77
Romanian (80)	109	0.12
Russian (129)	734	0.80
Scandinavian (115)	196	0.21
Scotch-Irish (597)	1,673	1.82
Scottish (870)	2,672	2.91
Serbian (30)	30	0.03
Slavic (6)	6	0.01
Slovak (13)	27	0.03
Slovene (8)	20	0.02
Soviet Union (0)	0	<0.01
Swedish (481)	1,098	1.19
Swiss (148)	591	0.64
Turkish (31)	49	0.05
Ukrainian (17)	81	0.09
Welsh (80)	373	0.41
West Indian, ex. Hispanic (72)	159	0.17
Bahamian (0)	0	<0.01
Barbadian (0)	0	<0.01
Belizean (8)	50	0.05
Bermudan (0)	0	<0.01
British West Indian (0)	15	0.02
Dutch West Indian (0)	0	<0.01
Haitian (0)	0	<0.01
Jamaican (47)	55	0.06
Trinidadian/Tobagonian (9)	24	0.03
U.S. Virgin Islander (0)	0	<0.01
West Indian (8)	15	0.02
Other West Indian (0)	0	<0.01
Yugoslavian (56)	91	0.10

Hispanic Origin	Population	%
Hispanic or Latino (of any race)	21,121	22.85
Central American, ex. Mexican	1,176	1.27
Costa Rican	33	0.04
Guatemalan	229	0.25
Honduran	56	0.06
Nicaraguan	317	0.34
Panamanian	95	0.10
Salvadoran	424	0.46
Other Central American	22	0.02
Cuban	164	0.18
Dominican Republic	28	0.03
Mexican	15,753	17.04
Puerto Rican	846	0.92
South American	374	0.40
Argentinean	37	0.04
Bolivian	13	0.01
Chilean	18	0.02
Colombian	67	0.07
Ecuadorian	37	0.04
Paraguayan	13	0.01
Peruvian	175	0.19
Uruguayan	1	<0.01
Venezuelan	11	0.01
Other South American	2	<0.01
Other Hispanic or Latino	2,780	3.01

Race*	Population	%
African-American/Black (9,510)	11,312	12.24
Not Hispanic (9,187)	10,590	11.46
Hispanic (323)	722	0.78
American Indian/Alaska Native (846)	2,206	2.39
Not Hispanic (510)	1,448	1.57
Hispanic (336)	758	0.82
Alaska Athabascan *(Ala. Nat.)* (1)	1	<0.01
Aleut *(Alaska Native)* (8)	20	0.02
Apache (24)	76	0.08
Arapaho (0)	0	<0.01
Blackfeet (10)	62	0.07
Canadian/French Am. Ind. (2)	8	0.01
Central American Ind. (0)	3	<0.01
Cherokee (69)	382	0.41
Cheyenne (1)	2	<0.01
Chickasaw (10)	16	0.02
Chippewa (9)	34	0.04
Choctaw (23)	87	0.09
Colville (1)	4	<0.01
Comanche (2)	11	0.01
Cree (1)	8	0.01
Creek (20)	52	0.06
Crow (1)	4	<0.01
Delaware (6)	7	0.01
Hopi (2)	4	<0.01
Houma (0)	0	<0.01
Inupiat *(Alaska Native)* (4)	8	0.01
Iroquois (5)	23	0.02
Kiowa (2)	5	0.01
Lumbee (0)	0	<0.01
Menominee (0)	0	<0.01
Mexican American Ind. (53)	104	0.11
Navajo (17)	64	0.07
Osage (2)	17	0.02
Ottawa (3)	4	<0.01
Paiute (9)	17	0.02
Pima (1)	7	0.01
Potawatomi (8)	11	0.01
Pueblo (2)	15	0.02
Puget Sound Salish (0)	0	<0.01
Seminole (2)	24	0.03
Shoshone (2)	6	0.01
Sioux (19)	49	0.05
South American Ind. (4)	14	0.02
Spanish American Ind. (6)	10	0.01
Tlingit-Haida *(Alaska Native)* (4)	6	0.01
Tohono O'Odham (2)	8	0.01
Tsimshian *(Alaska Native)* (3)	3	<0.01
Ute (3)	9	0.01
Yakama (0)	0	<0.01
Yaqui (7)	20	0.02
Yuman (0)	4	<0.01
Yup'ik *(Alaska Native)* (1)	2	<0.01
Asian (5,606)	8,485	9.18
Not Hispanic (5,378)	7,690	8.32
Hispanic (228)	795	0.86
Bangladeshi (0)	3	<0.01
Bhutanese (0)	0	<0.01
Burmese (20)	25	0.03
Cambodian (20)	28	0.03
Chinese, ex. Taiwanese (620)	1,024	1.11
Filipino (3,048)	4,581	4.96
Hmong (5)	6	0.01
Indian (521)	618	0.67
Indonesian (9)	27	0.03
Japanese (416)	1,116	1.21
Korean (239)	491	0.53
Laotian (46)	70	0.08
Malaysian (1)	5	0.01
Nepalese (3)	3	<0.01
Pakistani (28)	42	0.05
Sri Lankan (0)	0	<0.01
Taiwanese (25)	40	0.04
Thai (74)	187	0.20
Vietnamese (287)	400	0.43
Hawaii Native/Pacific Islander (532)	1,282	1.39
Not Hispanic (436)	1,004	1.09
Hispanic (96)	278	0.30
Fijian (9)	22	0.02
Guamanian/Chamorro (187)	372	0.40
Marshallese (1)	1	<0.01
Native Hawaiian (155)	556	0.60
Samoan (107)	173	0.19
Tongan (25)	36	0.04
White (61,301)	66,853	72.33
Not Hispanic (50,811)	54,459	58.92
Hispanic (10,490)	12,394	13.41

*Notes: † The Census 2010 population figure is used to calculate the percentages in the Hispanic Origin and Race categories. Ancestry percentages are based on the 2006-2010 American Community Survey population (not shown); ‡ Numbers in parentheses indicate the number of people reporting a single ancestry; * Numbers in parentheses indicate the number of persons reporting this race alone, not in combination with any other race; Please refer to the Explanation of Data for more information.*

Vallejo

Place Type: City
County: Solano
Population: 115,942

Ancestry	Population	%
Afghan (27)	27	0.02
African, Sub-Saharan (2,811)	3,554	3.06
African (2,389)	3,101	2.67
Cape Verdean (0)	12	0.01
Ethiopian (74)	74	0.06
Ghanaian (0)	0	<0.01
Kenyan (32)	32	0.03
Liberian (39)	58	0.05
Nigerian (20)	20	0.02
Senegalese (0)	0	<0.01
Sierra Leonean (0)	0	<0.01
Somalian (203)	203	0.17
South African (0)	0	<0.01
Sudanese (0)	0	<0.01
Ugandan (0)	0	<0.01
Zimbabwean (0)	0	<0.01
Other Sub-Saharan African (54)	54	0.05
Albanian (0)	0	<0.01
Alsatian (0)	0	<0.01
American (1,774)	1,774	1.53
Arab (123)	303	0.26
Arab (0)	98	0.08
Egyptian (0)	19	0.02
Iraqi (34)	34	0.03
Jordanian (0)	0	<0.01
Lebanese (23)	53	0.05
Moroccan (0)	0	<0.01
Palestinian (44)	44	0.04
Syrian (0)	33	0.03
Other Arab (22)	22	0.02
Armenian (132)	195	0.17
Assyrian/Chaldean/Syriac (0)	0	<0.01
Australian (31)	74	0.06
Austrian (26)	63	0.05
Basque (0)	19	0.02
Belgian (9)	30	0.03
Brazilian (8)	59	0.05
British (141)	256	0.22
Bulgarian (64)	79	0.07
Cajun (0)	0	<0.01
Canadian (79)	175	0.15
Carpatho Rusyn (0)	0	<0.01
Celtic (28)	37	0.03
Croatian (54)	76	0.07
Cypriot (0)	0	<0.01
Czech (36)	123	0.11
Czechoslovakian (50)	79	0.07
Danish (69)	328	0.28
Dutch (163)	784	0.68
Eastern European (52)	52	0.04
English (1,833)	4,762	4.10
Estonian (0)	0	<0.01
European (2,049)	2,852	2.46
Finnish (34)	163	0.14
French, ex. Basque (223)	1,427	1.23
French Canadian (103)	355	0.31
German (2,061)	6,925	5.97
German Russian (0)	0	<0.01
Greek (209)	399	0.34
Guyanese (0)	0	<0.01
Hungarian (42)	153	0.13
Icelander (0)	0	<0.01
Iranian (82)	96	0.08
Irish (1,291)	5,673	4.89
Israeli (0)	0	<0.01
Italian (1,030)	2,932	2.53
Latvian (0)	16	0.01
Lithuanian (41)	168	0.14
Luxemburger (0)	14	0.01
Macedonian (0)	0	<0.01
Maltese (0)	50	0.04
New Zealander (0)	0	<0.01
Northern European (107)	107	0.09
Norwegian (524)	1,107	0.95
Pennsylvania German (53)	67	0.06
Polish (269)	898	0.77
Portuguese (370)	926	0.80
Romanian (37)	37	0.03
Russian (183)	423	0.36
Scandinavian (62)	125	0.11
Scotch-Irish (247)	1,264	1.09
Scottish (336)	1,119	0.96
Serbian (0)	0	<0.01
Slavic (0)	9	0.01
Slovak (35)	87	0.07
Slovene (0)	12	0.01
Soviet Union (0)	0	<0.01
Swedish (158)	632	0.54
Swiss (55)	265	0.23
Turkish (0)	16	0.01
Ukrainian (73)	183	0.16
Welsh (38)	363	0.31
West Indian, ex. Hispanic (209)	443	0.38
Bahamian (0)	0	<0.01
Barbadian (0)	0	<0.01
Belizean (0)	13	0.01
Bermudan (0)	0	<0.01
British West Indian (43)	43	0.04
Dutch West Indian (0)	0	<0.01
Haitian (14)	58	0.05
Jamaican (39)	210	0.18
Trinidadian/Tobagonian (55)	61	0.05
U.S. Virgin Islander (0)	0	<0.01
West Indian (58)	58	0.05
Other West Indian (0)	0	<0.01
Yugoslavian (44)	131	0.11

Hispanic Origin	Population	%
Hispanic or Latino (of any race)	26,165	22.57
Central American, ex. Mexican	3,861	3.33
Costa Rican	25	0.02
Guatemalan	787	0.68
Honduran	159	0.14
Nicaraguan	629	0.54
Panamanian	97	0.08
Salvadoran	2,135	1.84
Other Central American	29	0.03
Cuban	186	0.16
Dominican Republic	33	0.03
Mexican	18,611	16.05
Puerto Rican	906	0.78
South American	507	0.44
Argentinean	29	0.03
Bolivian	18	0.02
Chilean	39	0.03
Colombian	110	0.09
Ecuadorian	29	0.03
Paraguayan	16	0.01
Peruvian	215	0.19
Uruguayan	11	0.01
Venezuelan	31	0.03
Other South American	9	0.01
Other Hispanic or Latino	2,061	1.78

Race*	Population	%
African-American/Black (25,572)	28,918	24.94
Not Hispanic (24,876)	27,466	23.69
Hispanic (696)	1,452	1.25
American Indian/Alaska Native (757)	2,467	2.13
Not Hispanic (453)	1,713	1.48
Hispanic (304)	754	0.65
Alaska Athabascan *(Ala. Nat.)* (1)	1	<0.01
Aleut *(Alaska Native)* (1)	6	0.01
Apache (23)	95	0.08
Arapaho (3)	3	<0.01
Blackfeet (7)	81	0.07
Canadian/French Am. Ind. (5)	10	0.01
Central American Ind. (3)	8	0.01
Cherokee (83)	421	0.36
Cheyenne (0)	4	<0.01
Chickasaw (5)	22	0.02
Chippewa (3)	11	0.01
Choctaw (27)	118	0.10
Colville (1)	1	<0.01
Comanche (1)	12	0.01
Cree (1)	8	0.01
Creek (3)	27	0.02
Crow (1)	1	<0.01
Delaware (0)	1	<0.01
Hopi (3)	13	0.01
Houma (0)	0	<0.01
Inupiat *(Alaska Native)* (0)	0	<0.01
Iroquois (3)	15	0.01
Kiowa (3)	3	<0.01
Lumbee (1)	1	<0.01
Menominee (0)	0	<0.01
Mexican American Ind. (71)	144	0.12
Navajo (29)	79	0.07
Osage (0)	6	0.01
Ottawa (1)	5	<0.01
Paiute (3)	8	0.01
Pima (2)	4	<0.01
Potawatomi (2)	3	<0.01
Pueblo (9)	13	0.01
Puget Sound Salish (1)	2	<0.01
Seminole (2)	26	0.02
Shoshone (1)	5	<0.01
Sioux (21)	67	0.06
South American Ind. (1)	4	<0.01
Spanish American Ind. (5)	6	0.01
Tlingit-Haida *(Alaska Native)* (2)	8	0.01
Tohono O'Odham (1)	5	<0.01
Tsimshian *(Alaska Native)* (1)	1	<0.01
Ute (2)	2	<0.01
Yakama (1)	2	<0.01
Yaqui (1)	10	0.01
Yuman (1)	7	0.01
Yup'ik *(Alaska Native)* (0)	0	<0.01
Asian (28,895)	32,761	28.26
Not Hispanic (28,386)	31,408	27.09
Hispanic (509)	1,353	1.17
Bangladeshi (0)	0	<0.01
Bhutanese (0)	0	<0.01
Burmese (19)	38	0.03
Cambodian (66)	87	0.08
Chinese, ex. Taiwanese (1,078)	1,715	1.48
Filipino (24,451)	27,622	23.82
Hmong (21)	28	0.02
Indian (1,148)	1,395	1.20
Indonesian (56)	78	0.07
Japanese (286)	716	0.62
Korean (234)	365	0.31
Laotian (142)	184	0.16
Malaysian (10)	37	0.03
Nepalese (8)	9	0.01
Pakistani (112)	130	0.11
Sri Lankan (3)	4	<0.01
Taiwanese (33)	39	0.03
Thai (79)	114	0.10
Vietnamese (576)	695	0.60
Hawaii Native/Pacific Islander (1,239)	2,436	2.10
Not Hispanic (1,159)	2,103	1.81
Hispanic (80)	333	0.29
Fijian (130)	190	0.16
Guamanian/Chamorro (451)	866	0.75
Marshallese (0)	0	<0.01
Native Hawaiian (135)	523	0.45
Samoan (283)	463	0.40
Tongan (90)	133	0.11
White (38,064)	44,045	37.99
Not Hispanic (28,946)	32,800	28.29
Hispanic (9,118)	11,245	9.70

*Notes: † The Census 2010 population figure is used to calculate the percentages in the Hispanic Origin and Race categories. Ancestry percentages are based on the 2006-2010 American Community Survey population (not shown); ‡ Numbers in parentheses indicate the number of people reporting a single ancestry; * Numbers in parentheses indicate the number of persons reporting this race alone, not in combination with any other race; Please refer to the Explanation of Data for more information.*

Victorville

Place Type: City
County: San Bernardino
Population: 115,903

Ancestry	Population	%
Afghan (29)	29	0.03
African, Sub-Saharan (703)	968	0.90
African (508)	753	0.70
Cape Verdean (0)	0	<0.01
Ethiopian (0)	0	<0.01
Ghanaian (90)	110	0.10
Kenyan (0)	0	<0.01
Liberian (12)	12	0.01
Nigerian (93)	93	0.09
Senegalese (0)	0	<0.01
Sierra Leonean (0)	0	<0.01
Somalian (0)	0	<0.01
South African (0)	0	<0.01
Sudanese (0)	0	<0.01
Ugandan (0)	0	<0.01
Zimbabwean (0)	0	<0.01
Other Sub-Saharan African (0)	0	<0.01
Albanian (0)	0	<0.01
Alsatian (0)	0	<0.01
American (2,132)	2,132	1.97
Arab (398)	486	0.45
Arab (207)	207	0.19
Egyptian (159)	159	0.15
Iraqi (0)	0	<0.01
Jordanian (0)	0	<0.01
Lebanese (8)	96	0.09
Moroccan (0)	0	<0.01
Palestinian (0)	0	<0.01
Syrian (12)	12	0.01
Other Arab (12)	12	0.01
Armenian (182)	271	0.25
Assyrian/Chaldean/Syriac (18)	18	0.02
Australian (23)	177	0.16
Austrian (14)	75	0.07
Basque (0)	0	<0.01
Belgian (9)	45	0.04
Brazilian (0)	0	<0.01
British (120)	227	0.21
Bulgarian (0)	0	<0.01
Cajun (0)	0	<0.01
Canadian (34)	57	0.05
Carpatho Rusyn (0)	0	<0.01
Celtic (24)	24	0.02
Croatian (0)	36	0.03
Cypriot (0)	0	<0.01
Czech (32)	232	0.21
Czechoslovakian (11)	71	0.07
Danish (135)	279	0.26
Dutch (229)	1,095	1.01
Eastern European (0)	0	<0.01
English (1,947)	5,862	5.42
Estonian (0)	0	<0.01
European (370)	464	0.43
Finnish (0)	22	0.02
French, ex. Basque (209)	1,932	1.79
French Canadian (74)	247	0.23
German (2,248)	8,964	8.29
German Russian (29)	29	0.03
Greek (50)	207	0.19
Guyanese (9)	9	0.01
Hungarian (76)	284	0.26
Icelander (0)	0	<0.01
Iranian (138)	138	0.13
Irish (1,712)	7,408	6.85
Israeli (0)	0	<0.01
Italian (1,303)	4,701	4.35
Latvian (0)	0	<0.01
Lithuanian (171)	384	0.36
Luxemburger (0)	0	<0.01
Macedonian (0)	0	<0.01
Maltese (0)	0	<0.01
New Zealander (0)	0	<0.01
Northern European (39)	39	0.04
Norwegian (224)	656	0.61
Pennsylvania German (27)	54	0.05
Polish (293)	1,032	0.95
Portuguese (118)	564	0.52
Romanian (53)	53	0.05
Russian (106)	255	0.24
Scandinavian (0)	24	0.02
Scotch-Irish (307)	997	0.92
Scottish (217)	992	0.92
Serbian (0)	0	<0.01
Slavic (13)	13	0.01
Slovak (0)	9	0.01
Slovene (0)	28	0.03
Soviet Union (0)	0	<0.01
Swedish (134)	730	0.68
Swiss (0)	25	0.02
Turkish (0)	0	<0.01
Ukrainian (153)	182	0.17
Welsh (15)	272	0.25
West Indian, ex. Hispanic (252)	432	0.40
Bahamian (0)	0	<0.01
Barbadian (0)	0	<0.01
Belizean (167)	167	0.15
Bermudan (0)	0	<0.01
British West Indian (0)	0	<0.01
Dutch West Indian (0)	0	<0.01
Haitian (43)	162	0.15
Jamaican (15)	15	0.01
Trinidadian/Tobagonian (11)	40	0.04
U.S. Virgin Islander (0)	0	<0.01
West Indian (16)	48	0.04
Other West Indian (0)	0	<0.01
Yugoslavian (14)	34	0.03

Hispanic Origin	Population	%
Hispanic or Latino (of any race)	55,359	47.76
Central American, ex. Mexican	3,702	3.19
Costa Rican	115	0.10
Guatemalan	1,045	0.90
Honduran	245	0.21
Nicaraguan	311	0.27
Panamanian	106	0.09
Salvadoran	1,801	1.55
Other Central American	79	0.07
Cuban	399	0.34
Dominican Republic	58	0.05
Mexican	45,246	39.04
Puerto Rican	1,218	1.05
South American	745	0.64
Argentinean	94	0.08
Bolivian	24	0.02
Chilean	74	0.06
Colombian	232	0.20
Ecuadorian	106	0.09
Paraguayan	3	<0.01
Peruvian	172	0.15
Uruguayan	1	<0.01
Venezuelan	30	0.03
Other South American	9	0.01
Other Hispanic or Latino	3,991	3.44

Race*	Population	%
African-American/Black (19,483)	22,134	19.10
Not Hispanic (18,579)	20,470	17.66
Hispanic (904)	1,664	1.44
American Indian/Alaska Native (1,665)	3,164	2.73
Not Hispanic (754)	1,682	1.45
Hispanic (911)	1,482	1.28
Alaska Athabascan *(Ala. Nat.)* (1)	2	<0.01
Aleut *(Alaska Native)* (1)	2	<0.01
Apache (97)	174	0.15
Arapaho (3)	3	<0.01
Blackfeet (10)	114	0.10
Canadian/French Am. Ind. (5)	19	0.02
Central American Ind. (1)	3	<0.01
Cherokee (87)	417	0.36
Cheyenne (4)	9	0.01
Chickasaw (3)	13	0.01
Chippewa (22)	33	0.03
Choctaw (23)	81	0.07
Colville (4)	4	<0.01
Comanche (4)	14	0.01
Cree (2)	3	<0.01
Creek (7)	26	0.02
Crow (2)	3	<0.01
Delaware (2)	6	0.01
Hopi (3)	4	<0.01
Houma (0)	0	<0.01
Inupiat *(Alaska Native)* (9)	11	0.01
Iroquois (3)	16	0.01
Kiowa (4)	5	<0.01
Lumbee (5)	7	0.01
Menominee (0)	1	<0.01
Mexican American Ind. (132)	221	0.19
Navajo (83)	116	0.10
Osage (3)	10	0.01
Ottawa (0)	4	<0.01
Paiute (4)	10	0.01
Pima (23)	30	0.03
Potawatomi (4)	5	<0.01
Pueblo (37)	45	0.04
Puget Sound Salish (2)	2	<0.01
Seminole (1)	21	0.02
Shoshone (7)	12	0.01
Sioux (35)	60	0.05
South American Ind. (6)	15	0.01
Spanish American Ind. (11)	19	0.02
Tlingit-Haida *(Alaska Native)* (4)	4	<0.01
Tohono O'Odham (25)	35	0.03
Tsimshian *(Alaska Native)* (0)	0	<0.01
Ute (2)	5	<0.01
Yakama (3)	3	<0.01
Yaqui (22)	48	0.04
Yuman (24)	30	0.03
Yup'ik *(Alaska Native)* (0)	0	<0.01
Asian (4,641)	6,401	5.52
Not Hispanic (4,341)	5,516	4.76
Hispanic (300)	885	0.76
Bangladeshi (15)	16	0.01
Bhutanese (0)	0	<0.01
Burmese (2)	3	<0.01
Cambodian (164)	208	0.18
Chinese, ex. Taiwanese (366)	560	0.48
Filipino (1,939)	2,680	2.31
Hmong (2)	2	<0.01
Indian (404)	509	0.44
Indonesian (67)	110	0.09
Japanese (212)	541	0.47
Korean (495)	661	0.57
Laotian (30)	44	0.04
Malaysian (12)	19	0.02
Nepalese (10)	12	0.01
Pakistani (39)	61	0.05
Sri Lankan (13)	16	0.01
Taiwanese (49)	63	0.05
Thai (128)	224	0.19
Vietnamese (525)	603	0.52
Hawaii Native/Pacific Islander (489)	1,009	0.87
Not Hispanic (390)	711	0.61
Hispanic (99)	298	0.26
Fijian (7)	7	0.01
Guamanian/Chamorro (147)	237	0.20
Marshallese (0)	0	<0.01
Native Hawaiian (91)	254	0.22
Samoan (141)	243	0.21
Tongan (59)	80	0.07
White (56,258)	61,977	53.47
Not Hispanic (32,804)	35,431	30.57
Hispanic (23,454)	26,546	22.90

*Notes: † The Census 2010 population figure is used to calculate the percentages in the Hispanic Origin and Race categories. Ancestry percentages are based on the 2006-2010 American Community Survey population (not shown); ‡ Numbers in parentheses indicate the number of people reporting a single ancestry; * Numbers in parentheses indicate the number of persons reporting this race alone, not in combination with any other race; Please refer to the Explanation of Data for more information.*

Visalia

Place Type: City
County: Tulare
Population: 124,442

Ancestry	Population	%
Afghan (0)	0	<0.01
African, Sub-Saharan (291)	408	0.34
African (91)	208	0.17
Cape Verdean (0)	0	<0.01
Ethiopian (119)	119	0.10
Ghanaian (0)	0	<0.01
Kenyan (0)	0	<0.01
Liberian (0)	0	<0.01
Nigerian (81)	81	0.07
Senegalese (0)	0	<0.01
Sierra Leonean (0)	0	<0.01
Somalian (0)	0	<0.01
South African (0)	0	<0.01
Sudanese (0)	0	<0.01
Ugandan (0)	0	<0.01
Zimbabwean (0)	0	<0.01
Other Sub-Saharan African (0)	0	<0.01
Albanian (0)	0	<0.01
Alsatian (0)	0	<0.01
American (4,048)	4,048	3.39
Arab (301)	365	0.31
Arab (18)	46	0.04
Egyptian (10)	10	0.01
Iraqi (0)	0	<0.01
Jordanian (34)	34	0.03
Lebanese (134)	161	0.13
Moroccan (0)	0	<0.01
Palestinian (58)	58	0.05
Syrian (35)	44	0.04
Other Arab (12)	12	0.01
Armenian (364)	492	0.41
Assyrian/Chaldean/Syriac (71)	71	0.06
Australian (14)	14	0.01
Austrian (19)	88	0.07
Basque (20)	63	0.05
Belgian (5)	20	0.02
Brazilian (6)	6	0.01
British (106)	152	0.13
Bulgarian (18)	18	0.02
Cajun (0)	0	<0.01
Canadian (128)	264	0.22
Carpatho Rusyn (0)	0	<0.01
Celtic (47)	47	0.04
Croatian (16)	35	0.03
Cypriot (0)	0	<0.01
Czech (179)	339	0.28
Czechoslovakian (50)	74	0.06
Danish (92)	569	0.48
Dutch (853)	2,016	1.69
Eastern European (43)	51	0.04
English (2,295)	6,494	5.44
Estonian (0)	0	<0.01
European (1,008)	1,098	0.92
Finnish (38)	69	0.06
French, ex. Basque (264)	1,964	1.65
French Canadian (103)	207	0.17
German (3,292)	9,722	8.15
German Russian (0)	0	<0.01
Greek (151)	313	0.26
Guyanese (0)	0	<0.01
Hungarian (41)	113	0.09
Icelander (0)	0	<0.01
Iranian (108)	152	0.13
Irish (2,121)	6,968	5.84
Israeli (0)	0	<0.01
Italian (1,199)	3,089	2.59
Latvian (0)	14	0.01
Lithuanian (10)	10	0.01
Luxemburger (0)	0	<0.01
Macedonian (0)	0	<0.01
Maltese (0)	0	<0.01
New Zealander (0)	0	<0.01
Northern European (118)	176	0.15
Norwegian (420)	877	0.74
Pennsylvania German (0)	0	<0.01
Polish (121)	589	0.49
Portuguese (1,464)	2,411	2.02
Romanian (0)	44	0.04
Russian (119)	307	0.26
Scandinavian (67)	73	0.06
Scotch-Irish (332)	979	0.82
Scottish (414)	1,236	1.04
Serbian (0)	10	0.01
Slavic (0)	0	<0.01
Slovak (0)	38	0.03
Slovene (0)	0	<0.01
Soviet Union (0)	0	<0.01
Swedish (406)	1,130	0.95
Swiss (46)	296	0.25
Turkish (0)	0	<0.01
Ukrainian (5)	31	0.03
Welsh (59)	350	0.29
West Indian, ex. Hispanic (16)	70	0.06
Bahamian (0)	0	<0.01
Barbadian (0)	0	<0.01
Belizean (0)	0	<0.01
Bermudan (0)	0	<0.01
British West Indian (0)	0	<0.01
Dutch West Indian (0)	30	0.03
Haitian (0)	24	0.02
Jamaican (16)	16	0.01
Trinidadian/Tobagonian (0)	0	<0.01
U.S. Virgin Islander (0)	0	<0.01
West Indian (0)	0	<0.01
Other West Indian (0)	0	<0.01
Yugoslavian (10)	85	0.07

Hispanic Origin	Population	%
Hispanic or Latino (of any race)	57,262	46.02
Central American, ex. Mexican	857	0.69
Costa Rican	39	0.03
Guatemalan	190	0.15
Honduran	63	0.05
Nicaraguan	63	0.05
Panamanian	25	0.02
Salvadoran	472	0.38
Other Central American	5	<0.01
Cuban	117	0.09
Dominican Republic	22	0.02
Mexican	52,121	41.88
Puerto Rican	542	0.44
South American	336	0.27
Argentinean	66	0.05
Bolivian	12	0.01
Chilean	30	0.02
Colombian	73	0.06
Ecuadorian	25	0.02
Paraguayan	0	<0.01
Peruvian	85	0.07
Uruguayan	0	<0.01
Venezuelan	45	0.04
Other South American	0	<0.01
Other Hispanic or Latino	3,267	2.63

Race*	Population	%
African-American/Black (2,627)	3,627	2.91
Not Hispanic (2,166)	2,764	2.22
Hispanic (461)	863	0.69
American Indian/Alaska Native (1,730)	3,192	2.57
Not Hispanic (811)	1,696	1.36
Hispanic (919)	1,496	1.20
Alaska Athabascan *(Ala. Nat.)* (0)	1	<0.01
Aleut *(Alaska Native)* (1)	1	<0.01
Apache (87)	152	0.12
Arapaho (3)	3	<0.01
Blackfeet (18)	59	0.05
Canadian/French Am. Ind. (5)	7	0.01
Central American Ind. (2)	2	<0.01
Cherokee (174)	526	0.42
Cheyenne (6)	8	0.01
Chickasaw (24)	58	0.05
Chippewa (10)	15	0.01
Choctaw (66)	168	0.14
Colville (0)	0	<0.01
Comanche (11)	28	0.02
Cree (1)	7	0.01
Creek (18)	33	0.03
Crow (0)	0	<0.01
Delaware (0)	5	<0.01
Hopi (1)	1	<0.01
Houma (0)	0	<0.01
Inupiat *(Alaska Native)* (0)	1	<0.01
Iroquois (6)	28	0.02
Kiowa (0)	0	<0.01
Lumbee (5)	6	<0.01
Menominee (0)	0	<0.01
Mexican American Ind. (133)	215	0.17
Navajo (41)	76	0.06
Osage (1)	9	0.01
Ottawa (0)	0	<0.01
Paiute (25)	33	0.03
Pima (2)	6	<0.01
Potawatomi (23)	31	0.02
Pueblo (2)	4	<0.01
Puget Sound Salish (10)	10	0.01
Seminole (8)	25	0.02
Shoshone (2)	3	<0.01
Sioux (11)	53	0.04
South American Ind. (3)	6	<0.01
Spanish American Ind. (8)	13	0.01
Tlingit-Haida *(Alaska Native)* (1)	2	<0.01
Tohono O'Odham (3)	4	<0.01
Tsimshian *(Alaska Native)* (0)	0	<0.01
Ute (3)	3	<0.01
Yakama (1)	3	<0.01
Yaqui (30)	56	0.05
Yuman (1)	4	<0.01
Yup'ik *(Alaska Native)* (0)	4	<0.01
Asian (6,768)	8,272	6.65
Not Hispanic (6,421)	7,389	5.94
Hispanic (347)	883	0.71
Bangladeshi (5)	5	<0.01
Bhutanese (0)	0	<0.01
Burmese (33)	41	0.03
Cambodian (49)	70	0.06
Chinese, ex. Taiwanese (607)	812	0.65
Filipino (1,513)	2,116	1.70
Hmong (542)	594	0.48
Indian (658)	743	0.60
Indonesian (9)	21	0.02
Japanese (317)	569	0.46
Korean (191)	293	0.24
Laotian (1,027)	1,194	0.96
Malaysian (4)	4	<0.01
Nepalese (8)	8	0.01
Pakistani (106)	115	0.09
Sri Lankan (7)	16	0.01
Taiwanese (17)	31	0.02
Thai (1,056)	1,134	0.91
Vietnamese (261)	317	0.25
Hawaii Native/Pacific Islander (164)	469	0.38
Not Hispanic (129)	304	0.24
Hispanic (35)	165	0.13
Fijian (6)	21	0.02
Guamanian/Chamorro (54)	77	0.06
Marshallese (3)	3	<0.01
Native Hawaiian (45)	169	0.14
Samoan (18)	40	0.03
Tongan (6)	7	0.01
White (80,203)	84,982	68.29
Not Hispanic (55,081)	57,171	45.94
Hispanic (25,122)	27,811	22.35

*Notes: † The Census 2010 population figure is used to calculate the percentages in the Hispanic Origin and Race categories. Ancestry percentages are based on the 2006-2010 American Community Survey population (not shown); ‡ Numbers in parentheses indicate the number of people reporting a single ancestry; * Numbers in parentheses indicate the number of persons reporting this race alone, not in combination with any other race; Please refer to the Explanation of Data for more information.*

Vista

Place Type: City
County: San Diego
Population: 93,834

Ancestry	Population	%
Afghan (186)	186	0.20
African, Sub-Saharan (142)	241	0.26
African (142)	235	0.25
Cape Verdean (0)	0	<0.01
Ethiopian (0)	0	<0.01
Ghanaian (0)	0	<0.01
Kenyan (0)	0	<0.01
Liberian (0)	0	<0.01
Nigerian (0)	0	<0.01
Senegalese (0)	0	<0.01
Sierra Leonean (0)	0	<0.01
Somalian (0)	0	<0.01
South African (0)	0	<0.01
Sudanese (0)	6	0.01
Ugandan (0)	0	<0.01
Zimbabwean (0)	0	<0.01
Other Sub-Saharan African (0)	0	<0.01
Albanian (18)	18	0.02
Alsatian (0)	0	<0.01
American (1,756)	1,756	1.90
Arab (248)	328	0.35
Arab (85)	85	0.09
Egyptian (77)	77	0.08
Iraqi (0)	0	<0.01
Jordanian (6)	6	0.01
Lebanese (32)	83	0.09
Moroccan (12)	24	0.03
Palestinian (26)	26	0.03
Syrian (0)	17	0.02
Other Arab (10)	10	0.01
Armenian (50)	60	0.06
Assyrian/Chaldean/Syriac (0)	0	<0.01
Australian (45)	55	0.06
Austrian (60)	158	0.17
Basque (15)	32	0.03
Belgian (26)	76	0.08
Brazilian (32)	32	0.03
British (199)	402	0.43
Bulgarian (34)	34	0.04
Cajun (0)	0	<0.01
Canadian (80)	160	0.17
Carpatho Rusyn (0)	0	<0.01
Celtic (0)	11	0.01
Croatian (113)	146	0.16
Cypriot (0)	0	<0.01
Czech (57)	231	0.25
Czechoslovakian (29)	55	0.06
Danish (197)	504	0.54
Dutch (190)	1,628	1.76
Eastern European (59)	59	0.06
English (3,981)	8,982	9.71
Estonian (16)	16	0.02
European (750)	1,022	1.11
Finnish (76)	371	0.40
French, ex. Basque (385)	2,777	3.00
French Canadian (88)	522	0.56
German (3,264)	10,626	11.49
German Russian (0)	0	<0.01
Greek (175)	493	0.53
Guyanese (0)	0	<0.01
Hungarian (70)	252	0.27
Icelander (0)	32	0.03
Iranian (69)	69	0.07
Irish (1,906)	7,670	8.29
Israeli (9)	9	0.01
Italian (1,244)	3,548	3.84
Latvian (24)	30	0.03
Lithuanian (85)	135	0.15
Luxemburger (0)	0	<0.01
Macedonian (11)	11	0.01
Maltese (0)	0	<0.01
New Zealander (0)	0	<0.01
Northern European (47)	67	0.07
Norwegian (244)	992	1.07
Pennsylvania German (0)	9	0.01
Polish (367)	1,090	1.18
Portuguese (83)	339	0.37
Romanian (76)	114	0.12
Russian (198)	388	0.42
Scandinavian (70)	164	0.18
Scotch-Irish (462)	1,235	1.34
Scottish (513)	1,642	1.78
Serbian (103)	142	0.15
Slavic (29)	29	0.03
Slovak (21)	49	0.05
Slovene (0)	13	0.01
Soviet Union (0)	0	<0.01
Swedish (283)	1,353	1.46
Swiss (48)	211	0.23
Turkish (81)	81	0.09
Ukrainian (45)	96	0.10
Welsh (20)	536	0.58
West Indian, ex. Hispanic (49)	68	0.07
Bahamian (0)	0	<0.01
Barbadian (10)	10	0.01
Belizean (0)	0	<0.01
Bermudan (0)	0	<0.01
British West Indian (0)	0	<0.01
Dutch West Indian (0)	0	<0.01
Haitian (0)	0	<0.01
Jamaican (39)	39	0.04
Trinidadian/Tobagonian (0)	19	0.02
U.S. Virgin Islander (0)	0	<0.01
West Indian (0)	0	<0.01
Other West Indian (0)	0	<0.01
Yugoslavian (112)	213	0.23

Hispanic Origin	Population	%
Hispanic or Latino (of any race)	45,380	48.36
Central American, ex. Mexican	768	0.82
Costa Rican	42	0.04
Guatemalan	269	0.29
Honduran	91	0.10
Nicaraguan	45	0.05
Panamanian	65	0.07
Salvadoran	245	0.26
Other Central American	11	0.01
Cuban	131	0.14
Dominican Republic	42	0.04
Mexican	40,799	43.48
Puerto Rican	657	0.70
South American	442	0.47
Argentinean	56	0.06
Bolivian	20	0.02
Chilean	51	0.05
Colombian	134	0.14
Ecuadorian	65	0.07
Paraguayan	0	<0.01
Peruvian	82	0.09
Uruguayan	4	<0.01
Venezuelan	18	0.02
Other South American	12	0.01
Other Hispanic or Latino	2,541	2.71

Race*	Population	%
African-American/Black (3,137)	4,293	4.58
Not Hispanic (2,753)	3,552	3.79
Hispanic (384)	741	0.79
American Indian/Alaska Native (1,103)	1,958	2.09
Not Hispanic (336)	799	0.85
Hispanic (767)	1,159	1.24
Alaska Athabascan *(Ala. Nat.)* (3)	6	0.01
Aleut *(Alaska Native)* (1)	1	<0.01
Apache (16)	54	0.06
Arapaho (4)	6	0.01
Blackfeet (5)	26	0.03
Canadian/French Am. Ind. (0)	0	<0.01
Central American Ind. (6)	7	0.01
Cherokee (47)	172	0.18
Cheyenne (1)	1	<0.01
Chickasaw (7)	13	0.01
Chippewa (4)	19	0.02
Choctaw (9)	45	0.05
Colville (0)	0	<0.01
Comanche (1)	2	<0.01
Cree (0)	0	<0.01
Creek (2)	9	0.01
Crow (0)	0	<0.01
Delaware (10)	14	0.01
Hopi (4)	7	0.01
Houma (0)	0	<0.01
Inupiat *(Alaska Native)* (2)	7	0.01
Iroquois (3)	9	0.01
Kiowa (0)	4	<0.01
Lumbee (0)	0	<0.01
Menominee (0)	1	<0.01
Mexican American Ind. (224)	308	0.33
Navajo (35)	56	0.06
Osage (3)	6	0.01
Ottawa (0)	1	<0.01
Paiute (0)	2	<0.01
Pima (1)	3	<0.01
Potawatomi (12)	14	0.01
Pueblo (15)	20	0.02
Puget Sound Salish (0)	1	<0.01
Seminole (1)	7	0.01
Shoshone (0)	0	<0.01
Sioux (15)	34	0.04
South American Ind. (4)	9	0.01
Spanish American Ind. (26)	32	0.03
Tlingit-Haida *(Alaska Native)* (1)	1	<0.01
Tohono O'Odham (7)	10	0.01
Tsimshian *(Alaska Native)* (0)	0	<0.01
Ute (4)	5	0.01
Yakama (1)	2	<0.01
Yaqui (18)	26	0.03
Yuman (7)	8	0.01
Yup'ik *(Alaska Native)* (1)	2	<0.01
Asian (3,979)	5,717	6.09
Not Hispanic (3,806)	5,148	5.49
Hispanic (173)	569	0.61
Bangladeshi (8)	8	0.01
Bhutanese (0)	0	<0.01
Burmese (1)	1	<0.01
Cambodian (49)	59	0.06
Chinese, ex. Taiwanese (506)	740	0.79
Filipino (1,343)	2,105	2.24
Hmong (3)	3	<0.01
Indian (289)	356	0.38
Indonesian (10)	47	0.05
Japanese (445)	973	1.04
Korean (343)	456	0.49
Laotian (43)	67	0.07
Malaysian (3)	11	0.01
Nepalese (1)	2	<0.01
Pakistani (21)	25	0.03
Sri Lankan (28)	29	0.03
Taiwanese (31)	35	0.04
Thai (56)	84	0.09
Vietnamese (609)	693	0.74
Hawaii Native/Pacific Islander (677)	1,252	1.33
Not Hispanic (615)	1,013	1.08
Hispanic (62)	239	0.25
Fijian (5)	5	0.01
Guamanian/Chamorro (110)	188	0.20
Marshallese (0)	0	<0.01
Native Hawaiian (78)	362	0.39
Samoan (390)	572	0.61
Tongan (3)	11	0.01
White (59,551)	63,675	67.86
Not Hispanic (38,287)	40,368	43.02
Hispanic (21,264)	23,307	24.84

*Notes: † The Census 2010 population figure is used to calculate the percentages in the Hispanic Origin and Race categories. Ancestry percentages are based on the 2006-2010 American Community Survey population (not shown); ‡ Numbers in parentheses indicate the number of people reporting a single ancestry; * Numbers in parentheses indicate the number of persons reporting this race alone, not in combination with any other race; Please refer to the Explanation of Data for more information.*

Walnut Creek

Place Type: City
County: Contra Costa
Population: 64,173

Ancestry	Population	%
Afghan (0)	77	0.12
African, Sub-Saharan (172)	208	0.33
African (44)	44	0.07
Cape Verdean (0)	12	0.02
Ethiopian (128)	152	0.24
Ghanaian (0)	0	<0.01
Kenyan (0)	0	<0.01
Liberian (0)	0	<0.01
Nigerian (0)	0	<0.01
Senegalese (0)	0	<0.01
Sierra Leonean (0)	0	<0.01
Somalian (0)	0	<0.01
South African (0)	0	<0.01
Sudanese (0)	0	<0.01
Ugandan (0)	0	<0.01
Zimbabwean (0)	0	<0.01
Other Sub-Saharan African (0)	0	<0.01
Albanian (0)	0	<0.01
Alsatian (0)	0	<0.01
American (1,266)	1,266	1.98
Arab (492)	713	1.12
Arab (74)	100	0.16
Egyptian (36)	52	0.08
Iraqi (12)	12	0.02
Jordanian (0)	0	<0.01
Lebanese (69)	131	0.21
Moroccan (0)	36	0.06
Palestinian (0)	0	<0.01
Syrian (43)	115	0.18
Other Arab (258)	267	0.42
Armenian (208)	291	0.46
Assyrian/Chaldean/Syriac (39)	39	0.06
Australian (90)	121	0.19
Austrian (221)	512	0.80
Basque (0)	0	<0.01
Belgian (59)	111	0.17
Brazilian (47)	47	0.07
British (370)	684	1.07
Bulgarian (114)	114	0.18
Cajun (0)	0	<0.01
Canadian (84)	270	0.42
Carpatho Rusyn (0)	0	<0.01
Celtic (23)	37	0.06
Croatian (60)	136	0.21
Cypriot (0)	0	<0.01
Czech (34)	260	0.41
Czechoslovakian (45)	137	0.21
Danish (146)	613	0.96
Dutch (277)	1,152	1.81
Eastern European (171)	171	0.27
English (2,895)	10,308	16.15
Estonian (0)	33	0.05
European (1,176)	1,316	2.06
Finnish (128)	357	0.56
French, ex. Basque (262)	2,243	3.52
French Canadian (181)	247	0.39
German (2,945)	11,568	18.13
German Russian (0)	0	<0.01
Greek (212)	372	0.58
Guyanese (19)	19	0.03
Hungarian (106)	463	0.73
Icelander (0)	17	0.03
Iranian (917)	1,013	1.59
Irish (2,437)	8,805	13.80
Israeli (67)	67	0.11
Italian (1,553)	4,697	7.36
Latvian (80)	155	0.24
Lithuanian (131)	310	0.49
Luxemburger (16)	16	0.03
Macedonian (0)	0	<0.01
Maltese (47)	54	0.08
New Zealander (0)	11	0.02
Northern European (382)	409	0.64
Norwegian (400)	1,356	2.13
Pennsylvania German (0)	0	<0.01
Polish (660)	1,693	2.65
Portuguese (440)	1,058	1.66
Romanian (61)	144	0.23
Russian (1,356)	2,317	3.63
Scandinavian (130)	218	0.34
Scotch-Irish (492)	1,286	2.02
Scottish (461)	2,364	3.70
Serbian (68)	82	0.13
Slavic (0)	10	0.02
Slovak (30)	60	0.09
Slovene (24)	24	0.04
Soviet Union (0)	0	<0.01
Swedish (488)	1,765	2.77
Swiss (98)	484	0.76
Turkish (78)	113	0.18
Ukrainian (368)	529	0.83
Welsh (24)	501	0.79
West Indian, ex. Hispanic (0)	24	0.04
Bahamian (0)	0	<0.01
Barbadian (0)	24	0.04
Belizean (0)	0	<0.01
Bermudan (0)	0	<0.01
British West Indian (0)	0	<0.01
Dutch West Indian (0)	0	<0.01
Haitian (0)	0	<0.01
Jamaican (0)	0	<0.01
Trinidadian/Tobagonian (0)	0	<0.01
U.S. Virgin Islander (0)	0	<0.01
West Indian (0)	0	<0.01
Other West Indian (0)	0	<0.01
Yugoslavian (91)	133	0.21

Hispanic Origin	Population	%
Hispanic or Latino (of any race)	5,540	8.63
Central American, ex. Mexican	646	1.01
Costa Rican	29	0.05
Guatemalan	99	0.15
Honduran	25	0.04
Nicaraguan	155	0.24
Panamanian	43	0.07
Salvadoran	282	0.44
Other Central American	13	0.02
Cuban	98	0.15
Dominican Republic	18	0.03
Mexican	3,108	4.84
Puerto Rican	217	0.34
South American	810	1.26
Argentinean	105	0.16
Bolivian	35	0.05
Chilean	86	0.13
Colombian	159	0.25
Ecuadorian	40	0.06
Paraguayan	15	0.02
Peruvian	315	0.49
Uruguayan	19	0.03
Venezuelan	31	0.05
Other South American	5	0.01
Other Hispanic or Latino	643	1.00

Race*	Population	%
African-American/Black (1,035)	1,477	2.30
Not Hispanic (996)	1,349	2.10
Hispanic (39)	128	0.20
American Indian/Alaska Native (155)	582	0.91
Not Hispanic (99)	413	0.64
Hispanic (56)	169	0.26
Alaska Athabascan *(Ala. Nat.)* (1)	1	<0.01
Aleut *(Alaska Native)* (0)	2	<0.01
Apache (1)	12	0.02
Arapaho (0)	0	<0.01
Blackfeet (0)	6	0.01
Canadian/French Am. Ind. (0)	0	<0.01
Central American Ind. (0)	1	<0.01
Cherokee (19)	114	0.18
Cheyenne (0)	3	<0.01
Chickasaw (2)	5	0.01
Chippewa (1)	18	0.03
Choctaw (9)	24	0.04
Colville (0)	2	<0.01
Comanche (0)	6	0.01
Cree (0)	1	<0.01
Creek (4)	12	0.02
Crow (0)	4	0.01
Delaware (1)	2	<0.01
Hopi (0)	3	<0.01
Houma (1)	1	<0.01
Inupiat *(Alaska Native)* (1)	3	<0.01
Iroquois (3)	8	0.01
Kiowa (0)	0	<0.01
Lumbee (1)	1	<0.01
Menominee (0)	0	<0.01
Mexican American Ind. (13)	28	0.04
Navajo (1)	9	0.01
Osage (0)	1	<0.01
Ottawa (1)	1	<0.01
Paiute (0)	0	<0.01
Pima (1)	2	<0.01
Potawatomi (1)	2	<0.01
Pueblo (2)	3	<0.01
Puget Sound Salish (0)	0	<0.01
Seminole (0)	1	<0.01
Shoshone (0)	0	<0.01
Sioux (4)	17	0.03
South American Ind. (5)	12	0.02
Spanish American Ind. (2)	3	<0.01
Tlingit-Haida *(Alaska Native)* (2)	3	<0.01
Tohono O'Odham (0)	0	<0.01
Tsimshian *(Alaska Native)* (1)	1	<0.01
Ute (0)	0	<0.01
Yakama (0)	0	<0.01
Yaqui (0)	3	<0.01
Yuman (0)	0	<0.01
Yup'ik *(Alaska Native)* (0)	0	<0.01
Asian (8,027)	9,707	15.13
Not Hispanic (7,954)	9,499	14.80
Hispanic (73)	208	0.32
Bangladeshi (10)	10	0.02
Bhutanese (0)	0	<0.01
Burmese (17)	23	0.04
Cambodian (12)	21	0.03
Chinese, ex. Taiwanese (2,891)	3,426	5.34
Filipino (1,420)	1,875	2.92
Hmong (0)	0	<0.01
Indian (1,143)	1,257	1.96
Indonesian (33)	59	0.09
Japanese (733)	1,162	1.81
Korean (835)	976	1.52
Laotian (13)	17	0.03
Malaysian (9)	11	0.02
Nepalese (6)	6	0.01
Pakistani (85)	108	0.17
Sri Lankan (21)	23	0.04
Taiwanese (210)	249	0.39
Thai (66)	86	0.13
Vietnamese (159)	212	0.33
Hawaii Native/Pacific Islander (125)	288	0.45
Not Hispanic (114)	248	0.39
Hispanic (11)	40	0.06
Fijian (13)	16	0.02
Guamanian/Chamorro (22)	47	0.07
Marshallese (0)	0	<0.01
Native Hawaiian (21)	100	0.16
Samoan (15)	19	0.03
Tongan (35)	46	0.07
White (50,487)	52,951	82.51
Not Hispanic (47,170)	49,141	76.58
Hispanic (3,317)	3,810	5.94

*Notes: † The Census 2010 population figure is used to calculate the percentages in the Hispanic Origin and Race categories. Ancestry percentages are based on the 2006-2010 American Community Survey population (not shown); ‡ Numbers in parentheses indicate the number of people reporting a single ancestry; * Numbers in parentheses indicate the number of persons reporting this race alone, not in combination with any other race; Please refer to the Explanation of Data for more information.*

Watsonville

Place Type: City
County: Santa Cruz
Population: 51,199

Ancestry	Population	%
Afghan (14)	27	0.05
African, Sub-Saharan (44)	44	0.09
African (44)	44	0.09
Cape Verdean (0)	0	<0.01
Ethiopian (0)	0	<0.01
Ghanaian (0)	0	<0.01
Kenyan (0)	0	<0.01
Liberian (0)	0	<0.01
Nigerian (0)	0	<0.01
Senegalese (0)	0	<0.01
Sierra Leonean (0)	0	<0.01
Somalian (0)	0	<0.01
South African (0)	0	<0.01
Sudanese (0)	0	<0.01
Ugandan (0)	0	<0.01
Zimbabwean (0)	0	<0.01
Other Sub-Saharan African (0)	0	<0.01
Albanian (0)	0	<0.01
Alsatian (0)	0	<0.01
American (302)	302	0.61
Arab (34)	54	0.11
Arab (0)	10	0.02
Egyptian (0)	0	<0.01
Iraqi (0)	0	<0.01
Jordanian (0)	0	<0.01
Lebanese (0)	10	0.02
Moroccan (0)	0	<0.01
Palestinian (34)	34	0.07
Syrian (0)	0	<0.01
Other Arab (0)	0	<0.01
Armenian (0)	0	<0.01
Assyrian/Chaldean/Syriac (0)	0	<0.01
Australian (11)	11	0.02
Austrian (0)	0	<0.01
Basque (0)	0	<0.01
Belgian (18)	47	0.09
Brazilian (8)	8	0.02
British (10)	76	0.15
Bulgarian (0)	0	<0.01
Cajun (35)	35	0.07
Canadian (28)	28	0.06
Carpatho Rusyn (0)	0	<0.01
Celtic (36)	36	0.07
Croatian (119)	185	0.37
Cypriot (0)	0	<0.01
Czech (12)	75	0.15
Czechoslovakian (29)	98	0.20
Danish (24)	77	0.16
Dutch (0)	108	0.22
Eastern European (0)	0	<0.01
English (371)	1,157	2.33
Estonian (12)	12	0.02
European (136)	252	0.51
Finnish (22)	22	0.04
French, ex. Basque (90)	512	1.03
French Canadian (68)	147	0.30
German (551)	1,843	3.72
German Russian (0)	0	<0.01
Greek (13)	75	0.15
Guyanese (0)	0	<0.01
Hungarian (0)	16	0.03
Icelander (0)	6	0.01
Iranian (25)	47	0.09
Irish (274)	1,552	3.13
Israeli (0)	0	<0.01
Italian (350)	956	1.93
Latvian (0)	0	<0.01
Lithuanian (0)	0	<0.01
Luxemburger (0)	0	<0.01
Macedonian (0)	0	<0.01
Maltese (0)	0	<0.01
New Zealander (45)	45	0.09
Northern European (0)	21	0.04
Norwegian (163)	214	0.43
Pennsylvania German (0)	0	<0.01
Polish (25)	178	0.36
Portuguese (551)	730	1.47
Romanian (0)	0	<0.01
Russian (88)	217	0.44
Scandinavian (0)	0	<0.01
Scotch-Irish (74)	168	0.34
Scottish (30)	148	0.30
Serbian (0)	0	<0.01
Slavic (35)	35	0.07
Slovak (0)	9	0.02
Slovene (0)	0	<0.01
Soviet Union (0)	0	<0.01
Swedish (62)	208	0.42
Swiss (0)	41	0.08
Turkish (0)	0	<0.01
Ukrainian (0)	0	<0.01
Welsh (35)	45	0.09
West Indian, ex. Hispanic (0)	0	<0.01
Bahamian (0)	0	<0.01
Barbadian (0)	0	<0.01
Belizean (0)	0	<0.01
Bermudan (0)	0	<0.01
British West Indian (0)	0	<0.01
Dutch West Indian (0)	0	<0.01
Haitian (0)	0	<0.01
Jamaican (0)	0	<0.01
Trinidadian/Tobagonian (0)	0	<0.01
U.S. Virgin Islander (0)	0	<0.01
West Indian (0)	0	<0.01
Other West Indian (0)	0	<0.01
Yugoslavian (0)	0	<0.01

Hispanic Origin	Population	%
Hispanic or Latino (of any race)	41,656	81.36
Central American, ex. Mexican	361	0.71
Costa Rican	5	0.01
Guatemalan	50	0.10
Honduran	21	0.04
Nicaraguan	16	0.03
Panamanian	6	0.01
Salvadoran	256	0.50
Other Central American	7	0.01
Cuban	18	0.04
Dominican Republic	3	0.01
Mexican	39,083	76.34
Puerto Rican	84	0.16
South American	113	0.22
Argentinean	27	0.05
Bolivian	5	0.01
Chilean	7	0.01
Colombian	18	0.04
Ecuadorian	11	0.02
Paraguayan	1	<0.01
Peruvian	43	0.08
Uruguayan	0	<0.01
Venezuelan	1	<0.01
Other South American	0	<0.01
Other Hispanic or Latino	1,994	3.89

Race*	Population	%
African-American/Black (358)	607	1.19
Not Hispanic (200)	325	0.63
Hispanic (158)	282	0.55
American Indian/Alaska Native (629)	1,066	2.08
Not Hispanic (139)	330	0.64
Hispanic (490)	736	1.44
Alaska Athabascan *(Ala. Nat.)* (0)	0	<0.01
Aleut *(Alaska Native)* (0)	0	<0.01
Apache (27)	42	0.08
Arapaho (0)	0	<0.01
Blackfeet (4)	15	0.03
Canadian/French Am. Ind. (0)	0	<0.01
Central American Ind. (2)	5	0.01
Cherokee (21)	71	0.14
Cheyenne (0)	0	<0.01
Chickasaw (0)	1	<0.01
Chippewa (2)	6	0.01
Choctaw (6)	17	0.03
Colville (0)	0	<0.01
Comanche (5)	11	0.02
Cree (1)	2	<0.01
Creek (3)	7	0.01
Crow (0)	0	<0.01
Delaware (0)	1	<0.01
Hopi (7)	12	0.02
Houma (0)	0	<0.01
Inupiat *(Alaska Native)* (0)	1	<0.01
Iroquois (1)	2	<0.01
Kiowa (0)	0	<0.01
Lumbee (0)	0	<0.01
Menominee (0)	0	<0.01
Mexican American Ind. (169)	233	0.46
Navajo (6)	18	0.04
Osage (0)	0	<0.01
Ottawa (0)	0	<0.01
Paiute (0)	0	<0.01
Pima (1)	1	<0.01
Potawatomi (1)	3	0.01
Pueblo (11)	12	0.02
Puget Sound Salish (0)	0	<0.01
Seminole (0)	1	<0.01
Shoshone (1)	8	0.02
Sioux (3)	5	0.01
South American Ind. (3)	4	0.01
Spanish American Ind. (6)	13	0.03
Tlingit-Haida *(Alaska Native)* (0)	5	0.01
Tohono O'Odham (0)	1	<0.01
Tsimshian *(Alaska Native)* (0)	0	<0.01
Ute (0)	0	<0.01
Yakama (0)	0	<0.01
Yaqui (9)	16	0.03
Yuman (1)	1	<0.01
Yup'ik *(Alaska Native)* (1)	1	<0.01
Asian (1,664)	2,166	4.23
Not Hispanic (1,549)	1,769	3.46
Hispanic (115)	397	0.78
Bangladeshi (0)	0	<0.01
Bhutanese (0)	0	<0.01
Burmese (5)	5	0.01
Cambodian (7)	8	0.02
Chinese, ex. Taiwanese (201)	247	0.48
Filipino (827)	1,140	2.23
Hmong (1)	1	<0.01
Indian (104)	133	0.26
Indonesian (1)	4	0.01
Japanese (389)	487	0.95
Korean (45)	62	0.12
Laotian (2)	4	0.01
Malaysian (0)	0	<0.01
Nepalese (0)	0	<0.01
Pakistani (5)	6	0.01
Sri Lankan (2)	2	<0.01
Taiwanese (9)	11	0.02
Thai (5)	13	0.03
Vietnamese (22)	27	0.05
Hawaii Native/Pacific Islander (40)	155	0.30
Not Hispanic (22)	69	0.13
Hispanic (18)	86	0.17
Fijian (0)	2	<0.01
Guamanian/Chamorro (5)	10	0.02
Marshallese (0)	0	<0.01
Native Hawaiian (26)	87	0.17
Samoan (8)	17	0.03
Tongan (0)	0	<0.01
White (22,399)	24,243	47.35
Not Hispanic (7,038)	7,468	14.59
Hispanic (15,361)	16,775	32.76

*Notes: † The Census 2010 population figure is used to calculate the percentages in the Hispanic Origin and Race categories. Ancestry percentages are based on the 2006-2010 American Community Survey population (not shown); ‡ Numbers in parentheses indicate the number of people reporting a single ancestry; * Numbers in parentheses indicate the number of persons reporting this race alone, not in combination with any other race; Please refer to the Explanation of Data for more information.*

West Covina

Place Type: City
County: Los Angeles
Population: 106,098

Ancestry	Population	%
Afghan (0)	0	<0.01
African, Sub-Saharan (380)	422	0.40
African (237)	279	0.26
Cape Verdean (0)	0	<0.01
Ethiopian (0)	0	<0.01
Ghanaian (143)	143	0.14
Kenyan (0)	0	<0.01
Liberian (0)	0	<0.01
Nigerian (0)	0	<0.01
Senegalese (0)	0	<0.01
Sierra Leonean (0)	0	<0.01
Somalian (0)	0	<0.01
South African (0)	0	<0.01
Sudanese (0)	0	<0.01
Ugandan (0)	0	<0.01
Zimbabwean (0)	0	<0.01
Other Sub-Saharan African (0)	0	<0.01
Albanian (8)	8	0.01
Alsatian (0)	0	<0.01
American (1,760)	1,760	1.67
Arab (891)	1,030	0.98
Arab (202)	266	0.25
Egyptian (125)	171	0.16
Iraqi (0)	0	<0.01
Jordanian (0)	20	0.02
Lebanese (292)	292	0.28
Moroccan (0)	0	<0.01
Palestinian (50)	50	0.05
Syrian (222)	231	0.22
Other Arab (0)	0	<0.01
Armenian (88)	127	0.12
Assyrian/Chaldean/Syriac (0)	0	<0.01
Australian (0)	0	<0.01
Austrian (0)	144	0.14
Basque (16)	33	0.03
Belgian (0)	15	0.01
Brazilian (29)	85	0.08
British (57)	110	0.10
Bulgarian (0)	20	0.02
Cajun (0)	0	<0.01
Canadian (119)	192	0.18
Carpatho Rusyn (0)	0	<0.01
Celtic (0)	0	<0.01
Croatian (13)	31	0.03
Cypriot (0)	0	<0.01
Czech (14)	153	0.14
Czechoslovakian (10)	10	0.01
Danish (105)	319	0.30
Dutch (251)	616	0.58
Eastern European (0)	11	0.01
English (820)	2,948	2.79
Estonian (0)	0	<0.01
European (222)	306	0.29
Finnish (6)	60	0.06
French, ex. Basque (62)	795	0.75
French Canadian (42)	125	0.12
German (1,081)	4,587	4.35
German Russian (0)	88	0.08
Greek (45)	107	0.10
Guyanese (37)	37	0.04
Hungarian (76)	130	0.12
Icelander (0)	0	<0.01
Iranian (141)	141	0.13
Irish (411)	2,568	2.43
Israeli (25)	25	0.02
Italian (623)	2,082	1.97
Latvian (13)	13	0.01
Lithuanian (31)	80	0.08
Luxemburger (0)	0	<0.01
Macedonian (0)	0	<0.01
Maltese (0)	0	<0.01
New Zealander (0)	0	<0.01
Northern European (0)	0	<0.01
Norwegian (174)	622	0.59
Pennsylvania German (12)	12	0.01
Polish (119)	734	0.70
Portuguese (58)	177	0.17
Romanian (10)	20	0.02
Russian (249)	400	0.38
Scandinavian (9)	34	0.03
Scotch-Irish (184)	353	0.33
Scottish (83)	411	0.39
Serbian (7)	21	0.02
Slavic (0)	0	<0.01
Slovak (0)	0	<0.01
Slovene (18)	34	0.03
Soviet Union (0)	0	<0.01
Swedish (96)	624	0.59
Swiss (7)	109	0.10
Turkish (33)	59	0.06
Ukrainian (4)	47	0.04
Welsh (40)	130	0.12
West Indian, ex. Hispanic (176)	176	0.17
Bahamian (0)	0	<0.01
Barbadian (24)	24	0.02
Belizean (0)	0	<0.01
Bermudan (0)	0	<0.01
British West Indian (0)	0	<0.01
Dutch West Indian (0)	0	<0.01
Haitian (0)	0	<0.01
Jamaican (118)	118	0.11
Trinidadian/Tobagonian (0)	0	<0.01
U.S. Virgin Islander (0)	0	<0.01
West Indian (34)	34	0.03
Other West Indian (0)	0	<0.01
Yugoslavian (0)	31	0.03

Hispanic Origin	Population	%
Hispanic or Latino (of any race)	56,471	53.23
Central American, ex. Mexican	4,091	3.86
Costa Rican	145	0.14
Guatemalan	946	0.89
Honduran	235	0.22
Nicaraguan	611	0.58
Panamanian	85	0.08
Salvadoran	2,019	1.90
Other Central American	50	0.05
Cuban	517	0.49
Dominican Republic	29	0.03
Mexican	46,505	43.83
Puerto Rican	615	0.58
South American	1,506	1.42
Argentinean	219	0.21
Bolivian	52	0.05
Chilean	81	0.08
Colombian	331	0.31
Ecuadorian	302	0.28
Paraguayan	6	0.01
Peruvian	437	0.41
Uruguayan	20	0.02
Venezuelan	43	0.04
Other South American	15	0.01
Other Hispanic or Latino	3,208	3.02

Race*	Population	%
African-American/Black (4,741)	5,634	5.31
Not Hispanic (4,260)	4,748	4.48
Hispanic (481)	886	0.84
American Indian/Alaska Native (1,045)	1,789	1.69
Not Hispanic (232)	532	0.50
Hispanic (813)	1,257	1.18
Alaska Athabascan *(Ala. Nat.)* (0)	1	<0.01
Aleut *(Alaska Native)* (0)	0	<0.01
Apache (53)	86	0.08
Arapaho (0)	2	<0.01
Blackfeet (8)	34	0.03
Canadian/French Am. Ind. (2)	2	<0.01
Central American Ind. (5)	13	0.01
Cherokee (21)	110	0.10
Cheyenne (12)	14	0.01
Chickasaw (3)	9	0.01
Chippewa (3)	11	0.01
Choctaw (8)	24	0.02
Colville (1)	5	<0.01
Comanche (1)	1	<0.01
Cree (0)	2	<0.01
Creek (3)	7	0.01
Crow (1)	1	<0.01
Delaware (5)	5	<0.01
Hopi (10)	17	0.02
Houma (0)	0	<0.01
Inupiat *(Alaska Native)* (0)	1	<0.01
Iroquois (1)	8	0.01
Kiowa (1)	3	<0.01
Lumbee (3)	3	<0.01
Menominee (0)	0	<0.01
Mexican American Ind. (156)	214	0.20
Navajo (22)	65	0.06
Osage (0)	2	<0.01
Ottawa (0)	4	<0.01
Paiute (8)	10	0.01
Pima (12)	22	0.02
Potawatomi (1)	2	<0.01
Pueblo (12)	24	0.02
Puget Sound Salish (0)	0	<0.01
Seminole (1)	1	<0.01
Shoshone (0)	0	<0.01
Sioux (12)	33	0.03
South American Ind. (0)	3	<0.01
Spanish American Ind. (8)	12	0.01
Tlingit-Haida *(Alaska Native)* (0)	0	<0.01
Tohono O'Odham (13)	17	0.02
Tsimshian *(Alaska Native)* (0)	0	<0.01
Ute (0)	4	<0.01
Yakama (1)	1	<0.01
Yaqui (14)	39	0.04
Yuman (0)	2	<0.01
Yup'ik *(Alaska Native)* (0)	0	<0.01
Asian (27,333)	29,177	27.50
Not Hispanic (26,834)	27,998	26.39
Hispanic (499)	1,179	1.11
Bangladeshi (25)	27	0.03
Bhutanese (0)	0	<0.01
Burmese (152)	178	0.17
Cambodian (163)	236	0.22
Chinese, ex. Taiwanese (8,012)	9,089	8.57
Filipino (10,689)	11,726	11.05
Hmong (0)	0	<0.01
Indian (667)	775	0.73
Indonesian (311)	427	0.40
Japanese (731)	1,100	1.04
Korean (756)	843	0.79
Laotian (168)	202	0.19
Malaysian (21)	40	0.04
Nepalese (5)	9	0.01
Pakistani (122)	133	0.13
Sri Lankan (75)	82	0.08
Taiwanese (1,199)	1,347	1.27
Thai (403)	449	0.42
Vietnamese (2,790)	3,230	3.04
Hawaii Native/Pacific Islander (198)	520	0.49
Not Hispanic (142)	363	0.34
Hispanic (56)	157	0.15
Fijian (13)	25	0.02
Guamanian/Chamorro (31)	59	0.06
Marshallese (0)	0	<0.01
Native Hawaiian (59)	146	0.14
Samoan (58)	96	0.09
Tongan (6)	17	0.02
White (45,432)	48,953	46.14
Not Hispanic (16,196)	17,497	16.49
Hispanic (29,236)	31,456	29.65

*Notes: † The Census 2010 population figure is used to calculate the percentages in the Hispanic Origin and Race categories. Ancestry percentages are based on the 2006-2010 American Community Survey population (not shown); ‡ Numbers in parentheses indicate the number of people reporting a single ancestry; * Numbers in parentheses indicate the number of persons reporting this race alone, not in combination with any other race; Please refer to the Explanation of Data for more information.*

Westminster

Place Type: City
County: Orange
Population: 89,701

Ancestry	Population	%
Afghan (0)	0	<0.01
African, Sub-Saharan (55)	55	0.06
African (55)	55	0.06
Cape Verdean (0)	0	<0.01
Ethiopian (0)	0	<0.01
Ghanaian (0)	0	<0.01
Kenyan (0)	0	<0.01
Liberian (0)	0	<0.01
Nigerian (0)	0	<0.01
Senegalese (0)	0	<0.01
Sierra Leonean (0)	0	<0.01
Somalian (0)	0	<0.01
South African (0)	0	<0.01
Sudanese (0)	0	<0.01
Ugandan (0)	0	<0.01
Zimbabwean (0)	0	<0.01
Other Sub-Saharan African (0)	0	<0.01
Albanian (13)	13	0.01
Alsatian (0)	0	<0.01
American (864)	864	0.97
Arab (930)	1,012	1.14
Arab (12)	12	0.01
Egyptian (296)	306	0.34
Iraqi (0)	0	<0.01
Jordanian (192)	202	0.23
Lebanese (61)	113	0.13
Moroccan (0)	0	<0.01
Palestinian (100)	100	0.11
Syrian (42)	52	0.06
Other Arab (227)	227	0.26
Armenian (351)	419	0.47
Assyrian/Chaldean/Syriac (78)	78	0.09
Australian (0)	0	<0.01
Austrian (100)	184	0.21
Basque (0)	35	0.04
Belgian (26)	128	0.14
Brazilian (14)	96	0.11
British (102)	148	0.17
Bulgarian (0)	0	<0.01
Cajun (0)	0	<0.01
Canadian (139)	162	0.18
Carpatho Rusyn (0)	0	<0.01
Celtic (13)	27	0.03
Croatian (6)	69	0.08
Cypriot (0)	0	<0.01
Czech (18)	185	0.21
Czechoslovakian (0)	36	0.04
Danish (42)	308	0.35
Dutch (384)	1,064	1.20
Eastern European (27)	27	0.03
English (1,027)	3,721	4.18
Estonian (0)	0	<0.01
European (384)	509	0.57
Finnish (52)	146	0.16
French, ex. Basque (243)	1,370	1.54
French Canadian (273)	434	0.49
German (2,129)	6,040	6.79
German Russian (0)	0	<0.01
Greek (133)	197	0.22
Guyanese (0)	0	<0.01
Hungarian (125)	219	0.25
Icelander (0)	0	<0.01
Iranian (140)	140	0.16
Irish (978)	4,442	5.00
Israeli (0)	0	<0.01
Italian (1,086)	2,561	2.88
Latvian (8)	8	0.01
Lithuanian (43)	107	0.12
Luxemburger (0)	0	<0.01
Macedonian (0)	0	<0.01
Maltese (0)	0	<0.01
New Zealander (0)	0	<0.01
Northern European (45)	53	0.06
Norwegian (184)	615	0.69
Pennsylvania German (0)	21	0.02
Polish (329)	1,011	1.14
Portuguese (51)	138	0.16
Romanian (46)	46	0.05
Russian (125)	257	0.29
Scandinavian (12)	66	0.07
Scotch-Irish (225)	521	0.59
Scottish (129)	513	0.58
Serbian (26)	26	0.03
Slavic (11)	55	0.06
Slovak (58)	96	0.11
Slovene (0)	10	0.01
Soviet Union (0)	0	<0.01
Swedish (241)	829	0.93
Swiss (14)	81	0.09
Turkish (0)	25	0.03
Ukrainian (82)	145	0.16
Welsh (83)	264	0.30
West Indian, ex. Hispanic (14)	24	0.03
Bahamian (0)	0	<0.01
Barbadian (0)	0	<0.01
Belizean (5)	10	0.01
Bermudan (0)	0	<0.01
British West Indian (0)	0	<0.01
Dutch West Indian (0)	0	<0.01
Haitian (0)	0	<0.01
Jamaican (0)	5	0.01
Trinidadian/Tobagonian (0)	0	<0.01
U.S. Virgin Islander (0)	0	<0.01
West Indian (9)	9	0.01
Other West Indian (0)	0	<0.01
Yugoslavian (121)	142	0.16

Hispanic Origin	Population	%
Hispanic or Latino (of any race)	21,176	23.61
Central American, ex. Mexican	867	0.97
Costa Rican	70	0.08
Guatemalan	249	0.28
Honduran	80	0.09
Nicaraguan	58	0.06
Panamanian	30	0.03
Salvadoran	374	0.42
Other Central American	6	0.01
Cuban	213	0.24
Dominican Republic	7	0.01
Mexican	18,037	20.11
Puerto Rican	257	0.29
South American	579	0.65
Argentinean	69	0.08
Bolivian	22	0.02
Chilean	44	0.05
Colombian	122	0.14
Ecuadorian	72	0.08
Paraguayan	2	<0.01
Peruvian	229	0.26
Uruguayan	3	<0.01
Venezuelan	10	0.01
Other South American	6	0.01
Other Hispanic or Latino	1,216	1.36

Race*	Population	%
African-American/Black (849)	1,255	1.40
Not Hispanic (700)	1,003	1.12
Hispanic (149)	252	0.28
American Indian/Alaska Native (397)	980	1.09
Not Hispanic (132)	495	0.55
Hispanic (265)	485	0.54
Alaska Athabascan *(Ala. Nat.)* (0)	0	<0.01
Aleut *(Alaska Native)* (0)	0	<0.01
Apache (18)	46	0.05
Arapaho (0)	0	<0.01
Blackfeet (10)	50	0.06
Canadian/French Am. Ind. (0)	0	<0.01
Central American Ind. (1)	2	<0.01
Cherokee (26)	148	0.16
Cheyenne (0)	2	<0.01
Chickasaw (0)	11	0.01
Chippewa (6)	17	0.02
Choctaw (7)	20	0.02
Colville (0)	0	<0.01
Comanche (1)	4	<0.01
Cree (3)	4	<0.01
Creek (2)	9	0.01
Crow (0)	0	<0.01
Delaware (0)	0	<0.01
Hopi (0)	3	<0.01
Houma (0)	0	<0.01
Inupiat *(Alaska Native)* (0)	0	<0.01
Iroquois (7)	22	0.02
Kiowa (0)	1	<0.01
Lumbee (3)	9	0.01
Menominee (0)	0	<0.01
Mexican American Ind. (59)	84	0.09
Navajo (13)	27	0.03
Osage (0)	3	<0.01
Ottawa (0)	0	<0.01
Paiute (0)	0	<0.01
Pima (1)	1	<0.01
Potawatomi (1)	1	<0.01
Pueblo (4)	11	0.01
Puget Sound Salish (1)	1	<0.01
Seminole (0)	3	<0.01
Shoshone (0)	3	<0.01
Sioux (15)	20	0.02
South American Ind. (1)	3	<0.01
Spanish American Ind. (0)	0	<0.01
Tlingit-Haida *(Alaska Native)* (0)	4	<0.01
Tohono O'Odham (0)	0	<0.01
Tsimshian *(Alaska Native)* (0)	8	0.01
Ute (4)	5	0.01
Yakama (0)	0	<0.01
Yaqui (6)	14	0.02
Yuman (5)	5	0.01
Yup'ik *(Alaska Native)* (0)	0	<0.01
Asian (42,597)	44,192	49.27
Not Hispanic (42,414)	43,687	48.70
Hispanic (183)	505	0.56
Bangladeshi (21)	21	0.02
Bhutanese (0)	0	<0.01
Burmese (15)	17	0.02
Cambodian (232)	282	0.31
Chinese, ex. Taiwanese (1,856)	2,590	2.89
Filipino (1,129)	1,578	1.76
Hmong (97)	102	0.11
Indian (331)	468	0.52
Indonesian (46)	113	0.13
Japanese (854)	1,229	1.37
Korean (613)	673	0.75
Laotian (104)	138	0.15
Malaysian (0)	2	<0.01
Nepalese (0)	0	<0.01
Pakistani (100)	116	0.13
Sri Lankan (14)	14	0.02
Taiwanese (65)	81	0.09
Thai (155)	196	0.22
Vietnamese (36,058)	37,176	41.44
Hawaii Native/Pacific Islander (361)	695	0.77
Not Hispanic (324)	589	0.66
Hispanic (37)	106	0.12
Fijian (1)	1	<0.01
Guamanian/Chamorro (65)	104	0.12
Marshallese (0)	2	<0.01
Native Hawaiian (59)	191	0.21
Samoan (210)	285	0.32
Tongan (1)	7	0.01
White (32,037)	34,753	38.74
Not Hispanic (22,972)	24,556	27.38
Hispanic (9,065)	10,197	11.37

*Notes: † The Census 2010 population figure is used to calculate the percentages in the Hispanic Origin and Race categories. Ancestry percentages are based on the 2006-2010 American Community Survey population (not shown); ‡ Numbers in parentheses indicate the number of people reporting a single ancestry; * Numbers in parentheses indicate the number of persons reporting this race alone, not in combination with any other race; Please refer to the Explanation of Data for more information.*

Whittier

Place Type: City
County: Los Angeles
Population: 85,331

Ancestry	Population	%
Afghan (0)	0	<0.01
African, Sub-Saharan (6)	6	0.01
African (6)	6	0.01
Cape Verdean (0)	0	<0.01
Ethiopian (0)	0	<0.01
Ghanaian (0)	0	<0.01
Kenyan (0)	0	<0.01
Liberian (0)	0	<0.01
Nigerian (0)	0	<0.01
Senegalese (0)	0	<0.01
Sierra Leonean (0)	0	<0.01
Somalian (0)	0	<0.01
South African (0)	0	<0.01
Sudanese (0)	0	<0.01
Ugandan (0)	0	<0.01
Zimbabwean (0)	0	<0.01
Other Sub-Saharan African (0)	0	<0.01
Albanian (0)	0	<0.01
Alsatian (0)	0	<0.01
American (1,920)	1,920	2.26
Arab (426)	515	0.61
Arab (16)	47	0.06
Egyptian (125)	125	0.15
Iraqi (0)	0	<0.01
Jordanian (0)	0	<0.01
Lebanese (240)	284	0.33
Moroccan (45)	45	0.05
Palestinian (0)	0	<0.01
Syrian (0)	14	0.02
Other Arab (0)	0	<0.01
Armenian (547)	696	0.82
Assyrian/Chaldean/Syriac (0)	0	<0.01
Australian (20)	48	0.06
Austrian (49)	219	0.26
Basque (42)	42	0.05
Belgian (5)	18	0.02
Brazilian (29)	44	0.05
British (211)	295	0.35
Bulgarian (0)	0	<0.01
Cajun (0)	0	<0.01
Canadian (42)	108	0.13
Carpatho Rusyn (0)	0	<0.01
Celtic (24)	24	0.03
Croatian (48)	99	0.12
Cypriot (0)	0	<0.01
Czech (12)	89	0.10
Czechoslovakian (19)	54	0.06
Danish (169)	555	0.65
Dutch (170)	826	0.97
Eastern European (0)	0	<0.01
English (1,368)	5,341	6.28
Estonian (0)	0	<0.01
European (619)	842	0.99
Finnish (10)	20	0.02
French, ex. Basque (98)	1,309	1.54
French Canadian (68)	322	0.38
German (1,339)	6,448	7.59
German Russian (0)	0	<0.01
Greek (147)	286	0.34
Guyanese (0)	0	<0.01
Hungarian (18)	124	0.15
Icelander (0)	0	<0.01
Iranian (12)	38	0.04
Irish (919)	5,094	5.99
Israeli (9)	62	0.07
Italian (995)	2,781	3.27
Latvian (0)	0	<0.01
Lithuanian (0)	31	0.04
Luxemburger (0)	0	<0.01
Macedonian (26)	26	0.03
Maltese (0)	0	<0.01
New Zealander (0)	0	<0.01
Northern European (9)	9	0.01
Norwegian (150)	721	0.85
Pennsylvania German (0)	80	0.09
Polish (190)	766	0.90
Portuguese (120)	210	0.25
Romanian (47)	102	0.12
Russian (267)	612	0.72
Scandinavian (68)	105	0.12
Scotch-Irish (264)	823	0.97
Scottish (214)	1,041	1.22
Serbian (4)	47	0.06
Slavic (0)	0	<0.01
Slovak (0)	10	0.01
Slovene (11)	23	0.03
Soviet Union (0)	0	<0.01
Swedish (212)	644	0.76
Swiss (102)	153	0.18
Turkish (14)	34	0.04
Ukrainian (137)	164	0.19
Welsh (111)	366	0.43
West Indian, ex. Hispanic (27)	44	0.05
Bahamian (0)	0	<0.01
Barbadian (0)	0	<0.01
Belizean (0)	0	<0.01
Bermudan (0)	0	<0.01
British West Indian (0)	0	<0.01
Dutch West Indian (0)	0	<0.01
Haitian (18)	18	0.02
Jamaican (0)	17	0.02
Trinidadian/Tobagonian (9)	9	0.01
U.S. Virgin Islander (0)	0	<0.01
West Indian (0)	0	<0.01
Other West Indian (0)	0	<0.01
Yugoslavian (0)	45	0.05

Hispanic Origin	Population	%
Hispanic or Latino (of any race)	56,081	65.72
Central American, ex. Mexican	2,758	3.23
Costa Rican	152	0.18
Guatemalan	684	0.80
Honduran	125	0.15
Nicaraguan	313	0.37
Panamanian	40	0.05
Salvadoran	1,390	1.63
Other Central American	54	0.06
Cuban	410	0.48
Dominican Republic	30	0.04
Mexican	48,567	56.92
Puerto Rican	555	0.65
South American	904	1.06
Argentinean	188	0.22
Bolivian	54	0.06
Chilean	47	0.06
Colombian	192	0.23
Ecuadorian	156	0.18
Paraguayan	15	0.02
Peruvian	191	0.22
Uruguayan	14	0.02
Venezuelan	25	0.03
Other South American	22	0.03
Other Hispanic or Latino	2,857	3.35

Race*	Population	%
African-American/Black (1,092)	1,560	1.83
Not Hispanic (780)	967	1.13
Hispanic (312)	593	0.69
American Indian/Alaska Native (1,093)	1,750	2.05
Not Hispanic (226)	411	0.48
Hispanic (867)	1,339	1.57
Alaska Athabascan *(Ala. Nat.)* (0)	0	<0.01
Aleut *(Alaska Native)* (0)	0	<0.01
Apache (78)	138	0.16
Arapaho (0)	0	<0.01
Blackfeet (2)	11	0.01
Canadian/French Am. Ind. (0)	0	<0.01
Central American Ind. (6)	8	0.01
Cherokee (34)	107	0.13
Cheyenne (4)	7	0.01
Chickasaw (3)	12	0.01
Chippewa (8)	11	0.01
Choctaw (2)	22	0.03
Colville (0)	0	<0.01
Comanche (1)	11	0.01
Cree (0)	0	<0.01
Creek (12)	14	0.02
Crow (0)	0	<0.01
Delaware (0)	1	<0.01
Hopi (8)	11	0.01
Houma (0)	0	<0.01
Inupiat *(Alaska Native)* (0)	5	0.01
Iroquois (5)	6	0.01
Kiowa (8)	11	0.01
Lumbee (0)	0	<0.01
Menominee (1)	1	<0.01
Mexican American Ind. (157)	229	0.27
Navajo (58)	80	0.09
Osage (1)	2	<0.01
Ottawa (0)	0	<0.01
Paiute (0)	3	<0.01
Pima (1)	5	0.01
Potawatomi (3)	4	<0.01
Pueblo (33)	45	0.05
Puget Sound Salish (0)	0	<0.01
Seminole (2)	6	0.01
Shoshone (10)	15	0.02
Sioux (17)	26	0.03
South American Ind. (2)	6	0.01
Spanish American Ind. (6)	9	0.01
Tlingit-Haida *(Alaska Native)* (1)	1	<0.01
Tohono O'Odham (8)	13	0.02
Tsimshian *(Alaska Native)* (0)	0	<0.01
Ute (1)	2	<0.01
Yakama (0)	0	<0.01
Yaqui (26)	50	0.06
Yuman (4)	5	0.01
Yup'ik *(Alaska Native)* (0)	0	<0.01
Asian (3,262)	4,266	5.00
Not Hispanic (2,996)	3,517	4.12
Hispanic (266)	749	0.88
Bangladeshi (0)	0	<0.01
Bhutanese (0)	0	<0.01
Burmese (7)	7	0.01
Cambodian (47)	55	0.06
Chinese, ex. Taiwanese (657)	923	1.08
Filipino (879)	1,213	1.42
Hmong (1)	1	<0.01
Indian (193)	251	0.29
Indonesian (20)	45	0.05
Japanese (597)	954	1.12
Korean (361)	438	0.51
Laotian (8)	8	0.01
Malaysian (4)	8	0.01
Nepalese (12)	15	0.02
Pakistani (28)	36	0.04
Sri Lankan (9)	12	0.01
Taiwanese (85)	103	0.12
Thai (82)	103	0.12
Vietnamese (113)	149	0.17
Hawaii Native/Pacific Islander (123)	319	0.37
Not Hispanic (91)	199	0.23
Hispanic (32)	120	0.14
Fijian (0)	0	<0.01
Guamanian/Chamorro (28)	49	0.06
Marshallese (0)	0	<0.01
Native Hawaiian (36)	138	0.16
Samoan (35)	53	0.06
Tongan (12)	15	0.02
White (55,117)	58,349	68.38
Not Hispanic (24,126)	24,902	29.18
Hispanic (30,991)	33,447	39.20

*Notes: † The Census 2010 population figure is used to calculate the percentages in the Hispanic Origin and Race categories. Ancestry percentages are based on the 2006-2010 American Community Survey population (not shown); ‡ Numbers in parentheses indicate the number of people reporting a single ancestry; * Numbers in parentheses indicate the number of persons reporting this race alone, not in combination with any other race; Please refer to the Explanation of Data for more information.*

Woodland

Place Type: City
County: Yolo
Population: 55,468

Ancestry	Population	%
Afghan (13)	13	0.02
African, Sub-Saharan (20)	48	0.09
African (20)	48	0.09
Cape Verdean (0)	0	<0.01
Ethiopian (0)	0	<0.01
Ghanaian (0)	0	<0.01
Kenyan (0)	0	<0.01
Liberian (0)	0	<0.01
Nigerian (0)	0	<0.01
Senegalese (0)	0	<0.01
Sierra Leonean (0)	0	<0.01
Somalian (0)	0	<0.01
South African (0)	0	<0.01
Sudanese (0)	0	<0.01
Ugandan (0)	0	<0.01
Zimbabwean (0)	0	<0.01
Other Sub-Saharan African (0)	0	<0.01
Albanian (0)	30	0.05
Alsatian (0)	0	<0.01
American (1,242)	1,242	2.27
Arab (47)	93	0.17
Arab (0)	27	0.05
Egyptian (0)	0	<0.01
Iraqi (0)	0	<0.01
Jordanian (15)	15	0.03
Lebanese (9)	28	0.05
Moroccan (0)	0	<0.01
Palestinian (0)	0	<0.01
Syrian (0)	0	<0.01
Other Arab (23)	23	0.04
Armenian (0)	0	<0.01
Assyrian/Chaldean/Syriac (0)	0	<0.01
Australian (27)	41	0.07
Austrian (12)	45	0.08
Basque (44)	127	0.23
Belgian (0)	17	0.03
Brazilian (13)	13	0.02
British (27)	78	0.14
Bulgarian (0)	0	<0.01
Cajun (0)	11	0.02
Canadian (18)	50	0.09
Carpatho Rusyn (0)	0	<0.01
Celtic (0)	0	<0.01
Croatian (0)	75	0.14
Cypriot (0)	0	<0.01
Czech (26)	86	0.16
Czechoslovakian (10)	23	0.04
Danish (132)	471	0.86
Dutch (139)	651	1.19
Eastern European (80)	80	0.15
English (1,641)	4,976	9.08
Estonian (0)	0	<0.01
European (759)	930	1.70
Finnish (82)	219	0.40
French, ex. Basque (189)	991	1.81
French Canadian (35)	215	0.39
German (2,362)	7,272	13.27
German Russian (0)	0	<0.01
Greek (107)	138	0.25
Guyanese (0)	0	<0.01
Hungarian (42)	130	0.24
Icelander (15)	15	0.03
Iranian (8)	8	0.01
Irish (1,178)	4,734	8.64
Israeli (0)	0	<0.01
Italian (857)	2,425	4.43
Latvian (0)	0	<0.01
Lithuanian (9)	38	0.07
Luxemburger (0)	16	0.03
Macedonian (0)	0	<0.01
Maltese (0)	0	<0.01
New Zealander (0)	7	0.01
Northern European (36)	36	0.07
Norwegian (182)	700	1.28
Pennsylvania German (17)	17	0.03
Polish (117)	473	0.86
Portuguese (340)	616	1.12
Romanian (0)	0	<0.01
Russian (69)	227	0.41
Scandinavian (91)	123	0.22
Scotch-Irish (199)	892	1.63
Scottish (204)	1,047	1.91
Serbian (0)	0	<0.01
Slavic (0)	11	0.02
Slovak (15)	24	0.04
Slovene (0)	0	<0.01
Soviet Union (0)	0	<0.01
Swedish (159)	725	1.32
Swiss (44)	205	0.37
Turkish (20)	20	0.04
Ukrainian (107)	133	0.24
Welsh (12)	276	0.50
West Indian, ex. Hispanic (26)	62	0.11
Bahamian (0)	0	<0.01
Barbadian (0)	0	<0.01
Belizean (0)	0	<0.01
Bermudan (0)	0	<0.01
British West Indian (0)	0	<0.01
Dutch West Indian (0)	0	<0.01
Haitian (8)	16	0.03
Jamaican (18)	46	0.08
Trinidadian/Tobagonian (0)	0	<0.01
U.S. Virgin Islander (0)	0	<0.01
West Indian (0)	0	<0.01
Other West Indian (0)	0	<0.01
Yugoslavian (13)	13	0.02

Hispanic Origin	Population	%
Hispanic or Latino (of any race)	26,289	47.39
Central American, ex. Mexican	367	0.66
Costa Rican	10	0.02
Guatemalan	69	0.12
Honduran	109	0.20
Nicaraguan	36	0.06
Panamanian	16	0.03
Salvadoran	127	0.23
Other Central American	0	<0.01
Cuban	42	0.08
Dominican Republic	15	0.03
Mexican	24,330	43.86
Puerto Rican	183	0.33
South American	157	0.28
Argentinean	31	0.06
Bolivian	2	<0.01
Chilean	12	0.02
Colombian	35	0.06
Ecuadorian	12	0.02
Paraguayan	0	<0.01
Peruvian	46	0.08
Uruguayan	2	<0.01
Venezuelan	14	0.03
Other South American	3	0.01
Other Hispanic or Latino	1,195	2.15

Race*	Population	%
African-American/Black (855)	1,263	2.28
Not Hispanic (708)	954	1.72
Hispanic (147)	309	0.56
American Indian/Alaska Native (726)	1,468	2.65
Not Hispanic (332)	754	1.36
Hispanic (394)	714	1.29
Alaska Athabascan *(Ala. Nat.)* (1)	4	0.01
Aleut *(Alaska Native)* (1)	2	<0.01
Apache (16)	40	0.07
Arapaho (0)	0	<0.01
Blackfeet (5)	18	0.03
Canadian/French Am. Ind. (0)	1	<0.01
Central American Ind. (0)	2	<0.01
Cherokee (66)	222	0.40
Cheyenne (1)	3	0.01
Chickasaw (2)	6	0.01
Chippewa (5)	13	0.02
Choctaw (20)	60	0.11
Colville (0)	0	<0.01
Comanche (0)	6	0.01
Cree (0)	2	<0.01
Creek (3)	7	0.01
Crow (6)	7	0.01
Delaware (0)	0	<0.01
Hopi (4)	6	0.01
Houma (0)	1	<0.01
Inupiat *(Alaska Native)* (2)	5	0.01
Iroquois (3)	16	0.03
Kiowa (0)	0	<0.01
Lumbee (0)	0	<0.01
Menominee (0)	0	<0.01
Mexican American Ind. (65)	97	0.17
Navajo (15)	35	0.06
Osage (1)	2	<0.01
Ottawa (0)	0	<0.01
Paiute (10)	18	0.03
Pima (3)	5	0.01
Potawatomi (4)	7	0.01
Pueblo (3)	9	0.02
Puget Sound Salish (0)	0	<0.01
Seminole (0)	0	<0.01
Shoshone (10)	14	0.03
Sioux (12)	37	0.07
South American Ind. (2)	5	0.01
Spanish American Ind. (8)	9	0.02
Tlingit-Haida *(Alaska Native)* (3)	3	0.01
Tohono O'Odham (2)	2	<0.01
Tsimshian *(Alaska Native)* (0)	0	<0.01
Ute (0)	0	<0.01
Yakama (5)	5	0.01
Yaqui (12)	28	0.05
Yuman (0)	0	<0.01
Yup'ik *(Alaska Native)* (0)	0	<0.01
Asian (3,458)	4,220	7.61
Not Hispanic (3,385)	3,937	7.10
Hispanic (73)	283	0.51
Bangladeshi (0)	0	<0.01
Bhutanese (0)	0	<0.01
Burmese (0)	0	<0.01
Cambodian (31)	39	0.07
Chinese, ex. Taiwanese (533)	675	1.22
Filipino (519)	801	1.44
Hmong (36)	44	0.08
Indian (995)	1,139	2.05
Indonesian (0)	2	<0.01
Japanese (198)	346	0.62
Korean (51)	77	0.14
Laotian (12)	27	0.05
Malaysian (0)	0	<0.01
Nepalese (149)	162	0.29
Pakistani (615)	677	1.22
Sri Lankan (8)	11	0.02
Taiwanese (8)	12	0.02
Thai (26)	37	0.07
Vietnamese (123)	157	0.28
Hawaii Native/Pacific Islander (169)	386	0.70
Not Hispanic (141)	283	0.51
Hispanic (28)	103	0.19
Fijian (85)	105	0.19
Guamanian/Chamorro (19)	40	0.07
Marshallese (0)	0	<0.01
Native Hawaiian (21)	84	0.15
Samoan (7)	21	0.04
Tongan (2)	5	0.01
White (34,904)	37,319	67.28
Not Hispanic (23,368)	24,340	43.88
Hispanic (11,536)	12,979	23.40

*Notes: † The Census 2010 population figure is used to calculate the percentages in the Hispanic Origin and Race categories. Ancestry percentages are based on the 2006-2010 American Community Survey population (not shown); ‡ Numbers in parentheses indicate the number of people reporting a single ancestry; * Numbers in parentheses indicate the number of persons reporting this race alone, not in combination with any other race; Please refer to the Explanation of Data for more information.*

Yorba Linda

Place Type: City
County: Orange
Population: 64,234

Ancestry	Population	%
Afghan (0)	0	<0.01
African, Sub-Saharan (66)	96	0.15
African (0)	30	0.05
Cape Verdean (0)	0	<0.01
Ethiopian (0)	0	<0.01
Ghanaian (0)	0	<0.01
Kenyan (0)	0	<0.01
Liberian (0)	0	<0.01
Nigerian (23)	23	0.04
Senegalese (0)	0	<0.01
Sierra Leonean (0)	0	<0.01
Somalian (0)	0	<0.01
South African (26)	26	0.04
Sudanese (9)	9	0.01
Ugandan (0)	0	<0.01
Zimbabwean (0)	0	<0.01
Other Sub-Saharan African (8)	8	0.01
Albanian (6)	6	0.01
Alsatian (0)	0	<0.01
American (2,302)	2,302	3.66
Arab (694)	870	1.38
Arab (153)	153	0.24
Egyptian (70)	89	0.14
Iraqi (15)	60	0.10
Jordanian (6)	25	0.04
Lebanese (291)	374	0.59
Moroccan (0)	0	<0.01
Palestinian (25)	25	0.04
Syrian (0)	10	0.02
Other Arab (134)	134	0.21
Armenian (219)	319	0.51
Assyrian/Chaldean/Syriac (4)	69	0.11
Australian (0)	6	0.01
Austrian (74)	115	0.18
Basque (12)	21	0.03
Belgian (33)	63	0.10
Brazilian (0)	24	0.04
British (169)	296	0.47
Bulgarian (8)	8	0.01
Cajun (0)	14	0.02
Canadian (199)	388	0.62
Carpatho Rusyn (0)	0	<0.01
Celtic (0)	0	<0.01
Croatian (0)	109	0.17
Cypriot (0)	0	<0.01
Czech (118)	277	0.44
Czechoslovakian (66)	120	0.19
Danish (231)	720	1.14
Dutch (319)	1,479	2.35
Eastern European (53)	63	0.10
English (2,446)	8,660	13.76
Estonian (12)	12	0.02
European (928)	1,039	1.65
Finnish (11)	82	0.13
French, ex. Basque (251)	2,344	3.73
French Canadian (120)	343	0.55
German (2,869)	11,892	18.90
German Russian (0)	0	<0.01
Greek (192)	309	0.49
Guyanese (0)	0	<0.01
Hungarian (107)	528	0.84
Icelander (0)	0	<0.01
Iranian (705)	789	1.25
Irish (1,634)	7,899	12.56
Israeli (15)	25	0.04
Italian (1,737)	4,743	7.54
Latvian (8)	26	0.04
Lithuanian (43)	97	0.15
Luxemburger (0)	0	<0.01
Macedonian (6)	6	0.01
Maltese (0)	0	<0.01
New Zealander (0)	0	<0.01
Northern European (34)	34	0.05
Norwegian (340)	975	1.55
Pennsylvania German (0)	0	<0.01
Polish (384)	1,600	2.54
Portuguese (41)	129	0.21
Romanian (105)	217	0.34
Russian (218)	691	1.10
Scandinavian (100)	245	0.39
Scotch-Irish (261)	1,121	1.78
Scottish (512)	1,413	2.25
Serbian (95)	149	0.24
Slavic (74)	86	0.14
Slovak (28)	204	0.32
Slovene (0)	66	0.10
Soviet Union (0)	0	<0.01
Swedish (414)	1,571	2.50
Swiss (8)	281	0.45
Turkish (9)	9	0.01
Ukrainian (77)	267	0.42
Welsh (21)	629	1.00
West Indian, ex. Hispanic (24)	32	0.05
Bahamian (0)	0	<0.01
Barbadian (0)	0	<0.01
Belizean (0)	8	0.01
Bermudan (0)	0	<0.01
British West Indian (0)	0	<0.01
Dutch West Indian (6)	6	0.01
Haitian (0)	0	<0.01
Jamaican (18)	18	0.03
Trinidadian/Tobagonian (0)	0	<0.01
U.S. Virgin Islander (0)	0	<0.01
West Indian (0)	0	<0.01
Other West Indian (0)	0	<0.01
Yugoslavian (11)	87	0.14

Hispanic Origin	Population	%
Hispanic or Latino (of any race)	9,220	14.35
Central American, ex. Mexican	331	0.52
Costa Rican	39	0.06
Guatemalan	83	0.13
Honduran	21	0.03
Nicaraguan	58	0.09
Panamanian	14	0.02
Salvadoran	115	0.18
Other Central American	1	<0.01
Cuban	255	0.40
Dominican Republic	25	0.04
Mexican	6,884	10.72
Puerto Rican	200	0.31
South American	703	1.09
Argentinean	132	0.21
Bolivian	17	0.03
Chilean	33	0.05
Colombian	153	0.24
Ecuadorian	95	0.15
Paraguayan	2	<0.01
Peruvian	239	0.37
Uruguayan	16	0.02
Venezuelan	8	0.01
Other South American	8	0.01
Other Hispanic or Latino	822	1.28

Race*	Population	%
African-American/Black (835)	1,145	1.78
Not Hispanic (789)	1,032	1.61
Hispanic (46)	113	0.18
American Indian/Alaska Native (230)	634	0.99
Not Hispanic (120)	389	0.61
Hispanic (110)	245	0.38
Alaska Athabascan *(Ala. Nat.)* (1)	3	<0.01
Aleut *(Alaska Native)* (5)	5	0.01
Apache (8)	42	0.07
Arapaho (0)	0	<0.01
Blackfeet (3)	24	0.04
Canadian/French Am. Ind. (0)	2	<0.01
Central American Ind. (1)	1	<0.01
Cherokee (23)	110	0.17
Cheyenne (0)	0	<0.01
Chickasaw (4)	5	0.01
Chippewa (2)	14	0.02
Choctaw (20)	50	0.08
Colville (0)	0	<0.01
Comanche (1)	1	<0.01
Cree (0)	0	<0.01
Creek (6)	7	0.01
Crow (0)	0	<0.01
Delaware (0)	0	<0.01
Hopi (1)	3	<0.01
Houma (0)	0	<0.01
Inupiat *(Alaska Native)* (0)	1	<0.01
Iroquois (0)	3	<0.01
Kiowa (0)	0	<0.01
Lumbee (0)	0	<0.01
Menominee (0)	0	<0.01
Mexican American Ind. (9)	19	0.03
Navajo (6)	13	0.02
Osage (7)	7	0.01
Ottawa (0)	0	<0.01
Paiute (2)	5	0.01
Pima (7)	7	0.01
Potawatomi (0)	0	<0.01
Pueblo (1)	2	<0.01
Puget Sound Salish (0)	0	<0.01
Seminole (0)	4	0.01
Shoshone (0)	2	<0.01
Sioux (3)	15	0.02
South American Ind. (7)	10	0.02
Spanish American Ind. (2)	2	<0.01
Tlingit-Haida *(Alaska Native)* (0)	0	<0.01
Tohono O'Odham (0)	0	<0.01
Tsimshian *(Alaska Native)* (0)	0	<0.01
Ute (0)	2	<0.01
Yakama (0)	0	<0.01
Yaqui (4)	13	0.02
Yuman (0)	0	<0.01
Yup'ik *(Alaska Native)* (0)	0	<0.01
Asian (10,030)	11,494	17.89
Not Hispanic (9,957)	11,216	17.46
Hispanic (73)	278	0.43
Bangladeshi (13)	13	0.02
Bhutanese (0)	0	<0.01
Burmese (17)	21	0.03
Cambodian (61)	73	0.11
Chinese, ex. Taiwanese (1,860)	2,347	3.65
Filipino (1,273)	1,657	2.58
Hmong (0)	0	<0.01
Indian (1,421)	1,545	2.41
Indonesian (107)	158	0.25
Japanese (711)	1,147	1.79
Korean (1,966)	2,132	3.32
Laotian (16)	20	0.03
Malaysian (3)	11	0.02
Nepalese (0)	0	<0.01
Pakistani (223)	259	0.40
Sri Lankan (21)	21	0.03
Taiwanese (517)	555	0.86
Thai (120)	143	0.22
Vietnamese (1,257)	1,456	2.27
Hawaii Native/Pacific Islander (85)	245	0.38
Not Hispanic (78)	214	0.33
Hispanic (7)	31	0.05
Fijian (4)	6	0.01
Guamanian/Chamorro (17)	28	0.04
Marshallese (0)	0	<0.01
Native Hawaiian (33)	114	0.18
Samoan (9)	29	0.05
Tongan (0)	0	<0.01
White (48,246)	50,506	78.63
Not Hispanic (42,183)	43,720	68.06
Hispanic (6,063)	6,786	10.56

*Notes: † The Census 2010 population figure is used to calculate the percentages in the Hispanic Origin and Race categories. Ancestry percentages are based on the 2006-2010 American Community Survey population (not shown); ‡ Numbers in parentheses indicate the number of people reporting a single ancestry; * Numbers in parentheses indicate the number of persons reporting this race alone, not in combination with any other race; Please refer to the Explanation of Data for more information.*

Yuba City

Place Type: City
County: Sutter
Population: 64,925

Ancestry	Population	%
Afghan (0)	0	<0.01
African, Sub-Saharan (22)	35	0.06
African (22)	35	0.06
Cape Verdean (0)	0	<0.01
Ethiopian (0)	0	<0.01
Ghanaian (0)	0	<0.01
Kenyan (0)	0	<0.01
Liberian (0)	0	<0.01
Nigerian (0)	0	<0.01
Senegalese (0)	0	<0.01
Sierra Leonean (0)	0	<0.01
Somalian (0)	0	<0.01
South African (0)	0	<0.01
Sudanese (0)	0	<0.01
Ugandan (0)	0	<0.01
Zimbabwean (0)	0	<0.01
Other Sub-Saharan African (0)	0	<0.01
Albanian (0)	0	<0.01
Alsatian (0)	0	<0.01
American (3,200)	3,200	5.04
Arab (68)	178	0.28
Arab (66)	66	0.10
Egyptian (0)	0	<0.01
Iraqi (0)	0	<0.01
Jordanian (0)	0	<0.01
Lebanese (0)	110	0.17
Moroccan (0)	0	<0.01
Palestinian (0)	0	<0.01
Syrian (2)	2	<0.01
Other Arab (0)	0	<0.01
Armenian (158)	168	0.26
Assyrian/Chaldean/Syriac (0)	0	<0.01
Australian (0)	0	<0.01
Austrian (9)	15	0.02
Basque (29)	29	0.05
Belgian (0)	16	0.03
Brazilian (37)	99	0.16
British (70)	91	0.14
Bulgarian (0)	0	<0.01
Cajun (9)	9	0.01
Canadian (31)	126	0.20
Carpatho Rusyn (0)	0	<0.01
Celtic (10)	22	0.03
Croatian (0)	14	0.02
Cypriot (0)	0	<0.01
Czech (122)	283	0.45
Czechoslovakian (25)	259	0.41
Danish (151)	417	0.66
Dutch (217)	1,215	1.92
Eastern European (6)	18	0.03
English (1,338)	4,674	7.37
Estonian (0)	0	<0.01
European (549)	685	1.08
Finnish (41)	123	0.19
French, ex. Basque (259)	1,371	2.16
French Canadian (9)	110	0.17
German (2,173)	7,806	12.31
German Russian (0)	0	<0.01
Greek (54)	211	0.33
Guyanese (0)	0	<0.01
Hungarian (10)	25	0.04
Icelander (0)	0	<0.01
Iranian (12)	61	0.10
Irish (1,178)	5,955	9.39
Israeli (0)	0	<0.01
Italian (941)	2,285	3.60
Latvian (0)	0	<0.01
Lithuanian (39)	54	0.09
Luxemburger (0)	43	0.07
Macedonian (0)	0	<0.01
Maltese (14)	14	0.02
New Zealander (0)	0	<0.01
Northern European (46)	46	0.07
Norwegian (239)	688	1.08
Pennsylvania German (0)	0	<0.01
Polish (101)	533	0.84
Portuguese (543)	1,175	1.85
Romanian (16)	16	0.03
Russian (27)	262	0.41
Scandinavian (89)	254	0.40
Scotch-Irish (379)	754	1.19
Scottish (387)	1,100	1.73
Serbian (0)	15	0.02
Slavic (0)	7	0.01
Slovak (0)	64	0.10
Slovene (0)	0	<0.01
Soviet Union (0)	0	<0.01
Swedish (70)	554	0.87
Swiss (36)	248	0.39
Turkish (33)	42	0.07
Ukrainian (11)	72	0.11
Welsh (49)	268	0.42
West Indian, ex. Hispanic (18)	76	0.12
Bahamian (0)	0	<0.01
Barbadian (0)	0	<0.01
Belizean (0)	0	<0.01
Bermudan (0)	0	<0.01
British West Indian (0)	0	<0.01
Dutch West Indian (0)	9	0.01
Haitian (0)	0	<0.01
Jamaican (18)	53	0.08
Trinidadian/Tobagonian (0)	0	<0.01
U.S. Virgin Islander (0)	0	<0.01
West Indian (0)	14	0.02
Other West Indian (0)	0	<0.01
Yugoslavian (19)	148	0.23

Hispanic Origin	Population	%
Hispanic or Latino (of any race)	18,413	28.36
Central American, ex. Mexican	271	0.42
Costa Rican	22	0.03
Guatemalan	51	0.08
Honduran	24	0.04
Nicaraguan	56	0.09
Panamanian	18	0.03
Salvadoran	99	0.15
Other Central American	1	<0.01
Cuban	44	0.07
Dominican Republic	4	0.01
Mexican	16,488	25.40
Puerto Rican	262	0.40
South American	116	0.18
Argentinean	17	0.03
Bolivian	1	<0.01
Chilean	5	0.01
Colombian	27	0.04
Ecuadorian	7	0.01
Paraguayan	3	<0.01
Peruvian	51	0.08
Uruguayan	1	<0.01
Venezuelan	0	<0.01
Other South American	4	0.01
Other Hispanic or Latino	1,228	1.89

Race*	Population	%
African-American/Black (1,591)	2,255	3.47
Not Hispanic (1,425)	1,934	2.98
Hispanic (166)	321	0.49
American Indian/Alaska Native (909)	1,967	3.03
Not Hispanic (606)	1,363	2.10
Hispanic (303)	604	0.93
Alaska Athabascan *(Ala. Nat.)* (0)	1	<0.01
Aleut *(Alaska Native)* (0)	0	<0.01
Apache (21)	51	0.08
Arapaho (0)	0	<0.01
Blackfeet (6)	53	0.08
Canadian/French Am. Ind. (3)	6	0.01
Central American Ind. (0)	0	<0.01
Cherokee (187)	490	0.75
Cheyenne (0)	1	<0.01
Chickasaw (5)	12	0.02
Chippewa (19)	37	0.06
Choctaw (42)	84	0.13
Colville (0)	0	<0.01
Comanche (1)	5	0.01
Cree (0)	0	<0.01
Creek (11)	18	0.03
Crow (0)	0	<0.01
Delaware (0)	1	<0.01
Hopi (2)	10	0.02
Houma (0)	0	<0.01
Inupiat *(Alaska Native)* (0)	0	<0.01
Iroquois (2)	9	0.01
Kiowa (0)	1	<0.01
Lumbee (1)	1	<0.01
Menominee (2)	2	<0.01
Mexican American Ind. (68)	101	0.16
Navajo (7)	44	0.07
Osage (1)	5	0.01
Ottawa (1)	1	<0.01
Paiute (2)	5	0.01
Pima (0)	2	<0.01
Potawatomi (7)	12	0.02
Pueblo (7)	15	0.02
Puget Sound Salish (1)	1	<0.01
Seminole (0)	3	<0.01
Shoshone (3)	4	0.01
Sioux (13)	26	0.04
South American Ind. (7)	10	0.02
Spanish American Ind. (5)	6	0.01
Tlingit-Haida *(Alaska Native)* (2)	11	0.02
Tohono O'Odham (2)	4	0.01
Tsimshian *(Alaska Native)* (0)	0	<0.01
Ute (1)	1	<0.01
Yakama (0)	0	<0.01
Yaqui (7)	19	0.03
Yuman (3)	6	0.01
Yup'ik *(Alaska Native)* (0)	0	<0.01
Asian (11,190)	12,691	19.55
Not Hispanic (11,026)	12,264	18.89
Hispanic (164)	427	0.66
Bangladeshi (2)	5	0.01
Bhutanese (0)	0	<0.01
Burmese (7)	7	0.01
Cambodian (49)	60	0.09
Chinese, ex. Taiwanese (257)	370	0.57
Filipino (607)	1,004	1.55
Hmong (227)	235	0.36
Indian (8,863)	9,352	14.40
Indonesian (15)	30	0.05
Japanese (236)	452	0.70
Korean (140)	223	0.34
Laotian (34)	48	0.07
Malaysian (2)	2	<0.01
Nepalese (9)	9	0.01
Pakistani (363)	380	0.59
Sri Lankan (6)	11	0.02
Taiwanese (1)	6	0.01
Thai (43)	88	0.14
Vietnamese (162)	193	0.30
Hawaii Native/Pacific Islander (228)	501	0.77
Not Hispanic (206)	422	0.65
Hispanic (22)	79	0.12
Fijian (20)	33	0.05
Guamanian/Chamorro (136)	189	0.29
Marshallese (0)	0	<0.01
Native Hawaiian (34)	117	0.18
Samoan (13)	42	0.06
Tongan (1)	5	0.01
White (37,382)	40,458	62.31
Not Hispanic (30,755)	32,577	50.18
Hispanic (6,627)	7,881	12.14

*Notes: † The Census 2010 population figure is used to calculate the percentages in the Hispanic Origin and Race categories. Ancestry percentages are based on the 2006-2010 American Community Survey population (not shown); ‡ Numbers in parentheses indicate the number of people reporting a single ancestry; * Numbers in parentheses indicate the number of persons reporting this race alone, not in combination with any other race; Please refer to the Explanation of Data for more information.*

Yucaipa

Place Type: City
County: San Bernardino
Population: 51,367

Ancestry	Population	%
Afghan (0)	0	<0.01
African, Sub-Saharan (117)	480	0.96
African (27)	54	0.11
Cape Verdean (0)	0	<0.01
Ethiopian (0)	0	<0.01
Ghanaian (0)	0	<0.01
Kenyan (0)	0	<0.01
Liberian (0)	0	<0.01
Nigerian (90)	348	0.69
Senegalese (0)	0	<0.01
Sierra Leonean (0)	0	<0.01
Somalian (0)	0	<0.01
South African (0)	0	<0.01
Sudanese (0)	0	<0.01
Ugandan (0)	0	<0.01
Zimbabwean (0)	0	<0.01
Other Sub-Saharan African (0)	78	0.16
Albanian (34)	51	0.10
Alsatian (0)	0	<0.01
American (1,941)	1,941	3.86
Arab (232)	240	0.48
Arab (121)	121	0.24
Egyptian (14)	14	0.03
Iraqi (0)	0	<0.01
Jordanian (0)	0	<0.01
Lebanese (0)	8	0.02
Moroccan (0)	0	<0.01
Palestinian (0)	0	<0.01
Syrian (97)	97	0.19
Other Arab (0)	0	<0.01
Armenian (28)	78	0.16
Assyrian/Chaldean/Syriac (0)	0	<0.01
Australian (0)	0	<0.01
Austrian (30)	180	0.36
Basque (0)	0	<0.01
Belgian (16)	33	0.07
Brazilian (0)	0	<0.01
British (95)	154	0.31
Bulgarian (0)	0	<0.01
Cajun (0)	0	<0.01
Canadian (266)	438	0.87
Carpatho Rusyn (0)	0	<0.01
Celtic (17)	17	0.03
Croatian (0)	0	<0.01
Cypriot (0)	0	<0.01
Czech (13)	189	0.38
Czechoslovakian (45)	60	0.12
Danish (68)	284	0.57
Dutch (240)	1,181	2.35
Eastern European (0)	0	<0.01
English (1,519)	5,884	11.71
Estonian (17)	17	0.03
European (611)	723	1.44
Finnish (29)	83	0.17
French, ex. Basque (438)	2,075	4.13
French Canadian (152)	391	0.78
German (2,666)	9,803	19.52
German Russian (0)	0	<0.01
Greek (117)	366	0.73
Guyanese (0)	0	<0.01
Hungarian (18)	125	0.25
Icelander (18)	484	0.96
Iranian (76)	131	0.26
Irish (1,345)	5,798	11.54
Israeli (0)	0	<0.01
Italian (572)	2,392	4.76
Latvian (0)	0	<0.01
Lithuanian (37)	46	0.09
Luxemburger (0)	0	<0.01
Macedonian (13)	13	0.03
Maltese (0)	0	<0.01
New Zealander (0)	0	<0.01
Northern European (21)	21	0.04
Norwegian (235)	709	1.41
Pennsylvania German (0)	12	0.02
Polish (334)	1,193	2.38
Portuguese (202)	488	0.97
Romanian (151)	160	0.32
Russian (96)	240	0.48
Scandinavian (41)	143	0.28
Scotch-Irish (710)	1,302	2.59
Scottish (485)	1,330	2.65
Serbian (0)	0	<0.01
Slavic (0)	0	<0.01
Slovak (0)	0	<0.01
Slovene (15)	40	0.08
Soviet Union (0)	0	<0.01
Swedish (194)	1,102	2.19
Swiss (22)	53	0.11
Turkish (0)	0	<0.01
Ukrainian (34)	94	0.19
Welsh (107)	488	0.97
West Indian, ex. Hispanic (14)	80	0.16
Bahamian (14)	14	0.03
Barbadian (0)	0	<0.01
Belizean (0)	33	0.07
Bermudan (0)	0	<0.01
British West Indian (0)	0	<0.01
Dutch West Indian (0)	0	<0.01
Haitian (0)	0	<0.01
Jamaican (0)	33	0.07
Trinidadian/Tobagonian (0)	0	<0.01
U.S. Virgin Islander (0)	0	<0.01
West Indian (0)	0	<0.01
Other West Indian (0)	0	<0.01
Yugoslavian (120)	184	0.37

Hispanic Origin	Population	%
Hispanic or Latino (of any race)	13,943	27.14
Central American, ex. Mexican	374	0.73
Costa Rican	15	0.03
Guatemalan	151	0.29
Honduran	28	0.05
Nicaraguan	66	0.13
Panamanian	17	0.03
Salvadoran	95	0.18
Other Central American	2	<0.01
Cuban	91	0.18
Dominican Republic	19	0.04
Mexican	11,979	23.32
Puerto Rican	244	0.48
South American	184	0.36
Argentinean	53	0.10
Bolivian	6	0.01
Chilean	12	0.02
Colombian	40	0.08
Ecuadorian	25	0.05
Paraguayan	0	<0.01
Peruvian	35	0.07
Uruguayan	3	0.01
Venezuelan	5	0.01
Other South American	5	0.01
Other Hispanic or Latino	1,052	2.05

Race*	Population	%
African-American/Black (837)	1,230	2.39
Not Hispanic (736)	1,013	1.97
Hispanic (101)	217	0.42
American Indian/Alaska Native (485)	1,109	2.16
Not Hispanic (242)	650	1.27
Hispanic (243)	459	0.89
Alaska Athabascan *(Ala. Nat.)* (1)	1	<0.01
Aleut *(Alaska Native)* (0)	1	<0.01
Apache (13)	33	0.06
Arapaho (0)	0	<0.01
Blackfeet (2)	23	0.04
Canadian/French Am. Ind. (1)	2	<0.01
Central American Ind. (0)	2	<0.01
Cherokee (39)	201	0.39
Cheyenne (3)	9	0.02
Chickasaw (2)	7	0.01
Chippewa (8)	15	0.03
Choctaw (17)	55	0.11
Colville (0)	0	<0.01
Comanche (0)	4	0.01
Cree (0)	1	<0.01
Creek (0)	13	0.03
Crow (0)	0	<0.01
Delaware (1)	4	0.01
Hopi (1)	3	0.01
Houma (0)	0	<0.01
Inupiat *(Alaska Native)* (2)	3	0.01
Iroquois (5)	13	0.03
Kiowa (0)	0	<0.01
Lumbee (0)	0	<0.01
Menominee (2)	2	<0.01
Mexican American Ind. (49)	71	0.14
Navajo (15)	24	0.05
Osage (1)	5	0.01
Ottawa (4)	4	0.01
Paiute (0)	2	<0.01
Pima (4)	4	0.01
Potawatomi (1)	11	0.02
Pueblo (4)	9	0.02
Puget Sound Salish (0)	0	<0.01
Seminole (0)	4	0.01
Shoshone (0)	7	0.01
Sioux (14)	31	0.06
South American Ind. (0)	0	<0.01
Spanish American Ind. (1)	2	<0.01
Tlingit-Haida *(Alaska Native)* (5)	7	0.01
Tohono O'Odham (3)	3	0.01
Tsimshian *(Alaska Native)* (0)	0	<0.01
Ute (1)	2	<0.01
Yakama (0)	0	<0.01
Yaqui (20)	31	0.06
Yuman (0)	0	<0.01
Yup'ik *(Alaska Native)* (0)	0	<0.01
Asian (1,431)	2,027	3.95
Not Hispanic (1,358)	1,786	3.48
Hispanic (73)	241	0.47
Bangladeshi (9)	15	0.03
Bhutanese (0)	0	<0.01
Burmese (0)	0	<0.01
Cambodian (17)	32	0.06
Chinese, ex. Taiwanese (193)	270	0.53
Filipino (466)	698	1.36
Hmong (0)	0	<0.01
Indian (174)	219	0.43
Indonesian (67)	91	0.18
Japanese (59)	196	0.38
Korean (214)	267	0.52
Laotian (1)	4	0.01
Malaysian (5)	5	0.01
Nepalese (0)	0	<0.01
Pakistani (18)	20	0.04
Sri Lankan (7)	8	0.02
Taiwanese (7)	9	0.02
Thai (21)	46	0.09
Vietnamese (108)	126	0.25
Hawaii Native/Pacific Islander (74)	193	0.38
Not Hispanic (62)	151	0.29
Hispanic (12)	42	0.08
Fijian (0)	0	<0.01
Guamanian/Chamorro (7)	25	0.05
Marshallese (0)	0	<0.01
Native Hawaiian (34)	89	0.17
Samoan (18)	32	0.06
Tongan (3)	3	0.01
White (40,824)	42,728	83.18
Not Hispanic (33,866)	34,844	67.83
Hispanic (6,958)	7,884	15.35

*Notes: † The Census 2010 population figure is used to calculate the percentages in the Hispanic Origin and Race categories. Ancestry percentages are based on the 2006-2010 American Community Survey population (not shown); ‡ Numbers in parentheses indicate the number of people reporting a single ancestry; * Numbers in parentheses indicate the number of persons reporting this race alone, not in combination with any other race; Please refer to the Explanation of Data for more information.*

Ancestry Group Rankings

Afghan

Top 10 Places Sorted by Population
Based on all places, regardless of total population

Place	Population	%
Fremont (city) Alameda County	2,760	1.32
Los Angeles (city) Los Angeles County	2,434	0.06
San Diego (city) San Diego County	1,850	0.14
Concord (city) Contra Costa County	1,655	1.36
Elk Grove (city) Sacramento County	1,211	0.86
Irvine (city) Orange County	1,177	0.59
Union City (city) Alameda County	1,085	1.59
Tracy (city) San Joaquin County	953	1.20
San Jose (city) Santa Clara County	925	0.10
Hayward (city) Alameda County	826	0.58

Top 10 Places Sorted by Percent of Total Population
Based on all places, regardless of total population

Place	Population	%
Mountain House (cdp) San Joaquin County	284	3.79
Contra Costa Centre (cdp) Contra Costa County	155	2.77
San Antonio Heights (cdp) San Bernardino County	79	1.99
Ripon (city) San Joaquin County	251	1.82
Union City (city) Alameda County	1,085	1.59
Concord (city) Contra Costa County	1,655	1.36
Fremont (city) Alameda County	2,760	1.32
Tracy (city) San Joaquin County	953	1.20
Newark (city) Alameda County	474	1.13
Dublin (city) Alameda County	428	1.00

Top 10 Places Sorted by Percent of Total Population
Based on places with total population of 50,000 or more

Place	Population	%
Union City (city) Alameda County	1,085	1.59
Concord (city) Contra Costa County	1,655	1.36
Fremont (city) Alameda County	2,760	1.32
Tracy (city) San Joaquin County	953	1.20
Elk Grove (city) Sacramento County	1,211	0.86
Antioch (city) Contra Costa County	725	0.73
Milpitas (city) Santa Clara County	454	0.70
Manteca (city) San Joaquin County	416	0.64
Irvine (city) Orange County	1,177	0.59
Hayward (city) Alameda County	826	0.58

African, Sub-Saharan

Top 10 Places Sorted by Population
Based on all places, regardless of total population

Place	Population	%
Los Angeles (city) Los Angeles County	51,431	1.36
San Diego (city) San Diego County	15,315	1.19
Long Beach (city) Los Angeles County	10,870	2.35
Oakland (city) Alameda County	8,436	2.18
Richmond (city) Contra Costa County	5,853	5.72
San Jose (city) Santa Clara County	5,552	0.60
Carson (city) Los Angeles County	4,806	5.26
San Francisco (city) San Francisco County	4,541	0.58
Compton (city) Los Angeles County	4,191	4.38
Sacramento (city) Sacramento County	4,175	0.91

Top 10 Places Sorted by Percent of Total Population
Based on all places, regardless of total population

Place	Population	%
Olancha (cdp) Inyo County	89	43.84
Shelter Cove (cdp) Humboldt County	65	12.40
North Richmond (cdp) Contra Costa County	326	10.87
Davenport (cdp) Santa Cruz County	32	10.36
Middletown (cdp) Lake County	161	9.78
View Park-Windsor Hills (cdp) Los Angeles County	894	8.30
West Rancho Dominguez (cdp) Los Angeles County	361	6.27
West Athens (cdp) Los Angeles County	499	6.01
Ladera Heights (cdp) Los Angeles County	398	5.95
Lemoore Station (cdp) Kings County	455	5.77

Top 10 Places Sorted by Percent of Total Population
Based on places with total population of 50,000 or more

Place	Population	%
Richmond (city) Contra Costa County	5,853	5.72
Carson (city) Los Angeles County	4,806	5.26
Compton (city) Los Angeles County	4,191	4.38
Hawthorne (city) Los Angeles County	2,790	3.31
Vallejo (city) Solano County	3,554	3.06
Inglewood (city) Los Angeles County	3,108	2.82
San Leandro (city) Alameda County	2,077	2.51
Pittsburg (city) Contra Costa County	1,533	2.48
Antioch (city) Contra Costa County	2,459	2.47
Vacaville (city) Solano County	2,233	2.43

African, Sub-Saharan: African

Top 10 Places Sorted by Population
Based on all places, regardless of total population

Place	Population	%
Los Angeles (city) Los Angeles County	39,515	1.05
Long Beach (city) Los Angeles County	9,464	2.05
San Diego (city) San Diego County	5,572	0.43
Oakland (city) Alameda County	4,978	1.29
Richmond (city) Contra Costa County	4,973	4.86
Carson (city) Los Angeles County	4,332	4.74
Compton (city) Los Angeles County	4,112	4.29
Vallejo (city) Solano County	3,101	2.67
San Francisco (city) San Francisco County	3,031	0.38
Palmdale (city) Los Angeles County	2,924	2.00

Top 10 Places Sorted by Percent of Total Population
Based on all places, regardless of total population

Place	Population	%
Olancha (cdp) Inyo County	89	43.84
Shelter Cove (cdp) Humboldt County	65	12.40
North Richmond (cdp) Contra Costa County	326	10.87
Davenport (cdp) Santa Cruz County	32	10.36
Middletown (cdp) Lake County	161	9.78
View Park-Windsor Hills (cdp) Los Angeles County	694	6.45
West Rancho Dominguez (cdp) Los Angeles County	361	6.27
Lemoore Station (cdp) Kings County	455	5.77
Dunnigan (cdp) Yolo County	54	5.70
Point Reyes Station (cdp) Marin County	47	5.66

Top 10 Places Sorted by Percent of Total Population
Based on places with total population of 50,000 or more

Place	Population	%
Richmond (city) Contra Costa County	4,973	4.86
Carson (city) Los Angeles County	4,332	4.74
Compton (city) Los Angeles County	4,112	4.29
Vallejo (city) Solano County	3,101	2.67
Vacaville (city) Solano County	2,024	2.20
Long Beach (city) Los Angeles County	9,464	2.05
Hawthorne (city) Los Angeles County	1,719	2.04
Palmdale (city) Los Angeles County	2,924	2.00
Inglewood (city) Los Angeles County	2,163	1.97
Fairfield (city) Solano County	2,042	1.97

African, Sub-Saharan: Cape Verdean

Top 10 Places Sorted by Population
Based on all places, regardless of total population

Place	Population	%
Sacramento (city) Sacramento County	299	0.07
San Diego (city) San Diego County	270	0.02
Los Angeles (city) Los Angeles County	198	0.01
Oakland (city) Alameda County	115	0.03
Concord (city) Contra Costa County	114	0.09
Elk Grove (city) Sacramento County	106	0.08
San Jose (city) Santa Clara County	105	0.01
Fontana (city) San Bernardino County	96	0.05
Florin (cdp) Sacramento County	77	0.16
Santa Monica (city) Los Angeles County	67	0.08

Top 10 Places Sorted by Percent of Total Population
Based on all places, regardless of total population

Place	Population	%
Angwin (cdp) Napa County	44	1.18
Warm Springs (cdp) Riverside County	18	0.85
La Riviera (cdp) Sacramento County	35	0.31
Suisun City (city) Solano County	52	0.19
Florin (cdp) Sacramento County	77	0.16
Lathrop (city) San Joaquin County	28	0.16
Red Bluff (city) Tehama County	19	0.14
Lomita (city) Los Angeles County	25	0.12
Monrovia (city) Los Angeles County	41	0.11
Concord (city) Contra Costa County	114	0.09

Top 10 Places Sorted by Percent of Total Population
Based on places with total population of 50,000 or more

Place	Population	%
Concord (city) Contra Costa County	114	0.09
Elk Grove (city) Sacramento County	106	0.08
Santa Monica (city) Los Angeles County	67	0.08
Sacramento (city) Sacramento County	299	0.07
Lakewood (city) Los Angeles County	50	0.06
Fontana (city) San Bernardino County	96	0.05
Fairfield (city) Solano County	57	0.05
Napa (city) Napa County	36	0.05
Redondo Beach (city) Los Angeles County	32	0.05
Simi Valley (city) Ventura County	46	0.04

African, Sub-Saharan: Ethiopian

Top 10 Places Sorted by Population
Based on all places, regardless of total population

Place	Population	%
Los Angeles (city) Los Angeles County	3,896	0.10
San Jose (city) Santa Clara County	2,008	0.22
San Diego (city) San Diego County	1,985	0.15
Oakland (city) Alameda County	1,983	0.51
Santa Clara (city) Santa Clara County	692	0.62
Sacramento (city) Sacramento County	692	0.15
Anaheim (city) Orange County	642	0.19
San Francisco (city) San Francisco County	585	0.07
Elk Grove (city) Sacramento County	492	0.35
Santa Rosa (city) Sonoma County	491	0.30

Top 10 Places Sorted by Percent of Total Population
Based on all places, regardless of total population

Place	Population	%
Inverness (cdp) Marin County	29	2.10
Strawberry (cdp) Marin County	100	1.95
Culver City (city) Los Angeles County	456	1.17
Pinole (city) Contra Costa County	187	1.01
Lemon Grove (city) San Diego County	213	0.85
Hercules (city) Contra Costa County	182	0.79
Ladera Heights (cdp) Los Angeles County	53	0.79
La Palma (city) Orange County	110	0.71
Marina del Rey (cdp) Los Angeles County	65	0.71
Mayflower Village (cdp) Los Angeles County	37	0.63

Top 10 Places Sorted by Percent of Total Population
Based on places with total population of 50,000 or more

Place	Population	%
Santa Clara (city) Santa Clara County	692	0.62
Palo Alto (city) Santa Clara County	360	0.58
Oakland (city) Alameda County	1,983	0.51
Hawthorne (city) Los Angeles County	409	0.49
Richmond (city) Contra Costa County	474	0.46
Alameda (city) Alameda County	326	0.45
San Leandro (city) Alameda County	350	0.42
Inglewood (city) Los Angeles County	399	0.36
Elk Grove (city) Sacramento County	492	0.35
Santa Rosa (city) Sonoma County	491	0.30

African, Sub-Saharan: Ghanaian

Top 10 Places Sorted by Population

Based on all places, regardless of total population

Place	Population	%
Los Angeles (city) Los Angeles County	587	0.02
West Covina (city) Los Angeles County	143	0.14
Thousand Oaks (city) Ventura County	128	0.10
San Francisco (city) San Francisco County	123	0.02
Victorville (city) San Bernardino County	110	0.10
Downey (city) Los Angeles County	93	0.08
Oakland (city) Alameda County	79	0.02
San Diego (city) San Diego County	79	0.01
Santa Ana (city) Orange County	72	0.02
Hawthorne (city) Los Angeles County	69	0.08

Top 10 Places Sorted by Percent of Total Population

Based on all places, regardless of total population

Place	Population	%
West Athens (cdp) Los Angeles County	32	0.39
Signal Hill (city) Los Angeles County	34	0.32
Ladera Heights (cdp) Los Angeles County	20	0.30
San Pablo (city) Contra Costa County	67	0.23
Bay Point (cdp) Contra Costa County	35	0.17
West Covina (city) Los Angeles County	143	0.14
View Park-Windsor Hills (cdp) Los Angeles County	13	0.12
Stanford (cdp) Santa Clara County	15	0.11
Thousand Oaks (city) Ventura County	128	0.10
Victorville (city) San Bernardino County	110	0.10

Top 10 Places Sorted by Percent of Total Population

Based on places with total population of 50,000 or more

Place	Population	%
West Covina (city) Los Angeles County	143	0.14
Thousand Oaks (city) Ventura County	128	0.10
Victorville (city) San Bernardino County	110	0.10
Downey (city) Los Angeles County	93	0.08
Hawthorne (city) Los Angeles County	69	0.08
Highland (city) San Bernardino County	41	0.08
Tustin (city) Orange County	44	0.06
Chino Hills (city) San Bernardino County	35	0.05
Roseville (city) Placer County	48	0.04
San Bernardino (city) San Bernardino County	56	0.03

African, Sub-Saharan: Kenyan

Top 10 Places Sorted by Population

Based on all places, regardless of total population

Place	Population	%
San Ramon (city) Contra Costa County	336	0.50
Los Angeles (city) Los Angeles County	336	0.01
San Diego (city) San Diego County	160	0.01
Fairfield (city) Solano County	135	0.13
Rancho Cordova (city) Sacramento County	129	0.20
Long Beach (city) Los Angeles County	117	0.03
Oakland (city) Alameda County	115	0.03
Albany (city) Alameda County	113	0.63
Foothill Farms (cdp) Sacramento County	106	0.32
Novato (city) Marin County	101	0.20

Top 10 Places Sorted by Percent of Total Population

Based on all places, regardless of total population

Place	Population	%
Albany (city) Alameda County	113	0.63
Salida (cdp) Stanislaus County	78	0.53
San Ramon (city) Contra Costa County	336	0.50
Foothill Farms (cdp) Sacramento County	106	0.32
Angwin (cdp) Napa County	12	0.32
Ridgecrest (city) Kern County	73	0.27
Rancho Cordova (city) Sacramento County	129	0.20
Novato (city) Marin County	101	0.20
Ashland (cdp) Alameda County	42	0.19
Fairfield (city) Solano County	135	0.13

Top 10 Places Sorted by Percent of Total Population

Based on places with total population of 50,000 or more

Place	Population	%
San Ramon (city) Contra Costa County	336	0.50
Rancho Cordova (city) Sacramento County	129	0.20
Novato (city) Marin County	101	0.20
Fairfield (city) Solano County	135	0.13
Mountain View (city) Santa Clara County	74	0.10
Union City (city) Alameda County	45	0.07
Castro Valley (cdp) Alameda County	42	0.07
Berkeley (city) Alameda County	70	0.06
Hayward (city) Alameda County	66	0.05
Murrieta (city) Riverside County	48	0.05

African, Sub-Saharan: Liberian

Top 10 Places Sorted by Population

Based on all places, regardless of total population

Place	Population	%
Hayward (city) Alameda County	129	0.09
Milpitas (city) Santa Clara County	104	0.16
San Jose (city) Santa Clara County	94	0.01
Stockton (city) San Joaquin County	91	0.03
Oakland (city) Alameda County	89	0.02
Los Angeles (city) Los Angeles County	76	<0.01
Concord (city) Contra Costa County	64	0.05
San Rafael (city) Marin County	63	0.11
Burlingame (city) San Mateo County	62	0.22
Vallejo (city) Solano County	58	0.05

Top 10 Places Sorted by Percent of Total Population

Based on all places, regardless of total population

Place	Population	%
Burlingame (city) San Mateo County	62	0.22
Milpitas (city) Santa Clara County	104	0.16
Foster City (city) San Mateo County	46	0.15
Hercules (city) Contra Costa County	30	0.13
San Rafael (city) Marin County	63	0.11
Hayward (city) Alameda County	129	0.09
Concord (city) Contra Costa County	64	0.05
Vallejo (city) Solano County	58	0.05
Redding (city) Shasta County	34	0.04
Indio (city) Riverside County	26	0.04

Top 10 Places Sorted by Percent of Total Population

Based on places with total population of 50,000 or more

Place	Population	%
Milpitas (city) Santa Clara County	104	0.16
San Rafael (city) Marin County	63	0.11
Hayward (city) Alameda County	129	0.09
Concord (city) Contra Costa County	64	0.05
Vallejo (city) Solano County	58	0.05
Redding (city) Shasta County	34	0.04
Indio (city) Riverside County	26	0.04
Stockton (city) San Joaquin County	91	0.03
Oakland (city) Alameda County	89	0.02
Torrance (city) Los Angeles County	23	0.02

African, Sub-Saharan: Nigerian

Top 10 Places Sorted by Population

Based on all places, regardless of total population

Place	Population	%
Los Angeles (city) Los Angeles County	3,268	0.09
San Leandro (city) Alameda County	729	0.88
San Diego (city) San Diego County	658	0.05
Eastvale (cdp) Riverside County	565	1.15
Hayward (city) Alameda County	543	0.38
Oakland (city) Alameda County	542	0.14
Long Beach (city) Los Angeles County	528	0.11
Antioch (city) Contra Costa County	522	0.52
Santa Clarita (city) Los Angeles County	517	0.30
Hawthorne (city) Los Angeles County	447	0.53

Top 10 Places Sorted by Percent of Total Population

Based on all places, regardless of total population

Place	Population	%
Mountain House (cdp) San Joaquin County	123	1.64
View Park-Windsor Hills (cdp) Los Angeles County	137	1.27
Eastvale (cdp) Riverside County	565	1.15
El Sobrante (cdp) Contra Costa County	152	1.13
Ladera Heights (cdp) Los Angeles County	71	1.06
Loma Linda (city) San Bernardino County	205	0.90
San Leandro (city) Alameda County	729	0.88
Hercules (city) Contra Costa County	184	0.80
Fairview (cdp) Alameda County	73	0.74
Yucaipa (city) San Bernardino County	348	0.69

Top 10 Places Sorted by Percent of Total Population

Based on places with total population of 50,000 or more

Place	Population	%
San Leandro (city) Alameda County	729	0.88
Yucaipa (city) San Bernardino County	348	0.69
Colton (city) San Bernardino County	335	0.64
Hawthorne (city) Los Angeles County	447	0.53
Bellflower (city) Los Angeles County	402	0.53
Antioch (city) Contra Costa County	522	0.52
Carson (city) Los Angeles County	369	0.40
Hayward (city) Alameda County	543	0.38
Inglewood (city) Los Angeles County	415	0.38
Highland (city) San Bernardino County	180	0.34

African, Sub-Saharan: Senegalese

Top 10 Places Sorted by Population

Based on all places, regardless of total population

Place	Population	%
Los Angeles (city) Los Angeles County	164	<0.01
San Diego (city) San Diego County	141	0.01
Monterey (city) Monterey County	131	0.47
Claremont (city) Los Angeles County	83	0.24
San Leandro (city) Alameda County	33	0.04
Salinas (city) Monterey County	20	0.01
Mission Viejo (city) Orange County	17	0.02
Los Altos Hills (town) Santa Clara County	14	0.18
Newark (city) Alameda County	13	0.03
Richmond (city) Contra Costa County	11	0.01

Top 10 Places Sorted by Percent of Total Population

Based on all places, regardless of total population

Place	Population	%
Monterey (city) Monterey County	131	0.47
Claremont (city) Los Angeles County	83	0.24
Los Altos Hills (town) Santa Clara County	14	0.18
San Leandro (city) Alameda County	33	0.04
Newark (city) Alameda County	13	0.03
Mission Viejo (city) Orange County	17	0.02
Palm Springs (city) Riverside County	7	0.02
San Diego (city) San Diego County	141	0.01
Salinas (city) Monterey County	20	0.01
Richmond (city) Contra Costa County	11	0.01

Top 10 Places Sorted by Percent of Total Population

Based on places with total population of 50,000 or more

Place	Population	%
San Leandro (city) Alameda County	33	0.04
Mission Viejo (city) Orange County	17	0.02
San Diego (city) San Diego County	141	0.01
Salinas (city) Monterey County	20	0.01
Richmond (city) Contra Costa County	11	0.01
Los Angeles (city) Los Angeles County	164	<0.01
Oakland (city) Alameda County	10	<0.01
Alameda (city) Alameda County	0	0.00
Alhambra (city) Los Angeles County	0	0.00
Anaheim (city) Orange County	0	0.00

African, Sub-Saharan: Sierra Leonean

Top 10 Places Sorted by Population

Based on all places, regardless of total population

Place	Population	%
Los Angeles (city) Los Angeles County	121	<0.01
San Jose (city) Santa Clara County	117	0.01
Vacaville (city) Solano County	91	0.10
Castaic (cdp) Los Angeles County	52	0.29
Livermore (city) Alameda County	52	0.07
Ashland (cdp) Alameda County	38	0.17
Glendale (city) Los Angeles County	34	0.02
Manteca (city) San Joaquin County	28	0.04
Hawthorne (city) Los Angeles County	27	0.03
Long Beach (city) Los Angeles County	27	0.01

Top 10 Places Sorted by Percent of Total Population

Based on all places, regardless of total population

Place	Population	%
Castaic (cdp) Los Angeles County	52	0.29
Larkfield-Wikiup (cdp) Sonoma County	16	0.19
Ashland (cdp) Alameda County	38	0.17

Parkway (cdp) Sacramento County	15	0.11
Vacaville (city) Solano County	91	0.10
Livermore (city) Alameda County	52	0.07
Manteca (city) San Joaquin County	28	0.04
Hawthorne (city) Los Angeles County	27	0.03
Glendale (city) Los Angeles County	34	0.02
Berkeley (city) Alameda County	23	0.02

Top 10 Places Sorted by Percent of Total Population

Based on places with total population of 50,000 or more

Place	Population	%
Vacaville (city) Solano County	91	0.10
Livermore (city) Alameda County	52	0.07
Manteca (city) San Joaquin County	28	0.04
Hawthorne (city) Los Angeles County	27	0.03
Glendale (city) Los Angeles County	34	0.02
Berkeley (city) Alameda County	23	0.02
San Leandro (city) Alameda County	14	0.02
San Jose (city) Santa Clara County	117	0.01
Long Beach (city) Los Angeles County	27	0.01
Temecula (city) Riverside County	12	0.01

African, Sub-Saharan: Somalian

Top 10 Places Sorted by Population

Based on all places, regardless of total population

Place	Population	%
San Diego (city) San Diego County	4,090	0.32
La Presa (cdp) San Diego County	388	1.11
San Jose (city) Santa Clara County	324	0.04
La Mesa (city) San Diego County	233	0.41
Vallejo (city) Solano County	203	0.17
Lemon Grove (city) San Diego County	202	0.81
Elk Grove (city) Sacramento County	148	0.10
Oceanside (city) San Diego County	139	0.08
San Marcos (city) San Diego County	129	0.17
Oakland (city) Alameda County	105	0.03

Top 10 Places Sorted by Percent of Total Population

Based on all places, regardless of total population

Place	Population	%
Sunnyside (cdp) Fresno County	70	1.54
Campo (cdp) San Diego County	35	1.18
La Presa (cdp) San Diego County	388	1.11
Lemon Grove (city) San Diego County	202	0.81
La Mesa (city) San Diego County	233	0.41
San Diego (city) San Diego County	4,090	0.32
Vallejo (city) Solano County	203	0.17
San Marcos (city) San Diego County	129	0.17
Davis (city) Yolo County	91	0.14
East Pasadena (cdp) Los Angeles County	8	0.14

Top 10 Places Sorted by Percent of Total Population

Based on places with total population of 50,000 or more

Place	Population	%
La Mesa (city) San Diego County	233	0.41
San Diego (city) San Diego County	4,090	0.32
Vallejo (city) Solano County	203	0.17
San Marcos (city) San Diego County	129	0.17
Davis (city) Yolo County	91	0.14
Elk Grove (city) Sacramento County	148	0.10
Oceanside (city) San Diego County	139	0.08
Highland (city) San Bernardino County	44	0.08
Pomona (city) Los Angeles County	99	0.07
Lake Forest (city) Orange County	46	0.06

African, Sub-Saharan: South African

Top 10 Places Sorted by Population

Based on all places, regardless of total population

Place	Population	%
Los Angeles (city) Los Angeles County	1,463	0.04
San Diego (city) San Diego County	869	0.07
Irvine (city) Orange County	339	0.17
San Francisco (city) San Francisco County	247	0.03
San Jose (city) Santa Clara County	211	0.02
Fullerton (city) Orange County	198	0.15
Carmichael (cdp) Sacramento County	152	0.25
Sacramento (city) Sacramento County	149	0.03
Manhattan Beach (city) Los Angeles County	138	0.40
Newport Beach (city) Orange County	125	0.15

Top 10 Places Sorted by Percent of Total Population

Based on all places, regardless of total population

Place	Population	%
Cobb (cdp) Lake County	43	2.22
Running Springs (cdp) San Bernardino County	87	1.72
Crestline (cdp) San Bernardino County	112	1.25
Marin City (cdp) Marin County	35	1.24
San Juan Bautista (city) San Benito County	11	0.75
Felton (cdp) Santa Cruz County	22	0.49
Manhattan Beach (city) Los Angeles County	138	0.40
Loomis (town) Placer County	22	0.34
Pismo Beach (city) San Luis Obispo County	26	0.33
Laguna Beach (city) Orange County	69	0.30

Top 10 Places Sorted by Percent of Total Population

Based on places with total population of 50,000 or more

Place	Population	%
Carmichael (cdp) Sacramento County	152	0.25
Irvine (city) Orange County	339	0.17
Palo Alto (city) Santa Clara County	97	0.16
Fullerton (city) Orange County	198	0.15
Newport Beach (city) Orange County	125	0.15
Rocklin (city) Placer County	77	0.14
Murrieta (city) Riverside County	118	0.12
Laguna Niguel (city) Orange County	78	0.12
Mountain View (city) Santa Clara County	83	0.11
Tustin (city) Orange County	75	0.10

African, Sub-Saharan: Sudanese

Top 10 Places Sorted by Population

Based on all places, regardless of total population

Place	Population	%
San Diego (city) San Diego County	1,036	0.08
Los Angeles (city) Los Angeles County	184	<0.01
Long Beach (city) Los Angeles County	126	0.03
Fresno (city) Fresno County	109	0.02
Hawthorne (city) Los Angeles County	102	0.12
San Jose (city) Santa Clara County	81	0.01
Oakland (city) Alameda County	78	0.02
Mountain House (cdp) San Joaquin County	62	0.83
Santa Clara (city) Santa Clara County	60	0.05
Temecula (city) Riverside County	55	0.06

Top 10 Places Sorted by Percent of Total Population

Based on all places, regardless of total population

Place	Population	%
Mountain House (cdp) San Joaquin County	62	0.83
Ben Lomond (cdp) Santa Cruz County	11	0.18
Rosemont (cdp) Sacramento County	36	0.16
Hawthorne (city) Los Angeles County	102	0.12
Agoura Hills (city) Los Angeles County	23	0.11
Mead Valley (cdp) Riverside County	18	0.10
East San Gabriel (cdp) Los Angeles County	15	0.10
Rocklin (city) Placer County	48	0.09
San Diego (city) San Diego County	1,036	0.08
Ridgecrest (city) Kern County	20	0.07

Top 10 Places Sorted by Percent of Total Population

Based on places with total population of 50,000 or more

Place	Population	%
Hawthorne (city) Los Angeles County	102	0.12
Rocklin (city) Placer County	48	0.09
San Diego (city) San Diego County	1,036	0.08
Temecula (city) Riverside County	55	0.06
Mountain View (city) Santa Clara County	40	0.06
Santa Clara (city) Santa Clara County	60	0.05
Long Beach (city) Los Angeles County	126	0.03
Corona (city) Riverside County	40	0.03
Fairfield (city) Solano County	28	0.03
Redlands (city) San Bernardino County	23	0.03

African, Sub-Saharan: Ugandan

Top 10 Places Sorted by Population

Based on all places, regardless of total population

Place	Population	%
Los Angeles (city) Los Angeles County	491	0.01
Santa Rosa (city) Sonoma County	146	0.09
Rancho Cordova (city) Sacramento County	108	0.17
Temecula (city) Riverside County	76	0.08
Concord (city) Contra Costa County	66	0.05
Pittsburg (city) Contra Costa County	55	0.09
Arden-Arcade (cdp) Sacramento County	40	0.04
Hemet (city) Riverside County	37	0.05
Long Beach (city) Los Angeles County	29	0.01
San Bernardino (city) San Bernardino County	24	0.01

Top 10 Places Sorted by Percent of Total Population

Based on all places, regardless of total population

Place	Population	%
Rancho Cordova (city) Sacramento County	108	0.17
Santa Rosa (city) Sonoma County	146	0.09
Pittsburg (city) Contra Costa County	55	0.09
Temecula (city) Riverside County	76	0.08
Concord (city) Contra Costa County	66	0.05
Hemet (city) Riverside County	37	0.05
Arden-Arcade (cdp) Sacramento County	40	0.04
Rocklin (city) Placer County	14	0.03
Los Angeles (city) Los Angeles County	491	0.01
Long Beach (city) Los Angeles County	29	0.01

Top 10 Places Sorted by Percent of Total Population

Based on places with total population of 50,000 or more

Place	Population	%
Rancho Cordova (city) Sacramento County	108	0.17
Santa Rosa (city) Sonoma County	146	0.09
Pittsburg (city) Contra Costa County	55	0.09
Temecula (city) Riverside County	76	0.08
Concord (city) Contra Costa County	66	0.05
Hemet (city) Riverside County	37	0.05
Arden-Arcade (cdp) Sacramento County	40	0.04
Rocklin (city) Placer County	14	0.03
Los Angeles (city) Los Angeles County	491	0.01
Long Beach (city) Los Angeles County	29	0.01

African, Sub-Saharan: Zimbabwean

Top 10 Places Sorted by Population

Based on all places, regardless of total population

Place	Population	%
Stockton (city) San Joaquin County	118	0.04
Pasadena (city) Los Angeles County	105	0.08
Los Angeles (city) Los Angeles County	101	<0.01
Temecula (city) Riverside County	68	0.07
Santa Monica (city) Los Angeles County	46	0.05
San Lorenzo (cdp) Alameda County	44	0.19
San Diego (city) San Diego County	39	<0.01
Clayton (city) Contra Costa County	35	0.32
San Ramon (city) Contra Costa County	33	0.05
Camp Pendleton South (cdp) San Diego County	32	0.24

Top 10 Places Sorted by Percent of Total Population

Based on all places, regardless of total population

Place	Population	%
Clayton (city) Contra Costa County	35	0.32
Camp Pendleton South (cdp) San Diego County	32	0.24
San Lorenzo (cdp) Alameda County	44	0.19
Loma Linda (city) San Bernardino County	22	0.10
Pasadena (city) Los Angeles County	105	0.08
Temecula (city) Riverside County	68	0.07
Santa Monica (city) Los Angeles County	46	0.05
San Ramon (city) Contra Costa County	33	0.05
Stockton (city) San Joaquin County	118	0.04
Monterey (city) Monterey County	10	0.04

Top 10 Places Sorted by Percent of Total Population

Based on places with total population of 50,000 or more

Place	Population	%
Pasadena (city) Los Angeles County	105	0.08
Temecula (city) Riverside County	68	0.07
Santa Monica (city) Los Angeles County	46	0.05
San Ramon (city) Contra Costa County	33	0.05
Stockton (city) San Joaquin County	118	0.04
Corona (city) Riverside County	30	0.02
Irvine (city) Orange County	13	0.01
Los Angeles (city) Los Angeles County	101	<0.01
San Diego (city) San Diego County	39	<0.01
Anaheim (city) Orange County	9	<0.01

African, Sub-Saharan: Other

Top 10 Places Sorted by Population

Based on all places, regardless of total population

Place	Population	%
Los Angeles (city) Los Angeles County	1,031	0.03
San Diego (city) San Diego County	376	0.03
Oakland (city) Alameda County	310	0.08
San Jose (city) Santa Clara County	297	0.03
Long Beach (city) Los Angeles County	235	0.05
San Francisco (city) San Francisco County	218	0.03
Pittsburg (city) Contra Costa County	206	0.33
Anaheim (city) Orange County	189	0.06
Berkeley (city) Alameda County	172	0.16
Marina del Rey (cdp) Los Angeles County	149	1.62

Top 10 Places Sorted by Percent of Total Population

Based on all places, regardless of total population

Place	Population	%
Eucalyptus Hills (cdp) San Diego County	99	1.69
Marina del Rey (cdp) Los Angeles County	149	1.62
Angwin (cdp) Napa County	51	1.36
French Gulch (cdp) Shasta County	2	1.16
Mentone (cdp) San Bernardino County	42	0.47
Imperial Beach (city) San Diego County	116	0.44
Klamath (cdp) Del Norte County	3	0.34
Pittsburg (city) Contra Costa County	206	0.33
View Park-Windsor Hills (cdp) Los Angeles County	33	0.31
Carmichael (cdp) Sacramento County	120	0.19

Top 10 Places Sorted by Percent of Total Population

Based on places with total population of 50,000 or more

Place	Population	%
Pittsburg (city) Contra Costa County	206	0.33
Carmichael (cdp) Sacramento County	120	0.19
Hanford (city) Kings County	94	0.18
Lakewood (city) Los Angeles County	133	0.17
Berkeley (city) Alameda County	172	0.16
Yucaipa (city) San Bernardino County	78	0.16
Rosemead (city) Los Angeles County	79	0.15
Alameda (city) Alameda County	99	0.14
Upland (city) San Bernardino County	77	0.10
Escondido (city) San Diego County	133	0.09

Albanian

Top 10 Places Sorted by Population

Based on all places, regardless of total population

Place	Population	%
Los Angeles (city) Los Angeles County	335	0.01
Anaheim (city) Orange County	207	0.06
San Diego (city) San Diego County	193	0.02
San Francisco (city) San Francisco County	143	0.02
Santee (city) San Diego County	118	0.22
Rancho Cucamonga (city) San Bernardino County	114	0.07
Dana Point (city) Orange County	102	0.30
Carmichael (cdp) Sacramento County	102	0.17
Simi Valley (city) Ventura County	102	0.08
Glendale (city) Los Angeles County	95	0.05

Top 10 Places Sorted by Percent of Total Population

Based on all places, regardless of total population

Place	Population	%
Lucerne Valley (cdp) San Bernardino County	52	0.93
Piedmont (city) Alameda County	82	0.78
Rolling Hills Estates (city) Los Angeles County	33	0.41
La Riviera (cdp) Sacramento County	35	0.31
Dana Point (city) Orange County	102	0.30
Santee (city) San Diego County	118	0.22
Claremont (city) Los Angeles County	77	0.22
Truckee (town) Nevada County	34	0.21
Kensington (cdp) Contra Costa County	9	0.18
Carmichael (cdp) Sacramento County	102	0.17

Top 10 Places Sorted by Percent of Total Population

Based on places with total population of 50,000 or more

Place	Population	%
Santee (city) San Diego County	118	0.22
Carmichael (cdp) Sacramento County	102	0.17
Yucaipa (city) San Bernardino County	51	0.10
Alhambra (city) Los Angeles County	73	0.09
Simi Valley (city) Ventura County	102	0.08
Rancho Cucamonga (city) San Bernardino County	114	0.07
Thousand Oaks (city) Ventura County	92	0.07
Temecula (city) Riverside County	70	0.07
Anaheim (city) Orange County	207	0.06
Davis (city) Yolo County	40	0.06

Alsatian

Top 10 Places Sorted by Population

Based on all places, regardless of total population

Place	Population	%
Los Angeles (city) Los Angeles County	78	<0.01
San Jose (city) Santa Clara County	61	0.01
San Francisco (city) San Francisco County	49	0.01
Eureka (city) Humboldt County	35	0.13
Costa Mesa (city) Orange County	33	0.03
Concord (city) Contra Costa County	29	0.02
Rancho Palos Verdes (city) Los Angeles County	27	0.07
Ontario (city) San Bernardino County	25	0.02
Thousand Oaks (city) Ventura County	25	0.02
San Carlos (city) San Mateo County	23	0.08

Top 10 Places Sorted by Percent of Total Population

Based on all places, regardless of total population

Place	Population	%
Macdoel (cdp) Siskiyou County	5	3.40
Aptos Hills-Larkin Valley (cdp) Santa Cruz County	15	0.63
Del Mar (city) San Diego County	18	0.43
Cottonwood (cdp) Shasta County	10	0.33
San Miguel (cdp) Contra Costa County	9	0.27
Eureka (city) Humboldt County	35	0.13
Sierra Madre (city) Los Angeles County	13	0.12
Auburn (city) Placer County	15	0.11
Mill Valley (city) Marin County	13	0.09
San Carlos (city) San Mateo County	23	0.08

Top 10 Places Sorted by Percent of Total Population

Based on places with total population of 50,000 or more

Place	Population	%
Costa Mesa (city) Orange County	33	0.03
Arden-Arcade (cdp) Sacramento County	23	0.03
Concord (city) Contra Costa County	29	0.02
Ontario (city) San Bernardino County	25	0.02
Thousand Oaks (city) Ventura County	25	0.02
Berkeley (city) Alameda County	19	0.02
Vacaville (city) Solano County	17	0.02
Lake Forest (city) Orange County	16	0.02
Redlands (city) San Bernardino County	16	0.02
Citrus Heights (city) Sacramento County	14	0.02

American

Top 10 Places Sorted by Population

Based on all places, regardless of total population

Place	Population	%
Los Angeles (city) Los Angeles County	68,094	1.81
San Diego (city) San Diego County	32,627	2.54
Hawthorne (city) Los Angeles County	12,456	14.79
San Jose (city) Santa Clara County	11,998	1.30
Simi Valley (city) Ventura County	11,845	9.74
Orange (city) Orange County	10,395	7.72
Bakersfield (city) Kern County	8,205	2.47
San Francisco (city) San Francisco County	8,041	1.02
Sacramento (city) Sacramento County	7,542	1.64
Irvine (city) Orange County	7,327	3.68

Top 10 Places Sorted by Percent of Total Population

Based on all places, regardless of total population

Place	Population	%
Nicasio (cdp) Marin County	4	57.14
Camp Nelson (cdp) Tulare County	28	42.42
Sugarloaf Village (cdp) Tulare County	7	41.18
Bombay Beach (cdp) Imperial County	119	39.67
Kirkwood (cdp) Alpine County	41	37.27
Carmet (cdp) Sonoma County	11	35.48
Fellows (cdp) Kern County	55	33.95
Richvale (cdp) Butte County	65	31.86
Santa Susana (cdp) Ventura County	395	30.36
Industry (city) Los Angeles County	106	28.80

Top 10 Places Sorted by Percent of Total Population

Based on places with total population of 50,000 or more

Place	Population	%
Hawthorne (city) Los Angeles County	12,456	14.79
Simi Valley (city) Ventura County	11,845	9.74
Orange (city) Orange County	10,395	7.72
Chico (city) Butte County	5,798	6.81
Redding (city) Shasta County	5,979	6.69
Yuba City (city) Sutter County	3,200	5.04
Thousand Oaks (city) Ventura County	5,973	4.79
Upland (city) San Bernardino County	3,521	4.77
Carson (city) Los Angeles County	4,135	4.53
Newport Beach (city) Orange County	3,741	4.48

Arab: Total

Top 10 Places Sorted by Population

Based on all places, regardless of total population

Place	Population	%
Los Angeles (city) Los Angeles County	30,066	0.80
San Diego (city) San Diego County	10,030	0.78
San Francisco (city) San Francisco County	5,672	0.72
San Jose (city) Santa Clara County	4,802	0.52
El Cajon (city) San Diego County	4,795	4.90
Fresno (city) Fresno County	4,301	0.89
Glendale (city) Los Angeles County	4,218	2.19
Anaheim (city) Orange County	4,077	1.22
San Bernardino (city) San Bernardino County	3,403	1.63
Corona (city) Riverside County	3,365	2.24

Top 10 Places Sorted by Percent of Total Population

Based on all places, regardless of total population

Place	Population	%
Boulevard (cdp) San Diego County	11	35.48
Hat Creek (cdp) Shasta County	31	14.35
Victor (cdp) San Joaquin County	37	13.50
Kenwood (cdp) Sonoma County	58	12.55
Parklawn (cdp) Stanislaus County	95	11.99
Salmon Creek (cdp) Sonoma County	9	10.84
Samoa (cdp) Humboldt County	24	8.79
Elkhorn (cdp) Monterey County	122	7.09
Arvin (city) Kern County	1,089	5.94
East Pasadena (cdp) Los Angeles County	340	5.91

Top 10 Places Sorted by Percent of Total Population

Based on places with total population of 50,000 or more

Place	Population	%
El Cajon (city) San Diego County	4,795	4.90
Santee (city) San Diego County	1,287	2.43
Daly City (city) San Mateo County	2,327	2.33
Corona (city) Riverside County	3,365	2.24
Glendale (city) Los Angeles County	4,218	2.19
Chino Hills (city) San Bernardino County	1,497	2.01
South San Francisco (city) San Mateo County	1,248	2.01
Burbank (city) Los Angeles County	1,768	1.72
San Bernardino (city) San Bernardino County	3,403	1.63
Irvine (city) Orange County	3,229	1.62

Arab: Arab

Top 10 Places Sorted by Population

Based on all places, regardless of total population

Place	Population	%
Los Angeles (city) Los Angeles County	3,096	0.08
Fresno (city) Fresno County	1,720	0.36
San Francisco (city) San Francisco County	1,106	0.14
Bakersfield (city) Kern County	1,040	0.31
Daly City (city) San Mateo County	991	0.99
San Diego (city) San Diego County	944	0.07
Stockton (city) San Joaquin County	879	0.31
Arvin (city) Kern County	782	4.27
San Jose (city) Santa Clara County	698	0.08
Irvine (city) Orange County	667	0.33

Top 10 Places Sorted by Percent of Total Population

Based on all places, regardless of total population

Place	Population	%
Victor (cdp) San Joaquin County	37	13.50
Parklawn (cdp) Stanislaus County	95	11.99
Frazier Park (cdp) Kern County	108	4.51

Place	Population	%
Camanche North Shore (cdp) Amador County	35	4.50
Ducor (cdp) Tulare County	20	4.50
Arvin (city) Kern County	782	4.27
Strathmore (cdp) Tulare County	119	3.61
Pine Mountain Club (cdp) Kern County	36	2.47
Golden Hills (cdp) Kern County	183	2.13
Bret Harte (cdp) Stanislaus County	106	2.08

Top 10 Places Sorted by Percent of Total Population
Based on places with total population of 50,000 or more

Place	Population	%
Daly City (city) San Mateo County	991	0.99
South San Francisco (city) San Mateo County	363	0.59
El Cajon (city) San Diego County	560	0.57
Chino Hills (city) San Bernardino County	405	0.54
Fountain Valley (city) Orange County	252	0.46
Santee (city) San Diego County	219	0.41
Burbank (city) Los Angeles County	383	0.37
Camarillo (city) Ventura County	233	0.37
Fresno (city) Fresno County	1,720	0.36
Mission Viejo (city) Orange County	324	0.35

Arab: Egyptian

Top 10 Places Sorted by Population
Based on all places, regardless of total population

Place	Population	%
Los Angeles (city) Los Angeles County	6,033	0.16
Corona (city) Riverside County	1,103	0.73
Anaheim (city) Orange County	1,072	0.32
Huntington Beach (city) Orange County	1,048	0.55
San Jose (city) Santa Clara County	847	0.09
Santa Clarita (city) Los Angeles County	636	0.37
Downey (city) Los Angeles County	603	0.54
Bellflower (city) Los Angeles County	494	0.65
San Francisco (city) San Francisco County	483	0.06
Irvine (city) Orange County	463	0.23

Top 10 Places Sorted by Percent of Total Population
Based on all places, regardless of total population

Place	Population	%
Cloverdale (city) Sonoma County	221	2.69
Woodside (town) San Mateo County	112	2.14
Santa Rosa Valley (cdp) Ventura County	62	1.92
Citrus (cdp) Los Angeles County	189	1.87
Del Aire (cdp) Los Angeles County	145	1.51
Midway City (cdp) Orange County	116	1.49
Tiburon (town) Marin County	130	1.47
Lakeport (city) Lake County	68	1.40
West Menlo Park (cdp) San Mateo County	47	1.38
El Sobrante (cdp) Riverside County	114	1.02

Top 10 Places Sorted by Percent of Total Population
Based on places with total population of 50,000 or more

Place	Population	%
Corona (city) Riverside County	1,103	0.73
Paramount (city) Los Angeles County	364	0.67
Bellflower (city) Los Angeles County	494	0.65
Huntington Beach (city) Orange County	1,048	0.55
Downey (city) Los Angeles County	603	0.54
Chino Hills (city) San Bernardino County	371	0.50
Arcadia (city) Los Angeles County	275	0.49
Cupertino (city) Santa Clara County	227	0.40
Hawthorne (city) Los Angeles County	329	0.39
Santa Clarita (city) Los Angeles County	636	0.37

Arab: Iraqi

Top 10 Places Sorted by Population
Based on all places, regardless of total population

Place	Population	%
El Cajon (city) San Diego County	3,081	3.15
Los Angeles (city) Los Angeles County	1,444	0.04
San Diego (city) San Diego County	1,390	0.11
Glendale (city) Los Angeles County	715	0.37
Modesto (city) Stanislaus County	547	0.27
Spring Valley (cdp) San Diego County	475	1.74
Rancho San Diego (cdp) San Diego County	459	2.27
Bostonia (cdp) San Diego County	322	2.22
Riverside (city) Riverside County	258	0.09
Corona (city) Riverside County	239	0.16

Top 10 Places Sorted by Percent of Total Population
Based on all places, regardless of total population

Place	Population	%
Hat Creek (cdp) Shasta County	31	14.35
El Cajon (city) San Diego County	3,081	3.15
Rancho San Diego (cdp) San Diego County	459	2.27
Bostonia (cdp) San Diego County	322	2.22
Spring Valley Lake (cdp) San Bernardino County	154	2.02
Dunsmuir (city) Siskiyou County	36	2.02
Spring Valley (cdp) San Diego County	475	1.74
East Pasadena (cdp) Los Angeles County	86	1.50
Jamul (cdp) San Diego County	78	1.47
Granite Hills (cdp) San Diego County	43	1.26

Top 10 Places Sorted by Percent of Total Population
Based on places with total population of 50,000 or more

Place	Population	%
El Cajon (city) San Diego County	3,081	3.15
Glendale (city) Los Angeles County	715	0.37
Santee (city) San Diego County	148	0.28
Modesto (city) Stanislaus County	547	0.27
Daly City (city) San Mateo County	230	0.23
Corona (city) Riverside County	239	0.16
Santa Clara (city) Santa Clara County	174	0.15
Redwood City (city) San Mateo County	100	0.13
Roseville (city) Placer County	141	0.12
San Diego (city) San Diego County	1,390	0.11

Arab: Jordanian

Top 10 Places Sorted by Population
Based on all places, regardless of total population

Place	Population	%
Los Angeles (city) Los Angeles County	1,238	0.03
Fresno (city) Fresno County	708	0.15
Anaheim (city) Orange County	575	0.17
Riverside (city) Riverside County	367	0.12
Pasadena (city) Los Angeles County	356	0.26
San Francisco (city) San Francisco County	353	0.04
Bakersfield (city) Kern County	352	0.11
South San Francisco (city) San Mateo County	278	0.45
Livermore (city) Alameda County	250	0.32
San Bernardino (city) San Bernardino County	250	0.12

Top 10 Places Sorted by Percent of Total Population
Based on all places, regardless of total population

Place	Population	%
Charter Oak (cdp) Los Angeles County	142	1.53
Shingletown (cdp) Shasta County	31	1.49
Millbrae (city) San Mateo County	243	1.16
Woodside (town) San Mateo County	48	0.92
La Verne (city) Los Angeles County	243	0.78
Lemoore Station (cdp) Kings County	55	0.70
East La Mirada (cdp) Los Angeles County	67	0.66
Alondra Park (cdp) Los Angeles County	46	0.52
Chowchilla (city) Madera County	87	0.48
South San Francisco (city) San Mateo County	278	0.45

Top 10 Places Sorted by Percent of Total Population
Based on places with total population of 50,000 or more

Place	Population	%
South San Francisco (city) San Mateo County	278	0.45
Livermore (city) Alameda County	250	0.32
Santee (city) San Diego County	160	0.30
Pasadena (city) Los Angeles County	356	0.26
Westminster (city) Orange County	202	0.23
Menifee (city) Riverside County	163	0.22
San Ramon (city) Contra Costa County	141	0.21
Buena Park (city) Orange County	142	0.18
Anaheim (city) Orange County	575	0.17
Fountain Valley (city) Orange County	92	0.17

Arab: Lebanese

Top 10 Places Sorted by Population
Based on all places, regardless of total population

Place	Population	%
Los Angeles (city) Los Angeles County	8,079	0.21
San Diego (city) San Diego County	3,545	0.28
Glendale (city) Los Angeles County	2,062	1.07
San Jose (city) Santa Clara County	1,317	0.14
San Francisco (city) San Francisco County	1,112	0.14
San Bernardino (city) San Bernardino County	1,107	0.53
Pomona (city) Los Angeles County	935	0.63
Corona (city) Riverside County	845	0.56
Anaheim (city) Orange County	816	0.25
Riverside (city) Riverside County	789	0.26

Top 10 Places Sorted by Percent of Total Population
Based on all places, regardless of total population

Place	Population	%
Boulevard (cdp) San Diego County	11	35.48
Kenwood (cdp) Sonoma County	58	12.55
Salmon Creek (cdp) Sonoma County	9	10.84
Samoa (cdp) Humboldt County	24	8.79
Coarsegold (cdp) Madera County	50	3.11
East Pasadena (cdp) Los Angeles County	178	3.09
Camanche Village (cdp) Amador County	18	3.06
Aptos (cdp) Santa Cruz County	165	2.64
Hillsborough (town) San Mateo County	278	2.61
Green Valley (cdp) Solano County	40	2.51

Top 10 Places Sorted by Percent of Total Population
Based on places with total population of 50,000 or more

Place	Population	%
Glendale (city) Los Angeles County	2,062	1.07
Redondo Beach (city) Los Angeles County	545	0.83
Pomona (city) Los Angeles County	935	0.63
Yorba Linda (city) Orange County	374	0.59
Corona (city) Riverside County	845	0.56
Mission Viejo (city) Orange County	507	0.55
San Bernardino (city) San Bernardino County	1,107	0.53
Chino Hills (city) San Bernardino County	383	0.51
Burbank (city) Los Angeles County	470	0.46
Carlsbad (city) San Diego County	443	0.44

Arab: Moroccan

Top 10 Places Sorted by Population
Based on all places, regardless of total population

Place	Population	%
Los Angeles (city) Los Angeles County	2,098	0.06
San Diego (city) San Diego County	611	0.05
Beverly Hills (city) Los Angeles County	451	1.33
Palo Alto (city) Santa Clara County	181	0.29
Torrance (city) Los Angeles County	174	0.12
Westmont (cdp) Los Angeles County	155	0.50
Lakewood (city) Los Angeles County	149	0.19
Corona (city) Riverside County	148	0.10
Berkeley (city) Alameda County	136	0.12
San Francisco (city) San Francisco County	135	0.02

Top 10 Places Sorted by Percent of Total Population
Based on all places, regardless of total population

Place	Population	%
Beverly Hills (city) Los Angeles County	451	1.33
Rollingwood (cdp) Contra Costa County	26	0.89
Knightsen (cdp) Contra Costa County	9	0.58
Westmont (cdp) Los Angeles County	155	0.50
Saranap (cdp) Contra Costa County	17	0.35
Hawaiian Gardens (city) Los Angeles County	49	0.34
Pleasant Hill (city) Contra Costa County	104	0.32
Palo Alto (city) Santa Clara County	181	0.29
Santa Venetia (cdp) Marin County	14	0.27
Pacific Grove (city) Monterey County	39	0.26

Top 10 Places Sorted by Percent of Total Population
Based on places with total population of 50,000 or more

Place	Population	%
Palo Alto (city) Santa Clara County	181	0.29
Novato (city) Marin County	108	0.21
Lakewood (city) Los Angeles County	149	0.19
Alameda (city) Alameda County	119	0.16
Mountain View (city) Santa Clara County	101	0.14
Carmichael (cdp) Sacramento County	87	0.14
Torrance (city) Los Angeles County	174	0.12
Berkeley (city) Alameda County	136	0.12
Corona (city) Riverside County	148	0.10
Santa Monica (city) Los Angeles County	82	0.09

Arab: Palestinian

Top 10 Places Sorted by Population

Based on all places, regardless of total population

Place	Population	%
Los Angeles (city) Los Angeles County	947	0.03
San Diego (city) San Diego County	828	0.06
San Francisco (city) San Francisco County	705	0.09
San Bernardino (city) San Bernardino County	670	0.32
San Jose (city) Santa Clara County	587	0.06
Daly City (city) San Mateo County	555	0.56
Richmond (city) Contra Costa County	539	0.53
San Bruno (city) San Mateo County	471	1.17
Lodi (city) San Joaquin County	464	0.75
Elk Grove (city) Sacramento County	396	0.28

Top 10 Places Sorted by Percent of Total Population

Based on all places, regardless of total population

Place	Population	%
Orland (city) Glenn County	282	3.95
Spring Valley Lake (cdp) San Bernardino County	227	2.97
Villa Park (city) Orange County	95	1.63
Penryn (cdp) Placer County	12	1.60
San Bruno (city) San Mateo County	471	1.17
Lompico (cdp) Santa Cruz County	11	1.06
Galt (city) Sacramento County	200	0.87
Hillsborough (town) San Mateo County	84	0.79
Lodi (city) San Joaquin County	464	0.75
Morada (cdp) San Joaquin County	36	0.74

Top 10 Places Sorted by Percent of Total Population

Based on places with total population of 50,000 or more

Place	Population	%
Lodi (city) San Joaquin County	464	0.75
Daly City (city) San Mateo County	555	0.56
Richmond (city) Contra Costa County	539	0.53
South San Francisco (city) San Mateo County	320	0.52
San Bernardino (city) San Bernardino County	670	0.32
Elk Grove (city) Sacramento County	396	0.28
San Mateo (city) San Mateo County	265	0.28
Mountain View (city) Santa Clara County	193	0.27
Chino Hills (city) San Bernardino County	175	0.24
Antioch (city) Contra Costa County	229	0.23

Arab: Syrian

Top 10 Places Sorted by Population

Based on all places, regardless of total population

Place	Population	%
Los Angeles (city) Los Angeles County	2,954	0.08
San Diego (city) San Diego County	762	0.06
Lancaster (city) Los Angeles County	536	0.36
Pasadena (city) Los Angeles County	428	0.31
Burbank (city) Los Angeles County	409	0.40
Anaheim (city) Orange County	399	0.12
Fresno (city) Fresno County	363	0.07
Irvine (city) Orange County	346	0.17
Glendale (city) Los Angeles County	340	0.18
Glendora (city) Los Angeles County	283	0.57

Top 10 Places Sorted by Percent of Total Population

Based on all places, regardless of total population

Place	Population	%
Bayview (cdp) Contra Costa County	52	2.36
Arnold (cdp) Calaveras County	49	1.42
Round Valley (cdp) Inyo County	4	1.37
Aromas (cdp) Monterey County	27	1.16
Searles Valley (cdp) San Bernardino County	23	1.10
Rosedale (cdp) Kern County	159	1.07
San Martin (cdp) Santa Clara County	64	0.88
Ross (town) Marin County	15	0.75
Green Valley (cdp) Solano County	12	0.75
Willows (city) Glenn County	46	0.74

Top 10 Places Sorted by Percent of Total Population

Based on places with total population of 50,000 or more

Place	Population	%
Burbank (city) Los Angeles County	409	0.40
Lancaster (city) Los Angeles County	536	0.36
Pasadena (city) Los Angeles County	428	0.31
Redlands (city) San Bernardino County	208	0.30
West Covina (city) Los Angeles County	231	0.22
Chino (city) San Bernardino County	174	0.22
Highland (city) San Bernardino County	117	0.22
Orange (city) Orange County	268	0.20
Simi Valley (city) Ventura County	236	0.19
Yucaipa (city) San Bernardino County	97	0.19

Arab: Other

Top 10 Places Sorted by Population

Based on all places, regardless of total population

Place	Population	%
Los Angeles (city) Los Angeles County	4,177	0.11
San Francisco (city) San Francisco County	1,559	0.20
Oakland (city) Alameda County	1,520	0.39
San Diego (city) San Diego County	1,335	0.10
El Cajon (city) San Diego County	958	0.98
San Jose (city) Santa Clara County	695	0.08
Irvine (city) Orange County	600	0.30
Fremont (city) Alameda County	590	0.28
Long Beach (city) Los Angeles County	586	0.13
San Bernardino (city) San Bernardino County	571	0.27

Top 10 Places Sorted by Percent of Total Population

Based on all places, regardless of total population

Place	Population	%
Elkhorn (cdp) Monterey County	122	7.09
Rose Hills (cdp) Los Angeles County	133	4.55
Buttonwillow (cdp) Kern County	71	4.24
Norris Canyon (cdp) Contra Costa County	32	3.94
Woodlands (cdp) San Luis Obispo County	14	3.76
East Tulare Villa (cdp) Tulare County	35	2.80
Del Rio (cdp) Stanislaus County	30	2.53
East Richmond Heights (cdp) Contra Costa County	78	2.43
Shelter Cove (cdp) Humboldt County	11	2.10
Rodeo (cdp) Contra Costa County	163	1.79

Top 10 Places Sorted by Percent of Total Population

Based on places with total population of 50,000 or more

Place	Population	%
El Cajon (city) San Diego County	958	0.98
Santee (city) San Diego County	498	0.94
Walnut Creek (city) Contra Costa County	267	0.42
Oakland (city) Alameda County	1,520	0.39
Newport Beach (city) Orange County	297	0.36
Rancho Cordova (city) Sacramento County	205	0.32
Upland (city) San Bernardino County	227	0.31
Irvine (city) Orange County	600	0.30
Palo Alto (city) Santa Clara County	183	0.29
Fremont (city) Alameda County	590	0.28

Armenian

Top 10 Places Sorted by Population

Based on all places, regardless of total population

Place	Population	%
Los Angeles (city) Los Angeles County	73,256	1.94
Glendale (city) Los Angeles County	65,434	34.05
Burbank (city) Los Angeles County	12,490	12.16
Fresno (city) Fresno County	7,000	1.45
Pasadena (city) Los Angeles County	5,017	3.68
San Diego (city) San Diego County	3,045	0.24
Altadena (cdp) Los Angeles County	2,354	5.18
La Crescenta-Montrose (cdp) Los Angeles County	2,171	10.89
San Francisco (city) San Francisco County	2,149	0.27
Montebello (city) Los Angeles County	1,885	3.02

Top 10 Places Sorted by Percent of Total Population

Based on all places, regardless of total population

Place	Population	%
Glendale (city) Los Angeles County	65,434	34.05
Leggett (cdp) Mendocino County	13	19.12
Avery (cdp) Calaveras County	59	15.49
Burbank (city) Los Angeles County	12,490	12.16
La Crescenta-Montrose (cdp) Los Angeles County	2,171	10.89
Bieber (cdp) Lassen County	16	6.23
Castle Hill (cdp) Contra Costa County	81	6.10
Amador City (city) Amador County	7	5.47
Altadena (cdp) Los Angeles County	2,354	5.18
Meadow Valley (cdp) Plumas County	33	4.90

Top 10 Places Sorted by Percent of Total Population

Based on places with total population of 50,000 or more

Place	Population	%
Glendale (city) Los Angeles County	65,434	34.05
Burbank (city) Los Angeles County	12,490	12.16
Pasadena (city) Los Angeles County	5,017	3.68
Montebello (city) Los Angeles County	1,885	3.02
Los Angeles (city) Los Angeles County	73,256	1.94
Fresno (city) Fresno County	7,000	1.45
Rancho Cordova (city) Sacramento County	900	1.42
Clovis (city) Fresno County	984	1.08
Redondo Beach (city) Los Angeles County	659	1.00
Whittier (city) Los Angeles County	696	0.82

Assyrian/Chaldean/Syriac

Top 10 Places Sorted by Population

Based on all places, regardless of total population

Place	Population	%
Turlock (city) Stanislaus County	5,798	8.61
El Cajon (city) San Diego County	4,776	4.88
Modesto (city) Stanislaus County	2,553	1.26
San Jose (city) Santa Clara County	2,016	0.22
Los Angeles (city) Los Angeles County	1,479	0.04
Rancho San Diego (cdp) San Diego County	776	3.83
Jamul (cdp) San Diego County	465	8.74
San Diego (city) San Diego County	463	0.04
Spring Valley (cdp) San Diego County	448	1.64
Riverbank (city) Stanislaus County	350	1.61

Top 10 Places Sorted by Percent of Total Population

Based on all places, regardless of total population

Place	Population	%
Jamul (cdp) San Diego County	465	8.74
Turlock (city) Stanislaus County	5,798	8.61
El Cajon (city) San Diego County	4,776	4.88
Rancho San Diego (cdp) San Diego County	776	3.83
Empire (cdp) Stanislaus County	103	2.74
Bass Lake (cdp) Madera County	10	2.16
Bonita (cdp) San Diego County	242	1.72
Cambrian Park (cdp) Santa Clara County	54	1.66
Spring Valley (cdp) San Diego County	448	1.64
Riverbank (city) Stanislaus County	350	1.61

Top 10 Places Sorted by Percent of Total Population

Based on places with total population of 50,000 or more

Place	Population	%
Turlock (city) Stanislaus County	5,798	8.61
El Cajon (city) San Diego County	4,776	4.88
Modesto (city) Stanislaus County	2,553	1.26
Cupertino (city) Santa Clara County	168	0.30
San Jose (city) Santa Clara County	2,016	0.22
Santee (city) San Diego County	110	0.21
Palo Alto (city) Santa Clara County	126	0.20
Santa Clara (city) Santa Clara County	219	0.19
La Mesa (city) San Diego County	94	0.17
La Habra (city) Orange County	85	0.14

Australian

Top 10 Places Sorted by Population

Based on all places, regardless of total population

Place	Population	%
Los Angeles (city) Los Angeles County	2,486	0.07
San Diego (city) San Diego County	1,114	0.09
San Francisco (city) San Francisco County	954	0.12
Huntington Beach (city) Orange County	391	0.21
Sacramento (city) Sacramento County	357	0.08
Murrieta (city) Riverside County	295	0.31
Davis (city) Yolo County	269	0.41
Roseville (city) Placer County	256	0.22
Irvine (city) Orange County	256	0.13
Oakland (city) Alameda County	216	0.06

Top 10 Places Sorted by Percent of Total Population

Based on all places, regardless of total population

Place	Population	%
Martell (cdp) Amador County	40	26.14

Place	Population	%
Farmington (cdp) San Joaquin County	28	9.33
Bear Valley (cdp) Alpine County	5	7.46
Lucerne (cdp) Lake County	167	6.23
Valley Springs (cdp) Calaveras County	121	3.00
Indio Hills (cdp) Riverside County	41	2.95
Keswick (cdp) Shasta County	12	2.82
Amador City (city) Amador County	3	2.34
Inverness (cdp) Marin County	28	2.03
Norris Canyon (cdp) Contra Costa County	16	1.97

Top 10 Places Sorted by Percent of Total Population

Based on places with total population of 50,000 or more

Place	Population	%
Davis (city) Yolo County	269	0.41
Murrieta (city) Riverside County	295	0.31
Santa Barbara (city) Santa Barbara County	212	0.24
San Clemente (city) Orange County	147	0.24
Encinitas (city) San Diego County	133	0.23
Roseville (city) Placer County	256	0.22
Huntington Beach (city) Orange County	391	0.21
Santa Monica (city) Los Angeles County	188	0.21
Walnut Creek (city) Contra Costa County	121	0.19
Victorville (city) San Bernardino County	177	0.16

Austrian

Top 10 Places Sorted by Population

Based on all places, regardless of total population

Place	Population	%
Los Angeles (city) Los Angeles County	11,090	0.29
San Diego (city) San Diego County	3,861	0.30
San Francisco (city) San Francisco County	3,588	0.45
San Jose (city) Santa Clara County	1,045	0.11
Oakland (city) Alameda County	843	0.22
Thousand Oaks (city) Ventura County	836	0.67
Santa Monica (city) Los Angeles County	793	0.89
Huntington Beach (city) Orange County	728	0.39
Sacramento (city) Sacramento County	709	0.15
Long Beach (city) Los Angeles County	617	0.13

Top 10 Places Sorted by Percent of Total Population

Based on all places, regardless of total population

Place	Population	%
Floriston (cdp) Nevada County	14	51.85
Creston (cdp) San Luis Obispo County	19	28.36
Camptonville (cdp) Yuba County	26	13.83
Edgewood (cdp) Siskiyou County	4	8.16
Rutherford (cdp) Napa County	15	7.85
North San Juan (cdp) Nevada County	10	7.63
Kenwood (cdp) Sonoma County	35	7.58
Redway (cdp) Humboldt County	70	6.84
Bluewater (cdp) San Bernardino County	10	5.71
Coleville (cdp) Mono County	33	5.45

Top 10 Places Sorted by Percent of Total Population

Based on places with total population of 50,000 or more

Place	Population	%
San Rafael (city) Marin County	601	1.06
Santa Monica (city) Los Angeles County	793	0.89
Walnut Creek (city) Contra Costa County	512	0.80
Newport Beach (city) Orange County	601	0.72
Thousand Oaks (city) Ventura County	836	0.67
Carlsbad (city) San Diego County	596	0.60
Palo Alto (city) Santa Clara County	343	0.55
Novato (city) Marin County	272	0.54
Santa Barbara (city) Santa Barbara County	443	0.50
Berkeley (city) Alameda County	539	0.49

Basque

Top 10 Places Sorted by Population

Based on all places, regardless of total population

Place	Population	%
Bakersfield (city) Kern County	1,084	0.33
Los Angeles (city) Los Angeles County	741	0.02
San Francisco (city) San Francisco County	508	0.06
San Diego (city) San Diego County	498	0.04
Fresno (city) Fresno County	359	0.07
Stockton (city) San Joaquin County	280	0.10
Santa Barbara (city) Santa Barbara County	276	0.31
San Jose (city) Santa Clara County	259	0.03
Rancho Cucamonga (city) San Bernardino County	221	0.14
Pacifica (city) San Mateo County	213	0.58

Top 10 Places Sorted by Percent of Total Population

Based on all places, regardless of total population

Place	Population	%
Elmira (cdp) Solano County	22	14.38
Dillon Beach (cdp) Marin County	23	14.11
Sereno del Mar (cdp) Sonoma County	9	7.32
Keene (cdp) Kern County	17	5.38
Cowan (cdp) Stanislaus County	18	5.14
Davenport (cdp) Santa Cruz County	12	3.88
China Lake Acres (cdp) Kern County	55	3.54
Litchfield (cdp) Lassen County	3	2.91
Tranquillity (cdp) Fresno County	32	2.61
Mammoth Lakes (town) Mono County	206	2.57

Top 10 Places Sorted by Percent of Total Population

Based on places with total population of 50,000 or more

Place	Population	%
Bakersfield (city) Kern County	1,084	0.33
Santa Barbara (city) Santa Barbara County	276	0.31
Upland (city) San Bernardino County	202	0.27
San Ramon (city) Contra Costa County	176	0.26
Woodland (city) Yolo County	127	0.23
Rocklin (city) Placer County	115	0.21
Livermore (city) Alameda County	156	0.20
Carmichael (cdp) Sacramento County	123	0.20
Hemet (city) Riverside County	146	0.19
Arden-Arcade (cdp) Sacramento County	159	0.17

Belgian

Top 10 Places Sorted by Population

Based on all places, regardless of total population

Place	Population	%
Los Angeles (city) Los Angeles County	2,001	0.05
San Diego (city) San Diego County	1,571	0.12
San Francisco (city) San Francisco County	783	0.10
San Jose (city) Santa Clara County	693	0.07
Oceanside (city) San Diego County	420	0.25
Oakland (city) Alameda County	370	0.10
Santa Monica (city) Los Angeles County	300	0.34
Riverside (city) Riverside County	285	0.09
San Clemente (city) Orange County	278	0.46
Irvine (city) Orange County	271	0.14

Top 10 Places Sorted by Percent of Total Population

Based on all places, regardless of total population

Place	Population	%
Tecopa (cdp) Inyo County	6	5.94
Deer Park (cdp) Napa County	38	3.63
Edwards AFB (cdp) Kern County	103	2.89
Lewiston (cdp) Trinity County	33	2.66
Benbow (cdp) Humboldt County	13	2.28
Lone Pine (cdp) Inyo County	52	2.25
Grangeville (cdp) Kings County	13	2.17
Mesa (cdp) Inyo County	8	2.17
Zayante (cdp) Santa Cruz County	17	2.10
Trinity Center (cdp) Trinity County	4	1.91

Top 10 Places Sorted by Percent of Total Population

Based on places with total population of 50,000 or more

Place	Population	%
San Clemente (city) Orange County	278	0.46
Castro Valley (cdp) Alameda County	216	0.36
Santa Monica (city) Los Angeles County	300	0.34
Novato (city) Marin County	164	0.32
Oceanside (city) San Diego County	420	0.25
La Mesa (city) San Diego County	141	0.25
Rocklin (city) Placer County	133	0.25
Newport Beach (city) Orange County	192	0.23
Carmichael (cdp) Sacramento County	145	0.23
Palo Alto (city) Santa Clara County	141	0.23

Brazilian

Top 10 Places Sorted by Population

Based on all places, regardless of total population

Place	Population	%
Los Angeles (city) Los Angeles County	3,962	0.11
San Diego (city) San Diego County	2,350	0.18
San Francisco (city) San Francisco County	1,569	0.20
San Jose (city) Santa Clara County	683	0.07
Richmond (city) Contra Costa County	547	0.53
Huntington Beach (city) Orange County	450	0.24
San Bruno (city) San Mateo County	438	1.09
Anaheim (city) Orange County	387	0.12
Burlingame (city) San Mateo County	381	1.35
Clovis (city) Fresno County	350	0.38

Top 10 Places Sorted by Percent of Total Population

Based on all places, regardless of total population

Place	Population	%
Carrick (cdp) Siskiyou County	20	11.76
Lompico (cdp) Santa Cruz County	52	5.01
Channel Islands Beach (cdp) Ventura County	58	1.79
Tara Hills (cdp) Contra Costa County	71	1.54
Marin City (cdp) Marin County	40	1.42
Cayucos (cdp) San Luis Obispo County	40	1.40
Burlingame (city) San Mateo County	381	1.35
Santa Venetia (cdp) Marin County	69	1.35
Rio del Mar (cdp) Santa Cruz County	122	1.29
Lockeford (cdp) San Joaquin County	44	1.26

Top 10 Places Sorted by Percent of Total Population

Based on places with total population of 50,000 or more

Place	Population	%
Novato (city) Marin County	316	0.63
Richmond (city) Contra Costa County	547	0.53
Redondo Beach (city) Los Angeles County	302	0.46
Clovis (city) Fresno County	350	0.38
San Rafael (city) Marin County	180	0.32
Daly City (city) San Mateo County	311	0.31
San Clemente (city) Orange County	182	0.30
Concord (city) Contra Costa County	327	0.27
Huntington Beach (city) Orange County	450	0.24
Inglewood (city) Los Angeles County	264	0.24

British

Top 10 Places Sorted by Population

Based on all places, regardless of total population

Place	Population	%
Los Angeles (city) Los Angeles County	12,180	0.32
San Diego (city) San Diego County	6,683	0.52
San Francisco (city) San Francisco County	6,050	0.77
San Jose (city) Santa Clara County	3,157	0.34
Oakland (city) Alameda County	1,790	0.46
Long Beach (city) Los Angeles County	1,611	0.35
Thousand Oaks (city) Ventura County	1,514	1.21
Sacramento (city) Sacramento County	1,493	0.32
Fremont (city) Alameda County	1,345	0.64
Mission Viejo (city) Orange County	1,204	1.30

Top 10 Places Sorted by Percent of Total Population

Based on all places, regardless of total population

Place	Population	%
Johnsville (cdp) Plumas County	67	79.76
Kennedy Meadows (cdp) Tulare County	9	47.37
Bear Valley (cdp) Mariposa County	95	34.93
Twain (cdp) Plumas County	22	32.84
Jacumba (cdp) San Diego County	138	21.97
Elmira (cdp) Solano County	25	16.34
Salton Sea Beach (cdp) Imperial County	64	13.79
Woodlands (cdp) San Luis Obispo County	35	9.41
Pike (cdp) Sierra County	14	8.92
Kenwood (cdp) Sonoma County	37	8.01

Top 10 Places Sorted by Percent of Total Population

Based on places with total population of 50,000 or more

Place	Population	%
Palo Alto (city) Santa Clara County	1,004	1.61
Mission Viejo (city) Orange County	1,204	1.30
Mountain View (city) Santa Clara County	927	1.28
Laguna Niguel (city) Orange County	778	1.24

Place	Population	%
Thousand Oaks (city) Ventura County	1,514	1.21
San Rafael (city) Marin County	672	1.18
Lake Forest (city) Orange County	891	1.16
Encinitas (city) San Diego County	666	1.13
Redondo Beach (city) Los Angeles County	730	1.11
Walnut Creek (city) Contra Costa County	684	1.07

Bulgarian

Top 10 Places Sorted by Population

Based on all places, regardless of total population

Place	Population	%
Los Angeles (city) Los Angeles County	2,293	0.06
San Diego (city) San Diego County	474	0.04
San Francisco (city) San Francisco County	468	0.06
Sunnyvale (city) Santa Clara County	308	0.23
Sacramento (city) Sacramento County	304	0.07
Concord (city) Contra Costa County	294	0.24
San Jose (city) Santa Clara County	264	0.03
Lakeside (cdp) San Diego County	205	1.00
Chico (city) Butte County	187	0.22
El Dorado Hills (cdp) El Dorado County	148	0.34

Top 10 Places Sorted by Percent of Total Population

Based on all places, regardless of total population

Place	Population	%
Anchor Bay (cdp) Mendocino County	50	15.67
Meadow Valley (cdp) Plumas County	23	3.41
Middletown (cdp) Lake County	36	2.19
Lincoln Village (cdp) San Joaquin County	47	1.05
Belvedere (city) Marin County	22	1.04
Lakeside (cdp) San Diego County	205	1.00
Greenville (cdp) Plumas County	9	0.91
Sky Valley (cdp) Riverside County	16	0.87
McCloud (cdp) Siskiyou County	10	0.83
Meridian (cdp) Sutter County	3	0.75

Top 10 Places Sorted by Percent of Total Population

Based on places with total population of 50,000 or more

Place	Population	%
Concord (city) Contra Costa County	294	0.24
Sunnyvale (city) Santa Clara County	308	0.23
Chico (city) Butte County	187	0.22
Walnut Creek (city) Contra Costa County	114	0.18
Novato (city) Marin County	84	0.17
Mountain View (city) Santa Clara County	108	0.15
Baldwin Park (city) Los Angeles County	93	0.12
Palo Alto (city) Santa Clara County	76	0.12
Laguna Niguel (city) Orange County	72	0.11
Cupertino (city) Santa Clara County	55	0.10

Cajun

Top 10 Places Sorted by Population

Based on all places, regardless of total population

Place	Population	%
San Francisco (city) San Francisco County	219	0.03
San Diego (city) San Diego County	217	0.02
Long Beach (city) Los Angeles County	157	0.03
Los Angeles (city) Los Angeles County	153	<0.01
Bakersfield (city) Kern County	139	0.04
Camp Pendleton South (cdp) San Diego County	74	0.55
Oceanside (city) San Diego County	74	0.04
San Jose (city) Santa Clara County	68	0.01
Santa Clarita (city) Los Angeles County	56	0.03
Santa Rosa (city) Sonoma County	56	0.03

Top 10 Places Sorted by Percent of Total Population

Based on all places, regardless of total population

Place	Population	%
Sky Valley (cdp) Riverside County	40	2.18
Lakeport (city) Lake County	48	0.99
Camp Pendleton South (cdp) San Diego County	74	0.55
Weaverville (cdp) Trinity County	21	0.53
Guerneville (cdp) Sonoma County	23	0.51
Myrtletown (cdp) Humboldt County	18	0.38
Needles (city) San Bernardino County	11	0.22
Golden Hills (cdp) Kern County	18	0.21
Garnet (cdp) Riverside County	13	0.20
Marysville (city) Yuba County	23	0.19

Top 10 Places Sorted by Percent of Total Population

Based on places with total population of 50,000 or more

Place	Population	%
Hacienda Heights (cdp) Los Angeles County	47	0.09
Fountain Valley (city) Orange County	29	0.05
Rocklin (city) Placer County	29	0.05
Bakersfield (city) Kern County	139	0.04
Oceanside (city) San Diego County	74	0.04
Temecula (city) Riverside County	43	0.04
Antioch (city) Contra Costa County	40	0.04
Redding (city) Shasta County	35	0.04
Mission Viejo (city) Orange County	33	0.04
Colton (city) San Bernardino County	22	0.04

Canadian

Top 10 Places Sorted by Population

Based on all places, regardless of total population

Place	Population	%
Los Angeles (city) Los Angeles County	7,817	0.21
San Diego (city) San Diego County	3,425	0.27
San Jose (city) Santa Clara County	1,796	0.19
San Francisco (city) San Francisco County	1,697	0.22
Irvine (city) Orange County	1,087	0.55
Long Beach (city) Los Angeles County	887	0.19
Fresno (city) Fresno County	874	0.18
Huntington Beach (city) Orange County	799	0.42
Torrance (city) Los Angeles County	769	0.53
Anaheim (city) Orange County	756	0.23

Top 10 Places Sorted by Percent of Total Population

Based on all places, regardless of total population

Place	Population	%
Leggett (cdp) Mendocino County	10	14.71
Anchor Bay (cdp) Mendocino County	42	13.17
Terminous (cdp) San Joaquin County	23	5.62
Greenhorn (cdp) Plumas County	11	5.42
Paradise Park (cdp) Santa Cruz County	23	5.04
Alto (cdp) Marin County	28	4.84
Markleeville (cdp) Alpine County	13	4.74
Blacklake (cdp) San Luis Obispo County	51	4.27
Romoland (cdp) Riverside County	52	4.11
Bell Canyon (cdp) Ventura County	95	3.87

Top 10 Places Sorted by Percent of Total Population

Based on places with total population of 50,000 or more

Place	Population	%
Novato (city) Marin County	539	1.07
Yucaipa (city) San Bernardino County	438	0.87
Cathedral City (city) Riverside County	404	0.80
Santa Monica (city) Los Angeles County	592	0.67
Camarillo (city) Ventura County	418	0.66
Temecula (city) Riverside County	608	0.63
Newport Beach (city) Orange County	516	0.62
Yorba Linda (city) Orange County	388	0.62
Mission Viejo (city) Orange County	559	0.60
Thousand Oaks (city) Ventura County	725	0.58

Carpatho Rusyn

Top 10 Places Sorted by Population

Based on all places, regardless of total population

Place	Population	%
Los Angeles (city) Los Angeles County	80	<0.01
Los Altos (city) Santa Clara County	57	0.20
Escondido (city) San Diego County	49	0.03
Oakland (city) Alameda County	37	0.01
Long Beach (city) Los Angeles County	34	0.01
Citrus Heights (city) Sacramento County	19	0.02
San Bruno (city) San Mateo County	18	0.04
San Francisco (city) San Francisco County	16	<0.01
Redondo Beach (city) Los Angeles County	15	0.02
Newport Beach (city) Orange County	13	0.02

Top 10 Places Sorted by Percent of Total Population

Based on all places, regardless of total population

Place	Population	%
Los Altos (city) Santa Clara County	57	0.20
San Bruno (city) San Mateo County	18	0.04
Escondido (city) San Diego County	49	0.03
Citrus Heights (city) Sacramento County	19	0.02
Redondo Beach (city) Los Angeles County	15	0.02
Newport Beach (city) Orange County	13	0.02
Oakland (city) Alameda County	37	0.01
Long Beach (city) Los Angeles County	34	0.01
Torrance (city) Los Angeles County	13	0.01
Berkeley (city) Alameda County	11	0.01

Top 10 Places Sorted by Percent of Total Population

Based on places with total population of 50,000 or more

Place	Population	%
Escondido (city) San Diego County	49	0.03
Citrus Heights (city) Sacramento County	19	0.02
Redondo Beach (city) Los Angeles County	15	0.02
Newport Beach (city) Orange County	13	0.02
Oakland (city) Alameda County	37	0.01
Long Beach (city) Los Angeles County	34	0.01
Torrance (city) Los Angeles County	13	0.01
Berkeley (city) Alameda County	11	0.01
Los Angeles (city) Los Angeles County	80	<0.01
San Francisco (city) San Francisco County	16	<0.01

Celtic

Top 10 Places Sorted by Population

Based on all places, regardless of total population

Place	Population	%
Los Angeles (city) Los Angeles County	654	0.02
San Jose (city) Santa Clara County	243	0.03
Oakland (city) Alameda County	235	0.06
San Diego (city) San Diego County	224	0.02
Arden-Arcade (cdp) Sacramento County	205	0.23
Poway (city) San Diego County	204	0.43
San Francisco (city) San Francisco County	194	0.02
Fresno (city) Fresno County	183	0.04
Long Beach (city) Los Angeles County	170	0.04
Santa Clarita (city) Los Angeles County	157	0.09

Top 10 Places Sorted by Percent of Total Population

Based on all places, regardless of total population

Place	Population	%
Comptche (cdp) Mendocino County	21	21.88
Carrick (cdp) Siskiyou County	13	7.65
Keswick (cdp) Shasta County	24	5.63
Tupman (cdp) Kern County	4	3.36
Beckwourth (cdp) Plumas County	10	2.41
Corralitos (cdp) Santa Cruz County	49	1.82
Eldridge (cdp) Sonoma County	30	1.71
Cutten (cdp) Humboldt County	41	1.35
Bishop (city) Inyo County	51	1.33
Plymouth (city) Amador County	11	1.22

Top 10 Places Sorted by Percent of Total Population

Based on places with total population of 50,000 or more

Place	Population	%
Arden-Arcade (cdp) Sacramento County	205	0.23
Redwood City (city) San Mateo County	115	0.15
Santa Cruz (city) Santa Cruz County	89	0.15
Santa Clarita (city) Los Angeles County	157	0.09
Hanford (city) Kings County	45	0.09
Fullerton (city) Orange County	111	0.08
Berkeley (city) Alameda County	86	0.08
Richmond (city) Contra Costa County	73	0.07
Alameda (city) Alameda County	50	0.07
Mountain View (city) Santa Clara County	50	0.07

Croatian

Top 10 Places Sorted by Population

Based on all places, regardless of total population

Place	Population	%
Los Angeles (city) Los Angeles County	6,277	0.17
San Jose (city) Santa Clara County	1,692	0.18
San Francisco (city) San Francisco County	1,466	0.19
San Diego (city) San Diego County	1,378	0.11
Rancho Palos Verdes (city) Los Angeles County	990	2.38
Huntington Beach (city) Orange County	618	0.33
Long Beach (city) Los Angeles County	485	0.11
Sacramento (city) Sacramento County	483	0.11
Arden-Arcade (cdp) Sacramento County	471	0.52
Oakland (city) Alameda County	455	0.12

Top 10 Places Sorted by Percent of Total Population
Based on all places, regardless of total population

Place	Population	%
Inverness (cdp) Marin County	79	5.72
Bass Lake (cdp) Madera County	21	4.54
Lexington Hills (cdp) Santa Clara County	79	3.32
Corralitos (cdp) Santa Cruz County	89	3.31
Wilkerson (cdp) Inyo County	18	3.20
Acalanes Ridge (cdp) Contra Costa County	46	2.85
Bloomfield (cdp) Sonoma County	9	2.68
Lucerne (cdp) Lake County	65	2.43
Point Reyes Station (cdp) Marin County	20	2.41
Rancho Palos Verdes (city) Los Angeles County	990	2.38

Top 10 Places Sorted by Percent of Total Population
Based on places with total population of 50,000 or more

Place	Population	%
Novato (city) Marin County	269	0.53
Arden-Arcade (cdp) Sacramento County	471	0.52
Santa Monica (city) Los Angeles County	427	0.48
Redwood City (city) San Mateo County	342	0.45
Cupertino (city) Santa Clara County	228	0.40
Fountain Valley (city) Orange County	198	0.36
Huntington Beach (city) Orange County	618	0.33
Livermore (city) Alameda County	261	0.33
Pleasanton (city) Alameda County	224	0.33
Thousand Oaks (city) Ventura County	398	0.32

Cypriot

Top 10 Places Sorted by Population
Based on all places, regardless of total population

Place	Population	%
Santa Clara (city) Santa Clara County	115	0.10
Long Beach (city) Los Angeles County	94	0.02
Los Angeles (city) Los Angeles County	69	<0.01
Alameda (city) Alameda County	51	0.07
San Diego (city) San Diego County	51	<0.01
San Francisco (city) San Francisco County	50	0.01
South San Francisco (city) San Mateo County	34	0.05
South Pasadena (city) Los Angeles County	27	0.11
Rancho Cordova (city) Sacramento County	22	0.03
Carlsbad (city) San Diego County	18	0.02

Top 10 Places Sorted by Percent of Total Population
Based on all places, regardless of total population

Place	Population	%
South Pasadena (city) Los Angeles County	27	0.11
Santa Clara (city) Santa Clara County	115	0.10
Alameda (city) Alameda County	51	0.07
Stanford (cdp) Santa Clara County	10	0.07
South San Francisco (city) San Mateo County	34	0.05
Rancho Cordova (city) Sacramento County	22	0.03
Burlingame (city) San Mateo County	9	0.03
Long Beach (city) Los Angeles County	94	0.02
Carlsbad (city) San Diego County	18	0.02
Davis (city) Yolo County	11	0.02

Top 10 Places Sorted by Percent of Total Population
Based on places with total population of 50,000 or more

Place	Population	%
Santa Clara (city) Santa Clara County	115	0.10
Alameda (city) Alameda County	51	0.07
South San Francisco (city) San Mateo County	34	0.05
Rancho Cordova (city) Sacramento County	22	0.03
Long Beach (city) Los Angeles County	94	0.02
Carlsbad (city) San Diego County	18	0.02
Davis (city) Yolo County	11	0.02
San Francisco (city) San Francisco County	50	0.01
Santa Barbara (city) Santa Barbara County	12	0.01
Lakewood (city) Los Angeles County	11	0.01

Czech

Top 10 Places Sorted by Population
Based on all places, regardless of total population

Place	Population	%
Los Angeles (city) Los Angeles County	6,899	0.18
San Diego (city) San Diego County	5,144	0.40
San Francisco (city) San Francisco County	2,987	0.38
San Jose (city) Santa Clara County	1,653	0.18
Sacramento (city) Sacramento County	1,164	0.25
Huntington Beach (city) Orange County	1,079	0.57
Long Beach (city) Los Angeles County	854	0.18
Fresno (city) Fresno County	825	0.17
Irvine (city) Orange County	775	0.39
Oakland (city) Alameda County	719	0.19

Top 10 Places Sorted by Percent of Total Population
Based on all places, regardless of total population

Place	Population	%
Butte Meadows (cdp) Butte County	9	30.00
New Pine Creek (cdp) Modoc County	29	25.66
Twain (cdp) Plumas County	12	17.91
Plumas Eureka (cdp) Plumas County	32	13.68
Beckwourth (cdp) Plumas County	49	11.81
Port Costa (cdp) Contra Costa County	15	8.93
Spring Valley (cdp) Lake County	72	8.76
Anchor Bay (cdp) Mendocino County	27	8.46
Concow (cdp) Butte County	56	7.06
Tecopa (cdp) Inyo County	7	6.93

Top 10 Places Sorted by Percent of Total Population
Based on places with total population of 50,000 or more

Place	Population	%
Palo Alto (city) Santa Clara County	554	0.89
Santee (city) San Diego County	392	0.74
Santa Monica (city) Los Angeles County	602	0.68
Carlsbad (city) San Diego County	593	0.59
Redondo Beach (city) Los Angeles County	391	0.59
Santa Cruz (city) Santa Cruz County	337	0.58
Huntington Beach (city) Orange County	1,079	0.57
Cupertino (city) Santa Clara County	319	0.56
Laguna Niguel (city) Orange County	337	0.54
Thousand Oaks (city) Ventura County	661	0.53

Czechoslovakian

Top 10 Places Sorted by Population
Based on all places, regardless of total population

Place	Population	%
Los Angeles (city) Los Angeles County	1,806	0.05
San Diego (city) San Diego County	1,044	0.08
San Jose (city) Santa Clara County	484	0.05
San Francisco (city) San Francisco County	422	0.05
Long Beach (city) Los Angeles County	369	0.08
Sacramento (city) Sacramento County	294	0.06
Clovis (city) Fresno County	275	0.30
Yuba City (city) Sutter County	259	0.41
Redding (city) Shasta County	235	0.26
Anaheim (city) Orange County	234	0.07

Top 10 Places Sorted by Percent of Total Population
Based on all places, regardless of total population

Place	Population	%
Lytle Creek (cdp) San Bernardino County	148	20.00
College City (cdp) Colusa County	12	13.04
Aguanga (cdp) Riverside County	82	5.73
Santa Susana (cdp) Ventura County	73	5.61
Mi-Wuk Village (cdp) Tuolumne County	44	5.19
Sand City (city) Monterey County	8	3.42
Inverness (cdp) Marin County	43	3.12
Pine Canyon (cdp) Monterey County	51	2.55
Hasley Canyon (cdp) Los Angeles County	20	2.07
Mission Canyon (cdp) Santa Barbara County	40	1.88

Top 10 Places Sorted by Percent of Total Population
Based on places with total population of 50,000 or more

Place	Population	%
Yuba City (city) Sutter County	259	0.41
Clovis (city) Fresno County	275	0.30
Redding (city) Shasta County	235	0.26
Upland (city) San Bernardino County	191	0.26
Santa Barbara (city) Santa Barbara County	206	0.23
Carmichael (cdp) Sacramento County	133	0.22
Walnut Creek (city) Contra Costa County	137	0.21
Arden-Arcade (cdp) Sacramento County	180	0.20
Newport Beach (city) Orange County	167	0.20
Carlsbad (city) San Diego County	189	0.19

Danish

Top 10 Places Sorted by Population
Based on all places, regardless of total population

Place	Population	%
Los Angeles (city) Los Angeles County	9,510	0.25
San Diego (city) San Diego County	5,944	0.46
San Francisco (city) San Francisco County	3,739	0.47
San Jose (city) Santa Clara County	3,362	0.36
Fresno (city) Fresno County	2,292	0.47
Santa Rosa (city) Sonoma County	2,234	1.37
Huntington Beach (city) Orange County	1,987	1.05
Sacramento (city) Sacramento County	1,908	0.42
Roseville (city) Placer County	1,567	1.38
Oceanside (city) San Diego County	1,549	0.94

Top 10 Places Sorted by Percent of Total Population
Based on all places, regardless of total population

Place	Population	%
Edna (cdp) San Luis Obispo County	20	66.67
Washington (cdp) Nevada County	18	48.65
Shoshone (cdp) Inyo County	10	30.30
Butte Meadows (cdp) Butte County	9	30.00
Keeler (cdp) Inyo County	8	29.63
Gasquet (cdp) Del Norte County	154	26.92
Comptche (cdp) Mendocino County	21	21.88
Artois (cdp) Glenn County	27	19.01
Red Corral (cdp) Amador County	300	17.47
Tuttletown (cdp) Tuolumne County	147	17.40

Top 10 Places Sorted by Percent of Total Population
Based on places with total population of 50,000 or more

Place	Population	%
Petaluma (city) Sonoma County	845	1.49
Carlsbad (city) San Diego County	1,413	1.42
Livermore (city) Alameda County	1,107	1.41
Chico (city) Butte County	1,185	1.39
Roseville (city) Placer County	1,567	1.38
Santa Rosa (city) Sonoma County	2,234	1.37
San Rafael (city) Marin County	775	1.36
Novato (city) Marin County	675	1.34
Citrus Heights (city) Sacramento County	1,123	1.33
Rocklin (city) Placer County	663	1.22

Dutch

Top 10 Places Sorted by Population
Based on all places, regardless of total population

Place	Population	%
Los Angeles (city) Los Angeles County	17,897	0.47
San Diego (city) San Diego County	14,365	1.12
San Jose (city) Santa Clara County	7,446	0.80
San Francisco (city) San Francisco County	7,416	0.94
Sacramento (city) Sacramento County	4,826	1.05
Fresno (city) Fresno County	4,720	0.98
Long Beach (city) Los Angeles County	4,630	1.00
Huntington Beach (city) Orange County	4,608	2.44
Modesto (city) Stanislaus County	4,037	2.00
Bakersfield (city) Kern County	4,032	1.21

Top 10 Places Sorted by Percent of Total Population
Based on all places, regardless of total population

Place	Population	%
Weott (cdp) Humboldt County	76	43.18
Monterey Park Tract (cdp) Stanislaus County	109	39.07
Nipinnawasee (cdp) Madera County	239	30.14
Mendocino (cdp) Mendocino County	216	21.51
Verdi (cdp) Sierra County	37	20.00
Lake Almanor Peninsula (cdp) Plumas County	51	19.62
Palo Verde (cdp) Imperial County	20	18.69
Litchfield (cdp) Lassen County	18	17.48
Mountain Gate (cdp) Shasta County	211	16.14
Clarksburg (cdp) Yolo County	34	15.04

Top 10 Places Sorted by Percent of Total Population
Based on places with total population of 50,000 or more

Place	Population	%
Menifee (city) Riverside County	2,084	2.87
Bellflower (city) Los Angeles County	1,961	2.58
San Clemente (city) Orange County	1,526	2.51
Huntington Beach (city) Orange County	4,608	2.44

Citrus Heights (city) Sacramento County	2,006	2.38
Yorba Linda (city) Orange County	1,479	2.35
Yucaipa (city) San Bernardino County	1,181	2.35
Redlands (city) San Bernardino County	1,575	2.29
Redding (city) Shasta County	2,024	2.26
Hanford (city) Kings County	1,162	2.22

Eastern European

Top 10 Places Sorted by Population

Based on all places, regardless of total population

Place	Population	%
Los Angeles (city) Los Angeles County	14,001	0.37
San Francisco (city) San Francisco County	3,844	0.49
San Diego (city) San Diego County	2,599	0.20
Oakland (city) Alameda County	1,717	0.44
San Jose (city) Santa Clara County	1,162	0.13
Berkeley (city) Alameda County	1,046	0.96
Santa Monica (city) Los Angeles County	988	1.11
Irvine (city) Orange County	851	0.43
Thousand Oaks (city) Ventura County	674	0.54
Agoura Hills (city) Los Angeles County	663	3.26

Top 10 Places Sorted by Percent of Total Population

Based on all places, regardless of total population

Place	Population	%
Sleepy Hollow (cdp) Marin County	91	3.72
Sea Ranch (cdp) Sonoma County	27	3.37
Agoura Hills (city) Los Angeles County	663	3.26
Muir Beach (cdp) Marin County	9	3.11
Moss Beach (cdp) San Mateo County	68	2.97
Corralitos (cdp) Santa Cruz County	77	2.86
West Menlo Park (cdp) San Mateo County	93	2.73
Montara (cdp) San Mateo County	74	2.40
Stanford (cdp) Santa Clara County	327	2.29
Deer Park (cdp) Napa County	23	2.19

Top 10 Places Sorted by Percent of Total Population

Based on places with total population of 50,000 or more

Place	Population	%
Santa Monica (city) Los Angeles County	988	1.11
Berkeley (city) Alameda County	1,046	0.96
Palo Alto (city) Santa Clara County	452	0.72
San Rafael (city) Marin County	360	0.63
Redondo Beach (city) Los Angeles County	380	0.58
Thousand Oaks (city) Ventura County	674	0.54
Santa Cruz (city) Santa Cruz County	297	0.51
San Francisco (city) San Francisco County	3,844	0.49
Alameda (city) Alameda County	341	0.47
Oakland (city) Alameda County	1,717	0.44

English

Top 10 Places Sorted by Population

Based on all places, regardless of total population

Place	Population	%
Los Angeles (city) Los Angeles County	129,873	3.44
San Diego (city) San Diego County	92,418	7.20
San Francisco (city) San Francisco County	45,268	5.74
San Jose (city) Santa Clara County	42,150	4.56
Sacramento (city) Sacramento County	28,086	6.11
Fresno (city) Fresno County	24,262	5.01
Long Beach (city) Los Angeles County	23,359	5.06
Huntington Beach (city) Orange County	21,837	11.56
Bakersfield (city) Kern County	21,066	6.35
Riverside (city) Riverside County	18,993	6.32

Top 10 Places Sorted by Percent of Total Population

Based on all places, regardless of total population

Place	Population	%
Strawberry (cdp) Tuolumne County	64	100.00
Indian Falls (cdp) Plumas County	35	100.00
Trona (cdp) Inyo County	17	100.00
Whitehawk (cdp) Plumas County	12	100.00
Shoshone (cdp) Inyo County	23	69.70
Little River (cdp) Mendocino County	200	68.97
Coulterville (cdp) Mariposa County	109	67.28
Mount Laguna (cdp) San Diego County	42	63.64
Valley Ford (cdp) Sonoma County	52	60.47
River Pines (cdp) Amador County	322	56.10

Top 10 Places Sorted by Percent of Total Population

Based on places with total population of 50,000 or more

Place	Population	%
Newport Beach (city) Orange County	14,515	17.37
Carlsbad (city) San Diego County	16,407	16.45
Encinitas (city) San Diego County	9,494	16.16
Walnut Creek (city) Contra Costa County	10,308	16.15
Carmichael (cdp) Sacramento County	9,670	15.65
Rocklin (city) Placer County	8,010	14.76
San Clemente (city) Orange County	8,898	14.64
Redding (city) Shasta County	12,433	13.91
Yorba Linda (city) Orange County	8,660	13.76
Roseville (city) Placer County	15,474	13.60

Estonian

Top 10 Places Sorted by Population

Based on all places, regardless of total population

Place	Population	%
Los Angeles (city) Los Angeles County	347	0.01
San Francisco (city) San Francisco County	227	0.03
San Diego (city) San Diego County	164	0.01
Riverbank (city) Stanislaus County	135	0.62
Lancaster (city) Los Angeles County	110	0.07
Redwood City (city) San Mateo County	76	0.10
Oakland (city) Alameda County	65	0.02
Los Gatos (town) Santa Clara County	61	0.21
Berkeley (city) Alameda County	57	0.05
Inglewood (city) Los Angeles County	55	0.05

Top 10 Places Sorted by Percent of Total Population

Based on all places, regardless of total population

Place	Population	%
Alta (cdp) Placer County	11	2.14
Carmel-by-the-Sea (city) Monterey County	54	1.45
Chester (cdp) Plumas County	15	0.81
Riverbank (city) Stanislaus County	135	0.62
Ahwahnee (cdp) Madera County	13	0.62
Cazadero (cdp) Sonoma County	2	0.55
Lake California (cdp) Tehama County	13	0.50
Big Pine (cdp) Inyo County	7	0.42
Larkfield-Wikiup (cdp) Sonoma County	31	0.36
Larkspur (city) Marin County	37	0.31

Top 10 Places Sorted by Percent of Total Population

Based on places with total population of 50,000 or more

Place	Population	%
Redwood City (city) San Mateo County	76	0.10
Lancaster (city) Los Angeles County	110	0.07
Novato (city) Marin County	37	0.07
San Marcos (city) San Diego County	44	0.06
Redondo Beach (city) Los Angeles County	39	0.06
Berkeley (city) Alameda County	57	0.05
Inglewood (city) Los Angeles County	55	0.05
Santa Clara (city) Santa Clara County	53	0.05
Walnut Creek (city) Contra Costa County	33	0.05
Santa Barbara (city) Santa Barbara County	38	0.04

European

Top 10 Places Sorted by Population

Based on all places, regardless of total population

Place	Population	%
Los Angeles (city) Los Angeles County	33,149	0.88
San Diego (city) San Diego County	19,955	1.56
San Francisco (city) San Francisco County	15,818	2.00
San Jose (city) Santa Clara County	9,840	1.06
Santa Rosa (city) Sonoma County	6,559	4.03
Oakland (city) Alameda County	6,403	1.65
Long Beach (city) Los Angeles County	5,522	1.20
Sacramento (city) Sacramento County	5,277	1.15
Bakersfield (city) Kern County	3,718	1.12
Temecula (city) Riverside County	3,436	3.59

Top 10 Places Sorted by Percent of Total Population

Based on all places, regardless of total population

Place	Population	%
Lookout (cdp) Modoc County	11	44.00
Markleeville (cdp) Alpine County	100	36.50
Garberville (cdp) Humboldt County	231	35.87
Byron (cdp) Contra Costa County	417	34.75
June Lake (cdp) Mono County	198	33.67
Mono City (cdp) Mono County	26	33.33
Downieville (cdp) Sierra County	64	30.05
Shelter Cove (cdp) Humboldt County	149	28.44
Scotia (cdp) Humboldt County	169	25.92
Meadow Valley (cdp) Plumas County	170	25.22

Top 10 Places Sorted by Percent of Total Population

Based on places with total population of 50,000 or more

Place	Population	%
Davis (city) Yolo County	3,038	4.69
Palo Alto (city) Santa Clara County	2,712	4.34
Santa Cruz (city) Santa Cruz County	2,354	4.04
Santa Rosa (city) Sonoma County	6,559	4.03
Temecula (city) Riverside County	3,436	3.59
Novato (city) Marin County	1,496	2.96
Newport Beach (city) Orange County	2,427	2.90
Rocklin (city) Placer County	1,482	2.73
Carlsbad (city) San Diego County	2,706	2.71
Redondo Beach (city) Los Angeles County	1,770	2.68

Finnish

Top 10 Places Sorted by Population

Based on all places, regardless of total population

Place	Population	%
Los Angeles (city) Los Angeles County	2,919	0.08
San Diego (city) San Diego County	2,374	0.19
San Francisco (city) San Francisco County	1,264	0.16
San Jose (city) Santa Clara County	892	0.10
Redding (city) Shasta County	836	0.94
Fresno (city) Fresno County	640	0.13
Sacramento (city) Sacramento County	567	0.12
Roseville (city) Placer County	530	0.47
Santa Rosa (city) Sonoma County	527	0.32
Oakland (city) Alameda County	514	0.13

Top 10 Places Sorted by Percent of Total Population

Based on all places, regardless of total population

Place	Population	%
North San Juan (cdp) Nevada County	33	25.19
Taylorsville (cdp) Plumas County	16	13.11
Onyx (cdp) Kern County	12	9.30
East Quincy (cdp) Plumas County	222	8.20
Cleone (cdp) Mendocino County	46	6.56
Covelo (cdp) Mendocino County	81	6.01
Cold Springs (cdp) Tuolumne County	13	4.25
Junction City (cdp) Trinity County	49	4.01
Beckwourth (cdp) Plumas County	15	3.61
Caspar (cdp) Mendocino County	28	3.38

Top 10 Places Sorted by Percent of Total Population

Based on places with total population of 50,000 or more

Place	Population	%
Redding (city) Shasta County	836	0.94
Walnut Creek (city) Contra Costa County	357	0.56
Roseville (city) Placer County	530	0.47
Rocklin (city) Placer County	257	0.47
Redondo Beach (city) Los Angeles County	289	0.44
Vista (city) San Diego County	371	0.40
Woodland (city) Yolo County	219	0.40
Camarillo (city) Ventura County	243	0.38
Laguna Niguel (city) Orange County	228	0.36
Menifee (city) Riverside County	251	0.35

French, except Basque

Top 10 Places Sorted by Population

Based on all places, regardless of total population

Place	Population	%
Los Angeles (city) Los Angeles County	46,698	1.24
San Diego (city) San Diego County	32,028	2.50
San Francisco (city) San Francisco County	17,757	2.25
San Jose (city) Santa Clara County	14,068	1.52
Sacramento (city) Sacramento County	9,645	2.10
Long Beach (city) Los Angeles County	8,425	1.82
Fresno (city) Fresno County	7,784	1.61
Riverside (city) Riverside County	7,394	2.46
Huntington Beach (city) Orange County	6,793	3.60
Anaheim (city) Orange County	5,575	1.67

Top 10 Places Sorted by Percent of Total Population

Based on all places, regardless of total population

Place	Population	%
Oakville (cdp) Napa County	81	65.85
Miranda (cdp) Humboldt County	155	45.99
Albion (cdp) Mendocino County	94	41.96
Elk Creek (cdp) Glenn County	47	39.83
Valley Ford (cdp) Sonoma County	34	39.53
Little River (cdp) Mendocino County	104	35.86
East Shore (cdp) Plumas County	103	34.56
Swall Meadows (cdp) Mono County	125	31.49
Soda Springs (cdp) Nevada County	38	29.69
Las Flores (cdp) Tehama County	28	28.57

Top 10 Places Sorted by Percent of Total Population

Based on places with total population of 50,000 or more

Place	Population	%
Encinitas (city) San Diego County	2,779	4.73
Santa Cruz (city) Santa Cruz County	2,565	4.40
Petaluma (city) Sonoma County	2,369	4.18
Apple Valley (town) San Bernardino County	2,805	4.16
Santee (city) San Diego County	2,200	4.15
Yucaipa (city) San Bernardino County	2,075	4.13
Rocklin (city) Placer County	2,223	4.10
Newport Beach (city) Orange County	3,333	3.99
Chico (city) Butte County	3,374	3.96
Redding (city) Shasta County	3,512	3.93

French Canadian

Top 10 Places Sorted by Population

Based on all places, regardless of total population

Place	Population	%
Los Angeles (city) Los Angeles County	6,978	0.18
San Diego (city) San Diego County	5,134	0.40
San Francisco (city) San Francisco County	2,726	0.35
San Jose (city) Santa Clara County	1,741	0.19
Sacramento (city) Sacramento County	1,254	0.27
Long Beach (city) Los Angeles County	1,161	0.25
Riverside (city) Riverside County	1,155	0.38
Huntington Beach (city) Orange County	1,008	0.53
Oakland (city) Alameda County	1,004	0.26
Bakersfield (city) Kern County	934	0.28

Top 10 Places Sorted by Percent of Total Population

Based on all places, regardless of total population

Place	Population	%
Phillipsville (cdp) Humboldt County	32	41.56
Pioneer (cdp) Amador County	182	16.74
Pike (cdp) Sierra County	24	15.29
Hornbrook (cdp) Siskiyou County	40	14.81
Diablo Grande (cdp) Stanislaus County	37	12.98
California Pines (cdp) Modoc County	16	12.70
Little River (cdp) Mendocino County	36	12.41
Bodega (cdp) Sonoma County	21	10.14
Alderpoint (cdp) Humboldt County	18	8.57
Moss Landing (cdp) Monterey County	17	8.13

Top 10 Places Sorted by Percent of Total Population

Based on places with total population of 50,000 or more

Place	Population	%
Redondo Beach (city) Los Angeles County	574	0.87
Carlsbad (city) San Diego County	850	0.85
Santee (city) San Diego County	452	0.85
Encinitas (city) San Diego County	482	0.82
Murrieta (city) Riverside County	745	0.78
Yucaipa (city) San Bernardino County	391	0.78
Menifee (city) Riverside County	556	0.77
Apple Valley (town) San Bernardino County	497	0.74
Camarillo (city) Ventura County	467	0.73
Redding (city) Shasta County	635	0.71

German

Top 10 Places Sorted by Population

Based on all places, regardless of total population

Place	Population	%
Los Angeles (city) Los Angeles County	177,061	4.69
San Diego (city) San Diego County	140,941	10.99
San Francisco (city) San Francisco County	65,133	8.25
San Jose (city) Santa Clara County	61,487	6.65
Sacramento (city) Sacramento County	41,408	9.01
Fresno (city) Fresno County	39,420	8.14
Long Beach (city) Los Angeles County	33,099	7.17
Huntington Beach (city) Orange County	32,622	17.27
Bakersfield (city) Kern County	31,918	9.62
Riverside (city) Riverside County	29,153	9.70

Top 10 Places Sorted by Percent of Total Population

Based on all places, regardless of total population

Place	Population	%
Strawberry (cdp) Tuolumne County	64	100.00
Bucks Lake (cdp) Plumas County	23	100.00
Loma Mar (cdp) San Mateo County	44	72.13
Blairsden (cdp) Plumas County	23	69.70
Proberta (cdp) Tehama County	135	65.22
Boulevard (cdp) San Diego County	20	64.52
Valley Ford (cdp) Sonoma County	52	60.47
New Pine Creek (cdp) Modoc County	68	60.18
Eagleville (cdp) Modoc County	41	58.57
Bloomfield (cdp) Sonoma County	196	58.33

Top 10 Places Sorted by Percent of Total Population

Based on places with total population of 50,000 or more

Place	Population	%
Santee (city) San Diego County	11,882	22.43
Lodi (city) San Joaquin County	12,805	20.58
Redding (city) Shasta County	17,567	19.65
Yucaipa (city) San Bernardino County	9,803	19.52
Chico (city) Butte County	16,596	19.49
San Clemente (city) Orange County	11,693	19.24
Rocklin (city) Placer County	10,333	19.04
Citrus Heights (city) Sacramento County	15,987	18.95
Yorba Linda (city) Orange County	11,892	18.90
Carmichael (cdp) Sacramento County	11,501	18.61

German Russian

Top 10 Places Sorted by Population

Based on all places, regardless of total population

Place	Population	%
Los Angeles (city) Los Angeles County	145	<0.01
Stockton (city) San Joaquin County	117	0.04
Carson (city) Los Angeles County	88	0.10
West Covina (city) Los Angeles County	88	0.08
Redding (city) Shasta County	61	0.07
San Diego (city) San Diego County	53	<0.01
Foothill Farms (cdp) Sacramento County	50	0.15
Long Beach (city) Los Angeles County	50	0.01
La Mesa (city) San Diego County	43	0.08
Sacramento (city) Sacramento County	38	0.01

Top 10 Places Sorted by Percent of Total Population

Based on all places, regardless of total population

Place	Population	%
Graeagle (cdp) Plumas County	34	3.73
Auberry (cdp) Fresno County	26	1.18
Indianola (cdp) Humboldt County	10	0.97
Boronda (cdp) Monterey County	13	0.73
Salton City (cdp) Imperial County	9	0.64
Sunnyslope (cdp) Riverside County	20	0.41
Rouse (cdp) Stanislaus County	8	0.41
Loomis (town) Placer County	21	0.32
Burbank (cdp) Santa Clara County	13	0.26
Carmel Valley Village (cdp) Monterey County	12	0.26

Top 10 Places Sorted by Percent of Total Population

Based on places with total population of 50,000 or more

Place	Population	%
Carson (city) Los Angeles County	88	0.10
West Covina (city) Los Angeles County	88	0.08
La Mesa (city) San Diego County	43	0.08
Redding (city) Shasta County	61	0.07
Stockton (city) San Joaquin County	117	0.04
Pittsburg (city) Contra Costa County	23	0.04
Victorville (city) San Bernardino County	29	0.03
South San Francisco (city) San Mateo County	18	0.03
Lancaster (city) Los Angeles County	27	0.02
Fairfield (city) Solano County	19	0.02

Greek

Top 10 Places Sorted by Population

Based on all places, regardless of total population

Place	Population	%
Los Angeles (city) Los Angeles County	12,497	0.33
San Diego (city) San Diego County	5,154	0.40
San Francisco (city) San Francisco County	4,216	0.53
San Jose (city) Santa Clara County	3,018	0.33
Sacramento (city) Sacramento County	2,242	0.49
Long Beach (city) Los Angeles County	1,580	0.34
Oakland (city) Alameda County	1,246	0.32
Santa Clarita (city) Los Angeles County	1,243	0.72
Glendale (city) Los Angeles County	1,214	0.63
Huntington Beach (city) Orange County	1,199	0.63

Top 10 Places Sorted by Percent of Total Population

Based on all places, regardless of total population

Place	Population	%
Cassel (cdp) Shasta County	154	33.62
Kingvale (cdp) Nevada County	28	16.87
La Honda (cdp) San Mateo County	103	8.52
Dorrington (cdp) Calaveras County	35	6.10
Westwood (cdp) Lassen County	63	5.84
Middletown (cdp) Lake County	87	5.29
Shaver Lake (cdp) Fresno County	37	5.23
Emerald Lake Hills (cdp) San Mateo County	232	5.22
Woodacre (cdp) Marin County	61	4.88
Downieville (cdp) Sierra County	10	4.69

Top 10 Places Sorted by Percent of Total Population

Based on places with total population of 50,000 or more

Place	Population	%
Redwood City (city) San Mateo County	799	1.06
Chico (city) Butte County	808	0.95
Roseville (city) Placer County	1,029	0.90
Laguna Niguel (city) Orange County	557	0.89
San Mateo (city) San Mateo County	776	0.82
San Ramon (city) Contra Costa County	522	0.78
South San Francisco (city) San Mateo County	486	0.78
Novato (city) Marin County	396	0.78
Temecula (city) Riverside County	740	0.77
Thousand Oaks (city) Ventura County	929	0.75

Guyanese

Top 10 Places Sorted by Population

Based on all places, regardless of total population

Place	Population	%
Los Angeles (city) Los Angeles County	437	0.01
San Diego (city) San Diego County	260	0.02
Bakersfield (city) Kern County	121	0.04
Oakland (city) Alameda County	106	0.03
Lompoc (city) Santa Barbara County	80	0.19
Concord (city) Contra Costa County	71	0.06
Sunnyvale (city) Santa Clara County	69	0.05
Mira Loma (cdp) Riverside County	68	0.34
Palo Alto (city) Santa Clara County	68	0.11
Compton (city) Los Angeles County	64	0.07

Top 10 Places Sorted by Percent of Total Population

Based on all places, regardless of total population

Place	Population	%
Mira Loma (cdp) Riverside County	68	0.34
Malibu (city) Los Angeles County	38	0.30
Alondra Park (cdp) Los Angeles County	25	0.28
Big Bear City (cdp) San Bernardino County	31	0.26
Lompoc (city) Santa Barbara County	80	0.19
Sebastopol (city) Sonoma County	14	0.19
Emeryville (city) Alameda County	13	0.14
Fallbrook (cdp) San Diego County	35	0.12
Marina (city) Monterey County	23	0.12
Palo Alto (city) Santa Clara County	68	0.11

Top 10 Places Sorted by Percent of Total Population

Based on places with total population of 50,000 or more

Place	Population	%
Palo Alto (city) Santa Clara County	68	0.11
Fountain Valley (city) Orange County	59	0.11
Compton (city) Los Angeles County	64	0.07
Santa Monica (city) Los Angeles County	58	0.07

Place	Population	%
Menifee (city) Riverside County	53	0.07
Concord (city) Contra Costa County	71	0.06
Chico (city) Butte County	50	0.06
Lakewood (city) Los Angeles County	45	0.06
Sunnyvale (city) Santa Clara County	69	0.05
Inglewood (city) Los Angeles County	53	0.05

Hungarian

Top 10 Places Sorted by Population

Based on all places, regardless of total population

Place	Population	%
Los Angeles (city) Los Angeles County	16,285	0.43
San Diego (city) San Diego County	6,397	0.50
San Francisco (city) San Francisco County	3,416	0.43
Huntington Beach (city) Orange County	1,920	1.02
San Jose (city) Santa Clara County	1,873	0.20
Long Beach (city) Los Angeles County	1,825	0.40
Irvine (city) Orange County	1,365	0.69
Santa Clarita (city) Los Angeles County	1,257	0.73
Sacramento (city) Sacramento County	1,189	0.26
Santa Monica (city) Los Angeles County	1,147	1.29

Top 10 Places Sorted by Percent of Total Population

Based on all places, regardless of total population

Place	Population	%
McGee Creek (cdp) Mono County	17	58.62
Moskowite Corner (cdp) Napa County	39	29.77
Taylorsville (cdp) Plumas County	31	25.41
Cohasset (cdp) Butte County	124	15.84
Mabie (cdp) Plumas County	16	9.70
Avery (cdp) Calaveras County	34	8.92
Greenview (cdp) Siskiyou County	31	8.52
Chilcoot-Vinton (cdp) Plumas County	47	7.74
Kenwood (cdp) Sonoma County	35	7.58
Carnelian Bay (cdp) Placer County	21	7.22

Top 10 Places Sorted by Percent of Total Population

Based on places with total population of 50,000 or more

Place	Population	%
Santa Monica (city) Los Angeles County	1,147	1.29
Newport Beach (city) Orange County	870	1.04
Huntington Beach (city) Orange County	1,920	1.02
Mountain View (city) Santa Clara County	690	0.95
Thousand Oaks (city) Ventura County	1,124	0.90
Carlsbad (city) San Diego County	885	0.89
Redondo Beach (city) Los Angeles County	576	0.87
Yorba Linda (city) Orange County	528	0.84
Mission Viejo (city) Orange County	754	0.81
Encinitas (city) San Diego County	478	0.81

Icelander

Top 10 Places Sorted by Population

Based on all places, regardless of total population

Place	Population	%
Yucaipa (city) San Bernardino County	484	0.96
San Diego (city) San Diego County	408	0.03
Los Angeles (city) Los Angeles County	380	0.01
San Francisco (city) San Francisco County	223	0.03
Palmdale (city) Los Angeles County	204	0.14
Sacramento (city) Sacramento County	189	0.04
Jamul (cdp) San Diego County	152	2.86
San Jose (city) Santa Clara County	121	0.01
China Lake Acres (cdp) Kern County	120	7.73
San Ramon (city) Contra Costa County	116	0.17

Top 10 Places Sorted by Percent of Total Population

Based on all places, regardless of total population

Place	Population	%
China Lake Acres (cdp) Kern County	120	7.73
Jamul (cdp) San Diego County	152	2.86
Cobb (cdp) Lake County	49	2.53
Lake Riverside (cdp) Riverside County	24	1.70
Acalanes Ridge (cdp) Contra Costa County	26	1.61
Shell Ridge (cdp) Contra Costa County	21	1.52
Westhaven-Moonstone (cdp) Humboldt County	13	1.52
Pixley (cdp) Tulare County	39	1.32
Bethel Island (cdp) Contra Costa County	25	1.14
Point Reyes Station (cdp) Marin County	9	1.08

Top 10 Places Sorted by Percent of Total Population

Based on places with total population of 50,000 or more

Place	Population	%
Yucaipa (city) San Bernardino County	484	0.96
San Ramon (city) Contra Costa County	116	0.17
Palmdale (city) Los Angeles County	204	0.14
Carmichael (cdp) Sacramento County	88	0.14
Carlsbad (city) San Diego County	83	0.08
Chico (city) Butte County	64	0.08
Lakewood (city) Los Angeles County	64	0.08
Citrus Heights (city) Sacramento County	63	0.07
Santa Cruz (city) Santa Cruz County	38	0.07
Berkeley (city) Alameda County	68	0.06

Iranian

Top 10 Places Sorted by Population

Based on all places, regardless of total population

Place	Population	%
Los Angeles (city) Los Angeles County	51,547	1.37
Glendale (city) Los Angeles County	10,199	5.31
Beverly Hills (city) Los Angeles County	9,158	26.95
Irvine (city) Orange County	7,908	3.97
San Diego (city) San Diego County	7,595	0.59
San Jose (city) Santa Clara County	7,389	0.80
Laguna Niguel (city) Orange County	3,258	5.20
Santa Monica (city) Los Angeles County	2,587	2.92
Mission Viejo (city) Orange County	2,460	2.66
Newport Beach (city) Orange County	2,378	2.85

Top 10 Places Sorted by Percent of Total Population

Based on all places, regardless of total population

Place	Population	%
Drytown (cdp) Amador County	76	36.19
Beverly Hills (city) Los Angeles County	9,158	26.95
Ruth (cdp) Trinity County	27	17.88
Lexington Hills (cdp) Santa Clara County	193	8.12
Calabasas (city) Los Angeles County	1,747	7.70
Fairbanks Ranch (cdp) San Diego County	136	6.88
Acalanes Ridge (cdp) Contra Costa County	104	6.45
Camino Tassajara (cdp) Contra Costa County	109	6.32
Glendale (city) Los Angeles County	10,199	5.31
Laguna Niguel (city) Orange County	3,258	5.20

Top 10 Places Sorted by Percent of Total Population

Based on places with total population of 50,000 or more

Place	Population	%
Glendale (city) Los Angeles County	10,199	5.31
Laguna Niguel (city) Orange County	3,258	5.20
Irvine (city) Orange County	7,908	3.97
Santa Monica (city) Los Angeles County	2,587	2.92
Newport Beach (city) Orange County	2,378	2.85
Mission Viejo (city) Orange County	2,460	2.66
Cupertino (city) Santa Clara County	1,005	1.78
Walnut Creek (city) Contra Costa County	1,013	1.59
Burbank (city) Los Angeles County	1,583	1.54
Lake Forest (city) Orange County	1,167	1.52

Irish

Top 10 Places Sorted by Population

Based on all places, regardless of total population

Place	Population	%
Los Angeles (city) Los Angeles County	147,342	3.91
San Diego (city) San Diego County	108,215	8.44
San Francisco (city) San Francisco County	64,487	8.17
San Jose (city) Santa Clara County	46,086	4.98
Sacramento (city) Sacramento County	35,916	7.82
Long Beach (city) Los Angeles County	27,445	5.94
Fresno (city) Fresno County	26,731	5.52
Bakersfield (city) Kern County	25,483	7.68
Huntington Beach (city) Orange County	24,675	13.06
Riverside (city) Riverside County	20,754	6.91

Top 10 Places Sorted by Percent of Total Population

Based on all places, regardless of total population

Place	Population	%
Johnsville (cdp) Plumas County	84	100.00
Prattville (cdp) Plumas County	21	100.00
Whitehawk (cdp) Plumas County	12	100.00
Lake Davis (cdp) Plumas County	11	100.00
Milford (cdp) Lassen County	41	87.23
Monterey Park Tract (cdp) Stanislaus County	215	77.06
Mabie (cdp) Plumas County	125	75.76
Volcano (cdp) Amador County	120	67.80
Daphnedale Park (cdp) Modoc County	33	67.35
Iron Horse (cdp) Plumas County	155	56.78

Top 10 Places Sorted by Percent of Total Population

Based on places with total population of 50,000 or more

Place	Population	%
Petaluma (city) Sonoma County	9,046	15.96
Carmichael (cdp) Sacramento County	9,857	15.95
Roseville (city) Placer County	18,023	15.83
Santee (city) San Diego County	8,278	15.63
San Clemente (city) Orange County	9,417	15.50
Newport Beach (city) Orange County	12,812	15.33
Redding (city) Shasta County	13,432	15.03
Citrus Heights (city) Sacramento County	12,491	14.81
Chico (city) Butte County	12,531	14.72
Rocklin (city) Placer County	7,830	14.43

Israeli

Top 10 Places Sorted by Population

Based on all places, regardless of total population

Place	Population	%
Los Angeles (city) Los Angeles County	12,294	0.33
San Diego (city) San Diego County	990	0.08
Beverly Hills (city) Los Angeles County	920	2.71
Sunnyvale (city) Santa Clara County	796	0.58
San Jose (city) Santa Clara County	641	0.07
Irvine (city) Orange County	525	0.26
Calabasas (city) Los Angeles County	443	1.95
San Francisco (city) San Francisco County	437	0.06
Palo Alto (city) Santa Clara County	421	0.67
Thousand Oaks (city) Ventura County	384	0.31

Top 10 Places Sorted by Percent of Total Population

Based on all places, regardless of total population

Place	Population	%
Oakhurst (cdp) Madera County	260	7.97
Beverly Hills (city) Los Angeles County	920	2.71
Calabasas (city) Los Angeles County	443	1.95
East Richmond Heights (cdp) Contra Costa County	55	1.71
Cambrian Park (cdp) Santa Clara County	54	1.66
Markleeville (cdp) Alpine County	4	1.46
Agoura Hills (city) Los Angeles County	215	1.06
Lompico (cdp) Santa Cruz County	10	0.96
Los Altos Hills (town) Santa Clara County	68	0.87
Santa Venetia (cdp) Marin County	37	0.73

Top 10 Places Sorted by Percent of Total Population

Based on places with total population of 50,000 or more

Place	Population	%
Palo Alto (city) Santa Clara County	421	0.67
Cupertino (city) Santa Clara County	363	0.64
Sunnyvale (city) Santa Clara County	796	0.58
Los Angeles (city) Los Angeles County	12,294	0.33
Thousand Oaks (city) Ventura County	384	0.31
Santa Monica (city) Los Angeles County	277	0.31
Irvine (city) Orange County	525	0.26
Tulare (city) Tulare County	140	0.25
Santa Cruz (city) Santa Cruz County	135	0.23
Berkeley (city) Alameda County	214	0.20

Italian

Top 10 Places Sorted by Population

Based on all places, regardless of total population

Place	Population	%
Los Angeles (city) Los Angeles County	101,064	2.68
San Diego (city) San Diego County	61,669	4.81
San Jose (city) Santa Clara County	40,876	4.42
San Francisco (city) San Francisco County	38,913	4.93
Sacramento (city) Sacramento County	18,754	4.08
Fresno (city) Fresno County	16,181	3.34
Huntington Beach (city) Orange County	15,311	8.10
Long Beach (city) Los Angeles County	14,721	3.19
Santa Clarita (city) Los Angeles County	13,153	7.64
Riverside (city) Riverside County	12,257	4.08

Top 10 Places Sorted by Percent of Total Population
Based on all places, regardless of total population

Place	Population	%
Pierpoint (cdp) Tulare County	12	100.00
McGee Creek (cdp) Mono County	17	58.62
Carrick (cdp) Siskiyou County	93	54.71
Bridgeport (cdp) Mono County	207	51.49
Myers Flat (cdp) Humboldt County	42	46.15
Elmira (cdp) Solano County	70	45.75
Jenner (cdp) Sonoma County	45	45.45
Sunny Slopes (cdp) Mono County	86	43.43
Benton (cdp) Mono County	125	43.25
Weott (cdp) Humboldt County	73	41.48

Top 10 Places Sorted by Percent of Total Population
Based on places with total population of 50,000 or more

Place	Population	%
Novato (city) Marin County	5,410	10.72
Petaluma (city) Sonoma County	5,480	9.67
Rocklin (city) Placer County	4,789	8.82
Folsom (city) Sacramento County	6,013	8.71
Newport Beach (city) Orange County	7,119	8.52
San Clemente (city) Orange County	5,107	8.40
Pleasanton (city) Alameda County	5,716	8.38
Thousand Oaks (city) Ventura County	10,438	8.37
Huntington Beach (city) Orange County	15,311	8.10
San Mateo (city) San Mateo County	7,619	8.04

Latvian

Top 10 Places Sorted by Population
Based on all places, regardless of total population

Place	Population	%
Los Angeles (city) Los Angeles County	2,043	0.05
San Francisco (city) San Francisco County	632	0.08
San Diego (city) San Diego County	596	0.05
Oakland (city) Alameda County	201	0.05
Walnut Creek (city) Contra Costa County	155	0.24
San Jose (city) Santa Clara County	155	0.02
Vacaville (city) Solano County	143	0.16
Santa Monica (city) Los Angeles County	136	0.15
Agoura Hills (city) Los Angeles County	131	0.64
Irvine (city) Orange County	131	0.07

Top 10 Places Sorted by Percent of Total Population
Based on all places, regardless of total population

Place	Population	%
Stonyford (cdp) Colusa County	5	4.20
Shelter Cove (cdp) Humboldt County	20	3.82
Westwood (cdp) Lassen County	36	3.34
Los Ranchos (cdp) San Luis Obispo County	44	2.90
Camanche Village (cdp) Amador County	15	2.55
Acalanes Ridge (cdp) Contra Costa County	34	2.11
Coarsegold (cdp) Madera County	21	1.31
Jamul (cdp) San Diego County	67	1.26
San Antonio Heights (cdp) San Bernardino County	48	1.21
Mount Shasta (city) Siskiyou County	40	1.17

Top 10 Places Sorted by Percent of Total Population
Based on places with total population of 50,000 or more

Place	Population	%
Walnut Creek (city) Contra Costa County	155	0.24
Novato (city) Marin County	89	0.18
Vacaville (city) Solano County	143	0.16
Santa Monica (city) Los Angeles County	136	0.15
Redondo Beach (city) Los Angeles County	95	0.14
Encinitas (city) San Diego County	66	0.11
Cupertino (city) Santa Clara County	60	0.11
Norwalk (city) Los Angeles County	104	0.10
Hemet (city) Riverside County	78	0.10
Berkeley (city) Alameda County	100	0.09

Lithuanian

Top 10 Places Sorted by Population
Based on all places, regardless of total population

Place	Population	%
Los Angeles (city) Los Angeles County	6,875	0.18
San Diego (city) San Diego County	2,852	0.22
San Francisco (city) San Francisco County	1,821	0.23
Santa Monica (city) Los Angeles County	1,080	1.22
Oakland (city) Alameda County	701	0.18
San Jose (city) Santa Clara County	644	0.07
Huntington Beach (city) Orange County	629	0.33
Sacramento (city) Sacramento County	593	0.13
Torrance (city) Los Angeles County	536	0.37
Long Beach (city) Los Angeles County	463	0.10

Top 10 Places Sorted by Percent of Total Population
Based on all places, regardless of total population

Place	Population	%
Fiddletown (cdp) Amador County	20	24.10
Calpine (cdp) Sierra County	20	16.39
Swall Meadows (cdp) Mono County	46	11.59
Big Bend (cdp) Shasta County	10	10.99
June Lake (cdp) Mono County	33	5.61
Amador City (city) Amador County	7	5.47
Plumas Eureka (cdp) Plumas County	12	5.13
San Geronimo (cdp) Marin County	24	4.27
Aromas (cdp) Monterey County	91	3.93
Fort Washington (cdp) Fresno County	14	3.24

Top 10 Places Sorted by Percent of Total Population
Based on places with total population of 50,000 or more

Place	Population	%
Santa Monica (city) Los Angeles County	1,080	1.22
San Rafael (city) Marin County	450	0.79
Walnut Creek (city) Contra Costa County	310	0.49
Mission Viejo (city) Orange County	388	0.42
Torrance (city) Los Angeles County	536	0.37
Victorville (city) San Bernardino County	384	0.36
Newport Beach (city) Orange County	304	0.36
Laguna Niguel (city) Orange County	227	0.36
Simi Valley (city) Ventura County	422	0.35
Huntington Beach (city) Orange County	629	0.33

Luxemburger

Top 10 Places Sorted by Population
Based on all places, regardless of total population

Place	Population	%
Los Angeles (city) Los Angeles County	253	0.01
San Jose (city) Santa Clara County	168	0.02
San Diego (city) San Diego County	130	0.01
San Francisco (city) San Francisco County	126	0.02
Glendale (city) Los Angeles County	86	0.04
Huntington Beach (city) Orange County	73	0.04
Pinole (city) Contra Costa County	64	0.35
Orangevale (cdp) Sacramento County	56	0.16
East Hemet (cdp) Riverside County	48	0.24
Oakland (city) Alameda County	46	0.01

Top 10 Places Sorted by Percent of Total Population
Based on all places, regardless of total population

Place	Population	%
Woodlands (cdp) San Luis Obispo County	14	3.76
Camino Tassajara (cdp) Contra Costa County	38	2.20
Sleepy Hollow (cdp) Marin County	21	0.86
Pine Grove (cdp) Amador County	16	0.67
San Pasqual (cdp) Los Angeles County	8	0.39
Pinole (city) Contra Costa County	64	0.35
Cottonwood (cdp) Shasta County	10	0.33
Rainbow (cdp) San Diego County	6	0.32
Shingle Springs (cdp) El Dorado County	11	0.28
East Hemet (cdp) Riverside County	48	0.24

Top 10 Places Sorted by Percent of Total Population
Based on places with total population of 50,000 or more

Place	Population	%
Yuba City (city) Sutter County	43	0.07
Palo Alto (city) Santa Clara County	30	0.05
Glendale (city) Los Angeles County	86	0.04
Huntington Beach (city) Orange County	73	0.04
Menifee (city) Riverside County	26	0.04
Pasadena (city) Los Angeles County	37	0.03
Redding (city) Shasta County	31	0.03
Burbank (city) Los Angeles County	30	0.03
Napa (city) Napa County	26	0.03
Tustin (city) Orange County	23	0.03

Macedonian

Top 10 Places Sorted by Population
Based on all places, regardless of total population

Place	Population	%
Los Angeles (city) Los Angeles County	473	0.01
San Francisco (city) San Francisco County	156	0.02
Carlsbad (city) San Diego County	127	0.13
Anaheim (city) Orange County	87	0.03
Larkspur (city) Marin County	85	0.72
San Jose (city) Santa Clara County	65	0.01
Palmdale (city) Los Angeles County	63	0.04
North Lakeport (cdp) Lake County	56	1.58
Soledad (city) Monterey County	50	0.20
San Clemente (city) Orange County	50	0.08

Top 10 Places Sorted by Percent of Total Population
Based on all places, regardless of total population

Place	Population	%
North Lakeport (cdp) Lake County	56	1.58
Larkspur (city) Marin County	85	0.72
Cherry Valley (cdp) Riverside County	31	0.51
Shasta (cdp) Shasta County	8	0.51
Sierra Madre (city) Los Angeles County	42	0.39
Seacliff (cdp) Santa Cruz County	11	0.37
Fort Bragg (city) Mendocino County	18	0.25
Indian Wells (city) Riverside County	12	0.25
Soledad (city) Monterey County	50	0.20
Live Oak (cdp) Santa Cruz County	28	0.17

Top 10 Places Sorted by Percent of Total Population
Based on places with total population of 50,000 or more

Place	Population	%
Carlsbad (city) San Diego County	127	0.13
Rocklin (city) Placer County	48	0.09
San Clemente (city) Orange County	50	0.08
Camarillo (city) Ventura County	49	0.08
Cupertino (city) Santa Clara County	44	0.08
Palo Alto (city) Santa Clara County	39	0.06
Burbank (city) Los Angeles County	47	0.05
Palmdale (city) Los Angeles County	63	0.04
Berkeley (city) Alameda County	41	0.04
San Ramon (city) Contra Costa County	25	0.04

Maltese

Top 10 Places Sorted by Population
Based on all places, regardless of total population

Place	Population	%
San Francisco (city) San Francisco County	608	0.08
Los Angeles (city) Los Angeles County	279	0.01
San Bruno (city) San Mateo County	275	0.68
Danville (town) Contra Costa County	217	0.52
San Mateo (city) San Mateo County	203	0.21
Millbrae (city) San Mateo County	191	0.91
Roseville (city) Placer County	181	0.16
San Jose (city) Santa Clara County	179	0.02
Concord (city) Contra Costa County	166	0.14
San Diego (city) San Diego County	146	0.01

Top 10 Places Sorted by Percent of Total Population
Based on all places, regardless of total population

Place	Population	%
Pioneer (cdp) Amador County	37	3.40
Sleepy Hollow (cdp) Marin County	49	2.01
Timber Cove (cdp) Sonoma County	3	2.01
Alhambra Valley (cdp) Contra Costa County	13	1.58
Cazadero (cdp) Sonoma County	5	1.38
Half Moon Bay (city) San Mateo County	126	1.13
Hillsborough (town) San Mateo County	116	1.09
San Antonio Heights (cdp) San Bernardino County	41	1.03
Millbrae (city) San Mateo County	191	0.91
Potter Valley (cdp) Mendocino County	7	0.85

Top 10 Places Sorted by Percent of Total Population
Based on places with total population of 50,000 or more

Place	Population	%
San Mateo (city) San Mateo County	203	0.21
Petaluma (city) Sonoma County	99	0.17
Roseville (city) Placer County	181	0.16
Redwood City (city) San Mateo County	121	0.16

Place	Population	%
South San Francisco (city) San Mateo County	100	0.16
Concord (city) Contra Costa County	166	0.14
Cathedral City (city) Riverside County	70	0.14
Chico (city) Butte County	73	0.09
San Francisco (city) San Francisco County	608	0.08
Walnut Creek (city) Contra Costa County	54	0.08

New Zealander

Top 10 Places Sorted by Population

Based on all places, regardless of total population

Place	Population	%
Los Angeles (city) Los Angeles County	502	0.01
San Diego (city) San Diego County	193	0.02
Torrance (city) Los Angeles County	154	0.11
American Canyon (city) Napa County	129	0.73
San Francisco (city) San Francisco County	123	0.02
Palo Alto (city) Santa Clara County	103	0.16
Truckee (town) Nevada County	98	0.62
Santa Rosa (city) Sonoma County	96	0.06
Mill Valley (city) Marin County	83	0.61
Huntington Beach (city) Orange County	80	0.04

Top 10 Places Sorted by Percent of Total Population

Based on all places, regardless of total population

Place	Population	%
Mayfair (cdp) Fresno County	76	1.88
Day Valley (cdp) Santa Cruz County	26	0.80
American Canyon (city) Napa County	129	0.73
Truckee (town) Nevada County	98	0.62
Mill Valley (city) Marin County	83	0.61
Boulder Creek (cdp) Santa Cruz County	29	0.54
Sausalito (city) Marin County	35	0.50
Shaver Lake (cdp) Fresno County	3	0.42
La Ca±ada Flintridge (city) Los Angeles County	67	0.33
Del Monte Forest (cdp) Monterey County	14	0.33

Top 10 Places Sorted by Percent of Total Population

Based on places with total population of 50,000 or more

Place	Population	%
Palo Alto (city) Santa Clara County	103	0.16
Torrance (city) Los Angeles County	154	0.11
Hanford (city) Kings County	57	0.11
Laguna Niguel (city) Orange County	60	0.10
Santa Monica (city) Los Angeles County	76	0.09
Alameda (city) Alameda County	62	0.09
Santa Rosa (city) Sonoma County	96	0.06
Rocklin (city) Placer County	33	0.06
Costa Mesa (city) Orange County	55	0.05
Pleasanton (city) Alameda County	34	0.05

Northern European

Top 10 Places Sorted by Population

Based on all places, regardless of total population

Place	Population	%
San Francisco (city) San Francisco County	2,060	0.26
Los Angeles (city) Los Angeles County	1,975	0.05
San Diego (city) San Diego County	1,520	0.12
Santa Cruz (city) Santa Cruz County	1,071	1.84
San Jose (city) Santa Clara County	1,065	0.12
Oakland (city) Alameda County	853	0.22
Lafayette (city) Contra Costa County	511	2.15
Sacramento (city) Sacramento County	493	0.11
Long Beach (city) Los Angeles County	485	0.11
Walnut Creek (city) Contra Costa County	409	0.64

Top 10 Places Sorted by Percent of Total Population

Based on all places, regardless of total population

Place	Population	%
Little Grass Valley (cdp) Plumas County	23	100.00
Freeport (cdp) Sacramento County	10	50.00
Valley Acres (cdp) Kern County	35	6.23
Alhambra Valley (cdp) Contra Costa County	40	4.85
Woodacre (cdp) Marin County	50	4.00
Pasatiempo (cdp) Santa Cruz County	45	3.71
Lytle Creek (cdp) San Bernardino County	27	3.65
Hornbrook (cdp) Siskiyou County	9	3.33
Ruth (cdp) Trinity County	5	3.31
Summerland (cdp) Santa Barbara County	34	3.14

Top 10 Places Sorted by Percent of Total Population

Based on places with total population of 50,000 or more

Place	Population	%
Santa Cruz (city) Santa Cruz County	1,071	1.84
Walnut Creek (city) Contra Costa County	409	0.64
Palo Alto (city) Santa Clara County	369	0.59
Davis (city) Yolo County	337	0.52
Alameda (city) Alameda County	269	0.37
San Ramon (city) Contra Costa County	237	0.35
Pleasanton (city) Alameda County	234	0.34
Arden-Arcade (cdp) Sacramento County	285	0.31
Redding (city) Shasta County	275	0.31
Encinitas (city) San Diego County	183	0.31

Norwegian

Top 10 Places Sorted by Population

Based on all places, regardless of total population

Place	Population	%
Los Angeles (city) Los Angeles County	20,565	0.55
San Diego (city) San Diego County	16,955	1.32
San Jose (city) Santa Clara County	8,087	0.87
San Francisco (city) San Francisco County	7,582	0.96
Sacramento (city) Sacramento County	5,382	1.17
Long Beach (city) Los Angeles County	4,263	0.92
Huntington Beach (city) Orange County	3,981	2.11
Santa Clarita (city) Los Angeles County	3,508	2.04
Roseville (city) Placer County	3,331	2.93
Anaheim (city) Orange County	2,965	0.89

Top 10 Places Sorted by Percent of Total Population

Based on all places, regardless of total population

Place	Population	%
Mono City (cdp) Mono County	34	43.59
Bradley (cdp) Monterey County	33	41.25
Mount Laguna (cdp) San Diego County	24	36.36
Edna (cdp) San Luis Obispo County	10	33.33
Johannesburg (cdp) Kern County	66	26.29
Valley Home (cdp) Stanislaus County	85	17.60
Lodoga (cdp) Colusa County	38	17.12
Whitewater (cdp) Riverside County	107	16.19
Alleghany (cdp) Sierra County	8	15.09
Greeley Hill (cdp) Mariposa County	131	14.94

Top 10 Places Sorted by Percent of Total Population

Based on places with total population of 50,000 or more

Place	Population	%
Encinitas (city) San Diego County	1,880	3.20
Rocklin (city) Placer County	1,640	3.02
Roseville (city) Placer County	3,331	2.93
Folsom (city) Sacramento County	1,785	2.58
Chico (city) Butte County	2,139	2.51
Santee (city) San Diego County	1,295	2.44
Murrieta (city) Riverside County	2,314	2.42
Citrus Heights (city) Sacramento County	2,043	2.42
Redding (city) Shasta County	2,132	2.39
Carlsbad (city) San Diego County	2,375	2.38

Pennsylvania German

Top 10 Places Sorted by Population

Based on all places, regardless of total population

Place	Population	%
Los Angeles (city) Los Angeles County	440	0.01
San Diego (city) San Diego County	308	0.02
Clovis (city) Fresno County	122	0.13
Mammoth Lakes (town) Mono County	118	1.47
San Francisco (city) San Francisco County	111	0.01
Huntington Beach (city) Orange County	94	0.05
Santa Clara (city) Santa Clara County	93	0.08
Riverside (city) Riverside County	82	0.03
Fresno (city) Fresno County	82	0.02
Whittier (city) Los Angeles County	80	0.09

Top 10 Places Sorted by Percent of Total Population

Based on all places, regardless of total population

Place	Population	%
Penryn (cdp) Placer County	39	5.19
North San Juan (cdp) Nevada County	6	4.58
Cold Springs (cdp) Tuolumne County	12	3.92
Sky Valley (cdp) Riverside County	28	1.52
Mammoth Lakes (town) Mono County	118	1.47
Mount Shasta (city) Siskiyou County	50	1.46
Shasta (cdp) Shasta County	18	1.15
Kelly Ridge (cdp) Butte County	26	1.01
Oceano (cdp) San Luis Obispo County	77	0.98
Palo Cedro (cdp) Shasta County	10	0.98

Top 10 Places Sorted by Percent of Total Population

Based on places with total population of 50,000 or more

Place	Population	%
Clovis (city) Fresno County	122	0.13
Encinitas (city) San Diego County	69	0.12
La Mesa (city) San Diego County	62	0.11
Apple Valley (town) San Bernardino County	68	0.10
Whittier (city) Los Angeles County	80	0.09
Citrus Heights (city) Sacramento County	75	0.09
Hemet (city) Riverside County	71	0.09
Santa Clara (city) Santa Clara County	93	0.08
Vacaville (city) Solano County	71	0.08
Hesperia (city) San Bernardino County	63	0.07

Polish

Top 10 Places Sorted by Population

Based on all places, regardless of total population

Place	Population	%
Los Angeles (city) Los Angeles County	60,010	1.59
San Diego (city) San Diego County	26,533	2.07
San Francisco (city) San Francisco County	16,127	2.04
San Jose (city) Santa Clara County	8,895	0.96
Long Beach (city) Los Angeles County	6,373	1.38
Santa Clarita (city) Los Angeles County	5,110	2.97
Thousand Oaks (city) Ventura County	4,985	4.00
Huntington Beach (city) Orange County	4,968	2.63
Sacramento (city) Sacramento County	4,573	1.00
Oakland (city) Alameda County	4,296	1.11

Top 10 Places Sorted by Percent of Total Population

Based on all places, regardless of total population

Place	Population	%
Alleghany (cdp) Sierra County	21	39.62
Phillipsville (cdp) Humboldt County	29	37.66
Soda Springs (cdp) Nevada County	37	28.91
Ponderosa (cdp) Tulare County	16	26.67
Midpines (cdp) Mariposa County	209	24.56
Crowley Lake (cdp) Mono County	108	19.49
Fields Landing (cdp) Humboldt County	50	19.31
Sereno del Mar (cdp) Sonoma County	19	15.45
Nord (cdp) Butte County	43	13.56
Dorrington (cdp) Calaveras County	69	12.02

Top 10 Places Sorted by Percent of Total Population

Based on places with total population of 50,000 or more

Place	Population	%
Santa Monica (city) Los Angeles County	4,188	4.72
Thousand Oaks (city) Ventura County	4,985	4.00
Carlsbad (city) San Diego County	3,666	3.68
Mission Viejo (city) Orange County	3,283	3.54
Camarillo (city) Ventura County	2,076	3.26
Laguna Niguel (city) Orange County	2,004	3.20
Temecula (city) Riverside County	3,023	3.15
Redondo Beach (city) Los Angeles County	2,078	3.15
Encinitas (city) San Diego County	1,809	3.08
Santa Cruz (city) Santa Cruz County	1,760	3.02

Portuguese

Top 10 Places Sorted by Population

Based on all places, regardless of total population

Place	Population	%
San Jose (city) Santa Clara County	15,480	1.67
San Diego (city) San Diego County	9,505	0.74
Los Angeles (city) Los Angeles County	7,722	0.20
Modesto (city) Stanislaus County	7,250	3.59
Sacramento (city) Sacramento County	7,182	1.56
Fresno (city) Fresno County	5,315	1.10
Turlock (city) Stanislaus County	5,184	7.69
Fremont (city) Alameda County	4,754	2.27
San Francisco (city) San Francisco County	4,497	0.57
Hayward (city) Alameda County	4,390	3.10

Top 10 Places Sorted by Percent of Total Population
Based on all places, regardless of total population

Place	Population	%
Acampo (cdp) San Joaquin County	17	68.00
Wallace (cdp) Calaveras County	74	46.25
Cartago (cdp) Inyo County	23	42.59
Hilmar-Irwin (cdp) Merced County	2,015	40.32
Grangeville (cdp) Kings County	215	35.89
Stevinson (cdp) Merced County	82	34.31
Princeton (cdp) Colusa County	80	32.79
Sunny Slopes (cdp) Mono County	56	28.28
Trowbridge (cdp) Sutter County	42	27.81
Hardwick (cdp) Kings County	23	24.73

Top 10 Places Sorted by Percent of Total Population
Based on places with total population of 50,000 or more

Place	Population	%
Turlock (city) Stanislaus County	5,184	7.69
Tulare (city) Tulare County	4,347	7.63
Hanford (city) Kings County	3,147	6.02
Manteca (city) San Joaquin County	3,310	5.10
Tracy (city) San Joaquin County	3,855	4.85
Castro Valley (cdp) Alameda County	2,665	4.40
San Leandro (city) Alameda County	3,314	4.00
Livermore (city) Alameda County	2,934	3.74
Modesto (city) Stanislaus County	7,250	3.59
Santa Clara (city) Santa Clara County	3,654	3.25

Romanian

Top 10 Places Sorted by Population
Based on all places, regardless of total population

Place	Population	%
Los Angeles (city) Los Angeles County	10,676	0.28
San Diego (city) San Diego County	2,000	0.16
San Francisco (city) San Francisco County	1,943	0.25
Anaheim (city) Orange County	1,744	0.52
San Jose (city) Santa Clara County	1,307	0.14
Sacramento (city) Sacramento County	1,087	0.24
Riverside (city) Riverside County	1,063	0.35
Huntington Beach (city) Orange County	1,012	0.54
Modesto (city) Stanislaus County	791	0.39
Antelope (cdp) Sacramento County	714	1.56

Top 10 Places Sorted by Percent of Total Population
Based on all places, regardless of total population

Place	Population	%
Sunset Beach (cdp) Orange County	239	19.07
Greenview (cdp) Siskiyou County	29	7.97
Olivehurst (cdp) Yuba County	587	4.41
Stevinson (cdp) Merced County	9	3.77
Airport (cdp) Stanislaus County	53	3.33
Hidden Hills (city) Los Angeles County	82	3.25
Davenport (cdp) Santa Cruz County	10	3.24
Brookdale (cdp) Santa Cruz County	59	3.23
Mokelumne Hill (cdp) Calaveras County	22	2.99
Doyle (cdp) Lassen County	10	2.69

Top 10 Places Sorted by Percent of Total Population
Based on places with total population of 50,000 or more

Place	Population	%
Rancho Cordova (city) Sacramento County	682	1.08
Carmichael (cdp) Sacramento County	629	1.02
San Rafael (city) Marin County	425	0.75
Laguna Niguel (city) Orange County	421	0.67
Mission Viejo (city) Orange County	592	0.64
Citrus Heights (city) Sacramento County	533	0.63
Santa Monica (city) Los Angeles County	500	0.56
Huntington Beach (city) Orange County	1,012	0.54
Menifee (city) Riverside County	386	0.53
Anaheim (city) Orange County	1,744	0.52

Russian

Top 10 Places Sorted by Population
Based on all places, regardless of total population

Place	Population	%
Los Angeles (city) Los Angeles County	96,251	2.55
San Francisco (city) San Francisco County	21,435	2.72
San Diego (city) San Diego County	18,222	1.42
San Jose (city) Santa Clara County	6,163	0.67
Oakland (city) Alameda County	5,358	1.38
Santa Monica (city) Los Angeles County	5,142	5.80
Sacramento (city) Sacramento County	4,916	1.07
Long Beach (city) Los Angeles County	4,610	1.00
West Hollywood (city) Los Angeles County	4,501	12.99
Thousand Oaks (city) Ventura County	4,469	3.58

Top 10 Places Sorted by Percent of Total Population
Based on all places, regardless of total population

Place	Population	%
Creston (cdp) San Luis Obispo County	20	29.85
Hidden Hills (city) Los Angeles County	408	16.18
Nord (cdp) Butte County	50	15.77
Sereno del Mar (cdp) Sonoma County	19	15.45
Pajaro Dunes (cdp) Santa Cruz County	43	14.33
West Hollywood (city) Los Angeles County	4,501	12.99
Cartago (cdp) Inyo County	7	12.96
Little River (cdp) Mendocino County	36	12.41
River Pines (cdp) Amador County	71	12.37
Dorrington (cdp) Calaveras County	69	12.02

Top 10 Places Sorted by Percent of Total Population
Based on places with total population of 50,000 or more

Place	Population	%
Santa Monica (city) Los Angeles County	5,142	5.80
Palo Alto (city) Santa Clara County	2,425	3.88
Berkeley (city) Alameda County	4,125	3.77
Walnut Creek (city) Contra Costa County	2,317	3.63
Thousand Oaks (city) Ventura County	4,469	3.58
San Rafael (city) Marin County	2,027	3.56
Encinitas (city) San Diego County	1,863	3.17
Laguna Niguel (city) Orange County	1,915	3.06
Santa Cruz (city) Santa Cruz County	1,732	2.97
Mountain View (city) Santa Clara County	1,976	2.73

Scandinavian

Top 10 Places Sorted by Population
Based on all places, regardless of total population

Place	Population	%
Los Angeles (city) Los Angeles County	4,130	0.11
San Diego (city) San Diego County	2,796	0.22
San Francisco (city) San Francisco County	1,088	0.14
Sacramento (city) Sacramento County	989	0.22
San Jose (city) Santa Clara County	980	0.11
Corona (city) Riverside County	681	0.45
Long Beach (city) Los Angeles County	561	0.12
Riverside (city) Riverside County	548	0.18
Bakersfield (city) Kern County	543	0.16
Santa Rosa (city) Sonoma County	542	0.33

Top 10 Places Sorted by Percent of Total Population
Based on all places, regardless of total population

Place	Population	%
Avery (cdp) Calaveras County	61	16.01
Snelling (cdp) Merced County	8	5.67
Blacklake (cdp) San Luis Obispo County	61	5.10
Aromas (cdp) Monterey County	118	5.09
El Portal (cdp) Mariposa County	19	5.03
Red Corral (cdp) Amador County	78	4.54
Shelter Cove (cdp) Humboldt County	23	4.39
North Gate (cdp) Contra Costa County	22	4.26
Yosemite Valley (cdp) Mariposa County	14	3.88
Mono Vista (cdp) Tuolumne County	113	3.70

Top 10 Places Sorted by Percent of Total Population
Based on places with total population of 50,000 or more

Place	Population	%
Santa Cruz (city) Santa Cruz County	451	0.77
Encinitas (city) San Diego County	377	0.64
La Mesa (city) San Diego County	320	0.57
Arden-Arcade (cdp) Sacramento County	481	0.53
San Rafael (city) Marin County	293	0.51
Redding (city) Shasta County	428	0.48
Mountain View (city) Santa Clara County	343	0.47
Corona (city) Riverside County	681	0.45
Concord (city) Contra Costa County	517	0.43
Costa Mesa (city) Orange County	473	0.43

Scotch-Irish

Top 10 Places Sorted by Population
Based on all places, regardless of total population

Place	Population	%
Los Angeles (city) Los Angeles County	21,996	0.58
San Diego (city) San Diego County	17,899	1.40
San Francisco (city) San Francisco County	8,480	1.07
San Jose (city) Santa Clara County	7,094	0.77
Sacramento (city) Sacramento County	5,314	1.16
Long Beach (city) Los Angeles County	4,933	1.07
Fresno (city) Fresno County	4,450	0.92
Santa Clarita (city) Los Angeles County	3,817	2.22
Huntington Beach (city) Orange County	3,816	2.02
Bakersfield (city) Kern County	3,607	1.09

Top 10 Places Sorted by Percent of Total Population
Based on all places, regardless of total population

Place	Population	%
Indian Falls (cdp) Plumas County	35	100.00
Clipper Mills (cdp) Butte County	40	40.82
Sierra Village (cdp) Tuolumne County	55	36.18
Daphnedale Park (cdp) Modoc County	16	32.65
Sierra Brooks (cdp) Sierra County	58	27.62
Forbestown (cdp) Butte County	95	26.76
Smartsville (cdp) Yuba County	50	22.62
Lytle Creek (cdp) San Bernardino County	153	20.68
Verdi (cdp) Sierra County	38	20.54
Jenner (cdp) Sonoma County	19	19.19

Top 10 Places Sorted by Percent of Total Population
Based on places with total population of 50,000 or more

Place	Population	%
Newport Beach (city) Orange County	2,750	3.29
Petaluma (city) Sonoma County	1,773	3.13
Encinitas (city) San Diego County	1,740	2.96
Arden-Arcade (cdp) Sacramento County	2,677	2.94
Carmichael (cdp) Sacramento County	1,728	2.80
Davis (city) Yolo County	1,809	2.79
Chico (city) Butte County	2,302	2.70
Livermore (city) Alameda County	2,051	2.61
Santa Cruz (city) Santa Cruz County	1,514	2.60
Novato (city) Marin County	1,315	2.60

Scottish

Top 10 Places Sorted by Population
Based on all places, regardless of total population

Place	Population	%
Los Angeles (city) Los Angeles County	29,120	0.77
San Diego (city) San Diego County	24,212	1.89
San Francisco (city) San Francisco County	13,167	1.67
San Jose (city) Santa Clara County	9,176	0.99
Sacramento (city) Sacramento County	7,694	1.67
Long Beach (city) Los Angeles County	6,072	1.31
Huntington Beach (city) Orange County	5,014	2.65
Fresno (city) Fresno County	4,988	1.03
Bakersfield (city) Kern County	4,779	1.44
Santa Rosa (city) Sonoma County	4,346	2.67

Top 10 Places Sorted by Percent of Total Population
Based on all places, regardless of total population

Place	Population	%
Mount Laguna (cdp) San Diego County	42	63.64
Myers Flat (cdp) Humboldt County	49	53.85
Goodyears Bar (cdp) Sierra County	94	47.47
Darwin (cdp) Inyo County	14	46.67
Likely (cdp) Modoc County	23	36.51
Fields Landing (cdp) Humboldt County	93	35.91
Calpine (cdp) Sierra County	37	30.33
Soda Springs (cdp) Nevada County	38	29.69
Carmet (cdp) Sonoma County	9	29.03
Plumas Eureka (cdp) Plumas County	63	26.92

Top 10 Places Sorted by Percent of Total Population
Based on places with total population of 50,000 or more

Place	Population	%
Santa Cruz (city) Santa Cruz County	2,581	4.43
Encinitas (city) San Diego County	2,179	3.71
Walnut Creek (city) Contra Costa County	2,364	3.70
San Clemente (city) Orange County	2,113	3.48

Place	Population	%
Newport Beach (city) Orange County	2,846	3.41
La Mesa (city) San Diego County	1,903	3.38
Chico (city) Butte County	2,710	3.18
Arden-Arcade (cdp) Sacramento County	2,817	3.10
Davis (city) Yolo County	1,993	3.07
Livermore (city) Alameda County	2,365	3.01

Serbian

Top 10 Places Sorted by Population
Based on all places, regardless of total population

Place	Population	%
Los Angeles (city) Los Angeles County	1,315	0.03
San Diego (city) San Diego County	935	0.07
San Francisco (city) San Francisco County	435	0.06
San Jose (city) Santa Clara County	398	0.04
Sacramento (city) Sacramento County	312	0.07
Carlsbad (city) San Diego County	288	0.29
Long Beach (city) Los Angeles County	263	0.06
Irvine (city) Orange County	223	0.11
Burbank (city) Los Angeles County	198	0.19
Santa Clara (city) Santa Clara County	187	0.17

Top 10 Places Sorted by Percent of Total Population
Based on all places, regardless of total population

Place	Population	%
Mabie (cdp) Plumas County	16	9.70
Keene (cdp) Kern County	17	5.38
Bodega Bay (cdp) Sonoma County	30	3.83
Shingletown (cdp) Shasta County	58	2.78
Murphys (cdp) Calaveras County	53	2.28
Salton City (cdp) Imperial County	30	2.14
Bermuda Dunes (cdp) Riverside County	132	1.92
Contra Costa Centre (cdp) Contra Costa County	95	1.70
Deer Park (cdp) Napa County	12	1.15
Fieldbrook (cdp) Humboldt County	10	1.08

Top 10 Places Sorted by Percent of Total Population
Based on places with total population of 50,000 or more

Place	Population	%
Carlsbad (city) San Diego County	288	0.29
Yorba Linda (city) Orange County	149	0.24
Burbank (city) Los Angeles County	198	0.19
Mountain View (city) Santa Clara County	135	0.19
Santa Monica (city) Los Angeles County	163	0.18
Buena Park (city) Orange County	146	0.18
Santa Clara (city) Santa Clara County	187	0.17
Upland (city) San Bernardino County	118	0.16
Redondo Beach (city) Los Angeles County	106	0.16
Vista (city) San Diego County	142	0.15

Slavic

Top 10 Places Sorted by Population
Based on all places, regardless of total population

Place	Population	%
Los Angeles (city) Los Angeles County	742	0.02
San Francisco (city) San Francisco County	627	0.08
San Diego (city) San Diego County	468	0.04
San Jose (city) Santa Clara County	235	0.03
Sunnyvale (city) Santa Clara County	228	0.17
Rancho Palos Verdes (city) Los Angeles County	203	0.49
Santa Monica (city) Los Angeles County	167	0.19
Sacramento (city) Sacramento County	161	0.04
San Clemente (city) Orange County	160	0.26
Long Beach (city) Los Angeles County	157	0.03

Top 10 Places Sorted by Percent of Total Population
Based on all places, regardless of total population

Place	Population	%
Groveland (cdp) Tuolumne County	31	8.76
Lake of the Woods (cdp) Kern County	46	4.67
Janesville (cdp) Lassen County	34	2.82
Coffee Creek (cdp) Trinity County	5	2.82
Amador City (city) Amador County	2	1.56
San Simeon (cdp) San Luis Obispo County	8	1.46
Julian (cdp) San Diego County	21	1.39
Graeagle (cdp) Plumas County	10	1.10
Day Valley (cdp) Santa Cruz County	32	0.98
Needles (city) San Bernardino County	45	0.91

Top 10 Places Sorted by Percent of Total Population
Based on places with total population of 50,000 or more

Place	Population	%
San Clemente (city) Orange County	160	0.26
Santa Monica (city) Los Angeles County	167	0.19
Laguna Niguel (city) Orange County	117	0.19
Manteca (city) San Joaquin County	117	0.18
Sunnyvale (city) Santa Clara County	228	0.17
Redondo Beach (city) Los Angeles County	110	0.17
San Buenaventura (Ventura) (city) Ventura County	153	0.15
Lodi (city) San Joaquin County	90	0.14
Yorba Linda (city) Orange County	86	0.14
Berkeley (city) Alameda County	128	0.12

Slovak

Top 10 Places Sorted by Population
Based on all places, regardless of total population

Place	Population	%
Los Angeles (city) Los Angeles County	1,904	0.05
San Diego (city) San Diego County	1,472	0.11
San Francisco (city) San Francisco County	861	0.11
San Jose (city) Santa Clara County	702	0.08
Huntington Beach (city) Orange County	427	0.23
Oakland (city) Alameda County	359	0.09
Berkeley (city) Alameda County	220	0.20
Benicia (city) Solano County	211	0.78
Palos Verdes Estates (city) Los Angeles County	207	1.54
Costa Mesa (city) Orange County	207	0.19

Top 10 Places Sorted by Percent of Total Population
Based on all places, regardless of total population

Place	Population	%
Lake of the Woods (cdp) Kern County	37	3.75
Oak Glen (cdp) San Bernardino County	18	3.54
Ross (town) Marin County	44	2.20
Palos Verdes Estates (city) Los Angeles County	207	1.54
Penn Valley (cdp) Nevada County	17	1.46
Brooktrails (cdp) Mendocino County	44	1.26
Twain Harte (cdp) Tuolumne County	28	1.24
Burney (cdp) Shasta County	38	1.23
Bella Vista (cdp) Shasta County	26	1.13
Sleepy Hollow (cdp) Marin County	26	1.06

Top 10 Places Sorted by Percent of Total Population
Based on places with total population of 50,000 or more

Place	Population	%
Yorba Linda (city) Orange County	204	0.32
Encinitas (city) San Diego County	160	0.27
Huntington Beach (city) Orange County	427	0.23
Manteca (city) San Joaquin County	151	0.23
Laguna Niguel (city) Orange County	140	0.22
Santee (city) San Diego County	114	0.22
Redondo Beach (city) Los Angeles County	142	0.21
La Mesa (city) San Diego County	116	0.21
Berkeley (city) Alameda County	220	0.20
Mission Viejo (city) Orange County	181	0.20

Slovene

Top 10 Places Sorted by Population
Based on all places, regardless of total population

Place	Population	%
Los Angeles (city) Los Angeles County	730	0.02
San Diego (city) San Diego County	455	0.04
San Francisco (city) San Francisco County	400	0.05
Huntington Beach (city) Orange County	159	0.08
Santa Cruz (city) Santa Cruz County	158	0.27
Santa Clarita (city) Los Angeles County	137	0.08
Manhattan Beach (city) Los Angeles County	123	0.35
Sacramento (city) Sacramento County	120	0.03
Torrance (city) Los Angeles County	108	0.08
San Jose (city) Santa Clara County	107	0.01

Top 10 Places Sorted by Percent of Total Population
Based on all places, regardless of total population

Place	Population	%
Edwards AFB (cdp) Kern County	104	2.92
Isleton (city) Sacramento County	17	1.83
Diablo (cdp) Contra Costa County	18	1.68
Descanso (cdp) San Diego County	12	0.89
Portola Valley (town) San Mateo County	35	0.82
Chester (cdp) Plumas County	15	0.81
Mountain Ranch (cdp) Calaveras County	11	0.75
Yreka (city) Siskiyou County	50	0.65
Pine Mountain Lake (cdp) Tuolumne County	16	0.58
Mission Canyon (cdp) Santa Barbara County	11	0.52

Top 10 Places Sorted by Percent of Total Population
Based on places with total population of 50,000 or more

Place	Population	%
Santa Cruz (city) Santa Cruz County	158	0.27
Rocklin (city) Placer County	64	0.12
Novato (city) Marin County	58	0.11
Livermore (city) Alameda County	79	0.10
Napa (city) Napa County	73	0.10
Yorba Linda (city) Orange County	66	0.10
Camarillo (city) Ventura County	57	0.09
Huntington Beach (city) Orange County	159	0.08
Santa Clarita (city) Los Angeles County	137	0.08
Torrance (city) Los Angeles County	108	0.08

Soviet Union

Top 10 Places Sorted by Population
Based on all places, regardless of total population

Place	Population	%
Los Angeles (city) Los Angeles County	105	<0.01
San Francisco (city) San Francisco County	75	0.01
Hemet (city) Riverside County	34	0.04
San Diego (city) San Diego County	25	<0.01
Santa Monica (city) Los Angeles County	20	0.02
Laguna Woods (city) Orange County	14	0.09
Duarte (city) Los Angeles County	14	0.07
Manhattan Beach (city) Los Angeles County	13	0.04
Ben Lomond (cdp) Santa Cruz County	9	0.15
Ojai (city) Ventura County	9	0.12

Top 10 Places Sorted by Percent of Total Population
Based on all places, regardless of total population

Place	Population	%
Ben Lomond (cdp) Santa Cruz County	9	0.15
Ojai (city) Ventura County	9	0.12
Laguna Woods (city) Orange County	14	0.09
Duarte (city) Los Angeles County	14	0.07
Hemet (city) Riverside County	34	0.04
Manhattan Beach (city) Los Angeles County	13	0.04
Santa Monica (city) Los Angeles County	20	0.02
San Francisco (city) San Francisco County	75	0.01
Palo Alto (city) Santa Clara County	9	0.01
Fairfield (city) Solano County	7	0.01

Top 10 Places Sorted by Percent of Total Population
Based on places with total population of 50,000 or more

Place	Population	%
Hemet (city) Riverside County	34	0.04
Santa Monica (city) Los Angeles County	20	0.02
San Francisco (city) San Francisco County	75	0.01
Palo Alto (city) Santa Clara County	9	0.01
Fairfield (city) Solano County	7	0.01
Los Angeles (city) Los Angeles County	105	<0.01
San Diego (city) San Diego County	25	<0.01
Alameda (city) Alameda County	0	0.00
Alhambra (city) Los Angeles County	0	0.00
Anaheim (city) Orange County	0	0.00

Swedish

Top 10 Places Sorted by Population
Based on all places, regardless of total population

Place	Population	%
Los Angeles (city) Los Angeles County	23,723	0.63
San Diego (city) San Diego County	17,467	1.36
San Francisco (city) San Francisco County	8,924	1.13
San Jose (city) Santa Clara County	8,620	0.93
Sacramento (city) Sacramento County	5,613	1.22
Fresno (city) Fresno County	4,491	0.93
Huntington Beach (city) Orange County	4,208	2.23
Long Beach (city) Los Angeles County	4,170	0.90
Santa Clarita (city) Los Angeles County	4,096	2.38
Bakersfield (city) Kern County	4,065	1.22

Top 10 Places Sorted by Percent of Total Population

Based on all places, regardless of total population

Place	Population	%
Onyx (cdp) Kern County	78	60.47
Sattley (cdp) Sierra County	12	54.55
Verdi (cdp) Sierra County	98	52.97
Bear Valley (cdp) Alpine County	23	34.33
Acampo (cdp) San Joaquin County	8	32.00
Valley Ranch (cdp) Plumas County	38	31.93
Edgewood (cdp) Siskiyou County	15	30.61
Sierra City (cdp) Sierra County	175	29.12
Honcut (cdp) Butte County	148	25.87
Eagleville (cdp) Modoc County	15	21.43

Top 10 Places Sorted by Percent of Total Population

Based on places with total population of 50,000 or more

Place	Population	%
Santa Cruz (city) Santa Cruz County	2,135	3.66
Redding (city) Shasta County	3,053	3.42
Rocklin (city) Placer County	1,645	3.03
Novato (city) Marin County	1,525	3.02
Newport Beach (city) Orange County	2,439	2.92
Livermore (city) Alameda County	2,279	2.90
Carlsbad (city) San Diego County	2,833	2.84
Pleasanton (city) Alameda County	1,893	2.78
Walnut Creek (city) Contra Costa County	1,765	2.77
San Clemente (city) Orange County	1,632	2.69

Swiss

Top 10 Places Sorted by Population

Based on all places, regardless of total population

Place	Population	%
Los Angeles (city) Los Angeles County	5,328	0.14
San Diego (city) San Diego County	4,165	0.32
San Francisco (city) San Francisco County	3,264	0.41
San Jose (city) Santa Clara County	2,530	0.27
Sacramento (city) Sacramento County	1,686	0.37
Modesto (city) Stanislaus County	1,072	0.53
Fresno (city) Fresno County	1,010	0.21
Santa Rosa (city) Sonoma County	924	0.57
Santa Clarita (city) Los Angeles County	896	0.52
Oakland (city) Alameda County	856	0.22

Top 10 Places Sorted by Percent of Total Population

Based on all places, regardless of total population

Place	Population	%
Nicolaus (cdp) Sutter County	38	22.22
Trinity Village (cdp) Trinity County	20	15.63
Sierra City (cdp) Sierra County	79	13.14
Trinidad (city) Humboldt County	32	12.36
Burnt Ranch (cdp) Trinity County	23	9.91
Hat Creek (cdp) Shasta County	19	8.80
Oak Shores (cdp) San Luis Obispo County	18	8.29
Point Reyes Station (cdp) Marin County	67	8.06
Spaulding (cdp) Lassen County	13	7.56
June Lake (cdp) Mono County	41	6.97

Top 10 Places Sorted by Percent of Total Population

Based on places with total population of 50,000 or more

Place	Population	%
Petaluma (city) Sonoma County	697	1.23
Davis (city) Yolo County	722	1.11
San Rafael (city) Marin County	561	0.99
Newport Beach (city) Orange County	730	0.87
Mountain View (city) Santa Clara County	591	0.82
Carmichael (cdp) Sacramento County	509	0.82
Redondo Beach (city) Los Angeles County	523	0.79
Palo Alto (city) Santa Clara County	490	0.78
Walnut Creek (city) Contra Costa County	484	0.76
Redwood City (city) San Mateo County	556	0.74

Turkish

Top 10 Places Sorted by Population

Based on all places, regardless of total population

Place	Population	%
Los Angeles (city) Los Angeles County	3,354	0.09
San Diego (city) San Diego County	1,280	0.10
San Francisco (city) San Francisco County	721	0.09
Irvine (city) Orange County	612	0.31
Oakland (city) Alameda County	575	0.15
San Jose (city) Santa Clara County	539	0.06
San Mateo (city) San Mateo County	501	0.53
Torrance (city) Los Angeles County	459	0.32
Long Beach (city) Los Angeles County	288	0.06
Redwood City (city) San Mateo County	283	0.38

Top 10 Places Sorted by Percent of Total Population

Based on all places, regardless of total population

Place	Population	%
Summerland (cdp) Santa Barbara County	31	2.86
Contra Costa Centre (cdp) Contra Costa County	96	1.72
Gerber (cdp) Tehama County	14	1.51
Roseland (cdp) Sonoma County	63	0.98
Capitola (city) Santa Cruz County	91	0.93
Knights Landing (cdp) Yolo County	8	0.89
Marin City (cdp) Marin County	25	0.88
Cotati (city) Sonoma County	48	0.68
Burlingame (city) San Mateo County	181	0.64
North Tustin (cdp) Orange County	149	0.61

Top 10 Places Sorted by Percent of Total Population

Based on places with total population of 50,000 or more

Place	Population	%
San Mateo (city) San Mateo County	501	0.53
Redwood City (city) San Mateo County	283	0.38
Torrance (city) Los Angeles County	459	0.32
Irvine (city) Orange County	612	0.31
Santa Barbara (city) Santa Barbara County	226	0.26
Davis (city) Yolo County	163	0.25
San Rafael (city) Marin County	141	0.25
Fountain Valley (city) Orange County	136	0.25
Newport Beach (city) Orange County	204	0.24
Palo Alto (city) Santa Clara County	144	0.23

Ukrainian

Top 10 Places Sorted by Population

Based on all places, regardless of total population

Place	Population	%
Los Angeles (city) Los Angeles County	11,493	0.30
San Francisco (city) San Francisco County	4,917	0.62
San Diego (city) San Diego County	3,425	0.27
Antelope (cdp) Sacramento County	3,301	7.22
Rancho Cordova (city) Sacramento County	2,814	4.45
North Highlands (cdp) Sacramento County	2,401	5.63
Sacramento (city) Sacramento County	2,189	0.48
Citrus Heights (city) Sacramento County	1,833	2.17
San Jose (city) Santa Clara County	1,748	0.19
Foothill Farms (cdp) Sacramento County	1,082	3.30

Top 10 Places Sorted by Percent of Total Population

Based on all places, regardless of total population

Place	Population	%
Elverta (cdp) Sacramento County	634	12.57
Pajaro Dunes (cdp) Santa Cruz County	34	11.33
Vallecito (cdp) Calaveras County	48	8.92
Muir Beach (cdp) Marin County	24	8.30
Big Lagoon (cdp) Humboldt County	15	7.94
Antelope (cdp) Sacramento County	3,301	7.22
Bell Canyon (cdp) Ventura County	150	6.11
Mather (cdp) Sacramento County	274	6.09
North Highlands (cdp) Sacramento County	2,401	5.63
Rancho Cordova (city) Sacramento County	2,814	4.45

Top 10 Places Sorted by Percent of Total Population

Based on places with total population of 50,000 or more

Place	Population	%
Rancho Cordova (city) Sacramento County	2,814	4.45
Citrus Heights (city) Sacramento County	1,833	2.17
Carmichael (cdp) Sacramento County	819	1.33
Rocklin (city) Placer County	685	1.26
Santa Monica (city) Los Angeles County	957	1.08
Mountain View (city) Santa Clara County	680	0.94
Palo Alto (city) Santa Clara County	563	0.90
Arden-Arcade (cdp) Sacramento County	761	0.84
Carlsbad (city) San Diego County	832	0.83
Walnut Creek (city) Contra Costa County	529	0.83

Welsh

Top 10 Places Sorted by Population

Based on all places, regardless of total population

Place	Population	%
Los Angeles (city) Los Angeles County	10,583	0.28
San Diego (city) San Diego County	8,167	0.64
San Francisco (city) San Francisco County	3,806	0.48
San Jose (city) Santa Clara County	3,304	0.36
Sacramento (city) Sacramento County	2,314	0.50
Fresno (city) Fresno County	1,973	0.41
Long Beach (city) Los Angeles County	1,823	0.39
Huntington Beach (city) Orange County	1,786	0.95
Modesto (city) Stanislaus County	1,523	0.75
Santa Clarita (city) Los Angeles County	1,502	0.87

Top 10 Places Sorted by Percent of Total Population

Based on all places, regardless of total population

Place	Population	%
Prattville (cdp) Plumas County	21	100.00
Little River (cdp) Mendocino County	138	47.59
Likely (cdp) Modoc County	23	36.51
Randsburg (cdp) Kern County	9	21.43
Anchor Bay (cdp) Mendocino County	60	18.81
Vallecito (cdp) Calaveras County	87	16.17
Valley Acres (cdp) Kern County	85	15.12
Dillon Beach (cdp) Marin County	20	12.27
Honcut (cdp) Butte County	68	11.89
Bangor (cdp) Butte County	42	11.35

Top 10 Places Sorted by Percent of Total Population

Based on places with total population of 50,000 or more

Place	Population	%
Newport Beach (city) Orange County	1,134	1.36
Santa Monica (city) Los Angeles County	1,075	1.21
Santa Barbara (city) Santa Barbara County	1,017	1.16
Davis (city) Yolo County	742	1.14
Napa (city) Napa County	853	1.12
Petaluma (city) Sonoma County	636	1.12
Carmichael (cdp) Sacramento County	664	1.07
Santa Cruz (city) Santa Cruz County	617	1.06
Livermore (city) Alameda County	796	1.01
Yorba Linda (city) Orange County	629	1.00

West Indian, excluding Hispanic

Top 10 Places Sorted by Population

Based on all places, regardless of total population

Place	Population	%
Los Angeles (city) Los Angeles County	17,886	0.47
San Diego (city) San Diego County	2,607	0.20
Long Beach (city) Los Angeles County	1,815	0.39
Oakland (city) Alameda County	1,774	0.46
Inglewood (city) Los Angeles County	1,770	1.61
San Francisco (city) San Francisco County	1,316	0.17
Lancaster (city) Los Angeles County	1,053	0.70
Sacramento (city) Sacramento County	812	0.18
Westmont (cdp) Los Angeles County	768	2.45
Moreno Valley (city) Riverside County	717	0.38

Top 10 Places Sorted by Percent of Total Population

Based on all places, regardless of total population

Place	Population	%
Herlong (cdp) Lassen County	105	7.51
Humboldt Hill (cdp) Humboldt County	259	6.87
Derby Acres (cdp) Kern County	15	3.74
View Park-Windsor Hills (cdp) Los Angeles County	400	3.71
Yosemite Valley (cdp) Mariposa County	13	3.60
West Rancho Dominguez (cdp) Los Angeles County	178	3.09
Bodfish (cdp) Kern County	59	3.04
Mariposa (cdp) Mariposa County	62	2.92
Ladera Heights (cdp) Los Angeles County	173	2.59
Westmont (cdp) Los Angeles County	768	2.45

Top 10 Places Sorted by Percent of Total Population

Based on places with total population of 50,000 or more

Place	Population	%
Inglewood (city) Los Angeles County	1,770	1.61
Hawthorne (city) Los Angeles County	645	0.77
La Mesa (city) San Diego County	419	0.74

Place	Population	%
Lancaster (city) Los Angeles County	1,053	0.70
Rialto (city) San Bernardino County	572	0.58
Gardena (city) Los Angeles County	332	0.57
Compton (city) Los Angeles County	458	0.48
Los Angeles (city) Los Angeles County	17,886	0.47
Oakland (city) Alameda County	1,774	0.46
Rancho Cucamonga (city) San Bernardino County	698	0.43

West Indian: Bahamian, excluding Hispanic

Top 10 Places Sorted by Population

Based on all places, regardless of total population

Place	Population	%
Los Angeles (city) Los Angeles County	166	<0.01
Long Beach (city) Los Angeles County	92	0.02
Inglewood (city) Los Angeles County	88	0.08
San Diego (city) San Diego County	74	0.01
Clovis (city) Fresno County	66	0.07
Elk Grove (city) Sacramento County	44	0.03
Rancho Cucamonga (city) San Bernardino County	34	0.02
Antioch (city) Contra Costa County	33	0.03
Thousand Oaks (city) Ventura County	29	0.02
Redlands (city) San Bernardino County	23	0.03

Top 10 Places Sorted by Percent of Total Population

Based on all places, regardless of total population

Place	Population	%
Rodeo (cdp) Contra Costa County	18	0.20
Inglewood (city) Los Angeles County	88	0.08
Woodcrest (cdp) Riverside County	11	0.08
Clovis (city) Fresno County	66	0.07
Rancho San Diego (cdp) San Diego County	12	0.06
Elk Grove (city) Sacramento County	44	0.03
Antioch (city) Contra Costa County	33	0.03
Redlands (city) San Bernardino County	23	0.03
Yucaipa (city) San Bernardino County	14	0.03
Tehachapi (city) Kern County	4	0.03

Top 10 Places Sorted by Percent of Total Population

Based on places with total population of 50,000 or more

Place	Population	%
Inglewood (city) Los Angeles County	88	0.08
Clovis (city) Fresno County	66	0.07
Elk Grove (city) Sacramento County	44	0.03
Antioch (city) Contra Costa County	33	0.03
Redlands (city) San Bernardino County	23	0.03
Yucaipa (city) San Bernardino County	14	0.03
Long Beach (city) Los Angeles County	92	0.02
Rancho Cucamonga (city) San Bernardino County	34	0.02
Thousand Oaks (city) Ventura County	29	0.02
San Diego (city) San Diego County	74	0.01

West Indian: Barbadian, excluding Hispanic

Top 10 Places Sorted by Population

Based on all places, regardless of total population

Place	Population	%
Los Angeles (city) Los Angeles County	202	0.01
Rialto (city) San Bernardino County	159	0.16
Antioch (city) Contra Costa County	93	0.09
Fontana (city) San Bernardino County	72	0.04
San Diego (city) San Diego County	39	<0.01
El Segundo (city) Los Angeles County	28	0.17
Roseville (city) Placer County	28	0.02
Tracy (city) San Joaquin County	27	0.03
Marina (city) Monterey County	26	0.13
Carson (city) Los Angeles County	25	0.03

Top 10 Places Sorted by Percent of Total Population

Based on all places, regardless of total population

Place	Population	%
Bradbury (city) Los Angeles County	3	0.31
Camp Pendleton North (cdp) San Diego County	21	0.21
El Segundo (city) Los Angeles County	28	0.17
Rialto (city) San Bernardino County	159	0.16
Marina (city) Monterey County	26	0.13
Sierra Madre (city) Los Angeles County	13	0.12
Antioch (city) Contra Costa County	93	0.09
Palos Verdes Estates (city) Los Angeles County	12	0.09
Coalinga (city) Fresno County	8	0.06
Millbrae (city) San Mateo County	10	0.05

Top 10 Places Sorted by Percent of Total Population

Based on places with total population of 50,000 or more

Place	Population	%
Rialto (city) San Bernardino County	159	0.16
Antioch (city) Contra Costa County	93	0.09
Fontana (city) San Bernardino County	72	0.04
Walnut Creek (city) Contra Costa County	24	0.04
La Mesa (city) San Diego County	23	0.04
Hanford (city) Kings County	19	0.04
Tracy (city) San Joaquin County	27	0.03
Carson (city) Los Angeles County	25	0.03
Newport Beach (city) Orange County	24	0.03
Laguna Niguel (city) Orange County	17	0.03

West Indian: Belizean, excluding Hispanic

Top 10 Places Sorted by Population

Based on all places, regardless of total population

Place	Population	%
Los Angeles (city) Los Angeles County	8,719	0.23
Lancaster (city) Los Angeles County	876	0.59
Inglewood (city) Los Angeles County	711	0.65
Westmont (cdp) Los Angeles County	574	1.83
Hawthorne (city) Los Angeles County	341	0.41
Long Beach (city) Los Angeles County	336	0.07
San Pablo (city) Contra Costa County	330	1.13
Compton (city) Los Angeles County	308	0.32
Moreno Valley (city) Riverside County	236	0.13
Rialto (city) San Bernardino County	231	0.23

Top 10 Places Sorted by Percent of Total Population

Based on all places, regardless of total population

Place	Population	%
Herlong (cdp) Lassen County	70	5.00
West Rancho Dominguez (cdp) Los Angeles County178 3.09		
Westmont (cdp) Los Angeles County	574	1.83
San Pablo (city) Contra Costa County	330	1.13
Stevenson Ranch (cdp) Los Angeles County	167	0.99
Westlake Village (city) Los Angeles County	73	0.88
Armona (cdp) Kings County	25	0.82
Inglewood (city) Los Angeles County	711	0.65
Lancaster (city) Los Angeles County	876	0.59
Hawthorne (city) Los Angeles County	341	0.41

Top 10 Places Sorted by Percent of Total Population

Based on places with total population of 50,000 or more

Place	Population	%
Inglewood (city) Los Angeles County	711	0.65
Lancaster (city) Los Angeles County	876	0.59
Hawthorne (city) Los Angeles County	341	0.41
Gardena (city) Los Angeles County	203	0.35
Compton (city) Los Angeles County	308	0.32
Los Angeles (city) Los Angeles County	8,719	0.23
Rialto (city) San Bernardino County	231	0.23
Lakewood (city) Los Angeles County	153	0.19
Colton (city) San Bernardino County	96	0.18
Menifee (city) Riverside County	121	0.17

West Indian: Bermudan, excluding Hispanic

Top 10 Places Sorted by Population

Based on all places, regardless of total population

Place	Population	%
Los Angeles (city) Los Angeles County	118	<0.01
San Diego (city) San Diego County	46	<0.01
Oakland (city) Alameda County	39	0.01
Santee (city) San Diego County	17	0.03
Elk Grove (city) Sacramento County	15	0.01
Fairfax (town) Marin County	14	0.19
Calimesa (city) Riverside County	13	0.17
Union City (city) Alameda County	12	0.02
Rossmoor (cdp) Orange County	10	0.10
Arden-Arcade (cdp) Sacramento County	10	0.01

Top 10 Places Sorted by Percent of Total Population

Based on all places, regardless of total population

Place	Population	%
Fairfax (town) Marin County	14	0.19
Calimesa (city) Riverside County	13	0.17
Rossmoor (cdp) Orange County	10	0.10
Santee (city) San Diego County	17	0.03
Union City (city) Alameda County	12	0.02
Oakland (city) Alameda County	39	0.01
Elk Grove (city) Sacramento County	15	0.01
Arden-Arcade (cdp) Sacramento County	10	0.01
Pasadena (city) Los Angeles County	8	0.01
Rancho Cordova (city) Sacramento County	5	0.01

Top 10 Places Sorted by Percent of Total Population

Based on places with total population of 50,000 or more

Place	Population	%
Santee (city) San Diego County	17	0.03
Union City (city) Alameda County	12	0.02
Oakland (city) Alameda County	39	0.01
Elk Grove (city) Sacramento County	15	0.01
Arden-Arcade (cdp) Sacramento County	10	0.01
Pasadena (city) Los Angeles County	8	0.01
Rancho Cordova (city) Sacramento County	5	0.01
Los Angeles (city) Los Angeles County	118	<0.01
San Diego (city) San Diego County	46	<0.01
Santa Clarita (city) Los Angeles County	1	<0.01

West Indian: British West Indian, excluding Hispanic

Top 10 Places Sorted by Population

Based on all places, regardless of total population

Place	Population	%
Los Angeles (city) Los Angeles County	308	0.01
Temecula (city) Riverside County	198	0.21
San Diego (city) San Diego County	112	0.01
Ontario (city) San Bernardino County	107	0.06
Lompoc (city) Santa Barbara County	103	0.25
Long Beach (city) Los Angeles County	69	0.01
Costa Mesa (city) Orange County	61	0.06
Bellflower (city) Los Angeles County	56	0.07
Vallejo (city) Solano County	43	0.04
San Francisco (city) San Francisco County	36	<0.01

Top 10 Places Sorted by Percent of Total Population

Based on all places, regardless of total population

Place	Population	%
Calipatria (city) Imperial County	19	0.27
Lompoc (city) Santa Barbara County	103	0.25
Temecula (city) Riverside County	198	0.21
Rodeo (cdp) Contra Costa County	14	0.15
Lawndale (city) Los Angeles County	31	0.10
Rio Vista (city) Solano County	7	0.10
Galt (city) Sacramento County	18	0.08
Bellflower (city) Los Angeles County	56	0.07
Culver City (city) Los Angeles County	28	0.07
Ontario (city) San Bernardino County	107	0.06

Top 10 Places Sorted by Percent of Total Population

Based on places with total population of 50,000 or more

Place	Population	%
Temecula (city) Riverside County	198	0.21
Bellflower (city) Los Angeles County	56	0.07
Ontario (city) San Bernardino County	107	0.06
Costa Mesa (city) Orange County	61	0.06
Montebello (city) Los Angeles County	31	0.05
Vallejo (city) Solano County	43	0.04
Gardena (city) Los Angeles County	16	0.03
Glendale (city) Los Angeles County	31	0.02
Norwalk (city) Los Angeles County	21	0.02
Santa Monica (city) Los Angeles County	18	0.02

West Indian: Dutch West Indian, excluding Hispanic

Top 10 Places Sorted by Population

Based on all places, regardless of total population

Place	Population	%
Oildale (cdp) Kern County	206	0.63

Place	Population	%
Bakersfield (city) Kern County	201	0.06
Fresno (city) Fresno County	133	0.03
Porterville (city) Tulare County	109	0.21
San Buenaventura (Ventura) (city) Ventura County	75	0.07
Santa Clarita (city) Los Angeles County	75	0.04
San Diego (city) San Diego County	74	0.01
Los Angeles (city) Los Angeles County	71	<0.01
Mariposa (cdp) Mariposa County	62	2.92
Santa Paula (city) Ventura County	57	0.20

Top 10 Places Sorted by Percent of Total Population
Based on all places, regardless of total population

Place	Population	%
Derby Acres (cdp) Kern County	15	3.74
Mariposa (cdp) Mariposa County	62	2.92
Challenge-Brownsville (cdp) Yuba County	29	2.20
Loleta (cdp) Humboldt County	12	1.42
South Taft (cdp) Kern County	24	1.10
Mountain View (cdp) Contra Costa County	16	0.76
Shackelford (cdp) Stanislaus County	28	0.75
McCloud (cdp) Siskiyou County	8	0.66
Oildale (cdp) Kern County	206	0.63
Palermo (cdp) Butte County	26	0.57

Top 10 Places Sorted by Percent of Total Population
Based on places with total population of 50,000 or more

Place	Population	%
Porterville (city) Tulare County	109	0.21
San Buenaventura (Ventura) (city) Ventura County	75	0.07
Laguna Niguel (city) Orange County	44	0.07
Bakersfield (city) Kern County	201	0.06
Hanford (city) Kings County	28	0.05
Santa Clarita (city) Los Angeles County	75	0.04
Redding (city) Shasta County	38	0.04
Fresno (city) Fresno County	133	0.03
Elk Grove (city) Sacramento County	42	0.03
Torrance (city) Los Angeles County	38	0.03

West Indian: Haitian, excluding Hispanic

Top 10 Places Sorted by Population
Based on all places, regardless of total population

Place	Population	%
Los Angeles (city) Los Angeles County	1,526	0.04
San Diego (city) San Diego County	413	0.03
Petaluma (city) Sonoma County	229	0.40
View Park-Windsor Hills (cdp) Los Angeles County	207	1.92
Rohnert Park (city) Sonoma County	191	0.47
Victorville (city) San Bernardino County	162	0.15
Ridgecrest (city) Kern County	151	0.55
Wildomar (city) Riverside County	140	0.46
Rosamond (cdp) Kern County	123	0.72
East Los Angeles (cdp) Los Angeles County	104	0.08

Top 10 Places Sorted by Percent of Total Population
Based on all places, regardless of total population

Place	Population	%
View Park-Windsor Hills (cdp) Los Angeles County	207	1.92
Dixon Lane-Meadow Creek (cdp) Inyo County	40	1.50
Herlong (cdp) Lassen County	14	1.00
Mayflower Village (cdp) Los Angeles County	55	0.93
Rosamond (cdp) Kern County	123	0.72
Ahwahnee (cdp) Madera County	12	0.57
Ridgecrest (city) Kern County	151	0.55
Vine Hill (cdp) Contra Costa County	18	0.52
Rohnert Park (city) Sonoma County	191	0.47
Wildomar (city) Riverside County	140	0.46

Top 10 Places Sorted by Percent of Total Population
Based on places with total population of 50,000 or more

Place	Population	%
Petaluma (city) Sonoma County	229	0.40
La Mesa (city) San Diego County	89	0.16
Victorville (city) San Bernardino County	162	0.15
San Marcos (city) San Diego County	83	0.11
Richmond (city) Contra Costa County	101	0.10
El Cajon (city) San Diego County	94	0.10
Cupertino (city) Santa Clara County	54	0.10
Novato (city) Marin County	50	0.10
Alameda (city) Alameda County	65	0.09
Colton (city) San Bernardino County	46	0.09

West Indian: Jamaican, excluding Hispanic

Top 10 Places Sorted by Population
Based on all places, regardless of total population

Place	Population	%
Los Angeles (city) Los Angeles County	4,559	0.12
San Diego (city) San Diego County	1,036	0.08
Inglewood (city) Los Angeles County	766	0.70
San Francisco (city) San Francisco County	714	0.09
Oakland (city) Alameda County	705	0.18
Long Beach (city) Los Angeles County	557	0.12
Riverside (city) Riverside County	502	0.17
Sacramento (city) Sacramento County	376	0.08
Moreno Valley (city) Riverside County	353	0.19
Chula Vista (city) San Diego County	345	0.15

Top 10 Places Sorted by Percent of Total Population
Based on all places, regardless of total population

Place	Population	%
Yosemite Valley (cdp) Mariposa County	13	3.60
Strawberry (cdp) Marin County	89	1.73
View Park-Windsor Hills (cdp) Los Angeles County	155	1.44
Ladera Heights (cdp) Los Angeles County	90	1.35
March ARB (cdp) Riverside County	11	1.30
Pacheco (cdp) Contra Costa County	37	1.14
Granite Hills (cdp) San Diego County	37	1.08
Quartz Hill (cdp) Los Angeles County	101	0.97
Herlong (cdp) Lassen County	13	0.93
Lake Hughes (cdp) Los Angeles County	7	0.90

Top 10 Places Sorted by Percent of Total Population
Based on places with total population of 50,000 or more

Place	Population	%
Inglewood (city) Los Angeles County	766	0.70
San Rafael (city) Marin County	197	0.35
La Mesa (city) San Diego County	147	0.26
Palmdale (city) Los Angeles County	344	0.24
Hawthorne (city) Los Angeles County	201	0.24
Fairfield (city) Solano County	229	0.22
Carson (city) Los Angeles County	198	0.22
Palo Alto (city) Santa Clara County	126	0.20
Paramount (city) Los Angeles County	109	0.20
Moreno Valley (city) Riverside County	353	0.19

West Indian: Trinidadian and Tobagonian, excluding Hispanic

Top 10 Places Sorted by Population
Based on all places, regardless of total population

Place	Population	%
Los Angeles (city) Los Angeles County	631	0.02
Oakland (city) Alameda County	387	0.10
Humboldt Hill (cdp) Humboldt County	259	6.87
Long Beach (city) Los Angeles County	168	0.04
San Diego (city) San Diego County	156	0.01
San Francisco (city) San Francisco County	140	0.02
San Jose (city) Santa Clara County	140	0.02
Oxnard (city) Ventura County	104	0.05
Sacramento (city) Sacramento County	90	0.02
Manteca (city) San Joaquin County	83	0.13

Top 10 Places Sorted by Percent of Total Population
Based on all places, regardless of total population

Place	Population	%
Humboldt Hill (cdp) Humboldt County	259	6.87
Ladera Heights (cdp) Los Angeles County	66	0.99
Herlong (cdp) Lassen County	8	0.57
West Menlo Park (cdp) San Mateo County	17	0.50
Rodeo (cdp) Contra Costa County	38	0.42
Loma Linda (city) San Bernardino County	49	0.21
View Park-Windsor Hills (cdp) Los Angeles County	23	0.21
Stanford (cdp) Santa Clara County	26	0.18
Arcata (city) Humboldt County	29	0.17
Alondra Park (cdp) Los Angeles County	14	0.16

Top 10 Places Sorted by Percent of Total Population
Based on places with total population of 50,000 or more

Place	Population	%
Manteca (city) San Joaquin County	83	0.13
Gardena (city) Los Angeles County	75	0.13
Perris (city) Riverside County	74	0.12
Oakland (city) Alameda County	387	0.10
San Ramon (city) Contra Costa County	53	0.08
Elk Grove (city) Sacramento County	79	0.06
Lynwood (city) Los Angeles County	44	0.06
Oxnard (city) Ventura County	104	0.05
Vallejo (city) Solano County	61	0.05
Rowland Heights (cdp) Los Angeles County	26	0.05

West Indian: U.S. Virgin Islander, excluding Hispanic

Top 10 Places Sorted by Population
Based on all places, regardless of total population

Place	Population	%
Los Angeles (city) Los Angeles County	77	<0.01
Inglewood (city) Los Angeles County	46	0.04
Long Beach (city) Los Angeles County	37	0.01
San Diego (city) San Diego County	27	<0.01
Fontana (city) San Bernardino County	24	0.01
Chula Vista (city) San Diego County	16	0.01
Oakland (city) Alameda County	16	<0.01
San Bernardino (city) San Bernardino County	15	0.01
Bellflower (city) Los Angeles County	14	0.02
Ontario (city) San Bernardino County	12	0.01

Top 10 Places Sorted by Percent of Total Population
Based on all places, regardless of total population

Place	Population	%
Stanford (cdp) Santa Clara County	10	0.07
Inglewood (city) Los Angeles County	46	0.04
Bellflower (city) Los Angeles County	14	0.02
Antelope (cdp) Sacramento County	9	0.02
Long Beach (city) Los Angeles County	37	0.01
Fontana (city) San Bernardino County	24	0.01
Chula Vista (city) San Diego County	16	0.01
San Bernardino (city) San Bernardino County	15	0.01
Ontario (city) San Bernardino County	12	0.01
San Rafael (city) Marin County	8	0.01

Top 10 Places Sorted by Percent of Total Population
Based on places with total population of 50,000 or more

Place	Population	%
Inglewood (city) Los Angeles County	46	0.04
Bellflower (city) Los Angeles County	14	0.02
Long Beach (city) Los Angeles County	37	0.01
Fontana (city) San Bernardino County	24	0.01
Chula Vista (city) San Diego County	16	0.01
San Bernardino (city) San Bernardino County	15	0.01
Ontario (city) San Bernardino County	12	0.01
San Rafael (city) Marin County	8	0.01
Los Angeles (city) Los Angeles County	77	<0.01
San Diego (city) San Diego County	27	<0.01

West Indian: West Indian, excluding Hispanic

Top 10 Places Sorted by Population
Based on all places, regardless of total population

Place	Population	%
Los Angeles (city) Los Angeles County	1,476	0.04
San Diego (city) San Diego County	474	0.04
Oakland (city) Alameda County	426	0.11
Long Beach (city) Los Angeles County	407	0.09
San Francisco (city) San Francisco County	208	0.03
Sacramento (city) Sacramento County	191	0.04
Ontario (city) San Bernardino County	155	0.09
Berkeley (city) Alameda County	129	0.12
Rancho Cucamonga (city) San Bernardino County	127	0.08
Santa Clarita (city) Los Angeles County	123	0.07

Top 10 Places Sorted by Percent of Total Population
Based on all places, regardless of total population

Place	Population	%
Bodfish (cdp) Kern County	59	3.04
Escalon (city) San Joaquin County	58	0.82
Rosamond (cdp) Kern County	113	0.66
Valley Center (cdp) San Diego County	55	0.61
Hercules (city) Contra Costa County	120	0.52
North Richmond (cdp) Contra Costa County	11	0.37

Place	Population	%
El Segundo (city) Los Angeles County	58	0.35
Rancho Mirage (city) Riverside County	58	0.35
Citrus (cdp) Los Angeles County	35	0.35
Lemoore (city) Kings County	81	0.34

Top 10 Places Sorted by Percent of Total Population

Based on places with total population of 50,000 or more

Place	Population	%
La Mesa (city) San Diego County	95	0.17
Rancho Cordova (city) Sacramento County	98	0.15
Pleasanton (city) Alameda County	96	0.14
Folsom (city) Sacramento County	90	0.13
Berkeley (city) Alameda County	129	0.12
Oakland (city) Alameda County	426	0.11
Lakewood (city) Los Angeles County	84	0.11
Antioch (city) Contra Costa County	97	0.10
Santa Monica (city) Los Angeles County	92	0.10
Upland (city) San Bernardino County	76	0.10

West Indian: Other, excluding Hispanic

Top 10 Places Sorted by Population

Based on all places, regardless of total population

Place	Population	%
San Jose (city) Santa Clara County	38	<0.01
San Diego (city) San Diego County	34	<0.01
Los Angeles (city) Los Angeles County	33	<0.01
Rancho Cucamonga (city) San Bernardino County	23	0.01
San Marcos (city) San Diego County	22	0.03
El Cerrito (city) Contra Costa County	21	0.09
Stockton (city) San Joaquin County	21	0.01
San Dimas (city) Los Angeles County	18	0.05
Culver City (city) Los Angeles County	17	0.04
Fullerton (city) Orange County	16	0.01

Top 10 Places Sorted by Percent of Total Population

Based on all places, regardless of total population

Place	Population	%
El Cerrito (city) Contra Costa County	21	0.09
San Dimas (city) Los Angeles County	18	0.05
Culver City (city) Los Angeles County	17	0.04
Walnut (city) Los Angeles County	12	0.04
San Marcos (city) San Diego County	22	0.03
Belmont (city) San Mateo County	6	0.02
Granite Bay (cdp) Placer County	5	0.02
Rancho Cucamonga (city) San Bernardino County	23	0.01
Stockton (city) San Joaquin County	21	0.01
Fullerton (city) Orange County	16	0.01

Top 10 Places Sorted by Percent of Total Population

Based on places with total population of 50,000 or more

Place	Population	%
San Marcos (city) San Diego County	22	0.03
Rancho Cucamonga (city) San Bernardino County	23	0.01
Stockton (city) San Joaquin County	21	0.01
Fullerton (city) Orange County	16	0.01
San Jose (city) Santa Clara County	38	<0.01
San Diego (city) San Diego County	34	<0.01
Los Angeles (city) Los Angeles County	33	<0.01
Fresno (city) Fresno County	13	<0.01
Bakersfield (city) Kern County	9	<0.01
Alameda (city) Alameda County	0	0.00

Yugoslavian

Top 10 Places Sorted by Population

Based on all places, regardless of total population

Place	Population	%
Los Angeles (city) Los Angeles County	2,313	0.06
San Jose (city) Santa Clara County	1,585	0.17
San Diego (city) San Diego County	1,142	0.09
Sacramento (city) Sacramento County	900	0.20
San Francisco (city) San Francisco County	538	0.07
Huntington Beach (city) Orange County	514	0.27
Citrus Heights (city) Sacramento County	447	0.53
Bakersfield (city) Kern County	365	0.11
Elk Grove (city) Sacramento County	358	0.25
Roseville (city) Placer County	348	0.31

Top 10 Places Sorted by Percent of Total Population

Based on all places, regardless of total population

Place	Population	%
Calpine (cdp) Sierra County	41	33.61
Leggett (cdp) Mendocino County	5	7.35
Carnelian Bay (cdp) Placer County	21	7.22
McArthur (cdp) Shasta County	7	3.26
Meridian (cdp) Sutter County	13	3.25
Columbia (cdp) Tuolumne County	73	2.92
Beckwourth (cdp) Plumas County	12	2.89
Paradise (cdp) Mono County	8	2.83
Delleker (cdp) Plumas County	15	2.68
Alta Sierra (cdp) Nevada County	176	2.51

Top 10 Places Sorted by Percent of Total Population

Based on places with total population of 50,000 or more

Place	Population	%
Rocklin (city) Placer County	299	0.55
Citrus Heights (city) Sacramento County	447	0.53
Camarillo (city) Ventura County	301	0.47
Carmichael (cdp) Sacramento County	272	0.44
Pleasanton (city) Alameda County	252	0.37
Yucaipa (city) San Bernardino County	184	0.37
Napa (city) Napa County	257	0.34
Cupertino (city) Santa Clara County	194	0.34
Roseville (city) Placer County	348	0.31
Alameda (city) Alameda County	226	0.31

Hispanic Origin Rankings

Hispanic or Latino (of any race)

Top 10 Places Sorted by Population
Based on all places, regardless of total population

Place	Population	%
Los Angeles (city) Los Angeles County	1,838,822	48.48
San Diego (city) San Diego County	376,020	28.76
San Jose (city) Santa Clara County	313,636	33.16
Santa Ana (city) Orange County	253,928	78.25
Fresno (city) Fresno County	232,055	46.91
Long Beach (city) Los Angeles County	188,412	40.76
Anaheim (city) Orange County	177,467	52.78
Bakersfield (city) Kern County	158,205	45.53
Riverside (city) Riverside County	148,953	49.02
Oxnard (city) Ventura County	145,551	73.55

Top 10 Places Sorted by Percent of Total Population
Based on all places, regardless of total population

Place	Population	%
Cantua Creek (cdp) Fresno County	461	98.93
Mecca (cdp) Riverside County	8,462	98.66
Heber (cdp) Imperial County	4,197	98.18
Linnell Camp (cdp) Tulare County	832	98.00
Oasis (cdp) Riverside County	6,731	97.69
Lost Hills (cdp) Kern County	2,354	97.60
Parlier (city) Fresno County	14,137	97.54
Maywood (city) Los Angeles County	26,696	97.45
Walnut Park (cdp) Los Angeles County	15,543	97.35
Huntington Park (city) Los Angeles County	56,445	97.13

Top 10 Places Sorted by Percent of Total Population
Based on places with total population of 50,000 or more

Place	Population	%
Huntington Park (city) Los Angeles County	56,445	97.13
East Los Angeles (cdp) Los Angeles County	122,784	97.07
South Gate (city) Los Angeles County	89,442	94.75
Pico Rivera (city) Los Angeles County	57,400	91.20
Florence-Graham (cdp) Los Angeles County	57,066	90.03
Lynwood (city) Los Angeles County	60,452	86.64
Watsonville (city) Santa Cruz County	41,656	81.36
Baldwin Park (city) Los Angeles County	60,403	80.12
Montebello (city) Los Angeles County	49,578	79.32
Paramount (city) Los Angeles County	42,547	78.65

Central American, excluding Mexican

Top 10 Places Sorted by Population
Based on all places, regardless of total population

Place	Population	%
Los Angeles (city) Los Angeles County	415,913	10.97
San Francisco (city) San Francisco County	33,834	4.20
Long Beach (city) Los Angeles County	16,486	3.57
Oakland (city) Alameda County	15,387	3.94
Palmdale (city) Los Angeles County	14,815	9.70
San Jose (city) Santa Clara County	14,697	1.55
Santa Ana (city) Orange County	11,011	3.39
Daly City (city) San Mateo County	9,813	9.70
South Gate (city) Los Angeles County	9,777	10.36
San Diego (city) San Diego County	9,188	0.70

Top 10 Places Sorted by Percent of Total Population
Based on all places, regardless of total population

Place	Population	%
Mendota (city) Fresno County	2,885	26.19
Montalvin Manor (cdp) Contra Costa County	553	19.23
Rollingwood (cdp) Contra Costa County	478	16.10
North Richmond (cdp) Contra Costa County	551	14.82
Colma (town) San Mateo County	251	14.01
Cudahy (city) Los Angeles County	3,198	13.43
San Rafael (city) Marin County	7,740	13.41
Lennox (cdp) Los Angeles County	3,045	13.38
Westmont (cdp) Los Angeles County	4,034	12.66
San Pablo (city) Contra Costa County	3,235	11.10

Top 10 Places Sorted by Percent of Total Population
Based on places with total population of 50,000 or more

Place	Population	%
San Rafael (city) Marin County	7,740	13.41
Huntington Park (city) Los Angeles County	6,404	11.02
Los Angeles (city) Los Angeles County	415,913	10.97
South Gate (city) Los Angeles County	9,777	10.36
Hawthorne (city) Los Angeles County	8,547	10.14
Palmdale (city) Los Angeles County	14,815	9.70
Daly City (city) San Mateo County	9,813	9.70
Florence-Graham (cdp) Los Angeles County	5,736	9.05
South San Francisco (city) San Mateo County	5,381	8.46
Lynwood (city) Los Angeles County	5,761	8.26

Central American: Costa Rican

Top 10 Places Sorted by Population
Based on all places, regardless of total population

Place	Population	%
Los Angeles (city) Los Angeles County	3,182	0.08
San Diego (city) San Diego County	723	0.06
San Francisco (city) San Francisco County	487	0.06
Long Beach (city) Los Angeles County	467	0.10
Anaheim (city) Orange County	296	0.09
Downey (city) Los Angeles County	263	0.24
San Jose (city) Santa Clara County	258	0.03
Riverside (city) Riverside County	249	0.08
Rancho Cucamonga (city) San Bernardino County	245	0.15
Torrance (city) Los Angeles County	218	0.15

Top 10 Places Sorted by Percent of Total Population
Based on all places, regardless of total population

Place	Population	%
Keeler (cdp) Inyo County	1	1.52
Glen Ellen (cdp) Sonoma County	6	0.77
Bodega Bay (cdp) Sonoma County	8	0.74
Santa Susana (cdp) Ventura County	7	0.68
Paradise (cdp) Mono County	1	0.65
Indio Hills (cdp) Riverside County	5	0.51
June Lake (cdp) Mono County	3	0.48
Del Aire (cdp) Los Angeles County	47	0.47
Toro Canyon (cdp) Santa Barbara County	6	0.40
California Pines (cdp) Modoc County	2	0.38

Top 10 Places Sorted by Percent of Total Population
Based on places with total population of 50,000 or more

Place	Population	%
Downey (city) Los Angeles County	263	0.24
Hawthorne (city) Los Angeles County	169	0.20
Burbank (city) Los Angeles County	199	0.19
Whittier (city) Los Angeles County	152	0.18
Rancho Cucamonga (city) San Bernardino County	245	0.15
Torrance (city) Los Angeles County	218	0.15
Norwalk (city) Los Angeles County	158	0.15
West Covina (city) Los Angeles County	145	0.14
Chino (city) San Bernardino County	106	0.14
La Habra (city) Orange County	83	0.14

Central American: Guatemalan

Top 10 Places Sorted by Population
Based on all places, regardless of total population

Place	Population	%
Los Angeles (city) Los Angeles County	138,139	3.64
San Francisco (city) San Francisco County	6,154	0.76
San Rafael (city) Marin County	5,895	10.21
Oakland (city) Alameda County	5,223	1.34
Long Beach (city) Los Angeles County	5,134	1.11
Hawthorne (city) Los Angeles County	3,669	4.35
Palmdale (city) Los Angeles County	3,618	2.37
Inglewood (city) Los Angeles County	3,593	3.28
Anaheim (city) Orange County	3,474	1.03
Riverside (city) Riverside County	3,338	1.10

Top 10 Places Sorted by Percent of Total Population
Based on all places, regardless of total population

Place	Population	%
San Rafael (city) Marin County	5,895	10.21
Lennox (cdp) Los Angeles County	1,474	6.48
Lawndale (city) Los Angeles County	1,953	5.96
Westmont (cdp) Los Angeles County	1,440	4.52
North Richmond (cdp) Contra Costa County	165	4.44
Hawthorne (city) Los Angeles County	3,669	4.35
Cudahy (city) Los Angeles County	902	3.79
North Fair Oaks (cdp) San Mateo County	552	3.76
Santa Venetia (cdp) Marin County	160	3.73
Alondra Park (cdp) Los Angeles County	315	3.67

Top 10 Places Sorted by Percent of Total Population
Based on places with total population of 50,000 or more

Place	Population	%
San Rafael (city) Marin County	5,895	10.21
Hawthorne (city) Los Angeles County	3,669	4.35
Los Angeles (city) Los Angeles County	138,139	3.64
Inglewood (city) Los Angeles County	3,593	3.28
Huntington Park (city) Los Angeles County	1,822	3.14
San Mateo (city) San Mateo County	2,755	2.83
South Gate (city) Los Angeles County	2,629	2.79
Novato (city) Marin County	1,412	2.72
Florence-Graham (cdp) Los Angeles County	1,685	2.66
Lynwood (city) Los Angeles County	1,754	2.51

Central American: Honduran

Top 10 Places Sorted by Population
Based on all places, regardless of total population

Place	Population	%
Los Angeles (city) Los Angeles County	23,919	0.63
Long Beach (city) Los Angeles County	2,696	0.58
San Francisco (city) San Francisco County	2,611	0.32
San Jose (city) Santa Clara County	1,890	0.20
San Diego (city) San Diego County	1,293	0.10
Oakland (city) Alameda County	1,160	0.30
Pasadena (city) Los Angeles County	897	0.65
Ontario (city) San Bernardino County	793	0.48
Santa Ana (city) Orange County	663	0.20
Palmdale (city) Los Angeles County	656	0.43

Top 10 Places Sorted by Percent of Total Population
Based on all places, regardless of total population

Place	Population	%
Mendota (city) Fresno County	416	3.78
Edmundson Acres (cdp) Kern County	7	2.51
Industry (city) Los Angeles County	3	1.37
Benbow (cdp) Humboldt County	4	1.25
Cudahy (city) Los Angeles County	249	1.05
Big Bend (cdp) Shasta County	1	0.98
Westmont (cdp) Los Angeles County	298	0.94
Norris Canyon (cdp) Contra Costa County	9	0.94
Lennox (cdp) Los Angeles County	206	0.91
Huntington Park (city) Los Angeles County	487	0.84

Top 10 Places Sorted by Percent of Total Population
Based on places with total population of 50,000 or more

Place	Population	%
Huntington Park (city) Los Angeles County	487	0.84
Florence-Graham (cdp) Los Angeles County	505	0.80
Hawthorne (city) Los Angeles County	584	0.69
Pasadena (city) Los Angeles County	897	0.65
Los Angeles (city) Los Angeles County	23,919	0.63
Lynwood (city) Los Angeles County	420	0.60
Inglewood (city) Los Angeles County	649	0.59
Compton (city) Los Angeles County	571	0.59
Long Beach (city) Los Angeles County	2,696	0.58
South Gate (city) Los Angeles County	507	0.54

Central American: Nicaraguan

Top 10 Places Sorted by Population

Based on all places, regardless of total population

Place	Population	%
Los Angeles (city) Los Angeles County	15,572	0.41
San Francisco (city) San Francisco County	7,604	0.94
San Jose (city) Santa Clara County	2,917	0.31
Daly City (city) San Mateo County	2,764	2.73
Hayward (city) Alameda County	1,745	1.21
South San Francisco (city) San Mateo County	1,639	2.58
Antioch (city) Contra Costa County	1,269	1.24
Richmond (city) Contra Costa County	1,209	1.17
Oakland (city) Alameda County	1,156	0.30
Fontana (city) San Bernardino County	1,152	0.59

Top 10 Places Sorted by Percent of Total Population

Based on all places, regardless of total population

Place	Population	%
Rollingwood (cdp) Contra Costa County	123	4.14
Colma (town) San Mateo County	72	4.02
Montalvin Manor (cdp) Contra Costa County	104	3.62
Big Creek (cdp) Fresno County	6	3.43
Daly City (city) San Mateo County	2,764	2.73
South San Francisco (city) San Mateo County	1,639	2.58
Broadmoor (cdp) San Mateo County	107	2.56
Darwin (cdp) Inyo County	1	2.33
Monterey Park Tract (cdp) Stanislaus County	3	2.26
San Bruno (city) San Mateo County	824	2.00

Top 10 Places Sorted by Percent of Total Population

Based on places with total population of 50,000 or more

Place	Population	%
Daly City (city) San Mateo County	2,764	2.73
South San Francisco (city) San Mateo County	1,639	2.58
Pittsburg (city) Contra Costa County	879	1.39
Antioch (city) Contra Costa County	1,269	1.24
Hayward (city) Alameda County	1,745	1.21
Richmond (city) Contra Costa County	1,209	1.17
South Gate (city) Los Angeles County	983	1.04
Downey (city) Los Angeles County	1,092	0.98
San Francisco (city) San Francisco County	7,604	0.94
San Mateo (city) San Mateo County	910	0.94

Central American: Panamanian

Top 10 Places Sorted by Population

Based on all places, regardless of total population

Place	Population	%
Los Angeles (city) Los Angeles County	2,131	0.06
San Diego (city) San Diego County	1,018	0.08
San Francisco (city) San Francisco County	399	0.05
San Jose (city) Santa Clara County	371	0.04
Sacramento (city) Sacramento County	325	0.07
Long Beach (city) Los Angeles County	313	0.07
Oakland (city) Alameda County	301	0.08
Chula Vista (city) San Diego County	203	0.08
Moreno Valley (city) Riverside County	186	0.10
Fontana (city) San Bernardino County	179	0.09

Top 10 Places Sorted by Percent of Total Population

Based on all places, regardless of total population

Place	Population	%
Vernon (city) Los Angeles County	2	1.79
Victor (cdp) San Joaquin County	4	1.37
Mono City (cdp) Mono County	2	1.16
Bombay Beach (cdp) Imperial County	2	0.68
Johannesburg (cdp) Kern County	1	0.58
McClellan Park (cdp) Sacramento County	4	0.54
North Edwards (cdp) Kern County	5	0.47
View Park-Windsor Hills (cdp) Los Angeles County	39	0.35
Edwards AFB (cdp) Kern County	7	0.34
Stirling City (cdp) Butte County	1	0.34

Top 10 Places Sorted by Percent of Total Population

Based on places with total population of 50,000 or more

Place	Population	%
Hawthorne (city) Los Angeles County	130	0.15
La Mesa (city) San Diego County	75	0.13
Pasadena (city) Los Angeles County	170	0.12
Murrieta (city) Riverside County	121	0.12
Elk Grove (city) Sacramento County	175	0.11
Lancaster (city) Los Angeles County	170	0.11
Inglewood (city) Los Angeles County	119	0.11
Moreno Valley (city) Riverside County	186	0.10
Oceanside (city) San Diego County	175	0.10
Concord (city) Contra Costa County	119	0.10

Central American: Salvadoran

Top 10 Places Sorted by Population

Based on all places, regardless of total population

Place	Population	%
Los Angeles (city) Los Angeles County	228,990	6.04
San Francisco (city) San Francisco County	16,165	2.01
Palmdale (city) Los Angeles County	9,488	6.21
Oakland (city) Alameda County	7,246	1.85
San Jose (city) Santa Clara County	6,829	0.72
Long Beach (city) Los Angeles County	6,657	1.44
Santa Ana (city) Orange County	6,389	1.97
South Gate (city) Los Angeles County	5,407	5.73
Daly City (city) San Mateo County	5,000	4.94
Richmond (city) Contra Costa County	4,888	4.71

Top 10 Places Sorted by Percent of Total Population

Based on all places, regardless of total population

Place	Population	%
Mendota (city) Fresno County	2,411	21.89
Montalvin Manor (cdp) Contra Costa County	329	11.44
Rollingwood (cdp) Contra Costa County	257	8.66
North Richmond (cdp) Contra Costa County	316	8.50
Colma (town) San Mateo County	128	7.14
Cudahy (city) Los Angeles County	1,634	6.86
San Pablo (city) Contra Costa County	1,908	6.55
Westmont (cdp) Los Angeles County	2,044	6.42
Palmdale (city) Los Angeles County	9,488	6.21
Los Angeles (city) Los Angeles County	228,990	6.04

Top 10 Places Sorted by Percent of Total Population

Based on places with total population of 50,000 or more

Place	Population	%
Palmdale (city) Los Angeles County	9,488	6.21
Los Angeles (city) Los Angeles County	228,990	6.04
Huntington Park (city) Los Angeles County	3,381	5.82
South Gate (city) Los Angeles County	5,407	5.73
Florence-Graham (cdp) Los Angeles County	3,239	5.11
Daly City (city) San Mateo County	5,000	4.94
Richmond (city) Contra Costa County	4,888	4.71
South San Francisco (city) San Mateo County	2,897	4.55
Lynwood (city) Los Angeles County	3,154	4.52
Hawthorne (city) Los Angeles County	3,335	3.96

Central American: Other Central American

Top 10 Places Sorted by Population

Based on all places, regardless of total population

Place	Population	%
Los Angeles (city) Los Angeles County	3,980	0.10
San Francisco (city) San Francisco County	414	0.05
Long Beach (city) Los Angeles County	212	0.05
Oakland (city) Alameda County	156	0.04
San Diego (city) San Diego County	148	0.01
San Jose (city) Santa Clara County	138	0.01
South Gate (city) Los Angeles County	136	0.14
Compton (city) Los Angeles County	114	0.12
Santa Ana (city) Orange County	113	0.03
Santa Clarita (city) Los Angeles County	108	0.06

Top 10 Places Sorted by Percent of Total Population

Based on all places, regardless of total population

Place	Population	%
Loma Mar (cdp) San Mateo County	1	0.88
Camanche Village (cdp) Amador County	3	0.35
Independence (cdp) Inyo County	2	0.30
Idyllwild-Pine Cove (cdp) Riverside County	11	0.28
Lagunitas-Forest Knolls (cdp) Marin County	5	0.27
Buttonwillow (cdp) Kern County	4	0.27
Broadmoor (cdp) San Mateo County	10	0.24
Covelo (cdp) Mendocino County	3	0.24
Westmont (cdp) Los Angeles County	70	0.22
Colma (town) San Mateo County	4	0.22

Top 10 Places Sorted by Percent of Total Population

Based on places with total population of 50,000 or more

Place	Population	%
Florence-Graham (cdp) Los Angeles County	96	0.15
South Gate (city) Los Angeles County	136	0.14
Compton (city) Los Angeles County	114	0.12
Hawthorne (city) Los Angeles County	104	0.12
Huntington Park (city) Los Angeles County	71	0.12
Lynwood (city) Los Angeles County	78	0.11
Los Angeles (city) Los Angeles County	3,980	0.10
Baldwin Park (city) Los Angeles County	67	0.09
Daly City (city) San Mateo County	80	0.08
Pico Rivera (city) Los Angeles County	50	0.08

Cuban

Top 10 Places Sorted by Population

Based on all places, regardless of total population

Place	Population	%
Los Angeles (city) Los Angeles County	13,494	0.36
San Diego (city) San Diego County	2,694	0.21
Downey (city) Los Angeles County	2,283	2.04
San Francisco (city) San Francisco County	1,992	0.25
Glendale (city) Los Angeles County	1,513	0.79
Long Beach (city) Los Angeles County	1,264	0.27
San Jose (city) Santa Clara County	1,194	0.13
Burbank (city) Los Angeles County	1,087	1.05
Santa Clarita (city) Los Angeles County	1,053	0.60
Anaheim (city) Orange County	945	0.28

Top 10 Places Sorted by Percent of Total Population

Based on all places, regardless of total population

Place	Population	%
Del Aire (cdp) Los Angeles County	219	2.19
Bell (city) Los Angeles County	774	2.18
Downey (city) Los Angeles County	2,283	2.04
Waukena (cdp) Tulare County	2	1.85
Greenhorn (cdp) Plumas County	4	1.69
Herlong (cdp) Lassen County	4	1.34
Bradbury (city) Los Angeles County	12	1.15
Culver City (city) Los Angeles County	414	1.06
Burbank (city) Los Angeles County	1,087	1.05
Weott (cdp) Humboldt County	3	1.04

Top 10 Places Sorted by Percent of Total Population

Based on places with total population of 50,000 or more

Place	Population	%
Downey (city) Los Angeles County	2,283	2.04
Burbank (city) Los Angeles County	1,087	1.05
Hawthorne (city) Los Angeles County	752	0.89
South Gate (city) Los Angeles County	754	0.80
Glendale (city) Los Angeles County	1,513	0.79
Huntington Park (city) Los Angeles County	442	0.76
Torrance (city) Los Angeles County	882	0.61
Santa Clarita (city) Los Angeles County	1,053	0.60
Eastvale (cdp) Riverside County	277	0.52
Glendora (city) Los Angeles County	259	0.52

Dominican Republic

Top 10 Places Sorted by Population

Based on all places, regardless of total population

Place	Population	%
Los Angeles (city) Los Angeles County	1,602	0.04
San Diego (city) San Diego County	903	0.07
San Francisco (city) San Francisco County	289	0.04
San Jose (city) Santa Clara County	235	0.02
Long Beach (city) Los Angeles County	194	0.04
Chula Vista (city) San Diego County	193	0.08
Sacramento (city) Sacramento County	190	0.04
Oakland (city) Alameda County	183	0.05
Oceanside (city) San Diego County	154	0.09
Anaheim (city) Orange County	114	0.03

Top 10 Places Sorted by Percent of Total Population

Based on all places, regardless of total population

Place	Population	%
Mono City (cdp) Mono County	2	1.16
Monterey Park Tract (cdp) Stanislaus County	1	0.75
Carnelian Bay (cdp) Placer County	3	0.57

Place	Population	%
San Pasqual (cdp) Los Angeles County	10	0.49
Beale AFB (cdp) Yuba County	6	0.45
Fort Irwin (cdp) San Bernardino County	39	0.44
Mesa Verde (cdp) Riverside County	3	0.29
McClellan Park (cdp) Sacramento County	2	0.27
Lemoore Station (cdp) Kings County	19	0.26
Camp Pendleton South (cdp) San Diego County	24	0.23

Top 10 Places Sorted by Percent of Total Population
Based on places with total population of 50,000 or more

Place	Population	%
La Mesa (city) San Diego County	59	0.10
Oceanside (city) San Diego County	154	0.09
National City (city) San Diego County	54	0.09
Chula Vista (city) San Diego County	193	0.08
Temecula (city) Riverside County	77	0.08
Lakewood (city) Los Angeles County	63	0.08
San Diego (city) San Diego County	903	0.07
Inglewood (city) Los Angeles County	74	0.07
Hawthorne (city) Los Angeles County	55	0.07
Downey (city) Los Angeles County	70	0.06

Mexican

Top 10 Places Sorted by Population
Based on all places, regardless of total population

Place	Population	%
Los Angeles (city) Los Angeles County	1,209,573	31.89
San Diego (city) San Diego County	325,812	24.92
San Jose (city) Santa Clara County	268,538	28.39
Santa Ana (city) Orange County	230,381	70.99
Fresno (city) Fresno County	211,431	42.74
Anaheim (city) Orange County	154,554	45.96
Long Beach (city) Los Angeles County	151,983	32.88
Bakersfield (city) Kern County	137,102	39.46
Oxnard (city) Ventura County	136,991	69.22
Chula Vista (city) San Diego County	130,413	53.47

Top 10 Places Sorted by Percent of Total Population
Based on all places, regardless of total population

Place	Population	%
Cantua Creek (cdp) Fresno County	450	96.57
Lost Hills (cdp) Kern County	2,310	95.77
Heber (cdp) Imperial County	4,084	95.53
Chualar (cdp) Monterey County	1,135	95.38
Calexico (city) Imperial County	36,443	94.48
Three Rocks (cdp) Fresno County	232	94.31
Oasis (cdp) Riverside County	6,493	94.24
Rodriguez Camp (cdp) Tulare County	147	94.23
Planada (cdp) Merced County	4,260	92.93
Parlier (city) Fresno County	13,445	92.76

Top 10 Places Sorted by Percent of Total Population
Based on places with total population of 50,000 or more

Place	Population	%
East Los Angeles (cdp) Los Angeles County	111,441	88.10
Pico Rivera (city) Los Angeles County	51,337	81.56
Huntington Park (city) Los Angeles County	46,467	79.96
South Gate (city) Los Angeles County	73,677	78.05
Watsonville (city) Santa Cruz County	39,083	76.34
Florence-Graham (cdp) Los Angeles County	47,862	75.51
Lynwood (city) Los Angeles County	51,021	73.13
Madera (city) Madera County	44,444	72.37
Santa Ana (city) Orange County	230,381	70.99
Baldwin Park (city) Los Angeles County	52,803	70.04

Puerto Rican

Top 10 Places Sorted by Population
Based on all places, regardless of total population

Place	Population	%
Los Angeles (city) Los Angeles County	15,565	0.41
San Diego (city) San Diego County	8,220	0.63
San Jose (city) Santa Clara County	4,763	0.50
San Francisco (city) San Francisco County	4,204	0.52
Sacramento (city) Sacramento County	3,344	0.72
Long Beach (city) Los Angeles County	3,025	0.65
Oakland (city) Alameda County	2,737	0.70
Chula Vista (city) San Diego County	2,282	0.94
Hayward (city) Alameda County	2,232	1.55
Riverside (city) Riverside County	2,115	0.70

Top 10 Places Sorted by Percent of Total Population
Based on all places, regardless of total population

Place	Population	%
Paxton (cdp) Plumas County	1	7.14
Robinson Mill (cdp) Butte County	3	3.75
Coulterville (cdp) Mariposa County	7	3.48
Fort Irwin (cdp) San Bernardino County	291	3.29
Edwards AFB (cdp) Kern County	53	2.57
Camp Pendleton North (cdp) San Diego County	133	2.56
Camp Pendleton South (cdp) San Diego County	261	2.46
Centerville (cdp) Fresno County	9	2.30
Coleville (cdp) Mono County	11	2.22
Beale AFB (cdp) Yuba County	28	2.12

Top 10 Places Sorted by Percent of Total Population
Based on places with total population of 50,000 or more

Place	Population	%
Hayward (city) Alameda County	2,232	1.55
Pittsburg (city) Contra Costa County	890	1.41
Manteca (city) San Joaquin County	844	1.26
Brentwood (city) Contra Costa County	618	1.20
Antioch (city) Contra Costa County	1,204	1.18
Fairfield (city) Solano County	1,184	1.12
Tracy (city) San Joaquin County	906	1.09
Castro Valley (cdp) Alameda County	665	1.08
Victorville (city) San Bernardino County	1,218	1.05
Murrieta (city) Riverside County	1,025	0.99

South American

Top 10 Places Sorted by Population
Based on all places, regardless of total population

Place	Population	%
Los Angeles (city) Los Angeles County	49,352	1.30
San Francisco (city) San Francisco County	8,618	1.07
San Diego (city) San Diego County	8,220	0.63
San Jose (city) Santa Clara County	6,035	0.64
Long Beach (city) Los Angeles County	4,123	0.89
Anaheim (city) Orange County	3,763	1.12
Downey (city) Los Angeles County	3,506	3.14
Santa Clarita (city) Los Angeles County	3,311	1.88
Glendale (city) Los Angeles County	3,287	1.71
Rancho Cucamonga (city) San Bernardino County2,823 1.71		

Top 10 Places Sorted by Percent of Total Population
Based on all places, regardless of total population

Place	Population	%
Paxton (cdp) Plumas County	1	7.14
Rutherford (cdp) Napa County	7	4.27
El Rancho (cdp) Tulare County	5	4.03
Eagleville (cdp) Modoc County	2	3.39
Lawndale (city) Los Angeles County	1,092	3.33
Del Aire (cdp) Los Angeles County	330	3.30
Downey (city) Los Angeles County	3,506	3.14
Coffee Creek (cdp) Trinity County	6	2.76
Edna (cdp) San Luis Obispo County	5	2.59
Burbank (city) Los Angeles County	2,548	2.47

Top 10 Places Sorted by Percent of Total Population
Based on places with total population of 50,000 or more

Place	Population	%
Downey (city) Los Angeles County	3,506	3.14
Burbank (city) Los Angeles County	2,548	2.47
San Mateo (city) San Mateo County	2,228	2.29
Hawthorne (city) Los Angeles County	1,826	2.17
Tustin (city) Orange County	1,443	1.91
Santa Clarita (city) Los Angeles County	3,311	1.88
Lake Forest (city) Orange County	1,430	1.85
Redondo Beach (city) Los Angeles County	1,230	1.84
Torrance (city) Los Angeles County	2,540	1.75
Glendale (city) Los Angeles County	3,287	1.71

South American: Argentinean

Top 10 Places Sorted by Population
Based on all places, regardless of total population

Place	Population	%
Los Angeles (city) Los Angeles County	8,570	0.23
San Diego (city) San Diego County	1,322	0.10
San Francisco (city) San Francisco County	1,100	0.14
San Jose (city) Santa Clara County	666	0.07
Long Beach (city) Los Angeles County	650	0.14
Santa Clarita (city) Los Angeles County	621	0.35
Rancho Cucamonga (city) San Bernardino County	561	0.34
Glendale (city) Los Angeles County	539	0.28
Anaheim (city) Orange County	519	0.15
Irvine (city) Orange County	440	0.21

Top 10 Places Sorted by Percent of Total Population
Based on all places, regardless of total population

Place	Population	%
Edna (cdp) San Luis Obispo County	5	2.59
Rutherford (cdp) Napa County	3	1.83
Soda Springs (cdp) Nevada County	1	1.23
Bradbury (city) Los Angeles County	10	0.95
Oak Glen (cdp) San Bernardino County	6	0.94
Whitewater (cdp) Riverside County	6	0.70
Kirkwood (cdp) Alpine County	1	0.63
Las Flores (cdp) Orange County	36	0.60
California Pines (cdp) Modoc County	3	0.58
North El Monte (cdp) Los Angeles County	20	0.54

Top 10 Places Sorted by Percent of Total Population
Based on places with total population of 50,000 or more

Place	Population	%
Burbank (city) Los Angeles County	406	0.39
Downey (city) Los Angeles County	429	0.38
Santa Clarita (city) Los Angeles County	621	0.35
Redondo Beach (city) Los Angeles County	232	0.35
Rancho Cucamonga (city) San Bernardino County	561	0.34
Mission Viejo (city) Orange County	313	0.34
Lake Forest (city) Orange County	261	0.34
Santa Monica (city) Los Angeles County	271	0.30
Upland (city) San Bernardino County	222	0.30
Pasadena (city) Los Angeles County	404	0.29

South American: Bolivian

Top 10 Places Sorted by Population
Based on all places, regardless of total population

Place	Population	%
Los Angeles (city) Los Angeles County	2,561	0.07
San Jose (city) Santa Clara County	459	0.05
San Francisco (city) San Francisco County	416	0.05
Santa Ana (city) Orange County	398	0.12
San Diego (city) San Diego County	345	0.03
Tustin (city) Orange County	285	0.38
Anaheim (city) Orange County	211	0.06
Burbank (city) Los Angeles County	208	0.20
Orange (city) Orange County	157	0.12
Glendale (city) Los Angeles County	150	0.08

Top 10 Places Sorted by Percent of Total Population
Based on all places, regardless of total population

Place	Population	%
Tuttle (cdp) Merced County	2	1.94
Pajaro Dunes (cdp) Santa Cruz County	2	1.39
Lake of the Woods (cdp) Kern County	4	0.44
Clyde (cdp) Contra Costa County	3	0.44
Tustin (city) Orange County	285	0.38
Diablo (cdp) Contra Costa County	4	0.35
Upper Lake (cdp) Lake County	3	0.29
Bloomfield (cdp) Sonoma County	1	0.29
Temelec (cdp) Sonoma County	4	0.28
Centerville (cdp) Fresno County	1	0.26

Top 10 Places Sorted by Percent of Total Population
Based on places with total population of 50,000 or more

Place	Population	%
Tustin (city) Orange County	285	0.38
Burbank (city) Los Angeles County	208	0.20
San Mateo (city) San Mateo County	131	0.13
Santa Ana (city) Orange County	398	0.12
Orange (city) Orange County	157	0.12
Downey (city) Los Angeles County	134	0.12
Redwood City (city) San Mateo County	90	0.12
Lake Forest (city) Orange County	85	0.11
Santa Clara (city) Santa Clara County	105	0.09
Daly City (city) San Mateo County	87	0.09

South American: Chilean

Top 10 Places Sorted by Population
Based on all places, regardless of total population

Place	Population	%
Los Angeles (city) Los Angeles County	4,112	0.11
San Diego (city) San Diego County	876	0.07
San Francisco (city) San Francisco County	754	0.09
San Jose (city) Santa Clara County	632	0.07
Oakland (city) Alameda County	297	0.08
Long Beach (city) Los Angeles County	288	0.06
Santa Clarita (city) Los Angeles County	284	0.16
San Mateo (city) San Mateo County	258	0.27
Riverside (city) Riverside County	236	0.08
Glendale (city) Los Angeles County	230	0.12

Top 10 Places Sorted by Percent of Total Population
Based on all places, regardless of total population

Place	Population	%
Coffee Creek (cdp) Trinity County	6	2.76
Strawberry (cdp) Tuolumne County	2	2.33
Eagleville (cdp) Modoc County	1	1.69
Oak Shores (cdp) San Luis Obispo County	3	0.89
Albany (city) Alameda County	112	0.60
Stanford (cdp) Santa Clara County	81	0.59
Scotia (cdp) Humboldt County	5	0.59
Fieldbrook (cdp) Humboldt County	5	0.58
University of California Davis (cdp) Yolo County	31	0.54
Amador City (city) Amador County	1	0.54

Top 10 Places Sorted by Percent of Total Population
Based on places with total population of 50,000 or more

Place	Population	%
San Mateo (city) San Mateo County	258	0.27
Davis (city) Yolo County	123	0.19
Berkeley (city) Alameda County	201	0.18
Santa Clarita (city) Los Angeles County	284	0.16
Burbank (city) Los Angeles County	165	0.16
Redondo Beach (city) Los Angeles County	104	0.16
Torrance (city) Los Angeles County	221	0.15
Santa Monica (city) Los Angeles County	131	0.15
Richmond (city) Contra Costa County	136	0.13
Walnut Creek (city) Contra Costa County	86	0.13

South American: Colombian

Top 10 Places Sorted by Population
Based on all places, regardless of total population

Place	Population	%
Los Angeles (city) Los Angeles County	9,766	0.26
San Diego (city) San Diego County	2,214	0.17
San Francisco (city) San Francisco County	1,717	0.21
San Jose (city) Santa Clara County	1,266	0.13
Long Beach (city) Los Angeles County	1,037	0.22
Anaheim (city) Orange County	884	0.26
Glendale (city) Los Angeles County	841	0.44
Santa Clarita (city) Los Angeles County	773	0.44
Downey (city) Los Angeles County	733	0.66
Rancho Cucamonga (city) San Bernardino County	694	0.42

Top 10 Places Sorted by Percent of Total Population
Based on all places, regardless of total population

Place	Population	%
Paxton (cdp) Plumas County	1	7.14
Manchester (cdp) Mendocino County	3	1.54
Canby (cdp) Modoc County	4	1.27
Washington (cdp) Nevada County	2	1.08
Sand City (city) Monterey County	3	0.90
Del Aire (cdp) Los Angeles County	87	0.87
Rolling Hills (city) Los Angeles County	14	0.75
Downey (city) Los Angeles County	733	0.66
Burbank (city) Los Angeles County	677	0.66
Boulevard (cdp) San Diego County	2	0.63

Top 10 Places Sorted by Percent of Total Population
Based on places with total population of 50,000 or more

Place	Population	%
Downey (city) Los Angeles County	733	0.66
Burbank (city) Los Angeles County	677	0.66
Lake Forest (city) Orange County	454	0.59
Hawthorne (city) Los Angeles County	487	0.58
Mission Viejo (city) Orange County	446	0.48
Glendale (city) Los Angeles County	841	0.44
Santa Clarita (city) Los Angeles County	773	0.44
Rancho Cucamonga (city) San Bernardino County	694	0.42
Simi Valley (city) Ventura County	502	0.40
Pasadena (city) Los Angeles County	540	0.39

South American: Ecuadorian

Top 10 Places Sorted by Population
Based on all places, regardless of total population

Place	Population	%
Los Angeles (city) Los Angeles County	7,314	0.19
San Diego (city) San Diego County	737	0.06
Long Beach (city) Los Angeles County	679	0.15
Downey (city) Los Angeles County	678	0.61
San Francisco (city) San Francisco County	577	0.07
Glendale (city) Los Angeles County	542	0.28
Santa Clarita (city) Los Angeles County	509	0.29
Anaheim (city) Orange County	417	0.12
Fontana (city) San Bernardino County	415	0.21
Rancho Cucamonga (city) San Bernardino County	399	0.24

Top 10 Places Sorted by Percent of Total Population
Based on all places, regardless of total population

Place	Population	%
Downey (city) Los Angeles County	678	0.61
Del Aire (cdp) Los Angeles County	61	0.61
Lawndale (city) Los Angeles County	191	0.58
Crestmore Heights (cdp) Riverside County	2	0.52
Alondra Park (cdp) Los Angeles County	40	0.47
Santa Fe Springs (city) Los Angeles County	71	0.44
Fruitdale (cdp) Santa Clara County	4	0.43
Patton Village (cdp) Lassen County	3	0.43
Vina (cdp) Tehama County	1	0.42
Covina (city) Los Angeles County	186	0.39

Top 10 Places Sorted by Percent of Total Population
Based on places with total population of 50,000 or more

Place	Population	%
Downey (city) Los Angeles County	678	0.61
South Gate (city) Los Angeles County	348	0.37
Burbank (city) Los Angeles County	376	0.36
Hawthorne (city) Los Angeles County	280	0.33
Norwalk (city) Los Angeles County	325	0.31
Alhambra (city) Los Angeles County	249	0.30
Gardena (city) Los Angeles County	176	0.30
Santa Clarita (city) Los Angeles County	509	0.29
Glendale (city) Los Angeles County	542	0.28
West Covina (city) Los Angeles County	302	0.28

South American: Paraguayan

Top 10 Places Sorted by Population
Based on all places, regardless of total population

Place	Population	%
Los Angeles (city) Los Angeles County	180	<0.01
San Diego (city) San Diego County	52	<0.01
San Francisco (city) San Francisco County	43	0.01
San Jose (city) Santa Clara County	31	<0.01
Glendale (city) Los Angeles County	20	0.01
Vallejo (city) Solano County	16	0.01
Pacific Grove (city) Monterey County	15	0.10
Walnut Creek (city) Contra Costa County	15	0.02
Whittier (city) Los Angeles County	15	0.02
Carlsbad (city) San Diego County	14	0.01

Top 10 Places Sorted by Percent of Total Population
Based on all places, regardless of total population

Place	Population	%
Shell Ridge (cdp) Contra Costa County	3	0.31
Saranap (cdp) Contra Costa County	9	0.17
Stinson Beach (cdp) Marin County	1	0.16
Yountville (city) Napa County	4	0.14
Pacific Grove (city) Monterey County	15	0.10
Granite Hills (cdp) San Diego County	3	0.10
Bradbury (city) Los Angeles County	1	0.10
Borrego Springs (cdp) San Diego County	3	0.09
Talmage (cdp) Mendocino County	1	0.09
Los Ranchos (cdp) San Luis Obispo County	1	0.07

Top 10 Places Sorted by Percent of Total Population
Based on places with total population of 50,000 or more

Place	Population	%
Walnut Creek (city) Contra Costa County	15	0.02
Whittier (city) Los Angeles County	15	0.02
Montebello (city) Los Angeles County	10	0.02
Lake Elsinore (city) Riverside County	9	0.02
San Francisco (city) San Francisco County	43	0.01
Glendale (city) Los Angeles County	20	0.01
Vallejo (city) Solano County	16	0.01
Carlsbad (city) San Diego County	14	0.01
Vacaville (city) Solano County	13	0.01
Santa Rosa (city) Sonoma County	11	0.01

South American: Peruvian

Top 10 Places Sorted by Population
Based on all places, regardless of total population

Place	Population	%
Los Angeles (city) Los Angeles County	14,033	0.37
San Francisco (city) San Francisco County	3,260	0.40
San Jose (city) Santa Clara County	2,128	0.22
San Diego (city) San Diego County	1,901	0.15
Anaheim (city) Orange County	1,365	0.41
Downey (city) Los Angeles County	1,277	1.14
San Mateo (city) San Mateo County	1,163	1.20
Long Beach (city) Los Angeles County	1,109	0.24
Concord (city) Contra Costa County	1,056	0.87
Torrance (city) Los Angeles County	955	0.66

Top 10 Places Sorted by Percent of Total Population
Based on all places, regardless of total population

Place	Population	%
El Rancho (cdp) Tulare County	5	4.03
Rutherford (cdp) Napa County	4	2.44
Fort Bidwell (cdp) Modoc County	3	1.73
Eagleville (cdp) Modoc County	1	1.69
Richvale (cdp) Butte County	4	1.64
Lawndale (city) Los Angeles County	525	1.60
Derby Acres (cdp) Kern County	5	1.55
San Mateo (city) San Mateo County	1,163	1.20
Broadmoor (cdp) San Mateo County	48	1.15
Downey (city) Los Angeles County	1,277	1.14

Top 10 Places Sorted by Percent of Total Population
Based on places with total population of 50,000 or more

Place	Population	%
San Mateo (city) San Mateo County	1,163	1.20
Downey (city) Los Angeles County	1,277	1.14
Novato (city) Marin County	496	0.96
Hawthorne (city) Los Angeles County	768	0.91
Concord (city) Contra Costa County	1,056	0.87
Redwood City (city) San Mateo County	578	0.75
Gardena (city) Los Angeles County	439	0.75
Antioch (city) Contra Costa County	748	0.73
Daly City (city) San Mateo County	738	0.73
South San Francisco (city) San Mateo County	424	0.67

South American: Uruguayan

Top 10 Places Sorted by Population
Based on all places, regardless of total population

Place	Population	%
Los Angeles (city) Los Angeles County	697	0.02
San Diego (city) San Diego County	141	0.01
San Francisco (city) San Francisco County	118	0.01
Anaheim (city) Orange County	66	0.02
Fontana (city) San Bernardino County	54	0.03
Glendale (city) Los Angeles County	53	0.03
Long Beach (city) Los Angeles County	51	0.01
Santa Clarita (city) Los Angeles County	47	0.03
Santa Ana (city) Orange County	47	0.01
San Jose (city) Santa Clara County	45	<0.01

Top 10 Places Sorted by Percent of Total Population
Based on all places, regardless of total population

Place	Population	%
Alhambra Valley (cdp) Contra Costa County	4	0.43
Byron (cdp) Contra Costa County	5	0.39
Desert View Highlands (cdp) Los Angeles County	9	0.38

Place	Population	%
Ridgemark (cdp) San Benito County	4	0.13
Lake of the Woods (cdp) Kern County	1	0.11
Malaga (cdp) Fresno County	1	0.11
Lake California (cdp) Tehama County	3	0.10
Contra Costa Centre (cdp) Contra Costa County	5	0.09
Forestville (cdp) Sonoma County	3	0.09
Boron (cdp) Kern County	2	0.09

Top 10 Places Sorted by Percent of Total Population
Based on places with total population of 50,000 or more

Place	Population	%
Novato (city) Marin County	32	0.06
Santa Monica (city) Los Angeles County	36	0.04
Redondo Beach (city) Los Angeles County	29	0.04
Tustin (city) Orange County	29	0.04
Cathedral City (city) Riverside County	22	0.04
Fontana (city) San Bernardino County	54	0.03
Glendale (city) Los Angeles County	53	0.03
Santa Clarita (city) Los Angeles County	47	0.03
Costa Mesa (city) Orange County	35	0.03
Downey (city) Los Angeles County	29	0.03

South American: Venezuelan

Top 10 Places Sorted by Population
Based on all places, regardless of total population

Place	Population	%
Los Angeles (city) Los Angeles County	1,490	0.04
San Diego (city) San Diego County	525	0.04
San Francisco (city) San Francisco County	496	0.06
San Jose (city) Santa Clara County	350	0.04
Bakersfield (city) Kern County	259	0.07
Oakland (city) Alameda County	176	0.05
Long Beach (city) Los Angeles County	123	0.03
Sacramento (city) Sacramento County	118	0.03
Irvine (city) Orange County	115	0.05
Santa Monica (city) Los Angeles County	107	0.12

Top 10 Places Sorted by Percent of Total Population
Based on all places, regardless of total population

Place	Population	%
Loma Mar (cdp) San Mateo County	1	0.88
Madison (cdp) Yolo County	3	0.60
Lake Almanor West (cdp) Plumas County	1	0.37
Fields Landing (cdp) Humboldt County	1	0.36
Corralitos (cdp) Santa Cruz County	7	0.30
Minkler (cdp) Fresno County	3	0.30
Doyle (cdp) Lassen County	2	0.29
Lytle Creek (cdp) San Bernardino County	2	0.29
San Juan Bautista (city) San Benito County	5	0.27
Aguanga (cdp) Riverside County	2	0.18

Top 10 Places Sorted by Percent of Total Population
Based on places with total population of 50,000 or more

Place	Population	%
Santa Monica (city) Los Angeles County	107	0.12
Redondo Beach (city) Los Angeles County	61	0.09
Davis (city) Yolo County	58	0.09
Berkeley (city) Alameda County	91	0.08
Bakersfield (city) Kern County	259	0.07
Pasadena (city) Los Angeles County	100	0.07
Santa Clara (city) Santa Clara County	79	0.07
Palo Alto (city) Santa Clara County	44	0.07
Encinitas (city) San Diego County	39	0.07
San Francisco (city) San Francisco County	496	0.06

South American: Other South American

Top 10 Places Sorted by Population
Based on all places, regardless of total population

Place	Population	%
Los Angeles (city) Los Angeles County	629	0.02
San Francisco (city) San Francisco County	137	0.02
San Diego (city) San Diego County	107	0.01
San Jose (city) Santa Clara County	90	0.01
Santa Clarita (city) Los Angeles County	59	0.03
Long Beach (city) Los Angeles County	49	0.01
Rancho Cucamonga (city) San Bernardino County	47	0.03
Oakland (city) Alameda County	44	0.01
Fullerton (city) Orange County	43	0.03
Torrance (city) Los Angeles County	42	0.03

Top 10 Places Sorted by Percent of Total Population
Based on all places, regardless of total population

Place	Population	%
Moskowite Corner (cdp) Napa County	2	0.95
Castle Hill (cdp) Contra Costa County	4	0.31
Rough and Ready (cdp) Nevada County	3	0.31
Clarksburg (cdp) Yolo County	1	0.24
Alturas (city) Modoc County	5	0.18
Spreckels (cdp) Monterey County	1	0.15
Graton (cdp) Sonoma County	2	0.12
Armona (cdp) Kings County	4	0.10
Lake California (cdp) Tehama County	3	0.10
Belvedere (city) Marin County	2	0.10

Top 10 Places Sorted by Percent of Total Population
Based on places with total population of 50,000 or more

Place	Population	%
San Mateo (city) San Mateo County	39	0.04
Santa Clarita (city) Los Angeles County	59	0.03
Rancho Cucamonga (city) San Bernardino County	47	0.03
Fullerton (city) Orange County	43	0.03
Torrance (city) Los Angeles County	42	0.03
Downey (city) Los Angeles County	35	0.03
Daly City (city) San Mateo County	33	0.03
Burbank (city) Los Angeles County	31	0.03
Santa Monica (city) Los Angeles County	23	0.03
Redwood City (city) San Mateo County	22	0.03

Other Hispanic or Latino

Top 10 Places Sorted by Population
Based on all places, regardless of total population

Place	Population	%
Los Angeles (city) Los Angeles County	133,323	3.52
San Diego (city) San Diego County	20,983	1.60
San Jose (city) Santa Clara County	18,174	1.92
Fresno (city) Fresno County	13,849	2.80
San Francisco (city) San Francisco County	13,162	1.63
Long Beach (city) Los Angeles County	11,337	2.45
Bakersfield (city) Kern County	9,517	2.74
Santa Ana (city) Orange County	9,024	2.78
Sacramento (city) Sacramento County	8,674	1.86
Riverside (city) Riverside County	8,353	2.75

Top 10 Places Sorted by Percent of Total Population
Based on all places, regardless of total population

Place	Population	%
Bucks Lake (cdp) Plumas County	3	30.00
California City (city) Kern County	2,790	19.76
French Camp (cdp) San Joaquin County	490	14.51
Seeley (cdp) Imperial County	195	11.21
Sugarloaf Saw Mill (cdp) Tulare County	2	11.11
Fuller Acres (cdp) Kern County	100	10.09
Avenal (city) Kings County	1,486	9.58
Yolo (cdp) Yolo County	40	8.89
Monson (cdp) Tulare County	16	8.51
Sultana (cdp) Tulare County	65	8.39

Top 10 Places Sorted by Percent of Total Population
Based on places with total population of 50,000 or more

Place	Population	%
Florence-Graham (cdp) Los Angeles County	3,154	4.98
Delano (city) Kern County	2,583	4.87
Lynwood (city) Los Angeles County	3,006	4.31
Huntington Park (city) Los Angeles County	2,484	4.27
Palmdale (city) Los Angeles County	6,233	4.08
Lancaster (city) Los Angeles County	6,340	4.05
Hawthorne (city) Los Angeles County	3,332	3.95
San Bernardino (city) San Bernardino County	8,199	3.91
Watsonville (city) Santa Cruz County	1,994	3.89
Hesperia (city) San Bernardino County	3,423	3.80

Racial Group Rankings

African-American/Black

Top 10 Places Sorted by Population

Based on all places, regardless of total population

Place	Population	%
Los Angeles (city) Los Angeles County	402,448	10.61
Oakland (city) Alameda County	119,122	30.49
San Diego (city) San Diego County	104,374	7.98
Sacramento (city) Sacramento County	80,469	17.25
Long Beach (city) Los Angeles County	69,744	15.09
San Francisco (city) San Francisco County	57,810	7.18
Inglewood (city) Los Angeles County	50,219	45.79
Fresno (city) Fresno County	46,895	9.48
Stockton (city) San Joaquin County	41,432	14.20
Moreno Valley (city) Riverside County	39,019	20.18

Top 10 Places Sorted by Percent of Total Population

Based on all places, regardless of total population

Place	Population	%
View Park-Windsor Hills (cdp) Los Angeles County	9,907	89.45
Ladera Heights (cdp) Los Angeles County	5,079	78.16
West Athens (cdp) Los Angeles County	4,726	54.14
West Rancho Dominguez (cdp) Los Angeles County	3,055	53.89
Westmont (cdp) Los Angeles County	16,791	52.71
Inglewood (city) Los Angeles County	50,219	45.79
Marin City (cdp) Marin County	1,109	41.60
Willowbrook (cdp) Los Angeles County	12,749	35.43
North Richmond (cdp) Contra Costa County	1,294	34.81
Compton (city) Los Angeles County	32,800	34.01

Top 10 Places Sorted by Percent of Total Population

Based on places with total population of 50,000 or more

Place	Population	%
Inglewood (city) Los Angeles County	50,219	45.79
Compton (city) Los Angeles County	32,800	34.01
Oakland (city) Alameda County	119,122	30.49
Hawthorne (city) Los Angeles County	24,674	29.27
Richmond (city) Contra Costa County	29,796	28.73
Gardena (city) Los Angeles County	15,136	25.73
Carson (city) Los Angeles County	23,090	25.18
Vallejo (city) Solano County	28,918	24.94
Lancaster (city) Los Angeles County	35,558	22.70
Pittsburg (city) Contra Costa County	12,770	20.19

African-American/Black: Not Hispanic

Top 10 Places Sorted by Population

Based on all places, regardless of total population

Place	Population	%
Los Angeles (city) Los Angeles County	372,821	9.83
Oakland (city) Alameda County	114,212	29.23
San Diego (city) San Diego County	94,818	7.25
Sacramento (city) Sacramento County	74,051	15.87
Long Beach (city) Los Angeles County	65,067	14.08
San Francisco (city) San Francisco County	53,760	6.68
Inglewood (city) Los Angeles County	48,512	44.23
Fresno (city) Fresno County	41,526	8.39
Stockton (city) San Joaquin County	37,389	12.82
Moreno Valley (city) Riverside County	36,134	18.69

Top 10 Places Sorted by Percent of Total Population

Based on all places, regardless of total population

Place	Population	%
View Park-Windsor Hills (cdp) Los Angeles County	9,650	87.13
Ladera Heights (cdp) Los Angeles County	4,963	76.38
West Athens (cdp) Los Angeles County	4,588	52.56
West Rancho Dominguez (cdp) Los Angeles County	2,966	52.32
Westmont (cdp) Los Angeles County	16,314	51.22
Inglewood (city) Los Angeles County	48,512	44.23
Marin City (cdp) Marin County	1,072	40.21
Willowbrook (cdp) Los Angeles County	12,396	34.45
North Richmond (cdp) Contra Costa County	1,224	32.93
Compton (city) Los Angeles County	31,687	32.85

Top 10 Places Sorted by Percent of Total Population

Based on places with total population of 50,000 or more

Place	Population	%
Inglewood (city) Los Angeles County	48,512	44.23
Compton (city) Los Angeles County	31,687	32.85
Oakland (city) Alameda County	114,212	29.23
Hawthorne (city) Los Angeles County	23,386	27.74
Richmond (city) Contra Costa County	28,533	27.51
Gardena (city) Los Angeles County	14,571	24.77
Carson (city) Los Angeles County	22,263	24.27
Vallejo (city) Solano County	27,466	23.69
Lancaster (city) Los Angeles County	33,469	21.37
Pittsburg (city) Contra Costa County	11,831	18.70

African-American/Black: Hispanic

Top 10 Places Sorted by Population

Based on all places, regardless of total population

Place	Population	%
Los Angeles (city) Los Angeles County	29,627	0.78
San Diego (city) San Diego County	9,556	0.73
Sacramento (city) Sacramento County	6,418	1.38
Fresno (city) Fresno County	5,369	1.09
San Jose (city) Santa Clara County	5,303	0.56
Oakland (city) Alameda County	4,910	1.26
Long Beach (city) Los Angeles County	4,677	1.01
San Francisco (city) San Francisco County	4,050	0.50
Stockton (city) San Joaquin County	4,043	1.39
San Bernardino (city) San Bernardino County	3,056	1.46

Top 10 Places Sorted by Percent of Total Population

Based on all places, regardless of total population

Place	Population	%
McClellan Park (cdp) Sacramento County	28	3.77
Lanare (cdp) Fresno County	21	3.57
Herlong (cdp) Lassen County	9	3.02
Palo Verde (cdp) Imperial County	5	2.92
Delft Colony (cdp) Tulare County	12	2.64
Ripley (cdp) Riverside County	17	2.46
View Park-Windsor Hills (cdp) Los Angeles County	257	2.32
Parkwood (cdp) Madera County	51	2.25
Fort Irwin (cdp) San Bernardino County	181	2.05
Richvale (cdp) Butte County	5	2.05

Top 10 Places Sorted by Percent of Total Population

Based on places with total population of 50,000 or more

Place	Population	%
Inglewood (city) Los Angeles County	1,707	1.56
Hawthorne (city) Los Angeles County	1,288	1.53
Moreno Valley (city) Riverside County	2,885	1.49
Pittsburg (city) Contra Costa County	939	1.48
San Bernardino (city) San Bernardino County	3,056	1.46
Victorville (city) San Bernardino County	1,664	1.44
Rialto (city) San Bernardino County	1,387	1.40
Stockton (city) San Joaquin County	4,043	1.39
Sacramento (city) Sacramento County	6,418	1.38
Perris (city) Riverside County	922	1.35

American Indian/Alaska Native

Top 10 Places Sorted by Population

Based on all places, regardless of total population

Place	Population	%
Los Angeles (city) Los Angeles County	54,236	1.43
San Diego (city) San Diego County	17,865	1.37
San Jose (city) Santa Clara County	16,064	1.70
Fresno (city) Fresno County	14,161	2.86
Sacramento (city) Sacramento County	13,242	2.84
San Francisco (city) San Francisco County	10,873	1.35
Bakersfield (city) Kern County	9,097	2.62
Oakland (city) Alameda County	8,322	2.13
Long Beach (city) Los Angeles County	7,958	1.72
Stockton (city) San Joaquin County	7,284	2.50

Top 10 Places Sorted by Percent of Total Population

Based on all places, regardless of total population

Place	Population	%
Furnace Creek (cdp) Inyo County	18	75.00
Fort Bidwell (cdp) Modoc County	86	49.71
Klamath (cdp) Del Norte County	381	48.91
Covelo (cdp) Mendocino County	551	43.90
Nubieber (cdp) Lassen County	18	36.00
Posey (cdp) Tulare County	3	30.00
Happy Camp (cdp) Siskiyou County	336	28.24
Big Pine (cdp) Inyo County	476	27.11
Laytonville (cdp) Mendocino County	284	23.15
Benton (cdp) Mono County	63	22.50

Top 10 Places Sorted by Percent of Total Population

Based on places with total population of 50,000 or more

Place	Population	%
Redding (city) Shasta County	4,059	4.52
Madera (city) Madera County	2,471	4.02
Santa Rosa (city) Sonoma County	5,575	3.32
Chico (city) Butte County	2,666	3.09
Porterville (city) Tulare County	1,675	3.09
Yuba City (city) Sutter County	1,967	3.03
Santa Maria (city) Santa Barbara County	2,866	2.88
Fresno (city) Fresno County	14,161	2.86
Sacramento (city) Sacramento County	13,242	2.84
Hemet (city) Riverside County	2,237	2.84

American Indian/Alaska Native: Not Hispanic

Top 10 Places Sorted by Population

Based on all places, regardless of total population

Place	Population	%
Los Angeles (city) Los Angeles County	19,510	0.51
San Diego (city) San Diego County	10,117	0.77
Sacramento (city) Sacramento County	7,885	1.69
Fresno (city) Fresno County	6,241	1.26
San Francisco (city) San Francisco County	6,241	0.78
San Jose (city) Santa Clara County	6,164	0.65
Oakland (city) Alameda County	4,795	1.23
Bakersfield (city) Kern County	4,742	1.36
Long Beach (city) Los Angeles County	4,002	0.87
Stockton (city) San Joaquin County	3,819	1.31

Top 10 Places Sorted by Percent of Total Population

Based on all places, regardless of total population

Place	Population	%
Furnace Creek (cdp) Inyo County	18	75.00
Klamath (cdp) Del Norte County	328	42.11
Fort Bidwell (cdp) Modoc County	72	41.62
Covelo (cdp) Mendocino County	520	41.43
Nubieber (cdp) Lassen County	14	28.00
Happy Camp (cdp) Siskiyou County	303	25.46
Big Pine (cdp) Inyo County	444	25.28
Laytonville (cdp) Mendocino County	241	19.64
Benton (cdp) Mono County	53	18.93
Cherokee (cdp) Butte County	13	18.84

Top 10 Places Sorted by Percent of Total Population

Based on places with total population of 50,000 or more

Place	Population	%
Redding (city) Shasta County	3,383	3.76
Chico (city) Butte County	1,922	2.23
Yuba City (city) Sutter County	1,363	2.10
Santa Rosa (city) Sonoma County	3,221	1.92
Citrus Heights (city) Sacramento County	1,579	1.90
Carmichael (cdp) Sacramento County	1,114	1.80
Arden-Arcade (cdp) Sacramento County	1,628	1.77
Rancho Cordova (city) Sacramento County	1,126	1.74
Sacramento (city) Sacramento County	7,885	1.69
Clovis (city) Fresno County	1,616	1.69

American Indian/Alaska Native: Hispanic

Top 10 Places Sorted by Population
Based on all places, regardless of total population

Place	Population	%
Los Angeles (city) Los Angeles County	34,726	0.92
San Jose (city) Santa Clara County	9,900	1.05
Fresno (city) Fresno County	7,920	1.60
San Diego (city) San Diego County	7,748	0.59
Sacramento (city) Sacramento County	5,357	1.15
San Francisco (city) San Francisco County	4,632	0.58
Bakersfield (city) Kern County	4,355	1.25
Santa Ana (city) Orange County	3,956	1.22
Long Beach (city) Los Angeles County	3,956	0.86
Riverside (city) Riverside County	3,585	1.18

Top 10 Places Sorted by Percent of Total Population
Based on all places, regardless of total population

Place	Population	%
Posey (cdp) Tulare County	2	20.00
Fort Bidwell (cdp) Modoc County	14	8.09
Nubieber (cdp) Lassen County	4	8.00
Raisin City (cdp) Fresno County	30	7.89
Big Lagoon (cdp) Humboldt County	7	7.53
Klamath (cdp) Del Norte County	53	6.80
Canyondam (cdp) Plumas County	2	6.45
Tooleville (cdp) Tulare County	20	5.90
Greenfield (city) Monterey County	907	5.55
Moskowite Corner (cdp) Napa County	11	5.21

Top 10 Places Sorted by Percent of Total Population
Based on places with total population of 50,000 or more

Place	Population	%
Madera (city) Madera County	1,904	3.10
Santa Maria (city) Santa Barbara County	2,139	2.15
Oxnard (city) Ventura County	3,471	1.75
San Rafael (city) Marin County	996	1.73
Pico Rivera (city) Los Angeles County	1,037	1.65
Huntington Park (city) Los Angeles County	954	1.64
South Whittier (cdp) Los Angeles County	933	1.63
Fresno (city) Fresno County	7,920	1.60
Whittier (city) Los Angeles County	1,339	1.57
Porterville (city) Tulare County	851	1.57

Alaska Native: Alaska Athabascan

Top 10 Places Sorted by Population
Based on all places, regardless of total population

Place	Population	%
Los Angeles (city) Los Angeles County	49	<0.01
San Diego (city) San Diego County	39	<0.01
Modesto (city) Stanislaus County	16	0.01
Redding (city) Shasta County	15	0.02
Bakersfield (city) Kern County	11	<0.01
Long Beach (city) Los Angeles County	11	<0.01
Oakland (city) Alameda County	11	<0.01
Riverside (city) Riverside County	11	<0.01
Sacramento (city) Sacramento County	11	<0.01
San Jose (city) Santa Clara County	11	<0.01

Top 10 Places Sorted by Percent of Total Population
Based on all places, regardless of total population

Place	Population	%
Scotia (cdp) Humboldt County	3	0.35
Cazadero (cdp) Sonoma County	1	0.28
Glen Ellen (cdp) Sonoma County	2	0.26
El Portal (cdp) Mariposa County	1	0.21
Arnold (cdp) Calaveras County	5	0.13
Kelly Ridge (cdp) Butte County	3	0.12
Westwood (cdp) Lassen County	2	0.12
Willow Creek (cdp) Humboldt County	2	0.12
Rio Dell (city) Humboldt County	3	0.09
Dollar Point (cdp) Placer County	1	0.08

Top 10 Places Sorted by Percent of Total Population
Based on places with total population of 50,000 or more

Place	Population	%
Redding (city) Shasta County	15	0.02
Modesto (city) Stanislaus County	16	0.01
Chico (city) Butte County	6	0.01
Hemet (city) Riverside County	6	0.01
Vista (city) San Diego County	6	0.01
Palo Alto (city) Santa Clara County	5	0.01
Encinitas (city) San Diego County	4	0.01
Woodland (city) Yolo County	4	0.01
Colton (city) San Bernardino County	3	0.01
Highland (city) San Bernardino County	3	0.01

Alaska Native: Aleut

Top 10 Places Sorted by Population
Based on all places, regardless of total population

Place	Population	%
San Diego (city) San Diego County	51	<0.01
Los Angeles (city) Los Angeles County	35	<0.01
San Jose (city) Santa Clara County	33	<0.01
San Francisco (city) San Francisco County	30	<0.01
Santa Rosa (city) Sonoma County	21	0.01
Vacaville (city) Solano County	20	0.02
Sacramento (city) Sacramento County	20	<0.01
Stockton (city) San Joaquin County	17	0.01
Modesto (city) Stanislaus County	16	0.01
Long Beach (city) Los Angeles County	13	<0.01

Top 10 Places Sorted by Percent of Total Population
Based on all places, regardless of total population

Place	Population	%
Keswick (cdp) Shasta County	3	0.67
Klamath (cdp) Del Norte County	5	0.64
River Pines (cdp) Amador County	1	0.26
Bertsch-Oceanview (cdp) Del Norte County	6	0.25
Cohasset (cdp) Butte County	2	0.24
Green Acres (cdp) Riverside County	3	0.17
Edwards AFB (cdp) Kern County	3	0.15
Concow (cdp) Butte County	1	0.14
Lakeport (city) Lake County	6	0.13
Redwood Valley (cdp) Mendocino County	2	0.12

Top 10 Places Sorted by Percent of Total Population
Based on places with total population of 50,000 or more

Place	Population	%
Vacaville (city) Solano County	20	0.02
Santa Rosa (city) Sonoma County	21	0.01
Stockton (city) San Joaquin County	17	0.01
Modesto (city) Stanislaus County	16	0.01
San Bernardino (city) San Bernardino County	11	0.01
Elk Grove (city) Sacramento County	8	0.01
Orange (city) Orange County	8	0.01
Livermore (city) Alameda County	7	0.01
Redding (city) Shasta County	7	0.01
Tracy (city) San Joaquin County	7	0.01

American Indian: Apache

Top 10 Places Sorted by Population
Based on all places, regardless of total population

Place	Population	%
Los Angeles (city) Los Angeles County	1,531	0.04
San Jose (city) Santa Clara County	959	0.10
Fresno (city) Fresno County	648	0.13
San Diego (city) San Diego County	616	0.05
Sacramento (city) Sacramento County	476	0.10
Stockton (city) San Joaquin County	384	0.13
Bakersfield (city) Kern County	336	0.10
San Francisco (city) San Francisco County	271	0.03
Modesto (city) Stanislaus County	266	0.13
Riverside (city) Riverside County	256	0.08

Top 10 Places Sorted by Percent of Total Population
Based on all places, regardless of total population

Place	Population	%
Macdoel (cdp) Siskiyou County	4	3.01
Clear Creek (cdp) Lassen County	4	2.37
Smartsville (cdp) Yuba County	4	2.26
Sisquoc (cdp) Santa Barbara County	4	2.19
Lemon Cove (cdp) Tulare County	6	1.95
Anchor Bay (cdp) Mendocino County	6	1.76
Crescent Mills (cdp) Plumas County	3	1.53
Courtland (cdp) Sacramento County	5	1.41
California Pines (cdp) Modoc County	7	1.35
Herlong (cdp) Lassen County	4	1.34

Top 10 Places Sorted by Percent of Total Population
Based on places with total population of 50,000 or more

Place	Population	%
Whittier (city) Los Angeles County	138	0.16
South Whittier (cdp) Los Angeles County	91	0.16
Victorville (city) San Bernardino County	174	0.15
Hesperia (city) San Bernardino County	126	0.14
Hemet (city) Riverside County	109	0.14
Pico Rivera (city) Los Angeles County	90	0.14
Fresno (city) Fresno County	648	0.13
Stockton (city) San Joaquin County	384	0.13
Modesto (city) Stanislaus County	266	0.13
Manteca (city) San Joaquin County	87	0.13

American Indian: Arapaho

Top 10 Places Sorted by Population
Based on all places, regardless of total population

Place	Population	%
Pacifica (city) San Mateo County	25	0.07
Los Angeles (city) Los Angeles County	24	<0.01
San Francisco (city) San Francisco County	17	<0.01
Oakland (city) Alameda County	16	<0.01
San Diego (city) San Diego County	16	<0.01
Bakersfield (city) Kern County	13	<0.01
Lancaster (city) Los Angeles County	12	0.01
Hayward (city) Alameda County	10	0.01
Sacramento (city) Sacramento County	10	<0.01
Apple Valley (town) San Bernardino County	9	0.01

Top 10 Places Sorted by Percent of Total Population
Based on all places, regardless of total population

Place	Population	%
Delleker (cdp) Plumas County	3	0.43
Fairmead (cdp) Madera County	4	0.28
Big Pine (cdp) Inyo County	4	0.23
Beale AFB (cdp) Yuba County	3	0.23
New Cuyama (cdp) Santa Barbara County	1	0.19
Squirrel Mountain Valley (cdp) Kern County	1	0.18
Springville (cdp) Tulare County	1	0.11
Wofford Heights (cdp) Kern County	2	0.09
Challenge-Brownsville (cdp) Yuba County	1	0.09
Lenwood (cdp) San Bernardino County	3	0.08

Top 10 Places Sorted by Percent of Total Population
Based on places with total population of 50,000 or more

Place	Population	%
Lancaster (city) Los Angeles County	12	0.01
Hayward (city) Alameda County	10	0.01
Apple Valley (town) San Bernardino County	9	0.01
Pasadena (city) Los Angeles County	9	0.01
Roseville (city) Placer County	9	0.01
Carson (city) Los Angeles County	8	0.01
Concord (city) Contra Costa County	8	0.01
El Cajon (city) San Diego County	8	0.01
Hemet (city) Riverside County	8	0.01
Chico (city) Butte County	7	0.01

American Indian: Blackfeet

Top 10 Places Sorted by Population
Based on all places, regardless of total population

Place	Population	%
Los Angeles (city) Los Angeles County	966	0.03
Sacramento (city) Sacramento County	485	0.10
San Diego (city) San Diego County	426	0.03
Oakland (city) Alameda County	328	0.08
San Francisco (city) San Francisco County	284	0.04
San Jose (city) Santa Clara County	267	0.03
Stockton (city) San Joaquin County	229	0.08
Fresno (city) Fresno County	216	0.04
Long Beach (city) Los Angeles County	214	0.05
Bakersfield (city) Kern County	186	0.05

Top 10 Places Sorted by Percent of Total Population
Based on all places, regardless of total population

Place	Population	%
Lake City (cdp) Modoc County	2	3.28
Forbestown (cdp) Butte County	9	2.81
Hyampom (cdp) Trinity County	4	1.66

Jenner (cdp) Sonoma County	2	1.47
Tupman (cdp) Kern County	2	1.24
California Pines (cdp) Modoc County	6	1.15
Daphnedale Park (cdp) Modoc County	2	1.09
New Pine Creek (cdp) Modoc County	1	1.02
Greenview (cdp) Siskiyou County	2	1.00
Trowbridge (cdp) Sutter County	2	0.88

Top 10 Places Sorted by Percent of Total Population

Based on places with total population of 50,000 or more

Place	Population	%
Rancho Cordova (city) Sacramento County	77	0.12
Highland (city) San Bernardino County	62	0.12
Lancaster (city) Los Angeles County	168	0.11
Carmichael (cdp) Sacramento County	65	0.11
Sacramento (city) Sacramento County	485	0.10
Victorville (city) San Bernardino County	114	0.10
Redding (city) Shasta County	94	0.10
Antioch (city) Contra Costa County	89	0.09
Chico (city) Butte County	81	0.09
Santee (city) San Diego County	47	0.09

American Indian: Canadian/French American Indian

Top 10 Places Sorted by Population

Based on all places, regardless of total population

Place	Population	%
Los Angeles (city) Los Angeles County	119	<0.01
San Diego (city) San Diego County	53	<0.01
San Jose (city) Santa Clara County	45	<0.01
San Francisco (city) San Francisco County	42	0.01
Long Beach (city) Los Angeles County	30	0.01
Oakland (city) Alameda County	27	0.01
Fresno (city) Fresno County	21	<0.01
Sacramento (city) Sacramento County	21	<0.01
Victorville (city) San Bernardino County	19	0.02
Stockton (city) San Joaquin County	17	0.01

Top 10 Places Sorted by Percent of Total Population

Based on all places, regardless of total population

Place	Population	%
Loleta (cdp) Humboldt County	4	0.51
Occidental (cdp) Sonoma County	5	0.45
Proberta (cdp) Tehama County	1	0.37
Beckwourth (cdp) Plumas County	1	0.23
Coarsegold (cdp) Madera County	4	0.22
Cedarville (cdp) Modoc County	1	0.19
Jacumba (cdp) San Diego County	1	0.18
Groveland (cdp) Tuolumne County	1	0.17
Bend (cdp) Tehama County	1	0.16
Avery (cdp) Calaveras County	1	0.15

Top 10 Places Sorted by Percent of Total Population

Based on places with total population of 50,000 or more

Place	Population	%
Victorville (city) San Bernardino County	19	0.02
San Francisco (city) San Francisco County	42	0.01
Long Beach (city) Los Angeles County	30	0.01
Oakland (city) Alameda County	27	0.01
Stockton (city) San Joaquin County	17	0.01
Compton (city) Los Angeles County	13	0.01
El Cajon (city) San Diego County	13	0.01
Huntington Beach (city) Orange County	13	0.01
Lancaster (city) Los Angeles County	12	0.01
Moreno Valley (city) Riverside County	12	0.01

American Indian: Central American Indian

Top 10 Places Sorted by Population

Based on all places, regardless of total population

Place	Population	%
Los Angeles (city) Los Angeles County	1,602	0.04
Oakland (city) Alameda County	199	0.05
San Francisco (city) San Francisco County	144	0.02
Long Beach (city) Los Angeles County	78	0.02
San Diego (city) San Diego County	59	<0.01
San Rafael (city) Marin County	56	0.10
San Jose (city) Santa Clara County	51	0.01
Fresno (city) Fresno County	34	0.01
Inglewood (city) Los Angeles County	33	0.03
Riverside (city) Riverside County	32	0.01

Top 10 Places Sorted by Percent of Total Population

Based on all places, regardless of total population

Place	Population	%
Elkhorn (cdp) Monterey County	3	0.19
Spreckels (cdp) Monterey County	1	0.15
Irwindale (city) Los Angeles County	2	0.14
Crockett (cdp) Contra Costa County	4	0.13
Tara Hills (cdp) Contra Costa County	6	0.12
Caruthers (cdp) Fresno County	3	0.12
Sky Valley (cdp) Riverside County	3	0.12
Bolinas (cdp) Marin County	2	0.12
Camanche Village (cdp) Amador County	1	0.12
Interlaken (cdp) Santa Cruz County	8	0.11

Top 10 Places Sorted by Percent of Total Population

Based on places with total population of 50,000 or more

Place	Population	%
San Rafael (city) Marin County	56	0.10
Oakland (city) Alameda County	199	0.05
Los Angeles (city) Los Angeles County	1,602	0.04
Florence-Graham (cdp) Los Angeles County	26	0.04
Huntington Park (city) Los Angeles County	21	0.04
Inglewood (city) Los Angeles County	33	0.03
Richmond (city) Contra Costa County	31	0.03
El Monte (city) Los Angeles County	29	0.03
Rialto (city) San Bernardino County	27	0.03
Redwood City (city) San Mateo County	25	0.03

American Indian: Cherokee

Top 10 Places Sorted by Population

Based on all places, regardless of total population

Place	Population	%
Los Angeles (city) Los Angeles County	4,661	0.12
San Diego (city) San Diego County	2,342	0.18
Sacramento (city) Sacramento County	2,019	0.43
San Jose (city) Santa Clara County	1,622	0.17
Bakersfield (city) Kern County	1,444	0.42
San Francisco (city) San Francisco County	1,441	0.18
Fresno (city) Fresno County	1,408	0.28
Stockton (city) San Joaquin County	1,176	0.40
Modesto (city) Stanislaus County	1,004	0.50
Oakland (city) Alameda County	971	0.25

Top 10 Places Sorted by Percent of Total Population

Based on all places, regardless of total population

Place	Population	%
McClenney Tract (cdp) Tulare County	1	10.00
Montgomery Creek (cdp) Shasta County	11	6.75
North San Juan (cdp) Nevada County	16	5.95
New Pine Creek (cdp) Modoc County	5	5.10
Belden (cdp) Plumas County	1	4.55
Camptonville (cdp) Yuba County	7	4.43
Challenge-Brownsville (cdp) Yuba County	42	3.66
Klamath (cdp) Del Norte County	27	3.47
Orick (cdp) Humboldt County	12	3.36
Tecopa (cdp) Inyo County	5	3.33

Top 10 Places Sorted by Percent of Total Population

Based on places with total population of 50,000 or more

Place	Population	%
Yuba City (city) Sutter County	490	0.75
Redding (city) Shasta County	599	0.67
Citrus Heights (city) Sacramento County	439	0.53
Rancho Cordova (city) Sacramento County	341	0.53
Manteca (city) San Joaquin County	343	0.51
Modesto (city) Stanislaus County	1,004	0.50
San Buenaventura (Ventura) (city) Ventura County	536	0.50
Chico (city) Butte County	431	0.50
Carmichael (cdp) Sacramento County	303	0.49
Antioch (city) Contra Costa County	489	0.48

American Indian: Cheyenne

Top 10 Places Sorted by Population

Based on all places, regardless of total population

Place	Population	%
Los Angeles (city) Los Angeles County	77	<0.01
Sacramento (city) Sacramento County	46	0.01
San Diego (city) San Diego County	31	<0.01
Oakland (city) Alameda County	28	0.01
Fresno (city) Fresno County	22	<0.01
Long Beach (city) Los Angeles County	22	<0.01
Palmdale (city) Los Angeles County	16	0.01
Stockton (city) San Joaquin County	16	0.01
Torrance (city) Los Angeles County	16	0.01
San Jose (city) Santa Clara County	16	<0.01

Top 10 Places Sorted by Percent of Total Population

Based on all places, regardless of total population

Place	Population	%
Orick (cdp) Humboldt County	3	0.84
Bangor (cdp) Butte County	5	0.77
Kingvale (cdp) Nevada County	1	0.70
Montgomery Creek (cdp) Shasta County	1	0.61
Johannesburg (cdp) Kern County	1	0.58
Rancho Tehama Reserve (cdp) Tehama County	7	0.47
Hornbrook (cdp) Siskiyou County	1	0.40
Coloma (cdp) El Dorado County	2	0.38
Fort Jones (city) Siskiyou County	3	0.36
Jacumba (cdp) San Diego County	2	0.36

Top 10 Places Sorted by Percent of Total Population

Based on places with total population of 50,000 or more

Place	Population	%
Apple Valley (town) San Bernardino County	15	0.02
Yucaipa (city) San Bernardino County	9	0.02
Sacramento (city) Sacramento County	46	0.01
Oakland (city) Alameda County	28	0.01
Palmdale (city) Los Angeles County	16	0.01
Stockton (city) San Joaquin County	16	0.01
Torrance (city) Los Angeles County	16	0.01
San Bernardino (city) San Bernardino County	14	0.01
Santa Rosa (city) Sonoma County	14	0.01
West Covina (city) Los Angeles County	14	0.01

American Indian: Chickasaw

Top 10 Places Sorted by Population

Based on all places, regardless of total population

Place	Population	%
Los Angeles (city) Los Angeles County	207	0.01
San Diego (city) San Diego County	141	0.01
Bakersfield (city) Kern County	112	0.03
Sacramento (city) Sacramento County	96	0.02
San Francisco (city) San Francisco County	80	0.01
Modesto (city) Stanislaus County	76	0.04
Fresno (city) Fresno County	71	0.01
Visalia (city) Tulare County	58	0.05
San Jose (city) Santa Clara County	53	0.01
Oakland (city) Alameda County	45	0.01

Top 10 Places Sorted by Percent of Total Population

Based on all places, regardless of total population

Place	Population	%
Shoshone (cdp) Inyo County	1	3.23
Cherokee (cdp) Butte County	1	1.45
Hyampom (cdp) Trinity County	2	0.83
Bear Valley (cdp) Mariposa County	1	0.80
Lake Almanor West (cdp) Plumas County	2	0.74
C-Road (cdp) Plumas County	1	0.67
Mokelumne Hill (cdp) Calaveras County	4	0.62
Spaulding (cdp) Lassen County	1	0.56
Boron (cdp) Kern County	12	0.53
Plymouth (city) Amador County	5	0.50

Top 10 Places Sorted by Percent of Total Population

Based on places with total population of 50,000 or more

Place	Population	%
Visalia (city) Tulare County	58	0.05
Modesto (city) Stanislaus County	76	0.04
Carmichael (cdp) Sacramento County	22	0.04
Eastvale (cdp) Riverside County	21	0.04
Bakersfield (city) Kern County	112	0.03
Clovis (city) Fresno County	28	0.03
Citrus Heights (city) Sacramento County	27	0.03
San Buenaventura (Ventura) (city) Ventura County	27	0.03
Chico (city) Butte County	26	0.03
Lakewood (city) Los Angeles County	25	0.03

American Indian: Chippewa

Top 10 Places Sorted by Population

Based on all places, regardless of total population

Place	Population	%
Los Angeles (city) Los Angeles County	331	0.01
San Diego (city) San Diego County	238	0.02
San Jose (city) Santa Clara County	181	0.02
San Francisco (city) San Francisco County	167	0.02
Sacramento (city) Sacramento County	151	0.03
Long Beach (city) Los Angeles County	108	0.02
Oakland (city) Alameda County	80	0.02
Huntington Beach (city) Orange County	68	0.04
Fresno (city) Fresno County	68	0.01
Redding (city) Shasta County	63	0.07

Top 10 Places Sorted by Percent of Total Population

Based on all places, regardless of total population

Place	Population	%
Buena Vista (cdp) Amador County	6	1.40
Greenville (cdp) Plumas County	13	1.15
Volcano (cdp) Amador County	1	0.87
Madison (cdp) Yolo County	4	0.80
Phillipsville (cdp) Humboldt County	1	0.71
East Shore (cdp) Plumas County	1	0.64
Sand City (city) Monterey County	2	0.60
Spaulding (cdp) Lassen County	1	0.56
Amador City (city) Amador County	1	0.54
Elmira (cdp) Solano County	1	0.53

Top 10 Places Sorted by Percent of Total Population

Based on places with total population of 50,000 or more

Place	Population	%
Redding (city) Shasta County	63	0.07
Carmichael (cdp) Sacramento County	38	0.06
Yuba City (city) Sutter County	37	0.06
Santee (city) San Diego County	30	0.06
Chico (city) Butte County	46	0.05
Huntington Beach (city) Orange County	68	0.04
Santa Rosa (city) Sonoma County	62	0.04
Arden-Arcade (cdp) Sacramento County	34	0.04
Vacaville (city) Solano County	34	0.04
Lakewood (city) Los Angeles County	33	0.04

American Indian: Choctaw

Top 10 Places Sorted by Population

Based on all places, regardless of total population

Place	Population	%
Los Angeles (city) Los Angeles County	1,133	0.03
San Diego (city) San Diego County	487	0.04
Bakersfield (city) Kern County	467	0.13
Sacramento (city) Sacramento County	426	0.09
Fresno (city) Fresno County	411	0.08
Modesto (city) Stanislaus County	385	0.19
San Jose (city) Santa Clara County	371	0.04
San Francisco (city) San Francisco County	318	0.04
Oakland (city) Alameda County	282	0.07
Stockton (city) San Joaquin County	276	0.09

Top 10 Places Sorted by Percent of Total Population

Based on all places, regardless of total population

Place	Population	%
Kennedy Meadows (cdp) Tulare County	1	3.57
Farmington (cdp) San Joaquin County	5	2.42
Bear Valley (cdp) Mariposa County	3	2.40
River Pines (cdp) Amador County	9	2.37
Swall Meadows (cdp) Mono County	5	2.27
Mettler (cdp) Kern County	3	2.21
Cherokee Strip (cdp) Kern County	5	2.20
Clipper Mills (cdp) Butte County	3	2.11
Mount Hebron (cdp) Siskiyou County	2	2.11
Fellows (cdp) Kern County	2	1.89

Top 10 Places Sorted by Percent of Total Population

Based on places with total population of 50,000 or more

Place	Population	%
Modesto (city) Stanislaus County	385	0.19
Redding (city) Shasta County	175	0.19
Tulare (city) Tulare County	106	0.18
Clovis (city) Fresno County	150	0.16
San Buenaventura (Ventura) (city) Ventura County	155	0.15
Manteca (city) San Joaquin County	102	0.15
Visalia (city) Tulare County	168	0.14
Bakersfield (city) Kern County	467	0.13
Antioch (city) Contra Costa County	136	0.13
Yuba City (city) Sutter County	84	0.13

American Indian: Colville

Top 10 Places Sorted by Population

Based on all places, regardless of total population

Place	Population	%
Los Angeles (city) Los Angeles County	27	<0.01
Sacramento (city) Sacramento County	12	<0.01
Norwalk (city) Los Angeles County	9	0.01
Rancho Cucamonga (city) San Bernardino County	8	<0.01
San Francisco (city) San Francisco County	8	<0.01
Mexican Colony (cdp) Kern County	7	2.49
San Jose (city) Santa Clara County	7	<0.01
Camarillo (city) Ventura County	6	0.01
Bakersfield (city) Kern County	6	<0.01
Escondido (city) San Diego County	6	<0.01

Top 10 Places Sorted by Percent of Total Population

Based on all places, regardless of total population

Place	Population	%
Mexican Colony (cdp) Kern County	7	2.49
Palo Cedro (cdp) Shasta County	1	0.08
Ferndale (city) Humboldt County	1	0.07
Kelseyville (cdp) Lake County	2	0.06
Big Pine (cdp) Inyo County	1	0.06
Searles Valley (cdp) San Bernardino County	1	0.06
Boyes Hot Springs (cdp) Sonoma County	3	0.05
Kings Beach (cdp) Placer County	2	0.05
East Porterville (cdp) Tulare County	3	0.04
Durham (cdp) Butte County	2	0.04

Top 10 Places Sorted by Percent of Total Population

Based on places with total population of 50,000 or more

Place	Population	%
Norwalk (city) Los Angeles County	9	0.01
Camarillo (city) Ventura County	6	0.01
Clovis (city) Fresno County	5	0.01
Rocklin (city) Placer County	5	0.01
Carmichael (cdp) Sacramento County	4	0.01
Los Angeles (city) Los Angeles County	27	<0.01
Sacramento (city) Sacramento County	12	<0.01
Rancho Cucamonga (city) San Bernardino County	8	<0.01
San Francisco (city) San Francisco County	8	<0.01
San Jose (city) Santa Clara County	7	<0.01

American Indian: Comanche

Top 10 Places Sorted by Population

Based on all places, regardless of total population

Place	Population	%
Los Angeles (city) Los Angeles County	145	<0.01
San Jose (city) Santa Clara County	91	0.01
San Diego (city) San Diego County	79	0.01
Fresno (city) Fresno County	77	0.02
Bakersfield (city) Kern County	57	0.02
San Francisco (city) San Francisco County	47	0.01
Sacramento (city) Sacramento County	44	0.01
Santa Rosa (city) Sonoma County	39	0.02
Visalia (city) Tulare County	28	0.02
San Bernardino (city) San Bernardino County	27	0.01

Top 10 Places Sorted by Percent of Total Population

Based on all places, regardless of total population

Place	Population	%
Cherokee (cdp) Butte County	1	1.45
Bear Creek (cdp) Merced County	3	1.03
Newell (cdp) Modoc County	3	0.67
Lodoga (cdp) Colusa County	1	0.51
Coulterville (cdp) Mariposa County	1	0.50
Mount Hermon (cdp) Santa Cruz County	5	0.48
Gasquet (cdp) Del Norte County	3	0.45
Delleker (cdp) Plumas County	3	0.43
Hornbrook (cdp) Siskiyou County	1	0.40
North San Juan (cdp) Nevada County	1	0.37

Top 10 Places Sorted by Percent of Total Population

Based on places with total population of 50,000 or more

Place	Population	%
Citrus Heights (city) Sacramento County	25	0.03
Fresno (city) Fresno County	77	0.02
Bakersfield (city) Kern County	57	0.02
Santa Rosa (city) Sonoma County	39	0.02
Visalia (city) Tulare County	28	0.02
San Buenaventura (Ventura) (city) Ventura County	21	0.02
Clovis (city) Fresno County	18	0.02
Santa Barbara (city) Santa Barbara County	18	0.02
Redding (city) Shasta County	15	0.02
Santa Cruz (city) Santa Cruz County	13	0.02

American Indian: Cree

Top 10 Places Sorted by Population

Based on all places, regardless of total population

Place	Population	%
Los Angeles (city) Los Angeles County	66	<0.01
San Diego (city) San Diego County	40	<0.01
Sacramento (city) Sacramento County	39	0.01
San Francisco (city) San Francisco County	35	<0.01
San Jose (city) Santa Clara County	18	<0.01
Fresno (city) Fresno County	15	<0.01
Oakland (city) Alameda County	14	<0.01
Santa Rosa (city) Sonoma County	13	0.01
Long Beach (city) Los Angeles County	13	<0.01
Altadena (cdp) Los Angeles County	10	0.02

Top 10 Places Sorted by Percent of Total Population

Based on all places, regardless of total population

Place	Population	%
Furnace Creek (cdp) Inyo County	2	8.33
Floriston (cdp) Nevada County	2	2.74
Ruth (cdp) Trinity County	1	0.51
Lee Vining (cdp) Mono County	1	0.45
Graeagle (cdp) Plumas County	3	0.41
Benbow (cdp) Humboldt County	1	0.31
Lower Lake (cdp) Lake County	3	0.23
Jacumba (cdp) San Diego County	1	0.18
Squirrel Mountain Valley (cdp) Kern County	1	0.18
Copperopolis (cdp) Calaveras County	5	0.14

Top 10 Places Sorted by Percent of Total Population

Based on places with total population of 50,000 or more

Place	Population	%
Sacramento (city) Sacramento County	39	0.01
Santa Rosa (city) Sonoma County	13	0.01
Berkeley (city) Alameda County	8	0.01
El Cajon (city) San Diego County	8	0.01
Elk Grove (city) Sacramento County	8	0.01
Pasadena (city) Los Angeles County	8	0.01
Santa Cruz (city) Santa Cruz County	8	0.01
Vacaville (city) Solano County	8	0.01
Vallejo (city) Solano County	8	0.01
Lakewood (city) Los Angeles County	7	0.01

American Indian: Creek

Top 10 Places Sorted by Population

Based on all places, regardless of total population

Place	Population	%
Los Angeles (city) Los Angeles County	334	0.01
San Diego (city) San Diego County	163	0.01
Fresno (city) Fresno County	162	0.03
Bakersfield (city) Kern County	143	0.04
San Jose (city) Santa Clara County	115	0.01
Sacramento (city) Sacramento County	114	0.02
San Francisco (city) San Francisco County	108	0.01
Long Beach (city) Los Angeles County	98	0.02
Oakland (city) Alameda County	97	0.02
Modesto (city) Stanislaus County	85	0.04

Top 10 Places Sorted by Percent of Total Population

Based on all places, regardless of total population

Place	Population	%
Floriston (cdp) Nevada County	2	2.74
Herlong (cdp) Lassen County	4	1.34
Mount Hebron (cdp) Siskiyou County	1	1.05

Bodega (cdp) Sonoma County	2	0.91
Groveland (cdp) Tuolumne County	5	0.83
Trinidad (city) Humboldt County	3	0.82
Coleville (cdp) Mono County	4	0.81
Hood (cdp) Sacramento County	2	0.74
Edmundson Acres (cdp) Kern County	2	0.72
Monmouth (cdp) Fresno County	1	0.66

Top 10 Places Sorted by Percent of Total Population
Based on places with total population of 50,000 or more

Place	Population	%
Vacaville (city) Solano County	52	0.06
Rancho Cordova (city) Sacramento County	35	0.05
Bakersfield (city) Kern County	143	0.04
Modesto (city) Stanislaus County	85	0.04
San Bernardino (city) San Bernardino County	76	0.04
Redding (city) Shasta County	38	0.04
Carmichael (cdp) Sacramento County	26	0.04
Turlock (city) Stanislaus County	26	0.04
Rocklin (city) Placer County	24	0.04
Fresno (city) Fresno County	162	0.03

American Indian: Crow

Top 10 Places Sorted by Population
Based on all places, regardless of total population

Place	Population	%
Los Angeles (city) Los Angeles County	44	<0.01
Sacramento (city) Sacramento County	37	0.01
San Francisco (city) San Francisco County	23	<0.01
Oakland (city) Alameda County	22	0.01
San Diego (city) San Diego County	20	<0.01
Fresno (city) Fresno County	18	<0.01
Chula Vista (city) San Diego County	13	0.01
Stockton (city) San Joaquin County	12	<0.01
Burbank (city) Los Angeles County	11	0.01
West Sacramento (city) Yolo County	10	0.02

Top 10 Places Sorted by Percent of Total Population
Based on all places, regardless of total population

Place	Population	%
Stirling City (cdp) Butte County	4	1.36
Fairmead (cdp) Madera County	4	0.28
Delleker (cdp) Plumas County	2	0.28
Desert Shores (cdp) Imperial County	3	0.27
Mountain View Acres (cdp) San Bernardino County	8	0.26
Madison (cdp) Yolo County	1	0.20
Biggs (city) Butte County	3	0.18
Bangor (cdp) Butte County	1	0.15
Meadow Vista (cdp) Placer County	4	0.12
Catheys Valley (cdp) Mariposa County	1	0.12

Top 10 Places Sorted by Percent of Total Population
Based on places with total population of 50,000 or more

Place	Population	%
Sacramento (city) Sacramento County	37	0.01
Oakland (city) Alameda County	22	0.01
Chula Vista (city) San Diego County	13	0.01
Burbank (city) Los Angeles County	11	0.01
Santa Rosa (city) Sonoma County	10	0.01
Arden-Arcade (cdp) Sacramento County	9	0.01
Corona (city) Riverside County	9	0.01
Napa (city) Napa County	9	0.01
Bellflower (city) Los Angeles County	7	0.01
Brentwood (city) Contra Costa County	7	0.01

American Indian: Delaware

Top 10 Places Sorted by Population
Based on all places, regardless of total population

Place	Population	%
Los Angeles (city) Los Angeles County	80	<0.01
San Francisco (city) San Francisco County	38	<0.01
San Diego (city) San Diego County	26	<0.01
San Jose (city) Santa Clara County	25	<0.01
Sacramento (city) Sacramento County	20	<0.01
Stockton (city) San Joaquin County	19	0.01
Oakland (city) Alameda County	18	<0.01
Fresno (city) Fresno County	16	<0.01
Vista (city) San Diego County	14	0.01
Long Beach (city) Los Angeles County	13	<0.01

Top 10 Places Sorted by Percent of Total Population
Based on all places, regardless of total population

Place	Population	%
Randsburg (cdp) Kern County	3	4.35
Meridian (cdp) Sutter County	3	0.84
Valley Home (cdp) Stanislaus County	1	0.44
North San Juan (cdp) Nevada County	1	0.37
Toro Canyon (cdp) Santa Barbara County	4	0.27
Madison (cdp) Yolo County	1	0.20
Coloma (cdp) El Dorado County	1	0.19
Del Rey Oaks (city) Monterey County	3	0.18
Hayfork (cdp) Trinity County	4	0.17
Jackson (city) Amador County	7	0.15

Top 10 Places Sorted by Percent of Total Population
Based on places with total population of 50,000 or more

Place	Population	%
Menifee (city) Riverside County	12	0.02
San Rafael (city) Marin County	12	0.02
Lake Elsinore (city) Riverside County	8	0.02
Stockton (city) San Joaquin County	19	0.01
Vista (city) San Diego County	14	0.01
Huntington Beach (city) Orange County	12	0.01
Santa Rosa (city) Sonoma County	11	0.01
Alameda (city) Alameda County	10	0.01
Antioch (city) Contra Costa County	10	0.01
Elk Grove (city) Sacramento County	8	0.01

American Indian: Hopi

Top 10 Places Sorted by Population
Based on all places, regardless of total population

Place	Population	%
Los Angeles (city) Los Angeles County	163	<0.01
Riverside (city) Riverside County	59	0.02
San Jose (city) Santa Clara County	58	0.01
San Diego (city) San Diego County	57	<0.01
Fresno (city) Fresno County	45	0.01
Sacramento (city) Sacramento County	28	0.01
Bakersfield (city) Kern County	27	0.01
San Bernardino (city) San Bernardino County	27	0.01
Oakland (city) Alameda County	26	0.01
Anaheim (city) Orange County	25	0.01

Top 10 Places Sorted by Percent of Total Population
Based on all places, regardless of total population

Place	Population	%
Cherokee (cdp) Butte County	3	4.35
Concow (cdp) Butte County	5	0.70
Shell Ridge (cdp) Contra Costa County	3	0.31
Clearlake Riviera (cdp) Lake County	8	0.26
Taft Mosswood (cdp) San Joaquin County	4	0.26
Herald (cdp) Sacramento County	3	0.25
Covelo (cdp) Mendocino County	3	0.24
Vallecito (cdp) Calaveras County	1	0.23
Berry Creek (cdp) Butte County	3	0.21
Rough and Ready (cdp) Nevada County	2	0.21

Top 10 Places Sorted by Percent of Total Population
Based on places with total population of 50,000 or more

Place	Population	%
Riverside (city) Riverside County	59	0.02
Palmdale (city) Los Angeles County	23	0.02
Antioch (city) Contra Costa County	19	0.02
Norwalk (city) Los Angeles County	18	0.02
Alhambra (city) Los Angeles County	17	0.02
Downey (city) Los Angeles County	17	0.02
Hesperia (city) San Bernardino County	17	0.02
San Buenaventura (Ventura) (city) Ventura County	17	0.02
West Covina (city) Los Angeles County	17	0.02
Apple Valley (town) San Bernardino County	14	0.02

American Indian: Houma

Top 10 Places Sorted by Population
Based on all places, regardless of total population

Place	Population	%
San Diego (city) San Diego County	12	<0.01
Los Angeles (city) Los Angeles County	10	<0.01
Oakley (city) Contra Costa County	9	0.03
Paradise (town) Butte County	6	0.02
Manteca (city) San Joaquin County	5	0.01
San Francisco (city) San Francisco County	5	<0.01
Fontana (city) San Bernardino County	4	<0.01
San Jose (city) Santa Clara County	4	<0.01
San Leandro (city) Alameda County	4	<0.01
Gardena (city) Los Angeles County	3	0.01

Top 10 Places Sorted by Percent of Total Population
Based on all places, regardless of total population

Place	Population	%
Oakley (city) Contra Costa County	9	0.03
Lucerne Valley (cdp) San Bernardino County	2	0.03
Idyllwild-Pine Cove (cdp) Riverside County	1	0.03
Lake Isabella (cdp) Kern County	1	0.03
Paradise (town) Butte County	6	0.02
Golden Hills (cdp) Kern County	2	0.02
Manteca (city) San Joaquin County	5	0.01
Gardena (city) Los Angeles County	3	0.01
Bay Point (cdp) Contra Costa County	2	0.01
Santa Paula (city) Ventura County	2	0.01

Top 10 Places Sorted by Percent of Total Population
Based on places with total population of 50,000 or more

Place	Population	%
Manteca (city) San Joaquin County	5	0.01
Gardena (city) Los Angeles County	3	0.01
San Diego (city) San Diego County	12	<0.01
Los Angeles (city) Los Angeles County	10	<0.01
San Francisco (city) San Francisco County	5	<0.01
Fontana (city) San Bernardino County	4	<0.01
San Jose (city) Santa Clara County	4	<0.01
San Leandro (city) Alameda County	4	<0.01
Arden-Arcade (cdp) Sacramento County	3	<0.01
Fresno (city) Fresno County	3	<0.01

Alaska Native: Inupiat (Eskimo)

Top 10 Places Sorted by Population
Based on all places, regardless of total population

Place	Population	%
Los Angeles (city) Los Angeles County	56	<0.01
San Diego (city) San Diego County	41	<0.01
Sacramento (city) Sacramento County	27	0.01
Oakland (city) Alameda County	26	0.01
San Jose (city) Santa Clara County	26	<0.01
San Francisco (city) San Francisco County	22	<0.01
Redding (city) Shasta County	20	0.02
Santa Rosa (city) Sonoma County	20	0.01
Clearlake (city) Lake County	13	0.09
Huntington Beach (city) Orange County	12	0.01

Top 10 Places Sorted by Percent of Total Population
Based on all places, regardless of total population

Place	Population	%
Volta (cdp) Merced County	1	0.41
Happy Camp (cdp) Siskiyou County	4	0.34
Challenge-Brownsville (cdp) Yuba County	3	0.26
Lake Don Pedro (cdp) Mariposa County	2	0.19
Dollar Point (cdp) Placer County	2	0.16
San Andreas (cdp) Calaveras County	4	0.14
Weed (city) Siskiyou County	3	0.10
Camanche North Shore (cdp) Amador County	1	0.10
Upper Lake (cdp) Lake County	1	0.10
Clearlake (city) Lake County	13	0.09

Top 10 Places Sorted by Percent of Total Population
Based on places with total population of 50,000 or more

Place	Population	%
Redding (city) Shasta County	20	0.02
Sacramento (city) Sacramento County	27	0.01
Oakland (city) Alameda County	26	0.01
Santa Rosa (city) Sonoma County	20	0.01
Huntington Beach (city) Orange County	12	0.01
Lancaster (city) Los Angeles County	12	0.01
Victorville (city) San Bernardino County	11	0.01
Lakewood (city) Los Angeles County	10	0.01
Antioch (city) Contra Costa County	8	0.01
Carmichael (cdp) Sacramento County	8	0.01

American Indian: Iroquois

Top 10 Places Sorted by Population

Based on all places, regardless of total population

Place	Population	%
Los Angeles (city) Los Angeles County	321	0.01
San Diego (city) San Diego County	183	0.01
San Francisco (city) San Francisco County	133	0.02
San Jose (city) Santa Clara County	117	0.01
Oakland (city) Alameda County	95	0.02
Sacramento (city) Sacramento County	92	0.02
Long Beach (city) Los Angeles County	79	0.02
Fresno (city) Fresno County	44	0.01
Berkeley (city) Alameda County	43	0.04
Escondido (city) San Diego County	41	0.03

Top 10 Places Sorted by Percent of Total Population

Based on all places, regardless of total population

Place	Population	%
Montgomery Creek (cdp) Shasta County	2	1.23
Sisquoc (cdp) Santa Barbara County	2	1.09
Port Costa (cdp) Contra Costa County	2	1.05
Wallace (cdp) Calaveras County	3	0.74
Downieville (cdp) Sierra County	2	0.71
Vallecito (cdp) Calaveras County	3	0.68
Myers Flat (cdp) Humboldt County	1	0.68
Independence (cdp) Inyo County	4	0.60
Drytown (cdp) Amador County	1	0.60
Desert Center (cdp) Riverside County	1	0.49

Top 10 Places Sorted by Percent of Total Population

Based on places with total population of 50,000 or more

Place	Population	%
Berkeley (city) Alameda County	43	0.04
Arden-Arcade (cdp) Sacramento County	36	0.04
Carmichael (cdp) Sacramento County	24	0.04
La Mesa (city) San Diego County	23	0.04
Escondido (city) San Diego County	41	0.03
Simi Valley (city) Ventura County	40	0.03
Murrieta (city) Riverside County	32	0.03
San Buenaventura (Ventura) (city) Ventura County	32	0.03
Clovis (city) Fresno County	29	0.03
Alameda (city) Alameda County	22	0.03

American Indian: Kiowa

Top 10 Places Sorted by Population

Based on all places, regardless of total population

Place	Population	%
Los Angeles (city) Los Angeles County	49	<0.01
San Jose (city) Santa Clara County	25	<0.01
Fresno (city) Fresno County	21	<0.01
Porterville (city) Tulare County	19	0.04
Bakersfield (city) Kern County	19	0.01
San Diego (city) San Diego County	16	<0.01
Sacramento (city) Sacramento County	15	<0.01
Vineyard (cdp) Sacramento County	11	0.04
Whittier (city) Los Angeles County	11	0.01
Oakland (city) Alameda County	11	<0.01

Top 10 Places Sorted by Percent of Total Population

Based on all places, regardless of total population

Place	Population	%
Kingvale (cdp) Nevada County	1	0.70
Greenview (cdp) Siskiyou County	1	0.50
Tulelake (city) Siskiyou County	2	0.20
Wilkerson (cdp) Inyo County	1	0.18
Littlerock (cdp) Los Angeles County	2	0.15
Independence (cdp) Inyo County	1	0.15
Squaw Valley (cdp) Fresno County	4	0.13
Pacheco (cdp) Contra Costa County	4	0.11
Elizabeth Lake (cdp) Los Angeles County	2	0.11
Niland (cdp) Imperial County	1	0.10

Top 10 Places Sorted by Percent of Total Population

Based on places with total population of 50,000 or more

Place	Population	%
Porterville (city) Tulare County	19	0.04
Brentwood (city) Contra Costa County	8	0.02
Bakersfield (city) Kern County	19	0.01
Whittier (city) Los Angeles County	11	0.01
Oxnard (city) Ventura County	10	0.01
Pico Rivera (city) Los Angeles County	9	0.01
Rancho Cucamonga (city) San Bernardino County	9	0.01
Rancho Cordova (city) Sacramento County	8	0.01
Cathedral City (city) Riverside County	7	0.01
Livermore (city) Alameda County	7	0.01

American Indian: Lumbee

Top 10 Places Sorted by Population

Based on all places, regardless of total population

Place	Population	%
Los Angeles (city) Los Angeles County	59	<0.01
San Diego (city) San Diego County	45	<0.01
Sacramento (city) Sacramento County	19	<0.01
Riverside (city) Riverside County	12	<0.01
Oildale (cdp) Kern County	11	0.03
Hemet (city) Riverside County	11	0.01
San Francisco (city) San Francisco County	11	<0.01
San Jose (city) Santa Clara County	11	<0.01
Huntington Beach (city) Orange County	10	0.01
Long Beach (city) Los Angeles County	10	<0.01

Top 10 Places Sorted by Percent of Total Population

Based on all places, regardless of total population

Place	Population	%
Round Mountain (cdp) Shasta County	1	0.65
Valley Home (cdp) Stanislaus County	1	0.44
Carnelian Bay (cdp) Placer County	2	0.38
Bieber (cdp) Lassen County	1	0.32
Canby (cdp) Modoc County	1	0.32
Benbow (cdp) Humboldt County	1	0.31
Middletown (cdp) Lake County	4	0.30
Lindcove (cdp) Tulare County	1	0.25
Sierra Brooks (cdp) Sierra County	1	0.21
McCloud (cdp) Siskiyou County	2	0.18

Top 10 Places Sorted by Percent of Total Population

Based on places with total population of 50,000 or more

Place	Population	%
Rocklin (city) Placer County	9	0.02
Hemet (city) Riverside County	11	0.01
Huntington Beach (city) Orange County	10	0.01
Alhambra (city) Los Angeles County	9	0.01
Westminster (city) Orange County	9	0.01
Lakewood (city) Los Angeles County	8	0.01
San Clemente (city) Orange County	8	0.01
Antioch (city) Contra Costa County	7	0.01
Berkeley (city) Alameda County	7	0.01
Clovis (city) Fresno County	7	0.01

American Indian: Menominee

Top 10 Places Sorted by Population

Based on all places, regardless of total population

Place	Population	%
San Diego (city) San Diego County	19	<0.01
Los Angeles (city) Los Angeles County	18	<0.01
Anaheim (city) Orange County	10	<0.01
Camp Pendleton South (cdp) San Diego County	9	0.08
San Jose (city) Santa Clara County	9	<0.01
Sacramento (city) Sacramento County	7	<0.01
Hemet (city) Riverside County	6	0.01
Fresno (city) Fresno County	6	<0.01
Rancho Calaveras (cdp) Calaveras County	5	0.09
Milpitas (city) Santa Clara County	5	0.01

Top 10 Places Sorted by Percent of Total Population

Based on all places, regardless of total population

Place	Population	%
Princeton (cdp) Colusa County	2	0.66
Fieldbrook (cdp) Humboldt County	3	0.35
Cazadero (cdp) Sonoma County	1	0.28
Lower Lake (cdp) Lake County	3	0.23
Maxwell (cdp) Colusa County	2	0.18
Tuttletown (cdp) Tuolumne County	1	0.15
Walker (cdp) Mono County	1	0.14
Rancho Calaveras (cdp) Calaveras County	5	0.09
Aguanga (cdp) Riverside County	1	0.09
Camp Pendleton South (cdp) San Diego County	9	0.08

Top 10 Places Sorted by Percent of Total Population

Based on places with total population of 50,000 or more

Place	Population	%
Hemet (city) Riverside County	6	0.01
Milpitas (city) Santa Clara County	5	0.01
San Diego (city) San Diego County	19	<0.01
Los Angeles (city) Los Angeles County	18	<0.01
Anaheim (city) Orange County	10	<0.01
San Jose (city) Santa Clara County	9	<0.01
Sacramento (city) Sacramento County	7	<0.01
Fresno (city) Fresno County	6	<0.01
San Buenaventura (Ventura) (city) Ventura County	5	<0.01
Santa Rosa (city) Sonoma County	5	<0.01

American Indian: Mexican American Indian

Top 10 Places Sorted by Population

Based on all places, regardless of total population

Place	Population	%
Los Angeles (city) Los Angeles County	9,589	0.25
San Jose (city) Santa Clara County	1,697	0.18
Fresno (city) Fresno County	1,666	0.34
San Diego (city) San Diego County	1,561	0.12
Oxnard (city) Ventura County	1,377	0.70
San Francisco (city) San Francisco County	1,209	0.15
Santa Ana (city) Orange County	974	0.30
Oakland (city) Alameda County	945	0.24
Madera (city) Madera County	891	1.45
Santa Maria (city) Santa Barbara County	868	0.87

Top 10 Places Sorted by Percent of Total Population

Based on all places, regardless of total population

Place	Population	%
Raisin City (cdp) Fresno County	27	7.11
Tooleville (cdp) Tulare County	17	5.01
McGee Creek (cdp) Mono County	2	4.88
Greenfield (city) Monterey County	765	4.68
Moskowite Corner (cdp) Napa County	8	3.79
Cartago (cdp) Inyo County	3	3.26
Ford City (cdp) Kern County	112	2.62
Coloma (cdp) El Dorado County	13	2.46
Lee Vining (cdp) Mono County	5	2.25
New Pine Creek (cdp) Modoc County	2	2.04

Top 10 Places Sorted by Percent of Total Population

Based on places with total population of 50,000 or more

Place	Population	%
Madera (city) Madera County	891	1.45
Santa Maria (city) Santa Barbara County	868	0.87
Oxnard (city) Ventura County	1,377	0.70
Huntington Park (city) Los Angeles County	286	0.49
Watsonville (city) Santa Cruz County	233	0.46
San Rafael (city) Marin County	248	0.43
East Los Angeles (cdp) Los Angeles County	487	0.38
Fresno (city) Fresno County	1,666	0.34
Salinas (city) Monterey County	508	0.34
Florence-Graham (cdp) Los Angeles County	213	0.34

American Indian: Navajo

Top 10 Places Sorted by Population

Based on all places, regardless of total population

Place	Population	%
Los Angeles (city) Los Angeles County	1,260	0.03
San Diego (city) San Diego County	532	0.04
San Jose (city) Santa Clara County	476	0.05
Sacramento (city) Sacramento County	355	0.08
Long Beach (city) Los Angeles County	320	0.07
Fresno (city) Fresno County	294	0.06
San Francisco (city) San Francisco County	242	0.03
Stockton (city) San Joaquin County	233	0.08
Riverside (city) Riverside County	201	0.07
Oakland (city) Alameda County	184	0.05

Top 10 Places Sorted by Percent of Total Population

Based on all places, regardless of total population

Place	Population	%
Montgomery Creek (cdp) Shasta County	12	7.36
Fort Bidwell (cdp) Modoc County	5	2.89

Place	Population	%
Long Barn (cdp) Tuolumne County	2	1.29
Bradley (cdp) Monterey County	1	1.08
San Simeon (cdp) San Luis Obispo County	4	0.87
Mesa (cdp) Inyo County	2	0.80
Jacumba (cdp) San Diego County	4	0.71
Fall River Mills (cdp) Shasta County	4	0.70
Trinity Village (cdp) Trinity County	2	0.67
Mi-Wuk Village (cdp) Tuolumne County	6	0.64

Top 10 Places Sorted by Percent of Total Population

Based on places with total population of 50,000 or more

Place	Population	%
Victorville (city) San Bernardino County	116	0.10
Norwalk (city) Los Angeles County	96	0.09
Whittier (city) Los Angeles County	80	0.09
Tracy (city) San Joaquin County	71	0.09
Apple Valley (town) San Bernardino County	60	0.09
Sacramento (city) Sacramento County	355	0.08
Stockton (city) San Joaquin County	233	0.08
San Bernardino (city) San Bernardino County	165	0.08
Modesto (city) Stanislaus County	158	0.08
Moreno Valley (city) Riverside County	146	0.08

American Indian: Osage

Top 10 Places Sorted by Population

Based on all places, regardless of total population

Place	Population	%
Los Angeles (city) Los Angeles County	107	<0.01
San Diego (city) San Diego County	70	0.01
San Jose (city) Santa Clara County	35	<0.01
Sacramento (city) Sacramento County	30	0.01
Long Beach (city) Los Angeles County	29	0.01
San Francisco (city) San Francisco County	26	<0.01
Fresno (city) Fresno County	24	<0.01
Huntington Beach (city) Orange County	21	0.01
Stockton (city) San Joaquin County	21	0.01
Lake Forest (city) Orange County	20	0.03

Top 10 Places Sorted by Percent of Total Population

Based on all places, regardless of total population

Place	Population	%
Garey (cdp) Santa Barbara County	2	2.94
Keswick (cdp) Shasta County	2	0.44
Hyampom (cdp) Trinity County	1	0.41
Bombay Beach (cdp) Imperial County	1	0.34
Mountain Gate (cdp) Shasta County	3	0.32
Zayante (cdp) Santa Cruz County	2	0.28
Butte Valley (cdp) Butte County	2	0.22
Lenwood (cdp) San Bernardino County	7	0.20
Julian (cdp) San Diego County	3	0.20
Jacumba (cdp) San Diego County	1	0.18

Top 10 Places Sorted by Percent of Total Population

Based on places with total population of 50,000 or more

Place	Population	%
Lake Forest (city) Orange County	20	0.03
Chico (city) Butte County	18	0.02
Vacaville (city) Solano County	17	0.02
Manteca (city) San Joaquin County	12	0.02
Santee (city) San Diego County	12	0.02
San Diego (city) San Diego County	70	0.01
Sacramento (city) Sacramento County	30	0.01
Long Beach (city) Los Angeles County	29	0.01
Huntington Beach (city) Orange County	21	0.01
Stockton (city) San Joaquin County	21	0.01

American Indian: Ottawa

Top 10 Places Sorted by Population

Based on all places, regardless of total population

Place	Population	%
Los Angeles (city) Los Angeles County	24	<0.01
San Diego (city) San Diego County	22	<0.01
Hemet (city) Riverside County	15	0.02
Tulare (city) Tulare County	13	0.02
Lancaster (city) Los Angeles County	11	0.01
Desert Hot Springs (city) Riverside County	10	0.04
Antelope (cdp) Sacramento County	9	0.02
Napa (city) Napa County	9	0.01
Roseville (city) Placer County	8	0.01
Anaheim (city) Orange County	8	<0.01

Top 10 Places Sorted by Percent of Total Population

Based on all places, regardless of total population

Place	Population	%
Orick (cdp) Humboldt County	1	0.28
Knights Landing (cdp) Yolo County	2	0.20
Cutten (cdp) Humboldt County	4	0.13
Jackson (city) Amador County	5	0.11
Lower Lake (cdp) Lake County	1	0.08
Berry Creek (cdp) Butte County	1	0.07
Julian (cdp) San Diego County	1	0.07
Red Corral (cdp) Amador County	1	0.07
Willits (city) Mendocino County	3	0.06
Pine Hills (cdp) Humboldt County	2	0.06

Top 10 Places Sorted by Percent of Total Population

Based on places with total population of 50,000 or more

Place	Population	%
Hemet (city) Riverside County	15	0.02
Tulare (city) Tulare County	13	0.02
Lancaster (city) Los Angeles County	11	0.01
Napa (city) Napa County	9	0.01
Roseville (city) Placer County	8	0.01
Antioch (city) Contra Costa County	7	0.01
Carson (city) Los Angeles County	7	0.01
El Cajon (city) San Diego County	6	0.01
Indio (city) Riverside County	6	0.01
Mission Viejo (city) Orange County	6	0.01

American Indian: Paiute

Top 10 Places Sorted by Population

Based on all places, regardless of total population

Place	Population	%
Bakersfield (city) Kern County	214	0.06
Susanville (city) Lassen County	156	0.87
Sacramento (city) Sacramento County	107	0.02
Los Angeles (city) Los Angeles County	86	<0.01
Modesto (city) Stanislaus County	70	0.03
Fresno (city) Fresno County	67	0.01
San Diego (city) San Diego County	62	<0.01
Fort Bidwell (cdp) Modoc County	59	34.10
San Jose (city) Santa Clara County	58	0.01
Independence (cdp) Inyo County	46	6.88

Top 10 Places Sorted by Percent of Total Population

Based on all places, regardless of total population

Place	Population	%
Fort Bidwell (cdp) Modoc County	59	34.10
Benton (cdp) Mono County	39	13.93
Independence (cdp) Inyo County	46	6.88
Bridgeport (cdp) Mono County	30	5.22
Lee Vining (cdp) Mono County	11	4.95
Walker (cdp) Mono County	24	3.33
Tupman (cdp) Kern County	5	3.11
Tecopa (cdp) Inyo County	4	2.67
Cartago (cdp) Inyo County	2	2.17
Cedarville (cdp) Modoc County	10	1.95

Top 10 Places Sorted by Percent of Total Population

Based on places with total population of 50,000 or more

Place	Population	%
Bakersfield (city) Kern County	214	0.06
Manteca (city) San Joaquin County	33	0.05
Redding (city) Shasta County	33	0.04
Merced (city) Merced County	32	0.04
Tracy (city) San Joaquin County	32	0.04
Modesto (city) Stanislaus County	70	0.03
Visalia (city) Tulare County	33	0.03
Antioch (city) Contra Costa County	27	0.03
Rancho Cordova (city) Sacramento County	19	0.03
Woodland (city) Yolo County	18	0.03

American Indian: Pima

Top 10 Places Sorted by Population

Based on all places, regardless of total population

Place	Population	%
Los Angeles (city) Los Angeles County	152	<0.01
Riverside (city) Riverside County	51	0.02
San Diego (city) San Diego County	44	<0.01
Bakersfield (city) Kern County	41	0.01
Fresno (city) Fresno County	41	0.01
San Jose (city) Santa Clara County	38	<0.01
San Francisco (city) San Francisco County	36	<0.01
Sacramento (city) Sacramento County	33	0.01
Stockton (city) San Joaquin County	31	0.01
Victorville (city) San Bernardino County	30	0.03

Top 10 Places Sorted by Percent of Total Population

Based on all places, regardless of total population

Place	Population	%
Weott (cdp) Humboldt County	4	1.39
Peters (cdp) San Joaquin County	7	1.04
Olancha (cdp) Inyo County	1	0.52
Hood (cdp) Sacramento County	1	0.37
Bombay Beach (cdp) Imperial County	1	0.34
Niland (cdp) Imperial County	3	0.30
Needles (city) San Bernardino County	12	0.25
Davenport (cdp) Santa Cruz County	1	0.25
Val Verde (cdp) Los Angeles County	6	0.24
Stratford (cdp) Kings County	3	0.23

Top 10 Places Sorted by Percent of Total Population

Based on places with total population of 50,000 or more

Place	Population	%
Hanford (city) Kings County	25	0.05
Porterville (city) Tulare County	23	0.04
Victorville (city) San Bernardino County	30	0.03
Riverside (city) Riverside County	51	0.02
West Covina (city) Los Angeles County	22	0.02
Hesperia (city) San Bernardino County	20	0.02
Temecula (city) Riverside County	20	0.02
Norwalk (city) Los Angeles County	18	0.02
Indio (city) Riverside County	15	0.02
South Gate (city) Los Angeles County	15	0.02

American Indian: Potawatomi

Top 10 Places Sorted by Population

Based on all places, regardless of total population

Place	Population	%
Los Angeles (city) Los Angeles County	115	<0.01
San Diego (city) San Diego County	80	0.01
Sacramento (city) Sacramento County	54	0.01
Bakersfield (city) Kern County	52	0.01
San Jose (city) Santa Clara County	52	0.01
Fresno (city) Fresno County	47	0.01
Stockton (city) San Joaquin County	35	0.01
San Francisco (city) San Francisco County	34	<0.01
Visalia (city) Tulare County	31	0.02
Riverside (city) Riverside County	31	0.01

Top 10 Places Sorted by Percent of Total Population

Based on all places, regardless of total population

Place	Population	%
Waukena (cdp) Tulare County	3	2.78
Iron Horse (cdp) Plumas County	5	1.68
Cartago (cdp) Inyo County	1	1.09
Paskenta (cdp) Tehama County	1	0.89
Cressey (cdp) Merced County	3	0.76
Dutch Flat (cdp) Placer County	1	0.63
Big River (cdp) San Bernardino County	8	0.60
Orick (cdp) Humboldt County	2	0.56
Wilkerson (cdp) Inyo County	3	0.53
West Park (cdp) Fresno County	5	0.43

Top 10 Places Sorted by Percent of Total Population

Based on places with total population of 50,000 or more

Place	Population	%
Redding (city) Shasta County	29	0.03
Citrus Heights (city) Sacramento County	25	0.03
Chico (city) Butte County	22	0.03
Carmichael (cdp) Sacramento County	17	0.03
Visalia (city) Tulare County	31	0.02
Temecula (city) Riverside County	24	0.02
San Buenaventura (Ventura) (city) Ventura County	19	0.02
Apple Valley (town) San Bernardino County	15	0.02
Upland (city) San Bernardino County	15	0.02
Hesperia (city) San Bernardino County	14	0.02

American Indian: Pueblo

Top 10 Places Sorted by Population
Based on all places, regardless of total population

Place	Population	%
Los Angeles (city) Los Angeles County	493	0.01
San Diego (city) San Diego County	150	0.01
Barstow (city) San Bernardino County	131	0.58
San Jose (city) Santa Clara County	114	0.01
Long Beach (city) Los Angeles County	83	0.02
Oakland (city) Alameda County	83	0.02
San Francisco (city) San Francisco County	83	0.01
Sacramento (city) Sacramento County	81	0.02
Fresno (city) Fresno County	68	0.01
Riverside (city) Riverside County	66	0.02

Top 10 Places Sorted by Percent of Total Population
Based on all places, regardless of total population

Place	Population	%
Richvale (cdp) Butte County	10	4.10
New Cuyama (cdp) Santa Barbara County	5	0.97
Burnt Ranch (cdp) Trinity County	2	0.71
Tecopa (cdp) Inyo County	1	0.67
Barstow (city) San Bernardino County	131	0.58
Chilcoot-Vinton (cdp) Plumas County	2	0.44
Edmundson Acres (cdp) Kern County	1	0.36
Lenwood (cdp) San Bernardino County	10	0.28
Scotia (cdp) Humboldt County	2	0.24
Bayview (cdp) Contra Costa County	4	0.23

Top 10 Places Sorted by Percent of Total Population
Based on places with total population of 50,000 or more

Place	Population	%
Apple Valley (town) San Bernardino County	58	0.08
Whittier (city) Los Angeles County	45	0.05
Victorville (city) San Bernardino County	45	0.04
El Cajon (city) San Diego County	37	0.04
Rialto (city) San Bernardino County	36	0.04
Tracy (city) San Joaquin County	32	0.04
San Bernardino (city) San Bernardino County	61	0.03
Fontana (city) San Bernardino County	56	0.03
Murrieta (city) Riverside County	36	0.03
San Leandro (city) Alameda County	29	0.03

American Indian: Puget Sound Salish

Top 10 Places Sorted by Population
Based on all places, regardless of total population

Place	Population	%
San Diego (city) San Diego County	32	<0.01
Los Angeles (city) Los Angeles County	22	<0.01
Sacramento (city) Sacramento County	21	<0.01
Bakersfield (city) Kern County	14	<0.01
Torrance (city) Los Angeles County	13	0.01
San Francisco (city) San Francisco County	11	<0.01
San Jose (city) Santa Clara County	11	<0.01
Garden Acres (cdp) San Joaquin County	10	0.09
Visalia (city) Tulare County	10	0.01
Grass Valley (city) Nevada County	9	0.07

Top 10 Places Sorted by Percent of Total Population
Based on all places, regardless of total population

Place	Population	%
Fort Washington (cdp) Fresno County	3	1.29
West Point (cdp) Calaveras County	4	0.59
Clear Creek (cdp) Lassen County	1	0.59
Coffee Creek (cdp) Trinity County	1	0.46
Biola (cdp) Fresno County	6	0.37
Whitley Gardens (cdp) San Luis Obispo County	1	0.35
Buttonwillow (cdp) Kern County	3	0.20
Alturas (city) Modoc County	4	0.14
Walker (cdp) Mono County	1	0.14
Tarpey Village (cdp) Fresno County	5	0.13

Top 10 Places Sorted by Percent of Total Population
Based on places with total population of 50,000 or more

Place	Population	%
Brentwood (city) Contra Costa County	8	0.02
Torrance (city) Los Angeles County	13	0.01
Visalia (city) Tulare County	10	0.01
Encinitas (city) San Diego County	7	0.01
Manteca (city) San Joaquin County	7	0.01
Murrieta (city) Riverside County	7	0.01
Costa Mesa (city) Orange County	6	0.01
South Gate (city) Los Angeles County	6	0.01
Tulare (city) Tulare County	6	0.01
Carmichael (cdp) Sacramento County	5	0.01

American Indian: Seminole

Top 10 Places Sorted by Population
Based on all places, regardless of total population

Place	Population	%
Los Angeles (city) Los Angeles County	234	0.01
San Diego (city) San Diego County	114	0.01
Oakland (city) Alameda County	86	0.02
San Francisco (city) San Francisco County	68	0.01
Sacramento (city) Sacramento County	63	0.01
San Jose (city) Santa Clara County	54	0.01
Fresno (city) Fresno County	49	0.01
Long Beach (city) Los Angeles County	48	0.01
Stockton (city) San Joaquin County	46	0.02
Riverside (city) Riverside County	43	0.01

Top 10 Places Sorted by Percent of Total Population
Based on all places, regardless of total population

Place	Population	%
Goodyears Bar (cdp) Sierra County	1	1.47
Traver (cdp) Tulare County	8	1.12
Chinese Camp (cdp) Tuolumne County	1	0.79
Downieville (cdp) Sierra County	1	0.35
McArthur (cdp) Shasta County	1	0.30
Saticoy (cdp) Ventura County	3	0.29
Mad River (cdp) Trinity County	1	0.24
Hayfork (cdp) Trinity County	5	0.21
Sutter Creek (city) Amador County	5	0.20
Caspar (cdp) Mendocino County	1	0.20

Top 10 Places Sorted by Percent of Total Population
Based on places with total population of 50,000 or more

Place	Population	%
Vacaville (city) Solano County	24	0.03
Manteca (city) San Joaquin County	17	0.03
Tulare (city) Tulare County	15	0.03
Oakland (city) Alameda County	86	0.02
Stockton (city) San Joaquin County	46	0.02
Moreno Valley (city) Riverside County	36	0.02
Vallejo (city) Solano County	26	0.02
Lancaster (city) Los Angeles County	25	0.02
Visalia (city) Tulare County	25	0.02
Victorville (city) San Bernardino County	21	0.02

American Indian: Shoshone

Top 10 Places Sorted by Population
Based on all places, regardless of total population

Place	Population	%
Los Angeles (city) Los Angeles County	116	<0.01
San Diego (city) San Diego County	51	<0.01
Sacramento (city) Sacramento County	49	0.01
San Jose (city) Santa Clara County	46	<0.01
Bakersfield (city) Kern County	45	0.01
Fresno (city) Fresno County	36	0.01
Anaheim (city) Orange County	30	0.01
Long Beach (city) Los Angeles County	29	0.01
Oakland (city) Alameda County	29	0.01
Lancaster (city) Los Angeles County	25	0.02

Top 10 Places Sorted by Percent of Total Population
Based on all places, regardless of total population

Place	Population	%
Furnace Creek (cdp) Inyo County	15	62.50
Tecopa (cdp) Inyo County	7	4.67
Paradise (cdp) Mono County	5	3.27
Cartago (cdp) Inyo County	2	2.17
Chalfant (cdp) Mono County	6	0.92
Lanare (cdp) Fresno County	4	0.68
Camptonville (cdp) Yuba County	1	0.63
Fort Bidwell (cdp) Modoc County	1	0.58
Lone Pine (cdp) Inyo County	10	0.49
Ballico (cdp) Merced County	2	0.49

Top 10 Places Sorted by Percent of Total Population
Based on places with total population of 50,000 or more

Place	Population	%
Chico (city) Butte County	23	0.03
Woodland (city) Yolo County	14	0.03
Lancaster (city) Los Angeles County	25	0.02
Apple Valley (town) San Bernardino County	15	0.02
Citrus Heights (city) Sacramento County	15	0.02
Whittier (city) Los Angeles County	15	0.02
Arden-Arcade (cdp) Sacramento County	14	0.02
Carmichael (cdp) Sacramento County	14	0.02
Lake Elsinore (city) Riverside County	9	0.02
Porterville (city) Tulare County	9	0.02

American Indian: Sioux

Top 10 Places Sorted by Population
Based on all places, regardless of total population

Place	Population	%
Los Angeles (city) Los Angeles County	661	0.02
San Diego (city) San Diego County	335	0.03
San Jose (city) Santa Clara County	313	0.03
Sacramento (city) Sacramento County	302	0.06
San Francisco (city) San Francisco County	251	0.03
Oakland (city) Alameda County	213	0.05
Stockton (city) San Joaquin County	185	0.06
Long Beach (city) Los Angeles County	166	0.04
Fresno (city) Fresno County	149	0.03
Modesto (city) Stanislaus County	105	0.05

Top 10 Places Sorted by Percent of Total Population
Based on all places, regardless of total population

Place	Population	%
Darwin (cdp) Inyo County	2	4.65
Fort Bidwell (cdp) Modoc County	5	2.89
Paskenta (cdp) Tehama County	3	2.68
Daphnedale Park (cdp) Modoc County	4	2.17
Manchester (cdp) Mendocino County	3	1.54
Keddie (cdp) Plumas County	1	1.52
Martell (cdp) Amador County	4	1.42
Forbestown (cdp) Butte County	4	1.25
Richvale (cdp) Butte County	3	1.23
Elk Creek (cdp) Glenn County	2	1.23

Top 10 Places Sorted by Percent of Total Population
Based on places with total population of 50,000 or more

Place	Population	%
Chico (city) Butte County	89	0.10
Rancho Cordova (city) Sacramento County	56	0.09
Arden-Arcade (cdp) Sacramento County	76	0.08
Redding (city) Shasta County	71	0.08
Manteca (city) San Joaquin County	52	0.08
Citrus Heights (city) Sacramento County	62	0.07
Alameda (city) Alameda County	53	0.07
Carmichael (cdp) Sacramento County	42	0.07
Woodland (city) Yolo County	37	0.07
Sacramento (city) Sacramento County	302	0.06

American Indian: South American Indian

Top 10 Places Sorted by Population
Based on all places, regardless of total population

Place	Population	%
Los Angeles (city) Los Angeles County	595	0.02
San Francisco (city) San Francisco County	198	0.02
Oakland (city) Alameda County	134	0.03
San Jose (city) Santa Clara County	133	0.01
San Diego (city) San Diego County	106	0.01
Long Beach (city) Los Angeles County	77	0.02
Berkeley (city) Alameda County	47	0.04
Riverside (city) Riverside County	45	0.01
Sacramento (city) Sacramento County	43	0.01
Irvine (city) Orange County	31	0.01

Top 10 Places Sorted by Percent of Total Population
Based on all places, regardless of total population

Place	Population	%
El Nido (cdp) Merced County	6	1.82
Paradise Park (cdp) Santa Cruz County	2	0.51
Coulterville (cdp) Mariposa County	1	0.50

Place	Population	%
Lake Don Pedro (cdp) Mariposa County	5	0.46
Benton (cdp) Mono County	1	0.36
Spreckels (cdp) Monterey County	2	0.30
Littlerock (cdp) Los Angeles County	4	0.29
North El Monte (cdp) Los Angeles County	10	0.27
Davenport (cdp) Santa Cruz County	1	0.25
Meadow Valley (cdp) Plumas County	1	0.22

Top 10 Places Sorted by Percent of Total Population

Based on places with total population of 50,000 or more

Place	Population	%
Berkeley (city) Alameda County	47	0.04
Oakland (city) Alameda County	134	0.03
San Mateo (city) San Mateo County	27	0.03
Santa Monica (city) Los Angeles County	24	0.03
San Leandro (city) Alameda County	23	0.03
Hawthorne (city) Los Angeles County	22	0.03
Santa Cruz (city) Santa Cruz County	20	0.03
Cathedral City (city) Riverside County	16	0.03
Los Angeles (city) Los Angeles County	595	0.02
San Francisco (city) San Francisco County	198	0.02

American Indian: Spanish American Indian

Top 10 Places Sorted by Population

Based on all places, regardless of total population

Place	Population	%
Los Angeles (city) Los Angeles County	564	0.01
Santa Ana (city) Orange County	170	0.05
Livingston (city) Merced County	87	0.67
San Jose (city) Santa Clara County	82	0.01
Winton (cdp) Merced County	69	0.65
Sacramento (city) Sacramento County	65	0.01
Long Beach (city) Los Angeles County	62	0.01
Fresno (city) Fresno County	58	0.01
Riverside (city) Riverside County	52	0.02
San Diego (city) San Diego County	51	<0.01

Top 10 Places Sorted by Percent of Total Population

Based on all places, regardless of total population

Place	Population	%
Boonville (cdp) Mendocino County	9	0.87
Monument Hills (cdp) Yolo County	12	0.78
Livingston (city) Merced County	87	0.67
Winton (cdp) Merced County	69	0.65
Delhi (cdp) Merced County	46	0.43
Hood (cdp) Sacramento County	1	0.37
Avery (cdp) Calaveras County	2	0.31
Mono Vista (cdp) Tuolumne County	9	0.29
Boronda (cdp) Monterey County	4	0.23
Keene (cdp) Kern County	1	0.23

Top 10 Places Sorted by Percent of Total Population

Based on places with total population of 50,000 or more

Place	Population	%
Santa Ana (city) Orange County	170	0.05
Florence-Graham (cdp) Los Angeles County	34	0.05
Santa Maria (city) Santa Barbara County	40	0.04
East Los Angeles (cdp) Los Angeles County	33	0.03
Vista (city) San Diego County	32	0.03
Compton (city) Los Angeles County	31	0.03
Alhambra (city) Los Angeles County	28	0.03
Merced (city) Merced County	26	0.03
Cathedral City (city) Riverside County	16	0.03
Hacienda Heights (cdp) Los Angeles County	15	0.03

Alaska Native: Tlingit-Haida

Top 10 Places Sorted by Population

Based on all places, regardless of total population

Place	Population	%
San Diego (city) San Diego County	70	0.01
Los Angeles (city) Los Angeles County	69	<0.01
Sacramento (city) Sacramento County	55	0.01
San Jose (city) Santa Clara County	40	<0.01
San Francisco (city) San Francisco County	29	<0.01
Fremont (city) Alameda County	20	0.01
Redding (city) Shasta County	19	0.02
Stockton (city) San Joaquin County	18	0.01
Elk Grove (city) Sacramento County	17	0.01
Santa Rosa (city) Sonoma County	16	0.01

Top 10 Places Sorted by Percent of Total Population

Based on all places, regardless of total population

Place	Population	%
French Gulch (cdp) Shasta County	4	1.16
Nipinnawasee (cdp) Madera County	5	1.05
Long Barn (cdp) Tuolumne County	1	0.65
Orick (cdp) Humboldt County	2	0.56
Ruth (cdp) Trinity County	1	0.51
Coleville (cdp) Mono County	2	0.40
Hornbrook (cdp) Siskiyou County	1	0.40
Plymouth (city) Amador County	3	0.30
Forest Meadows (cdp) Calaveras County	3	0.24
Newell (cdp) Modoc County	1	0.22

Top 10 Places Sorted by Percent of Total Population

Based on places with total population of 50,000 or more

Place	Population	%
Redding (city) Shasta County	19	0.02
Livermore (city) Alameda County	14	0.02
Folsom (city) Sacramento County	12	0.02
Redwood City (city) San Mateo County	12	0.02
Yuba City (city) Sutter County	11	0.02
San Diego (city) San Diego County	70	0.01
Sacramento (city) Sacramento County	55	0.01
Fremont (city) Alameda County	20	0.01
Stockton (city) San Joaquin County	18	0.01
Elk Grove (city) Sacramento County	17	0.01

American Indian: Tohono O'Odham

Top 10 Places Sorted by Population

Based on all places, regardless of total population

Place	Population	%
Los Angeles (city) Los Angeles County	220	0.01
San Diego (city) San Diego County	69	0.01
San Jose (city) Santa Clara County	68	0.01
Fresno (city) Fresno County	62	0.01
Victorville (city) San Bernardino County	35	0.03
Bakersfield (city) Kern County	32	0.01
Oakland (city) Alameda County	29	0.01
Riverside (city) Riverside County	29	0.01
Chula Vista (city) San Diego County	28	0.01
Banning (city) Riverside County	27	0.09

Top 10 Places Sorted by Percent of Total Population

Based on all places, regardless of total population

Place	Population	%
Garden Farms (cdp) San Luis Obispo County	3	0.78
Fort Bidwell (cdp) Modoc County	1	0.58
Groveland (cdp) Tuolumne County	2	0.33
Grenada (cdp) Siskiyou County	1	0.27
Happy Camp (cdp) Siskiyou County	3	0.25
Winterhaven (cdp) Imperial County	1	0.25
Mariposa (cdp) Mariposa County	5	0.23
Keene (cdp) Kern County	1	0.23
Calwa (cdp) Fresno County	4	0.19
Alpaugh (cdp) Tulare County	2	0.19

Top 10 Places Sorted by Percent of Total Population

Based on places with total population of 50,000 or more

Place	Population	%
South Whittier (cdp) Los Angeles County	22	0.04
Victorville (city) San Bernardino County	35	0.03
Montebello (city) Los Angeles County	16	0.03
Hesperia (city) San Bernardino County	19	0.02
San Buenaventura (Ventura) (city) Ventura County	17	0.02
West Covina (city) Los Angeles County	17	0.02
Citrus Heights (city) Sacramento County	15	0.02
Whittier (city) Los Angeles County	13	0.02
Glendora (city) Los Angeles County	12	0.02
Huntington Park (city) Los Angeles County	12	0.02

Alaska Native: Tsimshian

Top 10 Places Sorted by Population

Based on all places, regardless of total population

Place	Population	%
Los Angeles (city) Los Angeles County	14	<0.01
Westminster (city) Orange County	8	0.01
San Francisco (city) San Francisco County	8	<0.01
Chico (city) Butte County	7	0.01
San Diego (city) San Diego County	7	<0.01
Antelope (cdp) Sacramento County	5	0.01
Redding (city) Shasta County	5	0.01
Sacramento (city) Sacramento County	5	<0.01
Larkfield-Wikiup (cdp) Sonoma County	4	0.05
Montebello (city) Los Angeles County	4	0.01

Top 10 Places Sorted by Percent of Total Population

Based on all places, regardless of total population

Place	Population	%
Redway (cdp) Humboldt County	3	0.24
Fort Jones (city) Siskiyou County	1	0.12
Larkfield-Wikiup (cdp) Sonoma County	4	0.05
Fairview (cdp) Alameda County	3	0.03
Grass Valley (city) Nevada County	2	0.02
Fruitridge Pocket (cdp) Sacramento County	1	0.02
Roseland (cdp) Sonoma County	1	0.02
Westminster (city) Orange County	8	0.01
Chico (city) Butte County	7	0.01
Antelope (cdp) Sacramento County	5	0.01

Top 10 Places Sorted by Percent of Total Population

Based on places with total population of 50,000 or more

Place	Population	%
Westminster (city) Orange County	8	0.01
Chico (city) Butte County	7	0.01
Redding (city) Shasta County	5	0.01
Montebello (city) Los Angeles County	4	0.01
Los Angeles (city) Los Angeles County	14	<0.01
San Francisco (city) San Francisco County	8	<0.01
San Diego (city) San Diego County	7	<0.01
Sacramento (city) Sacramento County	5	<0.01
Arden-Arcade (cdp) Sacramento County	4	<0.01
Elk Grove (city) Sacramento County	4	<0.01

American Indian: Ute

Top 10 Places Sorted by Population

Based on all places, regardless of total population

Place	Population	%
Los Angeles (city) Los Angeles County	48	<0.01
San Diego (city) San Diego County	22	<0.01
Sacramento (city) Sacramento County	21	<0.01
Fresno (city) Fresno County	20	<0.01
Long Beach (city) Los Angeles County	19	<0.01
Manteca (city) San Joaquin County	18	0.03
San Francisco (city) San Francisco County	18	<0.01
San Jose (city) Santa Clara County	17	<0.01
Concord (city) Contra Costa County	16	0.01
Riverside (city) Riverside County	16	0.01

Top 10 Places Sorted by Percent of Total Population

Based on all places, regardless of total population

Place	Population	%
Hood (cdp) Sacramento County	3	1.11
Fort Bidwell (cdp) Modoc County	1	0.58
Canby (cdp) Modoc County	1	0.32
Delleker (cdp) Plumas County	2	0.28
Lebec (cdp) Kern County	4	0.27
Cold Springs (cdp) El Dorado County	1	0.22
Bayview (cdp) Humboldt County	5	0.20
Crockett (cdp) Contra Costa County	6	0.19
Twain Harte (cdp) Tuolumne County	4	0.18
Groveland (cdp) Tuolumne County	1	0.17

Top 10 Places Sorted by Percent of Total Population

Based on places with total population of 50,000 or more

Place	Population	%
Manteca (city) San Joaquin County	18	0.03
Concord (city) Contra Costa County	16	0.01
Riverside (city) Riverside County	16	0.01
Stockton (city) San Joaquin County	15	0.01
Corona (city) Riverside County	12	0.01
Livermore (city) Alameda County	11	0.01
Santa Clarita (city) Los Angeles County	11	0.01
Santa Rosa (city) Sonoma County	10	0.01
Antioch (city) Contra Costa County	9	0.01
Rancho Cucamonga (city) San Bernardino County	9	0.01

American Indian: Yakama

Top 10 Places Sorted by Population
Based on all places, regardless of total population

Place	Population	%
Los Angeles (city) Los Angeles County	15	<0.01
San Diego (city) San Diego County	12	<0.01
Lodi (city) San Joaquin County	11	0.02
El Paso de Robles (Paso Robles) (city) San Luis Obispo County	7	0.02
Long Beach (city) Los Angeles County	7	<0.01
Oakland (city) Alameda County	7	<0.01
San Francisco (city) San Francisco County	7	<0.01
San Jose (city) Santa Clara County	7	<0.01
Madera (city) Madera County	6	0.01
Redondo Beach (city) Los Angeles County	6	0.01

Top 10 Places Sorted by Percent of Total Population
Based on all places, regardless of total population

Place	Population	%
Keeler (cdp) Inyo County	1	1.52
Hat Creek (cdp) Shasta County	1	0.32
San Geronimo (cdp) Marin County	1	0.22
Rail Road Flat (cdp) Calaveras County	1	0.21
Linden (cdp) San Joaquin County	3	0.17
Etna (city) Siskiyou County	1	0.14
Zayante (cdp) Santa Cruz County	1	0.14
Rancho Tehama Reserve (cdp) Tehama County	2	0.13
Klamath (cdp) Del Norte County	1	0.13
Burney (cdp) Shasta County	3	0.10

Top 10 Places Sorted by Percent of Total Population
Based on places with total population of 50,000 or more

Place	Population	%
Lodi (city) San Joaquin County	11	0.02
Madera (city) Madera County	6	0.01
Redondo Beach (city) Los Angeles County	6	0.01
Chico (city) Butte County	5	0.01
Woodland (city) Yolo County	5	0.01
Carmichael (cdp) Sacramento County	4	0.01
Folsom (city) Sacramento County	4	0.01
Manteca (city) San Joaquin County	4	0.01
Los Angeles (city) Los Angeles County	15	<0.01
San Diego (city) San Diego County	12	<0.01

American Indian: Yaqui

Top 10 Places Sorted by Population
Based on all places, regardless of total population

Place	Population	%
Los Angeles (city) Los Angeles County	647	0.02
Fresno (city) Fresno County	522	0.11
San Jose (city) Santa Clara County	354	0.04
San Diego (city) San Diego County	310	0.02
Sacramento (city) Sacramento County	207	0.04
Stockton (city) San Joaquin County	166	0.06
Bakersfield (city) Kern County	154	0.04
Long Beach (city) Los Angeles County	130	0.03
San Bernardino (city) San Bernardino County	108	0.05
Riverside (city) Riverside County	103	0.03

Top 10 Places Sorted by Percent of Total Population
Based on all places, regardless of total population

Place	Population	%
Clear Creek (cdp) Lassen County	4	2.37
Winterhaven (cdp) Imperial County	9	2.28
Gazelle (cdp) Siskiyou County	1	1.43
Soda Springs (cdp) Nevada County	1	1.23
Cromberg (cdp) Plumas County	3	1.15
Lemon Cove (cdp) Tulare County	3	0.97
Tehama (city) Tehama County	4	0.96
Linnell Camp (cdp) Tulare County	7	0.82
Raisin City (cdp) Fresno County	3	0.79
West Park (cdp) Fresno County	9	0.78

Top 10 Places Sorted by Percent of Total Population
Based on places with total population of 50,000 or more

Place	Population	%
Fresno (city) Fresno County	522	0.11
Pico Rivera (city) Los Angeles County	56	0.09
Hesperia (city) San Bernardino County	59	0.07
Redlands (city) San Bernardino County	47	0.07
South Whittier (cdp) Los Angeles County	42	0.07
Stockton (city) San Joaquin County	166	0.06
Rialto (city) San Bernardino County	63	0.06
Whittier (city) Los Angeles County	50	0.06
Manteca (city) San Joaquin County	37	0.06
Delano (city) Kern County	33	0.06

American Indian: Yuman

Top 10 Places Sorted by Population
Based on all places, regardless of total population

Place	Population	%
Needles (city) San Bernardino County	153	3.16
Los Angeles (city) Los Angeles County	105	<0.01
Riverside (city) Riverside County	48	0.02
San Diego (city) San Diego County	48	<0.01
San Jose (city) Santa Clara County	41	<0.01
Long Beach (city) Los Angeles County	37	0.01
Victorville (city) San Bernardino County	30	0.03
San Bernardino (city) San Bernardino County	27	0.01
Anaheim (city) Orange County	26	0.01
Fresno (city) Fresno County	26	0.01

Top 10 Places Sorted by Percent of Total Population
Based on all places, regardless of total population

Place	Population	%
Winterhaven (cdp) Imperial County	21	5.33
Needles (city) San Bernardino County	153	3.16
Alderpoint (cdp) Humboldt County	5	2.69
Crescent Mills (cdp) Plumas County	3	1.53
Miranda (cdp) Humboldt County	5	0.96
El Rancho (cdp) Tulare County	1	0.81
Desert Shores (cdp) Imperial County	7	0.63
Bluewater (cdp) San Bernardino County	1	0.58
West Park (cdp) Fresno County	5	0.43
Big River (cdp) San Bernardino County	5	0.38

Top 10 Places Sorted by Percent of Total Population
Based on places with total population of 50,000 or more

Place	Population	%
Victorville (city) San Bernardino County	30	0.03
Porterville (city) Tulare County	17	0.03
Colton (city) San Bernardino County	14	0.03
Riverside (city) Riverside County	48	0.02
Hemet (city) Riverside County	14	0.02
Apple Valley (town) San Bernardino County	11	0.02
Delano (city) Kern County	8	0.02
Long Beach (city) Los Angeles County	37	0.01
San Bernardino (city) San Bernardino County	27	0.01
Anaheim (city) Orange County	26	0.01

Alaska Native: Yup'ik

Top 10 Places Sorted by Population
Based on all places, regardless of total population

Place	Population	%
San Diego (city) San Diego County	20	<0.01
Los Angeles (city) Los Angeles County	17	<0.01
Fort Irwin (cdp) San Bernardino County	9	0.10
Rancho Cucamonga (city) San Bernardino County	9	0.01
Oroville (city) Butte County	6	0.04
Lompoc (city) Santa Barbara County	6	0.01
Elk Grove (city) Sacramento County	6	<0.01
Fountain Valley (city) Orange County	5	0.01
Hacienda Heights (cdp) Los Angeles County	5	0.01
Huntington Beach (city) Orange County	5	<0.01

Top 10 Places Sorted by Percent of Total Population
Based on all places, regardless of total population

Place	Population	%
Bertsch-Oceanview (cdp) Del Norte County	4	0.16
Fort Irwin (cdp) San Bernardino County	9	0.10
Pleasure Point (cdp) Santa Cruz County	4	0.07
Silver Lakes (cdp) San Bernardino County	4	0.07
Calistoga (city) Napa County	3	0.06
Rio Dell (city) Humboldt County	2	0.06
Carmel-by-the-Sea (city) Monterey County	2	0.05
Three Rivers (cdp) Tulare County	1	0.05
Oroville (city) Butte County	6	0.04
Yreka (city) Siskiyou County	3	0.04

Top 10 Places Sorted by Percent of Total Population
Based on places with total population of 50,000 or more

Place	Population	%
Rancho Cucamonga (city) San Bernardino County	9	0.01
Fountain Valley (city) Orange County	5	0.01
Hacienda Heights (cdp) Los Angeles County	5	0.01
Gardena (city) Los Angeles County	4	0.01
San Diego (city) San Diego County	20	<0.01
Los Angeles (city) Los Angeles County	17	<0.01
Elk Grove (city) Sacramento County	6	<0.01
Huntington Beach (city) Orange County	5	<0.01
San Francisco (city) San Francisco County	5	<0.01
Santa Rosa (city) Sonoma County	5	<0.01

Asian

Top 10 Places Sorted by Population
Based on all places, regardless of total population

Place	Population	%
Los Angeles (city) Los Angeles County	483,585	12.75
San Jose (city) Santa Clara County	326,627	34.53
San Francisco (city) San Francisco County	288,529	35.83
San Diego (city) San Diego County	241,293	18.46
Fremont (city) Alameda County	116,755	54.54
Sacramento (city) Sacramento County	98,705	21.16
Irvine (city) Orange County	91,896	43.27
Oakland (city) Alameda County	73,775	18.88
Stockton (city) San Joaquin County	71,852	24.63
Fresno (city) Fresno County	69,765	14.10

Top 10 Places Sorted by Percent of Total Population
Based on all places, regardless of total population

Place	Population	%
Monterey Park (city) Los Angeles County	41,284	68.50
Cupertino (city) Santa Clara County	38,503	66.04
Walnut (city) Los Angeles County	19,258	66.02
Milpitas (city) Santa Clara County	43,466	65.08
Cerritos (city) Los Angeles County	31,691	64.62
San Gabriel (city) Los Angeles County	24,672	62.12
Rosemead (city) Los Angeles County	33,107	61.58
Rowland Heights (cdp) Los Angeles County	30,088	61.41
Arcadia (city) Los Angeles County	34,416	61.06
Daly City (city) San Mateo County	59,093	58.44

Top 10 Places Sorted by Percent of Total Population
Based on places with total population of 50,000 or more

Place	Population	%
Monterey Park (city) Los Angeles County	41,284	68.50
Cupertino (city) Santa Clara County	38,503	66.04
Milpitas (city) Santa Clara County	43,466	65.08
Rosemead (city) Los Angeles County	33,107	61.58
Arcadia (city) Los Angeles County	34,416	61.06
Daly City (city) San Mateo County	59,093	58.44
Union City (city) Alameda County	38,427	55.28
Diamond Bar (city) Los Angeles County	30,478	54.87
Alhambra (city) Los Angeles County	45,395	54.63
Fremont (city) Alameda County	116,755	54.54

Asian: Not Hispanic

Top 10 Places Sorted by Population
Based on all places, regardless of total population

Place	Population	%
Los Angeles (city) Los Angeles County	465,942	12.29
San Jose (city) Santa Clara County	318,607	33.68
San Francisco (city) San Francisco County	283,435	35.20
San Diego (city) San Diego County	232,029	17.75
Fremont (city) Alameda County	115,097	53.76
Sacramento (city) Sacramento County	94,141	20.18
Irvine (city) Orange County	90,762	42.74
Oakland (city) Alameda County	71,892	18.40
Stockton (city) San Joaquin County	65,993	22.62
Fresno (city) Fresno County	65,854	13.31

Top 10 Places Sorted by Percent of Total Population
Based on all places, regardless of total population

Place	Population	%
Monterey Park (city) Los Angeles County	40,660	67.46
Cupertino (city) Santa Clara County	38,342	65.76
Walnut (city) Los Angeles County	18,976	65.05

Place	Population	%
Milpitas (city) Santa Clara County	42,929	64.27
Cerritos (city) Los Angeles County	31,229	63.68
San Gabriel (city) Los Angeles County	24,430	61.51
Rosemead (city) Los Angeles County	32,749	60.91
Rowland Heights (cdp) Los Angeles County	29,752	60.73
Arcadia (city) Los Angeles County	34,096	60.49
Daly City (city) San Mateo County	57,841	57.20

Top 10 Places Sorted by Percent of Total Population
Based on places with total population of 50,000 or more

Place	Population	%
Monterey Park (city) Los Angeles County	40,660	67.46
Cupertino (city) Santa Clara County	38,342	65.76
Milpitas (city) Santa Clara County	42,929	64.27
Rosemead (city) Los Angeles County	32,749	60.91
Arcadia (city) Los Angeles County	34,096	60.49
Daly City (city) San Mateo County	57,841	57.20
Union City (city) Alameda County	37,720	54.26
Diamond Bar (city) Los Angeles County	29,892	53.82
Fremont (city) Alameda County	115,097	53.76
Alhambra (city) Los Angeles County	44,579	53.65

Asian: Hispanic

Top 10 Places Sorted by Population
Based on all places, regardless of total population

Place	Population	%
Los Angeles (city) Los Angeles County	17,643	0.47
San Diego (city) San Diego County	9,264	0.71
San Jose (city) Santa Clara County	8,020	0.85
Stockton (city) San Joaquin County	5,859	2.01
San Francisco (city) San Francisco County	5,094	0.63
Sacramento (city) Sacramento County	4,564	0.98
Fresno (city) Fresno County	3,911	0.79
Chula Vista (city) San Diego County	3,739	1.53
Long Beach (city) Los Angeles County	3,127	0.68
Bakersfield (city) Kern County	2,380	0.68

Top 10 Places Sorted by Percent of Total Population
Based on all places, regardless of total population

Place	Population	%
Bucks Lake (cdp) Plumas County	3	30.00
Posey (cdp) Tulare County	1	10.00
Big Creek (cdp) Fresno County	7	4.00
C-Road (cdp) Plumas County	6	4.00
Niland (cdp) Imperial County	38	3.78
Davenport (cdp) Santa Cruz County	13	3.19
Drytown (cdp) Amador County	5	2.99
Guadalupe (city) Santa Barbara County	200	2.82
Country Club (cdp) San Joaquin County	263	2.80
Lincoln Village (cdp) San Joaquin County	114	2.60

Top 10 Places Sorted by Percent of Total Population
Based on places with total population of 50,000 or more

Place	Population	%
Stockton (city) San Joaquin County	5,859	2.01
Chula Vista (city) San Diego County	3,739	1.53
South San Francisco (city) San Mateo County	902	1.42
Delano (city) Kern County	698	1.32
Salinas (city) Monterey County	1,935	1.29
Elk Grove (city) Sacramento County	1,960	1.28
Tracy (city) San Joaquin County	1,064	1.28
Daly City (city) San Mateo County	1,252	1.24
Fairfield (city) Solano County	1,258	1.19
Vallejo (city) Solano County	1,353	1.17

Asian: Bangladeshi

Top 10 Places Sorted by Population
Based on all places, regardless of total population

Place	Population	%
Los Angeles (city) Los Angeles County	3,483	0.09
San Jose (city) Santa Clara County	576	0.06
San Diego (city) San Diego County	254	0.02
Anaheim (city) Orange County	240	0.07
Fremont (city) Alameda County	231	0.11
Glendale (city) Los Angeles County	182	0.09
Long Beach (city) Los Angeles County	180	0.04
Santa Clara (city) Santa Clara County	177	0.15
Rancho Cucamonga (city) San Bernardino County	144	0.09
Irvine (city) Orange County	136	0.06

Top 10 Places Sorted by Percent of Total Population
Based on all places, regardless of total population

Place	Population	%
Albion (cdp) Mendocino County	2	1.19
Muir Beach (cdp) Marin County	2	0.65
Loma Linda (city) San Bernardino County	93	0.40
Santa Susana (cdp) Ventura County	3	0.29
University of California Davis (cdp) Yolo County	15	0.26
Artesia (city) Los Angeles County	36	0.22
Hawaiian Gardens (city) Los Angeles County	30	0.21
Fruitdale (cdp) Santa Clara County	2	0.21
Santa Clara (city) Santa Clara County	177	0.15
Folsom (city) Sacramento County	99	0.14

Top 10 Places Sorted by Percent of Total Population
Based on places with total population of 50,000 or more

Place	Population	%
Santa Clara (city) Santa Clara County	177	0.15
Folsom (city) Sacramento County	99	0.14
Fremont (city) Alameda County	231	0.11
Tustin (city) Orange County	81	0.11
Cupertino (city) Santa Clara County	67	0.11
Redlands (city) San Bernardino County	71	0.10
Los Angeles (city) Los Angeles County	3,483	0.09
Glendale (city) Los Angeles County	182	0.09
Rancho Cucamonga (city) San Bernardino County	144	0.09
Milpitas (city) Santa Clara County	58	0.09

Asian: Bhutanese

Top 10 Places Sorted by Population
Based on all places, regardless of total population

Place	Population	%
Oakland (city) Alameda County	272	0.07
Arden-Arcade (cdp) Sacramento County	142	0.15
San Diego (city) San Diego County	81	0.01
Alameda (city) Alameda County	71	0.10
Los Angeles (city) Los Angeles County	36	<0.01
Carmichael (cdp) Sacramento County	24	0.04
Santa Clara (city) Santa Clara County	22	0.02
Stanford (cdp) Santa Clara County	10	0.07
Santa Barbara (city) Santa Barbara County	10	0.01
Sacramento (city) Sacramento County	8	<0.01

Top 10 Places Sorted by Percent of Total Population
Based on all places, regardless of total population

Place	Population	%
Arden-Arcade (cdp) Sacramento County	142	0.15
Marin City (cdp) Marin County	4	0.15
Alameda (city) Alameda County	71	0.10
Oakland (city) Alameda County	272	0.07
Stanford (cdp) Santa Clara County	10	0.07
Carmichael (cdp) Sacramento County	24	0.04
San Anselmo (town) Marin County	4	0.03
Santa Clara (city) Santa Clara County	22	0.02
San Pablo (city) Contra Costa County	7	0.02
Los Osos (cdp) San Luis Obispo County	3	0.02

Top 10 Places Sorted by Percent of Total Population
Based on places with total population of 50,000 or more

Place	Population	%
Arden-Arcade (cdp) Sacramento County	142	0.15
Alameda (city) Alameda County	71	0.10
Oakland (city) Alameda County	272	0.07
Carmichael (cdp) Sacramento County	24	0.04
Santa Clara (city) Santa Clara County	22	0.02
San Diego (city) San Diego County	81	0.01
Santa Barbara (city) Santa Barbara County	10	0.01
Chino (city) San Bernardino County	5	0.01
Folsom (city) Sacramento County	4	0.01
Los Angeles (city) Los Angeles County	36	<0.01

Asian: Burmese

Top 10 Places Sorted by Population
Based on all places, regardless of total population

Place	Population	%
Daly City (city) San Mateo County	2,023	2.00
San Francisco (city) San Francisco County	1,579	0.20
Fremont (city) Alameda County	1,450	0.68
Los Angeles (city) Los Angeles County	842	0.02
San Diego (city) San Diego County	824	0.06
San Jose (city) Santa Clara County	602	0.06
Alhambra (city) Los Angeles County	528	0.64
Oakland (city) Alameda County	377	0.10
Rosemead (city) Los Angeles County	376	0.70
Arcadia (city) Los Angeles County	376	0.67

Top 10 Places Sorted by Percent of Total Population
Based on all places, regardless of total population

Place	Population	%
Daly City (city) San Mateo County	2,023	2.00
South San Gabriel (cdp) Los Angeles County	65	0.81
Talmage (cdp) Mendocino County	8	0.71
Rosemead (city) Los Angeles County	376	0.70
Broadmoor (cdp) San Mateo County	29	0.69
Fremont (city) Alameda County	1,450	0.68
Arcadia (city) Los Angeles County	376	0.67
San Gabriel (city) Los Angeles County	261	0.66
Alhambra (city) Los Angeles County	528	0.64
Grangeville (cdp) Kings County	3	0.64

Top 10 Places Sorted by Percent of Total Population
Based on places with total population of 50,000 or more

Place	Population	%
Daly City (city) San Mateo County	2,023	2.00
Rosemead (city) Los Angeles County	376	0.70
Fremont (city) Alameda County	1,450	0.68
Arcadia (city) Los Angeles County	376	0.67
Alhambra (city) Los Angeles County	528	0.64
Monterey Park (city) Los Angeles County	279	0.46
Union City (city) Alameda County	314	0.45
Diamond Bar (city) Los Angeles County	166	0.30
South San Francisco (city) San Mateo County	168	0.26
El Monte (city) Los Angeles County	241	0.21

Asian: Cambodian

Top 10 Places Sorted by Population
Based on all places, regardless of total population

Place	Population	%
Long Beach (city) Los Angeles County	19,998	4.33
Stockton (city) San Joaquin County	11,429	3.92
San Jose (city) Santa Clara County	4,934	0.52
Fresno (city) Fresno County	4,798	0.97
San Diego (city) San Diego County	4,650	0.36
Los Angeles (city) Los Angeles County	4,280	0.11
Oakland (city) Alameda County	3,175	0.81
Modesto (city) Stanislaus County	2,752	1.37
Santa Ana (city) Orange County	1,818	0.56
San Francisco (city) San Francisco County	1,518	0.19

Top 10 Places Sorted by Percent of Total Population
Based on all places, regardless of total population

Place	Population	%
Signal Hill (city) Los Angeles County	927	8.42
Rouse (cdp) Stanislaus County	152	7.58
Long Beach (city) Los Angeles County	19,998	4.33
Stockton (city) San Joaquin County	11,429	3.92
West Modesto (cdp) Stanislaus County	138	2.43
Wheatland (city) Yuba County	84	2.43
Paradise (cdp) Mono County	3	1.96
Rosemead (city) Los Angeles County	994	1.85
Riverdale Park (cdp) Stanislaus County	19	1.68
Lakewood (city) Los Angeles County	1,317	1.65

Top 10 Places Sorted by Percent of Total Population
Based on places with total population of 50,000 or more

Place	Population	%
Long Beach (city) Los Angeles County	19,998	4.33
Stockton (city) San Joaquin County	11,429	3.92
Rosemead (city) Los Angeles County	994	1.85
Lakewood (city) Los Angeles County	1,317	1.65
Modesto (city) Stanislaus County	2,752	1.37
Bellflower (city) Los Angeles County	978	1.28
Monterey Park (city) Los Angeles County	676	1.12
Fresno (city) Fresno County	4,798	0.97
Oakland (city) Alameda County	3,175	0.81
Norwalk (city) Los Angeles County	743	0.70

Asian: Chinese, except Taiwanese

Top 10 Places Sorted by Population
Based on all places, regardless of total population

Place	Population	%
San Francisco (city) San Francisco County	181,707	22.57
Los Angeles (city) Los Angeles County	75,827	2.00
San Jose (city) Santa Clara County	67,093	7.09
San Diego (city) San Diego County	40,557	3.10
Oakland (city) Alameda County	37,235	9.53
Fremont (city) Alameda County	36,484	17.04
Alhambra (city) Los Angeles County	31,493	37.90
Monterey Park (city) Los Angeles County	29,537	49.01
Irvine (city) Orange County	25,177	11.85
Sacramento (city) Sacramento County	23,350	5.01

Top 10 Places Sorted by Percent of Total Population
Based on all places, regardless of total population

Place	Population	%
Monterey Park (city) Los Angeles County	29,537	49.01
San Gabriel (city) Los Angeles County	17,137	43.15
Temple City (city) Los Angeles County	13,931	39.18
Arcadia (city) Los Angeles County	21,744	38.58
Rosemead (city) Los Angeles County	20,548	38.22
Alhambra (city) Los Angeles County	31,493	37.90
San Marino (city) Los Angeles County	4,707	35.80
Rowland Heights (cdp) Los Angeles County	16,563	33.81
East San Gabriel (cdp) Los Angeles County	4,965	33.38
Walnut (city) Los Angeles County	9,242	31.68

Top 10 Places Sorted by Percent of Total Population
Based on places with total population of 50,000 or more

Place	Population	%
Monterey Park (city) Los Angeles County	29,537	49.01
Arcadia (city) Los Angeles County	21,744	38.58
Rosemead (city) Los Angeles County	20,548	38.22
Alhambra (city) Los Angeles County	31,493	37.90
Cupertino (city) Santa Clara County	14,930	25.61
Diamond Bar (city) Los Angeles County	12,547	22.59
San Francisco (city) San Francisco County	181,707	22.57
Hacienda Heights (cdp) Los Angeles County	11,348	21.00
Fremont (city) Alameda County	36,484	17.04
Daly City (city) San Mateo County	16,992	16.80

Asian: Filipino

Top 10 Places Sorted by Population
Based on all places, regardless of total population

Place	Population	%
Los Angeles (city) Los Angeles County	139,859	3.69
San Diego (city) San Diego County	92,828	7.10
San Jose (city) Santa Clara County	62,549	6.61
San Francisco (city) San Francisco County	43,646	5.42
Daly City (city) San Mateo County	36,028	35.63
Chula Vista (city) San Diego County	31,344	12.85
Vallejo (city) Solano County	27,622	23.82
Stockton (city) San Joaquin County	27,113	9.29
Long Beach (city) Los Angeles County	24,963	5.40
Carson (city) Los Angeles County	21,539	23.48

Top 10 Places Sorted by Percent of Total Population
Based on all places, regardless of total population

Place	Population	%
Daly City (city) San Mateo County	36,028	35.63
Bucks Lake (cdp) Plumas County	3	30.00
American Canyon (city) Napa County	5,572	28.64
Hercules (city) Contra Costa County	6,670	27.72
Colma (town) San Mateo County	473	26.40
Broadmoor (cdp) San Mateo County	1,075	25.74
Vallejo (city) Solano County	27,622	23.82
Carson (city) Los Angeles County	21,539	23.48
South San Francisco (city) San Mateo County	14,358	22.56
Union City (city) Alameda County	15,289	21.99

Top 10 Places Sorted by Percent of Total Population
Based on places with total population of 50,000 or more

Place	Population	%
Daly City (city) San Mateo County	36,028	35.63
Vallejo (city) Solano County	27,622	23.82
Carson (city) Los Angeles County	21,539	23.48
South San Francisco (city) San Mateo County	14,358	22.56
Union City (city) Alameda County	15,289	21.99
Milpitas (city) Santa Clara County	12,649	18.94
National City (city) San Diego County	10,695	18.26
Delano (city) Kern County	6,927	13.06
Chula Vista (city) San Diego County	31,344	12.85
Hayward (city) Alameda County	17,134	11.88

Asian: Hmong

Top 10 Places Sorted by Population
Based on all places, regardless of total population

Place	Population	%
Fresno (city) Fresno County	24,328	4.92
Sacramento (city) Sacramento County	16,676	3.57
Stockton (city) San Joaquin County	6,073	2.08
Merced (city) Merced County	4,741	6.00
Clovis (city) Fresno County	3,001	3.14
Florin (cdp) Sacramento County	2,933	6.17
Elk Grove (city) Sacramento County	1,789	1.17
Linda (cdp) Yuba County	1,742	9.80
Chico (city) Butte County	1,225	1.42
San Diego (city) San Diego County	1,166	0.09

Top 10 Places Sorted by Percent of Total Population
Based on all places, regardless of total population

Place	Population	%
Biola (cdp) Fresno County	249	15.34
Thermalito (cdp) Butte County	966	14.54
South Oroville (cdp) Butte County	726	12.64
Franklin (cdp) Merced County	744	12.10
Cherokee (cdp) Butte County	7	10.14
Linda (cdp) Yuba County	1,742	9.80
Trowbridge (cdp) Sutter County	20	8.85
Lemon Hill (cdp) Sacramento County	1,009	7.35
Fruitridge Pocket (cdp) Sacramento County	422	7.28
Florin (cdp) Sacramento County	2,933	6.17

Top 10 Places Sorted by Percent of Total Population
Based on places with total population of 50,000 or more

Place	Population	%
Merced (city) Merced County	4,741	6.00
Fresno (city) Fresno County	24,328	4.92
Sacramento (city) Sacramento County	16,676	3.57
Clovis (city) Fresno County	3,001	3.14
Stockton (city) San Joaquin County	6,073	2.08
Chico (city) Butte County	1,225	1.42
Elk Grove (city) Sacramento County	1,789	1.17
Rancho Cordova (city) Sacramento County	440	0.68
Visalia (city) Tulare County	594	0.48
Porterville (city) Tulare County	203	0.37

Asian: Indian

Top 10 Places Sorted by Population
Based on all places, regardless of total population

Place	Population	%
San Jose (city) Santa Clara County	46,410	4.91
Fremont (city) Alameda County	40,010	18.69
Los Angeles (city) Los Angeles County	38,574	1.02
Sunnyvale (city) Santa Clara County	22,285	15.91
San Diego (city) San Diego County	19,096	1.46
Santa Clara (city) Santa Clara County	16,412	14.09
Cupertino (city) Santa Clara County	13,415	23.01
San Francisco (city) San Francisco County	11,583	1.44
Irvine (city) Orange County	11,325	5.33
Sacramento (city) Sacramento County	10,700	2.29

Top 10 Places Sorted by Percent of Total Population
Based on all places, regardless of total population

Place	Population	%
Cupertino (city) Santa Clara County	13,415	23.01
Fremont (city) Alameda County	40,010	18.69
Sunnyvale (city) Santa Clara County	22,285	15.91
Livingston (city) Merced County	2,039	15.61
Yuba City (city) Sutter County	9,352	14.40
Norris Canyon (cdp) Contra Costa County	137	14.32
Santa Clara (city) Santa Clara County	16,412	14.09
Union City (city) Alameda County	8,570	12.33
Foster City (city) San Mateo County	3,593	11.75
San Ramon (city) Contra Costa County	8,468	11.74

Top 10 Places Sorted by Percent of Total Population
Based on places with total population of 50,000 or more

Place	Population	%
Cupertino (city) Santa Clara County	13,415	23.01
Fremont (city) Alameda County	40,010	18.69
Sunnyvale (city) Santa Clara County	22,285	15.91
Yuba City (city) Sutter County	9,352	14.40
Santa Clara (city) Santa Clara County	16,412	14.09
Union City (city) Alameda County	8,570	12.33
San Ramon (city) Contra Costa County	8,468	11.74
Milpitas (city) Santa Clara County	6,602	9.88
Pleasanton (city) Alameda County	5,476	7.79
Mountain View (city) Santa Clara County	4,612	6.23

Asian: Indonesian

Top 10 Places Sorted by Population
Based on all places, regardless of total population

Place	Population	%
Los Angeles (city) Los Angeles County	3,670	0.10
San Francisco (city) San Francisco County	1,349	0.17
San Jose (city) Santa Clara County	948	0.10
Loma Linda (city) San Bernardino County	929	3.99
San Diego (city) San Diego County	879	0.07
San Bernardino (city) San Bernardino County	769	0.37
Rancho Cucamonga (city) San Bernardino County	723	0.44
Alhambra (city) Los Angeles County	647	0.78
Fontana (city) San Bernardino County	503	0.26
Irvine (city) Orange County	498	0.23

Top 10 Places Sorted by Percent of Total Population
Based on all places, regardless of total population

Place	Population	%
Loma Linda (city) San Bernardino County	929	3.99
North El Monte (cdp) Los Angeles County	43	1.15
Burnt Ranch (cdp) Trinity County	3	1.07
Norris Canyon (cdp) Contra Costa County	10	1.04
Wallace (cdp) Calaveras County	4	0.99
Walnut (city) Los Angeles County	280	0.96
Rowland Heights (cdp) Los Angeles County	459	0.94
Colton (city) San Bernardino County	429	0.82
East San Gabriel (cdp) Los Angeles County	118	0.79
Alhambra (city) Los Angeles County	647	0.78

Top 10 Places Sorted by Percent of Total Population
Based on places with total population of 50,000 or more

Place	Population	%
Colton (city) San Bernardino County	429	0.82
Alhambra (city) Los Angeles County	647	0.78
Arcadia (city) Los Angeles County	422	0.75
Redlands (city) San Bernardino County	434	0.63
Diamond Bar (city) Los Angeles County	350	0.63
Chino Hills (city) San Bernardino County	389	0.52
Upland (city) San Bernardino County	371	0.50
Monterey Park (city) Los Angeles County	284	0.47
Rancho Cucamonga (city) San Bernardino County	723	0.44
West Covina (city) Los Angeles County	427	0.40

Asian: Japanese

Top 10 Places Sorted by Population
Based on all places, regardless of total population

Place	Population	%
Los Angeles (city) Los Angeles County	43,978	1.16
Torrance (city) Los Angeles County	18,532	12.74
San Diego (city) San Diego County	16,815	1.29
San Jose (city) Santa Clara County	16,322	1.73
San Francisco (city) San Francisco County	15,278	1.90
Irvine (city) Orange County	8,797	4.14
Sacramento (city) Sacramento County	8,759	1.88
Gardena (city) Los Angeles County	6,584	11.19
Long Beach (city) Los Angeles County	4,683	1.01
Huntington Beach (city) Orange County	4,451	2.34

Top 10 Places Sorted by Percent of Total Population
Based on all places, regardless of total population

Place	Population	%
Torrance (city) Los Angeles County	18,532	12.74
Gardena (city) Los Angeles County	6,584	11.19
Rancho Palos Verdes (city) Los Angeles County	3,577	8.59

Rolling Hills Estates (city) Los Angeles County	645	8.00
South San Gabriel (cdp) Los Angeles County	607	7.52
Rose Hills (cdp) Los Angeles County	190	6.78
Monterey Park (city) Los Angeles County	4,034	6.69
Buck Meadows (cdp) Mariposa County	2	6.45
Spring Garden (cdp) Plumas County	1	6.25
La Palma (city) Orange County	886	5.69

Top 10 Places Sorted by Percent of Total Population
Based on places with total population of 50,000 or more

Place	Population	%
Torrance (city) Los Angeles County	18,532	12.74
Gardena (city) Los Angeles County	6,584	11.19
Monterey Park (city) Los Angeles County	4,034	6.69
Cupertino (city) Santa Clara County	2,489	4.27
Irvine (city) Orange County	8,797	4.14
Redondo Beach (city) Los Angeles County	2,658	3.98
Fountain Valley (city) Orange County	1,817	3.28
San Mateo (city) San Mateo County	2,835	2.92
Palo Alto (city) Santa Clara County	1,831	2.84
Sunnyvale (city) Santa Clara County	3,950	2.82

Asian: Korean

Top 10 Places Sorted by Population
Based on all places, regardless of total population

Place	Population	%
Los Angeles (city) Los Angeles County	114,140	3.01
Irvine (city) Orange County	19,473	9.17
Fullerton (city) Orange County	16,004	11.84
San Diego (city) San Diego County	15,883	1.21
San Jose (city) Santa Clara County	12,929	1.37
Torrance (city) Los Angeles County	12,779	8.79
San Francisco (city) San Francisco County	11,558	1.44
Glendale (city) Los Angeles County	10,650	5.56
Buena Park (city) Orange County	8,001	9.94
Cerritos (city) Los Angeles County	7,451	15.19

Top 10 Places Sorted by Percent of Total Population
Based on all places, regardless of total population

Place	Population	%
La Crescenta-Montrose (cdp) Los Angeles County	4,058	20.65
La Palma (city) Orange County	2,656	17.06
Cerritos (city) Los Angeles County	7,451	15.19
La Ca±ada Flintridge (city) Los Angeles County	3,030	14.97
Cypress (city) Orange County	5,878	12.30
Fullerton (city) Orange County	16,004	11.84
Diamond Bar (city) Los Angeles County	5,961	10.73
Stevenson Ranch (cdp) Los Angeles County	1,764	10.05
Buena Park (city) Orange County	8,001	9.94
Irvine (city) Orange County	19,473	9.17

Top 10 Places Sorted by Percent of Total Population
Based on places with total population of 50,000 or more

Place	Population	%
Fullerton (city) Orange County	16,004	11.84
Diamond Bar (city) Los Angeles County	5,961	10.73
Buena Park (city) Orange County	8,001	9.94
Irvine (city) Orange County	19,473	9.17
Torrance (city) Los Angeles County	12,779	8.79
Gardena (city) Los Angeles County	3,636	6.18
Glendale (city) Los Angeles County	10,650	5.56
Cupertino (city) Santa Clara County	2,876	4.93
Chino Hills (city) San Bernardino County	3,662	4.90
Hacienda Heights (cdp) Los Angeles County	2,609	4.83

Asian: Laotian

Top 10 Places Sorted by Population
Based on all places, regardless of total population

Place	Population	%
Fresno (city) Fresno County	6,733	1.36
Sacramento (city) Sacramento County	6,675	1.43
San Diego (city) San Diego County	6,058	0.46
Stockton (city) San Joaquin County	3,581	1.23
Oakland (city) Alameda County	3,071	0.79
Richmond (city) Contra Costa County	1,886	1.82
San Jose (city) Santa Clara County	1,590	0.17
Merced (city) Merced County	1,482	1.88
Modesto (city) Stanislaus County	1,257	0.62
Visalia (city) Tulare County	1,194	0.96

Top 10 Places Sorted by Percent of Total Population
Based on all places, regardless of total population

Place	Population	%
Fields Landing (cdp) Humboldt County	17	6.16
Fruitridge Pocket (cdp) Sacramento County	291	5.02
Weed (city) Siskiyou County	109	3.67
Lemon Hill (cdp) Sacramento County	497	3.62
Montalvin Manor (cdp) Contra Costa County	86	2.99
Bayview (cdp) Contra Costa County	49	2.79
San Pablo (city) Contra Costa County	798	2.74
Tara Hills (cdp) Contra Costa County	140	2.73
Cottonwood (cdp) Shasta County	90	2.71
Florin (cdp) Sacramento County	1,128	2.37

Top 10 Places Sorted by Percent of Total Population
Based on places with total population of 50,000 or more

Place	Population	%
Merced (city) Merced County	1,482	1.88
Richmond (city) Contra Costa County	1,886	1.82
Sacramento (city) Sacramento County	6,675	1.43
Fresno (city) Fresno County	6,733	1.36
Redding (city) Shasta County	1,124	1.25
Stockton (city) San Joaquin County	3,581	1.23
Visalia (city) Tulare County	1,194	0.96
Oakland (city) Alameda County	3,071	0.79
Porterville (city) Tulare County	429	0.79
Modesto (city) Stanislaus County	1,257	0.62

Asian: Malaysian

Top 10 Places Sorted by Population
Based on all places, regardless of total population

Place	Population	%
San Francisco (city) San Francisco County	358	0.04
Los Angeles (city) Los Angeles County	342	0.01
San Diego (city) San Diego County	315	0.02
San Jose (city) Santa Clara County	304	0.03
Fremont (city) Alameda County	158	0.07
Sunnyvale (city) Santa Clara County	96	0.07
Irvine (city) Orange County	84	0.04
Milpitas (city) Santa Clara County	81	0.12
Arcadia (city) Los Angeles County	80	0.14
Santa Clara (city) Santa Clara County	71	0.06

Top 10 Places Sorted by Percent of Total Population
Based on all places, regardless of total population

Place	Population	%
Sunny Slopes (cdp) Mono County	1	0.55
Boronda (cdp) Monterey County	5	0.29
San Marino (city) Los Angeles County	24	0.18
San Miguel (cdp) Contra Costa County	6	0.18
Camino Tassajara (cdp) Contra Costa County	4	0.18
University of California Davis (cdp) Yolo County	10	0.17
East Pasadena (cdp) Los Angeles County	10	0.16
Del Rio (cdp) Stanislaus County	2	0.16
East Richmond Heights (cdp) Contra Costa County	5	0.15
Black Point-Green Point (cdp) Marin County	2	0.15

Top 10 Places Sorted by Percent of Total Population
Based on places with total population of 50,000 or more

Place	Population	%
Arcadia (city) Los Angeles County	80	0.14
Milpitas (city) Santa Clara County	81	0.12
Monterey Park (city) Los Angeles County	49	0.08
Fremont (city) Alameda County	158	0.07
Sunnyvale (city) Santa Clara County	96	0.07
Alhambra (city) Los Angeles County	57	0.07
Hacienda Heights (cdp) Los Angeles County	39	0.07
Cupertino (city) Santa Clara County	38	0.07
Santa Clara (city) Santa Clara County	71	0.06
Diamond Bar (city) Los Angeles County	31	0.06

Asian: Nepalese

Top 10 Places Sorted by Population
Based on all places, regardless of total population

Place	Population	%
San Francisco (city) San Francisco County	388	0.05
Los Angeles (city) Los Angeles County	387	0.01
Sunnyvale (city) Santa Clara County	305	0.22
Artesia (city) Los Angeles County	226	1.37
El Cerrito (city) Contra Costa County	222	0.94
Berkeley (city) Alameda County	211	0.19
Oakland (city) Alameda County	204	0.05
Woodland (city) Yolo County	162	0.29
Santa Rosa (city) Sonoma County	153	0.09
Fremont (city) Alameda County	152	0.07

Top 10 Places Sorted by Percent of Total Population
Based on all places, regardless of total population

Place	Population	%
Artesia (city) Los Angeles County	226	1.37
El Cerrito (city) Contra Costa County	222	0.94
Sonoma (city) Sonoma County	55	0.52
Albany (city) Alameda County	77	0.42
Woodland (city) Yolo County	162	0.29
Eldridge (cdp) Sonoma County	3	0.24
Davis (city) Yolo County	150	0.23
Mountain House (cdp) San Joaquin County	22	0.23
Sunnyvale (city) Santa Clara County	305	0.22
San Pablo (city) Contra Costa County	58	0.20

Top 10 Places Sorted by Percent of Total Population
Based on places with total population of 50,000 or more

Place	Population	%
Woodland (city) Yolo County	162	0.29
Davis (city) Yolo County	150	0.23
Sunnyvale (city) Santa Clara County	305	0.22
Berkeley (city) Alameda County	211	0.19
Mountain View (city) Santa Clara County	108	0.15
Alameda (city) Alameda County	99	0.13
South San Francisco (city) San Mateo County	61	0.10
Santa Rosa (city) Sonoma County	153	0.09
Castro Valley (cdp) Alameda County	53	0.09
Fremont (city) Alameda County	152	0.07

Asian: Pakistani

Top 10 Places Sorted by Population
Based on all places, regardless of total population

Place	Population	%
Los Angeles (city) Los Angeles County	3,973	0.10
Fremont (city) Alameda County	2,242	1.05
San Jose (city) Santa Clara County	2,131	0.23
Sacramento (city) Sacramento County	2,061	0.44
Stockton (city) San Joaquin County	1,904	0.65
Lodi (city) San Joaquin County	1,709	2.75
Irvine (city) Orange County	1,631	0.77
San Diego (city) San Diego County	1,132	0.09
Torrance (city) Los Angeles County	1,050	0.72
San Francisco (city) San Francisco County	1,012	0.13

Top 10 Places Sorted by Percent of Total Population
Based on all places, regardless of total population

Place	Population	%
Lodi (city) San Joaquin County	1,709	2.75
Live Oak (city) Sutter County	158	1.88
Camino Tassajara (cdp) Contra Costa County	41	1.87
Victor (cdp) San Joaquin County	5	1.71
Woodland (city) Yolo County	677	1.22
Bradbury (city) Los Angeles County	12	1.15
Fremont (city) Alameda County	2,242	1.05
Morada (cdp) San Joaquin County	40	1.04
Mountain House (cdp) San Joaquin County	96	0.99
August (cdp) San Joaquin County	78	0.93

Top 10 Places Sorted by Percent of Total Population
Based on places with total population of 50,000 or more

Place	Population	%
Lodi (city) San Joaquin County	1,709	2.75
Woodland (city) Yolo County	677	1.22
Fremont (city) Alameda County	2,242	1.05
Santa Clara (city) Santa Clara County	974	0.84
Irvine (city) Orange County	1,631	0.77
San Ramon (city) Contra Costa County	525	0.73
Torrance (city) Los Angeles County	1,050	0.72
Stockton (city) San Joaquin County	1,904	0.65
Union City (city) Alameda County	450	0.65
Eastvale (cdp) Riverside County	342	0.64

Asian: Sri Lankan

Top 10 Places Sorted by Population
Based on all places, regardless of total population

Place	Population	%
Los Angeles (city) Los Angeles County	2,358	0.06
San Jose (city) Santa Clara County	358	0.04
Torrance (city) Los Angeles County	266	0.18
San Diego (city) San Diego County	248	0.02
Anaheim (city) Orange County	237	0.07
Irvine (city) Orange County	217	0.10
Long Beach (city) Los Angeles County	212	0.05
San Francisco (city) San Francisco County	191	0.02
Pasadena (city) Los Angeles County	182	0.13
Fremont (city) Alameda County	172	0.08

Top 10 Places Sorted by Percent of Total Population
Based on all places, regardless of total population

Place	Population	%
Mono City (cdp) Mono County	1	0.58
Independence (cdp) Inyo County	3	0.45
East Pasadena (cdp) Los Angeles County	21	0.34
North El Monte (cdp) Los Angeles County	12	0.32
Boulevard (cdp) San Diego County	1	0.32
Norris Canyon (cdp) Contra Costa County	3	0.31
Charter Oak (cdp) Los Angeles County	27	0.29
Las Flores (cdp) Orange County	16	0.27
University of California Davis (cdp) Yolo County	15	0.26
Diablo (cdp) Contra Costa County	3	0.26

Top 10 Places Sorted by Percent of Total Population
Based on places with total population of 50,000 or more

Place	Population	%
Torrance (city) Los Angeles County	266	0.18
Pasadena (city) Los Angeles County	182	0.13
Lake Forest (city) Orange County	100	0.13
Arcadia (city) Los Angeles County	67	0.12
Gardena (city) Los Angeles County	66	0.11
Irvine (city) Orange County	217	0.10
Tustin (city) Orange County	73	0.10
Davis (city) Yolo County	64	0.10
Thousand Oaks (city) Ventura County	115	0.09
Folsom (city) Sacramento County	66	0.09

Asian: Taiwanese

Top 10 Places Sorted by Population
Based on all places, regardless of total population

Place	Population	%
San Jose (city) Santa Clara County	6,579	0.70
Irvine (city) Orange County	5,790	2.73
Los Angeles (city) Los Angeles County	5,282	0.14
Arcadia (city) Los Angeles County	4,846	8.60
Fremont (city) Alameda County	4,572	2.14
Rowland Heights (cdp) Los Angeles County	3,476	7.09
San Diego (city) San Diego County	3,400	0.26
Diamond Bar (city) Los Angeles County	3,162	5.69
Hacienda Heights (cdp) Los Angeles County	2,944	5.45
San Francisco (city) San Francisco County	2,806	0.35

Top 10 Places Sorted by Percent of Total Population
Based on all places, regardless of total population

Place	Population	%
San Marino (city) Los Angeles County	1,498	11.39
Arcadia (city) Los Angeles County	4,846	8.60
Rowland Heights (cdp) Los Angeles County	3,476	7.09
Walnut (city) Los Angeles County	2,064	7.08
Diamond Bar (city) Los Angeles County	3,162	5.69
Temple City (city) Los Angeles County	1,964	5.52
Hacienda Heights (cdp) Los Angeles County	2,944	5.45
East San Gabriel (cdp) Los Angeles County	809	5.44
Cupertino (city) Santa Clara County	2,753	4.72
Bradbury (city) Los Angeles County	47	4.48

Top 10 Places Sorted by Percent of Total Population
Based on places with total population of 50,000 or more

Place	Population	%
Arcadia (city) Los Angeles County	4,846	8.60
Diamond Bar (city) Los Angeles County	3,162	5.69
Hacienda Heights (cdp) Los Angeles County	2,944	5.45
Cupertino (city) Santa Clara County	2,753	4.72
Irvine (city) Orange County	5,790	2.73
Alhambra (city) Los Angeles County	1,866	2.25
Fremont (city) Alameda County	4,572	2.14
Monterey Park (city) Los Angeles County	1,233	2.05
Chino Hills (city) San Bernardino County	1,422	1.90
Palo Alto (city) Santa Clara County	1,061	1.65

Asian: Thai

Top 10 Places Sorted by Population
Based on all places, regardless of total population

Place	Population	%
Los Angeles (city) Los Angeles County	14,122	0.37
San Francisco (city) San Francisco County	2,879	0.36
San Diego (city) San Diego County	2,061	0.16
Long Beach (city) Los Angeles County	1,266	0.27
San Jose (city) Santa Clara County	1,178	0.12
Visalia (city) Tulare County	1,134	0.91
Sacramento (city) Sacramento County	784	0.17
Cerritos (city) Los Angeles County	651	1.33
Anaheim (city) Orange County	632	0.19
Irvine (city) Orange County	598	0.28

Top 10 Places Sorted by Percent of Total Population
Based on all places, regardless of total population

Place	Population	%
Aspen Springs (cdp) Mono County	2	3.08
Phillipsville (cdp) Humboldt County	4	2.86
Tonyville (cdp) Tulare County	9	2.85
Pine Flat (cdp) Tulare County	3	1.81
Cerritos (city) Los Angeles County	651	1.33
Mono City (cdp) Mono County	2	1.16
Lindsay (city) Tulare County	134	1.14
Lodoga (cdp) Colusa County	2	1.02
Walnut (city) Los Angeles County	294	1.01
Orosi (cdp) Tulare County	87	0.99

Top 10 Places Sorted by Percent of Total Population
Based on places with total population of 50,000 or more

Place	Population	%
Monterey Park (city) Los Angeles County	569	0.94
Visalia (city) Tulare County	1,134	0.91
Bellflower (city) Los Angeles County	552	0.72
Alhambra (city) Los Angeles County	561	0.68
Arcadia (city) Los Angeles County	301	0.53
Hacienda Heights (cdp) Los Angeles County	287	0.53
Burbank (city) Los Angeles County	538	0.52
Lakewood (city) Los Angeles County	386	0.48
Rosemead (city) Los Angeles County	235	0.44
Chino Hills (city) San Bernardino County	323	0.43

Asian: Vietnamese

Top 10 Places Sorted by Population
Based on all places, regardless of total population

Place	Population	%
San Jose (city) Santa Clara County	106,647	11.27
Garden Grove (city) Orange County	48,774	28.54
Westminster (city) Orange County	37,176	41.44
San Diego (city) San Diego County	36,713	2.81
Santa Ana (city) Orange County	24,260	7.48
Los Angeles (city) Los Angeles County	23,325	0.62
San Francisco (city) San Francisco County	16,075	2.00
Anaheim (city) Orange County	15,674	4.66
Fountain Valley (city) Orange County	11,861	21.44
Milpitas (city) Santa Clara County	11,042	16.53

Top 10 Places Sorted by Percent of Total Population
Based on all places, regardless of total population

Place	Population	%
Midway City (cdp) Orange County	3,651	43.03
Westminster (city) Orange County	37,176	41.44
Garden Grove (city) Orange County	48,774	28.54
Fountain Valley (city) Orange County	11,861	21.44
Rosemead (city) Los Angeles County	10,046	18.69
Milpitas (city) Santa Clara County	11,042	16.53
Stanton (city) Orange County	5,762	15.09
San Jose (city) Santa Clara County	106,647	11.27
San Gabriel (city) Los Angeles County	3,834	9.65
Vineyard (cdp) Sacramento County	2,380	9.58

Top 10 Places Sorted by Percent of Total Population
Based on places with total population of 50,000 or more

Place	Population	%
Westminster (city) Orange County	37,176	41.44
Garden Grove (city) Orange County	48,774	28.54
Fountain Valley (city) Orange County	11,861	21.44
Rosemead (city) Los Angeles County	10,046	18.69
Milpitas (city) Santa Clara County	11,042	16.53
San Jose (city) Santa Clara County	106,647	11.27
El Monte (city) Los Angeles County	9,667	8.52
Santa Ana (city) Orange County	24,260	7.48
Alhambra (city) Los Angeles County	5,348	6.44
Monterey Park (city) Los Angeles County	3,323	5.51

Hawaii Native/Pacific Islander

Top 10 Places Sorted by Population
Based on all places, regardless of total population

Place	Population	%
Los Angeles (city) Los Angeles County	15,031	0.40
San Diego (city) San Diego County	11,945	0.91
Sacramento (city) Sacramento County	10,699	2.29
San Jose (city) Santa Clara County	8,116	0.86
Long Beach (city) Los Angeles County	7,498	1.62
Hayward (city) Alameda County	6,708	4.65
San Francisco (city) San Francisco County	6,173	0.77
Oakland (city) Alameda County	3,574	0.91
Stockton (city) San Joaquin County	3,566	1.22
Modesto (city) Stanislaus County	3,467	1.72

Top 10 Places Sorted by Percent of Total Population
Based on all places, regardless of total population

Place	Population	%
East Palo Alto (city) San Mateo County	2,386	8.47
Furnace Creek (cdp) Inyo County	2	8.33
San Bruno (city) San Mateo County	1,934	4.70
Hayward (city) Alameda County	6,708	4.65
Darwin (cdp) Inyo County	2	4.65
Marina (city) Monterey County	903	4.58
Sunny Slopes (cdp) Mono County	8	4.40
Diablo Grande (cdp) Stanislaus County	30	3.63
McClellan Park (cdp) Sacramento County	26	3.50
Carson (city) Los Angeles County	3,088	3.37

Top 10 Places Sorted by Percent of Total Population
Based on places with total population of 50,000 or more

Place	Population	%
Hayward (city) Alameda County	6,708	4.65
Carson (city) Los Angeles County	3,088	3.37
San Mateo (city) San Mateo County	2,803	2.88
South San Francisco (city) San Mateo County	1,797	2.82
Fairfield (city) Solano County	2,503	2.38
Sacramento (city) Sacramento County	10,699	2.29
Union City (city) Alameda County	1,563	2.25
Elk Grove (city) Sacramento County	3,319	2.17
Vallejo (city) Solano County	2,436	2.10
Oceanside (city) San Diego County	3,428	2.05

Hawaii Native/Pacific Islander: Not Hispanic

Top 10 Places Sorted by Population
Based on all places, regardless of total population

Place	Population	%
Los Angeles (city) Los Angeles County	10,779	0.28
San Diego (city) San Diego County	9,844	0.75
Sacramento (city) Sacramento County	9,762	2.09
Long Beach (city) Los Angeles County	6,549	1.42
San Jose (city) Santa Clara County	6,460	0.68
Hayward (city) Alameda County	6,093	4.23
San Francisco (city) San Francisco County	5,432	0.67
Oakland (city) Alameda County	3,073	0.79
Elk Grove (city) Sacramento County	3,048	1.99
Modesto (city) Stanislaus County	2,976	1.48

Top 10 Places Sorted by Percent of Total Population
Based on all places, regardless of total population

Place	Population	%
Furnace Creek (cdp) Inyo County	2	8.33
East Palo Alto (city) San Mateo County	2,310	8.20

Darwin (cdp) Inyo County	2	4.65
Sunny Slopes (cdp) Mono County	8	4.40
San Bruno (city) San Mateo County	1,792	4.36
Hayward (city) Alameda County	6,093	4.23
Marina (city) Monterey County	805	4.08
Diablo Grande (cdp) Stanislaus County	29	3.51
Carson (city) Los Angeles County	2,773	3.02
Oakville (cdp) Napa County	2	2.82

Top 10 Places Sorted by Percent of Total Population

Based on places with total population of 50,000 or more

Place	Population	%
Hayward (city) Alameda County	6,093	4.23
Carson (city) Los Angeles County	2,773	3.02
San Mateo (city) San Mateo County	2,588	2.66
South San Francisco (city) San Mateo County	1,595	2.51
Sacramento (city) Sacramento County	9,762	2.09
Fairfield (city) Solano County	2,140	2.03
Elk Grove (city) Sacramento County	3,048	1.99
Union City (city) Alameda County	1,374	1.98
Vallejo (city) Solano County	2,103	1.81
Oceanside (city) San Diego County	2,962	1.77

Hawaii Native/Pacific Islander: Hispanic

Top 10 Places Sorted by Population

Based on all places, regardless of total population

Place	Population	%
Los Angeles (city) Los Angeles County	4,252	0.11
San Diego (city) San Diego County	2,101	0.16
San Jose (city) Santa Clara County	1,656	0.18
Long Beach (city) Los Angeles County	949	0.21
Sacramento (city) Sacramento County	937	0.20
Chula Vista (city) San Diego County	753	0.31
San Francisco (city) San Francisco County	741	0.09
Fresno (city) Fresno County	702	0.14
Stockton (city) San Joaquin County	697	0.24
Hayward (city) Alameda County	615	0.43

Top 10 Places Sorted by Percent of Total Population

Based on all places, regardless of total population

Place	Population	%
Monmouth (cdp) Fresno County	3	1.97
Martell (cdp) Amador County	5	1.77
Sereno del Mar (cdp) Sonoma County	2	1.59
Coulterville (cdp) Mariposa County	3	1.49
Cartago (cdp) Inyo County	1	1.09
McClellan Park (cdp) Sacramento County	7	0.94
Irwindale (city) Los Angeles County	13	0.91
Littlerock (cdp) Los Angeles County	11	0.80
Smith Corner (cdp) Kern County	4	0.76
Hood (cdp) Sacramento County	2	0.74

Top 10 Places Sorted by Percent of Total Population

Based on places with total population of 50,000 or more

Place	Population	%
Hayward (city) Alameda County	615	0.43
Manteca (city) San Joaquin County	266	0.40
Tracy (city) San Joaquin County	311	0.38
Fairfield (city) Solano County	363	0.34
Carson (city) Los Angeles County	315	0.34
South San Francisco (city) San Mateo County	202	0.32
Chula Vista (city) San Diego County	753	0.31
Vacaville (city) Solano County	278	0.30
National City (city) San Diego County	173	0.30
Vallejo (city) Solano County	333	0.29

Hawaii Native/Pacific Islander: Fijian

Top 10 Places Sorted by Population

Based on all places, regardless of total population

Place	Population	%
Sacramento (city) Sacramento County	3,244	0.70
Hayward (city) Alameda County	2,535	1.76
Modesto (city) Stanislaus County	1,355	0.67
Elk Grove (city) Sacramento County	1,279	0.84
Stockton (city) San Joaquin County	665	0.23
Florin (cdp) Sacramento County	500	1.05
San Jose (city) Santa Clara County	490	0.05
San Bruno (city) San Mateo County	441	1.07
Los Angeles (city) Los Angeles County	420	0.01
Santa Rosa (city) Sonoma County	419	0.25

Top 10 Places Sorted by Percent of Total Population

Based on all places, regardless of total population

Place	Population	%
Hayward (city) Alameda County	2,535	1.76
San Bruno (city) San Mateo County	441	1.07
Florin (cdp) Sacramento County	500	1.05
Mather (cdp) Sacramento County	43	0.97
Elk Grove (city) Sacramento County	1,279	0.84
West Sacramento (city) Yolo County	387	0.79
East Palo Alto (city) San Mateo County	208	0.74
Sacramento (city) Sacramento County	3,244	0.70
Vineyard (cdp) Sacramento County	173	0.70
Bayview (cdp) Contra Costa County	12	0.68

Top 10 Places Sorted by Percent of Total Population

Based on places with total population of 50,000 or more

Place	Population	%
Hayward (city) Alameda County	2,535	1.76
Elk Grove (city) Sacramento County	1,279	0.84
Sacramento (city) Sacramento County	3,244	0.70
Modesto (city) Stanislaus County	1,355	0.67
South San Francisco (city) San Mateo County	414	0.65
Union City (city) Alameda County	403	0.58
San Mateo (city) San Mateo County	390	0.40
Pittsburg (city) Contra Costa County	234	0.37
Rancho Cordova (city) Sacramento County	233	0.36
Arden-Arcade (cdp) Sacramento County	262	0.28

Hawaii Native/Pacific Islander: Guamanian or Chamorro

Top 10 Places Sorted by Population

Based on all places, regardless of total population

Place	Population	%
San Diego (city) San Diego County	3,999	0.31
Los Angeles (city) Los Angeles County	1,840	0.05
San Jose (city) Santa Clara County	1,396	0.15
Chula Vista (city) San Diego County	1,389	0.57
Fairfield (city) Solano County	1,013	0.96
Long Beach (city) Los Angeles County	937	0.20
Vallejo (city) Solano County	866	0.75
Sacramento (city) Sacramento County	707	0.15
San Francisco (city) San Francisco County	566	0.07
Oceanside (city) San Diego County	525	0.31

Top 10 Places Sorted by Percent of Total Population

Based on all places, regardless of total population

Place	Population	%
Daphnedale Park (cdp) Modoc County	4	2.17
Acampo (cdp) San Joaquin County	6	1.76
Volta (cdp) Merced County	4	1.63
McClellan Park (cdp) Sacramento County	10	1.35
Robinson Mill (cdp) Butte County	1	1.25
Marina (city) Monterey County	231	1.17
Suisun City (city) Solano County	321	1.14
Sunol (cdp) Alameda County	9	0.99
Concow (cdp) Butte County	7	0.99
Fairfield (city) Solano County	1,013	0.96

Top 10 Places Sorted by Percent of Total Population

Based on places with total population of 50,000 or more

Place	Population	%
Fairfield (city) Solano County	1,013	0.96
Vallejo (city) Solano County	866	0.75
Chula Vista (city) San Diego County	1,389	0.57
National City (city) San Diego County	303	0.52
Santee (city) San Diego County	276	0.52
La Mesa (city) San Diego County	241	0.42
El Cajon (city) San Diego County	404	0.41
Vacaville (city) Solano County	372	0.40
Lakewood (city) Los Angeles County	275	0.34
Hayward (city) Alameda County	470	0.33

Hawaii Native/Pacific Islander: Marshallese

Top 10 Places Sorted by Population

Based on all places, regardless of total population

Place	Population	%
Sacramento (city) Sacramento County	400	0.09
Costa Mesa (city) Orange County	177	0.16
San Diego (city) San Diego County	164	0.01
Parkway (cdp) Sacramento County	161	1.10
Garden Grove (city) Orange County	109	0.06
Lemon Hill (cdp) Sacramento County	84	0.61
Santa Ana (city) Orange County	82	0.03
Tustin (city) Orange County	77	0.10
Florin (cdp) Sacramento County	37	0.08
Elk Grove (city) Sacramento County	26	0.02

Top 10 Places Sorted by Percent of Total Population

Based on all places, regardless of total population

Place	Population	%
Clio (cdp) Plumas County	1	1.52
Parkway (cdp) Sacramento County	161	1.10
Lemon Hill (cdp) Sacramento County	84	0.61
East Porterville (cdp) Tulare County	23	0.34
Costa Mesa (city) Orange County	177	0.16
Tustin (city) Orange County	77	0.10
Sacramento (city) Sacramento County	400	0.09
La Riviera (cdp) Sacramento County	10	0.09
Florin (cdp) Sacramento County	37	0.08
Strathmore (cdp) Tulare County	2	0.07

Top 10 Places Sorted by Percent of Total Population

Based on places with total population of 50,000 or more

Place	Population	%
Costa Mesa (city) Orange County	177	0.16
Tustin (city) Orange County	77	0.10
Sacramento (city) Sacramento County	400	0.09
Garden Grove (city) Orange County	109	0.06
Santa Ana (city) Orange County	82	0.03
Elk Grove (city) Sacramento County	26	0.02
National City (city) San Diego County	12	0.02
San Diego (city) San Diego County	164	0.01
Huntington Beach (city) Orange County	24	0.01
Fremont (city) Alameda County	17	0.01

Hawaii Native/Pacific Islander: Native Hawaiian

Top 10 Places Sorted by Population

Based on all places, regardless of total population

Place	Population	%
Los Angeles (city) Los Angeles County	4,062	0.11
San Diego (city) San Diego County	3,194	0.24
San Jose (city) Santa Clara County	2,161	0.23
San Francisco (city) San Francisco County	1,489	0.18
Sacramento (city) Sacramento County	1,236	0.26
Long Beach (city) Los Angeles County	1,018	0.22
Oceanside (city) San Diego County	877	0.52
Stockton (city) San Joaquin County	800	0.27
Hayward (city) Alameda County	784	0.54
Fremont (city) Alameda County	735	0.34

Top 10 Places Sorted by Percent of Total Population

Based on all places, regardless of total population

Place	Population	%
Furnace Creek (cdp) Inyo County	2	8.33
Oakville (cdp) Napa County	2	2.82
Franklin (cdp) Sacramento County	3	1.94
Martell (cdp) Amador County	5	1.77
Sunny Slopes (cdp) Mono County	3	1.65
Trinity Center (cdp) Trinity County	4	1.50
Coulterville (cdp) Mariposa County	3	1.49
Hat Creek (cdp) Shasta County	4	1.29
Nord (cdp) Butte County	4	1.25
Timber Cove (cdp) Sonoma County	2	1.22

Top 10 Places Sorted by Percent of Total Population

Based on places with total population of 50,000 or more

Place	Population	%
Fairfield (city) Solano County	668	0.63

Place	Population	%
Vacaville (city) Solano County	556	0.60
Gardena (city) Los Angeles County	324	0.55
Hayward (city) Alameda County	784	0.54
Oceanside (city) San Diego County	877	0.52
Manteca (city) San Joaquin County	340	0.51
Union City (city) Alameda County	332	0.48
Tracy (city) San Joaquin County	393	0.47
Brentwood (city) Contra Costa County	238	0.46
Vallejo (city) Solano County	523	0.45

Hawaii Native/Pacific Islander: Samoan

Top 10 Places Sorted by Population

Based on all places, regardless of total population

Place	Population	%
Long Beach (city) Los Angeles County	4,513	0.98
San Francisco (city) San Francisco County	2,542	0.32
San Diego (city) San Diego County	2,490	0.19
Los Angeles (city) Los Angeles County	2,480	0.07
Carson (city) Los Angeles County	2,352	2.56
San Jose (city) Santa Clara County	1,954	0.21
Oceanside (city) San Diego County	1,781	1.07
Sacramento (city) Sacramento County	1,233	0.26
Anaheim (city) Orange County	1,023	0.30
Hayward (city) Alameda County	859	0.60

Top 10 Places Sorted by Percent of Total Population

Based on all places, regardless of total population

Place	Population	%
Darwin (cdp) Inyo County	2	4.65
Carson (city) Los Angeles County	2,352	2.56
Baker (cdp) San Bernardino County	13	1.77
Sereno del Mar (cdp) Sonoma County	2	1.59
East Palo Alto (city) San Mateo County	430	1.53
West Carson (cdp) Los Angeles County	293	1.35
Herlong (cdp) Lassen County	4	1.34
Marina (city) Monterey County	256	1.30
Twentynine Palms (city) San Bernardino County	299	1.19
Signal Hill (city) Los Angeles County	125	1.13

Top 10 Places Sorted by Percent of Total Population

Based on places with total population of 50,000 or more

Place	Population	%
Carson (city) Los Angeles County	2,352	2.56
Oceanside (city) San Diego County	1,781	1.07
Long Beach (city) Los Angeles County	4,513	0.98
Compton (city) Los Angeles County	735	0.76
South San Francisco (city) San Mateo County	473	0.74
Lakewood (city) Los Angeles County	534	0.67
Paramount (city) Los Angeles County	360	0.67
Bellflower (city) Los Angeles County	507	0.66
Vista (city) San Diego County	572	0.61
Hayward (city) Alameda County	859	0.60

Hawaii Native/Pacific Islander: Tongan

Top 10 Places Sorted by Population

Based on all places, regardless of total population

Place	Population	%
East Palo Alto (city) San Mateo County	1,526	5.42
Oakland (city) Alameda County	1,463	0.37
Sacramento (city) Sacramento County	1,382	0.30
San Mateo (city) San Mateo County	1,324	1.36
Hayward (city) Alameda County	719	0.50
Hawthorne (city) Los Angeles County	656	0.78
Los Angeles (city) Los Angeles County	649	0.02
San Bruno (city) San Mateo County	612	1.49
Redwood City (city) San Mateo County	539	0.70
San Jose (city) Santa Clara County	526	0.06

Top 10 Places Sorted by Percent of Total Population

Based on all places, regardless of total population

Place	Population	%
East Palo Alto (city) San Mateo County	1,526	5.42
San Bruno (city) San Mateo County	612	1.49
San Mateo (city) San Mateo County	1,324	1.36
North Fair Oaks (cdp) San Mateo County	157	1.07
Menlo Park (city) San Mateo County	326	1.02
Hawthorne (city) Los Angeles County	656	0.78
Redwood City (city) San Mateo County	539	0.70
Lennox (cdp) Los Angeles County	154	0.68
Cherryland (cdp) Alameda County	95	0.65
Lawndale (city) Los Angeles County	170	0.52

Top 10 Places Sorted by Percent of Total Population

Based on places with total population of 50,000 or more

Place	Population	%
San Mateo (city) San Mateo County	1,324	1.36
Hawthorne (city) Los Angeles County	656	0.78
Redwood City (city) San Mateo County	539	0.70
Hayward (city) Alameda County	719	0.50
South San Francisco (city) San Mateo County	250	0.39
Oakland (city) Alameda County	1,463	0.37
Pittsburg (city) Contra Costa County	235	0.37
Concord (city) Contra Costa County	380	0.31
Sacramento (city) Sacramento County	1,382	0.30
Mountain View (city) Santa Clara County	202	0.27

White

Top 10 Places Sorted by Population

Based on all places, regardless of total population

Place	Population	%
Los Angeles (city) Los Angeles County	2,031,586	53.57
San Diego (city) San Diego County	824,542	63.07
San Jose (city) Santa Clara County	442,231	46.75
San Francisco (city) San Francisco County	420,823	52.26
Fresno (city) Fresno County	263,929	53.36
Sacramento (city) Sacramento County	233,865	50.13
Long Beach (city) Los Angeles County	231,897	50.17
Bakersfield (city) Kern County	211,351	60.82
Anaheim (city) Orange County	189,689	56.41
Riverside (city) Riverside County	184,386	60.68

Top 10 Places Sorted by Percent of Total Population

Based on all places, regardless of total population

Place	Population	%
Salmon Creek (cdp) Sonoma County	86	100.00
Lake City (cdp) Modoc County	61	100.00
Alleghany (cdp) Sierra County	58	100.00
Lake Davis (cdp) Plumas County	45	100.00
Idlewild (cdp) Tulare County	43	100.00
Butte Meadows (cdp) Butte County	40	100.00
Prattville (cdp) Plumas County	33	100.00
Belden (cdp) Plumas County	22	100.00
Johnsville (cdp) Plumas County	20	100.00
Trona (cdp) Inyo County	18	100.00

Top 10 Places Sorted by Percent of Total Population

Based on places with total population of 50,000 or more

Place	Population	%
Redding (city) Shasta County	80,967	90.10
Newport Beach (city) Orange County	76,656	89.99
San Clemente (city) Orange County	56,749	89.34
Encinitas (city) San Diego County	52,974	89.01
Santee (city) San Diego County	46,684	87.40
Rocklin (city) Placer County	49,657	87.16
Carlsbad (city) San Diego County	91,202	86.59
Carmichael (cdp) Sacramento County	52,877	85.61
Chico (city) Butte County	73,535	85.32
Citrus Heights (city) Sacramento County	70,911	85.13

White: Not Hispanic

Top 10 Places Sorted by Population

Based on all places, regardless of total population

Place	Population	%
Los Angeles (city) Los Angeles County	1,148,305	30.28
San Diego (city) San Diego County	625,399	47.84
San Francisco (city) San Francisco County	358,844	44.56
San Jose (city) Santa Clara County	292,431	30.91
Sacramento (city) Sacramento County	175,948	37.72
Fresno (city) Fresno County	156,548	31.65
Long Beach (city) Los Angeles County	145,170	31.40
Bakersfield (city) Kern County	137,595	39.60
Huntington Beach (city) Orange County	133,155	70.08
Glendale (city) Los Angeles County	123,773	64.56

Top 10 Places Sorted by Percent of Total Population

Based on all places, regardless of total population

Place	Population	%
Lake City (cdp) Modoc County	61	100.00
Idlewild (cdp) Tulare County	43	100.00
Butte Meadows (cdp) Butte County	40	100.00
Prattville (cdp) Plumas County	33	100.00
Belden (cdp) Plumas County	22	100.00
Johnsville (cdp) Plumas County	20	100.00
Trona (cdp) Inyo County	18	100.00
Tobin (cdp) Plumas County	12	100.00
Graniteville (cdp) Nevada County	11	100.00
McClenney Tract (cdp) Tulare County	10	100.00

Top 10 Places Sorted by Percent of Total Population

Based on places with total population of 50,000 or more

Place	Population	%
Redding (city) Shasta County	75,994	84.57
Newport Beach (city) Orange County	71,976	84.49
Encinitas (city) San Diego County	48,279	81.12
Rocklin (city) Placer County	44,930	78.86
San Clemente (city) Orange County	49,759	78.33
Carmichael (cdp) Sacramento County	48,212	78.06
Carlsbad (city) San Diego County	81,860	77.72
Chico (city) Butte County	66,261	76.88
Santee (city) San Diego County	41,021	76.80
Walnut Creek (city) Contra Costa County	49,141	76.58

White: Hispanic

Top 10 Places Sorted by Population

Based on all places, regardless of total population

Place	Population	%
Los Angeles (city) Los Angeles County	883,281	23.29
San Diego (city) San Diego County	199,143	15.23
San Jose (city) Santa Clara County	149,800	15.84
Santa Ana (city) Orange County	127,132	39.17
Fresno (city) Fresno County	107,381	21.71
Anaheim (city) Orange County	92,199	27.42
Chula Vista (city) San Diego County	87,377	35.82
Long Beach (city) Los Angeles County	86,727	18.76
Riverside (city) Riverside County	75,368	24.80
Bakersfield (city) Kern County	73,756	21.23

Top 10 Places Sorted by Percent of Total Population

Based on all places, regardless of total population

Place	Population	%
Woodville (cdp) Tulare County	1,201	69.02
Calexico (city) Imperial County	23,931	62.04
Poplar-Cotton Center (cdp) Tulare County	1,476	59.76
Walnut Park (cdp) Los Angeles County	9,196	57.60
Firebaugh (city) Fresno County	4,340	57.49
Pico Rivera (city) Los Angeles County	35,921	57.07
Heber (cdp) Imperial County	2,378	55.63
Irwindale (city) Los Angeles County	783	55.06
Monterey Park Tract (cdp) Stanislaus County	73	54.89
El Rancho (cdp) Tulare County	68	54.84

Top 10 Places Sorted by Percent of Total Population

Based on places with total population of 50,000 or more

Place	Population	%
Pico Rivera (city) Los Angeles County	35,921	57.07
Huntington Park (city) Los Angeles County	30,678	52.79
East Los Angeles (cdp) Los Angeles County	65,446	51.74
South Gate (city) Los Angeles County	47,308	50.12
Montebello (city) Los Angeles County	29,942	47.91
South Whittier (cdp) Los Angeles County	25,691	44.95
Baldwin Park (city) Los Angeles County	31,924	42.35
Downey (city) Los Angeles County	46,331	41.45
Florence-Graham (cdp) Los Angeles County	25,217	39.78
Paramount (city) Los Angeles County	21,493	39.73

Climate

California Physical Features and Climate Narrative

PHYSICAL FEATURES. The State of California extends along the shore of the Pacific Ocean between latitudes 32.5° N. and 42° N. Its more than 1,340 miles of coastline constitute nearly three-fourths of the Pacific coastline of the conterminous United States. The total land area amounts to 158,693 square miles. With its major axis oriented in a northwest-southeast direction, the State is 800 miles in length. Its greatest east-west dimension at a given latitude is about 360 miles though its average width is only 250 miles. However, it spreads over more than 10° of longitude, a distance of 550 miles.

The topography of the State is varied. Included are Death Valley, the lowest point in the U.S., with an elevation of 276 feet below sea level, and less than 85 miles away, Mt. Whitney, the highest peak in the conterminous states, reaching to 14,495 feet above sea level. These wide ranges of altitude and latitude are responsible in part for the variety of climates and vegetation found in various areas of the State. Another significant factor is the continuous interaction of maritime air masses with those of continental origin. The combination of these influences results in pronounced climatic changes with short distances.

The Coast Range parallels the coastline from the Oregon border to just north of the Los Angeles Basin. It is generally no more than 50 miles from the coast to the crest of the range. The principal break in the Coast Range is at San Francisco Bay where a sea level opening permits an abundant inflow of marine air to the interior of the State under certain circulation patterns. In the northern end of the State, the Coast Range merges with the Cascade Range, farther inland, to create an extensive area of rugged terrain more than 200 miles in width. The Cascades, in turn, extend southeastward until they merge into the Sierra Nevada. The Sierra Nevada, like the Coast Range, lies parallel to the coast, but the crest over most of its length is about 150 miles inland. Thus, between the two ranges there is a broad, flat valley averaging 45 miles or more in width. In length the valley extends nearly 500 miles.

Both the extreme northeastern portion of California and the desert area of southern California east of the mountains lie within the Great Basin. The Great Basin extends from Utah to the Sierra Nevada and has no surface drainage to the ocean. It is an area of climatological extremes.

GENERAL CLIMATE. Along the western side of the Coast Range the climate is dominated by the Pacific Ocean. Warm winters, cool summers, small daily and seasonal temperature ranges, and high relative humidities are characteristic of this area. With increasing distance from the ocean the maritime influence decreases. Areas that are well protected from the ocean experience a more continental type of climate with warmer summers, colder winters, greater daily and seasonal temperature ranges, and generally lower relative humidities. Many parts of the State lie within a transitional zone, where conditions range between these two climatic extremes. Summer is a dry period over most of the State. With the northward migration of the semi-permanent Pacific high during summer, most storm tracks are deflected far to the north. In winter, the Pacific high decreases in intensity and drops further south, permitting storms to move into and across the State, producing widespread rain at low elevations and snow at high elevations.

The easternmost mountain chains form a barrier that protects much of California from the extremely cold air of the Great Basin in winter. The ranges of mountains to the west offer some protection to the interior from the strong flow of air off the Pacific Ocean. As a result, precipitation is heavy on the coastward or western side of both the Coast Range and the Sierra Nevada, and lighter on the eastern slopes. Temperature tends toward uniformity from day to day and from season to season on the ocean side of the Coast Range and in coastal valleys. East of the Sierra Nevada temperature patterns are continental in character with wide excursions from high readings to low. Between the two mountain chains and over much of the desert area the temperature regime is intermediate between the maritime and the continental models. Hot summers are the rule while winters are moderate to cold. In the basins and valleys adjoining the coast, climate is subject to wide variations within short distances as a result of the influence of topography on the circulation of marine air. The Los Angeles Basin and the San Francisco Bay area offer many varieties of climate within a few miles.

A dominating factor in the weather of California is the semi-permanent high pressure area of the north Pacific Ocean. This pressure center moves northward in summer, holding storm tracks well to the north, and as a result California receives little or no precipitation from this source during that period. In winter, the Pacific high retreats southward permitting storm centers to swing into and across California. These are the storms that bring widespread, moderate precipitation to the State. When changes in the circulation pattern permit storm centers to approach the California coast from a southwesterly direction, copious amounts of moisture are carried by the northeastward streaming air. This results in heavy rains and often produces widespread flooding.

There is another California weather characteristic that results from the location of the Pacific high. The steady flow of air from the northwest during the summer helps to drive the California Current of the Pacific Ocean as it sweeps southward almost parallel to the California coastline. However, since the mean drift is slightly offshore there is a band of upwelling immediately off the coast as water from deeper layers is drawn into the surface circulation. The water from below the surface is colder than the surface water, and as a result there is a semi-permanent band of cold water just offshore. The temperature of water reaching the surface from deeper levels ranges from about 49°F. in winter to 55°F. in late summer along the northern California coast, and from 57°F. to 65°F. on the southern California coast. Comparatively warm, moist Pacific air masses drifting over this band of cold water form a bank of fog which is swept inland by the prevailing northwest winds out of the high pressure center. In general, heat is added to the air as it moves inland during these summer months, and the fog quickly lifts to form a deck of low clouds that extend inland only a short distance before evaporating completely. Characteristically this deck of clouds extends inland further during the night and then recedes to the vicinity of the coast during the day.

PRECIPITATION. In the northern part of the State the months of heaviest precipitation are October through April. The rainy season becomes shorter in the southern part of the State, November through March marking the wet period here. During the rest of the year precipitation is infrequent and usually light. In the north and over the central and northern mountains there are usually from 60 to 100 days of precipitation per year, while in the southern desert there may be as few as 10 days. It is apparent, therefore, that the rainy season is made up of periods of stormy weather alternating with longer periods of pleasant weather. A typical winter storm situation brings intermittent rain over a period of from two to five days, followed by seven to 14 days of dry weather.

SNOWFALL. Snow has been reported at one time or another in nearly every part of California but it is very infrequent west of the Sierra Nevada except at high elevations of the Coast Range and the Cascades. In the Sierra Nevada, snow in moderate amounts is reported nearly every winter at elevations as low as 2,000 feet. Amounts and intensities increase with elevation to around 7,000 or 8,000 feet. Above 4,000 feet elevation snow remains on the ground for appreciable lengths of time each winter.

RELATIVE HUMIDITY. In general, relative humidities are moderate to high along the coast throughout the year. Inland humidities are high during the winter and low during the summer. Since the ocean is the source of the cool, humid, maritime air of summer, it follows that with increasing distance from the ocean, relative humidity tends to decrease. Where mountain barriers prevent the free flow of marine air inland, humidities decrease rapidly. Where openings in these barriers permit a significant influx of cool, moist air it mixes with the drier inland air, resulting in a more gradual decrease of moisture. This pattern is characteristic of most coastal valleys.

STORMS. Thunderstorms may occur in California at any time of the year. Near the coast and over the Central Valley there appears to be no prevailing season. The storms are usually light and infrequent. Over the interior mountain areas storms are more intense, and they may become unusually strong on occasion at intermediate and high elevations of the Sierra Nevada. Many California thunderstorms produce so little precipitation that range and forest fires often result from the lightning strikes. Heavy precipitation occasionally results. Some flash flooding has been reported as a result of thundershowers. Hail diameters from one quarter of an inch to one half inch are sometimes reported. Serious hail damage is infrequent. Tornadoes have been reported in California but with a frequency of only one or two per year. They are generally not severe, in many cases amounting to little more than a local whirlwind.

DROUGHT. Drought must be evaluated on a different basis than in other parts of the country. Typically there are extended periods every summer with little or no precipitation. This is the normal and expected condition. A deficiency of precipitation becomes significant in the State when the normal winter water supply fails to materialize.

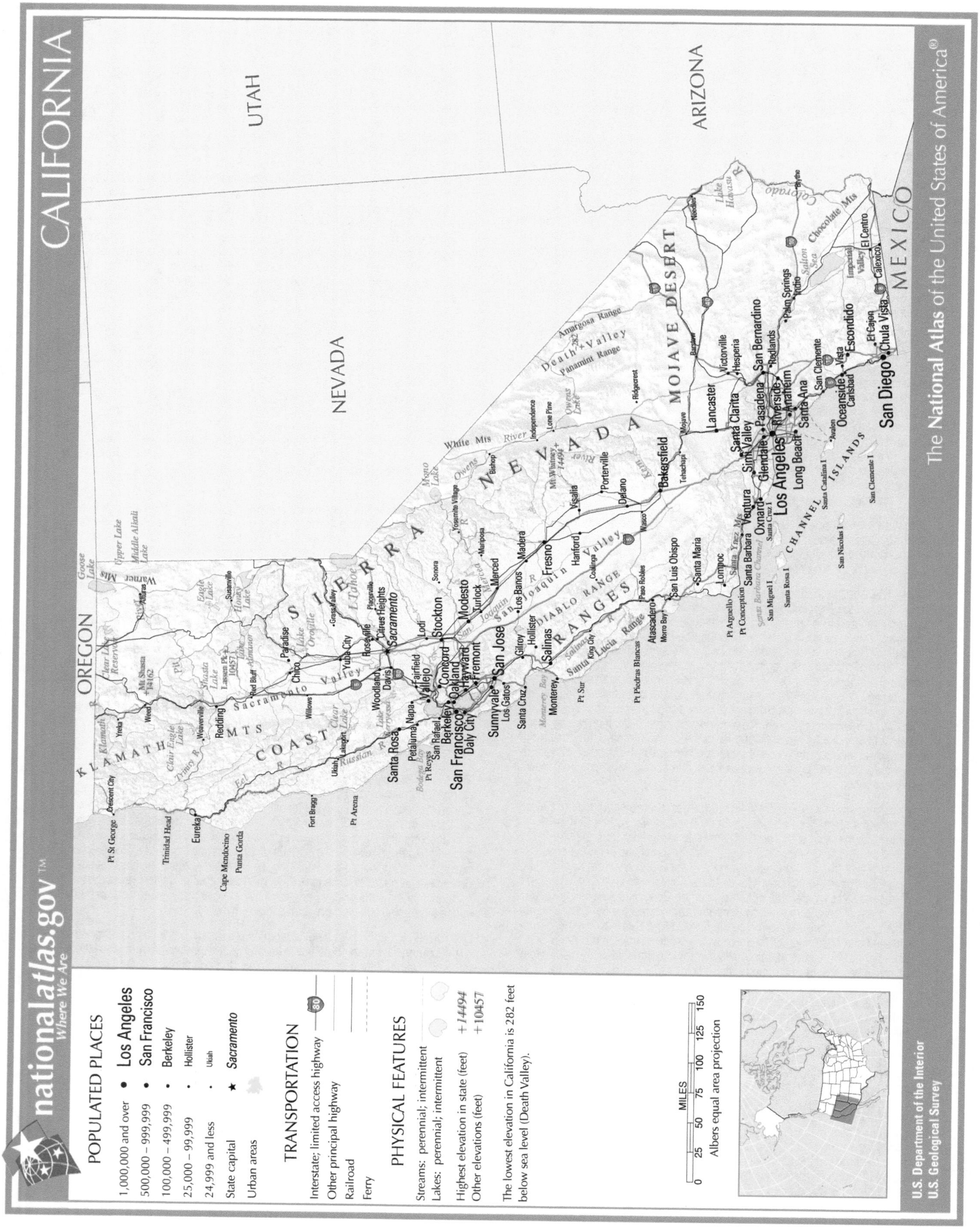

nationalatlas.gov™
Where We Are

CALIFORNIA

POPULATED PLACES

1,000,000 and over	•	Los Angeles
500,000 – 999,999	•	San Francisco
100,000 – 499,999	•	Berkeley
25,000 – 99,999	•	Hollister
24,999 and less	•	Ukiah
State capital	★	*Sacramento*
Urban areas		

TRANSPORTATION

Interstate; limited access highway 80

Other principal highway

Railroad

Ferry

PHYSICAL FEATURES

Streams: perennial; intermittent

Lakes: perennial; intermittent

Highest elevation in state (feet) +*14494*

Other elevations (feet) +10457

The lowest elevation in California is 282 feet below sea level (Death Valley).

MILES

0 25 50 75 100 125 150

Albers equal area projection

U.S. Department of the Interior
U.S. Geological Survey

The **National Atlas** of the United States of America®

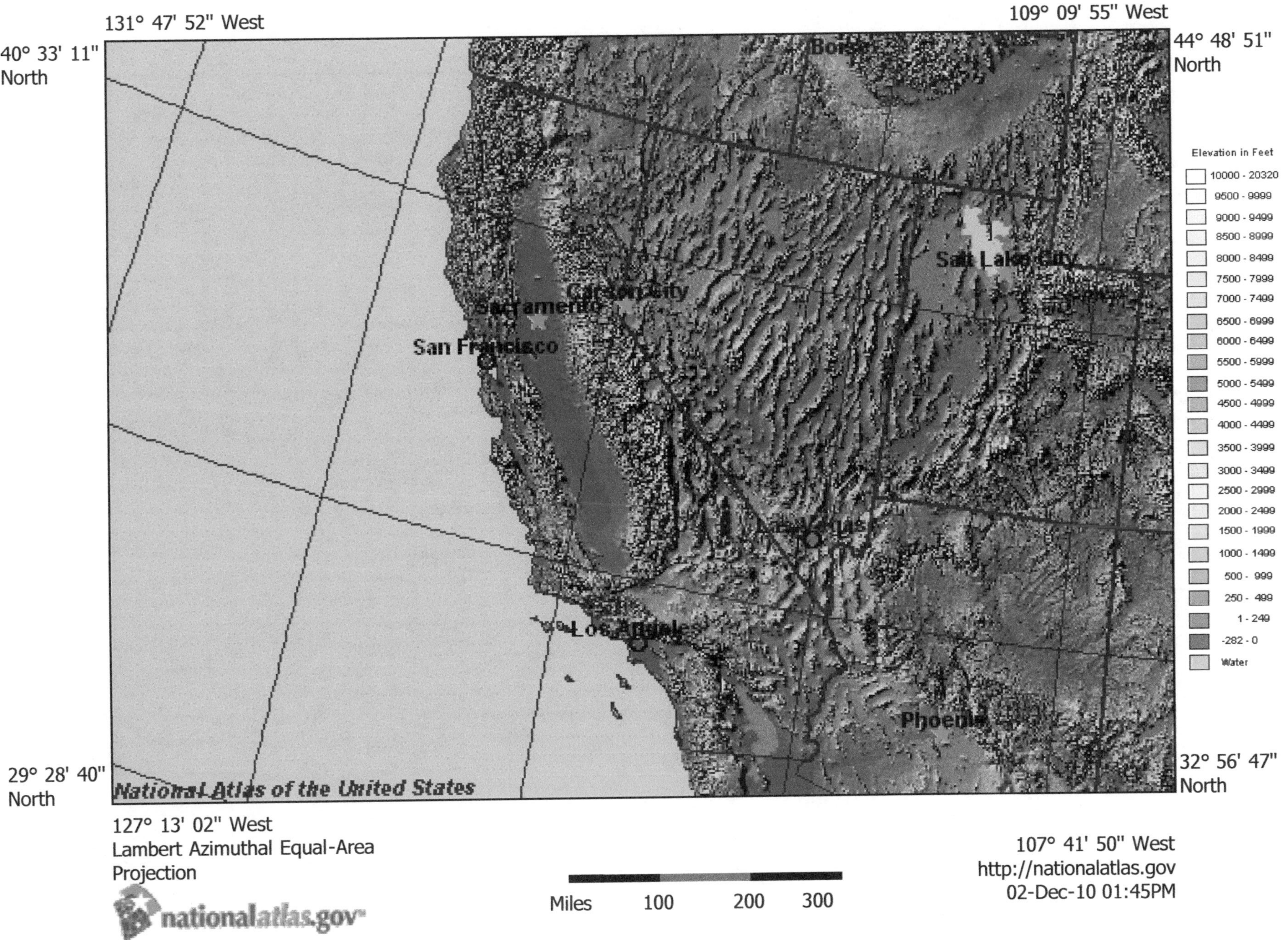
131° 47' 52" West
40° 33' 11" North
109° 09' 55" West
44° 48' 51" North
Sacramento
San Francisco
Salt Lake City
Phoenix
Elevation in Feet
10000 - 20320
9500 - 9999
9000 - 9499
8500 - 8999
8000 - 8499
7500 - 7999
7000 - 7499
6500 - 6999
6000 - 6499
5500 - 5999
5000 - 5499
4500 - 4999
4000 - 4499
3500 - 3999
3000 - 3499
2500 - 2999
2000 - 2499
1500 - 1999
1000 - 1499
500 - 999
250 - 499
1 - 249
-282 - 0
Water
29° 28' 40" North
National Atlas of the United States
32° 56' 47" North
127° 13' 02" West
Lambert Azimuthal Equal-Area
Projection
nationalatlas.gov
Miles 100 200 300
107° 41' 50" West
http://nationalatlas.gov
02-Dec-10 01:45PM

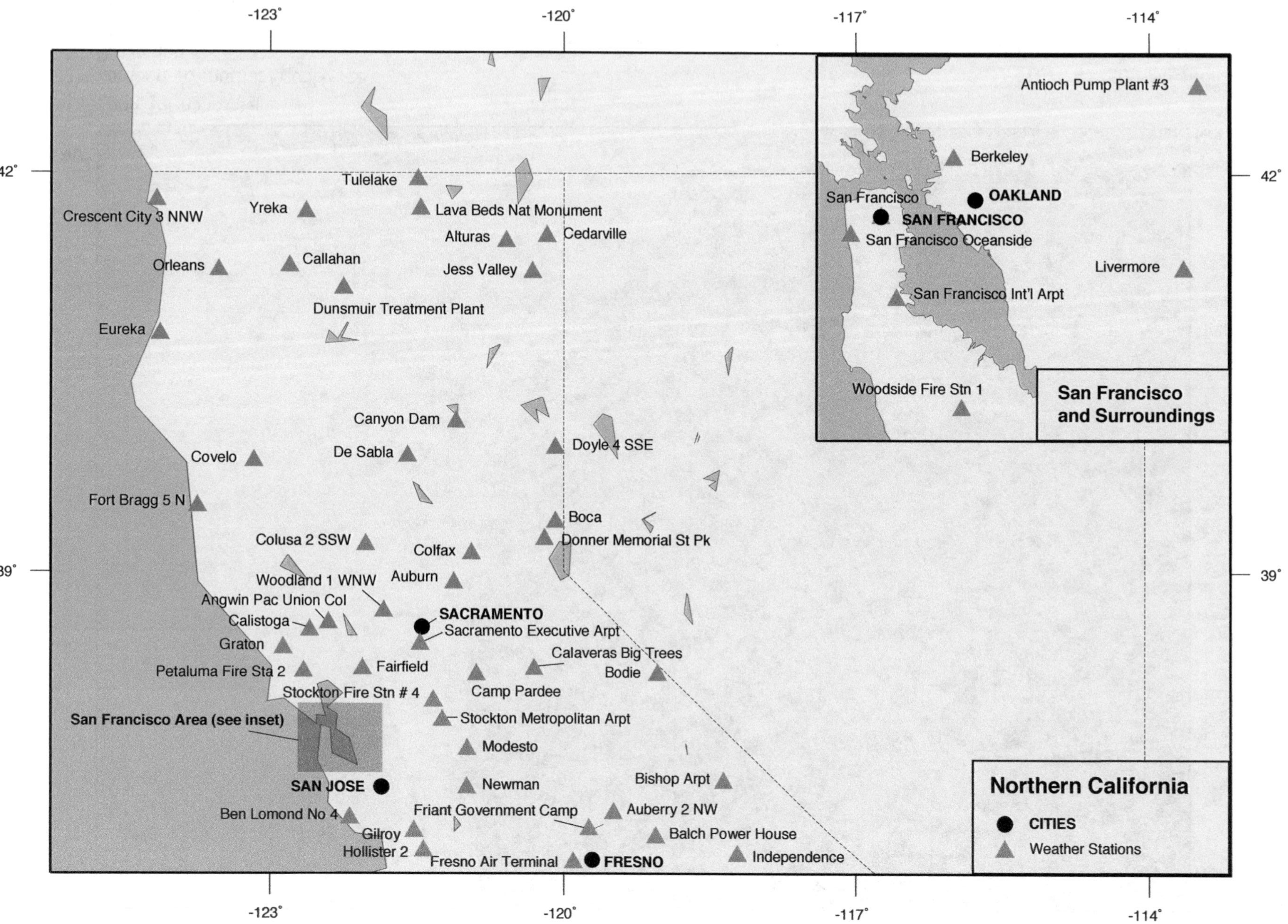

Northern California
CITIES
Weather Stations
San Francisco and Surroundings
Antioch Pump Plant #3
Berkeley
OAKLAND
San Francisco
SAN FRANCISCO
San Francisco Oceanside
Livermore
San Francisco Int'l Arpt
Woodside Fire Stn 1
Tulelake
Crescent City 3 NNW
Yreka
Lava Beds Nat Monument
Alturas
Cedarville
Orleans
Callahan
Jess Valley
Dunsmuir Treatment Plant
Eureka
Canyon Dam
Covelo
De Sabla
Doyle 4 SSE
Fort Bragg 5 N
Boca
Colusa 2 SSW
Donner Memorial St Pk
Colfax
Woodland 1 WNW
Auburn
Angwin Pac Union Col
SACRAMENTO
Calistoga
Sacramento Executive Arpt
Graton
Calaveras Big Trees
Petaluma Fire Sta 2
Fairfield
Bodie
Stockton Fire Stn # 4
Camp Pardee
San Francisco Area (see inset)
Stockton Metropolitan Arpt
Modesto
SAN JOSE
Newman
Bishop Arpt
Ben Lomond No 4
Friant Government Camp
Auberry 2 NW
Gilroy
Balch Power House
Hollister 2
Fresno Air Terminal
FRESNO
Independence
-123°
-120°
-117°
-114°
42°
39°

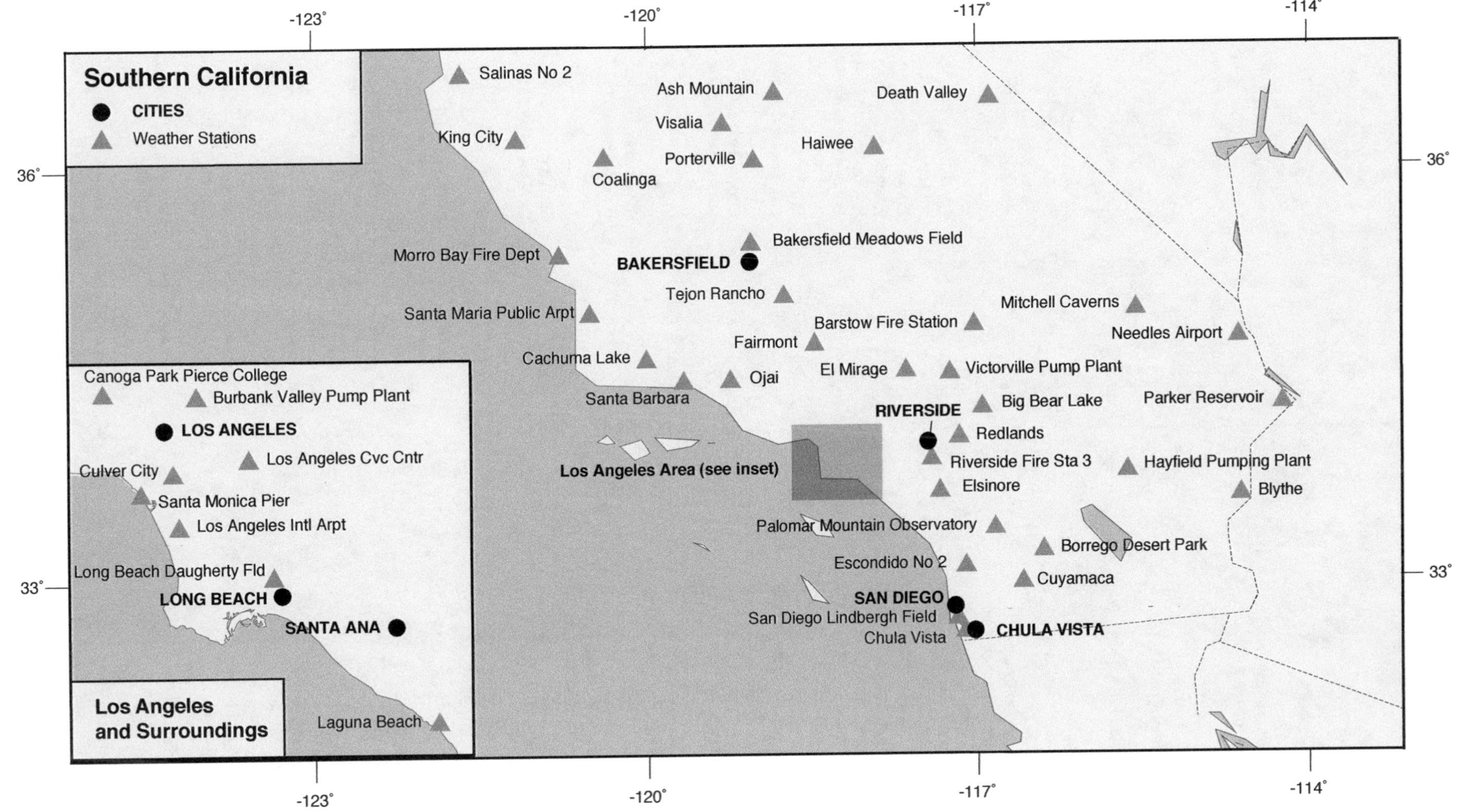
Southern California
CITIES
Weather Stations
Salinas No 2
King City
Coalinga
Ash Mountain
Visalia
Porterville
Haiwee
Death Valley
Bakersfield Meadows Field
BAKERSFIELD
Morro Bay Fire Dept
Santa Maria Public Arpt
Tejon Rancho
Mitchell Caverns
Barstow Fire Station
Needles Airport
Fairmont
Cachuma Lake
El Mirage
Victorville Pump Plant
Ojai
Santa Barbara
Big Bear Lake
Parker Reservoir
RIVERSIDE
Redlands
Riverside Fire Sta 3
Hayfield Pumping Plant
Los Angeles Area (see inset)
Elsinore
Blythe
Palomar Mountain Observatory
Borrego Desert Park
Escondido No 2
Cuyamaca
SAN DIEGO
San Diego Lindbergh Field
Chula Vista
CHULA VISTA
Canoga Park Pierce College
Burbank Valley Pump Plant
LOS ANGELES
Los Angeles Cvc Cntr
Culver City
Santa Monica Pier
Los Angeles Intl Arpt
Long Beach Daugherty Fld
LONG BEACH
SANTA ANA
Los Angeles and Surroundings
Laguna Beach
-123°
-120°
-117°
-114°
36°
33°

California Weather Stations by County

County	Station Name
Alameda	Berkeley
	Livermore
Butte	De Sabla
Calaveras	Calaveras Big Trees
	Camp Pardee
Colusa	Colusa 2 SSW
Contra Costa	Antioch Pump Plant #3
Del Norte	Crescent City 3 NNW
Fresno	Auberry 2 NW
	Balch Power House
	Coalinga
	Fresno Air Terminal
	Friant Government Camp
Humboldt	Eureka
	Orleans
Inyo	Bishop Arpt
	Death Valley
	Haiwee
	Independence
Kern	Bakersfield Meadows Field
	Tejon Rancho
Lassen	Doyle 4 SSE
Los Angeles	Burbank Valley Pump Plant
	Canoga Park Pierce College
	Culver City
	Fairmont
	Long Beach Daugherty Fld
	Los Angeles Civic Center
	Los Angeles Intl Arpt
	Santa Monica Pier
Mendocino	Covelo
	Fort Bragg 5 N
Modoc	Alturas
	Cedarville
	Jess Valley
Mono	Bodie
Monterey	King City
	Salinas No 2
Napa	Angwin Pac Union Col
	Calistoga
Nevada	Boca
	Donner Memorial St Pk
Orange	Laguna Beach
Placer	Auburn
	Colfax

County	Station Name
Plumas	Canyon Dam
Riverside	Blythe
	Elsinore
	Hayfield Pumping Plant
	Riverside Fire Sta 3
Sacramento	Sacramento Executive Arpt
San Benito	Hollister 2
San Bernardino	Barstow Fire Station
	Big Bear Lake
	El Mirage
	Mitchell Caverns
	Needles Airport
	Parker Reservoir
	Redlands
	Victorville Pump Plant
San Diego	Borrego Desert Park
	Chula Vista
	Cuyamaca
	Escondido No 2
	Palomar Mountain Observatory
	San Diego Lindbergh Field
San Francisco	San Francisco
	San Francisco Oceanside
San Joaquin	Stockton Fire Stn #4
	Stockton Metropolitan Arpt
San Luis Obispo	Morro Bay Fire Dept
San Mateo	San Francisco Int'l Arpt
	Woodside Fire Stn 1
Santa Barbara	Cachuma Lake
	Santa Barbara
	Santa Maria Public Arpt
Santa Clara	Gilroy
Santa Cruz	Ben Lomond No 4
Siskiyou	Callahan
	Dunsmuir Treatment Plant
	Lava Beds Nat Monument
	Tulelake
	Yreka
Solano	Fairfield
Sonoma	Graton
	Petaluma Fire Station 2
Stanislaus	Modesto
	Newman
Tulare	Ash Mountain
	Porterville
	Visalia

See User Guide for station inclusion criteria.

County	Station Name
Ventura	Ojai
Yolo	Woodland 1 WNW

California Weather Stations by City

City	Station Name	Miles
Anaheim	Laguna Beach	20.8
	Long Beach Daugherty Fld	14.9
	Los Angeles Civic Center	24.0
Antioch	Antioch Pump Plant #3	3.7
	Fairfield	24.1
	Livermore	22.3
Bakersfield	Bakersfield Meadows Field	5.7
Berkeley	Berkeley	0.4
	San Francisco Oceanside	15.7
	San Francisco Int'l Arpt	18.9
	San Francisco	11.4
Burbank	Burbank Valley Pump Plant	1.5
	Canoga Park Pierce College	13.8
	Culver City	12.1
	Los Angeles Intl Arpt	17.6
	Los Angeles Civic Center	10.4
	Santa Monica Pier	16.0
Carlsbad	Escondido No 2	11.2
Chula Vista	Chula Vista	2.2
	San Diego Lindbergh Field	10.2
Concord	Antioch Pump Plant #3	15.2
	Berkeley	15.5
	Fairfield	21.0
	Livermore	24.6
Corona	Elsinore	19.6
	Riverside Fire Sta 3	12.0
Costa Mesa	Laguna Beach	10.8
	Long Beach Daugherty Fld	18.7
Daly City	Berkeley	16.6
	San Francisco Oceanside	3.6
	San Francisco Int'l Arpt	6.1
	San Francisco	5.8
	Woodside Fire Stn 1	21.2
Downey	Burbank Valley Pump Plant	21.1
	Culver City	16.3
	Long Beach Daugherty Fld	7.4
	Los Angeles Intl Arpt	15.3
	Los Angeles Civic Center	9.7
	Santa Monica Pier	21.5
East Los Angeles	Burbank Valley Pump Plant	14.8
	Culver City	13.3
	Long Beach Daugherty Fld	13.6
	Los Angeles Intl Arpt	14.8
	Los Angeles Civic Center	3.9
	Santa Monica Pier	19.1
El Monte	Burbank Valley Pump Plant	20.0
	Culver City	21.7
	Long Beach Daugherty Fld	18.3
	Los Angeles Intl Arpt	23.4
	Los Angeles Civic Center	11.9

City	Station Name	Miles
Escondido	Escondido No 2	1.6
	Palomar Mountain Observatory	22.5
Fairfield	Fairfield	1.6
Fontana	Redlands	15.8
	Riverside Fire Sta 3	10.6
Fremont	Livermore	14.6
	San Francisco Int'l Arpt	23.3
	Woodside Fire Stn 1	16.5
Fresno	Fresno Air Terminal	3.9
	Friant Government Camp	15.4
Fullerton	Laguna Beach	24.2
	Long Beach Daugherty Fld	14.1
	Los Angeles Civic Center	21.1
Garden Grove	Laguna Beach	18.5
	Long Beach Daugherty Fld	12.9
	Los Angeles Civic Center	24.8
Glendale	Burbank Valley Pump Plant	5.7
	Canoga Park Pierce College	18.0
	Culver City	13.1
	Long Beach Daugherty Fld	23.3
	Los Angeles Intl Arpt	18.0
	Los Angeles Civic Center	7.9
	Santa Monica Pier	18.1
Hayward	Berkeley	18.4
	Livermore	17.1
	San Francisco Oceanside	23.9
	San Francisco Int'l Arpt	17.8
	San Francisco	21.2
	Woodside Fire Stn 1	17.5
Huntington Beach	Laguna Beach	16.0
	Long Beach Daugherty Fld	13.5
Inglewood	Burbank Valley Pump Plant	15.7
	Canoga Park Pierce College	20.1
	Culver City	5.2
	Long Beach Daugherty Fld	13.4
	Los Angeles Intl Arpt	3.4
	Los Angeles Civic Center	9.2
	Santa Monica Pier	9.3
Irvine	Laguna Beach	9.1
	Long Beach Daugherty Fld	23.5
Lancaster	Fairmont	16.4
Long Beach	Culver City	20.1
	Long Beach Daugherty Fld	1.9
	Los Angeles Intl Arpt	16.4
	Los Angeles Civic Center	17.4
	Santa Monica Pier	23.7
Los Angeles	Burbank Valley Pump Plant	5.5
	Canoga Park Pierce College	10.0
	Culver City	7.2
	Long Beach Daugherty Fld	24.3

See User Guide for station inclusion criteria.

City	Station Name	Miles
Los Angeles *(cont.)*	Los Angeles Intl Arpt	13.0
	Los Angeles Civic Center	11.2
	Santa Monica Pier	9.8
Modesto	Modesto	0.9
	Newman	23.9
	Stockton Metropolitan Arpt	21.1
Moreno Valley	Elsinore	19.0
	Redlands	8.9
	Riverside Fire Sta 3	8.6
Norwalk	Burbank Valley Pump Plant	24.5
	Culver City	19.7
	Long Beach Daugherty Fld	6.9
	Los Angeles Intl Arpt	18.3
	Los Angeles Civic Center	13.2
	Santa Monica Pier	24.8
Oakland	Berkeley	5.7
	San Francisco Oceanside	15.8
	San Francisco Int'l Arpt	15.7
	San Francisco	11.8
	Woodside Fire Stn 1	24.9
Oceanside	Escondido No 2	14.2
Ontario	Riverside Fire Sta 3	16.1
Orange	Laguna Beach	17.6
	Long Beach Daugherty Fld	19.2
Oxnard	Ojai	18.3
Palmdale	Fairmont	20.7
Pasadena	Burbank Valley Pump Plant	12.6
	Canoga Park Pierce College	24.9
	Culver City	18.1
	Long Beach Daugherty Fld	22.3
	Los Angeles Intl Arpt	21.7
	Los Angeles Civic Center	9.3
	Santa Monica Pier	23.6
Pomona	Riverside Fire Sta 3	22.6
Rancho Cucamonga	Redlands	23.3
	Riverside Fire Sta 3	16.5
Rialto	Redlands	12.2
	Riverside Fire Sta 3	11.3
Richmond	Berkeley	6.4
	San Francisco Oceanside	17.0
	San Francisco Int'l Arpt	22.8
	San Francisco	13.3
Riverside	Elsinore	19.5
	Redlands	14.9
	Riverside Fire Sta 3	1.6
Roseville	Auburn	15.2
	Sacramento Executive Arpt	20.7
Sacramento	Sacramento Executive Arpt	3.7

City	Station Name	Miles
Sacramento *(cont.)*	Woodland 1 WNW	20.3
Salinas	Gilroy	21.9
	Hollister 2	16.6
	Salinas No 2	2.2
San Bernardino	Big Bear Lake	24.9
	Redlands	8.6
	Riverside Fire Sta 3	13.5
San Buenaventura (Ventura)	Ojai	12.0
San Diego	Chula Vista	11.0
	Escondido No 2	22.9
	San Diego Lindbergh Field	4.2
San Francisco	Berkeley	12.0
	San Francisco Oceanside	3.8
	San Francisco Int'l Arpt	10.1
	San Francisco	0.6
	Woodside Fire Stn 1	24.8
San Jose	Ben Lomond No 4	19.6
	Woodside Fire Stn 1	22.7
Santa Ana	Laguna Beach	14.3
	Long Beach Daugherty Fld	17.5
Santa Clara	Ben Lomond No 4	19.7
	Livermore	24.3
	Woodside Fire Stn 1	16.3
Santa Clarita	Burbank Valley Pump Plant	18.5
	Canoga Park Pierce College	16.5
	Fairmont	20.0
Santa Rosa	Angwin Pac Union Col	17.0
	Calistoga	12.1
	Graton	8.6
	Petaluma Fire Station 2	13.0
Simi Valley	Burbank Valley Pump Plant	23.1
	Canoga Park Pierce College	11.6
	Santa Monica Pier	23.2
South Gate	Burbank Valley Pump Plant	18.4
	Culver City	12.3
	Long Beach Daugherty Fld	8.1
	Los Angeles Intl Arpt	11.4
	Los Angeles Civic Center	7.4
	Santa Monica Pier	17.5
Stockton	Antioch Pump Plant #3	23.2
	Stockton Metropolitan Arpt	7.2
	Stockton Fire Stn #4	1.1
Sunnyvale	Ben Lomond No 4	20.0
	Livermore	25.0
	Woodside Fire Stn 1	13.1
Thousand Oaks	Canoga Park Pierce College	17.7
Torrance	Burbank Valley Pump Plant	24.0
	Culver City	12.9
	Long Beach Daugherty Fld	10.2

See User Guide for station inclusion criteria.

City	Station Name	Miles
Torrance *(cont.)*	Los Angeles Intl Arpt	7.4
	Los Angeles Civic Center	16.1
	Santa Monica Pier	14.4
Vallejo	Berkeley	17.2
	Fairfield	13.9
	Petaluma Fire Station 2	25.0
Victorville	El Mirage	16.4
	Victorville Pump Plant	3.1
Visalia	Porterville	24.1
	Visalia	0.8
West Covina	Long Beach Daugherty Fld	20.9
	Los Angeles Civic Center	18.2

Note: Miles is the distance between the geographic center of the city and the weather station.

California Weather Stations by Elevation

Feet	Station Name
8,370	Bodie
6,790	Big Bear Lake
5,937	Donner Memorial St Pk
5,575	Boca
5,549	Palomar Mountain Observatory
5,399	Jess Valley
4,770	Lava Beds Nat Monument
4,693	Calaveras Big Trees
4,669	Cedarville
4,640	Cuyamaca
4,560	Canyon Dam
4,399	Alturas
4,390	Doyle 4 SSE
4,350	Mitchell Caverns
4,102	Bishop Arpt
4,035	Tulelake
3,950	Independence
3,825	Haiwee
3,185	Callahan
3,060	Fairmont
2,950	El Mirage
2,857	Victorville Pump Plant
2,709	De Sabla
2,625	Yreka
2,399	Colfax
2,319	Barstow Fire Station
2,169	Dunsmuir Treatment Plant
2,089	Auberry 2 NW
1,720	Balch Power House
1,714	Angwin Pac Union Col
1,708	Ash Mountain
1,424	Tejon Rancho
1,410	Covelo
1,370	Hayfield Pumping Plant
1,317	Redlands
1,292	Auburn
1,285	Elsinore
914	Needles Airport
839	Riverside Fire Sta 3
805	Borrego Desert Park
790	Canoga Park Pierce College
780	Cachuma Lake
750	Ojai
737	Parker Reservoir
669	Coalinga
658	Camp Pardee
654	Burbank Valley Pump Plant
600	Escondido No 2
488	Bakersfield Meadows Field
479	Livermore
419	Ben Lomond No 4
410	Friant Government Camp
399	Orleans
393	Porterville
379	Woodside Fire Stn 1

Feet	Station Name
370	Calistoga
333	Fresno Air Terminal
325	Visalia
319	King City
310	Berkeley
274	Hollister 2
270	Los Angeles Civic Center
268	Blythe
253	Santa Maria Public Arpt
200	Graton
193	Gilroy
174	San Francisco
120	Fort Bragg 5 N
115	Morro Bay Fire Dept
100	Los Angeles Intl Arpt
90	Modesto
89	Newman
68	Woodland 1 WNW
60	Antioch Pump Plant #3
56	Chula Vista
55	Culver City
49	Colusa 2 SSW
44	Salinas No 2
40	Crescent City 3 NNW
40	Fairfield
35	Laguna Beach
35	San Francisco Oceanside
30	Petaluma Fire Station 2
24	Long Beach Daugherty Fld
21	Stockton Metropolitan Arpt
20	Eureka
15	Sacramento Executive Arpt
14	Santa Monica Pier
13	San Diego Lindbergh Field
12	Stockton Fire Stn #4
7	San Francisco Int'l Arpt
4	Santa Barbara
-193	Death Valley

See User Guide for station inclusion criteria.

Bakersfield Meadows Field

Bakersfield, situated in the extreme south end of the great San Joaquin Valley, is partially surrounded by a horseshoe-shaped rim of mountains with an open side to the northwest and the crest at an average distance of 40 miles.

The Sierra Nevada mountains to the northeast shut out most of the cold air that flows southward over the continent during winter. They also catch and store snow, which provides irrigation water for use during the dry months. The Tehachapi Mountains, forming the southern boundary, act as an obstruction to northwest wind, causing heavier precipitation on the windward slopes, high wind velocity over the ridges and, at times, continuing cloudiness in the south end of the valley after skies have cleared elsewhere.

Because of the nature of the surrounding topography, there are large climatic variations within relatively short distances. These zones of variation may be classified as valley, mountain, and desert areas. The overall climate, however, is warm and semi-arid. There is only one wet season during the year, as 90 percent of all precipitation falls from October through April, inclusive. Snow in the valley is infrequent, with only a trace occurring in about one year out of seven. Thunderstorms seldom occur in the valley.

Summers are cloudless, hot and dry. Cotton, potatoes, grapes, and cattle are the principal agricultural products. Severe freezes seldom occur and there are occasional years with no frost at all in certain warm areas.

Winters are mild and semi-arid, yet fairly humid. December and January are characterized by frequent fog, mostly nocturnal, which prevails when marine air is trapped in the valley by a high pressure system. In extreme cases this fog may last continuously for two or three weeks. Another local characteristic is the occasionally warm, dry, southeast chinook wind that spills through the Tehachapi Pass during winter. This wind usually attains velocities of 30 to 40 miles an hour, sometimes reaching as high as 60 miles an hour.

During summer months northwest sea breezes frequent the Bakersfield area about twice weekly. When above normal temperatures prevail for several days, the gradient builds up sufficiently to draw in cooler air from the coastal section. During prolonged periods of drought this late afternoon breeze may carry varying amounts of dust, and thermal instability sometimes causes the dust to rise as high as 7,000 feet.

Based on the 1951-1980 period, the average first occurrence of 32 degrees Fahrenheit in the fall is December 11 and the average last occurrence in the spring is January 31.

Bakersfield Meadows Field *Kern County* Elevation: 488 ft. Latitude: 35° 26' N Longitude: 119° 03' W

	JAN	FEB	MAR	APR	MAY	JUN	JUL	AUG	SEP	OCT	NOV	DEC	YEAR
Mean Maximum Temp. (°F)	57.2	63.8	69.5	76.0	84.4	91.6	97.8	96.4	90.6	80.2	66.3	57.2	77.6
Mean Temp. (°F)	48.2	53.1	57.7	62.7	70.5	77.3	83.6	82.3	76.9	67.1	55.2	47.7	65.2
Mean Minimum Temp. (°F)	39.0	42.3	45.9	49.3	56.6	63.0	69.3	68.1	63.2	54.0	44.1	38.1	52.7
Extreme Maximum Temp. (°F)	82	87	94	101	107	110	112	112	109	103	88	81	112
Extreme Minimum Temp. (°F)	23	25	32	33	37	45	52	55	47	38	28	19	19
Days Maximum Temp. ≥ 90°F	0	0	0	3	9	19	28	26	18	4	0	0	107
Days Maximum Temp. ≤ 32°F	0	0	0	0	0	0	0	0	0	0	0	0	0
Days Minimum Temp. ≤ 32°F	5	1	0	0	0	0	0	0	0	0	1	6	13
Days Minimum Temp. ≤ 0°F	0	0	0	0	0	0	0	0	0	0	0	0	0
Heating Degree Days (base 65°F)	515	330	230	122	28	3	0	0	2	52	290	529	2,101
Cooling Degree Days (base 65°F)	0	0	11	60	206	379	583	542	366	125	3	0	2,275
Mean Precipitation (in.)	1.18	1.21	1.24	0.51	0.18	0.08	trace	0.05	0.08	0.28	0.63	0.83	6.27
Maximum Precipitation (in.)*	2.6	4.7	4.3	2.6	2.4	1.1	0.3	1.2	1.1	1.8	3.0	2.0	10.9
Minimum Precipitation (in.)*	trace	trace	trace	0	0	0	0	0	0	0	0	0	1.9
Extreme Maximum Daily Precip. (in.)	1.42	0.97	0.99	0.74	0.64	0.44	0.05	1.00	0.34	0.96	0.99	0.98	1.42
Days With ≥ 0.1" Precipitation	3	4	4	2	1	0	0	0	0	1	2	2	19
Days With ≥ 0.5" Precipitation	0	1	0	0	0	0	0	0	0	0	0	0	1
Days With ≥ 1.0" Precipitation	0	0	0	0	0	0	0	0	0	0	0	0	0
Mean Snowfall (in.)	***0.1***	na	na	na	na	na	na	na	na	na	na	na	na
Maximum Snowfall (in.)*	trace	trace	2	0	0	0	0	0	0	0	0	trace	2
Maximum 24-hr. Snowfall (in.)*	trace	trace	2	0	0	0	0	0	0	0	0	trace	2
Maximum Snow Depth (in.)	na	na	na	na	na	na	na	na	na	na	na	na	na
Days With ≥ 1.0" Snow Depth	na	na	na	na	na	na	na	na	na	na	na	na	na
Thunderstorm Days*	< 1	< 1	1	< 1	< 1	< 1	< 1	< 1	1	< 1	< 1	< 1	2
Foggy Days*	18	10	4	1	< 1	< 1	< 1	< 1	1	2	10	18	64
Predominant Sky Cover*	OVR	OVR	CLR	CLR	CLR	CLR	CLR	CLR	CLR	CLR	CLR	OVR	CLR
Mean Relative Humidity 7am (%)*	86	82	75	63	53	46	44	50	56	63	77	86	65
Mean Relative Humidity 4pm (%)*	61	50	42	33	27	23	21	24	28	33	48	61	38
Mean Dewpoint (°F)*	39	41	41	42	44	48	51	53	51	46	42	39	45
Prevailing Wind Direction*	E	E	NNW	NW	NW	NW	NW	NW	NW	NW	E	E	NW
Prevailing Wind Speed (mph)*	6	6	9	10	10	10	10	9	9	8	6	6	8
Maximum Wind Gust (mph)*	48	58	51	48	45	58	36	49	48	48	49	63	63

Note: (*) Period of record is 1948-1995

Bishop Airport

The station at Bishop is located at the Municipal Airport two and a half miles east of the town, one mile west of the Owens River, on the floor of the Owens Valley, which is orientated northwest to southeast and at this point is 12 miles wide, level, and semi-arid. Peaks of the 12,000 to 14,000 feet Sierra Nevadas are 25 miles west, and the 12,000 to 14,000 feet White Mountains are 10 miles east. The northern end of the valley is partly cut off by 6,000 to 8,000 feet mountains about 45 miles distant. The southern end of the valley makes a gradual descent to the Mojave Desert about 150 miles distant.

During the summer and autumn, the Mojave Desert causes an early morning and late evening northerly wind. Conversely, in the heat of the afternoon, it causes a southerly wind that is occasionally strong. Summer skies are mostly clear with thunderstorms from May through August. The days are hot and dry, the nights cool.

Winter and spring, although seasons of adverse weather, are quite mild. The skies are partly cloudy with the years greatest amounts of precipitation falling during the months of November through April. At times, strong northerly winds blow, especially in the spring during the months of February, March, and April. East and west winds frequently give pronounced warm mountain wind effects and turbulence.

During the winter and spring, strong westerly winds aloft, flowing over the Sierra Nevadas, create the Sierra Wave, known to sailplane pilots the world over.

Based on the 1951-1980 period, the average first occurrence of 32 degrees Fahrenheit in the fall is October 13 and the average last occurrence in the spring is May 7.

Bishop Airport *Inyo County* Elevation: 4,102 ft. Latitude: 37° 22' N Longitude: 118° 21' W

	JAN	FEB	MAR	APR	MAY	JUN	JUL	AUG	SEP	OCT	NOV	DEC	YEAR
Mean Maximum Temp. (°F)	53.8	57.6	64.8	72.2	81.7	91.3	97.9	95.8	87.4	75.7	62.3	53.3	74.5
Mean Temp. (°F)	38.3	42.0	47.9	54.1	62.9	71.0	77.0	74.7	67.0	56.4	44.8	37.4	56.1
Mean Minimum Temp. (°F)	22.8	26.3	30.9	36.0	44.1	50.7	56.0	53.6	46.6	36.9	27.3	21.5	37.7
Extreme Maximum Temp. (°F)	76	81	85	93	102	107	110	107	112	97	84	77	112
Extreme Minimum Temp. (°F)	1	3	9	17	26	29	34	40	26	18	8	-8	-8
Days Maximum Temp. ≥ 90°F	0	0	0	0	6	20	29	28	14	1	0	0	98
Days Maximum Temp. ≤ 32°F	0	0	0	0	0	0	0	0	0	0	0	0	0
Days Minimum Temp. ≤ 32°F	29	23	18	9	1	0	0	0	0	7	24	30	141
Days Minimum Temp. ≤ 0°F	0	0	0	0	0	0	0	0	0	0	0	0	0
Heating Degree Days (base 65°F)	821	644	524	323	117	19	1	0	43	268	598	847	4,205
Cooling Degree Days (base 65°F)	0	0	0	4	60	206	379	309	111	8	0	0	1,077
Mean Precipitation (in.)	1.03	0.94	0.53	0.26	0.19	0.19	0.17	0.13	0.19	0.26	0.51	0.65	5.05
Maximum Precipitation (in.)*	8.9	6.0	2.9	2.3	1.3	1.3	1.5	0.6	1.3	1.6	2.6	5.8	17.1
Minimum Precipitation (in.)*	0	0	0	0	0	0	0	0	0	0	0	0	1.8
Extreme Maximum Daily Precip. (in.)	4.00	1.24	1.75	1.58	0.58	0.68	0.38	0.42	1.25	1.58	1.30	2.67	4.00
Days With ≥ 0.1" Precipitation	2	2	1	1	1	0	1	0	1	1	1	1	12
Days With ≥ 0.5" Precipitation	1	1	0	0	0	0	0	0	0	0	0	0	2
Days With ≥ 1.0" Precipitation	0	0	0	0	0	0	0	0	0	0	0	0	0
Mean Snowfall (in.)	na	na	na	na	na	na	na	na	na	na	na	na	na
Maximum Snowfall (in.)*	23	32	15	9	2	0	0	0	0	2	4	13	57
Maximum 24-hr. Snowfall (in.)*	13	12	8	7	2	0	0	0	0	2	2	6	13
Maximum Snow Depth (in.)	na	na	na	na	na	na	na	na	na	na	na	na	na
Days With ≥ 1.0" Snow Depth	na	na	na	na	na	na	na	na	na	na	na	na	na
Thunderstorm Days*	0	0	< 1	< 1	1	2	5	2	1	1	0	0	12
Foggy Days*	1	1	1	0	1	0	0	0	0	0	< 1	2	6
Predominant Sky Cover*	CLR	CLR	CLR	CLR	CLR	CLR	CLR	CLR	CLR	CLR	CLR	CLR	CLR
Mean Relative Humidity 7am (%)*	71	68	58	44	39	34	35	39	43	52	63	68	51
Mean Relative Humidity 4pm (%)*	35	27	21	17	16	13	14	14	15	18	27	35	21
Mean Dewpoint (°F)*	19	20	19	20	27	31	36	35	31	25	21	19	25
Prevailing Wind Direction*	NW	N	N	N	N	S	S	S	S	S	N	N	N
Prevailing Wind Speed (mph)*	7	13	14	13	13	13	13	13	12	12	12	12	12
Maximum Wind Gust (mph)*	60	63	59	62	66	60	60	75	53	56	93	68	93

Note: (*) Period of record is 1948-1995

Eureka

Humboldt Bay is one-quarter mile north and one mile west of the station. There are no hills in Eureka of any consequence. The land slopes upward gently from the Bay toward the Coast Range, which begins about 3 miles east of the station and reaches the top of its first ridge approximately 10 miles to the east. The elevation of the ridge is 2,000 feet and extends in a semicircle from a point 20 miles north of Eureka to a point 25 miles south.

The climate of Eureka is completely maritime with high humidity prevailing the entire year. The rainy season begins in October and continues through April, accounting for about 90 percent of the annual precipitation. The dry season from May through September is marked by considerable fog or low cloudiness that usually clears in the late morning.

Temperatures are moderate the entire year. Although record highs have reached the mid 80s and record lows near 20 degrees, the usual yearly range is from lows in the mid 30s to highs in the mid 70s.

The principal industries are lumbering, fishing, tourism, and dairy farming. There is very little truck farming due to the low temperatures and lack of sunshine, however, the climate is nearly ideal for berries and flowers.

Based on the 1951-1980 period, the average first occurrence of 32 degrees Fahrenheit in the fall is December 10 and the average last occurrence in the spring is February 6.

Eureka *Humboldt County* Elevation: 20 ft. Latitude: 40° 49' N Longitude: 124° 10' W

	JAN	FEB	MAR	APR	MAY	JUN	JUL	AUG	SEP	OCT	NOV	DEC	YEAR
Mean Maximum Temp. (°F)	55.8	56.6	57.0	58.1	60.5	62.6	63.9	64.6	64.1	62.0	58.5	55.4	59.9
Mean Temp. (°F)	48.8	49.7	50.2	51.6	54.5	56.8	58.4	59.1	57.6	55.0	51.4	48.4	53.5
Mean Minimum Temp. (°F)	41.7	42.7	43.5	45.1	48.4	50.9	53.0	53.5	51.1	48.0	44.3	41.3	47.0
Extreme Maximum Temp. (°F)	78	80	76	80	83	81	76	82	86	87	78	75	87
Extreme Minimum Temp. (°F)	4	27	30	32	35	40	46	45	41	34	29	22	4
Days Maximum Temp. ≥ 90°F	0	0	0	0	0	0	0	0	0	0	0	0	0
Days Maximum Temp. ≤ 32°F	0	0	0	0	0	0	0	0	0	0	0	0	0
Days Minimum Temp. ≤ 32°F	2	1	0	0	0	0	0	0	0	0	1	2	6
Days Minimum Temp. ≤ 0°F	0	0	0	0	0	0	0	0	0	0	0	0	0
Heating Degree Days (base 65°F)	496	427	450	395	319	240	198	177	215	305	400	508	4,130
Cooling Degree Days (base 65°F)	0	0	0	0	0	0	0	1	1	1	0	0	3
Mean Precipitation (in.)	6.30	5.57	5.30	3.20	1.71	0.69	0.18	0.30	0.55	2.14	5.53	7.98	39.45
Maximum Precipitation (in.)*	13.9	10.8	11.2	10.7	6.0	2.6	1.2	3.4	3.3	13.0	16.6	14.1	67.2
Minimum Precipitation (in.)*	0.7	0.1	1.2	0.3	trace	trace	0	trace	trace	trace	0.3	0.5	21.1
Extreme Maximum Daily Precip. (in.)	3.21	2.47	2.41	1.74	1.74	1.07	0.89	1.57	0.99	2.18	4.37	6.79	6.79
Days With ≥ 0.1" Precipitation	11	10	11	7	4	2	0	1	1	5	10	12	74
Days With ≥ 0.5" Precipitation	5	4	4	2	1	0	0	0	0	1	4	5	26
Days With ≥ 1.0" Precipitation	2	1	1	0	0	0	0	0	0	0	2	2	8
Mean Snowfall (in.)	trace	0.2	trace	trace	0.0	trace	0.0	0.0	0.0	0.0	trace	0.1	0.3
Maximum Snowfall (in.)*	3	4	1	trace	0	0	0	0	0	0	trace	2	4
Maximum 24-hr. Snowfall (in.)*	2	2	1	trace	0	0	0	0	0	0	trace	2	2
Maximum Snow Depth (in.)	8	8	6	trace	0	trace	0	0	0	0	trace	3	8
Days With ≥ 1.0" Snow Depth	0	0	0	0	0	0	0	0	0	0	0	0	0
Thunderstorm Days*	1	1	< 1	< 1	< 1	< 1	< 1	< 1	< 1	< 1	1	1	4
Foggy Days*	13	11	10	12	13	16	22	22	21	21	15	15	191
Predominant Sky Cover*	na	na	na	na	na	na	na	na	na	na	na	na	na
Mean Relative Humidity 7am (%)*	na	na	na	na	na	na	na	na	na	na	na	na	na
Mean Relative Humidity 4pm (%)*	na	na	na	na	na	na	na	na	na	na	na	na	na
Mean Dewpoint (°F)*	na	na	na	na	na	na	na	na	na	na	na	na	na
Prevailing Wind Direction*	na	na	na	na	na	na	na	na	na	na	na	na	na
Prevailing Wind Speed (mph)*	na	na	na	na	na	na	na	na	na	na	na	na	na
Maximum Wind Gust (mph)*	69	60	58	53	60	51	47	38	49	49	69	62	69

Note: (*) Period of record is 1941-1995

The period of record for National Weather Service station data is 1980 – 2009 except where noted. See User Guide for detailed explanation of data.

Fresno Air Terminal

Fresno is located about midway and toward the eastern edge of the San Joaquin Valley, which is oriented northwest to southeast and has a length of about 225 miles and an average width of 50 miles. The San Joaquin Valley is generally flat. About 15 miles east of Fresno the terrain slopes upward with the foothills of the Sierra Nevada. The Sierra Nevada attain an elevation of more than 14,000 feet 50 miles east of Fresno. West of the city 45 miles lie the foothills of the Coastal Range.

The climate of Fresno is dry and mild in winter and hot in summer. Nearly nine-tenths of the annual precipitation falls in the six months from November to April.

Due to clear skies during the summer and the protection of the San Joaquin Valley from marine effects, the normal daily maximum temperature reaches the high 90s during the latter part of July. The daily maximum temperature during the warmest month has ranged from 76 to I15 degrees. Low relative humidities and some wind movement substantially lower the sensible temperature during periods of high readings. Humidity readings of 15 percent are common on summer afternoons, and readings as low as eight percent have been recorded. In contrast to this, humidity readings average 90 percent during the morning hours of December and January.

Winds flow with the major axis of the San Joaquin Valley, generally from the northwest. This feature is especially beneficial since, during the warmest months, the northwest winds increase during the evenings. These refreshing breezes and the normally large temperature variation of about 35 degrees between the highest and lowest readings of the day, generally result in comfortable evening and night temperatures.

Winter temperatures are usually mild with infrequent cold spells dropping the readings below freezing. Heavy frost occurs almost every year, and the first frost usually occurs during the last week of November. The last frost in spring is usually in early March. The growing season is 291 days.

Although the heaviest rains recorded at Fresno for short periods have occurred in June, usually any rainfall during the summer is very light. Snow is a rare occurrence in Fresno.

Fresno enjoys a very high percentage of sunshine, receiving more than 80 percent of the possible amounts during all but the four months of November, December, January, and February.

During foggy periods, sunshine is reduced to a minimum and fog frequently lifts to a few hundred feet above the surface of the valley, appearing as a heavy, solid cloud layer.

Fresno Air Terminal *Fresno County* Elevation: 333 ft. Latitude: 36° 47' N Longitude: 119° 43' W

	JAN	FEB	MAR	APR	MAY	JUN	JUL	AUG	SEP	OCT	NOV	DEC	YEAR
Mean Maximum Temp. (°F)	55.0	61.9	67.6	75.0	84.4	92.1	98.6	97.1	90.9	79.5	65.2	54.9	76.9
Mean Temp. (°F)	46.9	51.9	56.7	62.2	70.3	77.1	83.1	81.6	76.1	66.1	54.4	46.5	64.4
Mean Minimum Temp. (°F)	38.8	41.9	45.6	49.3	56.1	62.0	67.6	66.0	61.3	52.7	43.5	38.1	51.9
Extreme Maximum Temp. (°F)	78	80	87	100	107	110	113	112	107	102	85	77	113
Extreme Minimum Temp. (°F)	23	24	32	32	41	46	54	55	46	39	29	18	18
Days Maximum Temp. ≥ 90°F	0	0	0	2	10	20	29	28	18	4	0	0	111
Days Maximum Temp. ≤ 32°F	0	0	0	0	0	0	0	0	0	0	0	0	0
Days Minimum Temp. ≤ 32°F	6	2	0	0	0	0	0	0	0	0	1	6	15
Days Minimum Temp. ≤ 0°F	0	0	0	0	0	0	0	0	0	0	0	0	0
Heating Degree Days (base 65°F)	553	363	257	127	27	2	0	0	2	58	313	565	2,267
Cooling Degree Days (base 65°F)	0	0	6	49	197	372	568	521	343	100	1	0	2,157
Mean Precipitation (in.)	2.25	2.04	2.07	0.88	0.43	0.21	0.01	0.01	0.17	0.61	1.01	1.59	11.28
Maximum Precipitation (in.)*	8.6	6.0	7.2	4.4	1.6	1.6	0.2	0.3	1.2	2.2	3.5	6.7	21.6
Minimum Precipitation (in.)*	trace	trace	0	trace	0	0	0	0	0	0	0	0	6.1
Extreme Maximum Daily Precip. (in.)	1.88	1.87	2.38	1.39	1.11	1.80	0.22	0.06	0.85	1.50	1.05	1.64	2.38
Days With ≥ 0.1" Precipitation	5	5	5	2	1	0	0	0	1	1	3	4	27
Days With ≥ 0.5" Precipitation	1	1	1	1	0	0	0	0	0	0	1	1	6
Days With ≥ 1.0" Precipitation	0	0	0	0	0	0	0	0	0	0	0	0	0
Mean Snowfall (in.)	na	na	na	na	na	na	na	na	na	na	na	na	na
Maximum Snowfall (in.)*	2	trace	trace	0	0	0	0	0	0	0	trace	1	2
Maximum 24-hr. Snowfall (in.)*	2	trace	trace	0	0	0	0	0	0	0	trace	1	2
Maximum Snow Depth (in.)	na	na	na	na	na	na	na	na	na	na	na	na	na
Days With ≥ 1.0" Snow Depth	na	na	na	na	na	na	na	na	na	na	na	na	na
Thunderstorm Days*	< 1	< 1	1	1	1	< 1	< 1	< 1	1	1	< 1	< 1	5
Foggy Days*	23	15	8	3	1	< 1	< 1	< 1	1	5	17	23	96
Predominant Sky Cover*	OVR	OVR	CLR	CLR	CLR	CLR	CLR	CLR	CLR	CLR	CLR	OVR	CLR
Mean Relative Humidity 7am (%)*	92	91	86	75	63	56	54	61	69	77	88	92	75
Mean Relative Humidity 4pm (%)*	67	56	46	35	27	23	21	24	27	34	53	68	40
Mean Dewpoint (°F)*	40	42	43	44	46	49	53	54	52	47	43	40	46
Prevailing Wind Direction*	SE	NW	NW	NW	NW	NW	WNW	WNW	WNW	NW	NW	ESE	NW
Prevailing Wind Speed (mph)*	7	8	9	9	10	9	9	8	8	8	8	7	8
Maximum Wind Gust (mph)*	55	49	48	48	44	39	30	36	39	51	46	48	55

Note: (*) Period of record is 1949-1995

Long Beach Daugherty Field

The climate of the Long Beach Airport is considerably influenced by local topography, which plays a greater role in the climatic conditions at this station than the more general movements of pressure systems which dominate other sections of the country.

The Pacific Ocean, four miles south and 12 miles west, has a moderating effect on temperatures. The annual range of temperatures at the airport is much less than is experienced at stations further inland in the Los Angeles basin. Low coastal hills lie immediately between the station and the sea, the highest being Signal Hill, one and five eithths miles southwest and 498 feet above sea level. The Palos Verdes Hills, 11 miles west-southwest of the station, slope upward to 1,480 feet above sea level. These natural barriers between the ocean and the station cause slightly greater ranges of high and low temperatures locally than at stations on the coast. During the winter months high temperatures are usually in the upper 60s, and lows in the 40s. In the summer highs are in the 70s and low 80s, and lows in the high 50s.

Precipitation is sparse during the summer months, with an average of only about 0.60 inch for the months of May through October. The greatest rainfall occurs during the winter months. The coastal hills influence the local precipitation with greater amounts of rainfall occurring just one or two miles south and southwest of the station. Snow is an extremely rare phenomenon locally, although the San Gabriel Mountains are blanketed in the higher elevations much of the winter, and occasionally have snow down to the 2,500-foot level. Thunderstorms occur only sporadically at Long Beach.

The coastal hills to the southwest combine with the lowest mountain passes leading to the interior desert valleys east of the Los Angeles basin to produce a sea breeze from a westerly component in the afternoon and early evening hours. Occasionally, strong dry northeasterly winds descend the mountain slopes in the fall, winter, and early spring months, but ordinarily by-pass the station. Actually, the highest winds at Long Beach are recorded in association with the winter and spring storms which invade southern California from the Pacific.

During the summer months low clouds are quite common in the late night and morning hours at this station due to its proximity to the ocean. By late morning or early afternoon the clouds have disappeared and the balance of the day is sunny and comfortable. Here again is a moderating influence on summertime temperatures locally which is not so prominent at stations further inland where the coastal cloudiness arrives later, burns off earlier, and penetrates less frequently.

Long Beach Daugherty Field *Los Angeles County* Elevation: 24 ft. Latitude: 33° 50' N Longitude: 118° 10' W

	JAN	FEB	MAR	APR	MAY	JUN	JUL	AUG	SEP	OCT	NOV	DEC	YEAR
Mean Maximum Temp. (°F)	67.4	67.3	68.6	72.0	73.7	77.1	82.2	83.9	82.2	77.4	72.1	67.1	74.2
Mean Temp. (°F)	56.9	57.8	59.6	62.7	65.8	69.1	73.4	74.5	72.8	67.9	61.5	56.4	64.9
Mean Minimum Temp. (°F)	46.4	48.1	50.6	53.4	57.8	61.0	64.5	65.1	63.3	58.3	50.9	45.7	55.4
Extreme Maximum Temp. (°F)	93	91	98	105	104	109	107	103	108	109	98	89	109
Extreme Minimum Temp. (°F)	30	34	37	40	47	51	57	58	54	45	35	28	28
Days Maximum Temp. ≥ 90°F	0	0	0	1	1	1	4	6	5	3	1	0	22
Days Maximum Temp. ≤ 32°F	0	0	0	0	0	0	0	0	0	0	0	0	0
Days Minimum Temp. ≤ 32°F	0	0	0	0	0	0	0	0	0	0	0	0	0
Days Minimum Temp. ≤ 0°F	0	0	0	0	0	0	0	0	0	0	0	0	0
Heating Degree Days (base 65°F)	249	204	170	97	32	5	0	0	1	16	118	260	1,152
Cooling Degree Days (base 65°F)	4	6	10	34	61	134	267	302	240	112	20	2	1,192
Mean Precipitation (in.)	2.61	3.25	1.95	0.58	0.22	0.07	0.03	0.03	0.18	0.58	0.98	1.66	12.14
Maximum Precipitation (in.)*	12.8	9.4	8.8	4.4	2.3	0.9	0.2	2.0	1.4	1.6	6.0	5.3	27.7
Minimum Precipitation (in.)*	0	0	0	0	0	0	0	0	0	0	0	trace	2.8
Extreme Maximum Daily Precip. (in.)	3.75	2.78	3.46	1.61	1.17	0.86	0.27	0.33	1.39	1.97	1.77	3.05	3.75
Days With ≥ 0.1" Precipitation	4	5	4	1	0	0	0	0	0	1	2	3	20
Days With ≥ 0.5" Precipitation	2	2	1	0	0	0	0	0	0	0	1	1	7
Days With ≥ 1.0" Precipitation	1	1	0	0	0	0	0	0	0	0	0	0	2
Mean Snowfall (in.)	na	na	na	na	na	na	na	na	na	na	na	na	na
Maximum Snowfall (in.)*	trace	0	0	0	0	0	0	0	0	0	0	0	trace
Maximum 24-hr. Snowfall (in.)*	trace	0	0	0	0	0	0	0	0	0	0	0	trace
Maximum Snow Depth (in.)	na	na	na	na	na	na	na	na	na	na	na	na	na
Days With ≥ 1.0" Snow Depth	na	na	na	na	na	na	na	na	na	na	na	na	na
Thunderstorm Days*	< 1	1	1	< 1	< 1	< 1	< 1	< 1	< 1	< 1	< 1	< 1	2
Foggy Days*	14	12	11	8	7	8	8	9	12	14	15	15	133
Predominant Sky Cover*	CLR	OVR	CLR	CLR	OVR	CLR	CLR	CLR	CLR	CLR	CLR	CLR	CLR
Mean Relative Humidity 7am (%)*	77	79	80	77	76	78	79	80	81	80	76	75	78
Mean Relative Humidity 4pm (%)*	54	54	55	52	55	56	54	54	55	55	52	53	54
Mean Dewpoint (°F)*	42	44	46	48	52	56	60	61	59	54	46	42	51
Prevailing Wind Direction*	WNW	WNW	W	S	S	S	S	WNW	WNW	WNW	NW	WNW	WNW
Prevailing Wind Speed (mph)*	7	8	10	9	9	8	8	8	8	8	7	7	8
Maximum Wind Gust (mph)*	49	49	49	47	43	40	28	29	51	49	78	45	78

Note: (*) Period of record is 1949-1995

Los Angeles Civic Center

The climate of Los Angeles is normally pleasant and mild through the year. The Pacific Ocean is the primary moderating influence. The coastal mountain ranges lying along the north and east sides of the Los Angeles coastal basin act as a buffer against extremes of summer heat and winter cold occurring in desert and plateau regions in the interior. A variable balance between mild sea breezes, and either hot or cold winds from the interior, results in some variety in weather conditions, but temperature and humidity are usually well within the comfort level. The climate of the Los Angeles metropolitan area is marked by a difference in temperature, humidity, cloudiness, fog, rain, and sunshine over fairly short distances.

These differences are closely related to the distance from, and elevation above, the Pacific Ocean. Both high and low temperatures become more extreme and the average relative humidity becomes lower inland and up slopes. Relative humidity is frequently high near the coast, but may be quite low along the foothills. During periods of high temperatures, the relative humidity is usually below normal. Like other Pacific Coast areas, most rainfall comes during the winter with nearly 85 percent of the annual total occurring from November through March, while summers are practically rainless. Precipitation generally increases with distance from the ocean, from a yearly total of around 12 inches in coastal sections to the south of the city to over 20 inches in foothill areas. Destructive flash floods occasionally develop in and below some mountain canyons. Snow is often visible on nearby mountains in the winter, but is extremely rare in the coastal basin.

Prevailing winds are from the west during the spring, summer, and early autumn, with northeasterly wind predominating the remainder of the year. At times, the lack of air movement, combined with a frequent and persistent temperature inversion, is associated with concentrations of air pollution in the Los Angeles coastal basin and some adjacent areas. In fall, winter, and early spring months, occasional foehn-like descending Santa Ana winds come from the northeast over ridges and through passes in the coastal mountains. Sunshine, fog, and clouds depend a great deal on topography and distance from the ocean. Low clouds are common at night and in the morning along the coast during spring and summer, but form later and clear earlier near the foothills so that annual cloudiness and fog frequencies are greatest near the ocean, and sunshine totals are highest on the inland side of the city. The sun shines about 75 percent of daytime hours at the Civic Center. Light fog may accompany the usual night and morning low clouds, but dense fog is more likely to occur during the night and early morning hours of the winter months.

Los Angeles Civic Center *Los Angeles County* Elevation: 270 ft. Latitude: 34° 03' N Longitude: 118° 14' W

	JAN	FEB	MAR	APR	MAY	JUN	JUL	AUG	SEP	OCT	NOV	DEC	YEAR
Mean Maximum Temp. (°F)	68.6	69.2	70.4	73.3	75.1	78.9	83.8	84.8	83.4	79.0	73.3	68.3	75.7
Mean Temp. (°F)	59.2	60.2	61.7	64.4	67.1	70.5	74.6	75.4	74.1	69.7	63.5	58.8	66.6
Mean Minimum Temp. (°F)	49.8	51.2	52.9	55.5	59.1	62.1	65.4	65.9	64.8	60.4	53.8	49.3	57.5
Extreme Maximum Temp. (°F)	91	95	98	106	101	112	107	105	110	108	99	89	112
Extreme Minimum Temp. (°F)	35	34	39	40	50	52	57	58	54	48	39	33	33
Days Maximum Temp. ≥ 90°F	0	0	0	2	1	2	4	6	6	4	1	0	26
Days Maximum Temp. ≤ 32°F	0	0	0	0	0	0	0	0	0	0	0	0	0
Days Minimum Temp. ≤ 32°F	0	0	0	0	0	0	0	0	0	0	0	0	0
Days Minimum Temp. ≤ 0°F	0	0	0	0	0	0	0	0	0	0	0	0	0
Heating Degree Days (base 65°F)	188	152	124	74	23	3	0	0	0	9	81	196	850
Cooling Degree Days (base 65°F)	15	23	28	63	95	175	304	329	281	163	44	11	1,531
Mean Precipitation (in.)	3.21	4.08	2.57	0.87	0.27	0.06	0.01	0.04	0.24	0.62	1.02	2.02	15.01
Maximum Precipitation (in.)*	10.0	12.4	8.1	9.9	3.6	1.1	trace	0.4	5.7	2.3	6.0	8.5	31.3
Minimum Precipitation (in.)*	trace	0	0	trace	0	0	0	0	0	0	0	0	4.1
Extreme Maximum Daily Precip. (in.)	3.30	3.03	4.10	1.44	1.18	0.76	0.13	0.44	1.95	1.41	1.96	5.55	5.55
Days With ≥ 0.1" Precipitation	4	5	4	2	1	0	0	0	1	1	2	3	23
Days With ≥ 0.5" Precipitation	2	3	2	1	0	0	0	0	0	1	1	1	11
Days With ≥ 1.0" Precipitation	1	1	1	0	0	0	0	0	0	0	0	0	3
Mean Snowfall (in.)	na	na	na	na	na	na	na	na	na	na	na	na	na
Maximum Snowfall (in.)*	trace	0	0	0	0	0	0	0	0	0	0	0	trace
Maximum 24-hr. Snowfall (in.)*	trace	0	0	0	0	0	0	0	0	0	0	0	trace
Maximum Snow Depth (in.)	na	na	na	na	na	na	na	na	na	na	na	na	na
Days With ≥ 1.0" Snow Depth	na	na	na	na	na	na	na	na	na	na	na	na	na
Thunderstorm Days*	< 1	1	< 1	1	< 1	< 1	< 1	< 1	< 1	< 1	< 1	< 1	2
Foggy Days*	3	4	3	4	4	6	5	5	8	6	5	3	56
Predominant Sky Cover*	na	na	na	na	na	na	na	na	na	na	na	na	na
Mean Relative Humidity 7am (%)*	na	na	na	na	na	na	na	na	na	na	na	na	na
Mean Relative Humidity 4pm (%)*	na	na	na	na	na	na	na	na	na	na	na	na	na
Mean Dewpoint (°F)*	na	na	na	na	na	na	na	na	na	na	na	na	na
Prevailing Wind Direction*	na	na	na	na	na	na	na	na	na	na	na	na	na
Prevailing Wind Speed (mph)*	na	na	na	na	na	na	na	na	na	na	na	na	na
Maximum Wind Gust (mph)*	na	na	na	na	na	na	na	na	na	na	na	na	na

Note: (*) Period of record is 1921-1963

Los Angeles Int'l Airport

Predominating influences on the climate of the Los Angeles International Airport are the Pacific Ocean, three miles to the west, the southern California coastal mountain ranges which line the inland side of the coastal plain surrounding the airport, and the large scale weather patterns associated with Pacific storm paths. Marine air covers the coastal plain most of the year but air from the interior reaches the coast at times, especially during the fall and winter months. The coast ranges act as a buffer to the more extreme conditions of the interior. Pronounced differences in temperature, humidity, cloudiness, fog, sunshine, and rain occur over fairly short distances on the coastal plains and the adjoining foothills due to the local topography and the decreased marine effect further inland. In general, temperature ranges are least and humidity highest close to the coast, while precipitation increases with elevation.

The most characteristic feature of the climate of the coastal plain around the station is the night and morning low cloudiness and sunny afternoons which prevail during the spring and summer months and occur often during the remainder of the year. The coastal low cloudiness, combined with the westerly sea breeze, produces mild temperatures throughout the year. Daily temperature range is usually less than 15 degrees in spring and summer and about 20 degrees in fall and winter. Hot weather is not frequent at any season along the coast. When high temperatures do occur, the humidity is almost always low. Nighttime temperatures are generally cool but minimum temperatures below 40 degrees are rare and periods of over 10 years have passed with no readings below freezing at the airport. Prevailing daytime winds are from the west, but night and early morning breezes are usually light and from the east and northeast. Strongest winds observed at the station have been from the west and north following winter storms. During the fall, winter, and spring, gusty dry northeasterly Santa Ana winds blow over southern California mountains and through passes to the coast, but rarely reach L.A. International Airport.

Precipitation occurs mainly in the winter. Measurable rain may fall on about one day in four from late October into early April, but in three years out of four, traces or less are reported for the entire months of July and August. Thunderstorms do not occur often near the coast, but showers and thunderstorms are observed over the coastal ranges during the summer. Traces of snow have fallen at Los Angeles International Airport only a few times, melting as they fell.

Visibility at Los Angeles International Airport is frequently restricted by haze, fog, or smoke. Low visibilities are favored by a layer of moist marine air with warm dry air above and light winds. Light fog occurs at some time nearly every month, but heavy fog is observed least during the summer.

Los Angeles Int'l Airport *Los Angeles County* Elevation: 100 ft. Latitude: 33° 56' N Longitude: 118° 24' W

	JAN	FEB	MAR	APR	MAY	JUN	JUL	AUG	SEP	OCT	NOV	DEC	YEAR
Mean Maximum Temp. (°F)	65.9	65.7	65.6	68.0	69.4	72.1	75.4	76.4	75.9	73.9	70.3	66.0	70.4
Mean Temp. (°F)	57.4	57.9	58.7	60.9	63.4	66.3	69.6	70.4	69.6	66.6	61.8	57.3	63.3
Mean Minimum Temp. (°F)	48.9	50.1	51.7	53.8	57.3	60.4	63.7	64.4	63.2	59.2	53.2	48.6	56.2
Extreme Maximum Temp. (°F)	91	90	95	102	94	104	97	97	106	103	96	90	106
Extreme Minimum Temp. (°F)	33	35	39	42	49	51	53	56	54	45	39	34	33
Days Maximum Temp. ≥ 90°F	0	0	0	1	0	0	0	0	1	1	0	0	3
Days Maximum Temp. ≤ 32°F	0	0	0	0	0	0	0	0	0	0	0	0	0
Days Minimum Temp. ≤ 32°F	0	0	0	0	0	0	0	0	0	0	0	0	0
Days Minimum Temp. ≤ 0°F	0	0	0	0	0	0	0	0	0	0	0	0	0
Heating Degree Days (base 65°F)	234	201	197	135	65	15	0	0	2	24	113	233	1,219
Cooling Degree Days (base 65°F)	7	8	8	20	22	60	148	175	146	79	23	3	699
Mean Precipitation (in.)	2.79	3.45	1.97	0.66	0.22	0.08	0.03	0.06	0.21	0.51	1.09	1.80	12.87
Maximum Precipitation (in.)*	12.7	11.1	6.4	4.5	2.5	0.7	0.3	2.5	1.9	1.8	7.5	5.7	29.5
Minimum Precipitation (in.)*	0	0	0	0	0	0	0	0	0	0	0	0	3.1
Extreme Maximum Daily Precip. (in.)	3.50	3.10	2.55	1.35	0.77	0.74	0.28	1.00	1.66	1.45	1.69	4.53	4.53
Days With ≥ 0.1" Precipitation	4	5	4	2	1	0	0	0	0	1	2	3	22
Days With ≥ 0.5" Precipitation	2	2	1	0	0	0	0	0	0	0	1	1	7
Days With ≥ 1.0" Precipitation	1	1	0	0	0	0	0	0	0	0	0	0	2
Mean Snowfall (in.)	na	na	na	na	na	na	na	na	na	na	na	na	na
Maximum Snowfall (in.)*	trace	0	0	0	0	0	0	0	0	0	0	0	trace
Maximum 24-hr. Snowfall (in.)*	trace	0	0	0	0	0	0	0	0	0	0	0	trace
Maximum Snow Depth (in.)	na	na	na	na	na	na	na	na	na	na	na	na	na
Days With ≥ 1.0" Snow Depth	na	na	na	na	na	na	na	na	na	na	na	na	na
Thunderstorm Days*	< 1	1	1	< 1	< 1	< 1	< 1	< 1	< 1	< 1	< 1	< 1	2
Foggy Days*	11	10	8	7	6	6	7	8	9	11	11	11	105
Predominant Sky Cover*	CLR	CLR	CLR	CLR	OVR	OVR	CLR	CLR	CLR	CLR	CLR	CLR	CLR
Mean Relative Humidity 7am (%)*	70	72	76	76	77	80	80	82	81	76	69	68	76
Mean Relative Humidity 4pm (%)*	61	62	64	64	66	67	67	68	67	66	61	61	64
Mean Dewpoint (°F)*	42	44	46	49	53	56	60	61	59	54	46	42	51
Prevailing Wind Direction*	WSW	WSW	WSW	WSW	WSW	WSW	WSW	WSW	WSW	WSW	WSW	WSW	WSW
Prevailing Wind Speed (mph)*	9	9	10	10	10	10	9	9	9	9	9	8	9
Maximum Wind Gust (mph)*	51	56	62	59	49	40	31	33	39	46	60	49	62

Note: (*) Period of record is 1948-1995

Sacramento Executive Airport

Sacramento, and the lower Sacramento Valley, has a mild climate with abundant sunshine most of the year. A nearly cloud-free sky prevails throughout the summer months, and in much of the spring and fall. The summers are usually dry with warm to hot afternoons and mostly mild nights. The rainy season generally is November through March. About 75 percent of the annual precipitation occurs then, but measurable rain falls only on an average of nine days per month during that period. The shielding effect of mountains to the north, east, and west usually modifies winter storms. The Sierra Nevada snow fields, only 70 miles east of Sacramento, usually provide an adequate water supply during the dry season, and an important recreational area in winter. Heavy snowfall and torrential rains frequently fall on the western Sierra slopes, and may produce flood conditions along the Sacramento River and its tributaries. In the valley, however, excessive rainfall as well as damaging winds are rare.

The prevailing wind at Sacramento is southerly every month but November, when it is northerly. Topographic effects, the north-south alignment of the valley, the coast range, and the Sierra Nevada strongly influence the wind flow in the valley. A sea level gap in the coast range permits cool, oceanic air to flow, occasionally, into the valley during the summer season with a marked lowering of temperature through the Sacramento-San Joaquin River Delta to the capital. In the spring and fall, a large north-to-south pressure gradient develops over the northern part of the state.

Extreme hot spells, with temperatures exceeding 100 degrees, are usually caused by air flow from a sub-tropical high pressure area that brings light to nearly calm winds and humidities below 20 percent.

Thunderstorms are few in number, usually mild in character, and occur mainly in the spring. An occasional thunderstorm may drift over the valley from the Sierra Nevada in the summer. Snow falls so rarely, and in such small amounts, that its occurrence may be disregarded as a climatic feature. Heavy fog occurs mostly in midwinter, never in summer, and seldom in spring or autumn. An occasional winter fog, under stagnant atmospheric conditions, may continue for several days. Light and moderate fogs are more frequent, and may come anytime during the wet, cold season. The fog is the radiational cooling type, and is usually confined to the early morning hours.

Based on the 1951-1980 period, the average first occurrence of 32 degrees Fahrenheit in the fall is December 1 and the average last occurrence in the spring is February 14.

Sacramento Executive Airport *Sacramento County* Elevation: 15 ft. Latitude: 38° 30' N Longitude: 121° 30' W

	JAN	FEB	MAR	APR	MAY	JUN	JUL	AUG	SEP	OCT	NOV	DEC	YEAR
Mean Maximum Temp. (°F)	54.3	60.5	65.4	71.7	80.2	87.1	92.4	91.5	87.4	78.1	64.2	54.2	73.9
Mean Temp. (°F)	46.6	51.1	54.9	59.2	65.8	71.5	75.6	74.9	71.7	64.2	53.6	46.3	61.3
Mean Minimum Temp. (°F)	38.9	41.7	44.3	46.6	51.4	55.8	58.7	58.2	55.9	50.3	43.0	38.3	48.6
Extreme Maximum Temp. (°F)	74	76	88	95	105	108	112	110	108	104	85	72	112
Extreme Minimum Temp. (°F)	21	23	31	31	37	41	48	51	42	36	26	18	18
Days Maximum Temp. ≥ 90°F	0	0	0	1	6	12	21	19	13	3	0	0	75
Days Maximum Temp. ≤ 32°F	0	0	0	0	0	0	0	0	0	0	0	0	0
Days Minimum Temp. ≤ 32°F	5	2	0	0	0	0	0	0	0	0	1	6	14
Days Minimum Temp. ≤ 0°F	0	0	0	0	0	0	0	0	0	0	0	0	0
Heating Degree Days (base 65°F)	562	386	308	186	62	9	0	0	7	76	336	573	2,505
Cooling Degree Days (base 65°F)	0	0	1	18	95	211	335	313	214	58	1	0	1,246
Mean Precipitation (in.)	3.66	3.63	2.74	1.13	0.68	0.21	0.01	0.05	0.30	0.89	1.99	3.12	18.41
Maximum Precipitation (in.)*	9.7	8.8	8.1	4.2	3.1	1.3	0.8	0.6	2.8	7.5	7.4	12.6	33.4
Minimum Precipitation (in.)*	0.2	0.1	0	0	0	0	0	0	0	0	trace	0	5.6
Extreme Maximum Daily Precip. (in.)	2.99	2.63	1.85	1.49	1.67	1.14	0.37	0.32	1.79	2.94	2.08	2.12	2.99
Days With ≥ 0.1" Precipitation	7	7	6	3	2	1	0	0	1	2	4	6	39
Days With ≥ 0.5" Precipitation	2	3	2	1	0	0	0	0	0	1	1	2	12
Days With ≥ 1.0" Precipitation	1	1	0	0	0	0	0	0	0	0	0	1	3
Mean Snowfall (in.)	na	na	na	na	na	na	na	na	na	na	na	na	na
Maximum Snowfall (in.)*	trace	2	trace	trace	0	0	0	0	0	0	0	trace	2
Maximum 24-hr. Snowfall (in.)*	trace	2	trace	trace	0	0	0	0	0	0	0	trace	2
Maximum Snow Depth (in.)	na	na	na	na	na	na	na	na	na	na	na	na	na
Days With ≥ 1.0" Snow Depth	na	na	na	na	na	na	na	na	na	na	na	na	na
Thunderstorm Days*	< 1	1	1	1	< 1	< 1	< 1	< 1	< 1	< 1	< 1	< 1	3
Foggy Days*	22	14	8	3	1	< 1	< 1	1	2	7	16	22	96
Predominant Sky Cover*	OVR	OVR	CLR	CLR	CLR	CLR	CLR	CLR	CLR	CLR	CLR	OVR	CLR
Mean Relative Humidity 7am (%)*	91	89	85	78	72	67	69	74	75	81	87	91	80
Mean Relative Humidity 4pm (%)*	70	59	52	43	36	31	29	29	31	38	56	70	45
Mean Dewpoint (°F)*	39	42	43	44	47	50	53	53	51	47	43	39	46
Prevailing Wind Direction*	SE	SE	SW	SW	SW	SW	SSW	SSW	SSW	NNW	NNW	SE	SW
Prevailing Wind Speed (mph)*	9	9	10	10	12	13	10	10	10	10	9	9	10
Maximum Wind Gust (mph)*	53	46	47	45	51	45	37	33	38	40	56	51	56

Note: (*) Period of record is 1947-1995

San Diego Lindbergh Field

The city of San Diego is located on San Diego Bay in the southwest corner of southern California. The prevailing winds and weather are tempered by the Pacific Ocean. Temperatures of freezing or below have rarely occurred at the station since the record began in 1871, but hot weather, 90 degrees or above, is more frequent.

Dry easterly winds sometimes blow in the vicinity for several days at a time, bringing temperatures in the 90s and at times even in the 100s in the eastern sections of the city and outlying suburbs. As these hot winds are predominant in the fall, highest temperatures occur in the months of September and October. Records show that over 60 percent of the days with 90 degrees or higher have occurred in these two months. High temperatures are almost invariably accompanied by very low relative humidities, which often drop below 20 percent and occasionally below 10 percent.

A marked feature of the climate is the wide variation in temperature within short distances. In nearby valleys daytimes are much warmer in summer and nights noticeably cooler in winter, and freezing occurs much more frequently than in the city. Although records show unusually small daily temperature ranges, only about 15 degrees between the highest and lowest readings, a few miles inland these ranges increase to 30 degrees or more.

Strong winds and gales associated with Pacific, or tropical storms, are infrequent due to the latitude.

The seasonal rainfall is about 10 inches in the city, but increases with elevation and distance from the coast. In the mountains to the north and east the average is between 20 and 40 inches, depending on slope and elevation. Most of the precipitation falls in winter, except in the mountains where there is an occasional thunderstorm. Eighty-five percent of the rainfall occurs from November through March, but wide variations take place in monthly and seasonal totals. In each occurrence of snowfall only a trace was recorded officially.

As on the rest of the Pacific Coast, a dominant characteristic of spring and summer is the nighttime and early morning cloudiness. Low clouds form regularly and frequently extend inland over the coastal valleys and foothills, but they usually dissipate during the morning and the afternoons are generally clear.

Considerable fog occurs along the coast, but the amount decreases with distance inland. The fall and winter months are usually the foggiest. Thunderstorms are rare, averaging about three a year in the city.

San Diego Lindbergh Field *San Diego County* Elevation: 13 ft. Latitude: 32° 44' N Longitude: 117° 10' W

	JAN	FEB	MAR	APR	MAY	JUN	JUL	AUG	SEP	OCT	NOV	DEC	YEAR
Mean Maximum Temp. (°F)	65.7	65.8	66.2	68.3	69.2	71.6	75.5	77.1	76.4	73.4	69.6	65.4	70.3
Mean Temp. (°F)	57.7	58.6	60.0	62.4	64.6	67.1	70.8	72.3	71.1	67.2	61.8	57.2	64.2
Mean Minimum Temp. (°F)	49.7	51.4	53.8	56.5	60.0	62.6	66.0	67.4	65.7	61.0	54.0	48.9	58.1
Extreme Maximum Temp. (°F)	87	90	93	98	93	100	99	94	107	104	90	87	107
Extreme Minimum Temp. (°F)	35	38	42	45	50	54	59	60	53	48	39	34	34
Days Maximum Temp. ≥ 90°F	0	0	0	0	0	0	0	0	1	1	0	0	2
Days Maximum Temp. ≤ 32°F	0	0	0	0	0	0	0	0	0	0	0	0	0
Days Minimum Temp. ≤ 32°F	0	0	0	0	0	0	0	0	0	0	0	0	0
Days Minimum Temp. ≤ 0°F	0	0	0	0	0	0	0	0	0	0	0	0	0
Heating Degree Days (base 65°F)	222	179	154	91	41	9	0	0	0	12	103	236	1,047
Cooling Degree Days (base 65°F)	3	5	6	21	35	80	186	232	189	87	14	1	859
Mean Precipitation (in.)	2.05	2.34	1.87	0.76	0.14	0.07	0.03	0.02	0.15	0.50	0.98	1.37	10.28
Maximum Precipitation (in.)*	9.1	5.4	7.0	3.7	1.8	0.9	0.2	2.1	1.9	1.8	5.8	6.6	19.4
Minimum Precipitation (in.)*	trace	0	trace	0	0	0	0	0	0	0	0	trace	3.4
Extreme Maximum Daily Precip. (in.)	2.24	2.18	2.03	1.42	0.77	0.49	0.23	0.17	0.90	2.70	2.04	1.60	2.70
Days With ≥ 0.1" Precipitation	4	4	4	2	0	0	0	0	0	1	2	3	20
Days With ≥ 0.5" Precipitation	1	2	1	0	0	0	0	0	0	0	1	1	6
Days With ≥ 1.0" Precipitation	0	1	0	0	0	0	0	0	0	0	0	0	1
Mean Snowfall (in.)	na	na	na	na	na	na	na	na	na	na	na	na	na
Maximum Snowfall (in.)*	trace	0	0	0	0	0	0	0	0	0	0	trace	trace
Maximum 24-hr. Snowfall (in.)*	trace	0	0	0	0	0	0	0	0	0	0	trace	trace
Maximum Snow Depth (in.)	na	na	na	na	na	na	na	na	na	na	na	na	na
Days With ≥ 1.0" Snow Depth	na	na	na	na	na	na	na	na	na	na	na	na	na
Thunderstorm Days*	< 1	< 1	< 1	< 1	< 1	< 1	< 1	< 1	< 1	< 1	< 1	< 1	6
Foggy Days*	11	9	8	6	6	7	6	7	9	11	11	11	102
Predominant Sky Cover*	CLR	CLR	OVR	OVR	OVR	OVR	OVR	OVR	CLR	CLR	CLR	CLR	OVR
Mean Relative Humidity 7am (%)*	70	72	73	72	74	78	80	79	78	75	69	68	74
Mean Relative Humidity 4pm (%)*	58	58	59	60	64	66	66	66	65	64	60	58	62
Mean Dewpoint (°F)*	43	45	47	50	53	57	61	62	61	56	48	43	52
Prevailing Wind Direction*	NW	WNW	WNW	WNW	WNW	WNW	WNW	WNW	WNW	WNW	WNW	NW	WNW
Prevailing Wind Speed (mph)*	8	9	10	10	9	9	9	9	9	9	9	8	9
Maximum Wind Gust (mph)*	64	52	53	43	40	37	30	33	44	35	48	44	64

Note: (*) Period of record is 1948-1995

San Francisco Mission

San Francisco is located at the northern end of a narrow peninsula which separates San Francisco Bay from the Pacific Ocean. It is known as the air conditioned city with cool pleasant summers and mild winters.

Precipitation averages about 20 inches a year with pronounced wet and dry seasons, characteristic of its Mediterranean climate. Little or no rain falls from June through September while about 80 percent of the annual total falls from November through March. Snow and freezing temperatures are extremely rare. On average, thunderstorms occur on only two days each year. The average annual wind speed is about nine mph.

Sea fogs, and the low stratus clouds associated with them are most common in the summertime, but may occur at any time of the year. In the summer the temperature of the Pacific Ocean is much lower than the temperature inland, particularly in the Central Valley of California. This condition tends to enhance the sea breeze effect common to coastal areas. Brisk westerly winds blow throughout the afternoon and evening hours. The fog is carried inland by these westerly winds in the late afternoon and evening and then evaporates during the subsequent forenoon.

The complex topography of San Francisco causes complex patterns of fog and sun as well as temperature. A range of hills with elevations of nearly 1000 feet above sea level, bisects the city from north to south. This range partially blocks the inland movement of the fog, but gaps in the hills permit small masses of fog to pass through, further complicating the pattern.

Sunshine varies greatly from one part of the city to another, especially in the summer. Spring and fall are the sunniest seasons. The percent of possible summer sunshine varies from an estimated 25 to 35 percent at the ocean to 70 to 80 percent in the sunniest area.

The extent and behavior of the summertime fog on a particular day depends on several factors. A typical day would find the fog covering the entire city at sunrise and little wind. During the forenoon the skies become sunny in the eastern part of the city with some partial clearing reaching the ocean for a couple of hours in the early afternoon. By early afternoon the winds pick up and by late afternoon the fog is rolling inland again.

Temperature patterns in the city are the same as those of sunshine. In the winter there is little variation, with average maximums from 55 to 60 degrees and average minimums in the mid to upper 40s. Average temperatures rise until June and remain nearly constant through August with average maximums in the lower 60s near the ocean and upper 60s in the sunny eastern half of the city. Summer minimums range from 50 to 55. The warmest time of the year is September and October when the fog diminishes greatly.

San Francisco Mission *San Francisco County* Elevation: 174 ft. Latitude: 37° 46' N Longitude: 122° 26' W

	JAN	FEB	MAR	APR	MAY	JUN	JUL	AUG	SEP	OCT	NOV	DEC	YEAR
Mean Maximum Temp. (°F)	58.0	61.3	62.9	64.3	65.5	67.9	68.2	69.3	71.2	70.5	64.3	58.4	65.2
Mean Temp. (°F)	52.2	54.8	56.1	57.1	58.6	60.6	61.4	62.5	63.5	62.4	57.5	52.6	58.3
Mean Minimum Temp. (°F)	46.3	48.2	49.1	49.9	51.6	53.3	54.6	55.6	55.7	54.3	50.7	46.7	51.3
Extreme Maximum Temp. (°F)	74	81	87	94	101	103	103	98	100	102	83	73	103
Extreme Minimum Temp. (°F)	36	31	39	23	43	47	48	50	49	47	40	28	23
Days Maximum Temp. ≥ 90°F	0	0	0	0	0	1	0	0	1	1	0	0	3
Days Maximum Temp. ≤ 32°F	0	0	0	0	0	0	0	0	0	0	0	0	0
Days Minimum Temp. ≤ 32°F	0	0	0	0	0	0	0	0	0	0	0	0	0
Days Minimum Temp. ≤ 0°F	0	0	0	0	0	0	0	0	0	0	0	0	0
Heating Degree Days (base 65°F)	391	284	274	239	205	145	121	91	78	110	221	379	2,538
Cooling Degree Days (base 65°F)	0	1	3	10	13	19	18	21	40	36	4	0	165
Mean Precipitation (in.)	4.40	4.50	3.20	1.37	0.68	0.16	0.01	0.06	0.21	1.06	3.06	4.43	23.14
Maximum Precipitation (in.)*	10.7	10.1	9.0	5.5	4.0	1.4	0.2	0.5	2.1	5.5	8.2	11.5	43.8
Minimum Precipitation (in.)*	0.5	trace	trace	trace	0	0	0	0	0	trace	0	0	10.0
Extreme Maximum Daily Precip. (in.)	4.22	2.93	2.57	1.27	1.42	0.70	0.04	0.54	0.63	2.48	5.54	3.61	5.54
Days With ≥ 0.1" Precipitation	8	8	7	4	2	0	0	0	1	2	5	8	45
Days With ≥ 0.5" Precipitation	3	3	2	1	0	0	0	0	0	1	2	3	15
Days With ≥ 1.0" Precipitation	1	1	0	0	0	0	0	0	0	0	1	1	4
Mean Snowfall (in.)	na	na	na	na	na	na	na	na	na	na	na	na	na
Maximum Snowfall (in.)*	trace	trace	trace	0	0	0	0	0	0	0	0	1	1
Maximum 24-hr. Snowfall (in.)*	trace	trace	trace	0	0	0	0	0	0	0	0	1	1
Maximum Snow Depth (in.)	na	na	na	na	na	na	na	na	na	na	na	na	na
Days With ≥ 1.0" Snow Depth	na	na	na	na	na	na	na	na	na	na	na	na	na
Thunderstorm Days*	< 1	1	< 1	1	0	< 1	1	1	< 1	1	< 1	0	5
Foggy Days*	< 1	1	0	0	0	0	0	0	0	0	0	0	1
Predominant Sky Cover*	na	na	na	na	na	na	na	na	na	na	na	na	na
Mean Relative Humidity 7am (%)*	na	na	na	na	na	na	na	na	na	na	na	na	na
Mean Relative Humidity 4pm (%)*	na	na	na	na	na	na	na	na	na	na	na	na	na
Mean Dewpoint (°F)*	na	na	na	na	na	na	na	na	na	na	na	na	na
Prevailing Wind Direction*	na	na	na	na	na	na	na	na	na	na	na	na	na
Prevailing Wind Speed (mph)*	na	na	na	na	na	na	na	na	na	na	na	na	na
Maximum Wind Gust (mph)*	na	na	na	na	na	na	na	na	na	na	na	na	na

Note: (*) Period of record is 1921-1992

San Francisco Int'l Airport

The station is located in the central Terminal Building of the San Francisco International Airport, which is on flat filled tideland on the west shore of San Francisco Bay. The bay borders the airport from the north to the south-southeast. San Bruno Mountain, five miles to the north-northwest, rises to 1,300 feet. A north-south trending ridge of coastal mountains, four miles to the west, varies in elevation from 700 to 1,900 feet, being highest southward along the peninsula. The Pacific Ocean west of the ridge is six miles from the airport. A broad gap to the northwest of the station, between San Bruno Mountain and the coastal mountains, allows a strong flow of marine air over the station and dominate the local climate.

San Francisco Airport enjoys a marine-type climate characterized by mild and moderately wet winters and by dry, cool summers. Winter rains, occurring from November through March, account for over 80 percent of the annual rainfall, and measurable precipitation occurs on an average of 10 days per month during this period. However, there are frequent dry periods lasting well over a week. Severe winter storms with gale winds and heavy rains occur only occasionally. Thunderstorms average two a year and may occur in any month.

The daily and annual range in temperature is small. A few frosty mornings occur during the winter but the temperature seldom drops below freezing. Winter temperatures generally rise to the high 50s in the early afternoon.

The summer weather is dominated by a cool sea breeze resulting in an average summer wind speed of nearly 15 mph. Winds are light in the early morning but normally reach 20 to 25 mph in the afternoon.

A sea fog, arriving over the station during the late evening or night as a low cloud, is another persistent feature of the summer weather. This high fog, occasionally producing drizzle or mist, usually disappears during the late forenoon. Despite the morning overcast, summer days are sunny. On the average a total of only 14 days during the four months from June through September are classified as cloudy.

Daytime temperatures are held down both by the morning low overcast and the afternoon strengthening sea breeze, resulting in daily maximum readings averaging about 70 degrees from May through August. However, during these months occasional hot spells, lasting a few days, are experienced without the usual high fog and sea breeze. September, when the sea breeze becomes less pronounced, is the warmest month with highs in the 70s. Low temperatures during the summer are in the mid-50s.

San Francisco Int'l Airport *San Mateo County* Elevation: 7 ft. Latitude: 37° 37' N Longitude: 122° 24' W

	JAN	FEB	MAR	APR	MAY	JUN	JUL	AUG	SEP	OCT	NOV	DEC	YEAR
Mean Maximum Temp. (°F)	56.3	59.6	62.1	64.8	67.5	70.6	72.1	72.7	73.5	70.5	63.0	56.6	65.8
Mean Temp. (°F)	50.1	52.9	54.8	56.9	59.5	62.1	63.6	64.4	64.5	61.7	55.7	50.5	58.0
Mean Minimum Temp. (°F)	43.9	46.1	47.4	48.9	51.3	53.5	55.1	56.0	55.4	52.8	48.4	44.3	50.3
Extreme Maximum Temp. (°F)	72	77	83	92	97	105	105	100	100	99	80	71	105
Extreme Minimum Temp. (°F)	31	31	37	39	42	46	48	49	48	43	35	27	27
Days Maximum Temp. ≥ 90°F	0	0	0	0	0	1	1	0	1	0	0	0	3
Days Maximum Temp. ≤ 32°F	0	0	0	0	0	0	0	0	0	0	0	0	0
Days Minimum Temp. ≤ 32°F	0	0	0	0	0	0	0	0	0	0	0	0	0
Days Minimum Temp. ≤ 0°F	0	0	0	0	0	0	0	0	0	0	0	0	0
Heating Degree Days (base 65°F)	453	337	312	244	178	102	62	46	53	118	272	443	2,620
Cooling Degree Days (base 65°F)	0	0	1	6	13	22	26	33	44	22	1	0	168
Mean Precipitation (in.)	4.15	4.23	2.96	1.22	0.45	0.11	0.01	0.04	0.17	0.92	2.30	3.88	20.44
Maximum Precipitation (in.)*	11.3	9.5	9.0	6.4	3.8	0.9	0.3	0.7	2.3	7.3	7.9	12.3	38.3
Minimum Precipitation (in.)*	0.2	trace	0	trace	trace	trace	0	trace	trace	trace	trace	trace	8.7
Extreme Maximum Daily Precip. (in.)	5.59	2.92	1.83	1.54	1.03	0.60	0.09	0.56	0.88	2.64	2.26	3.16	5.59
Days With ≥ 0.1" Precipitation	7	8	7	3	2	0	0	0	1	2	4	7	41
Days With ≥ 0.5" Precipitation	3	3	2	1	0	0	0	0	0	1	2	3	15
Days With ≥ 1.0" Precipitation	1	1	0	0	0	0	0	0	0	0	1	1	4
Mean Snowfall (in.)	na	na	na	na	na	na	na	na	na	na	na	na	na
Maximum Snowfall (in.)*	2	trace	trace	0	0	0	0	0	0	0	0	trace	2
Maximum 24-hr. Snowfall (in.)*	2	trace	trace	0	0	0	0	0	0	0	0	trace	2
Maximum Snow Depth (in.)	na	na	na	na	na	na	na	na	na	na	na	na	na
Days With ≥ 1.0" Snow Depth	na	na	na	na	na	na	na	na	na	na	na	na	na
Thunderstorm Days*	< 1	< 1	< 1	< 1	< 1	< 1	< 1	< 1	< 1	< 1	< 1	< 1	5
Foggy Days*	17	12	7	4	4	3	4	4	6	9	12	17	99
Predominant Sky Cover*	OVR	OVR	OVR	CLR	CLR	CLR	CLR	CLR	CLR	CLR	CLR	OVR	CLR
Mean Relative Humidity 7am (%)*	87	86	82	79	78	77	81	83	82	83	85	86	82
Mean Relative Humidity 4pm (%)*	68	66	64	62	61	60	61	62	60	60	63	68	63
Mean Dewpoint (°F)*	42	44	44	45	47	50	52	53	52	50	46	42	47
Prevailing Wind Direction*	SE	WNW	WNW	WNW	WNW	WNW	WNW	WNW	WNW	WNW	WNW	WNW	WNW
Prevailing Wind Speed (mph)*	9	13	14	15	16	16	15	14	13	13	12	10	14
Maximum Wind Gust (mph)*	78	69	64	61	62	58	52	49	56	64	68	74	78

Note: (*) Period of record is 1945-1995

Santa Maria Public Airport

Santa Maria Valley is a flat, fertile valley opening on the Pacific Ocean where it is widest and tapering inland for a distance approximately 30 miles. The valley is 10 miles wide at the site of the station, which is located 13 miles inland at an elevation of 236 feet. It is bounded by the foothills of the San Rafael Mountains, the Solomon Hills, and the Casmalia Hills ranging from 1,300 to 4,000 feet.

Located 150 miles west-northwest of Los Angeles and 250 miles south of San Francisco, Santa Maria has a maritime climate, displaying characteristics of those of both neighbors. Year-round mild temperatures moving through gradual transitions characterize the climate more than do clearly defined seasons. The annual range of temperatures is about 13 degrees, while the daily temperature range is about 20 degrees for May through September and a few degrees higher from October through April.

Based on the 1951-1980 period, the average first occurrence of 32 degrees Fahrenheit in the fall is December 5 and the average last occurrence in the spring is March 15.

The rainfall season, typical of the mid-California coast, is in the winter. About three-fourths of the total annual rainfall occurs from December through March in connection with Pacific cold fronts and storm centers passing inland. During the remainder of the year, and particularly from June to October, the northward displacement and intensification of the semipermanent Pacific anticyclone produces a circulation resulting in little or no precipitation here. Thunderstorms are rare.

During most days, clear, sunny afternoons prevail. But under the influence of the Pacific high, considerable advective and radiative cooling frequently produces nightly low stratus clouds, known as California stratus, and early-morning fog. Both clouds and fog, however, are generally dissipated before noon.

The unequal daytime solar heating over land and ocean, in conjunction with the Pacific high, gives rise to a consistent and prevailing westerly sea breeze during most afternoons. The winds generally decrease to a calm by sundown. Thus the two factors of nighttime stratus and daytime sea breezes effectively combine to maintain relatively cool days and warm nights with little diurnal change.

Santa Maria Public Airport *Santa Barbara County* Elevation: 253 ft. Latitude: 34° 55' N Longitude: 120° 28' W

	JAN	FEB	MAR	APR	MAY	JUN	JUL	AUG	SEP	OCT	NOV	DEC	YEAR
Mean Maximum Temp. (°F)	64.3	64.9	65.7	68.1	69.3	71.4	73.7	74.0	74.6	73.8	69.5	64.5	69.5
Mean Temp. (°F)	52.0	53.3	54.4	56.1	58.4	61.0	63.8	64.2	63.8	61.2	56.2	51.7	58.0
Mean Minimum Temp. (°F)	39.6	41.7	43.1	44.1	47.5	50.6	53.9	54.3	52.9	48.5	42.9	38.9	46.5
Extreme Maximum Temp. (°F)	87	89	95	103	95	110	104	104	101	108	96	85	110
Extreme Minimum Temp. (°F)	21	23	28	31	36	39	44	45	41	34	27	21	21
Days Maximum Temp. ≥ 90°F	0	0	0	1	0	0	0	0	1	2	0	0	4
Days Maximum Temp. ≤ 32°F	0	0	0	0	0	0	0	0	0	0	0	0	0
Days Minimum Temp. ≤ 32°F	4	2	1	0	0	0	0	0	0	0	1	5	13
Days Minimum Temp. ≤ 0°F	0	0	0	0	0	0	0	0	0	0	0	0	0
Heating Degree Days (base 65°F)	398	325	322	265	203	122	56	45	64	133	262	404	2,599
Cooling Degree Days (base 65°F)	0	1	1	6	5	10	28	26	33	22	5	0	137
Mean Precipitation (in.)	2.68	3.08	2.67	0.93	0.32	0.05	0.03	0.02	0.14	0.54	1.27	1.84	13.57
Maximum Precipitation (in.)*	11.8	9.7	9.4	4.2	2.4	0.9	0.4	0.9	3.0	2.1	4.7	4.8	26.8
Minimum Precipitation (in.)*	trace	0	trace	trace	0	trace	0	0	0	0	0	trace	3.3
Extreme Maximum Daily Precip. (in.)	2.27	1.92	3.14	2.14	1.74	0.72	0.35	0.23	0.76	1.40	1.52	1.74	3.14
Days With ≥ 0.1" Precipitation	5	6	5	2	1	0	0	0	0	1	3	4	27
Days With ≥ 0.5" Precipitation	2	2	2	1	0	0	0	0	0	0	1	1	9
Days With ≥ 1.0" Precipitation	1	1	1	0	0	0	0	0	0	0	0	0	3
Mean Snowfall (in.)	na	na	na	na	na	na	na	na	na	na	na	na	na
Maximum Snowfall (in.)*	trace	trace	0	0	0	0	0	0	0	0	trace	trace	trace
Maximum 24-hr. Snowfall (in.)*	trace	trace	0	0	0	0	0	0	0	0	trace	trace	trace
Maximum Snow Depth (in.)	na	na	na	na	na	na	na	na	na	na	na	na	na
Days With ≥ 1.0" Snow Depth	na	na	na	na	na	na	na	na	na	na	na	na	na
Thunderstorm Days*	< 1	< 1	1	< 1	< 1	< 1	< 1	< 1	1	< 1	< 1	< 1	2
Foggy Days*	14	14	15	18	21	25	28	28	26	22	15	14	240
Predominant Sky Cover*	CLR	OVR	CLR	CLR	CLR	CLR	CLR	CLR	CLR	CLR	CLR	CLR	CLR
Mean Relative Humidity 7am (%)*	81	84	86	83	84	84	88	90	88	84	80	79	84
Mean Relative Humidity 4pm (%)*	59	62	63	61	61	60	61	62	63	61	60	58	61
Mean Dewpoint (°F)*	40	43	44	46	48	51	53	54	54	49	43	40	47
Prevailing Wind Direction*	WNW	WNW	WNW	WNW	WNW	WNW	WNW	WNW	WNW	WNW	WNW	WNW	WNW
Prevailing Wind Speed (mph)*	9	12	13	14	14	13	12	10	10	12	10	9	12
Maximum Wind Gust (mph)*	54	58	53	47	47	45	41	35	38	37	40	52	58

Note: (*) Period of record is 1954-1995

Stockton Metropolitan Airport

Stockton, the county seat of San Joaquin County, is located near the center of the Great Central Valley of California. It is on the southeast corner of the broad delta formed by the confluence of the San Joaquin and Sacramento Rivers. The surrounding terrain is flat, irrigated farm and orchard land, near sea level, with the rivers and canals of the delta controlled by a system of levees.

Approximately 25 miles east and northeast of Stockton lie the foothills of the Sierra Nevada, rising gradually to an elevation of about 1,000 feet. Beyond the foothills, the mountains rise abruptly to the crest of the Sierra, at a distance of about 75 miles, with some peaks here exceeding 9,000 feet in elevation. On a few days during the year, when atmospheric conditions are favorable, the downslope effect of a north or northeast wind can bring unseasonably dry weather to the delta area, but on the whole the Sierra Nevada has little or no effect on the weather of San Joaquin County. The Sierra Nevada does affect the area, however, to the extent that the entire economy of the Great Valley depends upon the water supplied by the melting snows in the mountains.

To the west and southwest, the Coast Range, with peaks above 2,000 feet, form a barrier separating the Great Valley from the marine air which dominates the climate of the coastal communities. Several gaps in the Coast Range in the San Francisco Bay Area, however, permit the passage inland of a sea breeze which fans out into the delta and has a moderating effect on summer heat, with the result that Stockton enjoys slightly cooler summer days than communities in the upper San Joaquin and Sacramento Valleys.

The summer climate in Stockton is characterized by warm, dry days and relatively cool nights with clear skies and no rainfall. Winter brings mild temperatures and relatively light rains with frequent heavy fogs.

The annual rainfall averages about 14 inches, with 90 percent of the precipitation falling from November through April. Thunderstorms are infrequent, occurring on three or four days a year. Snow is practically unknown in the Stockton area.

In summer, temperatures exceeding 100 degrees can be expected on about 15 days. During these hot afternoons the air is extremely dry, with relative humidities running generally less than 20 percent. Even on these hot days, however, temperatures will fall into the low 60s at night. In winter the nighttime temperature on clear nights will fall to or slightly below freezing, and will rise in the afternoon into the low 50s.

In late autumn and early winter, clear still nights give rise to the formation of dense fogs, which normally settle in during the night and burn off sometime during the day. In December and January, the so-called fog season, under stagnant atmospheric conditions the fog may last for as long as four or five weeks, with only brief and temporary periods of clearing.

Stockton Metropolitan Airport *San Joaquin County* Elevation: 21 ft. Latitude: 37° 54' N Longitude: 121° 14' W

	JAN	FEB	MAR	APR	MAY	JUN	JUL	AUG	SEP	OCT	NOV	DEC	YEAR
Mean Maximum Temp. (°F)	54.5	61.4	66.8	73.4	81.8	88.7	94.2	92.9	88.4	78.6	64.8	54.3	75.0
Mean Temp. (°F)	46.5	51.2	55.2	60.1	67.1	73.1	77.5	76.5	72.8	64.5	53.7	46.0	62.0
Mean Minimum Temp. (°F)	38.4	40.9	43.5	46.8	52.4	57.4	60.9	60.1	57.2	50.3	42.5	37.6	49.0
Extreme Maximum Temp. (°F)	71	77	87	100	107	110	115	109	106	101	84	72	115
Extreme Minimum Temp. (°F)	20	22	28	32	39	45	49	50	43	36	25	17	17
Days Maximum Temp. ≥ 90°F	0	0	0	1	7	14	23	21	14	3	0	0	83
Days Maximum Temp. ≤ 32°F	0	0	0	0	0	0	0	0	0	0	0	0	0
Days Minimum Temp. ≤ 32°F	7	3	0	0	0	0	0	0	0	0	2	8	20
Days Minimum Temp. ≤ 0°F	0	0	0	0	0	0	0	0	0	0	0	0	0
Heating Degree Days (base 65°F)	567	384	297	163	46	5	0	0	5	72	334	581	2,454
Cooling Degree Days (base 65°F)	0	0	1	22	119	253	396	363	246	63	1	0	1,464
Mean Precipitation (in.)	2.73	2.51	2.10	0.93	0.53	0.08	0.02	0.01	0.29	0.77	1.61	2.12	13.70
Maximum Precipitation (in.)*	7.1	6.0	6.5	3.5	2.3	0.7	0.6	0.8	3.0	2.2	6.2	8.0	26.6
Minimum Precipitation (in.)*	0.1	0	trace	0	0	0	0	0	0	0	0	trace	5.4
Extreme Maximum Daily Precip. (in.)	2.01	1.62	1.39	1.03	1.66	0.23	0.50	0.06	1.38	1.46	1.50	1.92	2.01
Days With ≥ 0.1" Precipitation	6	6	6	3	1	0	0	0	1	2	4	5	34
Days With ≥ 0.5" Precipitation	2	2	1	0	0	0	0	0	0	1	1	1	8
Days With ≥ 1.0" Precipitation	0	0	0	0	0	0	0	0	0	0	0	0	0
Mean Snowfall (in.)	na	na	na	na	na	na	na	na	na	na	na	na	na
Maximum Snowfall (in.)*	trace	trace	trace	trace	0	0	0	0	0	0	0	trace	trace
Maximum 24-hr. Snowfall (in.)*	trace	trace	trace	trace	0	0	0	0	0	0	0	trace	trace
Maximum Snow Depth (in.)	na	na	na	na	na	na	na	na	na	na	na	na	na
Days With ≥ 1.0" Snow Depth	na	na	na	na	na	na	na	na	na	na	na	na	na
Thunderstorm Days*	< 1	< 1	1	1	< 1	< 1	< 1	< 1	< 1	< 1	< 1	< 1	2
Foggy Days*	24	17	11	5	2	< 1	< 1	< 1	2	8	18	24	111
Predominant Sky Cover*	OVR	OVR	OVR	CLR	CLR	CLR	CLR	CLR	CLR	CLR	OVR	OVR	CLR
Mean Relative Humidity 7am (%)*	90	90	85	76	65	60	61	65	70	77	87	91	76
Mean Relative Humidity 4pm (%)*	70	60	51	41	33	29	26	28	31	37	59	71	45
Mean Dewpoint (°F)*	39	42	42	43	46	49	52	52	51	47	44	40	46
Prevailing Wind Direction*	SE	SE	WNW	WNW	W	W	WNW	WNW	WNW	NW	SE	SE	WNW
Prevailing Wind Speed (mph)*	9	9	9	9	10	12	10	9	9	9	9	9	9
Maximum Wind Gust (mph)*	60	53	52	45	49	43	32	37	39	54	49	54	60

Note: (*) Period of record is 1948-1995

Alturas *Modoc County* Elevation: 4,399 ft. Latitude: 41° 30' N Longitude: 120° 33' W

	JAN	FEB	MAR	APR	MAY	JUN	JUL	AUG	SEP	OCT	NOV	DEC	YEAR
Mean Maximum Temp. (°F)	43.5	47.0	53.4	59.9	68.8	78.4	88.6	87.7	79.4	66.8	50.5	42.1	63.9
Mean Temp. (°F)	30.7	33.6	39.2	44.0	51.7	59.1	66.3	64.7	57.4	47.2	36.4	29.9	46.7
Mean Minimum Temp. (°F)	17.9	20.1	25.0	28.0	34.4	39.9	44.0	41.6	35.3	27.5	22.2	17.6	29.5
Extreme Maximum Temp. (°F)	62	72	78	85	95	102	108	104	100	90	83	72	108
Extreme Minimum Temp. (°F)	-13	-33	-3	7	17	21	28	26	17	1	-17	-25	-33
Days Maximum Temp. ≥ 90°F	0	0	0	0	1	4	15	13	4	0	0	0	37
Days Maximum Temp. ≤ 32°F	2	1	0	0	0	0	0	0	0	0	1	3	7
Days Minimum Temp. ≤ 32°F	27	25	26	22	12	4	1	1	10	23	24	27	202
Days Minimum Temp. ≤ 0°F	2	1	0	0	0	0	0	0	0	0	0	2	5
Heating Degree Days (base 65°F)	1,055	882	792	624	409	192	52	64	230	546	854	1,082	6,782
Cooling Degree Days (base 65°F)	0	0	0	0	3	25	100	61	9	0	0	0	198
Mean Precipitation (in.)	1.30	1.26	1.47	1.21	1.42	0.75	0.26	0.33	0.54	0.85	1.62	1.35	12.36
Extreme Maximum Daily Precip. (in.)	1.20	1.28	1.99	1.60	1.20	1.12	1.03	0.87	1.00	1.22	1.08	1.00	1.99
Days With ≥ 0.1" Precipitation	4	4	5	4	4	2	1	1	1	3	5	4	38
Days With ≥ 0.5" Precipitation	0	0	0	0	1	0	0	0	0	1	1	0	3
Days With ≥ 1.0" Precipitation	0	0	0	0	0	0	0	0	0	0	0	0	0
Mean Snowfall (in.)	4.5	2.8	2.4	0.6	0.5	trace	trace	0.0	0.0	0.1	3.2	3.3	17.4
Maximum Snow Depth (in.)	21	10	9	4	4	0	trace	0	0	1	12	14	21
Days With ≥ 1.0" Snow Depth	4	3	1	0	0	0	0	0	0	0	3	4	15

Angwin Pac Union Col *Napa County* Elevation: 1,714 ft. Latitude: 38° 34' N Longitude: 122° 26' W

	JAN	FEB	MAR	APR	MAY	JUN	JUL	AUG	SEP	OCT	NOV	DEC	YEAR
Mean Maximum Temp. (°F)	53.2	55.9	60.4	66.1	73.6	80.4	86.0	85.3	81.6	72.3	59.5	52.8	68.9
Mean Temp. (°F)	45.9	47.7	50.6	54.4	60.3	65.7	70.4	69.7	67.6	60.9	51.0	45.6	57.5
Mean Minimum Temp. (°F)	38.5	39.5	40.7	42.5	47.0	50.9	54.8	54.2	53.5	49.5	42.5	38.4	46.0
Extreme Maximum Temp. (°F)	77	75	84	91	101	104	105	104	101	99	82	74	105
Extreme Minimum Temp. (°F)	25	20	24	27	29	36	40	42	39	30	25	16	16
Days Maximum Temp. ≥ 90°F	0	0	0	0	1	5	10	9	5	1	0	0	31
Days Maximum Temp. ≤ 32°F	0	0	0	0	0	0	0	0	0	0	0	0	0
Days Minimum Temp. ≤ 32°F	5	4	3	2	0	0	0	0	0	0	2	5	21
Days Minimum Temp. ≤ 0°F	0	0	0	0	0	0	0	0	0	0	0	0	0
Heating Degree Days (base 65°F)	587	482	443	322	181	71	15	17	44	164	414	596	3,336
Cooling Degree Days (base 65°F)	0	0	2	10	43	99	190	171	129	44	1	0	689
Mean Precipitation (in.)	7.43	8.32	5.63	2.32	1.46	0.30	0.01	0.06	0.38	2.03	5.06	7.95	40.95
Extreme Maximum Daily Precip. (in.)	5.67	7.40	6.14	3.08	2.29	1.36	0.16	0.44	1.56	4.04	4.50	5.57	7.40
Days With ≥ 0.1" Precipitation	9	9	8	5	3	1	0	0	1	3	7	9	55
Days With ≥ 0.5" Precipitation	5	5	4	1	1	0	0	0	0	1	3	5	25
Days With ≥ 1.0" Precipitation	2	3	2	1	0	0	0	0	0	1	2	3	14
Mean Snowfall (in.)	trace	trace	trace	trace	trace	0.0	0.0	0.0	0.0	0.0	0.0	0.1	0.1
Maximum Snow Depth (in.)	2	1	4	0	0	0	0	0	0	0	0	trace	4
Days With ≥ 1.0" Snow Depth	0	0	0	0	0	0	0	0	0	0	0	0	0

Antioch Pump Plant #3 *Contra Costa County* Elevation: 60 ft. Latitude: 37° 59' N Longitude: 121° 44' W

	JAN	FEB	MAR	APR	MAY	JUN	JUL	AUG	SEP	OCT	NOV	DEC	YEAR
Mean Maximum Temp. (°F)	53.9	60.2	***65.4***	71.9	79.1	***86.1***	91.7	90.2	86.2	77.4	64.0	54.5	***73.4***
Mean Temp. (°F)	46.3	51.3	***55.3***	60.0	66.2	***71.8***	75.5	74.3	71.6	64.8	54.5	46.6	***61.5***
Mean Minimum Temp. (°F)	38.7	42.4	***45.2***	48.0	53.1	57.6	59.2	58.3	57.0	52.2	44.9	38.5	***49.6***
Extreme Maximum Temp. (°F)	70	76	88	94	103	109	110	109	107	101	82	73	110
Extreme Minimum Temp. (°F)	23	25	32	29	40	35	44	47	41	39	28	20	20
Days Maximum Temp. ≥ 90°F	0	0	0	0	4	10	20	15	10	2	0	0	61
Days Maximum Temp. ≤ 32°F	0	0	0	0	0	0	0	0	0	0	0	0	0
Days Minimum Temp. ≤ 32°F	5	1	0	0	0	0	0	0	0	0	1	5	12
Days Minimum Temp. ≤ 0°F	0	0	0	0	0	0	0	0	0	0	0	0	0
Heating Degree Days (base 65°F)	572	381	***294***	165	56	***9***	0	0	6	68	311	565	***2,427***
Cooling Degree Days (base 65°F)	0	0	***1***	22	101	***221***	332	294	210	69	2	0	***1,252***
Mean Precipitation (in.)	2.90	2.70	***2.37***	0.77	0.45	0.09	0.02	0.02	0.18	0.54	1.60	2.39	***14.03***
Extreme Maximum Daily Precip. (in.)	2.80	2.33	***1.40***	***1.44***	***1.10***	0.58	0.40	0.35	0.66	1.75	2.34	2.20	***2.80***
Days With ≥ 0.1" Precipitation	6	6	***6***	2	***1***	0	0	0	1	1	4	5	***32***
Days With ≥ 0.5" Precipitation	2	2	***1***	0	0	0	0	0	0	0	1	2	***8***
Days With ≥ 1.0" Precipitation	1	0	***0***	0	0	0	0	0	0	0	0	0	***1***
Mean Snowfall (in.)	0.0	trace	0.0	0.0	0.0	0.0	0.0	0.0	0.0	0.0	0.0	0.0	trace
Maximum Snow Depth (in.)	0	trace	0	0	0	0	0	0	0	0	0	0	trace
Days With ≥ 1.0" Snow Depth	0	0	0	0	0	0	0	0	0	0	0	0	0

Ash Mountain *Tulare County* Elevation: 1,708 ft. Latitude: 36° 29' N Longitude: 118° 50' W

	JAN	FEB	MAR	APR	MAY	JUN	JUL	AUG	SEP	OCT	NOV	DEC	YEAR
Mean Maximum Temp. (°F)	58.7	62.1	65.4	71.1	81.1	90.5	98.7	98.0	92.0	81.0	67.1	58.8	77.0
Mean Temp. (°F)	48.0	50.9	53.9	58.5	67.2	75.6	83.1	82.3	76.4	66.5	54.8	47.9	63.8
Mean Minimum Temp. (°F)	37.2	39.7	42.3	45.7	53.3	60.7	67.5	66.6	60.8	52.0	42.5	36.9	50.4
Extreme Maximum Temp. (°F)	80	83	89	97	106	109	118	114	109	103	89	80	118
Extreme Minimum Temp. (°F)	22	22	28	28	34	42	50	51	45	31	25	17	17
Days Maximum Temp. ≥ 90°F	0	0	0	1	7	17	29	28	19	6	0	0	107
Days Maximum Temp. ≤ 32°F	0	0	0	0	0	0	0	0	0	0	0	0	0
Days Minimum Temp. ≤ 32°F	7	3	1	1	0	0	0	0	0	0	2	7	21
Days Minimum Temp. ≤ 0°F	0	0	0	0	0	0	0	0	0	0	0	0	0
Heating Degree Days (base 65°F)	521	391	340	218	73	11	0	0	7	74	307	522	2,464
Cooling Degree Days (base 65°F)	0	0	3	28	148	336	568	545	354	128	6	0	2,116
Mean Precipitation (in.)	5.13	4.78	4.65	2.21	1.13	0.41	0.11	0.06	0.46	1.38	2.76	3.62	26.70
Extreme Maximum Daily Precip. (in.)	3.50	4.02	2.73	3.15	1.96	2.15	0.80	1.03	2.70	3.74	3.85	2.91	4.02
Days With ≥ 0.1" Precipitation	7	7	7	4	2	1	0	0	1	2	4	5	40
Days With ≥ 0.5" Precipitation	4	3	3	1	1	0	0	0	0	1	2	3	18
Days With ≥ 1.0" Precipitation	2	2	1	0	0	0	0	0	0	0	1	1	7
Mean Snowfall (in.)	0.3	0.1	0.1	trace	0.0	0.0	0.0	0.0	0.0	0.0	0.2	0.1	0.8
Maximum Snow Depth (in.)	2	2	1	trace	0	0	0	0	0	0	6	trace	6
Days With ≥ 1.0" Snow Depth	0	0	0	0	0	0	0	0	0	0	0	0	0

The period of record for all cooperative weather station data is 1980 – 2009. See User Guide for detailed explanation of data.

Auberry 2 NW *Fresno County* Elevation: 2,089 ft. Latitude: 37° 05' N Longitude: 119° 30' W

	JAN	FEB	MAR	APR	MAY	JUN	JUL	AUG	SEP	OCT	NOV	DEC	YEAR
Mean Maximum Temp. (°F)	55.4	58.3	62.1	68.6	78.7	87.7	94.7	93.7	87.4	76.1	62.9	55.1	73.4
Mean Temp. (°F)	46.0	48.8	52.0	57.1	65.7	73.8	81.1	80.2	74.5	64.3	52.6	45.8	61.8
Mean Minimum Temp. (°F)	36.6	39.3	41.9	45.5	52.7	59.9	67.6	66.7	61.6	52.5	42.2	36.5	50.2
Extreme Maximum Temp. (°F)	79	76	85	94	103	104	109	109	105	100	85	76	109
Extreme Minimum Temp. (°F)	21	17	25	27	28	36	44	46	41	33	25	10	10
Days Maximum Temp. ≥ 90°F	0	0	0	0	4	14	26	24	14	2	0	0	84
Days Maximum Temp. ≤ 32°F	0	0	0	0	0	0	0	0	0	0	0	0	0
Days Minimum Temp. ≤ 32°F	8	4	2	1	0	0	0	0	0	0	2	8	25
Days Minimum Temp. ≤ 0°F	0	0	0	0	0	0	0	0	0	0	0	0	0
Heating Degree Days (base 65°F)	582	450	398	252	90	16	0	0	12	104	368	587	2,859
Cooling Degree Days (base 65°F)	0	0	2	21	119	287	508	479	305	90	2	0	1,813
Mean Precipitation (in.)	5.29	4.67	4.29	1.97	1.00	0.31	0.07	0.05	0.37	1.38	2.51	3.89	25.80
Extreme Maximum Daily Precip. (in.)	3.95	2.70	3.43	2.85	2.22	2.01	1.17	0.38	1.41	2.98	3.90	4.08	4.08
Days With ≥ 0.1" Precipitation	7	7	6	3	2	1	0	0	1	2	4	6	39
Days With ≥ 0.5" Precipitation	4	4	3	1	1	0	0	0	0	1	2	3	19
Days With ≥ 1.0" Precipitation	2	2	1	1	0	0	0	0	0	0	1	1	8
Mean Snowfall (in.)	0.4	0.3	0.7	0.1	0.0	0.0	0.0	0.0	0.0	0.0	trace	0.4	1.9
Maximum Snow Depth (in.)	2	4	1	2	0	0	0	0	0	0	0	8	8
Days With ≥ 1.0" Snow Depth	0	0	0	0	0	0	0	0	0	0	0	0	0

Auburn *Placer County* Elevation: 1,292 ft. Latitude: 38° 54' N Longitude: 121° 05' W

	JAN	FEB	MAR	APR	MAY	JUN	JUL	AUG	SEP	OCT	NOV	DEC	YEAR
Mean Maximum Temp. (°F)	54.5	58.5	62.5	67.8	76.4	84.5	91.6	90.7	85.2	75.7	62.0	54.6	72.0
Mean Temp. (°F)	46.1	49.4	52.4	56.7	64.2	71.2	77.5	76.6	72.1	63.9	52.7	46.0	60.7
Mean Minimum Temp. (°F)	37.6	40.3	42.5	45.6	51.9	57.7	63.4	62.5	58.9	52.0	43.4	37.4	49.4
Extreme Maximum Temp. (°F)	73	76	86	89	101	103	107	107	103	98	82	74	107
Extreme Minimum Temp. (°F)	23	22	29	30	35	43	48	35	43	32	29	16	16
Days Maximum Temp. ≥ 90°F	0	0	0	0	3	9	19	18	10	2	0	0	61
Days Maximum Temp. ≤ 32°F	0	0	0	0	0	0	0	0	0	0	0	0	0
Days Minimum Temp. ≤ 32°F	6	2	1	0	0	0	0	0	0	0	1	7	17
Days Minimum Temp. ≤ 0°F	0	0	0	0	0	0	0	0	0	0	0	0	0
Heating Degree Days (base 65°F)	579	434	385	255	108	24	1	1	17	104	363	582	2,853
Cooling Degree Days (base 65°F)	0	0	1	14	89	216	397	369	235	75	1	0	1,397
Mean Precipitation (in.)	6.19	6.44	5.70	2.70	1.53	0.38	0.03	0.07	0.60	1.66	4.27	6.01	35.58
Extreme Maximum Daily Precip. (in.)	4.75	3.98	3.22	2.40	2.94	1.20	0.58	0.47	1.43	2.96	3.38	***4.02***	***4.75***
Days With ≥ 0.1" Precipitation	8	8	8	4	3	1	0	0	1	2	6	7	48
Days With ≥ 0.5" Precipitation	4	4	4	2	1	0	0	0	1	1	3	4	24
Days With ≥ 1.0" Precipitation	2	2	2	1	0	0	0	0	0	1	1	2	11
Mean Snowfall (in.)	0.1	0.2	0.3	0.2	0.0	0.0	0.0	0.0	0.0	0.0	0.2	0.1	1.1
Maximum Snow Depth (in.)	0	2	3	2	0	0	0	0	0	0	0	2	3
Days With ≥ 1.0" Snow Depth	0	0	0	0	0	0	0	0	0	0	0	0	0

Balch Power House *Fresno County* Elevation: 1,720 ft. Latitude: 36° 55' N Longitude: 119° 05' W

	JAN	FEB	MAR	APR	MAY	JUN	JUL	AUG	SEP	OCT	NOV	DEC	YEAR
Mean Maximum Temp. (°F)	52.5	57.5	63.8	69.8	78.3	86.4	94.7	94.7	89.2	77.9	60.5	52.0	73.1
Mean Temp. (°F)	45.1	48.6	53.1	57.8	65.6	73.1	81.1	81.1	75.8	65.7	52.2	44.9	62.0
Mean Minimum Temp. (°F)	37.7	39.5	42.3	45.8	52.9	59.7	67.5	67.5	62.5	53.4	43.7	37.9	50.9
Extreme Maximum Temp. (°F)	69	77	88	92	103	106	112	110	108	102	82	68	112
Extreme Minimum Temp. (°F)	20	22	28	23	22	41	49	50	43	37	23	20	20
Days Maximum Temp. ≥ 90°F	0	0	0	0	3	12	25	25	16	3	0	0	84
Days Maximum Temp. ≤ 32°F	0	0	0	0	0	0	0	0	0	0	0	0	0
Days Minimum Temp. ≤ 32°F	5	3	1	0	0	0	0	0	0	0	1	5	15
Days Minimum Temp. ≤ 0°F	0	0	0	0	0	0	0	0	0	0	0	0	0
Heating Degree Days (base 65°F)	610	458	366	228	80	16	0	0	8	80	379	615	2,840
Cooling Degree Days (base 65°F)	0	0	2	20	106	264	506	507	339	107	1	0	1,852
Mean Precipitation (in.)	6.14	5.66	4.95	2.60	1.27	0.45	0.16	0.03	0.66	1.61	2.96	4.41	30.90
Extreme Maximum Daily Precip. (in.)	3.49	4.31	4.67	4.21	2.40	2.02	2.51	0.32	3.16	4.80	5.06	***5.16***	***5.16***
Days With ≥ 0.1" Precipitation	6	7	7	4	2	1	0	0	1	2	4	5	39
Days With ≥ 0.5" Precipitation	4	4	3	2	1	0	0	0	0	1	2	3	20
Days With ≥ 1.0" Precipitation	2	2	1	0	0	0	0	0	0	0	1	1	7
Mean Snowfall (in.)	0.0	0.0	0.0	0.0	0.0	0.0	0.0	0.0	0.0	0.0	0.0	0.0	0.0
Maximum Snow Depth (in.)	0	22	0	0	0	0	0	0	0	0	0	2	22
Days With ≥ 1.0" Snow Depth	0	1	0	0	0	0	0	0	0	0	0	0	1

Barstow Fire Station *San Bernardino County* Elevation: 2,319 ft. Latitude: 34° 53' N Longitude: 117° 01' W

	JAN	FEB	MAR	APR	MAY	JUN	JUL	AUG	SEP	OCT	NOV	DEC	YEAR
Mean Maximum Temp. (°F)	60.7	64.6	70.7	78.3	86.8	96.4	102.1	100.8	93.7	82.0	68.7	59.2	80.3
Mean Temp. (°F)	47.7	51.4	56.7	63.3	71.1	79.7	85.6	84.4	77.5	66.6	54.8	46.3	65.4
Mean Minimum Temp. (°F)	34.7	38.1	42.6	48.3	55.4	63.0	69.1	68.0	61.2	51.0	40.9	33.4	50.5
Extreme Maximum Temp. (°F)	78	87	92	98	107	112	115	112	109	101	89	76	115
Extreme Minimum Temp. (°F)	12	18	26	30	32	36	48	40	34	32	20	16	12
Days Maximum Temp. ≥ 90°F	0	0	0	3	14	25	31	30	23	6	0	0	132
Days Maximum Temp. ≤ 32°F	0	0	0	0	0	0	0	0	0	0	0	0	0
Days Minimum Temp. ≤ 32°F	11	6	2	0	0	0	0	0	0	0	4	15	38
Days Minimum Temp. ≤ 0°F	0	0	0	0	0	0	0	0	0	0	0	0	0
Heating Degree Days (base 65°F)	529	380	261	112	28	2	0	0	3	61	303	574	2,253
Cooling Degree Days (base 65°F)	0	1	11	69	225	450	647	609	384	117	4	0	2,517
Mean Precipitation (in.)	0.85	0.99	0.67	0.21	0.09	0.06	0.33	0.24	0.29	0.28	0.45	0.56	5.02
Extreme Maximum Daily Precip. (in.)	1.25	1.57	1.52	0.98	0.32	0.60	1.31	0.80	1.36	1.35	1.20	1.25	1.57
Days With ≥ 0.1" Precipitation	3	3	2	1	0	0	1	1	1	1	1	2	16
Days With ≥ 0.5" Precipitation	1	1	0	0	0	0	0	0	0	0	0	0	2
Days With ≥ 1.0" Precipitation	0	0	0	0	0	0	0	0	0	0	0	0	0
Mean Snowfall (in.)	0.0	0.0	trace	0.0	0.0	0.0	0.0	0.0	0.0	0.0	0.0	0.3	0.3
Maximum Snow Depth (in.)	0	0	trace	0	0	0	0	0	0	0	0	7	7
Days With ≥ 1.0" Snow Depth	0	0	0	0	0	0	0	0	0	0	0	0	0

The period of record for all cooperative weather station data is 1980 – 2009. See User Guide for detailed explanation of data.

Ben Lomond No 4 *Santa Cruz County* Elevation: 419 ft. Latitude: 37° 05' N Longitude: 122° 05' W

	JAN	FEB	MAR	APR	MAY	JUN	JUL	AUG	SEP	OCT	NOV	DEC	YEAR
Mean Maximum Temp. (°F)	61.5	63.7	67.3	72.0	76.6	81.8	85.1	85.8	84.4	78.2	67.9	60.8	73.8
Mean Temp. (°F)	49.4	51.4	53.9	57.0	61.1	65.1	67.9	68.1	66.6	61.3	53.8	48.7	58.7
Mean Minimum Temp. (°F)	37.1	39.0	40.4	42.1	45.6	48.3	50.7	50.4	48.7	44.3	39.7	36.6	43.6
Extreme Maximum Temp. (°F)	82	87	92	100	105	110	112	110	107	112	95	79	112
Extreme Minimum Temp. (°F)	20	20	27	29	33	35	40	40	37	30	25	15	15
Days Maximum Temp. ≥ 90°F	0	0	0	1	3	6	8	9	9	4	0	0	40
Days Maximum Temp. ≤ 32°F	0	0	0	0	0	0	0	0	0	0	0	0	0
Days Minimum Temp. ≤ 32°F	10	5	3	1	0	0	0	0	0	0	5	11	35
Days Minimum Temp. ≤ 0°F	0	0	0	0	0	0	0	0	0	0	0	0	0
Heating Degree Days (base 65°F)	478	378	339	240	139	49	11	9	31	133	331	498	2,636
Cooling Degree Days (base 65°F)	0	0	1	8	26	58	108	113	85	26	1	0	426
Mean Precipitation (in.)	10.04	10.18	7.10	3.07	1.21	0.24	0.03	0.06	0.27	2.29	5.91	9.55	49.95
Extreme Maximum Daily Precip. (in.)	11.47	5.40	4.38	3.79	3.05	0.86	0.61	0.72	0.98	8.61	5.80	8.43	11.47
Days With ≥ 0.1" Precipitation	8	9	8	4	2	1	0	0	1	2	6	9	50
Days With ≥ 0.5" Precipitation	5	6	5	2	1	0	0	0	0	1	3	5	28
Days With ≥ 1.0" Precipitation	3	3	2	1	0	0	0	0	0	1	2	3	15
Mean Snowfall (in.)	trace	0.1	trace	0.0	0.0	0.0	0.0	0.0	0.0	0.0	trace	0.1	0.2
Maximum Snow Depth (in.)	0	trace	trace	0	0	0	0	0	0	0	trace	trace	trace
Days With ≥ 1.0" Snow Depth	0	0	0	0	0	0	0	0	0	0	0	0	0

Berkeley *Alameda County* Elevation: 310 ft. Latitude: 37° 52' N Longitude: 122° 16' W

	JAN	FEB	MAR	APR	MAY	JUN	JUL	AUG	SEP	OCT	NOV	DEC	YEAR
Mean Maximum Temp. (°F)	***56.8***	59.9	***62.6***	65.3	68.3	72.1	72.6	72.7	***73.4***	70.9	***63.3***	57.0	***66.2***
Mean Temp. (°F)	***50.3***	52.8	***54.6***	56.6	59.4	62.4	63.3	63.7	***64.1***	61.6	***55.6***	50.4	***57.9***
Mean Minimum Temp. (°F)	***43.7***	45.7	***46.6***	47.8	50.4	52.7	54.0	54.7	***54.5***	52.2	***47.9***	43.7	***49.5***
Extreme Maximum Temp. (°F)	***77***	77	87	95	101	107	99	***98***	***99***	***99***	***82***	***73***	***107***
Extreme Minimum Temp. (°F)	***29***	34	33	36	41	45	47	***47***	***44***	***42***	***35***	***24***	***24***
Days Maximum Temp. ≥ 90°F	***0***	0	0	0	0	1	0	0	2	1	***0***	0	***4***
Days Maximum Temp. ≤ 32°F	***0***	0	0	0	0	0	0	0	0	0	***0***	0	***0***
Days Minimum Temp. ≤ 32°F	***0***	0	0	0	0	0	0	0	0	0	***0***	0	***0***
Days Minimum Temp. ≤ 0°F	***0***	0	0	0	0	0	0	0	0	0	***0***	0	***0***
Heating Degree Days (base 65°F)	***450***	338	***316***	255	180	99	73	61	***67***	127	***276***	447	***2,689***
Cooling Degree Days (base 65°F)	***0***	0	***2***	9	14	29	27	28	***45***	27	***2***	0	***183***
Mean Precipitation (in.)	***4.98***	5.45	***3.70***	1.68	0.87	0.15	0.01	0.07	0.27	1.31	***3.29***	4.92	***26.70***
Extreme Maximum Daily Precip. (in.)	***6.98***	3.20	***2.60***	2.27	***1.92***	0.57	0.13	***0.69***	***0.57***	***3.93***	***3.89***	***4.73***	***6.98***
Days With ≥ 0.1" Precipitation	***8***	8	***6***	4	2	0	0	0	1	2	***6***	7	***44***
Days With ≥ 0.5" Precipitation	***3***	4	***3***	1	0	0	0	0	0	1	***3***	3	***18***
Days With ≥ 1.0" Precipitation	***1***	2	1	0	0	0	0	0	0	0	***1***	1	***6***
Mean Snowfall (in.)	***0.0***	0.0	0.0	0.0	0.0	0.0	0.0	0.0	0.0	0.0	***0.0***	0.0	***0.0***
Maximum Snow Depth (in.)	***0***	0	***0***	0	0	0	0	***0***	***0***	***0***	***0***	***0***	***0***
Days With ≥ 1.0" Snow Depth	***0***	0	***0***	0	0	0	0	0	0	***0***	***0***	0	***0***

Big Bear Lake *San Bernardino County* Elevation: 6,790 ft. Latitude: 34° 15' N Longitude: 116° 53' W

	JAN	FEB	MAR	APR	MAY	JUN	JUL	AUG	SEP	OCT	NOV	DEC	YEAR
Mean Maximum Temp. (°F)	47.5	48.0	52.3	59.0	68.1	76.4	81.4	80.1	74.0	64.6	54.7	47.6	62.8
Mean Temp. (°F)	34.6	35.4	38.7	44.1	51.9	59.0	64.8	63.8	57.8	48.8	40.5	34.4	47.8
Mean Minimum Temp. (°F)	21.6	22.6	25.1	29.1	35.6	41.5	48.1	47.4	41.5	33.0	26.2	21.2	32.8
Extreme Maximum Temp. (°F)	71	72	74	82	87	90	94	92	85	85	74	68	94
Extreme Minimum Temp. (°F)	-1	-3	2	7	22	26	32	31	22	16	3	-8	-8
Days Maximum Temp. ≥ 90°F	0	0	0	0	0	0	1	0	0	0	0	0	1
Days Maximum Temp. ≤ 32°F	2	1	0	0	0	0	0	0	0	0	0	2	5
Days Minimum Temp. ≤ 32°F	29	26	28	22	10	2	0	0	2	14	25	29	187
Days Minimum Temp. ≤ 0°F	0	0	0	0	0	0	0	0	0	0	0	0	0
Heating Degree Days (base 65°F)	937	832	808	621	401	181	50	62	212	494	728	941	6,267
Cooling Degree Days (base 65°F)	0	0	0	0	0	7	51	33	3	0	0	0	94
Mean Precipitation (in.)	4.37	4.33	2.82	0.98	0.37	0.15	0.67	1.03	0.41	0.89	1.42	2.55	19.99
Extreme Maximum Daily Precip. (in.)	5.00	4.10	3.06	1.70	1.41	0.85	1.80	2.60	1.30	3.25	3.78	3.12	5.00
Days With ≥ 0.1" Precipitation	5	5	5	2	1	0	1	2	1	1	2	3	28
Days With ≥ 0.5" Precipitation	2	2	2	1	0	0	0	1	0	0	1	2	11
Days With ≥ 1.0" Precipitation	1	1	1	0	0	0	0	0	0	0	0	1	4
Mean Snowfall (in.)	15.2	15.8	15.3	3.9	0.6	trace	0.0	0.0	0.1	1.2	4.5	10.3	66.9
Maximum Snow Depth (in.)	na	na	na	***12***	***2***	***0***	***0***	***0***	***0***	na	na	na	na
Days With ≥ 1.0" Snow Depth	na	na	na	0	0	0	0	0	0	0	0	***3***	na

Blythe *Riverside County* Elevation: 268 ft. Latitude: 33° 37' N Longitude: 114° 36' W

	JAN	FEB	MAR	APR	MAY	JUN	JUL	AUG	SEP	OCT	NOV	DEC	YEAR
Mean Maximum Temp. (°F)	67.8	72.8	79.8	88.0	96.9	105.2	***108.7***	107.5	101.5	90.3	***75.4***	66.2	***88.3***
Mean Temp. (°F)	54.0	58.4	64.3	71.5	79.8	87.5	***93.1***	92.4	85.3	73.5	***60.4***	52.6	***72.7***
Mean Minimum Temp. (°F)	40.2	43.9	48.7	55.0	62.7	69.7	***77.4***	77.3	69.2	56.7	***45.5***	39.0	***57.1***
Extreme Maximum Temp. (°F)	84	93	100	115	114	122	122	118	116	111	95	85	122
Extreme Minimum Temp. (°F)	0	26	31	39	44	53	59	58	50	36	27	24	0
Days Maximum Temp. ≥ 90°F	0	0	3	13	24	29	30	30	26	17	0	0	172
Days Maximum Temp. ≤ 32°F	0	0	0	0	0	0	0	0	0	0	0	0	0
Days Minimum Temp. ≤ 32°F	3	1	0	0	0	0	0	0	0	0	0	4	8
Days Minimum Temp. ≤ 0°F	0	0	0	0	0	0	0	0	0	0	0	0	0
Heating Degree Days (base 65°F)	335	187	78	16	0	0	***0***	0	0	9	***148***	378	***1,151***
Cooling Degree Days (base 65°F)	0	7	63	219	467	680	***877***	858	616	281	***23***	0	***4,091***
Mean Precipitation (in.)	0.52	0.60	0.32	0.10	0.06	trace	0.20	0.52	0.45	0.15	0.23	0.52	3.67
Extreme Maximum Daily Precip. (in.)	1.21	1.76	***1.48***	0.75	0.70	0.04	1.22	2.18	2.56	***0.92***	1.27	1.23	***2.56***
Days With ≥ 0.1" Precipitation	1	2	1	0	0	0	0	1	1	0	1	1	8
Days With ≥ 0.5" Precipitation	0	0	0	0	0	0	0	0	0	0	0	0	0
Days With ≥ 1.0" Precipitation	0	0	0	0	0	0	0	0	0	0	0	0	0
Mean Snowfall (in.)	0.0	0.0	0.0	0.0	0.0	0.0	0.0	0.0	0.0	0.0	0.0	0.0	0.0
Maximum Snow Depth (in.)	0	0	0	0	0	0	0	0	0	0	0	0	0
Days With ≥ 1.0" Snow Depth	0	0	0	0	0	0	0	0	0	***0***	0	0	***0***

The period of record for all cooperative weather station data is 1980 – 2009. See User Guide for detailed explanation of data.

Boca *Nevada County* Elevation: 5,575 ft. Latitude: 39° 23' N Longitude: 120° 06' W

	JAN	FEB	MAR	APR	MAY	JUN	JUL	AUG	SEP	OCT	NOV	DEC	YEAR
Mean Maximum Temp. (°F)	42.5	45.6	51.1	58.3	67.0	75.7	84.6	83.9	77.0	66.4	52.1	42.6	62.2
Mean Temp. (°F)	27.0	29.9	35.6	41.3	48.6	54.9	61.2	59.9	53.6	45.6	35.8	28.3	43.5
Mean Minimum Temp. (°F)	11.4	14.2	20.0	24.4	30.1	34.0	37.8	35.9	30.2	24.7	19.4	14.0	24.7
Extreme Maximum Temp. (°F)	64	68	75	81	90	96	103	99	95	89	78	68	103
Extreme Minimum Temp. (°F)	-30	-43	-7	6	13	17	22	22	15	10	-9	-28	-43
Days Maximum Temp. ≥ 90°F	0	0	0	0	0	1	7	5	1	0	0	0	14
Days Maximum Temp. ≤ 32°F	3	2	0	0	0	0	0	0	0	0	1	3	9
Days Minimum Temp. ≤ 32°F	30	28	30	28	21	13	6	8	20	28	28	30	270
Days Minimum Temp. ≤ 0°F	6	3	0	0	0	0	0	0	0	0	0	3	12
Heating Degree Days (base 65°F)	1,171	985	905	703	503	301	135	162	335	595	870	1,131	7,796
Cooling Degree Days (base 65°F)	0	0	0	0	0	3	25	10	0	0	0	0	38
Mean Precipitation (in.)	3.45	3.35	2.88	1.23	0.97	0.55	0.51	0.38	0.76	1.35	2.65	3.89	21.97
Extreme Maximum Daily Precip. (in.)	2.99	2.82	2.38	1.28	1.65	0.98	2.00	1.00	1.23	2.28	2.33	3.95	3.95
Days With ≥ 0.1" Precipitation	6	5	6	4	3	2	1	1	2	3	5	6	44
Days With ≥ 0.5" Precipitation	2	2	2	1	0	0	0	0	0	1	2	3	13
Days With ≥ 1.0" Precipitation	1	1	1	0	0	0	0	0	0	0	1	1	5
Mean Snowfall (in.)	19.5	19.8	15.9	5.6	1.1	0.1	0.0	0.0	0.2	1.0	8.9	20.8	92.9
Maximum Snow Depth (in.)	54	70	55	31	3	2	0	0	2	5	25	55	70
Days With ≥ 1.0" Snow Depth	23	21	13	2	0	0	0	0	0	1	6	20	86

Bodie *Mono County* Elevation: 8,370 ft. Latitude: 38° 13' N Longitude: 119° 01' W

	JAN	FEB	MAR	APR	MAY	JUN	JUL	AUG	SEP	OCT	NOV	DEC	YEAR
Mean Maximum Temp. (°F)	40.3	41.1	44.9	51.3	61.5	70.4	77.5	76.8	70.1	60.2	48.6	41.1	57.0
Mean Temp. (°F)	23.2	24.6	28.6	35.0	43.2	50.6	56.3	54.9	48.4	39.7	30.6	23.9	38.3
Mean Minimum Temp. (°F)	6.1	8.0	12.3	18.7	24.9	30.9	35.0	33.0	26.7	19.2	12.6	6.6	19.5
Extreme Maximum Temp. (°F)	60	61	68	75	82	90	91	88	88	83	70	64	91
Extreme Minimum Temp. (°F)	-27	-33	-15	-6	2	6	12	12	4	-6	-21	-31	-33
Days Maximum Temp. ≥ 90°F	0	0	0	0	0	0	0	0	0	0	0	0	0
Days Maximum Temp. ≤ 32°F	6	5	3	1	0	0	0	0	0	0	2	5	22
Days Minimum Temp. ≤ 32°F	31	28	31	29	26	18	11	15	24	29	30	31	303
Days Minimum Temp. ≤ 0°F	9	7	3	0	0	0	0	0	0	0	3	9	31
Heating Degree Days (base 65°F)	1,289	1,136	1,120	892	668	425	265	305	491	776	1,024	1,267	9,658
Cooling Degree Days (base 65°F)	0	0	0	0	0	0	1	0	0	0	0	0	1
Mean Precipitation (in.)	1.68	1.70	1.44	0.86	0.77	0.74	0.63	0.49	0.48	0.58	1.11	1.42	11.90
Extreme Maximum Daily Precip. (in.)	2.80	1.42	2.41	1.22	1.42	1.49	2.10	1.10	1.23	1.55	1.95	1.26	2.80
Days With ≥ 0.1" Precipitation	4	4	4	3	2	2	2	2	2	2	3	4	34
Days With ≥ 0.5" Precipitation	1	1	1	0	0	0	0	0	0	0	1	1	5
Days With ≥ 1.0" Precipitation	0	0	0	0	0	0	0	0	0	0	0	0	0
Mean Snowfall (in.)	13.0	13.8	14.8	5.7	3.0	0.5	trace	trace	0.4	2.2	9.3	***13.2***	***75.9***
Maximum Snow Depth (in.)	45	78	63	46	23	2	trace	1	8	18	19	42	78
Days With ≥ 1.0" Snow Depth	27	26	26	13	2	0	0	0	0	1	9	24	128

Borrego Desert Park *San Diego County* Elevation: 805 ft. Latitude: 33° 14' N Longitude: 116° 25' W

	JAN	FEB	MAR	APR	MAY	JUN	JUL	AUG	SEP	OCT	NOV	DEC	YEAR
Mean Maximum Temp. (°F)	69.7	72.2	78.4	85.2	93.9	102.8	107.5	106.4	101.0	90.1	78.3	68.9	87.9
Mean Temp. (°F)	57.1	59.5	64.3	69.9	77.5	85.6	91.7	91.2	85.7	75.5	64.5	56.3	73.2
Mean Minimum Temp. (°F)	44.5	46.6	50.1	54.4	61.1	68.3	75.8	75.9	70.4	60.9	50.7	43.6	58.5
Extreme Maximum Temp. (°F)	89	95	101	111	115	122	121	119	117	113	98	87	122
Extreme Minimum Temp. (°F)	24	24	23	35	42	48	56	57	49	41	32	23	23
Days Maximum Temp. ≥ 90°F	0	0	3	11	23	28	31	31	28	18	2	0	175
Days Maximum Temp. ≤ 32°F	0	0	0	0	0	0	0	0	0	0	0	0	0
Days Minimum Temp. ≤ 32°F	1	0	0	0	0	0	0	0	0	0	0	1	2
Days Minimum Temp. ≤ 0°F	0	0	0	0	0	0	0	0	0	0	0	0	0
Heating Degree Days (base 65°F)	242	171	96	39	6	0	0	0	0	7	86	266	913
Cooling Degree Days (base 65°F)	6	21	81	192	402	624	834	818	628	340	79	4	4,029
Mean Precipitation (in.)	1.16	1.53	0.81	0.18	0.07	0.02	0.30	0.50	0.31	0.26	0.35	0.82	6.31
Extreme Maximum Daily Precip. (in.)	2.02	2.42	2.46	0.56	1.04	0.23	1.15	2.05	1.36	1.51	1.40	2.10	2.46
Days With ≥ 0.1" Precipitation	2	3	2	1	0	0	1	1	1	1	1	2	15
Days With ≥ 0.5" Precipitation	1	1	0	0	0	0	0	0	0	0	0	1	3
Days With ≥ 1.0" Precipitation	0	0	0	0	0	0	0	0	0	0	0	0	0
Mean Snowfall (in.)	0.0	trace	0.0	0.0	0.0	0.0	0.0	0.0	0.0	0.0	0.0	0.0	trace
Maximum Snow Depth (in.)	0	trace	0	0	0	0	0	0	0	0	0	0	trace
Days With ≥ 1.0" Snow Depth	0	0	0	0	0	0	0	0	0	0	0	0	0

Burbank Valley Pump Plant *Los Angeles County* Elevation: 654 ft. Latitude: 34° 11' N Longitude: 118° 21' W

	JAN	FEB	MAR	APR	MAY	JUN	JUL	AUG	SEP	OCT	NOV	DEC	YEAR
Mean Maximum Temp. (°F)	69.0	69.5	71.5	75.0	77.4	82.1	88.1	89.5	87.4	81.6	74.3	68.5	77.8
Mean Temp. (°F)	55.7	56.9	59.0	62.5	66.1	70.3	75.3	76.1	73.8	67.9	60.3	55.0	64.9
Mean Minimum Temp. (°F)	42.4	44.3	46.4	50.1	54.8	58.5	62.5	62.5	60.2	54.1	46.2	41.5	52.0
Extreme Maximum Temp. (°F)	93	92	98	105	107	110	110	110	111	108	98	89	111
Extreme Minimum Temp. (°F)	26	29	22	33	42	46	52	52	46	41	30	25	22
Days Maximum Temp. ≥ 90°F	0	0	1	2	3	5	13	15	12	6	1	0	58
Days Maximum Temp. ≤ 32°F	0	0	0	0	0	0	0	0	0	0	0	0	0
Days Minimum Temp. ≤ 32°F	1	0	1	0	0	0	0	0	0	0	0	1	3
Days Minimum Temp. ≤ 0°F	0	0	0	0	0	0	0	0	0	0	0	0	0
Heating Degree Days (base 65°F)	284	229	194	115	45	9	0	0	3	29	153	303	1,364
Cooling Degree Days (base 65°F)	3	7	15	48	88	174	327	349	275	124	17	2	1,429
Mean Precipitation (in.)	3.48	4.83	3.22	1.08	0.32	0.11	0.02	0.07	0.23	0.85	1.03	2.15	17.39
Extreme Maximum Daily Precip. (in.)	4.52	4.50	5.45	2.30	1.80	1.01	0.18	0.67	1.10	3.00	2.00	3.49	5.45
Days With ≥ 0.1" Precipitation	5	5	4	2	1	0	0	0	1	1	2	3	24
Days With ≥ 0.5" Precipitation	2	3	2	1	0	0	0	0	0	1	1	2	12
Days With ≥ 1.0" Precipitation	1	2	1	0	0	0	0	0	0	0	0	1	5
Mean Snowfall (in.)	0.0	0.0	0.0	0.0	0.0	0.0	0.0	0.0	0.0	0.0	0.0	0.0	0.0
Maximum Snow Depth (in.)	0	0	0	0	0	0	0	0	0	0	0	0	0
Days With ≥ 1.0" Snow Depth	0	0	0	0	0	0	0	0	0	0	0	0	0

The period of record for all cooperative weather station data is 1980 – 2009. See User Guide for detailed explanation of data.

Cachuma Lake *Santa Barbara County* Elevation: 780 ft. Latitude: 34° 35' N Longitude: 119° 59' W

	JAN	FEB	MAR	APR	MAY	JUN	JUL	AUG	SEP	OCT	NOV	DEC	YEAR
Mean Maximum Temp. (°F)	66.4	67.3	70.1	74.8	79.4	85.1	91.2	92.0	88.8	82.8	73.8	66.4	78.2
Mean Temp. (°F)	52.9	54.3	56.5	59.6	63.6	67.7	72.2	72.7	70.5	65.5	58.5	52.6	62.2
Mean Minimum Temp. (°F)	39.4	41.3	42.9	44.4	47.8	50.3	53.3	53.4	52.1	48.2	43.2	38.8	46.2
Extreme Maximum Temp. (°F)	87	92	95	105	104	113	112	112	112	110	100	87	113
Extreme Minimum Temp. (°F)	20	22	27	30	35	37	42	43	40	27	28	16	16
Days Maximum Temp. ≥ 90°F	0	0	0	2	4	9	18	20	14	8	1	0	76
Days Maximum Temp. ≤ 32°F	0	0	0	0	0	0	0	0	0	0	0	0	0
Days Minimum Temp. ≤ 32°F	4	2	1	0	0	0	0	0	0	0	1	4	12
Days Minimum Temp. ≤ 0°F	0	0	0	0	0	0	0	0	0	0	0	0	0
Heating Degree Days (base 65°F)	368	299	261	178	89	22	2	1	8	61	204	377	1,870
Cooling Degree Days (base 65°F)	0	3	5	23	52	112	232	247	180	84	15	0	953
Mean Precipitation (in.)	4.79	5.35	3.90	1.27	0.45	0.05	0.01	0.03	0.14	0.91	1.59	3.17	21.66
Extreme Maximum Daily Precip. (in.)	6.25	6.63	6.10	2.47	2.04	0.41	0.07	0.59	0.54	4.09	2.26	7.23	7.23
Days With ≥ 0.1" Precipitation	6	6	5	2	1	0	0	0	0	1	3	4	28
Days With ≥ 0.5" Precipitation	3	3	2	1	0	0	0	0	0	0	1	2	12
Days With ≥ 1.0" Precipitation	1	2	1	0	0	0	0	0	0	0	1	1	6
Mean Snowfall (in.)	0.0	0.0	0.0	0.0	0.0	0.0	0.0	0.0	0.0	0.0	0.0	0.0	0.0
Maximum Snow Depth (in.)	0	0	0	0	0	0	0	0	0	0	0	0	0
Days With ≥ 1.0" Snow Depth	0	0	0	0	0	0	0	0	0	0	0	0	0

Calaveras Big Trees *Calaveras County* Elevation: 4,693 ft. Latitude: 38° 17' N Longitude: 120° 19' W

	JAN	FEB	MAR	APR	MAY	JUN	JUL	AUG	SEP	OCT	NOV	DEC	YEAR
Mean Maximum Temp. (°F)	43.9	45.1	48.6	54.5	63.8	73.0	80.6	80.1	73.0	63.0	50.9	43.6	60.0
Mean Temp. (°F)	36.4	37.0	39.9	44.4	52.4	60.2	67.2	66.6	60.7	52.0	42.0	36.2	49.6
Mean Minimum Temp. (°F)	28.8	28.9	31.0	34.2	40.9	47.4	53.7	53.2	48.3	41.0	33.1	28.7	39.1
Extreme Maximum Temp. (°F)	62	68	72	82	93	91	95	98	92	88	73	65	98
Extreme Minimum Temp. (°F)	5	5	14	18	10	30	32	41	31	25	14	3	3
Days Maximum Temp. ≥ 90°F	0	0	0	0	0	0	2	1	0	0	0	0	3
Days Maximum Temp. ≤ 32°F	2	2	1	0	0	0	0	0	0	0	1	3	9
Days Minimum Temp. ≤ 32°F	23	21	19	13	4	0	0	0	0	4	14	23	121
Days Minimum Temp. ≤ 0°F	0	0	0	0	0	0	0	0	0	0	0	0	0
Heating Degree Days (base 65°F)	881	783	772	612	390	167	37	38	155	400	682	886	5,803
Cooling Degree Days (base 65°F)	0	0	0	0	5	30	113	96	31	4	0	0	279
Mean Precipitation (in.)	10.39	10.33	8.33	4.38	2.53	0.73	0.14	0.09	0.90	3.06	6.11	9.01	56.00
Extreme Maximum Daily Precip. (in.)	7.85	6.25	5.18	4.52	2.85	1.51	2.14	0.80	2.26	5.50	5.79	4.72	7.85
Days With ≥ 0.1" Precipitation	9	9	9	6	4	1	0	0	1	3	7	9	58
Days With ≥ 0.5" Precipitation	6	5	5	3	2	0	0	0	1	2	3	5	32
Days With ≥ 1.0" Precipitation	4	4	3	2	1	0	0	0	0	1	2	3	20
Mean Snowfall (in.)	22.9	25.6	23.8	11.1	1.7	0.1	0.0	0.0	trace	0.6	6.3	20.6	112.7
Maximum Snow Depth (in.)	***58***	***54***	na	***84***	1	trace	0	0	***0***	***7***	***20***	***36***	na
Days With ≥ 1.0" Snow Depth	***3***	***4***	***5***	***1***	0	0	0	0	0	0	1	2	***16***

Calistoga *Napa County* Elevation: 370 ft. Latitude: 38° 35' N Longitude: 122° 34' W

	JAN	FEB	MAR	APR	MAY	JUN	JUL	AUG	SEP	OCT	NOV	DEC	YEAR
Mean Maximum Temp. (°F)	***59.7***	63.9	67.8	***72.6***	79.6	86.4	92.4	91.5	88.2	79.8	***66.9***	***58.7***	***75.6***
Mean Temp. (°F)	***48.3***	51.4	54.3	***57.5***	63.1	68.4	72.6	71.8	69.2	62.5	***53.6***	***47.6***	***60.0***
Mean Minimum Temp. (°F)	***36.9***	38.9	40.8	42.4	46.6	50.4	52.8	52.1	50.1	45.2	***40.3***	***36.6***	***44.4***
Extreme Maximum Temp. (°F)	80	88	89	102	104	106	111	109	110	106	91	83	111
Extreme Minimum Temp. (°F)	18	17	21	20	29	35	37	38	35	27	21	12	12
Days Maximum Temp. ≥ 90°F	0	0	0	1	4	11	19	18	14	5	0	0	72
Days Maximum Temp. ≤ 32°F	0	0	0	0	0	0	0	0	0	0	0	0	0
Days Minimum Temp. ≤ 32°F	9	6	3	1	0	0	0	0	0	0	4	10	33
Days Minimum Temp. ≤ 0°F	0	0	0	0	0	0	0	0	0	0	0	0	0
Heating Degree Days (base 65°F)	***510***	379	328	***230***	107	25	2	2	15	111	***335***	***532***	***2,576***
Cooling Degree Days (base 65°F)	***0***	1	3	***13***	55	133	244	219	149	41	***1***	***0***	***859***
Mean Precipitation (in.)	7.48	8.03	5.69	2.04	1.31	0.27	0.03	0.07	0.33	1.98	4.59	8.05	39.87
Extreme Maximum Daily Precip. (in.)	5.80	8.10	5.63	2.17	2.30	1.03	0.53	0.83	1.18	3.06	3.58	5.90	8.10
Days With ≥ 0.1" Precipitation	8	8	7	4	2	1	0	0	1	3	5	8	47
Days With ≥ 0.5" Precipitation	4	5	4	1	1	0	0	0	0	1	3	5	24
Days With ≥ 1.0" Precipitation	2	3	2	0	0	0	0	0	0	1	1	3	12
Mean Snowfall (in.)	trace	trace	0.0	0.0	0.0	0.0	0.0	0.0	0.0	0.0	0.0	0.0	trace
Maximum Snow Depth (in.)	trace	trace	0	0	0	0	0	0	0	0	0	0	trace
Days With ≥ 1.0" Snow Depth	0	0	0	0	0	0	0	0	0	0	0	0	0

Callahan *Siskiyou County* Elevation: 3,185 ft. Latitude: 41° 19' N Longitude: 122° 48' W

	JAN	FEB	MAR	APR	MAY	JUN	JUL	AUG	SEP	OCT	NOV	DEC	YEAR
Mean Maximum Temp. (°F)	45.4	50.8	56.8	63.1	70.9	78.6	86.9	86.3	79.5	67.6	51.5	44.1	65.1
Mean Temp. (°F)	35.9	39.6	43.7	48.5	55.0	61.2	68.2	67.1	60.8	51.6	40.8	35.2	50.6
Mean Minimum Temp. (°F)	26.4	28.4	30.5	33.8	39.0	43.8	49.4	47.8	42.0	35.5	30.1	26.3	36.1
Extreme Maximum Temp. (°F)	65	72	76	86	98	100	103	102	98	90	75	64	103
Extreme Minimum Temp. (°F)	6	-1	14	19	25	23	30	34	27	16	11	-6	-6
Days Maximum Temp. ≥ 90°F	0	0	0	0	1	3	11	10	3	0	0	0	28
Days Maximum Temp. ≤ 32°F	1	0	0	0	0	0	0	0	0	0	0	1	2
Days Minimum Temp. ≤ 32°F	25	21	20	14	6	1	0	0	1	11	21	25	145
Days Minimum Temp. ≤ 0°F	0	0	0	0	0	0	0	0	0	0	0	0	0
Heating Degree Days (base 65°F)	896	711	654	489	312	140	28	30	144	410	720	917	5,451
Cooling Degree Days (base 65°F)	0	0	0	0	8	34	133	101	23	1	0	0	300
Mean Precipitation (in.)	3.45	2.84	2.15	1.28	1.30	0.79	0.46	0.31	0.44	1.24	2.97	3.99	21.22
Extreme Maximum Daily Precip. (in.)	4.36	2.42	2.23	1.17	1.86	1.21	1.03	2.51	1.01	1.99	2.22	3.98	4.36
Days With ≥ 0.1" Precipitation	7	6	5	3	3	2	1	1	1	3	6	7	45
Days With ≥ 0.5" Precipitation	2	2	1	1	1	0	0	0	0	1	2	2	12
Days With ≥ 1.0" Precipitation	1	1	0	0	0	0	0	0	0	0	1	1	4
Mean Snowfall (in.)	0.9	0.3	1.2	0.3	0.1	0.0	0.0	0.0	0.0	0.1	1.0	1.6	5.5
Maximum Snow Depth (in.)	11	12	0	1	0	0	0	0	0	0	5	10	12
Days With ≥ 1.0" Snow Depth	0	0	0	0	0	0	0	0	0	0	0	0	0

The period of record for all cooperative weather station data is 1980 – 2009. See User Guide for detailed explanation of data.

Camp Pardee *Calaveras County* Elevation: 658 ft. Latitude: 38° 15' N Longitude: 120° 52' W

	JAN	FEB	MAR	APR	MAY	JUN	JUL	AUG	SEP	OCT	NOV	DEC	YEAR
Mean Maximum Temp. (°F)	53.9	59.9	64.7	70.7	80.2	88.8	95.3	94.1	88.7	78.2	63.9	54.5	74.4
Mean Temp. (°F)	46.7	51.1	54.8	59.0	66.2	73.2	78.9	77.9	74.0	65.7	54.8	47.1	62.4
Mean Minimum Temp. (°F)	39.4	42.4	44.8	47.1	52.2	57.5	62.4	61.7	59.2	53.1	45.7	39.6	50.4
Extreme Maximum Temp. (°F)	71	75	85	99	108	108	113	111	106	102	83	73	113
Extreme Minimum Temp. (°F)	25	23	30	33	38	43	49	50	42	38	29	18	18
Days Maximum Temp. ≥ 90°F	0	0	0	1	5	14	25	23	15	3	0	0	86
Days Maximum Temp. ≤ 32°F	0	0	0	0	0	0	0	0	0	0	0	0	0
Days Minimum Temp. ≤ 32°F	4	1	0	0	0	0	0	0	0	0	0	4	9
Days Minimum Temp. ≤ 0°F	0	0	0	0	0	0	0	0	0	0	0	0	0
Heating Degree Days (base 65°F)	563	387	314	200	71	10	0	0	7	72	303	549	2,476
Cooling Degree Days (base 65°F)	0	0	2	24	114	260	436	407	282	98	3	0	1,626
Mean Precipitation (in.)	4.27	3.92	3.85	1.89	1.14	0.29	0.04	0.04	0.44	1.24	2.51	3.59	23.22
Extreme Maximum Daily Precip. (in.)	2.52	2.14	2.05	2.84	5.33	1.37	0.70	0.22	2.41	2.24	1.95	2.05	5.33
Days With ≥ 0.1" Precipitation	8	7	7	4	2	1	0	0	1	2	5	7	44
Days With ≥ 0.5" Precipitation	3	3	3	1	1	0	0	0	0	1	2	3	17
Days With ≥ 1.0" Precipitation	1	1	1	0	0	0	0	0	0	0	1	1	5
Mean Snowfall (in.)	0.0	0.0	0.0	0.0	0.0	0.0	0.0	0.0	0.0	0.0	0.0	0.0	0.0
Maximum Snow Depth (in.)	0	0	0	0	0	0	0	0	0	0	0	0	0
Days With ≥ 1.0" Snow Depth	0	0	0	0	0	0	0	0	0	0	0	0	0

Canoga Park Pierce College *Los Angeles County* Elevation: 790 ft. Latitude: 34° 11' N Longitude: 118° 34' W

	JAN	FEB	MAR	APR	MAY	JUN	JUL	AUG	SEP	OCT	NOV	DEC	YEAR
Mean Maximum Temp. (°F)	69.2	70.1	73.1	78.2	82.3	88.7	95.3	97.0	92.5	***84.8***	74.9	69.2	***81.3***
Mean Temp. (°F)	54.6	55.8	57.9	61.7	66.0	71.2	76.2	77.3	73.8	***67.3***	58.7	54.0	***64.5***
Mean Minimum Temp. (°F)	40.0	41.5	42.7	45.2	49.7	53.5	57.1	57.6	55.0	***49.6***	42.5	38.7	***47.8***
Extreme Maximum Temp. (°F)	92	94	101	105	113	113	115	116	114	***110***	97	93	***116***
Extreme Minimum Temp. (°F)	24	18	28	30	38	40	46	45	42	***35***	24	20	***18***
Days Maximum Temp. ≥ 90°F	0	0	1	5	7	15	25	27	19	***10***	2	0	***111***
Days Maximum Temp. ≤ 32°F	0	0	0	0	0	0	0	0	0	***0***	0	0	***0***
Days Minimum Temp. ≤ 32°F	4	3	1	0	0	0	0	0	0	***0***	1	5	***14***
Days Minimum Temp. ≤ 0°F	0	0	0	0	0	0	0	0	0	***0***	0	0	***0***
Heating Degree Days (base 65°F)	317	258	224	134	61	12	0	0	5	***40***	194	337	***1,582***
Cooling Degree Days (base 65°F)	3	4	10	42	100	204	355	390	275	***116***	12	1	***1,512***
Mean Precipitation (in.)	3.68	5.19	3.25	1.03	0.35	0.07	0.02	0.06	0.15	***0.89***	1.39	2.59	***18.67***
Extreme Maximum Daily Precip. (in.)	4.62	5.78	***6.06***	2.49	1.97	0.52	***0.17***	***0.54***	***0.75***	***3.20***	***2.33***	***4.62***	6.06
Days With ≥ 0.1" Precipitation	5	5	4	2	1	0	0	0	0	***1***	2	3	***23***
Days With ≥ 0.5" Precipitation	2	3	2	1	0	0	0	0	0	***0***	1	2	***11***
Days With ≥ 1.0" Precipitation	1	2	1	0	0	0	0	0	0	***0***	0	1	***5***
Mean Snowfall (in.)	0.0	trace	0.0	0.0	0.0	0.0	0.0	0.0	0.0	***0.0***	0.0	trace	***trace***
Maximum Snow Depth (in.)	0	0	0	0	0	0	0	0	0	***0***	0	trace	trace
Days With ≥ 1.0" Snow Depth	0	0	0	0	0	0	0	0	0	***0***	0	0	***0***

Canyon Dam *Plumas County* Elevation: 4,560 ft. Latitude: 40° 10' N Longitude: 121° 05' W

	JAN	FEB	MAR	APR	MAY	JUN	JUL	AUG	SEP	OCT	NOV	DEC	YEAR
Mean Maximum Temp. (°F)	40.4	43.9	50.2	57.5	67.8	76.0	84.2	83.5	76.5	64.3	48.6	40.2	61.1
Mean Temp. (°F)	32.2	34.6	39.2	44.5	52.8	59.8	66.5	65.4	59.4	49.8	39.0	32.3	48.0
Mean Minimum Temp. (°F)	24.0	25.2	28.1	31.4	37.8	43.6	48.8	47.3	42.3	35.3	29.2	24.3	34.8
Extreme Maximum Temp. (°F)	57	63	71	81	92	96	102	102	97	85	69	60	102
Extreme Minimum Temp. (°F)	-5	-10	8	14	23	27	34	31	26	19	9	-11	-11
Days Maximum Temp. ≥ 90°F	0	0	0	0	0	1	7	5	1	0	0	0	14
Days Maximum Temp. ≤ 32°F	3	1	0	0	0	0	0	0	0	0	0	3	7
Days Minimum Temp. ≤ 32°F	29	26	26	18	6	1	0	0	1	10	22	28	167
Days Minimum Temp. ≤ 0°F	0	0	0	0	0	0	0	0	0	0	0	0	0
Heating Degree Days (base 65°F)	1,011	853	793	610	374	173	46	52	176	465	775	1,008	6,336
Cooling Degree Days (base 65°F)	0	0	0	0	3	23	101	71	16	0	0	0	214
Mean Precipitation (in.)	6.09	6.64	5.18	2.62	1.61	0.75	0.16	0.19	0.71	2.10	4.53	6.49	37.07
Extreme Maximum Daily Precip. (in.)	4.10	3.22	3.41	2.49	2.15	1.18	0.60	1.07	1.97	2.74	3.42	3.79	4.10
Days With ≥ 0.1" Precipitation	9	9	8	5	4	2	0	1	1	3	7	9	58
Days With ≥ 0.5" Precipitation	4	4	4	2	1	1	0	0	1	2	3	4	26
Days With ≥ 1.0" Precipitation	2	2	2	1	0	0	0	0	0	1	1	2	11
Mean Snowfall (in.)	25.8	24.5	16.7	7.0	0.3	0.0	0.0	0.0	0.1	0.9	8.0	22.7	106.0
Maximum Snow Depth (in.)	115	101	95	50	4	0	0	0	2	4	31	72	115
Days With ≥ 1.0" Snow Depth	26	25	19	5	0	0	0	0	0	0	5	21	101

Cedarville *Modoc County* Elevation: 4,669 ft. Latitude: 41° 32' N Longitude: 120° 10' W

	JAN	FEB	MAR	APR	MAY	JUN	JUL	AUG	SEP	OCT	NOV	DEC	YEAR
Mean Maximum Temp. (°F)	40.7	44.4	51.1	57.4	66.7	76.5	86.9	86.0	77.5	64.9	48.8	40.1	61.7
Mean Temp. (°F)	30.9	34.2	39.9	45.4	53.7	62.0	70.7	69.1	60.5	49.4	37.5	30.3	48.6
Mean Minimum Temp. (°F)	21.0	24.0	28.8	33.4	40.6	47.4	54.5	52.1	43.3	33.9	26.3	20.4	35.5
Extreme Maximum Temp. (°F)	60	69	78	82	93	99	107	102	98	90	75	63	107
Extreme Minimum Temp. (°F)	-6	-17	-1	14	23	29	36	33	24	11	-5	-28	-28
Days Maximum Temp. ≥ 90°F	0	0	0	0	0	3	13	10	3	0	0	0	29
Days Maximum Temp. ≤ 32°F	5	2	0	0	0	0	0	0	0	0	1	5	13
Days Minimum Temp. ≤ 32°F	28	24	22	13	4	0	0	0	2	13	23	28	157
Days Minimum Temp. ≤ 0°F	0	0	0	0	0	0	0	0	0	0	0	1	1
Heating Degree Days (base 65°F)	1,051	864	770	580	356	143	23	26	167	477	817	1,070	6,344
Cooling Degree Days (base 65°F)	0	0	0	0	12	59	207	159	37	1	0	0	475
Mean Precipitation (in.)	1.61	1.28	1.39	1.24	1.21	0.67	0.20	0.26	0.44	0.79	1.75	1.66	12.50
Extreme Maximum Daily Precip. (in.)	2.38	1.92	1.34	1.00	1.22	1.86	0.76	0.85	1.37	1.31	1.48	1.21	2.38
Days With ≥ 0.1" Precipitation	4	4	4	4	4	2	1	1	1	3	5	5	38
Days With ≥ 0.5" Precipitation	1	0	0	0	0	0	0	0	0	0	1	1	3
Days With ≥ 1.0" Precipitation	0	0	0	0	0	0	0	0	0	0	0	0	0
Mean Snowfall (in.)	3.4	2.4	1.1	0.7	trace	trace	0.0	0.0	trace	0.1	1.8	3.7	13.2
Maximum Snow Depth (in.)	14	10	5	3	1	1	0	0	trace	3	10	17	17
Days With ≥ 1.0" Snow Depth	7	2	1	1	0	0	0	0	0	0	1	3	15

The period of record for all cooperative weather station data is 1980 – 2009. See User Guide for detailed explanation of data.

Chula Vista *San Diego County* Elevation: 56 ft. Latitude: 32° 38' N Longitude: 117° 05' W

	JAN	FEB	MAR	APR	MAY	JUN	JUL	AUG	SEP	OCT	NOV	DEC	YEAR
Mean Maximum Temp. (°F)	68.3	67.9	67.9	69.5	70.0	71.9	75.6	77.8	78.0	75.6	71.1	67.6	71.8
Mean Temp. (°F)	57.2	57.8	59.0	61.2	63.9	66.3	69.9	71.7	70.9	66.6	60.5	56.4	63.4
Mean Minimum Temp. (°F)	46.0	47.7	50.2	52.9	57.6	60.6	64.2	65.5	63.6	58.0	49.8	45.3	55.1
Extreme Maximum Temp. (°F)	90	90	95	102	95	97	100	96	108	106	96	84	108
Extreme Minimum Temp. (°F)	30	29	32	15	44	49	54	42	43	44	35	28	15
Days Maximum Temp. ≥ 90°F	0	0	0	0	0	0	0	0	1	1	0	0	2
Days Maximum Temp. ≤ 32°F	0	0	0	0	0	0	0	0	0	0	0	0	0
Days Minimum Temp. ≤ 32°F	0	0	0	0	0	0	0	0	0	0	0	0	0
Days Minimum Temp. ≤ 0°F	0	0	0	0	0	0	0	0	0	0	0	0	0
Heating Degree Days (base 65°F)	240	201	184	122	55	14	0	0	1	21	138	259	1,235
Cooling Degree Days (base 65°F)	3	4	5	15	26	59	161	215	185	79	10	0	762
Mean Precipitation (in.)	1.90	2.29	1.78	0.66	0.09	0.06	0.03	0.01	0.14	0.44	0.99	1.22	9.61
Extreme Maximum Daily Precip. (in.)	2.14	2.42	1.79	0.77	1.45	0.40	0.43	0.15	1.20	1.10	2.15	1.74	2.42
Days With ≥ 0.1" Precipitation	4	4	3	2	0	0	0	0	0	1	2	3	19
Days With ≥ 0.5" Precipitation	1	2	1	0	0	0	0	0	0	0	1	1	6
Days With ≥ 1.0" Precipitation	0	0	0	0	0	0	0	0	0	0	0	0	0
Mean Snowfall (in.)	trace	0.0	0.0	0.0	0.0	0.0	0.0	0.0	trace	0.0	0.0	0.2	0.2
Maximum Snow Depth (in.)	trace	0	0	0	0	0	0	0	trace	0	0	0	trace
Days With ≥ 1.0" Snow Depth	0	0	0	0	0	0	0	0	0	0	0	0	0

Coalinga *Fresno County* Elevation: 669 ft. Latitude: 36° 08' N Longitude: 120° 22' W

	JAN	FEB	MAR	APR	MAY	JUN	JUL	AUG	SEP	OCT	NOV	DEC	YEAR
Mean Maximum Temp. (°F)	58.9	65.2	71.4	78.1	87.3	94.4	100.2	98.8	93.4	82.9	68.5	59.5	79.9
Mean Temp. (°F)	48.2	52.9	57.6	62.5	70.7	77.5	83.5	81.8	76.6	66.8	55.1	47.9	65.1
Mean Minimum Temp. (°F)	37.4	40.5	43.7	47.0	54.1	60.5	66.8	64.7	59.8	50.6	41.7	36.2	50.2
Extreme Maximum Temp. (°F)	77	87	92	101	110	111	115	113	110	103	90	79	115
Extreme Minimum Temp. (°F)	17	21	29	31	38	41	44	51	44	30	26	11	11
Days Maximum Temp. ≥ 90°F	0	0	0	4	13	22	30	29	21	7	0	0	126
Days Maximum Temp. ≤ 32°F	0	0	0	0	0	0	0	0	0	0	0	0	0
Days Minimum Temp. ≤ 32°F	9	3	0	0	0	0	0	0	0	0	3	10	25
Days Minimum Temp. ≤ 0°F	0	0	0	0	0	0	0	0	0	0	0	0	0
Heating Degree Days (base 65°F)	515	337	232	122	26	2	0	0	3	53	293	524	2,107
Cooling Degree Days (base 65°F)	0	0	8	55	208	382	581	528	357	115	2	0	2,236
Mean Precipitation (in.)	1.91	1.74	1.48	0.47	0.26	0.07	0.01	0.03	0.18	0.39	0.52	1.07	8.13
Extreme Maximum Daily Precip. (in.)	2.59	1.99	3.74	1.09	1.55	0.70	0.08	0.25	0.98	1.19	1.15	1.39	3.74
Days With ≥ 0.1" Precipitation	4	4	3	1	1	0	0	0	0	1	2	3	19
Days With ≥ 0.5" Precipitation	1	1	1	0	0	0	0	0	0	0	0	1	4
Days With ≥ 1.0" Precipitation	0	0	0	0	0	0	0	0	0	0	0	0	0
Mean Snowfall (in.)	0.0	trace	0.0	0.0	0.0	0.0	0.0	0.0	0.0	0.0	0.0	0.0	trace
Maximum Snow Depth (in.)	0	trace	0	0	0	0	0	0	0	0	0	0	trace
Days With ≥ 1.0" Snow Depth	0	0	0	0	0	0	0	0	0	0	0	0	0

Colfax *Placer County* Elevation: 2,399 ft. Latitude: 39° 07' N Longitude: 120° 57' W

	JAN	FEB	MAR	APR	MAY	JUN	JUL	AUG	SEP	OCT	NOV	DEC	YEAR
Mean Maximum Temp. (°F)	54.7	56.8	60.4	66.0	74.7	83.0	90.9	90.2	84.7	74.1	60.0	53.6	70.8
Mean Temp. (°F)	44.9	46.7	49.5	54.0	61.6	69.0	75.9	74.8	69.7	60.6	49.7	44.2	58.4
Mean Minimum Temp. (°F)	35.1	36.4	38.4	41.9	48.4	54.9	60.8	59.4	54.6	47.0	39.2	34.8	45.9
Extreme Maximum Temp. (°F)	77	80	83	89	100	102	107	105	103	100	84	79	107
Extreme Minimum Temp. (°F)	18	15	24	22	30	38	44	44	36	31	22	14	14
Days Maximum Temp. ≥ 90°F	0	0	0	0	2	7	19	17	10	2	0	0	57
Days Maximum Temp. ≤ 32°F	0	0	0	0	0	0	0	0	0	0	0	0	0
Days Minimum Temp. ≤ 32°F	11	8	6	2	0	0	0	0	0	0	4	11	42
Days Minimum Temp. ≤ 0°F	0	0	0	0	0	0	0	0	0	0	0	0	0
Heating Degree Days (base 65°F)	616	512	475	331	158	42	3	1	34	170	453	637	3,432
Cooling Degree Days (base 65°F)	0	0	1	6	59	168	346	312	181	41	0	0	1,114
Mean Precipitation (in.)	7.98	8.45	6.93	3.22	1.72	0.62	0.05	0.14	0.82	2.38	6.02	8.25	46.58
Extreme Maximum Daily Precip. (in.)	4.18	5.90	3.80	2.88	2.00	1.86	0.82	0.93	2.06	2.61	3.99	4.20	5.90
Days With ≥ 0.1" Precipitation	9	9	9	5	3	1	0	0	1	3	7	9	56
Days With ≥ 0.5" Precipitation	5	5	5	2	1	0	0	0	0	2	4	5	29
Days With ≥ 1.0" Precipitation	3	3	2	1	0	0	0	0	0	1	2	3	15
Mean Snowfall (in.)	1.7	3.2	1.9	0.5	0.0	0.0	0.0	0.0	0.0	0.0	0.3	1.9	9.5
Maximum Snow Depth (in.)	0	16	1	trace	0	0	0	0	0	1	trace	5	16
Days With ≥ 1.0" Snow Depth	0	0	0	0	0	0	0	0	0	0	0	0	0

Colusa 2 SSW *Colusa County* Elevation: 49 ft. Latitude: 39° 12' N Longitude: 122° 01' W

	JAN	FEB	MAR	APR	MAY	JUN	JUL	AUG	SEP	OCT	NOV	DEC	YEAR
Mean Maximum Temp. (°F)	54.4	60.4	66.5	73.6	81.8	88.8	93.7	92.5	89.0	79.4	64.0	54.4	74.9
Mean Temp. (°F)	46.4	50.9	55.3	59.9	67.6	73.3	76.7	75.0	71.5	63.8	52.9	46.1	61.6
Mean Minimum Temp. (°F)	38.3	41.5	44.1	46.1	53.5	57.8	59.6	57.5	53.9	48.1	41.8	37.6	48.3
Extreme Maximum Temp. (°F)	75	78	88	98	106	108	111	111	108	105	85	72	111
Extreme Minimum Temp. (°F)	21	21	27	30	36	38	40	43	35	34	24	18	18
Days Maximum Temp. ≥ 90°F	0	0	0	1	7	14	23	21	15	4	0	0	85
Days Maximum Temp. ≤ 32°F	0	0	0	0	0	0	0	0	0	0	0	0	0
Days Minimum Temp. ≤ 32°F	6	2	0	0	0	0	0	0	0	0	2	7	17
Days Minimum Temp. ≤ 0°F	0	0	0	0	0	0	0	0	0	0	0	0	0
Heating Degree Days (base 65°F)	570	391	297	171	47	6	0	0	10	89	357	580	2,518
Cooling Degree Days (base 65°F)	0	0	3	24	136	263	369	317	211	59	1	0	1,383
Mean Precipitation (in.)	3.54	3.20	2.53	0.90	0.73	0.23	0.01	0.06	0.29	0.90	2.14	2.90	17.43
Extreme Maximum Daily Precip. (in.)	3.03	3.56	2.80	1.05	1.38	0.66	0.16	0.56	2.17	1.40	1.92	2.05	3.56
Days With ≥ 0.1" Precipitation	7	6	6	3	2	1	0	0	1	2	5	6	39
Days With ≥ 0.5" Precipitation	3	2	2	0	1	0	0	0	0	1	1	2	12
Days With ≥ 1.0" Precipitation	1	1	0	0	0	0	0	0	0	0	0	1	3
Mean Snowfall (in.)	0.0	0.0	0.0	0.0	0.0	0.0	0.0	0.0	0.0	0.0	0.0	trace	trace
Maximum Snow Depth (in.)	0	0	0	0	0	0	0	0	0	0	0	4	4
Days With ≥ 1.0" Snow Depth	0	0	0	0	0	0	0	0	0	0	0	0	0

The period of record for all cooperative weather station data is 1980 – 2009. See User Guide for detailed explanation of data.

Covelo *Mendocino County* Elevation: 1,410 ft. Latitude: 39° 49' N Longitude: 123° 15' W

	JAN	FEB	MAR	APR	MAY	JUN	JUL	AUG	SEP	OCT	NOV	DEC	YEAR
Mean Maximum Temp. (°F)	53.5	58.0	63.1	68.5	76.6	84.7	93.3	92.8	88.0	76.2	59.5	52.0	72.2
Mean Temp. (°F)	42.8	45.9	49.6	53.4	59.7	66.2	72.8	71.5	66.7	57.7	47.4	41.8	56.3
Mean Minimum Temp. (°F)	31.9	33.8	35.9	38.3	42.8	47.7	52.2	50.1	45.4	39.1	35.2	31.5	40.3
Extreme Maximum Temp. (°F)	78	82	88	94	104	106	110	115	107	104	82	70	115
Extreme Minimum Temp. (°F)	13	13	22	23	28	31	37	38	32	22	15	9	9
Days Maximum Temp. ≥ 90°F	0	0	0	0	3	9	22	22	14	3	0	0	73
Days Maximum Temp. ≤ 32°F	0	0	0	0	0	0	0	0	0	0	0	0	0
Days Minimum Temp. ≤ 32°F	17	13	10	5	1	0	0	0	0	4	12	17	79
Days Minimum Temp. ≤ 0°F	0	0	0	0	0	0	0	0	0	0	0	0	0
Heating Degree Days (base 65°F)	683	533	472	342	183	52	6	3	43	231	522	713	3,783
Cooling Degree Days (base 65°F)	0	0	0	2	26	96	253	211	102	12	0	0	702
Mean Precipitation (in.)	7.70	7.18	5.47	2.78	1.66	0.48	0.04	0.17	0.44	2.10	5.57	8.45	42.04
Extreme Maximum Daily Precip. (in.)	4.04	3.75	2.76	1.93	2.09	0.87	0.45	0.92	1.02	1.95	2.95	***5.70***	***5.70***
Days With ≥ 0.1" Precipitation	10	10	8	5	4	1	0	0	1	4	8	10	61
Days With ≥ 0.5" Precipitation	6	5	4	2	1	0	0	0	0	2	4	5	29
Days With ≥ 1.0" Precipitation	2	3	2	1	0	0	0	0	0	1	2	3	14
Mean Snowfall (in.)	0.6	0.5	0.1	0.1	0.0	0.0	0.0	0.0	0.0	0.0	0.1	0.4	1.8
Maximum Snow Depth (in.)	trace	0	1	trace	0	0	0	0	0	0	0	***0***	***1***
Days With ≥ 1.0" Snow Depth	0	0	0	0	0	0	0	0	0	0	0	0	0

Crescent City 3 NNW *Del Norte County* Elevation: 40 ft. Latitude: 41° 48' N Longitude: 124° 13' W

	JAN	FEB	MAR	APR	MAY	JUN	JUL	AUG	SEP	OCT	NOV	DEC	YEAR
Mean Maximum Temp. (°F)	55.0	56.0	56.6	58.3	60.9	63.3	65.7	66.0	65.7	62.8	57.3	54.5	60.2
Mean Temp. (°F)	47.9	48.7	49.4	50.9	53.7	56.2	58.6	59.0	57.5	54.7	50.3	47.3	52.9
Mean Minimum Temp. (°F)	40.8	41.4	42.2	43.6	46.4	49.0	51.5	51.8	49.3	46.5	43.4	40.1	45.5
Extreme Maximum Temp. (°F)	75	78	76	84	90	87	88	84	92	93	76	80	93
Extreme Minimum Temp. (°F)	24	24	28	30	34	37	40	40	37	29	27	19	19
Days Maximum Temp. ≥ 90°F	0	0	0	0	0	0	0	0	0	0	0	0	0
Days Maximum Temp. ≤ 32°F	0	0	0	0	0	0	0	0	0	0	0	0	0
Days Minimum Temp. ≤ 32°F	3	2	1	0	0	0	0	0	0	0	1	4	11
Days Minimum Temp. ≤ 0°F	0	0	0	0	0	0	0	0	0	0	0	0	0
Heating Degree Days (base 65°F)	524	454	476	415	344	259	193	181	220	316	433	541	4,356
Cooling Degree Days (base 65°F)	0	0	0	0	1	0	1	1	2	3	0	0	8
Mean Precipitation (in.)	10.25	8.73	8.88	5.65	3.29	1.71	0.37	0.56	1.05	4.37	9.67	13.23	67.76
Extreme Maximum Daily Precip. (in.)	***7.73***	***5.40***	na	na	na	***1.47***	***2.11***	2.00	***1.89***	na	na	na	na
Days With ≥ 0.1" Precipitation	11	10	11	8	5	3	1	1	2	5	10	12	79
Days With ≥ 0.5" Precipitation	6	5	5	3	2	1	0	0	1	3	6	7	39
Days With ≥ 1.0" Precipitation	3	3	2	1	1	0	0	0	0	1	3	4	18
Mean Snowfall (in.)	0.0	0.0	0.0	trace	0.0	0.0	0.0	0.0	0.0	0.0	0.0	0.0	trace
Maximum Snow Depth (in.)	0	0	0	0	0	0	0	0	0	0	0	0	0
Days With ≥ 1.0" Snow Depth	0	0	0	0	0	0	0	0	0	0	0	0	0

Culver City *Los Angeles County* Elevation: 55 ft. Latitude: 34° 01' N Longitude: 118° 24' W

	JAN	FEB	MAR	APR	MAY	JUN	JUL	AUG	SEP	OCT	NOV	DEC	YEAR
Mean Maximum Temp. (°F)	66.4	67.3	***68.7***	72.1	73.3	76.2	79.6	80.4	***79.4***	***75.9***	70.1	65.9	***72.9***
Mean Temp. (°F)	57.1	57.9	***59.6***	62.6	64.9	68.0	71.2	71.8	***70.7***	***66.6***	60.8	56.6	***64.0***
Mean Minimum Temp. (°F)	47.7	48.4	***50.4***	53.1	56.5	59.9	62.7	63.1	***62.0***	***57.3***	51.5	47.3	***55.0***
Extreme Maximum Temp. (°F)	87	90	***91***	105	97	107	102	103	110	104	96	90	***110***
Extreme Minimum Temp. (°F)	34	33	34	32	46	46	50	46	51	42	40	33	32
Days Maximum Temp. ≥ 90°F	0	0	0	1	0	1	1	1	2	1	0	0	7
Days Maximum Temp. ≤ 32°F	0	0	0	0	0	0	0	0	0	0	0	0	0
Days Minimum Temp. ≤ 32°F	0	0	0	0	0	0	0	0	0	0	0	0	0
Days Minimum Temp. ≤ 0°F	0	0	0	0	0	0	0	0	0	0	0	0	0
Heating Degree Days (base 65°F)	245	201	***170***	100	38	6	0	0	***1***	***26***	133	255	***1,175***
Cooling Degree Days (base 65°F)	4	6	***8***	35	43	103	199	217	***179***	***82***	14	1	***891***
Mean Precipitation (in.)	3.09	3.70	2.43	0.64	0.19	0.03	0.02	0.01	0.09	0.58	0.97	1.91	13.66
Extreme Maximum Daily Precip. (in.)	***3.19***	***4.04***	***4.10***	***1.98***	***1.06***	***0.34***	0.10	0.22	***0.61***	na	1.90	***2.60***	na
Days With ≥ 0.1" Precipitation	***5***	4	3	1	0	0	0	0	0	1	1	3	***18***
Days With ≥ 0.5" Precipitation	***2***	2	2	0	0	0	0	0	0	0	1	1	***8***
Days With ≥ 1.0" Precipitation	***1***	1	1	0	0	0	0	0	0	0	0	1	***4***
Mean Snowfall (in.)	trace	0.0	0.0	0.0	0.0	0.0	0.0	0.0	0.0	0.0	0.0	0.0	trace
Maximum Snow Depth (in.)	0	0	***0***	0	0	0	0	0	0	0	0	0	***0***
Days With ≥ 1.0" Snow Depth	0	0	0	0	0	0	0	0	0	0	0	0	0

Cuyamaca *San Diego County* Elevation: 4,640 ft. Latitude: 32° 59' N Longitude: 116° 35' W

	JAN	FEB	MAR	APR	MAY	JUN	JUL	AUG	SEP	OCT	NOV	DEC	YEAR
Mean Maximum Temp. (°F)	51.8	52.7	56.4	61.1	68.6	77.1	84.5	85.0	79.9	69.6	59.5	52.2	66.6
Mean Temp. (°F)	41.3	42.0	45.2	49.0	55.4	62.8	70.1	70.0	64.3	54.7	46.7	40.7	53.5
Mean Minimum Temp. (°F)	30.7	31.3	33.9	36.9	42.1	48.4	55.6	55.0	48.6	39.6	33.8	29.2	40.4
Extreme Maximum Temp. (°F)	74	74	80	86	92	98	103	99	99	91	80	75	103
Extreme Minimum Temp. (°F)	9	4	10	20	22	29	36	37	25	21	14	5	4
Days Maximum Temp. ≥ 90°F	0	0	0	0	0	1	6	7	2	0	0	0	16
Days Maximum Temp. ≤ 32°F	0	0	0	0	0	0	0	0	0	0	0	0	0
Days Minimum Temp. ≤ 32°F	20	17	13	7	1	0	0	0	0	4	13	21	96
Days Minimum Temp. ≤ 0°F	0	0	0	0	0	0	0	0	0	0	0	0	0
Heating Degree Days (base 65°F)	728	643	608	474	301	115	16	16	85	318	542	745	4,591
Cooling Degree Days (base 65°F)	0	0	0	0	8	55	180	179	71	5	0	0	498
Mean Precipitation (in.)	5.99	6.64	5.78	2.46	0.82	0.21	0.41	0.85	0.74	1.10	3.06	4.58	32.64
Extreme Maximum Daily Precip. (in.)	6.32	5.35	7.37	2.62	1.98	1.56	1.10	2.20	2.69	1.54	4.84	5.63	7.37
Days With ≥ 0.1" Precipitation	6	6	6	4	2	0	1	2	1	2	4	5	39
Days With ≥ 0.5" Precipitation	3	4	4	2	1	0	0	1	0	1	2	3	21
Days With ≥ 1.0" Precipitation	2	2	2	1	0	0	0	0	0	0	1	1	9
Mean Snowfall (in.)	4.6	6.6	6.5	2.8	0.1	0.0	0.0	0.0	0.0	trace	0.9	2.3	23.8
Maximum Snow Depth (in.)	13	28	24	12	0	0	0	0	0	trace	1	16	28
Days With ≥ 1.0" Snow Depth	2	1	2	0	0	0	0	0	0	0	0	1	6

The period of record for all cooperative weather station data is 1980 – 2009. See User Guide for detailed explanation of data.

De Sabla *Butte County* Elevation: 2,709 ft. Latitude: 39° 52' N Longitude: 121° 37' W

	JAN	FEB	MAR	APR	MAY	JUN	JUL	AUG	SEP	OCT	NOV	DEC	YEAR
Mean Maximum Temp. (°F)	52.6	55.1	59.6	65.4	73.9	82.6	90.4	89.9	84.2	73.2	58.3	51.3	69.7
Mean Temp. (°F)	42.6	44.4	47.7	52.2	59.5	66.7	72.9	72.1	67.1	58.4	47.3	41.8	56.1
Mean Minimum Temp. (°F)	32.5	33.7	35.7	38.9	44.9	50.7	55.4	54.3	49.9	43.7	36.2	32.4	42.4
Extreme Maximum Temp. (°F)	73	77	83	90	97	103	107	108	105	99	80	74	108
Extreme Minimum Temp. (°F)	12	11	20	22	27	31	39	38	30	19	15	6	6
Days Maximum Temp. ≥ 90°F	0	0	0	0	2	7	19	18	10	2	0	0	58
Days Maximum Temp. ≤ 32°F	0	0	0	0	0	0	0	0	0	0	0	0	0
Days Minimum Temp. ≤ 32°F	16	12	10	5	1	0	0	0	0	2	9	16	71
Days Minimum Temp. ≤ 0°F	0	0	0	0	0	0	0	0	0	0	0	0	0
Heating Degree Days (base 65°F)	689	576	530	382	200	63	7	5	57	224	526	711	3,970
Cooling Degree Days (base 65°F)	0	0	0	4	34	119	260	234	128	27	0	0	806
Mean Precipitation (in.)	11.56	12.06	9.42	4.89	2.88	0.94	0.05	0.15	1.14	3.52	7.65	13.61	67.87
Extreme Maximum Daily Precip. (in.)	8.37	7.72	5.99	3.60	2.93	1.76	0.62	1.22	***2.61***	3.36	4.92	7.85	***8.37***
Days With ≥ 0.1" Precipitation	11	10	10	7	4	2	0	0	2	4	8	10	68
Days With ≥ 0.5" Precipitation	6	7	6	3	2	1	0	0	1	2	5	7	40
Days With ≥ 1.0" Precipitation	4	4	4	2	1	0	0	0	0	1	3	5	24
Mean Snowfall (in.)	1.9	0.1	2.2	0.3	0.0	0.0	0.0	0.0	0.0	0.0	0.0	0.2	4.7
Maximum Snow Depth (in.)	30	0	15	13	0	0	0	0	0	0	1	7	30
Days With ≥ 1.0" Snow Depth	1	0	0	0	0	0	0	0	0	0	0	0	1

Death Valley *Inyo County* Elevation: -193 ft. Latitude: 36° 28' N Longitude: 116° 52' W

	JAN	FEB	MAR	APR	MAY	JUN	JUL	AUG	SEP	OCT	NOV	DEC	YEAR
Mean Maximum Temp. (°F)	66.9	73.4	81.7	90.5	100.5	109.8	116.4	114.7	106.5	92.8	77.1	65.4	91.3
Mean Temp. (°F)	53.0	59.5	67.7	76.0	86.2	95.1	101.8	99.8	90.7	76.7	62.2	51.5	76.7
Mean Minimum Temp. (°F)	39.1	45.5	53.7	61.4	71.9	80.3	87.1	84.9	74.9	60.6	47.3	37.5	62.0
Extreme Maximum Temp. (°F)	84	97	102	112	122	128	129	127	123	113	98	88	129
Extreme Minimum Temp. (°F)	0	26	26	23	46	54	67	66	55	37	30	22	0
Days Maximum Temp. ≥ 90°F	0	1	6	17	27	30	31	31	29	21	1	0	194
Days Maximum Temp. ≤ 32°F	0	0	0	0	0	0	0	0	0	0	0	0	0
Days Minimum Temp. ≤ 32°F	3	1	0	0	0	0	0	0	0	0	0	6	10
Days Minimum Temp. ≤ 0°F	0	0	0	0	0	0	0	0	0	0	0	0	0
Heating Degree Days (base 65°F)	365	169	45	8	1	0	0	0	0	5	128	412	1,133
Cooling Degree Days (base 65°F)	1	19	136	344	665	909	1,146	1,086	778	375	51	2	5,512
Mean Precipitation (in.)	0.36	0.47	0.33	0.13	0.05	0.03	0.09	0.13	0.21	0.07	0.17	0.17	2.21
Extreme Maximum Daily Precip. (in.)	0.99	0.99	0.96	1.47	0.30	0.40	0.28	0.66	1.11	0.40	0.80	0.55	1.47
Days With ≥ 0.1" Precipitation	1	1	1	0	0	0	0	0	1	0	0	1	5
Days With ≥ 0.5" Precipitation	0	0	0	0	0	0	0	0	0	0	0	0	0
Days With ≥ 1.0" Precipitation	0	0	0	0	0	0	0	0	0	0	0	0	0
Mean Snowfall (in.)	0.0	0.0	0.0	0.0	0.0	0.0	0.0	0.0	0.0	0.0	0.0	0.0	0.0
Maximum Snow Depth (in.)	0	0	0	0	0	0	0	0	0	0	0	0	0
Days With ≥ 1.0" Snow Depth	0	0	0	0	0	0	0	0	0	0	0	0	0

Donner Memorial St Pk *Nevada County* Elevation: 5,937 ft. Latitude: 39° 19' N Longitude: 120° 14' W

	JAN	FEB	MAR	APR	MAY	JUN	JUL	AUG	SEP	OCT	NOV	DEC	YEAR
Mean Maximum Temp. (°F)	40.5	42.7	47.6	54.1	63.7	72.5	81.2	81.0	73.9	62.7	48.7	39.4	59.0
Mean Temp. (°F)	28.1	29.8	34.6	40.1	48.0	54.9	61.6	61.1	54.8	45.6	35.7	27.7	43.5
Mean Minimum Temp. (°F)	15.6	16.8	21.5	26.1	32.3	37.3	42.0	41.3	35.6	28.6	22.7	16.0	28.0
Extreme Maximum Temp. (°F)	60	65	72	79	88	95	99	99	92	90	74	61	99
Extreme Minimum Temp. (°F)	-13	-27	-2	5	14	22	27	28	24	12	-3	-16	-27
Days Maximum Temp. ≥ 90°F	0	0	0	0	0	0	3	2	0	0	0	0	5
Days Maximum Temp. ≤ 32°F	5	3	2	0	0	0	0	0	0	0	2	6	18
Days Minimum Temp. ≤ 32°F	31	27	30	26	17	6	1	1	9	25	28	30	231
Days Minimum Temp. ≤ 0°F	1	1	0	0	0	0	0	0	0	0	0	2	4
Heating Degree Days (base 65°F)	1,137	989	941	734	522	300	125	130	301	593	871	1,148	7,791
Cooling Degree Days (base 65°F)	0	0	0	0	0	4	26	17	1	0	0	0	48
Mean Precipitation (in.)	6.82	6.53	5.61	2.51	1.74	0.74	0.33	0.42	0.95	2.02	4.99	6.69	39.35
Extreme Maximum Daily Precip. (in.)	4.04	4.36	4.56	2.29	2.40	0.77	1.50	1.31	1.55	3.50	3.31	6.00	6.00
Days With ≥ 0.1" Precipitation	9	8	8	5	4	2	1	1	2	3	7	8	58
Days With ≥ 0.5" Precipitation	4	4	4	2	1	0	0	0	1	1	3	4	24
Days With ≥ 1.0" Precipitation	2	2	2	0	0	0	0	0	0	0	2	2	10
Mean Snowfall (in.)	39.6	40.9	33.5	15.5	2.9	0.5	0.0	0.0	0.2	2.6	14.3	35.4	185.4
Maximum Snow Depth (in.)	68	94	76	74	46	4	0	0	2	12	32	62	94
Days With ≥ 1.0" Snow Depth	30	27	28	13	3	0	0	0	0	1	8	24	134

Doyle 4 SSE *Lassen County* Elevation: 4,390 ft. Latitude: 39° 58' N Longitude: 120° 05' W

	JAN	FEB	MAR	APR	MAY	JUN	JUL	AUG	SEP	OCT	NOV	DEC	YEAR
Mean Maximum Temp. (°F)	42.9	48.2	55.7	62.2	71.1	79.6	88.2	87.3	79.2	67.4	52.0	42.1	64.7
Mean Temp. (°F)	33.4	37.5	43.3	48.1	55.3	62.3	69.1	67.8	60.9	51.1	40.0	32.7	50.1
Mean Minimum Temp. (°F)	23.8	26.8	30.8	34.0	39.5	44.9	49.8	48.3	42.5	34.8	27.9	23.1	35.5
Extreme Maximum Temp. (°F)	70	70	80	85	95	101	104	104	98	89	75	66	104
Extreme Minimum Temp. (°F)	-4	-17	7	14	22	27	30	28	25	12	-2	-25	-25
Days Maximum Temp. ≥ 90°F	0	0	0	0	1	3	15	12	3	0	0	0	34
Days Maximum Temp. ≤ 32°F	3	1	0	0	0	0	0	0	0	0	1	4	9
Days Minimum Temp. ≤ 32°F	26	21	19	13	5	1	0	0	2	12	21	26	146
Days Minimum Temp. ≤ 0°F	0	0	0	0	0	0	0	0	0	0	0	1	1
Heating Degree Days (base 65°F)	973	770	665	501	302	119	21	24	146	423	743	995	5,682
Cooling Degree Days (base 65°F)	0	0	0	0	9	44	154	119	29	0	0	0	355
Mean Precipitation (in.)	2.15	2.32	1.87	0.90	0.97	0.66	0.36	0.30	0.65	0.97	2.34	2.43	15.92
Extreme Maximum Daily Precip. (in.)	3.58	4.48	4.13	1.44	1.30	1.73	2.15	0.95	1.05	2.38	3.63	4.06	4.48
Days With ≥ 0.1" Precipitation	4	3	3	3	3	2	1	1	2	2	4	4	32
Days With ≥ 0.5" Precipitation	1	1	1	0	0	0	0	0	0	1	1	1	6
Days With ≥ 1.0" Precipitation	1	1	0	0	0	0	0	0	0	0	1	1	4
Mean Snowfall (in.)	7.3	4.0	3.9	1.5	0.1	trace	0.0	0.0	0.2	0.2	2.5	6.8	26.5
Maximum Snow Depth (in.)	20	12	6	6	trace	trace	0	0	4	trace	12	22	22
Days With ≥ 1.0" Snow Depth	9	4	1	0	0	0	0	0	0	0	2	6	22

The period of record for all cooperative weather station data is 1980 – 2009. See User Guide for detailed explanation of data.

Dunsmuir Treatment Plant *Siskiyou County* Elevation: 2,169 ft. Latitude: 41° 11' N Longitude: 122° 16' W

	JAN	FEB	MAR	APR	MAY	JUN	JUL	AUG	SEP	OCT	NOV	DEC	YEAR
Mean Maximum Temp. (°F)	49.8	53.7	58.8	65.6	74.2	81.9	90.0	89.6	83.9	72.5	56.8	49.5	68.9
Mean Temp. (°F)	40.0	42.4	46.2	51.5	59.2	66.1	71.9	70.4	65.0	56.0	45.3	39.9	54.5
Mean Minimum Temp. (°F)	30.1	31.1	33.5	37.4	44.1	50.2	53.7	51.2	46.2	39.5	33.7	30.2	40.1
Extreme Maximum Temp. (°F)	70	78	83	92	99	102	108	109	106	99	82	75	109
Extreme Minimum Temp. (°F)	12	8	19	22	29	34	39	41	31	25	18	4	4
Days Maximum Temp. ≥ 90°F	0	0	0	0	3	7	18	17	10	1	0	0	56
Days Maximum Temp. ≤ 32°F	0	0	0	0	0	0	0	0	0	0	0	0	0
Days Minimum Temp. ≤ 32°F	23	18	14	6	0	0	0	0	0	2	14	23	100
Days Minimum Temp. ≤ 0°F	0	0	0	0	0	0	0	0	0	0	0	0	0
Heating Degree Days (base 65°F)	768	631	576	400	203	63	8	7	68	280	585	772	4,361
Cooling Degree Days (base 65°F)	0	0	0	1	31	102	230	183	76	9	0	0	632
Mean Precipitation (in.)	11.05	10.64	9.02	4.37	3.02	1.19	0.24	0.26	0.87	3.24	7.92	11.89	63.71
Extreme Maximum Daily Precip. (in.)	6.44	4.85	4.95	2.90	4.20	3.06	0.88	1.20	2.06	4.50	4.53	5.80	6.44
Days With ≥ 0.1" Precipitation	11	10	10	7	5	3	1	1	2	4	9	11	74
Days With ≥ 0.5" Precipitation	7	7	6	3	2	1	0	0	1	2	5	7	41
Days With ≥ 1.0" Precipitation	4	4	3	1	1	0	0	0	0	1	3	4	21
Mean Snowfall (in.)	8.0	7.5	4.5	0.5	0.0	0.0	0.0	0.0	0.0	trace	1.7	8.1	30.3
Maximum Snow Depth (in.)	30	20	15	5	0	0	0	0	0	trace	4	24	30
Days With ≥ 1.0" Snow Depth	10	5	2	0	0	0	0	0	0	0	1	6	24

El Mirage *San Bernardino County* Elevation: 2,950 ft. Latitude: 34° 35' N Longitude: 117° 38' W

	JAN	FEB	MAR	APR	MAY	JUN	JUL	AUG	SEP	OCT	NOV	DEC	YEAR
Mean Maximum Temp. (°F)	57.3	60.3	65.8	72.8	81.8	91.3	98.1	97.0	89.5	77.8	65.3	56.5	76.1
Mean Temp. (°F)	43.7	46.7	51.4	56.9	65.3	73.4	79.5	78.4	71.7	61.2	50.2	42.6	60.1
Mean Minimum Temp. (°F)	30.0	33.0	37.0	40.8	48.7	55.4	60.9	59.8	53.9	44.5	35.1	28.6	44.0
Extreme Maximum Temp. (°F)	75	82	88	95	104	110	112	108	103	95	84	78	112
Extreme Minimum Temp. (°F)	5	13	18	23	30	32	41	44	33	26	14	1	1
Days Maximum Temp. ≥ 90°F	0	0	0	1	7	20	29	28	17	3	0	0	105
Days Maximum Temp. ≤ 32°F	0	0	0	0	0	0	0	0	0	0	0	0	0
Days Minimum Temp. ≤ 32°F	21	13	7	3	0	0	0	0	0	1	10	22	77
Days Minimum Temp. ≤ 0°F	0	0	0	0	0	0	0	0	0	0	0	0	0
Heating Degree Days (base 65°F)	654	511	416	255	92	16	0	0	20	152	438	688	3,242
Cooling Degree Days (base 65°F)	0	0	1	17	107	273	458	423	230	41	0	0	1,550
Mean Precipitation (in.)	0.97	1.21	0.92	0.28	0.18	0.06	0.16	0.32	0.22	0.30	0.34	0.76	5.72
Extreme Maximum Daily Precip. (in.)	1.07	2.45	2.01	0.89	1.33	0.37	0.65	1.29	0.76	1.35	1.13	1.51	2.45
Days With ≥ 0.1" Precipitation	3	2	3	1	0	0	1	1	1	1	1	2	16
Days With ≥ 0.5" Precipitation	1	1	0	0	0	0	0	0	0	0	0	0	2
Days With ≥ 1.0" Precipitation	0	0	0	0	0	0	0	0	0	0	0	0	0
Mean Snowfall (in.)	0.2	0.2	0.2	trace	0.0	0.0	0.0	0.0	0.0	0.0	trace	0.7	1.3
Maximum Snow Depth (in.)	1	3	1	0	0	0	0	0	0	0	1	13	13
Days With ≥ 1.0" Snow Depth	0	0	0	0	0	0	0	0	0	0	0	0	0

Elsinore *Riverside County* Elevation: 1,285 ft. Latitude: 33° 40' N Longitude: 117° 20' W

	JAN	FEB	MAR	APR	MAY	JUN	JUL	AUG	SEP	OCT	NOV	DEC	YEAR
Mean Maximum Temp. (°F)	***66.0***	67.9	72.1	77.5	***83.8***	***90.9***	***97.8***	***98.8***	***93.4***	***83.4***	***72.4***	65.7	***80.8***
Mean Temp. (°F)	***52.6***	54.5	57.8	62.1	***68.3***	***73.7***	***79.5***	***80.7***	***76.2***	***67.6***	***57.8***	51.9	***65.2***
Mean Minimum Temp. (°F)	***39.1***	41.0	43.6	46.7	***52.7***	***56.5***	***61.1***	***62.5***	***59.0***	***51.9***	***43.1***	38.0	***49.6***
Extreme Maximum Temp. (°F)	91	92	98	103	109	112	114	115	111	106	96	88	115
Extreme Minimum Temp. (°F)	21	20	29	31	39	44	42	***51***	43	33	26	19	***19***
Days Maximum Temp. ≥ 90°F	0	0	1	4	8	16	25	***27***	19	7	1	0	***108***
Days Maximum Temp. ≤ 32°F	0	0	0	0	0	0	0	0	0	0	0	0	0
Days Minimum Temp. ≤ 32°F	4	2	1	0	0	0	0	0	0	0	1	4	12
Days Minimum Temp. ≤ 0°F	0	0	0	0	0	0	0	0	0	0	0	0	0
Heating Degree Days (base 65°F)	***378***	292	223	122	***31***	***5***	***0***	***0***	***2***	***36***	***218***	400	***1,707***
Cooling Degree Days (base 65°F)	***0***	1	8	41	***140***	***273***	***457***	***493***	***345***	***122***	***9***	1	***1,890***
Mean Precipitation (in.)	2.51	3.17	1.79	0.63	0.18	0.01	0.19	0.01	0.18	0.58	0.79	1.57	11.61
Extreme Maximum Daily Precip. (in.)	3.20	5.06	2.80	0.88	0.63	0.16	1.50	0.12	1.45	2.28	***1.63***	2.65	***5.06***
Days With ≥ 0.1" Precipitation	4	4	3	2	0	0	0	0	0	1	2	3	19
Days With ≥ 0.5" Precipitation	1	2	1	0	0	0	0	0	0	0	1	1	6
Days With ≥ 1.0" Precipitation	1	1	0	0	0	0	0	0	0	0	0	0	2
Mean Snowfall (in.)	0.0	0.0	0.0	0.0	0.0	0.0	0.0	0.0	0.0	0.0	trace	0.0	trace
Maximum Snow Depth (in.)	0	0	0	0	0	0	0	0	0	0	trace	0	trace
Days With ≥ 1.0" Snow Depth	0	0	0	0	0	0	0	0	0	0	0	0	0

Escondido No 2 *San Diego County* Elevation: 600 ft. Latitude: 33° 07' N Longitude: 117° 06' W

	JAN	FEB	MAR	APR	MAY	JUN	JUL	AUG	SEP	OCT	NOV	DEC	YEAR
Mean Maximum Temp. (°F)	***68.7***	69.1	***70.4***	***74.6***	***76.8***	82.0	87.3	***88.6***	***86.3***	***80.2***	***73.5***	69.0	***77.2***
Mean Temp. (°F)	***55.9***	56.9	***58.7***	***62.5***	***65.8***	70.0	74.8	***76.0***	***73.9***	***67.7***	***60.1***	55.4	***64.8***
Mean Minimum Temp. (°F)	***43.0***	44.6	***47.1***	***50.3***	***54.7***	58.1	62.2	***63.4***	***61.3***	***55.1***	***46.7***	41.7	***52.3***
Extreme Maximum Temp. (°F)	92	94	97	103	***103***	105	112	***109***	***108***	***105***	98	90	***112***
Extreme Minimum Temp. (°F)	25	27	32	36	***31***	41	52	***54***	***49***	***39***	30	26	***25***
Days Maximum Temp. ≥ 90°F	0	0	0	1	2	4	10	***13***	10	4	1	0	***45***
Days Maximum Temp. ≤ 32°F	0	0	0	0	0	0	0	***0***	0	0	0	0	***0***
Days Minimum Temp. ≤ 32°F	1	1	0	0	0	0	0	***0***	0	0	0	1	***3***
Days Minimum Temp. ≤ 0°F	0	0	0	0	0	0	0	***0***	0	0	0	0	***0***
Heating Degree Days (base 65°F)	***278***	226	***194***	***102***	***43***	6	0	***0***	***2***	***23***	***153***	292	***1,319***
Cooling Degree Days (base 65°F)	***2***	4	***7***	***34***	***74***	162	310	***349***	***274***	***113***	***13***	1	***1,343***
Mean Precipitation (in.)	3.15	3.54	2.74	1.11	0.24	0.13	0.09	***0.08***	0.21	0.60	1.25	1.65	***14.79***
Extreme Maximum Daily Precip. (in.)	***3.24***	***2.00***	***2.62***	***1.80***	***0.80***	0.75	0.74	***1.45***	***1.72***	***1.95***	***2.00***	***1.82***	3.24
Days With ≥ 0.1" Precipitation	5	5	4	3	1	0	0	***0***	0	1	3	4	***26***
Days With ≥ 0.5" Precipitation	2	2	2	1	0	0	0	***0***	0	0	1	1	***9***
Days With ≥ 1.0" Precipitation	1	1	1	0	0	0	0	***0***	0	0	0	0	***3***
Mean Snowfall (in.)	0.0	0.0	0.0	0.0	0.0	0.0	0.0	***0.0***	0.0	0.0	0.0	0.0	***0.0***
Maximum Snow Depth (in.)	0	0	0	0	***0***	0	0	***0***	***0***	***0***	0	0	***0***
Days With ≥ 1.0" Snow Depth	0	0	0	0	0	0	0	***0***	0	0	0	0	***0***

The period of record for all cooperative weather station data is 1980 – 2009. See User Guide for detailed explanation of data.

Fairfield *Solano County* Elevation: 40 ft. Latitude: 38° 16' N Longitude: 122° 04' W

	JAN	FEB	MAR	APR	MAY	JUN	JUL	AUG	SEP	OCT	NOV	DEC	YEAR
Mean Maximum Temp. (°F)	55.4	61.7	66.7	72.1	79.0	85.6	90.4	89.8	87.2	78.5	65.5	55.7	74.0
Mean Temp. (°F)	46.8	51.6	55.5	59.4	65.1	70.2	73.7	73.1	71.0	64.5	54.6	46.9	61.0
Mean Minimum Temp. (°F)	38.3	41.4	44.2	46.6	51.1	54.7	56.7	56.5	54.7	50.5	43.6	38.1	48.0
Extreme Maximum Temp. (°F)	74	79	87	97	111	111	114	111	109	102	87	77	114
Extreme Minimum Temp. (°F)	22	24	30	30	36	42	42	40	39	33	21	17	17
Days Maximum Temp. ≥ 90°F	0	0	0	1	5	10	16	15	12	3	0	0	62
Days Maximum Temp. ≤ 32°F	0	0	0	0	0	0	0	0	0	0	0	0	0
Days Minimum Temp. ≤ 32°F	5	1	0	0	0	0	0	0	0	0	1	6	13
Days Minimum Temp. ≤ 0°F	0	0	0	0	0	0	0	0	0	0	0	0	0
Heating Degree Days (base 65°F)	557	373	290	182	73	14	1	2	9	74	308	554	2,437
Cooling Degree Days (base 65°F)	0	0	2	20	82	176	276	260	195	66	2	0	1,079
Mean Precipitation (in.)	4.71	5.08	3.44	1.28	0.76	0.16	0.00	0.03	0.21	1.15	2.86	4.91	24.59
Extreme Maximum Daily Precip. (in.)	3.64	3.81	2.83	2.38	2.17	1.63	0.13	0.41	0.77	5.10	2.48	5.58	5.58
Days With ≥ 0.1" Precipitation	8	7	7	3	2	0	0	0	1	2	5	7	42
Days With ≥ 0.5" Precipitation	3	4	2	1	1	0	0	0	0	1	2	3	17
Days With ≥ 1.0" Precipitation	1	1	1	0	0	0	0	0	0	0	1	1	5
Mean Snowfall (in.)	0.0	0.0	0.0	0.0	0.0	0.0	0.0	0.0	0.0	0.0	0.0	0.1	0.1
Maximum Snow Depth (in.)	0	0	0	0	0	0	0	0	0	0	0	0	0
Days With ≥ 1.0" Snow Depth	0	0	0	0	0	0	0	0	0	0	0	0	0

Fairmont *Los Angeles County* Elevation: 3,060 ft. Latitude: 34° 42' N Longitude: 118° 26' W

	JAN	FEB	MAR	APR	MAY	JUN	JUL	AUG	SEP	OCT	NOV	DEC	YEAR
Mean Maximum Temp. (°F)	54.7	56.7	62.0	67.7	75.5	84.3	91.1	91.6	85.9	75.4	62.9	54.4	71.9
Mean Temp. (°F)	45.8	47.6	52.0	56.4	63.8	72.2	78.7	79.0	73.4	63.7	52.9	45.5	60.9
Mean Minimum Temp. (°F)	36.7	38.4	41.9	45.2	52.1	60.1	66.3	66.3	60.8	51.9	42.8	36.6	49.9
Extreme Maximum Temp. (°F)	75	78	87	93	100	108	111	107	105	96	84	77	111
Extreme Minimum Temp. (°F)	12	12	22	19	17	32	48	22	34	31	22	11	11
Days Maximum Temp. ≥ 90°F	0	0	0	0	3	10	19	20	12	2	0	0	66
Days Maximum Temp. ≤ 32°F	0	0	0	0	0	0	0	0	0	0	0	0	0
Days Minimum Temp. ≤ 32°F	8	5	3	1	0	0	0	0	0	0	2	8	27
Days Minimum Temp. ≤ 0°F	0	0	0	0	0	0	0	0	0	0	0	0	0
Heating Degree Days (base 65°F)	590	486	400	275	135	31	1	2	24	120	360	596	3,020
Cooling Degree Days (base 65°F)	0	0	4	24	103	253	435	443	283	86	3	0	1,634
Mean Precipitation (in.)	3.55	4.43	2.27	0.96	0.38	0.07	0.09	0.07	0.20	0.72	1.20	2.20	16.14
Extreme Maximum Daily Precip. (in.)	3.85	3.94	2.27	1.97	1.72	0.81	0.41	0.51	0.73	2.56	2.42	3.50	3.94
Days With ≥ 0.1" Precipitation	5	5	4	2	1	0	0	0	1	1	2	3	24
Days With ≥ 0.5" Precipitation	2	3	2	1	0	0	0	0	0	0	1	1	10
Days With ≥ 1.0" Precipitation	1	2	1	0	0	0	0	0	0	0	0	1	5
Mean Snowfall (in.)	trace	0.9	0.2	0.0	0.0	0.0	0.0	0.0	0.0	0.0	trace	1.9	3.0
Maximum Snow Depth (in.)	5	5	1	0	0	0	0	0	0	0	1	26	26
Days With ≥ 1.0" Snow Depth	0	0	0	0	0	0	0	0	0	0	0	0	0

Fort Bragg 5 N *Mendocino County* Elevation: 120 ft. Latitude: 39° 31' N Longitude: 123° 46' W

	JAN	FEB	MAR	APR	MAY	JUN	JUL	AUG	SEP	OCT	NOV	DEC	YEAR
Mean Maximum Temp. (°F)	54.8	56.1	57.5	59.3	61.9	64.3	66.4	66.5	66.0	63.4	58.1	54.3	60.7
Mean Temp. (°F)	47.5	48.5	49.5	51.0	53.6	56.0	57.8	58.1	57.3	54.8	50.4	47.1	52.6
Mean Minimum Temp. (°F)	40.2	40.9	41.5	42.7	45.2	47.7	49.2	49.6	48.6	46.1	42.6	39.9	44.5
Extreme Maximum Temp. (°F)	76	79	76	80	89	86	83	83	85	94	77	70	94
Extreme Minimum Temp. (°F)	26	24	29	30	35	37	38	42	38	33	29	18	18
Days Maximum Temp. ≥ 90°F	0	0	0	0	0	0	0	0	0	0	0	0	0
Days Maximum Temp. ≤ 32°F	0	0	0	0	0	0	0	0	0	0	0	0	0
Days Minimum Temp. ≤ 32°F	3	2	1	0	0	0	0	0	0	0	1	4	11
Days Minimum Temp. ≤ 0°F	0	0	0	0	0	0	0	0	0	0	0	0	0
Heating Degree Days (base 65°F)	536	461	472	412	348	264	215	209	225	313	432	547	4,434
Cooling Degree Days (base 65°F)	0	0	0	0	1	1	1	1	1	2	0	0	7
Mean Precipitation (in.)	7.07	7.06	5.94	3.10	1.73	0.58	0.10	0.22	0.45	2.34	5.27	8.30	42.16
Extreme Maximum Daily Precip. (in.)	3.84	3.06	2.93	2.21	1.78	1.74	0.33	2.05	1.16	3.78	2.55	4.36	4.36
Days With ≥ 0.1" Precipitation	11	11	10	7	4	1	0	0	1	4	9	12	70
Days With ≥ 0.5" Precipitation	5	5	4	2	1	0	0	0	0	2	4	6	29
Days With ≥ 1.0" Precipitation	2	2	2	1	0	0	0	0	0	1	1	3	12
Mean Snowfall (in.)	0.0	trace	trace	0.0	0.0	0.0	0.0	0.0	0.0	0.0	0.0	0.0	trace
Maximum Snow Depth (in.)	0	trace	trace	0	0	0	0	0	0	0	0	0	trace
Days With ≥ 1.0" Snow Depth	0	0	0	0	0	0	0	0	0	0	0	0	0

Friant Government Camp *Fresno County* Elevation: 410 ft. Latitude: 37° 00' N Longitude: 119° 43' W

	JAN	FEB	MAR	APR	MAY	JUN	JUL	AUG	SEP	OCT	NOV	DEC	YEAR
Mean Maximum Temp. (°F)	56.0	62.0	67.1	74.5	84.9	93.0	99.7	98.6	92.4	81.5	66.9	56.4	77.7
Mean Temp. (°F)	47.0	51.4	54.7	59.1	67.3	74.4	80.5	79.3	74.5	65.7	54.5	46.6	62.9
Mean Minimum Temp. (°F)	38.0	40.7	42.4	43.7	49.7	55.7	61.2	60.0	56.5	49.8	42.1	36.8	48.1
Extreme Maximum Temp. (°F)	77	79	88	99	108	109	114	114	108	102	87	79	114
Extreme Minimum Temp. (°F)	22	21	28	28	34	37	45	38	41	33	26	16	16
Days Maximum Temp. ≥ 90°F	0	0	0	2	10	21	29	29	20	6	0	0	117
Days Maximum Temp. ≤ 32°F	0	0	0	0	0	0	0	0	0	0	0	0	0
Days Minimum Temp. ≤ 32°F	6	2	1	1	0	0	0	0	0	0	2	8	20
Days Minimum Temp. ≤ 0°F	0	0	0	0	0	0	0	0	0	0	0	0	0
Heating Degree Days (base 65°F)	550	379	315	196	57	8	0	0	6	73	310	563	2,457
Cooling Degree Days (base 65°F)	0	0	3	26	137	296	487	452	297	101	3	0	1,802
Mean Precipitation (in.)	3.07	2.71	2.65	1.12	0.49	0.20	0.01	0.01	0.18	0.84	1.41	2.14	14.83
Extreme Maximum Daily Precip. (in.)	3.05	1.93	2.45	1.36	1.59	1.38	0.10	0.08	1.33	1.58	1.29	1.35	3.05
Days With ≥ 0.1" Precipitation	6	6	6	3	1	0	0	0	0	2	3	5	32
Days With ≥ 0.5" Precipitation	2	2	2	1	0	0	0	0	0	1	1	2	11
Days With ≥ 1.0" Precipitation	1	0	0	0	0	0	0	0	0	0	0	0	1
Mean Snowfall (in.)	0.0	0.0	0.0	0.0	0.0	0.0	0.0	0.0	0.0	0.0	0.0	0.0	0.0
Maximum Snow Depth (in.)	0	0	0	0	0	0	0	0	0	0	0	0	0
Days With ≥ 1.0" Snow Depth	0	0	0	0	0	0	0	0	0	0	0	0	0

The period of record for all cooperative weather station data is 1980 – 2009. See User Guide for detailed explanation of data.

Gilroy *Santa Clara County* Elevation: 193 ft. Latitude: 37° 00' N Longitude: 121° 34' W

	JAN	FEB	MAR	APR	MAY	JUN	JUL	AUG	SEP	OCT	NOV	DEC	YEAR
Mean Maximum Temp. (°F)	60.2	64.0	68.1	73.0	78.4	83.7	88.0	87.7	85.3	78.7	67.9	60.3	74.6
Mean Temp. (°F)	49.5	52.7	56.1	59.4	64.1	68.3	71.6	71.4	69.4	63.8	55.3	49.2	60.9
Mean Minimum Temp. (°F)	38.7	41.4	44.0	45.7	49.7	52.9	55.2	55.1	53.4	48.9	42.7	38.0	47.2
Extreme Maximum Temp. (°F)	79	86	90	100	106	110	112	112	104	107	94	76	112
Extreme Minimum Temp. (°F)	19	23	30	27	38	40	41	30	30	35	28	17	17
Days Maximum Temp. ≥ 90°F	0	0	0	1	3	6	11	11	9	4	0	0	45
Days Maximum Temp. ≤ 32°F	0	0	0	0	0	0	0	0	0	0	0	0	0
Days Minimum Temp. ≤ 32°F	7	3	0	0	0	0	0	0	0	0	2	7	19
Days Minimum Temp. ≤ 0°F	0	0	0	0	0	0	0	0	0	0	0	0	0
Heating Degree Days (base 65°F)	473	341	273	180	81	21	2	1	13	85	286	483	2,239
Cooling Degree Days (base 65°F)	0	0	3	19	59	127	214	208	151	56	2	0	839
Mean Precipitation (in.)	4.41	4.10	3.32	1.16	0.48	0.10	0.03	0.03	0.25	1.00	2.22	3.59	20.69
Extreme Maximum Daily Precip. (in.)	3.55	2.88	2.82	1.58	1.87	0.43	0.56	0.50	0.95	5.95	2.80	2.81	5.95
Days With ≥ 0.1" Precipitation	7	7	6	3	1	0	0	0	1	2	4	6	37
Days With ≥ 0.5" Precipitation	3	3	2	1	0	0	0	0	0	1	2	2	14
Days With ≥ 1.0" Precipitation	1	1	1	0	0	0	0	0	0	0	0	1	4
Mean Snowfall (in.)	0.0	0.0	0.0	0.0	0.0	0.0	0.0	0.0	0.0	0.0	0.0	0.0	0.0
Maximum Snow Depth (in.)	0	0	0	0	0	0	0	0	0	0	0	0	0
Days With ≥ 1.0" Snow Depth	0	0	0	0	0	0	0	0	0	0	0	0	0

Graton *Sonoma County* Elevation: 200 ft. Latitude: 38° 26' N Longitude: 122° 52' W

	JAN	FEB	MAR	APR	MAY	JUN	JUL	AUG	SEP	OCT	NOV	DEC	YEAR
Mean Maximum Temp. (°F)	57.4	62.1	66.1	70.6	76.0	81.5	83.6	83.9	83.0	77.7	66.4	57.5	72.2
Mean Temp. (°F)	46.7	50.0	52.9	55.7	60.2	64.4	66.3	66.4	65.0	60.3	52.5	46.4	57.2
Mean Minimum Temp. (°F)	36.0	37.9	39.5	40.8	44.3	47.3	49.1	48.8	46.9	42.9	38.6	35.2	42.3
Extreme Maximum Temp. (°F)	84	82	90	98	101	108	110	107	107	106	88	77	110
Extreme Minimum Temp. (°F)	19	17	25	28	33	35	38	40	34	29	23	14	14
Days Maximum Temp. ≥ 90°F	0	0	0	0	2	5	6	7	7	3	0	0	30
Days Maximum Temp. ≤ 32°F	0	0	0	0	0	0	0	0	0	0	0	0	0
Days Minimum Temp. ≤ 32°F	12	7	3	1	0	0	0	0	0	1	6	14	44
Days Minimum Temp. ≤ 0°F	0	0	0	0	0	0	0	0	0	0	0	0	0
Heating Degree Days (base 65°F)	560	417	370	275	162	64	27	24	51	157	367	571	3,045
Cooling Degree Days (base 65°F)	0	0	1	4	19	53	75	75	57	19	0	0	303
Mean Precipitation (in.)	8.22	7.88	5.69	2.29	1.31	0.30	0.01	0.08	0.33	1.91	5.28	8.10	41.40
Extreme Maximum Daily Precip. (in.)	5.72	4.94	6.49	3.19	2.33	1.39	0.09	1.40	0.97	2.79	3.35	6.70	6.70
Days With ≥ 0.1" Precipitation	10	9	8	5	2	1	0	0	1	3	7	9	55
Days With ≥ 0.5" Precipitation	5	5	4	2	1	0	0	0	0	1	4	5	27
Days With ≥ 1.0" Precipitation	3	3	2	0	0	0	0	0	0	1	2	3	14
Mean Snowfall (in.)	0.0	0.0	0.0	trace	0.0	0.0	0.0	0.0	0.0	0.0	0.0	0.0	trace
Maximum Snow Depth (in.)	0	0	0	trace	0	0	0	0	0	0	0	0	trace
Days With ≥ 1.0" Snow Depth	0	0	0	0	0	0	0	0	0	0	0	0	0

Haiwee *Inyo County* Elevation: 3,825 ft. Latitude: 36° 08' N Longitude: 117° 57' W

	JAN	FEB	MAR	APR	MAY	JUN	JUL	AUG	SEP	OCT	NOV	DEC	YEAR
Mean Maximum Temp. (°F)	54.1	57.8	64.7	72.0	81.9	90.9	96.8	95.7	88.3	77.7	64.0	53.7	74.8
Mean Temp. (°F)	41.4	44.7	50.6	56.9	66.0	74.4	80.4	79.2	71.8	61.7	49.8	41.3	59.9
Mean Minimum Temp. (°F)	28.7	31.6	36.5	41.8	50.3	57.7	63.8	62.6	55.2	45.7	35.5	28.9	44.9
Extreme Maximum Temp. (°F)	74	79	88	96	106	109	117	113	108	97	87	76	117
Extreme Minimum Temp. (°F)	-8	2	19	22	32	38	44	49	28	26	16	1	-8
Days Maximum Temp. ≥ 90°F	0	0	0	1	7	18	27	27	15	3	0	0	98
Days Maximum Temp. ≤ 32°F	0	0	0	0	0	0	0	0	0	0	0	0	0
Days Minimum Temp. ≤ 32°F	23	14	8	2	0	0	0	0	0	1	9	22	79
Days Minimum Temp. ≤ 0°F	0	0	0	0	0	0	0	0	0	0	0	0	0
Heating Degree Days (base 65°F)	723	568	439	252	79	10	0	0	16	142	450	727	3,406
Cooling Degree Days (base 65°F)	0	0	0	16	117	298	484	446	227	47	0	0	1,635
Mean Precipitation (in.)	1.25	1.60	1.07	0.33	0.20	0.08	0.38	0.32	0.25	0.21	0.58	0.92	7.19
Extreme Maximum Daily Precip. (in.)	2.35	1.44	2.65	0.73	0.58	0.50	1.03	1.53	1.60	0.76	1.86	1.68	2.65
Days With ≥ 0.1" Precipitation	3	3	2	1	1	0	1	1	1	1	1	2	17
Days With ≥ 0.5" Precipitation	1	1	1	0	0	0	0	0	0	0	0	1	4
Days With ≥ 1.0" Precipitation	0	0	0	0	0	0	0	0	0	0	0	0	0
Mean Snowfall (in.)	0.4	***0.3***	0.0	0.1	0.0	0.0	0.0	0.0	0.0	***0.0***	0.1	***0.4***	***1.3***
Maximum Snow Depth (in.)	na	na	na	na	na	na	na	na	na	na	na	na	na
Days With ≥ 1.0" Snow Depth	na	na	na	na	na	na	na	na	na	na	na	na	na

Hayfield Pumping Plant *Riverside County* Elevation: 1,370 ft. Latitude: 33° 42' N Longitude: 115° 38' W

	JAN	FEB	MAR	APR	MAY	JUN	JUL	AUG	SEP	OCT	NOV	DEC	YEAR
Mean Maximum Temp. (°F)	66.5	69.7	75.6	82.8	91.4	100.1	104.8	103.7	98.5	87.3	75.0	66.0	85.1
Mean Temp. (°F)	53.1	55.9	61.1	67.3	75.7	83.4	89.8	89.0	82.7	71.3	60.2	52.2	70.1
Mean Minimum Temp. (°F)	39.5	42.1	46.5	51.7	60.0	66.7	74.7	74.2	66.7	55.2	45.3	38.4	55.1
Extreme Maximum Temp. (°F)	84	91	99	105	111	119	119	116	113	108	94	84	119
Extreme Minimum Temp. (°F)	18	21	25	34	41	49	56	58	46	36	23	18	18
Days Maximum Temp. ≥ 90°F	0	0	1	7	20	27	31	31	26	13	1	0	157
Days Maximum Temp. ≤ 32°F	0	0	0	0	0	0	0	0	0	0	0	0	0
Days Minimum Temp. ≤ 32°F	5	3	1	0	0	0	0	0	0	0	1	7	17
Days Minimum Temp. ≤ 0°F	0	0	0	0	0	0	0	0	0	0	0	0	0
Heating Degree Days (base 65°F)	364	254	154	55	7	0	0	0	0	21	163	391	1,409
Cooling Degree Days (base 65°F)	1	5	40	128	346	559	774	751	539	221	26	1	3,391
Mean Precipitation (in.)	0.76	0.82	0.58	0.10	0.10	trace	0.25	0.68	0.33	0.24	0.27	0.58	4.71
Extreme Maximum Daily Precip. (in.)	1.80	1.27	1.63	0.39	1.62	0.06	1.45	2.70	2.80	1.04	1.08	3.00	3.00
Days With ≥ 0.1" Precipitation	2	2	1	0	0	0	0	1	1	1	1	1	10
Days With ≥ 0.5" Precipitation	0	1	0	0	0	0	0	0	0	0	0	0	1
Days With ≥ 1.0" Precipitation	0	0	0	0	0	0	0	0	0	0	0	0	0
Mean Snowfall (in.)	trace	0.0	0.0	0.0	0.0	0.0	0.0	0.0	0.0	0.0	0.0	0.0	trace
Maximum Snow Depth (in.)	trace	0	0	0	0	0	0	0	0	0	0	0	trace
Days With ≥ 1.0" Snow Depth	0	0	0	0	0	0	0	0	0	0	0	0	0

The period of record for all cooperative weather station data is 1980 – 2009. See User Guide for detailed explanation of data.

Hollister 2 *San Benito County* Elevation: 274 ft. Latitude: 36° 51' N Longitude: 121° 25' W

	JAN	FEB	MAR	APR	MAY	JUN	JUL	AUG	SEP	OCT	NOV	DEC	YEAR
Mean Maximum Temp. (°F)	59.9	62.6	65.9	70.3	74.1	78.3	80.8	81.5	81.1	76.6	67.1	59.6	71.5
Mean Temp. (°F)	49.1	51.8	54.3	57.3	61.0	64.7	67.0	67.5	66.7	62.2	54.5	48.6	58.7
Mean Minimum Temp. (°F)	38.1	40.9	42.5	44.3	48.0	50.9	53.1	53.6	52.3	47.7	41.8	37.4	45.9
Extreme Maximum Temp. (°F)	77	82	89	99	105	108	112	110	105	107	94	78	112
Extreme Minimum Temp. (°F)	20	20	25	27	37	38	44	45	40	34	24	14	14
Days Maximum Temp. ≥ 90°F	0	0	0	1	2	3	4	5	6	3	0	0	24
Days Maximum Temp. ≤ 32°F	0	0	0	0	0	0	0	0	0	0	0	0	0
Days Minimum Temp. ≤ 32°F	8	3	1	0	0	0	0	0	0	0	2	8	22
Days Minimum Temp. ≤ 0°F	0	0	0	0	0	0	0	0	0	0	0	0	0
Heating Degree Days (base 65°F)	488	367	327	235	147	63	26	18	32	117	310	503	2,633
Cooling Degree Days (base 65°F)	0	0	2	11	31	59	94	104	91	36	1	0	429
Mean Precipitation (in.)	2.89	2.85	2.24	0.88	0.39	0.06	0.04	0.01	0.21	0.69	1.60	2.11	13.97
Extreme Maximum Daily Precip. (in.)	2.82	2.33	2.05	1.43	0.88	0.50	0.61	0.18	1.30	2.31	1.86	2.00	2.82
Days With ≥ 0.1" Precipitation	6	6	6	3	1	0	0	0	0	2	4	5	33
Days With ≥ 0.5" Precipitation	2	2	1	0	0	0	0	0	0	0	1	1	7
Days With ≥ 1.0" Precipitation	0	1	0	0	0	0	0	0	0	0	0	0	1
Mean Snowfall (in.)	0.0	0.0	0.0	0.0	0.0	0.0	0.0	0.0	0.0	0.0	0.0	0.0	0.0
Maximum Snow Depth (in.)	0	0	0	0	0	0	0	0	0	0	0	0	0
Days With ≥ 1.0" Snow Depth	0	0	0	0	0	0	0	0	0	0	0	0	0

Independence *Inyo County* Elevation: 3,950 ft. Latitude: 36° 48' N Longitude: 118° 12' W

	JAN	FEB	MAR	APR	MAY	JUN	JUL	AUG	SEP	OCT	NOV	DEC	YEAR
Mean Maximum Temp. (°F)	55.8	59.5	66.5	74.0	83.9	93.2	99.6	97.9	90.3	78.2	64.8	54.8	76.5
Mean Temp. (°F)	42.4	46.1	52.0	58.7	68.2	76.8	82.6	80.7	73.6	62.1	50.1	41.5	61.2
Mean Minimum Temp. (°F)	29.0	32.7	37.6	43.4	52.4	60.3	65.7	63.4	56.8	46.0	35.4	28.2	45.9
Extreme Maximum Temp. (°F)	80	86	90	102	105	110	114	109	108	98	91	76	114
Extreme Minimum Temp. (°F)	9	12	16	21	30	38	43	49	40	27	16	-2	-2
Days Maximum Temp. ≥ 90°F	0	0	0	1	9	21	29	29	18	3	0	0	110
Days Maximum Temp. ≤ 32°F	0	0	0	0	0	0	0	0	0	0	0	0	0
Days Minimum Temp. ≤ 32°F	22	13	7	2	0	0	0	0	0	1	10	24	79
Days Minimum Temp. ≤ 0°F	0	0	0	0	0	0	0	0	0	0	0	0	0
Heating Degree Days (base 65°F)	693	529	397	211	59	8	0	0	9	138	441	721	3,206
Cooling Degree Days (base 65°F)	0	0	3	29	163	368	554	493	274	55	1	0	1,940
Mean Precipitation (in.)	1.09	1.15	0.64	0.21	0.11	0.17	0.10	0.12	0.16	0.21	0.68	0.75	5.39
Extreme Maximum Daily Precip. (in.)	2.18	2.06	2.57	0.50	0.40	0.93	0.40	0.71	0.56	1.05	3.05	1.58	3.05
Days With ≥ 0.1" Precipitation	2	3	1	1	0	0	0	0	0	1	1	2	11
Days With ≥ 0.5" Precipitation	1	1	0	0	0	0	0	0	0	0	0	0	2
Days With ≥ 1.0" Precipitation	0	0	0	0	0	0	0	0	0	0	0	0	0
Mean Snowfall (in.)	0.4	0.2	trace	trace	0.0	0.0	0.0	0.0	0.0	0.0	trace	***0.3***	***0.9***
Maximum Snow Depth (in.)	na	na	na	na	***0***	na	***0***	***0***	***0***	na	na	na	na
Days With ≥ 1.0" Snow Depth	na	na	na	na	***0***	na	***0***	***0***	***0***	na	na	na	na

Jess Valley *Modoc County* Elevation: 5,399 ft. Latitude: 41° 16' N Longitude: 120° 18' W

	JAN	FEB	MAR	APR	MAY	JUN	JUL	AUG	SEP	OCT	NOV	DEC	YEAR
Mean Maximum Temp. (°F)	42.1	44.3	49.1	55.1	64.4	73.2	83.4	82.7	76.1	63.7	49.2	41.3	60.4
Mean Temp. (°F)	31.2	32.9	37.2	41.9	49.8	57.1	65.4	64.3	58.0	47.9	37.2	30.5	46.1
Mean Minimum Temp. (°F)	20.5	21.7	25.4	28.5	34.9	41.0	47.3	45.8	39.7	32.0	25.1	19.6	31.8
Extreme Maximum Temp. (°F)	62	66	75	81	89	95	102	98	95	88	78	64	102
Extreme Minimum Temp. (°F)	-8	-28	1	6	18	21	29	30	19	8	-5	-26	-28
Days Maximum Temp. ≥ 90°F	0	0	0	0	0	1	5	5	1	0	0	0	12
Days Maximum Temp. ≤ 32°F	4	2	1	0	0	0	0	0	0	0	2	5	14
Days Minimum Temp. ≤ 32°F	28	25	26	22	11	3	0	0	5	16	24	27	187
Days Minimum Temp. ≤ 0°F	1	1	0	0	0	0	0	0	0	0	0	2	4
Heating Degree Days (base 65°F)	1,040	900	854	687	467	243	62	73	217	528	828	1,064	6,963
Cooling Degree Days (base 65°F)	0	0	0	0	2	12	80	57	14	0	0	0	165
Mean Precipitation (in.)	1.89	1.58	2.03	2.13	2.56	1.52	0.46	0.48	0.78	1.22	2.22	2.14	19.01
Extreme Maximum Daily Precip. (in.)	1.00	1.36	***1.68***	2.05	2.06	2.10	0.89	1.22	1.80	1.61	***1.21***	***1.30***	***2.10***
Days With ≥ 0.1" Precipitation	6	5	6	7	6	4	1	1	2	4	7	6	55
Days With ≥ 0.5" Precipitation	1	1	1	1	2	1	0	0	0	1	1	1	10
Days With ≥ 1.0" Precipitation	0	0	0	0	0	0	0	0	0	0	0	0	0
Mean Snowfall (in.)	12.0	10.0	11.9	10.1	4.2	0.4	0.1	0.0	0.2	2.5	10.8	13.1	75.3
Maximum Snow Depth (in.)	27	16	13	9	10	trace	trace	0	trace	5	12	18	27
Days With ≥ 1.0" Snow Depth	9	6	3	0	0	0	0	0	0	0	4	8	30

King City *Monterey County* Elevation: 319 ft. Latitude: 36° 12' N Longitude: 121° 08' W

	JAN	FEB	MAR	APR	MAY	JUN	JUL	AUG	SEP	OCT	NOV	DEC	YEAR
Mean Maximum Temp. (°F)	63.1	65.8	69.3	74.1	78.5	82.7	85.1	85.4	84.7	79.3	69.2	62.4	75.0
Mean Temp. (°F)	50.1	52.7	55.5	58.6	62.7	66.3	69.0	69.1	67.7	62.4	54.6	49.3	59.8
Mean Minimum Temp. (°F)	37.0	39.6	41.6	43.0	46.8	49.9	52.8	52.7	50.5	45.4	39.9	36.0	44.6
Extreme Maximum Temp. (°F)	83	86	93	104	106	112	111	109	111	109	93	84	112
Extreme Minimum Temp. (°F)	17	20	29	28	35	38	40	43	36	29	23	14	14
Days Maximum Temp. ≥ 90°F	0	0	0	2	3	6	7	7	8	4	0	0	37
Days Maximum Temp. ≤ 32°F	0	0	0	0	0	0	0	0	0	0	0	0	0
Days Minimum Temp. ≤ 32°F	9	5	2	0	0	0	0	0	0	0	5	12	33
Days Minimum Temp. ≤ 0°F	0	0	0	0	0	0	0	0	0	0	0	0	0
Heating Degree Days (base 65°F)	457	342	290	201	104	32	5	4	20	110	308	481	2,354
Cooling Degree Days (base 65°F)	0	0	2	15	39	79	135	137	106	36	2	0	551
Mean Precipitation (in.)	2.27	2.61	2.22	0.78	0.31	0.05	0.01	0.01	0.18	0.62	1.09	1.86	12.01
Extreme Maximum Daily Precip. (in.)	2.01	2.70	3.00	1.58	0.80	0.40	0.09	0.12	0.43	1.88	1.28	2.26	3.00
Days With ≥ 0.1" Precipitation	5	5	5	2	1	0	0	0	0	1	3	4	26
Days With ≥ 0.5" Precipitation	1	2	1	0	0	0	0	0	0	0	1	1	6
Days With ≥ 1.0" Precipitation	0	1	0	0	0	0	0	0	0	0	0	0	1
Mean Snowfall (in.)	0.0	0.0	0.0	0.0	0.0	0.0	0.0	0.0	0.0	0.0	0.0	trace	trace
Maximum Snow Depth (in.)	0	0	0	0	0	0	0	0	0	0	0	0	0
Days With ≥ 1.0" Snow Depth	0	0	0	0	0	0	0	0	0	0	0	0	0

The period of record for all cooperative weather station data is 1980 – 2009. See User Guide for detailed explanation of data.

Laguna Beach *Orange County* Elevation: 35 ft. Latitude: 33° 33' N Longitude: 117° 47' W

	JAN	FEB	MAR	APR	MAY	JUN	JUL	AUG	SEP	OCT	NOV	DEC	YEAR
Mean Maximum Temp. (°F)	***67.3***	67.9	68.8	71.4	***72.7***	74.8	78.7	79.7	79.4	***76.1***	71.2	67.1	***72.9***
Mean Temp. (°F)	***55.4***	56.3	57.7	60.2	***63.3***	65.8	69.3	69.8	68.9	***65.1***	59.2	54.9	***62.2***
Mean Minimum Temp. (°F)	***43.5***	44.7	46.6	49.0	***53.8***	56.7	59.8	59.9	58.4	***54.1***	47.1	42.8	***51.4***
Extreme Maximum Temp. (°F)	89	90	92	97	100	100	104	97	102	***98***	93	85	***104***
Extreme Minimum Temp. (°F)	27	30	32	35	39	39	43	49	45	***40***	28	30	***27***
Days Maximum Temp. ≥ 90°F	0	0	0	0	0	0	0	1	1	1	0	0	3
Days Maximum Temp. ≤ 32°F	0	0	0	0	0	0	0	0	0	0	0	0	0
Days Minimum Temp. ≤ 32°F	1	0	0	0	0	0	0	0	0	0	0	1	2
Days Minimum Temp. ≤ 0°F	0	0	0	0	0	0	0	0	0	0	0	0	0
Heating Degree Days (base 65°F)	***293***	242	222	146	***71***	26	3	2	9	***43***	174	306	***1,537***
Cooling Degree Days (base 65°F)	***1***	2	3	9	***25***	58	142	159	134	***53***	5	0	***591***
Mean Precipitation (in.)	2.63	3.53	2.13	0.92	0.22	0.11	0.05	0.03	0.26	0.62	1.21	1.96	13.67
Extreme Maximum Daily Precip. (in.)	2.45	3.00	2.97	***1.31***	0.54	0.88	0.32	0.16	1.01	2.20	***2.00***	***5.50***	***5.50***
Days With ≥ 0.1" Precipitation	4	5	4	2	1	0	0	0	1	1	2	3	23
Days With ≥ 0.5" Precipitation	2	2	2	1	0	0	0	0	0	0	1	1	9
Days With ≥ 1.0" Precipitation	1	1	1	0	0	0	0	0	0	0	0	0	3
Mean Snowfall (in.)	0.0	0.0	0.0	0.0	0.0	0.0	0.0	0.0	0.0	0.0	0.0	0.0	0.0
Maximum Snow Depth (in.)	0	0	0	0	0	0	0	0	0	***0***	0	0	***0***
Days With ≥ 1.0" Snow Depth	0	0	0	0	0	0	0	0	0	0	0	0	0

Lava Beds Nat Monument *Siskiyou County* Elevation: 4,770 ft. Latitude: 41° 44' N Longitude: 121° 30' W

	JAN	FEB	MAR	APR	MAY	JUN	JUL	AUG	SEP	OCT	NOV	DEC	YEAR
Mean Maximum Temp. (°F)	41.9	45.3	50.7	57.1	66.1	74.8	84.6	84.9	76.7	***64.7***	48.7	40.7	***61.4***
Mean Temp. (°F)	32.5	35.2	39.5	44.6	52.4	59.6	68.1	67.9	60.7	***50.5***	38.2	31.6	***48.4***
Mean Minimum Temp. (°F)	23.1	25.1	28.2	32.1	38.7	44.3	51.6	50.8	44.5	***36.1***	27.7	22.6	***35.4***
Extreme Maximum Temp. (°F)	60	68	75	88	94	98	103	102	99	89	74	64	103
Extreme Minimum Temp. (°F)	-1	-13	7	14	20	27	33	30	24	11	2	-18	-18
Days Maximum Temp. ≥ 90°F	0	0	0	0	0	2	9	8	2	0	0	0	21
Days Maximum Temp. ≤ 32°F	3	2	0	0	0	0	0	0	0	0	1	4	10
Days Minimum Temp. ≤ 32°F	28	24	23	16	7	2	0	0	2	10	22	28	162
Days Minimum Temp. ≤ 0°F	0	0	0	0	0	0	0	0	0	0	0	0	0
Heating Degree Days (base 65°F)	1,002	835	784	605	396	193	44	40	168	***447***	796	1,028	***6,338***
Cooling Degree Days (base 65°F)	0	0	0	0	12	36	148	137	44	***3***	0	0	***380***
Mean Precipitation (in.)	1.69	1.94	1.91	1.10	1.23	0.92	0.60	0.44	0.53	1.01	1.63	1.71	14.71
Extreme Maximum Daily Precip. (in.)	3.37	2.16	1.64	0.64	1.06	1.84	1.77	1.52	1.50	1.49	1.78	2.17	3.37
Days With ≥ 0.1" Precipitation	4	5	5	3	3	3	2	1	2	3	4	4	39
Days With ≥ 0.5" Precipitation	1	1	1	0	1	0	0	0	0	1	1	1	7
Days With ≥ 1.0" Precipitation	0	0	0	0	0	0	0	0	0	0	0	0	0
Mean Snowfall (in.)	10.1	7.7	7.5	3.3	1.1	0.1	trace	0.0	trace	0.3	4.5	8.6	43.2
Maximum Snow Depth (in.)	26	22	20	8	6	1	0	0	trace	2	17	20	26
Days With ≥ 1.0" Snow Depth	15	11	6	2	0	0	0	0	0	0	5	13	52

Livermore *Alameda County* Elevation: 479 ft. Latitude: 37° 40' N Longitude: 121° 46' W

	JAN	FEB	MAR	APR	MAY	JUN	JUL	AUG	SEP	OCT	NOV	DEC	YEAR
Mean Maximum Temp. (°F)	56.6	61.4	66.0	71.2	77.3	83.5	89.3	88.8	85.8	77.6	65.1	56.7	73.3
Mean Temp. (°F)	47.7	51.4	54.8	58.5	63.6	68.6	72.9	72.6	70.2	63.5	54.2	47.7	60.5
Mean Minimum Temp. (°F)	38.7	41.3	43.5	45.7	49.9	53.8	56.5	56.3	54.5	49.5	43.2	38.6	47.6
Extreme Maximum Temp. (°F)	73	77	88	96	104	109	112	110	110	106	86	71	112
Extreme Minimum Temp. (°F)	22	24	31	33	36	42	47	44	39	35	27	18	18
Days Maximum Temp. ≥ 90°F	0	0	0	1	3	8	16	15	11	3	0	0	57
Days Maximum Temp. ≤ 32°F	0	0	0	0	0	0	0	0	0	0	0	0	0
Days Minimum Temp. ≤ 32°F	6	3	0	0	0	0	0	0	0	0	1	6	16
Days Minimum Temp. ≤ 0°F	0	0	0	0	0	0	0	0	0	0	0	0	0
Heating Degree Days (base 65°F)	530	379	311	203	96	24	2	1	11	87	319	530	2,493
Cooling Degree Days (base 65°F)	0	0	1	14	59	140	255	243	172	49	1	0	934
Mean Precipitation (in.)	2.86	2.94	2.35	0.98	0.49	0.09	0.03	0.05	0.22	0.78	1.75	2.49	15.03
Extreme Maximum Daily Precip. (in.)	2.29	1.95	1.79	1.62	0.82	0.60	0.67	0.50	1.02	2.21	1.98	2.09	2.29
Days With ≥ 0.1" Precipitation	6	7	6	3	2	0	0	0	1	1	4	6	36
Days With ≥ 0.5" Precipitation	2	2	1	0	0	0	0	0	0	1	1	2	9
Days With ≥ 1.0" Precipitation	1	0	0	0	0	0	0	0	0	0	0	0	1
Mean Snowfall (in.)	0.0	0.0	trace	0.0	0.0	0.0	0.0	0.0	0.0	0.0	0.0	trace	trace
Maximum Snow Depth (in.)	0	0	trace	0	0	0	0	0	0	0	0	trace	trace
Days With ≥ 1.0" Snow Depth	0	0	0	0	0	0	0	0	0	0	0	0	0

Mitchell Caverns *San Bernardino County* Elevation: 4,350 ft. Latitude: 34° 57' N Longitude: 115° 33' W

	JAN	FEB	MAR	APR	MAY	JUN	JUL	AUG	SEP	OCT	NOV	DEC	YEAR
Mean Maximum Temp. (°F)	54.6	56.5	62.0	69.5	78.9	88.1	93.2	91.2	85.2	74.0	62.3	54.1	72.5
Mean Temp. (°F)	46.7	48.1	52.6	59.0	68.1	77.1	82.2	80.5	74.6	64.4	53.6	46.1	62.7
Mean Minimum Temp. (°F)	38.6	39.7	43.3	48.5	57.2	66.1	71.3	69.8	63.9	54.7	44.8	38.0	53.0
Extreme Maximum Temp. (°F)	73	81	83	89	98	105	110	106	100	97	82	75	110
Extreme Minimum Temp. (°F)	17	12	21	26	32	35	48	44	38	30	22	11	11
Days Maximum Temp. ≥ 90°F	0	0	0	0	3	14	24	20	8	1	0	0	70
Days Maximum Temp. ≤ 32°F	0	0	0	0	0	0	0	0	0	0	0	0	0
Days Minimum Temp. ≤ 32°F	5	4	2	1	0	0	0	0	0	0	2	6	20
Days Minimum Temp. ≤ 0°F	0	0	0	0	0	0	0	0	0	0	0	0	0
Heating Degree Days (base 65°F)	562	471	382	213	59	7	0	0	11	110	342	580	2,737
Cooling Degree Days (base 65°F)	0	0	5	39	162	377	540	489	305	97	5	0	2,019
Mean Precipitation (in.)	1.51	1.92	1.47	0.58	0.19	0.10	1.03	1.41	0.97	0.77	0.63	1.23	11.81
Extreme Maximum Daily Precip. (in.)	2.34	4.50	2.61	0.96	0.95	0.63	5.66	2.70	2.66	1.62	1.75	5.10	5.66
Days With ≥ 0.1" Precipitation	3	3	2	1	1	0	2	2	2	1	1	2	20
Days With ≥ 0.5" Precipitation	1	1	1	0	0	0	1	1	1	1	1	1	9
Days With ≥ 1.0" Precipitation	0	1	0	0	0	0	0	0	0	0	0	0	1
Mean Snowfall (in.)	0.3	0.3	0.6	0.1	trace	0.0	0.0	0.0	0.0	trace	0.1	0.8	2.2
Maximum Snow Depth (in.)	5	1	trace	trace	0	0	0	0	0	trace	6	***8***	***8***
Days With ≥ 1.0" Snow Depth	0	0	0	0	0	0	0	0	0	0	0	0	0

The period of record for all cooperative weather station data is 1980 – 2009. See User Guide for detailed explanation of data.

Modesto *Stanislaus County* Elevation: 90 ft. Latitude: 37° 39' N Longitude: 121° 00' W

	JAN	FEB	MAR	APR	MAY	JUN	JUL	AUG	SEP	OCT	NOV	DEC	YEAR
Mean Maximum Temp. (°F)	54.8	62.3	68.2	74.3	82.4	89.0	94.5	93.0	88.2	78.4	64.9	54.7	75.4
Mean Temp. (°F)	47.1	52.6	57.1	61.6	68.4	74.0	78.6	77.3	73.3	65.1	54.4	46.8	63.0
Mean Minimum Temp. (°F)	39.4	42.8	45.9	49.0	54.3	59.0	62.6	61.7	58.4	51.8	44.0	38.9	50.6
Extreme Maximum Temp. (°F)	75	80	87	100	107	111	113	108	105	101	88	75	113
Extreme Minimum Temp. (°F)	23	24	33	34	39	45	51	51	44	39	27	19	19
Days Maximum Temp. ≥ 90°F	0	0	0	2	7	15	24	22	14	2	0	0	86
Days Maximum Temp. ≤ 32°F	0	0	0	0	0	0	0	0	0	0	0	0	0
Days Minimum Temp. ≤ 32°F	4	1	0	0	0	0	0	0	0	0	1	5	11
Days Minimum Temp. ≤ 0°F	0	0	0	0	0	0	0	0	0	0	0	0	0
Heating Degree Days (base 65°F)	547	345	243	131	37	4	0	0	4	64	313	557	2,245
Cooling Degree Days (base 65°F)	0	0	4	37	148	282	427	389	260	76	2	0	1,625
Mean Precipitation (in.)	2.61	2.36	2.09	0.90	0.62	0.13	0.02	0.02	0.25	0.66	1.28	1.96	12.90
Extreme Maximum Daily Precip. (in.)	1.70	1.91	2.19	1.63	1.67	1.14	0.52	0.19	1.05	1.57	1.14	1.81	2.19
Days With ≥ 0.1" Precipitation	6	6	5	3	1	0	0	0	1	1	3	5	31
Days With ≥ 0.5" Precipitation	2	2	1	0	0	0	0	0	0	0	1	1	7
Days With ≥ 1.0" Precipitation	0	0	0	0	0	0	0	0	0	0	0	0	0
Mean Snowfall (in.)	na	na	na	na	na	na	na	na	na	na	na	na	na
Maximum Snow Depth (in.)	na	na	na	na	na	na	na	na	na	na	na	na	na
Days With ≥ 1.0" Snow Depth	na	na	na	na	na	na	na	na	na	na	na	na	na

Morro Bay Fire Dept *San Luis Obispo County* Elevation: 115 ft. Latitude: 35° 22' N Longitude: 120° 51' W

	JAN	FEB	MAR	APR	MAY	JUN	JUL	AUG	SEP	OCT	NOV	DEC	YEAR
Mean Maximum Temp. (°F)	62.5	62.9	63.5	64.4	63.5	64.2	65.8	66.5	67.5	68.4	66.7	62.4	64.9
Mean Temp. (°F)	52.5	53.5	54.3	55.0	55.9	57.3	59.3	60.0	59.9	59.3	56.6	52.3	56.3
Mean Minimum Temp. (°F)	42.4	44.0	45.0	45.6	48.2	50.3	52.7	53.4	52.4	50.1	46.4	42.2	47.7
Extreme Maximum Temp. (°F)	83	87	92	100	91	98	88	90	102	97	90	81	102
Extreme Minimum Temp. (°F)	23	25	32	34	34	39	35	40	41	37	31	22	22
Days Maximum Temp. ≥ 90°F	0	0	0	0	0	0	0	0	0	0	0	0	0
Days Maximum Temp. ≤ 32°F	0	0	0	0	0	0	0	0	0	0	0	0	0
Days Minimum Temp. ≤ 32°F	1	1	0	0	0	0	0	0	0	0	0	2	4
Days Minimum Temp. ≤ 0°F	0	0	0	0	0	0	0	0	0	0	0	0	0
Heating Degree Days (base 65°F)	382	320	326	298	278	228	173	154	158	185	253	386	3,141
Cooling Degree Days (base 65°F)	0	1	1	5	2	2	3	5	13	15	5	0	52
Mean Precipitation (in.)	3.42	3.85	3.27	1.07	0.42	0.08	0.03	0.05	0.24	0.77	1.40	2.50	17.10
Extreme Maximum Daily Precip. (in.)	3.70	2.63	8.82	2.55	2.23	0.63	0.22	0.67	1.05	1.98	1.49	2.51	8.82
Days With ≥ 0.1" Precipitation	6	7	5	3	1	0	0	0	1	2	3	5	33
Days With ≥ 0.5" Precipitation	2	3	2	1	0	0	0	0	0	0	1	2	11
Days With ≥ 1.0" Precipitation	1	1	1	0	0	0	0	0	0	0	0	1	4
Mean Snowfall (in.)	0.0	trace	0.0	0.0	0.0	0.0	0.0	0.0	0.0	0.0	0.0	0.0	trace
Maximum Snow Depth (in.)	0	trace	0	0	0	0	0	0	0	0	0	0	trace
Days With ≥ 1.0" Snow Depth	0	0	0	0	0	0	0	0	0	0	0	0	0

Needles Airport *San Bernardino County* Elevation: 914 ft. Latitude: 34° 46' N Longitude: 114° 37' W

	JAN	FEB	MAR	APR	MAY	JUN	JUL	AUG	SEP	OCT	NOV	DEC	YEAR
Mean Maximum Temp. (°F)	65.6	70.4	78.0	85.9	95.5	104.7	109.3	107.4	101.2	88.5	74.2	64.4	87.1
Mean Temp. (°F)	54.7	58.6	64.9	72.2	81.8	90.8	96.8	95.1	88.0	75.3	62.3	53.6	74.5
Mean Minimum Temp. (°F)	43.7	46.7	51.6	58.5	68.1	76.8	84.2	82.7	74.8	62.0	50.4	42.8	61.9
Extreme Maximum Temp. (°F)	85	92	99	106	114	121	125	121	115	109	92	80	125
Extreme Minimum Temp. (°F)	24	24	32	41	48	53	57	68	47	40	32	13	13
Days Maximum Temp. ≥ 90°F	0	0	2	11	24	29	31	30	28	15	0	0	170
Days Maximum Temp. ≤ 32°F	0	0	0	0	0	0	0	0	0	0	0	0	0
Days Minimum Temp. ≤ 32°F	1	0	0	0	0	0	0	0	0	0	0	1	2
Days Minimum Temp. ≤ 0°F	0	0	0	0	0	0	0	0	0	0	0	0	0
Heating Degree Days (base 65°F)	313	186	81	18	1	0	0	0	0	8	123	347	1,077
Cooling Degree Days (base 65°F)	1	12	84	243	529	780	992	940	698	333	50	1	4,663
Mean Precipitation (in.)	0.73	0.77	0.58	0.22	0.09	0.03	0.22	0.64	0.38	0.23	0.39	0.45	4.73
Extreme Maximum Daily Precip. (in.)	1.14	1.52	0.99	0.79	0.41	0.48	1.43	1.48	2.10	0.95	1.42	1.34	2.10
Days With ≥ 0.1" Precipitation	2	2	1	1	0	0	1	1	1	1	1	1	12
Days With ≥ 0.5" Precipitation	0	0	0	0	0	0	0	0	0	0	0	0	0
Days With ≥ 1.0" Precipitation	0	0	0	0	0	0	0	0	0	0	0	0	0
Mean Snowfall (in.)	***0.0***	na	na	na	na	na	na	na	na	na	na	na	na
Maximum Snow Depth (in.)	***0***	na	na	na	na	na	na	na	na	na	na	na	na
Days With ≥ 1.0" Snow Depth	***0***	na	na	na	na	na	na	na	na	na	na	na	na

Newman *Stanislaus County* Elevation: 89 ft. Latitude: 37° 19' N Longitude: 121° 01' W

	JAN	FEB	MAR	APR	MAY	JUN	JUL	AUG	SEP	OCT	NOV	DEC	YEAR
Mean Maximum Temp. (°F)	56.3	63.4	69.7	76.9	***85.1***	92.5	96.8	95.0	90.8	81.6	67.2	57.0	***77.7***
Mean Temp. (°F)	47.0	51.9	56.4	61.2	***68.6***	74.6	78.8	77.3	73.5	65.5	54.4	46.9	***63.0***
Mean Minimum Temp. (°F)	37.6	40.4	43.0	45.5	***52.0***	56.7	60.7	59.5	56.1	49.2	41.6	36.7	***48.3***
Extreme Maximum Temp. (°F)	76	80	96	101	***111***	112	116	111	108	104	86	74	***116***
Extreme Minimum Temp. (°F)	15	20	25	28	***35***	41	44	46	35	32	25	15	***15***
Days Maximum Temp. ≥ 90°F	0	0	0	2	***10***	20	27	26	18	5	0	0	***108***
Days Maximum Temp. ≤ 32°F	0	0	0	0	***0***	0	0	0	0	0	0	0	***0***
Days Minimum Temp. ≤ 32°F	8	3	0	1	***0***	0	0	0	0	0	3	9	***24***
Days Minimum Temp. ≤ 0°F	0	0	0	0	***0***	0	0	0	0	0	0	0	***0***
Heating Degree Days (base 65°F)	551	364	263	143	***35***	3	0	0	3	57	312	554	***2,285***
Cooling Degree Days (base 65°F)	0	0	3	36	***153***	300	434	388	264	79	1	0	***1,658***
Mean Precipitation (in.)	2.62	2.28	1.73	0.61	0.43	0.06	0.01	0.01	0.25	0.60	1.19	1.72	11.51
Extreme Maximum Daily Precip. (in.)	4.10	2.03	2.53	1.22	***1.70***	0.37	0.24	0.10	1.18	2.07	1.98	1.42	***4.10***
Days With ≥ 0.1" Precipitation	5	6	4	2	***1***	0	0	0	1	1	3	5	***28***
Days With ≥ 0.5" Precipitation	2	1	1	0	0	0	0	0	0	0	1	1	6
Days With ≥ 1.0" Precipitation	0	0	0	0	0	0	0	0	0	0	0	0	0
Mean Snowfall (in.)	0.0	0.0	0.0	0.0	0.0	0.0	0.0	0.0	0.0	0.0	0.0	0.0	0.0
Maximum Snow Depth (in.)	0	0	0	0	0	0	0	0	0	0	0	0	0
Days With ≥ 1.0" Snow Depth	0	0	0	0	0	0	0	0	0	0	0	0	0

The period of record for all cooperative weather station data is 1980 – 2009. See User Guide for detailed explanation of data.

Ojai *Ventura County* Elevation: 750 ft. Latitude: 34° 27' N Longitude: 119° 14' W

	JAN	FEB	MAR	APR	MAY	JUN	JUL	AUG	SEP	OCT	NOV	DEC	YEAR
Mean Maximum Temp. (°F)	67.9	68.6	70.6	75.4	78.1	82.7	89.1	90.6	88.1	81.4	73.2	67.4	77.8
Mean Temp. (°F)	52.5	53.8	55.9	59.6	63.2	67.3	72.6	73.1	70.7	64.5	57.0	51.7	61.8
Mean Minimum Temp. (°F)	37.0	39.1	41.2	43.9	48.3	51.8	56.0	55.5	53.3	47.5	40.8	36.0	45.9
Extreme Maximum Temp. (°F)	90	92	96	103	105	110	111	109	110	107	100	88	111
Extreme Minimum Temp. (°F)	19	22	28	29	36	39	44	42	39	31	24	16	16
Days Maximum Temp. ≥ 90°F	0	0	0	2	3	6	14	16	14	6	1	0	62
Days Maximum Temp. ≤ 32°F	0	0	0	0	0	0	0	0	0	0	0	0	0
Days Minimum Temp. ≤ 32°F	8	5	1	0	0	0	0	0	0	0	2	9	25
Days Minimum Temp. ≤ 0°F	0	0	0	0	0	0	0	0	0	0	0	0	0
Heating Degree Days (base 65°F)	382	311	278	174	96	31	1	1	14	73	238	404	2,003
Cooling Degree Days (base 65°F)	0	2	2	20	46	105	243	258	192	63	6	0	937
Mean Precipitation (in.)	4.74	5.64	3.65	1.18	0.44	0.08	0.04	0.05	0.20	0.93	1.64	2.74	21.33
Extreme Maximum Daily Precip. (in.)	7.10	5.60	4.82	2.67	1.45	0.80	0.43	0.97	0.80	3.14	4.89	4.65	7.10
Days With ≥ 0.1" Precipitation	5	5	5	2	1	0	0	0	0	1	2	3	24
Days With ≥ 0.5" Precipitation	3	3	2	1	0	0	0	0	0	0	1	2	12
Days With ≥ 1.0" Precipitation	1	2	1	0	0	0	0	0	0	0	0	1	5
Mean Snowfall (in.)	0.0	0.0	0.0	0.0	0.0	0.0	0.0	0.0	0.0	0.0	0.0	0.0	0.0
Maximum Snow Depth (in.)	0	0	0	0	0	0	0	0	0	0	0	0	0
Days With ≥ 1.0" Snow Depth	0	0	0	0	0	0	0	0	0	0	0	0	0

Orleans *Humboldt County* Elevation: 399 ft. Latitude: 41° 18' N Longitude: 123° 32' W

	JAN	FEB	MAR	APR	MAY	JUN	JUL	AUG	SEP	OCT	NOV	DEC	YEAR
Mean Maximum Temp. (°F)	51.3	56.8	63.4	70.1	77.2	83.9	92.1	91.9	86.5	73.1	56.9	49.9	71.1
Mean Temp. (°F)	43.7	47.4	51.8	56.2	61.9	67.4	73.6	73.0	68.3	58.9	49.0	43.0	57.8
Mean Minimum Temp. (°F)	36.0	37.8	40.2	42.2	46.6	50.9	55.1	54.1	49.9	44.6	41.0	36.0	44.5
Extreme Maximum Temp. (°F)	70	78	86	97	102	106	112	110	107	98	77	68	112
Extreme Minimum Temp. (°F)	12	16	27	29	31	38	43	39	35	27	21	5	5
Days Maximum Temp. ≥ 90°F	0	0	0	1	4	8	20	20	12	1	0	0	66
Days Maximum Temp. ≤ 32°F	0	0	0	0	0	0	0	0	0	0	0	0	0
Days Minimum Temp. ≤ 32°F	9	6	2	1	0	0	0	0	0	1	3	9	31
Days Minimum Temp. ≤ 0°F	0	0	0	0	0	0	0	0	0	0	0	0	0
Heating Degree Days (base 65°F)	654	492	402	262	133	36	3	1	26	196	474	677	3,356
Cooling Degree Days (base 65°F)	0	0	0	6	44	115	278	257	129	14	0	0	843
Mean Precipitation (in.)	8.81	7.47	6.38	3.58	2.30	0.89	0.19	0.35	0.74	3.28	7.71	10.83	52.53
Extreme Maximum Daily Precip. (in.)	4.50	3.07	2.64	1.88	***2.29***	1.85	1.18	3.15	1.65	3.63	5.46	4.69	***5.46***
Days With ≥ 0.1" Precipitation	11	10	10	7	5	2	0	1	2	5	11	13	77
Days With ≥ 0.5" Precipitation	6	5	5	2	1	1	0	0	0	2	5	7	34
Days With ≥ 1.0" Precipitation	3	3	2	1	1	0	0	0	0	1	2	4	17
Mean Snowfall (in.)	0.9	1.1	0.3	trace	trace	0.0	0.0	0.0	0.0	0.0	0.1	1.4	3.8
Maximum Snow Depth (in.)	2	4	trace	0	trace	0	0	0	0	0	trace	2	4
Days With ≥ 1.0" Snow Depth	0	0	0	0	0	0	0	0	0	0	0	0	0

Palomar Mountain Observatory *San Diego County* Elevation: 5,549 ft. Latitude: 33° 23' N Longitude: 116° 50' W

	JAN	FEB	MAR	APR	MAY	JUN	JUL	AUG	SEP	OCT	NOV	DEC	YEAR
Mean Maximum Temp. (°F)	50.7	51.0	55.8	61.7	69.4	78.1	84.0	83.8	78.5	67.9	57.5	50.5	65.7
Mean Temp. (°F)	43.0	43.1	46.7	51.4	58.6	67.0	73.4	73.6	68.4	58.6	49.2	42.9	56.3
Mean Minimum Temp. (°F)	35.3	35.2	37.6	41.1	47.7	55.9	62.4	63.2	58.0	49.3	40.9	35.3	46.8
Extreme Maximum Temp. (°F)	68	69	78	84	91	98	98	99	92	92	79	72	99
Extreme Minimum Temp. (°F)	14	12	18	19	20	30	39	41	34	30	19	17	12
Days Maximum Temp. ≥ 90°F	0	0	0	0	0	1	5	3	1	0	0	0	10
Days Maximum Temp. ≤ 32°F	1	1	0	0	0	0	0	0	0	0	0	1	3
Days Minimum Temp. ≤ 32°F	12	11	9	6	2	0	0	0	0	1	5	11	57
Days Minimum Temp. ≤ 0°F	0	0	0	0	0	0	0	0	0	0	0	0	0
Heating Degree Days (base 65°F)	674	611	559	406	229	66	5	3	48	221	468	678	3,968
Cooling Degree Days (base 65°F)	0	0	0	4	36	134	273	277	154	31	1	0	910
Mean Precipitation (in.)	5.67	6.74	4.79	1.73	0.58	0.13	0.37	0.84	0.54	1.11	2.40	3.31	28.21
Extreme Maximum Daily Precip. (in.)	***5.65***	***4.97***	9.58	2.42	2.19	1.42	1.50	1.65	2.26	6.20	4.86	na	na
Days With ≥ 0.1" Precipitation	5	6	4	3	1	0	1	1	1	2	3	3	30
Days With ≥ 0.5" Precipitation	3	4	3	1	0	0	0	1	0	1	2	2	17
Days With ≥ 1.0" Precipitation	2	2	2	1	0	0	0	0	0	0	1	1	9
Mean Snowfall (in.)	2.9	5.0	7.6	1.9	trace	trace	0.0	0.0	0.0	trace	0.8	3.9	22.1
Maximum Snow Depth (in.)	16	21	25	15	2	0	0	0	0	1	14	27	27
Days With ≥ 1.0" Snow Depth	3	3	2	1	0	0	0	0	0	0	1	2	12

Parker Reservoir *San Bernardino County* Elevation: 737 ft. Latitude: 34° 17' N Longitude: 114° 10' W

	JAN	FEB	MAR	APR	MAY	JUN	JUL	AUG	SEP	OCT	NOV	DEC	YEAR
Mean Maximum Temp. (°F)	65.8	70.4	77.4	85.2	94.6	103.5	107.7	106.3	100.4	88.6	74.9	64.8	86.6
Mean Temp. (°F)	54.8	58.9	65.3	72.5	81.8	90.4	95.5	94.2	88.0	76.0	63.0	53.9	74.5
Mean Minimum Temp. (°F)	43.8	47.3	53.1	59.8	69.0	77.2	83.3	82.1	75.5	63.3	51.1	42.9	62.4
Extreme Maximum Temp. (°F)	86	92	100	106	115	121	123	119	115	110	95	82	123
Extreme Minimum Temp. (°F)	30	27	35	41	50	56	64	67	53	38	36	25	25
Days Maximum Temp. ≥ 90°F	0	0	2	10	24	29	31	31	28	16	1	0	172
Days Maximum Temp. ≤ 32°F	0	0	0	0	0	0	0	0	0	0	0	0	0
Days Minimum Temp. ≤ 32°F	0	0	0	0	0	0	0	0	0	0	0	1	1
Days Minimum Temp. ≤ 0°F	0	0	0	0	0	0	0	0	0	0	0	0	0
Heating Degree Days (base 65°F)	310	181	80	18	1	0	0	0	0	8	113	338	1,049
Cooling Degree Days (base 65°F)	1	14	95	252	529	768	952	913	696	356	61	0	4,637
Mean Precipitation (in.)	1.09	1.10	0.80	0.19	0.08	0.01	0.47	0.64	0.61	0.43	0.39	0.64	6.45
Extreme Maximum Daily Precip. (in.)	2.35	1.75	1.02	1.01	0.51	0.12	1.80	1.47	2.02	1.49	1.77	0.98	2.35
Days With ≥ 0.1" Precipitation	2	2	2	1	0	0	1	1	1	1	1	1	13
Days With ≥ 0.5" Precipitation	1	1	1	0	0	0	0	0	0	0	0	0	3
Days With ≥ 1.0" Precipitation	0	0	0	0	0	0	0	0	0	0	0	0	0
Mean Snowfall (in.)	0.0	0.0	0.0	0.0	0.0	0.0	0.0	0.0	0.0	0.0	0.0	0.0	0.0
Maximum Snow Depth (in.)	0	0	0	0	0	0	0	0	0	0	0	0	0
Days With ≥ 1.0" Snow Depth	0	0	0	0	0	0	0	0	0	0	0	0	0

The period of record for all cooperative weather station data is 1980 – 2009. See User Guide for detailed explanation of data.

Petaluma Fire Station 2 *Sonoma County* Elevation: 30 ft. Latitude: 38° 16' N Longitude: 122° 39' W

	JAN	FEB	MAR	APR	MAY	JUN	JUL	AUG	SEP	OCT	NOV	DEC	YEAR
Mean Maximum Temp. (°F)	57.3	61.9	65.1	68.8	73.2	78.6	82.0	82.1	81.4	76.0	65.2	57.3	70.7
Mean Temp. (°F)	48.0	51.2	53.7	56.3	60.4	64.7	67.2	67.3	66.3	61.6	53.6	47.9	58.2
Mean Minimum Temp. (°F)	38.6	40.5	42.2	43.8	47.4	50.7	52.3	52.4	51.1	47.2	41.9	38.4	45.5
Extreme Maximum Temp. (°F)	80	81	87	97	100	107	107	104	103	106	87	79	107
Extreme Minimum Temp. (°F)	21	18	29	24	27	33	35	36	37	29	23	20	18
Days Maximum Temp. ≥ 90°F	0	0	0	0	1	3	4	5	6	2	0	0	21
Days Maximum Temp. ≤ 32°F	0	0	0	0	0	0	0	0	0	0	0	0	0
Days Minimum Temp. ≤ 32°F	6	3	1	0	0	0	0	0	0	0	3	7	20
Days Minimum Temp. ≤ 0°F	0	0	0	0	0	0	0	0	0	0	0	0	0
Heating Degree Days (base 65°F)	520	382	344	260	156	57	17	13	29	121	338	524	2,761
Cooling Degree Days (base 65°F)	0	0	0	5	21	53	91	91	74	23	1	0	359
Mean Precipitation (in.)	4.83	5.53	3.69	1.47	0.82	0.18	0.02	0.06	0.21	1.29	3.09	5.09	26.28
Extreme Maximum Daily Precip. (in.)	3.62	3.28	3.69	1.65	1.78	0.75	0.19	1.00	0.90	2.55	2.51	4.29	4.29
Days With ≥ 0.1" Precipitation	8	8	7	4	2	0	0	0	1	2	6	9	47
Days With ≥ 0.5" Precipitation	3	4	2	1	1	0	0	0	0	1	2	3	17
Days With ≥ 1.0" Precipitation	1	2	1	0	0	0	0	0	0	0	1	1	6
Mean Snowfall (in.)	0.0	trace	0.0	trace	0.0	0.0	0.0	0.0	0.0	0.0	0.0	0.0	trace
Maximum Snow Depth (in.)	0	trace	0	trace	0	0	0	0	0	0	0	0	trace
Days With ≥ 1.0" Snow Depth	0	0	0	0	0	0	0	0	0	0	0	0	0

Porterville *Tulare County* Elevation: 393 ft. Latitude: 36° 04' N Longitude: 119° 01' W

	JAN	FEB	MAR	APR	MAY	JUN	JUL	AUG	SEP	OCT	NOV	DEC	YEAR
Mean Maximum Temp. (°F)	58.3	65.0	70.8	77.4	85.5	92.9	98.0	97.3	92.3	82.9	68.4	58.5	78.9
Mean Temp. (°F)	48.4	53.5	58.2	63.3	70.3	77.0	82.3	81.2	76.4	67.4	55.6	47.9	65.1
Mean Minimum Temp. (°F)	38.4	41.9	45.6	49.0	55.0	61.0	66.4	65.1	60.4	52.0	42.7	37.3	51.2
Extreme Maximum Temp. (°F)	79	85	91	99	109	108	111	112	108	103	88	80	112
Extreme Minimum Temp. (°F)	24	23	32	32	38	45	51	52	45	33	27	16	16
Days Maximum Temp. ≥ 90°F	0	0	0	3	10	21	29	29	20	7	0	0	119
Days Maximum Temp. ≤ 32°F	0	0	0	0	0	0	0	0	0	0	0	0	0
Days Minimum Temp. ≤ 32°F	6	2	0	0	0	0	0	0	0	0	2	7	17
Days Minimum Temp. ≤ 0°F	0	0	0	0	0	0	0	0	0	0	0	0	0
Heating Degree Days (base 65°F)	508	320	215	109	27	2	0	0	2	44	280	523	2,030
Cooling Degree Days (base 65°F)	0	1	11	64	197	368	542	510	350	127	4	0	2,174
Mean Precipitation (in.)	2.20	1.97	2.16	0.92	0.42	0.11	0.02	0.01	0.20	0.49	1.24	1.46	11.20
Extreme Maximum Daily Precip. (in.)	1.50	1.15	1.49	1.09	1.59	0.80	0.22	0.08	0.92	0.78	1.32	1.13	1.59
Days With ≥ 0.1" Precipitation	5	5	5	3	1	0	0	0	0	1	3	4	27
Days With ≥ 0.5" Precipitation	2	1	1	1	0	0	0	0	0	0	1	1	7
Days With ≥ 1.0" Precipitation	0	0	0	0	0	0	0	0	0	0	0	0	0
Mean Snowfall (in.)	0.0	0.0	0.0	0.0	0.0	0.0	0.0	0.0	0.0	0.0	0.0	0.0	0.0
Maximum Snow Depth (in.)	3	0	0	0	0	0	0	0	0	0	0	0	3
Days With ≥ 1.0" Snow Depth	0	0	0	0	0	0	0	0	0	0	0	0	0

Redlands *San Bernardino County* Elevation: 1,317 ft. Latitude: 34° 03' N Longitude: 117° 11' W

	JAN	FEB	MAR	APR	MAY	JUN	JUL	AUG	SEP	OCT	NOV	DEC	YEAR
Mean Maximum Temp. (°F)	67.2	67.9	70.9	75.7	80.9	88.1	95.1	95.9	91.6	82.4	73.9	66.9	79.7
Mean Temp. (°F)	54.3	55.5	58.1	62.0	67.1	72.7	78.7	79.4	75.7	67.7	59.5	53.7	65.4
Mean Minimum Temp. (°F)	41.3	43.0	45.3	48.2	53.3	57.2	62.3	62.8	59.8	52.9	45.1	40.5	51.0
Extreme Maximum Temp. (°F)	93	92	97	106	109	109	118	113	112	110	98	86	118
Extreme Minimum Temp. (°F)	19	25	31	33	38	41	49	49	46	38	29	24	19
Days Maximum Temp. ≥ 90°F	0	0	1	3	6	14	26	27	19	7	1	0	104
Days Maximum Temp. ≤ 32°F	0	0	0	0	0	0	0	0	0	0	0	0	0
Days Minimum Temp. ≤ 32°F	1	1	0	0	0	0	0	0	0	0	0	2	4
Days Minimum Temp. ≤ 0°F	0	0	0	0	0	0	0	0	0	0	0	0	0
Heating Degree Days (base 65°F)	328	270	221	132	46	8	0	0	3	37	176	344	1,565
Cooling Degree Days (base 65°F)	2	4	14	49	118	245	433	454	330	128	19	1	1,797
Mean Precipitation (in.)	2.73	3.32	2.11	0.96	0.31	0.11	0.08	0.13	0.28	0.63	0.98	1.57	13.21
Extreme Maximum Daily Precip. (in.)	2.53	3.05	2.05	1.88	1.16	1.00	0.35	0.88	0.99	2.75	1.98	2.20	3.05
Days With ≥ 0.1" Precipitation	5	5	4	2	1	0	0	0	1	1	2	3	24
Days With ≥ 0.5" Precipitation	2	2	1	1	0	0	0	0	0	0	1	1	8
Days With ≥ 1.0" Precipitation	1	1	1	0	0	0	0	0	0	0	0	0	3
Mean Snowfall (in.)	0.0	0.0	0.0	0.0	0.0	0.0	0.0	0.0	0.0	0.0	0.0	0.0	0.0
Maximum Snow Depth (in.)	0	0	0	0	0	0	0	0	0	0	0	0	0
Days With ≥ 1.0" Snow Depth	0	0	0	0	0	0	0	0	0	0	0	0	0

Riverside Fire Sta 3 *Riverside County* Elevation: 839 ft. Latitude: 33° 57' N Longitude: 117° 23' W

	JAN	FEB	MAR	APR	MAY	JUN	JUL	AUG	SEP	OCT	NOV	DEC	YEAR
Mean Maximum Temp. (°F)	69.1	69.8	72.9	77.5	82.2	88.3	94.9	95.9	91.7	83.3	74.9	68.8	80.8
Mean Temp. (°F)	55.9	57.1	59.7	63.6	68.5	73.5	79.2	80.0	76.3	68.8	60.5	55.0	66.5
Mean Minimum Temp. (°F)	42.7	44.3	46.5	49.7	54.8	58.7	63.5	64.1	60.9	54.2	46.1	41.2	52.2
Extreme Maximum Temp. (°F)	92	91	99	105	110	111	116	113	112	109	98	89	116
Extreme Minimum Temp. (°F)	26	22	32	35	43	46	51	51	45	41	28	22	22
Days Maximum Temp. ≥ 90°F	0	0	1	4	6	14	25	26	18	8	1	0	103
Days Maximum Temp. ≤ 32°F	0	0	0	0	0	0	0	0	0	0	0	0	0
Days Minimum Temp. ≤ 32°F	1	1	0	0	0	0	0	0	0	0	0	2	4
Days Minimum Temp. ≤ 0°F	0	0	0	0	0	0	0	0	0	0	0	0	0
Heating Degree Days (base 65°F)	278	224	173	90	22	3	0	0	1	23	149	304	1,267
Cooling Degree Days (base 65°F)	3	5	17	57	139	265	448	471	348	146	20	2	1,921
Mean Precipitation (in.)	2.03	2.68	1.73	0.65	0.15	0.08	0.04	0.12	0.14	0.48	0.81	1.11	10.02
Extreme Maximum Daily Precip. (in.)	2.22	2.45	1.60	1.05	0.82	0.83	0.25	1.84	0.64	2.50	2.05	***2.16***	***2.50***
Days With ≥ 0.1" Precipitation	4	5	3	1	0	0	0	0	0	1	2	2	18
Days With ≥ 0.5" Precipitation	1	2	1	0	0	0	0	0	0	0	1	0	5
Days With ≥ 1.0" Precipitation	0	1	1	0	0	0	0	0	0	0	0	0	2
Mean Snowfall (in.)	0.0	0.0	0.0	0.0	0.0	0.0	0.0	0.0	0.0	0.0	0.0	0.0	0.0
Maximum Snow Depth (in.)	0	0	0	0	0	0	0	0	0	0	0	0	0
Days With ≥ 1.0" Snow Depth	0	0	0	0	0	0	0	0	0	0	0	0	0

The period of record for all cooperative weather station data is 1980 – 2009. See User Guide for detailed explanation of data.

Salinas No 2 *Monterey County* Elevation: 44 ft. Latitude: 36° 40' N Longitude: 121° 40' W

	JAN	FEB	MAR	APR	MAY	JUN	JUL	AUG	SEP	OCT	NOV	DEC	YEAR
Mean Maximum Temp. (°F)	62.8	64.4	65.8	67.7	68.8	70.6	71.6	73.1	74.7	73.6	68.0	62.7	68.7
Mean Temp. (°F)	52.2	54.0	55.3	57.0	59.2	61.4	63.1	64.3	64.2	61.7	56.5	52.0	58.4
Mean Minimum Temp. (°F)	41.5	43.4	44.8	46.2	49.5	52.1	54.6	55.3	53.7	49.7	44.8	41.3	48.1
Extreme Maximum Temp. (°F)	85	85	89	100	99	103	97	99	103	105	94	80	105
Extreme Minimum Temp. (°F)	22	26	31	32	37	42	43	45	42	36	27	24	22
Days Maximum Temp. ≥ 90°F	0	0	0	1	1	1	0	0	1	1	0	0	5
Days Maximum Temp. ≤ 32°F	0	0	0	0	0	0	0	0	0	0	0	0	0
Days Minimum Temp. ≤ 32°F	2	1	0	0	0	0	0	0	0	0	0	3	6
Days Minimum Temp. ≤ 0°F	0	0	0	0	0	0	0	0	0	0	0	0	0
Heating Degree Days (base 65°F)	391	307	294	242	181	113	68	44	53	121	254	396	2,464
Cooling Degree Days (base 65°F)	0	1	1	7	9	11	17	28	36	26	4	0	140
Mean Precipitation (in.)	2.98	3.01	2.61	0.97	0.40	0.09	0.03	0.04	0.14	0.67	1.67	2.27	14.88
Extreme Maximum Daily Precip. (in.)	2.96	2.38	***1.87***	1.06	***0.85***	0.47	0.67	0.35	1.03	1.50	2.05	***1.59***	***2.96***
Days With ≥ 0.1" Precipitation	5	6	5	3	1	0	0	0	0	1	3	5	29
Days With ≥ 0.5" Precipitation	2	2	2	0	0	0	0	0	0	1	1	1	9
Days With ≥ 1.0" Precipitation	1	0	0	0	0	0	0	0	0	0	0	0	1
Mean Snowfall (in.)	0.0	0.0	0.0	0.0	0.0	0.0	0.0	0.0	0.0	0.0	0.0	0.0	0.0
Maximum Snow Depth (in.)	0	0	0	0	0	0	0	0	0	0	0	0	0
Days With ≥ 1.0" Snow Depth	0	0	0	0	0	0	0	0	0	0	0	0	0

San Francisco Oceanside *San Francisco County* Elevation: 35 ft. Latitude: 37° 44' N Longitude: 122° 30' W

	JAN	FEB	MAR	APR	MAY	JUN	JUL	AUG	SEP	OCT	NOV	DEC	YEAR
Mean Maximum Temp. (°F)	***57.8***	59.8	60.1	60.5	60.6	62.0	62.9	63.9	***65.1***	***65.1***	62.4	***58.0***	***61.5***
Mean Temp. (°F)	***51.4***	53.2	53.6	54.4	55.5	57.1	58.5	***59.5***	***59.8***	***58.9***	55.6	***51.6***	***55.8***
Mean Minimum Temp. (°F)	***45.0***	46.5	47.1	48.3	50.3	52.2	54.0	***55.1***	***54.4***	***52.7***	48.8	***45.0***	***49.9***
Extreme Maximum Temp. (°F)	74	77	81	90	98	***87***	79	92	92	***91***	83	73	***98***
Extreme Minimum Temp. (°F)	29	31	29	35	40	***41***	46	***41***	31	***40***	36	26	***26***
Days Maximum Temp. ≥ 90°F	0	0	0	0	0	0	0	0	0	0	0	0	0
Days Maximum Temp. ≤ 32°F	0	0	0	0	0	0	0	0	0	0	0	0	0
Days Minimum Temp. ≤ 32°F	0	0	0	0	0	0	0	0	0	0	0	0	0
Days Minimum Temp. ≤ 0°F	0	0	0	0	0	0	0	0	0	0	0	0	0
Heating Degree Days (base 65°F)	***415***	327	346	314	290	232	197	***167***	***155***	***195***	277	***410***	***3,325***
Cooling Degree Days (base 65°F)	***0***	0	0	3	1	1	1	***3***	***6***	***10***	2	***0***	***27***
Mean Precipitation (in.)	***3.94***	4.17	2.75	***1.05***	***0.71***	***0.13***	0.01	***0.06***	0.13	***0.86***	***2.48***	4.01	***20.30***
Extreme Maximum Daily Precip. (in.)	***2.40***	3.90	***2.52***	***1.15***	***1.44***	***0.69***	0.07	***0.64***	***0.40***	na	***1.87***	***3.43***	na
Days With ≥ 0.1" Precipitation	***7***	8	6	***3***	***2***	***0***	0	***0***	0	***1***	***4***	7	***38***
Days With ≥ 0.5" Precipitation	***3***	3	2	***1***	***0***	***0***	0	***0***	0	***1***	***2***	2	***14***
Days With ≥ 1.0" Precipitation	***1***	1	0	***0***	***0***	***0***	0	***0***	0	***0***	***1***	1	***4***
Mean Snowfall (in.)	0.0	0.0	0.0	0.0	0.0	0.0	0.0	0.0	0.0	***0.0***	0.0	0.0	***0.0***
Maximum Snow Depth (in.)	0	0	0	0	0	***0***	0	***0***	0	***0***	0	0	***0***
Days With ≥ 1.0" Snow Depth	0	0	0	0	0	0	0	0	0	***0***	0	0	***0***

Santa Barbara *Santa Barbara County* Elevation: 4 ft. Latitude: 34° 25' N Longitude: 119° 41' W

	JAN	FEB	MAR	APR	MAY	JUN	JUL	AUG	SEP	OCT	NOV	DEC	YEAR
Mean Maximum Temp. (°F)	64.9	65.5	66.7	69.6	69.9	71.9	75.2	76.6	75.7	73.1	69.1	***65.3***	***70.3***
Mean Temp. (°F)	55.5	56.5	57.9	60.4	61.9	64.2	67.4	68.1	67.4	64.3	59.4	***55.5***	***61.5***
Mean Minimum Temp. (°F)	45.7	47.3	49.1	51.1	53.8	56.5	59.4	59.5	59.0	55.4	49.6	***45.6***	***52.7***
Extreme Maximum Temp. (°F)	89	89	96	101	97	103	105	96	98	102	95	***84***	***105***
Extreme Minimum Temp. (°F)	22	30	32	37	36	45	46	43	40	34	37	***26***	***22***
Days Maximum Temp. ≥ 90°F	0	0	0	1	0	0	0	0	1	1	0	***0***	***3***
Days Maximum Temp. ≤ 32°F	0	0	0	0	0	0	0	0	0	0	0	***0***	***0***
Days Minimum Temp. ≤ 32°F	0	0	0	0	0	0	0	0	0	0	0	***0***	***0***
Days Minimum Temp. ≤ 0°F	0	0	0	0	0	0	0	0	0	0	0	***0***	***0***
Heating Degree Days (base 65°F)	291	236	218	150	106	48	9	6	15	56	169	***289***	***1,593***
Cooling Degree Days (base 65°F)	2	2	5	17	18	32	90	109	92	41	8	***1***	***417***
Mean Precipitation (in.)	4.33	4.83	3.16	0.98	0.33	0.09	0.01	0.02	0.12	0.84	1.51	2.61	18.83
Extreme Maximum Daily Precip. (in.)	8.00	3.50	4.75	3.30	1.09	0.62	0.10	0.12	1.45	3.12	5.90	***3.75***	***8.00***
Days With ≥ 0.1" Precipitation	5	5	4	2	1	0	0	0	0	1	2	***3***	***23***
Days With ≥ 0.5" Precipitation	3	3	2	1	0	0	0	0	0	1	1	***2***	***13***
Days With ≥ 1.0" Precipitation	1	2	1	0	0	0	0	0	0	0	0	***1***	***5***
Mean Snowfall (in.)	0.0	0.0	0.0	0.0	0.0	0.0	0.0	0.0	0.0	0.0	0.0	0.0	0.0
Maximum Snow Depth (in.)	0	0	0	0	0	0	0	0	0	0	0	0	0
Days With ≥ 1.0" Snow Depth	0	0	0	0	0	0	0	0	0	0	0	0	0

Santa Monica Pier *Los Angeles County* Elevation: 14 ft. Latitude: 34° 00' N Longitude: 118° 30' W

	JAN	FEB	MAR	APR	MAY	JUN	JUL	AUG	SEP	OCT	NOV	DEC	YEAR
Mean Maximum Temp. (°F)	63.7	63.4	***63.0***	64.2	64.6	***66.8***	69.8	***70.4***	70.6	69.6	67.1	***63.8***	***66.4***
Mean Temp. (°F)	57.2	57.5	***57.8***	59.4	60.8	***63.4***	66.2	***66.8***	66.6	64.7	61.0	***57.2***	***61.6***
Mean Minimum Temp. (°F)	50.7	51.5	***52.7***	54.5	57.0	***60.0***	62.6	***63.2***	62.6	59.8	54.9	***50.6***	***56.7***
Extreme Maximum Temp. (°F)	84	89	85	99	86	***90***	84	***95***	89	99	91	85	***99***
Extreme Minimum Temp. (°F)	39	35	41	43	43	***51***	53	***55***	55	48	37	37	***35***
Days Maximum Temp. ≥ 90°F	0	0	0	0	0	0	0	***0***	0	0	0	0	***0***
Days Maximum Temp. ≤ 32°F	0	0	0	0	0	0	0	***0***	0	0	0	0	***0***
Days Minimum Temp. ≤ 32°F	0	0	0	0	0	0	0	***0***	0	0	0	0	***0***
Days Minimum Temp. ≤ 0°F	0	0	0	0	0	0	0	***0***	0	0	0	0	***0***
Heating Degree Days (base 65°F)	240	213	***220***	172	128	***59***	15	***12***	18	46	130	***238***	***1,491***
Cooling Degree Days (base 65°F)	7	7	***4***	11	6	***17***	60	***75***	73	44	18	***4***	***326***
Mean Precipitation (in.)	3.09	3.66	1.89	0.46	0.22	0.05	0.01	0.03	0.15	0.50	1.05	1.79	12.90
Extreme Maximum Daily Precip. (in.)	4.67	3.88	***2.65***	1.11	1.73	0.55	0.08	0.36	1.00	1.45	2.00	2.25	***4.67***
Days With ≥ 0.1" Precipitation	4	5	***3***	1	0	0	0	0	0	1	2	3	***19***
Days With ≥ 0.5" Precipitation	2	3	***1***	0	0	0	0	0	0	0	1	1	***8***
Days With ≥ 1.0" Precipitation	1	1	***1***	0	0	0	0	0	0	0	0	1	***4***
Mean Snowfall (in.)	0.0	0.0	0.0	0.0	0.0	0.0	0.0	0.0	0.0	0.0	0.0	0.0	0.0
Maximum Snow Depth (in.)	0	0	0	0	0	0	0	***0***	0	0	0	0	***0***
Days With ≥ 1.0" Snow Depth	0	0	0	0	0	0	0	***0***	0	***0***	0	***0***	***0***

The period of record for all cooperative weather station data is 1980 – 2009. See User Guide for detailed explanation of data.

Stockton Fire Stn #4 *San Joaquin County* Elevation: 12 ft. Latitude: 38° 00' N Longitude: 121° 19' W

	JAN	FEB	MAR	APR	MAY	JUN	JUL	AUG	SEP	OCT	NOV	DEC	YEAR
Mean Maximum Temp. (°F)	55.7	63.0	68.3	74.4	81.9	88.4	93.5	92.8	89.4	80.5	66.3	56.3	75.9
Mean Temp. (°F)	46.2	51.3	55.6	60.1	66.3	71.6	75.3	74.4	71.3	63.9	53.6	45.9	61.3
Mean Minimum Temp. (°F)	36.8	39.7	42.7	45.8	50.7	54.8	57.0	56.1	53.2	47.2	40.9	35.8	46.7
Extreme Maximum Temp. (°F)	72	78	87	99	106	110	112	110	105	102	85	73	112
Extreme Minimum Temp. (°F)	17	13	24	27	34	31	40	37	29	29	23	15	13
Days Maximum Temp. ≥ 90°F	0	0	0	1	6	13	22	21	15	4	0	0	82
Days Maximum Temp. ≤ 32°F	0	0	0	0	0	0	0	0	0	0	0	0	0
Days Minimum Temp. ≤ 32°F	9	4	2	0	0	0	0	0	0	0	3	9	27
Days Minimum Temp. ≤ 0°F	0	0	0	0	0	0	0	0	0	0	0	0	0
Heating Degree Days (base 65°F)	575	381	291	163	62	11	1	2	13	88	337	585	2,509
Cooling Degree Days (base 65°F)	0	0	3	23	109	216	326	302	211	62	1	0	1,253
Mean Precipitation (in.)	3.43	3.24	2.63	1.38	0.59	0.11	0.02	0.02	0.28	0.95	2.07	2.94	17.66
Extreme Maximum Daily Precip. (in.)	2.76	2.30	1.46	1.57	1.62	0.40	0.35	0.30	1.05	2.90	2.14	2.30	2.90
Days With ≥ 0.1" Precipitation	7	6	6	3	1	0	0	0	1	2	4	6	36
Days With ≥ 0.5" Precipitation	2	2	2	1	0	0	0	0	0	1	2	2	12
Days With ≥ 1.0" Precipitation	1	1	1	0	0	0	0	0	0	0	0	0	3
Mean Snowfall (in.)	0.0	0.0	0.0	0.0	0.0	0.0	0.0	0.0	0.0	0.0	0.0	0.0	0.0
Maximum Snow Depth (in.)	0	0	0	0	0	0	0	0	0	0	0	0	0
Days With ≥ 1.0" Snow Depth	0	0	0	0	0	0	0	0	0	0	0	0	0

Tejon Rancho *Kern County* Elevation: 1,424 ft. Latitude: 35° 02' N Longitude: 118° 45' W

	JAN	FEB	MAR	APR	MAY	JUN	JUL	AUG	SEP	OCT	NOV	DEC	YEAR
Mean Maximum Temp. (°F)	59.3	63.4	68.5	75.1	83.8	91.4	97.6	96.5	91.3	80.9	66.7	59.0	77.8
Mean Temp. (°F)	46.5	50.5	54.8	59.9	68.0	75.2	81.2	79.7	75.3	65.7	53.2	46.5	63.0
Mean Minimum Temp. (°F)	33.6	37.6	41.0	44.6	52.1	58.9	64.9	62.8	59.3	50.4	39.7	33.9	48.2
Extreme Maximum Temp. (°F)	82	84	89	100	109	108	113	109	108	101	90	81	113
Extreme Minimum Temp. (°F)	6	14	17	16	24	31	39	41	34	26	15	11	6
Days Maximum Temp. ≥ 90°F	0	0	0	2	8	18	27	27	19	5	0	0	106
Days Maximum Temp. ≤ 32°F	0	0	0	0	0	0	0	0	0	0	0	0	0
Days Minimum Temp. ≤ 32°F	13	6	3	2	0	0	0	0	0	1	4	12	41
Days Minimum Temp. ≤ 0°F	0	0	0	0	0	0	0	0	0	0	0	0	0
Heating Degree Days (base 65°F)	569	403	314	185	56	9	0	0	4	79	348	568	2,535
Cooling Degree Days (base 65°F)	0	0	3	38	155	320	511	462	319	108	2	0	1,918
Mean Precipitation (in.)	2.17	2.14	2.21	1.11	0.46	0.14	0.02	0.08	0.21	0.53	1.55	1.35	11.97
Extreme Maximum Daily Precip. (in.)	***2.19***	***1.68***	2.05	1.57	0.99	0.74	0.24	1.34	1.34	1.40	1.83	1.65	***2.19***
Days With ≥ 0.1" Precipitation	4	5	5	2	1	0	0	0	0	1	3	3	24
Days With ≥ 0.5" Precipitation	1	1	2	1	0	0	0	0	0	0	1	1	7
Days With ≥ 1.0" Precipitation	0	0	0	0	0	0	0	0	0	0	0	0	0
Mean Snowfall (in.)	0.0	0.0	0.0	0.0	0.0	0.0	0.0	0.0	0.0	0.0	0.0	trace	trace
Maximum Snow Depth (in.)	0	0	0	0	0	0	0	0	0	0	0	0	0
Days With ≥ 1.0" Snow Depth	0	0	0	0	0	0	0	0	0	0	0	0	0

Tulelake *Siskiyou County* Elevation: 4,035 ft. Latitude: 41° 57' N Longitude: 121° 28' W

	JAN	FEB	MAR	APR	MAY	JUN	JUL	AUG	SEP	OCT	NOV	DEC	YEAR
Mean Maximum Temp. (°F)	40.5	45.8	52.4	59.5	68.0	76.1	84.3	84.1	77.0	65.1	47.9	39.5	61.7
Mean Temp. (°F)	30.7	34.5	39.2	44.8	52.8	59.4	65.4	64.0	57.2	47.9	36.6	29.9	46.9
Mean Minimum Temp. (°F)	20.9	23.1	26.0	30.1	37.5	42.8	46.5	43.9	37.4	30.6	25.2	20.2	32.0
Extreme Maximum Temp. (°F)	60	69	76	84	95	96	101	102	99	89	71	59	102
Extreme Minimum Temp. (°F)	-14	-24	6	10	16	24	31	27	21	7	-9	-16	-24
Days Maximum Temp. ≥ 90°F	0	0	0	0	0	1	7	6	2	0	0	0	16
Days Maximum Temp. ≤ 32°F	4	2	0	0	0	0	0	0	0	0	1	5	12
Days Minimum Temp. ≤ 32°F	28	24	25	19	8	1	0	0	6	19	24	28	182
Days Minimum Temp. ≤ 0°F	1	1	0	0	0	0	0	0	0	0	0	1	3
Heating Degree Days (base 65°F)	1,055	857	792	599	378	183	60	74	234	524	846	1,083	6,685
Cooling Degree Days (base 65°F)	0	0	0	0	5	23	80	50	9	0	0	0	167
Mean Precipitation (in.)	1.37	1.18	1.14	0.98	1.10	0.82	0.34	0.33	0.49	0.79	1.35	1.41	11.30
Extreme Maximum Daily Precip. (in.)	1.20	1.32	1.32	1.03	0.82	1.28	1.05	1.37	1.22	0.84	1.21	1.65	1.65
Days With ≥ 0.1" Precipitation	5	4	4	3	4	2	1	1	1	2	4	4	35
Days With ≥ 0.5" Precipitation	0	0	0	0	0	0	0	0	0	0	0	1	1
Days With ≥ 1.0" Precipitation	0	0	0	0	0	0	0	0	0	0	0	0	0
Mean Snowfall (in.)	6.1	4.0	2.3	1.1	0.1	0.0	0.0	0.0	0.0	0.2	3.3	5.8	22.9
Maximum Snow Depth (in.)	21	11	4	2	0	0	0	0	0	1	5	10	21
Days With ≥ 1.0" Snow Depth	7	5	1	0	0	0	0	0	0	0	3	7	23

Victorville Pump Plant *San Bernardino County* Elevation: 2,857 ft. Latitude: 34° 32' N Longitude: 117° 18' W

	JAN	FEB	MAR	APR	MAY	JUN	JUL	AUG	SEP	OCT	NOV	DEC	YEAR
Mean Maximum Temp. (°F)	59.9	62.7	67.9	74.9	83.6	92.7	98.4	98.2	91.9	80.8	67.9	59.3	78.2
Mean Temp. (°F)	46.0	49.0	53.1	59.0	66.5	74.2	80.2	80.0	73.8	63.2	52.1	45.0	61.8
Mean Minimum Temp. (°F)	32.0	35.1	38.4	43.0	49.4	55.6	62.0	61.6	55.6	45.6	36.3	30.7	45.4
Extreme Maximum Temp. (°F)	79	84	93	100	108	111	116	112	113	101	88	79	116
Extreme Minimum Temp. (°F)	9	16	21	25	32	36	36	44	34	28	16	6	6
Days Maximum Temp. ≥ 90°F	0	0	0	2	9	20	27	28	20	6	0	0	112
Days Maximum Temp. ≤ 32°F	0	0	0	0	0	0	0	0	0	0	0	0	0
Days Minimum Temp. ≤ 32°F	18	10	5	1	0	0	0	0	0	1	9	20	64
Days Minimum Temp. ≤ 0°F	0	0	0	0	0	0	0	0	0	0	0	0	0
Heating Degree Days (base 65°F)	583	447	363	203	73	12	2	0	13	116	381	612	2,805
Cooling Degree Days (base 65°F)	0	0	3	29	127	294	479	471	283	67	1	0	1,754
Mean Precipitation (in.)	0.98	1.33	1.02	0.35	0.16	0.05	0.19	0.21	0.19	0.36	0.45	0.87	6.16
Extreme Maximum Daily Precip. (in.)	1.50	3.00	2.68	1.16	0.82	0.64	0.98	0.81	1.06	1.65	1.38	1.70	3.00
Days With ≥ 0.1" Precipitation	2	3	2	1	0	0	1	0	1	1	1	2	14
Days With ≥ 0.5" Precipitation	1	1	1	0	0	0	0	0	0	0	0	1	4
Days With ≥ 1.0" Precipitation	0	0	0	0	0	0	0	0	0	0	0	0	0
Mean Snowfall (in.)	trace	trace	0.0	0.0	0.0	0.0	0.0	0.0	0.0	0.0	0.0	0.0	trace
Maximum Snow Depth (in.)	0	0	0	0	0	0	0	0	0	0	0	0	0
Days With ≥ 1.0" Snow Depth	0	0	0	0	0	0	0	0	0	0	0	0	0

The period of record for all cooperative weather station data is 1980 – 2009. See User Guide for detailed explanation of data.

Visalia *Tulare County* Elevation: 325 ft. Latitude: 36° 20' N Longitude: 119° 18' W

	JAN	FEB	MAR	APR	MAY	JUN	JUL	AUG	SEP	OCT	NOV	DEC	YEAR
Mean Maximum Temp. (°F)	55.0	61.8	67.5	73.9	82.1	89.3	94.4	93.2	88.1	78.3	64.8	54.8	75.3
Mean Temp. (°F)	46.9	52.0	56.8	61.6	69.0	75.4	80.5	79.0	74.1	65.4	54.2	46.3	63.4
Mean Minimum Temp. (°F)	38.7	42.2	46.1	49.4	55.8	61.4	66.5	64.7	60.2	52.5	43.6	37.7	51.6
Extreme Maximum Temp. (°F)	79	81	87	97	105	107	108	105	104	98	86	78	108
Extreme Minimum Temp. (°F)	23	27	31	34	41	48	52	55	41	38	30	21	21
Days Maximum Temp. ≥ 90°F	0	0	0	1	6	15	25	23	13	2	0	0	85
Days Maximum Temp. ≤ 32°F	0	0	0	0	0	0	0	0	0	0	0	0	0
Days Minimum Temp. ≤ 32°F	4	1	0	0	0	0	0	0	0	0	0	6	11
Days Minimum Temp. ≤ 0°F	0	0	0	0	0	0	0	0	0	0	0	0	0
Heating Degree Days (base 65°F)	555	360	252	134	33	3	0	0	3	63	319	574	2,296
Cooling Degree Days (base 65°F)	0	0	5	41	164	320	486	440	284	82	1	0	1,823
Mean Precipitation (in.)	2.11	1.87	1.93	0.97	0.35	0.14	0.01	0.01	0.15	0.55	1.09	1.59	10.77
Extreme Maximum Daily Precip. (in.)	3.00	2.15	1.60	2.22	0.73	0.95	0.25	0.11	0.90	1.47	1.57	2.41	3.00
Days With ≥ 0.1" Precipitation	5	5	5	2	1	0	0	0	0	1	3	4	26
Days With ≥ 0.5" Precipitation	1	1	1	1	0	0	0	0	0	0	1	1	6
Days With ≥ 1.0" Precipitation	0	0	0	0	0	0	0	0	0	0	0	0	0
Mean Snowfall (in.)	0.1	0.0	0.0	0.0	0.0	0.0	0.0	0.0	0.0	0.0	0.0	0.0	0.1
Maximum Snow Depth (in.)	2	0	0	0	0	0	0	0	0	0	0	0	2
Days With ≥ 1.0" Snow Depth	0	0	0	0	0	0	0	0	0	0	0	0	0

Woodland 1 WNW *Yolo County* Elevation: 68 ft. Latitude: 38° 41' N Longitude: 121° 48' W

	JAN	FEB	MAR	APR	MAY	JUN	JUL	AUG	SEP	OCT	NOV	DEC	YEAR
Mean Maximum Temp. (°F)	54.5	60.4	66.7	73.6	82.2	90.0	95.2	94.1	89.9	79.0	64.5	54.6	75.4
Mean Temp. (°F)	47.0	51.5	56.2	61.0	68.0	74.1	77.6	76.6	73.8	65.4	54.5	46.7	62.7
Mean Minimum Temp. (°F)	39.4	42.5	45.6	48.3	53.8	58.2	59.9	59.0	57.7	51.9	44.4	38.8	49.9
Extreme Maximum Temp. (°F)	73	77	85	97	105	109	113	110	107	105	84	73	113
Extreme Minimum Temp. (°F)	23	25	32	33	39	46	49	50	47	38	28	19	19
Days Maximum Temp. ≥ 90°F	0	0	0	1	7	16	25	24	17	4	0	0	94
Days Maximum Temp. ≤ 32°F	0	0	0	0	0	0	0	0	0	0	0	0	0
Days Minimum Temp. ≤ 32°F	4	1	0	0	0	0	0	0	0	0	1	5	11
Days Minimum Temp. ≤ 0°F	0	0	0	0	0	0	0	0	0	0	0	0	0
Heating Degree Days (base 65°F)	551	376	272	149	40	4	0	0	3	62	310	559	2,326
Cooling Degree Days (base 65°F)	0	0	5	35	140	283	397	366	273	82	1	0	1,582
Mean Precipitation (in.)	4.27	4.51	3.00	1.29	0.64	0.16	0.01	0.07	0.37	1.05	2.37	3.55	21.29
Extreme Maximum Daily Precip. (in.)	3.18	3.39	2.15	2.70	2.03	0.47	0.11	0.97	2.74	2.74	2.13	3.60	3.60
Days With ≥ 0.1" Precipitation	7	7	6	3	2	1	0	0	1	2	4	6	39
Days With ≥ 0.5" Precipitation	3	3	2	1	0	0	0	0	0	1	2	2	14
Days With ≥ 1.0" Precipitation	1	1	1	0	0	0	0	0	0	0	0	1	4
Mean Snowfall (in.)	0.0	0.0	0.0	0.0	0.0	0.0	0.0	0.0	0.0	0.0	0.0	trace	trace
Maximum Snow Depth (in.)	trace	0	0	0	0	0	0	0	0	0	0	0	trace
Days With ≥ 1.0" Snow Depth	0	0	0	0	0	0	0	0	0	0	0	0	0

Woodside Fire Stn 1 *San Mateo County* Elevation: 379 ft. Latitude: 37° 26' N Longitude: 122° 15' W

	JAN	FEB	MAR	APR	MAY	JUN	JUL	AUG	SEP	OCT	NOV	DEC	YEAR
Mean Maximum Temp. (°F)	60.5	63.9	***68.2***	73.1	78.3	83.8	***88.5***	***88.7***	***86.2***	***79.3***	***67.1***	***60.2***	***74.8***
Mean Temp. (°F)	48.8	51.6	***54.7***	57.9	62.2	66.3	***70.1***	***69.8***	***68.0***	***62.5***	***53.8***	***48.5***	***59.5***
Mean Minimum Temp. (°F)	37.0	39.2	***41.2***	42.6	46.0	48.7	***51.6***	***50.9***	***49.8***	***45.6***	***40.4***	***36.9***	***44.2***
Extreme Maximum Temp. (°F)	84	84	91	99	105	***108***	114	114	108	***106***	***90***	***76***	***114***
Extreme Minimum Temp. (°F)	21	17	29	30	33	***36***	38	38	38	***30***	***23***	***20***	***17***
Days Maximum Temp. ≥ 90°F	0	0	0	1	3	7	12	12	9	***3***	0	0	***47***
Days Maximum Temp. ≤ 32°F	0	0	0	0	0	0	0	0	0	***0***	0	0	***0***
Days Minimum Temp. ≤ 32°F	10	4	1	0	0	0	0	0	0	***0***	3	10	***28***
Days Minimum Temp. ≤ 0°F	0	0	0	0	0	0	0	0	0	***0***	0	0	***0***
Heating Degree Days (base 65°F)	497	373	***313***	219	119	45	***8***	***6***	***22***	***107***	***331***	***503***	***2,543***
Cooling Degree Days (base 65°F)	0	0	***2***	11	39	90	***173***	***162***	***120***	***36***	***1***	***0***	***634***
Mean Precipitation (in.)	6.09	6.02	4.40	1.77	0.76	0.16	0.01	0.05	0.18	1.25	3.67	5.70	30.06
Extreme Maximum Daily Precip. (in.)	4.15	***3.21***	2.60	2.00	0.88	***0.86***	0.17	0.86	0.58	***2.70***	***3.53***	***4.64***	***4.64***
Days With ≥ 0.1" Precipitation	8	8	8	4	2	0	0	0	1	2	5	7	45
Days With ≥ 0.5" Precipitation	4	4	3	1	0	0	0	0	0	1	3	4	20
Days With ≥ 1.0" Precipitation	2	2	1	0	0	0	0	0	0	0	1	2	8
Mean Snowfall (in.)	0.0	0.0	0.0	0.0	0.0	0.0	0.0	0.0	0.0	0.0	0.0	0.0	0.0
Maximum Snow Depth (in.)	0	0	0	0	0	***0***	0	0	0	***0***	0	0	***0***
Days With ≥ 1.0" Snow Depth	0	0	0	0	0	0	0	0	0	***0***	0	0	***0***

Yreka *Siskiyou County* Elevation: 2,625 ft. Latitude: 41° 42' N Longitude: 122° 38' W

	JAN	FEB	MAR	APR	MAY	JUN	JUL	AUG	SEP	OCT	NOV	DEC	YEAR
Mean Maximum Temp. (°F)	45.9	51.4	57.9	64.1	73.4	81.6	91.7	91.2	83.1	70.3	53.0	44.8	67.4
Mean Temp. (°F)	35.3	39.1	43.9	49.1	56.8	63.7	71.7	70.8	63.5	52.8	40.9	34.6	51.9
Mean Minimum Temp. (°F)	24.7	26.6	29.9	34.1	40.2	45.8	51.8	50.4	43.8	35.2	28.8	24.3	36.3
Extreme Maximum Temp. (°F)	64	73	79	91	103	106	109	110	106	93	76	65	110
Extreme Minimum Temp. (°F)	6	-2	12	17	21	31	34	33	28	12	10	-5	-5
Days Maximum Temp. ≥ 90°F	0	0	0	0	3	7	20	20	9	1	0	0	60
Days Maximum Temp. ≤ 32°F	0	0	0	0	0	0	0	0	0	0	0	1	1
Days Minimum Temp. ≤ 32°F	27	23	22	12	4	0	0	0	1	10	22	27	148
Days Minimum Temp. ≤ 0°F	0	0	0	0	0	0	0	0	0	0	0	0	0
Heating Degree Days (base 65°F)	913	727	647	470	270	109	17	14	105	375	716	937	5,300
Cooling Degree Days (base 65°F)	0	0	0	1	24	78	232	201	66	3	0	0	605
Mean Precipitation (in.)	3.15	2.12	1.60	1.20	1.31	1.00	0.51	0.36	0.56	1.03	2.88	3.96	19.68
Extreme Maximum Daily Precip. (in.)	2.62	1.83	1.35	1.28	2.80	1.93	0.77	1.02	2.15	1.50	2.38	3.28	3.28
Days With ≥ 0.1" Precipitation	7	5	4	3	4	2	1	1	1	3	6	7	44
Days With ≥ 0.5" Precipitation	2	1	1	0	1	0	0	0	0	1	2	2	10
Days With ≥ 1.0" Precipitation	1	0	0	0	0	0	0	0	0	0	1	1	3
Mean Snowfall (in.)	3.7	2.5	0.8	0.2	trace	0.0	0.0	0.0	0.0	0.1	1.2	3.7	12.2
Maximum Snow Depth (in.)	14	10	1	***2***	0	***0***	0	0	0	***0***	5	12	***14***
Days With ≥ 1.0" Snow Depth	2	1	0	0	0	0	0	0	0	0	1	2	6

The period of record for all cooperative weather station data is 1980 – 2009. See User Guide for detailed explanation of data.

California Weather Station Rankings

Annual Extreme Maximum Temperature

Highest			Lowest		
Rank	Station Name	°F	Rank	Station Name	°F
1	Death Valley	129	1	Eureka	87
2	Needles Airport	125	2	Bodie	91
3	Parker Reservoir	123	3	Crescent City 3 NNW	93
4	Blythe	122	4	Big Bear Lake	94
4	Borrego Desert Park	122	4	Fort Bragg 5 N	94
6	Hayfield Pumping Plant	119	6	Calaveras Big Trees	98
7	Ash Mountain	118	6	San Francisco Oceanside	***98***
7	Redlands	118	8	Donner Memorial St Pk	99
9	Haiwee	117	8	Palomar Mountain Observatory	99
10	Canoga Park Pierce College	***116***	8	Santa Monica Pier	***99***
10	Newman	***116***	11	Canyon Dam	102
10	Riverside Fire Sta 3	116	11	Jess Valley	102
10	Victorville Pump Plant	116	11	Morro Bay Fire Dept	102
14	Barstow Fire Station	115	11	Tulelake	102
14	Coalinga	115	15	Boca	103
14	Covelo	115	15	Callahan	103
14	Elsinore	115	15	Cuyamaca	103
14	Stockton Metropolitan Arpt	115	15	Lava Beds Nat Monument	103
19	Fairfield	114	15	San Francisco	103
19	Friant Government Camp	114	20	Doyle 4 SSE	104
19	Independence	114	20	Laguna Beach	***104***
19	Woodside Fire Stn 1	***114***	22	Angwin Pac Union Col	105
23	Cachuma Lake	113	22	Salinas No 2	105
23	Camp Pardee	113	22	San Francisco Int'l Arpt	105
23	Fresno Air Terminal	113	22	Santa Barbara	***105***

Annual Mean Maximum Temperature

Highest			Lowest		
Rank	Station Name	°F	Rank	Station Name	°F
1	Death Valley	91.3	1	Bodie	57.0
2	Blythe	***88.3***	2	Donner Memorial St Pk	59.0
3	Borrego Desert Park	87.9	3	Eureka	59.9
4	Needles Airport	87.1	4	Calaveras Big Trees	60.0
5	Parker Reservoir	86.6	5	Crescent City 3 NNW	60.2
6	Hayfield Pumping Plant	85.1	6	Jess Valley	60.4
7	Canoga Park Pierce College	***81.3***	7	Fort Bragg 5 N	60.7
8	Elsinore	***80.8***	8	Canyon Dam	61.1
8	Riverside Fire Sta 3	80.8	9	Lava Beds Nat Monument	***61.4***
10	Barstow Fire Station	80.3	10	San Francisco Oceanside	***61.5***
11	Coalinga	79.9	11	Cedarville	61.7
12	Redlands	79.7	11	Tulelake	61.7
13	Porterville	***78.9***	13	Boca	62.2
14	Cachuma Lake	78.2	14	Big Bear Lake	62.8
14	Victorville Pump Plant	78.2	15	Alturas	63.9
16	Burbank Valley Pump Plant	77.8	16	Doyle 4 SSE	64.7
16	Ojai	77.8	17	Morro Bay Fire Dept	64.9
16	Tejon Rancho	77.8	18	Callahan	65.1
19	Friant Government Camp	77.7	19	San Francisco	65.2
19	Newman	***77.7***	20	Palomar Mountain Observatory	65.7
21	Bakersfield Meadows Field	77.6	21	San Francisco Int'l Arpt	65.8
22	Escondido No 2	***77.2***	22	Berkeley	***66.2***
23	Ash Mountain	77.1	23	Santa Monica Pier	***66.4***
24	Fresno Air Terminal	76.9	24	Cuyamaca	66.6
25	Independence	76.5	25	Yreka	67.4

Rankings include 25 highest/lowest stations. If state has less than 25 stations, all stations are included. The period of record is 1980–2009. See User Guide for detailed explanation of data.

Annual Mean Temperature

Highest			Lowest		
Rank	Station Name	°F	Rank	Station Name	°F
1	Death Valley	76.7	1	Bodie	38.3
2	Needles Airport	74.5	2	Boca	43.5
2	Parker Reservoir	74.5	2	Donner Memorial St Pk	43.5
4	Borrego Desert Park	73.2	4	Jess Valley	46.1
5	Blythe	***72.7***	5	Alturas	46.7
6	Hayfield Pumping Plant	70.1	6	Tulelake	46.9
7	Los Angeles Civic Center	66.6	7	Big Bear Lake	47.8
8	Riverside Fire Sta 3	66.5	8	Canyon Dam	48.0
9	Barstow Fire Station	65.4	9	Lava Beds Nat Monument	***48.4***
9	Redlands	65.4	10	Cedarville	48.6
11	Bakersfield Meadows Field	65.2	11	Calaveras Big Trees	49.6
11	Elsinore	***65.2***	12	Doyle 4 SSE	50.1
13	Coalinga	65.1	13	Callahan	50.6
13	Porterville	***65.1***	14	Yreka	51.9
15	Burbank Valley Pump Plant	64.9	15	Fort Bragg 5 N	52.6
15	Long Beach Daugherty Fld	64.9	16	Crescent City 3 NNW	52.9
17	Escondido No 2	***64.8***	17	Cuyamaca	53.5
18	Canoga Park Pierce College	***64.6***	17	Eureka	53.5
19	Fresno Air Terminal	64.4	19	Dunsmuir Treatment Plant	54.5
20	San Diego Lindbergh Field	64.2	20	San Francisco Oceanside	***55.8***
21	Culver City	***64.0***	21	Bishop Arpt	56.1
22	Ash Mountain	63.8	21	De Sabla	56.1
23	Chula Vista	***63.5***	23	Covelo	56.3
24	Visalia	63.4	23	Morro Bay Fire Dept	56.3
25	Los Angeles Intl Arpt	63.3	23	Palomar Mountain Observatory	56.3

Annual Mean Minimum Temperature

Highest			Lowest		
Rank	Station Name	°F	Rank	Station Name	°F
1	Parker Reservoir	62.4	1	Bodie	19.5
2	Death Valley	62.0	2	Boca	24.7
3	Needles Airport	61.9	3	Donner Memorial St Pk	28.0
4	Borrego Desert Park	58.5	4	Alturas	29.5
5	San Diego Lindbergh Field	58.1	5	Jess Valley	31.8
6	Los Angeles Civic Center	57.5	6	Tulelake	32.0
7	Blythe	***57.1***	7	Big Bear Lake	32.8
8	Santa Monica Pier	***56.7***	8	Canyon Dam	34.8
9	Los Angeles Intl Arpt	56.2	9	Lava Beds Nat Monument	***35.4***
10	Long Beach Daugherty Fld	55.4	10	Cedarville	35.5
11	Chula Vista	***55.1***	10	Doyle 4 SSE	35.5
11	Hayfield Pumping Plant	55.1	12	Callahan	36.1
13	Culver City	***55.0***	13	Yreka	36.3
14	Mitchell Caverns	53.0	14	Bishop Arpt	37.7
15	Bakersfield Meadows Field	52.8	15	Calaveras Big Trees	39.1
16	Santa Barbara	***52.7***	16	Dunsmuir Treatment Plant	40.1
17	Escondido No 2	***52.4***	17	Covelo	40.3
18	Riverside Fire Sta 3	52.2	18	Cuyamaca	40.4
19	Burbank Valley Pump Plant	52.0	19	Graton	42.3
20	Fresno Air Terminal	51.9	20	De Sabla	42.4
21	Visalia	51.6	21	Ben Lomond No 4	43.6
22	Laguna Beach	***51.4***	22	El Mirage	44.0
23	San Francisco	51.3	23	Woodside Fire Stn 1	***44.2***
24	Porterville	***51.2***	24	Calistoga	***44.4***
25	Redlands	51.0	25	Fort Bragg 5 N	44.5

Rankings include 25 highest/lowest stations. If state has less than 25 stations, all stations are included. The period of record is 1980–2009. See User Guide for detailed explanation of data.

Annual Extreme Minimum Temperature

Highest Rank	Highest Station Name	°F	Lowest Rank	Lowest Station Name	°F
1	Santa Monica Pier	***35***	1	Boca	-43
2	San Diego Lindbergh Field	34	2	Alturas	-33
3	Los Angeles Civic Center	33	2	Bodie	-33
3	Los Angeles Intl Arpt	33	4	Cedarville	-28
5	Culver City	32	4	Jess Valley	-28
6	Long Beach Daugherty Fld	28	6	Donner Memorial St Pk	-27
7	Laguna Beach	***27***	7	Doyle 4 SSE	-25
7	San Francisco Int'l Arpt	27	8	Tulelake	-24
9	San Francisco Oceanside	***26***	9	Lava Beds Nat Monument	-18
10	Escondido No 2	***25***	10	Canyon Dam	-11
10	Parker Reservoir	25	11	Big Bear Lake	-8
12	Berkeley	***24***	11	Bishop Arpt	-8
13	Borrego Desert Park	23	11	Haiwee	-8
13	San Francisco	23	14	Callahan	-6
15	Burbank Valley Pump Plant	22	15	Yreka	-5
15	Morro Bay Fire Dept	22	16	Independence	-2
15	Riverside Fire Sta 3	22	17	Blythe	0
15	Salinas No 2	22	17	Death Valley	0
15	Santa Barbara	***22***	19	El Mirage	1
20	Santa Maria Public Arpt	21	20	Calaveras Big Trees	3
20	Visalia	21	21	Cuyamaca	4
22	Antioch Pump Plant #3	20	21	Dunsmuir Treatment Plant	4
22	Balch Power House	20	21	Eureka	4
24	Bakersfield Meadows Field	19	24	Orleans	5
24	Crescent City 3 NNW	19	25	De Sabla	6

July Mean Maximum Temperature

Highest Rank	Highest Station Name	°F	Lowest Rank	Lowest Station Name	°F
1	Death Valley	116.4	1	San Francisco Oceanside	62.9
2	Needles Airport	109.3	2	Eureka	63.9
3	Blythe	***108.7***	3	Crescent City 3 NNW	65.7
4	Parker Reservoir	107.7	4	Morro Bay Fire Dept	65.8
5	Borrego Desert Park	107.5	5	Fort Bragg 5 N	66.4
6	Hayfield Pumping Plant	104.8	6	San Francisco	68.2
7	Barstow Fire Station	102.1	7	Santa Monica Pier	69.8
8	Coalinga	100.2	8	Salinas No 2	71.6
9	Friant Government Camp	99.7	9	San Francisco Int'l Arpt	72.1
10	Independence	99.6	10	Berkeley	72.6
11	Ash Mountain	98.7	11	Santa Maria Public Arpt	73.7
12	Fresno Air Terminal	98.6	12	Santa Barbara	75.2
13	Victorville Pump Plant	98.4	13	Los Angeles Intl Arpt	75.4
14	El Mirage	98.1	14	San Diego Lindbergh Field	75.5
15	Porterville	***98.0***	15	Chula Vista	***75.7***
16	Bishop Arpt	97.9	16	Bodie	77.5
17	Bakersfield Meadows Field	97.8	17	Laguna Beach	78.7
17	Elsinore	***97.8***	18	Culver City	79.6
19	Tejon Rancho	97.6	19	Calaveras Big Trees	80.6
20	Haiwee	96.8	20	Hollister 2	80.8
20	Newman	96.8	21	Donner Memorial St Pk	81.2
22	Camp Pardee	95.3	22	Big Bear Lake	81.4
22	Canoga Park Pierce College	95.3	23	Petaluma Fire Station 2	82.0
24	Woodland 1 WNW	95.2	24	Long Beach Daugherty Fld	82.2
25	Redlands	95.1	25	Jess Valley	83.4

Rankings include 25 highest/lowest stations. If state has less than 25 stations, all stations are included. The period of record is 1980–2009. See User Guide for detailed explanation of data.

January Mean Minimum Temperature

Highest			Lowest		
Rank	**Station Name**	**°F**	**Rank**	**Station Name**	**°F**
1	Santa Monica Pier	50.8	1	Bodie	6.1
2	Los Angeles Civic Center	49.8	2	Boca	11.4
3	San Diego Lindbergh Field	49.7	3	Donner Memorial St Pk	15.6
4	Los Angeles Intl Arpt	48.9	4	Alturas	17.9
5	Culver City	47.7	5	Jess Valley	20.5
6	Long Beach Daugherty Fld	46.4	6	Tulelake	20.9
7	San Francisco	46.3	7	Cedarville	21.0
8	Chula Vista	46.0	8	Big Bear Lake	21.6
9	Santa Barbara	45.8	9	Bishop Arpt	22.8
10	San Francisco Oceanside	***45.0***	10	Lava Beds Nat Monument	23.1
11	Borrego Desert Park	44.5	11	Doyle 4 SSE	23.8
12	San Francisco Int'l Arpt	43.9	12	Canyon Dam	24.0
13	Parker Reservoir	43.8	13	Yreka	24.7
14	Berkeley	***43.7***	14	Callahan	26.4
14	Needles Airport	43.7	15	Haiwee	28.7
16	Laguna Beach	***43.5***	16	Calaveras Big Trees	28.8
17	Escondido No 2	***43.0***	17	Independence	29.0
18	Riverside Fire Sta 3	42.7	18	El Mirage	30.0
19	Burbank Valley Pump Plant	42.4	19	Dunsmuir Treatment Plant	30.1
19	Morro Bay Fire Dept	42.4	20	Cuyamaca	30.7
21	Eureka	41.7	21	Covelo	31.9
22	Salinas No 2	41.5	22	Victorville Pump Plant	32.0
23	Redlands	41.3	23	De Sabla	32.5
24	Crescent City 3 NNW	40.8	24	Tejon Rancho	33.6
25	Blythe	40.2	25	Barstow Fire Station	34.7

Number of Days Annually Maximum Temperature ≥ 90°F

Highest			Lowest		
Rank	**Station Name**	**Days**	**Rank**	**Station Name**	**Days**
1	Death Valley	194	1	Bodie	0
2	Borrego Desert Park	175	1	Crescent City 3 NNW	0
3	Blythe	172	1	Eureka	0
3	Parker Reservoir	172	1	Fort Bragg 5 N	0
5	Needles Airport	170	1	Morro Bay Fire Dept	0
6	Hayfield Pumping Plant	157	1	San Francisco Oceanside	0
7	Barstow Fire Station	132	1	Santa Monica Pier	***0***
8	Coalinga	126	8	Big Bear Lake	1
9	Porterville	***119***	9	Chula Vista	2
10	Friant Government Camp	117	9	San Diego Lindbergh Field	2
11	Victorville Pump Plant	112	11	Calaveras Big Trees	3
12	Canoga Park Pierce College	***111***	11	Laguna Beach	3
12	Fresno Air Terminal	111	11	Los Angeles Intl Arpt	3
14	Independence	110	11	San Francisco	3
15	Elsinore	***108***	11	San Francisco Int'l Arpt	3
15	Newman	***108***	11	Santa Barbara	***3***
17	Ash Mountain	107	17	Berkeley	***4***
17	Bakersfield Meadows Field	107	17	Santa Maria Public Arpt	4
19	Tejon Rancho	106	19	Donner Memorial St Pk	5
20	El Mirage	105	19	Salinas No 2	5
21	Redlands	104	21	Culver City	7
22	Riverside Fire Sta 3	103	22	Palomar Mountain Observatory	10
23	Bishop Arpt	98	23	Jess Valley	12
23	Haiwee	98	24	Boca	14
25	Woodland 1 WNW	94	24	Canyon Dam	14

Rankings include 25 highest/lowest stations. If state has less than 25 stations, all stations are included. The period of record is 1980–2009. See User Guide for detailed explanation of data.

Number of Days Annually Maximum Temperature ≤ 32°F

Highest			Lowest		
Rank	**Station Name**	**Days**	**Rank**	**Station Name**	**Days**
1	Bodie	22	1	Angwin Pac Union Col	0
2	Donner Memorial St Pk	18	1	Antioch Pump Plant #3	0
3	Jess Valley	14	1	Ash Mountain	0
4	Cedarville	13	1	Auberry 2 NW	0
5	Tulelake	12	1	Auburn	0
6	Lava Beds Nat Monument	10	1	Bakersfield Meadows Field	0
7	Boca	9	1	Balch Power House	0
7	Calaveras Big Trees	9	1	Barstow Fire Station	0
7	Doyle 4 SSE	9	1	Ben Lomond No 4	0
10	Alturas	7	1	Berkeley	***0***
10	Canyon Dam	7	1	Bishop Arpt	0
12	Big Bear Lake	5	1	Blythe	0
13	Palomar Mountain Observatory	3	1	Borrego Desert Park	0
14	Callahan	2	1	Burbank Valley Pump Plant	0
15	Yreka	1	1	Cachuma Lake	0
16	Angwin Pac Union Col	0	1	Calistoga	0
16	Antioch Pump Plant #3	0	1	Camp Pardee	0
16	Ash Mountain	0	1	Canoga Park Pierce College	***0***
16	Auberry 2 NW	0	1	Chula Vista	0
16	Auburn	0	1	Coalinga	0
16	Bakersfield Meadows Field	0	1	Colfax	0
16	Balch Power House	0	1	Colusa 2 SSW	0
16	Barstow Fire Station	0	1	Covelo	0
16	Ben Lomond No 4	0	1	Crescent City 3 NNW	0
16	Berkeley	***0***	1	Culver City	0

Number of Days Annually Minimum Temperature ≤ 32°F

Highest			Lowest		
Rank	**Station Name**	**Days**	**Rank**	**Station Name**	**Days**
1	Bodie	303	1	Berkeley	***0***
2	Boca	270	1	Chula Vista	0
3	Donner Memorial St Pk	231	1	Culver City	0
4	Alturas	202	1	Long Beach Daugherty Fld	0
5	Big Bear Lake	187	1	Los Angeles Civic Center	0
5	Jess Valley	187	1	Los Angeles Intl Arpt	0
7	Tulelake	182	1	San Diego Lindbergh Field	0
8	Canyon Dam	167	1	San Francisco	0
9	Lava Beds Nat Monument	162	1	San Francisco Int'l Arpt	0
10	Cedarville	157	1	San Francisco Oceanside	0
11	Yreka	148	1	Santa Barbara	***0***
12	Doyle 4 SSE	146	1	Santa Monica Pier	***0***
13	Callahan	145	13	Parker Reservoir	1
14	Bishop Arpt	141	14	Borrego Desert Park	2
15	Calaveras Big Trees	121	14	Laguna Beach	2
16	Dunsmuir Treatment Plant	100	14	Needles Airport	2
17	Cuyamaca	96	17	Burbank Valley Pump Plant	3
18	Covelo	79	17	Escondido No 2	***3***
18	Haiwee	79	19	Morro Bay Fire Dept	4
18	Independence	79	19	Redlands	4
21	El Mirage	77	19	Riverside Fire Sta 3	4
22	De Sabla	71	22	Eureka	6
23	Victorville Pump Plant	64	22	Salinas No 2	6
24	Palomar Mountain Observatory	57	24	Blythe	8
25	Graton	44	25	Camp Pardee	9

Rankings include 25 highest/lowest stations. If state has less than 25 stations, all stations are included. The period of record is 1980–2009. See User Guide for detailed explanation of data.

Number of Days Annually Minimum Temperature ≤ 0°F

Highest			Lowest		
Rank	Station Name	Days	Rank	Station Name	Days
1	Bodie	31	1	Angwin Pac Union Col	0
2	Boca	12	1	Antioch Pump Plant #3	0
3	Alturas	5	1	Ash Mountain	0
4	Donner Memorial St Pk	4	1	Auberry 2 NW	0
4	Jess Valley	4	1	Auburn	0
6	Tulelake	3	1	Bakersfield Meadows Field	0
7	Cedarville	1	1	Balch Power House	0
7	Doyle 4 SSE	1	1	Barstow Fire Station	0
9	Angwin Pac Union Col	0	1	Ben Lomond No 4	0
9	Antioch Pump Plant #3	0	1	Berkeley	***0***
9	Ash Mountain	0	1	Big Bear Lake	0
9	Auberry 2 NW	0	1	Bishop Arpt	0
9	Auburn	0	1	Blythe	0
9	Bakersfield Meadows Field	0	1	Borrego Desert Park	0
9	Balch Power House	0	1	Burbank Valley Pump Plant	0
9	Barstow Fire Station	0	1	Cachuma Lake	0
9	Ben Lomond No 4	0	1	Calaveras Big Trees	0
9	Berkeley	***0***	1	Calistoga	0
9	Big Bear Lake	0	1	Callahan	0
9	Bishop Arpt	0	1	Camp Pardee	0
9	Blythe	0	1	Canoga Park Pierce College	***0***
9	Borrego Desert Park	0	1	Canyon Dam	0
9	Burbank Valley Pump Plant	0	1	Chula Vista	0
9	Cachuma Lake	0	1	Coalinga	0
9	Calaveras Big Trees	0	1	Colfax	0

Number of Annual Heating Degree Days

Highest			Lowest		
Rank	Station Name	Num.	Rank	Station Name	Num.
1	Bodie	9,658	1	Los Angeles Civic Center	850
2	Boca	7,796	2	Borrego Desert Park	913
3	Donner Memorial St Pk	7,791	3	San Diego Lindbergh Field	1,047
4	Jess Valley	6,963	4	Parker Reservoir	1,049
5	Alturas	6,782	5	Needles Airport	1,077
6	Tulelake	6,685	6	Death Valley	1,133
7	Cedarville	6,344	7	Blythe	***1,151***
8	Lava Beds Nat Monument	***6,338***	8	Long Beach Daugherty Fld	1,152
9	Canyon Dam	6,336	9	Culver City	***1,175***
10	Big Bear Lake	6,267	10	Los Angeles Intl Arpt	1,219
11	Calaveras Big Trees	5,803	11	Chula Vista	***1,235***
12	Doyle 4 SSE	5,682	12	Riverside Fire Sta 3	1,267
13	Callahan	5,451	13	Escondido No 2	***1,319***
14	Yreka	5,300	14	Burbank Valley Pump Plant	1,364
15	Cuyamaca	4,591	15	Hayfield Pumping Plant	1,409
16	Fort Bragg 5 N	4,434	16	Santa Monica Pier	***1,491***
17	Dunsmuir Treatment Plant	4,361	17	Laguna Beach	***1,537***
18	Crescent City 3 NNW	4,356	18	Redlands	1,565
19	Bishop Arpt	4,205	19	Canoga Park Pierce College	***1,582***
20	Eureka	4,130	20	Santa Barbara	***1,593***
21	De Sabla	3,970	21	Elsinore	***1,707***
22	Palomar Mountain Observatory	3,968	22	Cachuma Lake	1,870
23	Covelo	3,783	23	Ojai	2,003
24	Colfax	3,432	24	Porterville	***2,030***
25	Haiwee	3,406	25	Bakersfield Meadows Field	2,101

Rankings include 25 highest/lowest stations. If state has less than 25 stations, all stations are included. The period of record is 1980–2009. See User Guide for detailed explanation of data.

Number of Annual Cooling Degree Days

Highest			Lowest		
Rank	Station Name	Num.	Rank	Station Name	Num.
1	Death Valley	5,512	1	Bodie	1
2	Needles Airport	4,663	2	Eureka	3
3	Parker Reservoir	4,637	3	Fort Bragg 5 N	7
4	Blythe	***4,091***	4	Crescent City 3 NNW	8
5	Borrego Desert Park	4,029	5	San Francisco Oceanside	***27***
6	Hayfield Pumping Plant	3,391	6	Boca	38
7	Barstow Fire Station	2,517	7	Donner Memorial St Pk	48
8	Bakersfield Meadows Field	2,275	8	Morro Bay Fire Dept	52
9	Coalinga	2,236	9	Big Bear Lake	94
10	Porterville	***2,174***	10	Santa Maria Public Arpt	137
11	Fresno Air Terminal	2,157	11	Salinas No 2	140
12	Ash Mountain	2,116	12	Jess Valley	165
13	Mitchell Caverns	2,019	12	San Francisco	165
14	Independence	1,940	14	Tulelake	167
15	Riverside Fire Sta 3	1,921	15	San Francisco Int'l Arpt	168
16	Tejon Rancho	1,918	16	Berkeley	***183***
17	Elsinore	***1,890***	17	Alturas	198
18	Balch Power House	1,852	18	Canyon Dam	214
19	Visalia	1,823	19	Calaveras Big Trees	279
20	Auberry 2 NW	1,813	20	Callahan	300
21	Friant Government Camp	1,802	21	Graton	303
22	Redlands	1,797	22	Santa Monica Pier	***326***
23	Victorville Pump Plant	1,754	23	Doyle 4 SSE	355
24	Newman	***1,658***	24	Petaluma Fire Station 2	359
25	Haiwee	1,635	25	Lava Beds Nat Monument	***380***

Annual Precipitation

Highest			Lowest		
Rank	Station Name	Inches	Rank	Station Name	Inches
1	De Sabla	67.87	1	Death Valley	2.21
2	Crescent City 3 NNW	67.76	2	Blythe	3.67
3	Dunsmuir Treatment Plant	63.71	3	Hayfield Pumping Plant	4.71
4	Calaveras Big Trees	56.00	4	Needles Airport	4.73
5	Orleans	52.53	5	Barstow Fire Station	5.02
6	Ben Lomond No 4	49.95	6	Bishop Arpt	5.05
7	Colfax	46.58	7	Independence	5.39
8	Fort Bragg 5 N	42.16	8	El Mirage	5.72
9	Covelo	42.04	9	Victorville Pump Plant	6.16
10	Graton	41.40	10	Bakersfield Meadows Field	6.27
11	Angwin Pac Union Col	40.95	11	Borrego Desert Park	6.31
12	Calistoga	39.87	12	Parker Reservoir	6.45
13	Eureka	39.45	13	Haiwee	7.19
14	Donner Memorial St Pk	39.35	14	Coalinga	8.13
15	Canyon Dam	37.07	15	Chula Vista	9.61
16	Auburn	35.58	16	Riverside Fire Sta 3	10.02
17	Cuyamaca	32.64	17	San Diego Lindbergh Field	10.28
18	Balch Power House	30.90	18	Visalia	10.77
19	Woodside Fire Stn 1	30.06	19	Porterville	***11.20***
20	Palomar Mountain Observatory	28.21	20	Fresno Air Terminal	11.28
21	Ash Mountain	26.70	21	Tulelake	11.30
21	Berkeley	***26.70***	22	Newman	11.51
23	Petaluma Fire Station 2	26.28	23	Elsinore	11.61
24	Auberry 2 NW	25.80	24	Mitchell Caverns	11.81
25	Fairfield	24.59	25	Bodie	11.90

Rankings include 25 highest/lowest stations. If state has less than 25 stations, all stations are included. The period of record is 1980–2009. See User Guide for detailed explanation of data.

Annual Extreme Maximum Daily Precipitation

Highest			Lowest		
Rank	Station Name	Inches	Rank	Station Name	Inches
1	Ben Lomond No 4	11.47	1	Bakersfield Meadows Field	1.42
2	Morro Bay Fire Dept	8.82	2	Death Valley	1.47
3	De Sabla	***8.37***	3	Barstow Fire Station	1.57
4	Calistoga	8.10	4	Porterville	***1.59***
5	Santa Barbara	***8.00***	5	Tulelake	1.65
6	Calaveras Big Trees	7.85	6	Alturas	1.99
7	Angwin Pac Union Col	7.40	7	Stockton Metropolitan Arpt	2.01
8	Cuyamaca	7.37	8	Jess Valley	***2.10***
9	Cachuma Lake	7.23	8	Needles Airport	2.10
10	Ojai	7.10	10	Modesto	2.19
11	Berkeley	***6.98***	10	Tejon Rancho	***2.19***
12	Eureka	6.79	12	Livermore	2.29
13	Graton	6.70	13	Parker Reservoir	2.35
14	Dunsmuir Treatment Plant	6.44	14	Cedarville	2.38
15	Canoga Park Pierce College	***6.06***	14	Fresno Air Terminal	2.38
16	Donner Memorial St Pk	6.00	16	Chula Vista	***2.42***
17	Gilroy	5.95	17	El Mirage	2.45
18	Colfax	5.90	18	Borrego Desert Park	2.46
19	Covelo	***5.70***	19	Riverside Fire Sta 3	***2.50***
20	Mitchell Caverns	5.66	20	Blythe	***2.56***
21	San Francisco Int'l Arpt	5.59	21	Haiwee	2.65
22	Fairfield	5.58	22	San Diego Lindbergh Field	2.70
23	Los Angeles Civic Center	5.55	23	Antioch Pump Plant #3	***2.80***
24	San Francisco	5.54	23	Bodie	2.80
25	Laguna Beach	***5.50***	25	Hollister 2	2.82

Number of Days Annually With ≥ 0.1 Inches of Precipitation

Highest			Lowest		
Rank	Station Name	Days	Rank	Station Name	Days
1	Crescent City 3 NNW	79	1	Death Valley	5
2	Orleans	77	2	Blythe	8
3	Dunsmuir Treatment Plant	74	3	Hayfield Pumping Plant	10
3	Eureka	74	4	Independence	11
5	Fort Bragg 5 N	70	5	Bishop Arpt	12
6	De Sabla	68	5	Needles Airport	12
7	Covelo	61	7	Parker Reservoir	13
8	Calaveras Big Trees	58	8	Victorville Pump Plant	14
8	Canyon Dam	58	9	Borrego Desert Park	15
8	Donner Memorial St Pk	58	10	Barstow Fire Station	16
11	Colfax	56	10	El Mirage	16
12	Angwin Pac Union Col	55	12	Haiwee	17
12	Graton	55	13	Culver City	***18***
12	Jess Valley	55	13	Riverside Fire Sta 3	18
15	Ben Lomond No 4	50	15	Bakersfield Meadows Field	19
16	Auburn	48	15	Chula Vista	19
17	Calistoga	47	15	Coalinga	19
17	Petaluma Fire Station 2	47	15	Elsinore	19
19	Callahan	45	15	Santa Monica Pier	***19***
19	San Francisco	45	20	Long Beach Daugherty Fld	20
19	Woodside Fire Stn 1	45	20	Mitchell Caverns	20
22	Berkeley	***44***	20	San Diego Lindbergh Field	20
22	Boca	44	23	Los Angeles Intl Arpt	22
22	Camp Pardee	44	24	Canoga Park Pierce College	***23***
22	Yreka	44	24	Laguna Beach	23

Rankings include 25 highest/lowest stations. If state has less than 25 stations, all stations are included. The period of record is 1980–2009. See User Guide for detailed explanation of data.

Number of Days Annually With ≥ 0.5 Inches of Precipitation

Highest			Lowest		
Rank	Station Name	Days	Rank	Station Name	Days
1	Dunsmuir Treatment Plant	41	1	Blythe	0
2	De Sabla	40	1	Death Valley	0
3	Crescent City 3 NNW	39	1	Needles Airport	0
4	Orleans	34	4	Bakersfield Meadows Field	1
5	Calaveras Big Trees	32	4	Hayfield Pumping Plant	1
6	Colfax	29	4	Tulelake	1
6	Covelo	29	7	Barstow Fire Station	2
6	Fort Bragg 5 N	29	7	Bishop Arpt	2
9	Ben Lomond No 4	28	7	El Mirage	2
10	Graton	27	7	Independence	2
11	Canyon Dam	26	11	Alturas	3
11	Eureka	26	11	Borrego Desert Park	3
13	Angwin Pac Union Col	25	11	Cedarville	3
14	Auburn	24	11	Parker Reservoir	3
14	Calistoga	24	15	Coalinga	4
14	Donner Memorial St Pk	24	15	Haiwee	4
17	Cuyamaca	21	15	Victorville Pump Plant	4
18	Balch Power House	20	18	Bodie	5
18	Woodside Fire Stn 1	20	18	Riverside Fire Sta 3	5
20	Auberry 2 NW	19	20	Chula Vista	6
21	Ash Mountain	18	20	Doyle 4 SSE	6
21	Berkeley	***18***	20	Elsinore	6
23	Camp Pardee	17	20	Fresno Air Terminal	6
23	Fairfield	17	20	King City	6
23	Palomar Mountain Observatory	17	20	Newman	6

Number of Days Annually With ≥ 1.0 Inches of Precipitation

Highest			Lowest		
Rank	Station Name	Days	Rank	Station Name	Days
1	De Sabla	24	1	Alturas	0
2	Dunsmuir Treatment Plant	21	1	Bakersfield Meadows Field	0
3	Calaveras Big Trees	20	1	Barstow Fire Station	0
4	Crescent City 3 NNW	18	1	Bishop Arpt	0
5	Orleans	17	1	Blythe	0
6	Ben Lomond No 4	15	1	Bodie	0
6	Colfax	15	1	Borrego Desert Park	0
8	Angwin Pac Union Col	14	1	Cedarville	0
8	Covelo	14	1	Chula Vista	0
8	Graton	14	1	Coalinga	0
11	Calistoga	12	1	Death Valley	0
11	Fort Bragg 5 N	12	1	El Mirage	0
13	Auburn	11	1	Fresno Air Terminal	0
13	Canyon Dam	11	1	Haiwee	0
15	Donner Memorial St Pk	10	1	Hayfield Pumping Plant	0
16	Cuyamaca	9	1	Independence	0
16	Palomar Mountain Observatory	9	1	Jess Valley	0
18	Auberry 2 NW	8	1	Lava Beds Nat Monument	0
18	Eureka	8	1	Modesto	0
18	Woodside Fire Stn 1	8	1	Needles Airport	0
21	Ash Mountain	7	1	Newman	0
21	Balch Power House	7	1	Parker Reservoir	0
23	Berkeley	***6***	1	Porterville	***0***
23	Cachuma Lake	6	1	Stockton Metropolitan Arpt	0
23	Petaluma Fire Station 2	6	1	Tejon Rancho	0

Rankings include 25 highest/lowest stations. If state has less than 25 stations, all stations are included. The period of record is 1980–2009. See User Guide for detailed explanation of data.

Annual Snowfall

Highest Rank	Highest Station Name	Highest Inches	Lowest Rank	Lowest Station Name	Lowest Inches
1	Donner Memorial St Pk	185.4	1	Balch Power House	0.0
2	Calaveras Big Trees	112.7	1	Berkeley	***0.0***
3	Canyon Dam	106.0	1	Blythe	0.0
4	Boca	92.9	1	Burbank Valley Pump Plant	0.0
5	Bodie	***75.9***	1	Cachuma Lake	0.0
6	Jess Valley	75.3	1	Camp Pardee	0.0
7	Big Bear Lake	66.9	1	Death Valley	0.0
8	Lava Beds Nat Monument	43.2	1	Escondido No 2	***0.0***
9	Dunsmuir Treatment Plant	30.3	1	Friant Government Camp	0.0
10	Doyle 4 SSE	26.5	1	Gilroy	0.0
11	Cuyamaca	23.8	1	Hollister 2	0.0
12	Tulelake	22.9	1	Laguna Beach	0.0
13	Palomar Mountain Observatory	22.1	1	Newman	0.0
14	Alturas	17.4	1	Ojai	0.0
15	Cedarville	13.2	1	Parker Reservoir	0.0
16	Yreka	12.2	1	Porterville	***0.0***
17	Colfax	9.5	1	Redlands	0.0
18	Callahan	5.5	1	Riverside Fire Sta 3	0.0
19	De Sabla	4.7	1	Salinas No 2	0.0
20	Orleans	3.8	1	San Francisco Oceanside	***0.0***
21	Fairmont	3.0	1	Santa Barbara	0.0
22	Mitchell Caverns	2.2	1	Santa Monica Pier	0.0
23	Auberry 2 NW	1.9	1	Stockton Fire Stn #4	0.0
24	Covelo	1.8	1	Woodside Fire Stn 1	0.0
25	El Mirage	1.3	25	Antioch Pump Plant #3	Trace

Annual Maximum Snow Depth

Highest Rank	Highest Station Name	Highest Inches	Lowest Rank	Lowest Station Name	Lowest Inches
1	Canyon Dam	115	1	Berkeley	***0***
2	Donner Memorial St Pk	94	1	Blythe	0
3	Bodie	78	1	Burbank Valley Pump Plant	0
4	Boca	70	1	Cachuma Lake	0
5	De Sabla	30	1	Camp Pardee	0
5	Dunsmuir Treatment Plant	30	1	Crescent City 3 NNW	0
7	Cuyamaca	28	1	Culver City	***0***
8	Jess Valley	27	1	Death Valley	0
8	Palomar Mountain Observatory	27	1	Escondido No 2	***0***
10	Fairmont	26	1	Fairfield	0
10	Lava Beds Nat Monument	26	1	Friant Government Camp	0
12	Balch Power House	22	1	Gilroy	0
12	Doyle 4 SSE	22	1	Hollister 2	0
14	Alturas	21	1	King City	0
14	Tulelake	21	1	Laguna Beach	***0***
16	Cedarville	17	1	Newman	0
17	Colfax	16	1	Ojai	0
18	Yreka	***14***	1	Parker Reservoir	0
19	El Mirage	13	1	Redlands	0
20	Callahan	12	1	Riverside Fire Sta 3	0
21	Auberry 2 NW	8	1	Salinas No 2	0
21	Eureka	8	1	San Francisco Oceanside	***0***
21	Mitchell Caverns	***8***	1	Santa Barbara	0
24	Barstow Fire Station	7	1	Santa Monica Pier	***0***
25	Ash Mountain	6	1	Stockton Fire Stn #4	0

Rankings include 25 highest/lowest stations. If state has less than 25 stations, all stations are included. The period of record is 1980–2009. See User Guide for detailed explanation of data.

Number of Days Annually With ≥ 1.0 Inch Snow Depth

Highest

Rank	Station Name	Days
1	Donner Memorial St Pk	134
2	Bodie	128
3	Canyon Dam	101
4	Boca	86
5	Lava Beds Nat Monument	52
6	Jess Valley	30
7	Dunsmuir Treatment Plant	24
8	Tulelake	23
9	Doyle 4 SSE	22
10	Calaveras Big Trees	***16***
11	Alturas	15
11	Cedarville	15
13	Palomar Mountain Observatory	12
14	Cuyamaca	6
14	Yreka	6
16	Balch Power House	1
16	De Sabla	1
18	Angwin Pac Union Col	0
18	Antioch Pump Plant #3	0
18	Ash Mountain	0
18	Auberry 2 NW	0
18	Auburn	0
18	Barstow Fire Station	0
18	Ben Lomond No 4	0
18	Berkeley	***0***

Lowest

Rank	Station Name	Days
1	Angwin Pac Union Col	0
1	Antioch Pump Plant #3	0
1	Ash Mountain	0
1	Auberry 2 NW	0
1	Auburn	0
1	Barstow Fire Station	0
1	Ben Lomond No 4	0
1	Berkeley	***0***
1	Blythe	***0***
1	Borrego Desert Park	0
1	Burbank Valley Pump Plant	0
1	Cachuma Lake	0
1	Calistoga	0
1	Callahan	0
1	Camp Pardee	0
1	Canoga Park Pierce College	***0***
1	Chula Vista	0
1	Coalinga	0
1	Colfax	0
1	Colusa 2 SSW	0
1	Covelo	0
1	Crescent City 3 NNW	0
1	Culver City	0
1	Death Valley	0
1	El Mirage	0

Rankings include 25 highest/lowest stations. If state has less than 25 stations, all stations are included. The period of record is 1980–2009. See User Guide for detailed explanation of data.

Significant Storm Events in California: 2000 – 2009

Location or County	Date	Type	Mag.	Deaths	Injuries	Property Damage ($mil.)	Crop Damage ($mil.)
Riverside, San Bernardino, and San Diego County Mountains	03/04/00	Winter Storm	na	3	13	0.0	0.0
Interior Northern California	06/13/00	Excessive Heat	na	1	15	0.0	0.0
Bay Area	06/14/00	Excessive Heat	na	9	102	0.0	0.0
Tehama	09/29/00	Wild/Forest Fire	na	0	0	547.0	0.0
San Diego Co. Deserts and Coachella Valley	05/07/01	Excessive Heat	na	1	19	0.0	0.0
Kern County Mountains	01/03/02	Fog	na	1	15	0.8	0.0
Central and Southern San Joaquin Co. Valley	02/05/02	Fog	na	3	40	0.4	0.0
San Diego	02/10/02	Wild/Forest Fire	na	0	19	16.0	2.0
Tulare	08/01/02	Wild/Forest Fire	na	0	0	45.7	0.0
San Diego	08/01/02	Wild/Forest Fire	na	0	38	10.0	0.0
Los Angeles	09/01/02	Wild/Forest Fire	na	0	14	12.7	0.0
Los Angeles	09/22/02	Wild/Forest Fire	na	0	14	15.3	0.0
Southern California	01/05/03	High Wind	100 mph	2	11	3.2	28.0
San Diego	07/16/03	Wildfire	na	0	14	1.0	0.0
San Bernardino	10/21/03	Wildfire	na	0	35	50.0	0.0
San Diego	10/25/03	Wildfire	na	14	90	1,040.0	6.5
San Bernardino	10/25/03	Wildfire	na	4	5	696.4	0.0
San Diego	10/26/03	Wildfire	na	2	18	55.2	22.0
San Bernardino	11/01/03	Wildfire	na	2	7	278.6	0.0
San Diego	11/01/03	Wildfire	na	0	23	16.9	0.0
San Bernardino County Mountain	12/25/03	Landslide	na	14	10	5.0	0.0
San Bernardino County Mountain-Cajon Pass	04/01/04	Dense Fog	na	0	24	1.4	0.0
Riverside and San Diego County Valleys	05/02/04	Wildfire	na	0	18	8.0	0.0
San Bernardino	01/07/05	Heavy Rain	na	0	0	70.0	2.0
Los Angeles, Southern Santa Barbara, and Ventura Counties	01/10/05	Landslide	na	10	0	0.0	0.0
San Bernardino	02/18/05	Heavy Rain	na	0	0	40.0	0.0
Del Norte, Humboldt, Mendocino, and Trinity Counties	12/28/05	Landslide	na	0	0	55.9	0.0
Klamath and Russian River Basins	12/29/05	Flood	na	0	0	60.8	8.0
Napa	12/31/05	Flood	na	0	0	115.0	32.5
Marin	12/31/05	Flood	na	0	0	108.0	0.0
Sonoma	12/31/05	Flood	na	0	0	104.0	3.0
Marin	01/01/06	Flood	na	0	0	108.0	0.0
Sonoma	01/01/06	Flood	na	0	0	104.0	3.0
Coastal North Bay Area	03/11/06	Winter Weather	na	2	15	0.0	0.0
San Bernardino County Mountain-Apple and Lucerne Valleys	07/09/06	Wildfire	na	1	18	11.7	0.0
Interior Central California	07/16/06	Excessive Heat	na	46	18	0.1	492.4
Southern California	07/21/06	Excessive Heat	na	16	27	0.0	0.0
Santa Monica Mountains Recreational Area	01/08/07	Wildfire	na	0	0	60.0	0.0
Greater Lake Tahoe Area	06/24/07	Wildfire	na	0	3	500.0	0.0
San Diego County Coast	10/03/07	Landslide	na	0	0	48.0	0.0
San Diego County Valleys	10/21/07	Wildfire	na	8	61	75.0	0.0
San Diego County	10/21/07	Wildfire	na	0	0	50.0	0.0
Orange County Coast, Santa Ana Mountains and Foothills	10/21/07	Wildfire	na	0	16	10.0	0.0
San Diego County Valleys	10/22/07	Wildfire	na	0	5	151.1	15.0
San Bernardino County Mountain	10/22/07	Wildfire	na	0	9	65.0	0.0
San Bernardino County Mountain	10/22/07	Wildfire	na	0	1	50.0	0.0
San Diego County	10/23/07	Wildfire	na	0	15	5.0	0.0
Orange County Coastal Areas, San Bernardino and Riverside Counties	11/15/08	Wildfire	na	0	0	150.0	0.0
Santa Barbara County	05/05/09	Wildfire	na	0	30	17.0	0.0

Note: Deaths, injuries, and damages are date and location specific.

2015 Title List

Visit www.GreyHouse.com for Product Information, Table of Contents, and Sample Pages.

General Reference

An African Biographical Dictionary
America's College Museums
American Environmental Leaders: From Colonial Times to the Present
Encyclopedia of African-American Writing
Encyclopedia of Constitutional Amendments
Encyclopedia of Gun Control & Gun Rights
An Encyclopedia of Human Rights in the United States
Encyclopedia of Invasions & Conquests
Encyclopedia of Prisoners of War & Internment
Encyclopedia of Religion & Law in America
Encyclopedia of Rural America
Encyclopedia of the Continental Congress
Encyclopedia of the United States Cabinet, 1789-2010
Encyclopedia of War Journalism
Encyclopedia of Warrior Peoples & Fighting Groups
The Environmental Debate: A Documentary History
The Evolution Wars: A Guide to the Debates
From Suffrage to the Senate: America's Political Women
Global Terror & Political Risk Assessment
Media & Communications 1900-2020
Nations of the World
Political Corruption in America
Privacy Rights in the Digital Era
The Religious Right: A Reference Handbook
Speakers of the House of Representatives, 1789-2009
This is Who We Were: 1880-1900
This is Who We Were: A Companion to the 1940 Census
This is Who We Were: In the 1910s
This is Who We Were: In the 1920s
This is Who We Were: In the 1940s
This is Who We Were: In the 1950s
This is Who We Were: In the 1960s
This is Who We Were: In the 1970s
U.S. Land & Natural Resource Policy
The Value of a Dollar 1600-1865: Colonial Era to the Civil War
The Value of a Dollar: 1860-2014
Working Americans 1770-1869 Vol. IX: Revolutionary War to the Civil War
Working Americans 1880-1999 Vol. I: The Working Class
Working Americans 1880-1999 Vol. II: The Middle Class
Working Americans 1880-1999 Vol. III: The Upper Class
Working Americans 1880-1999 Vol. IV: Their Children
Working Americans 1880-2015 Vol. V: Americans At War
Working Americans 1880-2005 Vol. VI: Women at Work
Working Americans 1880-2006 Vol. VII: Social Movements
Working Americans 1880-2007 Vol. VIII: Immigrants
Working Americans 1880-2009 Vol. X: Sports & Recreation
Working Americans 1880-2010 Vol. XI: Inventors & Entrepreneurs
Working Americans 1880-2011 Vol. XII: Our History through Music
Working Americans 1880-2012 Vol. XIII: Education & Educators
World Cultural Leaders of the 20th & 21st Centuries

Education Information

Charter School Movement
Comparative Guide to American Elementary & Secondary Schools
Complete Learning Disabilities Directory
Educators Resource Directory
Special Education: A Reference Book for Policy and Curriculum Development

Health Information

Comparative Guide to American Hospitals
Complete Directory for Pediatric Disorders
Complete Directory for People with Chronic Illness
Complete Directory for People with Disabilities
Complete Mental Health Directory
Diabetes in America: Analysis of an Epidemic
Directory of Drug & Alcohol Residential Rehab Facilities
Directory of Health Care Group Purchasing Organizations
Directory of Hospital Personnel
HMO/PPO Directory
Medical Device Register
Older Americans Information Directory

Business Information

Complete Television, Radio & Cable Industry Directory
Directory of Business Information Resources
Directory of Mail Order Catalogs
Directory of Venture Capital & Private Equity Firms
Environmental Resource Handbook
Food & Beverage Market Place
Grey House Homeland Security Directory
Grey House Performing Arts Directory
Grey House Safety & Security Directory
Grey House Transportation Security Directory
Hudson's Washington News Media Contacts Directory
New York State Directory
Rauch Market Research Guides
Sports Market Place Directory

Statistics & Demographics

American Tally
America's Top-Rated Cities
America's Top-Rated Smaller Cities
America's Top-Rated Small Towns & Cities
Ancestry & Ethnicity in America
The Asian Databook
Comparative Guide to American Suburbs
The Hispanic Databook
Profiles of America
"Profiles of" Series - State Handbooks
Weather America

Financial Ratings Series

TheStreet Ratings' Guide to Bond & Money Market Mutual Funds
TheStreet Ratings' Guide to Common Stocks
TheStreet Ratings' Guide to Exchange-Traded Funds
TheStreet Ratings' Guide to Stock Mutual Funds
TheStreet Ratings' Ultimate Guided Tour of Stock Investing
Weiss Ratings' Consumer Guides
Weiss Ratings' Guide to Banks
Weiss Ratings' Guide to Credit Unions
Weiss Ratings' Guide to Health Insurers
Weiss Ratings' Guide to Life & Annuity Insurers
Weiss Ratings' Guide to Property & Casualty Insurers

Bowker's Books In Print® Titles

American Book Publishing Record® Annual
American Book Publishing Record® Monthly
Books In Print®
Books In Print® Supplement
Books Out Loud™
Bowker's Complete Video Directory™
Children's Books In Print®
El-Hi Textbooks & Serials In Print®
Forthcoming Books®
Large Print Books & Serials™
Law Books & Serials In Print™
Medical & Health Care Books In Print™
Publishers, Distributors & Wholesalers of the US™
Subject Guide to Books In Print®
Subject Guide to Children's Books In Print®

Canadian General Reference

Associations Canada
Canadian Almanac & Directory
Canadian Environmental Resource Guide
Canadian Parliamentary Guide
Canadian Venture Capital & Private Equity Firms
Financial Services Canada
Governments Canada
Health Guide Canada
The History of Canada
Libraries Canada
Major Canadian Cities

2015 Title List

Visit **www.SalemPress.com** for Product Information, Table of Contents, and Sample Pages.

Science, Careers & Mathematics

Ancient Creatures: Unearthed
Applied Science
Applied Science: Engineering & Mathematics
Applied Science: Science & Medicine
Applied Science: Technology
Biomes and Ecosystems
Careers in Business
Careers in Chemistry
Careers in Communications & Media
Careers in Environment & Conservation
Careers in Healthcare
Careers in Hospitality & Tourism
Careers in Human Services
Careers in Law, Criminal Justice & Emergency Services
Careers in Physics
Careers in Technology Services & Repair
Computer Technology Innovators
Contemporary Biographies in Business
Contemporary Biographies in Chemistry
Contemporary Biographies in Communications & Media
Contemporary Biographies in Environment & Conservation
Contemporary Biographies in Healthcare
Contemporary Biographies in Hospitality & Tourism
Contemporary Biographies in Law & Criminal Justice
Contemporary Biographies in Physics
Earth Science
Earth Science: Earth Materials & Resources
Earth Science: Earth's Surface and History
Earth Science: Physics & Chemistry of the Earth
Earth Science: Weather, Water & Atmosphere
Encyclopedia of Energy
Encyclopedia of Environmental Issues
Encyclopedia of Environmental Issues: Atmosphere and Air Pollution
Encyclopedia of Environmental Issues: Ecology and Ecosystems
Encyclopedia of Environmental Issues: Energy and Energy Use
Encyclopedia of Environmental Issues: Policy and Activism
Encyclopedia of Environmental Issues: Preservation/Wilderness Issues
Encyclopedia of Environmental Issues: Water and Water Pollution
Encyclopedia of Global Resources
Encyclopedia of Global Warming
Encyclopedia of Mathematics & Society
Encyclopedia of Mathematics & Society: Engineering, Tech, Medicine
Encyclopedia of Mathematics & Society: Great Mathematicians
Encyclopedia of Mathematics & Society: Math & Social Sciences
Encyclopedia of Mathematics & Society: Math Development/Concepts
Encyclopedia of Mathematics & Society: Math in Culture & Society
Encyclopedia of Mathematics & Society: Space, Science, Environment
Encyclopedia of the Ancient World
Forensic Science
Geography Basics
Internet Innovators
Inventions and Inventors
Magill's Encyclopedia of Science: Animal Life
Magill's Encyclopedia of Science: Plant life
Notable Natural Disasters
Principles of Chemistry
Science and Scientists
Solar System
Solar System: Great Astronomers
Solar System: Study of the Universe
Solar System: The Inner Planets
Solar System: The Moon and Other Small Bodies
Solar System: The Outer Planets
Solar System: The Sun and Other Stars
World Geography

Literature

American Ethnic Writers
Classics of Science Fiction & Fantasy Literature
Critical Insights: Authors
Critical Insights: New Literary Collection Bundles
Critical Insights: Themes
Critical Insights: Works
Critical Survey of Drama
Critical Survey of Graphic Novels: Heroes & Super Heroes
Critical Survey of Graphic Novels: History, Theme & Technique
Critical Survey of Graphic Novels: Independents/Underground Classics
Critical Survey of Graphic Novels: Manga
Critical Survey of Long Fiction
Critical Survey of Mystery & Detective Fiction
Critical Survey of Mythology and Folklore: Heroes and Heroines
Critical Survey of Mythology and Folklore: Love, Sexuality & Desire
Critical Survey of Mythology and Folklore: World Mythology
Critical Survey of Poetry
Critical Survey of Poetry: American Poets
Critical Survey of Poetry: British, Irish & Commonwealth Poets
Critical Survey of Poetry: Cumulative Index
Critical Survey of Poetry: European Poets
Critical Survey of Poetry: Topical Essays
Critical Survey of Poetry: World Poets
Critical Survey of Shakespeare's Sonnets
Critical Survey of Short Fiction
Critical Survey of Short Fiction: American Writers
Critical Survey of Short Fiction: British, Irish, Commonwealth Writers
Critical Survey of Short Fiction: Cumulative Index
Critical Survey of Short Fiction: European Writers
Critical Survey of Short Fiction: Topical Essays
Critical Survey of Short Fiction: World Writers
Cyclopedia of Literary Characters
Holocaust Literature
Introduction to Literary Context: American Poetry of the 20th Century
Introduction to Literary Context: American Post-Modernist Novels
Introduction to Literary Context: American Short Fiction
Introduction to Literary Context: English Literature
Introduction to Literary Context: Plays
Introduction to Literary Context: World Literature
Magill's Literary Annual 2015
Magill's Survey of American Literature
Magill's Survey of World Literature
Masterplots
Masterplots II: African American Literature
Masterplots II: American Fiction Series
Masterplots II: British & Commonwealth Fiction Series
Masterplots II: Christian Literature
Masterplots II: Drama Series
Masterplots II: Juvenile & Young Adult Literature, Supplement
Masterplots II: Nonfiction Series
Masterplots II: Poetry Series
Masterplots II: Short Story Series
Masterplots II: Women's Literature Series
Notable African American Writers
Notable American Novelists
Notable Playwrights
Notable Poets
Recommended Reading: 500 Classics Reviewed
Short Story Writers

2015 Title List

Visit www.SalemPress.com for Product Information, Table of Contents, and Sample Pages.

History and Social Science

The 2000s in America
50 States
African American History
Agriculture in History
American First Ladies
American Heroes
American Indian Culture
American Indian History
American Indian Tribes
American Presidents
American Villains
America's Historic Sites
Ancient Greece
The Bill of Rights
The Civil Rights Movement
The Cold War
Countries, Peoples & Cultures
Countries, Peoples & Cultures: Central & South America
Countries, Peoples & Cultures: Central, South & Southeast Asia
Countries, Peoples & Cultures: East & South Africa
Countries, Peoples & Cultures: East Asia & the Pacific
Countries, Peoples & Cultures: Eastern Europe
Countries, Peoples & Cultures: Middle East & North Africa
Countries, Peoples & Cultures: North America & the Caribbean
Countries, Peoples & Cultures: West & Central Africa
Countries, Peoples & Cultures: Western Europe
Defining Documents: American Revolution (1754-1805)
Defining Documents: Civil War (1860-1865)
Defining Documents: Emergence of Modern America (1868-1918)
Defining Documents: Exploration & Colonial America (1492-1755)
Defining Documents: Manifest Destiny (1803-1860)
Defining Documents: Post-War 1940s (1945-1949)
Defining Documents: Reconstruction (1865-1880)
Defining Documents: The 1920s
Defining Documents: The 1930s
Defining Documents: The American West (1836-1900)
Defining Documents: The Ancient World (2700 B.C.E.-50 C.E.)
Defining Documents: The Middle Ages (524-1431)
Defining Documents: World War I
Defining Documents: World War II (1939-1946)
The Eighties in America
Encyclopedia of American Immigration
Encyclopedia of Flight
Encyclopedia of the Ancient World
The Fifties in America
The Forties in America
Great Athletes
Great Athletes: Baseball
Great Athletes: Basketball
Great Athletes: Boxing & Soccer
Great Athletes: Cumulative Index
Great Athletes: Football
Great Athletes: Golf & Tennis
Great Athletes: Olympics
Great Athletes: Racing & Individual Sports
Great Events from History: 17th Century
Great Events from History: 18th Century
Great Events from History: 19th Century
Great Events from History: 20th Century (1901-1940)
Great Events from History: 20th Century (1941-1970)
Great Events from History: 20th Century (1971-2000)
Great Events from History: Ancient World
Great Events from History: Cumulative Indexes
Great Events from History: Gay, Lesbian, Bisexual, Transgender Events
Great Events from History: Middle Ages
Great Events from History: Modern Scandals
Great Events from History: Renaissance & Early Modern Era
Great Lives from History: 17th Century
Great Lives from History: 18th Century
Great Lives from History: 19th Century
Great Lives from History: 20th Century
Great Lives from History: African Americans
Great Lives from History: Ancient World
Great Lives from History: Asian & Pacific Islander Americans
Great Lives from History: Cumulative Indexes
Great Lives from History: Incredibly Wealthy
Great Lives from History: Inventors & Inventions
Great Lives from History: Jewish Americans
Great Lives from History: Latinos
Great Lives from History: Middle Ages
Great Lives from History: Notorious Lives
Great Lives from History: Renaissance & Early Modern Era
Great Lives from History: Scientists & Science
Historical Encyclopedia of American Business
Immigration in U.S. History
Magill's Guide to Military History
Milestone Documents in African American History
Milestone Documents in American History
Milestone Documents in World History
Milestone Documents of American Leaders
Milestone Documents of World Religions
Musicians & Composers 20th Century
The Nineties in America
The Seventies in America
The Sixties in America
Survey of American Industry and Careers
The Thirties in America
The Twenties in America
United States at War
U.S.A. in Space
U.S. Court Cases
U.S. Government Leaders
U.S. Laws, Acts, and Treaties
U.S. Legal System
U.S. Supreme Court
Weapons and Warfare
World Conflicts: Asia and the Middle East

Health

Addictions & Substance Abuse
Adolescent Health
Cancer
Complementary & Alternative Medicine
Genetics & Inherited Conditions
Health Issues
Infectious Diseases & Conditions
Magill's Medical Guide
Psychology & Behavioral Health
Psychology Basics

2015 Title List

Visit **www.HWWilsonInPrint.com** for Product Information, Table of Contents and Sample Pages

Current Biography
Current Biography Cumulative Index 1946-2013
Current Biography Monthly Magazine
Current Biography Yearbook: 2003
Current Biography Yearbook: 2004
Current Biography Yearbook: 2005
Current Biography Yearbook: 2006
Current Biography Yearbook: 2007
Current Biography Yearbook: 2008
Current Biography Yearbook: 2009
Current Biography Yearbook: 2010
Current Biography Yearbook: 2011
Current Biography Yearbook: 2012
Current Biography Yearbook: 2013
Current Biography Yearbook: 2014
Current Biography Yearbook: 2015

Core Collections
Children's Core Collection
Fiction Core Collection
Middle & Junior High School Core
Public Library Core Collection: Nonfiction
Senior High Core Collection

The Reference Shelf
Aging in America
American Military Presence Overseas
The Arab Spring
The Brain
The Business of Food
Conspiracy Theories
The Digital Age
Dinosaurs
Embracing New Paradigms in Education
Faith & Science
Families: Traditional and New Structures
The Future of U.S. Economic Relations: Mexico, Cuba, and Venezuela
Global Climate Change
Graphic Novels and Comic Books
Immigration in the U.S.
Internet Safety
Marijuana Reform
The News and its Future
The Paranormal
Politics of the Ocean
Reality Television
Representative American Speeches: 2008-2009
Representative American Speeches: 2009-2010
Representative American Speeches: 2010-2011
Representative American Speeches: 2011-2012
Representative American Speeches: 2012-2013
Representative American Speeches: 2013-2014
Representative American Speeches: 2014-2015
Revisiting Gender
Robotics
Russia
Social Networking
Social Services for the Poor
Space Exploration & Development
Sports in America
The Supreme Court
The Transformation of American Cities
U.S. Infrastructure
U.S. National Debate Topic: Surveillance
U.S. National Debate Topic: The Ocean
U.S. National Debate Topic: Transportation Infrastructure
Whistleblowers

Readers' Guide
Abridged Readers' Guide to Periodical Literature
Readers' Guide to Periodical Literature

Indexes
Index to Legal Periodicals & Books
Short Story Index
Book Review Digest

Sears List
Sears List of Subject Headings
Sears: Lista de Encabezamientos de Materia

Facts About Series
Facts About American Immigration
Facts About China
Facts About the 20th Century
Facts About the Presidents
Facts About the World's Languages

Nobel Prize Winners
Nobel Prize Winners: 1901-1986
Nobel Prize Winners: 1987-1991
Nobel Prize Winners: 1992-1996
Nobel Prize Winners: 1997-2001

World Authors
World Authors: 1995-2000
World Authors: 2000-2005

Famous First Facts
Famous First Facts
Famous First Facts About American Politics
Famous First Facts About Sports
Famous First Facts About the Environment
Famous First Facts: International Edition

American Book of Days
The American Book of Days
The International Book of Days

Junior Authors & Illustrators
Tenth Book of Junior Authors & Illustrations

Monographs
The Barnhart Dictionary of Etymology
Celebrate the World
Guide to the Ancient World
Indexing from A to Z
The Poetry Break
Radical Change: Books for Youth in a Digital Age

Wilson Chronology
Wilson Chronology of Asia and the Pacific
Wilson Chronology of Human Rights
Wilson Chronology of Ideas
Wilson Chronology of the Arts
Wilson Chronology of the World's Religions
Wilson Chronology of Women's Achievements